CONTENTS

Sections are arranged alphabetically, or chronologically, or have a detailed Table of Contents.

HISTORICAL
EVENTS

Chronicle of events from the earliest times to the present day. For events in pre-history the reader may also like to consult the relevant sections on geology and man's early ancestors in the Science section.

CHRONICLE OF EVENTS

Note.—For classical history and for the past millennium most dates are well established. For other periods there is sometimes considerable uncertainty. Many of the dates in ancient history are either dubious or approximate, sometimes both.

B.C.   **PREHISTORY**

4,600,000,000	Age of Earth.
3,300,000,000	Earliest known rocks (found in Greenland).
2,000,000,000	Life appears.
600,000,000	First large-scale occurrence of fossils.
30,000,000	Earliest ape fossils (Oligocene period—Fayum, Egypt).
20,000,000	Early ape fossils (Miocene period—*Proconsul*, E. Africa).
1,700,000	Earliest known hominids (Lower Pleistocene—*Australopithecus*, and *Homo habilis* S. Africa, E. Africa.) Oldowan culture—first stage of Palaeolithic or Old Stone Age (hunting and food-gathering) which persisted until end of Ice Age, *c.* 8,000 B.C.
400,000	*Homo erectus* stage (Java, China, Africa) with crude chopping tools and early hand-axes. Heidelberg jaw, Vertezöllös remains (Europe).
180,000	Ancestors of Neanderthalers and *Homo sapiens*, with advanced hand-axes (Europe: Steinheim and Swanscombe).
70,000	Neanderthalers (Europe, Asia, N. Africa). Rhodesian Man (S. Africa). Solo Man (Java). Flake tools.
40,000	First cold phase ends. Neanderthal race becoming extinct.
30,000	Second cold phase. *Homo sapiens* (modern man). Implements show significant advances: small knife-blades, engraving tools. Paintings and sculpture; magic rites and ceremonies. Cro-Magnons with Aurignacian culture.
18,000	Final culmination of last ice age. Aurignacian culture dying out to be replaced by Solutrean and then by the Magdalenian cultures. Great flowering of Palaeolithic art.
15,000	First immigrants from Asia to cross Behring Straits?
8,000	Last glaciers in Britain disappeared. Proto-Neolithic in Middle East. Agricultural settlements (*e.g.,* Jericho). Settled way of life leading eventually to such skills as weaving, metallurgy; inventions as ox-drawn plough, wheeled cart.
5,000	Britain becomes an island (land connection with continent severed by melting ice-sheets).

B.C. **CIVILISATION IN THE MIDDLE EAST**

4000	Susa founded.
3500	Sumerian civilisation flourishes. Cuneiform writing.
3100	First Egyptian Dynasty. Hieratic writing already perfected. Early Minoan Age (Crete). Pictorial writing, copper, silver, gold in use. Early Mycenaean civilisation begins.
2980	Memphis, capital of Egypt.

B.C.

2870	First settlements at Troy.
2850	Golden Age of China begins (legendary).
2700	Great Pyramid age in Egypt begins.
2400	Aryan migrations.
2371	Sargon founds Akkad: Akkadian empire.
2205	Hsia Dynasty begins in China (legendary).
2200	Middle Minoan Age: pottery, linear writing in pen and ink.
2100–1600	Building and rebuilding of Stonehenge.
1720–1550	Hyksos in Egypt. War chariots introduced. Hebrews entered Egypt (Joseph) *c.* 1600.
1751	Code of Hammurabi at Babylon.
1600	Late Minoan Age: Linear B script.
1600–1027	Shang Dynasty in China.
1546	18th Dynasty in Egypt commences. Civilisation at peak (under Tuthmosis III 1490). Chronology more certain.
1500	Powerful Mitanni (Aryan) kingdom in Asia Minor. Phoenicia thriving—trade with Egypt and Babylonia. Vedic literature in India.
1450	Zenith of Minoan civilisation.
1400	Ugarit (N. Syria) culture at its zenith. Cretan civilisation ends: Knossos burnt. Temple at Luxor built.
1379	Amenhotep IV (Akhnaten), the " heretic " Pharaoh.
1350	Zenith of Hittite civilisation.
1300	Israelite oppression (Rameses II): Exodus from Egypt (Moses). Phoenician settlements—Hellas and Spain (Cadiz). Tyre flourishing.
1250	Israelites invade Palestine (Joshua).
1200	Attacks on Egypt by " Peoples of the Sea ". Downfall of Hittite kingdom. Siege of Troy (Homeric). Beginning of sea-power of independent Phoenician cities. Probably all these are connected with Achaean and other migrations in Aegean area.
1115	Magnetic needle reputed in China.
1027–249	Chou Dynasty in China.
1005–925	Kingdom of David and Solomon: Jerusalem as Sanctuary.
1000	*Rig Veda* (India).
925–722	Israel and Judah divided.
900	Probably period of writing of Homer's epics.
893	Assyrian chronological records begin.
850	Foundation of Carthage (traditional).
781	Chinese record of an eclipse.
776	First Olympiad to be used for chronological purposes.
753	Foundation of Rome (traditional).
750	Greek colonists settling in Southern Italy.
745	Accession of Tiglath-Pileser III; Assyrian Power at its height.
722	Capture of Samaria by Sargon II: Israel deported to Nineveh.
683	Kingship abolished in Athens.
625	Neo-Babylonian (Chaldean) Empire (Nineveh destroyed 612).

B.C.
621 Publication of Athenian laws by Draco.

610 Spartan constitution, made rigid after Messenian Wars: later attributed to Lycurgus.

594 Athenian constitution reformed by Solon.

586 Capture of Jerusalem: Judah deported to Babylon (partial return 538).

561 Pisistratus tyrant of Athens.

560 Accession of Croesus—great prosperity of Lydia.

538 Babylon taken by Persians: Empire founded by Cyrus, soon covers almost all of civilised Middle East.

509 Foundation of Roman Republic (traditional).

508 Democratic constitution proclaimed in Athens.

500 Etruscans at height of their power in Northern Italy. Iron age beginning in Britain.

GREAT AGE OF GREECE

499 Revolt of Ionian Greek cities against Persian king Darius.

494 Secession of Plebeians from Rome. Tribunes established.

490 Battle of Marathon: Athenian repulse of Persian attack.

480 Death of Buddha. Battle of Thermopylae: Spartans under Leonidas wiped out by Persians. Battle of Salamis: Persian fleet defeated by Athenians under Themistocles; Persian invasion of Greece halted.

479 Battles of Plataea and Mycale: Greek victories by land and sea respectively destroy Persian invasion force. Death of Confucius.

477 League of Delos founded by Athens for defence against Persia; soon becomes Athenian Empire. (467 Naxos kept in by force.)

461 Pericles comes to power in Athens.

458 Cincinnatus saves Rome (traditional).

456 Death of Aeschylus.

447 Building of Parthenon begun.

431 Death of Phidias. Outbreak of Great Peloponnesian War between Athens and Sparta. Pericles "Funeral Oration" (according to Thucydides).

425 Death of Herodotus.

416 Massacre of Melos by Athenians.

415 Sicilian Expedition: flight of Alcibiades from Athens to Sparta.

413 Loss of entire Athenian expeditionary force at Syracuse.

406 Death of Euripides and Sophocles.

405 Battle of Aegospotami: Athenian navy destroyed by Sparta.

404 Athenian surrender to Sparta: beginning of Spartan hegemony in Greece.

403 Beginning of epoch of Warring States in China.

400 Death of Thucydides, Greek historian (?).

399 Execution of Socrates.

390 Occupation of Rome by Gauls under Brennus.

371 Battle of Leuctra: Spartans defeated by Thebans: beginning of Theban hegemony in Greece.

370 Death of Hippocrates of Cos (?).

347 Death of Plato.

338 Battle of Chaeronea: Greek city-states defeated by Philip II of Macedon, who becomes supreme in Greece.

336 Assassination of Philip of Macedon: accession of Alexander.

334 Alexander's invasion of Persian Empire. Battle of Granicus, first victory.

333 Battle of Issus: Alexander defeats Darius of Persia.

332 Alexander's siege and capture of Tyre, occupation of Egypt.

B.C.
331 Battle of Arbela (Gaugamela)—final defeat of Darius.

330 Death of Darius and end of Persian Empire. Alexander heir to civilisations of Middle East.

326 Battle of Hydaspes: Alexander conquers the Punjab.

323 Death of Alexander at Babylon. Beginning of Hellenistic Age in Middle East and Eastern Mediterranean. Ptolemy I founds dynasty in Egypt. Alexandria becomes intellectual centre of Hellenic world.

322 Death of Demosthenes.

321 Death of Aristotle. Maurya dynasty unites N. India.

312 Seleucus I founds dynasty in Asia.

300 Zeno the Stoic, Epicurus and Euclid flourishing.

ROME: CONQUESTS AND DECAY OF REPUBLICAN INSTITUTIONS

290 End of Third Samnite War. Rome dominates Central Italy.

280 Translation of Pentateuch into Greek.

275 Battle of Beneventum: Rome finally defeats Pyrrhus and the Greek cities of Southern Italy. Rome dominates all Italy.

274 Asoka becomes ruler of two-thirds of Indian sub-continent.

264 Beginning of First Punic War (Rome v. Carthage).

260 Battle of Mylae: first great Roman naval victory.

255 Defeat and capture of Regulus by Carthaginians.

250 "La Tène" Iron Age people invade Britain.

241 End of First Punic War. Sicily becomes first Province of Rome.

221 Kingdom of Ch'in completes conquest of all Chinese states under Shih Huang-ti.

218 Outbreak of Second Punic War: Hannibal crosses Alps.

216 Battle of Cannae: Hannibal wipes out great Roman army.

214 Great Wall of China constructed (by linking existing walls).

213 Burning of Chinese classics.

212 Capture of Syracuse by Romans and death of Archimedes.

207 Battle of Metaurus: defeat and death of Hasdrubal. End of Hannibal's hopes of overcoming Rome.

205 Roman provinces organised in Spain.

202 Battle of Zama: Hannibal defeated by Scipio Africanus. 202-A.D. 220 Han Dynasty in China.

201 End of Second Punic War. Rome dominates Western Mediterranean.

196 After defeating Macedon, Rome proclaims independence of Greek city-states. Death of Eratosthenes the geographer (?).

160 Death in battle of Judas Maccabaeus: Jewish revolt against Seleucids continues successfully.

149 Outbreak of Third Punic War.

146 Carthage destroyed. Roman province of Africa formed. Roman provinces of Macedonia and Achaea formed, and most of remainder of Greece reduced to vassal status.

134 First Servile War: Revolt of slaves in Sicily under Eunus. Suppressed 132.

133 Siege and destruction of Numantia by Romans. Tiberius Gracchus Tribune. Attempted land reforms. Murdered 132.

129 Roman province of Asia formed from lands bequeathed by Attalus of Pergamum.

124 Chinese Grand College to train Civil Service officials.

123 Caius Gracchus Tribune. Attempted land reforms. Murdered 121.

110 Chinese expansion to include most of southeast of modern China, under Emperor Wu Ti. Commercial activity in Indian Ocean.

B.C.

106   Jugurtha captured by Marius and Sulla.

104   Second Servile War: revolt of slaves in Sicily under Tryphon and Athenion. Suppressed 101.

102   Chinese expedition to Ferghana and possible knowledge of West.

101   Battle of Vercellae: Marius ends threat of Cimbri to Rome.

91   Social War: revolt of Italian cities against Rome. Suppressed 88. Roman franchise granted to most Italians.

88   Civil Wars of Marius and Sulla begin.

87   Massacre in Rome by Marius.

82   Proscriptions in Rome by Sulla.

75   Belgic invasion of south-eastern Britain.

73   Third Servile War: revolt of slaves in southern Italy under Spartacus the gladiator. Suppressed 71.

63   Conspiracy of Catiline exposed by Cicero.

60   First Triumvirate: Pompey, Caesar, Crassus.

58   Beginning of Caesar's conquest of Gaul.

55   Caesar's first British expedition: second, 54.

53   Battle of Carrhae: destruction of Roman army under Crassus by Persians.

52   Revolt of Vercingetorix against Caesar.

50   Migration to Britain of Commius and his followers.

49   Caesar crosses the Rubicon. Beginning of war against Pompey and the Senate.

48   Battle of Pharsalus: defeat of Pompey by Caesar.

46   Caesar's calendar reforms.

44   Murder of Caesar.

43   Second Triumvirate: Antony, Octavian, Lepidus.

42   Battle of Philippi: defeat and death of Brutus and his associates.

31   Battle of Actium: naval victory of Octavian over Antony and Cleopatra. Octavian unchallenged master of the Roman world.

THE ROMAN EMPIRE

27   Octavian given the title of Augustus by the Senate.

19   Death of Virgil.

8   Death of Horace

4   Assumed birth of Jesus.

A.D.

6   Civil Service Examination system in China.

9   Radical reforms by Wang Mang (short Hsin dynasty 9–23). Annihilation of Roman army under Varus by Teutonic tribesman under Arminius.

10   Cunobelinus reigning over much of south-east Britain from Colchester.

14   Death of Augustus.

17   Death of Livy.

18   Death of Ovid.

30   Crucifixion of Jesus.

43   Roman invasion of Britain under Aulus Plautius.

51   Caractacus taken to Rome as prisoner.

60   Revolt of Boudicca.

63   Death of St. Paul.

64   Great Fire of Rome.

65   Death of Seneca.

66   Jews of Palestine rebelled against Roman rule.

68   Death of Nero—end of Julio-Claudian line of Roman Emperors.

70   Jerusalem taken and Jewish revolt suppressed by Titus.

79   Destruction of Pompeii and Herculaneum by eruption of Vesuvius.

A.D.

80   Completion of Colosseum (Flavian Amphitheatre).

83   Battle of Mons Graupius: Agricola crushes Caledonians.

96   Accession of Nerva: first of the "Five Good Emperors."

97   Chinese expedition under Kang Yin (lieutenant of Pan Ch'ao) penetrates to Persian Gulf.

117   Death of Trajan, accession of Hadrian. Roman Empire at its greatest extent.

122   Beginning of Hadrian's Wall (Tyne–Solway) by Aulus Platorius Nepos.

135   Suppression of Bar-Cochba's revolt and Dispersion of Jews.

142   Construction of Antonine Wall (Forth–Clyde) by Quintus Lollius Urbicus.

180   Death of Marcus Aurelius, last of the "Five Good Emperors." Beginning of the "Decline" of the Roman Empire (Gibbon).

193   Praetorian guards murder Emperor Pertinax, sell Empire to highest bidder (Didius Julianus).

196   Clodius Albinus, governor, withdraws forces from Britain to support his attempt to become Emperor. Northern Britain overrun by barbarians.

208   Septimius Severus visits Britain to punish Caledonians (death at York 211).

212   Edict of Caracalla. Roman citizenship conferred on all free inhabitants of Empire.

220   End of Han Dynasty: China divided and frequently invaded for next three centuries.

227   Sassanid Empire in Persia.

230   Emperor Sujin—Japanese history emerging from legendary stage.

251   Goths defeat and kill Emperor Decius.

259   Break-away "Gallic Empire" set up: suppressed 273.

273   Defeat of Zenobia and destruction of Palmyra by Emperor Aurelian.

284   Accession of Diocletian, who reorganises Roman Empire (293) with rigid social laws and heavy taxation.

287   Carausius attempts to found independent "Empire of Britain": suppressed 297.

306   Constantine proclaimed Emperor at York.

313   Edict of Milan. Christianity tolerated in Roman Empire.

320   Gupta dynasty reunites India.

325   Council of Nicaea: first general Council of the Church.

367   Successful attack on Britain by Picts, Scots, Saxons.

369   Restoration of Roman authority in Britain by Theodosius.

378   Battle of Adrianople: Goths defeat and kill Eastern Roman Emperor Valens.

383   Magnus Maximus withdraws forces from Britain to support his attempt to conquer north-western part of Empire.

388   Magnus Maximus defeated and killed in Italy.

395   Death of Emperor Theodosius the Great: the division of the Empire into East and West at his death proves eventually to be the final one.

406   Usurper Constantine III withdraws forces from Britain to support his claims: probable end of Roman military occupation of Britain.

410   Sack of Rome by Alaric the Goth. Emperor Honorius tells Britons to arrange for their own defence.

THE BARBARIAN INVASIONS

415   Visigoths begin conquest of Spain.

419   Visigothic kingdom of Toulouse recognised by Roman government.

429   Vandals begin conquest of North Africa.

432   St. Patrick begins mission in Ireland.

A.D.
446   "Groans of the Britons"—last appeal to Rome (traditional).

451   Châlons: Attila the Hun repelled from Gaul by mixed Roman–Barbarian forces.

452   Attila's raid into Italy: destruction of Aquilea and foundation of Venice by refugees.

455   Rome pillaged by Vandals.

476   Romulus Augustulus, last Western Roman Emperor, deposed by Odovacar: conventionally the end of the Western Roman Empire.

481   Clovis becomes King of the Franks, who eventually conquer Gaul (d. 511).

493   Theodoric founds Ostrogothic Kingdom in Italy (d. 526).

515   Battle of Mount Badon: West Saxon advance halted by Britons, perhaps led by Arthur (?).

BYZANTIUM AND ISLAM

527   Accession of Justinian I (d. 565).

528   Code of Civil Law published by Justinian. Rule of St. Benedict put into practice at Monte Cassino (traditional).

534   Byzantines under Belisarius reconquer North Africa from Vandals.

552   Byzantine reconquest of Italy complete.

563   St. Columba founds mission in Iona.

568   Lombard Kingdom founded in Italy.

570   Birth of Mohammed.

577   Battle of Deorham: West Saxon advance resumed.

581–618   Sui Dynasty in China.

590   Gregory the Great becomes Pope.

597   St. Augustine lands in Kent.

605   Grand Canal of China constructed.

618–907   T'ang Dynasty in China: their administrative system lasts in essentials for 1,300 years.

622   Hejira or flight from Mecca to Medina of Mohammed: beginning of Mohammedan era.

627   Battle of Nineveh: Persians crushed by Byzantines under Heraclius.

632   Death of Mohammed: all Arabia now Moslem. Accession of Abu Bakr, the first Caliph.

634   Battle of Heavenfield: Oswald becomes king of Northumbria, brings in Celtic Christianity.

638   Jerusalem captured by Moslems.

641   Battle of Mehawand: Persia conquered by Moslems.

643   Alexandria taken by Moslems.

645   Downfall of Soga clan in Japan, after establishing Buddhism: beginning of period of imitation of Chinese culture.

650   Slav occupation of Balkans now complete.

663   Synod of Whitby: Roman Christianity triumphs over Celtic Christianity in England.

685   Nectansmere: end of Northumbrian dominance in England.

698   Carthage taken by Moslems.

711   Tarik leads successful Moslem invasion of Spain.

718   Failure of second and greatest Moslem attack on Constantinople. Pelayo founds Christian kingdom of Asturias in Northern Spain.

726   Byzantine Emperor Leo III begins Iconoclast movement: opposed by Pope Gregory II, and an important cause of difference between Roman and Byzantine churches.

THE HOLY ROMAN EMPIRE AND THE TRIUMPH OF CHRISTIANITY IN EUROPE: NORSEMEN AND NORMANS

732   Tours: Moslem western advance halted by Charles Martel.

735   Death of Bede.

750   Beginning of Abbasid Caliphate (replacing Omayyads).

A.D.
751   Pepin King of the Franks: founds Carolingian dynasty. Ravenna taken by Lombards: end of Byzantine power in the West.

754   Pepin promises central Italy to Pope: beginning of temporal power of the Papacy.

778   Roncesvalles: defeat and death of Roland.

786   Accession of Haroun-al-Rashid in Baghdad.

793   Sack of Lindisfarne: Viking attacks on Britain begin.

795   Death of Offa: end of Mercian dominance in England.

800   Coronation of Charlemagne as Holy Roman Emperor.

814   Death of Charlemagne: division of empire.

825   Ellandun: Egbert defeats Mercians and Wessex becomes leading kingdom in England.

827   Moslem invasion of Sicily.

840   Moslems capture Bari and occupy much of Southern Italy.

843   Treaty of Verdun: final division of Carolingian Empire, and beginning of France and Germany as separate states.

844   Kenneth MacAlpin becomes king of Picts as well as Scots: the kingdom of Alban.

862   Rurik founds Viking state in Russia: first at Novgorod, later at Kiev.

866   Fujiwara period begins in Japan. Viking "Great Army" in England: Northumbria, East Anglia and Mercia subsequently overwhelmed.

868   Earliest dated printed book in China.

872   Harold Fairhair King of Norway.

874   Iceland settled by Norsemen.

885–6   Viking attack on Paris.

893   Simeon founds first Bulgar Empire in Balkans.

896   Arpad and the Magyars in Hungary.

899   Death of Alfred the Great.

900   Ghana at the height of its power in North West Africa.

907–960   Five Dynasties in China: partition.

910   Abbey of Cluny founded: monastic reforms spread from here.

911   Rolf (or Rollo) becomes ruler of Normandy.

912   Accession of Abderrahman III: the most splendid period of the Omayyad Caliphate of Cordova (d. 961).

928   Brandenburg taken from the Slavs by Henry the Fowler, first of the Saxon Holy Roman Emperors.

929   Death of Wenceslas, Christian King of Bohemia.

937   Battle of Brunanburh: crowning victory of Athelstan. West Saxon kings now masters of England.

955   Battle of Lechfeld: Magyars finally defeated by Otto the Great and settle in Hungary.

960–1279   Sung Dynasty in China.

965   Harold Bluetooth king of Denmark, accepts Christianity.

966   Mieszko I, king of Poland, accepts Christianity.

968   Fatimids begin their rule in Egypt.

982   Discovery of Greenland by Norsemen.

987   Hugh Capet king of France: founder of Capetian dynasty.

988   Vladimir of Kiev accepts Christianity.

991   Battle of Maldon: defeat of Byrhtnoth of Essex by Vikings—renewed Viking raids on England.

993   Olof Skutkonung, king of Sweden, accepts Christianity.

1000   Leif Ericsson discovers North America.

1001   Coronation of St. Stephen of Hungary with crown sent by the Pope.

1002   Massacre of St. Brice's Day: attempt by Ethelred to exterminate Danes in England.

A.D.

1014 Battle of Clontarf: victory of Irish under Brian Boru over Vikings.

1016 Canute becomes king of England; builds short-lived Danish " empire."

1018 Byzantines under Basil II complete subjection of Bulgars.

1040 Attempts to implement Truce of God from about this time.

1046 Normans under Robert Guiscard in southern Italy.

1054 Beginning of Almoravid (Moslem) conquests in West Africa.

1060 Normans invade Sicily.

1066 Norman conquest of England under William I.

1069 Reforms of Wang An-Shih in China.

THE CRUSADES

1071 Manzikert: Seljuk Turks destroy Byzantine army and overrun Anatolia.

1073 Hildebrand (Gregory VII) becomes Pope. Church discipline and Papal authority enforced.

1075 Seljuk Turks capture Jerusalem.

1076 Kumbi, capital of Ghana, sacked by Almoravids: subsequent break-up of Ghana Empire.

1084 Carthusians founded by St. Bruno at Chartreuse.

1086 Compilation of Domesday Book.

1094 El Cid takes Valencia.

1095 Council of Clermont: Urban II preaches First Crusade.

1098 Cistercians founded by St. Robert at Citeaux.

1099 First Crusade under Godfrey of Bouilton takes Jerusalem.

1100 Death of William Rufus in the New Forest. Baldwin I: Latin Kingdom of Jerusalem founded.

1106 Tinchebrai: Henry I of England acquires Normandy, captures his brother Robert.

1115 Abelard teaching at Paris. St. Bernard founds monastery at Clairvaux.

1119 Order of Knights Templars founded.

1120 Loss of the White Ship and heir to English throne.

1122 Concordat of Worms: Pope and Emperor compromise on the Investiture Controversy, but continue to quarrel over other matters (Guelfs and Ghibellines).

1135 Stephen takes English crown: civil wars with Matilda and anarchy ensue.

1143 Alfonso Henriques proclaimed first king of Portugal.

1144 Moslems take Christian stronghold of Edessa.

1148 Second Crusade fails to capture Damascus.

1150 Carmelites founded about this time by Berthold.

1152 Accession of Emperor Frederick Barbarossa.

1154 Henry of Anjou succeeds Stephen: first of Plantagenet kings of England.

1161 Explosives used in warfare in China.

1169 Strongbow invades Ireland: beginning of Anglo-Norman rule. Saladin ruling in Egypt.

1170 Murder of Thomas Becket in Canterbury cathedral.

1171 Spanish knightly Order of Santiago founded.

1176 Battle of Legnano: Frederick Barbarossa defeated by the Lombard League. Italian autonomy established.

1185 Kamakura Period in Japan: epoch of feudalism: until 1333.

1187 Hattin: destruction of Latin kingdom of Jerusalem by Saladin.

A.D.

1189 Third Crusade launched: leaders—Frederick Barbarossa, Philip Augustus of France, Richard Lionheart of England.

1191 Capture of Acre by Crusaders.

1192 End of Third Crusade without regaining Jerusalem. Richard I seized and held to ransom in Austria on return journey.

1198 Innocent III becomes Pope.

1202 Fourth Crusade, diverted by Venetians takes Zara from Byzantines.

1204 Fourth Crusade captures Constantinople, founds Latin Empire. King John of England loses Normandy to France.

1206 Temujin proclaimed Gengiz Khan (Very Mighty King) of all the Mongols: soon controls all of Central Asia.

1208 Albigensian Crusade launched: the first against Christians.

1212 Battle of Las Navas de Tolosa: decisive victory of Spaniards over Moors. The Children's Crusade.

THE CULMINATION OF THE MIDDLE AGES

1215 Fourth Lateran Council: the authority of the mediaeval Church and Papacy at its zenith. Dominicans recognised by the Pope. Magna Carta extorted by barons from John.

1223 Franciscans recognised by the Pope.

1229 Emperor Frederick II, through diplomacy, recognised by Moslems as King of Jerusalem.

1230 Teutonic Knights established in Prussia.

1237 Golden Horde (Mongols) begin subjugation of Russia.

1241 Mongol incursions into Central Europe.

1250 St. Louis of France captured on his Crusade in Egypt. Mamelukes become rulers of Egypt. Mandingo king declares his independence of Ghana and embraces Islam.

1256 Conference of Baltic ports: the first form of the Hanseatic League.

1258 Provisions of Oxford: barons under Simon de Montfort force reforms on Henry III of England. Baghdad destroyed by Mongols.

1264 Battle of Lewes: Montfort's party become rulers of England.

1265 Simon de Montfort's Parliament. Battle of Evesham: defeat and death of de Montfort.

1274 Death of Thomas Aquinas.

1279-1368 Mongol Dynasty in China (Kublai Khan).

1281 Repulse of Mongol attack on Japan.

1282 Sicilian Vespers: rising of Sicilians against French ruler.

1284 Completion of Edward I of England's conquest of Wales.

1290 Expulsion of Jews from England. Death of Maid of Norway: Edward I begins attempts to rule Scotland.

1291 Fall of Acre: end of Crusading in Holy Land. Everlasting League of Uri: beginnings of Swiss Confederation.

1294 Death of Roger Bacon, the founder of experimental science.

1295 " Model Parliament " of Edward I (anticipated in 1275).

1308 Death of Duns Scotus.

THE DECLINE OF THE MIDDLE AGES

1309 Papacy moves to Avignon: beginning of the Babylonian Captivity.

1312 Suppression of Templars by king of France and Pope.

1314 Battle of Bannockburn: victory of Robert Bruce secures Scottish independence.

1321 Death of Dante.

1325 Zenith of Mandingo Empire of Mali (North West Africa) under Mansa Musa: superseded at end of 15th century by Songhai empire.

1327 Deposition of Edward II; subsequently murdered.

A.D.
1336 Ashikaga Period in Japan: great feudal lords semi-independent of authority of Shogun.

1337 Death of Giotto.

1338 Beginning of Hundred Years' War between England and France.

1340 Battle of Sluys: English capture French fleet.

1344 Swabian League: weakness of Imperial authority in Germany obliges towns to form leagues for mutual protection.

1346 Battles of Crecy and Neville's Cross: spectacular English victories over French and Scots.

1347 Calais taken by Edward III of England. Cola di Rienzi attempts to reform government of Rome: killed 1354.

1348 Black Death reaches Europe (England 1349, Scotland 1350).

1351 Statute of Labourers: attempt by English Parliament to freeze wages.

1353 Statute of Praemunire: restraints placed on Papal intervention in England.

1354 Ottoman Turks make first settlement in Europe, at Gallipoli.

1355 Death of Stephen Dushan: collapse of Serbian Empire which he had built.

1356 Battle of Poitiers: capture of King John of France by Black Prince. " Golden Bull " regulates Imperial elections in such a way as to place power in the hands of the German princes: valid until 1806.

1358 The Jacquerie: rising of French peasants.

1360 Peace of Bretigny: Edward III makes great territorial gains in France.

1362 English becomes the official language in Parliament and the Law Courts.

1363 Timur (Tamerlane) begins his career of conquest in Asia.

1368-1644 Ming Dynasty in China.

1370 Bertrand du Guesclin Constable of France: regains much territory from the English. Peace of Stralsund: Hansa in complete control of Baltic Sea.

1377 Pope returns to Rome: End of Babylonish Captivity.

1378 Disputed Papal Election: Beginning of Great Schism.

1380 Battle of Chioggia: decisive victory of Venice over Genoa. Battle of Kulikovo: Dmitri Donskoi of Moscow wins first major Russian victory over Golden Horde.

1381 Peasants' Revolt in England under Wat Tyler.

1384 Death of John Wyclif.

1385 Battle of Aljubarotta: Portugal safeguards independence from Castile.

1386 Battle of Sempach: Swiss safeguard independence from Habsburgs. Jagiello (Vladislav V) unites Lithuania and Poland.

1389 Battle of Kossovo: crushing defeat of Serbs and neighbouring nations by Turks.

1396 Battle of Nicopolis: " the last crusade " annihilated by Turks.

1397 Union of Kalmar: Denmark, Norway and Sweden united under one crown: dissolved 1448.

1398 Timur invades and pillages Northern India.

1399 Richard II deposed by Henry IV: first of the Lancastrian kings of England.

1400 Owen Glendower revolts in Wales. Death of Chaucer.

1401 De Haeretico Comburendo: the burning of heretics made legal in England.

1410 Battle of Tannenberg: Poles and Lithuanians break power of Teutonic Knights.

1415 Battle of Agincourt: great success of Henry V of England in France. Council of Constance ends Great Schism, burns John Hus.

1420 Treaty of Troyes: English claims to French throne recognised. Hussite Wars begin: Bohemian heretics defend themselves successfully.

A.D.
1429 Relief of Orleans by Joan of Arc.

1431 Burning of Joan of Arc.

1433 Rounding of Cape Bojador: first great achievement in exploration ordered by Henry the Navigator.

1434 Cosimo dei Medici begins his family's control of Florence.

1435 Congress of Arras: Burgundians withdraw support from England, in favour of France.

1438 Albert I becomes Emperor—the first Habsburg Emperor.

1440 Death of Jan van Eyck.

1450 Rebellion of Jack Cade against government of Henry VI of England.

1453 Battle of Castillon: final English defeat and end of Hundred Years' War. Constantinople taken by Turks: end of Byzantine or Eastern Roman Empire.

RENAISSANCE, DISCOVERIES, " NEW MONARCHIES "

1454 First dated printing from movable types in Europe: Papal indulgence printed at Mainz.

1455 First battle of St. Albans: beginning of Wars of the Roses.

1458 Mathias Corvinus becomes king of Hungary. George of Podiebrad becomes king of Bohemia.

1461 Battle of Towton: Yorkist victory in a particularly bloody battle. Louis XI becomes king of France.

1467 Charles the Bold becomes Duke of Burgundy.

1469 Marriage of Ferdinand of Aragon with Isabella of Castile: union of the main kingdoms of Spain. Lorenzo the Magnificent becomes ruler of Florence.

1470 Warwick (" The Kingmaker ") turns Lancastrian, dethrones Edward IV.

1471 Return of Edward IV: Lancastrians crushed at Barnet and Tewkesbury. Ivan III of Moscow takes Novgorod: Muscovy rising to supremacy in Russia.

1476 Caxton sets up his press at Westminster.

1477 Battle of Nancy: defeat and death of Charles the Bold: end of the greatness of Burgundy.

1479 Pazzi conspiracy against the Medici in Florence.

1481 Inquisition becomes active in Castile (1484 in Aragon).

1485 Battle of Bosworth Field: beginning of Tudor period in England.

1487 Lambert Simnel's rising fails.

1488 Bartholomew Diaz rounds Cape of Good Hope.

1491 Brittany acquired by King of France (by marriage).

1492 Rodrigo Borgia becomes Pope Alexander VI. Granada, last Moorish foothold in Western Europe, conquered by Spain. Christopher Columbus discovers the West Indies.

1493 Sonni Ali brings Songhai Empire to height of its prestige: Timbuktu renowned centre of literary culture.

1494 Italy invaded by French led by Charles VIII: beginning of Italian Wars and " modern " European diplomacy and international relations. Treaty of Tordesillas: Spain and Portugal agree to divide unexplored part of world: subsequently approved by Pope.

1496 Hapsburg–Spanish marriages: foundation of later empires.

1497 Perkin Warbeck captured by Henry VII (hanged 1499). John Cabot discovers Newfoundland.

1498 Savonarola burned. Vasco da Gama at Calicut: the sea route to India found.

1499 Amerigo Vespucci charts part of the South American coast.

A.D.

1500 Brazil discovered by Pedro Cabral.

1503 Casa de Contratación established at Seville; beginnings of Spanish colonial government. Fall of Caesar Borgia.

1507 Alfonso de Albuquerque becomes Viceroy of Portuguese Empire in the East.

1513 Accession of Pope Leo X, zenith of Renaissance Papacy. Machiavelli writes *The Prince*. Balboa discovers the Pacific (South Sea). Battle of Flodden: James IV of Scotland defeated and killed by English.

1514 Battle of Chaldiran: Turkish victory begins long series of wars between Turkish and Persian Empires.

REFORMATION, HAPSBURG–VALOIS WARS

1515 Francis I becomes king of France: victory of Marignano ends legend of Swiss invincibility. Thomas Wolsey becomes Lord Chancellor of England and Cardinal.

1516 Algiers taken by Barbarossa; beginning of the Corsairs.

1517 Martin Luther nails up his Ninety-five Theses: beginning of the Reformation. Turks conquer Egypt.

1519 Charles V inherits Hapsburg lands and elected emperor. Magellan begins first circumnavigation of the world. Death of Leonardo da Vinci.

1520 Suleiman the Magnificent becomes Sultan; Turkish power at its height. Field of Cloth of Gold; celebrated diplomatic meeting, spectacular but with no results.

1521 Mexico conquered by Hernando Cortes. Belgrade taken by the Turks. Diet of Worms; Luther commits himself irrevocably. Charles V divides his dominions: Austrian and Spanish Hapsburgs.

1522 Rhodes taken by the Turks; Knights of St. John move to Malta. Election of Adrian VI, last non-Italian Pope.

1523 Swedes expel Danish overlords, elect Gustavus Vasa King.   [1525).

1524 Peasants' War in Germany (suppressed

1525 Battle of Pavia: defeat and capture of Francis I by Imperialists.

1526 Battle of Mohács: Turkish victory ends Hungarian independence. Foundation of Danubian Hapsburg Monarchy (Hungarian and Bohemian crowns united with Austrian patrimony of Hapsburgs): Holy Roman Empire prolonged for 300 years. Battle of Panipat: Babar begins Moslem conquest of India, founds Mogul Empire.

1527 Sack of Rome by Imperialists. Italy under control of Charles V.

1529 Siege of Vienna by the Turks. Peace of Cambrai; pause in Hapsburg–Valois struggle, end of serious French intervention in Italy. Diet of Speyer: origin of the name Protestant.

1532 Peru conquered by Francisco Pizarro.

1533 Ivan IV (the Terrible) becomes Tsar. Marriage of Henry VIII and Catherine of Aragon declared null.

1534 Act of Supremacy: Henry VIII asserts control over English Church.

1535 Coverdale's English Bible printed. Execution of Thomas More and John Fisher.

1536 Execution of Anne Boleyn. Dissolution of smaller Monasteries by Henry VIII and Thomas Cromwell (remainder dissolved 1539). Pilgrimage of Grace: Northern rising because of religious grievances.   [de Quesada.

1538 Chibchas of Bogota conquered by Gonzalo

1540 Francisco de Coronado begins explorations in North America. Society of Jesus recognised by Pope.

1541 John Calvin regains authority in Geneva.

1542 First Portuguese reach Japan. New Laws of the Indies: first attempt to legislate for welfare of colonial natives, by Spanish government.

1543 Death of Copernicus.   [Reformation.

1545 Opening of Council of Trent: the Counter-

A.D.

1547 Death of Henry VIII: Somerset Protector in the name of the boy king, Edward VI.

1549 First English Book of Common Prayer. Kett's Rebellion in Norfolk, because of economic grievances.

1550 Deposition of Protector Somerset: Northumberland rules England.

1553 Lady Jane Grey proclaimed Queen by Northumberland on death of Edward VI: Mary I succeeds. Servetus burned by Calvin.

1555 Latimer and Ridley burned by Mary. Religious Peace of Augsburg: policy of *cuius regio, eius religio* accepted in Germany.

1556 Charles V abdicates imperial powers in favour of brother Ferdinand. Cranmer burned. Akbar becomes Mogul Emperor (d. 1605).

1557 Macao becomes permanent Portuguese port in China.

1558 Calais lost by English to French. Elizabeth I becomes Queen of England.

1559 Peace of Cateau-Cambrésis: end of Hapsburg–Valois duel.

RELIGIOUS WARS

1561 Mary, Queen of Scots, returns to Scotland.

1562 First War of Religion in France: wars continue intermittently until 1598.

1563 Thirty-nine Articles define Elizabethan Church settlement.

1564 Birth of Shakespeare; death of Michelangelo.

1565 Malta beats off Turks.

1567 Deposition of Mary, Queen of Scots. Alva in the Netherlands: severe rule.

1568 Flight of Mary, Queen of Scots, to England: imprisonment. San Juan de Ulua: defeat of Hawkins, and end of his slave-trading voyages. Beginning of Anglo-Spanish maritime feud. Revolt of Moriscos of Granada (suppressed 1570).   [England.

1569 Rebellion of Northern Earls (Catholic) in

1570 Elizabeth I anathematised by Pope.

1571 Battle of Lepanto: spectacular defeat of Turkish sea-power by Don John of Austria. Bornu (or Kanem) in Central Sudan at its zenith under Idris III.

1572 Dutch "Sea Beggars" take Brill. Massacre of St. Bartholomew in France. Polish Crown elective again, on death of Sigismund II.

1576 Catholic League formed in France, led by Guise family.   [1580).

1577 Drake begins voyage round world (returns

1578 Battle of Alcazar-Quivir: death of King Sebastian of Portugal. Parma re-establishes Spanish rule in Southern Netherlands.

1579 Union of Utrecht: seven northern provinces of Netherlands form what becomes Dutch Republic. Death of Grand Vizier Sokolli: decline of Turkish power begins.

1580 Philip II of Spain becomes king of Portugal.

1582 Gregorian Calendar (or New Style) introduced by Pope Gregory XIII.

1584 Assassination of William the Silent.

1585 Hidéyoshi Dictator of Japan: unification of the country. English intervention in Spanish–Dutch War.

1587 Execution of Mary, Queen of Scots. Drake " singes King of Spain's beard." Shah Abbas I (the Great) becomes ruler of Persia (d. 1629).

1588 Spanish Armada defeated.

1589 Death of Catherine de' Medici, Queen-Mother of France.

1591 Songhai Empire destroyed by troops from Morocco.

1593 Henry IV of France becomes Catholic.

1598 Edict of Nantes: French Protestants guaranteed liberty of worship. End of French Wars of Religion.

1600 English East India Company founded. Tokugawa Period begins in Japan (Ieyasu takes title of Shogun, 1603): lasts until 1868.

A.D.

1601 Rebellion and execution of Earl of Essex. Elizabethan Poor Law.

1602 Dutch East India Company founded.

1603 Irish revolts finally suppressed by Mountjoy. Accession of James VI of Scotland as James I of England: Union of English and Scottish Crowns.

1604 Hampton Court Conference: James I disappoints Puritans.

1605 Gunpowder Plot.

1607 Virginia colonised by London company: Jamestown founded.

1608 Quebec founded by Champlain.

1609 Twelve Years' Truce between Spain and United Provinces: Dutch independence in fact secured. Expulsion of Moriscos from Spain.

1610 Assassination of Henry IV of France.

1611 Plantation of Ulster with English and Scottish colonists. Authorised Version of the Bible in England.

1613 Michael Romanov becomes Czar: the first of the dynasty.

1614 Napier publishes his explanation of logarithms.

1616 Death of Shakespeare and Cervantes. Edict of Inquisition against Galileo's astronomy.

1618 " Defenestration of Prague ": Bohemian assertion of independence begins Thirty Years' War.

1620 Pilgrim Fathers settle in New England.

1624 " Massacre at Amboina ": English driven out of spice islands by Dutch. Richelieu becomes Chief Minister in France.

1628 Murder of Duke of Buckingham. Petition of Right by Commons to Charles I. Fall of La Rochelle: French Protestants lose political power. Harvey publishes his work on the circulation of blood.

1629 Charles I begins Personal Rule.

1630 Gustavus Adolphus of Sweden enters Thirty Years' War, turns tide against Imperialists.

1631 Sack of Magdeburg, one of the worst incidents of the Thirty Years' War.

1632 Battle of Lützen: death of Gustavus Adolphus.

1633 William Laud appointed Archbishop of Canterbury. Thomas Wentworth takes up his post as Lord Deputy of Ireland.

1634 Dismissal and murder of Imperialist general Wallenstein.

1635 John Hampden refuses to pay Ship Money.

1636 Japanese forbidden to go abroad.

1637 Russian pioneers reach shores of Pacific.

1638 Covenant widely signed in Scotland.

1639 First Bishops' War: Charles I comes to terms with Scots.

1640 Second Bishops' War: Charles I defeated by Scots. Long Parliament begins: abolition of Royal prerogatives. Great Elector (Frederick William) becomes ruler of Brandenburg. Revolt of Catalonia (finally suppressed 1659). Revolt of Portugal: Duke of Braganza proclaimed king.

1641 Japanese exclude all foreigners (except for small Dutch trading fleet). Massacre of Protestants in Ireland. Wentworth (Earl of Strafford) executed. Grand Remonstrance of Commons to Charles I.

1642 Charles I attempts to arrest the Five Members. Outbreak of English Civil War: first general engagement, Edgehill. Death of Richelieu.

1643 Mazarin becomes Chief Minister of France. Battle of Rocroi: French victory, end of Spanish reputation for invincibility. English Parliament agrees to Solemn League and Covenant, secures services of Scots army.

1644 Marston Moor: decisive battle of English Civil War. North lost to Charles I. Tippemuir: Montrose begins victorious Royalist

A.D.

campaign in Scotland. 1644-1911 Manchu Dynasty in China.

1645 Formation of New Model Army. Naseby: main Royalist army crushed. Battle of Philiphaugh: Montrose's army destroyed.

1646 Charles I surrenders to Scots.

1647 Charles I handed over to Parliament. Charles I seized by Army. Charles I flees to Carisbrooke Castle.

1648 Second Civil War: New Model Army defeats Scots and Royalists. " Pride's Purge ": Parliament refashioned by Army. Peace of Westphalia ends Thirty Years' War.

ASCENDANCY OF FRANCE

1649 Charles I executed. England governed as Commonwealth. Cromwell in Ireland. New Code of Laws in Russia completes establishment of serfdom.

1651 Battle of Worcester: Cromwell's final victory, now master of all Britain. First English Navigation Act. Hobbes' *Leviathan* published.

1652 Foundation of Cape Colony by Dutch under Van Riebeek. First Anglo-Dutch War begins (ends 1654).

1653 Cromwell dissolves Rump, becomes Protector.

1655 Major-Generals appointed to supervise districts of England. Jamaica seized by English.

1656 Grand Vizier Kiuprili: revival of Turkish government.

1658 Death of Cromwell.

1659 Peace of the Pyrenees: France replaces Spain as greatest power in Western Europe.

1660 Restoration of monarchy in Britain: Charles II. Royal Society founded.

1661 Death of Mazarin: Louis XIV now rules in person. " Clarendon Code ": beginning of persecution of Non-conformists in England.

1664 New York taken by English: Second Anglo-Dutch War ensues (ends 1667).

1665 Great Plague of London.

1666 Great Fire of London. Newton's discovery of law of gravitation.

1667 Dutch fleet in the Medway. War of Devolution begins: first of Louis XIV's aggressions.

1668 Portuguese Independence recognised by Spain.

1669 Death of Rembrandt.

1670 Secret Treaty of Dover between Charles II and Louis XIV. Revolt of peasants and Don Cossacks under Stenka Razin (suppressed 1671).

1672 Third Anglo-Dutch War begins (ends 1674). Murder of De Witt brothers: William of Orange becomes leader of Dutch against French invasion.

1673 Test Act deprives English Catholics and Non-conformists of public offices. Death of Molière.

1675 Battle of Fehrbellin: Swedes defeated by Great Elector; rise of Prussian military power. Greenwich Royal Observatory founded.

1678 " Popish Plot " of Titus Oates utilised by Shaftesbury and the Whigs to bring pressure on Charles II.

1679 Bothwell Brig: suppression of Scottish Covenanters. Habeas Corpus Act passed.

1680 Chambers of Reunion: Louis XIV uses legal arguments to complete annexation of Alsace.

1681 Oxford Parliament: Charles II overcomes his opponents, begins to rule without Parliament.

1683 Rye House Plot. Siege of Vienna by the Turks: last major Turkish attack on Europe.

1685 Sedgemoor: Monmouth's rebellion crushed by James II. Revocation of Edict of Nantes: persecution of French Protestants by Louis XIV.

A.D.
1688 Seven Bishops protest against James II's policy of toleration, and are acquitted. William of Orange lands in England: flight of James II. "The Glorious Revolution."

1689 Derry relieved: failure of James II to subdue Irish Protestants. Killiecrankie: death of Dundee and collapse of Highland rising. Bill of Rights defines liberties established by "Glorious Revolution."

1690 Locke's *Two Treatises on Government* published. Beachy Head: French victory over Anglo-Dutch fleet. Boyne: defeat of James II by William III.

1691 Capitulation of Limerick: surrender of Irish supporters of James II on conditions which are not fulfilled.

1692 Massacre of Glencoe: Government's "lesson" to Highlanders. La Hogue: Anglo-Dutch fleet regains command of the sea.

1693 National Debt of England begun.

1694 Bank of England founded.

1695 Press licensing abandoned: freedom of the press in England.

1696 Peter the Great sole Czar.

1697 Peace of Ryswyck between Louis XIV and William III. Peter journeys "incognito" to the West.

1699 Treaty of Karlowitz: great Turkish concessions to Austrians. Death of Racine.

1700 Great Northern War, involving all Baltic powers, begins (ends 1721). Battle of Narva: Russians defeated by Charles XII of Sweden. Death of Charles II of Spain: under French influence Louis XIV's grandson Philip of Anjou named successor.

1701 War of the Spanish Succession begins. Hungarian revolt led by Francis Rakoczi against Austrians. Elector of Brandenburg receives title of King of Prussia. Act of Settlement establishes Protestant Hanoverian Succession in England.

1703 Methuen Treaty between England and Portugal. St. Petersburg founded.

1704 Gibraltar taken by Rooke. Blenheim: Marlborough stops France from winning war.

1706 Ramillies: Marlborough's second great victory. Turin: Eugene defeats French in Italy.

1707 Almanza: Anglo-Austrian forces in Spain defeated by French under Berwick. Act of Union: English and Scottish Parliaments united. Death of Aurungzib, last powerful Mogul.

1708 Oudenarde: Marlborough's third great victory.

1709 Pultava: Charles XII's invasion of Russia smashed by Peter the Great. Malplaquet: Marlborough's fourth great victory—at great cost in lives.

1710 Tory government in England.

1711 Dismissal of Marlborough.

1713 Peace of Utrecht: England makes advantageous peace with Louis XIV. Bourbon king of Spain grants Asiento (monopoly of Spanish American slave trade) to England.

1714 Peace of Rastatt between France and Austria. Death of Queen Anne: accession of George I. Beginning of Hanoverian Dynasty in Britain. Whig oligarchy rules.

1715 Jacobite Rising defeated at Preston and Sheriffmuir. Death of Louis XIV. France under Regent Orleans.

ENLIGHTENED DESPOTS: FIRST BRITISH EMPIRE

1716 Septennial Act: English Parliament prolongs its life from three to seven years. Prince Eugène of Savoy defeated Turks at Petrovaradin (Yugoslavia).

1720 Collapse of Law's system of banking ("Mississippi Bubble") in France. "South Sea Bubble" in England.

A.D.
1721 Robert Walpole becomes first Prime Minister. Peace of Nystad: Sweden no longer a major power at end of Great Northern War. Russian gains.

1723 Death of Christopher Wren.

1727 First Indemnity Act for Non-conformists.

1729 Methodists begin at Oxford.

1730 Resignation from government of Townshend, who becomes agricultural pioneer.

1733 First Family Compact between Bourbon kings of France and Spain. Withdrawal of Walpole's Excise Bill. John Kay invents flying shuttle, first of the great textile inventions. Jethro Tull publishes *The Horse-Hoing Husbandry*, advocating new agricultural methods.

1738 Lorraine ceded to France.

1739 Nadir Shah with Persian army sacks Delhi, ruins Mogul power. War of Jenkins' Ear begins between Spain and Britain.

1740 Frederick II (the Great) becomes king of Prussia. Maria Theresa succeeds to Austrian dominions. Frederick seizes Silesia, begins War of the Austrian Succession.

1742 Fall of Walpole.

1743 Dettingen: George II, last British king to command his army in the field, defeats French.

1745 Fontenoy: Duke of Cumberland defeated by Marshal Saxe. Jacobite Rebellion under Prince Charles Edward: initial success, victory of Prestonpans, march to Derby.

1746 Culloden: Jacobites destroyed by Cumberland.

1748 Treaty of Aix-la-Chapelle: Frederick retains Silesia, elsewhere status quo.

1750 Death of J. S. Bach.

1751 First volume of the *Encyclopédie* published in France. Clive takes and holds Arcot: checks plans of Dupleix in Southern India. Chinese conquest of Tibet.

1752 Britain adopts New Style calendar.

1753 British Museum begun by government purchase of Sloane's collection.

1755 Lisbon earthquake. Braddock's defeat and death at the hands of French and Indians.

1756 Diplomatic Revolution (alliance of Austria with France) achieved by Kaunitz; Britain and Prussia perforce became allies. Seven Years' War begins. Minorca taken from British by French (Byng executed 1757). Black Hole of Calcutta: suffocation of many British prisoners.

1757 Pitt Secretary of State, main influence in British government. Rossbach: one of Frederick II's numerous victories against heavy odds. Plassey: Clive conquers Bengal.

1759 "Year of Victories" for Britain: Quebec, Minden, Lagos, Quiberon Bay. James Brindley designs Worsley–Manchester Canal: the beginning of this form of transport in Britain. Voltaire publishes *Candide*. Death of Handel.

1760 Wandewash: decisive defeat of French in India, by Coote.

1761 Panipat: Mahrattas heavily defeated by Afghans. Fall of Pitt.

1762 Catherine II (the Great) becomes Czarina. Rousseau's *Social Contract* and *Emile* published.

1763 Peace of Paris: British colonial gains, First British Empire at its height. Peace of Hubertusburg: Frederick II retains his gains. Pontiac's Conspiracy: failure of Red Indian attempt to destroy British power.

1764 John Wilkes expelled from Commons. James Hargreaves invents spinning jenny.

1766 Henry Cavendish proves hydrogen to be an element.

1768 Royal Academy of Arts founded.

1769 Richard Arkwright erects spinning mill (invention of water frame).

1770 Struensee comes to power in Denmark (executed 1772). "Boston Massacre." James Cook discovers New South Wales.

1772 First Partition of Poland between Russia, Prussia, and Austria.

A.D.

1773 Society of Jesus suppressed by Pope (restored 1814). Revolt led by Pugachov in Russia (suppressed 1775). "Boston Tea Party."

1774 Warren Hastings appointed first Governor-General of India. Treaty of Kutchuk Kainarji: great Turkish concessions to Russia. Karl Scheele discovers chlorine. Joseph Priestley's discovery of oxygen.

1775 Watt and Boulton in partnership at Soho Engineering Works, Birmingham. Lexington: first action in American War of Independence.

1776 American Declaration of Independence. Adam Smith's *Wealth of Nations* published.

1777 Saratoga: surrender of British army under Burgoyne to Americans.

1779 Beginning of great Franco-Spanish siege of Gibraltar (raised finally, 1783). Samuel Crompton invents spinning mule.

1780 Joseph II assumes sole power in Austria. Armed neutrality of maritime nations to restrain British interference with shipping.

1781 Joseph II introduces religious toleration, abolishes serfdom in Austria. Yorktown: surrender of British under Cornwallis to American and French forces.

1782 Battle of the Saints: Rodney's victory saves British West Indies.

1783 Treaty of Versailles: American independence recognised. Pitt the Younger becomes Prime Minister of Britain. First flights in hot-air (Montgolfier) and hydrogen (Charles) balloons.

1784 Death of Dr. Samuel Johnson.

1785 Edmund Cartwright invents the power loom.

1787 American Constitution drafted.

1788 Impeachment of Warren Hastings begins (ends 1795).

FRENCH REVOLUTION AND NAPOLEON

1789 Washington first President of U.S.A. French Revolution begins. Storming of the Bastille (July 14).

1790 Civil constitution of the Clergy in France.

1791 Flight of Louis XVI and Marie Antoinette to Varennes.

1792 Battle of Valmy: French Revolution saved from intervention of European kings. Denmark becomes first country to prohibit slave trade. France becomes a Republic.

1793 Louis XVI beheaded. Second partition of Poland.

1794 "Glorious First of June." Fall of Robespierre and end of Jacobin Republic. Negro revolt in Haiti led by Toussaint L'Ouverture.

1795 The Directory established. "Whiff of Grapeshot": Napoleon Bonaparte disperses Paris mob, Oct. 5. Batavian Republic set up by France.

1796 First Italian campaign of Bonaparte: victories of Lodi, Arcola.

1797 Treaty of Campo Formio: Bonaparte compels Austria to make peace. Britain left to fight France alone.

1798 Bonaparte goes to Egypt. Battle of the Nile. Vinegar Hill rebellion in Ireland suppressed.

1799 New coalition against France: Suvorov and Russians victorious in Italy. Bonaparte returns to France. *Coup d'état* of Brumaire, Nov. 9. Consulate set up.

1800 Parliamentary Union of Great Britain and Ireland.

1801 Treaty of Lunéville: Austria makes peace; great French gains in Germany.

1802 Peace of Amiens between Britain and France. *Charlotte Dundas*, first practical steamship, on Clyde.

1803 Insurrection in Ireland under Robert Emmet. Britain again at war with France.

A.D.

1804 Bonaparte becomes Emperor. Spain declares war against Great Britain. Serbian revolt against Turks under Kara George.

1805 Battle of Trafalgar, Nelson's great victory and death, Oct. 21. Battle of Austerlitz, Dec. 2.

1806 Death of Pitt, Jan. 23. Confederation of the Rhine: Napoleon's reorganisation of Germany, July 12. End of Holy Roman Empire, Aug. 6. Prussia overthrown at Jena. Napoleon declares Great Britain in a state of blockade—" Continental System."

1807 Slave trade abolished in British Empire. Treaty of Tilsit: with Alexander of Russia his friend, Napoleon controls all of Europe. Occupation of Portugal by French, to enforce Continental Blockade.

1808 Occupation of Spain by French. Spanish rising: guerrilla warfare. Peninsular War begins. Battle of Vimeiro (defeat of French by Wellington), Aug. 21.

1809 Battle of Corunna and death of Sir John Moore, Jan. 16. Attempted risings in Germany against Napoleon: Austria renews war. Treaty of Schönbrunn, Oct. 14.

1810 Self-government established in Argentina: first South American state to become independent of Spain.

1811 Massacre of Mamelukes at Cairo. Luddite riots.

1812 Retreat from Moscow: destruction of Napoleon's Grand Army.

1813 War of Liberation starts in Germany. Defeat of French by Wellington at Vitoria, June 21.

1814 Soult defeated by Wellington at Toulouse, April 10. Abdication of Napoleon, April 11; Louis XVIII king of France. Congress of Vienna (concluded June 1815) under guidance of Metternich. Resettlement of Europe, usually by restoration of kings. Germanic Confederation under Austrian supervision. Poland ruled by Czar. Kingdom of Netherlands to include Belgium.

THE OLD ORDER RESTORED

1815 Escape of Napoleon from Elba. Battle of Waterloo, June 18. Corn Law in Britain to safeguard agricultural interests by keeping up prices. Quadruple Alliance (Austria, Russia, Prussia, Britain) to maintain Vienna settlement and hold regular meetings (" Congress System ")—frequently confused with Holy Alliance, which was simply a declaration of Christian principles. Napoleon sent to St. Helena, Oct. 16.

1818 Bernadotte made king of Sweden (Charles XIV), Feb. 6.

1819 Singapore founded by Stamford Raffles. Beginnings of Zollverein (Customs Union) in Germany under Prussian influence. Parliamentary reform meeting at Manchester dispersed by military (" Peterloo "), Aug. 16.

1820 Death of George III, Jan. 29.

1821 Death of Napoleon at St. Helena, May 5.

1822 Congress of Verona: congress system breaks down with refusal of Britain (Canning) to intervene against revolutions.

1823 " Monroe Doctrine " announced by U.S.A. President, Dec. 2.

1824 Repeal of Combination Acts in Britain which had forbidden Trades Unions. Charles X king of France.

1825 Independence of all Spanish American mainland now achieved. Nicholas I Czar of Russia. First railway, Stockton to Darlington, opened.

1826 First crossing of Atlantic under steam by Dutch ship *Curaçao*. Menai suspension bridge opened.

1827 Battle of Navarino, Turkish and Egyptian fleet destroyed. Death of Beethoven.

1828 Death of Chaka, great Zulu conqueror.

1829 Greece independent. Catholic Emancipation Act in Britain. Metropolitan Police established.

A.D.

1830 Death of George IV, June 26. Louis Philippe ousts Charles X. Belgium breaks away from Holland. Russian Poland revolts ineffectually.

1831 First Reform Bill introduced by Lord John Russell. Leopold of Saxe-Coburg becomes king of independent Belgium. British Association founded. Faraday discovers electromagnetic induction.

1832 Reform Bill passed, June 7. Walter Scott, Jeremy Bentham, and Goethe die. Electric telegraph invented by Morse.

1833 Beginning of "Oxford Movement" in English Church. First government grant made to English schools. First British Factory Act.

1834 Poor Law Amendment Act: tightening up of relief in Britain. "Tolpuddle Martyrs" victimised to discourage British working-class movement. Carlist wars begin in Spain.

1835 Municipal Reform Act revises British local government. The word "socialism" first used. "Tamworth Manifesto" of Peel defines aims of Conservative Party.

1836 People's Charter states programme of Chartists. Great Trek of Boers from British South African territory. Texas achieves independence of Mexico.

1837 Queen Victoria succeeds to the throne.

1838 National Gallery opened.

1839 First Afghan war begins. Chartist riots at Birmingham and Newport. Anti-Corn Law League founded. Aden annexed by Britain.

1840 Penny postage instituted. Queen Victoria marries Prince Albert of Saxe-Coburg-Gotha. "Opium War" with China begins. Union Act gives Canada responsible government. Last convicts landed in New South Wales.

1841 Hong Kong acquired by Britain.

1842 Chartists present second national petition and put themselves at the head of strikes.

1846 Repeal of the Corn Laws. Peel resigns.

1847 British Museum opened.

REVOLUTIONS AND NEW NATIONS

1848 Monster meeting of Chartists on Kennington Common, procession abandoned, Apr. 10. General revolutionary movement throughout the Continent. Louis Philippe abdicates: French Republic proclaimed. Swiss Federal Constitution established after defeat of Sonderbund (Catholic secession movement). Rising in Vienna: flight of Metternich, accession of Francis Joseph. Nationalist risings in Bohemia and Hungary. Frankfurt Parliament: attempt to unite Germany on liberal principles. Communist Manifesto produced by Marx and Engels. U.S.A. makes great territorial gains from Mexico. Gold discovered in California.

1849 Collapse of revolutionary movements. Rome republic besieged by French (June 3), defended by Garibaldi, holds out until July 2. Austrians take Venice, Aug. 22. Repeal of old Navigation Laws. Punjab annexed by Britain.

1850 Cavour becomes Prime Minister of Piedmont. Don Pacifico affair: privileges of British citizenship at their highest defended by Palmerston.

1851 Great Exhibition in Hyde Park. First satisfactory submarine telegraph cable between Dover and Calais laid. Gold discovered in Australia.

1852 Independence of Transvaal recognised by Britain. Napoleon III Emperor of the French.

1853 Perry lands in Japan: beginning of Western influence. Russia and Turkey at war.

1854 War declared against Russia by France and Britain. Allied armies land in Crimea, Sept. 14 (Alma, Siege of Sevastopol, Balaklava, Inkerman). Orange Free State set up.

1855 Sardinia joins Britain and France against Russia. Fall of Sevastopol and end of Crimean War. Alexander II Czar of Russia.

A.D.

1856 Peace Treaty signed at Paris. Bessemer invents process for large-scale production of steel. Livingstone completes journey across Africa.

1857 Indian Mutiny. Relief of Lucknow. Canton captured by English and French.

1858 *Great Eastern* launched. Crown assumes government of India. Treaty of Aigun, by which China cedes Amur region to Russia.

1859 Darwin publishes *Origin of Species*. French support for Piedmont in war with Austria (Magenta, Solferino). Piedmont receives Lombardy. Harper's Ferry raid: John Brown hanged, Dec. 2.

1860 Garibaldi and the Thousand Redshirts in Sicily and Naples: most of Italy united to Piedmont. Vladivostok founded; Russia strongly established on N.W. Pacific.

1861 Abraham Lincoln takes office as Pres. of U.S. American Civil War commences with 11 states breaking away to form Southern Confederacy. Bull Run (July 21) Confederate success ends Federal hopes of easy victory. Victor Emmanuel proclaimed by first Italian Parliament as king of Italy. Emancipation of Serfs in Russia. Death of Prince Albert, Dec. 14.

1862 Bismarck becomes leading minister in Prussia. Garibaldi attempts to seize Rome but wounded at Aspromonte, Aug. 29. Cotton famine in Lancashire.

1863 Polish rising against Russia (suppressed 1864). French in Mexico. Battle of Gettysburg, July 1–3. Maximilian of Austria made emperor of Mexico.

1864 Cession of Schleswig-Holstein to Prussia and Austria. First Socialist International formed. Taiping rebellion in China ended. Federal army enters Atlanta, Sept. 2: General Sherman captures Savannah (" From Atlanta to the sea "), Dec. 22. Geneva Convention originated.

1865 Death of Cobden, Apr. 2. General Lee surrenders to Grant, Apr. 9. Lincoln assassinated, Apr. 14. Thirteenth Amendment to Constitution: slavery abolished in U.S. Death of Palmerston, Oct. 18. Lister introduces antiseptic surgery in Glasgow. Tashkent becomes centre of Russian expansion in Central Asia. Mendel experiments on heredity. William Booth founds Salvation Army.

1866 Austro-Prussian War over Schleswig-Holstein (" Seven Weeks War "). Prussian victory at Sadowa (July 3). Venice secured for Italy, who had, however, been defeated by Austrians at Custozza (June 24) and Lissa (July 20). Treaty of Prague, Aug. 23.

1867 North German Confederation founded. Emperor Maximilian of Mexico shot. Dominion of Canada established. Russia sells Alaska to America for $7 million. Garibaldi makes second attempt to seize Rome, but defeated by Pope with French support at Mentana, Nov. 3. Second Parliamentary Reform Bill passed (Disraeli " dished the Whigs ").

1868 Shogunate abolished in Japan: Meiji period of rapid Westernisation under Imperial leadership begins. Ten Years' War (1868–78); struggle for Cuban independence from Spain. Disraeli succeeds Derby as Prime Minister but defeated in general election by Gladstone, Nov.

1869 General Grant, Pres. of U.S. Irish Church disestablished. Suez Canal formally opened.

1870 Napoleon III declares war against Prussia, French defeated at Woerth, Gravelotte, and Sedan. Paris besieged. Rome and Papal states annexed to kingdom of Italy. Irish Land Act passed. Forster's Education Act puts elementary education within reach of all British children. Papal Infallibility announced.

1871 William I of Prussia proclaimed emperor of Germany at Versailles, Jan. 18. Paris capitulates, Jan. 28. Commune of Paris proclaimed, Mar. 28. Peace signed at Frankfurt-on-Main, May 10. Government troops enter Paris and

A.D.

crush Communards, May 28. Thiers President of the Republic, Aug. 31. Mont Cenis tunnel opened. Trade Unions in Britain legalised.

RIVAL IMPERIAL POWERS

1872   Secret ballot introduced in Britain. Death of Mazzini, Mar. 10.

1873   Death of Livingstone, May 4. Ashanti war.

1874   Disraeli succeeds Gladstone as Prime Minister.

1875   England purchases Khedive's shares in Suez Canal, Nov.

1876   Bulgarian massacres. Serbo-Turkish war. Bell invents the telephone. Custer defeated and killed in last large-scale Red Indian success. Porfirio Diaz in power in Mexico (until 1911).

1877   Victoria declared Empress of India. Transvaal annexed to British Empire. War between Russia and Turkey. Satsuma rebellion in Japan: final unsuccessful attempt to halt new ideas.

1878   Congress of Berlin: general Balkan settlement. Cyprus ceded to Britain. Second war with Afghanistan (ended 1880). Edison and Swan produce first successful incandescent electric light.

1879   Dual control (Britain and France) in Egypt. Zulu War. Gladstone's Midlothian Campaign. Tay Bridge destroyed, Dec. 28.

1880   Beaconsfield ministry succeeded by second Gladstone ministry. Transvaal declared a republic.

1881   British defeat at Majuba: independence of Transvaal recognised. France occupies Tunis. Gambetta becomes Prime Minister of France. Revolt of the Mahdi in the Sudan. Pasteur's famous immunisation experiment to show that inoculated animals can survive anthrax.

1882   Lord Frederick Cavendish, Irish Secretary, assassinated in Phoenix Park, Dublin, May 6. Triple Alliance (Germany, Austria, Italy) first formed. Alexandria bombarded, July 11. Cairo occupied by British troops, Sept. 14.

1883   National Insurance begun in Germany. Death of Wagner.

1884   Wolseley heads expedition to Khartoum to rescue Gordon. French establish complete protectorate in Indo-China. Evelyn Baring takes over administration of Egypt. Russians capture Merv. Berlin Conference defines rights of European Powers in Africa. Third Parliamentary Reform Bill. Parsons invents his turbine. Greenwich meridian internationally recognised as prime meridian. Fabian Society founded.

1885   Khartoum captured; Gordon slain, Jan. 26.

1886   Upper Burma annexed by Britain. Home Rule Bill defeated in Commons. All Indians in U.S.A. now in Reservations. Daimler produces his first motor car. Completion of Canadian Pacific Railway. Gold discovered in the Transvaal.

1887   Queen Victoria's Jubilee celebration, June 21.

1888   William II German Emperor. County Councils set up in Britain.

1889   Mayerling: tragic death of Prince Rudolf of Austria, Jan. 30. Flight of General Boulanger, after attempting to become master of France. Second Socialist International set up. Great London dock strike, Aug. 15–Sept. 16. Parnell Commission concludes sittings, Nov. 23 (129th day).

1890   Parnell ruined by divorce case: Irish politicians split. Sherman Anti-Trust Law: first attempt in U.S.A. to break cartels. Opening of Forth Bridge, Mar. 4. Bismarck resigns, Mar. 17. Caprivi succeeds. Heligoland ceded to Germany.

1891   The United States of Brazil formed.

1892   Panama Canal financial scandals in France.

1893   Home Rule Bill passes third reading in Commons, Sept. 1: Lords reject Bill, Sept. 8.

1894   Opening of Manchester Ship Canal, Jan. 1.

A.D.

Gladstone resigns, Mar. 3, Lord Rosebery succeeds. Armenian massacres by Turks: repeated at intervals for next quarter of century. Japan declares war against China. Dreyfus convicted of treason.

1895   Opening of Kiel canal, June 21. Rosebery resigns, June 22; Salisbury Ministry succeeds. Treaty of Shimonoseki: Japan gets Formosa, free hand in Korea. New Cuban revolution breaks out against Spanish. Marconi sends message over a mile by wireless. Röntgen discovers X-rays. Freud publishes his first work on psycho-analysis. Jameson Raid, Dec. 29.

1896   Jameson raiders defeated by Boers, Jan. 1. Adowa: Italian disaster at hands of Abyssinians, the first major defeat of a white colonising power by "natives." Gold discovered in the Klondike.

1897   Cretan revolt leads to Greek–Turkish War. Hawaii annexed by U.S.A. Queen Victoria's Diamond Jubilee, June 22. Great Gold Rush began.

1898   Port Arthur ceded to Russia. Spanish–American War. Maine, U.S. warship blown up in Havana harbour. Treaty of Paris, Dec. 10: Cuba freed, Puerto Rico and Guam ceded to U.S.A., Philippines surrendered for $20 million. Death of Gladstone, May 19. Battle of Omdurman, decisive defeat of Mahdists, Sept .2. Empress of Austria assassinated, Sept. 10. The Curies discover Radium.

1899   Boer War begins, Oct. 10.

1900   Boers attack Ladysmith, Jan. 6. Battle of Spion Kop, Buller repulsed with severe losses, Jan. 24. Relief of Kimberley, Feb. 15. Ladysmith relieved, Feb. 28. Mafeking relieved May 17. Boxer outbreak in China, May. Annexation of Orange Free State, May 26. Roberts occupies Johannesburg, May 31. "Khaki Election." Annexation of the Transvaal, Oct. 25. Australian Commonwealth proclaimed, Dec. 30.

1901   Queen Victoria dies, Jan. 22. Trans-Siberian Railway opened for single-track traffic.

1902   Anglo-Japanese Alliance, Jan. 30. Death of Cecil Rhodes, Mar. 26. Treaty of Vereeniging ends Boer War, May 31.

1903   Congo scandal: celebrated case of misrule and exploitation. Royal family of Serbia assassinated, May 29. First controlled flight in heavier-than-air machine—Orville and Wilbur Wright at Kitty Hawk, U.S.A., Dec. 17.

1904   Russo-Japanese War begins, Feb. 8. Japanese victory at Yalu River, May 1. British forces under Younghusband reach Lhasa, Aug. 3. Treaty with Tibet signed at Lhasa, Sept. 7.

1905   Port Arthur falls to Japanese, Jan. 3. "Bloody Sunday" massacre at St. Petersburg, Jan. 22. Destruction of Russian fleet under Rozhdestvenski at Tsushima by Admiral Togo (May). Treaty of Portsmouth (U.S.A.) ends Russo-Japanese war. Separation of Church and State in France. Norway separates itself from Sweden.

1906   General strike in Russia. San Francisco destroyed by earthquake and fire, Apr. 18. Simplon tunnel opened for railway traffic, June 1. First Duma (Parliament with limited powers) in Russia. Liberal "landslide" majority in Britain: Labour M.P.s appear. Movement for Women's Suffrage becomes active in Britain. Algeciras Conference: Franco-German crisis resolved in favour of France. Death of Ibsen. Vitamins discovered by F. G. Hopkins.

1907   New Zealand becomes a dominion.

1908   Annexation of Congo by Belgium. Young Turk revolution. Annexation of Bosnia and Herzegovina by Austria: severe rebuff for Russia. Asquith becomes Prime Minister of Britain.

1909   Old Age Pensions in Britain. Peary reaches North Pole. Blériot makes first cross-Channel flight. House of Lords rejects Lloyd George's budget. Union of South Africa formed. Henry Ford concentrates on producing Model T chassis: beginnings of cheap motors.

A.D.

1910 Accession of George V on death of Edward VII, May 6. Liberals win two General Elections. Labour Exchanges established in Britain. Death of Tolstoy and Florence Nightingale.

1911 Parliament Act: power of Lords decisively reduced. British M.P.s paid for first time. National Insurance in Britain. Great British rail strike. Tripoli taken from Turkey by Italy. Chinese Revolution. Amundsen reaches South Pole, Dec. 14.

1912 China becomes a Republic under Sun Yat Sen. *Titanic* disaster off Cape Race, Apr. 14–15. Great British coal strike. Scott's last expedition. Outbreak of Balkan Wars.

1913 Treaty of Bucharest: most of Turkey-in-Europe divided among Balkan states.

FIRST WORLD WAR

1914 Archduke Francis Ferdinand, heir to the Hapsburg thrones, assassinated at Sarajevo, June 28. Austria–Hungary declares war against Serbia, July 28. Germany declares war against Russia, Aug. 1. Germany declares war against France, Aug. 3. German invasion of Belgium: Great Britain declares war against Germany, Aug. 4. Great Britain declares war on Austria–Hungary, Aug. 12. British Expeditionary Force concentrated before Mauberge, Aug. 20. Battle of Mons; Japan declared war on Germany, Aug. 23. Battle of the Marne, Sept. 5–9. Trench warfare began on Aisne salient, Sept. 16. Three British cruisers (*Aboukir*, *Hogue*, and *Cressy*) sunk by one U-boat, Sept. 22. First Battle of Ypres, Oct. 12–Nov. 11. Raiding of German cruiser *Emden* until destroyed, Nov. 9. Battle of Coronel: German cruisers *Scharnhorst* and *Gneisenau* sink British cruisers *Good Hope* and *Monmouth*, Nov. 1. Great Britain declares war against Turkey, Nov. 5. Destruction of German squadron off Falkland Is., Dec. 8. British protectorate over Egypt proclaimed, Dec. 17. First Zeppelin appeared over British coast, Dec. 29.

1915 Turkish army defeated in Caucasus, Jan 5. Great Britain declared blockade of Germany, Mar. 1. Battle of Neuve Chapelle, Mar. 10–13. Naval attack on Dardanelles called off, Mar. 22. First landing of British, Australian, New Zealand troops on Gallipoli Peninsula, Apr. 25. Second Battle of Ypres, Apr. 22–May 25: Germans first used gas. Sinking of *Lusitania*, May 7. Battle of Aubers Ridge, May 9–25. Italy declares war on Austria, May 22. British Coalition Government formed, May 26. Italian army crosses Isonzo, June 2. Zeppelin destroyed by R. A. J. Warneford, June 7. Second landing of Allied troops at Suvla Bay. Italy declares war on Turkey, Aug. 20. Turks defeated at Kut-el-Amara, Sept 28. Serbia conquered by Austria and Bulgaria, Nov. 28. French and British troops occupy Salonika, Dec. 13. British troops withdraw from Anzac and Suvla, Dec. 20.

1916 Evacuation of Gallipoli completed, Jan 8. Opening of Battle of Verdun, Feb. 21. Sinn Fein rising in Ireland, Apr. 24. First Daylight Saving Bill passed. Fall of Kut, Apr. 29. Battle of Jutland, May 31. Brusilov's offensive in Galicia begins, June 4. Kitchener drowned when *Hampshire* struck mine, June 5. Battle of the Somme, July 1–Nov. 13: British losses: 420,000. Italians capture Gorizia, Aug. 10. Hindenburg and Ludendorff chiefs of German staff, Aug. 27. Rumania declares war against Austria and Germany, Aug. 27. Tanks first used by British, Sept. 15. Death of Francis Joseph of Austria, Nov. 21. Lloyd George forms War Cabinet, Dec. 6. Joffre replaced by Nivelle, early Dec.

1917 Unrestricted submarine warfare begins, Feb. 1. British troops occupy Baghdad, Mar. 11. Revolution in Russia, Mar. 12. U.S.A. declares war on Germany, April 6. Battle of Arras, Apr. 9–14: Vimy Ridge taken by Canadians, Apr. 10. Pétain replaced Nivelle, May 15. Messines Ridge taken by British, June 7. First American contingents arrive in France, June 26. Allenby assumes Palestine command, June 29. Third Battle of Ypres opened, July 31. Russia proclaimed a Republic, Sept. 15. British victory on Passchendaele Ridge, Oct. 4. French victory on the Aisne, Oct. 23. Caporetto: Italians severely defeated by Austrians. Oct. 24. Bolshevik Revolution, Nov. 7 (Oct. 25 O.S.). Passchendaele captured by British, Nov. 6. Balfour declaration recognised Palestine as "a national home" for the Jews, Nov. 8. Hindenburg Lines smashed on 10-mile front, Nov. 20. Fall of Jerusalem, Dec. 9. Russo-German armistice signed, Dec. 15.

1918 Treaty of Brest-Litovsk, Mar. 3. German offensive against British opened on Somme, Mar. 21. Battle of Arras, Mar. 21–Apr. 4. Second German offensive against British, Apr. 9–25. British naval raid on Zeebrugge and Ostend, Apr. 23. Foch appointed C.-in-C. Allied armies, Apr. 14. Peace signed between Rumania and Central Powers, May 7. *Vindictive* sunk in Ostend harbour, May 9. Last German offensive against French, July 15. British, Canadians, and Australians attack in front of Amiens, Aug. 8. Allenby destroyed last Turkish army at Megiddo, Sept. 19. Bulgarians signed armistice, Sept. 29. General Allied offensive in West began, Sept. 26. Germans accepted Wilson's Fourteen Points, Oct. 23. Great Italian advance, Oct. 24. Turkey surrenders, Oct 30. Austria accepts imposed terms, Nov. 3. Popular government in Poland (Lubin), Nov. 7. Revolutionary movement begins in Germany, Nov. 8. Kaiser abdicates and escapes to Holland, Nov. 9. Armistice signed by Germans, Nov. 11. Proclamation of Kingdom of Serbs, Croats and Slovenes in Belgrade, Dec. 1.

THE TWENTIES AND THIRTIES

1919 Peace Conference in Paris, Jan. 18. Einstein's theory of Relativity confirmed experimentally during solar eclipse, March 29. First direct flight across Atlantic by Sir J. Alcock and Sir A. W. Brown, June 15. Interned German fleet scuttled at Scapa Flow, June 19. Treaty of Peace with Germany signed at Versailles, June 28. Treaty of St. Germain: break-up of Austrian Empire, Sept. 10.

1920 Peace Treaty ratified in Paris. First meeting of League of Nations, from which Germany, Austria, Russia, and Turkey are excluded, and at which the U.S.A. is not represented. Prohibition in U.S.A. Peace Treaty with Turkey signed at Sèvres: Ottoman Empire broken up, Aug. 10. Degrees first open to women at Oxford Univ., Oct. 14.

1921 Riots in Egypt, May 23. In complete disregard of the League of Nations, Greece makes war on Turkey. Heligoland fortresses demolished, Oct. 14. Irish Free State set up by Peace Treaty with Britain, Dec. 6.

1922 Four-Power Pacific Treaty ratified by U.S. Senate, Mar. 24. Heavy fighting in Dublin, the Four Courts blown up, July 2. Defeat of Greek armies by the Turks, Aug.–Sept. Mussolini's Fascist "March on Rome," Oct. 28.

1923 French troops despatched to Ruhr, Jan. 11. Treaty of Lausanne, July 24. Earthquake in Japan, Tokio and Yokohama in ruins, Sept. 1. Rhine Republic proclaimed, Bavaria defies the Reich, Oct. 20. Turkish Republic proclaimed; Kemal Pasha, first President, Oct. 29.

1924 Lenin dies, Jan. 21. First Labour Ministry in Britain under MacDonald, Jan. 22; lasts 9 months. George II of Greece deposed and a Republic declared, Mar. 25. Dawes Plan accepted by London conference; Ruhr evacuation agreed to, Aug. 16.

1925 Hindenburg elected German President, Mar. 26. Treaty of Locarno signed in London, Dec. 1. Summer Time Act made permanent.

1926 Ibn Saud proclaimed king of the Hedjaz in Jeddah, Jan. 11. Evacuation of Cologne by British forces, Jan. 31. General strike in Britain.

1927 Lindbergh flies Atlantic alone, May 21.

1928 Earthquake in Greece, Corinth destroyed, Apr. 23. Capt. Kingsford-Smith flies the

A.D.

Pacific, June 9. General Nobile rescued by aeroplane from Arctic one month after disaster. June 24. Kellogg Pact accepted by Gt. Britain, July 18. German airship with 60 persons crosses Atlantic, Oct. 15. Women in Britain enfranchised.

1929 Second Labour Ministry under MacDonald. Graf Zeppelin makes numerous successful intercontinental flights. Commander Byrd flies over South Pole, Nov. 30. American slump and Wall Street crash.

1930 *R.101* destroyed in France on first flight to India, 48 lives lost, Oct. 5—end of British interest in airships.

1931 Great floods in China. Resignation of Labour Government and formation of Coalition under MacDonald.

1932 Manchuria erected into Japanese puppet state of Manchukuo, Feb. 18. Sydney Harbour Bridge opened, Mar. 19. Ottawa Imperial Conference.

1933 Hitler appointed Chancellor by Hindenburg, Jan. 30, and step by step gains supreme control. German Reichstag set on fire, Feb. 27.

1934 Dollfuss, Austrian Chancellor, murdered by Austrian Nazis, July 25. Death of Hindenburg, Aug. 2. Hitler becomes Dictator. Alexander of Yugoslavia assassinated in Marseilles, Oct. 9.

1935 Saar plebiscite for return to Germany, Jan. 13. Baldwin succeeds MacDonald as Prime Minister, June 7. War begins between Italy and Abyssinia, Oct. 3. Ineffectual economic "sanctions" by League of Nations against Italy, Nov. 18.

1936 Accession of King Edward VIII, Jan. 20. Repudiation of Locarno Treaty by Germany, Mar. 7. Remilitarisation of Rhineland, Mar. 8. Italian troops occupy Addis Ababa, May 5. Civil War breaks out in Spain, July 18. King Edward VIII abdicates after a reign of 325 days, Dec. 10. The Duke of York succeeds his brother as King George VI, Dec. 12.

1937 Coalition Ministry under Chamberlain, May 28. Japanese begin attempted conquest of China—" China incident," July 7.

1938 Austria annexed by Germany, Mar. 13. British navy mobilised, Sept. 28. Munich Agreement between Chamberlain, Daladier, Hitler, and Mussolini, Sept. 29.

1939

February 27 Great Britain recognises General Franco's Government.

March 16 Bohemia and Moravia annexed by Hitler and proclaimed a German Protectorate. 22 Memel ceded to Germany by Lithuania. 28 Anti-Polish press campaign begun by Germany.

April 1 Spanish War ends. 7 Italy seizes Albania. 14 First British talks with Russia. 27 Conscription introduced in Great Britain. 28 Hitler denounces Anglo-German Naval agreement and the Polish Non-Aggression Treaty.

May 12 Great Britain signs defensive agreement with Turkey. 22 Italy and Germany sign pact. 23 France and Turkey sign defensive agreement. 25 Anglo-Polish treaty signed in London.

July 10 Chamberlain re-affirms British pledge to Poland.

August 23 German-Soviet Pact signed by von Ribbentrop. 25 Japan breaks away from the Anti-Comintern Pact. 28 Holland mobilises. 31 British fleet mobilised.

SECOND WORLD WAR

September 1 Poland invaded by German forces. Great Britain and France mobilise. 1–4 Evacuation schemes put in motion in England and Wales: 1,200,000 persons moved. 2 Compulsory military service for all men in Britain aged 18 to 41. 3 War declared (11 a.m.) between Britain and Germany as from 5 p.m. 4 British liner *Athenia* sunk by submarine. R.A.F. raid the Kiel Canal entrance and bomb German warships. 6 First enemy air raid on Britain. 8 Russia mobilises. Russian troops on Polish border. 11 British troops on French soil. 17

A.D.

Russian troops cross the Polish frontier along its entire length. Russian and German troops meet near Brest Litovsk. 27 Capitulation of Warsaw. 29 Nazi-Soviet pact signed in Moscow approving partition of Poland.

October 14 *Royal Oak* sunk in Scapa Flow with a loss of 810 lives.

November 8 Bomb explosion in the Bürgerbräukeller at Munich after Hitler's speech. Germans using magnetic mines. 29 Diplomatic relations between Russia and Finland severed. 30 Finland attacked by Russia.

December 11 Italy leaves the League of Nations. 13 Battle of the River Plate: engagement of German warship *Admiral Graf Spee* by H.M. cruisers *Exeter*, *Ajax*, and *Achilles*. 14 Rejection by Russia of the League of Nations' offer of mediation in the Russo-Finnish war. Russia expelled from the League of Nations. 17 *Admiral Graf Spee* scuttles herself in the entrance of Montevideo harbour.

1940

February 14 Finnish advanced posts captured by Russians. 16 299 British prisoners taken off the German Naval Auxiliary *Altmark* in Norwegian waters. 26 Finns lose the island fortress of Koivisto. Finns retreat from Petsamo.

March 12 British ships to be fitted with a protective device against magnetic mines. Finland concludes a peace treaty whereby she cedes to Russia the Karelian Isthmus, the town of Vipuri and a military base on Hango Peninsula.

April 9 Invasion of Denmark and Norway by Germany. 15 British troops arrive in Norway. 19 British soldiers land in the Faroes.

May 2 British troops withdrawn from Norway. 10 Holland, Belgium and Luxembourg invaded by German forces. Parachute troops landed near Rotterdam. British troops cross the Belgian border. British troops land in Iceland. Rotterdam bombed. 11 National Government formed under Churchill. 13 Queen Wilhelmina arrives in London. 14 Rotterdam captured. Holland ceases fighting. Allied troops land near Narvik. 17 Belgian Government moves to Ostend. 24 German forces enter Boulogne. 27 Belgian army capitulates on the order of King Leopold. British forces to be withdrawn from Flanders. Narvik captured by Allied forces. 29 Ostend, Ypres, Lille and other Belgian and French towns lost to the Germans.

June Evacuation of British army from Dunkirk (May 27–June 4): 299 British warships and 420 other vessels under constant attack evacuate 335,490 officers and men. 5 Hitler proclaims a war of total annihilation against his enemies. 8 German armoured forces penetrate French defences in the West near Rouen. 10 Italy declares war on Great Britain and France. 14 Paris captured by German forces. 15 Soviet troops occupy Lithuania, Latvia and Estonia. 22 French delegates accept terms for an Armistice. 25 Hostilities in France cease at 12.35 a.m.

July 1 Channel Islands occupied by Germany. 3 French naval squadron at Oran immobilised. 10 Battle of Britain began.

August 19 British withdrew from British Somaliland. 25 British began night bombing of Germany.

September 6 King Carol of Rumania abdicates in favour of his son Michael. 7 London sustains severe damage in the largest aerial attack since war commenced. 15 Battle of Britain ends with British victory: German aeroplanes destroyed, 1,733; R.A.F. losses, 915. 23 Japanese troops enter Indo-China.

October 7 German troops enter Rumania. 28 Greece rejects an Italian ultimatum.

November 1 Greeks repel Italian attacks. 5 H.M.S. *Jervis Bay* lost defending Atlantic convoy from German warship *Admiral Scheer*. 11 Italian fleet at Taranto crippled by Fleet Air Arm. 14 Coventry heavily attacked, the Cathedral destroyed. 22 Albanian town of Koritza captured by the Greeks.

December 2 Bristol heavily bombed. 11 Sidi Barrani captured by British forces: beginning

A.D.

of Wavell's destruction of Italian forces in Cyrenaica. 29 City of London severely burned by incendiary bombs: Guildhall and eight Wren Churches destroyed.

1941

January 5 Bardia captured. **22** Tobruk captured by Australian troops.

February 7 Benghazi captured. **26** Mogadishu, capital of Italian Somaliland, occupied by Imperial troops. German mechanised troops in Libya.

March 4 British raid Lofoten Islands. **11** U.S. Lease and Lend Bill signed by Roosevelt. **27** Keren—main battle in British conquest of Abyssinia and Somaliland. **28** Cape Matapan: Italian fleet routed by British. **30** Rommel opens attack in N. Africa.

April 4 Addis Ababa entered by Imperial troops. **6** Greece and Yugoslavia invaded by German troops. **8** Massawa capitulates. **11** Belgrade occupied by German forces. **13** Bardia given up by British. Tobruk holds out. **24** Empire forces withdrawing from Greece. **27** Athens captured by the Germans.

May 2 Evacuation from Greece completed. **10** Rudolf Hess descends by parachute in Scotland. **20** Crete invaded by German air-borne troops. **24** H.M.S. *Hood* sunk. **27** German battleship *Bismarck* sunk; British forces withdraw from Crete.

June 2 Clothes rationing commences. **4** William II (ex-Kaiser of Germany) dies. **18** Treaty of friendship between Turkey and Germany signed. **22** Germany attacks Russia. **24** Russia loses Brest Litovsk.

July 3 Palmyra (Syria) surrenders to Allied forces. **7** U.S. forces arrive in Iceland. **9** General Dentz, the French High Commissioner in Syria, asks for Armistice terms. **25** Fighting round Smolensk.

August 25 British and Russian troops enter Persia. **27** The Dnepropetrovsk dam blown up by the Russians.

September 18 Crimea cut off from mainland. **19** Kiev entered by Germans.

October 6 German attack on Moscow. **16** Soviet Government leaves Moscow. Odessa occupied by German and Rumanian troops. **19** Taganrog on Sea of Azov captured by Germans. **26** Kharkov captured by the Germans.

November 14 *Ark Royal* sunk. **18** Libyan battle opens: Eighth Army's first offensive. **23** Bardia and Fort Capuzzo captured by British. **24** H.M.S. *Dunedin* torpedoed. **25** H.M.S. *Barham* sunk. **30** Russians re-take Rostov.

December 1 Points rationing scheme in force in Britain. **4** German attack on Moscow halted. **7** Japanese attack on Pearl Harbor. **8** Japanese forces land in Malaya. **9** British forces in Tobruk relieved. **10** H.M.S. *Repulse* and *Prince of Wales* sunk off Malaya by Japanese. Phillippines invaded by Japanese. **25** Hong-kong surrenders to Japanese.

1942

January 2 Manila and Cavite taken by Japanese. **23** Japanese forces land in New Guinea and the Solomon Islands.

February 9 Soap rationed. **12** Escape through English Channel of German ships *Scharnhorst*, *Gneisenau*, and *Prinz Eugen*. **15** Singapore surrenders to Japanese. **27** Battle of Java Sea.

March 9 Surrender of Java to Japanese.

April 15 George Cross awarded to the island of Malta.

May 4-8 Battle of Coral Sea. **7** Madagascar invaded by British forces. **7** U.S. forces sink **11** Japanese warships off the Solomon Islands. **30** Over 1,000 bombers raid Cologne. Canterbury bombed.

June 3-7 Midway Island: U.S. naval victory turns tide in Pacific. **20** Tobruk captured by the Germans.

July 16 R.A.F. make first daylight raid on the Ruhr.

August 6 Germans advancing towards the Caucasus. **10** American forces land in the Solomon

A.D.

Islands. **11** Malta convoy action (loss of H.M.S. *Eagle*, *Manchester*, *Cairo*, and one destroyer). **19** Raid on Dieppe. **23-25** Battle of Solomons.

September 6 Germans halted at Stalingrad.

October 23 El Alamein: Allied offensive opens in Egypt.

November 4 Rommel's army in full retreat. **5** Red Army holding firm at Stalingrad. **7** Allied invasion of N. Africa. **27** German forces enter Toulon. French Fleet scuttled.

December 2 First self-sustained, controlled nuclear chain reaction in uranium achieved by group working under Enrico Fermi at Chicago. **24** Admiral Darlan assassinated.

1943

January 6 German armies in the Caucasus and the Don elbow in retreat. **18** Leningrad 16-month siege ended. **23** Tripoli occupied by the Eighth Army. **27** American bombers make their first attack on Germany. **31** Remnants of the German army outside Stalingrad surrender.

February 9 Guadalcanal Island cleared of Japanese troops. **16** Kharkov retaken by the Russians.

March 1-3 Battle of Bismarck Sea. **23** 8th Army penetrates the Mareth Line.

May 7 Tunis and Bizerta captured by Allies. **12** All organised German resistance in Tunisia ceases. **16** Dams in the Ruhr breached by the R.A.F. **22** Moscow dissolves the Comintern.

June 3 French Committee for National Liberation formed in Algiers.

July 10 Allied invasion of Sicily. **25** Mussolini overthrown. **28** Fascist Party in Italy dissolved.

August 17 Sicily in Allied hands.

September 3 Italian mainland invaded. **7** Italy surrenders. **9** British and American troops land near Naples. **10** Rome seized by the Germans. **14** Salamaua captured from the Japanese. **23** *Tirpitz* severely damaged (sunk Nov. 12, 1944). **25** Smolensk taken by the Russians.

October 1 Naples taken. **25** Russians capture Dnepropetrovsk and Dneprodzerzhinck.

November 6 Kiev taken by the Russians. **26** Second Battle of Solomons. **28** Churchill, Roosevelt, and Stalin meet in Teheran.

December 2 Men between 18 and 25 to be directed to the mining industry by ballot in Britain. **26** Sinking of German battleship *Scharnhorst*.

1944

January 22 Allied landings at Anzio. **28** Argentina breaks with the Axis Powers.

February 1 American forces land on the Marshall Islands. **2** Russians penetrate Estonia.

March 15 Cassino (Italy) destroyed by Allied bombers.

May 9 Sevastopol captured by Russians. **18** Capture of Cassino and Abbey by Allies. **19** **50** Allied officers shot after escaping from a German prison camp. **30** Battle for Rome commences.

June 4 Allied forces enter Rome. King of Italy signs decree transferring his powers to Prince Umberto, his son. **6** *D-Day*: invasion of Europe (over 4,000 ships in invasion fleet). **7** Defeat of Japanese thrust at India, outside Imphal. **9** Heavy fighting near Caen. **12** First V-1 falls on England. **18** Cherbourg peninsula cut by the Americans. Russians break through the Mannerheim Line.

July 3 Minsk captured by Russians. **9** Caen captured by Allies. **20** "Bomb plot" on Hitler's life. **21** Guam captured by Americans.

August 1 Uprising in Warsaw. **4** Myitkyina falls to Allied forces. **15** Allied forces land in southern France. Marseilles taken. Rumania surrenders. **25** Paris liberated. Rumania declares war on Germany.

September 3 Allies in Belgium. **4** Antwerp and Brussels taken by Allies. Holland entered. Finland " ceases fire." **6** Bulgaria asks for an armistice. **7** Boulogne entered by Allies. Bulgaria declares war on Germany. **8** First V-2 falls on England. **11** Allied forces fighting on

A.D.

Reich territory. 17 Allied air-borne troops land near Arnhem. 22 First Battle of Philippines.

October 3 Warsaw rising crushed by the Germans. 5 British troops land on the mainland of Greece. 14 Athens occupied by Allies. 15 Hungary asks for armistice terms. 20 Aachen captured by the Americans. 25 Battle of Leyte Gulf: end of Japanese sea-power. 28 Second Battle of Philippines.

December 6 Civil war breaks out in Athens. 16 German forces counter-attack in the Ardennes: last German offensive in the West. 26 Budapest encircled by Russians.

1945

January 5 Organized fighting in Athens ceases. 11 U.S. forces land on Island of Luzon. 17 Warsaw captured by the Russians. 21 Russian troops in Silesia. 23 Burma road to China reopened.

February 4 Yalta conference. 14 Bombing of Dresden. 19 Americans land on Iwojima Island.

March 6 Cologne captured by Allies.

April 1 U.S. Invasion of Okinawa. 5 Russian Government denounces the Soviet-Japan neutrality pact. Japanese Cabinet resigns. 11 Russian Army enters Vienna after 7-day battle. 12 Death of President Roosevelt. 25 Berlin surrounded by Russian troops. 27 Russians and Americans link up in Germany. 28 Mussolini and his mistress shot by Italian partisans. 30 Hitler killed himself and his mistress.

May 2 German armies in Italy surrender. Berlin captured by the Russians. 3 Rangoon captured by British. 4 German forces in N.W. Germany, Holland and Denmark surrender. 8 End of World War II against Germany officially declared to be one minute past midnight (Tuesday). 28 Naval air attacks on Japan.

June 26 United Nations Charter signed at San Francisco.

July 5 Polish Government in Warsaw recognised by Allies. 26 Striking Labour victory in general election; Attlee became Prime Minister.

August 6 Atomic bomb first used against Japan: Hiroshima laid waste. 8 Russia declares war against Japan. 9 Russia advances into Manchuria. Nagasaki target for atomic bomb No. 2. 14 Japan surrenders unconditionally to the Allies. 17 Lend-Lease terminated.

September 2 Victory over Japan celebrated: end of Second World War.

"COLD WAR": AFRO-ASIAN INDEPENDENCE

October 9 U.S.A. to keep secret of manufacture of atomic bomb. 15 Laval executed.

November 20 Trial of major war criminals opens at Nuremberg.

1946

February 1 Mr. Trygve Lie elected Secretary-General of UNO.

April 19 League of Nations formally wound up.

June 5 Italy votes for Republic. 30 United States atom bomb tests at Bikini.

July 13 United States House of Representatives approves loan to Britain. 22 Bread rationing in Britain. British H.Q. in Jerusalem blown up. 24 Underwater atom bomb test at Bikini.

August 1 Peace Conference opens in Paris.

September 6 United Nations F.A.O. considers establishment of World Food Board.

October 16 Nuremberg sentences on Nazis carried out. Goering commits suicide. 23 General Assembly of the United Nations opens in New York.

November 10 Communists head poll in French General Elections.

December 2 Agreement signed for economic fusion of British and American zones in Germany.

A.D.
1947

January 1 British coal industry nationalised. 14 M. Vincent-Auriol elected first President of Fourth Republic.

March 15 Floods in England worst recorded. 24 Netherlands Government and Indonesian Cabinet sign agreement in Batavia for a United States of Indonesia.

April 1 School leaving age raised to 15 in Great Britain.

June 5 Inauguration of "Marshall Aid".

August 5 Dutch military action in Indonesia ends. 15 India and Pakistan assume Dominion Status. Viscount Mountbatten appointed Governor-General of India and Mr. Jinnah Governor-General of Pakistan. 29 Palestine Committee agrees British Mandate should end, majority report recommends partition.

September 22 First Atlantic automatic flight by U.S. pilotless aircraft.

October 6 Cominform, new international Communist organization, set up in Belgrade.

November 20 Marriage of Princess Elizabeth. 29 Palestine Committee of U.N. Assembly votes in favour of partition of Palestine into Jewish and Arab States.

December 15 Breakdown of 4-Power Conference on Germany. 30 King Michael of Rumania abdicates; Rumania becomes a People's Republic.

1948

January 1 British Railways nationalised. 4 Burma becomes independent Republic. 30 Mahatma Gandhi assassinated in New Delhi.

February 1 New Malayan federal constitution comes into force. 4 Ceylon Independence Act. 25 New Czechoslovak Government formed under Communist leadership.

March 10 Death of Jan Masaryk.

April 1 British electricity industry nationalised. 5 First European Aid shipments sail from America. 16 O.E.E.C. established.

May 3 Mr. Rajagopalachari appointed Gov.-Gen. of India in succession to Earl Mountbatten. 14 British Mandate for Palestine ended at midnight. Jews proclaim new State of Israel.

June 28 Yugoslavia expelled from Cominform; "Titoism" denounced.

July 1 "Berlin Airlift": American, British and French zones of Berlin supplied by air. 23 Malayan Communist party outlawed. 29 Bread rationing in Great Britain ends.

August 15 Republic of Korea proclaimed.

September 3 Death of Dr. Benes. 11 Death of Mohammed Ali Jinnah. 17 Count Bernadotte, U.N. Mediator for Palestine, assassinated.

October 30 Chinese Communist forces capture Mukden.

November 3 Mr. Truman elected U.S. President. 14 Birth of a son to Princess Elizabeth.

December 21 Republic of Ireland Bill signed in Dublin.

1949

March 15 Clothes rationing ends in Great Britain. 31 Russia protests against Atlantic Pact.

April 1 Newfoundland becomes part of Canada.

May 1 Gas Industry nationalised. 3 Ten-power conference in London establishes Council of Europe. 12 Berlin blockade lifted.

August 24 North Atlantic Treaty comes into force.

September 12 Professor Theodor Heuss elected first President of West German Republic. 21 General Mao Tse-Tung proclaims People's Republic of China.

October 2 Russia recognises newly-established Chinese People's Republic. 11 Herr Wilhelm Pieck elected first President of East German Republic.

December 8 Chinese Nationalist Government leaves mainland and sets up H.Q. in Formosa. 27 United States of Indonesia come into being.

1950

January 6 Britain recognises Communist Government of China; 24 Dr. Rajendra Prasad elected

A.D.

first President of Indian Republic; 26 New Constitution of Indian Republic comes into force.

February 14 30-year treaty of alliance between Russia and China signed in Moscow; 23 Labour Party wins General Election with narrow majority.

March 5 Lord Boyd Orr warns world that communism spreads where hunger prevails; 22 First of U.S. super-fortresses arrives in Norfolk.

April 1 Italy takes over from Britain administration of Somaliland; 13 First shipment of military aid to France under N.A. Pact unloaded at Cherbourg.

May 1 New Chinese marriage law abolishes polygamy and child marriages and gives both sexes equal rights; 19 Points rationing ends in Britain after 8 years; 25 Middle East Tripartite Declaration by Britain, France, and U.S.A.; 26 Petrol rationing ends in Britain.

June 25 N. Korean troops advance into S. Korea; Security Council calls for cease fire; 27 Pres. Truman orders U.S. air, and sea forces to support S. Korea and protect Formosa; U.N. Commission in Korea proposes neutral mediator; military assistance to S. Korea endorsed by Security Council; 30 Pres. Truman authorizes use of American ground troops in Korea.

July 2 American troops land in S. Korea; 8 Gen. MacArthur designated C.-in-C. of U.N. forces in Korea.

August 1 Security Council meets under chairmanship of M. Malik, the Soviet delegate; 7 American forces in Korea open offensive and halt drive on Pusan; 15 Princess Elizabeth gives birth to a daughter; severe earthquake in Assam; 17 Independence Day in Indonesia.

September 6 British troops in action in Korea; 9 Soap rationing ends in Britain.

October 9 U.N. forces across the 38th parallel in strength; 19 Sir Stafford Cripps retires from public life on account of illness; Pyongyang, N. Korean capital, captured by U.N. forces; 21 Princess Anne Elizabeth Alice Louise christened; 26 New Chamber of House of Commons opened at Westminster; 29 King Gustav V of Sweden dies.

November 2 Death of George Bernard Shaw aged 94; 6 Chinese forces from Manchuria reported fighting in Korea.

December 3 Mr. Attlee flies to Washington for talks with Pres. Truman; 4 Pyongyang occupied by Chinese; 19 Gen. Eisenhower appointed Supreme Commander of West European Defence Forces set up by Atlantic Powers; 25 Stone of Scone stolen from Westminster Abbey.

1951

January 30 U.N. Assembly rejects resolution of 12 Asian and Arab nations calling for 7-nation conference for peaceful settlement of Korean question; 31 Decree confiscating property of Alfred Krupp cancelled.

February 15 Vesting date for Iron and Steel.

April 11 Gen. MacArthur relieved of all his commands by Pres. Truman and replaced by Lt.-Gen. Ridgway; 13 Coronation Stone returned to Westminster Abbey.

May 2 Persian oil industry nationalized; Germany admitted to Council of Europe; 3 H.M. the King opens Festival of Britain from steps of St. Paul's.

June 23 M. Malik, Russian delegate to the U.N., appeals for settlement of Korean war.

July 1 Colombo plan comes into force; 9 State of war between Britain and Germany officially ended; 10 Armistice negotiations open at Kaesong; 17 King Leopold abdicates in favour of his son Baudouin, who becomes fifth King of the Belgians; 20 King Abdullah of Jordan assassinated.

September 1 Tripartite Security Treaty between U.S.A., Australia, and New Zealand signed in San Francisco; 8 Japanese Peace Treaty—to which Russia, China, and India are not

A.D.

parties—signed at San Francisco; Security Pact between Japan and U.S.A., providing for retention of American forces in Japan, also signed; 23 H.M. the King undergoes successful operation; 30 Festival of Britain ends.

October 8 Princess Elizabeth and Duke of Edinburgh leave for Canadian tour; 15 Egyptian Parliament passes unanimously Bills abrogating Anglo-Egyptian treaty of 1936 and 1899 Sudan Condominion Agreement; 16 Assassination of Liaquat Ali Khan; 25 General Election won by Conservatives with small majority.

November 5 Mr. Attlee receives the Order of Merit.

December 17 London foreign-exchange market reopens after 12 years; 24 Libya becomes independent state; 31 I.R.O. closes down.

1952

January 2 Mutual Security Agency replaces Economic Co-operation Administration; 31 Princess Elizabeth and Duke of Edinburgh leave London on first stage of Commonwealth tour.

February 6 King George VI died at Sandringham aged 56; 7 Queen Elizabeth II and the Duke of Edinburgh arrive home by air from Kenya; 15 Funeral of King George VI at Windsor; 21 Identity cards abolished.

March 20 South African Supreme Court rules invalid Dr. Malan's Act which places Cape coloured voters on separate electoral register.

April 11 H.M. the Queen declares that she wishes her children and descendants to bear the name of Windsor; 21 Death of Sir Stafford Cripps in Switzerland; 28 Japan regains status as sovereign and independent power.

May 5 H.M. the Queen takes up residence at Buckingham Palace; 27 Treaty setting up European Defence Community signed in Paris.

June 23 Power plants along Yalu River attacked by U.S. aircraft in biggest raid of Korean war.

July 7 American ship *United States* wins Atlantic Blue Riband; 19 Fifteenth Olympic Games held in Helsinki; 23 Military *coup d'état* takes place in Cairo.

August 1 Ratification of Bonn Agreement, by which W. Germany again becomes independent nation, and Treaty of Paris, which sets up the European Defence Community, approved by Government against Labour opposition; 16 Severe thunderstorms in Somerset and N. Devon cause rivers to flood; W. Lyn changes course bringing devastation to Lynmouth; 26 Passive resistance campaign against racial laws in S. Africa gains momentum.

September 2 Sir William Slim appointed Gov.-Gen. of Australia (from 1953); 8 New Egyptian Cabinet appoints Gen. Neguib military Gov.-Gen. of Egypt and approves land reforms.

October 3 Britain's first atomic weapon exploded in Monte Bello Islands, off N.W. Australia; 5 Tea derationed and decontrolled; 20 State of emergency declared in Kenya as a result of Mau Mau activities.

November 1 Reported explosion of U.S. hydrogen bomb at Eniwetok atoll in mid-Pacific; 4 Gen. Eisenhower, Republican candidate, wins sweeping victory in American Presidential election.

December 29 Fish recently caught off Madagascar confirmed as species of the prehistoric Coelacanth.

1953

January 20 Inauguration of General Eisenhower as 34th President of the United States; 31 Violent N.E. gales combined with surging high tides caused extensive flooding with loss of life along coasts of eastern England, the Netherlands, and Belgium.

February 4 Sweet rationing ended; 23 War-time deserters in Britain granted amnesty.

March 6 Marshal Stalin died, aged 74; 24 Death of Queen Mary at Marlborough House, aged 85; 31 Mr. Dag Hammarskjöld elected U.N. Sec.-Gen. in succession to Mr. Trygve Lie.

April 15 Dr. Malan's National Party again returned to power in S. Africa with increased

A.D.

majority; 24 Mr. Churchill created a Knight of the Garter by the Queen.

May 4 Duke of Edinburgh received his pilot's "wings"; 29 E. P Hillary and Sherpa Tenzing of the Everest Expedition led by Colonel John Hunt reached summit of Everest (29,002 ft.).

June 2 Coronation of H.M. Elizabeth II in Westminster Abbey amid scenes of magnificent pageantry; ceremony televised; 26 Republic of Egypt accorded *de facto* recognition by Britain.

July 4 German–Austrian Expedition reached summit of Nanga Parbat in the Himalayas; 13 De-nationalisation of British steel industry; 14 Royal Assent given to Central African Federation Bill; 27 Korean Armistice signed at Panmunjom.

August 9–12 Disastrous earthquakes in Greek Ionian Islands; 12 Explosion of Russian hydrogen bomb reported.

September 17 Bank rate reduced from 4 to 3½ per cent; 23 Royal Commission on Capital Punishment recommended that juries should decide whether death sentence or life imprisonment should be imposed on prisoners found guilty of murder, and that the M'Naghten Rules on insanity should be abrogated or amended; 26 Sugar rationing ended after nearly 14 years; 30 Professor Piccard in his bathyscaphe dived 10,000 ft. off Italian coast.

October 15 Sir Winston Churchill awarded 1953 Nobel Prize for Literature.

November 11 Great bell at Notre Dame rung by electricity for first time; 21 Piltdown skull, discovered in Sussex in 1911, found by anthropologists to be partial hoax; 23 The Queen and Duke of Edinburgh left in stratocruiser *Canopus* on first stage of 6-months' tour of Commonwealth.

December 1 Agreement signed for laying first transatlantic telephone cable; 23 M. René Coty elected Pres. of France at the 13th ballot; L. P. Beria, former chief of Soviet Secret Police, and six associates sentenced to death and shot; 25 The Queen gave her Christmas broadcast from Auckland; 31 Mildest December for 20 years, and before that for over 200 years.

1954

January 9 Self-government began in the Sudan; 12 M. Le Trouquer (Socialist) elected President of French National Assembly on retirement of M. Herriot; 16 M. René Coty became President of France in succession to M. Vincent Auriol; 31 Intense cold covered most of Europe.

February 3 The Queen and the Duke of Edinburgh arrived in Australia; First Parliament of newly formed Federation of Rhodesia and Nyasaland opened in Salisbury; 5 Britain's first "breeder" pile in operation at Harwell.

March 1 American hydrogen bomb exploded at Bikini; 22 London gold market reopened after 15 years.

April 1 The Queen and the Duke of Edinburgh left Australia; 3 Oxford won 100th Boat Race; 21 Russia joined UNESCO; 26 Conference on Far East opened in Palais des Nations, Geneva, Mr. Chou En-lai representing China; Russia joined I.L.O.

May 6 Roger Bannister ran the mile in under 4 min., the first man in the world to do so; 7 Fortress of Dien Bien Phu fell to Viet-Minh after siege of 8 weeks and final battle of 20 hours; 11 Bank rate reduced from 3½ to 3 per cent; 15 The Queen and the Duke of Edinburgh returned from their six-months' tour of the Commonwealth; 18 Liverpool Cotton Exchange reopened

June 1 Television licence fee raised from £2 to £3 a year; 2 Mr. John A. Costello (Fine Gael) elected Prime Minister of Ireland; 17 Indo-Chinese crisis brought M. Mendès-France to power in France; 22 First all-African Cabinet in British Africa appointed in the Gold Coast; 27 First electric power station using atomic energy began working in Soviet Union; 30 Eclipse of the sun.

July 3 All food rationing ended in Britain; 8 Mr. Nehru opened the world's longest canal

A.D.

(Bhakra–Nangal hydro-electric project); 27 Agreement reached in Cairo for withdrawal of British troops from Suez Canal Zone; 31 K2 (Mount Godwin Austen), second highest peak in the world, climbed by Italian team led by Prof. Ardito Desio of Milan Univ.

August 5 Persian oil dispute settled; 11 Cessation of hostilities in Indo-China after 8 years of fighting.

September 14 Sheffield–Manchester electrified railway opened.

October 14 Mr. Anthony Eden created a Knight of the Garter by the Queen; 19 Anglo-Egyptian Suez Canal Agreement.

November 1 French settlements in India passed under Indian control; 22 Death of Andrei Vyshinsky; 30 Sir Winston Churchill celebrated his 80th birthday and was presented by both Houses of Parliament with a portrait of himself by Graham Sutherland.

1955

January 27 Bank rate increased from 3 to 3½ per cent; 31 Princess Margaret left for tour of W. Indies.

February 8 Marshal Bulganin succeeded Mr. Malenkov as chairman of the Soviet Council of Ministers; 15 Plans to build 12 atomic power stations in Britain during next 10 years announced; 17 Britain to proceed with manufacture of hydrogen bombs; 24 Bank rate raised to 4½ per cent and restrictions on hire purchase announced; Dr. Albert Schweitzer appointed honorary member of the Order of Merit; Turco-Iraqi pact signed at Baghdad (Britain, Pakistan, and Persia acceded later).

April 5 Sir Winston Churchill resigned as Prime Minister; 6 Sir Anthony Eden succeeded as Prime Minister; 18 Afro-Asian conference (29 nations) opened at Bandung; Death of Dr. Albert Einstein; 29 Signor Gronchi elected President of Italy.

May 5 Ratification of London and Paris agreements completed; Germany attained full sovereignty and Western European Union came into being; 26 British general election resulted in Conservative majority of 59.

June 15 U.S. and Britain agreed to co-operate on atomic energy; 16 Revolt against the Perón government in Argentina.

July 9 Leading world scientists issued appeal for renunciation of war because of possible effects of hydrogen bomb; 18 Four-Power conference opened in Geneva (Pres. Eisenhower, Sir Anthony Eden, M. Faure, Marshal Bulganin), the first meeting between heads of Government since Potsdam, 1945; 27 Austrian State Treaty came into force.

August 8 International conference on peaceful uses of atomic energy opened in Geneva (1200 scientists from 72 countries attended).

September 16 Universal Copyright convention came into force, bringing U.S. into agreement with European countries; 19 General Perón resigned after rebels threatened to bombard Buenos Aires; 22 Independent television service began.

October 2 City of London became a "smokeless zone"; 12 British and Soviet warships exchanged courtesy visits; 20 Syria and Egypt signed mutual defence treaty; 23 Referendum on Saar European Statute gave victory to pro-German parties.

November 5 Vienna State Opera House re-opened; 23 *Hamlet* played on Russian stage by British company, the first since Tsarist times.

December 7 Mr. Attlee announced his retirement and was created an earl; 12 Completion of 830-mile pipeline through Urals, crossing 6 rivers; 14 Mr. Hugh Gaitskell elected leader of the Parl. Labour Party; 18 Anglo-American offer of financial assistance to Egypt in building Aswan High Dam; 24 In Christmas broadcast the Pope spoke of need to suspend nuclear test explosions.

1956

January 1 Sudan proclaimed an independent republic; 27 The Queen and the Duke of Edin-

A.D.

burgh left by air for 3 weeks' tour of Nigeria; 200th anniversary of birth of Mozart celebrated; Terrorist activity in Cyprus increasing.

February 1 Britain had coldest day since 1895; 13 Referendum in Malta resulted in vote in favour of integration with Britain; 16 House of Commons rejected by majority of 31 Government motion to retain death penalty; Bank rate increased from 4½ to 5½ per cent. (highest since 1932); 23 Remarkable sunflare caused increased cosmic radiation and long-wave radio disturbances; 25 M. Khrushchev in speech to Congress of Russian Communist Party denounced Stalin.

March 2 King Hussein of Jordan discharged Lieut.-Gen. J. B. Glubb; 5 Telephone weather forecast began; 9 Archbishop Makarios with leaders of Enosis movement in Cyprus deported to the Seychelles; 23 The Queen laid foundation stone of new Coventry Cathedral; Pakistan proclaimed an Islamic Republic within the Commonwealth.

April 6 Earl Attlee created Knight of the Garter; 11 Five-day week for Civil Servants announced; 18 Cease-fire between Israel and Egypt came into force; 29 French occupation of Indo-China ended after 80 years.

May 23 First atomic power station in Britain started working at Calder Hall; 24 2,500th anniversary of the death of Buddha celebrated in India; 31 May was the sunniest month at Kew since 1922 and the driest since 1896.

June 3 Third-class travel abolished on British Railways to conform to continental practice; 13 Last British troops left Suez; 24 Col. Nasser elected Pres. of Egypt.

July 20 Britain joined U.S.A. in withdrawing offer to help Egypt finance Aswan High Dam; 26 Pres. Nasser announced nationalisation of Suez Canal Company.

August 30 French troops arrived in Cyprus.

September 25 Newly-laid submarine telephone cable linking Britain and America opened to public service.

October 3 Bolshoi Ballet danced at Covent Garden; 15 Duke of Edinburgh left on world tour; 16 Prime Minister left with For. Sec. for Paris meeting; 17 The Queen opened Calder Hall, the world's first nuclear power station for commercial use; 19–21 New liberalised policy adopted by Central Committee of Polish United Workers' Party; M. Gomulka elected first secretary; 23 Insurrection broke out in Budapest and spread throughout country; 28 Pres. Eisenhower called upon Israel not to " endanger the peace "; 29 Israeli forces invaded Egypt and after 5 days' fighting had control of Sinai peninsula, heavy fighting at Abu Aweigila; 30 Britain and France issued 12-hour ultimatum to Israel and Egypt to cease fighting; Britain and France vetoed US resolution in Security Council calling upon Israel to withdraw behind armistice line; 31 Anglo-French offensive launched against military targets in Egypt.

November 2 UN Gen. Assembly called for immediate cease fire in Egypt; 4 Canadian resolution calling for international UN force for Middle East adopted; Soviet forces launched attack on Budapest to crush uprising; 5 Anglo-French airborne troops landed at Port Said; 6 Seaborne troops landed at Port Said; Pres. Eisenhower re-elected President with Congress controlled by Democrats; Anglo-French forces ceased fire at midnight; 7 Egypt accepted cease fire on UN conditions; 15 UN Emergency Force left Naples for Suez; 16 Suez Canal blocked by 49 ships; 17 First refugees from Hungary arrived in Britain; 22 Duke of Edinburgh opened 16th Olympic Games in Melbourne; 23 Sir Anthony Eden flew to Jamaica for rest cure; 24 UN for third time called upon Britain, France, and Israel to withdraw troops from Egypt.

December 5 140 people arrested in S. Africa for alleged treason; Anglo-French forces began to leave Port Said; 19 Lord Radcliffe's proposals for a constitution for Cyprus published; 29 Suez Canal clearing operation by UN salvage fleet began.

A.D.

1957

January 1 Anglo-Egyptian treaty of 1954 abrogated by Pres. Nasser as from October 31, 1956; Saar became tenth *Land* of German Federal Republic; Road Traffic Act came into force; 5 Eisenhower Doctrine for Middle East announced; 9 Resignation of Sir Anthony Eden as Prime Minister; 10 Mr. Harold Macmillan appointed Prime Minister; 16 Sadlers Wells Ballet group combined to form The Royal Ballet; Death of Signor Toscanini; 20 Mr. Gomulka's National Unity Front overwhelmingly returned in Polish general election; India's first atomic reactor, *Apsara*, inaugurated; 31 Trans-Iranian oil pipeline from Abadan to Teheran (600 m.) completed.

February 7 Bank Rate reduced from 5½ to 5 per cent; 15 Mr. Gromyko replaced Mr. Shepilov as Soviet Foreign Minister; 16 The Queen flew to Portugal on State visit and joined Duke of Edinburgh there who had just completed World tour; 22 Duke of Edinburgh granted title of Prince of the United Kingdom; 26 Indian resolution adopted by UN for " peaceful, democratic, and just solution " of Cyprus problem.

March 1 Mass protest in Tokio against nuclear weapon tests in Pacific; 5 Fianna Fail party under Mr. de Valera secured absolute majority in general election; 6 Ghana celebrated independence; Israeli withdrawal from Sinai completed; 11 Warning by WHO of genetic effects of radiation; 13 Anglo-Jordanian treaty of 1948 ended; 21 Homicide Act in force (death penalty retained only for five categories of " capital murder "); 25 European Common Market and Euratom treaties signed by France, Germany, Italy, and Benelux countries.

April 3 British Labour Party called for abolition of H-bomb tests; 4 No further call-ups for National Service after 1960; 8 The Queen and Prince Philip arrived in France on State visit; 9 Suez Canal cleared and opened to all shipping; 11 Agreement signed in London granting full internal self-government to Singapore from Jan. 1, 1958; 17 Archbishop Makarios arrived in Athens from exile; During the month appeals were made by the Pope, Dr. Schweitzer and Mr. Nehru for the banning of nuclear tests and weapons.

May 14 Petrol rationing (imposed 17.12.56) ended; 15 First British H-bomb exploded in Central Pacific near Christmas I.; 16 M. Spaak succeeded Lord Ismay as NATO Sec. Gen.; 18 The Queen and Prince Philip left for State visit to Denmark; 20 Death of Dr. Gilbert Murray.

June 1 New Copyright Act came into force; First drawing of Premium Bond prizes; 17 Historic decisions taken by US Supreme Court on matters relating to civil liberties; 19 Completion of British H-bomb tests in Pacific; 30 The IGY opened at midnight.

July 1 Women voted for the first time in Egypt's first general election since revolution of 1952; 17 Electricity Bill enacted appointing new Central Electricity Generating Board and Electricity Council in place of Central Electricity Authority; 18 President Mao Tse-tung's famous " Let 100 flowers blossom and 100 schools of thought contend " speech published; 25 Tunisia declared a republic; 31 Federation of Malaya Independence Act received Royal Assent.

August 1 Sir Christopher Hinton appointed chairman of new C.E.G.B., responsible for new nuclear power stations; 31 Royal Charter granted to Tangier by King of Morocco.

September 6 Disarmament discussions in London ended without agreement; 15 German general election (Dr. Adenauer re-elected Chancellor Oct. 22); 19 Bank Rate raised from 5 to 7 per cent.; 20 Death of Jean Sibelius, the Finnish composer; 30 Network Three introduced by B.B.C.

October 4 First earth satellite launched by Russia (180 lb. sphere, 23 in. diameter); 10 U.S.A. abolished fingerprinting for foreign visitors staying less than a year; 11 Largest radio tele-

A.D.

scope in world went into operation at Jodrell Bank for Manchester University; 14 The Queen opened Canadian Parliament in Ottawa; New road–rail double-decker bridge over Yangtse, one of largest in world, opened to traffic; 17 Endorsement of cheques no longer necessary save when negotiated.

November 3 Second earth satellite weighing half a ton launched into space by Russia with dog on board; 16 Russia announced construction of " scientific city " of 12 research institutes in Siberia; 20 Britain's first export order for nuclear power station for Northern Italy announced.

December 1 Latin 26-letter alphabet to be adopted in China; 4 Ninety people killed in railway accident in fog at Lewisham; 6 Attempt to launch earth satellite in the U.S.A. failed; *Sputnik I* completed its thousandth circuit of the Earth; 25 The Queen's Christmas broadcast televised for the first time; 31 The *Sputniks* were still circling the Earth, the first being expected to fall in the first days of January.

CO-EXISTENCE AND REALIGNMENT: THE NEW EUROPE

1958

January 1 Treaties establishing EEC (Common Market) and EAEC (Euratom) came into force; Metric system adopted throughout Japan; 3 Inauguration of West Indian Federation; Sir Edmund Hillary and New Zealand party reached South Pole; 4 *Sputnik I* disintegrated after completing 1,367 circuits of the Earth and travelling 43 million miles; 6 Mr. Thorneycroft resigned from Government after disagreement in Cabinet over pruning Budget estimates; 7 Mr. Macmillan left for six-week tour of Commonwealth; 8 Summit talks proposed by Marshal Bulganin and Notes sent to 19 States; 13 Over 9,000 scientists from 44 countries petition UN Sec. Gen. to end nuclear weapons tests; 20 Dr. Vivian Fuchs, leader of Commonwealth expedition, reached South Pole; 28 Abolition of licensed prostitution in Italy; 31 First American earth satellite *Explorer I* launched.

February 1 Union of Egypt and Syria in the United Arab Republic; 5 Continuation of Antarctic research for at least 5 years after end of IGY announced; 8 French aircraft bombed Tunisian frontier village of Sakhiet; 14 Merger of Iraq and Jordan under name of Arab Federation; 19 Worst colliery disaster in Indian history in West Bengal; 25 Campaign for Nuclear Disarmament launched under presidency of Lord Russell.

March 2 IGY Commonwealth Trans-Antarctic Expedition, led by Dr. Vivian Fuchs, completed first crossing of Antarctic (2,200 miles in 99 days); 8 Federal union between UAR and Yemen established; 14 Small test satellite, *Beta 1958*, successfully launched by US Navy; 20 Bank rate reduced to 6 per cent; 21 Opening of London planetarium, the first of its kind in Britain; 26 Third US earth satellite, *Explorer III*, successfully launched; 27 Mr. Khrushchev elected Prime Minister in succession to Mr. Bulganin; 31 Russian resolution to suspend nuclear tests; other powers invited to follow suit.

April 1 Abolition of legalised prostitution in Japan; 4 Campaign for Nuclear Disarmament organised 50-mile protest march from London to Atomic Weapons Research Establishment at Aldermaston, Berkshire; 17 Nationalist Party of S. Africa returned with increased majority.

May 1 Intense radiation belt in outer space discovered by US *Explorer* earth satellite; 10 Anti-government disturbances in Lebanon; 13 Military and colonist insurrection in Algeria; President of Italy paid state visit to Britain; 15 *Sputnik III* launched; New college to be built at Cambridge University (Churchill College); 22 Further reduction in Bank Rate to 5½ per cent.; 24 Nuclear reactor at Dounreay began working; 29 General de Gaulle accepted

A.D.

invitation to form a " Government of national safety."

June 1 General de Gaulle became Prime Minister of France; Clean Air Act banning emission of dark smoke came into force; 9 Gatwick Airport opened by the Queen; 19 Further cut in Bank Rate to 5 per cent.; New British plan for Cyprus announced; 20 London bus strike ended after 7 weeks; 21 Greek Government rejected British plan for Cyprus; 23 Ghana to be a republic.

July 1 Conference of scientists, including Russian delegation, met at Geneva to discuss ways of detecting nuclear tests; 14 Iraq monarchy overthrown, King Faisal assassinated; establishment of Republic; 15 US marines landed in Lebanon; 17 British troops flown to Amman in response to King Hussein's appeal; 24 First life barons and baronesses under Life Peerages Act named; 26 H.M. the Queen created her son, Charles, Prince of Wales.

August 1 British Government recognised Republic of Iraq; 5 U.S. nuclear submarine *Nautilus* surfaced after having passed under North Pole; 7 Litter Act came into force in Britain; 14 Bank Rate reduced to 4½ per cent.; 17 First attempt by America to launch moon rocket failed; Britain to resume nuclear tests on Christmas Island; 23 Bombardment by Chinese of Quemoy (Formosa Strait); 29 More American warships join Seventh Fleet in Formosa Strait.

September 1 International conference on peaceful uses of atomic energy opened in Geneva; 7 Britain successfully fired its first ballistic rocket (Black Knight) from Woomera; 15 Ambassadors of America and China met in Warsaw for discussions on Formosa crisis; 16 Relaxations in hire-purchase; 29 Referendum resulted in overwhelming victory for General de Gaulle; Lord Goddard retired as Lord Chief Justice; succeeded by Lord Justice Parker.

October 1 India began change to metric system; 2 French Guinea proclaimed Republic of Guinea after overwhelming vote for independence in French referendum; 8 Martial law in Pakistan; 9 Death of Pope Pius XII; 11 The London weeklies *John Bull* and *Illustrated* merged; US *Pioneer* space-rocket successfully launched (but failed to reach moon); 21 First women peers introduced to House of Lords; 28 State opening of Parliament and Queen's Speech televised; Cardinal Roncalli, Patriarch of Venice, elected as Pope John XXIII at age of 76; 31 Conference opened in Geneva (Russia, Britain, and the US) on suspension of nuclear tests.

November 20 Bank Rate reduced to 4 per cent.; 21 Work started on Forth road bridge, the largest suspension bridge in Europe; 27 Russian plan for withdrawal of troops and demilitarised free Berlin.

December 3 Last of four nuclear reactors at Calder Hall brought into operation; 17 Chinese leader, Mao Tse-tung, to resign as chairman of Republic but to retain party office; 18 US 4-ton missile fired into orbit; Empire Day to be known as Commonwealth Day; 21 General de Gaulle elected President of France; 27 Partial convertibility between £ and $ announced; UAR and Russia signed agreement on Russian co-operation in Aswan high dam project; 28 General de Gaulle announced devaluation of the franc.

1959

January 1 Batista Government in Cuba overthrown by revolutionary movement under Dr. Fidel Castro; 2 Russia launched planet round the sun (*Lunik I*); 3 Alaska became 49th state of American Union; 4 Mr. Mikoyan, Soviet Dep. Prime Min., arrived in Washington on 16-day visit; Rioting in Leopoldville; 7 Britain recognised new Cuban Government; 8 Gen. de Gaulle installed as first Pres. of Fifth French Republic; 10 Russian proposal for conference of 28 nations to draw up German Peace Treaty; 25 Oecumenical Council, the first since 1870, convened by Pope John XXIII.

A.D.

February 1 Votes for women rejected by Swiss national poll; **11** M. Vincent Auriol resigned from French Socialist Party; **21** Mr. Macmillan arrived in Moscow on official visit; **23** Archbishop Makarios returned to Cyprus after 3-year exile; Cyprus to become a republic with Greek Pres. and Turkish Vice-Pres.; **26** State of emergency declared in Southern Rhodesia; **27** Riots in Malta dockyard due to dismissal of workers.

March 3 American *Pioneer IV* went into planetary orbit round sun; State of emergency declared in Nyasaland; British scientists isolated basic molecule of penicillin; **17** Uprising in Lhasa against Chinese rule; Flight of Dalai Lama to India; **24** Iraq withdrew from Baghdad Pact.

April 5 Panchen Lama arrived in Lhasa to take over local government of Tibet; **8** Chair of Criminology founded at Cambridge; **14–16** Worst flood disaster of century in S. America; **27** Liu Shao-ch'i succeeded Mao Tse-tung as Chairman (President) of Chinese People's Republic.

May 1 Opening of Rajendra Bridge (6,074 ft.) over Ganges at Hathidah; **2** First Scottish nuclear power-station opened at Chapelcross; **15** Jodrell Bank radioed message to United States via moon; **28** Opening of Mermaid Theatre in City of London; **30** Auckland Harbour Bridge officially opened; **31** World's population (2,800 millions) increasing at rate of 45 millions a year.

June 8 U.S. Post Office made first successful delivery of mail by guided missile; **17** Mr. de Valera elected Pres. of Rep. of Ireland; Serious riots in African townships in Durban; **18** Five-year plan for Scottish Highlands announced; **24** World record price (£275,000) paid at Sotheby's for Rubens' *The Adoration of the Magi*; **26** St. Lawrence Seaway formally opened by the Queen and Pres. Eisenhower; **29** Norwegian Halden nuclear reactor in operation.

July 3 Tancarville road bridge near Le Havre, longest suspension bridge in Europe, opened; **4** Transatlantic record flight set up by Vickers *Vanguard* turbo-prop airliner (2,500 m. in 5¼ hrs.); **5** Recovery in good condition of 3 animals from outer space; **7** Litter Act passed making it an offence to drop litter; **21** Launching of first nuclear merchant ship *Savannah* by Mrs. Eisenhower.

August 16 The Street Offences Act came into force; **21** Baghdad Pact renamed Central Treaty Organisation; **22** First round-the-world service by British airliners inaugurated; **23** Announcement of plan for oil-pipeline network between Soviet Union and East European countries (completion 1963).

September 11 British loan made available for Malta dockyard. **13** Russian launched *Lunik II* which landed on moon; **15** Soviet atomic icebreaker *Lenin* made maiden voyage into Baltic; **25** Mr. Bandaranaike, Prime Min. of Ceylon, assassinated; **27** Typhoon in W. Japan (5,000 killed and missing, 1,000,000 homeless).

October 4 Russia fired *Lunik III*, which took photographs of back of moon; **8** General Election returned Conservatives with 100 overall majority; **10** End of one of longest droughts ever recorded in Britain; **24** Opening of new airport for Wellington, N.Z.; **29** Dublin's famous Abbey Theatre to be rebuilt (destroyed by fire 1951).

November 1 Basic travel allowance for British tourists ended; **2** First section of London-Yorkshire motorway (M1) opened to traffic; **5** Philip Noel-Baker awarded Nobel Peace Prize; **8** Sudan and U A.R. signed agreement on distribution of Nile waters; **14** Dounreay fast breeder reactor went into operation; **17** Announcement of discovery by American scientists of submarine plateau in Arctic Ocean; **19** Bank of England announced introduction of new series

A.D.

of bank notes (10s. £1, £5, £10); **21** British book exhibition opened in Moscow; **24** CERN's proton synchrotron at Geneva went into full operation; **27** Duke of Edinburgh opened Ghana's Academy of Learning in Accra; **28** Naval dockyard at Hong Kong closed after 80 years; **30** Inauguration of Italy's first nuclear research reactor.

December 1 Anglo-Russian cultural agreement signed in London; 12-power treaty on Antarctica signed in Washington; State of emergency in Cyprus ended; Bursting of dam at Fréjus killed 384 people; Pres. Eisenhower began tour of Europe, Asia, and Middle East; **5** Opening of 400-mile Sahara pipeline by French Prime Minister; **6** Inauguration of Panchet Hill Dam on Damodar R., Bihar; **10** Raising of school-leaving age to 16 recommended by Crowther Report; **14** Archbishop Makarios elected first Pres. of Cyprus; **15** New world speed record of 1,520 m.p.h. set up by U.S. Air Force pilot; **21** Marriage of Shah of Persia to Miss Farah Diba; **26** Soviet Antarctic expedition reached South Pole; **28** Yugoslavia's first nuclear reactor.

1960

January 1 Republic of Cameroun (formerly French Cameroons) became independent. **4** Albert Camus, French writer, killed in car crash. **7** Hirfanli Dam in Turkey opened, largest in Europe. **9** Work begun on Aswan High Dam. **12** State of emergency ended in Kenya after 8 years; **13** Nr. Aleksander Sidatov appointed to succeed Mr. J. Malik as Soviet Ambassador to Britain. **21** Bank rate increased to 5%. **23** M. Jacques Piccard and an American naval Officer descended 7 miles under Pacific in Marianas Trench. **24** Army rising in Algeria. **29** Broadcast of Pres. de Gaulle to nation contributed to collapse of military revolt.

February 3 Mr. Macmillan addressed S. African Parliament ("wind of change" speech). **13** First French atomic test in Sahara. **17** British agreement to U.S. ballistic missile early-warning system at Fylingdales Moor, Yorkshire. **19** Prince Andrew born. **29** Agadir destroyed by earthquake.

March 17 New £1 notes issued in Britain. **18** Last steam locomotive of British Railways named. **21** Sharpeville shooting in S. Africa when police fired on African gathering. **23** Mr. Khrushchev in Paris. **30** State of emergency in S. Africa.

April 1 U.N. Security Council adopted resolution deploring shootings in S. Africa. Dr. Hastings Banda, Pres. of proscribed Nyasaland African Congress, released from detention in S. Rhodesia. **5** Pres. de. Gaulle on state visit to Britain. **9** Attempt on life of Dr. Verwoerd. **13** *Blue Streak* as military weapon abandoned. **27** Rep. of Togo (former Togoland) came into being as independent state.

May 1 U.S. aircraft engaged in military reconnaissance flight over Soviet territory shot down. **6** Wedding of Princess Margaret and Mr. A. Armstrong-Jones in Westminster Abbey. **7** U.S. to resume underground nuclear tests; Mr. Leonid Brezhnev succeeded Marshal Voroshilov as Pres. of Soviet Union. **16** Opening and breakdown of Summit conference in Paris. **17** The Queen Mother officially opened Kariba Dam. **21** Earthquake disaster in Chile. **25** Everest climbed by 3 Chinese. Army seized control in Turkey. End of U.S. foreign aid to Cuba. **30** Death of Boris Pasternak.

June 10 Britain's first guided-missile destroyer *Devonshire* launched. Britain's nuclear power programme to be slowed down. **23** Bank rate raised to 6%. **25** Completion of second Saharan oil pipe-line (Edjelé to La Skirra on Tunisian coast). **26** British rule in Somaliland ended; Madagascar became independent state within French Community. **29** House of Commons rejected Wolfenden Committee's recommendations on homosexuality. **30** Belgian Congo

A.D.
became independent as the Congo Republic (Pres. M. Kasavubu, Prime Min. M. Lumumba).

July 1 Ghana proclaimed a Republic; Somali Republic came into being (merging of former British Somaliland and Italian Somaliland). **6** Army mutiny in Congo. Death of Aneurin Bevan. **11** Ivory Coast, Dahomey, Niger, and Upper Volta became independent. M. Tshombe, Congolese privincial leader, declared Katanga independent. M. Lumumba asked for U.N. help. **12** Congo (French), Chad and Central African Rep. became independent. **14** Sec. Council called for withdrawal of Belgian troops from Congo. **19–26** Royal Society Tercentenary celebrations.

August 2 Rawalpindi capital of Pakistan instead of Karachi. **8** Military *coup d'état* in Laos **9** Sec. Council called on Belgium to withdraw troops from Katanga and authorised U.N. troops to replace them. **16** End of British rule in Cyprus which becomes independent Republic. **25** Olympic Games opened in Rome. **29** Prime Minister of Jordan assassinated.

September 5 Announcement by Pres. Kasavubu that he had dismissed M. Lumumba as Prime Minister of Congo. **14** M. Lumumba appealed to U.N. for protection. **19** India and Pakistan signed Indus Waters Treaty. **23** Mr. Khrushchev led Soviet delegation to U.N. General Assembly in New York and criticised U.N. operations in Congo.

October 1 Federation of Nigeria became independent Member of the Commonwealth. **5** Labour Party Conference voted against Party's official defence policy. **14** Turkish trials of members of Menderes régime began. **21** Royal Navy's first nuclear submarine *Dreadnought* launched by the Queen. **27** Bank rate reduced to 5½%.

November 1 U.S. *Polaris* missile submarines to have base on Clyde. **3** Mr. Gaitskell re-elected leader of Parliamentary Labour Party **9** Senator John Kennedy elected Pres. of United States. **28** Islamic Republic of Mauritania proclaimed its independence.

December 1 Capture of M. Lumumba by Col. Mobutu's forces. **2** Archbishop of Canterbury visited the Pope at the Vatican. **3** Bank rate reduced to 5%. **14** Fighting in Vientiane, cap. of Laos, between right-wing and left-wing forces. **15** Marriage of King Baudouin of Belgium. **17** Revolt in Ethiopia crushed. **21** Strikes in Belgium. **27** Union of Ghana, Guinea, and Mali. **31** Farthing ceased to be legal tender.

1961

January 18 M. Lumumba, first Prime Min. of the independent Congo, sent to Katanga for imprisonment. **20** The Queen and the Duke of Edinburgh left for tour of India, Pakistan, Nepal and Iran; Mr. John Kennedy took office as 35th Pres. of the United States. **23** Portuguese liner *Santa Maria* seized in Caribbean by insurgents as protest against Salazar dictatorship. **26** Full diplomatic relations resumed between Britain and United Arab Republic. **31** M. Spaak resigned as Sec.-Gen. of Nato.

February 1 Increased National Health Service prescription charges announced. **3** Capt. Galvão hands over *Santa Maria* to Commander of Brazilian Navy in Recife. **5** Riots in Angola. **13** Death of M. Lumumba announced (violent demonstrations in many countries). **15** Total eclipse of the sun visible from Europe. **21** U.N. authorised the use of force " if necessary, in the last resort " to prevent civil war in Congo; measures also for withdrawal of foreign military personnel and mercenaries. **26** Death of King Mohammed V of Morocco; succeeded by elder son who becomes King Hassan II.

March 8 First of American nuclear-powered submarines carrying Polaris missiles arrived at Holy Loch; Death of Sir Thomas Beecham. **12**

A.D.
First winter ascent of the Eiger. **14** The New English Bible (New Testament) published. **15** Uprising of tribal groups in Angola, brutal retaliation of Portuguese by burning and bombing. **25** Russian satellite with dog aboard launched and brought safely back to earth. **29** Four-year South African treason trial ended with acquittal of accused.

April 9 Death of former King Zog of Albania. **11** Opening of trial of Adolf Eichmann in Jerusalem. **12** Major Yuri Gagarin made first flight into space and back. **17** Unsuccessful invasion of Cuba by rebel forces. **22** Insurrection of part of French army in Algeria; State of emergency declared in France. **23** Census held in Great Britain. **24** Gen. de Gaulle ordered blockade of Algeria. **25** Both sides in Laos agreed to cease-fire. **26** Collapse of mutiny in Algeria. **27** Independence of Sierra Leone.

May 1 Betting and Gaming Act came into force in Britain: betting shops opened. **5** Commander Alan Shepard made first American flight into space; The Queen and the Duke of Edinburgh visited Pope John XXIII at the Vatican. **12** Botvinnik regained world chess championship. **16** International conference on Laos opened in Geneva; Army in South Korea seized power. **17** Guildford Cathedral consecrated. **20** Talks opened at Evian between French government and Algerian provincial government (broke down July 18). **31** Gen. Trujillo, dictator of Dominican Republic, assassinated; South Africa became a Republic and withdrew from British Commonwealth.

June 1 N. Cameroons became part of Nigeria. **3** Meeting of Pres. Kennedy and M. Khrushchev in Vienna. **9** Security Council voted for Afro-Asian resolution calling upon Portugal to end repressive measures in Angola. **27** Enthronement of Dr. Ramsey as Archbishop of Canterbury in Canterbury Cathedral. **30** Portuguese refused to stop repressive measures in Angola.

July 1 British forces landed in Kuwait following appeal from ruler. **2** Death of Ernest Hemingway. **7** Soviet Trade Exhibition opened in London. **11** Major Yuri Gagarin, Russian pioneer of space travel, welcomed in London. **18** Over £9 million raised in Britain for 1960 World Refugee Year. **19** Fighting began between French and Tunisian forces over Bizerta naval base; U.K.–U.S. agreement to establish Missile Defence Alarm Station at Kirkbride. Cumberland. **21** U.S. launched its second space traveller (Capt. V. Grissom) 118 m. high, flight time 16 mins.; New Runcorn–Widnes Bridge opened over Mersey and Manchester Ship Canal (the largest span arch in Europe). **24** Bank rate rose to 7%. **30** Israel began construction of deep-sea port at Asdod.

August 4 International Monetary Fund placed £714 million at Britain's disposal. **6** Major Titov, Russia's second space man, circled earth 17 times before landing back near Moscow **13** Soviet sector of Berlin sealed off from Western sectors. **14** Jomo Kenyatta became a free man again. **15** U.N. recognised M. Adoula's government as the central government of the Congo. **16** Dr. Hastings Banda's Malawi Congress Party won control in the Nyasaland Legislative Assembly. **30** No agreement reached at Geneva on banning of nuclear tests. **31** Soviet announcement of resumption of nuclear weapons tests.

September 5 International conference on preservation of wild life opened at Arusha, Tanganyika; U.S. to resume underground nuclear tests. **18** Mr. Hammarskjöld killed in plane crash when flying from Leopoldville, to Ndola, to arrange cease-fire between U.N. and Katanga forces. **28** Syria seceded from the United Arab Republic.

October 1 S. Cameroons gained independence as part of Cameroun. **3** Mr. A. Armstrong-Jones created Earl of Snowdon. **4** Labour Party Conference voted against Polaris bases and German

A.D.

troops in Britain   5 Bank rate reduced to 6½%.
10 Volcanic eruption on Tristan da Cunha;
whole population evacuated to Britain.   14
Death of Chico Marx.   21 U.S. put into space,
amid world-wide protest, 350 million copper
needles for reflecting radio signals (they failed
to disperse into orbit).   23 Nobel Peace Prize
for 1960 awarded to South African, Albert
Luthuli; that for 1961 posthumously to Dag
Hammarskjöld.   30 Russia tested a bomb of
over 60 megatons amid world-wide protest.   31
Hurricane struck British Honduras, Belize devastated; Stalin's body removed from the Lenin
Mausoleum in Red Square.

November 2 Bank rate reduced to 6%.   3 U
Thant, Burma's chief representative at U.N.,
elected Acting Sec.-Gen. of U.N.; Birth of son
to Princess Margaret and Lord Snowdon;
7 Dr. Adenauer re-elected Chancellor of Fed.
German Rep. for fourth time.   8 Official
negotiations for entry of Britain into Common
Market opened in Brussels; Wales votes for
Sunday opening.   9 The Queen and the Duke
of Edinburgh left for tour of Ghana, Liberia,
and Sierra Leone.   20 Admission of Russian
Orthodox Church to World Council of churches.
23 South Africa's apartheid policy condemned
by U.N.

December 8 Cross-Channel submarine cable linking
electricity systems of England and France
officially inaugurated.   9 Tanganyika became
independent sovereign state; Russia broke off
diplomatic relations with Albania.   15 Adolf
Eichmann sentenced to death by Israeli court
for crimes against the Jewish people and
against humanity; Mr. Macmillan and Pres.
Kennedy met in Bermuda.   17 Indian troops
took over Portuguese colony of Goa.   19
Decimal coinage accepted in principle by British
government.   20 Mr. Adoula and Mr. Tshombe
agreed on Katanga's subordinate status.   27
Belgium and the Congo resumed diplomatic
relations.

1962

January 1 Western Samoa became independent.
10 Avalanche disaster in Peru.   11 Smallpox
outbreak in Britain.   15 Centigrade first used
in weather forecasts.   16 Death of R. H. Tawney.   24 T.U.C. decided to join "Neddy".   27
New world record for mile by New Zealander
Peter Snell (3 min. 54·4 secs.).

February 11 Death of Lord Birkett.   20 American
first manned orbital flight.

March 7 Franco-Algerian negotiations began at
Evian; Publication of Royal College of Physician's Report on dangers to health from
cigarette smoking.   8 Bank rate reduced to
5½%.   14 Opening of 17-nation disarmament
conference at Geneva.   19 End of Algerian
war.   28 Inauguration of Marlborough House
built by Wren, as Commonwealth Centre.

April 1 Government's "pay pause" ended.
5 Completion of Gt. St. Bernard road tunnel.
7 Strike in Asturias—first of many throughout
Spain.   8 French people voted in referendum
approving Algerian peace settlement.   11
Pres. Kennedy condemned U.S. steel industry
for raising prices.   13 International agreement
(40 countries) to stop oil pollution of seas and
beaches.   20 Gen. Salan, O.A.S. leader,
arrested by French in Algiers.   25 U.S. began
new series of atmospheric nuclear tests in
Pacific.   26 Britain's first satellite, Ariel,
launched from Cape Canaveral; Bank rate
down to 4½%.   30 Norway applied to join
Common Market.

May 6 Signor Segni elected Pres. of Italy; Canon-
isation of St. Martin de Porres of Lima (d. 1639),
first mulatto saint of the R.C. church.   8
Trolleybuses ran for last time in London.   13
Dr. Radhakrishnan elected Pres. of India.
25 Consecration of new Coventry Cathedral.   31
Eichmann executed in Israel; Dissolution of
The West Indies Federation.

June 5 Creation of University of Lagos.   14
Creation of European Space Research Organisation (ESRO).   15 Nuclear power station at

A.D.

Berkeley, Glos., began electricity supply to
national grid.   18 The Flying Scotsman made
centenary journey; Conservatives (Mr. Diefenbaker) won Canadian general election by small
majority.   23 Cease-fire in Laos.   24 Opening
of Punjabi University, India.   28 U.N. called
for more liberal constitution for S. Rhodesia.

July 1 Burundi and Rwanda became independent; French colonial rule in Algeria ended;
Commonwealth Immigrants Act came into
force.   3 Plan for British national theatre and
opera house accepted by L.C.C. and Government.   8 Pres. de Gaulle and Chan. Adenauer
attended Mass in Rheims cathedral.   10
Telstar, first experimental satellite in space
communications, launched—first live television
between U.S. and Europe.   20 Death of G. M.
Trevelyan, the historian.   26 Government
announce setting up of "Nicky".   30 Archbishop of Canterbury visited Moscow.   31
Rendezvous of U.S. nuclear submarines at
North Pole.

August 5 Russia began series of atmospheric
nuclear tests; Death of Marilyn Monroe, at age
36.   6 Jamaica became independent.   10
Abandonment of Blue Water missile.   11
British mountaineers scaled Russia's highest
peak (Mt. Communism).   11 and 12 Russia
launched two men into orbit (64 orbits and 48
orbits).   14 Completion of Mont Blanc tunnel
(7½ m.).   17 Pres. Kennedy's Bill on medical
care rejected by Senate.   20 Government
approval for construction of new underground
railway between Victoria and Walthamstow.
21 Maiden voyage of Savannah, world's first
nuclear-powered merchant ship.   27 U.S.
Mariner II launched towards Venus.   31
Trinidad and Tobago became independent.

September 3 Opening of Trans-Canada highway
(4,800 m. from St. John's, Newfoundland, to
Victoria, B.C.).   7 Life Presidency for Dr.
Nkrumah.   15 Iran assured Russia that no
foreign rocket bases would be permitted.   20
Zimbabwe African People's Union banned in
S. Rhodesia; Fighting between Chinese and
Indian troops on disputed N.E. frontier.   27
Overthrow of Imamate and republic proclaimed
in Yemen.   29 Canada launched her first
satellite, the Alouette, into orbit.   30 U.S. troops
enforced Fed. Government's order that Negro
student should enrol at Mississippi State
University.

October 3 6-orbit flight of U.S. astronaut.   9
Uganda became independent.   11 21st Oecumenical Council opened at Rome.   17 Opening
of Hyde Park Corner underpass; Electricity
for national grid generated at Dounreay reactor.
24 Commencement of U.S. naval quarantine
of Cuba.   28 Dismantling of missile base in
Cuba agreed by Russia; Gen. de Gaulle won
referendum for direct election of President.

November 1 Russia sent spacecraft on 7-month
journey to Mars.   6 Admiralty announced
record ocean depth by H.M.S. Cook in Mindanao
trench (37,782 ft.); Opening of Commonwealth
Institute (replaces Imperial Institute, S.
Kensington).   18 Death of Niels Bohr.   20
Cuba blockade ended.   21 Cease-fire declaration
by China on Sino-Indian border dispute (no
further hostilities occurred).   29 Announcement
of new Indo-Pakistan negotiations on Kashmir.
30 U Thant unanimously elected Sec.-Gen. of
U.N.

December 5 Soviet-American space research co-
operation agreement; Uprising in British prot.
of Brunei in protest to joining Fed. of Malaysia;
British nuclear device exploded underground in
Nevada.   9 Tanganyika became republic and
Dr. Julius Nyerere its first president.   12
British troops in control of Brunei uprising.   14
Signals from Mariner II as it passed within
21,000 miles of Venus; Eritrea became province
of Ethiopia; N. Rhodesia's first African domi-
nated government formed.   15 Sir Edgar
Whitehead's party lost to right-wing party in S.
Rhodesian general election.   17 Mr. Macmillan
left for meeting with Pres. Kennedy at Nassau,
Bahamas.   21 U.S. decision to abandon Sky

A.D.

bolt; offer of *Polaris* missiles for British submarines to form part of multilateral Nato nuclear force. **25** Europe snowbound with freezing temperatures. **28** Agreement in principle reached between China and Pakistan defining mutual boundary. **30** Worst snowstorms in England since 1881. **31** British Transport Commission replaced by British Railways Board (created by Transport Act, 1962), with Dr. Beeching as chairman.

1963

January 2 Gen. Lemnitzer succeeded Gen. Norstad as Supreme Allied Commander, Europe. **3** Bank rate reduced to 4 per cent. **14** Gen. de Gaulle's press conference repulsing Britain's entry to EEC and rejecting U.S. Polaris offer. **15** Official ending of Katanga secession. **18** Death of Hugh Gaitskell; Aden acceded to Fed. of S. Arabia. **29** Britain was refused entry to EEC; Death of Robert Frost, the American poet.

February 1 Nyasaland became self-governing protectorate. **6** Shipping restrictions on Cuba announced by U.S. Government. **8** Overthrow of Iraq government and execution of Gen. Kassim. **12** Seventeen-nation disarmament conference resumed in Geneva. **14** Harold Wilson elected leader of Labour Party. **19** Earthquake in Barce, Libya. **22** Unemployment figures showed 878,356, highest since 1947.

March 5-6 First frost-free night in Britain since Dec. 22. **8** Syrian government overthrown by military coup. **17** Typhoid broke out in Zermatt; First of Tristan da Cunha islanders returned home. **27** Publication of Beeching Report on British Railways.

April 5 Opening of Berkeley and Bradwell civil nuclear power stations. **6** Polaris missile agreement signed between U.S. and Britain. **8** Mr. Diefenbaker's Conservative Party defeated by Liberals in Canadian general election. **10** Pope John XXIII published his encyclical *Pacem in Terris*; New Zealand to change to decimal coinage in 1967; Loss of U.S. nuclear submarine *Thresher* with 129 lives. **17** Commissioning of Royal Navy's first nuclear-powered submarine, H.M.S. *Dreadnought*. **20** Execution of Julian Grimau, Spanish communist leader.

May 1 End of Dutch East Indies; New Guinea (West Irian) handed to Indonesia. **15** Twenty-two-orbit flight of Major Cooper of U.S. Air Force. **20** Petrosian won world chess title from Botvinnik; Life presidency for Pres. Sukarno of Indonesia.

June 1 New internal self-government constitution for Kenya came into force with Jomo Kenyatta as Kenya's first Prime Minister. **3** Death of Pope John XXIII. **11** Iraq resumed war against Kurds. **12** Rioting on big scale in Georgetown, British Guiana. **14-19** Bykovsky-Tereshkova space flights (first woman astronaut). **16** Resignation of Mr. Ben-Gurion. **20** House of Commons censure on Mr. John Profumo, former Sec. of State for War. **24** Zanzibar achieved internal self-government. **28** Inauguration in Nairobi of Univ. of East Africa. **30** Pope Paul VI crowned.

July 2 Franco-German Treaty of Co-operation came into force. **5** Sino-Soviet ideological talks began. **9** State visit of King and Queen of Greece to Britain. **26** Skopje destroyed by earthquake. **29** Pres. de Gaulle rejected Moscow test-ban treaty. **31** The Peerage Bill received Royal Assent; Security Council called on member states to impose partial arms embargo on Portugal.

August 1 Under Criminal Justice Act, 1961, minimum prison age raised to 17. **3** First successful solo climb on north wall of Eiger by Michel Darbellay. **5** Partial nuclear-test ban treaty signed in Moscow by America, Russia, and Britain. **7** Security Council resolution to stop sale and shipment of arms to S. Africa.

A.D.

8 Glasgow-London mail train robbery (£2·5 million). **16** Announcement of American-Soviet weather- and communications-satellite programme. **20** Mr. Khrushchev visited Yugoslavia. **21** Buddhists arrested and martial law imposed in South Vietnam. **28** Great Negro "freedom march" on Washington. **31** Death of George Braque, the French painter; The "hot-line" linking Kremlin with White House went into service.

September 5 Soviet-American co-operation in cosmic ray research in Antarctica announced. **15** Ben Bella elected first President of Algeria. **16** New state of Malaysia (Malaya, Singapore, North Borneo and Sarawak) came into being. **17** Malaysia broke off diplomatic relations with Indonesia; Fylingdales ballistic missile early warning station came into operation. **18** New Australian decimal currency to be introduced Feb. 1966. **19** Anglo-French report recommended rail tunnel as Channel link. **21** Reform of Roman Catholic Curia announced by Pope Paul VI. **23** Report on decimal currency advocated division of £1 into 100 units. **25** Denning report on Profumo affair published. **29** Reopening of Vatican Council; First buildings of University of East Anglia opened at Norwich.

October 1 Nigeria became a republic within the Commonwealth with Dr. Azikiwe its first President. **3** Honduras government overthrown by Army. **4** Hurricane Flora struck the Caribbean. **9** Vaiont dam disaster (N. Italy); the Kubaka of Buganda became first President of Uganda. **15** Dr. Adenauer retired after 14 years as Chancellor of Fed. German Republic; succeeded by Prof. Ludwig Erhard. **18** Mr. Macmillan resigned as Prime Minister; succeeded by the Earl of Home. **23** Robbins report on higher education published.

November 1 Diem oligarchy of S. Vietnam overthrown by military coup; First executions in S. Africa under the Sabotage Act of 1963. **7** Eleven German miners rescued after a fortnight underground; Sir Alec Douglas-Home elected at Kinross and W. Perthshire. **9** Train and mine disasters in Japan. **16** Greece began to release Communist prisoners taken during last war. **17** Temples of Abu Simbel to be removed and re-sited. **18** Opening of Dartford-Purfleet tunnel, linking Kent and Essex under Thames. **22** Assassination of President Kennedy in Dallas, Texas; Vice-President Lyndon Johnson sworn in as new President. **27** Publication of Buchanan report.

December 3 Britain's second nuclear submarine, the *Valiant*, launched. **4** Second session of Vatican Council ended. **10** Zanzibar became independent within the Commonwealth. **12** Kenya became independent within the Commonwealth. **22** Greek liner *Lakonia* caught fire and sank on cruise, off Gibraltar. **31** Dissolution of Federation of Rhodesia and Nyasaland.

1964

January 4-6 Pope Paul made pilgrimage to Holy Land; meeting between Pope and Patriarch of Constantinople. **9** Rioting in Panama. **12** Republican régime in Zanzibar. **20** Army mutiny in Tanganyika. **27** France recognized China; School-leaving age to be raised to 16 in 1970-71. **28** Riots in Salisbury, S. Rhodesia, after trial of Joshua Nkomo.

February 6 Anglo-French agreement on rail Channel tunnel announced. **11** Fighting between Greeks and Turks at Limassol, Cyprus. **27** Bank rate raised to 5%.

March 4 August Bank holiday to be moved to last Monday in month. **6** Death of King Paul of the Hellenes; son proclaimed King Constantine XIII. **10** Birth of Prince Edward. **11** S. Africa withdrew from I.L.O. **19** Opening of Great St. Bernard tunnel. **24** Stansted, Essex, provisionally chosen as site of London's

A.D.

third airport. 27 U.N. peacekeeping force in Cyprus operational; Severe earthquake and tidal wave in Alaska.

April 4 Dr. Leakey confirmed discovery in Tanganyika of *Homo habilis*; heavy fighting in Cyprus between Greek and Turkish communities. 5 Death of General MacArthur. 8 Shaikh Abdullah, former Prime Minister of Kashmir, released by Indian Government. 9 First Greater London Council election; Labour 64, Conservatives 36. 10 Mr. Macmillan declined earldom and Order of the Garter. 13 Mr. Ian Smith became Prime Minister of S. Rhodesia on resignation of Mr. Winston Field. 16 Sentences passed on 12 men found guilty in mail train robbery trial (two subsequently escaped from prison). 21 Opening of BBC-2. 23 Shakespeare quatercentenary celebrations. 27 Tanganyika and Zanzibar united (United Republic of Tanzania).

May 1 Birth of a daughter to Princess Margaret and Lord Snowdon. 9 Mr. Khrushchev's first visit to Egypt (completion of first stage Aswan High Dam). 22 State of emergency declared in British Guiana. 26 Typhoid outbreak in Aberdeen. 27 Death of Jawaharlal Nehru.

June 2 Mr. Lal Bahadur Shastri elected Prime Minister of India. 3 Senator Barry Goldwater defeated Mr. Nelson Rockefeller, in Republican Party's primary in California. 5 First flight into space of Britain's *Blue Streak* rocket (fired from Woomera). 9 Death of Lord Beaverbrook. 12 Life imprisonment imposed on Nelson Mandela and others in Rivonia trial, Pretoria; 20-year treaty of friendship signed between Soviet Union and E. Germany. 30 Last U.N. troops left Congo.

July 2 Enactment of U.S. Civil Rights Bill. 3–4 Foreign ministers of Iran, Pakistan and Turkey agreed to form Regional Co-operation for Development (R.C.D.) group. 6 Nyasaland became independent state of Malawi. 10 M. Tshombe succeeded M. Adoula as Prime Minister of the Congo. 15 Mr. Mikoyan succeeded Mr. Brezhnev as President of the Soviet Union. 17 Mr. Donald Campbell broke land-speed record on Lake Eyre with 403·1 m.p.h. 27 Last appearance of Sir Winston Churchill in House of Commons. 31 American *Ranger 7* hit moon after sending back over 4,000 pictures of surface.

August 2 U.S. destroyer attacked by N. Vietnam torpedo boats off N. Vietnam. 4 Nine French miners rescued after being trapped underground at Champagnole for 8 days; Bodies of three murdered civil rights workers found near Philadelphia, Mississippi. 5 Congolese rebels captured Stanleyville; U.S. air raid on N. Vietnam. 13 General Grivas, former EOKA leader took over supreme command of Cypriot National Guard. 13 Common Market set up by Arab League (Iraq, Jordan, Kuwait, Syria and U.A.R.) to come into force Jan. 1965.

September 2 Indonesian landings in Malaya. 4 Opening of new Forth bridge (largest suspension bridge in Europe). 7 People's Republic of the Congo declared by Congolese rebels. 14 Third session of Vatican Council opened (closed 21 Nov.). 20 Gen. de Gaulle began his tour of S. America. 21 Malta became independent within the Commonwealth after 164 years of British rule. 23 Maiden flight of supersonic TSR 2; Death of Harpo Marx, the comedian.

October 5 The Queen and the Duke of Edinburgh in Canada on week's visit. 10 Opening of Olympic Games in Tokyo. 12 Soviet 3-man spaceship launched on 24-hour flight. 14 1964 Nobel Peace Prize awarded to Dr. Martin Luther King. 15 Mr. Khrushchev replaced in posts of First Secretary of the CPSU and Prime Minister by Mr. Brezhnev and Mr. Kosygin respectively; General election in Britain: Labour won with overall majority of five. 16 Mr. Harold Wilson became Prime Minister; China exploded an atomic device. 22 M. Jean-Paul Sartre de-

A.D.

clined Nobel Prize for Literature. 24 Northern Rhodesia achieved independence as Republic of Zambia with Kenneth Kaunda as its first President; S. Rhodesia became officially known as Rhodesia. 26 Government proposed 15% import surcharge and export tax rebate to deal with balance of payments crisis. 29 Nobel Prize for Chemistry awarded to Prof. Dorothy Hodgkin.

November 2 Deposition of King Saud of Saudi Arabia and accession of his brother Faisal. 3 U.S. Presidential election: sweeping victory for President Johnson over Senator Goldwater. 5 Mr. Chou En-lai in Moscow for 47th anniversary of October revolution; Cease-fire in Yemen after two years of civil strife. 10 Australia to introduce selective compulsory service for military service overseas. 12 Grand Duchess Charlotte of Luxembourg abdicated in favour of her son. 17 Government to ban export of arms to S. Africa. 21 Opening of Verrazano-Narrows bridge spanning mouth of New York harbour, the world's longest bridge. 23 Bank rate rose to 7%. 24 Belgian paratroops landed at Stanleyville to rescue rebel-held hostages.

December 2 The Pope welcomed in Bombay. 5 Bishopsgate railway goods depot destroyed by fire. 12 Kenya became Republic within Commonwealth with Mr. Kenyatta as first President. 16 Statement of Intent on productivity, prices and incomes signed by Government, T.U.C. and Employers' organisations. 17 Free prescriptions from 1 February 1965. 28 Signor Saragat elected President of Italy. 31 Mr. Donald Campbell broke world water-speed record with speed of 276·33 m.p.h. on Lake Dumbleyung in W. Australia.

1965

January 7 Indonesia withdrew from U.N. 15 Child's body found (Dec. 11, 1964) in coffin in Stepney identified as that of Lady Anne Mowbray (1472–81), remains reinterred in Westminster Abbey; Prime Minister of Burundi assassinated. 20 Lyndon Baines Johnson inaugurated as 36th President of U.S. 21 Prime Minister of Iran assassinated. 24 Death of Sir Winston Churchill. 26 Hindi became official language of India with English an additional official tongue. 31 National Health prescription charges ended.

February 1 The Queen and Duke of Edinburgh in Ethiopia on state visit. 7 First U.S. retaliatory raids against N. Vietnam. 17 Pres. Johnson announced U.S. would continue " actions that are justified as necessary for defence of S. Vietnam." 18 Gambia became independent as 21st member of the Commonwealth. 24 U.S. jets bombed Vietcong in S. Vietnam. 25 Dr. Heenan, Archbishop of Westminster, created a cardinal.

March 3 Remains of Roger Casement, from Pentonville Prison, reburied in Dublin; Seretse Khama became Bechuanaland's first Prime Minister. 7 First of 3,500 American marines landed in S. Vietnam. 18 Alexei Leonov became first man to leave a spaceship and float in space. 19 Record price of 760,000 guineas paid at Christie's for Rembrandt's *Titus*. 23 First successful two-man manœuvrable flight by Grissom and Young in *Gemini III*; Dr. Dorothy Hodgkin awarded Order of Merit. 24 Successful completion of U.S. *Ranger* moon shot programme. 25 Defeat of Mrs. Bandaranaike in Ceylon elections; Mr. Senanayake became Prime Minister in Chile. 28 Earthquake in Chile.

April 1 Younger brother of King Hussein made heir to Jordan throne in place of his 3-year-old son. 6 Launching of *Early Bird* commercial communication satellite; Cancellation of TSR 2. 9 Fighting broke out between Indian and Pakistan forces in Rann of Kutch. 11 Tornadoes in mid-western U.S. 23 Opening of 250-mile Pennine Way, Britain's first long-distance foot-

A.D.
path from Edale in Derbyshire to Kirk Yetholm in Roxburghshire. **29** Australian troops to be sent to S. Vietnam.

May 8 Arrest of Sheikh Abdullah. **11** Cyclone and tidal wave disaster in E. Pakistan killing 16,000 people. **13** Conservatives made big gains in U.K. local government elections. **14** Inaguration of Kennedy memorial at Runnymede; China exploded second atomic bomb. **17** 31 miners killed in Welsh colliery disaster. **18** The Queen and the Duke of Edinburgh on 10-day state visit to Fed. German Republic. **20–29** Indian ascents of Everest. **28** 267 miners killed in Indian colliery disaster.

June 1 237 miners killed in Japanese colliery explosion. **3** Bank rate reduced to 6 per cent: Launching of U.S. *Gemini IV* with McDivitt and White. **4–7** Visit of Mr. Chou En-lai to Tanzania. **7** 128 miners killed in Yugoslav mine disaster. **19** Pres. Ben Bella of Algeria deposed by Revolutionary Council under Col. Boumedienne. **22** 700th anniversary of Parliament celebrated. **30** Cease-fire agreement in Rann of Kutch signed.

July 14 Adlai Stevenson died. **15** U.S. *Mariner IV* transmitted first close-up pictures of Mars; King Constantine of Greece dismissed his Prime Minister, Mr. Papandreou. **16** Opening of Mont Blanc tunnel. **19** Death of Syngman Rhee, former Pres. of S. Korea. **22** Sir Alec Douglas-Home resigned as leader of the Conservative Party; succeeded by Mr. Edward Heath (July 28). **26** Maldive Islands became independent. **30** U.S. Medical Care for the Aged Bill passed.

August 1 Radio and television licence fees increased; Television ban on cigarette advertising. **3** Creation of " The Queen's Award to Industry " for export and technological achievement. **5** Clashes on Kashmir border. **6** U.S. Voting Rights Bill passed. **9** Singapore seceded from Malaysia; **11** Negro riots in Los Angeles. **12** Appointment of first woman High Court judge. **21** U.S. *Gemini V* (Cooper and Conrad) launched. **24** Pres. Nasser and King Faisal signed cease-fire agreement in Yemen.

September 1 Pakistan forces crossed Kashmir cease-fire line. **2** Death of Sir Harry Hylton-Foster, Speaker of the House of Commons. **5** Death of Dr. Albert Schweitzer. **6** Indian forces invaded W. Pakistan and bombed Lahore. **12** American division 20,000 strong landed in S. Vietnam: General election in Norway: Labour Government defeated. **14** Second Vatican Council reconvened for 4th session. **21** British Petroleum struck oil in North Sea. **22** Cease-fire in Indo-Pakistan war.

October 1 Attempt to overthrow Pres. Sukarno of Indonesia: reprisals against communists. **4** The Pope addressed the U.N. Assembly. **8** Rhodesian independence talks failed. **11** Publication of Vinland Map, the only known example of mediæval Norse cartography. **13** Pres. Kasavubu of the Congo dismissed Mr. Tshombe. **17** Demonstrations throughout U.S. and in London against war in Vietnam. **19** Dr. Erhard re-elected Chancellor of Fed. Rep. of Germany. **22** Pakistan and India accept cease-fire call of Security Council. **26** Dr. Horace King elected Speaker of House of Commons. **23** Parliament passed Bill abolishing death penalty for murder.

November 8 New British colony of British Indian Ocean Territory set up. **11** UDI in Rhodesia: Britain declared régime illegal and introduced economic sanctions. **15** New land speed record of 600·6 m.p.h. set up in Utah by jet-powered car. **20** Security Council called on all states to sever economic relations with Rhodesia, and urged oil embargo. **25** General Mobuto deposed Pres. Kasavubu: France launched her first earth satellite.

December 1 R.A.F. Javelins arrived in Zambia. **4** *Gemini VII* (Borman and Lovell) launched. **8** The Second Vatican Council closed. **9** Mr.

A.D.
Mikoyan retired as President of the Soviet Union; replaced by Mr. Nikolai Podgorny. **15** Rendezvous in orbit between *Geminis VI* and *VII*. **17** Britain imposed oil embargo on Rhodesia; New forms of service for Anglican Church published. **19** General de Gaulle re-elected French President. **22** Death of Richard Dimbleby; 70 m.p.h. speed limit on British roads came into force. **27** Oil rig *Sea Gem* collapsed in North Sea. **28** 900th anniversary of Westminster Abbey celebrated.

1966

January 3 Indo-Pakistani summit talks in Tashkent with Mr. Kosygin as host. **9** Violent rioting in Nigeria. **10** Sudden death of Mr. Shastri in Tashkent. **11** Opening of Lagos Commonwealth Conference. **15** Army coup in Nigeria: Fed Prime Min. killed. **16** General Ironsi, C.-in-C. of Nigerian army, took over command to restore law and order; Death of Sergei Korolyov, Russian space scientist. **21** Smith régime in Rhodesia rejected Royal Prerogative commuting death sentences on two Africans. **22** Opening of Volta River project in Ghana. **24** Air India *Boeing* crashed into Mont Blanc; 177 killed. **31** U.S. bombing of N. Vietnam resumed after 37 days; British Government banned all trade with Rhodesia; Russia launched *Luna 9*.

February 3 Successful soft landing on moon by *Luna 9*. **17** Britain protested to S. Africa over petrol supplies to Rhodesia. **23** Death of Vicky, political cartoonist. **24** Army coup in Ghana while Dr. Nkrumah absent in Far East.

March 1 Russian rocket landed on Venus. **4** Britain recognised new régime in Ghana; Canadian *DC 9* crashed near Tokyo: 64 killed. **5** BOAC *Boeing* crashed near Tokyo: 124 killed; Nelson pillar in O'Connell Street, Dublin, blown up. **8** Severe earthquake in Hopeh, N. China. **11** Chi-Chi, the London Zoo's giant panda, flew to Moscow for union with An-An of the Moscow Zoo. **23** Historic meeting in Rome of Archbishop of Canterbury and the Pope. **25** Two of the team climbing north face of the Eiger reached summit. **31** British General Election: Labour victory with overall majority of 97.

April 3 Soviet *Luna 10* became the first lunar orbiter. **7** Recovery of U.S. hydrogen bomb lost off coast of Spain. **10** British Forces in Middle East instructed to stop any ship going to Beira with oil for Rhodesia: *Manuela* intercepted and boarded by British naval party and escorted away from Beira; Death of Evelyn Waugh, the novelist. **11** Students and militant Buddhists intensified campaign for return to civilian rule in S. Vietnam. **21** Opening of Parliament televised for first time. **30** Official support from Chou En-lai for " cultural revolution " to wipe out " bourgeois ideology " in all fields of culture.

May 9 China exploded third nuclear device. **16** Seaman's strike began (ended 1 July—biggest strike in England since the war and the first of its kind since 1911). **18** Talks between Britain and Spain opened over Gibraltar. **26** British Guiana became independent state of Guyana.

June 1 Peace talks between Malaysia, and Indonesia. **2** American *Surveyor I* made soft landing on moon; De Valera re-elected President of Irish Republic. **6** *Gemini 9*, manned by two astronauts, recovered after 45 orbits. **11** Commonwealth Day (the Queen's official birthday) to be observed on this date in future. **27** Death of Arthur Waley, translator.

July 3 Resignation of Mr. Frank Cousins as Minister of Technology over prices and incomes policy. **6** Malawi became a Republic within Commonwealth with Dr. Banda as its first President. **7** Sino-Tanzanian co-operation in joint shipping line. **14** Bank rate raised to 7 per cent; In by-election, Labour lost Carmarthen to Welsh Nationalist. **16** Prime Minister in Moscow for talks with Mr. Kosygin. **18** International Court of Justice ruled in favour of S.

A.D.

Africa; no violation of mandate of S.W. Africa.
20 Prime Minister announced six-month freeze
on wages, salaries, and prices. 21 Successful
landing of *Gemini 10*: docking manoeuvre and
space walk. 24 Common Market completed its
agricultural policy; 25 Report that Mao Tse-
tung had swum 9 miles in Yangtze R. 27 Retirement of M. Spaak from political life. 29
Mutiny by section of Nigerian army; General
Ironsi killed; U.S. aircraft attacked oil depots
near Hanoi and Haiphong. 30 World Cup
won by England.

August 1–2 Plenary session of Central Committee
of Chinese Communist Party: Marshal Lin Piao
officially recognised as Mao Tse-tung's successor. 3 Post Office to become public corporation.
4 Sir Edmund Compton named Britain's first
Parliamentary Commissioner (Ombudsman).
7 Opening of Salazar Bridge spanning Tagus
River (longest suspension bridge in Europe).
10 American *Orbiter I* launched—first U.S.
moon satellite; Public inspection of Cabinet
and other official documents to be allowed
after 30 years instead of present 50; Cabinet
reshuffle: Mr. George Brown became Foreign
Secretary. 11 Indonesian–Malaysian peace
agreement signed in Djakarta. 18 Mass rally
of Chinese Red Guards in Peking celebrating
the "cultural revolution," attended by Mao
Tse-tung, Lin Piao, and Chou En-lai; Tay road
bridge opened (longest road bridge in Britain).
Earthquake in E. Turkey: over 2,000 killed.
27 Francis Chichester set sail round world.
31 Decree restoring federal system of government to Nigeria announced.

September 1 Britannia airliner crashed at Ljubljana in Yugoslavia: 95 killed. 5 Selective
Employment Tax came into force. 6 Dr. Verwoerd assassinated in Parliament, Cape Town.
8 Opening of new Severn road bridge. 11 Dr.
Immanuel Jakobovits elected Chief Rabbi of
Commonwealth; Fourth French nuclear device
exploded over Mururoa. 13 Mr. John Vorster
chosen as S. Africa's new Prime Minister. 15
German submarine *Hai* sank off Dogger Bank.
16 Opening of new Metropolitan Opera House at
Lincoln Centre, New York; Launching of
Britain's first Polaris submarine. 19 Inauguration of Paris–Shanghai air service; Civil Rights
Bill providing housing integration defeated in
U.S. Senate. 28 Indonesia resumed U.N.
membership. 30 Sir Seretse Khama became
first President of Botswana.

October 1 Release of Speer and von Schirach from
Spandau, leaving only Rudolf Hess there. 2
Heavy casualties after cyclone and tidal wave
struck E. Pakistan; hurricane Inez in Caribbean.
4 Basutoland became independent kingdom of
Lesotho. 5 Part 4 of 1966 Prices and Incomes
Act came into effect, giving Government power
to freeze wages and prices. 21 Aberfan disaster
avalanche from coal tip slid down upon mining
village killing 144, including 116 children. 26
Brussels chosen as new headquarters of NATO
Council. 27 China's fourth nuclear test. 28
Channel Tunnel announced; Indonesia readmitted to U.N.

November 4 Italian floods: torrential rain caused
Arno to burst its banks into city of Florence; 9
"Hot line" between Paris and Moscow.
22 Organic Law of Spanish State provided for
appointment of Prime Minister. 23 Red
Guards demanded dismissal of Liu Shao-Ch'i,
China's Head of State. 26 Opening of the
Rance barrage; Australian General Election:
Liberal–Country Party Coalition Government
led by Mr. Harold Holt returned; New Zealand
General Election: Mr. Keith Holyoake's
National Party returned. 29 King Ntare of
Burundi overthrown. 30 Resignation of Dr.
Erhard, Western German Chancellor; Barbados
became independent.

December 1 Mr. Kosygin in France; Dr. Kiesinger
(Christian Democratic Union) took office as
Chancellor of German Federal Republic.
2 Meeting of Prime Minister and Mr. Ian Smith
of Rhodesia on board H.M.S. *Tiger* off Gibraltar: working document prepared; U Thant re-

A.D.

elected U.N. Sec.-Gen. for further five years.
5 Mr. Ian Smith and colleagues rejected working
document. 10 Opening of first stage of
Roseires dam on Blue Nile, Sudan. 16 U.N.
Security Council voted for British resolution
for mandatory sanctions (including oil) against
Rhodesia. 28 China exploded her fifth nuclear
bomb. 31 Death of Mr. Christian Herter,
former U.S. Sec. of State.

1967

January 4 Donald Campbell killed at Coniston
while trying to break own water speed record.
10 General Election in Bahamas (first all-
Negro Cabinet took office Jan. 16 under Mr.
Lynden O. Pindling). 11 Last detachment of
British troops left Sarawak. 13 Army took
over power in Togo. 15 Prime Minister and
Foreign Secretary in Rome for Common
Market talks. 18 Mr. Jeremy Thorpe, elected
Leader of Liberal Party following resignation
of Mr. Grimond. 20 Agreement on Soviet–
Japanese air service between Moscow and
Tokyo via Siberia. 26 Bank rate reduced to
6½ per cent. 27 Death of Marshal Juin;
Three American astronauts killed in fire during
ground test at Cape Kennedy.

February 6 Mr. Kosygin arrived in London. 7
Bush fire in Tasmania: 62 lives lost and heavy
damage. 9 Historic meeting between the
Queen and Mr. Kosygin at Buckingham Palace.
13 Agreement on a "hot line" between Kremlin and 10 Downing Street. 15 Chinese
authorities ordered dissolution of all "revolutionary organisations" and return of their
members to their own provinces. 19 Death of
Robert Oppenheimer, the American physicist.
22 Pres. Sukarno of Indonesia surrendered rule
to Gen. Suharto. 23 Trinidad and Tobago first
Commonwealth member to join Organisation of
American States. 26 Congress Party returned
to power in Indian elections but lost 8 states.
27 International treaty banning nuclear
weapons from outer space and prohibiting use
of Moon and other celestial bodies signed in
London, Moscow, and Washington.

March 6 Death of Zoltán Kodály, composer. 12
Mrs. Indira Gandhi re-elected Prime Minister
of India. 13 Gaullists gained bare majority in
French National Assembly. 16 Bank rate reduced to 6 per cent. 18 *Torrey Canyon* ran
aground off Land's End with 120,000 tons of
crude oil aboard. 22 Army in Sierra Leone
seized power. 28 *Torrey Canyon* bombed and
oil released and set on fire; Pope Paul issued
encyclical on duties of rich nations towards
poor nations. 29 Launching of France's first
nuclear submarine, *Le Redoutable*; Last link of
South-East Asia Commonwealth cable system,
inaugurated. 31 Death of Marshal Malinov-
sky, defender of Stalingrad.

April 13 Conservatives gained landslide victory in
GLC elections. 19 Death of Konrad Adenauer.
21 Army coup in Greece. 23 Col. Vladimir
Komarov, Soviet cosmonaut, killed after parachute failure. 27 Opening in Montreal of
Expo 67—Canada's 100th birthday international fair.

May 4 Bank rate reduced to 5½%. 8 Dr. Zakir
Hussain elected President of India. 11 Britain
presented application to join Common Market.
14 Opening of Liverpool's new R.C. cathedral.
19 U.N. peace forces removed from Egypt–
Israel border after request from Pres. Nasser.
22 Egypt closed Straits of Tiran to Israeli
shipping; Japan joined European Nuclear
Energy Agency's Reactor Programme. 23
J. Ryun (U.S.A.) broke his own world mile
record—3 min. 51·1 sec. 28 Francis Chichester
arrived in Plymouth. 30 Secession of Eastern
Region (Biafra) from Nigerian Federation;
Egypt and Jordan concluded five-year defence
agreement.

June 1 Gen. Moshe Dayan appointed Israeli
Defence Minister. 3–4 166 people killed in two
British air crashes, at Perpignan and Stockport.
5 Outbreak of six-day war in Middle East:

A.D.
lightning attack by Israel caused severe Arab losses and capture of territory, mainly from Egypt and Jordan. 6 E. African Economic Community formed by Kenya, Uganda and Tanzania. 8 U.N. called for immediate Middle East cease fire. 8–9 Riots in Hong Kong. 9 France's fishing limits extended to 12 miles. 10 Middle East fighting ceased; Soviet Union broke off diplomatic relations with Israel. 12 Soviet Union launched Venus spacecraft. 17 China exploded her first H-bomb. 19 Pres. Nasser took over as P.M. 23 Meetings between Pres. Johnson and Mr. Kosygin in Glassboro. New Jersey. 23–24 More violence in Hong Kong. 26 EEC Council of Ministers to refer British application for membership to EEC Commission: Mr. Kosygin visited Cuba; U.S.A. and Panama agreed treaty concerning Panama Canal. 28 Israel took over control of the Old City of Jerusalem. 30 End of period of severe economic restraint in Britain.

July 1 Mr. Tshombe kidnapped in mid-flight and arrested in Algeria; Colour television began in Britain on BBC-2. 2 Third French nuclear test at Muratoa atoll in Pacific. 7 Francis Chichester knighted by the Queen at Greenwich. 8 Police post in Hong Kong attacked by demonstrators from China. 10 Last use of steam engines on British Rail Southern Region; New Zealand changed to decimal currency. 12 Negro riots in Newark, N.J. 13 Public Record Act passed: public records now closed for only 30 years (from Jan. 1968). 14 Decimal Currency Act became law, providing for decimal currency in Britain in 1971. 15 Lake Palourde, sister ship of Torrey Canyon, arrested at Singapore as surety for oil pollution damage. 17 U.N. observers began operating on Arab-Israeli cease-fire line; London's first supersonic boom test. 18 Defence cuts announced: withdrawal from East of Suez by mid-1970s. 20 Latey Commission recommended that 18 should be legal age of majority. 21 Albert Luthuli killed in railway accident in S. Africa. 22 Earthquake in N.W. Turkey. 23 Negro riot in Detroit. 25 Pope Paul visited Istanbul, Izmir and Ephesus. 28 Vesting day of British Steel Corporation.

August 3 Aberfan tribunal report blamed N.C.B. for the disaster; Lord Robens' resignation not accepted. 13 U.S. bombed N. Vietnam 10 miles from Chinese border. 21 Britain began phased withdrawal of forces from Aden and S. Arabia.

September 3 Chinese Red Guards ordered to cease violence; Sweden's traffic changed from left to right. 10 Gibraltar referendum: overwhelming vote to stay with Britain. 13 U.S. announced an anti-ballistic missile system against China. 20 Launching on Clydebank of Cunard Liner Queen Elizabeth II. 27 Queen Mary arrived at Southampton at end of her last trans-atlantic voyage.

October 2 H.M.S. Resolution, Britain's first Polaris submarine, commissioned. 8 Death of Lord Attlee. 9 Road Safety Act dealing with drink and driving came into force; Che Guevara, Cuban revolutionary leader, killed in guerrilla fighting in Bolivia. 10 Outer Space Treaty ratified by 93 countries. 13 Tyne toll tunnel opened by the Queen. 16 Opening of new NATO H.Q. at Evère, Brussels. 18 Russian Venus 4 made first soft-landing on Venus. 19 American Mariner 5 passed within 2,000 miles of Venus; Bank Rate increased to 6%. 22 Big demonstrations against Vietnam war in Washington, London and other capitals. 24 Israel bombarded Egypt's Suez oil refineries. 25 Foot-and-mouth epidemic began at Oswestry. 26 Coronation of Shah of Iran; Anglo-French agreement on joint production of helicopters. 30 End of Canadian Expo 67; Old age pensions and other benefits increased in Britain; Russians performed first automatic link-up and separation of unmanned spacecraft.

November 9 Bank rate increased to 6½%; launching of U.S. giant Saturn 5 rocket. 14 State visit to Malta by the Queen. 18 Devaluation of

A.D.
Sterling by 14·3% to $2·40 to the £; Bank rate increased to 8%. 20 Professor Blackett and Sir William Walton awarded the O.M. 22 Security Council unanimously adopted British resolution requiring Israeli forces to withdraw from occupied Arab territory. 23 Indus water project inaugurated at Mangla Dam in W. Pakistan. 26 Lisbon area floods—464 dead. 27 End of eight-week unoffi.ial London dock strike. 29 Aden independent as Republic of South Yemen.

December 3 First human heart transplant operation at Cape Town. 13 King Constantine attempted unsuccessfully to overthrow the Greek military junta. 17 Mr. Harold Holt, Australian P.M., drowned in swimming accident. 19 France voted against negotiations for Britain's entry to EEC—Britain not to withdraw application. 20 Diplomatic relations resumed between Britain and Egypt.

1968

January 9 U.S. Surveyor spacecraft soft-landed on moon; Senator John G. Gorton elected P.M. of Australia. 14–15 Violent earth tremors in W. Sicily. 16 Prime Minister announced cuts in public spending. 23 Seizure by N. Korea of USS Pueblo off N. Korean coast.

February 11–12 U Thant in Moscow and London for talks on Vietnam. 13 U.S. planes bombed outskirts of Saigon. 18 Second Communist offensive in Vietnam; Introduction of British Standard Time. 19 Decision of Rann of Kutch Tribunal: nine-tenths to India and rest to Pakistan. 24 End of 25-day defence of Hué by Vietcong.

March 6 Africans in Rhodesia hanged in defiance of the Queen's reprieve. 12 Mauritius became independent. 14 Rush for gold in leading financial centres: U.S. Bank rate raised. Stock Exchange and Banks closed in Britain; Resignation of Mr. George Brown as Foreign Secretary. 17–18 Summit Meeting of Western Central Bankers: two-tier system for gold agreed. 21 Bank rate reduced to 7½%. 22 Resignation of Pres. Novotny of Czechoslovakia; Gen. Westmoreland, U.S. Commander in Vietnam, recalled to be Army Chief of Staff in Washington. 27 Yuri Gagarin killed in air crash. 30 Monetary Conference in Stockholm: special drawing rights scheme agreed, despite French non-co-operation.

April 4 Assassination of Martin Luther King at Memphis, Tennessee. 8 N. Vietnam agreed to direct talks with U.S. 16 Britain to withdraw from ELDO. 20 Pierre Trudeau became Liberal P.M. of Canada. 28 Extreme right-wing N.P.D. party won 12 seats in Baden-Württemberg state elections.

May 10 Violent clashes between students and security police in Paris. 13 Vietnam peace talks began in Paris. 17 French workers occupied factories. 18 Pres. de Gaulle cut short Romanian tour. 22 French National Assembly adopted amnesty after trade unions had agreed to negotiate with employers and Government. 29 U.N. Security Council adopted resolution imposing comprehensive mandatory sanctions against Rhodesia.

June 5–6 Senator Robert Kennedy shot and died in Los Angeles. 10 National Health prescription charge introduced. 14 Restrictions on entry into Britain by anyone connected with the Rhodesian régime. 15 Warsaw Pact manœuvres in Czechoslovakia. 26 Pierre Trudeau's Liberal Party won Canadian election. 30 Gaullists increased their majority in French election.

July 1 EEC abolished last internal industrial tariffs and common external tariff came into effect. 4 Fourth assembly of World Council of Churches; Mr. Alec Rose landed at Portsmouth after sailing single-handed round the world. 10 M. Couve de Murville replaced M. Pompidou as French P.M. 26 Government to

A.D.
remove Aberfan tips. 28 Serious riots in Mexico City. 29 Pope issued encyclical condemning all forms of artificial birth control; Summit Conference between Czech and Soviet leaders at Cierna.

August 3 Meeting at Bratislava between leaders of Czechoslovakia and other Warsaw Pact countries; death of Marshal Rokossovsky, Russian Second World War hero. 20 Soviet and Warsaw Pact forces entered Czechoslovakia. 22 The Pope visited Colombia, first papal visit to Latin America. 27 Death of Princess Marina, Duchess of Kent.

September 6 Swaziland independent. 11 Departure of Soviet troops from Prague. 13 High Court of Rhodesia ruled that the 1965 Constitution was legal. 15 Worst flooding in England since 1953. 16 Two-tier postal system began in Britain. 21–22 Clashes between students and police in Mexico City. 22 Successful recovery of Soviet *Zond 5* spacecraft after voyage round the moon. 26 Theatres Act, abolishing censorship, in force; Professor Marcello Caetano appointed P.M. of Portugal (Dr. Salazar ill). 27 French again vetoed British entry into Common Market.

October 1 Federal Nigerian troops captured Okigwi in Biafra. 5 Clashes between police and crowds in Londonderry (beginning of disturbances in N. Ireland). 9 H.M.S. *Fearless* talks on Rhodesia failed. 11 U.S. successfully launched *Apollo 7* 3-man moon rocket. 12 Olympic Games in Mexico City. 16 Treaty signed providing for stationing of Soviet troops in Czechoslovakia. 27 Czechoslovakia became a two-state federation; Massive demonstration march in London against Vietnam war. 31 Pres. Johnson ordered halt to bombing of N. Vietnam.

November 5 Mr. Richard Nixon won U.S. presidential elections. 12 Credit restrictions in France; Major policy statement by Mr. Brezhnev at Polish Party Congress—" a threat to a Socialist country is a threat to all Socialist countries." 15 New Greek Constitution came into force. 22 Stringent economy measures in France and higher taxation in Britain.

December 8 Royal Naval Dockyard in Singapore formally handed over to Singapore Government. 21–27 *Apollo 8* mission—Borman, Lovell and Anders made first lunar orbits. 28 China tested thermonuclear weapon. 28 Israeli commandos destroyed 13 Arab aircraft at Beirut after two Israeli airliners attacked by Arabs at Athens. 31 Maiden flights of Soviet TU-144 supersonic airliner.

1969

January 16 First manned docking operation in orbit by Soviet *Soyuz 4* and *5*. 20 Spain extended her territorial waters to 12 miles.

February 3 Assassination of Dr. Mondlane, Mozambique nationalist leader. 13 Arab attack on Israeli airliner at Zurich. 22 Vietnam Tet offensive began. 24 U.S. *Mariner* Mars spacecraft launched.

March 2 Maiden flight of French-built *Concorde*; Mrs. Golda Meir chosen as Israel's P.M.; Sino-Soviet clash on Ussuri River. 7 Opening of London's Victoria Line. 13 B.P. found Alaskan oil deposits. 18 U.S. offensive in S. Vietnam. 19 British troops landed with no opposition on Anguilla. 25 Resignation of Pres. Ayub Khan—succeeded by Gen. Yahya Khan.

April 1 Opening of China's ninth Communist Party Congress. 9 Maiden flight of British built *Concorde*. 14 Lin Piao declared Mao's successor. 17 Mr. Dubcek replaced as first Secretary of Czechoslovak Communist Party by Dr. Husak. 21 British Army units to guard key points in N. Ireland. 23 Biafran capital of Umuahia captured by Federal forces. 28 Gen. de Gaulle resigned as President of France after defeat on referendum.

A.D.
May 1 Maj. James Chichester-Clark became P.M. of N. Ireland after resignation of Mr. Terence O'Neill. 2 *Queen Elizabeth 2*'s maiden voyage began. 12 Voting age became 18. 16–17 Landing of Soviet spacecraft on Venus. 18–26 U.S. *Apollo 10* moon flight (Stafford, Young and Cernan). 27 Hungary ratified Nuclear Non-Proliferation Treaty.

June 5 World Communist Conference in Moscow. 15 M. Georges Pompidou elected President of France. 17 Boris Spassky became World Chess Champion. 18 Government dropped plans to put legal restraints on unofficial strikers in return for T.U.C. pledge to deal with disputes. 24 Resignation of Sir Humphrey Gibbs as Governor of Rhodesia.

July 1 Investiture of Prince Charles as 21st Prince of Wales at Caernarvon Castle. 3 Security Council censured measures taken by Israel to change status of Jerusalem. 5 Assassination in Nairobi of Tom Mboya. 8 Church of England rejected scheme for unity with Methodists; Methodists accepted it. 14 First major contingent of U.S. troops withdrawn from Vietnam. 21 Armstrong and Aldrin first men to land on the Moon at 3·56 a.m. (B.S.T.). 22 Prince Juan Carlos named future King of Spain by Gen. Franco. 24 Splashdown in Pacific of *Apollo 11*. 31 U.S. *Mariner 6* took photos of Mars; Pope Paul visited Kampala; Halfpennies ceased to be legal tender in Britain.

August 12 Three-day street battle in Londonderry after apprentice boys march. 19 Army took over security and police in N. Ireland.

September 1 King Idris of Libya deposed by military junta. 3 Death of Ho Chi-minh, President of N. Vietnam. 10 Barricades dismantled in Belfast and Army's " peace line " erected; Cameron Report *Disturbances in Northern Ireland*. 11 Meeting in Peking of Soviet and Chinese P.M.s. 23 Ton Duc Thang elected President of N. Vietnam; China carried out her first nuclear test underground. 28 Herr Brandt became Chancellor of W. Germany. 29 China exploded H-bomb.

October 1 Vesting day for new Post Office Corporation. 10 Hunt Committee report on N. Ireland recommended disarming police and disbanding B specials. 11–13 Group flight by Soviet *Soyuz* spacecraft and first experiment in space welding. 14 50p (10s.) piece introduced. 15 Mr. Dubcek resigned as President of Czechoslovak Federal Assembly; Peaceful demonstrations by millions of Americans against Vietnam war.

November 11 Owners of *Torrey Canyon* agreed to pay £1·5 million each to Britain and France for oil damage. 14 Launching of *Apollo 14* (Conrad, Gordon and Bean); Colour programmes began on BBC-1 and ITV. 15 Tanzania, Zambia and China agreed on construction of railway from Dar es Salaam to Zambia's copperbelt. 24 Soviet Union and U.S. ratified Nuclear Non-Proliferation Treaty. 25 U.S. renounced use of biological warfare.

December 1–2 EEC Summit Meeting at The Hague agreed on negotiations for British entry by June 1970. 2 Death of Marshal Voroshilov, former Soviet President. 11 European Conservation Year began. 16–18 Houses of Commons and Lords voted for permanent abolition of the death penalty. 19 Relaxation of U.S. trading restrictions with China. 27 Ruling Liberal Democratic Party won sweeping victory in Japanese General Election.

1970

January 12 Gen. Effiong proclaimed end of Biafran secession.

February 1 Pope reaffirmed celibacy as a fundamental law of the Latin church; Serious clash on Golan Heights between Israel and Syria. 3 Bertrand Russell died. 5 Special Public

A.D.

Order Act for N. Ireland passed. **11** Japan launched her first earth satellite. **15** Opening of Eilat to Ashkelon oil pipeline to by-pass Suez Canal. **17** Mrs. Meir, Israeli P.M. offered to halt attacks if Egypt agreed to respect the cease-fire.

March 2 Rhodesia proclaimed a republic. **4** French submarine *Eurydice* lost off Toulon. **5** Nuclear Non-Proliferation Treaty in force; Bank rate reduced to $7\frac{1}{2}\%$. **15** Expo-70 opened near Osaka, Japan; Assassination of Mr. Georgadis, Cypriot Minister of the Interior. **16** Publication of the complete *New English Bible*. **18** Prince Sihanouk overthrown in right-wing coup; Security Council resolution calling for an end to all relations between Rhodesia and U.N. member states. **19** Meeting of Federal Chancellor and E. German P.M. at Erfurt. **22** Publication of Rhodesian Church's *Crisis for Conscience* criticising recent Rhodesian legislation. **23** S. Africa banned from 1970 Davis Cup.

April 1 Murder of Count von Spreti, W. German Ambassador to Guatemala, by guerrillas. **8** Chinese–North Korean communiqué on America's new Asian policy; Israel bombed Nile delta. **10** U.S. Senate Foreign Relations Committee repealed Tonking Bay resolutions of 1964, used by Pres. Johnson to justify involvement in Vietnam. **18** Splashdown of *Apollo 13* after complex rescue operation (Lovell, Halse and Swigert). **21** Pres. Nixon announced withdrawal of another 150,000 U.S. troops from Vietnam in next year. **24** China launched her first satellite. **25** Russia launched eight Cosmos research satellites from one rocket. **28** ELDO decided to abandon British *Blue Streak* in favour of French rocket. **30** U.S. combat troops entered Cambodia.

May 1 Pres. Obote of Uganda nationalised all important export businesses. **4** Four students shot dead during demonstration at Kent state University, U.S.A. **12** Security Council resolution condemning Israeli military action in Lebanon. **15** S. Africa expelled from International Olympic Committee. **22** Britain cancelled S. African cricket tour.

June 4 Tonga independent. **7** Fighting for many days between Jordan troops and Palestinian guerrillas. **11** Drought of over 8 weeks in Borrowdale; warmest night in Britain for a century. **15** Pres. Kaunda banned coal imports from Rhodesia. **18** General Election in Britain; Conservative overall majority of 30. **19** Orbital space flight by Soviet cosmonauts in *Soyuz 9*. **21** Brazil won World Cup (Soccer). **23** Arrival of steamship *Great Britain* at Bristol from Falklands. **26** Mr. Dubcek expelled from Czechoslovak Communist Party. **29** British Government to end restrictions on sale of Council houses; Britain made third application to join EEC; Circular 10/70 issued, with Conservative policy on secondary education.

July 1 Division of W. Pakistan into four provinces. **6** Sir Alec Douglas-Home told Commons of Government's intention to resume arms sales to S. Africa. **20** Death of Mr. Iain Mcleod, Chancellor of the Exchequer. **23** Bill enacted to give pensions to people over 80 not entitled in present scheme; CS gas canisters thrown into Commons Chamber from Gallery. **30** Damages awarded to 28 deformed thalidomide children and their parents.

August 2 Army fired rubber bullets during Belfast disturbances. **7** Cease-fire in force along Suez Canal. **13** German-Soviet non-aggression treaty signed by Herr Brandt and Mr. Kosygin. **23** All marches in N. Ireland banned until Jan. 1971. **25** Indirect talks between Egypt, Israel and Jordan in New York, with U.N. mediator, Dr. Jarring.

September 2 Britain's Black Arrow rocket failed at Woomera. **4** World Council of Churches proposed financial aid to African guerrillas. **17** Civil War in Jordan between King Hussein's army and Palestinian guerrillas. **19** Syrian

A.D.

Army units intervened in Jordan. **22** Resumption of U.S. arms aid to Greece; Tunku Abdul Rahman resigned as Malaysian P.M. (succeeded by Tun Abdul Razak). **24** Soviet unmanned *Luna 16* brought back moon rock samples. **27** Agreement to end Jordan Civil War signed in Cairo by King Hussein, guerrilla leaders and leaders of eight Arab states. **29** Death of Pres. Nasser (later succeeded by Mr. Anwar Sadat).

October 15 Canonisation of 40 English and Welsh martyrs. **24** Dr. Salvador Allende, Marxist Socialist, elected President of Chile.

November 9 Death of Gen. de Gaulle. **17** Russia's *Luna 17* landed on moon with moon-walker which moved on surface. **20** U.N. voted to admit China but without necessary two-thirds majority. **21** U.S. bombed N. Vietnam after two-year halt.

December 7 Poland and W. Germany signed treaty recognising Oder-Neisse boundary; Elections in Pakistan. **15** Soviet *Venus 7* transmitted scientific information from surface of Venus. **18** Divorce became legal in Italy. **20** Mr. Gomulka resigned and was succeeded by Mr. Edward Gierek.

1971

January 1 Divorce Reform Act (1969) came into force; Kentucky mine disaster. **2** Ibrox Park disaster in Glasgow. **3** Open University on the air. **10** Highest ever January temperatures recorded in London. **14** Commonwealth Conference opened in Singapore. **15** Opening of Aswan High Dam. **19** Postal workers' strike began. **25** Pres. Obote of Uganda deposed by Maj. Gen. Amin, Army Commander.

February 4 Troop reinforcements sent to Belfast, after further violence; Financial collapse of Rolls Royce Ltd. **7** Male referendum in Switzerland gave women right to vote in national elections. **8** S. Vietnamese troops with U.S. air and artillery support crossed into Laos. **9** Earthquake in San Fernando valley, California. **15** Decimal Day in Britain. **21** March of over 100,000 trade unionists in London against Industrial Relations Bill. **22** Tornadoes hit Southern states of U.S.; British Government approved sale of seven helicopters to S. Africa against Security Council embargo. **24** Immigration Bill published, placing Commonwealth and alien immigrants under one system of control.

March 1 One-day strike by 1·5 million engineers against Industrial Relations Bill. **10** Mr. Gorton resigned as Australian P.M., replaced by Mr. William McMahon. **11** Landslide victory for Mrs. Gandhi in Indian General Election. **18** More troops to N. Ireland bringing total to 9,700. **19** S. Vietnam began withdrawal from Laos. **20** Resignation of Maj. Chichester-Clark as N. Ireland's P.M. (succeeded by Mr Brian Faulkner). **26** Civil war erupted in E. Pakistan after arrest of Sheikh Mujibar Rahman. **29** Lieut. Calley convicted of murder of 22 people in My Lai massacre in S. Vietnam. **30** Soviet Union agreed to outlaw germ warfare.

April 6 Death of Igor Stravinsky. **14** Direct telephone link between Britain and China opened after 22 years. **17** Egypt, Syria and Libya formed new Federation of Arab republics. **23** Launching of *Soyuz 10* (with three cosmonauts) to dock with Salyut space station in technical experiment to develop permanent base above Earth.

May 3 Resignation of Herr Ulbricht as First Secretary of East German Communist Party, in favour of Herr Erich Honecker. **6** Greece and Albania agreed to establish diplomatic relations, broken off in 1940. **10** Flotation of Deutsche Mark and Dutch guilder following Common Market currency crisis. **11** Vote for unity by Congregational and Presbyterian churches in England and Wales. **20-21** Heath-

A.D.
Pompidou talks on Common Market in Paris.
22 Earthquake in E. Turkey. **27** 15-year treaty of friendship and co-operation signed by Egypt and Russia. **31** Dissolution of Industrial Reorganisation Corporation, set up in 1966.

June 10 Lifting of 21-year embargo on trade with China by U.S. **21** Labour Party victory in Malta General Election, Mr. Dom Mintoff Prime Minister. **25** Death of Lord Boyd-Orr. **30** Russian space tragedy; Patsayev, Dobrovolsky and Volkov killed just before touchdown after 24 days in space.

July 1 Death of Sir Lawrence Bragg. **3** Opening of Erskine Bridge over Clyde. **6** Death of Louis Armstrong, jazz musician. **7** Publication of Government's *The United Kingdom and the European Communities* setting out terms for entry. **15** Chilean Government nationalised mining industry.

August 2 Lockheed Aircraft Corporation saved from bankruptcy by single Senate vote. **9** Internment without trial introduced in Northern Ireland; India signed treaty of friendship with Russia. **11** Trial in secret of Sheikh Mujibar Rahman, by Pakistan military court. **22** Right wing coup in Bolivia: Juan Torres replaced as President by Col. Hanzer. **23** Foreign Exchange markets reopened: sterling allowed to float upwards to new parity against the U.S. dollar.

September 2 Belfast explosions injured 40 people. **8** Australia cancelled S. African cricket tour after protests. **9** Parliament recalled for special debate on Northern Ireland. **11** Khrushchev died. **13** Attica prison stormed by U.S. police after riots: 40 killed. **24** Britain expelled 105 Russian diplomats for espionage. **27** Meeting of Prime Ministers Heath, Lynch and Faulkner at Chequers.

October 4 Labour Party Conference voted against Common Market terms by large majority. **9** Emperor Hirohito, on visit to Europe, given hostile reception at Amsterdam. **13** Conservative Party Conference voted overwhelmingly in favour of Common Market entry terms. **18** Prime Minister announced free vote for Conservatives on Common Market terms (Labour decided on a three-line whip on October 20). **23** India called up army reservists after further border friction with Pakistan. **26** U.N. General Assembly voted to admit China and expel Taiwan. **28** House of Commons (and Lords) voted in favour of joining Common Market on terms presented by Government: 69 Labour M.P.s voted with the Government. **31** Explosion at Post Office tower in London wrecked three floors.

November 13 U.S. *Mariner 9* went into orbit round Mars. **16** Compton Report on Interrogation in Northern Ireland found " some ill-treatment but no brutality." **24** Pakistan mobilised reserves for war. **25** Terms of Rhodesia settlement announced in London and Salisbury and at U.N.

December 3 Outbreak of Indo-Pakistan war after prolonged friction and many border disputes. **7** Libya nationalised B.P. oil investments in retaliation for British policy in Persian Gulf. **11** Mr. Geoffrey Rippon agreed terms with EEC for protection of fishing limits after Britain's entry. **16** Indian forces occupied Dacca. **17** End of Indo-Pakistan War. **18** Pres. Yahya Khan of Pakistan ousted and succeeded by Mr. Ali Bhutto; Group of Ten agreed on terms for re-alignment of currencies. **20-21** Heath–Nixon talks in Bermuda. **24** Signor Leone elected new President of Italy after 24 ballots. **29** British troops began withdrawal from Malta.

1972

January 1 Death of Maurice Chevalier. **9** *Queen Elizabeth* destroyed by fire in Hong Kong harbour; Miners' strike began with widespread power cuts and industrial disruption. **12** Sheikh Mujibar Rahman appointed Prime

A.D.
Minister of Bangladesh; Pearce Commission began work in Rhodesia. **13** Dr. Busia's government in Ghana overthrown. **22** Britain, Ireland, Norway and Denmark signed European Economic Community treaty. **30** " Bloody Sunday " in Londonderry: 13 civilians killed.

February 4 Britain recognised Bangladesh. **9** State of emergency in power crisis declared and large-scale power cuts began. **15** Over 1·5 million workers laid off at height of power crisis. **17** Second reading of European Communities Bill carried by only eight votes. **18** Wilberforce Enquiry's terms for settling the miners' dispute published. **21** President Nixon in Peking for talks. **22** Seven killed in IRA bomb explosion at Aldershot. **25** Miners voted to return to work.

March 4 Belfast restaurant explosion killed two and injured 136; Hovercraft capsized in Solent, killing five. **20** Dr. Sicco Mansholt appointed President of the European Commission; Six killed and 47 injured in bomb explosion in Donegal Street, Belfast. **26** New defence agreement signed between Britain and Malta. **29** Tutankhamun exhibition opened at the British Museum; Berlin Wall opened for the first time in six years; Transport and General Workers' Union fined for contempt by National Industrial Relations Court. **30** Direct rule came into force in Northern Ireland.

April 2 North Vietnamese troops mounted big offensive. **6** Scarman Tribunal reported on 1969 riots in Ulster. **10** 46 countries signed a convention outlawing biological weapons. **16** Launch of *Apollo 16* (Young, Mattingley and Duke). **17** Work-to-rule began on British Rail over pay claim. **18** Bangladesh admitted to the Commonwealth. **19** National Industrial Relations Court ordered 14-day cooling-off period in rail dispute; Widgery Report on " Bloody Sunday " published. **20** Transport and General Workers' Union fined further by National Industrial Relations Court for contempt. **23** French referendum showed majority in favour of the enlargement of the EEC.

May 3 Church of England Synod failed to reach required vote in favour of Anglican-Methodist union. **9** Black September hijackers killed at Lydda airport by Israeli soldiers. **13** Work-to-rule caused complete weekend shut-down of British Rail. **15** The Queen began state visit to France; Governor George Wallace of Alabama shot and wounded in Maryland. **18** Bomb disposal experts parachuted in mid-Atlantic to *Queen Elizabeth II* following bomb threat. **22** President Nixon arrived in Moscow for talks; Ceylon became the republic of Sri Lanka; Poet Laureate, Mr. C. Day Lewis, died. **23** Pearce Commission reported that the Rhodesians were not generally in favour of settlement proposals. **28** Duke of Windsor died in Paris.

June 4 Miss Angela Davis, a United States black militant, was acquitted after trial for murder, kidnapping and conspiracy. **5** Stockholm conference on the human environment opened. **6** 430 killed in Wankie Colliery explosion in Rhodesia. **12** Settlement of rail dispute. **16** A National Industrial Relations Court order against three London dockers was set aside by the Court of Appeal; 120 killed in tunnel rail crash near Soissons, France. Five burglars caught in Watergate building, Democratic Party's campaign H.Q. **18** BEA Trident crashed near Staines with loss of 118 lives. **20** Dr. Henry Kissinger in Peking for talks on Vietnam. **23** Government decision to " float " the pound.

July 5 M. Pierre Messmer became French Prime Minister after resignation of M. Chaban-Delmas; **30** patients killed in a fire at Coldharbour Hospital, Sherborne. **9** Ceasefire in Northern Ireland ended and six people were shot dead in Belfast. **12** Younger Report on privacy published. **18** Mr. Robert Carr became Home Secretary; Tripartite talks on combating inflation began. **21** Eleven people were killed and 130 injured in a series of bomb explosions

A.D.

in Northern Ireland; Five dockers committed to prison for contempt by National Industrial Relations Court. 22–28 Industrial action in support of dockers prevented publication of national newspapers. 28 Start of national dock strike following rejection of Jones–Aldington proposals for the modernisation of the docks. 31 " Operation Motorman " removed all barricades in Northern Ireland.

August 4 President Amin ordered expulsion of 40,000 British Asians in Uganda. 10 Housing Finance Act, 1972, came into operation. 22 International Olympic Committee expelled Rhodesia from the Olympic Games. 28 Prince William of Gloucester killed in air race crash.

September 1 Iceland extended fishing limits from 12 to 50 miles. 4 32 unions suspended by Trades Union Congress for registering under Industrial Relations Act. 5 Arab guerrillas held Israeli athletes hostage in Munich: the hostages, five guerrillas and a policeman were killed in gun battle at Fürstenfeldbruk airport. 8 Israeli aircraft struck at guerrilla bases in Syria and Lebanon. 17 First British Asian refugees arrived in England. 25 Darlington conference on the future of Northern Ireland opened. 26 Norway voted in a referendum against joining the European Economic Community. 29 Franks Committee report on secrecy published.

October 2 Denmark voted to join European Economic Community. 5 Congregational Church in England and Wales and Presbyterian Church of England combined to form the United Reformed Church. 10 Sir John Betjeman appointed Poet Laureate. 13 Bank rate abolished (now called minimum lending rate). 17 The Queen began state visit to Yugoslavia. 19 European summit conference opened in Paris. 24 President Heinemann of West Germany began state visit to England. 27 Mr. Cyril Smith won Rochdale by-election for the Liberal Party. 29 Three Olympic Games terrorists released by West Germany following a hijacking by Palestine guerrillas near Beirut.

November 6 Government imposed immediate 90-day freeze on prices, pay, rent and dividend increases. 7 President Nixon elected for a further term of office. 19 Herr Brandt re-elected in West German poll; Mr. Sean Mac-Stiofan, Chief of Staff of the Provisional IRA, arrested in Dublin and began hunger strike. 20 Silver Wedding anniversary of the Queen and Duke of Edinburgh. 22 Government defeated on new immigration rules; United States made biggest raids ever in Vietnam war. 25 Mr. Sean MacStiofan sentenced to six months' imprisonment.

December 2 Mr. G. Whitlam became first Labour Prime Minister in Australia since 1946. 4 Army seized power in Honduras. 5 Committee on Liquor Licensing published report suggesting lowering of minimum drinking age and more flexibility in opening hours. 6 End of Angry Brigade trial: four found guilty; Ireland voted to remove special position of the Roman Catholic Church from the constitution. 12 President Thieu rejected Vietnam peace terms. 18 United States resumed bombing of North Vietnam. 21 Treaty signed between West and East Germany. 22 Survivors found ten weeks after an air crash in the Andes. 23 Earthquake in Nicaragua devastated the capital Managua.

1973

January 1 Britain, Ireland and Denmark became members of the European Economic Community. 9 Rhodesia closed border with Zambia because of terrorist attacks. 15 Australian government announced its intention to end legal and judicial ties with Britain. 22 Ex-President Lyndon B. Johnson died in Texas; Major volcanic eruption in Iceland began; 180 people killed in Kano air crash. 27 Vietnam cease-fire agreement signed.

A.D.

February 1 The Common Agricultural Policy of the EEC came into operation. 5 First Protestant loyalists detained without trial in Northern Ireland. 7 One-day strike of loyalists in Northern Ireland. 8 Start of foreign exchange crisis. 12 First group of American prisoners released from North Vietnam; Dollar devalued by 10%. 21 Israeli fighters brought down a Libyan Boeing 727 with the loss of 104 lives. 23 Government granted heavy increases in food prices. 27 One-day strike of Civil servants. 28 One-day strike of ASLEF caused cancellation of all passenger train services.

March 1 Fine Gael and Labour Party coalition won Irish General Election: Mr. Liam Cosgrave became Prime Minister; Strike of hospital ancillary workers began; Mr. Dick Taverne won Lincoln by-election as a Democratic Labour candidate. 5 68 people died in mid-air collision over Western France: many world airlines suspended flights over France until end of strike of French air traffic controllers; EEC foreign exchange markets closed as a result of currency crisis. 8 One killed and 238 injured in two bomb blasts in central London. 9 Result of Northern Ireland referendum showed 591,820 in favour of retaining links with Britain, and 6,463 for links with the Republic. 10 Governor of Bermuda and his aide-de-camp murdered. 11 Gaullists and their allies won an absolute majority of seats in the French General Election. 16 ASLEF suspended industrial action. 18 Icelandic patrol vessel fired live shots across bow of a British trawler. 20 White Paper on future of Northern Ireland published: Northern Ireland Assembly to be elected by proportional representation. 23 Gas workers' ballot showed majority in favour of return to work. 26 Sir Noel Coward died. 29 Last American soldier left Vietnam.

April 1 VAT introduced in Britain; Phase 2 of counter-inflation policy came into operation. 6 Mr. Peter Niesewand, correspondent of the *Guardian* and B.B.C., was goaled in Rhodesia for an alleged breach of the Official Secrets Act (on appeal he was cleared of charges and released on 3 May). 8 Pablo Picasso died. 10 Israeli Forces raided guerrilla bases in Beirut and Southern Lebanon in reprisal. 12 Labour won control of the Greater London Council and the six other big conurbations. 13 Leaders of hospital ancillary workers recommended a return to work. 15 *Queen Elizabeth 2* sailed for Israel with unprecedented security precautions. 16 Sean MacStiofain released from goal

May 1 TUC day of protest against Government pay and prices policy. 7 President Nixon denied all knowledge of Watergate. 10 Elections held for 36 new metropolitan district councils. 11 Charges dismissed in Pentagon papers case in Washington. 14 Skylab space station launched. 15 Zambian troops shoot two Canadian tourists at Victoria Falls. 17 Senate Select Committee hearings on Watergate opened. 18 Royal Navy frigates sent to protect British trawlers in disputed 50-mile limit off Iceland. 21 Government announced cuts in public spending of £500m. in 1974/5. 25 Three American astronauts docked with crippled Skylab. 31 Mr. Erskine Childers succeeded Mr. de Valera as President of Ireland.

June 1 Greece declared a republic. 3 Russian Tupolev 144 crashed at Paris Air Show. 7 Skylab astronauts freed solar panels and saved mission. 9 Admiral Carrero Blanco became Prime Minister of Spain. 11 House of Lords ruled that 1971 Immigration Act was retrospective. 12 Car bomb killed six civilians in Coleraine. 21 Treaty between East and West Germany came into force; Mr Brezhnev and President Nixon signed agreement on arms limitation. 29 New Northern Ireland Assembly elected.

July 4 Rioting at Long Kesh prison in N. Ireland. 10 Reports of Portuguese military atrocities in Mozambique published in *The Times*. 20 Japanese airliner hijacked near Amsterdam and blown up at Benghazi after release of passengers.

A.D.

21 French exploded nuclear device at Mururoa atoll. 26 Liberals won by-elections at Ripon and Ely. 28 Second team of astronauts docked with Skylab. 30 18 miners killed in pit cage accident at Markham colliery in Derbyshire. 31 First sitting of Ulster Assembly ended in chaos.

August 2 Fifty killed in Sommerland fire at Douglas, Isle of Man; Commonwealth Prime Ministers' Conference opened in Ottawa. 3 Littlejohn brothers, goaled in Ireland, claimed they were working for Ministry of Defence. 7 Vice-President Agnew under investigation concerning possible criminal offences. 14 Mortgage interest rate rose to 10%; U.S. ceased bombing Cambodia. 19 Mr. George Papadopoulos became first President of Greece.

September 2 Professor J. R. R. Tolkien died. Death toll in Naples cholera outbreak rose to 11. 3 Dr. Henry Kissinger became U.S. Secretary of State. 7 Mr. Len Murray succeeded Mr. Vic Feather as TUC General Secretary. 10 Bombs in London stations injured 13 people. 11 Allende government overthrown in Chile: President Allende committed suicide when army took over: Lending restrictions imposed on banks; 12 Africans killed by police during riot in South African mine. 14 Mortgage rates rose to 11%. 15 Death of King Gustav of Sweden. 16 Mr. Tommy Herron, vice-chairman of UDA, found shot dead at Lisburn near Belfast. 17 Mr. Heath arrived in Irish Republic for talks on Ulster. 20 Bomb exploded in Chelsea barracks, 25 Skylab astronauts returned after 59 days in space. 29 Arab terrorists released three Soviet Jews held hostage at Vienna after government agreed to close transit camp.

October 6 Start of Arab-Israeli war: Israel attacked by Egypt across Suez Canal and by Syria on Golan Heights. 8 Mr. Heath launched Phase 3 of counter-inflation policy; Britain's first commercial radio station opened. 10 Mr. Spiro Agnew resigned as Vice-President of U.S.A. 12 General Peron became President of Argentina and his wife Vice-President. 16 Israeli tanks crossed Suez Canal; Government placed embargo on arms sales to Middle East. 17 Arab oil producers announced cut in oil supplies until Israel withdrew from occupied territories. 22 UN proposal for ceasefire agreed by Israel, Egypt and Jordan (marred by subsequent clashes). 26 Firemen began series of unofficial strikes. 31 Kilbrandon Report on the Constitution published; Three Provisional IRA leaders freed from Mountjoy prison by hijacked helicopter.

November 1 Electrical Power Engineers' Association began ban on out-of-hours work (called off Dec. 28). 8 End of " cod war " between Britain and Iceland: Britain to fish within 50-mile limit but with reduced annual catch; Conservatives held Hove and Edinburgh North in by-elections, Scottish Nationalists won Govan and Liberals Berwick. 12 Miners started overtime ban and ambulance drivers began selective strikes; Mr. Whitelaw outlawed two Protestant extremist groups. 13 Bank minimum lending rate increased to 13%. 14 Eight found guilty at Winchester in London car bombs trial; Six killed in explosion at ammunition factory in Birmingham; Wedding of Princess Anne and Captain Mark Philips. 16 Three more astronauts docked with Skylab. 17 Riots in Athens resulted in 11 deaths. 22 New 11-man Executive announced for Northern Ireland. 25 Army coup in Greece deposed President Papadopoulos: new Cabinet formed under Mr. Androutsopoulos.

December 1 Death of David Ben-Gurion. 5 50 mile/h speed limit imposed to conserve fuel. 6 Mr. Gerald Ford became Vice-President of U.S.A. 9 Tripartite talks on Northern Ireland ended in sufficient agreement to set up Council of Ireland in 1974. 11 Treaty normalising relations between W. Germany and Czechoslovakia signed in Prague. Resignation of Nelson Rockefeller as Governor of New York. 12 Rail drivers' union ASLEF began ban on

A.D.

overtime. 13 Further series of measures to conserve fuel announced: three-day working week from 31 December; cuts in electricity consumption. 17 Emergency budget included cuts in consumer credit and reduction in public expenditure. 20 Admiral Carrero Blanco, Prime Minister of Spain, assassinated in Madrid. 21 Geneva conference on Middle East opened. 23 Iran announced doubling of price of Persian Gulf oil. 26 Member of UDA beaten to death in Maze prison; Two more bombs in London. 27 Honorary West German consul in Belfast abducted. 28 Power engineers called off ban on out-of-hours working.

1974

January 1 Direct rule by U.K. Govt. in N. Ireland ended: New Ulster Executive took office; Mrs. Golda Meir won narrow victory in Israeli General Election. 6 Anti-terrorist security operation mounted at Heathrow; Further bomb attacks in London. 7 Mr. Brian Faulkner resigned as leader of the Unionist Party. 8 Lord Carrington became Secretary for Energy at head of new department. 9 Parliament recalled for two-day debate on energy crisis. 11 ASLEF policy of non-cooperation lifted, but ban on Sunday and rest day working continued. 15 One-day strike of ASLEF halted all rail services. 18 Israel and Egypt signed agreement on separation of forces. 19 Naval battle between China and S. Vietnam led to occupation of Paracel Is. by China. 22 Loyalists expelled from N. Ireland Assembly after angry scenes. 24 Publication of Pay Board's Report on Relativities (Cmnd. 5535). 27 Death of General Grivas, leader of Greek Cypriot movement for *enosis* (Union with Greece). 30 Non-stop air service between Peking and Moscow introduced.

February 4 12 killed in army coach explosion on M62 in Yorkshire: Miner's strike ballot showed 81% in favour of strike action. 7 Prime Minister called for General Election on 28 February. Island of Grenada achieved independence. 8 Skylab astronauts returned after record 84 days in space. 10 Miners' strike began. 11 ASLEF suspended industrial action. 12 Bomb attack on National Defence College. 13 Alexander Solzhenitsyn deported to the West. 24 £2 million Vermeer painting stolen from Kenwood House. 27 Mutiny by armed forces in Ethiopia (widespread unrest caused by famine). 28 Election in Britain resulted in no clear majority.

March 3 Turkish Airlines DC10 crashed with loss of 345 lives. 4 Mr. Edward Heath resigned and a minority Labour Government took office. 8 Inauguration of third Paris airport—the Charles de Gaulle. 9 Britain returned to five-day week. 11 Miners returned to work; Kenneth Littlejohn escaped from Mountjoy Prison, Dublin; Archbishop of Canterbury announced his retirement on 15 November. 20 Gunmen injured four in attempt to kidnap Princess Anne; Two soldiers accidentally shot by RUC; Government announced £21 million subsidy on bread. 22 Sir Alec Douglas-Home announced his retirement from politics. 26 Budget Day in Britain: increased pensions, extra food subsidies, higher income tax rates, indirect taxes on sweets, crisps, soft drinks, petrol, diesel fuel; gift tax to be introduced later in year. 29 Admission charges to museums and galleries in U.K. (in operation since 2 Jan.) abolished.

April 2 Death of M. Pompidou. 5 Death of Richard Crossman. 10 Resignation of Mrs. Golda Meir and her Cabinet after 5 years as Prime Minister. 11 Arab suicide squad in massacre attack on Israeli border community. 14 Heaviest fighting on Golan Heights and Mount Hermon since ceasefire in Oct. 1973. 15 President of Niger (since independence 1960) removed by Army coup. 18 Mr. Wilson visited N. Ireland. 20 Death of Ayub Khan. 23 Chair of peace to be created at London University to begin operating Sept. 1976. 24 General election in S. Africa: Nationalist Party returned for seventh successive time; Progressive

A.D.

Party won 6 seats. 25 Army uprising in Portugal: authoritarian régime in power since 1926 overthrown.

May 6 Resignation of Herr Brandt on discovery of chancellery aide spying for E. Germany; Portuguese junta offered ceasefire to African guerrillas. 8 Nurses began series of strikes in protest against low pay. 10 Defeat of former world chess champion, Boris Spassky, by Anatoly Karpov. 12 In referendum Italy voted to keep 3-year-old law legalising divorce (59·1% in favour, 40·9% against). 14 Dr. Donald Coggan, Archbishop of York, to succeed Dr. Ramsey as Archbishop of Canterbury in Nov: Dr. David Pitt (b. in Grenada) became first black GLC chairman. 15 General Spinola became President of Portugal; In Israeli village of Ma'alot schoolchildren killed when Israeli troops stormed school where children held hostage by Arab terrorists. 16 Herr Schmidt became Chancellor of West Germany. 16–17 Israeli reprisal air raids on Palestinian refugee camp in Lebanon. 19 State of emergency declared in N. Ireland because of Protestant general strike in protest against Sunningdale agreement; victory for M. Giscard d'Estaing in French general election. 22 Plan to establish a Council of Ireland postponed. 24 Death of Duke Ellington, jazz musician. 27 Inauguration of M. Giscard d'Estaing as President of France; M. Jacques Chirac Prime Minister; Army in N.I. took over power stations. 28 Collapse of N.I. executive. 29 Ulster Workers' Council called off strike; Assembly suspended: direct rule from Westminster resumed; Syria and Israel agreed to disengage forces on Golan Heights following 32-day mission of Dr. Kissinger.

June 1 Biggest explosion in Britain since war at Flixborough Nypro chemical works: 29 dead. 3 Mr. Rabin became Prime Minister of Israel; Michael Gaughan, Irish hunger striker, died at Parkhurst. 7 Price sisters ended their fast after 206 days; Valery and Galina Panov granted exit visas from Soviet Union. 10 Death of Duke of Gloucester. 15 Rival groups of left and right clashed in Red Lion Square, London: a university student died. 16 France exploded nuclear device in Pacific: Full diplomatic relations to be restored (after 7 years of hostility) between U.S. and Syria. 17 Bomb exploded beside Westminster Hall, injuring 11 people. 27 Foreign husbands and fiancés of British women to be allowed to live in Britain; Press and public to be excluded from wide range of matrimonial cases from 1 Oct. 27–3 July Brezhnew-Nixon Moscow summit meeting. 30 Martin Luther King's mother assassinated.

July 1 Death of General Peron of Argentina, aged 78. 3 Launch of Soyuz-14 which docked (5 July) with space station Salyut-3 (manned by Popovich and Artyukhin). 4 Swahili adopted as official language in Kenya in place of English. 9 Canadian general election gave Trudeau overall majority of 18. 10 Government announced choice of British-designed nuclear reactor for third stage of programme in 1980s. 12 Repeal of 1971 Industrial Relations Act. 13 Final Report of Ervin Senate Watergate Committee published. 15 Coup d'état in Cyprus by National Guard officers: President Makarios overthrown and replaced by Nicos Sampson. 17 Bomb exploded with no warning in Tower of London: one killed, 41 injured. 18 Maplin airport project cancelled; Abolition of Pay Board and end of statutory incomes policy. 20 Turkish invasion of Cyprus. 22 Ceasefire in Cyprus declared; Mini-Budget cut VAT to 8%. 26 Junta in Greece collapsed: Mr. Karamanlis returned to power; Glafkos Clerides interim-acting President of Cyprus. 24 Supreme Court ordered surrender of 64 White House tape recordings subpoenaed by Mr. Leon Jaworski, the Special Watergate prosecutor. 25 International Court of Justice in The Hague ruled that Britain not bound by Iceland's unilateral decision in 1972 to extend its rights from 12 to 50 miles. 26 Bomb exploded at Heathrow European terminal car park; French

A.D.

made official language of province of Quebec. 27–30 Three articles of impeachment adopted by Judiciary Committee of the House of Representatives against President Nixon. 30 British, Greek and Turkish foreign ministers signed a peace agreement in Geneva. 31 Abolition of the National Industrial Relations Court (NIRC).

August 3 Portugal to grant independence to her 3 African colonies: Angola, Mozambique, Guinea-Bissau. 5 President Nixon admitted he had withheld information on Watergate. 8 President Nixon resigned. 9 Mr. Gerald Ford sworn in as 38th President of USA; Extension of Italy's sea limits from 6 to 12 miles. 11 Half Bangladesh under water following monsoon floods: followed by famine and cholera epidemic. 14 Greek Prime Minister announced withdrawal of Greek armed forces from NATO. Failure of peace talks on Cyprus: Turks renewed offensive and took control of most of north-east third of island. 15 Collapse of Court Line left many holidaymakers stranded. 18 19 leading Provisionals broke out of Portlaoise top security prison. Egyptian girl of 13 swam English Channel, the youngest to do so. 20 President Ford named Mr. Nelson Rockefeller as Vice-President; Mr. F. A. Ahmed elected President of the Indian Union. 26 Death of Charles Lindbergh; Guinea-Bissau became independent. 29 Police broke up pop festival in Windsor Great Park.

September 1 U.S. Lockheed SR-71 crossed from New York to London in 1 h 55 m (3,490 miles). 2 New Conciliation and Arbitration Service (CAS) started work. 3 Two crew drowned when Mr. Heath's Morning Cloud was hit in Channel by huge waves. 4 Sikkim's status changed from Indian protectorate to associated state. 6 Wallace Rowling became Prime Minister of New Zealand following death of Norman Kirk. 8 President Ford granted full pardon to Richard Nixon. 12 Emperor Haile Selassie deposed by military command. 13 Bishop Blanch, Bishop of Liverpool, appointed Archbishop of York. 15 Dominant role for Frelimo in caretaker government in Mozambique (independence June 1975). 19 Hurricane Fifi struck Honduras: 8,000 dead; 600,000 homeless. 24 Portugal and India re-established diplomatic relations with Portugal recognising Indian sovereignty over Portuguese territories seized in 1961. 30 General Spinola resigned as President of Portuguese Republic; succeeded by General Francisco da Costa Gomes.

October 5 Death of Miguel Enriques, Chilean revolutionary, shot in battle with police; Two bombs in Guildford public houses killed five people and injured 70. 10 General Election in Britain: Labour returned with overall majority of 3. 15 Rioting in the Maze prison: fire destroyed many of the buildings; British space satellite UK5 launched off coast of Kenya. 18 Unit in Whitehall set up to prepare for devolution of power to Scotland and Wales. 22 Bomb exploded in Brooks's Club, St James's Street. 24 Death of David Oistrakh, Russian violinist and conductor. 26–29 Rabat summit meeting of Arab heads of state: PLO recognised as representative of Palestinians. 30 Muhammad Ali regained world heavyweight boxing title by knocking out George Foreman at Kinshasa. 31 Hostages held for six days at Scheveningen gaol freed by Dutch commandos.

November 2–3 Summit meeting between President Ford and Mr. Brezhnev at Vladivostok. 3 Strong reaction by hospital consultants to proposed phasing out of pay beds in National Health hospitals. 4 Judith Ward given 12 life sentences for causing M62 bomb blast deaths. 5 World Food Conference opened in Rome. 7 Two killed in bomb attack on Woolwich pubs. 8 Covent Garden market moved to new site at Nine Elms. 8 Ronald Milhench goaled for forging Mr. Harold Wilson's signature in land deals affair. 12 Budget day: increase in pensions; 25% VAT on petrol; £1,500 million relief to industry; UN General Assembly voted to exclude South Africa from meetings this session; Wolfson College, Oxford, opened.

A.D.
13 Yassir Arafat of the Palestine Liberation Organisation addressed UN General Assembly. **15** Dr. Donald Coggon succeeded Dr. Michael Ramsey as Archbishop of Canterbury. **17** Greece held first general elections since 1967: victory for Mr. Constantine Karamanlis; Mr. Erskine Childers, President of the Irish Republic, died. **21** 21 killed and 120 injured in bomb blasts in two Birmingham bars; Mr. John Stonehouse MP disappeared after going for a swim at Miami Beach. **24** Six charged with Birmingham bomb murders; Ethiopian military government announced execution of 60 former ministers. **25** Death of U Thant. **26** Plan for high-speed rail link between Folkestone and London abandoned for economy reasons. **27** Two bombs exploded in Chelsea. **29** Anti-Terrorism Bill proscribing the IRA and giving police wider powers received Royal Assent.

December 1 Two Irishmen charged with Guildford pub bomb outrage. **3** Defence cuts announced: £4,700 million over next 10 years. **5** Sir Don Ryder, Chief Executive of Reed International appointed Industrial Adviser to the Government; Appeal for £3·5 million to save fabric of Canterbury Cathedral; 90 people killed in Tehran when roof of Mehrabad airport terminal collapsed. **6** Government announced aid to British Leyland. **7** Archbishop Makarios returned to Cyprus. **8** Greeks voted against return to the monarchy and for a republic. **9** Energy saving programme announced: speed restrictions and reduced heating levels; Mr. Tanaka resigned as Prime Minister of Japan. **11** Mr. Ian Smith announced ceasefire with nationalist guerrillas and release of political prisoners in Rhodesia; House of Commons voted against restoration of capital punishment for terrorism. **15** 18 Residents died in fire at old people's home outside Nottingham. **18–22** New wave of bombs in London: outside Selfridges; at Harrods; and at the home of Mr. Edward Heath. **19** Petrol prices went up by 10p a gallon; Compensation to relatives of those killed on " Bloody Sunday " (1972) announced. **22** Ceasefire ordered by IRA over Christmas. **24** Mr. John Stonehouse found in Australia. **25** Devastation of Darwin, Australia, by cyclone Tracy.

1975

January 1 Watergate defendants Mitchell, Haldeman, Ehrlichman and Mardian found guilty of conspiracy and of obstruction of justice. **6** London Stock market index at lowest point of 146. **7** EEC finance ministers agreed on London scheme to recycle 12 billion petrodollars through IMF. **9** Mr. Elliot Richardson appointed Ambassador to UK. **13–17** China's Fourth National People's Congress: new state constitution adopted: post of Chairman (President) abolished; Mao Tse-tung named as Head of Forces. **20** Evacuation of some 9,000 Turkish Cypriot refugees from British base at Akrotiri. **23** Bomb attack on Europa hotel in Belfast; Referendum to be held on British Common Market membership before end of June. **24** Minimum lending rate reduced to 11%; Dr. Coggan enthroned 101st Archbishop of Canterbury; Pope represented at ceremony. **25** End of democracy in Bangladesh: Shaikh Mujibur Rahman became President of one-party state. **27** 24 hurt in terrorist bomb attacks in Manchester and London; President Sadat in Paris on arms deal; Government to introduce low-start mortgages for first-time home buyers; US Senate to set up Select Committee to investigate activities of CIA, FBI and other spying organisations; Khmer Rouge major offensive in Cambodia.

February 1 Death of Um Kalthoum, Egypt's popular singer. **4** Mr. Heath withdrew as leader of the Conservative Party after defeat by Mrs. Thatcher in first ballot for Tory leadership. **6** The Queen abandoned plan to spend £200,000 on modernising Sandringham. **7** Unemployment in US up to 8·2%, highest since 1941. **11** Mrs. Thatcher elected leader of the Conservative Party; Assassination of President of Malagasy.

A.D.
13 Wilson-Brezhnev summit meeting in Moscow began; Declaration by Turkish Cypriots of separate state in Cyprus. **14** Sir Julian Huxley and P. G. Woodehouse died. Reginald Maudling appointed Shadow Foreign Secretary. **18** Industry Bill given Second Reading (313 votes to 299). **25** Death of Nikolai Bulgarin, former Russian Prime Minister. **26** Government White Paper on organisation of Britain's EEC referendum published: result to be judged by simple majority. **28** Train at speed crashed into blind tunnel at Moorgate station, London Underground: 41 dead. Mildest winter in Britain since 1869.

March 4 Charles Chaplin knighted by the Queen. **5** Seaborne attack by Arab guerrillas on Tel-Aviv: 13 died including 7 terrorists. **6** End of OPEC meeting in Algiers: oil prices to be linked to inflation: agreement between Iran and Iraq. **10** South Africa ordered police units in Rhodesia to withdraw from anti-guerrilla activities; Workers' motorcycle cooperative at Meriden began work. **11** Agreement reached at EEC summit meeting at Dublin on renegotiation terms for Britain; Unsuccessful countercoup in Portugal: General Spinola fled. **13** Portugal's new Supreme Revolutionary Council headed by President Gomes took power. **17** Retreat of S. Vietnamese forces from Central Highlands after fall of Ban Me Thuot. **18** Mr. Wilson told Parliament of Cabinet's majority decision to recommend acceptance of renegotiation terms of Common Market membership (Cabinet vote 16–7 in favour); Herbert Chitepo, Rhodesian nationalist leader in exile (ZANU) assassinated in Lusaka. **22** Collapse of Kurdish uprisings in northern Iraq after Iranian withdrawal of support. **23** N. Vietnamese closed coast road between Hué and Da Nang; Breakdown of Dr. Kissinger's Middle East talks by failure to reach a new Egyptian–Israel accord. **25** Assassination of King Faisal of Saudi Arabia. **26** Evacuation of Hué by S. Vietnamese forces; Biological Weapons Convention came into force. **27** Death of Sir Arthur Bliss. **30** Da Nang abandoned by S. Vietnamese forces after panic and confusion; Suez Canal to be reopened 5 June 1975 but not yet to Israeli shipping.

April 1 Departure of Mashal Lon Nol from besieged capital Phnom Penh. **3** Death of Tung Pi-su, founder member of Chinese Communist Party. **5** Death of Chiang Kai-shek, aged 87. **9** Motion to approve EEC renegotiation White Paper carried by majority of 226 votes. **12** Death of Josephine Baker, aged 69. **16** Mr. Alexander Shelepin dropped from Soviet Politburo. **17** Phnom Penh government surrendered to Khmer Rouge: end of 5 years of civil war in Cambodia. **18** Death of Dr. Sarvepalli Radhakrishnan, second President of India, aged 86. **21** President Thieu resigned as N. Vietnamese forces encircled Saigon. **21–25** First European Nuclear Energy Conference held in Paris (47 countries represented). **23** Massive airlift of refugees from Vietnam to USA. **24** Government statement to Commons on British Leyland: Government to invest £1400 million over 8 years. **25** Elections in Portugal the first for 50 years: Socialist Party (PSP) 38% of votes, the largest single party; **29** Commonwealth Conference opened in Jamaica. **30** End of Vietnamese war, the longest conflict of the 20th century, when Saigon surrendered to Communist forces.

May 5 *Scottish Daily News* published, the first workers cooperative national newspaper. **12** US merchant vessel *Mayaguez* forced by Cambodian forces to anchor in Gulf of Thailand; Laos fell to Communists. **13** Britain recognised Provisional Revolutionary Government in S. Vietnam; Sterling sank to all-time low of 25·2% below Dec. 1971 levels; French franc to rejoin EEC's currency " snake ". **14** President Ford authorised air attacks on Cambodian patrol boats. **15** *Mayaguez* and crew rescued by US marines. **16** Entry into force of new local government structure in Scotland: 9 regional, 13 district and 3 island councils. **18** Filbert Bayi of Tanzania broke J. Ryun's 8-year-old mile record in Jamaica: 3 min 51 s. **21** Death

A.D.

of Barbara Hepworth, English sculptor. 27 Chinese team of 9 (including one woman) scaled Everest by North face. 29 Dr. Gustav Husak elected President of Czechoslovakia. 30 European Space Agency (ESA) set up (supersedes ELDO). 30–31 Coldest May night in Britain since records began.

June 2 Israeli decision to pull back further from Suez Canal; Snow fell in London for first time (in June) since reliable records began. 5 UK voted "Yes" by 2 to 1 majority in EEC referendum. 5 Reopening of Suez Canal to international shipping after 8 years of closure. 9 First live radio broadcast of House of Commons sitting. 12 Mrs. Gandhi convicted of illegally using Government officials in her campaign for Parliament in 1971. 15 Significant left-wing surge in Italian regional elections. 16 UK ended Simonstown Defence Agreement with S. Africa. 26 State of emergency declared by Mrs. Gandhi: 676 people arrested including 100 top political figures; British Government announced ending of Beira patrol now that Mozambique can itself impose sanctions against Smith regime. 30 £ fell to 29% of its Jan. 1971 value; Zambian economy put under state control: freehold land titles abolished. Sunniest June in London since records began.

July 1 Mr. S. S. Ramphal (Guyana's Minister of Justice) succeeded Mr. Arnold Smith (appointed 1965) as Commonwealth Secretary-General. 3 Watergate grand jury (in existence for 3 years) dissolved. 4 New Kurdish nationalist party formed in Iraq. 5 Cape Verde Islands achieved independence from Portugal. 6 Record wheat yield in China; Unilateral Declaration of Independence from France declared by Comoro Islands. 7 British Labour Party MPs attended European Parliament at Strasbourg. 8 School leaving date in England and Wales to be changed from end of summer term to Friday before Spring bank holiday. 11 Mr. Healey's statement of anti-inflation policy: £6 a week limit on pay increases till 1 Aug. 1976; Withdrawal of Socialist Party from Portuguese government; Independence of Portuguese São Tomé and Príncipe. 15 Launch of Apollo-Soyuz spacecraft for first international link-up. 16 £85,000 paid for Turner's " The Dark Rigi " at Sotheby's. 17 First link up of US astronauts and Soyuz cosmonauts in space when Apollo and Soyuz spacecraft successfully docked; 4 British soldiers in explosion in border area of N. Ireland—second such incident since cease-fire. Mineworkers' national executive committee gave support (14 to 10) to Government's anti-inflation policy; Fall of Portuguese coalition government; Portugal to receive no aid from EEC until democracy restored. 23 Approval of Mrs. Gandhi's emergency powers passed by both Houses of Parliament. 26 Salyut 4 space station landed after record time (63 days) in space; Turkish decision to close US air bases in protest against arms embargo. 29 Military coup in Nigeria deposed Gen. Gowon while he was in Kampala: new head of state Brigadier Murtala Mohammed; Lord Kearton head of new state oil combine (British National Oil Corporation); Expansion of British Rail's main line electrification programme under threat because of economic crisis. 30 Helsinki 35-nation summit conference on European security and cooperation; Gen. Gowon accepted defeat and pledged loyalty to new Government. 31 Britain recognised new Nigerian Government; Cabinda declared itself independent.

August 7 Hottest August day in London since records began in 1940 (32·3°C); Government plans to abolish tied cottages on farms and give 70,000 farmworkers protection of Rent Acts against eviction; Indian constitution amended to give Mrs. Gandhi fresh powers. 8 Pres. Costa Gomez swore in new Government in Portugal led by Prime Minister Gen. Goncalves; Death of Shostakovich, aged 68. 12 John Walker of New Zealand set world record for mile at 3 min 49·4 s. 15 Assassination of Muzibur Rahman of Bangladesh. 22 Opening of South Africa's Orange-Fish tunnel (50 miles long). 26–28 Meeting of Commonwealth

A.D.

Finance Ministers in Georgetown (Guyana). 27 Death of Haile Selassie, former Emperor of Ethiopia. 27–28 Bombs at Caterham and London. 28 Miners voted for Government/ TUC counter-inflation measures (pay increase limit of £6 a week). 29 Death of De Valera.

September 3 At Blackpool TUC Congress backed Government's £6 flat-rate pay policy. 4 Disengagement agreement negotiated by Dr. Kissinger signed between Egypt and Israel at Geneva. 5 Gen. Goncalves, Portugal's pro-Communist former Prime Minister, abandoned attempt to become commander-in-chief of armed forces. 9 Return after 5½ years of exile of Prince Sihanouk to Cambodia as titular head of state. 11 Soviet Union proposed international treaty banning all nuclear weapons tests. 14 Rembrandt's The Nightwatch severely slashed but not irreparably; The Pope canonised America's first native-born saint—Elisabeth Bayley Seton (1774–1821). 16 Independence of Papua New Guinea as 35th member of the Commonwealth. 24 Government announced £175m package of measures to check unemployment. Dougal Haston and Doug Scott climbed Everest by south-west face, the first ever successful assault by this route. 27 Execution of five political activists in Spain: 12 countries recalled their ambassadors in protest. 28 Gunmen took seven Italians as hostages in the Spaghetti House restaurant in London.

October 1 Three policemen shot dead in Madrid; Attorney General refused injunction by High Court to prevent publication of Crossman diaries. 3 End of the Spaghetti House siege: hostages released unharmed and captors surrendered; Dr. Herrema, a Dutch industrialist, kidnapped in Limerick, held captive at Monasterevin, near Dublin. 6 EEC broke off trade negotiations with Spain; In Argentina's guerrilla war, 30 people killed when troops fought guerrillas attacking army base and airport. 9 1975 Nobel peace prize awarded to Dr. Andrei Sakharov. 15 Iceland unilaterally extended its fishing rights from 50 to 200 miles; Archbishop of Canterbury launched campaign urging British people to rise to new sense of moral purpose. 17 " Cod war " talks between Britain and Iceland broke down. 20 Appointment of a Royal Commission to investigate the Health Service. 21 In Britain, unemployment rose to over one million for first time since the war; Inauguration at Teesside of first pipeline from Norwegian Ekofisk field. 23 Ceremony marking completion of track-laying of Tanzam railway (in full operation 1976) with tribute by Pres. Kaunda to Chinese assistance; Bomb placed under car of Mr. Hugh Fraser MP in London killed Professor Fairley, leading cancer expert; Nobel prize for literature awarded to Signor E. Montale. 25 Soviet Venus 10 soft-landed on Venus (Venus 9 landed on 22nd); 26 In Beirut, clashes between right-wing Christian Phalangists and left-wing Muslims developed into full-scale battles. 27 Alfred Herbert the machine tool group, taken over by the Government.

November 3 Major changes at top level in American government: dismissal of Dr. J. Schlesinger (Defence) and Mr. W. Colby (Director CIA); At Dyce, Aberdeenshire, the Queen formally inaugurated the flow of North Sea oil from the BP Forties field. 5 Chequers Meeting: Government, TUC, CBI and NEDC met to discuss strategy for regeneration of British industry; Reinforcement of Belize garrison in face of Guatemalan militancy. 7 Death of Cardinal Heenan; Mrs. Gandhi won her appeal in Supreme Court against corrupt electoral practice; Dr. Herrema released by kidnappers; IMF approached for £975m loan by Britain; Scottish Daily News closed down. 10 Independence of Angola after 500 years of Portuguese rule; UN General Assembly attacked Zionism as " a form of racism ": bitter Israeli reaction to accusation. 11 Australia's Labour Government, led by Gough Whitlam, dismissed by the Governor-General, Sir John Kerr; Opposition leader, Malcolm Fraser, appointed acting Prime Minister and

A.D.

general election called for 13 December; Number of civilians killed in N. Ireland since 1969 reached 1000. **12** One man killed and 15 injured when bomb exploded at Scott's Restaurant in Mount Street, London. **13** WHO announced eradication of smallpox in Asia. **14** Spain agreed to give up sovereignty of the Spanish Sahara by end of February 1976. **15** Leaders from Britain, United States, France, West Germany, Japan and Italy met at Rambouillet, near Paris, for 3-day summit conference on economic matters; Incidents with Iceland gunboats: arrival in Iceland of British minister. **18** President Nyerere on state visit to England; first official visit since he led Tanzania to independence in 1961. **20** Death of General Franco, aged 82; Ronald Reagan, former Governor of California, announced his candidature for Republican Party's nomination for the Presidency. **21** Anthony Crosland, Secretary for the Environment, announced 1% cut in Government grant towards councils' total expenditure in 1976. **22** Prince Juan Carlos crowned King of Spain. **25** British Government authorised the sending of three Royal Navy frigates to protect British tᵣ wlers fishing off Iceland; Surinam (Dutch Guiana) became independent. **27** Publication of White Paper on devolution for Scotland and Wales. Ross McWhirter, writer and publisher, shot dead by two gunmen at his home in north London. **28** Fretilin military forces in East Timor unilaterally declared the Portuguese colony independent. **29** New Zealand general election: Labour Party defeated by National Party. **30** UN Security Council agreed to renew for six months the mandate of UN peacekeeping force on Golan Heights; Republic of Dahomey, former French West African colony, changed name to People's Republic of Benin.

December 1 President Ford arrived in Peking for five-day visit; EEC heads of government met in Rome. **2** British Aircraft Corporation signed contract worth £186 million to supply Iran with Rapier anti-aircraft missile system. Five South Moluccan terrorists held passengers hostage in train hijacked in isolated part of Dutch countryside; Israeli attack on refugee camps in Lebanon: 77 killed. **3** Soviet Union's grain harvest of 137 million tonnes lowest for 10 years; King Savang Vatthana of Laos abdicated and the Government resigned. **4** End of detention without trial in N. Ireland after 4½ years. **10** First shots fired in "cod war". **11** House of Commons voted 361–232 not to restore death penalty; End of Balcombe Street siege in London: Mr. and Mrs. Matthews held in flat by IRA terrorists since 6 Dec. **12** Estate of Picasso valued at £650 million. **14** End of Dutch train siege at Beilen; Landslide victory in Australia for Malcolm Fraser's Liberal Country Party over Gough Whitlam's Labour Party. **16** Government announced measures costing £162.5 million to save Chrysler. **18** Announcement that 7 June 1977 would be the Bank Holiday to mark 25th anniversary of the Queen's accession; Education Bill compelling comprehensive school education published. **19** US Senate voted (against President Ford) to cut off aid to Angola. **26** Russia's supersonic Tupolov 144 began its first regular service. **29** Sex Discrimination and Equal Pay Acts came into force; Bomb explosion at La Guardia airport, New York.

1976

January 3 Weekend tidal wave and gales caused severe flood damage to east coast of England and northern Europe: sea defences after 1953 flood disaster held. **4** Five Roman Catholics killed in ambush by Protestant terrorists. **5** Machine-gun massacre of 10 Protestant textile workers at Whitecross, Armagh, by Catholic terror groups—worst sectarian murder since 1969. **6** MPLA offensive in Angolan civil war; British Army's "Spearhead Battalion" flown to S. Armagh as reinforcement. **7** Death of Sir Thomas Monnington, Pres. of Royal Academy; Strike of metro-workers in Madrid: other workers struck in sympathy. **8** Death of Chou

A.D.

En-lai, aged 77, for 26 years senior leader of China; Indian Government suspended freedom of speech, assembly and movement, the fourth suspension since emergency began. **10** Meeting in Addis Ababa of heads of state of Organisation for African Unity: deadlock over Angolan issue. **11** Iceland asked Dr. Luns, Sec. Gen. of NATO to mediate in "cod war". **12** Death of Agatha Christie, aged 85; Government to reconvene N. Ireland Convention from 3 Feb. (for 4 weeks). **13** Agreement signed between Zambia and Mozambique for construction of road and rail links. **14** Death of Tun Abdul Razak, Prime Minister of Malaysia; British Airways took possession of their first Concorde. **19** Icelandic Prime Minister invited to London for talks; Government majority of 158 at end of 4-day devolution debate. **20** UK unemployment 1,430,369 (inc. students): 6·1% of work force. **21** Concorde entered supersonic passenger service after 14 years' Anglo-French co-operation: simultaneous take-offs from London (to Bahrein) and Paris (to Rio de Janeiro). **22** Cease-fire announcement in Lebanon: Syrian peace plan; Seychelles to become independent 28 June; Government accepted Radcliffe Report on ministerial memoirs. **23** Sir Idwal Pugh to succeed Sir Alan Marre as Parliamentary Commissioner for Administration (Ombudsman); Death of Paul Robeson, aged 77. **27** Mr. Whitlam re-elected leader of Australian Labour Party; Clash in Spanish Sahara between Algerian and Moroccan forces; China to send official delegation to Brussels to negotiate trade agreement with EEC. **31** Most violent month in N. Ireland since 1969: 50 killed.

February 1 Death of Werner Heisenberg, German physicist, whose name is associated with the uncertainty principle. **2** Opening by the Queen of 310-acre National Exhibition Centre at Bickenhill, Birmingham; Iceland rejected Britain's proposals to end "cod war". **4** Licence granted for Concorde to land at Washington and New York for 16-month trial period. **11** Recognition of MPLA as legal government of Angola by OAU. **12** Workmen discovered a rose perfectly preserved, hidden in wall of Romsey Abbey in 1120, thought to be oldest botanical specimen found in Europe (the oldest was a posy recovered from Tutankhamun's tomb). **13** Assassination of General Murtala Mohammed, Nigerian head of state, in unsuccessful coup. **17** France first of Western countries to recognise MPLA as legal government of Angola; Sir Hugh Casson elected new President of Royal Academy; Abbot Basil Hume of Ampleforth to be next Archbishop of Westminster. **19** Iceland broke off diplomatic relations with Britain over fishing dispute. **23** Death of L. S. Lowry, Salford artist, aged 88.

March 3 Mozambique closed border with Rhodesia and implemented sanctions. **5** Mr. Dmitry Ustinov and Mr. Grigory Romanov to be full members of Soviet Politburo; Ulster Convention dissolved: direct rule from Westminster continued. **16** Resignation of Mr. Wilson as Prime Minister. **19** Official announcement of separation of Princess Margaret and Lord Snowdon. **24** Death of Lord Montgomery of Alamein; Senora Perón of Argentina deposed; Summit meeting in Lusaka of Presidents of Zambia, Tanzania, Botswana and Mozambique. **30** As from 1978 May Day to be a Bank Holiday.

April 5 Mr. James Callaghan became Prime Minister: defeated Mr. Michael Foot by 176 votes to 137 in final ballot for leadership of the Labour Party. **6** Community Land Act (passed 12 Nov. 1975) became effective. **9** Syrian regular forces advanced in Lebanon. **16** India raised minimum marriage ages from 18 to 21 (men) and 15 to 18 (women). **22** Mr. Harold Wilson appointed Knight of the Garter. **25** Portuguese parliamentary elections gave Dr. Mario Soares and his Socialist Party decisive lead. **26** Death of Marshal Grechko, Soviet Defence Minister. **27** Britain began exporting North Sea oil (from B.P.'s Forties field).

May 5 Fourth Unctad conference opened in Nairobi: Dr. Kissinger put forward constructive

A.D.

proposals for consumer-producer co-operation on commodities; TUC general council endorsed Chancellor's pay policy. **8** Mr. Brezhnev named a marshal of the army, the Soviet Union's highest military rank. **10** Resignation of Mr. Jeremy Thorpe as leader of the Liberal Party. **11** Suicide in prison of Frau Ulrike Meinhof, German anarchist leader. **12** Mr. Jo Grimond agreed to resume leadership of the Liberal Party for a temporary period. **17** Violent earthquake in Tashkent area of Soviet Central Asia. **24** Concordes from England and France flew to Washington for first time. **28** Soviet-American treaty controlling underground nuclear explosions for non-military purposes signed, providing for on-site verification. **29** South Africa to buy two nuclear power stations from France.

June 1 Interim agreement signed in Oslo ending " cod war " between Britain and Iceland; Intervention by Syrian troops in Lebanon to restore law and order. **5** Release of former Rhodesian Prime Minister, Mr. Garfield Todd, from house arrest. **7** Chancellor secured £3 billion stand-by credit from central banks of Europe and America. **9** Death of Dame Sybil Thorndike. **16** Riots began in African township of Soweto near Johannesburg against compulsory teaching of Afrikaans, exacerbated by pent-up grievances. **20–21** Italian general election:

	%	Seats
Christian Democrats	38·7	262
Socialists	9·6	57
Communists	34·4	228

(Signor Andreotti formed minority Christian Dem. Government July 29). **21** OECD adopted code of conduct on bribery and disclosure of information for multinational companies. **24** Vietnam reunified: recognition by Britain; **26** Pictures from Mars *Viking 1* gave rich geological data. **25** President Amin made life-president of Uganda. **25–28** Hottest consecutive four days in London with temperatures reaching 35°C (96°F). **26** Severe earthquake in Indonesian New Guinea. **27** Leaders from Britain, France, W. Germany, Italy, Canada, US and Japan met in Puerto Rico for second " economic summit " conference; Gen. Antonio Ramalho Eanes, Army Chief of Staff, elected President of Portugal. **29** Independence of Seychelles as republic within Commonwealth. **30** Mr. Dmitry Ustinov (who succeeded the late Marshal Grechko as Minister of Defence) promoted Marshal of the Soviet Union.

July 2 Government emergency powers to control water shortage in Britain. **4** Israeli attack on Entebbe airport to free 100 Israeli hostages from Air France Flight 139 from Tel Aviv hijacked by Palestinian extremists. **7** The Queen arrived in Washington for bicentennial celebrations; Death of Marshal Chu Teh, Grand Old Man of the Chinese Army; Mr. David Steel elected leader of the Liberal Party by party workers. **10** Explosion at Hoffman-La Roche's Seveso plant near Milan; poisonous chemical contaminated area of 7 km radius. **13** Mr. Roy Jenkins to be President of EEC Commission from Jan. 1977. **14** Official handing over to Tanzania and Zambia of Chinese-built Tanzam railway (1,860 km). **15** Governor Jimmy Carter of Georgia nominated presidential candidate by Democratic Convention; Senator Walter Mondale from Minnesota Mr. Carter's vice-presidential nominee. **16** Dr. Soares asked by Portuguese President Eanes to form government. **21** Mr. Christopher Ewart-Biggs, British Ambassador to Irish Republic, and a member of his staff, assassinated by landmine. **22** Death of archaeologist Sir Mortimer Wheeler. **28** Major earthquake (8·2 Richter scale), the worst since 1556, destroyed Chinese mining town of Tangshan: very heavy death toll; Britain broke off diplomatic relations with Uganda. **30** Partial amnesty granted by King Juan to Spanish political prisoners (about 650).

August 1 Trinidad and Tobago became independent republic within Commonwealth. **2** China reported another 15 earthquakes and over 100

A.D.

earth tremors. **4** Death of Lord Thomson of Fleet, owner of *The Times*; Renewed violence in South African township of Soweto. **6** Drought Act 1976 came into force. **7** *Viking 2* went into orbit round Mars. **8** Sortie by Rhodesian troops across Mozambique border. **12** Embattled Palestinian refugee camp of Tel al-Zaatar fell to right-wing Christian forces. **14** First mass rally of Women's Peace Movement in N. Ireland, formed by Mrs. Betty Williams and Miss Maireaed Corrigan. **16** Opening in Colombo of non-aligned nations' summit meeting: own monetary system sought; Spread of Black unrest in Cape Town's townships. **18** Soviet *Luna 24* made soft landing on surface of moon (S.E. part of Sea of Crises) to take soil samples with automatic scoop; Mr. Brian Faulkner, leader of the Unionist Party of N. Ireland, to retire from politics. **22** According to historical evidence drought in Britain worst for 500 years. **25** Hong Kong had heaviest rainfall (16 in.) for 15 years; Resignation of M. Chirac, Prime Minister of France; Unemployment figure (crude) in Britain rose above 1·5 million.

September 2 European Commission on Human Rights reported on charges against Britain brought by Irish Government: Britain guilty of torturing detainees in Ulster after introduction of internment in 1971 but cleared of charge of discrimination between Republican and Protestant extremists. **4** Meeting of Mr. Vorster and Dr. Kissinger in Zurich to find political solution to problems of Southern Africa. **6** Meeting of five African states around Rhodesia in Dar-es-Salaam. **8** High pressure system over Britain came to an end. **9** Death of China's great leader Mao Tse-tung, aged 82. **10** Mid-air collision of 2 airliners near Zagreb (one British, one Yugoslav), all 176 aboard killed. **11** Mourning ceremony in Peking began for Mao Tse-tung in the Great Hall of the People. **14** Meeting of Mr. Vorster and Mr. Smith in Pretoria to discuss Dr. Kissinger's proposals relating to Southern Africa. **19** Dr. Kissinger held weekend talks in Pretoria with Mr. Vorster and Mr. Ian Smith; India relaxed censorship of foreign journalists. **20** Convention signed by EEC members in Brussels for election of a 410-member European Parliament; Electoral defeat of Sweden's Social Democratic Party after 44 years in power; British minesweeper *Fittleton* sank after collision with frigate *Mermaid* on NATO exercise off Dutch coast. Mr. Dom Mintoff (Labour) won Malta's general election with majority of 3 seats. **22** Portugal became 19th member of Council of Europe. **24** Mr. Ian Smith announced acceptance of British and American proposals for majority rule in Rhodesia in two years. **29** Following two days of exceptional pressure on £, Chancellor applied to IMF for stand-by of £2·3 billion.

October 1 Roman Catholic Bishop of Umtali sentenced by Rhodesian court to 10 years' imprisonment for failing to report presence of guerrillas. **3** Welcome in Salisbury, Rhodesia, for nationalist leader, Bishop Muzorewa, who returned from exile; W. German Bundestag elections: ruling coalition of Social Democrats and Free Democrats (SPD–FDP) gained narrow victory over Christian Democrats (CDM) and Christian Social Union (CSU). **4** British Rail's high-speed train came into service on London-Bristol route. **6** MLR raised to 15%; Military coup in Thailand and the end of civilian rule after 3 years. **7** Sir Harold Wilson to head committee to investigate functioning of the City. **12** Official announcement of appointment of Hua Kuo-feng as Chairman of the Chinese Communist Party. **14** Death of Dame Edith Evans. **18** Revaluation of the Deutsche Mark took pressure off £. **19** Meeting of six Arab leaders in Saudi Arabian capital of Riyadh to draw up plans for ending civil war in Lebanon. **21** Mr. Michael Foot elected deputy leader of the Parliamentary Labour Party. **25** Official opening of the National Theatre by the Queen; Independence of the Transkei (international recognition withheld because seen as part of S. Africa's apartheid policy); New coalfield with 50 million tons of reserves located under

A.D.
Firth of Forth: **28** Conference on future of Rhodesia, chaired by Mr. Ivor Richard, opened in Geneva. **29** Opening of world's largest mining complex at Selby, Yorks. **30** EEC agreement on introduction of 200-mile Community fishing zone as from 1 Jan. 1977.

November 1 Top Premium Savings Bond increased from £75,000 to £100,000; Mr. Jimmy Carter elected President of the USA with Democratic majorities in both Houses. **7** Another earthquake in S.E. China near Kunming; Planting in Belfast of crosses for lives lost since 1969—a total of 1,662. **12** General strike in Spain. **13** Earth tremor near Peking; Formal end of civil war in Lebanon as Syrian troops (as part of Arab peacekeeping force) moved into heart of Beirut; US vetoed Vietnam's application for UN membership. **23** Tangshan (destroyed by earthquakes 28 July and 15 November) to be rebuilt in another location. **24** Earthquake in E. Turkey: at least 4,000 killed with injured survivors dying of exposure in freezing temperatures; Mr. Robert Anderson's American oil group, Atlantic Richfield, to take control of the *Observer*. **26** The Children Act 1976 came into force. **27** Rally in Trafalgar Square in support of N. Ireland Peace People. **30** Publication of Bill setting up Scottish and Welsh assemblies.

December 1 Angola admitted to UN as 146th member; Death of Marshal Ivan Yakubovsky, Soviet C.-in-C. of Warsaw Pact military alliance, aged 64. **4** Death of Benjamin Britten. **5** M. Jacques Chirac, former French Prime Minister, elected leader of new Gaullist movement, the Rassemblement pour la République, against alliance of socialists and communists. **13** First oil from Brent North Sea oilfield taken by tanker to Fawley for refining. **15** Government's mini-budget: fresh constraints on public spending. **16** Scotland and Wales to have referendum on devolution; Landslide victory for Mr. Michael Manley in Jamaica's general election; **11** OPEC members voted to increase oil prices by 10% on 1 Jan. 1977 and by a further 5% on 1 July 1977, Saudi Arabia to raise prices by only 5%. **17** MLR reduced to 14½%. Exchange of Vladimir Bukovsky, Soviet dissident, and Señor Corvalán, veteran leader of Chilean Communist Party; Mr. Ian Trethowan to succeed Sir Charles Curran as Director-General of BBC.

1977

January 1 Britain together with EEC countries extended fishing limits to 200 miles offshore (with effect from 1 April). **5** Figures released from International Wheat Council showed bumper crops in Soviet Union, N. America, India, China and Argentina (while world population increased by 67%, wheat production increased by 155%). **11** Chancellor announced agreement on safety net to solve problem of Britain's sterling balances. **12** Volcanic eruption in E. Zaïre: lava flow moved at 7 km/h on surrounding countryside; Executive of National Union of Mineworkers voted for Coal Board's retirement scheme: miners with 20 years' underground service to retire at 62. **13** Britain had heaviest snowfall for a decade. **14** Death of Lord Avon. **15** Opening of Festival of Arts and Culture (FESTAC 1977) in Lagos. **18** Mrs. Gandhi announced holding of general election in March; Mr. Ivor Richard arrived in Cape Town from Nairobi on second round of talks to find solution to Rhodesian problem. **19** Food riots in Egypt. **20** Inauguration of Mr. Jimmy Carter as 39th President of USA; Relaxation of emergency powers imposed by Mrs. Gandhi in 1975: censorship lifted and release of political prisoners. **21** MLR reduced by ¾% to 13¼%; President Carter pardoned "draft dodgers". **24** Collapse of second round of Rhodesian talks: Mr. Ian Smith rejected British proposals for transition to black majority rule. **26** Publication of Bullock Report on industrial democracy. **28** Despite Government ban on demonstrations in Spain, renewed violence. **31** Mr. Ivor Richard returned to London after end of his tour of Southern Africa;

A.D.
Earthquake in Soviet Central Asia near Tashkent; One of worst winters this century in Eastern States of USA.

February 2 Important NEDC meeting on industrial strategy; Britain had lowest strike record in 1975 for 9 years; Defection of Mr. Ram, senior member of Mrs. Gandhi's cabinet. **8** Diplomatic relations between Soviet Union and Spain resumed (for first time since Civil War); Soviet *Soyuz 24* docked with orbiting *Salyut 5* space laboratory one day after launch. **15** Deaths in England and Wales exceeded number of live births in 1976 (for first time since records began in 1837). **17** Uganda's Anglican archbishop and two cabinet ministers killed in mysterious circumstances while under arrest; Government to spend £6 million during next 4 years on solar energy research and development. **19** Death of Anthony Crosland, aged 58. **21** Dr. David Owen (aged 38) became Foreign Secretary. **22** British Government pressed for UN investigation into deaths in Uganda; Government defeated on guillotine motion to cut short debate of Devolution Bill. **23** Reports of large-scale massacres in Uganda of the Christian Achole and Lango tribes. **24** Rhodesian Government reduced Bishop Lamont's 10-year sentence to loss of citizenship and deportation; USA to cut aid to Ethiopia, Argentina and Uruguay because of human rights violations.

March 1 Mr. Callaghan's Government went into minority; Government to drop ship repairing section from aircraft and shipbuilding nationalisation Bill. **3** Death of Lord Faulkner, former N. Ireland Prime Minister. **4** Major earthquake in Transylvania, north of Bucharest (7·2 Richter scale); death toll estimated 1500. **7** The Queen arrived in Australia on her Jubilee tour; Landslide victory for Mr. Bhutto in Pakistan's national assembly election. **10** Astronomers observed (for first time) rings around Uranus as planet passed in front of a star; Mr. Callaghan in Washington for talks with President Carter. **13** French municipal elections: Alliance of left (Socialists and Communists) gained ground. **14** David McNee became Commissioner of the Metropolitan Police on retirement of Sir Robert Mark. **15** Sorin Crainic, aged 19, survived 252 hours under earthquake rubble in Bucharest. **16** Assassination of Lebanese left-wing leader, Kamal Jumblatt; **16–25** Dr. Castro's visit to Tanzania, Mozambique and Angola. **22** Resignation of Mrs. Gandhi after loss of seat in general election and defeat of Congress Party after 30 years in power; Earthquake in Iran (6·7 Richter scale) around Bandar Abbas. **23** Labour Government and Liberal Party's consultation agreement: Conservative motion of no-confidence defeated by 322 to 298. **24** Janata Government sworn in with Mr Moraji Desai as Prime Minister of India; Publication of Annan Committee's Report on future of broadcasting in Britain; **25** Summit meeting in Rome of EEC countries chaired by Mr. Callaghan. **26** Mr. Podgorny began visit to southern Africa. **27** World's worst aircraft disaster: collision on runway of two jumbo-jets (Pan Am and KLM) at Tenerife's Los Rodeos airport; 577 killed. **27–30** American Secretary of State, Mr. Cyrus Vance, in Moscow: rejection by Soviet Union of US proposals on arms control. **31** The Queen and Prince Philip arrived back home after 7-week tour of Australia and New Zealand; Stechford by-election won by Conservatives on swing of 17·4%; Britain to go ahead with Hawker Siddeley *Nimrod* aircraft to police waters around Britain as a result of no agreement by NATO countries on US Awacs project; MLR reduced by 1% to 9½%.

April 7 President Carter's nuclear energy policy statement: production of plutonium to end; reprocessing techniques and fast-breeder programme to slow down; Mrs. Margaret Thatcher began her visit to China. **11** Report of French air transport for Moroccan troops to Zaïre. **12** New British initiative on Rhodesia: Dr. David Owen, Foreign Secretary, arrived in Tanzania on his diplomatic tour of southern

A.D.

Africa. **15** MLR reduced to 9%. **18** Page written by Galileo in 1612 fetched record £17,500. **20** President Carter warned of profligate use of energy. **21** Imposition of martial law in Karachi, Hyderabad and Lahore following 6 weeks of political violence in Pakistan; Mr. Moss Evans chosen TGWU's general secretary in succession to Mr. Jack Jones (retired March 1978). **22** MLR reduced to 8¼% (lowest for 4 years); Norwegian Ekofisk Bravo oilfield disaster: oil rig pressure blow-out lasted 181 hours until stopped on 30 April. **28** Right to form independent trade unions granted by Spanish Government. **29** British Aerospace (based in Bristol) came into operation as public corporation; MLR reduced to 8¼%.

May 2 Zaïre suspended diplomatic relations with E. Germany; general strike in N. Ireland called by United Ulster Action Council, led by Rev. Ian Paisley and Mr. Ernest Baird. **3** US–Vietnam negotiations on establishment of normal relations and trade relations opened in Paris; RAF Canberra crashed into row of houses near Huntingdon, killing 3 children and crew of two; Gains for Scottish National Party in local government elections; HMS *Invincible*, anti-submarine cruiser, launched by the Queen at Barrow-in-Furness. **4** The Queen at Palace of Westminster to hear loyal addresses from Commons and Lords said " I cannot forget that I was crowned Queen of the United Kingdom of Great Britain and Northern Ireland ". **5** In local government elections in England and Wales, Conservative gains included Greater London Council, Merseyside, W. Yorkshire, Greater Manchester, W. Midlands, Derbyshire, Leicestershire, Northamptonshire, Nottinghamshire and Humberside; Death of Ludwig Erhard, former Chancellor of W. Germany, aged 80. **6** Power workers in N. Ireland refused to strike. **7** Downing Street Economic Meeting (third in series—Rambouillet 1975, Puerto Rico, 1976) attended by Carter (USA), Fukuda (Japan), Schmidt (W. Germany), Giscard d'Estaing (France), Callaghan (UK), Trudeau (Canada) and Andreotti (Italy); British Rail inter-city train claimed long-run world record (117¼ mile Bristol/London journey in 68·20 min). **11** Appointment of Mr. Peter Jay as British ambassador in Washington. **13** Collapse of Ulster 11-day strike despite widespread intimidation; Balance of payments moved into £111 million surplus in April, best figures for more than 5 years. **17** The Queen welcomed in Glasgow at beginning of Silver Jubilee tour of the United Kingdom; Israeli Labour Party defeated in general election after governing for 29 years: right-wing Likud Party, led by Mr. Menachem Begin, emerged as largest party. **18** International Commission of Jurists reported to UN horrifying massacres and murders in Uganda under Amin's rule (80,000 to 90,000 killed 1971–2). **19** Mr. Mondale and Mr. Vorster met in Geneva for talks on Southern Africa; Kenya imposed ban on big game hunting. **20** Last run of Orient Express from Paris to Istanbul. **23** South Moluccan terrorists in northern Holland held hostages in school and train sieges. **24** Departure of 74-year-old President Podgorny from Soviet Communist Party's Politburo. **25** U.S.S.R. enforced 200-mile fishing zone in Barents Sea; President Tito celebrated his 85th birthday and 30th anniversary of Yugoslav revolution. **27** Presidium of Supreme Soviet approved new draft constitution and text and music for a new national anthem. **30** Rhodesian forces overran guerrilla bases inside Mozambique.

June 1 Royal College of Physicians' Report on smoking and health said every cigarette shortens the habitual smoker's life by an average of 5½ min; Change in road traffic speed limits in UK: 70 mile/h, dual roads, 60 mile/h, single. **3** Four-day Conference on International Economic Co-operation (North–South dialogue) ended with limited success. **5** Bloodless coup in the Seychelles while President Mancham in London for Commonwealth Conference. **6** Derby designated a city to mark Silver Jubilee. **7** Silver Jubilee Thanksgiving celebrations with

A.D.

state pageantry in London. **8** Commonwealth Conference opened in London. **11** End of 11-day Dutch sieges by South Moluccan terrorists after storming of train and school by Dutch Marines and police: 2 hostages and 6 Moluccans died; Miners in Shantung province, E. China, unearthed bird fossil of the Miocene period beautifully preserved. **13** Inland letter rates increased: first-class 9p, second-class 7p. **15** General election in Spain, first since 1936: victory for Union of Democratic Centre (UCD) led by Prime Minister Suarez. **16** Mr. Brezhnev elected President of the Presidium of the Supreme Soviet; Britain severed last diplomatic link with Uganda; Irish Republic's coalition Fine Gael–Labour government defeated in general election by Mr. Jack Lynch's Fianna Fail. **17** Death of Werner von Braun, scientist who designed German V2 rocket and later US Saturn launching vehicle for *Apollo* missions. **26** Death of Lady Baden-Powell of the Girl Guides movement; Independence from France after 117 years of Djibouti (Afars and Issas). **28** Silver Jubilee Review of the Fleet by the Queen at Spithead. **30** Summit meeting of EEC met in London under chairmanship of Mr. Callaghan: commitment to achievement of " homeland " for the Palestinian people; Employment Secretary announced appointment of Court of Inquiry into Grunwick film processing plant dispute, one of the most bitter industrial disputes of recent times.

July 1 Expiry of South-East Asian Treaty (SEATO); Britain placed unilateral ban on herring fishing in North Sea. **4** Death of Vladimir Nabokov, novelist, aged 78. **5** Army took charge in Pakistan and deposed Mr. Bhutto: general election in October. **11** Trade union demonstration outside Grunwick factory. **12** Spanish peseta devalued by 20% against dollar; Statement by President Carter on production of the neutron bomb which would kill people by radiation while minimising blast effects; Verdict of High Court supported union recognition in Grunwick dispute (Court of Appeal later reversed the decision). **15** Chancellor of Exchequer's statement: earnings increase in next 12 months to be limited to 10%. **18** Mr. Ian Smith dissolved Rhodesian Parliament and called for general election on 31 August. **21** Mrs. Bandaranaike and her Sri Lanka Freedom Party suffered defeat in general election; Border clash between Libyan and Egyptian forces. **23** Official confirmation of Teng Hsiao-p'ing's reinstatement as senior Chinese leader. **31** Phase Two of Government's counter-inflation policy expired.

August 3 Death of Archbishop Makarios, aged 63. MLR reduced to 7⅓%. **8** Ethiopia stated that conflict with Somalia in Ogaden desert had reached dimensions of a full-scale war. **10** The Queen visited Belfast. **10** Conclusion of new Panama Canal Agreement: gradual takeover by Panama of the zone and canal by the year 2000. **13** National Front march in Lewisham, London, brought violent clashes. **18** Chinese Communist Party's 11th National Congress ended: Mao's policies not to be abandoned but applied less dogmatically. **23** UK unemployment (crude) rose to 1,635,832 (6.9%). **31** Mr. Spyros Kyprianou became President of Cyprus. **25** Scarman Report on Grunwick dispute recommended company to re-employ strikers, but company rejected report.

September 1 Dr. Owen presented Mr. Ian Smith with Anglo-American proposals for a Rhodesian settlement. **8** Miss Cynthia Nicholas, aged 19, set new record for two-way Channel swim (19 h 55 min). **12** Death of Mr. Steven Biko (aged 30), Black South African leader, while in detention in South Africa. **13** Death of the poet Robert Lowell, aged 60, and of the conductor Leopold Stokowski, aged 95. **16** Death of Maria Callas, Greek opera singer, aged 53; MLR reduced to 6%. **21** National Front's proposed march in Tameside, Greater Manchester, banned; EEC passed resolution on terms of employment of African labour in S. Africa—rights to unionisation and remuneration comparable to payments to non-Black people.

A.D.

25 Mr. F. Laker's first Skytrain service to New York began.

October 7 New constitution of Soviet Union replaced 1936 "Stalin" constitution; MLR reduced to 5¼%. **14** Death of Bing Crosby; MLR reduced to 5%. **16** The Queen began her Canadian Jubilee tour. **17** US Supreme Court ruled that Concorde could use New York's Kennedy airport. **17** W. Germany's special unit of border forces freed all 87 hostages from hijacked Lufthansa 737 at Mogadishu after 5-day ordeal: 3 of the hijackers killed. **18** 3 Baader-Meinhof prisoners in Stammheim gaol took their own lives. **19** Crackdown by South African authorities on " black " newspapers, anti-apartheid organisations and black leaders; kidnapped W. German industrialist, Dr. Hans-Martin Schleyer found dead in car on French-German border. **24** 66,000-tonne transatlantic liner *France* sold to Saudi Arabia for use as floating luxury hotel. **25** Joint European Torus Research Project (JET) to be sited at Atomic Energy Laboratories at Culham near Oxford; UK unemployment (crude) fell by 90,000 to 1,518,375 (6·4%) **31** Effective revaluation of the £: Government allowed it to float upwards.

November 1 Soviet supersonic airliner TU-144 went into service (Moscow–Alma Ata route); President Carter announced US withdrawal from International Labour Organisation (ILO); Soviet conductor Gennadi Rozhdestvensky appointed BBC's Symphony Orchestra's principal conductor. **2** The Queen ended her Caribbean tour and flew back from Barbados in Concorde; Opening of 60th anniversary celebration of Russian Revolution, President Brezhnev offered to halt nuclear tests and production of nuclear weapons. **4** Mandatory arms embargo imposed by UN Security Council against S. Africa; Confirmation of Palomar astronomer Charles Kowal's discovery of new body in solar system (Object Kowal), at present between orbits of Saturn and Uranus. **9** Severe Israeli retaliatory air attack on South Lebanese villages. **14** First day of firemen's strike after their claim for a 30% pay increase had been rejected: armed forces dealt with fires; Retirement pension increased from £15·30 to £17·50 (single person) and from £24·50 to £28 (married couple). **15** A son (Peter Mark Andrew) born to Princess Anne. **19** Historic meeting in Israel between President Sadat of Egypt and Prime Minister Menachem Begin of Israel; Coastal belt off Bay of Bengal hit by cyclone: estimated death toll 20,000–25,000. **20** President Sadat addressed the Israeli Knesset in Jerusalem. **22** UK unemployment (crude) fell for third successive month: 1,499,094 (6·4%); Concordes from London/Paris on inaugural commercial flights to New York (3,000-mile journey took 3¼ h). **23** Rhodesian bombing attack on guerrilla bases in Mozambique. **25** MLR raised by 2% to 7%. **26** Invitation by Egypt to Israel and all countries involved in Middle East crisis to attend Cairo summit to prepare way for Geneva peace conference. **29** Home Secretary granted amnesty for immigrants who had entered the country illegally before 1 Jan. 1976. **30** South African general election: Mr. Vorster's governing National Party vanquished both liberal and ultra right-wing political parties.

December 2 Biko inquest absolved S. African police although he died as a result of brain injuries inflicted while in custody, a verdict which outraged the civilised world. **8** Fall of Dr. Soares's minority Socialist Government in Portugal. **10** Resignation of Gough Whitlam as Australia's Labour leader after general election when Malcolm Fraser's Conservative coalition was returned. **12** Death of Lady Spencer-Churchill, aged 92. **14** Opening of Cairo conference with representatives from Egypt, Israel, US and UN; House of Lords dismissed appeal by Advisory, Conciliation and Arbitration Service (ACAS) in Grunwick dispute. **16** Extension of Piccadilly tube line to Heathrow

A.D.

opened by the Queen. **20** UK unemployment (crude) fell to 1,480,822; Earthquake in Iran around Zarand. **21** OPEC countries froze oil prices for next 6 months. **25** Summit meeting at Ismailia between President Sadat and Prime Minister Begin. **26** Death of Sir Charles Chaplin, aged 88.

1978

January 1 Air India jumbo jet crashed in sea off Bombay: all 213 people on board killed. **3** Indira Gandhi established new rival Indian National Congress; 100 houses destroyed in freak whirlwind in Newmarket, Suffolk. **4** Said Hammani, Palestine Liberation Organisation's London representative, shot dead in Mayfair; Mr. Callaghan began 10-day tour of Bangladesh, India and Pakistan; Victory for military regime in referendum in Chile. **5** Release of Andrei Klymchuk, British student held in Russia. **6** Historic Crown of St. Stephen returned to Hungary by the American Government; MLR reduced to 6⅜%. **9** Launching of a new daily newspaper *The Trib* in New York. **11** Executors of Lady Spencer-Churchill revealed that Graham Sutherland's portrait of Sir Winston (which he disliked) was destroyed by Lady Spencer-Churchill before her death. **12** Firemen called off strike (begun 14 November) for 30% increase in wages; acceptance of 10% rise now and a guaranteed future pay formula; £150 million contract to build warships for Egypt won by Vosper Thornycroft. **13** 1% reduction in mortgage interest rates to 8⅛%; Death of former US Vice-President Hubert Humphrey, aged 66, a much respected liberal, from cancer at his Minnesota home. **15** Michael Brearley, England's cricket captain, returned home from Pakistan after breaking his arm: Geoffrey Boycott appointed captain. **16** Official figures recorded a UK current account surplus in 1977 of £59 million, first surplus for a full year since 1972; Giulio Andreotti, Italian Prime Minister, resigned; Return of Soviet cosmonauts who had achieved the historic *Salyut* docking record on 11 January. **17** Britain informed her EEC partners that she would not be able to take part in direct elections to the European Parliament before 1979. **18** Sir Charles Villiers, the chairman of the British Steel Corporation, summoned by a representative of the Sergeant-at-Arms to attend and provide evidence to House of Commons Select Committee on Nationalised Industries. **19** First State of the Union address by President Carter: urged passing of the Energy Bill and pledged protection of the dollar; William Webster named as successor to Clarence Kelley as Director of the Federal Bureau of Investigation (FBI). **20** Official figures showed 1977 rate of inflation at 12·1%; Mario Soares reappointed Prime Minister of Portugal; Blizzards in eastern United States worst since 1969, with airports, schools and offices in New York closed. **21** Special Liberal Party Assembly voted 1727–520 to continue Lib-Lab pact until July; France beat England 15–6 in rugby international. **22** Representatives of Western powers met in Washington to review war in the Ogaden between Ethiopia and Somalia. **23** Government defeated in Commons over proposal to devalue " green pound " by 5%; Conservative motion proposing 7½% devaluation carried; Baron Edouard-Jean Empain, millionaire Belgian industrialist, kidnapped outside his Paris home. **24** Cosmos 954, a Soviet surveillance satellite, disintegrated in the atmosphere and fell to earth in the Northwest Territories of Canada. **25** Serious Government defeats on the Scottish Devolution Bill: amendments requiring minimum " Yes " vote of 40% on a turnout of 40% of the whole electorate carried, together with a third amendment which would allow the Orkney and Shetland Islands to opt out of devolution; British Government order placed for two British-built advanced gas-cooled reactors for the 1980s: one to be sited at Torness, East Lothian; Belize (formerly British Honduras) rejected proposals that it should cede territory to Guatemala as its price for independence. **26** Government majority of 177 on the guillotine motion on the European

A.D.

Assembly Elections Bill: State of emergency declared in Tunisia after the calling of a General Strike. **28** Severe blizzards swept Scotland: four people dead, whilst 70 rescued by helicopter from a stranded Inverness to Wick train. **29** Talks in Malta on future of Rhodesia with leaders of the Patriotic Front, Joshua Nkomo and Robert Mugabe; in Rhodesia itself, Ian Smith began negotiations for an internal settlement. **30** Mrs. Margaret Thatcher returned to the attack on present immigration policies: her speech widely condemned by leaders of the ethnic minorities.

February 1 Petrol shortages began as 80,000 tanker drivers started overtime ban; Heavy storms lashed the Channel: Norwegian oil rig *Orion* and the Seven Stones lightship adrift in the Channel. **3** Huge IRA ammunition dump found by security forces in Londonderry; US Government ordered the expulsion of the Vietnamese Ambassador to the United Nations for alleged espionage; Chairman of London Transport, Sir Kenneth Robinson, agreed to retire early. **4** Major Ethiopian offensive launched in the Ogaden: Somalia appealed to the West for aid. **5** John Lewis Partnership placed on the Government's " black list " for contravening pay guidelines. **6** The House of Commons decided that broadcasting of parliamentary proceedings should commence after Easter. **7** Severe snowstorms swept N.E. United States: over 40 people dead, with New York at a standstill and looting in Boston: Government majority of 14 in Commons for its policy of sanctions against companies breaking the pay guideline (the " black list "). **8** Japanese car manufacturers refused to restrict the sale of Japanese cars in Britain; mineworkers voted to accept 10% wage increase, thereby abandoning 92% pay claim; Ethiopian airstrike against Hargeisa and Berbera. **9** Somalia mobilised its forces. **11** Soviet officials expelled by Canada. **10** British Gas Corporation announced a freeze on gas prices until at least April 1979; Second Reading of Bill to prevent exploitation of children in pornographic films. **12** Contingency plans drawn up for restriction of Japanese imports. **13** Two people killed in explosion in Sydney, Australia, only hours before a conference of Asian and Commonwealth leaders due to open. **14** Government defeat on Scotland Bill: no referendum to be held in Scotland within three months of a general election polling day; Overtime ban by Shell tanker drivers ended; Italian Red Brigade terrorists shot Riccardo Palma, a well-known judge. **15** Further government defeats on Scotland Bill; New Zealand secured first-ever victory over England (by 72 runs) in the first Test Match of the series at Wellington; Closure announced of British Leyland assembly plant at Speke, with 3,000 redundancies. **16** Severe blizzards swept South Wales and West Country, the worst for 30 years; Leon Spinks beat Mohammed Ali to win world heavyweight boxing championship in Las Vegas. **17** Provisional IRA bombed restaurant at Comber; 12 people killed and 20 injured; Ban on casinos in Spain relaxed; Britain's rate of inflation in January fell to single figures, 9·9%. **18** Violence broke out against National Front youth rally in Birmingham. **19** Egyptian commandos stormed hi-jacked airliner at Larnaca airport in Cyprus: 15 commandos killed and 14 others injured; crisis in Egyptian–Cypriot relations. **20** British defence budget for 1978–79 to be £6,919 million—4·75% of Gross Domestic Product. **21** All-Party Speakers' Conference recommended increased Ulster representation at Westminster: number of seats to be increased from 12 to 17. **22** The Scotland Bill passed by the House of Commons (297 votes to 257); Ban imposed on projected National Front march through Ilford; Death of veteran Labour M.P., Marcus Lipton. **24** Unofficial action by members of National Graphical Association stopped production of *The Times*; Six people killed in explosion of railway wagons containing propane gas in Waverly, Tennessee. **25** Sweeping comeback for Mrs. Indira Gandhi in state elections in

A.D.

Karnataka and Andhra Pradesh. **26** Bruce Page appointed new editor of the *New Statesman*; First session since January 1975 of the Chinese National People's Congress opened in Peking. **28** Dickie Jeeps appointed successor to Sir Robin Brook as chairman of the Sports Council.

March 1 Three-man inquiry, headed by Mr. Justice Croom-Johnson, appointed to investigate huge losses incurred by the Crown Agents; £300 million export orders won by British aircraft industry in contract signed in Cairo. **2** Conservatives won the marginal Ilford North by-election on a 6·9% swing from Labour. **3** Internal settlement agreed in Rhodesia between Ian Smith and three black Nationalist leaders: majority rule to become effective by 31 December 1978: the Patriotic Front (the nationalist guerrillas) denounced the agreement and vowed to continue the guerrilla war; American record for length of time in space broken by Yuri Romanenko and Georgy Grechko (who had spent 84 days in *Salyut* 6); Landslide at Blackgang Chine on the Isle of Wight. **4** Wales retained the triple crown for third successive year. **5** Major Ethiopian offensive launched in the Ogaden: Somalia claimed Soviet and Cuban forces aiding the Ethiopian thrust. **6** Striking American coalminers ordered back to work for 80-day cooling off period by President Carter; Outcome of public inquiry into the Windscale nuclear plant in Cumbria recommended that it should go ahead. **8** Agreement reached in Italy on formation of new government to be headed by Giulio Andreotti; Prince Charles began 8-day visit to Brazil. **9** Two men trapped 355 feet under the North Sea in mini-submarine rescued; Ethiopian forces back in full control of the Ogaden: Somali regular forces withdrawn. **10** South African newspaper editor Percy Quoboza released after 5-months detention. **11** Major guerrilla raid into Israel; 35 killed and 80 injured by Arab terrorists who landed south of Haifa. **12** Swing to the Left in first round of the French parliamentary election: French Socialists and Communists formed united front for second round (19 March). **13** South Moluccan terrorists seized 71 hostages in Dutch town of Assen. **14** Dutch marines stormed South Moluccan terrorists in Assen: hostages released and terrorists captured. **15** Massive Israeli thrust into south Lebanon: Israeli tanks, troops and armour advanced towards the Litani river: many bases of Palestinian guerrillas obliterated. **16** Aldo Moro, five times Prime Minister of Italy, kidnapped by " Red Brigade " terrorists: five of his bodyguards killed; *Amoco Cadiz* supertanker ran aground off the Brittany coast: major pollution of Brittany coastal waters. **18** Mr Bhutto, former Prime Minister of Pakistan, sentenced to death by hanging; Wales beat France (16 points to 7) to win the " grand slam ". **19** French Left failed in second round of French elections: Government won 290 seats, the Opposition 200. **21** Stricter controls on immigration proposed by House of Commons select committee; 4-member executive council sworn in in Rhodesia. **22** House of Commons voted to go ahead with nuclear reprocessing plant at Windscale, Cumbria. **25** Oxford the victors in 124th University Boat Race: Cambridge boat sank. **27** Coalminers in America returned to work after 109-day strike; Namibian leader Chief Clemens Kapuuo assassinated. **28** Heavy fighting against terrorists along Mozambique–Rhodesia border. **29** Retirement of Jack Jones as Secretary of the Transport and General Workers Union: succeeded by Moss Evans; President Carter arrived in Venezuela on a tour which went on to include Brazil, Nigeria and Liberia.

April 1 *Lucius* won the Grand National (*Red Rum* three times winner of the race withdrew the previous day because of injury). **3** First regular radio broadcasts of proceedings in Parliament commenced. **4** Small bomb exploded in Communist Party headquarters in Covent Garden;

A.D.

House of Lords supported proportional representation for elections to the Scottish Assembly. 5 Government launched campaign to double the number of kidneys available for transplant. 6 HMS *Ark Royal* (commissioned 1955) left Plymouth on her final commission to the USA and the Caribbean. 7 First direct elections to the European Parliament fixed for 7–10 June 1979; President Carter announced that production of the neutron bomb would be deferred; Increase of 9·2% in the Civil List announced; Spillers announced closure of bread-making factories. 9 Attempted *coup* in Somalia crushed. 10 The Transkei, the first tribal homeland in South Africa to be granted independence, severed diplomatic links with South Africa. 11 Defection confirmed of Mr. Shevchenko, 47, senior Soviet diplomat at the United Nations; Blizzards and black ice returned to parts of Britain; Mr. Healey introduced his 13th Budget, containing proposals for a new low 25% tax band. 12 Ian Smith named the nine White Ministers in Rhodesia's transitional government; Gas explosion ripped through the Rutland Hotel, Leeds. 13 Labour retained the Glasgow Garscadden by-election; Release of 100 detainees from Wha Wha jail, near Gwelo, Rhodesia; Death announced of Lord Peddie. 14 Record turnover (52m shares) on Wall St; Jackson Tailors to close 30 shops. 16 Venice–Rome express derailed near Bologna, 45 killed; Pakistan President Haq flew to Saudi Arabia. 17 World Health Organisation (WHO) announced no cases of smallpox reported anywhere in the world during the previous year; Amnesty International and Caritas, the Roman Catholic Relief organisation offered to mediate to secure release of Aldo Moro. 18 Abolition of the death penalty in Spain; Temple of Augustus Caesar recovered from the island of Philae, now beneath the waters of the Nile; World's birthrate dropped to the lowest level in recorded history. 19 Renewal of riots in Turkish town of Malatya; Prince Andrew escaped unhurt from parachute jump mishap; Investigation announced into allegations of corruption in public life in Blackpool. 20 Labour retained Lambeth Central by-election. 21 South Korean Boeing 707 forced to land on frozen Soviet lake near Finnish border and two passengers killed. 22 Over 200 deaths from cholera epidemic in the Maldives. 23 Arrival of Herr Schmidt, West German Chancellor, in London. 24 The Speaker's ruling on the " Colonel B " case clamped down on any further use of Parliamentary privilege to name the man involved; French Government denied reports of a neutron bomb test; Death of Jacques Rueff, French economist and writer, in Paris, aged 81. 26 Arab terrorist attack on bus in Nablus in Israeli-occupied West Bank; More detainees freed in Rhodesia; 84th birthday in Spandau jail for Herr Rudolf Hess. 27 Disastrous collapse of Liberal votes in by-elections in Epsom and High Wycombe; President Daoud deposed in pro-Soviet *coup* in Afghanistan; John Ehrlichman, former Nixon aide, released from jail in Arizona. 28 Two boroughs, Redbridge and Sutton, directed to submit proposals for comprehensive education or face legal action; French bombers sent to Chad to resist rebel forces; Cocaine worth £2·2 million seized in Brussels.

May 1 First May Day holiday celebrated in

A.D.

Britain, in cold and dreary weather; Political storm over remarks made in Peking by Sir Neil Cameron, Chief, of Britain's Defence Staff; Three Senegalese UN troops killed by mine in Lebanon. 2 Terry Duffy elected President of the Amalgamated Union of Engineering Workers in succession to Hugh Scanlon (by 169,168 votes to 122,251); Ban on ZANU and ZAPU lifted in Rhodesia, but controversy raged over the dismissal of the black Justice Minister, Byron Hove; Death of Soviet composer Aram Khachaturian, 74, after a long illness. 3 SNP admitted setbacks in Scottish regional elections held the previous day. 4 Conservative gains in local elections held in check by Labour revival; Port of London revealed to be in serious financial difficulties; Experiment with 3-day-old embryos of mice, put into frozen suspended animation and stored at —196°C reported successful, with the mice now running around normally in a cage. 5 South African troops raided Angola, temporarily occupying the town of Cassinga; Cledwyn Hughes, chairman of the Parliamentary Labour Party, announced his intention to retire from politics at the next election 6 Ipswich won first-ever FA Cup, defeating Arsenal 1-0. 7 Oil slick from stricken Greek tanker *Eleni V* drifted towards Norfolk coast. 8 Oil slick polluted Norfolk beaches; Plot to invade the Seychelles uncovered. 9 Body of Aldo Moro, much-respected former Prime Minister of Italy and President of the Christian Democrats, found in Rome: universal condemnation of a despicable and callous murder. 10 Princess Margaret and the Earl of Snowdon to begin divorce proceedings; Labour suffered further defeats on the Budget—higher tax rates raised to £8,000; Resignation of Francesco Cossiga, Italian Interior Minister, in the wake of the Moro killing; Lady Hailsham killed in riding accident in Sydney, Australia. 11 Chinese and Russian troops clashed on the Ussuri River, an incident for which Russia subsequently apologised; Rioting in many towns in Iran; Death of Boris Khaikin, 73, Bolshoi Theatre conductor. 14 Death of Eric Treacy, the " Railway Bishop "; Fighting reported in Shaba province, Zaire, as a result of invasion by Angolan-based rebels. 15 Death of Sir Robert Menzies, Australian Liberal statesman. 18 Money supply grew by 16¼% over the past year. 20 Controversial new airport at Narita, Tokyo, officially opened. 21 French and Belgian paratroops in full control of Kolwezi in Zaire, but not before heavy loss of life among both white and black civilian population; Warmest April on record at the South Pole—an average temperature of −50°C 23 Number of unemployed in Great Britain fell for eighth consecutive month; Sir Bernard Docker died, aged 81. 24 Princess Margaret obtained a divorce from Lord Snowdon; Plans to reintroduce Sunday mail collection rejected by postmen. 25 David Steel the Liberal leader, announced that the Lib-Lab pact would terminate at the end of July. 27 Michelle Booth, the schoolgirl found unconscious beside the London–Reading railway in March, left hospital. 28 David Gower, 21-year-old Leicestershire cricketer, selected for the first Test Match against Pakistan. 29 Massive traffic jams as the Bank Holiday was celebrated in glorious sunshine. 31 Polling day in the Hamilton by-election, which was easily retained by Labour.

RELIGIOUS CALENDAR 1979

Epiphany	Jan. 6	Low Sunday	Apr. 22
Septuagesima Sunday	Feb. 11	Rogation Sunday	May 22
Quinquagesima Sunday	Feb. 25	Ascension Day—Holy Thursday	May 24
Ash Wednesday	Feb. 28	Whit Sunday—Pentecost	June 3
Quadragesima Sunday	Mar. 4	Trinity Sunday	June 10
Palm Sunday	Apr. 8	Corpus Christi	June 14
Good Friday	Apr. 13	First Sunday in Advent	Dec. 2
Easter Day	Apr. 15	Christmas Day	Dec. 25
Mohammedan New Year (1400)	Nov. 21	Ramadan, First day of	
Passover, First day of (Pesach)	Apr. 12	(tabular)	July 26
Feast of Weeks (Shebuoth)	June 1	Day of Atonement (Yom Kippur)	Oct. 1
Jewish New Year 5740 (Rosh Hashanah)	Sept. 22	Tabernacles, First day of (Succoth)	Oct. 6

PROMINENT PEOPLE

Glimpses of some of the famous people in the history of the world. See also Section E for composers; Section I for contemporary dramatists; Section M for prominent poets of the twentieth century.

PROMINENT PEOPLE

A

Abel, Sir Frederick (1826–1902), English military chemist, an authority on explosives. He and his friend James Dewar patented the propellant cordite (*see* Section L).

Abelard, Peter (1079–1142), one of the founders of scholastic moral theology, b. at Pallet (Palais) near Nantes. He lectured in Paris, where he was sought by students, though persecuted for alleged heresy. His main achievement was to discuss where others asserted. His love for Héloise, a woman of learning, ended in tragic separation and in a famous correspondence.

Abercrombie, Sir Patrick (1879–1957), architect and town-planner. He was consulted on the re-planning of Plymouth, Hull, Bath and other cities and produced a plan for Greater London, 1943.

Acton, 1st Baron (John Emerich Edward Dalberg Acton) (1834–1902), English historian. He planned the *Cambridge Modern History.*

Adam, Robert (1728–92), architect, one of four Scottish brothers. He developed a character-istic style in planning and decoration and his achievements in interior design include Hare-wood House, Yorks.; Osterley Park, Middlesex; Syon House, Middlesex; Kedleston Hall, Derbyshire; Luton Hoo, Bedfordshire; and Kenwood. *See* Neo-Classical Style, Section L.

Adams, John (1735–1826), succeeded Washington as president of the U.S.A. He was the first of the republic's ambassadors to England.

Adams, John Couch (1819–92), English mathema-tician and astronomer. He shared credit for the discovery of the planet Neptune (1846) with the French astronomer Leverrier, working independently.

Adams, Samuel (1722–1803), American revolution-ary statesman, b. Boston. He advocated " no taxation without representation " as early as 1765; promoted the " Boston tea-party "; and in 1776 signed the Declaration of Indepen-dence.

Adams, William (c. 1564–1620), navigator, b. Gillingham, Kent; the first Englishman to visit Japan. He found favour with the emperor Ieyasu, and an English and Dutch trading settlement was established till 1616.

Addams, Jane (1860–1935), American sociologist who founded Hull House, Chicago, in 1889.

Addison, Joseph (1672–1719), writer and Whig politician. He contributed to the *Tatler*, and was co-founder with Steele of the *Spectator*.

Adelard of Bath (c. 1090–c. 1150), English mathe-matician who translated into Latin the *Arith-metic* of Al-Kwarizmi and so introduced the Arabic numerals to the West (*see* L7).

Adenauer, Konrad (1876–1967), chancellor of the West German Federal Republic, 1949–63; founder and chairman of the Christian Democra-tic Party, 1945–66. To a defeated Germany he gave stable constitutional government and a place in the Western alliance. He promoted reconciliation with France but resisted accom-modation with Russia.

Adler, Alfred (1870–1937), Austrian psychiatrist, founder of the school of individual psychology. An earlier pupil of Freud, he broke away in 1911, rejecting the emphasis on sex, regarding man's main problem as a struggle for power to com-pensate for feelings of inferiority. *See* Adlerian psychology, Section J.

Adrian, 1st Baron (Edgar Douglas Adrian) (1889–1977), English physiologist. He shared with Sherrington the 1932 Nobel prize for medicine for work on the electrical nature of the nerve impulse. Pres. Royal Society 1950–5; Pres. British Association 1954; Chancellor Leicester Univ. 1958–71; Chancellor Cambridge Univ. 1967–75; O.M. 1942.

Adrian IV (Nicholas Breakspear) (d. 1159), pope 1154–59, the only English pope, b. near St. Albans. He crowned Frederick Barbarossa Holy Roman Emperor. Granted overlordship of Ireland to Henry II.

Aeschylus (525–456 B.C.), founder of Greek tragic drama. Of the many plays he wrote, only seven have come down to us, including *The Seven against Thebes*, *Prometheus Bound*, and a trilogy on Orestes.

Aesop (? 6th cent. B.C.), semi-legendary fabulist, originally a slave. The fables attributed to him probably have many origins.

Agassiz, Louis (1807–73), Swiss-American em-bryologist, author of *Lectures on Comparative Embryology*, intended for laymen, *Researches on Fossil Fishes*, and *Studies on Glaciers*. He was an opponent of Darwinian evolution.

Agricola, Gnaeus Julius (37–93), Roman governor of Britain, who subdued the country except for the Scottish highlands. His son-in-law Tacitus wrote his life.

Agrippa, Marcus Vipsanius (63–12 B.C.), Roman general.

Ahmad Khan, Sir Syed (1817–98), Indian educa-tionist and social reformer who founded what is now the Aligarh Muslim University.

Airy, Sir George Biddell (1801–92), English mathe-matician who was astronomer royal for over 40 years, 1835–81. He set up a magnetic observatory at Greenwich.

Akbar, Jalal-ud-din Mohammed (1542–1605), Mogul emperor of India, son of Humayun. He extended the imperial power over much of India, stabilised the administration, promoted commerce and learning; and, though a Muslim, respected Hindu culture and tolerated Christian missions. His reign saw a flowering of Mogul culture.

Akhenaten, the name adopted by the heretic pharaoh, **Amenhotep IV** (d. 1362 B.C.), who in-troduced a short-lived but influential religious and artistic reformation. He sought to convert his people from their polytheistic beliefs to a more compassionate religion based on the one supreme sun-god Aten (hence his name). His pacifism caused the temporary loss of most of Egypt's overseas territories. His wife was Nefertiti and he was succeeded by Tutankha-mun, who gave in to the conservative forces of the priesthood.

Alanbrooke, 1st Viscount (Alan Francis Brooke) (1883–1963), British field-marshal; chief of the imperial general staff 1941–46. Sir Arthur Bryant's *The Turn of the Tide* and *Triumph in the West* are based on his war diaries.

Alarcón, Pedro Antonio de (1833–91), Spanish novelist. His short story, *El Sombrero de tres picos* (The Three-Cornered Hat) became the subject of Falla's ballet and of Hugo Wolf's opera *Der Corregidor*.

Alaric I (376–410), Visigothic chief who, as first auxiliary to the Roman emperor Theodosius, later attacked the empire and sacked Rome in 410.

Alban, St. (d. c. 303), proto-martyr of Britain, con-verted by a priest to whom he had given shelter. He suffered under Diocletian at Verulam (now St. Albans), where in the 8th cent. King Offa of Mercia founded the abbey of that name.

Albert, Prince Consort (1819–61), son of the Duke of Saxe-Coburg-Gotha, married Queen Victoria in 1840. He helped the queen with political duties, projected the international exhibition of 1851, and in 1861 in a dispute with the United States advised a conciliatory attitude which averted war. He died of typhoid fever and is commemorated by the Albert Memorial in Kensington Gardens.

Albertus Magnus (Albert the Great) (1206–80), Dominican scholastic philosopher, b. Swabia. His interest in nature as an independent obser-ver marked the awakening of the scientific spirit. Among his pupils was Thomas Aquinas.

Alcibiades (c. 450–404 B.C.), Athenian general and statesman. Pupil and friend of Socrates, he was an egoist whose career brought Athens disaster. He was murdered in Phrygia.

Alcott, Louisa May (1832–88), American author of books for girls, notably *Little Women*.

Alcuin (735–804), English scholar, who settled on the continent and helped Charlemagne with the promotion of education. *See* Monasticism, Section J.

Aldred (d. 1069), Saxon archbishop of York who crowned William the Conqueror.

Aldrich, Henry (1647–1710), English composer of church music, theologian and architect. He designed Peckwater quadrangle at Christ Church, the chapel of Trinity College, and All Saint's Church, Oxford, and wrote the " Bonny Christ Church bells."

Alekhine, Alexander (1892–1946), world chess champion, 1927–35, 1937–46. He was born in Moscow and became a French citizen after the Russian revolution.

Alembert, Jean le Rond d' (1717–83), French mathematician and philosopher, one of the encyclopaedists, a leading representative of the Enlightenment.

Alexander of Tunis, Earl of (Harold Leofric George Alexander) (1891–1969), British field-marshal, b. Ireland. Directed retreat at Dunkirk 1940, and Burma 1942; C.-in-C. Allied Armies in Italy 1943–4; Supreme Allied Commander, Mediterranean 1944–5. Governor-general of Canada 1946–52.

Alexander II (1818–81), reforming Tsar of Russia, succeeded his father Nicholas in 1855. In 1861 he emancipated the serfs and in 1865 established provincial elective assemblies. Later his government became reactionary; he was assassinated by Nihilists; the pogroms followed.

Alexander the Great (356–323 B.C.), Greek conqueror. Educated by Aristotle, he succeeded his father Philip as king of Macedon in 336 B.C. He led the Greek states against Persia; and, crossing the Hellespont, he defeated Darius and sacked Persepolis. He captured Egypt and founded Alexandria. He penetrated to India. D. at Babylon. Centuries later legends formed round him.

Alexandra, Queen (1844–1925), daughter of Christian IX of Denmark, married the Prince of Wales (afterwards Edward VII) 1863.

Alfieri, Vittorio, Count (1749–1803), Italian poet and dramatist.

Alfonso the Wise (1221–84), king of León and Castile, known for his code of laws and his planetary tables. He caused the first general history of Spain to be written. Dethroned 1282.

Alfred the Great (849–99), king of Wessex who became a national figure. From the outset he had to repel Danish invaders. After years of effort he won the battle of Ethandun (Edington), and subsequently, probably in 886, made peace with Guthrum, leaving to the Danes the north and east. He built ships, was an able administrator, and promoted education, his own translations from the Latin being part of the earliest English literature.

Al-Kwarizmi (fl. c. 830), Persian mathematician said to have given algebra its name.

Allenby, 1st Viscount (Edmund Henry Hynman Allenby) (1861–1936), British general. He served on the Western front 1914–16, commanded in Palestine 1917–18, capturing Jerusalem on 9 December 1917.

Allende, Salvador (1908–73), Chilean radical leader, a Marxist democrat, who won the presidency 1970. He tried to bring social reform by democratic means but met his death resisting the military coup in which it is alleged the American CIA played a role.

Alleyne, Edward (1566–1626), actor and founder of Dulwich College.

Al-Mamun (813–33), caliph of Baghdad, son of Harun-al-Rashid. He built an observatory at Baghdad where observations were long recorded.

Ampère, André Marie (1775–1836), French physicist who propounded the theory that magnetism is the result of molecular electric currents. The unit of electric current is named after him.

Amundsen, Roald (1872–1928), Norwegian explorer, the first to navigate the north-west passage and to reach the south pole. Sailing in the fishing smack *Gjoa*, he made the north-west passage in 3 years, 1903–6, and in 1911 sailed to the antarctic in the *Fram*, reaching the pole on 14 December 1911, a month before his

English rival Scott. His attempt to rescue Nobile after his crash in the airship *Italia* cost him his life.

Anacreon (c. 560–475 B.C.), Greek lyric poet.

Anaxagoras (488–428 B.C.), Ionian philosopher who came to Athens 464 B.C. and inspired Pericles and the poet Euripides with his love of science. His rational theories outraged religious opinion, and, like Socrates (who differed from him) he was indicted for impiety.

Anaximander (611–547 B.C.), Miletan philosopher, pupil of Thales, the first among the Greeks to make geographical maps, and to speculate on the origin of the heavenly bodies. He introduced the sun-dial from Babylon or Egypt.

Anaximenes (b. c. 570 B.C.), the last of the Milesian school founded by Thales. For him the primal substance was air and he was the first to see the differences between substances in quantitative terms.

Andersen, Hans Christian (1805–75), Danish writer, especially of fairy tales such as *The Little Mermaid* and *The Ugly Duckling*, which are still widely read. He also wrote an autobiography *Mit Livs Eventyr*.

Anderson, Elizabeth Garrett (1836–1917), one of the first English women to enter the medical profession. She practised in London for many years and later became mayor of Aldeburgh, her native town, the first woman to hold the office of mayor.

Andrea del Sarto (1487–1531), Italian painter, b. Florence, the son of a tailor. Known as the " faultless painter," his chief works are the frescoes of the Annunziata at Florence and his Holy Families. He died of the plague.

Andrée, Salomon August (1854–97), Swedish explorer who attempted in 1897 to reach the north pole by balloon. In 1930 a Norwegian scientific expedition discovered the remains of the Andrée expedition on White Island, including a log-book, sketch maps, and diaries.

Andrew, St., one of the apostles of Jesus, brother of Simon Peter, whose festival is observed on 30 November. He became the patron saint of Scotland in the 8th cent.

Angelico, Fra (1387–1455), Italian painter. An exquisite colourist, Fra Giovanni (his Dominican name) painted especially religious frescoes, mainly at Florence and Rome.

Ångström, Anders Jöns (1814–74), Swedish physicist who studied heat, magnetism, and spectroscopy; hence the angstrom unit used for measuring the wavelength of light.

Anne, Queen (1665–1714), Queen of Gt. Britain and Ireland. A daughter of James II, she succeeded William III in 1702. The act of union with Scotland was passed in 1707. A well-intentioned woman without marked ability, she was influenced by favourites, at first by the Duchess of Marlborough but in the main she was guided by Tory and high church principles (she established Queen Anne's Bounty to improve church finances). Her reign was notable for literary output (Swift, Pope, Addison, Steele, Defoe), developments in science (Newton), architecture (Wren, Vanbrugh), and for the Duke of Marlborough's victories in war.

Anouilh, Jean (b. 1910), French playwright. *See* Section I.

Anselm, St. (1033–1109), Italian scholar who succeeded Lanfranc as archbishop of Canterbury. He resisted William II, but was able to work with the latter's successor, Henry I.

Anson, 1st Baron (George Anson) (1697–1762), English admiral who sailed round the world 1740–44, his squadron being reduced during the voyage from seven ships to one. An account was compiled by his chaplain.

Antoninus Pius (86–161), Roman emperor, successor of Hadrian. In his reign, which was peaceful, the Antonine wall between the Forth and the Clyde was built to protect Britain from northern attack.

Antonius Marcus (Mark Antony) (c. 83–30 B.C.), Roman triumvir. He supported Caesar, and after the latter's death was opposed by Brutus and Cassius, and defeated by Octavian; committed suicide. His association with the Egyptian queen Cleopatra is the subject of Shakespeare's play.

Antony, St. (c. 251–356), early promoter of monastic life. B. in Upper Egypt, he retired into the desert, where he was tempted, but attracted disciples and founded a monastery. Took part in the Council of Nicaea 325. (From his supposed help against erysipelas derives its name of St. Antony's fire.)

Apelles, 4th cent. B.C., Greek painter whose chief paintings, which have not survived, were of Alexander the Great holding a thunderbolt and of Aphrodite rising from the sea.

Apollinaire, Guillaume (Wilhelm Apollinaris Kostrowitzi) (1880–1918), French poet representative of the restless and experimental period in the arts before the first world war. He invented the term *surrealism* (*see* Section L). B. Rome of Polish extraction.

Apollonius of Perga (fl. 220 B.C.), Greek mathematician of the Alexandrian school, remembered for his conic sections; introduced the terms *ellipse*, *parabola*, and *hyperbola*.

Apollonius Rhodius (fl. 250 B.C.), scholar and poet of Alexandria and Rhodes, librarian at Alexandria. His epic *Argonautica* is about the Argonaut heroes.

Appert, Nicholas (1752–1841), sometimes known as Francois Appert, invented the method of preserving animal and vegetable foods by means of hermetically sealed cans or tins, and paved the way for the creation of a vast world industry.

Appleton, Sir Edward Victor (1892–1965), English physicist, best known as the discoverer of the ionised region of the upper atmosphere which became known as the Appleton layer. His researches led to the development of radar. Nobel prizewinner 1947.

Aquinas, Thomas, St. (c. 1225–74), scholastic philosopher and Dominican friar of Italian birth, whose philosophico-theological system (called Thomism) is still accepted by Catholic ecclesiastics. He understood Aristotle well and interpreted his thought in accord with Christian teaching. His most important works are *Summa contra Gentiles* and *Summa theologica*. *See also* God and Man, Section J.

Arago, Dominique François Jean (1786–1853), French astronomer and physicist, remembered for his discoveries in electromagnetism and optics.

Archimedes (287–212 B.C.), Greek mathematician, b. Syracuse, son of an astronomer; remembered for his contributions to pure mathematics, mechanics, and hydrostatics, notably the Archimedean screw for raising water, the conception of specific gravity, the doctrine of levers, and the measurement of curved areas. Not less than his scientific knowledge was his practical skill. He was killed by the Romans in the siege of Syracuse.

Argand, Aimé (1755–1803), Swiss physician, inventor of the lamp bearing his name, which was the first to admit a current of air to increase the power of the flame, by use of a chimney glass and circular wick.

Ariosto, Ludovico (1474–1533), Italian poet, author of *Orlando Furioso*.

Aristides (d. c. 468 B.C.), Athenian general and statesman, called "the just"; fought at Marathon.

Aristippus (c. 435–356 B.C.), founder of the Cyrenaic school of philosophy. He taught that man should aim at pleasure, but held that the pleasant was identical with the good.

Aristophanes (c. 444– c. 385 B.C.), Greek dramatist and comic poet, who satirised Athenian life. Among his plays are *The Clouds* and *The Birds*.

Aristotle (384–322 B.C.), Greek philosopher, pupil of Plato, after whose death in 347 he left Athens to become tutor to the young prince Alexander of Macedon. Subsequently at Athens he established his famous school in the garden known as the *Lyceum*, where he lectured in the *peripatos* (cloister) which gave his school of philosophy its name *Peripatetic*. He took the whole field of knowledge as his subject, giving it unity, and providing a philosophy which held its own for 2,000 years.

Arkwright, Sir Richard (1732–92), English inventor. A native of Preston, and originally a barber, he experimented with cotton-spinning machines. His "water frame" (run by water power), patented in 1769, was an early step in the industrial revolution. In 1790 he made use of Boulton and Watt's steam-engine. Rioters sacked one of his mills in 1779.

Armstrong, Neil (b. 1930), American astronaut, the first man to set foot on the moon, 20 July 1969.

Arne, Thomas Augustine (1710–78), English composer, remembered for *Rule, Britannia!* (from a masque called *Alfred*), and for Shakespearean songs such as *Where the Bee sucks*. He also wrote operas (women singers appeared in *Judith* in 1761) and oratorios.

Arnold. Thomas, (1795–1842), English headmaster, whose influence at Rugby (1828–42) gave it a high position among public schools.

Arrhenius, Svante August (1859–1927), Swedish chemist, one of the founders of modern physical chemistry. Received 1903 Nobel prize for originating the theory of electrolytic dissociation (ionisation).

Artaxerxes, the name borne by several ancient Persian kings. The first Artaxerxes, son of Xerxes, reigned 464–424 B.C.; he was succeeded by Darius II 424–404 B.C., who was followed by Artaxerxes II, who reigned until 358 B.C. Artaxerxes III, the last to bear the name, was a cruel and treacherous man and was poisoned in 338 B.C.

Arthur (c. 600), fabled Celtic warrior, whose feats, although referred to in passing in early Celtic writings, were first narrated in Geoffrey of Monmouth's *Historia* (c. 1135). In mediaeval times his legend developed an extensive literature, woven together by Sir Thomas Malory in his *Morte Darthur*, printed in 1485. Excavations are currently proceeding at South Cadbury, Somerset, the supposed site of his seat, Camelot.

Arundel, Thomas (1353–1414), archbishop of Canterbury 1396, and for a time lord chancellor. An enemy of heresy, he persecuted the Lollards.

Aske, Robert, leader of the Pilgrimage of Grace 1536, directed against the Henrician Reformation; executed 1537.

Asoka (c. 269–232 B.C.), Indian emperor and upholder of Buddhism. At first he expanded his empire by conquest, but on being converted to Buddhism rejected war and aimed at the good of his people. He sent Buddhist missionaries as far as Sri Lanka and Syria. Art flourished, and many rock inscriptions commemorate his doings.

Asquith, Herbert Henry, 1st Earl of Oxford and Asquith (1852–1928), Liberal prime minister 1908–16, having previously served under Gladstone. His government enacted social reforms including old-age pensions (1908) and unemployment insurance (1911), but as a war minister he had to give way to Lloyd George. He resigned leadership of his party in 1926. His daughter **Violet** (1887–1969), an eloquent speaker, was created a life peeress in 1964.

Asser, a Welsh monk of the 9th cent., traditionally author of a life of King Alfred.

Astor, John Jacob (1763–1848), founder of the millionaire family, was a native of Heidelberg, emigrated to America, and made a fortune by trading in fur.

Astor, Viscountess (Nancy Witcher Astor, *née* Langhorne) (1879–1964), the first woman M.P. to take her seat in the House of Commons, an American by birth, wife of the 2nd Viscount Astor.

Atatürk, Kemal (1881–1938), builder of modern Turkey. A fine soldier, he defended the Dardanelles against the British in 1915 and drove the Greeks out of Turkey in 1922. President of the Turkish Republic, and virtually dictator, 1923–38.

Athanasius, St. (296–373), upholder of the doctrine of the Trinity against Arius, who denied the divinity of Christ. He was bishop of Alexandria. He is not now thought the author of the creed which bears his name.

Athelstan (895–940), grandson of Alfred the Great, was crowned king of England in 925, and was the first ruler of all England.

Attila (406–53), invading king of the Huns from Asia. He defeated the Roman emperor Theodosius, and entered Gaul, but was defeated in 451 near Châlons-sur-Marne.

Attlee, 1st Earl (Clement Richard Attlee) (1883–1967), Labour prime minister 1945–51, having served as deputy to Churchill 1942–5. Called to the Bar in 1905, he lectured at the London School of Economics 1913–23, was mayor of

Stepney 1919, and parliamentary leader of his party 1935–55. His government helped to create a welfare society and granted independence to India. His writings include an autobiography, *As it Happened*, and *Empire into Commonwealth*.

Auchinleck, Sir Claude John Eyre (b. 1884), British field-marshal; G.O.C. North Norway 1940; C.-in-C. India 1941, 1943–7; Middle East 1941–2.

Auden, Wystan Hugh (1907–73), poet, b. in England and naturalised an American. Succeeded C. Day Lewis as professor of poetry at Oxford 1956–61. *See* Section M.

Auer, Leopold (1845–1930), Hungarian violinist and teacher; Mischa Elman and Jascha Heifetz were among his pupils.

Augustine of Canterbury, St. (d. *c.* 605), first archbishop of Canterbury. He was sent from Rome in 597 by Gregory the Great to convert the English peoples.

Augustus, Caius Octavianus (63 B.C.–A.D. 14), first Roman emperor. Nephew of Julius Caesar, he was for 12 years triumvir with Mark Antony and Lepidus; then reigned alone. His reign was notable for peace, and for writers like Horace and Virgil; hence Augustan age for a great period in literature (the title Augustus was given him by the Senate).

Aurelius, Marcus Antonius. *See* Marcus Aurelius Antoninus.

Auriol, Vincent (1884–1966), French politician. He voted against surrender in 1940, was interned and escaped to London in 1943. President of the Fourth Republic 1947–54.

Aurangzeb (1618–1707), Mogul emperor of India. Son of Shah Jehan, he obtained power by acting against his father and brothers. In his long reign the Mogul empire reached its fullest extent; but he estranged Hindus and Sikhs; and when he died his authority was in dispute and the Mogul empire broke up.

Austen, Jane (1775–1817), author of *Emma*, *Mansfield Park*, *Northanger Abbey*, *Persuasion*, *Pride and Prejudice*, and *Sense and Sensibility*. Though confining herself to the personal relations of the English middle classes, she combined artistry, accuracy, imaginative power, satiric humour, sense, and genuine feeling with the ability to create a range of living characters. She spent the first 25 years of her life at her father's Hampshire vicarage. She was un-married.

Austin, 1st Baron (Herbert Austin) (1886–1941), English motor manufacturer, pioneer of the small car—the 7-horsepower car—which he put on the market in 1921.

Avenzoar (Ibn Zuhr) (c. 1090–1162), Arab physician, b. Seville. His chief work was the *Tasir*.

Averroës (Ibn Rushd) (1126–98), Arab philosopher, b. Córdova. He believed in the eternity of the world (not as a single act of creation as demanded by the current theology of Islam, Christianity and Judaism, but as a continuous process) and in the eternity of a universal intelligence, indivisible but shared in by all. He expounded Aristotle to his countrymen, but his teaching was modified by Neoplatonism. He was a friend of Avenzoar.

Avicenna (Ali ibn-Sina) (980–1037), Arab philosopher and physician, of Bokhara, whose influence on mediaeval Europe was chiefly through his *Canon of Medicine*, in which he attempted to systematise all the medical knowledge up to his time.

Avogadro, Amedeo (1776–1856), Italian physicist, remembered for his hypothesis, since known as Avogadro's Law, that equal volumes of gases under identical conditions of temperature and pressure contain the same number of molecules.

Avon, Earl of. See Eden, Anthony.

Ayrton, William Edward (1847–1908), English electrical engineer, inventor of a number of electrical measuring instruments. His first wife, Matilda Chaplin Ayrton (1846–83), was one of the first woman doctors, and his second wife, Hertha Ayrton (1854–1923), became known for her scientific work on the electric arc and sand ripples and for her work for woman suffrage.

Ayub Khan, Mohammed (b. 1907–74), Pakistani military leader; president of Pakistan, 1958–69.

Azikiwe, Nnamdi (b. 1904), Nigerian statesman; president of Nigeria, 1963–6.

B

Baber, Babar or Babur (Zahir ud-din Mohammed) (1483–1530), founder of the Mogul dynasty which ruled northern India for nearly three centuries; a descendant of Tamerlane.

Bach, Johann Sebastian (1685–1750), composer. B. at Eisenach, Germany, he was successively violinist, church organist, and chief court musician. It was as organist at the Thomaskirche, Leipzig, that he composed the St. Matthew and the St. John Passion and the B minor Mass. His work was in the school of the contrapuntal style (especially the fugue and the chorale); after his day it lost favour, but during the last century it has gained ground continually. Personally he was contented and unwordly; latterly he became blind. His family was connected with music for seven generations. See Section E.

Bach, Karl Philipp Emmanuel (1714–88), 3rd son of the above, and one of the first experimenters in the symphonic and sonata forms.

Backhaus, Wilhelm (1884–1969), German pianist, gifted in interpreting classical and romantic concertos.

Bacon, Francis, Lord Verulam (1561–1626), English philosopher. He threw over Aristotelian deductive logic for the inductive method (*see* Baconian method, Section J); remembered for the impulse his writings gave to the foundation of the Royal Society (*c.* 1662). His chief work is the *Novum Organum*. His career as statesman under Elizabeth and James I was brought to an end by charges of corruption.

Bacon, Roger (c. 1219/20–94), founder of English philosophy, advocate of the value of observation and experiment in science. He first studied arts at Oxford but when he returned from lecturing in Paris he devoted himself to experimental science, especially alchemy and optics. He became a Franciscan friar in 1257. After his death he acquired a reputation for necromancy which was undeserved.

Baden-Powell, 1st Baron (Robert Stephenson Smyth Baden-Powell) (1857–1941), founder of Boy Scouts (1908) and Girl Guides (1910) to promote good citizenship in the rising generation; Chief Scout of the World 1921–41. As a young cavalry officer in the South African war he defended Mafeking.

Baer, Karl Ernst von (1792–1876), German naturalist, b. Estonia, founder of the science of embryology. He discovered the mammalian ovum (1827). An opponent of Darwin's theory.

Baffin, William (1584–1622), British navigator and explorer who in 1616 discovered the bay which separates the north-east coast of Canada from Greenland, which bears his name.

Bagehot, Walter (1826–77), English economist and journalist, editor of *The Economist*. Among his works are *The English Constitution*, *Physics and Politics*, and *Lombard Street*.

Baird, John Logie (1888–1946), Scottish television pioneer, inventor of the televisor and the noctovisor.

Baker, Sir Benjamin (1840–1907), English civil engineer. With Sir John Fowler he built the Forth bridge and the London Metropolitan railway. He designed the vessel which brought Cleopatra's Needle to London. In Egypt he was consulting engineer for the Aswan dam.

Baker, Sir Herbert (1862–1946), English architect who designed the Bank of England, Rhodes house, Oxford, and, with Sir E. Lutyens, New Delhi.

Bakst, Léon (1868–1924), Russian painter who designed scenery and costumes for Diaghilev's ballets.

Baldwin of Bewdley, 1st Earl (Stanley Baldwin) (1867–1947), Conservative prime minister, 1923–4, 1924–9, and 1935–7. His handling of the crisis over Edward VIII's proposed marriage ended with the king's abdication.

Balewa, Sir Abubakar Tafawa (1912–66), federal prime minister of Nigeria, 1960–6; murdered during the crisis of January 1966.

Balfour, 1st Earl (Arthur James Balfour) (1848–1930), statesman and writer. He was Conservative prime minister 1902–5. As foreign secretary under Lloyd George, he was responsible for a declaration on Palestine.

Balliol, John de (d. 1269), founder of Balliol College, Oxford; a regent for Scotland; sided with Henry III against his barons.

Balliol, John de (1249–1315), king of Scotland. Son of the above, he claimed the throne against Robert Bruce and was chosen by the arbitrator, Edward I of England, whose overlordship he acknowledged. Later, on renouncing homage, he was taken captive and d. in retirement. His son Edward Balliol (d. 1363) obtained the kingdom for a time, acknowledging Edward III of England and surrendering Lothian; but retired on an annuity, 1356.

Ball, John (d. 1381), English priest and a leader of the Peasants' Revolt, after which he was executed. The couplet When Adam delved, and Eve span, Who was then the gentleman? is attributed to him.

Balzac, Honoré de (1799–1850), French novelist of wide influence, and author of over eighty novels to which he gave the covering title of La Comédie Humaine, depicting the appetites and passions of the new social class born of the revolution and Napoleon.

Bancroft, Sir Squire (1841–1926), Victorian actor-manager.

Bandaranaike, Solomon West Ridgway Dias (1899–1959) socialist prime minister of Ceylon from 1956 until his assassination in 1959. His widow, Mrs. Sirimavo Bandaranaike, became the world's first woman prime minister, 1960–5, 1970–7.

Banks, Sir Joseph (1743–1820), an amateur scientist of wealth who accompanied Captain Cook on his expedition to the Pacific 1768–76. He left botanical collections to the British Museum.

Banting, Sir Frederick Grant (1891–1941), Canadian physician who with C. H. Best discovered insulin.

Bantock, Sir Granville (1868–1946), composer of songs, orchestral and choral music.

Barbarossa (Ital. = red beard), surname of two brothers who were Barbary pirates: Uruz (c. 1474–1518), was killed by Spaniards, and Khaireddin (c. 1483–1546) conquered Tunis for the Turks and died in Constantinople.

Barbirolli, Sir John (1899–1970), conductor of the Hallé Orchestra 1943–70; succeeded Toscanini as conductor of the New York Philharmonic Symphony Orchestra 1937–42.

Barbusse, Henri (1874–1935), French writer, author of the war novel Le Feu, which portrays in a starkly vivid way the experience of the common soldier.

Barham, Richard Harris (1788–1845), English humorist, author of The Ingoldsby Legends, written under his pen-name of Thomas Ingoldsby. His best-known poem is The Jackdaw of Rheims.

Barnardo, Thomas John (1845–1905), founder of homes for orphan-waifs; devoted himself to the protection, education, and advancement of destitute children.

Barrie, Sir James Matthew (1860–1937), Scottish author and dramatist. His novels include A Window in Thrums. Among his plays are Dear Brutus, The Admirable Crichton, and Peter Pan which gained great popularity with children.

Barrow, Isaac (1630–77), divine and mathematician, tutor of Sir Isaac Newton.

Barry, Sir Charles (1795–1860), architect of the houses of parliament at Westminster, the details of which were contributed by his assistant A. W. Pugin.

Barth, Karl (1886–1968), Swiss theologian, described by the late Pope John as a Protestant St. Thomas Aquinas.

Bartók, Bela (1881–1945), Hungarian composer. From an early age he was deeply interested in folk-song which inspired his researches into Hungarian and Rumanian peasant music. He left for America in 1940, where he lived precariously and apparently unhappily until the end of the war made a return possible, regrettably too late. See Section E.

Bartolommeo, Fra (di Paolo) (1475–1517), Italian painter. At first influenced by Savonarola, he later resumed painting. Some of his best work is at Lucca.

Bartolozzi, Francesco (1725–1815), Italian engraver, who settled in England and became a founder-member of the Royal Academy; noted for his stipple engravings.

Bashkirtseff, Marie (1860–84), a Russian girl, b. Poltava, in the Ukraine, writer of a famous diary.

Bassi, Agostino (1773–1856), Italian amateur microscopist who first suggested that infectious diseases might be caused by the invasion of the body by micro-organisms.

Batten, Jean Gardner (b. 1909), New Zealand airwoman who flew solo from England to Australia in 1934.

Baudelaire, Charles Pierre (1821–67), French poet of originality and sensitivity, best known for his Les Fleurs du Mal. His life was darkened by poverty and ill-health. He was also a talented draughtsman.

Bax, Sir Arnold (1883–1953), composer of numerous piano compositions, songs, and chamber works.

Baxter, Richard (1615–91), presbyterian divine and author; imprisoned after the Restoration. He wrote an autobiography.

Bayard, Pierre de Terrail, Seigneur de (c. 1474–1524), French knight, known as the "chevalier sans peur et sans reproche." He fought in campaigns against Italy and fell at the battle of Romagnano.

Bayle, Pierre (1647–1706), French philosopher, author of the Dictionnaire historique et critique (1697). His sceptical views influenced Voltaire and the encyclopedists of the 18th cent.

Baylis, Lilian Mary (1874–1937), manager of the Old Vic theatre from 1898 and of Sadler's Wells from 1931. Promoter of Shakespeare and of opera in English.

Beaconsfield. See Disraeli.

Beardsley, Aubrey Vincent (1872–98), black-and-white artist, who in a brief life published much work, some of it controversial (as in the Yellow Book).

Beatles, The (Paul McCartney (b. 1942), John Lennon (b. 1940), George Harrison (b. 1943), Ringo Starr (b. 1940)), a Liverpool pop group whose highly original and melodic songs held the attention of youth all over the world, especially during the period 1963–5 when they were in their prime.

Beatty, 1st Earl (David Beatty) (1871–1936), British admiral; succeeded Jellicoe as commander of the Grand Fleet 1916–19. Commanding the British battlecruisers, he fought the German fleet on 28 August 1914 in the Heligoland Bight, and on 31 May 1916 off Jutland.

Beaufort, Sir Francis (1774–1857), hydrographer of the navy, who introduced the wind scale (1805) which bears his name. See Section N.

Beaumont, Francis (1584–1616), and Fletcher, John (1579–1625), joint authors of many plays, including The Maid's Tragedy and Philaster.

Beaverbrook, 1st Baron (William Maxwell Aitken) (1879–1964), British newspaper owner and politician, a Canadian by birth. He gave energetic service as minister of aircraft production 1940–1. He controlled the Daily Express, Sunday Express, and Evening Standard, which sponsored his political campaigns.

Becket, Thomas (1118?–70), saint and martyr. An able chancellor, 1155–62, on becoming archbishop of Canterbury he made the position of the church his first care; and, coming into conflict with Henry II, was murdered in Canterbury cathedral. His shrine became a place of pilgrimage.

Beckett, Samuel (b. 1906), Anglo-Irish dramatist and novelist. Nobel prizewinner 1969. See Section I.

Becquerel, Antoine Henri (1852–1908), French physicist who in 1896 discovered radioactivity in uranium. Shared with the Curies the 1903 Nobel prize in physics.

Bede, the Venerable (673–735), English historian and scholar; lived at Jarrow. His chief work is his Ecclesiastical History to 731.

Beecham, Sir Thomas (1879–1961), English conductor and impresario. Founded the London Philharmonic Orchestra in 1931; introduced into England the operas of Richard Strauss, Russian operas, and the Diaghilev ballet; championed the music of Delius.

Beecher, Henry Ward (1813–87), American preacher and lecturer, whose church was at Brooklyn.

Beerbohm, Sir Max (1872–1956), critic and caricaturist, master of irony and satire. His works include *Zuleika Dobson* and *A Christmas Garland*, and he contributed to the *Saturday Review*.

Beethoven, Ludwig van (1770–1827), composer. B. at Bonn (his father being a tenor singer at the Elector's court), at 17 he went to Vienna, was recognised by Mozart, and eventually settled there; he never married; gradually he became deaf. In the development from simplicity to complexity of musical treatment, he stands midway between Mozart and Wagner; but in him were uniquely combined the power to feel and the mastery of musical resources necessary to express his feelings. Between the years 1805 and 1808 he composed some of his greatest works: the oratorio *Mount of Olives*, the opera *Fidelio*, and the *Pastoral* and *Eroica* symphonies besides a number of concertos, sonatas, and songs. The symphonies, nine in number, rank as the greatest ever written and the pianoforte sonatas and string quartets are unequalled in beauty. He died in Vienna at the age of 56. *See* Section E.

Behring, Emil von (1854–1917), German bacteriologist, founder of the science of immunology. Nobel prizewinner 1901.

Behring, Vitus (1680–1741), Danish navigator who entered the Russian service and in 1728 discovered the strait which bears his name.

Belisarius (505–65), Roman general under Justinian who fought against the Vandals, Ostrogoths, and Persians.

Bell, Alexander Graham (1847–1922), inventor, b. Edinburgh, emigrated to Canada in 1870, later becoming an American citizen. In 1876 he exhibited an invention which was developed into the telephone. He devoted attention to the education of deaf-mutes.

Bell, Gertrude Margaret Lowthian (1868–1926), the "uncrowned queen of Arabia," was a traveller in the Middle East; her knowledge proved of service to the British government in the first world war.

Bellamy, Edward (1850–98), American author of *Looking Backward*, a prophetic utopian novel.

Bellini, family of Venetian painters: Jacopo (*c.* 1400–70) and his two sons, Gentile (1429–1507), whose works include the *Adoration of the Magi* (National Gallery); and Giovanni (*c.* 1429–1516), brother-in-law of Mantegna, and teacher of Giorgione and Titian.

Bellini, Vincenzo (1801–35), Italian operatic composer; b. Sicily. *See* Section E.

Belloc, Hilaire (1870–1953), versatile writer whose works include *The Bad Child's Book of Beasts*, *The Path to Rome*, *Hills and the Sea*, *Cautionary Tales*, and historical studies of Danton, Robespierre, and Richelieu. B. in France, he became a British subject in 1902.

Bellow, Saul (b. 1915), American novelist and short-story writer. Nobel prizewinner 1976.

Belzoni, Giovanni Battista (1778–1823), Egyptologist. B. at Padua, he settled in England in 1803. His first interest was in hydraulics, and for this purpose he went to Egypt to Mehemet Ali. There he explored Thebes, Abu Simbel, and one of the pyramids, sending some sculptures to the British Museum.

Benavente y Martinez, Jacinto (1866–1954), Spanish dramatist, whose plays include *Los Intereses Creados* (Bonds of Interest). Nobel prizewinner 1922.

Benedict, St. (*c.* 480–*c.* 550), patriarch of western monasticism. B. at Nursia, and at first a hermit at Subiaco, he attracted numerous followers and grouped them in twelve monasteries. Later he went to Monte Cassino, where he formulated the Benedictine rule, of wide application in Western Christendom. *See* Monasticism, Section J.

Benes, Eduard (1884–1948), Czechoslovak statesman; co-founder with Thomas Masaryk of the Czech Republic after the break-up of the Austro-Hungarian monarchy (1918).

Ben Gurion, David (1886–1973), Zionist leader. He helped organise the Jewish Legion in 1918, and was prominently connected with the Labour movement in Palestine in between the world wars. Prime minister of Israel 1948–63.

Bennett, Enoch Arnold (1867–1931), English author, who wrote of the pottery towns where he was brought up. His novels include *The Old Wives' Tale*, *Clayhanger*, and *Hilda Lessways*.

Bennett, James Gordon (1841–1918), proprietor of the *New York Herald*. He sent out Stanley on an expedition to find Livingstone.

Bennett, Sir William Sterndale (1816–75), English composer, pianist and teacher, best known for his oratorio *The Woman of Samaria*, songs and piano pieces. Founded the Bach Society.

Bentham, Jeremy (1748–1832), utilitarian philosopher and writer on jurisprudence. His main works are *Government* and *Principles of Morals and Legislation*.

Bentley, Richard (1662–1742), classical scholar who did pioneer work in textual criticism.

Benz, Karl (1844–1929), German engineer whose motor car produced in 1885 was one of the first to be driven by an internal combustion engine.

Beresford, 1st Viscount (William Carr Beresford) (1768–1854), British general. He fought under Wellington in the Peninsular War and reorganised the Portuguese army.

Berg, Alban (1885–1935), Austrian composer whose best-known work is the three-act opera *Wozzeck*, based upon a drama by Buchner, which has become a modern classic.

Bergson, Henri Louis (1859–1941), French philosopher, exponent of the theory of creative evolution and the life force. Nobel prizewinner 1927. *See* Vitalism, Section J.

Bériot, Charles Auguste de (1802–70), Belgian violinist, whose wife was the operatic contralto Malibran. His son, Charles Wilfrid de Bériot (1833–1914) was a pianist and the teacher of Ravel.

Berkeley, George (1685–1753), idealist philosopher and critic of Locke. His spiritual outlook led him to believe that reality exists only in the eye of God, that it is undiscoverable by science, though it can be revealed by religion. His chief work is *Alciphron*. He was a master of prose. Of Irish birth, he became bishop of Cloyne.

Berlin, Irving (b. 1888), American composer of popular songs, b. Russia; pioneer of both ragtime and jazz music. His songs include *Alexander's Rag-time Band*, *Always*, *What'll I do?*; his musicals include *Annie Get your Gun* and *Call me Madam*.

Berlin, Sir Isaiah (b. 1909), British philosopher, b. Riga; Chichele Prof. of Social and Political Theory at Oxford 1957–67. His works include *Karl Marx*, *The Hedgehog and the Fox*, and *The Age of Enlightenment*. O.M. (1971).

Berlioz, Hector (1803–69), composer. B. near Grenoble, the son of a doctor, his romantic sensibility, taste for the grand (as in his *Requiem*), and response to literary influence made him a prime figure in the French romantic movement. His works include the symphony *Romeo and Juliet*, and the operas *Benvenuto Cellini* and *Beatrice and Benedict*. *See* Section E.

Bernadotte, Count Folke (1895–1948), nephew of the late King Gustav of Sweden. U.N. mediator for Palestine 1947. Assassinated by Jewish terrorists.

Bernadotte, Jean Baptiste (1764–1844), a French commander who served under Napoleon, and in 1810 was chosen heir to the throne of Sweden. In 1818 he succeeded as Charles XIV.

Bernal, John Desmond (1901–71), physicist, b. Ireland. Prof. of Physics, Birkbeck College, Univ. of London, 1937–63, Prof. of Crystallography, 1963–8. Author of *The Social Functions of Science*, *Science in History*, *The Origin of Life*. Lenin peace prize 1953.

Bernard, Claude (1813–78), French physiologist whose discoveries though not of immediate application paved the way for the work of Pavlov and Hopkins.

Bernard of Menthon (923–1008), patron saint of mountaineers. He founded Alpine hospices in the passes that bear his name.

Bernard, St. (1090–1153), abbot of Clairvaux, which became a chief centre of the Cistercian order. This order aimed at seclusion and austerity, and practised manual work. His writings had wide influence in Europe.

Bernhardt, Sarah (1844–1923), French tragedienne, b. Paris, daughter of a Dutch jewess. She became a member of the Comédie Française after the siege of Paris. Her first performance in London was in 1879. Her successes included *Phèdre*, *La Dame aux Camélias*, *Fédora*, *Théodora*, and *La Tosca*, and she produced and played in Racine and Molière.

Best, Charles Herbert (b. 1899), Canadian physiologist, who with F. G. Banting discovered the use of insulin in the treatment of diabetes.

Berthelot, Marcellin Pierre Eugène (1827–1907), French chemist and politician. He was the first to produce organic compounds synthetically.

Berzelius, Jöns Jakob (1779–1848), Swedish chemist, founder of electrochemical theory. His work was mainly concerned with the exact determination of atomic and molecular weights and he devised the system of chemical symbols in use today.

Bessemer, Sir Henry (1813–98), inventor of the process of converting cast-iron direct into steel. This revolutionised steel manufacture, reducing the cost of production and extending its use.

Betjeman, Sir John (b. 1906), English poet, author and broadcaster; succeeded C. Day Lewis as poet laureate 1972.

Bevan, Aneurin (1897–1960), British socialist politician, architect of the National Health Service which came into operation in 1948.

Beveridge, 1st Baron (William Henry Beveridge) (1879–1963), British economist who drew up the Beveridge Plan (1942), which formed the basis of the present social security services.

Bevin, Ernest (1881–1951), British trade union leader, who later became a forceful foreign secretary. He was assistant general secretary of the Dockers Union (his masterly advocacy of the London dockers' case in 1920 earned him the title of " the dockers' K.C."), later general secretary of the Transport and General Workers Union; Minister of Labour 1940–5, and Foreign Secretary 1945–51.

Beyle, Marie Henri. *See* Stendhal.

Bhave, Vinova (b. 1895), Indian reformer, leader of the Sarvodaya movement. A follower of Gandhi, in 1951 he began a walking mission to persuade landlords to help landless peasants.

Bichat, Marie François Xavier (1771–1802), French physiologist whose study of tissues founded modern histology. His theory was that life is " the sum of the forces that restrict death."

Biddle, John (1615–62), unitarian. He taught in Gloucester; was several times imprisoned for his controversial writings; and died of fever contracted in prison.

Binyon, Laurence (1869–1943), poet, art critic, and orientalist, who worked at the British Museum 1893–1933.

Birch, Samuel John Lamorna (1869–1955), English landscape painter in watercolour, known for his Cornish and Australian studies.

Birkbeck, George (1776–1841), founder of mechanics' institutes, first at Glasgow, later in London (the Birkbeck Institution developed into Birkbeck College, London University).

Birkenhead, 1st Earl of (Frederick Edwin Smith) (1872–1930), English lawyer and politician; lord chancellor 1919–22; secretary for India 1924–8.

Bishop, Sir Henry Rowley (1786–1855), English composer who wrote *Home, sweet Home*, glees, and operas.

Bismarck, Otto Eduard Leopold von, Prince Bismarck, Duke of Lauenburg (1815–98), Prusso-German diplomat and statesman, chief architect of the German empire. He was of Junker family. As Prussian ambassador at St. Petersburg (1859–62) and at Paris (1862), he learned to assess the European situation. He was recalled to Berlin by the king to become chief Prussian minister; and when the house of representatives would not pass a military bill he closed the house. He used a dispute over Schleswig-Holstein to bring about the defeat of Austria at Königgratz in 1866; and he provoked the Franco-Prussian war of 1870–1 when France was defeated at Sedan. Germany then became united under the military leadership of Prussia, with the king as emperor, instead of by the slower processes of democracy. He presided over the Berlin Congress of European powers in 1878. In 1884 he began a colonial policy. His authoritarian system, in spite of its inherent defects, was at least based on cautious and accurate assessment of power politics. This factor was not understood by William II, who succeeded as emperor in 1888, and dismissed the " iron chancellor " in 1890.

Bizet, Georges (1838–75), properly **Alexandre César Léopold**, French composer, chiefly remembered for his opera *Carmen* from the story by Merimée.

Björnson, Björnstjerne (1832–1910), Norwegian poet, dramatist and novelist. His work provides an image of Norwegian life from the period of the sagas (*Kong Sverre*) to contemporary problems (*Over Aevne*), and he wrote the national anthem.

Black, Joseph (1728–90), Scottish chemist. A professor first at Glasgow, later at Edinburgh, he was the first to undertake a detailed study of a chemical reaction. He laid the foundation of the quantitative science of heat and his discovery of latent heat was applied by Watt in improving his steam-engine.

Blackett of Chelsea, Baron (Patrick Maynard Stuart Blackett) (1897–1974), British physicist whose work on nuclear and cosmic ray physics gained him a Nobel prize in 1948; author of *Military and Political Consequences of Atomic Energy* (1948), *Lectures on Rock Magnetism* (1956), *Studies of War* (1962). Pres. British Assoc. 1956; Pres. Royal Society 1966–70; O.M. 1967.

Blackmore, Richard Doddridge (1825–1900), English novelist and author of *Lorna Doone*.

Blackstone, Sir William (1723–80), English judge. His *Commentaries on the Laws of England* is a classic.

Blackwood, Algernon (1869–1951), English novelist and writer of short stories.

Blackwood, William (1776–1834), originator of *Blackwood's Magazine*.

Blair, Robert (1699–1746), Scottish poet, author of *The Grave*.

Blake, Robert (1599–1657), Parliamentary general and an admiral in the Cromwellian navy in the Dutch and Spanish wars.

Blake, William (1757–1827), English poet, mystic, and artist, son of a hosier in Carnaby market, Soho. A solitary and deeply religious man, he had a hatred of materialism. He produced his own books, engraving on copper plates both the text of his poems and the illustrations. His *Book of Job* is a masterpiece in line-engraving in metal, his poems range from the mystical and almost incomprehensible to the delightfully simple *Songs of Innocence*. He has been called " the great teacher of the modern western world." His art is in many ways reminiscent of that of another rebel of the same day, the Spanish painter Goya.

Blanqui, Louis Auguste (1805–81), French revolutionary leader, master of insurrection. He invented the term " dictatorship of the proletariat," and his social theories, stressing the class struggle, influenced Marx. Active in 1830, 1848, and 1871, he spent 37 years in prison.

Blériot, Louis (1872–1936), French airman; the first to fly the English Channel from Calais to Dover, on 25 July 1909.

Bligh, William (1754–1817), sailor, b. Plymouth. He accompanied Cook 1772–4, and discovered bread-fruit; but was in 1789 cast adrift from *The Bounty* by his mutinous crew. As governor of New South Wales (1806) he fought to suppress the rum traffic.

Blind, Karl (1826–1907), German agitator, b. Mannheim. He was active in the German risings of 1848, and imprisoned; but escaped and settled in England, remaining in touch with men like Mazzini and Louis Blanc.

Bliss, Sir Arthur (1891–1975), English composer; succeeded Sir Arnold Bax as Master of the Queen's Musick 1953.

Bloch, Ernest (1880–1959), composer, whose music is characterised by Jewish and oriental themes. B. in Geneva, he became a naturalised American.

Blondin, Charles (1824–97), French rope performer, who crossed the Niagara Falls on a tight-rope.

Blücher, Gebhard Leberecht von (1742–1819), Prussian general. He fought against Napoleon, especially at Lützen and Leipzig; and he completed Wellington's victory at Waterloo by his timely arrival.

Blum, Léon (1872–1950), French statesman, leader of the French Socialist Party. His efforts strengthened the growth of the Popular Front and the campaign against appeasement of Hitler. He held office only briefly and was interned in Germany 1940–5.

Blumlein, Alan Dower (1903–42), British electronics engineer and inventor, chiefly remembered for his fundamental work on stereophony.

Blunden, Edmund Charles (1896–1974), English poet and critic; professor of poetry at Oxford 1966–8.

Blunt, Wilfrid Scawan (1840–1922), English poet and political writer who championed Egyptian, Indian, and Irish independence.

Boadicea (Boudicca), queen of the Iceni in eastern Britain, who fought against the Roman invaders, but was defeated in A.D. 61 and killed herself.

Boccaccio, Giovanni (1313–75), Italian author, father of the novel. He is chiefly known for his *Decameron* (set in the neighbourhood of Florence during the plague), and for his life of Dante.

Boccherini, Luigi (1743–1805) Italian cellist and composer of chamber music.

Bode, Johann Ehlert (1747–1826), German astronomer remembered for his theoretical calculation (known as Bode's law) of the proportionate distances of the planets from the sun.

Boethius (480–524) Roman scientific writer who translated the logical works of Aristotle and provided the dark ages with some elementary mathematical treatises.

Bohr, Niels Henrik David (1885–1962), Danish nuclear physicist whose researches into the structure of the atom gave him great authority in the world of theoretical physics. With Rutherford he applied the quantum theory to the study of atomic processes. Nobel prizewinner 1922.

Boieldieu, François Adrien (1775–1834), French composer especially of operas, including *La Dame blanche*.

Boileau-Despréaux, Nicolas (1636–1711), French literary critic and poet, best known for his *Satires*.

Boito, Arrigo (1842–1918). Italian poet and composer; he wrote the libretti of *Otello* and *Falstaff* for Verdi.

Boleyn, Anne (1507–36), queen of Henry VIII and mother of Queen Elizabeth. She was maid-in-waiting to Catherine of Aragon and her successor when Catherine's marriage was annulled. She failed to produce a male heir and was beheaded on a charge of adultery.

Bolivar, Simón (1783–1830), South American revolutionist, called the Liberator, b. Carácas. He led independence movements in the north-west of South America against Spanish rule, aiming at a South American federation. He founded Grand Colombia (now Venezuela, Colombia, Panama, Ecuador). Revered as a Latin-American hero.

Bonaventura, St. (1221–74), Franciscan theologian, b. Orvieto. His mystical theory of knowledge was in the Augustinian tradition.

Bondfield, Margaret Grace (1873–1953), as minister of Labour, 1929–31, she was the first woman to enter the cabinet and to be a member of the privy council.

Bondi, Sir Hermann (b. 1919), British mathematician and astronomer, b. Vienna; chief scientist to Min. of Defence, 1971–7, to Dept. of Energy, 1977–.

Bone, Sir Muirhead (1876–1953), architectural draughtsman and etcher, b. Glasgow; excelled in dry-point and drawings of intricate scaffolding; official war artist in both world wars.

Bonheur, Rose (1822–99),French painter of animals.

Boniface, St. (680–754), apostle of Germany. B. at Crediton, Devon, his name being Wynfrith, he became a Benedictine monk, and went as missionary to Friesland, securing papal approval. He founded Fulda Abbey and became archbishop of Mainz, but was martyred.

Bonnard, Pierre (1867–1947), French painter of landscapes, still life, and nudes, a colourist and skilled draughtsman.

Booth, Edwin Thomas (1833–93), American Shakespearean actor, brother of John Wilkes Booth who assassinated President Lincoln.

Booth, William (1829–1912), founder and first general of the Salvation Army, b. Nottingham. In 1865, with the help of his wife, Catherine Booth, he began mission work in the East End of London, which led to the creation in 1878 of the Salvation Army on military lines. It developed branches in many parts of the world. His son Bramwell (d. 1929) and his daughter

Evangeline were among his successors. See also Salvation Army, Section J.

Borges, Jorge Luis (b. 1899), Argentine poet, critic, and short story writer. Some of his work has been translated into English, including *A Personal Anthology* and *Labyrinths*.

Borgia, Caesar (1476–1507) Italian general. The son of Pope Alexander VI, at 17 he was suspected of murdering his brother. He became captain-general of the church, and made himself master of Romagna, the Marches, and Umbria. Banished by Pope Julius II he met his death fighting in Spain.

Borlaug, Norman Ernest (b. 1914), American wheat scientist, responsible for the "green revolution" (*see* Section L) which is transforming the agricultural prospects of the less-developed countries of the world. Nobel prize for peace 1970.

Borodin, Alexander Porfyrievich (1833–87), Russian composer who taught chemistry and founded a school of medicine for women. In a busy professional life he wrote two symphonies, two string quartets, the symphonic sketch *In the Steppes of Central Asia* and the opera *Prince Igor. See* Section E.

Borrow, George Henry (1803–81), English author, for many years agent for the British and Foreign Bible Society; in the course of his wanderings he studied gypsy life and wrote of his experiences in *Lavengro, Romany Rye, Bible in Spain.*

Bose, Subhas Chandra (1897–1945), Indian nationalist leader; killed in a plane crash.

Boswell, James (1740–95), Scottish author of *The Life of Dr. Johnson*, with whom he spent some years in intimacy. His own journals and letters recently published form an extensive literary collection.

Botha, Louis (1862–1919), South African soldier and statesman. In command of Transvaal forces 1899–1902 in the Boer war, he became prime minister of the Transvaal in 1907, and first premier of the Union of South Africa in 1910. In the 1914–18 war he conquered territory then under German rule.

Bottesini, Giovanni (1821–89), Italian double-bass player.

Botticelli, Sandro (*c.* 1445–1510), Italian painter. He worked under Fra Lippo Lippi, and was influenced by Savonarola. His art is delicate and poetic. His *Birth of Venus* is in the Uffizi Gallery, Florence, and his *Mars and Venus* in the National Gallery. He illustrated Dante's *Inferno.*

Bottomley, Horatio (1860–1933), English politician, journalist, and notorious financier, who died in poverty after serving a prison sentence for fraud.

Botvinnik, Mikhail (b. 1911), Russian chess player; world champion 1948–57, 1958–60, 1961–3. Retired 1965.

Boughton, Rutland (1878–1960), English composer of the opera *The Immortal Hour*, and writer on the history and philosophy of music.

Boult, Sir Adrian (b. 1889), conductor of the London Philharmonic Orchestra 1950–7, and of the B.B.C. Symphony Orchestra 1930–50. Musical Director B.B.C. 1930–42.

Boulton, Matthew (1728–1809), engineer who in partnership with James Watt manufactured steam-engines at his Soho works near Birmingham. He also minted a new copper coinage for Great Britain.

Bowdler, Thomas (1754–1825), issued for family reading expurgated editions of Shakespeare and Gibbon hence the term " bowdlerise."

Boyce, William (1710–79), London organist and composer, who also collected the works of English church composers. He was master of the orchestra of George III.

Boyd Orr, 1st Baron (John Boyd Orr) (1880–1971), British physiologist and nutritional expert. Director-general World Food and Agricultural Organisation 1945–8. Chancellor Glasgow Univ. 1946. Nobel prizewinner 1949.

Boyle, Robert (1627–91), English scientist who with Robert Hooke laid the foundations of the modern sciences of chemistry and physics. He established the law which states that the volume of a gas varies inversely as the pressure upon it, provided temperature is constant. His chief work is the *Sceptical Chymist* (1661).

B10

Bradley, Omar Nelson (b. 1893), American general. In the second world war he commanded in Tunis, Sicily, and Normandy, and was made chief of staff in 1948. Retired 1953.

Bradman, Sir Donald George (b. 1908), Australian cricketer who captained Australia in test matches against England 1936–48.

Bragg, Sir William Henry (1862–1942), English physicist. He held the chair of physics at Adelaide, Leeds, and London, and was professor of chemistry at the Royal Institution 1923–42. Pres. Royal Society 1935–40.

Bragg, Sir William Lawrence (1890–1971), son of the above. He succeeded Rutherford at the Cavendish laboratory, Cambridge, 1938–53. Dir. Royal Institution 1954–66. Shared with his father the 1915 Nobel prize for their fundamental work on X-rays and crystal structure.

Brahe, Tycho (1546–1601), Danish astronomer. At his island observatory at Uraniborg, provided by his sovereign, he carried out systematic observations which enabled Kepler to work out his planetary laws.

Brahms, Johannes (1833–97), composer. B. in Hamburg (son of a double-bass player), he did not marry, and led a simple life devoted to music; latterly he lived in Vienna. He was a friend of the Schumanns. *See Section E.*

Braille, Louis (1809–52), French educationist, who, as teacher of the blind, perfected his system of reading and writing for the blind. As the result of an accident when he was three years old he was himself blind.

Bramah, Joseph (1749–1814), English inventor of the safety-lock and hydraulic press which bear his name. He also invented the water-closet (1778) and a machine for printing the serial numbers on bank-notes.

Brandes, Georg Morris Cohen (1842–1927), Danish literary critic who exerted a vitalising influence on literature and art.

Brandt, Willy (b. 1913), first social democratic chancellor of the Federal Republic of Germany, 1969–74. His main achievements have been the Moscow and Warsaw treaties (1972) and the treaty between E. and W. Germany (1973) which recognised their sovereign existence.

Brangwyn, Sir Frank (1867–1956), artist of Welsh extraction, b. Bruges; first worked for William Morris making cartoons for textiles; he excelled in murals and in etching.

Breakspear, Nicholas. *See Adrian IV.*

Brecht, Bertold (1898–1956), German dramatist and poet, whose brilliant experimental theatre was characteristic of the period in Germany between the two world wars. Being a Marxist, he left Germany in 1933 for Russia, went to the U.S.A. in 1941, and returned to East Germany after the war. His plays include *The Three-penny Opera* (with music by Kurt Weill), *Mother Courage* and *The Caucasian Chalk Circle. See Section I.*

Brennan, Louis (1853–1932), inventor, b. Ireland. His inventions include a gyro-directed torpedo and a mono-rail locomotive on the gyroscope principle.

Breton, Andrée (1896–1966), French poet, founder of the surrealist literary movement in France and a close friend of Apollinaire.

Brewster, Sir David (1781–1868), Scottish physicist, noted for his research into the polarisation of light; invented the kaleidoscope. He helped to found the British Association for the Advancement of Science.

Brezhnev, Leonid Ilyich (b. 1906), succeeded Khrushchev as First Secretary of the Soviet Communist Party in 1964. In his years of office the Soviet Union has achieved strategic parity with the United States, society has become more stable and education and living standards have steadily improved.

Bridges, Robert (1844–1930), poet laureate 1913–30. His *Testament of Beauty* (1929) has been called "a compendium of the wisdom, learning and experience of an artistic spirit." His son Edward (d. 1969) was the head of the civil service from 1945.

Bridgewater, 3rd Duke of (Francis Egerton) (1736–1803), founder of British inland navigation by his canal, to the design of James Brindley (*q.v.*) from Manchester to his coal mines at Worsley, later extended to join the Mersey at Runcorn.

Bridie, James (pseudonym of Osborne Henry Mavor) (1888–1951), Scottish author and dramatist. The first of his many successful plays was *The Anatomist,* produced in 1931. Other plays include *Tobias and the Angel, Jonah and the Whale, Mr. Bolfrey, Dr. Angelus.*

Bright, Sir Charles Tilston (1832–88), English telegraph engineer who supervised the laying of the British telegraph network and the Atlantic cables (1856–8).

Bright, John (1811–89), radical Quaker statesman and orator, b. Rochdale: friend of Cobden, with whom he promoted the movement for free trade.

Brindley, James (1716–72), English canal builder, b. Derbyshire, of poor parents, apprenticed as a millwright. He was employed by the Duke of Bridgewater (*q.v.*) and designed and constructed the Bridgewater canal, carrying it over the R. Irwell by an aqueduct, the first of its kind. He also built the Grand Trunk canal linking the Mersey with the Trent.

Britten, Baron (Edward Benjamin Britten) (1913–76), English composer, closely associated with the Aldeburgh festival. O.M. 1965. *See Section E.*

Broca, Paul (1824–80), French pathologist, anthropologist and pioneer in neuro-surgery. He localised the seat of speech in the brain and originated methods for measuring brain and skull ratios.

Broch, Hermann (1886–1951), Austrian novelist, author of the trilogy *The Sleepwalkers.* Lived in U.S.A. after 1938.

Broglie, prominent family of Piedmontese origin; Victor Maurice (1647–1727), and François Marie (1671–1745) were marshals of France; Louis Victor, Prince de Broglie (b. 1892) received the Nobel prize for his work on quantum mechanics, and his brother Maurice, Duc de Broglie (1875–1960), also a physicist, is noted for his work on the ionisation of gases radioactivity, and X-rays.

Brontë, Charlotte (1816–55), forceful novelist, daughter of an Anglican clergyman of Irish descent, incumbent of Haworth, Yorkshire. She published under a pseudonym *Jane Eyre,* which was at once successful, and was followed by *Shirley* and *Villette.* Her sister Emily (1818–48) wrote poetry and also *Wuthering Heights*; and Anne (1820–49) wrote *Agnes Grey.*

Brooke, Rupert (1887–1915), English poet who died during the first world war, whose works, though few, showed promise and include the poems *Grantchester* and *If I Should Die.*

Brougham and Vaux, 1st Baron (Henry Peter Brougham) (1778–1868), English legal reformer; advocate of Queen Caroline against George IV; helped to found London university.

Brown, Sir Arthur Whitten (1886–1948), together with Sir John Alcock (d. 1919) in 1919 made the first transatlantic flight, crossing from Newfoundland to Ireland in 16 hr. 12 min.

Brown, John (1800–59), American abolitionist. His action in inciting Negro slaves to rebel in 1859 led to the civil war. He was hanged after failing to hold the U.S. arsenal at Harper's Ferry which he had captured. Known as "Old Brown of Osawatomie" and regarded as a martyr.

Browne, Charles Farrer (1834–67), American humorist who wrote under the pseudonym of Artemus Ward.

Browne, Hablot Knight (1815–82), English artist, the "Phiz" of many book illustrations, including Dickens's *Pickwick Papers.*

Browne, Sir Thomas (1605–82), author of *Religio Medici* and *Urne-Buriall* was born in London and practised in Norwich as a physician.

Browning, Elizabeth Barrett (1806–61), English poet. Owing to an injury in childhood, she spent her youth lying on her back, but her meeting with Robert Browning, whom she married, brought a remarkable recovery. In her lifetime her works were more read than those of her husband. They include *Cry of the Children, Sonnets from the Portuguese,* and *Aurora Leigh.*

Browning, Robert (1812–89), English poet. Because of his involved style his reputation grew only slowly. In *Strafford* and *The Blot on the 'Scutcheon* he attempted drama also. He married Elizabeth Barrett and lived mainly abroad. His works include *Dramatis Personae* and *The Ring and The Book.*

Bruce, Robert (1274–1329), Scottish national leader against Edward I and Edward II of England. Crowned king in 1306, after years of struggle he defeated Edward II at Bannockburn in 1314.

Bruce, William Spiers (1867–1921), Scottish polar explorer who led the Scottish national antarctic expedition in the *Scotia* 1902–4 and set up a meteorological station on the South Orkneys.

Bruch, Max (1838–1920), German composer and conductor, best known for his G minor violin concerto.

Bruckner, Anton (1824–96), Austrian composer and organist. *See* Section E.

Brummell, George Bryan (1778–1840), " Beau Brummell," fashion leader and friend of the Prince Regent (George IV).

Brunel, Isambard Kingdom (1806–59), English civil engineer, son of Sir Marc Isambard Brunel (1769–1849), whom he assisted in building the Thames (Rotherhithe) tunnel. He was engineer of the Great Western Railway and built the ocean liners, the *Great Western*, the *Great Britain* (brought back from the Falkland Is. to Bristol in 1970), and the *Great Eastern*. His other works include the Clifton suspension bridge over the R. Avon at Bristol and the Royal Albert bridge over the R. Tamar at Saltash.

Brunelleschi, Filippo (1377–1446), Italian architect, b. Florence; he adapted the ideals of the Roman period. Examples of his work in Florence include the Pitti Palace, the churches of San Lorenzo and San Spirito, and the cathedral dome.

Bruno, Giordano (1548–1600), Italian philosopher. A Dominican friar, he came to favour the astronomical views of Copernicus and was burnt at the stake.

Bruno, St. (*c.* 1032–1101), German monk, founder in 1084 of the Carthusian order at La Grande Chartreuse in the French Alps.

Brutus, Marcus Junius (85–42 B.C.), conspirator against Julius Caesar; later committed suicide.

Buchanan, George (1506–82), Scottish humanist who spent most of his life in France lecturing and writing Latin poems, plays, and treatises. Montaigne, Mary Queen of Scots, and James VI of Scotland were his pupils at various times.

Buchner, Eduard (1860–1917), German chemist, remembered for his work on the chemistry of fermentation. Nobel prizewinner 1907.

Büchner, Georg (1813–37), German dramatist. Dying at 24, his limited output (principally *Dantons Tod* and the fragment *Wozzeck*) is marked by power and maturity.

Buckle, Henry Thomas (1821–62), author of *The History of Civilisation in England*.

Buddha. *See* Gautama, Siddhartha.

Budge, Sir Ernest Alfred Wallis (1857–1934), archaeologist who conducted excavations in Mesopotamia and Egypt.

Buffon, Georges-Louis Leclerc, Comte de (1707–88), French naturalist, author of the *Histoire naturelle* (44 vols., 1749–1804).

Bulganin, Nikolai Alexandrovich (1895–1975), Soviet prime minister 1955–8; defence minister 1947–9, 1953–5. Retired 1960.

Bull, John (*c.* 1562–1628), English composer; possibly composer of *God save the Queen*.

Bülow, Hans Guido von (1830–94), German pianist and conductor. He married Liszt's daughter Cosima, who later left him to marry Wagner.

Bunsen, Robert Wilhelm (1811–99), German chemist, discoverer of the metals caesium and rubidium, and inventor of the Bunsen burner, battery, and pump. Made important observations in spectrum analysis.

Bunyan, John (1628–88), was originally a travelling tinker and is believed to have served in the Parliamentary army. He joined an Independent church in Bedford in 1655 and became a popular preacher. After the Restoration he was thrown into prison, and there wrote *The Pilgrim's Progress*. Of his 60 works, the best known after *Pilgrim's Progress* are *The Holy War*, *Grace Abounding*, and *Mr. Badman*. *See also* Allegory, Section M.

Burckhardt, Jacob Christoph (1818–97), Swiss historian, author of *The Civilisation of the Renaissance in Italy*.

Burghley, 1st Baron (William Cecil) (1520–98), English statesman. After holding office under her two predecessors, he was Queen Elizabeth I's secretary of state, 1558–72, and lord high treasurer, 1572–98.

Burke, Edmund (1729–97), Whig writer and political philosopher. B. in Dublin, he became secretary to Lord Rockingham and entered parliament in 1765. He advocated the emancipation (though not the independence) of th American colonies; and better administration in India; but was against the French revolution.

Burnet, Gilbert (1643–1715) bishop of Salisbury, b. Edinburgh. He wrote a *History of his Own Times*, which deals with many events of which he had personal knowledge.

Burnet, Sir John James (1859–1938), architect, b. Glasgow. The north front of the British Museum (King Edward's galleries) is his most important work in London.

Burney, Fanny (Madame D'Arblay) (1752–1840), originator of the simple novel of home life. Daughter of the organist, Dr. Burney, she published *Evelina* in 1778, and this brought her into court and literary society. She also wrote *Cecilia* and *Camilla*.

Burns, Robert (1759–96), Scottish poet. The son of a cottar, his first poems published in 1786 were at once successful, and he bought a farm. The farm failed, but he had a post as exciseman, and continued to write simply with tenderness and humour. Among his best-known poems are *Auld Lang Syne*, *Scots wa hae*, *Comin' through the rye*, and *The Banks of Doon*.

Burton, Sir Richard Francis (1821–90), British explorer and orientalist, who made a pilgrimage to Mecca and Medina in 1853 disguised as a Moslem. He explored Central Africa and translated the *Arabian Nights* (16 vols.).

Burton, Robert (1577–1640), English clergyman and scholar, author of *The Anatomy of Melancholy*.

Busoni, Ferruccio Benvenuto (1866–1920), pianist and composer of three operas (the last *Dr. Faust*, unfinished at his death), much orchestral and chamber music, and works for the piano. B. in Empoli, he lived in Germany. *See* Section E.

Butler, Joseph (1692–1752), English bishop, remembered for his *Analogy of Religion*, published in 1736 in reply to deistic attacks.

Butler, Nicholas Murray (1862–1947), American educationist who shared with the sociologist Jane Addams the 1931 Nobel peace prize.

Butler, Baron (Richard Austen Butler) (b. 1902), Conservative politician who brought in the Education Act of 1944 and helped secure Conservative acceptance of the welfare state. He took a leading part in drafting the *Industrial Charter* of 1947. " Butskellism " was the term applied to Conservative social and economic policies of the early fifties. Chancellor Sheffield and Essex Univs. Life peer 1965.

Butler, Samuel (1612–80), English verse-satirist, author of the poem *Hudibras* against the Puritans.

Butler, Samuel (1835–1902), English novelist and satirist, author of *Erewhon* and its sequel *Erewhon Revisited*. Other works include *The Fair Haven*, *Life and Habit*, and *Evolution Old and New*, in which he attacked Darwinism. His autobiographical novel *The Way of All Flesh* and his *Notebooks* were published after his death. He exhibited regularly at the Academy and was also a musician.

Butt, Clara (1872–1936), English contralto; made her début in London in 1892. She married Kennerly Rumford in 1900.

Buxton, Sir Thomas Fowell (1786–1845), English social reformer; succeeded Wilberforce as leader of the anti-slavery group in parliament.

Buys Ballot, Christoph Henrich Diedrich (1817–90), Dutch meteorologist who formulated the law which bears his name (an observer with back to wind in northern hemisphere has lower pressure to left; in southern hemisphere to right).

Byrd, Richard Evelyn (1888–1957), American rear-admiral, explorer and aviator. He flew over the north pole, 1926; and in 1929 made the first flight over the south pole. He made other polar expeditions in 1925, 1933–5, 1939 and 1946.

Byrd, William (1543–1623), English composer of church music, sacred choral music, string music, vocal and instrumental music; and a founder of the school of English madrigalists. He was organist of Lincoln cathedral at 20 and later of Queen Elizabeth's chapel royal. *See* Section E.

Byron, 6th Baron (George Gordon Byron) (1788–1824), English romantic poet who influenced European literature and thought. At 20 he published *Hours of Idleness*, which was violently attacked by the *Edinburgh Review*. This provoked his retaliatory *English Bards and Scotch Reviewers*, which caused a sensation. His *Childe Harold's Pilgrimage* appeared in 1812. His married life was unhappy. He went to help the Greeks in their struggle for independence and died at Missolonghi.

C

Cable, George Washington (1844–1925), American author and social critic. b. New Orleans, whose writings reflect the colour problems of his day: *Ole Creol Days, The Silent South.*

Cabot, John (1425–*c.* 1500), Genoese explorer who settled in Bristol and sailed westwards under letters-patent from Henry VII of England in 1497. Discovered Newfoundland and Nova Scotia, believing them to be part of Asia, and may have reached the mainland of America before Columbus did. His son:

Cabot, Sebastian (1474–1557), was born in Venice, and in 1509 in search of a north-west passage to Asia sailed as far as Hudson Bay. Entered Spanish service in 1512, and spent several years exploring the Plate and Paraná rivers. Re-entered English service in 1548 and organised expedition to seek a north-east passage to India, which resulted in trade with Russia. English claim to North America is founded on the voyages of the Cabots.

Cabral, Pedro Alvarez (*c.* 1467–*c.* 1520), Portuguese navigator, friend of Vasco da Gama, discovered Brazil, which he named " Terra da Santa Cruz."

Cadbury, George (1839–1922), liberal Quaker philanthropist of Cadbury Bros., mainly responsible for the pioneer garden city of Bournville.

Cadogan, Sir Alexander (1884–1968), English diplomat. He helped to draft the charter of the United Nations organisation and became Gt. Britain's representative on the Security Council.

Caedmon, the first English Christian poet, lived in the 7th cent. and, according to Bede, was first a cowherd and later a monk at Whitby. His poetry was based on the scriptures.

Caesar, Caius Julius (*c.* 101–44 B.C.), Roman general and writer. Under the declining republic, he was assigned in 61 the province of Gaul; in the course of pacifying it he invaded Britain (55 B.C.). Opposition in Rome to his career, mainly from Pompey, provoked him in 49 to the defiance of crossing the Rubicon with his army. He defeated Pompey, whom he pursued to Egypt, where he established Cleopatra as queen. At Rome he became dictator, and his reforms include the Julian calendar. He was murdered in 44. His career paved the way for Rome's becoming an empire under his nephew Octavian. His writings are masterly accounts of his wars.

Calderón de la Barca, Pedro (1600–81), Spanish dramatist, representative of contemporary Spanish thought, who also wrote court spectacles for Philip IV. Among his best-known works are *La Vida es Sueño* and *El divino Orfeo.*

Callaghan, James (b. 1912), Labour's fourth prime minister; elected parliamentary leader of the Labour Party, April 1976, following Sir Harold Wilson's resignation: elected for South Cardiff 1950; served as Chancellor of the Exchequer, Home Secretary, and Foreign Secretary in the Labour administrations, 1964–70, 1974–76.

Calvin, John (1509–64), French Protestant reformer and theologian. B. in Picardy, he broke with the Roman Catholic church about 1533, and subsequently settled in Geneva, where from 1541 he established a theocratic regime of strict morality. His theology was published in his *Institutes*; while, like Luther, he accepted justification by faith without works, he also believed in predestination. His doctrines spread on the continent, in Scotland and to some extent in England. *See* Calvinism, Section J.

Câmara, Helder Pessoa (b. 1909), Brazilian archbishop of Recife; critic of the economic imperialism of multinational companies and courageous campaigner for social reform in Latin America.

Camden, William (1551–1623), English antiquary and historian. His *Britannia* appeared in 1586.

Cameron, Sir David Young (1865–1945), Scottish etcher and landscape painter.

Cameron, Richard (1648–80), Scottish preacher who revolted in defence of the Solemn League and Covenant and was killed at Airds Moss (Ayrshire).

Cameron, Verney Lovett (1844–94), English explorer, the first to cross the African continent from east to west. He surveyed Lake Tanganyika and in 1872 went out to find Livingstone.

Camillus, Marcus Furius (4th cent. B.C.), Roman general. When the Gauls attacked in 387 B.C., he was made dictator and defeated them.

Camões, Luis Vaz de (1524–80), Portuguese poet, author of *Os Lusiadas,* an epic of Portuguese history and discovery.

Campbell, Colin, 1st Baron Clyde (1792–1863), Scottish general who was commander-in-chief in India during the Mutiny.

Campbell, Sir Malcolm (1885–1948), racing driver who held the land-speed record of 301 mile/h (1935) and water-speed record of 141·7 mile/h (1939). His son Donald held the water-speed record of 276·33 mile/h (1964); killed in 1967 at Coniston.

Campbell, Mrs. Patrick (Beatrice Stella Tanner) (1865–1940), English actress of beauty and wit, friend of G. B. Shaw.

Campbell, Thomas (1777–1844), Scottish poet, who at 22 published *The Pleasures of Hope.* His war poems include *Ye Mariners of England* and *The Battle of the Baltic.* He was one of the founders of University College, London.

Campbell-Bannerman, Sir Henry (1836–1908), Liberal statesman, prime minister 1905–8. His ministry included Asquith, Lloyd George, and Churchill.

Camus, Albert (1913–60), French writer native of Algeria. Preoccupied with the themes of the Stranger and the Absurd, the works for which he is particularly remembered are the philosophical essay *Le Mythe de Sisyphe,* the play *Caligula,* and the novel *L'Etranger.* Nobel prize for literature 1957. Killed in car crash. *See* Section I.

Canaletto (Antonio Canal) (1697–1768), Italian artist. B. at Venice, he painted views of his city. From 1746 to 1756 he worked mainly in London. Some of his work is in the National Gallery, and there is a collection at Windsor.

Canning, George (1770–1827), English statesman. He was an advocate of Catholic emancipation, and was the first to recognise the free states of South America.

Cannizzaro, Stanislao (1826–1910), Italian chemist who carried forward the work of Avogadro in distinguishing between molecular and atomic weights.

Canova, Antonio (1757–1822), Italian sculptor. B. at Venice, he infused grace into the classical style.

Canton, John (1718–72), English physicist and schoolmaster, the first to verify in England Franklin's experiments on the identity of lightning with electricity. He was the first to demonstrate that water is compressible and produced a new phosphorescent body (Canton's phosphorus) by calcining oyster shells with sulphur.

Canute (*c.* 994–1035), king of the English, Danes and Norwegians. The son of a Danish king, after some years of fighting he established himself as king of England and ruled with wisdom and firmness.

Capablanca, José Raoul (1888–1942). Cuban chess player, world champion from 1921 to 1927 when he was beaten by Alekhine.

Caractacus or Caradoc, a king in west Britain, who resisted the Romans in the first century. After capture he was freed by the emperor Claudius.

Carey, William (1761–1834), first Baptist missionary to India. An Oriental scholar, he published 24 translations of the scriptures.

Carissimi, Giacomo (1604–74), Italian composer, b. near Rome. He introduced more instrumental variety into the cantata and oratorio, and brought the recitative to perfection. His *Jephtha* is still in print, and there are collections of his works at Paris and Oxford. *See* Sec. E.

Carlyle, Thomas (1795–1881), Scottish author. Of peasant stock, he went to Edinburgh university, but later lived mainly in England where he lectured. He married Jane Welsh. His individual views pervade his historical writing. His best-known works include *Sartor Resartus*, *Heroes and Hero Worship*, *Cromwell's Letters and Speeches*, and the *French Revolution*.

Carnegie, Andrew (1835–1919), philanthropist b. Dunfermline; emigrated to America 1848; after early struggles established the Carnegie iron works. He made munificent gifts to Free Libraries and other educational work.

Carnot, Lazare Nicolas Marguerite (1753–1823), French military engineer, prominent in the French revolutionary wars, 1792–1802. His son, Sadi Carnot (1796–1832), was a physicist and engineer who worked on the motive power of heat, establishing the principle that heat and work are reversible conditions.

Caroline, Queen (1768–1821), was married to George IV when he was Prince of Wales. They soon separated, but when he became king in 1820, she tried to assert her position. The question came before parliament. In spite of some public sympathy she was unsuccessful.

Carrel, Alexis (1873–1944), American surgeon who won the Nobel prize in 1912 for his success in suturing blood vessels in transfusion and in transplantation of organs. A Frenchman by birth, he returned to France in 1939.

Carroll, Lewis. *See* Dodgson, Charles Lutwidge.

Carson, Baron (Edward Henry Carson) (1854–1935), Irish barrister, solicitor-general for Ireland 1892; attorney general 1915; first lord of the admiralty 1916–17; member of the war cabinet 1917–18. He led a semi-militant organisation against Home Rule.

Carson, Rachel (d. 1964), American biologist, remembered for *The Silent Spring*.

Carter, Howard (1873–1939), Egyptologist who was associated with Lord Carnarvon in discovering in 1922 the Tomb of Tutankhamun.

Carter, James Earl (b. 1924), American Democratic President 1977–; former Governor of Georgia.

Carter, Jacques (1494–1557), French navigator, b. St. Malo, who explored Canada, especially the gulf and river of St. Lawrence.

Cartwright, Edmund (1743–1823), English inventor of the power-loom, and also of a wool-combing machine, important steps in the weaving side of the textile revolution.

Cartwright, John (1740–1824), brother of the above; reformer and agitator against slavery.

Caruso, Enrico (1873–1921), Italian tenor, b. Naples.

Carver, George Washington (1864–1943), American Negro agricultural chemist of world repute.

Casabianca, Louis de (c. 1752–98), captain of the French flagship *L'Orient* at the Battle of the Nile. He and his ten-year-old son died together in the burning ship.

Casals, Pablo (1876–1973), Spanish cellist and conductor, son of an organist, b. Vendrell, Tarragona. He exiled himself from Spain in 1938 as a protest against dictatorship.

Casanova de Seingalt, Giacomo (1725–98), Italian adventurer, author of licentious memoirs.

Cassini, French family of Italian origin, distinguished for work in astronomy and geography. Through four generations (1671–1793) they were heads of the Paris Observatory.

Cassius, Caius Longinus, Roman general who opposed the dictatorship of Julius Caesar, and took part in his murder. He died in 42 B.C. after being defeated by Mark Antony.

Castlereagh, Viscount (Robert Stewart Castlereagh) (1769–1822), British minister of war and foreign secretary, who took a leading part in the Napoleonic wars. He was however unpopular and committed suicide.

Castro, Fidel (b. 1927), Cuban revolutionary. After two unsuccessful attempts he succeeded in 1959 in overthrowing a police-state. He has initiated reforms in agriculture, industry, and education, and repulsed American economic dominance. His acceptance of Russian support led to the " missiles crisis " of 1962.

Catchpool, E. St. John (b. 1890), first secretary of the English Youth Hostels Association, 1930–50; president of the International Federation, 1938–50.

Catherine, St. (4th cent.). Traditionally a virgin martyr in Alexandria, though not mentioned before the 10th cent. Legend represents her as tied to a wheel.

Catherine de' Medici (1519–89), Italian-born wife of Henry II and mother of three French kings (she was regent for Charles IX). Her antagonism to the Protestants may have led to the massacre of St. Bartholomew's day. She was able, and appreciated art and literature, but was unscrupulous and cruel.

Catherine of Aragon (1485–1536), first wife of Henry VIII of England, was daughter of Ferdinand and Isabella of Spain, and mother of Mary Tudor. When Henry VIII attempted to obtain papal dissolution of their marriage, and subsequently obtained an English declaration of its nullity (thus precipitating a movement towards the Reformation) she bore herself with dignity during her retirement.

Catherine the Great (1729–96), Empress Catherine II of Russia. Daughter of a German prince, she married in 1745 the future Peter III, a weakling, later deposed and murdered. Intelligent, cultivated, autocratic, she proved a capable ruler for a time but was hampered and opposed by the landed interests and, despite plans for reform, her reign was marked by imperialist expansion and extension of serfdom.

Cato, Marcus Porcius (234–149 B.C.), Roman statesman and writer. His tenure of office as censor was characterised by austerity and conservatism. He advocated opposition to Carthage. His writings deal with agriculture and history.

Catullus, Caius Valerius (c. 84–54 B.C.), Roman poet who wrote lyrics to Lesbia. His poems show sincere feeling and also Greek influence.

Cavell, Edith Louisa (1865–1915), English nurse who cared for friend and foe in Brussels in 1914–15 but was executed by the Germans for helping Allied fugitives to escape.

Cavendish, Henry (1731–1810), English scientist, a contemporary of Black, Priestley, Scheele, and Lavoisier, remembered for his investigations into the nature of gases. He discovered hydrogen and the chemical composition of water. He was the first to determine the weights of equal volumes of gases.

Cavour, Camillo Benso di (1810–61), Italian statesman, who, as premier of Piedmont, helped to bring about the unification of Italy.

Caxton, William (1422–91), the first English printer and publisher, a man of wide-ranging abilities. He probably learnt the art of printing at Cologne (1471–2), setting up his own printing press at Westminster (1476). He printed Chaucer's *Canterbury Tales*, Malory's *Le Morte Darthur* and Aesop's *Fables*. He was an accomplished linguist.

Cecil of Chelwood, 1st Viscount (Robert Cecil) (1864–1958), English politician who helped draft the Charter of the League of Nations. Nobel prize for peace 1937.

Cecilia, St. (2nd or 3rd cent.), patron saint of music. She is often represented playing the organ.

Cellini, Benvenuto (1500–71), Italian sculptor and goldsmith. B. at Florence, he worked for some years in Rome. His bronze statue *Perseus with the head of Medusa* is at Florence. His life was adventurous and he wrote an *Autobiography* which is revealing of himself and his time.

Celsius, Anders (1701–44), Swedish physicist and astronomer who invented the centigrade thermometer.

Ceresole, Pierre (1879–1945), Swiss founder of International Voluntary Service. He was by profession a teacher of engineering, and his pacifism led him to become a Quaker.

Cervantes, Saavedra Miguel de (1547–1616), Spanish novelist and dramatist, b. at Alcalá de Henares. He was injured at the battle of Lepanto, and thereafter struggled to earn a livelihood from literature. His *Don Quixote* describes the adventures of a poor gentleman, confused in mind, who on his horse Rosinante with his squire Sancho Panza seeks adventures; it satirised chivalry, but is also a permanent criticism of life. Of his plays only two survive.

Cézanne, Paul (1839–1906), French painter, b. in Aix-en-Provence, the son of a wealthy banker and tradesman. He developed a highly original style, using colour and tone in such a way as to increase the impression of depth. He said that he wanted "to make of Impressionism something solid and durable, like the art of the Museums." Like Giotto, six hundred years before, he more than any other artist determined the course European painting was to take. *La Vielle au Chapelet* and *Les Grandes Baigneuses* are in the National Gallery. He was a friend of Zola.

Chadwick, Sir James (b. 1891), English physicist, one of Rutherford's collaborators in the field of atomic research. Discovered the neutron in 1932, one of the main steps in the discovery of the fission process which led to the production of the atom bomb.

Chagall, Marc (b. 1889), Russian painter, b. at Vitebsk of Jewish parents, the forerunner of surrealism. He lives in Paris.

Chaliapin, Fedor Ivanovich (1873–1938), Russian opera singer, a bass with dramatic gifts.

Chamberlain, Joseph (1836–1914), English statesman. He began with municipal work in Birmingham. At first a Liberal under Gladstone, he became Conservative. He opposed Home Rule for Ireland, and was the first advocate of a partial return to protection.

Chamberlain, Neville (1869–1940), son of Joseph. He was prime minister 1937–40, when he appeased Hitler by the Munich agreement of 1938.

Chambers, Sir William (1726–96) British architect, b. Stockholm. He rebuilt Somerset House and designed the pagoda in Kew Gardens.

Chaminade, Cécile (1857–1944), French pianist and composer.

Champlain, Samuel de (1567–1635), French navigator who founded Quebec (1608), and discovered the lake known by his name.

Chantrey, Sir Francis Legatt (1781–1841), English sculptor who contributed statues to Westminster Abbey and St. Paul's. He left a fortune to the Royal Academy for the purchase of works of British art. The collection is in the Tate Gallery.

Chaplin, Sir Charles Spencer (1889–1977), first international screen star, with more than 50 years' achievement. B. in London, his mother was a music-hall singer and he made his début at five. In 1910 he went to the United States; and with the Keystone Company in Los Angeles (1914–15) he made films in which his early hardships are reflected in humour and sadness. His films include *Shoulder Arms*, *The Kid*, *The Gold Rush*, *City Lights*, *The Great Dictator*, *Modern Times*, and *Limelight*. In 1953 he went to live in Switzerland. *Autobiography* (1964).

Chapman, George (1559–1634), Elizabethan poet, dramatist, and translator of the *Iliad* and *Odyssey*. His best-known play is *Bussy d'Ambois*.

Chapman, Sydney (1888–1970), English mathematician and geophysicist, noted for his work on the kinetic theory of gases, geomagnetism, and solar and ionospheric physics. He was president of the special committee of the I.G.Y., 1957–8. An upper layer of the atmosphere and a crater on the far side of the moon are named after him.

Charcot, Jean Baptiste (1867–1936), French explorer, who in 1903–5 and 1908–10 commanded expeditions to the south polar regions. Charcot Island in the Antarctic is named after him.

Chardin, Jean Baptiste Siméon (1699–1779), French painter of still life and interior domestic scenes.

Chares (c. 300 B.C.), Greek worker in bronze from Rhodes, sculptor of the Colossus of Rhodes, one of the seven wonders of the world, which was destroyed in the earthquake of 225 B.C.

Charlemagne (742–814), Charles the Great. From being King of the Franks, he came to govern an empire comprising Gaul, Italy, and large parts of Spain and Germany, and was crowned Holy Roman Emperor.

Charles, Jacques Alexandre César (1746–1823), French physicist, the first to use hydrogen gas in balloons and who anticipated Gay-Lussac's law on the expansion of gases.

Charles Edward (Stuart) (1720–88), the Young Pretender (*i.e.*, claimant of the English throne),

grandson of James II, led an unsuccessful rising in 1745 and died in exile.

Charles I (1600–49), King of England, Scotland, and Ireland, succeeded his father James I in 1625. Personally sincere, and having an appreciation of art, he was yet ill-fitted to cope with the political problems of his time. His marriage with the French princess Henrietta Maria was unpopular. He supported Archbishop Laud's strict Anglicanism, and he also attempted to rule without parliament. Defeated in the Civil War which broke out in 1642, he spun out negotiations for a settlement till he was beheaded in 1649.

Charles II (1630–85), King of England, Scotland, and Ireland, son of Charles I; after the Civil War escaped to France, and returned in 1660 when the monarchy was restored. His religious sympathies were Roman Catholic and his personal life was amorous; but in political matters he was shrewd and realistic, and contrived not to "go on his travels" again. He promoted the development of the navy, but had to accept the laws enforcing religious conformity imposed by parliament.

Charles V (1500–58), Hapsburg ruler, succeeded his grandfather, Maximilian I, as emperor of the Holy Roman Empire, and as heir to Ferdinand and Isabella succeeded to the Spanish crown. His rivalry with Francis I of France led to prolonged war. He crushed a revolt of peasants in 1525. He presided in 1521 at the Diet before which Luther appeared, after which religious struggle continued in Germany till the Augsburg settlement of 1555. In that year he retired to a monastery in Spain.

Charles XII of Sweden (1682–1718), a brave but rash and ambitious general. He repelled Russian attacks at Narva in 1700, but subsequently pursuing military adventure he was defeated by Peter the Great at Poltava in 1709; and on invading Norway was killed at a siege.

Chateaubriand, François René, Vicomte de (1768–1848), French writer and diplomat. In a varied career he was at first an emigré, and later served as diplomat under both Napoleon and Louis XVIII. He was a friend of Mme. Recamier. His writings include *Mémoires d'outre-tombe*.

Chatham, 1st Earl of (William Pitt) (1708–78), English statesman and orator. His energetic conduct of the Seven Years War was an important contribution to English victory and to acquisitions in Canada and India at the peace (1763), though by then he was out of office. In the dispute with the American colonies he upheld their right to resist imposed taxation, and collapsed while making a last speech on this dispute.

Chatterton, Thomas (1752–70), English poet who tried to pass off his writings as newly discovered ancient manuscripts and killed himself at the age of 17.

Chaucer, Geoffrey (1340?–1400), English poet. His main work, *The Canterbury Tales*, gives a vivid picture of contemporary life.

Chekhov, Anton (1860–1904), Russian dramatist and short-story writer, whose plays include *The Cherry Orchard*, *Uncle Vanya*, and *The Three Sisters*. His stories include *The Steppe*, *The Sleepyhead*, *The Post*, *The Student*, and *The Bishop*. He was of humble origin and while a student at Moscow supported his family by writing humorous sketches and tales.

Cherubini, Luigi (1760–1842), Italian-born musician, for many years director of the Paris Conservatoire and composer of operas and church music.

Chesterfield, 4th Earl of (Philip Dormer Stanhope) (1694–1773), English statesman, whose *Letters* to his natural son, Philip Stanhope, are full of grace, wit, and worldly wisdom.

Chesterton, Gilbert Keith (1874–1936), English essayist, novelist and poet, who also wrote studies of Charles Dickens and Robert Browning. His best-known works include *The Napoleon of Notting Hill* and *The Ballad of the White Horse*.

Chevalier, Albert (1861–1923), English music-hall comedian known for his coster sketches.

Chevalier, Maurice (1889–1972), French stage and film actor.

Chiang Kai-shek (1887–1975), Chinese general. He at first fought for Sun Yat-sen. After the latter's death (1925), as commander of the

Kuomintang army, he attempted to unite China; but (involved as he was with business interests) he was more anxious to defeat the Communists than to repel the Japanese adventure in Manchuria in 1931. He was unable to establish peace and a stable, progressive régime; and in 1949 retired to Formosa after military defeat by the Communists. His widow is Mayling Soong.

Chichester, Sir Francis (1902–72), English seaman, who sailed his *Gipsy Moth IV* into Sydney harbour in 1966 after a 107-day voyage from Plymouth, and back again round the Horn.

Chippendale, Thomas (1718–79), designer of furniture, b. Otley, Yorks., son of a joiner. His designs are shown in *The Gentleman and Cabinet Maker's Director*, 1754.

Chirico, Giorgio de (b. 1888), painter associated with the surrealist school, born in Greece of Italian parents.

Chomsky, Noam (b. 1908), American theoretical linguist, professor of Linguistics, Massachusetts Institute of Technology; inventor of transformational grammar.

Chopin, Frédéric François (1810–49), Polish pianist and composer, son of a French father and Polish mother. He has been called " the poet of the piano " because of the originality and delicacy of his playing. He enjoyed Paris intellectual and musical society, was a friend of George Sand, and played in numerous concerts all over Europe. He died of consumption. *See* Section E.

Chou En-lai (1898–1976), Chinese revolutionary statesman, administrator and diplomat. He organised revolt in Shanghai 1927, later formed close partnership with Mao Tse-tung, took part in the " long march " 1934–5, becoming prime minister of the new China in 1949. Headed the Chinese delegation to the Geneva Conference of 1954.

Chrysostom, St. John (*c.* 347–407), preacher. Chrysostom means golden-mouthed. First at Antioch, and later as patriarch of Constantinople, he was an eloquent teacher; but by outspokenness he lost the Empress Eudoxia's favour and died from ill-treatment.

Chulalongkorn, Phra Paramindr Maha (1853–1910), Siamese reforming monarch.

Churchill, Lord Randolph Henry Spencer (1849–95), Conservative politician, who held brief office only. He was father of Winston Churchill.

Churchill, Sir Winston Leonard Spencer (1874–1965), British statesman and author, son of the last-named. He entered parliament in 1900. He served as a junior officer with the British forces abroad; and during the Boer War he acted as war correspondent. He held the following ministerial posts: Under-Secretary for the Colonies 1905–8; President of the Board of Trade 1908–10; Home Secretary 1910–11; First Lord of the Admiralty 1911–15, 1939–40; Chancellor of the Duchy of Lancaster 1915; Minister of Munitions 1917; Minister of War 1918–21; Minister of Air 1919–21; Secretary of State for the Colonies 1921–2; Chancellor of the Exchequer 1924–9; Prime Minister and Minister of Defence 1940–5; Prime Minister 1951–5. He was rector or chancellor of three universities. Cast in the heroic mould, he lived a full life. His main achievement was as leader of the British people in the second world war. His writings include a biography of his ancestor, Marlborough, and histories of the first and second world wars. He exhibited at the Royal Academy. Hon. American citizenship conferred 1963.

Cibber, Colley (1671–1757), a London actor and dramatist. His best comedies are *The Careless Husband* and *Love's Last Shift*. He wrote an autobiography.

Cicero, Marcus Tullius (106–43 B.C.), Roman orator and philosopher, many of whose letters and speeches survive. He held political office but was killed by the troops of the triumvirate.

Cid (El Campeador) (*c.* 1035–99), name given to the Spanish knight Rodrigo Diaz, a soldier of fortune who fought against Moors and Christians alike. Myth made him a national hero of knightly and Christian virtue.

Cierva, Juan de la (1895–1936), Spanish engineer who invented the autogiro.

Cimabue, Giovanni (Cenni di Pepo) (1240–1302), early Florentine painter. His only certain work is the St. John in Pisa cathedral.

Cimarosa, Domenico (1749–1801), Italian composer. His best-known opera is *Il Matrimonio Segreto*. He held revolutionary views.

Cimon (*c.* 512–449 B.C.), Athenian statesman and general, son of Miltiades. He defeated the Persian fleet at the mouth of the Eurymedon in 468. He worked for cooperation with other states, including Sparta.

Cipriani, Giambattista (1727–85), Italian painter of historical subjects who worked in London; a founder member of the Royal Academy.

Clair, René (b. 1898), French film producer, whose early films, full of wit and satire, include *Sous les Toits de Paris* and *A Nous la Liberté*.

Clare, John (1793–1864), Northamptonshire labourer who became a poet. *Poems Descriptive of Rural Life and Scenery*, and *The Village Minstrel* were among his publications. He died in the county lunatic asylum.

Clarendon, 1st Earl of (Edward Hyde) (1609–74), English statesman and historian. He was for some years chancellor to Charles II, and his daughter married the future James II, but he fell and died in exile. He wrote a *History of the Rebellion*.

Clark, Baron (Kenneth McKenzie Clark) (b. 1903), English art historian. He was director of the National Gallery 1934–45, Slade professor of fine arts at Oxford 1946–50, and chairman of the Arts Council 1953–60. Life peer 1969. Chanc. York University 1969. O.M. 1976.

Clarkson, Thomas (1760–1846) devoted his life to the abolition of slavery and shares with Wilberforce credit for the passing of the Act of 1807 abolishing the British slave trade.

Claude Lorrain (Gellée) (1600–82), French landscape painter. B. near Nancy, he settled in Rome. A close student of nature, he excelled in depicting sunrise or sunset, and founded a " picturesque " tradition.

Claudius (10 B.C.–A.D. 54), Roman emperor. After the murder of Caligula, he was proclaimed emperor almost accidentally by the Praetorian Guard. He was a sensible administrator. In his time the empire was extended to include Britain, Thrace, and Mauretania. He was probably poisoned by his wife Agrippina.

Clausewitz, Karl von (1780–1831), German military expert whose *Vom Kriege*, expounding his theories on war, dominated Prussia in the 19th cent.

Clemenceau, Georges (1841–1929), French statesman of radical views; twice premier, 1906–9, 1917–20. He was a defender of Dreyfus. In old age he presided at the peace conference of 1919, where he was hostile to Germany (" the Tiger ").

Cleopatra (69–30 B.C.), daughter of Ptolemy XI, the sixth queen of Egypt by that name, a brilliant, ambitious woman. In 51 she became joint sovereign with her younger brother Ptolemy XII. She was banished to Syria, but, obtaining the help of Caesar, regained the kingdom. She and Caesar became lovers, and in 47 she bore him a son Caesarion (later Ptolemy XIV). After Caesar's murder she returned to Egypt. She met the triumvir Mark Antony and bore him twins; he deserted his wife and broke with his brother-in-law Octavian (later Augustus). Antony and Cleopatra were, however, defeated in 31 B.C.; Antony fell upon his sword, and Cleopatra killed herself with an asp bite. Her life inspired Shakespeare's *Antony and Cleopatra* and Shaw's *Caesar and Cleopatra*.

Clive, 1st Baron (Robert Clive) (1725–74), English general who helped to lay the foundations of English power in India. B. near Market Drayton, he entered the service of the East India Company. He contemplated suicide, but Anglo-French rivalry, culminating in the Seven Years War, gave scope for his military powers in the siege of Arcot and the battle of Plassey. As a governor he showed administrative capacity. In his later life he was poor and unpopular.

Clovis (*c.* 465–511), Merovingian king of the Franks and a convert to Christianity. He defeated the Burgundians and West Goths, and fixed his court at Paris.

Clyde, Lord. *See* Campbell, Colin.

Cobbett, William (1763–1835), English controversialist. He is chiefly known for his *Rural Rides*, but also published a weekly *Political Register* from 1802.

Cobden, Richard (1804–65), English advocate of free trade. The son of a Sussex farmer, he led agitation against the laws restricting import of corn, and they were repealed in 1846. He was impoverished by his public work and was helped by subscription.

Cochrane, Thomas, 10th Earl of Dundonald (1775–1860), British seaman, who crippled a French fleet in Biscay (1809), aided the liberation of Chile and Peru from Spanish rule (1819–22), of Brazil from Portuguese rule (1823–5), and assisted the Greeks in their struggle to throw off the Turkish yoke (1827).

Cockcroft, Sir John Douglas (1897–1967), Cambridge nuclear physicist who shared with E. T. S. Walton the 1951 Nobel prize. They had worked together at Cambridge in the historic " atom-splitting " experiments beginning with the transmutation of lithium into boron. He was directly involved in Britain's first nuclear power programmes.

Cockerell, Christopher (b. 1910), English inventor of the hovercraft, which works on the aircushioning principle. *See* Hovercraft, Section L.

Cocteau, Jean (1891–1963), French writer and artist in widely varied forms of art.

Cody, Samuel Franklin (1861–1913), American aviator, the first man to fly in Britain (1,390 ft. on 16 Oct. 1908). He became a British subject in 1909. Killed while flying.

Cody, William Frederick (1846–1917), American showman, known as " Buffalo Bill," whose Wild West Show toured America and Europe.

Coggan, Donald (b. 1909), enthroned 101st archbishop of Canterbury, January 1975; archbishop of York 1961–74.

Cohn, Ferdinand Julius (1828–98) German botanist, founder of the science of bacteriology.

Coke, Sir Edward (1552–1634), English legal author, judge, and rival of Francis Bacon. His legal works are his *Reports* and *Institutes*.

Colbert, Jean Baptiste (1619–83), French statesman under Louis XIV, who fostered new industries, encouraged commerce, reformed the finances and established the navy on a sound basis. A patron of literature, science, and art.

Cole, George Douglas Howard (1889–1959), English economist and political journalist, professor of social and political theory at Oxford, 1944–57. Among his writings are *The Intelligent Man's Guide through World Chaos*, and *A History of Socialist Thought* (5 vols.).

Coleridge, Samuel Taylor (1772–1834), English poet, critic, and friend of Wordsworth, with whom he published *Lyrical Ballads*. His poems include *The Ancient Mariner*, *Christabel*, and *Kubla Khan*. His literary criticism is still valuable.

Coleridge-Taylor, Samuel (1875–1912), English composer, the son of a West African doctor practising in London and an Englishwoman. He is best known for his Hiawatha trilogy.

Colet, John (c. 1467–1519), English humanist and divine, founded St. Paul's School (1512). As scholar and friend of Erasmus he helped to bring the new learning to England.

Colette (Sidonie Gabrielle Claudine Colette) (1873–1954), French author of the *Claudine* stories, *Chéri* and *La Fin de Chéri*.

Collier, John (1850–1934), English painter noted for his " problem " pictures.

Collingwood, 1st Baron (Cuthbert Collingwood) (1750–1810), British admiral whose ship, the *Royal Sovereign*, led the fleet to battle at Trafalgar, and who on Nelson's death assumed command.

Collingwood, Robin George (1889–1943), English philosopher, historian, and archaeologist, associated with Oxford from 1908 to 1941. His philosophical thought is best studied in *Speculum Mentis*, *Essay on Philosophical Method*, *Idea of Nature*, and *Idea of History*.

Collins, Michael (1890–1922), Irish politician and Sinn Fein leader. He successfully organised guerrilla warfare, and mainly negotiated the treaty with Britain in 1921, but was killed in a Republican ambush on his return.

Collins, William (1788–1847), English landscape and figure painter.

Collins, William Wilkie (1824–89), son of the above; practically the first English novelist to deal with the detection of crime. *The Woman in White* appeared in 1860.

Colt, Samuel (1814–62), of Hartford, Connecticut, invented the revolver in 1835. It was used in the war with Mexico.

Columba, St. (521–97), founder of the monastery of Iona, b. Ireland. From his island shrine he made missionary journeys to the Highlands of Scotland.

Columbanus, St. (c. 540–615), Irish abbot who founded a number of monasteries in continental Europe. *See* Monasticism, Section J.

Columbus, Christopher (c. 1451–1506), Italian navigator, b. Genoa, who, prevailing upon Ferdinand and Isabella of Spain to bear the expense of an expedition, in 1492 discovered the Bahamas, Cuba, and other West Indian islands. In 1498 he landed on the lowlands of S. America.

Comenius, John Amos (1592–1670), Czech educationist and pastor, advocate of the " direct " method of teaching languages, of the use of pictures in education, and of equality of educational opportunity for girls.

Compton, Arthur Holly (1892–1962), American physicist whose work on X-rays established what is known as the Compton effect (1923). While professor of physics at the university of Chicago (1923–45) he helped to develop the atomic bomb. Nobel prizewinner 1927.

Compton, Karl Taylor (1887–1954), scientist-administrator, brother of the above. Pres. Massachusetts Institute of Technology 1930–48.

Compton-Burnett, Dame Ivy (1884–1969), English novelist whose books deal with family relationships and include *Pastors and Masters, Men and Wives, A House and Its Head, Mans rvant and Maidservant*.

Comte, August (1798–1857), French philosopher, founder of positivism. *See* Positivism, Section J.

Condé, Louis, Prince de (1621–86), French general who defeated Spain at Rocroi in 1643.

Confucius or **K'ung Fu-tse** (c. 551–478 B.C.), Chinese philosopher, founder of the system of cosmology, politics, and ethics known as Confucianism. He was not concerned with the supernatural, but appealed to reason and taught love and respect of one's fellows, superiority to ambition, charity, forgiveness, and repentance. *See* Confucianism, Section J.

Congreve, William (1670–1729), Restoration dramatist, whose witty plays include *The Way of the World* and *Love for Love*.

Conrad, Joseph (1857–1924), English novelist of Polish birth, whose parents were exiled to France for political reasons. He became master mariner in the British merchant service, and began to write novels after he left the sea in 1884. His novels include *Almayer's Folly*, *Lord Jim*, *Nostromo*.

Conscience, Hendrik Henri (1812–83), Flemish novelist who wrote *The Lion of Flanders*.

Constable, John (1776–1837), English landscape painter, b. East Bergholt, Suffolk. Unlike his contemporary Turner, who journeyed over the continent with his sketchbook, he found his scenes within a few miles of his home. His work was more popular in France than in England at the time and affected the Barbizon school and Delacroix. Examples of his work are in the National Gallery (including *The Hay Wain, Flatford Mill*, and *The Cornfield*), the Victoria and Albert, and the Tate (*The Valley Farm*).

Constant, Jean Joseph Benjamin (1845–1902), French painter of portraits and Oriental subjects.

Constantine (274–338), called " the Great ", the first Christian Roman emperor. He was proclaimed at York by the army in 306. He stabilised the empire after a period of decline, and founded a new capital at Constantinople. A Christian council was held under his auspices at Nicaea in 325, and he was baptised on his death-bed.

Cook, James (1728–79), English navigator, son of an agricultural labourer. He entered the Royal Navy and gained a high reputation for his scientific skill. He made voyages of discovery to New Zealand and Australia in the ships under his command, *Endeavour*, *Resolution*, and *Adventure*. He anchored at Botany Bay in 1770 on his first voyage and gave it that name because of the interesting plants found on its shores. He also surveyed the Newfoundland coast. In an attempt to find the north-west passage he was murdered at Hawaii.

Cooper, Sir Astley Paston (1768–1841), English surgeon and author of medical textbooks.

Cooper, James Fenimore (1789–1851), American novelist, who produced stirring stories of adventure, among them *The Spy*, *The Last of the Mohicans*, *The Pathfinder*, and *The Deer Slayer*.

Cooper, Samuel (1609–72), English miniaturist, represented with his brother Alexander (d. 1660) in the Victoria and Albert Museum. Among his miniatures is a portrait of Cromwell.

Copernicus, Nicolas (1473–1543), founder of modern astronomy, b. at Torun in Poland. He studied at Cracow and at a number of Italian universities before settling at Frauenburg in 1512 where he became canon of the cathedral. More of a student than a practical astronomer, he spent most of his private life seeking a new theory of the heavenly bodies. In his *On the Revolution of the Celestial Orbs*, published after his death, he broke with the past and put forward the novel theory that the planets, including the earth, revolve round the sun.

Coppée, François Joachim (1842–1908), French poet, novelist and dramatist.

Coquelin, Benoît Constant (1841–1909), and **Coquelin, Ernest** (1848–1909), (Coquelin aîné et cadet), brothers, were leading lights of the French theatre.

Corelli, Arcangelo (1653–1713), Italian composer and violinist, who established the form of the concerto grosso. *See* **Section E.**

Corneille, Pierre (1606–84), French dramatist, who ranks with Racine as a master of classical tragedy. *Le Cid*, *Polyeucte*, and *Le Menteur* marked a new era in French dramatic production.

Cornwallis, 1st Marquess (Charles Cornwallis) (1738–1805), British general who commanded the British forces which surrendered to the Americans at Yorktown in 1781, thus ending the war of independence. He was twice governor-general of India.

Corot, Jean Baptiste (1796–1875), French landscape painter.

Correggio, Antonio Allegri da (1494–1534), Italian painter, b. Correggio. His style anticipates the baroque. His *Ecce Homo* is in the National Gallery.

Cortés, Hernando (1488–1547), Spanish adventurer, b. Medellín, Estremadura, who captured Mexico for Spain, crushing an ancient civilisation.

Coulton, George Gordon (1858–1947), scholar and historian of the Middle Ages. In his *Five Centuries of Religion* he sets forth his interpretation of monastic history in England from the Conquest to the Reformation.

Couperin, a family of French musicians who were organists at St. Gervais, Paris, from about 1650 till 1826. **François Couperin** (1668–1733), called "Couperin the Great," is the best known today for his harpsichord music.

Cousin, Victor (1792–1867), French educationist and philosopher, founder of the eclectic school.

Cousins, Samuel (1801–87), English mezzotint engraver of plates after Reynolds, Millais, Landseer, and Hogarth.

Cousteau, Jacques-Yves (b. 1910), French underwater explorer, pioneer of aqualung diving.

Couve de Murville, Maurice (b. 1900), French diplomat; General de Gaulle's foreign minister 1958–68.

Coverdale, Miles (1488–1568), one of the early English reformers, b. Yorkshire, later to become bishop of Exeter. He assisted Tyndale in translating the Pentateuch and completed his own translation of the Bible in 1535. The Psalms still used in the Prayer Book and many of the phrases in the authorised version of 1611 are from his translation.

Cowper, William (1731–1800), English religious poet. His work is characterised by simplicity and tenderness. His best-known poems are *John Gilpin* and *The Task*.

Cox, David (1783–1859), English landscape painter. A collection of his works is in the Birmingham Gallery and the Tate Gallery.

Crabbe, George (1754–1832), English narrative poet of grim humour; author of *The Village* and *The Borough*.

Craig, Edward Gordon (1872–1966), son of Ellen Terry, producer and author of books on stagecraft.

Cranmer, Thomas (1489–1556), archbishop of Canterbury under Henry VIII, and Edward VI; an ardent promoter of the Reformation. On Mary's accession he at first consented to return to the old faith, but when called upon to make public avowal of his recantation, refused, and was burnt at the stake. His contributions were the English Bible and Book of Common Prayer.

Crichton, James (1560–82), Scottish adventurer who for his scholarly accomplishments was called "the admirable Crichton." He was killed in a brawl.

Cripps, Sir Stafford (1889–1952), British Labour statesman. A successful barrister, he relinquished practice for public work. As chancellor of the exchequer in post-war Britain, his programme was one of austerity, but his able exposition and single-minded purpose won him general support. Ill-health terminated his career.

Crispi, Francesco (1819–1901), Italian statesman, who aided Garibaldi and was later premier.

Crispin, St. (c. 285), martyr with his brother. By tradition they were Roman and became shoemakers, hence patron saints of shoemaking.

Croce, Benedetto (1866–1952), Italian philosopher and critic. His philosophy is expounded in the four volumes of *Filosofia dello Spirito* (which has been translated into English). He founded and edited *La Critica* in 1903, a review of literature, history, and philosophy. He was strongly opposed to fascism.

Croesus (d. c. 546 B.C.), last king of Lydia, reputed to be of immense wealth. Conquered and condemned to death by Cyrus, he was reprieved when Cyrus heard him recall Solon's saying "Call no man happy till he is dead."

Crome, John (1769–1821), English landscape painter, b. Norwich.

Cromer, 1st Earl of (Evelyn Baring) (1841–1917), British diplomat who, as British comptroller-general in Egypt from 1883 to 1907, did much to maintain order, improve the finances, and promote development. His *Modern Egypt* appeared in 1908.

Crompton, Samuel (1753–1827), English inventor of the spinning-mule (1779), which substituted machinery for hand work. He was b. near Bolton, a farmer's son, and benefited little by his invention.

Cromwell, Oliver (1599–1658), Protector of the commonwealth of England, Scotland, and Ireland. B. at Huntingdon, he represented Huntingdon in parliament. When civil war broke out, he served under the Earl of Essex; and then reorganised the parliamentary army, winning victories at Marston Moor and Naseby. Tortuous negotiations with Charles I could not be brought to an end, and he promoted the king's trial and execution in 1649. He defeated the Scots at Dunbar. When continued difficulties beset government he became Protector in 1653, but was soon obliged to govern by major-generals. His handling of Ireland enhanced the difficulties of that country. An able general and a strong character, he was personally tolerant (an Independent), sincere and devout; but he found himself in the revolutionary's dilemma— that there is no easy exit from a revolutionary situation; thus paradoxically he provoked English aversion to military rule.

Cromwell, Richard (1626–1712), son of the above, and his successor in the protectorate.

Cromwell, Thomas (1485–1540), English statesman, who succeeded Wolsey in the service of Henry VIII, and carried out the dissolution of the monasteries, but on his fall from favour he was executed.

Crookes, Sir William (1832–1919), English physicist who discovered the element thallium (1861) and invented the Crookes tube (1874) which was used by J. J. Thomson and others in their researches into the conduction of electricity in gases. He was also an authority on sanitation.

Cruikshank, George (1792–1878), caricaturist and book illustrator, whose work includes illustrations to *Grimm's Fairy Tales*, and *Oliver Twist*. Collections of his work are in the British Museum and the Victoria and Albert Museum.

Cummings, Bruce Frederick (1889–1919), English

zoologist and author of *Journal of a Disappointed Man.*

Cunard, Sir Samuel (1787–1865), founder of the Cunard line of steam ships. He was born in Nova Scotia, of a Welsh family of Quakers.

Cunningham of Hyndhope, 1st Viscount (Andrew Browne Cunningham) (1883–1963), British admiral in two world wars, b. Edinburgh. He served as commander-in-chief, Mediterranean, 1939–42 and Feb.–Oct. 1943; naval commander-in-chief for the Allied assault on North Africa 1942; first sea lord 1943–6.

Curie, Marie Sklodowska (1867–1934), first great woman scientist, b. Poland. Her father was a professor of physics at Warsaw. She came to Paris to study at the Sorbonne and married Pierre Curie (1859–1906), professor of physics. Thus began a fruitful collaborative career that led to the discovery of radium for which they shared the 1903 Nobel prize for physics. In 1911 Mme. Curie received the Nobel prize for chemistry. Pierre Curie was killed in an accident. *See also* Joliot-Curie.

Curzon of Kedleston, 1st Marquess (George Nathaniel Curzon) (1859–1925), statesman and administrator; viceroy of India 1898–1905; member of Lloyd George's war cabinet 1916–18; foreign secretary 1919–24.

Cuthbert, St. (*c.* 635–87), Celtic monk who became prior of Old Melrose (on the Tweed) and later of Lindisfarne. For a time he lived in seclusion on one of the Farne islands. The story of his life we owe to Bede.

Cuvier, Georges (1769–1832), French naturalist, noted for his system of classification of animals and his studies in comparative anatomy. His *Le Règne Animal* (1819) was a standard work for many years.

Cuyp Albert (1620–91), Dutch landscape painter of sea and river views.

Cyprian, St (d. 258), bishop of Carthage, and early Christian writer who was martyred.

Cyrus (559–529 B.C.), Persian emperor. He founded the Achaemenid line, having defeated the Medes. By conquering Lydia and Babylonia, he controlled Asia Minor. He was a wise and tolerant ruler, allowing the Jews to rebuild their temple.

D

Daguerre, Louis Jacques Mandé (1789–1851), French photographic pioneer, who invented the daguerrotype process. *See* Section L.

Daimler, Gottlieb (1834–1900), German inventor, with N. A. Otto of Cologne, of the Otto gas engine. The Mercédès car, exhibited at Paris in 1900, was named after the daughter of Emile Jellinek, Austrian banker and car enthusiast.

Dale, Sir Henry Hallett (1875–1968), English physiologist. He shared the 1936 Nobel prize for medicine for his work on the chemical transmission of nerve impulses.

Dalhousie, 1st Marquess of (James Andrew Broun Ramsay) (1812–60), governor-general of India. He annexed the Punjab and later other states; opened the civil service to Indians and acted against suttee.

Dalton, John (1766–1844), English chemist and mathematician, a Quaker teacher of Manchester. In 1808 in the first number of his *New System of Chemical Philosophy* (1808–27) the modern chemical atomic theory was first propounded by him. According to this the atoms of the chemical elements are qualitatively different from one another.

Damien, Father (1840–89), Belgian missionary priest, originally named Joseph de Veuster, who, witnessing the sufferings of the lepers confined on the Hawaiian island of Molokai, obtained permission to take charge, and remained there until he himself died of leprosy.

Damocles, 5th cent. B.C., Syracusan flatterer who pronounced the tyrant Dionysius the happiest of men. To illustrate the uncertainty of life, Dionysius invited him to a banquet, where a naked sword hung over his head by a hair. Hence the expression " Sword of Damocles " to mean impending danger or threat.

Damrosch, Walter Johannes (1862–1950), American conductor and composer, b. Breslau, Prussia. He promoted musical development in the U.S., especially while conductor of the New York Symphony Society which his father, Leopold Damrosch (1832–1885) had founded in 1878.

D'Annunzio, Gabriele (1863–1938), Italian poet, dramatist and nationalist. In 1919 he led a raid on Fiume and seized it, but was eventually forced to surrender. His bodyguard wore the black shirt which was to be the uniform of the Fascists.

Dante Alighieri (1265–1321), Italian poet, a figure of world literature. He was b. at Florence in a troubled period. Though he saw her but once or twice, he loved a lady whom he called Beatrice, who is believed to have been Bice Portinari who married Simone di Bardi; she died in 1290, after which Dante wrote his *Vita Nuova*. His next work *Convivio* was philosophical. He joined the party of the Bianchi, attained municipal office, but was imprisoned and in 1301 fled. His *Divina Commedia* is a description of hell, purgatory, and heaven, a work of moral edification, replete with symbolism. He d. at Ravenna.

Danton, Georges Jacques (1759–94), French revolutionary. To his eloquent lead in 1792 was largely due the defeat of the foreign forces attempting to quell the revolution. He was a member of the committee of public safety, and sought to modify the extremists, but was displaced by Robespierre and was subsequently executed.

D'Arblay. *See* Burney.

Darby, Abraham (1677–1717), member of the Quaker family of ironmasters of Coalbrookdale, Salop, who paved the way for the industrial revolution by developing iron metallurgy. His grandson Abraham (1750–91) built the first cast-iron bridge (1779) over the Severn at Coalbrookdale.

Darius I (548–486 B.C.), Persian king and founder of Persepolis. He extended the borders of the Persian empire beyond the Indus, and reorganised it into satrapies. He declared " God's plan for the earth is not turmoil but peace, prosperity and good government." On clashing with the Greeks, however, he was defeated at Marathon. Darius II was a natural son of Artaxerxes I and d. 405 B.C. **Darius III** (d. 331 B.C.) was the last of the Persian kings, and was defeated by Alexander and assassinated.

Darling, Grace Horsley (1815–42), English heroine who by putting off in a small boat from the lighthouse on one of the Farne islands, of which her father was keeper, saved the shipwrecked crew of the *Forfarshire.*

Darnley, Henry Stewart, Lord (1545–67), second husband of Mary, Queen of Scots (1565). He plotted the murder of her secretary, Rizzio, and was subsequently himself murdered. Through his son James I he is the ancestor of the Stuart monarchs.

Darwin, Charles Robert (1809–82), English naturalist, b. Shrewsbury, one of the pioneers of experimental biology. After returning from his formative voyage round the world as naturalist on the *Beagle* (1831–6), he spent nearly twenty years building up evidence for his theory of evolution before publishing it in *The Origin of Species* (1859). In it he argued that the evolution of present-day morphology had been built up by the gradual and opportunistic mechanism of natural selection. His ideas though welcomed by biologists aroused bitter controversy.

Daudet, Alphonse (1840–97), French writer who covered a wide range and whose works include *Lettres de mon Moulin, Robert Helmont,* and *Tartarin de Tarascon.*

David I (1084–1153), King of Scotland. As uncle of Matilda, daughter of Henry I of England, he supported her claim to the English crown, but was defeated. In Scotland he promoted unity and development.

David II (1324–71), King of Scotland. He was son of Robert Bruce. In invading England he was captured at Neville's Cross, 1346.

David, Sir Edgeworth (1858–1934), Australian geologist who accompanied Shackleton's antarctic expedition, 1907–9, leading the party that reached the south magnetic pole.

David, Jacques Louis (1748–1825), French painter of classical subjects and an ardent republican.

David, St., patron saint of Wales who lived in south Wales in the 6th cent.

Davidson, 1st Baron (Randall Thomas Davidson) (1848–1930), archbishop of Canterbury, 1903–28.

Davies, Sir Walford (1869–1941), English organist, composer, and broadcaster on music.

Davies, William Henry (1871–1940), Welsh poet. He spent some years tramping, both in England and America, and his work shows knowledge of and love for nature. He wrote *Autobiography of a Super Tramp*.

Da Vinci. See Leonardo.

Davis, Jefferson (1808–89), American civil war leader. B. in Kentucky, he was made president of the Confederate States when the civil war broke out. After the war he was tried for treason, but discharged. He wrote *The Rise and Fall of the Confederate Government*.

Davis, John (c. 1550–1605), Elizabethan explorer and discoverer of Davis's Strait, the channel between the Atlantic and Arctic oceans on the west of Greenland. Invented the backstaff, or Davis's quadrant.

Davitt, Michael (1846–1906). Irish nationalist. The son of a peasant who later came to England, he joined the Fenians, and in 1870 was sentenced to penal servitude. On his release he helped to found the Land League in 1879; was again imprisoned; and wrote *Leaves from a Prison Diary*. He was subsequently returned to parliament.

Davy, Sir Humphry (1778–1829), English chemist, b. Penzance. Much of his work found practical application, *e.g.*, the miner's safety lamp which still bears his name. His *Elements of Agricultural Chemistry* (1813) contains the first use in English of the word "element." He took Michael Faraday as his assistant at the Royal Institution.

Dawber, Sir Guy (1861–1938), English architect. As chairman of the Council for the Preservation of Rural England, he did much to bring about the restoration of buildings throughout the country.

Day Lewis, Cecil (1904–72), poet and critic; professor of poetry at Oxford 1951–6. He succeeded Masefield as poet laureate in 1968. *See Section M.*

Debussy, Claude Achille (1862–1918), composer and leader of the French Impressionist school in music. Among his works are *Suite bergamasque*, containing the popular *Clair de lune*; *L'Après-midi d'un Faune*, inspired by the poem of Mallarmé, and *La Mer*. He also wrote an opera *Pelléas et Mélisande* based on Maeterlinck's drama. *See also Section E.*

Defoe, Daniel (1660–1731), English political writer; also author of *Robinson Crusoe*, *Moll Flanders*, and a *Tour of Gt. Britain*. His *Shortest Way with Dissenters* brought him imprisonment.

De Forest, Lee (1873–1961), American inventor who was the first to use alternating-current transmission, and improved the thermionic valve detector by which wireless and sound films were made possible.

Degas, Edgar (1834–1917), French Impressionist painter and sculptor, son of a banker. He painted subjects from everyday life—dancers, café life, the racecourse.

De Gasperi, Alcide (1881–1954), Italian politician who founded the Christian Democrat Party and worked for European federation; prime minister 1945–53.

de Gaulle. See Gaulle, Charles de.

De Havilland, Sir Geoffrey (1882–1965), pioneer of civil and military aviation in Britain; designer of the famous Moth machines. His son was killed in 1946 while testing a plane.

Delacroix, Ferdinand Victor Eugène (1798–1863), French painter of the Romantic school.

De la Mare, Walter John (1873–1956), English poet and novelist whose work has a characteristic charm. Much of it was written for children.

Delane, John Thadeus (1817–79), editor of *The Times*, 1841–77, who did much to establish that paper's standing.

Delaroche, Paul (1797–1856), French historical painter.

Delibes, Clément Philibert Léo (1836–91), French composer of much graceful music, including operas, of which *Lakmé* is the best known, and ballets, among them *Coppélia*.

Delius, Frederick (1862–1934), English composer

of German parentage. His music, highly idiosyncratic in idiom, was more readily received in Germany than in England until promoted by Sir Thomas Beecham. *See Section E.*

Democritus (c. 470–c. 400 B.C.), one of the first scientific thinkers, pupil of Leucippus (fl. c. 440 B.C.). He took an atomic view of matter, denied the existence of mind as a separate entity, and counted happiness and inner tranquillity as important moral principles. His attitude was not shared by his contemporary, Socrates, nor by Plato and Aristotle, but was accepted by Epicurus. The atomic theory thus passed into the background for many centuries.

Demosthenes (385–322 B.C.), Greek orator who, by his *Philippics*, roused the Athenians to resist the growing power of Philip of Macedon.

De Quincey, Thomas (1785–1859), English essayist and critic; friend of Wordsworth and Southey. He wrote *Confessions of an Opium-eater.*

De Reszke, Jean (1853–1925) and **De Reszke, Edouard** (1856–1917), Polish operatic singers, the first a tenor, the second a baritone.

Derwentwater, 3rd Earl of (James Radcliffe) (1689–1716), leader of the English Jacobite movement for placing the pretender on the throne. He was defeated at Preston in 1715 and beheaded.

Descartes, René (1596–1650), French mathematician, pioneer of modern philosophy. Unconvinced by scholastic tradition and theological dogma, he sought to get back to why anything can be said to be true, which turned out to be a fruitful line of thought. The basis of his Cartesian philosophy is summed up in his own words, *cogito, ergo sum* (I think, therefore I am).

Desmoulins, Camille (1760–94), French revolutionary. He represented Paris in the National Convention, and wrote witty and sarcastic pamphlets and periodicals. He was an ally of Danton, and when Robespierre came to power he was arrested and executed on the same day as Danton.

Deutscher, Isaac (1907–67), Marxist historian, biographer of Stalin and Trotsky. B. in Poland, he joined the outlawed Polish Communist Party but was expelled for his anti-Stalinist views. In 1939 he came to London.

De Valéra, Eamon (1882–1975), Irish statesman, b. New York, son of a Spanish father and an Irish mother. He was imprisoned for his part in the Easter rising of 1916. He opposed the treaty of 1921; and in 1926, when the republican Fianna Fáil was founded, he became its president. Fianna Fáil won the election of 1932, and he then became president of the Executive Council, 1932–7; prime minister, 1937–48, 1951–4, 1957–9; president of the republic, 1959–73. He promoted Irish neutrality in the second world war encouraged the use of the Irish language, and in spite of early intransigence his leadership was moderate.

de Valois, Dame Ninette (b. 1898), Irish-born ballet dancer and choreographer. She toured Europe with Diaghilev, 1923–5, and in 1931 founded the Sadlers Wells Ballet School (now Royal Ballet School), of which she became director. *Autobiography* (1957).

Dewar, Sir James (1842–1923), chemist and physicist, a native of Kincardine. He succeeded in liquefying hydrogen, and invented the vacuum flask. The explosive cordite was the joint invention of himself and Sir Frederick Abel.

Dewey, John (1859–1952), American philosopher, psychologist, and educationist. A follower of William James, he was an exponent of pragmatism.

De Wit, Jan (1625–72), Dutch republican statesman, who carried on war with England and later negotiated the Triple Alliance, but was overthrown by the Orange Party and murdered.

Diaghilev, Sergei Pavlovich (1872–1929), Russian ballet impresario and founder of the Russian ballet. Among those associated with him are Anna Pavlova, Vaslav Nijinsky, Tamara Karsavina, Leonide Massine, Michel Fokine, the choreographer L. N. Bakst, the painter, and Igor Stravinsky, the composer.

Dickens, Charles (1812–70), popular English novelist of the 19th cent., with enormous output and capacity for vivid story-telling. Of humble origin, he was extremely successful.

His best-known works are perhaps *Pickwick Papers*, *Oliver Twist*, *A Christmas Carol* (this influenced the observance of Christmas), *Dombey and Son*, *David Copperfield*, *Little Dorrit*, and *Great Expectations*. He gave public readings from his works.

Dickinson, Emily (1830–86), American poet whose writing has a mystic quality. She lived a cloistered life and published almost nothing in her lifetime.

Dickinson, Goldworthy Lowes (1863–1932), English author, an interpreter and upholder of the Greek view of life.

Diderot, Denis (1713–84), French man of letters, critic of art and literature, and editor of the *Encyclopédie* (1713–84) to which many writers of the Enlightenment contributed.

Diemen, Anthony van (1593–1645), Dutch promoter of exploration. As governor-general in the Far East, he promoted Dutch trade and influence; and despatched Abel Tasman, who in 1642 discovered New Zealand and Van Diemen's Land (now Tasmania).

Diesel, Rudolf (1858–1913), German engineer, inventor of an internal combustion engine which he patented in 1893. *See also* L31.

Diocletian (245–313), Roman emperor and persecutor of Christianity. He divided the empire under a system of joint rule; later abdicated; and built a palace in Dalmatia.

Diogenes (412–322 B.C.), Greek cynic philosopher who lived in a tub and told Alexander to get out of his sunshine. He sought virtue and moral freedom in liberation from desire.

Dionysius the elder and younger, tyrants of Syracuse in the 4th cent. B.C.

Dirac, Paul Adrien Maurice (b. 1902), English physicist who shared with Erwin Schrödinger the 1933 Nobel prize for their work in developing Heisenberg's theory of quantum mechanics. Order of Merit (1973).

Disney, Walter Elias (1901–66), American film cartoonist, creator of Mickey Mouse. He is known for his *Silly Symphonies*, *Snow White and the Seven Dwarfs*, and *Pinocchio*.

Disraeli, Benjamin, Earl of Beaconsfield (1804–81), British statesman and novelist who helped to form modern Conservatism in England. The son of Isaac (q.v.), he published his first novel at 21, and later *Coningsby* and *Sibyl*, which helped to rouse the social conscience. He entered parliament in 1837 and was prime minister 1868 and 1874–80, when he arranged the purchase of shares in the Suez canal. He was rival of Gladstone and friend of Queen Victoria.

D'Israeli, Isaac (1766–1848), father of Benjamin (q.v.) and author of *Curiosities of Literature*.

Dobson, Austin (1840–1921), English writer of light verse and of 18th cent. biography.

Dodgson, Charles Lutwidge (1832–98). English writer. Under the pseudonym Lewis Carroll, he wrote poems and books for children, including *Alice in Wonderland*. In private life he was a lecturer in mathematics at Oxford.

Dolci, Carlo (1616–86), one of the last Florentine painters.

Dolci, Danilo (b. 1925), Italian architect who since 1952 has dedicated himself to the rehabilitation of the people of Sicily in their desperate poverty.

Dominic, St. (1170–1221), founder of the Friars Preachers or Black Friars. B. in Castile, he and his followers sought to teach the ignorant. In 1216 they were formed into an order and vowed to poverty. The order spread through Europe.

Domitian (Titus Flavius Domitianus) (A.D. 51–96), Roman emperor, son of Vespasian. He ruled despotically, aroused the hatred of the senate, and was assassinated as a result of a palace conspiracy.

Donatello (Donato di Niccolò) (c. 1386–1466), Italian sculptor, b. Florence, son of Niccolò di Betto di Bardo. He was the founder of modern sculpture, producing statues independent of a background, designed to stand in the open to be viewed from all angles. Among his masterpieces are the statues of *St. George* and *David* (in the Bargello, Florence) and his equestrian *Gattamelata* in Padua, the first bronze horse to be cast in the Renaissance.

Donizetti, Gaetano (1797–1848), Italian composer. The best known of his sixty operas are *Lucia di Lammermoor*, *La Fille du Régiment*, and *Don Pasquale*. *See* Section E.

Donne, John (1572–1631), English metaphysical poet and preacher (dean of St. Paul's). His poems and sermons, marked by passion, wit, and profundity of thought have received full publicity only in the present century. His writings include *Elegies*, *Satires*, *Songs and Sonnets*, *Problems and Paradoxes* and the *Holy Sonnets*.

Doré, Gustave (1833–83), French artist who painted scriptural subjects and illustrated Dante, Milton, and Tennyson.

Dostoyevsky, Feodor Mikhailovich (1821–81), Russian novelist, b. Moscow. As a result of his revolutionary activity he was sent to hard labour in Siberia. In his books, which include *Crime and Punishment*, *The Brothers Karamazov*, *The Idiot*, and *The Possessed*, he explored the dark places of the human spirit to a degree not previously attempted.

Douglas of Kirtleside, 1st Baron (William Sholto Douglas) (1893–1969), British airman; commanded Fighter command, 1940–2, Coastal command, 1944–5. A Labour peer.

Douglas, Norman (1868–1952), novelist and travel writer. A Scot, born in Austria, he made his home on the Mediterranean. His works include *South Wind*.

Doulton, Sir Henry (1820–97), English potter and the inventor of Doulton ware.

Dowden, Edward (1843–1913), English literary critic and Shakespearean scholar.

Dowding, 1st Baron (Hugh Caswell Tremenheere Dowding) (1882–1970), British airman; commanded Fighter command during the Battle of Britain period (1940).

Dowland, John (c. 1563–1626), English composer of songs with lute accompaniment. His son Robert succeeded him as Court lutanist to Charles I.

Doyle, Sir Arthur Conan (1859–1930), British writer, b. Edinburgh, creator of the detective Sherlock Holmes and of his friend and foil, Dr. Watson. He was trained as a doctor but gave up his medical practice in 1890 to devote himself to writing.

Doyle, Richard (1824–83), humorous artist on the staff of *Punch*.

D'Oyly Carte, Richard (1844–1901), English theatrical manager, who built the Savoy theatre and there produced Gilbert and Sullivan operas.

Drake, Sir Francis (c. 1540–96), English seaman. In 1577–80 he sailed round the world in the *Golden Hind*. In 1587 he destroyed a number of Spanish ships in Cadiz harbour; and under Lord Howard he helped to defeat the Spanish Armada in 1588.

Draper, John William (1811–82), American chemist, b. near Liverpool. He was the first, using Daguerre's process, to take a successful photograph of the human face (1840) and of the moon.

Dreiser, Theodore (1871–1935), American novelist of austere realism, author of *An American Tragedy*.

Dreyfus, Alfred (1859–1935), French victim of injustice. Of Jewish parentage, in 1894 he was accused of divulging secrets to a foreign power, and was sentenced by a military secret tribunal to imprisonment for life on Devil's Island in French Guiana. At a new trial in 1899 he was again found guilty. Efforts continued to be made on his behalf, and in 1906 he was entirely exonerated, restored to his rank in the army, and made a Chevalier of the Legion of Honour.

Drinkwater, John (1882–1937), English poet and playwright. His plays include *Abraham Lincoln* and *Oliver Cromwell*.

Drummond, William, Scottish poet and Royalist pamphleteer. He was laird of Hawthornden.

Drury, Alfred (1857–1944), English sculptor, especially of statues of Queen Victoria at Bradford and Portsmouth.

Dryden, John (1631–1700), prolific English poet and dramatist, who also wrote political satire (*Absalom and Achitophel*). He was hostile to the revolution of 1688, and thereafter mainly translated classical writers, including Virgil.

Du Barry, Marie Jeanne Bécu, Comtesse (1746–93), mistress of Louis XV of France and guillotined by the revolutionary tribunal.

Du Chaillu, Paul Belloni (1835–1903), traveller in Africa, who in 1861 and 1867 published accounts of his explorations. A French-American.

Dufferin and Ava, 1st Marquess of (Frederick Temple Hamilton-Temple Blackwood) (1826–1902), British diplomat, writer, and governor-general of Canada and viceroy of India.

Dulles, John Foster (1888–1959), U.S. Secretary of State in the Republican administration 1953–9. His foreign policy was inflexibly opposed to negotiation with Russia and to U.S. recognition of China.

Dumas, Alexandre (1802–70), French romantic novelist, among whose many works are *The Three Musketeers*, *The Count of Monte Cristo*, and *The Black Tulip*.

Dumas, Alexandre (1824–95), French dramatist, son of the above; author of *La Dame aux Camélias*.

Du Maurier, George (1834–96), contributor to *Punch* and author of *Trilby*.

Dundee, 1st Viscount (John Graham of Claverhouse), (1648–89), Scottish soldier (" Bonnie Dundee "). Employed to suppress the covenanters, he was defeated at Drumclog, but victorious at Bothwell Brig. At the revolution of 1688 he supported James II, and was killed in the (victorious) battle of Killiecrankie.

Dundonald, Earl of. *See* Cochrane, Thomas.

Duns Scotus, John (*c.* 1265–1308), Scottish scholastic philosopher, b. at Maxton near Roxburgh, opponent of Thomas Aquinas. He joined the Franciscans, studied and taught at Oxford and Paris, and probably d. at Cologne. He challenged the harmony of faith and reason.

Dunstable, John (*c.* 1380–1453), the earliest English composer known by name. He was a contemporary of the Netherlands composers Dufay and Binchois. *See* Section E.

Dunstan, St. (908–88), reforming archbishop of Canterbury. He lived through seven reigns from Athelstan to Ethelred, and was adviser especially to Edgar. Under him Glastonbury Abbey became a centre of religious teaching.

Dupleix, Joseph François (1697–1763), French governor in India. He extended French influence and power in the Carnatic, but his plans were frustrated by his English opponent, Clive. He was recalled in 1754 and died in poverty.

Dürer, Albrecht (1471–1528), German painter and engraver. B. at Nuremberg, he was (like his Italian contemporary, Leonardo) a man of intellectual curiosity and scientific insight. His best work is in his copper engravings, woodcuts, and drawings; the former include *The Knight*, *Melancholia*, and *St. Jerome in his Study*. He may be regarded as the founder of the German school and a pioneer of etching. Examples of his work are in the British Museum. He was the friend of Luther and Melancthon.

Durham, Earl of (John George Lambton) (1792–1840), served as governor-general of Canada after the disturbances of 1837, and in 1839 presented to parliament the *Durham Report*, which laid down the principle of colonial self-government.

Duse, Elenora (1861–1924) Italian tragedienne.

Duval, Claude (1643–70), notorious highwayman who came to England from Normandy and was eventually hanged at Tyburn.

Dvořák, Antonín (1841–1904), Czech composer whose music is rich in folk-song melodies of his native Bohemia. In 1884 he conducted his *Stabat Mater* in London. His *New World* symphony was composed in New York, where he was head of the National Conservatoire (1892–5). *See* Section E.

Dyson, Sir Frank Watson (1868–1939), English astronomer who was astronomer royal 1910–33, and astronomer royal for Scotland 1905–10.

Dyson, Sir George (1883–1964), English composer and writer. In *The New Music* he analyses the technique of modern schools of composition. He composed several choral works such as *The Canterbury Pilgrims* and *Nebuchadnezzar*.

E

Eastlake, Sir Charles Lock (1793–1865), English painter of historical and religious works.

Eastman, George (1854–1932), American inventor of the roll photographic film and the Kodak camera. His philanthropies were estimated at over $100 million.

Eck, Johann von (1486–1543), German Catholic theologian and opponent of Luther.

Eddington, Sir Arthur Stanley (1882–1944), English astronomer (Greenwich observatory 1906–13; Cambridge observatory 1914–44). His works include *The Nature of the Physical World*.

Eddy, Mrs. Mary Baker (1821–1910), American founder of the Church of Christ Scientist. Her *Science and Health with Key to the Scriptures* was published in 1875. *See* Christian Science, Section J.

Edelinck, Gerard (1640–1707), Flemish engraver, b. Antwerp, the first to reproduce in print the colour, as well as the form, of a picture.

Eden, Robert Anthony, 1st Earl of Avon (1897–1977), British statesman. He entered parliament in 1923; became foreign secretary in 1935 (resigning in 1938 over Chamberlain's negotiation with Mussolini and rebuff to President Roosevelt); deputy prime minister in 1951; succeeded Sir Winston Churchill in 1955. His Suez policy divided the country. He resigned for health reasons in 1957. Memoirs, *Facing the Dictators; The Reckoning;* and *Full Circle*. Earldom conferred 1961.

Edgar (943–75), King of England 959–75. He was advised by Archbishop Dunstan.

Edgar Atheling (*c.* 1060–*c.* 1130), was the lawful heir of Edward the Confessor, but in the Norman invasion he was unable to maintain his claim.

Edgeworth, Maria (1767–1849), Irish novelist, whose stories include *Castle Rackrent*, *The Absentee*, and *Belinda*.

Edinburgh, Duke of (Philip Mountbatten) (b. 1921), consort of Queen Elizabeth II. He relinquished his right of accession to the thrones of Greece and Denmark on his naturalisation in 1947 when he took the name of Mountbatten. He is the great-great-grandson of Queen Victoria, grandson of Admiral Prince Louis of Battenberg, and nephew of Earl Mountbatten of Burma. Pres. British Association 1951–2. Chancellor, Universities of Edinburgh, Wales, Salford and Cambridge.

Edison, Thomas Alva (1847–1931), American inventor of the transmitter and receiver for the automatic telegraph; the phonograph; the first practical incandescent lamp; and many devices for the electrical distribution of light and power. From being a newsboy on the railway and later a telegraph clerk, he became a master at applying scientific principles to practical ends. He set up a research laboratory (originally a barn) at Menlo Park, New Jersey, where his inventions were tested out.

Edmund II (Ironside) (980–1016), the son of Ethelred, king of the English, made a compact with Canute to divide England, but soon afterwards died.

Edward the Confessor (*c.* 1004–1066), English king who preceded the Norman Conquest and founded Westminster Abbey. He was canonised in 1161.

Edward the Elder (*c.* 870–*c.* 924), son of Alfred, succeeded him as king of the West Saxons in 899. He overcame the Danes and reoccupied the northern counties.

Edward I (1239–1307), King of England, succeeded his father Henry in 1272. Able and energetic, his legislation influenced the development of the land law, and he summoned parliamentary assemblies. A soldier, he conquered Wales, building castles, but could not maintain his hold on Scotland.

Edward II (1284–1327), succeeded his father Edward I as king of England in 1307 and was defeated by the Scots at Bannockburn. Weak and inept, he was murdered in 1327.

Edward III (1312–77), succeeded his father Edward II as king of England in 1327. Popular and ambitious for military glory, he began the Hundred Years War with France. He fostered the woollen industry. Latterly he became senile.

Edward IV (1442–83), able but dissolute Yorkist leader whose reign brought about a revival in the power of the monarchy, in English sea power, and in foreign trade (in which he himself took part). Spent 1470–71 in exile. Began rebuilding of St. George's chapel, Windsor. Patron of Caxton.

Edward V (1470–83), succeeded his father Edward IV at the age of 12 and was a pawn in the quarrels of baronial relatives. He and his brother were shut up in the Tower by his uncle, Richard, Duke of Gloucester, and there probably murdered, though exact proof has not been established.

Edward VI (1537–53), succeeded his father, Henry VIII, as king of England when in his tenth year. He was delicate and studious, and his government was carried on successively by the Dukes of Somerset and Northumberland; while under Archbishop Cranmer the prayer book was issued. He was induced to name Lady Jane Grey his successor.

Edward VII (1841–1910), King of Gt. Britain and Ireland. The son of Queen Victoria, he married Princess Alexandra of Denmark in 1863, and succeeded his mother in 1901. Interested mainly in social life and in international contacts, he visited India in 1875 and travelled much in Europe.

Edward VIII (1894–1972), King of Gt. Britain, succeeded his father George V 1936, and abdicated later that year because of disagreement over his proposed marriage. He was created Duke of Windsor, and was governor of the Bahamas 1940–45.

Ehrlich, Paul (1854–1915), German bacteriologist, who at Frankfurt-on-Main carried out work in immunology. He discovered salvarsan for the treatment of syphilis. Nobel prizewinner 1908.

Eiffel, Alexandre Gustave (1832–1923), French engineer, one of the first to employ compressed air caissons in bridge building. Among his works are the Eiffel Tower (1887–9) and the Panama Canal locks.

Einstein, Albert (1879–1955), mathematical physicist whose theory of relativity superseded Newton's theory of gravitation. He was born in Ulm of Jewish parents, lived for many years in Switzerland, and held a succession of professorial chairs at Zurich, Prague, and Berlin. In 1921 he was awarded the Nobel prize for his work in quantum theory. He was driven by the Nazis to seek asylum in America and became professor at the Institute for Advanced Study at Princeton 1933–45. In August 1939 at the request of a group of scientists he wrote to President Roosevelt warning of the danger of uranium research in Germany and stressing the urgency of investigating the possible use of atomic energy in bombs. *See* Relativity, Section F, Part II.

Eisenhower, Dwight David (1890–1969), American general and statesman. He was C.-in-C. Allied Forces, N. Africa, 1942–3; and in the European theatre of operations, 1943–5; and was Republican President, 1953–61.

Eisenstein, Sergei Mikhailovich (1898–1948), Russian film director of *The Battleship Potemkin*, *Alexander Nevsky*, and *Ivan the Terrible*.

Eleanor, Queen of Edward I. After her death in 1290 the king had memorial crosses erected at the twelve places where her body rested on its way from Grantham to Westminster.

Elgar, Sir Edward (1857–1934), English composer, especially of choral-orchestral works for festivals. His oratorios include *The Kingdom*, *The Apostles*, and *The Dream of Gerontius*; he also wrote the *Enigma Variations*, and the tone-poem *Falstaff*. *See* Section E.

Elgin, 7th Earl of (Thomas Bruce) (1766–1841), British diplomat who, with the object of saving them, conveyed some sculptures from the Parthenon in Athens to the British Museum.

Eliot, George (1819–80), pen-name of Mary Anne (later Marion) Evans, b. Warwickshire. Her novels include *Adam Bede*, *The Mill on the Floss*, *Silas Marner*, *Middlemarch*, and *Daniel Deronda*. Her works show deep insight. She lived with the writer George Lewes from 1854 until his death 25 years later. (Although Lewes had been deserted by his wife it was then not possible to obtain a divorce.) She brought up his three children.

Eliot, Thomas Stearns (1888–1965), poet and critic. He was born in St. Louis, Missouri, and became a British subject in 1927. His

poems include *Prufrock and Other Observations*, *The Waste Land*, *The Hollow Men*, *Ash Wednesday*, *Four Quartets*; his verse dramas *Murder in the Cathedral* and *The Family Reunion*. He described himself as "classicist in literature, royalist in politics, and Anglo-Catholic in religion". Nobel prizewinner 1948. *See* Sections I and M.

Elizabeth (b. 1900), Queen Consort of George VI, daughter of the 14th Earl of Strathmore. Before her marriage in 1923 she was Lady Elizabeth Angela Marquerite Bowes-Lyon. Chancellor, Universities of London and Dundee.

Elizabeth I (1533–1603), Queen of England, daughter of Henry VIII, succeeded her sister Mary in 1558. Politically and intellectually able and firm, though personally vain and capricious, she chose to serve her able men such as William Cecil; and her long reign was one of stability, victory over the Spanish, and adventure in the New World; while the Church of England was established, and literary output prepared the way for Shakespeare; it was however marred by the execution of Mary, Queen of Scots.

Elizabeth II (Elizabeth Alexandra Mary of Windsor) (b. 1926), Queen of Gt. Britain and N. Ireland, ascended the throne Feb. 1952 on the death of her father George VI. Her Consort, Prince Philip, Duke of Edinburgh, is the son of Prince Andrew of Greece and a descendant of the Danish royal family. They have four children: Charles, Prince of Wales (b. 1948), Princess Anne (b. 1950), Prince Andrew (b. 1960), and Prince Edward (b. 1964).

Ellis, Havelock (1859–1939), English writer whose *Studies in the Psychology of Sex* was influential in changing the public attitude towards sex. His books were published in America long before they were in England.

Emerson, Ralph Waldo (1803–82), American poet and essayist, b. Boston, member of the transcendentalist group of thinkers. Among his best-known poems are *Woodnotes*, *Threnody*, *Terminus*, *Brahma*, *The Problem*.

Emin Pasha, the name adopted by Eduard Schnitzer (1840–92), a German explorer associated with Gen. Charles Gordon in the Sudan as a medical officer; and governor of the Equatorial Province 1878–89, when he was menaced by the Mahdi and rescued by Stanley. He has contributed greatly to African studies.

Emmet, Robert (1778–1803), Irish patriot, led the rising of 1803, was betrayed, and executed.

Empedocles (*c.* 500–*c.* 430 B.C.), Greek philosopher, b. Agrigentum in Sicily, founder of a school of medicine which regarded the heart as the seat of life, an idea which passed to Aristotle, as did his idea that all matter was composed of four elements: earth, air, fire, and water.

Engels, Friedrich (1820–95), German socialist, son of a wealthy textile manufacturer, lifelong friend of Karl Marx, with whom he collaborated in writing the *Communist Manifesto* of 1848. Through him Marx acquired his knowledge of English labour conditions.

Epicurus of Samos (342–270 B.C.), refounded the atomic view of matter put forward by Democritus, and held that peace of mind comes through freedom from fear, the two main sources of which he regarded as religion and fear of death. The Epicureans were a rival sect to the Peripatetics and Stoics.

Epstein, Sir Jacob (1880–1959), sculptor, b. New York of Russian-Polish parents. His work includes *Rima*, in Hyde Park; *Day* and *Night* on the building of London Underground headquarters; *Genesis*, exhibited in 1931; *Lazarus*, in New College, Oxford; the *Madonna and Child* group in Cavendish Square, London; the figure of *Christ in Majesty* in aluminium in Llandaff cathedral; a sculpture for the T.U.C. headquarters in London; and a bronze group for Coventry cathedral.

Erasmus, Desiderius (1466–1536), Dutch Renaissance humanist, who spent several years in England and was the friend of Dean Colet and Sir Thomas More. He aimed at ecclesiastical reform from within and scorned the old scholastic teaching. He thus prepared the way for Luther. His *Praise of Folly* is still read.

Erhard, Ludwig (b. 1897), German economist and politician; succeeded Adenauer as Chancellor of the West German Federal Republic, 1963–7.

Essex, 2nd Earl of (Robert Devereux) (1566–1601), favourite of Queen Elizabeth I in her old age. Unsuccessful as governor-general of Ireland, he returned to England against the Queen's wish; plotted; and was executed.

Ethelbert, King of Kent at the close of the 6th cent., accepted Christianity on the mission of St. Augustine.

Ethelred II (c. 968–1016), King of England. Unable to organise resistance against the Danish raids, he was called the Unready (from Old Eng. uraed = without counsel).

Etty, William (1787–1849) English artist of historical and classical subjects.

Eucken, Rudolf Christoph (1846–1926), German philosopher of activism, which puts personal ethical effort above intellectual idealism. Nobel prizewinner 1908.

Euler, Leonhard (1707–83), Swiss mathematician, remembered especially for his work in optics and on the calculus of variations. He was called by Catherine I to St. Petersburg, where he was professor, 1730–41, and by Frederick the Great to Berlin, 1741–66. He became blind but continued his work.

Euripides (480–406 B.C.), Greek tragic dramatist, who is known to have written about 80 plays, of which 18 are preserved, including Alcestis, Medea, Iphigenia, and Orestes. He displayed a sceptical attitude towards the myths.

Eusebius (264–340), ecclesiastical historian. His Ecclesiastical History gives the history of the Christian church to 324. He also wrote a general history, Chronicon.

Evans, Sir Arthur John (1851–1941), English archaeologist, known for his excavations at Knossos in Crete and his discovery of the pre-Phoenician script.

Evans, Dame Edith Mary (1888–1976), versatile English actress who made her first appearance as Cressida in Troilus and Cressida in 1912.

Evelyn, John (1620–1706), cultured English diarist who gives brilliant portraits of contemporaries. He was a book collector and librarian and wrote Sylva, a manual of arboriculture. His magnificent library was sold by Christies in 1977.

Eyck, Jan van (c. 1389–1441), Flemish painter, whose best-known work is the altarpiece in Ghent cathedral. His brother Hubert (c. 1370–1426) is associated with him.

F

Fabius, the name of an ancient Roman family who over many generations played an important part in early Roman history. Quintus Fabius Maximus Verrucosus (d. 203 B.C.) saved Rome from Hannibal by strategic evasion of battle; hence his name Cunctator (delayer), and the term Fabian policy.

Fabre, Jean Henri Casimir (1823–1915), French naturalist, whose study of the habits of insects were delightfully recorded in his Souvenirs entomologiques.

Faed, name of two Scottish genre painters, Thomas (1826–1900), and John (1819–1902). A third brother, James, engraved their works.

Fahrenheit, Gabriel Daniel (1686–1736), German physicist, b. Danzig. He introduced c. 1715 the mercury thermometer and fixed thermometric standards.

Fairbairn, Sir William (1789–1874), Scottish engineer. In 1817 he took the lead in using iron in shipbuilding.

Fairfax, 3rd Baron (Thomas Fairfax) (1612–71), parliamentary general in the English civil war, and victor of Marston Moor. In 1650 he withdrew into private life.

Falconer, Hugh (1808–65) British botanist and palaeontologist, b. Forres, Scot.; physician to East India Co.; introduced tea into India.

Falla, Manuel (1876–1946), Spanish composer whose music is highly individual with a strong folk-song element. See Section E.

Faraday, Michael (1791–1867), English experimental physicist, founder of the science of electromagnetism. He was the son of a Yorkshire

blacksmith and at 13 became apprenticed to a bookseller in London. In 1813 he became laboratory assistant to Sir Humphry Davy at the Royal Institution, succeeding him as professor of chemistry in 1833. He set himself the problem of finding the connections between the forces of light, heat, electricity, and magnetism and his discoveries, translated by Maxwell (q.v.) into a single mathematical theory of electromagnetism, led to the modern developments in physics and electronics. He inaugurated the Christmas lectures for juvenile audiences at the Royal Institution.

Farman, Henri (1874–1958) French aviator, one of the pioneers of aviation, and a designer and builder of aeroplanes.

Farouk I (1920–65), King of Egypt, 1936–52. He was forced to abdicate as a result of the military coup of 1952.

Farrar, Frederick William (1831–1903), English clergyman, author of the schoolboy story Eric.

Faulkner, William (1897–1962), American novelist, whose series of novels, The Sound and the Fury, As I Lay Dying, Light in August, Sanctuary, depict the American South. Nobel prizewinner 1949.

Fauré, Gabriel Urbain (1845–1924), French composer and teacher. His works include chamber music, nocturnes, and barcarolles for piano, an opera Pénélope, some exquisite songs, and Requiem. Ravel was among his pupils. See Section E.

Fawcett, Millicent Garrett (1847–1929), educational reformer and leader of the movement for women's suffrage; one of the founders of Newnham College, Cambridge. She was the wife of the blind Liberal politician and economist, Henry Fawcett (1833–84).

Fawkes, Guy (1570–1606), a Yorkshire catholic, who with Catesby and other conspirators planned the Gunpowder Plot. Although warned, he persisted and was captured and hanged.

Fénelon, François de Salignac de la Mothe (1651–1715), archbishop of Cambrai and author of Telemachus.

Ferdinand V of Aragon (1452–1516), who married Isabella of Castile, and with her reigned over Spain, saw the Moors expelled from Spain, equipped Columbus for the discoveries that led to Spain's vast colonial possessions, and instituted the Inquisition.

Ferguson, James (1710–76), Scottish astronomer who, from being a shepherd-boy, educated himself in astronomy, mathematics, and portrait painting.

Fermi, Enrico (1901–54), Italian nuclear physicist whose research contributed to the harnessing of atomic energy and the development of the atomic bomb. Nobel prizewinner 1938.

Fichte, Johann Gottlieb (1762–1814), German philosopher of the nationalistic Romantic school who prepared the way for modern totalitarianism.

Field, John (1782–1837), Irish composer of nocturnes, pupil of Clementi and teacher of Glinka. His work served as a model for Chopin.

Fielding, Henry (1707–54), English novelist, author of Tom Jones, Joseph Andrews, and Amelia, as well as plays.

Fildes, Sir Luke (1844–1927), English painter and woodcut-designer.

Finsen, Niels Ryberg (1860–1904), Danish physician who established an institute for light therapy and invented the Finsen ultra-violet lamp. Nobel prizewinner 1903.

Firdausi, pen-name of Abu'l Kasim Mansur (940–1020), Persian poet, author of the epic Shah-Nama or Book of Kings.

Fisher of Lambeth, Baron (Geoffrey Francis Fisher) (1887–1972), archbishop of Canterbury, 1945–61; Headmaster of Repton School, 1914–32.

Fisher, Herbert Albert Laurens (1865–1940), English historian and educational reformer; author of A History of Europe.

Fisher, Sir Ronald Aylmer (1890–1962), British scientist who revolutionised both genetics and the philosophy of experimentation by founding the modern corpus of mathematical statistics.

FitzGerald, Edward (1809–83), English poet who translated the Rubaiyát of Omar Khayyám (1859).

Fitzroy, Robert (1805–65), British meteorologist who introduced the system of storm warnings which were the beginning of weather forecasts.

Flammarion, Camille (1842–1925), French astronomer, noted for his popular lectures and books which include *L'Astronomie Populaire*.

Flamsteed, John (1646–1719), the first English astronomer royal, for whom Charles II built an observatory at Greenwich (1675) where he worked for 44 years.

Flaubert, Gustave (1821–80), French novelist, and creator of *Madame Bovary*. His perfection of style was attained through unremitting effort. Other works were *Salammbô*, *L'Education sentimentale*, and *Bouvard et Pécuchet*.

Flaxman, John (1755–1826), English sculptor, b. York, employed as modeller by Josiah Wedgwood. He then took to monumental sculpture.

Flecker, James Elroy (1884–1915), English poet whose works include *Golden Journey to Samarkand*, *Hassan* (staged in London, 1923), and *Don Juan*, as well as many lyrics.

Fleming, Sir Alexander (1881–1955), Scottish bacteriologist who discovered the antibacterial enzyme lysozyme in 1922 and penicillin in 1928. Full recognition came during the war when Florey separated the drug now used for treatment from the original penicillin. Awarded Nobel prize for medicine jointly with Florey and Chain, 1945.

Fleming, Sir Ambrose (1849–1945), British scientist whose invention of the radio valve in 1904 revolutionised radio telegraphy and solved problems of radio-telephony. This eventually made possible high quality sound transmission, and thus led to broadcasting and television.

Fletcher, John (1579–1625), English dramatist who collaborated with Francis Beaumont (*q.v.*) in writing many pieces for the stage.

Flinders, Matthew (1774–1814), English navigator and explorer who made discoveries in and around Australia. He sailed through Bass Strait, so called in honour of his surgeon.

Florey, Baron (Howard Walter Florey) (1898–1968), British pathologist, b. Australia. Shared 1945 Nobel prize with Fleming and Chain for work on penicillin.

Foch, Ferdinand (1851–1929), French general, b. Tarbes. In the first world war he halted the German advance at the Marne (1914), and was engaged in the battles of Ypres (1914 and 1915) and the Somme (1916). In 1918 he became supreme commander of the British, French, and American armies and dictated the terms of Allied victory.

Fokine, Michel (1880–1944), Russian dancer, choreographer to Diaghilev's company, and creator of *Les Sylphides*, *Prince Igor*, *Scheherazade*, *Firebird*, and *The Spectre of the Rose*.

Fokker, Anthony (1890–1939), Dutch aircraft engineer, b. Java. The Fokker factory in Germany made warplanes for the Germans in the first world war.

Fonteyn, Dame Margot (Mme. Roberto de Arias) (b. 1919), prima ballerina of the Royal Ballet and acclaimed foremost English dancer.

Ford, Gerald R. (b. 1913), American Republican President 1974–7; automatically succeeded Richard Nixon when he resigned.

Ford, Henry (1863–1947), founder of Ford Motor Company (1903), of which he was president until 1919, when he was succeeded by his son, Edsel B. Ford (1893–1943). He was the pioneer of the cheap motor car.

Forester, Cecil Scott (b. 1899), English novelist, author of the *Captain Hornblower* series.

Forster, Edward Morgan (1879–1970), English novelist, author of *The Longest Journey*, *A Room with a View*, *Howards End*, *A Passage to India*. O.M. 1969.

Foscari, Francesco (*c.* 1372–1457), Doge of Venice and victor over Milan.

Fourier, Charles (1772–1837), French socialist who propounded a system of associated enterprise which utopian stimulated social reform.

Fourier, Jean Baptiste Joseph (1768–1830), French mathematical physicist. He played an active part in politics, holding administrative posts in Egypt and Isère, yet finding time for his own research, especially on the flow of heat along a conductor.

Fowler, Sir John (1817–98), was the engineer of the first underground railway (the London Metro-

politan) and with his partner, Sir Benjamin Baker, of the Forth bridge.

Fox, Charles James (1749–1806), English Whig statesman. Son of the 1st Lord Holland, he entered parliament at 19. He held office only for brief periods between 1770 and 1806, but he upheld the liberal causes of the day (American independence, the French revolution, and parliamentary reform), and was one of the impeachers of Warren Hastings. During a period of war and reaction his leadership inspired younger men.

Fox, George (1624–91), founder of the Society of Friends, son of a weaver of Fenny Drayton, Leicestershire.

Foxe, John (1516–87), English martyrologist, author of *History of the Acts and Monuments of the Church* (better known as *Foxe's Book of Martyrs*).

Frampton, Sir George James (1860–1928), English sculptor of the Peter Pan statue in Kensington Gardens and the Edith Cavell memorial.

France, Anatole (1844–1924), French writer, especially of short stories. Nobel prize 1921.

Francis I (1494–1547), King of France. Brilliant but ambitious and adventurous, he fostered learning and art, and met Henry VIII at the Field of the Cloth of Gold. His rivalry with the Emperor Charles V involved France in prolonged war, especially in Italy (he was captured at Pavia, 1525). He persecuted the Protestants.

Francis of Assisi, St. (1181/2–1226), founder of the Franciscan Order. Son of a wealthy cloth merchant, in 1208 he turned from a life of pleasure to poverty and the complete observance of Christ's teaching. He and his friars went about preaching the gospel by word and example, and the brotherhood increased rapidly. He was canonised in 1228.

Francis, Sir Philip (1740–1818), English politician, reputed author of the *Letters of Junius*.

Franck, César Auguste (1822–90), composer and organist, b. at Liege in Belgium. His music is romantic, mystical, and personal in idiom. Much of his composition is for the organ. *See* Section E.

Franco, Francisco (1892–1975), Spanish general and dictator. He led the Fascist rebellion against the Republican government (1936) and with German and Italian help ended the civil war (1939), since when he ruled Spain with utter ruthlessness.

Franklin, Benjamin (1706–90), American statesman. B. at Boston, he was at first a printer and journalist. He then took an interest in electricity, explained lightning as of electrical origin, and invented the lightning conductor. He was active in promoting the Declaration of Independence in 1773; he negotiated French support; and helped to frame the American constitution.

Franklin, Sir John (1786–1847), English Arctic explorer. His expedition in the *Erebus* and the *Terror* to find the north-west passage ended disastrously, and all attempts to find survivors failed.

Fraunhofer, Joseph von (1787–1826), optical instrument-maker of Munich, the first to map the dark lines of the solar spectrum named after him.

Frazer, Sir James George (1854–1941), Scottish anthropologist, b. Glasgow; author of *The Golden Bough*.

Frederick I (*c.* 1123–90), Holy Roman Emperor, nicknamed Barbarossa. A strong personality, he sought to impose his will on the city-states of northern Italy and the papacy, and was defeated at Legnano in 1176 but was more successful with a conciliatory policy (1183). He had also to contend with opposition at home. He died on the third crusade.

Frederick II (1194–1250), Holy Roman Emperor, grandson of the above, and son of the heiress of Sicily. Brilliant and enlightened, he attracted to his court in Sicily Jewish, Mohammedan, and Christian scholars; founded the university of Naples; was a patron of the medical school of Salerno; wrote a treatise on falconry; and commissioned a code of laws. Politically he was less successful, having trouble with the Lombard cities, and being involved with the papacy especially as regards his delay in going on crusade; but after negotiations with the sultan of Egypt he actually was crowned king of Jerusalem.

Frederick II (the Great) (1712–86), King of Prussia. Having inherited from his father a well-drilled army, in 1740 he seized Silesia from Austria, and retained it through the resulting war and the Seven Years war. He also took part in the partition of Poland. An able administrator and an outstanding general, he made Prussia powerful and strengthened its military tradition. He corresponded with Voltaire and he also played the flute.

French, Sir John, 1st Earl of Ypres (1852–1925), first British commander-in-chief in the first world war; replaced by Sir Douglas Haig in 1915.

Freud, Sigmund (1856–1939), psychiatrist and founder of psychoanalysis; b. Moravia, studied medicine in Vienna, where he lived until 1938 when the Nazi invasion of Austria sent him into exile in London where he died. His theories of the mind, based on years of investigation, illumined the way we think about ourselves, and had immense influence upon modern thought. *See* Psychoanalysis, Section J.

Friese-Greene, William (1855–1921), English inventor of the cinematograph. His first film was shown in 1890. He died in poverty.

Frobisher, Sir Martin (1535–94), first British navigator to seek the north-west passage from the Atlantic to the Pacific through the Arctic seas. He is commemorated in Frobisher's Strait. He also fought against the Spanish Armada.

Froebel, Friedrich Wilhelm August (1782–1852), German educational reformer, founder of the Kindergarten system.

Froissart, Jean (1337–1410), French author of *Chronicles* covering the history of Western Europe from 1307 to 1400, one of the chief sources for the history of the first half of the Hundred Years war.

Frost, Robert (1874–1963), American poet, author of *Stopping by Woods on a Snowy Evening*, *Birches*, *The Death of the Hired Man*, *After Apple-Picking*.

Froude, James Anthony (1818–94), English historian and biographer of Carlyle.

Fry, Christopher (b. 1907), English poet and dramatist of Quaker family; author of *The Lady's Not for Burning*, *Venus Observed*, *The Dark is Light Enough*, *Curtmantle*, and *A Yard of Sun*. *See* Section I.

Fry, Elizabeth (1780–1845), English prison reformer. She lived at Norwich and belonged to the Society of Friends.

Fry, Roger (1866–1934), English art critic and painter; introduced the work of Cézanne and the post-impressionists into England; author of *Vision and Design*.

Fuchs, Leonard (1501–66), German naturalist whose compendium of medicinal plants was for long a standard work. He was professor of medicine at Tübingen and the genus *Fuchsia* is named after him.

Fuchs, Sir Vivian Ernest (b. 1908), British geologist and explorer; leader of the British Commonwealth Trans-Antarctic Expedition 1957–8, the first to cross the Antarctic continent.

Fuller, Thomas (1608–61), English antiquarian and divine, author of *Worthies of England* and a *Church History of Britain*.

Fulton, Robert (1765–1815), American engineer who experimented in the application of steam to navigation, and in 1807 launched the *Clermont* on the Hudson.

Furniss, Harry (1854–1925), caricaturist, b. Wexford. He came to London as a young man, served on the staff of *Punch* and illustrated the works of Dickens and Thackeray.

G

Gade, Niels Vilhelm (1817–90), Danish composer. While studying at Leipzig he met Mendelssohn, whom he succeeded as conductor of the Gewandhaus orchestra.

Gagarin, Yuri Alexeyevich (1934–68), Soviet cosmonaut, the first man to be launched into space and brought safely back (12 April 1961). His flight was made in the front portion of a multi-

stage rocket which made a single circuit of the earth in 108 min. Killed in an air crash.

Gainsborough, Thomas (1727–88), English landscape and portrait painter, b. at Sudbury in Suffolk. His portraits are marked by informality and grace; examples are in the Tate Gallery.

Gaiseric or Genseric (c. 390–477), king of the Vandals, the ablest of the barbarian invaders of the Roman empire. He led his people from Spain into Africa, took Carthage, gained control of the Mediterranean by his pirate fleets, and sacked Rome in 455. He was a bigoted Arian.

Gaitskell, Hugh Todd Naylor (1906–63), Labour politician and economist. He represented Leeds South from 1945; was chancellor of the exchequer 1950–1; and leader of the Labour opposition 1955–63.

Galbraith, John Kenneth (b. 1908), American university professor of economics, b. Canada; author of *The Affluent Society* (1958), *The Liberal Hour* (1960), *The New Industrial State* (1967), *The Age of Uncertainty* (1977). He was ambassador to India 1961–3.

Galdós, Benito Pérez. *See* Pérez Galdós.

Galen, Claudius (131–201), physician, b. Pergamum (Asia Minor) of Greek parents. He systematised medical knowledge with his idea of purposive creation by the will of God; and thus discouraged original investigation. Many of his treatises survive, and his influence lasted for more than a thousand years.

Galileo (1564–1642), Italian scientist whose experimental-mathematical methods in the pursuit of scientific truth laid the foundations of modern science. He became professor of mathematics at Pisa university when he was 25 and lectured at Padua for 18 years. He made a number of fundamental discoveries, e.g., in regard to the hydrostatic balance, thermometer, magnet, telescope, and foreshadowed Newton's laws of motion. He detected the four major satellites of Jupiter, the ring of Saturn, and the spots of the sun. He proved the superiority of the Copernican over the Ptolemaic theory, and was imprisoned for so doing. He died the year Newton was born.

Galsworthy, John (1867–1933), English novelist and playwright, author of *The Forsyte Saga*, a series of novels dealing with the history of an upper middle-class family. Nobel prizewinner 1932.

Galton, Sir Francis (1822–1911), founder of eugenics, cousin of Darwin. His early work, *Meteorographica* (1863), contains the basis of the modern weather chart. He devised fingerprint identification, and was one of the first to apply mathematics to biological problems.

Galvani, Luigi (1737–98), Italian physician and physiologist, whose experiments at Bologna demonstrated the principle of animal electricity.

Gama, Vasco da (c. 1460–1524), Portuguese navigator who discovered the sea route to India in 1498 by doubling the Cape of Good Hope.

Gandhi, Indira (b. 1917), daughter of Nehru, succeeded Shastri in 1966 to become India's first woman prime minister. *See* Section C, Part II.

Gandhi, Mohandas Kamamchand (Mahatma) (1869–1948), Indian patriot, social reformer and moral teacher. From 1893 to 1914 he lived in South Africa opposing discrimination against Indians. In the movement for Indian independence after 1914 he dominated Congress, instituted civil disobedience, and advocated non-violence; and he sought to free India from caste. After independence he strove to promote the co-operation of all Indians but was assassinated on his way to a prayer meeting. His teaching of non-violence has had influence outside India.

Garbo, Greta (b. 1905), Swedish film actress of poetical quality. Her films included *Queen Christina* and *Ninotchka*.

Garcia, Manuel de Popolo Vicente (1775–1832), Spanish tenor, composer, and singing master. His son Manuel Patricio Rodriguez (1805–1906) was tutor to Jenny Lind. Both his daughters (Mme. Malibran and Mme. Viardot) were operatic singers, and his grandson and great-grandson baritones.

Garcia Lorca, Federico. *See* Lorca.

B26

Gardiner, Samuel Rawson (1829–1902), English historian of the Stuart period.

Garibaldi, Giuseppe (1807–82), Italian soldier and patriot, who with Mazzini and Cavour created a united Italy. In 1834 he was condemned to death for helping in a republican plot to seize Genoa, but escaped to S. America. He returned in 1848 to fight for Mazzini but was again forced to flee. In 1851 he returned and gave his support to Cavour, taking part in the Austrian war of 1859. In 1860 with a thousand volunteers he freed Sicily, took Naples, and handed over the Two Sicilies to Victor Emmanuel who was proclaimed king.

Garrick, David (1717–79), English actor and theatrical manager. Brought up at Lichfield, he was taught by Samuel Johnson.

Garrison, William Lloyd (1805–79), American philanthropist who worked to end slavery.

Gaskell, Mrs. Elizabeth Cleghorn (1810–65), English novelist, author of *Mary Barton*, *Cranford*, and a *Life of Charlotte Brontë*. She was brought up by an aunt in the little Cheshire town of Knutsford.

Gaulle, Charles de (1890–1970), French general and statesman, son of a headmaster of a Jesuit school; first president of the Fifth Republic 1959–69. He fought in the first world war until his capture in 1916. In the second world war he refused to surrender (1940) and raised and led the Free French forces, with headquarters in England. He came to political power in 1958; allowed Algerian independence in 1962 in face of an army and civilian revolt, initiated closer ties with West Germany (Franco-German treaty 1963), recognised Communist China, withdrew from NATO, building his own nuclear force, vetoed Britain's entry into the Common Market (1963 and 1967); and based his government on personal prestige and use of the referendum in place of parliamentary approval. He was taken by surprise by the rising of students and workers in 1968 and resigned after losing the referendum in 1969.

Gauss, Karl Friedrich (1777–1855), German mathematician. He spent most of his life at the university of Göttingen where he set up the first special observatory for terrestrial magnetism. He made major contributions to astronomy, mathematics, and physics. The unit of magnetic induction is named after him.

Gautama, Siddhartha (Buddha, the enlightened) (c. 563–c. 483 B.C.). B. near Benares, a rajah's son, he gave himself up to the religious life and attracted many disciples. Concerned with man's sorrow and suffering, he planned a movement which could be universally shared, in which kindness to others, including animals, took a leading part. His teaching is summarised in the "four noble truths" and the "eightfold path" (*see* Buddhism, Section J). After his death his teaching spread (with the help of the King Asoka) over much of India and through eastern Asia as far as Japan, and developed varying schools of thought. Buddhism is tolerant and also maintains that the good of the part is that of the whole; hence it is wrong to harm another or take life.

Gautier, Théophile (1811–72), French poet and novelist, author of *Mademoiselle de Maupin*.

Gay, John (1685–1732), English poet, author of *The Beggar's Opera* (set to music by Pepusch) and *Polly*.

Gay-Lussac, Joseph Louis (1778–1850), French chemist, who showed that when gases combine their relative volumes bear a simple numerical relation to each other and to the volume of their product, if gaseous (1808), *e.g.*, one volume of oxygen combines with two volumes of hydrogen to form two volumes of water vapour.

Ged, William (1690–1749), Scottish printer who patented stereotyping.

Geddes, Sir Patrick (1854–1932), Scottish biologist and a pioneer in town and regional planning, who invented the term conurbation.

Geikie, Sir Archibald (1835–1924), Scottish geologist. His brother James specialised in glacial geology.

Genghiz Khan (1162–1227), Mongol conqueror. After years of struggle to make good his succession to his father, he overran the greater part of Asia bringing devastation wherever he went.

Geoffrey of Monmouth (1100–54), chronicler,

b. Monmouth, later bishop of St. Asaph. His chronicle drew on his creative imagination.

George I (1660–1727), became King of Great Britain in 1714 as descendant of James I. His chief minister was Sir Robert Walpole. Himself personally undistinguished, his reign saw political development; and in spite of the Jacobite threat (rising in 1715) it began a period of dynastic stability.

George II (1685–1760), son of the above, succeeded in 1727, and survived a more serious Jacobite rising in 1745. His long reign helped the development of constitutional government, for he kept within the limitations of his powers and capacity; and it saw the extension of English power in India and North America.

George III (1738–1820), grandson of George II reigned 1760–1820. Sincere and well-intentioned, but not politically able, he suffered from mental illness due to intermittent porphyria. His reign saw a clash with John Wilkes, the rise of Methodism, and agrarian and industrial revolution; also the loss of the American colonies, the extension and the questioning of English power in India (Warren Hastings), and prolonged French wars.

George IV (1762–1830), eldest son of George III, reigned 1820–30, having become Prince Regent in 1812. Styled "the first gentleman of Europe," he is remembered for his interest in art and architecture. His married life was unfortunate, and the monarchy was at a low ebb; while his reign was a time of distress and of demand for reform.

George V (1865–1936), was the second son of Edward VII and Queen Alexandra, but became heir to the English throne on the death of his elder brother in 1892. He joined the Navy as a cadet in 1877. In 1893 he married Princess Mary of Teck. He succeeded in 1910 and discharged his office conscientiously. In 1932 he began the royal broadcast on Christmas Day and in 1935 celebrated his silver jubilee. His reign included the Kaiser's war, the emergence of the Irish Free State, and the first Labour government.

George VI (1895–1952), second son of George V, was called to the throne in 1936 on the abdication of his elder brother, Edward VIII. His personal qualities gained wide respect. His reign was marked by Hitler's war and rapid social change.

George, Henry (1839–97), American political economist whose "single tax" on land values as a means of solving economic problems is expounded in his *Progress and Poverty* (1879).

George, St., patron saint of England, adopted by Edward III. He is believed to have been martyred by Diocletian at Nicomedia in 303 (and not, as believed by Gibbon, to be confused with George of Cappadocia). The story of his fight with the dragon is of late date.

Gershwin, George (1898–1937), American jazz pianist and song-writer, composer of *Rhapsody in Blue* and the Negro folk-opera *Porgy and Bess*.

Gesner, Conrad (1516–65), Swiss naturalist, b. Zurich. In a series of magnificently illustrated volumes he gave a complete description of the animal and vegetable kingdoms.

Ghiberti, Lorenzo (1378–1455), Florentine sculptor whose bronze doors, beautifying the baptistery in Florence, were described by Michelangelo as fit for the gates of paradise.

Ghirlandaio, Domenico (1449–94), Florentine painter. Most of his frescoes are in Florence, including the cycle of the life of the Virgin and the Baptist in S. Maria Novella. Michelangelo began his apprenticeship in his workshop.

Giacometti, Alberto (1901–66), Swiss sculptor and painter, who worked mainly in Paris and produced abstract symbolic constructions.

Giap, Vo Nguyen (b. 1912). Vietnamese general who defeated the French at Dien Bien Phu (1954) and withstood American intervention in the Vietnam war which followed; deputy prime minister and commander-in-chief, North Vietnam.

Gibbon, Edward (1737–94), English historian of the *Decline and Fall of the Roman Empire*.

Gibbons, Grinling (1648–1720), English wood-carver and sculptor, b. Rotterdam, was brought to the notice of Charles II by Evelyn, the diarist. The choir stalls of St. Paul's and the carving in the Wren library at Trinity College, Cambridge, are his work.

Gibbons, Orlando (1583–1625), English composer

of church music, organist at the chapel royal. *See also* Section E.

Gide, André (1869–1951), French writer of many short novels in which he gives expression to his struggle to escape from his protestant upbringing (*Strait is the Gate*, *The Counterfeiters*). In his memoir *Si le grain ne meurt* he tells the story of his life up to his marriage. The narratives of his journeys in Africa led to a reform in French colonial policy. Nobel prizewinner 1947.

Gielgud, Sir John (b. 1904), English actor and producer, member of the Terry family, to whom the present popularity of Shakespeare is largely due. *See* Section I, Part I.

Gigli, Beniamino (1890–1957), Italian operatic tenor.

Gilbert, Sir Alfred (1854–1934), English sculptor and goldsmith. His sculptures include *Eros* in Piccadilly Circus.

Gilbert, Sir Humphrey (1537–83), English navigator. He was knighted by Queen Elizabeth for service in Ireland. In 1583 he discovered Newfoundland, but was drowned the same year.

Gilbert, William (1540–1603), English physician to Queen Elizabeth. His book *On the Magnet*, published in Latin in 1600, was the first major original contribution to science published in England.

Gilbert, Sir William Schwenck (1836–1911), English humorist and librettist of the Gilbert and Sullivan light operas. First known as author of the *Bab Ballads*, from 1871 he collaborated with Sir Arthur Sullivan, his wit and satire finding appropriate accompaniment in Sullivan's music. Their operas include *H.M.S. Pinafore*, *Patience*, *Iolanthe*, *The Mikado*, *The Gondoliers*, and *The Yeomen of the Guard*.

Gill, Eric (1881–1940), English sculptor and engraver, whose works include the *Stations of the Cross* (Westminster Cathedral), *Prospero and Ariel* (Broadcasting House), *Christ Driving the Money-changers from the Temple* (Leeds University). He also worked as a designer for printing (Gill Sans type), and the George VI stamps were his designs.

Gillray, James (1757–1815), English caricaturist who produced upwards of a thousand political cartoons.

Giotto di Bondone (1267–1337), Florentine artist. A pupil of Cimabue, he continued the development away from Byzantine tradition towards greater naturalism. His frescoes survive in the churches of Assisi, Padua, and Florence. He designed the western front of the cathedral at Florence and the campanile.

Gissing, George Robert (1857–1903), English novelist whose works deal with the degrading effect of poverty. The best known is *New Grub Street*.

Giulio Romano or **Giulio Pippi** (c. 1492–1546), Italian artist, was a pupil of Raphael. He was also an engineer and architect.

Gladstone, William Ewart (1809–98), English Liberal statesman. B. at Liverpool, he entered parliament in 1832 as a Tory and held office under Peel. From 1852 he served several terms as chancellor of the exchequer and was Liberal prime minister 1868–74, when his legislation included the education act of 1870, the ballot act, the disestablishment of the Church of Ireland and an Irish land act. In 1874 when Disraeli came to power, he temporarily withdrew, but made a come-back in 1879 with his Mid-Lothian campaign. He was again prime minister 1880–5, 1886 and 1892–4; he carried a parliamentary reform act, and advocated home rule for Ireland but was not able to carry it. His long life was one of moral stature and increasing advocacy of liberal causes. He was also a classical scholar and a writer on church matters.

Glazunov, Alexander Constantinovich (1865–1936), Russian composer, pupil of Rimsky-Korsakov. The first of his eight symphonies was composed when he was 16.

Glendower, Owen (c. 1350–c. 1416), Welsh chief, who conducted guerrilla warfare on the English border, and figures in Shakespeare's *Henry IV*.

Glinka, Mikhail Ivanovich (1804–57), Russian composer, first of the national school, best known for his operas, *A Life for the Tsar*, and

Russlan and Ludmilla, based on a poem by Pushkin. *See* Section E.

Gluck, Christoph Wilibald (1714–87), German composer, important in the development of opera. He studied in Prague, Vienna and Italy, and his first operas were in the Italian tradition; but with *Orfeo ed Euridice* (1762) his style became more dramatic. There followed *Alceste*, *Armide*, and *Iphigénie en Tauride* (his best-known work). *See* Section E.

Goddard of Aldbourne, Baron (Rayner Goddard) (1877–1971), Lord Chief Justice of England, 1946–58.

Godfrey of Bouillon (c. 1061–1100), Crusader on the first crusade, was proclaimed King of Jerusalem, but declined the title for that of Protector of the Holy Sepulchre.

Godiva, Lady (1040–80), English benefactress. According to tradition, she obtained from her husband Leofric, Earl of Chester, concessions for the people of Coventry by riding naked through the town.

Godwin, Earl ot the West Saxons (d. 1053), was the father of Edith, wife of King Edward the Confessor, and of Harold, last Saxon king.

Godwin, William (1756–1836), English political writer and philosopher, author of *Political Justice* (which criticised many contemporary institutions) and a novel *Caleb Williams*. He married Mary Wollstonecraft (1759–97), author of *A Vindication of the Rights of Women*; and their daughter, Mary Wollstonecraft Godwin (1797–1851) wrote *Frankenstein* and married Shelley.

Goethe, Johann Wolfgang von (1749–1832), German poet and thinker. B. at Frankfurt-on-Main, his first notable work was a romantic play, *Götz von Berlichingen*, followed by a novel *Werthers Leiden*. In 1776 he became a privy councillor to the Duke of Weimar, whom he served for many years. He had wide-ranging interests, and made discoveries in anatomy and in botany. Among his later writings are the play *Iphigenie* and the novel *Wilhelm Meister*, and he wrote many lyrics. His best-known work however is *Faust*, which was composed over many years; its theme is man's search for happiness. In later life he was a friend of Schiller.

Gogol, Nikolai Vasilievich (1809–52), Russian novelist and dramatist. His comedy, *The Government Inspector*, satirised provincial bureaucracy; and his novel, *Dead Souls*, deals with malpractice in the supposed purchase of dead serfs.

Goldsmith, Oliver (1728–74), Irish poet, dramatist and novelist. The son of a poor curate, he came to London in 1756, and eventually joined the circle of Dr. Johnson. He is best known for his novel *The Vicar of Wakefield* and his play *She Stoops to Conquer*.

Goncourt, Edmond Louis Antoine Huot de (1822–96) and **Jules Alfred Huot de** (1830–70), French brothers, remembered for their *Journal des Goncourts*, an intimate account of Parisian society spanning 40 years, and of documentary interest.

Góngora y Argote, Luis de (1561–1627), Spanish poet, b. Córdova. In *Polifemo* and *Soledades* he attempted to express the core of poetry in new experimental forms.

Goodyear, Charles (1800–60), American inventor who discovered the art of vulcanising rubber.

Goossens, Sir Eugene (1893–1962), English conductor and composer of Belgian descent. His compositions include the operas *Judith* and *Don Juan de Mañara*; brother of Léon, oboe virtuoso, and of Sidonie and Marie Goossens, harpists.

Gordon, Charles George (1833–85), Scottish soldier. After service in the Crimea and China, in 1873 he was made governor of the Equatorial provinces of Egypt; and he was a notable governor of the Sudan, 1877–80. When a rising was led by the Mahdi, he was sent out in 1884 to the garrisons in rebel territory and was killed at Khartoum.

Gordon, Lord George (1751–93), agitator, led No-Popery riots in London in 1780.

Gorky, Maxim (Alexey Maximovich Peshkov) (1868–1936), Russian writer. From the age of ten he worked at many trades from scullion on a Volga steamboat to railway guard, while learning to write; see *My Childhood*. His early work was romantic. He spent many years abroad, but returned in 1928, a supporter of the Soviet regime. His later work is marked by social realism.

Gosse, Sir Edmund (1849–1928), English poet and critic, known for his literary studies of the 17th and 18th centuries; and for his memoir *Father and Son.*

Gounod, Charles François (1818–93), French composer, known for his operas *Faust* and *Roméo et Juliette,* though his lyrical gifts are shown in earlier works, such as *Le Médicin malgré lui* and *Mireille.*

Gower, John (1325–1408), English poet of the time of Chaucer, author of *Confessio Amantis.*

Goya y Lucientes, Francisco José (1746–1828), Spanish painter and etcher, b. nr. Saragossa. He became court painter to Charles III in 1786. His portraits are painted with ruthless realism; his series of satirical etchings (*Los Caprichos* and the *Disasters of War*) expose man's inhumanity and express his hatred of the cruelty and reaction of his day. His work can best be seen in Madrid.

Grace, William Gilbert (1848–1915), English cricketer who scored 54,896 runs, including 126 centuries, and took 2,876 wickets. Scored 1,000 runs in May 1895; and three times made over 300 runs in an innings.

Grahame, Kenneth (1859–1932), Scottish writer of books for children, including *The Golden Age, Dream Days,* and *Wind in the Willows.*

Grahame-White, Claude (1879–1959), aviator and engineer, the first Englishman to gain an aviator's certificate, 1909.

Grant, Ulysses Simpson (1822–85), American general of the civil war, and president of the United States from 1869 to 1876.

Granville-Barker, Harley (1877–1946), English dramatist, actor, and producer, who promoted the plays of Ibsen, Shaw, and other serious writers. His own works include *The Voysey Inheritance.*

Grattan, Henry (1746–1820), Irish statesman, who struggled for Irish legislative independence and for Catholic emancipation (though himself a Protestant) and parliamentary reform; but unsuccessfully.

Graves, Robert Ranke (b. 1895), English writer, author of *Goodbye to All That,* written after the first world war; and of *I Claudius* and *Claudius the God;* besides poetry.

Gray, Thomas (1716–71), English poet, author of *Elegy written in a Country Churchyard* and *Ode on a Distant Prospect of Eton College.*

Greeley, Horace (1811–72), American newspaper editor, founder of the New York *Tribune* (1841).

Green, John Richard (1837–83), English historian, author of *Short History of the English People.*

Greenaway, Kate (1846–1901), English artist of children, especially for book illustrations.

Greene, Graham (b. 1904), English novelist and journalist, whose novels (*The Power and the Glory, The Heart of the Matter, The End of the Affair The Quiet American, Our Man in Havana, A Burnt-out Case, The Comedians, The Honorary Consul*), like his plays (*The Complaisant Lover*) and films (*Fallen Idol, The Third Man*) deal with moral problems in a modern setting.

Gregory, St. (c. 240–332), converted King Tiridates of Armenia and was thus founder of the Armenian church.

Gregory I (the Great), St. (c. 540–604), Pope 590–604, was the last great Latin Father and the forerunner of scholasticism. The main founder of the temporal power and the political influence of the papacy, he also maintained the spiritual claims of Rome, enforcing discipline, encouraging monasticism, defining doctrine, and adding to the music, liturgy, and canons of the Church. It was he who sent Augustine on a mission to England.

Gregory VII (Hildebrand) (c. 1020–85), Pope 1073–85. He strove for papal omnipotence within the church and for a high standard in the priesthood (especially by stamping out simony and clerical marriage). He also upheld the papacy against the Holy Roman Empire, and the emperor Henry IV did penance for three days in the snow at Canossa; but he had not quite the vision of Gregory I of an ideal theocracy embracing all states.

Gregory XIII (1502–85), Pope 1572–85; introduced the Gregorian calendar.

Gregory, James (1638–75), Scottish mathematician. He invented a reflecting telescope and was the first to show how the distance of the sun could be deduced by observations of the passage of Venus across the disc of the sun. Successive generations of the family reached distinction.

Grenville, Sir Richard (1541–91), English sea captain, who with his one ship engaged a fleet of Spanish war vessels off Flores in 1591, an exploit celebrated in Tennyson's ballad *The Revenge.*

Gresham, Sir Thomas (1519–79), English financier and founder of the Royal Exchange. Son of a Lord Mayor of London, he was an astute moneyfinder for four successive sovereigns, including Queen Elizabeth I. "Gresham's Law" is the statement that bad money drives out good.

Greuze, Jean Baptiste (1725–1805), French artist, known especially for his studies of girls. His *Girl with Doves* is in the Wallace Collection.

Grey, 2nd Earl (Charles Grey) (1764–1845), British Whig statesman under whose premiership were passed the Reform Bill of 1832, a bill abolishing slavery throughout the British Empire (1833), and the Poor Law Amendment Act, 1834.

Grey, Lady Jane (1537–54), Queen of England for a few days. The daughter of the Duke of Suffolk, she was put forward as queen by Protestant leaders on the death of her cousin, Edward VI; but overcome by the legal claimant, Mary Tudor, and executed.

Grieg, Edvard Hagerup (1843–1907), Norwegian composer, b. Bergen. He presented the characteristics of his country's music with strong accentuation. He is best known for his incidental music to *Peer Gynt.*

Griffin, Bernard William (1899–1956), Roman catholic archbishop of Westminster from 1944 until his death.

Griffith, Arthur (1872–1922), the first president of the Irish Free State, 1921; founder of the *Sinn Fein* movement.

Griffith, David Wark (1880–1948), American film producer, who introduced the close-up, the flash-back, and developed leading actors. His films include *Birth of a Nation,* and *Broken Blossoms.*

Grimm, the brothers Jakob Ludwig Karl (1785–1863), and Wilhelm Karl (1786–1859), German philologists and folk-lorists, best known for their *Fairy Tales.* Jakob published a notable philological dictionary, *Deutsche Grammatik.* The brothers also projected the vast *Deutsches Wörterbuch* which was completed by German scholars in 1961.

Grimthorpe, 1st Baron (Edmund Beckett Denison) (1816–1905), horologist who invented the double three-legged escapement for Big Ben (1854). For long known as Sir Edmund Beckett.

Gromyko, Andrei Andreevich (b. 1908), Russian diplomat who has served as foreign minister since 1957. He was ambassador to Britain 1952–3.

Grossmith, George (1847–1912), English actor. With his brother, Weedon Grossmith, he wrote *Diary of a Nobody.* His son, George Grossmith (1874–1935) was a comedian and introduced revue and cabaret entertainment into England.

Grote, George (1794–1871), English historian, author of a *History of Greece.*

Grotius (Huig van Groot) (1583–1645), Dutch jurist, the founder of international law. He was condemned to life imprisonment for religious reasons, but escaped to Paris, where he wrote *De Jure Belli et Pacis.*

Grouchy, Emmanuel, Marquis de (1766–1847), French general, who served under Napoleon; and after Waterloo led the defeated army back to Paris.

Grove, Sir George (1820–1900), English musicologist, author of *Dictionary of Music and Musicians.* By profession he was a civil engineer.

Guedalla, Philip (1889–1944), English historian, author of *The Second Empire, Palmerston,* and *The Hundred Days.*

Guevara, Ernesto "Che" (1928–67), revolutionary hero, b. Argentina. He took part in the Cuban guerrilla war and became a minister in the Cuban government 1959–65. He was killed while leading a band of guerrillas against American-trained Bolivian troops. ("Che" is Argentine for "chum".)

Guido Reni (1575–1642), Italian painter of the Bolognese school whose works are characteristic of the Italian baroque of his period and include the *Aurora* fresco in the Rospigliosi palace at Rome, and *Crucifixion of St. Peter* (Vatican).

Gustavus Adolphus (1594–1632), King of Sweden, the " Lion of the North." After a campaign in Poland he entered the Thirty Years' war in support of Swedish interests and Protestant distress, won the battle of Breitenfeld in 1631 and was killed in action the next year.

Gutenberg, Johann (c. 1400–68), German printer, b. Mainz, the first European to print with movable types cast in moulds. The earliest book printed by him was the Mazarin Bible (see L76).

Guy, Thomas (1644–1724), English philanthropist. A printer, he made money by speculation; and in 1722 founded Guy's Hospital in Southwark.

Gwynne, Nell (c. 1650–87), mistress of Charles II of England. Of Hereford origin, she sold oranges in London and became a comedienne at Drury Lane.

H

Haakon VII (1872–1957), King of Norway, was a Danish prince and elected on the separation of Norway from Sweden in 1905. He resisted the Nazi occupation.

Hadley, George (1685–1768). He developed Halley's theory of the trade winds by taking into account the effect of the earth's rotation and the displacement of air by tropical heat (1735).

Hadrian (76–138), Roman emperor. An able general, he suppressed revolts, and he was also a lover of the arts. He visited Britain c. A.D. 121 and built a protective wall between Wallsend-on-Tyne and Bowness-on-Solway.

Hafiz, pseudonym of Shams ad-Din Mohammed (d. c. 1388). Persian lyrical poet. His principal work is the *Divan*, a collection of short sonnets called *ghazals*. The sobriquet *Hafiz*, meaning one who remembers, is applied to anyone who has learned the Koran by heart.

Hahn, Otto (1879–1968), German chemist and physicist, chief discoverer of uranium fission, the phenomenon on which nuclear power and the atom bomb are based.

Hahnemann, Samuel Christian Friedrich (1755–1843), German physician who founded homoeopathy (treatment of disease by small doses of drugs that in health produce similar symptoms).

Haig, Douglas, 1st Earl of Bermersyde (1861–1928), British field-marshal, b. Edinburgh. He replaced French as commander-in-chief in France, 1915–19, leading the offensive in August 1918; and after the war presided over the British Legion.

Haile Selassie I (1891–1975), Emperor of Ethiopia 1930–74. He spent the years of the Italian occupation 1936–41 in England. Deposed 1974.

Hakluyt, Richard (1553–1616), English writer on maritime discovery. B. in Herefordshire, he spent some time in Paris. From 1582 (when *Divers Voyages* appeared), he devoted his life to collection and publishing accounts of English navigators, thus giving further impetus to discovery.

Haldane, John Burdon Sanderson (1892–1964), biologist and geneticist, noted not only for his work in mathematical evolutionary theory but for explaining science to the layman. He emigrated to India in 1957. He was the son of John Scott Haldane (1860–1936), b. Edinburgh, who studied the effect of industrial occupations upon health.

Haldane, 1st Viscount (Richard Burdon Haldane) (1856–1928), British Liberal statesman. As war minister in 1905 he reorganised the army and founded the Territorials.

Halévy, Ludovic (1834–1903) French playwright, who collaborated with Henri Meilhac in writing libretti for Offenbach and Bizet.

Halifax, 1st Earl of (Edward Frederick Lindley Wood) (1881–1959), British Conservative politician; foreign secretary during the period of appeasement of Germany; as Lord Irwin, viceroy of India 1926–31.

Halifax, 1st Marquess of (George Savile) (1633–95), English politician of changeable views, who wrote *Character of a Trimmer*.

Hallam, Henry (1777–1859), English historian, best known for his *Constitutional History*. He was father of Arthur Hallam, friend of Tennyson.

Hallé, Sir Charles (1819–95), German-born pianist and conductor, who settled in Manchester and organised an orchestra of high-class talent. He married the violinist Wilhelmine Neruda.

Halley, Edmond (1656–1742), English astronomer royal 1720–42. He published observations on the planets and comets, being the first to predict the return of a comet (see Section L). He furthered Newton's work on gravitation, setting aside his own researches. He made the first magnetic survey of the oceans from the naval vessel *Paramour*, 1698–1700. His meteorological observations led to his publication of the first map of the winds of the globe (1686).

Hale, George Ellery (1868–1935), American astronomer, after whom is named the 200-inch reflecting telescope on Mount Palomar.

Hals, Frans (c. 1580–1666), Dutch portrait painter, b. at Mechlin. He is best known for his *Laughing Cavalier* in the Wallace Collection, and for other portraits in the Louvre and at Amsterdam.

Hamilton, Alexander (1755–1804), American statesman and economist. With Madison and Jay he wrote the *Federalist* (1787). As secretary of the Treasury (1789–95) he put Washington's government on a firm financial footing and planned a national bank. He was the leader of the Federalists, a party hostile to Jefferson. He was killed in a duel.

Hamilton, Emma, Lady (*née* Lyon) (c. 1765–1815), a beauty of humble birth who, after several liaisons, was married in 1791 to Sir William Hamilton, British ambassador at Naples. There she met Nelson, and later bore him a child, Horatia.

Hammarskjöld, Dag (1905–61), world statesman. After an academic and political career in Sweden, in 1953 he became secretary-general of the United Nations, and aimed at extending its influence for peace, especially by initiating a U.N. emergency force in the Middle East. He was killed in an air crash while attempting to mediate in a dispute between the Congo and the secessionist province of Katanga. Posthumous Nobel peace prize.

Hammond, John Lawrence (1872–1949), English historian of social and industrial history, whose works (with his wife Barbara) include *The Town Labourer* and *The Village Labourer*.

Hampden, John (1594–1643), English parliamentarian and civil war leader. He refused to pay Charles I's illegal ship money in 1636. When civil war broke out, he raised a regiment and was killed on Chalgrove Field.

Hamsun, Knut, pen-name of Knut Pedersen (1859–1952), Norwegian author who in his youth struggled for existence, visited America twice and earned his living by casual labour. *The Growth of the Soil* won him the Nobel prize in 1920. Other great novels are *Hunger* and *Mysteries*.

Handel, George Frederick (1685–1759), German composer, son of a barber-surgeon to the Duke of Saxony; b. Halle, the same year as Bach; spent much of his life in England composing operas and oratorios. His operas, of which there are over 40, include *Atalanta, Berenice* and *Serse*, and his oratorios, of which there are 32, include *Saul, Israel in Egypt, Samson, Messiah, Judas Maccabaeus,* and *Jephtha*. Eight years before he died he became blind and relied upon his old friend and copyist John Christopher Smith to commit his music to paper. *See* Section E.

Hannibal (247–182 B.C.), Carthaginian general. He fought two wars against Rome. In the first he conquered southern Spain. In the second he overran Gaul, crossed the Alps, and defeated the Romans in successive battles, especially at Cannae. Thereafter his forces were worn down by Roman delaying tactics; he was defeated by Scipio at Zama and later poisoned himself.

Harcourt, Sir William Vernon (1827–1904), Liberal politician who revised death duties.

Hardicanute (1019–42), son of Canute, and last Danish king of England.

Hardie, James Keir (1856–1915), Scottish Labour leader, one of the founders of the Labour party. He first worked in a coal-pit; in 1882 became a journalist; and in 1892 was the first socialist to be elected to the House of Commons (for

(West Ham – South). He edited the *Labour Leader* 1887–1904. He was the first chairman of the parliamentary Labour party, 1906. A pacifist, he opposed the Boer war.

Hardy, Thomas (1840–1928), English novelist and poet, was trained as an architect and practised for some time, but became known in 1871 with *Desperate Remedies*. In 1874 his *Far from the Madding Crowd* was published. Following that came a series of novels, including *The Trumpet-Major*, *The Mayor of Casterbridge*, *Tess of the D'Urbervilles*, and *Jude the Obscure*. In 1908 he completed a dramatic poem, *The Dynasts*, whose central figure is Napoleon. His underlying theme is man's struggle against neutral forces, and he depicts the Wessex countryside.

Hargreaves, James (1720–78), English inventor, b. Blackburn. His spinning-jenny was invented in 1764 and became widely used, though his own was broken by spinners in 1768 and his invention brought him no profit.

Harkness, Edward Stephen (1874–1940), American banker and philanthropist, who in 1930 founded the Pilgrim Trust in Gt. Britain.

Harley, Robert, 1st Earl of Oxford and Mortimer (1661–1724), English statesman and collector of MSS. He held office under Queen Anne, and brought a European war to an end with the treaty of Utrecht. After the Hanoverian succession he lived in retirement, and formed the MSS. collection, now in the British Museum, which bears his name.

Harold II (1022–66), last Saxon king of England, was son of Earl Godwin. He was chosen king in succession to Edward the Confessor. He had at once to meet a dual invasion. He defeated the Norwegian king at Stamford Bridge; but was himself defeated by William of Normandy at the battle of Hastings (fought at Battle 1066).

Harriman, William Averell (b. 1891), American public official. He was adviser to President Roosevelt and later presidents especially on Marshall Aid and in connection with foreign affairs generally.

Harris, Joel Chandler (1848–1908), American author, creator of Uncle Remus and Brer Rabbit in Negro folk-tales.

Harrison, Frederick (1831–1923), English philosopher and lawyer, author of *The Meaning of History* and *The Philosophy of Common Sense*. He was president of the Positivist committee. *See* Positivism, Section J.

Harrison, John (1692–1776)—" Longitude Harrison," English inventor of the chronometer.

Harty, Sir Hamilton (1880–1941), composer and for some years conductor of the Hallé orchestra; b. County Down.

Harun al-Rashid (Aaron the Upright) (763–809), 5th Abbasid caliph of Baghdad. His court was a centre for art and learning, but he governed mainly through his vizier until the latter lost favour and was executed in 803. The *Arabian Nights* associated with him are stories collected several centuries later.

Harvey, William (1578–1657), English physician and discoverer of the circulation of the blood. B. at Folkestone, he studied at Padua while Galileo was there, and was physician to James I and Charles I. His treatise on circulation was published in Latin in 1628.

Hastings, Warren (1732–1818), English administrator in India. As governor-general for the East India Company he revised the finances, improved administration and put down disorder. On his return to England he was impeached for alleged corruption, and, though acquitted, lost his fortune in his own defence. Later however he received a grant from the company. Though he suffered unduly, his trial was important for the future as setting a high standard for Indian administration.

Hauptmann, Gerhart (1862–1946), German dramatist and novelist. B. in Silesia, he lived at first in Berlin and later abroad. His play *The Weavers* deals with a revolt of 1844 and has a collective hero. Other works include *Die versunkene Glocke*, *Der arme Heinrich*, and *Rose Bernd*. Nobel prizewinner 1912.

Havelock, Sir Henry (1795–1857), British general who helped to put down the Indian mutiny.

Hawke, 1st Baron (Edward Hawke) (1705–81), English admiral, who in 1759 defeated the French at Quiberon in a tremendous storm.

Hawkins, Sir John (1532–95), English sailor and slave-trader. In 1562 he was the first Englishman to traffic in slaves. He helped to defeat the Spanish Armada in 1588.

Hawthorne, Nathaniel (1804–64), American author. His works include *The Marble Faun*, *The Scarlet Letter*, *The House of the Seven Gables*.

Haydn, Franz Joseph (1732–1809), Austrian composer, belongs to the classical period of Bach, Handel, and Mozart. He has been given the title "father of the symphony." Much of his life was spent as musical director to the princely Hungarian house of Esterhazy. In 1791 and again in 1794 he visited London, where he conducted his Salomon symphonies. His two great oratorios, *The Creation* and *The Seasons*, were written in his old age. *See* Section E.

Hazlitt, William (1778–1830), English essayist and critic. His writings include *The Characters of Shakespeare's Plays*, *Table Talk*, and *The Spirit of the Age*. His grandson William Carew Hazlitt (1834–1913) was a bibliographer and writer.

Hearst, William Randolph (1863–1951), American newspaper proprietor who built up a large newspaper empire.

Heath, Edward (b. 1916), British statesman, leader of the Conservative Party 1965–75; prime minister 1970–4; leader of the opposition 1974–5.His unwavering faith in European unity was rewarded in 1972 by Britain's successful application for entry into the European Economic Community. In the contest for the leadership held in February 1975 he was defeated in the first ballot by Mrs. Thatcher and did not contest the second.

Hedin, Sven Anders (1865–1952), Swedish explorer of Central Asia; wrote *My Life as Explorer*.

Heenan, John Carmel (1905–76). English Roman Catholic prelate, archbishop of Westminster 1963–76; member of Sacred College (1965).

Hegel, Georg Wilhelm Friedrich (1770–1831), German idealist philosopher, b. Stuttgart, whose name is associated with the dialectic method of reasoning with its sequence of thesis –antitheses–synthesis. He studied theology at Tübingen with his friend Schelling. He taught philosophy at Jena, Nuremberg, Heidelberg, and Berlin. He produced an abstract philosophical system which was influenced by his early interest in mysticism and his Prussian patriotism. His doctrines were very influential in the 19th cent. and led to modern totalitarianism. He died of cholera. *See* Dialectical Materialism, Section J.

Heidenstam, Verner von (1859–1940), Swedish author and poet, leader of a new romantic movement. Nobel prizewinner 1916.

Heifetz, Jascha (b. 1901), Russian-born violinist, a U.S. citizen. He was the first musician to win a reputation in England by gramophone records before a personal appearance.

Heine, Heinrich (1797–1856), German lyric poet, b. Düsseldorf of Jewish parents. He lived mostly in Paris. His poems show profound beauty and subtlety of thought, but the satire and sometimes bitterness of his writings excited antagonism.

Heisenberg, Werner (1901–76), German physicist, noted for his theory of quantum mechanics and the Uncertainty Principle. Nobel Prizewinner 1932.

Helmholtz, Hermann von (1821–94), German physicist and physiologist. He published his *Erhaltung der Kraft* (Conservation of Energy) in 1847, the same year that Joule gave the first clear exposition of the principle of energy. His pupil Heinrich Hertz discovered electromagnetic radiation in accordance with Maxwell's theory.

Héloïse (c. 1101–64), beloved of Abelard (*q.v.*). Her letters to him are extant.

Hemingway, Ernest (1898–1961), American novelist of new technique and wide influence. His works include *A Farewell to Arms*, *Death in the Afternoon*, *For Whom the Bell Tolls*, *The Old Man and the Sea*. He committed suicide. Nobel prizewinner 1954.

Henderson, Arthur (1863–1935), British Labour politician, b. Glasgow. He worked mainly for disarmament, and was president of the World Disarmament Conference, 1932–5. Nobel peace prize 1934.

Henrietta Maria (1609–69), the daughter of Henry IV of France and wife of Charles I.

Henry, Joseph (1797–1878), American physicist and schoolteacher who independently of Faraday discovered the principle of the induced current. The weather-reporting system he set up at the Smithsonian Institution led to the creation of the U.S. Weather Bureau.

Henry I (1068–1135), King of England. The youngest son of William the Conqueror, he ascended the throne during the absence on crusade of his elder brother Robert of Normandy. His long reign brought order and progress, not entirely destroyed by the anarchy under his successor Stephen.

Henry II (1133–89), King of England. He was son of Matilda, daughter of Henry I, and Geoffrey Plantagenet, count of Anjou; and his lands stretched to the Pyrenees. He was a strong ruler to whom we largely owe the establishment of the common law system and permanent administrative reforms. His conflict with the Church brought about the murder of his archbishop Becket, a man of resolute character; and his later life was troubled by his unruly sons.

Henry III (1207–72), King of England, succeeded his father John in 1216. Himself devout and simple, his long reign was troubled by a partly factious baronial opposition.

Henry IV (1367–1413), grandson of Edward III and heir to the Duchy of Lancaster, became king of England in 1399. More solid and practical than his cousin Richard II, whom he had supplanted, he consolidated the government.

Henry V (1387–1422), son of Henry IV, succeeded his father as king of England in 1413. A successful commander, he renewed the French war and won the battle of Agincourt, but died young.

Henry VI (1421–71), son of Henry V, succeeded his father as king of England in 1422 as a baby. Gentle and retiring, he inherited a losing war with France. He founded Eton, and King's College, Cambridge. The Yorkist line claimed the crown from his (the Lancastrian) line, and the Wars of the Roses led to his deposition and death.

Henry VII (1457–1509) succeeded Richard III as king of England after defeating him in 1485. The first Tudor king, he was firm and shrewd, even avaricious; he built Henry VII's Chapel in Westminster Abbey, and encouraged John Cabot to sail to North America.

Henry VIII (1491–1547), King of England, succeeded his father Henry VII in 1509. A prince of the Renaissance, skilled in music and sports, he loved the sea and built up the navy. His minister Cardinal Wolsey fell when Henry, seeking divorce to obtain a legal heir, rejected papal supremacy and dissolved the monasteries. Ruthless and ostentatious, he executed Sir Thomas More, spent his father's accumulation, and in spite of six marriages left a delicate son to succeed.

Henry IV of France (Henry of Navarre) (1553–1610). Prior to becoming king, he was the leader of the Huguenots; and although on being crowned he became a Catholic, he protected the Protestants by the Edict of Nantes. He then became a national king, but was later assassinated by Ravaillac, a religious fanatic.

Henry the Navigator (1394–1460), Portuguese promoter of discovery, son of John I. His sailors discovered Madeira and the Azores.

Henschel, Sir George (1850–1934), singer, composer, and conductor. B. in Breslau, he became a naturalised Englishman in 1890. Founder and conductor of the London Symphony Concerts (1886).

Hepplewhite, George (d. 1786), English cabinetmaker whose name is identified with the style which followed the Chippendale period.

Heraclitus of Ephesus (c. 540–475 B.C.), Greek philosopher. His discovery of a changing world (he lived in an age of social revolution when the ancient tribal aristocracy was beginning to give way to democracy) influenced the philosophies of Parmenides, Democritus, Plato, and Aristotle, and later, of Hegel.

Herbert, George (1593–1633), the most purely devotional of English poets.

Hereward the Wake, the last Saxon leader to hold out against the Normans. His base in the fens was captured in 1071 but he escaped. His exploits were written up by Kingsley.

Herod the Great (c. 73–4 B.C.). At first governor of Galilee under the Romans, he obtained the title of king of Judaea in 31 B.C. The massacre of the Innocents reported in the New Testament is in keeping with his historical character.

Herodotus (c. 485–425 B.C.), Greek historian, called by Cicero the father of history. He travelled widely collecting historical evidence.

Herrick, Robert (1591–1674), English lyric poet. His poems include *Gather ye Rose Buds*, *Cherry Ripe*, and *Oberon's Feast*.

Herriot, Edouard (1872–1957), French Radical-Socialist statesman. A scholar, mayor of Lyons for more than a generation, three times prime minister, he resisted the German occupation, and was president of the National Assembly 1947–54.

Herschel, Sir John (1792–1871), British astronomer who continued his father's researches and also pioneered photography, a term introduced by him. One of his twelve children introduced fingerprints into criminology.

Herschel, Sir William (1738–1822), German-born astronomer who came to England from Hanover as a musician; father of the above. Unrivalled as an observer, and with telescopes of his own making he investigated the distribution of stars in the Milky Way and concluded that some of the nebulae he could see were separate star systems outside our own. He discovered the planet Uranus in 1781. His sister, Caroline Lucretia (1750–1848), compiled a catalogue of the clusters and nebulae discovered by him.

Hertz, Heinrich Rudolf (1857–95), German physicist, whose laboratory experiments confirmed Maxwell's electromagnetic theory of waves and yielded information about their behaviour.

Herzl, Theodor (1860–1904), founder of modern political Zionism, was b. Budapest. He convened a congress at Basle in 1897.

Hesiod (fl. c. 735 B.C.) Greek poet, author of *Work and Days*, which tells of life in the country.

Hill, Octavia (1838–1912), English social reformer concerned with the housing conditions of the poor, a pioneer in slum clearance in London; founder (with Sir Robert Hunter and Canon Rawnsley) of the National Trust.

Hill, Sir Rowland (1795–1879), originator of the penny postal system. He was secretary to the Postmaster-General 1846–54, then chief secretary to the Post Office until 1864.

Hindemith, Paul (1895–1963), German composer and viola player. He is associated with the movement for *Gebrauchsmusik*, which regarded music as a social expression. He incurred Nazi hostility and his later life was spent abroad. His numerous works include chamber works, songs, operas, ballet music, symphonies, and the oratorio *Das Unaufhörliche*. *See* Section E.

Hindenburg, Paul von (1847–1934), German field-marshal. In 1914 he defeated the Russians at Tannenberg. In his old age a national hero, he was president of the German Reich, 1925–34.

Hinshelwood, Sir Cyril Norman (1897–1967), English chemist. He shared with Prof. Semenov of Russia the 1956 Nobel prize for chemistry for researches into the mechanism of chemical reactions. Pres. Royal Society, 1955–60.

Hinton of Bankside, Baron (Christopher Hinton) (b. 1901), as managing director of the industrial group of the U.K. Atomic Energy Authority he played an important part in the building of Calder Hall. Chancellor University of Bath. O.M. 1976.

Hippocrates of Chios (fl. c. 430 B.C.), Greek mathematician, the first to compile a work on the elements of geometry.

Hippocrates of Cos (fl. c. 430 B.C.), Greek physician, whose writings are lost, but who is believed to have established medical schools in Athens and elsewhere, and to have contributed towards a scientific separation of medicine from superstition. Traditionally he is the embodiment of the ideal physician.

Hirohito, Emperor of Japan (b. 1901), acceded to the throne in 1926. In 1946 he renounced his legendary divinity. In 1971 he visited Europe.

Hitler, Adolf (1889–1945), German dictator, founder of National Socialism, b. in Austria, son of a customs official. He was in Vienna for 5 years with no regular work before going to Munich in

1913; enlisted in Bavarian infantry at outbreak of the Kaiser's war. At the end of the war conditions in Germany favoured the growth of a fascist movement and under his leadership the National Socialist (Nazi) party climbed to power. He became Reich chancellor in 1933 and on the death of Hindenburg in 1934 Führer; and commander-in-chief Wehrmacht 1935. Under his regime working class movements were ruthlessly destroyed; all opponents—communists, socialists, Jews—were persecuted and murdered. By terrorism and propaganda the German state was welded into a powerful machine for aggression. There followed the occupation of the Rhineland (1936), the annexation of Austria and Czechoslovakia (1938-9), the invasion of Poland and declaration of war by Great Britain and France (1939), the invasion of Russia (1941). Final defeat came in 1945; on 30 April he committed suicide as the Russian troops closed in on Berlin.

Hobbes, Thomas (1588–1679), English philosopher who published *Leviathan* in 1651. He favoured strong government and supported the supremacy of the state, but his arguments aroused antagonism even among royalists. He was a child of his age in his enthusiasm for scientific enquiry.

Hobhouse, Leonard Trelawney (1864–1929), English sociologist. His books include *The Theory of Knowledge, Morals in Evolution*, and *Development and Purpose*.

Ho Chi-minh (1892–1969), leader of the Vietnam revolutionary nationalist party of Indo-China, which struggled for independence from France during and after the second world war. His main purpose was to weld together the nationalistic and communistic elements in Vietnam. As president of North Vietnam he fought to extend his control over South Vietnam, defying the United States.

Hodgkin, Sir Alan (b. 1914), British biophysicist working in the field of nerve impulse conduction. During the second world war he worked on the development of radar. Pres. Royal Society, 1970-75. Nobel prizewinner, 1970; Chancellor Univ. of Leicester (1971), O.M. 1973.

Hodgkin, Dorothy Crowfoot (b. 1910), the third woman to win the Nobel prize in chemistry, awarded in 1964 for her X-ray analysis to elucidate the structure of complex molecules, notably penicillin and vitamin B-12. She and her team at the Dept. of Molecular Biophysics at Oxford succeeded in 1969 in determining the crystalline structure of insulin. Chancellor Bristol Univ.; Order of Merit (1965).

Hogarth, William (1697–1764), English engraver and painter, who satirised his time with character, humour, and power, especially in his *Harlot's Progress, Rake's Progress, Marriage à la Mode, Industry and Idleness*, and *The March to Finchley*.

Hogg, Quintin (1845–1903), educationist and philanthropist who purchased the old Polytechnic Institution in 1882 and turned it into a popular college providing education at moderate rates. His grandson, Lord Hailsham, was lord chancellor in the 1970-4 Conservative administration.

Hokusai, Katsushika (1760–1849), Japanese artist of the Ukiyo-e (popular school). He excelled in landscapes.

Holbein, Hans, the elder (c. 1465–1524), German painter, b. Augsburg, father of:

Holbein, Hans, the younger (1497–1543), German painter, b. Augsburg; settled in London 1532. He won the favour of Henry VIII, for whom he painted many portraits. He is also known for his series *The Dance of Death*.

Holden, Charles (1875–1960), British architect, designer of public buildings, including British Medical Asscn. Building, London; Underground Head Offices; Univ. of London Senate House.

Holden, Sir Isaac (1807–97), British inventor of woolcombing machinery.

Hölderlin, Johann Christian Friedrich (1770–1843), German poet, friend of Hegel. His works include the novel *Hyperion* and the elegy *Menon's Laments for Diotima*. In his middle years his mind became unhinged.

Holford, Baron (William Graham Holford) (1907–75). British architect and town-planner;

planned post-war redevelopment of City of London, including precincts of St. Pauls.

Holmes, Oliver Wendell (1809–94), American author. His writings include *Autocrat of the Breakfast Table, The Professor at the Breakfast Table*, and *The Poet at the Breakfast Table*.

Holst, Gustav Theodore (1874–1934), British composer of Swedish descent whose compositions include *The Planets* suite, *The Hymn of Jesus*, an opera *The Perfect Fool*, and a choral symphony. He was outstanding as a teacher. *See* Section E.

Holyoake, George Jacob (1817–1906), English social reformer and secularist. He wrote a history of the co-operative movement.

Holyoake, Keith Jacka (b. 1904), New Zealand politician and farmer; prime minister 1960–72.

Homer (c. 700 B.C.), epic poet. He is supposed to have been a Greek who lived at Chios or Smyrna, and has been regarded as the author of the *Iliad* and the *Odyssey*, though this is tradition rather than ascertained fact.

Hood, 1st Viscount (Samuel Hood) (1724–1816), British admiral who in 1793 was in command of the Mediterranean fleet and occupied Toulon.

Hood, Thomas (1799–1845), English poet. His poems include *The Song of the Shirt, The Dream of Eugene Aram* and *The Bridge of Sighs*. He was also a humorist and punster.

Hooke, Robert (1635–1703), English physicist. His inventions include the balance spring of watches. He was also an architect and drew up a plan for rebuilding London after the Great Fire. His *Diary* is published.

Hooker, Richard (1554–1600), English theologian, author of *Ecclesiastical Polity*. He was Master of the Temple, 1585–91. For his choice of words he was known as "Judicious Hooker".

Hopkins, Sir Frederick Gowland (1861–1947), English biochemist, pioneer in biochemical and nutritional research. He first drew attention to the substances later known as vitamins. Pres. Royal Society 1930–5. Nobel prize 1929.

Hopkins, Gerard Manley (1844–89), English poet of religious experience and of a style new in his day.

Hopkins, Harry (1890–1946), Franklin Roosevelt's personal assistant at foreign conferences, and in the New Deal and Lend-Lease.

Hopkinson, John (1849–98), English engineer. By developing the theory of alternating current and of the magnetic current in dynamos he paved the way to the common use of electricity.

Hoppner, John (1758–1810), English portrait painter, b. Whitechapel, of German parents.

Horace (Quintus Horatius Flaccus) (65–8 B.C.), Roman satirist and poet, son of a Greek freedman. He wrote *Satires, Epodes, Odes*, and *Epistles*. He fought on the republican side at Philippi, but lived to become poet laureate to Augustus.

Horniman, Annie Elizabeth Fredericka (1830–1937), founder of the modern repertory system in England. Her father F. J. Horniman founded the Horniman Museum.

Houdini, Harry (Erich Weiss) (1874–1926), American illusionist, son of a Hungarian rabbi. Famed for his escapes from handcuffs.

Housman, Alfred Edward (1859–1936), English poet, author of *A Shropshire Lad*; he was also a classical scholar. His brother Laurence (1865–1959) was a playwright and wrote *Little Plays of St. Francis* and *Victoria Regina*.

Howard, John (1726–90), English prison reformer. Imprisoned in France in wartime, he subsequently investigated English prisons, securing reforms; and later also continental prisons, dying in Russia of gaol fever.

Howard of Effingham, 2nd Baron (Charles Howard) (1536–1624), afterwards Earl of Nottingham; commanded the fleet which defeated the Spanish Armada (1588), and took part in the capture of Cadiz (1596).

Howe, Elias (1819–67), American inventor of the sewing machine.

Howe, Julia Ward (1819–1910), American suffragette, author of *Mine eyes have seen the glory*.

Howe, 1st Earl (Richard Howe) (1726–99), British admiral whose victories over the French in two wars included that off Ushant on 1 June 1794 (" the glorious first of June ").

Hua Kuo-feng (b. 1922), b. Hunan, succeeded Mao tse-Tung as Chairman of the Chinese Communist Party and leader of China, 1976. *See* Section C, Part II.

Hubble, Edwin Powell (1889–1953), American astronomer, noted for his work on extragalactic nebulae. With the 100-inch telescope on Mount Wilson he detected the Cepheid variables in Andromeda.

Hudson, Henry (d. 1611), English navigator credited with the discovery of the Hudson river and Hudson Bay, where mutineers turned him adrift to die. He was on a voyage to find a passage by the north pole to Japan and China. Nothing is known of his life before 1607.

Hudson, William Henry (1841–1922), naturalist, b. Buenos Aires of American parents, naturalised in England (1900). His books include *The Purple Land*, *Green Mansions*, and *Far Away and Long Ago*. Hyde Park bird sanctuary, containing *Rima* by Epstein, was established in his memory.

Huggins, Sir William (1824–1910), British astronomer who pioneered in spectroscopic photography, and was helped by his wife, Margaret Lindsay Murray (1848–1915).

Hughes, Thomas (1822–96), English novelist, author of *Tom Brown's Schooldays*, which is based on Rugby school.

Hugo, Victor Marie (1802–85), French poet, dramatist, and novelist, who headed the Romantic movement in France in the early 19th cent. His dramas include *Hernani*, *Lucrèce Borgia*, *Ruy Blas*, and *Le Roi s'amuse*. Of his novels *Notre Dame* belongs to his early period, *Les Misérables*, *Les Travailleurs de la mer*, and *L'Homme qui rit* were written while he was living in exile in Guernsey. Less well known is his skill as a graphic artist.

Humboldt, Friedrich Heinrich Alexander, Baron von (1769–1859), German naturalist and explorer whose researches are recorded in *Voyage de Humboldt et Bonpland* (23 vols., 1805–34), and *Kosmos* (5 vols., 1845–62).

Hume, David (1711–76), Scottish philosopher who developed the empiricism of Locke into the scepticism inherent in it. His main works are *Treatise of Human Nature* and *Dialogues Concerning Natural Religion*. He also wrote a *History of England*.

Hunt, Holman (1827–1910), English artist, one of the founders of the Pre-Raphaelite movement. His best-known picture is *The Light of the World*.

Hunt, Baron (John Hunt) (b. 1910), leader of the 1953 British Everest Expedition when Tenzing and Hillary reached the summit.

Hunt, Leigh (1784–1859), English poet and essayist. In 1813 he was fined and imprisoned for libelling the Prince Regent in *The Examiner*. He was a friend of Keats and Shelley.

Hutton, James (1726–97), an Edinburgh doctor who founded modern geological theory.

Huxley, Aldous (1894–1963), English novelist, author of *Brave New World*.

Huxley, Sir Julian (1887–1975), biologist and writer, grandson of T. H. Huxley and brother of Aldous; director of the London Zoo 1935–42; first director general of Unesco 1946–8; one of the founders of the International Union for the Conservation of Nature and of the World Wild Life Fund.

Huxley, Thomas Henry (1825–95), English biologist, b. Ealing. He started life as assistant-surgeon on H.M.S. *Rattlesnake* and during the voyage (1846–50) studied marine organisms. After the publication of Darwin's *Origin of Species* he became an ardent evolutionist and gave the first recognisably modern lecture on the origin of life to the British Association in 1870. He coined the term " agnostic " to distinguish a person who does not know whether God exists or not from the atheist who asserts there is no God. By his popular lectures and vigorous writings. *e.g.*, *Man's Place in Nature*, he made a real attempt to interest the public in the importance of science.

Huygens, Christian (1629–95), Dutch mathematician, physicist, and astronomer, son of the poet Constantijn Huygens (1596–1687); discovered the rings of Saturn, invented the pendulum

clock, and developed the wave theory of light in opposition to the corpuscular theory of Newton.

Hyde, Douglas (1860–1949), Irish scholar, historian, poet, and folk-lorist; first president of Eire in the 1937 constitution, 1938–45.

Hypatia of Alexandria, the only woman mathematician of antiquity. She excited the enmity of Christian fanatics, who raised an agitation against her, and she was murdered in A.D. 415.

I

Ibsen, Henrik Johan (1828–1906), Norwegian playwright and poet, who dealt with social and psychological problems and revolutionised the European theatre. His chief works are *Ghosts*, *The Wild Duck*, *The Master Builder*, *A Doll's House*, *Hedda Gabler* and the poetic drama, *Peer Gynt*.

Ingres, Jean Auguste Dominique (1780–1867), French historical and classical painter. His paintings include *La grande odalisque* in the Louvre.

Innocent III (c. 1160–1216), Pope 1198–1216. He asserted the power and moral force of the papacy over the Emperor Otto IV, Philip II of France, and John of England. He launched the fourth crusade, encouraged the crusade against the Albigensian heretics, and held the 4th Lateran council. His pontificate marks the zenith of the mediaeval papacy.

Inönü, Ismet (1884–1973), Turkish soldier and statesman; leader of the Republican People's Party founded by Kemal Atatürk; premier. 1923–38; president 1938–50 and 1961–5.

Ionesco, Eugene (b. 1912), French playwright of the Absurd. b. Romania, whose influential plays include *The Bald Prima Donna*, *The Chairs*, and *Rhinoceros*. *See* Section I.

Iqbal, Sir Muhammad (1877–1938), poet-philosopher, b. Sialkot (Pakistan). He wrote both poetry and prose in Urdu, Persian, and English, and his work is marked by mystic nationalism.

Ireland, John (1879–1962), English composer, popularly known for his setting of Masefield's *Sea Fever*, but also a composer of chamber music and sonatas for pianoforte and violin.

Irving, Sir Henry (1838–1905), English actor. At the Lyceum theatre from 1871, later with Ellen Terry, he gave notable Shakespearean performances, especially as Shylock and Malvolio.

Irving, Washington (1783–1859), American essayist, whose works include *Tales of a Traveller* and *The Sketch Book*, also biographies.

Isabella of Castile (1451–1504), reigned jointly with her husband, Ferdinand V of Aragon, over a united Spain, from which the Moors and the Jews were expelled. During their reign the New World was discovered.

Ismail Pasha (1830–95), grandson of Mehemet Ali, was Khedive of Egypt, and became virtually independent of the Sultan. Under him the Suez canal was made, but his financial recklessness led to Anglo-French control and to his own abdication.

Ismay, 1st Baron (Hastings Lionel Ismay) (1887–1965), British general who was chief of staff to Sir Winston Churchill in the second world war, and later the first secretary-general of NATO.

Ito, Hirobumi, Prince (1841–1909), Japanese statesman, four times premier, who helped to modernise his country. He was assassinated by a Korean.

Ivan the Great (1440–1505) brought the scattered provinces of Muscovy under one control and put an end to Tartar rule.

Ivan the Terrible (1530–84), crowned as first Tsar of Russia in 1547, was an autocratic ruler who consolidated and expanded Russia and entered into trading relations with Queen Elizabeth. He killed his own son.

J

Jackson, Andrew (1767–1845), American general who was twice president of the United States.

Jackson, Thomas Jonathan (1824–63), " Stonewall Jackson," was general on the Southern side in the American Civil War; killed at Chancellorsville.

Jacobs, William Wymark (1863–1943), English

novelist, b. London, author of humorous sea and other stories.

Jacquard, Joseph Marie (1752–1834), French inventor whose loom provided an effective method of weaving designs.

Jagellons, Lithuanian–Polish dynasty, which ruled Poland 1386–1572.

Jahangir (1569–1627), 3rd Mogul emperor and patron of art.

James I (1566–1625), King of England (1603–25) and, as James VI, King of Scotland (1567–1625). He was the son of Mary Stuart and succeeded to the English throne on the death of Elizabeth I. His reign saw the Gunpowder Plot of 1605 and the publication of the Authorised Version of the Bible, but it also marked an increasingly critical attitude of the Puritans towards the established church. Personally more of a scholar than a man of action, he was described as " the wisest fool in Christendom."

James II (1633–1701), King of England and, as James VII, King of Scotland (1685–8), was the younger son of Charles I. Personally honest, and an able admiral, he lacked political understanding; and when, having put down Monmouth's rebellion, he tried and failed to obtain better conditions for his fellow Roman Catholics, he was obliged in 1688 to flee the country.

James, Henry (1843–1916), American novelist, brother of William. He lived mainly in England. His work is noted for intellectual subtlety and characterisation, and includes *The American, Daisy Miller, The Portrait of a Lady, What Maisie Knew,* and *The Spoils of Poynton.*

James, William (1842–1910), American psychologist and philosopher, brother of Henry. He was a protagonist of the theory of pragmatism developed by his friend C. S. Peirce, and invented the doctrine which he called "radical empiricism." His major works are *The Principles of Psychology, The Will to Believe,* and *The Meaning of Truth.*

Janáček, Leoš (1854–1928), Czech composer and conductor, and student of folk music, b. in Moravia, son of a village schoolmaster, creator of a national style. His best-known opera is *Jenufa. See Section E.*

Jefferies, Richard (1848–87), English naturalist of poetic perception, b. in Wiltshire, author of *Gamekeeper at Home* and *The Life of the Fields.*

Jefferson, Thomas (1743–1826), American president, 1801–9. He created the Republican Party, by which the federalists, led by Hamilton, were overthrown, and helped to draft the Declaration of Independence. He tried unsuccessfully to bring an end to slavery.

Jeffreys, 1st Baron (George Jeffreys) (1648–89), English judge who held the " bloody assize " after Monmouth's unsuccessful rebellion. In 1688 he was sent to the Tower and there died.

Jellicoe, 1st Earl (John Rushworth Jellicoe) (1859–1935), British admiral. He fought the uncertain battle of Jutland in 1916, after which the German fleet remained in harbour. He was later governor-general of New Zealand.

Jenkins, Roy (b. 1920), British politician, b. Wales; Pres. EEC Commission 1977; served as Labour's Home Sec. 1965–7; Chanc. of Exchequer 1967–70.

Jenner, Edward (1749–1823), English physician, b. in Gloucs., pupil of John Hunter. His discovery of vaccination against smallpox (1798) helped to lay the foundations of modern immunology.

Jerome, Jerome Klapka (1859–1927), English humorous writer, author of *Three Men in a Boat.*

Jerome, St. (c. 331–420), scholar, whose translation of the Bible into Latin (the Vulgate) became for centuries the standard use.

Jesus Christ (c. 4 B.C.–A.D. 30), founder of Christianity, the son of Mary whose husband was Joseph, was born in a critical period of Jewish history. His home was at Nazareth in Galilee, but virtually nothing is known about his early life. When he was about 30 he began the mission which he believed to have been entrusted to him, proclaiming the Kingdom of God was at hand. His teaching is summarised in the Sermon on the Mount, and its main theme is love, especially for the poor and downtrodden. He was later crucified. The main source of his life is the New Testament. The title " Christ " comes from the Greek word *christos* = anointed, which is the Greek translation of the Hebrew title *Messiah.* Modern dating has amended the probable year of his birth.

Jiménez, Juan Ramón (1881–1958), Spanish lyric poet, author of *Platero y Yo.* Nobel prizewinner 1956.

Jinnah, Mohammed Ali (1876–1948), Pakistani statesman. B. at Karachi, he became president of the Muslim League, and succeeded in 1947 in establishing the Dominion of Pakistan, becoming its first governor-general.

Joachim, Joseph (1831–1907), Hungarian violinist and composer.

Joan of Arc, St. (Jeanne d'Arc) (1412–31), French patriot, called the Maid of Orléans; of peasant parentage (she was b. at Domrémy), she believed herself called to save France from English domination; and by her efforts Charles VII was crowned at Rheims in 1429. Captured by the English, she was burned as a heretic; but canonised in 1920.

Joffre, Joseph Jacques Césaire (1852–1931), French general. He was commander-in-chief of the French army in the 1914–18 war.

John, St., the Baptist (executed A.D. 28), the forerunner of Jesus Christ.

John, St., the Evangelist, one of the twelve apostles of Jesus Christ, a Galilean fisherman, son of Zebedee and brother of James; traditionally author of the fourth Gospel.

John (1167–1216), youngest son of Henry II, was King of England from 1199. Able but erratic and arbitrary, he lost Normandy. Baronial opposition to him, under the influence of Archbishop Stephen Langton, acquired a national character, and in 1215 he was obliged to seal Magna Carta (*see Section L*).

John of Gaunt (1340–99), Duke of Lancaster, son of Edward III and father of Henry IV.

John XXIII (1881–1963), elected Pope in 1958, succeeding Pius XII, was formerly Cardinal Angelo Giuseppe Roncalli, patriarch of Venice. He sought to bring the Church closer to modern needs and to promote Christian unity. His teaching is given in his encyclicals, *Mater et Magistra* and *Pacem in Terris.* He held an Ecumenical Council in 1962.

John, Augustus (1878–1961), British painter and etcher, b. in Wales; noted for his portraits, *e.g.,* Lloyd George, Bernard Shaw, T. E. Lawrence.

Johnson, Amy (1904–41), was the first woman aviator to fly solo from England to Australia. She lost her life serving in the Air Transport Auxiliary in the second world war.

Johnson, Lyndon Baines (1908–73), President of the United States, 1963–9. He became president on Kennedy's assassination and followed a progressive policy at home. but his achievements were clouded by the war in Vietnam.

Johnson, Samuel (1709–84), English lexicographer and man of letters, b. at Lichfield. His *Dictionary* was published in 1755, and was followed by *Rasselas, The Idler* (a periodical), and *Lives of the Poets.* He was a focus of London literary life of his day, and his biographer, James Boswell, has vividly portrayed his circle.

Johnston, Sir Harry (1858–1927), British explorer who led an expedition to Kilimanjaro.

Jókai, Mór (1825–1904), Hungarian novelist, author of *Black Diamonds.*

Joliot-Curie, Jean Frédéric (1900–58), and his wife **Irène** (1896–1956), French scientists who discovered artificial radioactivity. Nobel prizewinners 1935. Joliot-Curie was one of the discoverers of nuclear fission. Irène was the daughter of Pierre and Marie Curie. Both were communists, and both died from cancer caused by their work.

Jones, Ernest Charles (1819–69), English Chartist leader and poet.

Jones, Sir Harold Spencer (1890–1960), British astronomer royal, 1933–55. His major research was to determine the mean distance of the earth from the sun, 93,004,000 miles.

Jones, Inigo (1573–1652), architect of the English renaissance who studied in Italy and inspired the use of Palladian forms in England. His buildings include the banqueting hall in Whitehall and the queen's house at Greenwich. He also designed furniture and introduced the proscenium arch and movable scenery on the English stage.

Jonson, Ben (1573–1637), English poet and dramatist. His plays include *Every Man in his Humour*, *Volpone*, and *The Alchemist*; and his poems *Drink to me only with thine Eyes*. He also produced court masques.

Josephine, Empress (1763–1814), wife of Napoleon I, *née* de la Pagerie, she was previously married to the Vicomte de Beauharnais. She was divorced from Napoleon in 1809.

Josephus, Flavius (38–*c*.100), Jewish historian, author of *History of the Jewish War*.

Joule, James Prescott (1818–89), English physicist, pupil of Dalton, who researched on electromagnetism and determined the mechanical equivalent of heat. *See* **Section L.**

Jowett, Benjamin (1817–93), English scholar. He translated Plato's *Dialogues*, and he was an influential Master of Balliol College, Oxford.

Jowitt, Earl (William Allen Jowitt) (1885–1957), British Labour politician and lord chancellor. He wrote *The Strange Case of Alger Hiss*.

Joyce, James (1882–1941), Irish author, b. Dublin. His *Ulysses* gives a microscopic picture of a day in the life of two Irishmen, and flouted the conventions of his day. Other works include *Portrait of the Artist* and *Finnegans Wake*. He spent most of his life on the Continent.

Juin, Alphonse (1888–1967), French general who took part in the Allied invasion of Tunisia and the Italian campaign in the second world war.

Julian the Apostate (331–63), Roman emperor who tried to restore paganism in the empire. He was killed in war against Persia.

Jung, Carl Gustav (1875–1961), Swiss psychiatrist. A former pupil of Freud, he later formulated his own system of analytical psychology. *See* **Section J.**

Junot, Andoche (1771–1813), French general defeated by Wellington in the Peninsular War.

Jusserand, Jean Jules (1855–1932), French author and diplomat, who wrote on English literature and wayfaring life in the Middle Ages.

Justinian I (483–565), Roman emperor in the East. He and his wife Theodora beautified Constantinople, and his general Belisarius was successful in war. He codified Roman law.

Juvenal (60–140), Roman poet and Stoic, remembered for his *Satires*.

K

Kafka, Franz (1883–1924), German-speaking Jewish writer, b. Prague, whose introspective work, the bulk of which was not published till after his early death from tuberculosis, has had a notable influence on later schools, especially the surrealists. It includes the three novels *The Trial*, *The Castle*, and *America*, and some short stories.

Kālidāsa (c. A.D. 400), chief figure in classic Sanskrit literature. No facts are known about his life and date, but certain evidence places him in the 5th cent. Seven of his works survive: two lyrics, *Ritu-samhara* (The Seasons), and *Megha-dūta* (Cloud Messenger); two epics, *Raghu-vamśa* (Dynasty of Raghu) and *Kumarasambhava* (Birth of the War-god); and three dramas, *Śakuntalā*, *Mālavikāgnimitra*, and *Vikramorvaśīya*.

Kant, Immanuel (1724–1804), German philosopher, author of *Critique of Pure Reason* (1781), *Critique of Practical Reason* (1788), and *Critique of Judgement* (1790). He came from a Pietist family of Königsberg, where he lectured, but the Prussian government forbade his lectures as anti-Lutheran. He was influenced by the writings of his neighbour Hamann (*see* Romanticism, Section J) and by Rousseau and Hume, and his own work was of immense influence in shaping future liberal thought. He believed in the freedom of man to make his own decisions and considered the exploitation of man as the worst evil. In *Perpetual Peace* he advocated a world federation of states.

Kapitza, Pyotr (b. 1894), Russian physicist who worked on atomic research with Rutherford at the Cavendish Laboratory, Cambridge, and returned to Russia in 1935. Member of the Soviet Academy of Sciences and Fellow of the Royal Society.

Kauffmann, Angelica (1741–1807), Anglo-Swiss painter, a foundation member of the Royal Academy and the first woman R.A.

Kaulbach, Wilhelm von (1805–74), German painter who illustrated the works of Goethe and Schiller.

Kaunda, Kenneth (b. 1924), African leader of international standing, son of Christian missionaries. He has been president of Zambia since independence in 1964.

Kean, Edmund (1787–1833), English tragic actor. He made his name as Shylock.

Kean, Charles John (1811–68), English actor-manager, son of Edmund. He married Ellen Tree and in the 1850s played with her in spectacular revivals at the Princess's Theatre, London.

Keats, John (1795–1821), English poet who in his short life produced poems notable for richness of imagination and beauty of thought. They include *Odes*, *Isabella*, and *The Eve of St. Agnes*.

Keble, John (1792–1866), English clergyman associated with the Tractarian movement and author of *The Christian Year*. *See* Tractarianism. Section J.

Keller, Helen Adams (1880–1968), American author and lecturer who overcame great physical handicaps (blind and deaf before the age of two) to live an active and useful life.

Kelvin of Largs, 1st Baron (William Thomson) (1824–1907), British mathematician and physicist, b. Belfast, known for his work on heat and thermodynamics, and contributions to electrical science and submarine telegraphy. In the domain of heat he stands to Joule as Maxwell stands to Faraday in the history of electrical science, both bringing pre-eminently mathematical minds to bear on the results of experimental discoveries. He introduced the Kelvin or Absolute scale of temperature and was one of the original members of the Order of Merit.

Kemble, Fanny (1809–93), English actress. She came of a noted theatrical family, her father and uncle respectively being the actors Charles Kemble and John Philip Kemble, and her aunt, Mrs. Siddons.

Kempenfelt, Richard (1718–82), English admiral, who sank with his ship the *Royal George* together with 600 of the ship's company off Spithead through a shifting of the guns which caused it to capsize.

Kempis, Thomas à (1380–1471), name by which the German mystic Thomas Hammerken was known, was a monk of the Augustinian order, whose life was mainly spent at a monastery near Zwolle. He was the author of *The Imitation of Christ*.

Kennedy, John Fitzgerald (1917–63), President of the U.S.A., 1961–3, the youngest and the first Roman Catholic to be elected; son of a financier. He had world-wide pre-eminence and gave the American people a sense of purpose to meet the challenges of a scientific age. He opposed racial discrimination and initiated a new era in East–West relations; but his foreign policy sowed the seeds of the Vietnam war. He and his brother Robert were assassinated, the latter while campaigning for the presidency in 1968.

Kent, William (1684–1748), English painter, furniture designer, landscape gardener, and architect, protégé of Lord Burlington, whose buildings include the great hall at Holkham and the Horse Guards, Whitehall.

Kenyatta, Jomo (b. 1893), African leader who became president of Kenya in 1964.

Kepler, Johann (1571–1630), German astronomer and mystic, for a short time assistant to Tycho Brahe whose measurements he used in working out his laws of planetary motion, which are: 1. Planets move round the sun not in circles, but in ellipses, the sun being one of the foci. 2. A planet moves not uniformly but in such a way that a line drawn from it to the sun sweeps out equal areas of the ellipse in equal times. 3. The squares of the period of revolution round the sun are proportional to the cubes of the distances. The explanation of these laws was given by Newton; they dealt a death-blow to Aristotelian cosmology.

Keyes, 1st Baron (Roger John Brownlow Keyes) (1872–1945), British admiral who led the raid on Zeebrugge in 1918.

Keynes, 1st Baron (John Maynard Keynes) (1883–

1946), British economist, who was a Treasury representative at the Versailles peace conference, and published his views in *The Economic Consequences of the Peace*. His *Treatise on Money* (1930) and *The General Theory of Employment, Interest and Money* (1936) influenced economic thought all over the world.

Khrushchev, Nikita Sergeyevich (1894–1971), Russian statesman who became leader of the Soviet Union soon after the death of Stalin; first secretary of the Soviet Communist Party, 1953–64; prime minister, 1958–64. After the harsh years of the Stalinist régime he pursued a policy of relaxation both in home and foreign affairs. Relations with America improved but those with China became strained. Advances were made in scientific achievement, notably in the field of space research. In 1964 his posts were taken over by Leonid Brezhnev (first secretary) and Alexei Kosygin (prime minister).

Kierkegaard, Sören (1813–55), Danish philosopher and religious thinker, whose views have influenced contemporary existentialism. His main work is *Either–Or*.

King, Martin Luther (1929–68), American clergyman and Negro integration leader; awarded the 1964 Nobel peace prize for his consistent support of the principle of non-violence in the coloured people's struggle for civil rights. Assassinated at Memphis, Tennessee.

King, Mackenzie (1874–1950), prime minister of Canada, 1921–5, 1926–30, and 1935–48.

Kingsley, Charles (1819–75), English clergyman and novelist, author of *Hypatia*, *Westward Ho!*, *Hereward the Wake* and *The Water Babies*.

Kipling, Rudyard (1865–1936), British writer, b. Bombay. His vivid work portrays contemporary British rule in India and includes *The Light that Failed*, *Stalky and Co.*, *Kim*, and the *Barrack Room Ballads*. Among his books for children are the *Just So Stories*, *Puck of Pook's Hill* and the *Jungle Books*. Nobel prize 1907.

Kirchhoff, Gustav Robert (1824–87), German mathematical physicist, who with R. W. Bunsen discovered that in the gaseous state each chemical substance emits its own characteristic spectrum (1859). He was able to explain Fraunhofer's map of the solar spectrum. Using the spectroscope, he and Bunsen discovered the elements caesium and rubidium.

Kissinger, Henry (b. 1923), American Secretary of State 1973–7 and special adviser on national security affairs to Richard Nixon; inventor of shuttle-service diplomacy. Played active role in peace missions to the Middle East, Vietnam and Southern Africa and in SALT negotiations with the Soviet Union. Shared Nobel peace prize for 1973 with Le Duc Tho.

Kitchener of Khartoum, 1st Earl (Horatio Herbert Kitchener) (1850–1916), English general. In 1898 he won back the Sudan for Egypt by his victory at Omdurman. He served in the South African war; and in the first world war he was secretary of war, 1914–16. He was drowned on his way to Russia.

Klee, Paul (1879–1940), Swiss artist, whose paintings, in a restless, experimental period, are small-scale, delicate dream-world fantasies of poetical content.

Klemperer, Otto (1885–1973), German-born conductor, renowned as interpreter of the Beethoven symphonies. Expelled by the Nazis he became an American citizen and returned to Europe in 1946. He had been principal conductor of the Philharmonic Orchestra since 1959.

Kneller, Sir Godfrey (1646–1723), portrait painter, b. at Lübeck, who settled in England and was patronised by English sovereigns from Charles II to George I.

Knox, John (1505–72), Scottish reformer, b. near Haddington. While in exile at Geneva he was influenced by Calvin. On return to Scotland he was a leader of the reforming party against Mary, Queen of Scots. He wrote a *History of the Reformation in Scotland*.

Koch, Robert (1843–1910), German bacteriologist who discovered the bacillus of tuberculosis, and worked on cholera and cattle diseases.

Kodaly, Zoltán (1882–1967), Hungarian composer and teacher. He worked with Bartok in the collection of folk-tunes. *See* Section E.

Kokoschka, Oskar (b. 1886), Austrian portrait and landscape painter, a rare interpretative artist, who, after teaching in Dresden, in 1938 settled in England.

Koniev, Ivan Stepanovich (b. 1897), Russian general of the second world war and commander of the Warsaw Pact forces in the 1950s.

Korolyov, Sergei (1907–66), Russian space scientist, who designed the world's first earth satellite, the first manned spaceship and the first moon rocket.

Kosciusko, Tadeusz (1746–1817), Polish patriot. After experience gained in America in the War of Independence, he led his countrymen against Russia in 1792 and 1794 in opposition to the partition of Poland and was temporarily successful.

Kossuth, Louis (1802–94), Hungarian patriot, who in 1848 led a rising of his countrymen against the Hapsburg dynasty, but had to flee to Turkey and later to England.

Kosygin, Alexei Nikolayevich (b. 1904), succeeded Nikita Khrushchev as chairman of the Council of Ministers of the U.S.S.R. (prime minister) in 1964; formerly a deputy chairman of the State Economic Planning Commission, Gosplan.

Kreisler, Fritz (1875–1962), Austrian violinist, who composed violin music and an operetta. He became an American citizen in 1943.

Krenek, Ernst (b. 1900), Austrian composer of partly Czech descent, whose compositions cover a wide range, including the jazz opera *Jonny spielt auf*. He settled in America in 1938.

Kropotkin, Peter, Prince (1842–1921), Russian anarchist, geographer and explorer, who was imprisoned for favouring the political action of a working men's association, but escaped to England. He wrote on socialistic and geographical subjects. Returned to Russia in 1917.

Kruger, Stephanus Johannes Paulus (1825–1904), Boer leader, who in 1881 was appointed head of the provisional government against Britain, and later president. When the war of 1899–1902 turned against the Boers, he vainly sought help in Europe.

Krupp, Alfred (1812–87), founder of the German gun factories at Essen. He installed in a disused factory left him by his father a new steam-engine from England, began to make cast steel, and from 1844 specialised in armaments. The firm's factories made the Big Bertha guns which shelled Paris in 1918. His great-grand-son Alfried (b. 1907) was tried as a war criminal in 1948.

Krylov, Ivan Andreyevich (1768–1844), Russian writer of fables who has been called the Russian La Fontaine.

Kubelik, Jan (1880–1940), Czech violinist, son of a gardener at Michle, near Prague, who at the age of 12 played in public. His son Rafael (b. 1914), a conductor of international repute, was musical director of the Royal Opera House, Covent Garden, 1955–8.

Kublai Khan (1216–94), grandson of Genghiz Khan, was the first Mongol emperor of China. He extended the Mongol empire by conquest, and lived in unparalleled splendour. His court was described by Marco Polo and is the subject of a poem by Coleridge.

L

La Fayette, Marie Joseph Paul Roch Yves Gilbert du Motier, Marquis de (1757–1834), French soldier and statesman. He fought for the colonists in the American War of Independence; and in the 1789 French revolution he proposed a declaration of rights and was commander of the National Guard till his moderation made him unpopular. When the monarchy was restored he was an opposition leader, and took part in the revolution of 1830.

La Fontaine, Jean de (1621–95), French poet and fabulist, b. in Champagne, a friend of Molière, Boileau, and Racine, all brilliant writers of the reign of Louis XIV.

Lagerlöf, Selma (1858–1940), Swedish novelist and first woman member of the Swedish Academy. Nobel prizewinner 1909.

Lagrange, Joseph Louis, Comte (1736–1813), French mathematician, of Turin and Paris, whose interest in astronomy led him to distinguish two types of disturbance of members of the solar system, the periodic and the secular. He was called by Frederick the Great to Berlin to succeed Euler.

Lalande, Joseph Jerome LeFrançais de (1732–1807), French astronomer, author of *Traité d'astronomie.*

Lamarck, Jean Baptiste Pierre Antoine de Monet de (1744–1829), French biologist whose explanation of evolution was that new organs are brought into being by the needs of the organism in adapting to its environment and that the new characters acquired during its life-time can be passed on to the offspring through heredity, resulting in evolutionary change.

Lamb, Charles (1775–1834), English essayist, b. London. A clerk in the East India Office, he devoted his life to his sister Mary, who was of unstable mind. He is chiefly known for his *Essays of Elia,* and his letters, which have a blend of humour and tenderness.

Lambert, Constant (1905–51), English composer and critic, and conductor of Sadler's Wells ballet. His *Rio Grande* is in jazz idiom.

Landor, Walter Savage (1775–1864), English writer, b. Warwick, remembered for his *Imaginary Conversations* and poems.

Landseer, Sir Edwin (1802–73), English animal painter, b. London. He painted the *Monarch of the Glen* and designed the lions in Trafalgar Square.

Lane, Edward William (1801–76), English Arabic scholar, translator of the *Arabian Nights.*

Lanfranc (c. 1005–89), ecclesiastic. B. at Pavia, he became a prior in Normandy, and in 1070 archbishop of Canterbury, in which office he was energetic.

Lang, Andrew (1844–1912), Scottish man of letters, whose output includes *Myth, Ritual and Religion,* poems, fairy-tales, and fiction.

Lang, 1st Baron (Cosmo Gordon Lang) (1864–1945), was archbishop of Canterbury, 1928–42.

Langland, William (1330?–1400?), English poet, probably educated at Malvern, author of *Piers the Plowman.*

Langton, Stephen (1151–1228), archbishop of Canterbury, and adviser to the insurgent barons who induced King John to sign Magna Carta.

Lansbury, George (1859–1940), British Labour politician, founder of the *Daily Herald.* He improved London's amenities.

Lâo-Tsze (old philosopher) (c. 600 B.C.), traditional founder of Taoism in China. *See Section J.*

Laplace, Pierre Simon, Marquis de (1749–1827), French mathematician and astronomer, author of *Celestial Mechanics* (1799–1825). He advanced the hypothesis that the solar system had condensed out of a vast rotating gaseous nebula.

La Rochefoucauld, François, Duc de (1613–80), French writer, author of *Reflections and Moral Maxims.*

Lasker, Emanuel (1868–1941), German chess player, world champion, 1894–1921.

Lassalle, Ferdinand (1825–64), German socialist who took part in the revolutionary movement of 1848 and organised workers to press for political rights.

Lassus, Orlandus (Lasso, Orlando di) (c. 1532–94), Flemish composer and choirmaster, contemporary of Palestrina, writer of *chansons,* madrigals, and sacred music. *See Section E.*

Latimer, Hugh (c. 1485–1555), English Protestant martyr, became bishop of Worcester in 1535, and was executed under Queen Mary.

Laud, William (1573–1645), archbishop of Canterbury and adviser to Charles I. His attempts to get conformity for his high church policy made him unpopular and he was impeached and beheaded.

Lauder, Sir Harry (1870–1950), Scottish comic singer of wide popularity. He also wrote *Roamin' in the Gloamin'.*

Laval, Pierre (1883–1945), French politician who collaborated with the German occupation in the second world war and was subsequently tried and executed.

Lavery, Sir John (1856–1941), Irish portrait painter.

Lavoisier, Antoine Laurent (1743–94), French chemist, b. Paris, was the first to establish the

fact that combustion is a form of chemical action. We owe the word *oxygen* to him. He perished in the French Revolution.

Law, Andrew Bonar (1858–1923), Conservative politician, prime minister 1922–3.

Lawrence, David Herbert (1885–1930), English poet and novelist, b. Notts., a miner's son. He tried to interpret emotion on a deeper level of consciousness. His works, which have had wide influence, include *The White Peacock, Sons and Lovers, The Rainbow, Women in Love,* and *Lady Chatterley's Lover;* also plays. *See Section I.*

Lawrence, Sir Thomas (1769–1830), English portrait painter.

Lawrence, Thomas Edward (1888–1935) (Lawrence of Arabia), British soldier who led the Arabs against the Turks in the war of 1914–18, and wrote *The Seven Pillars of Wisdom.*

Leacock, Stephen (1869–1944), Canadian humorist.

Leavis, Frank Raymond (b. 1895), British critic, who edited *Scrutiny,* 1932–63, and whose works include *The Great Tradition, D. H. Lawrence, Novelist,* and *"Anna Karenina" and Other Essays.*

Lecky, William Edward Hartpole (1838–1903), Irish historian, author of *England in the Eighteenth Century.*

Leclerc, Jacques Philippe (Philippe, Comte de Hauteclocque) (1902–47), French general. He led a Free French force in Africa in the second world war and liberated Paris in 1944. He died in a plane crash.

Le Corbusier (1887–1965), pseudonym of Charles Édouard Jeanneret, Swiss architect, whose books and work (especially his Unité d'Habitation at Marseilles and the new Punjab capital at Chandigarh) have widely influenced town-planning.

Le Duc Tho (b. 1911), member of the Politburo of the N. Vietnamese Workers' Party who was his country's chief negotiator at the Vietnam truce talks 1970–3. He would not accept the 1973 Nobel peace prize awarded jointly with Dr. Kissinger until peace had "really been restored in S. Vietnam."

Lee of Fareham, 1st Viscount (Arthur Hamilton Lee) (1868–1947), British politician who presented Chequers Court to the nation as prime minister's residence.

Lee, Robert Edward (1807–70), American Confederate general in the Civil War, who made the surrender at Appomattox.

Lee, Sir Sidney (1859–1926), English critic, and joint editor of the *Dictionary of National Biography.*

Leech, John (1817–64), humorist artist, b. London, of Irish descent, contributed to *Punch.*

Leibnitz, Gottfried Wilhelm (1646–1716), German philosopher and mathematician, who invented the differential and integral calculus (1684) independently of Newton whose previous work on the same subject was not published until 1687. It was Leibnitz's nomenclature that was universally adopted.

Leicester, Earl of (Robert Dudley) (1538–88), English soldier, commanded English troops in the Netherlands, 1585–7, without much success, and in 1588 commanded forces assembled against the Armada. He was husband of Amy Robsart.

Leif Ericsson (fl. 1000), discoverer of Vinland on the north-east coast of America; b. Iceland, son of the Norse explorer, Eric the Red, who colonised Greenland.

Leighton, 1st Baron (Robert Leighton) (1830–96), English painter of wide popularity, whose works include *Paolo and Francesca.* He was also a sculptor.

Lely, Sir Peter (Pieter van der Faes) (1618–80), Dutch painter who settled in London and painted court portraits.

Lenin (Vladimir Ilyich Ulyanov) (1870–1924), Russian revolutionary leader and statesman. From 1893 to 1917 he worked underground in Russia and abroad for the revolutionary cause. During this time the Social-Democratic party was formed; within it developed an uncompromising revolutionary group, the Bolsheviks, and of this group Lenin was the leading spirit. In April 1917 he and his fellow exiles returned; after the November revolution he headed the new government having to face both war and

B38

anarchy. In 1921 his "new economic policy" somewhat modified the intensive drive towards planned industrial development. He was born in Simbirsk (now Ulyanovsk) on the middle Volga, the son of the local inspector of education. His body lies embalmed in Red Square, Moscow.

Leonardo da Vinci (1452–1519), Italian artist and man of science, son of a Florentine lawyer and a peasant. He described himself (when applying to Lodovico Sforza, Duke of Milan, for the post of city planner) as painter, architect, philosopher, poet, composer, sculptor, athlete, mathematician, inventor, and anatomist. His artistic output is small in quantity, and he is best known for his *Last Supper* in the refectory of Santa Maria delle Grazie in Milan and his *Mona Lisa* in the Louvre. He recorded his scientific work in unpublished notebooks written from right to left in mirror writing. The anatomy of the body (himself carrying out dissections), the growth of the child in the womb, the laws of waves and currents, and the laws of flight, all were studied by this astonishing man who believed nothing but had to see for himself. Although he was much admired, few people in his time had any notion of his universal genius.

Leoncavallo, Ruggiero (1858–1919), Italian composer of the opera *Pagliacci*.

Leonidas was king of Sparta at the time of the invasion of Greece by Xerxes (480 B.C.), and led the defence of the pass of Thermopylae, where he fell.

Lermontov, Mikhail Yurevich (1814–41), Russian poet and novelist, exiled to the Caucasus for a revolutionary poem addressed to Tsar Nicholas I on the death of Pushkin. He has been called the poet of the Caucasus. His novel *A Hero of Our Time* was written at St. Petersburg. He lost his life in a duel.

Le Sage, Alain René (1668–1747), French author, b. in Brittany, who wrote *Gil Blas* and *Le Diable Boiteux*. He was also a dramatist and his plays include *Turcaret*.

Lesseps, Ferdinand, Vicomte de (1805–94), French engineer who while serving as vice-consul at Alexandria conceived a scheme for a canal across the Suez isthmus; the work was completed in 1869. He also projected the original Panama canal scheme, which failed.

Lessing, Gotthold Ephraim (1729–81), German philosopher, dramatist, and critic, noted for his critical work *Laokoon* and his play *Minna von Barnhelm*.

Leucippus (fl. 440 B.C.), Greek philosopher, founder with Democritus of atomism, a theory of matter more nearly that of modern science than any put forward in ancient times. One of his sayings survives: "Naught occurs at random, but everything for a reason and of necessity."

Leverhulme, 1st Viscount (William Hesketh Lever) (1851–1925), British industrialist and philanthropist. He founded Lever Bros. which later became Unilever Ltd., and was a practical exponent of industrial partnership. He gave Lancaster House to the nation.

Leverrier, Urbain Jean Joseph (1811–77), French astronomer who, working independently of J. C. Adams of Cambridge, anticipated the existence of the planet Neptune which was later revealed by telescopic search.

Lévi-Strauss, Claude (b. 1908), French social anthropologist, b. Belgium, exponent of the theory of symbolic structures. He has written works on anthropology, religion, myths and language: *Les structures élémentaires de la parenté* (1949), *Tristes tropiques* (1955), *La Pensée Sauvage* (1963).

Lewis, Sinclair (1885–1951), American writer of novels satirising small-town life and philistinism. His works include *Main Street, Babbitt* (hence the term Babbitry), and *Elmer Gantry*. Nobel prizewinner 1931.

Liaquat Ali Khan (1895–1951), leader of the Moslem League (1946) and first premier of Pakistan in 1947. He was assassinated.

Lie, Trygve (1896–1968), Norwegian politician who became secretary-general of the United Nations, 1946–52.

Li Hung Chang (1823–1901), Chinese statesman, who though enlightened, was unable to secure

much modernisation and had to cede Formosa to Japan in 1895.

Lilburne, John (1614–57), English agitator and pamphleteer, leader of the Levellers in the Civil War period.

Linacre, Thomas (c. 1460–1524), English humanist and physician, who translated Galen's works and founded the College of Physicians.

Lincoln, Abraham (1809–65), American president. B. in Kentucky, he became a lawyer and was returned to Congress from Illinois in 1846. He was a leader of the Republican party which was formed in 1856 to oppose slavery. He became president in 1861, in which year the Confederate States proposed to withdraw from the Union, and war broke out. The phrase "government of the people, by the people, for the people" comes from his Gettysburg speech of 1863. He was assassinated in 1865.

Lind, Jenny (1820–87), Swedish singer, popular in Europe, and known as the Swedish nightingale. She founded musical scholarships.

Linnaeus (1707–78), Swedish botanist, remembered for his system of defining living things by two Latin names, the first being its *genus*, and the second its *species*. His method is expounded in *Philosophia Botanica* (1751). In 1757 he was ennobled as Karl von Linné. He studied, taught and died at Uppsala.

Lippi, Fra Filippo (1406–69), Italian artist, b. Florence. Frescoes in Prato cathedral are his main work. His son Filippino (1457–1504) finished Masaccio's frescoes in the Carmine, Florence, and executed others, for instance in Santa Maria Novella.

Lippmann, Gabriel (1845–1921), French physicist who invented a capillary electrometer and was a pioneer in colour photography. Nobel prizewinner 1908.

Lippmann, Walter (1889–1974), American journalist of influence, writing for the New York *Herald Tribune*, 1931–62.

Lipton, Sir Thomas Johnstone (1850–1931), Scottish business man and philanthropist. B. Glasgow, he emigrated to America, but returned to Scotland and established extensive chain-stores for groceries. He unsuccessfully competed in yachting for the America's Cup.

Lister, Baron (Joseph Lister) (1827–1912), English surgeon, son of J. J. Lister (1786–1869), an amateur microscopist. He founded antiseptic surgery (1865) which greatly reduced mortality in hospitals.

Liszt, Franz (1811–86), Hungarian pianist and composer. His daughter Cosima became the wife of Hans von Bülow and later of Wagner. *See Section E.*

Litvinov, Maxim (1876–1952), Russian diplomat, of revolutionary origin, who first as ambassador in London, then as commissar for foreign affairs, and 1941–3 ambassador to the U.S., gained respect and understanding for his country.

Livingstone, David (1813–73), Scottish explorer in Africa. He discovered the course of the Zambesi, the Victoria Falls and Lake Nyasa (now Lake Malawi), and roused opinion against the slave trade. At one time believed lost, he was found by Stanley (*q.v.*) on 10 Nov. 1871.

Lloyd-George of Dwyfor, 1st Earl (David Lloyd George) (1863–1945), Liberal statesman of Welsh origin. He was M.P. for Caernarvon, 1890–1944; and as chancellor of the exchequer he introduced social insurance, 1908–11. The war of 1914–18 obliged him to become a war premier (superseding Asquith), and he was subsequently one of the main figures at the peace conference. In 1921 he conceded the Irish Free State. His daughter, Lady Megan Lloyd George, was M.P. for many years, latterly for the Labour Party.

Locke, John (1632–1704), English liberal philosopher and founder of empiricism, the doctrine that all knowledge is derived from experience. His chief work in theoretical philosophy, *Essay Concerning Human Understanding*, was written just before the revolution of 1688 and published in 1690. Other writings include *Letters on Toleration, Treatises on Government*, and *Education*.

Lombroso, Cesare (1836–1909), Italian criminologist, whose *L'uomo delinquente* maintained the existence of a criminal type distinguishable from the normal.

Lomonosov, Mikhail Vasilievich (1711–65),

Russian philologist and poet who systematised Russian grammar and orthography.

London, Jack (1876–1916), American author of adventure tales such as *Call of the Wild*.

Longfellow, Henry Wadsworth (1807–82), American poet, popular in his lifetime, author of *The Golden Legend* and *Hiawatha*.

Lope de Vega Carpio, Félix (1562–1635), Spanish writer of immense output. First a ballad-writer, he took to play-writing and founded the Spanish drama. The number of his plays is said to have been 1,500, the earlier ones historical, the later ones dealing with everyday life; but most are lost.

Lorca, Federico Garcia (1899–1936), Spanish poet and dramatist of Andalusia. Among his works are *Llanto por Ignacio Sánchez Mejías*, an unforgettable lament on the death of a bull-fighter, and *Canción de Jinete* with its haunting refrain, " Cordoba, far away and alone." He was brutally murdered by Franco sympathisers at the outbreak of the civil war.

Louis IX (1214–70), St. Louis, King of France. Of saintly character (as described in Joinville's *Memoirs*), he also carried out practical reforms. He died on crusade.

Louis XIV (1638–1715), King of France. A despotic ruler, builder of Versailles, he also dominated the Europe of his day; but he sowed the seeds of future trouble for France by his exhausting wars. He revoked the Edict of Nantes which had given religious freedom to the Huguenots since 1598. His reign, however, was a great period for literature.

Louis XV (1710–74), King of France. Extravagant and self-indulgent, his reign marked a declining period for the monarchy, but produced some fine art.

Louis XVI (1754–93), King of France. Well-meaning but incapable, this king saw the outbreak of the French revolution of 1789, in which he and his queen Marie Antoinette were executed.

Louis, Joe (Joseph Louis Barrow) (b. 1914), American Negro boxer, who became world heavyweight champion in 1936, successfully defending his title 25 times.

Low, Archibald Montgomery (1888–1956), British scientist who worked in varied fields, including wireless, television, and anti-aircraft and anti-tank apparatus.

Low, Sir David (1891–1963), British cartoonist, b. New Zealand, associated with the *Evening Standard* and later the *Guardian*; creator of Colonel Blimp.

Lowell, Robert (1917–77), American poet, author of the verse play *The Old Glory*, and *Life Studies*, an autobiographical volume in verse and prose. *See* Section M.

Loyola, St. Ignatius (1491–1556), Spanish founder of the Jesuits, a missionary order working directly under the Pope.

Lucretius (99–55 B.C.), Roman poet, author of *De rerum natura*, a long philosophical poem advocating moral truth without religious belief.

Ludendorff, Erich (1865–1937), German general who directed German strategy in the first world war.

Lugard, 1st Baron (Frederick John Dealtry Lugard) (1858–1945), British colonial administrator in Africa, especially Nigeria, and exponent of the system of indirect rule through native chiefs.

Lukács, Georg (1885–1971), Hungarian writer, Marxist thinker and literary critic. His ideas are expounded in *History and Class Consciousness* (1923), *Studies in European Realism* (1946, Eng. tr. 1950), *The Historical Novel* (1955, Eng. tr. 1962).

Luther, Martin (1483–1546), German Protestant reformer. After spending time in a monastery, he was ordained priest (1507), and lectured at Wittenberg university. In 1517 he protested against the sale of indulgences; and when summoned before the Diet of Worms made a memorable defence. He was protected by the Elector of Saxony, and translated the Bible. German Protestantism culminated in the Augsburg confession (1530). *See also* Lutheranism, Section J.

Luthuli, Albert (1899–1967), African non-violent resistance leader, an ex-Zulu chief. Killed in train accident. Nobel prize for peace 1960.

Lutyens, Sir Edwin Landseer (1869–1944), English

architect both of country houses and public buildings; designed the cenotaph, Whitehall, and Liverpool Roman catholic cathedral.

Lyell, Sir Charles (1797–1875), Scottish geologist, whose *Principles of Geology* (1830–33) postulated the gradual geological change and helped to shape Darwin's ideas. His terminology—Pliocene (*Greek* = more recent), Miocene (less recent) and Eocene (dawn)—is still in use.

Lysenko, Trofim (1898–1976), Russian biologist who maintained that environmental experiences can change heredity somewhat in the manner suggested by Lamarck. After the death of Stalin his novel theories were severely criticised.

Lytton, 1st Baron (Edward George Earle Lytton Bulwer-Lytton) (1803–73), English novelist and playwright, author of *The Last Days of Pompeii*.

M

Macadam, John Loudon (1756–1836), Scottish inventor of the " macadamising " system of road repair.

MacArthur, Douglas (1880–1964), American general. He defended the Philippines against the Japanese in the second world war, and was relieved of his command in 1951 in the Korean war.

Macaulay of Rothley, 1st Baron (Thomas Babington Macaulay) (1800–59), English historian, poet and Indian civil servant. His poems include *Lays of Ancient Rome*. In India he was mainly responsible for education being given in English.

Macaulay, Zachary (1768–1838), anti-slavery agitator, father of the above.

Macbeth (d. 1057), Scottish king, married Gruoch, granddaughter of Kenneth, king of Alban. He was mormaer of Moray, succeeding Duncan in 1040 after killing him in fair fight. His reign of seventeen years was prosperous, but he was killed by Duncan's son, Malcolm, in 1057. Shakespeare's play is based on the inaccurate *Chronicle* of Holinshed.

MacDiarmid, Hugh (b. 1892), pseudonym of Christopher Murray Grieve, Scottish poet, leader of the Scottish literary renaissance; author of *A Drunk Man Looks at the Thistle*.

Macdonald, Flora (1722–90), Scottish Jacobite heroine who saved the life of Prince Charles Edward after the defeat at Culloden Moor in 1746.

Macdonald, Sir John Alexander (1815–91), Canadian statesman, first prime minister of the Dominion of Canada.

Macdonald, James Ramsay (1866–1937), Labour politician of Scottish origin, premier 1924 and 1929–31; also of a coalition 1931–5. His action over the financial crisis of 1931 divided his party.

Macdonald, Malcolm (b. 1901), son of above, has held positions overseas in the Commonwealth, the last as special representative in Africa.

Machiavelli, Niccolò (1467–1527), Florentine Renaissance diplomat and theorist of the modern state. His book *The Prince* (1513), dedicated to Lorenzo the Magnificent, is concerned with the reality of politics—what rulers must do to retain power. His *Discourses* is more republican and liberal.

Mackail, John William (1859–1945), British classical scholar, translator of the *Odyssey*.

Mackenzie, Sir Compton (1883–1972), British writer, whose works include *Carnival*, *Sinister Street*, and a monumental autobiography.

McLuhan, Herbert Marshall (b. 1911), Canadian author of a number of books on contemporary communications, including *The Gutenberg Galaxy*, *The Mechanical Bride*. *See* Section J.

Macmillan, Harold (b. 1894), British Conservative statesman, prime minister 1957–63; During his premiership came the crises of the Berlin Wall and the Cuban missiles (in which his personal diplomacy played an influential role), de Gaulle's veto to our entry into Europe, the signing of the Partial Test-Ban Treaty and his " wind of change " speech which hailed African independence. The final vol. of his memoirs was pub. 1973. Chancellor of Oxford University (1960). O.M. 1976.

McMillan, Margaret (1860–1931), Scottish educational reformer, b. New York, and pioneer (with her sister Rachel) of child welfare work in London and of open-air nursery schools.

Macneice, Louis (1907–63), British poet, playwright, and translator. *See* Section M.

Macready, William Charles (1793–1873), British actor and manager, especially associated with Shakespearean roles.

Maeterlinck, Maurice (1862–1949), Belgian man of letters, whose plays include *La Princesse Maleine, Pelléas et Mélisande*, and *L'Oiseau Bleu*. Nobel prizewinner 1911. He also did scientific work on bees.

Magellan, Ferdinand (c. 1480–1521). Portuguese navigator, and commander of the first expedition (1519) to sail round the world.

Mahler, Gustav (1860–1911), Austrian composer and conductor; a writer of symphonies and songs, a classical romantic, much influenced by Anton Bruckner and Wagner. *See* Section E.

Mahavira, Vardhamana Jnatriputra (6th cent. B.C.), Indian historical (as opposed to legendary) founder of Jainism, which teaches the sacredness of all life. *See* Jainism, Section J.

Maintenon, Françoise d'Aubigne, Marquise de (1635–1719), second wife of Louis XIV. Her first husband was the poet Scarron. On the king's death she retired to a home for poor girls which she had founded.

Makarios III (1913–77), Greek Orthodox archbishop and Cypriot national leader. Deported by the British to the Seychelles in 1956, he returned in 1957 to become president of the newly independent republic in 1960.

Malibran, Marie Félicité (1808–36), Spanish mezzosoprano.

Malik, Yakov Alexandrovich (b. 1906), Soviet diplomat; permanent representative at U.N. 1949–52, 1967– ; ambassador to Britain 1953–60; deputy foreign minister 1960–7.

Malory, Sir Thomas (c. 1430–71), English writer. From earlier sources and legends of King Arthur and the Knights of the Round Table, he compiled the *Morte Darthur* printed by Caxton in 1485.

Malraux, André (1895–1976), French novelist and politician. His works include *La Condition humaine, L'Espoir*, and *Psychologie de l'art* (tr. in 2 vols., *Museum without Walls*, and *The Creative Act*). Served under de Gaulle.

Malthus, Thomas Robert (1766–1834), English clergyman and economist who in his gloomy essay *The Principle of Population* contended that population tends to increase faster than the means of subsistence and that its growth could only be checked by moral restraint or by disease and war. *See* Malthusianism, Section J.

Manet, Edouard (1832–83), French painter. His impressionist pictures include *Olympia* and *Un bar aux Folies-Bergère* (the latter at the Courtauld).

Mann, Thomas (1875–1955), German writer who won world recognition at the age of 25 with his novel *Buddenbrooks*. His liberal humanistic outlook had developed sufficiently by 1930 for him to expose national socialism. He left Germany in 1933 to live in Switzerland, then settled in the U.S. Other works are *The Magic Mountain*, and the *Joseph* tetralogy. Nobel prizewinner 1929.

Mann, Tom (1856–1941), British Labour leader for more than fifty years.

Manning, Henry Edward (1808–92), English cardinal; archbishop of Westminster 1865–92. He was an Anglican churchman before he entered the church of Rome.

Mansfield, Katherine (Kathleen Beauchamp) (1890–1923), short-story writer, b. Wellington, New Zealand, whose work was influenced by the short stories of Chekhov. Her second husband was John Middleton Murry, literary critic.

Manson, Sir Patrick (1844–1922), Scottish physician, the first to formulate the hypothesis that the malarial parasite was transmitted by the mosquito. His joint work with Sir Ronald Ross rendered habitable vast areas of the earth hitherto closed.

Manuzio, Aldo Pio (1450–1515), Italian printer. founder of the Aldine press in Venice, which for just over a century issued books famed for their beautiful type and bindings.

Manzoni, Alessandro (1785–1873), Italian novelist and poet, b. Milan, whose historical novel *I Promessi Sposi* (The Betrothed) won European reputation.

Mao Tse-tung (1893–1976), Chinese national and Communist leader. B. in Hunan, of rural origin but university training, he understood how to win peasant support for a national and progressive movement. Attacked by Chiang Kai-shek, he led his followers by the "long march" to N.W. China, whence later they issued to defeat both Japanese and Chiang and proclaim a People's Republic in 1949, and later to promote the "great leap forward" of 1958–9 (the commune movement). He stood for an egalitarian democratic society, unbureaucratic, with revolutionary momentum. He was much to the fore in the "cultural revolution" which lasted from 1965 to 1969. See Section C, Part II, and Maoism, Section J.

Marat, Jean Paul (1743–93), French revolution leader, largely responsible for the reign of terror, and assassinated by Charlotte Corday.

Marconi, Guglielmo, Marchese (1874–1937), Italian inventor and electrical engineer who developed the use of radio waves as a practical means of communication. In 1895 he sent long-wave signals over a distance of a mile, and in 1901 received in Newfoundland the first transatlantic signals sent out by his station in Cornwall, thus making the discovery that radio waves can bend around the spherically-shaped earth. Nobel prizewinner 1909.

Marcus Aurelius Antoninus (121–80), Roman emperor and Stoic philosopher of lofty character, whose *Meditations* are still read.

Marcuse, Herbert (b. 1898), political philosopher. B. Berlin, he emigrated to the U.S. during the Nazi regime. A critic of Western industrial society, he sees the international student protest movement as the agent of revolutionary change.

Maria Theresa (1717–80), Empress, daughter of the Hapsburg Charles VI. Able and of strong character, she fought unsuccessfully to save Silesia from Prussian annexation. She promoted reforms in her dominions. She married the Duke of Lorraine and had 16 children.

Marie Antoinette (1755–93), Queen of France, was daughter of the above and wife of Louis XVI; accused of treason, she and her husband were beheaded in the French revolution.

Marie Louise (1791–1847), daughter of Francis I of Austria, became the wife of Napoleon and bore him a son (Napoleon II).

Marius, Caius (157–86 B.C.), Roman general who defended Gaul from invasion; later civil war forced him to flee from Rome, and on his return he took terrible revenge.

Mark Antony. See Antonius, Marcus.

Marlborough, 1st Duke of (John Churchill) (1650–1722), English general, victor of Blenheim, Ramillies, Oudenarde and Malplaquet. His wife, Sarah Jennings, was a favourite of Queen Anne.

Marlowe, Christopher (1564–93), English dramatist and precursor of Shakespeare. His plays include *Dr. Faustus, Tamburlaine the Great, Edward II*, and *The Jew of Malta*. His early death was due to a tavern brawl.

Marryat, Frederick (1792–1848), English author of sea and adventure stories, including *Peter Simple, Mr. Midshipman Easy*, and *Masterman Ready*. He was a captain in the Royal Navy.

Marshall, George Catlett (1880–1959), American general. He was U.S. chief of staff 1939–45, and originated the Marshall Aid plan for European reconstruction. Nobel prize for peace 1953.

Martial, Marcus Valerius (c. 40–104), Roman poet, b. in Spain, remembered for his epigrams.

Marvell, Andrew (1620–78), English poet and political writer. He was Milton's assistant and wrote mainly during the commonwealth.

Marx, Karl (1818–83), German founder of modern international communism, b. Trier of Jewish parentage. He studied law, philosophy and history at the universities of Bonn and Berlin, and later took up the study of economics. In conjunction with his friend Engels he wrote the *Communist Manifesto* of 1848 for the Communist League of which he was the leader. Because of his revolutionary activities he was forced to leave the continent and in 1849 settled in London. Here, mainly while living at 28 Dean Street, Soho, he wrote *Das Kapital*, a deep analysis of the economic laws that govern modern society. In 1864 he helped to found the first International. He ranks as one of the most original and influential thinkers of modern times. He was buried at Highgate cemetery. *See* Marxism, Section J.

Mary I (1516–58), Queen of England, was daughter of Henry VIII and Catherine of Aragon. A Roman Catholic, she reversed the religious changes made by her father and brother, and about 300 Protestants were put to death. She married Philip of Spain.

Mary II (1662–94), Queen of England with her husband the Dutch William III. As daughter of James II, she was invited to succeed after the revolution of 1688 and expelled her father.

Mary Stuart, Queen of Scots (1542–87), daughter of James V of Scotland and Mary of Guise, she laid claim to the English succession. She was imprisoned in England by Elizabeth and beheaded. Her husbands were the dauphin of France (d. 1560), Lord Darnley (murdered 1567) and Bothwell.

Masaryk, Jan Garrigue (1886–1948), Czech diplomat. The son of Thomas, he was Czech minister in London 1925–38, and foreign secretary while his government was in exile in London and after it returned to Prague, 1940–8.

Masaryk, Thomas Garrigue (1850–1937), Czech statesman and independence leader. He was the first president of Czechoslovakia, 1918–35.

Mascagni, Pietro (1863–1945), Italian composer of *Cavalleria Rusticana.*

Masefield, John (1878–1967), English poet. His best-known works are *Salt-Water Ballads* (as a boy he ran away to sea), and *Reynard the Fox.* He became poet laureate in 1930.

Maskelyne, John Nevil (1839–1917), English illusionist. He also exposed spiritualistic frauds.

Massenet, Jules Emile Frédéric (1842–1912), French composer of songs, orchestral suites, oratorios, and operas, among them *Manon* and *Thaïs.*

Massine, Léonide (b. 1896), Russian dancer, one of Diaghilev's choreographers. In 1944 he became a U.S. citizen.

Masters, Edgar Lee (1869–1950), American poet remembered for his *Spoon River Anthology.*

Matisse, Henri (1869–1954), French painter, member of a group known as *Les Fauves* (the wild beasts) for their use of violent colour and colour variation to express form and relief. A number of his paintings are in the Moscow Museum of Western Art.

Matsys (Massys), Quentin (1466–1530), Flemish painter, b. Louvain, settled Antwerp; he worked at a time when Italian influence was gaining ground. His *Money-changer and his Wife* is in the Louvre.

Maugham, William Somerset (1874–1965), British writer, b. Paris. He practised as a doctor till the success of *Liza of Lambeth* (1897), followed by *Of Human Bondage.* He was a master of the short story and his work reflects his travels in the East. In both world wars he served as a British agent.

Maupassant, Guy de (1850–93), French writer whose novels and short stories show penetrating realism. His stories include *Boule de Suif, La Maison Tellier,* and *La Parure* (The Necklace).

Mauriac, François (1885–1970), French writer whose novels deal with moral problems and include *Le Baiser au Lépreux* and the play *Asmodée.* Nobel prizewinner 1952.

Maurois, André (Emile Herzog) (1885–1967), French writer whose works include lives of Shelley and Disraeli.

Maxim, Sir Hiram Stevens (1840–1916), American inventor of the automatic quick-firing gun, perfected in London.

Maxton, James (1885–1946), Scottish Labour politician and pacifist; entered parliament 1922; chairman of I.L.P. 1926–31, 1934–9.

Maxwell, James Clerk (1831–79), Scottish physicist. He wrote his first scientific paper at 15, and after teaching in Aberdeen and London became first Cavendish professor of experimental physics at Cambridge. His mathematical mind, working on the discoveries of Faraday and others, gave physics a celebrated set of equations for the basic laws of electricity and magnetism. His work revolutionised fundamental physics.

Mazarin, Jules (1602–61), cardinal and minister of France was b. in Italy. In spite of opposition from the nobles, he continued Richelieu's work of building up a strong centralised monarchy.

Mazeppa, Ivan Stepanovich (1644–1709), Cossack nobleman, b. Ukraine (then part of Poland, before E. Ukraine passed to Russia, 1667). He fought unsuccessfully for independence allying himself with Charles XII of Sweden against Peter I of Russia (Poltava, 1709). According to legend he was punished for intrigue by being tied to the back of a wild horse and sent into the steppes. Byron wrote a poem about him.

Mazzini, Giuseppe (1805–72), Italian patriot. B. Genoa, he advocated a free and united Italy, and from Marseilles he published a journal, *Young Italy.* Expelled from the Continent, he took refuge in London in 1837. In 1848 he returned to Italy, and became dictator of the short-lived Roman republic, which was put down by French forces. His contribution to Italian unity was that of preparing the way.

Medawar, Sir Peter Brien (b. 1915), British zoologist, author of *The Art of the Soluble* and *The Future of Man;* president of the British Association 1969. Nobel prizewinner 1960.

Medici, Florentine family of merchants and bankers who were politically powerful and who patronised the arts. **Cosimo the Elder** (1389–1464) was for over 30 years virtual ruler of Florence. His grandson, **Lorenzo the Magnificent** (1449–92), poet, friend of artists and scholars, governed with munificence. His grandson, **Lorenzo,** was father of **Catherine de' Medici,** Queen of France (q.v.). A later **Cosimo** (1519–74) was an able Duke of Florence and then Grand-Duke of Tuscany, which title the Medicis held until 1737.

Méhul, Etienne Nicolas (1763–1817), French operatic composer. *Joseph* is his masterpiece.

Meitner, Lise (1878–1969), co-worker of Otto Hahn (q.v.) who interpreted his results (1939) as a fission process. A Jewish refugee scientist from Germany, she became a Swedish citizen in 1949.

Melanchthon, Philip (1497–1560), German religious reformer, who assisted Luther, and wrote the first Protestant theological work, *Loci communes.* He drew up the Augsburg confession (1530).

Melba, Nellie (Helen Porter Mitchell) (1861–1931), Australian soprano of international repute. b. near Melbourne.

Melbourne, 2nd Viscount (William Lamb) (1779–1848), English Whig statesman, was premier at the accession of Queen Victoria.

Mendel, Gregor Johann (1822–84), Austrian botanist. After entering the Augustinian monastery at Brünn he became abbot and taught natural history in the school. His main interest was the study of inheritance, and his elaborate observations of the common garden pea resulted in the law of heredity which bears his name. His hypothesis was published in 1866 but no attention was given to it until 1900. *See* Section F, Part IV.

Mendeleyev, Dmitri Ivanovich (1834–1907), Russian chemist, first to discover the critical temperatures. He formulated the periodic law of atomic weights (1869) and drew up the periodic table (*see* Section F), predicting the properties of elements which might fill the gaps. Element 101 is named after him.

Mendelssohn-Bartholdy, Felix (1809–47), German composer, grandson of Moses Mendelssohn, philosopher. He belongs with Chopin and Schumann to the early 19th cent. classic-romantic school, and his music has delicacy and melodic beauty. He was conductor of the Gewandhaus concerts at Leipzig for a time and often visited England. *See* Section E.

Mendès-France, Pierre (b. 1907), French politician, premier 1954–5, but defeated on his North African policy. He was a critic of de Gaulle.

Menuhin, Yehudi (b. 1916), American violinist, b. New York of Russian Jewish parentage. He first appeared as soloist at the age of seven and has international repute. Founded a School for musically gifted children.

Menzies, Sir Robert Gordon (1894–1978), Australian Liberal statesman, premier 1939–41, 1949–66.

Mercator, Gerhardus (Gerhard Kremer) (1512–94),

Flemish geographer who pioneered the making of accurate navigational maps. He worked out the map which bears his name in which meridians and parallels of latitude cross each other at right angles, enabling compass bearings to be drawn as straight lines.

Meredith, George (1828–1909), English writer, b. Portsmouth. His novels include *The Ordeal of Richard Feverel, The Egoist, Evan Harrington, Diana of the Crossways*, and *The Amazing Marriage*. His poetry has had renewed attention; the main works are *Modern Love* and *Poems and Lyrics of the Joy of Earth*.

Mesmer, Friedrich Anton (1733–1815), Austrian founder of mesmerism, or animal magnetism. See Mesmerism, Section J.

Mestrovic, Ivan (1883–1962), Yugoslav sculptor of international repute. He designed the temple at Kossovo. He later lived in England, and examples of his work are in London museums.

Metastasio, Pietro (Pietro Bonaventura Trapassi) (1698–1782), Italian librettist who lived in Vienna and provided texts for Gluck, Handel, Haydn, and Mozart.

Mechnikov, Ilya (1845–1916), Russian biologist who discovered that by " phagocytosis " certain white blood cells are capable of ingesting harmful substances such as bacteria (*see* Diseases of the Blood, Section P). For his work on immunity he shared the 1908 Nobel prize for medicine.

Michelangelo (Michelagniolo Buonarroti) (1475–1564), Italian painter, sculptor and poet. Of a poor but genteel Tuscan family, his first interest in sculpture came through his nurse, wife of a stone-cutter. He was apprenticed to Domenico Ghirlandaio. Like Leonardo, he studied anatomy, but instead of spreading his talents over a wide field, he became obsessed with the problem of how to represent the human body. In him, classical idealism, mediaeval religious belief, and renaissance energy met. Perhaps his most impressive work is the ceiling of the Sistine Chapel (a surface of about 6,000 square feet), the *Last Judgement* behind the chapel altar, his marble *Pietà* (St. Peter's), the statue of *David* (Academy, Florence), the great figure of *Moses* (San Pietro in Vincoli, Rome), and the four allegorical figures *Day, Night, Dawn, Twilight* (intended for the tombs of the Medici family at San Lorenzo, Florence).

Michelet, Jules (1798–1874), French historian who wrote a history of France in 24 vols. and of the revolution in 7 vols.

Michelson, Albert Abraham (1852–1931), American physicist, b. Poland. He collaborated with E. W. Morley in an experiment to determine ether drift, the negative result of which was important for Einstein. Nobel prizewinner 1907.

Mickiewicz, Adam (1798–1855), Polish revolutionary poet, author of *The Ancestors* and *Pan Tadeusz*.

Mill, John Stuart (1806–73), English philosopher. A member of Bentham's utilitarian school, he later modified some of its tenets. His main work is *On Liberty*, which advocates social as well as political freedom and warns against the tyranny of the majority. *The Subjection of Women* supported women's rights. He also wrote *Principles of Political Economy*. He was godfather to Bertrand Russell.

Millais, Sir John Everett (1829–96), English artist, b. Southampton; in his earlier years a pre-Raphaelite (*Ophelia*). Later works include *The Boyhood of Raleigh* and *Bubbles*. He married Mrs. Ruskin after the annulment of her marriage.

Millet, Jean François (1814–75), French painter of rural life, sometimes in sombre mood; his works include *The Angelus*.

Millikan, Robert Andrews (1868–1954), American physicist, who determined the charge on the electron and discovered cosmic rays. Nobel prizewinner 1923.

Milne, Alan Alexander (1882–1956), English humorist and poet whose work for children is still widely read.

Milner, 1st Viscount (Alfred Milner) (1854–1925), British administrator, especially in South Africa; author of *England in Egypt*.

Miltiades (d. 489 B.C.), one of the leaders of the Athenian army against the Persians at Marathon.

Milton, John (1608–74), English poet, author of *Paradise Lost*. B. in London, he wrote while still at Cambridge *L'Allegro, Il Penseroso, Comus*, and *Lycidas*. The Civil War diverted his energies for years to the parliamentary and political struggle, but during this period he defended in *Areopagitica* the freedom of the press. After he had become blind he wrote *Paradise Lost* and a sonnet *On His Blindness*.

Minot, George Richards (1885–1950), who with W. P. Murphy discovered the curative properties of liver in pernicious anaemia. Shared Nobel prize 1934.

Mirabeau, Gabriel, Honoré Victor Riquetti, Comte de (1749–91), French revolutionary leader. His writings and speeches contributed to the revolution of 1789.

Mistral, Frédéric (1830–1914), French poet, and founder of a Provençal renaissance. His works include *Lou Trésor dóu Félibrige* and a Provençal dictionary. Nobel prizewinner 1904.

Mithridates (c. 132–63 B.C.), King of Pontus, in Asia Minor; after early successes against the Romans was defeated by Pompey.

Modigliani, Amedeo (1884–1920), Italian painter and sculptor, b. Livorno. His portraits and figure studies tend to elongation and simplification. He lived mainly in Paris, in poverty, illness and disillusionment.

Moffat, James (1870–1944), Scottish divine who translated the Bible into modern English.

Mohammed (570–632), the founder of Islam, the religion of the Moslems, fled from Mecca to Medina in 622, from which date the Mohammedan era opens. By his constant preaching and proclaiming of the one and only deity Allah, he gathered round him a small and loyal, hard-fighting band of followers and was able to return to Mecca eight years later, an acknowledged conqueror. The sacred book of Islam, the *Koran*—though presented by him as an original revelation from the angel Gabriel—may in the main be traced to biblical and rabbinical sources. *See* Islam, Section J.

Molière (Jean Baptiste Poquelin) (1622–73), French playwright. B. in Paris, he gained experience as a strolling player, and subsequently in Paris, partly in the king's service, he wrote an unsurpassed series of plays varying from farce as in *Les Précieuses ridicules* to high comedy. Among his plays are *Tartuffe, Le Misanthrope, Le Bourgeois gentilhomme, Le Malade imaginaire*, and *Le Médécin malgré lui*.

Molotov, Vyacheslav Mikhailovich (b. 1890), Russian diplomat. He succeeded Litvinov as commissar for foreign affairs, 1939–49, and was chief representative of the Soviet Union at numerous post-war conferences. Expelled from the Communist Party 1964. He changed his name from Scriabin to Molotov (the hammer) early in his career to escape the imperial police.

Moltke, Helmuth, Count von (1800–91), Prussian general and chief of staff (1858–88) during the period when Prussia used success in three wars to unite Germany.

Mond, Ludwig (1838–1909), German chemist who in 1867 settled in England as an alkali manufacturer and in partnership with John Brunner successfully manufactured soda by the Solvay process.

Monet, Claude (1840–1926), French painter, leader of the Impressionists, the term being derived in 1874 from his landscape *Impression soleil levant*. He liked painting a subject in the open air at different times of day to show variation in light.

Monier-Williams, Sir Monier (1819–99), English Sanskrit scholar whose works include grammars, dictionaries, and editions of the *Sákuntalá*.

Monk, George, 1st Duke of Albemarle (1608–69), English general and admiral, whose reputation and moderation were mainly responsible for the return of Charles II in 1660.

Monmouth, Duke of (James Scott) (1649–85), English pretender, natural son of Charles II; centre of anti-Catholic feeling against succession of Duke of York (later James II). His troops, mostly peasants, were routed at Sedgemoor (1685) by John Churchill (later Duke of Marlborough). Beheaded on Tower Hill.

Monnet, Jean (b. 1888), French political economist, " father of the Common Market." He drafted the Monnet plan for French economic recovery (1947) and the plan for the establishment of the European Coal and Steel Community, of which he was president 1952–5.

Monroe, James (1758-1831), president of the U.S. He negotiated the purchase of Louisiana from France in 1803, and propounded the doctrine that the American continent should not be colonised by a European power. (At that time however the U.S. could not have enforced it.)

Montagu, Lady Mary Wortley (1689-1762), English writer. From Constantinople where her husband was ambassador she wrote *Letters* of which a complete edition was published 1965-7. She introduced England to the idea of inoculation against smallpox.

Montaigne, Michel de (1533-92), French essayist of enquiring, sceptical, and tolerant mind.

Montcalm, Louis Joseph, Marquis de (1712-59), French general, who unsuccessfully commanded the French at Quebec against Wolfe.

Montesquieu, Charles de Secondat, Baron de la Brède et de (1689-1755), French philosopher. His works include *Lettres persanes*, a satire on contemporary life; and *L'Esprit des Lois*, giving his political philosophy. The latter was based largely, but to some extent mistakenly, on English practice, and its influence led the U.S. constitution to separate the executive (President) from the legislature (Congress).

Montessori, Maria (1860-1952), Italian educationist, who developed an educational system based on spontaneity.

Monteverdi, Claudio (1567-1643), Italian composer who pioneered in opera. His chief dramatic work is *Orfeo* (1608). *See* Section E.

Montezuma II (1466-1520), last emperor of Mexico when the Spanish under Cortes invaded.

Montfort, Simon de, Earl of Leicester (*c.* 1208-65), English statesman. He led the barons in revolt against the ineffective rule of Henry III, but he differed from other rebels in that he summoned a parliamentary assembly to which for the first time representatives came from the towns. He was killed at Evesham.

Montgolfier, the name of two brothers, Joseph Michel (1740-1810) and Jacques Etienne (1745-99), French aeronauts who constructed the first practical balloon, which flew 6 miles.

Montgomery of Alamein, 1st Viscount (Bernard Law Montgomery) (1887-1976), British fieldmarshal; commanded 8th Army in North Africa, Sicily, and Italy, 1942-4; commanderin-chief, British Group of Armies and Allied Armies in Northern France, 1944. He served as Deputy Supreme Allied Commander Europe (NATO), 1951-8. His memoirs were published in 1958.

Montrose, Marquess of (James Graham) (1612-50), Scottish general. In the Civil War he raised the Highland clansmen for Charles I and won the battles of Tippermuir, Inverlochy, and Kilsyth; but was finally defeated and executed. He was also a poet.

Moody, Dwight Lyman (1837-99), American revivalist preacher, associated with Ira D. Sankey, the "American singing pilgrim."

Moore, George (1852-1933), Irish novelist, author of *Confessions of a Young Man, Esther Waters,* and *Evelyn Innes.*

Moore, Henry (b. 1898), English sculptor in semiabstract style, son of a Yorkshire coalminer. Examples of his work are to be seen in the Tate Gallery, St. Matthew's Church, Northampton, the Unesco building in Paris, and on an outside site opposite the House of Lords. O.M. 1963.

Moore, Sir John (1761-1809), British general, who trained the infantry for the Spanish Peninsular campaigns and conducted a brilliant retreat to Corunna, where he was mortally wounded after defeating the French under Soult.

Moore, Thomas (1779-1852), Irish poet, author of *Irish Melodies, Lalla Rookh* (oriental stories), and *The Epicurean* (novel). He also wrote a life of Byron.

More, Sir Thomas (1478-1535), English writer and statesman. In 1529 he succeeded Wolsey as lord chancellor, but on his refusal to recognise Henry VIII as head of the church he was executed. His *Utopia* describes an ideal state. He was canonised 1935.

Morgan, Sir Henry (*c.* 1635-88), Welsh buccaneer who operated in the Caribbean against the Spaniards, capturing and plundering Panama in 1671. Knighted by Charles II and made deputy-governor of Jamaica.

Morgan, John Pierpont (1837-1913), American

financier who built the family fortunes into a vast industrial empire.

Morland, George (1763-1804), English painter of rural life. His *Inside of a Stable* is in the National Gallery

Morley, 1st Viscount (John Morley) (1838-1923), English biographer and Liberal politician. He held political office, but is mainly remembered for his life of Gladstone. He also wrote on Voltaire, Rousseau. Burke, and Cobden.

Morley, Thomas (*c.* 1557-1603), English composer of madrigals, noted also for his settings of some of Shakespeare's songs. He was a pupil of Byrd, organist of St. Paul's cathedral, and wrote *Plaine and Easie Introduction to Practicall Music* (1597) which was used for 200 years.

Morris, William (1834-96), English poet and craftsman. His hatred of 19th-cent. ugliness, his belief in human equality, and in freedom and happiness for all, combined to make him a socialist, and he accomplished much for the improvement of domestic decoration. He was a popular lecturer, founded the Socialist League and the Kelmscott Press.

Morrison of Lambeth, Baron (Herbert Morrison) (1888-1965), British Labour statesman. From being an errand-boy, he rose to become leader of the London County Council. During the war he was Home Secretary, and he was deputy prime minister in a period of notable legislation, 1945-51.

Morse, Samuel Finley Breese (1791-1872), American pioneer in electromagnetic telegraphy and inventor of the dot-and-dash code that bears his name. He was originally an artist.

Mountbatten of Burma, 1st Earl (Louis Mountbatten) (b. 1900), British admiral and statesman. In the second world war he became chief of combined operations in 1942. As last viceroy of India, he carried through the transfer of power to Indian hands in 1947 and was the first governor-general of the dominion. He became first sea lord in 1955 and was chief of defence staff 1959-65.

Mozart, Wolfgang Amadeus (1756-91), Austrian composer. B. Salzburg, he began his career at four and toured Europe at six. In 1781 he settled in Vienna, where he became a friend of Haydn and where his best music was written. His genius lies in the effortless outpouring of all forms of music, in the ever-flowing melodies, in the consistent beauty and symmetry of his compositions, and in the exactness of his method. Among the loveliest and grandest works in instrumental music are his three great symphonies in E flat, G minor, and C (called the "Jupiter"), all written in six weeks in 1788. Three of the greatest operas in musical history are his *Marriage of Figaro* (1786), *Don Giovanni* (1787), and *The Magic Flute* (1791). His last composition, written under the shadow of death, was the *Requiem Mass*, a work of tragic beauty. *See* Section E.

Müller, Sir Ferdinand (1825-96), German-born botanist who emigrated to Australia, where he was director of the Melbourne Botanical Gardens, 1857-73, and whence he introduced the eucalyptus into Europe.

Mumford, Lewis (b. 1895), American writer on town-planning and social problems. His works include a tetralogy: *Technics and Civilisation, The Culture of Cities, The Condition of Man,* and *The Conduct of Life; The Myth of the Machine,* and *The Urban Prospect.*

Munkacsy, Michael von (1844-1900), Hungarian painter of historical subjects.

Munnings, Sir Alfred (1878-1959), English painter, especially of horses and sporting subjects.

Murdock, William (1754-1839), Scottish engineer and inventor, the first to make practical use of coal gas as an illuminating agent (introduced at the Soho works, Birmingham, 1800).

Murillo, Bartolomé Esteban (1617-82), Spanish painter, b. Seville, where he founded an Academy. His early works, such as *Two Peasant Boys* (Dulwich) show peasant and street life; his later paintings are religious, *e.g.,* the *Immaculate Conception* in the Prado.

Murray, Gilbert (1866-1957), classical scholar of Australian birth who settled in England. A teacher of Greek at the universities of Glasgow and Oxford, he translated Greek drama so as to bring it within the reach of the general public. His interest in the classics was begun by an English master's enthusiasm at his country school at Mittagong, New South Wales. He was a strong supporter of the League of Nations and the United Nations.

Mussolini, Benito (1883–1945), Fascist dictator of Italy 1922–43. From 1935 an aggressive foreign policy (Abyssinia and Spain) was at first successful, and in June 1940 he entered the war on the side of Hitler. Defeat in North Africa and the invasion of Sicily caused the collapse of his government. He was shot dead by partisans while attempting to escape to Switzerland.

Mussorgsky, Modest Petrovich (1839–81), Russian composer whose masterpiece is the opera *Boris Godunov* after the play by Pushkin. His piano suite *Pictures at an Exhibition* was orchestrated by Ravel. *See* Section E.

N

Nanak (1469–1538), Indian guru or teacher, who tried to put an end to religious strife, teaching that "God is one, whether he be Allah or Rama." His followers are the Sikhs. *See* Sikhism, Section J.

Nansen, Fridtjof (1861–1930), Norwegian explorer. In 1893 his north polar expedition reached the highest latitude till then attained—86° 14′. He published an account called *Farthest North*. He was active in Russian famine relief, 1921. Nobel peace prize 1922.

Napier, John (1550–1617), Scottish mathematician, b. Edinburgh, invented logarithms (published 1614) and the modern notation of fractions, improvements in the methods of mathematical expression which helped to advance cosmology and physics.

Napoleon I (Bonaparte) (1769–1821), French emperor and general, of Corsican birth (Ajaccio). Trained in French military schools, he became prominent in the early years of the revolution, with uncertainty at home and war abroad. In 1796 he became commander of the army in Italy and defeated the Austrians, so that France obtained control of Lombardy. He then led an expedition to Egypt but Nelson destroyed his fleet. After further Italian victories, he made a *coup d'état* in 1799, and in 1804 became emperor. Against continuing European opposition, he defeated the Austrians at Austerlitz, and his power in Europe was such that he made his brothers Joseph, Louis, and Jerome kings of Naples, Holland, and Westphalia; but in Spain he provoked the Peninsular War, and his armies were gradually driven back by the Spanish, helped by Wellington; while his invasion of Russia in 1812 ended in a disastrous retreat from Moscow; and in 1814 the Allies forced him to abdicate and retire to Elba. He emerged again in 1815 to be defeated at Waterloo and exiled to St. Helena. His government at home was firm and promoted some reforms (*e.g.*, legal codification), but the country was weakened by his wars. In Europe, in spite of the suffering caused by war, there was some spread of French revolutionary ideas, and equally a reaction against them on the part of authority. The imperial idea lingered in France, and Napoleon's remains were brought to Paris in 1840. He married first Josephine Beauharnais and second Marie Louise of Austria.

Napoleon II (1811–32), son of Napoleon I and Marie Louise.

Napoleon III (1808–73), son of Napoleon I's brother Louis. He returned to France in the revolution of 1848, and in 1851 came to power by a *coup d'état*. In his reign Paris was remodelled. His foreign policy was adventurous (the Crimean war, intervention in Mexico, war against Austria and Italy); but when he was manoeuvred by Bismarck into the Franco-Prussian war and defeated at Sedan he lost his throne and retired to England. His wife was the Spanish Eugénie de Montijo.

Nash, John (1752–1835), English architect who planned Regent Street, laid out Regent's Park, enlarged Buckingham Palace, and designed Marble Arch and the Brighton Pavilion.

Nash, Paul (1889–1946), English painter and designer, official war artist in both world wars. Best-known pictures are *The Menin Road* of 1918 and *Totes Meer* of 1941.

Nash, Walter (1882–1968), New Zealand Labour politician; prime minister 1957–60.

Nasmyth, James (1808–90), Scottish inventor of the steam-hammer, which became indispensable in all large iron and engineering works.

Nasser, Gamal Abdel (1918–70), leader of modern Egypt and of the Arab world. He led the 1952 army coup that deposed King Farouk, becoming president of the first Egyptian Republic in 1956 and of the United Arab Republic in 1958. His nationalisation of the Suez Canal in 1956 precipitated a short-lived attack by Britain and France. Israeli–Arab hostility led to the June war of 1967. He carried out reforms to bring his people out of feudal backwardness, including the building (with Russian help and finance) of the Aswan High Dam.

Needham, Joseph (b. 1900), British biochemist, historian of science, orientalist, author of the monumental work of scholarship *Science and Civilisation in China* (7 vols., 1954–).

Nehru, Pandit Jawaharlal (1889–1964), Indian national leader and statesman, first prime minister and minister of foreign affairs when India became independent in 1947. He studied at Harrow and Cambridge, and was for many years a leading member of the Congress Party, during which time he was frequently imprisoned for political activity. He played a part in the final negotiations for independence. Under his leadership India made technical, industrial, and social advances. In world affairs his influence was for peace and non-alignment. His daughter Indira became India's first woman prime minister in 1966.

Nelson, 1st Viscount (Horatio Nelson) (1758–1805), English admiral. Son of a Norfolk clergyman, he went to sea at 12 and became a captain in 1793. In the French revolutionary wars he lost his right eye in 1794 and his right arm in 1797. Rear-admiral in 1797, he defeated the French at Aboukir Bay in 1798. He was also at the bombardment of Copenhagen in 1801. In 1805 he destroyed the French fleet at Trafalgar, in which battle he was killed. His daring and decision made him a notable commander. He loved Emma Hamilton.

Nenni, Pietro (b. 1891), Italian socialist politician. He became secretary-general of his party in 1944, and was deputy prime minister, 1963–8.

Nernst, Walther Hermann (1864–1941), German scientist who established the third law of thermodynamics that dealt with the behaviour of matter at temperatures approaching absolute zero. Nobel prizewinner 1920.

Nero, Claudius Caesar (A.D. 37–68), Roman emperor, the adopted son of Claudius. He was weak and licentious and persecuted Christians. In his reign occurred the fire of Rome.

Newcomen, Thomas (1663–1729), English inventor, one of the first to put a steam-engine into practical operation. In 1705 he patented his invention, which was the pumping-engine used in Cornish mines until the adoption of Watt's engine.

Newman, Ernest (1868–1959), English music critic, whose chief work is the *Life of Richard Wagner*.

Newman, John Henry (1801–90), English priest and writer, who became a cardinal of the Roman church in 1879, and was a founder of the Oxford Movement. He is best remembered by his *Apologia pro Vita Sua* in which he described the development of his religious thought. He wrote *Lead, kindly Light*, set to music 30 years later by J. B. Dykes, and *The Dream of Gerontius*, set to music of Elgar. *See* J52.

Newton, Sir Isaac (1642–1727), English scientist, b. Woolsthorpe, Lincs. (the year Galileo died). He studied at Cambridge but was at home during the plague years 1665 and 1666 when he busied himself with problems concerned with optics and gravitation. Through his tutor Isaac Barrow he was appointed to the Lucasian chair of mathematics at Cambridge in 1669 and remained there until 1696 when he was appointed Warden, and later Master of the Mint. He was a secret Unitarian and did not marry. His three great discoveries were to show that white light could be separated into a sequence of coloured components forming the visible spectrum; to use the calculus (invented by him independently of Leibnitz) to investigate the forces of nature in a quantitative way; and to show by his theory of gravitation (for which Copernicus, Kepler and Galileo had prepared the way) that the universe was regulated by simple mathematical laws. His vision was set forth in the *Philosophiae Naturalis Principia Mathematica* of 1687, usually called the *Principia*. It was not until 200 years later that Einstein showed there could be another theory of celestial mechanics.

Ney, Michel (1769–1815), French general who served under Napoleon, especially at Jena, Borodino, and Waterloo.

Nicholas II (1868–1918), last emperor and Tsar of Russia, son of Alexander III. His reign was marked by an unsuccessful war with Japan (1904–5), and by the 1914–18 war. Ineffective and lacking ability, he set up a Duma in 1906 too late for real reform. Revolution broke out in 1917 and he and his family were shot in July 1918.

Nicholson, Sir William (1872–1949), English artist known for his portraits and woodcuts. His son, **Ben Nicholson, O.M.,** (b. 1894) is noted for his abstract paintings.

Nicolson, Sir Harold (1886–1968), English diplomat, author, and critic. His works include *King George V*; and *Diaries and Letters*. His wife was the novelist Victoria Sackville-West (1892–1962).

Niemöller, Martin (b. 1892), German Lutheran pastor who opposed the Nazi regime and was confined in a concentration camp. He was president of the World Council of Churches in 1961.

Nietzsche, Friedrich Wilhelm (1844–1900), German philosopher, in his younger years influenced by Wagner and Schopenhauer. His teaching that only the strong ought to survive and his doctrine of the superman are expounded in *Thus spake Zarathustra, Beyond Good and Evil,* and *The Will to Power.*

Nightingale, Florence (1820–1910), English nurse and pioneer of hospital reform, who during the Crimean war organised in face of considerable official opposition a nursing service to relieve the sufferings of the British soldiers, who called her " the lady with the lamp." Her system was adopted and developed in all parts of the world.

Nijinsky, Vaslav (1892–1950), Russian dancer, one of the company which included Pavlova, Karsavina and Fokine, brought by Diaghilev to Paris and London before the 1914–18 war. In *Les Sylphides, Spectre de la Rose* and *L'Après-midi d'un Faune* he won a supreme place among male dancers.

Nikisch, Arthur (1855–1922), Hungarian conductor of the Boston Symphony Orchestra, 1889–93. He was piano-accompanist to the Lieder singer, Elena Gerhardt.

Nimitz, Chester William (1885–1966), American admiral, commanded in the Pacific 1941–5; chief of naval operations 1945–7.

Nixon, Richard Milhous (b. 1913), Republican president (for two terms) of the U.S., 1969–74. In foreign affairs he negotiated the withdrawal of American troops from S. Vietnam and began a process of reconciliation with China and détente with the Soviet Union. But at home the Watergate conspiracies brought disgrace and an end to his presidency. His resignation in August 1974 rendered the impeachment process unnecessary; he accepted the pardon offered by his successor, President Ford. *See* The United States, Section C, Part II.

Nkrumah, Kwame (1909–72), Ghanaian leader, first premier of Ghana when his country achieved independence in 1957 and president in 1960. His government was spectacular and he promoted the Pan-African movement; but unsound finance and dictatorial methods led to his overthrow in 1966.

Nobel, Alfred Bernhard (1833–96), Swedish inventor and philanthropist. An engineer and chemist who discovered dynamite, he amassed a fortune from the manufacture of explosives; and bequeathed a fund for annual prizes to those who had contributed most to the benefit of mankind in the fields of physics, chemistry, medicine, literature and peace. *See* **L126–8.**

North, Frederick (1732–92), favourite minister of George III who held the premiership from 1770

to 1782. (He held the courtesy title of Lord North from 1752.) His incompetent foreign policy led to the American war of independence.

Northcliffe, 1st Viscount (Alfred Charles Harmsworth) (1865–1922), British journalist and newspaper proprietor, b. near Dublin. He began *Answers* in 1888 with his brother Harold, (later Lord Rothermere). In 1894 they bought the *Evening News,* and in 1896 the *Daily Mail.* In 1908 he took over *The Times.*

Northumberland, John Dudley, Duke of (1502–53), English politician who attempted to secure for his daughter-in-law Lady Jane Grey the succession to the throne after Edward VI.

Nostradamus or Michel de Notre Dame (1503–66), French astrologer and physician, known for his prophecies in *Centuries.*

Novalis, the pseudonym of Baron Friedrich von Hardenberg (1772–1801), German romantic poet and novelist, whose chief work is the unfinished *Heinrich von Ofterdingen.*

Nuffield, 1st Viscount (William Richard Morris) (1877–1963), British motor-car manufacturer and philanthropist, and until he retired in 1952 chairman of Morris Motors Ltd. He provided large sums for the advancement of medicine in the university of Oxford, for Nuffield College, and in 1943 established the Nuffield Foundation, endowing it with £10 million.

Nyerere, Julius (b. 1922), Tanzanian leader. He became first premier of Tanganyika when it became independent in 1961 and president in 1962. In 1964 he negotiated its union with Zanzibar.

O

Oates, Lawrence Edward (1880–1912), English antarctic explorer. He joined Scott's expedition of 1910, and was one of the five to reach the south pole; but on the return journey, being crippled by frost-bite, he walked out into the blizzard to die.

Oates, Titus (1649–1705), English informer and agitator against Roman catholics.

O'Casey, Sean (1884–1964), Irish dramatist whose plays include *Juno and the Paycock, The Silver Tassie, Red Roses for Me,* and *Oak Leaves and Lavender.*

Occam (Ockham), William of (c. 1270–1349), English scholar and philosopher and one of the most original thinkers of all time. He belonged to the Order of Franciscans, violently opposed the temporal power of the Pope, espoused the cause of nominalism and laid the foundations of modern theories of government and theological scepticism. *See* Occam's razor, Section J.

O'Connell, Daniel (1775–1847), Irish national leader. A barrister, he formed the Catholic Association in 1823 to fight elections; his followers aimed at the repeal of the Act of Union with England, and formed a Repeal Association in 1840; but the formation of the Young Ireland party, the potato famine, and ill-health undermined his position and he died in exile.

O'Connor, Feargus (1794–1855), working-class leader in England, of Irish birth. He presented the Chartist petition in 1848.

O'Connor, Thomas Power (1848–1929), Irish nationalist and journalist, sat in parliament 1880–1929 and founded the *Star.*

Oersted, Hans Christian (1777–1851), Danish physicist who discovered the connection between electricity and magnetism.

Offa (d. 796), king of Mercia (mid-England), was the leading English king of his day, and built a defensive dyke from the Dee to the Wye.

Offenbach, Jacques (1819–80), German–Jewish composer, b. Cologne, settled at Paris, and is mainly known for his light operas, especially *Tales of Hoffmann.*

Ohm, Georg Simon (1787–1854), German physicist, professor at Munich, who in 1826 formulated the law of electric current, known as Ohm's law, one of the foundation stones in electrical science. *See* Section L.

Olivier, Baron (Laurence Kerr Olivier) (b. 1907), British actor and director, especially in Shakespearean roles. He has also produced, directed, and played in films, including *Henry V, Hamlet,* and *Richard III*, and in television drama. In 1962 he was appointed director of the National Theatre (*see* Section I, Part II), and in 1970 received a life peerage.

Oman, Sir Charles William (1860–1946), English historian, especially of mediaeval warfare and of the Peninsular War. He also wrote memoirs.

Omar ibn al Khattab (581–644), adviser to Mahomet, succeeded Abu Bakr as 2nd caliph. In his reign Islam became an imperial power. He died at the hands of a foreign slave.

Omar Khayyám (*c.* 1050–1123), Persian poet and mathematician, called Khayyám (tent-maker) because of his father's occupation. His fame as a scientist has been eclipsed by his *Rubaiyat*, made known to English readers by Edward FitzGerald in 1859.

O'Neill, Eugene Gladstone (1888–1953), American playwright who, after spending his adventurous youth in sailing, gold-prospecting, and journalism, first won success in 1914 with the one-act play, *Thirst*. His later plays include *Anna Christie*, *Strange Interlude*, *Mourning Becomes Electra*, *The Iceman Cometh*. Nobel prizewinner 1936. *See also* Section I.

Orchardson, Sir William Quiller (1835–1910), Scottish painter, b. Edinburgh, best known for his *Napoleon I on board H.M.S. Bellerophon* and *Ophelia*.

Origen (*c.* 185–254), Christian philosopher and Biblical scholar, who taught at Alexandria and Caesarea, and was imprisoned and tortured in the persecution of Decius, 250. He drew on Greek philosophy as well as on the Hebrew scriptures in his exposition of Christian doctrine.

Orpen, Sir William (1878–1931), British painter of portraits, conversation pieces, and pictures of the 1914–18 war.

Ortega y Gasset, José (1883–1955), Spanish philosopher and essayist, known for his *Tema de Nuestro Tiempo* and *La Rebelión de Las Masas*.

Orwell, George (Eric Arthur Blair) (1903–50), English satirist, b. India, author of *Animal Farm* and *Nineteen Eighty-Four*.

Osler, Sir William (1849–1919), Canadian physician and medical historian, authority on diseases of the blood and spleen.

Ossietzky, Carl von (1889–1938), German pacifist leader after the first world war; sent by Hitler to a concentration camp. Nobel peace prize 1935.

Oswald, St. (*c.* 605–42), won the Northumbrian throne by battle in 633 and introduced Christianity there.

Otto I (the Great) (912–73), founder of the Holy Roman Empire (he was crowned king of the Germans in 936 and emperor at Rome in 962). The son of Henry I of Germany, he built up a strong position in Italy (as regards the papacy) and in Germany where he established the East Mark (Austria).

Otto, Nikolaus August (1832–91), German engineer who built a gas engine (1878) using the four-stroke cycle that bears his name.

Ouida (Maria Louise Ramé) (1939–1908), English novelist of French extraction, whose romantic stories include *Under Two Flags*.

Ovid (43 B.C.–A.D. 18), Latin poet (Publius Ovidius Naso), chiefly remembered for his *Art of Love* and *Metamorphoses*. He died in exile.

Owen, Robert (1771–1858), Welsh pioneer socialist, b. Montgomeryshire. As manager, and later owner, of New Lanark cotton mills he tried to put his philanthropic views into effect; other communities on co-operative lines were founded in Hampshire and in America (New Harmony, Indiana) but although unsuccessful they were influential in many directions. He challenged the doctrine of *laissez-faire*, inaugurated socialism and the co-operative movement, and foresaw the problems of industrial development.

P

Pachmann, Vladimir de (1848–1933), Russian pianist gifted in the playing of Chopin.

Paderewski, Ignace Jan (1860–1941), Polish pianist and nationalist. He represented his country at Versailles and was the first premier of a reconstituted Poland. He died in exile in the second world war.

Paganini, Niccolo (1782–1840), Italian violinist and virtuoso who revolutionised violin technique.

Paine, Thomas (1737–1809), English-born radical political writer, champion of agrarian reform. He spent the years 1774–87 in America helping the American revolutionary cause. On his return to England he wrote *The Rights of Man*, was condemned for treason, and had to flee to France. There he entered French politics, was sent to prison, and wrote *The Age of Reason*, advocating deism. His last years were spent in poverty in America.

Palestrina, Giovanni Pierluigi da (*c.* 1525–94), Italian composer of unaccompanied church music and madrigals. *See* Section E.

Palgrave, Sir Francis (1788–1861), English historian and archivist, an early editor of record series. His son Francis Turner Palgrave (1824–97) was a poet and critic and edited *The Golden Treasury*; while another son, William Gifford Palgrave (1826–88) was a traveller and diplomat.

Palissy, Bernard (*c.* 1510–89), French potter who discovered the art of producing white enamel, after which he set up a porcelain factory in Paris which was patronised by royalty.

Palladio, Andrea (1508–80), Italian architect, b. Padua, whose style was modelled on ancient Roman architecture (symmetrical planning and harmonic proportions) and had wide influence; author of *I Quattro Libri dell' Architettura*.

Palmer, Samuel (1805–81), English landscape painter and etcher, follower of Blake whom he met in 1824. *Bright Cloud* and *In a Shoreham Garden* are in the Victoria and Albert Museum.

Palmerston, 3rd Viscount (Henry John Temple) (1784–1865), English Whig statesman. At first a Tory, he was later Whig foreign secretary for many years, and prime minister 1855 and 1859–65. His vigorous foreign policy wherever possible took the lead and bluntly asserted English rights.

Pancras, St. (d. 304), patron saint of children, was (according to tradition) baptised in Rome where he was put to death at the age of fourteen in the persecution under Diocletian.

Pandit, Vijaya Lakshmi (b. 1900), sister of Nehru, was India's first ambassador to the Soviet Union (1947–9), and to the U.S. (1949–51), and the first woman to be elected president of the U.N. General Assembly (1954).

Panizzi, Sir Anthony (1797–1879), Italian bibliographer and nationalist. Taking refuge in England after 1821, he became in 1856 chief librarian of the British Museum, undertook a new catalogue and designed the reading room.

Pankhurst, Emmeline (1858–1928), English suffragette who, with her daughters Christabel and Sylvia, worked for women's suffrage, organising the Women's Social and Political Union.

Papin, Denis (1647–1714), French physicist and inventor. He invented the condensing pump, and was a pioneer in the development of the steam-engine. Not being a mechanic, he made all his experiments by means of models.

Paracelsus (Theophrastus Bombastus von Hohenheim) (1493–1541), Swiss physician whose speculations though muddled served to reform medical thought. He criticised the established authorities, Galen and Aristotle, and experimented and made new chemical compounds. His earliest printed work was *Practica* (1529).

Park, Mungo (1771–1806), Scottish explorer in west Africa, where he lost his life. He wrote *Travels in the Interior of Africa* (1799).

Parker of Waddington, Baron (Hubert Lister Parker) (1900–72) Lord Chief Justice of England 1958–70.

Parker, Joseph (1830–1902), English Congregational preacher, especially at what later became the City Temple.

Parnell, Charles Stewart (1846–91), Irish national leader. To draw attention to Ireland's problems, he used obstruction in parliament. He was president of the Land League but was not implicated in crimes committed by some members. His party supported Gladstone, who became converted to Home Rule. His citation in divorce proceedings brought his political career to an end.

Parry, Sir William Edward (1790–1855), English explorer and naval commander in the Arctic, where he was sent to protect fisheries and also tried to reach the north pole.

Parsons, Sir Charles Algernon (1854–1931)

English inventor of the steam-turbine, who built the first turbine-driven steamship in 1897.

Pascal, Blaise (1623–62), Frenchman of varied gifts, b. at Clermont-Ferrand. At first a mathematician, he patented a calculating machine. His *Lettres provinciales* influenced Voltaire. In 1654 he turned to religion, and his incomplete religious writings were published posthumously as *Pensées. See also* Jansenism, Section J.

Pasternak, Boris Leonidovich (1890–1960), Russian poet and writer. B. Moscow, he published his first poems in 1931. For some years his time was spent in translating foreign literature, but in 1958 his novel *Dr. Zhivago*, which describes the Russian revolution and is in the Russian narrative tradition, was published abroad, though banned in the Soviet Union. He was awarded a Nobel prize but obliged to decline it.

Pasteur, Louis (1822–95), French chemist, b. at Dôle in the Jura, whose work was inspired by an interest in the chemistry of life. His researches on fermentation led to the science of bacteriology and his investigations into infectious diseases and their prevention to the science of immunology. The pathological–bacteriological import of his researches came about mainly through his disciples (Lister, Roux, and others) and not directly, though all founded on his early non-medical investigations on organisms of fermentation, etc., which were of great importance in industry, and fundamentally. He spent most of his life as director of scientific studies at the Ecole Normale at Paris. The Institute Pasteur was founded in 1888.

Patmore, Coventry (1823–96), English poet. *The Angel in the House* deals with domesticity. Later he became a Roman catholic, and *The Unknown Eros* is characterised by erotic mysticism.

Patrick, St. (c. 389–c. 461), apostle of Ireland, was born in Britain or Gaul, and after some time on the continent (taken thither after his capture by pirates) went as missionary to Ireland, where after years of teaching and a visit to Rome he fixed his see at Armagh. He wrote *Confessions.*

Patti, Adelina (1843–1919), coloratura soprano, b. in Madrid of Italian parents, and of international repute.

Paul, St. (c. A.D. 10–c. 67), Jew to whom was mainly due the extension of Christianity in Europe. B. Tarsus (in Asia Minor), he was a Pharisee, and became converted about A.D. 37. His missionary journeys took him to the Roman provinces of Asia, Macedonia, and Greece (Rome had already had Christian teaching); and his epistles form nearly half the New Testament and were written before the gospels. He helped to develop both the organisation of the early church and its teaching. The date order of his epistles is to some extent conjectural. It is believed that he was executed in Rome. His Hebrew name was Saul.

Paul VI (Giovanni Battista Montini) (b. 1897), elected Pope in 1963 on the death of John XXIII. He was formerly archbishop of Milan. He visited the Holy Land in 1964.

Pauli, Wolfgang (1900–58), Austrian-born physicist who first predicted theoretically the existence of neutrinos (*see* F14). Nobel prizewinner 1945.

Pavlov, Ivan Petrovich (1849–1936), Russian physiologist, known for his scientific experimental work on animal behaviour, particularly conditioned reflexes and the relation between psychological stress and brain function. Nobel prizewinner 1904. *See* Q17–18.

Pavlova, Anna (1882–1931), Russian ballerina, b. St. Petersburg, excelling in the roles of *Giselle* and the *Dying Swan.*

Peabody, George (1795–1869), American philanthropist, a successful merchant who lived mainly in London. He supported exploration and education.

Peacock, Thomas Love (1785–1866), English novelist, b. Weymouth. His work, which is mainly satirical, includes *Headlong Hall* and *Nightmare Abbey.*

Pearson, Lester Bowles (1897–1972), Canadian politician, served as minister for external affairs 1948–57, and prime minister 1963–8. He supported the United Nations. Nobel peace prize 1957.

Peary, Robert Edwin (1856–1920), American arctic explorer, discoverer of the north pole (1909).

Peel, Sir Robert (1788–1850), English Conservative statesman, b. in Lancashire, son of a manufacturer. He first held office in 1811. With Wellington he enacted toleration for Roman catholics in 1829. As home secretary he reorganised London police. He developed a new policy of Conservatism, and in 1846, largely as a result of the Irish famine, he repealed the corn laws which protected English agriculture. He died from a riding accident.

Peirce, Charles Sanders (1839–1914), American physicist and philosopher of original mind, founder of the theory of pragmatism which was later developed by his friend William James. *See* Pragmatism, Section J.

Penfield, Wilder Graves (1891–1976), Canadian brain surgeon, author of *The Cerebral Cortex of Man, Epilepsy and the Functional Anatomy of the Human Brain.* O.M.

Penn, William (1644–1718), English Quaker and founder of Pennsylvania. The son of Admiral William Penn, he persisted in becoming a Quaker, and on receiving for his father's services a crown grant in North America he founded there Pennsylvania. He wrote *No Cross, No Crown.*

Penney, Baron (William George Penney) (b. 1909), British scientist. His nuclear research team at A.E.A. developed the advanced gas-cooled reactor (A.G.R.) chosen for the Dungeness " B " and Hinkley Point " B " power stations.

Pepys, Samuel (1633–1703), English diarist and naval administrator. His diary, 1660–69, was kept in cipher and not deciphered till 1825. It gives vivid personal details and covers the plague and fire of London. (The first complete and unexpurgated version of the diary was issued in 1970.)

Pereda, José María de (1833–1906), Spanish regional novelist (around his native Santander).

Pérez Galdós, Benito (1843–1920), Spanish novelist and dramatist, who has been compared to Balzac for his close study and portrayal of all social classes, especially in the series of 46 short historical novels *Episodios nacionales.* His longer novels, *Novelas españolas contemporáneas,* some of which are translated, number 31.

Pergolesi, Giovanni Battista (1710–36), Italian composer, best known for his humorous opera *La Serva Padrona* and his *Stabat Mater.*

Pericles (c. 490–429 B.C.), Athenian statesman, general, and orator, who raised Athens to the point of its fullest prosperity, and greatest beauty, with the Parthenon, Erechtheum, and other buildings; but he died in the plague which followed the outbreak of the Peloponnesian war.

Perkin, Sir William Henry (1838–1907), English chemist, b. London, who while seeking to make a substitute for quinine discovered in 1856 the first artificial aniline dye, mauve. His son, W. H. Perkin (1860–1929) was an organic chemist of note.

Perrin, Francis (b. 1901), French scientist and socialist; succeeded Joliot-Curie as High Commr. of Atomic Energy, 1951; professor of Atomic Physics, Collège de France, 1946, Nobel prizewinner 1926.

Persius Flaccus Aulus (A.D. 34–62), Roman satirist and Stoic philosopher.

Perugino, Pietro (1446–1524), Italian artist. He worked in the Sistine Chapel at Rome and he taught Raphael.

Pestalozzi, Johann Heinrich (1746–1827), Swiss educational reformer whose theories laid the foundation of modern primary education. His teaching methods were far in advance of his time. He wrote *How Gertrude Educates Her Children.*

Pétain, Henri Philippe (1856–1951), French general and later collaborator. In the first world war he was in command at Verdun, and between the wars he sponsored the Maginot line. In the second world war, when French resistance collapsed, he came to terms with Germany and headed an administration at Vichy. After the war he was sentenced to life imprisonment.

Peter I, the Great (1672–1725), emperor of Russia. Son of Alexei, he succeeded his brother after some difficulty. He reorganised the army, and, after coming to Deptford to learn shipbuilding, he created a navy. To some extent he western-ised Russian social life, and created a new capital at St. Petersburg (1703). In war with Charles XII of Sweden he was at first defeated, but later victorious at Poltava (1709). He married a peasant, Catherine, who succeeded him.

Peter the Hermit (c. 1050–1115), French monk who preached the First Crusade, originated by pope Urban II at the council of Clermont. He went on the crusade himself, but gave up at Antioch.

Petrarch, Francesco (1304–74), Italian poet, son of a Florentine exile. He is chiefly remembered for his poems *To Laura*, but he was also a scholar who paved the way for the Renaissance.

Petrie, Sir Flinders (1853–1942), British egyptolo-gist. He excavated in Britain (1875–90), Egypt (1880–1924), and Palestine 1927–38). See his *Seventy Years of Archaeology*.

Phidias (5th cent. B.C.), Greek sculptor especially in gold, ivory and bronze, worked at Athens for Pericles. No certain examples of his work are extant, but the Elgin marbles in the British Museum may be from his designs.

Philip II of France (1165–1223), son of Louis VII. He went on the Third Crusade with Richard I of England, but in France is mainly remembered for firm government, the recovery of Normandy from England, and the beautifying of Paris.

Philip II of Macedonia (382–336 B.C.), a successful commander, made his the leading military king-dom in Greece and was father of Alexander the Great.

Philip II of Spain (1527–98), succeeded his father Charles V in Spain and the Netherlands, also in Spanish interests overseas. In the Nether-lands his strict Roman catholic policy provoked a revolt which ended in 1579 in the independence of the United Provinces. He married Mary Tudor of England; and after her death sent the ill-fated Armada against Elizabeth in 1588.

Philip V of Spain (1683–1746), first Bourbon king, succeeded his uncle Charles II and was grandson of Louis XIV. His accession provoked Euro-pean war.

Phillip, Arthur (1738–1814), first governor of New South Wales. Under his command the first fleet of 717 convicts set sail from Britain to Australia, and with the founding of Sydney in 1788 colonisation of the whole country began.

Phillips, Stephen (1868–1915), English poet who wrote verse dramas, including *Paolo and Fran-cesca*.

Piast, first Polish dynasty in Poland until the 14th cent. and until the 17th cent. in Silesia.

Piazzi, Giuseppe (1746–1826), Italian astronomer who discovered Ceres, the first of the asteroids to be seen by man.

Picasso, Pablo Ruiz (1881–1973) Spanish painter, b. Málaga; received his early training in Catalonia and settled in Paris in 1903. He and Braque were the originators of Cubism (c. 1909). His influence over contemporary art is comparable with that exercised by Cézanne (q.v.) over the artists of his time. Perhaps the best-known single work is his mural *Guernica*, painted at the time of the Spanish civil war, expressing the artist's loathing of fascism and the horrors of war. His genius also found scope in sculpture, ceramics, and the graphic arts, and he designed décor costumes for the ballet.

Piccard, Auguste (1884–1962), Swiss physicist, noted for balloon ascents into the stratosphere and for submarine research. In 1960 his son Jacques made a descent of over 7 miles in the Marianas trench in the western Pacific in a bathyscaphe designed and built by his father.

Pilsudski, Joseph (1867–1935), Polish soldier and statesman who in 1919 attempted by force to restore Poland's 1772 frontiers but was driven back. From 1926 he was dictator.

Pindar (522–443 B.C.), Greek lyric poet.

Pinero, Sir Arthur Wing (1855–1934), English dramatist whose plays include *Dandy Dick*, *The Second Mrs. Tanqueray* and *Mid-Channel*.

Pirandello, Luigi (1867–1936), Italian dramatist and novelist whose plays include *Six Characters in Search of an Author*. Nobel prizewinner 1934.

Pissarro, Camille (1830–1903), French impression-ist painter of landscapes; studied under Corot.

Pitman, Sir Isaac (1813–97) b. Trowbridge, English inventor of a system of phonographic shorthand.

Pitt, William (1759–1806). English statesman. Younger son of the Earl of Chatham, he entered parliament at 21 and became prime minister at 24 in 1783 when parties were divided and the American war had been lost He rose to the position, and held office with scarcely a break till his death. An able finance minister, he introduced reforms, and would have gone fur-ther, but Napoleon's meteoric rise obliged him to lead European allies in a long struggle against France. He died worn out by his efforts.

Pius XII (1876–1958), elected Pope 1939. As Eugenio Pacelli, he was papal nuncio in Ger-many and later papal secretary of state. It has been argued that, as Pope in wartime, he could have taken a stronger line against Nazi war crimes.

Pizarro, Francisco (c. 1478–1541), Spanish adven-turer, b. Trujillo. After Columbus's dis-coveries, he conquered Peru for Spain, over-throwing the Inca empire. He was murdered by his men.

Planck, Max (1857–1947), German mathematical physicist, b. Kiel, whose main work was on ther-modynamics. In 1900 he invented a mathe-matical formula to account for some properties of the thermal radiation from a hot body which has since played an important role in physics. Nobel prizewinner 1918. *See* Quantum theory, Section L.

Plato (427–347 B.C.), Athenian philosopher, pupil of Socrates, teacher of Aristotle. He founded a school at Athens under the name of the Acade-my, where he taught philosophy and mathe-matics. His great work is his *Dialogues*, which includes the *Republic*, the longest and most celebrated. His known writings have come down to us and constitute one of the most influential bodies of work in history. *See also* Mind and Matter, Section J.

Playfair, 1st Baron (Lyon Playfair) (1818–98), a far-sighted Victorian who stood for the greater recognition of science in national life. He for-sook his profession as professor of chemistry at Edinburgh to enter parliament. Pres. British Association 1885.

Plimsoll, Samuel (1824–98), English social re-former, b. Bristol. He realised the evil of overloading unseaworthy ships, and as M.P. for Derby he procured the passing of the Merchant Shipping Act, 1876 which imposed a line (the Plimsoll Mark) above which no ship must sink while loading.

Pliny the Elder (A.D. 23–79), Roman naturalist, author of a *Natural History*. He died of fumes and exhaustion while investigating the eruption of Vesuvius. His nephew, **Pliny the Younger** (A.D. 62–113), wrote *Letters* notable for their charm and the insight they give into Roman life.

Plotinus (c. 203–c. 262), Greek philosopher, was the founder of Neoplatonism, which had con-siderable influence on early Christian thought. *See also* God and Man, Section J.

Plutarch (c. 46–120), Greek biographer, whose *Lives* portray 46 leading historical figures (in pairs, a Greek and a Roman whose careers were similar). Although based on myth his *Life of Lycurgus* about life in Sparta had a profound influence on later writers, e.g., Rousseau and the romantic philosophers He was educated at Athens but visited Rome.

Poe, Edgar Allan (1809–49). American poet and story-writer, b. Boston, Mass. His poems include *The Raven*, *To Helen*, and *Annabel Lee*, and his stories, often weird and fantastic, include *Tales of the Grotesque and Arabesque*.

Poincaré, Raymond Nicolas (1860–1934), French statesman. He was president 1913–20, and as prime minister occupied the Ruhr in 1923.

Pole, Reginald (1500–58), archbishop of Canter-bury, cardinal of the Roman church and antag-onist of the reformation. He opposed Henry VIII's divorce and went abroad in 1532, writing *De Unitate Ecclesiastica*; as a result of which his mother, Countess of Salisbury, and other rela-tives were executed. Under Queen Mary Tudor he became archbishop and died the year she did.

Pollard, Albert Frederick (1869–1948), English historian, especially of the Tudor period, and first director of the Institute of Historical Research.

Polo, Marco (1256–1323), Venetian traveller, who made journeys through China, India, and other eastern countries, visiting the court of Kubla Khan, and publishing an account of his travels.

Pompadour, Jeanne Antoine Poisson, Marquise de (1721–64), mistress of Louis XV of France, who exercised disastrous political influence.

Pompey (106–48 B.C.), Roman commander, who cleared the Mediterranean of pirates, and became triumvir with Caesar and Crassus.

Pompidou, Georges Jean Raymond (1911–74), French administrator and politician who succeeded de Gaulle as president 1969.

Pope, Alexander (1688–1744), English poet, b. London, of a Roman catholic family and largely self-educated. His brilliant satire was frequently directed against his contemporaries. He is especially remembered for *The Rape of the Locke*, *The Dunciad*, *Essay on Criticism*, and *Essay on Man*.

Popper, Sir Karl (b. 1902), British philosopher of science, b. Vienna; author of *The Open Society and Its Enemies* (1945), *Conjectures and Refutations* (1963), *Objective Knowledge* (1972). He rejects the doctrine that all knowledge starts from perception or sensation and holds that it grows through conjecture and refutation.

Pound, Ezra Loomis (1885–1972), American poet and writer on varied subjects, a controversial figure. He is noted for his translations of Provençal, Latin, Chinese, French, and Italian poets.

Poussin, Nicolas (1593–1665), French painter. He lived in Rome 1624–40, 1642–65. His *Golden Calf* is in the National Gallery.

Powys, John Cowper (1872–1964), English writer, best known for his novel *Wolf Solent* and his essays *The Meaning of Culture* and *A Philosophy of Solitude*. His brothers, Theodore Francis (1875–1953) and Llewelyn (1884–1939) were also original writers.

Prasad, Rajendra (1884–1963), Indian statesman, first president of the Republic of India, 1950–62.

Praxiteles (4th cent. B.C.), Greek sculptor, whose main surviving work is *Hermes carrying Dionysus*.

Preece, Sir William Henry (1834–1913), Welsh electrical engineer, associated with the expansion of wireless telegraphy and telephony in the United Kingdom. He was connected with Marconi and introduced the block system.

Prichard, James Cowles (1786–1848), English ethnologist who perceived that people should be studied as a whole. His works include *Researches into the Physical History of Mankind* and *The Natural History of Man*. He practised medicine.

Priestley, John Boynton (b. 1894), English critic, novelist, and playwright, b. Bradford. His works include the novels *The Good Companions*, *Angel Pavement*, and the plays *Dangerous Corner*, *Time and the Conways*, *I Have Been Here Before*, and *The Linden Tree*. O.M. 1977.

Priestley, Joseph (1733–1804), English chemist who worked on gases, and shared with Scheele the discovery of oxygen. A presbyterian minister, he was for his time an advanced thinker. In 1794 he settled in America.

Prior, Matthew (1664–1721), English poet. In early life he was a diplomat. He was a neat epigrammatist and writer of occasional pieces. His works include *The City Mouse and Country Mouse* and *Four Dialogues of the Dead*.

Prokofiev, Serge Sergeyevich (1891–1953), Russian composer, whose music has a strong folk-song element, rich in melody and invention. He has written operas: *The Love of Three Oranges*, *The Betrothal in a Nunnery*, *War and Peace*; ballets: *Romeo and Juliet*, *Cinderella*; symphonies, chamber music, and the music for Eisenstein's films *Alexander Nevsky*, *Ivan the Terrible*.

Protagoras (c. 480–411 B.C.), Greek philosopher, chief of the Sophists, noted for his scepticism and disbelief in objective truth, and for his doctrine that " man is the measure of all things."

Proudhon, Pierre Joseph (1809–65), French socialist. In 1840 he propounded the view that property is theft. His main work is *Système des contradictions économiques* (1846). He was frequently in prison.

Proust, Marcel (1871–1922), French psychological novelist, author of a series of novels known under the title of *A la recherche du temps perdu*. His works have been admirably translated into English by C. K. Scott Moncrieff.

Ptolemy of Alexandria (Claudius Ptolemaeus) (fl. A.D. 140), astronomer and founder of scientific cartography. In the *Almagest* he attempted a mathematical presentation of the paths along which the planets appear to move in the heavens. His other great work was his *Geographical Outline*.

Puccini, Giacomo (1858–1924), Italian composer, b. Lucca, whose operas include *Manon Lescaut*, *La Bohème*, *Tosca*, *Madam Butterfly*, and *Turandot* (completed by a friend).

Pupin, Michael Idvorsky (1858–1935), physicist and inventor (telephony and X-rays), b. Idvor, Hungary (now in Yugoslavia); went to America penniless 1874 to become professor of electromechanics at Columbia University.

Purcell, Henry (1658–95), English composer, b. Westminster, son of a court musician. He became organist of the chapel royal and composer to Charles II. His best works are vocal and choral. He also wrote for the stage. *See* Section E.

Pusey, Edward Bouverie (1800–82), English theologian, a leader of the Oxford or Tractarian movement with Keble and at first also with Newman, till the latter became Roman catholic. The movement aimed at revival. *See* Tractarianism, Section J.

Pushkin, Alexander (1799–1837), Russian writer, b. Moscow, whose place in Russian literature ranks with Shakespeare's in English. He wrote in many forms—lyrical poetry and narrative verse, drama, folk-tales and short stories. Musicians have used his works as plots for operas—the fairy romance *Russlan and Ludmilla* was dramatised by Glinka; the verse novel *Eugene Onegin* and the short story *The Queen of Spades* were adapted by Tchaikovsky, and the tragic drama *Boris Godunov* formed the subject of Mussorgsky's opera. Like Lermontov, who too was exiled, he was inspired by the wild beauty of the Caucasus. He was killed in a duel defending his wife's honour.

Pym, John (1584–1643), English parliamentary leader in opposition to Charles I. He promoted the impeachment of the king's advisers, Strafford and Laud.

Pythagoras (c. 582–500 B.C.), Greek philosopher, b. on the island of Samos, off the Turkish mainland, which he left c. 530 to settle at Croton, a Greek city in southern Italy. He was a mystic and mathematician, and founded a brotherhood who saw in numbers the key to the understanding of the universe.

Q

Quasimodo, Salvatore (1901–68), Italian poet of humanity and liberal views whose works include *La vita non e sogno*. Nobel prizewinner 1959.

Quesnay, François (1694–1774), French economist, founder of the physiocratic school who believed in *laissez-faire* and influenced the thought of Adam Smith. *See* Physiocrats, Section J.

Quiller-Couch, Sir Arthur Thomas (1863–1944), English man of letters, b. Bodmin, known as " Q." He edited the *Oxford Book of English Verse* and his works include *From a Cornish Window*.

R

Rabelais, François (c. 1495–1553), French satirist. At first in religious orders, he late studied medicine and practised at Lyons. His works, mainly published under a pseudonym, are full of riotous mirth, wit and wisdom. The main ones are *Gargantua* and *Pantagruel*.

Rachel, Élisa (Élisa Felix) (1821–58), Alsatian-Jewish tragic actress. Her chief triumph was in Racine's *Phèdre*.

Rachmaninov, Sergey Vasilyevich (1873–1943), Russian composer and pianist, b. Nijni-Novgorod (now Gorki), best known for his piano music, especially his *Prelude*. After the Russian revolution he settled in America. *See* Section E.

B50

Racine, Jean (1639–99), French tragic poet whose dramas include *Andromaque*, *Iphigénie* and *Phèdre*. An orphan, he was brought up by grandparents who sent him to Port Royal school where he acquired a love of the classics. In Paris he became a friend of Molière, whose company acted his first play, and of Boileau, with whom he became joint historiographer to Louis XIV. *Esther* and *Athalie* were written for Madame de Maintenon's schoolgirls.

Rackham, Arthur (1867–1939), English artist and book-illustrator, especially of fairy tales.

Radhakrishnan, Sir Sarvepalli (1888–1975), Indian philosopher and statesman, vice-president of India 1952–62, president 1962–7. He was at one time a professor at Oxford, and was chairman of Unesco in 1949.

Raffles, Sir Thomas Stamford (1781–1826), English colonial administrator who founded a settlement at Singapore in 1819. He was also a naturalist, and founded the London Zoo, being first president.

Raikes, Robert (1735–1811), English educational pioneer, whose lead in the teaching of children at Gloucester on Sundays led to an extensive Sunday School movement.

Raleigh, Sir Walter (1552–1618), adventurer and writer. He found favour at the court of Elizabeth I, helped to put down the Irish rebellion of 1580, and in 1584 began the colonisation of Virginia, introducing potatoes and tobacco to the British Isles. At the accession of James I he lost favour and was sent to the Tower, where he wrote his *History of the World*. Released in 1615 to lead an expedition to the Orinoco, he was executed when it failed.

Raman, Sir Chandrasekhara Venkata (1888–1970), Indian physicist whose main work has been in spectroscopy. For his research on the diffusion of light and discovery of the " Raman effect " (a phenomenon of scattered light rays) he was awarded the 1930 Nobel prize.

Rameau, Jean Philippe (1683–1764), French composer and church organist whose works on musical theory influenced musical development in the 18th cent.

Ramón y Cajal, Santiago (1852–1934), Spanish histologist who made discoveries in the structure of the nervous system. Shared 1906 Nobel prize.

Ramsay, Sir William (1852–1916), Scottish chemist, and discoverer with Lord Rayleigh of argon. Later he discovered helium and other inert gases, which he called neon, krypton, and xenon. Nobel prizewinner 1904.

Ramsey, Arthur Michael (b. 1904), archbishop of Canterbury, 1961–74. His previous career was: professor of divinity at Cambridge 1950–2; bishop of Durham 1952–6; archbishop of York 1956–61. Widely travelled, he worked hard for church unity; in 1970 he preached in South Africa.

Ranke, Leopold von (1795–1886), German historian, one of the first to base his work on methodical research. His chief work is a *History of the Popes*.

Raphael (Raffaello Santi) (1483–1520) of Urbino was the youngest of the three great artists of the High Renaissance. He was taught at Perugia by Perugino, and then at Florence he came under the influence of Leonardo and Michelangelo. Raphael's Madonnas, remarkable for their simplicity and grace, include the *Madonna of the Grand Duke* (Palazzo Pitti), the *Sistine Madonna* (Dresden) the *Madonna with the Goldfinch* (Uffizi) the *Madonna of Foligno* (Vatican), and the *Ansidei Madonna* (National Gallery). He painted the frescoes on the walls of the Stanza della Segnatura in the Vatican, and designed 10 cartoons for tapestries for the Sistine Chapel, 7 of which are on loan from the Royal Collection at the V. and A. After the death of Bramante he was appointed architect in charge of the rebuilding of St. Peter's.

Rasputin, Grigori Yefimovich (1871–1916), Russian peasant monk, who at the court of Nicholas II exerted a malign influence over the Tsarina through his apparent ability to improve the health of the sickly Tsarevich Alexis. He was murdered by a group of nobles.

Rathbone, Eleanor (1872–1946), social reformer who championed women's pensions and in her book *The Disinherited Family* set out the case for family allowances.

Ravel, Maurice (1875–1937), French composer, pupil of Fauré, one of the leaders of the impressionist movement. He wrote chamber music, piano pieces, songs, and ballet music, including *Daphnis et Chloé*, specially commissioned by Diaghilev. *See* Section E.

Rawlinson, Sir Henry Creswicke (1810–95), English diplomat and archaeologist. He made Assyrian collections now in the British Museum and translated the Behistun inscription of the Persian king Darius. He also wrote on cuneiform inscriptions and on Assyrian history.

Ray, John (1627–1705), English naturalist. A blacksmith's son, he went to Cambridge, travelled in Europe, and produced a classification of plants. He also wrote on zoology.

Rayleigh, 3rd Baron (John William Strutt) (1842–1919), English mathematician and physicist. He studied sound and the wave theory of light; and with Sir William Ramsay discovered argon. Nobel prizewinner 1904.

Read, Sir Herbert (1893–1968), English poet and art critic. His writings include *Collected Poems*, *The Meaning of Art*, and an autobiography, *Annals of Innocence and Experience*.

Reade, Charles (1814–84), English novelist. His chief work is *The Cloister and the Hearth*. He also wrote *Peg Woffington*, *It is Never too Late to Mend*, and *Griffith Gaunt*, aimed at social abuses. He tried unsuccessfully to write plays.

Réaumur, René Antoine Ferchault de (1683–1757), French naturalist who invented a thermometer of eighty degrees, using alcohol.

Récamier, Jeanne Françoise (*née* Bernard) (1777–1849), French beauty and holder of a noted salon. Her husband was a banker.

Regnault, Henri Victor (1810–78), French chemist and physicist, who worked on gases, latent heat, and steam-engines.

Reith, 1st Baron (John Charles Walsham Reith) (1889–1971), Scottish civil engineer, first director-general of the British Broadcasting Corporation 1927–38.

Rembrandt (Rembrandt Harmenszoon van Rijn) (1606–69), Dutch painter and etcher, b. Leiden, a miller's son, one of the most individual and prolific artists of any period. His output includes portraits, landscapes, large groups, etchings, and drawings. He settled in Amsterdam establishing his reputation with *The Anatomy Lesson*, painted in 1632. In 1634 he married Saskia, a burgomaster's daughter. *The Night Watch* was painted in 1642; it was not well received and Saskia died the same year, leaving the infant Titus. The path from relative wealth to lonely old age is depicted in his self-portraits. Caring little for convention or formal beauty, his work is characterised by bold realism and spiritual beauty, by vitality and simplicity. His understanding of the play of colour and the effects of light can give his pictures a mystical beauty, as in the atmospheric painting *The Mill*. His figures, even for religious pictures, were taken from real life, the Jews in the etching *Christ Healing* from the Jewish quarter where he lived. He met the misfortunes of later life by withdrawing from society and it was during this period of detachment that he produced his greatest works in portraiture, landscape, and biblical story.

Renan, Ernest (1823–92), French writer who, though unable to accept the orthodox viewpoint, wrote much on religious themes, especially a *Life of Jesus*.

Reni, Guido. *See* Guido Reni.

Rennie, John (1761–1821), Scottish civil engineer who built the old Waterloo and Southwark bridges and designed the granite London bridge which stood until recently. He also designed docks at London, Liverpool, Leith, Dublin, and Hull; constructed Plymouth breakwater; made canals and drained fens.

Renoir, Pierre Auguste (1841–1919), French impressionist painter, b. Limoges. His works include portraits, still-life, landscapes, and groups, including *La Loge*, *Les Parapluies*, *La première Sortie*, *La Place Pigalle*. He was later crippled with arthritis.

Reuter, Paul Julius, Freiherr von (1816–99), German pioneer of telegraphic press service, who in 1851 fixed his headquarters in London.

Reymont, Vladislav Stanislav (1868–1925), Polish novelist, author of *The Peasants*. Nobel prize-winner 1924.

Reynolds, Sir Joshua (1723–92), English portrait painter, b. Plympton, Devon. His portraits, which include *Mrs. Siddons*, are remarkable for expressiveness and colour and he was a sympathetic painter of children. He was first president of the R.A. from 1768 till his death.

Rhodes, Cecil John (1853–1902), English empire-builder. B. at Bishop's Stortford, he went to South Africa for health reasons and there prospered at the diamond mines. He became prime minister of what was then Cape Colony and secured British extension in what is now Rhodesia. He withdrew from politics after the failure of the ill-advised Jameson Raid of 1896 into the Transvaal. He bequeathed large sums to found scholarships at Oxford for overseas students.

Ricardo, David (1772–1823), English political economist of Jewish descent. By occupation a London stockbroker, he wrote a useful work, *Principles of Political Economy*.

Richard I (1157–99), succeeded his father Henry II as king of England in 1189. A patron of troubadours and a soldier (Lion-heart), he went on the third Crusade and took Acre, but could not recover Jerusalem from Saladin. On his return journey across Europe he was imprisoned and ransomed. He was killed in war with France.

Richard II (1367–1400), son of the Black Prince, succeeded his grandfather Edward III as king of England in 1377. Artistic and able, but erratic and egocentric, he personally at the age of fourteen met the Peasants' Revolt in 1381, making untenable promises. Latterly his rule became increasingly arbitrary, and he was deposed and imprisoned in 1399.

Richard III (1452–85), King of England, succeeded his brother, the Yorkist, Edward IV, in 1483, and is believed to have murdered his two nephews in the Tower. Shortly afterwards he was defeated and killed at Bosworth by the invading Earl of Richmond, who as Henry VII brought to an end the Wars of the Roses. Richard's character is disputed, but he was able and might have been a successful ruler.

Richardson, Sir Albert Edward (1880–1964), British architect, author of *Georgian Architecture*.

Richardson, Sir Owen Willans (1879–1959), English physicist who worked on thermionics, or emission of electricity from hot bodies. Nobel prizewinner 1928.

Richardson, Sir Ralph David (b. 1902), English actor who has worked at the old Vic, on the West End stage, and at Stratford-on-Avon, and appeared in films, including *South Riding*, *Anna Karenina*, and *The Fallen Idol*.

Richardson, Samuel (1689–1761), English author of *Pamela*, *Clarissa*, and *The History of Sir Charles Grandison*, exercised considerable influence on the development of the novel.

Richelieu, Armand Jean du Plessis, Duc de (1585–1642) French statesman, cardinal of the Roman church. As minister to Louis XIII from 1624 till his death, he built up the power of the French crown at home in central government, and by his military preparedness and active foreign policy gave France a lead in Europe.

Ridley, Nicholas (1500–55). English Protestant martyr, bishop of Rochester and later of London, was burnt with Latimer under Queen Mary Tudor.

Rienzi, Cola di (1313–54), Italian patriot, b. Rome, led a popular rising in 1347 and for seven months reigned as tribune, but had to flee, was imprisoned, and eventually murdered.

Rilke, Rainer Maria (1872–1926), German lyric poet, b. Prague. His work, marked by beauty of style, culminated in the *Duino Elegies* and *Sonnets to Orpheus*, both written in 1922, which gave a new musicality to German verse. His visits to Russia in 1899 and 1900 and his admiration for Rodin (who had been his wife's teacher) influenced his artistic career.

Rimbaud, Jean Nicolas Arthur (1854–91), French poet, b. Charleville, on the Meuse. In his brief poetic career (4 years from about the age of 16) he prepared the way for symbolism (*Bateau ivre*, *Les Illuminations*) and anticipated Freud (*Les déserts de l'amour*). He became in-

timate with Verlaine and at 18 had completed his memoirs, *Une saison en enfer*. He died at Marseilles.

Rimsky-Korsakov, Nikolai Andreyevich (1844–1908), Russian composer whose works include the operas *The Maid of Pskov*, *The Snow Maiden*, *Le Coq d'or*, and the symbolic suite *Scheherezade*. He was a brilliant orchestrator and rescored many works, including Borodin's *Prince Igor*.

Rizzio, David (1533?–66), Italian musician and secretary of Mary, Queen of Scots. He was murdered in her presence at Holyrood by her jealous husband, Darnley.

Robbia, Luca Della (1400–82), Florentine sculptor who introduced enamelled terra-cotta work.

Roberts of Kandahar, 1st Earl (Frederick Sleigh Roberts) (1832–1914), British general. He took part in the suppression of the Indian Mutiny, in the Afghan war (relieving Kandahar), and when put in command in South Africa in the Boer War he relieved Kimberley and advanced to Pretoria.

Robertson, Sir William (1860–1933), the only British soldier to rise from private to field-marshal. His son, Brian Hubert, 1st Baron (b. 1896) served in both world wars and was chairman of the British Transport Commission, 1953–61.

Robeson, Paul (1898–1976), American Negro singer, b. Princeton, especially remembered for his singing of Negro spirituals, and his appearance in works ranging from *Showboat* to *Othello*.

Robespierre, Maximilien Marie Isidoire de (1758–94), French revolutionary. A country advocate, b. Arras, he was in 1789 elected to the States General and in 1792 to the Convention. He became a leader of the Jacobins, the more extreme party which came to power under stress of war and after the king's execution in 1793. In this crisis, the Committee of Public Safety, of which he was a member and which used his reputation as a cloak, sent many to the guillotine. He opposed the cult of Reason and inaugurated the worship of the Supreme Being. In the reaction from the reign of terror he was denounced, tried to escape, but was guillotined.

Robinson, William Heath (1872–1944), English cartoonist and book-illustrator, especially known for his fantastically humorous drawings of machines.

Rob Roy (Robert McGregor) (1671–1734), Scottish freebooter who helped the poor at the expense of the rich, and played a lone hand in the troubled times of the Jacobite rising of 1715.

Robsart, Amy (1532–60), English victim (it is believed) of murder. The wife of Robert Dudley, Earl of Leicester, she was found dead at Cumnor Place. Her death was used by Scott in *Kenilworth*.

Rockefeller, John Davison (1839–1937), American philanthropist, b. Richford, N.Y. He settled in Cleveland, Ohio, and with his brother William founded the Standard Oil Company, making a fortune. His philanthropic enterprises are carried on by the Rockefeller Foundation. Nelson Rockefeller, Gov. of New York 1958–73, Vice-Pres. of the United States 1974–7, is his grandson.

Rodin, Auguste (1841–1917), French sculptor, b. Paris. His best-known works include *Le Penseur*, *Les Bourgeois de Calais*, the statues of Balzac and Victor Hugo, and *La Porte d'Enfer*, a huge bronze door for the Musée des Arts Décoratifs, which was unfinished at his death.

Rodney, 1st Baron (George Rodney) (1719–92), English admiral, who served in the Seven Years War and the War of American Independence; in the latter war he defeated the French fleet under de Grasse.

Roland de la Platière, Manon Jeanne (1754–93), a leading figure in the French revolution. Her husband Jean Marie (1734–93), belonged to the more moderate or Girondist party, and when threatened escaped; but she was imprisoned and executed. She wrote *Letters* and *Memoirs*.

Rolland, Romain (1866–1944), French author, whose main work is a ten-volume novel, *Jean-Christophe*, the biography of a German musician, based on the life of Beethoven, and a study of contemporary French and German civilisation. Nobel prizewinner 1915.

Romilly, Sir Samuel (1757–1818), English lawyer

and law-reformer, who aimed at mitigating the severity of the criminal law.

Rommel, Erwin (1891–1944), German general. He took part in the 1940 invasion of France, and was later successful in commanding the Afrika Korps till 1944. He committed suicide.

Romney, George (1734–1802), English artist, b. in Lancashire. He painted chiefly portraits, especially of Lady Hamilton, and lived mainly in London, but returned to Kendal to die.

Röntgen, Wilhelm Konrad von (1845–1923), German scientist who in 1895 discovered X-rays. Nobel prizewinner 1901.

Roosevelt, Franklin Delano (1882–1945), American statesman, a distant cousin of Theodore Roosevelt. During the first world war he held office under Wilson, and though stricken with poliomyelitis in 1921 continued his political career, becoming governor of New York in 1929 and U.S. president in 1933 (the first to hold office for more than two terms), till his death. A Democrat, he met the economic crisis of 1933 with a policy for a "New Deal" (*see* **Sec. L**). He strove in vain to ward off war. Towards other American countries his attitude was that of "good neighbour." After Pearl Harbor, he energetically prosecuted the war, holding meetings with Churchill and Stalin, and adopting a "lend-lease" policy for arms. He kept contact with his people by "fireside talks." His wife Eleanor (1884–1962) was a public figure in her own right, and was chairman of the U.N. Human Rights Commission 1947–51.

Roosevelt, Theodore (1858–1919), American president. Popular because of his exploits in the Spanish–American war, he was appointed Republican vice-president in 1900, becoming president when McKinley was assassinated, and was re-elected 1905. He promoted the regulation of trusts; and his promotion of peace between Russia and Japan gained the Nobel prize, 1906.

Rops, Félicien (1833–98), Belgian artist, known for his often satirical lithographs and etchings.

Ross, Sir James Clark (1800–62), Scottish explorer of polar regions, who accompanied his uncle Sir John, and himself discovered the north magnetic pole in 1831. He commanded the *Erebus* and *Terror* to the antarctic (1839–43), where his discoveries included the Ross ice barrier.

Ross, Sir John (1777–1856), Scottish explorer of polar regions, uncle of the above. He searched for the north-west passage and discovered Boothia peninsula.

Ross, Sir Ronald (1857–1932), British physician, b. India, who discovered the malaria parasite. He was in the Indian medical service, and later taught tropical medicine in England. Nobel prizewinner 1902.

Rossetti, Dante Gabriel (1828–82), English poet and painter, son of Gabriele (1783–1852), an exiled Italian author who settled in London in 1842. With Millais, Holman Hunt and others he formed the Pre-Raphaelite brotherhood which returned to pre-Renaissance art forms. His model was often his wife, Elizabeth Siddal. His poems include *The Blessed Damozel*. His sister Christina Georgina (1830–94) wrote poetry, including *Goblin Market*.

Rossini, Gioacchino Antonio (1792–1868), Italian operatic composer. *See* **Section E**.

Rostand, Edmond (1868–1918), French dramatist, whose *Cyrano de Bergerac* created a sensation in 1898.

Rothenstein, Sir William (1872–1945), English portrait painter. His son, Sir John (b. 1901), is an art historian and until 1964 was director of the Tate Gallery; he has written an autobiography.

Rothschild, Meyer Amschel (1743–1812), German financier, founder of a banking family, b. Frankfurt. His five sons controlled branches at Frankfurt, Vienna, Naples, Paris and London (Nathan Meyer, 1777–1836). Nathan's son, Lionel (1808–79), was the first Jewish member of the House of Commons.

Roubiliac, Louis François (1695–1762), French sculptor who settled in London and carved a statue of Handel for Vauxhall gardens and one of Newton for Trinity College, Cambridge.

Rouget de Lisle, Claude Joseph (1760–1836), French poet, author of words and music of the *Marseillaise*, revolutionary and national anthem.

Rousseau, Henri (1844–1910), influential French "Sunday" painter, called "Le Douanier" because he was a customs official; self-taught, he was for long unrecognised as an artist of considerable talent and originality; he used the botanical gardens for his jungle scenes.

Rousseau, Jean-Jacques (1712–78), French political philosopher and educationist, b. Geneva, herald of the romantic movement. After a hard childhood he met Mme de Warens who for some years befriended him. In 1741 he went to Paris where he met Diderot and contributed articles on music and political economy to the *Encyclopédie*. *La nouvelle Héloïse* appeared in 1760, *Emile*, and *Le Contrat Social* in 1762. *Emile* is a treatise on education according to "natural" principles and *Le Contrat Social*, his main work, sets forth his political theory. It begins, "Man is born free and everywhere he is in chains." Both books offended the authorities and he had to flee, spending some time in England. Later he was able to return to France. His views on conduct and government did much to stimulate the movement leading to the French Revolution. *See also* **Education, Section J.**

Rubens, Sir Peter Paul (1577–1640), Flemish painter. B. in exile, his family returned to Antwerp in 1587. He studied in Italy and visited Spain. His range was wide, his compositions vigorous, and he was a remarkable colourist. *Peace and War*, *The Rape of the Sabines*, and *The Felt Hat* are in the National Gallery. He was knighted by Charles I.

Rubenstein, Anton Grigorovich (1829–94). Russian pianist and composer, who helped to found the conservatoire at St. Petersburg (Leningrad); as did his brother Nicholas (1835–81) at Moscow.

Rücker, Sir Arthur (1848–1915), English physicist, who made two magnetic surveys of the British Isles, 1886, and 1891.

Ruisdael, Jacob van (*c.* 1628–82), Dutch painter of landscapes, b. Haarlem. Several of his works are in the National Gallery, including *Coast of Scheveningen* and *Landscape with ruins*. He was also a fine etcher.

Rupert, Prince (1619–82), general, son of Frederick of Bohemia and his wife Elizabeth, daughter of James I of England. He commanded the Royalist cavalry in the English civil war, but was too impetuous for lasting success. At sea he was defeated by Blake. He improved the art of mezzotinting and was the first governor of the Hudson's Bay Company.

Rusk, Dean (b. 1909), American politician, who has held various posts especially in connection with foreign affairs; a former Rhodes scholar.

Ruskin, John (1819–1900), English author and art critic, b. London. His *Modern Painters* in 5 volumes was issued over a period of years, the first volume having a strong defence of Turner. He helped to establish the Pre-Raphaelites. Other notable works include *The Seven Lamps of Architecture*, *The Stones of Venice* and *Praeterita*. *Unto this Last* develops his views on social problems, and he tried to use his wealth for education and for non-profitmaking enterprises. Ruskin College at Oxford, the first residential college for working people, is named after him. In 1848 he married Euphemia Gray, but in 1854 she obtained a decree of nullity and later married Millais.

Russell, 3rd Earl (Bertrand Arthur William Russell) (1872–1970), English philosopher, mathematician, and essayist, celebrated for his work in the field of logic and the theory of knowledge, and remembered for his moral courage, belief in human reason and his championship of liberal ideas. He published more than 60 books, including *The Principles of Mathematics* (1903), *Principia Mathematica* (in collaboration with A. N. Whitehead; 3 vols., 1910–13), *The Problem of Philosophy* (1912), *Mysticism and Logic* (1918), *The Analysis of Mind* (1921), *An Inquiry into Meaning and Truth* (1940), *History of Western Philosophy* (1945), and a number on ethics and social questions. His *Autobiography* (3 vols.) appeared 1967–9. He was the grandson of Lord John Russell and John Stuart Mill was his godfather. Nobel prize for literature 1950; O.M. 1949.

Russell, 1st Earl (John Russell), (1792–1878), English statesman, third son of the 6th Duke of Bedford. He had a large share in carrying the parliamentary reform bill of 1832. He was Whig prime minister 1846–52 and 1865–6. He was also a historian and biographer.

Russell of Killowen, 1st Baron (Charles Russell), British lawyer, b. Ireland; lord chief justice 1894–1900. He defended Parnell.

Rutherford, 1st Baron (Ernest Rutherford) (1871–1937), British physicist, b. New Zealand, eminent in the field of atomic research. His experiments were conducted at Manchester and Cambridge and attracted young scientists from all over the world. In 1911 he announced his nuclear theory of the atom and in 1918 succeeded in splitting the atom. His work prepared the way for future nuclear research.

Ruysdael, Jacob van. See **Ruisdael**.

Ruyter, Michiel Adrianszoon de (1607–76), Dutch admiral who ranks with Nelson. He fought against England and in 1667 caused alarm by sailing up the Medway as far as Rochester and up the Thames as far as Gravesend. He was mortally wounded at Messina.

S

Sachs, Hans (1494–1576), German poet, b. Nuremberg. A shoemaker, he wrote over 6,000 pieces, some dealing with everyday life, many (including *Die Wittenbergische Nachtigall*) inspired by the Reformation.

Sachs, Julius von (1832–97), German botanist, founder of experimental plant physiology. He demonstrated that chlorophyll is formed in chloroplasts only in light.

Sadat, Mohammed Anwar El (b. 1918), Egyptian statesman, President of Egypt since 1970. His visit to Israel in Nov. 1977 was a bold and courageous move in the cause of peace.

Sadi or **Saadi** (Muslih Addin) (c. 1184–1292), Persian poet, b. Shiraz, best known for his *Gulistan* (Flower Garden).

Sainte-Beuve, Charles Augustin (1804–69), French critic, b. Boulogne. He studied medicine, abandoning it for journalism, and after attempting to write poetry, turned to literary criticism. His work reveals the wide range of his intellectual experience and includes *Causeries du lundi* and *Histoire de Port-Royal*.

Saint-Just, Antoine (1767–94), French revolutionary, a follower of Robespierre and executed with him.

St. Laurent, Louis Stephen (b. 1882), Canadian politician, prime minister 1948–57.

Saint-Saëns, Charles Camile (1835–1921), French composer, for 20 years organist at the Madeleine. His compositions include symphonic and chamber music and the opera *Samson et Dalila*, which was produced by Liszt at Weimar in 1877. See **Section E**.

Saint-Simon, Claude, Comte de (1760–1825), French socialist, who in his *L'Industrie* and *Nouveau christianisme* prepared the way for much later thought.

Saintsbury, George Edward (1845–1933), English critic and literary historian.

Sakharov, Andrei Dimitrievich (b. 1921), Soviet nuclear physicist and human rights campaigner. Nobel prizewinner 1975.

Sala, George Augustus (1828–95), English journalist who contributed to *Household Words* and was a notable foreign correspondent.

Saladin (Salah-ad-din) (1137–93), sultan of Egypt and Syria and founder of a dynasty, who in 1187 defeated the Christians near Tiberias and took Jerusalem. This gave rise to the unsuccessful Third Crusade, in which Richard I of England joined. His great qualities were admired by his opponents, and his administration left many tangible signs in such matters as roads and canals.

Salazar, Antonio d'Oliveira (1889–1970), Portuguese dictator, having first been premier in 1932, a new constitution being adopted in 1933. He gave Portugal stability, but refused to bow to nationalism in Portuguese Africa and India.

Salimbene de Adamo (1221–c.1228), mediaeval chronicler, b. Parma, whose vivid description of life in the 13th cent. is embodied in his *Cronica*.

Salisbury, 3rd Marquess (Robert Arthur Salisbury)

(1830–1903), English Conservative statesman, prime minister 1885–6, 1886–92, 1895–1902, mainly remembered for his conduct of foreign affairs during a critical period, culminating in the Boer War. His grandson, **Robert Arthur, 5th Marquess** (1893–1972), led the Conservative opposition in the House of Lords.

Samuel, 1st Viscount (Herbert Samuel) (1870–1963), British Liberal statesman of Jewish parentage. He published philosophical works, including *Practical Ethics*.

Sand, George (1804–76), pseudonym of the French writer Armandine Lucie Dupin. Her publications are extensive and varied, and include the novel *Mauprat*, rural studies, and an autobiography *Histoire de ma vie*. She was associated with Alfred de Musset and Chopin.

Sandow, Eugene (1867–1925), German "strong man" who opened an Institute of Health in London.

Sanger, Frederick (b. 1918), British scientist noted for his work on the chemical structure of the protein insulin. Nobel prizewinner 1958.

Sankey, Ira David (1840–1908), American evangelist and composer, associated with Moody.

San Martin, José de (1778–1850), South American national leader in securing independence from Spanish rule to his native Argentina, Chile and Peru.

Santayana, George (1863–1952), American philosopher and poet, b. Madrid, of Spanish parentage. He was professor of philosophy at Harvard, 1907–12. His books include *The Sense of Beauty*, *The Life of Reason*, and *The Realms of Being*.

Santos-Dumont, Alberto (1873–1932), Brazilian aeronaut who in 1898 flew a cylindrical balloon with a gasoline engine. In 1909 he built a monoplane.

Sappho of Lesbos (fl. early 6th cent. B.C.), Greek poetess, of whose love poems few remain.

Sardou, Victorien (1831–1908), French dramatist popular in his day. Sarah Bernhardt created famous parts in *Fédora*, *Théodora* and *La Tosca*; *Robespierre* and *Dante* were written for Irving.

Sargent, John Singer (1856–1922), American painter, b. Florence, who worked mainly in England, especially on portraits.

Sargent, Sir Malcolm (1895–1967), popular British conductor, who conducted the Promenade Concerts from 1950 till his death, and succeeded Sir Adrian Boult as conductor of the B.B.C. Symphony Orchestra, 1950–7.

Sartre, Jean-Paul (b. 1905), French existentialist philosopher, left-wing intellectual, dramatist, essayist and novelist. His major philosophical work is *L'Etre et le Néant* and his plays include *Les Mouches*, *Huis Clos*, *Crime passionel*, *La Putain respectueuse*, and *Les Séquestrés d'Altona*. He was awarded (though he declined it) the 1964 Nobel prize. See **Section I**.

Sassoon, Siegfried (1886–1967), English poet and writer with a hatred of war. He is mainly known for *The Memoirs of a Foxhunting Man*, the first part of the *Memoirs of George Sherston*.

Savonarola, Girolamo (1452–98), Florentine preacher and reformer, a Dominican friar, who denounced vice and corruption not only in society but also in the Church itself, especially attacking Pope Alexander VI. He was excommunicated, imprisoned, and with two of his companions hanged and burned. His passion for reform made him impatient of opposition and incapable of compromise, yet he was a notable figure and commands the respect of later ages. George Eliot's *Romola* portrays him.

Scarlatti, Alessandro (1659–1725), Italian musician who founded the Neopolitan school of opera. He composed over 100 operas, 200 masses, and over 700 cantatas and oratorios. His son **Domenico** (1685–1757) was a harpsichord virtuoso whose work influenced the evolution of the sonata. The chief years of his life were spent at the Spanish court in Madrid. See **Section E**.

Scheele, Carl Wilhelm (1742–86), Swedish chemist, discoverer of many chemical substances, including oxygen (c. 1773—but published in 1777 after the publication of Priestley's studies).

Schiaparelli, Giovanni Virginio (1835–1910), Italian astronomer, noted for having detected certain dark markings on the surface of the planet Mars which he called canals.

Schiller, Johann Christoph Friedrich von (1759–1805), German dramatist and poet, b. Marbach in Württemberg, began life as a military surgeon. His play *The Robbers* with a revolutionary theme was successful in 1782 in Mannheim. After a stay at Dresden, where he wrote *Don Carlos*, and at Jena, where he wrote a history of the Thirty Years War, he became the friend of Goethe and removed to Weimar, where he wrote *Wallenstein, Mary Stuart, The Maid of Orleans* and *William Tell*, but died young. He is a leading figure in the European romantic movement.

Schirrmann, Richard (1874–1961), German originator of youth hostels. A schoolmaster, in 1907 he converted his schoolroom during holidays to a dormitory. The Verband für deutsche Jugendherbergen was founded in 1913, and the International Youth Hostels Federation in 1932, with Schirrmann as first president.

Schlegel, Friedrich von (1772–1829), German critic, b. Hanover, prominent among the founders of German romanticism, whose revolutionary and germinating ideas influenced early 19th–cent. thought. His brother, August Wilhelm (1767–1845), made remarkable translations of Shakespeare (which established Shakespeare in Germany), Dante, Calderón, and Camões.

Schliemann, Heinrich (1822–90), German archaeologist, who discovered Troy and excavated Mycenae.

Schnabel, Artur (1882–1951), American pianist of Austrian birth, regarded as a leading exponent of Beethoven's pianoforte sonatas.

Schoenberg, Arnold (1874–1951), Austrian composer of Jewish parentage who in 1933 was exiled by the Nazi regime and settled in America, teaching at Boston and Los Angeles. Among his works are the choral orchestral *Gurre-Lieder* and *Pierrot Lunaire*, a cycle of 21 poems for voice and chamber music. *See Section E.*

Schopenhauer, Arthur (1788–1860), German philosopher, b. Danzig, important historically for his pessimism, and his doctrine that will is superior to knowledge. His chief work is *The World as Will and Idea*. He regarded his contemporary Hegel as a charlatan.

Schubert, Franz Peter (1797–1828), Austrian composer, b. Vienna, the son of a schoolmaster, and a contemporary of Beethoven. He wrote not only symphonies, sonatas, string quartets, choral music and masses, but also over 600 songs of unsurpassed lyrical beauty. He might almost be called the creator of the German *Lied* as known today. He died in poverty in Vienna at 31 before his musical genius could reach its full flowering. *See Section E.*

Schumann, Robert Alexander (1810–56), composer of the early 19th cent. German romantic school. He wrote much chamber music, four symphonies, a piano concerto, and choral music, but it is his early piano pieces and songs that give constant delight. His wife Clara (1819–96) was one of the outstanding pianists of her time, especially as interpreter of Chopin. *See Section E.*

Schweitzer, Albert (1875–1965), Alsatian medical missionary, theologian, musician and philosopher, b. at Kayersberg. After publishing learned works, he resigned a promising European career to found at Lambaréné in French Equatorial Africa a hospital to fight leprosy and sleeping sickness and made it a centre of service to Africans. His funds were raised by periodic organ recitals in Europe. His motivation was not patronage but atonement. Nobel peace prize 1952. O.M. 1955.

Scipio, Publius Cornelius (237–183 B.C.), Roman general in the second Punic War, known as Scipio Africanus the elder. Scipio Africanus the younger (185–129 B.C.) was an adoptive relative and an implacable opponent of Carthage (destroyed 146).

Scott, Charles Prestwich (1846–1931), English newspaper editor. Under his editorship (1872–1929) the *Manchester Guardian* (now *The Guardian*) became a leading journal.

Scott, Sir George Gilbert (1811–78), English architect in the Gothic revival. He restored many churches and designed the Albert Memorial and the Martyrs' Memorial at Oxford.

Scott, Sir Giles Gilbert (1880–1960), English architect, grandson of above, designed the Anglican cathedral at Liverpool and planned the new Waterloo bridge.

Scott, Robert Falcon (1868–1912), English antarctic explorer. He led two expeditions: one 1901–4 which discovered King Edward VII Land; and another 1910–12 which reached the south pole and found the Amundsen records; but while returning the party was overtaken by blizzards and perished 11 miles from their base. *See also* Antarctic exploration, Sec. L. His son, Sir Peter Scott (b. 1909), is an artist and ornithologist, founder of the Severn Wild Fowl Trust; Chancellor Birmingham University.

Scott, Sir Walter (1771–1832), Scottish novelist and poet, b. Edinburgh. He was educated for the law, but came to know and love the Border country and his interests were literary; and in 1802–3 he issued a collection of ballads, *Border Minstrelsy*. Poems such as *Marmion* and *The Lady of the Lake* followed. His novels appeared anonymously, beginning with *Waverley* in 1814; and continuing with *Guy Mannering, The Antiquary, Old Mortality, Rob Roy*, and the *Heart of Midlothian*. From 1819 he turned also to English history, with *Ivanhoe* and *Kenilworth*. In 1826 he became bankrupt, largely as the fault of his publishing partner, and worked heroically to clear off debts.

Scott-Paine, Hubert (1891–1954), pioneer in the design and construction of aircraft and sea-craft.

Scriabin, Alexander (1872–1915), Russian composer and pianist, who relied to some extent on extra-musical factors such as religion, and in *Prometheus* tried to unite music and philosophy. *See Section E.*

Seeley, Sir John Robert (1834–95), English historian, author of a life of Christ, *Ecce Homo*.

Segovia, Andrés (b. 1894), Spanish concert-guitarist. He has adapted works by Bach, Haydn, Mozart, and other classical composers to the guitar.

Selfridge, Harry Gordon (1858–1947), American-born merchant who in 1909 opened a new style of department store in Oxford Street.

Semmelweis, Ignaz Philipp (1818–65), Hungarian obstetrician, a pioneer in the use of antiseptic methods, thus reducing the incidence of puerperal fever.

Seneca, Lucius Annaeus (c. 4 B.C.–A.D. 65), Roman stoic philosopher who was tutor to Nero, but lost favour and was sentenced to take his own life.

Senefelder, Alois (1772–1834), Bavarian inventor of lithography about 1796.

Severus, Lucius Septimius (146–211), Roman emperor, and a successful general. On a visit to Britain he suppressed a revolt, repaired Hadrian's Wall, and died at York.

Sévigné, Marie de Rabutin-Chantal, Marquise de (1626–96), French woman of letters. Her letters to her daughter Françoise written in an unaffected elegance of style give a moving picture of fashionable society in 17th cent. France.

Sgambati, Giovanni (1841–1914), Italian pianist (pupil of Liszt), composer and teacher, who revived interest in classical instrumental music in age of opera.

Shackleton, Sir Ernest Henry (1874–1922), British explorer, who made four antarctic expeditions; that of 1909 reached within 100 miles of the south pole. He died on his last expedition.

Shaftesbury, 7th Earl of (Anthony Ashley Cooper) (1801–85), English philanthropist largely responsible for legislation reducing the misery of the industrial revolution. He was for 40 years chairman of the Ragged Schools Union.

Shakespeare, William (1564–1616), England's greatest poet and dramatist, b. Stratford-on-Avon. Little is known of his career up to his eighteenth year, when he married Anne Hathaway. He came to London at the height of the English renaissance and soon became connected with the Globe theatre as actor and playwright. Thirty-eight plays comprise the Shakespeare canon. Thirty-six were printed in the First Folio of 1623 (the first collected edition of his dramatic works), of which eighteen had been published during his lifetime in the so-called Quartos. *Love's Labour's Lost* and *The Comedy of Errors* seem to have been among the earliest, being followed by *The Two Gentlemen of Verona*, and *Romeo and Juliet*. Then followed *Henry VI, Richard III, Richard II, Titus Andronicus, The Taming of the Shrew, King John, The*

B55

Merchant of Venice, A Midsummer Night's Dream, All's Well that Ends Well, Henry IV, The Merry Wives of Windsor, Henry V, Much Ado about Nothing, As You Like It, Twelfth Night. Then came some of his greatest plays, *Julius Caesar, Hamlet, Troilus and Cressida, Othello, Measure for Measure, Macbeth, King Lear, Timon of Athens, Pericles, Antony and Cleopatra, Coriolanus, Cymbeline, A Winter's Tale, The Tempest, Henry VIII,* and *The Two Noble Kinsmen.* In mastery of language, in understanding of character, and in dramatic perception, he has never been surpassed. Fresh interpretation of his work continues. *See* Section I.

Sharp, Granville (1735–1813), English abolitionist of slavery, and founder of the colony of Sierra Leone.

Shastri, Shri Lal Bahadur (1904–66), Indian politician who became prime minister of India after the death of Nehru in 1964. He died of a heart attack at the end of the Soviet-sponsored Tashkent talks.

Shaw, George Bernard (1856–1950), Irish dramatist who conquered England by his wit and exposure of hypocrisy, cant, and national weaknesses, and whose individual opinions found expression in musical criticism, socialist pamphlets and plays. His plays include *Man and Superman, Heartbreak House, Back to Methuselah, Saint Joan, The Apple Cart,* and *Buoyant Billions,* and most have important prefaces. In 1884 he joined the newly-born Fabian Society. Nobel prizewinner 1925.

Shelley, Percy Bysshe (1792–1822), English poet, b. Horsham. He was a master of language and of literary form, and a passionate advocate of freedom and of new thought. Sent down from Oxford for his pamphlet *The Necessity of Atheism,* he came under the influence of William Godwin; and, after his first marriage came to an unhappy end, married the latter's daughter, Mary Wollstonecraft, herself a writer. In the same year began his friendship with Byron. His works include *The Revolt of Islam,* the *Masque of Anarchy* (an indictment of Castlereagh), *The Cenci* (a play on evil), and *Prometheus Unbound,* besides lyrics such as *To a Skylark* and *Ode to the West Wind.* He was accidentally drowned while sailing near Spezzia.

Sheppard, Hugh Richard (Dick) (1880–1937), Anglican divine and pacifist. He made St. Martin-in-the-Fields a centre of social service and also founded the Peace Pledge Union.

Sheraton, Thomas (1751–1806), English cabinetmaker, b. Stockton, whose *Cabinetmaker's Book* promoted neo-classical designs.

Sheridan, Richard Brinsley (1751–1816), British dramatist. b. Dublin. He was a brilliant writer of comedies, especially *The Rivals, The Duenna, The School for Scandal,* and *The Critic.* He acquired and rebuilt Drury Lane theatre, which reopened in 1794, but was burnt down in 1809; and this, with his lack of business sense, brought him to poverty, in spite of his friends' efforts to help him. He was also in parliament where he made some notable speeches.

Sherman, William Tecumseh (1820–91), American general, who served especially in the Civil War. He took part in the battles of Bull Run and Shiloh, was appointed in 1864 to the command of the southwest, and with 65,000 men marched across Georgia to the sea. In 1865 he accepted Johnston's surrender.

Sherrington, Sir Charles Scott (1875–1952), English scientist, an authority on the physiology of the nervous system. His research led to advances in brain surgery. His principal work is *Integrative Action of the Nervous System* (1906). Shared with E. D. Adrian the 1932 Nobel prize.

Shirley, James (1596–1666), English dramatist. His tragedies include *The Traitor,* and his comedies *Hyde Park.* His death was hastened by the Great Fire.

Sholokhov, Mikhail Aleksandrovich (b. 1905), Russian novelist, author of *And Quiet Flows the Don.* Nobel prizewinner 1965.

Shostakovich, Dimitri (1906–75), Russian composer whose music is complex, profound, and deeply significant of the Soviet age in which he lived. His works include operas, ballets, symphonies, chamber music, and music for films. Hero of Soviet Labour 1966. *See* Section E.

Sibelius, Jean (1865–1957), Finnish composer imbued with national feeling. His works include seven symphonies, a violin concerto, and several tone poems, notably *Finlandia,* and some based on the Finnish poem *Kalevala. See* Section E.

Sickert, Walter Richard (1860–1942), British artist, b. Munich. He was influenced by Degas, and has himself influenced later painters. His *Ennui* is in the Tate Gallery.

Siddons, Sarah (1755–1831), English actress especially in tragic parts. She was daughter of the manager Roger Kemble and her reputation was almost unbounded.

Sidgwick, Henry (1838–1900), English philosopher who wrote *Methods of Ethics,* and who also promoted women's education, especially in the foundation of Newnham and Girton colleges.

Sidney, Sir Philip (1554–86), English poet and writer, best remembered for his *Arcadia, Apologie for Poetrie,* and *Astrophel and Stella,* all published after his death. He was killed at the battle of Zutphen, where he passed a cup of water to another, saying " Thy necessity is greater than mine."

Siemens, Sir William (1823–83), German-born electrical engineer who settled in England and constructed many overland and submarine telegraphs. He was brother of Werner von Siemens, founder of the firm of Siemens-Halske.

Sienkiewicz, Henryk (1846–1916), Polish novelist and short-story writer; best known of his historical novels is *Quo Vadis?.* Nobel prizewinner 1905.

Sikorski, Vladislav (1881–1943), Polish general and statesman, prime minister of the Polish government in exile (1939) and commander-in-chief of the Polish forces. Killed in an aircraft accident at Gibraltar.

Simpson, Sir James Young (1811–70), Scottish obstetrician who initiated the use of chloroform in childbirth.

Sinclair, Upton (1878–1968), American novelist whose documentary novel *The Jungle* on the Chicago slaughter yards caused a sensation in 1906.

Singer, Isaac Merritt (1811–75), American mechanical engineer who improved early forms of the sewing-machine and patented a single-thread and chain-stitch machine.

Sisley, Alfred (1839–99), French impressionist painter of English origin, who painted some enchanting landscapes, such as *Meadows in Spring* in the Tate Gallery. He was influenced by Corot and Manet.

Sitwell, Edith (1887–1964), English poet, a great experimenter in verse forms. *Gold Coast Customs, Façade* (set to music by William Walton) and *Still Falls the Rain* are probably best known. She had two brothers, Osbert (1892–1969) and Sacheverell (b. 1897), both poets and critics. *See also* Section M.

Slim, 1st Viscount (William Slim) (1891–1970), British general. He commanded the 14th Army in Burma, was chief of the Imperial General Staff 1948–52, and governor-general of Australia 1953–60.

Sloane, Sir Hans (1660–1753), British collector, b. Ireland. He practised in London as a physician. His library of 50,000 volumes and his collection of MSS. and botanical specimens were offered under his will to the nation and formed the beginning of the British Museum.

Slowacki, Julius (1809–49), Polish romantic poet, a revolutionary, he lived in exile in Paris. His work includes the poetic drama *Kordian, Balladyna* and *Lilli Weneda,* written in the style of Shakespeare; and the unfinished poem *King Spirit* which reveals his later mystical tendencies.

Smeaton, John (1724–92), English engineer; he rebuilt Eddystone lighthouse (1756–59), improved Newcomen's steam-engine, and did important work on bridges, harbours, and canals. He also invented an improved blowing apparatus for iron-smelting.

Smetana, Bedřich (1824–84), Czech composer, creator of a national style. He was principal conductor of the Prague National Theatre, for which he wrote most of his operas, including *The Bartered Bride* and *The Kiss.* Best known of his other compositions are the cycle of symphonic poems *My Country* and the string quartets *From My Life*. He became totally deaf in 1874, suffered a mental breakdown, and died in an asylum. *See Section E.*

Smiles, Samuel (1812–1904), Scottish writer, b. Haddington, in early life a medical practitioner, remembered for *Self Help* (1859), and his biographies of engineers of the industrial revolution.

Smith, Adam (1723–90), Scottish economist, b. Kirkcaldy. In Edinburgh he published *Moral Sentiments*. Later he moved to London, and his *Wealth of Nations* (1776) is the first serious work in political economy.

Smith, Sir Grafton Elliot (1871–1937), Australian anatomist who did research on the structure of the mammalian brain. His works include *The Evolution of Man*.

Smith, John (1580–1631), English adventurer who in 1605 went on a colonising expedition to Virginia and was saved from death by the Red Indian Pocahontas.

Smith, Joseph (1805–44), American founder of the Mormons. He claimed that the *Book of Mormon* was revealed to him. In 1838 feeling against the Mormons culminated in a rising and Smith was murdered. He was succeeded by Brigham Young. *See* Mormonism, Section J.

Smith, Sydney (1771–1845), Anglican divine and journalist, who founded the *Edinburgh Review* and supported Catholic emancipation.

Smith, William (1769–1839), English surveyor and canal-maker, the first to map the rock strata of England and to identify the fossils peculiar to each layer.

Smith, Sir William Alexander (1854–1914), Scottish founder of the Boys' Brigade (1883), the oldest national organisation for boys in Britain.

Smith, William Robertson (1846–94), Scottish biblical scholar whose " Bible " contribution to the 9th edition of *The Encyclopaedia Britannica* resulted in an unsuccessful prosecution for heresy.

Smollett, Tobias George (1721–71), Scottish novelist whose work is characterised by satire and coarse humour. His main novels are *Roderick Random, Peregrine Pickle*, and *Humphrey Clinker*.

Smuts, Jan Christian (1870–1950), South African statesman and soldier. B. in Cape Colony, during the Boer War he fought on the Boer side. He was premier of the Union 1919–24, 1939–48, and worked for cooperation within the Commonwealth and in the world, but his party was defeated in 1948 by the Nationalists under Malan.

Smyth, Ethel Mary (1858–1944), English composer and suffragette. Her main works are operas (*The Wreckers* and *The Boatswain's Mate*) and a *Mass in D*. She studied at the Leipzig Conservatory.

Snow, Baron (Charles Percy Snow) (b. 1905), English physicist and novelist, author of the essay *The Two Cultures of the Scientific Revolution*, and a sequence of novels *Strangers and Brothers* (11 vols.).

Snyders, Frans (1597–1657), Flemish still-life and animal painter who studied under Breughel.

Soane, Sir John (1753–1837), English architect who designed the Bank of England. He left the nation his house and library in Lincoln's Inn Fields (Soane Museum).

Sobers, Sir Garfield (b. 1936), West Indies and Nottinghamshire cricketer who ranks as one of the greatest all-rounders. Knighted 1975.

Socinus or Sozzini, Laelius (1525–62), Italian founder of the sect of Socinians, with his nephew Faustus (1539–1604). Their teachings resemble those of Unitarians.

Socrates (470–399 B.C.), Greek philosopher and intellectual leader, was the son of a sculptor of Athens. He distinguished himself in three campaigns (Potidaea, Delium, and Amphipolis). Returning to Athens, he devoted himself to study and intellectual enquiry, attracting many followers; through these, especially Xenophon and Plato, we know of his teachings, for he wrote nothing. In 399 B.C. he was charged with impiety and with corrupting the young, found guilty, and accordingly died by drinking hemlock; see Plato's *Apology, Crito*, and *Phaedo.*

Soddy, Frederick (1877–1956), English chemist, who in Glasgow about 1912 laid the foundation of the isotope theory, before the physicists became prominent in that field. Nobel prizewinner 1921.

Solon (638–558 B.C.), Athenian lawgiver, who in a time of economic distress cancelled outstanding debts, and introduced some democratic changes.

Solzhenitsyn, Alexander Isayevich (b. 1918), Russian novelist, b. Rostov-on-Don; author of *One Day in the Life of Ivan Denisovich*, a documentary novel depicting life in one of Stalin's prison camps where he spent many years of his life. He was expelled from the Soviet Writers' Union in 1969, and from his country in 1974. Nobel prizewinner 1970.

Somerset, Duke of (Edward Seymour) (1506–52), lord protector of England in the time of the young Edward VI, but he fell from power and was executed.

Sophocles (495–406 B.C.), Athenian dramatist, was awarded the prize over Aeschylus in 468. Of over a hundred plays of his, the only extant ones are *Oedipus the King, Oedipus at Colonus Antigone, Electra, Trachiniae, Ajax, Philoctetes.*

Sorel, Georges (1847–1922), French advocate of revolutionary syndicalism, author of *Reflections on Violence* (1905). The irrational aspects of his philosophy (derived from Bergson) appealed to Mussolini and the Fascists.

Soult, Nicolas Jean de Dieu (1769–1851), French general who fought under Napoleon in Switzerland and Italy, at Austerlitz, and in the Peninsular War.

Sousa, John Philip (1854–1932), American bandmaster and composer of some stirring marches.

Southey, Robert (1774–1843), English poet and historian. In 1803 he settled near Coleridge at Keswick, and in 1813 became poet laureate. His best work was in prose: histories of Brazil and of the Peninsular War; lives of Nelson, Wesley, and others.

Southwell, Robert (1561–95), English poet and Jesuit martyr, beatified 1929. His poems include *The Burning Babe.*

Spaak, Paul Henri (1899–1972), Belgian statesman, first president of the U.N. General Assembly in 1946 and of the Assembly of the Council of Europe, 1949–51; secretary-general of NATO, 1957–61.

Spartacus (d. 71 B.C.), Thracian rebel. A Roman slave and gladiator in Capua, he escaped and headed a slave insurrection, routing several Roman armies, but was defeated and killed by Crassus.

Speke, John Hanning (1827–64), British explorer. In 1858 he discovered the Victoria Nyanza; and in 1860 with J. A. Grant traced the Nile flowing out of it.

Spence, Sir Basil Urwin (1907–76), Scottish architect, mainly known for the new Coventry cathedral, and for Hampstead civic centre. He also brought a new approach to university buildings. O.M. 1962.

Spencer, Herbert (1820–1903), English philosopher. B. Derby, he was at first a civil engineer, then a journalist (sub-editor of the *Economist*), when he wrote *Social Statics*. He coined the phrase (1852) " the survival of the fittest " and his *Principles of Psychology* (1855), published four years before Darwin's *Origin of Species*, expounded doctrines of evolution. His ten-volume *Synthetic Philosophy* was issued over a period of thirty years.

Spencer, Sir Stanley (1891–1959), English artist of visionary power. His two pictures of the *Resurrection* are in the Tate Gallery. He also painted Cookham regatta.

Spengler, Oswald (1880–1936), German historicist who held that every culture is destined to a waxing and waning life cycle and that the West European culture was entering its period of decline. His principal work is *The Decline of the West*. His views prepared the way for national socialism.

Spenser, Edmund (1552–99), English poet, b. London and educated at Cambridge. His *Shepheards Calender* appeared in 1579. In 1580 he went to Ireland as the lord deputy's secretary, and later acquired Kilcolman castle, where he wrote most of his main work, *The Faerie Queene*. His castle was burnt in an insurrection in 1598, when he returned to London. He is called " the poet's poet."

Spinoza, Baruch (1632–77), Dutch philosopher, b. Amsterdam, whose parents came to Holland from Portugal to escape the Inquisition. An independent thinker, his criticism of the Scrip-

B57

tures led to his being excommunicated from the synagogue. He supported himself by grinding and polishing lenses. He owed much to Descartes but was mainly concerned with religion and virtue. His philosophical theories are set out in the *Ethics* which was published posthumously. In the light of modern science his metaphysic cannot be accepted but his moral teaching has enduring validity.

Spofforth, Reginald (1770–1827), English writer of glees, including *Hail, Smiling Morn.*

Spurgeon, Charles Haddon (1834–92), English Baptist who preached at the vast Metropolitan Tabernacle, London, from 1861 (burnt down 1898).

Staël, Anne Louise, Baronne de Staël-Holstein (1766–1817), French writer. Daughter of the finance minister, Necker, she married the Swedish ambassador, and kept a salon. Her *Lettres sur Rousseau* appeared in 1788. After the revolution she lived partly abroad, partly in France, and after a visit to Italy wrote her novel *Corinne* (1807).

Stalin (Joseph Vissarionovich Djugashvili) (1879–1953), Soviet statesman who for nearly 30 years was leader of the Russian people. He originally studied at Tiflis for the priesthood, but became an active revolutionary and took part in the civil war after 1917. After Lenin's death, he ousted Trotsky and became the outstanding figure. He modernised agriculture on socialist lines by ruthless means, and his series of five-year plans from 1929 made Russia an industrial power. On the German invasion in 1941 he assumed military leadership; and later attended Allied war conferences. After his death some of his methods and the "personality cult" were denounced by Khrushchev, and this had far-reaching results in other Communist countries. In his attack on "official" Marxism, George Lukács says Stalin "turned Marxism on its head" by making it into theories and strategies which fitted his own tactics of the day.

Stanford, Sir Charles Villiers (1852–1924), Irish composer of instrumental, choral, operatic, and other music.

Stanley, Sir Henry Morton (1841–1904), British explorer, b. Denbigh. He fought for the Confederates in the American Civil War. He then became a correspondent for the *New York Herald*, was commissioned to find Livingstone, and did so in 1871 at Ujiji, and with him explored Lake Tanganyika. In 1879 he founded the Congo Free State under the Belgian king. His works include *Through the Dark Continent* and an *Autobiography.*

Stark, Freya Madeline (b. 1893), British writer and explorer of the Arab world.

Steele, Sir Richard (1672–1729), British essayist, b. Dublin. He founded the *Tatler* (1709–11), to which Addison also contributed, and later the *Spectator* (1711–12) and the *Guardian* (1713).

Steen, Jan (1626–79), Dutch genre painter, b. Leiden, son of a brewer. *The Music Lesson* and *Skittle Alley* are in the National Gallery, the *Lute Player* in the Wallace collection.

Steer, Philip Wilson (1860–1942), English painter, especially of landscapes and of portraits.

Stefansson, Vilhjalmur (1879–1962), Canadian arctic explorer of Icelandic parentage; his publications include *Unsolved Mysteries of the Arctic.*

Stein, Sir Aurel (1862–1943), British archaeologist, b. Budapest. He held archaeological posts under the Indian government and explored Chinese Turkestan.

Stendhal, pseudonym of Marie Henri Beyle (1783–1842), French novelist, b. Grenoble. He was with Napoleon's army in the Russian campaign of 1812, spent several years in Italy, and after the revolution of 1830 was appointed consul at Trieste, and afterwards at Civitavecchia. In his plots he recreates historical and social events with imaginative realism and delineates character with searching psychological insight. His main works are *Le Rouge et le Noir*, and *La Chartreuse de Parme.*

Stephen (1105–54), usurped the crown of England from Henry I's daughter in 1135; and, after anarchy, retained it till his death.

Stephen, Sir Leslie (1832–1904), English writer, critic, and biographer. He edited the *Cornhill Magazine* (1871–82), and the *Dictionary of National Biography* (1882–91), and was the father of Virginia Woolf.

Stephenson, George (1781–1848), English engineer; a locomotive designer, b. at Wylam near Newcastle, a colliery fireman's son. As engine-wright at Killingworth colliery he made his first locomotive in 1814 to haul coal from mines. He and his son Robert built the *Locomotion* for the Stockton and Darlington Railway (1825), the first locomotive for a public railway. His *Rocket* at 30 miles an hour won the prize of £500 in 1829 offered by the Liverpool and Manchester Railway. He also discovered the principle on which the miners' safety lamp was based. He was the first president of the Institution of Mechanical Engineers.

Stephenson, Robert (1803–59), English engineer, son of the above, engineered railway lines in England and abroad, and built many bridges including the Menai and Conway tubular bridges and others overseas.

Sterne, Laurence (1713–68), English novelist and humorist. His main works are *Tristram Shandy* and *A Sentimental Journey.* He led a wandering and unconventional life, dying in poverty. His work helped to develop the novel.

Stevenson, Adlai (1900–65), American politician, an efficient governor of Illinois, 1949–1953; ambassador to the U.N., 1960–5, and unsuccessful presidential challenger to Eisenhower 1952 and 1956.

Stevenson, Robert (1772–1850), Scottish engineer and builder of lighthouses, who invented "intermittent" and "flashing" lights.

Stevenson, Robert Louis (1850–94), Scottish author, b. Edinburgh. He suffered from ill-health and eventually settled in Samoa. His main works are *Travels with a Donkey, Treasure Island, Kidnapped, Dr. Jekyll and Mr. Hyde*, and *The Master of Ballantrae.*

Stinnes, Hugo (1870–1924), German industrialist who built up a huge coalmining, iron and steel, and transport business, and later entered politics.

Stoker, Bram (Abraham Stoker) (1847–1912), Irish author of the horror story *Dracula* and *Personal Reminiscences of Henry Irving.*

Stokes, Sir George Gabriel (1819–1903), Irish mathematician and physicist to whom is due the modern theory of viscous fluids and the discovery that rays beyond the violet end of the spectrum (the ultra-violet rays) produce fluorescence in certain substances.

Stopes, Marie Carmichael (1880–1958), English pioneer advocate of birth control. Her *Married Love* appeared in 1918, and she pioneered birth control clinics.

Stowe, Harriet Beecher (1811–96), American author of *Uncle Tom's Cabin* (1852), written to expose slavery.

Strachey, John St. Loe (1901–63), English Labour politician and writer. He held office under Attlee, 1945–51.

Stradivari, Antonio (1644–1737), Italian maker of violins, b. Cremona, first in his art.

Strafford, 1st Earl of (Thomas Wentworth) (1593–1641), English statesman. He supported Charles I with a "thorough" policy, both as president of the north and as lord deputy in Ireland, where he introduced flax. His efficiency made him a special target when parliament met, and he was impeached and executed.

Strauss, David Friedrich (1808–74), German theologian, whose *Life of Jesus* attempted to prove that the gospels are based on myths.

Strauss, family of Viennese musicians. **Johann Strauss** (1804–49), the elder, was a composer of dance music, who with Joseph Lanner established the Viennese waltz tradition. His son, **Johann Strauss** (1825–99), the younger, although not so good a violinist or conductor as his father, was the composer of over 400 waltzes, which include *The Blue Danube* and *Tales from the Vienna Woods*. Two of his brothers, **Josef Strauss** (1827–70) and **Eduard Strauss** (1835–1916) were also composers and conductors.

Strauss, Richard (1864–1949), German composer and conductor, the son of a horn player in the opera orchestra at Munich. He succeeded von Bülow as court musical director at Meiningen. His works include the operas *Salome, Elektra*, and *Der Rosenkavalier* the symphonic poems *Don Juan, Till Eulenspiegel*, and *Don Quixote*, and many songs. *See* Section E.

Stravinsky, Igor (1882–1971), Russian composer and conductor, pupil of Rimsky-Korsakov.

His ballets, *The Fire Bird* (1910), *Petrushka* (1911), representative of his early romantic style, and the revolutionary *The Rite of Spring*, which caused a furore in 1913, were written for the ballet impresario Diaghilev. He adopted a neo-classical style in later works, for example, in the ballets *Pulcinella* and *Apollo Musagetes* and the opera-oratorio *Oedipus Rex*. He brought new vigour and freedom to rhythm and younger composers have been much influenced by his music. He became a French citizen in 1934 and a U.S. citizen in 1945. *See* Section E.

Strindberg, Johan August (1849–1912), Swedish writer of intense creative energy. His work is subjective and reflects his personal conflicts. He married three times but never happily. He produced some 55 plays as well as novels, stories, poems, and critical essays. *Lucky Peter, Gustav Adolf, Till Damascus, The Father, Miss Julie* are some of his plays.

Suckling, Sir John (1609–42), English poet, author of *Why so pale and wan?* He invented cribbage.

Sudermann, Hermann (1857–1928), German writer of plays and novels, including *Frau Sorge* (translated as Dame Care).

Sulaiman the Magnificent (1494–1566), sultan of Turkey, conquerer, and patron of art and learning, who dominated the eastern Mediterranean but failed to capture Malta.

Sullivan, Sir Arthur Seymour (1842–1900), Irish composer, mainly known for the music he wrote for light operas with W. S Gilbert as librettist, especially *The Pirates of Penzance, Patience, The Mikado, The Yeomen of the Guard* and *The Gondoliers.* He also wrote sacred music which was popular at the time. He and a friend discovered Schubert's lost *Rosamunde* music.

Sully, Maximilien de Béthune, Duc de (1560–1641), French statesman, finance minister to Henry IV. He also left *Memoirs.*

Sun Yat Sen (1867–1925), Chinese revolutionary, idealist and humanitarian. He graduated in medicine at Hong Kong, but after a rising failed in 1895 he lived abroad, planning further attempts, which succeeded in 1911 when the Manchus were overthrown and he became president. He soon resigned in favour of Yuan Shih-kai. His "Three Principles" were nationalism, democracy, and livelihood.

Sutherland, Graham Vivian (b. 1903), British artist. He painted the 80th birthday portrait of Sir Winston Churchill for parliament, and designed the tapestry for Coventry cathedral. O.M. 1960.

Swedenborg, Emanuel (1689–1772), Swedish author of *Arcana Coelestia, The Apocalypse Revealed, Four Preliminary Doctrines,* and *The True Christian Religion.* He claimed that his soul had been permitted to travel into hell, purgatory, and heaven. His works became the scriptures of the sect named Swedenborgians.

Sweelinck, Jan Pieterszoon (1562–1621), Dutch organist and composer of sacred music. In his fugues he made independent use of the pedals, and prepared the way for Bach. *See* Section E.

Swift, Jonathan (1667–1745), English satirist, b. Dublin of English parents. He crossed to England in 1688 to become secretary to Sir William Temple, and took Anglican orders, but did not obtain promotion. His *Tale of a Tub* and *The Battle of the Books* appeared in 1704. At first active in Whig politics, he became Tory in 1710, writing powerful tracts such as *Conduct of the Allies* (1711). In 1714 he retired to Ireland as Dean of St. Patrick's. His devoted women friends followed him—Hester Johnson (d. 1728), the Stella of his *Journal,* and Esther Vanhomrigh (d. 1723), the Vanessa of his poetry. Here he wrote his best work, including *Gulliver's Travels* (1726) and *The Drapier's Letters.*

Swinburne, Algernon Charles (1837–1909), English poet and critic. He first won attention with a play, *Atalanta in Calydon,* in 1865, followed by *Poems and Ballads.* Later followed *Songs before Sunrise, Bothwell,* and *Mary Stuart.* His criticism includes an essay on Blake.

Swithin, St. (d. 862), English saint, bishop of Winchester. Violent rain for 40 days fell in 971 when his body was to be removed to the new cathedral; hence the superstition as to rain on 15 July.

Syme, Sir Ronald (b. 1903), Camden Professor of Ancient History at Oxford, 1949–70; an authority on Tacitus. O.M. 1976.

Symonds, John Addington (1840–93), English author who wrote on the Italian Renaissance.

Synge, John Millington (1871–1909), Irish poet and playwright, author of *Riders to the Sea* and *The Playboy of the Western World.* He was a director of the Abbey Theatre.

T

Tacitus, Gaius Cornelius (*c.* 55–120), Roman historian. His chief works are a life of his father-in-law Agricola, and his *Histories* and *Annals.*

Taft, William Howard (1857–1930), United States president, 1909–13.

Tagore, Sir Rabindranath (1861–1941), Indian poet and philosopher who tried to blend east and west. His works include the play *Chitra.* Nobel prize 1913 (first Asian recipient).

Talbot, William Henry Fox (1800–77), English pioneer of photography which he developed independently of Daguerre. He also deciphered the cuneiform inscriptions at Nineveh.

Talleyrand-Périgord, Charles Maurice de (1754–1838), French politician and diplomat, led a mission to England in 1792 and was foreign minister from 1797 until 1807. He represented France at the Congress of Vienna.

Tallis, Thomas (*c.* 1510–85), English musician, with Byrd joint organist to the chapel royal under Elizabeth. He composed some of the finest of our church music.

Tamerlane (Timur the Lame) (1336–1405), Mongol conqueror. Ruler of Samarkand, he conquered Iran, Transcaucasia, Iraq, Armenia, and Georgia, and invaded India and Syria. He defeated the Turks at Angora, but died marching towards China. A ruthless conqueror, he was also a patron of literature and the arts. The line of rulers descended from him are the Timurids. He is the subject of a play by Marlowe.

Tarkington, Booth (1869–1946), American author of *Monsieur Beaucaire.*

Tarquinius: two kings of Rome came from this Etruscan family; Lucius the Elder (d. 578 B.C.); and Lucius Superbus, or the proud, (d. 510 B.C.) whose tyranny provoked a successful rising and brought an end to the monarchy.

Tartini, Giuseppe (1692–1770), Italian violinist, who wrote *Trillo del Diavolo.* He discovered the "third sound" resulting from two notes sounded together, a scientific explanation of which was later given by Helmholtz.

Tasman, Abel Janszoon (1603–59), Dutch navigator despatched by Van Diemen. He discovered Tasmania or Van Diemen's Land, and New Zealand, in 1642.

Tasso, Torquato (1544–95), Italian epic poet, b. Sorrento, author of *Gerusalemme Liberata.* He also wrote plays, *Aminta* and *Torrismondo.*

Tawney, Richard Henry (1880–1962), British historian, b. Calcutta, pioneer of adult education, and leader of socialist thought—the first critic of the affluent society. His works include *The Acquisitive Society, Equality, Religion and the Rise of Capitalism.*

Taylor, Sir Geoffrey Ingram (b. 1886), British scientist, noted for his work on aerodynamics, hydrodynamics, and the structure of metals. O.M. 1969.

Taylor, Jeremy (1613–67), English divine, b. Cambridge, author of many religious works, of which the chief are *Holy Living* and *Holy Dying.*

Tchaikovsky, Peter Ilyich (1840–93), Russian composer. His music is melodious and emotional and he excelled in several branches of composition. Among his works are the operas *Eugene Onegin* and *The Queen of Spades* (both from stories by Pushkin), symphonies, including the *Little Russian* and the *Pathétique,* ballets, including *Swan Lake, The Sleeping Beauty,* and *The Nutcracker,* the fantasies *Romeo and Juliet,* and *Francesca da Rimini,* the piano concerto in B flat minor, the violin concerto in D, and numerous songs. *See* Section E.

Tedder, 1st Baron (Arthur William Tedder) (1890–1967), British air marshal. From 1940 he reorganised the Middle East Air Force and later became deputy supreme commander under

Eisenhower for the invasion of Europe. He wrote an autobiography.

Teilhard de Chardin, Pierre (1881–1955), French palæontologist and religious philosopher. He went on palæontological expeditions in Asia, but his research did not conform to Jesuit orthodoxy, and his main works were published posthumously, *The Phenomenon of Man* and *Le Milieu Divin.*

Telemann, Georg Philipp (1681–1767), German composer, b. Magdeburg. His vitality and originality of form are appreciated today after a long period of neglect.

Telford, Thomas (1757–1834), Scottish engineer, originally a stonemason. He built bridges (two over the Severn and the Menai suspension bridge), canals (the Ellesmere and Caledonian canals), roads, and docks.

Tell, William, legendary Swiss patriot, reputedly required by the Austrian governor Gessler to shoot an apple from his son's head, and the subject of a play by Schiller. The story is late, but the Swiss confederation did first arise in the 14th cent. with Schwyz, Uri, and Unterwalden.

Temple, Frederick (1821–1902), English divine. He was headmaster of Rugby, 1857–69, and archbishop of Canterbury, 1897–1902.

Temple, William (1881–1944), English ecclesiastic, son of above, was a leading moral force in social matters and a worker for ecumenism. He was headmaster of Repton, 1910–14, and became archbishop of Canterbury in 1942.

Temple, Sir William (1628–99), English diplomat and writer, was instrumental in bringing about the marriage of Princess Mary with William of Orange. Swift was his secretary.

Templewood, 1st Viscount (Samuel John Gurney Hoare) (1880–1959), British Conservative politician. He piloted the India Act through the Commons while secretary for India, 1931–5; and as foreign secretary he negotiated an abortive pact with Laval.

Teniers, David, the elder (1582–1649), and the **younger** (1610–94), Flemish painters of rural life and landscape. The elder lived at Antwerp and the younger at Brussels.

Tenniel, Sir John (1820–1914), English book illustrator, especially for *Alice in Wonderland* and *Punch.*

Tennyson, 1st Baron (Alfred Tennyson) (1809–92), English poet-laureate, b. Somersby, Lincs. A master of language, his publications extended over 60 years, mirroring much of his age. *In Memoriam* reflects his grief for his friend Arthur Hallam. Apart from his lyrics, his longer works include *The Princess, Maud, Idylls of the King,* and *Enoch Arden.* Interest in his work is returning.

Terence, Publius Terentius Afer (c. 184–159 B.C.), a Latin poet and dramatist, an African (Berber), who rose from the position of a slave.

Teresa, St. (1515–82), influential Spanish religious reformer and writer, b. Avila, a woman of boundless energy and spiritual strength. She entered the Carmelite order about 1534, established a reformed order in 1562 (St. Joseph's, Avila), and also founded, with the help of St. John of the Cross, houses for friars. Her writings which rank high in mystical literature include *The Way of Perfection* and *The Interior Castle.*

Terry, Ellen Alice (Mrs. James Carew) (1848–1928), English actress, especially in Shakespearean parts with Sir Henry Irving, and in the plays of her friend Bernard Shaw.

Tertullian, Quintus (c. 160–220), Carthaginian theologian whose works, especially *Apologeticum,* have profoundly influenced Christian thought.

Tesla, Nikola (1856–1943), Yugoslav physicist and inventor; went to America 1883; pioneer in high-tension electricity.

Tettrazzini, Luisa (1871–1940), Italian soprano, especially successful in *Lucia di Lammermoor.*

Tetzel, John (c. 1465–1519), German Dominican preacher, whose sale of indulgences for St. Peter's building fund provoked Luther.

Thackeray, William Makepeace (1811–63), English novelist, b. Calcutta, author of *Vanity Fair, Pendennis, Esmond, The Newcomes, The Virginians, Philip,* and *Lovel the Widower.* He edited the *Cornhill Magazine* from the first number in 1860, his most notable contributions

being *Roundabout Papers.* He also wrote *Yellowplush Papers, The Book of Snobs,* and *The Four Georges* (lectures given in the United States).

Thales of Miletus (c. 624–565 B.C.), earliest of the Greek scientists, he created a sensation by his prediction of an eclipse of the sun, which was visible at Miletus in 585 B.C. He looked upon water as the basis of all material things, and in his mathematical work was the first to enunciate natural laws. *See also* God and Man, Section J.

Thant, Sithu U (1909–74), Burmese diplomat; secretary-general of the United Nations 1962–1972.

Thatcher, Margaret Hilda (b. 1925), leader of the Conservative Party 1975–; the first woman in Europe to lead a political party; entered parliament as member for Finchley 1959.

Themistocles (c. 523–458 B.C.), Athenian soldier and statesman. He fortified the harbour of Piraeus and created a navy, defeating the Persians at Salamis in 480 B.C. He prepared the way for later greatness, but fell from power and died in exile.

Theocritus (c. 310–250 B.C.), Greek poet, especially of pastoral subjects. His short poems came to be called *Idylls.*

Theodoric the Great (455–526), King of the East Goths, who conquered Italy. Himself an Arian, he practised toleration, and his long reign was peaceful and prosperous.

Theodosius the Great (346–95), Roman emperor of the East (the Empire being divided in 364). He was baptised as a Trinitarian, issuing edicts against the Arians, and after a judicial massacre at Thessalonica he did penance to (St.) Ambrose.

Theophrastus (c. 372–287 B.C.), Greek philosopher, who succeeded Aristotle as teacher at Athens and inherited his library. He is best known for his botanical works and his *Characters* (moral studies).

Thibaud, Jacques (1880–1953), French violinist, killed in an air crash.

Thierry, Augustin (1795–1856), French historian, known for his *History of the Norman Conquest.*

Thiers, Louis Adolphe (1797–1877), French statesman and historian. After a varied political career, he became president in 1871, helping to revive France after defeat. He wrote a history of the Revolution.

Thomas, Dylan (1914–53), Welsh poet, whose highly individual *Eighteen Poems* (1934) brought him instant recognition. There followed *Twenty-five Poems* and *Deaths and Entrances. Under Milk Wood,* a play for voices, has more general appeal. *See* Section M.

Thompson, Sir D'Arcy Wentworth (1860–1948), Scottish zoologist whose *On Growth and Form* (1917), written in lucid and elegant style, has influenced biological science. He was also a classical scholar.

Thomson, Sir George Paget (1892–1975), English physicist, son of Sir J. J. Thomson; author of *The Atom, Theory and Practice of Electron Diffraction, The Inspiration of Science.* Nobel prizewinner 1937.

Thomson, James (1700–48), Scottish poet who wrote *The Seasons* and *The Castle of Indolence.*

Thomson, James (1834–82), poet and essayist, b. near Glasgow, who wrote *The City of Dreadful Night.*

Thomson, Sir Joseph John (1856–1940), English physicist and mathematician, leader of a group of researchers at the Cavendish laboratory, Cambridge. He established in 1897 that cathode-rays were moving particles whose speed and specific charge could be measured. He called them corpuscles but the name was changed to electrons. This work was followed up by the study of positive rays which led to the discovery of isotopes, the existence of which had earlier been suggested by Soddy. Nobel prizewinner 1906.

Thoreau, Henry David (1817–62), American essayist and nature-lover, who rebelled against society and lived for a time in a solitary hut. His chief work is *Walden.* He was a friend of Emerson.

Thorez, Maurice (1900–64), French communist leader from 1930 and especially after the second world war.

Thorndike, Dame Sybil (1882–1976), English actress. She made her début in 1904, and played in Greek tragedies, in the plays of Shakespeare and Shaw, and in Grand Guignol. Her husband was Sir Lewis Casson.

Thornycroft, Sir William Hamo (1850–1925), English sculptor, whose works include a statue of General Gordon in Trafalgar Square.

Thorpe, Sir Thomas Edward (1845–1925), English chemist who researched in inorganic chemistry and with his friend Arthur Rücker made a magnetic survey of the British Isles.

Thorwaldsen, Bertel (1770–1844), Danish sculptor whose works include the Cambridge statue of Byron.

Thucydides (c. 460–399 B.C.), Greek historian, especially of the Peloponnesian War in which he himself fought. He was not merely a chronicler, but saw the significance of events and tried to give an impartial account. The speeches attributed by him to leaders include the beautiful funeral oration of Pericles.

Tiberius, Claudius (42 B.C.–A.D. 37), Roman emperor who succeeded Augustus. His early reign was successful but his later years were marked by tragedy and perhaps insanity. He is the Tiberius of Luke 3.1.

Tillett, Benjamin (1860–1943), English trade-union leader, especially of a dockers' strike in 1889 and a transport-workers' strike in 1911.

Tillotson, John (1630–94), English divine, a noted preacher who became archbishop of Canterbury in 1691.

Tindal, Matthew (1655–1733), English deist, author of *Christianity as old as the Creation*.

Tintoretto (1518–94), Venetian painter whose aim it was to unite the colouring of Titian with the drawing of Michelangelo. His numerous paintings, mostly of religious subjects, were executed with great speed, some of them on enormous canvasses. His *Origin of the Milky Way* is in the National Gallery. His name was Jacopo Robusti, and he was called Il Tintoretto (little dyer) after his father's trade.

Tippett, Sir Michael Kemp (b. 1905), English composer whose works include the operas *The Midsummer Marriage*, *King Priam*, and *Knot Garden*, and the song-cycles *Boyhood's End* and *The Heart's Assurance*. *See* Section E.

Titian (Tiziano Vecelli) (c. 1487–1576), Venetian painter. He studied under the Bellinis and was influenced by Giorgione, for example, in his frescoes at Padua. His mature style is one of dynamic composition and full colour, as in his *Bacchus and Ariadne* (National Gallery). Among his principal works are *Sacred and Profane Love* (Borghese Gallery, Rome), and some in the Prado, Madrid.

Tito (Josip Broz) (b. 1892), Yugoslav leader, b. Kumrovec. In 1941 he organised partisan forces against the Axis invaders, liberated his country, and carried through a communist revolution. In 1945 he became the first communist prime minister and in 1953 president. He has successfully pursued an independent line for his country. Order of Lenin (1972).

Titus (A.D. 39–81), Roman emperor, son of Vespasian, brought the Jewish war to a close with the capture of Jerusalem. He completed the Colosseum.

Tizard, Sir Henry Thomas (1885–1959), English scientist and administrator. He was chairman of the Scientific Survey of Air Defence (later known as the Tizard Committee) that encouraged the birth of radar before the second world war and turned it into a successful defence weapon. He was chief scientific adviser to the government, 1947–52.

Tocqueville, Alexis, Comte de (1805–59), French liberal politician and historian, author of *Democracy in America*, still relevant reading.

Todd, 1st Baron (Alexander Robertus Todd) (b. 1907), Scottish biochemist, noted for his work on the structure of nucleic acids. Nobel prizewinner 1957; Pres. Royal Society 1975. Chancellor Univ. of Strathclyde. O.M. 1977.

Tolstoy, Leo Nikolayevich, Count (1828–1910), Russian writer and philosopher, b. Yasnaya Polyana. Of noble family, he entered the army and fought in the Crimean War. Beginning with simple, natural accounts of his early life (*Childhood* and *Boyhood*), he proceeded to articles on the war, and so eventually to perhaps his best work, the long novel *War and Peace*, followed by *Anna Karenina*. Increasingly pre-

occupied with social problems, he freed his serfs before this was done officially, and refused to take advantage of his wealth. His later works include *The Kreutzer Sonata* and *Resurrection*. By many he was regarded as a moral teacher.

Tooke, John Horne (1736–1812), English politician and pamphleteer, was a supporter of Wilkes and later of Pitt. He was tried for high treason, but was acquitted.

Torquemada, Tomas de (1420–98), first inquisitor-general of Spain.

Torricelli, Evangelista (1608–47), Italian physicist, pupil of Galileo. He invented the barometer and improved both microscope and telescope.

Toscanini, Arturo (1867–1957), Italian conductor, b. Parma. He had a remarkable musical memory, and was at the same time exacting and self-effacing. He spent the second world war in exile.

Toulouse-Lautrec, Henri de (1864–1901), French painter, whose pictures portray with stark realism certain aspects of Parisian life in the nineties, especially the *Moulin Rouge* series. Many are in the Musée Lautrec at Albi.

Tovey, Sir Donald Francis (1875–1940), English pianist and composer. His compositions include chamber music, a piano concerto, and an opera *The Bride of Dionysus*; and his writings *Essays in Musical Analysis*.

Toynbee, Arnold (1852–83), English historian and social reformer. The settlement Toynbee Hall was founded in his memory.

Toynbee, Arnold Joseph (1889–1975), nephew of above, English historian, known mainly for his 10-volume *A Study of History*, an analysis of many civilisations. He was for 30 years director of the Institute of International Affairs.

Traherne, Thomas (c. 1636–74), English religious poet, b. Hereford; author also of *Centuries of Meditations*.

Trajan (c. 53–117), Roman emperor, was a successful general and firm administrator. He was born in Spain.

Tree, Sir Herbert Beerbohm (1853–1917), English actor-manager of the Haymarket theatre until 1897 when he built His Majesty's theatre. Sir Max Beerbohm was his half-brother.

Trenchard, 1st Viscount (Hugh Montague Trenchard) (1873–1956), British air-marshal. He served with the Royal Flying Corps in the first world war and became the first air marshal of the R.A.F. He was largely responsible for the R.A.F. college at Cranwell and was also concerned in establishing Hendon police college.

Trent, 1st Baron (Jesse Boot) (1850–1931), British drug manufacturer, b. Nottingham. He built up the largest pharmaceutical retail trade in the world, and was a benefactor of Nottingham and its university.

Trevelyan, George Macaulay (1876–1962), English historian, known for his *History of England* and *English Social History*.

Trevelyan, Sir George Otto (1838–1928), English liberal politician, father of above. He wrote a life of his uncle Lord Macaulay.

Trevithick, Richard (1771–1833), English mining engineer and inventor, b. near Redruth, Cornwall. His most important invention was a high-pressure steam-engine (1801) and he is commonly acknowledged as the inventor of the steam locomotive for railways.

Trollope, Anthony (1815–82), English novelist. His early life was a struggle, the family being supported by his mother's writings. His own career was in the post office, but by strict industry he produced many novels especially portraying clerical life (the *Barchester* series) and political life (the *Phineas Finn* series).

Trotsky, Leo (Lev Davidovich Bronstein) (1879–1940), Russian revolutionary, b. of Jewish parents in the Ukraine, one of the leaders of the Bolshevik revolution. As commissar of foreign affairs under Lenin he led the Russian delegation at the Brest-Litovsk conference. He differed from Stalin on policy, believing in "permanent revolution," according to which socialism could not be achieved in Russia without revolutions elsewhere, and was dismissed from office in 1925 and expelled from the Communist party in 1927. In 1929 he took up exile in Mexico where he was assassinated.

Trudeau, Pierre Eliott (b. 1919), Liberal prime minister of Canada since 1968.

Truman, Harry S. (1884–1972). U.S. President, 1945–53. He inherited the presidency on Roosevelt's death in 1945 when he took the decision to drop the first atom bomb, and he won the election of 1948. He intervened in Korea, dismissed General MacArthur, and aimed at raising standards in underdeveloped countries.

Tulsi Das (1532–1623), Indian poet whose masterpiece *Ram-Charit-Mānas* (popularly known as the *Rāmayana* and based on the Sanskrit epic of Vālmiki) is venerated by all Hindus as the Bible is in the West.

Turenne, Henri de la Tour d'Auvergne, Vicomte de (1611–75), French commander who was successful in the Thirty Years' War.

Turgenev, Ivan Sergeyvich (1818–83), Russian novelist, friend of Gogol and Tolstoy, who spent part of his life in exile. His works include *Fathers and Children, Smoke,* and *Virgin Soil.*

Turner, Joseph Mallord William (1775–1851), English landscape painter, b. London, a barber's son. He entered the Royal Academy and was at first a topographical watercolourist. Later he turned to oil and became a master of light and colour, achieving magical effects, especially in depicting the reflection of light in water. His works include *Crossing the Brook, Dido building Carthage, The Fighting Temeraire, Rain, Steam and Speed.* He also made thousands of colour studies. He encountered violent criticism as his style became more abstract which led to Ruskin's passionate defence of him in *Modern Painters.* He bequeathed his work to the nation (National and Tate Galleries, and the British Museum).

Tussaud, Marie (1760–1850), Swiss modeller in wax who learnt from her uncle in Paris, married a Frenchman, and later came to England where she set up a permanent exhibition.

Tutankhamun (d. *c.* 1340 B.C.), Egyptian pharaoh of the 18th dynasty, son-in-law of Akhenaten, whose tomb was discovered by Howard Carter in 1922, with the mummy and gold sarcophagus intact. He died when he was 18.

Twain, Mark (Samuel Langhorne Clemens) (1835–1910), American humorist. His *Innocents Abroad* was the result of a trip to Europe. His works include *A Tramp Abroad, Tom Sawyer, Huckleberry Finn,* and *Pudd'nhead Wilson.*

Tweedsmuir, 1st Baron (John Buchan) (1875–1940), Scottish author of biographies, historical novels, and adventure stories, including *Montrose* and *Thirty-nine Steps.* He was governorgeneral of Canada 1935–40.

Tyler, Wat (d. 1381), English peasant leader. He was chosen leader of the Peasants' Revolt of 1381 (due to various causes), and parleyed at Smithfield with the young king Richard II, but was killed.

Tyndale, William (c. 1494–1536), English religious reformer, translator of the Bible. He had to go abroad, where he visited Luther and his New Testament was printed at Worms. When copies entered England they were suppressed by the bishops (1526). His Pentateuch was printed at Antwerp, but he did not complete the Old Testament. He was betrayed, arrested, and executed. Unlike Wyclif, who worked from Latin texts, he translated mainly from the original Hebrew and Greek and his work was later to become the basis of the Authorised Version of the Bible.

Tyndall, John (1829–93), Irish physicist whose wide interests led him to research on heat, light, and sound, and on bacteria-free air and sterilisation. He discovered why the sky is blue ('Tyndall' effect) and pioneered popular scientific writing, *e.g., Heat as a Mode of Motion.* A mountaineer, one of the peaks of the Matterhorn is named after him.

U

Unamuno, Miguel de (1864–1936), Spanish philosopher, poet, essayist, and novelist, author of *El Sentimiento Trágico de la Vida* (The Tragic Sense of Life).

Ulanova, Galina (b. 1910), Russian ballerina, who made her début in 1928.

Undset, Sigrid (1882–1949), Norwegian novelist, daughter of an antiquary, author of *Jenny, Kristin Lavransdatter,* and *Olav Audunsson.* Nobel prizewinner 1928.

Unwin, Sir Raymond (1863–1940), English architect of the first garden city at Letchworth.

Ursula, St., said in late legend to have been killed by Huns at Cologne with many companions while on pilgrimage. It took rise from a 4th cent. inscription which simply referred to virgin martyrs.

Usher or Ussher, James (1581–1656), Irish divine who in 1625 became archbishop of Armagh, and whose writings include a long-accepted chronology, which placed the creation at 4004 B.C.

V

Valentine, St., was a Christian martyr of the reign of the emperor Claudius II (d. A.D. 270). The custom of sending valentines may be connected with the pagan festival of Lupercalia.

Valéry, Paul (1871–1945), French poet and essayist, strongly influenced by the symbolist leader, Mallarmé. His poems include *La jeune Parque, Charmes,* and *Le cimetière marin.*

Vanbrugh, Sir John (1664–1726), English architect and playwright. His buildings include Blenheim Palace and his plays *The Provok'd Wife.*

Vancouver, George (1758–98), British navigator who served under Captain Cook, also doing survey work, and who sailed round Vancouver island.

Vanderbilt, Cornelius (1794–1877), American merchant and railway speculator who amassed a fortune and founded a university at Nashville. His son, William Henry Vanderbilt (1821–85), inherited and added to it.

Van Dyck, Sir Anthony (1599–1641), Flemish painter, b. Antwerp. He studied under Rubens, travelled in Italy, and then settled in England with an annuity from Charles I. He excelled in portraits, especially of Charles I and Henrietta Maria, and of their court.

Vane, Sir Henry (1613–62), English parliamentary leader during the civil war period, though not involved in the execution of Charles I. He was executed in 1662.

Van Gogh, Vincent (1853–90), Dutch painter of some of the most colourful pictures ever created. With passionate intensity of feeling he painted without pause whatever he found around him—landscapes, still life, portraits; his was a truly personal art. His life was one of pain, sorrow, and often despair, and in the end he committed suicide.

Vauban, Sebastien de Prestre de (1633–1707), French military engineer, whose skill in siege works (*e.g.,* at Maestrict 1673) was a factor in the expansive wars of Louis XIV. He protected France with fortresses and also invented the socket bayonet.

Vaughan Williams, Ralph (1872–1958), English composer, b. Gloucestershire. After Charterhouse and Cambridge he studied music in Berlin under Max Bruch and, later in Paris, under Ravel. He wrote nine symphonies besides a number of choral and orchestral works, operas (including *Hugh the Drover, Riders to the Sea*), ballets, chamber music, and songs. He showed great interest in folk tunes. *See* Section E.

Velasquez, Diego (c. 1460–1524), Spanish conquistador, first governor of Cuba.

Velasquez, Diego Rodriguez de Silva y (1599–1660), Spanish painter, b. Seville, especially of portraits at the court of Philip IV, and also of classical and historical subjects. He made two visits to Italy (1629–31, 1649–51), studying the Venetian painters, especially Titian, which hastened the development of his style. Among his masterpieces are *The Maids of Honour, The Tapestry Weavers* (both in the Prado), the Rokeby Venus and a portrait of Philip IV (both in the National Gallery), the landscape views from the Villa Medici (Prado) and *Juan de Pareja* (sold in London in 1970 for £2·25 million).

Venizelos, Eleutherios (1864–1936), Greek statesman, b. Crete. He became prime minister in 1910 and held this office intermittently. He promoted the Balkan League (1912), forced the king's abdication (1917), and brought Greece into the war on the Allied side, securing territorial concessions at the peace conference, but his expansionist policy in Turkish Asia failed.

Verdi, Giuseppe (1813–1901), Italian composer, b. near Busseto in the province of Parma. His early works include *Nabucco*, *Ernani*, *I Due Foscari*, and *Macbeth*; a middle period is represented by *Rigoletto*, *Il Trovatore*, *La Traviata*, *Un Ballo in Maschera*, and *Don Carlos*; to the last period of his life belong *Aïda*, *Otello*, and *Falstaff* (produced when he was 80). *See Section E.*

Verlaine, Paul (1844–96), French poet, one of the first of the symbolists, also known for his memoirs and confessions. His works include *Poèmes saturniens*, *Fêtes galantes*, *Sagesse*, and *Romances sans paroles*. He was imprisoned for two years in Belgium for shooting and wounding his friend Rimbaud. He died in poverty in Paris.

Vermeer, Jan (1632–75), Dutch painter, b. Delft. His main paintings are of domestic interiors, which he makes into works of art, as in *Lady at the Virginals* (National Gallery). His reputation has grown during the last century.

Verne, Jules (1828–1905), French writer of science fiction, including *Five Weeks in a Balloon*, *Twenty Thousand Leagues Under the Sea*, *Round the World in Eighty Days*.

Vernier, Pierre (1580–1637), French inventor of the small sliding scale which enables readings on a graduated scale to be taken to a fraction of a division.

Veronese, Paolo (1528–88), Italian painter of the Venetian school, whose works include *Marriage Feast at Cana in Galilee*, *The Feast in the House of Simon*, and *The Presentation of the Family of Darius to Alexander*. His *Adoration of the Magi* is in the National Gallery.

Veronica, St., legendary woman who was said to hand her kerchief to Christ on the way to Calvary, to wipe his brow, and his impression was left on the kerchief. In its present form her legend dates from the 14th cent.

Verwoerd, Hendrik Frensch (1901–66), South African politician, b. Amsterdam, exponent of the policy of apartheid; prime minister 1958–66. He was assassinated.

Vespasian, Titus Flavius (A.D. 9–79), Roman emperor. He was sent by Nero to put down the Jews and was proclaimed by the legions. He began the Colosseum.

Vespucci, Amerigo (1451–1512), Florentine explorer, naturalised in Spain, contractor at Seville for Columbus. He later explored Venezuela. The use of his name for the continent arose through a mistake.

Vico, Giambattista (1688–1744), Italian philosopher of history and of culture, b. Naples. His ideas were developed in his *Scienza nuova* (science of history) but it was not until our own day that his originality as a thinker was fully recognised.

Victor Emmanuel II (1820–78), first king of Italy. King of Sardinia, he was proclaimed king of Italy in 1861 after the Austrians had been defeated and Garibaldi had succeeded in the south. Rome was added in 1870.

Victoria (1819–1901), Queen of the United Kingdom of Gt. Britain and Ireland and Empress of India, was granddaughter of George III and succeeded an uncle in 1837. In 1840 she married Prince Albert of Saxe-Coburg-Gotha, who died in 1861. Conscientious, hard-working, and of strict moral standards, she had by the end of a long life (jubilees 1887 and 1897) won the affection and respect of her subjects in a unique degree. Her reign saw industrial expansion, growing humanitarianism, literary output, and in the main prolonged peace; and by its close the British empire and British world power had reached their highest point.

Villeneuve, Pierre de (1763–1806), French admiral defeated by Nelson at Trafalgar and captured along with his ship, the *Bucentaure*.

Villon, François (1431–?1463), French poet, b. Paris, who lived at a turbulent time at the close of the Hundred Years War. After fatally stabbing a man in 1455 he joined the *Conquillards*, a criminal organisation. They had a secret language (the *jargon*) and it was for them that he composed his ballads. His extant works consist of the *Petit Testament* (1456),

originally called *Le Lais*, and the *Grand Testament* (1461), masterpieces of mediaeval verse.

Virgil (Publius Vergilius Maro) (70–19 B.C.), Roman epic poet, b. at Andes near Mantua, he went to Rome to obtain redress for the military confiscation of his farm. He was patronised by Maecenas, and wrote his pastoral *Eclogues*, followed by his *Georgics*. His best-known work, the *Aeneid*, deals with the wanderings of Aeneas after the fall of Troy till his establishment of a kingdom in Italy.

Vivaldi, Antonio (c. 1675–1743), Venetian composer, violin master at the Ospedal della Pieta. His output of orchestral works was prolific and Bach arranged some of his violin pieces for the harpsichord. *See Section E.*

Volta, Alessandro (1745–1827), Italian physicist of Pavia, who, working on the results of Galvani, invented the voltaic pile, the first instrument for producing an electric current. It provided a new means for the decomposition of certain substances. His name was given to the volt, the unit of electrical potential difference.

Voltaire (François Marie Arouet) (1694–1778), French philosopher and writer. His first essays offended the authorities, and he spent the years 1726–9 in England, where he wrote some of his dramas. Returning to France, he published his *Philosophical Letters*, which aroused the enmity of the priesthood. At this juncture, the Marquise du Châtelet offered him the asylum of her castle of Cirey, and for the next 15 years he made this his home, writing there his *Discources of Man*, *Essay on the Morals and Spirit of Nations*, *Age of Louis XIV*, etc. The marquise was a mathematician and taught him some science, thus helping him in his interpretation of Newton's *Principia*. To Voltaire we owe the story of the falling apple, also the dictum that Admiral Byng was shot "pour encourager les autres." He spent the years 1750–3 in Berlin at the invitation of Frederick the Great. In challenging accepted beliefs and traditions he prepared the way for the French revolution.

Vondel, Joost van den (1587–1679), Dutch poet who lived at Amsterdam. Most of his dramas are on biblical subjects, and the two most famous are *Jephtha* and *Lucifer*.

Voroshilov, Kliment Efremovich (1881–1969), Soviet general who commanded the Leningrad defences in 1941, and was U.S.S.R. president, 1953–60.

Vyshinsky, Andrei Yanuarievich (1883–1954), Soviet jurist and diplomat; conducted the prosecution of the Moscow treason trials, 1936–8; represented Russian interests at the U.N.

W

Wade, George (1673–1748), English general and military engineer who, after the rising of 1715, pacified the Scottish highlands, constructing military roads and bridges. In the 1745 rising Prince Charles' forces evaded him.

Wagner, Richard (1813–83), German composer, b. Leipzig. He achieved a new type of musical expression in his operas by the complete union of music and drama. He made use of the *Leitmotif* and was his own librettist. His originality and modernism aroused a good deal of opposition, and he was exiled for some years. But he was supported by loyal friends, including Liszt, the young King Ludwig of Bavaria, and the philosopher Nietzsche. He began the music of the *Ring des Nibelungen* in 1853, but it was not until 1876 that the whole of the drama (Rheingold, Valkyrie, Siegfried, Götterdämmerung) was performed at Bayreuth under the conductor Hans Richter. Other operas are *The Flying Dutchman*, *Rienzi*, *Tannhäuser*, *Lohengrin*, *Tristan und Isolde*, *Die Meistersinger von Nürnberg*, and *Parsifal*, a religious drama. He married Liszt's daughter Cosima, formerly wife of his friend Hans von Bülow. *See Section E.*

Waldheim, Kurt (b. 1918), Austrian diplomat; succeeded U Thant as secretary-general of the United Nations in 1972.

Waley, Arthur (1889–1966), English orientalist, known for his translations of Chinese and Japanese poetry and prose, being the first to bring the literature of those countries to the western world.

Walker, George (1618–90), hero of the siege of Londonderry in 1688, who kept the besiegers at bay for 105 days.

Wallace, Alfred Russel (1823–1913), British naturalist, b. Usk, Monmouth, joint author with Darwin of the theory of natural selection. In 1858, while down with illness in the Moluccas, he sent a draft of his theory to Darwin in England who was amazed to find that it closely agreed with his own theory of evolution which was on the point of publishing. The result was a reading of a joint paper to the Linnaean Society.

Wallace, Edgar (1875–1932), English novelist and playwright, known for his detective thrillers.

Wallace, Sir Richard (1818–90), English art collector and philanthropist, whose widow bequeathed his collection to the nation (Wallace Collection, Manchester Square, London).

Wallace, Sir William (c. 1274–1305), Scottish patriot. He withstood Edward I, at first successfully, but was defeated at Falkirk and executed.

Wallenstein, Albrecht von (1583–1634), German soldier and statesman during the Thirty Years War. An able administrator of his own estates, he sought the unity of Germany, but was distrusted and eventually assassinated.

Waller, Edmund (1606–87), English poet of polished simplicity, author of *Go, lovely rose*. He was able to agree with both parliamentarians and royalists.

Wallis, Sir Barnes Neville (b. 1887), British scientist and inventor whose many designs include the R100 airship, the Wellington bomber, the swing-wing aircraft, and the "bouncing bomb" that breached the Ruhr Dams in 1943.

Walpole, Horace, 4th Earl of Orford (1717–97), younger son of Sir Robert Walpole, English writer, chiefly remembered for his *Letters*, his *Castle of Otranto*, and his "Gothic" house at Strawberry Hill.

Walpole, Sir Hugh Seymour (1884–1941), English novelist, b. New Zealand. His works include *Fortitude*, *The Dark Forest*, and *The Herries Chronicle*.

Walpole, Sir Robert, 1st Earl of Orford (1676–1745), English Whig statesman, who came to office soon after the Hanoverian succession and is considered the first prime minister—a good finance minister, a peace minister, and a "house of commons man."

Walter, Bruno (1876–1962), German–American conductor, especially of Haydn, Mozart, and Mahler.

Walter, John (1776–1847), English newspaper editor. Under him *The Times*, founded by his father John Walter (1739–1812), attained a leading position.

Walton, Izaak (1593–1683), English writer, especially remembered for *The Compleat Angler*. He also wrote biographies of Donne, Hooker, and George Herbert.

Walton, Sir William Turner (b. 1902), English composer, whose works include concertos for string instruments, two symphonies, two coronation marches, *Façade* (setting to Edith Sitwell's poem), and an oratorio, *Belshazzar's Feast*. O.M. 1967.

Warbeck, Perkin (1474–99), Flemish impostor, b. Tournai, who claimed to be the younger son of Edward IV with French and Scottish backing, but failed and was executed.

Warwick, Earl of (Richard Neville) (c. 1428–71), "the kingmaker." At first on the Yorkist side in the Wars of the Roses, he proclaimed Edward IV king; but later changed sides and restored the Lancastrian Henry VI. He was killed at Barnet.

Washington, Booker Taliaferro (1858–1915), American Negro educationist, author of *Up from Slavery*. He became principal of Tuskegee Institute, Alabama.

Washington, George (1732–99), first U.S. president. B. in Virginia, of a family which originated from Northamptonshire, he served against the French in the Seven Years War. When the dispute between the British government and the Americans over taxation came to a head, he proved a successful general, and Cornwallis's surrender to him at Yorktown in 1781 virtually ended the war. In 1787 he presided over the Philadelphia convention which formulated the constitution, and was president 1789–97.

Watson, John Broadus (1878–1958), American psychologist, an exponent of behaviourism. *See* Behaviourism, Section J.

Watson-Watt, Sir Robert (1892–1973), Scottish physicist, who played a major part in the development of radar.

Watt, James (1736–1819), Scottish engineer and inventor, b. Greenock. He made important improvements to Newcomen's steam-engine by inventing a separate condenser (applying Black's discoveries (1761–4) on latent heat) and other devices based on scientific knowledge of the properties of steam. He was given support by Matthew Boulton, a capitalist, and settled down in Birmingham with him. He defined one horse-power as the rate at which work is done when 33,000 lb are raised one foot in one minute. He also constructed a press for copying manuscripts. The watt as a unit of power is named after him.

Watteau, Jean Antoine (1684–1721), French painter. He painted pastoral idylls in court dress. His works include *Embarquement pour Cythère* in the Louvre.

Watts, Isaac (1674–1748), English hymn-writer, author of *O God, our help in ages past*.

Watts-Dunton, Walter Theodore (1836–1914), English poet and critic, friend of Swinburne whom he looked after until his death in 1909. His works include *The Coming of Love* and *Aylwin*.

Waugh, Evelyn (1902–66), English satirical writer, author of *Vile Bodies*, *The Loved One*, *Brideshead Revisited*, *Life of Edmund Campion*, *The Ordeal of Gilbert Pinfold*, and an autobiography, *A Little Learning*.

Wavell, 1st Earl (Archibald Percival Wavell) (1883–1950), British general. He served in the first great war on Allenby's staff and in the second he commanded in the Middle East 1939–41, defeating the Italians; and in India 1941–3. He was viceroy of India 1943–7.

Webb, Matthew (1848–83), English swimmer, the first to swim the English Channel (1875).

Webb, Sidney James, Baron Passfield (1859–1947), and his wife **Beatrice**, née Potter (1858–1943), English social reformers and historians. They combined careful investigation of social problems (their books include *History of Trade Unionism* and *English Local Government*) with work for the future; they were members of the Fabian Society, launched the *New Statesman*, and helped to set up the London School of Economics. He held office in Labour governments.

Weber, Carl Maria Friedrich Ernst von (1786–1826), German composer, who laid the foundation of German romantic opera. His reputation rests principally on his three operas, *Der Freischütz*, *Euryanthe*, and *Oberon*. He was also an able pianist, conductor, and musical director. *See* Section E.

Webster, Daniel (1782–1852), American statesman and orator. He held office more than once and negotiated the Ashburton Treaty which settled the Maine–Canada boundary.

Webster, Noah (1758–1843), American lexicographer, who published an *American dictionary of the English language.*

Wedgwood, Dame Cicely Veronica (b. 1910), English historian, author of *William the Silent*, *Thomas Wentworth*, *The Thirty Years' War*, *The King's Peace*, *The Trial of Charles I*; a member of the Staffordshire pottery family. O.M. 1969.

Wedgwood, Josiah (1730–95), English potter, who at his Etruria works near Hanley produced from a new ware (patented 1763) pottery to classical designs by Flaxman, and gave pottery a new impetus.

Weill, Kurt (1900–50), German composer of satirical, surrealist operas, including *Die Dreigroschenoper* (librettist Brecht), and musical comedies, including *Lady in the Dark* and *One Touch of Venus*. In 1936 he settled in the United States. *See* Section E.

Weingartner, Felix (1863–1942), Austrian conductor, also a composer and writer of a text book on conducting.

Weismann, August (1834–1914), German biologist. He worked on the question of individual variability in evolution, stressing the continuity of the germ plasm and rejecting the idea of inheritance of acquired characteristics.

Weizmann, Chaim (1874–1952), Israeli leader, b. Pinsk. He came to England in 1903 and taught biochemistry at Manchester. He helped to draft the Balfour Declaration (1917), promising a Jewish national home, and was for many years president of the Zionists. In 1948 he became first president of Israel.

Wellesley, Marquess (Richard Colley Wellesley) (1760–1842), British administrator. He was a successful governor-general of India, and was brother of the Duke of Wellington.

Wellington, 1st Duke of (Arthur Wellesley) (1769–1852), British general. B. in Ireland, he joined the army and gained experience in India. In the Peninsular War he successfully wore down and drove out the invading French. When Napoleon escaped from Elba, Wellington defeated him at Waterloo. Thereafter he took some part in politics as a Tory, but in the last resort was capable of accepting change.

Wells, Herbert George (1866–1946), English author. B. London, he was at first a teacher. He believed in progress through science, and became one of the most influential writers of his time. His long series of books includes romances of the Jules Verne variety (*The Time Machine, The Island of Dr. Moreau, The Invisible Man*), sociological autobiography (*Love and Mr. Lewisham, Kipps, Tono-Bungay, The History of Mr. Polly, Mr. Britling Sees it Through*), and popular education (*Outline of History, The Science of Life, The Work, Wealth and Happiness of Mankind, The Shape of Things to Come, The Fate of Homo Sapiens*). He was an early and successful educator of the common man. He was also a founder member of the Fabian Society.

Wesley, Charles (1707–88), English hymnwriter. He was the companion of his brother John, and wrote over 5,500 hymns, including *Love divine* and *Jesu, lover of my soul*.

Wesley, John (1703–91), English evangelist and founder of Methodism (at first a system applied to friends of himself and his brother), b. at Epworth. After a trip to Georgia and after encountering Moravian influence, he began to teach on tour, covering in over 50 years more than 200,000 miles and preaching over 40,000 sermons. He made religion a live force to many ignorant folk of humble station who could only be reached by a new and direct challenge. He made a feature of the Sunday school and increased the use of music (the brothers' first hymnbook appeared in 1739). He did not plan separation from the Anglican church, though it was implicit in his ordination of a missionary, and it took place after his death. *See also* Methodism, Section J.

Westermarck, Edward Alexander (1862–1939), Finnish sociologist. His works include *History of Human Marriage, Origin and Development of the Moral Ideas*, and *The Oedipus Complex*.

Westinghouse, George (1846–1914), American engineer who invented an air-brake for railways (1868) called by his name, and pioneered the use of high tension alternating current for the transmission of electric power.

Westmacott, Sir Richard (1775–1856), English sculptor of Achilles in Hyde Park.

Wharton, Edith (1862–1937), American novelist and friend of Henry James. Her works include *House of Mirth* and *Custom of the Country*.

Whately, Richard (1787–1863), English archbishop of Dublin. He wrote treatises on *Rhetoric* and *Logic*.

Wheatstone, Sir Charles (1802–75), English physicist, one of the first to recognise Ohm's law. In 1837 he (with W. F. Cooke) patented an electric telegraph. He also introduced the microphone.

Wheeler, Sir Charles (1892–1974), English sculptor, especially on buildings. His autobiography is *High Relief*. P.R.A., 1956–66.

Whistler, James Abbott McNeill (1834–1903), American artist. B. at Lowell, he studied in Paris and settled in England. He reacted against the conventions of his day, and Ruskin's uncomprehending criticism of his work resulted in a lawsuit. Among his main works are studies of the Thames, and a portrait of his mother, now in the Louvre.

White, Sir George Stuart (1835–1912), British general who defended Ladysmith in the South African War.

White, Patrick (b. 1912), Australian novelist whose books include *The Aunt's Story, Riders in the Chariot, The Solid Mandala* and *The Eye of the Storm*. Nobel prizeman 1973.

Whitefield, George (1714–70), English evangelist, b. Gloucester. He was at first associated with the Wesleys, but differed from them on predestination. His supporters built him a "Tabernacle" in London, and he had other chapels elsewhere, but founded no lasting sect.

Whitgift, John (1530–1604), archbishop of Canterbury in the time of Elizabeth I (from 1583). His policy helped to clarify and strengthen the Anglican church.

Whitman, Walt (1819–92), American poet, b. Long Island. He led a wandering life and did hospital work in the Civil War. He aimed at forming a new and free American outlook. His works include *Leaves of Grass, Drum Taps*, and *Democratic Vistas*.

Whittier, John Greenleaf (1807–92), American Quaker poet, b. Haverhill, Mass. He wrote against slavery (*Justice and Expediency*), turning to poetry after the Civil War, especially remembered for *Snow-bound*.

Whittington, Richard (c. 1358–1423), English merchant. Son of a Gloucestershire knight, he became a London mercer and was mayor of London 1398, 1406, 1419. The cat legend is part of European folklore.

Whittle, Sir Frank (b. 1907), pioneer in the field of jet propulsion. The first flights of Gloster jet propelled aeroplanes with Whittle engine took place in May 1941

Whymper, Edward (1840–1911), English woodengraver and mountaineer. He was the first to climb the Matterhorn.

Widgery, Baron (John Passmore Widgery) (b. 1911), Lord Chief Justice of England, 1971–.

Wilberforce, William (1759–1833), English philanthropist, b. Hull. He was the parliamentary leader of the campaign against the slave trade, abolished in 1807. He then worked against slavery itself, but that further step was only taken in the year of his death.

Wilcox, Ella Wheeler (1855–1919), American writer of romantic sentimental verse.

Wilde, Oscar Fingall (1854–1900), Irish author and dramatist, son of a Dublin surgeon and leader of the cult of art for art's sake. His works include poems, fairy-tales, short stories, and witty comedies—*Lady Windermere's Fan, A Woman of No Importance, An Ideal Husband*, and *The Importance of Being Earnest*. In a libel action he was convicted of homosexual practices and imprisoned for two years, when he wrote *The Ballad of Reading Gaol*.

Wilder, Thornton Niven (1897–1975), American author and playwright. Among his books are *The Bridge of San Luis Rey* and *Ides of March*.

Wilkes, John (1727–97), English politician. A Whig, he violently attacked George III in his paper the *North Briton*, and as a result of unsuccessful proceedings against him, general warrants were determined illegal. He was again in trouble for obscene libel; his defiance of authority brought him popularity, and he was four times re-elected to parliament but refused his seat, until his opponents gave way. His motives were mixed, but he helped to establish freedom of the press.

Willcocks, Sir William (1852–1932), British engineer, b. India, who carried out irrigation works in India, Egypt, South Africa, and Mesopotamia. He built the Aswan dam (1898–1902).

Willett, William (1856–1915), English advocate of "daylight savings," adopted after his death.

William I of England (1027–87), the "Conqueror," Duke of Normandy, claimed the English throne as successor to Edward the Confessor, and defeated Harold II at Hastings in 1066. An able commander and a firm ruler, he crushed Saxon resistance, especially in the north, transferred most of the land to his Norman followers, and drew England into closer relations with the continent, as did his archbishop Lanfranc. He ordered the Domesday survey (*see* Section L).

William II of England (1056–1100), the Conqueror's son, surnamed Rufus, succeeded in 1187. Capricious and self-indulgent, his reign was troubled, and he was shot (by accident or design) while hunting in the New Forest.

William III of England (1650–1702), King of England, Scotland, and Ireland (1689–1702), son of William II of Orange and Mary, daughter of Charles I. He married Mary, daughter of the Duke of York (later James II) while stadtholder of Holland. In 1688, when James had abdicated and fled the country, he was invited to succeed and he and Mary became joint king and queen. The revolution of 1688 brought to England tolerance of Protestant worship, but William was mainly concerned with war against France, brought to an end in 1697.

William IV of England (1765–1837), third son of George III, succeeded his brother George IV in 1830; called the "sailor king." The reform bill of 1832 and other reform measures were carried without obstruction from him.

William I of Germany (1797–1888), King of Prussia and first German emperor. He succeeded to the throne in 1861 and continued resistance to reform, appointing Bismarck as chief minister, and supporting him through the Austro-Prussian and Franco-Prussian wars. His personal character was simple and unassuming.

William II of Germany, the Kaiser (1859–1941), King of Prussia and German emperor from 1888, was grandson of William I and of Queen Victoria. He was intelligent but impetuous, and believed in military power. He dismissed Bismarck. In 1914 his support of Austria helped to precipitate European war, and the resulting defeat brought his abdication, after which he lived in retirement at Doorn in Holland.

William the Silent (1533–1584), Dutch national leader. Prince of Orange, he led the revolt of the Protestant Netherlands against the rule of the Spanish Philip II. The union of the northern provinces was accomplished in 1579, and Spanish rule was renounced by 1584, in which year William was assassinated.

Williams, Sir George (1821–1905), founder of the Young Men's Christian Association.

Williamson, Malcolm (b. 1931), Australian composer, pianist and organist; succeeded Sir Arthur Bliss as Master of the Queen's Musick.

Wilson, Edmund (1895–1972), American critic, author of *Axel's Castle* (1931), *The Triple Thinkers* (1938), *The Wound and the Bow* (1941), *To the Finland Station* (1940), *The Shores of Light* (1952), *The Dead Sea Scrolls* (1955).

Wilson, Sir Harold (b. 1916), British statesman, leader parl. Labour Party 1963–76; prime minister 1964–70, 1974–6. Entered parliament 1945 as member for Ormskirk; elected for Huyton 1950. Returned twice, in 1964 and a decade later, to head a government facing a formidable balance-of-payments deficit. In Feb. 1974 returned to power at head of first minority government since 1929; in subsequent election Oct. 1974 secured narrowest overall majority in any election in recent history. Resigned March 1976. Founder of the Open University. Chancellor of Bradford University.

Wilson, Richard (1714–82), British landscape painter, b. Montgomeryshire. Admired by Turner and Constable.

Wilson, Thomas Woodrow (1856–1924), American statesman. He was U.S. president 1913–21, brought America into the first world war and advocated the League of Nations, but was not a successful negotiator at the peace conference and could not carry his country into the League. His administration introduced prohibition and women's suffrage.

Wingate, Orde Charles (1903–44), leader of the Chindit forces engaged behind the Japanese lines in Burma during the second world war.

Winifred, St., the 7th cent. patron saint of North Wales, said in late legend to have been killed by her rejected suitor, Prince Caradoc, but restored by her uncle.

Wiseman, Nicholas Patrick (1802–65), cardinal, b. in Spain of an Irish family. In 1850 on the restoration in England of the Roman Catholic hierarchy he became first archbishop of Westminster, and reorganised and developed his church in Great Britain.

Wittgenstein, Ludwig Josef Johann (1889–1951), Austrian linguistic philosopher whose main works were the *Tractatus Logico-Philosophicus* of his early period, much admired by Russell,

and the *Philosophical Investigations*.

Wodehouse, Pelham Grenville (1881–1975), English humorist. creator of Jeeves in the Bertie Wooster stories. He became a U.S. citizen.

Wolf, Friedrich August (1759–1824), German classical scholar, a founder of scientific classical philology.

Wolf, Hugo (1860–1903), Austrian song-writer. In his settings of over 300 German lyrics, including many of Mörike and Goethe, he achieved complete union of poetry and music. *See* Section E.

Wolfe, James (1727–59). British general, b. Westerham. He showed early promise in the Seven Years' War, and was given command of the expedition against Quebec, which in spite of its strong position he captured, but lost his life.

Wolsey, Thomas (c. 1475–1530), English cardinal. A butcher's son at Ipswich, he entered the church, becoming archbishop of York and cardinal, while in the same year (1515) he became Henry VIII's lord chancellor. But in spite of his ability he was unable to secure papal sanction for the king's divorce from Catherine of Aragon, and fell from power and died. He was the last of the great ecclesiastical statesmen of the Middle Ages.

Wood, Sir Henry Joseph (1869–1944), English conductor, founder of the Promenade Concerts which he conducted from 1895 till his death.

Woodcock, George (b. 1904), English trade union leader, T.U.C. general secretary 1960–69; first chairman of the Commission on Industrial Relations set up by the Labour government. 1969–71.

Woodville, Elizabeth (1437–91), wife of Edward IV. Her daughter Elizabeth married Henry VII.

Woolf, Virginia (1882–1941), English writer, daughter of Sir Leslie Stephen and wife of Leonard Woolf with whom she founded the Hogarth Press. Her works develop the stream-of-consciousness technique and include *To the Lighthouse, Mrs. Dalloway, The Waves, A Room of One's Own.*

Woolley, Sir Richard van der Riet (b. 1906), succeeded Sir Harold Spencer Jones as astronomer royal (England), 1956–72.

Wootton of Abinger, Baroness (Barbara Frances Wootton) (b. 1897). English social scientist; chairman Metropolitan Juvenile Courts 1946–62; deputy speaker of the House of Lords 1966–70. Her works include *Social Science and Social Pathology, Crime and the Criminal Law,* and an autobiography *In a world I never made.*

Wordsworth, William (1770–1850), English poet, b. Cockermouth. He went to Cambridge, and in 1798 with Coleridge issued *Lyrical Ballads*, a return to simplicity in English poetry. He settled at Grasmere with his sister Dorothy (1771–1855), to whose insight his poems owe much. Among his best works are his sonnets and his *Ode on the Intimations of Immortality,* besides his *Prelude.*

Wren, Sir Christopher (1632–1723), English architect, b. Wiltshire. After the great fire (1666) he prepared an abortive plan for rebuilding London, but did in fact rebuild St. Paul's and more than fifty other city churches, including St. Stephen, Walbrook, and St. Mary-le-Bow. Other works include Chelsea Hospital, portions of Greenwich Hospital, the Sheldonian theatre, Oxford, and Queen's College library, Oxford. He had wide scientific interests (he was professor of mathematics at Gresham College, London, and professor of astronomy at Oxford) and helped to found the Royal Society.

Wright, Frank Lloyd (1869–1959), American architect, initiator of horizontal strip and all-glass design. His influence has spread over the world. His buildings include the Imperial Hotel, Tokio, and the Guggenheim Museum, New York.

Wright, Orville (1871–1948), American airman who with his brother Wilbur (1867–1912) in 1903 was the first to make a controlled sustained flight in a powered heavier-than-air machine, flying a length of 852 ft. at Kitty Hawk, N.C.

Wyatt, James (1746–1813), English architect who built Fonthill Abbey.

Wyatt, Sir Thomas (1503–42), English poet who introduced the sonnet from Italy. He was also a diplomat.

Wyatt, Sir Thomas the younger (c. 1520–54), son of above, unsuccessfully led a revolt against Queen Mary on behalf of Lady Jane Grey.

Wycherley, William (1640–1715), English drama- tist of the Restoration period. A master of satiric comedy, his plays include *Love in a Wood*, *The Plain Dealer*, and (the best known) *The Country Wife*.

Wyclif, John (c. 1320–84), English religious re- former. He taught at Oxford, later becoming rector of Lutterworth. He insisted on inward religion and attacked those practices which he thought had become mechanical. His fol- lowers, called Lollards, were suppressed, partly for political reasons. The Wyclif Bible, the first and literal translation of the Latin Vulgate into English, was mainly the work of his academic followers at Oxford.

Wykeham, William of (1324–1404), English churchman. He held office under Edward III and became bishop of Winchester in 1367. He founded New College, Oxford, and Winchester School, and improved Winchester cathedral.

Wyllie, William Lionel (1851–1931), English mar- ine painter of *The Thames Below London Bridge*.

Wyspianski, Stanislav (1869–1907), Polish poet, dramatist and painter. His plays *The Wed- ding*, *Liberation*, and *November Night* treat of national themes.

X

Xavier, St. Francis (1506–52), "apostle of the Indies," b. at Xavero in the Basque country. He was associated with Loyola in founding the Jesuits, and undertook missionary journeys to Goa, Ceylon, and Japan. He died while plan- ning another to China.

Xenophon (444–359 B.C.), Athenian general and historian. He commanded Greek mercenaries under the Persian Cyrus, and on the latter's death safely marched the Ten Thousand home through hostile country. His chief works are the *Anabasis*, the *Hellenica*, and *Cyropaedia*.

Xerxes (c. 519–465 B.C.), King of Persia, was son of the first Darius. In 481 B.C. he started on an expedition against Greece when, according to Herodotus, he had a combined army and navy of over two and a half million men. He de- feated the Spartans at Thermopylae, but his fleet was overcome at Salamis. He reigned from 485 to 465 B.C. and met his death by assassination.

Ximénes de Cisneros, Francisco (1436–1517), Spanish statesman and churchman. He be- came cardinal in 1507; carried out monastic reforms; and directed preparation of a polyglot bible, the *Complutensian*; but as inquisitor- general he was fanatical against heresy. He was adviser to Queen Isabella; in 1506 regent for Queen Juana; and himself directed an expedition to conquer Oran and extirpate piracy.

Y

Yeats, William Butler (1865–1939), Irish lyric poet and playwright, b. near Dublin, a leader of the Irish literary revival. His plays were performed in the Abbey Theatre (which with Lady Gregory (1852–1932) he helped to found), and include *Cathleen Ni Houlihan*, *The Hour Glass*, and *Deirde*. His poetry is discussed in Section M. A complete edition of the *Collected Poems* appeared in 1950.

Yonge, Charlotte Mary (1823–1901), English novel- ist. Influenced by Keble, she wrote novels which faithfully reflect some aspects of Victor- ian life; one such is *The Daisy Chain*. She also wrote historical fiction such as *The Dove in the Eagle's Nest*.

Young, Brigham (1801–77), American Mormon leader, and president in 1844 after the founder's death. He was a main founder of Salt Lake City. He practised polygamy. *See also* Mormonism, Section J.

Young, Francis Brett (1884–1954), English novel- ist, author of *My Brother Jonathan* and *Dr. Bradley remembers*.

Young, James (1811–83), Scottish chemist, b. Glasgow, whose experiments led to the manu- facture of paraffin oil and solid paraffin on a large scale.

Young, Thomas (1773–1829), English physicist, physician and egyptologist, b. Somerset, of Quaker family. He established the wave theory of light and its essential principle of interference, put forward a theory of colour vision, and was the first to describe astigmatism of the eye. He was also largely responsible for deciphering the inscriptions on the Rosetta stone.

Younghusband, Sir Francis Edward (1863–1942), English explorer and religious leader. He ex- plored Manchuria and Tibet, and wrote on India and Central Asia. He founded the World Congress of Faiths in 1936 (*see* Section J).

Ypres, 1st Earl of. *See* French.

Ysaÿe, Eugène (1858–1929), Belgian violinist and conductor, noted chiefly for his playing of the works of Bach and César Franck.

Yukawa, Hideki (b. 1907), Japanese physicist, who received the 1949 Nobel prize for predict- ing (1935) the existence of the meson.

Z

Zadkiel (angel in rabbinical lore), pseudonym of two astrologers: William Lilly (1602–81) and Richard James Morrison (1794–1874).

Zadkine, Ossip (b. 1890), Russian sculptor in France, who makes play with light on concave surfaces. His works include *Orpheus* and the public monument *The De.truction of Rotterdam*.

Zaharoff, Sir Basil (1849–1936), armaments mag- nate and financier, b. Anatolia of Greek parents. He was influential in the first world war.

Zamenhof, Ludwig Lazarus (1859–1917), Polish- Jew who invented Esperanto. He was by profession an oculist.

Zeno of Citium (?342–270 B.C.), philosopher, founder of the Stoic system. He left Cyprus to teach in Athens.

Zeppelin, Ferdinand, Count von (1838–1917), German inventor of the dirigible airship, 1897– 1900. It was used in the first world war.

Zeromski, Stefan (1864–1925), Polish novelist, author of *The Homeless*, *The Ashes*, *The Fight with Satan*.

Zhukov, Georgi Konstantinovich (1896–1974), Soviet general, who led the defence of Moscow and Stalingrad and lifted the siege of Leningrad in the second world war, and accepted the German surrender in 1945. He continued to be active till 1957.

Zhukovsky, Vasily Andreyevich (1783–1852), Russian poet and translator of German and English poets. For many years he was tutor to the future Tsar Alexander II.

Zola, Emile Edouard (1840–1902), French novel- ist, b. Paris, of Italian descent. His series, *Les Rougon-Macquart*, portrays in a score of volumes (the best known of which are perhaps *L'Assommoir*, *Nana* and *Germinal*) the fortunes of one family in many aspects and in realistic manner. He had the moral courage to cham- pion Dreyfus.

Zorn, Anders Leonhard (1860–1920), Swedish sculptor, etcher, and painter.

Zoroaster (Zarathustra) (fl. 6th cent. B.C.), Per- sian founder of the Parsee religion. He was a monotheist, and saw the world as a struggle between good (Ahura Mazda) and evil (Ahri- man). *See* Zoroastrianism, Section J.

Zoshchenko, Mikhail (1895–1958), Russian writer of humorous short stories, which include *The Woman who could not Read and other Tales* and *The Wonderful Dog and other Stories*.

Zosimus (fl. c. 300), the first known alchemist. He lived in Alexandria.

Zuccarelli, Francesco (1702–88), Italian artist of fanciful landscapes. He spent many years in London and was elected a founder member of the R.A. (1768).

Zuckermann, Baron (Solly Zuckermann) (b. 1904), British biologist; chief scientific adviser to British governments: 1940–71. His publica- tions include *Scientists and War* and *The Frontiers of Public and Private Science*. O.M. 1968.

Zwingli, Ulrich (1484–1531), Swiss religious reformer. He taught mainly at Zurich, where he issued a list of reformed doctrines, less extreme than those of Calvin.

Zwirner, Ernst Friedrich (1802–61), German architect who restored Cologne cathedral.

BACKGROUND TO PUBLIC AFFAIRS

This section is in two parts. The first provides an up-to-date chronicle and analysis of recent changes in Britain, intended to put into perspective current political events. The second part provides a wide-ranging guide to events and movements elsewhere in the world.

TABLE OF CONTENTS

BACKGROUND TO PUBLIC AFFAIRS

This section is in two parts. The first outlines the political history of the United Kingdom since 1964. The second part provides a wide-ranging guide to events elsewhere in the world and takes stock of the changing patterns in international relations. The reader is invited to turn to Section D for key facts and figures relating to the British political system.

I. SURVEY OF THE BRITISH POLITICAL SCENE

BRITISH POLITICAL EVENTS 1964–78

The Political Situation in 1964.

By 1964 the Conservatives had been in office for 13 years and, in winning the 1959 General Election with a majority of 100 seats, had succeeded in increasing their parliamentary majority in three successive elections. However, economic and other difficulties led to a number of dramatic by-election losses in the early 1960s, and in 1963 Harold Macmillan had retired as Prime Minister, being replaced by the Foreign Secretary, Lord Home, who resigned his peerage and fought a by-election to enter the House of Commons. During 1963 also, following the death of Hugh Gaitskell, the Labour Party elected Harold Wilson as its leader.

1964 General Election.

Most of 1964 was dominated by electoral activity as the election was not held until almost the last possible date, in October. The result was a photo-finish. The large Conservative majority was wiped out but the Labour Party only had a majority of five over all other parties. However, after thirteen years in opposition, the Labour Party returned to office with Harold Wilson as Prime Minister. Although there was considerable doubt as to how long the new government could survive, it immediately started to take action to correct the serious economic situation it inherited, in particular a substantial balance of payments deficit.

New Conservative Leader.

The loss of the 1964 election and the popular appeal of the new Prime Minister convinced many Conservatives that a change of leader was necessary. Before tendering his resignation in 1965, Sir Alec Douglas-Home introduced a new procedure for the election of his successor by Conservative M.P.s. In the ensuing election Edward Heath was chosen to take his place.

1966 General Election.

Harold Wilson succeeded in exploiting his Party's position in Parliament to the full. As a result he was able to choose the date of the next election. This he did at the end of March 1966 and his tactical skill was rewarded by a convincing victory which gave Labour an overall majority of almost 100. However, the Government's fortunes soon changed with a serious deterioration in the economic situation. These problems and the harsh measures needed to deal with them dominated the life of the Government for the next three years. In July 1966 a severe deflationary package and a freeze on prices and incomes were introduced. These measures, however, failed to cure the problems and in November 1967 the Government was compelled to devalue the pound. This in itself necessitated further deflation. Economic policy thus produced tension between the trade unions and the Government and their relationship was further exacerbated by the attempt by the Government to introduce legislation to reform industrial relations, following the publication of a White Paper entitled "In Place of

Strife". After long and bitter negotiations, the Government agreed to withdraw its proposals in favour of an undertaking by the trade unions to introduce reforms themselves. All these difficulties were reflected in great unpopularity for the Government as its record of losing 15 by-elections, including some seats it had won easily in 1966, testifies.

A Reforming Government.

Despite these traumatic experiences in the economic field, the Labour Government succeeded in implementing a substantial programme of reform. In housing, education and the social services important changes were introduced; a start was made with reforming the institutions of government; and major developments occurred in industrial and regional policy. The Government also provided parliamentary time for the passage of private members' legislation to abolish capital punishment, to reform the divorce laws and to legalise abortion and homosexuality.

Foreign Affairs.

Three principal problems in foreign affairs confronted the Government. First, in 1965 Rhodesia declared independence unilaterally. Economic sanctions were introduced against the regime and Mr. Wilson made two unsuccessful attempts to negotiate with the rebel Prime Minister, Mr. Ian Smith. Secondly, the Government had to take decisions on Britain's relations with the European Economic Community. Although the Labour Party had opposed the Conservative Government's application, its attitude began to change after 1964 and, in May 1967, a second application was made to see what terms could be obtained. When France voted in December 1967 against the opening of negotiations, the application was left on the table. Thirdly, largely as a result of the pressing need to reduce defence expenditure, the Government decided to withdraw from our traditional role East of Suez.

The 1970 General Election.

By 1970 the Government had succeeded in restoring the balance of payments position. This was reflected in an increase in its popularity in the opinion polls. The local election results were also encouraging, with Labour regaining some of the ground it had lost in earlier years when its representation had been decimated. In this favourable climate, the Prime Minister decided to hold the election on 18 June.

On the eve of the poll, a Labour victory seemed certain. The opinion polls, with one exception (Opinion Research Centre), were predicting a Labour victory. The eventual result, however, was a 4·7 per cent swing to the Conservatives and their return to power with an overall majority of 30 over all other parties. The reasons for what appears to have been a last-minute change are complex, but the most accepted argument is that the publication of unfavourable trade figures just 3 days before polling day enabled the Conservatives to stir up anxiety about the cost of living and the economy.

A New Style of Government.

Right from the start, Mr. Heath made it clear that he intended his Government to be substantially different from Mr. Wilson's both in style and policies. Mr. Heath determined to shun the publicity and personal initiatives which had characterised Mr. Wilson's tenure of 10 Downing Street. For instance, he refused initially to intervene personally in industrial disputes. The Government's new policies had been outlined in the Conservative election manifesto and it used the parliamentary recess over the summer to prepare the details of its plans.

The New Policies.

In October 1970 the Government announced a number of major developments:

(1) *Reorganisation of the machinery of government*, including the creation of two new giant departments (Environment, and Trade and Industry) and a new advisory unit, the Central Policy Review Staff. Between 1970 and 1974 the Government also passed legislation reforming the structure of local government (implemented in England and Wales in 1974 and Scotland in 1975), the National Health Service (implemented in 1974) and the water industry (implemented in 1974).

(2) *Cuts in Public Expenditure*.—The Conservatives believed that government was intervening too much in the life of the nation and that too high a proportion of the nation's resources were committed to public expenditure. Following a major review of government activities, the Chancellor of the Exchequer announced that the Government planned to be more selective in its approach to the social services and to withdraw generally in its relations with private industry. Among the measures taken during 1970 and 1971 in this direction were the reform of the system of housing finance, the introduction of a new benefit for poor families and the dismantling of the machinery of intervention in industry.

(3) *Reform of Industrial Relations*.—One of the major issues of the Conservative election campaign had been the need to take stronger action to reform industrial relations. The Government published its proposals in October 1970 and, after a long and bitter parliamentary battle, the Industrial Relations Act became law in 1971. The provisions of the Act came into force during 1972. The Act was strongly opposed by an overwhelming majority of the trade unions, most of whom refused to register, as they were required by the Act in order to receive certain benefits it conferred, and initially they decided to boycott the institutions created by the Act, in particular the National Industrial Relations Court. However, following a number of controversial decisions, most unions decided that they should at least appear in order to defend themselves. Two of the Act's major features, the cooling-off period and the strike ballot, were first invoked by the Government in the course of a dispute between British Rail and the three rail unions in April/June 1972.

Industrial Unrest.

The first two and a half years of the Government's life were marked by widespread outbreaks of industrial unrest. This was the result of a number of factors. First, the Government's policy of confrontation as a means of limiting wage inflation led to a number of prolonged disputes, for instance, in the docks, in the electricity power industry and by local authority manual workers. Trade union opposition to the Industrial Relations Act produced a number of one-day stoppages and unofficial strikes of longer duration. These problems were aggravated by persistently high levels of unemployment especially in certain regions. Finally, after 1972, there was industrial action in protest against the Government's prices and incomes policy. In 1972 there were three serious disputes, involving the miners, the railwaymen and the dockworkers.

The Government's About-Turn.

1972 was not a happy year for the Government. We have already seen that it was a year of confrontation with the trade unions. It was also a year in which the pressure of circumstances, especially the problems of unemployment and inflation, forced the Government to abandon many of the initiatives it had started in 1970 and to adopt policies similar to those which it had attacked so vehemently when it had been in Opposition. This was particularly the case in three fields:

(1) *Regional policy*.—Faced with the twin problems of low levels of industrial investment and persistent unemployment in the regions, the Chancellor of the Exchequer announced in his 1972 Budget that the Government was substantially increasing government assistance to private industry and that, in the development areas, investment grants were to be reintroduced.

(2) *Consumer Protection*.—Although in 1970 the Government had brought about the demise of the Consumer Council, by 1972 it had come round to the view that some form of statutory consumer protection was necessary. Consequently, a new office, that of Director-General of Fair Trading, was created in 1973 and a new committee established to protect the interests of consumers.

(3) *Prices and Incomes Policy*.—Despite its strong opposition to the Labour Government's prices and incomes legislation and its initial refusal even to contemplate such a policy, the continuing problem of inflation placed the Government under increasing pressure to introduce some kind of prices and incomes policy. During the autumn tripartite talks were held between the Government, the TUC and the CBI in the search for voluntary agreement on prices and incomes restraint, but these broke down at the beginning of November. Consequently, the Government came to the conclusion, albeit reluctantly, that they would have to introduce legislation to give effect to their proposals. A 90-day standstill was imposed on wages and salaries, dividends, rates and rents, and prices and charges for goods and services were similarly frozen. Provision was made for firms which claimed that their costs had risen so much for it to be impracticable for them to be absorbed to apply to the Government for permission to increase prices. The prices of fresh food and of imported raw materials were excluded from the freeze.

Entry into Europe.

Negotiations with the EEC started immediately after the General Election of 1970. After a long series of talks in Brussels and a summit meeting between President Pompidou and Mr. Heath in Paris in May 1971, a formula was found to which Britain and the Six could agree. On this basis the House of Commons took the decision in principle to join the EEC on 18 October 1971, when the Conservative Government, opposed by some of its back-benchers but supported by 69 Labour pro-marketeers and five of the Liberals, had a majority of 112. Legislation to give effect to this decision was passed after a long parliamentary struggle in September 1972. Thus, twelve years after the first application had been made, Britain joined the Common Market on 1 January 1973.

Phases Two and Three.

The standstill on prices and incomes was extended until the end of April 1973 when it was replaced by the second phase of the Government's counter-inflation policy. Under Phase Two wage increases were limited to £1 per week plus 4%, with an overall ceiling of £250 per annum. Prices and dividends continued to be controlled as during the standstill. To enforce these controls the Government created two new statutory bodies, the Pay Board and the Price Commission. Phase Two was opposed by the TUC, which decided not to nominate members to serve on the new controlling bodies nor to co-operate in the implementation of the Government's policy. During the summer of 1973 bilateral talks took place between the Government and both the CBI and the TUC on what measures should succeed Phase Two in November 1973. In October the Government published its plans in a Green Paper, and these were put into practice with a few modifications. On prices the basis of control was unchanged, but there was some tightening of the regulations. On incomes, however, a more complex formula was introduced permitting a choice between a 7% increase, with a maximum of £350 per year, or an increase of £2·25 per week. In addition, higher increases could be awarded by the Pay Board on various grounds such as the removal of anomalies or the necessity of working " unsocial " hours. New Year's Day was also declared to be a public holiday.

The Oil Crisis.

The implementation of Phase Three took place against a rapidly changing economic situation. In the aftermath of the Arab-Israeli war of October 1973, problems arose in the supply of oil, on which Britain depends for 50% of her energy. First, the Arab oil producers decided to boycott some countries and to restrict supplies to most others. British imports were cut by 15%. Second, all the oil exporting countries decided to increase the price of crude oil dramatically. Shortage of petrol produced panic among many motorists leading to long queues and even violent scenes at some garages. The Government took the precaution of issuing ration coupons but managed to avoid introducing rationing, relying instead on voluntary restraint.

Deepening Economic Crisis.

The increased cost of oil imports and the reduction in supplies adversely affected both the balance of payments and industrial output. The economic situation was further weakened by the decision of the National Union of Mineworkers (NUM) in November 1973 to implement a ban on overtime and weekend working in support of a pay claim in excess of Phase Three. The rapidly deteriorating fuel situation was aggravated by an out-of-hours working ban by electricity power engineers which limited the ability of the Central Electricity Generating Board to cope with shortages at various power stations. Consequently on 13 November the Government declared a State of Emergency. Orders were enacted restricting space heating by electricity, except in the home and certain other places, and prohibiting the use of electricity for advertising, displays or floodlighting. The position worsened still further following the decision of the Amalgamated Society of Locomotive Engineers and Firemen (ASLEF) to ban Sunday, overtime and rest-day working. This had the effect of disrupting the delivery of coal to power stations as well as causing a considerable amount of inconvenience to passengers, especially in the South-East. The Government refused to make an offer to the miners outside the terms of Stage Three and was therefore compelled to introduce a package of tougher measures to deal with the crisis. Most important, as from 1 January, electricity was only provided to industry on three specified days per week. In addition a 50 mile/h speed limit was introduced on all roads, a maximum heating limit was imposed on all commercial premises and offices and television was required to close down at 10.30 p.m. each evening. The Chancellor of the Exchequer also announced large cuts in public expenditure and tighter controls on consumer credit.

Miners' Strike and the February 1974 Election.

Following an overwhelming vote in a pithead ballot, the NUM decided to intensify its industrial action by calling a national strike as from 10 February. Before the strike began, however, the Prime Minister announced that he had asked the Queen to dissolve Parliament so as to hold a general election on 28 February. For the Government, the main issue of the election was the attempt by a trade union to use its industrial strength to defeat the policy of the elected government. The Labour Party, however, attempted to widen the campaign to include the Government's general record since 1970. There was also general interest in the performance of the Liberals following a series of dramatic by-election successes in 1972 and 1973.

Minority Labour Government.

At the dissolution, Mr. Heath had had an overall majority of 16 in the House of Commons. As the results came in on election night it was clear that he was going to lose this and that the result was

going to be very close. Eventually the result was as follows:

Labour	301
Conservative	296
Liberal	14
Others	24

In this situation Mr. Heath did not offer his resignation immediately but entered into discussions with Mr. Jeremy Thorpe, the Leader of the Liberals, to see if the basis existed for the formation of a coalition. No agreement, however, was reached and Mr. Heath resigned on 4 March. The Queen then asked Mr. Wilson to form a government which he agreed to do without obtaining the support of any other parties. Immediate steps were taken to settle the miners' dispute and to end the three-day working week.

The Social Contract.

Although leading a minority government, Mr. Wilson knew that the other parties would be reluctant to force another election immediately. The Government was therefore able to make a start in implementing its programme. Most of its domestic policies were included in the *Social Contract*, a package of measures agreed between the Labour Party and the Trades Union Congress in 1973. Most important were the measures to control inflation. In return for the abolition of the Pay Board and all associated statutory controls on pay, which occurred in July 1974, the trade unions agreed voluntarily to restrain wage increases. Other measures included the repeal of the Industrial Relations Act 1971, the introduction of food subsidies, the strengthening of price controls and increased payments to old-age pensioners.

October 1974 Election.

Despite the Government's success in exploiting its parliamentary position, it was clear that it would seek a new mandate from the electorate at an early opportunity. Following the publication of a large number of statements of policy during the summer, the Prime Minister sought a dissolution of Parliament for polling to take place on 10 October. The Labour Party remained ahead in the opinion polls throughout the campaign and this was confirmed in the results, but its margin was rather smaller than predicted. Labour only obtained a majority of three over all other parties. However its position was in fact considerably stronger than this because of the fragmented nature of the Opposition.

Conservative Leadership.

Although many Conservatives were critical of Mr. Heath's leadership, his support was not tested immediately after the February election because of the proximity of another general election. However, after the October election Mr. Heath decided to establish a committee, under the chairmanship of Lord Home, to review the procedure for electing the leader of the Conservative Party. It proposed a number of changes which were adopted for the election, held in February 1975. In the first ballot, Mrs Margaret Thatcher defeated Mr. Heath but failed to win the required majority. Mr. Heath then withdrew, announcing his intention of returning to the backbenches, and in the second ballot Mrs. Thatcher secured an overall majority.

European Renegotiation.

The Government was committed to seek a fundamental renegotiation of the terms of entry into the European Economic Community and to consult the British people as to whether the new terms should be accepted. In April 1974 Mr. Callaghan outlined to the Council of Ministers the terms which Britain wished to change, the most important of which were the contribution to the Community budget, the effect of the Common Agricultural Policy, the need to safeguard the interests of the Commonwealth and developing countries and the promotion of regional development. After concluding successful negotiations on most of these points the Cabinet voted to recommend continued membership and this view was endorsed by 67·2% of those who voted in a referendum held in June 1975.

Counter-Inflation Programme.

Despite the agreement of the trade unions voluntarily to restrain wage increases, the rate of inflation accelerated so much that by the middle of 1975 it had reached 25% per annum. In July 1975, the Government was therefore compelled to introduce a limit of £6 a week on pay settlements for people earning up to £8,500 a year, with no increase for those earning more. This policy remained voluntary but the Government announced that employers who increased pay by more than the limit would have not only the excess but the whole pay increase disallowed for the approval of price increases under the Price Code and it warned that if the limits were exceeded it would have to seek statutory powers of enforcement. The Government also undertook to maintain strict price controls and to continue and extend the payment of food subsidies.

Rising Unemployment.

The measures taken by the Government to reduce the rate of inflation, implemented during a serious world-wide recession, led to a sharp rise in unemployment such that in January 1976 1·3 million were out of work. Various steps were taken to provide additional employment but, short of major reflationary measures which were ruled out on other grounds, there was little that the Government could do. Preparations were made, however, to facilitate the development of the economy when conditions permitted. In November 1975 the Government published a new industrial strategy designed to ensure that assistance was given to those sectors of the economy with good prospects. Its difficulties, however, were highlighted in the following month when it had to launch a major rescue to avert the closure of Chrysler car production in Great Britain. Earlier in the year the Government had purchased 95% of the shares of British Leyland as part of a package of measures of financial support.

Pay and Prices.

Although the £6 limit, which was observed without exception, succeeded in reducing the rate of inflation, it was clear that further pay restraint was needed. In his 1976 Budget the Chancellor announced various tax reliefs conditional upon agreement being reached on a voluntary pay limit for another year. Such an agreement was made in May with a new limit curbing average wage increases to 4½% in the year starting in August 1976. Price controls were also maintained, but there was some relaxation to encourage industrial investment.

Resignation of Harold Wilson.

In March 1976 Harold Wilson, to everyone's surprise, announced his intention of resigning as Prime Minister. Six candidates were nominated to succeed him and, after three ballots, James Callaghan was declared the winner, defeating Michael Foot by 39 votes, and he became Prime Minister on 5 April. A number of changes were made in the Cabinet and four senior ministers, including Ted Short and Barbara Castle, retired. Ted Short remained Deputy Leader of the Labour Party until October when he was succeeded by Michael Foot. Harold Wilson, who remained an M.P., received a knighthood from the Queen in recognition of his services to the country as the longest-serving Prime Minister this century.

Cuts in Public Expenditure.

During 1976 a vigorous campaign was mounted in favour of cuts in public expenditure. Concern that the Government was borrowing excessively to finance this spending also led to weakness of sterling on the foreign exchange markets. In July, to avert a further fall in the value of sterling, substantial cuts were announced in the Government's spending plans for 1977–8 and interest rates were raised to record levels. These measures were not sufficient however, to prevent a dramatic slide in the £ during the autumn which forced the Government to seek a $3,900 million loan from the International Monetary Fund. To obtain this assistance, further cuts in public expenditure, amounting to £3,000 m. over the next two years, and increases in taxation were imposed in December. The Government also introduced new and tighter " cash limits " over public spending.

Lords v. Commons.

Despite these economic problems, the Government proceeded with one of the largest legislative programmes ever introduced in a single session. Most of it was also controversial, and strong opposition was encountered in the House of Commons, where the Government's small majority was frequently threatened, and in the House of Lords The Lords attempted to make major changes in six bills, but the conflict eventually centred around two bills: the Dock Work Regulation Bill and the Aircraft and Shipbuilding Industries Bill. The former was returned to the Commons with its main provision transformed by the Lords, but the defection of two of its own backbenchers prevented the Government restoring its original proposal. Disagreement over the latter was not resolved by the time Parliament was prorogued and the bill to nationalise the aerospace and shipbuilding industries therefore had to be reintroduced at the beginning of the 1976–7 session. It became law in March 1977 but only after the Government had made substantial concessions.

Devolution.

In October 1974 the Scottish National Party secured 30·4% of the Scottish vote, winning 11 seats, and Plaid Cymru won 10·8% of the Welsh vote, winning 3 seats. The SNP also came second in 42 constituencies, 35 of them held by Labour. These successes brought the question of devolution to the centre of political debate and the Government announced its intention of setting up assemblies in Scotland and Wales. Both parties are split on this issue. Traditionally the Labour Party, and particularly its Scottish members, have opposed devolution, but with a few prominent exceptions in both Scotland and Wales, the Party supports the Government's proposals. The Conservatives have supported the creation of a Scottish assembly since the late 1960s, but in 1976 decided officially to oppose the Government's plans. A number of senior Conservatives, however, dissented from this apparent change of policy. In December 1976 the Scotland and Wales Bill was given a Second Reading by a majority of 45, the Government having secured the votes of most Labour MPs by promising to hold referenda before bringing the assemblies into existence. To get the Bill through its Committee Stage, which had to be taken on the floor of the House of Commons, the Government had to introduce a " guillotine " motion, but this was defeated by 29 votes in Feburary 1977, with back-bench Labour rebels joining Conservatives and Liberals.

Lib/Lab Pact.

By-election losses meant that by 1976 the Government had lost its overall majority. Its failure to make progress with the devolution bill also meant that it could no longer count upon the support of the Nationalists. In this situation, the Conservatives in March 1977 put down a motion of no confidence in the Government. Faced with the prospect of defeat, the Government entered into an agreement with the Liberal Party, initially until the summer. It therefore succeeded in defeating the Conservative motion with a comfortable majority of 24. In July the agreement was renewed for the next session of Parliament provided that the Government maintained the fight against inflation. Under its terms both parties retain their independence for electoral purposes and in the House of Commons, but the Liberals have agreed to support the Government in return for formal consultations on government policy and some specific undertakings on subjects such as direct elections to the European Assembly and devolution.

Stage Three.

One of the reasons behind Liberal support for the Government was their belief that it would be able to agree to a further year of pay restraint with the TUC. Negotiations took place during the early part of the summer but the TUC refused to agree to a limit on settlements, believing that there should be an immediate return to free collective bargaining subject only to an undertaking that settlements should last for twelve months. The Government, however, announced unilaterally in July 1977 its own pay guidelines which stated that the general level of settlements should be such that the nation's earnings would increase during 1977–78 by no more than 10%. In contrast to the first two years of pay policy, these guidelines led to a considerable number of industrial disputes. Most serious was the nine-week strike of firemen between November 1977 and January 1978 during which fire services were provided by the armed forces.

Political Tension.

1977 saw violent scenes in various parts of Britain. One problem was the rise of the National Front, a party calling among other things for a halt to immigration and the repatriation of many coloured residents. Its activities in holding marches and demonstrations, particularly in areas with large coloured populations, were opposed by many groups and resulted in clashes between its supporters and those of the extreme left, for instance in Lewisham and in Birmingham during August. There were also violent scenes in north London outside the Grunwick film-processing factory as the trade union movement organised a mass picket in connection with the firm's refusal to recognise the right of its employees to belong to a trade union.

Foreign Affairs.

For the first six months of 1977 it was Britain's turn to hold the Presidency of the EEC. This burden, along with many others, was one of the causes of the sudden death of the Foreign Secretary, Anthony Crosland, in February 1977. He was succeeded by one of his junior ministers, Dr. David Owen, who at the age of 37 was the youngest person in this office since Sir Anthony Eden in the 1930s. One of the first problems he had to face was the situation in Rhodesia. Following the breakdown of constitutional talks, held between October and December 1976 in Geneva, intensive diplomatic activity led to the publication of joint Anglo-American settlement proposals in September 1977. At the same time Ian Smith, the Rhodesian Prime Minister, also announced his intention of seeking an internal settlement with moderate African leaders.

Brighter Economic News.

The harsh economic measures taken by the Government in 1976 produced results more quickly than had been expected, and by the end of 1977 most indicators pointed to a dramatic change in the financial outlook. The balance of payments in the last part of the year was in surplus on both visible and invisible accounts; the pound was strong in relation to most other currencies and there had been massive increases in Britain's reserves; and the rate of inflation was falling steadily and was expected to be in single figures in the spring of 1978. However, unemployment remained at the very high level of 1·4 million and the growth in industrial output was still sluggish. None the less, the Chancellor of the Exchequer was able to cut taxes on two occasions during 1977 and interest rates fell progressively from their record levels of the previous year. One cause of this economic recovery was North Sea oil. The first oil was brought ashore in 1975, and by the end of 1977 50% of the country's needs were being met from this source.

The Parliamentary Position in January 1978.

The renewal of the Lib/Lab agreement was endorsed by the Liberal Assembly in September 1977, but its continuation was made conditional on there being substantial Labour support for the adoption of proportional representation for direct elections to the European Assembly. Although this was supported by a majority of Labour M.P.s, the House of Commons rejected it in a vote in December and the future of the agreement began to look in doubt. In any case, the Government's parliamentary position has been strengthened by the reintroduction of devolution proposals, this time as separate bills for Scotland and Wales. While these are proceeding through Parliament, under a timetable agreed in November, it is unlikely that the Nationalists will vote against the Government on an issue of confidence. However, the Government's position remains weak. Since the General Election it has lost 6 seats to the Conservatives in by-elections and one through the defection of Reg Prentice. In April. the Liberal leader announced that the Lib-Lab pact would terminate at the end of July. It is thus uncertain whether the Government will be able to choose the time of the next general election, which must take place by October 1979. Excluding the Speaker and his three deputies who do not vote, the state of the parties in June 1978 was:

	Seats
Labour	306
Conservative	282
Liberal	13
Scottish National	11
Ulster Unionist	6
Plaid Cymru	3
Scottish Labour	2
Other Northern Irish	6
Vacant (Penistone and Moss Side)	2

Major Legislation 1977.

Major legislation enacted during 1977 included:

Aircraft and Shipbuilding Industries Act 1977, brought the aircraft manufacturing and shipbuilding industries into public ownership to be owned and managed by two new public corporations, British Aerospace and British Shipbuilders.

Price Commission Act 1977, provided new powers for the control of prices including the selective investigation of price increases by a strengthened and expanded Price Commission.

Housing (Homeless Persons) Act 1977, imposed new responsibilities upon local authorities to provide housing for homeless persons and provide for financial assistance to be given to voluntary organisations concerned with homelessness.

Minibus Act 1977, removed from the scope of legislation relating to public service vehicles certain minibuses operated by bodies concerned with education, religion and other community activities.

Patents Act 1977, established a new law of patents, modifying existing law and giving effect to certain international conventions.

Post Office Act 1977, enlarged the size of the board of the Post Office Corporation so as to allow an experiment in industrial democracy.

Northern Ireland in Crisis.

Violence has erupted in Northern Ireland on various occasions since the implementation of the Government of Ireland Act of 1920. The latest troubles started in 1968. A new civil rights movement organised a number of marches which, although peaceful in intent, tended to become violent because of the involvement of extremists on both sides. During the summer of 1969 serious rioting in Belfast and Londonderry led the Government of Northern Ireland to ask for the assistance of British troops to prevent a breakdown of law and order. Although the arrival of the troops and the acceleration of the programme of reforms produced a temporary lull, the situation continued to deteriorate during 1970 and 1971. As a result, in March 1972 the UK Government decided to suspend the Government of Ireland Act and to impose " direct rule " from Westminster.

The table below sets out the main political events since the imposition of direct rule:

1973 March	Plebiscite held on the border. Boycotted by Catholic parties; 57·4% of electorate voted in favour of union with UK.
June	Election for new Assembly to replace Stormont Parliament. Discussions start on formation of a power-sharing executive.
December	Tripartite conference (UK Government, Northern Ireland Executive-designate and Irish Government) agrees to establish a Council of Ireland.
1974 January	Establishment of Executive comprising members of the Official Unionists, Social Democratic and Labour Party and Alliance Party.
February	UK General Election in which 11 out of the 12 seats were won by candidates opposed to the Executive.
May	Resignation of Executive following strike action initiated by Ulster Workers' Council. Direct rule resumed.
1975 May	Election for a Constitutional Convention, established to put forward recommendations on the future government of Northern Ireland.
1976 March	Following the failure of the Convention to produce a unanimous report and the rejection of the majority report by the UK Government, the Convention was dissolved.
August	Formation of Peace Movement which during the autumn held rallies and meetings in Northern Ireland, in Britain and overseas.
1977 May	10-day strike by Ulster Unionist Action Council in support of tougher action against the IRA and the implementation of the report of the Constitutional Convention. Strike ended without concessions from the UK Government.

Terrorism.

Since 1968–9 terrorist activity has persisted in Northern Ireland, and it has sporadically broken out in other parts of the United Kingdom. Over 1600 people have been killed in Northern Ireland and 20,000 injured. Since 1975 there have been many fewer bombings in Northern Ireland, the majority of the deaths being sectarian and inter-factional killings. There has also been a dramatic reduction in the level of violence in Britain, partly as a result of the sweeping emergency powers obtained by the Government in the wake of the Birmingham pub bombings in the autumn of 1974.

II. THE CHANGING WORLD SCENE

WESTERN EUROPE

FRANCE.

Gaullism without de Gaulle.

General de Gaulle died on 11 November 1970 at his home at Colombey-les-Deux-Eglises. He was 79. A somewhat Olympian figure, his main achievement had been to restore prestige and self-respect to France. Moreover the constitutional system which he introduced has survived the departure of the central figure about whom it was created (although the problem of what would happen if the President were faced with a hostile majority in the National Assembly remains unresolved). So has the party which he created to assist him in maintaining power. Part of the credit for this must go to the late President Pompidou, who while adhering to Gaullist traditions and stubbornly insisting on French interests revealed a cautious and pragmatic approach, shunning his predecessor's obsession with French grandeur. With this came a much needed revival of interest in economic and social matters. The most significant change was the ending of French hostility to Britain's entry to the EEC, culminating in the highly successful summit conference between M. Pompidou and Mr. Heath in May 1971—although this reversal was in fact initiated by de Gaulle himself. However as the parliamentary elections due in March 1973 approached the position of the Gaullists looked insecure. A referendum on expansion of the EEC gave only lukewarm endorsement to M. Pompidou's new policy, and the Gaullists were shaken by a series of scandals which led to the replacement of M. Chaban-Delmas by M. Messmer as Prime Minister. Moreover the Communist Party and the Socialists agreed on a common programme of government, thus forming the first Popular Front since 1934.

In fact the French electors came close in the first ballot to electing a Socialist-Communist coalition. However, in the second round, the Gaullists, and their Reformist allies led by M. Lecanuet, achieved a remarkable comeback. Although the left-wing parties almost doubled their parliamentary representation and the Gaullists suffered the heaviest losses, the Government parties retained an overall majority of 58 seats.

France under Giscard d'Estaing.

After a period of speculation about his failing health, President Pompidou died in April 1974. In the election to find his successor the official Gaullist candidate and former Prime Minister M. Chaban-Delmas was eliminated on the first ballot with a humiliating 15% of the vote. On the second ballot Valéry Giscard d'Estaing, leader of the centre-right Independent Republicans, only just defeated the candidate of the Left, M. Mitterand, by 50·8% to 49·2% of the vote. He appointed M. Chirac, who had been Gaullist Minister of the Interior under President Pompidou, as Prime Minister in a coalition widened to include all centre groupings. The President's programme included social reform and comprehensive anti-inflation measures. In January 1976 the first major reorganisation of government was carried out since M. Chirac's appointment as Premier. The coalition continued to be the basis for the President's support.

In August 1976, M. Chirac resigned as Premier and was replaced by M. Raymond Barre, one of the President's non-party supporters. M. Chirac had become frustrated by the policies pursued by the President and in December he announced a grand reform of the Gaullist Party, now to be known as the Assembly for the Republic. Together with right-wing disillusion, left-wing opposition to the government increased. M. Mitterand's near success in the Presidential election increased support for his socialist party and following gains for the Socialists and Communists in departmental elections M. Mitterand and the Communist Party leader, M. Marchais, resolved some differences and agreed on joint left-wing lists of candidates for the municipal elections held in March 1977. The alliance gained ground, capturing 58 major cities and towns. The successful candidacy of M. Chirac for the re-created post of mayor of Paris also produced problems in the ranks of the government coalition. In July agreement was reached between the parties of the governing majority on rules to be observed in the parliamentary election campaign in early 1978, and in September they issued a joint manifesto. However, the open estrangement continued between M. Chirac, on the one hand, and M. Barre and President Giscard d'Estaing, on the other. While the latter relied on the ambitious Barre

Plan for the economy, M. Chirac, and with him the Gaullist deputies, clearly rejected further sacrifices and unpopular measures.

At the same time the common front of the Left rapidly disintegrated. An attempt to update the Common Programme failed, mainly because of disputes about the Communists' ambitious nationalisation plans and their high estimate of the cost of the Common Programme. A real split between Communists and Socialists occurred in October 1977, especially on the issue of the continuation of the nuclear programme. Each party continued thereafter to pay lip-service to the joint programme, but each interpreted it in his own way. Meanwhile the Communists made it clear that they were not willing to play second fiddle in a government with the Socialists.

The Election of 1978.

In the first round of the General Election, on 12 March, the left polled well, despite a relatively poor performance by the Socialists (22·6% of the vote). In the second round, on 19 March, the Government romped home, winning 290 seats, the opposition taking 200. Once again, the " centre " had been victorious and the Left thwarted.

THE TWO GERMANYS.

Adenauer and West Germany.

The Federal Republic of Germany, founded in 1949, had as its first Chancellor Dr. Konrad Adenauer until his retirement in 1963 at the age of 86. His Christian Democrat government produced conditions of stability and confidence in which Germany rebuilt her shattered prosperity and a viable parliamentary democracy. His work in building a special relationship with France, culminating in a treaty of friendship, was a dramatic contrast to the long tradition of enmity towards France. But while he succeeded in building his country into the Western community he remained intransigent over German reunification within the boundaries of 1937, stressing West Germany's right to speak for the whole of Germany, including the Soviet Zone. The two states drifted steadily apart, and a seal was set on their division by East Germany's building of the Berlin Wall in 1961.

Erhard and Kiesinger.

Adenauer's successor Dr. Erhard had the prestige of having as economics minister been the main architect of West Germany's " economic miracle." As Chancellor from 1963 to 1966 he was a loyal supporter of the Atlantic Alliance—indeed it was held that he encouraged ties with the United States at the expense of the Franco-German friendship treaty, which had not lived up to the hopes reposed in it. This partly accounted for the enmity of the Bavarian wing of the Christian Democrats called the Christian Social Union (CSU), the party of Franz-Josef Strauss.

In 1966 a governmental crisis caused by the resignation of the junior partners in the coalition, the Free Democrats (FDP), led to the formation under Dr. Kiesinger of a Grand Coalition in which the Social Democrats (SDP) joined the CDU and so had their first taste of government on the national level since the Federal Republic's foundation. This helped to establish the SPD in the eyes of the electorate as a potential governing party.

The End of Christian Democratic Rule, 1969.

In the general election of September 1969 the SPD made significant gains in both votes and seats. Despite widespread publicity the extreme right-wing NPD (often referred to as Neo-Nazis) failed to qualify for any seats since it polled less than the necessary 5 per cent of the total votes. It is now virtually defunct. Thus the three-party system remained. Although the CDU was still the largest party, the SPD and FDP leaders agreed to form a coalition government with Herr Brandt, the SPD leader, as Chancellor and Herr Scheel, the FDP leader, as Foreign Minister.

Herr Brandt's achievement in reaching the Chancellorship was considerable, in view of his unpopularity in some quarters for having fled to Norway during the war and taken out Norwegian citizenship. However he had built up his reputation as Mayor of West Berlin.

Efforts to Improve Relations Between the Two Germanys.

The Brandt Government's main achievements were in the field of foreign policy. A radical development in 1970 was the two meetings between Chancellor Brandt and the East German Prime Minister, Herr Stoph. These showed that Herr Brandt had accepted the existence of two separate states within the German nation (although this fell short of East Germany's demand for complete recognition by Bonn). A treaty signed by West Germany and the Soviet Union in Moscow on 12 August stated that the borders of all European countries are inviolable, including that between the Federal and the Democratic Republics. Bonn implies that frontiers can still be changed by mutual agreement.

Bonn insisted that the ratification of the Moscow treaty and of the Warsaw treaty recognising the Oder–Neisse Line and normalising relations between West Germany and Poland depended on a satisfactory outcome of the Four-Power talks on Berlin. At last in September 1971 an agreement was signed by which the Soviet Union in turn accepted the realities which matter to the West. It recognised the rights of the Allies in Berlin and the city's special relations with the Federal Republic, which had been constantly disputed, especially by the East Germans. The free flow of traffic to and from Berlin, formerly unregulated and therefore a favourite object of disruption and escalation of tension, is now covered by an agreement for which the Soviet Union, rather than East Germany, can be held responsible. The representation abroad of West Berlin by the Federal Republic is now legally based. West Berliners can again visit the eastern part of the city and the GDR. The details of transit were left to be filled in by East and West Germany, and after the Russians had overcome East German recalcitrance the first treaty between the two German states was signed on 20 December 1971. The Brandt Government immediately initiated the ratification of the Moscow and Warsaw treaties, which was eventually achieved in May 1972 after prolonged antagonism from the opposition CDU and some former government supporters. Bonn stressed that the treaties were not an anticipation of a Peace Treaty and formed no legal basis for the existing frontiers, but this view was rejected by the USSR and Poland.

The way was now open for general agreements on traffic and for a general treaty between East and West Germany signed on 21 December 1972, which recognised the existence of two virtually sovereign German states. Though a shock for those who clung to the illusion of German unity, the treaty marked a new realism which promised greater contact between the two states and was therefore welcomed by a majority of Germans. The concessions extorted from the East Germans as a condition of signing the treaty considerably increased the numbers of West Germans and Berliners able to visit the East. The advantages gained by the GDR in terms of confirmation of its statehood and of the division of Germany for the foreseeable future are evident from the flood of countries (including Britain and France) which have recognised it since the signature of the treaty. Despite an attempt to have it declared unconstitutional, the treaty came into force in the summer of 1973. This was quickly followed by the admission of the two German states to the United Nations on 18 September. However the limits of détente were shown up by highly restrictive interpretations of the agreements by East Germany and by the latter's doubling of the sum visitors from West Germany and Berlin were required to exchange per day to 20 Marks, though it was later reduced. In pursuance of the Basic Treaty, Permanent Missions were opened in Bonn and East Berlin in May 1974.

1973 also saw the conclusion of a treaty normalising relations between West Germany and Czechoslovakia, long delayed by the Czech attempt to have the Munich Agreement of 1938 declared invalid " ab initio ". In 1975 agreements were signed between West Germany and Poland on the granting of credits to Poland, the payment of claims arising from the Second World War and the resettlement of ethnic Germans living in Poland. This was criticised as paying for emigration by the Opposition, who blocked it with their majority in the Upper house.

The SPD/FDP Coalition

In April 1972 a government crisis was brought about by defections from the government coalition mainly on the question of its Ostpolitik. This led to an early election in November 1972 as a result of which Chancellor Brandt's government was triumphantly returned to power. For the first time, the SPD became the largest party in the Bundestag and their position was strengthened by their coalition colleagues, FDP. However relations between them became strained as a result of demands from the left wing of the SPD.

In May 1974, following the arrest of Günther Guillaume, a Chancellery aide, who admitted spying for E. Germany, political responsibility for negligence was accepted by Chancellor Brandt who then resigned. His successor was the former finance minister Helmut Schmidt whose approach is marked by realism and pragmatism.

During 1974 the CDU made significant gains in elections in the Länder. Helmut Kohl, chairman of CDU, was accepted as its candidate for Federal Chancellor. In October 1976 federal elections to the Bundestag were held. The SPD–FDP coalition lost ground (see Table below) and based upon the fact that the CDU–CSU alliance was now the largest party in the Bundestag, Kohl attempted to claim the Chancellorship. However, with assurances from Hans Dietrich Genscher that the FDP would continue to support the SPD in a governing coalition, President Scheel was persuaded by Genscher and Brandt to ask Schmidt to continue as Chancellor.

Table : German election results for the Bundestag

	1976		1972	
	Seats	%	Seats	%
SPD .	214	42·6	230	45·9
CDU .	190	38·0⎫243, 48·6	224	44·8
CSU .	53	10·6⎭		
FDP. .	39	7·9	42	8·4
NPD .	—	0·3	—	0·6
Others .	—	0·6	—	0·3

During 1976 and 1977 the Social Democrats were weakened by a number of scandals in those Länder which were governed by them. Thus on 3 October 1976, as soon as voting closed in the Federal elections, Herr Oswald, Prime Minister of Hesse, resigned in the wake of the collapse of the state bank of Hesse following ill-judged financial speculation and amid accusations of accepting donations to SPD funds from dubious business sources. And later the Mayor of Berlin, Herr Schütz, felt obliged to resign after a series of scandals had compelled the resignation of some of his senators. During the same period the FDP, the small coalition partner of the SPD at federal level, formed coalition governments with the Christian Democrats in the Länder of Lower Saxony and the Saar. However, the ranks of the Federal Opposition were split following their defeat in the Federal elections by the decision of Franz-Joseph Strauss, leader of the Bavarian CSU, not to continue the joint parliamentary party in the Bundestag with the CDU which had been in existence since 1949. This decision was later reversed, although the CSU continued to threaten to form a " fourth party " throughout the Federal Republic.

Chancellor Schmidt's room for manoeuvre continued to be restricted by the opposition majority in the second chamber of the Federal parliament representing the governments of the Länder, and by the need to trim Social Democratic policies to the wishes of his coalition partner. However, his position was strengthened in the autumn of 1977 as a result of the firm stand taken against the Baader-Meinhoff terrorist group which kidnapped the chairman of the German employers' association, Hanns-Martin Schleyer, and later hi-jacked

a plane-load of German tourists. Although Herr Schleyer was later found murdered across the border in France, the German government was successful in a dramatic storming of the hi-jacked aeroplane at Mogadishu airport without loss of life among the hostages. The decisive action against the terrorists, and especially the suicide in prison of those leading Baader-Meinhoff members whose release had been demanded by the kidnappers, caused widespread anti-German demonstrations and acts of violence especially in Italy and France. But at home and in other parts of Europe Herr Schmidt's reputation was greatly enhanced.

East German Developments.

In October 1975 a wide-ranging 25-year Treaty of Friendship, Cooperation and Mutual Assistance was signed in Moscow. In May 1976 at the Ninth Congress of the Socialist Unity Party, the E. German leader Herr Honecker presented the General Committee report which reaffirmed close ties with the Soviet Union, reviewed economic and social developments and produced a new 5-year economic plan. The aims of the plan include increased national productivity and investment and closer economic integration with the Soviet Union and other COMECON countries. Following elections to the Volkskammer in October, the 5-year plan was endorsed and unanimous approval was given to the appointments of Herr Honecker as Chairman of the Council of State, Willi Stoph as Chairman of the Council of Ministers and Horst Sindermann as president of the Volkskammer.

Although an amendment was made to the new party programme allowing references to equality of religious beliefs, the position regarding religious and intellectual freedom remains unsatisfactory. Recent examples of this include the suicide of 2 clerics and the effective exiling of folksinger Wolf Biermann.

ITALY.

The centre-left coalition which has dominated recent Italian politics was formed in 1963 in an " opening to the Left " which brought Pietro Nenni's Socialists out of the wilderness with the Communists and into government. It was born of frustration with the inertia of the previous centre-right coalition. But it too had a long list of social reforms which it had failed to accomplish, though its problems came as much from dissensions within the Christian Democratic Party as between it and the Socialists. A major cause of the governmental crises which have afflicted post-war governments in Italy has been the increasing strength of the Communist Party and, until the 1976 elections, that of the Neo-fascists (MSI). The room for manoeuvre of the other parties was thus reduced. The elections of May 1972 were followed by the formation by Signor Andreotti of Italy's 34th post-war government, a coalition of the Christian Democrats (DC), Social Democrats (PSDI) and Liberals supported by the Republicans (PRI). In this " Government of the Centre " the Liberals were represented after a 15-year break and the Socialists (PSI) excluded for the first time since 1963.

After a series of parliamentary defeats and the withdrawal of Republican support, the Andreotti Government resigned in June 1973. Signor Rumor, the outgoing Minister of the Interior and former Prime Minister, was able to re-establish the Centre-Left coalition of Christian Democrats, Socialists, Social Democrats and Republicans. When a referendum on the legalisation of divorce in Italy was eventually held in May 1974, the result was a surprisingly substantial majority in favour of retaining the divorce laws, to the discredit of the Christian Democrats.

In the economic sphere Italy continues to be plagued by numerous strikes and by the seemingly intractable problems of the economically deprived south (Mezzogiorno). Particularly since the oil crisis there have been massive balance of payments deficits, rampant inflation, falling production and continuing bureaucratic paralysis. These economic problems and political unrest, manifested in bomb explosions and attacks on persons and property by extreme groups, on the left and especially the right, led to a further government crisis in late 1974. Signor Moro emerged as Prime Minister because he alone, among the DCs, retained some degree of credibility with parties of the left. A minority coalition of DCs and Republicans resulted.

In January 1976, the Socialists withdrew their support from the Government but reached an agreement with the DCs that they would abstain from voting against the Government. In April, faced with opposition to its abortion legislation, the falling value of the lira, increasing political violence and the exposition of bribery and corruption, the Moro government resigned. Elections were held in June, the main issue being the future pattern of government in Italy. The Communist Party, which had long demonstrated its independence from Moscow, had made significant gains in the regional, provincial and municipal elections in 1975 and had indicated its willingness to respect party pluralism and the transfer of power through elections. This position, together with the lowering of the voting age for the Chamber of Deputies, resulted in their share of the votes being increased from 27·1% in 1972 to 34·4% in the Chamber and from 28·3% in 1972 to 33·8% in the Senate. The strength of the DCs remained almost the same at about 38% in both Chambers. The full result, compared to 1972 for the Chamber of Deputies is set out below.

Chamber of Deputies

	1976		1972	
	Seats	%	Seats	%
DC . .	262	38·7	266	38·7
PCI .	228	34·4	179	27·1
PSI .	57	9·6	61	9·6
PSDI .	15	3·4	29	5·1
PRI	14	3·1	15	2·9
PLI .	5	1·3	20	3·9
MSI .	35	6·1	56	8·7
Others .	14	3·4	4	4·0

In July 1976, Signor Andreotti agreed to form a new minority government. Measures were taken to alleviate the economic crisis and protect the lira, including loans from the IMF and the EEC. The Communists provide tacit support for the Government, but are faced with the dilemma of either supporting measures with which they disagree or opposing them with the clear risk of economic and political collapse.

In July 1977 all the main Italian political parties, including the Communists but not the Neofascists, presented a common programme for curing the country's ills. Signor Andreotti emphasised that this did not bring Italy closer to a " historic compromise " (meaning Communist participation in the government). However, Signor Berlinguer, Secretary-General of the PCI, later reasserted the Communists' allegiance to the idea of a " historic compromise ", appealing to the evolving ideology of the European Communist Parties which is generally known as " Eurocommunism ". In Moscow in November he even proclaimed—in stark contradiction to Lenin—the thesis of a " non-ideological state ".

The Fall of Andreotti.

The Andreotti Government continued to steer Italy past the abyss of an economic catastrophe and bankruptcy of political confidence. But despite success in getting the balance of payments out of the red, it was acting against a background of an enormous budgetary deficit, mounting debt, increasing unemployment and an ever-growing incidence of terrorist attacks. The trade unions began to protest that restraint and sacrifice had brought them no benefits, and they and the Socialist Party began to advocate an emergency government of all the parties. The Republican Party had already called for the inclusion of the Communists, and in December 1977 the latter themselves explicitly demanded participation in a government of " national solidarity ".

Finally, it was the trade unions' threat of a general strike that brought about the resignation of Signor Andreotti. Italy thus finds itself in a deadlocked situation in which the Christian Democrats cannot govern without the Communists yet

cannot so far agree to govern with them. The Communists, on the other hand, can scarcely make further compromises while remaining excluded from power and still retain credibility with their supporters.

The Murder of Aldo Moro.

The assassination of Signor Aldo Moro, five times Prime Minister of Italy and one of the most respected Christian Democrats, by members of the Red Brigades in May 1978 was condemned as an act of barbarism by both Western and Communist countries.

PORTUGAL.

A military take-over in 1926 which brought Antonio Salazar to power inaugurated nearly fifty years of authoritarian rule. In 1968 Salazar was succeeded by Marcello Caetano who, despite slightly more liberal sympathies, maintained the instruments of oppression, including the hated Political Police (PIDE).

However, the dictatorship was overthrown by an almost bloodless military coup on 25 April 1974. Although the leadership of the seven-man " Junta of National Salvation " belonged to General Spinola, who became President, the coup was largely the work of middle-ranking officers whose experience in the long struggle against Nationalist forces in Portuguese Angola, Mozambique and Guinea had brought about profound dissatisfaction with the aims and methods of the Caetano government.

The new government initiated an impressive series of liberal measures, including the abolition of press censorship (later partially restored), the lifting of the ban on political parties, the abolition of the secret police, release of political prisoners and the promise of free elections. The right to strike and right of assembly were secured in August. Rapid progress was also made towards granting independence to Portugal's large African Territories. However after so many years of dictatorship it was not surprising that the preparations for democracy and the competition for power brought about a very unsettled situation. In September, after a split between left- and right-wing factions of the Junta and an alleged attempt at a counter-coup by General Spinola to reverse Portugal's leftward drift, the latter was replaced by General Costa Gomes and other conservatives were dismissed. Under pressure from the leftist Movement of the Armed Forces, impatient with the pace of reform, the officers of the Junta took over exceptional powers in February 1975.

The failure of an attempted *coup d'état* on 11 March 1975 resulted in General Spinola fleeing the country and the Armed Forces Movement's Revolutionary Council taking supreme power. A ban was imposed on three political parties, including the right-wing Christian Democrats, and the activities of the Popular Democrats were disrupted by left-wing elements.

In elections to a Constituent Assembly held in April 1975 (the first for fifty years) the Socialists under Dr. Soares emerged as the strongest party with 37% of the vote, while the Popular Democrats received 26% and the Communists only 12%. But there were no corresponding cabinet changes and the government continued with a programme of extensive nationalisation. Tension developed between the increasingly pro-Communist Armed Forces Movement and the Socialists and Popular Democrats, with both parties temporarily withdrawing from the coalition government. There was mounting indiscipline in the armed forces and in November 1975 some extreme leftist army units unsuccessfully attempted a putsch. In its wake the government under Pinheiro de Azevedo was able increasingly to promote law and order and in February 1976 a constitutional pact was reached between the army and the main political parties to reduce the powers of the former in the Supreme Revolutionary Council. After elections to the legislative assembly in April 1976, the Socialists remained the largest party and a new constitution was promulgated. On 27 June General Antonio dos Santos Ramalho Eanes, backed by the leading parties, was elected President with 61·5% of the vote. A new government was formed by Dr. Soares and a programme of economic measures was initiated to fight rampant inflation and high unemployment. The local election results at the end of 1976 indicated that a strong division still exists between the conservative north and the Communists in the south. Despite continuing support from Western Europe and a massive loan from the U.S., the position of Dr. Soares and the Socialists remained tenuous because of the virtually intractable economic problems. The international credits made available to Portugal in conjunction with the continuing programme of economic stabilisation were conditional upon a policy of austerity. However, the Social Democrats and the Centre finally refused to go along with Dr. Soares' economic programme, and in December 1977 his minority government was defeated. But the Social Democrats and Centre could not muster a majority on their own, while their agreement with the Communists could run no further than the defeat of the Socialist government. There was thus no solution without the Socialists, and despite Dr. Soares' evident opposition to coalition, a government was formed with the Centre in early 1978.

Meanwhile in March 1977 Portugal officially applied for membership of the EEC.

SPAIN.

The extremely bitter Civil War from 1936 to 1939, between, on the one hand, the republican forces which had been coming und r increasingly left-wing influence and, on the other, the Catholic and conservative National Front and the army which revolted under General Franco's leadership, resulted in a victory for the latter with the help of fascist Germany and Italy, which enabled Franco to dominate Spanish political life for three and a half decades. After remaining neutral during the Second World War Franco, despite cosmetic liberalisation measures and the temporary pushing into the background of the Falangist Party (Spanish Fascist Party), was ostracised by the United Nations and received no Marshall Aid. Even relations with the Vatican were strained (though the régime was certainly preferred to the anti-clerical Republican:), at least until a new Concordat was signed in 1953. However it became clear that the ostracism of Spain was having the unintended effect of helping to promote a defiant Spanish solidarity, and in 1953 the United States concluded bilateral agreements on defence and economic aid with Franco's government and two years later Spain was admitted to membership of the United Nations. Meanwhile the domestic scene in Spain was marked by political apathy, despite economic and other problems, and by a desire to avoid another civil war at all costs.

Franco had been grooming Prince Juan Carlos of the Spanish House of Bourbon-Parma to be his successor, despite Falangist opposition, and in 1966 an Organic Law declared Spain a monarchy though with a reigning monarch only after Franco's departure. At the same time provision was made for direct election of part of the Cortes, or parliament of estates of the realm, but on a restricted franchise and with candidates vetted by the Falangist movement. The Succession Law of July 1969 finally named Prince Juan Carlos as eventual successor of General Franco as Head of the Spanish State and King of Spain.

During the early 1970s Spain experienced increasing social and industrial unrest despite government repression; as well as terrorist activity by the Basque separatist movement ETA. This culminated in the assassination of the Prime Minister, Admiral Luis Carrero Blanco, in December 1973. He was succeeded by Sr. Arias Navarro. There followed a mixture of cautious attempts at liberalisation and retreat into repression. In December 1974 "political associations" (not parties) were legalised under certain conditions. But after industrial unrest and strikes, especially in the Basque provinces, to demand an amnesty for political prisioners, press censorship was intensified. In April 1975 after shootings of policemen a state of emergency was declared in two Basque provinces. The following month there came some liberalisation of local government as well as the introduction of a limited right to strike and labour legislation. However in August a new anti-terrorism law was followed by the

execution of Basque and Communist extremists, an action which provoked strong international protests.

In November 1975 the long dictatorship of General Franco finally came to an end when he died after a prolonged illness. However it soon became clear that the new king, Juan Carlos, was not going to make any sharp break with the past. Hence his confirmation of Sr. Arias Navarro as Prime Minister. He had to try to carry the intransigent Right with him in his reform plans, since they had a majority in the Cortes, the communes and the ministries and were determined not to give up their power. Only long-term plans were announced for repeal of the anti-terrorist law, amnesty for political prisoners and changes in the electoral law. Despite increasing toleration in practice of the activities at least of the Christian Democratic parties, the government lacked credibility with the rest of the population because of its desire not to provoke the right-wing opposition from the so-called "Bunker." It was faced with the dilemma of either suppressing strikes (such as the Madrid Metro Strike of January 1976) and so disavowing its democratisation programme, or permitting them and endangering the recession-bound economy.

Early in 1976 there were only vague indications of where and how elections would take place. However, in July Sr. Navarro was replaced by Sr. Adolfo Suárez Gonzáles who promised that the Government would be a "lawful promoter of a political process which is open to all" and an amnesty was offered for all political prisoners excluding those concerned with terrcrist offences. In November the Cortes approved plans for political reform which would replace the Cortes with a two-chamber parliament and in December, a referendum gave 94·2% support to the proposals. This was the first free vote in Spain since 1936. Unrest in the Basque regions continued as did discontent with the political situation evidenced by the assassination of Juan Villar and the kidnapping of Antonio Oriol, the Chief of the Council of State. In February Sr. Oriol was freed; responsibility for the kidnapping being claimed by GRAPO, an anti-fascist resistance group. In April 1977 the Communist Party was officially recognised thus raising the possibility of further right-wing violence and reaction.

The 1977 Election.

On 15 June 1977 the first free parliamentary elections for 41 years were held in Spain. This was a decisive step on the road from dictatorship to democracy, and in July the new two-chamber parliament replaced the old Cortes of General Franco. The strongest group was the "Union of the Democratic Centre" led by Sr. Suárez, who formed a minority government. The Socialist Workers' Party (PSOE) came a strong second, the Communist Party a weak third. The first task of the new government and parliament was the drawing up of a new democratic constitution. On 28 July Spain submitted its application to join the EEC. A serious economic crisis had been inherited from the last years of the Franco regime and the transitional period. But the most crucial issue for the future of the Spanish state was the regional problem. This applied not only to the Basque country, where the militant separatist organisation ETA had stepped up its terrorist activities. Both there and in Catalonia systems of "pre-autonomy" in anticipation of the new constitution were introduced in late 1977, setting Spain on the road from a strictly centralist to a federal state. The problem of whether the province of Navarre, which was divided on the question, should join the Basque region was left to be decided by referendum. Initiatives for pre-autonomy have been taken in other Spanish regions also.

EASTERN MEDITERRANEAN

GREECE.

On 21 April 1967 dictatorial power was seized in Greece by right-wing army colonels. They did so out of fear of the expected electoral victory of the Centre Union, under Mr. George Papandreou, which had increasing support from the Left.

Many politicians, journalists and others were arrested, often without charges being preferred. A rigid press censorship was imposed. The critical position of the 26-year-old King Constantine came to a head in December 1967 when after an abortive attempt to free himself of the military junta he went into exile in Rome.

In 1969 Greece withdrew from the Council of Europe when it became clear that a majority would vote for her suspension on the grounds of her repudiation of the values which the Council exists to uphold. The attitude of the United States, Greece's major protector, was crucial, but Mr. Papadopoulos managed to get the supply of heavy arms from the United States resumed in 1970 without naming a date for elections. In 1972 the régime's external position was strengthened by an agreement that Piraeus should become the home port of part of the US Sixth Fleet.

But the internal position was less secure. The foiling of an attempted naval mutiny in May 1973 was followed by the abolition of the monarchy and its replacement by a Presidential Republic. A referendum approved the change and elected Mr. Papadopoulos President. He then announced the abolition of martial law and of the Athens Special Military tribunal and an amnesty for all political crimes. But further trials of political opponents of the régime continued. In October 1973 President Papadopoulos appointed Mr. Spyros Markezinis, leader of the Progressive Party in the former Parliament, to form a civilian government. But bloody clashes between students and police in Athens led to the reimposition of martial law and mass arrests. On 25 November a bloodless military coup led by Brigadier Ioannides overthrew President Papadopoulos and Lieut.-General Gizikis replaced him as head of state. However the new régime commanded an even narrower basis of support than its predecessor and, in a fatal attempt to increase its popularity inside Greece, it moved steadily into a confrontation with Turkey.

The first dispute arose out of the discovery of oil in the Aegean near the island of Thasos and stirred old animosities as to the rights of the two countries over the Aegean. Turkey granted drilling rights outside Greek territorial waters but though Turkey maintained a conciliatory position the Greek Government became belligerent and uncompromising.

The Cyprus problem had been an even more emotive issue between Greece and Turkey. Yet Brigadier Ioannides decided to use the officers of the Greek National Guard on Cyprus in July 1975 in a coup to replace President Makarios with a régime controlled from Athens. This grossly unrealistic move was swiftly followed by the Turkish invasion of the island, and it transpired that Greece's military rulers had allowed the army to deteriorate to a point where it was unable to go to war. In this situation the President and the Armed Forces Commanders turned to the civilian politicians.

It was decided to call back the former premier, Mr. Constantine Karamanlis, to head a government of national unity. Mr. Karamanlis, who had been living in self-imposed exile in Paris since his defeat in the 1963 elections, returned to be greeted by tumultuous crowds celebrating the downfall of the junta.

The Restoration of Democracy in Greece.

Mr. Karamanlis's emergency coalition was no more capable than its predecessor of a military response to the Turkish challenge. However it was able to blame its impotence on the incompetence of the military régime whose apparatus it now began to dismantle.

Political detainees were freed. Greek citizenship was restored to those who had been stripped of it. The junta's constitution was scrapped and the 1952 Greek Constitution reintroduced. By mid-December more than 120,000 supporters of the junta had been removed from the state services. In October, ex-President Papadopoulos and his closest associates were banished to the island of Kea. Subsequently it was announced they they, along with Brigadier Ioannidis, would be charged with treason and with responsibility for the deaths at the Athens Polytechnic in November 1973.

Political parties—including the two Greek Communist parties—were allowed to operate freely again. Mr. Karamanlis set up his own New Democracy Party, while Mr. Mavros continued to lead the Centre-Union Party. The leftward leaning and volatile Mr. Andreas Papandreou, son of the now dead George Papandreou, formed PASOK—the Pan-Hellenic Socialist Union.

Only Colonel Papadopoulos was prevented from participating in the general elections which followed on 17 November 1974.

Mr. Karamanlis won a crushing victory, with the New Democracy Party taking more than 54% of the votes. Mr. Mavros's Centre Union received 20%, the Pan-Hellenic Socialist Union 13% and the Communists 8%.

Three weeks later in a referendum on the future of the monarchy the Greek people overwhelmingly rejected " crowned democracy " in favour of a presidential republic.

In January 1975 the Greek parliament ruled that the army's seizure of power on 21 April 1967 was a coup d'état and therefore illegal. The original coup leaders Ioannides and Papadopoulos and four other members of the junta were charged with revolt and high treason. Major trials began in the summer of 1975 and convictions soon followed.

A new republican constitution was adopted by the Greek parliament in June 1975 with the opposition abstaining. In ensuing Presidential elections Mr. Tsatsos, a friend of Mr. Karamanlis, was elected. In premature parliamentary elections held on 20 November 1977, Mr. Karamanlis' New Democracy Party suffered substantial losses. The strongest gains were made by the radical Pan-Hellenic Socialist Union of Mr. Andreas Papandreou, the greatest losses by the Centre Union. Amid prospects of a polarisation and radicalisation of politics, outside Parliament as well as inside, Mr. Karamanlis formed a new government coalition with a majority of 22. But he appeared unable to count any longer on closed ranks in his own party.

Greek Foreign Policy since the Junta.

Throughout the seven years of army rule, many Greeks regarded the United States as being responsible for the junta's survival. The invasion of Cyprus by Turkey generated a further upsurge in anti-American feeling and, on 15 August 1974, Mr. Karamanlis announced that Greece would withdraw from the military side of NATO in protest at the second Turkish military operation on the island. In December American bases and installations in the country, not belonging to NATO, were brought under " national control " though they continued to operate.

In contrast the new regime made determined efforts to restore its links with Western Europe, pressing for early acceptance as a full member of the Common Market and readmission to the Council of Europe. Despite the serious gap in NATO's southern flank which the departure of Greece created, it seemed likely that the country would maintain its pro-Western stance. In July 1976, formal negotiations were commenced for full membership of the EEC. Relations with neighbouring Balkan states were improved following a meeting on Balkan co-operation early in 1976.

The rising Pan-Hellenic Socialist Union is opposed to full EEC membership and to any Western military bases in Greece, as well as to the Karamanlis Government's policy of a return to the military organisation of NATO after satisfactory solution of the Cyprus and Aegean questions. It favours confrontation with Turkey.

TURKEY.

The military coup of 1960 and the liberal constitution promulgated under the caretaker junta in 1961 were followed by ten years of trying to reconcile democracy with rapid development—an increasingly difficult operation with the growth of extremists on the left and right. But in 1971 the army threw out the civilian government of Mr Demirel's Justice Party. Many arrests were made and constitutional reforms reduced civil liberties. After two years of disguised military rule, Parliament reasserted its initiative in 1973 by refusing to elect the Chief of Staff as President. Mr. Demirel was expected to return to power after the general elections in October, but a shock result produced major gains for Mr. Ecevit's Republican People's Party (approximately social democrat). After a period of deadlock Mr. Ecevit reached agreement to form a coalition with the Muslim-traditionalist National Salvation Party in January 1974. In the face of grave economic problems they maintained an increasingly shaky alliance until Mr. Ecevit resigned in September. Despite the national euphoria caused by the successes in Cyprus. Turkey's politics sank once more into a seemingly unbreakable deadlock. The right-wing parties could agree neither on the formation of a government nor on a date for early elections. They feared that Mr. Ecevit's success in Cyprus, which had reinvigorated his public popularity, would sweep him back to power. There followed several months without normal government but with rising political tension and pitched battles between leftist and rightist university students in an atmosphere reminiscent of the eve of the military coup in 1971. However in March 1975 a minority Nationalist Front cabinet of right-wing parties was formed under the leadership of Mr. Demirel. It faced a worsening economic crisis with inflation at 30%, high unemployment, reduced exports and a fall in the vital remittances from Turks working abroad, especially in West Germany.

In general elections held on 5 June 1977 Mr. Ecevit's Republican People's Party increased its share of the vote from 33·3% to 41·4%. Mr. Demirel's Justice Party from 29·8% to 36·9%. There was a corresponding decline of the smaller parties, including the Islamic National Salvation Party, which, however, remained apparently indispensable for any majority coalition. The exception was the rise to 6·4% of the vote by the National Action Party, a radical nationalist grouping. Mr. Demirel succeeded in constructing a government with a very narrow majority which included both these parties. In response to an alarming increase in terrorist activities and in the number of terrorist victims, stricter laws and judicial procedures were introduced. However, during the provincial elections in December, from which the opposition Republican People's Party emerged as clear victor, desertions from the Justice Party deprived Mr. Demirel of his majority. By the end of 1977 he found himself compelled to resign. Mr. Ecevit took over the task of forming a government, but though his was the largest party, he needed the support of ex-Justice Party members and parliamentary outsiders for an absolute majority.

Turkish Invasion of Cyprus.

After the Greek-inspired coup of 15 July 1974 which deposed, but failed to kill, President Makarios of Cyprus and replaced him with Nicos Sampson, a former gunman of the EOKA organisation which had fought for union of Cyprus with Greece, Mr. Ecevit tried in vain to persuade Britain to help restore the status quo under its obligations as a guarantor of the treaty setting up an independent Cypriot republic. Then on 20 July Turkish forces landed at Kyrenia in the north of Cyprus and after tough fighting established a secure foothold on the island.

The Turkish invasion triggered the rapid collapse of the Sampson regime in Nicosia and of the Colonels' dictatorship in Athens. Initially therefore it was greeted with support and approval by world opinion. But as events were to show, nationalist passions in both countries ruled out a speedy and peaceful settlement to the island's problems and as Turkey tightened her grip on the north of Cyprus, sympathy passed to the new governments in Athens and Nicosia.

Turkey's announced aim in Cyprus was the establishment of a bi-regional federation with a degree of geographical separation between the two communities. However, Mr. Karamanlis's first speech after his triumphant return to Athens rejected a federal solution for Cyprus, and Turkey thus went to the August peace talks in Geneva convinced that the Greeks did not seriously desire a settlement.

The early breakdown of the talks was thus more or less inevitable. Turkey immediately launched a second offensive to secure the 30% of the territory of the island which she claimed for its Turkish

community, advancing along a line stretching from Lefka in the West to Famagusta in the east.

Behind this Attila Line, as it became known, had lain 70% of the economic wealth of Cyprus and 40% of the Greek population. 180,000 Greek Cypriots fled before the Turkish army to the south of the island where they lived as refugees in the Troodos mountains. Under these circumstances it was difficult to imagine any Greek Cypriot Government accepting the new boundaries as the basis for a " bi-cantonal federation ".

In September 1975, talks were resumed between Mr. Denktash, the Turkish Cypriot leader and Mr. Glafkos Clerides, who was acting as President of Cyprus until the return of Archbishop Makarios. Several interruptions occurred after the discovery of mass graves of Turkish Cypriots murdered apparently by the Greeks, soon after the invasion. Nevertheless prisoners of war were exchanged and the diplomatic atmosphere eased.

Mr. Clerides had come to agree that the future of Cyprus must be settled in federal terms and a package deal was thought to have been agreed. When Archbishop Makarios returned to Cyprus in December 1975 a final political solution had not been reached and the Archbishop rejected any proposals which might lead to a partitioning of the island. Britain eventually allowed Turkish refugees living in British military bases in the Greek part of Cyprus to depart to the north of the island. The overwhelming majority of Turkish Cypriots were now concentrated in the Turkish-held sector of the island. Yet 8,000 Greek Cypriots were not allowed to return home despite assurances from Mr. Denktash that they would be able to do so. As a result of a decision of the US Congress to cut off aid to Turkey on 5 February 1975, the Turkish attitude became more intransigent leading to a proclamation eight days later by Mr. Denktash that the Turkish-held zone would be a federal state of the future Federal Republic of Cyprus. The Greeks, regarding this as an indication that there would be no prospect of returning refugees to their homes and that outright partition was near at hand, refused to negotiate with the Turks. Talks were in fact resumed although little progress was made during 1976. In April Mr. Clerides resigned his post as negotiator after the revelation of a secret agreement with Mr. Denktash of which Archbishop Makarios had not been informed. Mr. Denktash also resigned and was elected President of the Turkish Cypriot state. In January 1977 a major breakthrough occurred when Archbishop Makarios met Mr. Denktash in Nicosia, their first meeting in 13 years. After a second meeting the following month Archbishop Makarios said that there had been basic agreement that Cyprus should be an independent and non-aligned federal state with two communities; there was also agreement on some criteria for the distribution of territory between the two communities. However, further negotiations between the two sides held in Vienna under the aegis of the UN Secretary-General were fruitless, on account of wide disagreement about the amount of territory to be retained by the Turkish Cypriots.

The death of Archbishop Makarios on 3 August 1977 was a severe blow to Greek Cypriots. The President of the Greek Cypriot Parliament, Spyros Kyprianou, was proclaimed President for the period until the end of Makarios' term of office in February 1978. He pursued a neutralist course in alliance with the Socialists and Communists. After the successful outcome of the hard line taken by him in reaction to the kidnapping of his son by members of the fascist underground movement EOKA-B, his re-election was virtually certain.

Relations with Greece had not been improved when in July and August 1976 a Turkish oil-prospecting vessel began operations in the disputed area of the Aegean sea. Greek warships were sent to patrol the area and border troops were mobilized. A Greek application to the International Court of Justice for an injunction to prevent Turkish exploration was refused and attempts were made to negotiate a settlement of the dispute.

THE SOVIET UNION

A Turning Point in Soviet History.

Stalin died in 1953 and the struggle for succession then continued for five years. A triumvirate of successors, Malenkov, Molotov, and Beria had decided to give the post of party chief to Khrushchev, then a relatively harmless outsider, or so he was deemed by them. Beria, the all powerful police chief, was executed as a spy in 1953, Malenkov was forced to give up the premiership in 1954 and three years later both he and Molotov were expelled from the Central Committee. Khrushchev thereupon emerged with supreme powers.

In 1961 Khrushchev publicly and dramatically completed the process which he had begun in 1956, of finally rejecting the cult of Stalin. Stalin had made the Soviet Union a modern industrial society and a great armed power. But the arbitrary bureaucracy through which this had been achieved had, in Khrushchev's view, overrun itself. Radical changes became essential and Khrushchev attempted various steps—the scaling down of the secret police; the rebuilding of the administrative apparatus; the opening up of virgin lands; and a new theory that war was not inevitable. The legacy of the Stalinist era had been the concept of the " monolithic " party, which, however torn by internal conflict, must never allow any open division of opinion and free debate, much less the formation of any groups expounding distinctive views. But here de-Stalinisation brought little change.

Khrushchev was abruptly removed from power in October 1964 and replaced by Brezhnev and Kosygin.

The New Leadership.

A meeting of the Supreme Soviet in 1965 confirmed the principle of collective leadership, with Kosygin as Premier and Brezhnev General Secretary. The Brezhnev era has seen no re-Stalinisation as originally forecast, but there has been a retrenchment of the restrictive power of the establishment which had been disturbed by Khrushchev. The new balancing and compromising leadership style has strengthened both collective leadership and centralism. Critics of Brezhnev, including the conservative Pyotr Shelest and Voronov, were dropped from the Politburo and subsequently all the most important ministers including Andrei Gromyko (Foreign Secretary) and Marshal Grechko (Defence Minister) were brought into the Politburo. Tension between the party and state machinery was thus eased. In April 1975 Shelepin, at 56 the youngest member of the Politburo, was ousted. At the 25th Party Congress in February 1976, Brezhnev appeared fully in control and in May he was promoted to Marshal of the Soviet Union following the death of Marshal Grechko. The 5-year plan for the Soviet economy was presented in December 1975 and the disastrous agricultural situation is to be remedied by massive investment and better planning. Priority is to be given to heavy industry with the overall aim of raising the standard of living. The plan was endorsed in November by the Central Committee. In 1977 measures to promote competition were introduced as a spur to economic development.

In June 1977 Mr. Podgorny was replaced as Chairman of the Presidium of the Supreme Soviet (in practice Head of State) by Mr. Brezhnev, who combined the office with that of General Secretary of the Communist Party. This development was a blow to the principle of collective leadership. On 7 October a new Soviet constitution came into force, in time for the celebrations of the 60th anniversary of the Russian Revolution. It was presented by Mr. Brezhnev as corresponding to a developed, mature socialist society, and the first article declares the Soviet Union to be a " socialist state of the whole people ", following the fulfilment of the tasks of the " dictatorship of the proletariat ". The new constitution emphasises the leading role of the Communist Party, which was not mentioned in the previous constitution. Despite Mr. Brezhnev's official triumphs in 1977, there were signs by the beginning of 1978 that his continuing and perhaps worsening illness had cost him some power and influence.

Foreign Relations.

The historic rapprochement between the United States and China in 1971–2 met with a sharp condemnation of Chinese intentions by the Russians.

Yet Soviet–American negotiations over Berlin and the limitation of strategic armaments were speeded up and in May 1972, the first visit to Moscow of a US President (President Nixon) took place. A 12-point statement of principles to guide the future relationship between the two countries resulted and co-operation agreements were signed. Above all, agreements on the limitation of strategic nuclear weapons were also signed. Russia's declared eagerness for the holding of the European Security Conference indicated a new willingness to discuss mutual balanced force reductions in Europe with the West.

In June 1973 Mr. Brezhnev and other Soviet ministers visited the US. Co-operation agreements were signed and principles for further arms limitation and measures for the prevention of nuclear war were discussed. In the latter, they undertook to enter into urgent consultations if relations between them or between either and another country appeared to involve the risk of nuclear conflict.

The general policy of détente continued during 1974–5 with the visits of President Nixon in the summer of 1974 and of President Ford in November and trade agreements with Western European countries. In November 1977 Mr. Brezhnev proposed an agreement that all states should simultaneously cease production of nuclear weapons and call a moratorium on nuclear explosions for peaceful purposes. This was welcomed in Washington as removing some vital differences between the two countries.

Apart from relations with the United States, the Russians have tried to consolidate their position elsewhere by tying formerly non-aligned powers to themselves e.g., Egypt and India. However, in March 1976 the Treaty of Friendship and Co-operation with Egypt was abrogated following the Russians' refusal to supply arms and their demand for repayment of Egypt's debts. Later in the year relations were improved with the signing of a bilateral trade agreement.

Despite trade agreements with W. European countries, the new line taken by communist parties in those countries in support of democratic socialism and party pluralism, has been a blow to the Soviet claim to ideological leadership; renunciation of the principle of " proletarian internationalism " was severely condemned at the Party Congress in February. Efforts were made to strengthen relations with E. European countries. Mr. Brezhnev visited President Tito in Yugoslavia and the Warsaw Pact summit was held in Bucharest, Romania.

Dissidents.

Despite the agreement of the Soviet Union to the statement of the Conference on Security and Co-operation in Europe, concerning " respect for human rights and fundamental freedoms ", there have been persistent complaints about the treatment of the so-called " dissidents " and the restrictions on the right to emigrate. Prior to the Helsinki agreement, the famous writer and dissident Alexander Solzhenitsyn was expelled from the Soviet Union.

During 1976 several appeals were made by groups of dissidents for amnesty for those imprisoned for their political, religious or ideological views. In December 1976 Vladimir Bukovsky was released from prison in central Russia and was allowed to go to the West in return for the release of a Chilean, Luis Corvalán. Shortly afterwards the dissidents were blamed for a bomb explosion in the Moscow underground which killed several people. The most prominent of the remaining dissidents is Andrei Sakharov, a nuclear physicist who suffers continuous harassment and has recently been warned of possible prosecution for his activities. The Soviet Union has repudiated Western and Chinese claims that healthy political dissidents are declared mentally ill and consigned to mental hospitals.

EASTERN EUROPE

(For East Germany see The Two Germanys)

Background.

During the Second World War Czechoslovakia, Poland, Yugoslavia and Albania were occupied by Axis forces. Hungary, Romania and Bulgaria fought initially with the Axis powers. When they attempted to withdraw from the war they too underwent German occupation. Resistance movements of varying degrees of effectiveness developed in all the East European countries: the Yugoslav and Albanian movements succeeded in liberating their countries substantially by their own efforts. Elsewhere liberation was achieved by the Soviet army, as a result of which Communist regimes were established. The diplomatic prehistory of this takeover took place at the Moscow meeting of Stalin and Churchill in October 1944, which resulted in the "percentages" agreement on postwar spheres of interest, and the Yalta Conference of February 1945. Stalin's motives in extending Soviet power into East Europe were to create a buffer zone between the USSR and the West and to establish a system of economic exploitation under which allies fared little better than former enemies. However, the exercise was presented by the Communists as the consequence of genuine popular uprisings, and the constitutional label of "People's Democracies" was attached to the new regimes. Czechoslovakia, Romania and Yugoslavia have since taken the title of "Socialist Republics".

The monolithic unity which Stalin imposed upon Eastern Europe was breached in July 1948 by the expulsion of Yugoslavia from the Communist camp, a manoeuvre to unseat Tito which developed into a permanent rupture. Since then the Soviet Union has been unable to stem a movement towards "polycentrism", the desire of each Communist government to follow its "own road to socialism". This was demonstrated yet again at the Conference of European Communist Parties in July 1976. The USSR, however, has always been ready to resort to force to repress fellow Communist regimes if it fears they might move out of the Communist orbit altogether, as in Hungary in 1956 and Czechoslovakia in 1968.

With the exception of Czechoslovakia, which inherited an industrial base from the Austro-Hungarian Empire, these countries had underdeveloped agrarian economies before the Second World War and as suppliers of raw materials were dangerously susceptible to fluctuations in world trade and pressure from powerful neighbours. After the war, therefore, each country hastened to embark on a Stalinist course of collectivising agriculture and creating a heavy industry. Soviet aid facilitated this development, but also increased these countries' dependence on the USSR. Although a Communist international economic organisation (the Council for Mutual Economic Assistance, or " Comecon ") was created as early as 1949, Stalin preferred to see each satellite economically autarkic and linked to the USSR by bilateral agreements, and only since the sixties have genuinely integrative economic policies been implemented. These have met with some resistance, notably from Romania.

The East European Communist countries (except Albania and Yugoslavia) have been linked to the USSR in the Warsaw Pact military alliance since 1955.

Poland.

In June 1945 a Provisional Government of National Unity was set up in Warsaw which the Western Allies recognised instead of the pre-war government in exile in London. It was during this period that the foundations were laid for Poland's transformation into a People's Democracy, although there was vigorous armed resistance lasting into 1947. Poland's frontiers were redrawn by the Potsdam Agreement along the Curzon Line (thus losing territory to the USSR) and the Oder–Neisse Line (thus gaining territory from Germany). At the elections of January 1947 9 million votes out of 12·7 million were cast for the Communist-dominated "Democratic Bloc ". Opposition came only from the Polish Peasant Party, whose leader was subsequently forced into exile. In 1948 the Socialist Party was merged into the Communist Party.

With the Moscow-trained Bierut as President and Party Secretary the way was clear for full Communisation. The constitution of 22 July 1952 set the seal on this. During the wave of purges at the end of the forties of "rightists, nationalists and Titoists" Wladyslaw Gomulka

(then deputy premier) and other high-ranking leaders received prison sentences. But after Khrushchev's revelations to the Soviet Communist Party's 20th Congress in February 1956 and the death of Bierut in March a process of de-Stalinisation set in hastened by workers' riots in Poznań in June. In October Gomulka became Party leader and inaugurated a regime which granted considerable concessions. Collectivisation of agriculture was abandoned and more tolerance shown towards the Catholic Church, which commands a very wide adherence in Poland. Poland's efforts to obtain recognition for her Western border culminated in success in December 1970 when the West German Chancellor Willy Brandt signed a treaty affirming its inviolability.

At home the early promise of Gomulka's regime was not maintained into the sixties. There were attacks on the government from the right and Gen. Moczar led his "Partisans " faction in a bid for power in the Communist Party. This faction was not definitively dislodged until 1971. In 1968 a wave of student unrest was followed by an official campaign of anti-Zionism with strong undertones of anti-Semitism, and this led to the exodus of a number of intellectuals. Both attacks were repressed by Gomulka with an increasing insensitivity to the mood of the country. His government was finally toppled by the direct action of workers striking and rioting in the Baltic ports in December 1970, the immediate cause of which had been an increase in consumer prices. Gomulka was succeeded as Party leader by Edward Gierek, a popular trade unionist from the coal mining district of Silesia. Prices were frozen with the aid of Soviet subventions, but a second attempt to increase them in June 1976 led to more strikes and sabotage. Several workers received heavy prison sentences, some intellectuals formed a committee of protest and most price rises were temporarily withdrawn. By the beginning of 1978 the economic situation was at least as bad as in 1976. But despite the prospect of higher prices there was little sign of a threat of mass strikes. The ground had been better prepared, not least by concessions to the Roman Catholic Church, which retains a strength unparalleled in any other Communist state and a capacity for outspoken criticism of the regime.

Czechoslovakia.

Czechoslovakia functioned as a constitutional democracy between the wars, but her path to Communism was facilitated by the large number of Communist supporters (at the 1935 elections Communists had polled 10% of the vote), traditional pro-Russian sentiment dating from the Pan-Slavist movement, Beneš's inclination to rely on Soviet support in the bitterness following the 1938 Munich Agreement and the *fait accompli* of the Soviet prior presence as a liberation army. In May 1946 the Communists gained 38% of the electoral vote, more than twice as many as any other party, and their leader, Klement Gottwald, became prime minister of a coalition government. In February 1948 12 non-Communist ministers resigned in protest at the replacement of non-Communist members of the security forces. In an atmosphere of Communist-inspired workers' militancy Beneš was pressured into dropping the resigning ministers and approving a new cabinet of Communists and fellow-travellers. Jan Masaryk, veteran foreign minister since the government in exile, died in a fall from his window a few days later in suspicious circumstances. Communist-style elections were held in May 1948 resulting in an 89% majority for the government. Beneš resigned as president and was replaced by Gottwald. Under a new constitution of June 1948 Czechoslovakia became a People's Republic. The Gottwald government pursued a policy of ruthless repression. Party purges which began in 1950 resulted in the execution of Clementis and Slánský and the imprisonment of the Slovak Gustáv Husák among others, and paved the way for the emergence of Antonín Novotný as Party Secretary (1954) and President (1957). Even after the Khrushchev revelations the Party persisted in a hard Stalinist line, but by the sixties opposition was appearing in its own ranks, triggered by a serious deterioration in the economy. The 1961–5 Plan was abandoned and a more flexible system of planning and management was introduced in January 1967. Economic liberalisation led to an increasing pressure generally for political liberalisation and from Slovakia for more autonomy. In January 1968 a Slovak, Alexander Dubček, was elected to replace Novotný as Party Secretary (Novotný was later replaced as President by General Svoboda), and the era opened which has since been dubbed " the Prague Spring ", when an attempt was made to give Socialism " a human face ". Wide-ranging reforms were mooted in the Action Programme issued in April, but the Communist Party did not envisage relinquishing its commanding position in society. Fears that this was happening, however, led the USSR first to press for the abandonment of the Programme in a number of talks with the Czechoslovak leadership between May and August, and ultimately, in concert with the other Warsaw Pact powers except Romania, to occupy Czechoslovakia on 21 August in accordance with the " Brezhnev Doctrine " of " limited sovereignty ". Soviet efforts to set up a puppet government at first met with no success. The projected federalisation of the country into the twin republics of the Czech Lands and Slovakia went ahead in October, although plans for a similar federalisation of the Party were vetoed. Gradually, however, Dubček and his team were ousted from positions of influence, and Gustáv Husák, a partisan of " normalisation ", took over as Party Secretary in April 1969. Czechoslovakia repudiated its condemnation of the Warsaw Pact invasion in October 1969 and consented to the stationing of Soviet troops. Pro-Dubček personnel were hounded from the Party and their jobs (Dubček himself becoming a forestry official) and most of the reforms were abandoned. In May 1970 Czechoslovakia signed a 20-year treaty of friendship with the USSR. In December 1973 West Germany and Czechoslovakia signed a treaty annulling the Munich Agreement, thus normalising their relations. At the beginning of 1977, which had been heralded as " human rights year ", a dissident civil rights group " Charter '77 " was formed in Prague. By the end of the year Mr. Husák appeared to be increasingly isolated between the pragmatists, who criticised the backward state of the economy, and the orthodox hard-liners, who complained of weak leadership and lack of tough action action against the signatories of " Charter '77 ".

Hungary.

At the elections of November 1945 the Smallholder Party won an absolute majority, but at Soviet insistence a Communist was appointed to the key post of Minister of the Interior. As a result of a purge of allegedly fascist Smallholders and the enforced unification of the Social Democrats with the Communist Party the Communists increased their membership in the government at the 1947 and 1949 elections. The constitution of August 1949 made Hungary a People's Republic, and all power passed to the Communists under Mátyás Rákosi. Executions of " Titoist " Communists, notably László Rajk, took place in 1949. Cardinal Mindszenty, who refused to collaborate with the Communist authorities in their anti-church measures, was imprisoned (in 1956 he took refuge in the US legation, where he stayed until 1971). In July 1953 Rákosi was replaced by Imre Nagy as prime minister. The latter attempted to follow a " new course " but aroused the misgivings of Moscow and was expelled from office in April 1955. Rákosi took over again but was himself dismissed in July 1956, this time as a move in Khrushchev's game of wooing Tito. It was under his successor Gerő that the 1956 uprising flared up. On 23 October a vast procession of protest, initiated by students and originally peaceful, was roughly handled by Gerő and the police, and met force with force. The army joined the revolutionaries and Soviet forces were expelled from Budapest. A coalition government was formed under Nagy, and Soviet forces withdrew to the borders. However, on 1 November, after Nagy had proclaimed Hungary's withdrawal from the Warsaw Pact and asked for UN protection, Soviet forces re-entered the country. János Kádár, who had been imprisoned under Rákosi, formed a pro-Soviet alternative government on

3 November. On 4 November Soviet forces reached Budapest and Nagy took refuge in the Yugoslav embassy, whence he was subsequently abducted and murdered. Fighting continued for a fortnight before the uprising was suppressed, and there was a substantial exodus of refugees. The inaction of the Western powers, who were simultaneously preoccupied with the Suez crisis, definitively dispelled East European notions that the West might intervene in situations of this sort.

In its early days the Kádár regime promised many concessions, few of which were carried out. Kádár's achievement, however, has been in striking the right balance between reforming enough to satisfy the people without going far enough to arouse the anxieties of Moscow. In 1968 a " New Economic Mechanism " was introduced, and Kádár has eased political repression by reversing the militant Marxist maxim to form the less discriminatory " He who is not against us is for us ".

Romania.

Support for Romania's participation in the war on Hitler's side (except for the recovery of Bessarabia) was never wholehearted, and opposition to it was by no means confined to the left. In June 1944 the National Liberal Party and the National Peasant Party joined with the Social Democrats and Communists in a National Democratic Front which toppled Antonescu's government on 23 August 1944 and brought Romania into the war against Germany. An armistice with the USSR was signed on 12 September 1944. Although the Communist Party had only a little over 1,000 members at this time, the presence of Soviet occupation troops ensured that it and the Social Democrats received representation out of proportion to their numbers in the first postwar administration. In March 1945 a government was set up (excluding the National Liberals and National Peasants) headed by the Soviet fellow-traveller Petru Groza. The National Democratic Front claimed 79% of the votes cast at the November 1946 election, but its validity has been disputed. There followed the arrest of non-Communist politicians, the banning of the National Peasant Party and in December 1947 the abdication of King Michael and the proclamation of a People's Republic. Elections were held in March 1948 from a single list of candidates. A Soviet-type constitution was introduced in April. At the close of the forties a purge of Communists accused of " Titoism " opened. In 1952 Gheorghe Gheorghiu-Dej, Party leader since 1944, achieved supreme power in the government as well by engineering the removal of three ministers closely identified with Soviet interests. On his death in 1965 he was succeeded by Nicolae Ceausescu, who has pursued a steady path of self-aggrandisement, becoming in 1974 President of the State Council and the first holder of the newly created Presidency of the Republic.

In internal affairs rigid and orthodox, Romania began to develop an independent foreign policy in Gheorghiu-Dej's last years, and Ceausescu has continued this trend, maintaining friendly relations with China and Israel, becoming the first Soviet bloc country to recognise West Germany, and objecting to the Soviet invasion of Czechoslovakia. There are no Soviet troops in Romania. Although a full member of Comecon, Romania has blocked plans to integrate the Communist countries' economies for fear of becoming a second-class supplier of raw materials to the more industrialised members. Instead the Romanians are aiming for economic independence by pushing ahead with a massive industrialisation programme of their own. Another point at issue with the USSR is the latter's incorporation of Bessarabia, with its two-thirds Romanian population, as the Moldavian SSR. A high-point in this dispute was reached in May 1976: senior Soviet officials visited Romania and the Romanian army was " mobilised for manoeuvres ". Shortly after, Ceausescu stated that Romania had no territorial or other problems with the Soviet Union, and after a meeting with Brezhnev in August it was announced that there was a " growing identity of views " between the two leaders. This rapprochement is probably attributable to Romania's need for closer economic cooperation with the USSR as a result of economic difficulties at home and increasing indebtedness to the West.

Yugoslavia.

In their political and economic development, religion and culture the South Slav peoples (Slovenes, Croats, Serbs and Macedonians) have had separate and differing histories, and their unification since 1918 in one state has always been a risk. By the middle of 1944 the Partisans under the Moscow-trained Communist Josip Broz (Tito) had succeeded in liberating a large part of the country by their own efforts, and in October they assisted the advancing Soviet troops in the capture of Belgrade. At the elections of November 1945 the Communist-dominated People's Front gained 90% of the vote. Although opposition parties were handicapped in the election campaign, foreign observers declared these elections to be fair, and Tito commanded a lot of support from non-Communists as a Croat who would not embark on another round of Serbianisation, and as a successful and popular wartime leader. The new government proclaimed a federal People's Republic, adopted an intransigent attitude to the West and embarked upon a programme of Communisation which soon made Yugoslavia to all appearances the most Soviet-like of the satellites. Stalin, however, found Tito not subservient enough, and attempted to get him replaced as Party leader by expelling the Yugoslav Party from the Communist Information Bureau (Cominform), successor in all but name to the Communist International. This shocked the Yugoslav Communists as much as it surprised the West: Yugoslavia continued to protest its loyalty to Stalin and support the Soviet line in foreign affairs. Few Yugoslavs took a pro-Soviet position, however, in fact the unparalleled advantage of being able to identify the Communist Party with anti-Russian sentiment rallied people closer round Tito. In August 1949 the USSR broke off state relations with Yugoslavia, and Yugoslavia launched out on a course of independent Communism, surviving by securing economic aid from the West and abolishing the command economy at home. The institution of "workers' self-management" has transformed Yugoslavia's economy into a unique "market socialism" and has led to changes in the political structure embodied in the constitutions of 1963 and 1974.

In May 1955 Khrushchev made a visit to Belgrade in an attempt to win Yugoslavia back into the Soviet camp. Inter-government relations were re-established, but very much on Tito's terms: the joint "Belgrade Declaration" promised "non-interference in other countries' affairs for any reason whatever". Tito's return visit the following June re-established Party relations, and the "Moscow Declaration" issued then conceded that countries should be allowed to follow "their own roads to Socialism". Khrushchev and Tito, however, failed to reach agreement on Yugoslavia's place in the Communist community, and a growing division between them began to emerge against a background of "Titoist" nationalist disturbances in Poland and Hungary, hardening with the publication of a new Yugoslav Party Programme in April 1958, which the Soviets considered "revisionist". This hostile episode was terminated when the Soviet Union was looking around for allies at the outbreak of its dispute with China. A further inducement to the Soviet Union to mend its fences with Yugoslavia was the latter's influence among Third World countries as one of the founders of the non-alignment movement at the Belgrade Conference in September 1961. In 1965 Yugoslavia gained observer status in Comecon, and in 1967 Tito joined other Communist leaders in condemning Israel's alleged aggression against the Arabs. The drift towards closer relations with the USSR was temporarily halted by the Soviet invasion of Czechoslovakia in 1968. In the period of tension which followed there were some fears that Yugoslavia might be the next to be invaded. A territorial defence law was hurried through, and on 15 October 1968 US Secretary of State Dean Rusk reminded the USSR that the US considered Yugoslavia to be in a "grey zone" under NATO protection. These fears were shortlived: Brezhnev and Tito exchanged visits in 1971 and 1972, and in June 1976 Yugoslavia broke a long tradition by taking part in the Conference of European Communist Parties, albeit reiterating her independent stance. Soviet toleration of Yugoslavia has been made easier by the latter's recent adoption of a harder line at home. For all its democratisation of the state structure, the League of Communists retains a monopolistic grip on the levers of power. Challenging that has led to the persecution of intellectuals like Djilas, Mihajlov and the "Praxis" group of philosophers. An upsurge of Croat nationalism in the early seventies led to a widespread purge of Party and government officials. In a Yugoslavia split by ethnic dissensions after Tito's death it would be easy for the Soviet Union to re-establish its control over the area and gain access to the Adriatic, and there are some grounds for believing that discreet Soviet support has been offered to émigré Croat terrorist organisations. In 1974 and 1975 a number of groups of "Cominformists" (Yugoslav pro-Soviet Communists) were arrested, and in September 1974 a Soviet official was asked to leave. In November 1975 Yugoslav Party Secretary Dolanc complained to the Soviets about their interference, since when the anti-Cominformist campaign has been muted.

Albania.

Communism was imposed on feudal Albania by a handful of intellectuals acting in a long tradition of élitist rule. King Zog was deposed in absentia in January 1945. The wartime resistance movement had been captured by the Communists because of the support of Yugoslavia's Partisans, and Albania became a satellite of Yugoslavia until the latter's rupture with Stalin in 1948. Albania's security and economic development depend on having the favour of a more powerful ally, and in 1948 the Albanian leadership split into a pro-Yugoslav faction led by Koci Xoxe and a Stalinist faction under Party Secretary Enver Hoxha. The latter triumphed, Xoxe was executed and relations with Yugoslavia broken off. Privately the Albanian leaders considered Khrushchev's debunking of Stalin and particularly his wooing of Tito as a danger to their security, and when the Soviet–Chinese quarrel broke out in 1960 they made this view public and supported the Chinese position. Relations with the Soviet Union were broken off in 1961 and Albania became a client of China. Since 1971 there have seen some signs of dissension with China and of pro-Soviet activity at home. The remarkable stability of the leadership came to an end in 1974 with the sacking of the Minister of Defence Balluku, and in April 1976 two more ministers were sacked and Hoxha announced that an "anti-China group" had been smashed. However, in July 1977 the Party organ condemned the Chinese theory of the three Worlds as anti-revolutionary, contrary to the class struggle and protective of capitalism. After Chinese repudiation of this criticism it was renewed with increased vigour and there followed further signs of deteriorating relations, including the recall of Albanian students from China. Albania seems to be deliberately choosing isolation rather than accept compromises with what it sees as the new revisionism of China.

THE MIDDLE EAST

The Middle East War of 1967.

The third Arab–Israeli war began on 5 June 1967. In a pre-emptive strike Israel destroyed the air forces of Egypt, Jordan, and Syria in a few hours. She then destroyed their three armies in six days, occupying all Sinai to the banks of the Suez Canal (which was therefore closed, and remained so for 8 years), the west bank of the Jordan, and the Syrian hills above Galilee. The toll of human misery was immense: at least 300,000 refugees fled the occupied territories. As a consequence of the war, the Russians moved into the Middle East, backing the Arabs.

The Israeli case remained that peace could only be achieved through a negotiated settlement between the parties directly affected, which involves recognition of Israel as a nation-state. Furthermore, since neither the UN nor the four Powers could of themselves guarantee a settlement, Israel, in the interim period, must rely on her own resources to maintain her existence. The Arab governments continued to insist that Israel must first withdraw from the occupied areas before a settlement, or even recognition, could be considered. The Palestinian fedayeen organisation went further and refused to accept the state of Israel under any circumstances.

Obstacles to Peace.

The fighting continued in 1970, until the United States produced a peace initiative which led to a cease-fire between Egypt, Jordan and Israel. On 28 September the Arabs and Egypt lost their leader, President Nasser, who died of a heart attack. His successor, President Sadat, issued a warning that Israel must produce a timetable for withdrawal from the occupied territories.

Palestinian guerrillas were predictably hostile to peace initiatives, which they feared would frustrate their plan to establish a democratic state of Palestine in place of Israel. Their extreme line led to conflict with King Hussein's army, the guerrillas having used Jordan as their base for attacks on Israel. During 1970 King Hussein's position appeared to be very precarious, but after a major offensive Jordan was able to announce the total defeat of the guerrillas by July 1971.

Early in 1971 President Sadat indicated for the first time that Egypt would be prepared to sign a contractual peace treaty with Israel guaranteeing her inviolability and independence within secure and recognised boundaries. Israel in turn accepted the principle of withdrawal to " secure, recognised and agreed boundaries " to be established by a peace agreement, but rejected a retreat to the borders before the Six-day War. Mrs. Meir insisted on the retention of the Gaza strip, a united Jerusalem and the Golan Heights overlooking Syria. But 1971 also reaffirmed the willingness of the Great Powers to stand by their respective protégés. In May at the end of the visit of President Podgorny of the Soviet Union to Cairo, a 15-year treaty of friendship was signed in which the USSR undertook to continue to supply arms and training to the Egyptians. Later the United States agreed to resume deliveries of Phantom bombers to Israel, without the latter making far-reaching concessions to the Egyptians.

In June 1972 in a show of strength President Sadat announced the expulsion of all Soviet military experts from Egypt. The reasons he gave were disagreements about the type of Soviet armaments supplied to Egypt and delays in their delivery. The removal of the Russians should have made it easier for Israel to make concessions.

The Fourth Arab–Israeli War.

War suddenly broke out again on 6 October 1973 with simultaneous powerful Egyptian and Syrian offensives across the Suez Canal and on the Golan Heights. The Israelis were taken by surprise by the attack which came on the Day of Atonement, the holiest day of the Jewish year. The fighting was fierce and featured in Sinai one of the biggest tank battles in history. The Egyptians consolidated their position along much of the east bank of the Suez Canal and advanced some miles into Sinai. But a dramatic Israeli counter-attack established a major bridge-head on the west bank of the Canal, pushing well inland, destroying or capturing most of the Soviet SAM missile sites and re-establishing total air superiority. As the tide was turning in Israel's favour and the Egyptian Third Army of some 20,000 had been virtually caught in a pincer movement at the southern end of the front, a cease-fire was agreed in response to UN Security Council resolutions. On the northern front the Syrians also had considerable initial success, regaining most of the Golan Heights. But having contained the Egyptian assault the Israelis threw their weight against the Syrians and advanced to within 20 miles of Damascus before a cease-fire was agreed.

The Israelis thus more than overcame the paper situation by which their forces were vastly outnumbered and outgunned by the Egyptians and Syrians alone. During the war the USA began an " appreciable " airlift of military supplies to Israel to offset what was claimed had become a " massive " Soviet airlift to Egypt and Syria.

A third UN Security Council resolution approved the despatch of a UN peace-keeping force which would exclude military contingents from any of the permanent members. This defused the critical situation caused by American information that large Soviet forces might be sent to the Middle East, which had led to a world-wide alert of US forces. In November the mission of Dr. Kissinger to the Middle East worked out a cease-fire agreement—the first major agreement between Israel and an Arab country since 1949.

The Search for a Settlement.

This time the consequence of war was not new hostilities but on Kissinger's insistence and with Moscow's consent a peace conference, which was opened in Geneva by UN General Secretary Dr. Waldheim in December 1973, though the Syrians refused to take part. Both sides still have the means to attack again. But the war showed Israel that borders pushed forward by force give no absolute security and the Arabs that even a surprise attack with advanced Soviet weapons cannot wipe Israel off the map.

Despite advances for the right-wing Likud opposition in the elections at the beginning of 1974, making Mrs. Meir's Labour Alignment more dependent on the religious groups, Israel did make major concessions when on 18 January it signed with Egypt an agreement for the disengagement of their forces (negotiated by Dr. Kissinger commuting between the two countries). In return for the withdrawal of most of the Egyptian forces from the east bank of the Suez Canal, Israel undertook to evacuate the west bank (thus releasing the Egyptian Third Army) and withdraw from the east bank. Prisoners of war were exchanged between Egypt and Israel and the process of disengagement was completed by 4 March. A similar agreement between Syria and Israel was not achieved until 31 May after renewed heavy fighting. A UN Disengagement Observation Force was established and prisoners were repatriated.

Meanwhile full diplomatic relations had been restored between the United States and Egypt, and in June 1974 during President Nixon's visit to five Middle-East countries he was given a very enthusiastic reception in Cairo and agreements were signed for substantial economic aid to Egypt, including the area of nuclear energy.

A summit meeting of Arab Heads of State and representatives of the Palestine Liberation Organisation (PLO) in October 1974 was dominated by the dispute between Jordan and the PLO over which should be the legitimate representative of the Palestinian people of the Israeli-occupied West Bank of the Jordan. It resulted in a political victory for the PLO and in effect a commitment to the establishment of a separate Palestinian state after Israel withdrew. This inevitably complicated the search for a settlement. The following month the UN General Assembly, which had invited Yassir Arafat, leader of the PLO, to take part in its Middle East debate, gave him a hero's welcome and recognised the PLO as representing the Palestinians. This was accompanied by unrest among the Arab population of Israeli-occupied territory.

Meanwhile an escalation of tension in late 1974 brought Israel and Syria to the verge of active hostilities again and there was an intensification of the arms race with both sides seeking to replace losses in the 1973 war from traditional suppliers (which led to some improvement in Soviet–Egyptian relations). The breakdown of a further peace mission by Dr. Kissinger in March followed by the assassination of King Faisal of Saudi Arabia once again threw the long-term prospects for peace in the Middle East into serious doubt. Nevertheless June 1975 saw the reopening of the Suez Canal and in September a further limited agreement was signed by Israel and Egypt on military disengagement in the Sinai Peninsula, providing for Israeli withdrawal from some occupied territory in return for American commitment to Israel. The implementation of this agreement was completed in February 1976, and meanwhile Israeli ships were also allowed through the Suez Canal.

Terrorist Activities.

Since 1972 the Palestinian terrorists had resorted to desperate methods against Israelis including the attack on the Israeli Olympic team in Munich. During 1974 attacks within Israel intensified with the massacre of 20 Israeli children in a school at Ma'alot. Israeli reprisals included raids on Palestinian guerrilla bases in Lebanon. Some of the more extreme terrorists began to turn their anger on other Arabs. In December 1975 members of a group known as the Arm of the Arab Revolution seized 11 leading representatives in an attack on OPEC headquarters in Vienna. A statement was broadcast condemning Egypt and Iran and demanding sovereignty over oil resources for the benefit of the Arab people and the Third World. The hostages were eventually released, but the action was condemned by other Palestinian organisations.

In 1976 an Air France airbus was hijacked by members of the Haifa section of the Popular Front for the Liberation of Palestine, and made to fly to Entebbe, Uganda. The drama ended with an Israeli rescue raid to free the Israeli hostages after demands had been made for the release of "freedom fighters" imprisoned in Europe and Israel.

The Oil Crisis 1973–4.

During and after the war the Arabs began to make serious use of the dependence of much of the Western world on oil from the Middle East as a weapon to weaken support for Israel. The Organisation of Arab Petroleum Exporting Countries (OAPEC) decided to reduce production progressively until Israeli forces had withdrawn completely from territories occupied in June 1967 and the legal rights of the Palestinians had been restored. Several Arab countries also imposed a total ban on shipments to the USA and the Netherlands because of their support for Israel. The former ban affected some 6 per cent of American consumption: the latter also seriously affected other Western European countries whose oil normally came through Rotterdam.

In November the OAPEC countries decided to exempt EEC members except the Netherlands from the December cuts in appreciation of their communiqué of 6 November calling on Israel to end the territorial occupation which it had maintained since 1967, and recognising that any settlement must take account of the "legitimate rights of the Palestinians". This resolution aroused strong criticism in Israel. But Holland's subscription to it did not alter her position in Arab eyes.

Following a 70% price increase in October, the petroleum exporting countries (OPEC) in conference at Teheran in December decided to double the crude oil price. However on 23 December OAPEC agreed on a 10 per cent raising of production, leaving them 15 per cent under their October production level. Meanwhile in most oil-importing countries measures were introduced to restrict oil consumption, including reductions in heating levels, lower speed limits and bans on Sunday driving.

Confronted by this challenge, a conference of 13 major oil-consuming countries in Washington in February agreed (with France dissenting) on provisions for co-operation on energy policy. After the disengagement agreement between Israel and Egypt supplies to the USA and the Netherlands were resumed during 1974. The easing of supplies generally, though not of price, caused many of the restrictions on the use of oil to be lifted. But the non-oil-producing developing countries were far more vulnerable, and both the International Monetary Fund and the World Bank organised funds to aid them. In November, on the initiative of Dr. Kissinger, a working-party was set up to examine the question of recycling the massive surplus revenues of the OPEC countries, which had given them crucial economic power. An International Energy Agency was established in Paris under the auspices of the OECD by 16 oil-consuming countries to co-ordinate policy, especially by an oil-sharing scheme in times of supply difficulties. Although there is no shortage of oil, its vastly inflated price has seriously distorted the Western economies.

In December 1976 at the OPEC meeting in Qatar, the first split appeared in OPEC ranks led by Saudi Arabia. 11 members voted to raise prices by 10·4% on 1 January and by a further 5% on 1 July 1977. Saudi Arabia and the United Arab Emirates announced that they would raise their prices only 5% for the whole year. Whether

this position will be maintained by the Saudis will depend on progress at the North-South dialogue to be continued in Paris in the spring of 1978.

Lebanon: Civil War and Israeli invasion.

From April 1975 internal conflict between left-wing Moslems (including Lebanon-based Palestinian groups) and the Christian Phalangist Party escalated to full-scale civil war. The basic cause of the conflict appeared to be the inadequate representation of the Moslem community in government and resentment of the political and economic ascendancy of the Christians. As the fighting intensified, the Lebanese army was involved for the first time in September 1975. President Frangie's calls for a cessation of hostilities resulted in a series of abortive cease-fires. His failure to secure the agreement of Moslem leaders to his proposals for their involvement in government increased demands for his resignation which eventually took place in April 1976. In May, the Syrian-backed Mr. Elias Sarkis was elected in his place.

Throughout the war Syria backed the moderate groups and attempted in 1976 to involve other Arab States in a peace-keeping force. In July the "Damascus agreement" proposed Arab involvement through the calling and policing of a cease-fire and the regulation of Palestinian activities in Lebanon. After an initial set-back, the Arabs deterrent force increased and an effective cease-fire continues.

Prospects for Peace.

General elections held in Israel on 17 May 1977 resulted in the replacement of the long-standing Labour Government by the Likud Block, led by Menachem Begin. The former Defence Minister, Moshe Dayan, crossed over to the Likud Block and became Foreign Minister. This change of government appeared to herald a harder Israeli line towards the Arabs, especially as Mr. Begin had previously been one of the prime campaigners for a Greater Israel. And indeed when the United States said that representatives of the Palestinians must take part in reconvened Geneva peace negotiations, Israel rejected this on the grounds that a peace treaty must be worked out between states.

However, a dramatic new development occurred when President Sadat declared his willingness to explain his position as regards a Middle East settlement before the Knesset. The visit to Jerusalem took place on 19–21 November amid sharp criticism from Iraq, Syria, Libya (with whom Egypt had been involved in active hostilities in July), Algeria and the PLO. It produced agreement to pursue contacts and, among other things, on appropriate representation of the Palestinians in Geneva. But the most important thing was that such a visit, which had hitherto been unthinkable, took place at all. In mid-December negotiations were opened between Egyptian and Israeli diplomats, though it was doubtful whether the Israeli response had been sufficient to justify President Sadat's courageous move in the Arab world. At Christmas Mr. Begin met President Sadat again, this time on Egyptian soil at Ismailia on the Suez Canal. They agreed to regular meetings of the Defence and Foreign Ministers for negotiations on the details of a settlement. But the meeting ended without fundamental agreement on the elements of an overall solution: the evacuation not merely of Sinai but also of West Jordan and the Gaza Strip and the creation of a Palestinian State. Attempts, especially by the United States, to associate other Arab states with the talks had come to nothing, and President Sadat clearly showed signs of disappointment at the lack of Israeli concessions. However, Mr. Begin had problems even in his own Likud ranks, and when he produced his much-heralded peace plan he had to link it to a vote of confidence to get it accepted by his own party. The concessions it offered were real, if limited: withdrawal from Sinai and self-government in West Jordan. Moreover, there was general agreement on demilitarised zones under UN supervision. But the future of Israeli settlements south of the Gaza Strip and along the Gulf Coast on the western side of Sinai remained in dispute. Above all, the Palestine problem remains the kernel of any solution: as there had been major Israeli settlements there since 1967, Mr. Begin was able to offer no more than home rule. By early 1978 the euphoria had evaporated and the two sides were preparing for long, tough negotiations. The Israeli invasion of the Lebanon did nothing to help the prospects for a peace breakthrough.

SOUTH ASIA

Background.

In 1947 the British Empire in India was divided into 2 new states, broadly along communal lines—India and Pakistan. India is predominantly Hindu in religion, but the constitution of 1950 asserted its secularist, democratic republican nature. Pakistan resulted from the demand of the Muslim minority for its own separate state. The establishments of the two new states was marred by the slaughter of over 250,000 people as Hindus and Moslems struggled to transfer their homes. Disputes arose over the resources of the Raj and the strategically important state of Kashmir has remained a source of dissension.

India.

In January 1948 India's spiritual leader Mahatma Gandhi was assassinated. Jawaharlal Nehru, India's first prime minister, shared many of Gandhi's ideals. Unlike Gandhi, Nehru believed that economic progress would be achieved through western-style industrialisation and introduced five-year economic plans. India's economic problems also dictated a foreign policy of neutrality and nonalignment with the major powers.

In 1965 Mrs. Indira Gandhi (daughter of Jawaharlal Nehru) became Prime Minister. After a close election victory for the ruling Congress Party in 1967, Mrs. Gandhi faced the problems of opposition from the old guard of the Party in 1969 and terrorist activities in 1970. However, in 1971, the Party won a landslide election victory and plans for Socialist reforms were launched. Since the monsoon failure of 1972 and governmental attempts to remedy the severe food crisis, opposition to the Government increased. An anti-corruption campaign led by Jayaprakash Narayan was in part to blame for election losses in 1974–5 and a further setback was experienced when in June 1975, the Allahabad High Court declared Mrs. Gandhi's election null and void on the grounds that government officials had been involved in electioneering; she was debarred from office for six years. Mrs. Gandhi's appeal against the decision was subsequently upheld by the Supreme Court, but meanwhile a state of emergency was declared in June 1975. Opposition both inside and outside the government increased. Fundamental rights were suspended during the early months of 1976. In November wide powers were given to the Prime Minister. The state o emergency was accompanied by thousands of arrests without trial, a rigorous press censorship and a personal cult of Mrs. Gandhi and her son Sanjay, who was obviously her chosen successor. However, Mrs. Gandhi called elections for March 1977, in which she and the Congress Party suffered a resounding defeat at the hands of the opposition Janata coalition led by Mr. Morarji Desai, who subsequently became Prime Minister. This result was greeted as a triumph for democracy in India. The new government set about restoring basic rights, ending press restrictions and pursuing a foreign policy of neutrality and genuine nonalignment. The Bokaro Steel Agreement with the Soviet Union was renounced on the grounds of the latter's lack of the necessary know-how and negotiations were started with American firms. A campaign was launched against illiteracy, while the policy of compulsory sterilisation pursued by the previous government was rejected. Mr. Desai appeared to be trying to govern India more by persuasion than by strong leadership. But the governing parties were a coalition united by little more than their opposition to Mrs. Gandhi. The lack of direction was giving rise to increasing dissatisfaction by the end of 1977. Meanwhile the shadow of Mrs. Gandhi, who was put on trial in January 1978, continued to hang over India. The elections in Karnataka state, in February 1978, in which Mrs. Gandhi's own Congress Party

swept to power were a further reminder of her still powerful appeal.

Pakistan and Bangladesh.

After independence, Pakistan was beset by internal and external problems. India provided a constant external threat and there was resentment by East Pakistan of the political and economic domination by the western wing. Violent struggles resulted from the attempt to impose Urdu as the national language. Moreover, disunity among the western provinces provided continuing problems for the Government. Thirteen months after independence, Mohammed Ali Jinnah, Pakistan's leader died, and during the next decade there were many changes of government. The chaos was finally ended in October 1958 by a bloodless army coup resulting in the army dictatorship of General Ayub Khan. In 1960 he was formally elected President, and with the strong powers conferred on him by a new constitution in 1962 he instituted a series of reforms. After increasing opposition to Ayub Khan's leadership during the late 1960s, promises were made for a return to democracy. Elections were finally held in 1970 but not before the country had experienced martial law under General Yahya Khan who took over from Ayub Khan in March 1969.

Civil War.

As a result of the elections in December 1970, Sheikh Mujibur Rahman of the Awami League obtained a majority in the East and Mr. Bhutto of the People's Party triumphed in the west. Due to the greater population of the East, the Awami League commanded an overall majority, and insisted on a constitution which would give East Pakistan wide-ranging autonomy. Mr Bhutto opposed this and Civil War erupted on 26 March 1971 following the outlawing of the Awami League and the declaration of E. Pakistan as the independent republic of Bangladesh. The opposition was quickly suppressed, but involved the loss of thousands of innocent lives and created a severe refugee problem as many fled to India. Widespread disease and the cyclone disaster of November 1970 threatened a major famine in E. Pakistan.

War between India and Pakistan 1971.

Support for the Bangladesh guerrillas (Mukti Bahini) was provided by India and after charges and counter charges and incidents on the border between E. Pakistan and India in November 1971, a general offensive was launched. On 3 December India was put on a war footing following Mrs. Gandhi's demand for the withdrawal of Pakistani troops from Bangladesh. Bitter fighting occurred in both E. and W. Pakistan which was ended by Yahya Khan's acceptance of India's unilateral offer of a cease-fire.

The Aftermath.

On 20 December 1971 President Yahya Khan resigned and was replaced by Mr. Bhutto who released Sheikh Mujibur Rahman the following January. At the same time Pakistan left the Commonwealth as other members were about to recognise Bangladesh. (In April 1972 Bangladesh was admitted in place of Pakistan.) Peace negotiations with India were initiated to deal mainly with withdrawal from areas conquered in 1971 and the exchange of prisoners. The latter was only achieved after Pakistani recognition of Bangladesh. Diplomatic relations with India were finally re-established in May 1976. Internal problems within Pakistan arose with conflict in the provinces of Sindh and Baluchistan and have continued since then. Mr. Bhutto gradually introduced economic reform but throughout 1975 and 1976 unrest in the provinces and the outlawing of the Awami League led to approval of a declaration of a state of emergency. Elections were held in March 1977. Amid accusations of election malpractice, Mr. Bhutto claimed victory. Widespread unrest followed, with organised opposition to Mr. Bhutto being answered by the arrest of leading opposition politicians. Martial law was imposed in the major cities. The opposition

Pakistani National Alliance continued to demand the resignation of Mr. Bhutto and the holding of new elections. Finally, agreement was reached on new elections to be held in October, though there was still disagreement on measures for ensuring fairness. But on 5 July the army under General Mohammed Zia ul-Haq took over power, and Mr. Bhutto and other leading politicians were arrested. The General declared that his only aim was the holding of free and fair elections. These were fixed for October, and the politicians were released at the end of July. However, the expected return to democracy did not materialise, though in December the military government granted an amnesty to over 11,000 political prisoners.

Bangladesh.

After the release of Sheikh Mujibur Rahman in 1972, plans were announced to make Bangladesh a parliamentary democracy and to carry out large-scale nationalisation. In March 1973 the Awami League won all but 7 seats in the general elections. However, rising food prices, corruption among leading members of the Awami League and national disasters created widespread unrest. In 1975 a state of emergency was declared, fundamental civil rights were suspended and the parliamentary government was replaced by a presidential one party system under President Mujib. A series of radical reforms ensued causing resentment and opposition particularly from the army and in August 1975 the President and his family were killed in a military coup. Mr. Khandaker Moshtaque Ahmed succeeded to the presidency and began to reverse President Mujib's policies. In November 1975 a series of coups upset President Ahmed's government and that which replaced it under Brigadier Khalid Musharaf. Power passed to the hands of President Sayem and the chiefs of the armed services. Although steps were taken to restore normal conditions to Bangladesh and the ban on political parties was lifted in August 1976, the general elections planned for 1977 were later postponed indefinitely. In April 1977 President Sayem designated Major-General Zia ur-Rahman, the Chief Martial Law Administrator, as his successor and himself resigned. The latter released political prisoners and announced general elections for December 1978. Islam was officially made a basic principle of the state. On 30 May President Zia ur-Rahman's position was confirmed by referendum.

THE FAR EAST

CHINA.

On 1 October 1949, after the Communists had gained complete control of the Chinese mainland and the Nationalist forces of Chiang Kai-shek had retreated to Taiwan, the Chinese People's Republic was proclaimed under Chairman Mao Tse-tung. It claims sovereignty over one fifth of mankind, with a population of about 800 million.

The Cultural Revolution.

In 1966 Mao instigated China's remarkable "Cultural Revolution." Slogans and portraits of Mao Tse-tung appeared everywhere. Huge crowds of young people with red armbands thronged the streets in general excitement. Red Guards took a prominent part. Mao's essential teaching was disseminated by millions of copies of a little 300-page book of his selected writings, in a red plastic cover, carried by almost everyone and universally quoted, discussed, and preached. An objective of the movement was to stimulate the young who might otherwise take for granted the achievements of their elders made possible only by their past suffering and hunger. The revolution must be uninterrupted; the class struggle continued. This revolution emphasised rejection both of western capitalist technological society exemplified by Japan, and of "revisionism" leading to "bourgeois decay" as, it was claimed, had happened to Russia. But it developed into violent struggles between revolutionaries and reactionaries and then between the revolutionaries themselves. The Prime Minister, Chou En-lai, warned that industrial production was being

seriously affected. The situation remained very confused until 1968 when there was a gradual return to moderation. Of the 17 surviving members of the Politburo elected at the eighth Communist Party congress of 1956, 13 were declared "bourgeois reactionaries" during the cultural revolution. President Liu Shao-chi who had been Mao's right-hand man, was among those expelled from the party and was portrayed thereafter as the arch-villain at work in Chinese society.

Reconstruction.

The end of the Cultural Revolution was marked formally by the Ninth Congress of the Chinese Communist Party, which took place in Peking during April 1969 in conditions of great secrecy. The following years were devoted to restoring normal conditions. Disturbances caused by ultra-leftist organisations were firmly repressed; reorganisation was carried out of the Communist Party, whose structure had virtually disintegrated except in the army, and of the Communist Youth League, which had been supplanted by the Red Guards; a campaign was launched to increase production.

China and the World Powers.

Relations between China and the Soviet Union, already embittered by major ideological differences, were not improved when in 1969 serious clashes took place between Russian and Chinese troops on the Ussuri river boundary for control of the river islands. Relations mellowed in 1970 with exchanges of ambassadors and the signature of a new trade pact. However, in January 1974 the Chinese expelled Soviet diplomats accused of spying and the Russians responded in kind. Meanwhile relations with the West improved. In 1971 the 21-year embargo on the export of non-strategic goods by the US to the Chinese mainland was lifted. Then the UN voted to admit the People's Republic of China and the Republic of China (Taiwan) was expelled. Shortly afterwards President Nixon visited China where he was received by Mao Tse-tung and had many talks with Chou En-lai. In the final communiqué the common desire for understanding, peace and an increase in trade was stressed, but differences remained about the solution to current political and military problems, especially Taiwan. A further visit by an American president was made in December 1975 when President Ford and Dr. Kissinger had talks with Mr. Teng Hsiao-p'ing and Chairman Mao. In September 1975 official relations were established with the EEC.

In 1966 China announced that she had tested a guided missile with a nuclear warhead and further activities have taken place including underground tests and the explosion of a hydrogen bomb in 1969. These developments underline the need for China to be brought into arms control discussions.

Internal Political Developments.

In 1969 Defence Minister Marshal Lin Piao was formally named as Mao's successor. However, he was subsequently discredited and died in a plane crash in 1972 while trying to escape to the Soviet Union. Campaigns against Lin Piao and the philosopher Confucius began just before the Tenth Party Congress in 1973 and local political and military leaders were condemned. The Congress produced the election of 5 vice-chairmen by the Central Committee, whereas Lin Piao alone had been elected in 1969. Teng Hsiao-p'ing increasingly took over public duties from the ailing Chou En-lai. In January 1975 the National People's Congress adopted a new constitution which emphasised the role of the Communist Party and, among other things, abolished the office of President of the Republic. Command of the armed forces was transferred to the party chairman and the president's other prerogatives to the standing committee of the National People's Congress. Chou En-lai was appointed head of the new State's council, but in January 1976 he died.

He was succeeded by Hua Kuo-feng and not Teng Hsiao-p'ing as had been expected. It was suggested that Hua (later appointed to the Politburo to the Vice-Chairmanship of the Party in April 1976) was chosen as a compromise between the moderates and the radicals led by Chang Chun chiao and Chiang Ching (Mao's wife), on a question of priorities. The latter stress ideological purity and permanent revolution at the expense of internal development, while the moderates aim at political advancement through economic progress. During the early months of 1976 rioting occurred and campaigns were directed against the "capitalist roaders" despite Mao's directive that "stability and unity do not mean writing off class struggle ".

China after Mao.

On 9 September 1976 after leading China since 1949, Chairman Mao died at the age of 82. He was succeded by Hua Kuo-feng, who before he replaced Chou En-lai had been a security minister for one year and had previously only been known as an agricultural specialist in the southern province of Hunan. In the months after Mao's death, a vicious poster campaign was mounted against Chiang Ching (Mao's wife) and three others, Wang Hung-wen, Chang Chun-chiao and Yao Wen-yuan —known as the "gang of four". All four were arrested and the allegations against them included their planning to persuade the armed militia to take over the army and causing unrest by their backing of the Shanghai radicals. In their turn they were attacked as the real "capitalist roaders ".

Meanwhile Hua's image was built up through films and other propaganda. His colleagues were close associates of Chou En-lai and he appeared to have the support of the army. During 1977 Teng Hsiao-p'ing, who had been dismissed from his government and party posts in April 1976, was fully rehabilitated. Meanwhile, after a series of national conferences of practically all branches of the economy, new guidelines for a more pragmatic economic policy were worked out on the lines of Chou En-lai's basic programme as previously pursued by Teng Hsiao-p'ing.

Given the general focus on internal matters little change has been indicated in attitudes towards the outside world, especially the US. July 1977 saw a new agreement on trade and payments with the Soviet Union, but there has been no progress in the border dispute, and the slander campaign between the two countries continues.

JAPAN.

The new Japanese constitution of 1946 retained the emperor (who had renounced his claim to divinity) as " symbol of the state and of the unity of the people ", but provided for government by ministers responsible to a parliament elected by universal adult suffrage. It thus gave Japan fully representative institutions for the first time. Reforms were passed to achieve the growth of trade unions, the equality of women and a non-authoritarian educational system. The former rightist and militarist elements were deprived of much influence. On the other hand recognition of the need for economic recovery made the occupation authorities moderate in their reparations policy and in the deconcentration of the great zaibatsu monopoly firms.

Despite the prohibition of armed forces in the new constitution, the Korean War made the occupation authorities keen for limited Japanese rearmament. The result was the peace treaty signed by 48 nations at San Francisco in 1951 and a defence agreement with the USA providing for the continued maintenance of American bases in Japan. The new army, navy and air force were known as " self-defence forces ".

Economic and National Resurgence.

Relations were gradually resumed with Asian countries on the conclusion of treaties covering reparations, and full international recognition came with admission to the United Nations in 1956. Meanwhile Japan enjoyed rapid economic recovery. She has had a consistently high growth rate and sustained prosperity, while population control successfully reduced the undesirably high birth-rate.

This economic resurgence brought a new self-confidence and indeed nationalism, and some internal dissent. The attempts of successive

conservative governments to water down the reforms carried out under the occupation produced protests and violence from left-wing groups. The latter were also critical of the defence agreement with the United States, and here they found much public support on nationalist grounds. In 1960 the Kishi Government extracted some concessions in a revised agreement. But there were violent student demonstrations in Tokyo against the bases remaining at all. As a result the American President cancelled a planned visit and the Kishi Government resigned. This showed that Japan was no longer under US tutelage, but also that it had failed to achieve a consensus on its new role. Nevertheless when Japan acted as host to the Olympic Games in 1964 it symbolised her return to international status and to a sense of national identity and pride. Then in 1971 Emperor Hirohito visited seven Western European countries—the first Japanese sovereign ever to leave Japan during his reign.

By the peace treaty of 1951 Japan had given up her claims to her former colonies of Korea and Formosa, to the Kurile Islands (which went to the USSR), and to the Pacific islands mandated to it by the League of Nations. Okinawa and the neighbouring islands, which had been administered as integral parts of Japan, were taken over by the United States, though recognising Japan's residual sovereignty. In the 1960s Japan pressed for restoration, but the Americans regarded Okinawa as too important for their defence commitments. Finally, however, a treaty was signed in June 1971 providing for the return of Okinawa and the other Ryukyu Islands in 1972, with the retention of the use of some bases by US forces.

Japan's close ties with the United States made it difficult to achieve better relations with the Soviet Union and Communist China. However in the wake of President Nixon's initiatives Mr. Tanaka was able to make a historic visit to Peking and to achieve a rapprochement with the Soviet Union as well; though the problem of the Kurile Islands delayed the conclusion of a peace treaty.

Japan has also been striving for the conclusion of a treaty of peace and friendship with China, and in April 1977 the two countries signed a ten-year treaty on the promotion of economic and trade relations.

Internal Problems.

In 1969 Japan experienced the world-wide phenomenon of left-wing student demonstrations in a particularly violent form. They were directed especially against the United States.

Elections were held for the Lower House of the Diet in December 1972, soon after Mr. Tanaka had succeeded Mr. Sato as Prime Minister. The premature dissolution was probably prompted by the success of Mr. Tanaka's overtures to China and his desire for a mandate for his plan to overcome overcrowding and pollution by spreading industry and the population more evenly throughout the country by the building of modest new cities in less developed areas. The main opposition parties were the Japan Socialist Party (JSP), the Democratic Socialist Party (an offshoot from the JSP), the Japan Communist Party and Komeito (" Clean Government Party "). The JSP and the Communists strongly attacked increasing defence expenditure and the mutual security treaty with the USA; all called for greater emphasis on welfare policies. In the event Mr. Tanaka's Liberal Democratic Party, which had had 25 years of uninterrupted power, retained a large overall majority with 271 of the 491 seats. But significant gains were made by the left-wing parties, JSP increasing its share from 87 to 118 and the Communists from 14 to 38.

Mr. Tanaka resigned in December 1974 after allegations of corrupt business and political activities. He was replaced by Mr. Takeo Miki who also resigned at the end of December 1976 following internal party disagreements and an election defeat which split the Liberal Democratic party. His successor is Mr. Takeo Fukuda whose main task will be to put new life into the Japanese economy. The other major cause of political turmoil in Japan during 1976 was the revelation of large-scale bribery of leading Japanese politicians by American firms, particularly Lockheed, in order to promote the sale of their products. Mr. Tanaka's trial began at the end of January 1977 and could last several years. Mr. Fukuda has devoted much attention to promoting good relations with the countries of Southern and South-East Asia. His Minister of Justice resigned in protest when, following the hi-jacking of a Japan Airlines DC-8 by members of the Japanese " Red Army ", the government complied with the terrorists' demands for the release of nine members of the " Red Army " and payment of $6 million.

VIETNAM.

When Japan collapsed in 1945, the only organised troops in Vietnam were controlled by Ho Chi-minh, a Communist, who set up a Democratic Republic in the northern part of Vietnam. France was bent upon restoring her colonial empire in the south and the next year war broke out between the French and Ho Chi-minh, culminating in the dramatic siege and capture by Ho's forces of the fort of Dien Bien Phu in 1954. As a result of a 14-nation conference on Indo-China at Geneva in the same year Vietnam was partitioned after a cease-fire, the country to be united after tree elections. Laos and Cambodia became independent.

Unfortunately the United States refused to sign the agreement and South Vietnam refused to hold elections, but both affirmed that they would not use force to upset the agreement. There was thus a crystallisation into two Vietnams—Ho Chi-minh's Hanoi régime in the North and that of the Catholic nationalist Ngo Dinh Diem at Saigon in the South. By 1960 the Communist guerrillas in the South, known as the Vietcong, had set up a National Liberation Front. For eight or nine years a civil war was waged in South Vietnam against a very unpopular dictatorship. All that time it received United States military support while the North helped the rebels in the South. The position became increasingly untenable, and in 1963 the Buddhists rioted against the ruling Roman Catholic minority. The Diem régime which had savagely persecuted the Buddhists was overthrown by the military. In August 1964 two vessels of the US fleet were alleged to have been attacked in the Gulf of Tonking (off the North Vietnam coast) and American planes bombed North Vietnam installations as retaliation. This was the first of a series of bombing raids. In June 1965 the State Department gave authority to the American military commander to use troops in offensive operations against the Vietcong. An inquiry conducted by the US Senate Foreign Relations Committee in 1968 made it doubtful whether the alleged attacks on the two US destroyers in the Gulf of Tonking had ever taken place. This put a question mark against the constitutional legality of the war, as Congress had never declared war on North Vietnam.

After being advised by his officials that a military solution was impossible and that the only possible political solution was a negotiated settlement, President Johnson in March 1968 announced his partial bombing pause. Peace talks began in Paris in May, and by January 1969 the US, South Vietnam, North Vietnam, and the National Liberation Front (NLF) were sitting round a table. But little progress was made.

On 3 September 1969 Ho Chi-minh died after 24 years in power. His special achievement was the welding together of the two elements of nationalism and communism in Vietnam.

Growing opposition and disillusionment at home with the American rôle in the war, and the advent of Mr. Nixon to the Presidency brought an increased determination to reduce and eventually end the US military commitment in S.E. Asia. To this end a programme of " Vietnamisation " was launched by which the South Vietnamese were given the means to take on progressively a greater share of the burden.

On 26 January 1972 President Nixon revealed 2½ years of secret negotiations with the North Vietnamese and American concessions, including an offer of a massive reconstruction programme for the whole of Indo-China including N. Vietnam. He made a new 8-point peace offer which proposed total withdrawal of troops, simultaneous release of prisoners and neutrally organised elections in S. Vietnam. The plan was flatly rejected by N.

Vietnam, mainly because it failed to provide for the discarding of President Thieu.

North Vietnamese Offensive 1972.

On 30 March the North Vietnamese began a new offensive in which for the first time North Vietnamese forces fought conventionally in South Vietnam. They succeeded in taking the provincial capital Quang Tri and endangered the former imperial capital of Hué. The United States replied with ever heavier bombing of targets in N. Vietnam, supply routes and North Vietnamese units in the Demilitarised Zone and S. Vietnam. In May President Nixon announced the mining of Haiphong and other North Vietnamese ports. This brought a sharp denunciation by the Soviet Union (and China), but significantly none of the current bilateral negotiations was broken off.

Negotiations and Truce.

During the summer of 1972 the N. Vietnamese offensive failed: no major towns fell and the morale of the S. Vietnamese army held. This, combined with devastating American bombing, produced a more accommodating attitude from the Vietcong and the N. Vietnamese negotiators after many fruitless meetings between President Nixon's special adviser Dr. Kissinger and the leader of the N. Vietnamese delegation at the Paris peace talks, Le Duc Tho.

Despite set-backs, the negotiations did at last lead to the signature of a cease-fire agreement on 27 January 1973. By its terms US forces were to leave Vietnam within 60 days and there would be an exchange of prisoners of war. Vietnamese forces on both sides were to remain within their present territory. An international commission would supervise the observance of the agreement. Only vague outlines of a political settlement were included: principles for the reunification and neutrality of North and South and provisions for the people of S. Vietnam to exercise self-determination in supervised elections. The most serious omissions were its failure to mention any withdrawal of the N. Vietnamese forces in S. Vietnam, or even to define what territory was controlled by whom, and the fact that it applied only to S. Vietnam, not to Cambodia or Laos. But President Nixon claimed " peace with honour " and promised S. Vietnam continued support.

Both Vietnamese governments claimed the agreement as a victory. President Thieu gave up his objections and expressed satisfaction that Hanoi had been forced to recognise North and South Vietnam as two independent sovereign states. But he warned that the political struggle ahead could be even more dangerous than the war. Le Duc Tho commented that it could not be denied that there now existed in S. Vietnam " two administrations, two armies, two areas of control, and three political forces."

Vietnam was now a totally devastated country. The military casualties amounted to about 1,100,000 dead Vietnamese (and an unknown number of civilians) and 46,000 Americans. The United States had poured some $120 billion into Indo-China and suffered immense damage to its international authority. Yet the basic issue of the war remained unsettled: who has the right to govern S. Vietnam?

Neither War nor Peace.

Despite frequent and major infringements of the cease-fire the USA began withdrawal of its 23,000 soldiers still in Vietnam. An ultimatum to Hanoi was needed to procure the release of the remaining American prisoners, but finally 29 March 1973 marked the end of an era of US military presence in Vietnam. The agreements of the third international Vietnam conference in three decades meeting in Paris in March had little significance, as Saigon was alleging large-scale infiltration of troops and munitions into S. Vietnam. The attempts of the International Commission of Control and Supervision to enforce the cease-fire were proving largely ineffective. An agreement in June between Dr. Kissinger and Le Duc Tho in Paris on measures to ensure implementation of the ceasefire achieved a temporary sharp drop in the level of fighting. But talks between the S. Vietnamese Government and the Provisional Revolutionary Government on a political settlement remained fruitless: President Thieu would have no truck with anything approaching coalition government, and the Communists therefore refused to agree to elections. Then in January 1974 the increasingly offensive role of the Communist forces prompted President Thieu to put his troops on a war footing again.

Communist Victory.

In March and April 1975 as a result of increasing Vietcong pressure, South Vietnamese forces were withdrawn from the Central Highlands in order to strengthen the defence of more strategic towns. After the decisive battle of Xuan Loc in April 1975 and with Saigon encircled, President Thieu resigned. By the beginning of May the Communists had triumphed. During the latter half of 1975 an estimated 230,000 refugees left S. Vietnam. On 21 January 1976 the Military Management Committee handed over government to the People's Revolutionary Committee. Following the elections in April of a National Assembly for all Vietnam, the reunification of the country was proclaimed for the first time since 1859. A government for the Socialist Republic of Vietnam was formed by Mr. Phan van Dong and in December 1976 the first congress of the Vietnamese Communist party since 1960 was held. After a visit to Hanoi by an American delegation and a subsequent agreement by Vietnam to supply information on missing US soldiers, the United States finally withdrew their veto on Vietnamese membership of the United Nations.

LAOS AND CAMBODIA.

The war in Laos officially ended on 21 February 1973 with a standstill cease-fire agreement (leaving the Pathet Lao in control of two-thirds of the country). The formation of a coalition government was agreed after some US pressure on the rightists in the Vientiane Government.

In May 1975 after local fighting and left-wing demonstrations in Vientiane the right-wing ministers resigned and fled. Army units mutinied against right-wing officers and southern Laos was occupied by Pathet Lao forces. The American protégé Souvanna Phouma remained at the head of the coalition government until December when his half-brother Prince Souphanouvong proclaimed the existence of a People's Democratic republic with a government headed by Mr. Kaysone Phomvihan. A complete takeover by the Pathet Lao had not been expected until April 1976. In August 1976 a delegation from Thailand visited Vientiane and a 5-point communiqué for peaceful co-existence was signed. However, Laos now seems to have become almost totally dependent on Vietnam.

In Cambodia President Lon Nol proclaimed a state of emergency in March 1973: Prince Sihanouk's predominantly Communist forces had virtually cut off all supply routes to the capital Phnom Penh. The Republican Government was saved only by greatly intensified US bombing. However by dramatically cutting off all funds the US Congress forced an end to bombing raids on Cambodia by 15 August. Heavy fighting followed with the Sihanoukists just failing to take Kompong Cham.

During 1974 the military situation in Cambodia continued to deteriorate as the authority of the Lon Nol régime ceased to extend beyond Phnom Penh, Battambang and a few other centres. By January 1975 Khmer Rouge pressure had virtually isolated Phnom Penh, and the Mekong supply route had been cut. Increasing diplomatic recognition of the exiled Sihanouk régime followed. As Cambodia's plight became desperate, Lon Nol left the country in March 1975 and in April came surrender to the victorious Khmer Rouge Army.

All foreigners were swiftly expelled from Cambodia, and although information was scanty, apparently the whole population of Phnom Penh was sent to work in the fields to increase food production.

The victors were an uneasy alliance between the royalist followers of the exiled Prince Sihanouk and the Marxist Khmer Rouges. Prince Sihanouk remained as head of state with Penn Nouth as Prime Minister. After returning to Cambodia from Peking in September 1975 Sihanouk left soon afterwards on extensive travels. Elections were held on 30 March 1976 and the Prince resigned in April. He was replaced by Mr. Khieu Samphan and Penn Nouth's Government resigned to be followed by a new Cabinet under Mr. Pol Pot. In the early months of 1976 the entire population was mobilised in order to reconstruct the economy, but since then reports have reached the West of massive killings verging on genocide.

The pro-Chinese guerrilla movements in Thailand and Malaysia were naturally encouraged by these developments. Most countries in South-East Asia hastened to improve their relations with China and the other Communist countries of the area. The withdrawal of US forces from Thailand was accelerated at the behest of the Thais.

Conflict with Vietnam.

From September 1977 onwards several border clashes occurred between Vietnam and Cambodia. Information was difficult to obtain, particularly because Cambodia had virtually cut itself off from the rest of the world. But in December Hanoi appeared to have escalated the conflict into a concerted invasion. Cambodia broke off diplomatic relations and each side accused the other of long-standing violations of the frontier and massacres of the inhabitants of the frontier areas. Although the Soviet Union has supplied arms and aid to Vietnam, and China to Cambodia, the view that this conflict between Communists is a " proxy war " between Moscow and Peking is probably incorrect. Rather, it is a revival of the traditional enmity between the two neighbours. The Vietnamese, much the stronger in numbers and in arms, appear to have made initial advances into Cambodia but to have held back, preferring to seek dominant influence rather than open conquest.

AFRICA

ETHIOPIA AND SOMALIA.

Conflict in the Horn of Africa.

The Horn of Africa is the name given to the triangle of land which juts out on the east of the continent between the Indian Ocean and the Gulf of Aden. The two main countries which it comprises are Ethiopia, with a population of twenty-eight million, and the Somali Democratic Republic, with a population of three million. The third country of the Horn is the tiny state of Djibouti, the former French possession which became independent in June 1977. It has only 220,000 inhabitants, but is of great importance to Ethiopia, as 60% of her imports and 40% of her exports now pass through Djibouti.

The key to the significance of the Horn is its geographical position. It commands the entrance to the Red Sea, lies close to the oil supplies of the Persian Gulf and is a potential target for exploitation by the Soviet navy in the Indian Ocean. Events inside the Horn thus have considerable bearing on the economic and strategic interests both of neighbouring Middle East countries and of maritime states around the world.

The Dergue.

The politics of the Horn were thrown into the melting pot in 1974 when mutinies by soldiers demanding better pay and conditions led to the collapse of Haile Selassie's regime in Ethiopia. The Emperor himself was deposed in September 1974. Power passed into the hands of the Provisional Military Administrative Council, known as the Dergue. However, it failed to achieve any degree of governmental stability or to establish its authority in the country. There is continuing strife in Addis Ababa itself between the Dergue and its opponents, chiefly the Ethiopian People's Revolutionary Party.

The weakness of the central government gave a new impetus to the rebellion in the Ethiopian province of Eritrea. A former Italian colony, Eritrea was made a federated state of the Ethiopian Empire in 1952 and fully integrated ten years later. A secessionist movement, the Eritrean Liberation Front, grew up in the province. By 1976 there were some 15,000 guerrillas in action in Eritrea, equipped and trained by countries such as Syria, Libya and Iraq. Attempts by the Dergue in 1975 and 1976 to suppress the rebellion only served to unite the various factions on the opposing side. Liberation Front forces controlled the entire province, with the exception of the capital, Asmara, and the port of Massawa. In May 1978, however, Ethiopian troops, with Cuban assistance launched a major counter-offensive.

The Dergue's position worsened as a second military front developed in the south of the country. The Somali Democratic Republic, which became independent in 1960, claims the Ogaden desert region of Ethiopia, as well as Djibouti and parts of Kenya, and its constitution contains a commitment to reunite these " lost territories ". The turmoil in Ethiopia after the fall of Haile Selassie led the Somali Republic to foster a guerrilla movement in the Ogaden, the Western Somali Liberation Front. An offensive in June 1977 gave the guerrillas control of the southern Ogaden. Fighting was then concentrated on the seventy-mile road through the Marda Pass between Jijiga and Harar. In September the Somali-backed forces captured Jijiga and the Pass, and the fighting moved towards Harar. In early 1978, a major Ethiopian counter-attack recovered most of the Ogaden.

National and tribal rivalries in this corner of East Africa have long provided opportunities for outside powers to involve themselves in its affairs. When Britain ruled India the Red Sea was essentially a British sphere of influence, but since the 1950s the situation has become more complex. In 1953 the United States signed a mutual defence agreement with Ethiopia, and by 1974 the Americans had provided Haile Selassie with 400 million dollars worth of military aid. Western influence in Ethiopia was offset by Russian ties with the Somali Republic. Hostility to Ethiopia led the Somali Republic to turn to the Soviet Union for support, and in 1962 the two countries signed military and technical aid agreements. When the Soviet navy entered the Indian Ocean naval and communications facilities were established at Somali ports, particularly at Berbera.

The great power balance in the Horn was upset by the Ethiopian revolution and the switch in Russian support from the Somali Republic to Ethiopia. After a violent change of government in Addis Ababa in February 1977, the Dergue announced that it would henceforth buy arms from " socialist " countries.

Somalia Ousts Russians.

Nationalism inside the Horn proved to be a stronger force than a common ideology, and the Soviet Union's support for Ethiopia led to a breach with her former allies, the Somalis. On 13 November 1977 it was announced that President Barre of the Somali Republic had expelled the 6,000 Russian military and civilian advisers from his country, withdrawn all naval and military facilities and renounced his 1974 treaty of friendship with the Soviet Union. At the same time the Somali Republic broke off diplomatic relations with Cuba, whose troops were alleged to be fighting with the Ethiopians in the Ogaden. Increasing quantities of Russian military equipment have been transported to Ethiopia in preparation for counter-offensives in the Ogaden and Eritrea, and Russian naval vessels are reported to be supporting the Ethiopians in the defence of Massawa. The significance of Russian moves is not yet clear, but the West is at present reluctant to intervene in the hope that the end result will be a military stalemate which will bring about a negotiated settlement.

NIGERIA.

Tension between the main tribal groups (Hausa and Yoruba and Ibo) led to the assassination in 1966 by Ibo officers of the Hausa Prime Minister, Sir Abubakar Tafawa Balewa. General Ironsi, an Ibo soldier, tried to impose a unitary system of government but was murdered by non-Ibo soldiers. Civil war broke out in July 1967 after the seces-

sion of the Eastern Region under its Ibo leader, Colonel Ojukwu. This region became known as Biafra. Federal troops under the head of the new Federal Military Government, General Gowon, advanced into Biafra, cut the secessionists off from the sea and confined them to the Ibo heartland.

The Federal Military Government said that military operations would cease immediately if Colonel Ojukwu and his associates would agree to remain part of Nigeria and accept the new structure of the Federation based on the 12 states, including the South Eastern and Rivers States.

The end of the civil war after a period of apparent stalemate came at the beginning of 1970. Federal troops captured Owerri, headquarters of the secessionist régime, together with Uli airstrip through which relief supplies had reached Biafra. Colonel Ojukwu departed, leaving Colonel Effiong in charge of affairs. Colonel Effiong called on his troops to stop fighting and sued for peace.

Although he had promised a return to civilian rule, General Gowon announced its deferment in 1974. The first half of 1975 saw serious industrial unrest and highly inflationary pay increases, though Nigeria had a steadily increasing trade surplus because of her oil exports. In July 1975 General Gowon was deposed in a bloodless coup. The new head of state and commander-in-chief of the armed forces was Brigadier Murtala Mohammed. All former members of the Government and all state governors were dismissed. The plans of the new government included a timetable for return to civilian rule, the drafting of a new constitution, an anti-corruption drive and reduction of the armed forces. Steps were also taken to relieve the congestion in the port of Lagos. In February 1976 an attempted coup by officers was crushed but General Mohammed was killed. He was succeeded by General Olusegun Obasanjo who proceeded with his predecessor's policies. Port congestion was reduced and a strict economic programme placing emphasis on housing, health and agriculture was mounted. A new constitution was published in October 1976 and October 1979 is the projected date for the re-establishment of full democratic government.

In September 1977 elections to a constitutive assembly were held. All the candidates were independents because since the military take-over in 1966 all political parties had been banned. Nevertheless, these elections represented the punctual fulfilment of a further point in the Government's programme for a return to civilian government. The Assembly was opened on 6 October. After numerous bloody coups and the barbaric Biafran War, there are indeed signs of success for the military government. By the reorganisation of the country into 19 states, instead of four as previously, it became impossible for the political parties to dominate regions by identifying with the large tribes; there are hopes that the political parties, when they come, will cut across tribal divisions. Meanwhile, especially because of the oil boom, Nigeria has never been so prosperous.

UGANDA.

In August 1972 the President of Uganda, General Amin, announced that all Asians who held British passports (whose numbers were estimated at 57,000) must leave the country within 3 months. He accused them of sabotaging the economy and corruption and insisted that the economy must be in the hands of black Ugandans. Britain condemned this move as irresponsible and racist and reacted by suspending economic aid to Uganda. But she recognised her responsibility towards Asians with British passports and organised an air-lift. The expulsions were soon extended to Asians with Indian, Pakistani or Bangladesh passports, but these countries refused to accept the expellees. The Asians had played an indispensable rôle in the Ugandan economy, which must suffer from their departure, despite aid from Colonel Gaddafi in Libya.

General Amin had been strongly condemned by Presidents Nyerere of Tanzania and Kaunda of Zambia for racism of just the kind Africans deplore. There were actually brief military clashes on the Uganda–Tanzanian border in September 1972, and further allegations by Amin in 1974 that Tanzania and Zambia were planning an invasion of Uganda and supporting conspiracies by ex-President Obote.

Relations with Britain deteriorated when following British press reports of attempts to assassinate Amin and of brutal murders of prominent Ugandans, action was taken against British interests and all but 5 British diplomats were expelled in November 1974. In April 1975, General Amin said that he was ready to lift restrictions on the British High Commission. But relations were soured by the trial and sentence to death of Mr. Dennis Hills, a British lecturer, for treason and sedition. Only intense diplomatic activity including the mediation of President Mobutu of Zaïre and a visit to Kampala by Mr. Callaghan, then the British Foreign Secretary, secured a reprieve. In July 1976 a further dispute arose over the disappearance of Mrs. Dora Bloch, one of the hostages in the hijacked Air France airbus which landed at Entebbe airport. On 28 July Britain broke off diplomatic relations with Uganda, the first time this had been done with a Commonwealth country.

The Entebbe incident also caused friction with Kenya who had allowed Israel to use Kenyan facilities during the rescue operation.

Early in 1977 came reports of mass arrests and killings in Uganda. Amnesty International accused Uganda at the United Nations of serious breaches of human rights: the disappearance of at least 300,000 persons since 1971—including at least 50,000 murdered—torture in concentration camps, mass murders in the army and the systematic murder of Kenyan citizens in the wake of the Entebbe incident. After discovery of an alleged plot to stage a coup, Amin intensified persecution of opponents of the regime, especially among the Christian tribes of Lango and Acholi. The arrest and murder of the Anglican Archbishop of Uganda and two Christian Ministers was greeted with particular abhorrence abroad. Meanwhile Amin proposed to assume the titles of " Emperor " and " Son of God ". He offered the Soviet Union a military base in return for installation of a nuclear reactor. The excesses of General Amin were condemned by various African countries and Ghana broke off diplomatic relations. But there has been some restraint because of a wish not to upset the illusion of African unity. However the Commonwealth Conference in London in June, at which Britain had made it clear that General Amin would not be welcome, condemned the massive violations of basic human rights in Uganda. In September 1977 Amin banned all religious communities except the Anglicans, Roman Catholics, Orthodox and Moslems.

SOUTH AFRICA.

In South Africa Africans have no civil rights except in the " Bantustans ". These are some 200 pieces of land, making up about 13 per cent of the country's land area, specifically designated for African use. Elsewhere in South Africa, Africans may not vote, and they have no representatives in the South African Parliament or on any of the Provincial or Local Authorities. They may form Trades Unions but these are not recognised in law and take no part in industrial negotiations. Their right to strike is severely limited and they have no freehold rights of land or house ownership. Freedom of movement is restricted by influx-control laws governing movement between towns and between town and country. Regulations require them to carry a pass at all times. African industrial wages average a sixth of those of Whites, and foreign firms have also been blameworthy in this respect.

The Afrikaans-led Nationalist Party has been in power since 1948. In 1961 after a referendum they made South Africa a republic, fulfilling a Nationalist aspiration of fifty years standing.

The theory of the government's policy of " apartheid ", which owes much to the late Prime Minister, Dr. Verwoerd, looks forward to the eventual partition of South Africa as the only viable alternative to integration, which most Afrikaners regard as racial suicide. In practice, however, the government's policies are adapted to making a rigid caste system based on colour compatible with industrialisation and economic growth. Hence the increasing emphasis on the migrant labour system described by government ministers as " the cornerstone of our labour policy ". Africans are brought to work in industry and returned to the Reserves at the end of their contracts.

The government is unable to impose the taxes on White voters that genuine separate development would require. The Bantustans are therefore likely to remain overcrowded Labour reserves, and millions of Africans will always live and work in the " White areas ".

The implementation of apartheid legislation covering employment, housing and education after 1948 led to increasing African unrest, organised especially by the African National Congress (ANC). In 1959 the Pan Africanist Congress (PAC) broke from the ANC, and began to organise anti-pass law demonstrations. In March 1960 such a demonstration took place at the police station in the African township of Sharpeville. The police opened fire, killing 69 Africans and wounding over 180. The government declared a state of emergency and began mass arrests of African leaders. Strikes and mass marches of Africans continued for another week and the government then banned the ANC and PAC under the Suppression of Communism Act. Some African leaders went underground and organised a campaign of sabotage. But the security forces were able to infiltrate the organisations and in 1963 Nelson Mandela, the outstanding African leader, was captured with others and brought to trial. He was sentenced to life imprisonment.

Unrest among the Africans broke out again in 1973 with widespread strikes in Natal. In 1976 the worst riots since Sharpeville occurred in Soweto. The immediate cause was opposition to the compulsory use of Afrikaans as the medium of instruction in schools. The riots continued throughout the summer and spread to other areas. Student protest was reinforced by political strikes and despite conciliatory moves by the Government, discontent continues.

In 1974 independence was granted to the Transkei, a Bantu homeland, and in 1977 Bophutatswana became the second " Bantustan ". However, these states have not received international recognition.

Despite apparently growing African self-confidence, the White minority, overwhelmingly powerful and controlling the military and state machinery, remains determined to hold its privileged position. In 1974 there were some signs of change in South African attitudes both externally as well as internally. Mr. Vorster initiated talks with African nationalist leaders. With the significantly increasing involvement of Russian and Cuban forces in Angola, South African concern about the possibility of a Communist take-over led to the entry of South African troops from Namibia into Angola. The troops were withdrawn in 1976 following the MPLA victory. Mr. Vorster played a key role during Dr. Kissinger's visit to Africa and it appears that in the future South Africa's position will continue to be crucial to developments in Southern Africa.

Growing Repression in South Africa.

During 1977 the South African Government was faced with challenges to the apartheid system from various quarters. The Roman Catholic church opened its schools to all races and its Bishops' Conference published a 21-point programme for improving the situation of the Blacks. Several large American firms announced their intention of ending racial segregation in their South African branches and effecting full integration at work and in the canteen. And the European Community also laid down guidelines for firms operating in South Africa which required equality for Black workers. The reaction was mixed. In the spring, the threat of compulsory press censorship produced an agreement on voluntary self-censorship by the press. On the other hand, White political leaders in Natal announced in July that they wanted to investigate the possibility of an autonomous multi-racial government in the province. The following month plans were made public for a new South African Constitution whereby significant rights and participation would be extended to the Coloureds and the Indians but not to the Blacks, on the ground that they were covered by the Bantustan policy. These groups were to have parliaments with the same rights as that of the Whites, as well as a share (though not on a par with the Whites) in the election of a French-style President and in his Supreme Council of Ministers.

However, tension and violence increased following the deaths in prison of numerous Black activists who had been imprisoned without trial. Major riots were triggered off by the death of Steve Biko, the most popular Black leader, in whose case there were contradictions in the explanations given by the Minister of Justice and an inquiry showed severe head-wounds. In October the police raided 17 Black nationalist organisations and the Christian Institute, which was hostile to the regime: all were banned. This action represented a short-sighted snapping of the last threads of understanding between the races. Coming in the wake of steadily worsening relations between the United States and South Africa, it probably indicated that the latter had given up the attempt to placate Western opinion. General elections held on 30 November, in which Mr. Vorster's National Party won its greatest ever electoral victory with 135 seats out of 165, also suggested that Black unrest and world indignation over developments in South Africa had produced a dangerous attitude of defiance among Whites.

NAMIBIA.

Namibia (South West Africa) has been under South African control since it was wrested from Germany in the First World War. In 1920 the League of Nations mandated the territory to South Africa.

In 1964 the Odendaal Commission, set up by the SA government, recommended the effective integration of South West and South Africa with the mandated territory being divided into ten tribal Bantustans having home rule, and a White homeland consisting of 70 per cent of the land area. The response of the United Nations was a 1966 General Assembly resolution revoking South Africa's mandate on the grounds that she was extending apartheid to the territory and therefore not administering it in the interests of all its inhabitants. SA legislation in 1969 largely put the Odendaal recommendations into effect.

During the 1960s nationalist sentiment began to grow among the majority Ovambo tribe and a number of political parties were formed including the South West Africa People's Organisation (SWAPO). This party was banned and its leaders in exile have organised guerrilla infiltration of the territory. In December 1973 negotiations between the South African government and the UN Secretary-General Kurt Waldheim were broken off when it became apparent that the UN demand for independence for the whole territory under universal adult suffrage was irreconcilable with the South African plan of "independence" for a number of tribal Bantustans. In September 1974 the South African government declared itself ready to discuss the future of S.W. Africa and at a constitutional conference at the end of 1975 a declaration was signed promising independence in 3 years. SWAPO boycotted the conference and carried out intermittent guerrilla attacks during 1976, despite some attempt to facilitate their participation in a series of negotiations held during 1976. During 1977 five Western members of the UN Security Council held talks with Mr. Vorster. They demanded the inclusion of SWAPO in the independence process, the withdrawal of South African troops, the organisation of national elections under UN supervision and the release of all political prisoners. South Africa rejected UN supervision and troop withdrawal so long as the threat remained from the MPLA and the Cubans in neighbouring Angola. However, agreement was eventually reached that South Africa should appoint a General Administrator to govern Namibia by decree until elections were held for a constitutive assembly on an unrestricted party basis. By May 1978, however, an enduring settlement in Namibia had still not come about, despite increasing UN pressure on South Africa.

RHODESIA (ZIMBABWE).

In Rhodesia over five million Africans remain subordinate to 250,000 Whites. The 1961 Constitution provided for progressively increasing African representation in the Rhodesian Parliament. But a new White political party, the Rhodesian Front gained power at the 1963 elections on a platform of independence from Britain, opposition to the 1961 Constitution as too liberal, and opposition to proposals to repeal the Land Apportionment Act. The dissolution in December 1963 of the Federation of Rhodesia and Nyasaland led to the independence of Northern Rhodesia (as Zambia) and of Nyasaland (as Malawi) under majority governments and left Southern Rhodesia, renamed Rhodesia, as a self-governing colony with a White minority government. The Rhodesian Front leader, Winston Field, was replaced by Ian Smith after failing to obtain independence.

Unilateral Declaration of Independence.

Protracted negotiations took place between Mr. Smith and Mr. Wilson to reach a settlement in 1965. The latter took his stand on "five principles", including the stipulation that an agreed independence constitution should guarantee unimpeded progress to majority rule. But after winning all 50 White seats at the 1965 election, Mr. Smith made the unilateral declaration of independence from Britain on 11 November 1965. The British Government was thus confronted by an act of rebellion. However, it ruled out from the start the use of force. Mr. Wilson embarked on a policy of graduated economic sanctions, including an oil embargo; the objective being the emergence, under economic hardship, of a liberal alternative to the Smith régime. The UN Security Council later made sanctions mandatory, negotiations with the Smith regime proving fruitless. The white minority had found themselves unready to give the African majority reasonable prospects of education, jobs, political and civil rights. It was clear that what Mr. Smith objected to was majority rule in Rhodesia at any time. In 1969 a referendum led to Rhodesia being declared a republic. Under the republican Constitution, Whites were assured of a perpetual majority in the Senate and Africans could not hope for more than parity of representation in the lower House, and that in the indefinite future.

Stalemate and African Resistance.

Meanwhile exiled supporters of the banned African Nationalist organisations, Zimbabwe African People's Union (ZAPU) and Zimbabwe African National Union (ZANU), whose leaders Joshua Nkomo and Ndabaningi Sithole were imprisoned in Rhodesia, began armed incursions into Rhodesia from bases in Zambia in 1967 in co-operation with the South African ANC. As a result South African police were drawn in to help.

However sanctions were succeeding only in increasing rural unemployment and a shortage of foreign exchange and because of "leaks" through South Africa and the Portuguese territories, they were seen more as a bargaining counter than a solution. In 1971 agreement on a settlement was reached between Mr. Smith and Sir Alec Douglas-Home conditional upon the British Government being satisfied that it was acceptable to most Rhodesians. African parliamentary representation was to rise to parity with the whites and following a referendum and a Commission inquiry majority rule was expected to follow. However, a British Commission found the settlement unacceptable to the Africans. Sanctions therefore continued and guerrilla activity increased.

Further secret negotiations were held between Mr. Smith and Bishop Muzorewa, leader of the African National Council (ANC), but the proposals of the Government were rejected. Hopes of a solution to Rhodesia's problems were raised when Dr. Kissinger held a series of talks with African leaders and Mr. Vorster between April and September 1976. On 19 September Dr. Kissinger met Mr. Smith and on 24 September Mr. Smith broadcast his agreement to the "Kissinger package". He made it clear that he had no option but to accept. In essence the package provided for the establishment of an interim government, composed of a white-headed council of state and a black-led council of ministers, which would pave the way for majority rule within 2 years. In return steps would be taken to lift sanctions and end the guerrilla war. Black African leaders, including the so-called "front-line" presidents, rejected Smith's version of the agreement, but eventually a constitutional conference began in Geneva under the British chairmanship of Mr. Ivor Richard. The Africans were represented by the different nationalist leaders, Bishop Muzorewa (ANC), Joshua Nkomo (ZAPU), Robert Mugabe (ZANU) and Rev. Ndabaningi Sithole (ZANU). The talks foundered on the question of a date for majority rule and by December 1976 hopes for agreement on details had faded. Over Christmas, the "front line" presidents recognised Nkomo and Mugabe (now united as the Patriotic Front) as the representatives of Zimbabwe and Mr. Richard began a series of visits to African capitals in an attempt to negotiate a basis for the resumption of talks. His proposals which envisaged majority rule within 14 months with an interim government headed by a British "commissioner" were rejected by Mr. Smith who maintained adherence to his version of the Kissinger package.

Early 1977 saw the introduction of some measures for reducing racial discrimination in Rhodesia. However, at the same time the guerrilla war continued and intensified. In May Zambia declared that it was in a state of war with Rhodesia as a result of penetration of Zambian territory by Rhodesian troops " in hot pursuit ". Rhodesian troops also occupied some Mozambiquan territory for the purpose of eliminating terrorists. Meanwhile the increasingly insecure situation in Rhodesia was causing a growing exodus of whites. It became clear that Cuba was supplying arms to the Patriotic Front.

A visit to southern Africa by an Anglo-American negotiating team in July produced some progress, including an agreement on British supervision of the Rhodesian Government during a transitional period of three to six months before the holding of general elections. But a retrograde step followed when elections based on the old purely white electorate were called prematurely for 31 August. In these the Rhodesian Front won all of the 50 seats reserved for whites, and Mr. Smith said that he had a mandate to negotiate an " internal solution " with moderate black leaders. Talks later began with Bishop Muzorewa and Mr. Sithole, who disputed the primacy of the Patriotic Front and its support among the population.

A New Peace Plan.

On 1 September a new Anglo-American peace plan was published in Salisbury. Its basic elements were: return to legality with a transfer of power by the white minority government to Britain; an orderly and peaceful transition to independence in the course of the following year; free elections based on universal adult suffrage; the establishment by the British Government of a transitional government which would hold elections for an internationally recognised independent government; a temporary United Nations military presence; an independent constitution which would abolish discrimination and protect individual human rights and the independence of the courts; a large World Bank Development Fund for Zimbabwe under Anglo-American management. Britain was to nominate a Resident Commissioner to organise elections and act as commander-in-chief of the Rhodesian armed forces. The initial reaction of Mr. Smith was that the main items were mad and played into the hands of the so-called Patriotic Front, but he later modified this position. The Patriotic Front itself said that the plan aimed at establishing a neo-colonial state. However, the UN Security Council decided on the nomination of a representative to liaise with the British Resident Commissioner.

By December 1977 the so-called " front-line states " and the Patriotic Front under Nkomo and Mugabe agreed to negotiate with London for a peaceful transfer of power on the basis of the Anglo-American plan. They condemned the talks aimed at an " internal solution ". Meanwhile Mr. Ian Smith, after accepting the principle of universal adult suffrage for Rhodesia under certain conditions, reached agreement with the three leaders of African organisations inside Rhodesia (Bishop Muzorewa, Rev. Sithole and Chief Chirau) in March 1978 on Black majority rule by the end of 1978. The locally agreed settlement has been rejected by the UN Security Council.

MOZAMBIQUE AND ANGOLA.

Rebellion broke out in Mozambique in 1963 and intensified in Angola after 1966 forcing the Portuguese to pour in more troops. In 1973 their army in Africa numbered some 180,000 men of whom over a third were African (Portugal's population is some 9 million). Over half Portugal's annual budget went on defence, and conscription was lengthened to four years for all able-bodied men.

In countering guerrillas the Portuguese moved African villagers into fortified settlements so insulating them from insurgents. Non-Portuguese Catholic missionaries reported a series of atrocities in Tete when Africans were herded against their will and whole hamlets sympathetic to Frelimo (Front for the Liberation of Mozambique) were wiped out. Portugal denied these charges but following an international outcry in 1973, the civilian governor of Tete province was replaced.

Fighting in Mozambique and Angola intensified during 1973 and 1974, but cease-fires were called after an appeal by the new Portuguese government to the liberation movements for a cessation of hostilities. Agreements were reached for the independence of Guinea Bissau and Mozambique after President Spínola's statement in July on the independence of Portugal's African territories.

A transitional government was installed in Mozambique in September made up of Frelimo and Portuguese elements and full independence was scheduled for July 1975. However, the agreement led to serious racial unrest with white extremists attempting to proclaim UDI and thereby provoking a Black backlash. Nevertheless independence was granted on schedule. The Marxist-oriented government under President Machel produced plans to revolutionise the state machine and improve the economy. In December an attempt to overthrow President Machel was crushed. Relations with Portugal deteriorated and in February 1976 the capital Lourenço Marques was renamed Maputo.

Civil War in Angola.

Negotiations on Angola were held up because it had three rival liberation movements torn by dissension and because of serious racial violence in this the richest of the colonies, with great mineral wealth and hundreds of thousands of Portuguese settlers. However after the formation of a common front between the three liberation movements (MPLA, FNLA and UNITA) in January 1975 agreement was reached on independence in November 1975 and until then the establishment of a transitional government of all three plus representatives of the Portuguese Government.

But fighting continued, particularly between the FNLA and the Marxist MPLA, despite a truce agreement in March and became increasingly intense. During the summer of 1975 the MPLA gradually took over sole control of the capital Luanda, and UNITA joined the FNLA in operations against the MPLA. The latter held a central strip from the coast to the border with Zaïre, while UNITA held most of the South and FNLA the rest of the South and the northern provinces.

In the months before independence there was a massive departure of European settlers, leaving appalling economic problems for Angola. Meanwhile there was increasing evidence of the Soviet Union supplying the MPLA with tanks and artillery and of Soviet transport planes flying arms in to them. Several thousand Cuban soldiers also appeared on the MPLA side. The FNLA received support from China and some from the USA via Zaïre, though Congress soon put a stop to this by refusing further appropriations. South African troops were initially deployed to protect the Cunene River Dam project. In November the FNLA and UNITA formally established a joint military and political command, and two separate Angolan Republics were proclaimed, with rival governments being set up, by the MPLA in Luanda and by FNLA and UNITA in Huambo (formerly Nova Lisboa).

Full-scale civil war now developed. With

Soviet and Cuban support, the MPLA first brought the North under control pushing the FNLA back into Zaire. UNITA forces in the South were attacked and the South African forces which had advanced several hundred miles into Angola withdrew to patrol a 30-mile wide strip along the border. In February 1976, following the capture of Huambo, an MPLA victory was declared. UNITA forces under Dr. Jonas Savimbi and the FNLA under Mr. Holden Roberto continued guerrilla activities throughout 1976 while the MPLA attempted to bring the country back to normal.

Meanwhile Angola continues to have its own internal problems. In the enclave of Cabinda there was a movement for independence. Moreover, both of the former nationalist rivals to the MPLA showed signs of recovery. In August UNITA claimed significant successes in the continuing struggle in southern Angola, and in November it announced its intention of proclaiming an independent republic in the south of the country. President Neto was becoming ever more dependent on the Cubans, with whom a series of agreements on co-operation had been concluded.

Zaire.

In May 1978 an invasion of about 2000 Katangan exiles under the leadership of a " Congolese National Liberation Front " was launched from Angolan territory into the province of Shaba (formerly Katanga) in Zaire. Its aim was either to topple President Mobutu or to detach the copper-rich province from Zaire. However, in response to an appeal from Zaire and amidst the slaughter of both Black and white civilians, French and Belgian paratroopers were sent to Kolwezi, the town seized by the rebels.

THE UNITED STATES
Assassination of Kennedy.

The assassination of President Kennedy in November 1963 at Dallas, Texas, shocked the entire world. The youngest ever elected American President (43) when he succeeded Eisenhower, he had during his three years of office asserted his leadership and commitment to policies which promised increasing conciliation among nations. Lyndon B. Johnson, as Vice-President, automatically succeeded him.

The Presidential Election, 1968.

With memories of the rout of Goldwater in 1964, the Republican Party chose as its Presidential candidate Richard Nixon (who had once been Vice-President and a Presidential candidate). On the Democratic side the presidential race was thrown into confusion when President Johnson announced that he would initiate peace moves in Vietnam and lay down the presidency. Vice-President Humphrey entered the lists to become the chosen candidate for the Democratic Party. It was one of the most closely contested presidential elections in American history. But although securing only a small majority of the popular vote Nixon obtained 301 votes in the Electoral College against Humphrey's 191 and became the 37th President of the United States.

The Presidential Election 1972.

President Nixon's Democratic rival in the 1972 election was Mr. George McGovern, a " populist " with simple radical promises: an abrupt end to the Vietnam War, a radical reduction of the American military presence in Europe, and a better deal for Blacks and other disadvantaged minorities. His chief contender for the nomination, Governor George Wallace of Alabama, an advocate of strict segregation of the races, was severely wounded at an election meeting in May by an apparently deranged young white man. Mr. McGovern's programme was probably too radical and too vague for the electorate. Despite the scandal of the bugging of the Democratic Party Headquarters by men employed by the President's re-election committee, President Nixon was helped by an improving economy, by his decisive and adventurous diplomacy, and by progressive disengagement from Vietnam. The result on 7 November was the worst-ever defeat of a Democratic candidate: Nixon won in 49 of the 50 states. However the gains of the Republican Party in the simultaneous election for the House of Representatives were far from enough to give it a majority.

The Watergate Affair.

The Watergate scandal, which burst fully upon the United States during 1973, not merely shattered the credibility of President Nixon but caused a crisis in the whole American governmental system. Its effect was enhanced by Nixon's admission that he paid virtually no taxes in 1970–1 and by accusations that he granted favours to milk producers and the International Telephone and Telegraph (ITT) Corporation in return for election campaign contributions.

Two of those who had broken into and attempted to " bug " the offices of the Democratic Party in the Watergate Building in Washington in June 1972 were convicted in January 1973. The US Senate then set up a seven-man commission of enquiry under the chairmanship of Senator Ervin into what appeared to be a programme of illegal political espionage aimed at manipulating the democratic election process. Accusations and disclosures followed and the four main figures who emerged in the investigation of what became known as the " coverup " were among Nixon's closest associates. They were: Bob Haldeman (White House chief of staff), John Ehrlichman (Domestic Affairs adviser), John Mitchell (the Attorney-General), and John Dean (White House Counsel). Haldeman and Ehrlichman resigned in April, 1973, and John Dean was dismissed. He soon accused the President of having had full knowledge of the Watergate exploit in September 1972, three months after the break-in, and of having approved the cover-up attempts. Nixon maintained that he had first learned of it in March 1973 and denied having ever done anything towards covering up the affair.

In July 1973, it was revealed to the Senate Watergate Committee that Nixon had secretly been tape recording almost all of his White House conversations and telephone calls since before the break-in. If the tapes could be heard, they would indicate one way or the other the complicity of the President in the " coverup " which, rather than the break-in at Watergate itself, had become the central issue. A mammoth legal and political struggle over the tapes then ensued which was to last just over a year. The legal struggle centred on Federal Judge John Sirica who was presiding over the Federal Grand Jury. President Nixon resisted giving up the tapes on the grounds of confidentiality of staff deliberations and national security.

In the midst of the continuing crisis over Nixon's role, Vice-President Spiro Agnew resigned on 10 October 1973, shortly before pleading " no contest " to an income tax evasion charge. This incident led to the eventual appointment of Congressman Gerald R. Ford as Vice-President.

Events continued to work against the President. On 20 October, Attorney-General Elliot Richardson (Mitchell had resigned much earlier) and his deputy resigned after refusing to follow President Nixon's order to fire the Watergate Prosecutor, Archibald Cox. This incident became known as the " Saturday Night Massacre ". Controversy over the tapes and documents continued, including the revelation by the White House that an 18 minute gap existed in one of the most crucial tapes. These events culminated in July 1974, when the House Judiciary Committee adopted three articles of impeachment against President Nixon (only the second time that impeachment of a President had been recommended). These alleged that the President, in violation of his constitutional oath to uphold the law

(1) " engaged personally or through his subordinates or agents in a course of conduct or plan designed to delay, impede and obstruct the investigation " into the burglary at the Watergate building;

(2) " repeatedly engaged in conduct violating the constitutional rights of citizens " and impaired " the due and proper administration of justice and the conduct of lawful inquiries ".

(3) "failed without lawful cause or excuse to produce papers and things as directed by duly authorised subpoenas issued by the Committee".

This was followed by an admission by President Nixon that it was " clear that portions of the tapes of these June 23 conversations (with Haldeman, six days after the Watergate break-in in 1972) are at variance with certain of my previous statements." Though he remained committed not to resign, this statement unleashed demands for resignation or impeachment even among formerly staunch Republican supporters. Three days later, on 8 August, President Nixon finally announced in a televised broadcast his decision to resign (the first President ever to do so). But his statement did not include the expected confession of guilt. It was not the many breaches of the law by his subordinates but the affair of the tapes and his own abuse of executive privilege that destroyed Richard Nixon's credibility. By the end of his stubborn attempt to cling to power the nation was convinced of his complicity. He left America a legacy of shocked disillusionment with the sordid abuse of power by its political leaders and impaired respect for the highest office in the land.

America after Nixon.

On 9 August Vice-President Gerald Ford was sworn in as 38th President of the United States. He granted a controversial pardon to Mr. Nixon for " all offences against the United States " in order to spare the ex-President further suffering and the nation further divisive debate, but insisted there had been no "deal" involved. In January 1975 the Watergate cover-up trial resulted in the conviction of Ehrlichman, Haldeman and Mitchell for obstruction of justice and perjury.

President Ford had committed himself above all to combating inflation (" public enemy number one ") as well as to continuing the foreign policy of President Nixon. But in January 1975 he declared that the emphasis must be shifted because of the serious rise in unemployment (which was to reach 8 million in April 1975).

To many observers, the failure of American policy in Indo-China, the reverses suffered by Kissinger's attempts at Middle East peace and the trauma of Nixon's resignation seemed to indicate that a watershed in post-war American history had arrived—that America now needed a drastic reappraisal of her role in the world. In the wake of Watergate Congress began increasingly to challenge Presidential foreign policy, as with the " Jackson Amendment " to the Trade Treaty with the Soviet Union and the cutting off of military aid to Turkey. Its refusal to provide aid for Angola was clear evidence of the United States' new reluctance to become involved in foreign ventures. The increasing obstructionism of Congress was causing problems for President Ford with the Presidential election due in November 1976.

Revelation of Malpractices.

The CIA (Central Intelligence Agency) had been frequently accused of implication in operations to bring about a change in the political balance of some foreign countries (including the overthrow of President Allende in Chile in 1973) and of planning the assassination of political leaders to whose policies the United States strongly objected. Then in December 1974 allegations were made in the New York Times that the CIA in violation of its charter had conducted a vast illegal intelligence operation against adherents of the anti-war movement and other dissident groups inside the USA. President Ford established a commission headed by Vice-President Rockefeller to examine these allegations and recommend future safeguards. Both houses of Congress set up special committees to investigate the operations of the CIA, FBI and other intelligence and law enforcement agencies. The report of the Rockefeller Commission in June confirmed the allegations of large-scale spying on American citizens in the United States, including the opening of private mail, wire-tapping, room-bugging and infiltration of political groups (though generally with the aim of discovering foreign influence).

A further indirect result of Watergate was the discovery by a Senate Committee early in 1976 that many major American firms and particularly the Lockheed Aircraft Corporation had paid many millions of dollars in bribes to foreign officials, politicians and political parties to promote the sale of their products. This caused a sensation around the world, especially in those developed countries most affected, notably Japan, Italy and also the Netherlands in so far as the Queen's husband, Prince Bernhard, was alleged to be implicated. President Ford announced that he would establish a commission to investigate the practices of US firms in foreign countries.

However the question began to be raised whether the national, and especially the Congressional, mood of self-flagellation was not going too far, whether for the sake of a new political morality after Watergate all the sins whether of the CIA or of top American companies should be blazoned abroad, or whether the damage to American interests might be too great. Early in 1976 President Ford persuaded the House of Representatives not to publish the report of its committee on the activities of the CIA (though much had previously been leaked concerning such matters as CIA support of the Kurds in Iraq at the request of the Shah of Iran and on the orders of President Nixon and the payment of money to politicians and parties, particularly in Italy).

1976 Elections.

1976 became the year in which the country finally put Watergate and associated traumas behind it. With the election of a new President, the nation ended the year in a more positive mood than it had been since Nixon's re-election. Much of this spirit was symbolised by the nation's celebration of 200 years of independence which reached a climax on 4 July.

The year was dominated by the Presidential elections. President Ford had announced his intention to seek election to the office he then held by appointment, but barely won the Republican nomination over Ronald Reagan, former Governor of California. The Democrats had no single, obvious candidate and a free-for-all emerged among the possible challengers. At the beginning of the long primary election procedure to select the eventual candidate, Jimmy Carter, former Governor of Georgia, was a relative unknown outside the South. But he was eventually nominated with only token opposition. In the election itself Carter's massive early lead in the polls gradually dwindled until the outcome was called a " toss-up " by the pollsters. The result was close, although Carter had a larger popular majority than either Kennedy in 1960 or Nixon in 1968. In the electoral college, which constitutionally elects the President, the result was a margin of 56 votes for Carter.

President Carter.

Carter's election was both unusual and symbolic in a number of ways. The first President from the " deep south " since before the Civil War, some viewed Carter's election as the final act of reconciliation between North and South. Rising out of obscurity and possessing relatively little political experience, and having based much of his campaign on an attack on the Washington establishment, Carter was seen by some as a genuine Washington " outsider " not tied to any entrenched group.

In picking his Cabinet, however, Carter disappointed many of his supporters while reassuring the " establishment ". He did not pick as many women or blacks as many had hoped, but chose several former associates and many others who had served as officials in previous Democratic administrations. In domestic affairs he was expected to be a more activist President than his predecessor and acted immediately after his January 20 inauguration to propose measures to stimulate the US economy. During his first months in office he quickly set up a Department of Energy and proposed a drastic programme for energy saving. In nuclear energy policy he introduced many restrictions and promoted a search for greater safeguards. At the same time the proliferation of nuclear capacity abroad was discouraged. President Carter also sent to Congress an anti-inflation programme, though without wage or price controls, and a new welfare programme to benefit those unable to maintain themselves by work. He further initiated a bill providing that every kind of electronic surveillance, including telephone tapping, can take place only on the basis of a decision of a Federal judge; non-criminal investigations (as in the case of suspicion of espionage for a foreign power) were not exempted from this requirement as previously.

In foreign policy President Carter's emphasis on human rights proved a complicating factor in relations with the Communist states and with right-wing Latin American regimes. In November 1977 he signed the Foreign Aid Act denying aid to states which violated the human rights of their citizens.

the English-speaking minority in Quebec and the francophile minorities in the other provinces. When opening Parliament in Ottawa in October, the Queen appealed for unity and announced a proposed revision of the constitution to strengthen federalism in Canada. Mr. Trudeau proposed that a referendum on secession by Quebec should be held throughout Canada, and not merely in Quebec itself. Meanwhile the Quebec government was intensifying its relations with France, and when Mr. Lévesque visited Paris in November he was treated like a head of state. At the end of the year Mr. Trudeau said that he would accept an overwhelming majority vote in Quebec in favour of secession but that he would use force if necessary against any illegal unilateral declaration of independence.

CANADA

The relationship between the English and French speaking communities remains Canada's principal political problem. In 1970 the Quebec liberal party committed to federalism gained a clear majority in the elections, but the separatist Parti Quebecois took 25 per cent of the vote. The separatist movement lost some impact as the economic situation improved under the Liberal government. The kidnapping by the Front de Liberation du Québec of a British trade commissioner and the Quebec minister of Labour, Mr. Pierre Laporte (who was later found dead), prompted Mr. Pierre Trudeau, the Canadian prime minister, to invoke Canada's War Emergency Act But the Quebec separatist movement had been seriously weakened by the acts of terrorism.

In 1969 the Official Languages Act provided for equality between the two languages at federal level in parliament, government, and the courts. Bilingual districts could be established wherever the minority reached 10 per cent of the population and a Commission of Official Languages was to act as watchdog. In October 1971 Mr. Trudeau declared his allegiance to a policy of " multiculturalism within a bi-lingual framework." During 1974 there was great controversy in Quebec over legislation seeking to make French the sole official language of the Province and relegating English to an inferior position.

In parliamentary elections in October 1972 Mr. Trudeau's Liberal Party lost its overall majority and obtained only two seats more than the Progressive Conservative Party under Robert Stanfield, although it held its own in its stronghold of Quebec. Mr. Trudeau failed partly because rising unemployment had not prevented serious increases in the price of food, partly because of the failure of the experiment of the bilingual law. However he was able to form a government again with the parliamentary support of the small New Democratic Party (a Labour Party in all but name), which had also made gains. Further elections were held in 1974 after the Liberal Government had been defeated on a motion of no confidence in respect of the Budget. Mr. Trudeau succeeded with his argument against Mr. Stanfield that inflation was an international problem about which the Canadian Government could do little by itself.

As a result of deep concern about increasing economic dependence upon the US, Canada has strengthened its independent line in foreign policy. In 1971 Mr. Trudeau and Mr. Kosygin exchanged visits and wide-ranging co-operation agreements were concluded. A further economic agreement was signed in July 1976. In May 1976 nuclear aid to India was brought to an end due to the lack of safeguards over its use. Following 2 years of negotiations a framework agreement with the EEC was signed providing for non-preferential commercial and economic co-operation. The agreement is the first of its kind between the EEC and a major industrial state outside EFTA and was described as " a response to Canada's desire to diversify and extend external relations ".

In 1976 Mr. René Lévesque, a committed separatist, was elected Premier of Quebec. He later announced that a consultative referendum would be held before 1981 on the issue of independence for the province. A law passed in August 1977 provided that French should in future be the only official language in Quebec. Mr. Trudeau then sought Federal powers to protect the position of

LATIN AMERICA

Events since the early sixties in the major Latin American states are detailed individually below; perhaps the three most generalised phenomena are the trend towards industrialisation promoted locally by multi-national corporations, the emergence of a number of socialist experiments and of Cuban-style guerrilla movements, and the proliferation of military governments.

ARGENTINA.

The recent political history of Argentina has been dominated, even in his absence and after his death, by Juan Domingo Perón. During his eighteen years of exile (1955–1973) a succession of civilian and military regimes failed to break the loyalty of his followers, or to solve the problems posed by a series of worsening economic crises; his return, and death while in office, provoked a further crisis which led to a military intervention early in 1976.

The ousting of Perón in 1955 was followed by three years of military rule, but 1958 saw the installation of a civilian President, Dr. Arturo Frondizi. His attempt to introduce a stabilisation programme and to attract foreign capital into the country provoked an economic crisis in 1961, and his tolerance of Perónist politicians (who had supported his election, and who in 1962 won a majority of the seats contested in Congressional elections), led the military to depose him, rather than see Perón return. After a further military intervention, on 28 June 1966, the new President, General Ongania, reverted to policies of devaluation, wage control, and cuts in public spending, and his harsh suppression of labour and student opposition led to serious confrontations and the outbreak of guerrilla activity. He was deposed by Brigadier General Levingston on 8 June 1970. With the military increasingly divided, and unable to cope with civil unrest, and with the mounting guerrilla campaigns, Levingston was himself replaced by General Lanusse in March 1971. Convinced that the military could no longer rule the country, Lanusse called elections for early 1973, and in those elections the representative of the Perónist Justicualist Party, Dr. Hector Campora, emerged triumphant. Events thereafter moved swiftly. Perón returned permanently to Argentina in June, and less than a month later Campora resigned, and called new elections, while Lastiri remained as Provisional President. On 23 September, Perón was elected to the presidency with a vote of 62 per cent, and with absolute majorities in both houses of Congress, and on 12 October he was sworn in as President with his wife, Maria Estela Perón, as Vice-President. Rapidly approaching eighty, and in poor and failing health, Perón was no longer able to govern with vigour, or to control the widely disparate elements backing him. He suffered a heart attack on 29 June 1974, and after handing the Presidency on to his wife, he died on 1 July. Without political experience, and relying heavily on a close circle of personal advisers, Sra. Perón rapidly lost control of the political and economic situation. In early 1975 she gave wide-ranging responsibility to Lopez Rega, but was forced to dismiss him in July. When the new Economics Minister Celestino Rodrigo refused to grant a promised wage rise, a major crisis broke out. Sra. Perón departed briefly from office in September and October 1975, but returned amid rumours of an impending military coup. As inflation approached and passed 600 per cent per annum, and Sra. Perón's political support evaporated, the military reluctantly intervened, with General Jorge Videla taking power on 24 March 1976. Videla's attempts to follow a moderate line were undermined by guerrilla activity by the ERP (People's Revolutionary Army) and the Montoneros (although this abated significantly after a series of successes by the security forces, culminating in the death of ERP leader Roberto Santucho in July 1976), by the constant assassinations by right-wing terrorist groups (particularly the Argentinian Anti-Communist Alliance and the Liberation of America Commando), and by the hostility aroused by the very harsh economic measures taken to eliminate the balance of payments deficit and reduce inflation. By the end of 1976, Videla was faced with growing pressure from the right wing within the army, increasing combativeness from the once dominant trade unions, and continuing inflationary pressure. Measures were taken in January 1977 to control the labour unions, but there was little reason to believe that Argentina was at last emerging from the troubles of previous years.

In February 1977 evidence of widespread violations of human rights by the military regime was submitted to the United Nations by the Argentinian Human Rights Commission. This showed an alarming number of deaths, political prisoners and missing persons in the period since General Videla had come to power. Despite continuing attacks by the Montonero guerrillas, the shooting in June of the last of their leaders who still remained in Argentina itself marked the further disintegration of their military power.

A dispute which erupted between Argentina and Chile on ownership of certain small islands south of the Beagle Canal at Cape Horn was caused not only by national pride and a wish in both countries to distract popular attention from the domestic situation, but also by the desire to exploit the potential of the adjacent seas. After submission of the issue to arbitration by the British Crown, Argentina refused to accept the decision in favour of Chile and sent warships into the area.

BRAZIL.

Since 1964 Brazil has been governed by a series of military Presidents, and civilian political activity has been severely limited. Attempts by successive Presidents to liberalise the regime, whether sincerely intended or not, have so far failed, despite the considerable economic growth that has been achieved particularly since 1967; with the rapid growth rate now faltering, and a number of weaknesses becoming apparent in the " Brazilian economic model ", the prospects for a return to any form of civilian government in the near future must be slight.

The military seized power with remarkable ease in April 1964, closing a period of civilian rule which had lasted practically uninterrupted for seventy years, and a period of nearly twenty years of democratic politics. The ease with which the military established themselves in power owed much to the disarray of civilian politics, and the weakness of the Goulart regime, for Goulart's attempt to mobilise the masses in his favour upset not only his traditional opponents, but the more conservative members of his own fragile coalition. Once in power, Marshal Castelo Branco attempted to construct a stable regime with a degree of democratic accountability, but found himself caught between a vociferous " hard-line " sector in the armed forces and among civilian politicians, demanding wide-ranging repression of dissidents and the total destruction of the previous political system, and a shifting coalition of leading politicians seeking to capitalise on the discontent created by harshly deflationary economic policies by seeking more popular measures, and guarantees that the traditional electoral system would be respected. The harsh economic policies which Castelo Branco felt were necessary to solve the crisis inherited from previous regimes led to three years of recession and falling wages, and to a massive inflow of foreign capital into Brazil on favourable terms. The lack of popularity of the regime made electoral success improbable, and the hard-

liners insisted that political rights be withdrawn from an increasing number of politicians. After the gubernatorial elections of 1965, seen as a defeat for the government, all existing political parties were dissolved, and in their place ARENA, the government party, and MDB the " official " opposition party, were created by decree; state governors and the President were to be elected indirectly. While the Chamber of Deputies and the Senate continued to function, their role in government was practically eliminated. The dominance of the hard-line faction was confirmed by the succession to the presidency in 1967 of Marshal Arturo Costa e Silva, Castelo Branco's Minister of War, and while his presidency saw a shift in economic policy and the start of the " boom ", the political situation deteriorated steadily. In July 1967 former Presidents Goulart and Kubitschek joined dissident rightist Carlos Lacerda (former governor of Guanabara state, and an enthusiastic supporter of the 1964 coup) in an opposition Broad Front, which was banned in April 1968. Increasing problems with a weakened but hostile Congress led to its suspension in December 1968. In 1969 the presidency passed to General Garrastazu Médici. Carefully controlled elections in 1970 created a new congress, with ARENA winning substantial majorities in both houses, and claiming 21 of 22 governorships (with governors nominated by Médici, and " elected " by state assemblies). However, the declining economic situation, particularly after the spectacular increases in the price of oil, led to increasing opposition, and the MDB began to gain popularity. When General Ernesto Geisel, who succeeded Médici in 1974, allowed elections to take place with a greater degree of freedom, ARENA suffered considerable setbacks, and the project of liberalisation was halted. By 1976 inflation was mounting, the promises that wages would be allowed to rise substantially were brusquely withdrawn. Nationalist sectors within the army were annoyed by the opening of oil-fields to foreign companies; lack of finance threatened important development projects in steel and hydro-electric power, and the gains in export earnings due to significant diversification in the production of basic commodities, and the steady expansion of manufactured exports, were increasingly outstripped by the increased cost of oil and capital goods imports, and the growing burden of foreign debt, which by 1977 was absorbing an estimated 50 per cent of Brazil's export earnings. By early 1977 conflicts within the government led to the resignation of Trade and Industry Minister Severo Gomes, and pressure from industrialists for more open government and an expansion of the severely restricted domestic economy; meanwhile pressure was building up for further modifications to the already practically emasculated political system, as the question of the presidential succession in 1978 became a matter of public debate.

CHILE.

The trend towards military rule, and from constitutional government to dictatorship has been nowhere more marked and more tragic than in Chile; the Junta which seized power so bloodily in September 1973 still held power in 1977, but showed no sign of restoring the liberties it had destroyed when it came to power.

As long ago as 1958 Allende, the leader of the Chilean Socialist Party, narrowly failed to defeat the Conservative candidate, Jorge Alessandri in the Presidential elections; the subsequent rapid rise of the Christian Democrat Party, led by Eduardo Frei (and heavily backed by the CIA and American State Department) changed the face of Chilean politics. When the Conservative alliance collapsed in 1964, Frei was elected to the Presidency, and his young party gained control of Congress. Proclaiming a " revolution in liberty ", Frei however failed to push his ambitious reform programme through, and popular disenchantment led to rapidly declining support for his government, and to serious splits within the party, with a sector pledging alliance to the leftist opposition. In elections of historic importance in 1970, Socialist leader Allende, the candidate of the Popular Unity coalition (Unidad Popular) won a narrow victory over Alessandri in a bitterly contested three-way fight. Conspiratorial attempts to prevent his taking office, organised by conservative forces within Chile and within the Chilean military, and backed by the CIA, the United States Ambassador in Santiago, Korry, the ITT organisation (which stood to lose considerable holdings in Chile if planned nationalisation programmes went ahead), and by President Nixon himself, failed to prevent Christian Democrats in Congress voting with Popular Unity representatives to vote Allende into the Presidency on 4 November 1970. Throughout 1971 Allende enjoyed considerable popularity as he moved ahead with a land reform programme, the nationalisation of the US-owned copper companies, and of strategic sectors of the Chilean economy, and an expansionist economic programme based on rapidly growing real wages. But despite these apparent successes, several major problems were unresolved. Deep divisions within Allende's coalition were carried over into administration and government, popular initiatives consistently outran the willingness or capacity of the government to respond, foreign hostility exacerbated problems of finance and the supply of imports, and highlighted the dependence of the Chilean economy on external sources; most seriously, Allende's commitment to a "peaceful road to Socialism", combined with his inability to command a majority in Congress, and thus to enact legislation, led remorselessly to a position of stalemate and growing frustration. By 1972 growth was faltering and inflation soaring; a wave of strikes, co-ordinated by the opposition, late in 1972, led to the introduction of representatives of the armed forces into the cabinet. In March 1973, the Popular Unity coalition gained 44 per cent of the vote in the Congressional elections, but plans for the violent overthrow of the government were already underway. A failed coup in June was followed by an increasingly violent campaign of sedition and sabotage, and a further co-ordinated wave of strikes, particularly in the crucial transport sector; the Commander-in-Chief of the Armed Forces, General Prats, was forced to resign, and on 11 September 1973, the new High Command moved to overthrow Allende. He himself died besieged in the bombed Presidential Palace, and a military Junta took power, headed by General Augusto Pinochet. It is now officially recognised that thousands of Chileans died in the aftermath of the coup; many thousands more have passed through the hands of the security forces, with hundreds dying as a result of summary executions or prolonged torture. While an international campaign has drawn attention to the horrific human rights record of the Junta, the implacable pursuit of an orthodox monetarist policy has had only relative success in slowing inflation.

The depression was worst in 1975 with the GNP falling by a staggering 15 per cent; real wages have been drastically cut, investment has slumped, and unemployment reached 20 per cent during 1976. Agricultural production has steadily declined, although falling domestic consumption has made some exports possible. Early 1977 saw the beginning of an acute financial crisis, as the high cost of borrowing and the desperate need for credit combined to provoke a series of bankruptcies among financial institutions. Prospects for economic recovery seemed poor, but despite regular forecasts that he would be deposed, Pinochet continued to cling to power.

The Pinochet Referendum

In March 1977, on discovery of an alleged plot to overthrow the regime, all political parties were banned by government decree. However, in July General Pinochet announced that civilian government would be restored within eight years. 1977 brought signs of unrest in the light of an economic policy which had dramatically reduced inflation and improved production but at the expense of the living standards of the workers, many of whom were below the bread line. Despite threats of draconian punishments, strikes occurred and there was a general lack of civilian co-operation with the military regime. At the same time the Junta had difficulty in attracting foreign aid because of its notoriety for repression and terror. Partly as a result of a UN Resolution in December condemning the continued violation of human rights in Chile, a referendum was

organised for 4 January on the issue of support for General Pinochet and the legitimacy of his government. However splits became clear within the Junta on the wisdom of holding such a referendum. In the event emphasis was placed on the nationalist aspect of the referendum as a vote against foreign interference. The official result was a massive majority in support of the regime.

COLOMBIA.

Colombia's history of violence and instability notwithstanding, it has enjoyed until recently a brief period of relatively orderly if somewhat fragile civilian government, resulting from the Liberal–Conservative National Front coalition formed in 1958. Threatened from the start by slender electoral majorities, intra-party fractionalism, and the activity of left-wing guerrilla movements, as well as by the intransigence of traditional conservatives, the coalition has nevertheless managed to elect Liberal President Alberto Lleras Camargo in 1958, Conservative Guillermo Leon Valencia in 1962, Liberal Carlos Lleras Restrepo in 1966, Conservative Dr. Misael Pastrana Borrero in 1970 and Liberal Alfonso López Michelsen in 1974.

The narrow victory of Dr. Pastrana over ANAPO (the National Popular Front) led by ex-dictator turned populist General Rojas Pinilla (1953–7) in 1970 provoked widespread protest and disorder, while in concurrent Congressional elections the coalition National Front lost its majority dropping 53 of its 142 seats to the opposition groups. The army, brought back to prominence by its long campaigns against guerrillas, began to play an increasingly important role, particularly in the breaking of the general strike called in early 1971 to protest against rising unemployment. By May there were serious splits in both Conservative and Liberal parties, and in June Pastrana dismissed his cabinet, forming another from the right of each party. The atmosphere remained tense throughout the year, with troops occupying the National University in September. However, as the economy recovered from the mild recession of 1971 the political situation also eased; the coalition was able to approach the 1974 elections with some confidence; they turned out to be a particular triumph for the Liberals, for with Alfonso López Michelsen assuming the Presidency, his party achieved considerable majorities in the Senate and Chamber of Deputies. Cabinet posts were then shared between Liberal and Conservative politicians. However, despite the advantages accruing from an increasingly successful diversification into non-traditional exports, and from the rapid rise in the price of coffee (Colombia's major export) after the 1975 frost destroyed trees in Brazil, the political situation remained difficult through 1975 and 1976. A bank strike in early 1975 was followed by considerable disturbances in the National University, particularly in the Medical Faculty; these led to a doctors' strike in May, and to the dismissal of the radical Rector of the National University, Luis Carlos Pérez. A state of siege was declared on 6 June 1975. With Congressional and Municipal elections due to take place in April 1976, López Michelsen planned to discontinue the state of siege by the beginning of the year, but in the event splits in his own party over the choice of a candidate for the 1978 elections for the Presidency, combined with a scandal within the military arising from the conducting of a trial after the assassination of a senior General, and a wave of strikes and civil unrest, made this inadvisable. As the elections approached, public servants, bank workers, and teachers were again on strike, and the military occupation of the University in March was followed by a number of student deaths, while the dismissed Rector, Luis Carlos Pérez, emerged as the leftist candidate for 1978. The April elections were a defeat for the system as a whole, as only 25 per cent of those eligible to vote actually did so, and for Alfonso López Michelsen himself, for while the Liberal Party as a whole gained 50 per cent of the vote (to 40 per cent by the Conservatives), his faction within the party lost out to the "Group of Ninety" of Julio César Turbay, the Colombian Ambassador in Washington. The state of siege was lifted on 22 June, but was reimposed amid a new medical workers' strike, trouble in the University and a cabinet reorganisation. It remains to be seen whether Colombia's recent economic prosperity will be translated into political peace. In September 1977 a general strike took place against the President's economic and social policy.

CUBA.

Cuba, since the coming to power of Fidel Castro in the 1959 revolution, has caught the headlines when its impact on international politics has been most marked—with the Bay of Pigs invasion, the Missile Crisis, Che Guevara's disappearance from Cuba in 1965, his subsequent Bolivian campaign and his death at the hands of the Bolivian military, and, more recently, with the sending of Cuban troops to aid the MPLA in Angola; but in the meantime, significant developments have taken place within Cuba itself. While Cuba has moved firmly into the Socialist camp, there are indications that the relaxations in its isolation from the West may proceed further; meanwhile, however, despite ambitious plans for diversification, and despite considerable achievements in social policy, it remains heavily dependent on the production of sugar as its major export crop.

Cuba's alignment with the Soviet bloc was complete by the early sixties, although Castro continued to insist on supporting Latin-American guerrilla movements not supported by orthodox Communist parties in the region. During the same period, economic dependence on the USSR was enforced by the US blockade, and by the 1962 expulsion of Cuba from the Organisation of American States (OAS). The achievements of the revolution in health, education and housing are no longer a matter for dispute; and while some food rationing continues, starvation and abject poverty have disappeared. However, ambitious plans for vast programmes of public spending and social welfare have forced reliance on sugar to earn foreign exchange or trade goods from Russia, and after early denigrations of sugar, increasing efforts have been made to boost production, even at the expense of other sectors of the economy. This produced a crisis, which enabled the USSR to demand a fuller implementation of Soviet-aided central planning, and one result of this was the modification of earlier schemes of "moral incentives" and ruthlessly egalitarian wage structures, and their replacement by a system of material incentives for increases in labour productivity. Helped by these moves, by the rising price of sugar on world markets, and by a 1972 agreement that debts to the Soviet Union would be paid off only after 1986. the Cuban economy recovered well, recording a small trade surplus in 1974, and attracting a number of foreign loans in 1975. However, the rapid decline in the world price of sugar to extremely low levels by 1977 with little immediate prospect for improvement is substantial surpluses were still being produced, threatened steady growth once more, and caused a cutback in investment planned for the 1976–80 period.

During recent years, Cuba has moved towards the development of a system of popular government within a constitutional framework, though always in the context of a single party state. In 1973, a new system of local courts was set up with lay judges acting with legal guidance, and in 1974 an experiment in " popular power " took place in Matanzas province, with the election in June and July of a 68-member provincial assembly. The experiment was declared a success. and in 1975 a draft constitution was produced for discussion at local level. On 17 December 1975, 3,000 delegates gathered for the First Congress of the Cuban Communist Party, and heard Castro describe in detail various CIA plots to assassinate him, then announce that the new constitution would be submitted to a national plebiscite. It was thus tested in February 1976, and went into effect on the 24th of that month. In October 1976 indirect elections took place to provincial and national assemblies, as a prelude to the election of a council of state. The latter was constituted in December with Castro as its chairman.

Cuban intervention in Africa, and especially their military presence in Angola in support of the MPLA from 1975 onwards, marked a new adventurism in foreign relations. Official visits by Castro and other leading politicians were clearly designed to promote co-operation with the " progressive " states of East Africa. Arms were also supplied for the activities of the Patriotic Front in Rhodesia and for the " front-line states ". However, Cuba was also becoming increasingly obliged to take sides in struggles of Africans against other Africans, as opposed to whites or mercenaries as previously. This was the case in the conflict between MPLA and UNITA in Angola and that between Somalia and Ethiopia, as well as the invasion of Zaire from Angola. In some instances the Cubans found themselves supporting regimes whose reputation was not good even in Africa. In any case the widespread commitment of soldiers, advisers and money in Africa threatened to surpass Cuba's resources. This may have contributed to Castro's willingness to seek normalisation of relations with the United States, since Cuba was still suffering from the economic blockade, even though it had been considerably relaxed. In 1975 the USA had accepted the OAS decision to leave the question of relations with Cuba to individual states to decide, many Latin American states having already resumed relations despite the 1962 ban. As for the USA itself, substantial opposition remained in Congress to any rapprochement. Nevertheless, the Carter administration began by relaxing travel restrictions and the trade embargo, and diplomatic relations were restored during 1977.

MEXICO.

Mexico has for many years enjoyed a reputation for political stability and steady economic growth, and if the first of these seemed under threat when Luis Echeverria Alvarez inherited the presidency in 1970, the second seemed more in danger when he left it in 1976. However, the changes introduced by his successor, together with the huge oil deposits revealed early in 1977, may ensure the stability and prosperity of the Institutional Revolutionary Party (PRI) and of the country for the foreseeable future.

Echeverria came to the Presidency in 1970 in difficult circumstances, in the wake of the student massacre which preceded the 1968 Olympic Games, held in Mexico; he himself, as Minister of the Interior in the Diaz Ordaz government (1964–1970) had been partially responsible for the incident, and had to face considerable initial hostility, despite his being elected with 84 per cent of the popular vote. The complete dominance of the PRI itself was confirmed, with all sixty seats in the Senate, and practically ninety per cent of all seats in the Chamber of Deputies. In the first years of his administration however Echeverria presided over a period of rapid economic expansion, and inaugurated a political style marked by conciliation, liberalisation, and radical rhetoric. Countering the steady trend to the right of the PRI in the latter sixties, Echeverria gained considerable support. However, he antagonised the strong and conservative group of industrialists based on Monterrey, and failed to convince the student left of his sincerity in proposing reform. The price of his ambitious programme was a growing balance of payments deficit, and rates of inflation which while low by Latin American and even by recent British standards, were unusual in Mexico. 1972 saw a reform aimed at strengthening the small opposition parties in Mexico, by granting them a sliding quota of seats in the Chamber of Deputies if they obtained nationally a minimum share of the vote, and in 1973 Echeverria turned his attention to the international arena, promoting his " Third World " manifesto, the " Charter of Economic Rights and Duties of States ", engaging in prolonged overseas tours, and, on 31 May, calling jointly with the President of Guatemala for a " New Economic Order " to protect the legitimate interests of the Third World bloc. Meanwhile the domestic economy was suffering, shaken both by US inflation after the oil price rise. and by the demands of Echeverria's expansionist programme, which called for heavy state investment. Inflation in 1973 reached 18 per cent, and it was argued that the Mexican peso (unchanged at 12·5 to the dollar since 1954) was over-valued, and that exports were suffering as a result. Echeverria was confronted with a dual problem in the closing years of his administration – a deteriorating economic situation, and growing hostility from conservatives to his increasingly radical pronouncements and his statist policies.

Despite the problems, the PRI had no difficulty in choosing its candidate for the 1976 elections, or in winning them handsomely, and the surprise choice, Treasury Secretary José López Portillo, a man with little organised political support, but a close and long-standing friend of Echeverría himself, was duly elected on 4 July to take office on 1 December 1976.

Mexico's economic problems

The economic situation was, however, rapidly becoming more critical. In the wake of a Mexican vote in the United Nations equating Zionism with racism, Jewish associations in the United States declared a boycott on tourism in Mexico, and although it was short-lived, Mexico's income from tourism began to fall. A growing trade deficit, and heavy speculation against the peso, provoked an unexpectedly early devaluation in August 1976. By the time López Portillo took power, the peso had lost more than half its international value. Echeverría's parting gesture was to hand over to landless peasants 100,000 hectares of prime agricultural land in Northern Mexico. However, López Portillo came to office proclaiming that he would look more to the interests of private enterprise, and in the same month a federal court ruled that the land transfer was illegal. The peso made a slight recovery, but it remained to be seen whether Mexico could emerge from its pressing economic problems, or whether López Portillo could handle the political problems with which he had been presented. The first signs were that he was winning from the conservative labour unions some support for his policies.

PERU.

Until 1975 it seemed that the military regime which seized power in Peru in 1968 might be, in contrast to the regimes in power in 1975 in Argentina, Bolivia, Brazil, Chile and Uruguay a genuinely progressive and reforming force; these hopes were somewhat dashed by the replacement in 1975 of President Velasco by Morales Bermúdez and by an economic crisis which forced harsh policies in 1976. While many of the reforms of the revolutionary period, including the major nationalisations and the programme of land reform remained largely untouched, it appeared at the beginning of 1977 that the Government might be embarking on a policy of open repression.

The military intervention of October 1968 came after a troubled period in which the reforms promised by civilian President Fernando Belaúnde were soon blocked by a hostile Congress; as the economic situation worsened, the Government coalition (formed by the Popular Action Party and the Christian Democrats) collapsed in 1967. A substantial and unpopular devaluation in the same year was followed by the announcement late in 1968 of an agreement with the International Petroleum Company over ownership of disputed deposits and the pricing of crude oil; this provoked nationalists within the military, already dissatisfied with Belaúnde's inability to achieve reforms, to remove him from power and send him into exile. The government of General Juan Velasco immediately repudiated the agreements, and expropriated the IPC oil interests, then embarked on an ambitious programme of social and economic reform. The Government went on to establish state control over fishmeal, fish oil and minerals, and to set limits to the role foreign capital could play in Peru; it also developed a scheme of workers' participation in industry based on the concept of " industrial communities ", which were intended, over a period of years, to transfer the ownership of the enterprise to the workers themselves. It also set up SINAMOS (Office for Social Mobilisation), under General Leonidas Rodriguez, to organise and rally political support for the regime. By 1971 foreign oil companies were allowed into Peru again, and pressing debt problems led to attempts, unsuccessful until 1972, to obtain from major creditors a rescheduling agreement. Despite these problems,

and the ecological crisis which caused, in 1972 and 1973, the practical disappearance of the rich anchovy shoals on which the lucrative and expanding fishmeal industry depends. Velasco moved ahead with his programme of reforms, nationalising the fishmeal and fish oil industries in 1973, placing newspapers under government control in 1974, and nationalising the American Cerro de Pasco mining company at the end of that year. 1975 opened with the announcement that the agrarian reform programme, which had already placed the rich coastal sugar plantations under co-operative ownership, was to be extended; but a police strike, and possible coup attempt in February, followed by riots and widespread unrest, led to the declaration of a state of emergency. It came, however, as a surprise when Velasco, admittedly already seriously ill at the time, was replaced in a bloodless coup on 29 August 1975 by Prime Minister Morales Bermúdez, and despite initial claims that the continuity of the revolution was assured, it gradually became clear that a substantial shift to the right was taking place, and that *velasquistas* were being removed from positions of influence. An apparent attempt to seize power from the right by General Briceño on 13 February 1976 was foiled, but at the same time Morales Bermúdez was moving to strengthen private enterprise, to impose a programme of austerity in the face of threatened international insolvency, and to tempt back national and foreign investment. He offered an amnesty to former dissidents, but his attempt at rapprochement with the conservative forces of APRA (American Popular Revolutionary Alliance) was blocked by sectors of the army still hostile to their traditional opponents. By May it was apparent that the financial crisis was acute, and that Peru's only recourse was to seek an accommodation with her creditors on the terms available. On 28 June the sol was devalued by 31 per cent, and 1 July a national state of emergency was declared. A further attempt at a coup from the right was also foiled, but was followed on 16 July by the resignation of Prime Minister Fernández Maldonado; this signified the elimination of the *velasquistas* from positions of major influence. He was replaced as Prime Minister, War Minister and Commander-in-Chief of the Army by General Guillermo Arbulu Galliani. In November 1976 the announcement of the formation of a Socialist Revolutionary Party by Velasco supporters was announced; but in January 1977 founders of the party, including General Leonidas Rodriguez, were exiled.

In February, however, an outline plan for preparing free elections and a new constitution was published, under which political parties could resume their activities. President Morales Bermúdez later announced that elections would be held in 1980 and lifted the state of emergency. October 1977 saw the publication of the " Tupac–Amaru " Plan for social and political development up to 1980, and in November came a law providing for the holding of general elections to a constitutive assembly in June 1978, and the repeal of censorship provisions.

URUGUAY.

After a long history of democracy, prosperity, and advanced social welfare, Uruguay has become the victim of one of the most repressive and totalitarian regimes in Latin America, with its essentially pastoral economy in a state of extreme crisis.

The process of militarisation is relatively recent; total domination of the Government by the Colorado (Liberal) party only ended in 1958, when the Blanco (National) party, led by Luis Alberto de Herrera, came to power. It held power narrowly in the 1962 elections, but 1966 saw the return of the Colorados, and the reintroduction of the Presidential system, which had been abandoned in 1951 for a National Council of Government. President Jorge Pacheco Areco sought throughout his term of office to retain the presidency beyond 1971, but a referendum conducted simultaneously with the November 1971 elections failed to win popular acceptance for the idea; he had been involved throughout 1971 in attempts to gain special powers, largely to deal with the challenge presented by the Tupamaros, the urban guerrilla movement which had scored a number of spectacular successes in 1970 and 1971, culminating in the mass escape from Punta Carretas prison of 109 detainees, including the guerrilla leader Raúl Sendic himself. Pacheco's attempt to extend his own powers were blocked by Congress, and he narrowly escaped being impeached and removed from office. The November 1971 elections saw the emergence as President of the Colorado candidate, Juan Maria Bordaberry, confirmed by the Supreme Court in February 1972 and installed on 1 March. His first act in office was to order a massive devaluation of the currency, causing considerable discontent among the urban population. As Bordaberry sought to co-ordinate army and police activity to contain the threat from the Tupamaros (and succeeded in destroying the guerrilla group almost completely) the army began to play a more prominent role. In February 1973 the Army itself demanded an officially recognised role in government, and the National Security Council was formed, despite opposition from Congress and from the traditional political parties. On 27 June 1973, with the support of the army, Bordaberry dissolved Congress, declared a state of emergency, and continued to govern by decree and increasingly as a representative of the Armed Forces. On 29 October, the National University was closed. An atmosphere of increasing repression was made more difficult by rapid inflation throughout 1974, reaching over 100 per cent by the end of the year, while EEC regulations suspending imports of beef from outside the community threatened Uruguay's beef industry with disaster. Opposition grew throughout 1975, and detention and torture by the omnipresent security forces became more common; in November, these forces began a massive operation against suspected Communists, in which dozens of army officers were arrested, and as many again sought refuge in foreign embassies. Plans for elections were dropped and Bordaberry sought support from the army for his continuance in power beyond his constitutional term. Despite pressures from the marginalised political parties and from the United States Embassy for a return to a limited form of constitutionalism, the Army Commander-in-Chief announced on 18 May 1976 that Bordaberry would remain in the Presidency. However, in a remarkable *volte face*, the armed forces withdrew their support from Bordaberry a month later, and he was forced to resign. He was temporarily replaced by the 79-year-old head of the Council of State, Alberto Demichelli. On 14 July 1976, Dr. Aparicio Mendez, who had replaced Demichelli as the head of the Council of State, and was himself 71 years old, was chosen to succeed to the Presidency; he duly took office on 1 September. His first acts were to withdraw political rights from hundreds of Uruguayan citizens, and to dissolve the Supreme Court, announcing that its functions would henceforth be carried out by the Ministry of Justice. Subsequently the pro-US Minister of the Economy, Vegh Villegas, was forced to resign.

At the end of the year the United States Congress, annoyed at the course taken by the Uruguayan armed forces, voted to cut off military aid to Uruguay, and in February 1977 the Secretary of State of the new Carter administration, Cyrus Vance, told a Senate Committee that foreign aid to Uruguay had been cut by President Carter because of Uruguay's record of persistent human rights violations. With 3 million dollars of military credits already cut off, economic assistance to Uruguay fell from 220,000 to 25,000 dollars. It seems over-optimistic, however, to believe that Uruguay will enjoy democratic government again in the near future. When President Mendez announced that elections were planned for 1981, he said that only the traditional parties—the " Blancos " and the " Colorados " would be allowed to take part.

VENEZUELA.

The sub-continental trend towards military dictatorship has been reversed in Venezuela, which has been ruled by constitutionally elected civilian Presidents since the elections of 1959, which followed the overthrow in 1958 of the dictator Marcos Pérez Jiménez. Since then, Venezuela's increasing oil wealth has brought it consid-

erable prosperity, and a surge of industrial development.

Two parties have dominated recent Venezuelan politics. The first is the Democratic Action party (AD) which maintains a nationalistic stance but has moved steadily to the centre right after its founding as a radical alternative in 1941; the second is the Social Christian Party (COPEI) founded in 1946 to promote reformist policies favoured by currents within the Catholic Church. It is essentially a Christian Democrat party. Each of the parties has been dominated since its foundation by one man – the Democratic Action party by Romulo Betancourt, COPEI by Dr. Rafael Caldera.

During the first years of constitutional government, Venezuela was governed by coalitions. The winner of the 1959 Presidential elections, Romulo Betancourt, formed a coalition with COPEI, but his successor, Dr. Raúl Leoni, also of AD, when he came to power in 1964, governed in coalition not with COPEI, but with two smaller parties, the URD (Democratic and Republican Union Party), and the FND (National Democratic Front). In December 1968 the elections were won by Dr. Rafael Caldera, but although COPEI gained the Presidency, it had only a minority in Congress, and formed a working coalition with AD. Caldera attempted to put a stop to guerrilla activity which had been spreading through the country particularly after the Cuban Revolution; he legalised the Communist Party, and invited dissidents to express their views through the system but was unsuccessful in achieving an end to guerrilla activity. The run of coalitions was ended by the spectacular success of AD in the elections of December 1973; its candidate, Carlos Andrés Pérez, won the Presidency with practically 50 per cent of the vote, and the party won commanding majorities in Congress, with 183 seats in the Chamber of Deputies, and 42 in the Senate.

Venezuela was one of the founder members of OPEC, which was formed in January 1961 in the Venezuelan capital, Caracas, and measures were taken during the sixties to boost Venezuela's income from the operation of foreign-owned oil companies operating in Venezuela. In 1971 the state assumed a monopoly of sales of oil products within Venezuela, and the Oil Reversion Bill stipulated that all installations would be nationalised when existing contracts ran out in 1983. With the growing strength of OPEC, and the spectacular rise in the price of crude oil, stronger policies were however adopted, and on 29 August 1975, the year in which iron ore deposits and mining operations were also nationalised, a decree was published declaring that all installations and oil fields would become the property of the state on 1 January 1976. Over the same period, the increasingly nationalistic stance of the Government was shown in the growing international prominence of President Pérez as a spokesman for the interests of the Third World. Nationalisation went ahead smoothly as planned, with production being well maintained. Venezuela has vast proven reserves of oil.

Venezuela has recently abandoned its cautious policy of spending only from its own reserves, and announced plans early in 1976 to invest 14 billion dollars by 1978: this will require considerable borrowing on international markets, but there is unlikely to be any major problem in attracting loans.

Early in 1977 it was reported in the United States that in the past the CIA had made considerable personal payments to President Pérez, but such reports were unanimously denounced in Venezuela as an attempt to besmirch his considerable reputation as a nationalist, and to damage a leading opponent of United States policy.

AUSTRALIA AND NEW ZEALAND

In the sixties, the Liberal–Country coalition in Australia and the National Party in New Zealand were able to consolidate and extend their power at the expense of the Labour Party in each country. During 1968 and 1969 Labour opposition to participation in the Vietnam war increased in strength; this feeling combined with new leadership within each Labour party and, in Australia in particular, a feeling that the ruling party had

" lost its steam." But in the 1969 elections the ruling parties just maintained their leads.

With Britain joining the European Community, both Australia and New Zealand sought closer relations with their neighbours. New Zealand began a search for new markets for her agricultural products, especially in Japan and Latin America. Australia made an agreement with Japan on the peaceful use of atomic energy and one with Indonesia on the provision of defence and economic aid. Both countries have established diplomatic relations with China. On 1 November 1972 Mr. McMahon announced that the Australian High Commission in Britain would no longer be the responsibility of the Prime Minister's office but of the Foreign Office. This announcement came a day after publication of the new immigration regulations in Britain as a consequence of EEC entry: Australia pointed out that EEC citizens would now have easier entry to Britain than citizens of Commonwealth countries.

Elections in 1972 brought the long expected victories of the Labour Parties, under Mr. Gough Whitlam in Australia (who thus became the first Labour Prime Minister since 1949), and Mr. Kirk in New Zealand (succeeded by Mr. Rowling in 1974). Apart from a vote for new faces these victories perhaps contained some nationalist elements: old alliances were no longer found so useful. Both victors promised the end of conscription. Mr. Whitlam's government was returned with a reduced majority in 1974.

Both countries were foremost in the world-wide protests at the French nuclear tests carried out in the atmosphere on Mururoa Atoll in the South Pacific during the summer of 1973. Only after France announced in 1974 that in future tests would only be carried out underground did relations improve.

The greater participation in Asian affairs appears slowly to be moderating Australia's traditional immigration policies. Since 1945 some three million people have settled in the country of which almost half have had assisted passages. Over half have come from Britain and more than 100,000 from each of Italy, Greece, the Netherlands, and Germany. But more than 50,000 have been admitted from Asian and African countries including 16,000 Chinese and Japanese. From 1973 non-white racial characteristics no longer constitute an obstacle to immigration though in general immigration is permitted only for those with relations in Australia and for skilled workers. As from January 1975 white citizens of Britain, Ireland, Canada and Fiji require visas before visiting or settling in Australia, thus ending long-standing preferential treatment. (New Zealand had also introduced restrictions on British and Irish immigrants.)

During 1975 the opposition Liberal–Country majority in the Australian Senate blocked approval of the budget for months, thus condemning the Whitlam government to impotence. The deadlock was eventually broken by a very controversial decision of the Governor to dismiss the Prime Minister. The constitutional conflict which thus flared up, added to economic problems and dissension about the Government's socialist measures, poisoned the atmosphere of the ensuing election campaign. The election in December 1975 was won by the conservative opposition led by Mr. Malcolm Fraser. The Liberal–Country coalition won their largest majority in Australian political history. A new inner cabinet was created and to deal with economic problems a new Department of Productivity was established in November 1976 taking over the functions of other departments. A similar trend was experienced in New Zealand with the decisive defeat of the Labour government by the Nationalist party led by Robert Muldoon.

In 1977 the Governor-General of Australia, Sir John Kerr, resigned in the face of mounting criticism from Labour Party supporters and constitutional lawyers who disputed the legitimacy of his dismissal of Mr. Whitlam. However, after general elections called in December 1977 had resulted in Labour winning only one-third of the seats in the House of Representatives and a gain of 7% for the governing coalition, Mr. Whitlam himself retired from politics. This Liberal-Country victory was achieved despite growing unrest about unemployment.

DÉTENTE

The Partial Nuclear Test-Ban Treaty.

This important treaty was signed in Moscow in August 1963 between Britain, the USA, and the USSR who undertook not to conduct nuclear tests in three out of four possible spheres—in the atmosphere, in outer space and under water. The fourth possibility—underground tests—was not touched by the Treaty (but see below). The USA and Britain insist that since no foolproof method of identifying underground explosions has been devised, a ban would require a limited number of on-the-spot inspections. But Russia rejects this on the grounds that it would amount to espionage.

Treaty to Prevent Spread of Nuclear Weapons.

At the 18-power Conference at Geneva in 1967 a draft treaty was tabled by the US and USSR, which was then amended to meet some of the demands of the non-nuclear powers. In the UN General Assembly it was adopted by 95 votes to 4, with 21 abstentions. One of the countries that voted against was India which was dissatisfied with the guarantees against China. The Nuclear Non-Proliferation Treaty was signed in London, Moscow, and Washington on 1 July 1968. It came into force on 5 March 1970. In May 1975 a conference was held in Geneva to review the treaty. A large majority of countries have ratified or at least signed it. But of existing nuclear powers China and France have not signed, in common with several countries which are thought to have nuclear potential, such as Israel, Pakistan, Saudi Arabia, Spain and some South American countries.

Seabed Treaty.

A treaty was signed in February 1971 by the three nuclear powers, Britain, the US, and Russia, and by 64 other countries, banning nuclear weapons from the seabed. France and China did not sign.

Biological Weapons Convention 1972.

A treaty outlawing biological warfare was signed on 10 April 1972 by Britain, the US and Russia, banning the future production and requiring the destruction of stockpiles of agents of biological warfare. It came into force in March 1975.

Nuclear Arms and SALT.

A desire to attempt control of the burgeoning strategic arms stockpiles of the two superpowers has been an urgent goal ever since the Cuban missile crisis when the horrific possibility of nuclear war was brought to the forefront of men's fears. In 1969, formal bilateral negotiations began in Helsinki between the United States and Soviet Union. These Strategic Arms Limitation Talks (SALT) culminated in 1972 when President Nixon visited Moscow and with Mr. Brezhnev signed two important documents. The first, the ABM Treaty, limited the number of anti-ballistic missile defence systems that the two countries could construct. A 1974 protocol has further limited each side to one system each, and the US has now abandoned the one it had defending an ICBM (intercontinental ballistic missile) field. The Soviet Union maintains one, early technology ABM system around Moscow. The two countries were motivated to achieve these agreements not only by the enormous cost of the systems themselves, but also by the further offensive developments they would provoke in an attempt to overcome their defensive capabilities.

The second part of SALT I was an interim agreement on limiting strategic offensive weapons, which expires in October 1977. The Soviets were allowed a numerical superiority which was offset by US technological superiority, especially in the area of MIRV's (multiple independently targetable re-entry vehicles), which allow as many as 12 targets to be attacked with one missile. At a meeting between Mr. Brezhnev and President Ford at Vladivostok in November 1974, an agreement was reached that a ceiling of 2400 strategic nuclear delivery vehicles should be the basis of a

SALT II accord which would run until 1985, and would have to be reached before the interim agreement expired.

One of the major difficulties in SALT is the inability of negotiators and politicians to keep up with technological developments. The main sticking point in progress towards SALT II was the US development of the B-1 bomber and, more importantly, the cruise missile which is extremely accurate, cheap to build and small and therefore difficult to detect. On the Soviet side, the Backfire bomber worries US analysts.

In September 1977 SALT I was extended until such time as a SALT II agreement was reached. The latter is expected to be ready for signature during 1978, being made possible mainly by an envisaged play-off between cruise missiles and Backfire bombers. The aim is to interlock the ever more specific limitations on strategic arms so as to achieve that parity which was not brought about by SALT I because of the concession by the United States, relying on its own technological superiority, of numerical superiority of the Soviet Union.

WESTERN EUROPEAN ORGANISATIONS

The North Atlantic Treaty Organisation.

The founder members of the Pact in 1949 were Great Britain, the USA, Canada, France, Holland, Belgium, Luxembourg, Italy, Denmark, Norway, Iceland, and Portugal. The parties agreed that an armed attack against one or more of them in Europe or North America shall be considered an attack against them all and consequently they agreed that if such an armed attack occurs, each of them in exercise of the right of individual or collective self-defence recognised by the Charter of the UN, will assist the party so attacked. Greece and Turkey joined NATO in 1952. In 1966 France withdrew from NATO military organisations, though not from the Alliance.

The conflict over Cyprus between two of its members in 1974 was acutely embarrassing for NATO. Greece withdrew its armed forces from NATO in 1974, and during 1974–5 relations between the United States and Turkey deteriorated, particularly with the cutting off of US defence-aid and "nationalisation" of US bases in Turkey. NATO's south-eastern flank looked in considerable disarray.

With a gradual easing of tensions between Greece and Turkey over both the Aegean Sea and the Cyprus dispute, the situation improved, but still remains a crucial NATO problem.

The Search for Détente.

Force levels continue to be a major worry for the Alliance, whose conventional strength is so inferior to that of the Soviet bloc as to lead to a dangerous, and sometimes not very credible, reliance on nuclear weapons. Reductions of defence expenditure by Britain and other members create difficulties for NATO. There is also a wasteful reduplication of effort and resources and an impaired capacity for working together caused by the failure of the Alliance (unlike the Warsaw Pact) to co-ordinate arms production and procurement, since national interests predominate.

NATO policies continue to be based, sometimes rather uneasily, on the twin concepts of deterrence and détente. The latter aim prompted acceptance of a Conference on Security and Co-operation in Europe (CSCE), long campaigned for by the Soviet Union. NATO's preconditions for such a conference were met by the Berlin settlement and by the required progress in the talks between East and West Germany as well as the SALT negotiations (see above). Above all the USSR agreed to parallel talks on mutual and balanced force reductions in Europe (MBFR), as frequently proposed by NATO (an urgent subject in view of the threats by some countries to reduce unilaterally their commitment to NATO).

The CSCE finally opened in Helsinki in July 1973 with 35 foreign ministers taking part (representing all the European countries except Albania, plus the USA and Canada). The agenda concluded by the preparatory consultations was grouped under four heads: (1) Questions relating to security in Europe; (2) Co-operation in the fields of science and technology and of the environment; (3) Co-operation in humanitarian and other fields (the result of the insistence of the West and the neutral countries on the inclusion of self-determination and human rights in the catalogue of principles); (4) Follow-up to the Conference. In October the MBFR talks began in Vienna between NATO and the Warsaw Pact states.

The stage thus seemed set for decisive steps on multilateral détente. But the momentum was halted in a mass of detail. At the CSCE the West demanded 60 days' notice for manoeuvres and sizeable troop movements; the USSR refused to look more than 5 days ahead or to talk about troop movements at all. Moscow tried to turn "inviolability" of borders into "unchangeability", and raised the old barriers against proposals for the free movement of persons and information. The third and final stage of the Conference ended in August 1975. The MBFR talks (like SALT II: see above) were held up by Soviet insistence on superiority. The East European countries consider the present power relations in Central Europe with 770,000 NATO ground troops facing 925,000 of the Warsaw Pact (excluding Hungary) as balanced already. Moscow wants to stabilise this ratio at a lower level and proposes a 17% reduction on both sides between 1975 and 1977. The West demands 700,000 on each side, amounting to a 20% reduction for the Warsaw Pact, 10% for NATO. By December 1975 the West had shown willingness to include a reduction of their tactical nuclear weapons and air force strengths in exchange for reduced Warsaw Pact tank contingents.

As with SALT, talks came to a standstill in 1976 due largely to the US Presidential elections. President Ford even dropped the word "détente" from his vocabulary. During 1977 the main problem was discrepancies in the data on Warsaw Pact forces given by NATO and the Warsaw Pact.

The Council of Europe.

This body was formed in 1949 and now has 19 member nations. It has a Committee of Ministers and a Parliamentary Assembly. Headquarters are at Strasbourg. The Parliamentary Assembly is empowered to debate and make recommendations upon any matter which (i) is referred to it by the Committee of Ministers with a request for its opinion, or (ii) has been approved by the Committee. It consists of 147 members elected by their national parliaments, who sit grouped in political parties irrespective of their nationality. The Committee of Ministers is the Council's executive organ and is not responsible to the Assembly, but merely reports to it.

Future Role of the Council.—The Council remains in doubt about its future rôle, particularly now that Britain and the other candidates for Common Market entry have been admitted. Its condemnation of Greece in 1970 demonstrated that it has a claim to be the collective voice of European democratic opinion. (Greece had withdrawn when it became clear that a majority would vote for her suspension for repudiating the values which the Council exists to uphold. She was readmitted in 1974 after the return to democratic government.) It has a reasonably impressive record in encouragement of reciprocal social service arrangements, co-ordination of medical standards, harmonisation of law, and youth exchanges. In January 1977 all member states except Ireland and Malta signed an important convention on the suppression of terrorism. It can also hope to act as a bridge between the EEC countries and the other members.

Meanwhile the most important achievements of the Council have been in the implementation of the Human Rights Convention under which the member states guarantee the recognition of fundamental rights within their territories.

The European Free Trade Association.

In November 1958 France rejected the British proposals for linking the six European common-market nations with the eleven other OEEC countries in a free-trade area.

Thereupon seven countries outside the area of the Six formed a European Free Trade Association.

They were Great Britain, Austria, Denmark, Norway, Portugal, Sweden, and Switzerland. Between them tariffs on industrial goods were actually abolished faster than in the EEC, but member states retained separate external systems. The Seven were later joined by Finland as an associate member and Iceland as a full member. When EFTA was formed, its member nations confidently expected that the EEC would soon see the error of its ways and agree to the creation of a vast European free trade zone. In the event, EFTA members saw their error first, with three members of the original seven starting negotiations with the EEC in 1961. The same three once again began negotiations with the EEC in June 1970. In the event a national referendum in Norway decided against entry, but in joining the EEC Britain and Denmark left EFTA. However the others decided on maintaining co-operation in the EFTA framework, although they all also concluded agreements with the EEC on the phased establishment of a free |trade area. This came into force on 1 July 1977 and covers a market of 300 million people.

Organisation for Economic Co-operation and Development.

This body took the place of OEEC in 1961. Canada and the United States, who were associated members of OEEC, joined with the eighteen member countries of that body to set it up. Its broader objectives were to achieve in Europe the highest sustainable economic growth, employment, and standard of living; to contribute to economic development; and to expand world trade on a multilateral and non-discriminatory basis. Japan has also joined. It has recently been concerned with co-ordinating the responses of the oil-consuming countries to the world energy situation and in April in 1975 it also established a $25,000 million " safety net " fund for the mutual support of members in case of severe balance of payments difficulties arising from increased oil prices.

In January 1977 reports from the OECD warned of further energy crises for its members as a result of the continual growth in energy consumption.

The European Economic Community.

The EEC was formed in 1958, growing out of the European Coal and Steel Community, a supra-national body set up in 1952 for the co-ordination of coal and steel production in West Germany, Belgium, Holland, Luxembourg, France, and Italy. The EEC is unquestionably the strongest and most significant of all European organisations and the only one which provides any sort of basis for West European unity. Other bodies, such as the Council of Europe and the European Free Trade Area (EFTA) as well as regional associations like the Nordic Council and the Benelux Economic Union now stand outside the mainstream of European political and economic development.

The Treaty of Rome, 1957, which had established the European Economic Community defined (in Articles 2 and 3) the principles and objects for which the Community is to work. Those articles specify in detail the steps for creating a Common Market, for approximating the economic policies of member States, the promotion of harmonious development of economic activities, and raising the standard of living. But the aim of " closer relations between its member States " is stated without elaboration. It is into this gap that speculation is poured. No limit is set in the Treaty to the process of integration; on the other hand there is no commitment to join a Federation of Europe. While member States commit themselves to a common policy on a number of economic issues there will be co-ordination of national policies designed to take account of the needs of the rest of the Community.

The Organs of EEC.

The machinery of government of the European Economic Community consists of:

1. The Council of Ministers
2. The Commission
3. The Court
4. The Parliament or Assembly

The Council of Ministers issues regulations and decisions which are binding in law on all member States. It consists of one minister from each member State. Although the treaties provide for many decisions to be taken by an ordinary or qualified majority (the latter protecting the interests of the smaller states), in practice almost all decisions require unanimity.

The Council represents national interests. " If federation is unity in diversity, the Commission represents the unity and the Council the diversity. The balancing of individual interests and Community interests is accomplished by discussions between these institutions, culminating in the meetings of the Council of Ministers " (the words of Walter Hallstein, former President of the European Community).

The Commission.—Whereas the Council consists of politicians the Commission consists of permanent officials. It has 13 members—2 each from Britain, France, Germany and Italy, one from each of the other countries. They are the custodians of the supranational idea and are pledged to complete independence from national control. The business of the Commission is to further the general purposes of the treaties of the Communities and decisions are by majority vote. From the Commission flow two streams:

(a) Proposals, which it sends to the Council.

(b) Under powers of its own:

1. Decisions to named countries and binding on them.

2. Directives to named countries to achieve certain results, without specifying the means.

3. Recommendations and Opinions, which are not binding.

4. Authorisations without which many things are forbidden.

The Court, whose procedure is wholly Continental, consists of nine Judges appointed by Governments for a maximum of six years. Its word is final on the interpretation of the Treaty, on the rules made under the Treaty, and on the legality of all the actions of the organs of the Community.

European Parliament.—The Parliament or Assembly consists of nominated representatives of the national Parliaments, sitting according to party affiliation and not nationality. There are at present 198 representatives in all—36 members each from Britain, France, Italy, and the German Federal Republic; 14 each from Belgium and the Netherlands; 10 from Ireland and Denmark; six from Luxembourg. The European Parliament has no legislative or executive powers, but it debates all major policy issues, scrutinises legislation and has recently been granted control over a limited part of the Community's budget. Its members may question the Council and Commission. It can, by a two-thirds majority, enforce the resignation of the entire Commission. but the power to reappoint lies with the Council of Ministers. Plans were agreed for the doubling of members of the Parliament through direct elections in 1978. The British decision to elect British members by the traditional British system and not by proportional representation meant that the deadline could not be met.

Expansion of the EEC.

After a summit meeting of the Six in the Hague in December 1969 had agreed on the principle of enlargement of the Communities, Britain opened negotiations in June 1970 on its third attempt to join the Common Market. The application had been made by the Labour Government, but it fell to the new Conservative Government actually to begin the talks. Denmark, Norway, and the Rep. of Ireland had applied at the same time.

Progress in the negotiations was laborious until the Paris summit conference between Mr. Heath and President Pompidou in May 1971, which opened the way for British entry to the European Community. The two men declared themselves in agreement on the future shape of the Community—loose confederation (not a federal structure), respect for national interests, and the special position of the French language—as well as on Europe's relationship with the outside world and especially with the United States always a crucial point for the French. They also agreed on the phasing out of the rôle of sterling as a reserve currency and on safeguarding the interests of New Zealand and the Commonwealth sugar producers. The misjudgements and bitterness of the British " No " to the Coal and Steel Community and the EEC and the French " Non " to British entry in 1963 and 1967 had now been exorcised.

However it was not until 28 June 1971 in Luxembourg that M. Schumann, the French Foreign Minister and Mr. Rippon, the chief British negotiator, officially announced agreement on the detailed terms of entry. They were largely concerned with transitional arrangements for Britain's adaptation to the rules of the Common Market. They were accompanied by the Government's enthusiastic recommendation of this acceptance. On 28 October the House of Commons voted in favour of the principle of entry on these terms with a majority of 112, the Lords with a majority of 393. Some details remained to be worked out. Of the eventual terms of accession, apart from provisions for the representation of new members on the various Community bodies and arrangements for Commonwealth countries, the most important elements were provisions for adaptation to the Common Agricultural Policy, for adjustment to the customs union, for implementing the free movement of capital, and for contributions to the Community budget. On these terms the Treaty of Accession was signed in Brussels on 22 January 1972.

Referenda in Ireland and Denmark ratified their accession, but in Norway the voters decided against joining. In Britain, according to tradition, Parliament's decision was final, but the European Communities Bill, bringing existing EEC legislation into effect in Britain, was passed only after a bitter struggle. Britain, Denmark and the Irish Republic finally became members on 1 January 1973.

The Community in Crisis.

The first anniversary of the enlargement of the EEC found it in a serious state of crisis. The selfish refusal by Britain and France of solidarity with the Dutch in the oil crisis (of 1973) was a shock to their partners. Both countries rushed off to make bilateral deals with oil-producing countries, leaving West Germany and others no choice but reluctantly to follow suit. This made a nonsense of the simultaneous solemn commitment of the heads of government of the Nine in Copenhagen to work out a common energy policy and a common approach to the oil producing countries. France later refused to collaborate in the International Energy Agency formed by oil-consuming countries.

The ambitious Paris summit conference of 1972 had also committed the EEC to a regional policy, including the establishment of a Regional Development Fund by the end of 1973. But a disillusioned West Germany, tired of being the " milch cow " of the Community, insisted on restricting the fund to one-fifth of the £1,250 million demanded by Britain. An unnecessary row developed between the two at the end of 1973, especially after Britain vetoed progress on the energy question until Bonn would offer more. However both later modified their positions, and the Regional Development Fund finally came into being in 1975.

The serious balance of payments problems caused by the soaring oil prices, which called for increased EEC co-operation, in fact produced further disarray. Despite their frequent criticism of the failure of Britain, Ireland, and Italy to tie their currencies to the EEC joint float, the French acted blatantly to protect their national interests in January 1974 by letting their own currency float independently. This caused further dislocation of the Common Agricultural Policy and was a blow to hopes of economic and monetary union. Thus although unspectacular progress had continued, morale in the Community had reached a low ebb.

British Renegotiation.

Worst of all, the new British Labour Government in the spring of 1974 demanded major renegotiation of the terms of British membership and threatened to leave the Community if not given satisfaction. The four main areas concerned were the Common Agricultural Policy; the level of contributions to the Community budget; the Community's trade and aid policies towards Commonwealth and other developing countries; and how far the existing rules interfered with the British Government's ability to pursue independent regional and industrial policies. Increasing concentration by the EEC on the renegotiation issue brought most progress in other areas (including the fundamental aspects of agricultural and regional policy) to a halt. However by early 1975 arrangements had been worked out in most of the areas of renegotiation, including intermediate exemptions for Britain on sugar and beef; a plan whereby members would be eligible for reimbursements on their contributions to the EEC budget on the basis of their gross national product and economic growth; and generous terms for developing countries as described below. Although the concessions would probably have been obtained without dramatising them as renegotiation, the Community appeared to be prepared to go along with the British Government for British domestic consumption. In March 1975 a meeting of the European Council in Dublin settled the two outstanding renegotiation issues, contributions to the Community budget and continued access after 1977 for New Zealand dairy produce. On the former, a " correcting mechanism " was agreed on to prevent the development of situations unacceptable for a member state. For New Zealand there were improved provisions on prices, on quantities of butter and the possibility of some continuing imports of New Zealand cheese. In the light of the renegotiation the British Government decided, with a minority dissenting, to recommend that the British people should vote for remaining in the European Community. The result of the referendum, held in 1975 was a 67·2% " Yes " vote.

The EEC and Developing Countries.

The first major Community achievement for some time was the conclusion in February 1975 of the Lomé Convention on trade, economic co-operation and development between the EEC and 46 developing countries in Africa, the Caribbean and the Pacific (ACP), replacing the Yaoundé and Arusha Conventions. The agreement is unexampled in relations between industrial and developing countries and was described by the spokesman of the ACP countries as " revolutionary ". It guarantees them unrestricted access to Europe's markets for all their industrial and 84%of their agricultural produce and special terms for sugar. It also offers financial support from a European Development Fund trebled in volume, and guarantees to developing countries dependent on the export of a few primary products equalisation payments (repayable only by the richer) when export earnings suffer from price fluctuations on the world market. All that is asked in return is " most favoured nation " treatment under GATT, i.e. that the ACP countries should not treat the EEC worse than other trading partners. This agreement was a great achievement of the European Commission, and the generous treatment of mainly former colonies will further raise the Community's standing in the world (which is in any case higher than within its own borders). Other developing countries have since acceded to the Lomé Convention.

The Future of the EEC.

At the summit meeting of the heads of government of the Nine in Paris in October 1972 a statement of objectives was agreed. This included a programme, based on the previous Werner Plan, for achieving economic and monetary union, and affirmation of their " intention to transform before the end of the present decade . . . the whole complex of their relations into a European Union." Major issues remain unresolved. Thus there are sharp differences between France (and Denmark) and Germany (and Benelux) on the question of ultimately conferring supranational powers on community institutions, and the member nations are unready to undertake the pooling of political power which alone would make possible the fulfilment of their declarations. Reform of the confessedly unsatisfactory Common Agricultural Policy has continually been postponed, largely because both France and the German farmers gain so much from the present system. However Britain and Germany are pushing for major structural changes. *See also* Section G, Part IV.

Recently thought has been given to some issues not covered by the Treaty of Rome, such as the harmonisation of European foreign policies and defence. As a first step machinery was set up in 1971 for regular consultations on foreign policy matters. 1974 saw the beginnings of co-operation on the field of education and the adoption of a Community action programme on scientific and technological policy, with projects to be co-ordinated by a committee for scientific and technical research (CREST).

An institutional step forward was taken when the summit conference of heads of government in Paris in December 1974 agreed that the heads of government of member nations would in future meet at least three times a year to further political co-operation and co-ordinate diplomatic action. These meetings have been institutionalised as the " European Council ". At the same time there was a commitment to give up the practice of making agreement on all questions conditional upon unanimous consent, and a working party was to study the possibility of introducing a uniform Community passport. Meanwhile the European Parliament in 1975 received increased powers over the EEC's budget and direct elections are planned for 1978, though with a notable lack of enthusiasm in some countries including Britain.

The report by the Belgian Prime Minister, Mr. Tindemans, which had been commissioned by the EEC heads of government on the development of the EEC into a European Union, was published in January 1976. In line with the current mood it was sober and pragmatic, proposing that the European Council should be developed into a real decision-making centre with a parliament worthy of the name as counterweight. Much more controversial was the suggestion of a two-tier participation in the proposed economic and monetary union, allowing the weaker members to wait until their economics were capable of further integration. This inevitably raised again the bogy of " second class " membership of the Community.

During 1976 the Community announced a new fisheries policy which is based on a 200-mile economic zone around all member states' coasts known as the Community " pond ". Limits have been set on the amount of fish which can be caught by vessels from non-member states. Arrangements have still to be made for those member states particularly Ireland and the United Kingdom who have important fishing interests, and the major problem of policing any regulations remains unsolved.

The question of Greece's membership of the European Community had been revived after its return to democratic government, and early in 1976 the Commission argued that Greece should be accepted as a member only after a period of adjustment. However the Council of Ministers decided to accept Greece's full membership without preconditions and start negotiations forthwith. This appeared to be a key decision (even if not an explicit one) on the Community's future: enlargement was being given priority over integration, since the wider and more heterogeneous the Community, the more complicated will be the process of co-ordination and compromise and the prospects of working towards economic and monetary union between countries of widely differing economic strength.

1977 saw applications for membership of the Community from both Portugal and Spain. A meeting of EEC foreign ministers at Leeds Castle in Kent in May 1977 was therefore concerned particularly with the issue of enlargement. It produced agreement that in spite of the economic problems involved, especially in the agricultural field, all three applications should be given a favourable response for political reasons, in particular the strengthening of democratic development in the applicant countries. Negotiations were to be carried on with each country individually. Italy and especially France continued to have reservations about enlargement because of fear of competition in Mediterranean fruit, vegetables and wine. The French Communists and Gaullists even started a campaign against the entry of Spain, Portugal and Greece. It was therefore accepted by the Community that a very long transitional period would be necessary.

The member governments also agreed on the need for a reform of the decision-making processes of the EEC, especially in the Council of Ministers, not least in the light of the impending enlargement of the Community. It would be necessary to leave more decisions to be taken by the Permanent Representatives.

By the time Britain, Denmark and Ireland became full members of the EEC after the end of the five-year transitional period on 1 January 1978, the British Government had made itself unpopular with its partners in a number of ways. An informal meeting of the Foreign Ministers in October sharply criticised British policy towards the Community as expressed by Mr. Callaghan within the Labour Party, especially his emphasis on sovereignty and the right to determine economic and industrial policy independently and his welcoming of enlargement of the Community as lessening the dangers of over-centralisation and over-harmonisation. Britain's hindering of a common energy policy and unilateral measures for fishery protection within the 200-mile British economic zone have caused considerable ill-feeling. But the worst blow dealt by Britain to European unification was her frustration of the planned holding of direct elections to the European Parliament in May or June 1978. Although the other member states were able to complete the necessary legislative processes in time, further postponement became necessary with the British decision against applying a system of proportional representation and in favour of the traditional British simple majority system, with a consequent need for a lengthy process of drawing up large constituencies. Nevertheless, after prolonged deadlock on the site for the major nuclear fusion project JET (Joint European Torus), the Germans gave up their claim in favour of Culham in Oxfordshire. And when agreement was reached on a new European Unit of Account allowing for the changes of parity of European currencies since 1972, the other members agreed to a compromise for the United Kingdom, which had benefited so much from the old rate: its contribution was raised from 12·5% to 15·4%, and not to the 18% which would be its proper share.

The beginning of 1978 saw the start of the self-financing of the Community budget, in particular from contributions from national value added taxes and from the customs and levies imposed at the EEC's external frontiers.

POLITICAL COMPENDIUM

This new section provides a compact reference work of key facts and figures for an understanding of modern British politics. Readers will also find that the preceding section, *Background to Public Affairs*, complements this part of the book.

TABLE OF CONTENTS

POLITICAL COMPENDIUM

A. THE MONARCHY

The Queen is a constitutional monarch. In law she is the head of the executive, an integral part of the legislature, head of the judiciary, commander-in-chief of the armed forces and temporal head of the Church of England. In practice, the Queen's role is purely formal; she reigns, but she does not rule. In all important respects she acts only on the advice of her ministers. However, she still plays an important role symbolically as Head of State and Head of the Commonwealth.

Monarchs since 1900

1837–1901	Victoria
1901–1910	Edward VII
1910–1936	George V
1936	Edward VIII
1936–1952	George VI
1952–	Elizabeth II

B. GENERAL ELECTIONS

For electoral purposes the United Kingdom is divided into 635 constituencies each returning one M.P. to the House of Commons. All British subjects and citizens of the Irish Republic are entitled to vote provided they are 18 years old and over and are included on the electoral register which is compiled annually. The only exceptions are members of the House of Lords and those incapacitated through insanity or imprisonment. Anyone who is entitled to vote and aged at least 21 may stand as a candidate, the only exceptions being undischarged bankrupts, clergymen in the established church and the holders of certain other public offices. All candidates have to pay a deposit of £150, which is forfeited unless they receive one-eighth of the votes cast. In each constituency the winning candidate has only to obtain a simple majority.

General elections must be held every five years.

General Elections 1918–74
VOTES CAST (thousands)

	Conservative	Labour	Liberal	Communist	Plaid Cymru	SNP	Others
1918	4,166	2,546	2,753	—	—	—	1,296
1922	5,500	4,241	4,189	34	—	—	462
1923	5,538	4,438	4,311	39	—	—	260
1924	8,039	5,489	2,928	55	—	—	126
1929	8,656	8,390	5,309	51	1	—	243
1931	12,320	6,991	1,509	75	2	21	293
1935	11,810	8,465	1,422	27	3	30	273
1945	9,988	11,995	2,248	103	16	31	752
1950	12,503	13,267	2,622	92	18	10	290
1951	13,745	13,949	731	22	11	7	177
1955	13,312	12,405	722	33	45	12	313
1959	13,750	12,216	1,639	31	78	22	125
1964	12,023	12,206	3,093	46	70	64	168
1966	11,418	13,095	2,328	62	61	128	171
1970	13,145	12,198	2.117	38	175	307	384
Feb. 1974	11,910	11,646	6.059	33	171	632	958
Oct. 1974	10,501	11,457	5,347	17	166	840	897

SNP—Scottish National Party.

The Speaker has been regarded as a candidate of the party he represented before appointment.

SEATS WON

	Conservative	Labour	Liberal	Communist	Plaid Cymru	SNP	Others (GB)	Others (NI)	Total
1918	383	73	161	0	0	0	9	81	707
1922	344	142	115	1	0	0	10	3	615
1923	258	191	158	0	0	0	5	3	615
1924	412	151	40	1	0	0	10	1	615
1929	260	287	59	0	0	0	6	3	615
1931	521	52	37	0	0	0	3	2	615
1935	429	154	21	1	0	0	8	2	615
1945	213	393	12	2	0	0	16	4	640
1950	299	315	9	0	0	0	0	2	625
1951	321	295	6	0	0	0	0	3	625
1955	345	277	6	0	0	0	0	2	630
1959	365	258	6	0	0	0	1	0	630
1964	304	317	9	0	0	0	0	0	630
1966	253	364	12	0	0	0	0	1	630
1970	330	288	6	0	0	1	1	4	630
Feb. 1974	297	301	14	0	2	7	2	12	635
Oct. 1974	277	319	13	0	3	11	0	12	635

SNP—Scottish National Party.

Others: (NI) Ireland in 1918, Northern Ireland only 1922–74. Ulster Unionists regarded as Conservatives 1922–70

The Speaker has been regarded as an M.P. of the party he represented before appointment.

OPINION POLLS

Various organisations conduct regular surveys of public opinion on political matters, notably voting intention. The main polls and the newspaper and TV companies which publish the findings are listed below:

Poll	Outlets
Gallup	*Daily* and *Sunday Telegraph*
Opinion Research Centre	*The Times, Sunday Times* and *Evening Standard*
Louis Harris International	*Daily Express* and London Weekend TV
Marplan	*Sun* and *News of the World*
Business Decisions	*Observer*
National Opinion Polls	*Daily Mail*

By-Elections 1945–77

Parliament	Government	No. of By-elections	Changes	Con. +	Con. −	Lab. +	Lab. −	Lib. +	Lib. −	Others +	Others −
1945–50	Lab.	52	3	3	—	—	—	—	—	—	3
1950–51	Lab.	16	0	—	—	—	—	—	—	—	—
1951–55	Con.	48	1	1	—	—	1	—	—	—	—
1955–59	Con.	52	6	1	4	4	—	1	1	—	1
1959–64	Con.	62	9	2	7	6	2	1	—	—	—
1964–66	Lab.	13	2	1	1	—	1	1	—	—	—
1966–70	Lab.	38	16	12	1	—	15	1	—	3	—
1970–74	Con.	30	8	—	5	1	3	5	—	2	—
1974	Lab.	1	0	—	—	—	—	—	—	—	—
1974–77	Lab.	17	5	5	—	—	5	—	—	—	—

but may occur more frequently either because no government can command a majority in the House of Commons or at the request of the Prime Minister. If a seat falls vacant between general elections a by-election is held on a date usually chosen by the party which previously held the seat. Elections are generally held on Thursdays.

TURNOUT AND PARTY SHARE OF VOTES CAST

Turnout		Share of Poll (%)		
		Conservative	Labour	Liberal
1918	59	39	24	26
1922	71	38	30	29
1923	71	38	31	30
1924	77	48	33	18
1929	76	38	37	23
1931	76	59	32	7
1935	71	54	39	6
1945	73	40	48	9
1950	84	44	46	9
1951	83	48	49	3
1955	77	50	46	3
1959	79	49	44	6
1964	77	43	44	11
1966	76	42	48	9
1970	72	46	43	8
Feb. 1974	78	38	37	19
Oct. 1974	73	36	39	18

C. POLITICAL PARTIES

To understand the operation of the British system of government it is essential to appreciate the importance of the party system. Since the seventeenth century two parties have usually been predominant, at different times Tories and Whigs, Conservatives and Liberals, and since the 1930s Conservatives and Labour. Parties exist to form governments, and the path to this goal lies in the House of Commons, for the party which obtains a majority of seats has the right to have its leaders form the government. The other party forms Her Majesty's Opposition.

To this end parties in this century have been highly disciplined organisations. The opposition accepts that, unless the government's majority is very small, it is unlikely to defeat it in the Commons, and it thus sees its role as one of criticising government policy and setting forth an alternative programme which it hopes will win the support of the electorate at the next election.

Each of the major parties has an organisation within Parliament and one outside Parliament which exists to fight elections and to disseminate information about the party's policies.

Party Leaders.

The Conservative and Labour Party leaders are elected by the members of their parliamentary parties. The Liberal leader is elected by Liberal members throughout the country.

Present Leaders

Conservative	Mrs. Margaret Thatcher
Labour	Mr. James Callaghan
Liberal	Mr. David Steel
Scottish National Party	Mr. Donald Stewart
Plaid Cymru	Mr. Gwynfor Evans
Ulster Unionist	Mr. James Molyneaux

Past Leaders

Conservative Party Leaders

1900–2	Marquis of Salisbury
1902–11	A. Balfour
1911–21	A. Bonar Law
1921–22	A. Chamberlain
1922–23	A. Bonar Law
1923–37	S. Baldwin
1937–40	N. Chamberlain
1940–55	(Sir) W. Churchill
1955–57	Sir A. Eden
1957–63	H. Macmillan
1963–65	Sir A. Douglas-Home
1965–75	E. Heath
1975–	Mrs. M. Thatcher

Labour Party Leaders

1906–8	J. K. Hardie
1908–10	A. Henderson
1910–11	G Barnes
1911–14	J. R. MacDonald
1914–17	A. Henderson
1917–21	W Adamson
1921–22	J. Clynes
1922–31	J. R. MacDonald
1931–32	A. Henderson
1932–35	G. Lansbury
1935–55	C. Attlee
1955–63	H. Gaitskell
1963–76	H. Wilson
1976–	J. Callaghan

Liberal Party Leaders

1900–8	Sir H. Campbell-Bannerman
1908–26	H. Asquith
1926–31	D. Lloyd George

1931–35	Sir H. Samuel
1935–45	Sir A. Sinclair
1945–56	C. Davies
1956–67	J. Grimond
1967–76	J. Thorpe
1976–	D. Steel

Party Officers.

Conservative Party

Chairman of the Party Organisation
(appointed by the Leader of the Party)

1944–46	R. Assheton
1946–55	Lord Woolton
1955–57	O. Poole
1957–59	Viscount Hailsham
1959–61	R. Butler
1961–63	I. Macleod
1963	I. Macleod } Lord Poole
1963–65	Viscount Blakenham
1965–67	E. du Cann
1967–70	A. Barber
1970–72	P. Thomas
1972–74	Lord Carrington
1974–75	W. Whitelaw
1975–	Lord Thorneycroft

Chairman of Conservative (Private) Members'
Committee (or the 1922 Committee), which is
the organisation of back-bench Conservative
M.P.s

1945–51	Sir A. Gridley
1951–55	D. Walker-Smith
1955–64	J. Morrison
1964–66	Sir W. Anstruther-Gray
1966–70	Sir A. Harvey
1970–72	Sir H. Legge-Bourke
1972–	E. du Cann

Labour Party

General Secretary (appointed by the National
Executive Committee)

1944–62	M. Phillips
1962–68	A. Williams
1968–72	Sir H. Nicholas
1972–	R. Hayward

Chairman of the Labour Party
(elected annually by the National Executive
Committee)

1970–71	I. Mikardo
1971–72	A. Benn
1972–73	W. Simpson
1973–74	J. Callaghan
1974–75	F. Mulley
1975–76	T. Bradley
1976–77	J. Chalmers
1977–78	Miss J. Lestor

Chairman of the Parliamentary Labour Party
(until 1970 this post only existed when the
Labour Party was in government; a chairman
is now also elected when the Party is in
opposition)

1970–74	D. Houghton
1974	I. Mikardo
1974–	C. Hughes

Liberal Party

Head of Liberal Party Organisation

1936–52	W. Davies
1952–60	H. Harris
1960–61	D. Robinson
1961–65	P. Kemmis
1965–66	T. Beaumont
1966–70	P. Chitnis
1970–76	E. Wheeler
1976–	W. N. Hugh Jones

Scottish National Party—National Secretary: Miss M. Gibson.

Plaid Cymru—General Secretary: D. Williams.

National Front—Chairman of National Directorate: J. Tyndall.

Communist Party of Great Britain—Secretary: G. McLennan

D. PARLIAMENT

Parliament consists of the Queen, the House of Lords and the House of Commons. Over the centuries the balance between the three parts of the legislature has changed such that the Queen's role is now only formal and the House of Commons has established paramountcy over the House of Lords. Because of the party system the initiative in government lies not in Parliament but in the Cabinet. But Parliament, and especially the Commons, has important functions to play not only as the assembly to which the government is ultimately responsible but also in legitimising legislation, voting money and in acting as a body in which complaints may be raised.

House of Lords.

Composition. The House of Lords comprises over 1,100 peers, made up in 1976 as follows:

Hereditary Peers	822
Life Peers	254
Lords of Appeal	16
Archbishops and bishops	26

No new hereditary peers have been created since 1964. Less than 300 peers attend more than one-third of the Lords proceedings. Figures of party strengths in the Lords are not easy to obtain, but one source identified 283 Conservatives, 129 Labour and 37 Liberals in 1977.

Functions.

(1) Legislation. Some bills on subjects which are not matters of partisan controversy are initiated in the Lords. It also examines in detail many bills which originated in the Commons, but its part is limited by the Parliament Acts, under which it cannot require the Commons to agree to amendments nor delay a bill indefinitely.

(2) Debate. The Lords provides a forum for men and women, distinguished in most fields of national life, to discuss issues of importance free from the reins of party discipline.

(3) Court of appeal. The Lords is the highest court of appeal. Only the law lords take part in its legal proceedings.

House of Commons.

Composition. The House of Commons comprises 635 M.P.s elected to represent single-member constituencies (516 in England, 71 in Scotland, 36 in Wales and 12 in Northern Ireland). Its proceedings are presided over by the Speaker, who is elected by M.P.s at the beginning of each session. The present Speaker (May 1978) is a Labour M.P., Mr. George Thomas.

M.P.s sit on parallel rows of seats, known as benches, with those who support the government on one side of the chamber and the rest on the other side. Members of the government and the spokesmen of the Opposition are known as " front-benchers "; other M.P.s are " back-benchers ".

Functions.

(1) Legislation. There are two types of legislation—*public acts*, most of which are introduced by the government, but which can also be introduced by individual M.P.s and *private acts*, which confer special powers on bodies such as local authorities in excess of the general law and which are subject to special procedures.

All public legislation must pass through the following stages before becoming law:

First reading. The bill is formally introduced.

Second reading. The general principles of the bill are debated and voted.

Committee Stage. Each clause of the bill is debated and voted.

Report Stage. The bill is considered as it was reported by the committee, and it is decided whether to make further changes in individual clauses.

Third Reading. The bill, as amended, is debated and a final vote taken.

The Other House. The bill has to pass through the same stages in the other House of Parliament.

Royal Assent. The Queen signs the bill and it becomes law as an Act of Parliament.

(2) Scrutiny of government activities. There are a number of opportunities for the opposition and the government's own back-benchers to criticise government policy. They can question ministers on the floor of the House; they can table motions for debate and speak in debates initiated by the government; and they can take part in one of the select committees set up to scrutinise government activity.

Committees. The House of Commons uses committees to assist it in its work in various ways. They are of two types:

Standing Committees. A standing committee is a miniature of the House itself, reflecting its party composition, and consists of between 20 and 50 M.P.s. Its function is to examine the Committee Stage of legislation. Usually seven or eight such committees are needed.

Select Committees. A select committee is a body with special powers and privileges to which the House has delegated its authority for the purpose of discovering information, examining witnesses, sifting evidence and drawing up conclusions which are then reported to the House. A few select committees are established *ad hoc*, but the majority are semi-permanent, although the House can always wind them up at any time. In 1977/8 the most important select committees were:

Select Committees in 1977/8

Name	Chairman
European Legislation, etc.	Sir John Eden
Expenditure	Mr. James Boyden
Nationalised Industries	Mr. Russell Kerr
Overseas Development	Sir Geoffrey de Freitas
Parliamentary Commissioner for Administration	Mr. Anthony Buck
Privileges	Mr. George Strauss
Procedure	Sir Thomas Williams

Her Majesty's Government (in June 1978)

The Cabinet

Prime Minister, First Lord of the Treasury and Minister for the Civil Service	Mr. James Callaghan
Lord President of the Council and Leader of the House of Commons	Mr. Michael Foot
Lord Chancellor	Lord Elwyn-Jones
Chancellor of the Exchequer	Mr. Denis Healey
Secretary of State for the Home Department	Mr. Merlyn Rees
Secretary of State for Foreign and Commonwealth Affairs	Dr. David Owen
Secretary of State for Education and Science and Paymaster General	Mrs. Shirley Williams
Secretary of State for Energy	Mr. Anthony Wedgwood Benn
Secretary of State for Industry	Mr. Eric Varley
Secretary of State for the Environment	Mr. Peter Shore
Secretary of State for Northern Ireland	Mr. Roy Mason
Secretary of State for Scotland	Mr. Bruce Millan
Secretary of State for Wales	Mr. John Morris
Secretary of State for Defence	Mr. Frederick Mulley
Secretary of State for Employment	Mr. Albert Booth
Secretary of State for Social Services	Mr. David Ennals
Secretary of State for Trade	Mr. Edmund Dell
Lord Privy Seal and Leader of the House of Lords	Lord Peart
Minister of Agriculture, Fisheries and Food	Mr. John Silkin
Secretary of State for Prices and Consumer Protection	Mr. Roy Hattersley
Secretary of State for Transport	Mr. William Rodgers
Minister for Social Security	Mr. Stanley Orme
Chancellor of the Duchy of Lancaster	Mr. Harold Lever
Chief Secretary to the Treasury	Mr. Joel Barnett

Ministers not in the Cabinet

Minister of State, Ministry of Agriculture	Mr. Edward Bishop
Minister of State, Civil Service Department	Mr. Charles Morris
Minister of State, Ministry of Defence	Dr. John Gilbert
Ministers of State, Department of Education and Science	Mr. Gordon Oakes
	Lord Donaldson
Minister of State, Department of Employment	Mr. Harold Walker
Minister of State, Department of Energy	Dr. J. Dickson Mabon
Minister for Housing and Construction	Mr. Reginald Freeson
Minister of State for Sport and Recreation	Mr. Denis Howell
Ministers of State, Foreign and Commonwealth Office	Mr. Frank Judd
	Lord Goronwy-Roberts
	Mr. Edward Rowlands
Minister of State, Department of Health and Social Security	Mr. Roland Moyle
Ministers of State, Home Office	Lord Harris
	Mr. Brynmor John
Ministers of State, Department of Industry	Mr. Gerald Kaufman
	Mr. Alan Williams
Ministers of State, Northern Ireland Office	Lord Melchett
	Mr. Don Concannon
Minister of State for Overseas Development	Mrs. Judith Hart
Minister of State, Department of Prices and Consumer Protection	Mr. John Fraser
Minister of State, Privy Council Office	Mr. John Smith
Ministers of State, Scottish Office	Mr. Gregor Mackenzie
	Lord Kirkhill
Parliamentary Secretary, Treasury	Mr. Michael Cocks
Financial Secretary to the Treasury	Mr. Robert Sheldon
Minister of State, Treasury	Mr. Denzil Davies
Attorney General	Mr. Samuel Silkin
Solicitor General	Mr. Peter Archer

Principal Ministers 1900–'78

	Prime Minister	Chancellor of the Exchequer	Foreign Secretary	Home Secretary	Leader of the House of Commons
1900–2	Marquis of Salisbury	Sir M. Hicks-Beach	Marquis of Salisbury Marquis of Lansdowne	Sir M. White-Ridley C. Ritchie	A. Balfour
1902–5	A. Balfour *C.B.*	C. Ritchie A. Chamberlain	Marquis of Lansdowne	A. Akers-Douglas	A. Balfour
1905–8	Sir H. Campbell-Bannerman	H. Asquith	Sir E. Grey	H. Gladstone	Sir H. Campbell-Bannerman
1908–16	H. Asquith	D. Lloyd George R. McKenna	Sir E. Grey	H. Gladstone W. Churchill R. McKenna Sir J. Simon Sir H. Samuel	H. Asquith
1916–22	D. Lloyd George	A. Bonar Law A. Chamberlain Sir R. Horne	A. Balfour Earl Curzon	Sir G. Cave E. Shortt	A. Bonar Law A. Chamberlain
1922–23	A. Bonar Law	S. Baldwin	Earl Curzon	W. Bridgeman	A. Bonar Law
1923–24	S. Baldwin	N. Chamberlain	Earl Curzon	W. Bridgeman	S. Baldwin
1924	J. R. MacDonald	P. Snowden	J. R. MacDonald	A. Henderson	J. R. MacDonald
1924–29	S. Baldwin	W. Churchill	(Sir) A. Chamberlain	Sir W. Joynson-Hicks	S. Baldwin
1929–35	J. R. MacDonald	P. Snowden N. Chamberlain	A. Henderson Marquis of Reading Sir J. Simon	J. Clynes Sir H. Samuel Sir J. Gilmour	J. R. MacDonald
1935–37	S. Baldwin	N. Chamberlain	Sir S. Hoare A. Eden	Sir J. Simon	S. Baldwin
1937–40	N. Chamberlain	Sir J. Simon	A. Eden Viscount Halifax	Sir S. Hoare Sir J. Anderson	N. Chamberlain
1940–45	W. Churchill	Sir K. Wood Sir J. Anderson	A. Eden	H. Morrison Sir D. Somervell	C. Attlee Sir S. Cripps A. Eden

D8

Prime Minister	Chancellor of the Exchequer	Foreign Secretary	Home Secretary	Leader of the House of Commons
1945-51 C. Attlee	H. Dalton Sir S. Cripps H. Gaitskell	E. Bevin H. Morrison	C. Ede	H. Morrison C. Ede
1951-55 Sir W. Churchill	R. Butler	Sir A. Eden	Sir D. Maxwell-Fyfe G. Lloyd George	H. Crookshank
1955-57 Sir A. Eden	R. Butler H. Macmillan	H. Macmillan S. Lloyd	G. Lloyd George	R. Butler
1957-63 H. Macmillan	P. Thorneycroft D. Heathcoat Amory S. Lloyd R. Maudling	S. Lloyd Earl of Home	R. Butler H. Brooke	R. Butler I. Macleod
1963-64 Sir A. Douglas-Home	R. Maudling	R. Butler	H. Brooke	S. Lloyd
1964-70 H. Wilson	J. Callaghan R. Jenkins	P. Gordon Walker M. Stewart G. Brown M. Stewart	Sir F. Soskice R. Jenkins J. Callaghan	H. Bowden R. Crossman F. Peart
1970-74 E. Heath	I. Macleod A. Barber	Sir A. Douglas-Home	R. Maudling R. Carr	W. Whitelaw R. Carr J. Prior
1974-76 H. Wilson	D. Healey	J. Callaghan	R. Jenkins	E. Short
1976-79 J. Callaghan	D. Healey	A. Crosland D. Owen	R. Jenkins M. Rees	M. Foot
May 3 1979 M. Thatcher	Sir G. Howe	Lord Carrington	W. Whitelaw	N. St John-Stevas changed 1980 Sir Francis Pym

Public Accounts	Mr. Edward du Cann
Race Relations and Immigration	Mr. Frederick Willey
Science and Technology	Mr. Arthur Palmer
Statutory Instruments	Mr. Graham Page

E. CENTRAL GOVERNMENT

The executive work of central government is performed by the Prime Minister and the other ministers of the Crown. The power of executive action is not given to a government department as a corporate body but to the minister individually, who is responsible for the exercise of his duties legally to the Queen and politically to Parliament. For this reason, all ministers must be members of either the Commons or the Lords.

At the head of the government structure is the Cabinet, which consists of the leading members of the majority party in the Commons, selected by the Prime Minister. Most Cabinet ministers are the heads of government departments, which are staffed by civil servants, but there are usually some without departmental responsibilities. Although legally ministers are individually responsible for the exercise of government powers, politically it is accepted that the Cabinet is collectively responsible for government policy. It thus acts as one man, and a minister who disagrees with the cabinet must either resign or remain silent.

Size of the Government 1945–77

	Cabinet Ministers	Non-Cabinet Ministers	Junior Ministers	Total
1945	20	20	49	89
1950	18	22	44	84
1960	20	23	45	88
1965	23	33	55	111
1970	17	26	41	84
1975	24	31	54	109
1977	24	31	56	111

F. HER MAJESTY'S OPPOSITION

The leader of the largest party opposed to the government is designated Leader of Her Majesty's Opposition and receives an official salary. The leading spokesmen of the Opposition meet together as a committee and are generally known as the Shadow Cabinet. A Conservative Shadow Cabinet, officially known as the Leader's Consultative Committee, is selected by the leader of the party. Labour shadow cabinets, officially known as the Parliamentary Committee, are elected by the Parliamentary Labour Party, but the leader retains the right to invite members to take charge of particular subjects.

G. OTHER EXECUTIVE BODIES

A large number of semi-autonomous agencies have been established to carry out functions on behalf of the government, usually because a particular function is considered to be unsuitable for a normal government department. In this category are bodies such as the British Broadcasting Corporation and the Commission for Racial Equality which need to be insulated from the political process, and the nationalised industries, most of which are managed by public corporations so as to secure managerial flexibility. Some public control over these bodies is maintained by means of various powers which ministers possess.

National Health Service.

The National Health Service was created in 1948. Overall responsibility for the NHS rests with the Secretary of State for Social Services and the Secretary of State for Scotland. Managerial and operational responsibility, however, is delegated to various health authorities appointed by central government in consultation with local authorities and the health service professions. In England there are two tiers of authorities: 14 Regional Health Authorities and 72 Area Health Authorities. In Scotland and Wales the Scottish and Welsh Offices act as the regional tier and there are 14 Health Boards and 8 Area Health Authorities respectively.

H. THE CIVIL SERVICE

The civil service is the body of permanent officials who, working in the various departments, administer the policy of central government. It consists of some 746,000 people (2·9% of the working population), of whom 571,000 are non-industrial civil servants and the rest industrial workers in places such as the ordnance factories and naval dockyards. Over 70% of the civil service work outside Greater London, mainly in the regional and local offices of departments such as Health and Social Security, Employment and the Inland Revenue.

The political head of each department is a minister, but, as he often has no previous experience of the field to which he is appointed and his tenure of office may be fairly short-lived, great responsibility falls on the shoulders of the perman-

Her Majesty's Opposition (in June 1978)

The Shadow Cabinet

Leader of the Opposition	Mrs. Margaret Thatcher
Deputy Leader and Shadow Home Secretary	Mr. William Whitelaw
Overall responsibility for policy and research	Sir Keith Joseph
Agriculture	Mr. John Peyton
Consumer Affairs and Prices	Mrs. Sally Oppenheim
Defence	Sir Ian Gilmour
Devolution and House of Commons Affairs	Mr. Francis Pym
Education and Arts	Mr. Norman St. John-Stevas
Employment	Mr. James Prior
Energy	Mr. Tom King
Environment	Mr. Michael Heseltine
Foreign and Commonwealth Affairs	Mr. John Davies
Industry	Sir Keith Joseph
Northern Ireland	Mr. Airey Neave
Scotland	Mr. Edward Taylor
Social Services	Mr. Patrick Jenkin
Trade	Mr. John Nott
Treasury	Sir Geoffrey Howe
Wales	Mr. Nicholas Edwards
Leader of the Opposition, House of Lords	Lord Carrington
Without specific duties	Lord Hailsham
Chairman of the Party	Lord Thorneycroft
Chairman of Research Department	Mr. Angus Maude
Opposition Chief Whip	Mr. Humphrey Atkins

Major Nationalised Industries	*Chairman*
British Airways Board	Sir Frank McFadzean
British Gas Corporation	Sir Denis Rooke
British Railways Board	Sir Peter Parker
British Steel Corporation	Sir Charles Villiers
Electricity Council	Sir Francis Tombs
Central Electricity Generating Board	Mr. Glyn England
National Bus Company	Sir Freddie Wood
National Coal Board	Sir Derek Ezra
National Freight Corporation	Sir Daniel Pettit
Post Office Corporation	Sir William Barlow

Other Public Bodies	*Chairman*
National Enterprise Board	Sir Leslie Murphy
British Leyland Ltd.	Mr. Michael Edwardes
Rolls-Royce Ltd.	Sir Kenneth Keith
Advisory Conciliation and Arbitration Service	Mr. James Mortimer
British Broadcasting Corporation	Sir Michael Swann
Civil Aviation Authority	Mr. Nigel Foulkes
Commission for Racial Equality	Mr. David Lane
Equal Opportunities Commission	Lady Lockwood
Independent Broadcasting Authority	Lady Plowden
Health and Safety Commission	Mr. William Simpson
London Transport Executive	Mr. Ralph Bennett
Manpower Services Commission	Mr. Richard O'Brien
Price Commission	Mr. Charles Williams

ent civil servants in his department. Civil servants remain largely anonymous and their relationship with their minister is a confidential one. They are non-political in the sense that they serve both political parties impartially.

Civil Service Numbers

	Total	Industrial	Non-Industrial
1914	779,000	497,000	282,000
1938	581,000	204,000	377,000
1950	972,000	397,000	575,000
1960	996,000	359,000	637,000
1970	702,000	209,000	493,000
1977	746,000	175,000	571,000

Note: The drop in numbers between 1960 and 1970 is the result of the exclusion of Post Office staff, who ceased to be civil servants in 1969. Otherwise the size of the civil service grew by more than 50,000 between 1960 and 1970.

Senior Civil Servants

Head of the Home Civil Service

1945–56	Sir E. Bridges
1956–63	Sir N. Brook
1963–68	Sir L. Helsby
1968–74	Sir W. Armstrong
1974–78	Sir D. Allen
1978–	Sir I. Bancroft

Head of the Diplomatic Service

1945–46	Sir A. Cadogan
1946–49	Sir O. Sargent
1949–53	Sir W. Strang
1953–57	Sir I. Kirkpatrick
1957–62	Sir F. Hoyer Millar
1962–65	Sir H. Caccia
1965–69	Sir P. Gore-Booth
1969–73	Sir D. Greenhill
1973–75	Sir T. Brimelow
1975–	Sir M. Palliser

Permanent Secretary to the Treasury

1945–56	Sir E. Bridges
1956–60	{Sir N. Brook / {Sir R. Makins
1960–62	{Sir N. Brook / {Sir F. Lee
1962–63	{Sir N. Brook / {W. Armstrong
1963–68	{Sir L. Helsby / {(Sir) W. Armstrong
1968	{Sir W. Armstrong / {Sir D. Allen
1968–74	Sir D. Allen
1974–	Sir D. Wass

Secretary to the Cabinet

1938–47	Sir E. Bridges
1947–63	Sir N. Brook
1963–73	Sir B. Trend
1973–	Sir J. Hunt

Other Public Servants

The civil service constitutes only 12% of the public service. The remainder work as follows:

Local Government	37%
National Health Service	12%
Nationalised industries and other public bodies	39%

In all there were over 6 million employees in the public sector in 1976 (almost 25% of the total working population).

I. LOCAL GOVERNMENT

Local government in the United Kingdom is the creation of Parliament. Its structure is laid down by Parliament, and local authorities may only exercise those powers which Parliament either commands or permits them to exercise. Their functions include responsibility for all education services, except the universities, most personal welfare services, housing, public health, environmental planning, traffic management and transport, in each case subject to some central government control.

The structure of local government differs in England, Scotland and Wales. Within England there are also three different systems.

Next Elections.

England
County Councils (including Greater London Council), 1981
Metropolitan District Councils, 1979 (when a third of each council retires)
Non-metropolitan District Councils, 1979
London Borough Councils, 1982

Wales
County Councils, 1981
District Councils, 1979

Scotland
Regional (and Islands) Councils, 1982
District Councils, 1982

J. REDRESS OF GRIEVANCES

In the first instance most citizens who are aggrieved by the decision of a public body take up

First-tier Authorities

ENGLAND	Name	Population in 1975	Political control in 1978	Number of districts	Administrative capital
Greater London	GLC	7,111,500	Con.	32	London
Metropolitan Counties	Greater Manchester	2,708,900	Con.	10	Manchester
	Merseyside	1,588,400	Con.	5	Liverpool
	South Yorkshire	1,317,500	Lab.	4	Barnsley
	Tyne and Wear	1,192,600	Lab.	5	Newcastle-upon-Tyne
	West Midlands	2,777,500	Con.	7	Birmingham
	West Yorkshire	2,082,600	Con.	5	Wakefield
Non-Metropolitan Counties	Avon	919,600	Con.	6	Bristol
	Bedfordshire	489,500	Con.	4	Bedford
	Berkshire	658,300	Con.	6	Reading
	Buckinghamshire	501,800	Con.	5	Aylesbury
	Cambridgeshire	551,000	Con.	6	Cambridge
	Cheshire	910,900	Con.	8	Chester
	Cleveland	565,400	Con.	4	Middlesbrough
	Cornwall	397,200	Ind.	6	Truro
	Cumbria	473,800	Con.	6	Carlisle
	Derbyshire	887,400	Con.	9	Matlock
	Devon	936,300	Con.	10	Exeter
	Dorset	572,900	Con.	8	Dorchester
	Durham	607,600	Lab.	8	Durham
	E. Sussex	657,300	Con.	7	Lewes
	Essex	1,410,900	Con.	14	Chelmsford
	Gloucestershire	487,600	Con.	6	Gloucester
	Hampshire	1,449,700	Con.	13	Winchester
	Hereford and Worcester	585,600	Con.	9	Worcester
	Hertfordshire	938,100	Con.	10	Hertford
	Humberside	848,200	Con.	9	Hull
	Isle of Wight	110,700	Con.	2	Newport
	Kent	1,445,400	Con.	14	Maidstone
	Lancashire	1,369,200	Con.	14	Preston
	Leicestershire	836,500	Con.	9	Leicester
	Lincolnshire	521,300	Con.	7	Lincoln
	Norfolk	659,300	Con.	7	Norwich
	Northamptonshire	500,100	Con.	7	Northampton
	Northumberland	286,700	Con./ Ind.	6	Newcastle-upon-Tyne
	North Yorkshire	646,100	Con.	8	Northallerton
	Nottinghamshire	982,700	Con.	8	Nottingham
	Oxfordshire	539,100	Con.	5	Oxford
	Salop	354,800	Ind.	6	Shrewsbury
	Somerset	401,700	Con.	5	Taunton
	Staffordshire	988,400	Con.	9	Stafford
	Suffolk	570,000	Con.	7	Ipswich
	Surrey	1,000,700	Con.	11	Kingston-upon-Thames
	Warwickshire	471,800	Con.	5	Warwick
	West Sussex	623,100	Con.	7	Chichester
	Wiltshire	511,600	Con.	5	Trowbridge
WALES					
Counties	Clwyd	374,800	NOM (Con.)	6	Mold
	Dyfed	321,700	Ind.	6	Carmarthen
	Gwent	440,100	NOM (Lab.)	5	Cwmbran
	Gwynedd	224,200	Ind.	5	Caernarfon
	Mid Glamorgan	540,100	Lab.	6	Cardiff
	Powys	100,800	Ind.	3	Llandrindod Wells
	South Glamorgan	391,600	Con.	2	Cardiff
	West Glamorgan	371,700	Lab.	4	Swansea
SCOTLAND					
Regions	Borders	99,400	(Ind.)	4	Newton St. Boswells
	Central	269,300	(Lab.)	3	Stirling
	Dumfries and Galloway	143,700	NOM (Oth.)	4	Dumfries
	Fife	336,300	Lab.	3	Cupar
	Grampian	448,800	Con.	5	Aberdeen
	Highland	182,000	NP	8	Inverness
	Lothian	754,000	(Lab.)	4	Edinburgh
	Strathclyde	2,504,900	Lab.	19	Glasgow
	Tayside	402,000	(Con.)	3	Dundee
Islands Councils	Orkney	17,700	NP	—	Kirkwall
	Shetland	18,500	NP	—	Lerwick
	Western Isles	29,600	NP	—	Stornoway

NOM (Con.)—No overall majority (Conservatives the largest party)   NP—Non-party

Second-tier Authorities

	Number	Range of population	Party Control
England Metropolitan District Councils	36	172,000—1,084,000	Con. 18, Lab. 14, NOM 4.
Non-Metropolitan District Councils	296	24,000—420,000	Con. 165, Lab. 30, Other 35, NOM 54, NP 12
London Borough Councils	32	136,000—324,000	Con. 17, Lab. 14, NOM 1.
Wales District Councils	37	19,000—284,000	Con. 4, Lab. 7, Other 15, NOM 9, NP 2.
Scotland District Councils	53	9,000—881,000	Con. 8, Lab. 5, SNP 4, Other 10, NOM 20, NP 6.

NOM—No overall majority. NP—Non-party.

their complaint with the body concerned, either personally or in writing. If this does not satisfy them they have a number of options which vary according to the type of body and the nature of their complaint.

Central Government.

1. *M.P.s.* M.P.s may be contacted by letter, and many of them hold regular surgeries in their constituencies. On receipt of a complaint they can write to the minister in charge of the department concerned or ask a question in Parliament. If the complaint alleges maladministration (*e.g.,* arbitrary action, undue delay) this can be referred to the *Parliamentary Commissioner for Administration* (usually known as the Ombudsman) who is empowered to investigate complaints and report his findings to Parliament.

2. *Tribunals and inquiries.* In certain areas of government (*e.g.,* social security), special tribunals exist to adjudicate on disputes between citizens and government. In others (*e.g.,* planning) an inquiry can be set up. In both cases the machinery is less formal and more flexible than the ordinary courts.

3. *Courts of law.* On certain restricted matters (*e.g.,* that a public body has acted outside its lawful powers), citizens have recourse to the ordinary courts.

Local Government.

1. *Councillors.* Local councillors can be contacted in the same way as M.P.s. They can also refer complaints of maladministration to a *Commissioner for Local Administration* (or local Ombudsman). There are five commissioners, three in England and one each in Scotland and Wales, each investigating complaints in a particular part of the country.

2. *Tribunals and inquiries* (as above).

3. *Courts of law* (as above).

Other Public Bodies.

1. *National Health Service.* Each health authority has its own complaints procedure subject to a national code of practice. Complaints, other than those involving the exercise of clinical judgement, may be taken to the *Health Service Commissioner.* Special procedures exist for complaints against doctors.

2. *Nationalised Industries.* Each industry has a consumer council which exists both to take up individual complaints and to represent the views of consumers to the board of management for the industry (*e.g.,* The Post Office Users National Council, the Transport Users Consultative Committees).

Local Government Structure (showing numbers of authorities of each type)

	England			Wales	Scotland	
1st Tier	Metropolitan County Councils 6	Non-Metropolitan County Councils 39	Greater London Council 1	County Councils 8	Regional Councils 9	Islands Councils 3
2nd Tier	Metropolitan District Councils 36	Non-Metropolitan District Councils 296	London Borough Councils * 32	County District Councils 37	District Councils 53	
3rd Tier		Parish Councils 8,919		Community Councils	Community Councils	Community Councils

* Excluding the City of London.

Table derived from J. Stanyer and B. C. Smith, *Administering Britain* (Fontana, 1976), p. 119.

Local Government—Division of Functions

Service	England and Wales			Scotland
	Metropolitan areas	*Non-Metropolitan areas*	*Greater London*	
Education	District	County	Borough (except in inner London)[1]	Region
Personal social services	District	County	Borough	Region
Police and fire services	County	County	GLC[2]	Region
Planning	Shared	Shared	Shared	Shared
Highways	Shared	Shared	Shared	Shared
Environmental Health	District	District	Borough	District
Housing	District	District	Borough	District

Notes:

1. In Inner London a special body, the Inner London Education Authority, consisting of members of the GLC and the relevant boroughs, runs the education service.

2. The police service in London is the responsibility of the Home Secretary.

Parliamentary Commissioner for Administration.

1967–71	Sir Edmund Compton
1971–76	Sir Alan Marre (and Health Service Commissioner from 1973)
1976–	Sir Idwal Pugh (and Health Service Commissioner)

K. PRESSURE GROUPS

Large numbers of groups exist to exert pressure on government by direct consultation with ministers and civil servants, lobbying Parliament and general publicity campaigns. Some exist to defend interests such as labour, business or consumers; other promote particular causes such as the prevention of cruelty to children or the banning of blood sports. Of great importance in contemporary politics are the groups representing labour and business.

Trade Unions.

In 1976 11·8 million people, 46% of the working population, belonged to a trade union. The 12 largest unions were:

Business.

The peak organisation representing British business is the *Confederation of British Industry*, formed in 1965.

CBI Members in 1976

Industrial companies	10,075
Commercial companies	612
Public sector members	15
Employers' organisations and trade associations	157
Commercial associations	35
	10,894

Director-Generals of the CBI

1965–69	J. Davies
1969–76	C. Adamson
1976–	J. Methven

Business is also represented by large numbers of associations which promote the interests of individual industries and sectors (*e.g.*, the Society of Motor Manufacturers and Traders, the Retail Consortium, the Association of Independent Businesses).

	Members	Principal Officer
Transport and General Workers' Union	1,856,000	M. Evans
Amalgamated Union of Engineering Workers	1,435,000	H. Scanlon
National Union of General and Municipal Workers	881,000	D. Basnett
National Association of Local Government Officers	625,000	G. Drain
National Union of Public Employees	584,000	A. Fisher
Electrical, Electronic, Telecommunication and Plumbing Union	427 000	F. Chapple
Union of Shop, Distributive and Allied Workers	377,000	Lord Allen
National Union of Mineworkers	374,000	J. Gormley
Association of Scientific, Technical and Managerial Staffs	351,000	C. Jenkins
National Union of Teachers	285,000	F. Jarvis
Union of Construction Allied Trades and Technicians	278,000	G. Lloyd
Civil and Public Services Association	225,000	K. Thomas

110 trade unions, representing 89% of total union membership, are affiliated to the *Trades Union Congress*, which is the federal body of the trade union movement representing its views to government and others and giving assistance on questions relating to particular trades and industry.

TUC General Secretaries since 1946.

1946–60	(Sir) V. Tewson
1960–70	G. Woodcock
1970–74	V. Feather
1974–	L. Murray

L. THE MEDIA

1. Principal Newspapers

The principal national dailies, with their proprietors and circulation, are set out below.

There are also a number of provincial morning daily newspapers in England (*e.g.*, *The Birmingham Post and Gazette, The Liverpool Daily Post, The Yorkshire Post*). Scotland has five morning dailies, of which the most important are *The Scotsman, The Glasgow Herald* and *The Daily Record*. Wales has one, *The Western Mail*, and Northern Ireland two, *The News-Letter* and *Irish News*.

National Dailies	Proprietors	Circulation in 1976 (millions)	General political stance
Daily Express	Trafalgar House	2·6	Ind. Con.
Daily Mail	Associated Newspapers Ltd.	1·8	Ind. right-wing Con.
Daily Mirror	Reed Publishing Holdings Ltd.	3·9	Ind.
Daily Telegraph	Daily Telegraph Ltd.	1·3	Con.
Financial Times	Pearson Longman Ltd.	0·2	Finance, Ind.
Guardian	Guardian and Manchester Evening News Ltd.	0·3	Ind. Lib.
Morning Star	Morning Star Co-op Society	0·04	Comm.
Sun	News International Ltd.	11·9	Ind.
The Times	Times Newspapers Ltd.	0·3	Ind. Con.
National Sundays			
News of the World	News International Ltd.	5·1	Ind. Con.
Observer	Atlantic Richfield Co.	0·7	Ind.
People	Reed Publishing Holdings Ltd.	4·1	Ind.
Sunday Express	Trafalgar House	3·5	Ind. Con.
Sunday Mirror	Reed Publishing Holdings Ltd.	4·1	Ind.
Sunday Telegraph	The Sunday Telegraph Ltd.	1·4	Ind. Con.
Sunday Times	Times Newspapers Ltd.	2·8	Ind. Con.
London Evenings			
Evening News	Associated Newspapers Ltd.	0·6	Con.
Evening Standard	Trafalgar House	0·4	Ind. Con.

2. Broadcasting

British Broadcasting Corporation

Established in 1926 as a public service body and financed by licence fees paid by all owners of TV sets. It is directed by a board of governors appointed by the government.

Services: Radio—4 national networks; 20 local radio stations. TV—2 channels.

Chairman of the Board of Governors. 1973–. Sir Michael Swann

Director-General, 1977–. Mr. Ian Trethowan.

Independent Broadcasting Authority

Established in 1954 to licence programme contracting companies and to regulate their output. In 1972 its functions were extended to include local sound broadcasting. Independent broadcasting is financed by advertising revenue.

Services: TV—One channel, operated by 15 regional companies. A common news service is provided for all the companies by Independent Television News Ltd. Radio— 19 local radio stations.

Chairman of IBA, 1975–. Lady Plowden.

Director-General, 1970–. Sir Brian Young.

Editorially all brodcasting authorities are expected to show political balance. Both the BBC and the IBA have bodies with whom individuals and organisations may raise complaints.

M. WHO'S WHO IN BRITISH POLITICS

Benn, Anthony Wedgwood, b. 1925; M.P. (Lab.) since 1950 (except for short period between father's death and renunciation of the family peerage); Minister of Technology 1966–70, Secretary of State for Industry 1974–5 and for Energy since 1975; Member Labour Party NEC 1959–60 and since 1962.

Callaghan, James, b. 1912; M.P. (Lab.) since 1945; Chancellor of the Exchequer 1964–7, Home Secretary 1967–70, Foreign Secretary 1974–6, Prime Minister since 1976; Member Labour Party NEC since 1957, Treasurer 1967–76, Leader since 1976.

Carrington, Lord, b. 1919; Member of House of Lords since 1938; Leader of Opposition in the Lords 1964–70 and since 1974; Secretary of State for Defence 1970–4 and for Energy 1974; Chairman Conservative Party Organisation 1972–4.

Davies, John, b. 1916; Director-General CBI 1965–9; M.P. (Con.) since 1970; Secretary of State for Trade and Industry 1970–2, Chancellor of Duchy of Lancaster 1972–4; Shadow spokesman on foreign affairs since 1976.

Foot, Michael, b. 1913; M.P. (Lab.) 1945–55 and since 1960; Secretary of State for Employment 1974–6, Lord President of the Council and Leader of the Commons since 1976; Member Labour Party NEC since 1971, Deputy Leader since 1976.

Healey, Denis, b. 1917; M.P. (Lab.) since 1952; Secretary of State for Defence 1964–70, Chancellor of the Exchequer since 1974; Member Labour Party NEC 1970–5.

Heath, Edward, b. 1916; M.P. (Con.) since 1950; Chief Whip 1955–9, Minister of Labour 1959–60, Lord Privy Seal 1960–3, Secretary of State for Industry, Trade and Regional Development 1963–4, Prime Minister 1970–4; Leader of the Opposition 1965–70 and 1974–5; Leader Conservative Party 1965–75.

Howe, Sir Geoffrey, b. 1926; M.P. (Con.) 1964–6 and since 1970; Solicitor-General 1970–2, Minister for Trade and Consumer Affairs 1972–4; Shadow spokesman on social services 1974–5 and Treasury and Economic Affairs since 1975.

Joseph, Sir Keith, b. 1918; M.P. (Con.) since 1956; Minister of Housing and Local Government 1962–4, Secretary of State for Social Services 1970–4; Member of Shadow Cabinet since 1974 and spokesman on industry since 1977.

Owen, David, b. 1938; M.P. (Lab.) since 1966; Secretary of State for Foreign and Commonwealth Affairs since 1977.

Powell, Enoch, b. 1912; M.P. (Con. and later UUUC) since 1950 (except for 7 months in 1974); Minister of Health 1960–3; resigned from Conservative Party in 1974 joining United Ulster Unionist Coalition.

Prior, James, b. 1927; M.P. (Con.) since 1959; Minister of Agriculture 1970–2, Lord President of the Council and Leader of the Commons 1972–4; Shadow spokesman on employment since 1974.

Pym, Francis, b. 1922; M.P. (Con.) since 1961; Chief Whip 1970–3, Secretary of State for Northern Ireland 1973–4; Shadow spokesman on agriculture 1974–5 and on devolution and House of Commons affairs since 1976.

Rees, Merlyn, b. 1920; M.P. (Lab.) since 1963; Secretary of State for Northern Ireland 1974–6, Home Secretary since 1976.

Shore, Peter, b. 1924; M.P. (Lab.) since 1964; Secretary of State for Economic Affairs 1967–9, Minister without Portfolio 1969–70, Secretary of State for Trade 1974–6 and for the Environment since 1976.

Steel, David, b. 1938; M.P. (Lib.) since 1965; Leader Liberal Party since 1976.

Thatcher, Margaret, b. 1925; M.P. (Con.) since 1959; Secretary of State for Education and Science 1970–4; Leader of the Opposition since 1975.

Whitelaw, William, b. 1918; M.P. (Con.) since 1955; Lord President of the Council and Leader of the Commons 1970–2, Secretary of State for Northern Ireland 1972–3 and for Employment 1973–4; Chairman Conservative Party Organisation 1974–5; Shadow spokesman on employment 1974–5 and on home affairs since 1975.

Williams, Shirley, b. 1930; M.P. (Lab.) since 1964; Secretary of State for Prices and Consumer Protection 1974–6 and for Education and Science since 1976; Member Labour Party NEC since 1970.

Wilson, Sir Harold, b. 1916; M.P. (Lab.) since 1945; President of Board of Trade 1947–51; Prime Minister 1964–70 and 1974–6; Leader of Labour Party 1963–76.

N. NORTHERN IRELAND

From 1921 until 1972 Northern Ireland was governed under the scheme of devolution embodied in the Government of Northern Ireland Act 1920. This created the Northern Ireland Parliament, generally known as Stormont after its eventual location. Executive powers were formally vested in the Governor of Northern Ireland, but were in effect performed by a Prime Minister and small cabinet, responsible to Stormont.

The recent troubles in the province led the UK Government in 1972 to suspend the Government of Ireland Act. Since then, apart from a period of four months in 1974, Northern Ireland has been ruled direct from Westminster, the powers of government being vested in the Secretary of State for Northern Ireland. Most local government functions in Northern Ireland are performed either by the Secretary of State or by special boards. There are, however, 26 elected district councils with limited functions, mainly in the environmental field.

THE
WORLD OF
MUSIC

The art of music as it has developed in the Western world, with a glossary of musical terms and an index to composers. Special topics discussed include Festivals and Music Clubs and Societies.

TABLE OF CONTENTS

THE WORLD OF MUSIC

In writing this section no special knowledge on the part of the reader is assumed; it is for those who want to know about the history of music, how different styles evolved, and how one composer influenced another. It is a background to music as the science section is a background to science, and just as the latter cannot show the reader the colours of the spectrum but only tell of Newton's experiments and of the relationship between colour and wavelength, so in this section we can only describe man's achievements in the world of sound. But knowing something about a composer, his work, and when he lived can help to bring fuller understanding and enjoyment when listening to his music.

The section is in four parts:

I. Historical Narrative and Discussion

II. Glossary of Musical Terms

III. Index to Composers

IV. Special Topics

I. HISTORICAL NARRATIVE AND DISCUSSION

The history of music, like that of any people or art, is not one of uninterrupted progress towards some ideal perfection. For five centuries or more music in the West has achieved peaks of accomplishment in one style or another before society has dictated or composers have felt the need for something new and different. Thus Wagner's music-drama *Parsifal*, lasting five hours, is not necessarily a more rewarding work than what Monteverdi achieved in *Orfeo* 250 years earlier. More complex yes, more rewarding—well, that is for the listener to judge.

We must keep this in mind when considering the development of music from a starting point of, say, Gregorian chant down to the complicated structures of a Schoenberg in our own day. In this development there is no true dividing line between one period and another, nor must simplifying terms such as "classical" or "romantic" be taken too literally.

The earliest history of Western music as we know it today is closely bound up with the Church, for music had to be provided for services. The earliest Christian music was influenced by Greek songs, few of which unfortunately have survived, and by the music of synagogues, where the art of chanting originated. The modal system of the ancient Greeks was highly organised. The earliest Greek scale was from A to A and the four descending notes A,G,F,E became the basis of their musical theory, and it is from them that Western music learned to call notes after the letters of the alphabet. A scale can begin on any note and always includes two semitones upon which much of the character of a melody depends.

The Greek modes were based on the white notes only; the Dorian, Phrygian, Lydian, and Mixolydian began respectively on E,D,C, and B. Their character was thus decided by the position of the semitones, and they formed the basis, often corrupted, of the mediaeval modes. This system was transmitted through Latin writers such as Boethius and Cassiodorus, and through Arabic writers. The eight Church modes were not established until the 8th or 9th cent. These plagal modes, as they are called, started in each case, for technical reasons, a fourth below the authentic modes.

By the end of the 6th cent. Gregorian chant had developed so far that some sort of permanent record was required. *Neumes*, signs placed over the Latin text, were the earliest attempt at musical notation. Gradually lines came into use until a four-line stave was established, probably in the 11th and 12th cent., and with them clef signs, although the treble clef as we know it today did not appear until the 13th cent.

And what is this music—plainchant—like? It is an unaccompanied, single line of melody, which, when we have become used to its "antique" flavour is heard to have a wide range of spiritual and emotional expression, not excluding word painting. The texts used came from the Liturgy. These beautiful, extended lines of flowing, flexible melody can still be heard on Sundays in Roman Catholic cathedrals and churches.

Polyphony is Born.

The 10th cent. saw the appearance of a book called *Musica Enchiriadis* (whose authorship is disputed) which introduced theories about unison singing in which the melody is doubled at the fourth or fifth. Organum, or diaphony, is used to describe this method of writing, a term which confusingly could also be used for a kind of singing where melismatic melody was heard over a drone note on the organ. Rules came into fashion defining which intervals were allowed and which parts of the church services could be sung in more than one part. By the time of Guido d'Arezzo (c. 990–1050), a Benedictine monk who helped advance notation, contrary motion was permitted as the cadence was approached, another technical advance. Gradually the voices became more and more independent, and the third, so long considered a discord, came into use. Pérotin, of Notre Dame, was the first composer to write for three and four voices, and he and his great predecessor Léonin were the great masters of early polyphony. The proximity and spikiness of Pérotin's harmony is almost modern-sounding, and as with Gregorian chant, once we have adjusted ourselves to the sound, this music can be a rewarding experience.

Early Secular Music.

In mediaeval France, towards the end of the 11th cent., there developed what has become known as the age of the troubadours, poet-musicians. They were the successors to the *jongleurs*, or jugglers, and minstrels about whom we know little as practically none of their music has survived. The troubadours hymned the beauty of spring and of ladies. Contemporary with them in Germany were the Minnesingers. Their songs were mostly set in three modes. Adam de la Halle (d. 1287), because so much of his music survives, is perhaps the best known of the troubadours. He was a notable composer of *rondels*, an early form of round, of which the English *Sumer is icumen in*, written by a monk of Reading c. 1226, is a fine example. In that modes were used, the troubadours' music remained definitely akin to that of ecclesiastical hymns, although there is an undoubted feeling of our modern major scale in some of the songs.

Ars Nova.

The term *ars nova* derives partly from writings of Philippe de Vitry (1291–1361) who codified the rules of the old and the new music in a valuable treatise. This *new art* represented a freeing of music from organum and rhythmic modes, and an increase in the shape and form of melodic line. France was the centre of music during the 14th cent. and apart from Philippe de Vitry the leading composer was Guillaume de Machaut (1300–77), who wrote many secular works as well as a polyphonic setting of the Mass. His music is notable for its vigour and tenderness as well as for its technical expertise. Meanwhile in 14th-cent. Italy a quite separate branch of *ars nova* was developing. Imitation and canon were to be noted in the music of Italian composers, and choral forms such as the Ballata, Madrigal (which often included instrumental accompaniment) and Caccia (a two-voice hunting song in canon) were common. The greatest Italian composer of this period was the blind organist and lutenist Francesco di Landini (c. 1325–97). Italian pieces of the time, as compared with their French counterparts, are notable for their sensual rather than their intellectual qualities, a difference—it has been noted—between The Southern and The Northern New Art.

England was less affected by *ars nova*, but surviving music shows the influence of the Continent. Not until the 15th cent. did she begin to make a significant contribution to the history of music. Both John Dunstable (c. 1380–1453), who was no less eminent as a mathematician and an astronomer than as a musician, and his contemporary Lionel Power advanced the technique of music by their method of composition (use of the triad, for instance) and mellifluous style. Their musicianship was much appreciated on the Continent. Dunstable did away with the use of *cantus firmus*—a fixed melody—and increased the use of free composition.

After Dunstable the next great figure in European music was Guillaume Dufay (c. 1400–74), the most celebrated composer of the Burgundian school. His music is distinguished for its blend of flowing melody, cleverly wrought counterpoint and tender expressiveness. Much travelled, Dufay was a man of catholic outlook. Together with Dunstable and the Burgundian Gilles Binchois he bridged the gap between 14th cent. *ars nova* and the fully developed polyphony of the 15th cent.

Ars nova composers also showed an interest in secular music and many of their *rondeaux* and *chansons* (those of Binchois particularly) have been preserved. Personality began to play a distinguishing part in composition.

The results of Dufay's good work can be heard in the flowering of the Franco-Netherland school later in the 15th cent. Its two most notable representatives are Ockeghem (c. 1420–95) and his pupil Josquin des Prés (c. 1450–1521), who carried musical expressiveness even further than Dufay; their work can also be grand and majestic. Indeed Josquin's wide range, from the humorous to the dignified, partially accounts for his justly deserved high reputation. He was a master of counterpoint but tempered his mechanical ingenuity with imaginative insight.

Throughout the Renaissance choral music was breaking away, as we have seen, from its earlier bonds. The mediaeval tradition of having the *cantus firmus* in the tenor went by the board; the use of dissonance, when only two voices were used in mediaeval times, was abandoned in favour of euphony; and all the voices, democratically, came to share the musical lines. Composers also began to respect their texts; where words were previously fitted to the music, the reverse was now the case. In Josquin's music, indeed, we have the first attempts at symbolism: matching verbal ideas with musical ones. The importance of this musical renaissance has been realised only over the past twenty years. At last the Renaissance composers are coming to be seen not merely as historical figures relevant only in so far as their work culminated in the great classical composers, but as masters in their own right, whose music should be nearly as familiar to us as is that of a Mozart or a Beethoven.

With the exception of Dufay, little is known of the lives of the musicians so far mentioned. Most of them were in the service of royal or ducal households where they were in charge of the chapel choir, or else they worked in or around the great cathedrals, teaching at choir-schools. They were well rewarded for their services and their social position was probably high.

During recent years there has been an appreciable revival of interest in mediaeval music. Arguments continue about how much of it should be performed, but that is just one of the many indications that it is alive and not just part of the history of music. It can communicate, as the late David Munrow showed, just as well as music of later eras.

The Sixteenth Century.

By the 16th cent. music in England was a steadily expanding art and much encouraged. Music-making in the home was becoming quite the fashion in social circles. The Chapels Royal remained the chief musical centres but the music was changing with the development of new secular forms so that it was not so much religious as a part of life. Composers began their lives as choirboys and received a thoroughgoing education, both theoretical and practical.

Carrying on from where Josquin and his contemporaries left off, Palestrina in Italy, Victoria in Spain, Lassus in the Netherlands, and Byrd in England brought the polyphonic style to its zenith. At the same time came the rise of the madrigals, first in Italy, then in the Netherlands; and then the beginnings of instrumental music as it came to be known in the succeeding centuries.

The vocal composers began to use chordal (homophonic) as well as contrapuntal (polyphonic) methods of writing—examples are Victoria's *Ave Verum Corpus* and Palestrina's *Stabat Mater*—but polyphony was still the fullest most magnificent instrument of composition, as for instance in Byrd's *O Quam Gloriosum* which shows an eager response to the mood and to the inflection of the words in a kind of vocal orchestration. A feature of all these composers' music, but more especially that of Victoria (c. 1535–1611) and Palestrina (1525–94), is its serene simplicity and fervour of utterance. Palestrina was perhaps more spacious in his effects. Victoria the more passionate. How well we can imagine—and sometimes hear—their music resounding down the naves of the great cathedrals of Europe.

The music of Lassus (c. 1532–94) is distinguished both in sheer amount and in vitality. His mastery in the field of motets was unrivalled, encompassing a wide range of subject and mood. He and his fellow Flemish composers, Willaert, de Monte and Arcadelt, were also expert in the Madrigal, a form popular in Italy and England as well. The Madrigal was a contrapuntal setting of a poem, usually not longer than twelve lines, in five or six parts. The subject (of the poetry) was usually amorous or pastoral. It was a short-lived, but highly prolific vogue. Orlando Gibbons (1583–1625), Thomas Weelkes (c. 1573–1623), and John Wilbye (1574–1638) were the most prominent English exponents.

Instrumental Music.

By the end of the 14th cent. instrumental music began to become something more than mere anonymous dance tunes or primitive organ music. Instruments often accompanied voices, or even replaced them, so that the recorder, lute, viol, and spinet indoors, and sackbuts and shawms outdoors, had already been developed by the time instrumental music came to be written down. Gradually a distinction grew up between what was appropriate to the voice and what was suitable for instruments. Byrd, Gibbons, and Giles Farnaby in England, the great blind keyboard player, Cabezón (1510–66) in Spain, and Frescobaldi (1583–1643) in Italy produced valuable instrumental works. Perhaps the *Parthenia* and the *Fitzwilliam Virginal Book*, collections of Early English Keyboard music, give as fair a representative idea as any of the development of instrumental form at this time.

In chamber music musicians often played collections of dance tunes strung together to make a whole; or they chose fantasies (or " fancies "), where a composer altered a tune as he wished. Then there were sets of variations on a ground, that is a simple tune played over and over again on a bass viol.

As far as brass instruments are concerned, they were often used on festive occasions in spacious halls or in cathedrals. The Venetian composer Andrea Gabrieli (c. 1510–86) was the first to combine voice and instruments and his nephew Giovanni Gabrieli (1557–1612) carried the process further to produce sacred symphonies, often using antiphonal effects.

Drama in Music.

Not until the end of the 16th cent. did anyone begin to think about combining drama and music, and so " invent " the new art we know today as opera. A group of artistic intelligentsia met together in Florence and conceived the idea of reviving the ancient declamation of Greek tragedy. They took Greek mythological subjects, cast them in dramatic form, and set them to music, not in the choral polyphonic style of the Madrigal, but with single voices declaiming dialogue in music. The earliest examples of what was called *Dramma per Musica* were Peri's *Daphne* in 1597 (now lost) and his *Eurydice*, in which he co-operated with Caccini. The new style came to its full flowering with the appearance of Monteverdi (1567–1643), whose genius would surely have shone in any age.

Monteverdi's first opera, *Orfeo*, produced in 1607, is a landmark of dramatic expression, and it is nothing less than a catastrophe that so many of his later operas have been lost. His *Orfeo* provides the basic ground work for the operas of the next two centuries: recitative, accompanied recitative, and aria. His last opera *L'Incoronazione di Poppaea*, written when he was at the great age (for those days) of 75, succeeds in its aim of creating a free, fluid form, slipping easily from recitative to arioso and even aria without the strict, closed forms that were to be used in the 17th and 18th cent. He focuses attention to an almost unbelievable extent on character rather than situation. He creates real people with all their faults and foibles—the kittenish, sexually attractive Poppaea, the power-drunk, infatuated Nero, the noble Seneca, and the dignified, rejected empress Octavia. As recent productions have shown these characters leap from the musical page as if they had just been created, each unerringly delineated in musical terms. Only the vocal line, the continuo, and the very incomplete instrumental ritornelli parts have been preserved, but in sensitive, knowledgeable hands tonal variety in the shape of wind and string parts can be added, as we know certain instruments were available to the composer.

Monteverdi's successors were Cavalli (1602–76), Cesti (1623–69) and Stradella (1642–82), who gave the solo voice more and more prominence encouraged by the advent of the castrati's brilliant voices. These artificially created singers had a vogue and popularity similar to " pop " singers of today, fêted wherever they appeared. The aria became more extended and ornate, and dramatic verisimilitude gradually but inexorably took second place to vocal display. An aria was nearly always in *da capo* form, the first section being repeated after a contrasting middle one.

Sixteenth- and Seventeenth-century Church Music.

Of course, the invention of a new dramatic style affected church music too. The concentration on

the vertical aspect of music (homophony) as opposed to the horizontal (polyphony) led to the increasing importance of the voice in religious music. In Italy, it is true, there was the late-flowering, great madrigalist Carlo Gesualdo (1560–1614), whose harmonic daring still astonishes us today, but by 1600 the cantata was coming to replace older forms in church music. In its simplest form this was a story told in accompanied recitative. Giacomo Carissimi (c. 1604–74) was one of the first significant composers of this new form. He too was in on the birth of the oratorio, whose forerunner was the *sacra rappresentazione* (mystery or miracle play) of early 16th-cent Florence. Then in the mid-16th cent. St. Philip Neri brought in elements from popular plays on sacred subjects in his services in Rome, designed to hold the attention of youth—rather as certain parsons have tried with " pop " services today. Emilio del Cavalieri (c. 1550–1602) and Carissimi developed the form adding arias and choral movements, omitting actual representation. Alessandro Scarlatti (1660–1725), whose oratorios bear a close resemblance to his operas, brought oratorio to its zenith in Italy.

Heinrich Schütz (1585–1672), Bach's great predecessor, was the founder of German church music. His historical place has never been called into question but only in recent times have the intrinsic merits of his own music come to be recognised. He studied with Giovanni Gabrieli in his youth and later came under the influence of Monteverdi, so it was not surprising that he brought Italian ideas across the Alps to Germany and wrote the first German opera *Daphne*, now sadly lost. He also introduced his country to the Italian declamatory style and to the new kind of concertato instrumental writing. But his dramatic religious works were his greatest contribution to musical development. He wrote with a devout intensity, bringing to life the scriptural texts by closely allying his urgent music to the words. His three settings of the Passions—Matthew, Luke, and John—paved the way for Bach's even more remarkable works in this genre. Two contemporaries of Schütz, Johann Hermann Schein (1586–1630) and Samuel Scheidt (1587–1654), were both important figures in German Reformation music.

Lully, Purcell, and Seventeenth-century Opera.

France resisted the tide of Italian opera, although paradoxically it was an Italian, Jean-Baptiste Lully (c. 1632–87), who charted the different course of French opera which was from the beginning associated with the court ballet. His musical monopoly during the reign of Louis XIV was put to good use. In his thirteen operas the libretto, usually on classical, allegorical themes, plays a vital part in the composition, which is therefore less clearly divided between recitative and aria than in Italian opera. The orchestration and the ballets assume greater importance than in the traditional Italian form. It was, in short, a more realistic, less stylised art.

In England, opera developed out of the entertainment known as the Masque, a succession of dances, accompanied by voices and instruments and often incorporated in a drama or spectacle. Henry Lawes's (1596–1662) setting of Milton's *Comus* is probably the most famous of these entertainments. The *Venus and Adonis* of John Blow (1649–1708) can be called the first English opera because here the music is gradually gaining the ascendancy over the spoken word. However, it was Purcell (c. 1659–95), Blow's pupil, with *Dido and Aeneas*, who really gave dramatic life to the new medium by giving his characters a true musical personality that was subtler than anything the mere spoken word could achieve. The grief-laden lament of the dying Dido " When I am laid in earth " has an expressive power, achieved by extraordinarily bold harmonic effects, never before and seldom since achieved. The opera was in fact written for a young ladies' boarding school. Purcell followed it with several outstanding semi-operas—such as *The Fairy Queen* (to Dryden's text). His untimely death at the age of 36 probably robbed us of several full-length operas—and perhaps a consequence of this was that English music after him did not develop as it should have done.

His verse anthems and much of his instrumental music, especially the Fantasias, are also rich in imaginative mastery through his original use of harmony and counterpoint. However, a great deal of his pieces were written for a specific occasion and many of the odes are set to impossibly trite texts. At least his genius was fully acknowledged in his own day, and he was appointed organist in Westminster Abbey where he was buried with due pomp. He is said to have died through catching cold when locked out of his own house at night.

Vivaldi and the Rise of Instrumental Music.

Out of the dance suites popular in the 16th cent. and the beginning of the 17th (known in Italy as the *Sonata da Camera*) developed the concerto. This began as two groups of instrumentalists compared and contrasted with each other as in Giovanni Gabrieli's *Sonata piano e forte*. With Arcangelo Corelli (1653–1713) the concerto grosso took a more definite shape, alternating a solo group of instruments with the main body of strings in three or more contrasting movements. Giuseppe Torelli (1658–1709), Francesco Geminiani (1687–1762) and Tommaso Albinoni (1671–1750) were other notable contributors to the form, but none of the composers so far mentioned has today achieved the popularity of the priest Antonio Vivaldi (c. 1678–1741), himself a violinist, who had at his disposal the orchestra at the Ospedale della Pieta in Venice. The young women at this music school also contributed the vocal side of the concerts there of which there are many descriptions. One says: "They sing like angels, play the violin, flute, organ, oboe, cello, bassoon—in short no instrument is large enough to frighten them . . . I swear nothing is so charming than to see a young and pretty nun, dressed in white, a sprig of pomegranate blossom behind one ear, leading the orchestra, and beating time with all the grace and precision imaginable." For this body, Vivaldi wrote about 500 concertos which maintain a remarkably even quality, but "The Four Seasons " are perhaps the most felicitous.

Meanwhile organ music was advancing rapidly in technique. Girolamo Frescobaldi (1583–1643) and Jan Pieterszoon Sweelinck (1562–1621) wrote works that provided the foundation of the Italian and Northern German schools of organ music. Their ricercares gradually developed into the fugue, a vein so richly mined by Bach. Among their successors the most notable figure before Bach was Johann Pachelbel (1653–1706).

Other keyboard music, especially for the harpsichord, was the particular province of France; and Jean-Philippe Rameau (1683–1764) and François Couperin (1668–1733) were both masters of keyboard style and harmonic invention. They wrote many pieces of subtle charm and exquisite craftsmanship.

Bach (1685–1750).

The two giant figures of Bach and Handel bestride the first half of the 18th cent. Their differences are perhaps greater than their similarities. Bach wrote essentially for himself (although of course, he had to satisfy his employers at Cöthen and Leipzig) while Handel was composing to please his wide public. Bach was a provincial, always remaining in central Germany; Handel was widely travelled. Bach was devoutly religious, almost ascetic; Handel was more a man of the world. They never met.

To summarise Bach's vast output in a short space is virtually impossible. One can only try to distil the flavour of his music. He brought the art of polyphony to the highest pitch of mastery that has ever been achieved or is ever likely to be achieved. In his famous " Forty-Eight " and " the Art of the Fugue " he explored all the fugal permutations of the major and minor keys. At the same time his music rose above technical brilliance to achieve, especially in his organ music,

the two Passions, many of the church cantatas, and the B minor Mass, intense emotional and expressive power. The cantatas, from his Leipzig appointment (1723) onwards, were integrated into the services. They consisted usually of a chorus based on a Lutheran hymn tune, recitatives, several extended arias, and a concluding chorus usually a straightforward version of the hymn tune in which the congregation joined. There are some two hundred of these works and they contain a wealth of comparatively unknown and sometimes even unrecognised beauties. The St. John and the St. Matthew Passion extend these procedures to a grand scale, an Evangelist telling the new Testament story in vivid recitative, the chorus taking the part of the crowd, soloists pondering in arias on the meaning of the Gospel, and Jesus's words being sung by a bass. Anyone who has heard either of these works well performed cannot help but dismiss from his mind any idea of Bach as a mere dry-as-dust musical mathematician. In the St. Matthew Passion, every suggestion in the text that can possibly be illustrated by a musical equivalent is so illustrated. The Old Testament Pharasaic law is represented by strict musical forms such as the canon; Christ's sayings are given noble arioso life; and the arias reflect truly the New Testament's compassionate message. Technically the work is a marvel; expressively it is eloquent. The B minor Mass, although it contains borrowings from many of his own works, still stands as a satisfying monumental whole in which Bach's choral writing achieved a new richness, the adaptations being in accord with their new setting.

Bach's instrumental music, especially the violin concertos and the unaccompanied works for violin and cello, not only show the immense range of his powers but also contain many of his deeper thoughts, whereas the orchestral suites and the Brandenburg concertos are more extrovert, particularly the rhythmically exuberant fast movements.

Bach closes an era—that of the later contrapuntalists—by achieving the *ne plus ultra* in fugal composition; his last, incomplete work. The Art of the Fugue, is evidence of that. In recent years there has been a trend towards playing Bach's music on original instruments of his time (or replicas) and singing it with appropriately sized, all-male choirs.

Handel (1685–1759).

During his lifetime Handel was far more widely recognised as a great composer than Bach, and his music, unlike Bach's, maintained its place in popular esteem until the re-discovery of Bach and the dominance of the symphony placed Handel somewhat in the background.

During the latter part of the 19th cent. Handel's name was mainly associated with mammoth, anachronistic performances of a small sample of his oratorios at the Crystal Palace and elsewhere in England. In his lifetime these works, and all his other pieces in the genre, were sung by a small choir who were outnumbered by the instrumental players. Over the past few years authentic-sized performances of his oratorios and a revival of interest in his operas have revealed the real Handel, unknown to our grandparents.

The operas were neglected partly because the vocal prowess they required—and which the castrati so brilliantly supplied—was no longer available and because their dramatic life, at least according to 19th- and early 20th-cent. tenets, hardly existed. Now it is realised that this neglect has deprived us of an unending stream of glorious melody and of much daring harmony. But perhaps it is in the hitherto disregarded oratorios, such as *Semele*, that Handel's innate dramatic sense and musical range are to be heard gloriously fulfilled, and the pastoral serenade *Acis and Galatea* is surely one of the most delightful scores ever composed.

Handel was a colourful, imaginative orchestrator, and this can be heard both in his accompaniment to vocal music and in his concerti grossi, op. 3 and 6, the earlier set exploiting a diversity of interesting string and wind combination. In his writing he was at home in a polyphonic or homophonic style as his superb choruses show. His organ concertos, of which he was the "inventor" (to quote a contemporary source), were often played between the acts of his oratorios. They are alternately expressive and exuberant pieces calling for some virtuosity from the player. His occasional works, such as the Water Music and Fireworks Music show his ingenuity in extending the range of the typical 17th cent. suite to serve a particular occasion.

Handel's working life was mostly spent in England where his Italian operas were acclaimed. In the years between his arrival here in 1711 and 1729 he wrote nearly thirty operas. It was only when the public tired of these and his reputation slumped that he turned to oratorio with equal success.

Bach and Handel between them crowned the age of polyphony that had lasted for two hundred years or more. After them, it is hardly surprising that composers began looking for a new style, already anticipated in the music of Rameau and particularly Dominico Scarlatti (1685–1737), whose harpsichord sonatas foreshadowed the classical sonata form that was to dominate music for the next two hundred years. The change in musical style about 1750 was partly the result of a change in musical patronage. Bach was the last great composer to earn his living through being employed by the church. The new patrons were the nobility who liked to have a composer on hand to write for the various evening entertainments of the time. For this purpose the princes and dukes had their own orchestras and their own small opera houses. The music required had to be elegant, formal, galant. Haydn was exceptionally fortunate in having an employer, Prince Nicholas of Esterhazy, who allowed him to write more of less as he wished so that he was able to develop symphonic form into something more than a pleasing way of passing an evening.

The early symphonists, culminating in Haydn, broke away from Bach's contrapuntal treatment of the orchestra. Instruments now came to be treated in a more colourful manner according to their particular timbre. The court of Mannheim had an orchestra of a standard unheard hitherto, and Johann Stamitz (1717–57) and his son Karl (1745–1801) influenced the great composers who were to follow in their footsteps. The composition of their orchestra was flexible, oboes, flutes, and horns often being added to the standard string section. Bach's son Carl Philipp Emanuel (1714–88) added to and developed symphonic and sonata form, especially as regards keys and subjects.

Haydn and Mozart.

These two figures dominate the second half of the 18th cent. as Bach and Handel did the first. In a brief space only a general picture can be presented of their huge output and influence. Of Haydn's 104 symphonies (there may even be others) nearly all are worthy of study and hearing. The craftsmanship is always remarkable, the invention ever new. Indeed without Haydn's harmonic daring or his melodic ingenuity, the even greater symphonic thought of Beethoven would have been impossible: Haydn laid the groundwork on which his successor built towering edifices. A work such as the 93rd symphony in D is typical of his mature style with its searching introduction, powerfully wrought, earnestly argued first movement, beautiful Largo and resourceful bustling finale. Haydn did not fight shy of contrapuntal writing: the development section of this symphony's first movement and the finale are evidence of that, but it was only as an integral part of a predominantly homophonic technique.

Mozart's symphonies are not so different in from from Haydn's but—and this must be a subjective judgment—he put more emotional feeling into his. Nobody could listen to the heart-

searching first movement of his 40th symphony without being deeply moved. It was in his final three works in the medium that Mozart brought his symphonic art to perfection, and these obviously had an effect on Haydn's later symphonies written after them. For passion and tenderness contained within a classical form these late symphonies, and many other of Mozart's works, have yet to be surpassed.

Haydn, who has been rightly termed "the Father of the Symphony", was also the founder of the string quartet—perhaps the most perfect, because the most exactly balanced, form of musical expression. The four instruments—two violins, viola, and cello—discuss, argue, commune with each other over the whole gamut of feeling. In his quartets Haydn's mastery of structure is even more amazing than in his symphonies. Mozart's quartets (especially the six devoted to Haydn) and even more his quintets achieve miracles of beauty in sound, nowhere more so than in the first movement of the G minor (his most personal key) quintet. The two late piano quartets show how the piano can be ideally combined with strings. His clarinet quintet is also a masterly work.

Haydn did not leave any concertos of consequence. Mozart's, especially those for piano, are among his greatest works. As a brilliant clavier player himself, he showed a consummate skill in writing for the keyboard. Although the instrument he knew was slightly less advanced than the piano today, his concertos call for virtuosity in execution, yet they are as searching in emotional content as the late symphonies and quartets. Indeed the C major concerto (K. 467) and the C minor (K. 491) may be said to hold the quintessential Mozart. As well as twenty (mature) piano concertos, Mozart wrote six for the violin, four for the horn, and eighteen others, but none of these, delightful as they are, can be placed in quite the same class.

Of their church music, Haydn's sixteen masses and his oratorios—The Creation and The Seasons (both late works)—are perhaps more worthy of attention than Mozart's various masses, but we must not forget Mozart's final work—the Requiem or the serene late Motet Ave Verum Corpus.

Eighteenth-century Opera.

Mozart—for many the first great opera composer—did not, of course, create his masterpieces out of nothing. In France, Lully was followed by Rameau (1683–1764), who carried on his tradition of using classical themes but developed a more flexible style of recitative and greatly increased vividness of expression. But it was Gluck (1714–87) who more than anyone broke out of the straitjacket of the now ossified Italian form of opera—dominated by the singer—and showed just what could be achieved in moving human terms. Drama in music really came of age with his Orfeo e Euridice (1762), Alceste (1767) and Iphigénie en Tauride (1779). His simplicity and poignancy of expression were not lost on Mozart.

Meanwhile in Germany a kind of opera called Singspiel appeared during the 18th cent. Breaking away from classical themes, mundane stories were told in dialogue and music.

Until quite recently Haydn's operas were dismissed as unworthy representations of his genius but, chiefly through the enlightening efforts of the Haydn scholar, H. C. Robins Landon, some of his fifteen surviving works in the medium have been successfully revived. They have proved to be perfectly viable for the stage and, especially in the ensembles, full of that delightful invention to be found in the rest of his opus, if on a less fully developed scale. Still as musical drama they inevitably fall far short of Mozart's achievements, for the younger composer seems to have had an instinctive feeling for the stage. Into his operas he poured his most intense, personal music. He vividly portrays the foibles, desires, loves, and aspirations of mankind.

The earlier, immature stage pieces of his youth led to such works as Lucio Silla (1772) and La

Finta Giardiniera (1775) with their first glimpses of the glories to come. His first indubitably great opera is *Idomeneo* (1781). Despite its unpromisingly static plot, *Idomeneo* reveals Mozart's stature through its ability to breathe new life into a conventional *opera seria* form. Though influenced by Gluck it is yet more human and touching in its musical expression. To succeed this Mozart wrote a much more frivolous piece *Die Entführung aus dem Serail*. Stemming from the *Singspiel* tradition, it none the less creates real-life characters who have much charming music to sing.

After three lesser pieces Mozart embarked on his four masterpieces—*Le Nozze di Figaro* (1786), *Don Giovanni* (1787), *Cosi fan tutte* (1790), and *Die Zauberflöte* (1791).

Figaro, as well as being a delightful comedy, explores more fully than any previous opera situation and character, which find expression in beautiful arias and in two finales of symphonic proportion. In *Don Giovanni*, less satisfactory as a dramatic structure, the range of musical characterisation and insight into human motives is widened still further. *Cosi* lyrically but humorously expresses the follies of love. Mozart could not help but love his characters and his music for them is at one and the same time amusing and heartfelt. *Die Zauberflöte*—The Magic Flute—displays Mozart's deep-felt sympathy for his fellow men and of truth in an opera of great spiritual strength. Nor has opera any more loveable personality than the birdcatcher Papageno. Mozart's final opera *La Clemenza di Tito*, extolling imperial magnanimity, has never achieved the success or popularity of his other maturer stage works, though it contains much excellent music, and has recently been revived with honour in several opera houses.

Beethoven.

Mozart was the last major composer to depend, to any large extent, on private patronage for his living, and even he left the service of the Archbishop of Salzburg because he could not stand the restrictions imposed on his freedom. Henceforth composers would have to stand on their own two feet with all the advantages (liberty) and disadvantages (lack of security) that implied. Beethoven (1770–1827) was the first such composer of importance.

Although his work is usually divided into three periods, that division is somewhat too arbitrary, for no other composer in history, with the possible exception of Wagner, has shown such a continual development of his genius. Coming at just the right moment in musical history, he crowned the achievements of Haydn and Mozart with music of the utmost profundity of thought and feeling that looks back to its classical heritage and forward to the romantic movement of the 19th cent. His influence on musical thinking and writing is incalculable.

His first period shows his strong melodic gifts and the beginning of his individuality in developing form and structure to suit his own ends and match his particular genius. Unusual keys are explored, unusual harmonic procedures employed. With the "Eroica" (his third symphony) he established his position as a great composer. The unity of purpose he here achieved within a long and diverse structure is truly staggering, even today. In the first movement alone the formal invention and cogency went far beyond what even Mozart had achieved in his "Jupiter" symphony, and the second movement—a vast funeral March—has an overwhelmingly tragic emotional content. But the "Eroica" was followed by six equally great symphonies, each one as varied, as inventive, as unified as the others. The ninth symphony is significant for both its length and its finale. Here Beethoven crowns three superb instrumental movements with a choral movement that, as well as summing up all that has gone before, expresses in music the joy in existence more ecstatically than any other work.

The burning intensity of Beethoven's genius is just as evident in his chamber music. His quartets are the product of a revolutionary age in which the social graces and formal restraint of the 18th cent. were thrown off in a search for a more personal mode of expression. The early op. 18 set, and the Razoumovsky quartets, op. 59, go even beyond the range of Haydn's and Mozart's works in the medium but it was in his late quartets, his final musical testament, that Beethoven refined and distilled his art for posterity. No words can possibly describe their unique quality, but any and every chance should be taken to make their acquaintance: the effort required will be more than amply rewarded.

The early piano concertos do not reach quite that level of attainment, but the last three, together with the violin concerto, are on a par with the finest of the symphonies and quartets, as well as being considerable tests of the performers' technique. The Triple Concerto for piano, violin, and cello is an unusual and rewarding work. Beethoven's grandest choral work—and one of the most noble in existence—is the Mass in D (*Missa Solemnis*). Its vast scale and sublime utterance often defeat performers, but when it is successfully done there is no more spiritually uplifting experience for the listener, except perhaps Beethoven's only opera, *Fidelio*. This simple escape story was transformed by Beethoven's creative fire into a universal symbol of liberty, the composer identifying himself with the struggle for freedom from tyranny and release from darkness.

Beethoven lived in a period of war and revolution. A passionate believer in the brotherhood of man and in liberty, he was shocked to find his ideals thrown over by revolutionaries-turned-dictators. His own tragedy of deafness, which came upon him at the moment of his triumph, nearly submerged him, but in the end he won through and produced the string of masterpieces from the "Eroica" onwards. Hope springing from despair, love from hatred, victory over defeat, these are the unquenchable legacies left by Beethoven.

The Romantic Movement.

Inevitably, the Romantic movement in literature that burst forth about 1800 was bound to have its counterpart in music. And so it was. Breaking the classical bonds, composers such as Schubert, Schumann, Liszt, and Berlioz sought a new freedom in musical expression. Form became of less importance than content; and that content often had literary connections. For their purposes a larger orchestra was needed and supplied, but the miniature, the song especially, because of its very personal connotation, was also a favourite form.

Schubert (1797–1828)—described by Liszt as "the most poetic of musicians"—is perhaps the greatest lyrical genius in musical history. In him the Viennese tradition and influence of Haydn, Mozart, and Beethoven reached its zenith. The song was always Schubert's starting point, so it is hardly surprising that his reputation as a song writer has never been impaired but in his symphonic and instrumental works too it is always his inexhaustible fund of melody that first calls for attention. Nobody could listen to his "Trout" quintet, for piano and strings, his octet, his fifth symphony, or his song cycle *Die Schöne Müllerin* without being enchanted and invigorated by the sheer tunefulness of the music. But there is much more to Schubert than this: his understanding of the possibilities of harmonic change, his grasp of orchestral coloration (in the great C major symphony, for instance), his free use of sonata structure.

Although Mozart, Haydn, and Beethoven had all contributed to the song as an art form, it was with Schubert that it achieved its first full flowering. If he had written nothing but his songs, his place in the musical firmament would be assured. With his *Erlkönig* in 1815 the German *Lied* came of age and from then until the end of his life he wrote more than six hundred songs, hardly a dud among them. Whether it is the charm of *Heiden-röslein*, the drama of *Der Doppelgänger* or the numbed intensity of the *Winterreise* cycle, Schubert unerringly went to the heart of a poet's meaning; indeed he often raised poor verses to an inspired level by his settings. And for the first time the pianist shares a place of equal importance with the singer.

There is only room to mention one or two other composers, some of them wrongly neglected, who were roughly contemporaries of Beethoven and Schubert: the Czech Dussek (1760–1812), who like Beethoven bridges the classical-romantic gulf, Boccherini (1743–1805), the two Italian opera composers Cimarosa (1749–1801) and Paisiello (1740–1816), the Frenchman Méhul (1763–1817) and the German Hummel (1778–1837).

Weber (1786–1826) lacked Beethoven's energy and constructive powers and Schubert's sheer lyrical profundity, but he is an important figure, especially in the field of opera, where his *Der Freischütz* and *Oberon* led the way to a more flexible, dramatically realistic form of opera. His vivid imagination exactly fitted the new romantic mood abroad. The sheer beauty in the melodic shape of his music is also not to be denied. His instrumental works are attractive but insubstantial.

Mendelssohn and Schumann.

Mendelssohn (1809–47) was the civilised craftsman among the Romantic composers. A boy genius—many of his finest works were written before he was twenty—he maintained the importance of classical form while imbuing it with his own affectionate brand of poetic sensibility. His third and fourth symphonies—the "Scottish" and "The Italian"—(and possibly the fifth "The Reformation"), his string quartets (some of which go deeper than the rest of his music), octet, violin concerto, first piano concerto, and of course, the incidental music to "A Midsummer Night's Dream" represent his tidy yet effervescent style at its most winning.

Schumann (1810–56) is less easy to categorise. His early romantic flame was burnt out by some flaw in his intellectual and/or emotional make-up, and his inspiration seems to have declined in later years. No matter, by then he had given us the marvellous song cycles of 1840, an ever fresh piano concerto, many fine piano solos, including the mercurial, popular *Carnaval* and several symphonies, which, if not structurally perfect, contain much lovely music. The joys and sorrows of love and the feeling for natural beauty are all perfectly mirrored in these charming, lyrical works, and in the genial piano quintet.

Romantic Giants.

Berlioz (1803–69) and Liszt (1811–86) are the two most typical representative composers of the Romantic era. Both have always been controversial figures, with ardent advocates and opponents either unduly enthusiastic or unfairly derogatory. Berlioz might be termed the perfect painter in music. With an uncanny mastery of orchestral sound he could conjure up the countryside, the supernatural and the historical with the utmost ease. He based his music on the "direct reaction to feeling" and a desire to illustrate literature by musical means. That his technical expertise was not always the equal of his undoubted genius, can be heard in many of his larger works such as the dramatic cantata *The Damnation of Faust* and the dramatic symphony *Romeo and Juliet*, yet most people are willing to overlook the occasional vulgarity for the ineffable beauty of his many fine pages, but brutal cuts in his music, such as are often made in, for instance, his epic opera *The Trojans* only have the effect of reducing the stature of his works. We must accept him, warts and all. Anyone who has seen the two parts of *The Trojans*, presented complete in one evening at Covent Garden, will realise that Berlioz knew what he was about.

His output is not quantitatively large but includes several monumental works, as well as *The Trojans*. The *Requiem* ("Grand Messe des Morts") requires a tenor solo, huge chorus and orchestra, and brass bands, although Berlioz uses these forces fastidiously. The *Symphonie funèbre et triomphale* calls in its original form, for choir brass, and strings. But Berlioz was just as happy writing on a smaller scale as his exquisite song cycle, to words of Théophile Gautier, *Nuits d'Été*, shows. Gautier perhaps summed up better than anyone Berlioz's singular talent: "In that renaissance of the 1830s Berlioz represents the romantic musical idea, the breaking up of old moulds, the substitution of new forms for unvaried square rhythms, a complex and competent richness of orchestration, truth of local colour, unexpected effects in sound, tumultuous and Shakespearian depth of passion, amorous or melancholy dreaminess, longings and questionings of the soul, infinite and mysterious sentiments not to be rendered in words, and that something more than all which escapes language but may be divined in music."

During his lifetime Liszt was fêted and honoured not only by his musical colleagues but by the world at large, which idolised him and his piano. Then his reputation took a plunge from which it has only recently recovered. To be sure much of his early music is glitter and gloss, but his symphonies and tone poems—especially the Faust Symphony, the Dante Symphony (both, of course, inspired by literature), and *Orpheus* and *Prometheus*—and his late piano works show that he was an extraordinary harmonic innovator. The piano sonata in B minor brings his romantic, wilful temperament within a reasonably stable, pianistic form, and as such is a landmark in the repertory of the instrument. Liszt's output was prodigious, but the inquiring listener should explore the more original of his compositions already mentioned to form a true picture of his fertile genius.

Chopin.

Chopin (1810–49) was the master of the keyboard, par excellence. His development of the technical and expressive capabilities of the piano is unique in musical history. His inventive powers were poured out with nervous passionate energy and in a highly individual style through twenty astonishing, possibly agonised years of creative activity before his early death. A Chopin melody, limpid, transparent, singing, can be recognised easily by anyone, but his style gradually developed into something more subtle, more satisfying than pure melody. He took the greatest care of every detail so that any alteration, however small, upsets the perfect balance of his work. His poetic sensibility can be found in any of his works; for his constructive ability we must turn to the Ballades, the B minor Sonata, and the Barcarolle, while the Preludes and Studies blend technical powers and emotional expressiveness in ideal proportions.

Nineteenth-century Opera.

After Mozart's operas and Beethoven's *Fidelio* the medium might have been expected to decline. Instead it took on a new, if different, lease of life that culminated in Verdi's extraordinary output.

Rossini (1792–1868) created a world of exuberant high spirits in his operatic works that are as cheerful and heart-warming today as they were a hundred or more years ago.

He always worked in and around the lyric theatres of Italy and between 1810 and 1830 poured out a stream of works, not all of which can be expected to be masterpieces. However, *Il Barbiere di Siviglia*, *L'Italiana in Algieri*, *La Cenerentola* and *Le Comte Ory* will always delight audiences as long as opera houses exist. Although these works are difficult to sing really well, their vitality and charm can never be submerged even by poor voices or indifferent staging.

His German contemporaries were critical of his confidence and frivolity, but his works show a consistency of invention and an irresistible tunefulness that anyone might envy. In recent years, there has also been a renewed interest in his more serious operas—*Otello* (1816), *La Gazza Ladra* (1817), *Semiramide* (1823), *La Siège de Corinthe* (1820), and *Guillaume Tell* (1829)—which were certainly surpassed in dramatic power by his successors but which nevertheless are not to be despised or neglected.

William Tell, to give it its more popular title, was his last work for the stage although he lived on for nearly forty years in retirement in Paris, scene of many of his greatest successes. There he enjoyed good living, dispensing *bons mots*, and occasionally composing trifles. An exception is the unpretentious *Petite Messe Solennelle*, written originally for soloists, chorus, a harmonium, and two pianos. Rossini later orchestrated it, but he would not allow it to be performed during his lifetime. The first public performance was on 28 February 1869, as near as possible to the 78th anniversary of the composer's birth on Leap Year Day 1792.

In contrast to the mercurial Rossini, Vincenzo Bellini (1801–35) was an exquisite, romantic figure dealing with exquisite, romantic stories, an operatic equivalent to Chopin, who much admired him. His delicate, sinuous vocal line (in the arias) and brilliant acrobatics in the final sections (cabalettas) require singers of the utmost accomplishment to do them justice, although his music is never as florid as Rossini's. His most typical and popular works are probably *La Sonnambula* (1831), *Norma* (1831) and *I Puritani* (1835). The first is a tender, homely country story, the second an almost heroic lyrical drama of sacrifice, and the third a rather unsatisfactory historical story redeemed by its appealing music. In the past few years singers of the calibre of Maria Callas, Joan Sutherland, Guiletta Simionato, and Marilyn Horne have brought Bellini's operas a popularity almost equal to that they enjoyed at the time they were written.

Gaetano Donizetti (1797–1848) was an even more prolific operatic composer than Rossini. He wrote at least 75 works, mostly for the Italian stage, several of which, such as *Alfredo il Grande* or *Emilia di Liverpool*, are never likely to be revived, but during the past few years, with the renewed interest in what are called the *Ottocento* operas, many of his serious operas have been resuscitated and found as enjoyable in performance as his more frequently heard comedies.

He was a well-grounded musician and although his invention is often criticised for being too tied to the conventions of his day performances often belie his reputation, his dramatic instinct proving sure. *Lucia di Lammermoor*, because of the chances it offers to a coloratura soprano with tragic pretensions, has always held the stage and of late *Lucrezia Borgia*, *Anna Bolena*, *La Favorita*, and *Poliuto* have all been successfully revived. Of his lighter works, the comedies *L'Elisir d'Amore* and *Don Pasquale* have never declined in popularity. One of his last works was *Linda di Chamounix* (1842) which he wrote for Vienna where it aroused such enthusiasm that the Emperor appointed him Court Composer and Master of the Imperial Chapel.

French Opera.

The taste in Paris was for more and more lavish productions. Following Spontini (1774–1851), whose works were comparatively austere, came Halévy (1799–1862) and Giacomo Meyerbeer (1791–1864) whose operas contain all the ingredients that came to be expected of "Grand Opera "—spectacle, huge ensembles, showpieces for the soloists, and extended, if superfluous ballet. Drawing from Italian, German, and French traditions Meyerbeer's music contained everything the public wanted, yet today they are seldom revived, perhaps because his creative powers were essentially derivative, yet when they *are* given, operas like *Les Huguenots*, *Le Prophète*, and *L'Africaine* still have the power to fascinate and his influence on his successors, notably Wagner, was considerable.

Verdi.

Italian opera in the 19th cent. culminated in the works of Giuseppe Verdi (1813–1901), who rose from a peasant background to become his country's most noted composer, as well as something of a natural hero during the period of the Risorgimento. His earliest works, indeed, often roused his hearers to patriotic fervour. For instance, *Nabucco* (1842), with its theme of an oppressed people seeking deliverance, was treated as a symbol of the Italians' fight for freedom.

Musically, Verdi developed out of all recognition during the course of his long career. The continuously flowing structure of his last two operas *Otello* and *Falstaff* is very far removed from the start–stop formulas, inherited from his predecessors, of his first works, yet even they are touched, in harmonic subtleties, orchestral felicities, and a sense of drama, by a spark of genius, a burning inspiration that sets him apart from all other operatic composers. *Ernani* (1844), *I due Foscari* (1844), and *Luisa Miller* (1849) all have foretastes of glories to come even if as a whole they are flawed dramas, and these "galley years", as Verdi himself later described them, gave him the essential know-how to produce his later, greater operas, as well as establishing him incontrovertibly as the most popular Italian composer of the time.

However, it was with *Rigoletto* (1851), *Il Trovatore* (1853), and *La Traviata* (1853) that Verdi first really staked his claim to immortality. In these pieces his increasing dramatic mastery is married to a wonderful flow of lyrical melody, at the same time controlled by a fine musical sensibility. They were followed by four operas— *Simon Boccanegra* (1857), *Un Ballo in Maschera* (1858), *La Forza del Destino* (1862) and *Macbeth* (revised version, 1865)—in which Verdi overcame complexities of story line by his continually developing musical powers. This period is crowned by *Don Carlos* (written for the Paris Opéra 1867) a masterly exercise in combining private and public situations in a single, grand, and characterful work. In some respects Verdi never surpassed the subtlety of his writing in this opera. *Aïda* (1871) carried on the process but the characterisation in this ever-popular piece is less refined than in *Don Carlos*, if the grandeur of the design is more spectacular.

The success of *Otello* (1887) owes nearly as much to the skill of Boito whose literary ability combined with musical knowledge (he was himself a composer) presented Verdi with an ideal libretto for his seamless music in which the drama moves inevitably to its tragic end. Recitative, aria, ensemble are fused in a single, swiftly moving music-drama, which in its very different way equals that of Wagner. *Falstaff* (1893) achieves the same success in the field of comic opera, a brilliant, mercurial ending to a distinguished career. If Verdi had written only these two final masterpieces his place in musical history would be assured.

Brahms.

Brahms (1833–97) has justly been described as "a romantic spirit controlled by a classical intellect," for while complying with most of the formal regulations of sonata form he imbued them with an emotional content that accorded with his time. Indeed Schumann declared that he was the "one man who would be singled out to make articulate in an ideal way the highest expression of our time."

Perhaps in his chamber music will be found the quintessence of his art. The piano and clarinet quintets, the two string sextets, the horn trio, and the violin sonatas all are designed on a large scale yet the expression remains intimate, the design and structure clear.

The symphonies and concertos, though, remain his most popular works; they are part of the solid repertory of every orchestra and most piano and violin players in the world. Their high seriousness, constant lyrical beauty, and control of form are deeply satisfying. They do not provide the extremes of passion and excitement provided by his contemporaries, but their study provides continuous absorption and delight. The double concerto for violin and cello deserves a mention as a unique work in music.

Brahms wrote more than two hundred songs in which the desire for melodic beauty takes precedence over the words and meaning. Many are set to poor poetry, but hidden away are still some unexplored treasures, and the Four Serious Songs, at least, are tragic masterpieces. In a lighter vein the two sets of *Liebeslieder Walzer* for four voices are irresistible. The choral Requiem, too, is a fine work.

Bruckner.

In recent years Bruckner's reputation *vis-à-vis* his great contemporary Brahms has been enhanced in England. The old conception of him as a naïve Austrian unable to grasp the fundamentals of symphonic architecture has died hard, and the prevailing popularity of his grandest works is at last gaining him his rightful place in the 19th-cent. firmament. The nine symphonies and the masses are his chief claim to immortality. They contain melodies of unforgettable beauty, symphonic paragraphs of unparalleled grandeur, and an appreciation of formal development that, though different, is as equally valid as that of Brahms. The movements of his symphonies are long and he often pauses, as if for breath and to admire the scenery, before he reaches the climactic peak of his musical journey. His idiom is best approached by a newcomer to his work through the fourth and seventh symphonies as they are perhaps the easiest to understand, but the fifth, sixth, eighth, and ninth (unfinished) are just as beautiful—and cogently argued—once one has acquired the knack, so to speak, of listening to his music. Most of these works are now to be heard in their original form, stripped of the veneer of "improvements" suggested to the diffident composer by his friends.

The masses, which translate Bruckner's symphonic ideas to the choral plain, and Bruckner's delightful string quintet are worth investigating.

Wagner.

Praised only this side of idolatry by his admirers, unmercifully criticised by his detractors, Richard Wagner (1813-83) is perhaps the most controversial composer in musical history. And so it was bound to be with such a revolutionary figure, whose writings, other than his music, contain, to say the least, dubious theories and whose operas, composed to his own libretti, broke the bonds of the form as known until his time. He regarded music-drama as a fusion of all the arts—music, literature, painting—in one unity. With *The Ring of the Nibelungs* he achieved his purpose; no other work of art has ever tried to encompass the whole of existence. Today, and surely forever, musicians, philosophers, and writers will argue over its meaning, and each age will reinterpret it according to its own lights.

But before he reached this pinnacle of achievement, Wagner gradually transformed opera—through *Rienzi*, *The Flying Dutchman*, *Tannhäuser*, and *Lohengrin*—so that a new mould was fashioned to take what he wanted to pour into it. He introduced the *Leitmotiv*, a musical theme that could be associated with a particular person, situation, or idea, each time it occurred. Slowly he developed the musical form so that the drama could unfold continuously without breaks for arias. By the time he began to write *Tristan and Isolde* and *Die Meistersinger*, he had perfected his methods and had he never undertaken *The Ring* that tragedy and that comedy would have assured him his place in the musical firmament. Indeed, *Die Meistersinger* is considered a masterpiece even by those who are not willing or prepared to accept the rest of the Wagnerian ethos.

The length and complexity of these operas, and of *Parsifal*, a work of unique beauty in spite of certain *longueurs*, means that it is almost essential to prepare oneself by homework, with libretti and records, before attempting to assimilate them in the opera house. The added effort is well worth while for the ultimate musical satisfaction they bring because Wagner was more than an operatic reformer: he opened up a new harmonic language (especially in the use of chromaticism) that was logically to develop into the atonality of the 20th cent.

Wolf.

As Wagner was the culmination of the 19th cent. symphonic and operatic tradition, so Hugo Wolf (1860-1903) summed up, if he did not surpass, the achievements in song-writing of Schubert, Schumann, and Loewe (1796-1869).

Wolf was a lonely, pathetic man. He lived much of his life in poverty, and eventually lost his reason and died of an incurable disease. These circumstances account perhaps for his almost feverish bursts of creative activity, which were also the outward sign of his burning genius. His greatest contributions to the art of *Lieder* were his extraordinary insight into the poet's meaning and the harmonic means by which he heightened the expression of the words. He raised the importance of the piano part even higher than had Schumann, and in some of his songs the vocal part takes the form of a free declamation over a repeated idea in the piano. However, in the main the vocal and piano parts are interweaved with great subtlety, and he unerringly matched the very varied moods of the poems he chose to set. His greatest creative period was between early 1888 and early 1890 when songs poured from his pen daily—more than 50 settings of the German poet Mörike, 20 of Eichendorff, more than 50 of Goethe, and more than 40 of Heyse and Geibel (the Spanish Song-book). Later he composed songs from Heyse's Italian Song-book and the three Michelangelo sonnets. And the range of his creative understanding was wide, taking in the almost wild passion of the Spanish songs, the humanity and humour of the Italian love-songs, the titanic power of *Prometheus* (Goethe), the varying moods of the Mörike book, and the intangible power of the Michelangelo sonnets. There are almost inexhaustible riches here for the inquiring mind to discover. Outside *Lieder*, Wolf's output is small, but it includes a sadly neglected opera, *Der Corregidor*, the Italian Serenade for string quartet (alternatively for small orchestra) and a tone poem *Penthesilea*.

Ernest Newman, his greatest champion, summed up his work most aptly: "Wolf practically never repeats himself in the songs; every character is drawn from the living model. It is a positively Shakespearian imagination that is at work—Protean in its creativeness, inexhaustibly fecund and always functioning from the inside of the character or the scene, not merely making an inventory from the outside."

National Movements.

During the course of the 19th cent., alongside the emergence of national political identity, came the rise of nationalism in music, fertilising traditional Western—that is basically German—musical forms with folk material. Of these groups the Russian is certainly the most important, if not the most vital.

Glinka (1804-57) was the first important Russian composer of the national school and, although his two operas *A Life for the Tsar* (sometimes called *Ivan Susanin*) and *Russlan and Ludmilla* are strongly influenced by Italian models, they do introduce Russian song and harmony into the texture. He undoubtedly influenced Borodin (1833-87), Cui (1835-1918), Balakireff (1837-1910), Mussorgsky (1839-81) and Rimsky-Korsakov (1844-1908)—the so-called "Five" of 19th-cent. Russian music. However, each was very much of an individualist too. Borodin was a lecturer in chemistry who wrote in his spare time. His two symphonies, two string quartets led up to his most notable work, the opera *Prince Igor*, left incomplete at his death. Balakireff, friend and adviser to the rest of the group, wrote little himself, but his orchestral works and the piano fantasia, *Islamey*, are worthy of investigation.

Modest Mussorgsky (1839–81) is today seen as the most important and inspired of " The Five." More than the others he used Russian song and Russian speech as the basis of his operas in which he portrayed the lives and destinies of his own people. Although his capacities were seriously impaired by an uncongenial job, poverty, and drinking, he produced two great operas, *Boris Godunov* and *Khovanshchina*, and another *Sorochintsy Fair* that is immensely enjoyable. *Boris* should be given in its original, with spare orchestration, but more often than not it is heard in Rimsky-Korsakov's more elaborate revision. In any case the opera exists in various versions, none of them necessarily the right one: what is important is to hear it in one or the other because of its great portrayal of Boris's personality set against the background of the Russian people, unforgettably presented in choral outbursts. *Khovanshchina* was completed by Rimsky-Korsakov, *Sorochintsy Fair* by Tcherepnin (although other versions also exist). Mussorgsky's songs explore a new vein of naturalistic vocal declamation. Each of the four *Songs and Dances of Death* is a miniature drama worthy of Wolf, although of course in a quite other idiom. The *Nursery* songs miraculously conjure up a child's world as seen from a child's point of view. Many of the individual songs, the *Sunless* cycle too, should be investigated.

Rimsky-Korsakov (1844–1908) is perhaps a less attractive figure because so much of his music seems heartless or merely decorative, but this judgment is probably made on the strength of hearing *Shéhérazade* and the *Capriccio Espagnol* a few too many times. Such of his 15 operas as are played evince a (literally) fantastic mind and lyrical vein, and it is a pity that *Sadko*, *The Snow Maiden*, and *The Tsar's Bride*, at least, are not heard more often.

Tchaikovsky.

Peter Ilyich Tchaikovsky (1840–93) is a more universally admired figure than any of " The Five " and his music is indubitably closer to the mainstream than theirs in that it adheres more nearly to Western European forms. His popularity is due to his unhesitating appeal to the emotions and to his tender, often pathetic melodic expression. His lyrical gift is stronger than his sense of architecture, as he himself admitted. Yet his later symphonies—the fourth, fifth, and sixth (the *Pathétique*)—are all cogently enough argued and invigorating, as can be heard in the hands of a conductor willing to emphasise their formal power rather than their tendency towards sentimentality: the orchestral craftsmanship is also superb. The three piano concertos and the violin concerto offer rare opportunities for virtuoso display within a reasonably dramatic structure and his various overtures are always exciting to hear.

The three ballets—*The Sleeping Beauty, Swan Lake*, and *Nutcracker* show Tchaikovsky's skill on a smaller and perhaps more congenial scale, but only two of his operas—*Eugene Onegin* and *The Queen of Spades*—survive in regular performance. They demonstrate his ability to delineate character and his always eloquent melodic invention. His songs often felicitously capture a passing mood or emotion.

Bohemia (Czechoslovakia).

The Czech national school is dominated by two composers—Smetana (1824–84) and Dvořák (1841–1904). In his own country Smetana holds a unique position as the father of his country's music—which is remarkable when you consider that he lived in a country that was then under Austrian rule and never spoke the Czech language perfectly. Yet his music is filled with the spirit of Czech history and national life, and many of his operas, his most important contribution, deal purely with national subjects. The reawakening of interest in things national, after Austria's defeat by Italy in 1859, led to the establishment of a Provisional Theatre in 1862 and Smetana's first opera *The Brandenburgers in Bohemia* was produced there in 1866, but its success was eclipsed by the enormous popularity of *The Bartered Bride*, which appeared the same year. Its melodic charm, lively characterisation and cosy humour have carried it round the world and it is the one Smetana opera to be in the repertory of most opera houses. However, his next opera *Dalibor* (1868) is considered by some authorities as his masterpiece. It is conceived on a heroic scale, and frequently rises to great dramatic heights. His later operas include *Libuše* (1872) a solemn festival tableau, *The Two Widows* (1874), a delightful comedy, *The Kiss* (1876), *The Secret* (1878), and *The Devil's Wall* (1882).

His main orchestral work *Má Vlast* (My Country), written between 1874 and 1879, is a cycle of six symphonic poems nobly depicting the life and legends of his country. He composed only three mature chamber works—an elegiac piano trio, written in 1855 in memory of the death of his eldest daughter, and two string quartets, both autobiographical. The first in E minor (1876)—" From My Life "—tells of his youth and aspirations until a terrible, screeching E in *allissimo* describes the onset of deafness; the second in D minor, sadly neglected, was described by the composer as an attempt to explain the " whirlwind of music in the head of one, who has lost his hearing," and was probably influenced by Beethoven's later music.

Dvořák combined a fecund melodic gift with an intelligent grasp of structure. His symphonies and chamber music are mostly written in classical form, yet the works are imbued with a spontaneity and freshness that have not lost one whit of their charm over the years.

He wrote nine symphonies and, although only the last three or four are regularly performed, they are mostly mature works, several of which, for instance No. 7 in D minor (formerly known as No. 2) reach a tragic grandeur at times. They are all orchestrated in a masterly way and are full of delightful detail. Dvořák wanted to show that a Brahms could come out of Bohemia—and he succeeded in doing so while maintaining a definitely individual flavour, strongly influenced by natural rhythms.

He wrote three concertos, one each for piano, violin, and cello. The earlier ones are interesting without being quite in the first flight of the composer's output, but the cello concerto of 1895 is perhaps the composer's crowning achievement—warm, mellifluous, romantic.

He wrote chamber music throughout his long creative life. Some of the early works are weak and derivative, but the later string quartets, the " Dumky " trio, and the piano quartet and quintet are expressive and full of unforced invention. Dvořák felt himself somewhat hampered when setting words, nevertheless his *Stabat Mater* and *Te Deum* are both deeply felt choral works and he wrote songs throughout his career, many of them very fine indeed. He wrote ten operas, but only *Rusalka* (1901) has gained a foothold outside Czechoslovakia.

Janáček.

The Moravian composer Leoš Janáček (1858–1928) spent most of his life in Brno as a working musician. His music has recently come to be recognised as some of the most original written in the past hundred years. His operas, in which he closely followed the inflection of the speech of his native land, are his finest works. Over the score of his last opera, *From the House of the Dead*, he wrote the words " In every human being there is a divine spark ", and it is this deep love of humanity that permeates all his works. Of his operas *Kátya Kabanová* (1921) and *The Cunning Little Vixen*

(1924), the *Makropoulos Affair* (1926), and *From the House of the Dead* (adapted from a Dostoyevsky novel, 1928) are the most important and they have all been produced in Britain in recent years. His original genius is self-evident in all of them.

Among his orchestral works *Taras Bulba* and *Sinfonietta* should be noted, and his two string quartets, very difficult to play, should be better known. The song cycle, *Diary of one who has disappeared*, for tenor, contralto, and three female voices with piano, and the Glagolithic Mass contain music of much expressive beauty.

Hungary.

The Hungarian musical outburst came somewhat later than that in other countries. Its great figure is Bela Bartók (1881–1945) who, as well as being a national figure, has proved an influential composer in the whole of 20th-cent. music. His mind was full of folk music, but it was transmuted by his strongly personal style and powerful intellect into something highly original. His music is tense and volatile but this restlessness is sometimes relieved by a kind of other-wordly, ethereal lyricism, as in the lovely slow movements of his quartets.

Bartók was affected as much by the musical innovations of Debussy and Stravinsky (see below) as by East European, notably Magyar, folk music and many of his works are an attempt to meld the two.

The most important part of his output is undoubtedly his string quartets which cover most of his creative life. To this intimate form he confided his personal innermost thoughts and in it conducted his most far-reaching musical experiments, thereby extending its boundaries beyond anything previously known. As with Beethoven's late quartets many of Bartok's rely on organic or cyclic development while remaining just within the laws of classical form. As Mosco Carner puts it, " For profundity of thought, imaginative power, logic of structure, diversity of formal details, and enlargement of the technical scope, they stand unrivalled in the field of modern chamber music."

The most important of his orchestral works are the three piano concertos, of which the first two are harsh and uncompromising, and fiendishly difficult to play, while the third, written in 1945, is mellower and more diatonic. The second violin concerto (1937–8) shows the various elements of Bartók's style in full flower, by turns exuberant, passionate, and brilliant. The *Music for Strings, Percussion and Celesta* (1937) is remarkable for its strange sonorities and its fascinating texture. The *Concerto for Orchestra* (1944) is more immediately appealing and again shows the composer in complete command of a large canvas. Of the piano works *Mikrokosmos* (1935) and the sonata for two pianos and percussion (1937) are worth investigating.

His chief stage pieces are *The Miraculous Mandarin* (1919), a harsh, cruel ballet which drew appropriately dramatic music from the composer, and the opera *Duke Bluebeard's Castle* (1911), a luscious, original score that makes one regret that he wrote no more operas later in his career.

Kodály (1882–1967) was from early years closely associated with Bartók and with him collected Hungarian folk melodies using many of them in his music. He worked in many forms and the more important of his works are the *Peacock Variations* for orchestra, the choral *Psalmus Hungaricus* and *Te Deum*, The *Dances of Galánta*, and the opera *Háry János*, and the sonatas for cello and for unaccompanied cello.

Sibelius, Nielsen and Grieg.

Among Scandinavian composers the Finn Jean Sibelius (1865–1957) and the Dane Carl Nielsen (1865–1931) are outstanding. Sibelius is a lone northern figure ploughing his own furrow

oblivious or, at any rate, ignoring the unusual developments that were taking place in Central Europe, yet his seven symphonies are strong as granite, honest, rugged works that will undoubtedly stand the test of time. They are not by any means all similar in mood, or even form. The first is very much influenced by Tchaikovsky and Borodin, the second and third show a more personal style developing, the fourth is terse and tragic, the fifth lyrical, bright, and lucid; the sixth is perhaps most typically Sibelian in its evocation of primeval nature, and the seventh—in one continuous movement—is a more purely abstract piece, notable for its structural logic and the grandness of its themes. The violin concerto is the most easily understood of the composer's main works and has a grateful part for the soloist.

The tone poems *The Swan of Tuonela*, *Pohjola's Daughter*, *En Saga*, *Night Ride and Sunrise*, *The Bard*, and *Tapiola* uncannily evoke the icy words of the legends of the far north, and the primeval forces of nature. Sibelius's one string quartet *Voces Intimae* and many of his songs are worth hearing too. His music, reviled in some quarters during the 1950s, has now been restored to favour, and seems to be enjoyed again by critics and the general public alike.

Carl Nielsen (1865–1931) is another individualist. His six symphonies, like Sibelius's seven, are the most important part of his output, but whereas Sibelius was dealing with a huge, uninhabited northern landscape, Nielsen is more friendly and serene in his music, which is seldom forbidding, always inventive, throwing a new light, through unusual ideas about harmony, structure and tonality, on traditional forms. He also wrote highly individual concertos for the flute and clarinet, four string quartets and two operas— the dramatic, rather Brahmsian *Saul and David* (1902) and a delightful comedy, *Maskarade* (1906), full of lyrical music.

The Norwegian composer Edvard Grieg (1843–1907) was essentially a miniaturist whose range of feeling was not wide but whose music is always gentle and appealing. His most notable works are the romantic piano concerto, the atmospheric incidental music to Ibsen's play *Peer Gynt*, the charming Lyric Suite, and the small piano pieces. Not an important composer, then, but always an attractive one.

Elgar and the English Revival.

After the death of Purcell there is hardly a name in English music worth speaking of until the 19th cent. when Hubert Parry (1848–1918) and Charles Villiers Stanford (1852–1924), actually an Irishman, led a revival. Their music is seldom heard today, but their pioneer work paved the way for Edward Elgar (1857–1934). Although all were influenced by Brahms they nevertheless managed to establish a new English tradition that has been carried on in our own day. Elgar's symphonies are laid out on a grand, leisurely scale and they are both eloquent and exhilarating. His violin concerto has an elegiac slow movement as has the glorious cello concerto and both contain many fine opportunities for the soloist. The cello concerto is as appealing a work as any by Elgar expressing his innermost thoughts. His *Enigma Variations* are a series of portraits in sound of his friends, but there is another overall theme to go with them that has never been identified. This has not prevented the work from becoming Elgar's most popular, not surprisingly when one considers its charm and melodiousness. Three other orchestral pieces that should not be neglected are his symphonic study *Falstaff*, a many-sided musical picture of the Fat Knight, and the overtures *Cockaigne*, a happy evocation of London, and *In the South*, inspired by a visit to Italy. His three late chamber works, written when he was 61, are reticent, economic pieces that remove any misconception of Elgar as a bombastic composer. His songs are mostly feeble, but the oratorios, notably *The Dream of Gerontius*, show the composer's ability to control a large canvas. The composer himself wrote over the score of *Gerontius*,

' This is the best of me "—a verdict with which we can readily agree.

The French Impressionists.

César Franck (1822–90) was the main figure in mid-19th-cent. musical France and his influence spread even wider than his music of which only the D minor Symphony, the Symphonic Variations for piano and orchestra, the piano quintet, and the violin sonata are likely to be encountered today. The leading French opera composers of that time were Gounod (1818–93), Bizet (1838–75) and Massenet (1842–1912). Gounod's *Faust*, Bizet's *Carmen* (composed just before his untimely death when he caught cold after a swim) and Massenet's *Manon* all retain a deserved place in the repertory; each is a well-judged mini-drama unafraid of romantic ardour and forceful, histrionic strokes. Some of Massenet's other numerous operas, such as *Werther* and *Don Quichotte*, have enjoyed a revival in recent years.

Concurrently with similar movements in French painting and poetry came the French Impressionist composers at the end of the 19th cent. Their leader—and one of the great seminal forces of modern music—was Claude Debussy (1862–1918). His aim was to capture a mood or sensation, and he did that by more or less inventing a fresh system of harmony using a whole-tone scale, unusual chords, and by creating in the orchestra new, highly personal textures—there is no mistaking the Debussy idiom once you have heard at least one piece by him. His impressionistic style did not lead him, however, to abandon form as some have suggested, and his main works are just as closely organised as those by classical German composers. His music is sensuous and poetic yet nearly always structurally satisfying as well.

His reputation, at least with the general musical public, rests largely on his orchestral music, a few piano pieces and his only opera *Pelléas et Mélisande*. *La Mer* is a scintillating evocation of the sea in all its moods; *Nocturnes*, *Images*, and *Prélude à l'Après-midi d'un Faune* exactly suggest different places, times, moods—the " Iberia " and " Gigues " sections of *Images*, calling to mind respectively the spirit of Spain and the flickering light of a rainy English night. *Pelléas*, based on a Symbolist drama by Maeterlinck, tells a story of love, jealousy, and murder in predominantly restrained yet emotionally loaded terms. It is an elusive original work that has no predecessor or successor. Intensely atmospheric, rivetingly beautiful, it weaves an irresistible spell over the listener.

Debussy's chamber music is unjustly neglected. His string quartet (1893) was one of the first works in which he displayed his new and strange world of sound, and the three late sonatas, one for violin, one for cello, and the third for flute, viola, and harp are elliptical, compressed pieces which seem to be questing disjointedly into new regions of sound. His songs too, are worthy of investigation, and his piano music, especially the twenty-four Preludes and some of the shorter pieces, contain some of his most imaginative and original ideas and thoughts.

Gabriel Fauré (1845–1924) is a difficult figure to place. He lived through all kinds of musical revolutions yet they seemed to affect the character of his work very little. He has never been, and is never likely to be, a widely known or popular composer, yet his music has a reticence and delicacy that is very appealing. Despite his dreamy, retiring art he was not a recluse, but a very sociable man.

He was content with forms as he found them, but he imbued them with a very personal, human style. Perhaps his art is best heard in his songs. They are not overtly passionate or dramatic but the long, sinuous melodies and subtle harmonies are exquisitely wrought. Of the song-cycles, *La Bonne Chanson*, *Cinq Mélodies* (Verlaine), *Le Chanson d'Eve*, and *L'Horizon Chimérique* are best known. The last written in 1922, when the composer was seventy-seven, is a beautiful setting

of words by a soldier killed in the first World War. There are also many remarkable single songs, many of them settings of poems by Verlaine. His opera *Pénélope*, based on the classical heroine, is unjustly reglected.

He wrote few orchestral pieces, but the *Ballade* for piano and orchestra and the *Pavane* are among his most typical, and delicate compositions, and his outstanding piano music, modelled on Chopin's, includes Nocturnes, Impromptus, and Barcaroles. His chamber music covers more than half a century from the violin sonata of 1876 to the string quartet written the year he died. In that period he composed two piano quartets, two piano quintets, another violin sonata and two cello sonatas, the later works failing to show quite the unforced lyrical grace of the earlier ones. Perhaps Fauré is best approached with the first piano quartet, a charming, easily assimilated work, and the beautiful choral *Requiem*.

Saint-Saëns (1835–1921), an accomplished, cultivated musician, has had a " bad press " but his craftsmanship, as displayed in his symphonies, concertos, and *Samson et Dalila* (one among his 12 operas) is not to be despised.

Henri Duparc (1844–1933), despite a very long life, is known today only for a group of songs he wrote before he was forty. They are among the most emotionally direct yet tasteful melodies ever written. Paul Dukas (1865–1935) is another figure off the beaten track, as it were. He, too, is known only for a handful of compositions. He was strongly influenced by Vincent d'Indy (1851–1931) and the school who strongly opposed Debussy's new ideas, yet he could not help but come under Debussy's spell. Dukas's one great work is his opera *Ariane et Barbe-Bleue*, the text adapted from a Maeterlinck play written with the composer in mind.

Maurice Ravel (1875–1937), a pupil of Fauré, followed in Debussy's footsteps, although his later pieces were more ascetic. Indeed, he was one of the most fastidious of composers, always seeking, and often finding, artistic perfection. The works he wrote before 1918 are definitely of the Impressionist School and it would be difficult to imagine more beautiful sounds than are to be found in the ballet *Daphnis et Chloé*, in the song-cycle *Shéhérazade*, and the piano fantasy *Gaspard de la Nuit*. His first style was summed up in the A minor piano trio (1915). In his later music Ravel was struggling, not always successfully, to keep up with new developments such as jazz and atonality. The piano concerto, for instance, shows very strongly the influence of jazz.

Outstanding orchestral works of his, other than *Daphnis* are *Rapsodie espagnole* (1907), *La Valse* (1920), a sumptuous evocation of the Vienna waltz, and the ever-popular *Boléro*. Two chamber works, besides the trio, are masterpieces—the string quartet (1902–3) and the Introduction and Allegro for Harp, String Quartet, Flute, and Clarinet. This Septet composed in 1906, ravishes the senses with magical sound.

Ravel's piano pieces are perhaps his most notable contribution to music, combining an extraordinary feeling for the instrument's technical possibilities with the sensibility of a Chopin, and in this field *Jeux d'eau*, *Miroirs*, and *Ma Mère l'Oye*, all written just after the turn of the century, come very close to the perfection of *Gaspard de la Nuit*. His songs show his unusual appreciation of the need to fuse poetic and musical values, and he set exotic poems for preference. The song-cycle *Histoires naturelles* (1906) is an acutely observed setting of five poems about birds and animals; *Cinq Mélodies populaires Grecques* (1907) are charming settings of Greek folk songs; *Trois Poèmes de Mallarmé* (1913), *Chansons Medécasses* (1926), are suitably exotic settings of three poems by an 18th-cent. Creole poet called Parny. Finally in 1932 came *Don Quichotte à Dulcinée*, three poems by Paul Morand, Ravel's last composition.

Ravel wrote two operas—the slight but moderately amusing *L'Heure espagnole* (1907), nicely orchestrated in a faintly and appropriately Spanish style and *L'Enfant et les Sortilèges* (1925) to a story by Colette, a delicious fantasy about a naughty child who gets his due punishment for tormenting animals and destroying furniture.

Spain.

Felipe Pedrell (1841–1922) has been aptly described as the midwife of Spanish nationalist music. As a musicologist and teacher he strongly influenced the two main composers of the school, Manuel de Falla (1876–1946) and Enrique Granados (1867–1916). Falla's output was not large and most of it was written about the time of the first World War. He had spent the years before the war in Paris and there he naturally came under the influence of Debussy. Debussy wrote Spanish music without ever having been to Spain but so true was it that even to Falla, born and bred in Andalusia, it had new things to say. He was able to take something from Debussy and blend it with his own highly individual style, evoking in his music all the passion and gaiety of his native land. Perhaps his most typical works are the two ballets *Love the Magician* (1915) full of Spanish atmosphere, and *The Three-Cornered Hat* (1919). The opera *La Vida Breve* (1905), despite its weak libretto, has much appeal, especially when the leading rôle is sung by such a vibrant artist as Victoria de los Angeles. The Seven Popular Spanish Songs (1914) conjure up the vivacity and smouldering passion at the heart of the country's character, as does *Nights in the Garden of Spain* (1916), an evocative piece for piano and orchestra. His later works, especially the harpsichord concerto of 1926, show Falla tending towards a less ebullient, more neo-classical style. His second opera *Master Peter's Puppet Show* (1923) is a miniaturist work, refined and intense. His third opera *Atlantida*, left unfinished at his death, was completed by his pupil Ernesto Halffter and first staged in 1962. It is a long work, more a dramatic cantata than an opera, and as such a rather unwieldy epic.

Granados, who was drowned when his ship was torpedoed by the Germans in 1916, was perhaps a more restrictedly Spanish composer than Falla, but his music is unfailingly attractive, and surely others of his seven operas, besides *Goyescas* (which is heard occasionally), deserve to be rescued from oblivion. *Goyescas* itself is especially famous for the second interlude and opening of Act III—*La Maja y el Ruiseñor* (The lover and the nightingale), a haunting, sinuous melody for soprano, sometimes heard in its original form as a piano solo. He wrote a set of *Tonadillas*. A tonadilla is a type of Spanish song popular in the 18th cent., and Granados's set ably and enchantingly recaptures a lost age of grace and character. His exciting Spanish Dances are heard in both their piano and orchestral form.

The chief claim to fame of Albéniz (1860–1909) is *Ibéria*, masterly descriptive pieces for piano. Turina (1882–1949), not altogether successfully, attempted a more cosmopolitan style, but his most often heard music, especially that for guitar, is typically Spanish.

The Late German Romantics.

While composers such as Debussy, Sibelius, Stravinsky, and Schoenberg (see below for the latter pair) were striking out along new paths, Richard Strauss (1864–1949) continued in the trend of 19th-cent. German composers; he was the tradition's last great figure. At least two of his operas—*Salome* and *Elektra*—were considered shocking at the time, but today we can hear that they are essentially big-scale, romantic works—natural successors to Wagner's—however startling the harmonies may once have seemed.

If Strauss did not achieve the granite intellectual greatness of Beethoven or Wagner, there is no denying his melodic genius and powers of fertile invention which overlaid the streak of vulgarity and inflation in his musical make-up. His first outstanding achievement was in the field of the symphonic poem, where he carried the work of composers such as Liszt and Berlioz to its logical conclusion. Starting with *Don Juan* in 1888 and ending with *Sinfonia Domestica* in 1903 he wrote a series of kaleidoscopic works, full of enormous vitality, endless melody, and fascinating orchestration. The most easily assimilated—and the most popular—are *Don Juan* and *Till Eulenspiegel* but some of the longer works, notably *Also Sprach Zarathustra* (based on Nietzsche's prose poem) and *Don Quixote* (based, of course, on Cervantes's great work) will reward the persistent, inquiring mind with long hours of enthralled listening. Other works sound somewhat dated in their bombastic over-confidence, though Strauss's skill in composition seldom flagged at this stage of his long creative career. The symphonic poems all tell something of a story usually based on a literary source, but it is not essential to the enjoyment of the music to know what this is, although it may be helpful.

Strauss's reputation is even more solidly based on his fifteen operas, the earliest of which *Guntram* was first performed in 1894, the last, *Capriccio*, in 1942. During these years the essentials of Strauss's style changed little, though it became very much more refined as the years passed. His first operatic period ended with the violent, sensual tragedies *Salome* (1905) and *Elektra* (1909), the latter being his first collaboration with his chief librettist Hugo von Hofmannsthal. Then came their unique *Der Rosenkavalier* (1911), which filters the charm and the decadence of 18th-cent. Vienna through early 20th-cent. eyes. This was followed by *Ariadne auf Naxos* (1912). Originally intended to be given after Molière's *Le Bourgeois Gentilhomme*, it was later presented (1916) without the play but with an amusing Prologue, written by von Hofmannsthal. *Die Frau ohne Schatten* is the most grandiose result of the Strauss–Hofmannsthal partnership. It is a complex psychological allegory, but Strauss's contribution is not on as consistently lofty a level as is his librettist's. *Intermezzo* (1924), which has a libretto by Strauss himself, is a largely autobiographical domestic comedy, which has lately gained in reputation as a compact, charming piece. With *Die Aegyptische Helena* (1928), an opera on a mythical theme, and *Arabella* (1933), another sensuous Viennese comedy, the Strauss–Hofmannsthal collaboration ended on account of the librettist's death. Strauss then wrote *Die Schweigsame Frau* (1935) to a libretto by Stefan Zweig, based on a play by Ben Jonson, and *Friedenstag* (1938), *Daphne* (1938)—a beautiful opera—and *Die Liebe der Danae* (written 1938–40) with Josef Gregor as librettist. His swan-song was *Capriccio*, a dramatisation of the old argument about the relative importance of words and music in opera. The libretto is by the conductor Clemens Krauss and the opera, a serene, melodious work, was a fit end to a great operatic career.

However, Strauss went on composing till nearly the end of his life, adding a group of late orchestral pieces to his already large catalogue of works. The *Metamorphosen* for 23 solo string instruments, is probably the best of these. During his long creative career he wrote numerous songs, many of them, such as *Morgen*, *Wiegenlied* and *Ruhe, meine Seele* of surpassing beauty.

Other notable figures in German music at this time were Max Reger (1873–1916), a somewhat ponderous but highly accomplished composer who, in a quarter of a century of creative life, wrote more than 150 works, of which his sets of variations, his piano concerto, and chamber music are probably the most impressive. Hans Pfitzner (1869–1949), another German traditionalist, is chiefly remembered today for his opera *Palestrina*, about events, now known to be spurious, in the life of the 16th-cent. Italian composer.

Twentieth-century Music.

Mahler.

Gustav Mahler (1860–1911), the Austrian Jewish composer, is one of the most important figures in 20th-cent. music. In a sense he bridges the gulf between the late Romantics, who were tending more and more towards chromaticism and away from established key relationships, and the atonalists, who abandoned key signatures entirely. His detractors maintain that his inflation of allegedly banal Viennese beer-house music to unheard-of lengths rules him out of court as a serious writer. His admirers would claim that his music encompasses the whole of life in enormous, valid structures. The truth, if truth there be, perhaps lies somewhere in between: if his material does not always justify the length of his symphonies, and if there are occasional imperfections and *longueurs*, these shortcomings are worth enduring with for the sake of the depth of utterance, the humanity and the poetry of the great pages. He admitted himself that " I cannot do without trivialities," but it is out of these impurities that he forged his titanic victories.

His music is undoubtedly best approached through his songs, where the words force him to discipline his wide-ranging vision. *Lieder eines fahrenden Gesellen* (1884), to his own words *Kindertotenlieder* (1901–4), to poems by Rückert, and some individual songs perfectly relate words to music, and are all of a poignant loveliness. Similarly *Das Lied von der Erde* (1908), especially the last of the six songs, is a touching farewell to the world, nobly expressed.

The ten symphonies, however, are Mahler's most impressive legacy to posterity. They are almost impossible to characterise briefly so vast are they in terms of both length and variety. The first, fourth and ninth are probably the easiest to grasp but the fifth, sixth and seventh, despite flaws, contain some of his most awe-inspiring conceptions. The second and third, both of which use soloists and chorus, are revolutionary in orchestration and structure; they both try, inevitably without complete success, to carry out the composer's dictum, " a symphony should be like the world—it must contain everything." The eighth is even more gargantuan, but as in all Mahler's work size does not mean loss of clarity or an overloading of the structure. Part one—a mighty choral invocation—is a visionary setting of the mediaeval hymn *Veni Creator Spiritus*. Part two, which incorporates adagio, scherzo, and finale in one, is a setting of the final scene of Goethe's *Faust*. Until recently all of Mahler's unfinished tenth symphony that was ever performed was the Adagio, but the musicologist and Mahler scholar, the late Deryck Cooke, completed the symphony to critical and popular acclaim during the 1960s and thus added a noble, and also optimistic epilogue to the Mahler opus. The debate over the quality of Mahler's music is likely to continue: one fact, however, that cannot be gain-said is his popularity with an ever-increasing audience, largely made up of young people. There must be something in his uncertainty and intense self-inquiry that accords with the mood of the youthful mind.

Schoenberg and the Second Viennese School.

Arnold Schoenberg (1874–1951) revolutionised Western music by his twelve-note theory—a system which uses all the notes of the chromatic scale " and denies the supremacy of a tonal centre," as Schoenberg himself puts it. This serial technique of composition, as it is commonly called, naturally sounds strange to an ear acclimatised to music written, as it were, with a home base, but Schoenberg and his disciples Berg and Webern showed that the system could produce works that were something more than mere intellectual exercises. None of the more recent advances in music would have been possible, even thinkable, without Schoenberg's pioneer work.

Schoenberg always regarded himself as much as a composer as a theorist or teacher, and his works are supposed to appeal as much to the emotions as to the intellect, although to be understood they do, of course, require the listener's concentrated attention. To appreciate how his ideas developed it is necessary to hear first his pre-atonal music, such as the *Gurrelieder* (1900–1) and *Verklärte Nacht* (1899), in which he carried Wagnerian chromaticism to extreme lengths. The *Gurrelieder*, in particular, is a luxuriant, overblown

work that shows the Wagnerian idiom in an advanced stage of decay, in spite of many beautiful pages of music. In his succeeding works the feeling of tonality began to disappear until in the Three Piano Pieces (opus 11), of 1909, he finally rejected tonality, although the new 12-note scheme is not yet evident; traces of the old order can still be heard. The succeeding works were mostly short, highly compressed, and very expressive. Schoenberg was reaching out for a new system, which would " justify the dissonant character of these harmonies and determine their successions." By 1923 he had formulated his 12-note system and the Five Piano Pieces (opus 23), and the Serenade (opus 24) of that year, can thus be considered the first works that used a note-row as the fundamental basis of their composition. Between 1910 and 1915, however, the Russian composer Alexander Skryabin (1872–1915) had attempted to define a new method of composition of his own employing the " mystic chord " of ascending fourths, but his scheme proved comparatively abortive when compared with Schoenberg's. Josef Hauer (1883–1959) also developed a 12-note system which he propounded in 1919 and he always considered himself, rather than Schoenberg, as the true founder of the system. He later worked out a system of tropes (*i.e.*, half-series of six notes).

To return to Schoenberg, in later works he shows much more freedom and assurance in the use of his system. The wind quintet (1924), the Variations for Orchestra, opus 31 (1927–8), the third (1926), and fourth (1936) string quartets, and the string trio (1946) are modern classics of their kind: they require concentrated listening and a degree of understanding of the unfamiliar style of composition. The set of songs with piano *Das Buch der hängenden Gärten* (opus 15), written in 1908, *Pierrot Lunaire*, opus 21 (1912) and the Four Songs, opus 22 (1913–14) provide a kind of bridge between tonality and atonality that the adventurous mind should cross. The monodrama *Erwartung* (1909) is another fascinating work, but perhaps the unfinished *Moses and Aaron* (1932) is Schoenberg's masterpiece as its production at Covent Garden in 1965 showed. Here, for certain, the composer matched his obvious intellectual capacities with an evident emotional content and managed to combine *Sprechgesang* (speech-song) and singing with a real degree of success.

It is only in recent years that Schoenberg's music has had a real chance to make its mark through the essential prerequisite of frequent performance. If his idiom now seems approachable, and a reasonably natural outcome of late 19th-cent. developments, it is perhaps because other, more recent composers have extended the boundaries of sound much further.

Schoenberg's two most respected disciples were Anton Webern (1883–1945) and Alban Berg (1885–1935). Webern's output is small, reaching only to opus 31, and many of his works are very brief. They are exquisitely precise, and delicate almost to a fault. He was trying to distil the essence of each note and in so doing carried the 12-note system to its most extreme and cerebral limit. His music has often been described as pointillist in the sense that one note is entirely separated from the next, there being little discernible melody. Beyond Webern's music, there is indeed the sound of nothingness, and he was rightly described during his lifetime as the " composer of the *pianissimo espressivo*". In his later works, Webern tended towards a strict, and often ingenious use of form and the Variations for Orchestra of 1940 are a good example of this and of his delicacy of orchestration. Webern's influence has perhaps been greater than the impact of his own music, even though he has had no direct successor.

Berg's music is much more accessible. Like Webern his total output was not large, but nearly all his works are substantial additions to the repertory. He is also the directest link between Mahler and the second Viennese School, as Mahler's music influenced him strongly. He studied with Schoenberg from 1904 to 1910. His music is more intense, more lyrical, and less attenuated in sound than Schoenberg's or Webern's. His humanity and abiding compassion can be heard most strongly in his finest opera *Wozzeck* (1925) and his violin concerto (1935), written as an elegy on the death of Manon Gropius, a beautiful 18-year-old girl. Both works are very carefully designed yet formal considerations are never allowed to submerge feeling, and the note-row is fully integrated into the structure.

Both *Wozzeck* and the unfinished but rewarding *Lulu* are concerned with society's outcasts who are treated with great tenderness in both operas. The later work is entirely dodecaphonic, all the opera's episodes being based on a theme associated with Lulu. Between these operas Berg wrote the highly complex Chamber Concerto for piano, violin, and thirteen wind instruments (1925) and the expressive Lyric Suite (1926). Among his early works the Seven Early Songs (1908–9) and the concert aria *Der Wein* (1929) are notable.

Stravinsky.

Igor Stravinsky (1882–1971) was another vital figure in 20th-cent. music. If his influence has been in quite another and perhaps less drastic direction than Schoenberg's it is hardly less important. Indeed, future musical historians may consider his achievement the more significant. He has been compared with the painter Picasso in his almost hectic desire to keep up with the times, yet, although he wrote in a number of very different styles over a period of fifty years, every work of his is stamped with his own definitive musical personality. His most revolutionary and seminal work is undoubtedly *The Rite of Spring* (written for the ballet impresario Diaghilev), which caused a furore when it first appeared in 1913, and although it no longer shocks, the rhythmical energy, the fierce angular thematic material, and the sheer virtuosity of the orchestration will always have the power to excite new audiences. Before *The Rite* Stravinsky had written two ballets for Diaghilev—*The Firebird* and *Petrushka*—that are no less filled with vitality and new, albeit not so violent, sounds. During the next thirty years Stravinsky wrote a series of ballet works, gradually becoming more austere and refined in composition. *Apollo* (1928) and *Orpheus* (1947) belong among his most attractive scores.

Stravinsky did not confine himself in stage works to the ballet. *The Nightingale* (1914) is a charming, early opera; *The Soldiers Tale* (1918) is a witty combination of narration, mime, and dance; *Les Noces* (1923) is a concise, original choreographic cantata for soloists and chorus; *Oedipus Rex* (1927) is a dignified version of the Sophocles play, which can be staged or given on the concert platform; either way it is a moving experience. *Perséphone* (1934), a melodrama for reciter, tenor, chorus, and orchestra is an appealing, lucid score. After the war his most important stage work by far was *The Rake's Progress* (1951), with a libretto by W. H. Auden and Chester Kallman. This fascinating opera is deliberately based on 18th-cent. forms and the music itself is neo-classical, always attractive, sometimes haunting.

Stravinsky was no laggard in writing for the concert-platform either. The finest of his orchestral pieces are probably the fervent choral *Symphony of Psalms* (1930), the violin concerto (1931) and the aggressive compact Symphony in three movements (1945). Of his chamber music the octet (1923), a duo concertant (1932), and septet (1952) are probably the most important, but no piece, even the dryest and most pedantic, is without redeeming features.

Stravinsky is often thought of as an aloof, detached figure. He has been castigated for his lack of lyrical warmth. But in spite of his own professed desire to drain his music of specific emotion, craftsmanship and originality, often with a strange other-worldly beauty added, are unmistakably there throughout his many scores. Quirky and annoying he may be, dull never.

Busoni and Puccini.

Italian music in the early part of the century was dominated by two very different composers—Ferruccio Busoni (1866–1924) and Giacomo Puccini (1858–1924). Busoni is a difficult figure to place. His austere, intellectual power is never called in question, but he seldom, if ever, succeeded in translating his technical prowess into altogether successful compositions. We can admire the strength, honesty, and often beauty of such works as his huge piano concerto (1903–4), *Fantasia Contrappuntisca* (1912)—for piano solo—and his unfinished opera *Doktor Faust* without ever capitulating to them entirely. None the less, it has to be admitted that those who have studied his music closely have always fallen completely under his spell. In style his music is anti-Romantic and often neo-Classical yet he was an ardent admirer of Liszt and more especially of Liszt's realisation of the possibilities of the pianoforte. Busoni, himself a great pianist, carried on where Liszt had left off in his own piano music, in which form and expression often find their perfect balance. *Doktor Faust* is undoubtedly his most important opera but *Die Brautwahl* (1908–10) and *Turandot* (1917) have many points of interest too.

Puccini's *Turandot*—his last opera—is a much grander version of the same Gozzi fable and the culmination of this great opera composer's work. His achievement is at an almost directly opposite pole to Busoni's. Not for him the severity or intellectuality of his contemporary. He sought and found an almost ideal fusion of straight-forward lyricism and dramatic truth. His music unerringly follows the pathos and passion of the stories he sets and all his characters " live " as human beings. That, and his abundant flow of easy, soaring melody, are the reasons for his immense popular success, unequalled by any other 20th-cent. composer. Whether it is the pathetic Mimi (*La Bohème*—1896) and Cio-Cio-San, (*Madam Butterfly*—1904), the evil Scarpia, (*Tosca*—1900), the cunning Schicchi (*Gianni Schicchi*—1918), the ardent Rodolfo (*La Bohème*) and Cavaradossi (*Tosca*), or the ice-cold Turandot (*Turandot*—1926). Puccini's musical characterisation is unfailing. And he backs his *verismo* vocal writing with an orchestral tissue that faithfully reflects the milieu of each opera, for instance, Japanese for *Butterfly*, Chinese for *Turandot*, while never losing his particular brand of Italian warmth. His orchestration is always subtle and luminous.

Other Italian composers who wrote operas in the *verismo* style of Puccini were Leoncavallo (1858–1919), Mascagni (1863–1945), and Giordano (1867–1948). Mascagni's *Cavalleria Rusticana* and Leoncavallo's *Pagliacci* have formed an inseparable bill and a regular part of the repertory in most opera houses.

Prokofiev, Shostakovich, and Rachmaninov.

Sergey Prokofiev (1891–1953) spent part of his creative life in his native Russia, part of it (1918–34) abroad, mostly in Paris. His early music, apart from the popular Classical Symphony (1916–17) tended to be acid and harsh, but on his return to Russia his style, though still frequently satirical, became warmer, more Romantic. The third piano concerto (1917) and the second symphony (1924) are good examples of the former period, the ballets *Romeo and Juliet* (1935) and *Cinderella* (1941–4) and the fifth (1944) and sixth (1949) symphonies of the latter. His music gives the impression of immense rhythmical energy, as in the outer movements of several of his nine piano sonatas, but this fierce drive is often leavened by the soft, wistful lights of his slow movements. His second string quartet (1941), perhaps, presents all the elements of his music in the kindest light.

His strong leaning towards fantasy and mordant parody is felt in his earlier operas *The Love of the Three Oranges* (1921) and *The Fiery Angel* (1922–5). *War and Peace* (1941–2), written in the face of strong pressure from the Soviet authorities, is an epic work that catches unerringly the mood of Dostoyevsky's vast novel.

Dmitri Shostakovich (1906–75) also suffered from attacks on his style. He had to conform to Stalin's requirements for writing music, but he survived and continued to produce music of universal appeal, as, for example, his later string quartets. Like Prokofiev, his music falls into two very distinct styles: one humorous and spiky, the other intense, very personal and often large-scale in its implications. Not all his symphonies reach the expressive depths of numbers one, five, six, eight, ten and fourteen, but they all have rewarding passages, and his violin and cello concertos are of high quality. He also wrote fifteen string quartets, a piano quintet (an attractive piece) and two operas: the satirical *The Nose* (1930) and *Katerina Ismailova* (1934, revised 1959), originally known as " Lady Macbeth of Mtensk."

Although Sergey Rachmaninov (1873–1943) was born in Russia, he left his home country in 1918, disliking the Soviet régime, and lived mostly in Switzerland and the United States. His music is chiefly notable for its Romanticism, nostalgic melody, nervous energy and, in the piano works, its opportunities for displays of virtuosity. The first three piano concertos, the third symphony, the piano preludes, and the Rhapsody on a theme of Paganini, are his most typical and attractive works, and many of his songs are touching and beautiful. He wrote three operas.

Modern French Music.

French music after Debussy and Ravel was dominated by the slighter composers known as *Les Six*, the most important of whom were Arthur Honegger (1892–1955, Swiss born), Darius Milhaud (1892–1974) and Francis Poulenc (1899–1963). Each has contributed music of some wit and charm to the repertory. They were influenced by Erik Satie (1866–1925), an eccentric but interesting figure, who wrote works with odd titles such as *Three Pear-Shaped Pieces*. His music is entirely unsentimental, often ironic.

Much more revolutionary has been the work of Olivier Messiaen (b. 1908), who has turned to Indian music and, above all, to bird-song for inspiration. He first came to notice as a composer of organ music. Then his *Quatuor pour la fin de temps*, written in captivity between 1940 and 1942, his long piano pieces, based on bird-song (often literally) and his gigantic *Turangalîla* symphony show him experimenting with complex rhythms, strange sonorities (using unusual instruments such as the Ondes Martenot in the symphony), and considerably widening music's horizons. Edgar Varèse (1885–1965) cultivated an even broader spectrum of sound, employing electronic instruments to complement and contrast with traditional ones. Pierre Boulez (b. 1925), a pupil of Messiaen, bases his extremely complex works on mathematical relationships. His music, other than that for the piano, mostly calls for a variety of percussion instruments often combined with the soprano voice in evocations of French poetry (Mallarmé in particular). The resulting timbre and sonorities are intriguing even when the structural basis of the music is but dimly perceived. In recent years, he has devoted most of his time to conducting rather than composing.

Modern German Music.

Kurt Weill (1900–50) is chiefly known for his socio-politically pointed operas, such as *Die Dreigroschenoper* (1929), *Mahagonny* (1929), *Der Jasager* (1930), and *Happy End* (1929), all effective works on the stage, and for his particular brand of brittle, yet fundamentally romantic music. His influence on later composers has been considerable.

Carl Orff (b. 1895) has written chiefly for the stage. His music is rhythmically insistent, avoids counterpoint, and is deliberately, even self-consciously straightforward. Most frequently heard is his *Carmina Burana*, lively, rumbustious choral settings of mediæval poems.

Paul Hindemith (1895–1964) in his later years wrote in a strictly tonal, often neo-classical idiom, after being one of the most advanced intellectuals of his time. As well as many chamber and orchestral works, he wrote three formidable operas: *Die Harmonie der Welt*, *Cardillac* and *Mathis der Maler*.

Karlheinz Stockhausen (b. 1928), a pupil of Messiaen, is another extreme innovator. He more than anyone puts electronics to musical use. His scores are a maze of diagrams and instructions, which really need the composer's presence for their true interpretation. It is too early to say whether his music is evidence of a passing vogue or a real step forward in musical ideas.

Hans Werner Henze (b. 1926) has rebelled against the musical climate in Germany, and now lives in Italy, yet his music combines the intellectuality of the modern German schools with the lyricism of Italian music. He has written five symphonies, though none follow the traditional form, and nine operas, among them three impressive large-scale works, *König Hirsch* (1952–5), *The Young Lord* (1965) and *The Bassarids* (1966), to an Auden–Kallman libretto. His more recent work, as exemplified in *The Raft of Medusa* and certain stage works of a non-operatic nature, show him adopting a much more revolutionary style conditioned by his adherence to extreme left-wing views. This culminated in his opera written for Covent Garden, *We Come to the River* (1976), employing several stages and three separate instrumental groups.

American Music.

It was not until the 20th cent. that American music really got under way and an American school came into being. With the possible exception of MacDowell (1861–1908) no earlier composers are remembered or played today. Many composers of the American school have, of course, taken their cue from Europe but the influence of American jazz and folk-song is also recognisable in some of their music. Aaron Copland (b. 1900) is probably the most important figure on the current scene, and such works as *Appalachian Spring*, *Billy the Kid*, and his third symphony have gained a certain amount of international recognition and popularity. Samuel Barber (b. 1910) works along traditional lines and his music, like Copland's, is essentially diatonic. He has contributed to all the usual forms (symphony, concerto, sonata), most recently to opera with *Vanessa* (1958) and *Antony and Cleopatra* (1966), which opened the new Metropolitan Opera House in New York's Lincoln Centre. Roy Harris (b. 1898) has written seven symphonies and several concertos which include folk elements.

Charles Ives (1874–1954) has recently been recognised as the most original American composer. While carrying on a highly successful career in insurance, Ives yet managed to anticipate in his works, all written before 1920, many of the innovations which were later " invented " in Europe. His orchestral music is much influenced by the sounds, such as brass bands, which he heard in his native New England as a boy. His *Three Places in New England* and *The Unanswered Question* have a beautiful, elusive quality about them. In his five symphonies and *Concord* sonata we notice the working of an original mind employing polytonality and polyrhythms in larger and more complex works. An element of improvisation is sometimes introduced, another anticipation of latter-day technique. Ives is unlikely ever to become a popular composer—his music is too complicated and eclectic for that—but his importance as a prophet is surely established.

Modern English School.

The amazing 20th cent. revival of music in England owes much to Ralph Vaughan Williams (1872–1958) and Gustav Holst (1874–1934). Vaughan Williams's music is today suffering a decline in reputation, but the best of his symphonies (one, four, five, and six), his Fantasia on a theme by Tallis, his ballet *Job*, and the best of his choral and chamber music have a sturdiness that will no doubt weather the whim of passing fashion. His music alternates between the forceful and the contemplative and both moods are expressed in a distinctive musical vocabulary, based on modalism and 16th-cent. polyphony.

Holst was a more enigmatic figure, but his influence has undoubtedly been greater. Only his suite *The Planets* and the choral *The Hymn of Jesus* have established themselves as repertory works, but his bold harmonic experiments and the austerity, even mysticism, of his style as heard in the orchestral pieces *Egdon Heath, Beni Mora*, and the opera *Savitri* are perhaps more typical of this contemplative original composer. His daughter Imogen, a conductor, has done much to promote understanding of her father's music. Contemporaries who deserve much more than a passing reference are John Ireland (1879–1962) and Sir Arnold Bax (1883–1953), who wrote seven symphonies.

Frederick Delius (1862–1934) was the only important English disciple of the French impressionist school. He lived in France from 1888 onwards. His most important works are the atmospheric tone-poems for orchestra, such as *Brigg Fair*; the vocal and orchestral *A Mass of Life, Sea Drift* and *Appalachia*, and the opera *A Village Romeo and Juliet*.

Of the more recent generation of English composers the most important are undoubtedly Benjamin Britten (1913–76) Sir Michael Tippett (b. 1905), Alan Rawsthorne (1905–71), and Sir William Walton (b. 1902). Britten did more than anyone to establish English music on the forefront of the international stage. Much of his music seems to have an immediate appeal to large audiences and certainly his many stage works earned him a quite exceptional prestige both at home and abroad. *Peter Grimes* (1945), *Billy Budd* (1951), *Gloriana* (1953), *A Midsummer Night's Dream* (1960) all, in their very different ways, show his consummate mastery of stage technique and the first two are also moving human documents. His opera for television, *Owen Wingrave*, is a masterly adaptation of the Henry James short story. On a smaller scale he has achieved as much with his chamber operas— *The Rape of Lucretia* (1946), *Albert Herring* (1947), and *The Turn of the Screw* (1954, based on a Henry James novel)—and with the three Parables for Church Performance—*Curlew River* (1964), *The Burning Fiery Furnace* (1966) and *The Prodigal Son* (1968). His operatic output was crowned by *Death in Venice* (1973), also a personal expression of his love for the tenor Peter Pears who sang Aschenbach. If he had written nothing else, those dramatic works would have marked him out as a composer of outstandingly imaginative gifts.

But there is more—the choral works culminating in the *War Requiem* (1962), his various song cycles written for Pears, the *Serenade* for tenor, horn, and strings, *Nocturne* for tenor and orchestra, the three Canticles, and the Spring Symphony are further evidence—in very different media—of both his intense emotional commitment and his technical skill. While being strongly influenced by such composers as Schubert, Verdi, Mahler, and Berg, his style is entirely his own: it is a musical personality that manages to combine, as it has been said, "a deep nostalgia for the innocence of childhood, a mercurial sense of humour and a passionate sympathy with the victims of prejudice and misunderstanding."

This last quality is particularly evident also in Tippett's emotional makeup as expressed in his music, especially in one of his earliest successes, the choral work *A Child of Our Time* (1941), which shows both his compassion and his ability to write on a large scale. But Tippett is as much a mystic and searcher as a composer and he is constantly seeking new and different ways of widening his listeners' horizons, as may be heard in the exceedingly complex *Vision of St. Augustine* (1965), which tellingly sets to music the striving to understand the " beyond " of Augustine's words.

Tippett has also sought new means of musical expression as he has shown in his second opera *King Priam* (1962), very spare and pointed in idiom, and in the concerto for orchestra (1962). These works, his piano concerto (1956) and second symphony (of three)—a luminous work—and his three string quartets, are very difficult to perform —and to get to know—but the effort to understand

the composer's wide-spanning mind is always richly rewarded. However, perhaps a newcomer to his music does better to approach him through the more straightforward earlier works, the concerto for double string orchestra (1939), the Fantasia Concertante on a theme of Corelli (1953) —a lyrically poetic piece—or the song cycles *Boyhood's End* (1943) and *Heart's Assurance* (1957). The quality of his allegorical opera *The Midsummer Marriage* (1952), in spite of its involved libretto (by the composer), is now better appreciated since its more recent revival. *The Knot Garden*, also concerned with the inner life of the spirit and the external world, was first performed at Covent Garden in 1970. Tippett is an uncompromising individualist, writing without fear or favour, perhaps considerably in advance of his time in thought and achievement.

Rawsthorne's style is admirably direct and honest. Eschewing the latest fashions in music he ploughed his own furrow of deeply felt writing. His ideas are argued out with considerable lyrical force, and his astute regard for form does not hide the underlying emotional content of his music nor the touch of wit that pervades some of his more lively movements. Among his most important accomplishments are his three string quartets, violin concerto, two piano concertos, and the quintet for piano and wind instruments.

Walton's outstanding contribution was made before the second World War in music that was alternately gay and romantic. The irreverent *Façade* (1923) for speaker and chamber orchestra falls into the former category, the poetic viola concerto (1929) into the second. His first symphony (1934–5) is an arresting, dramatic score, and the oratorio *Belshazzar's Feast* (1931) is a landmark in choral music. Since the war his works have never quite recaptured the same urgency of expression. His sole full-length opera, *Troilus and Cressida* (1954) was revised with success in 1976.

Elisabeth Lutyens (b. 1906) is Britain's leading twelve-note composer. For long shunned by the musical establishment, she has now been accepted as an important and seminal figure in the history of 20th-cent. music. Her output has been large and includes numerous works for unusual, small groups of instruments, often combined with a solo voice. Benjamin Frankel (1906–73), Edmund Rubbra (b. 1901), Sir Arthur Bliss (1891–1975), and Lennox Berkeley (b. 1903) are other composers of note among the senior school of living British composers. Egon Wellesz (1885–1970), Austrian-born, settled in Britain in 1939. He wrote operas, choral works, symphonies, and chamber music, and taught widely. There is a thriving junior school of British composers who have already made their mark, among them Alexander Goehr, Richard Rodney Bennett, Malcolm Williamson, Harrison Birtwistle, and Nicholas Maw, each of whom has written one or more operas. Roger Smalley and John Taverner, still younger, also seem to have promising futures before them. Williamson was created Master of the Queen's Musick, in succession to Bliss, in 1975.

Where Does the Future Lie?

It is anybody's guess which way music will develop during the next few decades. Are older forms quite outmoded, as some recent innovators suggest, and does the future therefore lie with the electronic music and/or percussive sounds—of Boulez, Stockhausen, Luigi Nono (b. 1924), and their disciples? Or will what has been recognised as musical sound for several generations adapt itself to the new mood abroad? Has atonalism still something to offer or was it a passing phase, already dated and out of fashion? Perhaps the only answer that can be given with certainty is that, as with other centuries, a dozen or so composers' music will survive to delight later generations and that these geniuses will be found among composers who do and say what they must in music without regard to fashion, patronage, or fear of what anyone writes about them. May they be worthy of their rich heritage.

II. GLOSSARY OF MUSICAL TERMS

A. Note of scale, commonly used for tuning instruments.

Absolute Music. Music without any literary descriptive or other kind of reference.

A Capella. Literally " in the church style." Unaccompanied.

Accelerando. Quickening of the pace.

Accidental. The sign which alters a note by a semitone, *i.e.*, ♯ (sharp) raises it; ♭ (flat) lowers it; ♮ restores a note to its original position.

Accompaniment. Instrumental or piano part forming background to a solo voice or instrument that has the melody.

Ad. lib. (L. *ad libitum*). Direction on music that strict time need not be observed.

Adagio. A slow movement or piece.

Aeolian mode. One of the scales in mediæval music, represented by the white keys of the piano from A to A.

Air. A simple tune for voice or instrument.

Alberti bass. Rhythmical accompanying figure made up by splitting a chord. Used extensively in 18th-cent. music and associated with the Italian composer Alberti.

Allegretto. Not quite so fast as *Allegro*.

Allegro. Fast, but not too fast.

Alto. An unusually high type of male voice; also the vocal part sung by women and boys with a low range.

Ambrosian Chant. Plainsong introduced into church music by St. Ambrose, bishop of Milan (d. 397), and differing from Gregorian chant.

Andante. At a walking pace, not so slow as *Adagio* nor as fast as *Allegretto*.

Animato. Lively.

Answer. Second entry in a fugue, usually in the dominant.

Anthem. Composition for use in church during a service by a choir with or without soloists.

Antiphonal. Using groups of instruments or singers placed apart.

Appoggiatura. An ornament consisting of a short note just above or below a note forming part of a chord.

Arabesque. Usually a short piece, highly decorated.

Arco. Direction for string instruments to play with bow.

Aria. Vocal solo, usually in opera or oratorio, often in three sections with the third part being a repeat of the first. An *Arietta* is a shorter, lighter kind of aria.

Arioso. In the style of an aria; halfway between aria and recitative.

Arpeggio. Notes of a chord played in a broken, spread-out manner, as on a harp.

Ars antiqua. The old mediæval music, based on organum and plainsong, before the introduction of *Ars nova* in 14th cent.

Ars nova. Musical style current from 14th cent., more independent than the old style in the part-writing and harmony.

Atonal. Not in any key; hence *Atonality*.

Aubade. Morning song.

Augmentation. The enlargement of a melody by lengthening the musical value of its notes.

Ayre. Old spelling of *air*.

B. Note of scale, represented in Germany by *H*.

Bagatelle. A short, generally light piece of music. Beethoven wrote 26 Bagatelles.

Ballad. Either a narrative song or an 18th-cent. drawing-room song.

Ballade. Instrumental piece in story-telling manner. Chopin wrote 4.

Ballet. Stage entertainment requiring instrumental accompaniment; originated at French court in 16th and 17th cent.

Bar. A metrical division of music; the perpendicular line in musical notation to indicate this.

Barcarolle. A boating-song, in particular one associated with Venetian gondoliers.

Baritone. A male voice, between tenor and bass.

Baroque. A term applied, loosely, to music written in the 17th and 18th cent., roughly corresponding to baroque in architecture.

Bass. The lowest male voice; lowest part of a composition.

Bass Drum. Largest of the drum family, placed upright and struck on the side.

Bassoon. The lowest of the woodwind instruments, uses double reed.

Beat. Music's rhythmic pulse.

Bel canto. Literally " beautiful singing "—in the old Italian style with pure tone and exact phrasing.

Berceuse. Cradle song.

Binary. A piece in two sections is said to be binary in form. The balance is obtained by a second phrase (or section) answering the first.

Bitonality. Use of two keys at once.

Bow. Stick with horsehair stretched across it for playing string instruments.

Brass. Used as a collective noun for all brass or metal instruments.

Breve. Note, rarely used nowadays, with tone value of two semibreves.

Bridge. Wood support over which strings are stretched on a violin, cello, guitar, etc.

Buffo(a). Comic, as in *buffo bass* or *opera buffa*.

C. Note of scale.

Cabaletta. Final, quick section of an aria or duet.

Cadence. A closing phrase of a composition or a passage, coming to rest on tonic (key note).

Cadenza. Solo vocal or instrumental passage, either written or improvised, giving soloist chance to display technical skill to audience.

Calando. Becoming quieter and slower.

Canon. Device in contrapuntal composition whereby a melody is introduced by one voice or instrument then repeated by one or more voices or instruments, either at the same pitch (canon at the unison) or at different intervals (canon at the fifth, for example).

Cantabile. Song-like, therefore flowing and expressive.

Cantata. Vocal work for chorus and/or choir.

Cantilena. Sustained, smooth melodic line.

Cantus firmus. Literally " fixed song." Basic melody from 14th to 17th cent., around which other voices wove contrapuntal parts.

Canzonet. Light songs written in England c. 1600.

Carillon. A set of bells in tower of church, played from a keyboard below.

Carol. Christmas song.

Castrato. Artificially-created male soprano and alto, fashionable in 17th and 18th cent. (The castration of vocally gifted boys prevailed in Italy until the 19th cent.)

Catch. A part-song like a round, in vogue in England from 16th to 19th cent.

Cavatina. An operatic song in one section, or a slow song-like instrumental movement.

Celesta. Keyboard instrument with metal bars struck by hammers.

Cello. Four-stringed instrument, played with bow, with a bass range. Comes between viola and double bass in string family.

Cembalo. Originally the Italian name for the dulcimer, but sometimes applied to the harpsichord.

Chaconne. Vocal or instrumental piece with unvaried bass.

Chamber Music. Music originally intended to be played in a room for three or more players.

Chanson. Type of part-song current in France from 14th to 16th cent.

Chant. Singing of psalms, masses, etc., in plainsong to Latin words in church.

Choir. Body of singers, used either in church or at concerts.

Chorales. German hymn tunes, often made use of by Bach.

Chord. Any combination of notes heard together *See also* Triad.

Chording. Spacing of intervals in a chord.

Chorus. Substantial body of singers, usually singing in four parts.

Chromatic. Using a scale of nothing but semitones.

Clarinet. Woodwind instrument with single reed in use since mid-18th cent.

Clavichord. Keyboard instrument having strings struck by metal tangents, much in use during 17th and 18th cent. as solo instrument.

Clavier. Used in German (*Klavier*) for piano, in England for any stringed keyboard instrument.

Clef. Sign in stave that fixes place of each note.

Coda. Closing section of movement in Sonata form.

Coloratura. Term to denote florid singing.

Common chord. *See* Triad.

Common Time. Four crotchets to the bar, 4/4 time.

Compass. Range of notes covered by voice or instruments.

Composition. Piece of music, originated by a composer's own imagination; act of writing such a piece.

Compound time. Any musical metric not in simple time.

Con Brio. With dash.

Concert. Public performance of any music.

Concertato. Writing for several solo instruments to be played together.

Concerto. Work for one or more solo instruments and orchestra.

Concerto grosso. Orchestral work common in 17th and 18th cent. with prominent parts for small groups of instruments.

Concord. Opposite of discord, *i.e.,* notes that when sounded together satisfy the ear. (Conventional term in that its application varies according to the age in which one lives.)

Conduct. To direct a concert with a baton.

Consecutive. Progression of harmonic intervals of like kind.

Consonance. Like Concord.

Continuo. Bass line, used in 17th- and 18th-cent. music, for a keyboard instrument, requiring special skill from performer.

Contralto. A woman's voice with a low range.

Counterpoint. Simultaneous combination of two or more melodies to create a satisfying musical texture. Where one melody is added to another, one is called the other's counterpoint. The adjective of counterpoint is contrapuntal

Counter-tenor. Another name for male alto.

Courante. A dance in triple time.

Crescendo. Getting louder.

Crook. Detachable section of tubing on brass instruments that change the tuning.

Crotchet. Note that equals two quavers in time value.

Cycle. Set of works, especially songs, intended to be sung as group.

Cyclic form. Form of work in two or more movements in which the same musical themes recur.

Cymbal. Percussion instrument; two plates struck against each other.

D. Note of scale.

Da Capo (abbr. D.C.). A *Da Capo* aria is one in which the whole first section is repeated after a contrasting middle section.

Descant. Additional part (sometimes improvised) sung against a melody.

Development. Working-out section of movement in sonata form. *See* Sonata.

Diatonic. Opposite of chromatic; using proper notes of a major or minor scale.

Diminished. Lessened version of perfect interval, e.g., semitone less than a perfect fifth is a diminished fifth.

Diminuendo. Lessening.

Diminution. Reducing a phrase of melody by shortening time value of notes.

Discord. Opposite of concord, *i.e.,* notes that sounded together produce a clash of harmonies.

Dissonance. Like discord.

Divertimento. A piece, usually orchestral, in several movements; like a suite.

Dodecaphonic. Pertaining to 12-note method of composition.

Dominant. Fifth note of major or minor scale above tonic (key) note.

Dorian Mode. One of the scales in mediæval music, represented by the white keys on the piano from D to D.

Dot. Placed over note indicates staccato; placed after note indicates time value to be increased by half.

Double bar. Two upright lines marking the end of a composition or a section of it.

Double bass. Largest and lowest instrument of violin family; played with bow.

Drone bass. Unvarying sustained bass, similar to the permanent bass note of a bagpipe.

Drum. Variety of percussion instruments on which sound is produced by hitting a skin stretched tightly over a hollow cylinder or hemisphere.

Duet. Combination of two performers; composition for such a combination.

Duple time. Time in which main division is two or four.

Dynamics. Gradations of loudness or softness in music.

E. Note of scale.

Electronic. Term used to describe use of electronic sounds in music.

Encore. Request from audience for repeat of work, or extra item in a programme.

English horn (*Cor anglais*). Woodwind instrument with double reed of oboe family.

Enharmonic. Modulation made by means of change of note between sharps and flats, although note remains the same (E flat becomes D sharp, for example).

Ensemble. Teamwork in performance; item in opera for several singers with or without chorus; a group of performers of no fixed number.

Episode. Section in composition usually divorced from main argument.

Exposition. Setting out of thematic material in a sonata-form composition.

Expression marks. Indication by composer of how he wants his music performed.

F. Note of scale.

False relation. A clash of harmony produced when two notes, such as A natural and A flat, are played simultaneously or immediately following one another.

Falsetto. The kind of singing by male voices above normal register and sounding like an unbroken voice.

Fanfare. Flourish of trumpets.

Fantasy. A piece suggesting free play of composer's imagination, or a piece based on known tunes (folk, operatic, etc.).

Fermata. Pause indicated by sign ⌒ prolonging note beyond its normal length.

Fifth. Interval taking five steps in the scale. A perfect fifth (say, C to G) includes three whole tones and a semitone; a diminished fifth is a semitone less, an augmented fifth a semitone more.

Figure. A short phrase, especially one that is repeated.

Fingering. Use of fingers to play instrument, or the indication above notes to show what fingers should be used.

Flat. Term indicating a lowering of pitch by a semitone, or to describe a performer playing under the note.

Florid. Term used to describe decorative passages.

Flute. Woodwind instrument, blown sideways. It is played through a hole, not a reed. Nowadays, sometimes made of metal.

Folksong. Traditional tune, often in different versions, handed down aurally from generation to generation.

Form. Course or layout of a composition, especially when in various sections.

Fourth. Interval taking four steps in scale. A perfect fourth (say, C to F) includes two whole tones and a semitone. If either note is sharpened or flattened the result is an augmented or a diminished fourth.

Fugato. In the manner of a fugue.

Fugue. Contrapuntal composition for various parts based on one or more subjects treated imitatively but not strictly.

G. Note of scale.

Galant. Used to designate elegant style of 18th-cent. music.

Galliard. Lively dance dating back to 15th cent. or before.

Gavotte. Dance in 4/4 time, beginning on third beat in bar.

Giusto. Strict, proper.

Glee. Short part-song.

Glissando. Rapid sliding scales up and down piano or other instruments.

Glockenspiel. Percussion instrument consisting of tuned steel bars and played with two hammers or keyboard.

Grace note. See Ornament.

Grave. In slow tempo.

Grazioso. Gracefully.

Gregorian Chant. Plainsong collected and supervised mainly by Pope Gregory (d. 604).

Ground bass. Figure on theme used as bass in a composition and constantly repeated without change.

Guitar. Plucked string instrument of Spanish origin, having six strings of three-octave compass.

H. German note-symbol for *B.*

Harmony. Simultaneous sounding of notes so as to make musical sense.

Harp. Plucked string instrument of ancient origin, the strings stretched parallel across its frame. The basic scale of C flat major is altered by a set of pedals.

Harpsichord. Keyboard stringed instrument played by means of keyboard similar to a piano but producing its notes by a plucking, rather than a striking action.

Homophonic. Opposite of polyphonic, *i.e.,* indicated parts move together in a composition, a single melody being accompanied by block chords, as distinct from the contrapuntal movement of different melodies.

Horn. Brass instrument with coiled tubes. Valves introduced in 19th cent. made full chromatic use of instrument possible.

Hymn. Song of praise, especially in church.

Imitation. Repetition, exactly, or at least recognisably, of a previously heard figure.

Impromptu. A short, seemingly improvised piece of music, especially by Schubert or Chopin.

Improvise. To perform according to fancy or imagination, sometimes on a given theme.

In alt. The octave above the treble clef; *in altissimo,* octave above that.

Instrumentation. Writing music for particular instruments, using the composer's knowledge of what sounds well on different instruments.

Interlude. Piece played between two sections of a composition.

Intermezzo. Formerly meant interlude, now often used for pieces played between acts of operas.

Interval. Distance in pitch between notes.

Ionian mode. One of the scales in mediæval music, represented on piano by white keys between C and C, identical therefore to modern C major scale.

Isorhythmic. Term applied to motets of 14th and 15th cent. where rhythm remains strict although melody changes.

Jig. Old dance usually in 6/8 or 12/8 time.

Kettledrum (It. pl. *Timpani*). Drum with skin drawn over a cauldron-shaped receptacle, can be tuned to definite pitch by turning handles on rim, thus tightening or relaxing skin.

Key. Lever by means of which piano, organ, etc., produces note; classification, in relatively modern times, of notes of a scale. Any piece of music in major or minor is in the *key* of its tonic or keynote.

Keyboard. Term used to describe instruments with a continuous row of keys.

Key-signature. Indication on written music, usually at the beginning of each line, of the number of flats or sharps in the key of a composition.

Kitchen Department. Humorous term for percussion section of an orchestra.

Lament. Musical piece of sad or deathly significance.

Largamente. Spaciously.

Largo. Slow.

Leading-motive (Ger. *Leitmotiv*). Short theme, suggesting person, idea, or image, quoted throughout composition to indicate that person, etc.

Legato. In a smooth style (of performance, etc.).

Lento. Slow.

Libretto. Text of an opera.

Lied. (pl. *Lieder*). Song, with special reference to songs by Schubert, Schumann, Brahms, and Wolf.

Lute. String instrument plucked with fingers, used in 15th- and 16th-cent. music especially.

Lydian mode. One of the scales in mediæval music, represented by white keys of piano between F and F.

Lyre. Ancient Greek plucked string instrument.

Madrigal. Contrapuntal composition for several voices, especially prominent from 15th to 17th cent.

Maestoso. Stately.

Major. One of the two main scales of the tonal system with semitones between the third and fourth, and the seventh and eighth notes, identical with 16th-cent. Ionian mode.

Mandolin(e). Plucked string instrument of Italian origin.

Manual. A keyboard for the hands, used mostly in connection with the organ.

Master of the King's (or Queen's) Musick. Title of British court appointment, with no precise duties.

Melisma. Group of notes sung to a single syllable.

Mélodie. Literally a melody or tune; has come to mean a French song (cf. German *Lied*).

Metronome. Small machine in use since the beginning of the 18th cent., to determine the pace of any composition by the beats of the music, *e.g.*, $\downarrow = 60$ at the head of the music indicates sixty crotchets to the minute.

Mezzo, Mezza. (It. = " half ") *Mezza voce* means using the half voice (a tone between normal singing and whispering). *Mezzo-soprano*, voice between soprano and contralto.

Minim. Note that equals two crotchets in time value.

Minor. One of the two main scales of the tonal system (cf. major), identical with 16th-cent. Aeolian mode. It has two forms—the harmonic and melodic, the former having a sharpened seventh note, the latter having the sixth and seventh note sharpened.

Minuet. Originally French 18th-cent. dance in triple time, then the usual third movement in symphonic form (with a contrasting trio section) until succeeded by scherzo.

Mixolydian mode. One of the mediaeval scales represented by the white keys on the piano from G to G.

Modes. Scales prevalent in the Middle Ages. *See* Aeolian, Dorian, Ionian, Lydian, Mixolydian, Phrygian.

Modulate. Changing from key to key in a composition, not directly but according to musical " grammar ".

Molto. Much, very; thus *allegro molto*.

Motet. Sacred, polyphonic vocal composition. More loosely, any choral composition for use in church but not set to words of the liturgy.

Motive, motif. Short, easily recognised melodic figure.

Motto. Short, well-defined theme recurring throughout a composition, cf *Idée fixe* in Berlioz's *Symphonie Fantastique.*

Movement. Separate sections of a large-scale composition, each in its own form.

Music drama. Term used to describe Wagner's, and sometimes other large-scale operas.

Mutes. Devices used to damp the sound of various instruments.

Natural (of a note or key). Not sharp or flat.

Neo-classical. Term used to describe music written mostly during the 1920s and 30s in the style of Bach or Mozart.

Ninth. Interval taking nine steps, *e.g.*, from C upwards an octave and a whole tone to D.

Nocturne. Literally a " night-piece ", hence usually of lyrical character.

Nonet. Composition for nine instruments.

Notation. Act of writing down music.

Note. Single sound of specified pitch and duration; symbol to represent this.

Obbligato. Instrumental part having a special or essential rôle in a piece.

Oboe. Woodwind instrument with double reed, descended from hautboy; as such, in use since 16th cent., in modern form since 18th cent.

Octave. Interval taking eight steps of scale, with top and bottom notes having same " name ": C to C is an octave.

Octet. Composition for eight instruments or voices.

Ondes Martenot. Belongs to a class of melodic instruments in which the tone is produced by electrical vibrations controlled by the movement of the hands not touching the instrument.

Opera. Musical work for the stage with singing characters, originated in early years of 17th cent.

Opera seria. Chief operatic form of 17th and 18th cent., usually set to very formal librettos, concerning gods or heroes of ancient history.

Operetta. Lighter type of opera.

Opus. (abbr. *Op.*) With number following *opus* indicates order of a composer's composition.

Oratorio. Vocal work, usually for soloists and choir with instrumental accompaniment, generally with setting of a religious text.

Orchestra. Term to designate large, or largish, body of instrumentalists originated in 17th cent.

Orchestration. Art of setting out work for instruments of an orchestra. To be distinguished from *Instrumentation (q.v.)*.

Organ. Elaborate keyboard instrument in which air is blown through pipes by bellows to sound notes. Tone is altered by selection of various stops and, since the 16th cent., a pedal keyboard has also been incorporated.

Organum. In mediaeval music a part sung as an accompaniment below or above the melody or plainsong, usually at the interval of a fourth or fifth; also, loosely, this method of singing in parts.

Ornament. Notes that are added to a given melody by composer or performer as an embellishment.

Overture. Instrumental introduction or prelude to larger work, usually opera. Concert overtures are simply that: *i.e.*, work to be played at start of a concert.

Part. Music of one performer in an ensemble; single strand in a composition.

Part-song. Vocal composition in several parts.

Passacaglia. Composition in which a tune is constantly repeated, usually in the bass.

Passage. Section of a composition.

Passion. Musical setting of the New Testament story of Christ's trial and crucifixion.

Pastiche. Piece deliberately written in another composer's style.

Pavan(e). Moderately paced dance dating from 16th cent. or earlier.

Pedal. Held note in bass of composition.

Pentatonic Scale. Scale of five notes—usually piano's five black keys or other notes in the same relation to each other.

Percussion. Collective title for instruments of the orchestra that are sounded by being struck by hand or stick.

Phrygian Mode. One of the scales of mediaeval music, represented by the white keys on piano from E to E.

Piano. Soft, abbr. *p*; *pp* = *pianissimo*, very soft; instrument, invented in 18th cent., having strings struck by hammer, as opposed to the earlier harpsichord where they are plucked. The modern piano has 88 keys and can be either " upright " (vertical) or " grand " (horizontal).

Pianoforte. Almost obsolete full Italian name for the piano.

Pitch. Exact height or depth of a particular musical sound or note.

Pizzicato. Direction for stringed instruments, that the strings should be plucked instead of bowed.

Plainchant, Plainsong. Mediaeval church music consisting of single line of melody without harmony or definite rhythm.

Polka. Dance in 2/4 time originating in 19th cent. Bohemia.

Polonaise. Polish dance generally in 3/4 time.

Polyphony. Combination of two or more musical lines as in *counterpoint.*

Polytonality. Simultaneous use of several keys.

Postlude. Closing piece, opposite of Prelude.

Prelude. Introductory piece.

Presto. Very fast. *Prestissimo.* Still faster.

Progression. Movement from one chord to next to make musical sense.

Quartet. Work written for four instruments or voices; group to play or sing such a work.

Quaver. Note that equals two semiquavers or half a crotchet.

Quintet. Work written for five instruments or voices; group to play or sing such a work.

Rallentando. Slowing down.

Recapitulation. Section of composition that repeats original material in something like its original form.

Recitative. Term used for declamation in singing written in ordinary notation but allowing rhythmical licence.

Recorder. Woodwind instrument, forerunner of flute.

Reed. Vibrating tongue of woodwind instruments.

Register. Set of organ pipes controlled by a particular stop; used in reference to different ranges of instrument or voice (*e.g.*, chest register).

Relative. Term used to indicate common key signature of a major and minor key.

Répétiteur. Member of opera house's musical staff who coaches singers in their parts.

Rest. Notation of pauses for instrument in composition, having a definite length like a note.

Retrograde. Term used to describe a melody played backwards.

Rhapsody. Work of no definite kind with a degree of romantic content.

Rhythm. Everything concerned with the time of music (*i.e.*, beats, accent, metre, etc.) as opposed to the pitch side.

Ritornello. Passage, usually instrumental, that recurs in a piece.

Romance, Romanza. Title for piece of vague song-like character.

Romantic. Term used vaguely to describe music of 19th cent. that has other than purely musical source of inspiration.

Rondo. Form in which one section keeps on recurring.

Rubato. Manner of performing a piece without keeping strictly to time.

Sackbut. Early English name for trombone.

Saxophone. Classified as wind instrument, although made of brass, because it uses a reed.

Scale. Progression of adjoining notes upwards or downwards.

Scherzo. One of two middle movements, usually third, in four-movement sonata form. Displaced minuet in this form at beginning of 19th cent.

Score. Copy of any music written in several parts.

Second. Interval taking two steps in scale, *e.g.*, C to D flat, or to D.

Semibreve. Note that equals two minims or half a breve.

Semiquaver. Note that equals half a quaver.

Semitone. Smallest interval commonly used in Western music.

Septet. Composition for seven instruments or voices.

Sequence. Repetition of phrase at a higher or lower pitch.

Serenade. Usually an evening song or instrumental work.

Seventh. Interval taking seven steps in the scale.

Sextet. Composition for six instruments or voices.

Sharp. Term indicating a raising of pitch by a semitone.

Shawm. Primitive woodwind instrument, forerunner of oboe.

Simple time. Division of music into two or four beats.

Sinfonietta. Small symphony.

Sixth. Interval taking six steps in the scale.

Solo. Piece or part of a piece for one performer playing or singing alone.

Sonata. Term to denote a musical form and a type of composition. In *sonata form* a composition is divided into exposition, development and recapitulation. A *sonata* is a piece, usually, for one or more players following that form.

Song. Any short vocal composition.

Soprano. Highest female voice.

Sostenuto. Sustained, broadly.

Sotto voce. Whispered, scarcely audible, applied to vocal as well as instrumental music.

Sprechgesang. (Ger. Speech-song.) Vocal utterance somewhere between speech and song.

Staccato. Perform music in short, detached manner.

Staff. Horizontal lines on which music is usually written.

Stop. Lever by which organ registration can be altered.

String(s). Strands of gut or metal set in vibration to produce musical sounds on string or keyboard instruments. Plural refers to violins, violas, cellos, and basses of orchestra.

Study. Instrumental piece, usually one used for technical exercise or to display technical skill, but often having artistic merits as well (*e.g.* Chopin's).

Subject(s). Theme or group of notes that forms principal idea or ideas in composition.

Suite. Common name for piece in several movements.

Symphony. Orchestral work of serious purpose usually in four movements, occasionally given name (*e.g.*, Beethoven's " Choral " symphony).

Syncopation. Displacement of musical accent.

Tempo. Pace, speed of music.

Tenor. Highest normal male voice.

Ternary. A piece in three sections is said to be in ternary form. The balance is obtained by repeating the first phrase or section (though it need not be exact or complete) after a second of equal importance.

Tessitura. Compass into which voice or instrument comfortably falls.

Theme. Same as *subject* but can also be used for a whole musical statement as in " theme and variations."

Third. Interval taking three steps in scale.

Time. Rhythmical division of music.

Timpani. See Kettledrum.

Toccata. Instrumental piece usually needing rapid, brilliant execution.

Tonality. Key, or feeling for a definite key.

Tone. Quality of musical sound; interval of two semitones.

Tonic Sol-fa. System of musical notation to simplify sight-reading.

Transcribe. Arrange piece for different medium, instrument, or voice than that originally intended.

Transition. Passage that joins two themes of sections of a composition.

Transpose. Perform a piece at different pitch from that originally intended.

Treble. Highest part in vocal composition; high boy's voice.

Triad. A chord consisting of a note with the third and fifth above it, e.g., C–E–G. A common chord is a triad of which the 5th is perfect, e.g., C–E–G or C–E flat–G. Thus major and minor triads are common chords.

Trio. Work written for three instruments or voices; group to play or sing such a work.

Trombone. Brass instrument with slide adjusting length of tube.

Trumpet. Metal instrument of considerable antiquity; modern version has three valves to make it into a chromatic instrument.

Tuba. Deepest-toned brass instrument with three or four valves.

Twelve-note. Technique of composition using full chromatic scale with each note having equal importance. Notes are placed in particular order as the thematic basis of works.

Unison. Two notes sung or played together at same pitch.

Valve. Mechanism, invented in early 19th cent. to add to brass instruments allowing them to play full chromatic scale.

Variation. Varied passage of original theme. Such variations may be closely allied to or depart widely from the theme.

Verismo. Term to describe Italian operas written in " realist " style at the turn of this century.

Vibrato. Rapid fluctuation in pitch of voice or instrument. Exaggerated it is referred to as a " wobble " (of singers) or tremolo.

Viol. String instrument of various sizes in vogue until end of 17th cent.

Viola. Tenor instrument of violin family.

Violin. Musical four-string instrument, played with bow of violin family, which superseded viol at beginning of 18th cent.

Virginals. English keyboard instrument, similar to harpsichord of 17th and 18th cent.

Vivace. Lively.

Voluntary. Organ piece for church use, but not during service.

Waltz. Dance in triple time, fashionable in 19th cent.

Whole-tone scale. Scale progressing by whole tones. Only two are possible, one beginning on C, the other on C sharp.

Xylophone. Percussion instrument with series of wood bars tuned in a chromatic scale and played with sticks.

Zither. String instrument laid on knees and plucked. Common in Central-European folk music.

III. INDEX TO COMPOSERS

IV. SPECIAL TOPICS

FESTIVALS

The term derives from the Latin *festivitas* (merriment), and was used as early as the Renaissance to describe celebrations with music at royal courts to mark special occasions as, for example, the meeting of Francis I and Pope Leo X at Bologna in 1515. In more recent times the term was employed to describe grand musical occasions, usually dedicated to the greater glory of one particular composer. In Austria there were Haydn Festivals right at the end of the composer's life (1808–11), in Germany a Beethoven Festival in 1845, in England Handel Festivals beginning in 1862. The oldest of festivals still in existence is the Three Choirs, dating back to the first half of the 18th century. Bayreuth, begun by Wagner in 1876, is the most venerable of international events, and has its own purpose-built theatre for the performance of his operas. A year later the first Mozart Festival was held in Salzburg. Munich began its opera festival in 1901. The Florence Maggio Musicale was established in 1933. The Glyndebourne Festival in Sussex, England, started solely with Mozart's operas in 1934. The big expansion in festivals did not start until after the second World War, the first major new festival being in Edinburgh in 1947. Today the coinage has been badly debased, in the sense that any small town will call the most minor musical or theatrical occasion a festival, and many of the major ones have become unduly commercialised.

These are clearly divided between those that are wide-ranging and cosmopolitan in flavour and those that are specialised, either hymning the achievements of a single composer or else reflecting the style of one or two people. Into the first category go Salzburg and Edinburgh the largest events of their kind comprising all the arts. In recent years Salzburg has been dominated by the conductor-producer Herbert von Karajan who has directed most of the operas in the larger of the two main opera houses. He has also established a Salzburg Easter Festival, which is under his sole control, and presents one major production each spring. At the summer festival he has shared the honours with the veteran Karl Böhm, who has specialised in the operas of Mozart and Richard Strauss. Concerts are given by several major world orchestras every summer and by visiting soloists of international repute.

The first Mozart festivals were held at Salzburg between 1877 and 1910. Operas and concerts were conducted by such famous figures of the time as Mahler, Hans Richter, Richard Strauss, Felix Mottl, and Karl Muck. Later the famous director Max Reinhardt was a main influence on the festival. During the 1920s and 1930s, Strauss, Clemens Krauss, and Bruno Walter conducted memorable performances of Mozart and other operas. Toscanini appeared there in 1935 and 1937. The festival was resumed after the war in 1946 with Wilhelm Furtwängler as the leading light. In 1960 the Grosses Festspielhaus was opened. It has one of the largest and widest stages in the world.

Edinburgh was the brainchild of Glyndebourne, which presented the opera there during the first five years of the festival, again from 1953 to 1955. Since then there have been visits from companies from all over the world, augmented in recent years by performances from the Scottish Opera company. All these have to be squeezed on to the small stage of the King's Theatre pending the promised new opera house. As costs have soared that has become something of a mirage. Edinburgh has also played host to almost every orchestra of consequence, and about five of these give concerts there every year in the Usher Hall. Chamber music and recitals appear at the Freemasons' Hall and at Leith Town Hall. Rudolf Bing was the festival's first director and he has been succeeded by, among others, Lord Harewood and Peter Diamand. Various attempts have been made, especially by Harewood, to give the festival a theme or a purpose; none has proved lasting and the festival has continued along its somewhat amorphous way.

Benjamin Britten and his friend, the tenor Peter Pears, started the Aldeburgh Festival on the Suffolk coast in 1948. Their taste dominated the early years of the festival, which also saw the premiers of many Britten works, although by no means to the exclusion of the music of other modern composers. The conversion of the Maltings at Snape into a concert hall greatly increased the possibilities of the festival, and Britten lived long enough to conduct several unforgettable performances in the new building. In latter years he also welcomed several Soviet artists, and wrote works for, as well as playing with, Richter, Rostropovich and Vishnevskaya. The festival has always maintained a pleasingly informal and local atmosphere. This festival with its purpose and profile should be a model for others. Bath, like Aldeburgh, has its surroundings to recommend it, but it has not yet established such a true identity. Directors have included Beecham, Menuhin, Tippett, and most recently Sir William Glock, formerly head of music at the BBC. Cheltenham (for new music) and King's Lynn are other significant English post-war festivals. The Three Choirs and Leeds Triennial Festivals have a much longer history, both based on strong choral traditions. They continue to flourish.

Bayreuth, the oldest and most worthwhile of the German festivals, is a classic example of an event devoted wholly to the works of a single composer and thus having a continuing raison d'être. The festival celebrated its centenary in 1976, and could look back on a history of almost uninterrupted activity, apart from the period of the two world wars and of uninterrupted direction by the Wagner family. The composer's widow Cosima was in charge from 1883 until 1908 when her son Siegfried took charge. On his death in 1930 his widow Winifred succeeded him. Her friendship with Hitler threw a cloud over the festival lifted by her sons Wieland and Wolfgang, who revolutionised the staging of their grandfather's music-dramas from 1951 onwards. In the centenary year, a young Frenchman Patrice Chereau altered the pattern of the stagings once again with his modernistic ideas. Both changes caused a furore. The opera house at Bayreuth is an ideal design for seeing and hearing. It was copied at Munich's Prinzregententheater in 1901 when the Munich Festival started with the intention of presenting Wagner's works, but today performances are given in the rebuilt National Theatre and in the renovated 18th-cent. Cuvilliés Theatre. The festival tends to concentrate on the works of its native son, Richard Strauss, and on Mozart, with some excursions into the modern repertory. This is a good example of a basically home-orientated festival. The West Berlin Festival in September each year is more internationally based. Wiesbaden, held in May, has a history going back to 1900; it calls on predominantly local talent. In East Germany, the Handel Festivals at the composer's birthplace of Halle have been held steadily since 1951.

In Italy the spectacular yearly seasons in the Verona Arena (July–August), begun in 1913, are not actually called festivals but qualify as such. The repertory consists mainly of large-scale pieces from the Italian repertory sung by leading singers of the day. The Maggio Musicale Fiorentino, held as its title would suggest in May, was originally a biennial event but became annual in 1938, and has continued as such, apart from a war-time break, ever since. Again the repertory has been chiefly Italian, but there have been occasional experiments in other territory. The events are spread through May and the beginning of June. Spoleto, a little like Aldeburgh, is the brainchild of Gian-Carlo Menotti, the Italian American composer, and its performances (since its inception in 1958) take place in the attractive Teatro Nuovo and Teatro Melisso in the little hillside town in Umbria. Newish works and youngish artists are given prominence, and many youthful Americans are always in attendance.

In Austria, besides Salzburg, festivals are regularly held at Vienna (May–June), a kind of extension of the usual season with many extra opera and concert performances, and at Bregenz (July–August), where the lakeside theatre is unique. Operetta is a particular feature of this festival, which was started in 1956.

The attraction of a beautiful site is also one of the advantages of the Aix Festival, held every July in the open-air theatre of the Archbishop's Palace since 1948. Mozart and other 18th-cent. works has been the speciality there, but of late more 19th-cent. works have been given. France also has a number of smaller festivals among them the piano feast at Tours whose mastermind is Richter, and it attracts all the world's leading players to the attractive barn where the recitals take place. Other European festivals of note take place at Lucerne, Montreux, Zurich, Stockholm, Copenhagen, Prague, Athens, Savonlinna (Finland), Helsinki, Dubrovnik, Wexford.

In the United States the main festival is that at Santa Fé, held in the large, partially open-air theatre. Its moving spirit is John Crosby, and his choice of operas is wide-ranging. The festival is steadily gaining in prestige as the seasons go by, and may before long rival some of the best European events. At Caramoor (New York State), a kind of Glyndebourne-like Festival is held. The Marlboro Festival, begun by Rudolf Serkin and friends, is a training as much as a performing event, and it encourages young players, who come to perfect their craft. Other American festivals are held at Tanglewood, Hollywood Bowl, Newport, Ravinia Park (nr. Chicago), and Wolf Trap (nr. Washington DC). In Australia Adelaide now holds a biennial festival of the Arts.

THE GRAMOPHONE

Although the beginnings of recording stretch back well into the 19th century, its enormous potential did not begin to be realised until about 1900. In the 1890s some recording was done on cylinder machines, but it was eventually Emil Berliner's disc reproducer that won the day. The Gramophone and Typewriter Company (later HMV) was established in 1898, and by 1902 its roster of artists included besides the already indispensable Caruso (it has been said with truth that "Caruso made the gramophone, and the gramophone Caruso "), Chaliapin, Calvé, Battistini, to whom was soon to be added the legendary Patti, recorded in 1906 in her Welsh castle, Melba, De Luca Tamagno, indeed most of the reputable operatic artists of the age. In those days of pre-electrical recording, the voice was predominant, as it was impossible to record an orchestra around the horn with any kind of fidelity. In fact, many of the earliest discs were cut with only piano accompaniment.

However, surprisingly early (1906–14), a number of operas were recorded in some kind of complete form. They may sound comic today, but the achievement for its time was considerable. Electrical recording replaced the acoustic process in the middle of the 1920s. Already in the early part of the decade, some symphonies had been recorded, albeit often in abbreviated form. Now, with the new method, recording of the orchestral repertory began in earnest, while several operas were committed to disc for the first time, including sizeable chunks of the Wagnerian works. In the Italian repertory there were often rival versions of the same work made by the two main companies of the time, HMV and Columbia.

The advent of so many records began gradually to change the whole musical climate. Whereas in the past, the public had learnt their music through practical music-making in the home, often in piano reductions of orchestral and operatic scores, they now began to get to know music through the record, and naturally there were losses as well as gains in the process. There is no substitute for practical music-making: on the other hand, the enormous pleasure records have brought to millions is not to be denied. The danger has lain in using records as what has been aptly called "wallpaper music ", that is as merely a background to other activities; as such it does an injury to compositions intended to demand wholehearted attention.

With the advent of the long-playing disc in 1950, the possibilities for recording received perhaps an even bigger boost than at the coming of the electrical process. It was now possible to contain most of the works in the symphonic and chamber repertory on one disc and most operas on two or three. Almost immediately the whole range of works was re-recorded for the new medium, and a further, if not quite so drastic, revision was called for with the introduction of the stereo process in 1958–9. Today there is a wider catalogue of music available to the ordinary person in the home than at any previous time. At the same time, the study of past recording achievements is becoming almost a history on its own, as musicians come to realise that in the eighty years of the gramophone styles in singing and playing have changed—and changed more than once. Listening to Melba in opera or Pachmann on the piano is in itself an instruction in performing practices at the beginning of the century.

One of the first benefits from the advent of LP was the recording of much pre-classical (i.e., pre-1700) music. Gradually the music of Monteverdi and his great predecessors became readily accessible and also acceptable to the general public, whereas they had previously been the preserve of specialists. In the classical period the cantatas of Bach, formerly a virtually closed book to all but Bach experts, began to be recorded in large numbers. All the piano sonatas of Haydn, all his symphonies and quartets, all Mozart's piano concertos were projects realised during the 1970s. In the early 1960s the whole of Wagner's Ring, always considered an impossible task became available owing to the enterprise of John Culshaw of Decca, which often led the field in widening the recorded repertory. Soon it was followed by three or four other complete sets of the huge work, while all the other Wagnerian operas were also recorded, as were, almost needless to say, the major operas of Mozart, soon succeeded by his early works in the genre. There followed the first recording of many of Verdi's early operas to supplement the already released issues of his mature works. This led to the investigation of other early 19th-cent. opera, in particular the operas of Bellini and Donizetti. If the modern repertory, Britten excepted, received less than its due, that only reflected the comparative lack of interest from the general public in music of its own time. Even so, a good number of avant-garde works were recorded, and the 20th cent. as a whole was well treated: not only were the works of such important traditional figures as Sibelius, Elgar, and Nielsen recorded but also all the major works of Stravinsky, Schoenberg, Berg, and Webern, affording in all a comprehensive view of the century's achievements. Britten, while he was alive, supervised the recording of his works, and conducted most of his operas on disc himself, although sadly not Gloriana, while after his illness his last opera, Death in Venice, was entrusted to Steuart Bedford. Other British music of recent times was almost as generously treated.

The policy of some companies to delete records when they were not selling in sufficient numbers deprived the catalogue of many important issues. At the same time, HMV and Deutsche Grammophon, who hold in their archives the bulk of historic material, began to realise their responsibilities, and issued many successful boxes of classic performances. In this way, Elgar conducting Elgar, Beecham conducting Delius, the ancient records of Patti, Caruso, and Melba, the more recent ones of Maggie Teyte, the discs of Bayreuth singers from 1902 onwards were all issued in large-scale and well-annotated boxes.

Boxes indeed became the order of the day. All Mahler's symphonies, all of Bruckner's, all Mozart's string quarters, all Schubert's piano sonatas and so on were issued in boxes, fulfilling an apparently insatiable demand for comprehensive compilations and the saving in price that went with them. While the number of sets of Beethoven symphonies available surpassed all bounds, each seemed to find its market. The record industry became big business, but at the same time did not neglect its duty as an educational influence.

To accompany the revolution in recording, there has to be a complementary one in equipment, what became known in the record trade as "hardware". From the primitive horn of the early years of the century to the most complex set-ups, costing hundreds of pounds, of today is a huge step, although the objective, the most lifelike representation of what is enshrined on the records, remains the same. The early days of electrical recording saw the coming of the "radiogram", large consoles containing radios and gramophones as the name suggests. They were succeeded, in the early days of LP, by separate components of turntable, pick-up, amplifier, and loudspeakers, often unsightly but doing their job efficiently. While the specialist continued to concentrate on individual sections in the days of stereo and then quadrophonic (the invention, not widely disseminated, of the mid-1970s), the ordinary listener

was offered what was called "music-centres", which tried to incorporate some kind of "hi-fi" within a smaller space. The development of small but highly competent loudspeakers was a great gain in space-saving and looks.

A less welcome result of the record revolution has been the search for a spurious perfection. By the use of innumerable tape edits of several "takes" in recording sessions it has been possible to hear more exact performances of any work than would ever be possible in a concert hall or opera house, but such near-perfection has often been achieved at a severe cost to spontaneity and life in recorded interpretations. Another drawback is the following: people who hear near-ideal opera casts or solo-conductor partnerships in their home become disillusioned when they cannot encounter, for financial reasons, similar standards in live performances. The record industry would argue that they are able to give to the public something that they would never otherwise hear, and often at a very reasonable cost, that indeed the home has become the true opera house or concert hall; but it is simply not possible to have such performances if the live side of music-making is in a state of atrophy. An element of artificiality, even falsity, is therefore present in today's developments in the field of the gramophone. However, more live performances are now being recorded, and one must hope that a modus vivendi between the needs of record-makers and the existence of full-blooded interpretations will be found.

The most recent development in recorded music has been the arrival of the cassette as a potent rival to the disc. Easier to manage, easier to reproduce, it for long suffered from the disadvantage of more restricted sound, as compared with the record. That difficulty has been largely overcome, and more and more collectors now run a cassette machine in tandem with their record-player, even if they have not entirely replaced the one with the other.

INSTRUMENTS OF THE ORCHESTRA

The standard orchestra for symphonic music consists of four primary sections: strings, woodwind, brass, and percussion. The strings subdivide into violins, firsts and seconds; violas; cellos; double-basses. The wind subdivide into flutes (principal and second); piccolo; oboes (principal and second); clarinet (ditto); bassoon (ditto); bass-clarinet; double-bassoon; cor anglais. Not all compositions contain parts for piccolo and cor anglais, or bass clarinet and double-bassoon nor in 18th-cent. music, for clarinets. Some conductors insist on doubling the number of the main wind parts in tutti passages (i.e., passages where the whole orchestra is playing), in order that there should be a balance between the wind and the (usually large) string departments, consisting of fourteen first violins, fourteen seconds, twelve violas, ten cellos, and eight basses.

The brass subdivides into horns (four); trumpets (three or more); trombones (two tenor, one bass); tuba. For works by Bruckner and Wagner the "Wagner tuba" is used in addition to the other instruments. The percussion section is infinitely variable. Its most common components are the harp, timpani (or kettledrum), xylophone and tubular bell, which define pitch, and the cymbal and triangle, which are of indefinite pitch. To these are added more exotic instruments for many modern scores. Indeed, many of these make a feature of percussion sounds. Most of the main instruments have their attributes defined in the glossary.

A symphony orchestra indicates the full-scale, standard orchestra heard in the big concert halls. A chamber orchestra is a smaller body, sometimes containing strings only, but augmented by outside wind and brass players as pieces demand. Most chamber orchestras sometimes have as few as six first violins, with the remainder of the orchestra reduced accordingly.

MUSIC CLUBS AND SOCIETIES

There are many ways for the amateur to take part in making music. The oldest established is undoubtedly the choral society. There is hardly a district in Britain that does not have its own amateur choir (they are fully listed in the *British Music Yearbook*), ranging from the major London choruses such as the Royal Choral Society and Bach Choir, the two longest established, the New Philharmonia Choir, the London Philharmonic Choir, and the London Symphony Chorus to the small local groups. Most meet once a week to practise for three or four events through the season. Standards required vary, of course, according to the aspirations and range of each body. Similar organizations exist throughout Britain in the orchestral field. In the United States choirs and orchestras are more likely to be based on universities or on religious organizations, although more widely based groups also exist.

Music Clubs and Societies meet up and down Britain. They promote either live concerts by professionals and/or amateurs, or illustrated lectures by visiting speakers, or a combination of both. They are mostly under the umbrella of the National Federation of Music Societies or the National Federation of Gramophone Societies. There are also operatic societies, which as the name suggests, exist for the promotion of that specific branch of music; they, too, have their national association. Then there are, particulary in Northern Britain, brass bands, many of which compete yearly in major championships.

For young people there are equivalent organisations, the main one being the National Youth Orchestra. That supplements the orchestras of the country. For a younger age group there are various schools specialising in musical tuition and the specialised choir schools. Those are supplemented by the various competitions held throughout the country, with prizes given, for all forms of musical attainments. In several cases financial awards are given for further study, often abroad. The most famous among these are the Kathleen Ferrier Memorial Scholarship (for singers), the Leeds Piano Competition (triennial) and the Rupert Foundation (for conductors). In addition, there are many international competitions in Europe and various courses, generalised or specialised, for holiday music study. These are often open to people of all ages as well as to students. Many universities in this country run extra-mural courses, and the Open University runs a degree course from Milton Keynes. Most local authorities have Senior Music officials, and they run courses of adult education in music.

The main music periodicals are *The Musical Times*, *Music and Musicians*, *Opera*, *The Gramophone*, *Records and Recordings*, and *Classical Music*, all except the last (which is weekly) appear monthly. There are many other, more specialised magazines, several of them concerning themselves with particular instruments, or other aspects of music.

THE WORLD OF SCIENCE

A contemporary picture of scientific discovery, designed to explain some of the most important ideas in astronomy, physics, chemistry, biology and to give some account of recent research in various fields.

TABLE OF CONTENTS

THE WORLD OF SCIENCE

In Parts I, II, and III the inanimate universe is described. This is the domain of cosmology, astronomy, geology, physics, and chemistry. There are already many interesting links which join this realm to that of the living and make it difficult to say where the boundary lies. Nevertheless it is still convenient to accord to the biological and social sciences three separate chapters, IV, V and VI. In Part VII our intention is to give some short accounts of recent developments in both science and technology. They are usually contributed by scientists actively engaged in these, their own special fields.

I. ASTRONOMY AND COSMOLOGY—THE NATURE OF THE UNIVERSE

The universe includes everything from the smallest sub-atomic particle to the mightiest system of stars. The scientific view of the universe (not the only view but the one we are concerned with here) is a remarkable achievement of the human mind, and it is worth considering at the outset what a " scientific view " is, and what is remarkable about it.

A scientific view of something is always an intimate mixture of theories and observed facts, and not an inert mixture but a seething and growing one. The theories are broad general ideas together with arguments based on them. The arguments are designed to show that, if the general ideas are accepted, then this, that, or the other thing ought to be observed. If this, that, or the other actually are observed, then the theory is a good one; if not, then the theoreticians have to think again. Thus theoretical ideas and arguments are continually subjected to the severe test of comparison with the facts, and scientists are proud of the rigour with which this is done. On the other hand, theories often suggest new things to look for, i.e., theories lead to predictions. These predictions are frequently successful, and scientists are entitled to be proud of that too. But it follows that no theory is immutable; any scientific view of any subject may, in principle, be invalidated at any time by the discovery of new facts, though some theories are so soundly based that overthrow does not seem imminent.

A remarkable aspect of the scientific view of the universe is that the same principles are supposed to operate throughout the whole vastness of space. Thus the matter and radiation in stars are not different from the matter and radiation on earth, and their laws of behaviour are the same. Therefore theories hard won by studies in terrestrial physics and chemistry laboratories are applied at once to the whole cosmos. Astronomy and cosmology are spectacular extensions of ordinary mechanics and physics.

LOOKING AT THE UNIVERSE

The universe is observable because signals from it reach us and some manage to penetrate our atmosphere.

First, there are waves of visible light together with invisible rays of somewhat longer (infra-red) and somewhat shorter (ultra-violet) wavelengths. These waves show us the bright astronomical objects and, to make use of them, astronomers have constructed telescopes of great power and precision backed up with cameras, spectroscopes, and numerous auxiliaries. The most powerful telescope is the 236·2-inch reflector at Mount Semirodriki in the Soviet Union. The earth's atmosphere acts as a distorting and only partially transparent curtain and the erection of telescopes on satellites is beginning to extend optical telescope performance significantly.

Secondly, there are radio waves of much longer wavelength than light. Radiotelescopes are sensitive radio receivers with specialised aerial systems. The scientific stature of modern radioastronomy

was emphasised by the award in 1974 of the Nobel Physics Prize to two Cambridge radioastronomers, Ryle and Hewish.

Other types of radiation reach the earth from outer space. Cosmic radiation consists of fundamental particles, including protons (F16) of extremely high energy, moving at velocities very close to that of light. These particles can be detected by Geiger counters and by their tracks on photographic plates. X-rays and neutrinos (F16) are also generated by certain classes of astronomical objects (F5). With the recent advent of satellite-borne detectors and apparatus buried in deep mines, new facets of cosmic-ray astronomy, X-ray astronomy, and neutrino astronomy are now rapidly deepening our knowledge of the nature of the universe and of the violent processes by which galaxies as well as individual stars and planetary systems evolve (F6, F7).

Great Distances and Large Numbers

To visualise the immense scale of the universe is almost as much a problem for the scientist as for the layman. The conventional shorthand is to express 1,000 as 10^3; 1,000,000 as 10^6. On this scale the earth is $1·496 \times 10^8$ km away from the sun. Concorde, for example, the world's fastest airliner, took about 3½ hours to travel 5,000 km from London to New York. The "Viking" spacecraft in 1976 took just over a year to travel the 200 million km to Mars. These distances, however, are minute by comparison with the distance even to the nearest star, Proxima Centauri, some 4×10^{13} km away. This distance is more conveniently expressed in terms of the travel time of light itself. With a velocity of nearly 300,000 km per second, in a year light travels about $9·46 \times 10^{12}$ km. The distance to Proxima Centauri is therefore $4·2$ light years. Even this distance, enormous on our terrestrial scale, is a small cosmic distance. The diameter of our galaxy is about 10^5 light years, while the most distant objects yet observed are an incredible $1·4 \times 10^{10}$ light years distant.

PLANETS, STARS AND GALAXIES

The Solar System

The earth is the third, counting outward of nine planets revolving in nearly circular orbits round the sun. Some of their particulars are given in the Table (F8). The sun and its planets are the main bodies of the solar system. Mainly between the orbits of Mars and Jupiter revolve numerous small bodies—the minor planets or asteroids, the largest of which, Ceres, is only 800 km in diameter. Apart from these, the solar system is tenuously populated with particles varying in size from about a micron (10^{-6} m) to hundreds of metres in diameter. Some of these objects collide with the earth's atmosphere. The smaller fragments (micro-meteors) are too small to be visible. Larger particles (meteors), about 1 mm up to tens of cm, cause the phenomena known as "shooting stars" when they burn up at about 100 km altitude. Even larger chunks, of rocky or iron composition, cause the rare and brilliant fireballs, some of which survive their high-speed flight through the earth's atmosphere and may later be recovered. Such objects (meteorites) are very important, providing examples of extra-terrestrial rocks, and thus giving the composition of some of the most primitive material left in the solar system. Collisions with very large meteorites (or small asteroids) are now, fortunately, very rare. However, the large meteorite crater in Arizona is one recent reminder that such collisions still occur, although much less frequently now than earlier in the history of the planetary system. The surfaces of Mercury, the Moon, Mars, and Venus still show the scars from collisions with a multitude of objects of up to tens of km in diameter.

Comets are still enigmatic objects which, from time to time, provide a spectacular sight. Probably, they consist of a small nucleus (1–10 km diameter) of a compact, frozen conglomerate of dust and the so-called "icy" materials—H_2O, NH_3, CH_4, CO_2, etc. In their highly elliptical orbits, they spend most of their life at great distances from the sun, where the temperature is very low because of the feeble solar radiation, so that all the "icy" materials are solid. Periodically, when each comet returns to the inner parts of the solar system, the increasing solar radiation heats the surface layers, evaporating the volatile ices, which carry the surface dust away from the comet nucleus. After this heating and evaporation process, the ultra-violet component of sunlight further breaks down the parent "icy" molecules, a process known as photo-dissociation, and many molecules become ionised. Solar-radiation pressure, acting on the dust constituents, and the solar wind acting on the ionised constituents, form the gigantic cometary tails which may reach 2×10^8 km in length—larger than the radius of the earth's orbit. See also L28.

The sun itself is a dense, roughly spherical mass of glowing matter, 1,392,000 km across. Its heat is so intense that the atoms are split into separated electrons and nuclei (F11) and matter in such a state is called plasma. At the sun's centre the temperature has the unimaginable value of about 13 million degrees Centigrade (a coal fire is about 800°C). Under such conditions the atomic nuclei frequently collide with one another at great speeds and reactions occur between them. The sun consists largely of hydrogen and, in the very hot plasma, the nuclei of hydrogen atoms interact by a series of reactions whose net result is to turn hydrogen into helium. This is a process which releases energy just as burning does, only these nuclear processes are incomparably more energetic than ordinary burning. In fact, the energy released is great enough to be the source of all the light and heat which the sun has been pouring into space for thousands of millions of years.

Emerging from the sun and streaming past the earth is a "solar wind" of fast-moving electrons and protons (F11) whose motion is closely linked with the behaviour of an extensive magnetic field based on the sun. In fact, the region round the sun and extending far into space past the earth is full of complex, fluctuating particle streams and magnetic fields which interact with planetary atmospheres causing, among other things, auroras and magnetic storms.

Stars

In colour, brightness, age, and size the sun is typical of vast numbers of other stars. Only from the human point of view is there anything special about the sun—it is near enough to give us life. Even the possession of a system of revolving planets is not, according to some modern views, very unusual.

No star can radiate energy at the rate the sun does without undergoing internal changes in the course of time. Consequently stars evolve and old processes in them give rise to new. The exact nature of stellar evolution—so far as it is at present understood—would be too complex to describe here in any detail. It involves expa-

sion and contraction, changes of temperature, changes of colour, and changes in chemical composition as the nuclear processes gradually generate new chemical elements by reactions such as the conversion of hydrogen to helium, helium to neon, neon to magnesium, and so on. The speed of evolution changes from time to time, but is in any case very slow compared with the pace of terrestrial life; nothing very dramatic may occur for hundreds of millions of years. Evidence for the various phases of evolution is therefore obtained by studying many stars, each at a different stage of its life. Thus astronomers recognise many types with charmingly descriptive names, such as blue giants, sub-giants, red and white dwarfs, supergiants.

The path of stellar evolution may be marked by various explosive events. One of these, which occurs in sufficiently large stars, is an enormous explosion in which a substantial amount of the star is blown away into space in the form of high-speed streams of gas. For about a fortnight, such an exploding star will radiate energy 200 million times as fast as the sun. Japanese and Chinese (but not Western) astronomers recorded such an occurrence in A.D. 1054, and the exploding gases, now called the Crab nebula, can still be seen in powerful telescopes and form a cloud six or seven light-years across. While it lasts, the explosion shows up as an abnormally bright star and is called a *supernova*.

Groups of Stars

It is not surprising that ancient peoples saw pictures in the sky. The constellations, however, are not physically connected groups of stars but just happen to be patterns visible from earth. A conspicuous exception to this is the Milky Way, which a telescope resolves into many millions of separate stars. If we could view the Milky Way from a vast distance and see it as a whole we should observe a rather flat wheel of stars with spiral arms something like the sparks of a rotating Catherine wheel. This system of stars is physically connected by gravitational forces and moves through space as a whole; it is called a *galaxy*.

The galaxy is about 10^5 light-years across and contains roughly 10^{11} stars. An inconspicuous one of these stars near the edge of the wheel is our sun; the prominent stars in our night sky are members of the galaxy that happen to be rather near us. Sirius, the brightest, is only 8·6 light-years away, a trivial distance, astronomically speaking.

The galaxy does not contain stars only, there are also clouds of gas and dust, particularly in the plane of the galaxy. Much of the gas is hydrogen, and its detection is difficult. However, gaseous hydrogen gives out radio waves with a wavelength of 21 cm. Radio telescopes are just the instruments to receive these, and workers in Holland, America, and Australia detected the gas clouds by this means. In 1952 they found that the hydrogen clouds lie in the spiral arms of the galaxy, and this is some of the strongest evidence for the spiral form.

Another important feature of the galactic scene is the weak but enormously extensive magnetic field. This is believed to have an intimate connection with the spiral structure.

Around the spiral arms, and forming part of the galaxy, are numerous globular clusters of stars. These are roughly spherical, abnormally densely packed, collections of stars with many thousands of members. Because of its form and density, a globular cluster may be assumed to have been formed in one process, not star by star. Thus all its stars are the same age. This is of great interest to astronomers, because they can study differences between stars of similar age but different sizes.

Galaxies

One might be forgiven for assuming that such a vast system as the galaxy is in fact the universe; but this is not so. In the constellation of Andromeda is a famous object which, on close examination, turns out to be another galaxy of size and structure similar to our own. Its distance is given in the table (F8). The Milky Way, the

Andromeda nebula, and a few other smaller galaxies form a cluster of galaxies called the Local Group. Obviously it would not be so named except to distinguish it from other distinct groups, and it is indeed a fact that the universe is populated with *groups*, or *clusters*, of *galaxies*. A cluster may contain two or three galaxies, but some contain thousands. So far as the eye of the telescope and camera can see, there are clusters of galaxies.

On a photograph a galaxy is a nebulous blob without the hard outline that a single star produces. Such nebulæ were formerly thought to be inside the Milky Way, but, after controversy, it was established that many of them were separate distant galaxies. By about 1920 it was known that there were at least half a million galaxies, and with the advent of the 100-in. Mt. Wilson telescope this number rose to 10^8 and has been increased further by the 254-cm telescope which can see out to a distance of 7×10^9 light-years. Through the powerful telescopes the nearer galaxies reveal their inner structures. Photographs of galaxies are among the most beautiful and fascinating photographs ever taken, and readers who have never seen one should hasten to the nearest illustrated astronomy book. Most galaxies have a spiral or elliptical structure but about 2 per cent have peculiar wisps and appendages. Some galaxies are strong emitters of radio waves.

The Expanding Universe

Two discoveries about galaxies are of the utmost importance. One is that, by and large, clusters of galaxies are uniformly distributed through the universe. The other is that the distant galaxies are receding from us.

How is this known? Many readers may be familiar with the Doppler effect first discovered in 1842. Suppose a stationary body emits waves of any kind and we measure their wavelength, finding it to be L cm. Now suppose the body approaches us; the waves are thereby crowded together in the intervening space and the wavelength appears less than L; if the body recedes the wavelength appears greater than L. The Austrian physicist, J. Doppler (1803–53), discovered this behaviour in sound waves, and it explains the well-known change of pitch of a train whistle as it approaches and passes us. The same principle applies to the light. Every atom emits light of definite wavelengths which appear in a spectroscope as a series of coloured lines—a different series for each atom. If the atom is in a receding body all the lines have slightly longer wavelengths than usual, and the amount of the change depends uniquely on the speed. Longer wavelengths mean that the light is redder than usual, so that a light from a receding body shows what is called a "red shift." The speed of recession can be calculated from the amount of red shift.

It was the American astronomer, V. M. Slipher, who first showed (in 1914) that some galaxies emitted light with a red shift. In the 1920s and 1930s the famous astronomer E. Hubble (1889–1953) measured both the distances and red shift of many galaxies and proved what is now known as Hubble's Law. This states that the speed of recession of galaxies is proportional to their distance from us. This does not apply to our neighbours in the Local Group, we and they are keeping together. Hubble's Law has been tested and found to hold for the farthest detectable galaxies; they are about 7×10^9 light-years away and are receding with a speed $\frac{2}{3}$ of that of light.

The expansion of the universe does not imply that the Local Group is the centre of the universe —from any other viewpoint in the universe Hubble's Law would also be valid, and the distant galaxies would, similarly, all appear to be rapidly receding.

One possible implication of this most exciting scientific discovery is that, if the galaxies have always been receding, at an early time they must have been closer together. We can calculate that about 10^{10} years ago all the matter of the universe must have been packed densely together. The truth or otherwise of this hypothesis is the most

fundamental question of cosmology, and its testing still drives the quest to explore the universe, by larger and more sensitive telescopes, to the greatest possible distances.

Quasars, Pulsars and Black Holes

In November 1962 Australian radio astronomers located a strong radio emitter with sufficient precision for the Mt. Palomar optical astronomers to identify it on photographs and examine the nature of its light. The red shift was so great that the object must be exceedingly distant; on the other hand it looked star-like, much smaller than a galaxy. By the beginning of 1967 over a hundred of these objects had been discovered and other characteristics established, such as strong ultra-violet radiation and inconstancy, in some cases, of the rate at which radiation is emitted. Not all of these so-called quasars are strong radio emitters; some show all the other characteristics except radio emission. It has been estimated that the " quiet " kind are about a hundred times more numerous than the radio kind. One great problem here is: how can such relatively small objects generate such inconceivably great amounts of energy that they appear bright at such huge distances? So far this is unanswered; these quasi-stellar objects are a great mystery, though they are generally held to be an important pointer towards a deeper understanding of cosmology.

Late in 1967 while investigating quasars, Cambridge radio astronomers discovered pulsars, a new type of heavenly body. Their characteristic is the emission of regular pulses of radio waves every second or so. A pulsar in the Crab nebula has a repetition rate even faster—about 1/30 sec— and it follows that pulsars must be very small bodies little if at all bigger than the Earth.

The existence of such small bodies raises again the problem of the ultimate fate of evolving stars. Much depends on their mass because this determines how strong the inward pull of gravity is. For a star to be at least temporarily stable the inward pull must be balanced by an outward pressure. In the sun this is the pressure of the burning hydrogen (F8) and the resulting average density is about 1·4 times that of water (Table, F7). In some stars the inward pressure is so great that collapse proceeds until it is balanced by a different type of outward pressure that sets in when electrons and atomic nuclei are forced into proximity. Stars so formed are the " white dwarfs ". They are millions of times denser than the sun—" a matchbox of their matter would weigh a ton "— and they are very small though not small enough to be pulsars. The latter are now generally thought to be a million times denser even than white dwarfs and to consist largely of neutrons (see F11). Such bodies are called neutron stars and their gravity is balanced by the outward pressure of tightly packed neutrons.

Could the tendency of a massive star to fall inwards ever be so great that no outward pressure known to physics would suffice to balance it? Apparently it could! Many astrophysicists now hold on theoretical grounds that such a gravitational collapse could create a high density object whose gravitational field would be too strong to allow anything—including light waves—ever to leave the body. Such hypothetical objects are called " black holes " because, light and other signals being unable to emerge from them, their matter has literally disappeared from view. Black holes could be detected by the disturbance their gravitational attraction causes to neighbouring visible stars and also because atoms attracted by the black hole should emit intense X-rays before falling so far in that they too disappear into the black hole. Both of these detection methods have led some astronomers to conjecture (by 1973) that there is a black hole in the constellation Cygnus. The theory of gravitational collapse raises profound and unresolved problems about our physical concepts. The relation between gravitation and the other forces of nature (F18) is called into question.

Very recently, it has been conjectured that black holes, formed by the " death " of individual stars, and perhaps even on a massive scale at the centre of large and dense galaxies, have been responsible for " devouring " a very significant proportion of the total mass of the universe. Since this " devoured " mass is invisible by direct observation, we may have considerably underestimated the average density, and thus the total gravitational field of the universe. This underestimate may even be great enough to cast serious doubts as to whether the present expansion of the universe (F5) may be slowed, and eventually reversed, by gravitational forces.

THE ORIGIN AND DEVELOPMENT OF THE UNIVERSE

Scientists can only attempt to explain the universe by relating its observable structure to the features predicted by alternative theories of its origin and development. The time span of all our observations of the Cosmos is so small by comparison with the lifetime of the universe (more than 10^{10} years). Also, contrary to many other scientific disciplines, it is impossible to repeat the " experiment," under controlled conditions. We must, therefore, explore the evolution of the universe by using the fact that light from the most distant galaxies has taken about 10^{10} years to reach us, thus providing us with a crucial, if tantalisingly remote and thus indistinct, view of the universe at a much earlier epoch.

Evolutionary Theories

Several models of the universe have been based on Einstein's theory of General Relativity (F17). Observation strongly suggests that matter on a very large scale is uniformly distributed throughout the universe. Einstein's equations may be solved to predict the evolution of the universe. Of all possible solutions, corresponding to many possible expanding, static, or contracting universes, observations enable us to reject many, since the universe is observed to expand at present. Even so, there is a spectrum of solutions which vary from a continuous and indefinite expansion at the present rate to an eventual slowing and subsequent contraction to a dense state, again in the distant future, which hints at a " pulsating " universe. It is assumed that the initial dense state corresponds to the " origin " of the universe, while pulsating solutions might indicate the possibility of a repeated " origin " in the distant future (10^{11} years?). The exact form of Einstein's equations, the average density of matter throughout the universe, and the structure of the younger universe obtained from observations of the most distant galaxies are all crucial components in predicting the real future behaviour of the universe and, as yet, it is not possible to be certain whether the present expansion will or will not ever be slowed or reversed.

The Steady-State Theory

As an alternative to the Evolutionary theory based on Einstein's equations, Bondi, Gold, and Hoyle (1948) suggested the so-called " Steady-State " theory. This theory has no initial dense state or " origin " and, on a large scale, the density of galaxies and stars is always as at present. To permit this possibility, they proposed that matter—hydrogen atoms—is continuously created throughout space at a rate sufficient to compensate for the present observed expansion of the universe. Thus the average density of matter would always remain constant.

The Formation of Galaxies and Stars

On any theory of the universe, some explanation has to be found for the existence of clusters of galaxies. In all theories galaxies condense out from dispersed masses of gas, principally hydrogen. Once a huge gas cloud becomes sufficiently condensed to be separately identifiable as a galaxy, further condensation goes on inside it. It is believed on theoretical grounds that it could not condense into one enormous star but must form many fragments which shrink separately into clusters of stars. In these clusters many stars, perhaps hundreds or thousands or even millions, are born at once. A small cluster, visible to the

naked eye, is the Pleiades. The Orion nebula, visible as a hazy blob of glowing gas in the sword of Orion, is the scene of much star-forming activity at present.

According to the Evolutionary theory the " initial dense state " consisted of very hot plasma in a state of overall expansion. The expanding plasma was both cooling and swirling about. The random swirling produces irregularities in the distribution of the hot gas—here it would be rather denser, there rather less dense. If a sufficiently large mass of denser gas happened to occur, then the gravitational attraction between its own particles would hold it together and maintain its permanent identity, even though the rest of the gas continued to swirl and expand. Such a large mass would gradually condense into fragments to become galaxies, the whole mass turning into a cluster of galaxies.

The Changing Scene

The 1960s witnessed revolutionary developments in both observational and theoretical astronomy. For example, it now seems agreed after some years of uncertainty that remote sources of radio waves are more abundant the weaker their intensity. This strongly suggests that they are more abundant at greater distances. Thus the universe is not *uniform* as the original steady-state theory prescribed. Since greater distances correspond to earlier times, any extra abundance of objects observed at the greater distance means that the universe was denser in its younger days than now. This favours an evolutionary theory of the universe.

The same theory requires that the initial dense state of the universe—aptly christened " the primaeval fireball "—should contain intense electromagnetic radiation with a distribution of wavelengths characteristic of the high temperature. As the fireball, *i.e.*, the universe, expanded over a period of about 10^{10} years it cooled, and one feature of this process is that the wavelengths of the radiation increase and their distribution becomes characteristic of a much lower temperature. In fact, the wavelengths should now be concentrated round about 1 mm to 1 cm (corresponding to about $-270°$ C) and the radiation should approach the earth uniformly from all directions. Radiation just like this has recently been detected by extremely sensitive instruments both at ground-based observatories and flown from balloon payloads high in the earth's atmosphere—above most of the water vapour and other constituents which interfere with such delicate observations. This " microwave background " radiation appears to be " cosmological," and thus supports strongly the evolutionary or " Big Bang " theory as opposed to the " Steady-State " theory, which cannot rationally explain the radiation.

The Formation of the Chemical Elements

A stable nucleus is one that lasts indefinitely because it is not radioactive. There are 274 known kinds of stable atomic nuclei and little likelihood of any more being found. These nuclei are the isotopes (F12) of 81 different chemical elements; the other elements, including, for example, uranium and radium are always radioactive. Some elements are rare, others abundant. The most common ones on earth are oxygen, silicon, aluminium, and iron. However, the earth is rather atypical. It is especially deficient in hydrogen, because the gravitational attraction of our small planet was not strong enough to prevent this very light gas from escaping into space.

It is possible to examine the chemical constituents of meteorites and to infer the composition of the sun and other stars from the spectrum of the light they emit. By such means, the conclusion has been reached that 93% of the atoms in our galaxy are hydrogen, 7% are helium; all the other elements together account for about one in a thousand atoms. A glance at the Table of Elements (*see* end of Sec.) will show that hydrogen and helium are two of the lightest elements: they are in fact the two simplest. The problem is to explain how the heavier chemical elements appear in the universe at all. It is here that a fascinating combination of astronomy and nuclear physics is required.

We have already referred to the fact that the energy radiated from the sun originates in nuclear reactions which turn hydrogen into helium. Why is energy given out? To answer this question we note that nuclei are made up of protons and neutrons (F11). These particles attract one another strongly—that is why a nucleus holds together. To separate the particles, energy would have to be supplied to overcome the attractive forces. This amount of energy is called *binding energy* and is a definite quantity for every kind of nucleus. Conversely, when the particles are brought together to form a nucleus the binding energy is *released* in the form of radiations and heat. Different nuclei consist of different numbers of particles, therefore the relevant quantity to consider is the *binding energy per particle*. Let us call this B. Then if elements of *high* B are formed out of those of *low* B there is a *release* of energy.

Now B is small (relatively) for light elements like lithium, helium, and carbon; it rises to a maximum for elements of middling atomic weight like iron; it falls again for really heavy elements like lead, bismuth, and uranium. Consequently, energy is released by forming middleweight elements either by splitting up heavy nuclei (" nuclear fission ") or by joining up light ones (" nuclear fusion ").

It is the latter process, fusion, that is going on in stars. The fusion processes can be studied in physics laboratories by using large accelerating machines to hurl nuclei at one another to make them coalesce. In stars the necessary high velocity of impact occurs because the plasma is so hot. Gradually the hydrogen is turned into helium, and helium into heavier and heavier elements. This supplies the energy that the stars radiate and simultaneously generates the chemical elements.

The very heavy elements present a problem. To form them from middleweight elements, energy has to be *supplied*. Since there is plenty of energy inside a star, a certain small number of heavy nuclei will indeed form, but they will continually undergo fission again under the prevailing intense conditions. How do they ever get away to form cool ordinary elements, like lead and bismuth, in the earth? One view links them with the highly explosive supernovae, to which we have already referred (F4 (2)). If the heavy elements occur in these stars the force of the explosion disperses them into cool outer space before they have time to undergo the fission that would otherwise have been their fate. The heavy elements are thus seen as the dust and debris of stellar catastrophes. This view is in line with the steady-state theory, because supernovae are always occurring and keeping up the supply of heavy elements. In the evolutionary theory some of the generation of elements is supposed to go on in the very early stages of the initial dense state and to continue in the stars that evolve in the fullness of time. It cannot be claimed that the origin of the chemical elements is completely known, but we have said enough to show that there are plausible theories. Time and more facts will choose between them.

The Formation of the Planets

Precisely how the planetary system was formed is still not understood in detail. From extremely precise observations of the movements of some nearby stars, it seems certain that other planetary systems occur among our stellar neighbours. By inference, it is thus probable that among certain classes of stars, planetary systems are very common throughout the universe.

Two other facts are crucial for any theory of planetary system formation. First, all the planetary orbits lie within a few degrees of the same plane and near to the equatorial plane of the sun. These orbits lie nearly in the plane perpendicular to the axis of rotation of the sun, their rotations about the sun all being in the same direction and their axes of rotation, with two exceptions (Venus and Uranus), being close to the polar axis of their orbit planes, and in the same sense as their orbital rotation about the sun. Secondly, there is a very

strong inverse correlation between planetary distance from the sun and the planet's mean density, particularly if the correct allowance is made for the effects of gravitational compression in the deep interiors of planets (greater in large than in small planets).

Rather than theories which would place planetary formation as either the random collection of pre-formed planets by the sun in its path through the galaxy or as the consequence of a very near encounter between our sun and another star, it is now generally believed that the origin of the planetary system (and most of the satellites, etc.) was a direct consequence of the process which originally formed the sun.

As the primaeval solar nebula contracted, to conserve angular momentum, its rotation rate increased, and a diffuse equatorial disk of dust and gas formed. In the cold outer region (10–20° K) of this disk, all materials except helium and possibly hydrogen could readily condense on dust particles. Near the centre the temperature was higher, increasingly so as the proto-sun heated up, initially by the energy released by its gravitational contraction and, later, by the thermo-nuclear processes F4(1).

Within this rotating and swirling disk of gas and dust, the process of accretion proceeded. Low-velocity collision between dust particles from time to time allowed larger particles to be created, composed of a mixture of the heavier elements and also the " icy " materials, particularly so in the colder outer regions where more of the " ices " were in a frozen state. Virtually our only information on the composition of such particles comes from detailed study of meteorites and from spectroscopic observation of comets. Eventually rocks of the size of centimetres, metres, and even kilometres were built up in this way. The build-up, controlled by low-velocity collisions, particularly of " sticky " materials, and also by electrostatic charges, was, at all times, however, moderated by occasional destructive high-velocity collisions. The relatively high viscosity of the dust and gas mixture throughout the disk must have been very important in producing a relatively uniform, rotational motion throughout the disk.

When " rocks " a few kilometres in size had been created new factors became important. Gravitational forces firstly increased the capacity of the larger " rocks " to accrete additional dust and smaller particles and, secondly, allowed some retention of material after even high-velocity collisions which would have destroyed smaller pieces. The next stage is possibly the most difficult to model. Within a relatively uniform disk containing large numbers of rocks up to a few kilometres in diameter mixed within the residual dust and a large amount of gas, and extending to well outside Pluto's orbit, a small number of massive planets were formed. Some debris now remains as the comets and asteroids; however this debris and all the major planets, including the massive Jupiter, represent in total only a very small percentage of the original material of the solar nebula which was not condensed to form the sun.

It would appear that relatively quickly, during a period of 10^7 or 10^8 years, the large numbers of kilometre-sized objects, by collision and mutual gravitational attraction, formed the nuclei of the present planets and probably, in most cases, their major satellites also, in orbits relatively similar to their present ones. The planet-building process was most efficient at distances from the sun corresponding to the present orbits of Jupiter or Saturn, a compromise between temperature decreasing with distance from the sun, allowing a greater percentage of the total material to be solid and thus available for accretion, and density of material being greater closer to the sun.

The outer or " Jovian " planets must have grown quickly, sweeping up hydrogen and helium gas as well as solid particles. Closer to the sun, the " icy " materials, still mainly in gaseous form, could not contribute very significantly to the initial accretion process, so that only smaller planets could form. Owing to their smaller mass, gravitational field and thus lower " escape velocity," they were only able to accrete a small proportion of the heavier gas present within the inner part of the solar system. Thus, at present, these

THE SOLAR SYSTEM

	Mean distance from Sun (millions of km)	Diameter km	Period of Revolution	Average density (water = 1)	Number of Satellites
Sun	—	1,392,000			
Mercury	57·9	4,880	88 days	5·4	0
Venus	108·2	12,104	224·7 days	5·2	0
Earth	149·6	12,756	365·26 days	5·5	1
Mars	227·9	6,787	687 days	3·9	2
Jupiter	778·3	142,800	11·86 years	1·3	13
Saturn	1,427	120,000	29·46 years	0·7	10
Uranus	2,869·6	51,800	84·01 years	1·2	5
Neptune	4,496·6	49,500	164·8 years	1·7	2
Pluto	5,900	6,000	247·7 years	?	0

Note: Chiron, an object recently discovered orbiting the sun between Saturn and Venus has not been given " planet " status due to its small size.

" terrestrial " planets are much denser than the outer ' Jovian " planets, much smaller in size, and contain very little hydrogen or helium. The planet-building process was probably ended by two factors: the gravitational disruptive effect of the planets already formed and the enhanced " solar wind " of the young sun, which swept much of the residual dust and gas out of the solar system.

Before the process was complete, however, the gravitational energy released by the material falling onto the proto-planets plus the radioactive heating of short-lived isotopes present at the time of planetary formation were responsible for melting most of the bodies of the planets and probably all the larger satellites and asteroids. This process allowed gravitational segregation of denser and lighter materials within the planets, and the production of the core, mantle and crustal regions of each of the terrestrial planets. Long after the dust and gas were driven from the solar system and the planet surfaces cooled and solidified, the residual larger rocks and asteroids, of which enormous numbers were originally still present, continued to be swept up by each of the planets. The record of this violent stage of the solar system's development can still be seen in the saturation cratering observed on the Moon, Mercury, and Mars.

In the past decade, direct space exploration, by manned spacecraft to the Moon, by sophisticated automatic " lander " spacecraft to Mars and Jupiter, has enormously increased our knowledge and understanding of each individual planet and of its structure, composition, and evolution. The recent Mars–" Viking " project, Pioneer 11, *en route* to Saturn, and " Voyager ", now on its way to Jupiter and Uranus, will provide much more information about our planetary system, its formation and evolution. The future contributions to be made by ground-based telescopes should, however, not be neglected, having been responsible for the important recent discoveries of a new ring system of Uranus and of Chiron.

THE EARTH

Structure

The earth has the shape of a slightly flattened sphere, with an equatorial radius of 6378 km and a polar radius 21 km less. Its mass can be calculated from Newton's Law of Gravitation and from measurements of the acceleration due to gravity, and is $5·97 \times 10^{24}$ kg. The average density follows from these two figures and is about 5·5 grams per cubic centimetre. This is nearly twice the density of typical rocks at the surface, so there must be very much denser material somewhere inside, and the earth must have a definite internal structure.

This structure can be investigated using shock waves from earthquakes or large explosions. These are received at recording stations at different distances from their source, having penetrated to varying depths within the earth, and their relative times of arrival and characteristic forms enable the deep structure to be worked out. This consists of three main units, a core at the centre with a radius about half that of the earth, the mantle outside this, and the thin crust, about 35 km thick under the continents and 5 km thick under the oceans, forming a skin surrounding the mantle.

The composition of these three units can be deduced by observation and inference. For example, meteorites which arrive at the earth's surface from other parts of the solar system consist of three main types, composed of iron-nickel alloy, stony silicates, and a mixture of iron and silicates. Could these have originated from the break-up of some planet like the earth? If so, then perhaps the core of the earth is made up of iron-nickel alloy and the mantle of magnesium-rich silicates. Experiments on the physical properties of these materials at high pressures show strong similarities with the measured properties of the earth's interior. In addition, rocks composed of magnesium-rich silicates are found at the earth's surface in places where material seems to have come from great depth, such as in the debris from volcanic explosions. These may be direct samples of the earth's mantle.

Core, Mantle and Crust

By these arguments, and by many others, a picture can be built up of the internal structure of the earth. The core is composed of iron-nickel

SOME ASTRONOMICAL DISTANCES
(1 light-year = $9 46 \times 10^{..}$ km).

Object	Distance from Earth (light-years).	Velocity of recession (km per second).	Object.	Distance from Earth (light-years).	Velocity of recession (km per second).
Sun	$1·6 \times 10^{-5}$	—	Andromeda Galaxy	$1·5 \times 10^{6}$	—
Nearest star (Proxima Centauri)	4·2	—	Galaxy in Virgo	$7·5 \times 10^{7}$	1,200
Brightest star (Sirius)	8·6	—	Galaxy in Gt. Bear	10^{9}	14,900
Pleiades	340	—	Galaxy in Corona Borealis	$1·3 \times 10^{9}$	21,600
Centre of Milky Way	$2·6 \times 10^{4}$	—	Galaxy in Bootes	$4·5 \times 10^{9}$	39,300
Magellanic clouds (the nearest galaxies)	$1·6 \times 10^{5}$	—	Very remote quasi-stellar object	$\sim 1·5 \times 10^{10}$	$\sim 240,000$

alloy. It is liquid at the outside, but contains a solid inner core of radius about one-fifth of that of the earth. Convection currents flowing in the liquid part give rise to the earth's magnetic field. Outside this the mantle is solid, and is made up mainly of magnesium–iron silicates of various kinds. By studying its physical properties through earthquake wave observations, the mantle may be divided into several zones, of which the most important is the asthenosphere. This is the part of the mantle between 70 and 300 km depth in which volcanic lavas are formed. In this region the mantle is everywhere quite near to the temperature at which it begins to melt, and is thus rather soft compared with the rest of the mantle. The presence of a soft asthenosphere accounts for many of the surface features of the earth, mountain belts and ocean basins, that make it so very different from cratered planets such as the Moon and Mars.

The sharp boundary between mantle and crust is called the Mohorovicic Discontinuity. Above it, the crust is different under continents and oceans. The thick continental crust has a composition that can broadly be called granitic, while the thin oceanic crust is poorer in silicon, sodium, and potassium and richer in calcium, iron, and magnesium. The continental crust has been built up over thousands of millions of years by welding together mountain belts of different ages, while the oceanic crust is made up of basalt lavas and is nowhere older than 250 million years.

Rocks

Rocks are naturally occurring pieces of the solid earth. If you take a rock and break it up into grains, then separate the grains into different heaps of like grains, each heap will consist of grains of the same *mineral*. For example, the kind of rock called granite can be divided into glassy grains of the mineral quartz, milky white or pink grains of the mineral feldspar, shiny black flakes of the mineral biotite, and shiny colourless flakes of the mineral muscovite. Both biotite and muscovite belong to the mica group of minerals. Each different mineral has a well-defined composition or range of composition, and a definite and characteristic arrangement of the atoms that compose it. There are several thousand known kinds of minerals, but only fifty or so are at all common.

There are three main kinds of rock; igneous rocks, formed by the solidification of molten lava; sedimentary rocks, formed from material laid down under gravity on the earth's surface; and metamorphic rocks, formed by heating or reheating of either of the other kind of rock. Each of these broad groups may be further subdivided. When *igneous rocks* solidify deep inside the earth, they cool slowly and large crystals have time to form. Coarse-grained igneous rocks such as granites are known as plutonic igneous rocks. Conversely the rapidly cooled fine-grained igneous rocks that form the volcanic lavas, such as basalts and rhyolites, are called volcanic igneous rocks. *Sedimentary rocks* can be divided into three kinds: Clastic sediments are those formed from mechanically abraded and transported fragments of pre-existing rocks and include sandstone, mudstone, and clay. Organic sediments are those composed, as are most limestones, of fragments of organically produced material such as shells, wood, and bone. Chemical sediments are formed by direct chemical action and include, most typically, salt deposits formed by evaporation of sea water. *Metamorphic rocks* are more difficult to subdivide. They are usually classified on the basis of their original composition and/or the maximum pressure and temperature to which they have been subjected. Chemical reactions in metamorphic rocks give rise to successions of minerals as the pressure and temperature change, so that examination of a metamorphic rock will often allow one to say how deeply it was buried and how hot it was.

Age of Rocks

There are two distinct ways of estimating the age of rocks. The first gives the *relative age*. It is based on the principle that in a sequence of sediments, older rocks lie underneath and younger ones above, that igneous rocks are younger than the rocks they intrude, and that folded rocks are formed earlier than the earth movements that fold them. Correlation of a sequence of rocks in one place with those in another is made by fossil faunas and floras. Thus a complete scale of relative ages can be built up, stretching back to the first rocks containing fossils (see the table in Part IV). The *age in years* can, on the other hand be measured by using radioactive elements (Part II) contained in rocks. If the amount of a radioactive element present is measured, and the amount of the product of radioactive decay can also be found, then, using the known rates of decay, the time since the product started to accumulate (defined for this purpose as the age in years) can be measured. This method is particularly useful for studying rocks that do not contain fossils (igneous and metamorphic rocks, or those too old to contain fossils). By similar methods, the *age of the earth* can be obtained. This turns out to be about $4 \cdot 6 \times 10^9$ years. The rocks containing the first fossils are $2 \cdot 5 – 3 \times 10^9$ years old, while organised life in abundance first appeared about $0 \cdot 6 \times 10^9$ years ago.

The Continents and the Ocean Floor

The outer part of the earth, namely, the asthenosphere and the solid mantle and crust overlying it, the lithosphere, is in a state of restless movement, and it is this movement that gives rise to the formation of oceans, continents, and mountain belts. The surface of the earth can be divided into a number of rigid plates of lithosphere, which move apart, or together, or slide past one another. Some of these plates are very large, such as the one which contains all of North America, all of South America, and about half of the Atlantic Ocean. Others are no more than a few thousand square kilometres in size. But they are all moving about relative to one another like ice floes in pack-ice. Where two plates move apart, hot material rises from the asthenosphere to fill the gap, partly melts, and gives rise to a chain of volcanoes and a thin volcanic crust. This is how ocean basins form and grow larger. In the Atlantic, the Mid-Atlantic Ridge marks the line along which plates are moving apart, and where new ocean is being formed. Long narrow pieces of ocean such as the Red Sea and the Gulf of California mark where a continent has just begun to split apart, and a new ocean is forming. Where two plates slide past one another, a great tear fault results. Such a fault is the San Andreas fault which runs from the Gulf of California to San Francisco. Jerky movement on this fault gave rise to the great San Francisco earthquake of 1906 and could give rise to another earthquake there at any time.

Where two plates move together, the result depends on the nature of the crust forming the plates. If at least one of the plates is oceanic, the oceanic crust dips down into the mantle and slides away to great depths until it eventually merges with the asthenosphere. Along this dipping sheet of crust, strong earthquakes occur and frictional heating of the sheet leads to melting and the production of quantities of lava. Examples of such boundaries are the Andes, where the Pacific Ocean bed dips beneath South America, and Indonesia, where the Indian Ocean bed dips below Asia. When both plates are continental, on the other hand, the crust is too thick and buoyant to slide into the mantle, and a collision results, giving rise to a fold mountain chain. Eventually the movement grinds to a halt, the plates weld together, and the fold mountains become dormant. The Himalayas were formed in this way from the recent collision of India and Asia. The evidence that has led to these conclusions is too complex to summarise here. It comes from a study of rock magnetism, earthquakes, the flow of heat from inside the earth and even from the shapes of the continents, that must match across the oceans by which they have been split apart. Confirmation has come from a series of holes drilled in the ocean which has shown how the crust becomes younger towards the centres of the oceans.

Rates of movement of plates have been calculated, ranging from a few millimetres a year to ten centimetres a year. The faster movements can be measured directly on the ground by such simple techniques as looking at the displacement of railway lines, walls, and roads, but the slower ones, and those beneath the oceans must be measured by more indirect geophysical methods. The mechanism by which this movement takes place is still unknown. Are the plates pulled by their sinking edges, or pushed by their rising edges, or moved by some other means? But it cannot be doubted that the movement does happen, and that it holds the key to the development of the earth's crust since the time it was first formed.

The Rest

There is a lot more to the study of the earth than has been possible to set down here. The oceans, the atmosphere, and the rocks of the crust all interact with one another in their development in a complex way. The surface of the earth has gradually changed as life has evolved over thousands of millions of years and ice ages have come and gone, changing the surface again and again. Just as important is the economic potential of the earth, on which we depend for all of our energy and all raw materials. This section has given the basic framework within which such further investigations are carried out, to help the reader understand as he reads more widely.

II.   PHYSICS—THE FUNDAMENTAL SCIENCE OF MATTER

WHAT PHYSICS IS ABOUT

Anyone compelled by curiosity or professional interest to look into contemporary journals of pure physics research is soon struck by the fact that the old text-book division of physics into " heat, light, sound, electricity, and magnetism " has become very blurred.

Two different, though complementary, sections can be distinguished. First, there is the physics concerned with the properties of matter in bulk, with solids, liquids, and gases, and with those odd but very important substances, such as paints, plastic solutions, and jelly-like material, which are neither properly solid nor liquid. In this vast domain of physics questions like this are asked: Why is iron magnetic, copper not? What happens when solids melt? Why do some liquids flow more easily than others? Why do some things conduct electricity well, others badly, some not at all? During the last century, particularly the last few decades, it has become clear that such questions can be answered only by raising and solving others first. In particular, we must ask: (i) Of what nature are the invisible particles of which matter is composed? and (ii) How are those particles arranged in bulk matter?

The first of these two questions has generated the second major category of modern physics: this is the physics of particles and of the forces that particles exert on each other. In this field which represents science at its most fundamental questions like this are asked: If matter is composed of small units or particles, what are they like? How many kinds of particle are there? Do the particles possess mass? electric charge? magnetism? How do the particles influence each other? How can their motion be described and predicted?

The discussion which follows has been divided into two main parts (1) Particles and Forces, and (2) The Properties of Matter in Bulk, with part (1) describing the miscroscopic structure of matter and part (2) its macroscopic properties.

PARTICLES AND FORCES

Aristotle to Newton

The inference that matter should be composed of small particles or atoms originated, it is true, in classical times. The atomic idea was an attempt to solve the age-old problem of matter and its peculiar properties. The ancients had provided themselves with two solutions to the problem of matter:

(i) The theory of the four elements (earth water, fire, air), from which all different forms of matter were composed by selecting different ratios of the four ingredients. This approach had been used by traditional philosophy and was adopted by Aristotle.

(ii) The theory of atomism which postulated the existence of atoms and empty space.

Atomism remained very much in the background in the development of Western Science and persisted even longer in the Arab world. The idea that matter is composed of " small units " was in reality forced into the mental development of mankind by the repeated application of the process of dimension halving. By the time of Newton atomism had come to the fore and Newton considered that God had made the Universe from " small indivisible grains " of matter. Nevertheless, the search for the " philosopher's stone " was still in the seventeenth century, the main pursuit of many scientists, but the new chemistry of the seventeenth century made use of atomistic concepts. Newton's physics was a mechanics concerning particles in a vacuum and when Boyle described his gas law (i.e., Pressure × Volume is constant at a fixed temperature) he visualised matter as composed of particles with specific qualitative properties. It was, of course, the advance of experimental techniques which enabled scientists to test ideas and theories on the nature of matter.

Dalton and Atomic Theory

The modern view of atomism need be traced no farther than the beginning of the nineteenth century when Dalton and his contemporaries were studying the laws of chemical combination using precise weighing techniques. By that time the distinctions between elements, compounds, and mixtures were already made. Compounds and mixtures are substances which can be separated into smaller amounts of chemically distinguishable constituents. Elements (see end of Sec.) cannot be so divided. In a mixture the components may be mixed in any proportion and sorted out again by non-chemical means. In a compound the elements are combined in fixed proportions by weight. This last fact gives the clue to atomic theory.

Dalton pointed out that the fixed combining weights of elements could easily be explained if the elements consisted of atoms which combined in simple numerical ratios, e.g., 1 atom of element A with one of B, or one of B with two of C, and so on. For instance, 35·5 g of chlorine combine with 23·0 g of sodium to make 58·5 g of ordinary salt. If we assume one atom of chlorine links with one of sodium, then the atoms themselves must have weights in the ratio 35·5 to 23·0. This turns out to be consistent with the combining weights of chlorine and sodium in all other compounds in which they both take part. Sometimes two elements combine in several different proportions by weight. But this is easily explained by assuming that the atoms link up in a variety of ways e.g., one iron atom with one oxygen, or two irons with three oxygens, or three irons with four oxygens. Then the three different combining proportions arise from the three different numbers of atoms, using in each case the same ratio of oxygen atom weight to iron atom weight.

Atomic Weight

Over the century and a half since Dalton, these ideas have been repeatedly tested by chemical experiments. No one now doubts that every chemical element has atoms of characteristic weight. By convention the number 12·0000 is ascribed to carbon and called its " atomic weight." The atomic weights of other atoms are expressed by giving their ratio to that of carbon, *e.g.*, hydrogen, 1·008; iron, 55·85. These numbers are only ratios; the real weight of one single oxygen atom is 2·7 × 10⁻²³ g.

Valency

That the combinations of atoms in definite proportions was necessary to produce compounds, or more correctly molecules, was known from 1808. The reason why only one atom of sodium and one of chlorine was required to produce one molecule of salt was unknown. Further the seemingly odd combinations of two atoms of hydrogen (H) with one of oxygen (O) to give water (H_2O), while only one atom of hydrogen could combine with chlorine to give hydrogen chloride (HCl) could not be explained. This situation was not resolved until around 1860, when the chemical formulae of many molecules were known. It was then discovered that homologies existed in the elements, for example the series Na, K, Rb, Cs, or Fl, Cl, Br, I, and this culminated in the Periodic Table of the elements (see end of Section). The valency of an atom was determined by its position in the periodic table and determined by the number of electrons (see below) which the atom has orbiting its nucleus. Atoms combined to form molecules in a manner which maintained the number of " active " electrons in a stable grouping of 2, 8, or 18. For example, sodium has one active electron and chlorine seven, therefore the combination NaCl gives the stable grouping of eight; hydrogen has one and oxygen six, hence it requires two atoms of hydrogen and one of oxygen to give one stable molecule, H_2O. Other more complicated molecular structures and types of bonding between atoms are dealt with in the chemistry section. This discovery of particles smaller than the atom itself was necessary to fully comprehend the nature of valency in atomic combinations.

J. J. Thomson and the Electron

Matter is electrically uncharged in its normal state, but there exist many well-known ways of producing electric charges and currents—rubbing amber, or rotating dynamos, for example. It is therefore necessary to have some theory of electricity linked to the theory of matter. The fundamental experiment in this field was made by J. J. Thomson when, in 1897, he discovered the electron.

If you take two metal electrodes sealed inside a glass vessel and if the pressure of the air is reduced from atmospheric pressure, 76 cm of mercury, to 1 mm of mercury by mechanical pumping and then a high voltage, several kilo-volts, is applied to the electrodes, the negative electrode emits a " radiation " which causes the walls of the tube to glow. The rays are called *cathode rays*. The discovery of the electron was essentially a clarification of the nature of cathode rays. Thomson showed that they were streams of particles with mass and negative electric charge and a general behaviour unlike any other atomic particle known at that time. The importance of this discovery for the world of science cannot be overestimated, and its technical progeny are in every home and factory in X-ray machines, television tubes, and other devices.

Rutherford-Bohr Atom

Since the electrons emerge from matter, they are presumably parts of atoms. The relation between the negative electrons and the positively charged constituents of matter was elucidated by the great experimenter Rutherford and the great theoretician Bohr. Their work, just before the First World War, showed that the positive charge, together with almost all the mass, is concentrated in the central core or nucleus of the atom about which the very light-weight electrons revolve. The diameter of an atom is about 10⁻⁸ cm, roughly one three-hundred-millionth part of an inch. The central nucleus has a diameter about 10,000 times smaller still. The nucleus and the electrons hold together because of the electric attraction between them.

The positive charge of the nucleus is responsible for holding the electron in the region of space around the nucleus. The electrostatic Coulomb force, if left on its own would quickly attract the electrons into the nucleus but since the electrons move in orbits, circular and elliptical, they experience an outward centrifugal force which balances the inward electrostatic force. The mechanism is similar to that which holds the earth in orbit around the sun, only here a gravitational force replaces the effect of the Coulomb force.

At this stage work could, and did, go on separately along several different lines:

    (i) Electrons could be studied on their own. Nowadays the handling of beams of electrons of all sizes and intensities has become a major branch of technology.

    (ii) The nucleus could be treated as a special problem, and this led to the mid-century flowering of nuclear physics, to the atomic bomb, and to nuclear power.

    (iii) The behaviour of electrons in the atom could be analysed; this is the great domain of atomic physics which spreads into many other sciences as well.

Volumes have been written about each of these three fields, but we can spare only a few lines for each.

The Electron

Electrons are expelled from solids by light, heat, electric fields, and other influences. It has therefore been possible to study beams of electrons on their own *in vacuo*. Electrons inside matter, either as constituents, or temporarily in transit, can also be observed by their innumerable effects. These observations all show the particles to be indistinguishable one from another; all electrons are the same wherever they come from. They have a definite mass (9·11 × 10⁻²⁸ g), a negative electric charge, a magnetic moment, and a " spin " (intrinsic rotatory motion). No one has ever subdivided an electron or obtained an electric charge smaller than that on one electron. The electronic charge is therefore used as a basic unit of charge in atomic physics. The electron has come to be the best known of all the " fundamental particles." It is now used in research as probe for studying the structure of matter, for which it is ideally suited, since it is very much smaller than an atom. A whole field of electron-scattering research which studies the nature and structure of solids, liquids, and gases is being actively conducted in many laboratories.

The Nucleus

The early research programmes in nuclear physics were greatly facilitated by the occurrence in nature of certain unstable (radioactive) nuclei which emit fast-moving fragments. The latter can be used as projectiles to aim at other nuclei as targets; the resulting impacts yield much valuable information. This technique still dominates nuclear physics, though nowadays the projectiles are artificially accelerated by one or other of the large costly machines designed for the purpose.

The most important early discovery was that the nucleus consists of two types of fundamental particle—the positively charged *proton* and the electrically neutral *neutron*. These two are of nearly equal mass (about 1,800 times that of the electron), and like electrons, have a magnetic moment and spin. The proton charge is equal to the electron charge, though opposite in sign. Consider a moderately complex nucleus like that of iron. This usually has 30 neutrons and 26 protons. Its atomic weight therefore depends on the total number of neutrons plus protons, but the total charge depends only on the number of protons—called the *atomic number*. The latter is denoted by Z while the total number of neutrons plus protons is called the *mass number* and denoted by M. A species of nucleus with given values of Z and M is called a *nuclide*. Z is also the number of electrons in the atom, since the atom as a whole is electrically neutral. The atomic number determines the chemical nature of the atom (see below).

so that by altering the number of *neutrons* in a nucleus we do not change the chemical species. It is therefore possible to find—and nowadays to make—nuclei of the same element which nevertheless differ slightly in weight because they have different numbers of neutrons. These are called *isotopes*. Iron isotopes are known with 26, 27, 28, 29, 30, 31, 32, and 33 neutrons, but all have 26 protons. Thus a set of isotopes consists of the various nuclides that have the same Z but different M's.

When the atomic properties of isotopes are measured it is found that small, hyperfine differences in the motions of the electrons around the respective nuclei exist. These result from the different total spin of the isotopes and its effect on the orbiting electrons. This influence of atomic properties by nuclear effects is important in that it provides a link between different fields of research.

Stable Nuclides

The protons and neutrons in a nucleus are bound together by strong forces called *nuclear forces*. In many cases, the forces are so strong that no particles ever escape and the nucleus preserves its identity. There are two hundred and seventy-four different combinations of neutrons and protons of this kind, and they are called the *stable nuclides*. The earth is largely composed of such stable nuclides, because any unstable ones have, in the course of time, spontaneously broken up into stable residues.

Nevertheless, there are some unstable nuclei left on earth. They give rise to the phenomenon of radioactivity which was discovered by Becquerel in 1893.

Unstable Nuclides: Radioactivity

Becquerel found that certain chemicals containing uranium gave off rays capable of blackening a photographic plate, and shortly afterwards Marie and Pierre Curie discovered more substances, including radium, which produce similar but stronger effects. By now, about fifty chemical elements having radioactive properties are known to exist on earth, some, like radium, being strongly radioactive, others, like potassium, being so weak that the radiations are difficult to detect. These are called the *natural radioactive nuclides*.

The main facts about radioactivity are as follows: it is a *nuclear* phenomenon and (with minor exceptions) proceeds quite independently of whatever the electrons in the atom may be doing. Thus, the radioactivity of an atom is not affected by the chemical combination of the atom with other atoms, nor by ordinary physical influences like temperature and pressure. The radioactivity consists of the emission by the substance of certain kinds of rays. The early workers, Rutherford being the giant among them, distinguished three kinds of rays labelled α, β, and γ. These are described below. Whatever kind of ray is examined, it is found that the radiation from a given sample decreases gradually with time according to a definite law which states that the intensity of radiation decreases by half every T seconds. The number T, called the half-life, is constant for each radioactive material, but varies enormously from substance to substance. For instance, radium decreases its activity by a half every 1,622 years, whereas the half-life of one of the polonium isotopes is about 0.3×10^{-6} sec.

α-, β-, and γ-rays

The three most well-known types of radioactive emission are quite distinct from one another.

(i) α-rays or α-particles consist of two protons and two neutrons bound together. They are ejected from the radioactive nucleus with one of several well-defined speeds. These speeds are high, often of the order 10^9 cm per sec. Two protons and two neutrons are the constituents of the nucleus of helium, and α-particles are thus fast-moving helium nuclei.

(ii) β-rays are moving electrons. They may emerge from their parent nucleus with any speed from zero to a definite maximum. The maximum speed often approaches that of light, and is different for each isotope. The electron has a

positively charged counterpart, the positron (see below), and β-rays are sometimes positrons. To distinguish the two cases, the symbols $\beta-$ and $\beta+$ are used. The naturally occurring β-radiations are almost all $\beta-$.

(iii) γ-rays travel with the speed of light because they are in fact electromagnetic waves differing from light only in the extreme shortness of their wavelength. They have no electric charge.

It is unusual, though not unheard of, for the same radioactive substance to emit both α- and β-rays. On the other hand, γ-rays frequently accompany either α- or β-rays.

γ-rays pass through matter easily; in fact, they are extra penetrating X-rays. α-rays can be stopped by thin sheets of tissue paper. α-rays brought to rest pick up a pair of electrons from the surrounding matter and become neutral helium atoms, and helium gas from this source is consequently found imprisoned in certain radioactive rocks. β-rays are intermediate in penetrating power between α- and γ-rays.

We must now try to interpret these observations.

Radioactive Disintegration

A nucleus is a collection of neutrons and protons interacting with each other and possessing collectively a certain amount of energy. Just as some human organisations lose their coherence if they accept too many members, so nuclei can remain stable only if (i) the total number of particles is not too great, and (ii) neutrons and protons are there in suitable proportions. Radioactive nuclei are the ones for which either or both these conditions do not hold. Sooner or later such nuclei eject a fragment, thus getting rid of some energy they cannot contain. This is called a *radioactive disintegration*, and the fragments are the α-, β-, and γ-rays. α-emission relieves a nucleus of two neutrons and two protons and some energy; γ-emission simply carries off excess energy without altering the number or kind of particles left behind. β-emission is more complicated. There are no electrons normally present in a nucleus, but they are suddenly created and explosively emitted if a neutron changes into a proton; positive electrons are similarly generated if a proton changes into a neutron. β-emission is therefore a mechanism for changing the ratio of protons to neutrons without altering the total number of particles.

Both α- and β-emission change the Z of a nucleus, and the product, or daughter nucleus, is a different chemical element. α-emission also changes the M. It might happen that the daughter nucleus is unstable, in which case it too will disintegrate. Successive generations are produced until a stable one is reached. Part of such a family tree is shown below. The symbols above the arrows show the kind of rays emitted at each stage, the figures are the mass numbers, M, and the names and symbols of chemical elements can be found at the end of the Section.

$$U^{238} \xrightarrow{\alpha} Th^{234} \xrightarrow{\beta} Pa^{234} \xrightarrow{\beta} U^{234} \xrightarrow{\alpha} Th^{230} \xrightarrow{\alpha}$$
$$Ra^{226} \xrightarrow{\alpha} Rn^{222} \xrightarrow{\alpha} Po^{218} \xrightarrow{\beta} Pb^{214} \xrightarrow{\beta} Bi^{214} \xrightarrow{\beta}$$
$$Po^{214} \xrightarrow{\alpha} Pb^{210} \xrightarrow{\beta} Bi^{210} \xrightarrow{\beta} Po^{210} \xrightarrow{\alpha} Pb^{206}$$
(Pb^{206} is stable lead).

This family exists naturally on earth, because the head of the family, U^{238}, has so long a half-life (4.5×10^9 years) that there has not yet been time enough since its formation for it to have disappeared.

Artificial Radioactivity

Nowadays many new radioactive isotopes can be man-made. All that is required is to alter the M or Z (or both) of a stable isotope to a value which is incompatible with stability. The means for doing this is *bombardment, i.e.,* stable nuclei are exposed to the impacts of atomic particles such as streams of protons from an accelerator, the neutrons in an atomic reactor, or simply the α-particles from another radioactive substance.

The new material is called an *artificially radioactive isotope*. Artificial radioactivity is not different in kind from that of the naturally radioactive substances, but the half-lives are usually on the short side. Indeed, the isotopes in question would exist in nature but for the fact that their short half-lives ensured their disappearance from the earth long ago.

Suppose a piece of copper is exposed to the intense neutron radiation in an atomic reactor at Harwell.

The more abundant of the two stable isotopes of ordinary copper has thirty-four neutrons and twenty-nine protons (*i.e.*, $Z = 29$, $M = 63$). In the reactor many (not all) of these nuclei absorb a neutron, giving an unstable copper nucleus with $Z = 29$, $M = 64$. When removed from the reactor the specimen is observed to be radioactive with a half-life of 12·8 hours. It is somewhat unusual in that it gives out both β^- and β^+ rays. Some nuclei emit electrons, leaving a daughter nucleus with one more positive charge than copper, *i.e.*, a zinc nucleus ($Z = 30$, $M = 64$). One neutron has become a proton, and the resulting zinc nucleus is stable. The others emit positrons, leaving behind a nucleus in which a proton has been turned into a neutron ($Z = 28$, $M = 64$); this is a stable nickel nucleus. The overall process is one example of the artificial transmutation of the chemical elements which is now a commonplace of nuclear physics. It was first discovered by Irene and Frederick Joliot-Curie in 1934.

Lack of a Complete Theory

Consider now a collection of, say, one million radioactive nuclei of the same kind. It is impossible to tell exactly when any one of them will disintegrate; it is a matter of chance which ones break up first. All we know is that, after a time equal to the half-life, only a half a million will survive unchanged. In general, the more excess energy a nucleus has, the more likely it is to break up, and therefore the shorter the half-life of that particular nuclear species. In principle, to calculate the half-life theoretically, one would have to have a reliable theory of nuclear forces and energies. This is still being sought after, so it is probably fair to say that while the laws of behaviour of radioactive isotopes are well and accurately known, the *explanation* of this behaviour in terms of the properties of protons and neutrons is by no means complete.

Nuclear Fission—Chain Reaction

A discovery important not just for nuclear physics but for the whole of mankind was made by Hahn and Strassman in 1939. This was the discovery of nuclear fission in uranium. One of the natural isotopes of uranium is an unstable one, U^{235}, with 143 neutrons and 92 protons. It normally shows its instability by emitting α- and γ-rays. If uranium is bombarded with neutrons, some U^{235} nuclei temporarily gain an extra neutron, which makes them even less stable. This they show by splitting into two roughly equal parts, called fission fragments, together with two or three neutrons. There are two highly important things about this disintegration. One is that the two or three neutrons can promote further disintegrations in other uranium nuclei, and the process can therefore be self-propagating: it is then called a *chain reaction*. The other is that the total mass of the fission products is less than that of the original nucleus. This mass difference does not disappear without trace; it turns into energy according to a formula referred to in a paragraph below (F18(1)).

Nuclear Fusion

The ability of two light nuclei to combine and form a heavier nucleus is called fusion. A reaction of this nature does not form a chain process but proceeds in singly induced reactions. A typical fusion reaction is the formation of a helium nucleus (mass 3) from two deuterium nuclei which are made to collide at an energy of 60 keV (speed of $2 \cdot 410^6$ m/s)

i.e., $^2D_1 + {}^2D_1 \rightarrow {}^3He_2$ (0·82 meV) + n(2·45 meV)

where the $^3He_2$ particle has kinetic energy of 0·82 meV and the free neutron has free kinetic energy of 2·45 meV. This type of reaction is exoenergetic, the additional kinetic energy coming from the tighter binding of the nucleus in ^3He than in the two separate deuterium nuclei. The energy released in this form of nuclear reaction is much more than that in a fission process and is responsible for the emitted energy of the sun which burns hydrogen to form helium.

Applications of Nuclear Reactions

The world has two uses for the energy released in nuclear reactions:

(1) nuclear weapons;
(2) nuclear power plants.

The only nuclear bombs to be used in anger employed the fission chain reaction proceeding at a rapid rate which quickly becomes uncontrollable and produces a tremendous explosion. The second generation of nuclear warhead uses the fusion reaction, which is initiated by a fission-reacting detonator to produce an even more destructive blast. The third generation of nuclear warhead uses the large flux of very energetic neutrons to kill biological material, but the blast effect is essentially zero, hence attacks with neutron bombs leave most non-biological material and structures intact.

In the second application the nuclear fission process is controlled to provide a constant source of energy to drive turbines which produce electricity. The harnessing of the fusion process is the subject of a special topic at the end of the Section. Both uses represent epoch-making technical achievements, but mankind has yet to show itself capable of bearing sanely the burden of responsibility which nuclear physicists have laid upon it. One thing is certain: the discoveries will not cease. Already, other fissionable elements have been made and used; new chemical elements have been created; nuclear plants (" atomic piles ") have stimulated great demands for new materials that will stand the heat and radiation inside the reactor, and this promotes research in other fields of science; irradiation inside an atomic pile gives new, and potentially useful properties to old materials; nuclear power drives ships and submarines. It is difficult to write even briefly about contemporary nuclear physics without feeling keenly the ambiguity of its powerful promises.

Atoms.

A nucleus surrounded by its full complement of electrons is an electrically neutral system called an atom. Neither the atom as a whole, nor its nucleus, counts as a " fundamental particle " because either can be subdivided into more elementary parts, thus:

atom $\longrightarrow$ electrons + nucleus $\longrightarrow$ electrons + neutrons + protons

The chemical identity of the atoms of a given element, which was Dalton's key idea, depends entirely on the number and motion of the electrons. For example, the simplest element, hydrogen, has one proton for a nucleus, and one electron. The latter is comparatively easily detached or disturbed by the electric forces exerted by neighbouring atoms, consequently hydrogen is reactive chemically, *i.e.*, it readily lends its electron to build chemical structures with other equally co-operative elements. The second element, helium, has a nucleus of two protons and two neutrons; outside are two electrons in a particularly stable arrangement. Both electrons orbit the nucleus in the same spacial orbit, but with their spin directions opposite and at 90° to the plane through the nucleus and the electrons. This pair of electrons is so difficult to disarrange that the special name of closed shells has been coined to cover such cases. The fact that two electrons can be present in the same orbit is only possible if their spins are anti-parallel (Pauli Exclusion Principle). In the case of a stable group of eight electrons they arrange themselves in groups of two and their spins antiparallel. Helium with its closed shell will not react chemically, whereas hydrogen, which has an open shell of only one electron, will react very quickly with other atoms.

As the nuclear charge increases, different electron arrangements of greater or lesser stability succeed one another, with every so often a closed shell corresponding to one of the chemically inert gases neon, argon, xenon, krypton.

Such considerations, pursued in sufficient detail, enable atomic physics to account for all the differences and similarities among the chemical elements and, in principle at least, for all other facts of chemistry as well.

Ions

Changes in the atomic properties of an atom are accomplished by altering the position of any electron from one orbit to another. In the limit when an electron is completely removed from the atom, leaving it positively charged, the atom is said to be ionised and is called a positive ion. An atom can be singly or multiply ionised up to a level equal to the number of electrons existing in the neutral atom. In addition, atoms can, through distortion of the existing electrons, accept an additional electron and become negative ions. These can be formed in a resonance scattering process and exist only for life-times of only 10^{-14}s or be formed by chemical reactions. The roles played by negative and positive ions in the upper atmosphere of the earth and stellar atmospheres have been of special interest to atomic physicists since the 1930s.

Maxwell and Electromagnetic Waves

Atoms are held together by the electric attraction of the nucleus for the electrons. Finer details of atomic behaviour depend on the magnetic moments of the particles. Any moving charged particle gives rise to magnetic effects, and in the dynamo a coil moving in a magnet produces an electric current. It can be seen therefore that electric and magnetic phenomena are intimately linked. Any region of space subject to electric and magnetic influences is called an *electromagnetic field*.

In 1862, before the discovery of the electron, Maxwell, while still in his twenties, had perfected a general theory of the electro-magnetic field. This theory today still describes correctly almost all electro-magnetic phenomena. The elegance of this theory is difficult to appreciate, but it alone was the only theory of pre-twentieth-century physics which satisfied the prerequisites of Einstein's relativity theory (1905), *i.e.*, inherent in its structure was the concept of relativistic invariance. *Inter alia*, he proved that disturbances in the electric and magnetic conditions at one place could be propagated to another place through empty space, with a definite velocity, just as sound waves are propagated through air. Such electromagnetic disturbances in transit are called *electromagnetic waves*, and their velocity turned out experimentally to be the same as that of light and radio waves—which was a decisive argument to show that both of these phenomena are themselves electro-magnetic waves.

Einstein and Photons

In the years between about 1900 and 1920 this view was upset by Planck, Einstein, Millikan, and others, who focused attention on phenomena (radiant heat, photoelectricity) in which light behaves like a stream of particles and not at all like waves. A wave and a particle are two quite different things, as anyone will admit after a moment's contemplation of, say, the ripples on a pond and a floating tennis ball. The acute question was: is light like waves or particles?

Theoretical physicists have devised means of having it both ways. To say that light behaves as particles means that the waves of the electromagnetic field cannot have their energy subdivided indefinitely. For waves of a given frequency, there is a certain irreducible quantity of energy that must be involved whenever light interacts with anything. This quantity is the product $h\nu$ where ν is the frequency and h is a constant named after Planck. Each such unit

is called a *quantum of the electromagnetic field* or a *photon* and is counted as one of the fundamental particles. Frequencies and wavelengths vary widely. Typical wavelengths are: radio—hundreds or thousands of metres; radar—a few centimetres; visible light—5 × 10^{-5} cm; X-rays—10^{-8} cm.

De Broglie and Particles

Since it seemed possible to attribute particle properties to electro-magnetic waves, then why not associate wave properties with particles. If an electron (mass m) is travelling with a velocity of v cm/s, then De Broglie (1923) suggested that its characteristic wavelength would be given by the relation $mv\,\lambda = h$; for example if $v = 10^6$ cm/s, $m = 9 \times 10^{-28}$ g, $h = 6\cdot610^{-27}$ erg-seconds, then $\lambda = 7,500$ Å, which is the same wavelength as red light. This proposal was confirmed in 1927 by Davisson and Germer when they showed that electrons could produce diffraction, a property until then only associated with light. These wave-like properties are now known to exist for all particles, and we now consider a particle with momentum mv to behave like a wave of wave-length $\lambda = h/mv$.

De Broglie made his revolutionary assertion in his doctoral thesis, and his examiners were so uneasy about the validity of the hypothesis that they were prepared to fail the young man in his examination. Happily for De Broglie, Einstein was visiting that particular university and he was asked his opinion of the idea; his reply ensured success for De Broglie and saved the examiners from future embarrassment.

Molecules

Electrical attractions and interactions of various kinds can cause atoms to combine with each other or themselves to form molecules. Two similar atoms, say hydrogen, combining to form the homonuclear diatomic molecule H_2, while two different atoms, hydrogen and chlorine, will form a heteronuclear diatomic molecule HCl. Molecules have a wide range of complexity, from simple pairs of atoms to highly intricate spirals and chains composed of thousands of atoms. The biological basis of all life is, of course, molecular in both origin and function.

Excited Atoms

Like nuclei, atoms, when given excess energy (insufficient to ionise them), will absorb the energy in one of the electrons, which is then displaced from its equilibrium state to a state (or orbit) of higher energy. It will remain there for typically 10^{-8} seconds before returning to its equilibrium position with the excess energy being emitted as light. The time an atom remains in its excited state can exceed 10^{-8} seconds; lifetimes of 0·1 second are known, and these metastable states are prevented by the atomic properties of the atom from decaying quickly to their equilibrium states. The colour of the light emitted is characteristic of the atom involved, with the more energetic transitions giving blue light while the less energetic transitions give red light. Hence the emitted colour (or wavelength) of the light can be used as a tool for chemical identification and study of the various transition probabilities in atoms.

Herein lies the explanation of innumerable natural and technical phenomena, such as the colours of glowing gases whether they exist in the sun and stars, in aurora, or in street-lamps and neon signs. Herein also lies the reason for the importance of spectroscopy, which is the study of the characteristic radiation from excited states for spectroscopy is not only a useful tool for the chemical identification of substances (" spectroscopic analysis ") but was one of the main routes along which twentieth-century physicists broke through to a knowledge of the inner nature of the atom.

Forces in Nature

Nature uses four, possibly five, apparently different forces to make one particle interact with another. The weakest force is gravity which, although present at all particle interactions, is insignificant in atomic and nuclear interactions. Gravity controls the mass distribution in the universe and the force has an infinite range of interaction.

The electric force which also has an infinite range of interaction is much stronger than the gravitational force and is responsible for the binding forces inside atoms by the attraction of nuclei for electrons.

Inside the nucleus two types of interaction take place which require different forces for their existence:

(1) the forces which hold neutrons and protons together in the nucleus and this is the strong force, and

(2) the weak force which controls the changes in charge state of nucleons, e.g., the β-decay process when a neutron in a nucleus changes into a proton with the ejection of an electron is control led by the weak force.

Both these nuclear forces are short-range with their radius of influence approximately 10^{-13} cm, with the weak force acting on all matter and the strong force acting on nucleons only. In today's parlance the strong force will act only on particles which are single multiples of quarks (see later). Since quarks exist (or more precisely, since their existence has been deduced), then it is necessary to have a force through which they can interact.

The fifth force of the universe is postulated to be the colour force which operates only on quark particles and has a mode of interaction which prevents a normal range restriction being placed on it. The proton, i.e., the nucleus of atomic hydrogen, is composed of three quarks which move about freely within the shell of the proton; only when one quark tries to escape across the boundary of the proton does it experience the colour force which rebinds into the proton. Before we discuss further the interactions of these forces we must describe the range of particles which exist in physics.

Elementary Particles

When considering the word elementary in this context the reader should be wary of thinking that it implies some degree of absoluteness. The elementary mass of any particular particle is always highly qualified and subject to change. When a particle is discovered physicists measure its properties, i.e., mass, electric charge, and spin, and determine which of the five forces to which it is subject. In addition, its life-time must be determined to see if the particle is stable or only a transient particle which will break up into other particles. The life-times of unstable particles are extremely short, ranging from 10^{-17} s to 10^{-21} s, and it is debatable if a particle which lasts only for 10^{-21} s should be called a particle. Generally non such short-lived particles are called resonances which are produced in an interaction which is only a step to the final product.

The rudimentary classification of particles is into four groups:

(1) photons
(2) leptons
(3) mesons
(4) baryons

All particles have an anti-particle which has the same mass but opposite charge as the real particle, the only exception being the photon, which is its own anti-particle and forms a group on its own. The leptons (electron, muon, and neutrino) form a stable group of particles and do not react to the strong or colour forces. This group of particles, and the photon, are perhaps the most fundamental of all particles. The mesons are unstable particles and (as will be seen later) exist only to act as a means which enables nucleons to interact with each other. They are subjected to the strong nuclear force. All particles heavier than the proton are called baryons, every one of them, except the proton, is unstable in some degree, and a vast number of them are known. Only a few are listed in the Table on page F16.

Mesons and baryons are collectively called hadrons. All of these unstable particles have been detected either in the cosmic flux falling on the earth or produced in the very high energy accelerating machines in Europe, the USA, and the USSR.

Strangeness

Some particles have long life-times $\sim10^{-9}$ s, which is much larger than that encountered normally. Particles which possessed these long life-times were called "strange." Strangeness describes not a new property of matter but a different quality of matter which persists long enough to enable that particle to engage in strong nuclear-force interactions. Hence strangeness does not persist indefinitely. The decay of a strange particle into other particles with the abolition of strangeness proceeds via the weak nuclear force. The strange (and doubly strange) particles form highly symmetrised shapes when combined with non-strange particles. The pattern itself does not explain anything, but the underlying theory, known as Group Theory, does indicate by symmetry arguments which particle should be necessary to form a complete group. This mathematical procedure had a resounding success in 1964 when it predicted the existence of a triply strange particle known as "omega minus." The organisation of particles according to their properties of mass, spin, and strangeness in groups is now only an organisation exercise, and it will not tell us anything about the composition of nucleons.

Interactions of Particles

The method by which atomic, nuclear, and sub-nuclear particles interact is via the exchange of energy which can be considered as a particle exchange. The interaction between electric charges proceeds by the exchange of photons. For example, two charges feel each other by one charge emitting a photon which interacts with the second charge. Since the electric force has infinite range, its force-carrying particle has zero mass. The same criteria apply in the gravitational force, where the graviton is the particle which carries the force effect between particles of matter. Since the weak, strong, and colour forces are short-range, then their force-carrying particles have finite masses. The weak force uses W particles of variable mass energy, the strong force uses mesons, mass energy 1,865 and 2,020 MeV, as the means of communicating the force of interaction between nucleons. The quarks interact via the colour force, which is carried by gluons (mass at present unknown), which also feel the force themselves. The colour force does not distinguish between or acknowledge the existence of strangeness and charm.

The variable mass energy of the W particles $(W^{\circ} \ W^{+} \ W^{-})$, which ranges from zero to 3 GeV mass-energy, has enabled the weak and electric forces to be combined into one force in which the weak force is only an aspect of the electric force. The extension of this combination to include all the forces in one force system places one at the edge of knowledge on the frontiers of physics. No such extension has as yet been made.

Quarks

The stability of the leptons contrasts sharply with the instability of the hadrons (excepting the proton), and this as well as other things has led physicists to consider that all hadrons were composed from different combinations of yet undiscovered particles. Gellmann has postulated the existence of three particles from which the nucleons, mesons, and hence all hadrons are composed. These "new" particles are attributed with fractional electric charges of $+\frac{2}{3}$, $-\frac{1}{3}$, and $-\frac{1}{3}$ of the electron charge. The particles were called quarks. The name quark was taken from the novel Finnegan's Wake by James Joyce, the meaning of which is obscure, which is perhaps appropriate, but as students of Joyce will know, quark means "non sense," and other interpretations as to its meaning, such as the "sound of seagulls" or "quarts" are wrong. The three

SOME MEMBERS OF THE ATOMIC FAMILY

The numbers in brackets after the name denote first the electric charge and second, the mass. The charge on an electron is counted as -1 unit and the electron mass as $+1$ unit. Thus $(+1, 207)$ means the particle has a positive charge of 1 unit and a mass 207 times that of the electron.

The mass energy of an electron is 0·51 MeV, hence conversion to mass energies can be made by multiplying the given mass by 0·51. Thus the muon has a mass energy of 106 MeV. Note: the letter M is used to denote quantities of millions and the letter G to denote quantities of thousand of millions.

Photon (0, 0)	A quantum of electromagnetic radiation, *e.g.*, light, X-rays, γ-rays. The concept was introduced by M. Planck in 1900 when he described the emission of light as taking place in " packets " rather than in a steady stream. The energy of a photon is proportional to the frequency of the radiation and inversely proportional to the wavelength.

Leptons

Electron (−1, 1)	Discovered by J. J. Thomson in 1897. The number of orbital electrons in an atom determines its chemical properties. Actual rest mass = $9·1 \times 10^{-28}$ g. Emitted as β-rays by some radioactive nuclei. A stable particle.
Positron (+1, 1)	Positive counterpart or, " anti-particle," to the electron. Predicted theoretically by P. A. M. Dirac in 1928 and first discovered in cosmic rays by C. D. Anderson in 1932. Emitted as β-rays by some radioactive nuclei. When positrons and electrons collide they usually annihilate each other and turn into γ-rays; consequently, positrons only last about 10^{-10} sec. within ordinary matter, but are stable in isolation.
Neutrino (0, 0) and Anti-neutrino (0, 0)	These particles travel with the speed of light and are distinguished from one another by the relation of their spin to their direction of motion. A neutrino is emitted with the positron during positive β-decay; and an anti-neutrino with the electron during negative β-decay. Their interaction with matter is extremely slight. First postulated by Pauli in 1933 and detected in 1956. π-meson decay also produces neutrinos and anti-neutrinos but in 1962 it was proved experimentally that these are a different species. Thus there are two kinds of neutrino each with an anti-neutrino. All these particles are distinguished from photons by having different spin.
Muon (±1, 207)	Similar to, but heavier than, the electron and positron; disintegrates into electron (or positron if positive) + neutrino + anti-neutrino.

Mesons

Pion (±1, 273) or (0, 264)	The π-meson. Charged pions decay either into muons and neutrinos or into electrons and neutrinos. Neutral pions decay into γ-rays, into " positron-electron pairs," or both. Pions are intimately connected with nuclear forces, *i.e.*, with the " strong " interaction.
Kaon (±1, 966) or (0, 974)	The K-mesons. These decay in many different ways producing other mesons, electrons, and neutrinos.

Baryons

Proton (+1, 1836·1)	The positively-charged constituent of nuclei; the hydrogen nucleus is one proton. Fast-moving protons occur in cosmic rays. Does not spontaneously disintegrate.
Anti-proton (−1, 1836·1)	Negative anti-particle of the proton. Its existence was long suspected. Artificially produced and detected for the first time in 1955. Will react with the proton to produce pions or kaons.
Neutron (0, 1838·6)	Discovered by J. Chadwick in 1932. The neutral constituent of nuclei. When free it spontaneously disintegrates into a proton, an electron, and an anti-neutrino, after an average lifetime of about 18 minutes. Passes through matter much more easily than charged particles.
Anti-neutron (0, 1838·6)	The anti-particle of the neutron from which it is distinguished by properties connected with its magnetic moment and spin. Will react with neutron to produce pions or kaons.
Lambda Particle (0, 2183)	Discovered in 1947. Decays into proton plus pion.
Sigma Particle (0 or ±1; about 2330)	Various modes of disintegration, producing neutrons, protons, mesons and lambda particles.
Omega Particle (±1, 3272)	Predicted by recent theory and discovered at Brookhaven, New York, in 1964.
Psi Particle (0, about 6100)	Discovered independently by two laboratories in the USA 1974. Still under intensive study.

quarks were called up, down, and strange and have the properties given in the Table below:

Name	charge	spin	mass-energy (MeV)
up	$+\frac{2}{3}$	$\frac{1}{2}$	336
down	$-\frac{1}{3}$	$\frac{1}{2}$	338
strange	$-\frac{1}{3}$	$\frac{1}{2}$	540

These particles interact with each other via the colour force. Hence it can be seen that by taking different combinations of quarks, different hadrons can be built up. For example, the proton is two up quarks and one down, the neutron is two down and one up. The simplicity of this system can be appreciated, but the only experimental evidence to support the existence of quarks is indirect. No one has yet isolated a single quark! Many scientists are seeking ways to produce and detect them, but as yet (1978) no claims have stood the test of scrutiny. Of course as well as the three quarks up, down, and strange, there are the corresponding anti-quarks.

The K-mesons, for example, are composed of a quark and an antiquark either with the spins of the two quarks aligned parallel to give a net spin of one, or aligned antiparallel to give a net spin of zero. The charges $+1$, -1, and 0 are simply determined by selecting the correct combination of up and down quarks.

Charm

In the quest to unite the weak and electric forces, theoreticians were forced to introduce yet another new particle into the quark family. This was a charmed quark with charge $+\frac{2}{3}$. The four members of the quark family seemed now to be symmetrical with the four members of the lepton group (electron, muon, and two neutrinos). Since the charmed quark had charge $+\frac{2}{3}$ and mass of 1,500 MeV, it could simply replace the up quark as a building brick in nucleons to produce charmed matter. For example, by replacing the up quark in a proton and a meson by a charmed quark we get a charmed proton and a charmed meson. The first experimental evidence of the existence of charm was obtained by the high-energy physics group at University College, London, working at CERN laboratory, when they established the existence of " a neutral current interaction " in neutrino scattering experiments. Although " naked " charm has never been detected, charmed mesons (masses of 1,865 and 2,020) have been detected by the SPEAR laboratory in USA and charmed anti-protons have also been detected with masses of 2,260 MeV. The experimentally determined masses are in sufficient agreement with theory to confirm the existence of the charmed quark. If a charmed quark combined with an anti-charmed quark it would form a particle of mass 3,000 MeV (3 GeV), and this has been given the name of the Gipsy particle. Several laboratories in 1976 reported the possible existence of a particle of this mass energy, and called it either a J particle or psi particle. The uncertainty has now been resolved and the existence of the Gipsy has been confirmed. It can exist in an excited state of 3·7 GeV, from which it decays by gamma-ray emission to a value of 3·1 GeV, the predicted value. It can further change its spin state and decay to a mass energy value of 2·8 GeV. The building bricks of matter now seemed complete!

Quarks and Pre-Quarks (Preons)

The final picture of the structure of matter is not yet complete, and indeed theorists have added two further quarks to the family of four called truth and beauty, although to date (1978) no experimental evidence of their existence is available. It is further postulated that even the quarks are composed of only two different particles called preons. All of this is only theoretical, and we must wait for the definite isolation of a single quark to settle the matter.

QUANTUM THEORY AND RELATIVITY

Quantum Theory

In our discussion of the nature of the various particles in physics we have alluded to them as being classified with well-defined sizes and weights. Of course, once we consider the physics of matter on a scale which is smaller than that of our everyday comprehension, then the classical physics of Newton is insufficient and we must use quantum physics. In the atomic region of reality we are again faced with the problem of indivisibility where the Greeks stopped their thinking and called the smallest particles of the universe atoms. Today we know that each separate particle is composed of a definite amount of energy, and the larger the particle, *i.e.*, the more energy it is composed of, the easier it is to detect. We also know that the exchange of force between nucleons is carried by particles and that this inchangeability between mass and energy is a reality of quantum theory. To see this more fully we must realise that quantum theory rests on the theory of measurement! If a particle, of any type or structure, is composed of an amount of energy $\triangle E$, then it is necessary to make measurements on it for a certain minimum time before it is detected. This minimum time $\triangle t$ is given by the equation $\triangle E$. $\triangle t \leqslant \hbar$, where $\hbar$ is Planck's constant divided by 2π; hence it can be seen that the smaller $\triangle E$, then the longer a measurement must be made to detect the particle. Correspondingly, the time of measurement itself introduces an uncertainty, $\triangle E$, in the energy of the particle. As well as the parameters $\triangle E$ and $\triangle t$, a particular physical event can be expressed in terms of its momentum p and position q, and these can also be expressed in a relationship as $\triangle p \; \triangle q \leqslant t$. Hence one can ask at what position in space, q, is a particular particle with momentum p? Or what exactly is the wavelength of a wave? It may be thought that the first question cannot reasonably be asked of a wave nor the second of a particle, but bearing in mind the dual roles of particles and waves discussed earlier, then these questions can be interchanged. We know that electrons behave both as particles and waves. Since electrons have something in common with both, one question cannot be answered precisely for electrons without ignoring the other; alternatively, both questions can be given an imprecise answer. As the wavelength of electrons is intimately connected with their speed, one has to accept an accurate knowledge of the speed (wavelength) and ignorance of position, or the converse, or *inaccurate* knowledge of both. This is the famous Heisenberg Uncertainty Principle. Quantum theory is a set of mathematical rules for calculating the behaviour of fundamental particles in accordance with the Uncertainty Principle. In spite of its equivocal-sounding name, the principle has led to an enormous increase in the accuracy with which physical phenomena can be described and predicted. Quantum theory includes all that previous theories did and more.

Quantum theory grew up in the same epoch as the Theory of Relativity. Heroic attempts have been made to combine the two, but with only partial success so far. Relativity is concerned with all motion and all physical laws, but its characteristic manifestations occur only when something is moving with nearly the velocity of light. Quantum theory is likewise all-embracing, but its typical phenomena almost always occur when something on the minute atomic scale is in question. Consequently, the vast majority of everyday mechanics needs no more than the classical theory laid down by Newton, which is neither relativistic nor quantum.

Relativity

Historically, relativity grew out of attempts to measure the speed with which the earth moved through that hypothetical medium called the ether, which was supposed at that time to be the bearer of light waves. To take a simple analogy: sound waves travel through still air with a certain definite speed, v. If you move through the air with speed v' towards oncoming sound waves, they will pass you at the speed $v + v'$. Michelson and Morley, in their celebrated experiment of 1887, failed to find the corresponding behaviour on the part of light. This is so important an experiment that it has been repeated, and repeatedly discussed, ever since. In October 1958 the latest and most accurate confirmation of the Michelson–Morely result was announced. It seems as if light always travels with the same speed relative to an observer, however fast he moves relative to anything else. Einstein put it this way: two observers moving with any constant velocity relative to each other will always agree that light travels past them at the same speed; this speed is denoted by c, and is approximately 186,000 miles per second.

It should be remembered that the limiting value of the velocity of light in relativity is a postulate introduced by Einstein not a conclusion which the theory provides. There may exist forms of matter which can travel faster than light!

Nevertheless, the postulate that the maximum velocity encountered in the universe is c, logically developed, leads to remarkable conclusions. For instance: if you walk from tail to nose of an aircraft at 4 m.p.h. and the plane is receding from me at 300 m.p.h., then you recede from me at 304 m.p.h. " Common sense," Newton, and Einstein would all agree on this. But if you could walk at 0·25c and the plane moved at 0·5c, the Newtonian mechanics would give your recession speed as 0·75c, whereas Einsteinian relativity would give about 0·67c. Although at the everyday speed of 300 m.p.h., the disagreement, though present in principle, is absolutely negligible, at speeds near that of light it becomes very pronounced. Many experiments show that the relativity answer is right.

Equivalence of Mass and Energy

The most famous consequence of relativity theory from which we derive benefit is the knowledge that mass can be converted into energy. The amount of energy, E, which can be derived from a given mass, m, of any type of material is given by the celebrated e uation $E = mc^2$. If we take one gram of ash and convert it into the free energy of which it is composed we would get 10^8 kilowatts of power, sufficient to heat 15 houses for a year. The heat provided by the material which produced the ash is equivalent to that obtained from burning a single match. The massive energy released by $E = mc^2$ has been demonstrated in the power of nuclear weapons, but this energy has also been put to peaceful uses in nuclear-powered electricity generating stations.

In fundamental particle physics the masses of particles were always expressed in units of mass energy using $E = mc^2$ as the conversion equation. This is a matter of convenience from the realisation that mass is simply a condensed form of energy. The mesons which are the force-exchanging particles in the strong interaction have a mass energy of approximately 130 MeV, which is equivalent to a real mass of only 210^{-26} grams. The energy of the sun is provided by the conversion of real mass into light energy through thermonuclear fusion processes.

Mass and Rest Mass

The concept of mass is not a simple idea to grasp, for as we have seen, the mass of a body which is at rest is equivalent to its inherent latent energy. Further complications and interpretations arise when the body starts moving and its mass is no longer necessarily a constant quantity.

A stationary body can be observed to have a mass called its *rest mass*. If the body moves, it has energy of motion and therefore, according to Einstein's mass–energy equation, it increases its mass. Mass thus depends on speed, but in such a way that there is very little change unless the speed approaches that of light. Many experiments on atomic particles demonstrate this. The interesting question now arises: do all fundamental particles have rest mass? or do some have mass derived solely from their energy? The answer appears to be that photons and neutrinos have no rest mass; all other particles have. The Table on F16 gives their rest masses.

Special theory of relativity

The mathematical development of Einstein's ideas, leading to the conclusions just referred to, constitutes the Special Theory of Relativity.

Stated more generally, the theory raises the question whether two observers in uniform relative motion could ever detect, as a result of their relative speed, any difference in the physical laws governing matter, motion, and light. To this, Special Relativity answers: No. The detailed theory involves special consideration of the results the two observers would obtain when measuring (i) the spatial distance, and (ii) the time interval, between the same two events. It turns out that they would not agree on these two points. They would agree, however, on the value of a certain quantity made up jointly of the spatial distance and the time interval in a somewhat complex combination. The intimate mixture of space and time in this quantity has led to the treatment of the three space dimensions and time on an equivalent footing. Hence the frequent references to time as the " fourth dimension." Minkowski devised an extremely elegant presentation of relativity theory by using an extension of ordinary geometry to four dimensions. A line drawn in his four-dimensional space represents the path of a particle in space and time, *i.e.*, the whole history of the particle. Thus the movement of particles in the ordinary world is turned into the geometry of lines in Minkowski's four-dimensional world of " space–time."

General Relativity and Gravitation

In 1915, 10 years after the publication of the Special Theory of Relativity, Einstein published his theory of General Relativity. This apparently innocuous extension of the ideas of special relativity to include accelerated relative motion opened up new and difficult fields of mathematical complexity which, when solved, enabled Einstein to include gravitation in the theory. In discussing the physics of atomic, nuclear, and sub-nuclear particles, we did not include the effect of the gravitational force, since in relation to the Electric, Weak, Strong, and Colour forces it is extremely small and can be neglected in the discussion of the structure of matter but not in the discussion of astronomical problems and the movements of large-scale electrically uncharged bodies.

It has been usual, ever since Newton, to say that two bodies of mass m_1 and m_2, separated by a distance r attract one another with a force proportional to $m_1 m_2/r^2$. This is Newton's inverse square law of gravitation which explains the movements of planets and comets and the falling to earth of an apple from a tree.

The apple's fall is accelerated, and we observe this by noting its position relative to certain marks fixed with respect to us, and by timing it with some sort of clock. This system of location in space and time may be called out " frame of reference." We therefore assert that, in our frame of reference, the apple falls down with an acceleration which Newton saw no alternative but to attribute to a thing called gravitational attraction. Galileo had shown that *all* bodies fall with the same acceleration at all points, and we can now rephrase this by saying that in our frame of reference there is a constant gravitational attraction or *uniform gravitational field*. (This last statement and Galileo's demonstration only refer strictly to points fairly near the earth's surface; at greater distances the gravitational field decreases and is therefore not uniform.)

Now suppose a collection of falling bodies is observed by us and an intelligent creature, designated C, inhabits one of them. C has his own frame of reference fixed relative to him and we have ours fixed relative to us. In C's frame neither his own body, nor any of the others, is accelerated, and therefore he has no reason to suppose a gravitational force is acting on them. We have, therefore, the following situation:

(i) in our frame, fixed relative to us, we find all the bodies falling subject to a gravitational pull;

(ii) in C's frame, undergoing accelerated fall relative to us, no gravitational field is apparent to C.

It looks, therefore, as if one has only to choose the correct frame of reference for the measurements in order to remove the need for any assumptions about the existence of gravitational fields. This is a simple illustration of the connection between gravitation and frames of reference for the measurement of space and time. Einstein's General Theory of Relativity extends this to cover non-uniform gravitational fields and shows that what Newton taught us to call the gravitational field of material bodies is better thought of as a peculiarity of the space and time in the neighbourhood of such bodies. Since space–time, as we mentioned above, can be expressed in geometrical terms, Einstein has transformed the theory of gravitation into an exercise (a difficult one) in the geometry of space–time. Other physicists, in Einstein's tradition, are trying to turn *all* physics into geometry, but no one knows whether this is really feasible.

All this abstruse work is much more than a demonstration of mathematical power and elegance. Observable phenomena which fall outside the scope of Newton's theory of gravitation are accounted for by relativity. One is the small but definite discrepancy between the actual orbit of the planet Mercury and the predictions of Newton's theory. Another is the effect of a gravitational field on the wavelength of light emitted by atoms. Similar atoms in different places in a gravitational field emit radiations with slightly different wavelengths. For example, the light from an atom in the intense field of a star should have slightly longer wavelength than the corresponding light from an atom on earth. This effect has always proved very difficult to detect with certainty. However, Einstein's prediction was verified with moderate accuracy in 1960 by a very subtle method which was purely terrestrial in its operation. The atoms being compared were placed at the top and bottom of a water tower and the difference in their emission was detected by means that belong rather to nuclear physics than to astronomy.

Quantum Theory and Relativity Combined

The atomic family table refers to " antiparticles." The theory which first introduced such things in 1934 is due to the Cambridge physicist Dirac and was epoch-making. Dirac conceived an equation to describe the motion of electrons subject to the laws of both quantum theory and relativity. His achievement was thus to synthesise these two great ideas. The spin of the electron was originally a supposition that helped to make sense of spectroscopic observations of light emitted from atoms. Dirac's equation made spin a logical consequence of the union of relativity and quantum theory. Perhaps even more important was the brilliant inference that the equation for the electron implied the existence of another particle having the same mass and spin but with a positive instead of a negative electric charge. This object is called the electron's antiparticle and is now well known as a positron.

Every particle is now believed to imply an antiparticle, so it is conceivable that the universe could have been (but isn't) an anti-universe, *i.e.*, all the electrons and protons might have been positrons and antiprotons and so on. The laws of physics would still have been applicable, however.

The gravitational force has an infinite range and therefore its force-carrying particles must travel at the speed of light. The graviton is the name of the particle which transmits the gravitational force between bodies with mass. To date (1978) no experiment has detected the existence of gravitations which are the postulated quanta of gravitational waves. There is an exact analogy between photons, the quanta of electro-magnetic radiation, and gravitations.

Conservation Laws

If charged particles interact, then it is found that the amount of electric charge existing after the reaction is the same as that which existed before the event. This is called the law of conservation of charge. Many other conservation laws exist in physics, *e.g.*, conservation of mass energy, angular momentum, linear momentum, and other more abstruse conservation laws exist in particle physics, *e.g.*, conservation of baryons, leptons, strangeness, isotopic spin, and parity. The last three conservation laws listed have been found to have a limited jurisdiction, and the violation of parity in the weak interaction was a great surprise to physicists.

Any reader who looks in a mirror knows that the left- and right-hand sides of his face are interchanged in the image. Fortunately mirrors do not also turn the image upside down, but, if they did, the face would then have undergone what is called " a parity transformation." A screwdriver driving a right-handed screw downwards becomes, on parity transformation, a screwdriver driving a left-handed screw upwards. The law of conservation of parity is a way of asserting that any physical process that goes on in the world could equally well go on—obeying the same laws—in a parity transformed world. There is nothing left-handed that does not in principle have a right-handed counterpart.

For many years this belief was strongly held. It came as something of a shock when, in 1957, after theoretical proposals by Lee and Yang in America, Wu and co-workers proved that parity was not always conserved. To understand Wu's experiment, we must recall that nuclei can have intrinsic spin. Suppose the axis of spin were downwards into the page and the rotation were suitable for driving an ordinary screw into the page. Then Wu showed that beta-rays from such a nucleus are emitted *preferentially upwards, i.e.*, against the direction of travel of the screw. The parity transformed version of this would have the beta-rays preferentially emitted in the same direction as the travel of the screw and, if parity is conserved, this process would happen too. But it does not. If the beta-rays in the experiment had been emitted in equal numbers up and down, then the parity transformed version would have had this feature too, and thus parity would have been conserved.

Modern research on elementary particles is greatly concerned to find out which types of process obey which conservation laws. The parity surprise is only one of the stimulating shocks that this type of work is heir to.

Conclusion

Over a century's development of the atomic ideas has brought a progressive, if jerky, increase in the mathematical precision of the theories. In some fields of particle physics, observations to one part in a million, or even better, can be explained, to that level of accuracy, by the existing theories. At the same time, however, the theories have lost visual definition. An atom as an invisible but none the less solid billiard ball was easy enough; so was a light wave conceived like a sound wave in air. Even after Rutherford, an atom consisting of a miniature solar system merely exchanged the solid billiard ball for a system of revolving billiard balls and was no great obstacle to visualisation. But since quantum theory and the Uncertainty Principle, every unambiguous visualisation of fundamental wave-particles leaves out half the picture, and although the electrons are in the atom, we can no longer represent them in definite orbits. The moral seems to be that visualisation is unnecessary, or at best a partial aid to thought.

THE PROPERTIES OF MATTER IN BULK

One of the most obvious and at the same time most wonderful things about the properties of matter is their great variety. Think of air, diamond, mercury, rubber, snow, gold, pitch, asbestos. . . . Even the differences of state of the same chemical substance are remarkable enough, ice, water, and steam, for example. One of the aims of physics is to reach an understanding of all these different properties by explaining them in terms of the behaviour of the particles discussed in the previous section (F10–19). The widespread success with which this imposing programme has been carried out indicates the maturity of physics. It is difficult to think of any major property of matter in bulk for which there is not some attempted theoretical explanation, though future physicists will no doubt regard some present-day theories as rudimentary or incorrect.

Physics, Statistics, and Thermodynamics

Take a number equal to the population of London, multiply it by itself, and multiply the product by another million. The answer is about the number of molecules in 1 cubic centimetre of ordinary air. They are constantly moving about and colliding with one another. Even if the nature of the molecules and their laws of motion were perfectly understood, it would clearly be impracticable to calculate the exact paths described by each particle of so vast an assembly. This difficulty brought into being a whole branch of physics concerned with calculating the overall or average properties of large numbers of particles. Just as statisticians will provide the average height, income, expectation of life, and so on, of the population of London, without knowing everything about every individual, so statistical physicists can work out average properties of molecules or atoms in large groups. This important branch of physics is called *Statistical Mechanics*. It was founded in the nineteenth century by Maxwell, Boltzmann, and Gibbs and is still being actively developed.

Consider now all the molecules in 1 cubic centimetre of air contained in a small box. They are continually bombarding the walls of the box and bouncing off. This hail of impacts (it is actually about 10^{23} impacts per square centimetre per second) is the cause of the pressure which the gas exerts against the walls of the box. Now suppose we pump air in until there is twice as much as before, though the box is still the same size and at the same temperature. This means that the density of the gas (*i.e.*, the mass of 1 unit of volume) has doubled. We should now expect twice as many impacts per second on the walls as before, and consequently twice the pressure. We therefore arrive at a conclusion that, if the volume and temperature are constant, the pressure of a gas is proportional to its density. This is one of the simplest statistical arguments that can be checked against observation; in fact, it stands the test very well.

Heat, Temperature, and Energy

The proviso about the temperature remaining the same is an important one for the following reason. In the nineteenth century there was much discussion about the nature of heat. To Joule we owe the now well-established view that heat is equivalent to mechanical work. In one of his experiments, in the 1840s, the work necessary to rotate paddle wheels against the resistance of water in a tank generated heat that caused a slight rise in the temperature of the water. Joule found out exactly how much work was equivalent to a given quantity of heat. However, one can do other things with work besides generate heat; in particular, work creates motion, as when one pushes a car. Bodies in motion possess a special form of energy, called kinetic energy, which is equal to the work done in accelerating them from a state of rest. We have, then, three closely connected ideas: work, heat, and kinetic energy. Now according to the views of the nineteenth century, which are still accepted, any heat given to a gas simply increases the kinetic energy of its molecules; the hotter the gas, the faster its molecules are moving. If, therefore, the gas in our box is allowed to get hotter, there is an increase in molecular speed, and the impacts on the walls become correspondingly more violent. But this means the pressure increases, so we have another law: if the density remains the same, the pressure increases if the temperature does.

Laws of Thermodynamics

Such considerations as these have been pursued with great elaboration and subtlety. The notions

of heat, temperature, energy, and work—familiar but vague in everyday life—have been given precise definitions, and the relations between them have been enshrined in the Laws of Thermodynamics. Enshrined is perhaps a suitable word, because these laws are so soundly and widely based on experimental results that they have greater prestige than any others in physics. If any proposed physical law comes in conflict with thermodynamics then so much the worse for that law—it has to be revised. It is sometimes asserted that no one is properly educated who does not understand the Second Law of thermodynamics. We cannot, therefore, leave this section without at least stating the two best known thermodynamic laws:

First Law: *If any physical system is given a quantity of heat, and if the system performs some work, then the energy of the system increases by an amount equal to the excess of heat given over work done.* This law asserts that heat, energy, and work are convertible one into the other, and that all such transactions balance exactly. This is one form of a principle accepted as fundamental in all science, *viz.*, the Principle of the Conservation of Energy, according to which energy can never be created or destroyed, but only changed from one form to another.

Second Law: *It is impossible to make an engine which will continuously take heat from a heat source and, by itself, turn it all into an equivalent amount of mechanical work.* In fact, all engines which produce work from heat—steam engines for example—always use only a fraction of the heat they take in and give up the rest to some relatively cool part of the machine. The Second Law makes this obligatory on all work-from-heat devices. This statement of the Second Law has an engineering ring about it and, indeed, it arose from the work of the nineteenth-century French engineer Carnot. Nevertheless, it can be rephrased in very abstract terms, and has been applied with unbroken success to all fields of science involving the transfer of heat and allied matters. It sets a definite limit to the kinds of physical process that can be conceived to take place. Nothing has been known to contravene it.

The States of Matter

The molecular motion in gases has been referred to in the previous section. Tacitly it was assumed that each molecule acted independently of all others, except that collisions occurred between them. In reality, molecules exert attractive forces on one another and, if a gas is cooled so that molecular movements become relatively sluggish, a time comes when the attractive forces succeed in drawing the molecules close together to form a liquid. This process is called condensation.

The molecules in a liquid are packed tightly together and they impede each others' movements. On the other hand, movement still persists, and the molecules struggle about like people in a milling crowd. Besides wandering about, the molecules vibrate. These motions represent the energy contained in the liquid.

The fact that the molecules, though irregularly packed, can still slip past one another and move from place to place, explains the essential property of liquids that distinguishes them from solids—ability to flow. As a matter of fact, although the rather vague assertion that in a liquid molecules are irregularly packed would be generally accepted, there is no agreed opinion on what the irregularity is actually like. Indeed, not only the precise structure of liquids, but the theory of liquids in general, is fraught with such considerable mathematical difficulties that the liquid state is much less well understood than the solid or gaseous.

Most solids are crystals. The popular idea of a crystal is of something which has a more or less regular geometrical form with faces that shut in the light—like snowflakes or gems. However, crystallinity really depends on a regular inner pattern of the atoms, and may or may not show itself on the visible surface. A lump of lead, for example, is crystalline, though it may not look it.

The actual arrangement of the atoms in a crystal can be extremely complex. Some are quite simple, however. The largest model of a crystal structure must surely be the 400-ft. "Atomium" building in the 1958 Brussels Exhibition. This consisted of eight balls, representing atoms, situated at the corners of a cube, and one more ball exactly in the middle. Imagine this repeated in all directions so that every ball is the centre of a cube whose corners are the eight neighbouring balls. This is known to crystallographers and physicists as the "body-centred cubic structure"; it is the actual arrangement of atoms in iron, sodium, chromium, and some other metals. If every ball, instead of being the centre of a cube, were the centre of a regular tetrahedron (a solid figure with four equal triangular faces), and had its four neighbours at the corners of the tetrahedron, then we should have the "diamond structure." This is how the carbon atoms are arranged in diamonds.

In crystals the atoms are locked into a regular ordered structure by attractive forces which give the solid its rigidity and prevent it from flowing. The atoms are so close together that any attempt to press them closer involves crushing or distorting the atoms—a process they resist strongly. This explains why solids (and liquids too) are so difficult to compress. Gases can easily be compressed because there is so much space between the molecules.

The distinction between solid and liquid is not so sharp as is commonly supposed. A lump of dough will not bounce, but is plastic; a steel ball-bearing is very elastic and bounces excellently, but one cannot mould it in the fingers. Neither dough nor steel qualifies for description as a liquid. There are, however, substances which can be moulded like plasticine into a ball that will then bounce very well on the floor like an elastic solid, and finally, if left on a flat table, will spread into a pool and drip off the edge like a liquid. There is no point in trying to force such things into rigid categories. One may say instead that for short, sharp impacts the material behaves like an elastic solid, but under long-sustained forces it flows like a liquid. The properties of these, and many other anomalous materials, are increasingly engaging the attention of those who study the science of flow—*rheology*. It is interesting to see how many familiar and important materials exhibit peculiar rheological behaviour—paint, dough, ball-pen ink, cheese, unset cement, and solutions of nylon and other plastics are only a few examples.

Inside a Crystalline Solid

We now return to our wallpaper analogy of crystal structure and give some free play to our visual imagination.

Suppose we have walls papered with a regular pattern of, say, roses, fuchsias, and green leaves. These represent the different kinds of atoms in the solid. Careful observation shows that the whole pattern is shimmering. The flowers and leaves are not stationary, but are undergoing slight random oscillations about their proper positions. In a crystal these movements are called thermal vibrations, and are never absent. The hotter the crystal, the more the vibration, and at a high enough temperature the vibrations become so great that the atoms get right out of position and the pattern disappears altogether, *i.e.*, the crystal melts. Thermal vibrations are essential to the theory of solids, and are responsible for numerous physical properties.

Next we note something extraordinary about some of the papered walls. On these the paper has been hung in irregular patches fitted together like a not very well-made jig-saw puzzle. Lines of roses which should be vertical are horizontal in some patches, oblique in others. This represents the situation in most ordinary solids, for they consist of many small pieces of crystal irregularly packed together. Such material is called *polycrystalline*, and the small pieces are *crystal grains*. Crystal grains may be almost any size, sometimes visible to the naked eye, as often on galvanised iron.

However, on one wall, we see excellent regularity and no obvious patches at all. The physicist would call this a *single crystal*, and several techniques exist for preparing them. Natural single crystals can be found, and there are some beautiful large single crystals of rock salt. But on examining the single crystal wall closely, we find a number of places where the paperhanger has failed to make adjacent pieces register perfectly—there is a slight disjointedness. This occurs in real single crystals, and the line along which the structure fails to register is called a *dislocation*. These are much studied by physicists because of their bearing on the mechanical properties of solids, on the yielding of metals under strong stress, for instance.

This by no means exhausts the possibilities of the wallpaper analogy; several other phenomena can be found. For example, in a place where there should be a fuchsia there is actually a daffodil—something completely foreign to the pattern. Or perhaps a small wrongly shaped leaf is jammed between the proper leaves in a place that should really be blank. These represent chemical impurity atoms. The first is called *substitutional*, because it occupies the position of an atom that should be there, the second is called *interstitial*, because it does not. Substitutional impurities of indium metal, deliberately added to the semi-conductor silicon, make possible the manufacture of transistors (*see* Section L). Some steels derive their valuable properties from interstitial carbon atoms within the iron pattern.

What physicists call a vacancy would occur if a flower or leaf were simply missing. Remembering that all the atoms are vibrating, we should not be surprised if occasionally an atom jumps into a neighbouring vacancy if there happens to be one, *i.e.*, the atom and the vacancy change places. Later this may occur again. In the course of time, a rose which was near the ceiling may make its way to the floor by jumping into vacant rose positions when they occur near enough. This process, which the physicist calls *diffusion*, is also analogous to the game in which numbers or letters can be moved about in a flat box because there is one vacant space to permit adjustment. The more vacancies there are in a crystal, the faster diffusion occurs. It is, in fact, very slow in solids, but is nevertheless evidence that apparently quiescent materials are really internally active.

Metals, Electricity, and Heat

There is ample evidence that inside metals there are large numbers of free electrons. To illuminate this statement let us take sodium metal as an example. One single sodium atom has a nucleus with eleven protons; there are therefore eleven electrons in the atom. The outermost one is easily detached, leaving a positively charged sodium ion behind. We may think of these ions arranged in the three-dimensional pattern characteristic of sodium crystals. It is the same as the iron structure previously described. The detached electrons, one per atom, occupy the spaces in between. The usual metaphor is that the structure of ions is permeated by a "gas" of electrons. Like all visualisations of fundamental particles, this must be taken as a rough approximation. The important point is that the electrons in the gas are not bound to individual atoms but may wander freely about the crystal, hindered only by the collisions they make with the vibrating ions.

This is the picture as it appeared to physicists of the first decade of this century, and we can explain many properties of metals with it. Naturally the theory has developed greatly since then, thanks to the great work of Lorentz, Sommerfeld, and Bloch; it now relies heavily on quantum theory, but it is surprising how little violence is done to modern ideas by the simple picture we are using.

The free electrons move randomly in all directions at thousands of miles per hour. If the metal is connected across a battery it experiences an electric field. Electrons are negatively charged particles, and are therefore attracted to the electrically positive end of the metal. They can move through the metal because they are free; this flow is not possible to those electrons which remain bound to the ions. The function of the battery is to keep the flow going and, for as long as it is going, it is the electric current.

The flow of electrons is not unimpeded. They

constantly collide with the ions and are deflected from the path of flow. This hindrance is what the electrician calls *electrical resistance*. The electric force, due to the battery or a dynamo, accelerates the electrons, thus giving them extra energy; but they lose this to the ions at collisions because the ions recoil and vibrate more than before. The net effect of innumerable collisions is to increase the thermal vibrations of the ions, *i.e.*, to make the metal hotter. This is the explanation of the fact well known to every user of electric irons; that electric current heats the conductor. If a strong current is passed through a wire, the heating is so great the wire glows, as in electric-light bulbs, or melts and breaks, as in blown fuses.

If one end of a metal rod is heated we soon feel the heat at the other end; metals are excellent thermal conductors. This is because the mobile free electrons carry the heat energy down the rod, passing it on to the ions by colliding with them. Substances without free electrons cannot do this, nor can they conduct electricity well; so we have, in the free electrons, an explanation of the fact that the good electrical conductors are the good heat conductors. For technical purposes, it would be useful to have electrical insulators that would conduct heat well, and *vice versa*; but this is almost a contradiction in terms, and one can only compromise.

Non-conductors and Semi-conductors

There are some elements, and numerous compounds, in which all the electrons are so tightly bound to their parent atoms that free electron flow is impossible. These materials are electrical and thermal insulators.

Let us return to our sodium atom. It readily loses its outer electron, forming a positive ion. The ion is very stable; indeed, its electron arrangement resembles the "closed shell" belonging to the inert gas neon. The chlorine atom, on the other hand, would have a very stable structure, resembling the inert gas argon, if only it could be given one extra electron to complete the closed shell. If the outer sodium electron were given to a chlorine atom we should have two stable ions, one positive and one negative. These would then attract each other and form a compound. This is just how common salt, sodium chloride, is formed, and its crystals consist of a regular network of alternate sodium and chlorine ions. As all the electrons are bound to ions, it is not surprising that salt will not conduct electricity or heat to any appreciable extent. Not all insulating compounds are built on this pattern, but all have structures which bind the electrons tightly.

We have seen (F20) that Nature does not permit a hard-and-fast distinction between solids and liquids; nor does she between conductors and insulators. Over a hundred years ago, Faraday knew of substances which would conduct electricity, but rather badly. A common one is the graphite in pencils. Such are the elements selenium, germanium, and silicon, and a considerable number of compounds. Such substances are called semi-conductors.

Semi-conductors conduct badly because they have so few free electrons, many thousands of times fewer than metals. In very cold germanium—say, 200 degrees below freezing—all the electrons are tightly bound to atoms and the substance is an insulator. It differs from normal insulators in that, on warming it, the gradually increasing thermal vibration of the crystal detaches some of the electrons, for they are only moderately tightly bound. The warmer the crystal becomes, the more of its electrons become detached and the better it conducts electricity. By about the temperature of boiling water, there are so many freed electrons that conduction is moderately good, though less good than in metals. This is basic semi-conductor behaviour. Because transistors were made of germanium, and because they are of such great technical importance, more knowledge has accumulated about germanium than about any other material. *See also* Transistor, Section L.

Magnetism

The most important thing about magnetism is that it is inseparably connected with electricity. Oersted showed this in July 1820, when he deflected a magnetic compass needle by passing an electric current through a wire near it. Since then, many experiments have shown that wherever a current flows there will certainly be a magnetic field in the surrounding space. The laws of this are very well known now—they are the Maxwell equations previously referred to (F14). However, most people first meet magnetism when, as children, they pick up pins with a magnet. Where is the electricity here? and what is a magnet?

The explanation of magnetism exemplifies beautifully the technique of explaining the bulk properties of matter in terms of fundamental particles. In the atoms the electrons are moving, and a moving electric charge constitutes an electric current. Therefore each moving electron is a tiny source of magnetism. It does not immediately follow that every atom is a source of magnetism because it might—and often does—happen that the magnetic effect of different electrons in the atom cancel out. In helium atoms, for example, the two electrons have equal but opposed magnetic effects. Nevertheless, some atoms and ions have a net effect called their *magnetic moment*. This simply means they behave like tiny magnets. Crystals containing such atoms will be magnetic, though the magnetism is much weaker than in ordinary magnets because the different atoms largely annul one another's effects. In a very limited number of crystals, however, the magnetic ions act on one another in a special way which forces all the atomic magnets to point in the same direction. The total effect of many co-operating atoms is very strong and the crystal becomes what we normally call a magnet. Iron acts like this, so do cobalt and nickel, the rarer elements gadolinium and dysprosium, and a fair number of alloys. On the whole, this behaviour, which is called *ferromagnetism*, is very rare. The reason for the co-operation of all the atomic magnets is not explained to everyone's satisfaction yet, though the key idea was given by Heisenberg in 1928.

In the section dealing with the electron it was pointed out that every electron has an *intrinsic* magnetic moment. This is in addition to any effect simply due to the electron's motion round a nucleus. The net effects of ions are therefore partly due to the intrinsic magnetism of electrons. In the ferromagnetic metals the latter is by far the most important contribution. Thus we pick up pins, and benefit from magnets in other ways, because innumerable fundamental particles act in co-operation for reasons that are still somewhat obscure. It is interesting to ask whether the electrons responsible for magnetism are the same free electrons that allow the metals to conduct electricity. It is thought not.

We are accustomed to think of magnets as metallic. Actually the magnet originally discovered by the Chinese was the mineral lodestone, which is a non-metallic oxide of iron. Nowadays a number of non-metallic magnets are made. They are called *ferrites*, and some are insulators and some are semi-conductors. The combination of magnetism and insulation is technically very valuable in radio, radar, and other applications. The explanation of ferrite behaviour is related to that of metallic ferromagnetism, but is not the same.

Conclusion.

The aim of the second part of this account of physics is to show how our conception of fundamental particles allows us to build theories of the properties of matter. This very aim shows that the two " major divisions " of physics referred to at the beginning (F10) are divided only in the way that labour is divided by co-operating workers to lighten the task. For the task of physics is a very great one—no less than to explain the behaviour of matter; and since the universe, living and inanimate, is made of matter, physics must necessarily underlie all the other sciences.

III. THE WORLD OF THE CHEMISTS

WHAT CHEMISTRY IS ABOUT

The science of chemistry is concerned with the properties of atoms, the laws governing their combination to form molecules, and, more generally, with the behaviour of materials composed of large numbers of molecules. Thus chemistry borders on or, rather, interpenetrates physics—a fact illustrated by the existence of professional journals devoted to "chemical physics" and "physical chemistry." Physics is more concerned with the fundamental nature of matter and radiation; chemistry concentrates on the ways in which atoms combine, or can be made to combine, with each other to form innumerable compounds. Chemistry also merges with the life sciences where it deals, as in biochemistry, with the properties of the complex molecular building blocks of living organisms, e.g., proteins, carbohydrates, nucleic acids. Because of its comprehensiveness, the science of chemistry has been subdivided into what were at one time convenient sub-sciences, e.g., organic chemistry, electrochemistry, but here too the borderlines are becoming progressively blurred. Our task here will be to outline some of the ideas in use by present-day chemists.

ELEMENTS AND COMPOUNDS

Electron Shells and Stability

The reader will find in Part II a brief description of the atom and definitions of atomic number, atomic weight, isotope, and other terms. The simplest atom is hydrogen (H) with atomic number 1. Some common elements with their chemical symbols and atomic numbers are:— carbon (C) 6; oxygen (O) 8; sodium (Na) 11; chlorine (Cl) 17; calcium (Ca) 20; silver (Ag) 47; and uranium (U) 92. Let us now consider atoms in more detail.

The electrons in atoms move in well-defined *orbits* and the orbits fall into well-defined groups called *shells*. If all the orbits in a shell have electrons actually present in them the shell is *filled* or *closed* and this confers on the shell an unusual stability or inertness. Conversely, unfilled shells lead to activity and the electrons in the incompletely filled shells largely determine the chemical and physical properties of the element and are responsible for the combination of atoms to form molecules. The inner shell, i.e., the one nearest the nucleus, can accommodate only two electrons (the element helium has just that number) and the next two shells can hold eight each. Large atoms, e.g., lead, radium, have many filled shells and, subject to special exceptions, the general rule is that the inner shells are the filled ones and the outer shell may be incomplete. Elements which have equal numbers of electrons in their outer shell resemble each other. Thus the elements with complete electronic shells are chemically unreactive gases, e.g., argon and neon (minor constituents of the atmosphere). Elements with just one electron in the outer shell are highly reactive metals, e.g., sodium and potassium, whereas those with just one electron too few are also reactive but are not metals, e.g., chlorine, bromine, iodine.

Molecules, Ions, and Bonds

The general tendency of matter is for those changes that are possible to go on happening until a lasting arrangement or *stable state* is reached. Atoms with closed shells are stable but atoms with unfilled shells can achieve stability in several ways, of which two are as follows:

(i) Electron sharing

When atoms share electrons, the resulting structure, composed of several atoms, is known as a molecule. The simplest case is the molecule of hydrogen, composed of two atoms each contributing one electron. Thus each atom will have a share of two electrons which is the number required to fill completely the inner shell. The shared electrons constitute a *chemical bond* and confer stability on the resulting hydrogen molecule.

A more complex molecule is carbon tetrachloride, CCl_4. Here the carbon atom with four electrons in its outer shell is bonded to four chlorine atoms each of which needs one electron to complete a set of eight. Thus by sharing the electrons each of the five atoms can form a complete shell of eight electrons. The properties of the resulting molecular species do not usually bear any resemblance to the constituent atoms. Whereas molecular chlorine is a gas and carbon is a solid, carbon tetrachloride is a liquid which finds application as a dry cleaning fluid.

(ii) Electron transfer

Another method of completing electron shells is by transfer of one or more electrons from an atom with one or two electrons in its outer shell to one with that number too few. Thus sodium, with one electron in its outer shell, will combine with chlorine, deficient in one electron. This results in two electronically stable species (ions), both of which carry net electric charges. Thus the sodium will now have a net positive charge of 1 unit (11 protons, 10 electrons), whereas the chlorine has an excess negative charge (17 protons, 18 electrons). Because of these electric charges, solutions of ionic substances conduct electricity and this property is utilised in industrial processes such as electroplating and in the extraction of metals from their ores.

Thus the electrons which participate in the formation of chemical bonds are those in partly-filled shells (valence electrons), and the simplest and most stable type of bonds are those in which two electrons are shared (a covalent bond) and those in which there is a net transfer of electrons (an ionic bond). Sometimes, in order to attain a complete electronic shell, a chemical bond will require the sharing of four or even six electrons. The resulting molecules are highly reactive and will readily, and sometimes violently, combine with other molecules or atoms to achieve the greater stability associated with the two-electron covalent bond.

Molecules must not be envisaged as rigid assemblies of atoms with electrons uniformly distributed around the various nuclei. The properties of molecules are best acccounted for by imagining the atomic nuclei to be vibrating about mean positions—the bonds acting like spiral springs, holding the nuclei together. The electrons form a mobile cloud of negative charge which sorrounds the nuclei. The valence electrons, constituting the bond between pairs of atoms, also have no fixed location but fluctuate about mean positions, more or less along the line joining the atoms. Although the electrons are shared, their mean position is not usually halfway between the two atoms but depends on the relative atomic sizes and charges. In the carbon–chlorine bond of carbon tetrachloride the valence electrons are subjected to electrical attractions due to 17 positive charges on the chlorine nucleus and 6 positive charges on the carbon nucleus. Although the forces due to the chlorine nucleus are partially compensated for by the intervening negative charges of the complete electronic shells, they are stronger than the forces from the carbon nucleus, and the valence electrons are therefore pulled towards the chlorine atom which thus attains a net negative charge, leaving the carbon with a corresponding positive charge. The magnitude of this charge is less than that of an ion, and the carbon–chlorine

Polar

Non - polar
Carbon tetrachloride   Ammonia   Water

Fig. 1. The arrangement in space of molecules CCl_4, NH_3, and H_2O.

bond should be symbolised $\overset{+}{C} - \overset{-}{Cl}$ to emphasise that separate positive and negative charges of equal magnitude are embodied in the structure, and are attracting each other as well as causing an electric field outside the molecule.

A pair of equal and opposite charges like this is called a *dipole* and is the electrical analogue of the ordinary magnet which has north and south *poles* instead of charges. Chemical bonds made with dipoles are called *polar bonds*. Most molecules, both simple and complex, are bound with polar bonds, but in the case of CCl_4 the four bonds are symmetrically arranged in space so that the electric effects of the dipoles cancel each other outside the molecule which therefore does not, as a whole, act like a dipole. On the other hand, the bond dipoles in a molecule may not cancel in this way (Fig. 1) in which case the whole molecule will possess the properties of a dipole *e.g.*, when subjected to an electric field it will rotate to align itself with the field just as a compass needle will line up with a magnetic field.

Atomic and Molecular Weights

The masses of the electron and proton were determined early in the 20th century by ingenious experiments. The electronic mass is extremely small, about 9×10^{-28}g and the mass of a hydrogen atom is 1.7×10^{-24}g, which indicates that the proton is 1,837 times heavier than the electron and that the mass of the atom is almost completely confined to the nucleus.

The molecular weight of a compound is the sum of the atomic weights of all the constituent atoms, *e.g.*, water (H_2O) and ethyl alcohol (C_2H_5OH) have molecular weights 18 and 46 respectively. This means that the alcohol molecule weighs more than the water molecule in the ratio 46 to 18. If therefore we take 18 g of water and 46 g of alcohol, both quantities will contain the same number of molecules. Similarly, 1 litre of water with 342 g of sugar dissolved in it, and 1 litre with 58.5 g of salt, will again contain the same number of dissolved molecules because the molecular weights of sugar ($C_{12}H_{22}O_{11}$) and salt ($NaCl$) are 342 and 58.5 respectively. In each case the number of grams taken is numerically equal to the molecular weight and this amount is called 1 *mole* of a substance or the *gram molecular weight*.

The word mole may also be used for atoms or ions and means, in general, that amount of molecules (or atoms or ions, as the case may be) such that the total number of them is equal to the number of atoms in 12 g of carbon (F11(1)). This number, called Avogadro's number, is approximately 6×10^{23}. Thus one mole of any substance contains 6×10^{23} molecules of that substance and this fact makes the mole a very useful unit both in theory and practice.

Forces between Molecules

Something has already been said (F20–21) about the differences between solids, liquids, and gases and we may now put the question: what forces are responsible for the organisation of molecules in liquids or solids and their disorganisation in the gaseous state? Questions of this kind are of profound interest to chemists, physicists, and biologists.

unpolarized

polarized

Fig. 2. Mutual polarisation of molecules by distortion of their electron clouds.

The forces which act between molecules depend mainly on the fact that the electrons orbiting a molecule form a mobile cloud of negative charge. If a polar molecule is brought up to another molecule, then the latter will become polarised, *i.e.*, its electronic cloud will be displaced with respect to the nucleus. This is shown in Fig. 2 and it is apparent that the formerly non-polar molecule has acquired a temporary polar character. In this state it will be able to polarise other nearby molecules, and the ease with which molecules are polarised depends on how strongly the electrons are held in position by the nuclear charge, and this in turn depends on the mean distance between the nucleus and the electronic cloud. Thus, the larger the molecule, the more easily the electron cloud can be distorted by a nearby dipole and hence the stronger are the intermolecular forces. These forces are attractions or *binding forces*. They can be disrupted by violent vibratory or other motions whose source is heat, as when a solid is first melted and then boiled and its molecules fly off in all directions to form a gas. Since strong attractions are due to ease of polarisation, the latter must influence the melting and boiling points of substances.

As a general rule substances composed of small molecules have low boiling points and are gaseous at room temperature and atmospheric pressure, because when they approach each other during a collision, the forces they exert upon one another are not strong enough to produce cohesion and condensation. Examples of this type of behaviour are hydrogen and helium which boil at −253°C and −269°C respectively. Larger molecules are likely to be liquid at ordinary temperature, and if the forces between them are even stronger, they may be solid. Thus carbon tetrachloride, which contains five atoms, boils at 77°C, whereas glucose, with 24 atoms ($C_6H_{12}O_6$)

is a solid, melting at 146°C. Chemical compounds which are ionic in character are usually crystalline solids with high melting points (e.g., common salt, quicklime) because ions, possessing permanent charges, exert stronger forces on one another than do molecules.

Metals and Salts

It has already been explained that chemical elements are conveniently classified according to the number of electrons in the outer shell, because it is mainly those electrons which participate in chemical reactions and make bonds. Thus elements with 1, 2, or at most 3 electrons in the outer shell (e.g., sodium, calcium, aluminium respectively) will undergo reactions which enable them to lose those electrons, i.e., they will attempt to form ionic compounds. These elements are metallic, and when solid or liquid, conduct heat and electricity. On the other hand, elements which need 1 or 2 electrons to form a complete shell (e.g., chlorine, oxygen respectively) can also form ionic compounds by reacting with a metal, though these elements are themselves classed as non-metals and can be gases, liquids, or solids at room temperature. When a metal atom combines with one or more atoms of non-metal, the resulting ionic compound is termed a salt. Common salts of the metal sodium are the chloride, carbonate, and sulphate. Ot er examples of industrially important salts are silver bromide (used in photographic films), calcium sulphate (plaster of paris), and magnesium sulphate (epsom salts.)

Metals do not normally occur in the pure state in nature but are found as compounds (ores), sometimes of a complex structure. The science of metallurgy is concerned with the extraction of metals from their ores, and with their properties and uses. Since many metals possess useful mechanical and electrical properties, they find use as materials of construction, and hence the knowledge of their properties and behaviour under different conditions is of great importance. One need onl remember the imperfectly understood phenomenon of metal fatigue which led to the crashes of the early Comet aircraft to appreciate how vital is the contribution of metallurgy to the process of engineering.

Although metals can be mixed with other metals to form alloys, the large majority of metallic compounds are the salts in which the metal is present as positive ion (cation), and the negative ion (anion) is composed of one or several non-metallic elements. Common anions are the chloride, bromide, iodide, nitrate, sulphate, phosphate, and carbonate. Metals with simple electron structures can form only one type of ion. Thus sodium, with one outer shell electron forms Na^+ and 1 electron; calcium with two outershell electrons forms Ca^{++} and 2 electrons. There are, however, a number of metals with more complex electronic structures, involving partially filled inner electronic shells and these can exist in a variety of ionic forms. They include many metals which find application as structural materials, e.g., iron, copper, gold, platinum, nickel, chromium. For instance, iron can exist as Fe^{++} or Fe^{+++} and the process of removing a further electron from Fe^{++} is termed oxidation, and any chemical reagent which is capable of bringing about such a process is an oxidising agent. Conversely the addition of an electron is called reduction and the reagent which can give up an electron is a reducing agent. Thus the conversion of Fe^{++} to Fe^{+++} is achieved by an oxidising agent which is itself reduced in the process. Processes involving the transfer of one or several electrons are called Redox (reduction-oxidation) reactions and are of great importance in many branches of chemical technology and biochemical processes.

The non-metals which feature in the anions of salts include the well-known and industrially important elements, sulphur, phosphorus, iodine, bromine, and the common gases oxygen, nitrogen, and chlorine. Table 1 (F26) provides a summary of the classification of a few of the more common elements according to the number of electrons in their outer shell. Although some of these elements, e.g., aluminium, undoubtedly possess metallic properties and others, e.g., nitrogen, are non-metals, the dividing lines are not always so clearly defined and most of the compounds formed by elements near the centre of Table 1 are of the covalent type.

ACIDS AND BASES

pH Values

Hydrogen occupies a unique position in Table 1 According to its electronic structure it can be classified with sodium and potassium, as having one electron in its outer shell. It therefore readily forms cations, H^+, but it can hardly be called a metal. Having lost its electron, what remains is a proton (F10), a single positive charge. Thus we can compare sodium chloride, Na^+ Cl^-, with H^+ Cl^-, but whereas sodium chloride exists in ionic form in the solid and liquid states and in solution, HCl is a covalent gas in the pure state, but readily ionises in solution, because the H^+ does not exist on its own, but attaches itself to a solvent molecule. Thus when HCl is dissolved in water, it ionises and the H^+ combines with the water: $HCl + H_2O \rightarrow (H^+ \ H_2O) + Cl^-$. This is a typical example of what is known as an acid-base reaction, an acid being defined as a substance which in solution can produce one or several protons (hydrogen ions), and the base as being a substance which can accept protons from an acid. In the above reaction HCl is the acid and H_2O the base, and the reaction consists of the transfer of the proton from acid to base. Other common acids include sulphuric acid ($2H^+ + SO_4^{--}$) and nitric acid ($H^+ + NO_3^-$). When ammonia (NH_3), a covalent gas, is dissolved in water, an acid base reaction also occurs: $NH_3 + HOH \rightarrow (NH_3.H^+) + OH^-$. Here water acts as acid, since it donates a proton to the ammonia, forming NH_4^+, the ammonium ion. When a proton is removed from water, the remainder, a negatively charged ion, is called the hydroxyl ion, OH^-. It has now been established that water can act either as an acid or a base, and in pure water two molecules of water can react: $H_2O + H_2O = (H^+ \ H_2O) + OH^-$, so that one molecule behaves as an acid and the other as a base. This phenomenon is called self-ionisation and also occurs in other solvents.

The extent to which water ionises is very small, thus 1 litre of " pure " water contains 10^{-7} moles each of H^+ and OH^- ions. However, when a stronger acid, i.e., one that can produce more hydrogen ions than water, is added, the concentration of hydrogen ions increases and that of OH^- ions decreases correspondingly, so that the product of the amounts of H^+ and OH^- ions will always be constant and equal to 10^{-14} (see law of chemical equilibrium). It is important to be able to compare the strengths of acid solutions and this is done by reference to the concentration of hydrogen ions. The numerical measure is obtained by taking minus the logarithm of the hydrogen ion concentration and this number is called the pH value of the solution. Thus in pure water, the hydrogen ion concentration is 10^{-7} moles per litre and the pH value is therefore 7.

Vinegar, which is a dilute solution of acetic acid in water, has a hydrogen ion concentration of about 10^{-4} moles per litre; its pH is 4. Thus, solutions with a pH value below 7 are acidic (they contain an excess of hydrogen ions) and those with a pH value greater than 7 are basic (they contain an excess of OH^- ions). Many chemical and most biological reactions are extremely sensitive to small changes in the pH and steps must frequently be taken to adjust the pH to an optimum value for a given reaction. This is achieved by means of substances known as buffers, which have the capacity of mopping up or producing hydrogen ions and to maintain a constant pH. An example of this buffering action is the prevention of stomach acidity by the use of bicarbonates.

THE HYDROGEN BOND AND WATER

Where hydrogen is covalently bonded to a small, fairly strongly electronegative atom, i.e., one which requires 1, 2, or 3 electrons to fill its outer shell, the one electron which can be supplied by hydrogen is not shared equally by the two

TABLE 1

ELECTRONS IN OUTER SHELL (VALENCE ELECTRONS)

1	2	3	4	5	6	7	8
Hydrogen							
	Magnesium	Aluminium	Carbon	Nitrogen	Oxygen		Neon
Sodium	Calcium		Silicon	Phosphorus	Sulphur	Chlorine	Argon
Potassium						Bromine	
Silver	Radium					Iodine	

Metals
Positive ions

Covalent

Non-metals
Negative ions
or covalent

atoms but is pulled closer to the electronegative atom. The most common examples of this phenomenon are liquid water and ice. Here the electronegative atom is oxygen, as shown in **Fig. 3.** The dots represent the outer shell electrons of oxygen and the crosses the electrons contributed by hydrogen. The oxygen atom 1 exerts a strong pull on the lone electron supplied by the hydrogen, so that at the position of the oxygen atom 2 it appears as though the hydrogen is in fact an ion (H^+), devoid of electrons, and since a pair of electrons of oxygen atom 2 are already pointing in the direction of this hydrogen atom, a weak bond will be formed. Thus the " hydrogen bond " consists of one hydrogen atom between two oxygen atoms. The actual strength of such a bond is only about 10 per cent of that of an ordinary covalent bond, and not very much energy is required to disrupt it. In terms of most chemical reactions the hydrogen bond is therefore not of great significance, but it is vital in reactions which occur with small changes in energy, *i.e.*, biochemical reactions, where the making and breaking of hydrogen bonds is frequently of supreme importance. It must also be

FIG. 3. Formation of a hydrogen bond between neighbouring water molecules.

borne in mind that all biological reactions take place in an aqueous medium which is highly

hydrogen-bonded and it is well known that water is the essential substrate for all life processes, although it is not always appreciated that water is also the most anomalous of chemical compounds. It is one of very few substances that are denser in the liquid than in the solid state (ice floats on water) and it is unique in that upon heating the liquid from its melting point to 4°C, a further contraction takes place. From our discussion on intermolecular forces it is apparent that a chemical compound made up of small molecules, being not very easily polarised, should exist in the gas state at ordinary temperature, and this is the case for other substances whose molecules have approximately the same dimensions as those of water, *viz.*, CO_2 (carbon dioxide), NH_3, and HCl. The abnormal physical properties of water are due to the extensive hydrogen bonding which exists in its liquid and solid forms. Indeed, ice is the most perfectly hydrogen-bonded structure, and liquid water appears to retain some of this regular crystalline order, the main difference being that such crystalline regions are short-lived, forming and melting many million times every second. Nevertheless a snapshot of short enough exposure would no doubt reveal ice-like regions in liquid water.

ORGANIC CHEMISTRY—THE CHEMISTRY OF CARBON COMPOUNDS

Of all the hundred-odd elements which are now known and whose properties have been studied in detail, carbon is unique in the manner in which it can combine with itself to give rise to very large molecules (polymers) which can have molecular weights of several millions. Carbon compounds form the basis of the substances which make up living organisms, and thus the chemistry of carbon compounds is known as organic chemistry. Reference to **Table 1** (above) shows that carbon is capable of forming 4 covalent bonds, and the simplest organic compound is methane, CH_4 (the main constituent of North Sea gas). The hydrogen atoms are capable of being replaced by other

TABLE 2

Class of Compound	Elements	Example	Origin or Use
Hydrocarbon	C,H	Octane Benzene	Nat. oil deposit, fuel Coal tar, solvent, and raw material
Alcohols	C,H,O	Ethyl alcohol	Formed by fermentation of sugar
Amides	C,H,O,N	Acetamide	Constituents of synthetic polymers, *e.g.*, nylon
Lipids	C,H,O	Olive oil	Found in plant seeds, used as food energy
Carbohydrates	C,H,O	Sugar, starch, cellulose	Occur in Nature—sources of energy and plant structural materials
Amino acids	C,H,N,O,(S)	Glycine, alanine	Building blocks of proteins
Steroids	C,H,O	Cholesterol	Hormone substances
Terpenes	C,H,O	Geraniol	Occur in Nature—perfumes

atoms or groups of atoms, including carbon. Thus by replacing one of the C—H bonds by a C—C bond, $CH_3.CH_3$ (or C_2H_6) can be obtained. This process can continue and result in long chains of carbon atoms and the compounds so obtained form a series whose general formula is C_nH_{2n+2}, where n is any whole number. The compound C_8H_{18} is known as octane and forms the basis of petrol. The larger members of the series are the paraffin waxes. Starting again from methane and replacing one hydrogen atom by oxygen + hydrogen so that the carbon is covalently bonded to the oxygen, methyl alcohol, CH_3OH is obtained. Once again this is the first member of a series, the alcohols, whose second member, C_2H_5OH (ethyl alcohol), forms the basis of all alcoholic drinks.

In addition to ordinary 2-electron covalent bonds carbon also forms bonds involving 4 and 6 shared electrons. These bonds are much less stable than the ordinary covalent bonds so that compounds possessing them are extremely reactive. Carbon atom chains can also form side branches or closed rings, usually containing 5 or 6 carbon atoms. Furthermore, the important group of aromatic compounds are based on benzene, C_6H_6, in which the 6 carbon atoms form a planar ring and each has one hydrogen atom bonded to it. The remaining electrons form a mobile pool, so that the whole molecule is easily polarised and can be made to react with many other substances. It follows that a large variety of compounds can be obtained using only the elements carbon, hydrogen, and oxygen. If the elements nitrogen, phosphorus, sulphur are included, as well as chlorine, bromine, and iodine, the number of possible compounds becomes even larger. Table 2 provides some examples of classes of organic compounds and their occurrence in nature or their industrial application.

To achieve the growth of molecules by the elongation of the carbon chains is not usually feasible technically, although in nature this is a common process, brought about by enzymes (F27(2)). However, some molecules, especially those with four or six electron bonds, can react with one another to form polymers. In addition many molecules can be made to react (condense) to form more complex molecules with the elimination of a simple molecule, such as water or ammonia. Examples of the latter type of polymer are the proteins which are composed of amino-acid units (Table 2), the polysaccharides (carbohydrates), such as starch and cellulose, made up of condensed sugar molecules (Table 2), and synthetic condensation polymers of acids and alcohols known as polyesters, e.g., Terylene. Additional polymers also figure largely in chemical technology, examples being polyvinyl chloride (PVC), polyolefines (e.g., polythene) and polystyrene.

CHEMICAL REACTIONS

Laws Governing Chemical Reactions

Large amounts of energy are locked up within molecules and some of this energy is used up in chemical reaction. Like other forms of energy (e.g., electrical and mechanical) it is subject to certain laws, such as the law of conservation of energy which states that energy cannot be created or destroyed, but can be converted from one form to another. Thus, part of the chemical energy during the reaction may be converted into heat, and this is frequently the case (F20).

Another very important law deals with the extent to which a chemical reaction will proceed. The reaction of nitrogen with hydrogen, which combine to give ammonia, forms the basis of the fixation of atmospheric nitrogen in the manufacture of fertilisers. The two gases combine in the molecular ratio of 1 : 3, two molecules of ammonia being produced, i.e., $N_2 + 3H_2 = 2NH_3$. However, ammonia also decomposes to form nitrogen and hydrogen, and at a certain stage the rates of the two opposing reactions will be equal and the mixture is then said to be at equilibrium. The position of the equilibrium, i.e., the amount of ammonia formed, can be influenced by changes in temperature, pressure, or the amounts of the reacting substances, and the law of chemical equilibrium states that, if any factor governing an equilibrium is altered, then the equilibrium will shift in an attempt to counter the imposed alteration. Thus, in the ammonia synthesis, if ammonia is removed then more nitrogen and hydrogen will react in trying to re-establish the equilibrium. Furthermore, the reaction between hydrogen and nitrogen proceeds with the evolution of heat, so, if the temperature of the gas mixture is raised (i.e., heat is added) then the equilibrium will readjust itself in an attempt to nullify the imposed change, and accordingly some ammonia will decompose into hydrogen and nitrogen, because this process absorbs heat.

The laws governing the influence of temperature, pressure, and chemical composition on reactions are termed chemical thermodynamics and the effects described can be calculated in quantitative terms. Some of the problems of chemical engineering are concerned with maximising yields of chemical reactions, while at the same time reconciling the necessary conditions with the economics of the process, e.g., cost of plant, materials, and fuel.

One other important consideration is the speed with which chemical reactions proceed, and the time taken to reach equilibrium (chemical kinetics). This cannot be predicted by the laws of chemical thermodynamics. According to thermodynamic calculations, gaseous hydrogen and oxygen will react to form liquid water, but this reaction can be so slow that even in a million years not very much water would be formed.

Catalysts.

Molecules react as a result of collisions, during which the energy due to the collision must be channelled into the chemical bond which is to be broken or to be made. Although at ordinary pressure and temperature molecules collide many million times every second, if all these collisions were to result in chemical reaction, then all reactions would occur with explosive violence. In fact, only a very small number of collisions are of a high enough energy for reaction to take place. This energy, termed the energy of activation, is therefore an important factor controlling the rate of a chemical reaction. The combination of hydrogen and oxygen normally has a large energy of activation and the two gases do not react to form water, although thermodynamics predicts that the reaction is feasible. Reaction rates can be increased, i.e., the activation energy lowered, if certain solids are added, on which one or several of the reacting species are adsorbed. The bond formed between the added solid (e.g., platinum) and the reacting gas is strong enough to weaken other bonds in the molecules, so that, on collision with another molecule, reaction takes place more readily. The solid which itself does not participate in the chemical reaction, is called a catalyst. Its function is to promote chemical reactions between substances which, because of the high activation energy, would not react in its absence. Catalysts find applications not only in many industrial processes but are also extensively used by living organisms, where they are called enzymes. Current theories hold that the reacting molecule fits into a hole or groove, like a key into a lock, on the enzyme protein where it is held while the reaction takes place; an example of an enzyme catalysed reaction is the breakdown of starch by the body. This consists of several steps, each of which is controlled by its own specific enzyme. These biological catalysts are much more efficient than those used in synthetic reactions, both in their specificity and in the lowering of the energy of activation (i.e., the increase in the reaction rate). Sometimes a foreign molecule which bears a similarity to the molecule whose reaction is to be catalysed, will combine with a catalyst. If this foreign molecule is very strongly held by the catalyst then the latter can no longer perform its function and is said to be poisoned. This is also true for enzymes: e.g., carbon monoxide and cyanides act as poisons by combining with certain important enzymes and thus inhibit the biochemical reactions on which the functioning of organs depends.

SOME USEFUL APPLICATIONS OF CHEMISTRY

The application of basic chemical and physical principles to the manufacturing industries has led to the technological revolution which began at the turn of the century and is still gathering momentum. Although it is impossible to cover fully the areas in which the chemical sciences find application, a few of the more important fields are noted below:

Electrochemistry

Electrochemistry deals with processes in which chemical energy is converted into electrical energy or *vice versa*. The most common examples are the dry battery and the lead storage battery (L15), although the generation of electricity by fuel cells (L47) is fast becoming of industrial importance. Conversely, if a current is passed through an ionic solution, a chemical reaction will take place, and this principle is employed in the electrolytic refining of metal ores and in metal plating processes.

Surface Chemistry

Surface chemistry is based on the fact that solid and liquid surfaces have properties which are different from those of matter in the bulk state. A molecule A situated in the bulk interacts with its neighbours, but the various forces will cancel, as shown in Fig. 4. For a molecule B in the

SURFACE

FIG. 4—Surface Forces: molecules within the solid (or liquid) are subject to balanced forces, but for molecules in the surface there is a resultant downward force.

surface there is a net inward pull. The surface is therefore a high energy state and thermodynamics predicts that substances will try to minimise their total surface area. In a liquid this leads to the formation of spherical drops. The solid, on the other hand, will attract vapours and liquids which deposit surface films and thus reduce its surface energy. One application of adsorbed films, catalysis, has already been discussed.

Surface effects become significant in processes where the ratio of surface area to bulk volume is large, for instance, where matter is finely dispersed. This is the case in the technology of paints, printing inks, detergency, dairy products, air and water pollution, and solutions of polymers. The above-mentioned properties are also utilised in processes which involve the deposition of substances on surfaces, *e.g.*, textile finishing (water- and crease-proofing), metal coating, herbicides, cosmetics, and adhesives. Perhaps the most important field in which surface behaviour is one of the determining factors is biology. All living cells are separated from each other by membranes, and nutrients and other chemicals are adsorbed on, and diffuse through, these membranes, the nature and action of which are as yet very imperfectly understood (F33).

Photochemistry

Like other forms of energy, light, both visible and ultraviolet, can cause chemical changes to take place and, conversely, some reactions will give rise to the emission of radiation, *e.g.*, fluorescence. The ultimate source of most of the energy on earth is the radiation from the sun which, by the process of photosynthesis (F32), can be converted by green plants into the chemical energy stored in coal, oil, and carbohydrates.

The mechanism of photosynthesis is one of the most baffling problems in chemical kinetics.

In photography a film of gelatin, in which are embedded small grains of silver bromide, is exposed to light, when a " latent image " is formed. This is believed to consist of submicroscopic specks of silver in some of the grains, but the mechanism of its formation is still uncertain. The latent image can be " developed " into a negative image (silver) which is then " fixed " by dissolving away the unreduced silver bromide.

Analytical Chemistry

This is an important branch of Chemistry and deals with the identification and quantitative estimation of substances, often in complex mixtures. Where a quantitative analysis is to be achieved, the component under study has first to be separated in the pure state and then a suitable method must be found to determine its concentration in the mixture. In earlier days most analytical techniques were based on chemical reactions which were specific for the compound to be separated. Thus, sodium chloride and sodium sulphate can be separated by making use of the fact that many metal sulphates are insoluble in water, so that if a solution of, say, barium chloride is added to the mixture, barium sulphate will precipitate as solid and can be removed from the sodium chloride by filtration. If the amount of mixture initially used and the amount of precipitated barium sulphate are known, then, from the chemical formulae for barium and sodium sulphates, $BaSO_4$ and Na_2SO_4, it is easy to calculate the percentage of sodium sulphate in the original mixture.

During the last 25 years chemical analytical techniques have gradually been superseded by much more refined physical methods. Most important among these are the spectroscopic methods which can distinguish between small differences in energies associated with the vibrational motions of different chemical bonds. Some of these techniques not only measure energy differences but can detect minute amounts of energy, such as the energy liberated by a burning candle at a distance of 1 mile.

The detection, identification, and sometimes the quantitative estimation of very minor constituents of mixtures is frequently of great importance in industrial processes and products. For instance the presence of 1 g of iron in a ton of edible oil will rapidly cause the oil to turn rancid. Another example of the importance of traces of chemical compounds is provided by flavour and aroma of foodstuffs and perfumes. Frequently the characteristic, agreeable odour of a product is due to minute concentrations of one or several fairly simple organic compounds which at higher concentrations possess a quite unpleasant odour. The isolation of these compounds from natural products such as fruit or flowers and their identification provides a continuous challenge to the ingenuity of the analytical chemist.

Conclusion

It will now be readily seen that the science of chemistry covers a large field which extends from the very simple molecules, such as H_2O, to the complex naturally occurring molecules with molecular weights of several millions. It involves very fundamental studies, ranging from the nature of the forces between atoms and the how and why of apparently simple chemical reactions, to the very applied problems encountered in the manufacture of high-strength construction materials. Among new fields which have developed rapidly during recent years petroleum chemicals rank high. This industry, which is centered on the oil companies, produces a large variety of substances, such as detergents, polymer raw materials, solvents, dyestuffs, fats and waxes, from by-products obtained during oil refining. Pharmaceutical chemistry, too, is rapidly developing and attempts are being made not only to synthesise new drugs but to gain a better understanding of the mechanism of drug action.

Probably the most significant developments during the next twenty years will occur in the field of biochemistry. The elucidation of the structure and genetic functions of nucleic acids and some proteins has provided the impetus for further investigation into the chemistry and physics of these and other biologically active molecules. Other outstanding problems which may well be solved in the not too distant future include the mechanism of membrane action, muscle contraction and nerve impulse propagation in molecular terms. Where a hundred years ago the sciences of physics, chemistry, and biology parted

ways to follow their own separate paths, they are now seen to be converging and the areas of overlap are gradually increasing, as the molecular concepts of chemistry are providing a means of studying biological processes in terms of established physical laws and mechanisms. This part of the story will now be taken up in the section that follows.

IV. BIOLOGY—THE SCIENCE OF LIFE

WHAT BIOLOGY IS ABOUT

Biology embraces the study of all living things which exist on earth at the present time and also the recognisable remains of those that are extinct. Living things or organisms range from the apparently simple micro-organisms such as viruses and bacteria to the largest animals and plants.

Living Processes

The enormous variation and complexity of living processes make the task of understanding and defining life a very difficult one. Every living organism undergoes continual physical and chemical changes which, in spite of their diversity, are referred to as the metabolism of the organism. Metabolism involves the processing of food materials, the production of waste products, and all the intermediate stages between these whereby energy and matter are provided for the operation, maintenance, and growth of the organism. These reactions are under very exact chemical or nervous control at every stage and can be slowed down or speeded up as the need arises. Thus the organism can react to changes in the environment in which it lives, adjusting its activities in relation to the external changes. Finally, organisms can reproduce either in an identical or very slightly modified form. In this process new individuals are produced and the species continues to survive. Differences between offspring and parents can, under certain circumstances, act cumulatively over many generations and so form the basis of evolutionary change in which new species of organism are ultimately formed.

Molecular Biology

It has been evident for many years that the most fundamental aspects of these living processes occur in basic structural units known as cells. We shall examine this level of organisation first before we attempt to look at the larger questions of the organisation of multicellular animals and plants and their interactions in groups or populations. The study of living processes at the molecular and cell level has been given a tremendous impetus in recent years by the advent of new techniques which enable microscopic and submicroscopic parts of cell to be examined. Physicists, chemists, and mathematicians have found themselves working alongside biologists in this field and several of the very notable advances have been made by physical scientists. At this level of organisation the traditional division of Biology into Botany, the study of plants, and Zoology, the study of animals, has little meaning. Even the more recent Genetics, the study of inheritance, Biophysics and Biochemistry, concerned with the physics and chemistry of organisms, and Cytology, the study of cell structure, are losing such identity as they may once have had. Molecular biology is a term frequently used in describing this rapidly expanding and fascinating field of research.

EVOLUTION

Introduction.—It is commonly thought that the great 19th cent. naturalist Charles Darwin was the first person to suggest that life had continually evolved. However, the idea that species of living organisms could change over long periods of time

was considered by some Greek writers and, much later, by the Frenchmen Buffon and Lamarck at the end of the 18th cent. Further, the work of the 18th cent. geologists such as James Hutton and William Smith provided a basis without which Darwin's contribution would have been impossible. Hutton showed that the earth's surface had undergone prolonged upheavals and volcanic eruptions with consequent changes in sea level. This implied that the earth was much older than had previously been supposed. Smith developed a method of dating the geological strata by means of the fossils found in them and demonstrated that widely different types of animals and plants existed at different periods of the earth's history. As described in the previous section a general picture is presented of the evolution of organisms from the simple to the complex and from the aquatic to the terrestrial environment. These discoveries were in conflict with the Biblical account in the book of Genesis and, although various attempts were made to explain them away or discredit them, it became abundantly clear that through millions of years life has been continually changing, with new species constantly arising and many dying out. Before considering Darwin's major contribution to the theory of evolution it will be appropriate to outline briefly the various lines of evidence which indicate that, in fact, evolution has taken place.

The Evidence for Evolution

1. *The Geological Record.*—It has already been pointed out that successively younger rocks contain fossil remains of different and relatively more complex organisms. The spore-bearing plants preceded the gymnosperms and the angiosperms arose much later. Similarly in the vertebrate series the fish appeared before the amphibia which were followed by the reptiles and later by the air breathing, warm-blooded birds and mammals. On a more restricted level the rocks provide even greater support for the occurrence of evolution. For example, the evolution of the horse has been worked out in great detail from the small Eohippus which was about a foot high and had four digits on the forefeet and three on the hind feet to the large one-toed animal living today. However, such complete series are rare and the geological record is very incomplete. There are a number of gaps, particularly between the major groups of organisms. No satisfactory fossil evidence is known of the ancestors of the angiosperms (F43) and although some may be discovered it could be that they did not grow in conditions which favoured their preservation as fossils. On the other hand, Archæopteryx provides an indisputable link between the reptiles and the birds.

Another important point should also be made about the geological record. Although we talk about the age of fishes, the age of reptiles and so on it must be emphasised that these are the periods during which particular groups were abundant or even dominant. Each group probably originated many millions of years before it became widespread. Further, some groups, such as the giant reptiles and the seed-ferns, died out completely whereas others, the fishes and true ferns for example, are still common today. However, even in the latter groups there is evidence that they have continued to evolve so that many fishes and ferns that exist today are very different from those of the Devonian and Carboniferous periods (F48). On the other hand, the geological record also shows that some species, for example the

Maiden-hair tree, have remained unaltered for many millions of years.

2. *Geographical Distribution.*—Nearly all the marsupials or pouched mammals are found in the Australian continent which was cut off from the mainland about 60 million years ago. All the fossil evidence indicates that at that time the eutherian or placental mammals did not yet exist. The marsupials are the only naturally occurring mammals in Australia (F37(1)) but since the isolation of the continent the group has given rise to a large number of species very similar in appearance to those which evolved elsewhere in the world among the eutherian mammals. There are marsupials which look like wolves, dogs, cats and squirrels; yet they have no close biological relationships to these animals. Further, some marsupials such as the kangaroos have evolved which are unlike any other creatures in the rest of the world. Quite clearly the isolation of Australia so long ago has resulted in the evolution of these distinct types. A similar small-scale effect of isolation was studied by Darwin in the Galapagos islands where each has its own distinct flora and fauna which differ also from those of the S. American mainland.

3. *Anatomy.*—The comparative study of the development and mature structure of the mammalian body provides much evidence that all the species have evolved from a single ancestral stock. Although the arm of an ape, the leg of a dog, the flipper of a whale and the wing of a bat appear very different externally they are all built on the same skeletal plan. It would be difficult to explain such similarities unless they had all evolved from a common type. There is also evidence that the early development of an animal recapitulates its biological history to a certain extent. For example, the gill slits found in fish are formed during the early stages in the development of a mammal although later they disappear. Finally, apparently useless vestigial structures sometimes occur which would be inexplicable unless regarded in the light of an evolutionary history. In man a small appendix and vestiges of a third eyelid occur but these are functionless although in other animals such structures are well developed and functional, *e.g.*, the appendix in the rabbit.

4. *Human Selection.*—During his brief history on earth modern man has continually selected and bred animals and plants for his own use. We have only to look at the various breeds of dogs which have been developed from a single wild type to see that under certain circumstances great structural divergence can occur in a species even in a relatively short time.

The Darwinian Theory of Evolution.—Darwin amassed a great deal of information such as that outlined above which convinced him that evolution of life had taken place over millions of years. His was the first real attempt to collect all the evidence scientifically and no other satisfactory alternative explanation of all the facts he presented has been proposed. Perhaps even more important was his attempt to explain *how* evolution had actually occurred. He published his theory after many years of work in his book *The Origin of Species by Means of Natural Selection* in 1859. Some of his ideas have since been modified owing to our increased knowledge of genetics but they are so important that it is worth while recounting the main points of his theory.

1. *The Struggle for Existence.*—It is clear that in nature there is a severe struggle for existence in all animals and plants. Over a period of time the number of individuals of a species in a given community does not vary greatly. This implies that the number of progeny which survive to become mature breeding individuals more or less replaces the number of mature ones that die. Generally speaking the reproductive output of a species is much greater than this. For example, a single large foxglove plant may produce half a million seeds each one of which is potentially capable of giving rise to a new individual. Obviously nearly all the progeny die before reaching maturity and

the chance of any single one surviving is very remote.

2. *Variation.*—The individuals of any generation of human beings obviously differ from one another and such differences are found in other organisms. No two animals of the same species (except perhaps for identical twins) are exactly alike and when a large number of individuals are examined it is clear that they vary considerably in structure, colour, activity and so on. Darwin also pointed out that generally these variations were passed on from one generation to the next, for example, the children of tall parents tend to grow tall.

3. *Survival of the Fittest.*—If there is an intense struggle for existence in their natural environment among individuals of a species having different characteristics, those which are best " fitted " to a given set of conditions are most likely to survive to maturity. These will reproduce and the features which enabled them to survive will be passed on to their offspring. This process is liable to continue and a species will become better adapted to its environment.

4. *Natural Selection.*—Over a long period of time the environment of a given species is never stable but will change in various ways. As it does so the characters which best fit the individuals to the changed environment will be selected (not consciously of course) and the species will change. The environment may change only in part of the range of the species and thus lead to divergence and the production of a new species alongside the old one.

Darwin and Lamarck.—Darwin pictured evolution as a slow continuous process with natural selection operating on the small inheritable variations found between the individuals of a species which are undergoing intense competition. This neglects the important effect of the environment on the growth and structure of the individual. It is obvious that external conditions will affect the development of an organism, for example the effect of various soil conditions on the growth of a plant or the amount of food material available to an animal. Lamarck maintained that the characters acquired by an individual owing to the effect of its environment could be passed on to its offspring. Undoubtedly characters are acquired by the individual during its growth but in spite of many attempts to prove otherwise no experiments have been done which prove conclusively that these are inherited by the offspring. Thus Lamarck's theory that evolution has occurred by the inheritance of acquired characters is not generally acceptable today.

Neodarwinism

Darwinism received something of a setback during the early years of modern genetics. There did not seem to be much in common between the large mutations studied by geneticists and the small continuous variations which Darwin thought were the basic material upon which selection acted. With time, it became evident that not all mutations are large in their effects and that much of the continuous variation which occurs does indeed have a genetic basis. Mathematicians such as J. B. S. Haldane and Sewall Wright showed that even very small selective advantages would cause genes to spread throughout populations as the generations passed by. Experiments and observations on natural populations showed that evolution—seen as progressive, adaptive genetic change—does indeed occur today. For example, the proportion of dark-coloured moths has greatly increased in many areas where smoke pollution occurs, as a result of predation by birds on the now more obvious light forms. Again, many pest insects have evolved genetic resistance to the insecticides used to attack them, as a result of the intense selection pressure for such resistance.

GENETICS

Mendelism

Genetics is the study of the mechanisms of the hereditary process. Modern genetics began with the experiments of Gregor Mendel, an Austrian monk, in 1865. He studied the inheritance of different factors in peas by crossing different strains and counting the numbers of plants with different characters in the succeeding generations.

In one experiment Mendel crossed peas with round seeds with peas having wrinkled seeds. All of the offspring (known as the " first filial " or F1 generation) had round seeds. Mendel allowed these plants to pollinate themselves, and then measured the characteristics of their offspring (the F2 generation). There were 5,474 round-seeded plants and 1,850 wrinkled-seeded plants in the F2 generation, a ratio of very nearly three to one. The character of roundness can be described as being " dominant " over the " recessive " character of wrinkledness.

In order to explain his results Mendel suggested that the characters of roundness and wrinkledness were determined by particulate factors (now called *genes*), and that each plant possessed two genes for each feature. Suppose the gene for roundness is *A* and that for wrinkledness is *a*. Then the parental plants in Mendel's experiment will be represented by *AA* (round seeds) and *aa* (wrinkled seeds). The gametes (the ovules and the sperm nuclei of the pollen grains) will be *A* and *a* respectively. When these combine to form the F1 generation they will produce plants with the genetic constitution *Aa*. Both male and female gametes of the F1 generation are then of the two types *A* and *a*, and these can combine, on self-pollination, in four different ways:

F1	male gamete	female gamete	F2
	A	*A*	*AA*
Aa	*A*	*a*	*Aa*
	a	*A*	*Aa*
	a	*a*	*aa*

The individuals of the F2 generation will thus have genetic constitutions of *AA*, *Aa* and *aa* in the approximate proportions 1:2:1. Since both *AA* and *Aa* individuals have round seeds, the ratio of round-seeded plants to wrinkled-seeded plants will be about three to one, which indeed it is.

Mendel's results were ignored for many years until their rediscovery at the beginning of this century. Mendelian ratios were then found to govern inheritance in a large number of other cases, such as coat colour in rabbits and cattle, and white eyes and other characteristics in the fruit fly *Drosophila*. In other cases characteristics are governed by more than one set of genes so the simple mathematical relationships are obscured. This occurs in quantitative features, such as yield in crop plants and weight in animals.

Chromosome Theory

The chromosomes are dark-staining filaments which, as we shall see later, can be observed in the nucleus at cell division. Their behaviour was described in the nineteenth century, but it was not clear what their function was. After the rediscovery of Mendel's work, Sutton suggested that the genes are carried on chromosomes, since the observed behaviour of the chromosomes corresponded very well with the theoretical behaviour of Mendel's factors.

Further evidence for the chromosome theory of inheritance came from study of the phenomenon known as sex-linkage, in which the expression of a gene depends upon the sex of the individual in which it is found. Haemophilia in man, for example, is a hereditary disease which is normally found only in males, although it is clear that females can act as carriers (Queen Victoria was one, since one of her sons, three of her grandsons and seven of her greatgrandsons were haemophiliacs). Cytological study shows that there is one pair of chromosomes which differ in the two sexes. In the female (in man and most animals) the two chromosomes of this pair are similar and are known as the X chromosomes. In the male one of these is replaced by a much smaller Y chromosome. Hence recessive genes which are found on only one X chromosome are expressed in the male, since there is no other dominant gene present. A female haemophiliac would have haemophilia genes on both X chromosomes; this could only arise from a carrier mother and a haemophiliac father, a very rare occurrence.

In recent years it has become clear that chromosomes are composed largely of the DNA molecules of the cell nucleus, to be discussed in a later section. And since it has become evident that genes are DNA molecules, we now have a firm chemical basis for the assumption that genes are carried on chromosomes. Genetics has thus to some extent become a branch of molecular biology.

Mutations

Sometimes a DNA molecule may not replicate itself exactly during the process of cell division. When this happens the gene which it constitutes has changed its character so as to produce a difference effect when expressed in the individual organism. Such a change is known as a gene mutation. It seems likely, for example, that Queen Victoria's haemophilia gene arose as a mutation in herself or in her mother. Mutations, as we shall see, are of vital importance in providing the genetic variation upon which evolutionary selection can act.

The frequency with which mutations occur is increased by certain chemicals and by ionising radiation. Hence the need for caution in exposing the body to X-rays and to radioactive materials, and the concern over the possible genetic effects of radioactive waste from power stations and from military testing programmes.

THE CELL

Cells were first seen in 1665 by Robert Hooke when he looked at a piece of cork under his primitive microscope. It was not until 1839, however, that Schlieden and Schwann produced the cell doctrine which visualised the cell as both the structural and functional unit of living organisation. Exceptions may be found to the cell doctrine. For example, some protozoa, algae, and fungi show very complex internal organisation but are not divided into cells; they are usually called acellular organisms. The viruses also constitute a difficulty since in many ways they are intermediate between living and dead matter. They are absolutely dependent on cells of other organisms for their continued existence. Outside living cells they are inert molecules which may take a crystalline form. Inside a host cell, however, they become disease-producing parasites which multiply and show many of the other properties of living organisms. They are minute and lack the complex organisation usually associated with cells. Notwithstanding their somewhat ambiguous position, the viruses are often treated as though they were single cells or parts of cells and their extreme simplicity has made them ideal material for many types of research at this level. The bacteria also lack some of the properties of cells but the differences are not so clearly defined as they are in the case of viruses.

Structure and Function of Cells

Though the constituent cells of a multicellular organism are usually specialised to perform particular functions, they have a great many features in common. The cell is often said to be made up of a substance called protoplasm, a term for the fundamental material of life which dates from the 19th cent. Protoplasm has two main constituents, the cytoplasm and the nucleus, and is bounded on the outside by a cell or plasma membrane. Plant cells generally have an additional wall composed primarily of cellulose and used for support. The nucleus is the controlling centre of the cell and has rather limited metabolic capabilities. The cytoplasm contains various subunits which operate to produce energy and new cell structure during the normal metabolism of the cell.

Cells take up the raw materials for metabolism through the cell membrane from extracellular fluid which surrounds them. The nutrients include carbohydrates, fats, proteins, minerals, vitamins, and water. Fats and carbohydrates are important principally as sources of energy, though both types of compound are found in permanent cell structure. Proteins are complex substances of high molecular weight which contain nitrogen in addition to the carbon, hydrogen, and oxygen found in the other compounds. They are of fundamental importance in the structure and function of the cell and are built up of a number of simple nitrogen-containing organic molecules called amino acids. There are twenty amino acids occurring commonly in nature so that the number of possible combinations in large protein molecules is quite clearly enormous. A group of proteins whose significance is well established are the enzymes which are the catalysts of chemical reactions in living cells. Each enzyme will control and speed up a specific reaction even though it is present in very small amounts and is usually unchanged at the end of the process. A large number of inorganic mineral salts are essential for cells to function normally. Some, such as sodium, potassium, and calcium salts, are needed in considerable quantity; others are required only in trace amounts and these include iron, copper, and manganese. The trace elements are usually important constituents of enzyme systems. Vitamins are also necessary in very small amounts and it seems reasonable to conclude that their function is also a catalytic one in parts of some enzyme systems.

I. CYTOPLASM

For a long time cytoplasm was thought to be a homogeneous and structureless substrate in which enzymes occurred as part of a general colloidal system. With the refinement of techniques such as electron microscopy and ultracentrifugation, more and more identifiable components have been found within the cytoplasm. It now seems certain that the material other than these recognisable particles is not a structureless matrix but a highly organised and variable complex.

Mitochondria and Oxidation

Mitochondria vary in shape from cylindrical rods to spheres and in size from 0·2 to 3·0 microns. When seen in the living cell they are in constant motion. The whole structure is enclosed within a thin double membrane, the inner layer of which is thrown into folds extending across the central cavity of the mitochondrion and dividing it into small chambers. The function of mitochondria is to provide energy for the reactions of the rest of the cell. Almost the whole machinery for the oxidation of foodstuffs is to be found in the mitochondria. Slight damage to the mitochondrion will render it unable to carry out a complete cycle of oxidative processes. Destruction of parts of the double membrane system prevents the production of energy-rich phosphate bonds in adenosine triphosphate (ATP) in which energy is stored and transported about the cell.

Chloroplasts and Photosynthesis

Chloroplasts are particles found in cells in the green parts of plants, in fact they contain the green pigment which is called chlorophyll. They are involved in the process known as photosynthesis in which energy absorbed from light is used to synthesise carbohydrates from carbon dioxide and water, oxygen being formed as a by-product.

Chloroplasts are disc-shaped or flat ellipsoids from 2 to 20 microns across, possessing a complex structure which in many ways is reminiscent of that found in mitochondria. A typical double membrane surrounds the structure and the inside is made up very largely of a stack of discs consisting of paired membranes connected at their ends to form closed systems. This seems to be a further development of the type of lamellated structure seen dividing the central cavity of a mitochondrion. The chlorophylls and other pigments, such as the orange yellow carotenoids, seem to be arranged in layers a single molecule thick in the chloroplast discs so that they are maximally exposed to light.

The importance of this process whereby plants can make use of the energy in sunlight to fix carbon dioxide and produce carbohydrates is quite clear. The whole animal population of the world, including man, is dependent on plants for food since even the meat-eating carnivores prey upon herbivores. Although scientists continue to make efforts to produce adequate food materials from simple compounds, there is still no better machinery known for doing this than the plant cell. Man is dependent on photosynthesis not only for his supplies of food but also for much of his fuel, since much of the combustible material removed from the earth is of plant origin.

Endoplasmic reticulum, Ribosomes, and Protein Synthesis.

A network of elaborate and oriented double membranes existing within parts of the cytoplasm can be seen in the electron microscope. In the space between the pairs of double membranes small granules are visible, either free in the space or attached to a membrane. The whole system is called the endoplasmic reticulum. When the cell is homogenised and centrifuged the endoplasmic reticulum appears as the microsomal fraction. Biochemical analysis after separation of the membranous from the granular components reveals that the former is composed largely of phospholipids and cholesterol, which are compounds closely related to fats, and the latter of ribonucleic acid (RNA).

Nucleic Acids

The term nucleic acid covers a class of substances, usually of great complexity, built up from smaller units called nucleotides. Each nucleotide consists of a base, united to a sugar, in turn united to phosphoric acid. Nucleotides are joined together in a linear fashion by means of the phosphoric acid residues to form a chain from which the bases project at right angles. Two types of sugar are found in naturally occurring nucleic acids and these are the ribose of RNA and the desoxyribose of desoxyribonucleic acids (DNA). We shall return to the latter when the nucleus is considered. Four nitrogen-containing bases occur in nucleic acids and in RNA—adenine, cytosine, guanine, and uracil. In DNA the uracil is replaced by thymine.

Protein Synthesis

There is good evidence that RNA is manufactured exclusively within the nucleus and subsequently moves out into the cytoplasm. Some of it, called ribosomal RNA, unites with protein to form the granules, or ribosomes, of the endoplasmic reticulum. Another form, called messenger RNA, also migrates from the nucleus to associate with ribosomes but does not become incorporated into their permanent structure. It is also well established that the ribosomes are closely linked with protein synthesis in the cell because radioactive amino acids, when fed to an animal, are always found first in the ribosomes before any other cell structure. The specification for a particular protein is not carried on the ribosome which is merely the factory for making these complex molecules. It is thought that messenger RNA carries instructions from the nucleus which specify exactly the protein to be synthesised at a ribosome. This is done by means of a code in which a " triplet " of three nucleotide bases codes one amino acid (Fig. 1). Thus on a long molecule of RNA, three adjacent uracil bases would specify an amino acid called phenylalanine. If these were followed on the RNA molecule by one uracil and two guanines then the amino acid tryptophan would be specified and this would be joined to the phenylalanine. In this way complex protein molecules can be built up according to instructions emanating from the nucleus for each of the 20 different amino acids.

This system is responsible for building and maintaining much of the organisation of the cytoplasm. All the enzymes, for example catalysing every reaction within the cell will be specified and built up on the appropriate RNA template. The understanding of protein synthesis is of fundamental importance to the whole of biology and has particular significance in studies on cancer where cell growth becomes abnormal.

The Golgi Apparatus

The characteristic features of the Golgi apparatus are numbers of large vacuoles or spaces

Fig. 1. This shows a portion of a molecule of messenger RNA, associated with a ribosome and synthesising a protein. Adenine specifies Uracil (U), Cytosine specifies Guanine (G), Thymine specifies Adenine (A), and Guanine specifies Cytosine (C). The ribosome is moving down the messenger RNA strand "reading" the triplet code. Amino acid 4, which is phenylalanine specified by UUU, has just been joined to three other amino acids and its carrier RNA released to the cytoplasm. Amino acid 5, tryptophan specified by UGG, is attached to its carrier RNA and in position ready to be joined to the protein chain by the ribosome. Amino acid 6, methionine specified by UAG is attached to its carrier RNA but has not been brought into position on the messenger RNA strand. Other amino acids and carrier RNA molecules exist free in the cytoplasm and have not yet associated.

bordered by closely packed layers of double membranes. The latter look very much like the membranes of the endoplasmic reticulum but do not have the ribosome particles along their edge. They are therefore known as "smooth" membranes in contrast to the "rough" membranes of endoplasmic reticulum. The function of the Golgi apparatus may be associated with secretory activity of the cell.

Cell Membrane

Though the cell membrane plays a most vital part in regulating what can enter and leave the cell, it remains rather poorly understood. It is thought to consist of a double layer of lipid molecules with a layer of protein probably outside the lipid. Fairly large molecules seem to be able to penetrate the membrane in relation to their fat solubility, which would support the hypothesis of its lipid framework. Small molecules and ions appear to penetrate in relation to their size, the smaller ones getting through more readily than the larger. This suggests that pores of a certain size exist in the membrane.

The cell membrane has mechanisms which can move ions and other substances against concentration differences either into or out of the cell. A fine microelectrode can be pushed into a cell and the electrical potential of the inside determined with respect to the outside. In all the cells studied so far there is a potential difference across the membrane which is produced by the non-uniform distribution on either side of ions, parti-

cularly those of sodium, potassium, and chloride. Though these potentials have been studied in animal and plant cells generally, they are best known from the work on nerve cells where sudden changes in the membrane potential are the basis of nerve impulses. The basic process which produces the nerve impulse in any region of the nerve fibre has been shown to be a sudden increase in permeability of the membrane to sodium ions in that region. Transmission from one nerve cell to the next takes place at a special region called a synapse and when an impulse reaches this region it causes the release of a small amount of chemical transmitter substance which diffuses to the membrane of the adjacent cell. There it combines with the membrane in such a way as to change its permeability to ions and so produce a response in the second cell. A number of transmitter substances have now been identified and many of them are related chemically to tranquillisers and other drugs affecting the nervous system.

II. NUCLEUS

The main regions of the nucleus are the surrounding nuclear membrane, a mass of material known as chromatin, and a small sphere called the nucleolus. The nuclear membrane is a double structure very much like the membranes of the cell surface and endoplasmic reticulum. Suggestions have been made that these membranes are continuous at some regions within the cell. The status of chromatin was in doubt for many years. Light microscope studies reveal very little structure in the nucleus until the time when the cell is preparing for, and undergoing, division or mitosis. At this time a number of discrete double strands, the chromosomes, are revealed by virtue of their chromatin content—the material stains heavily with basic dyes.

Cell Division

During division the chromosomes behave in regular and recognisable sequence. In the first stage called prophase they appear and at the same time the nuclear membrane breaks down. Next, in metaphase, the chromosomes become arranged across the equator of a spindle-shaped collection of fibrils which appears in the area formerly outlined by the nucleus. Then follows anaphase in which the two threads of each chromosome, the chromatids, move to opposite poles of the spindle. Finally in the last stage, telophase, nuclear membranes are formed round the two separate collections of chromosome material and the cytoplasm itself divides into two. Thus two cells are formed each containing the same number of chromosomes as the parent and the cells enter a period of rest, or interphase, between divisions. During interphase the chromatin material disappears.

Genes

These are the elements which contain all hereditary information and the medium whereby hereditary features are transmitted from one cell to the next, either in the same organism or from parents to offspring via the fertilised egg. Experiments indicated that the same genes always occupy the same position on chromosomes and this really demands a structural continuity through the life of the cell. The chromosomes undoubtedly persist, but it is still not certain why or how they change so as to become visible during division. One suggestion has been that the nucleic acids of which they are very largely made up condense during the period of prophase. In the resting nucleus the chromosomes may be much more swollen and occupy much of the nucleus.

The problem that has attracted the most attention and is possibly the most fundamental that biology has to offer is that of the nature of the genes. The important material of the genes is known to be deoxyribonucleic acid (DNA), made up of nucleotides as is RNA, though in this case the bases are adenine, cytosine, guanine, and thymine. The DNA molecule is large and complex. Two long chains of nucleotides are known to coil round in a double helix with the pairs of bases on each helix directed towards one another and linked by means of hydrogen bonds (Fig. 2). Furthermore, if adenine is the base on one chain, thymine must be its partner on the other and similarly guanine can link only with cytosine. Because of this pairing of bases there is sufficient information in a single chain of nucleotides to resynthesise the double helix once more. Thus if we examine a section of a single strand of the helix and find bases in the order adenine, thymine, guanine, adenine, cytosine, we can predict that in similar positions on the other strand we shall find thymine, adenine, cytosine, thymine, guanine. The capacity of one half of a DNA molecule to specify the othe half exactly, enables the system to be self-replicating in a way that is essential in a hereditary transmitter and fits in well with what is known of chromosome behaviour during cell division.

Transmission of Genetic Information

Long before the structure and significance of the DNA molecules was known, geneticists were finding that alterations in a gene, known as a mutation, usually affected a particular chemical reaction and this in turn caused the changes seen in the organism as a whole. The effect was due to the failure to synthesise a necessary enzyme and so the hypothesis " one gene = one enzyme " gathered currency. This view has now been extended to include proteins other than enzymes and it is now certain that specific genes control the synthesis of specific proteins. The DNA of the genes transmits the instructions about protein synthesis to the ribosomes via messenger RNA. In the nucleus, messenger RNA is made with specific base sequences in its molecule by using DNA as the template; thus a group of three adjacent adenine bases in DNA would produce a group of three adjacent uracil bases in the synthesised RNA and this would lead to the specification of phenylalanine at the ribosome as we have seen. Only one of the two strands in the DNA double helix participates in the production of RNA.

FIG. 2. A portion of a DNA molecule showing how it is made up of two strands of nucleotides. Each nucleotide consists of a base, which may be Adenine (A), Thymine (T), Guanine (G), or Cytosine (C), united to the Pentose Sugar, Desoxyribose (S), in turn joined to Phosphoric Acid (P). The nucleotides are linked through the phosphoric acid groups. The two strands are held together by hydrogen bonds between bases, adenine linking only with thymine, and guanine only with cytosine. They are twisted round each other so that the molecule is in the form of a double helix.

The processes involved in nuclear control and the transmission of information from cell to cell is summarised in the aphorism " DNA makes RNA and RNA makes protein." The system of carrying that information in the base sequences of DNA molecules has become known as the " genetic code." A remarkable landmark in the study of DNA occurred when, towards the end of 1967, Kornberg and his colleagues managed to synthesise a virus DNA in a test tube. The synthesised molecules proved to be capable of infecting bacteria in the same way that the naturally occurring virus would. The DNA was synthesised using an extracted virus DNA molecule as template and attaching nucleotides by means of appropriate enzymes. The newly made molecules were then separated from the template. It can hardly be claimed that this is the creation of life in a test tube since the template was extracted from a living virus. The experiment suggests many possibilities in experimental modification of the genetic constitution of an organism with all the far-reaching ethical consequences.

MULTICELLULAR ORGANISATION

It is axiomatic, if evolutionary theory is accepted, that in the course of very long periods of time there has been a general change in multicellular organisation from the simple aggregation of cells with little individual differentiation, to the highly specialised and differentiated cells and tissues seen in complex animals and plants. It is fascinating to speculate on the environmental variations and internal mechanisms which together produced this result. The problem is so vast, however, that a complete analysis is impossible and even a statement of the sequence of changes is in many cases highly controversial.

Another aspect of becoming multicellular, where the problems offer more hope of analysis, is that the complex organisation must be built up in the lifetime of each animal or plant from the single-celled stage of the fertilised egg. We have already seen how cells can divide repeatedly, handing on self-replicating chromosomes so that each cell is apparently identical. If this were really so then division of the fertilised egg would result in an unorganised mass of cells showing no differentiation. The essential problems in development are: (1) how is the smooth succession of shape changes produced during cell division so that an appropriate and recognisable end product is reached?; (2) how do the cells differentiate during this temporal sequence so that those which form part of the eye, say, are different from those of liver and blood?

Method of Development

There are some important differences in the method of development in animals and plants. In animals there tends to be a relatively short period during which the basic structure is produced and after which growth, repair, and replacement may cause adjustment rather than major change. In higher plants, on the other hand, the apical regions of both roots and shoots remain in a permanently embryonic state and add material, which then differentiates, in a continuous process throughout the life of the plant. In spite of these differences—and in any case there are many exceptions—the two main problems in development are essentially similar in both animals and plants.

A great deal of work has been done on animal development since this takes place in a fairly stereotyped way during a short period of time. The fertilised egg of an animal divides in such a way as to form a hollow ball of cells, the blastula, which folds in on itself to produce a two-layered sac, the gastrula. A third layer, the mesoderm, is now added between the two layers, known as ectoderm on the outside and endoderm on the inside. At this stage much of the animal's basic structure is established. Many aspects of this orderly sequence can be explained in terms of specific adhesive properties of cells, so that a cell will stick to others of the same type but not to unrelated types. Other mechanical properties such as elasticity, particularly in surface layers, are important in maintaining shape and producing appropriate changes during processes when one layer is folded in on another. Why cells should have the different physical properties necessary to produce an integrated whole embryo is not known, but certainly it cannot be thought that every cell has an absolutely fixed constitution and therefore a predetermined role in development. Large parts of developing embryos can be removed in early stages and their places taken by remaining cells so that intact organisms are still produced. One is led to conclude that the surroundings of a cell have a great deal of influence on the way it reacts and that there is a great deal of adaptability in the developing system, especially in its early stages.

Formation of Specialised Tissues

These points lead us on to the second major question concerning the differences which appear progressively in cells during development so that specialised tissues are ultimately formed. This is essentially a problem in the regulation of gene activity since we know that each cell division produces daughter cells which are genetically identical. It seems likely therefore that instructions are carried on the chromosomes to cope with all requirements of the organism, but that in specialised cells only a small fraction of this full potential is realised. For a long time embryologists have known that egg cytoplasm shows regional differences which make identical nuclei behave differently, and it is thought that regional cytoplasm can in some way control gene activity. Techniques for the transplantation of nuclei in developing frog embryos have been perfected and it has been possible to put a nucleus from an intestinal cell of a tadpole into an enucleate egg. The egg will go on to develop normally even though its nucleus came from a fully specialised cell derived from endoderm. The embryo will form blood and muscle from the mesodermal layer and all the other components of an organism, under the influence of a nucleus which normally would have produced none of these things. One can conclude that all the genes are present, even in the nuclei of specialised cells, but that they have to be placed in a suitable cytoplasmic environment in order to be activated. Similar nuclear transplantation experiments indicate that genes can be " turned off " as well as " turned on " by an appropriate cytoplasmic environment, even though the nuclei come from cells which are so specialised as to stop dividing. The components of cytoplasm which control gene activity are still quite unknown.

A study of cell differentiation and the development of multicellular organisation leads us to the view that, important though the nucleus and its genes are in controlling cell activity, an integrated organism is the result of complex interactions between its constituent cells and between the cytoplasm of those cells and their nuclei.

THE CLASSIFICATION OF ORGANISMS

It was clear to the biologists of the 17th cent. that animals and plants could be fitted into different groups or species. John Ray, a leading biologist of the day, defined a species as a group of individuals capable of interbreeding within the group. This criterion, with its corollary that a species is reproductively isolated from organisms outside the group, has survived more or less unchanged to the present day. The early workers also saw that some species were very similar to one another while others were obviously dissimilar. Systems of classification based on the similarities and differences were drawn up so that all organisms could be fitted into an orderly scheme and species could be given names in accordance with the scheme. The most famous collector and classifier was the Swede, Linnaeus, who established his reputation in the 1730s. A very large number of animals and plants are known by the names given to them by Linnaeus.

Systematics, as the study of species and of higher groups of classification is called, acquired a new significance after Darwin and the Theory of Evolution. From the biological point of view the most satisfactory classification became one which reflected the evolution of the organisms classified. Such a system, based on the phylogeny or evolutionary history of a group, is called a natural classification. It is not always easy to produce because ancestral types tend to become extinct and the problem then becomes one of reconstructing a whole branching system when only the ends of the branches are known. A great deal of the work on systematics has, of necessity, to be done on museum specimens which may be fossils or material preserved in some way by the collectors. The biological criterion of reproductive isolation cannot be used to define a species when the only available representatives are in a preserved state. In this case the scientist must resort to an assessment of structural differences in an attempt to decide whether two organisms are of different or the same species. In recent years computer techniques have been used to compare large numbers of structural differences between groups of animals or plants. Physiological and biochemical characteristics are also becoming part of the armoury of the 20th cent. systematist. All these techniques have led to the realisation that even the species cannot be regarded as a static point in an evolutionary pattern. Some species die out and others arise as conditions in the environment slowly change.

When the systematist shifts his attention to the higher levels of classification the problems are just as great as at the species level. Different species having features in common can be grouped together into genera, genera into families, families into orders, orders into classes, and classes into phyla. The dividing lines between different groups at all levels is always difficult and in the final analysis somewhat arbitrary since at these levels we do not have any biological criterion such as exists for the species. The evolutionary status of the larger groups is also poorly defined. Many are now recognised to be polyphyletic, which is to say that there are several main evolutionary lines running right through the group.

THE ANIMAL KINGDOM

The animal kingdom is divided into about 24 large groups or phyla though the number varies between different classifications. Ten of the more important phyla are listed below.

1. Protozoa.—Microscopic, unicellular forms of great variety. Some may have more than one nucleus and others form colonies. Many are able to swim by waving hair-like flagella or cilia Others move by putting out extensions of the body or pseudopodia into which the rest of the body then flows. Protozoa are found in the sea, in fresh water and in the soil. Some are parasitic and cause important diseases in animals and man such as sleeping sickness and malaria.

2. Porifera.—Sponges. Very primitive multicellular animals whose cells display considerable independence of one another. Largely marine. The body which may become branched and plantlike is supported by a framework of spicules and fibres. The bath sponge is the fibrous skeleton of certain species.

3. Coelenterates.—Hydra, jellyfish, sea anemones, corals. Simple animals which have a body only two cells thick surrounding a gut cavity with a single opening to the outside. Largely marine. Many are colonial. Coral reefs are formed from the calcareous skeletons of these animals.

4. Platyhelminths.—Flatworms, which are free living in water, and liver flukes and tapeworms, which are parasitic. A third, solid block of cells, the mesoderm, has been developed between the two layers of cells seen in the coelenterates. A simple gut may be developed and the reproductive system is complex especially in the parasitic forms.

5. Nematodes.—Roundworms. The body is smooth and pointed at each end. Some of the most numerous and widespread of all animals. Free living in all environments and parasitic in practically all groups of plants and animals. At the same level of complexity as the Platyhelminths.

6. Annelids.—Segmented worms such as earthworms, marine worms and leeches. A system of spaces, the body cavity, is developed in the mesoderm so that movements of the main body of the animal and movements of the gut become more or less independent. Digestive, excretory, circulatory, nervous and reproductive systems are all well developed.

7. Arthropods.—A very large, diverse and important group of animals which includes crustaceans such as crabs, shrimps and water fleas; myriapods, such as centipedes and millepedes; insects; and arachnids, such as spiders and scorpions. The arthropods show many of the developments seen in annelids and in addition they possess a jointed, hard exoskeleton. Paired appendages grow out from the segments of the body and form antennae, mouth parts, walking legs, etc. The muscles within the skeleton are able to exert a fine control over the movement of the appendage. In order to grow these animals have to shed the exoskeleton periodically.

8. Molluscs.—Mussels, clams, oysters, squids, octopods and snails. Complex body form but somewhat different from annelid–arthropod type. Unsegmented body protected by shell which is variously developed in different types. It forms two valves in mussels and oysters, a spiral structure in snails, is reduced and internal in squids and completely lost in octopods.

9. Echinoderms.—Starfish, brittle stars, sea cucumbers, sea urchins, and sea lilies. All marine and all radially symmetrical, usually with five radii. Completely unlike the other advanced, major groups. Circulatory, excretory and nervous systems differently developed. Locomotion and feeding by means of hundreds of tube feet projecting from under surface.

10. Chordates.—Sea squirts, Amphioxus, fish, amphibia, reptiles, birds and mammals. Segmented animals which at some stage in their life have gill slits leading from pharynx to the outside and a supporting notochord from which, in all chordates except sea squirts and Amphioxus, is developed a vertebral column or backbone. Those animals with a backbone are commonly referred to as vertebrates, *all* those without as invertebrates. These are obviously names of convenience having no phylogenetic significance since they lump together totally unrelated phyla in one case and align these with a part of a single phylum in the other. The vertebrates have been investigated more completely than any other animals because of their direct structural and functional relationship with man himself. There are five well defined classes which are listed below. The first vertebrates were the fish and from them came the amphibia. The amphibia gave rise to the reptiles and both birds and mammals evolved from different reptilian stock.

(a) Fish

Cold blooded, aquatic animals breathing by means of gills. Sharks, rays and dogfish belong to a group known as the elasmobranchs characterised by a skeleton made of cartilage. Bony fish, most of them in a group called the teleosts, include almost all the fresh water fish and the common marine fish such as cod. mackerel, plaice, herring, etc.

(b) Amphibia

Cold blooded, more or less terrestrial animals which have to return to water to breed. Five fingered limbs are developed in place of the fins of fish. The egg hatches into a tadpole larva which is aquatic and breathes by gills. At metamorphosis the larva changes into the terrestrial adult which possesses lungs. Some amphibia such as the axolotl may become sexually mature as a larva and so never metamorphose into the adult. The class includes newts, salamanders, frogs and toads.

(c) Reptiles

Cold blooded and terrestrial. These animals do not return to water to breed because they have an egg with a relatively impermeable shell containing the food and water requirements of the developing embryo. There is no larval stage. Present day reptiles such as lizards, snakes and crocodiles are all that remains of a tremendous radiation of dinosaur-like creatures which occurred in the Mesozoic (F48).

(d) Birds

Warm blooded and adapted for aerial life. The characteristic feathers act both to insulate the body against heat loss and to provide the airfoil surfaces necessary for flight. The birds are an astonishingly uniform group and show less diversity of structure than much lower classification categories (*e.g.*, the teleosts) in other classes. The relationships of the 19,000 or more species of bird are difficult to establish because of this uniformity. It is clear that the flightless forms such as the ostrich are primitive and that the penguins are also in a separate category but the typical modern birds are classified in a large number of rather arbitrary orders. About half of all the known species are placed in one enormous order called the Passeriformes or perching birds.

(e) Mammals

Warm blooded animals which have been successful in a tremendous variety of habitats. Mammals are insulated from the environment by the characteristically hairy and waterproofed skin. They are, with two exceptions, viviparous which means that their young are born alive and in typical mammals at an advanced stage of development. In the marsupials of Australia the young are born at an early stage and transferred to a pouch where they develop further. The two exceptions referred to are primitive monotreme mammals known as the duck-billed platypus and spiny ant-eater and these animals lay eggs. The young of mammals are suckled by means of the milk producing mammary glands. The mammals include aquatic whales and dolphins, hoofed ungulates, flesh eating carnivores, rodents and insectivores, the aerial bats, and the tree climbing primates to which man himself belongs.

THE PHYSIOLOGY OF ANIMALS

Some basic features of cell organisation have already been dealt with, and in unicellular animals all life processes, such as respiration, movement, growth and reproduction, proceed in the single cell. However in multicellular animals cells are of various types, constituting distinct tissues and organs which perform special functions in the body. Although each cell has its own complex metabolism there must be co-ordination between cells forming special tissues and between the tissues which form the whole organism in order for the body to function efficiently. The study of these functional interrelationships at the tissue and organism level of organisation is the province of the physiologist.

1. Movement, Fibrils and Skeletons

(a) Muscles.—The prime movers in almost all animal movement are large protein molecules in the form of microscopic fibrillar threads. In some way not yet fully understood these fibrils can convert the chemical energy stored in the high energy phosphate bonds of ATP into mechanical energy. In the long, thin cells forming the muscles of animals, it has been discovered that there are two sets of fibrils, one formed of a protein called myosin, the other of actin, arranged in a regular, interdigitating fashion. When the muscle contracts the fibrils slide past one another so that, although the fibrils themselves do not change in length, the muscle as a whole develops tension and shortens. Fine bridges extend from the myosin fibrils to attach on to the actin and it is here that the conversion of chemical to mechanical energy goes on.

(b) Skeletons.—In order for muscles to work effectively it is necessary for them to operate in some sort of skeletal system. Contraction but not relaxation is an active process; muscles must be arranged in antagonistic pairs so that one muscle can extend the other. A skeleton also provides a system of levers so that the muscles can do work against the environment in an efficient manner. A simple type of skeleton found in fairly primitive animals is the hydrostatic system of coelenterates and worms. Here the animal can be thought of as a fluid filled bag or tube which can change shape but whose volume remains constant. By contraction of circular muscles the tube will become long and thin and conversely contraction of longitudinal muscles makes the tube short and fat. Examination of an earthworm will demonstrate how alternating waves of activity of this type passing from head to tail can move the animal over the ground. The earthworm shows an advance over

the simplest systems because the hydrostatic tube is broken up into small units by the segmentation of the body. This makes local responses possible. The next advance to be seen is the development in animals such as arthropods and vertebrates of a firm skeleton to which muscles are directly attached. The skeleton can then be used to support the body and to engage the environment. It seems to matter little whether an endoskeleton (vertebrates) or exoskeleton (arthropods) is developed since in both cases a tremendous radiation of fins for swimming, legs for walking and wings for flying can be seen. However in other respects these two types of skeleton show significant differences. The exoskeleton for example offers more protection than the endoskeleton while apparently setting an upper size limit. All the really big animals have endoskeletons.

(c) Cilia.—Fibrillar systems are also seen in the fine hair-like cilia which project from the surface of some cells. Cilia are important in a number of ways. They are the organelles of movement in many Protozoa, they are used to produce water currents past the bodies of some aquatic animals, and they are of great importance in moving fluid within the body of almost all animals. They beat in a regular fashion, the effective stroke being accomplished with the cilium held straight out from the surface and the recovery stroke with the cilium flexed at the base.

2. Feeding

All animals must take in and digest food materials. As well as water they require complex organic substances, proteins, fats and carbohydrates, together with small amounts of salts and vitamins. These materials are obtained by eating the dead bodies of plants and other animals. They are taken into the alimentary canal and there broken down or digested by enzymes into simpler, soluble amino acids, sugars and fatty acids. These substances are absorbed and distributed to various parts of the body where they are used in cell metabolism (F31-2) or stored for future use.

Many animals, called macrophagous feeders, take in relatively large masses of food. Some such as frogs and snakes swallow their food whole, but many break it up first. Arthropods have modified appendages arranged round the mouth for cutting, some molluscs have a rasp-like radula with which to scrape off particles, and many mammals break up their food with jaws and teeth. The teeth are usually well adapted to the type of food. Carnivores have large, sharp canines, premolars and molars with which to tear the flesh of the prey, fish eating seals have small peg-like teeth to grip the fish and herbivorous ungulates have flat grinding teeth with which they break up hard plant material.

In contrast, microphagous feeders collect small particles of food material from the environment by continuous filtration. In bivalve molluscs and many marine worms water currents are produced by beating cilia. Food is trapped within the confined space through which the water flows by means of a plentiful supply of sticky mucus in the filtering region. Some crustacea use fine hairs to sieve off food material, often from water currents created by the swimming movements. The most startling of filter feeders is the whalebone whale. As the whale swims forward a stream of water flows in at the front of the mouth and out at the sides via sheets of whalebone which filter off the organisms on which the animal feeds. Though macrophagy seems to favour the attainment of larger size there are exceptions! Another type of particulate feeding is seen in those animals which eat deposits of detritus as do many worms. Finally some animals take in only soluble food materials. These fluid feeders include internal parasites like the tapeworm which absorb substances over the surface of the body, and insects such as the aphid with sucking mouth parts.

3. Respiration. Gills, Lungs and Tracheae

All living cells respire and remain alive only if supplied with oxygen. In a multicellular body however, many cells are remote from the oxygen of the environment and the need arises for an efficient respiratory system by which oxygen can be taken up and carbon dioxide released. In addition a circulatory system is necessary to transport the oxygen to and from the respiring cells.

(a) Simple Gas Exchange Systems

Animals such as protozoa which because of their size have a high surface area to volume ratio do not need special structures for gas exchange. Diffusion over the whole body surface ensures an adequate supply of oxygen. Much larger animals such as earthworms also find it possible to rely on diffusion alone, partly because their consumption of oxygen is fairly low, and partly because their bodies are permeable all over. For various reasons most animals restrict the permeability of the outer layers of the body and under these conditions special respiratory areas have to be developed.

(b) Gas Exchange in Water

Aquatic animals, except those such as whales breathing at the surface, have to obtain their oxygen from the supplies which are dissolved in the water. This presents several problems because water is a dense medium, there is not a lot of oxygen in solution, and its diffusion rate is low. For these reasons there is a surprising functional uniformity in gill systems and they are very different from lungs. Gills are fine, finger-like processes with a good blood supply which are held out in a water stream. The water current is brought very close to the gill filaments so that the length of diffusion pathway for oxygen is minimal. There is a " counter current " flow of water and blood so that the water containing most oxygen comes into contact with the blood just leaving the gill. This ensures that most of the oxygen can be transferred from water to blood through the thin gill cells. The efficiency of " counter current " systems is well known to the engineer but they were invented by aquatic animals long before they were by man. These features can be seen in the gills of molluscs, crustacea and fish. The pumping devices which maintain the water currents also operate economically. Flow is maintained in crustacea by appendages modified to form beating paddles, in many molluscs by ciliary movement, and in fish by the operation of a double pump in mouth and opercular cavities. In almost all cases there is a continuous current over the gills, the water coming in one way and going out another. Thus the animal avoids reversing the flow with the consequent waste of energy in accelerating and decelerating a large mass of water. Fish, for example, take water in at the mouth and force it out through the gill slits (sharks) or operculum (teleosts).

(c) Gas Exchange in Air

Air breathing animals do not encounter these problems since the medium is less dense, contains a great deal (20%) of oxygen and diffusion rates are high. Lungs are therefore in the form of sacs whose walls are well supplied with blood. The area of the walls may be increased by folding so that the lung becomes spongy and full of minute air spaces called alveoli where the gas exchanges goes on. Only the main airways receive fresh air as the lung expands; oxygen is renewed in the alveoli by diffusion. Ventilation of the lung is accomplished by a tidal flow of air in and out of the same tubular opening known as the trachea. The actual ventilating mechanism varies in different animals. In the amphibia for example air is forced into the lungs when the floor of the mouth is raised with the mouth and nostrils shut. The lungs are emptied by elastic recoil and by lowering the floor of the mouth. Higher vertebrates use a costal pump which changes the volume of chest and lungs by movements of the ribs. This change in volume is further assisted in mammals by the diaphragm, a sheet of muscle which lies beneath the lungs and separates thorax and abdomen. In many animals sound producing organs are associated with the lungs and trachea. The larynx is a vocal organ in frogs, some lizards, and most notably mammals. In birds voice production takes place in the syrinx situated further down at the base of the trachea.

A completely different respiratory system is seen in insects. Branching tubes, known as tracheae, run throughout the body and carry oxygen directly to the cells without the intervention of a blood system. The tracheae communicate with the outside world via a series of holes called spiracles. Although the main tubes may be actively ventilated, diffusion in the system accounts for a large part of the movement of oxygen between the outside world and cells.

4. Circulation

In simple, small animals there is no blood system and dissolved oxygen, nutrients and other materials move about the body solely by diffusion, assisted to a certain extent by streaming movements of protoplasm within the cells. In larger animals a transport system is necessary to convey materials about the body and in many, but not all, it is in the form of a blood system. Blood systems are of two types, closed and open.

(a) Open Systems

In an open circulatory system blood is pumped from the heart into a few major arteries but these very quickly give way to large tissue spaces or sinuses so that the tissues and organs of the body are directly bathed in blood. Blood flows slowly from the sinuses back to the heart. Both mollusc and arthropods possess an open system.

(b) Closed Systems

In a closed system blood is pumped round the body in a branching network of arteries, and comes into contact with tissues and cells via very thin walled vessels called capillaries. Substances diffuse into and out of the blood through capillary walls. From capillaries, blood enters the veins and so returns to the heart. Blood flow in the tubes of a closed system is much more brisk and blood pressures tend to be higher than in an open system. In annelids the closed system is fairly simple with a vessel above the gut in which blood moves forward connecting to one below in which blood moves backwards. The blood is pumped by peristaltic contraction of the vessels and this system must be regarded as the precursor of a localised pump. Simple hearts are in fact seen in some annelids.

In vertebrates a well defined heart is always present, situated ventrally at the level of the forelimbs. In fish there is a single auricle and ventricle and the latter pumps blood directly to the gills. From the gills the blood is collected into a dorsal aorta which then branches to serve the rest of the body. Associated with the development of lungs and loss of gills in the tetrapods, we see a progressive modification of this simple pattern. The most posterior gill vessel is taken over as the lung or pulmonary artery and slowly a completely separate circuit evolves. This involves the division of the single heart into right and left sides, the former pumping blood to the lungs and the latter to the body. In the birds and mammals where the division is complete the system can be seen to be functionally satisfactory. Blood flows along the following route: left auricle to left ventricle, to body, to right auricle, to right ventricle, to lungs, to left auricle, and so on. Thus blood charged with oxygen in the lungs returns to the heart before being pumped to the body.

(c) Function of the Blood

Most of the materials transported by the blood such as nutrients, waste materials and hormones are carried in solution in the plasma. The respiratory gases, oxygen and carbon dioxide, are present in greater quantity than would be possible if they were in simple solution. Carbon dioxide is carried in the form of bicarbonate and oxygen combines with blood pigment. The best known blood pigment is haemoglobin which is found in a variety of animals and gives the red colour to blood. When oxygen is present in high concentration, as it is in the lungs, combination occurs to give oxyhaemoglobin. If the concentration of oxygen is low, as it is in the tissues, dissociation occurs and oxygen is given off leaving reduced haemoglobin. Carbon monoxide will combine more readily than oxygen with haemoglobin so that in carbon monoxide poisoning the blood cannot transport oxygen. The haemoglobin of vertebrates is contained in high concentration in red blood corpuscles. The amount of haemoglobin and, hence, oxygen carried is greater than if the pigment is not in corpuscles. In mammals the oxygen carrying capacity of blood is thirty times that of a similar quantity of water. Other blood pigments are the blue haemocyanin found in crustacea and molluscs, and the violet haemerythrin found in some worms. Also present in the blood are various types of white corpuscle which are part of the defence mechanism of the body and ingest invading bacteria. Special blood proteins such as fibrinogen, causing clot formation, and antibodies effective against foreign substances occur in the plasma.

5. Excretion, Ionic Regulation and Kidney Tubules

As the chemical reactions included under the erm metabolism proceed, so numerous waste products accumulate. The most important of these are compounds containing nitrogen, such as ammonia, urea and uric acid, arising from the use of protein as an energy source. In terrestrial animals they are removed from the blood by the kidney. The basic unit of a kidney is the tubule; in worms these tubules are not concentrated into a solid kidney but occur, a pair in every segment, right down the body. The kidney tubule begins with an end sac, corpuscle or funnel which is closely associated with the body cavity or the blood system. Fluid is filtered from the body cavity or blood into the corpuscle whence it passes to the tubule proper. During passage down the tubule, useful materials are reabsorbed through the tubule cells into the blood whereas unwanted materials remain and pass to the outside world.

Although it is usual to think of kidney function being primarily one of nitrogenous excretion, it is quite common to find that in aquatic animals the kidneys are hardly used for this purpose. In these animals the tubules are primarily concerned in regulating the salt and water levels in the body, nitrogenous wastes being eliminated by diffusion through any permeable surface. In fresh water for example all animals have osmotic problems since the body fluids have a much greater osmotic pressure than the environment. Water tends to enter the body and salts tend to leave. Fresh water animals produce large quantities of very dilute urine, filtering off a lot of blood plasma into the tubules but reabsorbing all wanted materials including the invaluable salts. Fresh water crustacea, molluscs and fish all possess tubules of different morphology which show very similar functional properties.

Different environmental conditions impose different demands on the osmotic and ionic regulating machinery. In very dry conditions, such as in deserts, it is obviously of advantage to reabsorb as much water from the tubule as possible. All animals do this but it is interesting that only birds and mammals have discovered the secret of so concentrating the urine that its salt concentration is higher than that in the blood. This is done by means of a hairpin-like loop in the tubule called the Loop of Henle, another example of a counter current device.

6. Co-ordinating Systems

Overall co-ordination of the animal's body, so that it functions as a whole and reacts appropriately to environmental changes, is largely the province of two systems, one chemical or hormonal, the other nervous. In one respect these are systems for homeostasis, that is for preserving the *status quo*, in spite of considerable environmental fluctuation. Paradoxically they can also initiate change as, for example, one can see in the daily repertoire of complicated behaviour patterns produced by almost any animal.

(a) Nervous Systems

(i) *Sensory Information*

Before appropriate reactions can be produced to any stimulus it is necessary to measure its intensity, position, duration and, most important, character. This is done by sense organs which are usually specialised to receive stimuli of a single modality or character. Thus photoreceptors detect light, mechanoreceptors detect mechanical disturbance and chemoreceptors detect specific chemicals. In all cases the sense organs produce a message about the stimulus in the form of nerve impulses (see **F33**—Cell Membrane) which travel up the nerve from the sense organ to the rest of the nervous system. Change of stimulus intensity is usually signalled as a change in frequency of nerve impulses. The position of the sense organ which is active indicates the position of the stimulus within or without the body. The duration of the repeated discharge of nerve impulses indicates the duration of the stimulus.

(ii) *Simple Networks*

The simplest type of nervous system is the network of interconnected nerve cells (neurones) found in the coelenterates. Branching processes of the nerve cells communicate with neighbouring processes at special regions called synapses (F33). Quite complicated behaviour is possible even with this relatively simple system. If a sea anemone is prodded violently it will close up equally violently, showing that activity has spread throughout the network. If it is tickled gently it will respond with local contractions around the site of stimulation. The movements of feeding and locomotion are very delicately performed at appropriate times.

(iii) *Central Nervous Systems*

In the majority of animals all the nerve cells tend to become collected into a solid mass of tissue referred to as a central nervous system (C.N.S.). Within the mass the nerve cells are interconnected via synapses in the same way as in a nerve net. The connexions with sense organs and muscles are made via long processes called axons. Numbers of axons are usually bound together with connective tissue to form a nerve trunk. In annelids and arthropods the C.N.S. is seen as a ventral cord lying beneath the gut with a swelling or ganglion in each segment of the body. In molluscs, the ganglia are usually more closely grouped around the oesophagus, with the possible provision of a pair of ganglia further back in the viscera. Vertebrates possess a dorsal nerve cord which is uniform in diameter and not ganglionated, though nerves emerge from it in a segmental fashion. The segmental nerves arise in two separate bundles or roots. The dorsal root is made up entirely of sensory nerves conveying information to the C.N.S. The ventral root consists of motor nerves which convey nerve impulses to the muscles of limbs and alimentary canal together with other effector organs such as glands.

(iv) *Reflexes*

A reflex, in which stimulation of a sense organ or sensory nerve results in the almost immediate contraction of a muscle, is the simplest type of C.N.S. activity. Reflexes have been studied in all animals but the best known ones can be seen in frogs, cats, dogs, and sometimes humans. The very simplest is the stretch reflex, in which a stretched muscle is made to contract by activity coming into the C.N.S. from stretch receptors in the muscle. The activity is relayed directly to the motor neurones of the muscle concerned, making them active and thus causing the muscle to contract. This reflex is monosynaptic, *i.e.* there is only the single synaptic connexion between sensory nerve and motor neurone. The knee jerk in humans is a stretch reflex, the stretch being caused by hitting the muscle tendon as it passes over the knee. Much of the recent work on reflexes has been done on this simple system, notably by Eccles. The flexor reflex, which is seen as the sudden withdrawal of a limb from any painful stimulus, is more complicated. Although the stimuli may vary, the withdrawal response is always accomplished by contraction of flexor muscles which bring the limb in towards the body. The reflex is polysynaptic, i.e. several intermediate neurones connect the sensory nerves through to the motor neurones. More complicated still is the scratch reflex in which an animal is made to scratch its flank in response to an irritation or tickling in that region. This reflex demonstrates some of the more involved properties of the C.N.S. For example a dog will continue to scratch for a time after the tickling has stopped, so that the C.N.S. must continue to be active in the absence of sensory stimulation. This has been called after-discharge.

v) The Brain

The C.N.S. functions in a more complicated way than is suggested by study of the reflexes and most of these higher activities are co-ordinated by the brain. A greater condensation of neurones is seen at the front end of the C.N.S. of all animals because of the larger numbers of sense organs in that region. Brains, which become the dominant part of the C.N.S., can be seen in arthropods, molluscs and vertebrates. The close association with sense organs is illustrated by the vertebrate brain which is divided into three regions: (a) forebrain (nose), (b) midbrain (eye) and (c) hindbrain (ear and taste). However, the brain is much more than a relay station for these stimulus modalities and it receives information from other parts of the body via the spinal cord. All this information is correlated and activity patterns initiated and transmitted to appropriate regions. In lower vertebrates, the roof of the midbrain (the optic tectum) is the important correlation centre and its effectiveness has been well established in studies on instinct and learning in fish. Another region of the brain of importance in all vertebrates is a dorsal upgrowth of the hindbrain called the cerebellum. This is a motor co-ordinating centre which ensures that all activities are performed in a smooth and well balanced way by the muscles and limbs of the body. In reptiles, the forebrain begins to take over the correlation role and in mammals this development reaches its peak in the cerebral cortex. In man the cortex overshadows the rest of the brain and contains some 1,000,000,000 neurones. It is easy to see the magnitude of the problem of understanding a system of this complexity. The bee's brain with far, far fewer cells can initiate complicated behaviour such as the hive dances. The possibilities offered by the human cortex seem vastly greater, though they are often realised in ways which give cause for concern. At the moment it would be quite impossible to build a computer with the properties of the human brain. To do this in the future would depend on major advances in computer technology and even greater advances in the knowledge of central nervous systems.

(b) Hormonal Regulation

Many aspects of an animal's metabolism are regulated, not by the nervous system, but by specific chemical signals known as hormones which are circulated in the blood stream. Growth, carbohydrate metabolism, salt balance, activity of ovaries and testes and their associated structures, and colour change are all regulated in some way by hormones. The substances are secreted by endocrine glands or ductless glands as they are often called. The important endocrine glands in vertebrates are the thyroid, parathyroid, adrenal, pancreas, the sex glands, and the pituitary.

In the past the endocrine and nervous systems were regarded as exerting an independent control in slightly different functional areas of the body. It is clear now that the integration of the two systems is much greater than was formerly envisaged and in vertebrates is accomplished through the pituitary gland. Secretions of this gland regulate almost all other endocrine glands and the secretions of the pituitary are either produced in the C.N.S. with which it is directly connected or are controlled by C.N.S. secretions. An astonishing, parallel development of other neurosecretory systems, such as those of the pituitary, has been found in a variety of animals and in all types the neurosecretory organ complex is the dominant endocrine gland of the body. In crustacea the so-

called X organ complex found within the eyestalk, and in insects neurosecretory cells connecting to the corpora cardiaca glands, occupy the functional position of the vertebrate pituitary. They all regulate growth, metabolism and reproductive physiology, either directly or through the mediation of other endocrine glands.

7. Animal Behaviour

In discussing the nervous system we have already dealt with simple mechanisms such as the reflex. Very much more complicated are the instinctive and learned patterns of behaviour which are studied by animal psychologists and ethologists such as Lorenz and Tinbergen.

(a) Instinct

Instinct is inborn behaviour which does not have to be learnt and is usually performed in a stereotyped way. For example a gull will retrieve an egg taken out of its nest by shovelling it back with the underside of its beak. The gull will never replace an egg in its nest in any other way, for example by using a wing or leg, and once it has begun a retrieval it will usually continue the movements back to the nest even though the egg is taken away. An instinctive behaviour pattern is triggered off by a particular stimulus or " releaser " which may be a very small part of the total environment. A male stickleback will attack a very crude model with a red belly but will not attack an exact model without it. The red underside appears to be a much more important stimulus than general shape. A particular instinctive pattern cannot always be elicited and the reaction of an animal very largely depends on when the behaviour was last produced. The longer the time that elapses, the easier it is to trigger off the instinctive pattern until eventually it may appear in the absence of an appropriate set of environmental circumstances.

(b) Learning

Learning is that behaviour acquired during the organism's lifetime as a result of experience. Evidence of learning has been seen in many animals from worms upwards though, as might be expected, the more complicated types of learning are found only in those animals with elaborate nervous systems. A simple type of learning is seen when an animal, upon repeated exposure to a stimulus, gradually decreases the normal response which is usually one of flight, until eventually the response may disappear completely. This process is called habituation. More complex are the conditioned reflexes, which were first discovered by Pavlov. In these an animal can in some way connect a conditioned stimulus such as a bell, with an unconditioned stimulus such as meat, so that eventually it salivates when the bell is rung. Trial and error learning of the type needed to be successful in running a maze is more complicated still. In this there is a retrospective element because the reward at the end of the maze comes after all the responses. Many animals can run mazes but the white rat has been extensively used in experiments of this nature and there is a huge literature on this one animal. A final category of learning can be called insight learning; in this an animal shows evidence of resolving a new problem without trial and error. This type of learning involves the perception of relations between different parts of the environment and though there may be examples in arthropods and molluscs the clearest evidence of it is seen in the behaviour of birds and mammals.

8. Reproduction

A single animal may live for a short or long time, but eventually it dies, and the continuance of the species is dependent upon reproduction. Some protozoa, such as Amoeba, reproduce asexually by the simple division of the cell to produce two new individuals. Asexual reproduction also occurs in some coelenterates, such as jelly-fish, in which there is an alternation of sexual and asexual generations. However, the vast majority of animals only reproduce sexually.

This involves the fusion of two cells, the gametes, produced by adult individuals, and each zygote thus formed develops into an individual of the next generation. The gametes are of two kinds, the large, spherical, immobile ova produced by the female gonad or ovary and the much smaller motile sperms produced by the male gonad or testis. The motility of the sperms helps them to reach the passive ovum, which contains food reserves to support the early development of the embryo.

Worms.—The flat worms, particularly parasitic forms, have complicated life cycles, and many are hermaphrodite, *i.e.*, each individual has both male and female organs. Cross-fertilisation usually occurs, the sperms from one worm being introduced into the female duct of another. The round worms are unisexual, and internal fertilisation also occurs. Of the annelids the polychaete worms are unisexual, but the ova and sperms are shed into the sea, where fertilisation takes place. However, *Lumbricus* and the leeches are hermaphrodite, cross-fertilisation takes place and the eggs are laid in cocoons.

Arthropods.—Many crustacea are unisexual, though the sedentary barnacles are hermaphrodite. Internal fertilisation may occur, but in the crabs and crayfish pairing takes place and the sperms are deposited on the tail of the female. When the eggs are shed they become fertilised and remain attached to the abdominal appendages. Most crustacea have motile larval stages into which the eggs first develop. In *Daphnia*, the water-flea, parthenogenesis sometimes occurs, *i.e.*, the eggs develop without being fertilised. The sexes are separate in the arachnida and there are usually no larval stages except in the primitive king-crabs. The insects are also unisexual, and the fertilised eggs are laid after copulation. In some, *e.g.*, dragon-flies, an immature nymph similar to the adult is formed, but in flies, beetles, moths, and many others the egg hatches into a larval form. This then develops into a pupa, from which the final adult or imago is produced. In the social ant's nest the workers are sterile females with large heads, reduced eyes, and no wings. The males and queens are winged, and insemination of the latter occurs during the " nuptial " flight.

Molluscs and Echinoderms.—Most lamellibranchs are unisexual, although some species of scallops and oysters are hermaphrodite. There are motile larval forms, and in the swan mussel, *Anodonta*, the larvae develop in the mantle cavity of the parent and when liberated become attached to the gills or fins of fish, where they remain parasitic for some time. Some gasteropods are unisexual, but the slugs and snails are hermaphrodite. In the latter cross-fertilisation occurs, the two approaching snails being stimulated to copulate by firing small sharp darts of calcium carbonate into each other. The echinoderms are unisexual, and fertilisation takes place in the sea. The egg first develops into a ciliated larval form.

Vertebrates.—The sexes are always separate in the vertebrates. In some cartilaginous fish, *e.g.*, dogfish, internal fertilisation occurs and the eggs are laid in protective sacs. In contrast, the bony fish shed ova and sperms into the water, where fertilisation takes place. Although pairing may take place in the amphibia, fertilisation occurs in water, and there is usually an aquatic larval stage. The reptiles, birds, and mammals are independent of water for fertilisation, as copulation takes place and the sperms from the male are introduced directly into the female. Most reptiles and all birds lay eggs with hard shells. Development of the embryo in marsupial mammals begins in the female uterus, but is continued in a ventral pouch which surrounds the teat of the mammary gland. In the two living species of monotreme mammals the eggs are incubated in a similar pouch. Finally, in the eutherian mammals the embryo develops in the female uterus and is born at an advanced stage.

Diversity of Sexual Reproduction.—This brief survey will give some idea of the diversity of sexual reproduction in animals. External fertilisation is very much a matter of chance, and large numbers of gametes are produced which offset the great losses of gametes and embryos that this method involves. Internal fertilisation is more certain, and is also independent of external water—an important factor in land animals. In vertebrates particularly there is increase in the care of the young by the parents, involving the development of characters of behaviour as well as those of structure. Some fish lay their eggs in holes or nests which are protected by the male. Similarly, a few frogs build nests, while others carry the eggs about. The eggs of birds require a constant high temperature for their development, and they are usually incubated by the parents. After hatching the young are fed and guarded by the parents until they can leave the nest and fend for themselves. In the eutherian mammals the embryos are attached to the uterus wall by the placenta, *via* which food materials pass from the mother. The period of gestation is long, and after birth the young are supplied with milk from the mother until they are weaned and can feed themselves. Another feature in mammals is the period of " childhood " during which they play and learn and are protected and fed by their parents. The internal fertilisation, internal development, and care and protection of the young after birth which is so conspicuous in the higher vertebrates results in the reduction of losses during the vulnerable embryonic and young stages, and in consequence relatively few progeny are produced by a pair of individuals.

THE PLANT KINGDOM

There are various ways in which the main classes of the plant kingdom can be grouped, but a simple, up-to-date arrangement is given in the chart. Vascular plants are often known as the *Tracheophyta* because they all possess woody conducting elements. These are absent in non-vascular plants, and the bacteria, fungi, and algæ are often called *Thallophyta, i.e.*, they have a relatively simple plant body or thallus. Many of the bryophytes also possess a thallus, but in some there is a stem bearing leaves, although a true vascular system is absent. Many thallophytes are aquatic, whereas the tracheophytes are mostly land plants in which the development of woody tissues can be related to the attainment of the land habit as the plant kingdom evolved. However, the chart should not be taken as indicating the evolutionary relationships of the various groups. It is more a convenient arrangement which reflects the relative complexity of the plant body.

1. Bacteria.—This is a vast group of minute organisms of very simple structure. They are spherical or rod shaped and may exist as separate cells, some species being motile, or as long chains or irregular masses. Their minute size makes the elucidation of their structure very difficult. There is a wall of complex composition, and cytoplasm which contains glycogen and fat. Electron-microscope studies have revealed the presence of structures which appear to consist of nuclear material. Multiplication is by simple division, which may take place very rapidly. For example, *Bacillus subtilis* can divide every 20 minutes, so that in 8 hours a single cell may give rise to 16 millions. Recent research indicates that a sexual process may also occur. Bacteria can survive unfavourable conditions by producing a resistant spore within the cell. They do not possess chlorophyll, though a few are pigmented. Most obtain their food already formed, and are thus either saprophytes or parasites. The saprophytic bacteria occupy a vital position in the living world. They are responsible for most of the decay of dead organic matter, and it has been truly said that without them the surface of the earth would soon become completely covered with the dead bodies of animals and plants. Bacteria also play a vital part in the circulation of nitrogen in nature. By breaking down organic material, ammonia is released and ammonium carbonate is formed in the soil. This is oxidised by other bacteria to form nitrates, which can be absorbed

Plant Kingdom

Non-vascular Plants   Vascular Plants

Bacteria   Fungi   Algae   Bryophyta   Psilopsida   Sphenopsida   Lycopsida   Pteropsida

Filicinae   Gymnospermae   Angiospermae

Monocotyledones   Dicotyledones

by plants again. Yet other bacteria can "fix" atmospheric nitrogen, and one species, *Rhizobium leguminosum*, occurs in the root nodules of the pea plant. Such plants are often grown on poor soils and ploughed in, thus improving the fertility of the soil. The parasitic bacteria are also of great importance, as they are responsible for many diseases of plants, animals, and man.

2. **Fungi.**—This is a large group of plants, none of which contain chlorophyll. Hence, like the bacteria, they are either parasites on other living plants and animals or saprophytes which live on dead organic matter. Some are unicellular aquatic plants, but many have a body called a mycelium composed of many branched threads or hyphæ. In the higher fungi (*e.g.*, toadstools, bracket fungi, and puff-balls) complex reproductive structures are formed. All fungi produce spores. In the aquatic species these may be motile, but the majority form minute, airborne spores. The spore output is often very great, and a single mushroom may produce 1,800 million spores. Some fungi are serious diseases of crop plants, such as potato blight and wheat rust.

3. **Algae.**—These are essentially aquatic plants which contain chlorophyll. They range from microscopic forms to the large seaweeds. The green algae (*Chlorophyceæ*) live mostly in fresh water and may be unicellular, motile or non-motile, or filamentous, though a few found in tropical seas are more complex. The brown algae (*Phœophyceæ*) are mostly seaweeds which possess a brown pigment, fucoxanthin, which masks the green chlorophyll. They include the bladder-wracks (*Fucus*) and kelps (*Laminaria*) of our coasts and the seaweeds which form dense floating masses over hundreds of square miles of the Sargasso Sea. Other groups are the red algae (*Rhodophyceæ*), mostly seaweeds of delicate form, the unicellular motile diatoms (*Bacillariophyceæ*), and the blue-green algae (*Cyanophyceæ*). All algae possess unicellular reproductive organs. Various types of life cycle occur, the most complex being found in the red algae.

4. **Bryophyta.**—These are the liverworts (*Hepaticæ*) and the mosses (*Musci*). They are all small plants characterised by a sharply defined life-cycle. This consists of an alternation of generations, the "plant" being a gametophyte bearing sex organs. The latter are multicellular, the female archegonium containing a single stationary ovum and the male antheridium producing many motile sperms. The latter are released and swim in water to the archegonium, where fertilisation takes place. After this a sporophyte is formed which is always dependent on the gametophyte and never becomes free living. The sporophyte usually consists of an absorbing foot buried in the tissue of the gametophyte and a stalk or seta bearing at the top a single sporangium. In many mosses this is a complex structure with hygroscopic teeth which move apart only when dry, thus releasing the minute spores only when conditions are suitable for their dissemination in the air. The bryophytes are of little economic importance, and may be looked upon as an evolutionary side-line. However, they occupy suitable "niches" in many plant communities, and species of the bog-moss *Sphagnum* cover large areas where rainfall is high.

5. **Psilopsida.**—This is a small group of primitive, vascular, spore-bearing plants. Its only living representatives are two rare genera of the Southern Hemisphere. However, a number of fossil forms are known from the Devonian period. The best known are those found in the chert at Rhynie in Scotland. The plants are excellently preserved, and their internal structure can be easily seen. They were probably marsh plants with prostrate and erect leafless stems, although *Asteroxylon* had simple leaves.

6. **Sphenopsida.**—The only living members of this group are about twenty-five species of horse-tails (*Equisetum*). In the Carboniferous period many tree forms existed (*e.g.*, *Calamites*), the remains of which are very common in coal deposits.

7. **Lycopsida.**—In the Carboniferous period the tree clubmosses were also prominent members of the forests (*e.g.*, *Lepidodendron*). They often reached 30m in height, were branched or un-branched, and had large simple leaves. They also had extensive root systems. The only living members belong to a few genera of small her-baceous clubmosses, such as *Lycopodium* and *Selaginella*. Like the true mosses, they have an alternation of generations, but the elaborate plant with stem, leaves, and roots is the sporophyte, and the gametophyte is very small. In *Lyco-podium* only one kind of spore is produced, and the resultant gametophyte is bisexual. *Sela-ginella* produces numerous small microspores which give rise to the very reduced male game-tophytes and motile sperms and the few large megaspores which produce the female game-tophytes. The latter are formed within the megaspore wall, which splits to allow the sperms to reach the small archegonia.

8. **Filicinae.**—These are the true ferns, which in some classifications are put with the horsetails and clubmosses in the Pteridophyta or vascular cryptogams (*i.e.*, vascular plants without seeds). The ferns have a long fossil history, and remains very similar to the living Royal ferns (*Osmunda*) are known from the Carboniferous. The ferns are widespread and particularly abundant in tropical forests. The majority are herbaceous perennial plants, but a few are aquatic, and there are some tree ferns, which may reach 6 m in height. Most ferns possess a stem bearing roots and large leaves or fronds. The plant is the sporophyte and produces numerous spores in sporangia borne on the fronds. Each spore gives rise to a minute green free-living gametophyte known as the prothallus, which bears the archegonia and antheridia. After fertilisation a young sporo-phyte develops, which at first draws nourishment from the prothallus. Thus, as in the *Bryophyta*, external water is essential for the motile sperms to swim in, and there is a clearly defined alternation of generations, but the sporophyte is a complex independent plant, and the gametophyte is reduced though free-living.

9. **Gymnospermae.**—These were the dominant land plants in the Mesozoic era, although fossil re-mains are found as far back as the Devonian. The living members still form large forests in the North Temperate regions. They are mostly tall evergreen trees with roots, stems, and small leaves. The conifers include the pines (*Pinus*), larches (*Larix*), and yews (*Taxus*). The cycads

are a relic group of tropical plants with thick, unbranched trunks and large fern-like leaves. The maiden-hair tree of Japan (*Ginkgo biloba*) has also had a long geological history. Another interesting Gymnosperm is *Metasequoia*, a genus well known to palaeobotanists. In 1948 a few living specimens were found in a remote area of China. Seeds were collected and plants are now being grown in botanical gardens all over the world. The Gymnosperms are characterised by the production of " naked " seeds, which are usually borne on cones. The male pollen grains, which are equivalent to the microspores of *Selaginella*, are carried by wind to the ovule of the female cone. The pollen germinates and the pollen tube carries the male gametes to the reduced archegonia borne on the female prothallus, which, unlike those of the ferns, is retained within the ovule on the parent plant. After fertilisation an embryo is formed, the prothallus becomes the food store or endosperm, and the outer part of the ovule becomes the seed coat. The cycads and *Ginkgo* retain a primitive feature in that the male gametes are motile and they swim to the archegonia from the pollen tube.

10. Angiospermae.—The apparent sudden rise of the Angiosperms in the Cretaceous period is still the " abominable mystery " it was to Darwin. Various suggestions have been put forward, but nothing definite is known about the origin of the group. The Angiosperms or flowering plants are now the dominant group over most of the land surface of the earth, and at least 250,000 species are known. Apart from the natural vegetation, the majority of our crop and garden plants are Angiosperms. They occur in every type of habitat and range in form from gigantic trees to minute plants, such as the duck-weeds. Some are climbers, others succulents, and a number have reverted to the aquatic habit. Although most possess chlorophyll, a few are partial (*e.g.*, Mistletoe) or complete parasites (*e.g.*, Dodder).

Flower, Fruit and Seeds.—The diagnostic feature of the group is the production of seeds, which are completely enclosed within the female part of the flower, the ovary. Basically a flower is a short reproductive shoot which bears several whorls of lateral organs. At the base are several, often green, protective sepals forming the calyx, and above this are the often brightly coloured petals of the corolla. Within this are the stamens of the androecium or male part of the flower. Centrally is the female gynoecium of one or more carpels containing the ovules. The parts of the flower may be free, as in the buttercup, or fused together. In many species the petals are fused (sympetalous), the stamens are borne on the corolla (epipetalous), and the carpels are fused to form a compound gynoecium (syncarpous). The stamens possess anthers, which produce pollen grains. These are shed and carried by insects or wind to the receptive stigmas of the carpels. Each produces a tube which grows down the style to the ovary and enters an ovule. The ovule is a complex structure containing an ovum and a primary endosperm nucleus. Two male nuclei are discharged from the pollen tube, one fuses with the ovum and the other fuses with the primary endosperm nucleus. After this " double fertilisation " an embryo is formed which is embedded in the nutritive endosperm and the outer tissues of the ovule form the seed coat or testa. The ovary of the carpel develops into the fruit containing the seeds. Fruits are of various kinds, being either dehiscent and opening when mature to release the seeds or indehiscent, with a succulent or dry wall. The indehiscent fruits are shed as a whole, and often contain only a single seed. Seeds and fruits show great variation in structure, and often have adaptations assisting dispersal. Some have hairs or wings which aid wind dispersal, whereas others have hooks or are sticky and are transported by animals. Some have flotation devices and may be carried a great distance from the parent plant by water. Seeds vary in size from the microscopic seeds of orchids to those of the double coconut, which may weigh 18 kg. Only about 10% of the weight of a seed is water, and the embryo, although alive, is dormant. The bulk of

a seed consists of stored food material, commonly fats or starch and proteins, which may be contained in the endosperm surrounding the embryo, although in some species the endosperm is absorbed during seed development and the food is stored in the one or two swollen seed leaves or cotyledons of the embryo.

Classification of Flowering Plants.—John Ray (1627–1705) was the first botanist to recognise the two great divisions of the Angiosperms—the dicotyledons with two seed leaves and the monocotyledons with only one. This primary division of the flowering plants has stood the test of time and is still recognised. Other differences are also found between the two groups. The dicotyledons usually have net-veined leaves and the floral parts are in fours or fives, whereas the monocotyledons usually have leaves with parallel veins and the floral parts are in threes.

THE PHYSIOLOGY OF PLANTS

Some of the fundamental differences between animals and plants can be ascribed to the ways in which the two groups of living organisms satisfy their requirements for food material. In a simple way at least, an animal can be thought of as a mobile gastro-intestinal tract which is highly specialised to search out and receive food in convenient, concentrated packets. In typical land plants, however, a quite different organisation exists because the organic nutrition is based on the process of photosynthesis in which carbon dioxide from the air is combined with water from the soil to form simple carbohydrates. An expanded foliage system is necessary to absorb carbon dioxide and to expose the photosynthetic pigment, chlorophyll, to sunlight. Similarly, an expanded root system is needed to absorb the other ingredients of nutrition, water and mineral salts, from the soil.

The work of the plant physiologist is devoted to understanding the functional relationships between these two expanded systems of root and shoot. The production of carbohydrates by photosynthesis has already been discussed (F28). Absorption and transport of water and mineral salts from root to leaf and transport of the synthesised organic compounds from leaves to other parts of the plant continue to be challenging problems. In addition, the physiologist is concerned with the progressive elaboration of root and shoot as the plant grows. Plants show much less specialisation of their cells into discrete tissues and organs than do animals and they also retain special areas, at root and shoot tips for example, where new cells are added to the structure throughout the life of the plant. In some cases whole plants can be regenerated from very few cells taken almost anywhere from a growing plant body. The orderly regulation of growth and differentiation is thus a basic property of much plant tissue.

1. Movement of Solutes and Water

The movement of water and inorganic solutes in a plant is primarily upwards from the roots where they are absorbed, to the leaves or growing regions where evaporation of water or the use of both water and salts occurs. Water and inorganic ions permeate freely through the cell walls and air spaces of the more peripheral cells of the roots. Equilibrium is established between the insides of cells in this region and the water and salts outside, water tending to enter by osmosis and the salts by diffusion or active transport. Increase in cell volume which would be caused by continual influx of materials is, of course, restricted by the inextensible cell wall. In the centre of the root is a region packed with the specialised conducting tissues called xylem and phloem. These form continuous channels through the root and into the shoot and clearly serve for the conduction of water and substances in solution. In the root this central region is separated from the more peripheral tissue by a single layer of cells, the endodermis. The endodermal layer can actively pump water and salts from the outer regions through into the longitudinal conducting strands of, in this case, the xylem. Evidence for this pumping activity can be seen in the exudation of liquid from the base of a plant stem cut close to ground level. In some cases pressures of 8 to 10 atmospheres have been generated in roots as a result of the pumping action of the endodermal cells.

Water is also moved up a plant by forces generated in the leaves. Constant evaporation from the walls of leaf cells, both on the surface and within the substance of the leaf, causes loss of water from the plant. The process is called transpiration and, within limits, the plant can control transpiration rate by regulating the ease with which water-saturated air passes to the exterior through perforations in the leaf surface called stomata. The diameter of these apertures can be regulated by movements of guard cells surrounding the stomatal openings. Loss of water from the leaf cells is made good by withdrawing more water from the xylem elements within the leaves and stem of the plant. Cohesive forces between water molecules prevent the continuous water columns within the xylem from breaking. The net result is that water is drawn up the stem as transpiration occurs in the leaves. Considerable suction pressures have been measured by suitable manometer systems attached to the cut stems of actively transpiring plants. In addition materials such as dyes or radioactive isotopes have been followed as they move up the conducting xylem vessels at rates which can usually be related to the rate of transpiration.

2. Movement of Organic Substances

The organic substances, whose site of manufacture is primarily in the leaves, have to be distributed to the rest of the plant body. It is thought that a second conducting tissue, the phloem, is mainly responsible for the distribution of these materials in solution. Phloem is found as a layer of tissue to the outside of the xylem vessels in a plant stem. It consists of conducting cells which are rather different from those of the xylem, which serve, as we have seen, mainly in the transport of water and salts. Whereas xylem tissues are composed of dead cells whose cell walls form effective longitudinal conducting channels, phloem is made up mainly of living cells. Elements called sieve tubes are the most important conducting cells in phloem and, during the initial stages of differentiation, a sieve tube has a full complement of cytoplasm and cell organelles. Later differentiation sees the protoplasmic structures break down, but even in mature sieve tubes protoplasmic strands join through the perforated ends of adjacent cells and may extend longitudinally through the conducting elements.

Ringing experiments in which a complete ring of phloem is cut from the outside of a plant, provide evidence of the tissue's function in longitudinal conduction of carbohydrates. Sugars accumulate above such a ring but not below it. Samples of fluid taken from sieve tubes have also revealed high concentrations of carbohydrates in the sap. The method used to obtain such samples is very ingenious. Several aphids (insects such as green fly) are known which parasitise the phloem translocation channels of plants. The aphid is allowed to insert its stylet tip into the phloem vessels and is then anaesthetised and cut off the inserted stylet. Sap exudes from the stylet stump and can be collected and analysed.

3. Growth

Growth is usually, but not always, thought of as involving increase of size as measured by length, volume, or weight. In these terms any unit in a plant, whether root, shoot or fruit would follow a sigmoid growth curve with growth starting slowly, then speeding up, before finally slowing down at maturity leading on to death. Growth may also be considered as an increase in the number of cells, or an increase in substances such as water, protein or DNA in the growing system, or an increase in complexity of organisation.

The organisation of growth, no matter how it is measured, presents a number of interesting problems. In the first divisions of a fertilised egg, all cells divide. Very soon this property becomes localised, polarity is established, and the young embryo develops a shoot tip and a root tip. These have then become discrete regions of cell division. The cells behind them cease active division, enlarge by developing large vacuoles and form mature plant tissue. A circular strand of dividing tissue, called the cambium, is left in the stem between differentiated xylem and phloem. The cambium is responsible for growth in girth. The acquisition of polarity has far-reaching consequences, for the behaviour of a shoot tip is very different from that of a root. The shoot tip, for example, gives rise to leaf cells with photosynthesising chloroplasts and it grows upwards away from gravity and towards light. The root tip gives rise to cells which absorb salt and water, and it grows towards gravity and away from light.

Quite a lot is known about the mechanisms which regulate growth by cell enlargement in the regions behind the actively dividing tips. Cell enlargement is achieved by the secretion of water and solutes to form a substantial vacuole within the cell, thus causing an overall increase of volume and expansion of the cell wall. The degree of enlargement is affected by external stimuli such as light and gravity, producing the differential growth patterns seen when plants orientate to these stimuli. Substances, called plant hormones or auxins, are now known to be produced at the growing apex and to move back causing vacuole formation in the actively elongating region. The distribution of auxin is affected by light or gravity so that the plant will turn towards or away from the stimulus. Indoleacetic acid is the active growth substance occurring naturally in many plants. Several man-made substances are also effective and are widely used as weedkillers. Evidence is also accumulating to show that a group of substances exists in plants to control cell division, just as auxins regulate cell enlargement.

ECOLOGY—THE STUDY OF LIVING ORGANISMS IN THEIR ENVIRONMENT

So far we have examined biological organisation at the level of the cell through to the whole, multicellular organism. The important branch of biology which deals with the relationship between living organisms and their environment must now be considered. Living organisms and the physical environment in which they exist form what is termed an ecosystem. Obviously it would be possible to regard the whole world as a giant ecosystem, though for purposes of study it would be extremely unrewarding and impractical to adopt such an extreme attitude. A pond, a rocky or sandy shore, a forest, and a peat bog are examples of ecosystems on a somewhat smaller scale, possessing different properties and containing populations of animals and plants that are different both in number of individuals and in species represented. The ecologist seeks to understand why a particular species is present in certain numbers in an ecosystem in terms of that species' interaction with all other living organisms (biotic factors) and with the physical (abiotic) factors of the ecosystem.

1. Abiotic Factors

All living organisms will show ranges of tolerance for abiotic factors such as temperature, humidity, salinity, oxygen levels, amount of light, etc. Clearly, if any factor in the environment moves outside the range of tolerance of a species, it becomes limiting for that particular species which is then excluded from the environment. Within the range of tolerance there will be an optimum value for each abiotic factor at which a species will survive best.

There is not a firm line separating suitable and unsuitable environments, but rather a steady shift from optimum values into conditions in which an organism finds it more and more difficult to survive. The interaction of different abiotic factors in an environment produces a complex situation which will make the environment suitable for one species but will exclude another species having slightly different abiotic optima from the first, even though the conditions are not outside the tolerance ranges of either species. Thus trout and carp show considerable overlap in the ranges of temperature, oxygenation of the water, and speed of water current in which they can survive and it is possible for both species to live in the same pool or tank. In the wild, however, they tend to form part of different ecosystems because trout have a lower temperature optimum, need more oxygen, and are more active than carp. Trout are found in rapidly-flowing, cool, unpolluted chalk streams whereas carp live best in shallow lakes which are somewhat warmer and rather stagnant.

One of the most important abiotic factors in an environment is the nature of the substrate upon or within which an organism moves and settles.

(a) The Terrestrial Environment.—Soil is the commonest substrate for terrestrial organisms. Particle sizes, ranging from the coarsest gravel soils, through sands and silts to the finely textured clays, have extensive effects on the flora and fauna of any area. Coarsely textured soils are obviously penetrated most easily both by roots and by soil animals. Soils of this type also allow the rapid movement of water and soil gases, but they have the serious disadvantage of poor water retention. The level at which water saturation occurs is known as the water table and is an important abiotic factor. The terrestrial environment tends on the whole to dehydrate organisms and there is always a marked dependence on water supplies.

Soil characteristics also vary with depth. A vertical section through any soil is referred to as its profile and has considerable bearing on the ecosystems in which the soil is involved. The layers, or horizons, of a soil profile vary enormously from one soil to another. Below a surface layer of organic debris one can, in general terms, distinguish a layer of soil from which substances have been leached (A horizon), soil containing the leached-out substances from the layer above (B horizon), the weathered parent material (C horizon), and finally the parent rock or some other stratum beneath the soil (D horizon).

Humus, which is formed from animal and plant remains and is located in the lower parts of the A profile, is of great importance in providing food for soil organisms and chemical elements such as nitrogen, phosphorus, and calcium for plant growth. It is also important in maintaining good soil structure and, though inorganic fertilisers can supply chemical elements, they have little or no effect on structure. Soil requires careful cultivation, and structure is easily disturbed by such things as heavy farm machinery. The smearing of soils by spinning tractor wheels as wet land is ploughed, or the winter harvesting of crops such as sugar beet in adverse conditions, eventually leads to the creation of impermeable layers with the disastrous exclusion of oxygen and oxygen-consuming organisms.

(b) The Aquatic Environments.—Marine and freshwater environments together cover more than 75 per cent of the earth's surface and, since they can be occupied throughout their entire depth, offer a much greater volume of living space than does the land. There is only a slight difference between the density of water and of living tissues, so that the bodies of aquatic organisms are very largely supported by the environment and do not need strong woody stems or powerfully muscled limbs to hold them up. Water has a high specific heat, which means that large amounts of heat are needed to raise its temperature. The result is that aquatic environments tend to show much smaller fluctuations in temperature than the terrestrial ones. In general, the larger the volume of water the smaller are the fluctuations in temperature, and so the fauna and flora of the oceans will not show wide temperature tolerance, whereas that of small pools will, but in neither case will the tolerance be so great as that shown by many terrestrial forms. Oxygen and carbon dioxide concentrations are very different in water and in air and this has led in animals to the development of gill

systems for gas exchange rather than the lungs, or lung-type structures, of terrestrial forms. Gas concentrations are also variable from one aquatic environment to another, making them suitable for the support of different fauna and flora.

An important difference between the sea and freshwater is seen when their salt concentrations are determined. This is usually done experimentally by measuring the temperature at which the medium freezes, because a well-established relationship exists between the salt concentration in a solution and the extent to which the freezing point is lowered below that of the solvent (in this case distilled water) alone. Thus, freshwater freezes at 0 °C or just below whereas sea water, with its high salt content, freezes at −1·9 °C, and a mixture of half fresh and half sea water freezes at −0·95 °C. Organisms living in fresh or in sea water face quite dissimilar problems in osmotic and ionic regulation. Life evolved originally in the sea and the salt concentration in the blood of marine molluscs, crustaceans, and echinoderms, for example, produces precisely the same freezing point depression as does sea water itself. Marine organisms have, on several occasions in the course of their evolution, moved into freshwater. Representatives of the worms, crustaceans, molluscs, and vertebrates have all independently invaded this very dilute habitat. What is more, all these animals show approximately the same types of modification to cope with the change. Their outer layers, in the main, become impermeable and the salt concentration of their blood is reduced considerably (to a freezing point of −1·0 °C in fish and to a spectacularly low level in the freshwater mussel, depressing the freezing point to a mere −0·2 °C). The kidneys become enlarged and produce a large volume of dilute urine. By these means freshwater animals can cut down loss of their salts to the dilute medium and can also remove the large volume of water that enters their bodies by osmosis. It is interesting that all terrestrial vertebrates, including the mammals, have retained a salt concentration in their blood of about half the seawater level and this is partly attributable to their freshwater ancestry. The transition between seawater and freshwater was achieved via brackish water estuaries and the organisms which live under brackish water conditions today are of great interest in showing how tolerance of substantial fluctuations in salinity can be achieved. The ultimate development of salinity tolerance is seen in such animals as the salmon and eel which move from fresh to salt water and back again during their life cycle.

2. Biotic Factors

(a) Associations between Organisms.—No organism can be considered to be independent of any other organism in an ecosystem but in some cases close associations of various types can be developed between different species or different members of the same species.

Commensalism is an association which benefits one member but has little effect on the other. Small organisms can live within the protective covering offered by a larger individual, as, for example, commensal crabs living within the shell of some species of oyster.

Symbiosis is a somewhat closer association in which both members benefit, as do certain species of green algae and the coelenterates in whose body tissues they live. The algae are protected and the coelenterates benefit from the food produced by the photosynthetic plant. Some symbiotic organisms are unable to survive outside the association. The lichens which are associations of algae and fungi, are examples of this type of symbiosis, as are some of the food-processing micro-organisms together with the animals in whose intestinal tracts they live.

Social animals. In some cases animals of the same species form social groups in which co-operative effort and division of labour makes them more successful in exploiting a particular environment. Social development is most obvious among certain insects such as termites, ants, wasps, and bees, and among the vertebrates. Social organisation in these groups may lead to the development of different behaviour patterns and ultimately, as in ants and bees, for example, to the evolution of a variety of structural modifications so that different castes are recognisable.

Parasitism. Not all associations are of mutual benefit and when one organism becomes sufficiently specialised so that it can live successfully on materials extracted from another, the latter is always adversely affected. Parasites, by causing disease in, and sometimes the death of, the host, can influence population growth and size. Important groups are bacteria, protozoa, fungi, nematodes (roundworms), and platyhelminths (tapeworms and liver flukes). Viruses are also important disease-producing agents which are incapable of an independent existence outside the cells of the host and utilise the host cell's metabolic pathways directly to synthesise new virus material.

Many parasites (and other pests which may disturb the comfort and health of man) can now be controlled to some extent, and, for a variety of reasons, such control procedures have extensive effects on the ecosystems involved. The regulation of some bacterial parasites by means of antibiotics, and control of the insect vectors of organisms such as the malaria parasite by means of insecticides, have both been important factors in the increase in human population. Though the beneficial effects of pest control of all types are clear, the process is not without its difficulties and dangers. Indiscriminate use of many chemical agents has led to the development of resistant strains. In any group of organisms, some will naturally be more resistant to a pesticide or antibiotic than others and these will be the survivors of any treatment that is less than totally effective. They will form the breeding stock for subsequent generations and so progressively more and more resistant types will evolve. Thus, there are now many strains of bacteria resistant to penicillin and other antibiotics. Even more alarming is the recent discovery that this resistance can be transferred in an infective way between bacteria of different species. Another complication associated with chemical control is that the agent concerned frequently affects a wide spectrum of organisms, including those that are in no sense injurious to man or his crops. Thus DDT kills bees and other pollinating insects unless its application to a crop is very precisely timed. In addition, the accumulation of quantities of chlorinated hydrocarbons such as DDT in the environment is known to have an injurious effect on organisms other than insects. Because these chemicals are broken down very slowly they now form a serious problem in environmental pollution.

Predation. A less direct association than that between parasite and host is the one which exists between predators and the prey which they capture and kill. However, interactions in both parasitism and predation have features in common, particularly those affecting population numbers. If the abundance of prey increases, the effort and time required for a capture is reduced so that the rate of predation must also go up. Eventually, however, predators do not respond to further increases in prey; because they are satiated, or for some other behavioural reason, a maximum predation rate is reached in a population of a certain size. Increased prey density also tends to result in larger numbers of predators, produced either by aggregation from outside areas or by increased reproduction rate. The density of predators then begins to have its limiting affect on the rate of predation. The total response may lead to stability in numbers but more often periodic oscillations in the number of both predators and prey are seen.

(b) **The Food Factor.**—Plants are the ultimate source of organic food for all animals. The most important food plants are those capable of photosynthesis (F23) in which organic material is synthesised from carbon dioxide and water, using radiant energy from the sun to drive the reaction.

Food Chains. Plants are eaten by herbivores which in turn are eaten by carnivores. It is possible to see many such sequences, called food chains, in all ecosystems. For example, in the open sea, green algae are the important photosynthetic organisms; these are eaten by a small crustacean, *Calanus,* which in turn forms a large part of the diet of the herring. Feeding relationships are usually of much greater complexity than is suggested by a simple food chain. Thus, Calanus represents about 20 per cent of the herring's diet but it is also eaten by many other marine animals as well. For example, it forms about 70 per cent of the total diet of larval sand eels. The larval eels are eaten in turn by the herring and may form 40 per cent of its diet. Because an animal's diet is usually quite varied and one species of animal or plant may be part of the food of a wide range of different animals, interactions are set up which are referred to as food webs. The more knowledge there is about a particular food web, the more complex it becomes. However, for general comparative purposes it is possible to disregard the detail of species and to group together all organisms with similar food habits. When this is done a relationship known as pyramid of numbers often appears in which organisms at the base of a food chain (the primary producers) are extremely abundant, while those at the apex (the final consumers) are relatively few in number.

Productivity. The validity of using numbers of individuals in such an analysis is often open to question, especially when ecosystems are to be compared. For example, a comparison between numbers of herring and numbers of whales as final consumers in two pyramidal systems is not very informative. This difficulty is partially overcome by using estimates of the total weight (biomass) of organisms at each level rather than their number. Even this has disadvantages because determinations of biomass give a measure of the amount of material present at any one time (the standing crop) but give no indication of the amount of material being produced or the rate of its production (the productivity). In some parts of the sea, for example, the biomass of small animals forming the zooplankton is greater than that of the plant life or phytoplankton on which it depends for food. This seems to contravene the pyramid concept. However, the rate of production of new material by the phytoplankton is very much greater than by the zooplankton so that, if taken over a year, the total amount of plant material produced would far exceed the total production of animal material. Productivity is a concept of great practical and theoretical importance. It may be determined in terms of the actual organic material produced in an area over a set period of time or, more usefully, in terms of the amounts of energy transferred and stored at each food level, again over a set period of time.

Under natural conditions only 1 to 5 per cent of the light falling on a plant is converted by its photosynthetic system into chemical energy contained in the material of its tissues. Similarly herbivores which consume plants will pass on to their predators only some 10 per cent of the energy contained in the plant material they eat. These low values for photosynthetic efficiency and ecological efficiency respectively are due to the fact that most of the energy appears as heat during the metabolic reactions needed to sustain life and only a small amount is incorporated into new tissue. It is easy to see that the form of a pyramid of numbers can be explained in terms of low ecological efficiency, as can the observation that a food chain rarely has more than five links. The loss of energy at each stage must mean that each succeeding stage becomes smaller and smaller in number and that the number of stages is severely limited.

Human Population and Food. The present very large increase in human population and the predicted rise from 3,300 million in 1968 to 6,000 million in the year 2000 has led to a pressing need for the controlled exploitation of food resources in the world. Consideration of the processes of energy transfer suggests that man should be mainly herbivorous. They also suggest that present agricultural crops, with the possible exception of sugar cane, do not achieve as high a primary productivity as that encountered in some natural ecosystems. Crops rarely achieve complete plant cover of the land throughout the growing season so as to trap the maximum amount of sunlight. It would be necessary to mix crops to do this effectively and there would then be complicated harvesting problems.

If man remains an omnivore, as he almost certainly will, then his domestic food animals will continue to be herbivorous as they are at present, though whether they will be the same herbivores is less easy to predict. Beef cattle raised on grassland convert only 4 per cent of the energy in the plants of their environment into similar chemical energy in their tissues. At the present time intensive farming practices are being empoyed to improve conversion, usually by harvesting plant material, processing it, and bringing it to the animals which are housed in special buildings. This cuts down on the wastage of plant food because it can be grown under better conditions and less of it is consumed by animals other than the cattle. Careful breeding and the limitation of the period over which livestock is raised to that of maximum growth efficiency have also contributed to conversions of some 35 per cent, achieved in the case of broiler chickens and calves. The moral problems raised by these methods and the circumstances which make them necessary give rise to widespread concern.

Fish are also an important part of man's diet and again an understanding of the ecology of food fish is important in running efficient fisheries. Many populations have been overfished so that returns have gone down in spite of intensified fishing effort. The fisheries scientist is concerned to discover the limit at which the maximum number of fish can be taken without depleting the population year by year. Research is also going on into possible methods of enclosing and farming areas of the sea or estuaries.

Population Dynamics

Factors such as those outlined above interact to determine the size and character of any population of living organism. Study of the numbers of organisms in a population, together with their change and regulation, forms a branch of the subject of considerable practical importance known as population dynamics.

Numbers of animals and plants tend to increase up to the capacity of the environment, at which stage some essential resource will exert a limiting effect. The rate of increase will be determined by the balance between reproduction rate and mortality. As Malthus appreciated, adults of any organism tend to replace themselves by a greater number of progeny and, in the absence of losses by mortality and other factors, there is a vast potential for increase in all populations. If an organism doubles its number in a year, there will be a 1,000-fold increase in 10 years, and a 10 million-fold increase in 20 years. Increase of this type soon leads to shortages and overcrowding so that mortality goes up, the net rate of increase diminishes, and finally an equilibrium is reached with no further increase in number. The change from low to high numbers with the passage of time follows an S-shaped curve, starting slowly, becoming faster and faster, and then slowing down to equilibrium.

When a population reaches equilibrium, the numbers are kept at a steady level by factors such as competition for food, refuge, or space. These factors are said to be density-dependent because greater numbers in the population intensify the competition and increase mortality, lower numbers decrease competition and favour survival. Abundance is therefore regulated by density-dependent processes arising from interactions, first, between individuals making up the population, and secondly, between the population under consideration and other populations whose members may be competitors, predators, or food. The level of abundance at which this regulation occurs may vary greatly and will be determined, at least in part, by general environmental factors such as temperature, rainfall, amount of sunlight, the nature of the vegetation, and so on.

Human population is increasing rapidly at the present time, mainly because of the fall in death-rate. Food production is also increasing, but in some areas of the world supply and requirement are so evenly matched that drought or war are inevitably followed by a famine. Though the human population has not yet reached the stage of equilibrium, it is clear that ultimately it must be subject to forces of regulation similar to those that control populations of other organisms. Birthrate cannot exceed death-rate indefinitely in any living organism. By limiting the size of families it is possible for man to achieve a population equilibrium at levels lower than those at which regulative factors such as famine or aggression must begin to operate. Rational control of birth-rate seems to offer the best chance of averting a global population disaster.

THE GEOLOGICAL RECORD

The various stages in the history of the earth can be read by the geologists in the strata or layers of rock laid down since the planet began to solidify, and it is in these rocks, too, that the record of life upon earth may be traced.

No Life Rocks.—The earliest rocks in the record are known as the Azoic (no life) rocks, because they show no trace of living things, and these layers are of such thickness that they occupy more tnan half of the whole record. That is to say, for more than half of the earth's history nothing living existed upon any part of the globe. For millions of years the surface of our planet was nothing but bare rock without soil or sand, swept by hot winds exceeding in violence the wildest tornadoes of today, and drenched by torrential downpours of tropical rain which, as we have seen elsewhere, gradually tore away the surface to form sandy sediments at the bottom of the seas. In such ancient rocks pushed above the surface by later upheavals we can still trace the marks of primeval oceans as they rippled upon the barren shores or of raindrops which left their imprint perhaps 1,500 million years ago.

Primitive Sea-life.—As we move upwards through the strata, however, traces of life begin to appear and steadily increase as we come to the more recent levels. The earliest signs appear in what is known as the Early Paleozoic Age (or by some writers as the Proterozoic Age), when we find the fossilised remains of small shellfish, sea-weeds, and trilobites—the latter were creatures somewhat like the plant-lice of modern times. All these primitive animals and plants lived in the shallow tidal waters of ancient seas ; for as yet life had not invaded either the dry land or the deep oceans. It is, of course, clear that these creatures of Early Paleozoic times were not the first living things: they were merely the first creatures capable of leaving fossilised remains, and without doubt must have had more primitive ancestors—amœbic-like forms, jellyfish, bacteria, and so on whose bodies were too soft to leave any traces in the record of the rocks.

The Age of Fishes.—Towards the end of the Early Paleozoic Era, in what we now know as the Silurian period, there arose a new form of life : the first backboned animals, primitive fishes somewhat similar to the sharks of today ; and in the division of the Upper Paleozoic Era known as the Devonian, they had come to multiply so greatly that this is frequently described as the Age of Fishes.

First Land Animals and Plants.—It is about this time, too, that we begin to find traces of animal and plant life upon the dry land. Both animals and plants had acute problems to solve before it became possible for them to live out of water; for both animals and plants had hitherto been supported by the surrounding water and respired by removing oxygen dissolved in the water. In land animals this problem was solved by a long series of adaptations from gills to lungs. Plants were able to invade the land because of the evolution of an impermeable outer cuticle which prevented water loss and also the development of woody tissues which provided support and a water-conducting system for the whole plant body.

Amphibia and Spore-bearing Trees.—The first type of vertebrates (backboned animals) to live upon dry land was the group of amphibia in the Carboniferous Age, which is today represented by the newts, frogs, toads, and salamanders. In all these forms the eggs give rise to a tadpole stage with gills which lives for some time entirely in water. Later the gills give place to a primitive form of lung which enables the animal to live upon land. Even so, amphibia are restricted more or less to swampy or marshy land, and without a damp environment they would dry up and shrivel to death. The most abundant forms of plant life in the Carboniferous period were the tree-like horsetails, clubmosses, and ferns, the fossilised tissues of which are found in the coal measures and are burned as household coal. But these plants also, as in the case of the amphibia, could exist only amongst the swamps and marshes, and life, although it had freed itself from the necessity of existence in the waters of the earth, still had to return to the water in order to reproduce itself. The highlands and the deeper waters of the planet were still empty of living things. Although the Carboniferous period had been a period of warmth and abundance, the Paleozoic Era came to an end with a long cycle of dry and bitterly cold ages. Such long-term climatic changes were due, it is now supposed, to such factors as changes in the earth's orbit, the shifting of its axis of rotation, changes in the shape of the land masses, and so on. Long before the Ice Ages of more recent times, there are records in the rocks of alternating periods of warmth and cold as far back as the Azoic and Early Paleozoic Eras. This long cold spell at the close of the Paleozoic era came to an end about 220 million years ago, and was succeeded by a long era of widely spread warm conditions—the Mesozoic Era, the so-called Age of Reptiles.

The Mesozoic Era.—The reptiles first appeared in the Permian, but it was during the Mesozoic era that they became the dominant group of animals. The giant reptiles included the stegosaurus, the gigantosaurus, the diplodocus, and many other kinds which were far larger than any land animals living today. Some, for example the diplodocus, were 100 ft. long, although they were vegetarian in habit and were preyed upon by other almost equally huge flesh-eating reptiles. Some species, such as the plesiosaurs and icthyosaurs, became secondarily aquatic, while the pterodactyl possessed wings with which it could glide and perhaps fly short distances. However, they all differed from the amphibia in that they had hard, dry skins, their lungs were more efficient, fertilisation was internal due to the development of copulatory organs, and they laid eggs with hard, protective shells.

It was also during the Mesozoic era that the warm-blooded birds arose. The birds, like the reptiles, lay eggs with hard shells, and they have several internal features found in the reptiles. The fossil bird Archæopteryx, three specimens of which have been found in Germany, lived in the Jurassic period. Although it was obviously a bird, it retained many reptilian features. Earliest mammals are recognised in rocks of the late Palaeozoic but in the Mesozoic considerable evolution of the group took place. The fossil Trituberculata which are also found in the Jurassic, are believed to be related to forms from which both the marsupial and placental mammals arose. Although insects were present as far back as the Carboniferous, it was in the Mesozoic that many of the groups we know today first appeared.

Great changes also took place in the plant cover of the land during this era. The spore-bearing giant horsetails and tree clubmosses declined and were replaced by gymnosperms—trees bearing naked seeds. One large group of these, the cycadeoids, has become extinct, but the conifers and a few of the once abundant cycads still remain. The flowering plants or angiosperms also made their appearance, and towards the end of the Cretaceous their evolution was extremely rapid. In fact, many of the fossil leaves found in rocks of Cretaceous age are indistinguishable from those of some present-day flowering plants.

A New Era.—But, perhaps 150 million years later, all this seemingly everlasting warmth and sunshine, the lush tropical life, the giant reptiles who had ruled the world, were wiped out by a new period of bitter cold which only the hardy species could survive. A new Era known as the Caenozoic was beginning, ushered in by a period of upheaval and volcanic activity, following which the map of the world came to resemble more closely the picture we know today. The cold period may have lasted several million years, and the main species to survive it were those which had come into existence towards the end of the Mesozoic Era, the seed-bearing flowering plants, the birds, and the mammals. The once all-powerful reptiles from this time onwards are represented only by the comparatively few and relatively small reptilian species of today: the snakes, lizards, crocodiles, and alligators. It was at this time, too, that, long after the creation of the mountains of Scotland and Norway (the so-called Caledonian revolution), or even of the Appalachian mountains (the Appalachian revolution), there arose the great masses of the Alps, the Himalayas, the Rocky Mountains, and the Andes. These are the mountain chains of the most recent, the Caenozoic revolution. Initially, as we have seen, the climate of the Caenozoic Era was cold, but the weather grew generally warmer until a new period of abundance was reached, only to be followed at the end of the Pliocene by a period of glacial ages generally known as the First, Second, Third, and Fourth Ice Ages.

THE GEOLOGICAL TIME SCALE

ERAS	PERIODS	AGE (millions of years)	LIFE
CAENOZOIC	Pleistocene	1	Man
	Pliocene		
	Miocene	25	Birds, Mammals and modern plants
	Oligocene		
	Eocene	70	
MESOZOIC	Cretaceous	135	Dinosaurs, Cycads; Earliest Birds; Ammonites and Sea-urchins
	Jurassic	180	
	Triassic	225	
PALAEOZOIC	Permian	270	First mammals; Early reptiles
	Carboniferous	350	Amphibians, tree-ferns, first insects
	Devonian	400	Fishes, first land plants
	Silurian	440	Mainly invertebrate animals; no life on land. Trilobites and graptolites
	Ordovician	500	
	Cambrian	600	

PRE-CAMBRIAN (also PROTEROZOIC, ARCHAEOZOIC) 2,000 Life emerges
4,600 Age of Earth

V. SCIENCES OF MAN

PHYSICAL ANTHROPOLOGY

MAN'S EARLY ANCESTORS

In the early Tertiary the earth's climate was generally warmer than it is today and extensive tropical forests covered much of North America and Europe as well as Africa and Asia. It is from geological deposits in these northern latitudes that the earliest fossil remains clearly attributable to the Primate order of mammals have been found. Three Families are represented in the Palaeocene period: the Carpolestidae, the Phenacolemuridae and the Plesiadipidae; the first two exclusively North American but the third known also from Europe. Most of the remains are of teeth and pieces of jaw but other parts of the skull and even bones from the rest of the skeleton have been preserved of some species. All the forms show many primitive characteristics as is to be expected in such early forms; more surprisingly they show little similarity in their special characteristics with later families, but they are judged to be Primate on the basis of the morphology of their molar teeth. By the next geological period, the Eocene, however, fossils are to be found which are fairly certainly the ancestors of present-day Primates. The Families known from the Eocene are the Adapidae, from which the Lemurs were probably descended, the Tarsiidae, containing the ancestor of the present-day *Tarsius*, the Anaptomorphidae which seem to have become extinct at the end of the Eocene and the Omomyidae, representatives of which seem to have given rise to the higher primates or Anthropoidea. The Palaeocene and Eocene primates along with the extant lemurs, lorises and tarsiers are referred to taxonomically as "prosimians". Little is known of their evolution after the Eocene until the Pleistocene, partly because of poor conditions for fossilisation where they lived, but partly also because they experienced a marked reduction in numbers following competition with evolving rodents and their own anthropoid descendants. Today the lemurs are confined to the island of Madagascar where they escaped this competition; the lorises have a restricted distribution in tropical Africa and Asia and are nocturnal in habit and the tarsier is confined to some of the islands in the East Indies.

The first definite anthropoids are known from the Oligocene period, mainly from deposits of a former swamp in the Fayum of Egypt. Among the fossils here have been identified the first Old World Monkeys (Cercopithecoidea) in *Parapithecus* and *Apidium*; the first gibbons (Hylobatidae) in *Aeolopithecus*; and the earliest ancestor of the Great Apes (Pongidae) in *Aegyptopithecus*. It has also been suggested that a form known only from a few teeth and a lower jaw *Propliopithecus* might represent the origin of the lineage giving rise to man, but this is now thought to be unlikely. Some Oligocene fossils are also known from South America and appear to be the beginnings of the New World Monkeys (Ceboidea) which are probably descended from New World prosimians and have evolved quite separately from Old World anthropoids.

From the Miocene, which follows the Oligocene, remains of a number of different apes have been found in East Africa, India (the Siwalik hills) and parts of Europe. Most are collectively referred to as the *Dryopithecinae* and still retain many monkey-like characteristics. Their skeleton indicates that they ran and jumped through the branches of trees, as most monkeys tend to do, but intermittently they probably moved by swinging from their arms; a mode of locomotion termed semi-brachiation. Present-day apes, the Orang, the Chimpanzee and the Gorilla are almost certainly descended from the Dryopithecinae. The group, however, is also seen as containing the ancestors of the human or hominid lineage. With regard to the early divergence of this lineage a fossil, known as *Ramapithecus* and found in both India, East Africa (where it was first called *Kenyapithecus*), Turkey and Europe is important. It is known only from teeth and jaws, but in contrast with apes these show a rounded shape to the dental arcade, small canine teeth and spatulate shaped incisors; all of which are hominid characters. It is surmised that *Ramapithecus* lived on seeds and had probably given up an arboreal life for a terrestrial one, and what is more, in becoming terrestrial had adopted an erect bipedal mode of locomotion. The fossil is dated to *c.* 14–10 million years ago. Mention should also be made here of another fossil anthropoid known best from Pliocene deposits in Italy: *Oreopithecus*. This, in a well-preserved skeleton, shows many features of bipedalism, but other characteristics, particularly of the teeth indicate that it is not closely related to man but is rather an aberrant ape.

Major Features of Primate and Human Evolution

The distinctive characteristics of Primates arise from the fact that all species in the group either themselves live in trees or have had ancestors which were tree-living. They, therefore, show, though to varying degrees, a number of arboreal adaptations.

1. Special development of the limbs

The arboreal environment is characterised by being not only three-dimensional but also irregular and precarious. Animals in it therefore require special mechanisms for hanging on to branches and moving through trees. Primates have adapted to these needs by evolving thumbs and big toes which are opposable to the other digits so as to form grasping organs. Associated with this is the tendency to replace claws with nails and the development of friction pads on the palmar surface of hands and feet. A considerable flexibility and wide range of movement is evolved in the forelimb and primates have the ability to sit back on their haunches and explore the irregularity in their environment with their hands, thus emancipating the forelimb from a solely locomotor function. The grasping hand can also be used for collecting food and transferring it to the mouth.

2. Development of special senses

Unlike terrestrial environments the world of the trees is not a world of smells and the sense of olfaction tends to be poor in Primates. Concomitantly there is a reduction in the snout, also made possible by the development of the hand. On the other hand, vision becomes an increasingly important sense and the eyes of Primates tend not only to be large but also to move from a lateral position on the skull on to the front of the face. Eventually there is overlapping in visual fields and the evolution of stereoscopy. In higher Primates colour vision arises. Tactile sense is also increased and balance and fine movement are improved. These changes in the senses are reflected in brain structure and size and Primates tend characteristically to have large brains for their body size.

3. Reduction in offspring number

The arboreal environment because of its precarious nature puts a premium on parental care and if there are many offspring to be cared for dissipation of parental effort may lead to none surviving. The arboreal environment is thus one of the few where animals who reduce their litter size can have a higher reproductive fitness than those with large litters. Primates typically give birth to only one or two offspring at any one time. This also means that there is little or no competition between offspring and therefore no premium for rapid development. Primates tend to be characterised by slow maturation and a long dependence on parents.

Clearly many of the features we see in man are an extension of his Primate heritage. But man, of course, has his own very distinctive characteristics. Anatomically these are to be seen particularly in his adaptations to a terrestrial bipedal existence, his much reduced face and jaws and his greatly enlarged brain. In evolution it would seem that it was the acquisition of the bipedalism which was critical. Why man's ancestors abandoned an arboreal habit is obscure, though there must have been a particular terrestrial ecological niche available, perhaps grain eating. Why in becoming terrestrial these same ancestors became bipedal is also unknown. Other Primates, such as the baboons and their relatives on re-colonising the ground continued to be quadrupedal. Perhaps the fact that the dryopithecine apes were semi-brachiators and therefore in many ways pre-adapted to an erect posture was significant. But whatever the explanation bipedalism, superimposed upon a Primate heritage, offered important evolutionary opportunities. This is not because bipedalism itself is a particularly effective means of locomotion but rather that it completes a Primate tendency of emancipating the forelimbs from locomotor function. They could therefore be used for many other purposes. One of the most important of these was tool use and subsequently tool-making. When early hominids colonised the terrestrial habitat they had few inbuilt defence mechanisms and the ability to use stones, sticks and bones to ward off carnivores and other predators must have been of considerable survival value, as has been shown by observation of present-day chimpanzees when they are on the ground. The ability was enhanced and extended as it became possible to fashion these natural objects into shapes for particular purposes, and throughout the later stages of hominid evolution there is evidence of increasing refinement of the use of stone and flints in the making of tools. Initially of use in defence, the tools became of value in offence, and there is evidence quite early in hominid evolution of a lineage changing from the traditional herbivorous diet of Primates to a carnivorous one, indicating the adoption of a hunting mode of life. Tool making must have been one of the practices which favoured the development of language, and, since it came to require fine manipulative skill, hand and brain evolved together; particularly those parts of the brain concerned with precise motor control and tactile sensation. Man is sometimes defined as the tool-making animal and although other creatures use tools and some fashion them at least occasionally, only man makes tools of a consistent and repeated pattern. Another consequence of freeing of the forelimbs through bipedalism was that carrying became so much easier. Thus food and other materials could be carried over considerable distances and this facilitated the establishment of a home base. Perhaps even more importantly the human infant could be carried in its mother's arms and held close to her body, allowing a much closer and intimate relationship between mother and child than is possible in other animals. The human infant is born in a very immature state; in part because of the limitations to the size of the birth canal imposed by the demands of bipedalism. It is therefore long dependent on maternal care. This raises problems in a hunting economy where nursing mothers become dependent upon males for the catching and providing of food. It has been argued that the evolution of the particular form of reproductive cycle found in man, in which the female is receptive to the male throughout most of her menstrual cycle should be seen as a means of ensuring that a hunting male will provide for his female and offspring. Certainly the type of behaviour found in many monkeys in which a female in heat abandons her offspring to consort with dominant males would not be compatible with survival of the human baby.

In recent years a great deal of attention has been devoted by physical anthropologists to studying the behaviour and ecology of many different Primates, especially Old World Monkeys and Apes. One of the aims of this has been to try and understand the origins of human sociality. Except in the most general of terms little can be said definitively about this, mainly, of course, because the non-human Primates have themselves evolved since the time they shared common ancestry with man. And even among quite closely related forms an immense diversity of social structures exists. But these new ethological studies have added a fascinating dimension to physical anthropology and allow a much more functional interpretation of Primate variety than was possible before.

THE HOMINID LINEAGE

Australopithecinae

This group of creatures are presumed to be descended from a form like *Ramapithecus* and lived during Pliocene and Lower Pleistocene periods. They are well known from many finds made by R. Dart, R. Brown and J. T. Robinson in South Africa and more recently from East Africa, where L. S. B. Leakey and his family have been the main discoverers. For a number of years controversy raged as to whether they were apes or hominids: the brain size is small, in most cases well within the ape range, and they have heavy projecting jaws and large teeth. However they also show a number of human characteristics; their canine teeth were not projecting dagger-like structures; their jaw movement was a rotatory grinding one not just directly up and down as in apes and most importantly, as evidenced from their post-cranial skeleton, they were terrestrial bipeds. In East Africa at least, there is also evidence that they made stone tools.

The taxonomy of the Australopithecines has been a source of great confusion. In South Africa the fossils were recovered from various former caves in Botswana and the Transvaal and those from a particular cave were given a distinct scientific name: *Australopithecus africanus* from Taung, *Australopithecus prometheus* from Makapansgat, *Pleisianthropus transvaalensis* from Sterkfontein, *Paranthropus robustus* from Kromdrai and *Paranthropus crassidens* from Swartkrans. Today it is generally agreed that only two forms are represented and that they are probably distinct only at the species level. They are known as *Australopithecus robustus* representing the forms previously known as *Paranthropus* and *Australopithecus africanus* the rest. The former, as its scientific name suggests, was a heavy rugged creature and, on the evidence of its extremely large premolar and molar teeth, was probably herbivorous. *A. africanus* was a much more gracile creature and, it is surmised, may well have been an active hunter.

A major problem in discussing the evolutionary significance of the South African australopithecines has been the difficulty in establishing accurately their age, since they were found in limestone breccias which cannot be geologically dated with present techniques. The situation is much better in East Africa where the fossils are found in or nearby igneous rocks which can be dated, particularly by the potassium/argon method. This indicates that australopithecine forms existed as long as 5 million years ago and occupied the region till 1·5 million years ago. The major sites from which specimens have been recovered are Olduvai Gorge in Tanzania, East of Lake Rudolph in Kenya and Omo and Afar in Ethiopia. Again there is evidence of two distinct forms as in South Africa; one robust, such as the well-represented "Nutcracker man" *Zinjanthropus boisei* (now known as *A. boisei* or *A. robustus boisei*) from Bed I at Olduvai Gorge; and the other gracile and comparable to *A. africanus*. At Olduvai Gorge, where it occurs in Bed I and the lower part of Bed II with dates ranging from 1·9 million—1·6 million the gracile form is more advanced than in South Africa with a larger braincase and more human teeth and has been termed *H. habilis*. It was almost certainly the maker of the Olduvan pebble culture and its advance on the South African form is probably because it was later in time. However, an anomaly which has not yet been explained is the discovery at East Rudolph of a form known as ER 1470 which appears more advanced, particularly in its large cranial capacity, than any other australopithecine and yet has a date of around 2·5–2 million years.

Homo erectus

Although evolution along a lineage is a process of slow and gradual change, it is necessary taxonomically to divide the continuum into stages. When the fossil record is incomplete the gaps in it are used for separating the stages, but as these gaps are filled by further discovery the divisions become increasingly arbitrary. Bearing this difficulty in mind we can refer the stage of human evolution after the australopithecines (probably from a form like *A. africanus*) to *Homo erectus*. Most of the finds of this species are dated to the upper part of the Lower Pleistocene and to the Middle Pleistocene period. *H. erectus* is character-ised by very thick skull bones, the development of heavy bony ridges, particularly above the eye region, and neither chin nor forehead. However the brain is much larger than in australopithecines and with a cranial capacity of 1,000 cc or more, *H. erectus* is intermediate between australopithe-cines and *H. sapiens*. Further the post-cranial skeleton is essentially indistinguishable from modern man and *H. erectus* was fully bipedal and made complex stone tools.

The first finds of *H. erectus* were made in middle Pleistocene river terrace deposits in Java at the end of the last century by E. Dubois. They were named *Pithecanthropus erectus*. Subsequently further fossils of the same form were recovered in the region, and some remains showing parti-cularly primitive features were recovered from Lower Pleistocene strata. Most of the latter were originally named *P. robustus* but a particularly massive jaw fragment termed *Meganthropus palaeojavanicus* shows australopithecine features. In 1927 and 1929 the first remains of Pekin Man (long known as *Sinanthropus pekinensis*) were found in Chou kou Tien cave near Pekin. These remains tend to show some advances on the Javanese fossils such as larger cranial capacities but otherwise are very similar. Although the first finds of *H. erectus* were in Asia it is now known that the species had a wide distribution in the Old World and remains now attributed to it have been recovered in Europe, at Heidelberg, Germany; Vertesszöllös, Hungary and Petrolona, Greece, and in Africa at Ternifine, Algeria; Sidi Abderrahman, Morocco (both initially called *Athanthropus mauritanicus*) and Olduvai Gorge, Tanzania. Some very recent discoveries in East Africa also indicate that *H. erectus* may have evolved much earlier than was formerly thought and been present 1·75 million years ago. It may thus be contemporaneous with late australo-pithecines.

Prior to the Middle Pleistocene all the varieties of primates, including hominids, had been con-fined to the tropical parts of the world. Now with cultural advances including knowledge of fire, man was able to leave the tropical areas and to utilise the space and resources of the more northerly parts of the Old World. Both at Chou kou Tien and Vertesszöllös there is clear evidence of the use of fire.

GEOLOGICAL DATING

It is evident that establishing the geological age of a fossil is critical to understanding fully the evolutionary significance of the remains. Most desirable is an ageing in years, termed absolute dating, where the results of tests are expressed as years " before present " or " b.p.", where " pre-sent " is taken as the year A.D. 1950. Where absolute dating is not possible, it is often still use-ful to know whether a particular fossil is older, younger or contemporaneous with other fossils. Establishing this is known as relative dating.

Radiometric Methods

The main methods of absolute dating are radio-metric and depend upon the fact that radioactive elements break down at a constant and known rate to other non-radioactive elements. The potas-sium-argon method, which has been associated with the East African hominids, depends upon the fact that the radioactive isotope of potassium K-40, which occurs in rocks of igneous origin, decays to the gas argon 40 and has a half-life of $1·3 \times 10^9$ years. It has been used for the absolute dating of deposits between 230,000 and 26 million

years old. For more recent fossils, up to about 50,000 years, the carbon-14 method can be used. This depends upon the constant rate of decay of the rare radioactive isotope of carbon, C-14, to normal carbon, C-12, and since bone contains car-bon, it is possible to date the actual fossil rather than the deposits in which the remains have been found.

Fluorine Method

One method of relative dating is called the fluorine method, depending as it does on the fact that bone progressively takes up fluorine from the waters percolating through deposits. The rate depends upon the concentration of fluorine in these waters, but if in one particular place some bones have high fluorine contents and others low, the former are likely to be the older. Relative dating may also be deduced from the depths at which fossil bones are found in undisturbed strata. An extension of this principle has been much used in the relative dating of fossil hominids in northern Eurasia, which in the second half of the Pleistocene was subjected, like North America, to a series of ice ages interrupted by periods when conditions became milder and at times even tropical. There were four major advances of the ice, often named from the Alpine ice sheets as Günz (the first), Mindel, Riss and Würm, and three major inter-glacials. Further, conditions ameliorated once during the course of the first three ice ages and twice during the Würm to form the so-called interstadial periods. The sequence is well repre-sented in the geology of many regions and forms a framework for the relative dating of various fos-sils.

NEANDERTHAL MAN

The most distinctive forms of Neanderthal Man, often known as classical Neanderthal man, have been recovered from deposits in Europe and sur-rounding regions dated to the time of the Würm I glaciation. Gibraltar was the site of the first discovery, but it was the skull fragment recovered from the Neander valley in Germany which gave the group its name. Other important sites of dis-covery are Spy (Belgium), La Chapelle-aux-Saints, La Ferrassie, Le Moustier and La Quina (France), Monte Circeo (Italy), Shanidar (Iraq), Mt. Carmel and Amud (Israel) and Teshik Tash (Uzbekistan). The main features of classical Neanderthal man are a long, narrow, low braincase, with a sloping forehead and a heavy bar of bone above the orbits; heavy faces with poor development of a cheek region, and the absence of a chin. However, al-though the general appearance of the skull has been described as " brutish ", the cranial capacity of classical Neanderthal man was at least as large as that of modern man, and the post-cranial skele-ton is completely modern in its anatomy. The bony remains are typically found associated with a distinctive flint industry, known as the Mouseer-ian industry, which occurs widely in Europe, the Near East and North Africa.

Progressive Neanderthal Man

The forms that precede classical Neanderthal man in the region show to varying degrees nean-derthaloid features, but these, surprisingly, tend to be less extremely developed, and most of the skulls look more like modern man than do the classical neanderthals. Important examples from the last interglacial are Ehringsdorf (Germany), Saccopastore (Italy), Fontechevade (France) and from the second or Great Interglacial, Steinheim (Germany) and Swanscombe (England). Al-though only the parietal and occipital bones of Swanscombe man are known, they are almost indistinguishable from modern man. This group of fossils is often referred to as Progressive Nean-derthal man. The paradox of early forms being more advanced than later forms has not been satisfactorily explained. The most widely held view is that there was a reversal of an evolutionary trend in Europe, under the influence of the cold of the Würm I glaciation and the isolation of the region which occurred with the expansion of the ice sheets. But as already noted classical nean-derthalers are not confined to Europe, and the features of the group do not appear to be cold adaptations. Perhaps more likely in the view that there were two (and possibly more) linkages from *Homo erectus*; a southern one evolving rapidly towards modern man, which only moved into Europe when the climate was warm, and a northerly linkage, evolving more slowly, which occupied the colder regions of Eurasia. In support of this view is the fact that not only do the remains from the Würm I glaciation appear primitive but also do those few which are known from the Riss glacial period at Abri-Suard and Arago in France. Further, more or less contemporaneous with classical neanderthal man, on the southern border of Europe were forms, like those recovered at Jebel Ighoud (Morocco), Jebel Quafza (Palestine) and the Skhul cave at Mount Carmel (Israel), which appear to represent the final transformation of progressive neanderthal man into modern man as we know him.

Rhodesian Man

Although not particularly neanderthaloid, two other types of remains should be mentioned here. Rhodesian man was first known from a completely preserved cranium found at Broken Hill, Zambia. It is remarkable in that whereas the skull is quite modern there are enormous brow ridges, comparable with an ape, and an extremely receding forehead region. Whilst only one specimen was known, some suggested it might be pathological, but an almost identical skull was later found at Saldanha Bay in South Africa. Until recently, Rhodesian man was thought to be about 40,000 years old and thus younger than the European neanderthals; it is now thought, however, to be considerably older.

Solo Man

Solo man is known from a number of crania from the later river terraces of the Solo river in Java. Apart from having larger cranial capacities, the remains are not unlike Javanese *Homo erectus*, and Solo man may well be the direct descendant of *Homo erectus* in the region.

MODERN MAN

With the retreat of the ice at the end of the Würm I glaciation, men, indistinguishable skeletally from present-day man, appear to have moved into Europe and replaced the classical neanderthalers. Whether there was any intermixture is uncertain; it is customary nowadays to include modern man and all the various forms of neanderthal man in the single species *Homo sapiens*, which would imply that intermixture would be possible. But if this happened it must have been on a small scale, since there is little evidence of any neanderthal features in the men of the Upper Palaeolithic: the latter derive their name from their stone tools which are infinitely superior to the mousterian flakes of the neanderthalers. In the stone industries of the Upper Palaeolithic—the Aurignacian, Solutrean, Magdelenian and others—one finds delicately constructed knife blades, arrow heads and engraving tools. This is also the time of the first cave paintings and clear evidence of the development of artistic tendencies. It is the first time too when the dead were buried. The economy, however, was still based on the hunting and gathering of foodstuffs, and crop cultivation and animal domestication were unknown.

Important Sites

A number of sites have been discovered in Europe which have yielded skeletal remains from this period. Among the more important are Combe-Capelle in the French Dordogne, which provides the earliest known skull (approximately 34,000 years B.P.); Cro-Magnon and Chancelade also in the Dordogne; Oberkassel in Germany, Brünn in Czechoslovakia and Paviland near Swansea in Wales.

Remains of modern man also begin appearing around this time in other parts of the Old World. The oldest comes from the Niah cave in Sarawak with a C^{14} date of 40,000 B.P. The upper cave at Chou kon Tien near Pekin has yielded a number of skulls. Then from Africa, mainly East and South, come a host of remains; the dating of many of these is not certain but most if not all are probably contemporaneous with the men of the European Upper Palaeolithic. Important sites from Southern Africa are Boskop, Cape Flats, Fish Hoek, Florisbad, Matjes River and Springbok Flats and from Eastern Africa, Elmenteita, Kanam, Kanjera and Omo. Interestingly none of the remains of this period in Africa show features like modern Negroes. The earliest remains from Australia have recently been recovered from Lake Mungo in New South Wales with a date of about 25,000 years B.P. Other, but less old, Australian sites as Kow Swamp and Keilor and the remains from these at least are clearly like modern aborigines in form. The earliest known skeletal remains from the New World date about 12,000 B.P., e.g., Tepexpan, Mexico, but from the finds of stone tools it is estimated that man first started occupying the Americas some 15,000–20,000 years ago, and that he came in a series of migrations from North East Asia across the Bering Straits.

Mesolithic Period

The Palaeolithic or Old Stone Age of Europe and many other parts of the world gradually gave way to the Mesolithic, from which there is evidence of domestication of the dog and the making of basketry; and this, in its turn, is transformed in the Neolithic or New Stone Age, when man first began cultivating plants and domesticating animals for food and transport, thus freeing his nutrition from the restrictions of the natural environment. In the Old World the Neolithic started in the Middle East some 10,000 years ago and rapidly spread in all directions. It developed again separately, however, in the New World. Until the Neolithic, man was a rare species; despite the fact that for many thousands of years he had been anatomically indistinguishable from present-day man. With the Neolithic, however, there began a dramatic increase in human numbers.

THE RACES OF MAN

The species *Homo sapiens*, like most other biological species, shows not only temporal variation, but at any one time, spatial or geographical variation as well. And much of this variation is hereditary in nature. Many attempts have been made to classify present-day mankind into races on the basis of this hereditary variation. In the past these attempts tended to be based on readily visible external features such as head shape, hair form and skin colour, but these characters are often affected by the environment in which individuals grow and develop, and even the hereditary component to their variation is complex and in no case fully understood. Typically, within any one population these characters show quantitative variation of a Normal or Gaussian form and it is not possible to place individuals into discrete categories, such as tall and short; the majority of a population are intermediate. When two populations are compared in such characters they usually show considerable overlap in their distributions and refined statistical methods may be necessary to reveal differences.

Racial Classifications

In recent years racial classifications have more commonly been based upon biochemical characters, often of the blood, since this tissue is most easily obtained, which show discrete rather than quantitative variation. The genetics of these characters is often relatively simple and has been determined, and differences in the environment in which people develop can be ignored. Populations are characterised in terms of the frequencies with which particular genes occur in them. There can be no doubt that classifications of mankind into races on the basis of either type of character express real features of human geographical variation, but inevitably they do so in a somewhat artificial if not misleading manner; they create the impression that the species is naturally partitioned into discontinuous groups, whereas changes from one region to another are often gradual rather than abrupt transitions. Further there is little precise concordance between the geographical distribution of different hereditary characters, and often distributions show no similarity with one another. Classifications based upon just a few characteristics are therefore likely to be quite different; and in racial taxonomy it is necessary to consider as much of the hereditary variation as possible. Bearing all these difficulties in mind, racial classifications can be useful, particularly in communication, but race is best seen as a phenomenon which needs to be explained, rather than as an explanation for other things.

Mendelian Population

Race is most accurately defined in population terms. A Mendelian population is a reproductive community of individuals who share in a common gene pool. Races are Mendelian populations which differ in the composition of their gene pools. More classically, race has been defined as a group of people who have the majority of their physical attributes in common. Three levels of differentiation of Mendelian populations or races are sometimes distinguished: (1) Geographical, (2) Local and (3) Micro-geographical.

Geographical Races

This is a collection of Mendelian populations such as occupy whole continents or large islands and are separated from one another by major geographical barriers to movement such as mountains, deserts and seas. Examples are the Negroes of Africa, the Caucasians of Europe, India and the Middle East, the Mongoloids of Eastern and S.E. Asia, the Australoids of Australia and neighbouring islands and the Amerindians of the New World.

Local Races

These are sub-populations within Geographical Races, frequently corresponding with particularly isolated and distinct breeding populations. Examples include the tribes within the Amerindian Geographical Race, and such groups as the Basques, the Ainu and Gypsies.

Micro-Races

These are the numerous distinct populations which are not clearly bounded breeding populations and can be distinguished only statistically. Much of the variation within the British Isles falls into this category.

ANTHROPOMETRY

Both individuals and populations of individuals vary in their size and shape, and anthropometry represents the different measuring techniques, usually made with calipers, which are used to analyse this physical variation as it occurs both in the living body and in the skeleton. From the early 19th cent. anthropometry has been a mainstay of physical anthropology, and particular attention has been devoted to the skeleton, since one of the main problems has been in establishing the evolutionary descent of the different races and skeletal remains constitute the most direct evidence of earlier populations. Many measurements have been devised, but the ones most commonly taken are of stature, head length and head breadth. For many years the latter two were especially favoured and used to calculate the cranial index (on the skull) or the cephalic index (on the living) by expressing the breadth as a percentage of the length. Long heads, with low cephalic indices (below 75) are termed dolichocephalic, while round heads with high indices (above 81) are termed brachycephalic. The intermediates are said to be mesocephalic.

Differing Features

Anthropometric features vary widely among the world's populations. Thus while the Nilotes of the Sudan have an average stature of 1·78 m, the African pygmies average only 1·36 m. There is little systematic pattern to the geographical distribution of stature itself, but it is a component determining the relationship between body volume and skin surface area, which shows a very distinct distribution. In people in cold regions, skin surface area is low in relation to volume, whereas in hot regions it tends to be high. This is explained

by the need to conserve body heat in arctic environments and to dissipate heat in the tropics. Because he follows this pattern man is said to observe the ecological rules of Bergmann and Allen. The causes for the variation in head shape are not known, though there is evidence that brachycephaly has been increasing in frequency since Upper Palaeolithic times. Nowadays, dolichocephalic heads are prevalent among Australian Aborigines while brachycephaly is extremely prevalent among mongoloid peoples.

Although there is a heritable component to most anthropometric variation, the nature of the environment in which an individual grows and develops can also be important. This has been shown by comparing migrants to new environments and their offspring, with parental populations.

PIGMENTATION

Variation in the colour of hair, skin and eyes is mainly due to differences in the amount and distribution of the black pigment melanin, which even causes the " blueness " of eyes when overlain with unpigmented tissues which defract light. The variation typically has a strong hereditary component, especially in eyes, but immediate environmental experience can have an important effect, as for example in skin tanning on exposure to ultra-violet radiation. Traditionally colour differences were described either in subjective terms or else by reference to matching standards. Both procedures presented serious limitations in reliability and in comparability of results. Recent years have witnessed the use of much more satisfactory objective procedures, involving spectrophotometers in hair and skin colour studies. These instruments record the percentage of light of a number of known specified wavelengths reflected from a surface relative to the reflectance from a pure white surface. In general, the darker the specimen, say of hair, the lower the percentage of light which it reflects. Using such instruments, precise and reliable quantitative estimations of hair and skin colour are possible and the genetic basis of the traits may be clarified and comprehended. There is some evidence that the skin colour differences between Europeans and Africans are due to three or four pairs of major genes. Dark skins confer advantages in sunny areas, since they protect the body against the harmful effects of ultraviolet radiation, minimising sunburn and the incidence of skin cancer. Light skins are advantageous in cloudy areas with low insolation, since they facilitate the body's synthesis of Vitamin D, thus reducing the incidence of rickets. The correlation between dark pigmentation and high levels of solar radiation is high, but it is impossible to state how much of the geographical distribution of skin colour mirrors the spread of dark- and light-skinned peoples from one or two sources and how much of the patterning is due to independent adaptations in many human groups in the past.

PHYSIOMETRIC OBSERVATIONS

These cover a diversity of phenomena, ranging from characters like colour blindness, ability to taste phenylthiocarbamide and fingerprints, whose variation is entirely or almost entirely hereditary, to characters like heat and cold tolerance and physiological adaptations to high altitude whose state is very largely a function of the environment in which an individual is living.

Red–green colour blindness is a sex-linked recessive character; males being far more commonly affected than females. Within Britain percentages of colour-blind males (which represents the frequency of this colour-blind gene) range from 5·4 in N.E. Scotland to 9·5 in S.W. England. Traditional societies, and particularly those still practising a hunter–gatherer economy, show much lower frequencies; and it may be presumed that colour blindness is a severe handicap under such a life-style. It has, in fact, been shown that red–green colour-blind individuals have difficulty in following a blood spoor on grass.

The tasting of P.T.C. is controlled by two genes T and t, the former being dominant. TT and Tt individuals normally experience a bitter taste sensation when they sip P.T.C. solution; tt individuals either cannot taste the substance at all or else only in very strong concentrations. The tt individuals are termed Non-tasters; TT and Tt individuals are termed Tasters. High frequencies of Non-tasters (exceeding 38%) occur in parts of Wales and Orkney, while low values (approximately 24%) occur in North Lancashire and Northumberland. A clue to the selective significance of this trait is provided by the excess of Non-tasters among individuals with nodular goitres (thyroid abnormalities). Non-European populations usually have lower percentages of Non-tasters than the British figures quoted. Thus, for example, the Jivaro Indians in the Amazonian lowlands of Ecuador contain but 1–2% of Non-tasters, as do the Chinese and many African Negro groups.

Finger-prints are one form of dermatoglyphic variation which also occurs on the palms of the hands, the soles of the feet and the toes. They arise as a series of epidermal ridges which form patterns on the surface of the stratum corneum of the skin. There is a strong genetic determination of these patterns, but the precise mode of inheritance is not known. Nor is it known why individuals and populations show this variation, or indeed why different patterns are found on the different fingers. In some pathologies, however, *e.g.*, Down's syndrome, there is marked abnormality of the dermatoglyphics.

The physiological variations in heat, cold and altitude adaptation tells us little or nothing about race, but they do indicate how remarkably adaptable the human being is, and help to explain why man has been able to colonise every type of terrestrial environment on earth.

BLOOD GROUPS

Attributes of the blood have increasingly been used in anthropological genetics because their mode of inheritance is relatively simple. One such set of attributes comprises the blood groups, which are complex chemical substances found in the wall of the red blood cell. These substances are antigenic and can be detected through their reactions with antibodies. A number of quite different blood group systems are now known. The first to be discovered, and still the most important in blood transfusion, is the ABO system. Whereas the antibodies to the other systems are only obtainable through immunisations, those to the ABO system are naturally occurring in human blood serum. The ABO system basically involves three genes, A, B and O (though there are sub-types of A). Every individual inherits two of these genes from parents, and so the genotype (genetic constitution) must be one of the following: AA, AO, BB, BO, AB, or OO. O is recessive to both A and B, and thus there are four possible phenotypes (genetic constitutions detectable by blood grouping): A, B, AB and O.

The ABO genes constitute a polymorphic system, that is several genes occur with frequencies such that the least frequent of them occurs with a frequency exceeding that due to mutation alone. Certain selective advantages and disadvantages of the ABO genes in human populations are known. Thus stomach cancers are more frequent among individuals of group A than they are in the population at large. Again, duodenal ulcers are almost 40% more common among persons of blood group O than in individuals of the other ABO groups.

Both on a global and on a local scale, the ABO genes display marked racial variation. Within Britain A varies from 31 to 53%, increasing in frequency from North to South; O varies from 38 to 54%, increasing in frequency from South to North. B shows less variation, though it is most prevalent in the Celtic areas. The regional fluctuations are not random but systematic and statistically highly significant despite the enormous migration within Britain during the last few hundred years, which might well have masked or minimised the underlying variability.

Globally the ABO variation is also striking. Thus the percentage of the blood group B exceeds 30 among the Mongoloids of Central and East

Asia, but the B gene is virtually absent in the Australian Aborigines, the American Indians and in the Basques. Many Amerindian tribes are 100% O; some others have very high A frequencies.

The Rhesus blood group system is more complicated and involves a number of closely linked genes. One pair of genes in this series determines whether an individual is rhesus positive, Rh+ (DD or Dd), or rhesus negative, Rh− (dd). The system is important in pregnancy, since if a mother is Rh− and her baby Rh+, any blood of the baby which crosses into the mother's blood stream can lead her to synthesise anti-Rh+ antibody. This will then cross the placenta and cause the baby's blood to haemolise; a condition known as erythroblastos foetalis and often fatal. First pregnancies are rarely affected, but subsequent ones often are, though in the last decade effective treatment has been discovered. Prior to this there was strong natural selection against the Dd heterozygote which should lead to the least frequent of the two genes in a population being eliminated. Nevertheless, many populations are polymorphic for these rhesus characteristics. In many parts of North West Europe and Africa the Rh− frequency is around 15%, and among the Basques it rises towards 40%. It is absent, however, from Amerindians, Australian Aborigines and most Eastern Asians.

An examination of the occurrence of the M and N genes of the MNS blood group system shows that most populations have an M frequency of 0·5–0·6. However, a higher frequency is found among Amerindians, Eskimos and some of the peoples of North East Asia; while N is higher in Australian Aborigines, New Guineans and Melanesians. In fact, there is a gradient of gene frequency known as a cline, around the Pacific. On the other hand, the S-linked gene is very rare among the aboriginal people of Australia, but it occurs at a frequency of some 20% in the native population of New Guinea.

Anthropologically the Diego system is of special interest, because it indicates affinity between Amerindian populations and the peoples of Eastern Asia. Other blood group systems include Kell, Duffy, Kidd, Lutheran, P, Xg; the last of these being a sex-linked character.

HAEMOGLOBIN

Haemoglobin, the red respiratory pigment of the red blood cell, exists in alternative forms in man, and these are genetically controlled. The frequencies of some of the genes which control haemoglobins vary markedly among human populations. The principal technique used to show variant haemoglobins is electrophoresis—the movement of charged particles in an electric field.

Normal human haemoglobin comprises two different haemoglobins, A and A2. An interesting variant of A is haemoglobin S. This may be indicated by electrophoresis and also by a sickling test. Red cells containing haemoglobin S placed in an oxygen-free atmosphere assume sickle shapes. Individuals who have inherited one S gene (AS heterozygotes) have a mild, non-fatal anaemia—the sickle-cell trait. Homozygous SS individuals suffer from the severe sickle-cell anaemia, which is usually fatal before maturity. Some abnormal haemoglobins including S, E and C have high frequencies and their existence, since all of them are deleterious to some extent, provides opportunities for viewing the action of natural selection and gene flow in human populations. Haemoglobin S reaches very high frequencies among some populations in southern Asia and particularly in much of tropical Africa (10–40%), despite its severe effect on individual viability and fertility. Haemoglobin C is most prevalent in northern Ghana and contiguous areas, while Haemoglobin E is found principally in South East Asia, with frequencies as high as 27% in Cambodia.

Homozygous SS individuals hardly ever live to transmit the S gene, and without a compensatory effect the gene would be totally lost except for certain cases possibly occurring as mutations. Compensation is through positive selection in favour of AS individuals who are more resistant to and so protected from falciparum malaria. Again AS females might be more fertile than AA females in certain populations, and this again would help to maintain the high S frequencies.

In addition to the genes which affect the chemical structure of the protein chains in haemoglobin, there are others which determine the rate of synthesis of those chains. These are the so-called thalassemia genes, and some of them also reach polymorphic proportions despite disadvantage in the homozygous state. Cooley's anaemia, which is common in certain Mediterranean countries, is an example. It would appear that this variation is also due to malaria; in Sardinia Cooley's anaemia is confined to lowland villages and does not occur in the mountains, where anopheline mosquitoes cannot breed.

OTHER SEROLOGICAL ATTRIBUTES

In addition to the blood groups and haemoglobin examples, many other polymorphisms are now known from human blood, and all of these show variation between populations as well as within them. In the serum of the blood are found the haptoglobins (proteins that bind the haemoglobin of old and broken-down red blood cells), transferrins (proteins in the blood sera used in transporting iron within the body) and the Gm groups (inherited variety within the structure of antibody molecules). The white blood cells carry the HLa antigens, so important in tissue and organ transplantation, and within the red blood cells a large number of genetically determined differences in enzyme structure have been discovered; examples include phosphoglumutase, adenylate kinase, acid phosphatase and glucose-6-phosphate dehydrogenase (which is particularly interesting, since it is a sex-linked character which, like the haemoglobins, appears to be important in resistance to malaria).

The extent of this variety is remarkable. It is now estimated that the average individual is heterozygous at 16% of his genetic loci (*i.e.*, sites of the genes). Taking the very conservative estimate that there are only 50,000 genes in man (a gene for this purpose being defined as a segment of DNA coding for a protein), this means that on average 8,000 gene loci carry different genes. With this level of variety the probability of two individuals being genetically alike, apart from identical twins, is astronomically low.

Analysing the causes for this incredible genetic variety is one of the central problems in anthropological genetics today. The factors which can determine the frequency of genes in populations are mutation, natural selection, movement and gene flow, genetic drift and founder effects. Further, differences between populations will only arise if they are to some extent geographically or socio-culturally isolated from each other. Gene mutation is a point change in the DNA code, and it constitutes the most fundamental factor acting upon gene frequencies. The mutation rate, or the rate of this alteration in the basic chemical structure of the gene, is evidently the same in all human populations. Whether or not a new gene remains in the population after its initial appearance depends upon the action of other evolutionary agencies. Thus, for example, natural selection, which is any environmental force that promotes the reproduction of certain members of the population who carry certain genes, at the expense of all the other members. Natural selection favours those genes which place their possessors at a reproductive advantage and tend to eliminate those genes that place the individual at an initial or long-term disadvantage. An example as simple as the amount of melanin present in the skin is entirely appropriate. High melanin concentrations inhibit the natural production of vitamin D by irradiation, and thus brings about vitamin D deficiency rickets and subsequent pelvic disproportions which may adversely interfere with pregnancy and a normal delivery.

Without doubt many of the characteristics used to identify groups of people or races have come into being through the forces of natural selection. A population whose members have shared the same gene pool for many generations and who are all descendants of a common ancestry has more than likely occupied the same geographical area and has thus responded to the same environment for a long period of time. If the environment has changed over the generations it may be assumed that natural selection has been at work, retaining some mutations, eliminating others and in any event changing the gene frequencies. Thus many genes now in the pool of a particular population were established through natural selection many generations ago. Unfavourable genes in an individual cannot be modified or corrected, and it is unlikely, especially if their effects are major, that they will be transmitted to the next generation. Rather, carriers of these inbuilt genetic errors will have a lower probability of reproducing than those without them, so that the next generation will have a higher proportion of individuals without the genetic defects and the generation following that an even higher proportion and so on. Population survival depending on genetic adaptation can only be effected through differential reproduction of genetically different individuals over the course of a number of generations.

The physical constitution of a population can also be influenced by gene flow which occurs when genes are transferred from one population to another. The carriers of these genes may arrive in great numbers and inundate the previously existing gene pool. On the other hand, the rate of genetic transfer may be slow but persistent over a protracted period. It is very unlikely that any human population ever remains totally genetically isolated over many generations despite geographical and/or socio-cultural barriers.

Recently there has been a striking increase in mobility, almost worldwide. Movement is the great homogenising force in evolution, for although it increases the variety within populations, it decreases the differences between populations. And the bicycle as well as the motor car and aeroplane can be shown to have had an effect. Racial and social barriers are also breaking down; in Brazil, for example, almost half the genes in the so-called Black group are of European origin, and in American Blacks the proportion is nearly a quarter.

Unless mutation, natural selection and gene flow are operating on a population, the gene frequencies within it will remain unchanged through successive generations, at least in large populations. In small populations, on the other hand—the situation prevailing during most of man's evolution—the genetic state of affairs is quite different, since the changes of gene frequencies may have nothing to do with selective advantages and disadvantages. In such populations the gene frequencies may oscillate due to random factors, such as the greater fertility, by chance, of one or two females, or disasters killing many men from one kin group, and the like. Similarly, only a small and unrepresentative sample of people may be involved in the founding of a new population. When this happens the genetic difference is said to have arisen from " founder effect ". In this context it is necessary to refer to the effective size of a population, that is, the percentage of the total population actually carrying out reproduction. In any human population many individuals are either too old or too young to be involved in reproduction, and many who are of the appropriate biological and cultural age may not be reproducing. It has, for instance, been estimated that about 60% of the population of the U.S.A. will reproduce the entire next generation. In hunter-gatherer and simple agricultural societies the effective population is frequently below 100, and drift can produce marked changes in gene frequency in a single generation. Whether or not it does act, however, depends also on whether the genetic alternatives affect the probabilities of survival and reproduction, *i.e.*, whether there is any natural selection. There is much debate at the moment on the extent to which neutral genes occur.

HUMAN ECOLOGY

While the main concerns of physical anthropologists are still the unravelling of the course of human evolution and explaining the patterns of present-day hereditary variation, recently, considerable attention has also been devoted to analysing the nature of all the interactions between man and his environment, whether they are genetically determined or not. This is broadly the field of human ecology and is as much concerned with the effects of the environment of man in industrial societies as in traditional societies. Much has been established of the ways human beings adapt physiologically to heat, cold, altitude; react to noise, pollution, crowding and stress; meet their nutritional requirements with different economies; and cope, culturally as well as biologically, with disease and other hazards in their environments. Even without his unique cultural and technical skills the human organism is remarkably adaptable; man's heat tolerance, for example, exceeding that of most tropical mammals, perhaps because for much of his evolution he was a tropical daylight hunter. But there is evidence that some of the diseases that appear to be increasingly common in modern industrial societies may be due to the fact that the environment has changed too much and too rapidly from that which prevailed throughout most of human existence. The flight/fight stress hormone response, for example, so adaptive in the context of a hunter-gatherer lifestyle, is probably contributing considerably to the increase in coronary heart disease in the sedentary urban man.

Human ecologists have also approached the problem of how whole communities interact with their environment. A study of energy flow through a Quechua Indian community in the Andes revealed that it was most economical to have large numbers of children. They could tend the flocks of animals, on which the community primarily depends for its food, as well as adults, but expended less energy in undertaking these tasks. Analysing the economy of energy, care and reproduction, risk and change is likely to be one of the major interests of future physical anthropologists.

THE STUDY OF SOCIAL ANTHROPOLOGY

What the Subject is About

Social anthropology is concerned with the way men live as members of ordered societies. It has been described as a branch of sociology, or as the sociology of the simpler peoples. Neither description is wholly correct. A social anthropologist seeks to identify the *structure* of the society he studies and the *processes* of social interaction within it. His method is direct contact—what has been called "participant observation." Therefore he must deal with a unit small enough to be manageable with this technique. Nation-states, such as sociologists commonly work among, are too large. Most social anthropologists have done their work in what we call "small-scale" societies; that is, peoples who lacked such media of communication as writing or money, let alone mechanical means of transport, until these were brought to them from Europe. A social anthropologist may choose to work in some section of a society that possesses those techniques—in the ancient countries of the East or in Europe or America. In that case he confines himself to a microcosm such as a village or a factory. When he is writing of societies alien to his own and that of most of his readers he is obliged to describe their *culture* as well as their social relationships, since without such a description his readers would not be able to picture, or even understand, the social rules that are his main subject of study; this would be superfluous for a sociologist taking modern machine society for granted. Culture has been called the raw material out of which the anthropologist makes his analysis of social structure. It is the sum total of standardised ways of behaving, of lore and technique, of belief and symbolism, characteristic of any given society. The founders of social anthropology as now practised in Britain were B. Malinowski and A. R. Radcliffe-Brown.

The Notion of Roles

All the world, as Shakespeare said, is a stage, and this is a key metaphor for social anthropologists. Every individual does indeed play many parts, not consecutively but all together; for every social relationship carries with it the expectation of society that the parties to it will behave in approved ways. Father and children, ruler and subject, buyer and seller, husband and wife; every one of these words is the name of a *role* to be played by the person it describes. The playing of roles involves the recognition of claims and obligations as well as appropriate modes of behaviour in personal contacts. All these rules are called *norms*; when they are concerned with rights and obligations they are *jural norms*. A social norm is what people think ought to happen; unlike a statistical norm, it may or may not be what happens in the majority of cases.

Kinship and Marriage

In societies of simple technology most roles are *ascribed*; that is, the parts people will play in life are given them at birth by the fact of their parentage and of the group of which this makes them members. In other words, the most important principle of organisation is *kinship*. W. H. R. Rivers called this " the social recognition of biological ties." The ties in question can be called genealogical; they all derive from the recognition of common ancestry. Such ties may be fictitious, as when a child is adopted. But in the vast majority of cases the relationships that are recognised are actually biological.

No man can recognise for social purposes all the individuals with whom he has a common ancestor somewhere in the past, or even know of their existence; their number increases with every generation. In every society a selection is made, from the whole universe of genealogically related persons, of certain categories towards which an individual recognises specific obligations and on whom he can make specific claims. Such *corporate groups* of kin have a permanent existence; they recruit new members in each generation in accordance with recognised rules. Kin groups are concerned largely with the transmission of property, and for this and other purposes they recognise the common authority of a senior man; they are also religious groups, performing together rituals directed to their common ancestors.

The common patrimony of a kin group normally consists in land or livestock; in societies of more advanced technology it may be a boat, as in Hong Kong, or even, as in Japan, a family business. It may have non-material resources too, such as the right to supply chiefs or priests for the society as a whole; this may be put conversely as the right to hold political or religious office. Those who share a common patrimony have a common interest in preserving and increasing it. Wrongs done by their members to outsiders are compensated from their collective resources, and they have joint responsibility for seeking compensation if one of their own members is injured, particularly in the case of homicide.

Descent

Kin groups may be recruited according to a number of principles. A principle widely followed in small-scale societies is that of *unilineal descent*; that is, group membership is derived from one parent only, either the father (*patrilineal* or *agnatic*) or the mother (*matrilineal*). Property is *administered* by men in either system, but in the matrilineal system it is *inherited* from the mother; hence its control passes from a man to the sons of his sisters. In a unilineal system every individual recognises kin linked to him through the parent from whom he does not trace his descent; this is the principle of *complementary filiation*. The complementary kin are *matrilateral* where the descent rule is patrilineal, *patrilateral* where it is matrilineal. A unilineal descent group is called a *lineage*.

Descent can also be traced *cognatically*; that is, all descendants of a common ancestral pair may be recognised as forming one *kindred*. In such a system there is no permanent group patrimony; people inherit a share of the property of both their parents, and this is often conferred upon them when they marry, while their parents are still living. Or all the inhabitants of a village may share rights in its rice-fields or fishing ponds; a man chooses among what kin he will live, but he can have rights in one village only. In such a system there are no continuing groups defined by descent; the permanent group is territorial, consisting in the inhabitants of the village.

Marriage

Kinship status is defined by legitimate birth, and this in its turn by legal marriage. There are always rules against marriage with specified categories of kin, though these are not necessarily near kin. Some societies consider that the ideal marriage is that between the children of a brother and a sister; if such marriages are repeated through the generations they create a permanent link between two lineages. Marriage between members of the same lineage is nearly always forbidden; this is expressed in the term *lineage exogamy*. The general effect of the prohibitions is to spread widely through a society the links created by marriage, links that impose an obligation of friendship on groups that without them would be mutually hostile.

In a matrilineal system women bear children for their own lineage; it is expected that they should be fathered by a man who has married their mother according to the approved procedure, but a child's lineage membership is not affected by the marriage of its mother. But in a patrilineal society wives must be brought from outside to bear children for the group. Associated with this fact is the payment of *bridewealth*, which used to be mistakenly interpreted as the purchase of wives. This payment is what fixes the status of a woman's children; all those she bears while the bridewealth is with her lineage are reckoned as the children of the man on whose behalf it was paid, even if he is dead and she is living with another partner. In a matrilineal society the making of gifts is part of the marriage procedure, but they are of slight economic value in comparison with bridewealth. The difference is correlated with the difference in what the husband acquires by the marriage; in both cases he gains the right to his wife's domestic services and sexual fidelity, but where bridewealth is paid he can also count her children as his descendants and call on their labour when he needs it.

In societies where most roles are ascribed by the fact of birth, marriage is the most important field in which there is freedom of choice. But the choice is commonly exercised not by the couple but by their lineage seniors, who are more concerned with alliances between lineages than with the personal feelings of the pair. *Polygamy*, or the simultaneous marriage of a man to more than one woman, is permitted in lineage-based societies; indeed it is the ideal, though only a minority of men attain it. One reason why it is valued is that it enables a man who has the resources necessary for successive bridewealth payments to build up a network of alliances.

Authority Systems

Every society has some arrangements for the maintenance of order, in the sense that force may be used against those who infringe legitimate rights. In every society theft, adultery, and homicide are treated as offences. Where no individual has authority to punish these on behalf of the community, *self-help* is the approved course. Lineage membership is significant here; a man who is wronged will go with his kin to seek redress (for a theft or adultery) or vengeance (for the homicide of a kinsman). Vengeance can be bought off by the payment of compensation; but because the taking of life is a serious matter in the most turbulent of societies, there must also be a solemn reconciliation, with a sacrifice to the ancestral spirits, between the lineages of killer and victim. The recognition of an appropriate method of dealing with injuries has been described as " the rule of law " in its simplest form.

Within a lineage the senior man is expected to settle quarrels, and the ancestral spirits are believed to punish with sickness juniors who do not listen to him. When quarrels break out between members of different lineages, their elders may meet and seek a solution. Where there is no hereditary authority individuals may attain positions of leadership in virtue of their powers of mediation by persuasion.

In addition to the maintenance of rights, most societies require at some time arrangements for the organisation of collective activities. It is possible for there to be no ascribed role of organ-

iser; in such a case leadership is a matter of competition. Competitive leadership in economic activities is characteristic particularly of the very small societies of New Guinea. What is needed here is not only powers of persuasion but resources to reward the participants. The very important principle, to be discussed later, that every gift ought at some time to be returned, is the basis of their position. A man who can put others in his debt can call upon their labour. It may take a long time to build up the necessary resources for acknowledged leadership, and leadership may be lost to a rival and is not necessarily passed to an heir.

Responsibility both for law and order and for collective activities may be shared on recognised principles among the whole adult male population. This is done where society is organised on the basis of *age*, a system widely found in east and west Africa. In such a system all adult men pass through a series of stages at each of which appropriate tasks are allotted to them. In its simplest form the division is made into " warriors " and " elders ". This principle may be complicated in various ways, but the essence of it is that men in their prime are responsible for activities requiring physical strength, impetuosity, and courage, while their elders have the task of mediating in disputes, discussing public affairs, and performing sacrifices to the ancestors. Men in the warrior grade are the fighting force, and may also have the police functions of summoning disputants and witnesses before the elders, and seizing property from a man who has been adjudged to pay compensation and does not do so voluntarily. Sometimes specific public works are allotted to them, such as rounding up stray cattle or clearing weeds from paths or springs. It is also possible for community responsibilities to be shared in more complicated ways, as for example among the Yakö of Nigeria, where the adherents of particular religious cults are believed to call on the spirit which they worship to punish persons guilty of particular offences.

Where there are hereditary chiefs, both public works and the maintenance of law and order are the responsibility of the chief and his subordinate officials. Resources are accumulated for public purposes by the collection of tribute, and labour is obtained for public works by the recognition of the principle that persons in authority can claim the labour of those subject to them. Expectations are attached to the role of chief as to any other. Chiefs are expected to dispense justice fairly, to be generous to the poor, to reward loyalty, and to be successful in war, and they are reminded of these expectations in the course of the elaborate rituals performed at their accession. The prosperity of the whole land is commonly held to be bound up with the health of the chief and the favourable attitude towards him of supernatural beings. He may be obliged to obey all kinds of ritual restrictions to this end; for example it was believed of the ruler of Ruanda, in east Africa, that he must not bend his knee lest the country be conquered. Chiefs are either themselves responsible for the performance of ritual on behalf of the whole populace or must maintain priests to do this.

Social anthropologists have recently turned their attention to the process of competition for the commanding roles which any society offers. Some would claim to have discarded the idea of structure altogether in favour of that of process; yet the structure must be taken into account as the set of rules in accordance with which the game is played. There are societies where it is the rule that on the death of a chief his sons must fight for the succession, to test who is the strongest and has the largest following. There are others where the rule of succession may seem to be clear, and yet there can always be dispute as to who fits it best. Sometimes people pursue the struggle for power by accusing their rivals of witchcraft; sometimes by massing their followers behind them in a show of strength before which their adversaries retire; the first is the method of the Ndembu in western Zambia, the second that of the Pathans in the Swat Valley in Pakistan. Such confrontations occur at moments of crisis, but the process of building up support is going on all the time. The study of these processes is among the most interesting new developments in social anthropology.

Economic Systems

The typical methods of subsistence in societies of simple technology are food-gathering (hunting and collecting roots and berries), herding, and agriculture. The domestication of animals and plants came relatively late in man's history; without it there could have been no permanent settlement, no cities, no civilisation. But the life of those food-gatherers who still exist is not a hard one; they can get an adequate diet in a very short working week. The three modes of subsistence should not be thought of as forming a historical series; moreover, there are many varieties of each, depending on the nature of the environment and the techniques used.

We shall never know what brought about the "agricultural revolution" or why the greater number of our ancestors chose the harder, but more productive, life of cultivators. This may have been somehow made necessary by the pressure of population in certain areas. Nor shall we know when and how trade and exchange began. We can reject the argument of Adam Smith that people first provided themselves with enough to eat and then began to exchange the products of specialists for surplus food. Exchanges are made among and between peoples who suffer from periodic famines, and the objects which are most valued are not exchanged for food.

These exchanges are not conducted, however, through the medium of a currency which enables people to calculate the relative value of goods of different kinds, as does money in a commercial society. Certain goods can be exchanged only for certain others—in the highlands of New Guinea, for example, shells and the plumes of rare birds. This has led to much controversy on the question whether primitive peoples can be said to have money. Of course, if money is defined as a universal medium of exchange, they do not. But some modern anthropologists find that too strict a definition, and prefer to say that, whereas modern currencies are "general-purpose money," societies of simple technology have different kinds of "special-purpose money"—strings of shells, hoe-blades, iron bars and the like, which are used only in a limited range of transactions.

It is certainly true, however, that money of this kind cannot be made the means of very exact calculations of profit and loss. It is often assumed that where there is no such common medium of exchange people do not make any economic calculations, and dispose of their property in ways that are the reverse of business-like. The principal reason why this assumption is made is the great importance attached in societies of simple technology to the making of gifts. The essential difference between a gift and a commercial exchange is that no return is stipulated. In the commercial world goods are sold, services hired, at a price, and anyone who fails to pay has broken a contract and is liable to be punished. The obligation to return a gift is a moral one. Moreover, to compete in the giving of gifts seems at first sight the very opposite of competition in the acquisition of wealth. But in most societies people who have a surplus of wealth like to have a reputation for generosity; only in the affluent world of machine production people feel the need to have many more material possessions before they begin to think in terms of surplus.

The exchange of gifts plays a particularly large part in the societies of Melanesia, where men form partnerships for the express purpose of giving and receiving valuable objects, and earn prestige at least as much by giving as by receiving. This exchange of valuables, mostly shell ornaments, is so important that it has a name in the language of each society. The first such exchange system to be described by an anthropologist was the *kula* of the Trobriand Islands, observed by Malinowski. An important man had a partner in an island on either side of his own home; from one he received armbands and returned necklaces, from the other he received necklaces and returned armbands. These objects did not become part of a store of wealth for any man; nobody could hold one long before it was time to pass it on to his partner. To receive his gift a man sailed by canoe to his partner's home; he was there welcomed peaceably, and while he was making his formal visit the crew were bartering their goods on the shore with the local populace. Thus the *kula* partnership had the nature of a political alliance; it was a means of maintaining peaceful relations between populations which would otherwise have been hostile.

In the highland area of New Guinea identical objects are exchanged, so that the relative value of amounts given and received can be calculated. In some parts the ideal is that a return gift should be twice the original one. Naturally it is no small achievement to carry on a prolonged series of exchanges at such a rate. Very few men manage it, and those who do are the acknowledged leaders of their community. For each large gift he has made a man wears a little bamboo stick hung round his neck; thus his munificence is publicly proclaimed. A new partnership is initiated by making the minimum gift. Men make these partnerships with others not bound to them by kinship, notably with their relatives by marriage. Each partnership extends the range within which a man can count on friendly treatment. So widespread is the idea that gifts should be repaid, and services rewarded, after some delay, and at the discretion of the man making the return, that where the highland people have taken to growing coffee for sale, the large-scale planters do not pay wages but employ young men for planting who get their return by coming to them later for help in difficulties. Of course the young men would stop giving their work if they judged that the return was not adequate.

Gift-giving, then, is an investment, but not one that produces a direct material return. One anthropologist, R. F. Salisbury, has called it an investment in power. The second classic example of the uneconomic use of goods is the *potlatch* practised by the Kwakiutl and kindred tribes of the northwest coast of America. This was a public distribution of goods at which the recipients had to be given their gifts in strict order of rank. The giver earned prestige and power by the scale of his gifts, by his knowledge of the correct rank order, and by the famous deeds (*potlatches* and others) which he was able to claim as feats of himself and his ancestors. Rivals for precedence would assert their claim by vying with each other in the amounts they distributed. The Kwakiutl way of avenging an insult was what has been called the "rivalry gesture." The man who thought he had been insulted actually destroyed valuable property by throwing it on a fire, or into the sea, and his enemy had to match him in destruction or be humiliated.

Certainly this is not turning resources to material advantage. No more is the giving of a very expensive dinner-party in London or New York. But equally certainly, it is not done without calculation. In the affluent society people display their superior affluence because this demonstrates their prestige rating, just as in the *potlatch*; and they keep on good terms, through the hospitality they offer, with people from whom they may later seek a return in professional dealings, rather as in the Melanesian gift-exchanges. In fact a substantial proportion of the incomes of people in European societies who are by no means affluent goes into the making of gifts—to parents, to kin, to friends, to persons who have helped one or given one hospitality; gifts which are given as a matter of moral obligation. The difference between the uses to which resources are put in societies of simple and of complex technology is one only of degree. The proportion that is devoted to securing non-material advantages is higher in the small-scale societies, and so is the proportion of gift-giving to commercial exchange. In gift-giving there is no bargaining, but there is a clear expectation of return. The initiation of new social relationships by the making of gifts is not by any means confined to New Guinea. Bride-wealth which legitimises children is the most widespread example. Pastoral peoples in East Africa also make gifts of stock to selected friends in distant parts. The friend on his home ground is a sponsor for his partner, and he is expected to make return gifts from time to time, and may be asked for a beast if his partner is in difficulties. One could think of such an arrangement as a type of insurance.

A small number of social anthropologists have

specialised in the study of the economic systems of small-scale societies, and have asked whether the concepts devised for the analysis of monetary economies—such notions, for example, as capital and credit—can be applied to people who gain their livelihood directly from the resources of their immediate environment. Starting from the assumption that there is always some choice in the allocation of resources, they have observed how these choices are actually made in the societies where they have worked. They have asked how the value of such goods as are obtained by barter is measured; how labour is obtained, how directed and how rewarded for such enterprises as the building of a canoe or a temple, which call for the co-operation of large numbers. They have examined the use of media of exchange, asking how far any of these fulfil the functions that we associate with money.

The general conclusion of these studies is that peoples of simple technology are perfectly capable of rational calculation in the allocation of their resources, even though their calculations are rough by comparison with those of the entrepreneur in an industrial society. They know what to regard as an adequate return when they are bartering goods. They withhold goods from consumption when they are planning an enterprise; that is to say, a man who proposes to initiate such an activity as canoe-building, arranges to be able to feed his labour force.

Religion

At a time when people questioned whether " primitive " societies could be said to have religion, E. B. Tylor offered as a " minimum " definition of religion " the belief in spiritual beings." All societies of simple technology have such beliefs, and think that unseen personalised beings influence the course of nature by direct intervention, causing rain to fall if they are pleased with the actions of men and withholding it if they are angry, sending sickness as a punishment and so forth. In the great majority of such societies the most important spirits to be worshipped are those of dead ancestors. But there may also be a belief in gods responsible for particular aspects of the world, to whom offerings are made for protection or success in their special fields. Many preliterate peoples believe in a "high god" from whom all other spirits derive their power, and one school of anthropology sees this as evidence of an original state of higher religious consciousness from which man has declined; but this view is not widely held.

Rituals involving groups of people are commonly performed on occasions when changes of status are to be signalised. A child becomes a member of society not by being born, but at a naming or showing ceremony. A youth or girl becomes adult at initiation. Marriage, which makes a couple into potential parents and links their kin groups, is another such ritual.

In funerary rites the dead person is made into an ancestor, and his heir adopts his social personality and his responsibilities. The accession of a man to political office is surrounded by ritual, and chiefs frequently observe annual rites at the time of harvest, when it is the season, not the person, that is changing. These are *confirmatory* rituals, designed to keep society and the world on an even course. When something goes wrong, a drought or epidemic or an individual sickness, *piacular* rituals are performed to make peace with the spirits responsible for the disaster.

An essential aspect of many of these religions is the belief in witchcraft—that is that it is possible for humans to harm others merely by hating them. Witchcraft supplies an explanation of undeserved misfortune. Diviners employ a multitude of techniques (which anthropologists rather inaccurately call oracles) to detect whether a disaster is a merited punishment or is due to witchcraft.

Every small-scale society has its myths—stories which tell how the world as people know it came to be. Sometimes their ritual re-enacts the myth; often the myth tells how the ritual was first performed and thereby gives a reason for its continuance. Then there are myths telling how death and evil came into the world. Some myths lend authority to the existing social order, and

particularly to the claims of ruling groups, by telling how the social structure was divinely ordained. Under the influence of the French anthropologist Lévi-Strauss, many anthropologists are beginning to see both myths and the symbolism of ritual as man's earliest attempt to order intellectually the world of his experience.

The existence of ultra-human beings on whom the affairs of men depended was universally taken for granted until a very short time ago. As long as this belief was held, the established order in any society was supported by the tenets of religion. But there are also revolutionary religions. In recent years anthropologists have been inspired by the many new religions that have arisen in developing territories to give more attention to this side of the subject. Notably in Melanesia, a succession of prophets have appeared with a message announcing the imminent coming of an ideal world from which all hardships would be banished, including the subjection of the indigenous peoples to colonial rulers. These events turned the attention of anthropologists, along with sociologists and historians, to the study of similar movements in the past, and we now have a considerable body of literature on such subjects as " the religions of the oppressed."

Closer study of traditional religions from this point of view has shown that they also often include symbolic reversals as part of their regular ritual. The high are brought low and the humble exalted. In his ritual installation a chief may be beaten and abused by his subjects, or a rite that confirms his authority may include a simulated rebellion. Women may assume for a day the garb and authority of men. There is a temporary suspension of the rules and cultural forms which differentiate the members of the ritual congregation. This may go as far as " ritual licence ", in which actions that at other times are offences liable to punishment, notably sexual promiscuity, are permitted and must not be made a reason for quarrels. Or it may be simply that the participants are masked, stripped naked, or dressed identically. Such rituals affirm their common membership, or communitas, as it has been called, and where they express not merely unity and equality, but the reversal of high and low, they remind the powerful that they must not abuse their power. Rites of this kind form a phase in complex rituals. They are followed by a re-affirmation of the accepted order in its ideal form, where hierarchical relations maintain order without promoting injustice. This theory would interpret the new " subversive " religions as the response to situations in which the injustices of the powerful have gone too far for the re-assertion of communitas to be possible.

Social Change

No doubt all the societies that anthropologists have studied have been gradually changing throughout the centuries when their history was not recorded. But they experienced nothing like the rapidity of the changes that came to them when they were brought under the rule of European nations and introduced to mass production and a money economy. The effect of this has been in essence to widen the range of choice in the relationships that people can form. A man may choose to be dependent on an employer rather than on work in co-operation with his kin or village mates. He is more likely to rise in the world by going to school and getting a city job than by earning the respect of the villagers or the approval of a chief. Small-scale societies are now becoming merged in larger ones and the close ties of the isolated village are loosened. In the newly created industrial areas new specialised associations are formed to pursue professional and other interests. The social insurance that kinship provided is lacking, and it has not as yet been replaced by what the state offers in the highly industrialised societies. The minority that has whole-heartedly adopted the values of the industrialised world now produces the political rulers of new states. They are impatient to carry the majority along the same road, but there are profound conflicts of value between them and the still largely illiterate masses.

The first studies of this type of social change

were mainly interested in the effects of intrusive influences on traditional institutions in rural areas. Later, attention was turned to social relationships in the cities which have come into being, or greatly increased in size and population, as a result of the development of commerce and industry. Recent work is largely concerned with the extent to which immigrants to the cities preserve their sense of a distinctive home origin. Immigrant populations which have abandoned all their traditional customs often preserve a strong sense of a common identity which differentiates them from their neighbours, and sometimes they even create a myth of the possession of " special customs " that has no foundation in fact. This sense of a particularly close relationship between people from the same place of origin is called *ethnicity*. It has been argued that when the members of an *ethnic group* are in a privileged position they appeal to the sense of ethnicity to close the ranks against outsiders. The less fortunate might be more likely to unite on a non-ethnic basis to improve their position. Divisions based on ethnicity cut across those based on social class. This is a field in which the interests of social anthropologists and sociologists overlap. The conclusions drawn from studies in African cities could be, and no doubt will be, tested against work among immigrant populations in Europe and America.

Recent Trends in Social Anthropology

Structural Anthropology, as it has been developed in France by Lévi-Strauss, has the aim of establishing the universal characteristics of cultural, that is rule-governed, human behaviour, as opposed to the natural, instinctive behaviour of non-human species. Lévi-Strauss finds the distinguishing feature of man in communication by symbols, and holds that the way in which symbols are constructed reflects the structure of the human brain. As he uses the term social structure, it means the system of symbols by which a given society comprehends the world of its experience.

According to Lévi-Strauss communication is an exchange, and for him all exchange is communication. The prohibition of incest, which represents to him man's first move from natural to cultural life, obliges men to exchange their sisters, giving them to other men as wives. Then they exchange goods for goods or services. But for Lévi-Strauss the most important exchange is that of messages, and his central interest is in the codes in which the messages are embodied. Every code is an arbitrary set of symbols, the meaning of which depends on the way in which they are related. A code is based on a logical structure, so that social structure is the structure of a socially accepted code. It should be noted that the existence of the structure is not demonstrated independently of the code, but deduced from it, while the nature of the code is deduced from the supposed nature of the structure.

For the principles of structure Lévi-Strauss turns to the linguists, notably Roman Jakobson, according to whom all speech-sounds can be analysed into pairs of opposites; it is by recognising these opposites that children learn to speak and to distinguish meaning. Lévi-Strauss argues that the structure of the human brain leads men to classify the objects of their experience into opposites, then finding mediating terms to link the opposites. The recognition of differences is in his view the basis of classification, more important than the recognition of similarities. In totemism, a phenomenon which many anthropologists have tried to explain, awareness of differences between social groups is expressed by associating them with different animals. Exogamous descent groups, the groups which exchange sisters, are commonly called by the names of animal species. Each group has its totem animal, and they often believe that they must not eat this animal. The rules attached to these animal names form a code which can be decoded as: " We, Elephants, are different from them, Lions ", not because either group is *like* elephants or lions, but because the groups differ as species differ. Any contrasting species would do; there is no intrinsic relation between Elephants and elephants just as there is none between the sounds of a word and its meaning. Totemism, then, is an arbitrary code to express the principles on which a society is organised.

Lévi-Strauss' most massive work is devoted to the interpretation of myth. In his view the material of myth comes from the unconscious. He has made an extensive study of the myths of Amerindian peoples, and has found that stories in which the incidents are superficially dissimilar lead to the same conclusion (convey the same message), and on the way deal with oppositions (or contradictions) between rules or necessary facts of life and human wishes. The episodes of myths are the symbols of the code, and they can be combined in many different ways, but always according to an underlying, unconscious logic (structure). To explain this logic he draws comparisons with music and with mathematics. A musical note has no meaning in itself, only as an element in a melody or a chord. A musical composition plays with modifications or transformations of themes or harmonies, and just as a theme can be transposed into a different key, so a message can be conveyed in images that may refer to the objects of all the different senses: sight (light and darkness), taste (cooking—the first volume of his great book on myths is called *The Raw and the Cooked*), hearing (noise and silence) and so on. Note that all these codes are concerned with contrasts. From mathematics Lévi-Strauss takes the idea of a system of algebraic signs which can be combined in many permutations. Ultimately the theory of myth tells us that the important socially prescribed relations between persons of different status can be represented as relations between animal species, between kinds of food, between kinds of sound and silence, smells and tastes, aspects of landscape or any of these in combination.

According to Lévi-Strauss, although the deep structure of thought is unconscious, the classification of observed phenomena is conscious, and is the first activity of the human mind. Hence he rejects the view that peoples of simple technology are interested in natural phenomena only in so far as these have practical uses.

Cognitive Anthropology was first taken up as a special field in America, where its pioneers were Ward Goodenough, Charles E. Frake and Harold Conklin. It has much in common with the structuralism of Lévi-Strauss, but its practitioners are not interested in myths, and the majority make less extensive claims than he does. Some of them do believe that studies of the way in which different peoples classify the objects of their experience should lead to the discovery of universal cognitive principles, but they do not seek to reduce all categories to binary oppositions: rather they talk of *contrast sets*.

Studies in cognitive anthropology began with the examination of kinship terms by the method known as *componential analysis*. Instead of asking what relatives were grouped together under a designation found in English kinship, such as " father " or " brother ", cognitive anthropologists looked for the essential *components* of any kin term, and found these to be sex, generation, and lineal or non-lineal relationship to the speaker or the person referred to by the term. This method was considered to give a truer picture of the principles according to which people group their relatives.

Cognitive anthropology has also been directed to other *domains* of experience, that is fields to which a distinguishable vocabulary is observed to apply; for example, to the classification of colours or of disease, but most of all to that of flora and fauna, or folk taxonomy, as this is called. These studies elucidate not only the principles according to which people group and distinguish the objects of their environment but also the factual knowledge they have of them.

Marxist anthropology has developed along with a general revival of interest in Marxist theory largely inspired by the new interpretation of Marxism introduced by the French writer Louis Althusser, not himself an anthropologist. The leading anthropological theorist in this field is

Maurice Godelier, also in France. Like Lévi-Strauss, Marxists look for the unperceived structural laws on which all society rests, but they look in another direction. They find their answer in the *relations of production*, that is in the manner in which production is organised, and in particular the distribution of the resources which make production possible. They apply to the study of pre-capitalist societies the analysis which Marx himself made of capitalism, and seek to place the primitive and peasant societies of today, and also some vanished societies of which there are records, in their place in a line of developing social formations, each a transformation of its predecessor. Thus Marxist anthropology is in a sense an historical study, and can be contrasted with functional analysis in which societies are taken as they are when the observer sees them and treated, as Malinowski put it, as "going concerns". A functionalist study asks what keeps a society going; hence Marxists regard such studies as essentially conservative.

For Marxists a *social formation* is a combination of the forces of production and the relations of production. The forces of production consist in labour power and technical knowledge, and in the way production is organised. The relations of production are the relations between those who control the means of production—land or machines —and those who supply their labour power. Those who control the means of production are able to determine what share of the product shall go to the workers, and invariably they take more than a fair share. The state exists to practise this *extraction of surplus value*, as it is technically called. Accepted religious beliefs and other systems of ideas are not, as Lévi-Strauss and the cognitive anthropologists would have it, attempts to organise experience; they are delusions which conceal from the workers the way in which they are exploited. One social formation gives way to another when its *internal contradictions*—conflicts, incompatibilities—become too acute to be contained within the existing system. All aspects of a society are linked to the relations of production. Hence Marxist anthropologists do not admit the validity of cross-cultural comparisons between different institutions, such as kinship, economics, politics or religion, and argue that only social formations can be compared.

Thus they have given much more attention than earlier anthropologists to societies of hunters and gatherers, where nobody is dependent on others for the weapons that are the sole means of production. As soon as the means of production are appropriated by one section of society, the opposition of classes is observed. This change took place in the Neolithic period, when the invention of agriculture led to the recognition of rights in land. Even in those systems in which land is regarded as the common property of a group, the senior man or men who control its use are in a position to exploit their juniors, so that there are class divisions among kinsmen. It is also sometimes argued that where people believe that specialists in magic can influence the weather, or promote the growth of crops as the Trobriand magicians observed by Malinowski do, their knowledge is indispensable to production, and so they, too, make the workers dependent on them and can exploit them.

Marxist anthropologists make use of the ethnographic work of Malinowski and his pupils, who looked, as Malinowski had taught them, for the importance of reciprocity in exchange. Lévi-Strauss also discusses this in his theory of the exchange of women as the basis of kinship systems. But Marxists are concerned with inequalities rather than reciprocities in exchange, inequalities that those who own the means of production can impose. Thus they would not agree with Malinowski's followers that there is any reciprocity in a state between rulers and ruled, that subjects pay tribute and rulers make their return both by maintaining order and in direct economic terms by the redistribution of wealth.

The study of ecology combines the work of anthropologists with that of human geographers and many natural scientists. It is associated with the name of the American anthropologist Julian Steward. Ecologists study the relations between society, technology and environment. They differ from the biologists who invented the term "ecology" in that they examine man's modification of his environment as well as his adaptation to it. Early ecological work concentrated on food-gathering populations who modify their environment very little, but it was soon extended to societies of pastoralists and cultivators.

Ecological studies have practical implications in various directions. They throw light on the success or failure of policies that are intended to raise standards of living, for example by persuading or compelling nomad pastoralists to become settled cultivators. A type of enforced change which has become widespread is the resettlement of populations whose homes have been flooded by the damming of rivers for hydro-electric projects; here the alteration in the environment is sudden and dramatic, quite unlike the effects of the unplanned changes of the past. It is usually accompanied by attempts to create a new environment that will make higher standards of living available, through housing schemes, new educational facilities, the introduction of new crops or farming methods, and so on. The proliferation of such schemes has been said to provide the anthropologist with a "laboratory situation" in which both policies and reactions can be compared. By combining ecological with medical studies it is possible to consider the prevalence of malnutrition or parasitic diseases in relation not only to the non-human environment but also to social groupings and norms which render certain populations, and particular categories within such populations, more vulnerable than others to these health hazards.

Another meeting-ground between anthropology and the natural sciences is in the new interest of sociologists in ethology, the study of the evolution of social behaviour. The classical exponents of this study have been Tinbergen in Holland and Lorenz in Austria. Close observation of the interaction between individuals and groups among non-human species has led many ethologists to conclude that animal populations may appropriately be regarded as societies. They hope to learn what tendencies among humans are genetically determined and so may not be amenable to deliberate attempts at social change. A subdivision of this study, human ethology, concentrates on minute details of behaviour with the aim of identifying gestures, facial expressions and the like that are found in all cultures, and so may be supposed to spring from affective systems common to all humanity. Yet a narrower subdivision is child ethology. Some anthropologists believe that these studies offer the key to the question What is Man? What are the characteristics that distinguish him from other animals, and how in fact did natural selection enable him to develop them?

These studies are still in their infancy, and in their present state they are vulnerable to some dangers. It is difficult, perhaps impossible, to use in the description of behaviour language which does not assume that what is described is social, the very question that the ethologists are asking. The assumption may be made unconsciously, but if it is consciously recognised it is possible to guard against it. The language used may also lead to the attribution to non-human animals of reactions that are specifically human (*anthropomorphism*). Zoologists may too readily assume that all human behaviour can be reduced to those reactions which are transmitted in our evolutionary heredity, forgetting that the processes of social conditioning are much more elaborate in man than in other animals. Anthropologists on their side may be too ready to seek the kind of interpretation of non-human behaviour that supports their *a priori* idea of the nature of man, *e.g.*, whether he is essentially aggressive or pacific, competitive or co-operative.

VI. MAN AND HIS ENVIRONMENT

THE CHALLENGE TO MANKIND

I. INTRODUCTION

We are now more than ever aware that we live in a world where events in one place affect people thousands of miles away. A dramatic example of this inter-relationship was the oil crisis that followed the Arab–Israel war of October 1973. The oil producers of the world, led by the Arab states, welded their organisation OPEC into an effective cartel which raised the price of oil to consumers fivefold by the end of 1974. This sudden action rocked the economies of countries one after another and increased the threat of world recession. In a country like India, dependent on importing oil, the extra drain on foreign exchange curbed her other imports, notably fertilisers. Another example can be drawn from the turn of the century. Successful synthesis of indigo by Professor Adolf Bayer of Munich in 1880 created havoc within a generation in the Indian villages depending on the cultivation of the natural indigo plant. Export of indigo from India fell from 187,000 tons in 1895–6 to the pitiful level of 11,000 tons in 1913–14 as synthetic production developed into a thriving industry in Europe: success in one part of the world meant economic devastation in another. Today we have reached the stage where we must take account of both the wider repercussions of new developments and also the consequences in using up irreplaceable resources.

In this part of the Science Section we shall be looking at key aspects of the environment in which we live—quality of life, population, food, energy, pollution. We shall see them as inter-acting parts of a system which includes all living things, the air, water and soil, accessible parts of the earth's crust and the exchange of radiation with the rest of the universe, the most important being the receipt of vast amounts of energy from the sun. Whether we can meet the challenge of living in equilibrium with our environment depends entirely upon ourselves. Those of us living in the "developed" (or "industrialised" or "advanced") countries have a great responsibility in finding lasting solutions to the problems since we have

* greater wealth

* more technology

* better educated populations

than many of those in the less-developed (or "underdeveloped" or "poor") countries whose poverty limits the extent to which they can help themselves.

The reader may like to refer to Section G (Part III) for a review of the economic problems of the less-developed countries.

An informal international group of scientists and economists known, because of their first meeting place, as the Club of Rome, have made a series of studies since 1968 of the effects of unrestrained economic and population growth. Their first report, "The Limits of Growth" by Professor Dennis Meadows of the Massachusetts Institute of Technology, warned of mass starvation and of mineral resources becoming exhausted if present trends continued. Other researchers criticised aspects of his methods and of his choice of relationships for the equations used in the computer exercises on which those conclusions were based. Further work published under the title "Mankind at the turning point" by M. Mesarovic and E. Pestel (1974) continued to rely on computer analyses of the future interplay between population, resources and the environment. But this is based on dividing the world into ten interacting regions, then examining results of a number of hypotheses (or "scenarios") in each case considered in terms of attempts to resolve problems by conflict or by co-operation. Scenarios based on conflict assume that individual nations or regions try to act on their own; those based on co-operation show regions of the earth banding together in a concerted attack on problems regardless of political, social and other differences. Both this and a later report (5th Report: "Goals for Mankind" 1977) confirm analytically that it is essential for nations to overcome their animosities, work closely together, make short-term sacrifices for long-term gains and share access to resources.

II. QUALITY OF LIFE

Some people would say that one of the main objectives of human activity is to achieve a better standard of living or a more congenial environment and not only for ourselves but for others less well off. The concept "quality of life" is difficult to define as it depends upon the criteria used as to what is desirable for human welfare. There is no correlation between level of income and level of cultural development (we have only to think of Ancient China and modern Kuwait). One writer suggests "we have to find ways of creating and maintaining a civilisation and at the same time to keep people fully employed earning their living producing the right kinds of goods in conditions that foster human attitudes." However, the results of some changes in our way of life can be objectively measured, and it is on these that we shall later dwell.

Ultimately, however, all attempts to define the quality of life must include "recognition of the inherent dignity and of the equal and inalienable rights of all members of the human family" set out in the Universal Declaration of Human Rights adopted in 1948 by the United Nations. This states that all human beings are born free and equal in dignity and rights, naming among these the right to life, liberty and security of person, freedom from slavery, from torture or degrading treatment, from arbitrary arrest, from arbitrary interference; it also names freedom of movement, of thought, conscience, religion, opinion, the right to take part in government and of equal access to public service; in the economic and social spheres it covers the right to social security, to work, to rest and leisure, to a standard of living adequate for health and well-being, including food, clothing and medical care and to education. The list of rights concludes with an article referring to everyone's duties to the community for free and full development of his personality subject to such limitations as are determined by law solely for the purpose of securing due recognition and respect for the rights and freedoms of others and of meeting the just requirements of morality, public order and the general welfare in a democratic society.

Policies directed at ensuring that man lives in equilibrium with his environment must be kept consistent with these humane and reasonable requirements. For example, it would not be acceptable to argue that the need to conserve resources demanded that consumption levels should be kept low in the countries that are at present poor; nor would it be consistent with the view that all human beings are equal to suggest that population should be more severely controlled in the poorer developing countries than in the richer developed ones. These are not "abstract" issues. They arose very forcefully at the World Food Conference and the World Population Conference, both held in 1974.

Broadly, the aspects of the quality of life that are felt to be most relevant in the developing countries are those dealing with such basics as food, health services, shelter, employment, education, which are generally seen as linked with industrialisation and technological development. The industrialised countries tend to interpret the issues in terms of preventing pollution of air, water and land, reducing noise, reclaiming land that has become an eyesore, cleaning up the residues of the industrial past, renewing the older towns and building the newer ones in aesthetically pleasing styles, minimising damage to the surroundings in new municipal, social and industrial building or activity. Social reformers add that these concerns should include providing for those with disadvantages—the poor, the sick, the physically and mentally handicapped, and above all the child in need of care.

Several of the industrialised countries now have projects in progress to improve the *quality of working life*, particularly for workers engaged in operations likely to induce stress. What types of operations would these be? They are production or clerical jobs involving forced uniform pacing, especially when the pace is rapid; repetitiveness and very short time cycles leading to monotony, triviality and meaninglessness in work; large impersonal structures of organisation and also objectives which seem distant and unreal. To combat these undesirable features, Dr. N. A. B. Wilson in 1973 in a report published by the UK Government (" On the quality of working life ") recommended re-arrangements to induce the worker to be less passively subordinate, more versatile, more self-directed and to link this with making all desirable work behaviour obviously rewarding. Generally, the efforts at job enrichment start by giving the worker more variety, making him part of a group with shared responsibility and some degree of autonomy. Such programmes are being actively promoted by the UK Department of Employment. Measures of the results, in addition to replies to questionnaires, will be the effects on absenteeism, quality of products, proportion of rejects, rate of turnover of staff, labour disputes and other indices.

Another aspect receiving attention in many countries is protecting the health of workers at work. The EEC have proposals for a planned programme of social reform of employment conditions which, they specify, must include the interests of immigrant workers in Europe. In the UK under the Health and Safety at Work Act 1974 the conditions of virtually all employed persons in the country now come under one unified control, a Health and Safety Commission was established, and a series of Codes of Practice to supplement regulations and give practical guidance are being introduced.

Habitat: 1976 UN Conference on Human Settlements.

In June 1976 the UN held a conference on human settlements under the title of Habitat. It resulted in a declaration and two groups of recommendations. Its Vancouver Declaration reflected a major commitment on the part of Governments and the international community to improve the quality of life for all peoples. Recommendations for specific action to put this into effect were grouped into those for national action and others demanding international co-operation. Major attention was given to the right of all people to a pure supply of water—an apparently simple provision that is nevertheless denied to a large proportion of the world's population. A further UN conference in 1977 devoted wholly to this single, important issue, endorsed the goal of adequate drinking water and sanitation facilities for all people by the year 1990. It called for international measures to support efforts by poorer countries to achieve this goal.

Arms and Disarmament

A further factor affecting the quality of life is the continuing build-up of armaments and the anxieties produced notably by the growing stocks of nuclear arms and of " improved " methods for delivering them on to enemies. This has been systematically documented in a series of reports by the Swedish-government-sponsored Stockholm International Peace Research Institute (SIPRI). The period from 1970 has been declared by the UN as the Disarmament Decade; the General Assembly during 1975 examined a number of relevant reports including a comprehensive study of nuclear-weapon-free zones. Nevertheless, the continuing build-up of arms, wasting human resources and threatening ever more devastating wars, provoked the UN to arrange for May/June 1978 a Special Session of the General Assembly devoted to disarmament.

III. POPULATION

In recent years there has been a growing realisation that the rapid increase in population is exerting pressures on existing resources, aggravating many social problems, especially attempts to combat poverty in developing countries. Significant of these worldwide anxieties was the holding of the first world intergovernmental conference on population in August 1974 under the auspices of the United Nations. It nevertheless proved to be a controversial subject since many countries placed more emphasis on industrial and technological development as the solution to their problems of rapidly rising population than on campaigns for population control. The final Plan of Action adopted was based on striving to reconcile these two policy approaches.

1. Background

The basic worrying demographic trend is that world population is growing by 2% a year; if this rate is sustained it will result in the doubling of world population every 35 years. Within this overall figure regional rates vary and national rates range from a negative rate to well over 3%. Generally, the rapid increase reflects decline in death rate while birth rate either does not decline or does so much more slowly. Nevertheless in the developing countries death rate remains high. In Africa average expectation of life is estimated by the UN to be less than 40 years and one baby in four dies before its first birthday. As the Plan reveals, many couples are unable to exercise the right to have the number of children they desire. Poor economic conditions, social norms, inadequate knowledge of effective methods of family regulation, unavailability of contraceptive devices result in a situation where couples have more children than they desire or feel they can properly care for. High birth rate means that in developing countries 41% of the population is under the age of 15. Though population of the rural areas continues to grow, that of town areas is increasing so fast that for the first time in history the majority of the world's people will be living in urban areas by the end of the century. Very often this movement takes place in an uncontrolled fashion accompanied by overcrowding, unemployment, slums and deterioration of the environment.

Change in fertility rate takes some decades before it has any effect on the growth rate of the population. Thus the demographers calculate that even if the developing countries now had on average only a little over 2 children per family—the replacement level—their population would still grow until the latter half of the next century; this effect is sometimes called " demographic inertia ". The Plan urged countries wishing to affect their population growth to anticipate future demographic trends and take appropriate decisions on plans for economic and social development well in advance.

2. Principles and Objectives

Formulating and implementing population policies was declared to be the sovereign right of each nation. A statement of principles opened by setting the aim of development to be the improvement of the levels of living and the quality of life of the people. Development was seen as playing a crucial role in affecting population trends so that population policies were elements of development policies. As we noted above, the conference decided that these should be consistent with human rights, individual freedom, justice and the survival of national, regional and minority groups; furthermore " respect for human life is basic to all human societies ". Other principles adopted included:

* couples have the basic human right to decide freely and responsibly the number and spacing of their children

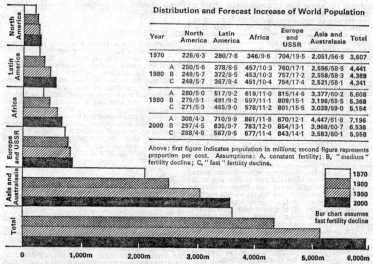

Distribution and Forecast Increase of World Population

Year		North America	Latin America	Africa	Europe and USSR	Asia and Australasia	Total
1970		226/6·3	280/7·8	346/9·6	704/19·5	2,051/56·8	3,607
1980	A	250/5·6	378/8·5	457/10·3	760/17·1	2,596/58·5	4,441
	B	249/5·7	372/8·5	453/10·3	757/17·2	2,558/58·3	4,389
	C	248/5·7	367/8·4	451/10·4	754/17·4	2,521/58·1	4,341
1990	A	280/5·0	517/9·2	619/11·0	815/14·6	3,377/60·2	5,608
	B	275/5·1	491/9·2	597/11·1	809/15·1	3,196/59·5	5,368
	C	271/5·3	465/9·0	578/11·2	801/15·5	3,039/59·0	5,154
2000	A	308/4·3	710/9·9	861/11·9	870/12·1	4,447/61·8	7,196
	B	297/4·5	635/9·7	783/12·0	854/13·1	3,968/60·7	6,536
	C	288/4·8	567/9·5	677/11·4	843/14·1	3,583/60·1	5,958

Above: first figure indicates population in millions; second figure represents proportion per cent. Assumptions: A, constant fertility; B, "medium" fertility decline; C, "fast" fertility decline.

All three of these projections, first published by the World Bank (Finance and Development, vol. 10. no. 4), assume declining mortality rates. The concept of fertility is based on the number of births during a woman's reproductive period, at current rates.

"Constant" fertility assumes that rates will remain at their present levels until 2000. "Fast" decline assumes that rates will fall by between 1 and 3 per cent annually until replacement level is reached, and could amount to a halving of the rate in 30 to 40 years.

* the family is the basic unit of society

* women have the right to complete integration in the development process

* consideration must be given to natural resources, the environment, food supply, minimising waste

* because of growing interdependence of nations, international strategies must enable the under-privileged to attain an early improvement in living conditions.

3. Recommendations for Action

Countries which consider their growth rate hampers their goals of promoting human welfare were invited to consider adopting population policies. It will be noted that this is far from a rousing call for campaigns to restrict population growth. The wording deliberately adopted throughout was neutral so that it could be interpreted to cover those said to desire population growth as well as those wishing to restrict it. The UN's "low variant projections"—reflecting assumptions about successful progress in development and implementing population policies—are based on the world rate of population growth declining from 2% to about 1·7% by 1985. These projections presume decline in the birth rate of the developing countries as a whole from the present level of 38 per thousand to 30 per thousand in 1985; that in the developed countries is projected as remaining at 15 per thousand. Achievement of these levels was recognised as requiring substantial national effort in both socioeconomic and population policies, supported on request by adequate international assistance.

Countries "which consider their birth rate detrimental to their national purposes" were invited to consider setting goals. Among recommendations adopted were:

* efforts to reduce mortality levels

* encouraging family planning

* ensuring full participation of women in the educational and general life of their countries on an equal basis with men

* as part of promoting knowledge recommending a population census in each country between 1975 and 1985

* inviting all countries to co-operate in a World Fertility Survey

In addition to recommending actions in areas directly concerned with possible control of population size there was strong emphasis on the indirect factors which are thought to have reduced birth rates dramatically in the richer countries, notably promoting the status of women.

4. Recommendations for Implementation

The Plan recommended continuous monitoring of population trends and policies by the UN, biennially beginning in 1977 and more comprehensively every 5 years after 1979. All this should be closely co-ordinated with the Strategy for the Second United Nations Development Decade.

In relation to world resources the conference expressed concern over disproportionate consumption in some countries which were asked to reduce such consumption and to refrain from any action that would adversely affect the ability of developing countries to promote their own development. Countries were urged to participate fully in the food conference (discussed later), giving priority to food and fertiliser production and consideration as to how shortages could best be overcome by national effort, regional and international co-operation.

The UN General Assembly has continued to monitor progress, receiving reports from the committees responsible. UN has supported a range of relevant researches and training courses in family-planning administration though all on a scale that appears to some observers to be small in relation to global trends and needs. The latest major review is entitled "Concise Report on the

World Population Situation in 1970–1975 and Its Long Range Implications " (UN E/5624).

For public information, the UN publishes a Population Newsletter.

As part of its aid programme, the UK in 1977/8 contributed £3m. to the UN Fund for Population Activities and £1·5m. to the International Planned Parenthood Federation.

5. " Social and political change may prove to be the key, the only key, to solving the population problem "

This quotation comes from Robert Cassen, Fellow of the Institute of Development Studies (University of Sussex). According to this analysis health, education, employment and reduced birth and death rates are all intimately connected. In the short run family planning is the only thing that has much effect, since other policy measures are slow to operate, difficult to pursue. Dr. Cassen's conclusion in advance of the conference was much the same as the compromise decisions reached. If the rich countries " are concerned about population growth in the Third World, we should be working much harder to create an international order more favourable to the elimination of poverty." In a nutshell, where we pursue trade and other policies that perpetuate poverty, we help to perpetuate high birth rates.

6. Britain is one of the Crowded Countries

Though these discussions tend to centre on the problems of poor countries remote from our shores, Britain is very directly involved in population problems.

POPULATION DENSITY 1975

	Person/sq km
England and Wales	326
Belgium	321
Netherlands	334
USA	23
USSR	11
France	97

Source UN Demographic Yearbook 1975.

Bernard Benjamin, Professor of Actuarial Science at the City University, has analysed the effects of allowing the British population of 54½ million to fall steadily until it reaches 35 million in helping reduce the strain on world resources, while easing our own crowding and the scramble for land and housing. His conclusion is that this is likely to be achieved without any real economic difficulty. It should be added that there is already a marked fall in births. Live births in England and Wales were 867,000 in the year ending June 1965 compared with an estimated 585,000 in 1976 (when deaths numbered 598,494). The balance of migration is outward and we lost some 41,000 emigrants in 1975, resulting in an overall decline in population. This trend in migration is expected to continue, and is included in projections. However, there have been previous periods in the country's history when trends have been markedly changed and there is some evidence that births may in fact be about to rise. The Office of Population Censuses and Surveys expects a fall in the total population of England and Wales of nearly 300,000 over the years 1976–82 (from 49·2m. to 48·9m.), but from 1982 onwards the population is estimated to grow steadily to a total of 50½m. in 2001 and over 51m. in 2016. For the UK as a whole the corresponding figures are from 54½m. in 1976, through a small fall, to 56½m. in 2016. The situation is thus one of uncertainty. Meanwhile an organisation has been set up in Britain called Population Concern, supporting voluntary family planning programmes throughout the world and any projects that work towards stabilising world population by means which also promote human welfare, personal freedom and the quality of life. They quote analyses showing that Britain has now lost the special world privileges it once had, so that the British people are now once again exposed to the penalties normally incurred when population outstrips resources. And the officially sponsored, though advisory, Report of the Population Panel (Cmnd. 5258,

1973) advocated a stationary population for Britain, with greater availability of reliable methods of contraception. In 1976 a Cabinet Office discussion paper " Future World Trends " warned that resources currently devoted to these problems are inadequate.

IV. FOOD

Projecting the present growth rates for population, food production and demand, the UN estimates that the vast majority of the developing countries will have a deficiency of 85 million tons each year by 1985. Urgent action was therefore proposed to the 1974 World Food Conference to prevent these developments and find a way of avoiding millions of people in the Third World dying of starvation during the next few years.

1. Demand

Demand for food is calculated to grow at 2·5% per annum; 2·0% represents population increases as quoted above and 0·5% increased purchasing power. But these overall figures are composed of a growth rate of only 1·6% in the developed countries and 3·7% in developing ones. Despite this expected growth there would still be some 34 countries by 1985 with a total of 700 million people where the intake of food energy per head on the average would fall short of basic nutritional requirements. For cereals (providing the bulk of human food) the projections are for demand to grow from 1,200 million tonnes in 1970 to 1,700 million tonnes in 1985; 300 million of the increase would be needed in poorer countries.

2. Supply

Here the basis for projections was felt to be less sure but growth rates were estimated at 2·4% for the developed, 2·6% for the developing countries and up to 3·5% for Eastern Europe and the USSR. These figures suggest approximate balance between supply and demand. But this would ignore fluctuations due to bad years. World stocks are now so low that bad harvests would have catastrophic effects. Furthermore, when a bad harvest occurs in a country with some financial resources they go out and buy, thus aggravating the supply position for others with similar crop failures but fewer other resources.

3. Malnutrition

The human cost of the inadequate food supplies at present is assessed by the UN as resulting in malnutrition for some 400 million people. In the report to the conference this condition was described as " the daily physical privation of fellow human beings, adversely affecting health and physical growth and seriously reducing the capacity of children to learn and adults to work." Overall no fewer than 61 countries were reckoned to have a deficit in food supplies in 1970. In the Far East, Near East and Africa this was considered to mean that up to a quarter of the population suffered from under-nutrition.

Furthermore the Food and Agriculture Organisation of the United Nations (FAO) has sponsored a Protein–Calorie Advisory Group to ensure that in food planning adequate attention is paid also to nutritional balance. They draw attention to the value of including in the diet such sources of protein as fish from the sea or from aquaculture, and recommend attention being given to exploiting Antarctic krill (little-known shrimp-like animals). They also reinforce the advice of the voluntary aid organisations such as War on Want and Oxfam that mothers in developing countries should be encouraged to continue breast feeding babies rather than weaning them on to infant foods too early and this was endorsed by a resolution of the 27th World Health Assembly. PAG has also drawn attention to the value of coconut flour, notably in the Philippines, as a food resource with many desirable characteristics for blending into foods to raise protein intake. To assess both current situations and the value of nutrition programmes, the Group has proposed a group of indicators to be used concurrently. They are mortality at individual ages 1, 2, 3 and 4; proportion of low birth weights; height at school entry age; age at menarche.

4. 1974 World Conference Conclusions

Results of the 1974 World Food Conference disappointed many observers, though the mere fact that it was held at all indicated the level of world concern. Its President assessed its work as having only sketched the beginnings of a world food policy. And Mr. Sayed Marei, its Secretary-General, was disappointed that wealthier countries had not offered sufficient help to countries already suffering from famine. Though the issues concerned people starving to death, there were political disputes among the assembled nations on the aid issue. The USA has in the past made large quantities of food available as aid. At this conference they stated that they would also expect a number of the newly-rich oil exporting countries to be willing to help finance the necessary food aid programme. These were to ensure forward planning of food aid, including at least ten million tons of grains as food aid every year and supplementary arrangements for other foods such as oils, oilseeds and dairy products.

Four principal recommendations to emerge from the proceedings were:

1. establishing a World Food Council to co-ordinate the activities of various international agencies;

2. creating an international fund for agricultural development to channel investment toward improving agriculture in the developing world;

3. agreeing on a co-ordinated system of cereal reserves as a world food security system; these reserves would be nationally held but supported by a service of worldwide information and detection of food shortage;

4. providing, on a three-year forward planning basis, both commodities and finance for food aid to a minimum level of ten million tons of grains a year and other foods, as stated above.

The final declaration included a pledge that "within a decade no child will go to bed hungry, that no family will fear for its next day's bread" and a statement that "every man, woman and child has the right to be free from hunger and malnutrition". These are, of course, historic declarations of intent demanding local and international efforts to reverse the trends discernible over the last few years.

5. World Situation 1978

In 1978 there were some signs of hope. A billion (US) dollar international fund was set up for agricultural development with a "first imperative" of assisting the food-deficit nations to feed themselves. The second imperative was to ensure food security for the world by building a grain reserve of ½m. tons of grain to prevent mass tragedies of starvation such as those in earlier years in the Sahel and in Bangladesh. The Fund has a unique governing structure with equal votes for OECD countries, OPEC countries and the recipient countries. Its chairman Mr. A. R. Tanco, urging faster progress, asked governments to reduce spending on arms to provide resources to help developing countries increase their food production.

Under the present UK Government, a "central objective" of aid policy has become promotion of development in country areas where the overwhelming majority of the poor of the Third World live, and thus to aid in increasing world food production. This is not an imposed view; it has been adopted as a consensus decision at the Commonwealth Ministerial Meeting on Food Production and Rural Development in 1975. Estimates for the UK gross aid programme for 1977/78 (all aspects, not only food) were £623m.

However, the extensive use of grain—suitable

for human consumption—for feeding animals has rightly been severely criticised. The World Development Movement accuses Britain and other rich meat-eating countries of supporting famine by buying grain to feed the animals. In more restrained terms similar criticism has been voiced by Dr. H. C. Pereira, F.R.S., Chief Scientist, Ministry of Agriculture.

If we were willing to obtain more protein from grain and reduce our consumption of meat we could contribute to world food supplies—and reduce our import bill.

6. Fertilisers and Pesticides.

Prices of fertilisers were generally four times as much in 1974 as in 1971, a major influence being the big rise in oil prices. In addition critical shortages of fertilisers and pesticides, and of quality seeds were reported by the UN as impeding efforts to increase food production in the poorer parts of the world. Even taking into account heavy investment in fertiliser manufacturing plants, world production of nitrogenous and phosphate fertilisers in 1980–81 was estimated to be likely to fall short by 19 million nutrient tons of the projected needs of almost 97 million. The FAO in mid-1974 set up an International Fertiliser Supply Scheme seeking to mobilise financial and technical assistance for buying fertilisers and for making them in developing countries. However, little has been reported of its success. FAO also call for better organised use of plant, animal and human wastes, estimating that these sources in developing countries could supply up to eight times more nutrient than the total they now consume of inorganic fertilisers.

Pests are reckoned to consume about a third of the crops of the developing countries and FAO have urged reserve stocks of pesticide and equipment for applying them, as well as the organisation of training courses and of industries to manufacture pesticides.

Output could be expanded by *quality seeds*. FAO recommends expanding their international Seed Industry Development Programme and also establishing stocks of these in various areas of the world; improved seeds are seen as a relatively cheap and simple input that can lead to higher yields and to plants with greater disease resistance. Some successes in this area have been achieved but on a limited scale.

7. Credit Facilities

Credit facilities may seem remote from this subject but they are of crucial importance to poor farmers. Without them the farmers cannot take advantage of the new technological package of better seeds, fertilisers and pesticides. FAO assess, for example, that in south Asia the average small farmer spends $6 per hectare a year when he should be spending between $20 and $80 according to crop. To purchase the means of increasing his output the farmer needs credit. Governments of developing countries should therefore expand credit and ensure that it reaches the smaller farmer.

8. Aquaculture

Noted briefly above, this is the production of freshwater and marine organisms by the equivalent of farming methods. The UN Protein-Calorie Advisory Group (PAG) estimates that it now contributes annually about 6 million tons of food in the world valued at $2,500 million. It could be greatly expanded and could contribute particularly to the nutrition of landlocked countries. Eel, shrimp and some oysters have long been cultivated for the luxury market but common carp, Chinese and Indian carp, milkfish and mussels have been reared for local human consumption. PAG gives the figures in the table as conservative estimates, stressing the economic as well as nutritional importance in the Philippines, Korea, Indonesia. To expand this valuable source of food they recommend more research, better data on fish eggs, larvae and juveniles, genetic improvement, disease control, predator and competitor control, training in the expertise, issuing instruction material and training

WORLD PRODUCTION BY AQUACULTURE

(excluding sport, bait and ornamental fish and pearls.)

Species	Annual production, thousands of tons
Finfish . . .	3,680
Shrimps and prawns .	14
Oysters . . .	711
Mussels . . .	180
Clams . . .	56
Other molluscs . .	20
Seaweeds . . .	373
Total	**5,034**

Source: PAG Bulletin, Vol. IV, No. 2

teachers, the so-called extension workers who give technical advice and assistance—the whole being run as an international programme.

9. The Intermediate Technology (IT)

Appropriate Technology (as some prefer to call the concept) is beginning on a small scale to contribute to improving farming in poorer countries. This is based on the view that it is impracticable and even damaging to transfer technology (tools, equipment, organisation) directly from industrialised countries to developing ones. Consequently, they argue, modern knowledge should be applied *not* to developing inferior technology but to assisting in developing technologies appropriate to the developing countries themselves with the co-operation of those living there. In farming, applying IT offers wide opportunities for diversifying and upgrading rural life, especially if new and improved farming equipment can be locally manufactured and serviced. For example, field projects in Zambia and Nigeria have resulted in innovations, including planting machines for maize and other crops, weeders, improved animal-drawn equipment; in India they have introduced an improved version of a thresher first designed in Iran; in Chad, improved pit silos for safely preserving crops to keep as cattle feed. In all cases, the design is at a suitable price level for the country concerned, developed by their own countrymen and at a level of complexity suited to local skills.

This approach was endorsed in the UN World Economic Survey 1974 and by Dr. Kurt Waldheim, Secretary-General of the UN, in his report to the UN Seventh Special Session 1975; in this he urged a New International Economic Order to aid in spreading the benefits of technological progress to all countries equitably. For the less-developed countries, the greatest impact is likely to be in rural areas.

This is of the greatest significance since the UN Industrial Development Organisation (UNIDO) is actively promoting industrialisation of developing countries. The theme that developing countries should evolve their own technology is an important part of the UN conference on science and technology for development in 1979. *See also* F73(2).

V. ENERGY

Until recently interest in energy sources on a practical industrial scale centred on coal, oil and gas. These of course remain the main sources in projections in terms of decades ahead but it is significant that a Survey of Energy Resources prepared for the World Energy Conference 1974 opened with a wider theme. All energy in its various forms of use is traceable to four sources which are, it pointed out:

1. solar radiation

2. subterranean heat from radioactive decay

3. inertial forces from gravitational and rotational phenomena

4. nuclear reactions releasing energy from fission or fusion of atomic nuclei.

Mankind has had a long period of dependence on the irreplaceable stores of energy derived from past solar radiation. Now there is active interest and research into the possibilities of utilising power derived from all of the above sources, which are effectively inexhaustible. A further significant feature was the theme of the conference itself "The economic and environmental challenges of future requirements". The grouping of its subject matter was equally indicative of present anxieties, for sections were devoted to relating energy to population, to environmental constraints and to recovery of resources as well as the more traditional subjects of energy conversion, transport and utilisation. This reflects the growing concern by the general public at the profligate use of many natural resources, particularly in the industrially advanced parts of the world. Other features of concern have been the heavy and growing dependence of the developed countries on oil, a large part of which comes from a politically unstable region. The oil crisis of 1973–4 led all consumer countries to take urgent measures to speed the search for other sources of energy and to seek economies in use. Correspondingly, the subject matter of the World Energy Conference in 1977 was "The Availability and Rational Uses of Energy Resources."

The growth in world production and the marked differences in usage in different parts of the world are shown in the table.

1. Energy Consumption: the growing problem.

Global energy needs have not only been growing but accelerating (up to the time of the exceptional events of 1973/4). In the inter-war years the figures rose by about $1\frac{1}{2}\%$ a year, in the 'fifties by nearly 5% a year, and in the 'sixties by $5\frac{1}{4}\%$ a year. In recent years (until 1974) demand for oil alone has grown at 7% a year. But coal production has remained constant, the decline in production in Western Europe (including the UK) being counterbalanced by increased output in the USA, USSR and Eastern Europe. The world market for energy is dominated by the USA where energy consumption per head per year is the highest in the world, roughly double that of any other developed country. Meanwhile two-thirds of the world's inhabitants living in the developing countries use so little per head that they consume only about one-tenth of global supplies.

Nuclear energy, hailed as the great hope early in the 'fifties has not as yet lived up to its early promise. Though reactors have so far operated at high levels of safety, their use has led to extensive debate internationally about possible future risks, including the liability to exploitation militarily by terrorist groups. The UK was the first country to generate electricity from nuclear stations on an industrial scale (1956) (*see* Section L). Of other possible sources only hydroelectricity makes any appreciable contribution. A barrage scheme (*see* Tidal Power, Section L) is already in operation on the River Rance in France and is the subject of research in England (the Severn estuary is particularly appropriate because its range from high to low tide is very large). Such a scheme could make an important contribution to electricity generation and storage but the cost would be high. Solar energy and geothermal energy are in use only to a very limited extent.

An immediate result of the oil price rise was a decline in global oil consumption in two successive years—1974 and 1975—reversing the consistent well-established long-term trend. On a world scale, total energy consumption was estimated by BP in its statistical review as having risen by less than 1% in 1975 compared with the preceding year. This was composed of a large proportionate rise (a small absolute one) in contribution by nuclear power and rises in solid fuels and water power.

In the UK, a separate Department of Energy was set up in January 1974 to concentrate on "energy problems arising from developments in the supply and price of oil". Energy and conservation problems were also examined by the

National Economic Development Office (NEDO) and by the so-called Think-Tank—the Central Policy Review Staff—in published reports. As the table shows, energy consumption fell but analysis of the causes was complicated by the poor levels of economic activity which reduces the demand for energy. Policy measures taken include establishing greater public control in respect of offshore oil and gas development, supporting a 10-year investment programme in the coal industry to provide 42 million tons of new coal-producing capacity by 1985 with a target for that year by the NCB of 150 million tons (including opencast) thus ending the rundown of the industry, provisionally increasing nuclear-powered generating of electricity, and a programme of energy conservation. For the longer term, the Department of Energy sought to stimulate wide public discussion of the issues—by issuing a series of informative reviews—including the contentious question of whether to proceed with constructing a Fast Breeder Reactor. From 1980 onwards North Sea oil (100–140 million tons p.a.) should meet our oil needs. Meanwhile the Social Science Research Council is promoting work on energy economics to ensure that this aspect is adequately taken into account and that the problem is not treated purely as one of technology.

UK ENERGY CONSUMPTION IN MILLION TONS COAL EQUIVALENT

	1973	1974	1975	1976
oil . . .	161	150	134	132
coal . . .	131	116	118	120
gas . . .	44	52	54	58
nuclear . .	10	12	11	13
hydroelectric .	2	2	2	2
Total	348	332	319	325

2. The Future

World-wide, energy demand is expected to grow at 3·3% p.a., so that demand in 1990 will be double that in 1970. There are grave anxieties about reserves of petroleum—where output is likely to be declining in about 2 decades. Possibilities of increasing gas output are in dispute. Coal has very large reserves, but difficulties are anticipated in trying to raise output quickly. Greatly increased dependence on nuclear energy seems inescapable.

For Britain, an important discussion document was published by the Advisory Council on Research and Development for Fuel and Power (ACORD) as Energy Paper No. 11 (London, HMSO, 1976). This accepted the widely-held view that the UK would be self-sufficient in energy throughout the 1980s due to large supplies of oil, coal and gas, with a supplement from nuclear reactors. Yet it warned that it would be a "grave mistake" to lapse into complacency. The breathing space should be used to improve the efficiency of energy use and to establish technologies upon which this country's future is likely to depend. After examining several possible lines of future development of policy, it concludes that we need

* more attention to coal utilisation and conversion

* high priority to technologies connected with North Sea oil and gas expanded nuclear technology

* wider R & D on "alternative sources" (solar, wind, wave and tidal power, waste materials, geothermal and—longer-term—nuclear fusion)

* new technology for gas and liquid fuel from coal

* improving efficiency in converting primary fuel to electricity

* major effort on energy-saving with economic equipment

An ingenious idea quoted by the Programmes Analysis Unit is calcining limestone to give CO_2, reacting this with hydrogen obtained in nuclear reactors by decomposing water, and thus yielding methanol fuel. Alternatively, the hydrogen might be used directly as the fuel. There are many critics of growing dependence on nuclear reactors since these create plutonium—a poisonous material and one that can be used to make devastatingly destructive bombs; thus distributing reactors disseminates potential nuclear explosive material. The Secretary of State for Energy, Tony Benn, has stated that he welcomes extensive public debate on the human/political/economic/technology issues involved. Among the discussion documents published in 1977 were "Energy Policy Reviews" and "Working Document on Energy Policy for the Energy Commission". Broadly they indicate that UK will have to place increased emphasis on: conservation; coal; nuclear power.

3. Other Research Areas

In the new situation of vastly increased energy cost, work on "alternative sources" has been greatly stimulated. Throughout the industrialised countries there are small groups working on projects applying particularly wind and solar power. In addition, in several countries there are now major officially funded projects in these and similar types of area—now removed from characterisation as "cranky" and accepted into the fold of formal scientific/technological develop-

WORLD ENERGY CONSUMPTION AND POPULATION, BY MAJOR REGIONS, 1950, 1960, 1970.

	1950		1960		1970	
Region	Population (million)	Consumption per capita (million Btu)	Population (million)	Consumption per capita (million Btu)	Population (million)	Consumption per capita (million Btu)
North America .	166·1	221·9	198·7	245·1	226·2	329·3
Canada .	13·7	197·6	17·9	217·0	21·4	328·9
United States .	152·3	224·3	180·7	248·0	204·8	329·3
Western Europe .	302·4	57·8	326·5	79·8	356·4	134·3
Oceania . . .	12·2	73·0	15·4	90·8	19·2	127·7
Latin America .	161·9	14·8	212·4	23·3	282·0	32·4
Asia (excl. Communist)	805·4	4·7	970·6	8·5	1,231·3	16·9
Japan . .	82·9	21·0	93·2	39·4	103·4	108·9
Other Asia .	722·5	2·9	877·4	5·2	1,127·9	8·5
Africa . .	217·0	6·0	276·0	7·8	349·5	10·5
USSR and Comm.						
Eastern Europe .	269·8	47·6	312·9	83·0	348·4	128·5
USSR . .	180·0	46·8	214·4	83·5	242·8	131·8
Eastern Europe .	89·7	49·2	98·5	82·0	105·6	120·9
Communist Asia .	569·8	2·2	677·5	9·7	795·6	14·2
WORLD . .	2,504·5	30·7	2,989·9	41·5	3,608·6	59·4

Source: J. Darmstadter. Royal Society conference "Energy in the 1980s", pub. 1974.

ment. In 1976, Dr. W. Marshall FRS, then Chief Scientist at the UK Department of Energy, reported on the assessments of the Energy Technology Support Unit; the table shows the possible contributions to UK energy supplies in the year 2000.

These are regarded largely as research projects during the next few years; it is reckoned to take decades before new technology in energy can make a worthwhile contribution. The programme on solar energy also involves the Department of the Environment who have responsibility for housing; it will also incorporate material from a detailed review by the UK section of the International Solar Energy Society. There are, however, informed critics of the view that greater energy supplies will continue to be needed to support economic growth; broadly these place emphasis on more conservation and recovery of discharged heat at present wasted notably in generating electricity. They also suggest that we may be approaching saturation of the market for energy in some areas. Studies along these lines are in progress in the Energy Research Group at the Open University. Also, during 1977, the Department of Energy launched a major conservation campaign—including subsidies to those improving efficiency of energy use and promoting research projects.

4. Energy and Environment in the Less-developed Countries

At its meeting in 1975 the Governing Councils of UNEP requested its Director to give high priority to establishing in typical rural areas in Asia, Africa and Latin America demonstration centres for harnessing locally available renewable sources of energy. Their grounds were recognition that small amounts of energy for cooking, desalination of water, lighting, could alleviate some of the conditions of abject poverty. Sources suggested were solar, wind, hydro-, biogas from organic wastes, planting quicker-growing trees. The aim was " to enhance the quality of life ".

VI. ECONOMIC GROWTH

1. Is Growth Desirable?

Until recently the value of economic growth was little questioned. It was assumed that increases in national output were desirable and would improve standards of living. Until the last decade or so, the availability of resources received relatively little attention. But in recent years these concepts of the value of economic growth have come under attack generally on the grounds that world resources will be quickly depleted, that a large part of the increased volume of products are worthless baubles and there should be more emphasis on re-distribution to give a more socially just society between and within countries. In the Introduction we quoted the main conclusions of the weighty, though unofficial, Club of Rome on the risks of exhausting resources and of major economic catastrophes unless all countries co-operate in the use of world resources.

A so-called " Blueprint for Survival ", published in the UK in 1972, contended that if current trends are allowed to persist the breakdown of society and the irreversible disruption of the life-support systems on this planet are inevitable. The principal defect of the industrial way of life with its ethos of expansion, according to this critique, is that it is not sustainable. It will end either in a succession of famines, epidemics, social crises and wars or under human control in a succession of humane and measured changes. Policy advo-

cated was to move towards a stable society based on:

1. minimum disruption of ecological processes;

2. maximum conservation of materials and energy;

3. a population in which recruitment equals loss;

4. a social system in which the individual can enjoy, rather than feel restricted by, the first three conditions.

Thoughtful reaction has been that these criticisms draw attention to real major problems, that the dire consequences are over-stated but that the pressures are valuable in speeding up corrective trends already emerging in response to world difficulties as noted earlier.

However, there have been strong hostile reactions from the poorer countries, illustrated by the comments of Dr. Abdel-Rahman, Executive Director of UN Industrial Development Organisation. Examining the possibility of reducing consumption in the developing countries, he understandably commented " if it goes on the average any lower it will mean starvation, famine and actual death for hundreds of millions today and in the next 25 years ". It would also increase tension between advanced countries with decreasing population and developing countries with increasing population at relatively lower standards of living. He therefore urged for developing countries accelerated and effective industrialisation. This in essence formed the subject of the UN Special Session 1975.

The UN is strongly committed to promoting technical co-operation for the developing countries and the UN Development Programme reported that in 1975 these activities exceeded a value of $1 (US) billion. They ranged from a small irrigation project in Mali to a 133 acre industrial park in El Salvador with 52 factory sites. This programme plans " new dimensions " of expansion of efforts in response to varied needs of countries in diverse stages of development.

From within the economically advanced countries comes the reply to queries on exhausting resources that there will be compensating adjustments. Increasing scarcity will raise prices, speed the search for new sources, justify working leaner and more remote sources, increase the pressure for re-cycling and speed the search for substitutes; all these reactions invalidate the assumptions on which estimates are based for the period in which existing resources are being exhausted. On the proposal for aiming at zero economic growth the counter-arguments—for example by Fremont Felix in World Markets of Tomorrow—are that this zero economic growth would actually hinder social progress, deny minority groups the chance to improve their positions, deny all under-privileged groups the opportunity to better their lots, deny to all countries the resources for more schools, universities and hospitals and to continue the fight against pollution and other environmental ills. Furthermore, he contends that the historical trends after the earliest stages of industrialisation are for the rate of growth to decline and for the consumption of electrical energy per unit of growth also to decline; growth is not in fact exponential, but diminishing. Dr. Wilfred Beckerman (in his book In Defence of Economic Growth) carries this counter-attack further. The developed countries with higher rates of growth (W. Germany, Denmark, Norway, Sweden) provide much more generous social insurance programmes—16% of

Source	Form of use	Annual mtce *	Growth beyond 2000
Solar			
i. Solar heating	heat	5	large
ii. Fuel from plants . .	fluid fuel	3	uncertain
Geothermal	heat	4	modest
Wind	electrical	6	small
Tides	electrical	3–10	small
Waves	electrical	15	very large

* mtce = million tons coal equivalent

NON-FERROUS METALS. RATE OF USE AND RECOVERY 1973

	Aluminium	Copper	Lead	Zinc	Platinum
UK consumption . . .	668,000 tonnes	699,000 tonnes	364,000 tonnes	391,000 tonnes	18·7 tonnes (600,000 troy oz)
Approximate scrap recovery as a proportion of consumption . .	26%	37%	62%	21%	58%

the National Product—than those with lower ones such as UK and USA which allot only 9% to these purposes. What is more, these types of expenditure tend to rise at 2½ times the growth rate of per capita National Product. Ironically he asks whether a starving man, say in Calcutta, in an unpleasant environment, would prefer an improved environment or a square meal. In the light of the situation described above (IV) this is a valid question. On mineral resources, Beckerman argues that priority must be given to current human welfare; there is no " correct " rate of usage, since things are for people; we might even be using resources too slowly. Concerning our duties to posterity, it can be added that since each successive generation has been richer than its predecessors and has successfully found ways of meeting its increased needs of goods and energy, this concern may well be misplaced.

Nevertheless the views of the critics of growth have led to many re-appraisals. Typical of the newer mood was the comment by Denis Healey, Chancellor of the Exchequer, in his 1974 autumn Budget speech favouring improvement in the standard of living but adding " the senseless accumulation of material goods of exactly the same type as the Western world had been producing since the war can no longer be regarded as the only guarantee of human happiness or the only measure of economic success."

In fact, during 1974 to 1977 the industrialised countries did suffer reductions in economic wealth due to both the recession and the greatly increased oil prices. But it is generally expected that economic growth will shortly be resumed.

2. War on Waste: re-cycling

Throughout the developed world there is growing interest in the re-use of materials, largely because of anxieties about resources in relation to economic growth, but also on more limited normal grounds of economy. And of course within companies and trades, industrial scrap is already extensively savaged and re-used. In the UK the Government in 1974 launched a campaign with a Green Paper entitled " War on Waste ". This discussed specifically problems in recovering ferrous metals, non-ferrous metals, paper, glass, plastics, rubber and other materials. The Government set up a Waste Management Advisory Council, and a special group to promote collecting waste paper for re-cycling. They planned to extend research and to study financial incentives, disincentives, grants, awards and regulations. Appeals were issued to local authorities, commercial firms, voluntary organisations and industry to increase efforts. A major difficulty—the Green Paper picked it out as a " critical factor "—is the instability of markets for recovered materials. The Government declared that it would consult the relevant industries so as to provide a firmer basis for the long-term development of the reclamation industry associated with more stable conditions, longer term contracts and less movement in prices. For bulk wastes that might be of industrial interest they also set up a waste exchange market dealing (in confidence) with offers or requests in this field without disclosing company details at the enquiry stage. It might be assumed that the normal working of industry would ensure that efforts were made to extract values from wastes or to sell it. But the Warren Spring Laboratory reports that its investigations showed that industry often did not know what it was throwing away. This laboratory in fact operates a Waste Recovery Service to aid industry in assessing the possibilities.

Overall the scale of the problem can be seen from the fact that in 1973 Britain produced 20 million tonnes of household and trade refuse, with an approximately equal quantity produced by industry, far larger quantities of mining and quarry waste, plus further agricultural waste. Much of this, it is now considered, could be put to use, producing economic wealth without any drain on resources, often improving the environment, often also reducing dependence on imports.

An officially commended scheme is operated by the charity Oxfam with a national collection of rag waste from their Oxfam shops and a central sorting depot run in co-operation with the local authority at Kirklees. They are also running an intensive segregated waste collection in the nearby area which is reported to have had a very good response.

The first published study of the WMAC has put forward to the government a set of recommendations to encourage waste paper collection by local authorities to overcome their reluctance based on the " critical factor " noted above which has led to losses in some cases and therefore local criticism. The theme of re-cycling has been taken up by many countries and by the UN. For example, a UN conference (organised by the Economic Commission for Europe for Sept. 1978) arranged to examine economic, technological and environmental aspects covering 21 topics.

VII. POLLUTION

Responding to worldwide anxieties about this subject the UN held a conference at Stockholm in 1972 on the human environment. Though dealing with many other aspects, it gave major attention to pollution risks. Since then the UN Environment Programme (UNEP) has established an earthwatch system of global monitoring and information services to provide early warning of environmental risks and providing governments with access to the latest scientific knowledge to deal with them. It gave high priority to monitoring radionuclides resulting from nuclear tests. It also adopted a number of decisions concerned with the preservation of the marine environment. (For completeness it should also be mentioned that it launched a major attack on the advance of deserts, with programmes to restore productivity of arid areas to prevent a future Sahel-type tragedy.)

In November 1973 the EEC similarly adopted an Environmental Action Programme. Items on which they have promoted action include reducing the amount of lead in petrol, of sulphur in diesel oil, and preparing for decisions on air pollution by sulphur compounds and dusts by starting a programme of exchanging information on them as the basis for a survey. However at this stage sulphur trioxide and suspended particles in air are the only pollutants under systematic and intense surveillance in every EEC state. Using the British Food Research Association as their agents, EEC are also investigating N-nitroso compounds in the environment; they will check the levels of nitrites, nitrates and amine precursors in root crops, grains, fruits, water supplies and elsewhere, including any relevant pesticide residues.

Within the UK considerable progress has been made because of public awareness and official pressures, though there can never be justification for complacency. The booklet " Clean Air Today " (issued by the Department of the Environment) presents photos—for example of Widnes at the end of the 19th cent. and today—and diagrams to illustrate how remarkably the air has improved over the last couple of decades. Domestic smoke emissions estimated at about 1·3 million tons p.a. in 1953 were reckoned at below

0·4 million by 1975 as a result of the Clean Air Act 1956 (a pioneering step by the UK) and changing social habits, notably the switch from crude coal burning in inadequate appliances to refined fuels, smokeless solid fuels and greatly improved appliances if the user chose to stay with coal. Sulphur dioxide *emissions* have slightly increased with time but strangely enough the amount in the air has fallen. From power stations it is discharged from very tall chimneys and the Scandinavian countries contend that the oxides of sulphur are being carried over the North Sea to them. This is disputed by the UK authorities and the problem is under study. Other theories include the suggestion that they are brought down sorbed on to particles. The Warren Spring Laboratory operates the National Survey of Smoke and Sulphur Dioxide and conducts research on, for example, pollutants in rain and other pollution topics. Other bodies involved in work on pollution are the Meteorological Office, the Ministry of Agriculture, Fisheries and Food, the National Environmental Research Council and the Atomic Energy Research Establishment.

Increasing concern about pollution from motor vehicles has resulted in a detailed survey by Warren Spring Laboratory of roadside levels of vehicle pollutants in five cities. The great spur to all this work in Britain was the London " smog " of 1952 when the death rate was doubled for that period. Some have compared the pressure for clean air just after this catastrophe to that for clean water supply and adequate sewerage of the 19th cent.

An important self-inflicted source of lethal pollution is smoking. A series of medical-statistical reports have pinpointed smoking as the largest single cause of both bronchitis and lung cancer (*see* Section P). This is evidently more severe a factor than air pollution, in general, today, since the Report on Air Pollution of the Royal College of Physicians in 1970 found evidence of association between *air* pollution and lung cancer to be *in*conclusive. It is reported that under present conditions—in sharp contrast to those in the more polluted ones of twenty years ago—there is very little correspondence between periods of heavier air pollution and mortality and sickness rates.

Radioactivity in the air and in milk is constantly monitored and, after rising to a peak, has steadily fallen since the signing of the agreements on banning atmospheric tests of nuclear weapons. When France and China carried out their nuclear tests, the effects were noted worldwide in surges of increased radioactivity.

A series of reports on river pollution has demonstrated a welcome improvement in river water quality. For example, by 1975, two-thirds of industrial and sewage effluent discharged to rivers was classed as " satisfactory ". Sewage flows are receiving better treatment, whilst discharges of sewage to estuaries are also being controlled.

Pesticides used for non-agricultural purposes have been more closely supervised since 1974, in the same way as those used in agriculture; food storage and related areas are already covered by the Pesticides Safety Precautions Scheme. And —reverting to international aspects—the FAO maintain a running control on hazards to health arising from contamination of foods with pesticide residues. In the UK the British Ecological Society seeks, among other objectives, to promote control of crop pests by biological means so avoiding environmental hazards from pesticides. The need for research into pollution of the stratosphere and its effects on the ozone layer (which protects our health and our crops from potentially harmful ultra-violet radiation) is now recognised.

Though this is very much a recent story of increasing awareness and of great advances in combating pollution, *eternal vigilance* remains the watchword. The large expansion in generation of electricity by nuclear power carries grave risks of greater quantities of radiation contaminating the biosphere. So does the conduct of two major powers (China and France) in carrying out nuclear explosions in the atmosphere. And the growing risks of 20 million tonnes of manufactured organic chemicals entering the environment annually (largely due to the development of the petrochemical industries) have received the attention of the Royal Society. The Health and Safety at Work Act 1974 also places some responsibility on industry for dealing with pollution problems arising from their activities. Research Associations are correspondingly beginning to introduce environmental services to aid industry in adjusting their processes to prevent possible ill-effects; and this ties in of course with pressures for re-cycling, for economising in world resources and for ending the casual throwaway attitude.

Disclosures of irresponsible casual dumping of toxic materials in dumps that were both unsightly and suspected to drain to water-courses led to the passing of the Deposit of Poisonous Waste Act 1972, which gave local authorities greatly increased powers to control this potentially lethal danger. Controls were further extended under the Control of Pollution Act 1974. There are now specialist companies willing to take such offensive and poisonous wastes and treat them before depositing them in protected areas. And the Warren Spring Laboratory advises companies, placing heavy emphasis on the possibilities of recovering values from waste. New features in recent years have been attention to controlling smells and controlling noise. Both have been the subject of special researches and surveys, then of government circulars urging action by local authorities. Further reflecting the mood of the times is the fact that in all new projects considered, even those arising from the crisis in energy supplies, a high priority is given to avoiding pollution or even despoiling the environment. Thus these considerations have been urged in respect of bringing in the oil from below the continental shelf around Britain (contaminating the sea, damaging Scottish coastal areas of outstanding natural beauty) in a way that would not have been a feature of the discussions in earlier periods.

VIII. APPRAISAL

Final decisions on the relative weight to be given to environmental issues are heavily influenced by value judgments. There are no correct, fixed or final answers. For starving people, the urgent necessity is food, and beyond that the facilities and means for making a living by their own efforts, with self-respect. But once man emerges beyond the stage of meeting his most basic needs, it becomes possible to make choices of how to live, what proportion of resources to give to keeping the air and water pure, land and coastlines attractive and inviolate, factories landscaped. Yet much of this is dependent on the mood of public opinion. In making the necessary decisions, the public needs to have information and knowledge of the technical possibilities for each case, the consequences of adopting particular options and also the consequences of drift without a strategic policy. In many of the topics discussed in this section, life and death are at stake. This is obvious for food, but no less so for preventing smog or the death from hyperthermia of old people unable to afford enough fuel. These are the most dramatic aspects of examining how we can learn to live in the modern world. But at a less critical level, action or inaction in respect of the environment affects our enjoyment of life, as, for example, in determining whether we look out on to a squalid tip or, after restoration, on to an attractive landscape; whether resources are used to pile up personal baubles or better social amenities: whether we are content to over-feed (particularly on meat which wastes grain) and risk later world upheavals or alter our mode of life to aid some re-allocation of food to those in need: whether part of our population should continue to spend their working days in almost mindless tedium or be stimulated to take an active interest in what they do.

Apart from calling a halt to the ceaseless accumulation of un-needed further personal possessions by those with spare, disposable income, such options mean contributing to (relatively small) changes in personal behaviour. If salvage from municipal refuse is widely introduced, we may be called upon to give support by sorting our domestic refuse, keeping some things like paper and metals separate. And fuel and space economies may turn us towards more use of public transport and less use of our precious personal cars. In attempting to provide a background, this section has striven to put forward a fair selection of the facts and issues, guided throughout by the major considerations that we in the UK share the surface of the planet with the

whole community of mankind and that we must accept the statement of the UNEP Governing Council in April 1975 ... that the issues of population, resources, environment and development are inter-related problems ... that environmental management implies sustainable development of all countries aimed at meeting basic human needs without transgressing the outer limits set to man's endeavours by the biosphere.

VII. SPECIAL TOPICS

DEVELOPMENT ANTHROPOLOGY

Introduction

The word development became a technical term in colonial administration with the implementation in the British territories of the Colonial Development and Welfare Act of 1940. With the passing of this measure Britain abandoned the principle that colonial territories should be self-supporting, and made available from British revenues grants for projects expected to improve the standard of living of the local populations. "Welfare" implied the expansion of social services: "development" was investment calculated to increase productivity. After the Second World War a similar policy was introduced in France, and as former colonial territories became independent the United States and the United Nations also contributed funds for their development; the United Nations proclaimed a "development decade" in 1960. The motives behind these policies were various; governments sought to extend their political influence, their trading relations and opportunities for their nationals, but a humanitarian element was also present. The development of resources had always been the aim of colonial powers, but now the emphasis was on the development of peoples.

The Problems of Development

In a sense anthropologists have been interested in problems of development from the time when, under the influence of Malinowski, British anthropologists turned from the reconstruction of the past to what he called "the anthropology of the changing African". African was taken as the type because it was the International African Institute, supported by large American grants, which supplied the bulk of the funds made available for research in anthropology in the period between the two world wars. Malinowski's pupils observed the effects that European penetration had had on African and other populations, and tended to concentrate on those which had been adverse. For a time they deplored economic development altogether, but they came to realise that the changes introduced by colonial rule were irreversible. They also had to recognise the fact that Western science and technology could and should be used for the benefit of non-Western peoples, particularly to raise standards of health and nutrition. Their attention was now focused on small-scale innovations with these aims, such as had of course always been attempted under colonial rule. The "community development" projects which had some vogue in West Africa in the period just before independence aimed at making such improvements through the efforts of the people expected to benefit from them, with some assistance from governments. Independent India adopted a community development policy which involved the division of the whole country into development areas under officials of the central government. Since the improvements sought were of a kind that any anthropologist would approve, it now became our task to explain the indifference or resistance which they so often encountered. Some also looked critically at the explanations in terms of "peasant conservatism" that were offered by people who were interested in

development but not versed in anthropological theory.

The Awareness of Poverty

The interest in development which was manifested after the Second World War arose from a new awareness of the poverty of many millions of people in those newly independent countries that began to be called "under-developed", and later from the recognition that population was increasing faster than natural resources. These poorer countries were contrasted with the highly industrialised ones, which were assumed to be "developed", and it was further assumed that their problem was simply that too little capital had been invested in industry. Hence external finance was offered for development programmes which aimed at rapid industrialisation, and the next assumption made was that this would increase national productivity, as it often did, and thus would automatically raise standards of living. It proved, however, to do little to alleviate the poverty of the peasant majorities of the populations concerned.

Food Production

Attention then turned to the possibility of increasing food production, and peasant incomes along with it, by introducing more efficient methods of farming. Since most anthropologists have worked among rural populations, it is here that they might be expected to have something to contribute, and that their advice has in fact sometimes been sought. An anthropologist may, for example, be appointed as a member of a UN development team; or a private company may engage one as consultant, as was done when copper was discovered on the island of Bougainville and the inhabitants were not satisfied with the compensation they were offered for the expropriation of their land. Sometimes one has been asked to comment on an elaborate multiple project such as the damming of a river for a hydro-electric scheme and the resettlement of the people whose homes would be flooded, and has been able to indicate situations that would have to be taken into account and persuade the planners to work to a slower timetable.

But more often anthropologists have come on the scene after a plan has been carried through, and have been able to see the various ways in which the results have differed from what was expected, and sometimes reasons why it has failed altogether—if, for example, a farm project does not attract or hold settlers.

The Colson–Scudder Survey

A well-known example of a study which was begun before the change that was planned and continued after it, is that made by Elizabeth Colson and the ecologist Thayer Scudder of the 56,000 Gwembe Tonga who were moved from their homes when the Kariba Dam was built on the Zambezi River. They made a detailed study of the Gwembe social organisation and adaptation to the environment in their traditional homes, and returned when the move was still a recent drama in most people's lives, and at intervals in later years. Their final study contrasted the adaptation to the move made by two village communities whose home environments had been very different and who had been moved to new sites only a few miles apart.

In their study of the resettlement process they called attention to the hardships that had been caused by requirements of technicians which were allowed to override consideration for human values. The height of the dam was raised after the preparations for resettlement had begun, so that the area to which many people had agreed to move was flooded and they had to be sent elsewhere. Those who had furthest to go had to be moved *en bloc* in a single day because the Public Works Department could only release the number of lorries needed for one day. New sites were not provided with water in time for the move, as had been promised.

This list of grievances illustrates both a failure to co-ordinate the activities of different technical departments of government and a lack of imaginative sympathy. But it also indicates that the agents of change must work within the limits of their technical resources. It would have been quite impracticable in this case, for example, for Public Works to transport several thousand people over 100 miles by a shuttle service, picking up families or even whole villages as and when they were ready to move. After all, the Kariba Dam had not been conceived as an operation to benefit the Gwembe Tonga. Anyone who is convinced that a project must go through can argue that the people who are affected will settle down after a temporary upset; and in a sense they do, as they come to take their new circumstances for granted.

Nevertheless, if those in authority think it important not to impose unnecessary hardships on those who are subject to their decisions, this detailed account of an exercise which is likely to be repeated in some form where dams are built, populations moved from disaster areas, refugees settled and so on, is a record to which they can look to see what mistakes they might avoid.

The Weinrich Study

A comparable study is that made by Dr' A. H. K. Weinrich (Sister Mary Aquina) of the African response to the various policies pursued by the government of Rhodesia with the aim of improving African farming. Certain areas of land have been earmarked for purchase by Africans who are required to show that they are efficient farmers. Others have been irrigated and are offered on lease to farmers who have to follow a closely controlled programme of work. The largest proportion of the area of land allotted to African occupation is " tribal trust land ", where, after an attempt to enforce fixed standards of cultivation, the authorities fell back on the educational work of missionaries and extension officers. Dr. Weinrich investigated communities holding land in each of these three ways, and concluded that no great improvement in cultivation could be observed in any, except in the case of a minority of men and women who had followed courses of training to qualify as " master farmers ". Her own conclusions were drastic: that *all* rights to agricultural land, including those of Europeans, should be conditional on efficient cultivation, and that every African cultivator should be held individually responsible for a specified area of land. Much more attention should be given to the education of peasant farmers in place of attempts at coercion, and farming communities should be given a say in the management of their own affairs. At the time when her findings were published, Rhodesian politics had not reached their present (1978) critical stage, but whatever type of government emerges they will have to deal with the problems that she has analysed.

These two examples are of action taken in territories where policy was dominated by European settler interests. Few such territories remain today, and it is the professed aim of the rulers of all the new states to seek the welfare of the indigenous populations. In such a context an anthropologist could be in a stronger position. If his views were asked in advance, he might be able to say that an apparently beneficial scheme would not really be so; or that it would need to overcome specific difficulties arising from existing power structures or modes of co-operation; or that the benefits would be lost if they were not accompanied by technical instruction (for instance, in the

control of irrigated water supplies or the maintenance of pumps).

A difficulty in organising co-operation between anthropologists and development agents lies in the different time-scales with which they work. An anthropologist does not expect to speak with confidence about the people he studies until he has worked with them for at least a year. No doubt a development plan takes a year to complete, but once it has been adopted it is expected to be put into operation as soon as possible. Time-tables are drawn up, and even if deadlines are seldom met, there must be an attempt to meet them. In any event, decisions have to be taken at the moment when problems arise. Occasionally an anthropologist has actually been put in charge of a small-scale project and has had to face this dilemma.

Some would say, then, that the studies made after the event to explain failure or disappointment form the most valuable contribution of social anthropology; they are there as warnings or lessons for future planners, provided the planners will read them—but this is a risky assumption. Others would say that development agents should learn the elements of social anthropology as part of their training, and if they did, " village level " or " rural development " workers would certainly be more sensitive to the reception of their activities by villagers.

Intermediate Technology

Where there are the best prospects for fruitfu co-operation is in the introduction of small-scale improvements such as are sometimes called " intermediate technology ". Such improvements can sometimes be made by people who have made no academic study of anthropology at all, if they have enough local knowledge. It was an anthropologist working with a WHO team who pointed out that apparently simple additions to children's diet were far beyond the means of urban workers in Jakarta, but it was a doctor in India who discovered how to make existing food sources far more nutritious.

A field that anthropologists are only now beginning to enter is that of the traditional contribution of women to the farm and household economy. The exhortations and demonstrations of agronomists have commonly been directed to men, and men have been persuaded—sometimes—that methods involving harder work will bring in higher returns; it is not often noticed that the women may be doing the harder work while the men get the price of the crop. A move is now being made to train women for anthropological fieldwork among their own compatriots. They will have the general knowledge of social structure that must be the basis of any research, but they will concentrate their attention on women and on those aspects of co-operation in the household that have generally been taken for granted in the past. What are the chores that occupy a woman's day and how could they be lightened by the adoption of simple labour-saving devices? What are their ideas on the health and feeding of children and on the treatment, or recourse for aid, in sickness? How much independence of decision do they have, and in what contexts? One outcome of these studies is expected to be a fuller understanding of women's attitudes towards child-bearing and family receptiveness or resistance to the idea of family planning which is now beginning to be considered so urgently important in heavily populated countries. *See also* **F67(1)**.

The Anthropology of Development

A distinction has been drawn between " development anthropology ", that is anthropology in the service of development and " the anthropology of development ", or the study of interactions between all persons concerned in development, those who intend to bring benefits as well as the supposed beneficiaries. Studies of the latter type would depart from that focus on the reaction of intended beneficiaries which has been the main interest of anthropologists up to now, and would examine not only the motives of development planners but the interactions between the representatives of different interests engaged in planning. In the two African examples cited here,

F74

the benefit of the peasant cultivators was not the primary aim; the Kariba Dam was intended to provide electric power for industry, the various Rhodesian land policies, as Dr. Weinrich repeatedly emphasises, to enable an African population to subsist within limits set by the interests of a European one. Other plans are forced on governments by one crisis or another. But in addition, closer analysis would show how the competing interests of different technical agencies may influence the content of any development scheme and will certainly influence the allocation of resources within it. Governments are not the only empire-builders; divisions within them also seek to extend their power, and every expert thinks the most important benefits are those that depend on his own expertise (anthropologists are no exception). The most effective study of this kind that has been made is the work not of an anthropologist but of a political scientist, Robert Chambers, who followed in detail the history of the Mwea land settlement that was initiated in Kenya just before independence. He, however, was not solely interested in description as opposed to prescription; he travelled through Africa looking at settlement schemes, and concluded that the most important prerequisite for success was to keep government provision to the minimum and rely on self-help. But, brilliant as his analysis of the planning process is, it does not tell anyone how to plan better. It just throws light on human weakness and suggests the impossibility of making a perfect plan. A good many anthropologists would hope to offer more, even if they had to confine themselves to limited aspects of a plan.

GENETIC ENGINEERING

Introduction

The genetic information of most organisms is encoded along the length of long molecules of deoxyribonucleic acid (DNA). The fundamental units of inheritance, the *genes*, are discrete segments of these long molecules, and the information they carry is required for synthesis of the different proteins that constitute the tissues and enzymes of an organism.

Chromosomes

Although DNA is universal, nature has devised strict barriers to prevent exchange of DNA between different species. Indeed, without such barriers, the species could never have evolved. In plant and animal cells the DNA is complexed with protein and organised into linear structures known as chromosomes which are present in the nucleus of every cell. The number of chromosomes, their length and the order of the genes within them is characteristic for each species. New forms of genes constantly arise as a result of rare mutations, and this gives rise to the genetic variation which exists in all natural populations. This variation is constantly tried out in new combinations as a result of reassortment and exchanges between chromosomes during sexual reproduction. But sexual reproduction is only possible between individuals of the same species.

Manipulation of Genetic Material

Manipulation of genetic material is not a new concept. From earliest times man has unconsciously exploited sexual reproduction to select a combination of genetic characteristics in plants and animals which are of either economic advantage or purely aesthetic value to himself. In the present century, a knowledge of the mechanism of inheritance together with the discovery that certain chemicals or types of irradiation increase natural mutation frequencies has greatly improved breeding techniques. However, any breeding programme which relies on sexual reproduction can only lead to exchange of DNA between different individuals of the same species.

Current research in genetics, for which the term *genetic engineering* has been introduced, can break down nature's species barriers. Biochemists have now devised techniques which enable them to cut out genes from the isolated DNA of one organism and to insert these genes into the isolated DNA

molecules of another organism. When introduced into a suitable cell, these hybrid DNA molecules are replicated and their genes are expressed. Obviously such a technology could only have been developed with a full understanding of the structure and properties of DNA molecules and the ability to handle DNA in the test tube.

DNA Structure

DNA has a relatively simple structure as shown in Fig. 2.(F34) The basic building blocks are *nucleotides*. Each nucleotide consists of a sugar molecule, a phosphate group and one of four organic bases *Adenine* (A), *Thymine* (T), *Guanine* (G) or *Cytosine* (C). Each nucleotide is joined to the adjacent nucleotide by a chemical bond between the phosphate group and the sugar molecule to give a polynucleotide chain. A DNA molecule is composed of two polynucleotide chains which are held together by weak hydrogen bonds between the bases. These bonds are very specific, A always bonds with T and G always bonds with C. This means that A in one chain is always opposite T in the other chain, and similarly G is always opposite C. Although the two chains of the molecule are not identical they are said to be *complementary*, and it is usual to refer to the order of nucleotide bases along the length of the molecule in terms of base pairs.

The specificity of base pairing is extremely useful when DNA molecules are handled in the test tube. If a solution of DNA is heated to 80 °C the hydrogen bonds between the bases are broken and the two chains fall apart. If the solution is cooled slowly the hydrogen bonds reform between A and T and G and C and the two halves of the molecule can fit back together again. Any single DNA chains which have a complementary base sequence will fit together whatever their source. It is this important property which has made it possible to join different DNA molecules for the purpose of genetic engineering.

The Genetic System of Bacteria

At the present time the technology of genetic engineering relies on using the cells of bacteria as the recipient environment for replicating the hybrid DNA molecules created in the test tube. Of necessity, DNA which normally replicates in bacterial cells is one component in the system and enzymes from bacterial cells provide the tools to implement the techniques.

Bacteria are simple organisms compared with plants and animals, and their genetic material is more amenable to manipulation. The entire genetic information for a bacterium is contained in a single chromosome which is a circular molecule of DNA some 4 million base pairs in length. Some cells, however, carry additional genes in extra genetic elements called *plasmids*. Plasmids are circular molecules of DNA, much smaller than the chromosome, and these replicate as independent units in the cell. The extra genes they carry can often prove advantageous to the cell. Some plasmids have the ability to transfer themselves from one cell to another by cell contact and, even more important, may transfer themselves from the cell of one species to that of another species.

The genes which make bacteria resistant to antibiotics are carried in plasmids. Resistance plasmids are a heterogeneous group. Small plasmids carrying only a single resistance gene can exist independently or join up with other plasmids to create larger molecules which carry genes to inactivate a whole range of clinically used antibiotics. Some plasmids can actually recombine their DNA with the bacterial chromosome. A plasmid found in the gut bacterium *Escherichia coli*, for example, can exist as an independent circular molecule or become inserted into the larger circle of the bacterial chromosome. Insertion is reversible, and on resuming its independent state the plasmid may take with it a chromosome gene. Such a plasmid has become a vector for the chromosome gene because it will take it into other cells, even into the cells of other bacterial species. There the gene will be replicated as part of the plasmid DNA and even be expressed by having its protein synthesised in a new cell environment.

A number of small DNA viruses which infect *Escherichia coli* cells may also act as vectors for carrying bacterial genes. For example, the chromosome of the virus *lambda* has many features in common with the plasmid found in *E. coli*. Only the *lambda* chromosome enters a bacterial cell on infection. This may replicate many times with full expression of its genes to produce new complete virus particles, or it may become inserted into the chromosome and remain dormant. On leaving the chromosome it may pick up a bacterial gene and so become a vector. When a vector virus infects a new cell it will express the bacterial gene and, because many copies of the virus DNA can be synthesised, the bacterial gene will exist in many copies also and amplified amounts of its protein can be synthesised.

Artificially Constructed Vectors

Naturally occurring vector plasmids and viruses have proved immensely useful for studying the structure and function of individual bacterial genes isolated from the rest of the chromosome. A logical development from such naturally occurring vectors is to create artificially vectors which carry and express any bacterial gene the geneticist wants to study. Even more exciting is the prospect of creating vectors which carry not a bacterial gene, but a gene from an entirely different source such as man. This could open up the possibility of growing vats of bacteria capable of synthesising large amounts of such valuable proteins as insulin or viral antigens (which could be used as vaccines) or the clotting factor missing in people suffering from haemophilia. Certainly it would be cheaper than the methods used to obtain these proteins at present.

Artificial vectors have to be made in the test tube and a number of requirements must be met.

1. A method of breaking isolated DNA molecules so that they can be joined together again.
2. A small circular vector DNA molecule which is capable of replicating itself and can be opened to insert a DNA fragment from a different source.
3. A method of introducing the vector into a functional bacterial cell and a method of identifying cells carrying the vector.

Breaking and Rejoining DNA Molecules

Bacterial cells contain a number of enzymes which act to break, repair or extend DNA molecules. These are all vital for genetic engineering. Joining DNA molecules is technically more difficult than breaking them. Fortunately there are enzymes which cut DNA molecules in such a way as to leave " sticky " ends which can join together again. These enzymes are called *restriction enzymes*, and their normal function is to destroy foreign DNA that gains entrance to a bacterial cell. They are another of nature's tricks to prevent DNA from different sources recombining, but they are extremely valuable in the test-tube system.

Certain restriction enzymes recognise a specific base-pair sequence and only cut the DNA molecule at this sequence. One of these enzymes recognises the following sequence:

$$— — \overset{\downarrow}{G} \quad A \quad A \quad T \quad T \quad C \quad — —$$
$$— — C \quad T \quad T \quad A \quad A \quad \underset{\uparrow}{G} \quad — —$$

This sequence has a symmetrical arrangement of the bases in the two chains of the DNA molecule, and it is this which creates " sticky " ends when the molecule is cut. The enzyme does not cut the chains opposite each other but between the G–A positions marked by the arrows. The broken ends of the two chains are both left with an unpaired AATT sequence. Since these sequences are complementary, the two ends can fit together again and remain joined by the bonds which will form between the A and T bases.

DNA molecules from two quite different sources can be cut and joined using this restriction enzyme. By using the same enzyme to cut the DNA molecule all the fragments produced have the same " sticky " AATT ends.

When the two sources of DNA are mixed, there will be random joining of " sticky " ends and some of the joined molecules will be hybrids. The joining process can be completed by adding another enzyme (*DNA ligase*) which repairs the chemical bond between the sugar molecule and the phosphate group.

Not all restriction enzymes leave " sticky " ends when they cut DNA molecules, so another technique has been developed to add on " sticky " ends. Using an enzyme which can add nucleotides to one chain of the DNA molecule only, a sequence of A nucleotides is added to the molecules from one source. The same enzyme is then used to add a sequence of T nucleotides to the molecules from the other source. The As will bond with the Ts when the two types of DNA are mixed, so joining the different molecules together. The final sealing step is again done by adding DNA ligase. The advantage of this technique is that all the molecules which join form hybrids.

Vector Molecules and Selection Procedures

The construction of hybrid DNA molecules is the essential step required for making vector molecules. One might ask why a vector molecule is necessary. Why cannot one simply introduce a fragment of DNA containing a foreign gene into a bacterial cell and have it replicated? The answer is that a DNA molecule which is capable of replicating has a unique point in the base sequence from which replication always starts. Fragments of DNA produced by enzyme action will not contain this unique sequence, so there will be no way in which they can be replicated. They can be replicated if they are inserted into a molecule which has the replication sequence—this is one role of the vector. The other role of the vector is to provide genes whose function can be detected in bacterial cells.

Small plasmids which carry antibiotic resistance genes make excellent vector molecules. Let us consider how the properties of such a plasmid can be exploited. The plasmid contains genes which confer resistance to two antibiotics, kanamycin and tetracycline. A restriction enzyme can be used which cuts the plasmid molecule at only one position to open the circle and leave " sticky " ends. The sequence the enzyme recognises lies inside the gene for tetracycline resistance. The same enzyme is used to produce fragments of a foreign DNA molecule. The fragment has the correct sticky ends to fit the ends of the opened plasmid molecule and can become inserted to close the plasmid. Of course the cut ends of the plasmid can fit back together again so a mixture of hybrid plasmids and reconstituted plasmids will be formed.

The plasmids can be introduced into bacterial cells (not containing a plasmid) if the walls of the bacterial cells are first made permeable by treatment with a calcium salt. After culturing the bacteria it remains to determine which cells are replicating a hybrid plasmid and which a reconstituted plasmid. This is the reason for having the resistance genes in the plasmid. Cells replicating only a reconstituted plasmid will have gained resistance to both kanamycin and tetracycline. Cells replicating a hybrid plasmid will only be resistant to kanamycin. This is because the foreign DNA fragment has been inserted inside the gene for tetracycline resistance and has inactivated it by cutting it in half. It is a simple procedure to test samples of cells on growth media containing one or both antibiotics to find out which they are resistant to.

The chromosome of the *lambda* virus also makes an excellent vector. It does, however, require that the chromosome be modified and shortened before foreign DNA is inserted. The chromosome has to be packaged into the protein coat of the mature virus particle and there is a limit to how long the chromosome can be (108% of the normal length). Fortunately the central region of the chromosome is not essential for replication and can be cut using a restriction enzyme, and a foreign DNA fragment can be inserted in its place. The hybrid *lambda* chromosomes produced can then be introduced into bacterial cells which have been treated to make their walls permeable. These will replicate to produce many copies of the hybrid DNA which will be packaged into new virus particles. The vector viruses will be distinguishable from reconstituted viruses because they have lost normal viral functions. They are also distinguishable from reconstituted ends of the viral chromosome because these molecules are too short to be packaged.

These two examples illustrate the essential steps in vector construction and selection of bacterial cells replicating the vector. Naturally many other systems have been developed.

Vectors with Animal Genes

Scientists have demonstrated the success of the techniques described. Fragments representing all the genes of *Escherichia coli* have now been inserted into plasmids and viruses providing a bank of cultures which can be used to amplify individual genes in order to study their base sequence and their properties. The controlling regions in DNA which switch genes on and off have also been isolated into vectors, and much will be learned from the sequence of these.

To introduce an animal gene into a vector presents the problem of how to find the gene in the first place. Fragmentation of human DNA would yield some million fragments. Whilst technically possible to introduce all these fragments into vectors, screening for the right gene would be a daunting job.

In exceptional cases the DNA base pair sequence of particular genes makes it relatively easy to separate them from other genes on the basis of density (a lot of A–T pairs makes the DNA fragment light). This has made it possible to purify genes which encode part of the ribosome structure (ribosomes are the machinery which make proteins in the cell). The first animal genes to be replicated in bacterial cells were the ribosome genes of a toad and a fruit fly.

Another approach is actually to make the gene. The first step in making proteins in the cell is the transfer of gene information into a messenger molecule. The messenger is not DNA but a very similar molecule, ribonucleic acid (RNA). RNA is single stranded and has a uracil (U) base replacing thymine. The enzyme which makes the messenger puts the RNA nucleotides together sequentially using one chain of the DNA molecule as template. The specific pairing between the RNA and DNA bases (A–U and G–C) ensures that the messenger sequence is complementary to the DNA chain. Interestingly, there is an enzyme (*reverse transcriptase*) which can actually reverse this step and use the messenger RNA molecule to make a complementary DNA chain. This will constitute half the DNA segment of the gene. Its partner chain can be made using another enzyme (*DNA polymerase*). Once " sticky " ends have been attached, this man-made gene can be inserted into a vector molecule.

Man-made genes for mammalian globin, immunoglobin and insulin have been inserted into plasmid vectors and have been replicated inside bacterial cells. Unfortunately their proteins were not synthesised. This is because the messenger RNA molecule contains only the information for protein structure; it does not contain a copy of the control sequences in DNA which operate to switch on gene expression. This final problem was overcome very recently (December 1977). Biochemists synthesised the gene for a human brain hormone, somatostatin, and attached this gene to part of a bacterial gene which had its control switch attached. When inserted into a vector a composite protein was synthesised from which active somatostatin could be cleaved by chemical treatment.

The potential benefits of genetic engineering are considerable. In the future it may be possible to find suitable vectors to introduce genes into plant and animal cells. This could provide cells with extra functions or replace defective functions.

Biological Hazards

There has been much debate about the possible hazards of replicating foreign DNA in bacterial cells. It is conceivable that a fragment introduced into a plasmid may carry a potentially harmful gene which produces a toxic product. This would be no problem in the laboratory, but the usual host cell for vector plasmids is the harmless *Escherichia coli* which lives in our gut. If such bacteria were poured down the drain they could end up in a human population. The problem could be exacerbated by the fact that the selection procedures for recovering plasmid vectors makes use of their antibiotic resistance genes. Even if the plasmid carried only one or two resistance genes it could meet and join into a larger plasmid with multiple resistance genes. The very first DNA chromosome to be used in recombinant DNA research in 1972 was that of a small animal virus which causes tumours, SV40. The investigators concerned were soon in a position to replicate potential tumour-inducing genes in *Escherichia coli* cells. They did not attempt it because they considered the risks too great. How serious the hazards are is not known, but the National Institute of Health in the United States and the Genetic Manipulation Advisory Group in Great Britain have introduced stringent regulations concerning safety precautions and the types of experiments which can be conducted. To minimise the risks still further, biologists are developing strains of bacteria which are debilitated by gene mutations. If these are used as host cells for culturing vector molecules there is no chance that they could survive outside the laboratory. Biologists are taking care to see that the potential benefits of this new technology are not marred by catastrophe.

ELECTRICITY FROM THERMONUCLEAR FUSION

Introduction

The demands for electricity are increasing on a global basis and if the need for electrical power continues as it seems destined to do then there is the definite probability that in the 21st cent. the electricity generating capacity of the Earth will be unable to satisfy the needs of the population. Unless new methods of converting other existing forms of energy into electricity are developed the availability of electric power in 30 years' time will fall short of the universal demand. It is this need for new sources of energy to replace the world's finite, and hence exhaustible, supply of available fossil fuels (*i.e.*, coal, gas, oil) which has forced scientists to investigate the possibility of using controlled thermonuclear fusion to provide a domestic energy source.

Electricity supply is something which we all take for granted, an adaptable supply of power which is both clean and convenient. Nevertheless, these particular 20th-cent. prerequisites are only apparent, since the production of electricity entails all the inconvenience which we would associate with a less sophisticated energy supply, for example the combustion of fossil fuels or the rotation of water wheels. In a power-generating station the electrical output is derived from a turbine which is forced into mechanical motion by a pressure differential established between its input and output. This pressure differential can be produced by a flow of water through the mechanical veins of the turbine which will force it into relative motion with respect to a fixed multi-solenoid system. This rotary movement of the magnetic section of the turbine relative to the rest of the turbine induces a flow of electric current in coils of the turbine; a procedure similar to that used in a simple bicycle dynamo. Hence we can convert the potential energy of a water flow into electricity, and this is the principle of the method used in hydro-electrical power generating stations. Norway, with its abundant fast-flowing water supply, is able to produce 99% of its electricity requirement (7×10^{10} kWh) using this technique. The mechanical motion of the turbine is the essential link between the ingoing form of power and the electrical output. Turbines can also be driven by high-temperature gas flow and steam as well as water flow. The production of steam is easily affected by burning a fossil fuel, and this method of electricity production is used in the UK to provide approximately 90% of the requirement.

It is important to note that the description

" Power Generating " as conventionally applied to electricity producing stations is incorrect, and the word generating should be replaced by the more applicable word " converting ", since the electrical power output has been derived from a different power input. In addition to the combustion of fossil fuels to produce high-pressure steam to drive a turbine, a direct mechanical drive can be obtained by using the naturally occurring motions of tides, winds and water waves. Specially designed turbines are used in these cases. These different sources can be used as power inputs suitable for conversion into electrical power; current research programmes at several laboratories are actively assessing the relative merits of these alternative sources of energy.

Exploitation of the radiant energy of the sun has not yet been sufficiently developed to rate as an independent direct energy supply source. Solar-heated panels can operate in a domestic water-heating system as a pre-heater raising the water temperature by a few degrees centigrade. The direct electrical output which can be obtained from a photo-responsive semiconductor devices constitutes a low power source and has been used only in unmanned space craft.

So far we have only considered the use of the bulk properties of matter as a source fuel for a power converting plant, but nuclear properties can also be effectively utilized. Since the establishment of Einstein's famous mass-energy equation $E = mc^2$ and its demonstration at the end of the Second World War, civilisation has been aware of the vast energy release occurring in a chain fission reaction. Control of the fission process by moderating the flux of neutrons which initiate the break up of a nucleus has enabled present-day nuclear-fuelled power converting stations to produce electrical power from the energy released in a uranium fission reaction. The decrease in total mass $\triangle m$ of the nuclei involved in the fission reaction does not disappear, but is transmuted into a definite quantity of energy. This energy is used as heat to produce steam, which then drives the turbines in the conventional manner.

Several nuclear power fuelled electricity converting plants are operational in the UK providing a total of 28×10^9 kWh to the national grid. This method of power conversion has since its inception demonstrated that although the principle of the method is cost-effective, the nuclear waste produced by a fission reaction is difficult to deal with. The radioactive waste, which can in some cases have a lifetime of 1,000 years, must be re-treated to remove the radioactivity, or held in a sealed store for the duration of its life. This is an expensive business, and hence reduces the cost-effectiveness of the fission reactor. The fission reactor also produces, as one of the end products, plutonium, which is used in the most destructive of present-day nuclear weapons. Hence an additional expense derived from security precautions is also present on the debit side of the balance sheet. " Dirty " nuclear reactions, as they are euphemistically called, have presented more problems than they have solved, and the present generation of physicists is seeking ways of producing electrical power by using a fusion nuclear reaction to fuel the turbines. fusion reaction has the definite advantage that it is " clean ", with no dangerous radioactive waste products being produced. In order to have sufficient power for the 21st cent. the governments of the EEC have selected the Culham Laboratory in the UK as the European Centre for Fusion Research with the directive to produce a commercially viable Fusion Reactor by the year 2000. This historic commitment by European Governments on the advice of the European scientific community has been entitled the JET Programme (Joint European Torus).

Fusion Process

The massive energy released in a hydrogen bomb explosion, which is in fact an uncontrolled fusion reaction, must be harnessed and effectively regulated before it can function as a commercial source of usable power. The large amounts of energy released in a fusion reaction derive from the combination of two lighter elements to form a stable heavier element which contains less binding energy than the two separate elements. The energy required to break deuterium into a neutron and a proton is its binding energy (see Nuclear Energy, L88). The reduction in the total binding energy is the source of the emitted energy, and it is the conversion of hydrogen into helium which is responsible for most of the energy produced in the sun and other stars. There are several possible fusion reactions, each requiring different experimental conditions, which could be used to provide the source of energy, but the one which requires the least stringent operational conditions is that between deuterium (D) and tritium (T). Here two heavy isotopes of hydrogen have a fusion reaction equation given by

$$D^1 + T^3 \to He^4 + n^1 + 17 \cdot 6 \text{ MeV}$$

where a stable helium nucleus is produced with a neutron. The $17 \cdot 6$ MeV kinetic energy which is released from the reduction in the total binding energy of the system is shared between the neutron ($14 \cdot 1$ MeV) and the alpha particle ($3 \cdot 5$ MeV). In order to overcome the electrostatic repulsion between the deuterium and tritium nuclei, they must be made to collide at very high velocities. At kinetic energies of 10 keV the mutual coulomb repulsion between the two positively charged nuclei can be overcome and the fusion D–T reaction is able to proceed. It is of course a relatively simple matter to accelerate beams of deuterium and tritium nuclei in particle accelerators to energies of 10 keV and let them collide and hence produce alpha particles and neutrons, but in this mode more energy is consumed by the acceleration than is produced from the reaction. This method of overcoming the coulomb repulsion is commercially ineffective. In order to proceed with a commercially cost-effective system it is generally agreed by all physicists that the fusion reaction should take place in a high-temperature plasma which should be heated to a temperature of one hundred million degrees Kelvin (10^8 °K). In such a thermonuclear plasma where the temperature corresponds to particle kinetic energies of approximately 10 keV all the atoms will be fully ionised, since the temperature corresponds to three times the total ionisation potential of most atoms, and the plasma will be a highly conducting medium.

When referring to the temperature of a plasma we are in fact stating the ionic temperature, derived from the equation $\frac{1}{2}mv^2 = \frac{3}{2}kT$, and this is not the same as the electron temperature as one would expect from the principle of the equipartition of energy. In fact, in a thermonuclear plasma the ionic temperature is greater than the electron temperature, since the ions gain energy from the nuclear reaction, whereas in a normal electrical discharge the electron temperature is greater than the ion temperature.

The problems encountered in producing electricity from the D–T reaction should not be minimised. Firstly, the fuel, i.e., deuterium and tritium, must be available in sufficient quantity to maintain the reaction, secondly, the plasma must be maintained at an extremely high temperature and finally, a means must be devised to convert the energy released into electricity.

Deuterium is a naturally occurring isotope found in heavy water, but tritium is an artificial isotope, and therefore must be manufactured on site to maintain the D–T reaction. It is possible using the flux of neutrons from the D–T reaction to produce tritium via a fission reaction with lithium which is both plentiful and stable. The reaction equation is

$$Li^6 + n^1 \to T^3 + He^4 + 4 \cdot 8 \text{ MeV}$$

hence the tritium is recycled and the inert helium is the only waste product. Even with the required fuel available in sufficient quantity the problem of heating the plasma to 10^8 °K and maintaining it at this temperature against the competing energy loss processes is formidable. If the plasma cools to below the ignition temperature the D–T reaction will stop. In addition at such high temperatures containment of the plasma in any physical container is impossible, as the material from which the container is made will melt on contact with the plasma. Happily, since the

F78

plasma is fully ionised, it can be contained inside a metal container by confining it using high-intensity magnetic fields such that the plasma does not physically touch the walls of the container. Such an arrangement is called a "magnetic bottle". The final major technical problem is to design an efficient cost-effective fusion reactor which will produce electricity cheaply from the energy released in the D–T reaction.

We will now examine separately these three main divisions of the overall project.

Plasma Containment

The charged particles of a fully ionised plasma can be confined by a magnetic field. If a set of circular coils or a solenoid generates a magnetic field, then the plasma moving along the axis of the solenoid will spiral around the magnetic lines of force. The helix angle which the plasma flow makes with the direction of the magnetic field depends of course on the initial angle of inclination of the plasma flow direction with the axis of the solenoid. Such a system has the serious disadvantage that, since it is open-ended, it will lose the plasma after one transit along the solenoid length. To prevent this loss the open-ended coil system can be bent to form a circle and the plasma can therefore circulate around the torus indefinitely. The magnetic field which confines the plasma in its journey around the torus is the toroidal field. In JET a set of 32 coils will produce a mean field of 4 Tesla at the centre of the plasma. This single magnetic field, however strong, still cannot retain all the plasma within its grasp indefinitely. There will always exist a non-uniform magnetic field distribution across the minor diameter of the torus and this will cause a drift of part of the plasma outwards to the walls of the vacuum chamber. Plasma escaping from the magnetic bottle in this manner will consequently reduce the plasma temperature.

In order to prevent this diffusion it is necessary to introduce a further magnetic field, the poloidal field, which encircles the toroidal field path. This poloidal field can be produced by helical conductors outside the vacuum or by a direct current flow in a solid superconducting ring which is levitated in the plasma. (The use of physical supports to position and hold the ring outside of the torus would cause a very rapid fall in plasma temperature.) Both these systems have been used, but neither is sufficiently strong to contain the plasma at a high enough temperature and density to enable the fusion reaction to take place. Magnetic fields which are used to confine and compress plasmas are generally referred to as *pinches*.

In the strongest pinches the poloidal field is produced by an induced toroidal plasma current flow which also heats the plasma by ohmic heating. Two types of toroidal pinches can be used for fusion work; one where the plasma is pinched by the poloidal field and a weak spatially varying toroidal field and two the tokamak system, where the plasma is stabilised by a constant very strong toroidal field and a weak poloidal field. The tokamak magnetic field pinch is the most favoured method of obtaining the plasma conditions required for a fusion reaction.

The confining magnetic fields are very costly, and hence they must be used to a high efficiency. The ratio of the magnetic field that exists in the plasma to the field that the containment system imposes on the plasma is called the β factor. A low β factor indicates that the magnetic fields are being used inefficiently, which means that the magnetic pressure produced on the plasma by the confining field greatly exceeds the pressure required adequately to contain the plasma. Typical operating values of β are 0·03 in most tokamaks.

The toroidal geometry of the plasma is generally circular, but in JET the cross-section of the plasma will be D-shaped to allow maximum efficiency to be made of the magnetic field configuration. It will be possible in JET to maintain poloidal currents of 3 million amps with toroidal currents of 44 million amps, the poloidal current being produced by a 2,000-ton transformer with a primary coil diameter of 10 m.

Heating the Plasma

The plasma in a tokamak is partly heated by the current (44 million amps) flowing in the plasma. This current flow is slightly impeded by the small resistance in the plasma, and hence some of the energy which drives the current around the torus is transferred to the plasma by ohmic heating. However, as the plasma temperature increases its inherent resistance decreases and ohmic heating becomes less effective. Hence on its own this method of heating is insufficient to raise the plasma temperature to 10^8 °K and auxiliary methods must be used in conjunction with it to obtain the temperature required to sustain a thermonuclear reaction. Heating the plasma essentially means raising the kinetic energy of the ions which form the plasma, and this can be done directly by injecting into the glowing plasma high-energy hydrogen atoms from an external source. By accelerating protons to between 50 and 150 keV in an ion accelerator and then converting the fast-moving protons into hydrogen atoms by adding electrons to them (i.e., charge exchange process) we obtain a flux of high-energy neutral particles. These can then simply penetrate the magnetic bottle and readily enter the plasma. Once inside the magnetic confining fields they are ionised in the high-temperature plasma already existing in the torus and further increase the plasma temperature. It will be possible using this technique to inject 10 megawatts of heating power into the plasma by using several injectors. Improvements in the efficiency of neutral particle injection devices will enable greater heating power to be transferred to the plasma in this manner.

Other modes of plasma heating which could be used are radio-frequency heating, at an harmonic of the ion cyclotron frequency, and the firing of high-power carbon dioxide laser pulses into the plasma.

Even considering the idealised case where the plasma is completely confined by the magnetic bottle the plasma can still cool as a result of different processes occurring inside the plasma itself. The bombardment of the walls of the vacuum chamber by energetic particles escaping from the plasma will cause an "evaporation" of material from the inner vacuum surfaces. These "impurity" particles enter the plasma and cause large energy losses via radiation processes. The lower Z materials are much less efficient in reducing the plasma temperature than higher Z impurity atoms, and hence the materials used in the construction of the tokamak must be carefully selected. Nevertheless, even a very small concentration of any "impurity" atoms will significantly reduce the plasma temperature. In addition, energy losses also occur due to the thermal gradient which is established in the plasma. Since the outer edge of the plasma is cool (approximately 10^4 °K), there is a drift of particles down the thermal gradient from the centre of the plasma to the outer edge. It is not possible to remove this loss effect, but it can be minimised by adjusting the plasma surface area and the thermal gradients to give the minimum size for an operational torus.

In order that the plasma should perform satisfactorily as an efficient burner of deuterium and tritium, then the net energy released must be greater than the energy used in heating plus that associated with the intrinsic losses. If the plasma temperature (T) can be maintained at 10^8 °K, the ion number density (n) increased to 10^{14} cm⁻³ and the plasma confined for approximately one second against all inherent instabilities, then the fusion reaction will proceed. The product of number density and confinement time (T) is the limiting operational condition and must exceed 10^{14} s cm⁻³ in order to sustain the thermonuclear reaction.

Fusion Reactor System

Once the thermonuclear reaction is in process the flux of high-energy neutrons coming from the deuterium–tritium fusion must be harnessed to produce electricity. In the typical reactor design envisaged, the neutron flux, which is the energy source produced by the burning of the nuclear fuel, will be absorbed in a 1-metre-thick blanket of lithium surrounding the torus. Since the neutrons are electrically neutral, they are not confined by the " magnetic bottle ", and consequently the lithium will heat up as the kinetic energy of the neutron is dissipated in its thickness. The energy deposited in the primary attenuating material can readily be removed by heat exchange and used to drive turbines and hence produce electricity in the conventional manner. The lithium blanket also functions in a secondary role as a source of tritium. The neutrons, as well as kinetically slowing down in the lithium blanket, react with the lithium nuclei to produce tritium and helium. This tritium can then be recycled to be used as fuel to maintain the thermonuclear fusion process in the plasma.

The whole process is conceptually simple, but several aspects of the physics involved and the technology required are unknown. The neutron flux could damage the vacuum container wall, and since the whole apparatus is radioactive when running, this could make it impossible to repair quickly. In addition, it is uncertain which type of vacuum material will produce the least amount of impurity in the plasma. The final decision to use a ceramic (low Z) material or a heavy element material (molybdenum or tungsten) has yet to be made. The massive stresses, equivalent to several thousand tons, placed on the whole mechanical structure by the high-intensity magnetic field interactions will impose severe engineering design criteria. It is hoped that these questions will be answered by the experimental conditions produced by JET and that the optimum design criteria for an operational fusion reactor will be determined in several years time.

Energy Conversion

The production of electricity is the conversion of one form of energy to another. The physics involved in explaining each step of the processes embraces the bulk, nuclear and atomic properties of matter. The electrical output is obtained by utilising the different states and phases of matter in the transition of mass-energy to electrical energy. To see this involvement of the whole range of physics we will briefly recap the processes in a Thermonuclear Electricity Generating Reactor.

Nuclear particle physics is required to explain the fission process of deuterium and tritium with the release of alpha particles and neutrons. The production of 17·6 MeV in the form of kinetic energy from the reaction is an example of relativistic mass-energy transformation, and the control of the processes in the torus is governed by the photon and particle flux in the plasma. The operation of the torus utilises the atomic properties of matter as exemplified in a high-temperature plasma; the control of the plasma temperature, density and stability is accomplished using the classical bulk properties of electromagnetic theory to produce the toroidal pinch.

The retardation of the neutrons in the surrounding attenuator produces heat which is removed by heat exchanges working on classical thermodynamical principles as applied to the bulk properties of matter. The conversion of the heat into steam is a simple phase-change of matter, and again the bulk property of the motion of steam is used to drive the turbine.

The conversion of this mechanical motion into electricity is described by the atomic properties of electrical current flow produced by electromagnetic induction. This link of bulk property and atomic property is of paramount importance; by moving a magnet inside a conducting coil we can produce a flow of electrons in the coil which constitutes the electric current supply. Hence the momentum of the mechanical motion is transferred to the dynamics of electron flow in conducting matter.

It is the bulk properties of matter which provide the link between the burning of the nuclear fuel and the mechanical motion of the turbine, and again, coupled with the atomic states of matter, in producing the flow of electric charge. The full range of the states of matter is therefore involved in the production of a usable electricity supply.

Conclusion

The quest by scientists to provide a source of " clean " nuclear energy for domestic use is now at a turning point. The experimental determination of the exact operational conditions required for a complete fusion reactor will be given in several years by JET. Then with the building of the first full-scale production fusion reactor we can be assured of a cheap (half the current cost) supply of electrical power beyond the 21st cent.

THE COMMUNICATIONS REVOLUTION

Pioneers of Television

Even when their years of painstaking and dedicated research seemed about to be rewarded, it is doubtful whether the pioneers of television dreamed that they were sowing the seeds of a world revolution in communications; that from a tiny audience of about one thousand for the opening of the BBC Television Service in 1936 would grow, within some forty years, millions witnessing the momentous events of their time in their own homes.

Like many other discoveries, the creation of television was the result of successive, interrelated inventions rather than a single act. The names of Paul Nipkow in Germany, Boris Rosing in Russia and A. A. Campbell Swinton in Britain have gone down with many others in the history books as the founding fathers.

But if the birth of television was attended by a number of midwives, the greatest impetus for its modern development as a means of spreading information and entertainment came from only one—John Logie Baird, a Scotsman, in the early twenties.

Baird

The initially crude system he developed was based on Nipkow's device for scanning an object mechanically, using a large spinning disc punched with a series of holes. With this and other apparatus, including a lens bought from a cycle shop and some Government surplus valves, he was able to transmit the shadow of a Maltese cross, cut out of cardboard, over a distance of about two feet.

Returning to London, he set up his equipment in an attic in Frith Street, Soho, and it was here, in October 1925, that success came. The dummy's head he was using suddenly showed up on the screen as a detailed image instead of a blur, and he was able to repeat the exercise with a living subject, an office boy from the floor below.

After further successful demonstrations and the publicity they attracted, Baird managed to persuade the infant British Broadcasting Corporation to make one of its stations available outside normal radio programme times so that regular television test transmissions could be made. After much negotiation these began in September 1929, the first one being watched by an audience of fewer than thirty people.

Initially, because only one wavelength was available, sound and vision had to be transmitted separately, in two-minute sequences, from the Baird studio in Long Acre, London, through the BBC transmitter on the roof of Selfridge's store in Oxford Street. It was not until the following year, when two wavelengths were allotted, that the first synchronised transmissions became possible. But even as the BBC was becoming sufficiently impressed to take co-operation a stage further to the extent of providing a studio at the newly opened Broadcasting House, formidable rivals to Baird were appearing on the scene.

EMI (Electrical and Musical Industries)

The impetus for all-electronic television as opposed to Baird's mechanical system came from EMI (Electrical and Musical Industries, Ltd.), which was formed in 1931 as a result of a merger between the Gramophone Company and a number of other organisations. At the head of the research team was Isaac Shoenberg, a Russian-born scientist who had settled in England in 1914.

Within a short time EMI and the Marconi company had agreed to merge their television interests, and for a while they concentrated on developing and improving the mechanical system. That was only a temporary phase; before long they had turned their attention to the theory of scanning the picture electronically by a team of cathode rays, as conceived independently by both Campbell Swinton in England and Rosing in St. Petersburg. One of Rosing's pupils was Vladimir Zworykin, who later left Russia for America. His contribution was the "Iconoscope", a camera tube which took in the principles of electronic scanning and was therefore much more sensitive to light. From that development was to come the "Emitron" camera.

The BBC engineers who saw the demonstrations were impressed by the result—better defined pictures and a reduction in the flicker of the mechanical system, though by now the Nipkow disc and 30-line picture had been overtaken by a mirror-drum device and 240 lines. Against such formidable and wealthy opposition, Baird seemed to be struggling. For a time he introduced a technique called the intermediate film process. The programme was filmed as for the cinema and the film fed through a continuous processing plant, to be transmitted, still dripping, just over a minute later. He also used, under licence, an electronic system developed by an American inventor, Philo T. Farnsworth.

As the competitors were fighting it out, the Government stepped in and ordered a Committee to examine the whole future of television in Britain. After six months' deliberation the Committee recommended, in January 1935, that the BBC should undertake the provision of a television service, just as it had done with radio. The Committee recommended a two-year trial period during which the Baird and Marconi–EMI methods would be transmitted on alternate weeks. The Baird system operated on 240 lines, 25 pictures per second, with sequential scanning, the Marconi–EMI system on 405 lines, 25 pictures per second, with interlaced scanning, producing a picture of high quality.

As a result of experience gained from these transmissions, the Committee recommended in February 1937 the adoption of the Marconi–EMI 405-line system as the British standard, and the services from Alexandra Palace continued until the outbreak of war, when the station closed down because it was feared the tall television mast would be of help to enemy aircraft. Alexandra Palace reopened to provide a television service for London in June 1946.

The Medium Comes of Age

Just as the greatest interest in television prewar had been aroused by the crowning of George VI in 1937, so, it could be said, the first milestone of the post-war era was the coronation of his daughter, Elizabeth, sixteen years later. For the first time a British domestic television audience outnumbered those for radio—and by very nearly two to one. Twenty-three million people are thought to have been watching television on 2 June 1953, against the twelve million estimated to have followed the radio commentary; another one and a half million saw the pictures live in Europe, an achievement which hastened the creation of a European network for the regular exchange of programmes. One American network, determined to be first with the coronation pictures, filmed the BBC's coverage off the television tube, developed it in special portable tanks and then flew it to America in a chartered plane, editing on the way. From Boston the film was played into the network. But they were still beaten. One of their rivals won by taking a "feed" from Canadian Television of the BBC's own film, which reached the other side of the Atlantic with the co-operation of the Royal Canadian Air Force and a relay of RAF Canberra jet bombers.

The long Coronation broadcast was hailed as a spectacular triumph for the BBC, yet ironically the Corporation's monopoly was about to come to an end. The Conservatives, forming their first post-war Government, were committed to the introduction of a competitive element into British television. The principles were enshrined in the Television Act of 1954, which created the Independent Television Authority. To this body was given the responsibility of building and operating the transmitters and selecting the companies to provide programmes on a regional basis. The

finance was to come from the sale of advertising time. Not that ITV was born without a fight, between those who contemplated the arrival of "commercial" television with horror and those who believed the time had come for the BBC to be shaken out of what they saw as its complacency.

On 22 September 1955, after an opening ceremony at Guildhall, the first ITV programmes were transmitted by Associated-Rediffusion from their new studios near Wembley Stadium. By the end of the next year more than half the population of Britain could receive the new programmes. For a while the pioneer companies lost money, but soon ITV's mass appeal brought the audiences and the advertisers flocking, and spending on television advertising rocketed from about £11 million in 1965 to more than £60 million within four years.

By the late 'fifties television had become an enormously popular past-time. The number of television licences began to outstrip those for radio only, a process speeded up by the introduction of a third channel, BBC-2, in 1964. Television's popularity coincided with a sharp decline in cinema audiences, which fell from their 1946 peak of 1,635 million to 288 million in 1966; the number of cinemas dropped by almost a third, to below 1,850, over the same period.

The leap forward in the spread of television was accompanied by increasing interest in the programmes and events being transmitted in other countries. The exchange of film presented no particular problem, but the exchange of television signals was something else because of the number of lines contained in the various systems. At that time Britain was still transmitting on its 405-line standard, the United States on 525 and the French on 819. An internationalism of sorts was possible by pointing a television camera working on one line standard at a monitor showing pictures made up of another, but there was a certain loss of quality. Just the same, in July 1952, the BBC and French television, ORTF, co-operated in a week of programmes from Paris; West Germany, France and Holland took the coronation transmission successfully the following year. Within another few months the European Broadcasting Union had formalised the link into an eight-nation network called "Eurovision".

In 1958 experiments began for exchanging newsfilm, with five services participating. In 1961 a daily Eurovision News Exchange was established, soon to blossom into a three-times-daily service through the EBU's administrative headquarters in Geneva and a technical centre in Brussels. In 1976 more than 6,300 news items were originated for the network, about half by the members themselves, the rest coming from similar organisations like OIRT, the EBU's East European equivalent, and the big international newsfilm agencies.

The EBU also opened a New York office to cope with satellite transmissions to the continent, but in the early days the BBC had to get its news pictures from America either by air freight or, for really important occasions, through "Cablefilm", a system developed by its own engineers. Transmission was through the transatlantic telephone cable at the rate of about an hour and a half for every minute of film, and the sound had to be sent separately, to be synchronised with the film before it could be transmitted. The last major use of Cablefilm was on 22 November 1963, when the Kennedy assassination pictures were shown in a special late-night bulletin about four hours after the shooting in Texas. But by then the system had already been overtaken and a new era in international co-operation was about to begin.

Television in the Seventies

It was as early as 1945, in a now famous article in the magazine *Wireless World*, that the science-fiction writer Arthur C. Clarke foreshadowed the possibility of using man-made satellites for long-distance radio communication, but it was not until the sixties that it actually happened. The momentum came from the United States, where President Kennedy had already made a national commitment to the rapid development of space exploration.

The principle of the communications satellite was to beam the television picture from one point on earth to another, using an orbiting satellite to pick up, amplify and re-transmit the signals to their destination. The first satellite capable of putting that principle into practice between continents was *Telstar*, launched in July 1962. Its effectiveness was strictly limited; for only a few minutes during each two-and-a-half-hour orbit was it within receiving range of ground stations in North America and Europe. Nevertheless, it had shown the way, and its success led to discussions about the establishment of an international system. These in turn resulted in the founding of the International Telecommunications Satellite Organisation (Intelsat) in August 1964. By 1978 over one hundred countries had joined, most of whom are represented by their national organisations responsible for telecommunications. How much each pays towards operating costs, research and development depends on the use it makes of the system.

The first Intelsat satellite was named *Early Bird*, which carried one television signal or 240 telephone calls; by 1969 a global system had been established in time to bring to some 600 million viewers throughout the world the historic pictures of Neil Armstrong walking on the moon, just before 4 a.m., London time, on Monday, 21 July. This world coverage was achieved by positioning satellites 22,300 miles above the Atlantic, Pacific and Indian oceans; each one takes twenty-four hours to complete a single orbit and so appears to be stationary. In theory, three are enough, but the busy Atlantic region needs two to cope with all the traffic, and spare satellites are on station in case of breakdown.

As technology has advanced, so each new generation of satellites has been developed to carry a greater capacity—telephone, telex and computer data as well as television. The system (end 1977) includes three satellites in the Intelsat IV-a series, which have an average capacity of 6,250 voice circuits plus two television channels; the seven in the Intelsat V series, the first of which is due to be launched in 1979, will each carry 12,000 telephone conversations plus television.

The world's television news services have come to rely on the system to bring to their audiences " same-day " coverage of events occurring almost anywhere in the world. Film or electronically-gathered material can be edited using the facilities of local television stations and then transmitted via the nearest ground station. Where permanent sites do not exist or would be over-burdened, temporary ones can be constructed for special occasions, as the wealthy American networks have combined to do several times, President Nixon's 1972 visit to China among them.

Hand-in-hand with the improved sophistication of world communications has come increased flexibility for producers—the invention of a reliable recording system so that television programmes, or at least parts of them, can be made at the times most convenient for those involved in them. In the early days of television every studio production had to be broadcast " live " at its scheduled time of transmission, creating obvious difficulties for all concerned. One step forward came with the introduction of tele-recording, a system of filming productions off television monitors. This was successful enough, but it was still necessary to process the film in the conventional way, which meant inevitable delays before a programme could be pronounced satisfactory. What was needed to overcome this was a method comparable to that which allowed quarter-inch sound tapes to be replayed immediately on completion of the recording. Achieving this for sound *and* picture on the same machine proved a great deal more difficult, notably because of the speed of tape necessary to keep the picture steady when replayed. Eventually, in 1956, the Ampex company of America marketed a machine which appeared to solve the problem. This utilised a tape moving at only 15 inches a second, the picture being recorded across its width of two inches.

Before long both independent television and the BBC introduced the system into Britain and videotape recording (VTR) had soon found its place as one of the most valuable weapons in any producer's armoury. Now it became possible to assemble casts at mutually convenient

times and record programmes for transmission any time in the future; complicated productions, calling on myriad sources—outside broadcasts, film, studio and art-work—could also be conducted without the ever-present worry of flaws; mistakes were wiped out by re-recording. Edited highlights of great state occasions, sport and other events, became the vogue. The instant play-back facility offered by videotape was also of tremendous advantage to news and current affairs programmes, which became able to receive contributions from other sources—regional stations, other studios or from abroad—in time for replaying at pre-selected points.

Today, very few programmes are transmitted live, and even many of those which start their lives on film are transferred to videotape for transmission and archive preservation. The tapes themselves are of 90 minutes duration and can be replayed scores of times without loss of quality. Editing, once possible only by physical cutting and splicing, has now achieved a very high degree of sophistication with the introduction of invisible electronic methods by which chosen sequences are re-recorded from one machine to another.

VTR machines able to record and transmit in colour have also become commonplace. Although Baird had worked on colour television in the twenties, it was not until 1953 that the United States Federal Communications Commission settled for a standard which was also compatible with black-and-white transmissions. This was named NTSC, after the National Television System Committee, but progress remained slow, largely because of the initially high cost of colour productions in relation to the number of sets sold.

In Europe, attempts were made early on to agree a common standard for colour, although the issue was complicated by Britain's 405-line system at a time when 625 lines for greater definition had been more widely adopted. There was also the problem that France, with SECAM, and West Germany, with PAL, had both developed variants of the American system. With no agreement in sight, the British opted for PAL and 625 lines, declaring their intention of phasing out 405-line transmissions some time during the eighties.

The BBC became the first European service in colour when its second channel, BBC-2, televised the Wimbledon tennis championships of 1967. Within two years all three domestic channels were transmitting colour programmes on 625 lines, and the popularity of colour became such that of the 18 million licences sold in the year ended March 1977, very nearly million were for colour.

The coming of colour also opened a new era of inventiveness for studio productions. To the established systems of set construction and back-projection techniques adopted by producers was added Colour Separation Overlay (otherwise known as Chromakey), which takes pictures from two separate sources and merges them into one, creating an illusion of completeness. The most regular users of the system are the daily television news programmes, where the presenter in the studio appears to be set against a frequently changing pictorial background. In fact, he or she is being " seen " by one camera in front of a backcloth of a plain colour (usually blue), on to which a picture from a second source is fed electronically. In this way the BBC's Nine O'Clock News was able to create the impression that its newscasters was sitting not in a studio but in the newsroom; the newsroom picture was provided by one camera and the picture of the newscaster in the studio some distance away by another. CSO has given producers a whole new range of technical tricks. It can be used effectively with still or moving pictures and, as development continues to a point where more than two sources can be employed, is capable of becoming a substitute for expensively built studio sets.

The rapid spread of television to most corners of Britain also made it possible to establish a unique partnership between the medium and education on a direct basis. The Open University, an independent and degree-awarding system of higher education for adults, began its foundation course in 1971 with television and radio programmes produced by the BBC for the University; in 1976 more than 35 hours of television a week were being transmitted for the students. The British Post Office has also made use of television with the introduction of "Confravision", a system which enables conferences to take place on a closed-circuit link between five cities.

While much effect has also gone into the development of large-screen television, advance has been made towards the truly portable set. This is "Microvision", made by a British firm based in Cambridgeshire. And whereas Baird's first "Televisor" showed its 30-line picture two and a half inches high and one and a half across, it was encased in a large cabinet; Microvision's two-inch diagonal screen is built into a receiver which measures four inches by about six and a half and weighs no more than a 35-mm still camera.

A View of the Future

Despite the major advances of the past few years, an enormous potential remains for further development of the present system of satellite communications. The future is seen to lie in broadcasting to small communities, perhaps direct to single homes equipped with miniature versions of the dish aerials which identify the conventional large-scale ground stations of the world.

This is one of the ways in which the viewer may eventually escape from the rigidity of programme schedules, for the drift is towards television as a more personalised home entertainment and information centre, with the reception of normal programme output only one of its functions. Growing use is being made of the systems for making recordings on cassettes containing one-inch or smaller width videotape for replaying through the ordinary domestic receiver at times which suit the consumer rather than the planner. Timing devices are incorporated to allow selected programmes to be recorded automatically and it is also possible to watch the output of one channel while the VCR is recording another. At first the system was so expensive it was confined largely to educational or community use, but VCRs have recently begun to filter into the home for purely domestic purposes, and the hope is that as sales increase prices will come down. The cassettes themselves, though capable of re-use, remain fairly expensive, and a cheaper method of home viewing has also been developed, with the picture carried in grooves or pits on discs which resemble long-playing records.

The television screen is also being used for electronic versions of football and other games; the time is fast approaching when the use of the screen for displaying written information will become equally commonplace. For some time a development of computer technology has allowed engineers to make use of some of the "empty" lines which exist in the normal 625-line picture to transmit test signals or other information without disturbing the viewer. In October 1972 the BBC announced that it had taken that facility a stage further by using two of the spare lines in each inter-laced field to transmit information for translation into written words on the screen.

The BBC christened its system CEEFAX (Seeing Facts) because it saw an eventual public service being concerned primarily with the kind of data business and domestic users seemed likely to want at their fingertips—news headlines, weather forecasts, share prices, sports results and so on—at times which were convenient to them.

The Independent Broadcasting Authority entered the field in April 1973 with a similar system which it called ORACLE (Optical Reception of Announcements by Coded Line Electronics). A generic term for both, Teletext, emerged, and after a further year's discussion between the broadcasting authorities and the set manufacturers, so did a common standard, making it possible for both BBC and IBA services to be received on the same set. The receivers themselves have to be specially adapted to "decode" the signals into a display format. A pocket-calculator-sized keypad is used to switch from normal programmes and then to select the required subjects, which are broken down into "pages" accommodating up to 24 rows of text with a maximum of 40 characters each. Subjects can be spread over extra pages which change automatically after a reasonable interval for reading.

Teletext's information is provided by special editorial units and fed into computers for transmission. The pages are broadcast in succession, each one taking up to about a quarter of a second to transmit, so a complete one hundred page "magazine" takes less than twenty-five seconds.

Government approval for regular public services of CEEFAX and ORACLE was given in November 1976, but the cost of building the teletext decoder unit into the conventional set has only just begun to reach the point where passing interest is likely to be translated into purchase or rental. Even so, one estimate is that by the end of 1978 about 50,000 teletext-equipped sets will be in use, with the expectation that more will follow.

A similar service to teletext is "Viewdata", the British Post Office system for linking computerised information to the screen by use of the telephone. Again the information is displayed in the form of written characters or simple diagrams such as weather maps, but this time the emphasis is on a much more personalised service, for which the consumer would have to pay.

The information is summoned by telephone call and then made to appear on the screen by means of the teletext-style keypad. A national network of computers is envisaged, storing data fed in by information-provider organisations offering services which might range from the non-commercial (weather forecasts, railway time-tables, etc.) to the highly expensive (specialist financial statistics). The knowledge available to the system is theoretically limitless, for the international satellite network could be used to link the subscriber and his telephone with the data banks of other countries. At the other extreme, Viewdata can be very localised, storing messages in much the same way as the telephone answering device. Development also includes an alphanumeric push-button attachment enabling subscribers to type in their own communications.

In the summer of 1978 the Post Office plans to test the potential market more thoroughly by providing the service in London, Birmingham and Norwich. About 1,500 people are being selected to take part, about three-quarters of them domestic users, with access to about sixty thousand pages of information. The Post Office are already so confident about the appeal of the system that they have announced the opening of a public service in the first quarter of 1979.

With such diversions available to the viewer, the broadcasting authorities will not be able to stand still if they are to retain significant audiences for conventional programme schedules, and at least one recent development suggests that they are aware of the potential competition. This is in the field of news and current affairs, where the battle to bring matters of importance to the screen without delay is beginning to be won by an innovation called Electronic News Gathering (ENG). This consists of a small, very lightweight television camera unit usually operated by two people. It is much easier to handle than the still cumbersome cameras normally used for outside television work and, as the pictures are taken electronically, does away with the chemical processing stage associated with film. This second advantage is particularly important in news work, where processing and editing cannot be carried out within much under an hour.

ENG pictures can be transmitted live, beamed back to base for recording and editing, or recorded on to the unit's own videotape cassette machine, to be edited on the spot or collected by messenger for return to headquarters. The American networks are rapidly turning to the system as a replacement for news gathering by film, which some stations are now abandoning entirely as too slow and costly. The BBC introduced ENG on a one-year experimental basis in the autumn of 1977, but even if that trial proves successful, it seems certain that they and other broadcasting organisations, particularly in Europe, will feel it important to retain some film capacity indefinitely. For them, the dilemma will come when ENG-equipped American units, based abroad, become able to transmit their material home by satellite (and back again) before domestic film crews, working on their own doorstep, clear processing. The other side of the coin is that it may

Teletext

TELETEXT Information collated by specially created editorial units is fed into computers and then broadcast on some of the spare lines available in the normal 625-line television picture. The signals are decoded by an adaptor fitted to the receiver and appear on the screen in the form of written "magazine pages". Selection of individual pages is made by a key-pad, the size of a pocket calculator.

Electronic News Gathering

ELECTRONIC NEWS GATHERING (ENG) Lightweight television camera system ideal for the coverage of news events Pictures from two-member crew can be: (1) beamed back to the studio via a mobile radio link for "live" transmission or recording and editing; (2) recorded on to a videotape cassette on site; (3) recorded and returned to base by messenger while the unit remains on location.

not be too long before laboratories able to process film quickly will be confined, in America, to the big cities.

But the so-called "Lightweight Revolution" is by no means over. There are still technical hurdles to be overcome and there remains the human problem involved in making such fundamental change. Baird would have relished that challenge.

CHEMICALS FROM COAL

The Past

From the middle of the 19th cent. coal became the main source of organic chemicals and of ammonia for about 100 years throu hout the industrial world. Then oil became cheaper than coal and petroleum became the most important feedstock. But now there is renewed interest in using coal for making chemicals—using different, modern techniques. What, in essence, were the old methods?

The chemicals were produced originally as by-products of processes heating coal in the absence of air ("carbonisation processes") to make gas and coke. The benzole, coal tar, naphthalene and ammoniacal liquor formed at the same time were first treated as nuisances. In due course they became the bases for chemical industries yielding such materials as benzene, toluene, xylene and higher aromatics, pyridine bases, phenolics and a range of very useful oils. Even the residue of distilling coal tar—the pitch—proved to be useful for it is adhesive, waterproof and durable. Tar, after some refining, was in demand as a protective paint, a water-proofing agent and for making lamp-black, in the early days.

Later, separation processes were improved. Today, virtually no coal is carbonised *primarily* for gas and coal tar is derived from coke-ovens operated to meet the need for coke in making iron. The gas of course is used and the coal tar refined by distillation and sometimes additional operations to the range of products shown in Fig. 1. Overall in Britain coal now provides about 5% of our organic chemicals. But the proportion varies for individual compounds. In 1975, for example, about 16% of benzene and over 20% of the toluene came ultimately from coal.

A century ago, ammonia was recovered from the ammoniacal liquors. Later, ammonia was also produced from coke—reacted with air to make producer gas ($CO + N_2$) and, in parallel, with steam to yield water gas ($CO + H_2$). After further stages, the nitrogen and hydrogen went on to the converters forming ammonia. Today in Britain most ammonia is made by reactions with natural gas as the source of hydrogen.

COAL TAR, ITS PRODUCTS AND THEIR MAIN USES

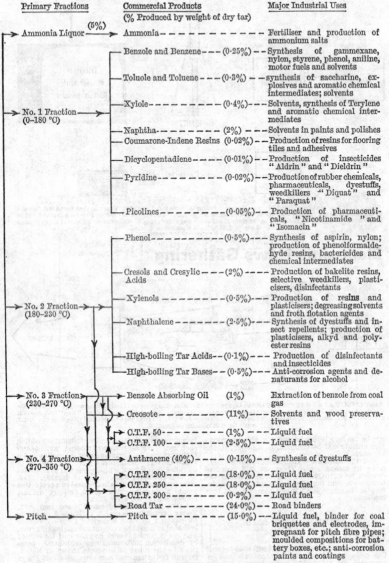

Primary Fractions	Commercial Products (% Produced by weight of dry tar)	Major Industrial Uses
Ammonia Liquor (5%)	Ammonia	Fertiliser and production of ammonium salts
No. 1 Fraction (0–180 °C)	Benzole and Benzene (0·25%)	Synthesis of gammexane, nylon, styrene, phenol, aniline, motor fuels and solvents
	Toluole and Toluene (0·3%)	synthesis of saccharine, explosives and aromatic chemical intermediates; solvents
	Xylole (0·4%)	Solvents, synthesis of Terylene and aromatic chemical intermediates
	Naphtha (2%)	Solvents in paints and polishes
	Coumarone-Indene Resins (0·02%)	Production of resins for flooring tiles and adhesives
	Dicyclopentadiene (0·01%)	Production of insecticides "Aldrin" and "Dieldrin"
	Pyridine (0·02%)	Production of rubber chemicals, pharmaceuticals, dyestuffs, weedkillers "Diquat" and "Paraquat"
	Picolines (0·05%)	Production of pharmaceuticals, "Nicotinamide" and "Isomacin"
No. 2 Fraction (180–230 °C)	Phenol (0·5%)	Synthesis of aspirin, nylon; production of phenolformaldehyde resins, bactericides and chemical intermediates
	Cresols and Cresylic Acids (2%)	Production of bakelite resins, selective weedkillers, plasticisers, disinfectants
	Xylenols (0·5%)	Production of resins and plasticisers; degreasing solvents and froth flotation agents
	Naphthalene (2·5%)	Synthesis of dyestuffs and insect repellents; production of plasticisers, alkyd and polyester resins
	High-boiling Tar Acids (0·1%)	Production of disinfectants and insecticides
	High-boiling Tar Bases (0·5%)	Anti-corrosion agents and denaturants for alcohol
No. 3 Fraction (230–270 °C)	Benzole Absorbing Oil (1%)	Extraction of benzole from coal gas
	Creosote (11%)	Solvents and wood preservatives
	C.T.F. 50 (1%)	Liquid fuel
	C.T.F. 100 (2·5%)	Liquid fuel
No. 4 Fraction (270–350 °C)	Anthracene (40%) (0·15%)	Synthesis of dyestuffs
	C.T.F. 200 (18·0%)	Liquid fuel
	C.T.F. 250 (18·0%)	Liquid fuel
	C.T.F. 300 (0·2%)	Liquid fuel
	Road Tar (24·0%)	Road binders
Pitch	Pitch (15·0%)	Liquid fuel, binder for coal briquettes and electrodes, impregnant for pitch fibre pipes; moulded compositions for battery boxes, etc.; anti-corrosion paints and coatings

FIG. 1 From *Coal Carbonization Products*, by Donald McNeil

There was also some short-lived interest—notably in Germany and in Britain—in making petrol from coal by reacting the solid fuel with hydrogen. These processes too were swept aside by cheaper feedstocks. Only in South Africa, today, are there major chemical industries based on coal because the fuel there is so exceptionally cheap. There, coal is transformed into gas, purified to a mixture of carbon monoxide (CO) and hydrogen (H_2) and these reacted to make ultimately petrol, waxes, lubricating oil, detergents, pharmaceuticals and others.

Petroleum—Current Feedstock

From about the 1930s in the USA and around the 1950s in Europe and Japan, it was petroleum that largely took over as feedstock for organic chemicals and for ammonia. For the world as a whole over 90% of organic chemicals derive from this source. The six major organic chemicals (often called in the industry, base chemicals, since others are formed from them) are ethylene, propylene, butadiene, benzene, toluene and xylenes. How they are obtained is shown in the diagrams in Fig. 2 and Fig. 3.

In these, the terms C_2 and C_3 gases mean ethane and propane, amylenes are the same as the compounds usually quoted as pentenes, and the naphthenes are cycloparaffin hydrocarbons, generally derivatives of cyclopentane (C_5H_{10}) and cyclohexane (C_6H_{12}). From this range of base chemicals are now made industrial solvents, plasticisers, plastics and rubber moulding materials and other chemical intermediates as well as pharmaceuticals and detergents.

The renewed interest in swinging back to coal as the starting point is based on two inter-linked forward estimates. They are:

1. Supplies of petroleum (and natural gas) are expected to peak during the next two decades and then decline.

2. As they start to decline, their prices are expected to rise in real terms compared to coal (and to other commodities).

For these reasons petroleum companies throughout the world have started to buy in to coal where this is commercially possible; both they and gas companies are sponsoring research and development (R & D) on coal conversion processes.

Making Coal More Versatile

Though coal can be satisfactorily handled on a large scale, many consumers prefer the convenience of liquid and gaseous fuels; furthermore, in some applications, such as driving cars and lorries, it is virtually essential to supply the fuel in a form that can directly substitute for those obtained from petroleum. Both for these reasons, and in order to produce larger yields of chemicals than are obtained from carbonisation, coal must be converted. The essence of the chemical transformation needed is shown clearly in the table below:

Fuel	Carbon % by weight	Hydrogen % by weight	Ratio H/C
Bituminous coal	75–92	5·6– 4·0	0·057
Crude oil	84–88	14·5–11·5	0·15
Methane	75	25	0·33

Lower olefins & diolefins—petroleum sources of manufacture

(Shell)
Fig. 2.

Aromatics—main petroleum sources of manufacture

(Shell)

FIG. 3.

Notes:
1. The fuels contain other constituents, notably oxygen and nitrogen in coal, sulphur in both coal and oil.
2. Since oil and coal are ranges of materials, their compositions can be given only as ranges.
3. Where ranges are given, the ratios H/C are calculated from the mid-points.
4. Methane, main constituent of many natural gases (including North Sea gas), is a chemical compound of defined composition.

Clearly the ratio of hydrogen to carbon is much higher in the liquid fuel and higher still in the gaseous one than in coal. Consequently, converting coal into the other products means either introducing more hydrogen and/or separating off compounds with a higher proportion of hydrogen, leaving behind a carbon-rich residue. The hydrogen may be supplied either as such or in the form of steam. The steam is obviously cheaper, but its reaction with carbon absorbs heat; in turn this means that heat must be generated in the reactor in order to sustain the reaction between coal and steam. This heat may be provided by supplying oxygen, or by air which is cheaper but dilutes the resulting gases with its nitrogen.

It is attempts to resolve the dilemmas indicated by these contradictory features of the key reactions, and to raise the thermal efficiency of conversion, that account for the wide variety of processes under development. Often the processes may be adapted to produce materials sold as "chemicals", or as "fuels", or combinations of the two. The essential technologies may be grouped as follows:

A. Introducing More Hydrogen

1. Research projects on adding hydrogen include processes where it is applied under pressure and sometimes in multiple stages to:

coal simultaneously heated to decompose it; the combined process is called "hydropyrolysis";

coal mixed into a slurry with oils derived from coal;

coal simultaneously with extraction with high-

pressure gas to increase the yield of liquid products;

pyrolysis liquids to produce lighter, more volatile, more valuable fractions;

products of extracting coal with organic liquids or with high-pressure gases to yield lighter, more valuable fractions;

residues after other treatments: these residues are of high molecular weight and are "cracked" to smaller molecules, in a method called "hydrocracking".

2. Other projects use steam for adding the hydrogen—usually with air or oxygen burning part of the coal to provide heat. They normally convert most of the coal into gas and are called "gasification". The gases may contain methane, carbon dioxide, carbon monoxide, hydrogen and nitrogen after removal of sulphur compounds. Further treatments may be designed to result in fuel gases, alcohols or the range of products of the Fischer-Tropsch reactions of CO with hydrogen. If the gases are intended for fuels they may be used on site as low or medium heating value sources (100 to 500 Btu/cu ft or 3·7 to 18·6 MJ/cu m) or upgraded to a fuel rich in methane as Substitute Natural Gas (SNG) of 1000 Btu/cu ft or 37·3 MJ/cu m.

One exciting version of these processes, though yielding only low-value gas, is in underground gasifying of coal in the seam; this has attracted much interest, but so far no economic success.

B. Separating "Hydrogen-rich" Compounds

1. *Pyrolysis.* Major improvements are being made in methods of heating coal in the absence of air. In the current conventional way of carbonising in coke ovens yields of volatile products may be around 25%, but the proportion can be increased by rapid methods of heating, ranging up to the use of electrical plasma for a few seconds, or even fractions of a second.

2. *Extraction with Liquid Solvents.* When coal is treated at raised pressure and temperature with anthracene oil, almost 90% of it can be removed leaving a high carbon residue (and incombustible mineral matter).

3. *Extraction with "Super-critical" Gas.* Coal

extracted with gases at very high pressure and high temperature (in conditions known as " supercritical " when the gas cannot be compressed to a liquid), yields a rich range of compounds thought to be present in the coal and not products of chemically breaking it down.

How Soon?

For the UK all the categories of products—gas fuels, liquid fuels and chemicals—have been assessed with few exceptions to be uneconomic, *at this stage*. Yet work continues for the reasons indicated above—petroleum and gas sources will be exhausted in decades and will become more expensive as we approach that time. The main area where it is currently profitable to develop products from coal is by improving carbonisation processes and working up the products. Thus, the National Coal Board's Central Research Establishment (CRE) have extended and improved the range by developing fire retardants based on ammonium sulphate for treating timber, paper and for fire extinguishers. From the phenols of tar new foam boards have been developed of phenol-formaldehyde; other phenolic resins form the basis for electrically insulating varnishes. High-speed carbonisation results in forming acetylene as a basis for many chemical syntheses.

In the USA, which has by far the world's largest programme of coal conversion (as part of the world's largest energy programme), the situation is much more urgent. There are already shortages of natural gas, and the administration is striving to reduce the dependence on imported oil and gas. Several demonstration plants on a commercial scale are planned for the next few years. Among the first of these is a " slagging gasifier " developed in Britain by British Gas from a Lurgi plant originally designed in Germany. In this, coal is reacted with steam and oxygen to form a mixture of gases; after purification, they are passed through a " methanator " in which they are converted to an SNG rich in methane (Fig. 4). The reaction is operated at such a high temperature that the ash melts to a slag and is tapped off in this condition—hence the name. The UK modifications rendered the plant capable of dealing with a much wider range of coals and greatly raised the efficiency. Other US demonstration plants under design include one based on hydrogenation where the hydrogen will probably come from a reactor applying the carbon/(steam + oxygen) reaction, and a further one using pyrolysis. In these programmes they emphasise the importance of making them " environmentally acceptable " before they will receive official support and approval.

Around the world are over 50 plants of 3 main types currently converting coal into gas in countries where conditions make the conversion economic and/or governments are interested in order to reduce dependence on imported fuels. All 3 are of German design. The Winkler process treats coal with oxygen and steam in a so-called fluid bed where the coal is suspended in a stream of gas. In the Lurgi process (mentioned above), the bed of coal descends slowly with reaction in a counter-current of steam and oxygen, at pressures between 20 and 30 atmospheres. The third of the types of plant already in use is called the Koppers-Totzek and is markedly different. At opposite sides of the reaction chamber are burners —one each side—facing each other. Fine coal is entrained in a stream of oxygen and steam at roughly atmospheric pressure and reacts at high speed in the chamber at higher temperatures than in the other processes, namely around 1,800 °C.

The gases are used directly as fuel, or enriched as fuel, or as a basis for synthesis. It is a set of Lurgi gas generators that are used in South Africa to provide the gases used there for synthesis of organic chemicals, while Koppers-Totzek gasifiers produce gas for synthesising ammonia.

For the UK the coal industry estimates that we should have commercial coal refineries early in the 1990s. That is the time when it is thought likely that oil and gas prices will have risen to appropriate levels, and the full technological development of the selected best processes should have been completed.

Coalplexes—Linking All Uses of Coal

Could it improve efficiency and the economics of processes if several different applications of coal were integrated? For many years there has been interest in a more limited sense in linking together the generating of electricity with heating by applying the discharged heat. This has proved most successful in industry, where both kinds of demand are under one management. A survey sponsored by the Department of Energy found that it would not be economic for the UK for homes, shops, schools and offices.

Nevertheless, studies have been made to determine if integration could be carried further with advantage. With coal as the fuel, integration could combine in the same plant such features as:

    processing the coal leaving a high-carbon residue;
    working up the products yielding gas and liquid fuels;
    working up the products yielding chemicals;
    generating electricity by burning the solid residue from processing;
    salvaging discharge heat from both processing and from generating electricity.

Schemes of this kind (Fig. 5) will need to incorporate features making for flexibility, since it will not be realistic to assume that demand for all the products and services produced will always be available in the desired quantities and ratios. These are challenging ideas which have not yet been turned into practicality.

Coal Research—an International Activity

A network of organisations in addition to extensive personal contact between researchers ensures that ideas and results in coal processing are exchanged (though there are naturally limitations on commercial grounds). Under the aegis of the UN, the Economic Commission for Europe (ECE) has a Coal Committee which brings together countries of East and West Europe.

FIG. 4. The Production of SNG from coal by the Slagging Gasification route (British Gas)

In reactor (A), excess CO is reacted with steam to produce CO_2 and H_2, adjusting the ratio of H_2 to CO to 3. Then CO_2 is removed (B) and the mixture goes forward for methane synthesis by the reaction $CO + 3H_2 = CH_4 + H_2O$

The European Coal and Steel Community (linked with the EEC) supports coal research from levies on the industry controlling progress by appropriate international committees of its own member countries. In addition, 19 countries drawn largely from West Europe, with the addition of the USA, Japan, Canada and some others, constitute the International Energy Agency which has a very active Working Group on Coal Technology, where the UK provides the chairman and has responsibility for leading the group.

Supplementing these arrangements are separate agreements between countries and companies. For instance, the NCB has such agreements with the Soviet Union, the Electric Power Institute of the USA and with others; at the British Gas Development Centre, the work on the slagging gasifier was funded by a consortium of US companies with participation of Lurgi of West Germany. A further example is the contract between the US and West German governments to harmonise projects for processes yielding liquids from coal . . . and there are many others.

Broadly, coal researchers now comment that there has been a big improvement in attitude from the former atmosphere of reserve and secrecy. Today it is evident from the web of international agreements that coal interests regard co-operation in research and development (covering mining, and coal combustion as well as coal conversion to other fuels and chemicals) as the key to future prosperity for the industry; they seem equally confident that demand for coal and for processes will ensure that this co-operation can be handled without damage to commercial advantage. Naturally the closer the projects to practical working plant, the more likely it is that the collaboration will be on a confidential, licensing basis. Yet overall it is clear that these are very active fields of research at all levels—from fundamental science to practical development—and the agreements are helping to minimise duplication of efforts, making the research more economical in time and effort.

Fig. 5.
One possible Coalplex. This layout is based on the COED pyrolysis process. A rich gas is produced by pyrolysis, the tar is hydrogenated to synthetic crude oil using hydrogen generated by the carbon/steam gasification reaction from residual char; unconsumed char is converted to produce gas which is converted to clean fuel gas to fire a combined-cycle generating system, while the inert flue gas from the boiler is used as the fluidising gas for the first pyrolysis stage. Electricity generated is used to supply the heat for the carbon/steam gasification reaction in the electro-gasifier stage. (After P. F. M. Paul, N.C.B.)

ELEMENTS

Element (Symbol)	Atomic Number	Atomic Weight	Valency
actinium (Ac)*	89	227	
aluminium (Al)	13	26·9815	3
americium (Am)*	95	243	3, 4, 5, 6
antimony (Sb)	51	121·75	3, 5
argon (A)	18	39·948	0
arsenic (As)	33	74·9216	3, 5
astatine (At)*	85	210	1, 3, 5, 7
barium (Ba)	56	137·34	2
berkelium (Bk)*	97	247	3, 4
beryllium (Be)	4	9·0122	2
bismuth (Bi)	83	208·980	3, 5
boron (B)	5	10·811	3
bromine (Br)	35	79·004	1, 3, 5, 7
cadmium (Cd)	48	112·40	2
calcium (Ca)	20	40·08	2
californium (Cf)*	98	251	
carbon (C)	6	12·0111	2, 4
cerium (Ce)	58	140·12	3, 4
caesium (Cs)	55	132·905	1
chlorine (Cl)	17	35·453	1, 3, 5, 7
chromium (Cr)	24	51·996	2, 3, 6
cobalt (Co)	27	58·9332	2, 3
copper (Cu)	29	63·546	1, 2
curium (Cm)*	96	247	
dysprosium (Dy)	66	162·50	3
einsteinium (Es)*	99	254	
erbium (Er)	68	167·26	3
europium (Eu)	63	151·96	2, 3
fermium (Fm)*	100	253	
fluorine (F)	9	18·9984	1
francium (Fr)*	87	223	1
gadolinium (Gd)	64	157·25	3
gallium (Ga)	31	69·72	2, 3
germanium (Ge)	32	72·59	4
gold (Au)	79	196·967	1, 3
hafnium (Hf)	72	178·49	4
helium (He)	2	4·0026	0
holmium (Ho)	67	164·930	3
hydrogen (H)	1	1·00797	1
indium (In)	49	114·82	3
iodine (I)	53	126·904	1, 3, 5, 7
iridium (Ir)	77	192·2	3, 4
iron (Fe)	26	55·847	2, 3
krypton (Kr)	36	83·8	0
lanthanum (La)	57	138·91	3
lawrencium (Lw)*	103	257	
lead (Pb)	82	207·19	2, 4
lithium (Li)	3	6·941	1
lutetium (Lu)	71	174·97	3
magnesium (Mg)	12	24·305	2
manganese (Mn)	25	54·9380	2, 3, 4, 6, 7
mendeleevium (Mv)*	101	256	
mercury (Hg)	80	200·59	1, 2
molybdenum (Mo)	42	95·94	3, 4, 6
neodymium (Nd)	60	144·24	3
neon (Ne)	10	20·17	0
neptunium (Np)*	93	237	4, 5, 6
nickel (Ni)	28	58·71	2, 3
niobium (Nb)	41	92·906	3, 5
nitrogen (N)	7	14·0067	3, 5
nobelium (No)*	102	254	
osmium (Os)	76	190·2	2, 3, 4, 8
oxygen (O)	8	15·9994	2
palladium (Pd)	46	106·4	2, 4, 6
phosphorus (P)	15	30·9738	3, 5
platinum (Pt)	78	195·09	2, 4
plutonium (Pu)*	94	244	3, 4, 5, 6
polonium (Po)*	84	210	
potassium (K)	19	39·102	1
praseodymium (Pr)	59	140·907	3
promethium (Pm)*	61	145	3
protactinium (Pa)*	91	231	
radium (Ra)*	88	226	2
radon (Rn)*	86	222	0
rhenium (Re)	75	186·2	
rhodium (Rh)	45	102·905	3
rubidium (Rb)	37	85·47	1
ruthenium (Ru)	44	101·07	3, 4, 6, 8
samarium (Sm)	62	150·35	2, 3
scandium (Sc)	21	44·956	3
selenium (Se)	34	78·96	2, 4, 6
silicon (Si)	14	28·086	4
silver (Ag)	47	107·870	1
sodium (Na)	11	22·9898	1
strontium (Sr)	38	87·62	2
sulphur (S)	16	32·064	2, 4, 6
tantalum (Ta)	73	180·947	5
technetium (Tc)*	43	99	6, 7
tellurium (Te)	52	127·60	2, 4, 6
terbium (Tb)	65	158·925	3
thallium (Tl)	81	204·37	1, 3
thorium (Th)	90	232·038	4
thulium (Tm)	69	168·934	3, 4
tin (Sn)	50	118·69	2, 4
titanium (Ti)	22	47·90	3, 4
tungsten (see wolfram)			
uranium (U)	92	238·03	4, 6
vanadium (V)	23	50·942	3, 5
wolfram (W)	74	183·85	6
xenon (Xe)	54	131·30	0
ytterbium (Yb)	70	173·04	2, 3
yttrium (Y)	39	88·905	3
zinc (Zn)	30	65·37	2
zirconium (Zr)	40	91·22	4

* In the cases of these elements, which are very rare or not found in nature, but have been artificially prepared, atomic weight in the chemical sense is meaningless; the integral mass of the most stable isotope known is given.

Note: In 1961 the isotope of Carbon-12 replaced Oxygen as a standard, the weight of its atom being taken as 12. This change of standard has meant a slight adjustment in atomic weights from the old chemical scale.

The new elements with an atomic number higher than that of uranium 238 (element 92) are termed Transuranics.

GAS LAWS

The Perfect or Ideal Gas Law: $pV = nRT$
where n is the number of moles in volume V at pressure p and absolute temperature T, and R is a universal constant.

Van der Waals' equation: $\left(p + \dfrac{a}{V^2}\right)(V - b) = nRT$
where a and b are constants, different for each gas.

PERIODIC TABLE OF THE ELEMENTS

Transition metals →

Noble metals

GROUP → Period ↓	1A Alkali metals	2A Alkaline earth metals	3B	4B	5B	6B	7B	8	8	8	1B	2B	3A	4A	5A	6A	7A	0 Inert gases
1	1 H 1·00797																	2 He 4·0026
2	3 Li 6·941	4 Be 9·0122											5 B 10·811	6 C 12·0111	7 N 14·0067	8 O 15·9994	9 F 18·9984	10 Ne 20·17
3	11 Na 22·9898	12 Mg 24·305											13 Al 26·9815	14 Si 28·086	15 P 30·9738	16 S 32·064	17 Cl 35·453	18 Ar 39·948
4	19 K 39·103	20 Ca 40·08	21 Sc 44·956	22 Ti 47·90	23 V 50·942	24 Cr 51·996	25 Mn 54·938	26 Fe 55·847	27 Co 58·933	28 Ni 58·71	29 Cu 63·546	30 Zn 65·37	31 Ga 69·72	32 Ge 72·59	33 As 74·922	34 Se 78·96	35 Br 79·904	36 Kr 83·80
5	37 Rb 85·47	38 Sr 87·62	39 Y 88·905	40 Zr 91·22	41 Nb 92·906	42 Mo 95·94	43 Tc 99	44 Ru 101·07	45 Rh 102·905	46 Pd 106·4	47 Ag 107·870	48 Cd 112·40	49 In 114·82	50 Sn 118·69	51 Sb 121·75	52 Te 127·60	53 I 126·904	54 Xe 131·30
6	55 Cs 132·905	56 Ba 137·34	57 La* 138·91	72 Hf 178·49	73 Ta 180·947	74 W 183·85	75 Re 186·2	76 Os 190·2	77 Ir 192·2	78 Pt 195·09	79 Au 196·967	80 Hg 200·59	81 Tl 204·37	82 Pb 207·19	83 Bi 208·980	84 Po 210	85 At 210	86 Rn 222
7	87 Fr 223	88 Ra 226	89 Ac† 227															

* Lanthanides (see L72)

58 Ce 140·12	59 Pr 140·907	60 Nd 144·24	61 Pm 145	62 Sm 150·35	63 Eu 151·96	64 Gd 157·25	65 Tb 158·925	66 Dy 162·50	67 Ho 164·930	68 Er 167·26	69 Tm 168·934	70 Yb 173·04	71 Lu 174·97

† Actinides (see L8)

90 Th 232·038	91 Pa 231	92 U 238·03	93 Np 237	94 Pu 244	95 Am 243	96 Cm 247	97 Bk 247	98 Cf 251	99 Es 254	100 Fm 253	101 Md 256	102 No 254	103 Lw 257

Roman type—metals
Italic type—semiconductors
Bold type—non-metals

These designations refer to the normal materials, usually at room temperature. Processes like heating or compressing can turn metals into insulators and vice versa.

BACKGROUND TO ECONOMIC EVENTS

The aim of this section is to help the ordinary reader to follow economic events as they happen, and to understand the controversies that accompany them.

TABLE OF CONTENTS

BACKGROUND TO
ECONOMIC EVENTS

This section is divided into four parts. Part I gives a brief description of the most important problems of economic policy. Part II is concerned with a more detailed survey of the British economy and the way in which it operates. In the course of this survey, the specialised terms used by economists are explained, and the attempt is made to present an intelligible summary of the information, facts, and figures relevant to an understanding of economic events. There are five main sub-sections: International Trade and Payments; Employment, Production, and Industry; Incomes, Wages, and Prices; Money, Banking, and Finance; and Economic Aspects of the Public Services. Part III outlines the main economic problems faced by the less developed countries, and the economic policies of Britain and other developed countries towards the less developed world. Some suggestions for further reading are given at the end of Parts II and III. Part IV is written as shortly before publication as possible, and contains a survey of recent developments in the British economy.

I. CENTRAL PROBLEMS OF ECONOMIC POLICY

Unemployment.

Between the wars, unemployment was Britain's most urgent economic problem. Quite the worst slump was that of the early 1930s: in 1932, nearly 3 million workers were without a job. But in no year between 1919 and 1939 were there fewer than a million workers unemployed. Economists make a distinction between *structural* unemployment and *cyclical* unemployment. Structural unemployment appears when the structure of industry gets out of line with the pattern of demand for industrial products. In Britain, unemployment was particularly severe and persistent in areas which were dependent on the coal, textile, and shipbuilding industries, and some sections of the engineering industry. Cyclical unemployment appears when there is a general decline in the level of demand for goods and services, which leads to a decline in the employment of workers producing those goods and services. In the slump years unemployment was so high because of a combination of structural and cyclical unemployment: in the best years, unemployment was largely structural.

Unemployment means waste. Men willing to work, who could produce valuable goods and services, are idle: the economy produces fewer goods and services than it is capable of producing. Unemployment also means hardship and low standards of living for those out of work, and for their families. The avoidance of mass unemployment has been accepted as a primary objective of economic policy by all political parties. It is only with the advent in the 1970s of new and greater problems of inflation and the balance of payments that this commitment has faltered. Cyclical unemployment can be tackled through measures to increase total spending by consumers, by investors, and by the Government. The problem which has daunted Governments in recent years is that such expansionary policies may not be possible without fuelling inflation and worsening the deficit in the balance of payments.

There have been ups and downs in unemployment in the post-war years, but these have been very slight until recently, compared to those before the war. In most post-war years, less than 2 per cent of the working population was unemployed —a sharp contrast with the 11 per cent for 1937 and the 22 per cent for 1932. But there are still areas of the country where structural unemployment is serious. In Northern Ireland, for example, despite the efforts which have been made to attract new industries, unemployment ranged between 6 and 10 per cent in the last decade.

Inflation.

A characteristic of the British economy in post-war years has been a persistent rise in prices and money incomes. For example, between 1950 and 1970, retail prices went up by about 52 per cent or—expressed as an annual rate—by 4·3 per cent per annum, export prices rose by 40 per cent (or 3·4 per cent per annum), and weekly wage rates by about 67 per cent (5·3 per cent per annum). However, these rates of increase were somewhat slower than the corresponding rates in the immediately post-war decade, or the annual inflation of 14 per cent between 1970 and 1976. Inflation can be harmful in various ways. Firstly, it is associated with an arbitrary redistribution of purchasing power. Prices rise for everyone, but some members of the community are better placed than others to secure increases in their money incomes which offset, or more than offset, the rise in the price of the goods and services they buy. The feeling that particular groups are falling behind, in that their money incomes have not risen as fast as those of other groups, is a source of much unrest and discontent. Secondly, and crucially for the British economy, an inflation of prices makes it more difficult to achieve a satisfactory balance of payments. As prices of our exports rise, it becomes harder to sell them in foreign markets; and as imports become cheap in comparison with goods produced at home there is a tendency to buy more of them.

Two main explanations have been advanced to account for the inflation which has occurred. The first stresses the role of an excess of demand or spending power in the economy—of too much money chasing too few goods, and so leading to a rise in prices. The inflationary problem is seen as the obverse of the cyclical unemployment problem: the latter involves a deficiency of spending, and the former an excess. Those who consider an excess of demand (*demand-pull*) to be an important factor in the inflationary situation favour policies designed to reduce purchasing power: for example, the reduction of spendable income by levying higher taxes, or the reduction of spending financed through borrowing by making credit more expensive or more difficult to get. The second stresses the role of an excessive increase in incomes: it is argued that prices have risen mainly because costs have increased faster than productivity (*cost-push*). Those who take this view favour measures to restrain or control increases in wages, profits, rents, and other forms of income. Neither explanation excludes the other. Many would agree that both demand-pull and cost-push factors have contributed—with different strengths at different times—to the inflationary spiral in prices and incomes, and that measures both to control demand and to restrain or control incomes may be necessary.

But it is easier to specify in general terms the measures needed to combat inflation than it is to apply policies which are successful in practice. In particular, policy measures to restrain or control wage increases are difficult to reconcile with widely-accepted procedures of collective bargaining.

The Balance of Payments.

Britain is heavily dependent on imports. This country must import food: it cannot produce enough food within its borders to feed its population. Many of the raw materials necessary for its industry have to be purchased from abroad. Furthermore, some manufactured goods produced in other countries will be purchased because they are cheaper or more attractive than similar goods produced at home. All these goods, and our imports of services, have to be paid for in foreign currency. Foreign currency is earned by exporting goods and services to other countries. It is not, however, considered sufficient to earn enough foreign currency from our exports to pay for our imports. The objective is to earn considerably more than that, so that we have a surplus of foreign currency available to pay off external debts, to build up our external assets by investing abroad, to enable us to lend and give aid to underdeveloped countries, and to increase our foreign exchange resources.

Since the war, our balance of payments position has been precarious. Exports have increased considerably, but so have imports; and the margin of safety has been so narrow that unfavourable turns of events have led to crises in the balance of payments. In several years, our earnings from the export of goods and services have not even been sufficient to cover our payments for imports, and in almost none has the surplus been as large as is considered necessary. With the balance of payments delicately poised even in favourable years, and with corrective action necessary in crisis years, economic policies have been much influenced by our foreign trade problems. It is easy to say that most of the problems would disappear, or would become less urgent, if we could achieve a major expansion of our exports. But most export markets are highly competitive, and we cannot expect to sell more unless the price, quality, and terms of delivery of our goods and services are at least as attractive as those of our rivals in export markets.

Economic Growth.

Taking a longer view, the most important objective of internal economic policy must be to raise the standard of living. The standard of living can increase only if more goods and services are produced per head of population. In a fully-employed economy, the main source of increased output is a higher productivity—output per person—of the working population.

British living standards have until recently been rising: the output of goods and services per head of population increased by about 21 per cent between 1960 and 1970; i.e. by 2 per cent per annum on average. Nevertheless, many economists are of the opinion that the rate of growth of output and productivity can be, and should be, increased. In particular, they point out that our rate of growth compares unfavourably with that achieved by some other countries. The potentialities for higher productivity are enormous. In many United States industries, output per person employed is twice or more than yet attained in Britain. Higher productivity will require more and better capital equipment, and better planning and organisation in the use of labour and machinery.

Less Developed Countries.

Britain and the other developed countries of the world have important responsibilities towards the less developed countries. The poorest two-thirds of the world's population account for only a sixth of total world income and output, while two-thirds of world income accrue to the richest sixth of world population, a category which includes Britain. The poorest two-thirds suffer from poverty, hunger, malnutrition, debilitating diseases, and widespread illiteracy. To make matters worse, most of the poor countries are experiencing a rapid growth of population. Output has to rise as fast as population just to prevent standards of living from falling, and an increase in standards of living requires an even faster growth of output.

Few of these countries can hope to solve the increasing problems they face without active and generous help from developed countries. This help must take many forms. Financial aid in the form of grants or loans in order to place resources at the disposal of less developed countries which they would otherwise not be able to obtain; technical aid to assist in the solution of the many technical problems which have to be solved; trading policies which do not hinder underdeveloped countries from getting the imports they need or from selling their exports—these are all activities in which Britain should play her part. In particular, Britain must contribute to the development of the underdeveloped countries of the Commonwealth. *See* Part III.

The Inter-relationship of Economic Problems.

Each of the problems briefly described above is extremely complex. The difficulties of achieving successful solutions are further aggravated by the fact that the problems are inter-related in such a way that measures which are helpful for one problem can make others more difficult to solve. For example, a reduction of purchasing power might be considered helpful in the control of inflation, and might ease balance of payments problems by reducing—or slowing down the increase of—imports. But it could also lead to an increase in unemployment, and to a slowing down in the rate of growth of the economy. Or again, a reduction in aid to less developed countries could make it easier to balance our external accounts, but such action could hardly be reconciled with our responsibilities towards less developed countries. In the next section, particular aspects of the British economy are considered in some detail; the final section discusses the main features of the development of the economy in recent years.

The Worsening Economic Climate.

In the mid-1970s, after 30 years of rapid growth and unprecedented prosperity for the major Western economies, the prospects for continued growth became much less favourable. This resulted partly from the acceleration of inflation in many countries, bringing with it insecurity and militancy in industrial relations. However, the main cause was the remarkable increase in the price of oil, a fuel on which the Western economies had become heavily dependent. This produced a strong burst of inflation; and, because much of the oil revenue accruing to producers could not be spent, gave rise to an unprecedented balance of payments problem and a very severe world recession. There was a danger that, through a lack of international co-ordination and of business confidence and through misplaced attempts by countries to cure their immediate economic problems by means of deflation, mass unemployment on the scale of the 1930s would again appear. In the changing situation both the problems of economic policy and the inter-relationships between them became more difficult.

II. SURVEY OF THE BRITISH ECONOMY

1. INTERNATIONAL TRADE AND PAYMENTS

International Trade.

(i) Imports and Exports.

In 1976 the United Kingdom bought from abroad goods to the value of £31,000 million, or about £560 per head. Food was a large item on this bill, accounting for 16 per cent of the total. Fuel, largely oil, cost about 18 per cent, basic materials for industry 10 per cent, and manufactured goods (including a large number of semi-manufactured goods bought for further processing) 54 per cent. This last category of imports has increased sharply in recent years. In 1954 it represented only 20 per cent in an import bill of only £3,359 million. All this can be seen in the table.

UNITED KINGDOM IMPORTS AND EXPORTS

Imports of goods (c.i.f.)	£ million.		Percentage of total.	
	1954.	1976.	1954.	1976.
Food, drink, and tobacco . .	1,314	4,983	39	16
Basic materials .	1,015	3,218	30	10
Fuels and lubricants .	329	5,645	10	18
Semi-manufactures	513	8,044	15	26
Finished manufactures	174	8,853	5	28
TOTAL * . .	3,359	31,155	100	100
Exports of goods (f.o.b.)				
Food, drink, and tobacco . .	154	1,692	6	7
Basic materials .	101	776	4	3
Fuels and lubricants .	151	1,255	6	5
Metals . .	338	2,345	13	9
Engineering products .	1,007	10,125	38	39
Textiles .	324	934	12	4
Other manufactured goods .	490	7,934	18	31
TOTAL * . .	2,650	25,770	100	100

* The column figures do not add up to the totals because the former exclude postal packages.

There are three main determinants of the level of British imports. One is the competitiveness of British with foreign producers. Britain imports those commodities which—at the ruling exchange rate between the pound and foreign currencies—can be bought more cheaply from foreign than from home producers. Secondly, the level of imports depends on the extent to which free trade is prevented by tariffs on imported goods or by other devices. Thirdly, as total incomes in the economy expand, there is a general increase in the demand for goods and services, including imports. Therefore imports can be expected to vary with the total incomes in the country, known as the *national income*.

Whereas in 1954 imports amounted to 23 per cent of national income, in 1976 the proportion was 32 per cent. One reason for this rise is the liberalisation of trade among the industrialised countries during the post-war period, and the tendency for trade in manufactures among these countries to increase. An example is the formation of the *European Economic Community* in 1956 and Britain's entry to it in 1973 (*see* G45). Another reason is the great increase in the price of oil which occurred in the 1970s. Britain's oil import bill rose from £900 million in 1970 to £5,500 million in 1976. On the other hand, there has been a sluggish demand for other *primary products* such as food and raw materials. The British spend little of their additional income on food, and the development of synthetic substitutes and new products has slowed down the growth in demand for raw materials.

Since the exports of one country must be the imports of another, the same factors in reverse, foreign competitiveness, access to foreign markets, and the level of foreign incomes determine the level of British imports. In 1976 these amounted to over £25,000 m of which no less than 83 per cent were manufactures, mainly engineering products. In 1954 it was true to say that Britain gained from trade by exporting manufactures, in which she had a *comparative advantage*, in return for food and raw materials, which she was not suited to produce. This is still partly true; but increasingly—with the growth of trade and specialisation among the major economies—Britain gains from trade by exporting those manufactures in which her producers specialise and importing other

manufactures. Among the main manufacturing exports are cars and commercial vehicles, tractors, aircraft and aircraft engines, finished steel, various forms of machinery, woollen fabrics, man-made fibres, and chemicals; among the main manufactured imports are wood products, aluminium, newsprint, cars, and aircraft. With the expansion of British oil production, the pattern of trade continues to show rapid change (*see* G41(2)).

(ii) The Terms of Trade.

The value of trade increased roughly ten-fold between 1954 and 1976. This increase can be separated into two components, price and volume, of which price has been the more important. The ratio of the average price of exports to that of imports is known as the *terms of trade*; and a rise in the price of exports relative to imports indicates an improvement in the terms of trade. Thus, when we note in the table that the terms of trade improved by some 20 per cent between 1954 and 1970 we mean that, in 1970, 20 per cent less exports by volume would have been needed to buy the same amount of imports as in 1954. This improvement in the terms of trade reflects the fact that the prices of many primary products —food and raw materials such as wool, cocoa, rubber, tea, and oil—tended to stagnate in world markets over this period (*see* G32–3). The subsequent worsening of the terms of trade reflected the commodity boom and the oil price increase which occurred in the 1970s (*see* G40).

VISIBLE TRADE: VOLUME AND PRICES

	1970 = 100	
	1954	1976
Value		
Imports	37	345
Exports	33	319
Volume		
Imports	47	134
Exports	52	139
Price		
Imports	79	289
Exports	63	240
Terms of trade	80	83

(iii) The Volume of Trade.

Superficially it would appear that any improvement in the terms of trade raises the value of British exports relative to imports. However, this is not always true: faster inflation in Britain, leading to a more rapid increase in export prices, would harm rather than help the balance of payments. If the prices of our export goods rise faster than the prices of our competitors in overseas markets it becomes progressively more difficult to sell our exports. Conversely, inflation in Britain makes it progressively more difficult to compete with imports. Growth in the volume of imports exceeded that in exports during the period 1954–70. The trade balance may well be harmed by a rise in the price of imported primary products (as it was after 1970); but the balance of trade in manufactures is worsened by an improvement in their terms of trade (as happened before 1970).

In the post-war period there was a considerable fall in Britain's share of world exports: from 20 per cent of exports of manufactures in 1954 to 16 per cent in 1961, to 12 per cent in 1967, the year of sterling devaluation, and to the lowest figure of 9 per cent in 1976. Britain's main competitors in export markets—and particularly Germany and Japan, with respectively 21 and 15 per cent of the total in 1976—were more successful in expanding their exports. Britain's competitive position in manufacturing has been persistently eroded over the years.

The Balance of Payments.

The *balance of payments* is an account of the total transactions of one country with the rest of the world. To illustrate the balance of payments and its components, the British accounts are presented in the table: accounts for a good year, 1970, and for a bad year, 1976. A detailed examination of recent movements in the British balance of payments is made in Part IV (see G38).

BALANCE OF PAYMENTS OF THE
UNITED KINGDOM, 1970 AND 1976
(£ millions)

	1970	1976
Exports (f.o.b.) . . .	8,121	25,416
Imports (f.o.b.) . . .	8,146	28,987
Visible balance . .	−25	−3,571
Invisible balance . .	+720	+2,166
of which: private services .	+684	+2,598
military . .	−285	−750
other government transfers and services .	−201	−796
interest, profit and dividends .	+825	+1,831
Current balance . . .	+695	−1,405
Official long-term capital .	−205	−158
Net private investment .	49	−49
of which: Overseas investment in U.K. . .	+838	+2,051
U.K. investment overseas . .	−789	−2,100
Other capital flows . .	+728	−2,607
Balancing item . .	+20	+591
Balance for official financing	+1,420	−3,628
Net borrowing from I.M.F. .	−134	+1,018
Net borrowing from other monetary authorities .	−1,161	−34
Net borrowing by public sector . . .	—	+1,791
Drawings on (+) or additions to (−) reserves . .	−125	+853
Total official financing .	−1,420	+3,628

(i) The Balance of Visible Trade.

The *balance of (visible) trade* is the difference between exports and imports of goods. It is said to be in *surplus* if exports exceed imports and in *deficit* if imports exceed exports. In estimating the balance of trade it is important that imports and exports be valued on the same basis. The normal method in the trade returns is to measure imports *c.i.f.* (cost, insurance, and freight) and exports *f.o.b.* (free on board). In other words import prices are shown to include the cost of transporting them to Britain, and exports are valued at the prices when loaded in British ports. Our table shows both imports and exports *f.o.b.*

Britain's visible balance is normally in deficit. The trade balance in 1970 was one of the best achieved in recent years. On the other hand, the year 1976 produced the largest deficit ever recorded. In that year Britain's trade was heavily in deficit to her EEC partners, to the United States, and to the oil-exporting countries.

(ii) Patterns of Trade.

The United States is Britain's largest trading partner, with 10 per cent of total British trade (exports plus imports) in 1976, followed by West Germany (8 per cent), the Netherlands and France (both 7 per cent), Ireland and Sweden (both 4 per cent). Britain's EEC partners as a group accounted for no less than 36 per cent of her trade, and the rest of Western Europe for 16 per cent. Three groups of countries—North America, the oil-exporting countries, and other less developed countries—each accounted for 13 per cent British trade in that year.

(iii) The Balance on Current Account.

The chronic deficit in the balance of visible trade has in normal years been offset by a surplus in the *balance of invisible trade*. This relates to international transactions in services as opposed to goods. It comprises four main groups of transactions. The first covers receipts from non-residents *less* payments to non-residents for services such as shipping, civil aviation, tourism,

insurance, and financial services. The second covers receipts from foreign governments in respect of military bases in the country *less* payments by this country in respect of military bases abroad. The third covers receipts of gifts and grants made to this country, *less* gifts and grants made by this country. The fourth includes all receipts of interest, dividends, and profits earned on overseas investment *less* interest, dividends, and profits paid out on foreign investment in this country.

The *balance on current account* is the sum of the balances on visible and invisible trade. We see that in 1970 there was a surplus and in 1976 a large deficit.

(iv) Capital Flow.

It is not sufficient simply to avoid deficits on current account. It has been the Government's objective to earn a surplus in order to finance investment abroad, to repay foreign debts previously incurred, and to build up reserves of gold and foreign exchange which can help to tide us over periods of deficit in the future. In fact a surplus of the magnitude aimed at by the government was only rarely achieved.

The capital account of the balance of payments contains net official long-term capital movements (*e.g.*, inter-government loans to less developed countries), net private investment abroad (being the difference between investment abroad by United Kingdom residents and investment by foreigners in the United Kingdom). Both these items are normally in deficit and tend to be long-term movements.

There are also large, short-term capital flows, sometimes referred to as *monetary movements*. These include trade credits, changes in sterling reserves held by foreign governments, and Eurodollar transactions. Such funds can be highly volatile, moving out of a currency if there is a risk of its devaluation or depreciation and into it if there is a chance of appreciation or if other currencies are suspect. Therefore, monetary movements often accentuate a surplus or deficit in the other items of the balance of payments; as happened both in 1970 and 1976.

(v) Balance for Official Financing.

The book-keeping identity of international payments and receipts may be illustrated by reference to the year 1976. In that year the United Kingdom had a record deficit on current and capital account of no less than £4,200 million. In other words, there was a net demand to transfer funds from sterling into other currencies. In theory, the supply and demand for foreign exchange could be equated in the market provided that the monetary authorities made no attempt to regulate the exchange rate (see G8). But an excess demand for foreign exchange of this magnitude would have involved an unprecedented fall in the value of sterling. Indeed, the monetary authorities did permit the market price for sterling to fall—from $2·0 to the pound in January 1976 to $1·7 in December—and yet a deficit of £4,200 had still to be financed from official sources. Total net official financing recorded was in fact £3,600 million, so that there must have been an unrecorded capital inflow of £600 million, known as the *balancing item*.

(vi) Foreign Exchange Reserves.

A deficit can be financed through an increase in liabilities, *i.e.* by government borrowing from abroad, or by a reduction in assets, *e.g.* a depletion of the official gold and foreign-exchange reserves. The gold and foreign-exchange reserves are used to finance payments abroad which cannot be financed in any other way: they are a last line of defence in international trade. We see that the imbalance in 1976 was financed partly through borrowing from the International Monetary Fund, partly through foreign currency borrowing by nationalised industries, and only partly by running down the reserves.

The official reserves of gold and foreign currencies amounted to £2,420 million at the end of 1976. There are bound to be imbalances in international trade and payments, and the function of these reserves is to tide over temporary imbalances by increasing reserves in favourable periods and running down reserves in unfavourable periods. If reserves are not sufficient to withstand temporary pressures, measures to protect the reserves will have to be taken—*e.g.*, raising interest rates and tightening up monetary policies generally—and these measures may create unemployment and recession, and restrict the growth of the economy.

Correcting a Deficit.

If an imbalance in international payments persists, the deficit cannot be met indefinitely from official financing. At some stage the Government must take action to remove the deficit. What action can it take? There are a number of alternatives available, each with its advantages and disadvantages, and economic opinion is by no means unanimous on the choice of policy. Let us consider each of these alternatives in turn.

(i) Variation of the Exchange Rate.

The *exchange rate* is the ruling official rate of exchange of pounds for dollars or other currencies. It determines the value of British goods in relation to foreign goods. Under the post-war Bretton Woods arrangements (*see* G9), Britain and other countries maintained a constant value of their currencies in terms of gold, permitting only very minor fluctuations of the exchange rate about its par value. However, persistent balance of payments deficits or surpluses caused occasional adjustments of the official exchange rate, the response to persistent deficit being *devaluation* and to persistent surplus *upvaluation*. In 1972 the major countries adopted a system of fluctuating exchange rates. However, exchange rates are not permitted to fluctuate entirely freely, *i.e.*, so that the market supply and demand for foreign exchange are continuously equated. While the monetary authorities permit the foreign-exchange market to influence the exchange rate, they are prepared to intervene in the national interest in the market (by buying or selling their currency) and so to keep the exchange rate within bounds. Given some flexibility in the exchange rate, a tendency for a deficit to arise is thus met by a *depreciation* of sterling, and an incipient surplus by *appreciation*.

If the pound is devalued or if it depreciates in terms of other currencies, British exports (which are paid for in pounds) become cheaper to foreigners and British imports (paid for by purchasing foreign currency) become more expensive to holders of pounds. In this way a fall in the value of the pound can improve the British balance of payments position by encouraging exports and discouraging imports.

If the pound is devalued or if it depreciates in terms of other currencies, British exports (which are paid for in pounds) become cheaper to foreigners and British imports (paid for by purchasing foreign currency) become more expensive to holders of pounds. In this way a fall in the value of the pound can improve the British balance of payments position by encouraging exports and discouraging imports.

But there are certain disadvantages attached to devaluation (or depreciation). The prospect of devaluation results in a speculative outflow of capital funds: and one fall may be taken as a sign that there will be a further fall in the future. Moreover, the rise in the price of imports of raw materials and consumption goods results in higher costs and prices and then in wage demands to maintain the British standard of living. It is possible that inflation will in this way neutralise the beneficial effects of devaluation.

The probable effect of a devaluation in Britain is initially to *worsen* the balance of trade, because the sterling price of imports is likely to be raised by more than that of exports. After about six months the effect of the devaluation on quantities —curbing imports and expanding the volume of exports—dominates, and the balance of trade improves. However, the improvement is maintained only if fiscal and incomes policies can prevent the devaluation from feeding through to domestic prices and costs and so both neutralising the gain in competitiveness and exacerbating inflation.

The pound was devalued in 1949, when an official exchange rate of £1 = $2·8 was established, and again in 1967, to a rate of £1 = $2·4. During 1971, when, as a result of the dollar crisis, exchange rates were allowed to fluctuate, the rate varied between £1 = $2·4 and £1 = $2·5. After the devaluation of the dollar in December 1971, the rate with gold remained unchanged, but the exchange rate with dollars became £1 = $2·6. After June 1972 the value of sterling in relation to other currencies was allowed to *float*. It fluctuated, but the tendency was to float downwards: by end May 1978 the pound equalled $1·81 (*see* G40).

(ii) Exchange Controls and Convertibility.

A currency is fully *convertible* if it can be freely exchanged for any other currency, or for gold, at the ruling rates of exchange. Exchange controls impose restrictions on convertibility by limiting the powers of holders of a currency to exchange their holdings for other currencies or gold. In the early post-war period there was a world-wide shortage of dollars: if sterling had been convertible, there would have been a rush to obtain dollars, with the consequence that Britain's reserves would soon have been exhausted. In fact, a premature attempt to establish sterling convertibility in 1947 led to such a drain on reserves that strict exchange controls had to be re-imposed.

Exchange controls on residents can be enforced by requiring that earnings of foreign currencies (*e.g.*, the proceeds from the sale of exports) be handed over to the exchange control authority—the Bank of England acts as the Government's agent—in exchange for sterling; and by permitting the exchange of sterling for foreign currencies (*e.g.*, to enable the purchase of imports) only for transactions approved by the exchange control authority.

By restricting convertibility the Government can make it more difficult for funds to move into or out of sterling. In this way the Government can impede capital movements, *e.g.*, British private investment abroad, or it can restrict current spending abroad, *e.g.*, on foreign holidays.

(iii) Import Controls and Tariffs.

Import controls impose limitations on the quantity or value of goods which are permitted to enter a country; tariffs are duties levied on imported goods so that the price of those goods to consumers in a country is higher than the price received by the foreigners supplying the goods. In the early post-war years, Britain maintained strict import controls over a wide range of goods. These were gradually dismantled during the 1950s.

All countries impose tariffs. Some tariffs are primarily intended to raise revenue for the Government, and others are primarily intended to protect home industries by raising the price of competing goods from abroad. The rights of countries to raise tariffs, or to operate tariffs in a discriminatory way (*i.e.*, to offer lower tariffs on goods from some sources than on similar goods from other sources), are closely circumscribed by the rules of the *General Agreement on Tariffs and Trade* (GATT). The object of the GATT is to work towards free trade, especially through a reduction in tariffs. In the post-war period GATT held several major conferences, at which bargaining to reduce tariffs was attended by modest success. The most significant moves towards free trade in this period were on a regional basis.

The disadvantage of introducing import controls or tariffs to correct a deficit in the balance of payments is that the benefits of free trade are lost. Moreover, there is always the possibility of retaliation by Britain's trading partners. Yet, import controls or tariffs may well be preferable to another measure which has been used to correct a deficit, deflation. Britain's powers to impose tariffs and quotas on imports were greatly circumscribed in 1973 by her accession to the European Economic Community, since this requires free trade within the community and a common external tariff. *See* G42(1).

(iv) Deflation.

Throughout the post-war period the U.K. balance of payments was far from secure. As a result, domestic economic policies were much influenced by balance of payments considerations. Devaluation was turned to only as a last resort. The movement in the 1950s and 1960s was towards greater freedom of trade. By ruling out devaluation and trade restrictions, the authorities had to fall back on *deflation* of the economy to correct periodic deficits. In other words, the Government took measures to discourage demand and so cut back incomes and employment. By reducing demand in general, the authorities secured a fall in demand for imports. However, it was necessary to cut back national income by many times the ensuing fall in imports. Deflation is a painful method of correcting a deficit: not only does it have a direct effect on the level of incomes and employment, but it is also liable to slow down the rate of growth of the economy. This can happen because deflation can weaken the incentive to expand productive capacity by investing in new plant, machinery, and other capital goods.

The problem which faced British policy-makers attempting to raise the rate of economic growth was this: as total demand for goods and services expands, it is difficult to prevent growth in the demand for imports and diversion of exports to the home market, particularly when home industries reach the limit of their productive capacity. Yet if consequent balance of payments difficulties are met by restrictions on total demand, it is difficult to maintain the investment necessary for growth in the productive capacity of the economy. The main need during the 1970s was the same as that in the two previous decades: to achieve an expansion of exports relative to imports so as to secure economic growth without running into balance of payments difficulties.

The international monetary system is partly to blame for the British decisions to resort to periodic deflation of the economy. The use of sterling as a reserve currency has subjected the balance of payments to violent swings in short-term capital flows. Moreover, if there is a world-wide shortage of *international liquidity*, *i.e.*, gold and foreign exchange reserves, this means that countries have an incentive to maintain a surplus in their balance of payments and so increase their reserves. In this situation surplus countries do not help to correct an imbalance in foreign transactions: the burden of correcting the imbalance is placed on the deficit country. If the Government of the deficit country is unable effectively to devalue its currency or to impose trade restrictions, it has to deflate the economy.

The International Monetary System.

(i) International Liquidity.

Imbalance in payments between countries is financed by transfers of gold or foreign-exchange reserves. These reserves are known as *international liquidity*. Their basic characteristic is general acceptability: they can perform their function only if they retain the confidence of those engaged in international transactions. Near the end of 1977 gold accounted for 14 per cent of total international liquidity, foreign-exchange reserves for 75 per cent, drawing rights on the International Monetary Fund (IMF) for 8 per cent, and special drawing rights on the IMF for 3 per cent. Each of these will be described below.

(ii) The International Monetary Fund.

The *International Monetary Fund* was set up at Bretton Woods in 1944 with the object of working towards free trade at stable exchange rates. Under the original agreement establishing the Fund, members agreed to make their currencies convertible into other currencies and gold at fixed rates of exchange, and agreed not to impose exchange or import controls without the permission of the Fund.

The function of the Fund is to make foreign-exchange resources available to members which run into balance of payments difficulties. Each member country has a deposit (called its quota), paid partly in gold and partly in its own currency,

with the Fund. The size of the deposit is fixed in relation to the country's share in world trade. In return, it is granted certain automatic drawing rights, which entitle it to borrow foreign currencies from the Fund. The Fund has power to make larger loans, and to grant standby credits to be drawn on if required. Before the Fund will make such loans and credits available it has to be satisfied that the borrowing country is taking appropriate action to correct the balance-of-payments disequilibrium.

(iii) Gold.

Gold played a central role in the international monetary system during the 1950s and 1960s. Central banks were prepared to buy and sell gold at a fixed price in terms of their currencies, and gold was exchanged among them in settlement of imbalances. Until 1968 the central banks operated a *gold pool* in the London market whereby such exchanges were made. The price of gold was held for many years at \$35 per fine ounce. However, this fixed price in the face of rising costs of gold production meant that gold supply could not increase rapidly enough to provide the international liquidity needed to finance expanding world trade.

It was not clear, however, that an increased price of gold was the best solution to this problem. First, it would help those countries most which needed help least—those with large gold reserves. It would represent a victory for gold hoarders and speculators, and so act as a stimulus to further hoarding and speculation in the future; the United States had no incentive to help in particular the gold-producing countries Russia and South Africa; and finally, it would represent a sheer waste of economic resources: gold had no intrinsic value. The moves since 1968 to *demonetise* gold are described in Part IV.

(iv) An International Currency?

The domestic currency of the United Kingdom is not backed by gold: on a one-pound note the Governor of the Bank of England promises to pay the bearer on demand the sum of one pound—another pound note! Yet, within Britain, there is complete confidence in the currency, because it is generally acceptable and so convertible into goods and services. Just as gold no longer backs the domestic currency, there is no need for gold in settlement of international payments. All we need is a generally acceptable international currency, *i.e.*, one in which all currencies have confidence.

Such a currency could be created by an international authority constituted for this purpose; and it could be made available to deficit countries, which could then pay their creditors in the new currency. In this way the shortage of international liquidity could be made good, and indeed gold—Keynes' " barbarous relic "—could be supplanted. There are various difficulties with such a scheme. It involves some loss of national autonomy and the vesting of considerable power in the international authority issuing the paper currency. Decisions have to be made as to which countries should receive the new currency, and in what quantities. And there is a fear that it will enable reckless governments to pursue inflationary policies without the discipline imposed by shortage of reserves, and that their inflation will be infectious. Many variations on the basic scheme have been devised in an attempt to surmount these—largely political—objections.

The first, very limited, step towards the creation of an international currency—the issue by the IMF of small quantities of *special drawing rights* between 1970 and 1972—is described in Part IV (see G42(2)).

(v) Foreign Exchange Reserves.

Two national currencies are widely used in settlement of international payments: the pound and the dollar. The pound has performed this function since the First World War, but the dollar has become the main reserve currency since the Second World War. Surplus countries are prepared to hold short-term debt in pounds or dollars —so earning a rate of interest—confident that their future trading deficits can be financed by payment of these currencies. These holdings are known as the *dollar* and *sterling balances*. They can perform their function only if there is confidence that they can be converted into other currencies and hence into goods and services at current exchange rates.

The United States ran a large and persistent payments deficit during the 1950s and 1960s. This was made possible by the willingness of the creditor countries to build up their dollar balances. Indeed, this increase in dollar balances was the main source of new international liquidity during that period. But there is necessarily a limit to such a process: by the late 1960s dollar balances actually exceeded the United States gold reserves. The weakness in the balance of payments of the United States has in fact added to the problem of international liquidity. The deficits have produced periodic fears that the dollar would be devalued; and this has resulted in speculation against the dollar. The problems which have beset the dollar in recent years are explained in Part IV (*see* **G43**).

(vi) The Sterling Balances.

Governments and individuals may hold balances in sterling (*e.g.*, Treasury bills, Government stocks, and bank accounts) for many reasons. Some countries reckon to keep a high proportion of their reserves in the form of sterling balances. It is convenient to hold sterling to finance trading transactions because sterling is widely acceptable in settlement of trading debts. Sterling balances are also held privately to the extent that they are considered a safe way of holding liquid assets. It is profitable to hold sterling if the rate of interest paid on balances in London is higher than that paid in other financial centres, provided that the interest-rate differential is not offset by an expectation that sterling will be depreciated in terms of other currencies.

At the end of 1976 the sterling balances totalled £6,120 million—well in excess of the official reserves, which stood at £4,120 million. £2,640 million was held by central banks, with the oil-exporting countries accounting for more than half.

An increase in the sterling balances enables Britain to finance an adverse balance of payments without reducing her gold and dollar reserves. Conversely, a reduction in sterling balances can impose a drain on reserves even if there is no adverse balance. The fear that the pound would depreciate in value makes it unlikely that Britain would be able to finance a persistent payments deficit through an increase in the sterling balances. The sterling balances thus tend to move perversely, so accentuating movements in the reserves.

It is ironical that Britain's position as an international currency country makes it more and not less difficult to rely on a running down of reserves to meet a temporary deficit in the balance of payments. British Governments have been concerned to reduce the size of the sterling balances in recent years, and in this they have had the support of the international community. Attempts to run down the sterling balances and to make them less volatile are described in Part IV (*see* **G41**).

(vii) The Eurodollar Market.

The Eurodollar market is a market for bank deposits which are denominated in foreign currencies. It derives its name from the fact that most of the banks which accept these foreign currency deposits are in Europe (including Britain) and most of the deposits are denominated in U.S. dollars. The Eurodollar market has grown at remarkable speed. A phenomenon of the 1960s, the market involved deposits of $9 billion in 1964 and $37 billion in 1969, and reached $48 billion in 1975. The reason for that growth was the profitability of Eurodollar transactions. Banks found that, particularly if only large units of money were handled, they could profitably borrow funds in country A and lend in country B, while paying interest rates higher than those paid in country A and charging rates lower than those charged in country B. Its growth was helped by the continuous deficit in the United States balance of payments, since this meant that banks and institutions received dollars which they were

willing to hold and lend. London is very important in the Eurodollar market.

The Eurodollar market—involving great mobility of short-term dollar balances—creates problems for the regulation of economic activity. The market affects the rates of interest and the availability of credit in different countries, and money movements can thwart both restrictive and expansionist monetary policies.

2. EMPLOYMENT, PRODUCTION, AND INDUSTRY

Population.

In June 1976 the population of the United Kingdom was estimated to be 55·9 million—49·2 m. in England and Wales, 5·2 m. in Scotland, and 1·5 m. in Northern Ireland. Since 1971 the population has increased by only 0·5 per cent. The crude birth rate (the number of live births per 100 people) has averaged about 1·3 over the 1970s, whilst the crude death rate has been little short of 1·2. More people have migrated from the United Kingdom than have migrated to this country.

The official estimate of the population of the United Kingdom in the year 2001 is 57·5 million. But prediction of future trends is difficult. For instance, it depends on immigration and emigration policies, the effect of improving medical services on the average length of life, trends in the age at which people marry, advances in techniques of birth control, and attitudes towards desirable family size. This projection is based on the belief that there will be a continued small outward migration from Britain, and that the birth rate will exceed the death rate, though by a smaller amount than at any time since the Second World War.

It is sometimes said that Britain is an over-populated island. However, the apparent increase in overcrowding may be more the result of increasing prosperity, *e.g.*, the impact of the motor car on our environment, than of increasing population.

The Labour Force.

Of the total population only some are of *working age*, *i.e.*, between the minimum school leaving age of 16 (15 before 1973) and retiring age—65 years for men and 60 for women. Of course, not all those of working age do work and not all those above working age have retired. In 1976, when the total population of the United Kingdom was 56·0 million, the labour force was 25·9 million. Of males who were aged 16 or over, 84·5 per cent were in the labour force, compared with only 49·5 per cent of females. The labour force is defined to include not only those who are gainfully employed (as employees or self-employed) but also the unemployed who are looking for work. Students and housewives are excluded unless they do some work for cash. One feature of the past decade or so has been a slight fall in the number of adult males going out to work, a fall which it is expected will continue until the early 1980s. It is caused by an increasing number of students and by more people retiring early. Those factors also affected the number of women going out to work, but they have been more than offset by a rising participation of married women. This increasing trend is again expected to continue until the early 1980s.

Most of the labour force work for wages and salaries as employees. Of the total for the United Kingdom in June 1976 of 26·0 million, 1·9 m. were employers or self-employed, 0·3 m. were in the Forces, 22·5 m. were employees and 1·3 m. were registered as unemployed. So less than half the population who are at work have to produce not only for themselves but also for the rest of the population who are either not in the labour force or who are unemployed.

The table shows the industries in which people work. Some 3·3 per cent of the total work in the *primary sector* (agriculture and mining) and 46 per cent in the *production industries*, 32 per cent being in manufacturing (the main production industry). As an economy develops there is a tendency for employment in the primary sector to decline at the expense of the production industries. At high levels of income a large

DISTRIBUTION OF WORKING POPULATION, UNITED KINGDOM, JUNE 1976
(Thousands)

Primary Industries:	
Agriculture, forestry, and fishing	395
Mining and quarrying	348
TOTAL	743
Production Industries:	
Construction	1,308
Gas, electricity, and water	353
Transport and communication	1,475
Manufacturing	7,246
of which:	
food, drink, and tobacco	714
chemicals and allied industries	423
metal manufacture	469
engineering	1,818
shipbuilding	185
vehicles	744
textiles	513
clothing and footwear	381
paper, printing, and publishing	542
other manufacturing	1,457
TOTAL	10,382
Services:	
Distributive trades	2,723
Financial, business, professional and scientific services	4,757
Catering, hotels, etc.	850
Miscellaneous services	1,449
National government service	660
Local government service	966
TOTAL	11,405
GRAND TOTAL	22,530

proportion of income is spent on services, and employment in services expands as a proportion of the total. Thus, in 1955 services accounted for only 36 per cent of total employment; whereas by 1976 the proportion had risen to 51 per cent.

Employment and Unemployment.

In 1976 an average of 1,270,000 persons—5·3 per cent of the labour force—were unemployed in the U.K. In most post-war years the average was lower than 1·5 per cent. Even in January 1959, the worst month of the 1950s, the rate rose only to 2·8 per cent, and in February 1963—an exceptional month owing to weather—to 3·9 per cent. These contrast with an average figure in 1937, the best year of the 1930s, of 11 per cent, and with a figure of 22 per cent at the bottom of the slump in 1932. The low unemployment of the post-war years was not maintained in the late 1960s. Unemployment grew to reach the remarkable level of 928,600 (4·1 per cent of the labour force) in January 1972. It then started to fall back with the general economic recovery, only to start rising again as the economy moved back into recession. By 1976 the unemployment rate exceeded 5 per cent.

UNEMPLOYMENT AND VACANCIES
(United Kingdom, thousands)

	Unemployment.† (Annual Average)	Vacancies. (Annual Average)	Unemployment as a percentage of total employees
1932*	2,829	n.a.	22·1
1937	1,482	n.a.	10·9
1962	454	150	2·0
1964	393	222	1·7
1966	353	257	1·5
1968	564	190	2·5
1970	602	188	2·6
1972	855	147	3·7
1974	600	303	2·6
1976	1,270	121	5·3

* Figures relate only to population insured against unemployment.
† Excluding school-leavers.

Until the late 1960s 1–1·5 per cent unemployment was somewhere near the practicable minimum; for some unemployment is more or less inevitable. Some seasonal rise in unemployment in the winter must be expected, e.g., in seaside towns, and for this reason unemployment in January is half a per cent or so higher than in June. Moreover, some unemployment is bound to be involved in job-changing and as the demands of industries change. " Full employment " means that there should be about as many jobs vacant as there are workers looking for jobs. A large excess of vacancies is evidence of inflationary pressure in the labour market, for it means that the employers needing workers to meet the demands for their products will have to compete with each other by bidding up wages. Most commentators feel that the practicable minimum level of unemployment has increased since the late 1960s. One explanation of this is that as the fixed costs (like National Insurance contributions) of employing workers have gone up, so employers have been more careful to economise on labour. Another possible explanation is that workers who are unemployed take longer to find a new job, since they may have drawn redundancy pay (since the Redundancy Payments Act of 1965) or they may be drawing earnings-related unemployment benefit, the earnings-related supplement having been introduced in 1966. A final possibility is that many of the unemployed have skills which are redundant in an economy where the structure of industry is changing. Experts still disagree about the relative importance of these several explanations.

To some extent unemployment figures are misleading, as not all unemployed workers are eligible for unemployment benefit under the National Insurance Scheme. Most married women who go out to work normally opt not to pay the full National Insurance contributions, so that, when they become unemployed, they just drop out of the " working population." Unemployment figures definitely understate the seriousness of recessions, as they do not count all the persons who would like to have, but cannot find, jobs.

Regional Unemployment.

A peculiarly dreadful feature of the inter-war years was the emergence of the depressed areas—the regions of the country where a third of the men had not had a job for a year or more. Such extreme regional unemployment has not recurred in the post-war period: only in Northern Ireland was unemployment very high. Between 1954 and 1976 unemployment there ranged between 6 and 10 per cent. Nevertheless, regional inequalities exist.

PERCENTAGE OF WORKERS UNEMPLOYED, BY REGIONS

	Annual average 1965	October 1976
North	2·5	7·2
Yorkshire and Humberside	1·1	5·2
East Midlands	0·9	4·6
East Anglia	1·3	4·8
South East	0·8	4·2
South West	1·5	6·4
Wales	2·5	7·0
West Midlands	0·7	5·3
North West	1·6	6·6
Scotland	2·9	6·9
Great Britain	*1·4*	*5·5*
Northern Ireland	6·1	9·8

In October 1976 the proportion of all workers unemployed in Great Britain was 5·5. But the table shows a lower proportion was unemployed in the South East, East Anglia, and East and West Midlands, and that there was a much higher proportion unemployed in the North and West of England, in Wales, Scotland, and Northern Ireland. Moreover, the labour shortage of 1965 was not shared equally; unemployment remained at 2·5 per cent or above in the North, Wales, Scotland, and Northern Ireland. In this situation checks have to be placed on the economy before full employment is reached, because in the booming areas vacancies far exceed unemployment.

DECREASE IN EMPLOYMENT IN SELECTED INDUSTRIES, 1950–1976

	Thousands	Per cent.
Textiles . . .	538	49
Mining and quarrying .	508	59
Shipbuilding . .	123	40
Agriculture, forestry, and fishing . .	530	57

One of the main reasons for the regional pattern of unemployment is that certain industries and services, in which big changes have been taking place, tend to be grouped in specific regions. Most of our early industrial centres had to be established close to coal, iron ore, and adequate water supplies. But employment in many long-established industries has recently been declining. The scale of this contraction can be seen from the table. On the other hand new and growing industries, and their related offices, have been concentrated in Greater London, the South East, and the Midlands. The growth of services, too, has centred on the areas where industry is booming and population is increasing. In the absence of government intervention, the process would tend to become cumulative, and regional inequalities would grow rather than diminish.

Regional Planning.

There are essentially two ways of tackling the problem of regional imbalances; taking jobs to the people or bringing people to the jobs. In so far as the latter alternative is chosen, the Government should encourage the mobility of labour, e.g., through retraining schemes or a rehousing subsidy. However, the migration of population may damage community life in the denuded areas, and cause congestion, housing shortages, and overcrowding in the booming regions. The Government can create employment opportunities in the relatively depressed regions in various ways. It can try to induce expanding industries to set up new plants in these regions by offering tax incentives; it can authorise additional expenditure on public works —e.g., by accelerating road-building programmes —to provide additional employment; it can place orders for the goods it needs—e.g., defence contracts—where work is required. It can also use physical controls on expansion in the better-off areas; since 1947 factory building over a particular size, which has been changed from time to time, has required the granting of an *Industrial Development Certificate*.

(i) Labour's Policy.

On taking office in October 1964, the Labour Government made regional planning the responsibility of its Department of Economic Affairs. Britain was divided into eight regions, with the intention of producing a plan for each region. The Government also established two kinds of planning body: regional economic planning Councils and Boards to advise on and co-ordinate the planning of each region.

Labour Government policy to cure regional unemployment took the following forms. Various measures to defer public construction programmes excluded the *Development Areas*. Fiscal incentives to locate industry in the depressed regions were given, e.g., the cash grants provided in 1966 for new plants and machinery in manufacturing were at twice the national rate in the Development Areas. By contrast, office building in the main conurbations, London and Birmingham, was strictly limited. To encourage the mobility of

labour, the Government introduced redundancy compensation and achieved some expansion in both public and private training facilities. In 1967 regional differentials in the selective employment tax were also introduced. Under this scheme manufacturers in Development Areas were paid £1·50 per week for each full-time adult male employee and lower amounts in respect of other workers, so giving the Development Areas a wage cost advantage in manufacturing of 5–10 per cent.

In 1965/6 special assistance to industry in the Development Areas was only £29 million. The estimate for the financial year 1970/1 was £309 million; taking the form mainly of the Regional Employment Premium and investment grants.

(ii) Conservative Policy.

In 1970 the incentive to invest in the Development Areas was affected by the Conservative Government's replacement of cash grants by a system of initial allowances against tax. Whereas cash grants had been 40 per cent of investment in plant and machinery in Development Areas and 20 per cent in other areas, there was now to be free depreciation in Development Areas and 60 per cent initial allowances in other areas.

Early in 1972, with the national unemployment rate no less than 4·0 per cent, unemployment rates in Northern Ireland, Scotland, Wales and Northern England had reached appalling levels. At the time of the Budget the Government produced a White Paper on regional development. In the Budget the Chancellor had introduced free depreciation throughout the country on all investment in plant and machinery (see G47); the previous preferential treatment of investment in Development Areas was therefore ended. Instead *regional development grants*, in the form of cash payments towards investment in plant, machinery and buildings, were introduced. These were to be made by *regional industrial development boards*, at rates equal to 22 per cent of investment expenditure in Special Development Areas and 20 per cent in Development Areas and Intermediate Areas. The Government also proposed in four years to triple expenditure on retraining facilities, and to pay a worker who had undergone retraining a rehousing grant of £600 if he moved house to take a new job; and also £400 to any worker in an assisted area who moved house to take a new job. It should be remembered, however, that strong measures were necessary merely to replace the Labour Government's system of cash grants, and the Regional Employment Premium which was to be phased out beginning in 1974. Though R.E.P. was retained by the incoming Labour Government, it was finally replaced by more selective measures in 1977 (see G50).

Slumps normally affect the poorest regions most. This was not so in the recession of 1974–1975. Between mid-1974 and mid-1975 unemployment rose by 47 per cent in the development regions, as against 81 per cent in the unassisted areas. It is doubtful whether this was due to government regional policy. It is more likely to be attributable to the following factors. North Sea oil created jobs in Scotland and the North East. Nationalised industries, which tend to be concentrated in the poor areas, cut back their labour force by relatively little. The slump in the demand for consumer durables and cars badly affected production and therefore employment in one of the better-off areas—the West Midlands.

Though regional problems remain, recent studies have shown that IDC's, financial incentives, and REP have to a limited extent mitigated them.

National Income.

Gross domestic income (GDY) is the sum total of incomes received for the services of labour, land, or capital in a country. Gross domestic product (GDP) is the money value of all the goods and services produced in the country. So as to avoid double-counting, only the *value added* at each stage of production is included: firms' purchases of goods and services from other firms are excluded. The revenue from selling the GDP is either paid out to the hired factors of production—labour, land, and capital—or retained in the form of profits. Therefore, provided it is calculated net of taxes on goods produced, GDP must equal GDY. To estimate gross national income (GNY) from GDY it is necessary to add the net income—such as profits and interest—received from abroad. If an allowance is made for wear and tear of the nation's capital equipment, i.e., for *capital consumption*, we arrive at net national income, better known as the *national income*.

In 1976 the national income of the United Kingdom was £96,676 million, implying a national income per head of £1,726. In 1955 the corresponding figures had been £15,523 million and £305 per head. However, only part of the increase in value was due to an increase in the quantity of goods and services produced; some of the increase simply reflected a rise in prices. It is important to calculate changes in the volume of output—known as *real output*—as well as changes in its value. Real output is calculated by the statistical device of constructing an index number. This is done by calculating the volume of goods and services provided in each year and then valuing these goods and services at the prices found in one particular year. Thus between 1955 and 1976 the money value of national income rose by 522 per cent, whereas real income increased by only 64 per cent, and the difference represented a rise in prices.

The Quality of Life.

In real terms national income per head rose by 49 per cent between 1955 and 1976, or by 1·2 per cent per annum. National income per head is the most useful indicator of the standard of living. However, this measure is necessarily a crude one. For instance, it cannot take into account new and better products, e.g., television, man-made fibres, faster flight, long-playing records, or the lowly plastic bucket; nor does it indicate changes in the distribution of income between rich and poor; nor in the length of working week.

Data of national income per head may also conceal important changes in the "quality of life", e.g., in our physical environment. This is affected by such things as traffic congestion, noise, water- and air-pollution. Between 1960 and 1975 the number of cars on British roads more than doubled, from 5·5 million to 13·7 million; the number of road goods vehicles with unladen weight exceeding 8 tons growing almost ten-fold over the same period. Movement of civil aircraft over Britain doubled during the 1960s and increased by another 40 per cent in the first half of the 1970s, whilst some aircraft tended to become noisier. On the other hand, air in London has become cleaner: in the period 1949–54 there were on average 1·29 hours of winter sunshine per day, whereas in the period 1964–69 the average was 1·66 hours.

Industrial Production.

It is fairly easy to measure output in the main manufacturing industries, and in many of the other industries producing goods. It is much more difficult to do so for the service industries: the output of a doctor or a teacher is not easily measured. So each month the Central Statistical Office calculates the *index of industrial production* covering the main production industries. Industrial production is thus an early indicator

of economic trends (*see* G46), but it is prone to fluctuate more than the other components of GDP.

Manufacturing industry accounts for nearly three-quarters of industrial production. Within manufacturing the following industries have expanded most rapidly—chemicals, which include drugs, plastics, cosmetics and detergents, coal and petroleum products, including oil refining, and instrument and electrical engineering. The slowest growing manufacturing industries are textiles, clothing, leather and shipbuilding, which are losing their markets to cheaper competitors. Those industries in which demand has stagnated tend to be the industries in which output per employee, i.e. productivity, has stagnated.

International Comparisons.

In recent years Britain's GDP has grown less rapidly than that of almost any other major Western country. The British economy is also characterised by a relatively slow growth of output per head, i.e., productivity. Britain has fallen behind many of the European countries in terms of income per head. Some comparisons with other countries are made in the table. However, these may be misleading because incomes are converted into pounds at official exchange rates, and these need not reflect relative costs of living.

Many explanations of Britain's poor performance have been suggested, and there is by no means agreement on this matter among economists. It has been argued that the U.K.—like the U.S.A.—has a highly advanced economy in which there is a relatively high demand for services: and that it is difficult to raise productivity in the large services sector. Another argument is that Britain has been hampered by its slowly growing labour force, which has restricted growth not only in output but also in output per man. The reason given is that an expanding labour force needs to be equipped with additional plant and machinery so that its capital equipment tends to be newer on average than that used by a static labour force, and thus more up-to-date and efficient.

Some commentators have put the blame on the inefficiency of our business management; some on our educational system, biased towards the humanities; some on the social milieu which looks down on money-making as a career; some on over-manning and other restrictive practices of trade unions. A good deal of attention has also been paid to the proportion of output which different countries devote to *investment*, i.e., expenditure on commodities—such as plant and machinery—for use in future production. These investment ratios are shown in the table. With the exception of the U.S.A., all countries have investment ratios considerably higher than in the U.K., with correspondingly higher growth rates of output and productivity. Since investment in dwellings contributes very little to growth, it may be appropriate to exclude this investment: however, similar results are obtained. This leads to the hypothesis that Britain's growth rate could be raised if a higher proportion of output were devoted to investment, particularly in plant and machinery. There is probably some truth in many of these explanations, and it is unlikely that any one remedy will be sufficient to raise the British growth rate.

AN INTERNATIONAL GROWTH LEAGUE TABLE

	Percentage change per annum, 1958–60 to 1970–72			Fixed investment as percentage of GDP, 1960s.	Income per head, 1972 £ p.a.
	Output.	Employ-ment.	Output per head.		
Japan	10·6	1·3	9·3	32	1,042
France	5·5	0·4	5·1	24	1,449
W. Germany	4·7	0·2	4·5	26	1,605
Italy	4·5	−0·6	5·1	21	845
U.S.A.	4·4	1·8	2·6	17	2,126
U.K.	3·1	0·2	2·9	18	1,066

Investment.

In 1976 gross investment in capital assets amounted to £23,427 million in the United Kingdom. This was about 21 per cent of the GNP. The net addition to the nation's stock of capital assets was just over half of total investment, and just under half the total was needed to offset the wastage of assets already in use, *i.e.*, to make good the *capital consumption*.

There are four main kinds of investment: plant and machinery, vehicles, dwellings, and other construction. In 1976 the four categories accounted for 35, 10, 20, and 35 per cent respectively. Investment may also be analysed by the purpose for which it is used. Social services such as education and health (6 per cent) take a surprisingly small proportion of total investment. Distribution and other service industries (15 per cent) and public corporations take a large proportion: investment in electricity, gas, and water alone accounts for over 6 per cent of the total. It is clear that some sectors of the economy are more capital-intensive than others. Manufacturing investment accounts for 17 per cent of the total. This is small in relation to the contribution of manufacturing to output, and has declined in recent years. However, many of the fast-growing manufacturing industries—*e.g.*, chemicals, electronics, steel—use much machinery and equipment per unit of output produced. These capital-intensive plants cannot pay unless they are worked at near full capacity. With the growing capitalisation of industry it is increasingly necessary to introduce shift work.

Increasing Investment.

The proportion of total output invested—the *investment ratio*—is lower in Britain than in other countries with faster growth rates of output and productivity; and there is reason to believe that a higher proportion would improve the growth rate to some extent (*see* G13). But in a fully employed economy it is not possible to increase investment expenditures without curtailing other forms of expenditure, notably private and public consumption. This curtailment would have to be brought about by increasing taxation or encouraging people to save or by pruning public services. Yet the very act of restricting private consumption may induce private firms to *reduce* their investment expenditures.

In 1976, 75 per cent of total investment in the United Kingdom was carried out in the private sector, 23 per cent by public authorities and 20 per cent by the public corporations. The Government has more control over investment in the public sector than in the private sector. Governments do possess various policy measures by which to influence private investment (*see* G22–7, 46–52) but private investment is volatile and highly dependent on businessmen's expectations, especially their expectations about the future growth of their markets. It is no easy matter to raise the British investment ratio.

If a higher investment ratio could be achieved, a faster rate of economic growth—and therefore higher consumption in the future—would involve a sacrifice in current consumption. A choice must be made between the loss in current consumption and the ensuing gain in future consumption. Of course not all consumption expenditure is equally important to the standard of living: some would argue that if British defence expenditure was pruned to permit more investment, there would be no loss to set against the future gain.

The Finance of Investment.

Any business is allowed to charge as a cost the depreciation of its assets. Normal depreciation allowances are based on the original cost of the asset and on its expected useful life. In a time of price inflation depreciation allowances will not provide sufficient finance to permit the replacement of assets at higher prices, and there are many supporters of depreciation allowances being based on replacement costs. Many firms do set aside extra funds specifically to cover these extra replacement costs.

Governments have, however, adopted certain fiscal devices to encourage replacement and net investment. Soon after the war initial allowances were introduced. Under this system firms were permitted to charge against profits in the first year of its life 20, or at times 40, per cent of the cost of any new equipment, and the system amounted to a loan of the tax saved in the first year, repaid over the life of the asset. In 1954 initial allowances for machinery were replaced by a system of investment allowances, under which a firm could charge against profits 20 per cent of the cost of any new machine, with the difference that all ordinary depreciation allowances were still chargeable. So the investment allowance was a grant, not a loan, of the saved tax. In 1966, initial and investment allowances on new plant and machinery in three sectors—manufacturing, mining, and shipping—were replaced by cash grants. Other plant and machinery and industrial building received higher initial allowances. In 1970 the Conservative Government reintroduced initial allowances in place of investment grants but in 1972 tried to encourage investment by granting free depreciation (*see* G47 (2).

Depreciation allowances and government allowances and grants for investment are sufficient to cover more than half of investment (excluding dwellings) by the private sector, and to cover a minor part of public (non-housing) investment. The residue of investment, and housebuilding, has to be provided from other sources of funds. Companies rely mainly on retained profits, which are often larger, taking companies as a whole, than their net investment. Other sources of company finance are borrowing in financial markets and the issue of company shares. Much public investment must be financed by the Treasury.

Automation.

Accompanying the accumulation of capital is a tendency towards automation in production. With automation, much of the manual semi-skilled work should come to an end. So far the impact of automation has been small. The main use has been in the office, where computers can carry out far more efficiently much of the routine calculating, recording, and checking operations previously done by clerks. But it will continue to spread, and must do so if the growth in incomes is to continue. This revolution will take many decades to effect. It raises no spectre of widespread redundancy; but it does mean that over the years more and more emphasis will need to be laid on the training of workers for skilled work, and indeed on raising the general level of education.

Monopoly and Competition.

A trend to increasing size and increasing capitalisation has been going on now for many decades, and in the process it has changed the face of British industry. In the early 19th century the typical firm was the owner-managed textile mill. Then in the 1860s and 1870s came the discovery of cheap methods of making steel, with the consequential immense growth in the engineering industries. Most of the chemical industry is still newer, and there are a number of entirely 20th cent. industries such as aircraft and electronics.

In the capital-intensive industries the big firm predominates. In some it has become almost a monopoly; in others the pattern is of a few firms, all large. In 1970 the top British companies —each with sales exceeding £1,000 million— included oil firms (British Petroleum and Shell), tobacco firms (British American Tobacco and Imperial Tobacco), chemical firms (Imperial Chemical Industries and Unilever) and one in the motor industry (British Leyland Motor Corporation). There is evidence that the extent of *concentration* of British industry—according to measures such as the proportion of the output of an industry produced by the largest three firms—has increased steadily since 1945. Concentration increased particularly rapidly in the 1960s. There are two possible reasons for such an increase. The first is the natural growth of already large firms; the second is because of merger activity. This latter factor has been the more important in Britain.

Competition goes on, but it has changed its form. In the old days competition was largely by price. Now it is largely by advertising and by variations in the quality and other features of the product—detergents and motor cars being good examples. In many industries, groups of firms producing similar products entered into agreements which had the effect of restricting competition, for example through schemes for price-fixing. The effect is to increase the price to the consumer and to reduce the amount of output available. Some authorities have estimated that the total "welfare" loss because of this is relatively small, and have argued that our major concern should be over the dangers of large corporations having substantial political power because of their size, and over their using this power to force the Government into unwise decisions about, for example, subsidising inefficient management.

Regulation of Monopoly and Competition.

(i) Restrictive Practices Court.

The Restrictive Trade Practices Acts of 1956 and 1968 outlawed many of the main forms of restrictive agreements to prevent competition. Collective price fixing was declared to be illegal unless the industry could show that the practice brought substantial benefit to the public. Collective price-fixing was the system under which a central association for the industry lays down minimum prices at which members may sell. Usually such a system was backed by arrangements for collective boycotts, under which members of the association would refuse to sell goods to wholesalers or retailers who broke the rules. Collective boycotts were also found in industries without collective price-fixing, one common purpose being to make sure that retailers did not sell a manufacturer's products below his recommended price. This form of collective resale price maintenance was also outlawed by the Acts.

Under the Acts any restrictive agreements of several specified kinds had to be registered with the Registrar of Restrictive Practices. He then had to decide whether there was a *prima facie* case for the discontinuation of the agreement, and, if he thought there was, the case was referred to a Restrictive Practices Court, containing both judicial and lay members. For an agreement to be upheld, the agreeing parties had to prove to the Court that the agreement conferred some substantial benefit on the public which outweighed any injury it did to the public. A 1976 Act extended this legislation to cover service industries.

(ii) Resale Prices Act.

The Act of 1956 permitted individual manufacturers to enforce *resale price maintenance* (r.p.m.) for their own products. Few suppliers would want the publicity of enforcing r.p.m. through the courts, but individual suppliers could still put some commercial pressure on price-cutters, *e.g.*, by offering less favourable terms or by refusing them supplies. The Resale Prices Act of 1964 prohibited all methods of enforcing minimum resale prices. However, goods which had been registered in due time with the Registrar of restrictive trading agreements or had been approved by the Restrictive Practices Court, were exempted, temporarily in the former case and permanently in the latter. For r.p.m. to be approved by the Court, it must be shown that some ensuing benefit to customers (*e.g.*, of increased quality or more retail outlets) outweighs any detriment. It is also lawful to withhold supplies to retailers selling goods at a loss to attract customers.

As a result of the Act r.p.m. has ceased to be a common practice, and has largely been replaced by "recommended" retail prices, which are in effect maximum prices. This practice has been investigated by the Monopolies Commission, which found that it was not always against the public interest.

(iii) The Monopolies Commission.

The Restrictive Practices Acts left untouched the industries in which one firm is dominant: these remained the responsibility of the Monopolies Commission. This is an independent administrative tribunal, established in 1948, with powers to investigate and decide whether a monopoly (defined in terms of market share) is contrary to the "public interest." The Commission reports on industries referred to it by the Department of Trade and Industry (formerly the Board of Trade) and makes recommendations.

The Monopolies and Mergers Act of 1965 strengthened control over monopolies and mergers. With regard to monopolies, the Government wished to provide itself with legal powers of enforcement: previously monopolies had been expected to comply voluntarily with the findings of the Monopolies Commission. The Act also permitted the Government to refer a merger or a proposed merger to the Monopolies Commission in cases where the merger would lead to monopoly (defined as control of at least one third of the market) or would increase the power of an existing monopoly, or where the value of the assets taken over exceeded £5 million.

In interpreting the public interest, the Monopolies Commission has criticised monopolies for various practices, *e.g.*, if they attempt to deter entry to the industry, or earn abnormally high profit rates, or show weakness in research and innovation.

(iv) The Industrial Reorganisation Corporation.

Mergers may lead to monopoly and to the abuse of monopoly power. But it would be wrong to presume that mergers are always bad: mergers— by facilitating research and other economies of large-scale production—may increase industrial efficiency. For this reason the *Industrial Reorganisation Corporation* (IRC) was set up in 1966 under Government auspices. Its functions were to promote industrial reorganisation in the interests of industrial efficiency, *e.g.*, by enabling industries to achieve economies of scale or by reorganising inefficiently managed firms. It assisted firms in agreed regroupings and could intervene to encourage a particular takeover which, in its estimation, was in the public interest. However its objective in making loans was to "prod" and not to "prop" inefficient firms. It supported mergers in electronics, trawling, nuclear power, mechanical engineering, and other industries. In 1970 the Conservative Government decided to wind up the IRC. However, some of the proposed functions of the National Enterprise Board, set up in 1975, were similar to those performed by the IRC (*see* G51).

(v) Restrictive Labour Practices.

Restrictive labour practices—which result in the "over-manning" of plant or the "under-employment" of men—are common in British industry. These stem from such causes as the fear of redundancy and unemployment, anxiety to preserve a craft skill threatened by technical progress, the desire to work at overtime rates, and sometimes just inertia. Governments have made attempts to eliminate this underemployment. In its incomes policy the Labour Government specifically made *productivity agreements*— agreements to change working practices in return for higher pay—an exception to the norm laid down for wage increases (*see* G55). One of the objectives of the Conservative Government taking office in 1970, in condoning and maintaining the recession in the economy, was to achieve a "shakeout" of underemployed labour. The "self-financing productivity" exception in the 1977–8 incomes policy had as one of its aims the reduction of restrictive practices. The permanent elimination of restrictive labour practices requires more enlightened management, more union co-operation, and more Government measures to promote the mobility of labour between occupations.

(vi) The Fair Trading Act.

The 1973 Fair Trading Act placed the previously dispersed responsibilities for overseeing competition policies in the hands of a civil servant—the Director General of Fair Trading. The Monopolies Acts of 1948 and 1965 were repealed and replaced by rather more comprehensive rules. Monopoly was now defined as control of one quarter of the market instead of one third. For the first time local monopolies were made subject to control. The Director General of Fair Trading —as well as the Department of Trade and Industry—was enabled to refer monopoly situations to the Monopolies Commission; though it was still only the Department which could make references on mergers. Additionally the Director General took over the functions of the Registrar of Restrictive Practices. The Act also gave him responsibilities for general consumer protection, and set up a new body to assist in that aim—the Consumer Protection Advisory Committee. In 1977 the Government announced a review of its general policy. There were two main concerns. The first was to examine the conflict between controlling mergers for fear of malpractice and encouraging them to stimulate efficiency. The second was to investigate whether, in projected mergers, the burden of proof be put more on to the firms involved to show that no significant harm to the consumer would ensue.

Nationalised Industries.

Nationalised industry accounts for over 10 per cent of British production. Local authorities also run some services, e.g., bus transport and water provision. In many cases—e.g., the railways, gas, electricity, and postal services— these industries are natural monopolies, in which the provision of competing services would obviously be wasteful. They were thus obvious candidates for public ownership. With the exception of steel—de-nationalised 1951–53 and re-nationalised in 1967—nationalisation was for a long time not extended into manufacturing industry. The post-1974 Labour Government nationalised the shipbuilding and aerospace industries, and established the British National Oil Corporation and the National Enterprise Board (see G51), with powers to take holdings in private industry.

The nationalised industries are required normally to cover their costs, and to earn a target rate of return on their investment. However, it is government policy that subsidies can be made for some services which are justified on social grounds, e.g., grants are made to British Rail to continue unremunerative rail services. Cross-subsidisation of non-commercial services by commercial services within a nationalised industry is discouraged, and costing according to the *marginal cost* of a service is encouraged. To give an example of marginal costing: once all the gas production equipment and gas pipes have been installed the cost incurred in supplying additional gas is low; thus consumers are charged a low price per unit of gas consumed and, to avoid a financial loss, the Gas Boards make a standing charge to cover overheads.

The nationalised industries are voracious users of capital, as they are nearly all highly-capitalised industries (see **G14**). Until 1956 they raised new capital, when they wanted it, by borrowing on the Stock Exchange; this fixed interest stock being guaranteed by the Treasury. Since then the nationalised industries have drawn directly on the Exchequer for most of their capital. In 1971–75, for example, £5,700 million was raised from the government, and £1,600 million from other (mainly overseas) sources. This system has been criticised. The advocates of equity issue have pointed to the strain it puts on the Exchequer and the possibility of nationalised industries cutting investment when surpluses fall or become deficits because of the ensuing difficulties in meeting interest obligations. It is also said that nationalised industries have suffered from their dependence on the Exchequer. In times of balance of payments crises the nationalised industries have been forced by the Government to cut back their planned expansion, sometimes at serious cost of disorganisation. But any alternative system of financing would also be open to criticism. *See also* **G58**.

3. INCOMES, WAGES, AND PRICES

Personal Income.

National income is a measure of the total income accruing to the residents in a country in return for services rendered (see **G12**). It therefore consists of the sum of wages, salaries, profits, and rents. But not all this income accrues to persons, e.g., companies do not distribute all their profits to shareholders and some nationalised industries earn profits. This is part of national income but not of *personal income*. On the other hand, some personal incomes are not payments for services rendered. Such incomes are called *transfer incomes* to emphasise that their payment does not add to the national income, but only transfers income from one recipient to another. Included in this category are retirement pensions, family allowances, and student grants. In the United Kingdom in 1976 income accruing to companies and public corporations and not distributed exceeded £15,219 million, but the central and local governments made transfer payments of nearly £13,000 million to the personal sector; so that personal income (£112,350 million) was slightly more than gross national income (£110,259 million).

Personal Disposable Income.

Not all personal income is available for spending. In 1976 the State took 16 per cent of personal income in *direct taxation*, i.e., income tax and surtax; and 7 per cent went as National Insurance contributions, which being compulsory are in effect a form of tax. The remaining 77 per cent of personal income—called *personal disposable income*—was available for spending. However, not all disposable income need be spent on consumer goods and services: income can instead be saved. There are many possible motives for saving, e.g., to meet future contingencies, for a future purchase such as a house or car, for retirement, or for the income to be derived from saving. Saving as a fraction of personal disposable income was fairly steady in 1971 at between 7 and 9 per cent, but from 1972 increased appreciably, and in 1976 was nearly 15 per cent.

Types of Personal Income.

Compare the sources of personal income in Britain in 1938 and in 1976. We see in the table that the share of income from employment increased considerably, especially that of wages and salaries. The share of salaries grew relative to that of wages, not because average salaries rose faster than average wages but because the number of salaried workers expanded rapidly. With the development of the Welfare State there was an increase in the percentage of incomes derived from public grants—pensions, social security payments, student grants, etc.

SOURCES OF PERSONAL INCOME, 1938 AND 1976
(As percentage of total)

	1938	1976
Income from employment of which:	59·5	70·0
wages and salaries .	55·5	59·8
Forces' pay .	1·5	1·3
employers' contributions*	2·5	8·9
Income from self-employment of which:	12·5	9·1
professional persons .	2·0	1·5
farmers .	1·5	2·1
others .	9·0	5·5
Income from property .	22·5	9·3
Grants from public authorities .	5·5	11·6

* To National Insurance and other superannuation schemes.

The types of income which fell as a percentage of the total are incomes of self-employed persons— a diminishing group—and incomes from property. During the war and for several years afterwards property incomes changed little—the effects of rent control, excess profits tax, and low interest rates were such that these incomes did not rise, while other incomes increased sharply. Subsequently there was a rise, as rent control on some property was lifted and as interest rates increased. In the latter part of the 1960s there was a growing recession in the economy. There was also an acceleration in the rate of wage increases but often prices could not be raised correspondingly because of the need to keep British products competitive with those of other countries. These developments contributed to a squeezing of the share of profits in national income. We see that the share of property incomes (profits, interest, and rents) in 1976 was less than half of what it had been in 1938. Over this third of a century there was a fundamental redistribution of income away from property-owners towards employees.

Inequality of Income.

In the tax-year 1974/75 nearly one seventh of income-receivers had incomes under £1,000 and one third under £1,500. The richest 47 per cent received 69 per cent of total income, the richest 17 per cent received 35 per cent, and the top 3 per cent received 12 per cent of the total. Thus Britain is far from being an egalitarian society. Income is still unevenly distributed, but not so unevenly as before the war, when the top 1 per cent received 16 per cent of total income.

Taxes on income are of course highly progressive, rising sharply as income increases. Those with no incomes pay no income tax, and in so far as they are pensioners, no compulsory contributions either. We see from the table that the proportion of income paid in direct taxes is about 6 per cent on incomes under £1,000 per annum, is 16 per cent in the income range £2,000-2,999, and is 42 per cent on incomes over £10,000.

This tax burden somewhat changes the distribution of incomes. After tax the top 17 per cent received 32 per cent of income and the top 3 per cent 9·5 per cent. But the redistributive effect of taxation must not be overstressed: the levelling of incomes before tax has been of greater importance in making Britain rather more egalitarian than has been taxation policy.

WEALTH OF INDIVIDUALS IN BRITAIN, 1974

Range of net wealth. (£000)	As percentage of total.	
	Number of cases.	Value of wealth (£m).
0·9	18·1	1·3
1–2·9	25·4	5·5
3–4·9	11·8	5·5
5–9·9	21·9	19·3
10–14·9	11·5	16·9
15–19·9	4·0	8·5
20–24·9	2·2	6·0
25–49·9	3·4	13·8
50–99·9	1·2	9·8
100–199·9	0·4	5·9
200–	0·1	7·5
Total	18·837m	£157,100m

Income and Spending Power.

In various ways figures for incomes alone underestimate the degree of inequality in British society. First, incomes are defined for income tax purposes. Any allowed expenses are excluded; and for the self-employed and the higher ranks of management the expense allowance now adds substantially to spending power. Second, if one buys an asset which then rises in value one gains extra spending power. Such capital gains can be very important to the wealthy in periods of boom in ordinary share prices, land prices and house prices—as experienced in Britain in the 1950s and 1960s. Yet only in 1965 did capital gains become taxable and even then the rate of tax on capital gains was low in relation to the rate on additional income.

Inequality of Wealth.

Spending power depends not only on income and capital gains but also on the sheer amount of capital owned. Data on the ownership of capital in Britain have to be estimated indirectly from information arising in connection with the payment of death duties, supplemented by information from capital transfer tax returns and therefore cannot always be relied upon. An alternative method is to estimate the stock of wealth by working back from information on investment income, but this approach is also prone to error. However, it appears from the table that individuals owning more than £10,000—just over a fifth of all individuals—owned two thirds of total wealth in 1974, while the richest 5 per cent owned 37 per cent of the total. And this in spite of a growing tendency for the rich to pass on their capital before death to avoid death duties (now capital transfer tax). The vast majority own very little, and Britain is still far from being a property-owning democracy. There is a natural tendency for the inequality of wealth to grow because the higher income groups tend to save a higher proportion of their income, and so to accumulate capital more readily. The Government by capital transfer tax has had to neutralise this tendency. There is some evidence that in the last decade the inequality of wealth has been reduced. Between 1962 and 1973 the share of the wealthiest 1 per cent fell from 27 to 22 per cent of total wealth, and that of the wealthiest 25 per cent from 79 to 73 per cent.

Wages and Salaries.

In 1976 no less than 70 per cent of personal income was paid in the form of wages and salaries. The distinction between the two is very much a matter of convention; many salary-earners now earn less than wage-earners, and a more important

GROSS WEEKLY EARNINGS,
GREAT BRITAIN
(Median earnings, adults. April 1977)

	Manual	Non-Manual
Men . . .	£68·2	£81·1
Women . . .	£42·6	£49·2

BRITISH INCOMES BY SIZE, 1973/74

Range of incomes before tax.	As percentage of total.			Rate of tax as percentage.
	Number of incomes.	Incomes before tax.	Incomes after tax.	
–£999	14·5	5·3	6·0	5·6
£1000–1499	19·0	10·8	11·6	11·5
£1500–1999	19·1	15·2	15·8	14·2
£2000–2999	30·1	33·4	34·2	15·6
£3000–4999	14·2	23·4	23·0	18·8
£5000–9999	2·5	7·3	6·5	26·6
£10,000–19,999	0·6	3·3	2·3	41·5
£20,000–	0·1	1·5	0·7	63·3
Total . . .	20·842m	£45,907m	£37,862m	17·5

division is between those salary-earners who are paid monthly and the rest. Even though weekly-paid staff do not now earn more than wage-earners, they may still in effect be better off; for they generally work shorter hours, are more likely to be covered by private superannuation schemes, and usually work in better conditions. The table shows the earnings of manual and non-manual workers.

Earnings by Occupation.

Different occupations command different pay, as the table shows. The figures are of *median* earnings, *i.e.*, the earnings of the middle worker within each occupation when workers are arranged in descending order of pay. The structure of pay reflects in part the amount of responsibility which the different jobs entail. The differentials reflect

MEDIAN GROSS WEEKLY EARNINGS OF FULL-TIME ADULT MALE EMPLOYEES, BY SELECTED OCCUPATION, APRIL 1976.

	£ per week
Medical practitioner	123·3
University teacher	120·4
Architect	100·8
General manager	93·9
Engineer, civil or structural	87·7
Primary teacher	86·3
Works or production manager	83·8
Accountant	81·9
Furnaceman	76·3
Coal miner, face-trained	75·1
Policeman (below sergeant)	74·8
Docker, stevedore	74·4
Electrician, maintenance	71·6
Railway engine driver	69·7
Compositor	67·5
Bus conductor	65·3
Plumber, pipe fitter	62·7
Postman, mail sorter	61·5
Bricklayer	60·4
Telephonist	59·3
Dustman	56·4
Junior clerk	54·8
Hospital porter	54·2
Unskilled building worker	53·6
Butcher, meat cutter	46·0
Shop assistant	45·1
General farm worker	43·6
Total workers	**65·8**
of which: *Manual*	**62·1**
Non-manual	**73·9**

also the ease of entry into various occupations. This in turn depends on the degree of specialised knowledge, skill or talent required, and in a few cases it depends on the extent to which artificial barriers to entry have created scarcity. The structure of pay is also influenced, of course, by the degree of organisation and bargaining strength of workers in different occupations.

Within the manual occupations the difference between skilled, semi-skilled and unskilled pay is now small. There has been a narrowing over the years. This was most marked during the war, in the years immediately after the war and since 1970 when skilled workers were only granted the same flat rate advances as unskilled.

Occupational differentials have been a major source of industrial strife in some industries. In engineering, for instance, there has been continued conflict between unions with membership largely among the skilled and those with membership largely among the less skilled, over what forms demands for wage increases should take. On the railways there has been similar strife. Because of the importance placed on occupational differentials in collective bargaining there exist powerful rigidities in the structure of earnings in Britain.

Earnings by Industry.

Even within the manual occupations there are significant differences in earnings among industries. These are associated with the bargaining strength of different groups of workers, with the prosperity of the industry, and with the average skill levels required in production. Coal mining is one of the highest paying industries. Manufacturing industries also pay relatively well. Public administration (including local government roadmen and the like) is a low-wage sector.

Earnings by Sex.

The table also shows very significant earnings differences within each industry between men and women. There are two possible reasons why women are paid less than men. One is that they are crowded into lower-paying occupations. This may be because their attachment to the labour force is weak, and therefore neither they nor their employers have much incentive to invest in training. The second reason is that they may have lower pay than men within the same occupation. The Equal Pay Act (1970) obliged a firm to pay men and women, who are doing the same job, the same wage by the end of 1975. In 1970 women in manual occupations had average earnings which were only half those of men, but by 1976 this figure had risen to over 60 per cent. This change is explained by the impact of the Act and by flat rate general increases agreed under incomes policies.

Overtime and Short-time.

The earnings of any individual worker depend on many factors, and are usually well above the basic wage rate payable for a *standard working-week*. They include overtime earnings; and over-time working is common for men. In most weeks about 1½–2 million operatives in manufacturing—about a third of the total—will be working over-time to the extent of 8 to 9 hours. Even in 1971—a year of high unemployment—the average amount of overtime worked by full-time male manual employees over all industries was 6 hours per employee (including those who worked none); with the average standard working-week being 40 hours, the average hours actually worked were therefore 46. The average working-week has fallen very little since before the war, although the standard week has been significantly reduced. In

AVERAGE WEEKLY EARNINGS OF MANUAL WORKERS IN CERTAIN INDUSTRIES (£p)
(April 1977)

	Men	Women
Paper, printing and publishing	78·4	46·8
Chemicals	77·2	45·5
Mechanical engineering	74·0	49·7
Food, drink and tobacco	72·6	46·4
Textiles	67·1	42·0
All manufacturing*	74·2	45·0
Transport and communication	76·6	56·1
Distributive trades	60·5	38·7
All industries*	71·5	43·7

* Including industries not listed.

most industries it was cut from 48 to 44 hours soon after the war, a 42-hour week was introduced between 1960 and 1962, and there was a movement towards a 40-hour standard working-week in the late 1960s.

Short-time, the working of less than the standard week, has not been common since the war. It has been important in particular industries at particular times; but even at the end of 1971—with a national rate of unemployment of over 4 per cent—it was far smaller than overtime. Then 100,000 operatives in manufacturing were on an average short-time of 12 hours a week—a total 1·2 million hours lost as against 12·8 million hours of overtime in the same week.

Earnings and Rates.

Overtime is not, however, the main reason why earnings exceed minimum wage-rates; for most workers earn very much more than the minimum in the standard working-week. One reason is payment by results, the system of payment under which the worker's wage depends partly on output. A common form is still the piecework system, under which pieceworkers are paid a fixed low rate per hour for each hour worked plus a fixed piecework price for each operation performed; but increasingly employers tend to prefer, as a more effective incentive, some scheme under which the bonus payment is related to the output of a larger group or to that of a whole factory. With such incentive schemes, earnings rise as productivity rises, and, as usually such workers also participate in advances in wage-rates negotiated between employers and unions, the gap between earnings and wage-rates tends to widen for them. So workers not paid on incentive systems press for similar advances for themselves, and in times of booming trade get them under a wide variety of names and forms—merit payments, lieu rates, compensation bonuses, etc.

Between 1955 and 1976 wage-rates rose by 449 per cent and earnings by 514 per cent. The advance in rates was more than the rise in prices, which was 265 per cent, but for much of the period anyone who actually earned the minimum rate throughout was not much better off. Earnings, on the other hand, rose considerably more than prices, so that a major source of the extra real income of the working class is to be found in the widening gap between earnings and rates.

Wage Negotiation.

In Britain there were c. 12 million trade union members in 488 unions in 1975. Most of these unions are very small, almost 326 having less than 2,500 members, but 25 have a membership of over 100,000. The main job of unions is collective bargaining with employers, and in most industries most employers also belong to associations which bargain collectively on their behalf. Some big firms, however, prefer to remain outside the associations, and strike their own bargain with the unions. Before the war many firms tried to encourage the formation of Company Unions, i.e., of unions confined to employees of a single firm; but this is now uncommon. In some lowly paid trades—catering, baking, dressmaking, agriculture and others—minimum wages are fixed by Wages Boards or Councils set up by the Department of Employment: and representatives of the workers and employers, and independent members, meet together to reach agreement on the settlement to be recommended to the Minister. But over most of industry the aim of collective bargaining is to reach voluntary agreement, and the Department of Employment intervenes only when no agreement is reached. In 1974 the Labour Government set up the *Advisory Conciliation and Arbitration Service* (A.C.A.S.) to provide independent mediation and arbitration services.

The usual pattern of negotiation is like this. First, the union puts in a claim for an all-round increase, usually much larger than it expects to get. Then after a time the employers reply, often offering a much smaller increase, and sometimes none at all. They then argue round a table until either they reach agreement or they definitely fail to reach agreement. If the latter happens the next step varies considerably from industry to industry. Many industries have their own "conciliation" machinery, in which outsiders try to help the two sides to reach agreement. Some, though not many, also have their own "arbitration" machinery, in which outsiders can recommend a solution of the dispute, which is sometimes binding and sometimes not. It depends on what the two sides have agreed on in advance. Many industries have no machinery of their own and until 1974 depended on the general facilities the Minister responsible could offer. Since then they have relied on the services of the A.C.A.S. Just as neither unions nor employers were obliged to

call in the Minister, so now they are under no obligation to call in the A.C.A.S.: the unions may opt to put pressure on the employers immediately either by strike action, or by banning overtime or piecework, or by other action.

After the Second World War plant bargaining developed as an increasingly important supplement to industry-wide bargaining in many sectors of the economy. Initially this was largely informal bargaining, with shop-stewards (unpaid lay trade union officials at the plant level) negotiating with management about, for example, special rates for working new machines. It is this, which to a large degree was responsible for the growing gap between wage rates and earnings. The Donovan Commission, which was set up to inquire into the state of industrial relations and which reported in 1968, also saw it as the major cause of many of Britain's industrial relations problems, such as a high level of strike activity. Realising that it was impossible to put the clock back, the Commission recommended that plant bargaining procedures should be formalised, giving, for instance, proper channels for the resolution of wage disputes. Since then there has indeed been an increase in *formal* plant negotiations, with many plants now setting their own wage rates and using national agreements purely as a minimum benchmark. This development has probably improved the climate of industrial relations.

It, however, did little to increase the Government's power to control wages directly or to impose agreements—if anything quite the reverse. The recent attempts to introduce compulsion in wage-determination are described in Part IV.

Strikes.

The strike is the unions' weapon of last resort. Most unions maintain strike funds in order to support their members when they call them out on strike; but these funds are small, and strike pay is usually very much below normal wages. So unions cannot afford to call strikes irresponsibly, and major official strikes are uncommon. In most years there will be one or two, but not more, and the total number of working-days lost is usually negligible—less than one day per head. Even in the industry affected the lost working-days are usually made up in the following weeks by overtime. Nevertheless, the big strikes are important; for the success or failure of one big strike can affect the results of all the other collective bargaining under way at the time.

Most strikes are neither large nor official nor about wages. An official strike is one called by a union, usually by decision of the national executive, and is usually the result of collective bargaining about wages. But unofficial strikes called by local leaders are often about other matters. Few of the big unofficial strikes which have plagued the docks since the war were about wages; rather they reflected job insecurity and the poor state of labour relations in that industry. Much the same may be said about the continual strikes in shipbuilding, many of them caused by demarcation disputes concerning which jobs should be done by which type of skilled worker. Other strike-prone industries are mining and vehicles. In most industries there are very few strikes, and even in shipbuilding, with the worst record of disputes, losses average little more than one day a year. But strikes are often a symptom of industrial trouble—frequently occurring in industries with stagnant productivity and declining employment. They are sometimes really a form of industrial protest, and employers have to bear their share of the blame.

From the mid 1950s the number of strikes in Britain tended to increase, except in coal mining. In 1969 and 1970 there was a huge jump in both the number of stoppages and working days lost. After that industrial disputes fell to a more normal level. But is Britain particularly strike prone compared with other countries? Making allowances for the size of their labour forces, Sweden and West Germany have fewer strikes and lose fewer working days than Britain. The United States has less strikes, but the ones they have are very large, and thus they lose more working days than the U.K. The strike records of Australia

WAGES AND PRICES
(1955=100)

	Weekly wage rates.	Weekly earnings.	Index of retail prices.	Real wage rates.	Real earnings.
1950	73	68	77	96	91
1955	100	100	100	100	100
1960	124	130	114	109	114
1965	151	175	136	112	129
1970	202	250	170	119	147
1976	549	614	365	150	168

and France are most comparable with the U.K.'s.

In its Industrial Relations Act of 1971 the Conservative Government laid down new laws for the regulation of industrial relations and for the curbing of strikes. However, the Act was repealed by the incoming Labour Government in 1974. Since then there has been a panoply of legislation. The main elements of this have been the Trade Unions and Labour Relations Act, the Employment Protection Act, and the Trade Unions and Labour Relations (Amendment) Act. As well as increasing legal protection for the individual employee and extending trade union immunities and rights, this legislation has been concerned to improve industrial-relations practice. The belief behind the legislation is that this can be done by machinery which ensures, for example, that employers formally recognise unions for collective bargaining purposes and that unions have greater access to information to enable them to negotiate about issues (such as a firm's investment plans) which previously ignorance had precluded them from doing.

Prices and Real Incomes.

The aim of a trade union is to get for its members a higher standard of living, and its success depends on the extent to which wage advances exceed the rise in the cost of living. Prices rose very rapidly (by over 30 per cent) between 1949 and 1953, and earnings only just kept ahead in this period. But since then *real earnings* (*i.e.*, the command which money earnings have over goods and services) rose steadily until 1974. Since then there has been some interruption to this trend (*see* Part IV).

Price Changes.

In the calculation of real wages it is usual to make use of the *index of retail prices*, commonly called the cost-of-living index. The index is calculated monthly by the Department of Employment, and it naturally has an influence on the course of wage negotiations. Indeed, up to 1958 it was probably the dominant influence and sometimes automatic adjustment for cost-of-living was written into wage agreements.

The table shows how consumers allocate their expenditure among different commodities in Britain, and how the prices of these commodities

have moved over time. Almost 30 per cent of expenditure in 1970 was on food; and housing, fuel, and light between them accounted for 18 per cent. Drink and tobacco represented 11 per cent; and expenditure on transport and vehicles no less than 12 per cent. Comparing the allocation of expenditure in 1952 and in 1970, we see in particular the growing importance of housing and the declining importance of food in household budgets.

Price changes have not been the same for all types of goods. For instance between 1956 and 1970, when the total index rose by 65 per cent, housing went up by 122 per cent and fuel and light by 90 per cent; but the prices of food, clothing and especially durable household goods rose less than the average. It is partly the fall in the *relative* price of food and partly the fact that as people grow richer they choose to spend less of their income on food which accounts for the declining share of food in total expenditure.

The general retail price index is calculated by weighting each of the commodity price indexes by the proportionate importance of that commodity in total expenditure in a particular year, and then summing all the indexes, *i.e.*, the general index is a *weighted average* of its constituent indexes. A different pattern of expenditure would mean a different set of weights, and hence a different cost-of-living index. For instance, the poor—and particularly pensioners—spend a higher proportion on the basic necessities: food, fuel and light, and housing. It is possible that the cost-of-living rose more for the poor than for the rich over these years.

The cost-of-living index has not risen evenly in Britain. There were spurts of rapid inflation in the periods 1950–52 and 1954–56, followed by a decade of relatively little inflation (averaging 2·9 per cent per annum). After 1967, however, the rate of inflation accelerated, rising progressively from 2·5 per cent per annum between 1966 and 1967 to 7·1 per cent between 1971 and 1972.

The Causes of Inflation.

(i) Import Prices.

Prices charged in the shops are determined by a great many factors, over many of which the Government has little or no control. First among these is the price of imports. Prices of imported

INDEX OF RETAIL PRICES
(January 1956 = 100)

	1952 Weight*.	1970 Weight*.	Monthly average index.					
			1950	1955	1960	1965	1970	1975
Food	399	298	98	98	107	124	155	320
Drink	78	66	}94	100	98	127	156	343
Tobacco	90	64		98	112	146	169	251
Housing	72	119	83	98	132	169	222	396
Fuel and light	66	61	65	92	117	150	190	362
Durable household goods	62	60	80	94	98	107	129	213
Clothing and footwear	98	86	83	98	104	114	132	223
Transport and vehicles	—	126	—	—	118	135	167	319
Services	91	55	73	97	115	147	200	374
Other goods	44	65	77	96	120	140	183	324
All items	*1000*	*1000*	*74*	*97*	*111*	*132*	*165*	*304*

*i.e., proportionate importance of items in total expenditure in 1952 and in 1970.

food and raw materials are determined in the world markets, in which Britain is only one of many purchasers. In the raw material markets the U.S.A. is usually the dominant purchaser, and prices depend greatly on the level of economic activity there. In the food markets British purchases are more important, since the U.S.A. grows most of its own food, and is a large exporter of some foods. Prices in raw material markets are continually changing, and can fluctuate wildly. For instance, the average price of copper rose 70% between 1972 and 1973, and almost halved in six months during 1974. The free market price of sugar quadrupled in the period from October 1973 to October 1974. The big increases in commodity prices occurred during the Korean war and in the well-synchronised world boom of 1972 and 1973 (see G40–1). The sharp increases in the prices of primary commodities contributed to British inflation at these times, but for most of the post-war period the rise in import prices has been less rapid than the domestic inflation. Imports cannot be primarily blamed for the continuing inflation, nor for the acceleration of inflation after 1967 (see G54). The source has to be looked for in the tendency of wages, salaries, profits, and other incomes to rise faster than real output; and this they have done in almost every year since the war.

(ii) Demand-Pull Inflation.

An alternative explanation of inflation is that it arises not so much from increased costs as from demand pressures increasing prices and profits. If there is an increase in aggregate demand for goods and services in the economy, how does the economy respond? If it is operating at less than full employment, producers are able to expand their production to meet the additional demand. But if full employment has already been achieved, it is the price level and not production which rises. Given an excess demand for goods and services, there is competitive bidding for the limited supplies and producers are able to sell at higher prices. A more sophisticated version of this argument recognises that full employment cannot be precisely defined: rather, there are degrees of less or more unemployment. Bottlenecks appear in different firms and industries at different stages; so that any increase in demand is met by an increase in both prices and production. But the lower the rate of unemployment, the more does the response take the form of price increases.

A variant of the demand-pull theory is the so-called *quantity theory of money*, in which inflation is seen as a response to an increase in the supply of money: there is too much money chasing too few goods. The theory dates back at least to David Hume, but it was generally discredited as a result of the writings of Maynard Keynes in the 1930s. However, it was recently revived by Milton Friedman and has received some measure of acceptance among economists in the United States (see G26).

The evidence for the demand-pull theory of inflation in Britain is very slight. No doubt there are times at which demand contributes to inflation in the economy as a whole or in particular sectors. Thus, for instance, the great shortages during and immediately after the war would no doubt have generated rapid demand inflation had it not been for rationing and price controls; and the spurt of inflation between 1954 and 1956 was associated with a very high pressure of demand. On the other hand, inflation has occurred even in periods of relatively high unemployment. Moreover, the method by which most firms price their products is on the basis of their costs; so that most prices are not directly sensitive to the pressure of demand. A more plausible mechanism by which demand might influence prices indirectly is through its effect on wages.

(iii) Wages and Inflation.

When a trade union negotiates a wage advance for all or most employees in an industry, firms will immediately consider whether they should increase their prices to cover their increased wage-costs. As it is common practice for firms to fix the selling prices of their products by first calculat-

ing the direct cost of labour and of materials, and then adding on a percentage to cover overhead costs and profits, they will tend to want to raise their prices not only to cover the cost of the wage advance, but also to cover their percentage addition. Moreover, in deciding whether or not their customers will stand for such increases, firms will be influenced by the knowledge that their competitors have to pay the increased wages too, and will probably therefore be raising their prices. So industry-wide wage advances—and changes in costs of materials—are particularly likely to be passed on to the consumer; and, as wage-earners are also consumers, to generate further demands for wage advances to cover the increased prices. Profits per unit also go up under this tendency to set prices on a *cost-plus* basis; but it is the wage advance which tends to set the spiral off, by providing the opportunity for price increases.

Once this spiral gets going, it is very hard to stop it. In general, the requirement is that wage earnings should not rise faster than productivity (output per man). But as in some industries productivity is very slow to rise, and as it would be unfair and impracticable to exclude their workers from participating in any general rise in the standard of living, this requirement means that in industries with a rapid growth of productivity wage advances should be kept well below the rate of rise of productivity. For two reasons this is rather difficult. First, rising productivity often raises the wages of some workers in these industries automatically, because they are paid by results or through some incentive scheme. The rise of wages from this source takes the form of a tendency on the part of earnings in these industries to rise faster than wage-rates; but that does not mean that all employees benefit, or that the unions in these industries will not press for the same rate of increase in wage-rates as is achieved in the slowly-growing industries. Second, employers in the rapidly-growing industries have far less reason to resist demands for wage increases than those in slowly-growing industries. Indeed, they are quite likely to bid up wages in order to get the labour they need, rather than to try to hold down wages.

There are therefore major problems in preventing a faster rise in wages than in productivity, with its consequence of rising prices. And once a wage-price spiral has started, the problems become more acute because unions and employers become accustomed to substantial annual advances in money wages. A main source of continuing price inflation has been the tendency of money wages to continue to advance at a rate that was appropriate when the cost-of-living was going up sharply, but ceased to be appropriate in later years.

(iv) The Phillips Curve.

Even if wage behaviour is primarily responsible for inflation, the pressure of demand may still be important. If unemployment is low and unfilled vacancies high, there is competitive bidding among employers to obtain or retain their workers. Moreover, with the economy booming the bargaining strength of trade unions increases: employers are more willing to concede wage demands. These possibilities have led economists to postulate—and indeed to measure—the so-called *Phillips Curve* relationship: the lower the level of unemployment, the faster the rate of increase in wages. Such a relationship has been found to exist in the British economy over some periods. But events after 1967 reveal the danger of postulating "general laws" in economics: inflation accelerated despite high and growing unemployment (see G53). Clearly, changes in the cost-of-living, expectations for the future, Government policies and the degree of militancy of trade unionists can all have a significant influence on wage behaviour; and the level of demand may at times be relatively unimportant. There are many schools of thought attempting to explain this, but it is possible to discern two general approaches. The first is that trade unions behave reactively. In other words, they respond in their wage demands to their expectations about prices and Government policies. The second is that, as well as responding to their perception of the events they face, they act in a more initiatory way—to fulfil, for example, aspirations (developed perhaps over a long period of time) about what their real earnings, and therefore their share of the national cake, should be. In striving to realise these aspirations, they may be relatively unaffected by concern over rising unemployment.

The Effects of Inflation.

British Governments have been concerned about inflation mainly because of its effects on British competitiveness, and hence on the balance of payments. If our costs rise relative to competitors' costs, British exporters find it more difficult to compete in foreign markets if they raise their prices; and if they keep prices down in order to compete, this implies their having to accept lower profit margins on exports than on sales in the home market, and so discourages exporting.

But inflation can have other harmful consequences. It often produces a redistribution of income, with the strong gaining at the expense of the weak, *i.e.*, the poorly organised workers and the pensioners. In inflationary conditions income gains can appear to result not so much from work or sacrifice as from ingenuity and speculation and the exercise of economic and political power. Inflation can breed uncertainty, insecurity and industrial unrest. For instance, during the rapid inflation of 1970 the number of strikes was up by 60 per cent on the annual average for 1960–66, and the number of working days lost was up by 250 per cent. This was partly a cause but also partly an effect of the inflation.

Government Policy against Inflation.

There are several possible methods of attack on the inflationary spiral of wages and prices. Their usefulness will depend on the causes of the inflation.

One policy appropriate to most inflations, and also helpful to other objectives of economic policy, is to achieve a faster rate of productivity growth. The faster the growth of average productivity the faster can average incomes rise without an increase in average prices. Only if faster growth in productivity raised the growth of money wages proportionately would the inflation not be reduced. Comprehensive and detailed government control of wages except as an emergency policy was thought for a long time to be impractical for political and institutional reasons, as was comprehensive and detailed control of prices. Experience suggested that such detailed policy, except as a temporary general " freeze ", would be very difficult to operate and, if successful, would involve a major loss of flexibility in the economy. At the other extreme, general exhortations to unions to exercise restraint on wages, and to manufacturers to exercise restraint on prices, were thought to have little effect. After 1974 more people began to think that a semi-permanent incomes policy might in fact be a viable policy tool. This development is discussed in Part IV.

The Government can attempt to regulate inflation by controlling purchasing power through its monetary and fiscal policies, the nature of which will be examined below. There is a danger that curbing demand also curbs the growth of output and productivity in the economy; so conflicting with other objectives of economic policy. Moreover, there is no certainty that inflation is sensitive to the rate of unemployment over the politically acceptable range of unemployment; and experience in Britain after 1967 suggests that it is not.

There is no easy solution—difficulties and disadvantages are attached to every measure for controlling inflation. In Part IV we shall discuss the solutions which have been attempted since 1960.

4. MONEY, BANKING AND FINANCE

Economic Objectives and Demand Management.

The various economic objectives—full employment, balance of payments equilibrium, the control of inflation, *etc.*—which, as mentioned in Part 1, have been shared by all post-war British Governments, are all to a greater or a lesser extent dependent for their attainment upon the type of *demand management* policy pursued by the government. By this is meant the policy, or set of policies, with which the government seeks to regulate the total level of expenditure on goods and services. The latter is the sum of consumption and investment expenditure by both the private sector (firms and consumers) and the public sector (the government and the nationalised industries). If the resulting level of aggregate demand for output is greater than the amount which can be produced with the economy's resources the result will be shortages leading to inflation and/or an increased demand for imports. If the level of demand is not high enough, on the other hand, the result will be a waste of resources, *i.e.* workers will be unemployed and capital equipment will be underutilised. Hence it is crucial for the government to keep the pressure of demand at an appropriate level by regulating the various types of expenditure making up the total.

Fiscal and Monetary Policy.

One way in which the government can attempt to regulate demand is by fiscal policy, *i.e.* the regulation of taxes and public expenditure (*see* G46). If the government believes, for example, that the level of demand is too high, it may seek to reduce it by raising taxes whilst leaving public expenditure unchanged, thereby reducing its *budget deficit* (*i.e.* the excess of public spending over tax revenue). Since the private sector's expenditure plans are financed partly out of its after-tax income and partly out of borrowing, an increase in taxes will generally reduce private sector expenditure, so that total expenditure then falls if public expenditure is held constant. Conversely, the government can cut taxes or increase public spending if it wants to expand the economy by increasing total expenditure.

However, fiscal policy of this type is not independent of *monetary policy*, *i.e.* the regulation of interest rates or the stock of money in the economy. For example, if the government increases public spending it has to pay for the various resources which this involves. The finance may come from additional taxes, but if the government does not raise taxes the extra expenditure then has to be paid for in one of two ways: either the government increases its borrowing from the private sector by issuing government stock in return for money to pay for public expenditure; or the government prints new money for this purpose. In the latter case the supply of money is increased; in the former case interest rates will generally be increased, since the private sector will probably require higher interest rates if it is to be induced to lend extra funds to the government.

Economic Controversies.

Thus changes in the government's " fiscal stance " (*i.e.* the size of its Budget deficit) necessarily involve monetary changes in the form of interest rate and/or money supply changes. There is a great deal of controversy amongst economists about what sort of monetary policy the government should follow—*i.e.* how it should finance its budget deficit—and about the importance of monetary policy as an influence upon the level of demand for output. Broadly speaking, the so-called " monetarist " school of economists, the leading exponent of which is Professor Milton Friedman, believes that the supply of money (and its rate of increase) is the main determinant of the level of demand. They therefore argue that the government must control the rate of growth of the money supply: if it grows too fast, so will aggregate demand, with consequent inflationary and balance of payments problems. The implication is that a large Budget deficit must be financed by borrowing—even if this causes a large rise in interest rates—rather than by a rapid expansion of the money supply. In contrast, the so-called " Keynesian " school of economists, following the lead of the late J. M. Keynes, does not believe that changes in the money supply necessarily have a very large or predictable impact upon aggregate demand, and they are therefore less concerned than monetarists about financing a Budget deficit by expanding the money supply. They tend to stress the harm that might result from allowing interest rates to rise.

The remainder of this section describes the working of Britain's monetary system, and the various types of monetary policy followed since the war, and shows why there is so much controversy amongst economists about this aspect of economic policy.

The Definition of " Money ".

Although most people probably have a clear idea of what they understand by " money ", it is in fact an extremely difficult concept to define with precision. Economists tend to define it as anything which is readily acceptable as a means of payment. Evidently "money" in this sense constitutes " cash "—banknotes and coins—and also current account bank deposits, since possession of the latter allows the drawing of cheques which, normally, are a universally acceptable means of payment. The total of cash and current account deposits at any given time is one possible definition of the supply of money existing at that time: it is known as " M1 ", and also as the " narrowly-defined " money supply, since an alternative definition—known as " M3 "—embraces other types of bank accounts (deposit accounts, foreign currency accounts, and public sector accounts) as well as the components of M1. The argument in favour of M3 is that cheques can in practice be drawn on the additional types of account which it includes and that they therefore constitute " money " as defined.

The fact that the money supply can be defined in more than one way poses an obvious problem for monetarists. If it is important to control the money supply, which of the possible monetary aggregates is to be controlled? (Methods of control are outlined below.) This is of some practical importance, since M1 and M3 often grow at different rates. In 1972 and 1973, for example, M3 grew much more rapidly than M1; in 1975 and 1977 the position was reversed. Thus ensuring that, say, M1 grows at a predetermined rate does not necessarily ensure any particular pattern or rate of growth of M3; but it may be that M3 exerts a greater impact on aggregate demand than does M1. The evidence is ambiguous: at some times M1 seems to have been more important, at other times M3. The evidence can also be interpreted as showing that the money supply, however defined, does not have a particularly important or predictable effect upon overall demand—the Keynesian view. It is because the evidence is ambiguous and consistent with several different views, that disagreements between different schools of thought can persist.

Liquidity.

Another problem of definition is that neither M1 nor M3 includes accounts at institutions other than banks, e.g. Post Office accounts, building society accounts. Whilst it is true that cheques cannot be drawn on such accounts—so that they do not in themselves constitute a means of payment in the way that bank accounts do—it is the case that in practice cash—which is a means of payment—can be withdrawn on demand from building societies, etc. If the government controls M1 (or M3) as a means of controlling aggregate demand, therefore, its policy may be circumvented if, say, people run down building society accounts in order to increase their current expenditure. Many Keynesians regard this as a crucial objection to the idea of controlling aggregate demand by controlling the money supply (whether M1 or M3). They argue that what matters for the control of aggregate demand is not "money" but the economy's stock of liquid assets, i.e. assets which can readily be converted into "money", and hence into potential expenditure on current output.

Evidently the sort of accounts at building societies, etc., mentioned above constitute highly liquid assets. (By definition " money " itself is completely liquid.) Other types of financial asset—e.g. long-dated government stock, known as gilt-edged securities (see below)—are less liquid, since although the owner of such assets can easily exchange them for money, he cannot confidently predict the price at which he can do so. For example, he may have to sell at a time when the market price of government stock is unusually low, so that he realises relatively little money from the sale. Thus " liquidity " refers not only to the speed with which assets can be sold, but also to the predictability of the amount of money which the sale will realise. In practice, there is a liquidity spectrum, i.e. a whole range of different types of asset, each possessing a different degree of liquidity. The spectrum includes not only financial assets but also real assets—houses, capital equipment, etc.—the latter being highly illiquid, e.g. selling a house takes a long time, involves high transactions costs, and the sale price is unpredictable.

Liquidity and Expenditure.

There is a crucial difference between Keynesians and monetarists about the working of the liquidity spectrum. Keynesians believe that firms and consumers regard " money " and non-money liquid assets as good alternatives to one another in as much as both provide security, predictability, etc. That is, there is on the Keynesian view a high degree of substitutability between money and other liquid financial assets; and, in contrast, a relatively low degree of substitutability between money and real assets. Monetarists, on the other hand, assume the reverse: relatively high substitutability between money and real assets, relatively low substitutability between money and other financial assets. These different assumptions imply different effects if the government increases the money supply. Monetarists argue that much of the extra money is spent directly on real assets, i.e. there is a strong effect upon aggregate demand for real output. Keynesians argue, in contrast, that much of the extra money is spent on acquiring other financial assets, i.e. the direct effect upon aggregate demand for real output is relatively low. This is not the end of the matter in the Keynesian viewpoint, however: for the increase in demand for financial assets will tend to push up their prices where these are determined in the markets, as in the case of, e.g. gilt-edged securities, and this will tend to lower interest rates. (This happens because gilt-edged securities pay a fixed sum of money each year as interest; hence their proportional interest rate falls as their price rises, and this tends to push down interest rates elsewhere.) When interest rates fall this increases aggregate demand for real output because borrowing—which, as noted above, finances part of private expenditure—now becomes more attractive. Hence an increase in the money supply eventually increases demand for real output in the Keynesian approach; however, the mechanism is less direct than the monetarist one, and the size of the eventual increase in demand is likely to be smaller if, as many Keynesians argue, the demand for output is not very responsive to changes in interest rates.

In the monetarist view, then, changes in the money supply have a strong, direct impact upon aggregate demand; in the Keynesian view, the impact is mainly indirect—being exerted through interest rate changes—and probably weaker. Thus monetarists stress the need to control the money supply regardless of what then happens to interest rates; Keynesians, at least until recently, have tended to argue for stabilising interest rates, regardless of what this implies for the money supply, since this makes it easier for the government to manage the National Debt and the interest charges involved.

The National Debt and Government Borrowing.

In 1977 the National Debt—roughly speaking, the total indebtedness of the government, excluding local government—stood at £68,000 million, equivalent to roughly 0·6 times the annual value of national income (a higher ratio than in most comparable countries). This huge total of indebtedness is mainly the result of vast government borrowing during the war. However, the total continues to rise year by year, reflecting continued government borrowing (although as a proportion of national income it has fallen in the past decade).

The government borrows in several different ways. First, the issue of new bank-notes is a form of borrowing: as seen above, it can be used to finance a budget deficit. Second, it borrows from foreign governments (*see* **G9**). Third, it borrows from companies through tax reserve certificates, whereby company taxes are paid when the taxable profits are earned rather than at the later date when the taxes become legally due. Fourth, it borrows from private individuals through the various forms of national savings, *e.g.* Post Office accounts.

These four types of borrowing result in *non-marketable debt*, *i.e.* an individual who has a Post Office account cannot sell it in the market to another individual. Two other types of borrowing—gilt-edged securities and Treasury Bills—result in *marketable debt*, *i.e.* an individual who owns gilt-edged securities can sell them in the market to someone else. In practice, most gilt-edged and all Treasury Bills are held by institutions—banks, discount houses, etc.—rather than by private individuals. However, whereas Treasury Bills, representing short-term (usually three months) loans to the government are liquid assets (*i.e.* they can quickly be cashed at a predictable price), gilt-edged are illiquid. They represent promises to repay a certain sum of money at a specified date, *e.g.* government stock issued in 1977 had repayment dates ranging from 1979 to 1998, and the average time to repayment of all stock held in the market is about 12 years. Occasionally stock is issued without a repayment date. Owners of such stock are in effect promised a fixed annual interest payment for ever. At any time prior to repayment gilt-edged can be traded, and there is a large market for such trading in which the market price (as opposed to the fixed repayment price) varies widely.

Interest Rates and Debt Financing.

As already seen, such variations in gilt-edged market prices cause changes in interest rates on all financial assets. Aside from the effects on aggregate demand, interest rate changes themselves have a large impact upon the financing of the National Debt, and hence upon overall public expenditure. For example, if restrictions on the growth of the money supply cause interest rates to rise, this increases the interest charges which the government has to pay on its existing debts. Furthermore, the accompanying fall in the market price of government stock may cause potential buyers of new issues of stock to anticipate further falls (*i.e.* further increases in interest rates), in which case they will be reluctant to purchase the stock—and the government unable to finance its budget deficit—unless and until these further changes occur. When they do, the interest charges on the National Debt are further increased; and the market may still be unsettled, excepting yet further changes.

It is problems of this sort which lead many Keynesians to advocate a policy of promoting stable (or at least slowly changing) interest rates—an " orderly market " for financial assets—rather than a predetermined growth rate of the money supply. In other words, Keynesians see monetary policy mainly as a means of easing the financing of the National Debt rather than as a means of controlling aggregate demand. Monetarists object on the grounds that the government cannot in practice stabilise interest rates in this manner. They argue that although the government may be able to stabilise or even reduce interest rates in the short run by a rapid expansion of the money supply, this expansion will itself *increase* interest rates in the longer run. This is because, on the monetarist approach, the monetary expansion increases demand for real output, which in turn generally increases the rate of inflation. If this causes people to expect a higher future rate of inflation, gilt-edged stock then becomes less attractive to investors because of the associated decline in the anticipated real value of its fixed edged therefore falls, which pushes its price down and thus its effective interest rate up. This continues until the effective interest rate has risen sufficiently to offset the higher expected inflation. Interest rates elsewhere tend to get bid up at the same time, since banks, building societies, *etc.*, have to protect their own reserves.

Monetarists therefore distinguish between the *nominal* interest rate, *i.e.* the current money value of the interest rate, and the *real* interest rate, *i.e.* the nominal rate minus the expected rate of price

inflation on real output. They argue that firms and consumers are concerned about the real, not the nominal, interest rate; in this case nominal rates must inevitably rise if inflation increases—which it will do, on the monetarist argument, if the government, in pursuing a Keynesian policy of stabilising interest rates, over-expands the money supply. Hence the monetarists produce a paradox: a monetary policy which seeks to hold interest rates down may instead cause them to rise.

The Trend of Interest Rates in Britain.

It is difficult to deny that some element of the monetarist view of interest rates has operated in the post-war period, especially in more recent years. The accompanying table shows the course of (nominal) interest rates and yields on certain types of financial assets since the war. It can be seen that with the exception of the yield on Ordinary Shares—which is considered later—all rates have shown a trend increase. Since inflation and therefore, in all probability, inflationary expectations have shown a similar trend increase, the rise in nominal interest rates is broadly consistent with the monetarist position. Note particularly the tendency for all rates to peak around 1975–76 and then to decline in 1977. This is consistent with the view that the great rise in inflation in the early 1970s (*see* **G53**) pushed up inflationary expectations, which in turn pushed up interest rates; and that the apparent success of the incomes policy introduced in July 1975 (*see* **G57**) in reversing the rise in inflation led to a similar fall in inflationary expectations and then in interest rates. Note also that the 15 per cent Minimum Lending Rate announced in October 1976, although a post-war record in nominal terms, was probably equivalent to a substantially *negative real* interest rate, given the high inflation rate then operating.

PERCENTAGE YIELD ON FINANCIAL ASSETS
(Range during period)

	Bank rate*	Treasury Bill rate	Long-dated government stock	Industrial ordinary shares dividend yield
1945–50	2	½	2–3	3½–5½
1951–55	2½–4½	1–4	3½–5½	4½–7
1956–60	4½–7	3–6½	5–6	4–7
1961–65	4½–7	3½–7	5–7	4–6
1966–70	5½–8	5½–8	6½–10	3–6
1971–75	6–13	5½–11½	7½–17½	3–12
1976	9½–15	8½–14½	13–16	5–8
1977	5–12	4½–13½	10½–14	5–6

* Minimum lending rate from October 1972.

Although the broad trend of interest rates is consistent with the monetarist view, however, more detailed examination of the evidence also gives some support to the Keynesian approach. For it appears that interest rates adjust relatively slowly to changes in inflationary expectations; and also, that they do not adjust *exactly*—they may adjust proportionately more or less than the change in expectations. There may thus be a good deal of scope for a Keynesian policy of stabilising interest rates in the short and medium term; over a longer period, however, there are reasonable grounds for believing that attention also needs to be paid to controlling the money supply—something which is now accepted, to a greater or a lesser degree, by nearly all Keynesians.

The Commercial Banks.

If the government does adopt the monetarist approach of seeking to control the money supply rather than interest rates, its main need is to find ways of influencing the behaviour of the commercial banks, known in England as the clearing banks. For as seen above, the main component of the money supply is the deposits of the clearing

LONDON CLEARING BANKS, OCTOBER 1977
(£ million)

Eligible liabilities	Eligible reserve assets		Percentage of eligible liabilities
22,080	Balances with Bank of England	356	
	Money at call	1,107	
	UK and N. Ireland Treasury Bills	460	
	Other bills	489	
	British government stock up to 1 year	526	
	Total	2,938	13·3

Total liabilities	Assets		Percentage of total liabilities
38,618	Cash	727	1·9
	Eligible reserve assets	2,938	7·6
	Special and supplementary deposits	649	1·7
	Advances	14,310	37·1
	Investments	2,365	6·1
	Foreign currency assets	5,518	14·3
	Other*	12,111	31·3
	Total	38,618	

* Includes loans in the British market and miscellaneous assets in sterling and foreign currency.

banks, regardless of whether M1 or M3 is the chosen definition.

In Britain there are four main banks with one or more branches in every town. Each of them earns profits by borrowing at low or zero rates of interest—anyone holding a bank account is in effect making a loan to his bank—and lending out part of the resulting funds at higher interest rates. In normal circumstances—i.e. unless there is a run on the banks—not all deposits will be withdrawn at once; therefore the banks need keep only a small proportion of their deposits in the form of cash. This proportion is known as the *cash ratio* and until 1971 the Bank of England required it to be at least 8 per cent. Also, between 1951 and 1971 the Bank of England requested that the banks held liquid assets—Treasury Bills, comercial bills, and money at call and short notice as well as cash—equal to at least 30 per cent of deposits. This was known as the *liquidity ratio*.

In 1971 the government introduced a new policy, generally known as *Competition and Credit Control*, which redefined the liquidity ratio and lowered it to 12½ per cent, this being the banks' required ratio between what were defined as *eligible reserve assets* and *eligible liabilities*. The former comprise balances with the Bank of England, Treasury Bills, some commercial bills and local authority bills, and gilt-edged stock with less than one year to maturity. Eligible liabilities are, after various minor adjustments, sterling deposits. Note particularly that cash holdings are not included in eligible reserve assets. The accompanying table shows the balance sheet of the London clearing banks in October 1977, operating under the 1971 rules.

Controlling the Commercial Banks.

The commercial banks can " create " money because of their ability to accept deposits far in excess of their cash and liquid asset holdings; as economists would say, because they operate under a *fractional reserve system*. If a bank provides an overdraft facility to a customer who then draws cheques on the facility, the recipients of these cheques pay the proceeds into their bank accounts which are thereby enlarged; and this represents an increase in the money supply, since the enlarged accounts can be used to finance additional transactions. Thus any increase in the banks' eligible reserve assets allows them to expand loans, overdrafts, etc.—and thereby the money supply—until eligible liabilities (sterling deposits) have increased by 8 times as much, in order to restore the 12½ per cent reserve ratio.

The government can therefore control the money supply by controlling the components of banks' eligible reserve assets—broadly speaking, their liquid assets. A reduction in the latter can be engineered in various ways. *Open market operations* involve the Bank of England's selling more gilt-edged than it otherwise would; this reduces the banks' liquidity, since, as already seen, gilt-edged are not regarded as liquid assets, so that their purchase involves a drain of liquidity from the banks. At the same time, as already seen, it will generally involve a rise in interest rates. The Bank of England may also put pressure on the banks' liquidity by pushing up interest rates directly *via* an increase in Minimum Lending Rate (known as Bank Rate until 1972); such an increase tends to trigger similar increases in all short-term interest rates, thus making liquid (short-term) assets attractive to a variety of potential purchasers as well as the banks, who may therefore find their own holdings squeezed.

Another technique of monetary control is known as *Special Deposits*, which were introduced in 1960. The idea is that banks are required to place deposits with the Bank of England which, although they earn interest, do not count as liquid assets. Thus the banks' liquidity position is threatened and they may have to reduce advances to preserve their required reserve ratio. As the accompanying table shows, Special Deposits, together with Supplementary Deposits, were 1·7 per cent of total assets in 1977. (Supplementary Deposits were introduced in 1973: the Bank of England declares a permitted maximum rate of growth of interest-bearing deposits over a stated period of time, and any bank which exceeds this rate has to lodge additional special deposits at the Bank of England, on which no interest is paid.)

A fourth method of control is often called " *moral suasion* ", and was much used in the 1960s The government issues direct requests to banks about both the amount of advances to issue to customers and their direction (*e.g.* giving priority to exporting firms over domestic consumers). Under this heading of direct controls by the government also come *hire purchase* controls: a tightening of H.P. deposit and repayment terms can exert a strong and immediate effect upon borrowing, although the impact is mainly upon the relatively narrow sector of the economy producing consumer durables.

The 1971 changes already referred to abolished direct controls and placed the emphasis of policy upon controlling credit through the redefined reserve ratio. It also imposed this reserve ratio on *all* banks—not just on the clearing banks, as had previously been the case—and also on Finance Houses (where a 10 per cent ratio was applied); special deposits could now also be called from these institutions as well as from the clearing banks. There were two reasons for this widening of controls. First, it was felt unfair to the clearing banks to subject them to controls which did not apply to potential competitors. Second, it was seen as a means of rationalising, and obtaining greater control over, an increasingly complicated market for credit: in the previous two decades institutions other than clearing banks had grown in importance as sources of credit, and it had become increasingly anomalous not to seek to influence the whole of the market.

The Stock Exchange.

Whilst short-term credit is mostly provided by banks and Finance Houses, long-term borrowing by companies is undertaken through the Stock Exchange. Firms in the private sector of the economy issue three main types of security on the Stock Exchange. *Debenture Stock* is simply a fixed-interest loan. *Preference Stock* is a fixed-interest loan with provisions for waiving the interest if no profits are earned. The most important type, representing the great majority of holdings, are *Ordinary Shares*. The owner of an Ordinary Share is, legally, a part-owner of the company concerned, with a right to participate in any net profits which it makes (though he has no legal right to any particular level of dividend or interest payment).

In contrast to government stock, a significant proportion of Ordinary Shares is owned by private individuals. However, a growing proportion is owned by insurance companies and pension funds, which have grown in importance as private superannuation schemes have become more widespread. It is likely that the market for Ordinary shares, like that for government stock, will eventually be completely dominated by such large institutional investors.

The attraction of Ordinary Shares to the investor wanting an outlet for his savings is that because they represent a part ownership of the firm concerned, their prices and dividends are likely to rise as the value of the firm increases. This is so whether the firm's value increases in real terms, because it is expanding, or simply in money terms, because of general inflation. Thus Ordinary Shares generally represent a reasonable " hedge " against inflation—unlike fixed-interest securities such as gilt-edged. It is for this reason that, as seen in the earlier table, the dividend yield on Ordinary Shares does not tend to rise with inflation: the demand for Ordinary Shares does not necessarily fall if inflation increases, so that their prices and yields are not affected in the same way as those of gilt-edged and other fixed-interest securities by changes in inflation rates.

The one major deviation of dividend yields and share prices in the post-war period occurred in 1974, when Ordinary Share prices were for a time so depressed that dividend yields rose to 12 per cent (see earlier table). However, this almost certainly reflected the crisis of profitability and liquidity in British industry in 1974 (*see* G48) rather than the rapid inflation of that year; though the latter was in part responsible for a more indirect manner, since it helped to create the liquidity crisis. Apart from 1974, however, dividend yields were virtually no higher in the 1970s than in the 1950s or 1960s, despite much higher inflation rates.

Monetary Policy in Britain.

(i) The Keynesian Era.

Until 1968 British monetary policy was in practice strongly Keynesian in the sense described earlier. That is, the government was mainly concerned with attempting to stabilise interest rates in order to facilitate the management of the National Debt. For although successive governments several times embarked on a policy designed to reduce the rate of growth of the money supply by squeezing banks' liquidity, each such phase of policy was ended when the government concerned found itself unable to countenance the resulting rise in interest rates. This occurred when the banks sought to replenish their liquid assets by selling their gilt-edged holdings, particularly those nearing maturity; the banks preferred to do this rather than call in advances, since the latter were generally more profitable. In practice, it was usually the Bank of England which bought the gilt-edged being unloaded by the banks, thereby undoing the effects of its own monetary squeeze.

In effect, therefore, the Bank of England's priority was to support gilt-edged prices and keep interest rates down, without worrying too much about money supply. Such a policy is often called " permissive " monetary policy, *i.e.* the government supplies whatever amount of money will permit trading to take place at a given set of interest rates, as opposed to laying down a target rate of monetary growth and sticking to it. In adopting a " permissive " monetary policy successive governments were reflecting the intellectual spirit of the times. In the twenty years after the war Keynesian ideas were dominant: the money supply was regarded as a relatively unimportant influence upon aggregate demand, which was best regulated by fiscal methods. Thus large Budget deficits were financed by rapid monetary growth. The high point of Keynesian influence was probably marked by the publication in 1959 of the Report of the Radcliffe Committee on the working of the monetary system. This took a strongly Keynesian line, emphasising the importance of liquidity and suggesting that " money " as such was not merely unimportant as an influence on economic activity, but more or less incapable of precise definition.

(ii) The Monetarist Revival.

Keynesian ideas began to come under increasingly strong intellectual challenge from monetarists in the 1960s, and this has been reflected in the gradual change of policy to a predominantly monetarist stance. The first hint of this came in 1968, when the then Chancellor of the Exchequer, Roy Jenkins, expressed in a " Letter of Intent " to Britain's creditors, the International Monetary Fund, the intention of controlling the growth of the money supply in order to control aggregate demand and thereby help to push the balance of payments into surplus following the 1967 devaluation. The fact that an explicitly monetarist approach was thus made the centrepiece of policy for the first time reflected not only the growing intellectual influence of such ideas in Britain, but also (and probably more importantly) their influence in the I.M.F., which has traditionally favoured the setting of monetary targets.

This trend towards monetarism appeared to have been strengthened by the 1971 measures described earlier: these removed support from the gilt-edged market in order to focus attention upon the control of money and credit. In practice, however, these measures were followed in 1972–73 by a vast expansion of the money supply —M3 rose at an annual rate of nearly 30 per cent— which was the reverse of the policy advocated by monetarists (or indeed by most Keynesians). Other measures adopted at this time—moral suasion in an attempt to limit lending for property development; subsidies to building societies to hold down their interest rates—were also incompatible with the monetarist view that the market should operate freely within a framework of monetary control. Thus in the period 1972–73 policy may have become more monetarist in form, but it was certainly not monetarist in substance.

More recently the monetarist approach has become much more strongly entrenched in policymaking, especially since Britain's application for large I.M.F. credits in the autumn of 1976 (see G41). The government has since then laid down annual target growth rates in M3: for fiscal year 1977–78 the target was to keep the growth of M3 within the range 9–13 per cent. The implication was that if the government's budget deficit was too large to be financed by monetary expansion within that range, the remainder would have to be financed by sales of gilt-edged, even if these sales could be achieved only by large increases in interest rates. In practice, the government found it easy to make very large sales of gilt-edged in 1977, even though interest rates were *falling* from the peak rates which, as seen earlier, they reached in 1976. This may have been because of the effect of short-term " extrapolative " expectations of the type mentioned earlier; *i.e.* if investors see interest rates falling—gilt-edged prices rising— they may expect this trend to continue in the near future, in which case they are keen to buy gilt-edged quickly.

Easy sales of government debt in 1977 may also have resulted from the " market becoming monetarist "; *i.e.* the large institutional investors in the market may themselves have been influenced by monetarist ideas so that they expect falling interest rates (and therefore rising gilt-edged

THE COST OF PUBLIC SERVICES
(£ million)

Expenditure.	1960.	1975.	Percentage increase 1960–75.	Percentage of total 1975.
Defence	1,612	5,189	222	9·5
External relations	172	687	299	1·3
Roads, transport and communication	739	3,997	441	7·3
Industry and trade	562	5,285	840	9·7
Research	99	395	299	0·7
Agriculture, forestry and fishing	324	1,702	425	3·1
Housing	490	4,291	776	7·9
Environmental services	332	2,405	624	4·4
Libraries, museums and arts	30	289	863	0·5
Police and prisons	150	1,166	677	2·1
Education	917	6,840	646	12·6
National health service	861	5,260	511	9·7
Social Security benefits	1,488	8,918	499	16·4
School meals, milk and welfare foods	85	397	367	0·7
Local welfare services and child care	58	1,050	1,710	1·9
Debt interest	1,165	4,513	287	8·3
Other expenditure	316	2,081	559	3·8
Total expenditure	9,400	54,465	479	100·0

prices) to result from a policy of tight control of the money supply. If this is the case, such a policy therefore encourages them to buy gilt-edged quickly before its price rises; and the resulting heavy pressure of demand itself causes such prices to rise and thus pushes down the interest rate.

For this effect to be important, monetarist ideas would have had to become the prevailing orthodoxy, at least amongst investors in financial markets. It is not clear to what extent this is the case in Britain; however, it very probably applies in the United States, where financial markets react strongly, quickly, and in a monetarist direction to short-term movements in the money stock. This has itself become a problem—since the markets may over-react to short-run disturbances—and is one reason for the American adoption of *rolling targets* for monetary expansion; *i.e.* the target annual growth rate for the money stock is revised, say, every few months—which allows temporary disturbances to be incorporated into a new annual target on the assumption that they can be offset later in the new annual period. The more British financial markets become monetarist, the more likely it is that the British government will also adopt the technique of rolling targets as its method of monetary control.

5. ECONOMIC ASPECTS OF THE PUBLIC SERVICES

The Cost of Public Services.

In 1975 total public expenditure was £54,465 million, about £973 per head. Of this total the central government spent about two-thirds, the local authorities about a quarter, and the public corporations' investment programme was responsible for the remaining one-twelfth. Total public expenditure increased six-fold between 1960 and 1975; and rose as a proportion of the national income from 45 to 56 per cent.

The Government collects in revenue considerably more than it spends itself, but transfers funds to the local authorities, to the National Insurance Fund, and to the nationalised industries. The expenditure of the public sector as a whole generally exceeds its revenue, and the difference is met by net borrowing.

A breakdown of public expenditure is shown in the table. Not all categories of expenditure expanded at the same rate: expenditure on industry and trade (mainly the investment of public corporations and capital grants to the private sector), environmental services (water, sewerage, public health, parks, etc.), police and prisons, social security benefits, education, libraries, museums and arts, and local welfare services and child care increased faster than the total; and expenditure on defence, external relations, the agricultural subsidy, roads, transport and communication, research, and debt interest fell behind the total. Nevertheless, defence expenditure

accounted for 9·5 per cent of the total (*i.e.* 5·4 per cent of national income) in 1975.

Council Housing.

Expenditure on council housing amounted to 7·9 per cent of public expenditure in 1975. Housing expenditure consists of two quite different items. There is the capital cost of building new council houses. This is financed out of borrowing by local authorities, both from the Government and from the market. There is also a recurrent cost, in the form of subsidies on counci lhousing. This represents the difference between the cost of housing, including the cost of borrowing, and rents received on council housing.

Up to 1957 the Government contracted to pay a flat subsidy per year on every council house built. From 1957, government subsidies were no longer paid on ordinary new council houses, but in 1961 were reintroduced, in a form intended to encourage councils to charge higher rents on their existing houses. The Labour Government substantially increased the subsidy in 1967.

The 1972 Housing Finance Act made major changes to the system of council housing finance. Councils were in future to charge " fair rents "—the likely market rent for a dwelling if supply and demand for rented accommodation were in balance in the area concerned. The Government was also prepared to finance a rent rebate scheme whereby people in need, both council tenants and private tenants, could claim a rebate according to a formula based on family size and income. A slum clearance subsidy was also to be paid to councils and—to encourage housebuilding—a " rising costs " subsidy whereby the additional costs resulting from council house building were to be subsidised. The system of " fair rents " was ended by the Housing Rents and Subsidies Act of 1975. Under the new Act most Government help would go to new building, the acquisition of land and housing and improving the stock of council housing. Additionally the 1975 Community Land Bill was designed after a period of about five years to give local authorities the power to acquire all land for development at prices based on its value in current use as distinct from its value for development.

The Housing Market.

Government housing policy must be seen in terms of the housing market as a whole. In 1976 there were some 20·6 million dwellings in the United Kingdom, 53 per cent being owner-occupied, 32 per cent being council houses, and the remaining 15 per cent privately rented. The importance of owner-occupation has grown and that of private renting has declined: in 1960 they had accounted for 42 per cent and 32 per cent of the total respectively.

This switch is largely the result of Government

policy. Rent controls have meant that there is little incentive to build houses for renting, nor even to maintain existing rented houses: in 1971 over half the dwellings which had been declared "unfit" in England and Wales were privately rented. On the other hand, Government has given considerable tax advantages to owner-occupiers. Owner-occupied houses are exempt from the capital gains tax introduced in 1964, and owner-occupiers can also obtain tax relief on mortgage-interest payments. Since the abolition of the Schedule A tax in 1961—whereby owner-occupiers paid tax on the rental income imputed to their houses—this tax relief on interest payments must be justified as an inducement to home-ownership; but it is also a considerable subsidy to owner-occupiers, who tend to be the relatively well-off. In the tax-year 1976/77 the British Government gave tax-relief of £1,100 million to house-mortgagees; averaging £206 for each of the 5·3 million owner-occupiers benefiting. This total was only 20 per cent less than the whole of the public subsidy on council housing in the same year.

The year 1953 was a peak for public sector housebuilding in the United Kingdom when 262,000 council dwellings were completed. There was a trough in 1961 (122,000), a peak in 1967 (211,000) and a subsequent fall to 113,000 in 1973, followed by a recovery to 169,000 in 1976. By contrast, the number of private dwellings completed rose steadily from 65,000 in 1953 to a peak of 226,000 in 1968. Thereafter the number fell back to an annual average of slightly less than 200,000 in the early 1970s, and still further to 150,000 a year in 1974–76. The total number of dwellings completed reached a peak of 436,000 in 1968, the total falling back to 279,000 in 1974 and recovering to 324,000 in 1976.

Over the 15 years 1955–70 the rate of inflation in the price of modern existing houses averaged 5 per cent per annum: somewhat faster than the rise in the cost of living. After 1970 there was a great surge in house prices: between December 1970 and December 1972 the average rise was no less than 30 per cent per annum. There are various reasons for this remarkable inflation. Partly it reflected the rapid acceleration of general inflation; in such times it is sensible to hold one's wealth in the form of assets which will appreciate in value. It also reflected the decline in house-building after 1968, and a slowing-down in the rate at which building land became available. The precise timing of the inflation resulted from the sudden and large increase in the availability of building society mortgages. And as the inflation grew, so optimistic expectations helped to raise house prices still further. By 1974 the rate of increase had slowed down considerably and the average price of existing houses for that year as a whole was less than 10 per cent higher than in 1973. The rate of increase slowed even further in 1975 and 1976.

Education.

Educational expenditure rose by no less than 646 per cent between 1960 and 1976, and accounted for 13 per cent of public expenditure in 1976. Between 1961 and 1976 enrolment in all schools in the United Kingdom increased by 28 per cent. In addition, expenditure rose because the more expensive types of education—secondary schools and universities—expanded more rapidly. University enrolment increased from 174,000 in 1965/66 to 269,000 in 1975/76. In that year there were also about the same number of people enrolled for advanced courses at polytechnics and other institutions of further education. More children stayed on at school after reaching the school-leaving age of 15. This percentage increased again with the raising of the school-leaving age to 16 in 1973. For instance, the number of children aged 16 and over at school in the United Kingdom rose from 13 per cent of the 16–18 age-group in 1961 to 26 per cent in 1976.

In December 1972 the Conservative Government published a White Paper setting out plans for the expansion of education over the next decade. More emphasis was to be placed on nursery schooling for the 3- and 4-year-olds: within 10 years it would be available to all children whose parents want them to attend. There would be a school building programme to replace the bad old school buildings. Teacher training would be expanded to reduce pupil-teacher ratios further. Higher education would be expanded less rapidly than in the previous decade, and the emphasis would be placed on polytechnics and other non-university colleges.

It is increasingly recognised that education can be an economic investment for the future just as much as capital formation in, say, machinery or roads. There is a " private return " on " investment in education ", which takes the form of higher earnings over the lifetime of the person educated; and there is a " social return " on public resources devoted to education, being the greater contribution to the national product which trained and educated people can make. The Government published a consultative Green Paper in October 1976. The main theme of this was that greater attention should be paid to fitting children and students to do a job of work. To achieve this, changes in the school curricula were suggested, as was stronger liaison between schools and industry.

Social Security.

There are two forms of social security: *National Insurance* and *supplementary benefits.*

(i) National Insurance.

Under this scheme employees receive rights to unemployment benefit, sickness benefit, retirement pensions, widows' benefits, injury and disablement benefits, etc. For instance, in 1975 553 thousand persons received unemployment benefit, 1·0 million received sickness benefit, there were 8·0 million retirement pensioners and 500 thousand receiving widows' benefits. Weekly rates are laid down for each benefit, e.g. in late 1977 a weekly rate of £14·70 was paid to a single person receiving unemployment benefit or sickness benefit. The basic rate was increased according to the number of dependants: £9·70 for one adult, so much for the first child, etc. In 1966 an earnings-related supplement was introduced for benefits paid to persons between 18 and 65 (men) or 60 (women): the supplement in 1976 being one-third of average weekly earnings between £11 and £30 and 15 per cent of any earnings lying between £30 and £69, and a maximum total benefit, including increases for dependants, of 85 per cent of earnings.

By far the most important benefit is the retirement pension, paid as of right to contributors on retirement. Individuals may increase their rate of pension by staying on at work after the minimum retiring age of 65 for men and 60 for women. In November 1977 the Chancellor raised retirement pensions to £17·50 per week for single persons and to £28 for a married couple.

(ii) The Financing of National Insurance.

The main source of finance for National Insurance payments is the National Insurance Fund. These funds are built up largely from the compulsory weekly National Insurance contributions which most of the adult population have to pay and which amounted to £8,426 million in 1976. In April 1975 there was a fundamental change in the system of contributions. The basic scheme prior to that date is described in what follows. For employees, both employer and employee pay a contribution. The self-employed also pay contributions of smaller size than the sum of the employer's and employee's contribution, but they are not entitled to unemployment benefit and one or two other benefits. Most non-employed persons, other than married women and the retired, have to pay still lower benefits. Weekly contributions include a contribution to the cost of the National Health Service. Both ordinary and contracted-out workers pay a graduated contribution on their earnings between £15 and £105 per week to meet the cost of the earnings-related supplements introduced in 1966.

The National Insurance Scheme is an odd mixture of insurance and tax. The levels of contributions, when the scheme started in 1948, were fixed on the actuarial principle that contributions by or on behalf of an individual plus a specified

State contribution should on average suffice to pay for the benefits to which he was entitled. But the scheme did not allow for inflation and a rising standard of living, and a succession of increases granted in the rate of pensions has put an end to this actuarial probity. Instead the principle became established that the rate of contributions in each year, together with a minor transfer from the Government, should equal the total benefits paid out in that year.

iii) Reform of Pensions.

There are nearly eight million pensioners in Britain. 25 per cent of these are kept out of poverty only by receiving a supplementary pension: it is estimated that another 10 per cent are entitled to a supplementary pension, but do not draw it. Many of the remainder find their living standards considerably reduced from when they were working. This is because the existing state retirement pension is inadequate. There are some occupational pension schemes which offer a better income, but these are rather restricted in their coverage, being available to many more non-manual than manual workers. Like personal savings, many of them also tend to have only limited safeguards against inflation. In an era of rapidly rising prices, the pensioner is at a particular disadvantage. Widows form the poorest groups among them, with about 60 per cent of them needing to draw a supplementary pension.

A scheme for graduated pensions was introduced for employees in 1961. Under the scheme there were two kinds of employees—*ordinary* and *contracted-out*. In the case of contracted-out workers, their employer (on whom the decision whether to contract out rested) had to institute a private superannuation scheme that gave at least as favourable terms as the new State scheme, including the provision that rights under the scheme should be transferable up to the limits of the State scheme. Transferability was the guarantee that the individual did not lose his pension rights when he changed his job. For ordinary workers the contribution depended on earnings. Until April 1975, those earning less than £9 a week paid a flat-rate contribution, which was lower than that paid by contracted-out workers. Those earning more than £9 paid in addition a percentage of the amount by which earnings exceeded £9 up to a limit of £62 and in return received the right to an increased pension on retirement.

In 1969 the Labour Government made proposals in a White Paper to replace the National Insurance Scheme by a new scheme of superannuation and social insurance, in which both contributions and benefits would be related to the earnings of the individual. It argued that the existing scheme failed to provide security in old age. The new earnings-related contributions would be mostly higher than contributions under the existing scheme, especially among higher earners; and in return higher pensions and other benefits would be paid.

An important feature of the proposed scheme was that benefits were to take into account both changes in prices and in general living standards. Thus, for instance, a contributor who received earnings equal to the national average throughout his working life would receive a pension calculated on the national average earnings at the time he reached pension age, not on the money he received over his working life. Some two-thirds of employed men were contracted out, *i.e.*, in occupational pension schemes, in 1970. The Government intended that these schemes should continue to exist together with the State scheme, and it proposed to allow for partial contracting out of the State scheme.

These plans lapsed with the change of Government in 1970. The Conservative Government announced its proposals for reform in a White Paper published in 1971. It considered that the costs of earnings-related benefits would be too great; instead it favoured earnings-related contributions for basically flat-rate pensions. In addition it wished to encourage contracting out, so that almost all employees would also be members of a private occupational pension scheme, in which pensions would be related to past contributions. The Government recognised that it would have to ensure that occupational pension

rights were transferable between jobs. Like the previous Government, it envisaged a legal guarantee that State pensions would be revised every two years. It also envisaged that the share which the State provides from taxation for National Insurance—about 18 per cent of contributions in 1970—would be maintained. Again the plan lapsed with the change of government.

Meanwhile the Government had become aware of the need for a frequent adjustment of pension rates in an era of high inflation. In early 1975 the full pension entitlement was £10 for a single person and £16 for a married couple. In November 1977 the rates stood at £17·50 for a single person and £28 for a married couple. The real need, however, was for fundamental reform. Yet another new scheme went before Parliament in February 1975, and to some extent the scheme has been implemented. The idea is for a two-tier pension. The bottom tier is a common flat-rate for everyone. The top tier is earnings related—that is, it is a fixed proportion of the pensioner's previous earnings. Because of the flat-rate element, a low earner will be able to expect a pension which is a higher percentage of his working income than that obtained by a higher earner. Contributions to the scheme will be earnings related. The pensions will be fully protected against inflation, and women will enter the scheme on the same footing as men. There was an obvious emphasis on the need to protect women from poverty in retirement, after the death of the husband. There will be a maximum pension entitlement and a maximum contribution. For this reason among others, the Government plans to encourage new and improved occupational schemes, to exist alongside the state scheme. It is hoped that the scheme will come to full maturity in twenty years, this long delay reflecting the formidable difficulties in financing the plan. In the meantime fully earnings-related contributions started in 1975. These replaced flat-rate National Insurance payments and graduated pension contributions.

(iv) Poverty in Britain.

Despite the existence of National Insurance there are many people in Britain whose income falls below that which the Government regards as adequate. These people are supported from Government revenues by means of *supplementary benefits*, before 1966 known as *National Assistance*. It is a fault of the National Insurance Scheme that so many have required this assistance. In 1976 there were no less than 3 million recipients of supplementary benefits, of whom nearly two-thirds—1·7 million—were persons over pension age. Another 260 thousand were sick and disabled 680 thousand unemployed and 310 thousand women with dependent children. About a quarter of those on National Insurance retirement pensions also received supplementary benefits.

Supplementary benefits ensure that a certain minimum weekly income is maintained: in late 1977, in the case of a single pensioner £17·90, a pensioner couple £28·35, and an unemployed man with wife and children aged 4 and 7, £34·40. In addition an allowance for housing expenditure is paid. The operation of social security is illustrated in the following example, utilising the data and regulations in force in 1975. Take a worker earning the average weekly gross earnings for adult male workers in November 1975. Assume that this individual has a wife and two children aged 4 and 8 years. While he is working his gross income is supported by National Insurance contributions and income tax, and supplemented by family allowance; his net income being £46·32. If he becomes unemployed or sick, he receives National Insurance benefit, including an earnings-related supplement, and family allowance; his net income being £33·35. But after 6 months the earnings-related supplement lapses: he receives only £25·01 in National Insurance benefits, and is eligible for supplementary benefits to raise his income to £30·57 plus an allowance for housing expenditure. A major fault with the supplementary benefits scheme was that they could not be paid to those in employment whose earnings were below the benefit level, and if such persons became unemployed they could claim benefits only up to their normal earnings level. The *Family*

Income Supplement was introduced in 1971 to alleviate hardship amongst low earners, but it has been estimated that only half of those eligible have claimed F.I.S.

Public Revenue.

We see from the table below that, of the sources of revenue, personal income tax, National Insurance contributions and taxes on capital were the most buoyant over the decade. No less than 54 per cent of the total public revenue in 1976 came from taxes on income; more than half of this being personal income tax. Taxation of profits amounted to only 3 per cent of total public revenue. Taxes on expenditure accounted for 26 per cent of the total. It is interesting to note the growing importance of *direct taxation* (taxes on income) relative to *indirect taxation* (taxes on expenditure on goods and services) over the decade.

Two commodities in particular were heavily taxed: alcoholic drink and tobacco. Together they accounted for almost 10 per cent of public revenue. These commodities are singled out partly for social reasons and partly because—in economists' jargon—the demand for them is *inelastic*; *i.e.*, the public reduces its consumption of drink and tobacco only slightly in response to a rise in their price. Indirect taxation—taking the form of excise duties and purchase taxes (value added tax after 1973)—was spread unevenly over the different sorts of expenditure. In 1970 taxation increased the price of cigarettes by 203 per cent; drink by 69 per cent; consumer durables such as cars by 26 per cent; the running of cars (*e.g.*, petrol) by 93 per cent; clothing by 10 per cent; and food hardly at all. For goods and services in general, tax raised prices by 23 per cent on average. The introduction of Value Added Tax in 1973 tended to even out the incidence of indirect taxes on different goods and services.

The Budget.

Each year in April the Chancellor of the Exchequer announces his Budget for the coming fiscal year. The most important and most difficult task in drawing up the Budget is to decide on the size of deficit to aim for. The deficit is the excess of public expenditure over public revenue; and it has to be financed by borrowing from the private sector. A large deficit is reflationary; sometimes that may be required to get the economy out of recession. A small deficit—and even more, a surplus—is deflationary, and is a means of holding a demand-pull inflation in check (*see* G20). In 1970 there was a small surplus, and thus the net borrowing requirement was negative (£−18m). Since then the borrowing requirement has become increasingly large.

The calculation of the precise deficit or surplus

needed is a chancy business; for the level that is required depends on the amount of saving and on the amount of spending out of credit that people intend to do—and this is not easily predictable. It also depends on the change in the foreign balance. Nor can the Chancellor be sure his figures are right: estimating next year's revenue, and even next year's expenditure, by the Government is difficult enough, but he needs to estimate also the likely trends of private income and expenditure, without really reliable information as to what they were in the past year. The introduction of advance *cash limits* on a large proportion of expenditure in 1976 was meant to give the Government greater control over projected spending (*see* G49).

Nevertheless, fiscal policy—running large deficits when economic activity is low, and small ones when it seems to be excessively high—is the most important action through which the economy can be kept on an even keel. Monetary policy may help; but the Budget decision of the Chancellor on changes in taxation and public expenditure is the key one.

6. SOURCES OF STATISTICS, AND SOME SUGGESTIONS FOR FURTHER READING

The non-specialist will find that most of the statistics he needs are given in the *Annual Abstract of Statistics*, published every year by Her Majesty's Stationery Office. This comprehensive document includes figures on population, social conditions, education, labour, production, trade and balance of payments, national income and expenditure, wages and prices, and many other topics. For more up-to-date information, reference should be made to the *Monthly Digest of Statistics* which has a similar coverage and gives month-by-month figures. A selection of the more important series, presented in a manner which can more easily be understood by the layman, is given in another Stationery Office publication, *Economic Trends*, also issued monthly.

Fuller information on labour problems is given in the *Department of Employment Gazette*, on trade in *Trade and Industry*, and on financial matters in the *Bank of England Quarterly Bulletin*. These three periodicals include discussions on the statistics presented. An important new Government annual publication in 1970 was *Social Trends*, containing articles and detailed statistics on social and economic conditions in Britain.

For an analysis of developments in the economy see the official *Economic Report*, published just before the Budget by the Treasury, and the *Economic Review*, a private publication issued by the National Institute for Economic and Social Research. To explain economic events and policy, the Treasury publishes a monthly *Economic Progress Report*, available free of charge to the

SOURCES OF PUBLIC REVENUE

Revenue.	1960. £m	1976. £m	Percentage increase 1960–76.	Percentage of total revenue 1976.
Taxes on income	3,626	27,150	649	54·3
of which paid by:				
personal sector	1,991	16,635	736	33·3
companies	612	1,396	128	2·8
national insurance contributions	913	8,426	823	16·8
Taxes on capital	236	885	275	1·8
of which:				
death duties	236	359	52	0·7
capital gains tax	—	494	—	1·0
Taxes on expenditure	3,391	13,197	289	26·4
of which levied on:				
alcohol	400	2,221	455	4·4
tobacco	818	2,027	148	4·1
rates	771	4,540	489	9·1
Surplus of public corporations	534	4,678	776	9·4
Other revenues	901	4,099	354	8·2
Total revenue	8,688	50,009	476	100·0
Net borrowing	710	8,497		
Total expenditure	9,398	58,506		

public. The periodic *British Economic Survey* (Oxford University Press) contains up-to-date articles on aspects of the economy.

For a comprehensive and systematic introduction to the British economy the reader is referred to A. R. Prest and D. J. Coppock, *The U.K. Economy: a Survey of Applied Economics* (Weidenfeld and Nicolson). Easier to read is S. Brittan *Steering the Economy* (Penguin).

An entertaining account of economic ideas and their application is found in Michael Stewart, *Keynes and After* (Penguin). Other Pelicans include Joan Robinson, *Economic Philosophy*, and J. Pen, *Modern Economics*. A thorough explanation of international monetary affairs is given in Fred Hirsch. *Money International*

(Allen Lane) or Brian Tew, *The Evolution of the International Monetary System 1945–77* (Hutchinson). E. J. Mishan in *Growth: The Price We Pay* (Staples Press) produces an interesting criticism: of economists' and politicians' " obsession " with economic growth and affluence. A. B. Atkinson examines inequality in Britain in *The Economics of Inequality* (Oxford).

Readers with an appetite for economic theory may wish to try the introductory books *Economic Theory* by G. B. Richardson (Hutchinson) and *Introduction to Positive Economics* by R. G. Lipsey (Weidenfeld and Nicolson). A recent book which combines a discussion of economic theory and of the British economy is *The Economic System in the UK*, edited by D. Morris (Oxford).

III.   THE LESS DEVELOPED ECONOMIES

Income Levels.

Two-thirds of the world's population live in dire poverty—a poverty which can scarcely be imagined by those accustomed to the standards of living attained in the relatively few developed countries of the world. The orders of world inequality may be seen from the table comparing annual income per capita by region, converted into pounds sterling at official exchange rates. These figures are only very approximate because exchange rates are misleading indicators of purchasing power and because the averages conceal considerable income inequalities within some regions and countries. Nevertheless, it is clear that poverty is widespread in the world. The alleviation of this poverty is widely recognised as the most important economic—and indeed political—task of the second half of the twentieth century.

NATIONAL INCOME PER CAPITA BY REGION, 1970

	(£ p.a.)
North America	1,788
Oceania	894
Europe	873
Latin America	217
Middle East	155
Africa	79
Asia (excl. Japan)	46

What is a Less Developed Country?

There are no less than 140 countries comprising the so-called " Third World," known variously as " less developed " or " developing " or " underdeveloped " or " poor " countries. There is a great diversity among them, and yet they have a number of features in common. Foremost among these is their poverty, but even poverty is not universal: some of the oil-producing countries such as Saudi Arabia, Kuwait and Libya have achieved very high levels of income per capita while retaining many of the other characteristics of less developed countries.

Most of the developing countries are primarily agricultural economies, with the bulk of the population engaged in *subsistence agriculture*. For many millions of peasant farmers the primary objective is to produce enough food for their family to subsist. India is a classic example, with no less than 70 per cent of its 574 million people dependent on agriculture for a living. Most less developed countries have only a small industrial sector as yet: it is rare for the output of the manufacturing sector to exceed 10 per cent of the gross domestic product. The main exceptions to this rule are the successful exporters of labour-intensive manufacturing goods, such as Hong Kong, Singapore and Puerto Rico. Many of the less developed countries lack the necessary ingredients for successful industrialisation—capital, skills and entrepreneurship.

The developing countries vary enormously in

size—from the teeming masses of India and China to scores of countries with less than a million people, including Bahrain, Botswana, Fiji, Gabon, Mauritius and many West Indian islands. The development problems and possibilities facing large and small countries are very different. The small size of most developing economies forces them to concentrate on the production of one or two primary products for world markets. Their high degree of specialisation and heavy dependence on exports and imports makes these economies dangerously vulnerable to the vagaries of world trade and the world economy.

Enough has been said to show that, apart from their poverty, the less developed countries have other economic characteristics and problems in common. However, it is dangerous to generalise because there are also important differences. In particular, they vary in their degree of development and in their potential for development. A semi-industrialised, urbanised country such as Argentina has little in common with an utterly backward country such as Chad, and the economic prospects for an oil-rich country such as Iran are far brighter than for a country with few natural resources such as Tanzania.

Population Growth.

Many underdeveloped countries are experiencing an unprecedented population explosion: annual rates of increase of between 2 and 3 per cent—which double population in as little as 35 and 24 years respectively—are common. This is a phenomenon of the last three decades. Death rates have fallen sharply in response to improved health services and modern methods of control, *e.g.*, the eradication of malaria through DDT spraying. On the other hand, birth rates have been kept up by such factors as tradition, social prestige, religion, the need for security in old age and a lack of facilities for family planning.

POPULATION SIZE, GROWTH AND DENSITY BY REGION

	Population 1975 (m).	Growth rate 1965–75 (% p.a.).	Density 1975 (per sq. kilo).
North America	237	1·0	11
Europe	473	0·6	96
U.S.S.R.	255	1·0	11
Oceania	21	2·0	3
Africa	401	2·7	13
Latin America	324	2·7	16
China	839	1·6	86
India	598	2·1	182
Other Asia	819	2·5	56
World Total	3,967	1·9	29

The table indicates that over half the world's population lives in Asia, and that the developed regions account for under a third of the total. Apart from Australasia (into which immigration is high) the developed countries show slower rates of population growth than Africa, Latin America and Asia. The figures of population density may easily be misleading, since they take no account of the nature of the area, *e.g.*, deserts are included. But it is clear that Asia is more densely populated than Africa or Latin America.

The Population Problem.

In many developing countries there is population pressure on the land, and many people want more land for farming. Population density is a hindrance in agricultural economies, but not necessarily in industrial economies: because it is industrialised and has accumulated much capital, Europe can support at a high standard of living a population more concentrated even than that of Asia.

As a result of rapid population growth the pressure of population on the land has increased. The consequences have been far more serious in countries such as Bangladesh (with a population density of 497 people per square kilometre in 1973) or India (175 per sq. km) than in Zambia (6 per sq. km) or Brazil (12 per sq. km). In those countries with abundant land the expanding population can spread into unused areas; but as land becomes increasingly scarce, less and less productive land must be brought into cultivation and soil erosion and loss of fertility become major problems. A substantial increase in output is required to prevent a fall in per capita income as population grows, and an even greater increase is required if living standards are to be improved. Between 1963 and 1973 food production in the developing countries as a group increased by 28 per cent, but per capita food production fell by 2 per cent.

Even in those countries with plenty of land a rapid increase in population can have harmful effects. For instance, it diverts scarce investment resources away from directly productive investments such as factories and irrigation projects so as to meet the needs of the expanding population for more schools, hospitals, housing, cities and other public services.

Problems of Agriculture.

There are many millions of peasant farmers throughout the Third World eking out a subsistence from the soil. The margin between what can be produced and what is required to support life is narrow: the failure of crops because of drought, floods or pests can lead to famine unless food is quickly supplied from outside the area affected. For instance, relief action by the international community was too slow to prevent the drought which struck the Sahel area of Africa in 1973 and 1974 from claiming some 100,000 lives, endangering future income by destroying seeds and livestock, and breaking up rural communities.

Agricultural production may be held back by a shortage of land, or by the use of primitive tools and methods of cultivation (which may in turn be due to a lack of farming knowledge and skills or to a lack of funds for investment in land improvement or equipment), or by an unjust system of land tenure which deprives the farmer of incentive to raise his production. Perhaps all these problems must be tackled simultaneously.

The Green Revolution.

A technology is being introduced which can increase the yields from foodgrains by 50 per cent or more in tropical areas. This new technology is commonly thought to have caused a *green revolution*. It consists of new high-yielding seeds, largely for wheat and rice. Not only are the yields per acre higher but also shorter cropping cycles permit multiple cropping. The new technology economises on land and, being labour-intensive, provides more farm employment.

However, we cannot assume that it is going to solve the problem of foodgrain shortage in the underdeveloped countries. As yet, the new seeds are less resistant to drought, floods and disease. To be effective, they require substantial inputs of fertiliser and of water: in many areas expensive irrigation will be essential to their success. More-over, the fact that fertiliser and water are complementary inputs has meant that the green revolution has caught on—and been encouraged by governments—among the larger, more prosperous farmers in the better-watered, more prosperous regions. This is true of, *e.g.*, Mexico, Pakistan and the Philippines. Unless governments ensure that the benefits of the green revolution are widely spread, the effect might even be to harm small peasant farmers by increasing the competition from large farmers.

Land Reform.

There are many forms of land tenure in less developed countries. In black Africa communal or tribal ownership of land is common, with members of the community or tribe receiving rights to use the land individually. In parts of Asia and Latin America, there is private ownership of land, which—particularly where the land is densely populated—has often led to great inequality of land ownership. In some cases land tenure is characterised by absentee landlords and sharecropping tenants. The development of large estates produces a class of landless labourers.

The need for land reform varies according to the circumstances. In most cases the main argument is for greater social justice. In some cases it may be possible also to expand production by redistributing land more evenly or by giving land to share-cropping tenants and so improving their incentives. On the other hand, large farmers may have access to technology, skills and capital which small farmers lack: there is a danger that greater equity will be achieved only at the expense of efficiency. Hence the need to ensure that land reform is accompanied by a package of measures, *e.g.*, education, training and advice, and credit for fertiliser, tools and land improvements. Few governments have succeeded in implementing serious land reform programmes. The main reason is that the system of land tenure in a country often reflects the balance of political power: land reform invariably faces political opposition from entrenched interests. By the same token, a successful land reform may alter the balance of political power so as to facilitate broad-based development.

Case-study of Land Reform.

Egypt provides a case-study of relatively successful land reform. It began in 1952 after the overthrow of a régime which relied heavily on the support of big landlords. It was necessary because of the gross inequality of land ownership and the acute shortage of arable land in Egypt. In 1952 more than 2 million families, making up two-thirds of land proprietors, held no more than an acre each and only 13 per cent of the land in total; whereas 12,000 families, each with more than 50 acres, owned a third of agricultural land. A ceiling was imposed on the size of family holding and gradually brought down, and the requisitioned land redistributed to landless families and small farmers. Yet progress was slow: only 14 per cent of agricultural land had been redistributed by 1971 and only the richest and the poorest were affected. An important element in the success of the reforms was the formation of state-supervised co-operatives which organised cultivation, channelled credit and marketed produce. Agricultural yields rose significantly, particularly after 1960.

A grave problem facing the poor in agriculture which land reform cannot solve is population growth, currently estimated in Egypt to be 2·2 per cent per annum. Between the census years 1947 and 1966, the rural population increased from 12·6 million to 17·7 million people.

Exports of Primary Products.

Almost all underdeveloped countries export primary products (foodstuffs, industrial raw materials or minerals) and import manufactured goods, especially the capital goods (plant, machinery and vehicles) required for development. This international division of labour has recently operated to the disadvantage of the underdeveloped countries. The world demand for their primary products has increased only very slowly. This is because people spend just a small part of their additional income on food (*e.g.*, tea, coffee, cocoa), because synthetic substitutes have been developed for many raw materials (*e.g.*, rubber, cotton, jute), because developed countries protect their own agriculture (*e.g.*, sugar) and because demand in the developed countries has moved towards commodities with low raw material content (*e.g.*, from heavy industries to services).

In consequence, the general trend has been for the prices of primary products to fall in relation to those of manufactured goods. This was an important cause of the improvement in Britain's terms of trade (*see* **G6**). The reverse of the coin was a deterioration in the terms of trade of many underdeveloped countries, *i.e.*, they could now buy fewer imports for a given quantity of exports. Primary commodities exported by developing countries actually decreased in price on average by 12 per cent over the period 1957–62, and increased by only 2 per cent between 1962 and 1970. Most poor countries benefited from the soaring prices of various commodities in world markets during 1972 and 1973. These were years of world economic boom, food shortages and speculative purchasing of primary commodities. However, the non-oil-producing developing countries suffered as a result of the oil price rise after October 1973. The world recession of 1974 and 1975 depressed primary commodity prices, and inflation in developed countries increased the price of manufactured imports (*see* **G43**). Unsatisfactory prices of primary commodities (other than oil) have contributed to the shortage of foreign exchange which restricts investment expenditure in many less developed countries.

The prices of various primary products tend to fluctuate violently from one year to another. Many underdeveloped economies depend heavily on the exports of one or two commodities. For instance, coffee is the most important product in Brazil, cotton in Egypt, copper in Zambia, sugar in Cuba, cocoa in Ghana and rice in Burma. Fluctuations in the world price of its main export cause instability in the export revenues of a country, and this in turn can produce fluctuations in income throughout its domestic economy.

Problems of Industrialisation.

In those underdeveloped countries where there is population pressure on the land, alternative employment has to be created in industry or services. Even in countries with a surplus of land, if there is heavy dependence on one or two primary products, industrialisation provides a means of diversifying the economy.

But industrialisation is not an easy course. Because the margin between agricultural production and food consumption is narrow, the surplus from the agricultural sector exchangeable for the products of other sectors—*e.g.*, industry and services—is small; *i.e.*, the demand for the goods and services produced by other sectors is low. A second constraint on industrialisation is imposed by competition from abroad: new industries in an underdeveloped country have to compete with established industries in developed countries, which have the advantage of experience, a trained labour force and markets big enough for them to reap all the potential economies of large-scale production.

Industrialisation Strategies.

One means of overcoming the small size of market is to export manufactures to the developed countries. Developing countries with cheap labour are likely to have a comparative advantage in the manufacture of relatively labour-intensive commodities. A number of less developed countries have had remarkable success in following this strategy, *e.g.*, Hong Kong, Taiwan, South Korea, Mexico and Puerto Rico. Among their successful activities are textiles, clothing and labour-intensive components of electronic equipment. However, the markets for such products are limited—so that not all developing countries can succeed—and the developed countries often impose protective tariffs. Another form of manufacturing is the processing of primary products before exporting them. Here developing countries sometimes face the problem that tariffs are

higher on the processed than on the unprocessed products.

A means of overcoming competition from the industries of the developed countries is by nurturing an infant industrial sector behind tariff walls—which is how the United States and Germany developed their industries in the face of British competition in the nineteenth century. A number of developing countries have adopted this strategy. However, it has its drawbacks. Sometimes the "infants" never grow up, and vested interests press for continued protection. Import-substituted industrialisation often means that raw materials or semi-processed goods are imported for local processing. There is a danger that fluctuations in export proceeds will periodically curtail imports of necessary intermediate goods. The under-utilisation of capital in the manufacturing sector because of foreign exchange shortages has frequently occurred in countries such as India, Sri Lanka and Ghana.

Unemployment and Underemployment.

Unemployment and underemployment occur on a very considerable scale in both the rural and the urban areas of developing countries. Consider first the rural case. Because farm work is normally shared, underemployment—disguised unemployment—is more common than open unemployment. People work for only a part of the day or year. Where land is scarce, underemployment is chronic: people would like to work more if only they had more land. Unless the yield from the land can be raised, growth in population causes greater underemployment and reduces income per head on the land. Where land is abundant, underemployment is a seasonal phenomenon. People are fully employed in the busy season—harvesting and planting—but underemployed at other times of the year.

In the towns open unemployment is common with people queueing for *modern sector* jobs at the labour exchanges and at the factory gates. Rates of urban open unemployment in excess of 10 per cent are frequently recorded, *e.g.*, in Ghana, Colombia, Puerto Rico, Trinidad, Sri Lanka and the Philippines. Few developing countries can afford unemployment benefits, so that job-seekers remain openly unemployed only until their savings are used up or support by their relations is withdrawn. Then they have to scrape out a subsistence in the urban *traditional sector* while waiting and hoping for something better. Underemployment is rife in the easily entered traditional sector activities such as petty trading, hawking, beer brewing, fetching and carrying. A shoeshiner may be on the streets for ten hours a day but have only a couple of customers. The more people enter these activities, the further average income per worker is depressed. In many less developed countries this self-employment in the traditional sector accounts for the majority of urban workers.

Migration to the Cities.

Urbanisation is proceeding at an unprecedented pace in much of the Third World. Rural people are being drawn to the cities at a rate well in excess of the capacity of the cities to absorb them productively. The reason for this migration might be economic or social. The economic explanation runs in terms of an income differential between the urban and the rural areas. Relatively unskilled wages in the modern sector of the economy—often governed by minimum wage legislation or trade union bargaining—can be well above the incomes to be derived from peasant agriculture. People go to the towns in search of modern sector wage jobs, although they may actually end up underemployed in the low-income traditional sector. Rural–urban migration may be a social phenomenon: rural people are attracted by the facilities and "bright lights" of the cities. The recent expansion of education in many countries may also play a part, since a high proportion of the migrants are school leavers.

Whatever the reasons the consequences are socially harmful and politically explosive. Shanty towns and slums proliferate in the cities and their outskirts; poverty, disease and crime flourish.

Employment Creation.

As recognition has grown that unemployment, in its open and disguised forms, is both high and rising in many of the developing countries, so the objective of creating productive employment has received higher priority. For various reasons the growth of modern sector employment has been tardy and has lagged behind the growth of output. One reason is that the modern sector normally uses capital equipment and technology which is imported from the developed countries. This means that, even in countries with cheap and abundant labour, the most profitable techniques of production are often highly capital-intensive, so that the amount of scarce investment funds required to equip a worker is high. Hence the case for developing an *intermediate technology* which is both profitable and suited to the needs of the underdeveloped countries.

There is some danger that the establishment of capital-intensive factories may actually have existing labour-intensive production. For instance, sandals can be made by small cobblers using local leather (or old car tyres) or by a large plant using imported plastic materials: a new factory employing a few machine operators might displace many more traditional craftsmen who have no alternative employment opportunities. Governments, by encouraging or discouraging particular forms and areas of investment, have the power to influence the growth of employment. In the rural areas the encouragement and organisation of labour-intensive developmental or community projects can assist in harnessing the one abundant resource which almost all developing countries possess: unskilled labour.

Educated Manpower.

Many underdeveloped countries are faced with the dual problem of unskilled labour surpluses and scarcities of skilled and educated manpower. The problem is particularly acute in some of the recently independent countries of Africa. To give an extreme example: at the time of its independence in 1964, Zambia had only 100 Zambian university graduates and 1,200 secondary school graduates in a population of 3·5 million. In such countries the great shortage of educated and skilled people enables them to earn high incomes—with the result that there is a very unequal distribution of income. And even in countries where surpluses have developed, the existence of an international market for professional people such as doctors and engineers helps to keep up their earnings: these countries suffer from a " brain drain " to the developed world.

Because teachers are educated people, education in underdeveloped countries can be very expensive. In Uganda in the 1960s only 45 per cent of the children in the relevant age-group were at primary school and only 2 per cent were at secondary school. Yet the salary bill paid to their teachers exceeded 2 per cent of the gross domestic product. In such circumstances it is difficult to meet the demands for universal primary education; especially if the sort of primary education provided does not enable children to become better farmers.

Economic development is not just a matter of capital accumulation: it requires also an increase in educated manpower. Not only more knowledge but also new habits and attitudes—*e.g.*, attitudes towards risk-taking, hard work and thrift. Education—of the right sort and with suitable content—is generally acknowledged to be important for development, although the benefits of education cannot be quantified at all satisfactorily.

On the other hand, there are developing countries whose problem is now surplus rather than shortage of educated manpower. Such cases are common in Asia, *e.g.* India, Sri Lanka and the Philippines. The high financial returns accruing to the educated have generated powerful pressures for the expansion of state education, to which governments have acceded. Rapid expansion in quantity has frequently been accompanied by decline in quality of education. Some governments have found that it is easier to expand an educational system than it is to expand an economy, and shortages have given way to surpluses.

The response to surplus may take various forms: unemployment of the educated, or displacement of the less educated from their jobs, so pushing the unemployment down the educational ladder, or pressures on government to create unnecessary jobs for the educated in the public service. In this last case—true of Egypt—scarce resources are doubly wasted.

Economic Aid.

The gap between living standards in the underdeveloped areas of the world and in the areas already developed has tended to widen in recent years. In the 1950s real income per capita rose in the developed countries by 2·7 per cent per annum on average, and in the less developed countries by 2·3 per cent per annum. It was through a growing world recognition of the situation that the 1960s were designated " The United Nations Development Decade." But between 1960 and 1970 these rates of growth widened to 3·8 and 3·0 per cent per annum respectively. World inequalities continued to increase: hence the " Second United Nations Development Decade " in the 1970s.

The main industrial countries—organised as a 17-member *Development Assistance Committee* (DAC)—have provided economic aid to the developing countries. The total net flow of economic assistance from the DAC countries was $40 billion (about £18 billion) in 1976. Roughly $23·3 billion of this was net private investment and $13·7 billion official aid from governments. A third of the net *official development assistance* (ODA) was contributed by the United States: the other principal donors were France, West Germany, Japan, Canada and Britain in that order.

The DAC nations have accepted three aid targets. One is that the net flow of private and official resources combined should exceed 1 per cent of each country's gross national product. In 1973 only 5 of the 17 countries had achieved this percentage. The second target is that net ODA should exceed 0·7 per cent of GNP: not one country managed this in 1973. The third target, more generally achieved, concerns the " grant element "—the extent to which ODA contains an element of grant as opposed to commercial loans.

Although the money value of ODA increased between 1963 and 1973, in real terms it remained roughly constant. As a proportion of the combined GNP of the DAC countries, it fell from 0·51 per cent to 0·30 per cent over the decade. By their own standards the countries of the First World were failing to assist the Third World on an adequate scale. Yet, with the oil crisis and world recession, the situation has worsened. Many of the developing countries are in greater need of assistance, and in the developed countries the unprecedented balance of payments deficits and the fall in real incomes has made the provision of aid more difficult. Nevertheless, some improvement in the flow of aid did occur between 1973 and 1976. The total net flow of resources from DAC countries to developing countries increased from 0·79 to 0·97 per cent of GNP, and net ODA increased slightly to 0·33 per cent of GNP.

Forms of Aid.

Aid to the developing countries takes many forms, it serves many purposes and it is given for many reasons. Underdeveloped countries need aid to provide finance for development projects; to provide foreign exchange with which imports for development purposes can be bought; and to provide the trained manpower and technical knowledge they lack. The motives of the donor are not always humanitarian. " Aid " can take a military form; it can be used to prop up an incompetent or unjust government, or to buy support in the cold war. Nor is aid always beneficial to the recipient country. It may be wasted on ill-conceived or prestige projects, or cause the government simply to relax its own efforts. Sometimes schools or hospitals are built with aid but there is a lack of local revenues with which to staff and run these institutions. Concern over donor's motives and instances of waste has led some people to react against aid-giving. However, the correct remedy is not to cut off aid but rather to prevent its misuse.

Donor governments may finance specific projects, or they may contribute to the general pool of funds available for expenditure by the governments of underdeveloped countries. But financial aid is not always enough. Many underdeveloped countries need technical assistance in planning their development, to ensure that development possibilities are exploited and that scarce resources are used to best advantage. Hence the many schemes for providing experts by individual countries and by the technical agencies of the United Nations, such as the Food and Agriculture Organisation (FAO), the World Health Organisation (WHO), the International Labour Organisation (ILO), the United Nations Educational, Scientific and Cultural Organisation (UNESCO), the Technical Assistance Board (UNTAB) and so on. Hence also the schemes for educating and training people from the developing countries.

Foreign Private Investment.

One possible form of aid is private investment by firms from developed countries. These investments—setting up branch factories, for example—are concentrated in those projects which appear profitable to the investor. However, it is a characteristic of underdevelopment that there are few openings for profitable investment. Most of the U.K. private investment overseas, for example, has been concentrated in relatively highly developed countries of the world. Private investment cannot be relied upon to provide an adequate flow of resources.

Indeed, it has been questioned whether private investment constitutes aid to less developed countries at all. Its opponents argue that the benefits are often small or even negative: foreign-owned firms repatriate high profits and avoid tax by means of royalty payments to the parent company or unrealistic pricing of their transactions with the parent company; and these firms deter local enterprise. Supporters of foreign investment point to the high political risks which necessitate high profits in order to attract investors to developing countries, and question whether resources are available for any alternative path to development. A form of compromise which has become common in the Third World is a partnership arrangement between multinational companies and the host country's government.

British Aid.

The table shows how British assistance to developing countries has grown over the years, and how it has measured up to the international aid targets now accepted by the British Government. The first target is that the total net financial flow to developing countries should exceed I per cent of GNP. The large but fluctuating flows of private capital meant that this target was achieved in 1975 and in some previous years. The second target is for a net official development assistance (ODA) in excess of 0·7 per cent of GNP. We see that British ODA as a percentage of GNP was only slightly more than half of the officially accepted target in 1976, and was lower than it had been ten years previously. The table also shows that ODA has grown in value; in 1976 it exceeded £8 per head of British population. However, if we allow for inflation by expressing official aid in real terms, we see that the volume of aid has stagnated.

Government aid may be divided into multilateral aid and bilateral aid. Multilateral aid is given through the medium of the international development institutions; bilateral aid is given directly to the developing countries. Multilateral aid constituted over a quarter of total British aid in 1976. Three-quarters of British bilateral disbursements in 1976 took the form of grants, and the rest were loans. Most of the loans were fairly " soft ", with maturity averaging 25 years and the rate of interest averaging 2 per cent. About half of expenditure on aid is formally tied to the purchase of British goods and services. Other aid is not tied formally, and may be used directly to finance local expenditure; but when it is used to finance imports directly,

it has to be spent on British goods if these are available on competitive terms. Multilateral aid is untied. The tying of aid tends to raise the costs to developing countries; but it also enables countries with precarious foreign balances—such as the United Kingdom—to be more generous.

Aid takes the form not only of financial but also of technical assistance. Government expenditure on technical assistance amounted to a third of net bilateral disbursements in 1976. At the end of 1976 British technical assistance personnel overseas totalled 7,700 (excluding volunteers recruited by voluntary societies); about 1,000 administrators, 3,600 teachers, 900 agricultural advisers, 600 doctors and medical workers, and 1,700 involved in the economy.

All British official aid is channelled and co-ordinated by the Ministry of Overseas Development (ODM). In addition there are various private associations concerned with promoting development, such as Oxfam, War on Want and the World Development Movement.

The World Bank.

The International Bank for Reconstruction and Development (IBRD) known as the *International Bank* or as the *World Bank*, is an agency of the United Nations established in 1945. It has the primary function of making funds available to assist developing countries. Member nations agreed to subscribe quotas—fixed in much the same way as the quotas for the IMF—to the Bank. In fact, only a small proportion of the quotas has been called up by the Bank; the major part of the Fund's resources are borrowed—on the security of the remainder of the quotas—in financial centres.

Usually, loans are made to finance specific projects of investment in underdeveloped countries; and the Bank will normally make a loan only if it is satisfied that the investment will yield a revenue sufficient to enable the payment of interest on the loan, and the repayment of the sum lent. In 1976 the Bank made loans to the value of over $3,200 million. Thus a sizeable amount of lending is channelled through the Bank, but it is clear that some projects of great value to underdeveloped countries cannot be financed in this way, because they would not yield returns quickly or large enough to meet the Bank's requirements for interest and repayment. Accordingly a new institution, the *International Development Association*, was set up in 1960 with the power to make loans at low rates of interest and with more generous repayment conditions. The IDA contributes towards the development of education and agriculture ($1,300 million in 1974).

UNCTAD.

In 1964 the United Nations Conference on Trade and Development (UNCTAD) was held. For the first time the poorer nations of the world—77 were represented—came together to act as a pressure group on trading matters. The Conference made the following recommendations. Developing countries should be given free access to world markets for their manufactures and semi-manufactures by the elimination of quotas and tariffs. International *commodity agreements* should be made for each major primary commodity in world trade, to stabilise commodity prices. Compensation schemes—whereby countries are compensated for the declining prices of their primary products—were recommended for consideration. The Conference also resolved that the developed countries should aim to provide at least 1 per cent of their national income as aid for the underdeveloped countries.

Nothing concrete resulted from the 1964 Session: no significant trade measures in favour of the developing countries were taken, and the international transfer of financial resources diminished in relation to the income of the developed countries. A second Session of the Conference was held in 1968. Again, no action resulted from the Session; but the developed countries did accept more firmly the principle of discrimination in favour of developing countries in trade and shipping, and the 1 per cent target for aid. Progress was subsequently made in introducing tariff

FINANCIAL FLOWS FROM BRITAIN TO DEVELOPING COUNTRIES, 1964–1976

| | Net total flows, official and private | | Net official development assistance. | | |
	£m.	% of GNP.	£m.	% of GNP.	£m. (1970 prices).
1964	328	0·98	176	0·53	201
1967	287	0·72	173	0·44	203
1970	520	1·02	186	0·36	186
1973	601	0·82	246	0·34	187
1974	1010	1·22	307	0·37	200
1975	1062*	1·02*	389	0·37	197
1976	1204*	0·98*	462	0·38	205

* Excluding considerable long-term foreign currency lending by British banks.

preferences on poor countries' exports of some manufactures to rich countries.

UNCTAD III, held in Chile in 1972, appeared to be more a political tournament than a constructive Conference. Perhaps the most promising outcome was the greater likelihood of a future link between SDRs and international aid; *i.e.,* the issue of the new international paper currency to less developed countries—so easing the problems both of international liquidity and of development (*see* G42(2)).

The Impact of the Oil Price Rise.

In October 1973, during the Arab–Israeli war, the members of the Organisation of Petroleum Exporting Countries (OPEC) cut supplies of oil and increased their prices drastically. The price of oil subsequently rose fourfold above its initial level. By acting as a cartel to control supplies the OPEC countries were able to maintain the higher prices without surpluses accumulating and a competitive price war breaking out. The impact on all countries was great (*see* G43): on a number of less developed countries it was disastrous.

Some idea of the magnitude of the problem can be given by expressing the *additional* oil bill in 1974 as a percentage of the total import bill and of the GNP in 1973 of various countries. For Uruguay the figures were 39 and 4·9 per cent respectively, for Thailand 26 and 5·4, for South Korea 20 and 9·0, and for Turkey 19 and 3·3 per cent. The bout of inflation in the industrial countries resulting from the oil crisis meant that the developing countries also had to pay more for their other imports. They were further hit by the world recession generated by the oil crisis, because the resultant fall in world demand produced a slump in the prices of primary commodities. Between June 1974 and June 1975 the primary commodity exports (other than oil) of developing countries fell in price by nearly 40 per cent, and their imports of manufactures rose in price by 40 per cent. The developing countries had to cut back on the volume of their imports, to the detriment of development programmes. However, they were partly cushioned by the emergency loans provided through the *oil facility* scheme introduced by the IMF.

Of course, a number of less developed countries benefited from the oil price increases. These included the five rich countries (Saudi Arabia, Kuwait, Qatar, Abu Dhabi and Libya), whose levels of income per capita now exceed those in the industrial countries. Their use of the new revenues is limited by the ability of their economies to absorb them: for that reason they continue to need technical assistance. How they use their unabsorbed oil revenues can greatly affect the economies of both developed and developing countries. Other, less wealthy, oil-producing countries—including Iran, Iraq, Venezuela, Indonesia and Nigeria—have much larger populations and more absorptive capacity. They now have an opportunity to transform their economies with the oil revenues.

Reappraisal of Development and Aid Policies.

By the mid-1970s it was generally recognised that there was a case for a drastic reappraisal of development policies and of aid priorities. One of the important considerations was the new situation created by the increased price of oil.

Many developing countries would require substantially more aid to offset its various adverse effects. The success of OPEC in raising the oil price aroused the hopes and expectations of developing countries producing other primary commodities that they too could improve their terms of trade with the developed world. A " New International Economic Order " was envisaged by the General Assembly of the United Nations, in which the formation of producers' associations and new commodity agreements could play a part. These were the main issues debated, but with little agreement being reached, in the fourth session of UNCTAD held in May 1976.

Other factors calling for a reappraisal of policies included a growing recognition of the precarious food situation in many developing countries, and an increased awareness of large and growing income inequalities both within and among the developing countries.

Growing Indebtedness.

The external indebtedness of the developing countries has grown alarmingly in the 1970s, particularly since 1973. In nominal terms debt has grown at 20 per cent per annum and in real terms by nearly 10 per cent per annum. Debt servicing obligations increased from $9 billion in 1970 to $32 billion in 1976. For non-oil developing countries as a whole, debt and debt service amounted to 20 and 3 per cent of GNP respectively in 1976.

These developments have caused concern that countries will be unable to meet their obligations. They can be expected to lead to requests to the lending governments for debt relief. Such requests coming from the poorest countries will be difficult to refuse. However, in the case of the much increased private debt, default is increasingly likely. Many of the less developed countries have yet to adjust fully to their worsened economic and trading position since 1973, an adjustment which in some cases may prove intolerable.

The Food Crisis.

In the last couple of decades food production in the developing countries has done no more than keep pace with the growth of population. F.A.O. projections of demand and supply over the decade 1975–85 indicate no increase in food production per capita in the developing countries. Many developing countries have become net food importers, and this trend is likely to continue. In the period 1970–72 food imports represented no less than 14 per cent of the total imports of the less developed countries.

The years 1972–74 were ones of poor harvests in various parts of the developed and developing world. Famines occurred in the Sahel area of Africa, in Bangladesh and in parts of India. In response to vast imports of grain by the Soviet Union and many other countries, world grain stocks were reduced to very low levels and the price of grain rocketed. At the same time an acute shortage of fertiliser emerged, and its price also soared. These circumstances led to the calling of a World Food Conference in 1974.

The Conference foresaw the possibility of inadequate food supplies and famines in the developing countries in future years. It called for a building up of world food stocks and increased emergency *food aid*—aid provided in the form of foodstuffs. However, the long-run solution was seen to come from a fundamental attack on the problems of agricultural development. In response, most of the DAC donor countries decided to increase very substantially their aid to agriculture in the recipient countries.

Concern for food shortages leads inexorably to the population issue. Although the urgency of the problem of rapidly expanding population is not appreciated in some developing countries, growing attention is being paid to the economic benefits of population planning, *e.g.*, with the calling of the World Population Conference in 1973. Aid for family planning increased tenfold between 1965 and 1973; but in 1973 it still represented only 2·3 per cent of total aid.

Inequality Within Countries.

The growth performance of the less developed countries taken together—growth of GNP per capita of 2·3 per cent per annum in the 1950s and 3·0 per cent in the period 1960–75—is good by the standards of the past, although worse than the corresponding performance of the developed countries. However, in many less developed countries these growth rates have been achieved without any apparent improvement in the lot of the masses.

The majority of the people are engaged in agriculture in the rural areas, whereas much of the development has taken place in industry and services in the urban areas. A minority of people have benefited—industrialists, bureaucrats, educated and skilled workers, organised labour in the modern sector of the economy—but the poor living in the urban slums, often in open or disguised unemployment, and the enormous numbers in the rural areas have been little affected by development. In many countries the fruits of development have not been widely spread. It is a growing criticism that development policies have been biased towards industry and towards the cities, and that rural people in agriculture have been neglected. This outcome may be a reflection of the uneven distribution of political power within a developing country.

Increasingly, the growth of GNP per capita as a goal of development has been questioned, both within the less developed countries and among national and international aid agencies. Both recipient and donor governments have recently shown a greater concern for poverty, employment creation and social equity. Many donors have modified their aid policies to try to reach the poor. Of course, this redirection coincides to a considerable extent with the increased concern for agricultural development.

Basic Needs.

A direction in which international thinking has moved is towards the acceptance of a *Basic Needs* strategy of development. Essentially the aim is to alleviate absolute poverty, *i.e.* to meet minimum standards of food, shelter, clothing and safe drinking water, and to satisfy certain other basic human needs. It is proposed that these standards be reached not so much by means of welfare transfers as by enabling the poor to help themselves through productive employment. The minimum standards are inevitably subjective, there are economic and political obstacles to the fulfilment of basic needs, and the approach does not translate easily into specific policies. Nevertheless, the basic needs strategy may have an impact on the priorities both of aid agencies and of recipient governments.

Inequality Among Countries.

Not all less developed countries have fared equally well in recent years. In particular, there appears to be a tendency for disparities among less developed countries to widen. Dividing such countries into the 46 with GNP per capita of less than £85 ($200) and the 96 with GNP per capita above £85 in 1972, we find that no less than half

of the poorer group failed to raise average income per capita by more than 1 per cent per annum between 1960 and 1972, whereas only a tenth of the less poor group failed to do so. The countries which have performed well tend to be semi-industrialised and able to respond to opportunities for exporting manufactures to the developed countries, or to be well endowed with mineral or oil resources. Recent growth success stories include Brazil, Colombia, South Korea, Taiwan, Mexico and Turkey. Some of these are on the way to becoming self-reliant economically.

The poorest countries—25 of which have been designated the *least developed countries*—are experiencing the greatest difficulty in escaping from the vicious circle of poverty. A growing recognition of their problem has led the DAC countries to reallocate aid in favour of the least developed countries, and to offer aid on more concessionary terms to these countries.

Revision of British Aid Policies.

The revision of DAC aid policies mentioned above also occurred in the British aid programme. In 1974 the British Government began to direct more of its aid towards the poorest developing countries, and all future ODA to countries with a GNP per capita of less than $200 (£85) per annum was to take the form of outright grants. A Disaster Unit was established to respond to emergencies. Aid for family planning was stepped up. Increasing weight would be placed on rural development and the expansion of agricultural production, in particular on helping the poor in rural areas, *e.g.*, small farmers and landless labourers. The proportion of net bilateral ODA going to the poorest group of countries in fact rose from 48 to 54 per cent between 1973 and 1976.

Some Suggestions for Further Reading.

For an introduction to the subject the reader is referred to Jagdish Bhagwati, *The Economics of Underdeveloped Countries* (World University Library). A recent book concerned with international disparities, and addressed to the general reader, is *Development in a Divided World*, edited by Seers and Joy (Pelican). An interesting account of life in rural India is found in Kusum Nair, *Blossoms in the Dust* (Duckworth). On Asia the reader may wish to dip into the three volumes of Gunnar Myrdal entitled *Asian Drama: An Enquiry into the Poverty of Nations* (Allen Lane, The Penguin Press). A helpful introduction to African problems is found in Andrew M. Kamarck, *The Economics of African Development* (Praeger). On South America there is Celso Furtado, *Economic Development of Latin America* (Cambridge University Press). Introductory books on particular topics include G. K. Helleiner, *International Trade and Economic Development* and Peter Dorner, *Land Reform and Economic Development* (both Penguins).

The Overseas Development Institute has published a number of pamphlets on aid topics, including *World Development Handbook*, *British Development Policies* and *Volunteers in Development*. The Ministry of Overseas Development has compiled a handbook of *British Aid Statistics* (H.M.S.O.). A recent publication of the World Bank, *The Assault on World Poverty* (Johns Hopkins), examines the causes of poverty, especially in the rural areas, and the remedies. The Organisation for Economic Co-operation and Development, comprising all the major non-communist developed countries, publishes an Annual Review of aid and development entitled *Development Co-operation* (O.E.C.D.).

An interesting quarterly publication of the I.M.F. and the World Bank, *Finance and Development*, is available free of charge: applications should be sent to *Finance and Development*, I.M.F. Building, Washington, D.C. 20431. U.S.A.

IV. RECENT DEVELOPMENTS IN THE BRITISH ECONOMY

1. INTERNATIONAL DEVELOPMENTS

The Balance of Payments.

The balance of payments problem has dominated events in the British economy in recent years. It is therefore important to analyse the balance of payments in some detail; to understand why the balance of payments has been a problem; and to see its effects on economic policy. The balance of payments and its components are explained in detail on G6–8. The balance of payments in each year since 1964 is shown in the table below.

The 1964 Crisis.

We begin our story at a familiar point: with the British balance of payments heavily in deficit and under severe pressure. The late 1950s and early 1960s saw a decline in British competitiveness. The British share in world exports of manufactures fell steadily, and there was a rapid increase in imports of manufactured goods. The record current account deficit of 1964 was made worse by the sharp pre-election boom which depleted stocks and diverted demand to imports as domestic bottlenecks were reached. After the General Election of October 1964 the new Labour Government took immediate remedial action. This included a *temporary import surcharge* on all imports of manufactures and semi-manufactures, and a system of *export rebates*, representing the indirect taxes paid in Britain by British exporters.

The deficit on capital account was no less than that on current account. The United Kingdom was not an attractive investment proposition. A crisis arose in the second half of the year, when an outflow of short-term capital—a "flight of hot money"—took place in the expectation that a devaluation would be necessary to cure the worsening imbalance. Once this feeling developed, the process became cumulative: the greater the outflow, the more likely it seemed that Britain would be forced to devalue. A great deal of sterling was offered for sale by speculators holding pounds—the "Gnomes of Zurich"—and by British and foreign importers and exporters. In order to prevent the price of sterling from falling below the official minimum limit to the exchange rate of £1 = $2.78 (*i.e.*, to "support sterling") the Bank of England was itself forced to buy pounds. To do this the Bank had to draw on the country's reserves of gold and foreign exchange. The vast drain on the reserves could not be allowed to continue, and in late November, Bank Rate was

raised by 2 per cent to 7 per cent. The aim of this measure was to lure back short-term capital funds with the high rate of interest, and also to convince speculators that the pound would not be devalued. Speculators were not convinced, however, and the crisis continued. Two days later it was announced that an enormous loan totalling over £1 billion (*i.e.* £1,000 million) would be made available to Britain from all the leading Western central banks. This news was sufficient to slow down the speculative outflow, and by the close of 1964 the selling had come to an end.

Events leading to Devaluation.

The current account improved gradually in 1965 and again in 1966. Nevertheless, there was still a substantial deficit in total currency flow, which had somehow to be financed. Confidence in the pound remained weak and was further upset by the seamen's strike in May and June. Yet another flight of short-term capital occurred, and this led the Government in panic to introduce a policy of deflation, in a package-deal known as the "July measures" (*see* G47). To improve the balance of payments directly, the personal travel allowance outside the Sterling Area was reduced to £50 per annum. The fall in demand resulting from the deflationary policy, together with a wage-freeze introduced at the same time (*see* G55), helped to improve the trade balance, but of course at a cost of more unemployment and slower growth.

The trade gap widened to a record level in 1967. No single factor can be held responsible, but the following contributed: a continued decline in competitiveness, the removal of the temporary import surcharge, the building up of imported stocks which had been depleted, and the exceptionally slow growth of world production in 1967 (which meant that demand in the countries importing British goods was fairly stagnant). With the trade returns deteriorating, sterling came under unremitting speculative pressure, reaching a climax in November.

Devaluation of the Pound, 1967.

The Government recognised that action would have to be taken to improve the balance of payments, and to obtain further foreign loans to protect the depleted reserves. The alternatives were: deflation, import controls, tariffs and devaluation. Simple deflation to reduce imports was ruled out politically as the economy was now already in recession. Import controls and tariffs would meet

	1964	1965	1966	**1967**	1968	1969
Exports (f.o.b.)	4,521	4,848	5,204	5,139	6,282	7,075
Imports (f.o.b.)	5,019	5,071	5,268	5,693	6,649	7,231
Visible balance	−498	−223	−64	−554	−667	−156
Invisible balance	+145	+196	+167	+256	+395	+616
Current balance	−353	−27	+103	−298	−272	+460
Official long-term capital	−116	−85	−81	−59	+17	−99
Net private investment	−256	−130	−39	−96	−160	−6
Other capital flows	+71	−111	−503	−445	−863	−60
Balancing item	−41	—	−72	+227	−132	+392
Balance for official financing	−695	−353	−591	−671	−1,410	+687
Net borrowing from IMF*	+357	+489	+15	−339	+506	−30
Other net borrowing*	+216	+110	+610	+895	+790	−613
Change in reserves*	+122	−246	−34	+115	+114	−44
Total official financing	+695	+353	+591	+671	+1,410	−687

* A plus sign denotes a rise in liabilities or a fall in assets, and a minus sign a fall in liabilities or a are included as changes in the official reserves.

with resistance from Britain's competitors and the GATT, and tariffs had been tried in 1964 without success. The Government decided to devalue the pound.

The case for devaluation is a mixed one (see G8). It makes imports more expensive in relation to home-produced goods, and so demand for manufactured goods shifts away from imports; but in the case of food and raw materials, Britain must continue to import these essentials at the higher price because there are no domestic substitutes. It is possible, therefore, that devaluation will actually raise the import bill. However, export receipts should be increased by a greater amount: Britain exports its products in a highly competitive market, so that the reduced price of British goods in terms of foreign currencies should lead to a considerable increase in the amount of exports.

This improvement in the trade balance depends on Britain being able to retain at least part of the price advantage gained by devaluation. However, since devaluation raises the price of imported goods, it raises the cost of living both directly and indirectly, e.g., imported raw materials rise in price, so increasing production costs, which are passed on as higher prices. The trade unions react to this cut in the standard of living by demanding wage increases. In this way a spiralling inflation can occur which entirely neutralises the gain from devaluation. Devaluation makes an incomes policy both more difficult and more important (see G54-7).

In November 1967, the pound was devalued by 14·3 per cent, from $2.8 to $2.4 to the £. Devaluation was anticipated by speculators, and on the day before, there was a run on the pound said to be greater than any previously experienced. The devaluation was unfortunately delayed by the need to achieve international co-operation so as to prevent a flurry of competitive devaluations. It was also agreed among central bankers that Britain should be given credits of up to $3 billion, including $1·4 billion standby credit from the IMF (see G9 and 10). This credit protected the reserves against speculation; but it would have to be paid back out of balance of payments surpluses over the next few years.

Devaluation increases the demand for domestically produced goods and services: imports are replaced by local substitutes and foreign demand for British goods increases. This switch in demand requires also a switch in scarce resources—labour and capital—into the exporting and import substituting industries, if the new demand is to be met. To release resources for these industries it is necessary to reduce the demand for resources elsewhere in the economy. Accordingly, the devaluation was accompanied by a series of deflationary measures (see G47).

Improvement after Devaluation.

In his Letter of Intent to the IMF immediately after devaluation, the Chancellor stated the

Government's aim to improve the balance of payments by at least £500 million a year. However, progress after devaluation was initially disappointing: the current account deficit for 1968 was only slightly less than that for 1967. Moreover, this improvement came in the invisible account: the trade gap actually widened.

The balance of payments was transformed in 1969, improving strongly throughout the year. British exports were helped by the rapid increase in world trade. The volume of imports hardly rose, partly because of the import deposit scheme, introduced in November 1968, by which importers were required to deposit with H.M. Customs for a period of six months money equal to half (later reduced) of the value of certain imports.

The improvement in the balance of payments enabled the Government in 1970 to abolish the restrictions on travel expenditure and the import deposit scheme. The balance of payments continued to improve, and in 1971, for the first time in many years, the British share of world exports of manufactures rose. On the other hand, the growth of imports was constrained by the stagnation of the economy. Most unusually for Britain, the visible trade balance showed a large surplus in 1971.

The surplus on current account was no less than 500 million in 1969, £700 m. in 1970 and £1 000 m. in 1971. This improvement occurred both in visibles and invisibles. Between 1968 and 1971 the trade balance improved by over £900 m. and the invisible balance by nearly £400 m.; its most improved components being private services (e.g., financial, insurance and travel services) and net income from abroad. The total currency flow was transformed from an enormous deficit in 1968 (when the authorities were forced to borrow £1·3 billion) to surpluses of £740 m. in 1969, £1·42 b. in 1970 and no less than £3·35 b. in 1971, some of which represented short-term capital flight from the dollar.

Was the improvement in the balance of payments after 1968 an indication that the policy of devaluation had eventually succeeded? The efficacy of devaluation can only be judged after a few years, and then with difficulty since we need to know what would have happened in the absence of devaluation. Economists have not produced a unanimous answer. The National Institute for Economic Research has suggested that the current account surplus of £600 million in 1970 might have been over £400 m. smaller (£300 m. less on invisible trade) had it not been for devaluation. Undoubtedly the balance of payments was aided by the depressed state of the economy.

Britain's Debt Repayments.

At the end of 1968 the British Government had short- and medium-term debts outstanding to central banks and the IMF of no less than £3·4 billion. This represented about 10 per cent of the

1964-77 (£ MILLION)

1970	1971	1972	1973	1974	1975	1976	1977
8,121	9,061	9,449	12,115	16,538	19,461	25,416	32,176
8,146	8,781	10,151	14,468	21,732	22,664	28,987	33,788
−25	+280	−702	−2,353	−5,194	−3,203	−3,571	−1,612
+720	+778	+807	+1,431	+1,629	+1,502	+2,166	+1,577
%695	+1,058	+105	−922	−3,565	−1,701	−1,405	−35
−205	−274	−255	−254	−276	−288	−158	−168
+49	+216	−610	−196	+1,129	+336	−49	+1,046
+881	+2,194	+299	+417	+743	+155	−2,607	+3,937
+20	+272	−680	+184	+323	+33	+591	+2,596
+1,420	+3,271	−1,141	−771	−1,646	−1,465	−3,628	+7,376
−134	−554	−415	—	—	—	+1,018	+1,113
−1,161	−1,181	+864	+999	+1,751	+810	+1,757	+1,112
−125	−1,536	+692	−288	−105	+655	+853	−9,588
−1,420	−3,271	+1,141	+771	+1,646	+1,465	+3,628	−7,363

rise in assets. From July 1972 transactions with IMF affecting the U.K. reserve position in the Fund national income in 1968 and compared with gold and foreign exchange reserves of only £1·0 billion. The continued improvement in the balance of payments after 1968 and the first allocation of Special Drawing Rights (*see* G42) enabled the steady reduction of outstanding debts. The vast balance of payments surplus of 1971 eliminated almost all of these debts, and indeed the Bank of England lent to foreign monetary authorities under the "swap agreement" among central banks. The British reserves rose to the record level of over £2·7 b. early in 1972. By the end of 1972 the official short- and medium-term indebtedness was nil.

Renewed Balance of Payments Problems.

The competitive position of the United Kingdom was weakened after 1971 by an inflation more rapid than in other countries (*see* G53) and by the dollar devaluation of 1971 (*see* G43). These developments contributed to the sharp deterioration in the balance of payments which occurred in 1972. There were sharp increases in demand for such consumer goods as cars and colour television sets—no doubt set off by the abolition of hire-purchase restrictions in 1971 (*see* G47)—and the inability of domestic producers to expand their production correspondingly both constrained exports and accelerated imports. The import bill was also up on account of a rapid increase in the world prices of a number of primary products, especially of such foodstuffs as beef, wheat, sugar and coffee. The trade balance deteriorated from a surplus in 1971 to a record deficit in 1972; and the current account was just in balance. A large private capital net outflow occurred, so that there was a deficit of over £1·1 billion in the total currency flow.

Floating of the Pound.

The deterioration in the balance of payments contributed to a large outflow of short-term funds in mid-1972, which culminated in a sterling crisis and a floating of the pound in June. This was the first time that sterling had been allowed to float since a period in the 1930s, and it represented a contravention of the increasingly criticised IMF system (*see* G43). The pound floated downwards after June, from about $2.60 = £1 to an average value of roughly $2.40 during 1973, and to a low of below $2.30 in early 1974. It fluctuated between $2.30 and $2.40 until June 1975 when the rate dropped to $2.20. The downward slide continued, and in March 1976 the pound fell below $2.00 for the first time and continued to slide. Sterling depreciated even further in relation to such currencies as the mark, the franc and the yen, as the dollar was itself devalued in 1971 and 1973 (*see* G43).

The falling value of the pound was of no immediate assistance to the balance of payments: experience suggests that the improvement occurs only after a lag of a year or two. In the meantime the devaluation pushed up the domestic price of imports of raw materials and foodstuffs, so raising both the costs of production and the cost of living. The downward floating of the pound made a counter-inflation policy both more difficult and more important (*see* G54–7).

Inflation in Commodity Markets.

The current account of the balance of payments deteriorated sharply in 1973, to reach the unprecedented deficit of £1·12 billion. Exports did reasonably well, rising by 25 per cent in terms of value and by 11 per cent in terms of volume. However, the import bill soared, increasing by no less than 41 per cent. Import volume increased by 14 per cent, reflecting the rapid upsurge of the economy during 1972, and the emergence of shortages and a need for stockbuilding during 1973. More important was the higher price of imports: up by an average of 26 per cent between 1972 and 1973. This period witnessed a remarkable inflation in the prices of various primary products in world markets. To give some examples, between the first quarter of 1972 and the last quarter of 1973 average price increases in major world markets were as follows: cocoa 173 per cent, copper 115 per cent, cotton 127 per cent,

rubber 123 per cent, wool 138 per cent and zinc 308 per cent.

This unprecedented jump in primary commodity prices stemmed from the sharp and well-synchronised expansion of the major industrial economies during 1972 and 1973, and it was assisted by some speculative buying as a hedge against inflation. Commodity prices generally reached their peak in the second quarter of 1974. Food prices continued to rise after this, while the prices of other commodities, especially fibres and metals, fell as the world economy moved into recession.

The Oil Crisis.

An event of great importance to Britain and to other industrial countries was the decision of the Arab oil-producing states, taken in October 1973, to restrict oil supplies and to raise oil prices. The restriction of supplies was initiated as a short-run political weapon in the Arab–Israeli conflict; but it revealed a potential for obtaining higher prices which had not previously been exploited by the Organisation of Petroleum Exporting Countries (OPEC). In the past the world demand for oil had grown very rapidly—by about 8 per cent per annum between 1960 and 1973—but it had been successfully met by expansion of production. A slower growth of oil supply in relation to demand produces scarcity and a rocketing of price. Alternative sources of energy cannot be developed—and thus the demand for oil cannot be curtailed or even its growth retarded—for many years: little can be done about the prices charged by OPEC until the 1980s. However, maintenance of high prices depends on the ability of the OPEC group to restrict oil supplies to the market despite the incentive of each individual country to take advantage of the high prices by expanding its sales.

It seemed initially that the oil restrictions would produce physical shortages in the economy which would harm production and require rationing and direct controls. By February it appeared that demand would be met, but only at a much higher price. Between September 1973 and January 1974 the oil-producing governments raised their "take" on a barrel of crude oil from $1.75 to $7.00, and the import price was increased from $3.45 to $8.70 a barrel, *i.e.*, an increase of 150 per cent. Comparing 1974 with 1973 the price of oil imported into Britain almost trebled.

Oil and the Balance-of-Payments.

Largely because of higher import prices Britain's current balance deteriorated sharply in 1974. The value of imports rose by about 50 per cent. This was all accounted for by price increases, and not only oil prices: imported basic materials rose in price by 47 per cent, semi-manufactures by 42 per cent, and food by 28 per cent. Meanwhile the price of exports increased by 30 per cent but, because of world inflation, this involved little loss of competitiveness. In 1974 Britain recorded her worst ever current account deficit: no less than £3·65 billion. It represented a worsening of over £2·5 billion; in fact the additional oil bill amounted to £2·8 billion. The deficit was of an order of magnitude—no less than 5 per cent of GDP—which made the deficits of previous crisis years appear puny.

In the wake of the oil crisis the world economy moved into severe recession (*see* G43). To this the British economy was no exception: real GDP stagnated in 1974 and fell in 1975. The domestic recession reduced the demand for imports, which fell in volume by 8 per cent in 1975. With rapid inflation at home and abroad, both exports and imports again rose sharply in price. The world recession made it difficult for OPEC to raise oil prices further (although an increase of 10 per cent was announced late in 1975); and the depressed state of world demand caused the prices of primary commodities actually to fall. Britain therefore benefited from a 6 per cent improvement in the terms of trade. Moreover, British exports suffered less than the exports of most other countries, falling in volume by only 3 per cent in 1975; and the British share of world exports of manufactures rose slightly, against the long-run trend. The net result of these changes was that the current account deficit of the balance of payments was halved, to £1·7 billion, in 1975.

In 1976 the world economy began to emerge from its severe recession, and output of the OECD countries grew by 5 per cent on average. This helped the British balance of payments; despite this, the current account deficit, at £1·5 billion, did little more than mark time. Exports rose by 30 per cent in value and by 8 per cent in volume; they were assisted by the depreciation of sterling and by the domestic price controls which encouraged producers to switch to foreign markets. The import bill rose by 35 per cent and import volume by 9 per cent. There was a particularly large increase in imports of cars: British producers appeared unable to expand production to meet the demand. Although the current account was no worse in 1976, the deficit in total currency flow rose to no less than £3·6 billion. To understand the reason we must examine the way in which the oil deficits have been financed and movements of the exchange rate.

Financing the Deficit.

In 1974 the oil exporting countries financed the largest part of the current account deficit by adding £2·2 billion to their sterling balances. There was also an unusual net inflow of private investment and considerable public sector borrowing in the Eurodollar market. The reduced deficit of 1975 actually posed a greater problem of financing, because the oil producers were less willing to accumulate balances in sterling. Britain's foreign exchange reserves fell by £500 million, the Government borrowed another £500 million in the Eurodollar market and announced that it would borrow £1 billion from the IMF in 1976.

Interest rates were kept high in London during 1975 to attract short-term capital and to discourage its withdrawal. However, during 1975 the rate of inflation in Britain was some 15 per cent above the average for the OECD countries: it became increasingly clear that sterling would have to be depreciated further. In March and April 1976 speculative outflows of funds forced the authorities to intervene strongly in the foreign exchange market by selling foreign exchange, and even then the pound depreciated substantially to a new low level. The British economy had again become precariously dependent on creditors and speculators.

In March the value of the pound fell below $2.00: in the space of two months it depreciated by 9 per cent. The pound slipped further with large withdrawals of officially held sterling balances, until it was checked in June by the announced agreement of a $5·3 billion standby credit facility made available to the Bank of England by the "Group of Ten" countries; this would be available for six months. With the trade returns worsening, sterling came under pressure again in September and October. The exchange rate slid to a low point of $1·57 in October, and the Bank of England's minimum lending rate (see G25) was raised to the unprecedented level of 15 per cent. Drawings on the credit facility exceeded $1 billion, and these had to be repaid in December. Accordingly, the Government applied to the IMF to draw on the United Kingdom's credit tranche of $3·9 billion. The successful conclusion of these negotiations in January 1977, and the borrowing of more than $1 billion from the IMF, helped to restore confidence. However, the terms of the agreement involved some loss of control over domestic affairs: in his Letter of Intent to the IMF, the Chancellor agreed to restrictions on the rate of domestic credit expansion (dce) and on the public sector borrowing requirement (psbr) (see G50).

Over the year 1976 the pound depreciated by some 15 per cent against other currencies. However, with the British rate of inflation running at 16 per cent and well above that in the other major countries, the ensuing gain in competitiveness was small.

The Sterling Balances.

The official sterling holdings (see G10) have been very volatile in recent years. They rose sharply after the oil crisis, as oil funds were invested in

Britain; early in 1975 they amounted to £4·9 billion. In 1976, however, much of the oil money was withdrawn during the bouts of speculation against the pound, and the sterling balances fell by some £1·1 billion over the year to reach £2·6 billion in December. It had become increasingly necessary to reduce the vulnerability of the British economy to fluctuations of this sort.

The IMF agreement of January 1977 was followed by the successful negotiation of a "safety net" for the officially held sterling balances. The new facility, for an amount of $3 billion, was to operate with the support of various major central banks. Under the scheme, the British Government offers official holders of sterling the opportunity to convert all or part of their holdings into medium-term foreign currency bonds. But in addition, the UK is able to draw on the credit facility in respect of any other net reductions in the official sterling holdings.

North Sea Oil.

In 1974 the "oil deficit" in the balance of payments was £3·4 billion, in 1975 £3·1 billion, and in 1976 £3·0 billion. This is to be contrasted with a current account deficit (including oil) in these years of £3·4 billion, £1·5 billion, and £1·4 billion, respectively. The future course of the British balance of payments depends crucially on the rate of expansion of British oil production. The official forecast was that the net effect of North Sea oil production on the current account would rise steadily from a negligible sum (£90 million) in 1976 to some £5·4 billion (3 per cent of the GNP) in 1980, when Britain would be self-sufficient in oil. Of course, such a forecast involves many imponderables, including the price of oil itself. This depends on the ability of the OPEC cartel to survive and on the growth of world demand (influenced by the pace of economic recovery) in relation to supply (influenced by the development of new fields such as the North Sea and Alaska).

The Return to Surplus, 1977.

In 1977 an improvement in the "oil deficit" of £1·1 billion accounted for nearly all the improvement in the current account: the current account moved into slight surplus. The volume of imports increased very little, but the substitution of British production for imported oil was largely responsible for this success. Imports of manufactured goods rose fast even though domestic manufacturers had the capacity to produce more. Imports of cars rose by no less than 26 per cent, reflecting the supply difficulties of the British motor industry. Fortunately the volume of manufactured exports also rose sharply in 1977, by a proportion (8 per cent) well above the growth rate of world trade in manufactures. Probably this reflected the gain in competitiveness resulting from the depreciation of sterling in 1976.

The improvement in the current account, assisted by high interest in London and speculation against the dollar, produced a heavy demand for sterling in late 1977. There was a large increase in short-term sterling balances, much of it recorded in the "balancing item" (see G38). The demand for sterling was met in part by the willingness of the monetary authorities to let the exchange rate rise. From its lowest level of £1 = $1·58 in October 1976, it rose to $1·75 in October 1977 and to $1·94 in March 1978. This revaluation helped to curb domestic inflation by keeping down the sterling price of imported goods, but it was likely also to have a delayed harmful impact on the competitive position of the manufacturing sector. Thus the official concern to prevent an inflow of short-term capital, and so prevent an expansion of the money supply, could have harmful consequences.

Balance of Payments Prospects.

It is important to realise that the current account for 1977 would have been heavily in deficit had the British economy not been in such serious recession. World economic recovery should increase the demand for British exports, although it could also worsen the British terms of trade by raising the prices of primary commodities. It is the growth of exports, together with the terms of trade, which puts a ceiling on the growth of imports if the current account deficit is to be eliminated. Since the expansion of the economy raises the demand for imports, the foreign exchange constraint on imports in turn limits the extent to which production and employment can be permitted to increase. The balance of payments will therefore act as the crucial constraint on the growth of the economy in the next few years.

Economic forecasters charting the likely course of the economy up to 1980 have drawn pessimistic conclusions, despite the expected gains from North Sea oil. If resources are to be released for correcting the balance of payments and for investment, there will have to be very severe restriction on the growth of real wages, private consumption and public expenditure. Unless this restriction is accepted by the community, the rate of unemployment in Britain might actually have to rise above the 6·0 per cent level reached at the end of 1977. If a 2·5 per cent unemployment rate is to be restored by 1980, very substantial improvement in the balance of payments will be necessary. For this to be achieved, inflation will have to be curbed drastically, and either further depreciation of the exchange rate or the imposition of import controls seems all too likely.

Fear has been expressed that the economy will not be reflated sufficiently as the balance of payments improves. With the expansion of British oil production and the consequent improvement in the balance of payments, the government may allow the exchange rate to rise in response to upward pressures. The danger is that the manufacturing sector will become increasingly uncompetitive, and that the effect of this on manufacturing production and employment will be serious.

Should Imports be Controlled?

Pressure was brought to bear on the British Government to ease the balance of payments and unemployment problems by imposing import duties or quotas. The Government acceded to these pressures in a selective and minor way. For instance, in 1975 new quota levels on cotton yarn and man-made fibre imports from certain countries, and a licensing system for imports of television tubes and colour television sets, were introduced. However, in his budget of April 1976, the Chancellor rejected general and semi-permanent controls on manufactured goods: they would infringe treaty obligations to the GATT and the EEC, and he feared that they would lead to retaliation and the danger of an international trade war.

The economics profession, as on so many issues, is by no means in agreement on the relative merits of devaluation and import controls for remedying Britain's balance of payments deficit. The protagonists of import controls point to their scope for selectivity, e.g., permitting concentration on manufactures and excluding raw materials and food, to the possibility of using price controls to avoid subsequent price increases in the sheltered industries, and to the avoidance of financial crises which would result from the prospect of devaluation. The devaluationists, on the other hand, argue that import controls are more likely to provoke retaliation by other countries, that controls breed inefficiency in production, that selective controls need to be very substantial to have the same impact as devaluation, and may have to be progressively intensified.

Foreign Investment.

One of the more successful items in the UK balance of payments has been net interest, profit, and dividends from private sources. In 1976 the net figure was a £1·83 billion surplus, to be compared with £0·76 billion a decade before. Much of this is made up of the overseas earnings of British companies.

Should the British Government discourage or encourage private investment abroad? An economic study has suggested that for every £100 of British investment abroad, British exports immediately increase by about £11, i.e., there is an initial drain on the balance of payments of £89. The average rate of profit on capital overseas is thereafter about £8 per annum, or only £5 if capital appreciation is allowed for. The short-term balance of payments loss must therefore be weighed against the long-term gain. The importance of the short-term considerations depends on the state of the balance of payments, e.g., if more investment overseas causes the Government to take deflationary measures the national cost is great.

The Rise of Multinational Companies.

The remarkable expansion since 1960 of international investment, both by foreign companies in the United Kingdom and by British companies abroad, reflects the growing importance of *multinational companies* in the world economy. Some 165 multinationals account for 80 per cent of British private investment abroad. The multinationals tend to dominate the world markets for technologically advanced products. They account for no less than 60 per cent of trade in manufactures in the developed world. Their financial and market power, their global investment strategies, and their ability to avoid national taxation pose a challenge to the economic sovereignty of national governments.

Reform of the International Economic System.

The international monetary system and international liquidity are explained on G9–10. The main problem facing the international economic system during the 1960s was an increasing shortage of international liquidity in the face of expanding world trade. This gave a deflationary twist to the world economy and threatened the continuation of free trade. In the 1970s the focus moved to the problems of world inflation and to the international imbalance caused by the increased price of oil, and the resultant threat to economic growth. We trace the issues and events as they unfolded.

The Group of Ten.

The main function of the IMF has been to provide deficit countries with loans, to be repaid over a certain period (*see* G9–10). The amount of these credit facilities has been increased over time, but the level has remained low in relation to needs, and the IMF facility has therefore been supplemented in various ways. In order to increase the resources available to neutralise the movements of short-term funds which so disrupted the balance of payments at that time, the IMF initiated a scheme for a "Lenders' Club" in 1961. According to the scheme, the main trading countries—the *Group of Ten*—undertook (subject to some control by lending countries over the use of the funds) to make available substantial loans to the IMF for relending to countries of the Group suffering an outflow of short-term funds.

Special Drawing Rights.

In 1967 the members of the IMF agreed in principle to a scheme according *special drawing rights* (SDRs) to member countries, and in 1970 the scheme came into operation. SDRs are distributed annually to all members in proportion to their quotas with the IMF. They initially had a fixed value in terms of gold, and are generally accepted as a means of payment. Thus a deficit country can use its SDRs to buy the currency of the countries with which it has a deficit, and the surplus countries, in accumulating SDRs, earn a rate of interest on them. This is a movement towards an international paper currency, since the SDRs, unlike IMF loans, do not have to be repaid: they are a permanent addition to international reserves. Allocations were made in 1970, 1971, and 1972; none has been made since then. The scheme was launched on a scale which is small in relation to the size of the problem: the value of SDRs amounted to $10 billion, or 4 per cent of total world reserves, in early 1977. However, it is expected that the SDR will eventually become the principal reserve asset of the international monetary system. The IMF, in its statistics, now values all reserves, including gold and dollars, in terms of SDRs.

The Gold Crisis.

The United States ran a large and persistent payments deficit in the 1950s and 1960s. This was initially financed through the willingness of foreigners to run up dollar balances. However, distrust of the dollar grew, and between 1960 and 1967 U.S. gold reserves were run down, from $19·5 billion to $12·1 b. After the devaluation of sterling in November 1967, the interest of speculators transferred from the pound to the dollar. Since many speculators expected the devaluation of the dollar in terms of gold to be followed by a corresponding devaluation of other currencies there was a growing demand for gold.

With growing speculation against the dollar, the system could not be continued without endangering the U.S. gold reserves. The central bankers gathered for a crisis meeting in Washington in March 1968, and decided to terminate the gold pool (see G9). They introduced two markets for gold, with private transactions taking place in the free market at a price determined by supply and demand, and transactions among central banks taking place in the official market at the official gold price. The United States was now prepared to convert dollars into gold only for central banks, i.e., to finance a deficit only on its current plus long-term capital account. In this way speculation against the dollar could be controlled; but the problem of the U.S. deficit on current and long-term capital account was still to be solved. The free market price of gold initially rose in response to speculative demand, but, after a currency realignment in 1969, tension in the foreign-exchange markets was relaxed and the price fell back to $35 per fine ounce.

The Dollar Crisis.

In 1970 the deficit in the United States balance of payments rose to a record level. This was financed by creditor countries increasing their dollar balances. They had little choice: a large-scale conversion of dollar balances would force the United States to renounce its obligation to supply gold to central banks at $35 per ounce. It became increasingly clear that if the United States failed to reduce its deficit, e.g., by restricting capital outflows or military expenditures abroad, the creditor countries would either have to go on financing American deficits by accumulating dollars or allow their currencies to appreciate in terms of the dollar.

In May 1971, in response to speculative capital movements mainly from the United States to West Germany, the deutschmark was allowed to float upwards, i.e., the authorities allowed its price to rise above the official ceiling. But massive speculation against the dollar continued and in August the United States Government imposed a surcharge on imports and suspended the convertibility of dollars into gold. Currencies of the major trading countries were then allowed to float upwards against the dollar by varying amounts.

Adjustment of Exchange Rates.

The Smithsonian Agreement of December 1971 set the seal in the biggest realignment of exchange rates for nearly a quarter of a century. After negotiations among the Group of Ten it was agreed that the United States would withdraw its surcharge and devalue the dollar against gold if other countries would revalue upwards or at least not devalue. In terms of gold Japan revalued by 8 per cent, West Germany by 5 per cent, 44 countries including the United Kingdom and France did not alter their exchange rates, and 44 countries, all underdeveloped, followed the United States in devaluing by 8 per cent. It was also agreed that there should be a period of greater flexibility in exchange rates, with countries being allowed to alter their exchange rates by 2¼ per cent from the par value in each direction.

The year 1972 saw a rise in the free market price of gold to almost $70 per fine ounce—well above the new official rate of $38. This development reflected the doubts of speculators that the new exchange rates would be permanent. The pound came under speculative pressure in June; and this, combined with a deteriorating balance of payments and the imminence of accession to the

EEC, led the British Government to float the pound downwards (see G39). Various countries—including Britain, West Germany, Italy and Japan—took measures to try to control speculative capital flows. Partly to prevent speculative capital outflows, interest rates were raised competitively by various governments during the year.

Despite the devaluation of the dollar in December 1971 the U.S. balance of payments on current account actually deteriorated in 1972. Speculation against the dollar broke out early in 1973: the West German central bank was believed to have taken in no less than $6 billion in ten days despite its capital controls. The chief foreign exchange markets were closed, and in February the dollar was devalued by 10 per cent and the Japanese yen—the strongest currency—was allowed to float upwards. In March the EEC countries agreed that their currencies would float jointly against the dollar, but with the currencies of Britain, Ireland and Italy—then in balance of payments difficulties—temporarily floating independently. In early 1974 France left the joint EEC float. Though individual governments intervened to stop their currencies changing value too rapidly or too far, it would be true to say that the international monetary system had entered a new era of flexible exchange rates.

Oil and the International Balance of Payments.

In 1973 the oil-producing countries exported oil worth $27 billion, and their surplus on current account was $13 billion. Their surplus for 1974 was estimated at $56 billion. This surplus involved a corresponding deficit for the oil-importing countries as a group. Such a transformation in the international balance of payments was unprecedented in its scale and speed. It involved a massive transfer of purchasing power from consumers to producers of oil. Since only a small part of the additional oil revenue was spent, this had a severe deflationary effect on the world economy. This effect was not remedied, and it was even compounded by the restrictive monetary and fiscal policies introduced by many of the major countries to stem their oil-induced inflation and balance of payments deficits.

The oil-producing countries have to invest their surplus funds abroad, so that there is a corresponding surplus on the capital account of the oil importing group of countries. However, it is unlikely that the current account deficit of each individual country will be offset by a corresponding capital inflow. There is a danger that these funds will be highly mobile between recipient countries, thus introducing considerable instability in the currency flows of the western oil consumers. There is also a danger that each country will take undesirable and self-defeating measures, e.g., deflation and import controls, to improve its own current account.

The Response to Oil Deficits.

Faced with these problems, the major industrial countries agreed in 1974 that capital transfers among themselves should be used to overcome individual imbalances. Despite this, many governments took restrictive measures to combat both domestic inflation and their balance of payments deficits. In 1974 and 1975 the industrial countries experienced the worst economic recession of the post-war period. For instance, the level of industrial production in the OECD group of countries was 10 per cent lower at the end of 1975 than it had been at the end of 1973. At the end of 1975, unemployment rates were 8 per cent in the United States, 7 per cent in Canada, 5 per cent in Britain, and 4 per cent in France and West Germany.

The economic recession meant that the price of primary products fell—on average by 13 per cent between 1974 and 1975—and the price of oil could not be raised much further. As a result, the terms of trade of the developed countries improved in 1975. The recession also brought a sharp fall in their imports—by 8 per cent in volume terms in 1975—while the OPEC countries increased their imports very rapidly. The net effect was that the OECD countries returned to near balance on current account in 1975. In November the leaders of the six major non-communist countries held a summit meeting in France and agreed to various forms of economic co-ordination and co-operation, *e.g.*, rejecting protectionist, retaliatory beggar-my-neighbour trade policies.

Financing the Oil Deficits.

The OPEC group ran a surplus on current account of $56 billion in 1974 and $32 b. in 1975. The United Kingdom attracted $21 b. of these funds in 1974 but only $4 b. in 1975, the United States received $11 b. and $6 b., other countries $21 b. and $17 b., and international organisations $3·5 b. and $4 b. respectively. This last mainly represents the oil producers' financing of the IMF's *oil facility*: a loan fund intended to help countries cope with their oil deficits. By the end of 1975 drawings on the oil facility exceeded $5 billion.

In 1975 the OECD group formally established a *recycling* fund which would be used to help member countries in balance of payments difficulties: since most of the oil surpluses are invested within the OECD group, inter-governmental transfers of funds are possible. In January 1976 the IMF agreed to give all its member countries a temporary increase in borrowing rights of 45 per cent. These various methods of financing oil deficits provide a temporary accommodation but they do not obviate the need for a long-run correction of the new imbalance in world trade and payments.

Tardy World Recovery.

In 1976 the world economy began gradually to recover from the recession, and the output of the OECD countries as a whole increased by 5 per cent over the year. Unemployment remained high, but was lowest in those countries (*e.g.*, West Germany) which were able to " export " their unemployment by repatriating migrant workers. The effect of renewed expansion was to reopen the current account deficit of the OECD, to increase the OPEC trade surplus, and to reduce a little the large deficit of the less developed countries as their terms of trade improved.

The world recovery of 1976 proved to be short-lived. The growth rate of the OECD economies dropped again to 3·6 per cent in 1977. Only in the United States and Japan did it exceed 4 per cent; Western Europe was firmly in recession. The recession meant that world trade was sluggish: in that way recession was infectious among countries. While the United States had a huge deficit on current account of SDR 16 billion, West Germany had a surplus of SDR 3 billion and Japan a surplus of no less than SDR 9 billion. It was crucially important that these surplus countries take action to expand their economies and upvalue their currencies, so alleviating the balance-of-payments difficulties of other countries and enabling them to grow more rapidly.

Yet this was not the only problem. Even the serious recession of the OECD countries did not prevent them from running an overall current account deficit of SDR 28 billion in 1977—much of it with OPEC—while the OPEC countries ran a surplus of SDR 36 billion. Many deficit countries borrowed heavily from public or private international sources to cope with their oil deficits. They assumed that their oil deficits were not a normal imbalance requiring domestic adjustment policies, and were relying on a reflation of the world economy to permit repayment of their debts. Unfortunately, the large surplus of the oil producers is likely to be exacerbated by world expansion, implying a corresponding deficit in the rest of the world which will somehow have to be accommodated. It is this problem of a greater trade deficit, together with the fear that expansion will fuel inflation, which is likely to restrain the growth of the major economies up to 1980. The problem is greatest for those deficit countries which cannot attract OPEC funds. It can be alleviated to the extent that the deficit country governments recycle such funds among themselves in accordance with the needs of individual deficit countries. The case for international co-ordination of policies is clear.

SDRs and Gold.

By the end of 1977, total international reserves were valued at 248 billion SDRs. Of this gold accounted for 36 b. SDRs, foreign exchange for 186 b. SDRs, IMF drawing rights for 18 b. SDRs, and SDRs for 8 b. Originally the SDR had been set equal to the par value of the U.S. dollar, but when the dollar was devalued the SDR maintained its value in terms of gold (SDR1 = 0·889 grammes of fine gold = $1.206). With the general floating of exchange rates after March 1973, the volatility of the SDR in terms of currencies conflicted with the aim of developing it as the principal reserve asset of a reformed international monetary system, and its adoption as the unit of account for all IMF transactions. The IMF therefore introduced, as from July 1974, a new system of valuation based on the value of a group of 17 major currencies in specified proportions. In March 1978 the dollar was worth 0·81 SDRs.

The rapid inflation and great uncertainty in the world economy contributed to the speculative demand for gold; this raised its price many times over in the free market. In December 1974 the London gold price exceeded $180 per fine ounce. However, the IMF in 1975 decided that the official price of gold should be abolished, and that it would auction 25 million oz (equivalent to a year's production) over a period of 4 years. The profits from the sale of the gold would go as aid to less developed countries. The effect of this decision was to depress the free market price of gold, which fell to under $130 in April 1976. It was agreed that central banks should be allowed to buy and sell gold among themselves and on the open market at free market prices, as opposed to the old official price, provided that there is no net accrual of gold by the countries concerned.

In March 1978 the price of gold again exceeded $180. Gold flourishes in times of uncertainty and expected inflation.

Experience of Exchange-rate Flexibility.

One of the advantages claimed for greater flexibility in exchange rates is that it diminishes the need for international liquidity. Variations in exchange rates should reduce the size of imbalances and therefore the resources required to tide over deficits.

However, it is not clear from recent experience that greater exchange-rate flexibility can produce equilibrium in international payments. It seems that the balance of payments takes a long time—perhaps two or three years—to adjust to a depreciation of the exchange rate. In the meantime there might be wage increases to compensate for the increase in the cost of living brought about by the depreciation, which in turn tend to neutralise the depreciation. For instance, between the date of the Smithsonian agreement in 1971 and February 1978 the pound had depreciated against other currencies by 35 per cent, the dollar by 10 per cent, the yen had appreciated by 24 per cent and the deutschmark by 46 per cent. Yet, because of their different rates of inflation, the signs were that the British current balance and the competitiveness of British goods were no stronger relative to the German than they had been in December 1971. One of the worrying features of the flexible exchange-rate system is that it not only permits but also generates a far wider spread of inflation rates among the major countries.

Reform of the IMF.

A major amendment of the IMF's Articles of Agreement was proposed in 1976, which would have the effect of formalising the end of the Bretton Woods system. For the amendment to take effect it must be accepted by a high proportion of the member countries. The proposals formally permit member countries freedom to choose their exchange-rate arrangements, including floating, so departing from the par value system. In line with the objective of reducing the role of gold in the international monetary system, the amendment abolishes an official price for gold or its use as a denominator in exchange arrangements, it eliminates obligations to transfer or receive gold under the Articles, and allows for the disposition of part of the Fund's holdings of gold. The objective is to make the SDR the principal reserve asset of the international monetary system. The amendment contains adequate powers for the Fund to increase the value of SDRs in circulation and to raise their yield to one which is more competitive with those on other reserve assets.

Prospects for Further Reform.

The movements in the 1970s towards greater control of " hot money " flows, greater flexibility of exchange rates, and increased international liquidity helped to correct international imbalances. But there were various reasons for believing that they would not provide a permanent solution. Reasons have been given above for questioning whether exchange-rate flexibility can cope with the international imbalances of the 1970s. Moreover, the amount of short-term funds and the scope for speculation with them is greater than ever. The surpluses of the OPEC countries —with their *increase* in funds totalling $175 billion in the four years 1974–77—present a considerable problem. International companies, with structures that span exchange control barriers, have accumulated vast sums which they move about in search of security and profit. These developments, together with the growth of the Eurodollar market (*see* G10), makes control of short-term capital flows very difficult and gives rise to the possibility of exaggerated and destabilising movements in international exchange rates.

International liquidity grew very rapidly during the early 1970s, mainly because the United States deficit was financed by other countries accumulating dollars. But the fact that dollar holdings were not in general convertible meant that the apparent increase in liquidity was to a large extent illusory.

The severe imbalance in international payments resulting from the oil crisis made it all the more important that there be further reform to help in the correction of such imbalances without sacrificing full employment, trade and economic growth.

The European Economic Community.

The *European Economic Community* (EEC), otherwise known as the Common Market, was set up by the Treaty of Rome, ratified in 1958. It consisted of six full members—Belgium, France, Holland, Italy, Luxembourg, and Western Germany. Britain had participated in the negotiations which led up to its formation, and had argued in favour of a looser " free trade area " without a common external tariff, and excluding trade in agricultural products. No compromise acceptable to the Six was found, and Britain joined with six other European countries—Austria, Denmark, Norway, Portugal, Sweden, and Switzerland—in forming the *European Free Trade Area* (EFTA).

Economic Arrangements of the EEC.

The EEC forms a common market with no tariffs or trade controls within it and a Common External Tariff (CET). There is a Common Agricultural Policy (CAP), which is maintained by a system of variable import levies setting *threshold prices* on imports of agricultural products from outside the Community, and by means of *intervention prices* at which agricultural products of the Community are purchased. The intervention price is slightly higher than the threshold price of a product. The EEC has a large Budget required mainly for supporting the CAP, *i.e.*, for subsidising Common Market farmers. There is free movement of both capital and labour within the Community, and a certain degree of fiscal harmonisation.

Prospects for Economic Union.

In 1970 the Commission of the European Economic Community published the Werner Plan, a report on the establishment of economic and monetary union of the EEC. The plan aimed at transferring within a decade the principal economic decisions from the national to the Community level, and at establishing within the Community complete freedom of movement of goods, services, persons and capital, with fixed and constant rates of exchange between national currencies or, preferably, a common currency. A centre of decision for economic policy would be established and made responsible to a European parliament.

These proposals have far-reaching economic and political implications, since they involve a considerable reduction of national sovereignty. For instance, the loss of power to correct balance of payments deficits by means of trade controls or variation in the exchange rate implies either that the deficit country's currency should be generally acceptable to its creditors (so that the country within the Community—like a region within a country—simply cannot have a balance of payments problem), or the country must resort to deflation. And even if there is a common currency, it is very likely that resources will concentrate in some regions of the Community to the neglect of other regions, possibly those far from the main centres of production and consumption. Complete mobility of resources is likely to produce a regional problem within the Community just as it can produce a regional problem within a country. But the Community may not, to the same extent as a country, possess the political power and determination required to remedy the problem. It is not surprising, therefore. that the Werner Plan has been pursued in only limited respects and that its eventual implementation is not certain: economic union cannot precede political union.

Mr. Roy Jenkins, President of the European Commission, since taking office has pressed for monetary union and a common European currency: the issue is alive.

The Terms of British Entry.

After the resignation in 1969 of General de Gaulle, who had vetoed British membership of the EEC, the path was clear for British entry. In 1971 entry terms were negotiated and published in a White Paper.

Tariffs and trade between Britain and the Community were to be eliminated and the CET imposed on imports from other countries; the changes would be made gradually over five years. Britain also agreed to introduce the CAP in the first year of membership and gradually to raise both threshold and intervention prices over five years. In the meantime, to ensure that prices to producers were equated, levies and compensation payments would be made on agricultural trade between Britain and the rest of the Community. It was agreed that Britain should eventually contribute to the Community Budget according to its share of the total GNP of the Community. Thus Britain would build up its contribution over five years from 9 per cent to about 20 per cent of the total. Britain also had to follow all the EEC countries in introducing a *value added tax*.

The high British customs duties on oil, alcholic beverages, and tobacco could be retained and yet avoid contravention of the Treaty of Rome by becoming internal taxes.

Accession to the Community 1973.

The United Kingdom acceded as a full member of the EEC on 1 January 1973. Two of Britain's EFTA partners—Ireland and Denmark—joined on the same date, so forming an expanded Community of nine countries. The economic ties with the Sterling Area were weakened and those with the Community strengthened. For instance in 1972 the Government relaxed restrictions on direct investment by British firms in the EEC and introduced controls on capital transactions with the Overseas Sterling Area. In 1972 trade with the original six members of the EEC accounted for about 23 per cent of total British trade, trade with the EFTA partners about 13 per cent. and with the Commonwealth 19 per cent. After accession, trade with the EEC expanded sharply and the proportion of trade with the former EFTA countries and the Commonwealth fell. Excluding trade with the oil-exporting countries, British trade with the original six members rose from 25 per cent of the total in 1972 to 30 per cent in 1974.

It was on the issue of monetary union that the first major economic problem for Britain arose after entry. In conformity with the Werner Plan (above), the Community agreed in March 1973 to fix the exchange rates between member currencies and to float them together against the dollar (*see* G43). Britain and Italy—then in balance of payments difficulties—insisted that they be permitted temporarily to float independently. There is a danger that the right to vary exchange rates be withdrawn from member countries without there being uniformity in other policies. If there is to be a monetary union, there should also be conformity in industrial relations and incomes policies! For if inflation is more rapid in Britain than in her partner countries, and if Britain is prevented from adjusting the exchange rate or imposing import restrictions against her partners to correct the ensuing balance of payments deficit the Government might see no alternative but to deflate the economy: stagnation could ensue.

In fact, the " snake in the tunnel "—*i.e.*, Community currencies being permitted to fluctuate against each other only within limited bands—has not proved a success. Countries other than Britain, including France, have dropped out.

Labour Government Policy.

The Labour Party in opposition had criticised the terms of British entry to the EEC negotiated by the Conservative Government. When it came to power in 1974 the Labour Government was determined to renegotiate terms. The Government wanted major changes in the CAP and in the method of financing the Community Budget, and other safeguards of British and Commonwealth interests. Some concessions were negotiated, *e.g.*, in the contributions to the Community Budget and on New Zealand butter. Moreover, the Lomé Convention of March 1975 effectively safeguarded the interests of most poor Commonwealth countries. It was left to the British electorate to vote in a referendum in June 1975 on the renegotiated terms. There was an overwhelming vote in favour of the United Kingdom remaining a member of the EEC: 67 per cent voted " yes " and 33 per cent " no."

The Green Pound.

It is in the British interest that the CAP—with its heavy support of Common Market farmers—be reformed. Community funds are available to protect farmers by buying excess food and building up stocks of food if the free market price falls below the intervention price. As a result " food mountains " have developed, surviving even the drought of 1976, *e.g.*, in the autumn of that year the stockpile of milk products amounted to 1·3 million tonnes.

Nevertheless, the British contribution to the EEC Budget has been much smaller than expected. The *net* contribution (payments *less* benefits) was £104 million in 1973, £31 million in 1974, and there was a net gain of £54 million in 1975. Britain gained from " monetary compensation amounts," *i.e.*, refunds associated with the difference between the values of the pound in the foreign exchange markets and the *green pound*. The green pound is the agreed exchange rate between the pound and the other Community currencies which is used in calculating contributions to the Budget. As the market value of the pound has floated below the agreed green pound rate, so the United Kingdom has had the difference refunded. A devaluation of the green pound increases the prices paid to British farmers but raises the prices of EEC foodstuffs to British consumers.

2. INTERNAL DEVELOPMENTS
Government Stabilisation Policies.

Since the war successive governments have attempted to *stabilise* the economy, *i.e.* to prevent fluctuations in the level of economic activity as measured by, for example, the degree of utilisation of capital equipment or the rate of growth of output. To this end governments have adopted monetary and fiscal policies (*see* G22) designed to keep aggregate demand growing at a steady rate. This involves a " counter-cyclical " policy, *i.e.* if total demand appears to be growing too rapidly the government adopts more restrictive monetary

and fiscal policies, and *vice versa*. However, counter-cyclical policies are difficult to operate: it is not easy to determine whether or not total demand is at the right level at any particular time, nor is it easy to predict how rapidly or to what extent changes in government policies will affect the economy. As a result there is always the danger that governments will make mistakes in both the size and the timing of counter-cyclical policies.

Economic Fluctuations.

The accompanying table shows that governments have not been able to eliminate fluctuations in the economy. Indeed, some economists believe that the magnitude of disturbances has actually been exacerbated as a result of persistent errors in the size and timing of policies. The table shows that the period 1961–62 was one of recession, 1963–65 upswing and boom, 1966–67 stagnation, 1968 slight reflation, 1969–71 recession and growing unemployment, 1972–73 sharp upswing, and 1974–76 recession. Industrial production was more unstable than GDP and investment more unstable still.

An Electoral Cycle 1958–65?

The sharp pre-election boom of 1958–60 was accompanied by a worsening balance of payments.

ECONOMIC FLUCTUATIONS IN THE BRITISH ECONOMY 1962–77

	Percentage change over previous year in:			
	GDP*	Industrial* Production	Private* manufacturing investment	Number† unemployed
1962	1·2	1·1	−8·1	36·0
1963	3·3	3·4	−12·2	23·7
1964	6·1	7·7	12·7	−33·6
1965	2·7	2·9	10·0	−13·8
1966	1·7	1·1	3·2	9·4
1967	1·8	0·6	−3·0	54·8
1968	4·2	6·0	3·0	4·8
1969	2·0	2·8	7·0	−1·2
1970	1·7	0·1	7·7	6·2
1971	1·5	0·3	−6·5	29·4
1972	2·9	2·2	−12·6	10·5
1973	5·7	7·2	0·8	−29·3
1974	−0·7	−2·7	15·7	−0·6
1975	−1·7	−5·1	−14·0	59·0
1976	1·1	0·5	−4·9	39·0
1977	0·9	0·2	5·0	9·2

* At constant prices.
† Average number unemployed during the year.

After the General Election of 1959 economic policy became increasingly deflationary. For instance, in July 1961 the Chancellor introduced a collection of restrictive measures, primarily intended to ease the critical foreign balance, but not without effect on the domestic economy. Bank rate was raised, a 10 per cent surcharge on indirect taxation—the *regulator*—was imposed, the increase in Government spending was cut, and the banks were required to increase their special deposits at the Bank of England.

The recession continued during 1961 and 1962, and in early 1963 there was substantial under-utilisation of capacity in many branches of industry. Consequently the economy could respond to the expansionary April budget: national output rose by 6 per cent over the year. By 1964 the economy was beginning to show signs of strain, and there was a rapid deterioration in the balance of trade. However, the 1964 budget was again reflationary, and both industrial production and consumption expenditure responded. By the end of 1964 there were reports of growing labour shortage and the balance of payments was heavily in deficit (*see* G38). Nothing was done about it, however, until after the General Election of October. The incoming Government attempted to tackle the balance of payments directly, without recourse to deflation. Its first budget was not deflationary, and full employment was maintained up to and beyond the General Election of 1966.

On the basis of British experience in the decade prior to 1966, it is apparent that either General Elections were timed to coincide with booms or that booms were timed to coincide with elections, or a little of both! The evidence points to the existence of an electoral trade cycle, in which booms were determined by politics and recessions by the balance of payments.

Stagnation 1966-71.

Balance of payments difficulties eventually produced a deflation of the economy. In mid-1966, during yet another run on the pound, the Government panicked. In its " July measures " the Government raised indirect taxation 10 per cent and introduced a variety of deflationary measures. As a result, the economy went into recession in the second half of 1966. Employers now began to lay off workers, and unemployment rose from 1·3 per cent of the labour force in early 1966 to average 2·3 per cent in 1967.

Despite growing unemployment the Chancellor produced a " no-change " April Budget in 1967. The balance of payments prevented him from taking reflationary measures. The balance of payments deteriorated, and, since further deflation was politically unacceptable, the Government devalued the pound. Devaluation was itself strongly reflationary—increasing demand for exports and for import-substitute goods—and had to be accompanied by measures to release resources for these industries. Taxes were raised and monetary restrictions imposed. Further cuts in government spending were announced in December, and again in January, when future defence spending was considerably reduced because of the decision to withdraw forces from East of Suez, and the planned rise in the school-leaving age from 15 to 16 was put off until 1972.

The 1968 budget was highly deflationary. The Chancellor increased taxation to yield an additional £920 million per annum. Most of this came from indirect taxation, with purchase tax and taxes on spirits, wines, tobacco, vehicles, and petrol all raised. Partly to gain support for the incomes policy, the Chancellor raised family allowances and placed a heavy " special levy " for one year on unearned income above £3,000 per annum. In deflating the economy the Chancellor was attempting to reduce private consumer demand so as to free resources for the export market and for replacing imports. His strategy was to produce an overall balance of payments surplus of the order of £500 million before resuming growth, and in this way to break the vicious circle of " stop-go."

In February 1969 Bank Rate was raised, partly to help reduce bank lending and partly to retain short-term funds in London: owing to the shortage of international liquidity (*see* G42) central banks competed for short-term capital by raising their discount rates. The April budget was somewhat restrictive; additional taxation was raised mainly by increasing corporation tax to 45 per cent. The budget continued the strategy of improving the balance of payments at the expense of consumption. In June the Chancellor published a Letter of Intent to the IMF stating his intention to limit the annual increase in *domestic credit expansion* to £400 million. Domestic credit expansion is defined as the increase in the money supply adjusted for changes resulting from external transactions. In fact domestic credit expansion turned out to be negative in the financial year 1969/70: credit was extremely tight except for the manufacturing sector. The growth of the economy in 1969 was slight, output being about 2 per cent up on 1968. Investment and consumption stagnated, and the main impetus for expansion came from exports.

In 1970, with the balance of payments improved and an election not far ahead, the Chancellor reduced taxation. Even then, because expenditure was to be restrained and income tax receipts rise with the inflation, he expected a Government budget surplus of £620 million. It could not be claimed that this was an electioneering budget: output was planned to rise by 3·5 per cent in the

next year. But the period of severe restraint on private consumption was over.

In October the new Conservative Government announced cuts in both public expenditure and taxation. There was to be a 2·5p cut in the standard rate of income tax and a cut in corporation tax. Prescription charges and dental charges were increased, the subsidy on welfare milk was ended, the price of school meals was raised, and the system of import levies on farm produce was extended. These changes involved a redistribution of income away from the poor. However, a *family income supplement* (FIS) was introduced to provide a cash benefit for poor families with children (*see* G29-30). Although real output grew by only very little in 1970, the Chancellor did not take any measures which would have an immediate reflationary effect.

With business profits and liquidity down and business confidence weak, private investment was low and the economy continued to stagnate. The 1971 budget, therefore, was somewhat reflationary with tax reductions of £550 million in the financial year 1971-72. The Chancellor claimed as his objective an increase in output of about 3 per cent per annum. The main measures were a further cut in corporation tax to 40 per cent, an increase in the tax allowances for children, a reduction in surtax particularly for very high income earners, and a general increase in national insurance benefits and contributions. The economy did not appear to respond to the budget measures, and further but minor reflationary action was taken during the year.

1971 was also a year of important monetary changes. The Bank of England abolished the ceiling for lending by banks and repaid outstanding special deposits. Associated with the large inflow of short-term funds from abroad, the money supply expanded rapidly and Bank Rate fell from 7 per cent to 5 per cent. Many interest rates were thus below the rate of price inflation, so that the effective rate of interest incurred on borrowing could actually be negative! In September the Bank of England introduced new techniques of monetary control which are outlined in G25. Also the Government removed all restrictions on hire-purchase, credit sale and rental agreements.

Reflation 1972-73.

By early 1972 the economy was still depressed, and with total unemployment approaching one million the Government was under increasingly heavy pressure to take additional reflationary action. One reason why the Government resisted this pressure for so long was undoubtedly its concern to reduce the rate of inflation. However, it also seems likely that it had underestimated both the degree of recession in 1971 and the speed with which the 1971 budget measures would stimulate output and employment.

In March 1972, therefore, the Government introduced a highly reflationary budget aimed at stimulating an annual growth rate of 5 per cent. Tax reductions of £960 million were combined with a number of other measures: old age pensions and other National Insurance benefits were increased (though this was financed by increased National Insurance contributions on earnings); rates of purchase tax were reduced in anticipation of its abolition and replacement by a *value added tax* in addition private investment was encouraged by the introduction of *free depreciation—i.e.* an allowance of 100 per cent of investment spending against income liable to tax in the year of the investment—for all investment in plant and machinery, and a 40 per cent initial allowance for expenditure on industrial building.

The expansionary fiscal stance was financed by a rapid growth of the money supply until mid-1972, and this kept interest rates down. Despite this, and the Budget's tax incentives, investment remained depressed, and the main impact of the budget was on consumption, especially on consumer durables, which rose very rapidly throughout 1972. This weakened the balance of payments by increasing the demand for imported consumer goods. As a result the Government faced contradictory pressures by early 1973. On the one hand, it needed to protect the balance of payments by slowing down the growth of consumption demand (whilst, if possible, continuing to encourage increased investment); on the other hand, the economy still appeared to be operating below capacity, with under-utilised capital equipment and over 700,000 unemployed workers.

The Government decided to compromise by maintaining roughly an unchanged policy aimed at a further 5 per cent growth over 1973. To this end the budget of March 1973 was "neutral," *i.e.* it neither added to nor reduced the pressure of demand. However, the net effect of the various expansionary measures adopted since 1971 had been a large increase in the public sector borrowing requirement, which was projected to be £4·4 billion in the financial year 1973–4. To meet this large deficit the Government relaxed the monetary restraint which it had imposed in the latter half of 1972; thus the continuing budget deficit was financed by rapid growth of the money supply. As pointed out earlier (*see* G25), such a policy is likely eventually to cause rises in interest rates and in inflation. Interest rates did rise in 1973–74 —thereby reducing the chances of a rise in investment—but inflation was held in check by the incomes policy which the government had introduced in November 1972 (*see* G56).

Despite the government's continued expansionary policy, output growth slowed down in 1973, coming almost to a halt by the end of the year. This was mainly due to "bottlenecks," *i.e.* shortages of labour in particular sectors and with special skills and also of materials and components. These occurred despite the fact that unemployment was still more than 500,000 (though vacancies had risen to a record 360,000 by the end of the year). Since domestic output could not keep pace with the growth of demand, imports continued to rise and the balance of payments to worsen, the problem being much exacerbated by the dramatic rises in the price of oil and of many other imported goods. In December 1973 the Government was forced to bring in an emergency budget which reduced the pressure of demand by cutting public spending—a reduction of £1·2 billion was planned for 1974–75 by reimposing hire purchase and other credit controls.

The 1972–73 period represents a classic illustration of the difficulties of stabilisation policy. After delaying reflation for too long the Government then expanded much too rapidly, with disastrous consequences for inflation and the balance of payments. However, whilst this is clear with the benefit of hindsight, it was not obvious at the time: in 1972 most economists broadly approved the Government's expansion strategy, since there was insufficient information about the current state of the economy, and about the likely effects of policy changes, for a sound judgement to be made about the appropriate degree of expansion.

Slumpflation 1974–78.

The period 1974–78 was one of "Slumpflation": a remarkable combination of the most rapid inflation, the deepest recession and the worst balance-of-payments deficit of the post-war period. All these problems were, primarily, a legacy of the over-expansionary policies of 1972–73.

1974.

1974 saw a simultaneous failure to meet all four main policy objectives—of adequate economic growth, full employment, a stable balance of payments and stable prices. The volume of consumer spending fell for the first time in 20 years, GDP rose year-on-year by only a small amount, and by January 1975 over 700,000 people were unemployed, 140,000 more than at the beginning of the previous year. Despite this, the balance of payments deficit on current account was the largest ever recorded (*see* G40), and retail prices in January 1975 were over 19 per cent higher than in January 1974 (*see* G53). Production in the first quarter fell by 5 per cent. affected as it was by the three-day working week, imposed by the Government in response to the overtime ban and subsequent strike in the coal mining industry (*see* G56).

With the fall in production there was a running down of stocks, a diversion of exports to the home market and a sharp increase in imports. The trade deficit increased to unprecedented levels;

nearly £1·3 billion in the first three months. The miners' strike was settled and full-time working was restored by the incoming Labour Government in March.

Because the oil-producing countries could absorb only a small part of their increased balance of payments surpluses, and because any feasible reduction by western countries of their oil consumption could make only a relatively minor impact on the surpluses, the British Government felt that industrial countries should agree to collectively run current account deficits and finance them by borrowing from the oil producers (*see* G44). This was the alternative to taking strongly deflationary measures which could only exacerbate the recession.

Three weeks after taking office the new Chancellor presented his first budget. Overall, the budget was only mildly deflationary in its intended effect on demand. Taxation was to be raised by about £1·5 billion. The standard rate of income tax was raised by 3p to 33p in the pound and the income at which higher rates were to be paid was lowered; but personal tax allowances and child allowances were increased. Corporation tax was raised to 52 per cent, and employers were to pay a higher flat rate contribution to finance the higher National Insurance benefits announced in the budget (*see* G28). The Chancellor announced various measures to reduce tax avoidance. Tax relief of interest payments would apply only to the interest on a mortgage of up to £25,000 in respect of an owner-occupier's main house. The main forms of additional planned expenditure were higher retirement pensions, £500 million additional subsidies on basic foodstuffs, and provision for an expanded local authority housing programme. The Chancellor announced very large increases in the prices of coal, electricity, steel, postage and rail fares, in order to reduce the growing need for State subsidisation of these nationalised industries. As it turned out, this express intention to run down the level of subsidies (except on food) did not materialise; some price increases were delayed until 1975.

The second budget of the year, in July, was mildly expansionary. Value added tax was reduced from 10 per cent to 8 per cent; the Regional Employment Premium (*see* G12) was doubled; dividend controls also were eased. The main aim of yet another supplementary budget of November was to bring relief to companies which were suffering heavy taxation on "paper profits." These had resulted from inflation driving up the value of their stocks of goods and materials, which meant an increase in their declared profits. It was argued that at least part of this was an unreal increase, because the cost of replacing these stocks had gone up *pari passu*. The budget also eased some of the provisions of the Price Code (*see* G56), increased VAT on petrol to 25 per cent, made minor income tax concessions, and announced an increase in pensions and related benefits and in family allowances.

Though GDP recovered from its first quarter level, the recovery was very weak, and over the year as a whole it was virtually stagnant. This reflected mainly the weakness of private sector demand, since public expenditure rose through the year. Consumers' expenditure was down slightly. The demand for cars fell sharply, reflecting the higher cost of petrol. Factors affecting the more general sluggishness of consumption were the stricter hire-purchase controls introduced late in 1973 and the negligible rise in personal disposable income through 1974. The biggest slump in demand was in private investment. Though investment in manufacturing rose by nearly 10 per cent, housing investment shot down by nearly 25 per cent. Investment in the construction, distribution and other service industries also fell. Stockbuilding was lower than in 1973.

1975.

The picture in early 1975 was, therefore, a gloomy one. Weak or even falling output and also sales in the fourth quarter of 1974 was reflected in the unemployment figures. By February 1975 736,700 (or 3·2 per cent of the workforce) were unemployed. Despite this significant weakening in the pressure of demand, inflation showed little sign of slowing down.

One of the most alarming features of the situation was the massive increase in the public sector financial deficit. In the financial year 1974–75 it had risen to £5·5 billion, and was forecast to reach £8·9 billion in 1975–76. This latter figure would represent more than 10 per cent of the value of our total national output. This huge deficit was partly due to inflation affecting both the income and expenditure sides of the account, and thus magnifying the existing deficit. But it also represented a real increase in public expenditure.

In the budget of April 1975 the Chancellor announced that he planned to cut back the public deficit to 8 per cent of national output in 1975–76 and to 6 per cent in 1976–77. To do this he increased taxation in 1975, and aimed to reinforce this by cutting back public spending in the following year, to the tune of £900 million. Defence spending was to be cut as were food and housing subsidies. Subsidies on nationalised industry prices were to be reduced in 1975, and probably phased out altogether in 1976. Income tax rates were raised by 2p in the pound, so bringing the standard rate up to 35p. This was partly offset by increasing the amount of income which could be earned before tax was levied. Though the standard rate of VAT remained at 8 per cent, it was raised to 25 per cent on most domestic electrical appliances, radios, television sets, hi-fi equipment, cameras, furs, jewellery, and on other " luxury " goods. Excise duties were raised substantially. The company sector, already in difficulties, did not suffer as much as the personal sector. Corporation Tax was unchanged, and no surcharge on advance payment was levied. There was to be some slight further relief from the Price Code provisions. More money was made available for retraining workers, and a temporary employment subsidy was planned to encourage the deferment of redundancies. Some capital gains tax relief was announced for farmers and small businessmen. A new scheme of family allowances was proposed for the future, which, amongst other things, would give an allowance for the first child.

This was one of the harshest of recent budgets. Yet it would be hard to call it excessively restrictive. It still meant the biggest peacetime deficit in government accounts on record, and was intended to cut the flow of spending in the economy by only about £330 million by the end of 1975. The hope was that it would create enough spare capacity to enable the U.K. to take advantage of the expected upswing of world trade in 1976.

Though there was some recovery of world trade towards the end of the year, it was less strong than had been expected. The volume of U.K. exports fell between 1974 and 1975. The major components of domestic demand also declined. Although real personal disposable income was slightly higher consumers' expenditure on durable goods declined and saving increased. Thus the ratio of saving to real personal disposable income rose to 14 per cent, compared with 13 per cent in 1974, which was itself a very high figure. One explanation for this is that people were trying to restore the real value of their assets which had been eroded by inflation. Another is that people felt exceptionally uncertain in the face of rising unemployment. Uncertainty about the future together with very low profit margins and a severe liquidity shortage explained negative stockbuilding (i.e., a running down of stocks) by industrialists and also the fall in manufacturing investment. Investment as a whole remained more or less stable because of an increase in private housebuilding and investment in mining and quarrying. The current spending of public authorities expanded in volume terms—and, because of inflation, very rapidly in value terms—but not sufficiently to offset the fall in private demand. Despite the rapid inflation, the money supply grew by only 8 per cent over the year. As a result of the contraction in real demand, GDP fell by 1·7 per cent and industrial production by 5 per cent.

1976.

Although there was some evidence of recovery, the economy was still in deep recession in early 1976. Unemployment was still rising and in February 1976 exceeded 1·2 million. In that month the Chancellor announced a £215 million package designed to create or save 70,000 jobs. Money was put into industrial investment and construction, and into the temporary employment subsidy and a job creation scheme. Inflation, though it eased off, was still uncomfortably high compared to that suffered by our major competitors. The problem faced by the government was to prevent any recovery leading to higher inflation and to further balance of payments difficulties.

The Budget of April 1976 was broadly neutral in its intent. The Chancellor's intention was to give a mild stimulus to the economy by encouraging the demand for consumer durables, while at the same time keeping a tight hold on inflationary pressure. The higher VAT rate (which applied to consumer durables and luxury goods) of 25 per cent was halved to 12½ per cent, but the duty on beer, spirits, wine, cigarettes, cigars and petrol was increased. Pensions were to be increased from November (see G28), and Family Income Supplement (see G29) was to be raised from July. The temporary employment subsidy was increased from £10 to £20, and the scheme was extended by 4½ months until the end of December 1976. An extra £40 million was made available for various industrial schemes receiving government aid. The profit level at which smaller companies qualify for the preferential rate of corporation tax was raised and tax relief for stock appreciation was continued. In the field of personal taxation age allowances were increased by £60 for single people and by £130 for married couples. The child allowance was raised by £60.

There were two novel aspects to the Budget. The first was an offer of tax cuts, through increased personal allowances, but conditional upon obtaining trade union agreement to a new round of the incomes policy. The second major innovation was in the control of public expenditure. In the tax year 1975–76 both government revenue and, even more so, spending increased by more than had been anticipated in the 1975 Budget. The result was that the public sector's borrowing requirement was £10,770 million, representing 11 per cent of GNP; this was 16 per cent above the predicted level. The unanticipated increase was partly a result of the recession being more severe than was thought likely and consequently higher social security payments and the like; but probably more important was inflation magnifying the difference between revenue and expenditure. The borrowing requirement for 1976/7 was forecast at £11,960 million, which it was expected would be a smaller proportion of GNP than the 1975/6 deficit. When Supply Estimates were presented with the Budget, they were calculated on the basis of price levels prevailing at the time. As inflation proceeded, therefore, Supplementary Estimates were needed and of course the greater the inflation the greater this unplanned expenditure. The introduction of strict advance cash limits was therefore announced. Three quarters of central government expenditure other than social security benefits, was to be subject to these. There would also be stricter control of grants to local government and of the spending of nationalised industries.

During the course of the year, inflation moderated (see G53) and there was a slight rise in output, which was 1·6 per cent higher in the last quarter of 1976 than in the last quarter of 1975. The fastest rising component of demand was exports, whose volume increased by 8½ per cent. Consumers' expenditure rose by ½ per cent, despite a fall of 1½ per cent in real personal disposable income. This meant a fall in the personal savings ratio, from 14 per cent in 1975 to 12 per cent in 1976—still a high level compared to the 1960s. Spending increased most on durable goods, especially cars and motor-cycles, and was financed by borrowing. There was a rise in net credit extended for the first time in two years. Most other items of consumer spending were stagnant. Investment fell by 4 per cent, there being particularly large falls in manufacturing industry and private services. There was, however, some recovery in the second half of the year. There was also some fall in stocks held, especially in manufacturing, which implied that employers were far from sanguine about the immediate prospects for economic recovery. Despite the moderate increase in demand, there were still large margins of unused capacity, and unemployment rose to 1·42 million in February 1977: an unprecedentedly high level for the post war period.

Later in the year, the Chancellor took further measures. In July he announced £1 billion cuts in previous public spending estimates for 1977/78, whilst a further £1 billion was pruned off the estimates for that year in a December mini-budget. This budget also announced 10 per cent increases in alcohol and tobacco duties from 1 January 1977, and the sale of some of the government stake in British Petroleum. This latter decision was confirmed in the March 1977 Budget, with the Government still holding 51 per cent of the shares.

Many commentators argued that during the year fiscal policy, as it had been known, ceased to exist. It was no longer primarily seen as the instrument with which to manage domestic demand fluctuations. Rather the concern was with controlling the public sector borrowing requirement, with reducing cost inflation and the balance of payments deficit, and at the end of the year with satisfying our IMF creditors by imposing limits on both the public sector borrowing requirement (p.s.b.r.) and domestic credit expansion (d.c.e.). Certainly the Government achieved some measure of success in reducing p.s.b.r. From a figure of £10·5 billion in 1975, which represented over 11 per cent of GNP, in 1976 it was brought down to £10·3 billion or less than 10 per cent of GNP. Cash limits on public spending were undoubtedly in large part responsible for this success. Early in 1977 it was announced that they would be extended to some items of expenditure not previously covered, such as new housing investment and slum clearance. Monetary policy was not so successfully controlled, and for a period in the summer of 1976 the money supply was expanding at a rate of almost 30 per cent per annum. Over the year as a whole, however, it rose by about 10 per cent. The restriction in the latter part of the year, in the face of a huge p.s.b.r. pushed up interest rates: in October the Bank of England's minimum lending rate rose to a record 15 per cent.

1977.

In early 1977, then, the economy was still in recession. Output growth was sluggish, and unemployment had not started to fall. The rate of inflation, though lower than it had been a year earlier, was still uncomfortably high in comparison with our major competitors. The Government was committed to strict limits on the public sector borrowing requirement and on domestic credit expansion, as a result of the IMF loan and subsequent " safety net " arrangements.

In the March 1977 Budget the Chancellor announced that he hoped to cut p.s.b.r. to £8·5 billion for the 1977/78 financial year. There were to be tax cuts of £1·29 billion, to be achieved by raising tax thresholds and increasing personal allowances also. He also promised to reduce the standard rate of income tax from 35p in the pound to 33p, if satisfactory agreement could be reached with the trade unions on a new stage of incomes policy from August. This would take another £960 million off the tax bill. V.A.T. remained unchanged. but the duties on such items as cigarettes and the vehicle excise tax were increased. Corporation tax was not altered, though extra relief was given to small companies, whilst the scheme for relief on stock appreciation was continued. The temporary employment subsidy, which had been due to expire, was extended for the whole 1977/78 tax year. The Government calculated that the scheme had so far saved 200,000 jobs. They regarded such direct policies against unemployment as effective and safer than general reflation, which might have alarming inflationary consequences.

Some of these budget proposals were subsequently defeated in Parliament and replaced by new provisions, the most significant being a further increase in personal allowances. Moreover, Parliament also voted for a proposal that, in future, personal allowances should be indexed against inflation, i.e. that they should be increased annually in line with the increase in prices and money incomes, thereby making it impossible for the Government to, in effect, increase taxation by

failing to preserve the real value of personal allowances. Faced with these defeats, which effectively meant larger tax cuts than it thought desirable, the government decided to reduce income tax only to 34p in the pound, though this was not made conditional on agreement on pay policy with the unions: by then it had already become clear that no agreement would be reached.

In October a further budget was introduced. This raised personal allowances still further, by the amount required to index them against inflation over the tax year 1977–78 (so that the Government was, in effect, meeting the indexation requirement six months earlier than was necessary); gave a tax-free bonus of £10 to old age pensioners; and foreshadowed a £400 million increase in public expenditure on construction after April 1978. The measures amounted to a fiscal stimulus of £1 billion. The reason for their introduction was the realisation that the p.s.b.r. was turning out to be lower than had been planned at the time of the April budget, so that some increase in the budget deficit was permissible within the monetary targets laid down in April. The reason for the fall in the p.s.b.r. was partly due to lower public expenditure as a result of the fall in interest rates and therefore of debt interest payments, and partly due to revenue being higher than expected. With the new measures, the revised estimate for the p.s.b.r. was £7·5 billion in 1977–78.

The economy continued to stagnate throughout 1977. Total real output rose hardly at all; and a small increase in total final demand occurred only because of rapidly rising exports (an increase of 7½ per cent in volume) and some restocking. Private and public consumption and gross fixed investment all fell (though private manufacturing investment rose). Unemployment continued to rise: by the end of the year it stood at over 1·4 million. Real personal disposable income fell by about 2 per cent over the year as a whole, though the two halves of the year were significantly different in this respect: by the middle of the year, when Stage Two of the incomes policy came to an end, real income had fallen by about 5 per cent since mid-1976, but in the second half of 1977 there was some increase. This was helped by the continued fall in the rate of price inflation, which by the end of the year had dropped to about 13 per cent. During the year the balance-of-payments current account moved into surplus, though the size of the surplus was only small because imports rose rapidly—by 4½ per cent in volume—despite sluggish demand.

Throughout the year the emphasis of economic policy, as in 1976, was on meeting monetary targets, controlling the p.s.b.r., and reducing cost inflation. By the beginning of 1978 it was clear that the monetary target for fiscal year 1977–78— a 9–13 per cent growth in M3 (*see* G23)—would not be significantly breached; in the event annual growth turned out to be almost exactly 13 per cent. The p.s.b.r. turned out well below the forecast level, even after the October tax cuts, as public spending was over 4 per cent below the budgeted amount. Since, as already noted, inflation continued to fall, policy in 1977 could be judged reasonably successful on these criteria. The major problem was, of course, the continued stagnation in the " real " economy, *i.e.* in levels of output and employment; it was clear by the end of the year that the improvement in the economy's financial position had not so far spilled over to real variables.

1978.

At the beginning of 1978, therefore, the economy remained in recession. With the balance of payments in surplus and the inflation rate continuing to fall, there appeared to be some possibility of a mild reflation; however, the scope for this was limited by the need to maintain strict monetary guidelines in accordance with I.M.F. requirements, and by the expectation that any significant expansion of demand would cause a very large increase in imports and hence push the economy back into balance-of-payments deficit. Also, there was widespread recognition of the need to avoid the mistakes of 1972–73, when demand was expanded much too rapidly.

In the April Budget, therefore, the Chancellor

proceeded cautiously, cutting taxes by £2 billion with the aim of stimulating demand by enough to add ½ per cent to output growth, the target for which was set at 3 per cent over the year. There were hints from the Government that an additional stimulus might be given later in the year, depending upon trends in the balance of payments and in inflation.

The main tax changes in the budget were increases in personal allowances and the introduction of a new lower rate of 25p in the pound income tax on the first £750 of taxable income. The idea of taxing a band of income at a lower rate had been part of the tax system until 1969, when it was abolished because of its administrative inconvenience. Its reintroduction represented an attempt to alleviate some aspects of the "poverty trap" (see G29) by reducing the marginal tax rate paid by poorer families. Other changes included increases in retirement pensions and in unemployment and sickness benefits to take effect in November; a series of increases in child benefit allowances in April and November of 1978 and April 1979 (this being concurrent with the phasing out of child tax allowances); some widening of the bands of income to which higher rates of tax apply; a series of changes in corporation tax, capital gains tax, capital transfer tax, and V.A.T. designed to help small businesses and the self-employed; and help for "profit-sharing" in industry by allowing companies from 1979–80 onwards to allocate up to £500 of shares to any one employee tax-free. No changes were made in rates of V.A.T. or any other indirect tax, or in corporation tax.

The budget was accompanied by targets for p.s.b.r. and for the rate of monetary growth over 1978–79. The p.s.b.r. ceiling was set at £8·5 billion, and an 8–12 per cent target rate of growth for sterling M3 was adopted, to be reviewed after six months. Minimum lending rate was raised from 6½ to 7½ per cent in an attempt by the Government to reassure financial markets that its monetary and fiscal targets would be adhered to even if they required higher interest rates. Many investors were worried that the p.s.b.r. target would only prove compatible with the monetary target at the expense of significant increases in interest rates. They were also concerned about the possibility of increases in the inflation rate later in the year, perhaps triggered off by large pay settlements. It was clear, therefore, that the course of pay negotiations over the year remained crucial to the Government's economic strategy.

Prospects for Economic Growth.

There has not only been dissatisfaction with the uneven way in which the economy has grown. There has also been increasing dissatisfaction with the rate of growth achieved in the economy since the war. The economies of most other industrial countries have expanded at a much faster rate (see G13). To try to improve our growth performance, the Labour Government introduced the National Plan in 1965. By setting a target annual rate of growth until 1970, it aimed to bolster firms' expectations and hence their investment and to co-ordinate their decisions. Unanticipated balance of payments difficulties meant that the Plan was short-lived, but some of the institutions associated with the Plan survived. The National Economic Development Council had been established in 1962 to stimulate a more systematic study of the problems involved in securing a faster rate of growth. Twenty-one Economic Development Committees for different industries were set up under its umbrella.

(i) The National Enterprise Board.

In 1974 The Labour Government published a White Paper entitled The Regeneration of British Industry, setting out ideas which found their legislative expression in the Industry Act of 1975. Underlying this Act was the feeling that private enterprise, on its own, had not done enough to stimulate a high rate of growth. The Act aimed to remedy this by setting up the National Enterprise Board. Its proposed functions were to assist the establishment, development or maintenance of any industrial enterprise or industry, to extend public ownership into profitable areas of

manufacturing, to promote industrial democracy in undertakings controlled by it, and to hold and manage the securities of any other property in public ownership. The Board was not, without the consent of the Minister for Industry, to acquire shares if this would give the Board control of more than 30 per cent of the voting rights of the company, or to invest more than £10 million in the shares of any one company. The Board's borrowings were to be limited to £700 million, which could be increased to £1,000 million by order. These sums are very modest in relation to the market value of the share capital of major British firms. Funds for aid which the Minister directed the Board to give were to be additional to the above figures. Both the Minister and the Treasury were to ensure that the Board earned an "adequate" return on capital employed. The Act also contained provisions for the compulsory disclosure of information by firms both to the Minister and to trade unions. It also introduced the idea of voluntary planning agreements, which private companies might enter into with the Government. In return such companies would be assured of regional development grants at the rates prevailing at the time the agreement was made.

Critics argued both that the Act was doctrinaire socialism and that it was not proved that such state intervention would have more favourable effects than the workings of free private enterprise. As presently financed, it is clear that the National Enterprise Board cannot proceed much further with the extension of public ownership, since it has available only small funds. Guidelines issued in early 1976 further restricted its ability to act without reference to the Secretary of State for Industry. He had to be consulted in all cases involving share purchases of more than £½ million if shareholders objected. Some measure of greater independence was given to the NEB in December 1976, when it was allowed to make loans or guarantees or engage in joint ventures without informing the Secretary of State, where the cost was less than £10 million, and where no new significant policy issues arose. From February 1978 the NEB was allowed to sell off investments up to the value of £1 million without the Secretary of State's permission.

Even before the NEB was effectively operational, state acquisitions in the private sector had proceeded apace. Normally the Government had provided help to ailing companies on condition of taking a shareholding, under the provisions of the Conservatives' 1972 Industry Act. State holdings in eight companies were handed over to the NEB at its inception. These companies were British Leyland, Rolls-Royce, Cambridge Instruments, Ferranti, Herbert, Brown-Boveri-Kent, Dunford and Elliott, and ICL. The NEB acquired shareholdings in another fourteen companies by early 1977. By early 1978 only one planning agreement—with Chrysler—had been concluded.

(ii) An Approach to Industrial Strategy.

In 1975 a White Paper, entitled An Approach to Industrial Strategy, set out the Government's general views on planning for growth. It envisaged a systematic and continuing study of the past performance of thirty or so sectors of manufacturing, assessing the implications for medium-term growth assumptions. It further suggested consultations about these studies between government and industry at the national, industry, and company level. In February 1978 thirty-nine of the sectoral working parties presented their reports. These reports were full of suggestions, particularly on how to improve export performance. But at present it is too early to say whether anything practical will come of them. Though in early 1978 the Government was still talking of its "industrial strategy," it is tempting to conclude that the strategy comprised little but discussion.

There was, however, one area where the 1975 Industry Act had practical consequences. This was in the introduction of schemes of financial assistance to industry. By the end of 1976 nine sectors were benefiting from this provision of the Act. They were wool textiles; ferrous metals; machine tools; clothing; paper and board;

poultry; meat processing; printing machinery; textile machinery; and red-meat slaughterhouses. Other sectors have received funds since then. The assistance has been directed towards modernisation and improvement of productivity; for example, £10 million was given to encourage new investment in the instrumentation and automation industry. Nevertheless, there is concern that some of the money is going into sectors which even improvements would be unlikely to make internationally competitive.

(iii) British Oil Production.

The discovery of oil in British waters has implications for Britain's long-term growth prospects. The oil crisis of 1973 and the subsequent rocketing of the price of oil drove the economy into recession and engendered concern about Britain's medium-term growth rate. Whilst these early fears may have been somewhat exaggerated, so also might expectations of a bonanza in the late 1970s from oil production in British waters. Though by early 1976 extraction of British oil had fallen behind schedule, it was still expected that by 1980 production would be enough for the U.K. to be almost self-sufficient. But there were a number of doubts about the costs of exploitation and about the extent to which the Government would have already mortgaged future returns by heavy borrowing abroad. It was uncertain how long after 1980 the U.K. would continue to be self-sufficient. Production was expected to rise very fast until the early 1980s, and then, at best, to increase at only a slow rate. Since the domestic demand for oil was not expected to slow down in this way, the U.K. was likely to become dependent on imports once again.

Meanwhile the Government was trying to ensure that the state got a substantial share of the returns from offshore oil extraction. A major concern was the large degree of foreign ownership of the oil companies involved in the operations. In February 1975, therefore, a Bill was introduced into Parliament, which proposed a *petroleum revenue tax* of 45 per cent and royalties of 12½ per cent. Corporation tax was to be deducted from the residue at the standard rate. It was envisaged that this would allow the oil companies a 20 per cent return on capital. Concern had been expressed that such a tax system would discourage exploitation of the "marginal fields", that is the smaller oil-fields which might not justify the huge initial expenditure needed to make them productive. Several safeguards were, therefore, proposed. No petroleum revenue tax would be levied until a field had earned back 175 per cent of its capital outlay. Fields returning less than 30 per cent on investment after paying p.r.t. would have the tax refunded. There was also to be discretionary provision to return all or part of the 12½ per cent royalties. The Government reiterated its intention to press for 51 per cent state participation in the oil-fields, which it proceeded to do through the agency of the British National Oil Corporation.

In March 1978 the Government published a White Paper, *The Challenge of North Sea Oil.* In this it was estimated that by the mid 1980s North Sea Oil would increase national income by £6 billion per year and improve the balance of payments to the tune of £8 billion per year. Perhaps more crucially the annual benefit to government revenue was expected to be £4 billion. The crucial issue was how this extra revenue was to be used. The White Paper designated four priorities: more resources for industrial investment; funds for energy conservation and new energy investment; the reduction of the level of personal taxation; the improvement of certain essential services. It was clear that the Government believed that North Sea oil provided it with an opportunity to stimulate sustained growth, and the first two of the four priorities were obviously designed with this in mind. How far reality would coincide with intention remained to be seen, but the authorities were well aware of the connection between energy policy and growth performance. Meanwhile their major worry on the energy front was the fast rate of extraction of North Sea gas. Many people felt that this meant that gas was being sold too cheaply, and thus was threatening the market for coal and nuclear power, which were the two

fuels on which medium-term energy policy was based.

(iv) Pressures on the Industrial Sector.

Between 1961 and 1974 employment outside industry increased by over one third relative to employment in industry; *i.e.* employment grew much faster in private services and in public services and utilities. This larger non-industrial sector imposed extra demands on industrial production. Capital goods for investment in the industrial sector had to be provided from the output of the industrial sector, whilst more industrial production was needed for consumers employed in the services and elsewhere. Thus less was left over for investments in industry itself and for industrial exports. This meant an inadequate growth of industrial capacity. Thus when the Government attempted to stimulate the economy, bottlenecks quickly developed and imports of consumer goods increased rapidly. The result was balance of payments difficulties, which were only partially alleviated by increasing exports of services like insurance, and therefore the government took deflationary action. This vicious circle could only be broken by an upsurge in industrial investment, which was prevented by declining profitability.

Some commentators have argued that the problem was a direct result of the growth in public sector employment. This had to be paid for either by workers or private employers, and trade unions made sure that it was the employers; if, for example, income tax was raised, this was passed on in successful wage demands. The result was declining profitability. This analysis is at best speculative. It is not, for example, at all evident that public sector employment has grown nearly as rapidly as implied. In certain activities such as local government there was a very rapid growth, but overall the ratio of public sector to total employment increased only modestly—from 23·9 per cent in 1961 to 27·2 per cent in 1974. Similarly over the same period public sector spending increased only from 21·5 per cent to 26·8 per cent of gross domestic product. On the other side it was argued that such figures understate the true change: the spending figures are in constant prices; in current money terms the change was more striking because of the *relative price effect, i.e.*, items like teachers' and civil servants' salaries rising faster than the general price level. The figures also exclude transfers from people who produce to those who do not, such as pensioners. Finally, it was argued that the claim of the public sector on output which could be sold increased by almost 50 per cent between 1961 and 1974 thus reducing the resources available for industrial investment. If such arguments are borne out by further investigations, a conflict between industrial growth and the humanitarian aims of society—such as the provision of health services and of education—may arise. But before that argument begins, research will be needed into how productively the extra resources apparently claimed by the public sector have been used.

Inflation.

(i) Wages and Prices.

Retail prices continued to edge upwards in the 1960s and 1970s (*see* G20–1). In 1977 they were 235 per cent higher than in 1963. Very little of this increase can be attributed to an increase in import prices. To explain the inflation we must look at the behaviour of labour costs. Between 1963 and 1977 the nationally negotiated weekly wage rates rose by 324 per cent, and weekly earnings—including overtime payments and payments negotiated on the factory floor—by 344 per cent. Since the increase in productivity during this period was slow, income from employment per unit of output (indicating labour costs per unit of output) rose by about 275 per cent. These increased costs were passed on to the public in the form of increased prices, so that real earnings rose by only 38 per cent. The table shows annual average prices, earnings, real earnings, and also real disposable incomes (*i.e.*, the purchasing power of total personal incomes after income tax), all as indexes with 1963 = 100.

AVERAGE RETAIL PRICES, WEEKLY
EARNINGS, REAL WEEKLY EARNINGS
AND REAL DISPOSABLE INCOMES
1963 = 100

	Retail prices	Weekly earnings	Real weekly earnings	Real disposable incomes
1964	103·3	107·1	103·7	103·9
1965	108·2	115·1	106·4	106·3
1966	112·5	122·5	108·9	108·6
1967	115·3	126·2	109·5	110·0
1968	120·7	136·8	113·3	112·0
1969	127·2	147·5	115·9	112·8
1970	135·3	164·4	121·5	116·8
1971	148·1	182·8	123·4	119·9
1972	158·6	205·7	129·7	128·7
1973	173·2	234·1	135·2	136·7
1974	201·0	275·2	136·9	138·1
1975	249·5	348·8	139·8	131·5
1976	288·9	403·2	139·6	140·6
1977	335·2	443·9	132·4	137·8

(ii) The Growing Inflation.

A disturbing feature of the table is the growth in the rate of inflation in Britain after 1967. Between 1968 and 1970 retail prices rose by an average of 5·9 per cent per year, between 1970 and 1971 by 9·5 per cent, between 1971 and 1972 by 7·1 per cent, between 1972 and 1973 by 9·2 per cent, between 1973 and 1974 by 16 per cent and between 1974 and 1975 by 24·1 per cent. The increase in average weekly earnings also accelerated.

Why was there this acceleration in the rate of inflation? In 1968 and 1969, it resulted partly from the increase in import prices consequent upon the devaluation of the pound in November 1967 (see G38), partly from the increase in indirect taxes introduced after devaluation in order to free resources for exports (see G47), and partly from the spurt in money wages when the Government's incomes policy weakened (see G55). But in 1970 the blame could be placed squarely on the " wage explosion ". Normally money wages rise more rapidly the greater the pressure of demand in the labour market (see G21). But with unemployment high in 1970, pressure of demand for labour could not be the explanation. Rather, the wage explosion appeared to reflect a general increase in militancy by trade unionists angered by the near-stagnation of real earnings and real disposable incomes after 1967 and possibly influenced by events in other countries (see below). Once begun it was maintained by the growth of expectations that prices would continue to rise rapidly.

In 1970 there was a sharp increase in real earnings (by 5 per cent), implying a decline in the share of profits. This share (gross trading profits as a proportion of domestic income) is normally low during a recession, but the share in 1970 dropped to 10 per cent compared with 14 per cent in the recession of 1962. The share rose in 1971 when the increase in labour costs had a delayed effect on prices: retail prices were up by no less than 9 per cent on 1970. There was a danger that this in turn might set off further wage demands and so maintain, or even accelerate, a vicious spiral of inflation. Indeed, that is what happened in 1972. Both wage and price increases accelerated, and the Government was forced to intervene in November by introducing a pay and price standstill (see G56). The inflation of 1972 was caused mainly by increased wage payments, although the effective devaluation of the pound in June and the rising world prices of food and raw materials also contributed, both directly to prices and indirectly through their effects on wage demands. The rising price of imports—particularly of food which accounted for half of the 10 per cent increase in the cost of living between end-1972 and end-1973 —was mainly responsible for the inflation during 1973, but labour costs also rose markedly. There was a temporary slowdown in the rate of inflation following the July 1974 budget, but apart from this it accelerated fairly steadily through 1974 as a whole. Whilst import prices had been the fastest growing item of costs for the two years up to the

middle of 1974, by then domestic wage and salary costs had taken over this role. Average earnings increased by no less than 25 per cent between the fourth quarters of 1973 and 1974. Since productivity growth was very slow, this meant a 23 per cent rise in labour costs. Government policy had some effect in dampening down the rate of inflation, both through the operation of the Price Code (see G56) and through increased subsidies.

(iii) The Attack on Inflation.

1975 saw an even higher rate of inflation than 1974. Average weekly earnings rose by nearly 27 per cent. Productivity fell and prices rose by about 25 per cent. Import prices made a smaller contribution to inflation than in the previous two years. They were 13 per cent higher than in 1974, much of this being the result of an 8 per cent fall in the value of sterling. Real earnings rose by 2·1 per cent, implying a further drop in the share of profits in domestic income to less than 6 per cent, after a larger fall from 9·7 per cent in 1973 to 6·6 per cent in 1974. But through 1975 inflation moderated. Average earnings started to slow down in the second quarter, and wholesale and retail prices followed with a lag. By the third quarter they were all increasing at about 15 per cent. The slowdown of average earnings started before the imposition of the £6 limit (see G57), and it has been suggested that this was caused by growing unemployment. Such an effect was, however, small compared with the direct impact of the £6 rule.

Domestic inflation moderated still further in 1976, retail prices being 16 per cent higher than in 1975. The main contributor to this was the deceleration in the rate of increase in labour costs. Average weekly earnings were over 15 per cent higher than in 1975. Real earnings were therefore slightly lower than in the previous year, implying some recovery in the share of profits in domestic income. By far the largest influence on the deceleration of wage inflation was the voluntary incomes policy, first the £6 limit and from August its successor, which aimed at a 4½ per cent increase in basic wage rates (see G57). In the last few months of the year price inflation showed a small increase. Whereas in July the retail price index was only 13 per cent higher than a year earlier, by December this figure was 15 per cent. This upturn is explained by the sharp fall in the value of the pound during the year putting up the cost of raw materials and fuel purchased by British industry. Over a year as a whole the largest price increases were in food, fuel, and light, and the smallest were in durable household goods, tobacco, and services.

Retail prices were 16 per cent higher in 1977 than in 1976, whilst earnings were only 10 per cent higher. Real earnings, therefore, fell by 5 per cent, and this meant some further recovery in the share of profits in national income. Real disposable income fell by the smaller amount of 2¼ per cent, because of the reduction of taxes in the April and October budgets. Productivity improved hardly at all during the year, and so the earnings increases meant a similar increase in labour costs per unit of output, these costs feeding through to prices.

There was a considerable contrast between the two halves of 1977. In the year to July 1977 prices rose at the rate of 17½ per cent, inflation being exacerbated by the depreciation of sterling in 1976, and further fed by the delayed impact of earnings increase of 14 per cent during Stage I of incomes policy, which ended in July 1976 (see G57). Since by early 1977 Stage II of incomes policy was holding earnings increases down to 10 per cent, real personal income was badly squeezed in the first half of the year. These lower increases in earnings together with the appreciation of sterling had their effect on retail prices in the second half of the year. By early 1978 price inflation had fallen below 10%. At the same time earnings had begun to inc.ease at the rate of about 15 per cent per annum. This, together with the 1977 tax cuts, meant an appreciable recovery in real personal income.

Thus by early 1978 price inflation had fallen back into single figures. A higher rate of increase seemed inevitable later in the year as the rise in earnings had its impact. How great this increase would be depended on two factors: first, the extent to which union demands were moderated by lower inflation and high unemployment; second, the success of the Government in achieving a new stage of incomes policy from August 1978.

(iv) International Inflation.

The acceleration of inflation in Britain coincided with similar trends in other countries, including the United States, Japan, W. Germany, France, and Italy, as the table shows. It is also apparent that inflation has generally been more rapid in the United Kingdom than in the other countries since 1968.

Was this the result of a series of coincidences; did the inflations have a common cause; or were they "contagious"? Both France and Italy had major strikes and subsequent "wage explosions"; Britain's inflation too was "cost-push" not "demand pull" in character (see G4); Japan and W. Germany experienced strong demand pressures; and in the United States the price increases could be explained as a lagged reaction to the demand pressure of 1966–69. Nevertheless, it is likely that inflation was to some extent transmitted from one country to another—particularly from the United States and particularly to small, trading countries—through its effects on the prices of imports and exports, and possibly through its effects on workers' expectations. In all countries, whatever the initial impetus to the inflation, expectations came to play an important role in sustaining it.

Policies against inflation were also similar. Heartened by the apparent success of the statutory wages and prices policies introduced in the United States in August 1971, a growing number of European countries, including the United Kingdom, introduced or tightened direct controls on pay and prices. But these policies did not prevent inflation from accelerating. The sharp increase in inflation experienced by all the major economies in 1973 reflected the rising prices of primary products in world markets. World inflation accelerated further during 1974 as the increased oil price had its full effect on costs and prices in the industrial countries. The high price of oil meant a transfer of purchasing power from its consumers to its producers, and therefore a fall in effective demand in industrialised countries. Many foreign countries exacerbated the consequent recession by much more restrictive fiscal and monetary policies than those employed by the British Government. The result was a fall in their inflation rates in the first half of 1975; and, though there was a renewed rise in the second half of the year, the rise of consumer prices in 1975 as a whole was somewhat lower than in 1974. Britain is the only one of the countries listed in the table whose inflation rate increased in 1975. In all major trading countries the inflation rate fell in 1976. In 1977 the inflation rate continued to fall in Japan and Germany; it rose in the United States and Italy, and remained more or less unchanged in Britain and France. Britain remains near the top of the inflation league table. Only Italy, of the countries listed in the table, had a higher rise in consumer prices.

Incomes Policy.

Britain's competitive position in world trade has deteriorated in relation to that of her main rivals the United States, West Germany, and France; this is one major reason for her recurrent balance of payments difficulties. The British share in total world exports of manufactures fell from 17·7 per cent to 12·3 per cent between 1959 and 1967; and further, to 8·8 per cent, between 1967 and 1975. There are essentially two methods of remedying this situation. We must secure either a relative fall in the external value of the pound, or a relative rise in its internal value. In other words, either there must be a devaluation of the pound in terms of other currencies, or we must have a policy to limit the increase in the British price-level. Up to 1967 the Government concentrated on the latter alternative; and attempts were made to introduce some form of *incomes policy*. In 1967 and from 1972 it allowed the pound to depreciate or float downwards; but incomes policy was still necessary if the devaluation was to be successful, and if harshly restrictive monetary and fiscal policies were to be avoided.

Other harmful effects of inflation, giving rise to the need for some form of incomes policy, are discussed on G21–2.

(i) The Pay Pause.

In July 1961 the Chancellor of the Exchequer called for a "pause" in wages, salaries, and dividend payments. Exhortations for restraint have been a familiar feature of ministerial statements for many years, but on this occasion the Government soon made it clear that it intended to use such power as it has to influence the amount and timing of wage and salary awards. It had the power to decide when the pay awards recommended by the Wages Councils—which fix minimum wages for 3½ million workers—should be implemented. The Government's power is strongest over workers which it directly or indirectly employs, e.g., civil servants, teachers, and Post Office workers. Their pay awards were cut back. The Government also had a limited influence on awards made in nationalised industries.

The "pay pause" came to an end in April 1962. It was envisaged as a temporary policy, and its effects are difficult to assess. It certainly postponed some wage awards which would otherwise have been made in that period, and it may have contributed to a stiffening of resistance to wage claims. But because the pause affected some groups of people more severely than others, this form of incomes policy was seen to be discriminatory.

(ii) The National Incomes Commission.

In February 1962 the Government issued a White Paper which outlined its incomes policy for the period after the pause. It stated that "the objective must be to keep the rate of increase in incomes within the long-term rate of growth of national production." The Government stressed that most of the arguments which had in the past been advanced in justification of wages and salary claims—e.g., increases in the cost of living, trends in productivity or profits in particular industries, and comparisons with levels or trends in other employments—should be given less weight; and that "general economic considerations"—i.e., the increases which the economy can afford given the prospective rate of increase in national production—should be given more weight. Late in 1962 the Government set up the *National Incomes Commission* (NIC). However, the powers of this body were limited. It had, for example, no power to cancel or modify a wage agreement on which it reported. NIC produced only 4 reports, and was wound up after the change in Government.

(iii) The National Board for Prices and Incomes.

In October 1964 the Labour Government's new Department of Economic Affairs was made responsible for achieving an incomes policy. The lessons of the past had been learned: the Government recognised that a successful incomes policy would require the support of both sides of industry. Its first objective was to achieve a "Joint Statement of Intent on Productivity, Prices and Incomes"; this was signed in December 1964. In this document the T.U.C. and the employers' organisations undertook to co-operate with the Government in producing an effective machinery for the implementing of an incomes policy.

It was Government policy that growth in earnings per employee should equal the planned growth in national output per employee of 3–3½ per cent per annum. Thus, in those industries (e.g., engineering) in which productivity growth exceeded this "norm", earnings should rise less rapidly than productivity, and in those industries (e.g., railways) in which productivity growth fell short of the norm, earnings could rise more rapidly than productivity. Moreover, prices would be expected to fall in industries such as

RISE IN CONSUMER PRICES

	1959–1972*	1972–1973	1973–1974	1974–1975	1975–1976	1976–1977
U.S.	2·8	6·2	11·0	9·1	5·8	6·5
Japan	5·5	11·7	23·2	11·7	9·4	8·2
France	4·2	7·3	13·7	11·7	9·6	9·5
W. Germany	3·0	6·9	7·0	6·0	4·5	3·9
Italy	3·9	10·4	19·4	17·2	16·5	19·4
U.K.	4·5	8·3	16·0	24·1	15·8	16·0

* Annual average.

engineering, and permitted to rise in industries such as railways. Growth in earnings per employee should exceed the norm only in exceptional cases; *i.e.*, as a reward for increasing productivity by eliminating restrictive working practices; if necessary to transfer labour from one industry to another; if earnings were too low to maintain a reasonable standard of living; or if a group of workers had fallen seriously out of line with earnings for similar work.

To make specific recommendations on the basis of this policy, the Government set up a *National Board for Prices and Incomes.* The Prices Review Division of the Board could investigate the price of any goods in the economy, and the Incomes Review Division had power to investigate all claims and settlements relating to wages, salaries and other incomes. In less than 5 years of operation the Board had produced over 150 reports on prices and earnings.

There was no statutory authority to enforce the recommendations of the Board: reliance was placed on voluntary methods and the power of persuasion and public opinion. However, in late 1965 the Government introduced a compulsory " Early Warning " system, whereby it was notified in advance of any intended increase in incomes or in certain prices. As a result, the Government and the Board had time to consider increases before they were put into effect.

(iv) The Prices and Incomes Standstill.

A voluntary incomes policy is very difficult to implement, since it depends on co-operation among Government, workers, and employers; moreover, co-operation among representatives at the top may be undermined by " wage-drift " at the factory level. Thus the annual average of weekly wage-rates rose by no less than 5 percentage points between 1965 and 1966. In fact all of this increase took place in the period before July 1966. Clearly the voluntary incomes policy was meeting with little success.

Therefore, as part of the July measures taken to deal with the balance of payments problem, the Government introduced a " prices and incomes standstill." Increases in prices and incomes were as far as possible avoided altogether until the end of 1966. The only exceptions in the case of incomes were pay increases resulting directly from increases in output (*e.g.*, piece-work or over-time earnings) and from genuine promotion or regular increments on a predetermined scale. Increases already negotiated but not yet implemented were deferred for 6 months. The first half of 1967 was a period of " severe restraint." Any price increases were carefully examined, and the norm for income increases was zero. Any increase in earnings had to be justified by one of the four conditions for exception, referred to above. To enforce its " freeze " the Government took the unprecedented step of asking Parliament for reserve powers (including penalties for offenders), which were to be used only if the need should arise. For the most part, there was a voluntary observation of the standstill; but from October 1966 the Government found it necessary to exercise its power of compulsion in a few cases, *e.g.*, laundry and dry cleaning charges, and a wage agreement in the electrical engineering industry. The power of compulsion lapsed in August 1967.

There then followed a year in which there was to be a " nil norm " except where increases in incomes could be justified by one of the four criteria listed above. The Government could no longer legally enforce its policy, but it did retain the power to delay price and pay increases, through

reference to the Board, by up to 7 months. Whereas the Government succeeded in slowing down the rise in wages and prices during the year in which it took compulsory powers, in the second half of 1967 weekly wage rates rose at an annual rate of 6 per cent. The advantage gained from the previous restraint was reduced but not entirely lost.

(v) Incomes Policy after Devaluation.

Incomes policy was made both more difficult and more important by the devaluation of the pound: more difficult in that devaluation involved a cut in the standard of living, and more important in that the trading benefit from devaluation should not be neutralised by inflation.

In April 1968 the Government published a White Paper outlining its policy for the period until the end of 1969. Wage increases had still to be justified by the four criteria, and there was a " ceiling " to increases in income of 3½ per cent per annum except for " productivity agreements " and low-paid workers. Price increases were permitted only as a result of unavoidable increases in cost per unit of output, and price reductions were required when costs fell. Dividend increases were also subject to the ceiling of 3½ per cent per annum, and home rent increases restricted. The Government intended to rely on the voluntary co-operation of unions and employers over pay; but it decided to lengthen its delaying powers for pay and price increases up to 12 months, and take powers to enforce price reductions recommended by the Board.

Between November 1967 and November 1968 the retail price index rose by 5·2 per cent, mainly due to the effect of devaluation on import prices. In the face of this rise in the cost of living the incomes policy met with firm resistance. In practice the nominal ceiling of 3½ per cent per annum rapidly became the normal increase. In the first year after devaluation basic wage rates rose by 6·0 per cent and average earnings by 7·5 per cent. Workers were able to protect themselves against this inflation and to increase slightly their real income.

During 1969 the process of wage and price inflation accelerated. In December the Government published a White Paper on its incomes policy for the period after 1969. It laid down a norm for wage increases of 2·5 to 4·5 per cent per annum: increases should exceed the upper limit only in exceptional circumstances, *e.g.*, in productivity agreements, in cases where an inappropriate pay structure is rationalised, *e.g.* by means of job evaluation, in the case of low-paid workers and in the achievement of equal pay for women. Comparisons with other workers should not be used, except in the case of public servants (*e.g.*, teachers and nurses) whose productivity cannot be measured and whose pay tends to fall behind that of the private sector. The limit on the increase in company dividends of 3·5 per cent per annum was ended and the Government's powers to delay the implementation of proposed wage and price increases were reduced. However, the incomes policy laid down in the White Paper was tempered by the imminence of a General Election and the recent cost of living increases; and it did not prevent a " wage explosion " occurring in 1970.

(vi) Conservative Policy.

On taking office in June 1970 the Conservative Government eschewed its predecessor's approach to incomes policy and disbanded the National

Board for Prices and Incomes. To curb the inflation it maintained the economy in recession and squeezed company liquidity, hoping in this way to weaken wage pressures and strengthen the resistances of employers. In addition it attempted to resist demands for wage increases in the public sector, at the cost of prolonging strikes, *e.g.*, in electricity supply, postal services and coal mining. In the former two cases it met with some success; in the case of the coal miners' strike early in 1972 the Government was unable to enforce its policy. In any case this form of incomes policy—like the "pay pause" of 1961—was both partial and discriminatory. The Government also intervened to curb price rises in the nationalised industries, *e.g.*, postal charges and steel prices. The main initiative on prices came from the Confederation of British Industry (CBI): in July 1971, it asked its members to avoid price increases over the next twelve months or to limit them to 5 per cent or less in unavoidable increases. Over 170 leading British companies agreed to comply.

The Government measures were by no means a sure remedy for the inflation spiral. Moreover, even its apparent strategy of deterring wage demands by maintaining high unemployment was dropped in the reflationary budget of 1972 (*see* **G47**). The Government appeared to be placing its faith in its Act for the Reform of Industrial Relations to solve the problem of wage inflation in the long run.

(vii) The Pay and Price Standstill.

In 1972 wage demands became more difficult to contain because of the increase in the cost-of-living resulting from the effective devaluation of the pound in June and the rise in world food prices during the year. There was a marked increase in the number and seriousness of strikes (*see* **G19**). This was fairly widespread, although the national miners' strike accounted for 10·8 million of the 23·9 million working days lost in 1972. Nevertheless, on average only very slightly more than one working day was lost per employee during the year. The principal cause of the rise in disputes was a sharp rise in disagreements over pay claims: this increase being both cause and effect of the rapid inflation. In the six months between the first and third quarters of 1972 average weekly earnings rose by no less than 7 per cent. It was inevitable that the Government should intervene. The expectation of an impending freeze now encouraged further wage and price increases, especially after the CBI's period of voluntary restraint had elapsed.

The Government first tried to achieve a tripartite voluntary agreement with the CBI and the TUC to combat inflation. After this attempt had failed, on 6 November the Conservative Government reversed its previous policy on inflation and introduced a Statutory Prices and Pay standstill. In effect there was a standstill on all prices of goods and services other than imports and fresh foods, a standstill on rents, on dividends, and on all negotiated wages and salaries including those previously negotiated but not yet in operation. The freeze was to last for 90 days, and possibly for a further 60 days. Offenders were liable to be fined.

(viii) The Price Commission and the Pay Board.

In early 1973 the Government formulated its policy for after the standstill in a series of documents, culminating in a Price and Pay Code. Two new agencies—a *Price Commission* and a *Pay Board*—were established to regulate prices, pay, dividends, and rent in accordance with the Price and Pay Code.

In Stage Two of the policy—lasting from the end of the pay standstill on 31 March until the autumn—the following criteria on pay were to apply. The total annual pay increase for any group of employees should not exceed £1 a week plus 4 per cent of the current pay bill excluding overtime. There was flexibility for negotiation of increases within a group: emphasis was to be on the lower paid and the maximum allowable increase was £250 a year. Exceptions to the limit were made for, *e.g.*, movement towards equal pay between the sexes, reduction in standard hours worked to not less than 40 hours a week,

increased annual holidays up to a three week maximum, personal increments and promotion, and some improved pension benefits. The Pay Board had to be notified of all settlements involving less than 1,000 employees but settlements involving more than 1,000 employees required its prior approval. It became an offence to strike or threaten to strike to force an employer to contravene an order of the Pay Board.

Prices in Stage Two could be increased only to take account of *allowable* cost increase:, and were to reflect only the percentage increases in these costs per unit of output since 1 October 1972. Moreover to allow for productivity growth, firms were permitted to pass on as price increases only a fraction of the increase in the wage costs allowed by the Code. Prices were also limited by the requirement that net profit margins should not exceed the average percentage level of the best two of the last five years. Exceptions were made for companies which could show that without higher profits their investment would be held back. Large firms had to give prior notice of price increases to the Price Commission, medium firms had to report regularly on prices, and small firms had to keep price records. Imports, fresh foods, auctioned goods, secondhand goods and interest charges were among the exemptions from the price controls. Dividends could not be raised by more than 5 per cent over the previous year. The standstill on business rents was extended into Stage Two.

One of the problems facing the price policy was the continued sharp rise in world food prices after the standstill was declared. This made public acceptance of the Government policy more difficult to achieve.

(ix) Stage Three.

Stage Three of the counter-inflation policy was announced in October 1973. Price controls were similar to those under Stage Two. Wage increases negotiated for any group of workers would be statutorily limited to an average of either £2·25 a week per head, or if preferred, 7 per cent per head, with a limit of £350 a year on the amount to be received by any one individual. However, further increases were permitted beyond these limits, to deal with certain specific matters: changes in pay structures, better use of manpower, efficiency schemes, "unsocial" hours, and progress towards equal pay for women. A novel aspect of the pay policy was the *threshold agreement* to safeguard against increases in the cost of living. It was possible for wage negotiators to bargain for a pay increase of up to 40p a week, payable if the retail price index reached 7 per cent above its level at the beginning of Stage Three, with up to another 40p a week for each percentage point it rose thereafter until the end of Stage Three in November 1974. Other countries, Canada for example, have recently experimented with various forms of *indexation* similar to threshold agreements. In Britain many people claimed that these agreements were responsible for a large part of the wage and price inflation of 1974. Indeed in a purely statistical sense this was correct. The threshold was triggered eleven times, which meant an extra £4.40 per week for anyone under the scheme. It was estimated that 10 million workers were covered by such arrangements by October 1974. The idea behind thresholds was that unions, when negotiating wage increases, might have unduly pessimistic expectations about inflation. By introducing automatic compensation, such expectations would be taken out of the bargaining situation. Without this compensation, it might be argued, many groups would have refused to settle under Stage Three terms, and their pay increases would have been just as large or even larger than the ones which they actually obtained.

(x) The Miners' Strike.

An increasing number of settlements were made under the Stage Three conditions; the number of workers covered rising to over 6 million by the end of February 1974. The National Union of Mineworkers, however, feeling strongly that their relative pay had fallen and recognising their new bargaining powers resulting from the oil crisis, refused to settle under Stage Three. A national overtime ban was begun in November. which in January 1974 became a national strike. In November the Government declared a State of Emergency and in January introduced a three-day week for industry in order to conserve coal and electricity (which depended on coal). It was unwilling to waive the Stage Three legislation in the miners' case, despite a declaration by the Trade Union Congress that its member unions would not invoke a settlement of the miners' dispute in support of their own claims. By using the maximum flexibility permitted in the legislation, *e.g.*, on payment for unsocial hours, the National Coal Board had been able to offer an average increase of some 17 per cent within the Stage Three rules. The Government referred the NUM claim to the Pay Board, for the Board to determine whether the miners constituted a special case which justified a further increase in their relative pay. The Government then called a General Election. The Pay Board reported just after the election, and recommended that an additional increase be paid, on the grounds that the long-run contraction of the industry would in future be reversed and that higher relative pay would be necessary to recruit and retain sufficient mineworkers. The incoming Labour Government settled with the miners on terms very similar to those recommended by the Pay Board.

(xi) The Social Contract.

The Labour Party came to power pledged to deal firmly with prices but to abandon statutory wage controls. It took early action on house rents and food prices, by means of controls and subsidies. The Pay Board was abolished and the policy of compulsory wage restraint thus finally ended in July 1974. The Price Code and the Price Commission were, however, retained.

During the February 1974 general election campaign an agreement between the TUC and the Labour Party was announced. This became known as the *social contract*, and formed the backbone of the Labour Government's attempts to stem wage inflation. The hope was that, in return for the repeal of the 1972 Industrial Relations Act, the TUC would be able to persuade its members to cooperate in a programme of voluntary wage restraint. In this way it was hoped to avoid the strains caused by formal incomes policies, which have always appeared to trade unionists to leave them without any role to play. Under a voluntary system they could still do their job—that is bargain about wage rates. The terms of the contract were that there should be a twelve-month interval between wage settlements; and that negotiated increases should be confined either to compensating for price increases since the last settlement, or for anticipated future price increases before the next settlement. An attempt by the TUC's general secretary to tighten up the interpretation of the contract, so that nothing was generally allowed apart from compensation for past increases, was unsuccessful.

(xii) Voluntary Restraint.

By early 1975 it was evident that this policy had failed. Some wage settlements were of the order of 30 per cent. In July 1975 the Government announced that there would be a limit of £6 per week on pay increases, £6 representing 10% of average earnings. There were to be no exceptions to this, and those earning more than £8,500 a year were to get nothing at all. The Government had the prior agreement of the TUC to such a policy, and the TUC agreed to try to persuade its members to comply. The policy was voluntary to the extent that there were no legal sanctions against individual unions, but in another sense there were very powerful sanctions. These operated through the Price Code. No firms could pass on in price rises any part of a pay settlement above the limit; this applied not only to the excess but to the whole of the increase. Apart from avoiding the threat of penalties on trade unionists, this form of sanctions had the advantage of covering all payments made at the plant level;

many previous incomes policies had been relatively successful at monitoring national negotiations, but had failed to keep a check on extra payments made below this level.

The £6 limit was due to lapse in July 1976, and the April 1976 Budget gave the first indications of a possible successor. The Chancellor announced that he would make cuts in the effective amount of tax paid by private individuals, if he could secure trade union agreement to a second year of pay restraint. Other countries, like Norway, have linked fiscal policy and incomes policy in this way. Its attraction was that it would allow an increase in take-home pay with the employers bearing less than half the cost. Therefore prices would rise by less and our competitive position deteriorate by less than if the whole increase had been achieved by putting up money wages. There were, however, those who felt that the integrity of Parliament was threatened by making taxation decisions conditional on trade union agreement. Be that as it may, agreement was reached with the TUC. From August 1976 more severe limits on pay operated than under the £6 limit. For those earning less than £50 a week, wage increases were limited to £2·50; for those earning between £50 and £80 the limit was 5 per cent, whilst those earning more than £80 could get no more than a £4 per week increase. Average earnings in August were about £75 per week, and the implied overall limit was about 4½ per cent.

There is no doubt that the pay policy was successful in holding down earnings. During the £6 policy, earnings rose by 14 per cent. An all-round increase of £6 would have meant a 10 per cent rise. Another 2 per cent can be explained by the implementation of agreements made before August 1975, by moves towards equal pay, and by increased overtime earnings. This leaves only 2 per cent unaccounted for. Some of this "slippage" was no doubt evasion of the limits. There is no reason to think that there was any greater slippage from the 4½ per cent policy, and during the year of its operation (until August 1977) earnings rose by only 9 per cent. It is unclear whether the success of the policy was due as much to the threat of Price Code sanctions and to the recession in the economy as to the voluntary co-operation of the trade unions. What is clear is that the threat of sanctions is greater in recession conditions and that such threats have a disproportionate impact on the larger firms, whose price and pay changes it is easier for the Government to monitor.

The 4½ per cent policy was due to lapse at the end of July 1977, and in the March 1977 Budget the Chancellor offered the prospect of tax cuts if trade union agreement to a new stage could be reached. In the event the TUC agreed to continue its support for the 12-month rule, whereby no union should attempt more than one settlement in a year. It could not, however, agree to a limit of a specific amount. In return the Government gave a modest reduction in income tax, and introduced a "voluntary" policy of its own. This new Stage III policy was to last until the end of July 1978 and aimed for a national earnings increase of no more than 10 per cent during this time. No specific limit was to be put on individual negotiations, but the Government reserved the right to impose sanctions on firms whose settlements appeared inconsistent with the national target. These sanctions might be exercised through the Price Commission's controls on profit margins (though it was expected that these would lapse in July 1978), through public purchasing policy and the placing of contracts, and through consideration of industrial assistance. The Government did stress, however, the possibility that larger increases could be obtained by self-financing productivity deals.

By the spring of 1978 it seemed that earnings increases during this stage of policy would turn out to be as high as 14 per cent. The Government was reasonably successful in holding the public sector down to near 10 per cent, though there were some costly productivity deals, particularly in coal mining. But the main problem was in the private sector. Though the majority of wage-rate increases were at about 10 per cent, earnings drift together with consolidation of the previous two years' increases in rates worked out for overtime, piece rates or shiftwork were pushing earnings increases way above 10 per cent. In addition, productivity deals were incorporated in about 30 per cent of agreements, in each case adding between 6 per cent and 10 per cent to pay. It is unclear how many of these deals involved genuine cost saving, or how sanctions discouraged false deals of this sort.

This relatively high increase in earnings was expected to cause prices to accelerate again from about mid-1978. The extent of this acceleration depended on the course of import prices and on whether a new stage of incomes policy was applied from August 1978. In the spring of 1978 Government thinking was certainly in favour of a continuance of incomes policy, but there were many problems. In order to get some public sector groups—e.g. the firemen and the police—to agree to only 10 per cent awards, large increases had been promised to them for the autumn of 1978. Also there was a continued desire of some groups to " correct " anomalies and squeezed differentials. The latter were partly responsible for a shortage of skilled labour in some sectors of the economy, which would of course threaten any economic recovery. A further great uncertainty was the prospect of a general election before the end of the year. If the Conservatives won an election they were thought likely to abandon incomes policy, in the belief that it interfered with the efficient operation of the labour market. Meanwhile, there were signs of industrial unrest, in that strike activity was substantially higher in 1977 and early 1978 than in the two previous years.

The Nationalised Industries.

A White Paper on the nationalised industries was published in April 1978. It is too early to judge whether it will have any real effect, but it contains two potentially important proposals. The first is that the Government intends to take powers to give the industries specific directions to do things that their boards will not do willingly. These powers will be used only sparingly and the industry concerned will be compensated for any cost. Though Governments in the past have intervened in " the national interest " (Heath, for instance, held down their prices to help his anti-inflation policy), this proposal formalises an important new principle. The second proposal is to change the way that the desirability of investment projects is judged. It will require them to earn a 5 per cent rate of return, discounting

price increases. This rate is thought to be that which the private sector can expect.

Is Britain Taxed Too Highly?

It is commonly throught that Britain labours under an excessive burden of taxation. The Treasury recently issued some international comparisons. Including all forms of taxation and social security payments, about 40 per cent of Britain's national income was taken in taxation in 1973/74. This is not very high by international standards. The figure is about 50 per cent for Denmark, Norway, Netherlands and Sweden. Even the West Germans, the French and Canadians pay more tax than we do. The Americans and Japanese pay less.

Britain is, however, more heavily dependent on direct taxation (that is taxation of income) than are other countries. Many feel that high marginal rates of tax discourage people from working harder or seeking promotion, but this issue is hotly debated. A move towards greater reliance on present indirect taxes, mainly VAT, would increase inequality unless the taxation were concentrated heavily on luxuries.

The Meade Committee Report.

A recent report by the Meade Committee is likely to prove influential. One of the main concerns of this committee was that the present system taxes income whatever use is made of it. Income tax usually hits the saver twice: on the income earmarked for saving and on the income generated by this saving. There are some forms of saving, however, which are given full or partial exemption from tax. These include payments into an approved pension scheme, life assurance premiums, interest on loans for house purchase, investment by companies. Payments for such items are deducted from taxable income (see Section H). The Committee felt that penalisation of some forms of saving but not others was unfair and distortionary. They discussed the possibility of a tax system based on expenditure. Income tax returns would be sent in as at present, but tax would be levied only on that proportion of income which was spent. Though the theoretical arguments of the Committee are undoubtedly correct, the complications and expense of introducing an expenditure tax system would be great. Our present tax-system is, therefore, likely to continue for some time.

MONEY
MATTERS

This new section, specially devised
for readers of Pears, provides a
concise but authoritative introduction to the complex problems
of money, investment and taxation.
There are sections covering such
everyday problems as buying a
house, insurance, income tax and
ways of saving.

TABLE OF CONTENTS

MONEY MATTERS

I. MONEY

1. SPENDING

Planning a Budget.

Most of us need some form of financial planning. Wages and salaries are usually paid in regular weekly or monthly instalments. The flow of expenditure, on the other hand, is normally much less even. Bills often seem to get lonely and like to arrive in batches. The way to deal with this problem is to work out an annual budget consisting of your major expenditures. An example is given in Table 1.

List the amounts you spent last year under each of the headings. As prices are likely to continue to rise, it is worth adding on a little extra to be on the safe side. In the example, average price increases of 10 per cent are allowed for. It is also sensible to add a small amount for unforeseen expenditure. Having calculated your estimated total bills for the forthcoming year, you can then calculate how much money has to be reserved each month or each week for these items.

Preparing a budget like this has a number of advantages. First of all, by planning in this way you can save money. For example, it is cheaper to pay car tax once a year rather than every four months. Annual season tickets are cheaper than monthly or quarterly ones. Also, it is usually cheaper to pay your insurance premiums in one go, rather than by instalments. A second advantage is that you have a clear idea of your major expenses, so you know how much money there is left over for day-to-day expenses. Thirdly, because the money can be put aside when you are paid, the cash is usually ready when the bills come in.

It is also possible to arrange this through a bank with a budget account. What happens is that you calculate your monthly expenses as above. The bank then transfers that amount each month from your current account (more on this below) to a separate budget account. A separate cheque book is provided for this account. When the bills come in, you simply write out a cheque for them. Using a bank in this way does have an advantage in that you can overdraw on the budget account if a lot of bills come in early in the year. The bank will, however, expect the account to run mainly in credit. There is also a charge for this service.

How Other People Spend their Money.

It is interesting to see how other people spend their money, with or without a budget. Table 1 shows the pattern of expenditure reported in 1976.

TABLE 1. *The Pattern of Expenditure in 1976*

	Percentage of reported expenditure.
Food	24·9
Housing	14·9
Fuel and light	5·7
Alcohol	5·1
Tobacco	3·7
Clothing and footwear	8·1
Durable household goods	6·6
Transport	13·2
Other	17·8
	100·0

Source: Central Statistical Office, *Social Trends*, 1977, p. 129.

These figures are only averages, as people have different spending patterns. For example, if you have just bought a house with a large mortgage, the proportion of your income going on housing would probably be much greater than 14·9 per cent.

Expenditure patterns also differ between different types of household. For example, households with three or more adults, but no children, reported spending 7·3 per cent of their income on alcohol. In contrast, households of one adult with children reported that, on average, they spent only 1·9 per cent of their income in this way.

Transport costs also vary a great deal. Households of one adult aged 65 or over spend only 3·9 per cent of their income on transport. Households of three or more adults spend over 16 per cent on this item. Food costs vary as well. The biggest spenders on food are families with four or more children (32·2 per cent of income). The smallest spenders are single adults aged under 65 years (20·7 per cent of income).

2. SPENDING ECONOMICALLY

Many forms of expenditure are almost unavoidable. Rent or mortgage payments, rates and water rates cannot usually be altered unless you move home. Nevertheless, in many other areas savings can be made.

As a general guide, the Consumers' Association publishes a monthly magazine *Which?*. This provides a great deal of information about the price and quality of different products. Information about subscriptions to this magazine can be obtained from *Which?*, 1, Caxton Hill, Hertford SG13 7LZ. Alternatively, it is available at libraries.

Food.

There are severa points to remember when buying food. First of all, larger shops often sell goods at lower prices than smaller shops. As most people know, supermarkets often sell their own brands of many products. " Own brands " are, on average, cheaper than the brands of leading manufacturers. For example, on items such as peas, baked beans, soup and soap powder, own brands can be up to 15 per cent cheaper. On some lines, such as washing-up liquid, the savings can be even greater. There is no reason to suppose that own brands are inferior. They are commonly produced in the same place as the branded products. Often, the only difference is the packaging—and the price.

Other savings can be made with stores' special offers. Things like washing powder and toothpaste will be needed sooner or later; so it can make sense to buy these items when an offer is on, rather than waiting until you have run out.

When comparing prices, it is worth bearing in mind that the quantity varies as well. It is, therefore, better to compare the *unit cost* of products. This is the cost per ounce or pound. Packaging can easily make something look larger than it actually is.

Domestic Appliances.

Like food, the price of domestic appliances varies. Much of the variation depends on the number of extras. For example, a basic gas or electric cooker costs something in the region of £130. Such a cooker would serve a family quite adequately. If, however, you want a model with extras, then the cost can be £250 or more. A second important factor is where the appliance is sold. The price of the same model can vary considerably from place to place, so it is very worthwhile shopping around. There may also be a delivery charge. Discount warehouses are usually the cheapest place to buy appliances. The sales can also make a substantial difference to the price. Most appliances are likely to be cheaper in both winter and summer sales. Fridges are often particularly good bargains in winter sales, for obvious reasons. There is nothing inferior about domestic appliances sold in sales. Traders usually want to clear their premises for new lines. They also realise that January and the summer would otherwise be very lean times for them.

A particular question often arises as to whether to rent or to buy a television set. The advantages of renting are that repairs and service calls are included in the rent. If the set breaks down it is also likely to be repaired more quickly than if you owned a set. And if it cannot be fixed straight-away the rental company will provide a substitute until the original is repaired. On the other hand, it is generally true that it is cheaper to buy in the long run. This is true even if you buy the set on hire purchase. And if you decide to dispose of the set, you can always sell it. (Provided, of course, that any HP payments have been completed.)

Cars.

Cars are very expensive to buy and to run. It is quite common for the annual cost of owning a car (including the drop in its secondhand value) to exceed £1,000. So it is worth thinking carefully about whether or not to buy a car. It may be cheaper to use taxis. They also have the advantage of removing any worries about parking, maintenance and drunken driving.

If you do decide to buy a car, the initial investment can be greatly reduced by buying a second-hand car. The value of most cars drops considerably in their first year. There are other advantages in buying second hand. A used car will have been run in and the teething troubles ironed out. However, if the car is more than three years old it must have an MOT (Ministry of Transport) test every year. The test is now very tough, so cars should be checked carefully before purchase.

If you do not get a guarantee from a reputable dealer you should consider having it examined by the A.A. or the R.A.C. They charge a fee for the service, but it may avoid a purchase you later regret. Alternatively, if faults are discovered it may enable you to negotiate a lower price.

Before setting out to buy a secondhand car it is sensible to study the market. Car price guides are widely available. They provide useful information on cars of different ages and condition. The two major sources of secondhand cars are professional dealers and private sellers. You are unlikely to get a bargain if you buy from a dealer, since they are very familiar with the value of used cars. If you buy privately you avoid the mark-up of the dealer, and so can expect to pay less. Even if you buy a new car, it can pay to ask for a discount, especially if you are paying cash. Dealers receive a sizeable discount on new cars. You may be able to persuade one to pass some of it on to you. Whatever sort of car you buy, new or old, you should give it a test drive. Even new cars are not immune from faults.

3. BORROWING

Under certain circumstances, it can be advantageous to borrow money. The biggest example in many peoples' lives is buying a house with the aid of a mortgage (*see* H12). On a much smaller scale most goods can be bought with the aid of credit. This does enable you to enjoy something without having to wait while you accumulate the cash to buy it outright. As prices rise, you may also be able to buy goods more cheaply through buying straightaway. And you save money buying things like season tickets annually. But there are some disadvantages with borrowing. Some people might find easy credit too much of a temptation and spend more than they can afford.

In addition, borrowing usually costs money. How much it costs depends on where the loan comes from. At the cheapest end of the scale are first mortgages and bank overdrafts. At the beginning of 1978 the mortgage interest rate was 8½ per cent and overdraft rates varied from 7 to 12½ per cent. At the other end of the scale are second mortgages, some hire-purchase arrangements and check trading. The rates of interest at the top end can be 25 per cent per year or even more. There are many sources of credit, so only the main ones will be discussed here.

Banks.

Banks offer three main types of loan: overdrafts, ordinary loans and personal loans. An overdraft is simply an agreement with your bank manager allowing you to overdraw on your account up to an agreed figure. There is no formal arrangement about the timing of repayments, though the agreement will normally be for a specified period. Ordinary and personal loans, on the other hand, are repaid on a regular basis.

Credit Cards.

Banks also provide credit cards. Barclays Bank operate the *Barclaycard* credit card system. The four other main banks, Lloyds, Midland, National Westminster and Williams and Glyn's have their own credit card—*Access*. Credit cards are very simple to use. When you buy something on credit you simply sign a voucher. You can also draw up to £30 in cash from a bank displaying the appropriate sign. Every month you are sent a statement showing how much you owe. You then have to repay a certain minimum amount. If you wish to pay more, or clear all the debt completely, you can.

There is no charge for obtaining an Access or Barclaycard. Nor is interest charged for the 25 days following the statement. If you pay off the debt within this time, therefore, the credit will have cost you nothing. If you do not, then interest is charged. With Barclaycard, interest is charged on the amount outstanding at the end of the 25 days. Access has a slightly different arrangement: interest is also charged on any outstanding balance, but from the date of the statement rather than the end of the interest-free period. The arrangements for amounts drawn in cash also differ. Barclaycard has a 2·5 per cent handling charge, but the 25 days free credit is still allowed. Access does not impose a handling charge, but charges interest from the date the cash was drawn.

The rate of interest charged fluctuates. At the time of writing (early 1978) Access charged 1·75 and Barclaycard 1·5 per cent per month. An interest rate of 1·5 per cent per month is equivalent to an annual rate of 19·5 per cent. However, if the interest-free period is taken into account the annual rate of interest is lower. How much lower depends on when you made the purchase. If the purchase was made just before the statement you may only get about 30 to 35 days free credit in all. If, however, the purchase was made, say, three weeks before the statement, you would get up to 51 days free credit. If the retailer is slow in sending details of the purchase to the credit card centre the interest-free period may be even longer. For this reason, it can be useful to have both an Access and a Barclaycard. If your statement dates differ, you can then use the card with the statement date furthest away. This will increase your interest-free period.

Barclaycard and Access can both be used overseas. Access in interchangeable with Eurocard and Mastercharge, two overseas credit cards Barclaycard is interchangeable with Visa.

If you lose a credit card, or have it stolen, you should inform the credit centre at once. You are liable if anyone dishonestly obtains goods with the card until the credit card centre is told of the loss of the card. However, provided the cardholder acts in good faith, both Access and Barclaycard limit this liability to £25.

Other Cards.

There are several other cards Two of the main ones are *American Express* and *Diners Club*. They have longer free credit periods than Access and Barclaycard, but they are accepted by fewer outlets in Britain. They also charge for the card itself. A number of other organisations operate credit card schemes. These include department stores, such as Debenhams and Harrods.

Hire Purchase.

The rates of interest on hire-purchase agreements are generally higher than those charged on bank or credit-card loans. To see this clearly, we should describe two ways of quoting interest rates. Salesmen often quote " flat " rates of interest. This refers to the difference between the cash price and the cost if bought on credit. For example, suppose you could buy a cooker for £100 cash, or £125 payable in monthly instalments for one year. The extra cost of buying on credit is £25. This gives an annual flat rate of interest of 25 per cent on the £100 borrowed. But this is not the real rate of interest. The reason is that from the first month some of the capital has been repaid. In fact, the average amount borrowed throughout the year is just over £50. The true rate of interest on the balance outstanding (rather than the original loan) is over 40 per cent in this example.

Insurance Companies.

If you have an insurance policy you may be able to borrow money from the insurance company on the strength of it. The policy would have to have a cash-in, or surrender value. The interest charged on such loans is often lower than other rates.

Check Trading.

Check trading is a simple form of credit used particularly in the main industrial towns of the North of England. The check trading company provides checks which can be used to buy goods in shops which accept them. The borrower repays the check trader in weekly instalments.

4. SAVING

There are several reasons why people save. They include the need to meet unforeseen expenditures, to provide for retirement or simply to buy large items such as a car. It is normally cheaper to pay cash rather than to buy on hire purchase. Although many people save only when they have money left over from their various outgoings, it is better to plan savings. That is, budget your income and expenditure and to regard savings as part of your regular outgoings. This allows capital to be built up on a regular basis.

Before deciding where to invest these savings there are factors that you should consider. The first is whether to invest for short or long periods of time. It is generally true that long-term savings attract a higher rate of interest. However, there are usually financial penalties or constraints that will restrict your ability to draw on the money when required. This loss of *liquidity* is important, since you may require money immediately to meet unforeseen expenditures.

You must also consider how taxation affects the income from your investments. This is considered in the section on taxation. Nevertheless, it is important to establish the tax position of different investments. For instance, the rates of interest offered by building societies are tax-paid. These rates may appear low in comparison with other rates, but if you are paying tax at the basic rate they can be quite advantageous. If you do not pay tax, then there are normally better investments, since you cannot claim back the tax already paid by the building society.

Another consideration is the rate at which prices are increasing; that is the rate of inflation. The saver is particularly concerned with what goods or services money will buy in the future. The important rate of return of an investment is not the nominal or money rate of interest but the real rate of interest. If, for example, an investment offers a return of 12 per cent per annum and the rate of inflation is 10 per cent per annum, the real rate of interest is 2 per cent per annum. The individual requires 10 per cent per annum merely to maintain the purchasing power of his capital.

The real rate of interest is very important during periods of inflation because it may well be negative. For example, if the nominal rate of interest is 7 per cent per annum and the rate of inflation is 10 per cent per annum the real rate of interest is minus 3 per cent per annum. This means that when the saver withdraws money in the future, it will not buy the same quantity of goods or services it would have when the investments were made.

Having considered these general points, we can now look at the specific forms of investment open to the saver.

National Savings.

These are schemes provided by the Government. They include The National Savings Bank, Savings Certificates, Retirement Certificates, British Savings Bonds, Premium Bonds and the Save-As-You-Earn Scheme.

The National Savings Bank.

This was formerly known as the Post Office Savings Bank. There are over 20,000 post offices in the U.K. where you can deposit or withdraw money. There are two types of account available:

Ordinary Accounts.

Anyone over the age of seven can open an account with a minimum of 25p. The maximum you are allowed in any one or a number of accounts is £10,000. The rate of interest is 5 per cent and the first £70 worth of interest is tax-free. This is equivalent to 7·57 per cent if you pay tax at the basic rate. You can therefore have up to £1,400 in your bank account before you pay any tax.

Interest is calculated on each complete £1 deposited for a full calendar month. The money begins to earn interest from the first day of the month after it is deposited. It does not earn interest on the month in which it is withdrawn. You should therefore try to deposit money towards the end of the month and withdraw at the beginning of the month.

Up to £30 a day can be drawn on demand from your account. The bank book will be retained if the withdrawal exceeds £20. This will also occur if you withdraw more than £10 twice in any one week. If you require more than £30 you will have to allow a few days before you get your money. This is because you must apply in writing. Alternatively, notice can be given by telegram for urgent withdrawals. A charge of the cost of the telegram is made. Greater flexibility in withdrawing money can be achieved by having more than one account. For example, if you have two accounts you can draw up to £60 on demand.

Money can be transferred to Giro accounts. Also, the payment of regular fixed amounts can be arranged, as long as the payments are not more frequent than once a month. Finally, crossed warrants are available for a minimum sum of £1. These are similar to cheques.

The advantage of the system is its accessibility, since there are post offices in almost every town and village, and they are open six days a week. It is cheap, since there are no bank charges and money earns interest. Also, small amounts of money are available on demand. The tax-free element makes ordinary accounts particularly attractive to high tax payers.

So, National Savings accounts are a good place to keep small amounts of money to meet unforeseen expenditures. On the other hand, the services offered are limited, when compared with banks for example.

Investment Accounts.

Like ordinary accounts, anyone over the age of seven can open an account. Children under seven can have one opened on their behalf. The minimum sum required to open an account is £1. The rate of interest is higher than an ordinary account and is at present 9 per cent per annum. This is liable to tax. The upper limit on deposits is £50,000. As with ordinary accounts, money earns interest on the final day of the month following that in which it was deposited. Money withdrawn does not earn interest in the month in which it is withdrawn.

There is no limit on the amount of money that can be withdrawn. However, notice of one month of the withdrawal is required. Investment accounts are better for long-term savers, although higher rates of interest can be obtained elsewhere. The rate of interest is more attractive to non-tax payers when compared with the rates offered by building societies, which are tax paid.

These accounts suffer from the general characteristic of most forms of national savings, in that the interest rates are slow to change. This is an important disadvantage while the rates of interest are rising, although an advantage when the rates of interest are falling.

National Savings Certificates.

There have been sixteen issues of these, but only one is on sale at any particular time. At present the fourteenth issue has been reintroduced but a seventeenth issue has been announced for June 1978. The minimum investment is £5 and the maximum £1,000. Instead of earning interest, the value of the certificate rises at an accelerating rate. With the fourteenth issue this is equivalent to a compound rate of interest of 7·6 per cent per annum. This is free of tax. If allowance is made for the basic rate of income tax, this is equivalent to 11·5 per cent gross. Table 2 shows how the value and yield (or interest) builds up.

TABLE 2. *The Value and Yield of the Fourteenth Issue of Saving Certificates*

Year.	Value of a unit at end of year.	Yield for one year (%).	Yield after No. of years (%).
1	1·06	6·00	6·00
2	1·13½	7·08	6·54
3	1·22½	7·93	7·00
4	1·34	9·39	7·6

The certificates are issued in units of a pound each. Thus, at the end of four years each unit becomes £1·34 (column 2). This is equivalent to a compound rate of interest of 7·6 per cent (column 4). So, for example, if you invest £100 (100 units) this becomes £134 in four years. To cash certificates you have to give eight days notice. If you do this before they mature, then the rate of interest or yield is considerably reduced. For example, if you cash them in at the end of two years the rate of interest is only 6·54 per cent (column 4).

You need not cash in certificates when they reach maturity. In most cases, however, it will pay to do so. The rates of interest currently paid on matured certificates can be obtained from most large post offices or the District Commissioner for National Savings. Again, anybody can hold certificates, including children under seven. They are available from post offices, commercial banks and Trustee Savings Banks. You will receive a holder's card and a registration number, which is then printed on all certificates that you hold. The card is necessary when you buy more certificates or cash them in. Saving certificates are therefore very attractive to long-term savers who pay tax, especially those in the higher brackets. However, for those who do not pay tax there are better rates elsewhere. They are obviously not suitable for those who require a regular income from their savings or for those who think they might need the money in the immediate future.

Index-linked National Saving Certificates Retirement Issue.

These are one of the superior forms of National Savings. Unfortunately, as the name suggests, they are limited to men over sixty-five and women over sixty. You do not have to be retired to hold them. Provided they have been held for at least a year, their value is based on the cost of living as reflected by the U.K. General Index of Retail Prices (R.P.I.). So the saver is protected from any falls in the value of money due to inflation. In addition, if held for a full five years, a bonus of 4 per cent is added.

Certificates are available in units of £10. You may hold up to £500 worth. The sum that you receive will be calculated in line with changes in R.P.I. between the months you purchased and

cashed the certificates. A repayment value chart, updated monthly, is on display at post offices. For example, if you hold £100 of certificates and the R.P.I. has risen 20 per cent during the period since purchase, you will receive at least £120. All repayments are tax free. Certificates are available from Post Offices and Trustee Savings Banks. The amount repaid will never be less than the purchase price.

These certificates are an attractive means of protecting the purchasing power of your savings. However, if inflation slows down it may be necessary to reconsider your position. If you have no spare savings to invest and you require a regular income or might need money in the immediate future, retirement certificates are not for you.

British Savings Bonds.

The present issue of savings bonds is the Jubilee Issue. It celebrates 60 years of national savings. The rate of interest of 8½ per cent is taxable, but if you hold them for a full five years, a tax-free bonus of 4 per cent on every £100 is paid. Almost anybody can hold savings bonds. They are sold in units of £5. The maximum that can be held is £10,000 and they can be bought from saving's banks post offices or from any bank. One month's notice must be given if you wish to cash your bonds. Interest is payable every six months. No interest is payable if they are held for less than six months.

Before investing in savings bonds it is best to shop around and see if other investments offer better rates. In particular, look at the rates offered by building societies. For high-rate tax-payers, savings bonds are particularly unattractive.

Premium Bonds.

Premium Bonds are one of the most popular forms of national savings. No interest is earned on the bond. Instead, you have a regular chance to win a tax-free cash prize each week and month. The monthly prize money is set by calculating one month's interest at the rate of 5½ per cent a year on all bonds eligible for the draw. A very cheap form of government borrowing!

Prize money is tax-free, but you have to hold the bonds for three clear months before you qualify for the draw. If you win you will be notified by post, so it is important to notify the Bonds and Stock Office of any change of address. Most newspapers publish the numbers of bonds winning prizes of £50 and over. A complete list is given every month in the *London Gazette* and is on display at the larger post offices. If you fail to claim a prize at the time of the draw this can be done later.

Premium Bonds can be bought at post offices and banks. Any person over the age of 16 can buy bonds. A parent or guardian can buy bonds on behalf of their children. You can cash in premium bonds at any time, for the same price as you paid. However, since you do not earn interest and because of inflation, the real value of your money will have fallen. Thus, premium bonds are not a suitable investment for your savings. They are a gamble, and only if you have some spare capital should you consider " investing " in some. The maximum holding is limited to £2,000.

Save As You Earn.

The present third issue of the Save As You Earn scheme is index-linked. This means that, like retirement certificates, your savings are protected from inflation. Anyone over the age of sixteen, whether earning a living or not, can save in the scheme. The minimum number of monthly contributions is sixty. You are therefore committing yourself for a minimum of five years. The monthly payments can be any amount in whole pounds from £4 to £20. This remains fixed for the period. You are allowed to miss up to six monthly contributions. When you miss one the whole contract is postponed by one month, and so on up to six. If you miss a seventh the contract is cancelled. Interest is then paid at the rate of 6 per cent per annum, tax free, on what has been paid in. You can stop the contract at any time and get your contributions back. If this is done within the first twelve months you get no interest. After a year, and before the completion date, you receive tax-free interest of 6 per cent per annum. Partial withdrawals of money are not allowed.

You may feel reluctant to commit yourself to the scheme because of the need to keep up the payments. Obviously you should not commit yourself to sums that put a strain on your resources. Additional contracts can be taken out as your financial position improves. More than one contract can be held provided that the total paid per month does not exceed £20. It is also better to have a number of contracts for small amounts, rather than one large contract. For example, instead of having one of £20 a month, have four of £5. This means that should you require money at any time, one or more of the contracts can be cancelled without affecting the others.

To take out a contract you need to fill in a form available from most banks and post offices. Check to see if your employer has a group scheme. Payments can be made through standing order on a bank account or National Giro account or in cash at the post office counter. With employer run schemes, payments can be made by automatic deductions from pay.

The contract runs for five years, after which the contributions are *individually* revalued on the following formula:

$$\frac{\text{Payment} \times \text{Repayment month index}}{\text{Payment month index}}$$

As an example, assume you are contributing £20 a month. The Retail Price Index (R.P.I.) on the first of the month following your contribution was 150 and after five years is 192. The first monthly contribution will be revalued at £25·60, *i.e.*, $£20 \times \frac{192}{150}$. If the index on the second contribution month was 151, then this contribution will be revalued at £25·43 and so on. These repayments are free of tax.

You can leave the money invested for a further two years. No further contributions are made during this period. At the end of two years the whole amount is revalued again. In addition, you will get a tax-free bonus which is equal to two monthly payments. For example, if you were saving £20 a month, your bonus will be £40. If you withdraw your money at any time before the fifth and seventh years you will only receive the value as at the end of five years. Should the R.P.I. fall, you will not receive back less than the total amount of your contributions. Save As You Earn is thus a very good scheme for saving regularly. It is particularly advantageous to higher-rate tax-payers. If you cannot spare even a small amount of money each month or you require a regular income from your savings, the S.A.Y.E. scheme is not for you.

Trustee Savings Banks.

Trustee Savings Banks have traditionally offered accounts similar to those offered by the National Savings Bank. However, they are now moving into the general area of banking, which will mean many changes in their activities. There are two accounts offered, savings and deposit accounts. New investors are encouraged to invest in deposit accounts as savings accounts are being phased out. The interest paid on deposit accounts is taxable. At present this is 6 per cent per annum. You can draw on demand up to £50 from any branch. Fairly large amounts can be withdrawn on demand from your local bank.

For more long-term savers there are term deposits. The fixed period is usually a year. The rate of interest is guaranteed for the period of the deposit. At present this rate is 7 or 8 per cent per annum, depending on the sum invested. Income tax is not deducted at source. Deposit accounts are a good place to keep money you may require at short notice. They are not a good place in which to build up your capital. In deciding whether to invest small amounts of money in a deposit account look at the rates offered by the National Savings Bank and the Building Societies. Remember, if you pay tax you should compare the gross or taxable equivalent rates offered by build-

ing societies and National Savings ordinary accounts.

Building Societies.

There are many building societies in the United Kingdom. Some of these are national, others local. All building societies are non-profit-making organisations. There is no difference in the security of your money as between the small and large societies. If you want to be absolutely sure, you should choose one that has Trustee Status and is a member of the Building Societies Association.

A variety of accounts is offered, and although the names might vary between societies, they are basically the same thing.

Interest rates quoted by building societies are tax-paid, hence the column which shows the taxable equivalent if you are paying tax at the basic rate. Non-tax-payers cannot claim back tax paid on interest. Interest rates tend to be higher for regular savings and the longer you are prepared to commit your money. The most popular way of saving with a building society is through a share account. These earn a higher rate of interest than deposit accounts, usually 0·25 per cent more. This is because, in the unlikely situation of a building society failure, deposit account holders have a prior claim on the assets of the society. The maximum that can be deposited is £15,000. Building societies do not normally require notice before withdrawing from share or deposit accounts unless the amounts are large. Interest is calculated daily and credited half-yearly.

Building societies offer a variety of investments, and it is important to pick those that suit your needs. The rates of interest offered tend to change slowly. This is an advantage when inflation is falling, but a disadvantage when inflation is rising. If you do not pay tax there are better investments. A final consideration is that those who have invested in a building society may get preferential treatment when it comes to getting a mortgage.

Clearing Banks.

Banks offer two main types of account, current and deposit. Current accounts are for everyday transactions, and they do not earn interest. These are discussed in the section on Banking. Deposit accounts earn interest.

The rates of interest offered on deposit accounts do tend to change more quickly than those offered by other schemes. This is because the deposit rate is based on Minimum Lending Rate (M.L.R.), which is announced each Friday by the Bank of England. The deposit rate is usually between 4½ and 3 per cent below the M.L.R. The current rate offered by the various banks is usually on display at the bank branches. Interest is paid daily and is taxable. There is no minimum or maximum amount that can be deposited. Although seven days notice of withdrawal is technically required, in practice you can withdraw fairly substantial sums on demand. If you do, you will usually lose seven days interest. You can only withdraw money at the branch at which you have an account. If you want ready access to your savings, deposit accounts can be attractive for small amounts of money. But you should look at the rates offered by National Savings, Trustee Savings Banks and Building Societies before choosing a deposit account with a bank.

Local Authority Loans.

Local authorities not only raise money through rates but also by borrowing from the public. They do this by advertising in the Press for loans or issuing loan stock quoted on the Stock Exchange. Most papers carry advertisements for these loans, particularly the Sunday papers. Loans are at a fixed rate of interest. The length of the loan is generally from two to five years, although you can sometimes lend for a year or less. The minimum that you can invest varies from authority to authority and can be as high as £1,000.

Different local authorities pay different rates of interest. It is therefore important to watch the newspapers carefully and not just consider investing in your own local authority. The rate of interest tends to be very attractive, especially to on-tax payers. However, tax at the basic rate is deducted from interest payments, and this must be claimed back by non-tax-payers. Interest is normally paid every six months. Generally, interest rates will be higher the longer the loans run for and the greater the minimum investment. Some of the smaller local authorities offer higher rates of interest. There is no difference in the security of such loans, since all loans are guaranteed.

It is important to bear in mind when considering whether to invest in local authority loans that you cannot normally regain your capital until the end of the investment period. Thus, local authority loans are excellent for long-term savers and for non-tax-payers. They are not for short-term savers.

Gilt Edged Securities.

As well as raising taxes to finance its expenditure, the Government borrows from the general public. It does this by issuing gilt-edged stock. There are basically two types of stock, redeemable and irredeemable. Redeemable or dated stocks are those that the Government has agreed to repurchase on a certain date. Usually, two dates are given. This means that the Government cannot redeem them before the first date, but it must redeem them on or before the last date. Each stock has a *par* or face value of £100. This is the amount that will be repaid on redemption. An example of a redeemable stock is the 8¼ per cent Treasury Stock 1987–1990. Stocks that the Government is not committed to redeem are called irredeemable or undated stocks. The 2½ per cent consol introduced after the Second World War is an example.

The cost of buying or selling securities will depend on whether you go through a stockbroker or through the Department for National Savings, Bonds and Stock Office. It is cheaper to use the National Savings Stock Office, although you can only deal in stocks that are on the National Stock Register. In addition, not more than £5,000 nominal value of any particular stock can be purchased in any one day. There is no limit to the total amount you may hold. Application forms may be obtained from Post Offices.

The interest or *coupon rate* on a stock is normally paid half-yearly. Some pay quarterly, which is particularly useful for old-age pensioners, for example. This is based on the nominal or par value. For example, the 8¼ per cent Treasury Stock pays £8·25 per year. However, the price that you pay for the stock will probably be less than par. The effective rate of interest or *running yield* will therefore be greater than 8¼ per cent.

Prices of stocks fluctuate so that their yield keeps in line with interest rates generally. This presents the possibility of a capital gain or loss. However, it is generally true that as the stock approaches redemption, the closer the price will be to par, and the smaller the capital gain. The further away redemption is, the lower the price of the stock, and hence the greater will be the capital gain if the stock is held to redemption. Government securities are a very marketable investment. They can be sold quickly if need be. Also, stocks are free of capital-gains tax if in your possession for more than one year. For larger sums of money, gilt-edged stock provides a good alternative to local authority loans.

Shares.

For the more adventurous, there is the possibility of investing in shares on the stock market. If you invest in shares it is advisable to " spread your risk." This means that you must have a varied and balanced collection of shares in your portfolio. To do this will require a lot of capital and knowledge of the market. So it is best to seek professional advice from a stockbroker or your bank manager. People with more limited means will be better advised to participate indirectly in the stock market by holding units in a unit trust.

Unit Trusts.

Unit trusts are a means of pooling resources. They do this by selling units, the proceeds of which are used to buy shares. This means that the individual has a share in a wide portfolio. Risk is reduced and he benefits from the expertise of the trust managers. The value of the units in the trust are worked out each day in line with changes in the value of the fund's stock-market investments. The prices of unit trusts are listed in most newspapers. Two prices are given, an offer (or buying) price and a bid (or selling) price. These prices are worked out according to a formula set by the Department of Trade. The offer price is usually between 5 and 6 per cent above the bid price. This is to help cover the costs of running the trust. In addition there is usually a small half-yearly or yearly charge. Units can be bought and sold without going through a stockbroker. They can be obtained directly from the managers or through your bank. The minimum value that can be purchased may be as low as £50, but this varies from trust to trust.

There are over 380 trusts. Some specialise in certain sectors of the stock market, for example commodities, whereas others are more general in their investment policy. To benefit from spreading risk it is wiser to invest in general trusts. Some trusts invest in shares which give a low income but which promise a high capital gain. Others invest in high-yielding shares with prospects of lower capital gains. It is important to choose a trust that best suits your requirements. Finally, in deciding which trusts to invest in, try to avoid the " chart-toppers." This performance may well be temporary, so it is safer to go for the trusts that exhibit a more steady performance. Several tax problems are avoided by investing in unit trusts rather than directly buying and selling shares. The dividends (which are normally paid twice yearly) have tax deducted at the basic rate. There is also a tax credit of 17 per cent on capital gains. This means that basic-rate tax-payers do not pay capital-gains tax when units are sold.

Life Assurance as Saving.

Life assurance policies provide an alternative method of saving regular amounts for long periods of time. The various policies are considered in the section on insurance.

5. BANKS

Most people are familiar with the high street banks. These are the clearing banks and are known as the Big Four. They are the National Westminster, Midland, Barclays and Lloyds. In addition, there are a number of smaller banks, such as Williams and Glyn's and the Co-operative Bank. There are also the National Giro and the Trustee Savings Banks. Banks offer a variety of services, and we begin by considering current accounts.

Current Accounts.

A current account is a safe and easy way of making and receiving payments. Many people automatically assume that they require a current account. If you make only a few payments each week or month and you are paid in cash it will probably be better to keep your money in an account with the National Savings Bank, Trustee Savings Bank or a building society (see the section on Saving). This is because money in current accounts, except those of the Co-operative Bank, does not earn interest. Indeed, as we will see later, you may have to pay in one way or another for the services provided.

Opening a Bank Account.

Opening an account is straightforward. You simply go into the local branch of the bank of your choice and tell the cashier or enquiries clerk that you want to open an account. The bank will want samples of your signature, and you will have to fill in a form giving your name and address. Finally, it will require you to give two references. These could be your employer and a friend with a bank account. You can open an account with as little as £1. To pay further amounts into your account, you simply fill in a form provided at the bank.

Making Payments.

With a current account you will receive a cheque book. This is used in making cash withdrawals from the bank or in making payments without using cash. A cheque is not money. It is merely a written instruction to the bank to pay an amount out of your account, to the person(s) named on the cheque. Cash can be obtained from your local branch. If you require cash from another you must make special arrangements or use a cheque card.

Cheque Cards.

Most retailers are reluctant to accept an unsupported cheque. This is because they do not know if you have sufficient money in your account for the bank to honour the cheque. And, of course, the cheque book may have been stolen. This problem is overcome by a cheque card. The card guarantees that the bank will honour cheques up to £50 regardless of the state of the customer's account. You have to be a reliable and well-established customer before your bank will give you a cheque card. A cheque drawn on a cheque card cannot be stopped or cancelled.

Cash Cards.

A major problem with people who work is access to the banks. Banks are only open between 9.30 a.m. and 3.30 p.m. from Monday to Friday. The major banks have various schemes whereby sums of money can be automatically dispensed outside the branch, twenty-four hours a day. The problem is that not all branches have these installed.

Standing Orders.

There are other ways of making payments apart from cheques. If asked, the bank will automatically make regular payments from your account. These "standing orders" are useful for paying such things as insurance premiums, subscriptions and mortgage repayments. The banks offer a cheaper alternative to standing orders, a bank budget account (see the section on Spending).

Cost of a Bank Account.

Charges are made for clearing cheques and putting through transactions on accounts. The rules are complicated and vary from bank to bank. Generally, if you keep a sizeable balance in your account you will escape charges. The charge for each cheque will vary from 6p to 10p, depending on the bank. With a current account you get a regular statement. This shows the amounts paid into your account (credits) and amounts paid out (debits).

Borrowing from your Bank.

You can borrow from your bank by either having an overdraft or a personal loan. An overdraft simply means that your current account is allowed to go from credit to debit, according to the amount agreed by your bank manager. This type of loan is usually for short periods and is the cheapest way of borrowing. However, banks prefer to lend you money by means of a personal loan. You get a lump sum and pay it off in fixed instalments. The interest charged tends to be higher than that charged on an overdraft. In addition to the services mentioned, banks provide a whole range of other services. These include deposit accounts (considered in the section on Saving), travel facilities, advice on investment, insurance and taxation, safe custody of items and many more. For further information on the additional services banks offer, contact your nearest branch.

The National Giro.

The National Giro was set up by the Government to provide a low-cost current-account bank service. When Giro started it was considerably cheaper to run compared with a current account at a bank. However, the difference is now small. Giro can be operated via the post or through the 21,000 Post Offices in the U.K. These are generally open six days a week. You therefore have access to your account for more days and for longer hours than you do with the commercial banks. Up to £50 can be withdrawn on demand every other business day at either of two post offices nominated by you. For larger sums, prior arrangements have to be made. Money can be transferred by means of a Giro transfer free to other Giro account holders. Also standing orders and statements are free. The problem with Giro is that it does not provide overdrafts, although there are arrangements for personal loans. In addition, there are many other services provided by the commercial banks but not by Giro.

Trustee Savings Bank.

Trustee Savings Banks are gradually taking on the identity of a clearing bank. They offer cheque accounts which are similar to current accounts. The advantage is that a cheque account is considerably cheaper than a current account. If you keep a minimum balance of £50 in your account during the six-month charging period, cheques and standing orders are free. Even if your balance falls below this, you are only charged 2½p for each cheque and standing order. Cheque cards for amounts up to £50 are also available. It has been the case that overdraft facilities have not been available. However, these are gradually being introduced.

Trustee Savings Banks also have many other services similar to those offered by the banks. These include deposit accounts, term deposits, personal loans, Save-As-You-Earn Schemes, unit trusts and the selling of Government stocks at low rates of commission. They thus offer a very competitive alternative to the clearing banks.

6. INSURANCE

Insurance is a contract to pay a premium in return for which the insurer will pay compensation in certain eventualities, for example, fire or theft. In effect, insurance is a means of sharing certain risks. The traditional forms of insurance are general insurance and life assurance. The latter is usually called " assurance " because the cover is given against the occurrence of an event which is inevitable.

Life Assurance.

Life assurance provides a capital sum to your estate in the event of your death. Some policies also combine a savings element so that you receive a lump sum if you survive the period. These are called endowment policies. All forms of life assurance are subject to tax concessions. As a general point, it is just as important that you do not overburden yourself with life assurance as it is to have some form of cover. If you have to give up or surrender your policy before it matures there are usually severe financial penalties. There are three basic types of life assurance: term assurance, whole-life assurance and endowment assurance.

Term Assurance.

This type of policy provides life assurance for a fixed period of time. Should you die during the term of the policy your estate will receive the sum assured. However, if you survive the period you receive nothing. There are variations on the basic type of term policy. A *decreasing term* policy, for example, is often necessary if you have a mortgage. The sum assured decreases as you pay off the mortgage.

Other types of policies include level and convertible term policies. With *level term* policies the sum assured remains fixed throughout the term of the policy. A *convertible term* policy has the additional option of being able to convert it to another kind of policy later on, if you so desire. Term policies provide the cheapest form of life cover.

Whole-Life Assurance.

With this type of policy you are normally

required to pay the premiums for the whole of your life-time. Like term assurance, the sum assured is paid out to your estate only on your death. Whole-life policies can either be with or without profits. A with-profits policy will be more expensive, since the sum received on your death will be the sum assured plus a share in the profits made by the company. Having to keep up the premiums after your retirement can be a problem, so *limited payment* policies are available. Premiums are paid until you reach a specific age, although life cover continues until your death. The premiums will be higher than for a straight whole-life policy.

Endowment Assurance.

Both whole-life and term policies provide benefit only on your death. With an endowment policy, benefit is still provided should you die before the maturity date of the policy. But if you survive this period you will receive the sum assured. Like whole-life policies, these policies can be with or without profits. Although the more expensive, with-profits endowment policies are the most popular form of life assurance in this country. Since the premiums are subject to tax relief, endowment policies are a useful way of combining life assurance with long-term saving. However, they do tend to be expensive, and the proportion of the premium used to provide death cover is small. This is because the chances of dying before the maturity date are usually low. Thus, the bulk of the premiums is used by the company to build up the capital sum on maturity.

Endowment policies are often used in conjunction with loans for house purchase, school fees and for providing for retirement. As well as with-profits investment policies, life assurance companies offer other investment policies. These include equity linked contracts, property bonds and policies linked to building societies. With equity contracts the bulk of the premium is used to purchase units in a unit trust (*see* **H8**). Property bonds are very similar, except the investment is in property.

General Insurance.

As mentioned earlier, this provides cover for an eventuality that may never happen. The types of general insurance considered here are for house and possessions, motor vehicles, sickness and medical insurance.

Insuring your House.

If you are buying a house on a mortgage the building society will insist that it is insured. The sum that you will have to insure your house for will probably be more than what you paid for it. This is because the insurance value will be related to the cost of rebuilding the house. It is therefore important to adjust the amount for which the house is insured periodically to keep pace with inflation. Alternatively, you can take out policies which are "index-linked." Although most policies give the same kind of cover, there is no standard house insurance. So you should check to see if your policy covers all eventualities. This is particularly important if your area is prone to such events as flooding or subsidence.

Insuring your Possessions.

Unless you have a combined policy, the contents of your home and other possessions will not be covered by your house insurance. In the past insurance companies have reimbursed the purchase cost of articles, less a charge for wear-and-tear. However, you can get policies that do not make this deduction.

House and Possessions.

If you are a tenant living in rented accommodation you should only buy policies that cover the contents of the house and leave the landlord to buy insurance for the buildings. For owner-occupiers, it is best to buy a combined policy of house and possessions. This has the advantage that it will be generally cheaper than buying two separate policies.

Motor Insurance.

Motor insurance is compulsory by law. However, only a basic minimum is compulsory, and many people prefer to take out more comprehensive policies. Insurance companies offer two main types of policy; third party and fully comprehensive insurance.

Third-Party Motor Insurance.

The additional cover provided by this type of policy is the cost of repairing the other driver's car. Also, if you incur legal costs in dealing with a claim, these will be reimbursed if your insurer approves your actions. Since third-party insurance does not cover damage to your car, it is only suitable if your car is fairly old.

Comprehensive Motor Insurance.

If your car is relatively new and hence more valuable, then you should consider a comprehensive policy. The most important additional benefit of such a policy is cover for loss or accidental damage to your car.

Sickness and Medical Insurance.

If you consider the benefits provided by the National Insurance schemes and the National Health Service to be inadequate, you can take out insurance that provides for you when ill. There are several schemes. *Hospital risk insurance* provides a sum only for the period you are in hospital. You may consider it best to have a *permanent health insurance*. This provides cover for the total period you are ill. In addition to providing an income for yourself when ill, there are schemes that provide for private medical treatment. The most well-known is the British United Provident Association (B.U.P.A.).

Buying Insurance.

Because of the bewildering variety of policies available it is often best to seek professional advice when buying insurance. This can be obtained from an insurance broker or your bank manager.

7. BUYING A HOUSE

Buying a house is very often preferable to renting a home. Your own house provides you and your family with a secure home. A house is also one of the soundest investments available to most people. The general tendency is for house prices to rise, and it is unusual for someone to lose money on a house, unless he sells it within a year or two. In addition, a house can be a very useful asset. For example, if you wish to move elsewhere the house can always be sold and the proceeds used to buy a home elsewhere. A house can be particularly valuable on retirement. With the mortgage paid off, the retired owner can choose from a number of possible courses of action. He could continue living in it rent free. If the house proved too large for retirement part of it could always be let out to provide some additional income. Alternatively, the owner could move to a smaller home and the difference in the value of the two houses would provide a useful capital sum.

For many people there is no satisfactory alternative to buying a home. Most people are unlikely to be offered council accommodation. Furthermore, a home owner is likely to find it much easier to move than a council tenant. Councils are often reluctant or unable to offer new accommodation when their tenants wish to move; whereas an owner occupier can always sell his house and buy another elsewhere.

Accommodation rented privately also has its disadvantages. Reasonably priced rented accommodation is becoming increasingly difficult to find. Tenants sometimes pay nearly as much, or even more, in rent than they would have to pay for a mortgage on similar property. And mortgage interest normally attracts tax relief whereas rent does not. Finally, rents are likely to rise as inflation continues. Mortgage repayments on the other hand, although they fluctuate from time to time, are related to the original loan and not to the current value of the property.

The basic drawback of buying a house is the cost of buying and selling. The costs can include solicitor's and surveyor's fees and (in the case of selling) an estate agent's fee. Normally there will be the costs of fitting out a new home—the cost of curtains is one example. These costs clearly mean that it is not advantageous to buy a home if you expect to move in the near future.

An obstacle for many people is cash. One hundred per cent mortgages are uncommon, and the buyer has to find the difference between the mortgage offered and the price of the house. There are also the other fees mentioned above. The position may be illustrated with an example. Mr. and Mrs. Smith agree to buy a house for £13,000. The Smiths' building society is prepared to lend them 95 per cent of the value of the property. In this case, the loan would be £12,350 which leaves the Smiths £650 to find. On top of the £650, the Smiths have to pay a valuation fee to the building society of, say, £30. The valuation fee is related to the value of the property so that the higher the value, the higher the fee. If the price of the house had exceeded £15,000 stamp duty would also have to be paid. The rates of the stamp duty are as follows:

Price of the house (£).   *Rate of stamp duty* (%).

15,000–20,000	$\frac{1}{2}$
20,001–25,000	1
25,001–30,000	$1\frac{1}{2}$
Over 30,000	2

Note that duty is levied on the total price of the house, and not just the excess over £15,000. So, for example, the stamp duty on a £20,000 house would be £100. The Smiths also decide to have a professional survey of the house done in order to see if there are any defects in the property. The surveyor's fee depends on how detailed the buyer wishes the survey to be. In this example the fee is £70. Finally, the Smiths receive a solicitor's bill for £150. The solicitor's charge will depend partly on the value of the house, and partly on how much work the solicitor has to do to transfer the house from the seller to the buyer.

Cost of the house	£13,000
Mortgage	£12,350
	650
Valuation fee	30
Survey fee	70
Solicitor's fee	150
	£900

In this example, therefore, the Smiths need at east £900 of their own money. Frequently the amount of money needed will be greater than this. For example, if the Smiths' mortgage were limited to 90 per cent of the value of the house they may have had to find at least £1,550.

It should also be borne in mind that more money is needed to furnish the house. A first-time buyer needs almost everything from curtains to a cooker, and from doormats to a dinner service. Not all of these things need to be bought straight away of course. Nevertheless, some items, such as something to sleep on, and to eat off, will be needed almost immediately.

So it can be seen that, unless one is likely to move in the near future, buying a house can be a sensible decision. The key thing is to save up a reasonable sum of money towards the various costs. The next step is choosing a house.

Choosing a House.

Given the price of houses, selecting your future home is clearly not a decision to be rushed. Possibly the first thing to do is to work out how much you can afford to pay. If you need a mortgage, building societies will give you a rough indication of the maximum amount they will lend. They cannot give a precise figure, however, because the amount a society will lend depends not only on your income but also the house itself. There is more on this below. The next stage is to decide where you would like to live. If you are not familiar with the area it pays to spend time studying a map in detail. That way you soon get an idea of the proximity of each area to your work,

to the nearest shopping centre and so on. It is also worth thinking carefully about the type of house you want. You may, of course, be influenced by what is available. Nevertheless, if you have a fairly clear idea of what you want a lot of time can be saved by eliminating houses that are obviously unsuitable. Features to think about include whether you want a house, bungalow or flat; the number of bedrooms you require and whether you want a large, medium or small garden.

The next move is to find out as much as possible about the current state of the home market. Estate agents are always delighted to deluge prospective home buyers with details of many properties. Many of them might be unsuitable for you, but they will begin to give you an idea of the value of different houses. You may also change your mind about the sort of house you want. Estate agents are not the only source of information about houses for sale. Houses are often advertised privately, usually in the local newspaper. And because the seller will be saving hundreds of pounds in estate agent's fees, you might be able to buy a house advertised privately for a bit less than if it were handled by an agent.

There are several other considerations that should be borne in mind. For example, if you are likely to have to move within a few years you may wish to buy a house which is relatively easy to resell. Such a house might be a fairly modern three-bedroomed semi-detached house which is close to shops and schools: rather than a " character " property in a remote area.

Buying a House.

The process of buying a house should not be rushed either. In fact, at this stage it is well to have two or three properties in mind. This reduces the disappointment should you fail to get your first choice. It also puts you in a better bargaining position over the price of the house. There is nothing sacred about the asking price. Sellers will often ask for a bit more than they think they will probably get. So, depending on the state of the market, it can often pay to offer less than the advertised price.

When a price is agreed, make it " subject to contract." Neither party is formally bound to the agreement until the contracts are actually signed. Before that happens there are a number of things to be done. First of all you will probably want a solicitor. It is not absolutely necessary to use a solicitor, but unless you are familiar with the procedure it is usually advisable to do so. If you need a mortgage the next thing to do is to give full details of the house you intend to buy to your building society manager. He will then arrange to have the property surveyed and valued. The purpose of this is to safeguard the building society's money by making sure that the house is a good investment. When the building society is ready it will inform you how much it is prepared to lend on the house. Your solicitor should then be instructed to complete the remaining formalities.

As soon as the solicitors are satisfied about the technicalities of the purchase the next stage is the signing and exchange of contracts. The contract is usually prepared in duplicate with one copy to be signed by the buyer and one by the seller. The buyer is normally expected to pay a deposit of 10 per cent of the purchase price when contracts are exchanged. The exchange of contracts legally commits both parties to the purchase. This commitment stands regardless of what happens thereafter. This is why it is important for you or your solicitor or both to find out as much as possible about the property before the contract is signed. The contract will contain a number of details, including the date on which the deal will be completed. The date is usually a few weeks ahead and allows both parties to make final arrangements before the house is actually handed over. On the completion date the balance of the purchase money is paid, and the purchaser can take possession of the house.

The length of time between finding a house of your choice and taking possession can vary considerably. It depends on the number of complications involved. If everything goes well it would probably take between eight and ten weeks to buy the house. Such is the process of buying a home.

However, for many people the major consideration is the mortgage. It is therefore worth describing mortgages in greater detail.

Mortgages.

A " mortgage " is a technical term meaning that certain rights over one's property are given to someone else as security for a loan. In other words, if you buy a house with a loan you give a mortgage as security. In everyday usage, however, a mortgage refers just to the loan, even though the property is still used as security. Even if you can afford to pay cash, it is often worthwhile buying a house with the aid of a mortgage. There are several reasons for this. First of all, if the house is to be your main residence the mortgage interest on the first £25,000 borrowed qualifies for tax relief. Secondly, as inflation continues the value of money declines, and so the real value of the mortgage also declines. As a result, the mortgage repayments will not tend to rise in line with inflation.

It is true that interest rates fluctuate, and that when they rise your mortgage repayments will rise as well. But sooner or later the rate of interest will fall again. In the meantime, higher interest payments are mitigated by higher tax relief. In addition, when interest rates rise it is sometimes possible to extend the repayment period, rather than increase the monthly repayments. There are several types of mortgage. Three of the main ones are: repayment mortgages, endowment mortgages and option mortgages.

Repayment Mortgages.

Repayment mortgages are usually the most straightforward. They are repaid in equal monthly instalments. Each payment consists partly of interest and partly of a repayment of capital. In the early years the repayments consist almost entirely of interest. As the loan is paid off, the interest element declines. This means that the tax relief is the highest in the early years of the mortgage.

The size of the monthly repayments depends on the rate of interest and the length of the repayment period. It also depends, of course, on the amount borrowed. For example, suppose you have a mortgage repayable over 25 years at a rate of interest of 10 per cent. In this case the gross monthly repayment for each £1,000 borrowed would be £9·18. However, the tax relief should also be considered. The actual amount of relief depends on the highest rate of tax you pay. Suppose you are subject to a basic rate of tax of 34 per cent. If the tax relief is then taken into account in the above example the net monthly cost of the mortgage in the first year would be £6·36 rather than £9·18. If you are subject to higher rates of tax the tax relief would be worth more to you, and the net monthly repayments correspondingly less.

Endowment Mortgages.

An " endowment mortgage " is a mortgage linked to an insurance policy. When the policy matures it pays off the mortgage. In the meantime you only pay interest on the loan. If you die before the end of the agreement the insurance policy would pay off the mortgage. Endowment mortgages cost more than repayment mortgages because of the premium for the insurance policy. In addition, most building societies charge an extra ½% or ¼% on endowment mortgages. Nevertheless, there are some advantages with endowment mortgages. First of all, tax relief is allowed on the insurance premium as well as the mortgage interest. Secondly, as with other insurance policies, it is possible to have a " with-profits " element in an endowment policy. This costs more, but it means that the insurance company not only guarantees to provide a minimum sum but also adds " bonuses " each year. The size of the bonus depends on the investment position of the company. When the policy matures the pay-out (including bonuses) will cover the mortgage and leave you with a substantial sum as well.

Option Mortgages.

The option mortgage scheme is designed to help people who do not pay sufficient tax to benefit fully from the tax relief associated with mortgage interest. Under this scheme the borrower pays a lower rate of interest, but loses his right to tax relief. The Government then subsidises the lender by the appropriate amount.

Where to Get a Mortgage.

The vast majority of mortgages are supplied by building societies. Local councils can also provide mortgages. But councils often limit their lending to people in certain categories, such as council tenants or those recognised as having a particular housing need. In addition, councils often charge higher rates of interest than building societies. So, clearly, the first place for most people to look for a mortgage is a building society. Councils, however, will sometimes lend money on property that building societies are reluctant to consider. This is particularly true of older houses. The reason is that many councils take the view that it is better to modernise many older properties rather than to demolish them. Some insurance companies also provide mortgages, but this is only a minor source of loans. Some employers, such as banks and building societies, will provide their employees with loans at favourable rates.

Getting a Mortgage.

The first thing to do is to plan ahead. As we have seen, you will probably need to put up a substantial sum of money of your own, so you should start saving as soon as possible. It can be advantageous to save by investing in a building society. When mortgage funds are in short supply societies are likely to consider their own investors before casual applicants. Building societies have fairly strong preferences about the sort of property they are prepared to lend on. For example, they are often very reluctant to lend on older property. In such cases local councils will often take a more liberal attitude. Many building societies are also reluctant to lend on flats. Nevertheless, the lending policies of building societies differ, so if you are turned down by one society, try another. It can also help to ask people who are likely to have close contacts with building societies. Estate agents, your solicitor or bank manager may each be able to suggest a possible source. If you are still unsuccessful, try the local authority.

How Much Can Be Borrowed?

The final question to be dealt with in this section is how much an individual will be allowed to borrow. As stated above, this partly depends on the value of the house concerned. But it also depends on the financial status of the borrower. Building societies have to safeguard their investors' money. Societies are careful not to lend more to anyone than they are likely to be able to repay. A person with a secure career may therefore be treated more favourably than a person whose future earnings are uncertain. Again, different societies have different policies. None the less, it is very rare for building societies to lend more than two and a half or three times their annual income. Most building societies will also take a spouse's income into account, but for a smaller proportion.

For example, suppose you went to a building society which was prepared to lend up to two and a half times your annual earnings plus an amount equal to your wife's annual income. If you earn £4,000 and your wife £3,000, the society would then be prepared to lend you up to £13,000:

Your income	£4,000	Maximum loan	£10,000
Wife's income	£3,000	Maximum loan	£3,000
		Combined Limit	£13,000

The extent to which your wife's income is taken into account depends on the building society. It can be as low as a quarter of her annual income.

II. TAXES

Taxation permeates almost every aspect of financial life. In addition, the entire subject is exceedingly complex, and the tax system is altered or amended at least once a year. All that will be attempted here, therefore, is a description of some of the most common situations faced by tax-payers. If your circumstances are more complicated you should consult your tax office, or take professional advice, or both.

For reasons which are largely historical, taxes are often divided into *direct* and *indirect* taxes. Direct taxes are paid to the Inland Revenue. There are five main types of direct taxation:

1. Income tax
2. Investment income surcharge
3. Capital gains tax
4. Capital transfer tax
5. Corporation tax

Indirect taxes are collected mainly by the Customs and Excise. They include:

1. Value added tax
2. Customs and excise duties
3. Car tax
4. Stamp duties

Stamp duties are, however, the responsibility of the Inland Revenue.

In terms of the amount of revenue raised, income tax is by far the most important tax. It is also the tax most likely to affect the average tax-payer directly.

8. INCOME TAX

If you are resident in the United Kingdom tax is levied on your income whether it originates in the UK or from overseas. Even if you are not resident, tax is still levied on any income you have which originates in the UK. Tax is charged for each year of assessment; that is the year from 6 April to the following 5 April.

Income Subject to Tax.

Most types of income are taxable, including the following:

Income from employment. This includes wages, bonuses, commission, tips and benefits in kind, such as the private use of the company's car.

Income from self-employment, business, professions and vocations.

Interest, dividends and annuities.

Rent.

Pensions.

Income not Subject to Tax.

A few types of income are not subject to tax. The main groups are:

The first £70 of interest per person received from ordinary deposit accounts in the National Savings Bank and the Trustee Savings Bank. However, the Government has decided that for Trustee Savings Banks the interest will become taxable after 20 November 1979.

Interest on National Savings Certificates and Index Linked Retirement Certificates. Also, interest from the Save-As-You-Earn scheme is exempt.

Unemployment benefit, sickness benefit, attendance allowance, maternity benefit, death grant and family income supplement.

Educational grants and awards.

" Golden handshakes " (severence payments and capital sums given on retirement) up to £5,000. Gratuities for service in the armed forces are also exempt.

War and disability pensions. 50 per cent of a war widow's pension is exempt.

Any wins from gambling, including Premium Bond prizes.

The capital element of annuity payments.

Luncheon vouchers (up to 15p a day).

Housing improvement grants from local authorities.

Allowances.

As most people know, there is also a system of allowances which may be deducted before tax is levied on the remainder of your income. The values of the allowances for the income tax years 1977–78 and 1978–79 are shown below in Table 3.

TABLE 3. *Allowances Against Gross Income in 1977–78 and 1978–79*

	1977–78. £	1978–79. £
Single person's allowance	945	985
Married man's allowance	1,455	1,535
Wife's earned income allowance (maximum)	945	985
Age allowance—single person	1,250	1,300
Age allowance—married man	1,975	2,075
Children:		
Aged not more than 11 years		
For the first child	196	100
For each subsequent child	170	100
Aged over 11 but not over 16 years		
For the first child	231	135
For each subsequent child	205	135
Aged over 16 (if receiving full-time education or training)		
For the first child	261	165
For each subsequent child	235	165
Additional personal allowance	510	550
Dependent relative allowance	100	100
Except if the claimant is a woman other than a married woman		
living with her husband	145	145
Housekeeper allowance	100	100
Daughter's services allowance	55	55
Blind person's allowance (each)	180	180

N.B. The figures for 1978–79 are those proposed by the Chancellor in the Budget of 11 April 1978. At the time of going to press, the Finance Bill had not become law and these figures are thus only *proposed* rates. It should also be noted that child allowances are gradually being replaced by child benefits paid to the mother.

After your allowances have been deducted, tax is payable on the rest.   (See Table 4.)

TABLE 4.   *Rates of Tax on Taxable Income, 1977/78 and 1978/79**

Rate of tax (%)	Slice of taxable income.	
	1977/78. £	1978/79. £
25	—	1–750
34		
the " basic rate "	1– 6,000	751– 7,000
40	6,001– 7,000	7,001– 8,000
45	7,001– 8,000	8,001– 9,000
50	8,001– 9,000	9,001–10,000
55	9,001–10,000	10,001–11,500
60	10,001–12,000	11,500–13,000
65	12,001–14,000	13,001–15,000
70	14,001–16,000	15,001–17,500
75	16,001–21,000	17,501–23,000
83	over 21,000	over 23,000

* These figures have been altered by the passage of the Finance Act.   The basic rate has been reduced to 33% and the threshold at which higher tax is paid has been raised.

Investment Income Surcharge.

In addition to these rates of income tax, investment income in excess of £1,500 (or £2,000 for tax-payers aged 65 or more) is subject to a further charge.   The rates for investment income surcharge in 1977/78 and 1978/79 are shown below.

TABLE 5.   *The Rates of Investment Income Surcharge in 1977/78 and 1978/79*

	Taxpayers aged 65 or over, investment income. £	Other taxpayers, investment income. £
The 1977/78 bands		
Nil	1–2,000	1–1,500
10%	2,001–2,500	1,501–2,000
15%	over 2,500	over 2,000
The 1978/79 bands		
Nil	1–2,500	1–1,700
10%	2,501–3,000	1,701–2,250
15%	over 3,000	over 2,250

9. ASSESSMENT AND COLLECTION

The administration of income tax is the responsibility of the Inland Revenue.   In practice, the job is divided into two parts: assessment and collection.   The " assessments " for tax are the responsibility of inspectors of taxes in over 750 tax offices spread throughout the country.   When an individual's tax has been assessed the information is then passed to a collector of taxes who actually sends out the bill.   If you receive a tax bill which you think is wrong you should contact the inspector.   The collector has no power to amend the bill, his job is simply to collect the amounts decided between you and the inspector.

The Tax Schedules.

For historical reasons, income is divided into six groups, known as " schedules."   These are:

1. *Schedule A:* Income from property.

2. *Schedule B:* Income from commercial woodlands.

3. *Schedule C:* Certain interest and annuities paid out of public revenue.

4. *Schedule D:* Income from trades, businesses and professions.   Also included are interest, rents and income not covered by other schedules.

5. *Schedule E:* This is the schedule that affects most people as it covers wages and salaries.   It also deals with pensions.

6. *Schedule F:* Dividends and other distributions made by companies.

Pay-As-You-Earn.

By far the largest schedule is Schedule E.   Nearly all Schedule E income is taxed through the Pay-As-You-Earn (PAYE) system.   PAYE is the method used to deduct tax from wages, salaries and some pensions.   In order to keep the deductions as accurate as possible, PAYE is operated on a cumulative basis.   This means that your earnings, tax paid and so on are accumulated throughout the tax year.   This is how it works.   At the beginning, or before the start of the tax year, your tax-free allowances are added up.   The total is then converted into a code number.   For example, if your allowances came to £1,661 and you are married, then your code number would be 166H.   The H suffix denotes that you are entitled to the married man's allowance.   (The H stands for the " higher " allowance).   If you are single or a working wife the suffix would be L (representing the " lower " single person's or wife's earned income allowance).   If there are special circumstances, for example if you had a second job, the suffix would probably be T.   There are also special suffixes for pensioners.   The main ones are P for single people, and V for married pensioners.   If your current code number is different from the previous one the tax office will send you a " Notice of Coding."   This will show the allowances the tax office has taken into account and how your code number has been calculated.   If you do not receive a notice of coding you may request one.   You should always check to see that you have received your full entitlement to allowances.   Your code number is also sent to your employer so he knows how much tax to deduct from your earnings.   It is worth noting that the higher your code, the lower the tax deducted from your pay.

It may be of interest to work through a simple example of PAYE operating.   Suppose that a person's allowances for the year amount to £1,040, and the appropriate code is issued to his employer.   The principle is that the annual allowances are divided by the number of pay periods in the year.   If an individual is paid weekly, therefore, his allowances are divided by 52.   In our example the individual would be granted £20 worth of allowances each week.   This weekly allowance is then accumulated as the tax year progresses.   Hence in, say, week 26 of the tax year the individual would be entitled to £520 worth of allowances.   At the same time, the PAYE system accumulates the amount of earnings received.   This enables the amount of tax to be deducted to be calculated accurately.   Suppose the individual in our example earned £60 in Week 1 of the tax year.   The employer knows from the code number that the person's allowances for that week amount to £20.   The employer then deducts this £20 from the £60 gross pay, which leaves £40 of " taxable pay ".   The next stage is to calculate the tax due on the £40.

To assist him in this process, the employer has two sets of tax tables.   The first table converts code numbers into weekly or monthly allowances.   After these allowances have been deducted from gross pay the second set of tables is used to calculate the tax due on the remaining pay.   In the example, there is £40 of taxable pay, so with a tax rate of 34 per cent, £13·60 would be deducted in tax.   Suppose that the wage in the second week was also £60.   Because of the cumulative feature, the value of the allowances would now be £40.   (£20 for the second week, plus £20 for the first week).   Cumulative pay would now be £120.   After deducting the allowances, taxable pay is now £80.   The second set of tables would now show a total of £27·20 due in tax.   However, £13·60 (" cumulative tax paid ") was deducted in week 1.   The amount of tax due in week 2, therefore, is a further £13·60 (£27·20 minus the £13·60 deducted in week 1).   This process then continues for the rest of the tax year.

PAYE has a number of advantages.   These include accurate deductions of tax.   The system can also repay tax during the year if the employee's pay falls substantially, for example if he becomes unemployed.   Repayments occur when the value of the allowances accumulates faster than gross pay. The system does not always work in this way. For example, suppose you fail to send your tax return back to the tax office. You may find that you are then put on the Emergency Code (E). This code only gives you allowances equal to the single person's allowance, so if you are entitled to more you will have too much tax deducted. This, of course, provides you with an incentive to sort out your tax affairs with the Inland Revenue.

Sometimes you may find that you have been put on what is known as a "week 1" basis. This means that tax is being deducted from your pay on a *non-cumulative* basis. In other words, every week is treated as though it were the first week of the tax year. One of the main results of the "week 1" basis is that it prevents tax repayments being made automatically if, say, your income falls through unemployment.

How to Check your Code Number.

As you can see from the above explanation, your code number is the factor that determines the amount of tax that is deducted from your pay. You can check your code number by examining your Notice of Coding. You should compare the allowances and expenses you claimed on your tax return with the ones listed on the Notice. One item which might appear on the Notice of Coding is "Tax unpaid for earlier years." This is to enable the tax office to collect outstanding tax by lowering the value of your code. The tax will then be collected slowly over the tax year rather than in one lump sum.

Appeals.

When your tax for the year is assessed you will be sent a Notice of Assessment. This is often not considered necessary if you are taxed under PAYE and your tax situation is straightforward, though you can still ask for one.

If you receive a Notice of Assessment which you think is wrong you must appeal within 30 days of the date appearing on the Notice. Appeals made after 30 days are normally allowed only if you can provide a satisfactory explanation such as being in hospital or abroad, and can show that the appeal was made without unreasonable delay. Most appeals are settled directly with the inspector. If you and the inspector cannot agree, then the case goes before the Commissioners of Income Tax. There are two types of Commissioners: the General Commissioners and the Special Commissioners. The General Commissioners are unpaid and recruited from members of the public. They sit with a clerk who provides advice on tax law. The Special Commissioners are professional civil servants who are experts in tax matters. It is often said that if your appeal is based on common sense, rather than the intricacies of tax law, you may do better to go to the General Commissioners. Each party pays its own costs for hearings before the Commissioners. If, however, the case is taken on to the High Court, or further, the loser usually pays the costs.

Taxation and Marriage.

When a couple marry, the wife continues to be treated by the tax office as a single person until the end of the tax year. The husband gets the full married man's allowance only if the wedding takes place at the beginning of the tax year (6 April) and 5 May. For weddings later in the year, the married man's allowance is reduced. The amount of the reduction depends on the number of complete months between the start of the tax year and the date of the wedding. For each complete month the allowance is reduced by 1/12th of the difference between the single person's and the married man's allowances.

After the end of the tax year the couple are normally treated as a single person (the husband). The husband is then responsible for completing the tax return in which he must include both his own income and his wife's. This arrangement means that many married couples are taxed more favourably than if they were single. The reason is that the husband gets the married man's allowance instead of the single person's allowance. The wife also loses her single person's allowance

but, if she works, she is entitled to the wife's earned income allowance.

The situation in 1978/79 is shown below:

Unmarried couple

Man	£985	single person's allowance
Woman	£985	,, ,, ,,
Total	1,970	

Married couple

Husband	£1,535	married man's allowance
Wife	£985	wife's earned income allowance
Total	£2,520	

If the wife has no earned income the husband cannot, of course, claim the wife's earned income allowance; just the married man's allowance of £1,535. On the other hand, if the wife works and the husband has no taxable income the couple are treated more favourably. This is because both the married man's allowance and the wife's earned income allowance can be set against the wife's earnings.

However, for couples with high incomes marriage can mean that they pay more tax than if they were single. The reason is that a married couple's incomes are added together. This means that they face a lower threshold for higher-rate tax and investment income surcharge than if they were single. Single people can earn up to £7,000 of *taxable income* before they become liable to higher rates of tax. They can also receive up to £1,700 of income from investment before investment income surcharge is levied. The same thresholds apply to married couples who are assessed jointly.

To reduce the problems of joint assessment, there are two sets of provisions for couples to be treated separately. The first is the *separate taxation* of the wife's earnings. The second is *separate assessment*. The two provisions are quite different and should not be confused.

Separate Taxation of Wife's Earnings.

Separate taxation applies only to the wife's earnings. Couples cannot choose to have the wife's investment income taxed separately. The only way to achieve that would be permanent separation. Separate taxation often involves both gains and losses. The gains arise because the couple may reduce their liability to higher rates of tax. The losses arise because the couple will lose the married man's allowance. It is difficult to be precise about the level of earnings at which it becomes worthwhile to chose separate taxation. It depends on the individual circumstances. Clearly you have to be paying tax at higher rates before any gains can be made. Usually both you and your wife have to have a substantial income before separate taxation leads to net gains. Further information is available in the Inland Revenue's pamphlet IR 13, *Taxation of Wife's Earnings.*

Separate Assessment.

Separate assessment does *not* affect the total amount of tax a couple has to pay. All that happens is that husband and wife get separate tax bills. There are two main reasons why couples may wish to be assessed separately. The first is that the husband may not wish to deal with the tax on his wife's income. This may be particularly true if the wife's income is much larger than the husband's. The second reason is that the wife may be entitled to a tax rebate in her own right. Unless separate assessment is chosen the rebate would be paid to the husband. Separate assessment may also be claimed for capital gains tax. It is also possible to be separately assessed *and* to have the wife's earnings taxed separately at the same time.

10. HOW TO COMPLETE A TAX RETURN

There are four main types of tax return:

1. *Form P1.* This blue form is mainly for people who earn a salary or a wage and do not have com-

plicated tax problems. For example, if your main source of income is your job, and you have small amounts of interest from your savings but no other income you will probably receive form Pl. (The "P" prefix, incidentally, stands for "Pay-As-You-Earn.").

The form Pl is simpler than some of the other forms. In fact, you are not even required to fill in your main earnings. This is because your employer tells the Inland Revenue directly how much you have earned. Most people who receive form Pl do not get one every year. When this happens, the reason is that the tax office is pretty sure that it has enough information to ensure you pay the right amount of tax without having to fill in a return every year. But, remember, it is your responsibility to tell the tax office if your tax liability changes as a result of a change in your circumstances.

For example, if you become entitled to a new allowance because, say, you have a new baby, you should tell the inspector. Nobody else will. Alternatively, if you begin to receive a new source of income you should also tell the inspector. He may well find out anyway. For instance, banks must inform the Inland Revenue of the interest they pay to depositors. Concealing income can lead to demands for back tax plus interest. You may also be liable to penalties.

2. Form 11P. This buff-coloured form is designed for people with more complicated circumstances. For example, if you have a job and some other outside earnings you will probably be sent form 11P. The form is similar to the form Pl, except that it asks for rather more detail.

3. Form 11. This white form is for the self-employed.

4. Form 1. Form 1 is buff coloured and designed for a number of categories of tax-payer. Most of the form is specifically designed for trustees, personal representatives and partnerships.

General Points.

It is very worthwhile keeping a tax file containing all the information relevant to your tax affairs. The whole process of completing a tax return is much simpler if you keep all the relevant documents close together. These documents include items such as: P60 (from your employer); dividend advice slips; receipts for expenses. You may also be asked by the inspector to submit detailed records supporting expense claims. A second point is to keep a copy of your return. A photocopy is perhaps the best method of doing this. Alternatively, you can keep a separate record of what you put in the return as you go along.

Keeping a copy of your return has two advantages. First of all it will help you deal with any questions the inspector may have about your return. Secondly, it will enable you to complete your next return more easily. The tax office usually compares your latest tax return with your previous one to see if you have forgotten something. So it is better if you spot any omissions first. If you get into difficulties with your return, you can always telephone or write to the tax office whose address appears on the front of the form. If you wish to call personally, most tax offices are open for public enquiries between 10 am and 4 pm. But remember to take your tax file with you. It does not matter if you wish to make a personal call and your tax office is hundreds of miles away. This is often the case with Londoners and people who work for large nationwide companies. You can always call at a local office and in London there are special PAYE enquiry offices. (Their addresses are in the telephone directory.) Most enquiries can be handled without recourse to your official file. If the file is needed, the Inland Revenue can arrange to have it sent to a local office.

The Return Itself.

As stated above, there are four main types of return. The tax return analysed in this section will be Form 11P. Whichever form you get, you should always read the accompanying notes. At

the time of writing the latest tax return to hand is Form 11P(1977). This return really covers two years. It refers to the income received in the year ended 5 April 1977, and the allowances you are entitled to in the year ended 5 April 1978. The convenient place to start is page 2 with income received.

INCOME.

Employments or Offices.

If you are an employee, you will receive a form P60 from your employer after 5 April each year. The P60 will show your total earnings and tax deducted under PAYE. It will do this even if you changed your job during the year. You should enter the total figure on the return, plus any bonuses, tips and so on. You should also enter any earnings from spare-time jobs. The same information should be entered for your wife. If you are sent form Pl you are not required to enter the earnings from your full-time job. Your employer will give this information to the tax office.

The tax treatment of overseas earnings is unusually complicated—even by income-tax standards! If you are going to work abroad you should enquire about the tax implications. One place to start is with the Inland Revenue's leaflets IR6, IR20 and IR25. As a very rough outline, the normal situation is that if you do part of your job in the UK and part overseas, all your income will be liable to UK tax. If 30 days or more (continuously or not) are spent abroad for your employer in any one year, tax relief is given on a quarter of that period's earnings.

Trade, Profession or Vocation.

Any profits you make from self-employment should be entered here. This section covers both partnerships and sole traders. The figure required is your net profit for your accounting year which ended in the twelve months to 5 April 1977. The figure should be supported by a statement of account. If you do not know what your profits are when you complete the return you should write "per accounts to be submitted." Your accounts should then be sent to the Inspector as soon as possible.

Social Security Pensions and Benefits.

Some pensions and most social security benefits are tax-free and do not have to be entered on the tax return. Further details of these are given in the notes accompanying the return. "Retirement pension or old people's pension" refers to the state retirement pension, and this must be entered. If you are approaching retirement you should inform the tax office. This will help the Revenue make sure that your tax affairs are kept up to date when you retire. Otherwise, it is possible that you may pay too much (or too little) tax until your affairs are sorted out.

Other Pensions.

If a pension is paid by a former employer it will usually be taxed through the PAYE system. At the end of the tax year, therefore, you should receive a form P60 showing the gross pension paid during the year. Only 50 per cent of a war widow's pension is taxable. Nevertheless, you should still enter the gross amount and leave it to the Inspector to make the adjustment. This section also covers pensions from abroad. Only 90 per cent of most overseas pensions are taxable, but again you should enter the gross amount. Normally overseas pensions are taxed on a preceding year basis. In other words, your current tax bill will be based on the pension you received during the previous tax year.

Property.

Rent can be treated in one of two ways. If the accommodation is furnished *and* the rent covers services such as meals and cleaning the income will be treated as *earned* income. If the accommodation is unfurnished *or* it is furnished and the rent does not cover services the rent will be treated as *investment* income. The figures required are those for total income, expenses and net income. It is only the last of these, the net income, that is taxable, and included in the taxpayers' total income. The details of property income should be presented in a separate statement.

The expenses that may be claimed include:

Rates and rent.

Repairs and maintenance.

Insurance for the structure and its contents (but not insurance against loss of rent).

Costs of providing services to tenants.

Wear and tear for furniture and fittings. The allowance is usually 10 per cent of the rent receivable.

Management expenses. This includes items such as agents' commission for letting the property or collecting the rent.

Dividends from United Kingdom Companies, etc.

Because dividends from UK companies and distributions from unit trusts are accompanied by a "tax credit," you do not have to pay basic-rate tax on them. However, you still have to enter the dividends and tax credits from each company or unit trust, in case you are liable to higher-rate tax or are entitled to a rebate. The necessary information will be shown on your dividend slips. If you do not have enough room, make out a separate list and submit it with the return. The totals should be entered on the return itself. One point should be made about unit trusts. Part of the first distribution you receive will be called *equalisation*. This is part of your capital, and so *should not* be entered on the return.

Other Dividends, etc.

This section requires you to enter the gross (before tax) amount of income from each source. Where tax has already been deducted from foreign income you should give the details.

Interest not Taxed before Receipt.

The first £70 of interest received from ordinary (but *not* investment) accounts with the National and Trustee Savings Banks is exempt from tax. Your wife is also entitled to a £70 exemption. You should still enter the total amount on the return. Interest from bank desposits accounts should also be entered. Provided it is over a certain minimum amount, banks are required to report to the Inland Revenue the amount of interest they have paid or credited to you. Bank interest is often overlooked by tax-payers and normally results in an enquiry from the Revenue. Bank interest is usually credited twice a year and, of course, you should enter the total of these two payments.

Untaxed Income from Abroad.

This section refers only to unearned income from overseas. (Foreign earnings, business income and pensions are dealt with in earlier sections.) You should enter the total amounts involved, whether or not they were actually remitted to the UK. You may deduct expenses incurred. If the income has already been taxed overseas you may be entitled to relief. Details are given in the Revenue's booklet IR6.

Interest from UK Building Societies.

Building society interest is "tax paid"—but this only saves you from tax at the basic rate. If you are liable to investment income surcharge or higher rates of tax you will have to pay more tax on the interest. The Inland Revenue will calculate the additional amount of tax payable. For this purpose, the interest payment will be *grossed up* to include the tax at the basic rate.

Any Other Profits or Income.

As you can guess, this section is for any source of income not covered elsewhere.

Alterations in Untaxed Income, etc.

The Inspector needs to know about changes in your untaxed income and your outgoings so that he can, if necessary, adjust your code number. This will enable your deductions of tax to be kept up to date. Such a change may, of course, also affect an assessment on other income.

OUTGOINGS.

Expenses in Employment.

The basic rule covering claims for employment expenses is that they must be incurred wholly, exclusively and necessarily in the performance of the duties of that employment. The rule is usually applied quite strictly. Thus, for example, travel expenses to and from work are not normally allowable because they are not incurred *in the performance* of the duties of the employment. Travelling expenses may be allowed, but only if incurred in the course of the employment.

Nevertheless, there are several types of expenditure which may be claimed. They include subscriptions to professional bodies, tools and some types of industrial clothing. Trade Unions often agree a fixed allowance with the tax office, but you can still claim for actual expenses if they exceed the agreed figure.

Interest on Loans.

Tax relief on interest paid is now very limited. Loans from a Building Society or a Local Authority for the purchase of your main residence qualify for relief. You do not have to enter the amount of interest paid to these organisations, as they will inform the tax office themselves. The only thing you need to do is to enter the name of the building society or local authority and your account number. Bank overdrafts do not qualify for tax relief. Nor do loans obtained with credit cards. However, the interest from a bank loan which is used to buy or improve your only (or main) residence does qualify for relief.

Capital Gains and Development Gains.

You should give details of the assets you have bought and sold during the tax year. Capital gains tax and how to calculate your gain or loss are discussed in greater detail in a separate section below. The taxation of development gains is extremely complex but unlikely to affect the average tax-payer. It will not, therefore, be dealt with here.

Allowances.

Unlike the income part of the return, which refers to income received in the previous year, the allowances section refers to your entitlement in the current year. Compared to some aspects of income tax, the allowances are relatively straightforward. You should be able to establish your entitlement by reading the official notes carefully. If not, ask at the tax office.

11. CAPITAL GAINS TAX

When you dispose of an asset or possession you may make a capital gains or a capital loss. An asset is property of any kind. It includes both property in the United Kingdom and property overseas. You are considered to have disposed of an asset if you sell it, lose it, exchange it or give it away. However, the transfer of a possession between a husband and wife who are not separated is not considered to be a disposal.

Capital Gains Tax.

The same tax year applies for capital gains tax as for income tax; that is the year running from 6 April to the following 5 April. Capital gains tax is payable if the *proceeds* of all your assets disposed of during the tax year exceed £1,000. The disposals of husband and wife are added together for this purpose. If the net proceeds exceed £1,000 tax is payable on the gains minus the losses.

Tax-free Gains.

The following assets are exempt from capital gains tax:

Your home (but see below).

Personal possessions, household goods and other chattels, provided that each item is worth £1,000 or less at the time of the disposal. A set of goods, for example a pair of vases, is counted as one item. (*Chattels* means tangible, movable property.)

Animals, private cars, caravans and boats. Also other chattels which are wasting assets; that is assets expected to last 50 years or less.

Life assurance policies.

National Savings Certificates, British Savings Bonds and Save-As-You-Earn.

British government stocks if owned for more than one year or inherited.

British money.

Foreign currency obtained for personal or family expenditure.

Winnings from betting or from Premium Bonds.

Gifts which you make to others during the tax year, provided that their total value is less than £100 for each recipient.

Gifts to charities.

Gifts to certain institutions such as the National Trust and the British Museum.

Your Own Home.

When you sell your house any capital gains you make will normally be exempt from tax. However, there are a number of circumstances in which you may get only partial exemption. For example, if you let out part of your home or used part of it for business you may not be allowed full exemption from capital gains tax. These circumstances are described in more detail in the Inland Revenue leaflet CGT 4, *Capital Gains Tax—Owner-occupied houses*. You should enter any gains from the disposal of your house on your tax return in case they are not wholly exempt.

Capital Losses.

Your capital gains can be reduced by deducting allowable losses. An allowable capital loss is usually one which would have been taxable if it had been a gain. For example, a loss on an item which is exempt, such as your car, would *not* be considered an allowable loss. If your losses exceed your gains in the tax year you can carry the balance forward to set against gains in future years. You can do this even if the proceeds of all your assets sold in the year are less than £1,000. If the proceeds are less than £1,000, there is no liability at all, and so the losses can be carried forward in their entirety. You can also deduct allowable expenditure from your capital gains (or add them on to your capital losses).

Working Out Your Gain.

Normally your capital gain (or loss) is the amount you receive when disposing of the asset *minus* the original amount you paid for it. If you give the asset away, the market value at the time of disposal is used instead. The same method is used if you were originally given the asset, or if you inherited it. There are special rules for assets which you owned before 6 April 1965. (This was the date that capital gains tax was introduced.) These rules usually mean that it is only the gain or loss since that date which counts.

Shares.

If you buy batches of the same share at different prices the cost of each share is considered to be the average cost. For example, suppose you purchase 100 shares in a company for £200. Three months later you buy a further 100 of the same shares for £300. You would then have a total of 200 shares which cost you £500. The average cost

is, therefore, £2·50 per share. When you come to sell all or some of these shares the calculation of your gain or loss will be based on this average cost.

The Rates of Capital Gains Tax.

Since 1965 net capital gains have been taxed at a flat rate of 30 per cent. There is an alternative method of calculating the tax, however. By this method half your gains up to a maximum of £2,500 are ignored, and the rest taxed as investment income. For most people, this alternative method of charging capital gains tax is the most favourable. Most people who pay the tax do so at 17 per cent, as half the gain is treated as tax-free, and the other half is taxed at the basic rate of 34 per cent.

In his budget speech on April 12, 1978, the Chancellor announced that he proposed to replace this alternative method of assessing capital gains tax with a new " small gains " relief. The proposals are that an individual's *gains* up to £1,000 in any year should be exempt and gains between £1,000 and £5,000 be charged at 15 per cent, that is at half the full rate. There are to be marginal provisions so that the full rate of tax will apply only to gains of £9,500 or more. It is also proposed that this new relief will apply to the tax year 1977/78 as well as to future years.

Unit Trusts and Investment Trusts.

There are special provisions for " authorised " unit trusts and " approved " investment trusts (this includes most unit and investment trusts). The effect of these provisions is that capital gains from investment and unit trusts are effectively tax-free for basic-rate tax-payers. If you are a higher-rate tax-payer you would pay tax at a reduced rate.

12. CAPITAL TRANSFER TAX

Capital transfer tax is a particularly complicated and technical tax. What is attempted here, therefore, is very much a summary. If you are not sure of your position you should consider obtaining professional advice. This is especially necessary with respect to capital transfer tax and trusts. Capital transfer tax was introduced in 1975 as a successor to estate duty. The old estate duty was imposed on property passing at death, but capital transfer tax also applies to assets given away during a person's lifetime.

The Tax.

Capital transfer tax is payable on gifts made after 26 March 1977. It is also imposed on the net value of a person's estate where death occurs after 12 March 1975. Certain gifts, most of which are listed below, are exempt from tax. All other gifts are taxable, and the Inland Revenue will keep a cumulative total of the gifts you make. The final stage of cumulation occurs with the inclusion of property passing at death. As soon as your cumulative total passes over the threshold for tax (£25,000 at the beginning of 1978) you become liable for tax. There are two tax scales. The first, Table 8, applies to transfers made during life. The second and higher-rate scale (Table 9) applies to transfers made at death. If you die within three years of making a taxable transfer, additional tax is payable to bring the tax on it up to the scale applicable on death.

Valuation.

The method of valuing assets is similar to that which applied for estate duty. Assets are usually valued at the price they would fetch on the open market at the time of the transfer. Some transfers, however, are exempt from tax. These can be divided into two groups: those exempt if the transfer is made during life, and those exempt whether the transfer was made in life or at death.

Exempt Transfers—Lifetime Gifts.

The following exemptions apply if the transfer is made during life.

Transfers up to £2,000 in any one year (unused relief may be carried forward for one year only).

Small gifts of up to £100 to any one recipient in any tax year.

Gifts made as part of normal expenditure.

Marriage gifts as follows:

Parent	£5,000 each
Grandparents	£2,500 each
Bride and groom	£2,500 to each other
Other people	£1,000 each

Other Exempt Transfers.

The following exemptions apply to transfers made either during life or at death:

The first £25,000 of transfers.

Transfers between husband and wife if both are domiciled in the United Kingdom.

Gifts to charities and political parties (unless made within one year of death, in which case the exemption is limited to £100,000 for charities and a further £100,000 for political parties). A " political party " is defined for this purpose as a party with two M.P.s, or one M.P. and not less than 150,000 votes for its candidates at the last general election.
Gifts for national purposes, etc. For example, gifts to the National Trust, National Gallery, universities and museums are exempt.

Other Relief.

There is also some relief for business assets, agricultural land and shares which represent a controlling interest in a company. In addition, a certain amount of relief is being extended to minority shareholdings in unquoted companies.

Working Out the Tax.

The tax is based on the amount the donor is financially worse off when he makes a gift. Liability is based on the *gross* value of the gift; that is the net gift *plus* the tax. This may be illustrated with an example. Suppose you are liable to capital transfer tax at a rate of 50 per cent. If you intend to give £3,000 after tax the cost to you will be £6,000. The value of the gift would be taken as £6,000, so that £3,000 is due in tax and £3,000 is left as the net gift. For this reason when you make a gift you should make clear who is to be responsible for the tax: you or the recipient. If you simply give an asset away, then you as the donor will be primarily liable for tax. In the above example a net gift of £3,000 meant a tax bill of £3,000 for the donor. If the recipient had agreed to pay the tax on the £3,000 he would have paid £1,500 in tax and kept £1,500.

Transfers in Life.

The application of capital transfer tax can be illustrated with a further example. Suppose your

TABLE 6.   *Rates of Tax on Lifetime Transfers*

Slice of transfer. £		Rate (%).	Cumulative tax at maximum of each slice (£).
0 to	25,000	NIL	NIL
25,001	30,000	5	250
30,001	35,000	7½	625
35,001	40,000	10	1,125
40,001	50,000	12½	2,375
50,001	60,000	15	3,875
60,001	70,000	17½	5,625
70,001	90,000	20	9,625
90,001	110,000	22½	14,125
110,001	130,000	27½	19,625
130,001	160,000	35	30,125
160,001	210,000	42½	51,375
210,001	260,000	50	76,375
260,001	310,000	55	103,875
310,001	510,000	60	223,875
510,001	1,010,000	65	548,875
1,010,001	2,010,000	70	1,248,875
over	2,010,000	75	—

first taxable transfer was a gift of £30,000. Table 6 shows that the transfer would result in a tax liability of £250. This would leave a net gift of £29,750. Now suppose you make a second taxable transfer, this time of £5,000. This would be added to your previous gift with the result that you would now face a tax rate of 7½ per cent. The tax payable on this second gift, therefore, is £375 leaving a net gift of £4,625.

Capital Transfer Tax at Death.

On your death, capital transfer tax is charged as if you transferred the *net value* of your estate the moment before you expired. The higher rate scale applying to transfers on death is shown in Table 7. The net value of your estate is the gross value of your assets minus certain deductions. These deductions include funeral expenses, debts and legal and professional fees owing at death. Any liability for income tax and capital gains tax up to the date of death may also be deducted.

TABLE 7.   *Rates of Tax on Transfers made at Death*

Slice of transfer. £		Rate (%).	Cumulative tax at maximum of each slice (£).
0 to	25,000	NIL	NIL
25,001	30,000	10	500
30,001	35,000	15	1,250
35,001	40,000	20	2,250
40,001	50,000	25	4,750
50,001	60,000	30	7,750
60,001	70,000	35	11,250
70,001	90,000	40	19,250
90,001	110,000	45	28,250
110,001	130,000	50	38,250
130,001	160,000	55	54,750
160,001	510,000	60	264,750
510,001	1,010,000	65	589,750
1,010,001	2,010,000	70	1,289,750
over	2,010,000	75	—

Administration and Collection.

The responsibility for the administration of capital transfer tax lies with the Inland Revenue. The procedures for assessment, appeals and penalties are similar to those for income tax. Payment of the tax is due at the end of the sixth month after the transfer is made, or at the end of the following April, whichever is the later. Tax arising on death is payable at least on an estimated basis before probate is granted. Overdue tax is subject to an interest charge of 6 per cent per annum for transfers at death, and 9 per cent for lifetime transfers.

13. VALUE ADDED TAX

If you have a business with a taxable turnover of £10,000 a year or more you must register for value added tax (VAT) with the Customs and Excise.

How VAT Works.

Whenever a taxable person is supplied with taxable goods or services VAT is payable. The amount of tax will be shown separately on the tax invoice received from the suppliers. A simple tax invoice will show, for example:

Goods supplied	£10·00
VAT at 8%	£00·80
Total payable	£10·80

When, in turn, the taxable person sells his products to his customers he charges them VAT. However, he is able to take credit for the VAT already paid to his suppliers. The balance is then payable to the Customs and Excise.

An example will illustrate the principle. At the end of the accounting period (every three months) our trader, John Smart, makes a return to the Customs and Excise. In it, he adds up his total sales (£10,000) and the amount of VAT charged to his customers (£800). John also adds up the cost of his supplies (£6,000) and the VAT paid on them (£480).

Total sales for the period	£10,000
VAT received	£800
Total inputs for the period	£6,000
VAT paid	£480
Balance payable to the Customs and Excise	£320

John's accounts then show that the VAT received by him (£800) is more than the VAT paid by him (£480). The difference (£320) is payable to the Customs and Excise. VAT is collected at each stage of production where the product is bought and sold. The idea is that the tax should be passed on to the final customer. This can be shown by tracing the progress of a good on the final stages of its journey to the customer.

	Price.	VAT.	Amount received by Customs and Excise.
Wholesaler buys good from manufacturer	£10	£00·80	£00·80
Wholesaler sells good to retailer	£20	£1·60	
Wholesaler pays VAT to Customs and Excise			£00·80 (£1·60 minus £00·80)
Retailer sells good to consumer	£30	£2·40	
Retailer pays VAT to Customs and Excise			£00·80 (£2·40 minus £1·60)
Customer pays	£30 plus £2·40 VAT		
Customs and Excise receive			£2·40

In the examples so far it has been assumed that the rate of VAT was 8 per cent. This, in fact, was the standard rate in 1977/78. There is also a higher rate (of 12½ per cent in 1977/78). In addition, some goods are exempt and others are "zero-rated" (see below). To allow for the needs of economic management, the Treasury is empowered to increase or decrease the rates of VAT by up to 25 per cent during the financial year.

Goods Subject to Higher Rate VAT.

The main categories of goods subject to higher rate VAT (12½ per cent) are: domestic appliances (but not ovens, water heaters, telephones and tools); radio and television sets, gramophones and tape recorders; boats and aircraft; caravans weighing less than 2,030 kg; photographic equipment; furs; jewellery; petrol.

Zero-rated Goods.

Goods that are "zero-rated" are in principle subject to VAT, but the rate applying to them is zero. This means that while VAT is not charged on these goods and services, traders can still recover any VAT paid on their supplies. The effect of this arrangement is that zero-rated goods and services should be entirely free of VAT. Exports, for example, are relieved of VAT in this way. The main categories of zero-rated goods are: food (but not items such as petfoods, ice cream, chocolates, alcoholic drinks and "meals out"); water; books and journals; talking books for the blind and handicapped and wireless sets for the blind; newspaper advertisements; news services; fuel and power; construction of buildings; transport; gold and banknotes; drugs, medicines, medical and surgical appliances (but only if purchased on a prescription); exports; goods supplied by charities; clothing and footwear for young children and crash helmets.

Goods and Services that are Exempt from VAT.

Exempt goods and services are not subject to VAT, even in principle. However, traders cannot take credit for any VAT paid on the supplies used to produce exempt goods and services. These items include: land (but not land used for things like camping sites and parking space); insurance; postal services (but not telephone, telegram or telex services); betting, gaming and lotteries (but gaming machines and the income from them are taxable); finance; education; health; burial and cremation services.

Registration.

Traders with a turnover of less than £10,000 per year are not required to register with the Customs and Excise. It may, however, be in their interests to do so. Where a trader pays more VAT for his supplies than he receives from his customers he may be entitled to a rebate. Such a rebate can only be claimed by registered traders. Businesses which should be registered but are not, remain liable for tax on their supplies, but they are not allowed to charge their customers VAT, or to claim any repayments. They are also liable to penalties.

Exempt Businesses.

Businesses which are exempt are those with turnovers of less than £10,000 and those producing only exempt goods and services. Exempt businesses are not required to keep VAT records or make returns or charge their customers VAT. If they register voluntarily they are no longer exempt.

THE CONTEMPORARY THEATRE

Since the 1950s our stage has seen far-reaching changes. Influential foreign plays long neglected have been produced here for the first time and contemporary writers, both indigenous and foreign, have experimented with new techniques and been concerned with urgent social problems. This section is concerned with the revival in the theatre, the differing types of drama, and with premières of the most outstanding plays of the last 25 years.

TABLE OF CONTENTS

THE CONTEMPORARY THEATRE

This section concerns the English theatre since 1950 and since a shared experience between actors and playgoers has long been vital to the full enjoyment of drama it is limited to plays acted live to a live audience. There are four sections:

I. INTRODUCTION

Although recently some of our most popular plays have been Ayckbourn's clever social comedies in the style of the " well-made play " between the wars, yet the work of many eminent dramatists has been very different in theme and technique. The theme of Hampton's *Savages* and Fugard's *Sizwe Bansi* was social injustice in other continents and Shaffer's *Equus* explored the anguish of the disturbed personality. The visual image of Beckett's *Not I* and *That Time* was a dimly lit mouth and young writers like Brenton and Hare constantly use surprising images as they question our social structure.

Such plays are more fully appreciated in the context of the many innovations in drama dating from the mid-1950s and this section is concerned with the more significant plays of this period.

The Function of Dramatic Art.

It is not the function of art to make a statement but to induce an imaginative response, and the spectator receives not an answer to a question but an experience.

Drama, like the other arts, gives expression to that subtle and elusive life of feeling that defies logical definition. By feeling is to be understood the whole experience of what it feels like to be alive—physical sensations, emotions, and even what it feels like to think.

This flux of sensibility cannot be netted down in logical discourse, but can find expression in what Clive Bell, when discussing the visual arts, called " significant form. "

The contemporary philosopher, Susanne Langer, in her book, *Feeling and Form*, has developed Clive Bell's concept, arguing that all artistic form is an indirect expression of feeling. The artist, be he painter, poet, or dramatist, creates an image, a form that gives shape to his feeling, and it is for the sensitive recipient to interpret its significance.

The especial province of drama, as was pointed out by Aristotle, is to create an image, an illusion of action, that action " which springs from the past but is directed towards the future and is always great with things to come." Both tragedy and comedy depict such action and the conflict which it normally entails.

The Therapeutic Effect of Drama.

One of the achievements of serious drama is to create an image that will objectify and help to resolve deep human conflicts.

Most people have at some time or another come away from a fine play feeling in some inexplicable way exhilarated and released, and it has long been recognised that drama can have a beneficial, even a therapeutic effect.

It is easy to understand the exhilarating effect of comedy but extremely difficult to comprehend that of tragedy. In the 4th cent. B.C. Aristotle claimed that tragedy accomplishes a beneficial purgation of pity and terror (see **The Aristotelian Play**) and Helen Gardner in *Religion and Litera-*

ture, 1971, again examines the paradox as to why a dramatisation of catastrophe should give us some kind of release and satisfaction. Discussing such influential theories as those of Hegel, Bradley, Schopenhauer, Nietzsche, Unamuno and Niebuhr, she elucidates the tragic conflict as opposition between such contraries as man and fate, man's incompatible ideals and inner conflicts, reason and emotion. She concludes that the power of tragedy lies in reconcilement of harshly discordant contraries—the passionate protest at inevitable suffering and its agonised acceptance—which realised together have power to console.

Helen Gardner's book is especially relevant to-day for she denies tragic stature to the modern serious play. Studying two of those rare periods productive of tragedy, she points out that social and religious conditions in 5th cent. Athens had a parallel in Elizabethan London. In both cultures a consciousness of guilt and sin and the need for propitiation and salvation involved a conviction that human action was profoundly significant, helping to create a climate propitious to tragedy which Helen Gardner following Aristotle defines as " the imitation of a complete action. "

Today's climate she considers adverse. The contemporary metaphysical despair and sense of meaninglessness together with post-Freudian emphasis on " sickness " rather than wrong-doing have helped to erode a sense of responsibility for actions, so that today's serious play is either eventless, pathetic rather than tragic, or as in the " theatre of cruelty " (*q.v.*), preoccupied with violent event for event's sake, while the unrelieved despair inevitably lacks that conflict of protest and acceptance, which exhilarates and consoles.

Another distinguished woman critic, Muriel Bradbrook, has put forward a most interesting psychological explanation of the effect of serious drama on the audience. She suggests that in watching a mature play we are encouraged to sympathise with many different characters at one and the same time, and it may be that the imaginative effort entailed has a corresponding movement in the unconscious mind. There, at the most primitive level, is an " internal society ", the petrified infantile images of father, mother and siblings, to which we are linked by inflexible attitudes. It may be that the sympathetic response to the playwright's images of these figures helps us to relax our rigid attitudes towards them so that the internal pattern of relationships shifts, and we experience a sense of release and a new access of energy.

It is noteworthy also that drama can be fully appreciated only in a public performance, a social event demanding the co-operation and understanding between author, players and audience. Because it can flourish only in a community, normally a city, it has been called the metropolitan art.

The Constituents of Drama.

Drama is a complex art in that it uses two very different kinds of ingredient or material, one speech, the literary constituent, the other the gesture movement, and confrontation of actors on an actual stage. Speech is man's most precise, subtle, and mature means of expression. Gesture and confrontation, which he shares to some degree with animals, is more primitive and some of the power of drama is its fusion of civilised speech and primitive gesture into one organic whole.

It is just possible to conduct brief scenes using only one of these media. The chorus in Shakespeare's *Henry V* is virtually confined to speech and there is in Galsworthy's *Justice*, revived in 1968, a moving wordless scene, showing a criminal in solitary confinement that is reputed to have led to amendment of the penal code.

Perhaps the more primitive gesture has the greater emotional force, but words made permanent in the literary script have constituted the commanding form of drama. Even the wordless mime is given permanence by the script.

The Ritual Element.

While speech and the confrontation of actors are essential to full drama, there is an element that has sometimes been neglected and that is ritual, perhaps the most primitive and evocative of all. The early tragedy of Greece was probably organically connected with the religious ritual of Dionysus and the matrix was song and dance. Similarly in England the origins of drama are to be found in church liturgy and ritual and civic occasion, both of which used procession, pageantry, costume, and symbolic insignia to great effect and also clowning which served as comic relief.

There have naturally been few dramatists able to combine literary ability, a sense of stage situation and skill in the use of ritual. The enduring power of Shakespeare is due to his manifold genius in that he could deploy inimitable poetry, swift action, and such ritual enrichments as royal processions, crowning and dethroning, duelling and wrestling, masque, pageantry, song and dance.

The Background of Modern Drama.

The happy fusion of excellence which is to be found in Shakespeare's plays is extremely rare, for it demands not only a versatile genius but also a receptive audience and a suitable building. By the Restoration the delicate balance was already disturbed and by the middle decades of the 19th cent. popular taste had all but banished literature from the stage. The disorderly audiences of the time demanded only spectacular and sensational theatrical and musical effects, and in the vast monopoly theatres of Drury Lane and Covent Garden they could hardly have heard, let alone appreciated, good dialogue. The managers discouraged men of genius, so that poets like Browning, who had no practical knowledge of the theatre, produced wordy "closet dramas" which were virtually unactable. while the popular theatrical melodramas like *Maria Marten* or *Murder in the Red Barn*, are today unreadable.

With the gradual establishment of smaller theatres. catering for a sober middle-class audience, men of talent again began to write for the stage. It was the turn of literature to take command, and more popular and traditional techniques such as music and clowning were now banished to the music-hall and pantomime.

T. W. Robertson, Henry Arthur Jones and Pinero all furthered the trend towards realism but it was the genius of Ibsen that set a high standard of excellence for the literary and realistic play of middle-class life. He expressed profound insight into personal and social problems in finely constructed plays, the overtones of poetic universality being conveyed in symbolism that was usually verbal.

Able writers, like Granville Barker and Galsworthy, although they lacked the poetic power of Ibsen, firmly established in England a similar type of literary play, realistic, well-constructed, serious-minded, concerned with the middle class and almost exclusively verbal.

Some of the few exceptions to this type of play are to be found in Shaw. Like Shakespeare, he was not only a literary genius. He was also well acquainted with stage-production and although, much too wordy in old age, in his best comedies he combined some of the wittiest dialogue in English drama along with the delightful shocks and surprises of total theatre. Androcles' engaging Lion belongs to the same family as Titania's Ass.

But Shaw in his prime was unique, and between the wars the verbal, realistic play was perpetuated by such writers as Maugham and Coward. Not over-concerned with psychological or social issues, they used it to portray the leisured classes.

By the 'forties the conventional West End play had come to imitate not life but photography. Confined to the proscenium arch and realistic to the last trivial detail, it presented a prosaic picture of middle- and upper-class life, with stereotyped situation, demanding only stock responses and lacking interest in ideas, poetic intensity, and genuine wit. With the star cast and the long commercial run, theatre-going had become not an artistic experience but a social occasion.

Apart from the novel comedies of such writers as Rattigan and the verse plays of T. S. Eliot and Fry, it was the revivals of the classics, English and European, that were bringing genuine drama to the stage. Shakespeare could be enjoyed not only at Stratford and the Old Vic, but in the West End. It was largely due to Gielgud that Shakespeare was now a box-office draw.

Gielgud's fine histrionic sense, and his highly sensitive and poetic interpretation had earned him that rare distinction of being the Hamlet of his generation. As actor and producer, working with other fine artists, such as Edith Evans, Peggy Ashcroft, Olivier, Guinness and Scofield, Gielgud later confirmed his success. Enthralling interpretations of plays by Shakespeare, Webster, and the like, demonstrated that the classics could have a wide popular appeal.

Such achievements reminded audience and aspiring playwright that there are many other dramatic styles than fashionable realism and so may even have helped to further the dramatic revival that began in the 'fifties.

The Modern Revival.

Although artistic work overflows the tidy schemes of chronology, it is helpful to distinguish two main phases of contemporary drama, beginning with plays produced during the first sudden outburst of creativity.

The decade beginning 1955.

Many new playwrights first became known during an exciting decade. There were British premières of plays by continental writers such as Brecht, Ionesco, Genet, Dürrenmatt, Frisch, Vian, Hochhuth and Weiss and by the American Albee. British dramatists who soon established their reputation included Beckett, Osborne, Behan. Pinter, N. F. Simpson, Mortimer, Wesker, Arden, Shaffer, Saunders and Bolt. Most of these fortunately, still continue to write.

It is never easy to identify causes of artistic renewal but one reason was that young men like Wesker injected new vigour into jaded realism by using it to express the stresses of the working people they knew. Hence the settings in shabby basements and attics (*see* Neo-realism). It was in such a setting in Osborne's *Look Back in Anger* (*q.v.*) that there suddenly exploded that blast of confused and impotent anger which expressed the frustration of many of his contemporaries.

More far-reaching was the general awareness among avant-garde playwrights that verbalism was not enough, and their readiness to experiment with the resources of "total theatre". Here the way had been shown by scholarly research into the history of the theatre which gave dramatists confidence to revive valid techniques such as song, music and clowning that the early 20th cent. had banished to the music-hall.

The most vital stimulus was the challenge of genius. Brecht's Epic Theatre (q.v.) offered a more free and fluid form than that of the "well-made play" (q.v.) and his novel uses of traditional theatrical devices (such as song, masks extravagant costume and settings, direct address to the audience) were quickly adapted by dramatists like Arden, Bolt and Osborne.

Meanwhile Ionesco, whole-hearted devotee of the Theatre of the Absurd (q.v.), introduced monsters like the rhinoceros and exploited stage properties like empty chairs to satirise man's frightened and empty existence. He was soon followed by Saunders and by Simpson, whose weighing-machines symbolised the dominance of imagination by machinery. Devices recently restricted to pantomime were reviving.

A pervasive and growing influence was that of Artaud's demand for a Theatre of Cruelty (q.v.). This is both the most novel and the most atavistic type of theatre, for it attempts to re-create in modern terms that primitive, even barbaric ritual from which drama evolved. It was clearly exemplified in 1964 in a play by Weiss (q.v.) and in England is still best known in translations.

Developments since 1965.

One of the most interesting aspects of theatre was a fresh topical approach to Shakespeare.

Some critics and producers have traced in his plays the bleak disenchantment of post-war Europe, owing much to the Polish critic, Jan Kott, whose book *Shakespeare, our Contemporary*, was published here in 1964.

Kott, who lived through the Nazi tyranny and the Stalinist occupation of Poland, urges that the power-politics of twentieth century Europe have their counterpart in the Wars of the Roses and the Tudor disturbances. He finds in Shakespeare's Histories and Tragedies, what he terms the "Grand Mechanism" of history, the blood-stained struggle for power and claims that Shakespeare "condemns war by showing up the Feudal butchery."

The series, "The Wars of the Roses", which was produced for the B.B.C. during 1965–6 by Peter Hall and John Barton with the R.S.C., vividly demonstrated the crime-ridden lust for power and the Feudal butchery. Meanwhile at Stratford and the Aldwych, the production of *Henry V* showed the king, grimy and battle-scarred, leading a tattered army, plagued by corrupt camp-followers. Played on a bare, gaunt stage, grey, metallic and cavernous, it was strikingly similar in tone and significance to Brecht's *Mother Courage*, running concurrently at the Old Vic.

Shakespearean comedy was also approached afresh. In Clifford Williams' enchanting production for the National Theatre in 1967 of *As You Like It*, with an all-male cast, the women's parts were not taken as in Shakespeare's time by boys with unbroken voices but by young men. Williams was aware of the unorthodox theories expressed in Kott's *The Bitter Arcadia*. Kott observing the almost identical appearance of modern youths and girls was reminded of those Shakespearean comedies where the girl appears disguised as a youth. He argues that their theme is that of the sonnets—" the impossibility of choice between the youth and the woman, the fragile boundary between friendship and love . . . the universality of desire which cannot be contained or limited to one sex."

The sober fact remains that Shakespeare is not our contemporary. Historical accuracy of presentation is comparatively recent and the text can even be illuminated by anachronism as in Brook's production of *A Midsummer Night's Dream* with techniques borrowed from Persia. The plays can even be abbreviated as in most productions of *Hamlet*.

But violations such as Nahum Tate's notorious happy ending to *King Lear* now appear ridiculous. Helen Gardner castigates as "outrageous arrog-

ance" attempts to present Shakespeare as "our contemporary," an existentialist confounding "the tragic" with "the meaningless", and sacrificing poetry to spectacle and violence.

Recent perspectives.

Meanwhile there have since 1965 been diverse influences from abroad through plays by Soyinka, Duras, Jarry, Fugard, Feiffer, Lowell, Triana and Chayavsky. A new generation of British dramatists has become prominent including Mercer, Bond, McGrath, Storey, Terson, Nichols, Wood, Hampton and Stoppard. Some have experimented in fresh dramatic genres and techniques but generally speaking the most novel contribution of native authors and producers has been a new candour in the presentation of social problems.

Joe Orton, whose best play had been produced in 1964, popularised a peculiar brand of "black comedy" (q.v.).

A more serious innovation was the "theatre of fact". *The Investigation* of Peter Weiss set an example for plays which constitute a kind of "documentary" of the stage, the dramatist endeavouring to present objectively a selection of the actual events of contemporary history. But however detached, selection involves bias.

One of the most sober of such factual plays, Kipphardt's on Oppenheimer, followed Weiss in presenting a judicial enquiry. Later examples were Hare's *Fanshen*, 1975, and Brook's production of *The Ik*, 1976.

The R.S.C. also carried out an experiment in a new genre, that of "Director's Theatre", and the involvement of the audience was certainly the purpose of *US*, directed by Peter Brook as a direct assault on our apathy concerning the war in Vietnam.

A refreshing candour in the approach to social problems has been evident in plays involving biting criticism of the military mentality and recourse to war, notably McGrath's *Bofors Gun*, Vian's *The Generals' Tea Party*, and Charles Wood's *Dingo* and "*H*".

Meanwhile the pressing international problem of relations between black and white has been illuminated in plays by Fugard and Lowell.

Illness both physical and mental is now frankly presented. Peter Nichols in 1967 used remarkable theatrical skill in revealing the effects on the parents of the incurable illness of a spastic shild. His ironic *The National Health* (1969) was set in a grim hospital ward.

It is no longer unusual to see a play depicting the distressed mind. Storey's touching work *Home* (1970) is set in the grounds of a mental hospital. Both he and Mercer have been concerned with the malaise of a generation educated beyond the parents.

There has steadily developed a sympathetic attitude towards sexual deviation. In 1965 *A Patriot for Me*, Osborne's uncompromising portrait of a homosexual, could be performed only privately. But in 1968 Christopher Hampton's *Total Eclipse* was devoted to a candid exploration of the historic relationship between Verlaine and Rimbaud.

The abolition in September 1968 of the Lord Chamberlain's powers of theatre censorship removed official taboos on the dramatist's freedom of expression, which are now conditioned by the public's response. There has been an increasing vogue for four-letter words and sexual reference. The revue *Oh! Calcutta!* (1970), sponsored by Tynan, included a representation of sexual intercourse and total nudity. The taboo on stage nakedness was broken. Although nudity has proved commercially successful the plays in which it is employed have been unremarkable.

Four-letter words are now a commonplace. Chaucer used them precisely and effectively and after Victorian repression they needed a good airing. In realistic plays such as Whitehead's they give a valid impression of actual speech. Pinter is very conscious of the explosive force of an erotic taboo word suddenly erupting to the surface and for that very reason uses it rarely. Lesser playwrights have used such words freely so as to shock, when they show diminishing returns, and degenerate into a modish gutter slang and like false money depreciate the vocabulary.

In the avant garde Living Theatre coherent narrative sequence is discarded in favour of a series of "happenings"—disparate theatrical images, involving movement, mime, inarticulate cries, rhythmic sound and music. These are frequently violent, sometimes in a talented company surprising and beautiful, but often unintelligible. Living Theatre is often imbued with the spirit of Artaud's "Theatre of Cruelty". Sometimes "audience participation" is invited, actors and spectators mingling with each other both on stage and in the auditorium.

Recently much experimental work has made its appearance on the Fringe. An increasing number of enterprising companies—such as McGrath's 7.84—have presented plays in shabby makeshift quarters such as basements, disused rooms and pubs. Some were founded some time ago, such as the Unity, N.W.1, 1937, or the Traverse Theatre, Edinburgh, 1963. Recently there have been successful pub theatres like the King's Head, Islington, and the Bush, W.12. A fortunate few have good modern buildings such as the Cockpit, 1970, the Soho Poly, and the Half Moon of 1972, all in London.

The late '60s and early '70s have seen a rise in the importance of provincial theatres, with many new ones being opened in towns such as Exeter, Colchester and Worcester. More established provincial theatres, particularly the Nottingham Playhouse, have combined programmes of neglected classics with premières of important new plays.

Criteria of Judgment.

How can the value of novel and experimental plays be estimated? The ultimate test of time is obviously impossible and some of the critical principles by which traditional drama has been interpreted are no longer relevant.

The first canon of criticism is that every art form determines the criteria by which it is judged,

and the good dramatic critic does not approach any play with a pontifical set of rules but endeavours to keep an open mind.

Since artistic form is an expression of human feeling, the first encounter with a work of art should be in a mood of extreme receptivity, so that one may be aware of the feeling implicit in the work, however novel or even bizarre the expression may be. The initial reaction to drama should be intuitive.

The nature and quality of the implicit feeling can then be considered. Is it an original and genuine response to experience, or perfunctory and stereotyped, is it intense or diffuse, profound or shallow, subtle or commonplace, reasoned or irrational?

Drama is an especially complicated art, in that part of its material being words, it may also involve discussion of ideas. This discussion, however, should not be mistaken for a statement of the author's convictions. In a good play it is an expression of his characters' *feeling* about ideas.

Another enquiry concerns the appropriateness and beauty of the form in which the feeling is conveyed. Many consider that Beckett's *Waiting for Godot*, while lacking the tragic greatness of *King Lear*, conveys its implicit mood, and that each play is an image of man, disillusioned, adrift, assailed by despair in an alien universe. This recognised, the critic's task is to explore the form of the two plays. Apart from the fact that they both use a most improbable fable, they could hardly be more different. Yet in either case the form of the play has artistic significance and appropriateness and repays analysis, and here again the critic needs to be flexible.

The most searching question to be asked of a play is whether it is life-enhancing, whether it gives delight or deepens understanding.

Most difficult to estimate are those plays like *Lear* or *Godot*, which express a mood of despair. But if man's honesty and endurance are ultimately affirmed, the play is not negative in import. Lear begs forgiveness and the tramps still wait. Similarly a biting satire may be positive if it helps to clear away old wood. A facile optimism may be a betrayal.

Ideally the best way to know a play is first to see it on the stage, when its theatrical qualities can be enjoyed, and later to read it at leisure, when its literary value can be appreciated.

II. EMINENT THEATRICAL GROUPS

We are greatly indebted to a few enterprising and devoted groups—chiefly repertory companies and theatre clubs—which help to keep drama alive.

Foremost are the Royal Shakespeare Company and the National Theatre, which have earned an international reputation by their superb productions of both classics and new plays. Some groups, such as the English Stage Company and the Traverse Theatre, Edinburgh, have been particularly concerned with new dramatists.

Many repertory theatres do exciting work and there is a comprehensive list in the *Stage Year Book*.

The Royal Shakespeare Company.

When Peter Hall was appointed managing director in January 1960 he decided to supplement the annual season of Shakespeare at Stratford-on-Avon by a continuous repertory of classical and contemporary plays at the Aldwych, and in 1962 to hold a special experimental season at the Arts Theatre.

Under the directors, Peter Hall, Peter Brook and Paul Scofield, a brilliant team of over 100 actors was gathered together and the imaginative direction and artistic perfection of the ensemble playing became world famous.

Each year at the Aldwych arresting Shakespearean productions from Stratford alternate with other classics and stimulating modern work. There have been new experimental plays by native writers, such as Beckett, Mercer, Pinter, Saunders and Whiting. Stimulating foreign playwrights have included Albee, Arrabal, Brecht, Chayavsky, Duras, Dürrenmatt, Feiffer, Gorky, Günter Grass, Hochhuth, Triana and Weiss. Their work is discussed in Part IV.

The annual World Theatre Season, organised by Peter Daubney, has given a unique opportunity for seeing ensembles from other countries with apparatus for simultaneous translation.

The National Theatre.

Sixty years after Granville Barker and William Archer had formulated plans for a National

Theatre, the inaugural production of *Hamlet* took place on 22 October 1963 at its temporary home, the Old Vic.

Laurence Olivier already appointed director, the nucleus of a distinguished company was formed and soon established its high reputation for exquisite ensemble playing, guest artists also appearing on occasion.

The intention was to build up a large repertoire of classical and modern plays from all countries and the wide and varied list included works by Euripides, Shakespeare, Ben Jonson, Webster, Congreve, Farquhar, Molière, Feydeau, Pinero, O'Neill, Strindberg, Shaw, O'Casey and Brecht. Contemporary dramatists represented were often Arden, Arrabal, Griffiths, Miller, Nichols, Peter Shaffer, Stoppard and Wood.

The imaginative quality of production and acting was enthusiastically acclaimed by packed houses and the scenery was often breathtaking.

In April 1973 Peter Hall became co-director with Olivier and in the autumn assumed full responsibility.

In March 1976 the new National Theatre on the South Bank at last opened. It has three auditoria. The Lyttelton, with its proscenium arch familiar in England during the last 300 years, opened first, later The Olivier, with the type of stage used in Greek and Elizabethan times, but the smaller Cottesloe was not ready till 1977.

The English Stage Company.

Formed to promote contemporary drama, the company acquired in 1956 a long lease of the Royal Court with George Devine (d. 1965) as director and Tony Richardson as assistant. Declaring themselves a Writers' Theatre, they were extraordinarily successful in sponsoring new playwrights, such as Arden, Bond, Osborne, N. F. Simpson, Storey and E. A. Whitehead. The première of *Dingo* by the promising Charles Wood, was seen here, as were new plays by established authors like Beckett and Wesker. New plays appeared by stimulating foreign writers, including Ionesco, Genet, Sartre and Arthur Miller.

An interesting departure was to present for the first time seminal plays from the past, including the first Brecht staged in London and work by Jarry and Wedekind. In 1968 D. H. Lawrence's plays were at last produced.

In 1973 the Court was particularly successful with premières by Brenton and Hampton, and from '73 to '74 with 3 plays by Fugard, acted by his South African black collaborators.

These writers are all discussed in Part IV.

The Mermaid Theatre.

It was largely due to the efforts of Bernard Miles that in 1959 the City of London's first new theatre since Shakespeare's time was opened at Blackfriars. Commerce, industry and the general public had generously given money, the City Corporation had granted the site at a peppercorn rent and the surviving walls of a blitzed warehouse had been used as the shell for a delightful little theatre of 499 seats with an open stage, based on that of Shakespeare's day.

The Mermaid is now part of the City's artistic life with foyer exhibitions, films, concerts, and lectures. The enterprising " Molecule Club " for children uses ingenious theatrical means to demonstrate basic scientific principles.

The Mermaid has a fine varied record of productions, including British premières of works by Brecht, Camus, and O'Casey. There have been revivals of Shakespeare, Ford, Dekker, Beaumont and Fletcher and Shaw, and of foreign plays by Ibsen, Pirandello, Henry James Lessing and Euripides. Lowell's *Benito Cereno* (*q.v.*) and James Joyce's *Exiles* (*q.v.*) both had their premières here.

The National Youth Theatre.

Originating in Alleyn's School and the enterprise of Michael Croft, the N.Y.T. fosters in young people an appreciation of theatre, whether as audience or performers. Since 1959 it has performed annually in the West End and abroad. In 1971 Camden Council generously offered the N.Y.T. fine permanent headquarters—the new Shaw Theatre.

Terson (*q.v.*) has written for the N.Y.T. plays specially commissioned, admirably suited to the company and enthusiastically received. Since 1975 the N.Y.T. has also produced plays by Barrie Keefe.

Theatre Workshop and Joan Littlewood.

Between 1953 and 1961 Joan Littlewood as director of Theatre Workshop at Stratford East introduced several new playwrights, including Behan. Spontaneity, pseudo-Brechtian techniques and social commitment rather than careful construction were the hall-marks of her work, her masterpiece being *Oh What a Lovely War* (M). This paradoxically used a period piece brilliantly to satirise the tragic futility of the first world war.

In 1967 Littlewood directed *MacBird* and *Mrs. Wilson's Diary*. *MacBird* (P), by Barbara Garson, is an American parody on *Macbeth* in doggerel blank verse, attacking the American " Establishment ", under Lyndon Johnson. Unfortunately Joan Littlewood made such alterations to the text that the satirical parallel with Shakespeare was blurred. *Mrs. Wilson's Diary* (M), in form a jolly prewar musical, was described by its authors, Ingrams and Wells, as " an affectionate lampoon " on the Wilson administration.

In 1970 Joan Littlewood returned to Stratford East, where she has produced Hill's *Forward Up Your End* and Wells' *The Projector*, set in Walpole's age but suggesting parallels with the collapse of flats at Ronan Point.

III. GLOSSARY OF DRAMATIC TERMS

Absurd Drama.

The Theatre of the Absurd, originating in Paris, was introduced here through the plays of Beckett and translations of Ionesco and Vian. It has had considerable impact on Pinter, N. F. Simpson, Saunders and Stoppard, while absurdist plays by the Americaan Albee and the Swiss Frisch have also been produced here.

The concept of the Absurd was first formulated by Camus to indicate the discrepancy between human reason and aspiration and an indifferent and hostile universe. But like Sartre he expressed his convictions through the traditional dramatic form.

Not every playwright of the Absurd is an existentialist and many are more concerned with an irrational human society than with the universe. What they have in common is a technique. All have discarded traditional realism and express absurdity through images that are themselves absurd, including bizarre situations and objects, both sad and comic, as aged parents consigned to dustbins.

There is in the Absurd an element of Surrealism and Dr. Bradbrook has suggested that a better term might be Theatre of Dream, for it is the unconscious dream mind that juxtaposes objects and incidents that in the waking state have no connection, such as a rhinoceros in a provincial street. Pinter seems to have an intuitive awareness of the hinterland of dream, while Simpson makes a conscious manipulation of Surrealism.

Frisch has ably demonstrated that the Absurd can be an effective vehicle for satire and absurdist writers like Ionesco and Simpson have satirised the modern corruption of language by salesmen and politicians, using conversations of vapid emptiness to demonstrate its breakdown and relying more on ludicrous objects and situations, thus extending the range of total theatre.

The Aristotelian Play.

Brecht and Ionesco have disparagingly referred somewhat inaccurately, to "Aristotelianism". Strictly speaking, this means the concept of tragedy which Aristotle first analysed in his *Poetics*, basing it primarily on the poetic tragedies of Sophocles, especially the *Oedipus Rex* (P), c. 425 B.C. The Aristotelian concept, revived since the Renaissance, has obviously been much modified, but certain basic principles can still be discerned.

Aristotle claims that poetry in general aims at that rational pleasure which is part of the good life. He defines tragedy as the imitation of an action. By imitation he does not mean the description of an actual happening but of one that is possible. Hence the poetic licence whereby the dramatist may adapt historical material to his own theme.

Aristotle stresses that the action should be complete in itself and have inner coherence. Tragedy must have an intelligible beginning, a middle necessitated by the beginning and which itself necessitates the end. "The story ... must represent one action, a complete whole, with its several incidents so closely connected that the transposal or withdrawal of any one will disjoint and dislocate the whole."

The action should be of some magnitude, with "incidents arousing pity and fear wherewith to accomplish the purgation of such emotions." Here is Aristotle's celebrated doctrine of purgation or "catharsis" which has been variously interpreted, some considering that something like a ceremonial purification is intended, with an ethical end in view, others that bodily or psychological relief from tension is meant.

Aristotle emphasised the paramount importance of action or plot, the characters being revealed in and through the action. The kind of plot recommended is one where the hero is an eminent man, neither inordinately good nor bad, whose misfortune is brought upon him by some error of judgment.

Here is the germ of the splendid Renaissance tragedy concerned with the fall of princes and also of the modern finely constructed play, such as Ibsen's *Ghosts*. Such a play has classical symmetry, the beginning, middle and end, becoming in modern parlance the exposition, development and climax or dénouement. It has its own organic unity and inevitability. But although many writers, such as Sartre, still work within the classical disciplines many have discarded the traditional form.

Brecht and his followers have repudiated the whole pattern in favour of a sequence of self-contained episodes strung along a narrative thread, where ironic detachment supersedes the emotional involvement and catharsis of Greek tragedy.

In this day of the common man few are concerned with the fall of princes, and it is interesting to examine some of the more striking modern plays and to ask how far they stand up to the Aristotelian canon. Should a new concept of tragedy be evolved, that of potentiality unrealised, not a fall from greatness but a failure to rise?

Black Comedy.

Orton (*q.v*) popularised a genre in which human suffering is presented as comic. The basic technique is the shock of violent juxtapositions both in language and incident. Death, mental illness, murder, sexual perversion, suddenly excite laughter because they are conveyed in deadpan jests and genteel terms, or are promptly succeeded by the bathos of farce. Like circus clowning, the style has some value, especially in satire, but it easily stifles compassion.

The Brechtian or Epic Play.

Many British dramatists have felt the pervasive influence of the Bavarian Brecht (*q.v.*), who developed a new kind of Epic or narrative play of debate, with a loose sequence of episodic scenes linked by commentary or songs. Discarding realism, Brecht attempted not to arouse the onlooker's emotions but to stimulate him to think about social issues and to take left-wing action. In the event his ambiguous central situation appealed to deeper levels of experience.

There have been several instances of the ambiguous protagonist, but English playwrights have tended to adopt not the political intentions but the style of the Epic genre. Esslin has said that Shaffer in *The Royal Hunt of the Sun* has joined "Bolt, Arden and John Whiting of *The Devils* in the select group of British dramatists who have genuinely benefited from the conception of epic ... techniques in drama."

Theatre of Cruelty.

In 1938 Antonin Artaud published *The Theatre and its Double*, a collection of essays and letters, which forms the theoretic basis of the Theatre of Cruelty, his central purpose being a ritual of cruelty to exorcise fantasies.

Professor Brustein has described how Artaud hated industrial civilisation, believing, like Freud and D. H. Lawrence, that it stifled instinctual life. He claimed that the theatre, as the heart of a common culture, should enact a primitive ritual of cruelty, a sacrificial frenzy and exaltation. In this way it would bring to the surface and exorcise the spectator's latent anarchy, violence, and eroticism, serving as an "outlet for repressions".

Artaud's theories have yet to be proved. Anthropology has shown that a sacrificial blood ritual was long practised by primitive tribes without diminishing man's urge to cruelty, as is poetically conveyed in Edith Sitwell's *Gold Coast Customs* (see **M**, Part II). A modern dramatic enactment can certainly make us aware of repressed violent impulses but does it clear them away?

As to technique, Artaud envisaged a total theatre appealing to total man, primarily visual, where the all-important director would deploy "music, dance, plastic art, pantomime, mimicry, gesticulation, intonation, architecture, scenery and lighting" to induce a state of trance. Attacking the inadequacy of a pallid conceptual language, Artaud demanded that dramatic language should have an emotional and incantatory effect.

Genet fulfils Artaud's demands and in England the specific Theatre of Cruelty has been best represented by his plays, the *Marat Sade* of Weiss, Triana's *The Criminals* and *The Architect and the Emperor of Assyria* of Arrabal. But the methods of production advocated by Artaud have had a wide and pervasive influence on the movement towards total theatre.

Expressionism.

The genre flourished in Germany after the first world war, where its chief exponents were Kaiser and Toller, and in Czechoslovakia in the plays of Capek. O'Neill and O'Casey have also occasionally experimented with Expressionism.

Reacting from Realism with its insistence on individual psychology and the detailed representation of actual life, Kaiser, Toller and Capek deliberately rejected the particular in favour of the typical. Living at a time of social upheaval they were preoccupied with the class struggle and with man's fear of the encroaching machine.

Their subject was social flux and clash and they sought to project on to the stage the aspirations and fears of large social groups or of the generality of mankind.

Their characters are types, sometimes even symbolic figures such as the Nameless one representing the mob in Toller's *Man and the Masses*. Their décor is stylised with occasional use of film, the dialogue staccato and the brief scenes are characterised by mass movement and swift action.

Allardyce Nicoll carefully distinguishes between the aims and the methods of Expressionism. He considers that although some impressionistic plays of Strindberg and later subjective writers sometimes employ similar techniques they cannot justly be considered as expressionist because their aim is to reveal subjective feelings.

Naturalism.

Naturalism in drama may be regarded as a special case of Realism, and it is not easy, nor perhaps always desirable, to make a sharp distinction between the two.

Naturalistic drama attempts to record as faithfully as possible the actual experiences of life, however banal, and to present life, undistorted by the playwright's theories or too much concern for artistic form. The virtues of Naturalism are fidelity and spontaneity. Its danger is that it may keep so close to life as to lose artistic form and tension, becoming the stage version of the tape recorder. *See* Slice-of-Life Play.

Zola in the 1870s propounded the principles of Naturalism. Distrusting both the play of ideas and the well-constructed play as tending to impose on life a falsifying pattern, he urged that drama should record as objectively as possible the actual course of man's life, especially the way it is conditioned by environment.

Strindberg's *Miss Julie*, 1888, is an essay in Naturalism but the genre is found in its most accomplished form in the Russian theatre, especially in Stanislavsky's production at the Moscow Art Theatre of the plays of Chekhov and in 1902 of Gorky's *The Lower Depths*.

Neo-Realism.

There is nothing new in dramatic Realism (*q.v.*) as such. What is novel is the realistic presentation of the shabby lodgings and streets of the underprivileged. Gorky in *The Lower Depths* was perhaps the first dramatist to reveal the wretched condition of the destitute and this play influenced O'Neill's *The Iceman Cometh*. Their production in London, with a starkly realistic background, had some effect on those modern plays where the kitchen-sink and dustbin were as much in vogue as was formerly the fashionable drawing-room.

Any worthwhile play has significance far beyond its milieu and modern neo-realistic plays vary greatly in theme and purpose. Several playwrights like Wesker have themselves been workers and their plays are an authentic interpretation of their own culture, once inaccessible to the middle-class audience. The fact that their work is occasionally loose in structure may be attributable to the influence of Naturalism (*q.v.*) or to the author's unacademic background. The advent of this fresh and vigorous drama from a group that has seldom been articulate is most valuable.

Realism.

Writers of realistic drama, such as Galsworthy attempt to create a stage illusion of actual life, usually through the medium of the well-constructed play. It is not always easy to distinguish between Realism and Naturalism—its extreme form—but one salient difference is that the latter tends to discard organised plot as imposing a false pattern on the flux of life.

The Satirical Play.

Recent years have seen heartening revivals of plays by Shaw, triggered off by Stage Sixty's production of *Widowers' Houses*, with its topical relevance to Rachmanism. There followed a long succession of Shaw revivals.

Shaw has found few successors, for genuine satire is a most demanding art. Subjective hostility and negative criticism are not enough. The motive power in Ibsen and Shaw was rational indignation, a most difficult fusion of strong emotion and objective reasoning, and their satire was constructive in that it implied and indicated positive values. It was also characterised by a precise aim at a specific target. Vague and wholesale denunciation diffuse a disagreeable tone which has a boomerang effect for it becomes associated not with the targets but with the playwright himself.

The graces of satire are detachment, irony and wit and it flourishes apparently in a stable society such as that of the 18th cent. which produced Swift and Voltaire. The European upheavals of the last half century have been unpropitious for satire and it is significant that the best plays in this genre, those of Frisch and Dürrenmatt, have come from neutral Switzerland.

The " Slice of Life " Play.

Here is an extreme kind of Naturalism, where the author has been so anxious to preserve fidelity to the natural spontaneity of living, that he has all but discarded form, as having a cramping and distorting effect.

Verse Drama.

During the 20th cent. several attempts have been made to revive drama in verse—the normal vehicle for the Renaissance playwright. Although the verse plays of Shakespeare and his contemporaries, kept alive in excellent revivals, still rise like the Himalayas above the contemporary scene, the dramatist today who tries to use verse has not the benefit of an unbroken tradition. T. S. Eliot and Christopher Fry succeeded in getting their verse plays on the stage but at the moment the most successful poetic drama achieves its effect through poetic prose and the theatrical poetry of its situation and stage imagery. Beckett Arden and Pinter have captured this poetry.

The finest verse play seen on the English stage for many years is Robert Lowell's *Benito Cereno*.

The Well-made Play.

The term " well-made play " was frequently used in a derogatory sense. Eric Bentley has pointed out that the " well-made play " is a form of classical tragedy, degenerate in that although the plot is ingeniously contrived, with arresting situation, intrigue and suspense, the play is mechanical and devoid of feeling.

IV. INDIVIDUAL DRAMATISTS

This part, alphabetical in arrangement, includes representative plays of dramatists whose work, whether English or in translation, has had its British première since 1950. Unless otherwise stated the quotation of date and actor refers to the British première.

Some less expensive editions are referred to thus: F: Faber and Faber. M: Methuen. P: Penguin. Inexpensive acting editions can usually be obtained from French's Theatre Bookshop, 26 Southampton Street, W.C.2.

Arthur Adamov (1908–1970).

Adamov first wrote plays such as *Professor Taranne* (P), which translate his own personal neuroses into images of the absurd, until with the propagandist *Paolo Paoli* he adopted a Brechtian technique. His *Spring 1871*, an epic panorama of the Paris Commune, had its world première in London in 1962.

Edward Albee (b. 1928).

The American Albee is a brilliant satirist, master of a hostile dialogue of barbed intellectual wit, and an adept in utilising diverse styles. He was adopted by wealthy foster parents and his major plays express the claustrophobia, the emptiness that may lurk behind the deceptively secure façade of wealth.

His early plays include the absurdist *Zoo Story* (P) and *The American Dream* (P), and the realistic *The Death of Bessie Smith*.

Who's Afraid of Virginia Woolf? 1964. P

A brilliant and scarifying satire on sterility in an American campus uses a ritual movement. George and Martha, named after the Washingtons, are an unsuccessful and childless middle-aged couple. They cherish a fantasy " son ", whom George, to spite Martha, symbolically " murders " during a drunken night party, when they attack each other and their guests (a young couple also childless) with ferocious mental cruelty.

A Delicate Balance. 1969. P.

An icy surface glasses over treacherous depths in the well-to-do home of Tobias (Hordern) and Agnes (Peggy Ashcroft) and the play begins and ends with her virtual monologue—phrased with the elegance of a Henry James—on how it will be if she goes mad.

Agnes holds the " delicate balance " of polite manners, while tolerant Tobias is now ineffectual and her alcoholic sister Claire persists in her sarcastic utterance of unwelcome truths. The most galling, obliquely hinted at, is that Tobias is more drawn to Claire than to Agnes.

Their son long since dead, and Tobias having then withdrawn from Agnes, their sole offspring is the neurotic Julia, who now returns home at the breakdown of her fourth marriage.

Suddenly their " oldest friends ", Harry and Edna, arrive seeking asylum from some inexplicable terror of " nothing ". Bewildered, but courteous, the hosts accept their guests, but after Julia has threatened to shoot the " intruders ", Agnes forces Tobias to realise that they bring " the plague ".

Tobias, unable to discard his last ideal of friendship, begs them to stay, while telling them this truth, but they depart, realising that they demand a sacrifice they themselves could not make.

Here is a microcosm of a society where love and friendship have died, humanism crumbles, and little but polite diplomacy survives, often a vehicle for fear and hostility. In tone it is a bitter inversion of the Apocryphal *Tobit*, with its touching pictures of religious faith, family love

and neighbourliness, and the " entertaining of Angels unaware ".

The literary provenance in subject and style is Eliot's *Family Reunion*, where another Harry, fleeing the furies, comes to a Wishwood, also dominated by a woman whose husband had loved her sister, like Claire also a visionary. But in Eliot the visionary is healer not destroyer and Harry departs to " follow the bright angels. "

With literary subtlety Albee exposes the " panic and emptiness " in a society losing its confidence and sense of values.

Tiny Alice. 1970.

A " metaphysical melodrama " of great emotional tension, possibly personal, is at surface level, like Dürrenmatt's *The Visit* (q.v.), a satire on materialism, with the victim sold to Mammon. It has another facet, the schema being primitive magic, the sexual initiation and ritual sacrifice of the victim. Here Albee draws on techniques of the Theatre of Cruelty (q.v.). There are also echoes of T. S. Eliot's *The Cocktail Party* (q.v.) and of Lewis Carroll's *Alice*.

A brilliant first scene initiates a bargain between two astute and unsavoury men, literally " of the same school ", who detest each other—the Cardinal, corrupt representative of the Church, and the Lawyer, emissary of Miss Alice, embodiment of Croesus. She is to confer immense wealth on the Church on condition that the lay brother Julian shall collect it.

With Julian, the gentle and compassionate protagonist, a deeper theme is developed, the distinction between actuality and symbol. His ideals being service, obedience and possible martyrdom, Julian has fought against accepting illusion and a false god, the puppet made in man's image, instead of God the Creator.

But in Miss Alice's echoing castle he is confronted and confused by an extraordinary image, a huge model, an exact replica of the castle, and within it a tiny model of the model Sometimes events within castle and model synchronise.

The play's sinister dimension now becomes clearer, as Miss Alice, her brutal lover, the lawyer, and the butler, a former lover, plan, with the acquiescence of the cardinal, to entrap Julian. Their purpose is consummated as Miss Alice by witchery and her appeal " Help me ", seduces Julian, when she utters the cry " Alice. " (On the satirical plane this may signify that only by orgasm can the millionairess realise her identity).

Later, after Julian's marriage to Alice by the reluctant cardinal, the four participants in the plot circle round Julian drinking to " the ceremony " and " Alice." Julian is now told that Miss Alice is an illusion, a surrogate for the real Alice who is within the model. Refusing to accept this, he is callously shot by the lawyer and left to die alone, slumped against the model.

The disparate elements in this exciting and disturbing play are not perfectly fused. Although Miss Alice experiences conflict between her " awesome " rôle and genuine tenderness for Julian, the characters are, with the exception of the complex Julian, two-dimensional. He, in his shy integrity, is touchingly portrayed. But his problem of faith although clinically scrutinised is not penetrated. This is especially apparent in his ambiguous and over-long dying soliloquy.

The work is meticulously plotted and worded, motifs, gestures, and phrases poetically recurring with ironic and suggestive shifts of meaning.

All Over. 1971.

In the handsome room of a dying celebrity there " gather " his Wife aged seventy-one, his Mistress, a fading voluptuous beauty for whom he had twenty years ago deserted the Wife, his Best Friend with whom the Wife had had a brief affair on her husband's desertion, and his Son and Daughter. The characters are not named.

The Wife's question, " Is he dead yet? " opens the play and her chilly clinical detachment is reflected in the older generation's dispassionate reminiscences. The Wife's haughty aloofness is a defence against desperate emotion, but she does not disguise her contempt for her ineffectual Son and unstable Daughter. The only event and climax of Act 1 is the unhappy Daughter's revengeful attempt to let the waiting Pressmen into the room.

Only at the death does the Wife's control crumble, as, discovering she loves no one but her husband, she breaks down sobbing. She may even realise that the plight of her children may not be unconnected with the parents.

But characterisation in depth is not the mainspring here, for Albee has attempted to endistance and universalise the situation. There are many references to ritual and echoes of T. S. Eliot's *The Family Reunion*. But in *All Over* the power of communal emotion which inspires the ritual of death is lacking. There is little love and no religious awe, and ritual has dwindled to convention.

This is a static play, like the fifteenth-century *Everyman*, a paradigm of the human predicament but enacted now in a " sad and shabby time ".

Counting the Ways. A Vaudeville. 1977.
The title is from *Sonnets from the Portuguese.*

In a duologue a middle-age man and wife, whose love is fading, recall their earlier experiences in elegant, mannered style best suited to the small stage.

Jean Anouilh (b. 1910).

Anouilh is a playwright of remarkable theatrical versatility and skill. Following Giraudoux, he has frequently employed classical themes, as in *Eurydice* (M), and *Antigone*, 1949 (M), with Olivier and Vivien Leigh. More recently he treated historical figures. Saint Joan in *The Lark* (M), and Becket in the play of that name (M). The play within a play is a favourite expedient of his and he used it again in *The Fighting Cock* (M).

Anouilh's outlook is deeply pessimistic. A recurring theme is that purity is incompatible with experience of life and many of his protagonists say, " No." His plays fall into two categories—the fatalistic *pièces noires* and the romantic fantasies *pièces roses*. Anouilh's amoral attitude has been reflected in many West End successes.

Aleksei Arbuzov (b. 1908).

The Russian producer and playwright Arbuzov has been writing since 1930.

The Promise. 1966.

In the Chekhovian tradition *The Promise* is a moving and positive work free from both illusion and despair. During the siege of Leningrad two boys and a girl contrive to survive in a bombed house, and here in brief episodic scenes their hardship, gaiety, and the slow awakening of love are shown with a delicate and touching naturalism.

Four years later Lika must choose between the two men and although she loves the engineer Marat she chooses the dependent, poetic Leonidik. The decision brings fulfilment to no one and finally Leonidik courageously summons back Marat and leaves him and Lika together.

Produced in 1976 were *Evening Light, Once Upon a Time* and *Old World*—humane and scrupulously non-political plays.

John Arden (b. 1930).

Arden is a vigorous and gifted playwright, who has experimented with a variety of subjects and methods, sometimes too original and complex to find quick acceptance.

He has the rare gift of the poet and his diction is often richly suggestive and evocative. He has said in interview that plays should use speech in

the way that a poet uses individual images and that the playwright " should *form* language rather than just report it ", so that even colloquial speech is given a tension and dramatic rhythm.

With the exception of *The Island of the Mighty* Arden's major work has been produced before 1967 and since some more recent plays have differed in approach and key it is appropriate first to discuss his earlier work.

His characters have been full-blooded and rich in human contradictions, and he has sympathetically brought to life even such bogeys as Herod and King John. He has chosen to dwell on some ambiguous personality, where generosity conflicts with violence, and to consider the problems of directing man's unruly vitality.

His favourite theme has been the dispute between instinctual energy and good government and he has pleaded the case cogently for both sides, giving no facile judgment or direct " message " unless it be " the recognition of the fallibility of man ". Thus although, like Brecht, he is deeply concerned with social and political issues, he remained politically " uncommitted." He has above all been the dramatist of the dilemma.

There has been a fruitful cross-fertilisation of Arden's interest in current events and his literary studies; and his historical plays, like Brecht's *Mother Courage*, have combined a fine sense of period and a sharp relevance to some current issue.

His plays have been poetic in structure, depending in part on the recurrent image and metaphor and, like Arthur Miller in *The Crucible*, he has skilfully devised for each an appropriate dialect of time and place. At the same time he has a keen sense of theatre, and has successfully adapted techniques from Miracle plays, Elizabethan drama, music-hall, puppet stage, and Brechtian epic play.

Apart from *The Island of the Mighty*, most of Arden's recent plays have been more theatrical in effect. They lack his poetic intensity both in style and structure, despite a more lavish use of verse and song. They are still much concerned with social problems but there is not the same many-angled approach and personalities are often deliberately presented in caricature.

Live Like Pigs. 1958. P.

Seventeen realistic scenes full of comic and frightening incident reveal how fatal conflicts develop between households at different social levels in a new housing estate. Street ballads in Brechtian style preface some scenes.

The Happy Haven. 1960. P.

Here, in a good-tempered satirical fable, enlivened by a dash of magic, Arden touches on problems of longevity.

Doctor Copperthwaite, the superintendent of the Happy Haven, an old people's home, is, like a mediaeval alchemist, bent on producing an Elixir of Life and Youth, intending to use his five unsuspecting patients as guinea-pigs. But outwitted by them he is himself transformed into a small boy.

The theme is childishness. The egocentric demands of the very old are seen as amusing childish foibles, while Doctor Copperthwaite brings childishness on himself.

In form the play is an extended puppet show. The characters wear masks, the set is formalised.

Serjeant Musgrave's Dance. 1959. M.

For a fine play, which explores the ethical dilemma of war, Arden drew on two sources—contemporary events in Cyprus and a journal written by a deeply devout N.C.O. during the Crimean War. He has fused his material into vivid incidents, which he projects against the background of a fictitious colonial war of the 1880s.

In a frost-bound colliery town there arrive three private soldiers, led by the dominating Serjeant Musgrave. They claim to have come recruiting but are in fact deserters from a colonial war.

In spite of his rigid sense of military duty, Musgrave had been horrified by the terrible fivefold reprisals taken by the British for the assassination of a comrade, Billy Hicks. Believing himself to be God's agent, he has now come to Billy's town, obsessed by one purpose, to expose war's horrors.

Exhibiting Billy's skeleton in the market-place, he at first wins sympathy in his denunciation of atrocities. Then bewildered by his own confused "logic", he demands twenty-five deaths in return for the five taken by the British and turns the Gatling on the astonished crowd.

Suddenly, with the thaw, the Dragoons arrive and Musgrave finds himself awaiting execution, stunned that no one has learned the lesson he yearned to teach.

Fierce incident and macabre surprise are used for a play of ideas which enunciates no facile answer. It is typical of Arden's fair and non-doctrinaire approach that the dilemma of the religious man in face of war should be embodied in the fanatical and confused Musgrave. This has sometimes misled the audience, but the spirit of compassion implicit throughout the play is clearly revealed in the gentle, pacific Private Attercliffe, also to be executed with Musgrave. The women's parts are also significant expecially that of Mrs. Hitchcock, the owner of the inn, who visits Musgrave in prison and shows him how he had erred in trying to use war itself to end war. In his darkest despair she gives him hope, and he accepts wine from her.

The complex play weaves together many tensions; harsh discord between colliery owner and strikers; contention between the three privates, each of whom is strongly individualised; the discrepancy between a woman's love and the careless soldier's life; Musgrave's own bitter inner struggle.

The dialogue has a wonderful period character and the soldiers' ballads and lyrical songs occur with complete naturalness.

The Workhouse Donkey. 1963. M.

Styled by Arden as a "vulgar melodrama", this ample Brechtian play shows jockeying for power in a northern town between the Tory Alderman Sweetman, a wealthy brewer, and Alderman Butterthwaite (Frank Finlay), the Labour ex-mayor. Both attempt to manipulate the police and to enlist the support of the electorate, represented by the shifty turncoat Doctor Blomax, until all these four elements of the community are deeply corrupted.

Butterthwaite, called "the workhouse donkey" because born in the workhouse, is the dominating Rabelaisian character. A Dionysiac figure, he is drunken, lecherous and amoral, yet devotedly loyal and generous. Finally in an attempt to help the treacherous Blomax he robs the Borough safe and brings disaster on himself and the town.

The personality of the late Mr. Joseph D'Arcy of Dublin inspired much of the play.

Armstrong's Last Goodnight. 1964. M.

The old "Ballad of Johnie Armstrang", c. 1603, forms the framework of a play concerning the dilemmas of government. Armstrong of Gilnockie, the Scots Border laird, freebooter and rebel, is invited to a meeting by the young Scottish King James V and then treacherously hanged. Arden has introduced into this stark story the historical character of the king's herald, Sir David Lindsay, poet and politician, and shows him at first striving by devious diplomatic expedients to persuade Armstrong (Albert Finney) to loyalty, before he finally advises force. The play is diversified by minor characters and incidents which overcomplicate the impressive ballad line.

The introduction of Lindsay was suggested to Arden by his reading of Conor Cruise O'Brien's book *To Katanga and back*, for he was struck by "a basic similarity of moral" between 20th-cent. Africa and 16th-cent. Scotland, the rôle of O'Brien being similar to that which he invents for Lindsay.

Arden makes free use of Elizabethan pageantry and of Brechtian ballad-singing and the setting is the mediaeval convention of "simultaneous mansions", Gilnockie, the Border, and the Court all being formally represented on the stage at one and the same time.

Arden "constructed" a dialect to suggest place and period, but it is difficult to follow.

Left-handed Liberty. 1965. M.

Commissioned by the Corporation of the City of London to write a play to commemorate the 750th anniversary of Magna Carta, Arden presents the historical facts with very little transposition and addition.

He approaches his theme of liberty from an unusual angle, showing the aftermath of Runnymede in the apparent failure of the Charter, and demonstrating that the agreement had to take place in people's minds before it could become effective.

Arden does not present a clash of black and white. John is a rounded character, a slippery villain, but shrewd and energetic and gifted with the Plantagenet charm, while some of the barons are coarse and unscrupulous fighters.

The use of stylised scene emblems gives mediaeval colour to the simple staging and Arden has again invented a suitable dialect.

The Royal Pardon. 1967. M.

A play for young teenagers, was written in collaboration with Arden's Irish wife Margaretta D'Arcy.

Squire Jonathan. 1968.

In a grim Gothic tower, centuries ago, threadbare old Jonathan, descended from kings, gloats over his treasure chest, suspicious of the Dark Men outside and desiring the White Woman. A foolish, clumsy blonde, she appears wearing a chastity belt and eventually refusing his jewels, goes to the Dark Men. The play, was interpreted as an image of Britain's current situation, Jonathan dressed as Wilson and the White Woman like a Britannia or Boadicea.

The Hero Rises Up. 1968. M.

Written with his wife, this burlesque of melodrama is a sardonic enquiry into the motivation and deeds of Nelson, and the very differing reactions he occasioned. The authors use the racy style of period ephemera, such as street ballads, broadsheets and caricature and "stage spectacles of sensational splendour" like "tuppence-coloured prints".

The Ballygombeen Bequest. 1972.

Arden and his wife assert exploitation in Galway. An absentee English landlord so takes advantage of the tourist trade inflating the price of land that he evicts the ignorant lccal smallholder.

Although Arden disclaims the rôle of activist, this play of protest, conveyed in pantomime style, has been called his first "agit prop" work.

The Island of the Mighty. 1972. M.

A play written as a television trilogy for the B.B.C. went unproduced and Arden collaborated with his wife in the long work produced by the R.S.C.

The Celtic Arthurian legends and the *Golden Bough* form a misty background to Arden's convincing picture of what were probably the harsh realities of life in the chaotic Dark Age that succeeded Rome's withdrawal from Britain.

The Romano-British Arthur, now nearing seventy, is a limping hero who has striven for thirty years to maintain order during the break-up of a civilisation. Nominally Christian and boasting Imperial descent he cherishes the Roman ideals of "justice, restraint of power and protection of the weak". He relies on his highly disciplined but ageing armoured cavalry, the loyalty of the handsome young Medraut, his nephew, and the diplomacy of Merlin.

Merlin, a subtle and complex personality, shares Arthur's ideal of unity but is increasingly distressed by war's cruelties. A radical young pagan poet, Aneurin, is concerned with the oppression of obscure individuals and the poets act as commentators offering differing insights.

Britain is ravaged by persistent English raids and torn internally by rival chieftains, blood feuds and vengeful bandits, while the indigenous matriarchal fertility religions, suppressed by the Romans, linger secretly in distorted forms.

Again Arden skilfully presents the interplay of social forces through arresting individuals such as the turbulent roving brothers Balin and Balan, dispossessed by the English, and the pathetic young bondwoman, passed like a chattel from man to man.

The commanding theme is land hunger. Arthur realises that Britain's chief peril is the remorseless English attacks, but unable to persuade the British to unite all he can do is to fight to preserve *some* patch of fertile ground. But he is gradually worn down by British disunity, the growing ambition of Medraut and his own inner conflicts.

Arthur's final undoing is the resurgence of the matriarchal pagan cults. This is early foreshadowed in the frightening annual fertility rituals of a desperately poor tribe of pagan Picts, the Wild Cats, who assume weird cat masks. The captured Balan becoming consort to the princess has to fight his lame predecessor and is himself ritually lamed. But the avaricious old queen, finding his brother Balin shipwrecked, orders that this ritual be re-enacted prematurely. The doomed brothers fight and kill each other and the fertility magic is also lost.

Arthur is similarly destroyed. For reasons of political expediency he marries the mischievous young Gwenhwyvar. Taught by the crone Morgan, Arthur's sister, that she represents the ancient cult, Gwenhwyvar sets her sign on Medraut who is wildly acclaimed by the people. But due ceremony has been neglected and as Medraut announces that he will claim Imperial rule Morgan despairingly tears to shreds her symbolic green fertility robe.

Meanwhile Arthur has gradually revealed that he also has been involved in the ancient superstition and that Medraut is in fact his son by ritual incest, instigated by Morgan. In a final catastrophic battle Medraut and Arthur destroy each other and the way is wide open for the English invasion. As Merlin has forseen, five hundred years of history were " swept away to nowhere in a pagan bog of blood and mud " and Merlin loses his reason.

The play is alive with a host of convincing characters, complex inter-relationships, violent unruly emotion and exciting incident. The dialogue is clearly individualised and with some few exceptions has both a period flavour and an immediate freshness. The style varies between prose and verse with some passages of poetic intensity and power, especially in the weird and erotic sequences, and it conjures up a landscape of Roman ruins, wildwood and desolate shore. Interspersed are ballads, some almost doggerel, others like genuine early ballads, are richly suggestive, especially the final refrain.

Some incidents seem superfluous and it is confusing that in a confessedly anti-imperialist play Arthur should be the centre of the action.

The play has been called untidy, but " tidiness " would be inappropriate in this image of civilisation in breakdown. Arden has so orchestrated his themes that there is a poetic resonance in its design.

It is regrettable that the play could not be shown as planned, as a trilogy, when the complexities of its rich and intricate tapestry could be gradually assimilated and its relevance to our own divided and hungry world fully realised.

Fernando Arrabal (b. 1932).

Born in Spanish Morocco, Arrabal was early involved in cruelty. He was four years old when the Spanish Civil War broke out and his father was condemned to thirty years' imprisonment. When he was nine Arrabal was told that his father had escaped. He never heard of him again. The father, whom he had deeply loved, had been completely abandoned by his mother and this harrowing experience is given dramatic expression in *The Two Executioners*, P. He retains vivid memories of the Civil War, the mass executions and the cries of tortured prisoners and says that in schooling and religion he was " brought up on sado-masochism ". When of

age he broke free from his extraordinary mother and in 1955 he moved finally to France.

Arrabal's work is in the tradition of Spanish surrealism, and even before reading Ionesco and Beckett he wrote plays considered as absurdist. " His main preoccupation," says Esslin, " is with the absurdity of ethical and moral rules. He looks at the world with the incomprehension of a child that simply cannot understand the logic of conventional morality." His work, which is " a highly disturbing mixture of innocence and cruelty ", has been much influenced by Artaud's Theatre of Cruelty and from 1962 he developed his ritualistic theatre as a Panic Ceremony, so called after the god Pan.

Arrabal has also experimented with abstract drama. The *Orchestration Théâtrale* of 1959 attempted to create a dramatic spectacle devoid of human content and consisting solely in the manipulation of three-dimensional shapes—some mechanical and others moved by dancers—to the accompaniment of coloured diagrams.

Arrabal's work is increasingly characterised by surrealist fantasy and the grotesque. Disclaiming imagination, he has said, " What I do is to copy my memories or my dreams ... almost exactly, without changing a word."

The Architect and the Emperor of Assyria. 1971.

After terrifying intensity of noise the lordly Emperor descends from the skies calmly announcing to a cowering man whom he later dubs his architect that he is the sole survivor.

The situation recalls *The Tempest*, the Emperor, like Prospero, an embodiment of civilisation, the Architect an amalgam of Caliban and Ariel, a primitive, at first ignorant even of language, yet retaining magical powers over nature.

These two, the sole inhabitants of a desert island, play out an unending repetition of sado-masochistic fantasies, springing from infantile traumas. All but naked they circle each other in balletic movement and mime, instantaneously exchanging such rôles as master, persecutor, judge, lover and mother.

In Act I the Emperor is usually dominant, though sometimes sobbing for comfort in the arms of his " mummy ". In Act II he is judged by the Architect for murdering his own mother whom he gave to his dog to eat. He demands the same punishment and is killed and eaten by the Architect, who in his cannibalism sucks in the Emperor's civilisation but loses his former magical power.

Again come darkness and deafening noise, but this time the Architect descends, taking over the Emperor's rôle.

As in Triana's more disciplined *The Criminals*, the dramatic movement is cyclical, the remorseless, self-destroying recurrence of obsession, especially guilt-ridden hate and dependence on the mother. The play has some root in anthropology and recalls Artaud's theories, exposing man's most grisly unconscious motivation and deploying a most extensive range of theatrical devices. Garcia, the producer, used brilliant lighting and baroque music.

Tense and exciting, the work can yet have a shattering effect on the audience, which is implicity called on to play the exhausting rôle of untrained and helpless psychiatrist. The basic subject is that of Aeschylus' *The Eumenides*—matricide pursued by guilt. But the Greek tragedy exhilarates and achieves an Aristotelian catharsis.

And They Handcuffed the Flowers. 1973.

The title is derived from words of Lorca who in 1936 was executed by fascists. The play was stimulated by requests that the playwright would bear witness to what he had seen during his few weeks of political imprisonment in 1967 but its chief source of inspiration is his anguished childhood.

Apart from a few casual references and brief readings by a little girl sitting on a stool, few factual details about prison life emerge for Arrabal is preoccupied with the terrible distortion of the psyche caused by long years of incarceration. His three principal characters are the three inmates of a prison cell now degraded by their inhuman conditions. Their pathological urges are enacted in sado-masochistic fantasies, religious and sexual, in which the prison chaplain, hated because evasion of mass is punished by solitary confinement, is ritually castrated, the mass is parodied, there is a pornographic Christ and harsh grotesque whores invade the scene.

In contrast to the extravagant surrealist fantasies, the simplicity of some direct questions is all the more effective. " Who invented the prison? Animals don't have them."

Alan Ayckbourn (b. 1939).

Ayckbourn is a successful writer of social comedy, an acute observer of human folly and of trivial middle-class snobbery. He has assured theatrical expertise and is adept in farcical timing and contriving ingenious incident and comic rejoinder. His craftsmanlike plays include *Relatively Speaking*, 1967, *How the Other Half Loves*, 1970, *Time and Time Again*, 1972, and *Absurd Person Singular*, 1973.

The Norman Conquests. 1974. (P).

The play is a dazzling trilogy of three farcical comedies: *Table Manners*, *Living Together* and *Round and Round the Garden*. The action is simultaneous and interlocking, the offstage events of one play providing the material of the others. Each is limited to either dining room, living room or garden of the same house, and they span the family weekend of six people. Spinster Annie is entertaining her capable sister Ruth, married to philandering Norman, her brother with his bossy, prudish wife Sarah, and her own suitor, incredibly slow-witted Tom. Norman has persuaded Annie to an illicit weekend, but is foiled by Sarah. Piqued he attempts to persuade Sarah herself to join him and finally misinterprets Ruth's attempts to bring him to his senses as passion for himself and is rejected by all three.

Absent Friends. 1975.

Colin's fiancee has been lost at sea, and Paul, whose wife Colin had once courted, invites him to meet friends of bachelor days. Much empty jocularity is a smoke-screen for hurt feelings.

Confusions. 1976.

Five actors present five characteristic sketches.

Bedroom Farce. 1977.

By selective lighting three contrasting bedrooms in different houses are shown and the hilarious sequence depicts the extraordinary pursuits of four couples during one night. The Victorian first bedroom is that of Ernest and Delia, parents of Trevor, married to disturbed Susannah. After an anniversary dinner they munch pilchards on toast and read *Tom Brown's Schooldays!*

In the small second room Malcolm and Kate play practical jokes until suddenly the guests arrive for the housewarming. Trevor and Sue come separately and fight violently. Malcolm tries to eject Trevor, but Sue sees him kissing his old flame Jan.

In the affluent third bedroom Jan's husband Nick is helpless with a strained back and she returns to haul him clumsily back to bed. Trevor arrives, insisting on confessing his kiss to an indifferent Nick, and Malcolm, furious with Trevor, is at 3 a.m. angrily using a " do-it-yourself " kit to make a dressing table that collapses! Only at dawn is harmony restored.

Just Between Ourselves. 1977.

Genial Dennis tries to sell the Morris Minor in the garage to Neil. In his non-stop enthusiastic sales-talk he fails to see the strain in his wife Vera. Exuberant comedy ends as she breaks down.

Samuel Beckett (b. 1906).

Beckett, an Anglo-Irishman, who has made his home in France, is both novelist and the most distinguished of the English dramatists of the Absurd. His world is drastically limited, peopled chiefly by old men awaiting their death, and conceived with the suggestiveness of the true poet.

His work is poetic in its verbal imagery, sometimes as searching and macabre as that of Webster, and his dramatic prose has an underlying rhythm often more flexible and effective than that of Eliot's verse. In structure his plays have a poetic symbolism, like that of James Joyce, Beckett's close friend, and their striking visual imagery has a kind of theatrical poetry, as for instance the two tramps at the foot of a bare tree in *Waiting for Godot*. It is remarkable that so literary a playwright should also have succeeded with the wordless mime play.

Beckett's chief weakness as a dramatist is that the action and visual imagery are frequently too static, as in the motionless dustbins in *End Game*, much less effective theatrically than Ionesco's movable chairs.

Waiting for Godot. 1955. F.

This tantalising and compelling tragi-comedy, Beckett's masterpiece, originally written in French and produced in Paris in 1953, was later translated and performed in more than twenty countries.

Character and incident are pared to the bone and only a skeleton situation remains. At evening, on a desolate road, bare but for a single tree, two wretched tramps, Vladimir and Estragon, nicknamed Didi and Gogo, wait for a mysterious Mr. Godot. As they while away the time with desultory talk and clowning, a tragi-farcical diversion is provided by the entry of Pozzo and Lucky, bullying master and wretched slave, and a boy later brings a message that Mr. Godot cannot come but will arrive the next evening After discussing whether or not they shall hang themselves from the tree, the tramps decide to go away for the night, but remain on the spot.

Act II presents " Next day same place," the only difference being that the tree has sprouted a few leaves, and the basic pattern of Act I is repeated.

Although by the skilful use of music-hall techniques Beckett presents his tramps in the guise of amusing clowns, they are at the same time pathetically human as they waver between suicide and irrational hope. A fretful affection has kept them together over fifty years, and their dispositions are complementary, possibly even representing different aspects of the one personality.

Pozzo and Lucky, another pair of contrasting characters, are portrayed more farcically. The loud, confident Pozzo drives Lucky in as if he were a beast of burden. Lucky carries in his mouth the whip with which he is beaten and humbly obeys every insolent command. He dances for Pozzo and even thinks for him. In their second appearance Pozzo is blind and Lucky dumb.

They may be considered personifications respectively of master and slave, worldly materialism and higher values, the physical and the intellectual, body and soul, or the two aspects of a sado-masochistic relationship.

The play as a whole is a most complex dramatic symbol expressing man's anxiety and suffering as to his origin and destination.

The uncertainty is symbolised by the characters' confusion as to even the physical actualities of time and place. but the dominating symbol is the tramps' doubt as to Godot's identity and purpose.

To equate Godot with God is inadequate, yet the play has Christian references. A tree is frequently used as an emblem of the Cross. Beckett, questioned about his theme, quoted Saint Augustine. . . . " Do not despair; one of the thieves was saved. Do not presume; one of the thieves was damned."

Beckett neither affirms nor denies Saint Augustine's statement but inverts it into a question, more distressing than direct denial. Can we any longer accept the existence of divine grace and judgment? It is a question such as this that gives to the play its symbolic shape of doubt, and which is cogently expressed in the theatrical image of two outcasts at the foot of a tree, a tree of life which puts forth leaves, a tree of death which they contemplate using as a gallows.

Yet the significance of the play is even deeper than an exploration of religious doubt, its appeal wider and more contemporary. The anguished uncertainty of the 20th cent. is whether life has any meaning whatsoever.

Some have considered it to be written from the point of view of existentialism: continuing vainly to hope for a supernatural revelation, the tramps lack the courage to come to terms with the nothingness of our existence and the need to choose and create our own destiny.

A Jungian psychologist, Eva Metman, has made a similar interpretation, remarking, " Godot's function seems to be to keep his dependents unconscious."

" Habit is a great deadener," says Vladimir. If Beckett's play enables the audience to escape the drug of habit and to face this image of anguish and so find some relief, then it may have the therapeutic value of that inner knowledge advocated by Freud and Jung.

It is not a play for those who cannot bear to suffer. When performed in San Francisco Gaol, the first play there for forty-four years, it held its audience of fourteen hundred convicts spellbound. They realised that each must find his own personal message. All knew that it spoke to those who must suffer and wait.

Endgame. 1958. F.

Also re-created from the French, this play again depicts a static situation. In a single, claustrophobic room, the selfish, materialistic Hamm, who keeps his senile and legless parents in dustbins, is now paralysed and blind and dependent on his servant Clov, who longs to leave him. But if Clov should leave, both would die, for Hamm owns the only store of food in a devastated and dead world. Finally Clov sees outside what may be a small boy, " a potential procreator," and he prepares for departure but remains immobile.

The play like poetry can be interpreted in several ways. Since Hamm and Clov are mutually dependent, it probably represents tension between complementary aspects of personality, Hamm sensation and emotion, and Clov intellect. As Clov has vision and sees the boy, the situation suggests the struggle of the mystic endeavouring to escape from a deadening materialism to a vital awakening of the spirit. It may also depict a period of traumatic depression when the whole external world seems dead and unreal. The play's overall impression is that of the dissolution of the personality in death, both personal and global.

Endgame lacks the wry humour of *Godot*.

Krapp's Last Tape. 1958. F.

In the briefest sketch, Krapp, a solitary, decrepit, unsuccessful old man listens to his own autobiographical tape-recording of thirty years ago, but the moment of miraculous insight that commemorates is now so meaningless to him that he switches off that section of the recording and broods on a description of his love-making.

Beckett employs a most effective stage device to pose contemporary queries as to the limitations of verbal communication and the continuity of personal identity.

Happy Days. 1962. F.

Winnie, buried to her waist in a mound of earth, assiduously tries to fill in the time between the waking bell and the bell for sleep with the routine of nail filing, with rummaging in her capacious bag, with memories of her first kiss and of her husband's proposal and with a flood of talk adjuring cheerfulness, " ah yes . . . great mercies ". In rare moments with bent head and breaking voice she says, " What *is* one to do? All day long. Day after day ", but soon, lifts her head with a smile—" The old style! "

She shows tender concern for her husband, Willie, whose bald head topped by a boater is just visible behind the mound. " . . . just to know you are within hearing and conceivably on the semi-alert, is—er—paradise enow," she says, overjoyed at his rare and monosyllabic replies. To his answer, " It ", she cries, " Oh you are going to talk to me today. This is going to be a happy day!"

In a brief second act Winnie is buried to her neck. Willie " dressed to kill " in a morning coat crawls from behind the mound and collapses while trying to reach her. She is shocked that he may have gone out of his " poor old wits ". Just audibly he says, " Win ", and the happy expression grows on her face.

It is possible to conjecture several interpretations, the most obvious being that of the woman becoming paralysed by illness and unable any longer to make contact with or help the husband who appears to have psychological difficulties. Poor Willie had always been in " dire need of a hand ". In her bag is the revolver he had asked her to take from him. Now he can barely communicate, hardly crawl and has to reverse into a hole which shelters him, an image suggesting Beckett's recurring theme of a desire to regress to childhood and the womb.

The theme is suffering but the surface of the play is rich comedy.

Play. 1964. F.

Beckett's own directions best describe the striking imagery of a brief one-act play. " Three identical grey urns . . . From each a head protrudes, the neck held fast in the urn's mouth . . . They face undeviatingly front throughout the play. Faces so lost as to age and aspect as to seem almost part of the urns."

The heads are those of a man between two women, apparently his wife and mistress. With impassive faces and normally toneless voices each utters a monologue. At first there builds up a vivid and amusing picture of a man who had passionately loved two women who were possessive and bitterly jealous. When the man suddenly disappears from an impossible situation the voices become dim and lower, for all three are left isolated living in a limbo of obsessive memory and sadness, touched by pity.

The imprisoning urns effectively symbolise their self-absorbed condition.

Not I. 1973. F.

In a play of only fifteen minutes Beckett pares every thing down to bare essentials. On a dark stage there is a dimly lit mouth appearing totally disconnected from the rest of the body and downstage a faintly visible Auditor, intent on Mouth, cloaked, silent and all but immobile.

Mouth (Billie Whitelaw) pours forth a flood of disjointed phrases, voicing the anguish of a woman nearing seventy to whom she persistently refers as " She ". Some few facts emerge. Born prematurely and deserted by the mother she had been an unloved waif with " no love of any kind " and " practically speechless . . . all her days ".

One early April morning " wandering in a field " she had suddenly experienced some extraordinary shock, finding herself barely sentient and aware only of darkness with a beam of light " ferreting around " and a " dull roar in the skull ".

Later, came thoughts that she was being punished, that she was " not suffering " at any rate " so far " and then the sudden realisation that " words were coming " and that " a voice she did not recognise . . . at first " must be her own, followed by the sensation of her mouth actually moving, " mouth on fire " but " no idea what she's saying " and with " the brain . . . raving away on its own . . . trying to make sense of it . . . or make it stop ".

The frenzied monologue is four times punctuated by a vehement disclaimer that Mouth is speaking of herself, when, as if in answer to questions she cries, " what? . . . who? . . . no! . . . she! " while the silent Auditor raises and drops his or her arms in a gesture of hopeless compassion. The play expresses complete despair save that the closing words suggest a desperate courage as Mouth gasps, " not knowing . . . what to try " but " no matter . . . keep on . . . hit on it in the end " while her repetition of religious phrases is no longer accompanied by harsh laughter but may express acceptance, " God is love . . . tender mercies . . . new every morning ".

The monologue has some basis in commonplace fact and it might be interpreted as occasioned by a stroke or as expressing the agony of an autistic or schizophrenic personality. But the play has a much wider and deeper reference, for it is a poignant dramatic image of the lonely anguish of man enmeshed in the dark enigma of human suffering and desperately seeking meaning.

Footfalls and *That Time.* 1976.

Footfalls. Mrs. Winter was in her forties when May (Billie Whitelaw) was born. When the mother was bedridden May nursed her devotedly. Now locked in her past May paces rhythmically up and down, the dim light concentrated on her feet although her dead mother's voice implores her, " Will you never have done revolving it all? " Such are the few theatrical images. *That Time.* Dimly lighted an old man's face is immobile, while three unseen voices disjointedly represent his past.

Brendan Behan (1923–64).

Behan, a Dubliner, had only two plays produced in his life. *The Quare Fellow,* 1956 (M), is set in a prison the day before the hanging of a brutal fratricide and is incidentally an effective plea for the abolition of capital punishment. *The Hostage,* 1958 (M), is set in a Dublin brothel where a captured young Cockney soldier expects death during Irish political strife. Both were given shape by Joan Littlewood. *Richard's Cork Leg,* 1972 (M), lacks her sense of tension. The personnel of Behan's plays are generally wildly eccentric and their world randy and bizarre, relying on a vivid impressionistic style and lively ribald speech—an innovation in the '50s.

Alan Bennett (b. 1914).

Bennett was a participant in the witty, satirical revue, *Beyond the Fringe.*

Forty Years On. 1968. F.

The retiring Head (Gielgud) of Albion House is entertained by a cavalcade of British history devised by his radical successor and acted by the boys. The play's loose organisation allows satirical skits on the middle class and public schools, where Bennett indulges his special talent for parody.

Getting On. 1971. F.

George, a middle-aged Labour M.P., his youthful enthusiasm for the welfare state disregarded, voices Bennett's free-wheeling satire on current trends in picturesque idiom, biting, witty, comic, sometimes merely facetious.

Habeas Corpus. 1973. F.

Mrs. Swabb, sturdy daily help, presents her employers as caricatures in the style of seaside postcards.

Most are preoccupied with their bodily idiosyncracies. The ageing Dr. Wickstead still desires his female patients, his wife contemplates her menopause with consternation, his son Dennis is hypochondriac, his spinster sister Constance is wretched because she is flat-chested. Of their guests, Sir Percy Shorter is irate that his name matches his short stature and lovely Felicity has just become pregnant from a chance encounter.

The action is a whirl of accidents, assignations, intrigue and mistaken identities, ending in an improbable double marriage. Felicity gladly marries Dennis for, unknown to himself, he has only three months to live, and Constance glamorous in her falsie bra has found an ardent suitor.

Bennett ingeniously uses the classical ingredients of farce, transforming them by his wryly caustic wit. The far-fetched comparison and outrageous statement delivered in a flat prim tone are now his hallmark.

The Old Country. 1977.

Hilary (Guinness) and his wife play Elgar records and talk of English interests: country towns and food, King's College carols, Anthony Powell, *The Times.*

This disarming setting preludes the revelation that Hilary, once a treacherous F.O. official, had

defected to Russia to escape arrest. Their first visitors, vaguely drawn, are another English traitor and his Russian wife.

They are then confronted by Hilary's strident sister and her husband, Duff, eminent in the Establishment, who from ulterior motives tries to persuade Hilary to return.

The situation occasions precise satire of English bourgeois mannerisms. Hilary, elegantly ironic, discusses the English love of irony. He caustically dismisses E. M. Forster on betrayal, and asks of Solzhenistsyn, " which is worse, five years in a camp or three pages in *The Listener*? " With equal skill Bennett mimics Duff's empty platitudes. Although negative, this ingenious satire exposes the aridity of treason and self-interest.

Steven Berkoff.

Berkoff began on the Fringe, later establishing the London Theatre Group. Aiming at the " magical " he uses techniques of music hall, vaudeville, dance and mime. In 1977 he had three plays produced at the Cottesloe, free adaptations of *The Fall of the House of Usher* and Kafka's *Metamorphosis* and an original play, *East,* a furious protest at the waste of the East End of his childhood.

Robert Bolt (b. 1914).

Earlier work such as *The Flowering Cherry* (1957) was realistic, but Bolt has successfully tried other genres, including a children's play *The Thwarting of Baron Bollingrew,* 1965. Liking plays in which " people have ideas as well as predicaments ", he holds the balance of discussion fairly and his own convictions are clear only in the outcome.

The Tiger and the Horse. 1960.

The title is from Blake's " The Tygers of wrath are wiser than the horses of instruction ". Dean, master of an Oxbridge College, a well-balanced man whose philosophy is detachment is the " horse ". His wife Gwen, evidently disturbed, and passionately concerned to sign a petition for nuclear disarmament is the " tiger ". Eventually Dean, to save her from mental breakdown, bravely identifies himself with her, thereby deserting his philosophy and career. It is typical of Bolt's dialectic that it is Gwen who stresses the value of social idealism which he endorses.

A Man for All Seasons. 1960. P.

Bolt attempts to give his characters heroic dimension by striking back into history. Believing that our need today is a sense of personal individuality, he chooses as his hero of " selfhood " Sir Thomas More. He consciously uses dramatic licence to adapt history to his own purpose, for More's theory of conscience was not subjective and existentialist but that of Aquinas. Hence some inconsistency in his portrayal.

More is described by a contemporary as " a man for all seasons ", flexibly adjusted to Renaissance society yet preserving an inner core of unassailable integrity. Suspected of a critical attitude to Henry VIII's divorce, he uses his skill in " the thickets of the law " resolutely refusing to swear the oath to the Act of Succession that would have released him from the Tower and the block, because for him perjury means the loss of the soul, the self. His constancy is contrasted with the growing corruption of Rich, whose final perjury sends More to his death.

More's situation is like that of Brecht's Galileo, and Bolt uses a bastardised version of Brecht's style Episodic scenes are strung along a strong thread of intellectual argument while a commentator, the Common Man, with costumes from his property basket takes a succession of minor parts, throwing into relief More's steadfastness.

Bolt, like Brecht, believing that beauty of language is a means of " alienation " combines fine passages from More with his own appropriate use of wit and imagery, using images of land and sea the transcendental.

Gentle Jack. 1963.

Bolt contrasts plutocratic society with natural spontaneity and its potential violence.

Vivat! Vivat Regina! 1970.

The play has two " heroines "—Elizabeth I and Mary Queen of Scots. In the same predicament, the conflict between royal statecraft and woman's desire for husband, child, and heir, they are in temperament sharply contrasted. Mary is shown as sophisticated, sensuous, passionate and self-willed, ruthlessly conniving at plots to murder her rival. Elizabeth, listening to Cecil and Walsingham, foregoes her love for Leicester in the interest of the realm.

Since the period spanned is virtually that of Mary's return from France until her execution (with a hint of England's coming victory over the Armada) she is the main dramatic focus although Elizabeth's astute dialogues with her advisers are more interesting.

Bolt does not attempt the subtle complexity of *A Man For All Seasons* but he cleverly employs emblematic properties, such as thrones, pulpits, desks and heraldic blazons so that with selective lighting the action shifts unhindered through space and time.

State of Revolution. 1977. H.

The play's framework is an anniversary address on Lenin, *c.* 1930, by the humane Lunacharsky, who also, rather confusingly, participates in past events.

To Bolt, member of the C.P. from 1942 to 1947, Lenin was a " great man ", because he " withstood tensions of absolutely irreconcilable demands ". When in 1910 in Gorky's home, Lunacharsky reads a thesis, applauded by fellow activists, that Marxism is compatible with love, Lenin alone, bullying and cajoling, insists that their only ethic is " unconditional class hatred " and " unconditional human love " a " dirty dream ". The play's theme is the tension between these views.

Skilful lighting ensures a swift sequence of events: Lenin's startling arrival in 1917, heartening news of the Kronstadt meeting convincing him that deserters form his proletariat, his signing of the Brest Litovsk treaty.

Act II shows growing problems, peasants shot for hoarding grain, the revolt of the Kronstadt group and their terrible extermination. Gorky, stigmatising the Revolution " merely ferocious ", leaves. During Lenin's illness rivalry between Stalin and Trotsky grows, and despite Lenin's testament, Stalin succeeds him. Lunacharsky concludes his anniversary address.

Bolt's ambitious canvas involves omissions and over-simplifications. There is too much verbal debate, and save for the arresting figure of the brawny Kronstadt sailor Zhelnik, no representation of the peasantry.

Edward Bond (b. 1915).

Bond had an unfortunate start. The son of a London labourer, he said that his relationship with his family " was one of total suspicion ", and his education at a Secondary Modern School "consisted of one evening " when he was taken to *Macbeth*. Generalising from scant experience he asserted, " There's really no difference between our State prisons and our State schools ", as both train " alienated slaves " to fit into society.

Bond shares the dismay of most sensitive people at contemporary violence, industry's drab monotony and stifling of individuality. Interviews have given the impression that after *Saved* much early work was motivated by the need to exorcise his own emotional problems, and there was an uneasy alliance between his strange and powerful intuitive images and the tenuous fable fabricated to rationalise them. He first adopted a naïve Romantic anarchy, asserting " Society . . . makes all men animals ". But in *The Sea* there were signs that he was beginning to recognise individual responsibility.

Bond appears to have read widely, not always with discrimination, even in drama. Opinions on

him are divided. Some critics rate him highly and he is valued in Eastern Europe.

Saved. 1965. M.

The portrayal of a baby murdered in London by the gang of its putative father caused some protest. Others likened the play to a realistic social document. The use of delinquents' argot and the speech of the inarticulate obscures some issues.

Early Morning. 1968.

Such archetypal figures as parents, nurse, grown-ups and siblings appear as famous Victorians. The last scene is a nightmare of mutual cannibalism, indicating oral eroticism and sadism. Esslin judged it as absurdist, with an underlying " seriousness and poetic power ". Yet Wardle says Bond writes like an angry omnipotent baby, presenting a " solipsistic muddle " meriting case study rather than criticism.

Narrow Road to the Deep North. 1968. M.

The play set in seventeenth-century Japan shows a repressive native regime, overthrown by another, representing Western imperialism, supported by missionary zeal inculcating a Puritan sense of sin, the " message " apparently being that government is per se evil. Eventually a naked man rises from the river, recalling the Romantic myth of the " noble savage " Dogma muffles the play's moving plea for individuality.

Black Mass. 1970.

In memory of Sharpeville, Bond writes a satire of a corrupt priest.

Lear. 1971. M.

Bond drastically alters the basic situation and story line of Shakespeare's *King Lear*, whittling it down to a political fable, and he presents a symbolic object, a huge wall, representing man's possessiveness, fear and aggression.

The furious Lear visits the wall which he is erecting against two hostile dukes, whereupon one of the workers is promptly executed, and his two daughters, Bodice and Fontanelle, provocatively announce their marriage to the dukes. They soon make away with their husbands, seizing power and defeating Lear, who is left wretched and vagrant. Cordelia, a priest's daughter, who had been urging her husband to erect a fence (evidently a microcosm of the wall), is now in command of victorious guerrilla forces. She has the sisters killed and Lear blinded by a " scientific device." He lives on, accompanied by the ghost of Cordelia's husband, who experiences a second death. Finally, Lear, feebly attempting to dismantle the wall which Cordelia now feverishly maintains, is shot dead.

The horror of gruesome maimings and killings indicates that Bond is beginning to recognise that evil is inherent in man but still argues that contemporary life is bearable to no one " unless he'd been made morally insane " by our education and the pressure to conform.

Bond eventually resorts to crude verbalism, as when Lear says, " We have only one thing to keep us sane; pity, and the man without pity is mad." But this is moral preaching not drama.

In *King Lear* Shakespeare did not have to resort to preaching, for his play is permeated by loyalty and compassion which reach their apotheosis in the tender reconciliation of Lear and Cordelia. *King Lear.* IV. 7.

Bond however says, " The Cordelia figure was very unsatisfactory in Shakespeare . . . He can't deal with her. My view is that she is a moralised person and moralised people are not good people." As criticism this is poppycock.

The Sea. 1973. M.

Bond enters new territory in a play which although bizarre has a realistic setting, an East

Coast village in 1907, dominated by the imperious Mrs. Rafi (Coral Browne), a wealthy widow. It begins with the drowning of Colin, the fiancé of her niece Rose, and his death is the pivot of the play.

The village draper Hatch, who faces bankruptcy through Mrs. Rafi's capricious cancelling of orders, is becoming paranoic and suffers hallucinations. He had been on the beach the night Colin drowned and repelled his friend Willy who yet survived. When Mrs. Rafi again cancels a commission he threatens her. Eventually as she conducts Colin's strange cliff-top funeral he attacks her and is taken away mad.

The play described as a comedy has a long and irrelevant farcical scene. There is also satiric comedy at the funeral which changes to the macabre as Colin's ashes are spilled and pelted at Hatch.

The spirit of comedy is more evident in a new sympathy for the individual. The grief of the bereaved Rose and Willy and their growing love are tenderly depicted and their decision to marry and leave the village sounds a new note of hope.

The theme of *The Sea* is the crippling of human nature by a social élite but the indications in *Lear* that evil is not solely attributable to society is here explicitly expressed by one who acts as commentator: " People are cruel and boring and obsessed."

Bingo. 1973. M.

In *Bingo* or " scenes of money and death " Bond again limits himself to a precise locality and period, Stratford-on-Avon in the early seventeenth century, and his portrayal of Shakespeare the man finds support in an interpretation of an extant document and in literary tradition.

Bond seizes on the oft-discussed anomaly between the humane spirit of reconciliation that animates *The Winter's Tale* and the shrewd business acumen of the owner of New Place, and his Shakespeare is a deeply divided and withdrawn man, sensitive and concerned for the suffering of the poor yet trapped by his own desire for gain. He allows the ruthless William Coombe, predecessor of the modern property-developer, to secure his agreement to the enclosure of common land regardless of the impoverishment of the common people seen in the homeless woman who strays into his garden, is flogged for vagrancy and later hanged.

Shakespeare's wealth brings him nothing but increasing disillusion and despair. His daughter Judith, grown bitter, is harshly obsessed with what he may bequeath her. Ben Johnson comes to Stratford to borrow money and persuade him to return to the theatre but fails on both counts and Shakespeare stumbles home from their drinking bout, carrying the fatal potion Jonson has just handed him. Locking the bedroom against his furious wife he slips the famous will under the door and dies wretchedly on the floor.

In a letter to *The Times* Bond stated that " the contradictions in Shakespeare are those in our own society " and his more disciplined focus certainly gives the play a sharper relevance.

The Fool. 1975.

Although Bond makes free use of " poetic licence " in distorting and inventing characters, his play is broadly based on the life of the Northamptonshire poet, John Clare (1793–1864), labourer and herdsmen.

Bond early contrasts him with a fellow peasant, " Darkie ", who scorns Lord Milton's patronage. Clare is absorbed in poetry and although engaged to Patty has a brief affair with Mary, Milton's servant. Meanwhile enclosures are impoverishing the villagers and the rebellious " Darkie " is eventually hanged.

Act II shows Clare in London, patronised by the litterati; but his poems prove too radical in politics, too frank about love. Clare is quickly dropped. A London patron brings back quantities of unsold books and Milton has him permanently assigned to an asylum.

Clare's thwarted genius gives Bond a moving human story and his political " message " is the more effective for the discipline.

Bertold Brecht (1898–1956).

Perhaps the most original and vigorous dramatist and producer of the century the Bavarian Brecht, was remarkable in his command of both literary and theatrical genius.

His practice and theory underwent constant modification. Early plays, like *Baal*, written to provide entertainment, reveal a satiric and anarchic attitude, and in 1928 the ironic *The Threepenny Opera* (P), made him famous. From 1930 onward his work became explicitly communistic, marked by the rejection of the individual in favour of a social ideal. But although Brecht always remained " committed " to Marxist ideology, most of his later plays, written after his withdrawal from Nazi Germany, are less didactic than humanist in spirit and it is by these mature works that he is best known in Britain.

After 1949 Brecht consolidated the famous Berliner Ensemble in East Berlin, where he developed his influential techniques of production.

The most permanent feature of Brecht's mature drama are the Epic form and the *Verfremdung*, or " alienation " effect, both developed in reaction to the traditional dramatic form, which he dubbed " Aristotelian ". He considered that the closely constructed Aristotelian play, which encourages the audience's emotional participation in the action, syphons off the spectator's emotion, leaving him a passive and acquiescent member of society.

According to Brecht, the drama should be not ritual but debate. The spectator should be a detached observer, calmly investigating the view of the world that confronts him. rationally considering arguments and stimulated to decisive social action. It is taken for granted that he will find the solution to problems in communism.

Brecht therefore developed his " Epic ", or narrative play, loosely constructed with a sequence of individual scenes, functioning as independent dramatic illustrations or quotations to the narrative.

He uses a variety of techniques to establish the narrative tone, such as an actual story-teller on the stage, explanatory verses relayed before the scenes, and banner headlines which foretell the events to be portrayed. Although by throwing the action thus into the past tense, he discards the lure of suspense, his dramatic intelligence, vigour, and inventiveness excite lively interest and curiosity.

To break down the traditional identification of the spectator with the action, Brecht developed his celebrated " alienation " effect, devising techniques to keep him at a critical distance. This implies using an image that suddenly makes the familiar appear strange and novel to the onlooker, so that he is shocked into recognising its significance.

His productions were thus avowedly non-realistic and theatrical, sometimes appearing like an inspired charade. He used not only direct narration but direct address to the audience, formalised settings and properties, masks and stylised make-up, sometimes grotesque in character. His text, " scarcely more than prompter's copy," was freely adapted during rehearsal, so that an acquaintance with the pattern of Brecht's mime and gesture is often necessary to the full understanding of his plays.

Few find in Brecht's mature work the plea for communism that he intended, and many of his protagonists, designed as exponents of capitalist villainy, appeal strongly to the sympathy. The compelling and fascinating central ambiguity can be ascribed, as Esslin has pointed out, to the tension between Brecht's conscious reason and the unconscious emotional experience on which every creative writer must intuitively draw. This profound tension is the major source of Brecht's power.

Brecht's influence has been pervasive, especially through the plays written between 1937 and 1945, the first to be produced here. He has left his mark on Arden, Bolt, Whiting and Joan Littlewood and his plays, major and minor, are still being revived. Above all his iconoclastic attitude and his fertile experiment have been invaluable in encouraging a new and empirical approach to drama.

Esslin's book *Brecht: a Choice of Evils*, 1959, is authoritative.

Baal. Written 1918.

The amoral vagabond poet, Baal (O'Toole), driven by instinct and emotion, expresses the subjective experience of the youthful Brecht.

Man is Man. Written 1924–25.

An amusing comedy marks the turning point between the anarchic hedonism of plays like *Baal* and didactic Marxism. Three raffish soldiers, losing a fourth, persuade a pacific, gentle companion to take his identity. Through their manipulation he becomes a fierce, aggressive soldier. The theme of brain-washing is apparent.

Saint Joan of the Stockyards. Written 1929–30.

Mauler, a Chicago canned-meat capitalist, trying to outdo competitors causes suffering to the workers. Joan, a simple evangelist, identifies herself with them. She offers to carry a communist letter urging a general strike, but realising that violence will be involved fails to deliver it. Joan, dying, recants saying that without violence the world cannot be changed, but the capitalists drown her words and she is canonised. There are interesting parallels with Shaw's play. Brecht returned to the subject in *The Visions of Simone Machard*, 1941–3, where Joan is pictured working with the French Resistance and her suffering drives her insane.

Galileo. Written 1938–9. M.

Brecht intended Galileo's recantation as an image of the scientist's allowing the State to assume authority over science. It has also been interpreted as Galileo's cunning expedient, allowing him to continue research.

Mother Courage. Written 1939. M.

In his panorama of war's futility, Brecht designed Mother Courage—a camp follower in the Thirty Years' War—as an epitome of the haggling profiteer. But his intuitive understanding of this dynamic, maternal figure, bereaved eventually of all three children, has endowed her with an ambiguous fascination.

The Good Person of Szechwan. Written 1938–40. M. P.

Shen Te (Peggy Ashcroft), the benevolent prostitute, has to disguise herself as Shui Ta, the harsh task-master, in order to survive in an unjust commercial society.

Puntila. Written 1940–1.

The drunken generosity of the mean landowner, Puntila, designed by Brecht to highlight his harshness when sober, has however given him an attractive inconsistency. The chauffeur who rejects Puntila's daughter, is a Schweikian character.

The Resistable Rise of Arturo Ui. Written 1941.

The late British première, 1967, of a minor play vividly illuminates Brecht's principles and method. The Chicago thug, Ui, and his cronies burlesque Hitler and his entourage and the horror of Nazism is offset by the brilliant clowning by Rossiter of Ui's abject cowardice and monstrous arrogance. The play successfully parodies Shakespeare's verse, especially in *Richard III*, but the picture of Chicago gangsters as vegetable dealers is unconvincing.

The Caucasian Chalk Circle. Written 1944–5. M. P.

The prologue to this delightful fairy-tale constitutes an overt plea for communism rare in Brecht's later work. The rascally judge Adzak, who takes bribes from the rich and gives judgment in favour of the poor, is one of Brecht's typical contradictory characters.

The Days of the Commune. Written 1948–49.

A late play presents Paris between January and May 1871. In Montmartre liberal leaders of the Communards refrain from taking the Bank of France and restrain the workers from marching to Versailles against Thiers. Consequently they are killed while Thiers watches the city burn. The Communards are sentimentalised, and the Bourgeoisie, Thiers and Bismarck caricatured. The theme is an interesting debate on whether violence can be justified and on what grounds.

Howard Brenton (b. 1942).

Brenton who began on the Fringe first wrote short plays like *Revenge*, *Fruit* and *Christie in Love*, tailored for the small touring company. He has said, " One of my blazing faults is that I understand the ' agit ' but I have difficulty with the ' prop '." But his struggle to clarify his ideas of a just society can be more telling than overt propaganda.

Lay By. 1971

Brenton and Hare (*q.v.*) collaborating with five others dramatised a laconic newspaper account of a case of fellatio. The play is a sensational portrayal of perversion, pornography and drug addiction. The three chief characters are later found together in a mortuary. A gruesome surrealist ending is intended as satire on society's callous indifference to the individual.

Brassneck. 1973. M.

Brenton and Hare (*q.v.*) " wrote the play line by line together ". " Brassneck " means " impudence " with " criminal inference " and the play is a sweeping indictment of civic corruption in a Midland town between 1945 and 1973, through three generations of the Bagley family. Their progress is synchronised with post-war England's decline by topical background photographs and song.

The parvenu Bagley with a shady solicitor and venal Tory house-agent forces his way to civic power through property speculation, the Masonic Lodge, the Conservative Club and the golf club. Members of these institutions, moved by self-interest admit the new Labour M.P. and the Marxist mayor, Bagley's toady. All work in collusion.

In the second generation, Roderick, a dubious architect, through calculated gift and pre-arranged tender extends the family fortunes. Suddenly he is bankrupt, his bribery disclosed and accomplices involved. In generation three, Sidney, Etonian spiv and brothel owner, with his family and cronies launches a combine in Chinese heroin.

Despite some improbabilities and complexities, the play maintains a variety of incident, bravura and pace.

Magnificence. 1973. M.

In an interesting and original political play three high-spirited young men and two women decide to attract attention to the plight of the homeless by squatting in an empty house. Their leader is Jed. There follows a struggle with a bailiff who evicts them and accidentally kicks a girl, causing a miscarriage, thus enraging Jed and sparking off a wish for revenge.

Act One is followed by Jed's remarkable speech describing how after nine months in prison he emerges as a Marxist Leninist.

He decides that the assassination of " Alice ", a Tory minister, shall be his " magnificent " protest against the establishment. But the gelignite fails to go off. Alice cunningly tries to undermine Jed's confidence with hospitable drinks. Then the gelignite explodes accidentally and kills them both. His fellow squatter Cliff speaks Jed's epitaph. What horrifies Cliff is not the violence but the tragic waste of effort that could have been diverted to constructive political action.

Magnificence explores " the question of individual terrorism ". Brenton has said that his emotional sympathy is with Jed's urge to " disrupt the spectacle " and expose the " obscene parade " of the privileged establishment. But it is Cliff's insight that he endorses.

The Churchill Play. 1974.

The play is set in 1984 at the Churchill camp for internees. The spokesman is tough Sergt. Baxter who after fighting the Irish in Ulster had fought the English at home. When a new liberal doctor suggests that the internees act a play for visiting M.P.s they grasp this outlet for their bitterness and also the chance of a break-out. The subject is Churchill. The theme is that like the human body so can the state contract fatal ills and the Churchill cult encouraged neglect of our democratic freedom. The play poses unanswered questions and theatrically follows Weiss's *Marat Sade.*

Weapons of Happiness. 1976.

In 1952 Josef Frank was executed after the Stansky trial in Czechoslovakia, but Brenton imagines him alive and working in a London factory where the workers unsuccessfully stage a sit-in on learning that the business is to be closed and they dismissed.

Frank is through a woman unwillingly drawn into the protest, and when the workers escape down a sewer " dies " of a heart attack while for a moment Stalin's tanks are seen entering Prague. Finally the factory hands consider taking over a disused farm. Brenton neatly contrasts the experienced European communist of 1952, his reluctant phantom and the English workers.

Epsom Downs. 1977.

Brenton's first comedy presents, like Frith's *Derby Day,* the heterogenous types who attend the Derby, such as drunken Labour peer, gipsy, evangelist, Cockney, owner, trainer, jockey mounted on the shoulders of a naked man, stable boy and policeman. The central characters are a straitened family who risk their savings at five to one on a winner ridden by Piggott, and depart to buy a council house. As a Left-wing gesture Brenton shows the protesting ghost of Emily Davison, suicide suffragette, but the device lacks dramatic force. The Joint Stock Company's production used only nine actors, swiftly changing parts. Some illusion of a crowd was created at the crisis of the race by the sudden surge of litter over the Downs.

Peter Brook (b. 1925). Director.

US (or ambiguously *U.S.*). 1966.

US is a collaboration between director, actors, designers, musicians, and writers in an attempt to confront the Vietnam war and to involve the audience.

Brook admits anti-American bias.

The First Act is a violent theatrical assault on apathy. Brook re-employs techniques from Weiss's *Marat-Sade* and alternates utmost stillness, as in the initial mime of a Buddhist self-immolation, with loud music and noise. In the hideous uproar and confusion of a bombing raid at the climax a giant war-effigy from the proscenium crashes across the stage. Shattering assault is succeeded in Act Two by a penetration in depth, its centre being a dialogue between a white man about to burn himself alive and a girl whose cold, detached criticism gradually gives way to a bitter indictment of English parochial indifference. In an ambiguous poetic finale an actor silently releases butterflies, one of which he burns.

This daring and controversial use of theatre directly to involve the emotion of the audience in confrontation with contemporary political tragedy marked a new departure.

The Ik. 1976.

Peter Brook (whose last major experiment had been *Orghast,* where the actors communicated ceremony by gesture and non-verbal sound) produced *The Ik* as a dramatisation from Colin Turnbull's anthropological study, *The Mountain People,* scripted by Denis Cannen and Colin Higgins who use Turnbull as the Investigator. The appalling story is of a group of hunters between Kenya and Uganda whose grounds have become a nature reserve, consigning them to an almost barren area.

Vividly shown is the shocking degradation where food is the sole concern. Children aged 3 are discarded and the old (aged 30) turned out to die. Even the priest is deserted by his son. Save for a private reverence for the mountain the tribe is devoid of spiritual sense and ritual. An effective contrast is the unusual migration of one tribe to be closer to the Sudan, where food is less scarce, the people hospitable and ritual survives.

Brook stresses the danger of any society, including our own, where communal ritual declines.

Albert Camus (1913–60).

The French existentialist philosopher and novelist, Camus, first enunciated the concept of the Absurd as whatever is incompatible with man's desire for reason, justice, happiness and purpose. Like Sartre, Camus expressed his views through the traditional dramatic form, and the plays most familiar here were those written before he had moved on to a more humanistic philosphy. They include *Caligula* (P), *Cross Purposes* (P) and *The Price of Justice.*

Paddy Chayevsky (b. 1923).

The Latent Heterosexual. 1968.

This American play begins as a hilarious caricature of homosexuality and drug addiction as embodied in the outrageous poet, Morley. His novel has just earned him $72,000 and his accountant advises him to evade taxation by a token marriage and by turning himself into a Corporation.

The marriage, to an expensive prostitute, is a sensational success, but soon the Corporation usurps Morley's personal identity. Almost paralysed, he makes a frantic effort to liberate himself and can find his only resource in suicide.

The remorseless and impressive final scenes change the tone of the play and constitute a serious satire on the atrophy of the human personality by Big Business.

Marguerite Duras (b. 1914).

The French novelist and script-writer of the film *Hiroshima Mon Amour,* has a sensitive flair for dialogue and for exploring the ebb and flow of feeling. Her naturalistic plays move subtly towards their climax, often the agony of parting, as in the one-act *La Musica,* 1966 (P).

Days in the Trees. 1966.

The theme of the play, virtually a trio, is the love–hate relationship between mother (Peggy Ashcroft) and son. She had indulged her own emotions by conniving at his playing truant for " whole days in the trees," so that he is now incapable of love for anyone else. Finally, the ageing woman admits to herself his callous egoism and misery, as now a gambler and pimp he lives contemptuously with the devoted girl for whom he procures.

The Lovers of Viorne. 1971.

Marguerite Duras returns to the subject of an earlier play, *The Viaduct*—an actual murder committed in provincial France in the 1940s when a married woman killed her husband and disposed of the corpse by dropping dismembered portions from a viaduct on to passing trains.

Apart from changing the identity of the victim to a deaf-mute cousin, housekeeper to the couple, Duras keeps closely to the facts and concentrates on penetrating the motive.

This demanding play is almost exclusively verbal and spare in design. After a loudspeaker announcement of the discovered crime an impersonal " Interrogator " probes the husband about the twenty-year barren marriage and in Act II he questions the wife herself, Claire Lannes (Peggy Ashcroft), apathetic yet deeply suffering.

He elicits complementary pictures of their meaningless existence, devoid of emotion or thought, the husband finding a cold response to his early love, the wife obsessed by thoughts of the former lover who had destroyed her religious faith, exasperated by the stifling house and revolted by her cousin's cooking.

Duras has spoken of " their totally asphyxiated life " saying, " the silence between them has to be destroyed. "

It is significant that the victim is the deaf and dumb cousin.

Suzanna Andler. 1971.

For many years Suzanna (Eileen Atkins) has brought her children to the same rented house for the summer but now she contemplates change.

In the off-season an agent shows her over a larger empty villa, again in St. Tropez. She worries about the expense but gradually deep levels of anxiety are disclosed. Married for seventeen years Suzanna had long accepted the infidelities of the wealthy husband who still cares for her, but recently she has agreed to a brief affaire with Michel, a rough and struggling journalist, which involves her in new emotional conflicts. Confused as if in a dream she struggles with that paralysis of will that often accompanies suffering, as she strives to come to terms with her tenderness for her husband and the need she and her aggressive lover now feel for each other although they have little else in common.

This sensitive play reveals with faithful naturalism the loneliness and anguish of indecision. As literature and vocally it is exquisite. Theatrically it is less successful for apart from brief meetings with the agent and a confidante and a long telephone conversation with her husband, Suzanna's indecisive encounter with Michel provides the only external action. A radio production with Vivien Merchant as Suzanna indicated that radio is the play's ideal medium.

Friedrich Dürrenmatt (b. 1921)

The German-Swiss Dürrenmatt acknowledges the Greek dramatists, Shakespeare, and Swift as major influences. He describes his work as " theatre of paradox ", revealing " precisely the paradoxical effects of strict logic. " He is an unsparing critic of contemporary society, whose dangerous tendencies he exposes in striking and bizarre fictions, reminiscent of the later Shaw.

The Marriage of Mr. Mississippi. 1959.

An extravaganza poses the opposition between two principles carried to their logical and farcical extreme. One is a passion for the law of Moses, interpreted as retributive justice. The other is pure Marxism. The two characters embodying these principles, together with a Quixotic lover, are manipulated and destroyed by an unscrupulous politician.

The Visit.

An old multi-millionairess revisits her birthplace and offers the inhabitants £1,000,000 to murder her former lover, who had denied her paternity order. Gradually persuading themselves that they are acting justly they comply.

Dürrenmatt cleverly maintains suspense in his withering satire on love of money, hypocrisy and the sycophancy of press and radio.

The Physicists. 1963.

Dürrenmatt has said that this arresting play is not so much about the hydrogen bomb as about society itself and the impossibility of escaping the consequences of one's thinking.

The central character, attempting to suppress scientific discoveries that may lead to the hydrogen bomb, retires to a private asylum pretending to be in contact with King Solomon. There he is first in danger of two spies, pretending to the delusion that they are Einstein and Newton, and eventually of the mad proprietress whose use of his discoveries will lead to the destruction of the human race.

The Meteor. 1966.

Another play of paradox has as hero a man who wishes to die but cannot.

Schwitter (Patrick Magee), famous dramatist and Nobel prizewinner, already proclaimed dead in hospital, returns to the garret of his youth to die. In vain. As the old egoist swaggers, drinks, makes love, one by one those who touch his orbit meet their death.

The symbolism is unclear. Is Schwitter the egoistic kind of artist who feeds on the lives of others? The most effective incident—his dialogue with an ancient tart—cynically suggests that his art also has been prostitution, for he too has supplied artificial emotion to meet public demand.

The chief weakness of the play is that the surprise wears thin. An original idea adequate to a one-act play has been inflated too far.

T. S. Eliot (1888–1965). *See also* Section M.

In his attempt to revive poetic drama the distinguished poet, T. S. Eliot, was moved by deeply religious and social aims, modestly regarding his work as experimental, " that of the first generation only. " The verse he evolved was of a flowing poetic rhythm, " close to contemporary speech " and based on natural stress. Normally he used a line with three stresses and varying length.

In his two plays of the 'thirties Eliot had adopted the ritualistic themes and patterns of Greek drama and had achieved a certain tragic intensity. But the *Cocktail Party* inaugurated a new style, the theme still being Christian redemption and the plot deriving from Greek drama, but the idiom, that of the fashionable comedy of manners. In spite of subtle organisation the liaison has been an uneasy one.

It is curious that the creator of Prufrock should seem unable fully to animate his dramatis personae. This is partly because their inspiration is literary, partly because they are used to illustrate Anglican doctrine and to convey a message. Nor do they belong to the impeccable background against which they are so carefully placed.

The wealth and subtlety of reference of these plays and the beauty of the language make them a delight to the reader, but they are less compelling on the stage.

The Cocktail Party. 1949. F.

This play, revived in 1968, has its literary origin in Euripides' tragi-comedy *Alcestis*, the demi-god Hercules being replaced by Reilly, the psychiatrist, whose intervention breaks the back of the play, for it is not easy to sympathise with people who let their actions be so directed.

The Confidential Clerk. 1953.

Described as " high farce ", this play derives from another tragi-comedy of Euripides, the *Ion*, whose theme of parents seeking their lost children reappears in Terence, Plautus and Shakespeare.

The Elder Statesman. 1955.

Eliot here returns to a tragedy, the *Oedipus at Colonus* of Sophocles, but the youthful peccadilloes of Lord Claverton appear pallid compared with the patricide and incest of Sophocles' protagonist.

Jules Feiffer.

Feiffer, the New York strip-cartoonist of international fame, now writes plays.

Little Murders. 1967. P.

The blustering Newquist family of New York embody what Feiffer has called the " national paranoia " in face of " random violence ", and when the daughter, Patsy, introduces her fiancé, Alfred, who is so strong that he never retaliates, they are incredulous. But Patsy is killed by some stray bullet, Alfred adopts the Newquist ethos, and the family is happily united sniping down harmless passers by.

The main theme is clear. " Man hates war but is fascinated by it. . . . Peace is a Sissy." The play began as a novel, which may account for the plethora of other stimulating ideas which are never fully integrated, and also for some highly entertaining satirical vignettes not entirely relevant.

God Bless. 1968.

This Shavian satire scintillates with dramatic and verbal paradox, epigram and ironic understatement, and improves on reading.

It is timed in " the immediate future," with America waging war in three continents, and is set in the library of the Liberal Brackman (Dotrice), America's " oldest elder statesman."

On his 110th birthday he is cynically dictating the record of his shilly-shallying career, used by Feiffer as an image of the American Liberal compromise as a betrayal of principle, a " sellout ". His narrative is punctuated by teletype and television presentations of mounting insurrection off-stage. Then two heavily armed agitators, for Peace and Civil Rights, formerly Brackman's Harvard students, enter, soon to be followed by the President himself.

As forty-six cities go up in flames, the President reveals that the agitators have actually been financed by him as a tactic to shake up Congress! But the " tactic has gotten out of hand " and while Civil War breaks out the four men settle down to effect yet another compromise. The revolutionaries insist on bombing ten cities, but the President is to decide which ten!

The play operates as an urgent warning.

Max Frisch (b. 1911).

Frisch, a German-Swiss who has been influenced by Shaw and Brecht, dramatises current issues in ingenious, apt and witty parables that have a lucid economy of outline.

The Fire-Raisers. 1961. M.

A delightful Absurdist satire on bourgeois self-delusion and ineptitude shows Biedermann (Alfred Marks) persuading himself that he can cajole the incendiaries about to set fire to his house by inviting them to a good dinner. The situation is analogous to that of Benes of Czechoslovakia who included communists in his government, and to that of the Germans who connived at Hitler.

Andorra. 1964. M.

An incisive and moving satire on the vicious pervasiveness of antisemitism shows the Andorrans' betrayal of the lad Andri, reputedly a Jewish foundling, to the invading totalitarian state. Andri is in fact a Gentile and his assumption of Jewish traits is an example of identity imposed from without by society.

Christopher Fry (b. 1907).

Fry, widely acclaimed in the 'forties for bringing verse back to the stage, has written comedies and religious plays, the latter culminating in A Sleep of Prisoners, 1951, commissioned for enactment in churches during the Festival of Britain.

Fry devises ingenious situations, often in terms of poetic fable, informed by implicit affirmation and hope, lightly and gaily conveyed. His special talent is the creation of a dramatic atmosphere, unique to each play. But like Love's Labours Lost they tend to be too static and are carried by the dynamic and magic of verse. His delightful early verse was sometimes too lavish and discursive and with Curtmantle he began to use a plainer style with brief, telling images.

His mature work completes the quartet of the Seasons that had begun with the Spring comedy, The Lady's Not for Burning, 1948, O.U.P., and Venus Observed, 1950, O.U.P., an unusual and felicitous comedy of Autumn.

The Dark is Light Enough. 1954.

In a play of Winter an eccentric and saint-like old Countess (Edith Evans) gives asylum to men of both sides in the Hungarian rising of 1948. The theme of non-intervention is presented with an elegance that saves it from didacticism.

Curtmantle. 1962.

A vigorous play has as tragic protagonist Henry II, shown as an imperious autocrat, brilliant, generous and headstrong. Redeeming England from anarchy by his firm foundation of Common Law, he yet makes the tragic error of promoting as Archbishop his tried friend, Becket, who then proves intransigent and inconsistent and triumphs by his martyrdom.

With remarkable skill Fry incorporates the truly tragic hero and emotional power of the Aristotelian play (q.v.) in a work modern in structure. The main themes interpenetrate: the progressive discovery of Henry's contradictory personality in his relations with Becket, his people, and the wife and sons who deserted him, and the " interplay of different laws." The drama moves swiftly through the years 1158–89, the events successfully telescoped as in William Marshall's memory.

Some prose is appropriately used and the poetry is disciplined and vivid.

A Yard of Sun. 1970.

It is July 1946 in Siena, time of the first postwar Palio, that tense horse-race, which is also a " galvanic liturgy of life." In war's aftermath two neighbouring families strive towards renewal.

In one there are still brothers' conflicts to be resolved. Angelino's eldest son, the rebellious Roberto, ex-Partisan, now a devoted doctor, is scathingly scornful of easy-going Luigi, failed politician and Blackshirt, and also of the long-missing Edmondo, who suddenly turns up. A war-profiteer, Edmondo is smugly eager to use his financial expertise to contrive the families' fortunes.

Unwillingly Roberto is stirred by Edmondo's dazzling wife, embodiment of the passionate excitement of the Palio. But her husband's machinations go comically awry and they soon depart.

Roberto now realises that he loves the simple Grazia, daughter of the neighbour Giosetta, whose putative husband has just returned from a concentration camp, and now believes in his duty to return to his legal invalid wife. There is a hint of union between Giosetta and Angelino.

Although the scheme of this quiet, humorous comedy is somewhat too neat and flat it is true to its theme of resurgence. The fruits of Autumn may come. The poetic imagery well expresses the differing personalities and the volatile Italian temperament.

Athol Fugard (b. 1932).

Fugard, an Afrikaner, has now emerged as one of the most remarkable playwrights writing in English.

He left the University of Cape Town before completing his degree in Philosophy and spent two years as a seaman in the Far East, subsequently working in Europe. Economic circumstances obliged him to direct and act in his own plays and he had his own theatre group in Port Elizabeth, but he has now given up acting and hopes soon to devote himself entirely to writing.

As a liberal Fugard is in a most difficult situation. His roots and source of inspiration are in his Afrikaans kinship and his over-riding drive is to reveal to South Africans the " social circumstances that do terrible things to people," apartheid being one of these circumstances. He depicts them with unsparing realism and while constantly facing the risk of police interference and taboo he has tried "to be as courageous as possible . . . in indicting a social system ", his aim being " to get plays performed not banned ". Although the social implications of his plays seem inescapable, they do reach the stage in South Africa, for they are not committed to political criticism. Indeed they rise above it and perhaps it is the tensions that inhibit emotional self-indulgence that give to his work its characteristic fusion of passionate caring and disciplined objectivity.

A dominant theme is the human courage that survives appalling odds, a courage especially evident in women such as Milly, Lena and Hester. He is especially skilful in his handling of confrontation between two people who are closely involved emotionally, some complete plays being limited to a cast of two. The playwright Fugard most admires is Samuel Beckett.

In about 1963 seven men from New Brighton, the black ghetto in Port Elizabeth, asked his help in starting an amateur drama group, which became the precursor of several other groups of black actors, who, because of *apartheid* can play to black audiences only. The Serpent Players presented works of Brecht, Genet, Strindberg, Sophocles and Euripides and became the seed-bed of a remarkable partnership in creative writing between Fugard and the black South Africans John Kani and Winston Ntshona. Their *Sizwe Bansi* and *The Island* when brought to England in 1973–4 were enthusiastically received.

The Blood Knot. 1966. P.

Of two brothers belonging to the mixed race of " Cape Coloureds ", one " tries for white. " The dialogue between them, both comic and naïve, and fraught with intense love and hate, is a microcosm of the terrible strains imposed by racial segregation.

People Are Living There. 1970. O.U.P.

In a shabby Johannesburg kitchen, the slatternly landlady, Milly, just deserted by her lover, frenziedly tries to whip up a party for her fiftieth birthday. The only guests are her lodgers, a " retarded poor white, " and a student immersed in Sartre's anguish.

They get down to the grim " rock bottom " of mutual self-knowledge, of society's indifference to poverty, of the loss of joy in the aging process, measured by the frail chiming of a shaky clock. Only Milly's outburst of laughter at the ridiculous spectacle of the whole animal world saves their precarious companionship.

This compassionate play recalls Sartre's *In Camera* but has a more valid conclusion than Sartre's dictum, " hell is other people. "

Boesman and Lena. 1971.

Uprooted from their shanty town near Port Elizabeth, the aging coloured couple, Boesman and Lena, can find no other refuge than a succession of rubbish dumps.

" We're whiteman's rubbish, " exclaims Boesman. " He can't get rid of his rubbish. He throws it away, we pick it up. Wear it. Sleep in it. Eat it. We're made of it now. His rubbish is people. "

When they encounter an old and dying Kaffir, Boesman adopts the bullying tone of the *baas*, but Lena tries to befriend him only to find that he speaks an obscure dialect and they cannot communicate.

In spite of inhuman conditions, Lena, like Milly in *People are Living There*, somehow preserves some courage and resilience.

In an authentic film version Fugard himself takes the part of Boesman.

Hello and Goodbye. 1973.

The scene is the slum home of the Smits, poor whites in Port Elizabeth.

Hester, now on the streets, returns unexpectedly to search for and claim from her brother Johnny her share of the compensation paid to their father, who having lost a leg in an industrial accident was also crippled by resentment and self-pity. Tough and forceful she obliges her neurotic brother to fetch from the father's bedroom all the cardboard boxes which when searched disclose nothing but the ugly and worthless cast-offs from their squalid past. These like the furniture in Miller's *The Price* focus the emotional strain between the two; Johnny having given up personal ambition to act as nurse has identified himself with the invalid

father, Hester with the mother, the patient bread-winner.

Eventually Hester is shocked to find the bedroom empty for Johnny had deliberately hidden from her the fact that the father had died. Suddenly moved, she asks Johnny to come away with her. But he, a victim of agoraphobia symbolically takes his father's crutches and adopts his defeated pose.

As in *The Blood Knot* Fugard skilfully used a taut dualogue to reveal the pain of conflict between siblings but this later play lacks the wider resonance of the social suffering endemic in *apartheid*.

Sizwe Bansi is Dead. 1973.

Sizwe is a triumph of collaboration, both dramatic and racial, between Fugard and two members of the black Serpent Players, John Kani and Winston Ntshona, who are also the only actors. The piece is rooted in the personal experience of these two men, given shape by the literary talent of Fugard, and it creates a wonderful illusion of spontaneous dramatic interchange, story-telling and mime. Kani and Ntshona, who appear professionally for the first time, give a dazzling performance. They play the three characters while incidental figures are brilliantly conjured up by lightning impersonations. The action is continuous, the simple set being quickly adaptable to change of locale.

Initially it is the one room " Photographic Studio " of Styles (Kani). In a richly humorous monologue he recalls the day when the anxious bosses at the Ford plant, where he once worked for six years, ordered frenzied and long overdue cleaning and safety precautions in hasty preparation for an unexpected visit by Ford himself. They had called on Styles to translate their exhortations to the workers and their injunctions to " Smile ", and he re-enacts with relish his highly individual interpretation and mimics their fawning reaction to Ford's three-minute entry.

Now proudly independent in his studio Styles confides his desire to take photographs that will confirm the black man's dream of self-respect and give him a symbol of permanent identity.

Robert timidly enters for a photograph to send his wife. Styles gives him confidence posing him with a cigarette in one hand and a fancy pipe in the other, and as the flashbulb goes for a second snapshot there is a blackout and a flashback to Robert's past, when Kani now takes on the part of Buntu.

Robert's real name is Sizwe Bansi. A bewildered countryman, he has walked from his famished village to Port Elizabeth in search of work and has been picked up in a police raid, but is too simple to realise that his Passbook is now stamped with an order to return home. Buntu befriends him and eventually gets across the harsh complications of the Pass Laws. Then Buntu stumbles over the corpse of one Robert Zwelima, and urges the reluctant Sizwe for the sake of his starving family to adopt Robert's Passbook with its work permit. He rehearses Sizwe in his new role by improvising possibly risky encounters and drilling into his mind the new identity number. " Burn that into your head, my friend . . . It's more important than your name. " Buntu wishes him luck as long as he " stay out of trouble. " " Impossible, Buntu. Our skin is trouble. "

But Sizwe agrees to try and the play closes as again in the " Studio " he jauntily responds to Styles' encouragement, " Now smile Robert . . . Smile . . . Smile . . . "

An enthralling play brings home the massive hypocrisy and ruthlessness of a regime that would mutilate and reduce manhood to an identity number and a set of finger prints. Yet the work is devoid of self-pity and has none of that stridency which sometimes mars the British play of protest. In their warmth and generosity, their creativity and sense of humour, the black people find the rueful courage to survive and beyond courage evince even a rare " gaiety transfiguring all that dread. "

The Island. 1973.

Like *Sizwe Bansi* the play was devised by Fugard and the two actors Kani and Ntshona.

The setting is a prison recalling the notorious Robben Island to which some members of the Serpent Players had been relegated. The two prisoners are locked by their isolation into a symbiotic relationship which they describe as a "marriage", hating each other as they toil digging and carting sand, comforting each other huddled in their cell. When John learns that his ten years' sentence has been reduced and he will be free in three months, Winston at first joyfully hugs him but then is overcome by jealousy.

But John urges Winston to go forward with the rehearsal for a prison concert of their version of *Antigone*, and notwithstanding Winston's pathetic drag, their performance gives a universal significance to their incarceration.

Statements After an Arrest Under the Immorality Act. 1974.

In South Africa sexual relationship between white and black or coloured is illegal. A brief play shows the tenderness and anguish of a married coloured man and his white mistress. Their privacy is harshly shattered as, still naked, the re photographed and interrogated by police.

Dimetos. 1975.

A daring experimental play uses Camus' notebooks. Dimetos, engineer, has retired to a "remote province" where he becomes aware of his "guilty love" for his niece Sophia. Danilo arrives to persuade his return, but Dimetos arranges that Danilo shall try to assault Sophia while he watches. She, learning this, hangs herself. Finally, Dimetos goes mad. His opening and closing words stress the theme of this abstruse work, that gravity is the law that holds the universe in balance.

Jean Genet (b. 1910).

The French Genet, abandoned as a child, has lived as social outcast and criminal and, while politically "uncommitted", has mirrored his bitter repudiation of society in plays of frightening impact.

His dramatis personae have been the rejected, murderers (*Deathwatch* (F)), despised servants (*The Maids* (F)), prostitutes (*The Balcony* (F)), Negroes (*The Blacks* (F)), and Algerian peasants (*The Screens*). These have realised their fantasies of sex, power, violence, and revenge only by compulsive ritual acts, so that sequences of arresting ceremonial, sometimes Absurdist, replace character study and coherent plot.

In his destructive scorn of contemporary society, his recourse to rituals of violence, and his incantatory language, Genet satisfies the requirements of Artaud's Theatre of Cruelty.

The Maids. 1956. F.

Two sisters, maids to a fine lady, continually take it in turn to enact the rôle of mistress and maid so that each can vent her envy and rancour on the mistress. When their plot to murder the mistress misfires, one of them herself drinks the poisoned cup of tea.

Their compulsive charade, designed originally for a cast of young men, mirrors the obsessive and self-destroying conflict of envious love and hate in the mind of the outsider.

Triana's *The Criminals* has a similar theme and technique.

The Balcony. 1957. F.

This censored play had its world première at the Arts Theatre Club. It opens in a brothel, where the frequenters enact their fantasies of power by dressing up as bishop, judge, or general, until after an abortive revolution they are called upon by the Court to impersonate these authorities in actuality. Eventually the defeated revolutionary leader visits the brothel to enact the part of Chief of Police, who is then satisfied that his image also has been established in popular regard. The film gives a softened version of the play.

The Screens. 1973.

A rather sprawling play to be acted against movable screens with a cast of ninety-seven and lasting five hours was with Genet's permission presented in three hours with a cast of nine, the adaptor being Howard Brenton (*q.v.*).

Written in 1961 it differs from Genet's previous plays in representing his views on a specific issue, the French-Algerian conflict of 1954–62 and attacks colonialism as represented by decadent exploiters and cruel, sexually perverted soldiers. But the revolution of the wretched Algerian peasants is focused on yet another of Genet's rejected outcasts, the treacherous criminal Said, driven by his mother "to go to extremes" and so impoverished that he can marry only the ugliest girl.

There is an uneasy juxtaposition of political incidents with obsessive fantasies of sex and power, and the play is less concentrated and effective than earlier work.

Maxim Gorky (1868–1936).

The delayed première here of *The Lower Depths* produced 1902, by Stanislavsky, showing the despair of the destitute in a bleak dosshouse, awoke interest in Gorky's later plays. *Enemies*, 1971, M., depicts industrial conflict in the Bardins' factory near their country estate. Bardin, a gentle liberal, reluctantly agrees to the demands of his reactionary partner, who is shot. The play reveals the dismay of employers aware that the workers are now their "enemies".

Summerfolk. 1974.

The summerfolk, who rent summer cottages are the rising professional bourgeoisie, who, lacking purpose, fritter their time in gossip, quarrels, drink, theatricals and seduction. In contrast are an able woman doctor, Maria Lvovna, with her emancipated daughter, and Varvara (wife of a drunkard). Two visitors arrive, Shalimov once a writer admired by Varvara, but now a poseur, and the wealthy self-made industrialist Dvoetoche. Eventually Varvara escapes with her younger brother, who will join Dvoetoche in Siberia to build schools and hospitals. The 1977 version rearranged the order of scenes.

Trevor Griffiths.

The Party. 1974.

In the expensive flat of an impotent young husband a heterogeneous group of left-wingers meet during the French uprising of students and workers of May 1968. They indulge in interesting political monologue and there is little action.

Comedians. 1975.

Emphasing the need for humanity in today's permissive and often cruel atmosphere, the famous ex-comedian Eddie Waters tries to train a few students as stand-up comics for the brief interludes tolerated in working men's clubs—the shabby setting of the play. An agent's scout is set to spot talent, but the attempts of all save one miscarry. Especially hurtful to Waters is the failure of his favourite pupil Gethin, who has violently accused a dummy pair in evening dress, piercing the woman so that "blood" flows. The play ends as Waters and Gethin discuss Gethin's methods and intentions, and the relation of comedy to cruelty.

Günter Grass (b. 1927).

Grass, a notable German novelist and author of some early absurdist plays, has recently written propaganda for the Social Democratic Party of Federal Germany.

The Plebians Rehearse the Uprising. 1968.

Produced here first by amateurs in 1968, and then by the R.S.C. in 1970, *The Plebians* is set in a theatre in East Berlin. The date, 17 June 1953, is that of the spontaneous yet formidable rising of the workers in East Germany against the Ulbricht régime.

The play imagines a situation in which the Boss, clearly a counterpart of Brecht the dramatist-producer, is rehearsing his Germanised version of *Coriolanus*, whose protagonist is the aristocrat, who, spurning the rebellious plebians, all but betrays his country.

Into the Boss's theatre intrude rebellious workers, asking him to write a manifesto which will give coherence to their inarticulate demands. But the dramatist who has indefatigably urged intelligent revolution, scorns their amateur incompetence. Despite the advice of his wife, he temporises.

Finally, moved by the enthusiasm of a girl, herself inspired by Katrin in Brecht's *Mother Courage* (*q.v.*), the Boss resolves to support the uprising. But already the Russian tanks are moving in. Bitterly he realises that he has himself played the part of Coriolanus.

The play reflects not only Grass's disquiet about Brecht's rôle in a satellite dictatorship. It concerns the predicament of the modern artist—that of Grass himself—as to whether art or political commitment should take precedence. A significant minor incident in the play is that the response of the University to the workers' cry, "Intellectuals, Solidarity", is merely to bar their windows. Grass clearly indicates that the lack of effective support of artists and intellectuals for the revolution they advocate results in a tragic cleavage in the nation—hence the sub-title, *A German Tragedy*.

Christopher Hampton (b. 1946).

When Did You Last See My Mother? 1960. F.

Hampton frankly explores homosexuality.

Total Eclipse. 1968. F.

The story of Verlaine's passionate infatuation for the younger poet Rimbaud (prototype of Brecht's Baal) is dispassionately and convincingly presented, almost like a chronicle, the opening and closing scenes being particularly skilful.

The Philanthropist. 1970. F.

An ingenious comedy, ironic parallel of Molière's *The Misanthropist* (M), is " set in the near future " in the room of a bachelor don, Philip, the " philanthropist. "

In an arresting *coup de théâtre* an aspiring dramatist, trying to convince Philip and his friend Donald of the likelihood of his protagonist's suicide, unfortunately blows out his own brains.

Shortly afterwards a dinner party for six occasions some brilliantly precise and apt repartee. As in Molière, the characters are boldly contrasted. Philip, a literal-minded philosophy don, disclaims critical judgment, but is fascinated by words in isolation, his lonely pastime devising anagrams. He is terrified of hurting people, but his mumbling evasions give more offence than Don's trenchant criticisms.

The evening culminates in comic fiasco. Philip, too imperceptive to realise that his fiancée, Celia, wants to stay, lets her be " taken home " by an unscrupulous acquaintance, and out of pique she sleeps with him. Meanwhile Philip is too timid to refuse the nymphomaniac, Araminta, who stays the night " under conditions too appalling to relate. "

Next day, Celia, having discovered Araminta at breakfast, returns again to break off her engagement with one too weak to control her. Philip, crestfallen, decides to approach Liz, only to find that she has spent the night with Don!

Harking back to Scene 1, Philip transposes " Imagine the theatre as real " into " I hate thee, sterile anagram. " Then, taking a cigarette and a small pistol, he goes to join Don and Liz. Is this ambiguous finale a token suicide, Philip having previously given up smoking for fear of cancer, or does the transposed anagram indicate a new fruitful involvement in life?

A theme shared with Molière is the foibles of the age, in Molière courtly hypocrisy, in Hampton growing indifference to violence. Hampton's characters are of the same metal as their prototypes but the coin is reversed. The idealistic misanthropist, Alceste, rebukes flatterers, even his beloved, the coquettish Célimène, finally deciding to withdraw from society. The gentle Philip, diffidently condones even the " frivolous " Celia. The play is too derivative to be entirely self-subsistent but Hampton skilfully incorporates a penetration of Philip's complex nature into his meticulously structured comedy.

Savages. 1973. F.

A play informed by an icy indignation is grounded in topical political events and in Hampton's personal experience. After reading how the Indians of the upper Amazon were being progressively exterminated so that their land might be developed by speculators, Hampton visited Brazil to investigate. He set his play in the Brazil of 1970–1, when during a brief revolutionary movement foreign diplomats of four different countries were kidnapped.

Hampton invents a fifth, West (Scofield), a British diplomat, collector and translator of Indian myths. West is seized by urban guerrillas revolting against a brutal fascist military dictatorship in cahoots with American speculators. A series of scenes between West and his captor Carlos form the framework of the play.

Handcuffed to a bed the sceptical liberal diplomat is confronted by an enthusiastic and friendly Marxist and their sophisticated and ironic dialogue reveals their growing personal sympathy and opposed ideology—Carlos's dedication to action and West's stance as humane observer. The kidnapping is in fact the diplomat's first close contact with Brazil, for hitherto he has thought only in a " distanced " way, typical, considers Hampton, of the English people.

To Carlos obsessed by the massive squalor of a country where wealth is owned by three per cent of the people, the plight of the Indians is a " marginal problem " but West is aware of their systematic extermination by violent murder and by such gifts as poisoned food. Interspersed with discussion are film-style flashbacks demonstrating the Indians' predicament, one depicting the infamous hunting party of 1963, whose simple expedient was the mass murder of the villagers and firing of their homes. Scattered scenes of West's translations and the enactment of myths lack cumulative impact.

The climax of the play is Carlos's reluctant shooting of West followed by a scene of the ruthless bombing raid exterminating a whole tribe during their ritual fertility ceremony.

The ambiguous title, indicating that the savages are the " civilised " exploiters, is underlined by contrasting public concern at West's assassination with indifference to mass genocide.

Treats. 1976.

Ann's lover Dave, a loutish, promiscuous journalist, is in Cyprus when the conventional Patrick supplants him in her flat but is eventually rejected in favour of Dave. The play had a mixed reception.

David Hare (b. 1947).

Hare is one of our younger experimental writers and has on occasion collaborated with Brenton (*q.v.*).

Slag. 1970.

Hare claims that his play set out " to show what was good about women " but admits that it ends up " as rather a vicious slur on them. "

Slag relies on parody of girls' schools, women's lib. and political jargon.

What Happened to Blake. 1970.

A pantomime-style dramatisation of William Blake's career distorts the quality of his life.

The Great Exhibition. 1972.

Like *Slag* the play deals with self-isolated members of the middle class.

Hammett, once a reasonably energetic Labour M.P., can now find no motive for action but simply stays in his flat brooding on his life's futility. His disillusioned wife entertains a disaffected boyfriend and together they smoke pot. When she leaves Hammett, in a desperate resort to action he exposes himself on Wimbledon Common but without effect save on his wife's best friend. Hare combines a picture of existentialist despair with some farcical comedy and random satire.

Knuckle. 1974.

A fast-moving play is in the style of a Mickey Spillane private-eye thriller. Curly is a tough gun-runner from Peru, yet he returns to his home town Guildford to unravel the mysterious death of his sister, who had disappeared from there and been seen in Surbiton and Eastbourne before her deserted clothes had been discovered in a lonely spot. He is unable to learn anything even from their father, a suave, wealthy merchant-banker, or the dead girl's lover, but at last he accidentally realises the truth through his relationship with Jenny, a hostess in Guildford's night club.

Hare has daringly used parody to satirise the forces of ruthless materialism and corruption that have distorted life's values not in distant Peru but Surrey.

Fanshen. 1975.

Fanshen means "to turn over" and Hare, writes a convincing resumé of William Hinton's 700-page documentary of how between 1945 and 1949 the people of Long Bow in Shensi turned over to Chinese communism.

Using nine people as a microcosm of the village, with occasional advisers from the Party, Hare shows the peasants' mounting revenge against the extortionate landlord and more gradually an honest evaluation of their own possessions.

Teeth n' Smiles. 1975.

Hare emphasises the social gulf between a rock group playing for a Cambridge May ball and the privileged members of college.

Rolf Hochhuth (b. 1931).

Hochhuth, like his predecessor Schiller, is specially interested in the historical play.

The Representative. 1963. M. P.

A verse play exposes the failure of Pope Pius XII, Christ's " representative ", to protest against Nazi massacres of Jews. Films of Auschwitz horrors are used.

Soldiers. 1968.

Hochhuth's inordinately long play had its genesis in his horror and protest at the bombing of non-combatants. It is set symbolically at Coventry Cathedral but contains a realistic play-within-the-play, the only part produced in 1968.

This is timed for the crucial months, May to July, 1943, and historical persons are assigned fictional parts. Hochhuth embodies his theme by presenting Cherwell as the " eminence grise " who advocates to Churchill (John Colicos), the commanding protagonist, a policy of ruthless saturation bombing. The theme is counterpointed by the suggestion that success in modern warfare demands not only barbarity but treachery. This is given personal urgency in Churchill's confrontation with his ally, the Polish General Sikorski, whose intransigent hostility to Russia was proving a threat to our precarious alliance with Stalin.

Hochhuth's sensational insinuation that Churchill connived at Sikorski's death is a striking and poignant dramatic image and is defended by some critics on the grounds that a play is an agreed fiction. Hochhuth himself, however, claims to have seen secret evidence and has by

some been sharply criticised for traducing Churchill when he cannot produce this.

In the final Act, Bishop Bell is presented in a fictional impassioned protest to Churchill against civilian atrocities, but the arguments assigned to him do not unfortunately proceed to their logical conclusion that modern warfare is *per se* an atrocity and here the moral pressure of the play is dissipated.

Hochhuth boldly handles his dominant theme while organising the intricate political detail in a gripping and enthralling way. The presentation of historical characters is remarkably convincing and Churchill emerges as an idiosyncratic, massive and tragic hero, fully aware of his moral dilemmas and ironically prescient of his rôle as the servant of history in winning a war that destroyed the balance of Europe.

Ödön von Horvath (1901–38).

Tales from the Vienna Woods. 1977. F, idiomatically translated by Christopher Hampton (*q.v.*).

Insistent Strauss waltzes and a spectacular cabaret in Vienna, 1931, balance the dubious relationships and intrigues of the backstreets. The butcher Oskar has long wooed gentle Marianne, but at a picnic celebrating their engagement she succumbs to the specious charm of Alfred, gigolo and punter. He warns her to love " sensibly ", for being moneyless he " couldn't take the responsibility " of a broken engagement. Too infatuated to listen Marianne flings back Oscar's ring.

Disowned by her father, deserted by Alfred, rejected by the church she appears naked in a cabaret to support her baby, who is taken to Wachau and dies through the deliberate neglect of Alfred's vengeful grandmother. Marianne, now embittered, accepts Oskar's love, which he had warned her she would " never escape ".

Horvath presents a social kaleidoscope. The principal characters are seen in the round.

Eugene Ionesco (b. 1912).

Ionesco differs from Camus (*q.v.*) and Sartre (*q.v.*) in expressing his conviction of life's absurdity in images that are themselves absurd.

In 1948, after learning English from a primer Ionesco dramatised its platitudes in *The Bald Prima Donna*, and singled out those aspects of contemporary life that remained the chief targets of his ridicule. They include the empty myopic life of the petit bourgeois and the dessication of language, now " clichés, empty formulas and slogans ".

Ionesco's sense of absurdity is rooted in his concern for the flight from reason, potentially both tragic and absurd. He believes that by dramatising his own inner anguish he can reveal a universal experience. Naturally therefore he has little interest in specific social issues and has deliberately repudiated " committed " didactic drama.

An iconoclast, he has challanged realism, plot, the Aristotelian play, consistent characterisation, motivation and the distinction between tragedy and comedy.

Discarding so much, Ionesco has evolved a new technique of shock tactic, using most ingenious theatrical devices to express his convictions. He attempts " to go right down to the very basis of the grotesque, the realm of caricature . . . to push everything to paroxysm, to the point where the sources of the tragic lie. To create a theatre of violence—violently comic, violently tragic."

A charactistic technique is the use of proliferating material objects, which externalise the anxieties of his characters—an accumulation of chairs or eggs, for instance, or an expanding corpse. He hopes thus " to make the stage settings speak: to translate action into visual terms; to project visible images of fear, regret, remorse, alienation. "

The discarding of proved theatrical techniques is risky. Shock tactics are successful only as long as they surprise by their novelty. It is a measure of Ionesco's talent that he continues to invent the novel and arresting.

In two of his later plays, *Rhinoceros* and *Exit the King*, the nihilism for which Ionesco has been criticised has been relieved by the assertion of the human value of fortitude.

Ionesco's plays were introduced into England in the 'fifties and they have had a marked and specific impact on English drama, especially on Simpson and Saunders. Although Pinter has a philosophy and style all his own, his early work is based on similar presuppositions.

The Bald Prima Donna. Written 1948.

Characters from an English language manual come to life and pour out their clichés in a " parody of a play ", which Ionesco first considered to be a " tragedy of language ", but which proved theatrically very funny. The first dialogue between husband and wife is now a classic.

Thus Ionesco, almost by accident, wrote the first of many satirical exposures of the sterile language of those who live a merely mechanical existence.

The Lesson. Written 1950. P.

A nervous old professor coaches an eager young girl. Elaborately " proving " the impossibility of communicating by words, he arbitrarily decides what various words shall mean, until he rapidly gains assurance and eventually rapes and murders his pupil, the fortieth that day.

Ionesco illustrates the prostitution of language as a means to power, the sexual element in power, and the sadism lurking in the teacher-pupil relationship and indeed in all authority.

Jack. Written 1950.

Urged by his conventional family to settle down to married life, the Bohemian son, Jack, resists Roberte, the proposed bride, because having only two noses she is not ugly enough. He eventually succumbs to Roberte II with three noses. Ionesco parodies submission to bourgeois conformity.

The Chairs. Written 1951. P.

An ancient concierge and his wife prepare for a crowd of guests who are to hear his final message to posterity. As the totally invisible guests arrive the couple fetch more and more chairs for them, until with the entry of the professional orator who is to pronounce the message, they jump into the sea. But the orator is deaf and dumb and his writing on the blackboard is a meaningless jumble.

The empty chairs constitute a most effective theatrical image for man's failure to communicate, and the dumb orator makes the record of a lifetime seem utterly futile. It may also suggest how meaningless can be the words of author and actor. Ionesco says, " The theme of the play is nothingness made concrete."

Victims of Duty. Written 1952.

By transforming a detective into a psychoanalyst, Ionesco argues that there is little difference between the psychological drama and the mere detective play.

Amédée. Written 1953. P.

A corpse in the flat of a married couple, constantly growing at a frightening rate, is a gruesome and appropriate image of their dead love.

Rhinoceros. Written 1958. P.

More and more rhinoceroses appear in a small provincial town. They are the inhabitants who, one after the other, want to be turned into these thick-skinned, aggressive animals. Finally only Bérenger (Olivier) resists the urge to conform.

The terrifying lure of conformity is here skilfully and movingly illustrated.

Exit the King. Written 1963.

In an agnostic counterpart of the 15th cent.

Everyman, Ionesco shows King Bérenger (Alec Guinness), in his disintegrating palace, reluctantly submitting to the process of dying, his final resource being fortitude alone. This dramatic elegy, inspired by the final scenes of Richard II, is designed with bold simplicity, presenting man's mortal dissolution with unflinching honesty and a tenderness new in Ionesco.

Alfred Jarry (1873–1907).

Ubu Roi. 1966. M.

In 1896, Jarry initiator of the " Pataphysics " movement, scandalised Paris with his startling *Ubu Roi*, precursor of Absurd drama.

The characters appear as grotesque puppets, shocking and comic. The shameless, greedy Ubu caricatures both Macbeth and bourgeois vulgarity and in his brutal conquest of Poland becomes a monstrous prototype of ruthless cruelty.

James Joyce (1882–1941). *See also* Section M.

Exiles. P.

Joyce's only play, rejected by both Yeats and Shaw, was wonderfully justified under Pinter's direction in 1970.

Its theme is the agony of mind and spirit engendered by a courageous attempt to live beyond the confines of law, convention and habit. Richard Rowan returns to Dublin, a famous writer, after nine years' voluntary exile. He brings Bertha, his wife by common-law, who had devotedly left Ireland with him, and their little son, Archie.

Rowan again meets Beatrice, who has always loved him and with whom he has for years corresponded voluminously about his work. From complex motives, partly to assure himself that Bertha's union with him is still absolutely free of conventional ties, he encourages her growing intimacy with his old friend and disciple, Robert. But Bertha, who in her simplicity is envious of Beatrice's education and subtlety of mind, feels rejected and confused, Robert that he is acting in an underhand way, and Richard that he must be ever wounded by doubt as to their fidelity.

Only parental feeling for Archie and Bertha's profound tenderness for Richard save them. For Bertha, with " something wiser than wisdom in her heart," has an intuitive insight beyond Richard's probing manipulating intelligence. Since Richard is to some degree a self-portrait, objective self-criticism is remarkable.

This taut and close-knit play in " three cat and mouse acts," where the past " is present here now, " recalls Ibsen.

Heiner Kipphardt.

In the Matter of J. Robert Oppenheimer. 1966. M.

The play, already performed in 23 capitals, concerns Oppenheimer, " father of the A bomb. " The source is documentary, the 3,000 pages of proceedings before the Personnel Security Board of the US Atomic Energy Commission in 1954.

A hearing taking over a month with 40 witnesses has been condensed and shaped so that evidence is represented by only 6 witnesses. Kipphardt's aim was to follow Hegel in stripping away the adventitious circumstances so that the essential situation clearly emerges. He has made a few additions and all deviations from the literal documents are based on historical data.

The play therefore has an extraordinary authenticity and grip while the central dilemmas are lucidly presented. As *The New Scientist* pointed out, it is for the audience to answer the searching questions raised. Was Oppenheimer, with his communist connections, a security risk? Can a scientist work with state authorities and keep his integrity? Is he responsible for the use made of his discoveries?

D. H. Lawrence (1885–1930).

In 1968 at the Royal Court Peter Gill staged three Lawrence plays in a special season acclaimed by the critics. They were *A Collier's Friday Night* (P), *The Daughter in Law* (P) and *The Widowing of Mrs. Holroyd* (P).

They depict Lawrence's Nottinghamshire mining community and share the themes already familiar through the contemporary *Sons and Lovers*, moving foward with a leisurely naturalism, undisturbed by any forced plot.

Robert Lowell (b. 1917). *See also* Section M.

The first dramatic work of the distinguished American poet, Robert Lowell, is *The Old Glory*, a trilogy of plays in free verse based on stories of Hawthorne and Melville. Their unifying motif is the flag.

Benito Cereno.   1967.

The third and best play of Lowell's trilogy is based on a short story by Melville.

About 1800, while off Trinidad, Delano, Captain of an American trader, observes that a Spanish trader, the *San Domingo*, is in great difficulties and generously goes to her aid.

Captained ostensibly by Benito Cereno, the *San Domingo* is in fact in the hands of her cargo of revolted slaves who have spared his life only that he may navigate them back to Africa. The effete and exhausted Cereno lives at the knife point at the hands of Babu, their wily leader.

Delano fails to realise this, for Cereno dare not speak plainly, and the American is too opaque and self-assured to interpret hints. Only when Babu openly defies him is he enlightened, but too late. The only safe course now left is open violence and instantly his seamen massacre all the Negroes.

In a final ominous incident the last survivor, Babu, cries out " The future is with us " before Delano empties his pistol into the Negro's body, crying, " This is your future."

This truly poetic play in lucid verse is rich in themes and suggestive power and austere in design, while mimes, rituals and masques are used with ironic significance. The Director, Jonathan Miller, envisaged it as a kind of inverted *Tempest*, the Spanish ship a black magic island and Cereno a drugged Prospero held captive by Babu, and he produced it in the formal and stylised manner of opera.

The play was also relevant to America's dilemma, domestic and foreign, including her ambiguous attitude to the contemporary Negro.

Prometheus Bound.   1971.

Lowell has adapted the first and only surviving play of Aeschylus's trilogy, where Prometheus, whose name means " forethought " and who had stolen fire from heaven for the benefit of mankind, is manacled to a crag at the command of a vengeful and violent Zeus.

Jonathan Miller's stylised production emphasised the tragic significance for today of an archetypal myth—the situation of one who refuses to compromise with arbitrary dictatorship and is consigned to solitary imprisonment and torture.

John McGrath (b. 1935).

Early realistic plays were critical of some aspects of society and during the early seventies McGrath became a committed writer identifying himself with a leading fringe group the 7·84 Theatre Company, so called because 7 per cent of the people in the country were said to own 84 per cent of the wealth. The Company is convinced that the underprivileged are also exploited culturally by mass media that erode their sense of values, and it aims to give workers both self-confidence and lively entertainment.

Events while Guarding the Bofors Gun.   1966.   M.

In situation, McGrath's masculine and dis-

ciplined play is a realistic counterpart of Giles Cooper's radio fantasy *Mathry Beacon*.

The futility of military routine is exposed with steely irony as, on a freezing night in Germany, during the Cold War, seven men guard the obsolete Bofors gun. The frustrating situation also engenders personal conflict. The uncontrollable desperado O'Rourke defies Lance Bombardier Evans. An insecure boy of 18, Evans is so obsessed by the hope that promotion may provide him a way of escape to England that he connives at insubordination. Finally O'Rourke's reckless suicide destroys them both.

Bakke's Night of Fame.   1968.

It is the prisoner's last night in an American condemned cell. Bakke, condemned for an apparently motiveless murder, enjoys being as provocative as possible. He entangles the priest with his contention that society is demanding not justice but revenge. His constant demand is that he shall meet his " buddy " the executioner, whom he so needles that the man is provoked to a violent outburst, gloating over his imminent task. Bakke, triumphant, has proved his point.

Plugged In.   1972.

The theme of three original one-act plays is the massive indifference of monopoly capitalism to individual human need. Free from didacticism they work indirectly, played in a cartoon-like setting of giant contemporary objects such as a Daz packet, symbolic of mass production, an Ionesco-like absurdity which in the first two plays is reflected in the dramatic situation. Both of these derive power from the association of the latent violence inherent in capitalism with loveless sexuality, repression and licence.

In *Plugged In*, the best of the trio, Kay, wife of a managing director, wearily sits on a street bench and obsessively recites disconnected newspaper reports of violence and disaster. She is joined by Derek, a sympathetic young working man who, preferring country walks, refuses to work more than one week in three.

He cannot stem her recital until his account of how in anger he had beaten his mistress excites Kay's own erotic masochistic feelings. Of her newspapers she cries, " I feel plugged in to history . . . taken over, crushed, by many many men . . . I need pain. It stops me suffering "; of her husband she says, " At night he drinks cocoa."

In this, the most powerful of the three plays, Kay is presented with psychological insight.

Fish in the Sea.   1975.

The subject, like the sit-in at Fisher Bendix, is the occupation by the workers of a factory that would otherwise be dismantled. The play, set fictionally in Liverpool, shows the varied repercussions in the complex left-wing family of the Maconochies and the daughters' suitors. Only the last part of the play culminates in the sit-in. Songs abound.

Little Red Hen.   1976.

A young girl is enthusiastic for Scots Nats but Granny recalls for her the socialist leaders of the twenties, Maclean, Maxton, Gallacher, the Scots Nats being represented as a middle-class phenomenon, their M.P.s " Bay City Rollers of Westminster ". The girl is won for socialism and becomes a " little red hen ". The play concludes as a working-class family less badly off is, however, inert before the tele. The didactic propaganda is less effective than the imaginative indirect approach of *Plugged In*.

Out of Our Heads.   1977.

Here the pub, not the tele, is blamed for inertia. Despite the efforts of Davey, energetic communist shop steward, the workers prefer drink in the *Brewers Arms* to branch meetings. He vainly tries to convert Harry, his old school friend now a drunken lout, but a flash back to Harry's school days shows him an obstinate fool even then. Scenes of Bacchic revels in other cultures provide lively diversion.

David Mercer (b. 1928).

Since 1961 Mercer has written television plays and also the film-script *Morgan or a Suitable Case for Treatment*. His first stage play, *Ride a Cock Horse*, was produced in 1965. He is concerned with the psychological predicament of today's able, educated young man of artisan origin (a reflection of his own situation as son of a Yorkshire engine-driver). He usually depicts him as estranged from his parents, disorientated and childless.

Originally drawn to Marxism, Mercer has recently said that whatever the society he is examining, " whether the Vatican or the Kremlin," he is most concerned with the individual " who's catching the muck that's flying off the ideological fan," but he has not yet successfully dramatised this concern on the stage.

Belcher's Luck. 1966.

The rickety English class structure is the framework of a complex play.

On his ramshackle country estate, contemptuously served by his former batman, Belcher, Sir Gerald is becoming senile, Helen, his icy, avaricious niece, persuades Belcher to goad her uncle to his death so that they may together inherit the property. She then scornfully dismisses Belcher in favour of Victor, his bastard son.

Victor, expensively educated by Sir Gerald, is mentally unstable and impotent, but this familiar Mercer figure is now on the periphery. The conflict between the chaste and physically timid Sir Gerald and the coarse and drunken Belcher has become the compelling focus.

After Haggerty. 1970. M.

Bernard Link, dejected after two unsuccessful marriages, suddenly finds his new flat invaded by the vociferous American Claire, deserted wife of the former tenant Haggerty. She brings her baby. Idiosyncratic " decorators " from " Rely-On " add to the comic confusion.

Meanwhile rather stereotyped flashbacks in the form of monologue reveal emotional stalemate; Bernard, international drama critic, addresses his parochial engine-driver father (invisible to the audience); and the adoring heiress, Claire, talks to the indifferent and anarchical Haggerty (also unseen).

Bernard's weary embarrassment is intensified by the unheralded arrival of his father, prejudiced and censorious, yet pathetic.

The play ends with two acts of cruelty. An empty coffin arrives from Haggerty indicating his demise, and Bernard, exasperated by his father's mental atrophy, symbolically hangs the funeral wreath round his neck.

A latent topic is disillusion with communism and violent protest, but Mercer's favourite theme, the alienation of artisan father and educated son, finds no resolution. The dialogue is vigorous and inventive, especially in invective.

Flint. 1970. M.

The play presents the improbable situation of a kindly septuagenarian Kensington vicar, Flint (Michael Hordern), agnostic since ordination, whose sexual obsessions and irregularities have long been the scandal of the diocese.

While conducting his latest affair in the vestry with the teen-age Dixie, a Liverpool Irish " scrubber " from Holloway gaol, already pregnant by another, Flint inadvertently sets the vestry on fire. Meanwhile his wife, hysterically crippled since her honeymoon, sets fire to the church. She is then murdered by her sister, formerly Flint's mistress, who promptly goes mad. Flint and Dixie escape abroad on his motor-bike and side-car. While she is in labour by the roadside, he helplessly crashes into an ammunition lorry and is killed.

Mercer has claimed that Flint's " humanity is more valuable and more deserving of our love and compassion than the institution to which he belongs." But to contrast the hero, presented as endearing, with some stagy clerics is unconvincing demonstration. Recent revivals of Shaw make *Flint* look paltry as a " play of ideas ",

especially as the individuals who " catch the muck " are the vicar's hapless women!

There is melodrama in plenty and some lively farcical comedy, but wordy meditations, virtually monologues, clog the action.

Duck Song. 1974. M.

Maurice, 71, wealthy, inept, is an artist passé, terrified of death. He reluctantly supports his brother Herbert, 61, formerly an expert cracksman, Herbert's daughter Jane, " an angry psychiatrist ", and her unemployed lover. On this ménage there intrude first a burglar, Herbert's latest accomplice, then Herbert's ex-wife from America, now thrice married. She introduces her young lover Lee, alias Swift Arrow, a Red Indian, their only luggage being a buffalo head on a pole like a totem. The act ends in a blinding flash of light.

The second act shows the same scene but devoid of furniture and Lee, now in Red Indian dress, meditates on the Indians' virtual extinction (as indicated by the buffalo head) and foresees a similar fate for the white imperialists. There is a series of desultory conversation and monologues as each expresses his regrets, disillusion, sense of futility and uncertainty. In this limbo death is apparently impossible, for three people are deliberately murdered without any effect, and the play ends amid signs of final cataclysm as all mournfully cluster around the totem unable even to sing their " swan song ".

Themes include art, imperialism, sex and love, confusion and disintegration, but characters and situation are unconvincing and the fable obscure.

Arthur Miller (b. 1915).

Arthur Miller, an admirer of Ibsen, shares his strong sense of moral purpose and of the individual's responsibility to the community. This is balanced by a sympathetic understanding of the insecurity of the individual in modern society.

Miller's characters, deeply felt and realised, are fallible men who suffer through their own errors of character or judgment in social conditions which are incomprehensible, indifferent, or even hostile to them.

A recurrent pattern is that of paternal responsibility within a patriarchal family unit, and the father's distress as he sees his errors hurting wife and sons. But the sense of responsibility flows outwards to society as a whole, of which the family is but the growing point. Significantly—apart from the benign mother-figures—Miller's most balanced characters are lawyers.

His plays are well constructed, the dialogue economic and telling, and he has progressed from the realism of *All My Sons*, published 1947, to much freer experimental techniques, while the prose style has become more fluid and eloquent.

Death of a Salesman. Published 1949. P.

A compassionate and finely-balanced play exposes the impingement of hire-purchase commercialism on the ageing salesman, Willy Loman, a weak, foolish, and deeply affectionate man, and also reveals his overwhelming sense of guilt towards wife and sons. The play is worked out on two planes, the inexorable present and Willy's past which obsessively enacts itself within his mind. The film version with Frederic March, is excellent.

The Crucible. Published 1953. P.

In 1949 Marion Starkey's *The Devil in Massachusetts* dealt with a witch-hunt in Salem in 1692, and pointed out its relevance to our own age, also rent by " ideological intensities." In 1952 the activities of McCarthy gave it a special urgency.

In this powerful play Miller uses this historical incident to depict not an indifferent society but one in which positive evil is unleashed. The evils he explores are the persecution of a minority and the interference of the Establishment in the individual conscience.

Characteristically Miller focuses attention on the plain man, John Proctor, and he invents his former adultery with Abigail, so that the play is not a partisan manifesto but a study of the complex contradictions of actual life. The self-righteous fanaticism of the persecutors and Proctor's own growth in self-knowledge and courage are faithfully and poignantly portrayed.

A View From the Bridge. 1956. P.

Eddie Carbone, a Brooklyn docker, is so gripped by jealous possessiveness of his wife's niece, that he eventually betrays her two kinsmen, illegal immigrants, to the Authorities.

In a play of repressed sexual passion, with hints of incest and homosexuality, Miller shows mastery of a kind of situation new to him and the heightening tension is realised in taut and disciplined sequences.

A lawyer, Alfieri, acts as a Greek chorus but is powerless to intervene, for Eddie infringes something more primitive than the legal code and it is by the primitive vendetta that he is eventually killed.

Incident at Vichy. 1966. P.

Miller here turns to the responsibility of society for the individual in a play which exposes the latent racial hostility which even the best men may unconsciously harbour.

The example he takes is antisemitism, the place and time Vichy in 1942, the scene a bleak anteroom within sound of a railway, where sealed trucks are deporting Jews to the furnaces of Auschwitz. Here a group of men and a boy, Jewish suspects, await investigation. There is an atmosphere of chill horror and suspense as each tries to summon up his own pitiful defence against the premonition of the ghastly journey he must embark on, once he is summoned behind the closed door.

Eventually only two men remain, the two most aware and articulate, Doctor Leduc, a Jewish analyst (Anthony Quayle) and Von Berg (Alec Guinness), the only Gentile of the group, a cultured and humane Viennese Prince, who is horrified by the vulgarity and barbarism of the Nazis.

In their final dialogue Doctor Leduc convinces the Prince of his unconscious antisemitism and the Prince gives his safe-conduct to the doctor.

A subsidiary theme of the play is the way society imposes extrinsically an identity on the individual, in this instance, as in Frisch's *Andorra*, the rôle of victim on the Jewish people. Through Leduc, Miller also criticises the Jews' acceptance of their rôle.

This disturbing play makes the greatest demands on the emotions, intelligence and humanity of the audience, who like the Prince to some degree undergo psycho-analysis. But the play is also characterised by a fine restraint. As in Aeschylus' *Agamemnon* the violence takes place behind closed doors, with the significant difference that in Miller's play the chorus and victims are identical.

The Price. 1969.

Two brothers confront each other in an attic crowded with the heavy furniture of their dead father, a financier ruined in the Depression. Its imminent sale is the occasion of their first encounter in sixteen years.

Victor Franz, who had given up a scientific career to support his father, is now a policeman at retiring age but too immobilised by his past to begin a new career in spite of the hysterical pressure of his wife. Walter, a surgeon, in his slick pursuit of success has had a prolonged breakdown and a broken marriage. The " price ", ostensibly that of the furniture, is the price each has paid for his decision in life and its inexorable results.

The brothers ruthlessly dissect and probe back to the motivation of their choice. Walter is forced to admit calculated callousness but drives Victor to realise that his sense of social responsibility was also flawed, for he had sentimentally sacrificed his potentiality to a disingenuous father too cowardly to work again.

But no reconciliation ensues, Victor angrily refusing the dubious job which Walter offers as a salve to conscience.

Miller describes his play as stripped to the skeletal structure of two lives, the home the dead husk from which they had developed. But the characters are complex and through the Ibsenlike situation runs a thread of delightful and significant comedy. Solomon, a ancient Jew, survivor of wildly differing professions and four marriages, is the furniture appraisor and embodies the resilience lacking in the Franzes. When he falls, he bounces. He shrewdly decides to buy all the furniture at a fair price and at curtain fall sits gleefully in the chair of the beaten father, chuckling exuberantly at his decision to begin life afresh.

The play is realistic, but the muted significance of various remnants of bric-a-brac is symbolic in effect. Organised with meticulous artistry, it is lucid and profound, and rich in the wisdom of experience distilled. Acted without a break it holds the audience absorbed.

John Mortimer (b. 1923).

Mortimer, a barrister, first won success with his short plays, such as *The Dock Brief*, 1957, and *Lunch Hour*, 1960 (M). Here his talents are seen at their best, especially his gift for seizing on an unusual encounter between " the lonely, the neglected, the unsuccessful ", whom he envisages in realistic settings of shabby gentility, and he is particularly sympathetic to those who allow their fantasy to swamp actuality.

But the moment of insight that gives pathos to his short plays is not enough to illuminate those of full length, like *What Shall We Tell Caroline?* and *The Wrong Side of the Park*, which lack substance. *Two Stars for Comfort*, 1960 (M), is also unsatisfactory. *The Judge*, 1967, (M), and *A Voyage Round My Father*, 1970 (M), were more successful.

Peter Nichols.

Nichols has long been interested in music-hall and revue and he expertly deploys their techniques of direct address to the audience. He successfully uses one of the dramatis personae as an ironical commentator able to step easily in and out of the action.

He has a remarkable talent for conveying with comedy and compassion the sharp pain that can underlie the absurdities of personal relationships and he is intelligently concerned with specific social problems.

A Day in the Death of Joe Egg. 1967. F.

Nichols has shown remarkable sensitivity and skill in developing his theme—the especial difficulties of monogamy when the only child, a ten-year-old girl, is hopelessly spastic. He uses comic techniques of revue as the parents re-enact their frustrating encounters with doctors and clergy. But below the jesting facade grows the realisation that the wife's compulsive maternity blinds her to her husband's needs and that his endurance is crumbling.

Nichols has a spastic child and says " It's a play about marriage. . . . Not autobiographical."

The National Health. 1969. F.

In a bleak men's ward in a decaying hospital the staff are reasonably competent but faceless. Interpolated are brief TV scenes of *Nurse Norton's Affair*, a burlesque of the rosy view of the medical profession as seen on popular TV.

The vignettes of the consultant, the chaplain, and the visitor, have the pungency of revue. The male nurse acts as compère to the whole, and also as devil's advocate who maliciously destroys the beginning of a positive relationship between a neurotic but protective schoolmaster and the alcoholic he is helping.

The play has the sharp comedy associated not with impartial enquiry but with astringent criticism. It has been seen as an image of Britain's own condition.

Forget-me-not Lane. 1971. F.

In a brisk comedy Nichols deftly spans the generations, for middle-aged Frank slips in and out of the action as he watches his adolescent self played simultaneously by a young actor, and ruefully and sardonically interprets his war-time experiences. As the only child of a divided home he had reacted against his Puritanical, absurdly unsuccessful father, Charles, joining his easy-going mother in revue entertainments for the troops. Preoccupied with sex, but too shy to respond to the overtures of Ursula (later his wife) he indulged in fantasy.

Later Frank faces the breakdown of his own marriage, and caught in " the genetic trap " finds himself echoing Charles' mannerisms. Too late he understands his pathetic father. Motifs from 1971 reappear later.

Chez Nous. 1974. F.

In realistic comedy Nichols exposes the malaise of an affluent, permissive group.

Dick, 40, a paediatrician, has written a book advocating sexual freedom at puberty. By changing the title to The Nubile Baby and providing a provocative dust-jacket his publishers have promoted this to a best-seller and he and his homely wife Liz have bought and modernised the farm in France they previously rented.

Here they again welcome Phil and Di their " oldest friends ". While through the war Dick had chastely waited for Di, she had faithlessly married Phil, now pining for a son, and strains soon show.

Nichols adroitly places successive shocks: first that the hosts have acquired a fourth child, baby Sammy. Then Liz blurts out that Sammy is son to their eldest daughter Jane, now 14. Last a French peasant tells Dick that he recognises Phil as Jane's lover. Long pent-up recriminations ensue, Dick indignant and cheated, Phil torn between shame and pride in paternity, his longing to adopt Sammy opposed by Di's disdain and Liz's maternity, Dick urging Di to join in a romantic elopement. But neither Di nor Dick can finally cut adrift, and in a muddled compromise the couples agree to share Sammy between them.

Dick echoes Frank, gnawed by vain regrets but now presented with greater detachment.

Privates on Parade. 1977. F.

After the atypical The Freeway, 1974, Nichols presents hilarious comedy. " The Song and Dance Unit S.E. Asia " is playing in Singapore about 1950. Their " Captain " Terri is an outrageous " Queen ", happiest in drag, impersonating Dietrich et. al., lavish in sexy innuendo and prattling of Clementina Attlee and Jessica Christ. Other types are sharply drawn, the genial, foul-mouthed " Corporal " Bonny, RAF men Kevin and Eric, and Sylvia the promiscuous Eurasian of 24, who seduces Steve the idealist young recruit.

The blimpish Major Giles, proclaiming a Christian campaign against Communism, leads the company into the Malayan jungle. Here the plot creaks badly, for the brutal RSM Reg, who had sold arms to Communists and, suspecting Sylvia and Steve's cognisance, faked his own death, stole Giles' plans and ambushed the concert party. Bonny is killed and others wounded.

" Keeping rubber safe for Britain " is poor recompense to the wounded who board the ship home, Kevin now impotent, Eric, like Dick, returning to a faithless fiancée, Steve ominously married to Sylvia. Last Reg, dressed as a Chinese, slinks aboard. The gay romp ends with astringent implications, but the play lacks depth.

Eugene O'Neill (1888–1953).

Although O'Neill's work belongs to the first half of the century, three of his later works had their delayed première here in the 'fifties, two of them making a great impression.

The Iceman Cometh. Published 1947.

In a naturalistic play, whose prototype is Gorky's The Lower Depths, down-and-outs await the arrival of the dionysiac Hickey. But Hickey has just murdered his wife and his abortive attempt to rouse them from " pipe dreams " to reality leaves them sunk even more deeply than before in drink and self-deceit.

Long Day's Journey Into Night. Published 1955.

An avowed autobiographical play depicts O'Neill's family on the day when his mother (Gwen Ffrangcon Davies) relapses into drug addiction and Eugene learns that he must leave the doomed circle for a sanatorium. As it was there that he chose his vocation, this constitutes the one note of hope in a deeply mournful reverie. The Freudian love-hate relationships are unfolded with tender understanding.

Joe Orton (1933–67).

Orton was a successful commercial exponent of black comedy who also won praise from serious critics especially for his dialogue.

His range is narrow and he is preoccupied with crime, perverted sexuality, and violence portrayed without inhibition as hilariously comic, sometimes with satiric effect. The macabre plots occasion a flow of deadpan repartee, normally smutty, sometimes merely facetious, often very apt and funny indeed, always a parody of the genteel. Nearly all Orton's characters speak alike and are as undifferentiated in their lingo as in their lack of morality.

The satire is in the form of caricature or parody and apart from its implications it is almost impossible to discover in Orton any expression of human value or aspiration. It is not always easy to discriminate between the unsavoury matter of his plays and the expertise and aplomb with which it is manipulated, and some feel that he defaces the image of life.

Entertaining Mr. Sloane. 1964. P.

The handsome young wastrel, Sloane, already a murderer, finds a cosy refuge with Kath. A slattern of forty, she smothers him with motherliness and, sexually insatiable, she seduces him from the first night. Her brother, Ed, a homosexual, soon employs Sloane as his " chauffeur ". When Sloane tries to escape their possessiveness, his brutal murder of their father puts him into their power and they agree quite literally to share him, each having him for six months at a time.

The play scores by a skilfully handled plot, an ironic " poetic justice " and the sly and genteel euphemisms of the salacious dialogue, and it won the London Critics Variety Award as the best play of 1964.

Loot. 1966. M. P.

Helped by his accomplice a young criminal secretes the loot from a burglary in his mother's coffin. This is the key situation in a macabre and complicated farce, which is also an exuberant caricature of funeral ritual, of a police which is represented as hamhanded and venal, and of cheap detective fiction. The characters are cardboard puppets manipulated by the plot and the play is notable for the fact that vice is completely triumphant.

Crimes of Passion. 1967. M.

A double bill consists of The Ruffian on the Stair, 1966, Orton's first play, and The Erpingham Camp. 1967. Frequent and fussy scene changes betray their origin in radio and television respectively.

The Ruffian on the Stair. 1967. M.

The occupants of the room are Mike, a criminal living with an ex-prostitute, Joyce. The intruder is a boy ostensibly seeking revenge for his brother with whom he had lived in homosexual incest, and whom Mike had murdered. He is in fact seeking his own death and provokes Mike to murder him by pretending that he has seduced Joyce.

The Erpingham Camp. 1967. M.

A satire on holiday camps shows an uprising of the merrymakers who eventually kill Erpingham. The ebullient parody has some highly comic incidents. Orton's sketch lacks complexity and Erpingham meets his fate because he is stupid and dictatorial.

What the Butler Saw. 1969. M.

A farce in a psychiatric clinic is typically Orton in its discrepancy between decorous speech and indecent behaviour. In the original production pace and invention seemed to flag but a revival by the Royal Court in 1975 revealed the play's inherent potential.

John Osborne (b. 1929).

Osborne is endowed with considerable theatrical talent and a torrential rhetoric, most effective in impetuous monologue and in hostile denunciation.

These gifts were at once apparent in *Look Back in Anger*, 1956, where the protagonist, Jimmy Porter, makes a strident attack on the assumptions and values of the middle class. The play was perfectly timed and its success immediate, for Jimmy voiced the pent-up frustrations of the radicals of his generation, baffled by the complacence of an establishment which had muddled through two wars and left them without any sense of security or direction. Moreover, the frisson of surprise at sight of Jimmy's shabby provincial attic delighted playgoers jaded by the convention of stage drawing-room.

Osborne had broken new ground and for some years went on to experiment, attempting in 1957 and 1961 Brechtian techniques. But his two plays of 1968 are conventional in both structure and plushy, affluent settings, while the heady tirade of invective has dwindled, as the characters spew out a bitter personal malaise in disconnected complaint.

Osborne is most successful in the portrayal of his dominating and eloquent protagonists, like Archie Rice, Bill Maitland and Laurie. Even when disorganised by self-pity they convince us as we watch them driven on by sado-masochistic urges to destroy both themselves and their circle. A succession of famous actors have brought them unforgettably to life. But the other dramatis personae, serving as "feed", are often presented perfunctorily, distinguishable only by a few mannerisms and in the assertions of their fellows. This kind of characterisation is damaging to structure. Dramatic confrontation is spasmodic so that the play becomes slack. Time has disclosed Osborne's tenuous grip on structure generally. His expositions are sometimes maladroit or even misleading, the development desultory and the climax superimposed.

The mood of Osborne's protagonists, rejection of the present and sentimental nostalgia for the era of Britain's imperial and colonial power, has now invaded the minor characters, so the play tends to be uniformly negative and sometimes downright dreary. Such an idiom cannot be defended as satire, which is positive in its implications.

Look Back in Anger. 1956. F.

Jimmy Porter, product of "white-tile" university, has married Alison a colonel's daughter and their misalliance triggers off his furious diatribe against her and her family. When she returns to her parents because pregnant, her friend Helena promptly becomes Jimmy's mistress, until Alison, having lost her baby returns and is reduced to grovelling to Jimmy before they can resume their unstable relationship.

The play, with its fusion of sexual and social tension, made an immediate impact on Osborne's contemporaries. It cleverly synthesises a strident denunciation of Alison and of the privileged classes, so that Jimmy's marriage is like a token rape and plunder of the establishment, the excitement given a sensational fillip by his liaison with Helena.

Jimmy's torrential rhetoric is inebriating and

the surprises well judged, but the surrounding characters are too compliant to be convincing. This dramatic defect and the author's ambivalent attitude to Jimmy himself, give a false authority to an immature and wantonly destructive protagonist.

The Entertainer. 1957. F.

Osborne here attempts to use the Brechtian device of "endistancing", employing a framework of music-hall scenes, where Archie Rice (Olivier), a seedy comedian, tries to hold the stage with tawdry patter and songs in a dubious show with nudes called "Rock'n Roll New'd Look." These are intended to "endistance" realistic scenes of Archie's shabby home. But the "endistancing" device serves little purpose for the overall mood of unquestioned disillusion "whooped up" by drink and patter is in both planes unrelieved. Querulous complaint that England has lost the glory and glamour of Edwardian days is crystallised on the realistic plane by the report of the death of Archie's son at Suez and in the music-hall by the presentation of a nude Britannia, wearing only her helmet.

Luther. 1961. F.

Luther is a less subjective work, although Osborne again takes for his hero a rebel, the son of an unsympathetic mother, and emphasises the emotional and not the intellectual sources of Luther's protests.

The play is imitative of Brecht's *Galileo* both in its loose "epic" structure and also in the attempt to present the protagonist in an equivocal light. The first two acts give a sympathetic and leisurely portrayal of Luther's early conflicts of conscience and vigorous attack on superstition while in the third act he is hurriedly presented as having treacherously let down the peasants who had been encouraged to rise against the Emperor. But the political reasons for Luther's dilemma are not even hinted at and we are invited not to think, as in *Galileo*, but to condemn while ignorant of relevant facts. Structurally this sudden *volte face* is most damaging to the play.

The most effective scenes, such as Tetzel's selling of indulgences and Martin's sermon at Wittenberg are splendid rhetoric, without a word of dialogue and directed straight at the audience.

Skilful period production and the acting of Albert Finney as Luther made the play theatrically effective.

Two Plays for England. 1962.

Two slight plays make a double bill. *The Blood of the Bambergs*, a send-up of royal weddings, and *Under Plain Cover*, an attack on press sensationalism, rely on parody and mimicry.

Inadmissible Evidence. 1964. F.

The play provides the sensational spectacle of a middle-aged solicitor, Bill Maitland (Nicol Williamson), obsessed with sex, and disintegrating under the influence of drink and drugs.

The play opens with a dream sequence as Maitland is tried in the court of his own mind. What follows is his rancid outpouring of self-pity, as during forty-eight hours, he is progressively deserted by staff, clients and mistress. Maitland's flagellation of himself and his fate is unrelieved.

A Patriot for Me. 1965.

The protagonist of a play, produced privately, is Redl, a distinguished army officer of the Austro-Hungarian Empire, who through his homosexuality is blackmailed into becoming a spy for Tsarist Russia.

Osborne is here objective and ironic. He uses a series of brief scenes with significant juxtaposition of characters and swift dialogue. The first act, showing Redl's gradual discovery of his nature is discriminating and adroit and the drag ball which opens Act Two is an astonishing *tour de force*.

Act Three shows a decline of tension as Redl, now a spy, himself declines, his fibre coarsened through a sequence of sordid infidelities by male lovers and prostitutes. His final unmasking and suicide is almost a foregone conclusion.

A Bond Honoured. 1966.

Osborne, in a free translation of *La Fianza Satisfecha*, is said to have distorted Lope de Vega's play.

Time Present. 1968. F.

The protagonist, Pamela, is a neurotic actress. Emotionally strangled by the familiar " Electra complex ", an exaggerated devotion to her father, a once famous actor, now dying off-stage, she is unable to establish any satisfactory human relationship, in spite of love affairs and the friendship of the devoted Constance, a successful Labour M.P., in whose flat she is living.

Pamela's role is static and verbal; reiteration of her shallow scheme of values (a preference for style over vulgarity), sentimental reminiscences of her father and a relentless spate of contemptuous and indiscriminate derision. Phrased in modish argot some gibes have a bitter wit, pleasing to the prejudices of the illiberal.

Pamela's alienation, which should arouse compassion, becomes tiresome because of the play's apparent assumption that her outpourings have objective value.

The Hotel in Amsterdam. 1968. F.

United by fear and dislike of their employer, a film magnate, cryptically referred to as K.L., three couples retreat to a luxury hotel in Amsterdam as a hide-out from his encroachments.

They pass the weekend in denouncing K.L., drinking, and exchanging desultory jokes and complaints about homosexuals, mothers and " the working class ", until the unwelcome arrival of a relative and the news that K.L. has killed himself disturb the tenuous camaraderie.

Such a structure is perfunctory. Only the garrulous and petulant Laurie (Scofield) is individualised and the characters reveal and discover little of value about themselves or each other.

A revealing sidelight is that Laurie fancies himself as an authority on " the creative process ", boasting, " What I do, I get out of the air." Is this Osborne's method?

West of Suez. 1971. F.

In a sub-tropical island, formerly British, an expatriate couple entertain her family; three sisters, two with husbands, and her father, Wyatt (Ralph Richardson), once a distinguished writer.

The relatives and a host of supernumeraries drift in and out, usually preceded by a dissection of their deficiencies, but Wyatt firmly holds the centre. Now a television sage, he is a consummate poseur, effusively professing that consideration for others which he conspicuously lacks and pathetically anxious for adulation.

He and his coterie are privileged but bored and uneasy, " perched between one civilisation and the next ", and nostalgically recalling army officer life in India.

The play is without incident until a sudden melodramatic finale. First a hippie American student makes a violent verbal onslaught and almost immediately armed islanders enter and gun Wyatt down.

Osborne obviously follows Chekhov in depicting a decaying and powerless society but fails to catch Chekhov's humane portrayal of the complex and subtle relationships within a closely knit group.

Later plays, *A Sense of Detachment,* 1972 (F), *The End of Me Old Cigar,* 1975, and *Watch it Come Down,* 1976, did not enhance Osborne's reputation.

Alexander Ostrovsky (1823-86).

The eminent Russian playwright is unfortunately little known in this country.

The Storm. 1966.

Written in 1859, Ostrovsky's fine realistic play portrays a social group unfamiliar to us, the petty tradesmen of an isolated township, who are avaricious, ignorant and bigoted.

The widow, Kabanovna, is a warped and ruthless matriarch, who saps the vitality of her weak son and cruelly tyrannises over his hapless wife, Katerina. The lonely, susceptible girl yields to the love of a young stranger from Moscow. Then sheltering in a church during a violent storm, she is overcome by superstitious dread and remorse. She confesses and later kills herself.

Harold Pinter (b. 1930).

The versatile Pinter, one of our foremost playwrights, began as an actor and also directs plays and films.

He exerts an almost hypnotic effect over his audience with his uncanny sense of tension and the telling pause. Whether his novel situations find resolution in final surprise or disturb with teasing uncertainty, they have a satisfying elegance of design.

His art developed quickly and two main phases can now be distinguished. The plays culminating in *The Caretaker,* 1960, were concerned with the underprivileged and showed a growing sense of compassion. His later plays were much concerned with sexual dominance and jealousy, the background usually sophisticated, the attitude detached.

Whatever the subject, the plays have a poetic resonance, due in part to Pinter's intuitive understanding of man's subconscious life, especially his memories and fears. The basis is actuality. As a Jewish boy growing up in East London he had personal experience of hostility and aggression, intensified by his knowledge of Europe's suffering Jewry.

His recurring image is of a room that is invaded and he has said, " I don't think it is all that surrealistic and curious because surely this thing of people arriving at the door has been happening in Europe in the last twenty years. Not only the last twenty years, the last two to three hundred."

But his basic situation is so striking, that, like poetry, it can be interpreted on more than one level. Those periods of private anxiety, when the distraught individual holds on precariously to some tiny foothold, also image the predicament of the whole human race, where existence is threatened by ungovernable forces. Like Kafka, whom he admires, Pinter expresses vividly the feeling of some inscrutable menace from some vague hinterland invading humdrum human life.

Some of the disturbing fascination Pinter exerts is due to the state of uncertainty he creates but the questions posed have become increasingly significant. He deliberately rejects the Ibsenite rôle of the omniscient, for people's memories are inconsistent and it is particularly difficult to be precise about people's inner lives and motives, especially if they are inarticulate.

Pinter has affinities with dramatists of the absurd and is closest in feeling to Beckett. He shares with Ionesco an awareness that tragedy can co-exist with comedy, saying " Even tragedy is funny."

Pinter is a stylist in dialogue, especially in Cockney and the shabby genteel, in clichés and non-sequiturs. He records talk rather than conversation, what Martin Buber calls " monologue disguised as dialogue ". His characters' monologues are spiced with boasting as each strives for ascendancy.

The theme of power over others is indeed the keynote of much of his best work.

Esslin's study " *The Peopled Wound* " (M. 1970), is scholarly and illuminating.

Pinter's early one-acters include *The Room,* 1957 (M), which includes some insignificant factual contradictions and ends in melodrama, and *The Dumb Waiter,* 1960 (M and P), which shows Ben and Gus, hired assassins, harrassed by an Ionesco-like dumb-waiter, while awaiting their victim in a basement. It is then revealed that Ben is deputed to kill Gus.

The Birthday Party. 1958. M.

In Pinter's first full-length play, the room is in a shabby boarding-house kept by the motherly Meg. Here Stanley, who claims to have been a concert pianist, has taken refuge, until he is suddenly unnerved by the arrival of a sinister pair, the specious Goldberg and the brutal McCann. They subject Stanley to a fantastic catechism, a parody of brain-washing, and during his phoney and ludicrous birthday party he is blindfolded and his glasses broken—symbolic of destruction of vision. Next morning the pair lead Stanley away, conventionally dressed, incapable of speech, his personality disintegrated.

The menace here is economically sustained, and the fact that the identity of the three main characters is never revealed adds to the terror. Some see Stanley as the political refugee; some, since he was a pianist, as the artist made to conform. But by its deliberate lack of definiteness, the play has a wide reference to all who seek refuge from a hostile world.

The Caretaker. 1960. M.

The play is set in a junk-filled room, where the kindly Aston lives in his brother's derelict house. He brings home an old tramp, Davies, who grudgingly agrees to stay as " caretaker " and then tries to encroach further by playing off one brother against the other, until finally rejected by both.

In a naturalistic background Pinter has created two unforgettable characters, presented in psychological depth with reference to their past, and has depicted their failure to come to terms with compassion and restraint.

Davies is one who bites the hand that feeds him. His very identity is suspect for he passes under an assumed name, having " left his papers " years ago " at Sidcup. " But he never retrieves them. Aston haltingly tells Davies how he once had periods of unique lucidity, now destroyed by a terrifying shock-treatment in mental hospital, but Davies' only reaction is later to threaten him. It is remarkable that when Aston finally rejects Davies' last encroachment the plight of the tramp should seem as pitiful as Aston's own, Pinter having wisely rejected his first intention to end the play with the violent death of Davies.

This mature play shows a man actually opening the door to his fears and mastering them. Aston in his long speech faces the wrong done to him by " people ". His unique vision destroyed, his only creative outlet has been tinkering with his junk, but as he tries to break out of his isolation by befriending another crippled human being, he unhappily meets a man so twisted by his own suffering and resentment that he cannot respond. Some find in Aston a moving image of the mystic and artist in man whose creative insight is destroyed by an imperceptive and mechanical society.

There followed four short plays, *A Slight Ache* and *A Night Out*, 1961 (M), and then two with a chic setting, *The Collection*, 1962 (M), and *The Lover*, 1961 (M).

The Homecoming. 1965. M.

Teddy, a Doctor of Philosophy in an American University, brings his wife, Ruth, on a surprise visit to his former home in North London, where Max, his widowed father, still lives with his two younger sons, Lenny and Joey. It is gradually revealed that Ruth before her marriage had been a " model " and the family decide to keep her as their common mistress, while the brutal Lenny, a pimp, arranges that she shall earn her keep as a prostitute.

Because this is presented with clinical detachment, the audience is induced to suspend emotion. Only at the last moment is this cool acceptance shattered when Max, aged 70, crawls sobbing to Ruth asking to be kissed and the audience is shocked into feeling the degradation.

On the surface the play is a disillusioned glance at life. It may also be interpreted as a fantasy of sexual gratification, which in a dream state escapes the taboo of ethical and humane feeling. The use of some accepted sex symbols and the slow and trance-like acting, especially that of Ruth, is dream-like and the final shock is analogous to waking up and realising what the dream has implied.

It is possible also to see in Teddy an acquiescent Hamlet. He returns home from a foreign university to find marital infidelity, for it is disclosed that his mother had been unfaithful with an uncle figure and Hamlet's scornful words to Ophelia suggest that Ruth may represent her.

Landscape and *Silence.* 1969. M.

Beckett's influence is apparent in two short plays, where inconclusive words and action are pared to the bone and whose theme is personal isolation. Both recall *Krapp's Last Tape* in their repetitive memories of past love.

Landscape, originally broadcast, is set in the kitchen of a country house, where the middle-aged caretaker appears to be telling his wife (Peggy Ashcroft) of the day's commonplace events and recalls an infidelity. She, absorbed in dreaming of a former tender encounter on the sea-shore, ignores him.

Silence is even more spare and brief. Ellen sits between two men. Both have loved her in vain, although she has all but forgotten them. They are almost immobile, their only speech interlacing, fragmentary memories of love. These are redolent of the country, mostly at nightfall. The men are faintly characterised and setting is discarded in favour of " three areas ". *Silence* recalls Beckett's *Play*. Pinter was later to develop further the theme of nostalgic memory.

The Tea Party and *The Basement.* 1970. M.

Two plays originally seen on television were perfectly suited to the medium since both make swift transitions from objective happenings to subjective fantasies. They were however translated as faithfully as possible to the stage. Both involve the theme of encroachment.

The Basement, written first, is like a chic version of *The Caretaker*. A fastidious bachelor, Law, welcomes to his flat an old friend, Stott, who brings his girl friend. Both promptly take possession, even of the host's bed. Law alternates between friendly chat and suppressed fantasies, such as romantic seduction of the girl and violent duelling with Stott. The play suddenly concludes with rôles reversed, Law being the visitor demanding admittance.

The Tea Party centres on Disson, a middle-aged plumbing tycoon. Just before his marriage to a young woman socially his superior, he engages a new secretary, Wendy, with whom he is soon infatuated. But his patronising wife comes to the office as his secretary, and he suspects an incestuous liaison between her and her parasite brother.

Since wife, secretary and even he as husband have each a curious distorted double, Disson's vision, not surprisingly, becomes confused. A single table-tennis ball appears to him as two and he can only touch Wendy when blindfolded. His hysterical blindness culminates, at an office tea party, in complete loss of sight. Poor Disson had from the outset been blind to his social position and his sexual needs.

The play has echoes of *The Birthday Party*, but now all on a fashionable level.

Old Times. 1971. M.

Deeley and his wife Kate await the first visit of Anna, her friend in London twenty years before. As Deeley jestingly questions the laconic Kate he is startled to learn that the two girls " lived together ", and the waiting Anna then comes forward from the symbolic half-light.

In an exchange of conflicting memories Deeley and Anna begin to strive for possession of Kate, even in retrospect.

In the second act Deeley alone with Anna insists that he recognises her as the girl he had picked up at a pub. Anna's riposte is that she was then wearing Kate's underwear so that his memory of the two girls becomes more confused.

His jealousy of Anna, inflamed by her talk of her expensive home, flares out in anger at her mention of the word " passion ". But Kate remains withdrawn until a strange final speech.

She had, she says, seen Anna lying dead in their room with earth on her face and her place taken by a man. She had tried to plaster his face with earth but he had resisted. Is this Kate's rejection of both rivals? Anna turns to go. Deeley sobs silently. Then brightly lit all three are seen as in their opening conversation, as though locked together by their past.

Pinter has skilfully fused the themes of nostalgia and sexual rivalry.

No Man's Land. 1975.

Hirst (Richardson), a wealthy alcoholic in his sixties, once man of letters, brings home a seedy contemporary Spooner (Gielgud), self-styled poet. Spooner trying to insinuate himself into this luxurious home offers himself as friend. Hirst, drunk, says, "No man's land . . does not move . . or change . . or grow old . . remains . . forever . . icy," falls and crawls away. Alone Spooner is startled by the arrival of two tough, scornful men servants, and realises he must struggle with them also for ascendancy. Hirst, returning, professes not to know Spooner, and is plied with drink by the servants, who lead him away, threatening Spooner violently and plunging the room into darkness.

Next day Hirst claims Spooner as one of his Oxford set, their friends' photographs still preserved in his albums. But they quarrel, the servants return and Spooner makes his supreme effort. He could revive the nostalgia embalmed in "the albums", act as chef and secretary to Hirst, who would be chief guest at his poetry readings. The bodyguard stand dumbfounded. At last Hirst's ambiguous reply is, "Let us change the subject, for the last time. What have I said?" By sleight of words one servant traps him, saying, "So that nothing else will happen for ever."

Spooner replies with Hirst's own words, telling him he is in no man's land. "I'll drink to that," replies Hirst.

The audience was gripped by the play's uncertainties, manoeuvring and menace.

Stephen Poliakoff.

Poliakoff speaks for young folk who feel urban society is dehumanised.

City Sugar. 1975.

Nicola works in a dull Leicester super store, permeated by programmes of her hero, disc jockey Brazil. He encourages her phone-calls and she reaches his final competition, but is gratuitously humiliated before he cynically moves on to London.

Strawberry Fields. 1977.

Charlotte, strawberry blonde, and frenetic Ken, both of the "English People's Party" travel north along the neon-lit motorways. They pick up a hitch-hiking teacher, Nick, indifferent to their jargon. At the end of Act I a policeman asks to search Charlotte's bag. Taking out a gun, she kills him. In Act II Ken decamps and Charlotte, realising that Nick does not credit her paranoid fantasies of imminent civil war, shoots him and goes on alone. The play has a nightmare suspense.

Terence Rattigan (1911-1977).

Rattigan is expert in the well-made light comedy. Later, more serious works include The Deep Blue Sea, 1952 revived 1977, and Ross, 1960.

A Bequest to the Nation. 1970.

Spanning Nelson's last days in England the play's theme is conflict between his infatuation for Emma and his duty, to which she generously yields. Nelson's schoolboy nephew is cleverly used to embody duty, to act as link with Lady Nelson and as the "juvenile sensibility" which focuses Emma's tipsy decline.

In Praise of Love. 1973.

In a double bill a thirty-minute curtain raiser proved unsuccessful, while many critics considered the second play one of Rattigan's best.
Before Dawn.
An unfortunate inversion of Puccini's Tosca represents the chief of police successfully seducing the heroine while her lover faces execution. It is further marred by some awkward puns.
After Lydia.
Lydia is married to the literary critic, gruff Sebastian. She disguises the fact that she is dying of leukæmia, unaware that he already knows. Each suffers in trying to save the other pain. Finally Lydia can face death, secure in the realisation of her husband's love.

Cause Célèbre. 1977.

Founded on a trial of 1935, the play concerns Alma Rattenbury of Bournemouth, 38 and infatuated with her 17-year-old handyman, who murders her elderly husband. Tried as his accomplice, she is, despite adverse public opinion acquitted, but commits suicide. Rattigan complicates his effective trial scene and the plot by the invention of a forewoman of jury, hostile to Alma.

David Rudkin.

David Rudkin won a drama award for the most promising playwright of 1962. But it was not until 1973 that any other reckonable stage play appeared. He has wide and unusual interests, uses words evocatively, and has the power of creating an uncanny sense of suspense and the macabre. His plays are deeply felt but sometimes overloaded in theme.

Afore Night Come. 1962. P.

Revived by the R.S.C. in 1974, the play shows a Midland pear orchard, where a gang of superstitious pickers prepare to re-enact a gruesome fertility murder. Chance witnesses are threatened with the asylum from which the pathetic Johnny has been allowed out for only a few hours to act as carter.

During a tense afternoon the gang ominously focus their hostility on a filthy old tramp who they believe brings misfortune and blight. Increasingly agitated Johnny incoherently tries to persuade Larry, a casual student worker, to escape with him but is repulsed. Then "afore night come" the gang plunge their knives into the tramp's body, score it with the cross and then behead and bury it, their grisly ritual once more accomplished.

But in giving him his fountain pen Larry transforms Johnny's shame to radiant confidence.

Cries from Casement as his bones are brought to Dublin. 1973.

A radio play, somewhat disappointing when staged, concerns Roger Casement the F.O. diplomat secretly in league with the Sinn Fein and executed as a traitor. When his bones are taken to Dublin for ceremonial reburial he emerges from his coffin to describe and re-enact his life. Rudkin, connecting Casement's espousal of rebellion with his homosexual experiences in Black Africa, sees him as an outsider. The play ends with a plea for Irish unity.

Ashes. 1974.

The title is symbolic. In their desperate efforts to have a child Colin and Anne undergo a humiliating sequence of tests and advice and the strain of a "pregnancy at risk". In the maternity ward Anne suffers hysterectomy, her uterus consigned to ashes. Even an application to adopt is refused.

There is then a sudden change of subject, with little structural connection but expanding the theme. Colin, returned from Belfast, tells of the death of a Protestant uncle, in "an atrocious anagram of people". His cousin says, "We shall fight till Ulster is in ashes ", but Colin, unable to concur, feels rejected as " tribal son " and connects this with his own childlessness.

The Sons of Light. 1976.

An inordinately long play, springing from a deep personal struggle, was thrice rejected both by the R.S.C. and the National, before a short version of over 3 hours was produced at Newcastle University.

The scene is a blighted island where from a monstrous ikon Nebewohl forces his slave gang to work in an underworld of agony and death. Finally the evangelical son of a new pastor urges the gang to destroy the false ikon, the island is torn by a tremendous geological upheaval and its inhabitants freed.

Jean-Paul Sartre (b. 1905).

The plays of the French philosopher Sartre (see J18) can be fully appreciated only in the light of his atheistic existentialist convictions. As a communist Sartre vindicates violence and his protests against the absurdity of existence, especially that of the bourgeoisie, are expressed not as Ionesco's in images themselves absurd but through the medium of the well-made play.

Influential British premières seen since 1950 include *Lucifer and the Lord* (P), *Nekrassov* (P) and *Altona* (P).

James Saunders (b. 1925).

In Saunders' very early work, as *Alas Poor Fred* and *Ends and Echoes*, 1960, the influence of Ionesco is apparent. But his most promising work was in the '60s. In *Next Time I'll Sing to You*, 1963, on the hermit of Canfield who died in 1942, Saunders uses the style of Pirandello's *Six Characters* to explore the theme of solitude. In *A Scent of Flowers*, 1964, the protagonist is a young girl who, because of a moral conflict, has just committed suicide. It shows her touching encounters with friends and relatives from whom she had vainly sought help. *The Borage Pigeon Affair*, produced in 1969 by amateurs, was seen as an image of Enoch Powell's protests at immigration. But in 1975 it was produced by professionals with stress on the lively and amusing conflict between a Labour Councillor who keeps pigeons in his attic to the indignation of the Borage Medical Officer of Health, a Conservative Councillor, a situation further distorted by the media.

Anthony Shaffer (b. 1926).

The playwright, once a barrister, is twin brother of Peter Shaffer (*q.v.*). In *Sleuth*, 1970, a famous writer of stories about a wealthy amateur detective plans to outwit his wife's lover, and inviting him to their country house he there emulates his own fictional hero.

Shaffer combines an ingenious detective thriller all suspense and surprise with a witty parody of the genre he presents. *The Murderer*, 1975, proved less successful.

Peter Shaffer (b. 1926).

Shaffer is an assured and ingenious dramatist whose first success was with the realistic well-made play and who has since 1964 moved on to freer modes of composition.

His plays operate successfully on two levels: they offer insight into the subtleties of personal relationships, especially into the difficulties of adjustment between people of different cultural background, and they also involve discussion of ideas.

Shaffer's early realistic plays include the skilful *Five Finger Exercise*, 1958 (P), and *The Private Ear and The Public Eye*, 1962, two spare tri-

angular plays both demonstrating the influence of artistic taste on the relationship between the sexes.

The Royal Hunt of the Sun. 1964.

A sweeping " epic " drama of Pizarro's fantastic conquest of Peru skilfully uses, as narrator, " old Martin ", who watches his own boyhood as page to Pizarro. Shaffer deploys " total theatre " in dazzling ceremonial, processions and masks, in ritual dancing, mime and strange, metallic music.

There is rich thematic material in the clash of " two immense and joyless powers, " in the conflict of Christianity and Sun worship. Personal tragedy develops in the mutual attraction felt by the grizzled Pizarro (Colin Blakeley) and the young Inca, Atahualpa (Robert Stephens). Captor and prisoner, they painfully seek for the god in each other and the Inca accepts death both as a sacrifice to friendship and the final test of his faith.

Black Comedy. 1965.

A highly successful brief comedy frankly uses an effective device of Chinese theatre. During a party the lights fail and the stage, although supposed to be in darkness, is still fully illuminated so that the ludicrous behaviour of the dramatis personae is visible only to the audience.

The Battle of Shrivings. 1970.

In a return to realistic drama, Shaffer shows the conflict between the eminent philosopher, Sir Gideon, a humanist and pacifist who believes in human perfectibility and his friend and guest, Mark, a famous and amoral poet. A painful weekend together results in a deliberate contest of wills, in which both win but both are broken. This attempt to dramatise the discrepancy between man's ideals and his personal relationships proved too wordy and contrived.

Equus. 1973.

In attempting to penetrate the motive of a shocking crime of which he had been told, Shaffer has created a compelling work of art.

Dysart (Alec McCowen), overworked child psychiatrist in a provincial hospital, accepts as patient Alan Strang, a part-time stable boy who has inexplicably blinded six horses. Shaffer's vivid imagination has been brilliantly interpreted in John Dexter's inventive production.

An open stage with a palisaded square within a circle and selective lighting are so skilfully deployed that they instantly indicate such diverse locations as the stable, the psychiatrist's consulting room, Alan's hospital cubicle, the Strangs' home, a beach, and often two locations at the same time, so that Dysart's interviews with Alan and others melt into enactment of the deeds he is uncovering.

Alan's well-meaning parents are incompatible, his mother religious, his father a self-educated atheist. The boy's first memorable experience had been on a beach when a stranger took him onto his horse, until his ecstatic ride was roughly interrupted by his parents. His fascination with horses was fostered by his mother's constant re-reading of a favourite story and also of splendid Biblical passages such as that from Job. Thus Alan's erotic and religious emotions become fused. A harrowing picture in his bedroom of Christ on the way to Calvary was torn down by his outraged father and replaced by one of a horse gazing directly at the onlooker, and Alan came to worship this image of Equus the chained god, devising his own ritual of obeisance and self-flagellation.

He had no chance to ride until he found a weekend job as a stable boy. There he would fondle his favourite horse, Nugget, like a lover and one night in every three weeks would gallop naked and bareback in a lonely field, in secret ecstasy.

One night the stable girl excited Alan by taking him to a blue film, where to his dismay he saw his respectable father. She then attempted to seduce Alan in the stable, but unsuccessfully, for he was agonised by his treachery to Equus. Driving the girl away he vainly implored forgiveness from Nugget's implacable stare and in desperation stabbed out the eyes of all six horses in the stable.

Since the audience watch Dysart's meetings with Alan's parents and his gradual winning of the boy's confidence and at one and the same time the actual events which he elicits, the play is a gripping detective story and fascinating psychiatric study.

But the extraordinary relationship between doctor and patient gives it a special depth. For Alan has the psychotic's instinct for sensing Dysart's own problems and throughout presents an urgent challenge. For Dysart's own life is devoid of sexual or religious passion, his marriage sterile, his only contact with the intuitive life he values his prim annual holidays in Greece. In his own terrible nightmare he sees himself as a masked priest sacrificing children and tearing out their entrails. He has lost faith in his vocation and says that in bringing Alan back to the drab normal he is destroying his capacity for reverence and rapture.

Some critics have assumed that Dysart's estimate of his own worth is that of Shaffer and that the playwright is decrying psychiatry itself. This is a misreading, for the wise and humane woman J.P., who first brings Alan to Dysart feels only gratitude for pain banished and Shaffer, acknowledging his debt to the advice and expert comment of a distinguished child psychiatrist says, " I have also come to perceive that psychiatrists are an immensely varied breed . . . Dysart is simply one doctor in one hospital."

N. F. Simpson (b. 1919).

N. F. Simpson's plays of the Absurd are in the peculiarly English vein of Lewis Carroll and Edward Lear, a world of surrealist fantasy, non-sequitur and nonsense. It is almost a contradiction in terms to organise such material coherently and to do so in a full-length play is a *tour de force* which Simpson brought off in his *One Way Pendulum.* His best work ridicules the mechanical and conventional existence, the attenuation of feeling, of the little suburban home, his usual milieu.

The Resounding Tinkle.   1957.   P.   F.

A most unusual play, which pokes fun at suburban life, discards plot, progress and characterisation, and the uniform dialogue is one continuous flow of clever verbal paradoxes and non-sequiturs. The apologetic " author " appears at intervals and in the final act there is a parody discussion of the play by a panel of " critics "—devices used by Ionesco in *The Shepherd's Chameleon.* Simpson's verbal agility is exhilarating, but some find the play over-cerebral.

One Way Pendulum.   A Farce in a New Dimension.   1959.   F.

Here Simpson has devised a framework built of whimsy and yet firm enough to carry its own logic and to be dramatically satisfying. The characters are drawn simply, but consistently, each with his own " humour " in the manner of Ben Jonson and the dialogue is a close parody of banal family interchange.

The play concerns a suburban family, the Groomkirbys, whose son, Kirby, is teaching a collection of weighing-machines to sing the Hallelujah Chorus. His ineffectual father is combining his two favourite hobbies of law and " do it yourself " carpentry, by building an enormous model of the Old Bailey in the living-room, where the phlegmatic mother pays a charwoman to eat up the " left-overs ".

Finally a trial takes place in the Old Bailey and Kirby is convicted of murdering forty-three people in order that he may wear black, the weighing-machines being part of a complicated device to cause a holocaust of death.

The main theme of the play is the tyranny of things, which is exemplified by the absurd Ionesco-like objects. These are treated with the respect due to human beings while human beings are treated as things, and father and son are so obsessed by things that they cannot get into touch with one another.

The tyranny of mechanical routine and social custom is also indicated. Kirby will only eat when a cash-register rings and will only wear black when it is sanctioned by funeral convention.

The anxiety and guilt which result from a starved and mechanical existence are finally symbolised in the nightmare parody of a trial scene in the final act.

Although the stage objects are novel and intriguing and can be assigned a clear meaning they lack the suggestive power of Ionesco's chairs or rhinoceroses. Contrived rather than intuitive, they illustrate more than they illuminate the human condition. But the play is an original and successful experiment and the implied comment on the unconscious assumptions and compulsive habits of the Groomkirbys has a wide reference.

The Cresta Run.   1965.

A play about counter-espionage proved disappointing, partly because its mockery is directed at a schoolboy dream rather than at a general malaise, partly because it lacks the bold structural outline of *One Way Pendulum.* Even the absurd objects—keys, codes, disguises—are trivial compared with the " Old Bailey ". Simpson has also lost some of the claustrophobic compulsion of his earlier plays by his constant switching of the action from the home of the suburban couple to the Ministry and back again.

It is unfortunate that a promising latent theme —the compulsion felt by the Security man to divulge his secret information—is swamped by trivia, while the best jest is only a casual aside—the suggestion that in England Intelligence should logically be in the hands of private enterprise!

Was He Anyone?   1972.   F.

On a cargo-boat, " several sizes too small for him ", Whitebrace, a bookie's runner, absent-mindedly runs into the sea. He treads water for over a year, while his plight is elaborately discussed by bureaucratic and charitable organisations and is depicted on the media.

So that he may improve himself culturally while waiting he is given a baby-grand on which he learns to play. The World's National Help-You-Out Week professes concern, the P.M. hopes to gain popularity with photographs of himself shaking hands with the wife and cruise ships stop to watch her husband's struggles. Eventually a private citizen thinks to throw a life-belt, but it causes concussion and death.

Appropriately the actress playing Mrs. Whitebrace is the only one of the cast not to change rôles during the play. The other six, as in a cabaret, quickly impersonate a number of figures devious, foolish or pompous.

A lively surrealistic comedy satirises popular voyeurism and the procrastination of official and charitable organisations in helping " the drowning man ".

Wole Soyinka (b. 1934).

Soyinka, a Nigerian and an English graduate, is an admirer of Brecht, Arden and Dürrenmatt.

The Road.   1965.

The Road, set in a drivers' haven in Nigeria successfully produced with a large cast of coloured actors, later won a Dakar award.

The Lion and the Jewel.   1966.   O.U.P.

In a lively comedy, presented by the Ijinle Company of African actors, the jewel is Sidi, the belle of a Yoruba village. Elated at being photographed for a glossy magazine, she rejects both the native schoolmaster and the old chieftain, the Lion, until cunningly seduced by him she exultantly joins his harem.

Native culture, with vivid ritual dance and music, is presented as more alluring and virile than European, which is mocked both in amusing mimes and in the shabby, ineffective schoolmaster infatuated with Western gadgets.

Tom Stoppard (b. 1937).

Stoppard is a shrewd observer and the most versatile, ingenious and witty of all our playwrights.

Rosencrantz and Guildenstern are Dead. 1966. F.

Stoppard's diverting play is a gloss on *Hamlet* and he dovetails snatches of Shakespeare's tragedy with his own action or rather inaction, for his archetype is Beckett's *Waiting for Godot.*

He humorously chooses as protagonists the two nonentities, Rosencrantz and Guildenstern. Summoned inexplicably to Elsinore, they hang about, always on the fringe of great events they do not understand, passing the time, like Shakespearean jesters, in witty word play and fruitless speculation as to their situation and destiny.

Their predicament is a suggestive image of the bewilderment of the ordinary man faced with world events beyond his grasp and, at a deeper level, with the existential problem of man's very being on this earth, and the imminence of death.

The rehearsal of the Players creates a further film of unreality and illusion.

The play is too long, the second act not sufficiently contrasted, but it is remarkable that so derivative a play should be so delightfully fresh and original.

Enter a Free Man. 1968. F.

The family situation of an " inventor " of unworkable gadgets, though funny and pathetic, is inadequate for a full-length play.

The Real Inspector Hound. 1968. F.

A crisp burlesque of a ridiculous " whodunnit " with a corpse ignored stage centre, uses the device of a play within a play. Interest is focused on two critics, each nursing his own obsession. Finally, at the ringing of the stage telephone one follows the other on to the stage, where both are shot.

After Magritte. 1970. F.

Fascinated by Magritte's surrealist painting, Stoppard tries to emulate him theatrically. Within the confines of the well-made play he uses several of Magritte's motifs, plus his own favourite, the detective, even inventing logical causation for the bizarre sequence. The playlet is an ingenious *jeu d'esprit.*

Jumpers. 1972. F.

In a hilarious farce Stoppard fuses zany, incongruous incidents, sizzling verbal wit and the serious theme of credibility. Sceptical of claims to certainty, he parodies the contortions of philosophy, the pretensions of psychiatry and political dogma as gymnastics.

The scene is the flat of George Moore (Hordern), a dishevelled Professor of Moral Philosophy, and the action, set on a revolving stage, shifts swiftly from one room to another. His wife is the lovely Dorothy or Dotty (Diana Rigg), a musical comedy star suffering nervous breakdown, for, since the landing on " that Juney old moon ", she can no longer sing her romantic songs with conviction.

In her sumptuous bedroom Dotty receives Archie, the suave, immaculate Vice Chancellor, her lover and opportunely her psychiatrist, while in his study George dictates to his secretary.

At a party thrown by Dotty celebrating a Radical-Liberal *coup d'état*, Archie compères a performance by his " jumpers ", gymnast philosophers such as logical positivists and linguistic analysts, for Archie professes strict rationalism. They form a human pyramid, but at its base McFee, Professor of Logic, is shot dead and Dotty is left alone with the body, later seen hanging inside a cupboard door.

This symbolic collapse of the coherence of modern philosophy is paralleled by George's verbal fumblings on the credibility of God and moral absolutes. Oblivious of the murder, he dictates his refutation of McFee's contribution to the annual symposium on " Man—good, bad or in-

different? " George retains some faith in man's ability to discern moral values by intuition and since " to sustain the attention of rival schools of academics by argument alone is tantamount to constructing a Gothic arch out of junket ", he plans to demonstrate his points with Zeno's bow and arrow, a specially trained tortoise, Pat, and a hare, Thumper (*cf.* jumper).

Dotty suspected of McFee's murder is questioned by Inspector Bones, an ardent fan, who arrives with a bouquet, since he can hardly arrest her by " Interflora ". But Archie, whose jumpers have now disposed of the body in a plastic bag, is also Dotty's lawyer and the coroner, and easily manipulates Bones.

A further dimension is given by political events, for the Rad–Libs are rationalising even the Church and have appointed an agnostic Archbishop. " It's like the chairman of the Coal Board believing in oil."

The progress of the lunar landing, seen on a television screen, gives an even more remote perspective. The two amoral astronauts, Scott and Oates, had fought each other for survival. For Dotty, this makes earth's morality parochial. But McFee, reminded of the self-sacrifice of the Antarctic Captain Oates, had ruefully admitted that if irrational altruism is a possibility, his logical arguments were " up a gum tree ".

George at last discovers that he has unwittingly shot Thumper, and in his dismay crunches Pat underfoot and collapses sobbing.

The contrast between Archie, cocksure and cynical opportunist, and ineffectual George, oddly engaging sympathy in his desperate search for moral certainty, effectively dramatises an underlying concern with genuine values. These, like the identity of the murderer, remain unidentified. To use stock situations like cuckolded husband and detection of murder as vehicle for erudite parody is a *tour de force.*

Travesties. 1974.

Staying in Zürich in 1917 are 3 men destined to influence our culture, the Rumanian poet Tristan Tzara (a founder of Dadaism which affected Surrealism), Lenin and James Joyce, while at the British Consulate is youthful Henry Carr, who had accepted Joyce's invitation to participate in a production of *The Importance of Being Earnest.* So much is factual but round this nub Stoppard spins complex webs of fantasy, these being the reminiscences of Carr, both as an old man remembering and as a youthful participant, and these recollections form the framework of the play.

Stoppard invents a friendship between Carr and Tzara resembling that between Wilde's Algy and Jack, and the names of the girls are Gwendolen (Carr's sister) and Cecily. Fitting settings for their wit and persiflage are the private drawing rooms of Tzara and Joyce. Another setting is Zürich library where Tzara works at one table, concocting his random verses, Joyce at another dictating part of *Ulysses* to Gwendolen, and Lenin and his wife, planning the historic secret return to revolted Russia, are unsuccessfully spied on by Carr.

Again a play of Stoppard's displays his fertile invention and verbal wit, and his interest in Surrealism and the absurd, this time linked with a serious subject. Its full appreciation demands considerable erudition.

Dirty Linen and New-Found-Land. 1967. F.

In a *jeu d'esprit* satire and farce fuse as members of a Parliamentary Select Committee on Promiscuity in High Places eventually have to investigate their own liaisons with their own secretary, Miss Gotobed, who has been " going through the ranks like a lawnmower in knickers." Two Home Office men then take over their room and in *New-Found-Land* discuss the application for naturalisation from public-spirited American Ed Berman; " A theatrical farmer with buses on the side doing publishing work in a beard," sighs one. But Berman becomes British and the re-assembled Select Committee eludes a scandal.

Every Good Boy Deserves Favour. 1977.

Under an unqualified psychiatrist, Alex (McKellen), friend of a dissident, is held in a Soviet asylum. In his cell is mad Ivanov (John Wood), who imagines he is conducting his own music. Alex endures Ivanov's obsession, a dangerous, fruitless hunger strike and torture. Although it would release him, he steadily refuses to admit madness, even when his little son, caught up in Ivanov's lunacy (" a trombone is the longest distance between two points "), tries to persuade him. Finally a K.G.B colonel, confusing the men's names, asks Ivanov if dissidents are kept in asylums and Alex whether he is conducting an orchestra, and both are judged sane. Alex's disinterested altruism would have given George Moore of *Jumpers* (*q.v.*) better evidence for his case than did Pat and Thumper!

The play was produced for one day only by the R.S.C. at the Royal Festival Hall. The prisoners occupied a small space with two beds in the midst of an orchestra, for which Previn composed and conducted Ivanov's imaginary score.

David Storey (b. 1933).

Storey, also a novelist, is the son of a Yorkshire miner and helped to support himself at the Slade by playing professional Rugby for Leeds. He wrote the film-script for his own novel, *This Sporting Life*, and Lindsay Anderson, while directing it encouraged him to revise his discarded play, *Arnold Middleton*.

Anderson has directed Storey's four subsequent plays and the imaginative rapport between producer and playwright has led to their being interpreted with singular insight and restraint.

One theme in Storey's work, as in Mercer's, is the stress felt by the educated offspring of working folk. Many plays involve reference to mental trouble or instability and he is much interested in the theories of R. D. Laing.

The plays are grounded in every-day life, frequently in Storey's own experience. Yet they have become increasingly poetic in approach, in that their significance is consciously ambiguous, and " escapes and refuses definitions. " Storey deliberately leaves " all the options open. " He also says that, if on reading something through, he " knows completely what it is all about, then it is dead, " but if it mystifies him then it has " taken on an independent life of its own. "

Storey is refreshingly versatile in subject and approach and each new work shows a growing mastery and maturity. A genuine and unassuming artist, he is now one of our best playwrights.

The Restoration of Arnold Middleton. 1967. P.

Arnold, a young schoolmaster (as Storey once was) is a jesting eccentric, his latest acquisition an outsize suit of armour introduced during the play's revision. But Arnold's clowning disguises the fact that he is going mad.

The theme is reminiscent of Mercer's *Morgan*, with the gorilla suit, but the exuberant comedy tends to blur the issue and the interpretation of the hero's instability and lightning recovery is inadequate.

In Celebration. 1969. P.

Three sons return home to celebrate the fortieth wedding anniversary of their parents, doting collier husband and complacent matriarch, who considers herself his social superior.

With first-hand realism Storey conveys the disorientation and embarrassed filial feeling of sons educated beyond their origins. The eldest brother, the iconoclastic Andrew, is hell-bent on tearing down the family facade and tries to force on stolid Colin and sensitive Steven his theory that their ambitious mother had distorted their lives into a false respectability to appease her own sense of guilt. When six months pregnant, she had felt obliged to marry the collier father and after the firstborn had died at the age of seven, she had tried to commit suicide.

After an extravagant dinner at the local hotel Andrew lashes the bewildered father with his scorn and only the concerted efforts of Colin and Steven can help to reassure the old man and get Andrew away next morning before he can confront the mother.

The psychological motivation is not fully credible but this compassionate and close-knit play, with the past haunting the present, recalls Ibsen, especially since Andrew is an ignoble counterpart of Gregers Werle in *The Wild Duck*.

The Contractor. 1969. P.

Five men leisurely assemble and later dismantle a huge tent for the wedding of the contractor's daughter, while members of the family drift in and out. The workers' banter and taunts and the family casual talk hint at hidden hurts, but the focus of the play is the actual work on the tent—as in Ionesco a " thing "—presented here with no absurdity or phantasy but with almost the faithfulness of documentary, for Storey can draw on his own experience of the job.

The image is however metaphorical and because the play cannot " be confined to any one definition, " Storey finds it one of his most satisfying works. He sometimes sees it as " somehow related to the decline and falling away of capitalist society " or " as a metaphor for artistic creation. " Yet " it still continues to make sense—and complete sense—as the story of these men who put up this tent and that's that. "

Home. 1970. P.

Sitting at a garden table, on the only two chairs available, two aging gentlemen, Jack (Ralph Richardson) and Harry (Gielgud), gently and diffidently make conversation. Jack, slightly more dapper, and prone to pointless family anecdote, usually takes the initiative in their exchange of dated clichés and banalities. The broken phrases refer to wives now separated, ambitions unfulfilled, the clouds, but real communication can only be unspoken and there is sad irony in Jack's, " So rare these days nowadays to meet someone to whom one can actually talk."

When these leave, their places are taken by two rough, " Cor blimey " women, full of prurient innuendo and scandal, and when the gentlemen return and courteously escort " the ladies " to " corn beef hash ", it has gradually become apparent that this is a mental " home ". Act II begins with the entry of a leucotomised young man who aimlessly shifts the furniture about.

The play, heart-breaking in its naturalistic fidelity to human inadequacy, is handicapped by some monotony of incident and dialogue. But, like Beckett's *Godot*, also a strange quintet, it works through poetic suggestion. The ironic title and the furniture, inadequate for 2000 people, are significant as is the apparently irrelevant juxtaposition of phrases, which are in themselves ambiguous metaphors. (" This little island." " Shan't see its like." " Oh, no." " The sun has set." " Couple of hours.")

But the decline and vitality (perhaps that of England herself) is most potently expressed by the unadorned shape of the play, the decline of the day from morning to evening, the sky overcast, the rain that of the old men's silent tears.

The Changing Room. 1971. P.

Storey can rely on his own memories of Rugby League football when he paints the bare, chilly, changing room. Opened up by the caretaker, a muttering old pensioner, it is gradually taken over by the players, clearly individualised and arriving in ascending order of their social status, to be treated by the masseur, advised by the trainer, briefly encouraged by the Chairman, until changed into their kit they stand as a team, silent for a moment before trotting down the tunnel to the icy pitch and the roar from the stands.

The second act includes the brief half-time when the battered players, committed by their common hazard and purpose are now welded into a corporate body. In the third, exultant after victory, they joke and bath in easy comradeship until with his everyday clothes each man assumes his separate identity and only the caretaker is left.

Storey here develops and refines the deceptively easy naturalism and the novel pattern of *The Contractor*, but peripheral and rather conventional interest such as that of the Contractor's family, which intrudes on the work scene, is now pared away and Storey wholly commits himself to the recreation of men thrown together by the exigencies of their job yet temporarily finding themselves a community.

To create out of such simple materials and means a shapely and invigorating work of art is a remarkable achievement.

Cromwell. 1973. Cape.

In a play which took shape in 1968–9, a time of conflict in Vietnam and Ireland, Storey abandons naturalism for a kind of dramatic fable, where brief, swiftly-moving scenes, occasionally using some verse, depict " people wandering through woods and a war ". Although Cromwell is never mentioned the setting suggests the Ireland of his time.

Amid the refugees, rigid partisans and turncoats of a confused guerrilla war, the protagonist Proctor emerges as a man of principle, constantly searching for the right course of action. Two amiable Irish layabouts, shameless opportunists, serve as a foil to Proctor and their comic lackadaisical backchat acts as cynical running commentary on his devotion to ideals. He is fighting on behalf of dispossessed Catholics but disillusioned by the futility of inconclusive reprisals he withdraws from war, marries Joan and finds deep satisfaction in restoring her ravaged farm. Then, because he gives shelter to some wounded anarchist Levellers the farm is devastated a second time by the Protestants and their child killed.

After bitter heart searching, Proctor finally eschews all political and social ideology and in a final scene a boatman ferries him and Joan across a river. Storey says that the scene indicates " just the transference from one kind of life to another ", although it may be interpreted both literally and also symbolically as purification and absolution.

Storey's theme is the irrelevance of theoretical and political standpoints and he has said that " it has become immaterial which side you choose to be on ". Yet the value of integrity is stressed as paramount and the boatman significantly refuses to carry the layabouts, who " hang like leeches ", for " hands which always receive can offer nought ".

An interesting play of ideas suffers from structural imbalance, for there is an extremely long and leisurely first act while Proctor's deepest conflicts are hurried into brief and rather obscure final scenes. There are literary echoes from Dante and Bunyan but Storey says Shakespeare is his only model.

The Farm. 1973.

The play reverts to the realistic style of *In Celebration*. It is dominated by the rough Yorkshire farmer, Slattery, who after a dangerous stroke still drinks inordinately.

After a lifetime of toil he is angered and bewildered by the sterility of his offspring. Three daughters still live at home. Two are teachers in their thirties, Wendy early separated from her husband and Jenny restlessly seeking one, while Brenda, aged twenty-three, a fierce and naïve subvertionist, is still supported by her father. Slattery is passionately scornful of the son Arthur, a poet manqué, idolised by his mother. Now twenty-one, he has left home and drifts impecuniously from job to job.

One night Wendy finds that Arthur has returned unexpectedly. He is shaking with apprehension and next morning tells his father he is about to marry Alison, a divorced woman of forty-two. Slattery, incredulous and furious, lashes him with invective yet agrees to receive Alison that evening. But Arthur's courage fails and he arrives late and alone. Slattery's paroxysm of rage is such that he almost collapses and during the night the despondent Arthur leaves as unobtrusively as he had come.

Next morning a brief final scene shows Slattery genially welcoming to the breakfast table Brenda's diffident suitor, who has at last found courage to come openly to the house.

The play is looser in texture than *In Celebration* and the portrayal of the sisters rather flat and repetitive. But the frustration of their unfulfilled lives is peripheral, although probably stemming from the mutually destructive relationship between father, mother and son. Slattery gradually betrays his misery that his wife has withheld from him the love she has lavished on Arthur and in his final outburst he even accuses his son of trying to supplant him by deliberately contriving an emotional shock that will cause his death. Storey's compassionate presentation of this Oedipal situation is powerful and moving'.

Life Class. 1973.

In a play related to his novel *A Temporary Life* Storey portrays a mixed group of students in a shabby Yorkshire art college drawing a nude woman from the life.

Their teacher Allott, the educated son of working folk, and unhappily married, is a failed artist, deeply alienated. His attitude to his students is ironic and remote.

Their personalities and attitudes to their task differ widely and Allott's provocative questions on the woman as artist, the place of art in modern society and its relation to illusion and reality are unanswered. He remains aloof even when two of his randiest students apparently rape the model, but the act like art itself is also a simulation. Summarily dismissed by his conventional and rigid Principal, Allott is still nonchalantly unperturbed.

Critics differ in their estimates. Some consider that this third play in his once novel genre (the naturalistic portrayal of a group at work) is becoming conventional. Others see deeper implications.

Peter Terson (b. 1932).

Terson is a prolific writer with a talent for fertile, fluent dialogue, which immediately establishes personalities and relationships His most successful work has been done in co-operation with two directors, Cheeseman and Croft.

In 1963, while working in the Vale of Evesham, Terson first contacted Cheeseman, director at Stoke-on-Trent, who encouraged him to write several plays located in the Vale. A recurrent theme is the mysterious power of nature and, as in Rudkind's *Afore Night Come* (*q.v.*), a sinister theme often runs through them. They include *A Night to Make the Angels Weep*, 1963; *The Mighty Reservoy*, 1964 (P); *I'm in Charge of These Ruins*, 1966; *All Honour Mr. Todd*, 1966 and *Mooney and His Caravans*, 1967 (P).

Later Cheeseman produced plays which broke new ground, *The Samaritan*, 1971 (begun 1968) and *But Fred Freud is Dead*, 1972 (written 1964). Both involve a sympathetic and wittily accurate picture of an emotionally insecure man who overcompensates with a false bravura. Cheeseman rightly considers Terson's greatest gift is " his capacity to write in a way that is both very funny and profoundly serious at the same time ".

Terson became nationally known through his remarkable collaboration with Michael Croft, director of the NYT. He writes about youngsters with affectionate zest and exuberant humour, vividly aware of the lack of opportunity offered them by society.

Terson's plays tailored for the NYT include: *Zigger-Zagger*, 1967 (P), which depicts the Dionysiac frenzy of a young football crowd; *The Apprentices*, 1968 (P); *Fuzz*, 1969; *Spring-Heeled Jack*, 1970; *Good Lads at Heart*, 1971, showing conflict between modern and authoritarian methods in an approved school; *Geordies' March*, 1972, where apprentices encounter unexpected setbacks when marching to London from Sunderland to protest at a fatal accident to one of their fellows.

In 1977 came *Family Ties*, two similar one-acters in which parents now appear, as disgruntled working-class fathers protest about their offsprings' shortcomings. The dads are well drawn, the mums conventional.

Jose Triana (b. 1931).

Triana, born in Cuba, has written several plays.

The Criminals. 1967.

The first Cuban play staged here depicts three adults, a brother and his two sisters, acting out fantasies of childhood, hatred of thwarting parents, which culminate in a frenzied ritual of their murder at the end of Act One. The trial of the children in Act Two gradually develops into an enactment of the parents' mutual detestation. As the curtain falls the ritual begins afresh.

This intense play, in the genre of " Theatre of Cruelty " (*q.v.*), has less wealth of imagery than Weiss's *Marat-Sade* but a greater universality of reference than Genet's world. It may have been influenced by the work of Arrabal.

Triana shows great psychological insight; children's play is often a dramatic projection of their inner conflicts and at all ages the sterile process of fantasy gives only temporary relief and must be exhaustingly repeated. The most significant moment of the play is when the word " love " is timidly offered as an alternative only to be rejected.

An apt parallel to Triana's vision was the contemporary Reith lecture (26 Nov. 1967), when Dr. Leach, the social anthropologist, criticised our unthinking acceptance of the inward turning family life, where " The parents fight: the children rebel." " The strain is greater than most of us can bear," and the source of our social discontents.

Triana's play shows it as a potent source of man's aggression. Some critics have seen in it implications of Castro's resistance to the dominance of America.

Boris Vian (1920–59).

The French Vian was influenced by the Absurdist approach of Ionesco.

The Empire Builders. 1962. M.

Man's futile flight from death is imaged in a family trying to escape from a terrifying noise by moving up to a higher and higher floor and meaner quarters. Eventually the father alone reaches the attic, where he dies.

The General's Tea Party. 1966. P.

Written in 1951, Vian's biting, absurdist satire on the military mentality represents his general behaving like a small boy, afraid of Mama, and asking his playfellows—other generals—to tea. After deciding that war would be a nice idea, they then select the target—prophetically Algeria.

Frank Wedekind (1864–1918).

The plays of the German Wedekind, a passionate amoralist, are preoccupied with the mysterious power of sex and in their intensity they sporadically break through the bounds of realism into fantasy and symbolism—techniques later to be deployed in Expressionism (*q.v.*).

Spring's Awakening. 1863.

Published in 1891, the play which concerns the lyrical rapture and the agony of puberty, is a fervid indictment of a disastrous and repressive " morality ", of secretive or hypocritical parents and grotesquely tyrannical schoolmasters.

Finally in a scene of nightmare fantasy, the ruined adolescent, Melchior, searching for the grave of his sweetheart, dead through an abortion, is encountered by the ghost of his suicide friend and is himself only restrained from the same fate by the symbolic Man in the Mask.

Lulu. 1970.

Lulu is the title given by Peter Barnes to his adaptation of two plays, *Earth Spirit*, 1895, and its sequel *Pandora's Box*, 1903.

Wedekind's protagonist, Lulu, the incarnation of the instinctual life, symbolises sexual passion in its beauty, rapture and terror. In her narcissism and uninhibited passion she destroys all who become hopelessly infatuated with her.

In Barnes's Act I, corresponding to *Earth Spirit*, Lulu causes the death of her first husband by shock, the suicide of the second and shoots the third, Schön.

In Act II, the sequel, she gradually degenerates to amateur prostitute, still adored by two ruined devotees, a lesbian countess and Schön's son. To him she has been successively foster-sister, step-mother and mistress, the incarnation of a Freudian dream. These two also die and she is herself assassinated by a pervert casual client.

Barnes's adaptation neglects the mystery and pathos of the original. Fantasy is abruptly succeeded by grotesque bathos as in black comedy (*q.v.*).

The Marquis of Keith. 1974.

The protagonist is an imposter and adventurer. The familiar theme is the conflict of sexuality and pleasure, with ethics.

The Singer. 1976.

The play satirises society captivated by a Wagnerian tenor's sex appeal, rather than his art.

Peter Weiss (b. 1916).

The German-speaking Weiss has adopted Swedish nationality and Marxist doctrine.

The " Marat Sade." 1964.

The full title of this verse play, one of the most impressive exemplifications of Artaud's Theatre of Cruelty, is *The Persecution and Assassination of Jean-Paul Marat as Performed by the Inmates of the Asylum of Charenton under the Direction of the Marquis de Sade*! As the title indicates this complex work operates on receding planes of cruelty, thus exciting in the audience that vivid experience of violence which is the aim of Artaud.

Artaud's demand for primitive ritual which shall exorcise repressed fantasy is met by Corday's threefold visit and murder of Marat and also by the lunatics' frenzied miming of the ceremony of the guillotine—a background motif to the whole play. The use of pantomime and gesticulation on the open stage satisfy Artaud's demands for spectacle, for " poetry in space."

Peter Brook pointed out that these elements are not inconsistent with a Brechtian " alienation "—achieved by the device of a play within a play, the protesting comments of the director of the asylum, the intellectual debates between Sade and Marat and the ribald songs of a grotesque quartet of zanies. The effect is an inextricable blend of the comic and the violent.

The Investigation. 1965.

A documentary of the Frankfurt War Crime Trials, edited by Weiss, had a multiple première in East and West Germany and at the Aldwych. Described by Weiss as an " Oratorio in 11 Cantos ", after Dante's *Inferno*, it indicts the millions, including the German monopoly capitalists, who tacitly supported the Nazi atrocities.

At the first impact the grisly facts leave an overwhelming impression of horror. It is remarkable that the author's restraint and dignity in presenting them and the formal austerity of his design have in retrospect the effect of catharsis.

The Song of the Lusitanian Bogey. 1969.

A passionate indictment of Portuguese colonial exploitation and oppression of Angola recalls in some of its techniques Peter Brook's *US*. It was splendidly acted by the New York Negro Ensemble.

Arnold Wesker (b. 1932)

Wesker's work is best understood in the light of his Jewish background and his didactic socialism. He is no naïve optimist but has always represented the tension between idealism and practicality and is most trenchant in his criticism of characters like Ronnie who reveal this dichotomy.

His sense of dramatic structure is erratic but he sometimes evinces an exhilarating sense of stage movement. His chief weakness is diction and he succeeds best in plays like *Roots*, *Chips* and *Golden City* where the use of an unaccustomed idiom necessitates disciplined study. The reportage of the voluble converse of some Jewish people is all too easy for him and in some plays action is drowned in a garrulous flood.

After 1962 he devoted much energy to the founding of Centre 42 to bring good art to the masses, and their own apathy has been his greatest disappointment especially as he is member of a race which highly values education and culture.

Wesker first worked as a chef in Norwich, London and Paris, but soon achieved fame through the "kitchen sink" naturalism of his trilogy of plays.

The first, *Chicken Soup with Barley*, 1958 (P), shows a Jewish socialist family, the Kahns, on 4 October 1936, helping to prevent Mosley's march through the East End. It concludes in 1957 with the disillusion of the vacillating son Ronnie at the Russian invasion of Hungary. The theme of the play is "caring", not only politically but in the home, for the stalwart mother must cope with the inertia of Ronnie and of her shiftless husband.

In *Roots*, 1959 (P), Beatie, who is engaged to Ronnie, revisits her Norfolk family (the coarse roots of her origin), ignorant, prejudiced and inarticulate. Although she fails to understand him Beatie constantly parrots Ronnie's teaching about the power of words, or "bridges" to communicate ideas. Then on the day he is to arrive she receives a letter saying their marriage would not work. Beatie, galvanised by shock and ecstatic with self-realisation, discovers that she is at last speaking thoughts of her own. This play, the best of the trilogy, is well-constructed, the characters convincing and the concept of "roots" and "bridges" develop organically from the situation.

I'm Talking about Jerusalem. 1960. P.

Kahn's daughter and her husband Dave go to Norfolk to put into practice the ideas of William Morris, but find they cannot compete with factory products and in 1960 return to London, Dave's self-respect contrasting with the bitter cynicism of a friend. But he is not sufficiently commanding to save a play weak in structure.

The Kitchen. 1959. P.

In a two-acter, Wesker draws on his experience as a chef to give a vivid impression of a day in the kitchen of Marango's restaurant. The play is notable for its skilful contrasts in pace and movement. The quiet morning quickens to a frenzy of anxiety at lunch-time, and the doldrums of the afternoon are succeeded by the sudden outburst of a German who goes beserk.

The swirling vortex is a microcosm of the world, where men with their casual contacts find themselves in a situation beyond their grasp. The play ends with the dramatic irony of Marango's failure to perceive that work and food alone cannot satisfy man's desires.

Chips with Everything. 1962. P.

In *R.U.R.* the Expressionist playwright Capek used robots as dramatis personae. In *Chips with Everything* Wesker illustrates the process whereby military discipline can reduce both men and officers to robot-like uniformity.

A squad of nine R.A.F. conscripts are subjected to a battery of bullying abuse from the corporal and pychological manipulation by the officers, until, their personal identity submerged, they learn to move as one mechanical unit and pass out to the blaring of a military band playing "God Save the Queen".

Wesker employs a new stylised, streamlined technique which appropriately shares some of the techniques of expressionism. Type characters are used and the identity of the recruits, with two exceptions, indicated very lightly. The dialogue is usually staccato while brief, symbolic scenes such as square bashing, bayonet practice and the comic mime of stealing coke succeed one another rapidly, an instance of Wesker's command of stage movement.

As to the two recruits presented in more detail: the plight of the gentle Smiler broken and suffering gives pathos to the play without disturbing its tone, but the somewhat unconvincing predicament of Thompson is treated with too much detail to be in key. The son of a general, he is at first resistant to authority and seems to be trying to assume leadership of the squad, but accused by them of "slumming" and assailed by the officers' blandishments he finds the habits of those who can "eat chips with everything" too distasteful for him and he suddenly capitulates and assumes officer's uniform.

The overall effect is tense and powerful for the audience facing the same direction as the recruits cannot avoid feeling the obliterating effect of the military machine.

The Four Seasons. 1965. P.

Wesker deliberately ignoring "any recognisable social context" indicates his milieu of old house and garden only symbolically. He limits his characters to a man and woman whose previous marriages had floundered and they live together from winter to the following autumn. The play relies on lyrical interchange followed by alienation but even the final quarrel is too unmotivated to convince. Wesker forgetting that drama is the imitation of an action is attempting the impossible.

Their Very Own and Golden City. 1966. P.

The driving force of a vigorous play may be Wesker's own frustrated struggle to realise a communal artistic ideal in Centre 42, intended to make good art accessible to the people.

The opening dream-like scene in Durham Cathedral in 1926 shows Andrew Cobham and fellow apprentices with Jessie his future wife, when Andy is so exhilarated by the soaring splendour that he is inspired to his life work as architect. This seminal experience is flashed forward and developed in the early part of the play as if nurturing his vision of the twelve Golden Cities he is inspired to design where the centre shall not be the town hall but museums, art galleries and theatres.

When he is already married an aristocratic girl, Kate, befriends him and holds him determinedly to his purpose. Future householders enthusiastically finance the buildings of one city but Andy is so frustrated by ten years of fruitless waiting for the T.U.C. that he yields to Kate's persuasion and compromises his principles by accepting support from a Tory minister and a capitalist industrialist.

Similarly Andy's private life is jeopardised, for Kate scorns Jessie from whom he is gradually estranged. Eventually knighted and a member of the Establishment, he is seen a cantakerous old man playing bridge with his three influential friends while Jessie sews. A final scene is a sad ironic flash-back to the Cathedral, where the youngsters discover themselves locked in until one door is discovered open, symbolic perhaps of Wesker's fears and hopes.

He ably portrays the dilemma of the socialist artist caught between an obscurantist labour movement and the privileged Establishment which fosters cultural values. He uses with assurance techniques worked out in *Chips* integrating a panorama of social trends with type characters, but here those at the heart of the play are realised in depth.

In spite of some mawkish phrases in the Cathedral and some over-long political speeches the dialogue is usually sharp and incisive.

The Friends. 1970.

A Jewish death-bed scene was sentimental.

The Old Ones. 1972.

Kaleidoscopic scenes show "defiant old age" in a much troubled Jewish family. But when Sarah joins the next generation in acting the joyful Succoth ritual some confident release results.

The Wedding Feast. 1977.

The play adapted from a Dostoevsky story shows in Act I Louis Litvanov at 52 entertaining his staff, while a journalist narrator punctuates the dialogue. Louis, son of an immigrant Jewish cobbler, has founded in Norwich a thriving shoe factory, and as idealistic socialist indulged his workers' every outrageous demand. His staff warn that his paternalism is self-deception and that the workers want to keep their distance. He is left worrying whether he is peasant or tycoon. Self-confidence returns when he presents shoes for the wedding of his secretary's brother, Knocker White, but he gatecrashes the reception to the acute embarrassment of all.

A whirling Act II of richly orchestrated comedy is triggered off by the sheepish accident-prone Knocker, dismayed at entertaining the boss, and by family idiosyncracies and bickering. The dominant theme is the immense gulf that isolates Louis, his inept toasts, his patronisingly buying champagne and his embarrassment at the risqué jokes and gestures. In tipsy Act III the journalist and Louis fight drunkenly and then in the "shoe game" the workers' suppressed malaise accelerates until Louis, blindfolded, is violently beaten with shoes until he passes out. At dawn he shuffles into the room, his fact hardening as he (not necessarily Wesker) mutters, "Yes, that's the way it has to be."

The first act's use of narrator is somewhat clumsy, but once the realistic party begins the play proceeds vigorously to its climax. Relevence to vexed industrial relations is obvious, but this is no agit-prop manifesto, but an incisively honest drama of a lonely, generous, but sentimentally obtuse man who makes a painful blunder.

E. A. Whitehead.

Whitehead has asserted his conviction that a new pattern of mating and breeding should now be found. His plays are stark and sincere but narrow in scope, their limited verbal idiom monotonous.

The Foursome. 1971. F.

Two youths take two girls they have successfully picked up the previous evening to a sandy hollow of the beach but they are sexually frustrated and infuriated by the girls' sham reluctance. The dialogue of the men's bawdy taunts and the girls' prurient and prudish repartee is seldom relieved.

Alpha Beta. 1972. F.

A vigorous two-character play spanning nine years shows a working-class married couple in their thirties suffering the inexorable collapse of their marriage. Frank (Albert Finney) feeling trapped by convention and children, Nora grimly refusing divorce, they fight physically, until both are worn down. Finally Frank, now 38, can envisage freedom in two years time under the new Act. Nora sardonically asks, "Free for what?"

Old Flames. 1975.

Edward entertained by Sally on her houseboat is disturbed to find three other guests, his deserted wife, his ex-wife and his mother. Edward disappears and the women frankly discuss their hostility to men. Eventually pieces of flesh are brought in from the kitchen. Marriage has already been stigmatised in *Alpha Beta* as "ritual slaughter" and this extraordinary, surrealistic ending to a realistic play suggests a nightmare misogony which Whitehead feels can only adequately be conveyed by cannibalism.

Mecca. 1977.

In a Moroccan holiday camp, fortified with barbed wire, six Britons can experiment with, and volubly discuss, their own sexual frustrations and the others' peculiarities. But when the natives rape one of the women xenophobia takes over. Two men attack a boy, probably innocent, who dies. Only by buying their way out can the party escape. Whitehead seems to have enlarged his territory but not his vision.

John Whiting (1915–63).

John Whiting was an original playwright preoccupied with the theme of self-destruction. He was slow to find his own style but his last two subtle plays are still influential, despite his early death.

A Penny for a Song, 1951, written at a time of personal happiness, is an agreeable whimsy depicting two wealthy eccentric brothers preparing to repel Napoleon with such gadgets as a homemade fire engine. *Saints Day,* an earlier play not performed until 1951, shows an angry octogenerian, once a famous revolutionary poet, but the play becomes swamped by extraneous action and melodrama.

Marching Song. 1954. P.

In a play much concerned with the existentialist stress on the inescapability of choice, Whiting returns to the theme of self-destruction.

The setting is generalised—a wealthy house "above a capital city in Europe." Rupert Forster, formerly a general, who seven years previously had inexplicably lost a decisive battle, here meets his dilemma. He must either face a trial, which might cause political unrest, or commit suicide. The choices are represented by two people.

In Act II Forster encounters Dido, a young woman who revives his sense of humanity and will to live. She represents the female side of personality, the Jungian anima; and her name recalls the Dido of the *Aeneid,* who by her love deflected Aeneas from the path of military duty.

In Act III he has a very different meeting with Captain Bruno, the embodiment of military ambition. To him Forster at last confesses the cause of his fatal defeat. He had been so overcome with compassion for children whom he had destroyed while they were impeding his tanks that he had been unable to follow up his advance. Bruno stigmatises the delay as military error and guilt and Forster commits suicide rather than face disgrace and imprisonment.

This is a strongly constructed play, its dominating theme worked out with single-minded austerity. Forster's reversion to his original decision to commit suicide gives it a circular movement. It is concerned to clarify judgment and in the contrast between military code and humane ethic is stimulating and relevant.

The Devils. 1962. P.

Suggested to Whiting by Peter Brook, this intricate and distinguished play is based on Aldous Huxley's *The Devils of Loudun,* which treats of an actual case of suspected diabolism in France between 1623 and 1634.

Whiting employs two focal points. One is Grandier (Richard Johnson), again a man who invites his own destruction, a worldly and sensual priest who is yet gifted with a rare religious insight and compassion. The other is a hunchback prioress (Dorothy Tutin). Although she has not met Grandier, she becomes obsessed by fantasies of his amorous adventures and her resulting hysteria, which spreads throughout the convent, is suspected as diabolical possession, instigated by Grandier. Richelieu, for political reasons, uses this as a pretext to get rid of him. Grandier, in spite of excruciating torture and degradation, the prelude to his being burnt alive, struggles to retain his faith.

In its subject and theme *The Devils* is strikingly similar to Miller's *The Crucible.*

There are significant differences. Whiting's intricate play is not realistic but Brechtian in style, with a series of brief episodes and a commentary by a sewerman, whose ironic and sceptical remarks counterpoint Grandier's eloquence. Its final note is one of harsh pessimism, as the sewerman tells the prioress that Grandier's bones are being prized by the crowd as superstitious "charms".

The final act presents an almost unbearable spectacle of a barbarous ritual of physical torture as the maimed and twitching Grandier is paraded in public procession through the streets.

Tennessee Williams (b. 1914).

Since 1950 the works of the American playwright seen here, have included, *The Rose Tatoo*, 1951 (P), *Cat on a Hot Tin Roof* 1955 (P) and *Suddenly Last Summer* 1958 (P), with its crescendo of violence. Williams' plays often breathe the atmosphere of the deep south and he is preoccupied with the inner emotions of his vulnerable people, a prey to guilt, aggression and despair, and caught in a web of relationships which they only break at great cost. Especially poignant are Williams' picture of life's pathetic failures.

The Two Character Play. 1967.

Believing them to be mad, a touring company desert their fellow actors Felice and Clare. This brother and sister then hysterically enact Felice's work, *The Two Character Play*, that may perhaps mirror their own unhappy relationship.

Small Craft Warnings. 1973.

In Monk's foggy bar on the Pacific his customers are misfits and failures, such as a disqualified doctor, Violet, a sensual nymphomaniac, the sensual Bill supported by Leona (Elaine Stritch) in her trailer. But when Leona discovers Violet trying to seduce Bill her fury is lacerating. The play loses impetus when Monk devises some facile solutions. Only Leona, rejecting Bill, resumes her vagrant life.

The Red Devil Battery Sign. 1977.

In Dallas sexual deviation jostles with political melodrama as the Red Battery Man, leader of international terrorists, plans to assassinate the next President but two.

Charles Wood (b. 1932).

Descended from actors and once a regular soldier, Wood has made stage and army the province of his plays. He skilfully devises for each an appropriate dialogue.

The triple bill *Cockade*, 1963, was concerned with the army and *Fill the Stage with Happy Hours*, 1966 (P), set in a tatty provincial theatre was, says Wood, "about theatrical failure" and serves as a contrast to *Veterans*.

Dingo. 1967. P.

Wood employs Expressionism to present a phantasmagoria of the last War, beginning in the desert and grinding through Stalag to the unconditional surrender of Germany. It is an assault on the emotions and sensations in a passionate attempt to bring home war's physical horror and spiritual attrition, Wood exposing latent jingoism and political expedience and the futile heroism they exact.

The scurrilous words matter less than certain persistent images: the ranker, Dingo, epitome of bitter disillusion; Tanky, rendered simple-minded because he was powerless to release his mate, screaming to death in a flaming tank; an ENSA comedian who serves to parody Churchillian rhetoric, and breezy morale-boosting of High Command; a young subaltern, dressed as a blonde in a bikini for a concert party designed to cover an escape from Stalag, and now, with Tanky, lolling dead from the barbed wire.

The play is sprawling but powerful, attacking the idea that Britain's rôle was disinterested. It was fought, says Dingo, "for all the usual reasons."

"H". 1969. M.

Wood's subject is the heroic march of the elderly General Havelock, or "H", during the Mutiny. His column vastly outnumbered and decimated by disease, he yet relieved Cawnpore and won twelve desperate battles before relieving Lucknow where he died of dysentery.

A chivalrous Christian and a disciplined commander, Havelock yet ordered some of the terrible reprisals then current, hanging mutinous sepoys or shooting them alive from the mouths of cannon. His equivocal behaviour helps to focus Wood's own conflicting impulses, his fascination with military discipline and his horror at war's bestiality, so that the play is more unified than *Dingo*.

The core of the play is irony, centred in the action of the protagonist. But the irony proliferates, as in the contrast between the stylised Victorian language and the brutal deed, and unconnected episodes sometimes distract and confuse.

The fact that Havelock's aide-de-camp is his own son suggests the tender perspective of home. Resolute in courage and obedience, the son differs from his father in opinion and faith and his eventual confession of Christianity at Havelock's death gives pathos to the scene.

The Brechtian epic style is well suited to the simple episodic structure. Brechtian devices are also used:—direct address to the audience, map titles and symbolic emblems, such as the simple blood-stained floor and awning, conveying the Indian atrocities at Cawnpore, and the deliberate theatricality of short scenes projected within a little replica of the popular travelling stage.

Although Havelock on the surface resembles the Brechtian ambiguous protagonist, he does not attain the commanding stature of a Galileo or a Mother Courage.

Veterans. 1972. M.

Wood has imagined his own play *H* being filmed in Turkey near the Hellespont and the filming of his screenplay, *The Charge of the Light Brigade*, has given him an authentic background.

The play is set in or near the small Greek amphitheatre of Prieria and the veterans are two famous actors, Sir Geoffrey Kendle (John Gielgud) as Havelock, and d'Orsay (John Mills), as Outram. Sir Geoffrey spends nearly all day waiting, tired and frustrated. His conversation with his jealous friend d'Orsay and the younger star, Bryan, " a curled young man ", is that of the green room but uncovers some of their problems. The tenuous action consists in their transient contact with each other, and with the exuberant young director. d'Orsay is early sent off the set for indecent exposure, Bryan walks off in dudgeon and Sir Geoffrey, as he says " fell off " the rickety rostrum on which he had been directed to climb, only to find that producers and camera crew had all unaccountably vanished.

What emerges is a delightful dramatic portrait of Sir Geoffrey, generally believed to represent Gielgud himself. Idioms of speech and personal idiosyncracies are painted in affectionate detail— the unflinching honesty about others at odds with innate courtesy and concern, the *faux pas* hastily withdrawn, above all the integrity and self-effacing modesty of the true artist.

The play especially appeals to theatrical cognoscenti but it has another dimension. It is, says Wood, "about the failure of theatrical success" and it comically exposes the absurdities of costly film epics. The setting in the Greek theatre is effective visual irony and the final impression is of the futility of a mammoth enterprise that leaves the ancient site littered with indestructible plastic cups tossed everywhere among the Hittite débris.

Jingo. 1975.

The play, set in the last days of Singapore, centres round the promiscuous Gwendoline and her relations with her ex-husband and lover and with her present husband, an impotent and masochistic brigadier, reiterating his fatuous denigration of the Japs. As satire it is sadly out of date.

IDEAS &
BELIEFS

This section explains many of the
ideas and beliefs that have dominated men's minds during the centuries.   The arrangement is alphabetical and the subjects fall broadly
into four groups: religious, philosophical, political, and off beat cults
and ideas.

IDEAS AND BELIEFS

THIS section explains many of the ideas and beliefs which people have held at different periods in history. Beliefs may be true or false, meaningful or totally meaningless, regardless of the degree of conviction with which they are held. Since man has been moved to action so often by his beliefs they are worth serious study. The section throws a vivid light on human history.

Man has always felt a deep need for emotional security, a sense of "belonging." This need has found expression in the framing of innumerable religious systems, nearly all of which have been concerned with man's relation to a divine ruling power. In the past people have been accustomed to think of their own religion as true and of all others as false. Latterly we have come to realise that in man's religious strivings there is common ground, for our need in the world today is a morality whereby human beings may live together in harmony.

There is also to be found in man an irresistible curiosity which demands an explanation of the world in which he finds himself. This urge to make the world intelligible takes him into the realm of science where the unknown is the constant challenge. Science is a creative process, always in the making, since the scientist's conjectures are constantly being submitted to severe critical tests. Basic scientific ideas are discussed in Section F.

A

Activists, those in a political movement who insist on taking active steps towards their objectives rather than merely putting forward a programme. Lately activism has become an increasingly common facet of political life. This is probably because the undeniably rapid social changes which are taking place across the world at the moment are not generally being followed by appropriate shifts in political structures and ideals.

Acupuncture, a quasi-medical system originating in China and based on the supposedly therapeutic effects of implanting fine gold needles in the spinal cord and other specific parts of the body. The site of needle implantation is decided according to traditional texts. The apparent lack of any logical relationship between the implantation sites and any known physiological or anatomical systems within the body has caused acupuncture to be held in low regard by Western medicine. Indeed it is certainly true that acupuncture and other similar practices tend to flourish in parts of the world where orthodox medicine has made little progress or where doctors and trained staff are scarce.

Recent years however have seen a curious and unexpected revival of interest in acupuncture in Europe and America, prompted in large part by the considerable press publicity which has surrounded a number of major surgical operations performed without anaesthesia upon human patients and which have been witnessed by sceptical Western specialists. Considerable controversy still surrounds acupuncture and is likely to continue for many years—possibly because it is hard to envisage a theory to explain its effects which is consistent with orthodox medicine. No doubt the immensely powerful effects of suggestion and hypnosis need to be taken into account. Some recent discoveries on the psychology and physiology of pain which show that severe wound pain may be alleviated by electrical stimulation of the nerve endings in the site of the wound may also have some relevance. It is tempting to take the line that acupuncture is based on some "forgotten" or "hidden" medical system and to assume that it is only because Western scientists are blinkered and hide-bound that it is not being incorporated in a big way into European and American hospitals. But there are always two sides to an argument; whereas the first reports from Western specialists visiting China were filled with grudging acceptance and genuine puzzlement, more recent visitors have brought back a subtly different story. One of the world's leading experts on pain, for example, who has himself witnessed acupuncture-based surgery, reports four significant findings: (1) contrary to earlier reports, patients *are* sedated, sometimes heavily so, before surgery; (2) those patients who do go for surgery using acupuncture are only chosen after a fairly rigorous selection procedure to see whether they have complete faith in the method; (3) acupuncture does not appear to work with children; and (4) its use appears to be on the decline in the major hospitals in China. Despite this rather sceptical analysis, it is clear that the full story about acupuncture, its nature and its practical value has not yet been told.

Adlerian Psychology. In 1911 the Viennese psychoanalyst Alfred Adler (1870–1937) together with his colleague Carl Gustav Jung broke with their friend Sigmund Freud over disputes concerning the latter's theoretic approach to psychoanalysis. Jung and Adler were themselves shortly also to part company, each to set up and develop his own "school" of psychoanalysis. Adler's system of psychotherapy is based on the idea, not of sex as a driving force as in the case of Freud, but on the concept of "compensation" or a drive for power in an attempt to overcome the "inferiority complex" which he held to be universal in human beings. The child naturally feels inferior to adults, but bullying, making him feel insignificant or guilty or contemptible, even spoiling, which makes him feel important within the family but relatively unimportant outside, increases this feeling. Or the child may have physical defects: he may be small or underweight, have to wear glasses, become lame, be constantly ill, or stupid at school. In these ways he develops a sense of inferiority which for the rest of his life he develops a technique to overcome.

This may be done in several ways: he may try to become capable in the very respects in which he feels incompetent—hence many great orators have originally had speech defects; many painters poor eyesight; many musicians have been partially deaf; like Nietzsche, the weakling, he may write about the superman, or like Sandow, the strong man, be born with poor health.

On the other hand he may overdo his attempt and overcompensate. Hence we have the bully who is really a coward, the small man who is self-assertive to an objectionable degree (Hitler, Napoleon, Stalin, and Mussolini were all small men) or the foreigner who like three of these men wanted to be the hero of his adopted country—Hitler the Austrian, Napoleon the Italian, Stalin the Georgian.

But what about the man who can do none of these things, who continues to fail to compensate? He, says Adler, becomes a neurotic because neurosis is an excuse which means "I could have done so-and-so but . . . ." It is the unconscious flight into illness—the desire to be ill. Adler's treatment involves disclosing these subterfuges we play on ourselves so that we can deal with the real situation in a more realistic way. Adlerian psychoanalysis still attracts supporters, but its golden days were when the founder was at the head of the movement in the U.S.A., when his views were considered to provide a more "acceptable" theory of the mind than the enormously controversial theories of Freud with their strong sexual orientation.

Adventists, a group of American religious sects, the most familiar being the Seventh-Day Adventist Church, which observes Saturday as the true Sabbath. With more than a million members throughout the world, it shares with other Adventists a belief in the imminent second coming of Christ (a doctrine fairly widespread in the U.S.A. during the early decades of the 19th cent. when the end of the world was predicted by William Miller for 1843, then for 1844). Modern Adventists content themselves with the conviction that the " signs " of the Advent are multiplying, the " blessed event " which will solve the world's ills. Believers will be saved, but the sects differ as to whether the unjust will be tortured in hell, annihilated, or merely remain asleep eternally.

Agnosticism. *See* God and Man.

Albigenses, also known as Cathari. French heretical sect (named after the town of Albi in Provence) which appeared in the 11th cent. to challenge the Catholic Church on the way true Christians should lead their lives. They followed a life of extreme asceticism in contrast to the local clergy and their faith was adopted by the mass of the population, especially in Toulouse. Condemned as heretics by Pope Innocent III, the sect was exterminated in the savage Albigensian Crusade (1208–29), initially led by Simon de Montfort. (In his thoroughness, de Montfort also succeeded in destroying the high culture of the Troubadors.)

Alchemy, ancient art associated with magic and astrology in which modern chemistry has its roots. The earliest mention of alchemy comes from ancient Egypt but its later practitioners attributed its origins to such varied sources as the fallen angels of the Bible, to Moses and Aaron, but most commonly to Hermes Trismegistus, often identified with the Egyptian god Thoth, whose knowledge of the divine art was handed down only to the sons of kings (cf. the phrase " hermetically sealed "). Its main object was the transmutation of metals. Egyptian speculation concerning this reached its height during the 6th cent. in the Alexandrian school. Brought to Western Europe by the Moslems, one of its most famous Arab exponents was Jabir (*c.* 760–*c.* 815), known to the Latins as Geber, who had a laboratory at Kufa on the Tigris. One school of early Greek philosophy held that there was ultimately only one elemental matter of which everything was composed. Such men as Albertus Magnus (1206–80) and Roger Bacon (1214–94) assumed that, by removing impurities, this *materia prima* could be obtained. Although Bacon's ideas were in many ways ahead of his time, he firmly believed in the philosopher's stone, which could turn base metals into gold, and in an elixir of life which would give eternal youth. Modern science has, of course, shown in its researches into radioactivity the possibility of transmutation of certain elements, but this phenomenon has little bearing on either the methods of the alchemist or the mysteries with which he surrounded them. In line with the current considerable revival of interest in the occult, alchemy appears to be staging a comeback, at least as a literary if not an experimental topic.

Anabaptists. *See* Baptists.

Analytical Psychology, the name given by Carl Gustav Jung (1875–1961) of Zürich to his system of psychology which, like Adler's (*see* Adlerian Psychology), took its origin from Freud's psychoanalysis from which both diverged in 1911. Briefly, Jung differed from Freud: (1) in believing that the latter had laid too much emphasis on the sexual drive as the basic one in man and replacing it with the concept of *libido* or life energy of which sex forms a part; (2) in his theory of types: men are either extrovert or introvert (*i.e.* their interest is turned primarily outwards to the world or inwards to the self), and they apprehend experience in four main ways, one or other of which is predominant in any given individual—sensing, feeling, thinking, or intuiting; (3) in his belief that the individual's unconscious mind contains not only repressed material which, as Freud maintained, was too unpleasant to be allowed into awareness, but also faculties which had not been allowed to develop—*e.g.*, the emotional side of the too rational man, the feminine side of the too masculine one; (4) in the importance he attaches to the existence of a

collective unconscious at a still deeper level which contains traces of ancient ways of thought which mankind has inherited over the centuries. These are the *archetypes* and include vague primitive notions of magic, spirits and witches, birth and death, gods, virgin mothers, resurrection, etc. In the treatment of neuroses Jung believed in the importance of (*a*) the present situation which the patient refuses to face; (*b*) the bringing together of conscious and unconscious and integrating them.

In the 1940s and 50s interest in Jung's ideas waned, at least in academic circles, as the emphasis among experimental psychologists shifted closer and closer to the " hard " scientific line. This was also true in the field of psychoanalysis where the Jungian as opposed to the Freudian point of view became progressively less popular. At the present time this trend is beginning to reverse, and while Jung's offbeat views on astrology, telepathy, etc., are still unfashionable, a reappraisal of the significance of his views on the nature of the unconscious is taking place and many psychologists feel that his contribution to our understanding of the nature of human mental processes has been greatly underrated. *See also* Psychoanalysis.

Anarchism, a political philosophy which holds, in the words of the American anarchist Josiah Warren (1798–1874), an early follower of Robert Owen, that " every man should be his own government, his own law, his own church." The idea that governmental interference or even the mere existence of authority is inherently bad is as old as Zeno, the Greek Stoic philosopher, who believed that compulsion perverts the normal nature of man. William Godwin's *Enquiry Concerning Political Justice* (1793) was the first systematic exposition of the doctrine. Godwin (father-in-law of Shelley) claimed that man is by nature sociable, co-operative, rational, and good when given the choice to act freely; that under such conditions men will form voluntary groups to work in complete social harmony. Such groups or communities would be based or equality of income, no state control, and no property; this state of affairs would be brought about by rational discussion and persuasion rather than by revolution.

The French economist Proudhon (1809–65) was the first to bring anarchism to the status of a mass movement. In his book *What is Property?* he stated bluntly that " property is theft " and " governments are the scourge of God." He urged the formation of co-operative credit banks where money could be had without interest and goods could be exchanged at cost value at a rate representing the hours of work needed to produce each commodity. Like Godwin, he disapproved of violence but, unlike Marx, disapproved of trades unions as representing organised groups.

In communistic anarchism these ideas were combined with a revolutionary philosophy, primarily by the Russians Michael Bakunin (1814–76) and Peter Kropotkin (1842–1921) who favoured training workers in the technique of " direct action " to overthrow the state by all possible means, including political assassination. In 1868 anarchists joined the First International which broke up a few years later after a bitter struggle between Bakuninists and Marxists. Subsequently small anarchist groups murdered such political figures as Tsar Alexander II of Russia, King Humbert of Italy, Presidents Carnot of France and MacKinley of America, and the Empress Elizabeth of Austria.

Anarchism and communism differ in three main ways: (1) anarchism forms no political party, rejects all relationship with established authority, and regards democratic reform as a setback; (2) communism is against capitalism, anarchism against the state as such; (3) both have the final goal of a classless society, but anarchism rejects the idea of an intermediate period of socialist state control accepted by communism. Philosophical anarchists, such as the American writer Henry David Thoreau (1817–62), were primarily individualists who believed in a return to nature, the non-payment of taxes, and passive resistance to state control;

in these respects Thoreau strongly influenced Gandhi as did the Christian anarchist Tolstoy.

Anarchism has traditionally been criticised as being impractical—*e.g.*, in a non-authoritarian society, who is going to look after the sewers or clean the streets?—and there is a good deal of force to this argument. In fact anarchistic ideas became progressively less fashionable in the first half of this century. A curious and probably significant revival of interest has taken place in the past decade, however, probably because of a growing sense of disillusion, particularly on the part of young people, with the progress of orthodox political systems. *See also* Syndicalism.

Anglicanism, adherence to the doctrine and discipline of the Anglican Church, as the genuine representative of the Cathlic Church. *See* Church of England.

Anglo-Catholicism. To Queen Elizabeth I the Church of England was that of the " middle way " in which human reason and commonsense took their place beside Scripture and Church authority. The extent to which these various factors are stressed creates the distinctions between " high " and " low " church. Anglo-Catholics tend to reject the term " Protestant " and stress the term " Catholic " and, although few accept the infallibility of the Pope. some Anglo-Catholic churches have introduced much or all of the Roman ritual and teach Roman dogmas. *See* Catholicism, Tractarianism.

Animism. To early man and in primitive societies the distinction between animate and inanimate objects was not always obvious—it is not enough to say that living things move and non-living things do not, for leaves blow about in the wind and streams flow down a hillside. In the religions of early societies, therefore, we find a tendency to believe that life exists in all objects from rocks and pools to seas and mountains. This belief is technically known as *animatism*, which differs from *animism*, a somewhat more sophisticated view which holds that natural objects have no life in themselves but may be the abode of dead people, spirits, or gods who occasionally give them the appearance of life. The classic example of this, of course. is the assumption that an erupting volcano is an expression of anger on the part of the god who resides in it. Such beliefs may seem absurd today, but it is worth realising that we are not entirely free of them ourselves when we ascribe " personalities " of a limited kind to motor cars, boats, dolls, or models which incur our pleasure or anger depending upon how well they " behave."

Anthropomorphism, the attribution of human form, thoughts or motives to non-human entities or life forms from gods to animals. At one end this can be summed up in the once widespread image of God as a " white-bearded old gentleman sitting on a cloud." At the other end is the very common tendency to invest domestic animals and pets with man-like wishes and personalities. At both extremes the belief could be seriously misleading. Firstly, it could be very unwise to assume that God, if he exists, necessarily thinks as humans do and has human interests at heart. Secondly, we shall learn very little about animal behaviour if we look upon them as mere extensions of our own personality, and we do them less than justice if we see them simply as human beings or diminutive intelligence.

Anthroposophy, a school of religious and philosophical thought based on the work of the German educationist and mystic Rudolf Steiner (1861–1925). Steiner was originally an adherent of Madame Blavatsky's theosophical movement (*cf* Theosophy) but in 1913 broke away to form his own splinter group, the Anthroposophical Society, following ideological disputes over the alleged " divinity " of the Indian boy Krishnamurti. Steiner was much influenced by the German poet and scientist, Goethe, and believed that an appreciation and love for art was one of the keys to spiritual development. One of the first tasks of his new movement was the construction of a vast temple of arts and sciences, known as the Goetheanum, to act as the headquarters of the society. This structure, which was of striking and revolutionary architectural

style, was unfortunately burnt down in 1922 to be replaced by an even more imaginative one which today is one of the most interesting buildings of its kind in the world. Anthroposophy, which ceased to expand greatly following its founder's death, is nevertheless well-established in various parts of the world with specialised, and often very well equipped, schools and clinics which propagate the educational and therapeutic theories of the movement. These, which include the allegedly beneficial powers of music, coloured lights, etc., have made little impact on modern educational ideas. but the schools have acquired a reputation for success in the training of mentally handicapped children, though one suspects that these successes are due to the patience and tolerance exercised in these establishments rather than to the curative value of colour or music " therapy " itself. Despite its apparent eccentricities, anthroposophy has made its mark on art and architecture, the outstanding modern painter Kandinsky, for example, being particularly influenced by Steiner's ideas and teachings.

Anticlericalism, resentment of priestly powers and privileges, traceable in England to Wyclif's insistence in the 14th cent. on the right of all men to have access to the Scriptures. The translation of the Bible into the common tongue was a great landmark in the history of the Bible and the English language. Wyclif's principles were condemned by the Roman Church of his time but were readily accepted during the Reformation. Tudor anticlericalism arose from motives ranging from a greedy desire to plunder the riches of the Church to a genuine dislike of the powers of the priesthood whose spiritual courts still had the right to decide on points of doctrine or morals in an age when the layman felt he was well able to decide for himself. In innumerable ways the Church was permitted to extort money from the laity. It is generally agreed, says Trevelyan, that the final submission of church to state in England was motivated quite as much by anticlericalism as by Protestantism. The rise of the Reformed churches in England satisfied the people generally and anticlericalism never became the fixed principle of permanent parties as happened in France and Italy from the time of Voltaire onwards.

Antisemitism, a term first applied about the middle of the last century to those who were anti-Jewish in their outlook. Although this attitude was prevalent for religious reasons throughout the Middle Ages, modern antisemitism differed (*a*) in being largely motivated by economic or political conditions, and (*b*) in being doctrinaire with a pseudo-scientific rationale presented by such men as Gobineau (1816–82) and Houston Stewart Chamberlain (1855–1927), and later by the Nazi and Fascist " philosophers." Beginning in Russia and Hungary with the pogroms of 1882 it gradually spread south and westwards where, in France, the Dreyfus case provided an unsavoury example in 1894. Thousands of Jews from Eastern Europe fled to Britain and America during this period; for in these countries anti-semitism has rarely been more than a personal eccentricity. During the last war the murder of six million Jews by the Nazis and their accomplices led to a further exodus to various parts of the world and finally to the creation of the state of Israel.

The individual Jew-hater makes unconscious use of the psychological processes of projection and displacement: his greed or sexual guilt is projected on to the Jew (or Negro or Catholic) because he cannot bear to accept them as his own emotions, and his sense of failure in life is blamed on his chosen scapegoat rather than on his own inadequacy.

But there are social causes too and politicians in some lands are well versed in the technique of blaming unsatisfactory conditions (which they themselves may have in part produced) upon minority groups and persuading others to do the same. Historically, the Jew is ideally suited for this role of scapegoat: (1) in the Middle Ages when usury was forbidden to Christians but not to Jews, the latter often became moneylenders incurring the opprobrium generally associated with this trade (*e.g.*, to the simple-minded Russian peasant the Jew often represented, not only the " Christ-killer," but also the moneylender or small shopkeeper to whom he owed money); (2) many trades being closed to Jews, it was natural that they concentrated in others, thus arousing suspicions of " influence " (*i.e.* Jews are felt to occupy a place in certain trades and professions which far exceeds their numerical proportion to the population as a whole); (3) even with the ending of ghetto life, Jews often occupy *en masse* some parts of cities rather than others and this may lead to resentment on the part of the original inhabitants who begin to feel themselves dispossessed; (4) Jews tend to form a closed society and incur the suspicions attached to all closed societies within which social contacts are largely limited to members; marriage outside the group is forbidden or strongly disapproved of, and the preservation, among the orthodox, of cultural and religious barriers tends to isolate them from their fellow citizens. Discrimination, hateful as it is, does not come from one side only and it is such barriers as these that help to maintain an old and cruel folly. *See* Racism, Zionism, Judaism.

Anti-vivisection, opposition to scientific experimentation upon live animals based, according to its supporters, both on the moral grounds of the suffering imposed, and on the less secure claim that many doctors and scientists of repute have rejected the value of information gained in this way. It is true that the protagonists of the movement during its early days in the mid-19th cent. included a number of eminent physicians and surgeons, but few today—whatever their moral scruples—would deny the value of the results obtained. Without animal experiments we would be unable to test out new drugs for safety before using them on human beings. There are in Britain two or three large national anti-vivisection societies and several smaller ones. Much of their work is co-ordinated through the British Council of Anti-Vivisection Societies. Animal experimentation is controlled by Act of Parliament which makes obligatory the possession of licences by experimenters, inspection of laboratories by the Home Office, and the issue of annual returns of experiments. Many people would like the number of experiments on animals reduced and the law changed to prohibit any experiment in which there is any risk of inflicting suffering. A recent opinion survey showed that while the public approves of medical experiment it strongly disapproves of animals being used for the testing of cosmetics and other chemicals which have nothing to do with medical research. Reform of the Cruelty to Animals Act 1876 has been called for in view of the enormous increase in the number and variety of live animal experiments.

Apartheid, an Afrikaans word meaning " apartness," referred to by South African Government spokesmen as " separate development " or " self-development." To others it means the system of total racial discrimination between black and white South Africans—the permanent inhabitants of the country—as enforced by the Nationalist Party since it came to power in 1948. Some degree of racial segregation has existed in South Africa since the earliest days of colonialism in the mid-17th cent. and the policy was continued by the United Party under Smuts and Hertzog from 1934 onwards though it was never a political issue. This changed when the National Party gained power and oppressive measures against the non-white segment of the population have grown steadily under Malan, Strydom, Verwoerd, and Vorster. *Apartheid* involves the beliefs in racial purity and *baaskap*, or white supremacy. It means keeping vast African populations in a condition of helotry. Thousands of families are broken up by the pass laws. The official policy of the South African Government is to create separate self-governing black states in which the Africans would be guided to self-government and, it is claimed, eventually to independence. The first so-called Bantu reserve was set up in the Transkei in 1962. But Africans with 70 per cent of the population would have only about 13 per cent of the land, and the poorest land at that; cities and mineral areas would remain the reserve of the whites. Total *apartheid* or complete separation of the black and white races in South Africa remains unlikely to be realised since mining, the main industry of the country, is based on low-paid African labour.

The sports boycott, the conflict between the churches and the government, and the economic need to make more use of African labour, could bring an impetus for change. The increasing economic power of some of the black African states – Nigeria for example, is rich in oil resources – and the elimination of " Europeanism " from the Arab cultures of the North, has led to a steady erosion of the power-base of the white dominant countries such as South Africa and Rhodesia. Inevitably, *apartheid* has shown signs of reaction in response to these external pressures. More recent events, including the suppression of the Soweto riots and the death of Steve Biko, have increasingly isolated South Africa even from her erstwhile Western allies.

See also Africa, Section C, Part II.

Aquarius, one of the twelve " signs of the Zodiac." This has recently achieved special significance in the mythology of our time because of the pronouncements of astrologers that the world is shifting out of the 2000-years-old cycle of the Age of Pisces, the fish, into that of Aquarius the water-carrier. The exact date of the transition is a matter of astrological controversy, but the consensus is that it began in 1960 and will be completed sometime in the 24th century. The Aquarian Age is predicted to be one of peace and harmony, replacing the era of strife which, ironically, has marked the dominance of the Christian symbol of the fish. Such speculations are totally without scientific backing and are mentioned here only to draw attention to the grip which astrological and other mythical concepts still have on human thinking. One of the first spaceships to carry man to the moon, for example, was named Aquarius by its crew. *See also* Astrology.

Arianism, formed the subject of the first great controversy within the Christian Church over the doctrine of Arius of Alexandria (d. 336) who denied the divinity of Christ. The doctrine, although at first influential, was condemned at the Council of Nicaea (325), called by the Emperor Constantine, at which Arius was opposed by Athanasius, also of Alexandria, who maintained the now orthodox view that the Son is of one substance with the Father. Arius was banished and the heresy had died out by the end of the 4th cent., but disbelief in the divinity of Christ has formed part of the doctrine of many minor sects since, notably in Unitarianism (*q.v.*).

Assassins, a sect of Moslem Shi'ites, founded by the Persian Hasan i Sabbah (*c.* 1090), which for more than two centuries established a rule of terror all over Persia and Syria. The coming of the Mongols in 1256 destroyed them in Persia and the Syrian branch suffered a similar fate at the hands of the then Mamluk sultan of Egypt, *c.* 1270. It was a secret order, ruled over by a grand master, under whom the members were strictly organised into classes, according to the degree of initiation into the secrets of the order. The devotees, belonging to one of the lower groups, carried out the actual assassinations under strict laws of obedience, and total ignorance of the objects and ritual of the society. It is believed that the latter were given ecstatic visions under the influence of hashish, whence the term *hashshashin*, which became corrupted to " assassin."

Associationism. In psychology, the Associationist school of the 19th cent. accepted the association of ideas as the fundamental principle in mental life. It was represented in Britain by the two Mills and Herbert Spencer, in Germany by J. F. Herbart (1776–1841). To these, mental activity was nothing but the association of " ideas " conceived of as units of both thought and feeling—the emotion of anger or the perception of a chair were both " ideas "—and apart from them the self did not exist. Personality was simply a series of these units coming and going, adding to or cancelling each other out, in accordance with rigid and mechanistic scientific laws.

Astrology was once the best available theory for explaining the course of human life and bears much the same historical relationship to astronomy as alchemy does to chemistry. Originally it was divided into the two branches of Natural Astrology which dealt with the movements of the heavenly bodies and their calculations, and Judicial Astrology which studied the alleged influence of the stars and the planets on human life and fate. It was the former that developed into modern astronomy; the latter was, and remains, a primitive myth.

Astrology owes most to the early Babylonians (or Chaldeans) who, being largely nomadic in an environment which permitted an unobstructed view of the sky, readily accepted the idea that divine energy is manifested in the movements of the sun and planets. Gradually this concept became enlarged and the relative positions of the planets both in relation to each other and to the fixed stars became important together with the idea of omens—that, if a particular event occurred whilst the planets were in a particular position, the recurrence of that position heralded a recurrence of the same sort of event. Soon the planets became associated with almost every aspect of human life. They were bound up with the emotions, with parts of the body, so that astrology played quite a large part in medicine up to late mediaeval times. Not only was the position of the planet to be considered but also the particular sign of the zodiac (or house of heaven) it was occupying, and it was believed possible to foretell the destiny of an individual by calculating which star was in the ascendant (*i.e.* the sign of the zodiac nearest the eastern horizon and the star which arose at that precise moment) at the time of his birth. Astrology was popular among the Egyptians, the Romans (whose authorities found the Chaldean astrologers a nuisance and expelled them from time to time), and during the Middle Ages when astrologers were often highly respected.

Despite the apparent absurdity of astrological beliefs—for example, how could the pattern of light from stars billions of miles away possibly influence the temperament of single individuals on earth—a substantial number of intelligent and well-educated people take its study in all seriousness. The most interesting "convert" was the psychologist and philosopher, Carl Jung, who conducted a complex experiment in which he compared the "birth signs" of happily married and divorced couples and claimed to find that those most favourably matched in astrological terms were also those more likely to have permanent wedded bliss. Jung's findings were subsequently shown to have been based on a simple statistical fallacy, which did not prevent the brilliant but eccentric psychologist from offering them up as evidence in support of his own theory of "synchronicity" (**J51**), an involved and vaguely metaphysical notion which suggests that events in the universe may be significantly related in a "non-causal" fashion. To add fuel to the controversy however, the French mathematician, Michel Gauquelin, has recently offered up fresh data which apparently supports the general astrological view. In a carefully controlled study he noticed statistically significant correspondences between certain astrological signs and the professions of a large number of Frenchmen whose birth time and date were accurately recorded. Gauquelin claims to have repeated his study on a second large sample of his fellow countrymen, though he has been unable to use English people as the exact times of birth are not recorded on their birth certificates! This apparent shot in the arm for astrology is still a matter of great scientific controversy, though Gauquelin's work has been given support from the distinguished British psychologist, H. J. Eysenck, who has pronounced his statistical data to be incontrovertible. Both scientists, however, carefully refrain from discussing the implications of these curious findings, and the controversy will no doubt increase rather than decrease in the near future.

Atheism. *See* God and Man.

Atlantis, a mythical continent supposed to have lain somewhere between Europe and America and a centre of advanced civilisation before it was inundated by some great natural catastrophe in pre-Christian times. There is little, if any, serious historical or archaeological evidence for its existence, but the legend of the Golden Land destroyed when the waters of the Atlantic closed over it has remarkable staying power and is believed by large numbers of people. Plato wrote convincingly about the wonders of Atlantis in his dialogues *Timaeus* and *Critias*, while other writers gave suggested that the biblical story of the Flood is based on fragmentary accounts of the Atlantean deluge. The lost continent is also of occult significance, largely as the result of the writings of W. Scott-Elliott whose book, *The Story of Atlantis* (recently re-published by the Theosophical Society), alleged that by clairvoyance he had been able to contact the spirits of Atlanteans who had been destroyed because of their addiction to black magic. There even exists in Britain today a minor but ardent religious group, the "Atlanteans," who hold that Atlantis still exists today, but on a differen metatphysical plane, and that it is possible to communicate with it via individuals with supposedly mediumistic powers (*see* Spiritualism). Members of the Atlanteans meet regularly to hear "trance addresses" by one of the high priests of Atlantis, Helio-Arconaphus. Such beliefs are essentially harmless and merely reflect the great variety of religious attitudes which human beings enjoy.

Atomism. In philosophy, the atomists were a group of early Greek thinkers, the most important of whom were Leucippus (fl. *c.* 440 B.C.) and his younger contemporary Democritus (*c.* 460–370 B.C.). Prior to these men, although it had been agreed that matter must be composed of tiny ultimate particles and that change must be due to the manner in which these mingled or separated from each other, it was supposed that there existed different types of particle for each material—*e.g.* for flesh, wood, hair, bone. The atomists taught that atoms were all made of a single substance and differed only in the connections (pictured as hooks, grooves, points, etc.) which enabled them to join each other in characteristic ways. Theirs was the first move towards modern atomic theory and a predecessor of the modern concept of chemical linkages.

Authoritarianism, a dictatorial form of government as contrasted with a democratic one based on popular sovereignty. Its alleged advantages are the avoidance of the delays and inefficiency said to be characteristic of the latter.

Automatism, the production of material, written or spoken in "automatic" fashion—*i.e.*, apparently not under the conscious or volitional control of the individual. This psychologically perplexing phenomenon has occurred from time to time throughout the history of literature and art, and while it has occasionally produced work of great merit (much of William Blake's poetry, Coleridge's "Kubla Khan," etc.) the bulk of it is indifferent and often simply rubbish. Spiritualists claim that the work is produced under the direct guidance of the spirit world, and their argument has recently attracted considerable attention through the compositions of the pianist Rosemary Brown who, with little or no academic background in musical theory, has produced a number of "original" piano pieces allegedly composed by Beethoven, Mozart, etc., from the astral plane. While few music critics doubt Mrs. Brown's honesty and integrity, most consider her work to be clever pastiche and barely comparable in quality to the masterworks of the dead composers. Nevertheless automatism wants some explaining, and most psychologists today defer judgement, taking the view that it serves to remind us of the fund of material which lies in the unconscious mind, and which is prone to pop up from time to time without warning. Rather similar is the case of Matthew Manning, a young English student who produces clever and artistically intriguing drawings and sketches, allegedly guided by the hands of famous dead artists.

B

Baconian Method, the use of the inductive (as opposed to the deductive or Aristotelian) method of reasoning as proposed by Francis Bacon in the 17th cent. and J. S. Mill in the 19th cent. Deduction argues from supposedly certain first principles (such as the existence of God or Descartes's " I think, therefore I am ") what the nature of the universe and its laws *must* be, whereas the only means of obtaining true knowledge of the universe, in Bacon's view, was by the amassing of facts and observations so that when enough were obtained the certain truth would be known in the same way that a child's numbered dots in a playbook joined together by a pencilled line create a picture. However, this is not the way science progresses in practice (*see* **F3(1)**). Bacon underrated the importance of hypothesis and theory and overrated the reliability of the senses. In discussing the scientific tradition, Sir Karl Popper in his book, *Conjectures and Refutations,* says: " The most important function of observation and reasoning, and even of intuition and imagination, is to help us in the critical examination of those bold conjectures which are the means by which we probe into the unknown." Two of the greatest men who clearly saw that there was no such thing as an inductive procedure were Galileo and Einstein.

Bahá'i Faith, a faith which teaches the unity of all religions and the unity of mankind. It arose in Iran from the teachings of the Bab (Mirza Ali Mohammed, 1820–50) and the Bahá'u'lláh (Mirza Husain Ali, 1817–92), thought to be manifestations of God, who in his essence is unknowable. Emphasis is laid on service to others. It has communities in many states and is surprisingly strong in England with a substantial following among university students. Its aims—universal peace, love, fellowship, etc. —are so laudable that it is hard to disagree with anything in the movement. On the other hand it is equally hard to see what it can offer, apart from more good intentions, over and above the teaching of more orthodox religious systems. The movement is now guided and administered by an elected order, " The Universal House of Justice ".

Baptists, a Christian denomination whose distinctive doctrines are that members can only be received by baptism " upon the confession of their faith and sins " and that " baptism in no wise appertaineth to infants." Baptism is therefore by total immersion of adults. Modern Baptists base their doctrines upon the teaching of the Apostles and some hold that the Albigenses (*q.v.*) maintained the true belief through what they regarded as the corruption of the Roman Church in mediaeval times. On the other hand any connection with the Anabaptist movement during the Reformation is rejected and the beginning of the modern Church is traced to John Smyth, a minister of the Church of England who in Amsterdam came under the influence of the Arminians (*q.v.*) and Mennonites. Smyth died in 1612 when the first Baptist church in England was built at Newgate. This, the " General " Baptist Church, rejected Calvinistic beliefs and held the Arminian doctrine of redemption open to all, but some years later a split occurred with the formation of the " Particular " Baptist Church which was Calvinist in doctrine. In 1891 the two bodies were united in the Baptist Union and today the sect is spread throughout the world notably in the United States.

The Anabaptist movements of Germany, Switzerland, and Holland also practised adult baptism in addition to a primitive communism and demanded social reforms. Persecuted by both Catholics and Protestants, their leader, Thomas Münzer, and many others were burned at the stake (1525). However, this sect was noted for its violence under a religious guise, and its taking over of the state of Münster in 1533 was characterised by wild licentiousness, since, as Antinomians, they believed that the " elect " could do no wrong. A revival begun by Menno Simons (d. 1561), a Dutch religious reformer, led to the formation of the Mennonite sect which, whilst rejecting infant baptism, gave up the objectionable features of the Anabaptists. This reformed sect still exists as small agricultural groups in the original strongholds of the movement and in the United States.

Beat Generation, a term first used by the American writer Jack Kerouac (d. 1969), author of *The Town and the City* and *On The Road,* to define various groups spread across the face of the country, but notably in New York and San Francisco, who, belonging to the post-war generation, represented a complex of attitudes. Briefly, these were: rejection of the values of the past and lack of conviction in the possibility of a future for humanity—hence an acceptance of nothing but the immediate present in terms of experience and sensations; rebellion against organised authority, not out of any political conviction (as in the case of anarchism), but rather from lack of any interest or desire to control events, nature, or people; contempt for the " Square "—the orthodox individual who, stuck firmly in his rut, " plays it safe " and remains confident of the rightness and decency of his moral values. *See* **Beat Poets, Section M.**

The Beat Generation of the 1940s and 50s gave way to the Love generation or Flower people, with their flowers, beads, and cowbells. Their social philosophy was the same—living in the present, unconventionally, seeking personal freedom, believing drugs to be essential, claiming to be acting against the rat race, dissociating themselves from politics, taking a superficial interest in the religions of the East, borrowing much of their language, music, and ideas on dress from the American " hippy "; yet believing in the creation of a new and gentler society based on different forms and values.

Both the Beat and Love generations were forerunners in America of an increasing and certainly welcome social awareness on the part of American students. This led in turn to the " campus revolutions " which were disruptive in their early stages but were also influential as part of the wave of public protest against the American involvement in Vietnam.

Behaviourism, a school of psychology founded in 1914 by J. B. Watson (1878–1958), an animal psychologist at Johns Hopkins University, Baltimore. Its main tenet was that the method of introspection and the study of mental states were unscientific and should be replaced by the study of behaviour. When animals or human beings were exposed to specific stimuli and their responses objectively recorded, or when the development of a child, as seen in its changing behaviour, was noted, these alone were methods which were truly scientific. Watson contributed an important idea to psychology and did a great deal towards ridding it of the largely philosophical speculations of the past. But he also went to absurd extremes, as in his view that thought is nothing but subvocal speech, consisting of almost imperceptible movements of the tongue, throat, and larynx (*i.e.,* when we think, we are really talking to ourselves), and his further opinion that heredity is, except in grossly abnormal cases, of no importance. He claimed that by " conditioning," the ordinary individual could be made into any desired type, regardless of his or her inheritance.

The work of Ivan Pavlov had begun about 1901, but was unknown in America until about ten years later, and it was through another Russian, Vladimir Bekhterev, that the concept of " conditioning " was introduced into the country. Bekhterev's book *Objective Psychology,* describing his new science of " reflexology," was translated in 1913 and played a great part in the development of Behaviourist ideas. The conditioned reflex became central to Watson's theory of learning and habit formation (*e.g.,* he showed that a year-old child, at first unafraid of white rats, became afraid of them when they came to be associated with a loud noise behind the head). Finally all behaviour, including abnormal behaviour, came to be explained in terms of conditioned responses; these were built up by association on the infant's three innate emotions of fear, rage, and love, of which the original stimuli were, for the first, loud noises and the fear of falling; for the second, interference with freedom of movement; and for the third, patting and stroking.

Because of its considerable theoretical simplicity and its implicit suggestion that human behaviour could be easily described (and even modified or controlled), Pavlovian psychology appeared very attractive to the Communist regime in Russia, and before long it became the "official" dogma in universities and research laboratories. Whereas in America and Western Europe its severe limitations became gradually apparent, in Russia these were ignored or disguised for ideological reasons with the inevitable outcome that Soviet psychology failed to evolve and, at one stage, seemed to be no more than a pallid offshoot of physiology. The recent liberalisation which has been taking place throughout Soviet society has led to a considerable broadening of scientific horizons and Pavlovian ideas are no longer looked upon with such unquestioning reverence. In non-Communist countries simple Watsonian behaviourism has evolved into more sophisticated studies of animal learning, largely pioneered by the Harvard psychologist, Skinner. These techniques, which have shown that animals, from monkeys to rats, may be taught to solve a remarkable range of physical problems (such as pressing complex sequences of buttons or levers to escape from a cage) have themselves turned out to be rather disappointing in terms of advancing our general understanding of the workings of the human and animal brain. There is a growing feeling among psychologists that the real keys to the understanding of mankind will only be found through the study of man himself, and not of his simpler animal cousins. *See also* **Gestalt Psychology** and Q18–20.

Benthamism. *See* Utilitarianism.

Black Power. The division of the world's population into races is now generally agreed by scientists to have arisen as the result of climatic and environmental pressures—the darker, more highly pigmented peoples tending to be better equipped to withstand higher solar output than the fairer, more northerly based types. For various reasons, again largely climatic and environmental, the first great advances in civilisation came from the temporary ascendancy over the black or near-black. Until quite recently—not much more than a century ago—the technological gulf between white and black was so vast that the negroid races were often held in slavery by the Europeans and while such a thought might be repugnant to most today, attitudes to coloured people still reflect a notion of inherent white "superiority" which it is easy to deny intellectually but difficult to shake off emotionally. In the U.S.A., the most advanced and at the same time the most tormented multi-racial society in the world, the role of the substantial negroid population has changed dramatically in the last hundred years, shifting from that of slave to friendly servant, and then to near, or theoretical, equal. With this shift has come a corresponding change in the black community's view of itself, from relief at being no longer slaves, to gratitude at being allowed to do the menial jobs in the American society. More recently, with advances in educational opportunity and increasing political liberalisation, the attitude of the Negro in the U.S.A. has shifted yet again—from subservience to intellectual and physical equality, and even, perhaps, to inherent superiority. This new stand, rare at first, but spreading rapidly across America and other parts of the world throughout the 1960s, has crystallised in the concept and ideology of "Black Power," a movement of growing significance and importance in modern society. It is hard to trace the moment at which this formally emerged but one of its first expressions was the use by Negroes of the phrase "Black is beautiful," an apparent wakening of the belief that their colour, physique, features, hair, etc., were in no way aesthetically inferior to those of Europeans. Suddenly, in Negro communities it became no longer fashionable to straighten hair artificially, to bleach the skin or even to copy white American clothing, social habits, speech, and mannerisms. Alongside this highly important psychological jump—a rejection of the white man's social patterns—came an increasing

rejection of his political machinery as well, a belief that the black races should have political autonomy and power of their own and not as part of an integrationist evolution of Caucasian societies.

The Black Power movement at this moment has no formal political representation in the United States, largely because it spurns the normal democratic approach of offering up candidates for election, but its strength and growing potency is well understood by enlightened American politicians who take careful account of its views on current or proposed "racialist" legislation. Its present strategy is a declared one of attaining black supremacy and autonomy rapidly by violence and revolution if necessary, and it has supporters in all sections of the Negro population—and among many of the younger whites as well. In the late 60s when the Black Power movement was in its most aggressive phase of expansion, there were real fears that open conflict, almost of civil war dimensions, might break out in American cities, but increasing liberalisation and better opportunities for social advancement and education for Negroes has slightly dulled its sense of purpose. The early 70s in fact have seen a dramatic change in the state of the Negro, with blacks penetrating middle-class and professional strata of society – medicine, law, politics, business, science etc.—at a rate which would have seemed incredible 20 years ago. Urban ghettoes, however, still exist and provide numerous flashpoints for black-white conflict—the city of Boston is a particularly good example—but most observers (black and white) now view the future with more optimism than pessimism. However, the fact that America is fast becoming the best integrated country in the world is at least partly due to the conflicts and injustices which launched Black Power into being.

Bolshevism, an alternative name for Communism (*q.v.*), usually used in the West in a derogatory sense. When the Russian Social Democratic Party at a conference held in London in 1903 split over the issue of radicalism or moderation, it was the radical faction headed by Lenin (who subsequently led the 1917 Revolution and became first Head of State of the Soviet Union) which polled the majority of votes. The Russian for majority is *bolshinstvo* and for minority *menshinstvo*; hence the radicals became known as Bolsheviki and the moderates as Mensheviki, anglicised as Bolsheviks and Mensheviks. *See* Communism, Marxism.

British Israelites, a religious group who hold the race-theory that the English-speaking peoples (of the White Race) are the lineal descendants of the "lost Ten Tribes" of Israel (deported by Sargon of Assyria on the fall of Samaria in 721 B.C.). They believe the Anglo-Saxons to be God's "Chosen People" in the literal sense of the term as it is used in the Old Testament by whom the world will be brought in readiness for the Millennium. The official organisation is the British–Israel World Federation of which the official journal is the *National Message*. Some British Israelites have the notion that the future can be foretold by the measurements of the Great Pyramid.

Buchmanism. *See* **Moral Re-Armament.**

Buddhism, one of the great Oriental religions. It arose against the background of Hinduism in north India in the 6th cent. B.C., its founder (real or legendary) being the Hindu prince Siddhartha Gautama, known as the Buddha or "Enlightened One." Distressed by the problem of human suffering from which even death allowed no escape—since Buddha accepted the Hindu doctrine of a cycle of lives—he left his palace and his beloved wife and child to become a religious mendicant and ascetic, studying without success for six years the beliefs of Brahmin hermits and self-torturing recluses. After this fruitless search he sat down under a tree (the Bo-tree) and finally came to understand the cause and cure of suffering. The result of his meditations are enshrined in the "four noble truths" which are: (1) that existence is unhappiness; (2) that unhappiness is caused by selfish desire or craving; (3) that desire can be destroyed; (4) that it can be destroyed by following the "noble eightfold path" whose steps are: right views; right desires; right speech, plain and truthful; right conduct, including abstinence not only from immorality but also from taking life, whether human or animal; right livelihood, harming no one; right effort, always pressing on; right awareness of the past, the present, and the future; and lastly, right contemplation or meditation. The more man acquires merit by following these rules in his chain of lives, the sooner is *Nirvana* attained; he loses his individuality, not by annihilation, but " as the dewdrop slips into the shining sea," by merging with the universal life.

Buddhism teaches the way of liberation through ethics and discipline. A universal God plays no part in this religion, and in many Buddhist nations no word exists for the concept which was neither affirmed nor denied by Buddha himself but simply ignored. Nor did Buddha claim to be other than a man, although much superstition entered the religion at a later date; prayers were made to Buddha, ritual developed, sacred relics preserved under stupas, and the belief in a succession of Buddhas introduced; the sacred writings (*Tipitaka*) are divided into three parts: for the layman, the monks, the philosophers. They were produced by devotees at three councils—the first held immediately after the death of Buddha at the age of 80, the last at the order of King Asoka in 244 B.C. The founder himself wrote nothing.

Buddhism spread to Sri Lanka, Nepal, Tibet, Mongolia, Indo-China, Burma, Siam, China, and Japan, although on the whole losing influence in India. In Tibet, Buddhism developed into Lamaism (*q.v.*). In Sri Lanka and Burma it persisted in its pure form (the Hinayana), while in China and Japan it developed into the Mahayana with its bodhisattvas and avatars.

Bushido, the traditional code of honour of the Samurai or Japanese military caste corresponding to the European concept of knighthood and chivalry from which it took its separate origin in the 12th cent. Even today it is a potent influence among the upper classes, being based on the principles of simplicity, honesty, courage, and justice which together form a man's idea of personal honour.

C

Cabala, originally a collection of Jewish doctrines about the nature of the Universe, supposedly handed down by Moses to the Rabbis, which evolved into a kind of mystical interpretation of the Old Testament. Students of the history of religious belief have found its origins to be in fact extremely obscure, and some aspects appear to have been lifted from ancient Egyptian sources. Skilled Cabalists hold that the system contains a key to biblical interpretation based on the numerical values of the words and letters of the Scriptures which reveal hidden depths of meaning behind the allegorical Old Testament stories.

Calvinism, the branch of Protestantism founded basically (although preceded by Zwingli and others) by Jean Chauvin (1509–64), who was born in Noyon in Picardy. John Calvin, as he is usually called, from the Latin form of his name, Calvinius, provided in his *Institutions of the Christian Religion* the first logical definition and justification of Protestantism, thus becoming the intellectual leader of the Reformation as the older Martin Luther was its emotional instigator. The distinctive doctrine of Calvinism is its dogma of predestination which states that God has unalterably destined some souls to salvation to whom " efficacious grace and the gift of perseverance " is granted and others to eternal damnation. Calvinism, as defined in the Westminster Confession, is established in the Reformed or Presbyterian churches of France, Holland, Scotland, etc., as contrasted with the Lutheran churches, and its harsh but logical beliefs inspired the French Huguenots, the Dutch in their fight against Spanish Catholic domination, and the English Puritans. The rule set up under Calvin's influence in Geneva was marred by the burning at the stake of the anatomist Servetus for the

heresy of " pantheism," or, as we should say, Unitarianism.

Perhaps its greatest single influence outside the Church was the result of Calvinist belief that to labour industriously was one of God's commands. This changed the mediaeval notions of the blessedness of poverty and the wickedness of usury, proclaimed that men should shun luxury and be thrifty, yet implied that financial success was a mark of God's favour. In this way it was related to the rise of capitalism either as cause or effect. Max Weber, the German sociologist, believed that Calvinism was a powerful incentive to, or even cause of, the rise of capitalism (*q.v.*); Marx, Sombart, and in England, Tawney, have asserted the reverse view—that Calvinism was a result of developing capitalism, being its ideological justification.

Capitalism is an economic system under which the means of production and distribution are owned by a relatively small section of society which runs them at its own discretion for private profit. There exists, on the other hand, a propertyless class of those who exist by the sale of their labour power. Capitalism arose towards the end of the 18th cent. in England where the early factory owners working with small-scale units naturally approved of free enterprise and free trade. But free enterprise has no necessary connection with capitalism; by the beginning of this century monopolies were developing and state protection against foreign competition was demanded. Capitalism is opposed by those who believe in socialism (*q.v.*), first, for the moral reasons that it leads to economic inequality and the exploitation of labour and the consuming public, and that public welfare rather than private profit should motivate the economic system; secondly, for the practical reason that capitalism leads to recurrent economic crises. The recent world economic crisis has led to great hopes on the part of Marxists and Communists that capitalism is now involved in its final death throes. It is worth commenting, however, that the European war of the 1940s, the great depression of the 30s, the first world war and the Russian Revolution were also, in their turn, confidently held up by Communists as heralding capitalism's imminent collapse.

Cartomancy, the art of telling fortunes or predicting the future by playing cards or by the Tarot pack. The elegant Tarot cards number 78 in all and are probably mediaeval in origin. They are rich in symbolism and include trump cards depicting the devil, the pope, death, the moon, the wheel of fortune, etc., and are an interesting part of our cultural mythology. There is no evidence whatsoever that they can be used in any objective way to divine the future, and professional fortune tellers and clairvoyants who use them almost certainly rely on a little native, basic psychology to achieve their results.

Catholicism. For those who are not Roman Catholics the term " Catholic " has two separate meanings. The more general refers to the whole body of Christians throughout the world, the more specific refers to a particular view of Christianity. In this latter sense the Church of England, the Orthodox Eastern Churches, and others consider themselves " Catholic " meaning that (*a*) they belong to Christ's Church as organised on an accepted basis of faith and order; (*b*) they insist on the necessity of " liturgical " worship through established forms (*e.g.*, baptism, holy communion); (*c*) they emphasise the continuity of Christian tradition by the use of ancient creeds (*e.g.*, the Apostles' Creed, the Nicene Creed) and regard the ministry as a succession (Apostolic succession) deriving from early practice. In this sense there is thought to be no necessary contradiction between Catholicism and Protestantism regarded as a renewal of the Church in the 16th cent. by an appeal to the Scriptures as interpreted by the early Fathers of the Church. This definition obviously excludes Quakers, Christian Scientists, and many Nonconformist sects.

The Roman Catholic Church is the religious organisation of all those who acknowledge the bishop of Rome as head of the Christian

Church, recognizing him as the lawful successor of St. Peter, who was the apostle appointed by Christ to be the head of the Church. Whereas in the Protestant Churches prayer and preaching play a central part (each individual soul seeking direct communication with God), in Roman Catholic worship the central service is the Mass, or Holy Eucharist, the seven sacraments (baptism, confirmation, eucharist, penance, extreme unction, orders, and marriage) being administered by a special priesthood. Church discipline and organisation are strong and authoritarian. *See* Papal Infallibility.

Characterology, the attempt made over many centuries to classify people into personality types on the basis of physical or psychological characteristics. The first attempt was made by Hippocrates in the 5th cent. B.C. who classified temperaments into the *sanguine* (or optimistic), the *melancholic*, the *choleric* (or aggressive), and the *phlegmatic* (or placid); these were supposed to result from the predominance of the following " humours " in the body: red blood, black bile, yellow bile, or phlegm respectively. Theophrastus, a pupil of Aristotle, described, with examples, thirty extreme types of personality (*e.g.* the talkative, the boorish, the miserly, etc.); these were basically literary and imaginative but about the same time " physiognomy " arose which attempted to interpret character from the face. Physiognomy became of importance again during the Renaissance and there are still those today who believe in it in spite of the fact that, broadly speaking, there is no connection whatever between facial features and personality (*i.e.* although it may be possible to tell from the features that a man is an idiot or some extreme abnormal type and some idea of character may be obtained from an individual's characteristic facial expressions, it is not possible to tell (as Johann Lavater, the best-known physiognomist of the late 18th cent. believed) from the shape of the nose, height of the brow, or dominance of the lower jaw, whether anyone is weak, intellectual, or determined). The contention of the 19th cent. Italian criminologist Cesare Lombroso that criminals show typical facial characteristics— prominent cheekbones and jaw, slanting eyes, receding brow, large ears of a particular shape— was disproved by Karl Pearson early this century when he found that 3,000 criminals showed no significant differences of features, carefully measured, from a similar number of students at Oxford and Cambridge.

It has, however, been noted that people in general tend to be intellectual or emotional, inward- or outward-looking, and this observation is reflected in the classifications of the Scottish psychologist, Alexander Bain (d. 1903), into intellectual, artistic, and practical; Nietzsche's Apollonian and Dionysian types; William James's " tender " and " tough-minded "; and C. G. Jung's introvert and extrovert. Careful experiments have shown that these are not clear-cut and that most individuals fall in between the extremes.

Some connection has been found between temperament and body-build. The German psychiatrist Ernst Kretschmer (b. 1888) showed that manic-depressive patients and normal people who are extroverted and tend to alternate in mood (as do manic-depressives to an exaggerated degree) were usually short and stout or thick-set in build; schizophrenics and normal people, who both show shyness, serious or introverted reactions, were usually tall and slender. The former of " pyknic " body-build are " cyclothyme " in temperament, the latter with " schizothyme " temperament are of two bodily types—the tall and thin or " asthenic " and the muscularly well-proportioned or " athletic." The American Sheldon has confirmed these observations on the whole and gone into further details. According to him the basic body types are: (1) *endomorphic* (rounded build), corresponding to Kretschmer's pyknic, normally associated with the *viscerotonic* temperament (relaxed, sociable); (2) *mesomorphic* (squarish, athletic build), normally associated with the *somatotonic* temperament (energetic, assertive); and (3) *ectomorphic* (linear build) normally associated with the *cerebrotonic* temperament (anxious, submissive, restless). Glandular and metabolic factors have considerable effect on human personality and also, to some extent, on physique. It is not too surprising, therefore, to find an association between body build (or " somatotype " as Sheldon termed it) and general mood. However, Sheldon's original clear-cut and oversimplified categories of body-type are no longer looked upon as reliable indicators of personality.

Chartism, a socialistic movement in England (1837–55) which attempted to better the conditions of the working classes. Named after " The People's Charter " of Francis Place (1838), its programme demanded: (1) universal manhood suffrage; (2) vote by ballot; (3) equal electoral districts; (4) annual parliaments; (5) payment of members; (6) abolition of their property qualifications. Chartism was supported by the Christian socialists (*q.v.*), J. F. D. Maurice (1805–72), and Charles Kingsley (1819–75) with certain qualifications. The movement, the first mass organisation of the industrial working class, had considerable influence on the evolution of socialist ideas in England. It is worth noting that its demands—with the exception of the unworkable " annual parliament "— have largely been met today, though at the time they were thought by many to be both outrageous and impossible.

Chauvinism, a term applied to any excessive devotion to a cause, particularly a patriotic or military one. The word is derived from Nicholas Chauvin whose excessive devotion to Napoleon made him a laughing-stock.

Chirognomy, the attempt to read character from the lines in the hand (as contrasted with chiromancy or palmistry, in which an attempt is made to tell the future in the same way) is an ancient practice which, like astrology (*q.v.*) has no discernible scientific basis but a very considerable popular following. As with astrology, where it is hard to see what kind of link could exist between the constellations and human behaviour, so it is equally hard to see how the configuration of lines on the hand could be paralleled by psychological attributes. This argument might be thought of as irrelevant if palmistry, etc. actually had predictive power, but the plain fact is that when put to a scientific test, practitioners of these arts turn out to show no abilities beyond those with which a normally perceptive individual is equipped.

Chiropractic, the art of manipulation of the joints, in particular the spine, as a means of curing diseases, is a slightly fashionable quasi-medical practice. Few qualified doctors employ its questionable principles though, as with its near-neighbour osteopathy, it seems on occasions to be a useful complement to medical treatment. Much controversy surrounds the status of practitioners of fringe medicine of this kind. In America osteopathy (bone manipulation), which seems to be beneficial in many cases for the condition known as prolapsed or " slipped" disc, is becoming gradually merged into ortho-dox medical practice.

Christadelphians, a religious denomination formed in the U.S.A. about 1848 at the time of the American Civil War by John Thomas, an Englishman from London. They claim to represent the simple apostolic faith of the 1st cent., and, in common with many other sects, hold that they alone interpret the Scriptures truly. They believe that Christ will return soon to set up the Kingdom of God with Jerusalem as its capital. In social life Christadelphians keep to themselves and hold aloof from organisational activities, though they do take an interest in political events if only from the point of view of their belief in biblical prophecy.

Christianity, the religion founded by Jesus Christ whose teaching is found in the New Testament's four Gospels. Simple as His creed may seem it soon became complicated by the various ways in which Christians interpreted it, and the differences within the early Church are reflected in the numerous Councils held to define truth from heresy. The Eastern Church of the Byzantine Empire from the 5th cent. onwards had differed in various ways from the See of Rome and by 1054 the breach became permanent. The 16th cent. Reformation was the other great break in the unity of the Church and once Protestantism had given in effect the right to each man to interpret the Scriptures in his own way, the tendency to fragmentation increased so that, by 1650, there were no fewer than 180 sects, mostly dogmatic and intolerant towards each other. Today there are many more, some of which are mentioned in this section under the appropriate headings. Nevertheless there are signs today that the trend of disunity is being reversed. The modern ecumenical movement, which has its roots in the great missionary movement of the 19th cent., aims to bring about a reunion of Christendom by uniting Christians throughout the world on the simple basis of the acceptance of Jesus Christ as God and Saviour, *i.e.*, on the basis of Christian fellowship. The movement finds expression in the World Council of Churches (*q.v.*). The Christian life is expressed in the words of Christ: "Thou shalt love the Lord thy God with all thy heart and thy neighbour as thyself." For many it is the humanitarian side of Christianity that has meaning today: to accept responsibility for others, as well as for oneself. *See* chart, below.

Christian Science, a religious denomination founded by Mary Baker Eddy (1821–1910), an American lady who sought to organise a church which would reinstate primitive Christianity and its lost element of healing. The sacred books of the movement are the Bible and *Science and Health with Key to the Scriptures* (1891), a revision of *Science and Health*, first published by Mrs. Eddy in 1875. Its main tenets (quoting from an official Christian Science source) are "that nothing is real save God and His spiritual creation, including man in His image and likeness; that man's essential nature is spiritual and wholly good; that matter, evil, disease and sickness are unreal—illusions existing only through ignorance of God. Therefore Christian Scientists renounce for themselves medicine, surgery and drugs and rely on healing through prayer."

The name of the movement seems misleading since it has nothing to do with any of the natural sciences of which Mrs. Eddy had no first-hand knowledge. In using the word, Mrs. Eddy meant

that the teaching and acts of Jesus were rooted in unchanging divine law. Mrs. Eddy was at first interested in Spiritualism and afterwards, having been a patient of a faith-healer named Quimby, claimed to have been divinely healed.

There is a good deal of controversy about the efficacy of the Christian Science methods. In principle believers argue that if one has total, unquestioning faith in the healing power of Christ, then all sickness will be revealed as illusion and vanish. The trouble of course is that total faith is almost impossible to achieve, and hence even Christian Scientists inevitably fall ill and die. This makes the Church's argument irrefutable, but there is some evidence that the argument is convincing fewer individuals than it once did. On the other hand the growth of interest in "divine healing" within the more orthodox churches has led to a softening of barriers between Mrs. Eddy's splinter group and the hard-core Christian religions. Christian Science may well fade away after handing over to orthodoxy its single key concept.

Christian Socialism, a movement launched in 1848, a year of revolutions throughout the continent, by a group in England designed to commit the Church to a programme of social reform. The leaders, notably J. F. D. Maurice, Charles Kingsley (both Anglican clergymen), and John Ludlow were deeply moved by the wretched conditions of the British working class and the two priests had, indeed, given active support to the Chartist movement (*q.v.*). However, all insisted that socialism in its existing forms ignored the spiritual needs of mankind and must be tempered with Christianity. Tracts were written to expose the sweated industries, the consequences of unrestrained competition, and the evils following the enclosure system; but, more concretely, Christian socialism fostered co-operative workshops and distributive societies based on those of the Rochdale pioneers, organised a working-man's college and set up elementary classes for education. It also supported the trade-union movement's right to organise and bargain for its members.

The traditions of Christian socialism have

Early Christian Church

(Church of the Roman Empire)
4th cent.

3rd–7th cent. Schisms in the East.
Controversies concerned with the relation of Jesus Christ to God and to man: Arianism, Nestorianism Monophysitism, Monotheletism

Nestorian Church   Armenian Church   Jacobite Church   Coptic Church

Great Schism 1054

Western Christendom
Latin
Rome

Eastern Christendom
Greek
Constantinople

Mediaeval Inquisition began c. 1231

Spanish Inquisition began 1481

Orthodox Eastern Church

Counter Reformation and Inquisition at Rome, 16th cent.   *Reformation,* 16th–17th cent.   *Renaissance* 15th cent.

Roman Catholic Church   Protestantism   Humanism

Moravians   Lutherans   Calvinists   Church of England   (*Henry VIII's break with Rome* 1534. *Excommunication of Elizabeth* 1570)

Presbyterians

Nonconformism

Baptists   Congregationalists   Methodists   Evangelicals   Modernists   Anglo-Catholics been carried on by the Fabian Society, by adherents of Guild Socialism, and by individuals who reject Marx's teaching of revolutionary change, and seek to bring it about by the methods of action through political parties, education, and encouragement of the unions. They believe that Christ's teachings can only be fully realised in a new society since Christianity implies social responsibility, and material factors are admitted to have an important bearing on the ability to lead a truly religious life. *See also* Fabian Society, Guild Socialism.

Church of England. There is some evidence of possible continuity with the Christianity of Roman Britain, but in the main the Church derives from the fusion of the ancient Celtic church with the missionary church of St. Augustine, who founded the See of Canterbury in A.D. 597. To archbishop Theodore in 673 is ascribed its organisation in dioceses with settled boundaries, and in parishes. St. Augustine's church was in communion with Rome from the first, but the Church of England was not brought within papal jurisdiction until after the Norman conquest, and was at no time under the complete domination of Rome. It remains the Catholic Church of England without break of continuity, but during the Reformation the royal supremacy was accepted and that of the pope repudiated. It is the Established Church (*i.e.*, the official church of the realm), crowns the sovereign, and its archbishops and bishops in the House of Lords can act as a kind of " conscience of the state " at every stage of legislation. The policy of religious toleration has been accepted since the 16th cent. The Church is organised in two ecclesiastical provinces (Canterbury and York) and 43 dioceses. Its form of worship is embodied in the Book of Common Prayer.

The Anglican Communion comprises the churches in all parts of the world which are in communion with the Church of England. All the bishops of the Anglican Communion meet every ten years in the Lambeth Conference (first held in 1867), over which the Archbishop of Canterbury by custom presides as *primus inter pares*. The theme of the 1968 Conference was " The Renewal of the Church," and for the first time observers and laymen were admitted.

Church of Scotland, the established national church of Scotland, presbyterian in constitution, and governed by a hierarchy of courts—the kirk-sessions, the presbyteries, the synods, and the General Assembly. *See* Presbyterianism.

Clairvoyance. *See* Telepathy.

Communism, ideally refers to the type of society in which all property belongs to the community and social life is based on the principle " from each according to his ability, to each according to his needs." There would be public ownership of all enterprises and all goods would be free. Since no such society as yet exists, the word in practice refers to the attempt to achieve such a society by initially overthrowing the capitalist system and establishing a dictatorship of the proletariat (Marx identified the dictatorship with a democratic constitution). Communists believe that their first task is the establishment of socialism under which there remain class distinctions, private property to some extent, and differences between manual and brain workers. The state is regulated on the basis " from each according to his ability, to each according to his work." Lenin applied Marx's analysis to the new conditions which had arisen in 20th-cent. capitalist society. Marxism–Leninism develops continuously with practice since failure to apply its basic principles to changed circumstances and times would result in errors of dogmatism. Mao Tse-tung worked out the techniques of revolutionary action appropriate to China; Che Guevara the guerrilla tactics appropriate to the peasants of Latin America. His counsel " It is not necessary to wait until conditions for making revolution exist; the insurrection can create them," was the opposite of Mao Tse-tung's " Engage in no battle you are not sure of winning," and Lenin's " Never play with insurrection." Two fundamental principles of communism are (1) peaceful co-existence between countries of different social systems, and (2) the class struggle between oppressed and oppressing classes and between

oppressed and oppressor nations. China, for example, holds that it is a mistake to lay one-sided stress on peaceful transition toward socialism otherwise the revolutionary will of the proletariat becomes passive and unprepared politically and organisationally for the tasks ahead.

In Russia the civil war developed *after* the revolution; in China the communists fought their civil war *before* they seized power; the Yugoslav partisans won their own guerrilla war during their stand against the fascist powers—differences which had important political consequences. Russia suffered three decades of isolationism and totalitarian suppression (" an isolated and besieged fortress ") before the death of Stalin. Then came a marked, if zigzagging shift towards " liberalisation." Mao Tse-tung held to the orthodox Leninist view about capitalism and communism, regarded *détente* as a dangerous illusion and compromise and " revisionism " as a fatal error. The ideological dispute which has developed since 1960 between these two great communist powers has been likened to the East–West schism in the Christian church. Today, communist parties in some countries, *e.g.*, Italy are taking the democratic road to socialism and believe that a communist government should be installed by the ballot box and not by force. *See also* Maoism, Marxism, Trotskyism, and Section C, Part II.

Confucianism. Confucius (Latinised form of K'ung-Fu-tzu) was born in 551 B.C. in the feudal state of Lu in modern Shantung province. He was thus a contemporary of Buddha, although nobody could have been more dissimilar. Where Buddha was metaphysical in his thought, Confucius was practical; Buddha was original, Confucius had hardly an original idea in his head; Buddha wanted to convert individuals to an other-worldly philosophy, Confucius wanted to reform the feudal governments of his time, believing that in this way their subjects would be made happier. Other religions have in their time, been revolutionary; Confucius was a conservative who wanted to bring back a golden age from the past. The only respect in which Confucius agreed with the Buddha was that neither was particularly interested in the supernatural, and God or gods played little part in their religions.

Much of his time was spent in going from the court of one feudal lord to another trying to impress them by his example. For he suffered from the curious belief that the example set by the ruler influences his subjects. He made much of etiquette, trembling and speaking in low tones before princes, at ease and polite with his equals, and behaving with " lofty courtesy " to his inferiors. Promoting the idea of " the golden mean," he was not impressed by heroic deeds or unusual people, and was greatly displeased when he heard that a truthful son had reported that his father had stolen a sheep: " Those who are upright," he said, " are different from this; the father conceals the misconduct of the son, and the son conceals the misconduct of the father." One feels that Confucius would have felt not at all out of place in an English public school. Virtue brings its own reward in this world, ceremonial is important, politeness when universal would reduce jealousy and quarrels; " reverence the spirits but keep them far off." Destiny decides to what class a man shall belong, and as destiny is but another name for Nature prayer is unnecessary, for once having received his destiny, a man can demand and obtain from Nature what he chooses—his own will determines all things. Chinese philosophy students today look upon Confucius as " a forefather of all reactionaries."

Congregationalists, the oldest sect of Nonconformists who hold that each church should be independent of external ecclesiastical authority. They took their origin from the Brownists of Elizabeth's days. Robert Browne (*c.* 1550–*c.* 1633), an Anglican clergyman, who had come to reject bishops, was forced with his followers to seek refuge, first in Holland and then in Scotland where he was imprisoned by the Kirk. In later life he changed his views and is disowned by Congregationalists because of his reversion to Anglicanism. His former views were spread by Henry Barrow and John Greenwood who, under an Act passed in 1592 " for the punishment of persons obstinately refusing to come to church " (and largely designed for the suppression of this sect), were hanged at Tyburn. They had preached (a) that the only head of the church is Jesus Christ; (b) that, contrary to Elizabethan doctrine, the church had no relationship to the state; (c) that the only statute-book was the Bible whereas the Articles of Religion and Book of Common Prayer were mere Acts of Parliament; (d) that each congregation of believers was independent and had the power of choosing its own ministers. The body fled once more to Holland and were among the Pilgrims who set sail in the *Mayflower* for America in 1620 whilst those who remained were joined by Puritans fleeing from Charles I. They became free once more to live in England under the Commonwealth only to be repressed again under Charles II. Finally full liberty of worship was granted under William III. In 1833 the Congregational Union of England and Wales was formed which had no legislative power. It had issued a Declaration of Faith by which no minister was bound; he was responsible to his own church and to nobody else. The sect is widespread both in Britain and the U.S.A. where it is held in special honour because of its connection with the Pilgrim Fathers. In 1972 the Congregational Church in England and Wales and the Presbyterian Church of England decided to unite to form the United Reformed Church. The majority of members who did not join comprise the Congregational Federation.

Conservatism. The term " Conservative " came into general use after 1834 in place of the older name of " Tory." The modern Conservative Party has its origins in the period of " Tory Democracy " introduced by Disraeli between 1874 and 1880. Originally the party of church, aristocracy and landed gentry, Conservatism has been increasingly supported since the turn of the century by large business interests. Under Baldwin, Conservative-dominated administrations held office for much of the inter-war period. The 1945 Labour victory caused the Conservative Party to undertake a basic review of its philosophy. From 1951 to 1964, Conservatives held office continuously, reaching a peak in Harold Macmillan's 1959 election victory. Though defeated by Labour in 1964 and 1966, the party regained power in 1970 under Edward Heath. The subsequent troubled administration, plagued with problems on the industrial front, ended with the February 1974 election. The subsequent defeat in October 1974, followed by the battle for the Conservative leadership, again caused the party to seek to review its philosophy as it had developed in recent years. Most particularly, sections of the party were disturbed over the party's approach to economic problems and its increasingly narrow electoral base.

On the continent, Conservatism has generally adopted a more right-wing stance, being identified with the established order and fearing most forms of social change. *See also* Section C, Part I.

Coptic Church, the sect of Egyptian Christians who, holding " Monophysite " opinions (*i.e.*, refusing to grant the two natures, God and Man, of Christ), were declared heretical by the Council of Chalcedon in 451. They practise circumcision and have dietary laws. Their language is a direct descendant of ancient Egyptian. Like the Armenians, they are regarded as an heretical branch of Eastern Christianity. Their religious head is the patriarch of Alexandria.

Cynics, a school of philosophy founded in the time of Alexander the Great by Diogenes. Choosing to live like a dog by rejecting all conventions of religion, manners, or decency, and allegedly living in a tub, Diogenes unwittingly brought on his school the title " Cynic," meaning not " cynical," as the word is understood today, but " canine." His teacher, Antisthenes, who had been a disciple of Socrates, decided, after the latter's death, that all philosophy was useless quibbling and man's sole aim should be simple goodness. He believed in a return to nature, despised luxury, wanted no government, no private property, and associated with working men and slaves. Far from being cynics

in the modern sense, Diogenes and Antisthenes were virtuous anarchists rather like old Tolstoy (except that in the practice of their beliefs they were more consistent).

D

Deism. *See* God and Man.

Demonism, Demons, and the Devil. Demons are ethereal beings of various degrees of significance and power which are believed to be implicated in men's good, but especially evil, fortune. They are common to most cultures. From the anthropological point of view the demon arose as a widespread concept in the following ways: (1) as a psychological projection into the outer world of man's own good or evil emotions and thoughts; (2) as a survival of primitive animism (*q.v.*), thus spirits are believed to haunt places, trees, stones, and other natural objects; (3) when by warlike invasion the gods of the vanquished become the devils of the conquerors (as when the Jews occupied Canaan); (4) as a primitive belief that spirits of the dead continue after death to hover near their former habitation, and not always entirely welcome to the living; (5) the conception of a supreme source of evil (the Devil or Satan) which took shape among the Jews during their sojourn in Babylon under the influence of Zoroastrianism (*q.v.*), a religion in which the struggle between the two spirits, Good and Evil, reached its height in the imagination of the ancient world. The Satan of the Old Testament was first regarded as one of God's servants (in the Book of Job he goes up and down the earth to see whether God's commands are obeyed), but when the Jews returned from their captivity he had become identified with Ahriman, the spirit of evil, who was in continual conflict with Ahura Mazda, the spirit of good. As Dr. Margaret Murray has pointed out, the primitive mind ascribed both good and evil to one power alone; the division into God and the Devil, priest and witch, belongs to a higher stage of civilisation. The worship of evil itself, or of its personification in Satan, is a curious practice which seems to have developed hand-in-hand with Christianity and to have received steady support from a small but measurable minority. Many of the ceremonies involved in Satanism or in the so-called Black Mass appear to have been no more than opportunities for sexual excesses of one kind or another—such indulgences being traditionally barred to devout Christians. The alleged power of sex as a form of magic was propagated by the talented but rather mad poet, Aleister Crowley (1875–1947), who scandalised pre-war Europe with his very well-publicised dabblings into Satanism. The self-styled " wickedest man in the world," Crowley was a pathetic rather than shocking figure and died a drug addict. He can hardly be said to have significantly advanced the cause of Demonology, though it has to be admitted that he tried very hard. *See also* Witchcraft, Magic.

Determinism and Free-will. The question of whether man is, or is not, free to mould his own destiny is one which has exercised the minds of philosophers since Greek mythology conceived of the Fates as weaving a web of destiny from which no man can free himself. Socrates emphasised that man could through knowledge influence his destiny whilst ignorance made him the plaything of fate; Plato went further in pointing out that man can, and does, defeat the purposes of the universe and its divine Creator. It is our duty to live a good life, but we can live a foolish and wicked one if we choose. Aristotle wrote " Virtue is a disposition or habit involving deliberate purpose or choice." If this were not so morality would be a sham.

The Problem for Theology. The last of the great philosophers of antiquity and one of the great influences in moulding Catholic theology was Plotinus (c. 204–70). Soul, he taught, is free, but once enmeshed in the body loses its freedom in the life of sense. Nevertheless, man is free to turn away from sensuality and towards God who is perfect freedom; for even when incarnated in matter the soul does not entirely lose the ability to rescue itself. This conception was carried over into the beliefs of the early Christian Apologists because it appeared to be in line with the teaching of Jesus that He had come to save man from sin. Sin implies guilt, and guilt implies the freedom to act otherwise; furthermore an all-good God cannot be responsible for the sin in the world which must be man's responsibility and this again implies freedom. Pelagius (*c*. 355–*c*. 425), a Welsh priest, not only believed in free-will but, questioning the doctrine of original sin, said that when men act righteously it is through their own moral effort, and God rewards them for their virtues in heaven. This belief became fairly widespread and was declared a heresy by the Church, being attacked notably by St. Augustine (354–430), a contemporary of Pelagius, who believed in predestination—that, since the sin of Adam, God had chosen who in all future history would be saved and who damned. This represents one tradition in Christianity: the determinism which leads to Calvinism (*q.v.*). St. Thomas Aquinas (1227–74), the greatest figure of scholasticism and one of the principal saints in the Roman Catholic Church, compromised between the two positions in the sense that, believing man to be free, he yet held that Adam's sin was transmitted to all mankind and only divine grace can bring salvation. But even when God wishes to bestow this salvation, the human will must co-operate. God foresees that some will not accept the offer of grace and predestines them to eternal punishment.

The Problem for Philosophy. With the Renaissance, thinkers began to free themselves from the domination of the Church and to study the world objectively and freely without preconceptions. But the more man turned to science, the more he discovered that the world was ruled by apparently inexorable laws and, since the scientist must believe that every event has a cause, he was led back to determinism. Man as part of the universe was subject to law too and all that existed was a vast machine. Francis Bacon (1561–1626) separated the fields of religion and science but left man subject completely to the will of God. Thomas Hobbes (1588–1679) was a rigid determinist and materialist although, having had trouble with the church in France whence, as a royalist, he had fled, he took care to announce that the Christian God is the Prime Mover.

Modern philosophy begins with René Descartes (1596–1650), a Frenchman who tried to reconcile the mechanical scientific universe of his time with the spiritual need for freedom. He did this by separating completely mind and body; the former, he said, is free, the latter completely determined. But, by admitting that the will can produce states of body, he was left with the problem of how this could happen—a problem which the so-called Occasionists solved to their own satisfaction by stating that the will is free and God so arranges the universe that what a person wills happens. Baruch Spinoza (1632–77), a Dutch Jew whose independence of thought had led to his excommunication from the Amsterdam Synagogue in 1656, was a complete determinist. He asserted that God and Nature are one, everything that happens is a manifestation of God's inscrutable nature, and it is logically impossible that things could be other than they are. Thus both Hobbes and Spinoza were determinists for entirely opposed reasons. The former as a materialist, the latter because he believed in the absolute perfection and universality of God. Yet the great religious mystic and mathematician Blaise Pascal (1623–62) held that, no matter what reason and cold logic may indicate, we *know* from direct religious experience that we are free. John Calvin (1509–64) and Martin Luther (1483–1546) were both determinists. *See* Calvinism, Lutheranism.

To the more practical British philosophers, John Locke (1632–1704) and David Hume (1711–76), free-will was related to personality. Locke believed that God had implanted in each individual certain desires and these determine the will; the desires are already there, but we use our will to satisfy them. Hume argued that a man's behaviour is the necessary result of his character and if he had a different character he would act otherwise. Accordingly, when a man's actions arise from his own nature and desires he is free. He is not free when external events compel him to act otherwise (*e.g.*, if he strikes another because his own nature is such he is free as he is not if he is compelled to do so against his desire). Leibnitz (1646–1716), although as a German metaphysical philosopher holding very different general views, said much the same thing—that choice is simply selecting the desire that is strongest. But most of the 18th cent. thinkers after Voltaire, with the great exceptions of Rousseau and the later German philosophers Kant, Fichte, Schopenhauer, and Hegel, who were initially influenced by him, accepted determinism. Rousseau (1712–78) began to stem the tide by his declaration that man is a free soul striving to remain free and only prevented from being so by society and the cold science which stifles his feeling heart. Once again the will became important as Kant (1724–1804) asserted that belief in freedom is a moral necessity although it cannot be proved by reason; the moral nature of man shows that there is a " transcendental " world beyond the senses where freedom applies. Fichte and Schelling found freedom in the Absolute ego or God of whom each individual was part and thus also free. Hegel (1770–1831) saw the whole universe as evolving towards self-awareness and freedom in man although this could only be fully realised in a society that makes for freedom. Even God himself only attains full consciousness and self-realisation through the minds of such individuals as are free. This is the goal of the dialectical process. (*See* Dialectical Materialism.)

The Scientist's View. For the scientist the law of cause and effect is a useful hypothesis since, by and large, it is necessary for him to assume that all events are caused. Nevertheless the modern tendency is to think in terms of statistical probability rather than relentless mechanistic causality, and, although the free-will problem does not concern the scientist as such, it is clear that freedom and determinism (assuming the terms to have any meaning at all) are not necessarily opposed. In sociology, for example, we *know* that certain actions will produce certain results upon the behaviour of people in general, *e.g.*, that raising the bank rate will discourage business expansion. But this does not mean that Mr. Brown who decides in the circumstances not to add a new wing to his factory is not using his free-will. Even in the case of atoms, as Dr. Bronowski has pointed out, the observed results of allowing gas under pressure in a cylinder to rush out occur because most of the atoms are " obeying " the scientific " law " relating to such situations. But this does not mean that some atoms are not busy rushing across the stream or even against it—they are, but the general tendency is outwards and that is what we note. Lastly, the modern philosophical school of Logical Analysis would probably ask, not whether Free-will or Determinism is the true belief, but whether the question has any meaning. For what scientific experiment could we set up to prove one or the other true? The reader will note that some of the philosophers mentioned above are using the words to mean quite different concepts.

Dialectical Materialism, the combination of Hegel's dialectic method with a materialist philosophy produced by Karl Marx (1818–83) and his friend Friedrich Engels (1820–95). It is the philosophical basis of Marxism (*q.v.*) and Communism (*q.v.*). " Dialectic " to the ancient Greek philosophers meant a kind of dialogue or conversation, as used particularly by Socrates, in which philosophical disputes were resolved by a series of successive contradictions: a thesis is put forward and the opposing side holds its contradiction or antithesis until in the course of argument a synthesis is reached in which the conflicting ideas are resolved.

From Thesis through Antithesis to Synthesis. Hegel in the 19th cent. put forward the view that this process applies to the course of nature and history as they strive towards the perfect state. But to him, as to the Greeks, the conflict was in the field of ideas. The " universal reason " behind events works through the ideas held by a particular society until they are challenged by those of another which supersedes them and in turn, usually by war, becomes the agent of universal reason until the arrival of a new challenger. Hegel therefore regarded war as an instrument of progress and his Prussian compatriots found no difficulty in identifying their own state as the new agent of progress by universal conquest. Feuerbach, Lassalle, and other early socialists were impressed by some of Hegel's ideas: *e.g.*, that societies evolved (with the assumption that finally their own ideal society would be achieved) and that truth, morals, and concepts were relative so that a type of society that was " good " at one time was not necessarily so at another. But Marx and Engels in effect turned Hegel upside-down, accepted his dialectic but rejected his belief that ideas were the motive force. On the contrary, they said, ideas are determined by social and economic change as a result of materialistic forces. (*See* Calvinism, where it is pointed out that the Marxist view is not that Calvin changed men's economic ideas but rather that a developing capitalism unconsciously changed his.) The historical materialism of Marxism purports to show that the inexorable dialectic determines that feudalism is displaced by capitalism and capitalism by creating a proletariat (its antithesis) inevitably leads to socialism and a classless society. The state, as a tool of the dominant class, withers away. Dialectical materialism is applied in all spheres. As a philosophy there is little to be said for it save that it has shown us the close dependence of man's thoughts upon current material and social conditions. But as a battle-cry or a rationalisation of Marxism it wields immense power over the minds of men. *See* Marxism.

Dianetics. *See* Scientology.

Diggers, one of the many sects which flourished under the Commonwealth (others were the Muggletonians, the Levellers, the Millenarians, and the Fifth Monarchy Men), so-called because they attempted to dig (*i.e.* cultivate) untilled land. Gerrard Winstanley, a profoundly religious man, and leader of the Diggers, believed in the economic and social equality of man and castigated the clergy for upholding the class structure of society. In his book *The True Leveller's Standard Advanced* (1649) he wrote: " Every day poor people are forced to work for fourpence a day, though corn is dear. And yet the tithing priest stops their mouth and tells them that ' inward satisfaction of mind ' was meant by the declaration ' the poor shall inherit the earth'. I tell you, the Scripture is to be really and materially fulfilled. You jeer at the name ' Leveller '; I tell you Jesus Christ is the Head Leveller."

Doukhobors, a religious sect of Russian origin, founded by a Prussian sergeant at Kharkov in the middle of the 18th cent., and now mainly settled in Canada. Like many other sects they belong to that type of Christianity which seeks direct communication with God and such bodies tend to have certain traits in common such as belief in the " inner light," opposition to war and authority in general, and often ecstasies which show themselves in physical ways such as shaking, speaking in strange tongues (glossolalia), and other forms of what to the unbeliever seem mass hysteria. Liturgy, ritual, or ceremony is non-existent. The Doukhobors were persecuted in Tsarist Russia, but in 1898 Tolstoy used his influence to have them removed to Canada where the government granted them uninhabited land in what is now Saskatchewan and seven or eight thousand settled down in peace which they enjoyed for many years. Recently, however, their practices have caused difficulties once more; for even the most tolerant government which is prepared to accept pacifism, total dependence on communally-owned agriculture, refusal to engage in commerce, non-payment of taxes, rejection of the marriage ceremony and separation " when love ceases," finds it difficult to tolerate, as civilisation advances ever closer to Doukhobor communities, their proneness to " put off these troublesome disguises which we wear "—*i.e.*, to walk about naked in the communities of their more orthodox

neighbours. What the future of the Doukhobors in their various sects (for even they have their differences) will be it is impossible to say, but it is difficult to believe that these simple people can long resist the pressure of modern civilisation.

Dowsing. *See* Radiesthesia.

Druidism, the religion of Celtic Britain and Gaul of which Druids were the priesthood. They were finally wiped out by the Roman general Suetonius Paulinus about A.D. 58 in their last stronghold, the island of Anglesey. There are two sources of our present beliefs in Druidism: (1) the brief and factual records of the Romans, notably Pliny and Julius Caesar, which tell us that they worshipped in sacred oak groves and presumably practised a religion doing reverence to the powers of nature which must have had its roots in early stone age times and had many cruel rites, *e.g.*, human sacrifice; (2) the beliefs put forward by William Stukeley, an amateur antiquarian who from 1718 did valuable work by his studies of the stone circles at Stonehenge and Avebury. However, influenced by the Romantic movement, he later put forward the most extravagant theories which unfortunately are those popularly accepted by those without archaeological knowledge today. Stonehenge and Avebury were depicted as the temples of the " white-haired Druid bard sublime " and an attempt was made to tie up Druidism with early Christianity, above all with the concept of the Trinity. In fact, these circles have no connection with the Druids. They may have made ceremonial use of them but recent evidence suggests that the megalithic stones at Stonehenge belong to a Bronze Age culture (2100–1600 B.C.). Nor have Druidism and Christianity any relationship. Almost nothing is known of the religion. Yet such were its romantic associations that, even today, one hears of " Druidic " ceremonies practised at the appropriate time of year on Primrose Hill in the heart of London (though whether seriously or with tongue in cheek one does not know). In Wales the name Druid survives as the title for the semi-religious leaders of the annual festivals of Celtic poetry, drama, and music known as Eisteddfods. Lingering, but now tenuous, druidic connections are to be found in all Celtic parts including Cornwall and Brittany, where Eisteddfods are also held.

Dualism, any philosophical or theological theory which implies that the universe has a double nature, notably Plato's distinction between appearance and reality, soul and body, ideas and material objects, reason and the evidence of the senses, which infers that behind the world as we perceive it there lies an " ideal " world which is more " real " than that of mere appearance. In religions such as Zoroastrianism or the Gnostic and Manichaeism heresies, it was believed that the universe was ruled by good and evil " principles "—in effect that there was a good God and a bad one. In psychology, dualism refers to the philosophical theories which believe mind and body to be separate entities. The opposite of dualism is monism which asserts the essential unity of the substance of the universe.

An essential problem in the dualistic view lies in the question as to how and where the two separate and distinct properties of the universe interact. Where, for example, does the " mind " actually mesh with the physical mechanics of the brain and body—where does the ghost sit in his machine? Descartes decided that mind and body must interact somewhere and he selected the pineal gland (an apparently functionless part of the brain) as the spot. But this did nothing to explain how two *totally different* aspects of nature can possibly influence each other, and today most philosophers and psychologists reject dualistic views of life and personality as posing more problems than they solve. *See also* Psychology, Occam's Razor.

E

Ecomovement. In the early 1970s widespread publicity was for the first time given to the urgent warnings of ecologists that the current exponential increase in (a) world population, (b) depletion of natural resources, and (c) pollution of the environment. could not continue without global catastrophe. The most significant single event in the evolution of what is now being known as the " ecomovement " was probably the publication of the Club of Rome's paper on *The Limits to Growth*. From this sprang a movement, unfortunately initially drawn only from the middle class and better educated, which aimed to reduce environmental pollution, the extravagances of advertising and needless waste of natural resources. Its first campaigns were directed against such obvious targets as disposable glass bottles and unnecessary packaging and wrapping in shops and supermarkets. The ecomovement also protests against industrial firms which pollute rivers and seas. against aircraft noise and waste in general. Its early campaigns were greeted with some derision but have achieved dramatic point with the world energy and economic crisis which developed towards the end of 1973. *See also* Section F.

Ecumenism, a world movement which springs from the Christian belief that all men are brothers and that the Christian Church should be re-structured to give reality to the belief. Christ's church exists not to serve its own members, but for the service of the whole world. Some see the answer in a united church of a federal type (unity in diversity), others in an organic structure with one set of rules. The period since the convening of the Second Vatican Council by Pope John has been one of fervent discussion among Christian theologians with the aim of promoting Christian unity. *See* World Council of Churches.

Education. Education was no great problem to primitive man, but as societies became more complex people began to ask themselves such questions as: *What* should young people be taught? *How* should they be taught? Should the aim of their education be to bring out their individual qualities or rather to make them good servants of the state?

The first teachers were priests who knew most about the traditions, customs, and lore of their societies and thus the first schools were in religious meeting places. This was notably true of the Jews who learned from the rabbis in the synagogue.

The Greeks. We begin, as always, with the Greeks whose city-states, based on slavery, educated men (not women) for the sort of life described in Plato's *Dialogues*—the leisured life of gentlemen arguing the problems of the universe at their banquets or in the market-place. This made it necessary to learn debate and oratory (or rhetoric) especially for those who proposed to take up politics. The Sophist philosophy taught the need to build up convincing arguments in a persuasive manner, to learn the rules of logic and master the laws and customs of the Athenians, and to know the literature of the past so that illustrations might be drawn from it. These strolling philosophers who taught for a fee were individualists showing the student how to advance himself at all costs within his community.

Socrates had a more ethical approach, believing that education was good in itself, made a man happier and a better citizen, and emphasised his position as a member of a group. His method of teaching, the dialectic or "Socratic" method, involved argument and discussion rather than overwhelming others by rhetoric and is briefly mentioned under Dialectical Materialism (*q.v.*). Today this method is increasingly used in adult education where a lecture is followed by a period of discussion in which both lecturer and audience participate; for psychologists have shown that people accept ideas more readily when conviction arises through their own arguments than when they are passively thrust down their throats.

Socrates' pupil Plato produced in his book *The Republic* one of the first comprehensive systems of education and vocational selection. Believing that essentially men have very different and unequal abilities he considered that in an idealistic or utopian society they should be put into social classes corresponding to these differences, and suggested the following method: (1) For the first 18 years of a boy's life he should be taught gymnastics and sports, playing and singing music, reading and writing, a knowledge of literature, and if he passed this course sent on to the next stage; those who failed were to become tradesmen and merchants. (2) From 18–20 those successful in the first course were to be given two years of cadet training, the ones thought incapable of further education being placed in the military class as soldiers. (3) The remainder, who were to become the leaders of society, proceeded with advanced studies in philosophy, mathematics, science, and art. Such education was to be a state concern, state supported and controlled, selecting men and training them for service in the state according to their abilities.

Plato's pupil Aristotle even suggested that the state should determine shortly after birth which children should be allowed to live and destroy the physically or mentally handicapped; that marriage should be state-controlled to ensure desirable offspring. However, in their time the leisured and individualistic Sophists held the field and few accepted the educational views of Plato or his pupil.

Rome. The Romans were not philosophers and most of their culture came from Greece. Administration was their chief aptitude and Quintilian (A.D. *c.* 35–*c.* 95) based his higher education on the earlier classical tuition in public speaking, but he is important for emphasising the training of character and for his humanistic approach to the method of teaching that caused his *Institutio oratoria* to be influential for centuries later—indeed one might almost say up to the time of the great Dr. Arnold of Rugby. Education, he believed, should begin early but one must "take care that the child not old enough to love his studies does not come to hate them" by premature forcing; studies must be made pleasant and interesting and students encouraged by praise rather than discouraged when they sometimes fail; play is to be approved of as a sign of a lively disposition and because gloomy, depressed children are not likely to be good students; corporal punishment should never be used because "it is an insult as you will realise if you imagine it yourself." The world became interested not in *what* he taught but *how* he taught it; he was the pioneer of humanistic education and character-training from Vittorino da Feltre (1378–1446) of Mantua, through Milton and Pope who commended his works, to the modern educationists who have studied their pupils as well as their books.

The Middle Ages: The Religious View. With the development of Christianity education once more became a religious problem. The earliest converts had to be taught Christian doctrine and were given instruction in "catechumenal" schools before admission to the group, but as the religion came increasingly into contact with other religions or heresies a more serious training was necessary, and from these newer "catechetical" schools, where the method used was the catechism (*i.e.*, question and answer as known to all Presbyterian children today), the Apologists arose among whom were Clement of Alexandria and the great Origen. From this time education became an instrument of the church and in 529 the Emperor Justinian ordered all pagan schools to be closed.

As typical of the best in mediaeval education whilst the lamp of civilisation burned low during the Dark Ages, after the fall of Roman power, and survived only in the monasteries, we may mention St. Benedict (*c.* 480–*c.* 547) of Monte Cassino. There, in southern Italy, a rule was established which became a part of monastic life in general. Monastic schools were originally intended for the training of would-be monks, but later others were admitted who simply wanted some education; thus two types of school developed, one for the *interni* and the other for *externi* or external pupils. Originally studies were merely reading in order to study the Bible, writing to copy the sacred books, and sufficient calculation to be able to work out the advent of holy days or festivals. But by the end of the 6th cent. the " seven liberal arts " (grammar rhetoric, dialectic, arithmetic, geometry, music, and astronomy) were added.

The Renaissance. The close of the Middle Ages saw the development of two types of secular school. One came with the rise of the new merchant class and the skilled trader whose "guilds" or early trade unions established schools to train young men for their trades but ultimately gave rise to burgher or town schools; the other was the court school founded and supported by the wealthy rulers of the Italian cities—Vittorino da Feltre (mentioned above) presided over the most famous at Mantua.

These Renaissance developments are paralleled in northern Europe by the Protestant reformers who, having with Martin Luther held that everyone should know how to read his Bible in order to interpret it in his own way, were logically committed to popular education, compulsory and universal. In theory this was intended for biblical study, but writing, arithmetic, and other elementary subjects were taught and Luther said that, even if heaven and hell did not exist, education was important. Universal education is a Protestant conception.

Views of Philosophers. From this period onwards people were free to put forward any ideas about education, foolish or otherwise, and to create their own types of school. Of English philosophers who theorised about, but did not practise, education we may mention the rationalist Francis Bacon (1561–1626) who saw learning as the dissipation of all prejudices and the collection of concrete facts; the materialist and totalitarian Hobbes (1588–1679) who, as a royalist, believed that the right to determine the kind of education fit for his subjects is one of the absolute rights of the sovereign power or ruler; the gentlemanly Locke (1632–1704) whose ideal was a sound mind in a sound body to be attained by hard physical exercise, wide experience of the world, and enough knowledge to meet the requirements of the pupil's environment. The end result would be one able to get on with his fellows, pious but wise in the ways of the world, independent and able to look after himself, informed but reticent about his knowledge. Classics and religious study were not to be carried to excess, since Locke held that these subjects had been overrated in the past. Locke's pupil was the well-to-do, civilised young man of the 17th cent. who knew how to behave in society.

Jean-Jacques Rousseau (1712–78), a forerunner of the Romantic movement (*q.v.*), which despised society and its institutions, put emotion at a higher level than reason. His book *Émile* describes the education of a boy which is natural and spontaneous. Society, he holds, warps the growing mind and therefore the child should be protected from its influences until his development in accordance with his own nature is so complete that he cannot be harmed by it. During the first 4 years the body should be developed by physical training; from 5 to 12 the child would live in a state of nature such that he could develop his powers of observation and his senses; from 13 books would be used and intellectual training introduced, although only in line with the child's own interests, and he would be given instruction only as he came to ask for it. Moral training and contact with his fellows to learn the principles of sympathy, kindness, and helpfulness to mankind would be given between 15 and 20. Girls, however, should be educated to serve men in a spirit of modesty and restraint. His own five children he deposited in a foundling hospital.

Summary. Broadly speaking, then, there have been four main attitudes to education: (1) religious, with a view to a life beyond death; (2) state-controlled education, with a view to uniform subservience to authority; (3) "gentlemanly" education, with a view to social graces and easy congress in company; (4) the "child-centred" education, which attempts to follow the pupil's inner nature. It is unnecessary to mention the ordinary method of attempting to instil facts without any considerable degree of co-operation between pupil and teacher in order that the former may, with or without interest, follow some occupation in adult life; for this the philosophers did not consider. Today there

remain the two fundamental principles: education for the advantage of the state and its ideology or education for individual development and freedom.

Four educationists of the modern period who have influenced us in the direction of freedom were Johann Pestalozzi of Switzerland (1746–1827) who, by trying to understand children, taught the "natural, progressive, and harmonious development of all the powers and capacities of the human being"; Friedrich Froebel (1782–1852) of Germany, the founder of the Kindergarten who, like Pestalozzi, was influenced by Rousseau but realised the need to combine complete personal development with social adjustment; Maria Montessori (1869–1952) whose free methods have revolutionised infant teaching; John Dewey (1859–1952) who held that the best interests of the group are served when the individual develops his own particular talents and nature.

Eleatics, the philosophers of Elea in ancient Greece who, at the time when Heraclitus (c. 535–475 B.C.) was teaching that change is all that exists and nothing is permanent, were asserting that change is an illusion. Of the three leaders of this school, Xenophanes asserted that the universe was a solid immovable mass forever the same; Parmenides explained away change as an inconceivable process, its appearance being due to the fact that what we see is unreal; and Zeno (the best-known today) illustrated the same thesis with his famous argument of the arrow which, at any given moment of its flight, must be where it is since it cannot be where it is not. But if it is where it is, it cannot move; this is based, of course, on the delusion that motion is discontinuous. The Eleatics were contemporaries of Socrates.

Empiricism. While not a single school of philosophy, empiricism is an approach to knowledge which holds that if a man wants to know what the universe is like the only correct way to do so is to go and look for himself, to collect facts which come to him through his senses. It is, in essence, the method of science as contrasted with rationalism (*q.v.*) which in philosophy implies that thinking or reasoning without necessarily referring to external observations can arrive at truth. Empiricism is typically an English attitude, for among the greatest empirical philosophers were John Locke, George Berkeley, and David Hume. *See* Rationalism.

Epicureanism. The two great schools of the Hellenistic period (*i.e.* the late Greek period beginning with the empire of Alexander the Great) were the Stoics and Epicureans, the former founded by Zeno of Citium (not to be confused with Zeno the Eleatic) (*q.v.*), the latter by Epicurus, born in Samos in 342 B.C. Both schools settled in Athens, where Epicurus taught that "pleasure is the beginning and end of a happy life." However, he was no sensualist and emphasised the importance of moderation in all things because excesses would lead to pain instead of pleasure and the best of all pleasures were mental ones. Pleasures could be active or passive but the former contain an element of pain since they are the process of satisfying desires not yet satiated. The latter involving the absence of desire are the more pleasant. In fact, Epicurus in his personal life was more stoical than many Stoics and wrote "when I live on bread and water I spit on luxurious pleasures." He disapproved of sexual enjoyment and thought friendship one of the highest of all joys. A materialist who accepted the atomic theory of Democritus, he was not a determinist, and if he did not disbelieve in the gods he regarded religion and the fear of death as the two primary sources of unhappiness.

Epiphenomenalism. *See* Mind and Body.

Erastianism, the theory that the state has the right to decide the religion of its members, wrongly attributed to Erastus of Switzerland (1524–83) who was believed to have held this doctrine. The term has usually been made use of in a derogatory sense—*e.g.*, by the Scottish churches which held that the "call" of the congregation was the only way to elect ministers at a time when, about the turn of the 17th and 18th cent., they felt that Episcopalianism was being foisted on them. "Episcopalianism" (*i.e.* Anglicanism) with its state church, ecclesiastical hierarchy, and system of livings presented by patrons was to them "Erastian" in addition to its other "unscriptural practices."

Essenes, a Jewish sect which, during the oppressive rule of Herod (d. 4 B.C.), set up monastic communities in the region of the Dead Sea. They refused to be bound by the scriptural interpretations of the Pharisees and adhered rigorously to the letter of Holy Writ, although with additions of their own which cause them by orthodox Jews today to be regarded as a break-away from Judaism. Among their practices and beliefs were purification through baptism, renunciation of sexual pleasures, scrupulous cleanliness, strict observance of the Mosaic law, communal possession, asceticism. Akin in spirit, although not necessarily identical with them, were the writers of Apocalyptic literature preaching that the evils of the present would shortly be terminated by a new supernatural order heralded by a Messiah who would reign over a restored Israel. The casting out of demons and spiritual healing formed part of these general beliefs which were in the air at that time. The sect has an importance far beyond its size or what has been known about it in the past since the discovery from 1947 onwards of the Dead Sea Scrolls (*see* Section L) of the Qumran community occupying a monastery in the same area as the Essenes and holding the same type of belief. These scrolls with their references to a "Teacher of Righteousness" preceding the Messiah have obvious relevance to the sources of early Christianity and have given rise to speculations as to whether Jesus might have been influenced by views which, like His own, were unacceptable to orthodox Jews but in line with those of the Dead Sea communities. At the very least they seem to show that early Christianity was not a sudden development but a gradual one which had its predecessors.

Ethical Church, a movement typical of 19th cent. rationalism which attempted to combine atheism (or at any rate the absence of any belief in a God which was inconsistent with reason or based on revelation) with the inculcation of moral principles. Prayers were not used and ordinarily the service consisted in the singing of edifying compositions interspersed with readings from poems or prose of a similar nature by great writers holding appropriate views. It terminated in a talk on an ethical or scientific theme. There is an Ethical Church in London and the South Place Institution where Moncure Conway preached from 1864 to 1897 still exists.

Ethnocentrism, the exaggerated tendency to think the characteristics of one's own group or race superior to those of any others.

Eugenics, a 19th-cent. movement largely instigated by the British scientist and mathematician, Sir Francis Galton. Galton argued that many of the most satisfactory attributes of mankind—intelligence, physical strength, resistance to disease, etc.—were genetically determined and thus handed down in the normal process of inheritance. From this he reasoned that selective mating of physical "superior" individuals, and its converse, the controlled limitation on the breeding of criminals or the insane, would lead inevitably to a progressive improvement in the overall standards of the human race. In their simplest form these proposals are incontestable, though they do of course introduce marked restrictions on the choice of the individual for marriage and procreation. Worse yet is the way in which the argument can be misapplied or elaborated—as it was in Nazi Germany—to include the sterilisation of alcoholics, confirmed criminals and even epileptics. Nevertheless there remains the feeling that there are some aspects of eugenics which intuitively at any rate make good sense and of course the widespread application of birth control is itself an enactment of eugenic principles.

Evangelicalism, the belief of those Protestant sects which hold that the essence of the Gospel consists in the doctrine of salvation by faith in the atoning death of Christ and not by good works or the sacraments; that worship should be "free" rather than liturgical through established forms; that ritual is unacceptable and superstitious. Evangelicals are Low Churchmen.

Evangelism, the preaching of the Gospel, emphasising the necessity for a new birth or conversion. The evangelistic fervour of John Wesley and George Whitefield (*see* Methodism) aroused the great missionary spirit of the late 18th and 19th cent. George Fox, founder of the Society of Friends (*q.v.*), was also an evangelist. Evangelists can be Low, High, or Middle Churchmen.

Existentialism, a highly subjective philosophy which many people connect with such names as Jean-Paul Sartre (b. 1905) or Albert Camus (1913–60) and assume to be a post-war movement associated with disillusion and a sordid view of life. However, existentialism stems from Sören Kierkegaard (1813–55), the Danish "religious writer"—his own description of himself—in such works as *Either/Or, Fear and Trembling,* and *Concluding Unscientific Postscript.* Between the two wars translations of Kierkegaard into German influenced Martin Heidegger's great work *Being and Time* and the other great existentialist Karl Jaspers; it has strongly influenced modern Protestant theology notably in Karl Barth, Reinhold Niebuhr, and Paul Tillich and beyond that field the French philosopher Gabriel Marcel, the Spanish writer Unamuno in his well-known *The Tragic Sense of Life,* and Martin Buber of Israel in his *I and Thou.* We have it on Heidegger's authority that "Sartre is no philosopher" even if it is to his works that modern existentialists often turn.

Existentialism is extremely difficult for the non-metaphysically-minded to understand; it deals, not with the nature of the universe or what are ordinarily thought of as philosophical problems but describes an attitude to life or God held by the individual. Briefly, its main essentials are: (1) it distinguishes between *essence, i.e.,* that aspect of an entity which can be observed and known—and its *existence*—the fact of its having a place in a changing and dangerous world which is what really matters; (2) existence being basic, each self-aware individual can grasp his own existence on reflection in his own immediate experience of himself and his situation as a free being in the world; what he finds is not merely a knowing self but a self that fears, hopes, believes, wills, and is aware of its need to find a purpose, plan, and destiny in life; (3) but we cannot grasp our existence by thought alone; thus the fact "all men must die" relates to the essence of man but it is necessary to be involved, to draw the conclusion as a person that "I too must die" and experience its impact on our own individual existence; (4) because of the preceding, it is necessary to abandon our attitude of objectivity and theoretical detachment when faced by the problems relating to the ultimate purpose of our own life and the basis of our own conduct; life remains closed to those who take no part in it because it can have no significance; (5) it follows that the existentialist cannot be rationalist in his outlook for this is merely an escape into thought from the serious problems of existence; none of the important aspects of life—failure, evil, sin, folly—nor (in the view of Kierkegaard) even the existence of God or the truth of Christianity—can be proved by reason. "God does not exist; He is eternal," was how he expressed it; (6) life is short and limited in space and time, therefore it is foolish to discuss in a leisurely fashion matters of life or death as if there were all eternity to argue them in. It is necessary to make a leap into the unknown, *e.g.,* accepting Christ (in the case of the Christian existentialist) by faith in the sense of giving and risking the self utterly. This means complete commitment, not a dependence on arguments as to whether certain historical events did, or did not, happen.

To summarise: existentialism of whatever type seems to the outsider to be an attitude to life concerning itself with the individual's ultimate problems (mine, not yours); to be anti-rationalist and anti-idealist (in the sense of being, as it seems to the believer, practical)—in effect it seems to say " life is too short to fool about with argument, you must dive in and become committed " to something. Sartre who calls himself an " atheist existentialist " is apparently committed to the belief that " hell is other people," but for most critics the main argument against existentialism is philosophy is that it often rests on a highly specialised personal experience and, as such, is incommunicable.

Existential Psychology, a new if rather diffuse movement in modern psychology with no specific founder but with a number of figures who have, perhaps against their will, acquired leader status. One of the key figures is the British psychiatrist, R. D. Laing, whose radical views on psychotherapy are counted as being heretical by the vast majority of his medical colleagues. Laing holds that many so-called neurotic and psychotic conditions are essentially not " abnormal " and merely represent extreme strategies by which an individual may adjust to environmental and personal stress. Instead of attempting to suppress or eliminate the psychosis in the traditional manner, one should lead the patient through it thus allowing the individual's " unconscious plan " for his own adjustment to be fulfilled.

Exorcism, the removal or ejection of an evil spirit by a ritual or prayer. It is easy to forget that the concept of insanity as representing a disorder of the brain, analogous to physical sickness of the body, is fairly recent in origin. Barely two centuries ago it was considered to be appropriate treatment to put lunatics into chains and beat them daily in the hope that the malevolent beings inhabiting them might be persuaded to depart. Tragically, many of the symptoms of severe forms of mental disorder induce such an apparent change in the personality of the individual as to suggest that an alien individual has indeed taken over their body, and this belief is still common in many parts of the world. Most religious systems have developed some ritual or set of rituals for expelling these demons, and while, not surprisingly, the practice of exorcism by the clergy has declined dramatically in the past century, it is still brought into play now and again in such circumstances as alleged hauntings, poltergeist phenomena, etc. From a scientific point of view, exorcism must be counted as a superstitious rite, but its suggestive power in cases of hysteria, and perhaps even more serious mental illnesses, cannot be completely ruled out. General interest in the topic has been stimulated in part by the resurgence of the practice of Black Magic and witchcraft, largely in the form of experimental dabbling by young people, who no doubt become disillusioned when it fails to live up to its promise. Testimony to the pulling-power of this remnant of our superstitious past is the fact that a sensational and terrifying novel, *The Exorcist*, which its author claimed was based on fact, topped the best-seller lists in 1972, and the even more horrific movie-version became one of the most successful (in box office terms) films of all time. The Church of England, incidentally, takes anything but a dismissive line on the matter, and in fact employs a number of ordained priests as " licensed exorcists ". These services are apparently much in demand.

F

Fabian Society. In 1848 (the year of *The Communist Manifesto* by Marx and Engels) Europe was in revolt. In most countries the workers and intellectuals started bloody revolutions against the feudal ruling classes which were no less violently suppressed; hence on the continent socialism took on a Marxist tinge which to some extent it still retains. But at the same time England was undergoing a slow but non-violent transition in her political and industrial life which led the workers in general to look forward to progress through evolution. Marxism never became an important movement in England even though it took its origin here.

There were many reasons for this: the agitation of the Chartists (*q.v.*); the writings of Mill, Ruskin, and Carlyle; the reforms of Robert Owen; the religious movement led by the Wesleys; the Co-operative societies; the Christian socialists. Furthermore legislation stimulated by these bodies had led to an extension of the franchise to include a considerable number of wage-earners, remedial measures to correct some of the worst abuses of the factory system, recognition of the trade unions, etc. This was the background against which the Fabian Society was founded in 1884 with the conviction that social change could be brought about by gradual parliamentary means. (The name is derived from Quintus Fabius Maximus, the Roman general nicknamed " Cunctator," the delayer, who achieved his successes in defending Rome against Hannibal by refusing to give direct battle.) It was a movement of brilliant intellectuals, chief among whom were Sidney and Beatrice Webb, H. G. Wells, G. B. Shaw, Graham Wallas, Sidney Olivier, and Edward Pease. The Society itself was basically a research institution which furnished the intellectual information for social reform and supported all contributing to the gradual attainment by parliamentary means of socialism.

The Webbs's analysis of society emphasised that individualist enterprise in capitalism was a hang-over from early days and was bound to defeat itself since socialism is the inevitable accompaniment of modern industrialism; the necessary result of popular government is control of their economic system by the people themselves. Utopian schemes had been doomed to failure because they were based on the fallacy that society is static and that islands of utopias could be formed in the midst of an unchanging and antagonistic environment. On the contrary, it was pointed out, society develops: " The new becomes old, often before it is consciously regarded as new." Social reorganisation cannot usefully be hastened by violent means but only through methods consonant with this natural historical progression—gradual, peaceful, and democratic. The Fabians were convinced that men are rational enough to accept in their common interest developments which can be demonstrated as necessary; thus public opinion will come to see that socialisation of the land and industries is essential in the same way that they came to accept the already-existing acts in respect of housing, insurance, medical care, and conditions of work.

The Society collaborated first in the formation of the Independent Labour Party and then with the more moderate Labour Party and the trade unions and Co-operative movement. But in general it disapproved of independent trade union action since change should come from the government and take political form. The class-war of Marx was rejected and so too was the idea of the exclusive role of the working class—reform must come from the enlightened co-operation of all classes—not from their opposition.

Faith Healing, the belief and practice of curing physical and mental ills by faith in some supernatural power, either allegedly latent in the individual (as with Christian Science) or drawn in some way from God. It is a characteristic of faith healing that it is supposed to be publicly demonstrable—*i.e.*, a " healer " will hold public meetings and invite sick people to come up to be cured on the platform. In the emotionally charged atmosphere which the healer generates, it is not unusual for people to show immediate and striking improvement in their illness, but the almost invariable rule is for relapses to occur within days or hours after the event. When remission is more permanent, the illness is generally hysterical in origin and will often return to the individual in some other form. Spiritualists claim that the healing in such cases is done not by " faith " but by direct intervention of the spirits of doctors, etc., who have died and passed on to another world. Perhaps the world's most famous faith healer in recent years was Harry Edwards (d. 1976), who had literally millions of letters from all parts of the world asking for the healing attention of his spirit guides. Many doctors, while remaining immensely sceptical about the origins and extent of this kind of therapy, are inclined to admit that it might have benefits when the sickness is mildly hysterical in origin. The real danger, of course, comes when patients seek unorthodox therapy before consulting their doctor.

Falangists. The Fascist Party of Spain founded in 1933 by José Antonio Primo de Rivera, son of the man who was dictator of the country from 1923 to 1930; he was shot by the Republicans. In 1937 the falangists who had shown unwelcome signs of social radicalism were merged with the other right-wing political groups to form the *Falange Española Tradicionalista y de las Juntas de Ofensive Nacional Sindicalistas* which replaced the Cortes (*i.e.* the Government) between 1939 and 1942 when the Cortes was reinstituted. The Falange is the only political party allowed in Spain. *See* Fascism.

Fascism. From the end of mediaeval times with the opening up of the world, the liberation of the mind and the release of business enterprise, a new spirit arose in Europe exemplified in such movements as the Renaissance, the Reformation, the struggle for democracy, the rise of capitalism, and the Industrial Revolution. With these movements there developed a certain tradition which, in spite of hindrances and disagreements or failures, was universally held both by right- and left-wing parties however strongly they might fail to agree on the best means of attaining what was felt to be a universal ideal. The hard core of this tradition involved: belief in reason and the possibility of human progress; the essential sanctity and dignity of human life; tolerance of widely different religious and political views; reliance on popular government and the responsibility of the rulers to the ruled; freedom of thought and criticism; the necessity of universal education; impartial justice and the rule of law; the desirability of universal peace. Fascism was the negation of every aspect of this tradition and took pride in being so. Emotion took the place of reason, the "immutable, beneficial, and fruitful inequality of classes" and the right of a self-constituted élite to rule them replaced universal suffrage because absolute authority "quick, sure, unanimous" led to action rather than talk. Contrary opinions are not allowed and justice is in the service of the state; war is desirable to advance the power of the state; and racial inequality made a dogma. Those who belong to the "wrong" religion, political party, or race are outside the law.

The attacks on liberalism and exaltation of the state derive largely from Hegel and his German followers; the mystical irrationalism from such 19th cent. philosophers as Schopenhauer, Nietzsche, and Bergson; from Sorel (*see* Syndicalism) came the idea of the "myth," and an image which would have the power to arouse the emotions of the masses and from Sorel also the rationale of violence and justification of force. But these philosophical justifications of fascism do not explain why it arose at all and why it arose where it did—in Italy, Germany, and Spain. These countries had one thing in common—disillusionment. Germany had lost the 1914-18 war, Italy had been on the winning side but was resentful about her small gains, Spain had sunk to the level of a third-rate power, and people were becoming increasingly restive under the reactionary powers of the Catholic Church, the landed aristocracy, and the army. In Marxist theory, fascism is the last fling of the ruling class and the bourgeoisie in their attempt to hold down the workers.

Italian Fascism. The corporate state set up by Benito Mussolini in Italy claimed to be neither capitalist nor socialist, and after its inception in 1922 the Fascist Party became the only recognised one. Its members wore black shirts, were organised in military formations, used the Roman greeting of the outstretched arm, and adopted as their slogan "Mussolini is always right." Membership of the Party was not allowed to exceed a number thought to be suited to the optimum size of a governing class and new candidates were drawn, after strict examinations, from the youth organisations.

The Blackshirts, a fascist militia, existed separately from the army and were ruled by Fascist Headquarters.

At the head of government was Mussolini, "Il Duce" himself, a cabinet of fourteen ministers selected by him and approved by the King to supervise the various functions of government, and the Grand Council or directorate of the Fascist Party, all the members of which were chosen by the Duce. Parliament, which was not allowed to initiate legislation but only to approve decrees from above, consisted of a Senate with life-membership and a Chamber of Fasci and Corporations composed of nominated members of the Party, the National Council of Corporations, and selected representatives of the employers' and employees' confederations. Private enterprise was encouraged and protected but rigidly controlled; strikes were forbidden, but a Charter of Labour enforced the collaboration of workers and employers whose disputes were settled in labour courts presided over by the Party. All decisions relating to industry were government-controlled (*e.g.*, wages, prices, conditions of employment and dismissal, the expansion or limitation of production), and some industries such as mining, shipping, and armaments were largely state-owned.

Italian fascism served as a model in other countries, notably for the German National Socialist Party, in Spain and Japan, and most European nations between the wars had their small Fascist parties, the British version led by Sir Oswald Mosley being known as the British Union which relied on "strong-arm tactics", marches and violence. The Public Order Act of 1936 was passed to deal with it. Although fascism in all countries has certain recognisable characteristics, it would be wrong to think of it as an international movement taking fixed forms and with a clearly thought-out rationale as in the case of communism. While there have been minor revivals of interest in Fascism in Italy—presumably as a counter-move against the considerable inroads being made by the Communist party in that country—Fascism's final remaining bastion in Europe—Spain—began to crumble with the death of its dictator, General Franco, in 1975.

See Falange, Nazism.

Fatalism. *See* Determinism.

Feedback Cult is the name given to a curious fad which began in America in 1970 and which is interesting because it incorporates complicated scientific equipment and experimental psychological methods into its practice. The basis of the cult is as follows: for nearly fifty years it has been known that the brain is the source of varied electrical signals of very low power which can be detected by attaching electrodes to the scalp and amplifying the pulses emitted. Much scientific controversy has surrounded these pulses, and their interpretation by skilled clinicians can lead to the detection of hidden cerebral disorders such as tumours, epileptic foci, etc. The presence of one particular rhythm, the so-called alpha wave, which beats at 14 cycles per second—is believed to be dependent upon whether or not the individual is "attending" to something, particularly in the visual field. It is this alpha rhythm, or rather its control, that is the basis of the feedback cult.

Within the past decade it has been discovered that when some people are connected to an electroencephalograph (the device which records brain rhythms) and are shown the recorded tracings of their own brain waves as they actually occur, they find it possible to modify and control the nature of the waves—the alpha in particular. This, a scientific curiosity rather than a major discovery, soon caught the attention of followers of yoga and other systems seeking enhanced relaxation, "mental discipline," etc. The argument was advanced that for centuries man had been seeking to exercise control over his own mental activities, without however having much opportunity to assess his success—or lack of it. The use of the EEG with the individual's brain waves "fed back" to him for inspection would remedy this. The result has been a sudden surge of lay interest in electroencephalography and a boom in the sale of small, portable EEG machines. Followers of the cult, who may sit for hours inspecting the output from their own brains and attempting to modity it at will, claim that the activity promotes mental " relaxation " and a greater and deeper understanding of their own personal problems. Psychologists are extremely dubious about the reality of this as mental therapy, and the feedback cult will probably die away as soon as some new and equally attractive scientific toy is developed.

Fetichism, originally a practice of the natives of West Africa and elsewhere of attributing magical properties to an object which was used as an amulet, for putting spells on others, or regarded as possessing dangerous powers. In psychology the term refers to a sexual perversion in which objects such as shoes, brassières, hair, etc., arouse sexual excitement.

Feudalism. The feudal system took its origins from Saxon times and broadly speaking lasted until the end of the 13th cent. It was a military and political organisation based on land tenure, for, of course, society throughout this period was based almost entirely on agriculture. The activities of men divided them into three classes or estates. The First Estate was the clergy, responsible for man's spiritual needs; the Second was the nobility, including kings and emperor as well as the lesser nobles; the Third was composed of all those who had to do with the economic and mainly agricultural life of Europe. The praying men, the fighting men and administrators, and the toilers were all held to be dependent on each other in a web of mutual responsibilities.

The theory of feudalism, although it by no means always worked out in practice, was as follows: the earth was God's and therefore no man owned land in the modern sense of the word. God had given the pope spiritual charge of men, and secular power over them to the emperor from whom kings held their kingdoms, and in turn the dukes and counts received the land over which they held sway from the king. Members of the Second Estate held their lands on the condition of fulfilling certain obligations to their overlord and to the people living under them, so when a noble received a fief or piece of land he became the vassal of the man who bestowed it. To him he owed military service for a specified period of the year, attendance at court, and giving his lord counsel. He undertook to ransom his lord when he fell into enemy hands and to contribute to his daughter's dowry and at the knighting of his son. In return the lord offered his vassal protection and justice, received the vassal's sons into his household and educated them for knighthood.

The system was complicated by the fact that large fiefs might be subdivided and abbots often governed church lands held in fief from nobles. The serf or toiling man dwelt on the land of a feudal noble or churchman where he rendered service by tilling the soil or carrying out his craft for his manorial lord in return for protection, justice, and the security of his life and land. He was given a share in the common lands or pastures from which he provided for his own needs. In the modern sense he was not free (although at a later stage he could buy his freedom) since he was attached to the soil and could not leave without the lord's permission. On the other hand he could neither be deprived of his land nor lose his livelihood. Feudal tenures were abolished in England by statute in 1660, although they had for long been inoperative. In Japan a feudal system existed up to 1871, in Russia until 1917, and many relics of it still linger on (e.g. the *mezzadria* system of land tenure in parts of Italy).

Flying Saucers. In June 1947 an American private pilot, Kenneth Arnold, saw a series of wingless objects flying through the air at a speed which he estimated at thousands of miles an hour. He later told the press that the objects " flew as a saucer would if you skipped it across the water," and the phrase " flying saucers " was erroneously born. What Arnold actually saw has never been satisfactorily explained—it was probably a flight of jet fighters reflecting the sun's rays in a way that made them appear as discs—but since that date literally hundreds

of thousands of people all over the world have reported the sighting of strange objects in the sky, coming in a bewildering range of shapes and sizes. Initially the American Air Force launched an official enquiry—Project Bluebook —to attempt to solve the mystery of these " unidentified flying objects " or " U.F.Os," which finally folded in 1969 after concluding that the bulk of the sightings were probably misinterpretations of natural phenomena and that there was no evidence for the commonly held view that earth was being visited by spacecraft trom some other planetary system. A rather similar conclusion was arrived at by the famous University of Colorado project—the Condon Committee—which published its findings in 1968. Despite this clear-cut official attitude, belief in the existence of flying saucers and their origin as alien space vehicles is exceedingly widespread and is held very strongly by people in all walks of life. In 1959 this striking social phenomenon attracted the attention of the psychologist C. G. Jung. He noticed that the press were inclined to report statements that saucers existed when made by prominent people and not publish contrary statements made by equally prominent people. He concluded that flying saucers were in some way welcome phenomena and in his brilliant little book, *Flying Saucers—a modern myth* he hypothesised that the U.F.O.s were the modern equivalent of " signs in the skies." It was Jung's contention that the saucers were looked upon as the harbingers of advanced alien civilisations who had come to save the world from its descent into nuclear catastrophe— archangels in modern dress in fact.

Whatever the validity of this imaginative view of U.F.O.s, it is undeniably true that they exercise a great fascination for millions of people, some of whom invest them with definite religious significance. The best example of the open incorporation of flying saucers into a religious belief system is to be found in the Aetherius Society, an international organisation with headquarters in Los Angeles but founded by a former London clerk, George King. Mr. King, who claims to be the mediumistic link between earth and the largely benevolent beings from outer space. regularly relays messages— notably from a Venusian known as Aetherius— to enthusiastic congregations at religious meetings. The sect, which is entirely sincere and dedicated in its beliefs, also makes pilgrimages to the tops of various mountains which have been " spiritually charged " with the aid of the spacebeings in their flying saucers.

Odd though such ideas may seem to most people, they can be readily understood within the context of the very marked decline in orthodox religious belief which we have seen in the past two decades. To an increasing number of people, many of whom feel a desperate need for spiritual guidance and enlightenment, the concepts of the traditionally Western religions seem somehow unsatisfactory. Many therefore turn to cults and splinter groups which use ideas and terminology which to them seem more at home in the twentieth century than those that sprung to life thousands of years ago. To members of the Aetherius Society, for example, the idea that Jesus Christ lives on Venus and rides around in a flying saucer is neither blasphemous nor ludicrous. As long as empty churches testify to the growing, if perhaps only temporary loss of contact between orthodox religions and the man-in-the-street, then one can expect such offbeat ideas as the cults surrounding flying saucers, and the science-fiction-like cult of Scientology (q.v.) to expand and flourish.

Fourierism. *See* Utopianism.

Freemasonry, a widespread, influential secret organisation of English origin. Although it can be traced back to the Middle Ages when itinerant working masons in England and Scotland were organised in lodges with secret signs for the recognition of fellow-members, modern freemasonry first arose in England in the early decades of the 18th cent. The first Grand Lodge was founded in London in 1716 and Freemasons' Hall was opened in 1776. With its clubs for discussion and social enjoyment (women were excluded) it met a need and became a well-known feature of English life. The movement quickly spread abroad to places which had direct trade links with England. The graded lodge structure, the social prestige conferred by membership, the symbolism, ritual and ceremony, and the emphasis on mutual help have had a lasting appeal. Interest in the occult had more appeal on the Continent than in England. Until a decade or so ago, membership conferred definite business and social advantages, particularly in small communities where the leading middle-class figures were generally members. Recently this advantage has markedly declined and freemason lodges nowadays tend to be little more than worthy charitable organisations. Fear of secret societies has given freemasonry many opponents; it was condemned by the Roman Catholic Church, banned by Fascist dictators, and denounced by the Comintern. The fact that the movement's influence on religious and economic matters is slowly waning may be evidenced by the recent rumours that the Roman Catholic Church was expecting to lift its ban on Freemasonry.

Freudian theory. *See* Psychoanalysis.

Friends, The Society of. *See* Quakers.

Fundamentalism is a term covering a number of religious movements which adhere with the utmost rigidity to orthodox tenets; for example the Old Testament statement that the earth was created by God in six days and six nights would be held to be factual rather than allegorical or symbolic. There is a strong minority undercurrent of support for various Fundamental religions, including such sects as Jehovah's Witnesses, the Seventh Day Adventists, etc. Although the holding of rigid beliefs in the literal truth of the Bible might seem to be frequently contrary to modern scientific findings, the fundamentalists at least do not have the problems of compromise and interpretation to face, and among many simple-minded and poorly educated people this is no doubt a great attraction.

G

Game Theory, an approach to understanding human and animal behaviour which takes the view that psychological insight is best gained by studying the decisions which all living things make constantly and which govern the course of their lives. It proposes that life is basically a strategic game following complex rules which can probably only be understood by a study of the "decision units" as and when they occur. Because one is dealing with highly variable animals controlled by highly complex brains, and not with simple clockwork or electro-mechanical systems, the study of the rules which operate in the game of life is enormously complicated and thus game theory has quickly taken off into advanced mathematics. Game theory, incidentally, can be used to apply to individual action or to the behaviour of groups. Little of any predictive value has been put forward by the protagonists of this approach, but the use of computers to tackle the complex mathematics involved may well lead to some interesting advances.

Gestalt Psychology. In the latter half of the 19th cent. it became evident to psychologists that in principle there was no good reason why "mental" events should not be just as measurable and manageable as "physical" ones. Intensive studies of learning, memory, perception, and so on were therefore undertaken and the beginnings of an empirical science of psychology were underway. In the early part of the 20th cent. the experiments of Pavlov (*see* Behaviourism) and his co-workers suggested that the behaviour of an animal, or even men, might ultimately be reduced to a descriptive account of the activities of nervous reflex loops—the so-called conditioned reflexes. With the publication of Watson's important book on Behaviourism in 1914 it looked as though the transfer of psychological studies from the field of philosophy to that of science could now take place. Actually the over-simplified picture of cerebral and mental pictures which Behaviourism offered

was rather comparable to the billiard ball view of the universe so fashionable in Victorian science. Just as Behaviourism implied that there was a fundamental building block (the conditioned reflex) from which all mental events could be constructed, so Victorian physics assumed that the entire universe could be described in terms of a vast collection of atoms pushing each other around like billiard balls. The development of nuclear physics was to shatter the latter dream and at the same time a challenge to the naïve "reflex psychology" came from the Gestalt experimental school.

The founders of this school were Max Wertheimer, Kurt Koffka and Wolfgang Köhler three young psychologists who in 1912 were conducting experiments—notably in vision—which seemed to expose the inadequacies of the behaviourist position. The Pavlov–Watson view, as we have said, implied that complex sensory events were no more than a numerical sum of individual nervous impulses. Wertheimer's group proposed that certain facts of perceptual experiences (ruled out of court as subjective and therefore unreliable by Watson) implied that the whole (*Gestalt*) was something more than simply the sum of its parts. For example, the presentation of a number of photographs, each slightly different, in rapid series gives rise to cinematographic motion. In basic terms, the eye has received a number of discrete, "still" photographs, and yet "motion" is perceived. What, they asked, was the sensory input corresponding to this motion? Some processes within the brain clearly *added* something to the total input as defined in behaviourist terms. An obvious alternative—in a different sense modality—is that of the arrangement of musical notes. A cluster of notes played one way might be called a tune; played backwards they may form another tune, or may be meaningless. Yet in all cases the constituent parts are the same, and yet their relationship to one another is evidently vital. Once again the whole is something more than the simple sum of the parts.

The implications of all this appeared to be that the brain was equipped with the capacity to organise sensory input in certain well-defined ways, and that far from being misleading and scientifically unjustifiable, human subjective studies of visual experience might reveal the very principles of organisation which the brain employs. Take a field of dots, more or less randomly distributed; inspection of the field will soon reveal certain patterns or clusters standing out—the constellations in the night sky are a good illustration. There are many other examples, and Wertheimer and his colleagues in a famous series of experiments made some effort to catalogue them and reduce them to a finite number of "Laws of Perceptual Organisation" which are still much quoted today. *See* Q19, Q21.

Ghosts, belief in ghosts is one of the most common features of supernatural and mystical philosophy. At its roots it is based on the assumption that Man is essentially an individual created of two separate and distinct substances, mind and body. Most religious systems hold to this dualistic view (*see* Dualism), arguing that whereas the body is transient and destructible, the mind or spirit is permanent and survives the death of its physical host. The discarnate spirit is normally assumed to progress to some other realm ("Heaven," "Nirvana," "The Spirit World," etc.) whereupon it loses contact with the mortal world. Occasionally, however, for one reason or another, the spirits may not progress and may become trapped and unable to escape the material world. Traditionally this is supposed to occur when the death of the individual is precipitated by some great tragedy —murder, suicide, etc.—when the site of the tragedy is supposed to be haunted by the earthbound spirit. Although the library of the Society for Psychical Research is crammed with supposedly authentic accounts of hauntings of this kind, scientific interest in ghosts has been waning rapidly in recent years. At one time, in particular in the latter part of the 19th cent., with the upsurge of scientific interest in Spiritualism (*q.v.*), there were even attempts to call up ghosts in the laboratory. These led to spectacular opportunities for fraud on the part of Spiritualist mediums and the like, but in the long run added little to the cause of science. As we have said, belief in ghosts is largely dependent upon a parallel belief that the mind or soul of man is something essentially separate from the body. With the decline in belief of this notion (it is now almost totally dismissed by most scientists and philosophers) has come an inevitable decline in belief in ghosts.

Gnosticism. Among the many heresies of early Christianity, especially during its first two centuries, was a group which came under the heading of Gnosticism. This was a system or set of systems which attempted to combine Christian beliefs with others derived from Oriental and Greek sources, especially those which were of a mystical and metaphysical nature, such as the doctrines of Plato and Pythagoras. There were many Gnostic sects, the most celebrated being the Alexandrian school of Valentius (fl. c. 136–c. 160). "Gnosis" was understood not as meaning "knowledge" or "understanding" as we understand these words, but "revelation." As in other mystical religions, the ultimate object was individual salvation; sacraments took the most varied forms. Many who professed themselves Christians accepted Gnostic doctrines and even orthodox Christianity contains some elements of Gnostic mysticism. It was left to the bishops and theologians to decide at what point Gnosticism ceased to be orthodox and a difficult task this proved to be. Two of the greatest, Clement of Alexandria and his pupil Origen, unwittingly slipped into heresy when they tried to show that such men as Socrates and Plato, who were in quest of truth, were Christian in intention, and by their lives and works had prepared the way for Christ. Thus they contradicted Church doctrine which specifically said *Extra ecclesiam nulla salus*—outside the Church there is no salvation.

God and Man. The idea of gods came before the idea of God and even earlier in the evolution of religious thought there existed belief in spirits (*see* Animism). It was only as a result of a long period of development that the notion of a universal "God" arose, a development particularly well documented in the Old Testament. Here we are concerned only with the views of philosophers, the views of specific religious bodies being given under the appropriate headings. First, however, some definitions.

Atheism is the positive disbelief in the existence of a God. Agnosticism (a term coined by T. H. Huxley, the 19th cent. biologist and contemporary of Darwin) signifies that one cannot know whether God exists or not. Deism is the acceptance of the existence of God, not through revelation, but as a hypothesis required by reason. Theism also accepts the existence of God, but, unlike Deism, does not reject the evidence of revelation (*e.g.*, in the Bible or in the lives of the saints). Pantheism is the identification of God with all that exists (*i.e.*, with the whole universe). Monotheism is the belief in one God, Polytheism the belief in many (*see also* Dualism).

Early Greek Views. Among the early Greek philosophers, Thales (c. 624–565 B.C.) of Miletus, in Asia Minor, Anaximander (611–547 B.C.), his pupil, and Anaximenes (b. c. 570 B.C.), another Miletan, were men of scientific curiosity and their speculation about the origin of the universe were untouched by religious thought. They founded the scientific tradition of critical discussion. Heraclitus of Ephesus (c. 540–475 B.C.), was concerned with the problem of change. How does a thing change and yet remain itself? For him all things are flames—processes. "Everything is in flux, and nothing is at rest." Empedocles of Agrigentum in Sicily (c. 500–c. 430 B.C.) introduced the idea of opposition and affinity. All matter is composed of the so-called four elements—*earth, water, air,* and *fire*—which are in opposition or alliance with each other. All these were materialist philosophers who sought to explain the working of the universe without recourse to the gods.

Socrates, Plato, and Aristotle. Socrates (470–399 B.C.) was primarily concerned with ethical

matters and conduct rather than the nature of the universe. For him goodness and virtue come from knowledge. He obeyed an "inner voice" and suffered death rather than give up his philosophy. He believed in the persistence of life after death and was essentially a monotheist. Plato (427–347 B.C.) was chiefly concerned with the nature of reality and thought in terms of absolute truths which were unchanging, logical, and mathematical. (*See* Mind and Matter.) Aristotle (384–322 B.C.) took his view of matter not from Democritus (atomic view) but from Empedocles (doctrine of four elements), a view which came to fit in well with orthodox mediaeval theology. Matter is conceived of as potentially alive and striving to attain its particular form, being moved by divine spirit or mind (*nous*). (An acorn, for example, is matter which contains the form "oak-tree" towards which it strives.) Thus there is a whole series from the simplest level of matter to the perfect living individual. But there must be a supreme source of all movement upon which the whole of Nature depends, a Being that Aristotle describes as the "Unmoved Mover," the ultimate cause of all becoming in the universe. This Being is pure intelligence, a philosopher's God, not a personal one. Unlike Plato, Aristotle did not believe in survival after death, holding that the divine, that is the immortal element in man, is mind.

Among the later Greek thinkers the Epicureans were polytheists whose gods, however, were denied supernatural powers. The Stoics built up a materialist theory of the universe, based on the Aristotelian model. To them God was an all-pervading force, related to the world as the soul is related to the body, but they conceived of it as material. They developed the mystical side of Plato's idealism and were much attracted by the astrology coming from Babylonia. They were pantheists. The Sceptics were agnostics.

From Pagan to Christian Thought. Philo, "the Jew of Alexandria," who was about 20 years older than Jesus, tried to show that the Jewish scriptures were in line with the best in Greek thought. He introduced the *Logos* as a bridge between the two systems. Philo's God is remote from the world, above and beyond all thought and being, and as His perfection does not permit direct contact with matter the divine *Logos* acts as intermediary between God and man. Plotinus (204–70), a Roman, and the founder of Neoplatonism, was the last of the great pagan philosophers. Like Philo, he believed that God had created the world indirectly through emanations—beings coming from Him but not of Him. The world needs God but God does not need the world. Creation is a fall from God, especially the human soul when enmeshed in the body and the world of the senses, yet (*see* Determinism) man has the ability to free himself from sense domination and turn towards God. Neoplatonism was the final stage of Greek thought drawing its inspiration from the mystical side of Plato's idealism and its ethics from Stoicism.

Christianity: The Fathers and the Schoolmen. It was mainly through St. Augustine (354–430), Bishop of Hippo in North Africa, that certain of the doctrines of Neoplatonism found their way into Christianity. Augustine also emphasised the concept of God as all good, all wise, all knowing, transcendent, the Creator of the universe out of nothing. But, he added, since God knows everything, everything is determined by Him forever. This is the doctrine of predestination and its subsequent history is discussed under Determinism.

In the early centuries of Christianity, as we have seen, some found it difficult to reconcile God's perfection with His creation of the universe and introduced the concept of the *Logos* which many identified with Christ. Further, it came to be held that a power of divine origin permeated the universe, namely the Holy Spirit or Holy Ghost. Some theory had to be worked out to explain the relationships of these three entities whence arose the conception of the Trinity. God is One; but He is also Three: Father, Son (the *Logos* or Christ), and Holy Ghost.

This doctrine was argued by the Apologists and the Modalists. The former maintained that the *Logos* and the Holy Spirit were emanations from God and that Jesus was the *Logos* in the form of a man. The Modalists held that all three Persons of the Trinity were God in three forms or modes: the *Logos* is God creating, the Holy Spirit God reasoning, and God is God being. This led to a long discussion as to whether the *Logos* was an emanation from God or God in another form; was the *Logos* of like *nature* with God or of the same *substance*? This was resolved at the Council of Nicaea (325) when Athanasius formulated the orthodox doctrine against Arius (*q.v.*): that the one Godhead is a Trinity of the same substance, three Persons of the same nature—Father, Son, and Holy Ghost.

St. Thomas Aquinas (1227–74), influenced greatly by Aristotle's doctrines, set the pattern for all subsequent Catholic belief even to the present time. He produced rational arguments for God's existence: *e.g.*, Aristotle's argument that, since movement exists, there must be a prime mover, the Unmoved Mover or God; further, we can see that things in the universe are related in a scale from the less to the more complex, from the less to the more perfect, and this leads us to suppose that at the peak there must be a Being with absolute perfection. God is the first and final cause of the universe, absolutely perfect, the Creator of everything out of nothing. He reveals Himself in his Creation and rules the universe through His perfect will. How Aquinas dealt with the problem of predestination is told under **Determinism**.

Break with Mediaeval Thought. Renaissance thinkers, free to think for themselves, doubted the validity of the arguments of the Schoolmen but most were unwilling to give up the idea of God (nor would it have been safe to do so). Mystics (*see* **Mysticism**) or near-mystics such as Nicholas of Cusa (*c.* 1401–64) and Jacob Boehme (1575–1624) taught that God was not to be found by reason but was a fact of the immediate intuition of the mystical experience. Giordano Bruno held that God was immanent in the infinite universe. He is the unity of all opposites, a unity without opposites, which the human mind cannot grasp. Bruno was burned at the stake in 1600 at the instigation of the Inquisition (a body which, so we are told, never caused pain to anyone since it was the civil power, not the Inquisition, that carried out the unpleasant sentences) for his heresy.

Francis Bacon, who died in 1626, separated, as was the tendency of that time, science from religion. The latter he divided into the two categories of natural and revealed theology. The former, through the study of nature, may give convincing proof of the existence of a God but nothing more. Of revealed theology he said: " we must quit the small vessel of human reason . . . as we are obliged to obey the divine law, though our will murmurs against it, so we are obliged to believe in the word of God, though our reason is shocked at it." Hobbes (d. 1679) was a complete materialist and one feels that his obeisance to the notion was politic rather than from conviction. However, he does mention God as starting the universe; in motion infers that God is corporeal but denies that His nature can be known.

From Descartes Onwards. Descartes (1596–1650) separated mind and body as different entities but believed that the existence of God could be deduced by the fact that the idea of him existed in the mind. Whatever God puts into man, including his ideas, must be real. God is self-caused, omniscient, omnipotent, eternal, all goodness and truth. But Descartes neglected to explain how mind separate from body can influence body, or God separate from the world can influence matter.

Spinoza (1632–77) declared that all existence is embraced in one substance—God, the all-in-all. He was a pantheist and as such was rejected by his Jewish brethren. But Spinoza's God has neither personality nor consciousness, intelligence nor purpose, although all things follow in strict law from His nature. All the thought of everyone in the world, make up God's thoughts.

Bishop Berkeley (1685–1753) took the view that things exist only when they are perceived, and this naturally implies that a tree, for example, ceases to exist when nobody is looking at it. This problem was solved to his own satisfaction by assuming that God, seeing everything, prevented objects from disappearing when we were not present. The world is a creation of God but it is a spiritual or mental world, not a material one.

Hume (1711–76), who was a sceptic, held that human reason cannot demonstrate the existence of God and all past arguments to show that it could were fallacious. Yet we must believe in God since the basis of all hope, morality, and society is based upon the belief. Kant (1724–1804) held a theory similar to that of Hume. We cannot know by reason that God exists, nor can we prove on the basis of argument anything about God. But we can form an idea of the whole of the universe, the one Absolute Whole, and personify it. We need the idea of God on which to base our moral life, although this idea of God is transcendent, *i.e.*, goes beyond experience.

William James (1842–1910), the American philosopher (*see* Pragmatism), held much the same view: God cannot be proved to exist, but we have a will to believe which must be satisfied, and the idea works in practice. Hegel (1770–1831) thought of God as a developing process, beginning with " the Absolute " or First Cause and finding its highest expression in man's mind, or reason. It is in man that God most clearly becomes aware of Himself. Finally Comte (1798–1857), the positivist, held that religion belongs to a more primitive state of society and, like many modern philosophers, turned the problem over to believers as being none of the business of science.

Golden Dawn, Order of, a strange but intellectually influential secret society founded in 1887 by three former Rosicrucians (*q.v.*). The Society, which was but one of the large number of occult organisations which flourished in the latter half of the 19th cent., was particularly interesting because it attracted so many scholarly eccentrics to its ranks. These included the poet W. B. Yeats, the actress Florence Farr, the writers Arthur Machen and Algernon Blackwood and the poetess Dion Fortune. A member with a less savoury reputation was the notorious Aleister Crowley who was ultimately expelled from the order for practising Black Magic. Essentially the movement, like others of its kind, professed to offer important secrets of occult knowledge, and taught its followers the basic principles of White, as opposed to Black Magic. Mainly harmless in their aims and activities, societies such as this served largely as pastimes for individuals of intellectual and academic standing who found the concepts and rituals of the Established Church too dull for their inquisitive minds. Most members of the Order of the Golden Dawn either became disillusioned when the white magic, which they had so arduously studied, failed to provide any genuine supernatural results and gave up in disgust, or broke away to form their own rival groups. Though these often had equally glamorous names and rituals, they tended to be no more successful and themselves vanished into the mists of obscurity. Today so-called White Magic has become fashionable with many young people, no doubt as the result of the almost total collapse of the authority of orthodox religion, but it is noticeable that such interest is generally to be found among the less well-educated and intelligent. White Magic had its intellectual heyday in the 19th cent. and it is unlikely ever to attract such sustained academic interest again.

Good and Evil.

Early Philosophers' Views. The early Greek philosophers were chiefly concerned with the laws of the universe, consequently it was common belief that knowledge of these laws, and living according to them, constituted the supreme good. Heraclitus, for example, who taught that all things carried with them their opposites, held that good and evil were like two notes in a harmony, necessary to each other. " It is the opposite which is good for us." Democritus, like Epicurus (q.v.), held that the main goal of life is happiness, but happiness in moderation. The good man is not merely the one who *does* good but who always *wants* to do so: " You can tell the good man not by his deeds alone but by his desires." Such goodness brings happiness, the ultimate goal.   On the other hand, many of the wandering Sophist teachers taught that good was merely social convention, that there are no absolute principles of right and wrong, that each man should live according to his desires and make his own moral code.   To Socrates knowledge was the highest good because doing wrong is the result of ignorance: " no man is voluntarily bad."   Plato and Aristotle, differing in many other respects, drew attention to the fact that man is composed of three parts: his desires and appetites, his will, and his reason.   A man whose reason rules his will and appetites is not only a good but a happy man; for happiness is not an aim in itself but a by-product of the good life. Aristotle, however, emphasised the goal of self-realisation, and thought that if the goal of life is (as Plato had said) a rational attitude towards the feelings and desires, it needs to be further defined. Aristotle defined it as the " Golden Mean "—the good man is one who does not go to extremes but balances one extreme against another.   Thus courage is a mean between cowardice and foolhardiness. The later philosophers Philo and Plotinus held that evil was in the very nature of the body and its senses.   Goodness could only be achieved by giving up the life of the senses and, freed from the domination of the body, turning to God, the source of goodness.

Christian Views. St. Augustine taught that everything in the universe is good.   Even those things which appear evil are good in that they fit with the harmony of the universe like shadows in a painting.   Man should turn his back on the pleasures of the world and turn to the love of God.   Peter Abelard (1079–1142) made the more sophisticated distinction when he suggested that the wrongness of an act lies not in the act itself, but in the intention of the doer: " God considers not what is done but in what spirit it is done; and the merit or praise of the agent lies not in the deed but in the intention."   If we do what we believe to be right, we may err, but we do not sin.   The only sinful man is he who deliberately sets out to do what he knows to be wrong.   St. Thomas Aquinas agreed with Aristotle in that he believed the highest good to be realisation of self as God has ordained, and he also agreed with Abelard that intention is important.   Even a good act is not good unless the doer intended it to have good consequences.   Intention will not make a bad act good, but it is the only thing that will make a good act genuinely good.

In general, Christianity has had difficulties in solving the problem of the existence of evil; for even when one accepts that the evil men do is somehow tied up with the body, it is still difficult to answer the question: how could an all-good God create evil?   This is answered in one of two ways: (a) that Adam was given free-will and chose to sin (an answer which still does not explain how sin could exist anywhere in the universe of a God who created everything); (b) by denying the reality of evil as some Christians have chosen to do (e.g., Christian Science q.v.).   The Eastern religions, on the other hand (see Zoroastrianism), solved the problem in a more realistic way by a dualism which denied that their gods were the creators of the whole universe and allowed the existence of at least two gods, one good and one evil.   In Christianity there is, of course, a Devil, but it is not explained whence his evil nature came.

Later Philosophic Views. Hobbes equated good with pleasure, evil with pain.   They are relative to the individual man in the sense that " one man's meat is another man's poison."   Descartes believed that the power to distinguish between good and evil given by God to man is not complete, so that man does evil through ignorance.   We act with insufficient knowledge and on inadequate evidence.   Locke, believing that at birth the mind is a blank slate, held

that men get their opinions of right and wrong from their parents.   By and large, happiness is good and pain is evil.   But men do not always agree over what is pleasurable and what not.   Hence laws exist and these fall into three categories: (1) the divine law; (2) civil laws; (3) matters of opinion or reputation which are enforced by the fact that men do not like to incur the disapproval of their friends.   We learn by experience that evil brings pain and good acts bring pleasure, and, basically, one is good because not to be so would bring discomfort.

Kant (see God and Man) found moral beliefs to be inherent in man whether or not they can be proved by reason.   There is a categorical imperative which makes us realise the validity of two universal laws: (1) " always act in such a way that the maxim determining your conduct might well become a universal law; act so that you can will that everybody shall follow the principle of your action; (2) " always act so as to treat humanity, whether in thine own person or in that of another, in every case as an end and never as a means."

Schopenhauer (1788–1860) was influenced by Buddhism and saw the will as a blind impelling striving, and desire as the cause of all suffering. The remedy is to regard sympathy and pity as the basis of all morality and to deny one's individual will.   This is made easier if we realise that everyone is part of the Universal Will and therefore the one against whom we are struggling is part of the same whole as ourselves.

John Stuart Mill and Jeremy Bentham were both representatives of the Utilitarian school, believing that good is the greatest good (happiness) of the greatest number (see Utilitarianism). Lastly, there is the view held mostly by political thinkers that good is what is good for the state or society in general (see State and Man).

Graphology, the study of the analysis of human handwriting.   There are two approaches to this topic and it is important to separate them clearly.   The first involves the attempt on the part of an expert to decide from looking at a signature (a) to whom it belongs, and (b) whether or not it is forgery.   This art is a legitimate, though tricky area of study, and graphologists have been called in as expert witnesses in courts of law.   The second approach involves attempts to detect such tenuous variables as character from a study of an individual's handwriting, and the facts here are altogether less clear. Psychologists find it difficult enough to assess character or personality in a face-to-face interview and even when they are equipped with a range of special tests.   The general opinion here would seem to be that some slight information might be revealed by a careful study of handwriting, but that the overall effect would be too unreliable for this kind of graphology to be of practical value.

Greater World Spiritualists.   Spiritualism, as an organised religion, holds the view that the human personality survives death, and that it is possible to communicate with the spirits of those who have died in the physical sense. Relatively little importance is attached to the divinity of Jesus Christ, which is of course the cornerstone of the Christian faith.   Some Spiritualists, however, hold a kind of halfway house position, believing both that Jesus was the son of God, and also that communication with the spirit world is not only possible but also a " lost aspect " of Christian teachings. The most significant group holding this view are the Greater World Christian Spiritualists' Association, founded in 1931.   Their teachings are based on trance addresses received through the mediumship of Winifred Moyes.   Despite the fact that her control in the spirit world was named "Zodiac," Christian Spiritualists claim that their philosophy is closer to the original teachings of Jesus than that of the orthodox Church today.

Guild Socialism, a British form of syndicalism (q.v.) created in 1906 by an architect, A. J. Penty, who was soon joined by A. R. Orage, S. G. Hobson, and G. D. H. Cole.   The background to the movement was the situation that, although at that time the Labour Party had 29 members in the House of Commons, a period of severe economic crisis had shown the government unwilling and the Labourites unable to do anything about it; the workers were resorting again to direct action to secure their demands and the democratic and constitutional methods to which the Fabians had partly persuaded them seemed to have failed. The guild socialists advocated a restoration of the mediaeval guild system as was being recommended by the French syndicalists whose programme involved a return to direct economic action, a functional industrial structure, return of craftsmanship, and distrust of the state. Guild socialists believed that value was created by society as a whole rather than by individuals singly, and that capitalist economists had recommended the acquisition of wealth without emphasising the social responsibilities which wealth should bring. The trade unions were to be organised to take over and run their own industries after nationalisation. Thus guild socialists were not only against capitalism but also against state socialism in which the state took over the control of industry. Political authority was held to be uncongenial to human freedom and therefore nothing was to be gained by the substitution of state bureaucracy for capitalist control. The National Guilds League, formed in 1915, advocated abolition of the wages system, self-government in industry and control by a system of national guilds acting in conjunction with other functional democratic organisations in the community. This body was dissolved in 1925, but the theories of guild socialism have undoubtedly influenced British socialism.

Gurdjieff, Russian–Greek mystic who set up an occult commune near Paris in the 1930s, to which were attracted a host of the intellectual and literary avant garde of the time. His teachings, which are immensely obscure, are presented in allegorical form in a lengthy philosophical novel, *All and Everything*, which has the peculiar sub-title "Beelzebub's Tales to his Grandson." Opinions as to the merits of Gurdjieff's ideas are strikingly varied: some commentators hold that he was one of the century's leading philosophers, others that he was a brazen confidence trickster with a vivid personality and the gift of making trivial observations sound pregnant with meaning. The truth probably lies somewhere in between the two extremes and, despite the fact that a number of highly intelligent individuals still espouse his cause two decades after his death, most people continue to find his books largely unreadable and his philosophy muddled and pretentious.

H

Heresy, originally meant a sect or school of thought holding views different from others (*e.g.*, Pharisees and Sadducees within Judaism). Later it came to mean beliefs contrary to orthodox teaching (*e.g.*, Arianism, Apollinarianism, Nestorianism).

Hinduism, the religion and social institutions of the great majority of the people of India. Hinduism has no fixed scriptural canon but its doctrines are to be found in certain ancient works, notably the *Veda*, the *Brahmanas*, the *Upanishads*, and the *Bhagavad-gita*. The dark-skinned Dravidians invaded India between about 3250 and 2750 B.C. and established a civilisation in the Indus valley. They were polytheists who worshipped a number of nature-gods; some elements of their beliefs persisted into Hinduism. They were subdued by a light-skinned Nordic people who invaded from Asia Minor and Iran about 1500 B.C. The language of these Aryan people was Vedic, parent of Sanskrit in which their religious literature (the Vedas) came to be written after many centuries of oral transmission.

The *Veda* or Sacred Lore has come down to us in the form of mantras or hymns of which there are four great collections, the best-known being the *Rig-Veda*. These Vedic Aryans worshipped nature-deities, their favourites being Indra (rain), Agni (fire), and Surya (the sun). Their religion contained no idolatry but became contaminated by the more primitive beliefs of the conquered Dravidians. Sacrifice and ritual became predominant in a ceremonial religion.

As a reaction a more philosophic form arose (c. 500 B.C.) with its scriptures in the *Upanishads*. At its highest level, known as Brahmanism, belief is in a subtle and sophisticated form of monotheism (Brahman is an impersonal, all-embracing spirit), but there is a tolerant acceptance of more primitive beliefs. Thus Vishnu (a conservative principle) and Siva (a destructive principle) grew out of Vedic conceptions. The two great doctrines of Hinduism are *karma* and transmigration. The universal desire to be reunited with the absolute (*atman* or Brahman) can be satisfied by following the path of knowledge. Life is a cycle of lives (*samsara*) in which man's destiny is determined by his deeds (*karma*) from which he may seek release (*moksa*) through ascetic practices or the discipline of Yoga (*q.v.*). Failure to achieve release means reincarnation—migration to a higher or lower form of life after death—until the ultimate goal of absorption in the absolute is reached.

In the great Sanskrit epic poems *Ramayana* and *Mahabharata* the deity takes three forms, represented by the divine personalities of Brahma, Vishnu, and Siva. There are also lower gods, demi-gods, supernatural beings, and members of the trinity may even become incarnate, as Vishnu became identified with Krishna, one of the heroes of the *Mahabharata* and the well-known *Bhagavad-gita*.

The ritual and legalistic side of Brahmanism is the caste system based on the elaborate codes of the *Law of Manu*, according to which God created distinct orders of men as He created distinct species of animals and plants. Men are born to be Brahmans, soldiers, agriculturists, or servants, but since a Brahman may marry a woman from any of these castes, an endless number of sub-castes arise.

Hinduism has always shown great tolerance for varieties of belief and practice. Ideas pleasant and unpleasant have been assimilated: fetichism, demon-cults, animal-worship, sexual-cults (such as the rites of *Kali* in Calcutta). Today, as would be expected in a country which is in the throes of vast social change, Hinduism itself is changing. Under the impact of modern conditions new ideas are destroying old beliefs and customs. *See also* Jainism, Sikhism.

Holy Rollers. Contrary to general belief there is no single individual religious group calling themselves Holy Rollers; rather this is a generic term referring to a number of minor revivalist groups whose members work themselves into an ecstatic frenzy in the course of religious worship. Swooning and fainting are probably the most popular methods of expressing this kind of religious ecstasy, but "speaking with tongues" (*i.e.*, babbling nonsense), snake handling (many believers die from snake venom as a consequence) and uncontrolled dancing are also featured. Athletic religious worship of this kind is of course of great interest to psychologists. Anthropologists are equally interested, for they see in such behaviour patterns vivid reminders—if such are needed—that mankind has a history that predates our present culture by millions and not just by thousands of years.

Homoeopathy, a branch of fringe medicine whose motto *Similia Similibus Curantur* (like cures like) sums up its controversial approach to therapy. In essence the homoeopathists claim that a disease can be treated by administering quite minute doses of a substance which produce symptoms (in the healthy person) similar to those induced by the disease itself. The founder and populariser of this unusual approach to medicine was the German Samuel Hahnemann who was born in 1775, a friend of the physician Mesmer who propagated hypnotherapy. Hahnemann lived to see his ideas spread across the civilised world and despite the grave theoretical difficulties implicit in the question of how the very minute dosages actually achieve any result at all, it remained a respectable approach of medicine until the latter half of the last century. Even today a number of qualified doctors still employ homoeopathic ideas within the framework of the national health service, and the late King George V was treated by the eminent homoeopathist, Sir John Weir, but it seems nevertheless to be in slow but steady decline. This is probably due not to any revealed deficiencies in homoeopathy itself, but rather to the extraordinary advances which have been made in orthodox medicine in the last few decades.

Humanism, the term applied to (1) a system of education based on the Greek and Latin classics; and (2) the vigorous attitudes that accompanied the end of the Middle Ages and were represented at different periods by the Renaissance, the Reformation, the Industrial Revolution, and the struggle for democracy. These include: release from ecclesiastical authority, the liberation of the intellect, faith in progress, the belief that man himself can improve his own conditions without supernatural help and, indeed, has a duty to do so. " Man is the measure of all things " is the keynote of humanism. The humanist has faith in man's intellectual and spiritual resources not only to bring knowledge and understanding of the world but to solve the moral problems of how to use that knowledge. That man should show respect to man irrespective of class, race or creed is fundamental to the humanist attitude to life. Among the fundamental moral principles he would count those of freedom, justice, tolerance and happiness.

Today the idea that people can live an honest, meaningful life without following a formal religious creed of some kind does not seem particularly shocking. It is an interesting gauge of the rapid change in social attitudes to religion that when, less than twenty years ago, the psychologist Margaret Knight tentatively advanced this thesis in a short B.B.C. talk, public opinion seemed to be outraged and both Mrs. Knight and the B.B.C. were openly attacked by the popular press for immoral and seditious teachings.

Hussites, the followers of John Hus, the most famous pupil of John Wyclif. He was the rector of Prague University and, although it is now by no means certain that his beliefs were heretical, he was condemned to death for heresy and burnt at the stake in 1415 at Constance whence he had come with a safe conduct issued by the Emperor Sigismund of Hungary. The latter based his action on the doctrine that no faith need be kept with heretics, but it is obvious that the main objection to Hus was his contempt for authority of any kind. After their leader's death, the Hussites became a formidable body in Bohemia and Moravia. They took up arms on behalf of their faith, their religion being strongly imbued with political feeling (hostility to Germanism and to the supremacy of the Roman Church). Their religious struggles for reform led to the Hussite Wars during which the movement splintered into several groups.

I

I Ching, the Chinese " Book of Changes " which is supposed to provide a practical demonstration of the truths of ancient Chinese philosophy. The method consists of casting forty-nine sticks into two random heaps, or more simply, of tossing three coins to see if there is a preponderance of heads or tails. The coins are cast six times whereupon the head-tail sequence achieved is referred to a coded series of phrases in the book, which are supposed to relate in some way to the question held in the mind when the sticks or coins are being cast. The phrases are without exception vague, and platitudinous remarks such as " Evil people do not further the perseverance of the superior man," etc., abound. Consequently it is not difficult to read into such amorphous stuff a suitable " interpretation " or answer to one's unspoken question. The I Ching might well be looked upon as an entertaining parlour game, but it is currently a great fad in Europe and America and is taken with great seriousness by an astonishing number of people.

Idealism, in a philosophical sense, the belief that there is no matter in the universe, that all that exists is mind or spirit. See **Mind and Matter** and **Realism**.

Illuminati, a secret society founded in 1776 by Adam Weishaupt, a Bavarian professor of canon law at Ingolstadt, in an attempt to combat superstition and ignorance by founding an association for rational enlightenment and the regeneration of the world. " He tried to give the social ideals of the Enlightenment realisation by conspiratorial means " (J. M. Roberts, *The Mythology of the Secret Societies*, 1972). Under conditions of secrecy it sought to penetrate and control the masonic lodges for subversive purposes. Among its members were Goethe and Schiller. The Order spread to Austria, Italy and Hungary but was condemned by the Roman Catholic Church and dissolved in 1785 by the Bavarian government.

Immortality. The belief in a life after death has been widely held since the earliest times. It has certainly not been universal, nor has it always taken a form which everyone would find satisfying. In the early stages of human history or prehistory everything contained a spirit (*see* Animism) and it is obvious from the objects left in early graves that the dead were expected to exist in some form after death. The experience of dreams, too, seemed to suggest to the unsophisticated that there was a part of man which could leave his body and wander elsewhere during sleep. In order to save space, it will be helpful to classify the various types of belief which have existed in philosophical thought regarding this problem: (1) There is the idea that, although *something* survives bodily death, it is not necessarily eternal. Thus most primitive peoples were prepared to believe that man's spirit haunted the place around his grave and that food and drink should be set out for it, but that this spirit did not go on forever and gradually faded away. (2) The ancient Greeks and Hebrews believed for the most part that the souls of the dead went to a place of shades there to pine for the world of men. Their whining ghosts spent eternity in a dark, uninviting region in misery and remorse. (3) Other people, and there were many more of these, believed in the transmigration of souls with the former life of the individual determining whether his next life would be at a higher or lower level. Sometimes this process seems to have been thought of as simply going on and on, by others (*e.g.*, in Hinduism and Buddhism) as terminating in either non-sentience or union with God but in any case in annihilation of the self as self. Believers in this theory were the Greek philosophers Pythagoras, Empedocles, Plato (who believed that soul comes from God and strives to return to God, according to his own rather confused notions of the deity. If it fails to free itself completely from the body it will sink lower and lower from one body to another.) Plotinus held similar views to Plato, and many other religious sects in addition to those mentioned have believed in transmigration. (4) The belief of Plato and Aristotle that if souls continue to exist after death there is no reason why they should not have existed before birth (this in part is covered by (3)), but some have pointed out that eternity does not mean " from now on," but the whole of time before and after " now "—nobody, however, so far as one knows, held that *individual* souls so exist. (5) The theory that the soul does not exist at all and therefore immortality is meaningless: this was held by Anaximenes in early Greek times; by Leucippus, Democritus, and the other Greek atomists; by the Epicureans from the Greek Epicurus to the Roman Lucretius; by the British Hobbes and Hume; by Comte of France; and William James and John Dewey of America. (6) The thesis, held notably by Locke and Kant, that although we cannot prove the reality of soul and immortality by pure reason, belief in them should be held for moral ends. (For the orthodox Christian view *see* God and Man, Determinism and Free-will.) From this summary we can see that many philosophies and religions with the important exceptions of Islam and Christianity without denying a future life do deny the permanence of the individual soul in anything resembling its earthly form (*see* Spiritualism, Psychic Research).

Imperialism, the practice by a country, which has become a nation and embarked upon commercial and industrial expansion, of acquiring and administering territories, inhabited by peoples usually at a lower stage of development, as colonies or dependencies. Thus the " typical " imperialist powers of the 19th cent. and earlier were Britain, Belgium, Holland, Spain, and Portugal, whilst Germany, Italy, and Japan, which either did not have unity during this period or adequate industrial expansion, tried to make good their lacks in this direction by war in the 20th cent. The term " imperialism " is not easy to define today (although often enough used as a term of abuse). There is economic imperialism exerted, not through armies, but through economic penetration. There is what may be described as ideological imperialism, *e.g.*, the anti-communist crusade that led America (in the name of freedom) into acts of appalling inhumanity in Vietnam; the dogmatism that led the Soviet Union into the invasion of Czechoslovakia. The Afrikaners in South Africa pass laws to permit the exploitation of the black and coloured peoples in their midst. Imperialism is a dangerous word and, before using it, we would do well to remember the retort of a British statesman who, when lecturing in America prior to Indian independence, was asked by an elderly matron " What are you going to do about the Indians? " " Which Indians, madam —ours or yours? "

Irrationalism. An attitude that puts emotion and passion before reason, and which can be exploited for dubious ends.

Islam, the religion of which Mohammed (570–632) was the prophet, the word signifying submission to the will of God. It is one of the most widespread of religions. Its adherents are called Moslems or Muslims. Islam came later than the other great monotheistic religions (Judaism and Christianity) and may be regarded in some respects as a heresy. Mohammed accepted the inspiration of the Old Testament and claimed to be a successor to Moses, and although he did not recognise Jesus as God, he did recognise Him as a prophet.

The sacred book of Islam is the Koran, the most influential book in the world next to the Bible. According to Islamic belief the words were revealed to the prophet by God through the angel Gabriel at intervals over a period of 20 years, first at his native Mecca, and then at Medina. The book is divided into 114 *suras* or chapters: all but one begin with the words: " In the name of Allah, the Merciful, the Compassionate." It is written in classical Arabic, and Moslems memorise much or all of it. The Koran superseded the Gospel as Mohammed superseded Christ. Its ethical teachings are high. The great advantage of Mohammedanism is that, like orthodox Judaism it is a literal-minded religion lived in everyday life. No Moslem is in any doubt as to exactly how he should carry on in the events of his day. He has five duties: (1) Once in his life he must say with absolute conviction: " There is no God but Allah, and Mohammed is His Prophet." (2) Prayer preceded by ablution must be five times daily—on rising, at noon, in mid-afternoon, after sunset, and before retiring. The face of the worshipper is turned in the direction of Mecca. (3) The giving of alms generously, including provisions for the poor. (4) The keeping of the fast of Ramadan, the holy month, during which believers in good health may neither eat nor drink nor indulge in worldly pleasures between sunrise and sunset. (5) Once in his life a Moslem, if he can, must make the pilgrimage to Mecca. In addition, drinking, gambling, and the eating of pork are forbidden and circumcision is practised. Polygamy is permitted, although decreasing; sexual relations outside marriage are disapproved of; marriage is only with the wife's consent; and divorce may be initiated by either husband or wife. A great advantage in the spread of Islam has been its lack of race prejudice.

Mohammed's main achievements were the destruction of idolatry, the welding of warring tribes into one community, the progress of a conquest which led after his death to the great and cultured empire which spread throughout the Middle East into north Africa, north India, and ultimately to Spain. That it did not spread all over Europe was due to the Muslim defeat by Charles Martel at Tours in 732.

J

Jainism. The Jains are a small Indian sect, largely in commerce and finance, numbering about 2 million. Their movement founded by Vardhamana, called Mahavira (the great hero), in the 6th cent. B.C. arose rather earlier than Buddhism in revolt against the ritualism and impersonality of Hinduism (*q.v.*). It rejects the authority of the early Hindu Vedas and does away with many of the Hindu deities whose place is largely taken by Jainism's twenty-four immortal saints; it despises caste distinctions and modifies the two great Hindu doctrines of *karma* and transmigration. Jain philosophy is based on *ahimsa*, the sacredness of all life, regarding even plants as the brethren of mankind, and refusing to kill even the smallest insect.

Jehovah's Witnesses, a religious body who consider themselves to be the present-day representatives of a religious movement which has existed since Abel " offered unto God a more excellent sacrifice than Cain, by which he obtained witness that he was righteous." Abel was the first " witness," and amongst others were Enoch, Noah, Abraham, Moses, Jeremiah, and John the Baptist. Pre-eminent among witnesses, of course, was Jesus Christ who is described in the Book of Revelation as " the faithful and true witness." Thus they see themselves as " the Lord's organisation," in the long line of those who through the ages have preserved on earth the true and pure worship of God or, as the Witnesses prefer to call Him, " Jehovah-God."

So far as other people are aware, the movement was founded by Charles Taze Russell (Pastor Russell) of Allegany, Pittsburgh, Pennsylvania, U.S.A. in 1881 under the name, adopted in 1896, of the Watch Tower Bible and Tract Society, which has continued as the controlling organisation of Jehovah's Witnesses. Its magazine, *The Watch Tower Announcing Jehovah's Kingdom*, first published in 1879, and other publications are distributed by the zealous members who carry out the house-to-house canvassing. The movement has a strong leadership.

Their teaching centres upon the early establishment of God's new world on earth, preceded by the second coming of Christ. Witnesses believe this has already happened, and that Armageddon " will come as soon as the Witness is completed." The millennial period will give sinners a second chance of salvation and " millions now living will never die " (the title of one of their pamphlets).

The dead will progressively be raised to the new earth until all the vacant places left after Armageddon are filled. There is, however, some doubt about the " goatish souls " who have made themselves unpleasant to the Witnesses, those who have accepted (or permitted to be accepted) a blood-transfusion contrary to the Scriptures, and others who have committed grave sins.

Every belief held by the movement, it is claimed, can be upheld, chapter and verse, by reference to the Scriptures. Witnesses regard the doctrine of the Trinity as devised by Satan. In both wars Witnesses have been in trouble for their refusal to take part in war and it is only fair to add that six thousand suffered for the same reason in German concentration camps.

Jensenism, name given to the minority group of psychologists and educationalists who, in general, support the view of the American professor, Arthur Jensen. The latter's studies of individual variation in learning and of the genetic factor in mental ability has led him to argue that heredity is more crucial in determining intellectual ability than environment. By implication this has put him and his colleagues at the centre of a divisive "race and intelligence" controversy which has acquired some political overtones. In 1973 Professor H. J. Eysenck was physically assaulted by students at a university lecture because he was reputed to be supporting the Jensenist position.

Jesus People, naïve and exhibitionist revival of interest in the teaching and personality of Jesus Christ which has recently featured as part of the American "Hippy" scene. The Jesus people or Jesus Freaks, as they are sometimes called, are generally white but not necessarily of an orthodox Christian background. The cult, like so many others of its kind seems to have developed in California and its adherents adopt the regimental attire (colourful costumes, long hair, beards, etc.) of the modern American Hippy, who is himself a descendant of the Beatnik (*see* Beat Generation). Apart from the fact that the long hair and beards are vaguely reminiscent of the Victorian pictorial representation of Jesus, the followers of the present-day cult would seem to have little genuinely in common with the ethos of Christianity, and the movement and its ideals appear to be superficial and probably transitory. A recent highly successful rock musical, "Jesus Christ, Superstar," blatantly cashes in on the Jesus Freak vogue.

Judaism, the religion of the Jews, the oldest of the great monotheist religions, parent of Christianity and Islam, the development of which is presented in the Old Testament. The creed of Judaism is based on the concept of a transcendent and omnipotent One True God, the revelation of His will in the *Torah*, and the special relation between God and His "Chosen People." The idea of Incarnation is rejected, Jesus is not recognised as the Messiah. The *Torah* is the Hebrew name for the Law of Moses (the Pentateuch) which, Judaism holds, was divinely revealed to Moses on Mount Sinai soon after the exodus of the Israelites from Egypt (1230 B.C.). Many critics deny the Mosaic authorship of the first five books of the Bible and believe them to be a compilation from four main sources known as J (Jahvist), E (Elohist), D (Deuteronomist) and P (Priestly Code), distinguished from each other by the name used for God, language, style, and internal evidence. From the historical point of view an important influence on Judaism may have been the monotheism of Akhenaten, the "heretic" Pharaoh (note, for example, the striking resemblance between Psalm 104 and Akhenaten's "Hymn to the Sun").

The Talmud is a book containing the civil and canonical laws of the Jews and includes the Mishna, a compilation from oral tradition written in Hebrew, and the Gemara, a collection of comments and criticisms by the Jewish rabbis, written in Aramaic. There are in fact two Talmuds: the one made in Palestine (the Jerusalem Talmud), finished at the beginning of the 5th cent., and the other made in Babylon, completed at the end of the 6th cent.

Judaism at the beginning of the Christian era had a number of sects: (1) the Pharisees (whose views include the first clear statement of the resurrection of the just to eternal life and the future punishment of the wicked) who held to the *Torah* and the universality of God; (2) the Sadducees, the upper class of priests and wealthy landowners, to whom God was essentially a national God and who placed the interests of the state before the *Torah*; they rejected ideas of resurrection and eternal life; (3) the Essenes (*q.v.*) who were regarded as a puritanical break-away movement by both parties. The views of the Pharisees prevailed.

Jewish writing continued through the years and some books were added to the *Torah*, among them the Three Major Prophets and certain books of the Twelve Minor Prophets. There were also the Apocalyptic writers who were unorthodox in their preaching of a divinely planned catastrophic end to the world with a "new Heaven and a new earth," preceded by a divine Messiah, and a future life—all of which beliefs influenced early Christianity. Judah Halevi of Toledo (c. 1085–c. 1140) and Moses Maimonides of Cordova (1135–1204) were the great Jewish philosophers.

Modern movements in Judaism stem from the Enlightenment, notably with Moses Mendels-

sohn in the 18th cent. who accepted, as was the tendency of the period, only that which could be proved by reason. He translated the Pentateuch into German thus encouraging German Jews to give up Yiddish and Hebrew for the language of the land and thereby preparing them for their vast contribution to Western civilisation. One of his disciples, David Friedländer (d. 1834) instituted "reform" Judaism. He wanted to eliminate anything that would hamper the relationships of Jews with their neighbours or tend to call in doubt their loyalty to their adopted state. A similar movement in America (1885) called for the rejection of dietary laws, the inauguration of Sunday services, and the repudiation of Jewish nationalism. Between "reform" and orthodoxy there arose the conservative movement which, in England, includes prayers in English in the service, does not segregate men and women in the synagogue, and translates the Law in a more liberal way. (The fact is that it would be almost impossible for a strictly orthodox Jew to live in a modern industrialised community at all.)

Judaism is essentially a social and family religion which, more than almost any other, concerns itself with the observances of every aspect of daily life. As in Islam (*q.v.*) details are laid down in the most minute way for the behaviour of the orthodox.

The home is the main Jewish institution and Jews, like Catholics, cannot surrender their religion. Circumcision takes place eight days after birth, and a boy becomes a man for religious purposes at his Bar Mitzvah at the age of thirteen. Women are spared most of this because their place in the home is considered sufficiently sacred. Among festivals are Passover, recalling the Exodus; Rosh Hashanah (the Jewish New Year), the anniversary of the Creation and the beginning of ten days of penitence ending with Yom Kippur (the Day of Atonement), a day of fasting spent in the synagogue; Purim, celebrating the deliverance of the Jews from Haman; and Chanukah, celebrating their victory against the Syrians under their leader Judas Maccabeus. A new and semi-religious festival is the Yom Haatzmaut, the anniversary of the birth of the new Jewish state of Israel.

K

Kabbala. *See* Cabala.

Ku Klux Klan. After the American Civil War (1861–65) southern conservatives and ex-Confederate leaders began to fear (as they had every reason to do) both Negro and poor White rule. Taxes were rising owing to radical legislation and the tax-burdened and disenfranchised planters finally took to illegal means to achieve their ends by trying to effect an alliance with the poor White and small farmer through appealing to his anti-Negro prejudice.

Hence the Ku Klux Klan was formed in 1866 as a secret society by a small group of Confederate veterans in Tennessee with the intention of frightening Negroes by dressing in ghostly white robes in the guise of the spirits of dead soldiers. But the movement spread like wild-fire throughout the South encouraged by small farmers and planters alike. General Nathan Bedford Forrest was appointed "Grand Wizard" of the Klan "empire" and in every community armed Klansmen riding at night horsewhipped "uppity" Negroes, beat Union soldiers, and threatened carpet-bag politicians (*i.e.*, fortune-hunters from the North). Soon several similar organisations arose, many of which did not stop at torture, burning property, and murder. In fact, although claiming to be a "holy crusade" the Klan was a vicious and contemptible organisation in which former Southern leaders trying to regain control deliberately set poor and middle-class Whites against the Negroes by appeal to race prejudice. Congress struck back with laws and intervention of Federal troops, and after a large number of convictions in South Carolina much of the violence stopped even if the feelings continued.

After the 1914–18 war the movement, dormant since 1900, revived as a sadistic anti-Negro, anti-Jewish, anti-Catholic society, spreading to the north as well as the south. By 1926, with its white-gowned hooligans and fiery crosses, the Klan began to subside once more. While it revived again in the mid-60s, the Klan has suffered a sensational loss of support in recent years as the notion of the essential inferiority of black people has wilted among the new generations of America.

Kuomintang, a Chinese Nationalist party founded in 1891 by Sun Yat Sen. It took part in the first Chinese revolution of 1911 and led the second the following year, dominating south China by 1930 and, under Chiang Kai-shek, who succeeded Sun Yat Sen on his death in 1925, conducted China's defence against Japanese invasion from 1937–45. Sun Yat Sen had attempted to found a democratic republic based on Western parliamentary democracy and in his famous *Testament* laid down the principles upon which the constitution of China should be based. In 1946, Sun Fo, the son of Sun Yat Sen, deplored the party's departure from the principles of social democracy and the welfare of the people in which his father had believed. Beginning as a movement largely inspired by Russia, the Kuomintang under Chiang Kai-shek degenerated into a reactionary and corrupt military oligarchy which, collapsing in 1949, was replaced by the Communist Party, leaving Chiang and his followers to rule Formosa (Taiwan) with American aid.

L

Lamaism, the religion of Tibet. Its beliefs and worship derive from the Mahayana form of Buddhism which was introduced into Tibet in 749. The emphasis laid by its founder on the necessity for self-discipline and conversion through meditation and the study of philosophy deteriorated into formal monasticism and ritualism. The Dalai Lama, as the reincarnated Buddha, was both king and high priest, a sort of pope and emperor rolled into one. Under him was a hierarchy of officials in which the lowest order was that of the monks who became as numerous as one man in every six or seven of the population. The main work carried out by this vast church-state was the collection of taxes to maintain the monasteries and other religious offices. Second in power to the Dalai Lama was the Panchen or Tashi Lama believed to be a reincarnation of Amitabha, another Buddha. The last Dalai Lama fled to India in 1959 when the Chinese entered his country. For a brief period following his departure, the Panchen Lama surprised the Western world by publicly welcoming the Communist invasion, but he later renounced the regime and the suppression of Lamaism in Tibet continued unchecked.

Levellers, an English military-politico-religious party prominent in the Parliamentary Army about 1647 which stood for the rights of the people *See* Diggers.

Liberalism. The Liberal Party is the successor to the Whigs (a nickname derived from *Whiggamore*, used in the 17th cent. for Scottish dissenters) of the 18th and 19th cents. Under Gladstone's two great ministries (1868–74; and 1880–85), and again under Campbell-Bannerman and Asquith (1906–14) much reforming legislation was enacted. The Asquith–Lloyd George split of 1916, and the advent of Labour as a major party after 1918, have caused the Liberals to be relegated as a smaller, third party. In the decade after 1945, there were times when the Liberal Party nearly disappeared altogether. But under Grimond's leadership, a revival followed the Orpington by-election triumph of March 1962. Another revival in 1972–3, with Jeremy Thorpe as leader, culminated in a Liberal vote of over 6 million in February 1974. Under David Steel the party entered into a Lib–Lab pact in 1976.

Liberal philosophy is moderately radical and progressive in terms of social reform. But the party strongly disapproves of state control or any form of monopoly, private or public. The main proposals favoured by the party are co-ownership in industry, proportional representation, greater protection of individual liberties, and separate Parliaments for Wales and Scotland.

Many younger members of the party hold views to the Left of official party policy. The phenomenon of " community politics " has owed much to these younger, radical Liberals.

Logical Positivism, a school of philosophy founded in Vienna in the 1920s by a group known as " the Vienna circle ": their work was based on that of Ernst Mach, but dates in essentials as far back as Hume. Of the leaders of the group, Schlick was murdered by a student, Wittgenstein came to Britain, and Carnap went to America following the entry of the Nazis. Briefly the philosophy differs from all others in that, while most people have believed that a statement might be (a) true, or (b) false, logical positivists consider there to be a third category; a statement may be meaningless. There are only two types of statement which can be said to have meaning: (1) those which are tautological, *i.e.*, those in which the statement is merely a definition of the subject, such as " a triangle is a three-sided plane figure " (" triangle " and " three-sided plane figure " are the same thing); and (2) those which can be tested by sense experience. This definition of meaningfulness excludes a great deal of what has previously been thought to be the field of philosophy; in particular it excludes the possibility of metaphysics. Thus the question as to whether there is a God or whether free-will exists is strictly meaningless, for it is neither a tautological statement nor can it be tested by sense experience.

Lollards, a body of religious reformers and followers of Wyclif who were reviled and persecuted in the reign of Richard II. The name " Lollard " comes from a Flemish word meaning " mutterer "—a term of contempt used to describe the sect. After his accession Henry IV renewed persecution of the group, even condemning one of his own personal friends, the Lollard leader Sir John Oldcastle, to be burnt at the stake.

Luddites, a group of peasants and working men who deliberately destroyed spinning and farm machinery in England in the early part of the 19th cent., fearing that such devices would destroy their livelihood. Their name was taken from the eccentric Ned Lud who had done the same in a less organised way two or three decades earlier. The Luddites' worst fears were of course not realised, for far from putting human beings out of work the industrial revolution created jobs for a vastly increased population. Luddism, dormant for over a century, is beginning to appear again, if in muted form. Public anxiety about the rapid growth in computer technology is manifesting itself in the form of such groups as the Society for the Abolition of Data Processing Machines, which while not of course dedicated to the physical destruction of computers, urge for social and even governmental checks on the development of such things as " data banks." These are vast computer memory stores listing comprehensive records concerning all the people living in a city or country and able to cross-reference them in a way that has never previously been possible. The arguments for and against such data banks and other developments in computer technology are beyond the scope of this section, but the rise of this 20th-cent. Luddism is of considerable historical and social significance.

Lutheranism. The Reformation had a long history before it became, under Luther and Calvin, an accepted fact. The mediaeval Church had held (as the Catholic Church holds today) that the sacraments were the indispensable means of salvation. Since these were exclusively administered by the clergy, any movement which attacked clerical abuses was forced by sheer necessity to deny the Church's exclusive control of the means of salvation, before it could become free from dependence on a corrupt priesthood. Hence the Albigenses and the Waldenses (qq.v.), the followers of John Hus and Wyclif (see Anticlericalism), were bound to deny the authority of the Church and emphasise that of the Bible. Luther began his movement primarily in order to reform the Church from its gross abuses and the famous ninety-five theses nailed to the door of the Church at Wittenberg in 1517 were not primarily theological but moral complaints dealing with the actual behaviour of the clergy rather than Church beliefs. But, unlike the earlier reformers, Luther had arrived at the right moment in history when economic individualism and the force of nationalism were bound, sooner or later, to cause the authorities in Germany to line up on his side. Thus he began with the support of the peasants who were genuinely shocked at the abuse of indulgences and other matters, but ended up by being supported by the noblemen who wanted to destroy the power of the pope over the German states and looked forward to confiscating the lands and property of the Church. When the peasants wanted the reform of actual economic abuses relating to the feudal system, Luther took the side of the nobles against them. The contemporary movement in Switzerland led by Ulrich Zwingli had no such secular support, and Zwingli was killed in 1531.

Martin Luther (1483–1546) was the son of a miner in Eisleben in Saxony, entered the order of Austin Friars in 1505, and later taught at the newly founded university of Wittenberg. After the publication of the theses the real issue so far as the Church was concerned was whether he was willing or not to submit to the authority of his superiors; Luther refused to compromise with his conscience in the famous words: " Here I stand; I can do no other." In a further statement Luther recommended the formation of a German national church, the abolition of indulgences and other means whereby Rome obtained money from Germany, and an end to the celibacy of the clergy. For this he was naturally excommunicated. His teaching was based on the German translation of the Bible, but he was by no means a fundamentalist: *e.g.*, he denied that the Book of Hebrews was written by Paul, would have nothing to do with the Apocrypha, and regarded the letter of James as " an epistle of straw." The Scriptures were open to all and could be interpreted by private judgment enlightened by the Spirit of God. Like Calvin, Luther was a predestinarian and determinist, but he was also a conservative and soon became alarmed about the position taken by many extremists once the Reformation was under way. He had really wanted the Church to reform itself, but when he alienated Rome he had perforce to rely more and more on the secular powers which finally resulted in the state-church form which became pronounced in Prussia and later elsewhere. Whereas Calvin wished the Church to be at least the equal of the State and in some respects its superior, Luther's rebellion resulted in the reverse, a state-controlled episcopalianism. *See* Calvinism, Presbyterianism.

Lycanthropy, the belief that men may, by the exercise of magical powers or because of some inherited affliction, occasionally transform into wolves. The so-called werewolf is an important feature of mid-European folklore and much the same can be said of the were-tigers and were-bears of Africa and the Far East. There is, needless to say, no such thing as a genuine werewolf known to biology, but it is not hard to see how legends of their existence could arise. There are a number of mental illnesses in which men may deliberately or unconsciously mimic the actions of animals and there are a number of endocrinological disorders which may cause gross changes in the features of the individuals, including the excessive growth of hair. In times when the physiological bases of such afflictions were not properly understood, sufferers from such complaints could easily be persuaded, either by themselves or others, that they were in fact wolfmen. Once the mythology of lycanthropy is established in a society, then of course it will be used by unscrupulous individuals for their own ends —for example revenge killings by people dressed as animals—thus helping to perpetuate the legend.

M

McLuhanism. According to Marshall McLuhan, a Canadian, and former professor of English at Toronto University, the *way* people communicate is more important than *what* they communicate: hence his famous slogan, " the medium is the message." There have been two great landmarks in human understanding since we learnt to speak and write: the invention of the printed book and the present electronic revolution. The printed word took us step by step along the linear, logical path to understanding; television comes at us from all directions at once. " Electronic circuitry has overthrown the regime of ' time ' and ' space ' ... Its message is Total Change." Thus the spectacle of the Chicago police force clubbing people outside the Democratic Convention in August 1968 was described by Alistair Cooke in a despatch to *The Guardian*, as " a terrifying demonstration of McLuhanism: the millions frozen with terror in front of their television screens." In his essay, " On Reading Marshall McLuhan," Dr. George Steiner (one of the first critics in England to understand him) writes: " Marshall McLuhan posits that Western civilisation has entered, or is about to enter an era of electromagnetic technology. This technology will radically alter the milieu of human perception, the reality co-ordinates within which we apprehend and order sense data. Experience will not present itself serially, in atomized or linear patterns of casual sequence, but in ' fields ' of simultaneous interaction." McLuhan's importance lies in alerting us to the present clash between two great technologies, the literate and the electromagnetic, and in his vision, beyond the present chaos, of a world drawn tighter together in a " global village " where identity will merge in collectivity and we shall all be able to co-operate for the common good instead of being split up into warring nations.

Magic, a form of belief originating in very early days and based on the primitive's inability to distinguish between similarity and identity. The simplest example would perhaps be the fertility rites in which it is believed that a ceremony involving sexual relations between men and women will bring about fertility in the harvest. Or the idea that sticking pins in an image of an individual will bring about harm or even death to the real person. Magic is regarded by some as a form of early science in that man in his efforts to control Nature had recourse to magical practices when the only methods he knew had failed to bring the desired results. It filled a gap. By others magic is regarded as an elementary stage in the evolution of religion. It can be said to have served a purpose there too. Yet magic differs from religion, however closely at times it may come to be related with it, in this important respect: religion depends upon a power *outside and beyond* human beings, whereas magic depends upon nothing but the casting of a spell or the performance of a ceremony—the result follows automatically.

The idea that " like produces like " is at the roots of imitative magic, and it is interesting to note that in some languages (*e.g.*, Hebrew and Arabic) there is no word for " resembles " or " similar to." Hence one says " All thy garments are myrrh " instead of " are *like* myrrh." It follows that an event can be compelled by imitating it. One engages in swinging, not for pleasure, but to produce a wind as the swing does; ball games are played to get rainy weather because the black ball represents dark rainclouds; other ball games, in which one attempts to catch the ball in a cup or hit it with a stick, represent the sexual act (as some gentlemen at Lords may be distressed to hear) and bring about fertility; in medicine until a few centuries ago herbs were chosen to cure a disease because in some respects their leaves or other parts looked like the part of the body affected (*e.g.*, the common wildflower still known as " eyebright " was used in bathing the eyes because the flower looks like a tiny eye). *See* Witchcraft, Demonism.

Malthusianism, the theory about population growth put forward by the Rev. Thomas Malthus (1766–1834) in *An Essay on Population* (1798). His three main propositions were: (1) " Population is necessarily limited by means of subsistence." (2) " Population invariably increases where means of subsistence increase, unless prevented by some very powerful and obvious checks." (3) "These checks, and the checks which repress the superior power of population, and keep its effects on a level with the means of subsistence, are all resolvable into moral restraint, vice and misery." In other words, no matter how great the food supply may become, human reproductive power will always adjust itself so that food will always be scarce in relation to population; the only means to deal with this is by "moral restraint" (*i.e.*, chastity or not marrying), "vice" (*i.e.*, birth-control methods), or misery (*i.e.*, starvation). More specifically, Malthus claimed that while food increases by arithmetical progression, population increase by geometrical progression. It is true that these gloomy predictions did not take place in Malthus's time largely owing to the opening up of new areas of land outside Europe, the development of new techniques in agriculture, the growth of international trade to poorer areas, the increased knowledge of birth-control, and developments in medical science which reduced the misery he had predicted. Furthermore, we now know that as a society becomes industrialised its birth-rate tends to fall. Nevertheless there are very few scientists who are not perturbed by the growth in the world's population which has increased from about 465 million in 1650 to 3,890 million today.

Manichaeism, an Asiatic religion which developed from Zoroastrianism (*q.v.*) and shows the influence of Buddhism (*q.v.*) and Gnosticism (*q.v.*), being founded by Mani, a Persian who was born in Babylonia, *c.* 216 A.D. Mani presented himself to Shapur I as the founder of a new religion which was to be to Babylonia what Buddhism was to India or Christianity to the West. His aspiration was to convert the East and he himself made no attempt to interfere directly with Christianity although he represented himself as the Paraclete (the Holy Ghost or "Comforter") and, like Jesus, had twelve disciples. His success in Persia aroused the fury of the Zoroastrian priests who objected to his reforming zeal towards their religion and in 276 Mani was taken prisoner and crucified.

Of Mani's complicated system little can be said here, save that it is based on the struggle of two eternal conflicting principles, God and matter, or light and darkness. Although its founder had no intention of interfering with the West, after his death his followers soon spread the religion from Persia and Mesopotamia to India and China. (Manichaeism flourished in China until the 11th cent.) It reached as far as Spain and Gaul and influenced many of the bishops in Alexandria and in Carthage where for a time St. Augustine accepted Manichaeism. Soon the toleration accorded it under Constantine ended and it was treated as a heresy and violently suppressed. Yet it later influenced many heresies, and even had some influence on orthodox Catholicism which had a genius for picking up elements in other religions which had been shown to appeal to worshippers provided they did not conflict unduly with fundamental beliefs.

Maoism is the branch of communism that reigns in China. It has been shaped by one of the most remarkable statesmen of modern times, Mao Tse-tung (1893–1976), who set the pattern of revolution for poor peasant societies and restored pride and confidence to his fellow countrymen after years of turmoil and brutality. Although Marxist theory guided the Chinese communists in their struggle for liberation from the old, bourgeois and feudal China, it was interpreted in a manner peculiar to China and developed to fit into the Chinese way of life and the "thoughts" of Chairman Mao. As early as 1926 Mao had pointed out that the Chinese proletariat had in the peasantry its staunchest and most numerous ally. "A rural revolution," he said, "is a revolution by which the peasantry overthrows the authority of the feudal landlord class." The struggles of 1925–49 (the Long March of the Red Army, the Anti-Japanese War, the Civil War against Chiang Kai-shek) were the foundations on which present-day China has been built. Maoism is against authoritarianism and for self-reliance; against bureaucracy and

for revolutionary momentum: against rivalry between individuals and for common effort. One of the great achievements has been the removal of poverty, ignorance and disease from China. Mao taught that struggle is necessary for the revolution to endure. "Running water does not go stale and door-hinges do not become worm-eaten," Mao reminded his comrades. "We must," he said, "make every comrade understand that the highest criterion for judging the words and deeds of the communists is whether they conform with the best interests and win the support of the broadest masses of the people." It remains to be seen what effect the death of Mao Tse-tung will have on Chinese communism and whether political direction will be towards the modernisation of China and away from "continuous revolution." *See also* China, Section C, Part II.

Marxism. The sociological theories founded by Karl Marx and Friedrich Engels on which modern communist thought is based. Marx and Engels lived in a period of unrestrained capitalism when exploitation and misery were the lot of the industrial working classes, and it was their humanitarianism and concern for social justice which inspired their work. They co-operated in 1848 in writing the *Communist Manifesto*, and in his great work, *Das Kapital* (1867), Marx worked out a new theory of society. He showed that all social systems are economically motivated and came as a result of technical and economic changes in methods of production. The driving force of social change Marx found to be in the struggle which the oppressed classes wage to secure a better future. Thus in his celebrated theory of historical materialism he interpreted history in terms of economics and explained the evolution of society in terms of class struggle. (*See* Dialectical Materialism.) "In the social production of their means of existence," he wrote, "men enter into definite and unavoidable relations which are independent of their will. These productive relationships correspond to the particular stage in the development of their material productive forces." Marx's theory of historical materialism implies that history is propelled by class struggle with communism and the classless society as the final stage when man will have emancipated himself from the productive process. Marx was the first to put socialism on a rational and scientific basis, and he foretold that socialism would inevitably replace capitalism. His prophecy, however, came to realisation not in the advanced countries as he had envisaged but in backward Russia and China. *See also* Communism.

Mesmerism, a rapidly vanishing name to denote the practice of hypnosis, which owes its popularity, though not its discovery, to the Austrian physician, Anton Mesmer (1733–1815). Mesmer's contribution was the realisation that a large number of what we would today call psychosomatic or hysterical conditions could be cured (or at least temporarily alleviated) by one or another form of suggestion. Mesmer himself relied on the idea of what he called "animal magnetism," a supposedly potent therapeutic force emanating from the living body which could be controlled by the trained individual. Mesmer used wands and impressive gadgetry to dispense the marvellous force and he effected a remarkable number of cures of complaints, hitherto looked upon as incurable or totally mysterious in origin—the most typical of these being hysterical blindness, paralysis or deafness, nervous skin conditions, and so on. Hypnosis, which is a valid if very poorly understood psychological phenomenon even today, would probably have been developed much further had not efficient general anaesthetics such as ether, nitrous oxide, etc., been discovered, thus greatly diminishing its role as a pain reliever in surgery. Mesmer, who was three parts charlatan, never really troubled to think deeply about the cause of his undoubted successes. The first man to treat hysteria as a formal class of illness and who made a scientific attempt to treat it with hypnosis was Ambrose Liébeault (1823–1904). He and his colleague Hippolyte Bernheim (1840–1919) believed: (*a*) that hysteria was produced by suggestion, and particularly by autosuggestion on the part of the patient, and (b) that suggestion was a normal trait found in varying degrees in everyone. These conclusions are true, but as Freud showed later are far from being the whole truth.

Messianism. Most varieties of religious belief rely on the assumption that the deity is a supernatural being either permeating the universe or dwelling in some other sphere, and normally inaccessible to man. Where divine intervention is necessary, the deity is traditionally believed to nominate a human being—in the case of Christianity, for example, Jesus is believed to be the actual son of God. Messianic cults introduce a novel variant on the traditional theme. In these a human being is held to be God himself. He may either nominate himself for this role, relying on his own personality or native talent to acquire the necessary following, or for one reason or another large numbers of people may alight on one individual and declare him the Messiah. While it might seem that beliefs of this kind would be confined to earlier epochs in man's recorded history, this is in fact not the case. In the past century, and even within recent decades, a number of individuals have been held by groups to be actually divine. Among these were the Dutchman Lourens van Voorthuizen, a former fisherman who declared himself to be God in 1950 and got large numbers to accept his claim; the Anglican priest Henry James Prince, who did much the same thing in 1850; and of course the famous Negro George Baker, who convinced hundreds of thousands of other Negroes that he was " Father Divine." To simple people the idea that God is to be found on earth and that one may even be personally introduced to him, is an obviously attractive one. The trouble is that all self-styled gods to this present date have sooner or later seriously disappointed their supporters by performing that most human of acts—dying.

Metapsychology. Not to be confused with parapsychology (q.v.). The branch or off-shoot of psychology which goes beyond empirical and experimental studies to consider such philosophical matters as the nature of mind the reality of free-will and the mind/body problem. It was originally used by Freud as a blanket descriptive term denoting all mental processes, but this usage is now obsolete.

Methodism, the religious movement founded by John Wesley in 1738, at a time when the Anglican Church was in one of its periodic phases of spiritual torpor, with the simple aim of spreading " scriptural holiness " throughout the land. Up to that time Wesley had been a High Churchman but on a visit to Georgia in the United States he was much impressed by the group known as Moravians (q.v.), and on his return to this country was introduced by his brother Charles, who had already become an adherent, to Peter Böhler, a Moravian minister in England. Passing through a period of spiritual commotion following the meeting, he first saw the light at a small service in Aldersgate in May 1738 " where one was reading Luther's preface to the Epistle to the Romans " and from this time forth all Wesley's energies were devoted to the single object of saving souls. He did this for fifty years and at the end of his life confessed that he had wasted fifteen minutes in that time by reading a worthless book. Even when he was over eighty he still rose at 4 a.m. and toiled all day long.

Soon Whitefield, a follower with Calvinist views, was preaching throughout the country and Charles Wesley was composing his well-known hymns; John's abilities at this time were taken up in organising the movement described as " People called Methodists." They were to be arranged in " societies " which were united into " circuits " under a minister, the circuits into " districts " and all knit together into a single body under a conference of ministers which has met annually since 1744. Local lay preachers were also employed and to maintain interest the ministers were moved from circuit to circuit each year. These chapel services were not originally meant to conflict with the Church of England of which Wesley still considered himself a member. They were purely supplementary, and it used to be the custom (before the

Methodists began to count themselves as Nonconformists) for Methodists to attend Church in the morning and Chapel in the evening.

The class-meeting was the unit of the organisation where members met regularly under a chosen leader to tell their " experiences " upon which they were often subjected to severe crossexamination. At the end of every quarter, provided their attendances were regular, they received a ticket of membership which entitled them to come to monthly sacramental services. If attendance was inadequate the name was removed from the list, without appearance on which nobody was deemed a member. The price of the ticket was " a penny a week and a shilling a quarter " but Wesley was not interested in receiving money from anyone who was not utterly devoted to the cause.

John Wesley introduced four other innovations, some of which were regarded by Churchmen who had previously been willing to commend his efforts in bringing religion to the poorer classes as dangerous: (1) He started the Sunday-school scheme and afterwards enthusiastically supported that of John Raikes, often regarded as the founder of the idea; this was of immense importance in the days before the Education Acts. (2) He reintroduced the Agapae or " love feasts " of the early Church which were fellowship meetings deepening the sense of brotherhood of the society. (3) He began to copy the open-air meetings of the eloquent Whitefield and soon unwittingly produced the most extraordinary results, finding that his sermons led to groans, tears, faintingfits, and all sorts of emotional expression. Even his open-air lay speakers produced like results and these came to be associated with Methodism and gave significance to the proud Anglican claim that *their* services would be " without enthusiasm." (4) After some hesitation he ventured to consecrate Dr. Thomas Coke, who was being sent as a missionary to America, as a bishop of his church. In addition to Wesley's religious work he was a great educator of the common man. Thus he introduced the cheap book and the church magazine, publishing books of any sort which he thought would edify and not harm even when the views expressed were different from his own—e.g., Thomas à Kempis's *Imitation of Christ* and works of history, biography, science, and medicine in some cases written by himself. In this way the movement with its cheap books and reading rooms had an influence far beyond its actual membership. Both the Anglican Church and the Evangelical movement of Wilberforce and others profited from Wesley's work. Some social historians, rightly or wrongly, have claimed that it was Wesley's influence among the working classes that spared England the revolutionary activity which characterised most other European countries during the first quarter of the 19th cent.

Methodism, especially after Wesley's death in 1791, began, like other movements, to develop schisms. There were the long-standing differences which the Baptist movement (q.v.) had shown too between Arminian and Calvinist sections—i.e., between those who did and those who did not accept the doctrine of predestination. In the case of the Methodists, this led to a complete break in 1811. Then there were differences associated with the status of the laity, or the relationship of the movement with the Anglican Church. The " Methodist New Connection " of 1797 differed only in giving the laity equal representation with the ministers but the more important break of the Primitive Methodists in 1810 gave still more power to the laity and reintroduced the " camp-meeting " type of service. In 1815 the Bryanites or " Bible Christians " were formed, and a further schism which was even brought before the law courts was ostensibly over the foundation of a theological college. The real reason, of course, was that the ministers were becoming more Tory, whilst the laity were becoming more Radical. Finally in 1932, at a conference in the Albert Hall in London, the Wesleyan Methodists, the Primitive Methodists, and the United Methodists became one Church, the Methodist Church.

Mind and Matter.

Early Greek Views: Idealism and Dualism.
Primitive peoples could see that there is a distinction between those things which move and do things by themselves and others, such as stones, which do not. Following the early state of Animism (*q.v.*), in which spirits were believed to have their abode in everything, they began to differentiate between matter or substance and a force which seems to move it and shape it into objects and things. Thus to the Greek Parmenides (fl. *c.* 475 B.C.), who was a philosopher of pure reason, thought or mind was the creator of what we observe and in some way not quite clear to himself it seemed that mind was the cause of everything. This is perhaps the first expression of the movement known as Idealism which says, in effect, that the whole universe is mental—a creation either of our own minds or the mind of God. But from Anaxagorus (488–428 B.C.) we have the clearer statement that mind or *nous* causes all movement but is distinct from the substance it moves. He does not, however, think in terms of individual minds but rather of a kind of generalised mind throughout the universe which can be used as an explanation of anything which cannot be explained otherwise. This is the position known as Dualism (*q.v.*) which holds that both mind and matter exist and interact but are separate entities.

Most people in practice are dualists since, rightly or wrongly, mind and body are thought of as two different things; it is the "commonsense" (although not necessarily the true) point of view. Plato in a much more complex way was also a dualist although he held that the world of matter we observe is in some sense not the genuine world. The real world is the world of ideas and the tree we see is not real but simply matter upon which mind or soul has imprinted the idea of a tree. Everything that exists has its corresponding form in the world of ideas and imprints its pattern upon matter. Mind has always existed and, having become entangled with matter, is constantly seeking to free itself and return to God.

Plato's pupil Aristotle had a much more scientific outlook and held that, although it was mind which gave matter its form, mind is not *outside* matter, as Plato had thought, but *inside* it as its formative principle. Therefore there could be no mind without matter and no matter without mind; for even the lowest forms of matter have some degree of mind which increases in quantity and quality as we move up the scale to more complex things.

So far, nobody had explained how two such different substances as matter and mind could influence each other in any way, and this remains, in spite of attempts to be mentioned later, a basic problem in philosophy.

Two later ideas, one of them rather foolish and the other simply refusing to answer the question, are typified by the Stoics and some members of the Sceptic school. The first is that only matter exists and what we call mind is merely matter of a finer texture, a view which as an explanation is unlikely to satisfy anyone; the other, that of some Sceptics, is that we can know nothing except the fleeting images or thoughts that flicker through our consciousness. Of either mind or matter we know nothing.

Renaissance Attitude. Christian doctrines have already been dealt with (*see* God and Man, Determinism and Free-will), and the past and future of the soul is dealt with under Immortality. Nor need we mention the Renaissance philosophers who were really much more concerned about how to use mind than about its nature. When they did consider the subject they usually dealt with it, as did Francis Bacon, by separating the sphere of science from that of religion and giving the orthodox view of the latter because there were still good reasons for not wishing to annoy the Church.

17th-cent. Views: Hobbes, Descartes, Guelincx, Spinoza, Locke, Berkeley. Thomas Hobbes in the 17th cent. was really one of the first to attempt a modern explanation of mind and matter even if his attempt was crude. As a materialist he held that all that exists is matter and hence our thoughts, ideas, images, and actions are really a form of motion taking place within the brain and nerves. This is the materialist theory which states that mind does not exist.

Thus there are three basic theories of the nature of mind and body: idealism, dualism, and materialism, and we may accept any one of the three. But, if we accept dualism, we shall have to explain precisely the relationship between body and mind. In some of his later writings Hobbes seems to suggest that mental processes are the effects of motion rather than motion itself; *i.e.*, they exist, but only as a result of physical processes just as a flame does on a candle. This theory of the relationship is known as *epiphenomenalism.*

Descartes, the great French contemporary of Hobbes, was a dualist who believed that mind and matter both exist and are entirely different entities; therefore he had to ask himself how, for example, the desire to walk leads to the physical motion of walking. His unsatisfactory answer was that, although animals are pure automatons, man is different in that he has a soul which resides in the pineal gland (a tiny structure in the brain which today we know to be a relic of evolution with no present function whatever). In this gland the mind comes in contact with the "vital spirits" of the body and thus there is interaction between the two. This theory is known as *interactionism,* and since we do not accept its basis in the function of the pineal gland, we are simply left with the notion of interaction but without the explanation of how it takes place.

One of Descartes's successors, Arnold Guelincx, produced the even more improbable theory of *psychophysical parallelism,* sometimes known as the theory of the "two clocks." Imagine you have two clocks, each keeping perfect time, then supposing you saw one and heard the other, every time one points to the hour the other will strike, giving the impression that the first event causes the second, although in fact they are quite unrelated. So it is with the body and mind in Guelincx's view, each is "wound up" by God in the beginning in such a way as to keep time with the other so that when I have the desire to walk, purely unrelated physical events n my legs cause them to move at the same time. A variety of this theory is *occasionism,* which says that whenever something happens in the physical world, God affects us so that we *think* we are being affected by the happening.

The trouble about all these theories is (*a*) that they really explain nothing, and (*b*) that they give us a very peculiar view of God as a celestial showman treating us as puppets when it would surely have been easier to create a world in which mind and matter simply interacted by their very nature. Spinoza, too, believed in a sort of psychophysical parallelism in that he did not think that mind and body interacted. But since in his theory everything is God, mind and matter are simply two sides of the same penny.

John Locke, another contemporary, thought of the mind as a blank slate upon which the world writes in the form of sensations, for we have no innate or inborn ideas and mind and matter do interact although he does not tell us how. All we know are sensations—*i.e.*, sense impressions. Bishop Berkeley carried this idea to its logical conclusion: if we know nothing but sensations, we have no reason to suppose that matter exists at all. He was, therefore, an idealist.

18th cent. Views: Hume, Kant. David Hume went further still and pointed out that, if all we know are sensations, we cannot prove the existence of matter but we cannot prove the existence of mind either. All we can ever know is that ideas, impressions, thoughts, follow each other. We do not even experience a self or personality because every time we look into our "minds" all we really experience are thoughts and impressions. Hume was quick to point out that this was not the same as saying that the self did not exist; it only proved that we cannot know that it does.

Kant made it clear that, although there is a world outside ourselves, we can never know what it is really like. The mind receives impressions and forms them into patterns which conform not to the thing-in-itself but to the nature of mind. Space and time, for example, are not realities but only the form into which our mind fits its sensations. In other words our mind shapes impressions which are no more like the thing-in-itself than the map of a battlefield with pins showing the position of various army groups at any given moment is like the battlefield. This, of course, is true. From physics and physiology we know that the sounds we hear are "really" waves in the air, the sights we see " really " electromagnetic waves. What guarantee do we have that the source is " really " like the impression received in our brain? Kant was the leader of the great German Idealist movement of the 18th cent. which in effect said: " why bother about matter when all we can ever know is mental? "

19th and 20th cent. Views. The Englishman Bradley, and the Frenchman Henri Bergson in the 19th and early 20th cent. both held in one form or another the belief that mind in some way creates matter and were, therefore, idealists, whereas Comte, the positivist (*q.v.*), and the Americans William James and John Dewey, held that mind is a form of behaviour. Certain acts (*e.g.*, reflexes) are " mindless " because they are deliberate; others which are intended may be described for the sake of convenience as " minded " (*i.e.*, purposeful). But like the majority of modern psychologists—insofar as they take any interest in the subject—they regarded mind as a process going on in the living body. Is there any reason, many now ask why we should think of mind as being any different in nature from digestion? Both are processes going on in the body, the one in the brain the other in the stomach and intestines. Why should we regard them as " things "? *See also* J43–4 and Section Q.

Mithraism, a sun-religion which originated in Persia with the worship of the mythical Mithra, the god of light and of truth. It was for two centuries one of early Christianity's most formidable rivals, particularly in the West since the more philosophical Hellenic Christianity of the East had little to fear from it. (Arnold Toynbee has described Mithraism as " a pre-Zoroastrian Iranian paganism—in a Hellenic dress "; Manichaeism as " Zoroastrianism—in a Christian dress ".) Mithraism was a mystery-faith with secret rites known only to devotees. It appealed to the soldiers of the Roman Army which explains its spread to the farthest limits of the Roman empire and its decline as the Romans retreated. The religion resembled Zoroastrianism (*q.v.*) in that it laid stress on the constant struggle between good and evil and there are a number of parallels with Christianity, *e.g.*, a miraculous birth, death, and a glorious resurrection, a belief in heaven and hell and the immortality of the soul, a last judgment. Both religions held Sunday as the holy day of the week, celebrated 25 December (date of the pagan winter solstice festival) as the birthday of the founder; both celebrated Easter, and in their ceremonies made use of bell, holy water, and the candle. Mithraism reached its height about 275 A.D. and afterwards declined both for the reason given above and, perhaps, because it excluded women, was emotional rather than philosophical, and had no general organisation to direct its course. Yet even today, from the Euphrates to the Tyne, traces of the religion remain and antiquarians are familiar with the image of the sun-god and the inscription *Deo Soli Mithrae, Invicto, Seculari* (dedicated to the sun-god of Mithra, the unconquered). Mithraism enjoyed a brief revival of popular interest in the mid-1950s when workers excavating the foundations of the skyscraper, Bucklersbury House in the City of London, found the well-preserved remains of a Roman Mithraic temple. A campaign to save the temple as a national monument resulted in its now being on open display on a site in front of the skyscraper.

Mohammedanism. See Islam.

Monasticism. When in the 4th cent. A.D. Constantine in effect united state and church there were naturally many who hastened to become Christians for the worldly benefits they expected it

to bring in view of the new situation. But there were others who, in their efforts to escape from worldly involvement, went into the deserts of North Africa and Syria to live as hermits and so in these regions there grew up large communities of monks whose lives of renunciation made a considerable impression on the Christian world. They were men of all types but the two main groups were those who preferred to live alone and those who preferred a community life. Among the first must be included St. Anthony, the earliest of the hermits, who was born in Egypt *c.* 250 and who lived alone in a hut near his home for fifteen years, and then in the desert for a further twenty. As his fame spread Anthony came forth to teach and advocate a life of extreme austerity, until by the end of his life the Thebaid (the desert around Thebes) was full of hermits following his example. (Not unnaturally, he was constantly assailed by lustful visions which he thoughtfully attributed to Satan.) In the Syrian desert St. Simeon Stylites and others were stimulated to even greater austerities and Simeon himself spent many years on the top of a pillar in a space so small that it was only possible to sit or stand. With some of these men it is obvious that ascetic discipline had become perverted into an unpleasant form of exhibitionism.

The first monastery was founded by Pachomius of Egypt *c.* 315 and here the monks had a common life with communal meals, worship, and work mainly of an agricultural type. In the Eastern part of the Empire St. Basil (*c.* 360) tried to check the growth of the extreme and spectacular practices of the hermits by organising monasteries in which the ascetic disciplines of fasting, meditation, and prayer, would be balanced by useful and healthy activities. His monasteries had orphanages and schools for boys—not only those who were intended for a monkish life. But the Eastern Church in general continued to favour the hermit life and ascetic extremes. Originally a spontaneous movement, the monastic life was introduced to the West by St. Athanasius in 339 who obtained its recognition from the Church of Rome and St. Augustine introduced it into North Africa beyond Egypt. The movement was promoted also by St. Jerome, St. Martin of Tours, who introduced it into France, and St. Patrick into Ireland. The monastery of Iona was founded by St. Columba in 566. But it must be remembered that the Celtic Church had a life of its own which owed more to the Egyptian tradition than to Rome. Unlike the more elaborate monasteries of the Continent those of the early Celtic Church were often little more than a cluster of stone bee-hive huts, an oratory, and a stone cross. It had its own religious ceremonies and its own art (notably its beautifully carved crosses and the illuminated manuscripts such as the Lindisfarne Gospel (*c.* 700) and the Irish Book of Kells dating from about the same time). The Scottish St. Ninian played a major part in introducing Egyptian texts and art to Britain where, mixed with Byzantine influences and the art of the Vikings, it produced a typical culture of its own. Strangely enough, it was the relatively primitive Celts who played almost as large a part in preserving civilisation in Europe during the Dark Ages as the Italians have since. It was St. Columbanus (*c.* 540–615) who founded the great monasteries of Annegray, Luxeuil, and Fontaine in the Vosges country, St. Gall in Switzerland, and Bobbio in the Apennines. So, too, it was the Anglo-Saxon Alcuin (*c.* 735–804) who was called from York by Charlemagne to set up a system of education throughout his empire; the most famous of the monastic schools he founded was at Tours. Among those influenced by him was the philosopher John Scotus Erigena.

Meanwhile from the south, as the disintegrating Roman empire became increasingly corrupt, St. Benedict of Nursia (*c.* 480–*c.* 543) fled the pleasures of Rome to lead a hermit's life near Subiaco. Here he founded some small monasteries, but *c.* 520 made a new settlement, the great monastery of Monte Cassino in southern Italy, where he established a " Rule " for the government of monks. This included both study and work and emphasised that education was necessary for the continuance of Christianity. As his influence spread his Rule was adopted by other monasteries, and schools became part of monastic life. It is not possible to describe the many different orders of monks and nuns formed since, nor the mendicant orders of friars (*e.g.*, Franciscans, Dominicans, Carmelites, Augustinians). In many ways even those outside the Roman Catholic Church owe much to the monastic movement. Monasticism, of course, is not peculiar to Christianity and forms a major aspect of Buddhism, especially in the form of Lamaism in Tibet (*q.v.*)

Montanism, a Phrygian form of primitive Puritanism with many peculiar tenets into which the early Christian theologian Tertullian (*c.* 150–*c.* 230) was driven by his extremist views that the Christian should keep himself aloof from the world and hold no social intercourse whatever with pagans. The sect had immediate expectation of Christ's second coming and indulged in prophetic utterance which they held to be inspired by the Holy Ghost but which their enemies put down to prompting by the Devil. In seeking persecution and martyrdom they antagonised the Church and were suppressed.

Moral Re-Armament, a campaign launched in 1938 by an American evangelist of Lutheran background, Frank N. D. Buchman (1878–1961), founder of the Oxford Group Movement, and at first associated with the First Century Church Fellowship, a fundamentalist Protestant revivalist movement. On a visit to England in 1920 Buchman preached " world-changing " through life-changing " to undergraduates at Oxford, hence the name Oxford Group. This revivalist movement was based on Buchman's conviction that world civilisation was breaking down and a change had to be effected in the minds of men.

Two of the Group's most typical practices were group confession of sins openly and the " quiet time " set aside during the day to receive messages from the Almighty as to behaviour and current problems. In the eyes of non-Groupers the confession (often of trivial sins) appeared to be exhibitionist and there was felt to be a certain snobbery about the movement which made it strongly conscious of the social status of its converts.

The Oxford Group gave way to Moral Re-Armament, the third phase of Buchmanism. M.R.A. men and women lay stress on the four moral absolutes of honesty, purity, love, and unselfishness. They believe they have the ideas to set the pattern for the changing world and, indeed, claim to have aided in solving many international disputes—political, industrial, and racial. Theologians complained of the Groups that their movement lacked doctrine and intellectual content; M.R.A. is no different in this respect.

The peak of public interest in M.R.A. was probably reached in the 1950s. Like so many movements of its kind it relied heavily for its motive force on the dynamism of its founder and leader. With the death of Dr. Buchman and the unexpected demise at an early age of his most promising protégé and successor-designate, the journalist Peter Howard, the movement began to lose its public impact.

Moravian Church, a revival of the Church of the " Bohemian Brethren " which originated (1457) among some of the followers of John Hus. It developed a kind of Quakerism that rejected the use of force, refused to take oaths, and had no hierarchy. It appears to have been sympathetic towards Calvinism but made unsuccessful approaches to Luther. As a Protestant sect it was ruthlessly persecuted by Ferdinand II and barely managed to survive. However, in the 18th cent. the body was re-established by Count Zinzendorf who offered it a place of safety in Saxony where a town called Herrnhut (God's protection) was built and this became the centre from which Moravian doctrine was spread by missionaries all over the world. Their chief belief (which had a fundamental influence on John Wesley—*see* Methodism) was that faith is a direct illumination from God which assures us beyond all possibility of doubt that we are saved, and that no goodness of behaviour, piety,

or orthodoxy is of any use without this " sufficient sovereign, saving grace."

Mormons, or **Latter-day Saints,** one of the very numerous American religious sects; founded in 1830 by Joseph Smith, the son of a Vermont farmer, who, as a youth, had been influenced by a local religious revival though confused by the conflicting beliefs of the various denominations. He said that while praying for guidance he had been confronted by two heavenly messengers who forbade him to join any existing church but prepare to become the prophet of a new one. Soon, in a series of visions, he was told of a revelation written on golden plates concealed in a nearby hillside. These he unearthed in 1827 and with the help of " Urim and Thummim " translated the " reformed Egyptian " characters into English. Described as the *Book of Mormon,* this was published in 1830 and at the same time a little church of those few who accepted his testimony was founded in Fayette, N.Y. In addition the first of Joseph Smith's " miracles "—the casting out of a devil—was performed. The *Book of Mormon* purports to be a record of early American history and religion, the American Indians being identified as the ten Lost Tribes of Israel, whose fate has never failed to attract the attention of those who prefer myth to fact (cf. British Israelites). Jesus Christ is alleged to have appeared in America after His ascension. Yet Smith's eloquence was able to influence quite educated people, including Sidney Rigdon with whom he went into business for a time. *Doctrine and Covenants* is the title of another book dealing with the revelations Smith claimed to have received. Soon the sect was in trouble with the community both because its members insisted on describing themselves as the Chosen People and others as Gentiles and because they took part in politics, voting as Smith ordered them to. Smith was constantly in trouble with the police. Therefore they were turned out from one city after another until they found themselves a dwelling-place at Nauvoo, Illinois, on the Mississippi.

That would probably have been the end of the story had not Smith been murdered in 1844 and thereby made to appear a martyr, and had there not appeared Brigham Young, a quite extraordinary leader, who stamped out warring factions and drove out the recalcitrant. While persecutions continued Brigham Young announced that it had been revealed that he must lead the faithful to Salt Lake, then outside the area of the United States. There followed the famous trek of more than a thousand miles across desert country in which he led the way, reaching his journey's end in the forbidding valley of the Great Salt Lake on 24 July 1847. By 1851 30,000 Mormons had reached the Promised Land. Here they held their own in a hostile environment and under the practical genius of their leader carried through a vast irrigation scheme and built Salt Lake City which still serves as the headquarters of their sect. In 1850 their pioneer settlement was made Utah Territory, and in 1896 incorporated in the Union. The church was strictly ruled by its leader who also looked after affairs of state for thirty years until his death in 1877.

Polygamy, although opposed by some Mormons, and only sanctioned by Brigham Young when Salt Lake City had been built, is the best-known of Mormon doctrines. It brought the sect into much disrepute and was renounced in 1890. Mormons are millenarians, believing that some time Christ will appear and rule for a thousand years.

There are two orders of priests or leaders: the Melchizedeks, or higher order, include the apostles or ruling elders, and the high priest; the Aaronic priesthood, or lower order, attends to the temporal affairs of the church as the Melchizedeks attend to the spiritual. Members abstain from alcohol, tobacco, coffee, and tea. The church lays stress on the importance of revelation through visions, on education to meet the social, spiritual, and cultural needs of its members, and on community welfare. Members of the Church of Jesus Christ of Latter-day Saints now number over three million in congregations throughout the world.

The Reorganised Church of Jesus Christ of Latter-day Saints with its headquarters at Independence, Missouri, has been separate and distinct since 1852.

Muggletonians, one of the many sects which arose during the Commonwealth but, unlike most of the others (**Levellers** (q.v.), **Diggers** (q.v.), Fifth-Monarchy Men, and the Millenarians) which tended to have a strongly political aspect, this was purely religious. Founded by two journeymen tailors, Lodowick Muggleton and John Reeve, who interpreted the Book of Revelation in their own peculiar way, it was decided that Reeve represented Moses, and Muggleton, Aaron. They also believed that the Father, not the Son, had died on the cross (an ancient heresy) but added the strange statement that He left Elijah in control during His period on earth. Rejecting the doctrine of the Trinity, they also asserted that God has a human body. Nevertheless, for a time, they had a large number of followers.

Mysticism, a religious attitude which concerns itself with direct relationship with God, "reality" as contrasted with appearance, or the "ultimate" in one form or another. All the higher religions have had their mystics who have not always been regarded without suspicion by their more orthodox members, and, as Bertrand Russell points out, there has been a remarkable unity of opinion among mystics which almost transcends their religious differences. Thus, characteristic of the mystical experience in general, have been the following features: (1) a belief in insight as opposed to analytical knowledge which is accompanied in the actual experience by the sense of a mystery unveiled, a hidden wisdom become certain beyond the possibility of doubt; this is often preceded by a period of utter hopelessness and isolation described as "the dark night of the soul"; (2) a belief in unity and a refusal to admit opposition or division anywhere; this sometimes appears in the form of what seem to be contradictory statements: "the way up and the way down is one and the same" (Heraclitus). There is no distinction between subject and object, the act of perception and the thing perceived; (3) a denial of the reality of time, since if all is one the distinction of past and future must be illusory; (4) a denial of the reality of evil (which does not maintain, e.g., that cruelty is good but that it does not exist in the world of reality as opposed to the world of phantoms from which we are liberated by the insight of the vision). Among the great mystics have been Meister Eckhart and Jakob Boehme, the German religious mystics of the 13th and 16th cent. respectively, Acharya Sankara of India, and St. Theresa and St. John of the Cross of Spain. Mystical movements within the great religions have been: the Zen (q.v.) movement within Buddhism; Taoism in China; the Cabalists and Hasidim in Judaism; the Sufis within Islam; some of the Quakers within Christianity.

Mystery Religions. See Orphism.

N

Natural Law, the specifically Roman Catholic doctrine that there is a natural moral law, irrespective of time and place, which man can know through his own reason. Originally a product of early rational philosophy, the Christian form of the doctrine is basically due to St. Thomas Aquinas who defined natural law in relation to eternal law, holding that the eternal law is God's reason which governs the relations of all things in the universe to each other. The natural law is that part of the eternal law which relates to man's behaviour. Catholic natural law assumes that the human reason is capable of deriving ultimate rules for right behaviour since there are in man and his institutions certain stable structures produced by God's reason which man's reason can know to be correct and true. Thus, the basis of marriage, property, the state, and the contents of justice are held to be available to man's natural reason. The rules of positive morality and civil law are held to be valid only insofar as they conform to the natural law, which man is

not only capable of knowing but also of obeying. Protestant theologians criticise this notion. Thus Karl Barth and many others hold that sinful and fallen man cannot have any direct knowledge of God or His reason or will without the aid of revelation. Another theologian Niebuhr points out that the principles of the doctrines are too inflexible and that although they are the product of a particular time and circumstance, they are regarded as if they were absolute and eternal. In fact, as most social scientists would also agree, there is no law which can be regarded as "natural" for all men at all times. Nor does it seem sensible to suppose that all or even many men possess either the reason to discern natural law or the ability to obey it; whether or not we accept man's free-will (and all Protestant sects do not), we know as a fact of science that people are not always fully responsible for their actions and some not at all.

Nazism, the term commonly used for the political and social ideology of the German National Socialist Party inspired and led by Hitler. The term *Nazi* was an abbreviation of National Socialist. Those in the Federal Republic today sympathetic to National Socialist aims are known as neo-Nazis. See Fascism.

Neoplatonism. See Determinism and Free-will and God and Man.

Nihilism, the name commonly given to the earliest Russian form of revolutionary anarchism. It originated in the early years of Tsar Alexander II (1818–81), the liberator of the serfs, who, during his attempts to bring about a constitutional monarchy, was killed by a bomb. The term "nihilist," however, was first used in 1862 by Turgenev in his novel *Fathers and Children.* See Anarchism.

Nominalism. Early mediaeval thinkers were divided into two schools, those who regarded "universals" or abstract concepts as mere names without any corresponding realities (Nominalists), and those who held the opposite doctrine (Realism) that general concepts have an existence independent of individual things. The relation between universals and particulars was a subject of philosophical dispute all through the Middle Ages.

The first person to hold the nominalist doctrine was probably Roscelin or Roscellinus in the late 11th cent., but very little is known of him and none of his works remains except for a single letter to Peter Abelard who was his pupil. Roscelin was born in France, accused twice of heresy but recanted and fled to England where he attacked the views of Anselm, according to whom Roscelin used the phrase that universals were a *flatus voci* or breath of the voice. The most important nominalist was the Englishman William of Occam in the 13th cent. who, once and for all, separated the two schools by saying in effect that science is about things (the nominalist view), whereas logic, philosophy, and religion are about terms or concepts (the Platonic tradition). Both are justified, but we must distinguish between them. The proposition "man is a species" is not a proposition of logic or philosophy but a scientific statement since we cannot say whether it is true or false without knowing about man. If we fail to realise that words are conventional signs and that it is important to decide whether or not they have a meaning and refer to something, then we shall fall into logical fallacies of the type: "Man is a species, Socrates is a man, therefore Socrates is a species." This, in effect, is the beginning of the modern philosophy of logical analysis which, to oversimplify, tells us that a statement is not just true or untrue, it may also be meaningless. Therefore, in all the philosophical problems we have discussed elsewhere, there is the third possibility that the problem we are discussing has no meaning because the words refer to nothing and we must ask ourselves before going any further "what do we mean by God," and has the word "free-will" any definite meaning?

Nonconformism, the attitude of all those Christian bodies which do not conform to the doctrines of the Church of England. Up to the passing of the Act of Uniformity in 1662 they were called "puritans" or "dissenters" and were often persecuted. The oldest bodies of nonconformists are the Baptists, Independents, and (in England) the Presbyterians; the Methodists, although dating from 1738, did not consider themselves nonconformists until some time later. The Presbyterians are, of course. the official Church of Scotland where it is the Anglicans (known as " Episcopalians ") who are the nonconformists, although not generally described as such.

O

Objectivism, a semi-political philosophy expounded by the American novelist, Ayn Rand, and interesting in as much as it was first propagated through two of her own best-selling novels. The thesis of Objectivism is the inherent suitability of the competitive capitalist system for the well-being and advancement of the human race. The seeds of man's destruction, Miss Rand believes, are to be found in the creeping menace of socialism, which by its tendency to encourage the individual to rely on the state rather than himself, undermines the dynamic power of human hard work and self-interest. In her first, and perhaps most significant novel, *The Fountainhead*, she tells the story of an unconventional and highly self-motivated architect, Howard Roark, who achieves world fame and success by a combination of hard work, talent, and refusal to compromise. Her second major novel, *Atlas Shrugged*, which is over 1100 pages long, pictures a world in which the " objectivists " (the hard-working, self-motivated, highly talented individuals in the human race) decide to pull out from society and set up a secret nation of their own. Left to its own devices, the world of socialist slackers and loafers slides into grey destruction. Objectivism seems to have arisen as a kind of counterblast to the growing tendency within some sections of the United States to decry capitalism as impersonal profiteering, and followers sport as their insignia a small badge depicting the dollar sign—the emblem incidentally of the secret states in *Atlas Shrugged*. The movement, which relies heavily on the talent and personality of its founder, has made little headway into formal American politics, but Miss Rand's books, which have sold literally by the millions, obviously touch a chord in many readers' minds.

Occam's Razor, the philosophical maxim by which William of Occam, the 14th cent. Franciscan has become best-known. This states in the form which is most familiar: " Entities are not to be multiplied without necessity " and as such does not appear in his works. He did, however, say something much to the same effect: " It is vain to do with more what can be done with fewer." In other words, if everything in some science can be interpreted without assuming this or that hypothetical entity, there is no ground for assuming it. This is Bertrand Russell's version. and he adds: " I have myself found this a most fruitful principle in logical analysis."

Occultism. *See* **Magic, Alchemy, Astrology,** and **Theosophy.**

Orangemen, members of an Irish society formed in Ulster in 1795 to uphold Protestantism. Their name is taken from King William III, Prince of Orange, who defeated James II at the Battle of the Boyne (1690), hence the enormous banners depicting " King Billy on the Boyne " carried in procession on 12 July each year. The Unionist Party of Northern Ireland (the ruling political party from 1921 to 1972) is largely maintained by the Orange Order. The Order has branches in many English-speaking countries but flourishes chiefly in Ulster.

Orgonomy, a pseudo-psychological theory advanced by the German psychiatrist Wilhelm Reich (1897–1957), a pupil of Freud, who was expelled from Germany for attacking the Nazis and who started life afresh in the U.S.A. like so many of his colleagues. Moving quickly away from orthodox psychoanalytic theories, Reich became increasingly obsessed with the view that all living things were permeated with a unique force or energy which he termed " orgone " and which he believed could be photographed and measured with a geiger counter. The key to the successful flow of orgone throughout the body was sexual intercourse and the resulting orgasm (hence " orgone "). Reich achieved a substantial following for his increasingly bizarre views and when he was sentenced to two-years' imprisonment in 1956 for alleged medical malpractice a " civil rights " controversy developed which has not died down to this date. His unfortunate and rather tragic death in prison has fanned the emotional issues and granted him the important role of martyr to his cause. There is presently a strong revival of interest in Reich and orgonomy, partly in tune with the general occult revival. A recent witty, but not totally unsympathetic film about his work " W R—Mysteries of the Organism " has drawn the attention of a large new audience to his teachings.

Orphism. The Greeks in general thought very little of their gods, regarding them as similar to human beings with human failings and virtues although on a larger scale. But there was another aspect of Greek religion which was passionate, ecstatic, and secret, dealing with the worship of various figures among whom were Bacchus or Dionysus, Orpheus, and Demeter and Persephone of the Eleusinian Mysteries. Dionysus (or Bacchus) was originally a god from Thrace where the people were primitive farmers naturally interested in fertility cults. Dionysus was the god of fertility who only later came to be associated with wine and the divine madness it produces. He assumed the form of a man or a bull and his worship by the time it arrived in Greece became associated with women (as was the case in most of the Mystery Religions) who spent nights on the hills dancing and possibly drinking wine in order to stimulate ecstasy; an unpleasant aspect of the cult was the tearing to pieces of wild animals whose flesh was eaten raw. Although the cult was disapproved of by the orthodox and, needless to say, by husbands, it existed for a long time.

This primitive and savage religion in time was modified by that attributed to Orpheus whose cult was more spiritualised, ascetic, and substituted mental for physical intoxication. Orpheus may have been a real person or a legendary hero and he, too, is supposed to have come from Thrace, but his name indicates that he, or the movement associated with him, came from Crete and originally from Egypt, which seems to have been the source of many of its doctrines. Crete, it must be remembered, was the island through which Egypt influenced Greece in other respects. Orpheus is said to have been a reformer who was torn to pieces by the Maenad worshippers of Dionysus. The Orphics believed in the transmigration of souls and that the soul after death might obtain either eternal bliss or temporary or permanent torment according to its way of life upon earth. They held ceremonies of purification and the more orthodox abstained from animal food except on special occasions when it was eaten ritually. Man is partly earthly, partly heavenly, and a good life increases the heavenly part so that, in the end, he may become one with Bacchus and be called a " Bacchus."

The religion had an elaborate theology. As the Bacchic rites were reformed by Orpheus, so the Orphic rites were reformed by Pythagoras (c. 582–c. 507 B.C.) who introduced the mystical element into Greek philosophy which reached its heights in Plato. Other elements entered Greek life from Orphism. One of these was feminism which was notably lacking in Greek civilisation outside the Mystery Religions. The other was the drama which arose from the rites of Dionysus. The mysteries of Eleusis formed the most sacred part of the Athenian state religion, and it is clear that they had to do with fertility rites also, for they were in honour of Demeter and Persephone and all the myths speak of them as being associated with the supply of corn to the country. Without being provocative, it is accepted by most anthropologists and many theologians that Christianity, just as it accepted elements of Gnosticism and Mithraism, accepted elements from the Mystery Religions as they in turn must have done from earlier cults. The miraculous birth, the death and resurrection, the sacramental feast of bread and wine, symbolising the eating of the flesh and drinking of the blood of the god, all these are common elements in early religions and not just in one. None of this means that what we are told about Jesus is not true, but it surely does mean: (a) that Christianity was not a sudden development; (b) that the early Church absorbed many of the elements of other religions; (c) that perhaps Jesus Himself made use of certain symbols which He knew had a timeless significance for man and invested them with new meaning.

Orthodox Eastern Church. There are two groups of Eastern churches: (1) those forming the Orthodox Church dealt with here which include the ancient Byzantine patriarchates of Constantinople, Alexandria, Antioch, and Jerusalem, and the national churches of Russia, Greece, Yugoslavia, Bulgaria, Rumania, etc. (although Orthodox communities exist all over the world and are no longer confined to geographical areas); (2) the churches which rejected Byzantine orthodoxy during various controversies from the 5th to the 7th cent., notably the Coptic church (q.v.) and the Armenian church. Although all Orthodox churches share the same doctrine and traditions they are arranged as national independent bodies each with its own hierarchy. They do not recognise the pope, and the primacy of the patriarch of Constantinople is largely an honorary one. Although claiming to be the One Holy, Catholic, and Apostolic Church its alleged infallibility rests on universal agreement rather than on any one individual, and agreement over the faith comes from the Scriptures interpreted in the light of the Tradition. The latter includes dogmas relating to the Trinity, Christology, Mariology, and Holy Icons; the testimony of the Fathers (St. Athanasius, St. Basil, St. John Chrysostom, St. Cyril of Alexandria, etc.); the canons or rules as formulated by the Councils and the Fathers. The Orthodox Church did not take part in the great Western controversies about the Bible, nor, of course, in the Reformation. Attempts have recently been made to improve relations between Rome and Constantinople: the two Churches agreed in 1965 to retract the excommunications cast on each other in A.D. 1054, which formalised the Great Schism.

Ouspensky, a contemporary of Gurdjieff (q.v.), Peter Ouspensky was another obscure mystic of Eastern European origin who believed he had an occult philosophical message to bring to the West. This he embodied in a series of lengthy books which are both humourless and self-indulgent.

Oxford Group. See Moral Re-Armament.
Oxford Movement. See Tractarianism.

P

Pantheism. See God and Man.
Papal Infallibility. The basis of papal infallibility is (a) that every question of morals and faith is not dealt with in the Bible so it is necessary that there should be a sure court of appeal in case of doubt, and this was provided by Christ when he established the Church as His Teaching Authority upon earth; (b) ultimately this idea of the teaching function of the Church shapes the idea of papal infallibility which asserts that the Pope, when speaking officially on matters of faith or morals, is protected by God against the possibility of error. The doctrine was proclaimed in July 1870.

Infallibility is a strictly limited gift which does not mean that the Pope has extraordinary intelligence, that God helps him to find the answer to every conceivable question, or that Catholics have to accept the Pope's views on politics. He can make mistakes or fall into sin, his scientific or historical opinions may be quite wrong, he may write books that are full of errors. Only in two limited spheres is he infallible and in these only when he speaks officially as the supreme teacher and lawgiver of the Church, defining a doctrine that must be accepted by all its members. When, after studying a problem of faith or morals as carefully as possible, and with all available help from expert consultants, he emerges with the Church's answer—on these occasions it is not strictly an answer, it is *the* answer.

Historically speaking, the Roman Catholic Church of the early 19th cent. was at its lowest ebb of power. Pope Pius IX, in fear of Italian nationalism, revealed his reactionary attitude by the feverish declaration of new dogmas, the canonisation of new saints, the denunciation of all modern ideals in the Syllabus of Errors, and the unqualified defence of his temporal power against the threat of Garibaldi. It is not too much to say that everything regarded as important by freedom-loving and democratic people was opposed by the papacy at that time. In 1870, after a long and sordid struggle, the Vatican Council, convened by Pius IX, pronounced the definition of his infallibility. Döllinger, a German priest and famous historian of the Church, was excommunicated because, like many others, he refused to accept the new dogma. It is difficult not to doubt that there was some connection between the pronouncement of the Pope's infallibility and his simultaneous loss of temporal power.

After the humanism of the Second Vatican Council (1962–5) the Pope's encyclical *Humanae Vitae* (1968), condemning birth control, came as a great disappointment to the many people (including theologians, priests, and laymen) who had expected there would be a change in the Church's teaching. The Church's moral guidance on this controversial issue, however, does not involve the doctrine of infallibility. (The Roman Catholic Church teaches that papal pronouncements are infallible only when they are specifically defined as such.) That there is unlikely to be any immediate softening of the Church's line on infallibility was made clear in July 1973 when the Vatican's Sacred Congregation for the Doctrine of the Faith published a document strongly reaffirming papal infallibility. The document also reminded Catholics of their obligation to accept the Catholic Church's unique claims to authenticity.

Parapsychology, the name given to the study of psychical research (q.v.) as an academic discipline, and chosen to denote the topic's supposed status as a branch of psychology. The impetus behind parapsychology came from the psychologist William MacDougall who persuaded Duke University in North Carolina, U.S.A., to found a department of parapsychology under J. B. Rhine. Throughout the 1930s and 40s the work of Rhine and his colleagues, who claimed to have produced scientific evidence for the existence of E.S.P., attracted world-wide attention. Increasing reservations about the interpretation of Rhine's results and an apparent lack of any readily repeatable experiments, however, gradually eroded scientific confidence in the topic. The academic status of parapsychology is at the present time exceedingly uncertain. Rhine retired from university life in 1965 and the world-famous parapsychology laboratory at Duke University was closed. On the other hand the American Association for the Advancement of Science recently admitted the Parapsychology Association (the leading organisation for professional parapsychologists) as an affiliated member society. An American government body, the National Institute of Mental Health, has also officially supported some medical research into alleged telepathic dreams, the first "official" grant support of this kind. In Britain a recent poll of readers in the weekly journal, *New Scientist*, revealed a very high interest in the subject matter of parapsychology, though no British university actively supports research into the topic. Stories of intensive parapsychological research in Soviet Russia are however without foundation and are not supported by Western parapsychologists who have visited Russia.

Parsees. See Zoroastrianism.
Pavlovian theory. See Behaviourism.
Pentecostalism, a religious movement within the Protestant churches, holding the belief that an essential feature of true Christianity is a vigorous and profound spiritual or mystical ex-

perience which occurs after, and seemingly reinforces the initial conversion. The origins of modern Pentecostalism appear to lie in the occasion on 1 January 1901 when a member of a Bible College in Topeka, Kansas, one Agnes N. Ozman, spontaneously began to speak in an apparently unknown language at one of the College's religious meetings. This " speaking in tongues " was assumed to be evidence of her conversion and " spirit baptism," and became a feature of most Pentecostal meetings in due course. The movement spread rapidly across America, particularly in rural communities, and also was a strong feature of Welsh religious life in the early part of the century. Pentecostal services are enthusiastic and rousing, with a strong emphasis on music and participation on the part of the congregation. Pentecostalism is evangelistic in nature and seems to be gaining in strength at the present time, at the expense of more orthodox and staid versions of Christianity. The fiery character Aimee Semple McPherson was one of its most prominent evangelists.

Phrenology, a psychological " school " founded in 1800 by two Germans, Franz Josef Gall and Johann Gaspar Spurzheim. Gall was an anatomist who believed there to be some correspondence between mental faculties and the shape of the head. He tested these ideas in prisons and mental hospitals and began to lecture on his findings, arousing a great deal of interest throughout both Europe and America, where his doctrines were widely accepted. Phrenology became fashionable, and people would go to " have their bumps read " as later men and women of fashion have gone to be psychoanalysed. Roughly speaking, Gall divided the mind into thirty-seven faculties such as destructiveness, suavity, self-esteem, conscientiousness, and so on, and claimed that each of these was located in a definite area of the brain. He further claimed that the areas in the brain corresponded to " bumps " on the skull which could be read by the expert, thus giving a complete account of the character of the subject. In fact, (a) no such faculties are located in the brain anywhere for this is simply not the way the brain works; (b) the faculties described by Gall are not pure traits which cannot be further analysed and are based on a long outdated psychology; (c) the shape of the brain bears no specific relationship to the shape of the skull. Phrenology is a pseudo-science; there is no truth in it whatever. But, even so, like astrology, it still has its practitioners.

Physiocrats. A French school of economic thought during the 18th cent., known at the time as Les Economistes but in later years named physiocrats by Du Pont de Nemours, a member of the School. Other members were Quesnay, Mirabeau, and the great financier Turgot. The physiocrats held the view, common to the 18th cent., and deriving ultimately from Rousseau, of the goodness and bounty of nature and the goodness of man " as he came from the bosom of nature." The aim of governments, therefore, should be to conform to nature; and so long as men do not interfere with each other's liberty and do not combine among themselves, governments should leave them free to find their own salvation. Criminals, madmen, and monopolists should be eliminated. Otherwise the duty of government is laissez-faire, laissez passer. From this follows the doctrine of free trade between nations on grounds of both justice and economy; for the greater the competition, the more will each one strive to economise the cost of his labour to the general advantage. Adam Smith, although not sharing their confidence in human nature, learned much from the physiocrats, eliminated their errors, and greatly developed their teaching.

Physiognomy. See Characterology.

Pietism, a movement in the Lutheran Church at the end of the 17th cent.—the reaction, after the sufferings of the thirty years' war, of a pious and humiliated people against learning, pomp and ceremony, and stressing the importance of man's personal relationship with God. The writings of Johann Georg Hamann (1730–88) who came from a Pietist family of Königsberg influenced Kierkegaard. The Pietist move-

ment was the root of the great Romantic movement of the 18th cent.

Plymouth Brethren, a religious sect founded by John Nelson Darby, a minister of the Protestant Church of Ireland, and Edward Cronin, a former Roman Catholic, in 1827. Both were dissatisfied with the lack of spirituality in their own and other churches and joined together in small meetings in Dublin every Sunday for " the breaking of bread." Soon the movement began to spread through Darby's travels and writings and he finally settled in Plymouth, giving the popular name to the " Brethren." Beginning as a movement open to all who felt the need to " keep the unity of the Spirit," it soon exercised the right to exclude all who had unorthodox views and split up into smaller groups. Among these the main ones were the " Exclusives," the Kellyites, the Newtonites, and " Bethesda " whose main differences were over problems of church government or prophetical powers. Some of these are further split among themselves. Readers of Father and Son by Sir Edmund Gosse, which describes life with his father, the eminent naturalist Philip Gosse, who belonged to the Brethren, will recall how this basically kind, honest, and learned man was led through their teachings to acts of unkindness (e.g., in refusing to allow his son and other members of his household to celebrate Christmas and throwing out the small tokens they had secretly bought), and intellectual dishonesty (e.g., in refusing for religious reasons alone to accept Darwinism when all his evidence pointed towards it).

Today, the majority of Brethren belong to the " Open Brethren " assemblies and, unlike the " Exclusives," hold that the Lord's Supper (a commemorative act of " breaking the bread " observed once a week) is for all Christians who care to join them. Baptism is required and Brethren believe in the personal premillennial second coming of Christ.

Poltergeist. allegedly a noisy type of spirit which specialises in throwing things about, making loud thumpings and bangings, and occasionally bringing in " apports," i.e., objects from elsewhere. Most so-called poltergeist activities are plain frauds, but the others are almost invariably associated with the presence in the house of someone (often, but not always a child) who is suffering from severe mental conflicts usually of a sexual nature. The inference is that those activities which are not simply fraudulent are either due to some unknown influence exuded by such mentally abnormal people, or that they are actually carried out by ordinary physical means by such people when in a state of hysterical dissociation—i.e., unconsciously. The second hypothesis is much the more probable. See Psychic Research.

Polytheism. See God and Man.

Positivism, also known as the Religion of Humanity, was founded by Auguste Comte (1798–1857), a famous mathematician and philosopher born in Montpellier, France. His views up to the end of the century attracted many and it would have been impossible throughout that time to read a book on philosophy or sociology that did not mention them, but today his significance is purely of historical interest. In his Cours de Philosophie Positive (1830) he put forward the thesis that mankind had seen three great stages in human thought: (1) the theological, during which man seeks for supernatural causes to explain nature and invents gods and devils; (2) the metaphysical, through which he thinks in terms of philosophical and metaphysical abstractions; (3) the last positive or scientific stage when he will proceed by experiment and objective observation to reach in time " positive truth."

Broadly speaking, there is little to complain of in this analysis; for there does seem to have been some sort of general direction along these lines. However, Comte was not satisfied with having reached this point and felt that his system demanded a religion and, of course, one that was " scientific." This religion was to be the worship of Humanity in place of the personal Deity of earlier times, and for it he supplied not only a Positive Catechism but a treatise on Sociology in which he declared himself the High Priest of the cult. Since, as it stood, the religion was likely to appear somewhat abstract to many, Comte drew up a list of historical characters whom he regarded as worthy of the same sort of adoration as Catholics accord to their saints. The new Church attracted few members, even among those who had a high regard for Comte's scientific work, and its only significant adherents were a small group of Oxford scholars and some in his own country. Frederic Harrison was the best-known English adherent and throughout his life continued to preach Comtist doctrines in London to diminishing audiences.

Pragmatism, a typically American school of philosophy which comes under the heading of what Bertrand Russell describes as a "practical" as opposed to a "theoretical" philosophy. Whereas the latter, to which most of the great philosophical systems belong, seeks disinterested knowledge for its own sake, the former (a) regards action as the supreme good, (b) considers happiness an effect and knowledge a mere instrument of successful activity.

The originator of pragmatism is usually considered to have been the psychologist William James (1842–1910) although he himself attributed its basic principles to his life-long friend, the American philosopher, Charles Sanders Peirce (1839–1914). The other famous pragmatist is John Dewey, best-known in Europe for his works on education (for although American text-books on philosophy express opinions to the contrary, few educated people in Europe have taken the slightest interest in pragmatism and generally regard it as an eccentricity peculiar to Americans). James in his book *The Will to Believe* (1896) points out that we are often compelled to take a decision where no adequate theoretical grounds for a decision exist; for even to do nothing is to decide. Thus in religion we have a right to adopt a believing attitude although not intellectually fully convinced. We should believe truth and shun error, but the failing of the sceptical philosopher is that he adheres only to the latter rule and thus fails to believe various truths which a less cautious man will accept. If believing truth and avoiding error are equally important, then it is a good idea when we are presented with an alternative to believe one of the possibilities at will, since we then have an even chance of being right, whereas we have none if we suspend judgment. The function of philosophy, according to James, is to find out what difference it makes to the individual if a particular philosophy or world-system is true: "An idea is ' true' so long as to believe it is profitable to our lives" and, he adds, the truth is only the expedient in our way of thinking . . . in the long run and on the whole of course." Thus " if the hypothesis of God works satisfactorily in the widest sense of the word, it is true." Bertrand Russell's reply to this assertion is: "I have always found that the hypothesis of Santa Claus ' works satisfactorily in the widest sense of the word '; therefore ' Santa Claus exists' is true, although Santa Claus does not exist." Russell adds that James's concept of truth simply omits as unimportant the question whether God really *is* in His heaven; if He is a useful hypothesis that is enough. "God the Architect of the Cosmos is forgotten; all that is remembered is belief in God, and its effects upon the creatures inhabiting our petty planet. No wonder the Pope condemned the pragmatic defence of religion."

Predestination. *See* Calvinism.

Presbyterianism, a system of ecclesiastical government of the Protestant churches which look back to John Calvin as their Reformation leader. The ministry consists of presbyters who are all of equal rank. Its doctrinal standards are contained in the *Westminster Confession of Faith* (1647) which is, in general, accepted by English, Scottish, and American Presbyterians as the most thorough and logical statement in existence of the Calvinist creed. The Church of Scotland is the leading Presbyterian church in the British Isles.

The Reformation in Scotland was preceded by the same sort of awareness of the moral corruption of the Roman Church as had happened elsewhere, but for various political and emotional reasons, which need not be dis-

cussed here, the majority of the Scottish people (unlike the English who had been satisfied with the mere exchange of Crown for Pope) were determined on a fundamental change of doctrine, discipline, and worship, rather than a reform of manners. The church preachers had learned their Protestantism not from Luther but from Calvin and their leader John Knox had worked in Geneva with Calvin himself and was resolved to introduce the system into Scotland. In 1557 the "Lords of the Congregation" signed the Common Band (*i.e.*, a bond or covenant) to maintain "the blessed Word of God and his congregation" against their enemies, and demanded the right to worship as they had chosen. However, the real date of the Scottish Reformation is August 1560 when Mary of Guise (the regent for Mary Queen of Scots who was not yet of age) died and the Estates met to settle their affairs without foreign pressure; the *Scots Confession* was drawn up and signed by Knox and adopted by the Estates.

The ideas on which the Reformed Kirk was based are found in the *Scots Confession*, the *Book of Discipline*, and the *Book of Common Order*, the so-called Knox's liturgy. Knox's liturgy, the same as that used in Geneva but translated into English, was used until Laud's attempt to force an Anglican liturgy on the Kirk led to an abandonment of both in favour of " free prayers."

The Presbyterian tradition includes uncompromising stress upon the Word of God contained in the Scriptures of the Old and New Testaments as the supreme rule of faith and life, and upon the value of a highly trained ministry, which has given the Church of Scotland a high reputation for scholarship and has in turn influenced the standard of education in Scotland. The unity of the Church is guaranteed by providing for democratic representation in a hierarchy of courts (unlike the Anglican Church, which is a hierarchy of persons). The local kirk-session consists of the minister and popularly elected elders (laymen). Ministers, elected by their flocks, are ordained by presbyters (ministers already ordained). Above the kirk-session is the court of the presbytery which has jurisdiction over a specified area; above that the court of synod which rules over many presbyteries; and finally the General Assembly which is the Supreme Court of the Church with both judicial and legislative powers, and over which the Moderator of the General Assembly presides. The function of the elders is to help the minister in the work and government of the kirk. The episcopacy set up by James VI and I, and maintained by Charles I was brought to an end by the Glasgow Assembly (1638), but General Assemblies were abolished by Oliver Cromwell and at the Restoration Charles II re-established episcopacy. The Covenanters who resisted were hunted down, imprisoned, transported, or executed over a period of nearly thirty years before William of Orange came to the throne and Presbyterianism was re-established (1690). Today Presbyterians no less than other Christian communities are looking at Christianity as a common world religion in the sense that the principles which unite them are greater than those which divide them. A small but significant step in the direction of international Christian unity was made in 1972 when the Presbyterian and Congregationalist Churches in England were merged to form the United Reformed Church. *See* Church of Scotland, Calvinism.

Protestant, the name first applied to those who favoured the cause of Martin Luther and who protested against the intolerant decisions of the Catholic majority at the second Diet of Speyer (1529), revoking earlier decisions of the first Diet of Speyer tolerating the Reformers in certain cases (1526). In general the name " Protestant" is applied to those Churches which severed connection with Rome at the time of the Reformation. The essence of Protestantism is the acceptance by the individual Christian of his direct responsibility to God rather than to the Church. *See* Lutheranism, Presbyterianism, Calvinism.

Psychedelism. For all his recorded history man

has relied upon drugs of one kind or another to make his life more tolerable. These have generally been central nervous system depressants— *i.e.*, alcohol, hashish, etc.—and their use in most societies has been brought under careful government control. Most societies have also at some stage experimented with the use of certain drugs of another class—the hallucinogens. These, far from having the mentally tranquillising characteristics of small doses of alcohol, provoke striking changes in mental alertness, frequently coupled with visionary or hallucinatory experiences. The confusion and disorientation which accompany such states has led to social disapproval of their use in Western countries, and the favoured " legal " drug for centuries has been alcohol. In the 1950s the novelist Aldous Huxley in his essay *The Doors of Perception* wrote of his experiences with the drug mescalin, a derivative of the South American peyotl and a powerful hallucinogen. Huxley put forward the hypothesis that mescalin had given him not only an entirely original psychological experience but had also significantly " heightened " his perceptual ability— a development of the greatest possible interest to artists, writers, and poets. Huxley's book had considerable impact, stimulating other creative individuals into similar experiments, not always with such euphoric results. In England the author Richard Ward reported some frightening moments under the drug LSD in his *A Drug-taker's Notebook* and Huxley amplified the unpredictable nature of the drug-experience in *Heaven and Hell*, published in 1956. Although such experiments were technically illegal, public interest had been considerably aroused and in the 1960s, when it became easy to synthesise the most effective of the hallucinogens, LSD, its use began to be common among certain sections of society. In 1964 a sensational scandal rocked the great American university of Harvard when senior members of the teaching staff, including the psychologist Timothy Leary, were dismissed for using LSD and encouraging students in its use. Unrepentant, Dr. Leary set up a community near New York from whence the cult of psychedelism was propagated.

Psychedelism—which is not really an organised system of belief, but rather an attitude of mind —preaches that through the controlled use of drugs, particularly of the hallucinogenic variety, an individual may be made aware for the first time of the rich fields of experience which lie latent in the unconscious mind. The exploration of these territories will have both a liberating and an enriching effect, the outcome being to " turn on " the individual to the total reality of mind. So convinced do many of the proponents of psychedelia become of the significance of the experience of the so-called LSD " trip," that they are inclined to urge non-trippers to experiment with the drug. Herein, of course, lies one obvious danger, for the drug LSD is potentially a toxic substance which needs to be administered in minute doses if it is not to cause madness or even death. There is also much uncertainty about the possible long-term effects of " tripping," many psychologists and scientists believing that it leads to a progressive disorientation and destruction of the personality, a disintegration of which the individual drug-taker is seldom aware. If there is a credit side to psychedelism it may lie in the clear, if limited, evolution in popular music, art, and design and to a lesser extent, literature which has been inspired by these excursions. The wave of interest in LSD and similar drugs is beginning to slacken off, possibly because of an increasing awareness of the possible grievous side-effects and of the largely illusory nature of the " insights " which the " trip " is supposed to provide. The controversial Dr. Leary, the movement's most literate and influential figure, has himself disavowed many of his original statements, and today warns young people against the indiscriminate use of drugs as an aid to insight or self-awareness.

Psychic Research is a general term for the various approaches to the scientific investigation of the paranormal, in particular supposed extra-sensory powers of the mind, but also manifestations such as ghosts, poltergeists, spiritualistic phenomena, etc. In recent years the word parapsychology has also come into use, particularly for the investigation of ESP in a laboratory setting, but it is really part of psychic research as the subject's fascinating history reveals.

For all recorded history, and no doubt very much earlier, man has been puzzled at his apparent ability to perceive features of the universe without the use of the normal senses— mind-to-mind contact, dreams about the future which come true, etc. He has also been intrigued by the notion that in addition to the natural world of people and things, there exists in parallel, a *supernatural* world of ghosts, spirits and other similar strange manifestations. Belief in such oddities was tremendously widespread and still forms one of the major casual conversational topics raised when people see each other socially today. Of course, until the 19th cent. or thereabouts such phenomena, while bizarre, unpredictable and possibly frightening, were not at odds with man's view of himself and his world as revealed through basic religious beliefs. Man was supposed to be in essence a supernatural being with eternal life, and the world was seen as the happy hunting ground of dynamic evil forces which could intervene directly in the lives of humans. The rise of material science in the 19th cent. however began to shake the orthodox religious framework, and as a result in due course scientists began to question the basis of all supernatural powers and manifestations, putting forward the reasonable argument: " if such things *are* real then they should be demonstrable in scientific terms—just as all other aspects of the universe are."

Once having advanced this argument, the next step was to carry it to its conclusion and set about the systematic investigation of the phenomena to see whether they *did* conform in any way to the immensely successful framework of 19th cent. science, and from this step psychic research was born. In fact one can date its origins rather precisely—to 1882 when a group of scholars formed the Society for Psychical Research in London—an organisation which still exists today. The first experiments in this slightly eccentric field of science were haphazard and tended to be confined to spiritualistic phenomena such as table tapping, mediumistic messages, ectoplasmic manifestations, etc. which were having a great wave of popularity among the general public at the time. In fact what one might term as the first phase of psychic research—it has gone through three phases in its history—was really heavily tied up with Spiritualism. Before ridiculing it for this, it is only fair to point out that many of the most eminent figures of the time—the great physicists Sir Oliver Lodge and Sir William Crookes, Alfred Russell Wallace, co-discoverer with Darwin of the theory of evolution by natural selection, the brilliant author and creator of Sherlock Holmes, Sir Arthur Conan Doyle, and many others—became convinced Spiritualists as the result of their early experiments. Nevertheless, despite the ardent support of such intellectual giants, medium after medium was in due course detected in fraud— sometimes of the most blatant kind—and the majority of scientists gradually became more critical and less likely to be taken in by even the subtlest of trickery. As a result, interest slowly shifted from the séance room to a different realm, and as it did so the first phase of psychic research drew to a close.

The second phase was, broadly speaking, the era of the ghost hunter. With the idea of spirits materialising in laboratories seeming intrinsically less and less credible, scientists began to study what struck them at the time to be basically more " plausible " matters— haunted houses, poltergeist phenomena and so on. For some reason the idea of a house dominated by a psychic presence as the result of some tragic history seemed (at the turn of the century) *somehow* scientifically and philosophically more acceptable than did the old spiritualist notions about direct communication with the spirit world. The key figure in the "ghost hunting" era was Mr. Harry Price, an amateur magician who became the scourge of fraudulent mediums, but who staked his name and credibility on the authenticity of the alleged poltergeist phenomena at Borley Rectory in Suffolk, which became world famous through his book, *The Most Haunted House in England*. The ancient rectory's catalogue of ghosts and marvels allegedly witnessed by numerous "reliable witnesses" seemed irrefutable. Unfortunately investigations by the Society for Psychical Research some years after Price's death now make it seem certain that Price was responsible for faking some of the Borley phenomena himself, and with these disclosures scientifically "respectable" ghost hunting took a nasty tumble. Thus, with an increasingly critical attitude developing among scientists, haunted houses and poltergeists gradually began to shift out of favour to usher in the third phase of psychic research.

The date of the commencement of this phase can be identified as 1927 when the Parapsychology Laboratory at Duke University in North Carolina was formed by Dr. J. B. Rhine. Here the emphasis was on laboratory studies along the traditional lines of experimental psychology; spirit forms and poltergeists were ignored in favour of the routine testing of literally thousands of people for telepathy, precognition (the ability to see into the future), etc., almost always involving card tests which could be rigidly controlled and the results statistically analysed. By the 1940s Rhine was claiming irrefutable evidence of telepathy achieved by these means, but once again critical forces began to gather and it was pointed out that results obtained in Rhine's laboratory rarely seemed to be replicable in other scientists' laboratories in different parts of the world. In fact the failure of ESP experiments of this kind to be easily repeatable has turned out to be crucial and has led to a growing scepticism on the part of uncommitted scientists who now question whether psychic research and parapsychology have really advanced our understanding of the world of the paranormal in any way. At the present time the topic is in a highly controversial phase; Rhine's university parapsychology laboratory has closed with his retirement, allegations of cheating and faking experimental results have been made against some parapsychologists (and apparently substantiated) and the topic is racked with controversy both internal and external. On the other hand public as opposed to scientific interest in the topic remains exceedingly high, though interest in the more sensational and bizarre phenomena, such as the alleged fork bending abilities of the Israeli Uri Geller, seems to be growing at the expense of the routine, admittedly dull, but at least scientifically controllable, card guessing experiments by Rhine.

To sum up the topic one could say that in a curious way, while the third phase of psychic research is now drawing to a close, the evidence suggests that a fourth phase is appearing, and that this may well feature a return to the study of the more sensational and dramatic phenomena characteristic of Uri Geller, and in its way so reminiscent of the Victorian séance room. If this is so, a century after its foundation the wheel will have turned full circle and psychic research will be back where it started, without in the opinion of most scientists, having solved any of the basic questions which it had set out to answer. *See* Poltergeist, Telepathy, Spiritualism.

Psychoanalysis, an approach to the study of human personality involving the rigorous probing, with the assistance of a specially trained practitioner, of an individual's personal problems, motives, goals and attitudes to life in general. Often, and quite understandably, confused with psychology (of which it is merely a part), psychoanalysis has an interesting historical background and has attracted the interest of philosophers, scientists and medical experts since it emerged as a radical and controversial form of mental therapy at the turn of the century. The traditionally accepted founder is the great Austrian Sigmund Freud, but he never failed to acknowledge the impetus that had been given to his own ideas by

his talented friend, the physiologist Joseph Breuer, who for most of his working life had been interested in the curious phenomena associated with hypnosis. Breuer had successfully cured the hysterical paralysis of a young woman patient and had noticed that under hypnosis the girl seemed to be recalling emotional experiences, hitherto forgotten, which bore some relationship to the symptoms of her illness. Developing this with other patients Breuer then found that the mere recalling and discussing of the emotional events under hypnosis seemed to produce a dramatic alleviation of the symptoms—a phenomenon which came to be known as *catharsis*. Breuer also noticed another curious side-effect, that his women patients fell embarrassingly and violently in love with him, and he gradually dropped the practice of "mental catharsis," possibly feeling that it was a bit too dangerous to handle. This left the field clear for Freud, whose brilliant mind began to search beyond the therapeutic aspects of the topic to see what light might be thrown on the nature of human personality and psychological mechanisms in general. The most important question concerned the "forgotten" emotional material which turned up, apparently out of the blue, during the hypnotic session. Freud rightly saw that this posed problems for the current theories of memory, for how could something once forgotten (a) continue to have an effect on the individual without his being aware of it, and (b) ultimately be brought back to conscious memory again. It must be remembered that at this time memory was considered to be a fairly simple process—information was stored in the brain and was gradually eroded or destroyed with the passage of time and the decay of brain cells. Once lost, it was believed, memories were gone for ever, or at best only partially and inaccurately reproducible. Furthermore, human beings were supposed to be rational (if frequently wilful) creatures who never did anything without thinking about it (if only briefly) beforehand and without being well aware of their reasons for so doing. It was within this framework that Freud had his great insight, one which many people believe to be one of the most important ideas given to mankind. This was simply the realisation that the human mind was not a simple entity controlling the brain and body more or less at will, but a complex system made up of a number of integrated parts with at least two major subdivisions—the conscious and the unconscious. The former concerned itself with the normal round of human behaviour, including the larger part of rational thought, conversation, etc., and large areas of memory. The latter was principally devoted to the automatic control of bodily functions, such as respiration, cardiac activity, various types of emotional behaviour not subject to much conscious modification and a large storehouse of relevant "memories" again not normally accessible to the conscious mind. Occasionally, Freud proposed, an exceedingly unpleasant emotional or otherwise painful event might be so troublesome if held in the conscious mind's store, that it would get shoved down into the unconscious or "repressed" where it would cease to trouble the individual in his normal life. The advantages of this mechanism are obvious, but they also brought with them hazards. With certain kinds of memory, particularly those involving psychological rather than physical pain—as for example a severe sexual conflict or marital problem—repression might be used as a device to save the individual from facing his problem in the "real" world, where he might be able ultimately to solve it, by merely hiding it away in the unconscious and thus pretending it did not exist. Unfortunately, Freud believed, conflicts of this kind were not snuffed out when consigned to the basements of the mind, but rather tended to smoulder on, affecting the individual in various ways which he could not understand. Repressed marital conflicts might give rise to impotence, for example, or even to homosexual behaviour. Guilt at improper social actions similarly repressed might provoke nervous tics, local paralysis, etc, etc. Following this line of reasoning, Freud argued that if the unwisely repressed material could be dredged up and the individual forced to face the crisis instead of denying it, then dramatic alleviations of symptoms and full recovery should follow.

To the great psychologist and his growing band of followers the stage seemed to be set for a dramatic breakthrough not only in mental therapy but also in a general understanding of the nature of human personality. To his pleasure—for various reasons he was never too happy about hypnosis—Freud discovered that with due patience, skill and guidance an individual could be led to resurrect the material repressed in his unconscious mind in the normal, as opposed to the hypnotic, state. This technique, involving long sessions consisting of intimate discussions between patient and therapist became known as psychoanalysis, and it has steadily evolved from its experimental beginnings in the medical schools and universities of Vienna to being a major system of psychotherapy with a world-wide following and important theoretical connotations. Psychoanalysis, as practised today, consists of a number of meetings between doctor and patient in which the latter is slowly taught to approach and enter the territory of his subconscious mind, and examine the strange and "forgotten" material within. A successful analysis, it is claimed, gives the individual greater insight into his own personality and a fuller understanding of the potent unconscious forces which are at work within him and in part dictating his goals.

Freud's initial ideas were of course tentative, and meant to be so. He was however a didactic and forceful personality himself, unwilling to compromise on many points which became controversial as the technique and practice of psychoanalysis developed. The outcome was that some of his early followers, notably the equally brilliant Carl Jung and Alfred Adler, broke away to found their own "schools" or versions of psychoanalysis, with varying degrees of success. Today, psychoanalysis is coming under increasingly critical scrutiny, and its claims are being treated with a good deal of reservation. Notable antagonists include the English psychologist Professor H. J. Eysenck who points out that there is little if any solid experimental data indicating that psychoanalysis is a valid method of treating or curing mental illness. Analysts respond by saying that their system is closer to an art than a craft and not amenable to routine scientific experiment. The controversy will no doubt continue for some time to come, but whatever its validity as therapy, the basic ideas behind psychoanalysis—notably the reality and power of the unconscious mind—are beyond question and have given human beings definite and major insights into the greatest enigma of all—the workings of the human mind. *See also* Section Q.

Psychokinesis (alternatively Telekinesis), the supposed faculty of the human mind to influence objects at a distance by "thought" or the act of will. Scientific evidence for the existence of PK (as it is abbreviated) is very slender indeed and people claiming to have witnessed it have probably been the victims of simple trickery or a skilful illusion. Almost 20,000,000 people watched an alleged demonstration of PK on British television in 1973 when a young Israeli, Uri Geller, purported to bend cutlery by mental power. Despite their spectacular appearance, such demonstrations have no scientific validity and little can be inferred about the powers of Mr. Geller and other similar claimants unless they have demonstrated their abilities to professional magicians, in order to have simple sleight of hand can be ruled out.

Psychometry, the supposed talent or faculty of divining something about the history and previous owners of an object by holding it in the hand. A common feature of modern Spiritualistic practice, and to a certain extent synonymous with clairvoyance, psychometry is based on an ancient magical assumption that objects somehow take on traces or "memories" of their surroundings which are detectable by specially sensitive individuals. Controlled scientific tests on people claiming to have this power have however proved totally negative. *See also* Psychic Research.

Pyramidology, a curious belief that the dimensions

of the Great Pyramid at Giza, if studied carefully, reveal principles of fundamental historical and religious significance. The perpetrator of this was a Victorian publisher, John Taylor, who discovered that if you divide the height of the pyramid into twice the side of its base you get a number very similar to pi—a number of considerable mathematical importance. Later discoveries in the same vein include the finding that the base of the pyramid (when divided by the width of a single casing stone) equals exactly 365—number of days in the year. Many books have been written on the interpretation of the dimensions of the pyramid, none of which has any scientific or archaeological validity. Pyramidology is simply a classic example of the well-known fact that hunting through even a random array of numbers will turn up sequences which appear to be "significant"—always provided that one carefully selects the numbers one wants and turns a blind eye to those that one doesn't! A peculiar variant of pyramidology has recently arisen through the publication of a claim that razor blades kept beneath a cardboard model of a pyramid never lose their cutting edge! Scientific tests have shown that this is not so, but the belief persists—implicit testimony to the mystical power of certain common emblems and symbols.

Pyrrhonism, a sceptical philosophy which doubts everything.

Q

Quakers, a religious body founded in England in the 17th cent. by George Fox (1624–91). The essence of their faith is that every individual who believes has the power of direct communication with God who will guide him into the ways of truth. This power comes from the "inner light" of his own heart, the light of Christ. Quakers meet for worship avoiding all ritual, without ordained ministers or prepared sermons; there is complete silence until someone is moved by the Holy Spirit to utter his message.

In the early days Quakers gave vent to violent outbursts and disturbed church services. Friends had the habit of preaching at anyone who happened to be nearby, their denunciation of "steeple-houses" and references to the "inner light," their addressing everyone as "thee" and "thou," their refusal to go beyond "yea" and "nay" in making an assertion and refusing to go further in taking an oath, must have played some part in bringing about the savage persecutions they were forced to endure. Many emigrated to Pennsylvania, founded by William Penn in 1682, and missionaries were sent to many parts of the world. The former violence gave way to gentleness. Friends not only refused to take part in war but even refused to resist personal violence. They took the lead in abolishing slavery, worked for prison reform and better education. As we know them today Quakers are quiet, sincere, undemonstrative people, given to a somewhat serious turn of mind. The former peculiarities of custom and dress have been dropped and interpretation of the Scriptures is more liberal. Although Quakers refuse to take part in warfare, they are always ready to help the victims of war, by organising relief, helping refugees in distress, or sending their ambulance units into the heat of battle.

Quietism, a doctrine of extreme asceticism and contemplative devotion, embodied in the works of Michael Molinos, a 17th cent. Spanish priest, and condemned by Rome. It taught that the chief duty of man is to be occupied in the continual contemplation of God, so as to become totally independent of outward circumstances and the influence of the senses. Quietists taught that when this stage of perfection is reached the soul has no further need for prayer and other external devotional practices. Similar doctrines have been taught in the Moslem and Hindu religions. *See* Yoga.

R

Racism, the doctrine that one race is inherently superior or inferior to others, one of the bases of racial prejudice. It has no connection whatever with the study of race as a concept, nor with the investigation of racial differences, which is a science practised by the physical anthropologist (who studies physical differences), or the social anthropologist (who studies cultural differences). Racism is simply a vulgar superstition believed in by the ignorant or mentally unbalanced, and it may be categorically stated as a scientific fact that racial superiority is a myth believed in by no scientist of repute. *See also* Race, Section L.

Radiesthesia, the detection, either by some "psychic" faculty or with special equipment, of radiations alleged to be given off by all living things and natural substances such as water, oil, metal, etc. The word radiesthesia is in fact a fancy modern name for the ancient practice of "dowsing," whereby an individual is supposed to be able to detect the presence of hidden underground water by following the movements of a hazel twig held in his hands. Dowsers, or water diviners, as they are sometimes called, claim also to be able to detect the presence of minerals and, hard though it may seem to believe, have actually been hired by major oil companies to prospect for desert wells—though without any notable successes. The theory of dowsing is that all things give off a unique radiation signal which the trained individual (via his twig, pendulum, or whatever) can "tune in" to, a theory which, while not backed up by any data known to orthodox sciences, is at least not too fantastically far-fetched. It is when radiesthesists claim to be able to detect the presence of oil, water, or precious metals by holding their pendulum *over a map* of the territory and declare that it is not necessary for them to visit the area in person to find the required spot that the topic moves from the remotely possible to the absurdly improbable. Some practitioners of this art state that they are able to perform even more marvellous feats such as determining the sex of chickens while still in the egg, or diagnosing illness by studying the movements of a pendulum held over a blood sample from the sick individual. Such claims when put to simple scientific test have almost invariably turned out as fiascos. Yet belief in dowsing, water-divining, and the like is still very widespread.

There is an important link between radiesthesia and the pseudo-science of *radionics*, which holds that the twig or pendulum can be superseded by complicated equipment built vaguely according to electronic principles. A typical radionic device consists of a box covered with knobs, dials, etc., by which the practitioner "tunes in" to the "vibration" given off by an object, such as a blood spot, a piece of hair, or even a signature. By the proper interpretation of the readings from the equipment the illness, or even the mental state, of the individual whose blood, hair, or signature is being tested, may be ascertained. The originator of radionics seems to have been a Dr. Albert Abrams who engaged in medical practice using radionic devices in America in the 1920s and 30s. The principal exponent in this country was the late George de la Warr who manufactured radionic boxes for diagnosis and treatment of illnesses, and even a "camera" which he believed to be capable of photographing thought. In a sensational court case in 1960 a woman who had purchased one of the diagnostic devices sued de la Warr for fraud. After a long trial the case was dismissed, the Judge commenting that while he had no good evidence that the device worked as claimed, he felt that de la Warr sincerely believed in its validity and thus was not guilty of fraud or misrepresentation.

Ranters, a fanatical antinomian (the doctrine that Christians are not bound to keep the law of God) and pantheistic sect in Commonwealth England. The name was also applied to the Primitive Methodists because of their noisy preaching.

Rationalism is defined as "the treating of reason as the ultimate authority in religion and the rejection of doctrines not consonant with reason." In practice, rationalism has a double significance: (1) the doctrine as defined above, and (2) a 19th cent. movement which was given to what was then known as "free-thought," "secularism," or agnosticism—*i.e.*, it was in

the positive sense anti-religious and was represented by various bodies such as the Secular Society, the National Secular Society, and the Rationalist Press Association (founded in 1899).

In the first sense, which implies a particular philosophical attitude to the universe and life, rationalism is not easy to pin down although, at first sight, it would appear that nothing could be simpler. Does it mean the use of pure reason and logic or does it mean, on the other hand, the use of what is generally called the "scientific method " based on a critical attitude to existing beliefs? If we are thinking in terms of the use of pure reason and logic then the Roman Catholic Church throughout most of its history has maintained, not that the whole truth about religion can be discovered by reason, but as St. Thomas Aquinas held, the basis of religion—*e.g.* the existence of God—can be rationally demonstrated. Nobody could have made more use of logic than the schoolmen of the Middle Ages, yet not many people today would accept their conclusions, nor would many non-Catholics accept St. Thomas's proofs of the existence of God even when they themselves are religious. The arguments of a First Cause or Prime Mover or the argument from Design on the whole leave us unmoved, partly because they do not lead us to the idea of a *personal God*, partly because we rightly distrust logic and pure reason divorced from facts and know that, if we begin from the wrong assumptions or premises, we can arrive at some very strange answers. If the existence of a Deity can be proved by reason, then one can also by the use of reason come to the conclusions, or rather paradoxes, such as the following: God is by definition all good, all knowing, all powerful—yet evil exists (because if it does not exist then it cannot be wrong to say "there is no God "). But if evil exists, then it must do so either because of God (in which case He is not all good) or in spite of God (in which case He is not all powerful).

Arguments of this sort do not appeal to the modern mind for two historical reasons: (1) many of us have been brought up in the Protestant tradition which—at least in one of its aspects—insists that we must believe in God by faith rather than by logic and in its extreme form insists on God as revealed by the "inner light "; (2) our increasing trust in the scientific method of observation, experiment and argument. Thus, no matter what Aristotle or St. Thomas may say about a Prime Mover or a First Cause, we remain unconvinced since at least one scientific theory suggests that the universe did not have a beginning and if scientific investigation proved this to be so, then we should be entirely indifferent to what formal logic had to say.

The secularist and rationalist movements of the 19th cent. were anti-religious—and quite rightly so—because at that time there were serious disabilities imposed even in Britain by the Established Church on atheism or agnosticism and freedom of thought. They are of little significance now because very little is left, largely thanks to their efforts, of these disabilities.

Finally, although most people are likely to accept the scientific method as the main means of discovering truth, there are other factors which equally make us doubt the value of " pure " logic and reason unaided by observation. The first of these is the influence of Freud which shows that much of our reasoning is mere rationalising—*e.g.*, we are more likely to become atheists because we hated our father than because we can prove that there is no God. The second is the influence of a movement in philosophy which, in the form of logical positivism or logical analysis, makes us doubt whether metaphysical systems have any meaning at all. Today, instead of asking ourselves whether Plato was right or wrong, we are much more likely to ask whether he did anything but make for the most part meaningless noises. Religion is in a sense much safer today than it ever was in the 19th cent. when it made foolish statements over matters of science that could be *proved* wrong; now we tend to see it as an emotional attitude to the universe or God (a "feeling of being at home in the universe," as William James put it) which can no more be proved or disproved than being in love.

Realism is a word which has so many meanings, and such contradictory ones, in various spheres, that it is difficult to define. We shall limit ourselves to its significance in philosophy. In philosophy, "realism" has two different meanings, diametrically opposed. (1) The most usual meaning is the one we should least expect from the everyday sense of the word—*i.e.*, it refers to all those philosophies from Plato onwards which maintained that the world of appearance is illusory and that ideas, forms, or universals are the only true realities, belonging to the world beyond matter and appearance—the world of God or mind. In early mediaeval times St. Thomas Aquinas was the chief exponent of this doctrine which was held by the scholastics as opposed to the Nominalists (*q.v.*). (2) In its modern everyday meaning "realism" is the belief that the universe is real and not a creation of mind, that there is a reality that causes the appearance, the "thing-in-itself" as Kant described it. Material things may not really be what they appear to be (*e.g.* a noise is not the "bang" we experience but a series of shock-waves passing through the atmosphere), yet, for all that, we can be sure that matter exists and it is very possible (some might add) that mind does not.

Reformation, the great religious movement of the 16th cent., which resulted in the establishment of Protestantism. John Wyclif (d. 1384), John Hus (d. 1415) and others had sounded the warning note, and when later on Luther took up the cause in Germany, and Zwingli in Switzerland, adherents soon became numerous. The wholesale vending of indulgences by the papal agents had incensed the people, and when Luther denounced these things he spoke to willing ears. After much controversy, the reformers boldly propounded the principles of the new doctrine, and the struggle for religious supremacy grew bitter. They claimed justification (salvation) by faith, and the use as well as the authority of the Scriptures, rejecting the doctrine of transubstantiation, the adoration of the Virgin and Saints, and the headship of the Pope. Luther was excommunicated. But the Reformation principles spread and ultimately a great part of Germany, as well as Switzerland, the Low Countries, Scandinavia, England, and Scotland were won over to the new faith. In England Henry VIII readily espoused the cause of the Reformation, his own personal quarrel with the Pope acting as an incentive. Under Mary there was a brief and sanguinary reaction, but Elizabeth gave completeness to the work which her father had initiated. *See* Lutheranism, Calvinism, Presbyterianism, Baptists, Methodism.

Renaissance is defined in the *Oxford English Dictionary* as: "The revival of art and letters, under the influence of classical models, which began in Italy in the 14th century." It is a term which must be used with care for the following reasons: (1) Although it was first used in the form *rinascita* (re-birth) by Vasari in 1550 and people living at that time certainly were aware that something new was happening, the word had no wide currency until used by the Swiss historian Jacob Burckardt in his classic *The Civilization of the Renaissance in Italy* (1860). (2) The term as used today refers not only to art in its widest sense but to a total change in man's outlook on life which extended into philosophical, scientific, economic, and technical fields. (3) Spreading from Italy there were renaissance movements in France, Spain, Germany, and northern Europe, all widely different with varying delays in time. As the historian Edith Sichel says: "Out of the Italian Renaissance there issued a new-born art; out of the Northern Renaissance there came forth a new-born religion. There came forth also a great school of poetry, and a drama the greatest that the world had seen since the days of Greece. The religion was the offspring of Germany and the poetry that of England."

The real cause of the Renaissance was not the fall of Constantinople, the invention of printing, or the discovery of America, though these were phases in the process; it was, quite simply,

money. The birth of a new merchant class gave rise to individualist attitudes in economic affairs which prepared the way for individualism and humanism. The new wealthy class in time became patrons of the arts whereas previously the Church had been the sole patron and controller. Thus the artist became more free to express himself, more respected, and being more well-to-do could afford to ignore the Church and even, in time, the views of his patrons.

It is true that art continued to serve to a considerable extent the purposes of faith, but it was judged from the standpoint of art. Mediaeval art was meant to elevate and teach man; Renaissance art to delight his senses and enrich his life. From this free and questing spirit acquired from economic individualism came the rise of modern science and technology; here Italy learned much from the Arab scholars who had translated and commented upon the philosophical, medical, and mathematical texts of antiquity, while denying themselves any interest in Greek art and literature. Arabic-Latin versions of Aristotle were in use well into the 16th cent. The Byzantine culture, though it had preserved the Greek tradition and gave supremacy to Plato, had made no move forward. But the Greek scholars who fled to Italy after the fall of Constantinople brought with them an immense cargo of classical manuscripts. The recovery of these Greek masterpieces, their translation into the vernaculars, and the invention of printing, made possible a completer understanding of the Greek spirit. It was the bringing together of the two heritages, Greek science, and Greek literature, that gave birth to a new vision. But it was not only Aristotle and Plato who were being studied but Ovid, Catullus, Horace, Pliny and Lucretius. What interested Renaissance man was the humanism of the Latin writers, their attitude to science, their scepticism.

The period *c.* 1400–1500 is known as the Early Renaissance. During this time such painters as Masaccio, Uccello, Piero della Francesca, Botticelli, and Giovanni Bellini were laying the foundations of drawing and painting for all subsequent periods including our own. They concerned themselves with such problems as anatomy, composition, perspective, and representation of space, creating in effect a grammar or textbook of visual expression. The term High Renaissance is reserved for a very brief period when a pure, balanced, classical harmony was achieved and artists were in complete control of the techniques learned earlier. The High Renaissance lasted only from *c.* 1500 to 1527 (the date of the sack of Rome), yet that interval included the earlier works of Michelangelo, most of Leonardo's, and all the Roman works of Raphael.

Ritualism, a tendency which, during the 19th cent., developed in the High Church section of the Church of England to make use of those vestments, candles, incense, etc. which are usually regarded as features of the Church of Rome. Since some opposition was aroused, a Ritual Commission was appointed in 1904 to take evidence and try to find some common basis on which High and Low Church could agree with respect to ceremonial. The report of 1906 in effect recommended the giving of greater powers to bishops to suppress objectionable practices. Although they are often associated together, it is worth while pointing out that there was no special connection between the Oxford Movement or Tractarians (*q.v.*) and Ritualism because Pusey disliked ritual and even Newman, who eventually went over to Rome, held extremely simple services at his church of St. Mary's.

Roman Catholic Church, the Christian organisation which acknowledges the Pope as the lawful successor of St. Peter, the apostle appointed by Christ to be the head of His Church. The reforming impulse at the Second Vatican Council (1962–5), summoned by Pope John, set in train movements towards religious unity and the reform and modernisation of the Church. Pope Paul made changes in the government and liturgy of the Church but refused to allow birth control, the marriage of priests and a greater role for women in the Roman Catholic Church. In fact the apparent trend towards increasing liberalism within the body of the Church has been reversed with a highly conservative papal pronouncement on sexual conduct which produced sharp controversy in the early part of 1976. The 1970s, incidentally, have shown a sharp decline in the number of worshippers at Roman Catholic Churches in Europe and America—a development of considerable significance in the light of the Roman Church's traditional solid support from its rank and file. *See also* Cardinals, Section L.

Romantic Movement or **Romanticism** is the name given not so much to an individual way of thinking but to the gradual but radical transformation of basic human values that occurred in the Western world round about the latter part of the 18th cent. It was a great breakthrough in European consciousness and arose through the writings of certain men living during the half-century or more following, say, 1760. It arose then because both time and place were propitious for the birth of these new ideas. There was a revolution in basic values—in art, morals, politics, religion, etc. The new view was of a world transcending the old one, infinitely larger and more varied.

To understand the Romantic movement it is necessary first to take note of the climate of thought preceding the great change; then to account for its beginning in Germany where it did (*see* Pietism) during the latter part of the 18th cent., and finally to appraise the writings of those men whose ideas fermented the new awakening. Briefly, the shift was away from French classicism and from belief in the all-pervasive power of human reason (the Enlightenment) towards the unfettered freedom that the new consciousness was able to engender. What mattered was to live a passionate and vigorous life, to dedicate oneself to an ideal, no matter what the cost (*e.g.*, Byron).

The ideas of the Enlightenment (*e.g.*, Fontenelle, Voltaire, Montesquieu) had been attacked by the Germans Hamann and Herder and by the ideas of the English philosopher Hume, but Kant, Schiller, and Fichte, Goethe's novel *Wilhelm Meister*, and the French Revolution all had profound effects on the aesthetic, moral, social, and political thought of the time. Friedrich Schlegel (1772–1829) said: " There is in man a terrible unsatisfied desire to soar into infinity; a feverish longing to break through the narrow bonds of individuality." Romanticism undermined the notion that in matters of value there are objective criteria which operate between men. Henceforth there was to be a resurgence of the human spirit, deep and profound, that is still going on.

Rosicrucians, an ancient mystical society founded in the 16th cent. by Christian Rosenkreuz which attempted to forge a theoretical link between the great Egyptian religions and the Church of Rome, drawing rituals and philosophy from both camps. The Society did not long survive the death of its founder (he managed to reach the age of 106 incidentally) but has been revived in succeeding centuries by a series of rivalling factions. Perhaps the most famous of these is the Rosicrucian Order (A.M.O.R.C.) which has become well-known in the Western world as a result of its heavy advertising in the popular press. Founded by the American H. Spencer Lewis, this offers a simple and good-natured doctrine preaching the Brotherhood of Man, the reincarnation of the soul and the immense latent potential of the human mind. As with many American-based organisations of this kind, the boundary between business and religion is hard to define. The A.M.O.R.C. Rosicrucian order, for example, proudly advertises that it is not a religion, and it is probably best summed up as a modern secret society which serves an important function in the lives of many people of mystical inclinations.

S

Salvation Army. The religious movement which in 1878 became known by this name arose from the Christian Mission meetings which the Rev. William Booth and his devoted wife had held in the East End of London for the previous thirteen years. Its primary aim was, and still is, to preach the gospel of Jesus Christ to men and women untouched by ordinary religious efforts. The founder devoted his life to the salvation of the submerged classes whose conditions at that time were unspeakably dreadful. Originally his aim had been to convert people and then send them on to the churches, but he soon found that few religious bodies would accept these " low-class " men and women. So it was that social work became part of their effort. Practical help like the provision of soup-kitchens, accompanied spiritual ministration. Soon, in the interests of more effective " warfare " against social evils, a military form of organisation, with uniforms, brass bands, and religious songs, was introduced. Its magazine *The War Cry* gave as its aim " to carry the Blood of Christ and the Fire of the Holy Ghost into every part of the world."

General Booth saw with blinding clarity that conversion must be accompanied by an improvement of external conditions. Various books had earlier described the terrible conditions of the slums, but in 1890 he produced a monumental survey entitled *In Darkest England and the Way Out*. From that time forward the Army was accepted and its facilities made use of by the authorities. Today the Army's spiritual and social activities have spread to countries all over the world; every one, no matter what class, colour, or creed he belongs to is a " brother for whom Christ died."

Sandemanians or **Glassites,** an obscure religious sect whose sole claim to fame is that one of its members was the great Michael Faraday, founder of the science of electromagnetism, who never failed to attend its Sunday services.

Sceptics. From Thales of Miletus (*c.* 624–565 B.C.) to the Stoics in the 4th cent. B.C. philosophers had been trying to explain the nature of the universe; each one produced a different theory and each could, apparently, prove that he was right. This diversity of views convinced the Sceptic school founded by Pyrrho (*c.* 360–270 B.C.) that man is unable to know the real nature of the world or how it came into being. In place of a futile search for what must be for ever unknowable, the Sceptics recommended that men should be practical, follow custom, and accept the evidence of their senses.

Schoolmen. From the time of Augustine to the middle of the 9th cent. philosophy, like science, was dead or merely a repetition of what had gone before. But about that time there arose a new interest in the subject, although (since by then Western Europe was entirely under the authority of the Catholic Church) the main form it took was an attempt to justify Church teaching in the light of Greek philosophy. Those who made this attempt to reconcile Christian beliefs with the best in Plato and Aristotle were known as " schoolmen " and the philosophies which they developed were known as " scholasticism." Among the most famous schoolmen must be counted John Scotus Erigena (*c.* 800–*c.* 877), born in Ireland and probably the earliest; St. Anselm, archbishop of Canterbury (1033–1109); the great Peter Abelard whose school was in Paris (1079–1142); Bernard of Chartres, his contemporary; and the best-known of all, St. Thomas Aquinas of Naples (1225–74), who was given the name of the " Angelic Doctor."

The philosophies of these men are discussed under various headings (God and Man, Determinism and Free-will), but being severely limited by the Church their doctrines differed from each other much less than those of later philosophical schools. However, one of the great arguments was between the orthodox Realists (*q.v.*) and the Nominalists (*q.v.*) and a second was between the Thomists (or followers of St. Thomas Aquinas) and the Scotists (followers of John Duns Scotus—not to be confused with John Scotus Erigena). The two latter schools were known as the Ancients, whilst the followers of William of Occam, the Nominalist, were known as the Terminalists. All became reconciled in 1482 in face of the threat from humanism of which the great exponent was Erasmus of Rotterdam (1466–1536) who hated scholasticism.

Scientology, an unusual quasi-philosophical system started by the American science-fiction writer L. Ron Hubbard, which claims to be able to effect dramatic improvement in the mental and physical well-being of its adherents. Originally developed in the United States as "Dianetics, the modern science of mental health," it was hailed in Hubbard's first book to be "a milestone for Man comparable to his discovery of fire and superior to his inventions of the wheel and the arch." Such extravagant statements exemplify the literature of the movement, which in the late 1950s began to expand in England when its founder came to live in East Grinstead. Followers of Dianetics and Scientology advance within the cult through a series of levels or grades, most reached by undertaking courses of training and tuition, payment for which may amount to hundreds and, in total, even thousands of pounds. These courses consist largely of specialised and complex mental exercises based on Hubbard's own variation of psychology and known as "processing" and "auditing." One of the principal goals of a Scientologist is the attainment of the state known as "Clear" (roughly speaking, one "cleared" of certain mental and physical handicaps) when it is believed he (she) will be a literally superior being, equipped with a higher intelligence and a greater command over the pattern of his (her) own life.

The Scientologists' claims that their movement is a genuine religion have generally been met with resistance from establishment bodies. In recent years the situation seems to have changed however, and acceptance of their claim is now much more widespread. Religious services moulded on the movement's philosophy are held, and the organisation is becoming involved in social work, notably the drug rehabilitation scheme known as Narconon.

Shakers, members of a revivalist group, styled by themselves "The United Society of Believers in Christ's Second Appearing," who seceded from Quakerism in 1747 though adhering to many of the Quaker tenets. The community was joined in 1758 by Ann Lee, a young convert from Manchester, who had "revelations" that she was the female Christ; "Mother Ann" was accepted as their leader. Under the influence of her prophetic visions she set out with nine followers for "Immanuel's land" in America and the community settled near Albany, capital of New York state. They were known as the "Shakers" in ridicule because they were given to involuntary movements in moments of religious ecstasy.

Central to their faith was the belief in the dual role of God through the male and female Christ: the male principle came to earth in Jesus; the female principle, in "Mother Ann." The sexes were equal and women preached as often as men at their meetings which sometimes included sacred dances—nevertheless the two sexes, even in dancing, kept apart. Their communistic way of living brought them economic prosperity, the Shakers becoming known as good agriculturists and craftsmen, noted for their furniture and textiles. After 1860, however, the movement began to decline and few, if any, are active today.

Shamans, the medicine men found in all primitive societies who used their magical arts to work cures, and protect the group from evil influences. The *shaman* was a man apart and wore special garments to show his authority. Shamanism with its magical practices, incantations, trances, exhausting dances, and self-torture is practised even today by tribes that have survived in a primitive state of culture.

Shiites or Shia, a heretical Moslem sect in Persia, opposed by the orthodox Sunnites. The dispute, which came almost immediately after the death of the Prophet and led to bitter feuding, had little to do with matters of doctrine as such, but with the succession. After Mohammed's death, there were three possible claimants: Ali, the husband of his daughter Fatima, and two others, one of whom gave up his claim in favour of the other, Omar. The orthodox selected Omar, who was shortly assassinated, and the same happened to his successor so Ali was passed over again. The Shiites are those who maintain that

Ali was the true vicar of the Prophet, and that the three orthodox predecessors were usurpers.

Shintoism, literally means "teaching of the Gods" and is the specifically Japanese splinter version of Buddhism with a strong bias towards ancestor worship and the divine powers of natural forces. Unusual in that it had no recognised founder nor written dogma, Shintoism permeated Japanese life in a most vigorous way until the defeat of the country at the hands of the Allied Powers in 1945. In the 1500 years of its existence the Shinto religion produced tens of thousands of unique and beautiful shrines throughout Japan. Vast numbers of these were destroyed by bombing in the war, but a tolerant decision by the American airforce spared the Shinto capital, Kyoto, from air-attack. Shintoism was disestablished by the American occupying forces in 1945 and the Emperor Hirohito "abdicated" his divine powers. Current dissatisfaction among many Japanese with the worldly extravagance of their heavily industrialised society has led to a recent revival of interest in their ancient and selfless religion.

Sikhism. The Sikh community of the Punjab, which has played a significant part in the history of modern India, came into being during a period of religious revival in India in the 15th and 16th cent. It was originally founded as a religious sect by Guru (teacher) Nanak (1469–1538) who emphasised the fundamental truth of all religions, and whose mission was to put an end to religious conflict. He condemned the formalism both of Hinduism and Islam, preaching the gospel of universal toleration, and the unity of the Godhead, whether He be called Allah, Vishnu, or God. His ideas were welcomed by the great Mogul Emperor Akbar (1542–1605). Thus a succession of Gurus were able to live in peace after Nanak's death; they established the great Sikh centre at Amritsar, compiled the sacred writings known as the *Adi Granth,* and improved their organisation as a sect. But the peace did not last long, for an emperor arose who was a fanatical Moslem, in face of whom the last Guru, Govind Singh (1666–1708), whose father was put to death for refusal to embrace Islam, had to make himself a warrior and instil into the Sikhs a more aggressive spirit. A number of ceremonies were instituted by Govind Singh; admission to the fraternity was by special rite; caste distinctions were abolished; hair was worn long; the word singh, meaning lion, was added to the original name. They were able to organise themselves into 12 *misls* or confederacies but divisions appeared with the disappearance of a common enemy and it was not until the rise of Ranjit Singh (1780–1839) that a single powerful Sikh kingdom was established, its influence only being checked by the English, with whom a treaty of friendship was made. After the death of Ranjit Singh two Anglo-Sikh wars followed, in 1845–46, and 1848–49, which resulted in British annexation of the Punjab and the end of Sikh independence. In the two world wars the Sikhs proved among the most loyal of Britain's Indian subjects. The partitioning of the continent of India in 1947 into two states, one predominantly Hindu and the other predominantly Moslem, presented a considerable problem in the Punjab, which was divided in such a way as to leave 2 million Sikhs in Pakistan, and a considerable number of Moslems in the Indian Punjab. Although numbering less than 2 per cent. of the population (c. 8 million) the Sikhs are a continuing factor in Indian political life. In 1966 the Punjab was divided on a linguistic basis—Punjabi-speaking Punjab and Hindi-speaking Hariana.

Socialism, is a form of society in which men and women are not divided into opposing economic classes but live together under conditions of approximate social and economic equality, using in common the means that lie to their hands of promoting social welfare. The brotherhood of man inspires the aims of socialism in foreign, colonial, social, and economic policies alike. The word "socialism" first came into general use in England about 1834 in connection with Robert Owen's "village of co-operation" at New Lanark. About the middle of the 19th cent., Charles Kingsley and others established a form of Christian socialism, and William Morris, John Burns, and others founded a Socialist League in 1886. With the development of trade unions the socialist movement took a more practical trend. Fabianism (*q.v.*) associated in its early days with the names of Beatrice and Sidney Webb and George Bernard Shaw, aims at the gradual reorganisation of society by creating intelligent public opinion by education and legislation. The British Labour Party believes in peaceful and constitutional change to socialism by democratic methods based upon popular consent. The Labour Government of 1945–51 initiated a major period of social reform and public ownership. Though beset by economic difficulties, the 1964–70 Labour Government continued a policy of radical reform. The minority Labour Government (of February–October 1974) and the subsequent administration have continued this process, particularly in the area of state intervention in industry, although not all sections of the party are united on the extent of public ownership and state intervention. *See also* Section C, Part I.

Southcottians, followers of Joanna Southcott, who died in 1814 shortly after announcing that (although over 50) she was about to give birth to a divine human being named Siloh. Miss Southcott certainly produced all the symptoms of pregnancy, and was even examined by the Royal physician who pronounced her unquestionably " with child." Although she even went " into labour," no child, divine or otherwise, appeared and she seems to have died of something rather close to a broken heart. Her interesting symptoms would today be classed as " hysterical pregnancy "—a not uncommon condition which may mimic real pregnancy in a remarkable way. Joanna's followers remained loyal to her memory, however, and a tiny sect still survives to this day. Shortly before her death, incidentally, she handed to followers a number of locked and sealed boxes which she indicated contained, among other things, the secret of the universe. These were only to be opened 100 years after her death and then in the presence of 12 bishops. In 1927 one of these boxes unexpectedly turned up and it was ceremoniously opened at the Caxton Hall before a public audience. The organisers had to make do with only one bishop as most of the country's senior clerics pronounced themselves to be too busy to attend. Perhaps it was just as well for Miss Southcott's marvellous box was found to contain only a few rare coins, a horse pistol, a woman's embroidered nightcap, and a slightly improper novel, *The Surprises of Love*. One of the most endearing qualities of Joanna Southcott must have been her sense of humour.

Spiritualism is a religion which requires to be distinguished from psychical research (*q.v.*) which is a scientific attempt carried on both by believers and non-believers to investigate psychic phenomena including those not necessarily connected with " spirits "—*e.g.*, telepathy or clairvoyance and precognition. As a religion (although for that matter the whole of history is filled with attempts to get in touch with the " spirit world ") Spiritualism begins with the American Andrew Jackson Davis who in 1847 published *Nature's Divine Revelations*, a book which is still widely read. In this Davis states that on the death of the physical body, the human spirit remains alive and moves on to one or another of a considerable range of worlds or " spheres " where it commences yet another stage of existence. Since the spirit has not died, but exists with full (and possibly even expanded) consciousness, there should be no reason, Davis argues, why it should not make its presence known to the beings it has temporarily left behind on earth. In 1847, the year of the publication of Davis's book, two young girls, Margaret and Kate Fox, living in a farmhouse at Hydesville, New York, began apparently to act as unwitting mediums for attempts at such between-worlds communication. The girls were the focus for strange rappings and bangs which it was alleged defied normal explanation and which spelt out, in the form of a simple

alphabetical code, messages from the spirits of " the dead." The Fox sisters were later to confess that they had produced the raps by trickery, but by that time the fashion had spread across the world and before long " mediums " in all lands were issuing spirit communications (often in much more spectacular form). In the late 19th cent. Spiritualism went into a phase of great expansion and for various reasons attracted the attention of many scientists. Among these were Sir William Crookes, Sir Oliver Lodge, Professor Charles Richet, Alfred Russell Wallace, to say nothing of the brilliant and shrewd creator of Sherlock Holmes, Sir Arthur Conan Doyle. Today many people find it astonishing that people of such brilliance should find the phenomena of the seance room of more than passing interest, but the commitment of the Victorian scientists is understandable if we realise that Spiritualists, after all, claim to do no more than demonstrate as fact what all Christians are called on to believe—that the human personality survives bodily death. Furthermore, at the time of the late 19th cent. peak of Spiritualism, much less was known about human psychology and about the great limitations of sensory perception in typical seance conditions, when lights are dimmed or extinguished and an emotionally charged atmosphere generated. Today the most striking phenomena of the seance room— the alleged materialisation of spirit people and the production of such half-spiritual, half-physical substances as ectoplasm—are rarely if ever produced at Spiritualist meetings. Some say that the most probable explanation for this is that too many fraudulent mediums have been caught out and publicly exposed for the profession to be worth the risks. The movement today, which still has a large and often articulate following, now concentrates on the less controversial areas of " mental mediumship," clairvoyance and the like, or on the very widespread practice of " spirit healing." Where people are not deliberately deluded by bogus mediums acting for monetary reward (a practice which largely died out with the " death " of ectoplasm) Spiritualism probably has an important role to play in the life of many people whose happiness has been removed by the death of a much loved relative or spouse. It certainly does not deserve the violent attacks that are often made on it by orthodox clergy who allege that Spiritualists are communicating not with the souls of the departed but with the devil or his emissaries. To many people today belief in the devil would be looked upon as somewhat odder than belief in the survival of the individual spirit after death.

State and Man. Most of the early civilisations such as those of Egypt and Babylonia were theocratic, that is to say, they were arranged in a hierarchy with, at the peak, a king who was also an incarnation of the god. Needless to say, in such circumstances there was no room for philosophising about the nature of the state and the relationship which ought to exist between state and citizens. As usual, we have to turn to ancient Greece for the beginnings of thought about this problem. We do so as briefly as possible since in general it is only the later philosophers whose work has much contemporary interest and, in any case, most people today realise that the political philosophy of a particular time is bound to reflect the actual conditions prevailing then and as such is of mainly theoretical interest today.

The Greek Approach. The early pre-Socratic philosophers Democritus and the Pythagorean school, for example, held that the individual should subordinate himself to the whole; they had no doubt that the citizen's first duty was to the state. The Greeks until the time of Plato were not really thinking in terms of individual rights, nor had they given much thought to what form the state should take—they simply accepted it. The first great attempt to describe the ideal state is to be found in Plato's *The Republic* which is referred to elsewhere (*see* Education). His pupil Aristotle did not try to form a utopia but made many comments on the nature of government. Thus, while agreeing that the state was more important than any individual person, he distinguished between good and bad states, and pointed out that to the extent that the state does not enable its citizens to lead virtuous and useful lives it is evil. A good constitution must recognise the inequalities between human beings and confer on them rights according to their abilities: among these inequalities are those of personal ability, property, birth, and status, as freeman or slave. The best forms of rule were monarchy, aristocracy, and democracy; the worst forms—tyranny, oligarchy (or rule of a powerful few), and ochlocracy (or mob-rule). The later Greek thinkers of Hellenistic times held two opposed points of view. The Epicureans (*q.v.*) taught that all social life is based upon self-interest and we become members of a group for our own convenience; therefore there are no absolute rights and laws—what is good is what members decide at that time to be good, and when they change their minds the law must change too. Injustice is not an evil in any god-given sense; we behave justly simply because if injustice became the general rule, we ourselves should suffer. The Stoics (*q.v.*), on the other hand, held that the state must dominate the individual completely and everyone must carry out, first and foremost, his social duties and be willing to sacrifice everything for it; but the state of the Stoics was no narrowly national one, but one that strove to become a universal brotherhood.

The Christian Approach. The orthodox Christian view is expressed in St. Augustine's book *The City of God.* Here it is held that the church, as the worldly incarnation of the City of God, is to be supreme over the state, and the head of the church is to be supreme over secular rulers. In addition it must be recognised that, whilst the secular ruler can make mistakes, the church does not, since it is the representative of God's kingdom on earth.

The Secular State. During the Renaissance (*q.v.*) people began to think for themselves and the results of their cogitations were not always pleasant; for it was during this time that many rulers, petty and otherwise, were seeking absolute authority. Two notable thinkers at this stage were Niccolo Machiavelli (1469–1527) in Italy and Thomas Hobbes (1588–1679) in England, where, of course, the Renaissance arrived later in history. Both supported absolute monarchy against the former domination of the church. The name of Machiavelli has become a by-word for any behaviour that is cunning and unscrupulous, but he was not really as bad as he is usually painted. It is, indeed, true that in his book *The Prince* he showed in the greatest detail the methods by which a ruler could gain absolute control and destroy civic freedom, but this despotism was intended as merely a necessary intermediate stage towards his real idea which was a free, united Italian nation wholly independent of the church. Hobbes was a materialist whose thesis was that man is naturally a ferocious animal whose basic impulse is war and pillage and the destruction of whatever stands in his way to gain his desires. But if he allowed himself to behave in this way his life would be " nasty, brutish, and short " so he creates a society in which he voluntarily gives up many of his rights and hands them over to a powerful ruler in his own interest. But having done this he must obey; even when the ruler is unjust, as he has no right to complain because anything is better than a return to his natural state. The religion of the king must be the religion of the people and the only things no ruler has the right to do is to cause a man to commit suicide or murder or to make him confess to a crime.

Views of Locke: Live and Let Live. John Locke (1632–1704) disagreed with these views. Man is naturally peaceful and co-operative and therefore social life comes readily to him. He sets up an authority in order to preserve the group and that is why laws are made; but the function of the state is strictly limited to maintaining the public good and beyond this men are to be left free. Therefore absolute power and the doctrine of the Divine Right of Kings were wrong because power ultimately rests with the people who have the right to make and break governments. It is also wrong that those who make the laws should be able to execute them. This is the important British doctrine of the separation of powers between the legislature and the executive which, in Britain and America, is regarded as one of the bases of democracy.

Rousseau's Social Doctrine. The only other views we need consider here are those of Jean-Jacques Rousseau (1712–78) and Herbert Spencer (1820–1903), since the views of the two important intervening figures, Hegel and Karl Marx, are dealt with elsewhere (*see* Dialectical Materialism) and after Spencer we come to a stage where political philosophy begins to merge with sociology and the social sciences. Rousseau is a puzzling figure. On the one hand he has been hailed as the prophet of freedom and on the other as the father of modern totalitarianism. His book *Social Contract* (1762) begins with the words: " Man is born free, and everywhere he is in chains." He says that he is in favour, not merely of democracy, but of direct democracy in which everyone has to give his assent to all measures as in the Greek city-states and in Geneva, of which city he was a citizen. (This method is still in force in respect of some measures in the Swiss cantons.) Natural society is based on a " social contract " or mutual agreement and Rousseau speaks of a " return to nature " which would ensure the sovereignty of the people at all times. Thus far, he seems to agree with Locke but soon we find that he is more akin to Hobbes, since (as we are learning in our own day) nothing is more tyrannical than the absolute rule of all the people. (Public opinion is more Hitlerian than Hitler.) As it turns out, then, the " social contract " consists in " the total alienation of each associate, together with all his rights, to the whole community " and " each of us puts his person and all his power in common under the supreme direction of the general will." Rousseau admired direct democracy in the small city-state, but if his doctrine is applied to large city-states, then the " general will " becomes absolute. It is in this sense that he is regarded as the forerunner of totalitarianism. Herbert Spencer is quoted only as an example of the inappropriate application of a biological theory to social issues. Influenced by Darwin's thesis of natural selection, he saw in society a struggle in which the fittest survived and the less fit perished. Each individual had the right to preserve himself, but in the case of human beings this depended upon group life in which, to some extent, each individual is limited by the rights of others. But this should not go too far, and he condemned the socialism of J. S. Mill which (*a*) would give over-much protection to the unfit, and (*b*) would give the state powers which it has no right to since the best government is the least government. In accordance with Darwinism free competition was essential.

Stoics, the followers of Zeno, a Greek philosopher in the 4th cent. B.C., who received their name from the fact that they were taught in the Stoa Poikile or Painted Porch of Athens. They believed that since the world is the creation of divine wisdom and is governed by divine law, it is man's duty to accept his fate. Zeno conceived virtue to be the highest good and condemned the passions. (*See* God and Man, State and Man, Determinism and Free-will for a more detailed account of their beliefs.)

Subud, a cultish movement surrounding the Javanese mystic Pak Subuh which established its headquarters in England in 1958 and made newspaper headlines because of alleged " miracle " cures of both psychological and physical ills. The basis of Subud (which is a contraction of three Sanskrit words, Susila Budhi Dharma, meaning " the right living of the soul ") is a single spiritual exercise, the *latihan*, in which the individual comes into contact with, or is overwhelmed by a metaphysical force of some kind which is supposed to produce great mental and physical changes. During the latihan people may make strange movements, some violent, and utter unusual cries or chants. Now better known in America than in Britain, Subud did not live up to the expectations of its early followers, many of whom were people of considerable intelligence and professional standing. It is of particular interest because it represents a unique incursion of a rather obscure Eastern cult into Western life, and suggests again that there is growing dissatisfaction in many quarters with orthodox religion and its contribution to the philosophy of the modern world.

Sunnites, the orthodox sect of Islam as contrasted with the Shiites or Shia (q.v.).

Swedenborgianism. The Church of the New Jerusalem, based on the writings of Emanuel Swedenborg (1688–1772), was founded by his followers eleven years after his death. The New Church is regarded by its members not as a sect but as a new dispensation bearing the same relationship to Christianity as Christianity does to Judaism.

Synchronicity, an attempt by the psychologist, Carl Gustav Jung, to explain the apparently significant relationship between certain events in the physical universe which seem to have no obvious " causal " link. This rather involved concept is easily understood if one realises that almost all scientific and philosophical beliefs are based on the notion that the continuous process of change which is taking place in ourselves and in the universe around us is dependent upon a principle known as causality. We can express this another way by saying that an object moves because it has been pushed or pulled by another. We see because light strikes the retina and signals pass up the nervous system to the brain. A stone falls to the ground because the earth's gravity is pulling it towards its centre. etc., etc. For all practical purposes every event can be looked upon as being " caused " by some other prior event and this is obviously one of the most important principles of the operation of the universe. Jung, however, felt that there is a sufficiently large body of evidence to suggest that events may be linked in a significant (i.e., non-chance) way without there being any true causal relationship between them. The classic example he held to be the supposed predictive power of astrology by which there appears to be a relationship between the stellar configurations and the personality and life-pattern of individuals on earth. Jung was scientist enough to realise that there could be no causal connection between the aspect of the stars and the lives of people billions of miles from them, yet felt the evidence for astrology was strong enough to demand an alternative non-causal explanation. The trouble with synchronicity, which has not made much impact on the world of physics or of psychology, is that it is not really an explanation at all but merely a convenient word to describe some puzzling correspondences. The real question, of course, is whether there really are events occurring which are significantly but not causally linked, and most scientists today would hold that there were probably not. Still it was typical of the bold and imaginative mind of Jung to tackle head-on one of the principal mysteries of existence and come up with a hypothesis to attempt to meet it.

Syndicalism, a form of socialist doctrine which aims at the ownership and control of all industries by the workers, contrasted with the more conventional type of socialism which advocates ownership and control by the state. Since syndicalists have preferred to improve the conditions of the workers by direct action, e.g. strikes and working to rule, rather than through the usual parliamentary procedures, they have been closely related to anarchists (q.v.) and are sometimes described as anarcho-syndicalists. Under syndicalism there would be no state; for the state would be replaced by a federation of units based on functional economic organisation rather than on geographical representation. The movement had bodies in the United Kingdom, where guild socialism (q.v.) was strongly influenced by its doctrines, in France, Germany, Italy, Spain, Argentina, and Mexico, but these gradually declined after the first world war losing many members to the communists. Fascism (q.v.) was also strongly influenced by the revolutionary syndicalism of Georges Sorel in making use of his concept of the " myth " of the general strike " as an emotional image or

ideal goal to spur on the workers; with Mussolini the " myth " became that of the state. Mussolini was also influenced by Sorel's doctrine of violence and the justification of force. Syndicalism had a certain influence in the Labour Party in its early days, but was crushed by men like Ernest Bevin who began to fear that by involving the workers in direct responsibility for their industries, it would put them at a disadvantage when bargaining for wages.

T

Taoism, a religion which, although in a degenerate state, is still one of the great Eastern creeds. Its alleged founder, Lao-tze, is said to have been born in Honan about 604 B.C.; he is also said to be the author of the bible of Taoism, the *Tao-te-ching,* or in English *The Way of Life,* and to have disapproved of Confucius. This, if true, would hardly be surprising; for Taoism is eminently a mystical religion recommending doing nothing and resisting nothing, whereas Confucianism (q.v.) is eminently a practical code of living and its founder insisted on intervening in everything to do with social life. But the truth as revealed by modern scholarship is rather different. We are told that the poems of the *Tao-te-ching* are anonymous and probably originated among recluses in lonely valleys long before the time of Confucius; they were collected and given form at some time late in the 3rd cent. B.C. and their authorship attributed to Lao-tze. It is entirely possible that no such person ever existed (unlike Confucius, who certainly did), but if there were such a man he appears to have used a pseudonym since " Lao " is not a surname but an adjective meaning " old " and it was customary to attribute important works to old men on account of their supposed wisdom. Lao-tze simply means " the old philosopher," and although the *Tao-te-ching* is one of the most remarkable and instructive books ever written it is as anonymous as the Border Ballads.

It is apparent that the religion learned both from the ancient Chinese mystics and from Brahmanism: *Tao,* the Way, is impalpable, invisible, and incapable of being expressed in words. But it can be attained by virtue, by compassion, humility, and non-violence. Out of weakness comes true strength whereas violence is not only wrong but defeats its own ends. There is no personal God and such gods as men imagine are mere emanations of *Tao* which gives life to all things. *Tao* is Being. Works are worthless and internal renunciation is far better than anything that follows from the use of force because passive resistance convinces the other from within that he is in error, whereas violence only compels the external appearance of conviction whilst inwardly the individual is as before. " It is wealth to be content; it is wilful to force one's way on others."

Later Lao-tze became a divinity and indeed one of a Trinity each worshipped in the form of idols (which the founder had hated). Soon there was worship of the forces of nature: the stars, the tides, the sun and moon, and a thousand other deities among whom Confucius was one. The purest mysticism and wisdom had been utterly corrupted by contact with the world.

Telepathy and Clairvoyance. Telepathy is the alleged communication between one mind and another other than through the ordinary sense channels. Clairvoyance is the supposed faculty of " seeing " objects or events which, by reason of space and time or other causes, are not discernible through the ordinary sense of vision. Such claims have been made from time immemorial but it was not until this century that the phenomena were investigated scientifically. The first studies were undertaken by the Society for Psychical Research, which was founded in 1882 with Professor Henry Sidgwick as its first president. Since then it has carried out a scholarly programme of research without —in accordance with its constitution—coming to any corporate conclusions. In America the centre of this research was the Parapsychology Laboratory at Duke University (*see* Parapsychology) where at one time it was claimed clear scientific evidence for extra-sensory perception (ESP) had been obtained. These claims have been treated with great reservation by the majority of scientists but despite the belief that the study of ESP was going into eclipse, there remains a small but measurable residue of interest in scientific research in this area. It would be odd if some scientists were not interested in ESP because of the enormous weight of anecdotal evidence which has built up over centuries to support it. The weakness of the scientific as opposed to the casual evidence is however exemplified by the failure of ESP researchers to produce a reliable " repeatable " experiment.

Theism. *See* **God and Man.**

Theosophy (Sanskrit *Brahma Vidya* = divine wisdom), a system of thought that draws on the mystical teachings of those who assert the spiritual nature of the universe, and the divine nature of man. It insists that man is capable of intuitive insight into the nature of God. The way to wisdom, or self-knowledge, is through the practice of Yoga (*q.v.*). Theosophy has close connections with Indian thought through Vedic, Buddhist, and Brahmanist literature. The modern Theosophical Society was founded by Mme H. P. Blavatsky and others in 1875, and popularised by Mrs. Annie Besant.

Tractarianism, a Catholic revival movement, also known as the **Oxford Movement** (not to be confused with the so-called Oxford Group), which had its beginnings at Oxford in 1833. The leaders included the Oxford high churchmen E. B. Pusey, J. Keble and J. H. Newman. Through the *Tracts for the Times* (1833–41), a series of pamphlets which were sent to every parsonage in England, they sought to expose the dangers which they considered to be threatening the church from secular authority. The immediate cause of the movement was the Reform Act (1832) which meant that the state was no longer in the safe keeping of Tories and Churchmen but that power was falling into the hands of Liberals and Dissenters. They advocated a higher degree of ceremonial in worship nearer the Roman communion. In *Tract 90* (the last) Newman showed how the Thirty-nine Articles themselves, which were regarded as the bulwark of Protestantism, could be made to square with Roman doctrine. It was obvious which direction the movement was taking and the romanizing tendency was widely resented. In 1845 Newman went over to Rome. Pusey and Keble persisted in their efforts to secure recognition of Catholic liturgy and doctrine in the Anglican Church. Catholicism of the Anglican type (*i.e.*, Catholic in ritual, ceremony, and everything save submission to the Pope) is termed Anglo-Catholicism (*q.v.*).

Transcendental Meditation, popularised in the West by the Maharishi Mahesh Yogi, who achieved sensational worldwide publicity by his " conversion " of the Beatles a few years ago. This is a simple meditational system which it is claimed is an aid to relaxation and the reduction of psychological and physical stress. It is reported that the technique can be taught in under five minutes provided that someone trained by the Maharishi is the teacher. The pupil or would-be meditator is given a mantra—a meaningless word which acts as a focal point for the imagination—and letting his thoughts flow freely while sitting in a comfortable position. Extraordinary claims are made on behalf of the system. As with most cults, religious and occult systems, there is an initial psychological benefit to anyone who becomes deeply involved. Nevertheless, apart from this simple " participation-effect," there is some evidence that the body's autonomic functions (heart rate, respiratory cycle, brain waves, etc.) can be modified by certain individuals including yogis. Whether it is ultimately beneficial to be able to modify these autonomic functions or not is another matter. The latest evidence from laboratory studies in fact shows that subjects in the most relaxed phase of TM are in fact in a (quite normal) stage of light sleep. *See also* **Feedback Cult.**

Transmigration of Souls. *See* **Immortality.** **Buddhism, Hinduism.**

Transubstantiation, the conversion in the Eucharist of the bread and wine into the body and blood of Christ—a doctrine of the Roman Catholic Church.

Trotskyism, a form of communism supporting the views of Leon Trotsky, the assumed name of Lev Bronstein (1879–1940) who, in 1924, was ousted from power by Stalin and later exiled and assassinated in Mexico. Trotsky held that excessive Russian nationalism was incompatible with genuine international communism and that Stalin was concentrating on the economic development of the Soviet Union to an extent which could only lead to a bureaucratic state with a purely nationalist outlook. After the Hungarian uprising in 1956, which was ruthlessly suppressed by the Soviet Armed Forces, a wave of resignations from Western Communist parties took place, many of the dissident elements taking to Trotskyism in its place.

U

Ufology, cultish interest in the study of strange and unexplained aerial phenomena (unidentified flying objects, hence UFOs). *See* **Flying Saucers.**

Underground, the name given to an increasingly well-organised group, mainly composed of young people, university students, etc., which propagates anti-establishment and often highly controversial views. Its history, and to some extent its aims, are obscure, but it is a force of increasing power in Western society and its evolution is worth watching with care. The 1960s were years of great metamorphosis in Europe and America with rapid changes taking place in our attitudes to war and peace, to sex and morals, to marriage and family, to church and state. For large sections of the population these changes have been too rapid and too radical by far, but for others they have been too slow. In particular, the liberalisation of the law on the so-called " soft drugs," notably marijuana, is advocated by a vocal and increasing minority of young people. The expression of their views has been finding outlet in magazines and newspapers, privately published and printed, which reach a wide circulation despite the disinclination of many newsagents to stock them. These publications, while frequently containing material of an obscene and, to many people, highly offensive nature, also contain articles, features, and poems by writers of repute, many of whom contribute regularly to more orthodox publications and yet are sympathetic to the " underground cause." The word underground here, incidentally, refers back to the " underground press " that published revolutionary material at great risk in Nazi-occupied territories during the last war. With the exception of the risqué magazine *Private Eye*, which is largely concerned with acid political satire, the first of the genuine underground newsheets was the *International Times* (IT) which was followed in due course by *Oz* and *Rolling Stone*. All three papers were strongly anarchistic in flavour, uneven in literary merit, openly in favour of legalising marijuana (" pot "), and generally quite scandalous to the middle-class and middle-aged. This is not the place to argue the pros and cons of the underground arguments, nor to decide whether our " permissive society " has gone too far or not yet far enough. The important message that the appearance of the whole underground movement implies is that young people, because of greater financial independence, wider opportunities for travel, better education, and easier access to communication channels, such as printing presses, radio transmitters, etc., are beginning to make their admittedly controversial views more widely publicised. Furthermore, this is a trend which will inevitably develop rather than diminish and in the absence of authoritarian repression, these forces will have an increasing impact on our lives. By 1973 however signs of the decline in the power of the underground seemed to be appearing. One of its leading publications *Oz* had folded and its " drop-out " arguments seemed to be appealing less and less to students and young people. The most likely reason for this is that the movement in its decade of vigorous life was successful in inducing a number of reforms ranging from the propagation of a more liberal attitude to what may be printed, spoken about or shown on stage and screen, and an acceptance by school and university authorities that students should have a greater voice in academic affairs. These reforms, whether welcome or not to the middle-aged and the middle class, have nevertheless reached fruition in the " permissive " society which in turn appears to have taken much of the steam out of the underground itself. *See also* Weathermen.

Unitarianism has no special doctrines, although clearly, as the name indicates, belief is in the single personality of God, *i.e.*, anti-trinitarian. This general statement, however, can be interpreted with varying degrees of subtlety. Thus unitarian belief may range from a sort of Arianism which accepts that, although Christ was not of divine nature, divine powers had been delegated to him by the Father, to the simple belief that Christ was a man like anyone else, and his goodness was of the same nature as that of many other great and good men. Indeed, today, many Unitarians deny belief in a personal God and interpret their religion in purely moral terms, putting their faith in the value of love and the brotherhood of man. The Toleration Act (1689) excluded Unitarians but from 1813 they were legally tolerated in England. Nevertheless attempts were made to turn them out of their chapels on the ground that the preachers did not hold the views of the original founders of the endowments. But this ended with the Dissenting Chapels Act of 1845. In America no such difficulties existed, and in the Boston of the 19th cent. many of the great literary figures were openly unitarian both in belief and name: *e.g.*, Emerson, Longfellow, Lowell, and Oliver Wendell Holmes.

Utilitarianism, a school of moral philosophy of which the main proponents were J. S. Mill (1806–73) and Jeremy Bentham (1748–1832). Bentham based his ethical theory upon the utilitarian principle that the greatest happiness of the greatest number is the criterion of morality. What is good is pleasure or happiness; what is bad is pain. If we act on this basis of self-interest (pursuing what we believe to be our own happiness), then what we do will automatically be for the general good. The serious failing of this thesis is (1) that it makes no distinction between the quality of one pleasure and another, and (2) that Bentham failed to see that the law might not be framed and administered by men as benevolent as himself. J. S. Mill accepted Bentham's position in general but seeing its failings emphasised (1) that self-interest was an inadequate basis for utilitarianism and suggested that we should take as the real criterion of good the social consequences of the act; (2) that some pleasures rank higher than others and held that those of the intellect are superior to those of the senses. Not only is the social factor emphasised, but emphasis is also placed on the nature of the act.

Utopias. The name " utopia " is taken from a Greek word meaning " nowhere " and was first used in 1516 by Sir Thomas More (1478–1535) as the title of his book referring to a mythical island in the south Pacific where he sited his ideal society. Since then it has been used of any ideal or fanciful society, and here a few will be mentioned. (The reader may recall that Samuel Butler's 19th cent. novel, describing an imaginary society in New Zealand where criminals were treated and the sick punished, was entitled *Erewhon* which is the word " nowhere " in reverse.) It should be noted that not all utopias were entirely fanciful—*e.g.*, Robert Owen's and François Fourier's beliefs, although found to be impractical, were, in fact, tried out.

Sir Thomas More. More wrote at a time when the rise of the wool-growing trade had resulted in farming land being turned over to pasture and there was a great wave of unemployment and a rise in crime among the dispossessed. More began to think in terms of the mediaeval ideal of small co-operative communities in which class interests and personal gain played

a decreasing part, a society which would have the welfare of the people at heart both from the physical and intellectual points of view. His utopia was one in which there was no private property, because the desire for acquisition and private possessions lay at the root of human misery. There was, therefore, only common ownership of land and resources. Each class of worker was equipped to carry out its proper function in the economic scheme and each was fairly rewarded, for its share in production so that there was neither wealth nor poverty to inspire conflict. Nobody was allowed to be idle, until the time came for him to retire when he became free to enjoy whatever cultural pleasures he wished, but, since the system was devoid of the waste associated with competition, the working day would be only six hours. There was to be compulsory schooling and free medical care for everybody, full religious toleration, complete equality of the sexes, and a modern system of dealing with crime which was free from vindictiveness and cruelty. Government was to be simple and direct by democratically-elected officials whose powers would be strictly limited and the public expenditure kept under close scrutiny. It will be seen that More was far in advance of his age, and to most democratically-minded people in advance of an earlier utopia, Plato's *Republic*, which is described under the heading of Education.

James Harrington. James Harrington published his book *The Commonwealth of Oceana* in 1656 and offered it to Oliver Cromwell for his consideration but without tangible results. Better than any other man of his time Harrington understood the nature of the economic revolution which was then taking place, and, like More, saw the private ownership of land as the main cause of conflict. He put forward the theory that the control of property, particularly in the shape of land, determines the character of the political structure of the state; if property were universally distributed among the people the sentiment for its protection would naturally result in a republican form of government. The Commonwealth of Oceana was a society " of laws and not of men "—*i.e.*, it was to be legally based and structured so as to be independent of the good or ill-will of any individuals controlling it. Thus there must be a written constitution, a two-house legislature, frequent elections with a secret ballot, and separation of powers between legislature and executive—all today familiar features of parliamentary democracy, but unique in his time.

Saint-Simon. The utopias of the late 18th and 19th cent. come, of course, into the period of the industrial revolution and of laissez-faire capitalism. Individual enterprise and complete freedom of competition formed the outlook of the ruling class. Naturally the utopias of this period tended to have a strongly socialist tinge since such theories are obviously produced by those who are not satisfied with existing conditions. Saint-Simon's *New Christianity* (1825) is one such, and by many, Claude Henri, Comte de Saint-Simon (1760–1825) is regarded as the founder of French socialism. His book urged a dedication of society to the principle of human brotherhood and a community which would be led by men of science motivated by wholly spiritual aims. Production property was to be nationalised (or " socialised " as he describes the process) and employed to serve the public good rather than private gain; the worker was to produce according to his capacity and to be rewarded on the basis of individual merit; the principle of inheritance was to be abolished since it denied the principle of reward for accomplishment on which the society was to be founded. Saint-Simon's proposals were not directed towards the poorer classes alone, but to the conscience and intellect of all. He was deeply impressed with the productive power of the new machines and his scheme was, first and foremost, intended as a method of directing that power to the betterment of humanity as a whole.

Fourier. François Marie Charles Fourier (1772–1837). although by conviction a philosophical anarchist who held that human beings are naturally good if allowed to follow their natural desires, was the originator of what, on the face of it, one would suppose to be the most regimented of the utopias. It consisted of a system of "phalanxes" or co-operative communities each composed of a group of workers and technicians assured of a minimum income and sharing the surplus on an equitable basis. Agriculture was to be the chief occupation of each phalanx and industrial employment planned and so carefully assigned that work would become pleasant and creative rather than burdensome. One of his ideas was that necessary work should receive the highest pay, useful work the next, and pleasant work the least pay. The land was to be scientifically cultivated and natural resources carefully conserved. Most of the members' property was to be privately owned, but the ownership of each phalanx was to be widely diffused among members by the sale of shares. Such "parasitic and unproductive" occupations as stockbroker, soldier, economist, middle-man and philosopher would be eliminated and the education of children carried out along vocational lines to train them for their future employment.

The strange thing was that Fourier's suggestions appealed to many both in Europe and the U.S.A. and such men (admittedly no economic or technical experts) as Emerson, Thoreau, James Russell Lowell, and Nathaniel Hawthorne strongly supported them. An American Fourier colony known as Brook Farm was established and carried on for eight years when it was dissolved after a serious fire had destroyed most of its property.

Robert Owen. Robert Owen (1771–1858), a wealthy textile manufacturer and philanthropist, established communities founded on a kind of utopian socialism in Lanarkshire, Hampshire, and in America. Of his New Lanark community an American observer wrote: "There is not, I apprehend, to be found in any part of the world, a manufacturing community in which so much order, good government, tranquillity, and rational happiness prevail." The workers in Lanark were given better housing and education for their children, and it was administered as a co-operative self-supporting community in Scotland. Later in life Owen returned to sponsoring legislation that would remove some of the worst evils of industrial life in those days: reduction of the working day to twelve hours, prohibition of labour for children under the age of ten, public schools for elementary education, and so on. But he lived to see few of his reforms adopted. He also promoted the creation of co-operative societies, the formation of trades unions, labour banks and exchanges, the workers' educational movement, and even an Anglo-American federation. There can be no doubt that, if he saw little result himself, he left the imprint of his convictions to benefit future communities who may not even know his name.

V

Vitalism, the philosophical doctrine that the behaviour of the living organism is, at least in part, due to a vital principle which cannot possibly be explained wholly in terms of physics and chemistry. This belief was at one time held strongly by the late Professor C. E. M. Joad and is implicit in Henri Bergson's (1859–1941) theory of creative evolution. It was maintained by Bergson that evolution, like the work of an artist, is creative and therefore unpredictable; that a vague need exists beforehand within the animal or plant before the means of satisfying the need develops. Thus we might assume that sightless animals developed the need to become aware of objects before they were in physical contact with them and that this ultimately led to the origin of organs of sight. Earlier this century a form of vitalism described as "emergent evolution" was put forward. This theory maintains that when two or more simple entities come together there may arise a new property which none of them previously possessed. Today biologists would say that it is the *arrangement* of atoms that counts, different arrangements exhibiting different properties, and that biological organisation

is an essentially dynamic affair, involving the lapse of time.

W

Wahabis, members of an Arabian sect of Islam which originated in the teaching of Muhammad Ibn 'Abd-al-Wahab, born at the end of the 17th cent. He was deeply resentful of the Turkish rule which, in addition to its tyranny, had brought about innovations in the religion which Muhammad regarded as a perversion of its original form. He proceeded to reform Islam to its primitive conditions and impressed his beliefs on Mohammed Ibn Saud, a sheikh who spread them with the aid of his sword. Under the successors of Ibn Saud the power of the Wahabis spread over much of Arabia where it is dominant today in Saudi Arabia. Its particular characteristic is that it refuses to accept symbolic or mystical interpretations of the words of the Prophet and accepts quite literally the teaching of Islam. It is, in fact, a sort of Moslem fundamentalism. Although crushed by the Turks in 1811–15, the movement remains an important element in Mohammedanism.

Waldenses, a movement also known as "The Poor Men of Lyons," founded by Peter Waldo of that city about the same time, and in the same part of southern France, as the Albigenses (q.v.) with whom, however, they had nothing in common. Their main belief was a return to Apostolic simplicity, based on reading the Bible in their own language; their doctrines were somewhat similar to those of the Mennonites and the Quakers. However, they did not wish to separate themselves from the Church and were oringally protected by several Popes until the Lateran Council of 1215 excluded them mainly for the crime of preaching without ecclesiastical permission. From this time they were subjected to persecution, yet maintained some contact with the Church until the Reformation when they chose to take the side of the Protestants. Situated mainly on the sides of the Alps, half in Piedmont and half in France, they were persecuted or not according to the contemporary political convenience of the Dukes of Savoy, and the major attempt to destroy them called forth Oliver Cromwell's intervention and the famous sonnet of Milton. In spite of torture, murder, deportation, and even the kidnapping of their children, to have them brought up in the Roman Catholic faith, the sect survived, and still exists, having been granted full equality of rights with his Roman Catholic subjects by Charles Edward of Piedmont in 1848.

Weathermen, the rather incongruous name for the most radical and volatile of the many groups making up the so-called "underground" in the United States of America. Unlike most of the loosely-structured organisations involved in the growing anti-establishment front, the Weathermen appear to have direct rather than anarchistic political goals, taking a stand far to the left of traditional politics. Their avowed aim is the total overthrow of the current American political structure, with specific and carefully planned acts of violence as the tools of their trade and the civil police force as one of their prime targets. This has led to a series of bomb explosions, often cunningly planned, and brutal murders of police patrolmen which have deeply shocked the average American citizen. A particularly sinister and ominous feature, to most people's eyes, is the fact that the Weathermen appear to be largely drawn from the highly intelligent and well-educated strata, many of them with well-to-do and/or academic backgrounds. Members of this group make no secret of their contempt for the intellect and political attitudes of the American middle-class, and claim to demonstrate the impotence of Society by their ability to commit flagrant acts of violence with such ease and the equal ease with which they subsequently escape detection and arrest. The elusive nature of the organisation and its uncertain background have led to a number of fantastic speculations about its true origins. One of the oddest of these is the notion, widely held in America, that the Weathermen are in reality financed and backed by the country's extreme *right*—as a means of discrediting in the public eye the slow but steady move towards socialism that seems to be developing there. The Weathermen appear to have ceased activity in the early 1970s, but bomb outrages in early 1975 were once more perpetrated in their name.

Witchcraft. There are various interpretations and definitions of witchcraft from that of Pennethorne Hughes who states that "witchcraft, as it emerges into European history and literature, represents the old paleolithic fertility cult, plus the magical idea, plus various parodies of contemporary religions" to that of the fanatical Father Montague Summers who says that Spiritualism and witchcraft are the same thing. A leading authority on witchcraft, however, the late Dr. Margaret Murray, distinguishes between Operative Witchcraft (which is really Magic (*q.v.*)) and Ritual Witchcraft which, she says, "embraces the religious beliefs and ritual of the people known in late mediaeval times as 'witches.'" That there were such people we know from history and we know, too, that many of them—the great majority of them women—were tortured or executed or both. Many innocent people perished, especially after the promulgation of the bull *Summis desiderantes* by Pope Innocent VIII in 1484. Himself "a man of scandalous life," according to a Catholic historian, he wrote to "his dear sons," the German professors of theology, Johann Sprenger and Heinrich Kraemer, "witches are hindering men from performing the sexual act and women from conceiving . . ." and delegated them as Inquisitors "of these heretical pravities." In 1494 they codified in the *Malleus Maleficarum* (Hammer of Witches) the ecclesiastical rules for detecting acts of witchcraft. Dr. Murray points out that there have ordinarily been two theories about witchcraft: (1) that there were such beings as witches, that they possessed supernatural powers and that the evidence given at their trials was substantially correct; (2) that the witches were simply poor silly creatures who either deluded themselves into believing that they had certain powers or, more frequently, were tortured into admitting things that they did not do. She herself accepts a third theory: that there were such beings as witches, that they really did what they admitted to doing, but that they did not possess supernatural powers. They were in fact believers in the old religion of pre-Christian times and the Church took centuries to root them out. That there existed "covens" of witches who carried out peculiar rites Dr. Murray has no doubt whatever. The first to show that witchcraft was a superstition and that the majority of so-called witches were people suffering from mental illness was the physician Johann Weyer of Cleves (1515–88). His views were denounced by the Catholic Church. Few people realise how deeply the notion of witchcraft is implanted in our minds and how seriously its power is still taken. For example, the Witchcraft Act was not repealed in this country until the 1950s. Furthermore, as recently as 1944, when the allied armies were invading Europe, the Spiritualist medium Mrs. Helen Duncan was charged with witchcraft and actually sent to prison—a prosecution which brought forth caustic comments from the then prime minister, Winston Churchill. *See also* Demonism.

Women's Liberation Movement, the name given to a loosely organised collection of women drawn from all ages and walks of life which appears to be emerging as a latter-day "supersuffragette" movement. Unlike the original suffragette movement, however, which advocated "Votes for Women," the 1970s' version seems to have less definite aims. The principal argument hinges on the fact that with the development of highly efficient methods of contraception (the "pill") women need no longer be "slaves" to their family commitments and the traditional dominant and decision-making role of the male in our society must go. At the same time there should be no more wage or job discrimination against women. The movement has been going from strength to strength in America and is acquiring definite power in local and state politics. In Europe it has made somewhat less dramatic inroads. To many spectators, the movement's bible is the witty if polemical book *The Female Eunuch* by the Australian author Germaine Greer. An equally amusing, if perhaps somewhat less serious counterblast *The Manipulated Man* by the German woman doctor. Esther Vilar, traitorously takes an anti-feminist line. A small victory for the feminist cause has been the slow advance of the abbreviation "Ms" as an acceptable alternative for Mrs or Miss. 1975 saw the passage, in the United Kingdom, of the "Equal Opportunities Act"—a development which would have delighted the suffragettes of half a century ago.

World Congress of Faiths, an inter-religious movement which aims to break down barriers between faiths. The first step was taken by the world's parliament of religions held in Chicago in 1893; similar gatherings were held subsequently at intervals in Europe; but the actual organisation was formed in 1936 by Sir Francis Younghusband; and now an annual conference is held and educational activity carried on.

World Council of Churches, a union of Christian Churches from all over the world (including the Churches of the Protestant, Anglican, and Orthodox traditions, but excluding the Roman Catholic Church), engaged in extending Christian mission and unity throughout the world. All Churches which "accept our Lord Jesus Christ as God and Saviour" are eligible. This modern ecumenical movement stems from the great World Missionary Conference held at Edinburgh in 1910. The World Council was founded in 1948 and meets for consultation from time to time In the light of the 1975 assembly in Nairobi, the Churches plan to monitor the suppression of human rights throughout the world.

Y

Yoga, a Hindu discipline which teaches a technique for freeing the mind from attachment to the senses, so that once freed the soul may become fused with the universal spirit (*atman* or Brahman), which is its natural goal. This is the sole function of the psychological and physical exercises which the Yogi undertakes, although few ever reach the final stage of *Samadhi* or union with Brahman which is said to take place in eight levels of attainment. These are: (1) *Yama*, which involves the extinction of desire and egotism and their replacement by charity and unselfishness; (2) *Niyama*, during which certain rules of conduct must be adopted, such as cleanliness, the pursuit of devotional studies, and the carrying out of rituals of purification; (3) *Asana*, or the attainment of correct posture and the reduction to a minimum of all bodily movement (the usual posture of the concentrating Yogi is the "lotus position" familiar from pictures); (4) *Pranayama*, the right control of the life-force or breath in which there are two stages at which the practitioner hopes to arrive, the first being complete absorption in the act of breathing which empties the mind of any other thought, the second being the ability almost to cease to breathe which allegedly enables him to achieve marvellous feats of endurance; (5) *Pratyahara* or abstraction which means the mind's complete withdrawal from the world of sense; (6) *Dharana* in which an attempt is made to think of one thing only which finally becomes a repetition of the sacred syllable OM; (7) *dhyana*, meditation, which finally leads to (8) *Samadhi* the trance state which is a sign of the complete unity of soul with reality.

Yoga is very old, and when the sage Patanjali (*c.* 300 B.C.) composed the book containing these instructions, the *Yoga Sutras*, he was probably collecting from many ancient traditions. Some of the claims made by Yogis seem, to the Western mind, frankly incredible; but in the West and especially in recent years Yoga methods have been used at the lower levels in order to gain improved self-control, better posture, and improved health. Whether it achieves these ends is another matter, but the genuine Yogi regards this as a perversion of the nature and purpose of the discipline.

Z

Zen Buddhism, a Buddhist sect which is believed to have arisen in 6th cent. China but has flourished chiefly in Japan; for some reason it has of recent years begun to attract attention in the West thanks to the voluminous writings of Dr. D. T. Suzuki and the less numerous but doubtless much-read books of Mr. Christmas Humphreys. But the fact that these writings exist does not explain their being read, nor why of all possible Eastern sects this particular one should be chosen in our times. What is Zen's attraction and why should anyone take the trouble to read about something (the word " something " is used for reasons that will become evident) that is not a religion, has no doctrine, knows no God and no after-life, no good and no evil, and possesses no scriptures but has to be taught by parables which seem to be purposely meaningless? One of the heroes of Zen is the fierce-looking Indian monk Boddhidharma (fl. *c.* 516–34) who brought Buddhism to China, of whom it is recounted that when the Emperor asked him how much merit he had acquired by supporting the new creed, the monk shouted at him: " None whatever ! " The Emperor then wished to know what was the sacred doctrine of the creed and again the monk shouted: " It is empty—there is nothing sacred ! " Dr. Suzuki, having affirmed that there is no God in Zen, goes on to state that this does not mean that Zen denies the existence of God because " neither denial nor affirmation concerns Zen." The most concrete statement he is prepared to make is that the basic idea of Zen is to come in touch with the inner workings of our being, and to do this in the most direct way possible without resorting to anything external or superadded. Therefore anything that has the semblance of an external authority is rejected by Zen. Absolute faith is placed in a man's own inner being. Apparently the intention is that, so far from indulging in inward meditations or such practices as the Yogi uses, the student must learn to act spontaneously, without thinking, and without self-consciousness or hesitation. This is the main purpose of the *koan,* the logically insoluble riddle which the pupil must try to solve. One such is the question put by master to pupil: " A girl is walking down the street, is she the younger or the older sister? " The correct answer, it seems, is to say nothing but put on a mincing gait, to *become* the girl, thus showing that what matters is the experience of being and not its verbal description. Another *koan*: " What is the Buddha? " " Three pounds of flax " is attributed to T'ung-shan in the 9th cent. and a later authority's comment is that " none can excel it as regards its irrationality which cuts off all passages to speculation." Zen, in effect, teaches the uselessness of trying to use words to discuss the Absolute.

Zen came to Japan in the 13th cent., more than five centuries after Confucianism or the orthodox forms of Buddhism, and immediately gained acceptance whilst becoming typically Japanese in the process. One of the reasons why it appealed must have been that its spontaneity and insistence on action without thought, its emphasis on the uselessness of mere words, and such categories as logical opposites, had an inevitable attraction for a people given to seriousness, formality, and logic to a degree which was almost stifling. Zen must have been to the Japanese what nonsense rhymes and nonsense books, like those of Edward Lear and Lewis Carroll, were to the English intellectuals. Lear's limericks, like some of the *koans,* end up with a line which, just at the time when one expects a point to be made, has no particular point at all, and *Alice in Wonderland* is the perfect example of a world, not without logic, but with a crazy logic of its own which has no relationship to that of everyday life. Therefore Zen began to impregnate every aspect of life in Japan, and one of the results of its emphasis on spontaneous action rather than reason was its acceptance by the Samurai, the ferocious warrior class, in such activities as swordsmanship, archery,

Japanese wrestling, and later Judo and the Kamikaze dive-bombers. But much of Japanese art, especially landscape gardening and flower-arrangement, was influenced similarly, and Zen is even used in Japanese psychiatry. The very strict life of the Zen monks is based largely on doing things, learning through experience; the periods of meditation in the Zendo hall are punctuated by sharp slaps on the face administered by the abbot to those who are unsatisfactory pupils. Dr. Suzuki denies that Zen is nihilistic, but it is probably its appearance of nihilism and its appeal to the irrational and spontaneous which attracts the Western world at a time when to many the world seems without meaning and life over-regimented. However, it has influenced such various aspects of Western life as philosophy (Heidegger), psychiatry (Erich Fromm and Hubert Benoit), writing (Aldous Huxley), and painting (Die Zen Gruppe in Germany).

Zionism, a belief in the need to establish an autonomous Jewish home in Palestine which, in its modern form, began with Theodor Herzl (1860–1904), a Hungarian journalist working in Vienna. Although Herzl was a more or less assimilated Jew, he was forced by the Dreyfus case and the pogroms in Eastern Europe to conclude that there was no real safety for the Jewish people until they had a state of their own. The Jews, of course, had always in a religious sense thought of Palestine as a spiritual homeland and prayed " next year in Jerusalem," but the religious had thought of this in a philosophical way as affirming old loyalties, not as recommending the formation of an actual state. Therefore Herzl was opposed both by many of the religious Jews and, at the other extreme, by those who felt themselves to be assimilated and in many cases without religious faith. Even after the Balfour Declaration of 1917, there was not a considerable flow of Jews to Palestine, which at that time was a predominantly Arab state. But the persecutions of Hitler changed all this and, after bitter struggles, the Jewish state was proclaimed in 1948. Today Zionism is supported by the vast majority of the Jewish communities everywhere (although strongly disapproved of in the Soviet Union as " Western imperialism ") and Zionism is now an active international force concerned with protecting the welfare and extending the influence of Israel.

Zoroastrianism, at one time one of the great world religions, competing in the 2nd cent. A.D. on almost equal terms from its Persian home with Hellenism and the Roman Imperial Government. Under the Achaemenidae (*c.* 550–330 B.C.) Zoroastrianism was the state religion of Persia. Alexander's conquest in 331 B.C. brought disruption but the religion flourished again under the Sassanian dynasty (A.D. *c.* 226–640). With the advance of the Mohammedan Arabs in the 7th cent. Zoroastrianism finally gave way to Islam. A number of devotees fled to India there to become the Parsees. In Persia itself a few scattered societies remain.

The name Zoroaster is the Greek rendering of Zarathustra, the prophet who came to purify the ancient religion of Persia. It is thought that he lived at the beginning of the 6th cent. B.C. He never claimed for himself divine powers but was given them by his followers. The basis of Zoroastrianism is the age-long war between good and evil, Ahura Mazda heading the good spirits and Ahriman the evil ones. Morality is very important since by doing right the worshipper is supporting Ahura Mazda against Ahriman, and the evil-doers will be punished in the last days when Ahura Mazda wins his inevitable victory.

The sacred book of this religion is the *Avesta.* If Zoroastrianism has little authority today, it had a very considerable influence in the past. Its doctrines penetrated into Judaism (*q.v.*) and, through Gnosticism, Christianity. The worship of Mithra by the Romans was an impure version of Zoroastrianism. Manichaeism (*q.v.*) was a Zoroastrian heresy and the Albigensianism of mediaeval times was the last relic of a belief which had impressed itself deeply in the minds of men.

GAZETTEER
OF THE
WORLD

An index and guide to the maps
with up-to-date descriptive matter,
together with a list of the sovereign
members of the Commonwealth
and British dependent territories,
and information on the reorganisation of local government in the
United Kingdom.

GAZETTEER OF THE WORLD

Measurement of Geographical Phenomena.

(1) Physical Features.

In using the gazetteer the reader should note that it is impossible to make absolutely correct measurements of geographical phenomena. For example, measurement of height of land above sea-level depends, in the first instance, upon the definition of the elusive concept of sea-level itself. This is constantly changing and so an arbitrary value of *mean sea-level* is normally used, but the value adopted varies from country to country. As a result, height above sea-level has inbuilt inconsistencies and inaccuracies. Similarly, the length of a river will depend upon the scale of the survey from which measurements are made. Large-scale maps and aerial photographs can show in great detail the sinuous course of rivers, whereas a map on a smaller scale must reduce the amount of information shown and thereby the apparent length. We hope to include in a later edition the results of a yet unpublished work by a commission of the United Nations which is attempting to define in precise terms the area of the world's seas and oceans.

The gazetteer now records the heights of mountains, lengths of rivers, and land and sea areas in metric units. English equivalents will be found on **K183** and p. 1 of the Atlas.

(2) Definition of Urban Area.

An even more difficult problem of measurement relates to the definition of the urban area of a town or city. It is possible to define the extent of urban areas in three major ways, by using (1) the administrative area, (2) the physically built-up area, and (3) the socio-geographic, metropolitan area. This latter concept is in many ways the most meaningful for it relates to the notion that a city exerts a strong influence over the population resident beyond its administrative or built-up boundary. For example, the city may provide employment opportunities or shopping and entertainment facilities for a population resident some distance away from it. In order to define " city " in these terms some means of measuring the degree of connection between it and its surrounding hinterland (the city-region) must be found and, needless to say, there is considerable disagreement among workers in this field as to what are the most suitable criteria to use. Different criteria produce different definitions and even the most recent measurements are obsolete within a short space of time. However, the real significance of this less tangible concept of " city " may be illustrated by the fact that the reform of local government in England rests in part upon the concept of the city-region.

The population figures given in the gazetteer normally relate to the city's administrative area. In the case of some large cities two figures are given—(1) for the administrative city, and (2) for the more extensive metropolitan area which surrounds and includes the administrative city.

The census of the United Kingdom is now based on the reorganised local government areas. Up-to-date population figures perforce refer to these areas which are both fewer in number and larger in size than their predecessors. As a result much local detail is lost in the most recent (post-1971) figures.

Place Names.

Where there have been recent changes in place names, the old name is given in brackets and a cross reference directs the reader to the new name. *See also* **K183.**

Reorganisation of Local Government in the United Kingdom.

The gazetteer has been modified to incorporate the new system of local government in the United Kingdom. Details of the changes will be found on **K186.**

Editor's Note to Readers.

As a result of the indeterminate and dynamic nature of geographical phenomena inconsistencies and inaccuracies are bound to occur in a gazetteer of this size. The editor welcomes comments and criticisms of the entries based upon local knowledge and will try to make the fullest possible use of information received from readers.

ABBREVIATIONS USED IN THE GAZETTEER

GEOGRAPHICAL NAMES

Ala. = Alabama
Ark. = Arkansas
ASSR = Autonomous Soviet Socialist Republic
Atl. Oc. = Atlantic Ocean
B.C. = British Columbia
Brit. = British
Cal. = California
Col. = Colorado
Conn. = Connecticut
ČSSR = Czechoslovak Socialist Republic
Del. Delaware
Eng. = England
Fla. = Florida
Fr. = French
Ga. = Georgia
Ill. = Illinois
Ind. = Indiana
Kan. = Kansas
Ky. = Kentucky
La. = Louisiana
Land = prov. (W. Germany)

Mass. = Massachusetts
Md. = Maryland
Me. = Maine
Mich. = Michigan
Minn. = Minnesota
Miss. = Mississippi
Mo. = Missouri
Mont. = Montana
N.B. = New Brunswick
N.C. = North Carolina
N.D. = North Dakota
Neth. = Netherlands
N.H. = New Hampshire
N.J. = New Jersey
N.M. = New Mexico
N.S.W. = New South Wales
N.T. = Northern Territory (Australia)
N.Y. = New York
N.Z. = New Zealand
Oblast = aut. prov. (USSR)
O.F.S. = Orange Free State
Okla. = Oklahoma

Okrug = aut. dist. (RSFSR)
Ore. = Oregon
Pac. Oc. = Pacific Ocean
Penns. = Pennsylvania
R.I. = Rhode Island
R.o.I. = Republic of Ireland
RSFSR = Russian Soviet Federal Socialist Republic
S.C. = South Carolina
Scot. = Scotland
S.D. = South Dakota
SSR = Soviet Socialist Republic
Tenn. = Tennessee
USA = United States of America
USSR = Union of Soviet Socialist Republics
Va. = Virginia
Vt. = Vermont
Wash. = Washington
W.I. = West Indies
Wis. = Wisconsin
Wyo. = Wyoming

OTHER ABBREVIATIONS

a. = area
admin. = administrative
agr. = agriculture
alt. = altitude
anc. = ancient
arch. = archaeological
a.s.l. = above sea-level
ass. = associated
aut. rep. = autonomous republic
bdy. = boundary
bldg. = building
bor. = borough
bdr. = border
C. = cape
c. = city; circa = about
can. = canton
cap. = capital
cas. = castle
cath. = cathedral
ch. = chief
cm = centimetres
co. = county
C.B. = county borough
col. = colony
colly. = colliery
comm. = commercial
conurb. = conurbation
cst. = coast
ctr. = centre
cty. = country
dep. = department
dist. = district
div. = division
E. = east or easterly
elec. = electrical
engin. = engineering
esp. = especially
est. = estimate
exp. = exports

F. = firth
fed. = federal
fish. pt. = fishing port
fortfd. = fortified
G. = Gulf
gen. = general
G.N.P. = gross national product
gr. = great, group
ha = hectares
gtr. = greater
hgst. = highest
I. = island
impt. = important
inc. = including
indep. = independent
inds. = industries
industl. = industrial
Is. = Islands
km = kilometres
km² = square kilometres
L. = lake
l. = length
lge. = large
l. gov. dist. = local government district
lgst. = largest
lt. = light
m = metres
machin. = machinery
met. a. = metropolitan area
met. co. = metropolitan county
mftg. = manufacturing
mkg. = making
mkt. = market
mm = millimetres
mnfs. = manufactures
mng. = mining
mtn. = mountain
mun. = municipality

N. = north or northerly
nat. = national
non-met. co. = non-metropolitan county
nr. = near
p. = population
par. = parish
penin. = peninsula
pref. = prefecture
prin. = principal
prod. = products
prot. = protectorate
prov. = province
pt. = port
R. = river
rep. = republic
residtl. = residential
rly. = railway
S. = south or southerly
shipbldg. = shipbuilding
sm. = small
spt. = seaport
st. = state
sta. = station
sub. = suburb
t. = town
Tan-Zam=Tanzania-Zambia rly.
terr. = territory
tr. = trade
trib. = tributary
Turk-Sib = Turkestan-Siberia rly.
univ. = university
U.D. = urban district
v. = village
W. = west or westerly
wat. pl. = watering place
wks. = works
wkshps. = workshops

A

Aachen (Aix-la-Chapelle), t., N. Rhine-Westphalia, **W. Germany;** anc. spa t. in coal-field dist.; industl., route ctr.; contains tomb of Charlemagne; p. (est. 1969) 176,800.

Aalen, t., Baden-Württemberg, **W. Germany;** on R. Kocher; iron, textiles, lens mkg.; p. (est. 1969) 34,773.

Aalst (Alost), t., E. Flanders, **Belgium,** 24 km N.W. Brussels; industl., comm. ctr. at rly. junc.; agr. tr.; p. (1968) 45,881.

Aarau, t., cap. of Aargau can., **Switzerland;** precision tools and instruments, shoes, textiles; hydroelectric power; p. (1969) 17,800.

Aare, R., Switzerland, flows through Brienz and Thun Ls., thence into Rhine; Aare gorges above Meiringen; lgst R. wholly in Switzerland, 290 km long.

Aargau, can., N. Switzerland; occupies lower Aare R. valley; agr. in valleys, wooded uplands; cap. Aarau; a. 1,404 km²; p. (1969) 422,000.

Aba, t., Nigeria; N.E. of Pt. Harcourt; mkt., palm oil processing; p. (1971) 158,330.

Abaco, Gt., I., Bahamas, **W.I.;** sheltered harbours, yachting; exp. crayfish; p. (est. 1969) 6,500.

Abādān, c., Iran; spt., major oil terminal and refining ctr. on A.I. in Persian G.; p. (est. 1971) 300,000.

Abakan, t., RSFSR, on R. A.; recent rly.; sawmilling, food inds.; p. (1970) 90,000.

Abashiri, t., N. cst. Hokkaido, Japan; impt. fishing base; p. (1970) 43,904.

Abbeville, t., N. France; on R. Somme; connected with Paris and Belgium by canals; sugarmilling, carpets, biscuits, beer; p. (1968) 25,702.

Abbots-Langley, v., Herts., Eng.; birthplace of Nicholas Breakspeare (Pope Adrian IV).

Åbenrå, spt., S.E. Jutland, **Denmark;** at head of A. fjord and admin. ctr. of S. Jutland prov.; vehicles, clothing, food processing; p. (1970) 20,264.

Abeokuta, t., Nigeria; cap. Ogun st.; N. of Lagos; palm oil, textiles; p. (est. 1971) 226,361.

Aberaeron, t., Ceredigion, Dyfed, S. Wales; p. (1971) 1,324.

Abercarn, t., Islwyn, Gwent, Wales; tinplate, knitting pins; former colliery t.; p. (1971) 18,468.

Aberconwy, l. gov. dist., Gwynedd, Wales; lower Conwy valley inc. ts. Conwy, Betws-y-Coed, Llanwrst and Llandudno; p. (est. 1976) 50,300.

Aberdare, t., Cynon Valley, Mid Glamorgan, Wales; on R. Cynon: wire cables; former coalmng; p. (1971) 37,760.

Aberdare Range, mtns., Nat. Park, Kenya; rise to 4,000 m; form a section of E. rim of Gr. Rift Valley; equable climate attractive to white settlers; camphor forests, fruit and pastoral agr. at higher alts.

Aberdeen, royal burgh, l. gov. dist., Grampian Reg., Scot.; between mouths of Rs. Dee and Don; impt. fishing pt. under competition from claims of rapidly growing N. Sea oil ind.; "granite-city"—much granite used in central bldgs.; univ., cath.; p. (1971) 182,071.

Aberdeen, t., S.D., USA; ctr. for wheat and livestock region; p. (1970) 26,476.

Aberdeenshire, former co., E. Scot. See **Grampian Region.**

Aberfeldy, burgh, Perth and Kinross, Scot.; in Strath Tay, 6 km below Loch Tay; mkt.; salmon and trout fishing resort; p. (1971) 1,537.

Abergavenny, t., Gwent, Wales; on R. Usk; scene of massacre of Welsh chiefs; light engin., concrete prods.; cattle mkt.; cas.; p. (1971) 9,388.

Abergele, t., Colwyn, Clwyd, Wales; p. (1971) 12,257.

Aberlour, Charlestown of, burgh, Moray, Scot.; on R. Spey, 19 km S. of Elgin; p. (1971) 763.

Abernethy, burgh, Perth and Kinross, Scot.; on R. Tay, once cap. of Pictish Kings; p. (1971) 698.

Abersoch, t., Gwynedd, Wales; yachting resort.

Abertillery, t., Blaenau Gwent, Gwent, Wales; collieries, tinplate; p. (1971) 21,140.

Aberystwyth, t., Ceredigion, Dyfed, Wales; on Cardigan Bay at mouth of R. Ystwyth; resort; cas., univ. college; Nat. Library of Wales; p. (1971) 10,680.

Abidjan, c., cap. of Ivory Coast; pt.; exp. palm oil, cocoa, copra, hardwood, rubber; oil refining at Vridi nearby; p. (est. 1964) 282,000 (met. a.).

Abilene, t., Texas, **USA;** univ.; agr. processing, oil refining; p. (1970) 88,433 (c.), 112,168 (met. a.).

Abilene, t., on Smoky Hill R. Kansas, **USA;** childhood home of Eisenhower; p. (1970) 6,661.

Abingdon, Vale of White Horse, Oxon., **Eng.;** mkt. t. on R. Thames; cars, leather gds.; mediaeval and Georgian bldgs.; p. (1971) 18,596.

Abingdon, t., Va., **USA;** timber inds., agr. processing and tr., tobacco; tourist ctr.; p. (1970) 4,376.

Abinger Hammer, v., Surrey, **Eng.;** former centre of Weald iron industry.

Abkhazskaya, aut. rep., Georgian SSR, **USSR;** borders Black Sea; sub-tropical crops, tourism; cap. Sukhumi; a. 8,599 km²; p. (1970) 487,000.

Abo. See **Turku.**

Abomey, anc. cap., Dahomey, former slave mkt.; cotton; p. (est. 1970) 34,000.

Abovyan, t., Armeniyan SSR, **USSR;** 16 km from Yerevan; new model t. founded 1963; planned p. 50,000.

Aboyne and Glentanner, par., Kincardine and Deeside, Scot.; on R. Dee nr. Ballater; Highland games; resort.

Abraham, Plains of, nr. Quebec, Canada; Wolfe's victory over French under Montcalm, 1759.

Abram, t., Gtr. Manchester, Eng.; engin.; p. (1971) 6,472.

Abrantes, t., Portugal, on Tagus R.; French won battle here in Napoleonic Wars, 1807.

Abruzzo Molise, region, central Italy; high limestone plateaux, narrow cstl. plain bordering Adriatic; poor agr., livestock; methane; forms part of Mezzogiorno; a. 15,229 km²; p. (1969) 1,202,071.

Abu Dhabi, I., emirate, lgst. of **United Arab Emirates;** S.E. Arabian pen.; rich oil reserves; a. 207,200 km²; p. (est. 1968) 46,375.

Abu Qir, v. on A. Bay, Egypt; site of anc. Canopus; Battle of the Nile fought in the Bay 1798; p. 7,086.

Abu Simbel, Nile Valley, Egypt; anc. temples carved out of solid sandstone, one to Rameses II and the other to his Queen; saved from waters of Lake Nasser.

Abydos, anc. t. of Phrygia, Asia Minor, in present Turkey; resisted Philip of Macedon; famed for story of Leander and Hero.

Abydus, ruined c., Upper Egypt; celebrated for its temple of Osiris.

Acajutla, spt., El Salvador; exp. coffee; cement, oil refining, fertilisers; p. (1960) 15,475.

Acapulco de Juárez, spt., Gro., **Mexico;** major modern resort in bay surrounded by steep mtns.; exp. agr. prods.; p. (1970) 174,378.

Accra, c., cap. of Ghana; spt.; univ.; airpt.; consumer gds.; p. (1970) 564,194 (c.), 738,498 (met. a. inc. Tema).

Accrington, t., Hyndburn, Lancs., Eng.; 32 km N. of Manchester; former cotton ctr.; textile machin., more diversified new inds.; p. (1971) 36,838.

Achill I., Mayo, **R.o.I.;** mtnous.; agr., fishing, tourism at Dugort and Keal; a. 148 km²; p. (1966) 3,598.

Acireale, spt., Sicily, Italy; cath.; sulphur springs, p. (est. 1968) 47,581.

Aconcagua, mtn., Andes, **Argentina;** highest peak of Western Hemisphere, alt. 6,956 m.

Aconquija, Nevada de, mtn. range, in E. Andes, N. **Argentina;** rises steeply from Chaco lowland to 5,500 m.

Acre. See **'Akko.**

Acre, st. E. Brazil; isolated within Amazon basin; cap. Rio Branco; a. 153,170 km²; p. (est. 1968) 204,081.

Acton. See **Ealing.**

Adamawa Highlands, Nigeria; rise to over 5,490 m; stock rearing.

Adam's Bridge, chain of sandbanks, 35 km long, in Palk Strait, between India and Sri Lanka; construction of rail causeway mooted.

Adana, t., Turkey; on Seijhan R.; agr. processing and tr.; cas.; cap. of A. prov.; 4th. t. of Turkey; p. (1965) 289,918 (t.), 347,093 (met. a.).

Adapazari, t., Turkey; rly. junction; agr. and tr. ctr., silk, linen; high-grade concentrate from low-grade iron ore deposits in Camdagi a.; p. (1970) 152,171.

Adda, R., N. Italy; flows through L. Como to R. Po.; agr. in wide valley above L. Como; 240 km long.

Addis Ababa, c., cap. of Ethiopia; at 2,440 m in central highlands; terminus of Djibouti rly., ctr. of coffee tr., light inds.; admin. ctr.; univ., palaces; p. (1971) 881,400.

Adelaide, c., spt., cap. of South Australia; on R. Torrens, which flows into G. of St. Vincent; transcontinental rly. connections; univ.; cars, steel tubes, electrical appliances, chemicals, sugar and oil refining; p. (1972) 16,331 (c.), 842,611 (met. a.).

Adélie Land (Terre Adélie), Antarctica; French terr. and dependency of Réunion.

Adelsberg, t., Yugoslavia. *See* Postojna.

Aden, spt., cap. of Democratic Rep. of Yemen; former Brit. col.; bay behind headlands of Aden t. and Little Aden, excellent anchorage; p. (est. 1970) 250,000 (met. a.).

Aden, G. of. W. Arabian Sea; one of most impt. shipping lanes in world; pts. of Aden, Berbera, Djibouti; length 880 km, width 480 km at mouth.

Adige, R., N. Italy; upper course forms impt. routeway through Alps between Italy and N.; flows via Verona to Adriatic; 360 km long.

Adirondack, mtns., USA; hgst. peak Mt. Marcy (1,630 m), average height 1,200 m; scenically attractive, ski resorts, sanatoria, iron ore deposits.

Adlington, t., Lancs., Eng.; nr. Chorley; former cotton spinning t.; p. (1971) 4,991.

Admiralty Is., 27 km of sm. coral Is., one lge. I., S.W. Pac. Oc.; N. of New Guinea; forms part of Bismarck Archipelago; Australian mandate; anc. civilisation; pearl fishing, coconuts; ch. t. Lorengau.; a. 2,072 km²; p. (1966) 20,202.

Adour, R., S.W. France; rises in Pyrenees, enters Bay of Biscay below Bayonne; 331 km long.

Adria, mkt. t., Rovigo, Italy; formerly on cst., now 22 km inland, old Etruscan c.; p. (est. 1968) 22,703.

Adrianople. *See* Edirne.

Adriatic Sea, branch of the Mediterranean, between Italy and Balkan Peninsula; forms G. of Venice on the N.; chief trading pts., Venice, Trieste, and Ancona on the N., Brindisi and Dürres on the S.; a. 134,680 km², 720 km long.

Adriatic Highway, Yugoslavia; cst. road (in need of repair) across Dinaric Alps motivated by tourist boom.

Adullam or Aidelma, Judean c. of Canaanite origin, S.W. Jerusalem, Israel, where David hid in cave from Saul.

Adur, l. govt. dist., West Sussex, Eng.; lower A. valley and ts. of Shoreham-by-Sea and Southwick; p. (est. 1976) 57,500.

Adwick le Street, t., South Yorks, Eng.; coal; home of George Washington's family; p. (1971) 18,000.

Adygeyskaya (Adygei), aut. region, RSFSR; in foothills of Caucasus; mainly agr. and lumbering; cap. Maykop; a. 7,599 km²; p. (1970) 386,000.

Adzharskaya, aut. rep., Georgian SSR, USSR; borders Turkey; mtnous.; sub-tropical crops; cap. Batumi; a. 2,849 km²; p. (1970) 310,000.

Aegades, gr. of rocky Is. off W. cst. of Sicily, Italy; ch. t. Favignana on I. of that name.

Aegean Is., between Greece and Turkey; called the Grecian Archipelago, inc. Crete, Cyclades, Sporades, and Dodecanese; a. 3,901 km².

Aegean Sea, branch of the Mediterranean; studded with Is., between Greece and Turkey; connected through the Dardanelles with Sea of Marmara and thence through the Bosporus Strait with the Black Sea; rich cultural history; coral sponge fishing; recent oil finds contested between Greece and Turkey; length 640 km, width 320 km.

Afan, l. govt. dist., West Glamorgan, Wales; comprises Glyncorrwg and Port Talbot; p. (est. 1976) 58,200.

Afars and Issas. *See* Djibouti.

Affric, Glen, Inverness, Scot.; 48 km S.W. of Inverness; hydroelectric power.

Afghanistan, rep. (1973), former kingdom, Asia; lies N. and W. of Pakistan; cap. Kabul; comm. ctrs. Kabul, Kandahar; mtnous.; ch. Rs., Kabul and Helm; intense summer heat, severe winter cold, scanty rainfall; races, Afghans, aboriginal hill-tribes; languages, official Persian, spoken Pushtu; religion, Islam; cereals, fruit, sheep, horses, camels; inds. carpets, woollens, silks; coal-mng. at Dara-i-Suf;

natural gas at Shibarghan; rich copper, lead, iron ore resources undeveloped; no rly. a. 647,500 km²; p. (est. 1969) 16,516,000.

Africa, second lgst. continent contains 22 per cent of world's land a. but only 8 per cent of p.; diverse physical and cultural conditions; plateaux interrupted in N. and S. by steeply folded, sharply eroded mtn. ranges and by mtn. massifs of Sahara and E. Africa; climate and vegetation vary from hot desert to equatorial rain forest and from Mediterranean woodland to tropical savannah; sparse but ethnically varied p., concentrated mainly along N.W. Mediterranean cst., Nile valley, cst. of W. Africa and N.E. of L. Victoria; little urbanisation; economic development hindered by colonial legacy and neo-colonial international companies, poorly developed transport network, poor soils, inadequate rainfall and low economic value of natural vegetation; schemes like Volta R. multipurpose development and the Cabora Bassa dam designed to alleviate this natural poverty; continent contains 40 per cent of world hydroelectric potential and is storehouse of non-energy producing minerals, but many are exported in unprocessed form; agr. predominant economic activity, except in industl. enclaves of Egypt, Rhodesia and S. Africa; 60 per cent land devoted to subsistence crops; 46 ctys. had achieved independence by 1977 compared with 4 in 1945; a. c. 30,259,000 km²; p. (est. 1975) 401,000,000.

Agadir, spt., S. cst. Morocco; wrecked by earthquake, 1960; new t. built S. of former c. in a. of greater geological stability; p. (est. 1970) 34,000.

Agana, cap. of Guam; reconstructed after second world war; p. (1970) 2,131 (exc. armed forces).

Agen t., cap. of Lot-et-Garonne, France; mkt. t.; aqueduct and bridge over Garonne R.; fruit tr. and processing; p. (1968) 37,470.

Agincourt, v., Pas-de-Calais, France; famed for battle in 1415 between English, led by Henry V and French under d'Albert; p. (1968) 220.

Agra, c., Uttar Pradesh, India; on Jumna R., 184 km S.S.E. of Delhi; formerly cap. of Mogul Empire; famous Taj Mahal mausoleum; univ.; footwear; p. (1971) 591,197 (c.), 634,622 (met. a.).

Agrigento, t., S. Sicily, Italy; spt., exp. sulphur, salt. Formerly Girgenti, founded Akragas, c. 580 B.C., famous for its temples; birthplace of Empedocles; p. (1969) 52,283.

Aguadilla, spt., Puerto Rico; exp. coffee and sugar; p. (1970) 21,087.

Aguascalientes, st., Mexico; on central plateau at 1,800 m; agr.; mineral springs; cap. A.; a. 6,472 km²; p. (1969) 316,000.

Aguascalientes, t., cap. of A. st. Mexico; alt. over 1,800 m; 416 km N.W. of Mexico City; wide range of local inds.; hot springs; p. (1970) 181,277.

Agulhas, C., rocky projection, 160 km E. of C. of Good Hope, most southerly point of Africa.

Ahlen, t., N. Rhine–Westphalia, W. Germany; on R. Werse; coalmng., metal and engin. wks.; p. (est. 1969) 45,175.

Ahmadabad, temporary cap. of Gujarat, India; Jain temple, mosques; univ.; impt. textile ctr.; oilfield at Nawagam nearby; p. (1971) 1,585,544 (c.), 1,741,522 (met. a.).

Ahmadnagar, c., Maharashtra, India; admin. ctr.; old Bahmani cap.; lge. tr. in cotton and silk gds.; p. (1971) 118,236 (c.), 148,405 (met. a.).

Ahvāz (Ahwāz), c., cap. of Khuzestan prov., Iran; airpt.; oil, aluminium, steel pipes; p. (est. 1971) 270,100.

Aigues-Mortes, t., Gard dep., France; on Rhône delta; canal ctr., once spt., now 5 km from Mediterranean; salt-works; much of mediaeval t. preserved; tourism; p. (1968) 4,197.

Aiguille d'Arves, mtn., Dauphiné Alps, S.E. France; 3 rock needles; hgst. alt. 3,511 m.

Aiguille du Midi, mtn., Mt. Blanc massif, S.E. France; rock needle, funicular rly.; alt. 3,845 m.

Aiguille Verte, mtn., Mt. Blanc massif, S.E. France, rock needle overlooking Chamonix; alt. 4,130 m.

Ailefroid, mtn., Dauphiné Alps, S.E. France; double summit; alt. 3,962 m.

Ailsa Craig, rocky I., Kyle and Carrick, Scot.; alt. 340 m; gannetry.

Ain, dep., France; in Jura; mainly agr., famous for pigs and poultry; a. 5,822 km²; p. (1968) 339,262.

Ain, R., France; trib. of R. Rhône, flows S.S.W. from Jura; hydroelectric power; 194 km long.

Airdrie, burgh, Strathclyde Reg., Scot.; 19 km E. of Glasgow; iron inds., brick and concrete wks., steel tubes, pharmaceutics; p. (1971) 37,740.

Aire, R., West Yorks., Eng.; trib. of Ouse; length 112 km.

Aireborough, t., West Yorks., Eng.; woollens; p. (1971) 29,477.

Aisne, dep., France; borders Ardennes; forested; mainly agr., sugar beet; sm. textile is.; cap. Laon; a. 7,423 km²; p. (1968) 526,346.

Aisne, R., N.E. France; navigation improved by regularisation; 240 km long.

Aitolia and Akarnania, Greece; mtnous. prov. on N. side G. of Patras; arable cultivation on cstl. plain; cap. Missolonghi; a. 5,390 km²; p. (1971) 228,719.

Aix-en-Provence, t., Bouches-du-Rhône, France; 29 km N. of Marseilles; old cap. of Provence; thermal springs; cultural and comm. ctr., agr., inds.; p. (1968) 93,671.

Aix-la-Chapelle. See Aachen.

Aix-les-Bains, health resort, Savoy, France; p. (1968) 20,718.

Aizuwakamatsu, t. N. Honshu, Japan; lacquer ware, candles; p. (est. 1971) 105,000.

Ajaccio, spt., cap. Corse du Sud, Corsica, France; tiber, flour, olive oil, tobacco; tourism; birthplace of Napoleon; p. (1968) 42,300.

Ajman, emirate, one of United Arab Emirates; p. (est. 1968) 4,000.

Ajmer, t., Rajasthan, India; salt extraction, vegetable oils; p. (1971) 262,851 (c.), 264,291 (met. a.).

Akhaia, prov., Greece; impt. currant producing a.; livestock; inc. pt. of Patras; a. 3,134 km²; p. (1971) 238,594.

Akhisar, t., Turkey; anc. Thyatira; in fertile agr. basin; p. (1965) 47,422.

Akita, pref., Japan; a. 11,663 km²; contains Japan's lgst. oilfield and copper mine; mtns. and fertile lowlands; p. (1970) 1,241,376.

Akita, c., Japan; cap. Akita pref.; old cas. t., pt; oil refining ctr., fertilisers, wood pulp; p. (est. 1971) 245,000.

'Akko (Acre), c., spt., Israel; famous for sieges during Crusades; withstood Napoleon for 61 days in 1799; pt. functions now assumed by Haifa; p. (est. 1970) 33,900.

Akmolinsk. See Tselinograd.

Akola, t., Maharashtra, India; cotton; p. (1971) 168,438.

Akosombo, pt., Ghana; pt. and new t. S. of L. Volta; textile factory being built; planned p. 50,000.

Akranes, t., Iceland; N. of Reykjavik; lge. cement wks.

Akron, c., Ohio, USA; lge. rubber mftg. ctr.; maize mills, woollens, machin., chemicals; univ.; p. (1970) 273,266 (c.), 673,485 (met. a.).

Aktyubinsk, t., N.W. Kazakh SSR, USSR; at S. end of Ural mtns.; ferro-alloys, engin., lignite, elec. power, chemicals, copper; p. (1970) 150,000.

Akureyri, t., N. Iceland; herring fishery, textiles, food processing; 2nd. t. of Iceland; p. (1970) 10,755.

Akyab, See Sittwe.

Alabama, st., USA; cap. Montgomery, ch. pt. Mobile; " cotton st.", cattle-rearing; fertilisers, chemicals, mng.; a. 133,667 km²; p. (1970) 3,373,006.

Alagôas, st., N.E. Brazil; hot, dry cattle rearing a., poor st. with low literacy rate; cap. Maceió; a. 28,648 km²; p. (1968) 1,400,248.

Alameda, spt. Cal., USA; on I. in San Francisco Bay; impt. naval and air base; pt. inds.; p. (1970) 70,968.

Aland Is. (Ahvenanmaa), group belonging to Finland at entrance of G. of Bothnia; a. 1,481 km²; p. (1968) 21,500.

Alaska, Arctic st., USA; separated from other sts.; bought from Russia (1868); mtnous.; furs, timber, salmon; major oil discoveries on N. slope present difficult ecological problems for exploitation; route of pipeline from Prudhoe Bay to Valdez now approved; new cap. Willow South; a. 1,518,776 km²; p. (1970) 294,607.

Alaska G. of, S. cst. A., USA.; semi-circular G. with precipitous csts.; oil in Cook Inlet and Controller B.; a. 5,000 km².

Alaska Highway, from Dawson Creek, B.C., Canada, to Fairbanks, Alaska, USA; 2,443 km long; built for second world war programme; main supply base and H.Q., Edmonton, Alberta.

Alaska Range, mtn. massif, S.A., USA; extends in arc of 640 km; separates S. cst. and N. tundra; S.E. flowing glaciers; many peaks over 3,000 m; Mt. McKinley, 6,182 m.

Alatau, mtns., bdy. of Kazakhstan, USSR; and Sinkiang, China; group of 5 ranges, outliers of Tien-Shan; alt. up to 4,600 m; highest peak Khan Tengri, 6,954 m.

Alava, Basque prov., N. Spain; ch. t. Vitoria; viticulture; a. 3,043 km²; p. (1970) 204,323.

Albacete, prov., S.E. Spain; stock-raising; a. 14,864 km². p. (1970) 335,026.

Albacete, t., cap. of A. prov., Spain; agr. mkt., fruit, saffron; p. (1967) 83,495.

Alba-Iulia, t., Romania; on R. Mures, formerly Carisburgh; union of Transylvania with Romania proclaimed here 1918; p. (1966) 22,225.

Albania, rep., S.E. Europe; lying along Adriatic, adjacent to Yugoslavia and Greece; politically aligned with China; recent industl. development with Russian and Chinese aid; food ch. ind.; petroleum reserves and refining, hydroelectric power, coal, chrome ore, copper, iron ore; fastest growing p. in Europe; cap. Tirana; a. 27,529 km²; p. (1973) 2,322,600.

Albano, crater L., Italy; tourist attraction 24 km S.E. of Rome; steep sides; a. 8 km².

Albany, mkt. t., Ga., USA; on Flint R.; agr. ctr.; cotton, food; p. (1970) 72,623.

Albany, c., cap. of N.Y. st., USA; R. pt. on Hudson R.; admin. and industl. ctr.; p. (1970) 113,857 (c.), 710,602 (met. a.).

Albany, t., W. Australia; pt. on King George Sound; fruit ch. exp.; founded (1826) as penal col.; p. (1972) 13,055.

Albert, L. See Mobutu Seso, L.

Alberta, prov., W. Canada; part of prairies; Rockies in W.; wheat, livestock, feed crops; coal less impt. with development of rich oil and gas resources; chemicals, timber; cap. Edmonton; a. 661,188 km²; p. (1976) 1,838,037.

Albertville. See Kalemi.

Albi, t., cap. of Tarn dep., France; cath., industl. and comm. ctr.; p. (1968) 46,613.

Ålborg, c., cap. of N. Jutland prov., Denmark; spt. on S. side of Lim fjord: shipbldg., cement, textiles; airpt. 11 km to N.W.; p. (est. 1970) 154,737.

Albula Alps, mtn. range, Rhaetian Alps, E. Switzerland; summits intersected by low passes; inc. several impt. Dolomitic peaks.

Albuquerque, t., N.M., USA; on Rio Grande; alt. 1,525 m, univ.; food prod., engin.; resort; p. (1970) 242,411 (c.), 313,829 (met. a.).

Albury, t., N.S.W., Australia; on Murray R.; wool sales; clothing; p. (1966) 32,029.

Alcalá de Henares, t., Spain; nr. Madrid; univ.; birthplace of Cervantes; p. (1970) 59,783.

Alcamo, t., Sicily, Italy; nr. ruins of anc. Segesra; p. (est. 1968) 42,758.

Alcatraz, I., Cal., USA; San Francisco Bay; former prison.

Alcoy, t., Spain; textiles, paper; p. (1970) 61,371.

Aldabra Is., Seychelles Rep.; 400 km N.W. of Malagasy Rep.; leased (1971-1985) to Royal Society for wildlife research (unique animal and plant species).

Aldan, R., E. Siberia, USSR; flows from Stanovoy Range to Lena R. via Tommot gold-mng. dist.; coal in lower course; 2,682 km long.

Aldeburgh, spt., Suffolk Coastal, Suffolk, Eng.; 48 km from Ipswich; famous for annual music festival; p. (1971) 2,793.

Alderley Edge, t., Cheshire, Eng.; residtl.; viewpoint N. over Cheshire plain; p. (1971) 4,458.

Aldermaston, Berkshire, Eng.; atomic weapons research ctr.

Alderney, I., Channel Is., Eng.; horticulture tourism; a. 794 ha; p. (est. 1973) 1,700.

Aldershot, t., Rushmoor, Hants., Eng.; bricks; lge. military camp; p. (1971) 33,311.

Aldridge, t., West Midlands, Eng.; plastics packing cases; expanded t.; p. with Brownhills (1971) 88.475.

Alençon, t., cap. of Orne dep., France; textiles; p. (1968) 31,656.

Aleppo, c., Syria; 2nd. c. of Syria; in limestone hills; univ.; mkt. and textile ctr.; p. (1970) 639,000.

Alès, t., Gard dep., France; sm. coalfield; chemicals; p. (1968) 42,818.

Alessandria, t., N. Italy; rly. ctr. on Tanaro R.; engin.; p. (est. 1968) 99,023.

Ålesund, spt. on Giske I., W. Norway, fishing, fish processing; airpt. on I. to N.; p. (1968) 38,544.

Aletsch, glacier, Switzerland; in Bernese Alps; lgst. in Europe; length 24 km.

Aletschhorn, mtn., Bernese Alps, Switzerland; alt. 4,198 m.

Aleutian Is.; Bering Sea, Alaska, USA; chain of over 150 Is. formed from partially submerged peaks of volcanic A. mtn. range; on earthquake belt; U.S. air base.

Alexander Archipelago, S.E. Alaska, USA; dense I. system; fjord scenery; well populated; furs, lumbering, fishing; a. 33,670 km².

Alexandria, ch. pt., Egypt; founded by Alexander the Great, 332 B.C.; floating dock; exp. cotton, wheat, rice, gum; second lgst. c. in Africa; p. (est. 1974) 2,146,000.

Alexandria, t., La., USA; p. (1970) 41,557.

Alexandria, c., spt., Va., USA; on Chesapeake Bay; indust. t.; p. (1970) 110,938.

Alford, t., East Lindsey, Lincs., Eng.; mkt.; brewing, food processing; p. (1971) 2,278.

Alfreton, t., Amber Valley, Derbys., Eng.; mkt. t.; formerly coal-mng.; hosiery, knitwear; p. (1971) 21,670.

Algarve, prov., anc. kingdom, Portugal; in extreme S. of cty . tourism, fishing, fruit; p. (est. 1970) 316,200.

Algeciras, spt., Spain; W. of Gibraltar on A. Bay; nearby Campo de Gibraltar scheme for social and economic development to break down Gibraltar's economic isolation; p. (1967) 73,292.

Algeria, indep. st. (1962), N. Africa; formerly under French rule; 13 deps.; fertile valleys, rugged mtns.; barren plateaux; Mediterranean climate; Berbers, Kabyles, Arabs, Tuaregs; cap. Algiers; wine, fruit, olive oil, tobacco; oil, natural gas and iron ore in Sahara; developing tourism; land reform in progress: a. 2,373,994 km²; p. (est. 1969) 13,349,000.

Algiers (renamed El Dzejair, 1972), pt., cap. c. of Algeria; old t. surmounted by 16th cent. Casbah (fortress); univ.; exp. wine, citrus fruit, iron ore; oil refining at Maison Carrée; airpt. at Maison Blanche, 16 km E. of c.; p. (1966) 903,530 (c.), 943,142 (met. a.).

Alhambra, Cal., USA; sub. Los Angeles; fruit mkt.; mftg.; p. (1970) 62,125.

Alicante, spt., cap of A. prov., Spain; wine, fruits; oil refinery; p. (est. 1969) 137,500.

Alice Springs, t., N.T., Australia; ch. t. of desert a.; major cattle raising ctr.; p. (1972) 11,118.

Aligarh, t., Uttar Pradesh, India; 128 km S.E. of Delhi; univ.; p. (1971) 252,314.

Alkmaar, t., Netherlands; impt. cheese mkt. on N. Holland canal; p. (1967) 48,561.

Allahabad, t. Uttar Pradesh, India; at confluence of Jumna and Ganges Rs.; univ.; Hindu pilgrimage ctr.; p. (1971) 490,622 (c.), 513,036 (met. a.).

Allegheny Mtns., USA; part of Appalachian system, inc. several parallel ranges; water-shed between Atlantic and Mississippi R. drainage; forested, tourism; average alt. 1,500 m.

Allegheny R., Penns., N.Y., USA, rises in A. mtns., flows to Ohio R.; Pittsburg met. a. on lower reaches where R. entrenched 120 m below plateau making urban development difficult; used for coal and oil transport; 520 km long.

Allen, Bot of, R.o.I.; peat bogs, peat cutting, cultivation; a. 958 km².

Allentown, t., Penns., USA; coal, textiles, cement; p. (1970) 210,301 (c.), 538,388 (met. a.).

Alleppey, spt., Kerala, S. India; on sand spit; coconut prods.; p. (1971) 160,166.

Allerdale, l. govt. dist., Cumbria, Eng.; cstl. dist. inc. Workington, Maryport, Cockermouth and Keswick; p. (est. 1976) 94,900.

Alliance, t., Ohio, USA; iron, steel, engin.; p. (1970) 26,547.

Allier, dep., France; N. of Massif Central; coal- and iron-mng.; mineral springs, wine, wheat; a. 4,786 km²; p. (1968) 386,553.

Alloa, sm. burgh, Clackmannan, Scot.; on N. bank of R. Forth; bricks, tiles, glass, distilling; p. (1971) 14,100.

Alma-Ata, c., cap. of Kazakh SSR, USSR; in foothills of Tien-Shan mtns.; univ.; comm. agr., and ind. ctr.; food processing, machin., printing; p. (1970) 730,000.

Almada, t., Portugal; on R. Tagus estuary opposite Lisbon; Salazar bridge (opened 1966) links it with Lisbon; p. (1970) 43,537.

Almelo, t., Overijssel, Neth.; 40 km S.E. of Zwolle; cotton textile mnfs.; p. (1968) 58,155.

Almeria, spt.. on G. of A., S.E. Spain; cath.; exp. grapes, oranges; p. (1967) 99.653.

Alnwick, t., l. gov. dist., Northumberland, Eng.; cas.; mkt. t.; p. (est. 1976) 27,600 (dist.).

Alor Star, t., cap. of Kedah, W. Malaysia; on main W. cst. road and rly.; p. 32,424.

Alost. See Aalst.

Alpes-de-Haute-Provence (Basses-Alpes), dep., S.E. France; mtnous., infertile a. bordering Italy; olives, wines; cap. Digne; a. 6,988 km²; p. (1968) 104,813.

Alpes-Maritimes, dep., S.E. France; ceded by Italy in 1860; ch. t. Nice; olives, wines, fruit; a. 3,737 km²; p. (1968) 722,070.

Alphen, t., S. Holland. Neth.; on Old Rhine, 16 km S.E. of Leiden; mkt. for dairy produce; p. (1967) 30,980.

Alps, hgst. mtns. in Europe; 960 km long, inc. 1,200 glaciers; separates S. and central Europe, forming a climatic divide; major tourist a., winter sports; hydroelec. power; main peaks Mont Blanc (4,814 m), Mont Rosa (4,641 m), Matterhorn (4,509 m).

Als, I., S. Denmark; in the Little Belt, a. 337 km²; linked to Jutland by bridge; p. (1965) 48,676.

Alsace-Lorraine, region, E. France; bordered to E. by W. Germany and Rhine R; incorporated into Germany at time of unification (1871), returned to France by Treaty of Versailles (1919); impt. iron-ore and iron and steel inds. in Lorraine; regional aid for economic development; well wooded.

Alsdorf, t., N. Rhine-Westphalia, W. Germany; 16 km N. of Aachen; tar-distillation plant; p. (est. 1969) 31,420.

Alston, t., Eden, Cumbria,†Eng.; in upper reaches of south Tyne in N. Pennines; limestone quarrying; p. with Garrigill (1971) 1,909.

Altai Mtns., Mongolia, USSR; border China; steppes and glaciers; silver and mercury; multi-purpose R. project at Kamenna-Obi; ctr. of USSR atomic ind. at Ust Kamenogorsk; stock-rearing; average alt. 3,000 m, hghst. alt. 4,656 m at Tabun Bogdo.

Altamira, caves, N. Spain; prehistoric shelters, paintings of animals (Magdalenian).

Altamura, t., Apulia, Italy; at foot of Apennines; wines, wool; cath.; p. (est. 1968) 45,988.

Altdorf, t., cap. of Uri can., Switzerland; rubber gds., wood workings; statue of William Tell and Tell Theatre; p. (1970) 8,647.

Altenahr, t., N. Rhine-Westphalia, W. Germany; site of anc. cas. of Counts von der Marck; metals, wine; p. (est. 1969) 31,891.

Altenburg, t., Leipzig, E. Germany; lignite mng., engin., metallurgy, mnfs. playing cards, textiles; p. (est. 1970) 46.737.

Alton, t., East Hants., Eng.; breweries, lt. engin.; p. (1971) 12,686.

Alton, t., Ill., USA; on Mississippi R.; oil refining; p. (1970) 39,700.

Altona, R. pt. of Hamburg, W. Germany; on the Elbe; chemical and fishing inds.; trawler pt.

Altoona, c., Penns., USA; rly. t.; p. (1970) 62,385 (c.), 134,142 (met. a.).

Altrincham, mkt. t., Trafford, Gtr. Manchester, Eng.; engin.; residtl.; p. (1971) 40,752.

Alva, burgh, Clackmannan, Scot.; at S. foot of Ochil Hills, 5 km N. of Alloa; woollens, printing fruit and fish canning; p. (1971) 4,180.

Alwar, c., Rajasthan, India; in hilly agr. region; former cap. of A. princely st.; fort, palace; p. (1971) 100,378.

Alyn and Deeside, l. govt. dist., Clwyd, Wales; inc. Connah's Quay, Buckley and Hawarden; p. (est. 1976) 70,300.

Amagasaki, c., Japan; nr. Osaka; chemicals polyethylene; iron and steel; oil refining; p. (est. 1971) 543,000.

Amalfi, spt., Italy; on G. of Salerno; tourist resort; fisheries; p. (est. 1968) 7,162.

Amapá, fed. terr., N. Brazil; on equator; tropical rain forest, sparse p.; a. 137,423 km²; p. (est. 1968) 109,076.

Amārah, Al, pt., Iraq; on left bank of R. Tigris 400 km below Baghdad; Arab t. and agr. mkt. at R. crossing; p. (1965) 104,000 (met. a.).

Amārapura, t., Burma; on R. Irrawaddy 10 m. S.W. of Mandalay; former cap.; craft inds.

Amarillo, t., Texas, USA; oil refining, creameries, meat packing; p. (1970) 123,973 (c.), 140,876 (met. a.). [p. (1965) 33,539.

Amasya, t., Turkey; on Yesil-Cekerek R.; tr. ctr.;

Amazon, gr. R., S. America; drains lgst. a. and carries more water than any other R. in world; main Andean headstreams Ucayali and Marañón from Peru unite to flow across Brazil to Atl. Oc., receiving waters of many Rs., inc. the Madeira; lgst. rain forest in world; ocean steamers penetrate to Iquitos, Peru, c. 3,680 km from mouth; a. drained c. 6 million km² of sparsely populated cty., mostly in Brazil; length 6,712 km, longest R. in world; basin inc. 40% of S. America; ocean pt. Belém.

Amazonas, lgst. st. of Brazil; isolated; tropical rain forest; tree prods.; cap. Manáus; a. 1,595,823 km²; p. (est. 1968) 921,390, (mainly Indian).

Amazonas, fed. terr., Venezuela; cap. Puerto Ayacucho on Orinoco R., isolated, tropical rain forest; a. 181,300 km²; p. (est. 1970) 12,831.

Amazonia, Peru, Columbia, Brazil; a. covered by Amazon R. and its tribs. and the surrounding lowland; thickly forested; underdeveloped.

Ambala, c., Haryana, India; cotton, flour; p. (1971) 102,493 (c.), 200,576 (met. a.).

Ambato, c., Ecuador; S. of Quito, on slope of Mt. Chimborazo; alt. 2,702 m; textiles, canned fruits, leather gds.; p. (1966) 89,541.

Amberg, t., Bavaria, W. Germany; mediaeval walled t. on R. Vils; specialist steels, textiles; p. (est. 1969) 42,300.

Amber Valley, l. gov. dist., Derbys., Eng.; S. of co., nr. Notts.; inc. Alfreton, Ripley, Heanor and Belper; p. (est. 1976) 106,000.

Ambès, t., Gironde, France; nr. Bordeaux; oil refining. [Windermere.

Ambleside, tourist ctr., Cumbria, Eng.; N. of L.

Amboise, t., Indre-et-Loire dep., France; 24 km E. of Tours; famous cas. and prison; p. (1968) 8,899.

Ambon, I., Moluccas, Indonesia; spices, coconuts; a. 818 km²; p. 73,000.

America, the lands of the Western hemisphere, comprising the continents of North and South America, separated by narrow Isthmus of Panama; most N. point over 14,400 km from C. Horn, the extreme S. point; p. (est. 1967) 479,000,000. See also North, South, and Central America.

Amersfoort, c., Utrecht, Neth.; walled c. on R. Eem; rapid growth of light inds.; p. (1968) 76,285.

Amersham, t., Bucks., Eng.; radiochemical ctr.; lt. inds., 17th cent. mkt. hall; p. (1971) 68,413 (dist.).

Ames, t., Iowa, USA; Iowa State Univ. of Science and Technology and many fed. and st. institutes; p. (1970) 39,505.

Amiens, c., cap. of Somme dep; major textile ctr. of France, on R. Somme; cath.; p. (1968) 117,888 (c.), 136,713 (met. a.).

Amirante Is., British group. Indian Ocean; S.W. of Seychelles.

Amlwch, t., Gwynedd, Wales; N. cst. of Anglesey; resort; pt.; oil terminal; p. (1971) 3,681.

Amman, c., cap. of Jordan; N.E. of Dead Sea; site of biblical Raboth Ammon; textiles, cement, tobacco; airpt.; univ.; p. (est. 1971) 520,700.

Ammanford, t., Dinefwr, Dyfed, Wales; anthracite, brick mkg.; p. (1971) 5,595.

Amoy (Xiamen), c., Fukien, China; rail link to Yingtang, Kiansi; tea, fruit, bricks; univ.; former treaty-pt.; p. (est. 1970) 400,000.

Ampthill, Mid Beds., Eng.; mkt. t.; p. (1971) 5,575.

Amravati, c., Maharashtra, India; cotton ctr., univ.; p. (1971) 193,800.

Amritsar, c., Punjab, N.W. India; Golden Temple sacred to Sikhs; trade ctr. for shawls and carpets; soaps, paints, engin.; p. (1971) 407,628 (c.), 458,029 (met. a.).

Amroha, t., Uttar Pradesh, India; pilgrimage ctr.; p. (1961) 68,965.

Amsterdam, spt., cap. of Netherlands; at junction of R. Amstel and the IJ; built on 96 Is. joined by 300 bridges, harbour at terminus of N. Sea canal can hold 1,000 ships; two univs., Royal Palace, Bourse; extensive tr.; exp. dairy prod., sugar, tobacco; shipbldg., diamond polishing, aeronautical, marine, elec. machin., oil refining; p. (1968) 857,635 (c.), 1,047,588 (met. a.).

Amu-Dar'ya (Oxus), R., marks boundary between USSR and Afghanistan; flows from Pamir mtns. to Aral Sea; Kara- and Kzyl-Kum deserts on either bank; rich in fish; irrigation in lower course; 1,395 km long.

Amur (Hei-Lung Chiang), major R. of E. Asia; flows from Mongolia between N.E. China and E. Siberia into Pac. Oc. opposite Sakhalin I.; with tribs. Argun and Ussuri forms lgst. R. frontier in world; crossed by Trans-Siberian rly. at Khabarovsk; 2,827 km long.

Anaconda, t. Mont, USA; one of lgst. copper mines in world; p. (1970) 9,771.

Anaheim, t., Cal., USA; tourism; Disneyland; p. (1970) 441,327 (c.), 1,409,335 (met a.).

Ahahuac, plateau, Mexico; average alt. 2,000 m; surrounded by higher cty. inc. volcano Popocatapetl (5,456 m); contains Mexico City, heartland of Aztec Mexico; a. c. 3,900 km².

Anambas Is., Indonesia; 240 km W. of W. Malaysia; little development; p. c. 12,000.

Anatolia (Asia Minor), penin. approx. coextensive with Turkey bounded by Black Sea (N.), Mediterranean (S.), Aegean (W.)

Anching, c., Anhwei prov., China; R. pt. on Yangtse; tr.|in agr. prods.; p. (est. 1970) 160,000.

Anchorage, t., Alaska, USA; timber, salmon fishing and canning; earthquake 28 Mar. 1964; spt.; airpt.; p. (1970) 48,081.

Ancona, spt., central Italy; on the Adriatic Sea; founded by Dorians, 1500 B.C.; sugar refineries, shipbldg.; p. (1969) 109,422.

Andalucia, region, covering southern Spain; Córdoba, Seville, Jaén and Granada, celebrated ctrs. in Moorish times; irrigation for wines, olives, fruits.

Andaman and Nicobar Is., Bay of Bengal; constituted a union terr., India, 1956; hilly remnants of drowned mtn. chain; primitive pygmy tribes; a. 8,327 km²; p. (1967) 80,000.

Anderlecht, t., residtl. and industl. sub. of Brussels, Belgium; p. (est. 1969) 104,157.

Andermatt, v., Uri, Switzerland; at foot of Mt. St. Gotthard; tourist ctr., winter health resort; p. (1970) 1,589.

Anderson, t., Ind., USA; car components; p. (1970) 49,061 (c.), 125,819 (met. a.).

Andes, gr. volcanic mtn. system, S. America; extends over 6,400 km from N.–S.; physical and climatic divide rising to over 6,000 m; densely populated; high tropical plateaux; rich in minerals; hgst. peak, Aconcagua (6,965 m).

Andhra Pradesh, st. S.E. India; cap. Hyderabad; inc. valleys of lower Godavari and Krishna Rs.; sugar, rice; a. 275,278 km²; (1971) 43,394,951.

Andizhan, c. Uzbek SSR, USSR; once residence of Khans of Khokan; industl. ctr.; in irrigation a.; cotton, silk; oil fields; p. (1970) 188,000.

Andorra, sm. mtn. st., E. Pyrenees; under joint suzerainty of French President and Bishop of Urgel (Spain); virtually indep.; livestock, wines, tobacco; tourism having fundamental social and economic consequences; alt. 900–3,000 m; a. 495 km²; p. (est. 1967) 15,000.

Andover, mkt. t., Test Valley, Hants., Eng.; prehistoric earthwks.; expanded t.; p. (1971) 25.538.

Andria, t., S. Italy; Roman remains, cath., palaces; p. (est. 1968) 76,482.

Andros, lgst. I., Bahamas; sponges, sisal, hemp; p. (est. 1969) 75,000.

Andújar, t., Spain; on Guadalquivir R.; mineral springs, pottery, soap, textiles, uranium plant; p. (1970) 31,464.

Angara, R., Siberia, USSR; trib. of Yenisey; navigable almost its entire length., rises nr. and flows through L. Baykal; length 2,080 km; hydro-electric power.

Angarsk, t., E. Siberia, USSR; on R. Angaar 32 km N.W. Irkutsk; engin. saw milling; p. (1970) 204,000.

Angel Falls (Salto del Angel), waterfall, Venezuela; nr. Ciudad Bolivar; 980 m drop.

Angerman, R., N. **Sweden** rises nr. Norwegian border, falls to G. of Bothnia; timber transport; 448 km long.

Angers, t., cap. of Maine-et-Loire dep., **France;** on R. Maine; mkt. t. for local produce, fruit, vegetables, Anjou wines, Cointreau; textiles; cath., cas.; p. (1968) 128,533 (t.), 163,191 (met. a.).

Angkor, c., **Cambodia;** jungle-covered ruins of c. from Khmer civilisation; discovered 1860.

Anglesey (Ynys Môn), former co., l. gov. dist., Gwynedd, **Wales;** separated from mainland by Menai Straits; former stronghold of Druids, attacked by Romans A.D. 61; mainly agr. and tourism; p. (est. 1976) 64,500.

Angola, People's Rep. of (Port. W. Africa), W. **Africa;** interior forms part of central African plateaux, bounded by transitional escarpments in W. which face on to narrow coastal plain; rainfall diminishes from N.–S. with consequent crop zoning: coffee, cotton, oil palm in N., corn, peanuts, sisal in drier interior, cattle in S., semi-desert in S.E.; economy dependent upon primary inds., especially agr.; coffee major exp., produced on foreign (mainly Portuguese) owned plantations; newly discovered oilfields; diamonds in remote N.E. Luanda dist.; iron ore mng. impt. at Cassinga; little mftg.; hydro-electric scheme on Cuarza R.; pts. on natural harbours impt. transhipment points for land-locked central African ctys.; indep. 1975, followed by civil war between rival guerrilla groups; cap. Luanda; a. 1,246,375 km²; p. (est. 1970) 5,466,600.

Angoulême, mftg. t., Charente, France; on R. Charente; cognac, paper; cath.; suffered during Huguenot wars; p. (1968) 50,883.

Angra do Heroismo, t., cap. admin. dist. Azores; pt. on Terceira I.; p. (est. 1970) 105,800 (dist.).

Angren, t., Uzbek SSR, USSR; E. of Tashkent; lgst. ctr. of lignite mng. in central Asia; p. (est. 1968) 94,000.

Anguilla I., Leeward Is., W.I.; dry climate, thin limestone soil; exp. cotton, salt; a. 91 km²; reverted to Brit. Crown after secession from St. Kitts–Nevis ass. st. 1967; plans for autonomy but future still unsettled; p. (est. 1967) 5,800.

Angus, l. gov. dist., former co., Scot.; part of Tayside Reg.; a. 1,937 km²; p. (1971) 84,660.

Anhwei, prov., E. central **China;** in delta region of Yangtse R.; a. 140,686 km²; cap. Hofei; soya-beans, rice, tea, coal and iron; p. (est. 1968) 35,000,000.

Aniakchak, volcano, S.W. Alaska, USA; rich variety of flora and fauna on crater floor; alt. 1,384 m.

Anjou, former prov. of France; mainly S. of lower R. Loire; ch. t. Angers.

Ankara, c., cap. of Turkey since 1923; alt.1,037 m; univ., cultural and admin. ctr.; p. (est. 1970) 1,162,000 (met. a.).

Anklesvar, t., Gujarat, India; natural gas, oil; gas pipelines to Ultaran and Barodi; p. (1961) 20,287.

'Annaba, spt., Algeria; on fertile plain; phosphates, iron and steel wks.; p. (1966) 152,006 (c.), 168,790 (met. a.).

Annaberg-Bucholz, t., Karl-Marx-Stadt, E. Germany; in Erz Mtns.; cobalt, tin, uranium mng.; p. (est. 1970) 27,892.

Annam, region, Vietnam; formerly within French Union; divided by 17th parallel bdy. (1957); a. 147,560 km²; ch. t. Hué.

Annamese Cordillera, cstl. mtn. range, Laos, Vietnam; N.–S. watershed between Mekong and S. China Sea, rising to 2,000 m in Ngoc Linh; forested; inhabited by hill tribes.

Annan, royal burgh, Annandale and Eskdale, Scot.; on R. Annan, 3 km from its mouth in Solway F.; Chapelcross reactor sta.; p. (1971) 6,051.   [academy; p. (1970) 29,592.

Annapolis, c., cap. of Maryland, USA; naval

Annapolis Valley, Nova Scotia, Canada; famous fruit growing a., especially for apples.

Annapurna, massif, Nepal; part of Himalayas; many glaciers in W. and N.W.; alt. 8,080 m.

Ann Arbor, c., Mich., USA; on the Huron; Univ. of Michigan.; motor lorries, farm implements, scientific instruments; p. (1970) 98,414 (c.), 230,128 (met. a.).

Annecy, t., **France;** dep. of Haute-Savoie; at lower end of beautiful L. Annecy; textiles, paper, watches; resort; p. (1968) 56,689.

Ansbach, t., Bavaria, W. **Germany;** machin.,

metallurgy, furniture indus.; rly. ctr.; p. (est. 1968) 30,768.

An-shan, c., Liaoning, N. **China;** at foot of Changpai Shan, 96 km S.W. of Mukden; lgst. iron and steel complex in China (fully automated steel plant), elec. and locomotive ind.; p. (1957) 805,000.

Antakya (Antioch), anc. c. S. Turkey; on R. Orontes; cap. of Hatay prov., major Roman cap. and early ctr. of Christian culture; p. (1965) 57,584.

Antalya, c., S.W. **Turkey;** spt. with shallow harbour from which Paul and Barnabas sailed to Antakya; tourism; p. (1965) 71,632.

Antarctica, plateau continent within A. circle; snow-covered, extensive ice sheets and glaciers; volcanoes and Is.; alt. 2,000–3,000 m; owned by U.K., Australia, N.Z., France, Norway but a. S. of 60° S reserved for peaceful international scientific research; a. 16 million km².

Antarctic Ocean, parts of Pac., Atl. and Indian Oceans, S. of 60°S.; cold and dangerous; no mammalian life other than whales.

Antibes, t., Alpes-Martimes, N. of Cap d. A., S.E. **France;** spt. on Fr. Riviera; exp. oranges; flowers for perfume mnfs.; resort; Roman remains; p. (1968) 48,013.

Anticosti, barren I. in G. of St. Lawrence, Quebec, **Canada;** well wooded game reserve, lumbering; 224 km by 45 km.

Antigua, anc. c. **Guatemala;** 32 km W. of Guatemala c.; former cap., destroyed by earthquake 1773; comm. ctr. in coffee dist.; notable colonial ruins; tourism; p. (1964) 21,984.

Antigua, Leeward gr., **W.I.;** aut. st. in ass. with Gt. Britain; semi-arid limestone; 75 per cent p. in N.E.; sugar, cotton, tourism; cap. St. Johns; a. (inc. Barbuda and Redonda) 440 km²; p. (1970) 65,000.

Antilles, Greater and **Lesser,** archipelago enclosing Caribbean Sea and G. of Mexico, **W.I.;** complex political structure, tropical climate and crops; a. c. 259,000 km².

Antioquia, mtnous. dep., **Colombia;** colonial mng.; agr. now more impt.; one of major p. clusters in Colombia inc. dep. cap. Medellin; a. 65,791 km²; p. (est. 1968) 2,828,000.

Antisana, volcano, central Ecuador; alt. 5,708 m.

Antofagasta, spt., Chile; cap., comm. and industl. ctr. of A. prov; exps. copper from Chuquicamata; situated in desert, water supply 240 km by adqueduct from Andes; p. (1970) 137,968.

Antony, t., Hauts-de-Seine, France; brick wks. toys; sub. of Paris; p. (1968) 56,878.

Antrim, former co.; l. gov. dist., N. **Ireland;** fertile lowland a., arable agr.; borders L. Neagh in S.W. and A. mtns. in N.E.; p. of former co. (est. 1971) 352,549.

Antrim, mkt. t., N. **Ireland;** on Lough Neagh; linen, nylon; p. (1966) 5,468.

An-tung c., Liaoning, **China;** pt. on R. Yalu, 24 km from mouth; Chinese frontier sta. on main rly. from China into N. Korea; mkt. for agr. prod.; lumbering; p. (est. 1968) 450,000.

Antwerp, low-lying prov., N. **Belgium;** grain, flax; a. 2,859 km²; p. (1968) 1,518,464.

Antwerp, spt., Belgium; on Scheldt R., 88 km from sea; major transit pt. for EEC, competes with Rotterdam; oil pt., refineries; diamonds; Gothic cath.; of artistic and historic interest; p. (est. 1969) 230,184 (c.), 673.040 (met. a.).

Anuradhapura, anc. cap., Sri Lanka; ctr. of Buddhism; comm. ctr of irrigated rice-growing a. in dry zone; p. (est. 1968) 30,000.

An-yang, c., Honan prov., China; coal. cotton ind.; former cap. of Shang dynasty; p. (est. 1970) 225,000.

Anzhero-Sudzhensk, t., S.W. Siberia, USSR; nr. Tomsk; coalmng., mng. equipment, pharmaceutics; p. (1970) 106,000.

Aomori, spt., N. Honshu, Japan; on A. Bay; cstl. tr. of timber, fish with Hokkaido; S. outlet of Sei-ken Tunnel between Honshu and Hokkaido; cap. of apple-growing A. prov.; p. (est. 1971) 250,000.

Aosta, t., cap. of Val d'Aosta, N. Italy; in valley of Dora Baltea at node of trans-Alpine routes; iron inds.; Mont Blanc road tunnel links to Chamonix, Switzerland, opened 1964; cath.; p. (1969) 35,577.

Apapa, spt., sub. of Lagos, Nigeria; on mainland opposite I. on which Lagos is situated; modern pt. terminus of W. Nigerian rly. system; exp. agr. prods.; imports industl. prods.

Apeldoorn, c., Gelderland, Netherlands; holiday resort; royal summer palace of Het Loo; p. (est. 1969) 122,287.

Apennines, mtn. " backbone " of Italy; rich in minerals inc. Carrara marble; cultivation on lower slopes; earthquakes, in S.; barrier to E.-W. communications; hgst. alt. 2,916 m, (Grand Sasso d'Italia); length N.-S. 1,280 km; width 120 km.

Apia, spt., N. Upolu, cap. of W. Samoa; exp. agr. prods.; p. (est. 1971) 30,593 (met. a.).

Apolda, t., Erfurt, E. Germany; ball-casting and museum; p. (est. 1970) 29,087.

Appalachian Mtns., parallel ranges between Atl. Oc. and Mississippi basin, stretching for 2,560 km from Me. to Ala., USA; afforestation, hydro-elec. power, coal in N., iron ore in S.; region of human poverty; average alt. 900 m; Mt., Mitchell 2,039 m.

Appenzell, can., N.E. Switzerland; divided into the half-cans. Appenzell Inner-Rhoden, a. 174 km², cap. Appenzell; p. (1970) 13,124; and Appenzell Ausser-Rhoden; textiles, agr.; a. 243 km², cap. Herisau; p. (1970) 49,023.

Appenzell, picturesque t., cap. of A. can., Switzer-land; on R. Sitter; lace, embroidery; p. (1970) 5,217.

Appian Way, anc. highway; runs from Rome to Campania and S. Italy.

Appleby, t., Eden, Cumbria, Eng.; mkt. t. on R. Eden; cas.; p. (1971) 1,946.

Appleton, c., Wis., USA; industl. c. in rich dairy dist.; p. (1970) 57,143.

Apsheron, peninsula, E. Azerbaydzhan SSR, USSR; on W. side of the Caspian; petroleum wells (nr. Baku) and mud volcanoes.

Apulia, region, S.E. Italy; hilly, cstl., pastoral plain; grain, fruits, livestock; wine, olive oil; a. 19,347 km²; p. (1969) 3,628,909.

Aqaba, t., Jordan's only spt. at head of G. of A., 88 km from Israeli Elat; exp. phosphates, imports petroleum; p. (est. 1964) 10,000.

Aqaba G., Red Sea, between Sinai Peninsula and Saudi Arabia; impt. Biblical waterway; few natural harbours, Dahab, Elat, Aqaba main pts; Elat ctr. of mng. a., and airpt.; length 160 km, width 24 km.

Aquila (L'Aquila), t., cap. of Abruzzi prov., Italy; on R. terrace of R. Aterno; mkt. and sm. inds. ass. with local farming; holiday resort; cath.; p. (1969) 58,845.

Aquitaine, Basin of, geographical region, S.W. France; to W. and S.W. of Central Massif, to N. of Pyrenees, bordered on W. by Atl. Oc.; warm, wet, oceanic climate; rich agr. lowland; inc. Landes, reclaimed sandy area; ch. ts. Bordeaux, Toulouse.

Arabia, peninsula, S.W. Asia; mainly desert pla-teau, lying between Red Sea and Persian Gulf; inc. Saudi Arabia, South Yemen, North Yemen, Oman, United Arab Emirates, Kuwait, Bahrain, Qatar; coffee, dates, gums, horses, camels; E. Arabia rich in oil reserves; a. 2,590,000 km²; p. 8,000,000.

Arabian Desert, E. Egypt; between R. Nile and Red Sea; alt. approx. 350–2,000 m; a. 207,200 km².

Arabian Mtns., ridge along W. and S.W. csts. of Arabia; volcanic, hgst. peaks in Yemen Arab Rep.; average alt. 1,500 m, rising to over 3,500 km.

Arabian Sea, N.W. part of Indian Oc., tr. in Arab dhows; width 2,880 km.

Aracaju, spt., cap. of Sergipe st., Brazil; sugar, soap, textiles, tanneries; p. (1970) 179,512.

Arad, new t. (1962) Israel; in Negev desert, nr. Beersheba; inds. to be based on gasfields at Zohar and Kanaim; chemicals.

Arad, t., Romania; industl., route ctr. on R. Mures; p. (est. 1969) 135,181.

Arafura Sea, N. of Australia, S.W. of Papua-New Guinea, and E. of Timor.

Aragua, sm. upland cstl. st., Venezuela; lies in densely populated industl., agr., urban and political region of cty.; tropical climate; good road network; cap. Maracay in fertile Aragua valley; a. 7,014 km²; p. (est. 1970) 429,344.

Araguaia R., Brazil; trib. of Tocatins R.; splits into 2 parts in middle course to form Banaral I.; rapids; length 1,800 km.

Arak, t. Iran; mkt. and agr. processing ctr. for surrounding region on Trans-Iranian rly.; carpets; p. (1966) 72,087.

Aral Sea (Aral'skoye More), inland sea with no outlet, USSR; fed by Amu-Dar'ya and Syr Dar'ya Rs.; sparse p. on shore but attempts to develop agr.; a. 63,805 km².

Aran Is.; Galway, R.o.I.; inc. anc. religious ctr. and I. of Inishmore; fishing; agr.; a. 47 km²; p. (1966) 1,612.

Arandelovac, t., Yugoslavia; industl. a. based on local sources of refractory clays; tourist resort.

Aranjuez, t., Spain; 18th cent. planned t. on R. Tagus; mkt. gardens; strawberries, asparagus; p. (1970) 29,548.

Ararat, volcanic mtn., Turkey; supposed resting-place of Noah's Ark.; 5,168 m.

Ararat, t., Victoria, Australia; on W. Highway; ctr. of fertile lava agr. a.; forestry; p. (1972) 8,317.

Aras (Araxes) R., flows from Bingöl Daǧlari mtns. (Turkey) to Caspian Sea forming long sections of USSR–Iran frontier; valley in rich fruit growing a.; home of anc. civilisation; length 880 km.

Araucania, terr., Chile; concentration of A. Indians, especially in Rio Tolten valley.

Arbroath, royal burgh, Angus cst., Scot.; engin., textiles, fishing; pt.; holiday resort; p. (1971) 22,586.

Arcachon, t., Gironde, S.W. France; on S. side of Bassin d'Arcachon, Bay of Biscay; fish. pt., oysters; resort; p. (1968) 15,755.

Arcadia, region of anc. Greece in Peloponnesus; tradition of pastoral agr. in dry a.; ch. c. was Megalopolis.

Arctic Ocean, almost landlocked sea extending from N. Pole to Atl. Oc.; flora and fauna of scientific interest; a. 14,089,600 km².

Ardabil, anc. c. in fertile agr. a., Azerbaijan, Iran; tr. and route ctr.; carpets; p. (1966) 83,546. [aluminium wks.

Ardal, t., Norway; on Sogne nord; site of Ardèche, dep. S. France; Cevennes Mtns.; olives, wine, silk, minerals; cap. Privas; a. 55,530 km²; p. (1968), 256,927.

Ardennes, hilly wooded region, Belgium, N. France, Luxembourg, rising to over 600 m; infertile; heavy fighting in both world wars.

Ardennes, dep., N.E. France; farming, woollens, iron; cap. Mézières; a. 5,250 km²; p. (1968) 309,380.

Ardglass, sm. t., Down, N. Ireland; one of N.I.'s impt. fishing pts.

Ardnacrusha, Clare, R.o.I.; power sta. on R. Shannon, 5 km N. of Limerick.

Ardrishaig, sm. spt., Argyll and Bute, Scot.; on Loch Gilp, at entrance to Crinan canal.

Ardrossan, burgh, Cunninghame, S.W. Scot.; resort and spt. on Firth of Clyde; oil storage, ship-bldg., road bitumen, engin.; p. (1971) 10,562.

Ards, l. gov. dist., N. Ireland; formerly part of Down; N. of Strangford L.; main t. New-townards.

Arecibo, spt., N. cst. Puerto Rico; sited in rich agr. a.; local hydro-elec. power; p. (1970) 72,283.

Arendal, spt. Norway; on Skagerrak; wood pulp, aluminium, shipping; p. (est. 1970) 11,831.

Arequipa, c., Peru; cap. of A. prov. and former Inca c.; impt. wool mkt.; alpaca wool inds.; growth point for prov. industl. development; copper mng. nearby; earthquakes frequent; p. (est. 1970) 194,700.

Arezzo, c., cap. of Arezzo prov., Tuscany, Italy; hill site in basin within Apennines at junc. of valley routes; in mediaeval times ctr. of learn-ing and the arts; birthplace of Petrarch and Vasari; Gothic cath.; mkt. for silk, wine, olives; p. (est. 1969) 85,954.

Arfon, l. gov. dist., Gwynedd, Wales; borders Menai Straits and inc. Bangor and Caernarvon; p. (est. 1976) 53,900.

Argenteuil, t., Val-d'Oise, France; N.W. sub. of Paris; industl., mkt. gardens; p. (1968) 90,929.

Argentina, fed. rep., S. America; 2nd. in a., 3rd. in p. of S. American sts.; p. predominantly of European origin and highly urbanised; varied relief and climate, inc. Andes, tropical N., Chaco, Pampas, Patagonia in S.; agr. less impt. internally than other S. American sts., yet pro-vides most of exp., inc. meat, wool, wheat, maize, cotton; petroleum, natural gas; cap. Buenos Aires; a. 2,797,109 km², p. (est. 1970) 23,360,000.

Argonne, hill ridge, S.E. Paris basin, France; composed of greensand; wooded; fighting in 2nd world war; alt. 300 m; a. c. 650 km².

Argos, c. of anc. Greece; N.E. Peloponnesus; leading c. in 7th cent. B.C. under King Pheidon.

Argostólion, cap. of Cephalonia I., Greece; shipbldg.; earthquake 1953; p. (1971) 7,521.

Argyll, former co., N.W. Scot.; now divided between Highland and Strathclyde Regs.

Argyll and Bute, l. gov. dist., Strathclyde Reg., Scot.; rural a. N.W. of Glasgow conurb.; a. 6,754 km²; p. (1971) 63,265.

Arhus, c., Denmark; prin. spt. on E. cst. Jutland; admin. ctr. of A. prov.; Gothic cath.; univ.; comm. and industl. ctr.; pt. processing inds., oil refining; p. (est. 1969) 111,266 (c.), 193,573 (met. a.).

Arica, spt., N. Chile, free zone; exp. tin, copper, sulphur mainly from Bolivia; rly. to La Paz and oil pipeline connects to Sica-Sica in Bolivia; p. (est. 1966) 63,160.

Ariège, dep., S. France; Pyrenees in S., fertile lowland in N.; livestock, fruit, iron, copper; cap. Foix; a. 4,900 km²; p. (1968) 138,478.

Arizona, st., USA; home of Apache Indians; much desert, rainfall increasing to E.; many lge. irrigation schemes for cotton, grain, fruit, vegetables; inc. Col. Plateau and Grand Canyon to N.; copper, lead mng. and refining; prin. ts. Phoenix (cap.), Tucson; huge meteorite crater nr. Winslow; a. 295,024 km²; p. (1970) 1,752,122.

Arkansas, st., USA; highland in N.W., inc. Ozark, Ouachita mtns.; lowland in S.E. where Arkansas R. and Mississippi alluvium; humid climate; cotton cultivation; bauxite, coal, petroleum; cap. Little Rock; a. 137,534 km²; p. (1970) 1,886,210.

Arkansas, R., USA; rises in Rockies, trib. of Mississippi; completion (1971) of 704 km waterway (17 dams and locks), opening Okla. and Ark. to sea; flows through impt. agr. as.; several major cs. on banks; length 2,334 km.

Arkhangel'sk, c., major spt., USSR; on E. side Dvina estuary, White Sea; lge. harbour kept open in winter by ice breakers; fishery headquarters; inds. from local softwood resources; engin.; hydro-elec. power; p. (1970) 343,000.

Arklow, U.D. spt., Wicklow, R.o.I.; fisheries, pottery; fertiliser plant under construction; resort; p. (1966) 6,056.

Arlberg, Alpine pass, 1,803 m; main western entry to Austria; rly. tunnel 10 km long.

Arles, t., Provence, S. France; on Rhône delta; anc. Roman t.; historic bldgs and monuments; Van Gogh and Gauguin painted here; p. (1968) 46,136.

Arlington, t., Texas, USA; aircraft, missiles; rapid expansion; p. (1970) 89,723.

Arlington, t., Va., USA; Arlington National Cemetery contains tombs of the Unknown Soldier and President Kennedy.

Arlon, t., cap. of Luxembourg prov., Belgium; p. (est. 1970) 14,343.

Armadale, burgh, West Lothian, Scot.; 16 km S.W. Linlithgow; p. (1971) 7,152.

Armagh, former co.; l. gov. dist., N. Ireland; lowland in N. rising to over 450 m adjoins R.o.I. border; mainly rural; p. of former co. (est. 1971) 133,196.

Armagh, t., A., N. Ireland; caths.; linen, whiskey; p. (est. 1971) 12,297.

Armavir, c., Krasnodar Terr., RSFSR, on Kuban R.; rly. junc.; engin.; food processing; p. (1970) 146,000.

Armenia, constituent rep., USSR; former a. divided between Turkey, Russia, Iran; rich mineral deposits, mineral inds.; sub-tropical agr.; hydro-elec. stas. under constr.; cap. Yerevan; a. 30,821 km²; p. (1970) 2,493,000.

Armenia, t., Colombia; coffee; p. (est. 1972) 172,300 (t.), 189,100 (met. a.).

Armentières, mftg. t., Nord, France; base of British operations against Lille in first world war; textiles; p. (1968) 28,469.

Armidale, t., N.S.W., Australia; univ.; caths.; ctr. of wool industry; p. (1966) 14,990.

Arnhem, c., cap. of Gelderland prov., Neth.; on R. Neder-Rhine; lge. tin smelter; lt. inds. using rubber and rayon; p. (est. 1969) 133,391 (c.), 268,987 (met. a.).

Arnhem Land, N. part of N.T., Australia; an aboriginal reserve.

Arno, R., central Italy; flows past Florence and Pisa into Mediterranean; Val d'Arno is the fruitful valley of the R.; length 120 km.

Arnold, t., Gedling, Notts., Eng.; almost continuous with Nottingham; hosiery, brick mkg.; p. (1971) 33,254.

Arnstadt, t., Erfurt, E. Germany; on R. Gera, 16 km S. of Erfurt; artificial silk, leather gds., engin.; p. (est. 1970) 28,762.

Aroostook, dist., New England, USA; produces 12 per cent of USA potatoes.

Arran, I., Cunninghame, Scot.; in Firth of Clyde; contains many summer resorts; a. 427 km²; p. (1971) 3,576.

Arras, t., cap. of Pas-de-Calais dep., France; historic cap. of Artois; renowned for tapestry; agr. mkt.; brewing, textiles, metal inds.; almost destroyed in first world war; p. (1968) 53,573.

Árta, t., cap. of Árta prov., Epirus. Greece; agr. tr. ctr.; Ambracia was its name in anc. Greece; p. (1970) 20,333.

Artemovsk, t., Ukrainian SSR, USSR; industl. ctr. in Donets Basin; salt, coal, iron, mercury; p. (est. 1969) 81,000.

Arthur's Seat, famous hill, Edinburgh, Scot.; 251 m.

Artois, former prov. of N. France; now mainly with dep. of Pas-de-Calais.

Aru Is., gr., Indonesia; S.W. of W. Irian; fertile; sago, rice, sugar, coconuts, tobacco; a. 8,402 km²; p. 18,139.

Aruba, I., Leeward Is., Neth. Antilles; oil refining, shipping; guano; voted for indep. from gr. (1977); a. 176 km²; p. (1968) 59,020.

Arun, l. gov. dist., West Sussex, Eng.; W. section of S. Downs and ts. of Arundel, Littlehampton and Bognor Regis; p. (1976) 111,600.

Arunachal Pradesh, new union terr. (1972), N.E. Assam, India; formerly N.E. Frontier Agency; in Himalayas bordering Tibet and Burma; tribal p.; cap. Itanagar; a. 81,424 km²; p. (est. 1971) 440,000.

Arundel, t., Arun, West Sussex, Eng.; mkt. t. on Arun R.; Arundel Castle, seat of Duke of Norfolk; p. (1971) 2,382.

Arusha, t., Tanzania; S.W. of Mt. Meru; mkt. for coffee; H.Q. of E. African Common Market; airpt. at 1,388 m (W. of t.); p. (1967) 32,452.

Aruwimi, R., Zaïre; trib. of R. Zaïre; route of Stanley's famous forest march in 1887; 992 km long.

Arvida, t., S. Quebec, Canada; aluminium plant; nearby Saguenay power development; p. (1971) 18,433.

Arvika, t., N. of L. Vänern, Sweden; agr. machin. and implements, pianos, organs; p. (est. 1970) 15,098.

Asahigawa, c., Hokkaido, Japan; on Ishikari R.; industl., comm. and rly. ctr. for gr. agr. region; p. (est. 1971) 305,000.

Asansol, t., W. Bengal, India; in Damodar valley; rly. junc.; coal mng., iron, steel; p. (1971) 155,968 (c.), 241,792 (met. a.).

Ascension I., part of Brit. col. St. Helena, 1,216 km to S.E.; volcanic; ch. settlement Georgetown; nesting place of sooty tern; Brit. earth satellite sta. (1966); airstrip known as Miracle Mile; some arable and pastoral agr.; a. 88 km²; p. (1967) 1,486.

Aschaffenburg, t., Bavaria, W. Germany; pt. on R. Main; cas.; synthetic fibres, scientific-based inds.; p. (est. 1969) 55,772.

Aschersleben, t., Halle, E. Germany; potash and lignite mng., chemicals, textiles, engin., horticulture; p. (est. 1970) 37,196.

Ascoli Piceno, cath. c., central Italy; cap. of A.P. prov.; lies in wooded hills; agr. inds.; (1969) 55,247.

Ascot, v., Berks., Eng.; famous racecourse at Ascot Heath.

Ashanti, admin. region, central Ghana; formerly powerful native st.; timber, cocoa, goldmines; cap. Kumasi; a. 24,390 km²; p. (1970) 1,477,397.

Ashbourne, t., West Derbys., Eng.; nr. Dovedale; mkt. t.; quarrying, milk processing; p. (1971) 5,575.

Ashburton, t., Teignbridge, Devon, Eng.; old mkt. t., S. gateway to Dartmoor; anc. stannary t.; p. (1971) 3,495.

Ashburton, t., S. Island, N.Z.; ctr. of gr. wheat growing dist;. p. (1971) 13,299.

Ashby-de-la-Zouch, t., North West Leics., Eng.; local coal-mng., hosiery; p. (1971) 8,291.

Ashby Woulds, t., North West Leics., Eng.; clay mng., pottery; p. (1971) 2,994.

Ashdod, pt., Israel; new modern deepwater pt. on Med. cst., 32 km S. of Jaffa.

Ashdown Forest, East Sussex, Eng.; heath and woodland; site of former iron industry

Asheville, c., N.C., USA; economic and cultural ctr. of mtnous. region; winter resort; glass; p. (1970) 55,444 (c.), 135,424 (met. a.).

Ashfield, l. gov. dist., Notts., Eng.; comprises Sutton-in-Ashfield, Hucknall and Kirkby A.; p. (est. 1976) 103,100.

Ashford, t., l. gov. dist., Kent, Eng.; mkt. t., rly. ctr.; agr. implements, beer, bricks; expanded t.; p. (est. 1976) 81,700 (dist.).

Ashikaga, c., Honshu, Japan; cultural ctr.; old silk-weaving ctr.; anc. school with library of Chinese classics; p. (est. 1971) 159,000.

Ashington t., Wansbeck, Northumberland, Eng.; coal mng.; p. (1971) 25,645.

Ashkhabad, c., cap. of Turkmen SSR, USSR; in foothills of Kopet-Dag mtns.; textiles, clothing, food processing; univ.; p. (1970) 253,000.

Ashland, t., Ky., USA; on R. Ohio; iron, steel, lumber, leather; p. (1970) 29,245.

Ashtabula, t., Ohio, USA; pt. on L. Erie handling iron ore, coal; many diversified inds.; p. (1970) 24,313.

Ashton-in-Makerfield, t., Gtr. Manchester. Eng.; nr. Wigan; former coal-mng.; p. (1971) 26,271.

Ashton-under-Lyne, t., Tameside, Gtr. Manchester, Eng.; textiles, lt. engin., rubber, tobacco; p. (1971) 48,865.

Asia, largest continent, extends over nearly one-third of the land surface of the earth; chief mtn. ranges, Himalayas, Kunlun, Tien Shan, Altai, Tibetan plateau; ch. Rs., Ob, Yangtze, Yenisey, Lena, Amur, Hwang-ho, Mekong; deserts, Arabia, Thar, Takla Makan, Gobi; some very fertile valleys and plains; climate very varied, extreme in N., monsoonal in S. and E.; gold, coal, oil, iron, manganese, antimony, tin; principal countries in Asia: Turkey in Asia, Israel, Jordan, Iran, Iraq, Afghanistan, India, Pakistan, Sri Lanka, Burma, China, Vietnam, Indonesia, Thailand, Malaysia, Korea, Japan, Bangladesh, Cambodia, Laos, Philippines, Korea, Syria, Lebanon, Taiwan, and Soviet Asia; industrialisation greatest in Japan, China, India, and Soviet Asia; a. c. 43,250,000 km²; p. (est. 1975) 2,256,000,000 (57 per cent of world total).

Asia Minor. See Anatolia.

Asir, dist., S.W. Saudi Arabia; desert cstl. plain with parallel A. mtns.

Askja, volcanic crater, L. and lava plain, E. Iceland; surrounded by Dyngju-fjöll Hills; alt. 1,450 m.

Asmara, c., Ethiopia; alt. 2,226 m; on rly.; textiles, matches, soap, brewing; p. (est. 1971) 240,700.

Asnières, t., sub. N.W. Paris, Hauts-de-Seine, France; regattas; p. (1968) 80,530.

Aspra Spitia, t. central Greece; new industl. t. close to Andikira Bay; aluminium wks.

Aspull, t., Gtr. Manchester, Eng.; nr. Wigan; former coal mng.; p. (1971) 7,510.

Assab, pt. on Red Sea, Ethiopia; oil refinery; p. (est. 1970) 14,900.

Assam, st., India; on Brahmaputra R.; valley enclosed by mtns.; forested; extensive tea plantations; rice, cotton, coal; oil development at Rudrasagar; former cap. Shillong; since 1956 4 new sts. carved out – Nagaland (1963), Meghalaya, Manipur, Tripura (1972), and union terrs. of Arunachal Pradesh and Mizoram (1972); a. (1972) 121,973 km²; p. (1972) 14,857,314.

Assen, t., prov. cap. Drenthe, Neth.; route ctr.; food processing; p. (1968) 39,040.

Assiniboine, R., Manitoba, Canada; joins Red R. at Winnipeg; 720 km long.

Assisi, t., Umbria, central Italy; 24 km S.E. of Perugia; birthplace of St. Francis; cath. and old cas.; p. (est. 1968) 24,755.

Assyria, gr. anc. empire, northern plain Mesopotamia (Iraq), cap. Neneveh; drained by R. Tigris; now mainly pastoral farming a.

Astara, pt., Azerbaydzhan, USSR; on Caspian Sea, at frontier with Iran; natural gas pipeline.

Asti, t., Italy; route, industl., comm. ctr.; cath.; sparkling wines; p. (1969) 75,032.

Astin Tagn, (Aerchin Shan), mtn range, S.. Sinkiang, China; N. branch of Kunlun mtn. system which separates Tibet from Turkestan; rises to 5,000 m.

Astrakhan', c., RSFSR; major air and sea pt. on delta of R. Volga, 80 km from Caspian Sea; handles petroleum, timber; lge. fishing fleet; caviar; food and pt. processing inds.; astrakhan fur; cap. A. oblast; univ.; p. (1970) 411,000.

Asturias, region and former kingdom, N.W. Spain; S. of Bay of Biscay; now Oviedo prov.; isolated from rest of Spain by Cantabrian mtns.; coalmng.

Asunción, c., cap. of Paraguay; at confluence of Rs. Paraguay and Pilcomayo; 25 per cent of p. of Paraguay in and around A.; admin., industl., comm. ctr.; cath.; p. (1968) 411,500 (met. a.).

Aswan, t., Upper Egypt; on Nile at first cataract; anc. name Syene. Aswan dam built 1902, 5 km S. of t., to control Nile flood; lge. cement plant; univ. proposed; p. (est. 1970) 201,500.

Aswan High Dam (107 m high) opened 1971, on R. Nile, Egypt, 6 km S. of old Aswan dam, has harnessed R. to bring electricity and irrigation to hundreds of vs. and prevent Nile's flood from being lost into Mediterranean. See also Nile.

Asyût, major c. of Upper Egypt; nr. A. dam on Nile R.; anc. Lycopolis; noted pottery, wood, ivory carving; caravan tr. ctr.; cap. of A. prov.; p. (est. 1970) 175,700.

Atacama Desert, N. Chile; arid coastal tract rich in nitrates; one of world's driest deserts.

Ataléia, t., Minas Gerais, Brazil; W. of Sierra des Aimorés; p. (est. 1967) 118,112.

Atami, t., Honshu, Japan; on Sagami Bay; seaside hot-spring resort; p. (1970) 51,281.

Atbara, t., Sudan; at confluence of Atbara R. with Nile; heavy inds.; international airpt.; p. (est 1969) 53,110.

Atbara R., or Black Nile, Ethiopia and Sudan; trib. of Nile; provides irrigation water for Sudan; length 1,264 km.

Athelney, hill, formerly encircled by marsh nr. Taunton, Somerset, Eng.; between the Rs. Tone and Parret; King Alfred's hiding-place.

Athens (Athinai), c., cap of Greece; on plain of Attica; admin., economic and cultural ctr.; varied mnfs., notably textiles; anc. c. of Greek art and learning; Acropolis and many splendid temples; univ.; airpt; p. (1971) 862,133 (c.), 2,530,207 (met. a.).

Athens, t., Ga., USA; univ.; cotton gds., lumber; p. (1970) 44,342.

Athens, t., Ohio, USA; univ.; coal, lt. inds.; p. (1970) 24,168.

Atherstone, t., North Warwicks., Eng.; N. of Coventry; mkt. t., coalmng, footwear, granite quarrying; p. (1971) 38,611.

Athlone, U.D., Westmeath, R.o.I.; on R. Shannon; radio sta.; textiles; p. (1966) 9,616.

Atholl, dist., N. Perth and Kinross, Scot.; extensive deer forests and grouse moors; a. 1,166 km².

Athos, peninsula, Khalkidhiki, N.E. Greece; Mt. Athos (2,034 m) at S. tip, known as Holy Mountain, home of monastic community; ch. t. Karves.

Athy, U.D., Kildare, R.o.I.; on Grand Canal; agr. machin.; p. (1968) 4,055.

Atitlán L., S.W. Guatemala; volcanic; famed for beauty; dense p. on shore; maize, fishing; a. 137 km².

Atlanta, c., st. cap. Ga., USA; univ.; cotton, paper, farm implements, printing, clothing; p. (1970) 487,553 (c.), 1,373,629 (met. a.).

Atlantic City, c., N.J., USA; summer resort, convention c.; p. (1970) 45,386 (c.), 170,492 (met. a.).

Atlantic Ocean, 2nd lgst ocean; a. est. 82,440,000 km²; connected to Pac. Oc. by Panama Canal; central ridge of volcanic activity runs S. from Iceland to Antarctic, some peaks emerging as Is. mainly in N. (e.g., Azores, Ascension, Tristan da Cunha); S. mainly a barren waste of water; chief deeps: Milwaukee Deep (9,225 m) nr. Bahamas and Nares Deep (8,531 m) nr. Puerto Rico.

Atlas, mtn. range, N.W. Africa; extends 2,400 km through Morocco, Algeria, to Tunisia; formed of several chains; mineralised, roads across passes; long been home of Berber ribes; average height 2,500–3,000 m; hgst. peak Jebel Toubkal, 4,141 m.

Atlixco Valley, t., **Mexico**; 16 km S.W. of Puebla; fertile volcanic soils; wheat, fruit, vegetables.

Attica, (Attiki), dep., **Greece**; agr., serving cap. Athens; a. 3,761 km²; p. (1971) 201,460.

Attleboro, c., Mass., **USA**; founded (1669) by immigrants from English Attleborough (Norfolk); jewellery, silverware; p. (1970) 32,907.

Attock, t., **Pakistan**; on Indus R. between Peshawar and Islamabad; oil wells, oil refining; impt. crossing of R. Indus.

Aubagne, t., Bouches-du-Rhône, **France**; bricks, tiles, corks, meat processing; p. (1968) 27,938.

Aube, dep., N.E. **France**; arid, infertile chalk in ctr. and N.W.; wooded and fertile S.E.; drained by Seine and A. Rs.; cap. Troyes; a. 6,024 km²; p. (1968) 270,325.

Aubervilliers, t., Seine-St. Denis, **France**; sub. of Paris; industl.; p. (1968) 73,808.

Auburn, t., N.Y., **USA**; shoes, woollens, farm implements; st. prison; p. (1970) 34,599.

Aubusson, t., Creuse dep., **France**; sited on Creuse R.; fine tapestries and carpets; p. (1968) 6,761.

Auch, t., cap. of Gers dep., **France**; agr. mkt., tr. in Armagnac brandy; agr. processing; p. (1968) 23,718.

Auchterarder, burgh. Perth and Kinross, **Scot.**; 24 km S.W. of Perth; health resort on S. slopes of vale of Strathearn; woollen inds.; p. (1971) 2,446.

Auchtermuchty, burgh, North East Fife, **Scot.**; at S. foot of Ochil Hills, 40 km N.E. of Alloa; distilling; p. (1971) 1,475.

Auckland, spt., c., N.I., **N.Z.**; lgst. c. in N.Z.; seat of government 1845–64; univ.; extensive tr. and shipping; univ.; sawmills, sugar refinery, shipbldg., glass; steelwks. projected 40 km S. of A., in Waikato iron sand a.; p. (1971) 151,567 (c.), (est. 1970) 603,500 (met. a.).

Auckland Is., uninhabited gr. of S. Pac. Oc.; 320 km off N.Z.; discovered by British (1806); fur seals; a. 606 km².

Aude, dep., S. **France**; mtnous.; fertile N., salt from S. cstl. lagoons; drained by A. R. to Mediterranean; cap. Carcassonne; a. 6,340 km² p. (1968) 278,323.

Audenshaw, t., Gtr. Manchester, **Eng.**; metals, leather, pharmaceutics; p. (1971) 11,887.

Aue, t., Karl-Marx-Stadt, E. **Germany**; 32 km S.E. of Zwickau; uranium mng., metallurgy, textiles; p. (est. 1970) 30,930.

Aughrim, v., Galway, **R.o.I.**; battle (1691) between William III and James II.

Augsburg, c., Bavaria, W. **Germany**; at confluence of Rs. Lech and Wertach; cath.; theological institute; major industl. ctr., textiles, engin.; route ctr.; p. (est. 1969) 213,000.

Augusta, t., Sicily, **Italy**; on E. cst. peninsula; gd. harbour used as naval base; fishing; lubricants; p. (est. 1968) 31,602.

Augusta, c., Ga., **USA**; pt.; on Savannah R. and boundary with S.C.; cotton, cotton-seed oil, chemicals, foundries; p. (1970) 58,483 (c.), 249,842 (met. a.).

Aulnay-sous-Bois, t., Seine-St. Denis, **France**; residtl. sub. of Paris; p. (1968) 61,758.

Aurangabad, t., admin. ctr., Maharashtra, **India**; textiles, grain tr.; p. (1971) 150,483 (t.), 165,253 (met. a.).

Aurès, mtn. massif, **Algeria**; Berber stronghold.

Aurignac, v., Haute-Garonne, S. **France**; at foot of Pyrenees; caves, paleolithic remains.

Aurillac, t., cap., mkt. t. for dep. of Cantal, **France**; cheeses, umbrellas, leather goods; p. (1968) 31,143.

Aurora, t., Ill., **USA**; rly. wks., foundries, office equipment; p. (1970) 74,182.

Aussig. See Usti Nad Labem.

Austin, st. cap., Texas, **USA**; educational and artistic ctr., st. univ.; food processing; international airpt.; p. (1970) 246,904 (c.), 289,597 (met. a.).

Australasia, div. of Oceania; inc. Australia, Tasmania, N.Z., New Guinea and neighbouring archipelagos.

Australia, Commonwealth of, lgst. I., smallest continent in world; forms part of Australasia;

Cook took possession for Britain 1770; Commonwealth proclaimed 1901; fed. of N.S.W., Victoria, Queensland, S.A., W. Australia, Tasmania; inc. also Cap. Terr. (Canberra) and N.T.; p. and inds. concentrated around cst. and in st. caps.; agr. economy (sheep, wheat, dairying) giving way to mineral inds. esp. in W.A. where lge. and diverse deposits abound; offshore petroleum deposits; N. cst. tropical, interior dry, S.E. cst. more moderate, Mediterranean climate in S.W.; mtns. in E. form Gr. Dividing Range separating E. cst. from interior, where plains drained by Murray-Darling and L. Eyre R. systems (used for hydroelec. power and irrigation); cap. Canberra; a. 7,686,884 km²; p. (1972) 12,728,461.

Australian Alps, from S. part of Gr. Dividing Range, between E. cst. and interior, **Australia**; extend for 320 km S.W. from Australian Cap. Terr. to Goulburn R. in Victoria; plateau with average height of 300–600 m; tablelands extend to 1,500 m; dense vegetation cover; popular tourist and naturalist a.

Australian Antarctic Terr., part of **Antarctica**; between 45° E. and 160° E. and S. of 60° S. excluding Adélie Land; research stas. of Mawson, Davis and Wilkes.

Australian Bight, Gr.; gr. cstl. indentation S. of Nullarbor Plain, **Australia.**

Australian Capital Territory, fed. terr. surrounding Canberra, seat of Fed. Govt. of **Australia**; predominantly pastoral; highest point Mt. Bimberi, 1,912 m; a. 2,432 km²; p. (1972) 143,843.

Austria, rep., **Europe**; after long and glamorous history under the Hapsburgs (L53), instability between A. and Hungary a cause of first world war; forcibly incorporated in German Reich, 1938, liberated 1945, recovered indep. 1955; almost entirely within Alps; drained mainly by Danube; continental climate; magnificent scenery generates a major tourist ind. but much food must be imported; forests and timber inds.; mineralised, iron-ore of Styria; hydroelec.; inds. located in ts.; cap. Vienna; a. 83,898 km²; p. (est. 1969) 7,371,000, mainly Roman Catholic.

Austria, Lower, st., **Austria**; impt. agr. a.; cap. Vienna; a. (excluding Vienna) 18,384 km²; p. (excluding Vienna) (est. 1968) 1,365,090.

Auvergne, old French prov. forming the present deps. of Puy-de-Dôme, Cantal and a small part of Haute-Loire; part of Massif Central; volcanic scenery; ch. t. Clermont-Ferrand.

Auvergne Mtns., mtns., central **France**; in N.W. of Central Massif; highest peak Puy de Sancy in Mt. Dore, 1,887 m; volcanic landscape.

Auxerre, t., cap. of Yonne dep., **France**; comm. and industl. ctr.; wine; tr.; Gothic cath.; p. (1968) 38,066.

Ava, c., **Burma**; on the Irrawaddy R.; former cap.; many pagodas, now ruins; bridge over R.

Avebury, v., Wilts., **Eng.**; mediaeval v. outside Neolithic circle and avenues, nr. Silbury Hill; lgst. prehistoric structure in England.

Aveiro, t., **Portugal**; on Vouga estuary, connected to sea by canal; fish. pt., salt from lagoons; p. (1963) 16,011.

Avellaneda, industl. sub. of Buenos Aires, **Argentina**; hides, wool; p. (1960) 329,626.

Avellino, t., cap. of A. prov., **Italy**; on motorway from Naples to W.; monastery; sulphur mng. and refining; hats; p. (est. 1968) 49,455.

Aversa, t. **Italy**; in fertile plain of Campania; agr and route ctr.; p. (est. 1968) 47,018.

Avesta, t., Kopparberg, **Sweden**; on Dal R.; iron, aluminium and charcoal wks.; p. (est. 1970) 28,545.

Aveyron, dep., **France**; on S.W. rim of Central Massif, inc. Causses limestones; extensive forests; grain, dairying, sheep; coal; cap. Rodez; a. 8,767 km²; p. (1968) 281,568.

Aviemore, t., Badenoch and Strathspey, **Scot.**; on R. Spey, 19 km S.W. of Grantown; rly. junction; winter sports.

Avignon, t., cap. of Vaucluse, dep., **France**; anc. Roman t. at crossing of R. Rhône; Provençal tourist ctr.; diversified inds. inc. wine tr.; p. (1968) 86,096 (t.), 139,134 (met. a.).

Avila, t., cap. of A. prov., **Spain**; in Old Castile; univ., cath.; mediaeval architecture; birthplace of St. Teresa; p. (1970) 30,938.

Avon, non-met. co., S. **Eng.**; based on Lower

Avon valley and Severnside; major ctrs. of p. at Bristol and Bath; pt. at Avonmouth; cstl. resort at Weston-super-Mare; bordered by Mendips in S.; a. 1,336 km²; p. (est. 1976) 920,200.

Avon, R., Avon/Wiltshire, Eng.; flows from Cotswolds to enter Bristol Channel at Avonmouth; spectacular limestone gorge between Bristol and the sea; length 128 km.

Avon, R., Warwicks, Eng.; flows past Stratford-on-A., to reach Severn R. at Tewkesbury; fertile agr. valley; string of ts. along course; length 152 km.

Avon, R., Wilts./Hants./Dorset, Eng.; flows past Salisbury into English Channel at Christchurch; length 112 km.

Avonmouth, outport of Bristol, at mouth of R. Avon, Eng.; docks; seed crushing, petrol refinery, non-ferrous metal and chemical plants.

Avranches, t., Manche, France; Normandy mkt. t.; cider and dairy produce; p. (1968) 11,102.

Awe, Loch, Argyll and Bute, Scot.; 13 km W. of Inveraray, bordered by Ben Cruachan; a. 41 km², length 40 km; salmon and trout fishing; hydroelec. sta. at Cruachan.

Axholme, Isle of, flat lowland a., Boothferry, N.W. Lincs., Eng.; W. of Trent R.; drained by Vermuyden in 17th cent.; p. (1971) 14,882 (dist.).

Axminster, t., East Devon, Eng.; brushes; flour and sawmills; carpet and press tool mftg.; p. (1971) 15,301 (dist.).

Ayacucho, t., Peru; cap. of A. dep.; founded by Pizarro in 1539; lies in equable fertile valley; p. (est. 1969) 27,000.

Aydin, t., Turkey; anc. Tralles; rly. and agr. tr. ctr. for surrounding a.; p. (1965) 43,289.

Aylesbury, co. t., Aylesbury Vale, Bucks., Eng.; mkt. t.; expanded t.; p. (1971) 41,288.

Aylesbury Vale, l. gov. dist., Bucks., Eng.; a. in N.W. of co. inc. Aylesbury and Buckingham; p. (est. 1976) 118,800.

Aylesford, mkt. t., Kent, Eng.; N.W. Maidstone.

Aylsham, t., Norfolk, Eng.; on R. Bure; p. with St. Faith's (1971) 60,168 (dist.).

Ayr, royal burgh, Kyle and Carrick, Scot.; pt. on F. of Clyde, 48 km S.W. of Glasgow; Burns born nearby; p. (1971) 47,896.

Ayrshire, former co., Scot.; now part of Strathclyde Region.

Aysgarth, v. Richmondshire, North Yorks., Eng.; on R. Ure in Wensleydale; famous waterfalls.

Ayutthaya, t., Thailand; former cap., on Menam Chao Phraya R. delta; p. (est. 1969) 40,352.

Azarbaijan, E. and W., provs., N. Iran; border USSR (Azerbaydzhan SSR) and Turkey; cap. (E.A.) Tabriz; p. (1967) 2,598,022; cap. (W.A.) Rezayeh; p. (1967) 1,087,702.

Azerbaydzhan, Transcaucasia, constituent rep. USSR; Caucasus and Lesser Caucasus separated by hot dry irrigated steppe; impt. oil ind.; 86,661 km²; p. (1970) 5,111,000.

Azores, Portuguese gr. of physically and climatically attractive Is. in mid-Atlantic about 1,440 km W. of Lisbon; partial indep. by regional gov. (1977); volcanic; fruit, wine; ch. spts: Ponta Delgada, Horta (a major whaling ctr.), Angra do Heroismo; U.S. air bases on Terceira I.; a. 2,569 km²; p. (est. 1970) 336,100.

Azov Sea (Azouskoye More), USSR; joins Black Sea by Kerch strait; receives Don R.; fisheries; a. 36,000 km².

Azpeitia, t., N. Spain; mineral springs; local quarrying; timber inds., agr. processing; p. (1970) 10,797.

Azraq Desert Nat. Park, Jordan; first Jordanian nat. park around oasis of Azraq, 96 km E. of Amman; a. 3,900 km².

B

Baalbek, c., Lebanon, S.W. Asia; old Heliopolis; ruins; tourism.

Bab-el-Mandeb, strait connecting Red Sea and Indian Oc.; dangerous but impt. shipping lane; length 32 km, width 27 km.

Babergh, l. gov. dist., S. Suffolk, Eng.; inc. Sudbury and Hadleigh; p. (est. 1976) 68,600.

Babol, t., Iran, Mazandaran prov.; airport; p. (1966) 49,973.

Babylon, anc. cap. of Babylonian Empire, in Euphrates valley about 96 km S. of Baghdad, Iraq.

Bačău, t., E. Romania; on R. Bistrita; oil, sawmilling, textiles; p. (1968) 79,079.

Bacolod City, t., Negros, Philippines; sm. pt.; exp. sugar; p. (1968) 156,900.

Bacton, v., Norfolk, Eng.; terminal for S. gasfields in N. Sea.

Bacup, t., Rossendale. S.E. Lancs., Eng.; 32 km N. of Manchester; textiles, felts, footwear; p. (1971) 15,102.

Badagri, t., W. of Lagos, Nigeria; on the Bight of Benin; formerly a gr. slave pt.; coir sacks.

Badajoz, lgst. prov., Spain; gr. reclamation scheme in progress; a. 21,624 km²; p. (1970) 687,599.

Badajoz, c., cap. of B. prov., W. Spain, in Estremadura; anc. fortress c.; transit tr.; p. (est. 1969) 112,836.

Badalona, t., sub. of Barcelona; Spain; p. (est. 1967) 139,223.

Baden, t., Switzerland; health resort, mineral springs; p. (1969) 15,700.

Baden-Baden, t., Baden-Württemberg, W. Germany; fashionable spa; p. (est. 1969) 39,074.

Baden-bei-Wien, wat. pl., Austria; 22 km S.W. of Vienna; p. (1961) 22,484.

Baden-Württemberg, Land, S. W. Germany; created 1952; bounded by Rhine in W., drained by Neckar and Donau R. systems; mtnous., inc. Black Forest and Swabian Jura; received much immigrant ind. from E. Europe, so encouraging prosperous and diversified industl. structure; several impt. industl. regions centred on Mannheim, Karlsruhe, and cap. Stuttgart; a. 35,750 km²; p. (1969) 8,910,000.

Bad Lands, S.D., USA; stretches of infertile badly eroded soil.

Badrinath, mtn. and t., Uttar Pradesh, India; pilgrim shrine of Vishnu.

Badulla, t., Sri Lanka; tea; anc. t.; rly. terminus; ctr. of tea estates; p. (est. 1968) 30,000.

Badwater, salt pool, Cal., USA; 85 m below sea-level, lowest point in N. America.

Baeza, t., S. Spain; anc. Moorish c.; olives, wine; p. (1970) 14,833.

Baffin B., between Greenland and Canada; joined to Atl. Oc. by Davis Strait, to Arctic Oc. by Nares Strait; open 4 months per year; B. I., in W., ctr. of Arctic research and communications; length 1,120 km, width 100–650 km.

Bagé, t, S. Brazil; ctr. of cattle tr.; p. (est. 1968) 90,593.

Baghdad, c., cap. of Iraq; anc. c. on R. Tigris; terminus Baghdad rly.; airport; univ.; textiles, gum, bricks, tiles, metal inds.; p. (1967) 1,169,655.

Baghdad, prov. or liwa, Iraq; between Iran and Syrian Desert; inc. some of the most fertile lands in the Tigris and Euphrates valleys; p. (est. 1967) 2,270,639.

Baghlan, t., Afghanistan; new industl. t. in ctr. of sugar producing a.; alt. 518 m; p. (est. 1971) 105,944.

Bagnolet, t., Seine-St. Denis, France; sub. of Paris; famous for " plaster of Paris " from local gypsum; textiles; p. (1968) 34,039.

Bagshot, t., Surrey Heath, Surrey, Eng.; heath of same name; historically old postal town, 42 km S.W. of London; residtl.; p. (1971) 27,021 (dist.).

Baguio, Luzon, N.W. of Manila, summer cap. of Philippines, alt. 1,500 m; gold mines; p. (est. 1969) 71,400.

Bahamas, indep. st. (1973) within Brit. Commonwealth, W.I., more than 700 coral atolls; subtropical climate; infertile but valuable tourist tr.; exp. crayfish; cap. Nassau; a. 11,406 km²; p. (1970) 168,812.

Bahawalpur, t., Pakistan; former cap. of B. princely st.; impt. bridging point over Sutlej R.; p. (est. 1969) 147,000.

Bahia, st., Brazil; cap. Salvador; cattle, cacao, sugar, coffee, tobacco; oil, extensive mineral deposits; a. 560,139 km²; p. (est. 1968) 6,914,658.

Bahia Blanca, spt., Argentina; industl. ctr., oil refining; prin. shipping point of S.; exp. oil, grain, wool, hides; p. (1970) 175,000 (met. a.).

Bahrain Is., indep. st. (1971) in Persian G.; low sandy Is., springs allow cultivation of dates; oil wells, oil and aluminium refining; trading ctr.; cap. Manamah; airpt. at Muharraq; a. 570 km²; p. (est. 1974) 220,000.

Baia, historic v., Campania, Italy; beautifully situated on Bay of Naples; celebrated Roman pleasure resort.

Baia-Mare, t., N.W. Romania; on Somesul R., in region mining copper, lead, zinc, gold, silver; mtn. resort; p. (1968) 68,077.

Baikal L. See Baykal L.

Baildon, t., West Yorks., Eng.; nr. Bradford; moorland resort; p. (1971) 14,690.

Baja, t., Hungary; impt. bridging point of R. Danube in Gr. Plain; p. (1966) 33,800.

Baja California. See Lower California.

Bakar, pt., Yugoslavia; S. of Rijeka; new pt. and oil harbour.

Bakersfield, t., Cal., USA; ctr. of oil prod. and refining; aircraft assembly; p. (1970) 67,955 (c.), 325,090 (met. a.).

Bakewell, t., West Derbys., Eng.; tourist ctr. Peak District; agr., mng.; p. (1971) 4,240.

Bakhchisaray, t., Crimea, Ukrainian SSR, USSR; old cap. of Tartar Khans; copper, leather; p. 16,000.

Bakhuis Gebergte mtns., W. Surinam; major aluminium complex based on local power and bauxite.

Bakony Wald, mtns., Hungary; forested; vine-yards; bauxite, manganese.

Baku, cap. of Azerbaydzhan SSR, USSR; pt. on Caspian Sea; univ.; oil-wells; oil pipeline connects with Batumi; shipbldg.; p. (1970) 847,000 (c.), 1,261,000 (met. a.).

Bala, t., Meirionnydd, Gwynedd, N. Wales; nr. Denbigh, lt. engin., resort; p. (1971) 1,580.

Bala, L., Meirionnydd, Gwynedd, N. Wales; drained by the Dee.

Balaklava, pt., S. Crimea, USSR; scene of the charge of the Light Brigade (1854); p. 2,000.

Balashov, t., Saratov area, RSFSR; on Khoper R.; engin., aircraft plant; p. (est. 1969) 76,000.

Balaton, L., lgst. in Hungary; a. 596 km²; long history of settlement in a.; shores forested; vineyards; tourism.

Balboa, t., Panama Canal Zone; pt. on Pac.; p. (1970) 2,568.

Balbriggan, spt., Dublin, R.o.I.; hosiery; p. (1966) 3,249.

Baldock, t., North Herts., Eng.; on N. edge of Chiltern Hills and Gr. N. Road; hosiery, malt-ing, lt. engin.; p. (1971) 6,270.

Baldwin, t., N.Y., USA; on S. Long I.; fisheries; p. (1970) 34,525.

Balearic Is., in Mediterranean Sea, Spain; inc. Majorca, Minorca, Ibiza, Formentera; limestone scenery and mild climate encourage tourism which has swamped Moorish influence; agr.; ch. t. Palma; a. 5,014 km²; p. (1970) 558,287.

Bali, I. off Java, Indonesia, in Lesser Sundas; equable climate, fertile soil, luxurious vegeta-tion; p. mainly engaged in agr.; noted native dancers; a. (inc. Lombok) 10,196 km²; p. (est. 1970) 2,247,000.

Balikesir, t., Turkey; rly. junc.; ctr. of fertile agr. region; p. (1965) 69,256.

Balikpapan, t., Kalimantan, Indonesia; new oil refinery; p. (1971) 137,340.

Balinag, t., Luzon, Philippines; rice, bamboo hats, mkt.; p. (est. 1969) 51,400.

Balkan Mtns., Bulgaria; fine alpine meadows, forested; tourism based on Sofia; average alt. 900–1,200 m, hgst. point Botev Peak, 2,377 m.

Balkan Peninsula, the easternmost of the three gr. southern peninsulas of Europe, between the Adriatic and Ionian seas on the W., and the Black Sea, Sea of Marmara and the Aegean Sea on the E., with an area of, roughly, 500,000 km²; includes Turkey, Yugoslavia, Bulgaria, Albania, Greece; ch. mtns.: Rodopi, Pindhus, Balkan; ch. Rs.; Danube, Maritsa, Vardar; ch. Ls.: Scutari, Okhrida.

Balkh. See Wazirabad.

Balkhash, t., Kazakh SSR, USSR; on N. shore of L.B.; smelting, esp. local copper; vermiculite deposits nearby, salt; p. (est. 1969) 77,000.

Balkhash, L., Kazakh SSR, USSR; receives Ili R., but has no outlet; salt water; fishing, salt-panning; a. 17,301 km².

Ballachulish, v., Argyll and Bute, Scot.; on S. shore of Loch Leven, N.E. of Oban; tourism; ferry across Loch Linnhe, new road bridge.

Ballarat, t., Victoria, Australia; 117 km N.W. of Melbourne, former gold-field dist.; mkt ctr.;

engin., timber, bricks, and tiles; caths.; p. (1972) 58,434.

Ballater, burgh, Kincardine and Deeside, Scot.; on R. Dee, 59 km S.W. of Aberdeen; tourist resort, mineral wells; nr. the royal Highland residence of Balmoral; p. (1971) 982.

Ballina, U.D., spt., Mayo, R.o.I.; agr. machin. salmon fishing; p. (1966) 6,187.

Ballina, t., N.S.W., Australia; at mouth of Richmond R.; resort, fishing; p. (1972) 6,133.

Ballinasloe, U.D., Galway and Roscommon, R.o.I.; agr. ctr.; cattle mkt.; terminus of Grand Canal; p. (1966) 5,826.

Ballinrobe, R.D., Mayo, R.o.I.; E. of Lough Mask; trout fishing; p. (1961) 13,492.

Ballybunion, resort, Kerry, R.o.I.; at mouth of R. Shannon; p. (1966) 1,160.

Ballycastle, spt., mkt. t., Moyle, N. Ireland; abbey and cas. ruins; seaside resort; p. (1966) 2,949.

Ballyclare, t., Newtownabbey, N. Ireland; paper, linen, dyeing, asbestos-cement prod.; p. (1966) 4,583.

Ballymena, mkt. t., l. gov. dist., N. Ireland; on R. Braid; linen and dyeing; p. (est. 1971) 16,487.

Ballymoney, mkt. t., l. gov. dist., N. Ireland; 64 km N.W. of Belfast; linen; p. (1966) 3,520.

Ballynahinch, t., Down, N. Ireland; 19 km from Downpatrick.

Ballyshannon, spt., Donegal, R.o.I.; at mouth of R. Erne; salmon fishery; resort; hydro-electric power plant; p. (1966) 2,233.

Balmoral Cas., Kincardine and Deeside, Scot.; royal residence, on R. Dee, 13 km W. of Ballater.

Balsas, R., and lowland, Mexico; R. flows E. to Pacific through rich agr. valley of Morelos; length 800 km.

Baltic Sea, an arm of Atl. Oc., opens into N. Sea by narrow channels between Denmark and Sweden; joined to Arctic by White Sea Canal; low. dune-backed cst.; shallowness, tendency to freeze reduce its importance for shipping; a. 414,000 km².

Baltic White Canal. See Volga Baltic Waterway.

Baltimore, industl. c., spt., Md. USA; fine harbour nr. head of Chesapeake B.; pt. processing and diversified inds.; steel wks. at Sparrow's Point; educational, cultural ctr., seat of Johns Hopkins univ.; many fine public bldgs. despite disastrous fire of 1904; p. (1970) 895,222 (c.), 2,045,200 (met. a.).

Baltoro Glacier, Karakoram Mtns., Pakistan; drains into tribs. of Indus; alt. 3,532 m.

Baluchistan, prov. (revived 1970), Pakistan; S. of Afghanistan; largely desert and rugged barren mtns.; cap. Quetta; cereals, potatoes, fruits, dates; new oil and natural gas discoveries; a. 137,011 km²; p. (1972) 2,409,000.

Bamako, cap. c. of Mali; impressive site at foot of escarpment on R Niger; admin. and agr. tr. ctr.; R. pt.; univ.; p. (est. 1970) 196,800.

Bamberg, c., Bavaria, W. Germany; cath.; textiles, elec., leather and engin. inds.; impt. R. pt.; p. (est. 1969) 69,303.

Bamburgh, t., Northumberland, Eng.; former cap. of Bernicia and Northumbria; cas.; birthplace of Grace Darling.

Banaba I. See Ocean I.

Banagher, v., Offaly, R.o.I.; impt. crossing of R. Shannon.

Banam, t., Cambodia; on Mekong R.; boat-bldg., rice milling; p. 28,000.

Banat, terr., Vojvodina, Yugoslavia; major source of petroleum, natural gas, vineyards, but eco-nomically backward.

Banbridge, t., l. gov. dist., N. Ireland; on Bann R.; linen; p. (1966) 6,551.

Banbury, mkt. t., Cherwell, Oxford. Eng.; 128 km from London; aluminium ind., furniture, printing, ladies' wear; expanded t.; p. (1971) 29,216.

Banchory, burgh, Kincardine and Deeside, Scot.; on R. Dee, 27 km S.W. of Aberdeen; p. (1971) 2,355.

Banda Is., volcanic gr. in Moluccas, in Banda Sea Indonesia; nutmegs and mace; a. 103 km².

Bandama, R., Ivory Coast; major power and irrigation scheme at Kossou Dam; length c. 320 km.

Bandar. See Masulipatnam.

Bandar 'Abbās, spt., S. Iran; airport; oil ex-ploration; new deepwater harbour; p. (1967) 163,133.

Bandar-e-Būshehūr (Bushire), spt., S.W. Iran; on Persian G., Iran's major pt.; petro-chem. complex project; p. (est. 1971) 40,000.

Bandar-e-Pahlavi, spt., N. Iran; on Caspian Sea; p. (1967) 59,737.

Bandar-e-Shāh, spt., N. Iran; on Caspian Sea, on rly. from Tehran; p. (1966) 13,081.

Bandar-e-Shāhpūr, spt., Iran, on Persian G., terminus of rly. from Tehran; petrochemical plant; p. (1966) 6,013.

Bandjarmasin, c., cap. of Kalimantan, Indonesia; pt. on Martapura R., nr. confluence with Barito R.; tr. ctr.; oil, timber, rubber, printing plant; p. (1971) 281,673.

Bandon, t., Cork, R.o.I.; on B.R.; agr. processing; p. (1966) 2,294.

Bandung, c., W. Java, Indonesia; industl. and tourist ctr.; tech. institute; radio sta. at nearby Malabar; p. (est. 1971) 1,114,000 (met. a.).

Banff Nat. Park, Canada; first Canadian Nat. Park; in Rocky Mtns.; variegated scenery, many tourist facilities; a. 6,695 km².

Banff, royal burgh, Banff and Buchan, Scot.; on Moray Firth at mouth of R. Deveron; fisheries; tourism; p. (1971) 3,723.

Banffshire, former co., Scot.; lge. part now forms Banff and Buchan l. gov. dist., Grampian Reg.; a. of dist. 1,525 km²; p. of dist. (1971) 73,880.

Bangalore, c., Karnataka, India; well-planned c., former Brit. military sta. and admin. H.Q.; route ctr.; textiles, engin.; p. (1971) 1,540,741 (c.), 1,653,779 (met. a.).

Bangka (Banka), I., between Sumatra and Kalimantan, Indonesia; tin; a. 11,942 km²; p. 280,000.

Bangkok (Krung Thep), cap. c., Thailand; pt. on Menam Chao Phraya R., 32 km from sea; built originally round canals; major industl. ctr.; royal palace, univ.; p. (1970) 2,132,000.

Bangladesh (East Pakistan), indep. sov. st., S. Asia; within Commonwealth (1972); occupies former Indian prov. of E. Bengal and E. part of Ganges delta; dense rural p. engaged in intensive farming of rice and jute; susceptible to flooding and cyclones, cstl. embankment project; open warfare between India and Pakistan (Dec. 1971) resulted in creation of indep. st.; cap. Dacca; a. 142,776 km²; p. (1975) 76,200,000 (+40 per cent since 1961).

Bangor, t., North Down, N. Ireland; spt. on S. shore of Belfast Lough, 16 km N.E. of Belfast; lt. inds.; carpets, hosiery; seaside resort; p. (est. 1971) 35,178.

Bangor, t., S. Me., USA; pt. of entry on Penobscot R.; timber inds., shoes; p. (1970) 33,168.

Bangor, t. Arfon, Gwynedd, Wales; pt. on S. shore of Menai Strait; cath., univ. college; lt. engin.; tourist ctr.; p. (1971) 14,526.

Bangui, c., cap. of Central African Empire; pt. on R. Ubangi; airpt.; p. (est. 1971) 187,000 (met. a.).

Bangweulu, L., Zambia; 240 km long, 128 km wide, contains 3 islands. Dr. Livingstone died at Illala. on S. shore of this L., in 1873.

Baniyas, spt., Syria; terminus of oil pipeline from Kirkuk, opened 1952.

Banja Luka, t., N. Bosnia, Yugoslavia; caths., mosques; recent industl. development; cellulose; rly. junc.; p. (1971) 89,866.

Banjul (Bathurst), t., cap. of Gambia; pt. at mouth of Gambia R., exp. groundnuts; airport; p. (1967) 31,800.

Banks I., Canada, Arctic Oc.; separated by McClure Strait from Melville I.

Banks Is., gr. of sm. is. in S. Pacific; N.E. of New Hebrides.

Banks Peninsula, on E. cst. of S.I., N.Z.

Banks Strait, separating Furneaux Is. from Tasmania, Australia.

Bankura, t., W. Bengal, India; on Hooghly R.; shellac, silk; p. (1961) 62,833.

Bann, Upper and Lower R., N. Ireland; rises in Mtns. of Mourne, and flows through Lough Neagh to Atlantic nr. Coleraine; length 144 km.

Bannockburn, moor, nr. Stirling, Scot.; Bruce's victory over Edward II on June 23–24, 1314, established Scotland's independence.

Banovici, basin, Yugoslavia; in Bosnia; brown coal.

Banská Bystrica, region, Slovakia, ČSSR; copper and silver mng., metal wks.; a. 9,230 km²; p. (est. 1968) 38,865 (commune).

Banstead, Surrey, Eng.; dormitory t.; p. (1971) 44,986. See Reigate.

Bantam, t. and dist., W. Java, Indonesia; suffered severely from fever and volcanic eruption; former pt. and sultanate; cattle rearing.

Bantry, t., Cork, R.o.I.; tweed; p. (1966) 2,341.

Bantry Bay, Cork, R.o.I.; Atlantic inlet; natural harbour utilised mainly by oil-storage depot.

Bar, spt., Dalmatian cst., Yugoslavia; terminal of new Belgrade-Bar rly.; p. 5,500.

Baracaldo, pt., N.E. Spain; rapidly growing industl. t. on Bilbão estuary; p. (est. 1967) 110,516. [(est. 1967) 105,090.

Baracoa, spt., Cuba; exp. bananas, coconuts; p.

Baranovichi, c., Belorussiya, USSR; admin. ctr. of agr. dist.; impt. rly. ctr.; p. (1970) 102,000.

Barataria Bay, S.E. Louisiana, USA; 56 km S. of New Orleans; ctr. of shrimp ind., petroleum extraction; picturesque stilt vs.; a. 466 km².

Barauni, t., N. Central Bihar, India; oil refining; oil pipelines to Gauhati, and Kanpur and from Haldia; p. (1961) 40,321.

Barbados, I., indep. sovereign st., within Brit. Commonwealth, W.I.; fertile soils; economy based on intensive agr. supporting dense p.; sugar, molasses, rum; fishing; tourism; cap. and spt. Bridgetown; a. 429 km²; p. (1969) 250,686.

Barbary Coast, gen. name applied to Mediterranean cst. of N. Africa between Strait of Gibraltar and C. Bon.

Barberton, t., Ohio, USA; S.W. of Akron; tyre mftg.; p. (1970) 33,052.

Barberton, t., Transvaal, S. Africa; developed from 19th cent. gold rush; ctr. of rich agr. dist.; p. (est. 1967) 13,200.

Barbican, dist., City of London, Eng.; inc. major housing scheme to attract p. back into c.; cultural amenities.

Barbizon, v., nr. forest of Fontainebleau, France; haunt of painters, especially those ass. with the Barbizon school.

Barbuda and Redonda, Is., Leeward Is., W.I.; dependencies of Antigua; sea-island cotton; a. 163 km²; p. (1960) 1,145.

Barcellona, t., N.E. cst., Sicily, Italy; mkt. t.; p. (est. 1968) 34,526.

Barcelona, c., cap. of B. prov., major spt. of Spain; industl. and comm. ctr., "Manchester of Spain", textiles and varied inds.; exp. agr. prod. inc. cork; cath., univ.; p. (est. 1969) 1,827,838.

Barcelona, t., N. Venezuela; cap. of Anzoátegui st.; agr. tr.; brewing; p. (est. 1970) 54,916.

Barcoo Creek. See Cooper's Creek.

Bardsey, I., Irish Sea; off cst. of Wales, nr. N. point of Cardigan Bay; lighthouse.

Bareilly, c., Uttar Pradesh, India; mkt., sugar refining, cotton mills, bamboo furniture; p. (1971) 296,248 (c.), 326,106 (met. a.).

Barents Sea, part of Arctic Oc., E. of Spitzbergen to N. Cape; impt. cod fisheries; oil potential.

Bari, c., cap. of B. prov., Apulia, Italy; spt. on Adriatic handling agr. prods.; agr. processing inds., oil refinery; p. (1969) 352,425.

Barinas, t., cap. of B. st., Venezuela; cattle, oil in surrounding Llanos; p. (est. 1970) 50,576.

Barisal, t., Bangladesh; nr. Tetulia at mouth of Ganges; river pt.; gr. damage and loss of life from cyclone 1965; p. (est. 1969) 79,300.

Barito R., Borneo, Indonesia; a. of swampland in lower valley; proposals to develop valley for rice cultivation; length c. 440 km.

Barking, outer bor., E. London, Eng ; on Rs. Roding and Thames; diversified inds. inc. huge R.side Ford motor wks.; high proportion of council housing; p. (est. 1976) 153,800.

Barlad, t., Moldavia, Romania; soap, textiles; p. (1966) 41,060.

Bar-le-Duc, t., cap. of Meuse dep., France; in picturesque Ornain valley; many fine old houses; varied inds.; p. (1968) 20,384.

Barletta, t., spt., Italy; diversified pt. processing inds.; wine tr.; p. (est. 1968) 75,097.

Barmouth, t., Meirionnydd, Gwynedd, Wales; pt. on Cardigan Bay; chemicals; resort; p. (1971) 2,103.

Barnard Castle, Teesdale, Durham, Eng.; mkt. t., resort; woollens, penicillin; cas.; p. (1971) 5,228.

Barnaul, t., W. Siberia, RSFSR; route ctr. in cotton-growing dist. nr. industl. Kuznetsk Basin; varied inds.; p. (1970) 439,000.

Barnet, former U.D., Herts., Eng.; now outer bor., Greater London; comprising Finchley,

Hendon, Barnet, East Barnet and Friern Barnet; p. (est. 1976) 305,200.

Barnsley, t., met. dist., South Yorks., Eng.; machin., plastics; carpets; coal-mng. ctr.; p. (est. 1976) 224,400 (dist.).

Barnstaple, North Devon, Eng.; mkt. t., pt. on R. Taw; seaside resort; p. (1971) 17,342.

Baroda, t., Gujarat, India; univ.; palaces, Hindu temples; natural gas pipeline from Ankleshwar; oil refining nearby at Jawaharnagar; p. (1971) 467,422.

Barquisimeto, t., Venezuela; well built c.; comm. ctr. for fertile agr. a.; p. (est. 1970) 281,600.

Barra Is., Outer Hebrides, Scot.; a. 901 km²; lighthouse on Barra Head; p. (1971) 1,088.

Barrancabermeja, R. pt., Colombia; oilfield, oil refining, paper mkg., petrochemicals; p. (est. 1972) 94,000 (t.), 106,000 (met. a.).

Barranquilla, t., Colombia; major spt. nr. mouth of Magdalena R.; impt. industl. ctr.; international airpt.; p. (est. 1972) 682,300 (t.), 693,900 (met. a.).

Barreiro, t., Setúbal, Portugal; on S. bank of Tagus estuary; agr. processing; p. (1970) 35.622.

Barrhead, burgh, Renfrew, Scot.; 11 km S.W. of Glasgow; p. (1971) 18,289.

Barrow, R., R.o.I.; rises in Slieve Bloom mtns.; flows to Waterford; navigable; linked to Dublin by canal from Athy; 192 km long.

Barrow-in-Furness, spt., l. gov. dist., Cumbria, Eng.; iron and steel ind. once based on local haematite ores; shipbldg., submarines; p. (est. 1976) 73,400 (dist.).

Barrow Point, most N. headland in Alaska, USA.

Barry, pt., Vale of Glamorgan, South Glamorgan, Wales; rapid growth in 19th cent. as outport of Cardiff; modern light inds., replacing coal and tinplate inds.; p. (1971) 41,578.

Barth, spt., Rostock, E. Germany; shipyard engin., furniture, sugar; p. (1963) 12,406.

Bartlesville, t. Okla., USA; oil refining, metal inds.; p. (1970) 29,683.

Barton-on-Humber, mkt. t., Glanford, Humberside, Eng.; anc. Eng. pt.; S. site of new Humber Bridge; p. (1971) 7,496.

Basel, c., cap. of B. can., 2nd. t. of Switzerland; cath., univ.; burial place of Erasmus; comm., industl. rly. ctr. at head of barge navigation on R. Rhine; p. (est. 1969) 213.200 (c.), 364,800 (met. a.).

Basel, can., Switzerland; divided into 2 half cantons: (1) B.—Stadt; in immediate vicinity of B.c.; cap. B.; a. 36 km²; p. (1969) 238,000; (2) B.—Land; on N. Jura slopes; watchmaking; cap. Liestal; a. 427 km²; p. (1969) 200,500.

Basford, t., Gedling, Notts., Eng.; outskirts of Nottingham; hosiery; p. (1971) 70,763 (dist.).

Bashkir (Bashirskaya) ASSR, occupies Belaya R. basin in S.W. Urals, RSFSR; impt. mng. and metal inds., inc. major oilfield; arable agr.; cap. Ufa; a. 143,486 km²; p. (1970) 3,819,000.

Basildon, t., l. gov. dist., Essex, Eng.; in lower Thames valley; new t. 1949; light inds.; p. (est. 1976) 141,700.

Basilicata, region, S. Italy; mtnous. in W., drains to G. of Taranto; arable agr.; a. 9,984 km²; p. (1969) 626,141.

Basingstoke, l. gov. dist., N. Hants., Eng.; 80 km W. of London; expanded t.; engin., light inds.; p. (est. 1976) 120,800 (dist.).

Basle. See Basel.

Basotho ba Borwa (S. Sotho) Bantu Terr. Authority, O.F.S., S. Africa; cap. Witzieshoek; a. 52,000 hectares; p. (est. 1969) 144,000.

Basque Provs., N. Spain; comprise 3 provs.: Alava, Guipuzcoa and Vizcaya where Basque language spoken; recent claims that French dep. of Pyrénées-Atlantiques should be inc. within an indep. Basque prov.; lgst. c. Bilbáo. p. (1970) 1,878,636.

Basra, t., Iraq; cap. of B. prov.; R. pt., 64 km from mouth of Tigris R., on main rly. from Baghdad; exp. agr. prods.; p. (1965) 310,950.

Bas-Rhin, dep., E. France; N. part of Alsace; extends to Rhine rift valley, inc. Vosges Mtns.; impt. agr. dist.; many industl. ts.; cap. Strasbourg; a. 4,791 km²; p. (1968) 827,367.

Bass Rock, lighthouse in Firth of Forth, opposite Tantallon Cas., E. Lothian, Scot.; gannetry.

Bass Strait, Australia; between Victoria and Tasmania; length 320 km; width 224 km.

Bassano del Grappa; cap. of Vicenza prov., on

R. Brenta, Italy; light and craft inds.; cath.; p. (est. 1968) 34,763.

Bassein, t., Burma; on mouth of Irrawaddy R., univ.; airfield; rice tr. and milling; p. (est. 1969) 175,000 (met. a.).

Bassenthwaite, L., L. Dist., Cumbria, Eng.; most N. of lge. Ls.; drained to Solway Firth by R. Derwent; length 6 km, width 1·6 km.

Basses-Alpes. See Alpes-de-Haute-Provence.

Basses-Pyrénées. See Pyrénées-Atlantique.

Basse-Terre, I., cap. of Guadeloupe, Fr. W.I.; pt.; p. (est. 1969) 16,000.

Basseterre, t., St. Kitts I., W.I.; cap. St. Kitts-Nevis-Anguilla ass. st.; pt.; sugar refining; p. (est. 1970) 14,133.

Bassetlaw, l. gov. dist., N. Notts., Eng.; lge. a. based on Worksop and East Retford; p. (est. 1976) 100,300.

Bastia, c. spt., cap. Haute Corse, N.E. Corsica, France; lgst. t. of Corsica; agr. exp. and inds.; tourism; p. (1968) 50,100.

Basutoland. See Lesotho.

Bata, t., ch. spt., Equatorial Guinea; cap. of Rio Muni prov.; airpt.; p. (1960) 27,024.

Bataan, peninsula and prov., W. Luzon, Philippines; mtnous.; inc. t. of Balanga; timber inds., oil refining.

Batangas, prov. and spt., S.W. Luzon, Philippines; oil refining; agr. tr.; p. (est. 1966) 102,100 (t.).

Batavia. See Djakarta.

Bath, c., l. gov. dist., Avon, Eng.; Roman baths, hot springs, medicinal waters; fine Regency architecture; univ.; elec. engin., metal inds.; p. (est. 1976) 83,100.

Bathgate, burgh, W. Lothian, Scot.; coal mng. automobile ind.; p. (1971) 14,224.

Bathurst, t., N.S.W. Australia; ctr. of mng. pastorial agr. and fruit dist. on Macquarie R.; light inds., tourism; p. (1972) 17,169.

Bathurst, I., off cst. of N.T., Australia; separated from Melville I. by Apsley Str.; aboriginal reserve; cypress pine milling.

Bathurst, t., N.B., Canada; pt. on Nipisiguit Bay; paper mill; salmon fishing; local mng.; p. (1971) 16,404.

Bathurst. See Banjul.

Bâtinah, Al, fertile coastal plain, Oman, Arabia; produces early-ripening dates famous for flavour.

Batley, t. West Yorks., Eng.; heavy woollens shoddy; p. (1971) 42,004.

Baton Rouge, st. cap., La., USA; on Mississippi; major tr. ctr.; univ.; oil refining, chemical plants; p. (1970) 161,783 (c.), 276,763 (met. a.).

Battambang, t., Cambodia; 288 km N.W. of Phnom-Penh; cotton mill; p. (1962) 38,846.

Battersea, dist., London, Eng.; S. of R. Thames; famous park; lge. power sta.; part of Wandsworth.

Batticaloa, t., cap. of E. Prov., Sri Lanka; on E. cst.; comm. ctr.; p. (est. 1968) 24,000.

Battle, t., Rother, East Sussex, Eng.; battle of Hastings 1066; abbey; p. (1971) 33,563 (dist.).

Battle Creek, t., Mich., USA; on Kalamazoo R.; engin., local cereal prod.; p. (1970) 39,931.

Batu Arang, t., Malaya; ctr. of only worked coalfield in Malaya; 45 km from Kuala Lumpur.

Batumi, t., spt. on E. shore of Black Sea; Georgian SSR, USSR; oil, engin., citrus fruits, tea; oil pipeline connects with Baku; resort; airpt; p. (1970) 101,000.

Bauchi, t., Nigeria; cap. Bauchi st.; ctr. of Jos plateau; tin-mng. ctr. [Canada.

Bauld, C., northernmost part of Newfoundland.

Bauru, t., São Paulo st., Brazil; comm. ctr.; food inds.; p. (1970) 120,178.

Bautzen, t., Dresden, E. Germany; on R. Spree; textiles, engin., iron inds.; cath.; p. (est. 1970) 43,670.

Bavaria (Bayern), Land, W. Germany; mtnous., bounded in S. by Alps, inc. Böhmerwald, Fichtelgebirge, Franconian Forest; main Rs. Danube and Main; fertile agr. valleys; forestry and agr.; economic life concentrated in ts., esp. cap. Munich, now a focus of p. immigration; rural beauty attracts tourist tr.; celebrated beer; a. 70,220 km²; p. (1967) 10,280,400.

Bavarian Alps, mtn. range, W. Germany, along Austrian border; Zugspitze (2,969 m) highest mtn. in W. Germany.

Bavarian Forest. See Böhmerwald.

Bawdwin, t., Burma; in Shan plateau; impt. mng. ctr.; wolfram, lead, zinc, silver, rubies.

Bayamón, t., Puerto Rico; in fertile valley; oil refining; p. (1970) 147,552 (t.), 156,192 (met. a.).

Baybay, t., Leyte, Philippines; impt. comm. pt.; p. (est. 1969) 70,200.

Bay City, t., Mich., USA; comm. pt. nr. head of Saginaw B.; fishing; pt. processing inds.; p. (1970) 49,075 (c.), 116,628 (met. a.).

Bayeux, t., Calvados, France; mkt. t.; cath. museum, Bayeux tapestry; p. (1968) 12,871.

Baykal, L. (Ozero Baykal), Siberia, RSFSR; sixth largest fresh-water L. in world; basin forms deepest depression in world (1,616 m); many pts. around shores but frozen Nov.–May; skirted by Trans-Siberian rly.; sturgeon, salmon; tourism; a. 35,483 km².

Bayonne, spt., Pyrénées-Atlantique, S.W. France; cath.; noted for invention of bayonet; Basque Museum; p. (1968) 42,743 (t.), 110,163 (met. a.).

Bayonne, t., N.J., USA; 10 km from New York; chemicals, oil refining; dry docks; p. (1970) 72,743.

Bayreuth, t., Bavaria, W. Germany; home of Wagner; famous for musical festivals in national theatre; p (est. 1969) 65,530.

Baytown, pt., S.E. Texas, USA; industl. t., oil refining and exp.; p. (1970) 43,980.

Beachy Head, chalk headland, S.W. of Eastbourne, East Sussex, Eng.; 175 m high.

Beaconsfield, t., l. gov. dist., Bucks., Eng.; residtl; home of Edmund Burke; p. (est. 1976) 62,600 (dist.).

Beardmore Glacier, Antarctica; one of world's lgst. valley glaciers; over 176 km in length.

Bear I (Björnöya I.), Norway; in Arctic Oc., 208 km S. of Spitzbergen; cod fisheries.

Bearsden, burgh, l. gov. dist. with Milngavie, Scot.; residtl.; p. (1971) 25,013.

Beas (Bias), R., Punjab, India; trib. of Sutlej R.; part of irrigation scheme ; marked limit of Alexander's advance into India, 327 B.C.

Beattock, pass, S. Uplands, Scot.; gives access from valley of R. Clyde to R Annan; used by main W. cst. rly. route from Carlisle to Glasgow and Edinburgh; alt. 309 m.

Beauce, region, central France; flat limestone plateau; arid, few surface streams; thin layer of loam (limon) permits agr.; impt. wheat growing a. (" the granary of France "); p. mainly grouped in vs. [Oc.

Beaufort Sea, off N. Alaska, USA; part of Arctic

Beaujolais, France; in upper Rhône valley, N.E. Massif Central; wine-growing dist.

Beaulieu, v., Hants. Eng.; on Beaulieu R.; Cistercian abbey; car museum.

Beauly, t., Inverness, Scot.; on B. R.; ruined priory.

Beaumaris, t., Anglesey, Gwynedd, N. Wales; pt. on Menai Strait; lt. engin.; resort; p. (1971) 2,096.

Beaumont, t.; 2nd. pt. of Texas, USA; ctr. of petrochemical inds.; p. (1970) 115,716 (c.), 306,016 (met. a.).

Beaune, t., Cote d'Or, France; mediaeval walled t.; ctr. of wine tr.; p. (1968) 17,377.

Beauvais, agr. mkt. t., cap. of Oise dep., N. France; cath.; Gobelin tapestry removed to Paris; p. (1968) 49,347.

Bebington, Wirral, Merseyside, Eng.; part of pt. of Liverpool; soap, chemicals, engin.; p. (1971) 61,488.

Becancourt, t., Quebec, Canada; on S. bank of St. Lawrence; integrated steel mill projected.

Beccles, Waveney, Suffolk, Eng.; mkt t. on R, Waveney S. of Broads; resort, agr. inds.; p. (1971) 8,015.

Béchar (Colom-Béchart) t., N.W. Algeria; airpt.; coal; p. (1966) 42,090.

Bechuanaland. See Botswana.

Beckum, t., N. Rhine-Westphalia, W. Germany; cement, chalk, engin. wks.; p. (est .1969) 22,189.

Beddington and Wallington. See Sutton.

Bedford, co. t., North Beds., Eng.; on R. Ouse, 80 km N. of London; gen. engin., inc. marine and elec., bricks, aero research; Bunyan imprisoned here: p. (1971) 73,064.

Bedfordshire, non-met. co., Eng.; co. t., Bedford; crossed by Chilterns; agr., mkt. gardening, brickmkg., cement, vehicles, engin.; a. 1,232 km²; p. (est. 1976) 491,700.

Bedfordshire, North, l. gov. dist., Beds., Eng.; a. inc. Bedford and surrounding rural a.; p. (est. 1976) 130,300.

Bedfordshire, South, l. gov. dist., Beds., Eng.;

close to Luton and inc. Dunstable and Leighton-Linslade; p. (est. 1976) 99,300.

Bedford Level, once over 162,000 ha of peat marsh in S. Fenland, Eng.; first successful draining initiated by Earl of Bedford 1634.

Bedlington, t., Wansbeck, Northumberland, Eng.; nr. Blyth; coal mng.; electronics; p. (1971) 28,167.

Bedloe's I., or Liberty I., N.Y. harbour, USA; on which the statue of Liberty stands.

Bedwas and Machen, t., Rhymney Valley, Mid Glamorgan, Wales; gas, coal and coke byprods.; new anthracite mine; p. (1971) 12,548.

Bedwellty, t., Islwyn, Gwent, Wales; elec. gds., car upholstery; p. (1971) 25,326.

Bedworth, t., Warwicks., Eng.; nr. Coventry; coal mng., limestone quarrying, engin., textiles; p. (1971) 40,535.

Bedzin, t., S. Poland; coalmng. t. in Upper Silesia; p. (1970) 42,800.

Beerenberg, mtn., Jan Mayen I., Norway, Arctic Oc.; one of lgst. volcanic cones in world; glaciated; alt. 2,546 m.

Beersheba, t., Israel; ctr. for development of the Negev; p. (1968) 69,500.

Beeston and Stapleford, Broxtowe, Notts., Eng.; sub. of Nottingham; engin., drugs, telephones; p. (1971) 63,498.

Bègles, t., Gironde, France; mtg.; p. (1968) 27,330.

Begovat, t., E. Uzbek SSR, USSR; on Syr Dar'ya R.; iron and steel wks.; hydroelectric power; p. (1967) 59,000.

Beira, spt., Moçambique; airpt; rly. runs inland to Salisbury (Rhodesia) and Blantyre (Malawi); exp. sugar, maize, cotton; oil pipeline to Umtali; p. (1960) 64,000.

Beirut, t., cap. of Lebanon; pt. on Mediterranean; anc. Phoenician c., now busy shipping and mercantile ctr.; silk, wool, fruits; 4 univs.; p. (1964) 700,000.

Beisan (Bet She'an), t., Israel; in Jordan valley, c. 90 m below sea level; archaeological finds date from 1500 B.C.; rebuilt since 1948 by Israelis; p. (est. 1970) 11,900.

Bejaia (Bougie), spt., Algeria; impt. tr. ctr.; exp. wood, hides; oil pipeline connection to Hassi-Messoud; p. (1967) 63,000.

Belaya Tserkov, t., N. Ukrainian SSR, USSR; agr. and comm. ctr.; p. (1970) 109,000.

Békéscsaba, t., Hungary; milling; rly. junc.; poultry processing plant; p. (1968) 53,000.

Belém, spt., cap. of Pará st., Brazil; comm. ctr., ch. pt. of Amazon basin (rubber, Brazil nuts, cacao, timber); univ.; p. (1970) 565,097.

Belfast, l. gov. dist., cap, of N. Ireland; pt. on Belfast Lough; Britain's lgst. single shipyard; linen mnf., rope, tobacco, distilling, aircraft, fertilisers, computers; oil refinery on E. side of harbour; univ.; Stormont Castle; p. (est. 1976) 385,000.

Belfort, t., cap. of Belfort dep., E. France, in Alsace; fortress t. between Jura and Vosges; heavy inds., rly. wks., cotton ind.; elec. engin.; p. (1968) 55,833.

Belfort (Territoire de), dep., France; ch. t. Belfort; a. 608 km²; p. (1968) 118,450.

Belgaum, t., Karnataka, India; cotton; alt. 760 m; Jain temples; p. (1971) 192,427 (t.), 213,872 (met a.).

Belgium, kingdom, N.W. Europe, comprises 9 admin. provs.; low-lying except in Ardennes in S.E.; very high density of p., intensive agr. and highly industl.; severe social and economic problems have resulted from decline of Sambre-Meuse coalfield and associated heavy engin. inds., similar difficulties in textile inds. in N.W.; industl. expansion on Kempenland coalfield in N.E. and around Brussels, Antwerp, and Ghent; heavily dependent upon foreign tr. for economic survival; member of EEC; major spt. of Antwerp competing with Rotterdam for hinterland of N. EEC; 2 language groups: Flemish (Dutch dialect) in N., French dialect in S. (Walloon a.); univs. at Brussels, Ghent, Liège, Louvain; cap. Brussels; a. 30,445 km²; p. (1970) 9,650,944.

Belgorod, t., RSFSR; N.W. of Kharkov, on N. Donets R.; rly. junc. in agr. region; p. (1970) 151,000.

Belgrade (Beograd), c., cap. of Yugoslavia; inland pt. on Danube at mouth of Sava R.; industl., admin. and cultural ctr.; univ.; airport; p. (est. 1969) 772,000.

Belitung or Billiton, I., between Sumatra and Kalimantan, Indonesia; tin; a. 4,832 km²; p. 102,375.

Belize (British Honduras), self-gov. Brit. col., Central America; proposed indep. postponed as result of internal discrder; heavy rainfall, hurricanes; tropical forests; poor agr., under-developed; fishing, pine, mahogany; new cap. Belmopen; a. 22,962 km²; p. (est. 1969) 120,000.

Belize, c. former cap. of Belize; mahogany, dye-woods, bananas; almost devastated by hurricane 31 Oct. 1961; cap. moved to Belmopan 80 km further inland; spt.; p. (1966) 38,482.

Bellary, c., Karnataka, India; fort; cotton processing and tr.; p. (1971) 125,183.

Bell Bay, pt., Tasmania, Australia; on bank of Tamar R.; modern pt. and site of aluminium refinery.

Bell, I., Newfoundland E. Canada; in Conception Bay, 32 km N.W. of St. Johns; impt. Wabana iron-ore deposits outcrop on N.W. cst., smelted on Pictou coalfield, Nova Scotia; a. 31 km².

Belle Isle Strait, Canada; between Newfoundland and Labrador, on N. shipping route to Canada from Europe.

Belleville, pt., L. Ontario, Canada; agr. processing; white marble nearby, cement; light inds.; p. (1971) 34,498.

Belleville, t., Ill., USA; industl. ctr., domestic prod., coal; air force training school; p. (1970) 41,699.

Belleville, t., N.J., USA; machin., chemicals; p. (1970) 37,629.

Bellingham, t., spt., Wash., USA; agr. distribution ctr.; timber inds.; salmon canning; p. (1971) 34,498.

Bellingshausen Sea, borders Antarctica; part of S. Pac.; ice floes obstruct passage.

Bellinzona, t., Switzerland; on R. Ticino; 22 km N. of Lugano; three castles built on hills dominating t.; rly. engin.; tourism; p. (1969) 21,049.

Bell Rock, (Inchcape I.), rock and lighthouse 19 km S.E. of Arbroath, Scot.

Belluno, t., cap. of B. prov., Venezia, N. Italy; route ctr. at S. foot of Dolomites; cath.; engin.; p. (1969) 34,129.

Belmopan, new cap., Belize; at geographic ctr. of cty.; replaces Belize.

Belo Horizonte, c., cap. of Minas Gerais st. Brazil; impt. inland c.; ctr. rich agr. and mng. region; steel mills, food inds., textiles, diamond cutting; oil pipeline from Guanabara; univ.; p. (1970) 1,106,722.

Beloretsk, t., Bashkir ASSR, RSFSR; in Ural Mtns. on Belaya R.; iron, metal inds.; p. (est. 1969) 66,000.

Belorussiyan SSR, constituent rep., USSR; low-lying; timber; agr. on drained marshes; peat; 209,790 km²; p. (1970) 9,003,000.

Belovo, t., W. Siberia, RSFSR; in Kuznetsk basin; coal mng. zinc. engin.; p. (1970) 108,000.

Belper, mkt. t., Amber Valley Derbys., Eng.; hosiery, textiles, oil wks., iron foundries; p. (1971) 16,665.

Belsen, v., 24 km N.W. of Celle, W. Germany; notorious second world war concentration camp.

Belterra, t., dist., Pará st., N.E. Brazil; nr. confluence of Tapajós and Amazon Rs; site of Fordlandia scheme.

Beltsy, t., Moldavian SSR, USSR; on trib. of Dniester R.; agr. ctr., food processing; p. (1970) 102,000.

Belvoir, Vale of, Melton, Lincs., Leics., Eng.; clay vale; cattle, sheep; Stilton cheese; recent discovery of valuable coal deposits.

Bembridge, v., E. cst., I. of Wight, Eng.; resort, yachting.

Benalla, t., dist., Victoria, Australia; pastoral and agr.; p. (1972) 8,235 (t.).

Benares. See Varanasi.

Benbecula I., Outer Hebrides, Western Isles, Scot.; between Is. of N. and S. Uist; airpt. in N.; fishing; a. 93 km²; p. 900.

Bendigo, c., Victoria, Australia; former goldmng. dist., gold rush 1851; food processing and tr.; varied inds.; p. (1972) 45,860.

Benevento, c., Campania, Italy; cap. of B. prov. which contains many Roman remains; cath.; agr. processing; p. (1969) 60,082.

Benfleet, t., Castle Point, Essex, Eng.; residtl.; p. (1971) 47,924.

Bengal, Bay of, part of Indian Oc. washing E.

shores of India and W. shores of Burma; receives waters of Rs. Krishna, Ganges, Brahmaputra, Irrawaddy.

Benghazi, joint cap. (with Tripoli) of Libya; spt. and airpt. on G. of Sirte; univ.; former Greek Hesperides; p. (est. 1970) 170,000.

Benguela, t., Angola, S.W. Africa; rly. runs inland to Zaire and Zambia; seaport now lost much tr. to Lobito; p. (est. 1969) 35,162.

Benha, t., Egypt; impt. mkt. t., rail and road ctr. in heart of cultivated a. of Nile delta 48 km N. of Cairo; airpt.; p. (est. 1970) 72,500.

Beni City, t., Nigeria; cap. of Benin st.; former notorious slave ctr.; p. (1971) 121,699.

Benin, People's Rep. of (Dahomey), W. Africa; indep. from France 1960; name changed 1975; limited transport system, agr. mainstay of comm. economy; exp. groundnuts, palm-kernels, palm oil via major pt. of Cotonou; some industl. development; brewing, chemicals, tobacco; equatorial climate, much tropical rain forest; cap. Porto Novo; a. 115,640 km²; p. (est. 1969) 2,640,000.

Beni Suef, t., Egypt; on Nile, 96 km S. of Cairo; ctr. of fertile agr. a.; carpets, cotton; p. (est. 1970) 99,400.

Ben Lawers, mtn., Perth and Kinross, Scot.; by Loch Tay; arctic and alpine flora; alt. 1,215 m.

Ben Macdhui, mtn., Kincardine and Deeside, Scot.; Cairngorm gr.; second highest peak in Brit. Is.; alt. 1,310 m.

Ben Nevis, mtn., Lochaber, Scot.; volcanic; hgst. peak in Brit. Isles alt. 1,344 m.

Benoni, t., Transvaal, S. Africa; gold mng. ctr.; engin.; p. (1970) 162,794.

Benrath, t., W. Germany; on Rhine R. nr. Düsseldorf; R. pt. and industl. t.; chemicals, machin.

Bensberg, t., N. Rhine–Westphalia, W. Germany; 16 km from Cologne; leather gds.; mainly residtl.; foundries; cas.; p. (est. 1969) 40,516.

Bensheim, t., Hesse, W. Germany; ctr. of fruit and wine dist. on E. edge Rhine valley; textiles, paper, metallurgy; p. (est. 1969) 26,975.

Bentley with Arksey, t., South Yorks., Eng.; p. (1971) 22,888.

Benton Harbor, t., Mich., USA; midway along E. cst. L. Michigan; p. (1970) 16,481.

Benue R., Nigeria-Cameroon; rises in Adamawa mtns.; forms ch. trib. of Niger R.; R. pts. and agr. tr.; length 1,392 km.

Ben Vorlich, mtn., Perth and Kinross, Scot.; alt. 983 m.

Benwell, t., Tyne and Wear, Eng.; sub. of Newcastle.

Ben Wyvis, mtn., Ross and Cromarty, Scot.; nr. Dingwall; alt. 1,046 m.

Ben-y-Gloe, mtn., Glen Tilt, Perth and Kinross, Scot.; alt. 1,120 m.

Beograd. See Belgrade.

Beppu, c., Kyushu, Japan; hot spring resort; p. (est. 1971) 124,000.

Berbera, pt., Somalia, on G. of Aden; exp. livestock from pastoral hinterland; new deep-sea pt. completed 1969; airport; p. (est. 1963) 12,219.

Berchtesgaden, v., W. Germany; mtn. resort 24 km S. of Salzburg; Hitler's mtn. retreat; tourism; potash.

Berck-Plage, resort, Pas-de-Calais, France, on Eng. Channel; p. (1968) 13,690.

Berdichev, t., Ukrainian SSR, USSR; ctr. of sugar a.; engin., lt. inds.; p. (est. 1969) 61,000.

Berdyansk, c., Ukrainian SSR, USSR; pt. on Sea of Azov; agr. ctr.; machin.; health resort; p. (1970) 100,000.

Bere Regis, mkt. t., Dorset, Eng.; Saxon royal residence.

Berezina, R., USSR; trib. of Dnieper; forms part of Baltic-Black Sea waterway; 608 km long.

Berezniki, t., E. European RSFSR; pt. on Kelva R., W. Urals; salt, chemicals, paper; p. (1970) 145,000.

Bergama, t., Turkey; anc. Pergamos, ruins; morocco leather inds.; agr. tr.; p. (1965) 24,113.

Bergamo, c., Lombardy, Italy; 54 km N.E. Milan; cath. and academy; silk industry; p. (1969) 125,310.

Bergen, spt., W. cst. Norway; univ.; most impt. comm. pt. in kingdom; shipping, fishing; mftg. inds.; birthplace of Grieg; p. (est. 1969) 115,964.

Bergen op Zoom, t., N. Brabant, Neth.; sugar refining, engin.; p. (1968) 38,489.

Bergerac, t., Dordogne, S.W. France; impt. bridge over Dordogne R.; mkt. for wines and luxury foods; anc. Huguenot stronghold; p. (1968) 28,015.

Bergisches Land, terr., N. Rhine-Westphalia, W. Germany; specialised iron and steel prod.; chemicals, machin.; inc. ts. of Solingen, Remscheid, Velbert, Wuppertal.

Bergisch-Gladbach, t., N. Rhine-Westphalia, W. Germany; 11 km E. of Cologne, paper, metallurgy, textiles; p. (est. 1969) 49,704.

Berhampur, t., Orissa, India; admin. and educational ctr.; p. (1971) 117,662.

Bergstrasse, region, Baden-Württemberg, W. Germany; fruit-growing.

Bering Current (Okhotsk Current, or Oyashio), ocean current, N. Pac. Oc.; flows through Bering Strait from Arctic, along E. cst. of Kamchatka and Japanese Is. Hokkaido, Honshu; relatively cold; moderate summer temperatures along csts. causes fogs.

Bering Sea, part of N. Pac. Oc. between Aleutian Is. and B. Strait; fishing; a. 2,274,020 km².

Bering Strait, narrow sea which separates Asia from N. America, and connects Bering Sea with Arctic Oc.; 58 km wide at narrowest part.

Berkeley, v., Gloucs., Eng.; nr. R. Severn, 24 km N. of Bristol; scene of murder of Edward II; civil nuclear power-sta.

Berkeley, c., Cal., USA; univ.; chemicals; now inc. in San Francisco; p. (1970) 116,716.

Berkhamsted, Dacorum, Herts., Eng.; mkt. t.; chemicals; cas. ruins, 17th cent. school; birthplace of William Cowper the poet; p. (1971) 15,439.

Berkshire, non-met. co., Eng.; chalk downland inc. Inkpen Beacon, White Horse Hills; drained by Thames and tribs.; residtl.; electronics, biscuits; dairying; Windsor Gr. Park; Ascot racecourse; a. 1,256 km²; p. (est. 1976) 659,000.

Berlin, c., former cap. of Germany, Europe; on Spree R.; divided into 4 occupied zones 1945; Soviet (now E. Berlin), British, American, French (now W. Berlin); W. Berlin forms enclave within E. Germany; focal point of escape attempts from E. to W. led to construction of "Berlin Wall"; W. Berlin major industl. ctr. aided by American and W. German capital; educational, cultural and tourist ctr.; relaxation of cold war adding to metropolitan character of c. as meeting place between E. and W.; wartime reconstruction has lagged in E. Berlin; p. (est. 1970) 2,134,256 (W. Berlin); 1,200,000 (E. Berlin).

Bermondsey. See Southwark.

Bermuda, Brit. gr. coral Is. (360 in no. of which 20 are inhabited) N. Atlantic; about 1,120 km E. of S.C.; Hamilton, on Long I. is the ch. t.; Brit. and US air and naval stas.; favourite winter resort for Americans; inds. attracted by tax incentives; no surface water; total a. 54 km²; p. (est. 1969) 52,000.

Bern, c., cap. of B. can. and fed. cap. Switzerland; on Aare R.; cath., univ.; textiles, musical instruments, chocolate; H.Q. of Postal Union; bear pit; p. (1969) 166,800 (c.), 258,000 (met. a.).

Bern, can., Switzerland; fertile valleys, dairying; watches; hydroelectric power; plans for separate can. in Jura reg.; a. 6,881 km²; p. (1969) 1,005,000.

Bernard, Great St., one of the Alps in the S. of the Valais, Switzerland; highest point 3,390 m; height of mtn. pass between Italy (Aosta) and Switzerland (Martigny), 2,477 m; famous hospice for travellers in monastery on mtn.; road tunnel completed 1962.

Bernard, Little St., one of Graian Alps, Savoy, S. of Mt. Blanc, France; pass traversed by Hannibal 218 B.C.

Bernburg, t., Halle, E. Germany; cas.; chemicals, salt mng.; p. (est. 1970) 45,322.

Bernese Oberland (Berner Alpen), alpine region, Switzerland; 35 peaks over 3,000 m inc. Finsteraarhorn and Jungfrau; tourist a. inc. resorts of Interlaken and Grindelwald.

Bernina Alps, Switzerland; alt. 4,050 m.

Berri, t., S. Australia; ctr. of irrigated fruit growing a. on R. Murray; wines; p. (1966) 2,224.

Berri, oilfield, Saudi Arabia; 72 km N.W. of Ras Tannura; the field extends offshore.

Berwick, l. gov. dist., former co., Borders Reg.,

S.E. Scot.; a. of sheep rearing and woollen inds. in S. Uplands; a. 875 km²; p. (1971) 17,200.

Berwick-upon-Tweed, l. gov. dist., Northumberland, Eng.; spt. on mouth of Tweed; border t.; fishing, lt. engin., tweeds, knitwear; cas. ruins; p. (est. 1976) 25,500 (dist.).

Besançon, t., cap. of Doubs dep., France; cath., observatory, univ.; farm implements, textiles; watch- and clock-making; birthplace of Victor Hugo; p. (1968) 113,220 (t.), 116,197 (met. a.).

Besche, t., Saarland, W. Germany; oil refining.

Beskids, W. and E., (Beskidy Zachodnie), mtn. range, Poland, ČSSR, E. Europe; northern range of Carpathian mtn. system, seldom exceeds alt. 1,200 m, many passes; forested; tourism; length 352 km.

Bessarabia, terr., ceded to USSR by Romania 1940, and now part of Moldavian SSR; agr. region. [33,428.

Bessemer, t., Ala., USA; iron and steel; p. (1970)

Bethany (El Azarieh), v., on Mt. of Olives 6 km W. of Jerusalem, Jordan.

Bethel, anc. c., the modern Beitin, Jordan; 16 km N. Jerusalem.

Bethesda, t., Arfon, Gwynedd, Wales; slate, lt. engin; p. (1971) 4,167.

Bethlehem, t., Jordan; 9 km S.W. Jerusalem; birthplace of Christ; p. (est. 1967) 16,313.

Bethlehem, t., Penns., USA; 80 km N. of Philadelphia; iron-wks.; univ.; p. (1970) 72,686.

Bethnal Green, dist., London, Eng.; in E. End of London; furniture, clothing; now in Tower Hamlets.

Béthune, t., Pas-de-Calais, France; rail and canal ctr. for coalfield; mkt. t.; p. (1968) 28,379 144,678 (met. a.).

Betteshanger, v., Kent, Eng.; on N. flank of N. Downs, 6 km W. of Deal; coal mng.

Bettws-y-Coed, t., Aberconwy, Gwynedd, Wales; waterfalls; tourism; p. (1971) 726.

Beuel, t., N. Rhine-Westphalia, W. Germany; on E. bank R. Rhine opposite Bonn; chemicals, furniture; p. (est. 1969) 38,668.

Beuthan. See Bytom.

Beverley, l. gov. dist., mkt. t., Humberside, Eng.; famous minster (13th cent.); agr. processing; p. (est. 1976) 106,700 (dist.).

Beverly, c., Mass., USA; footwear, machin.; p. (1970) 38,348.

Beverly Hills, t., Cal., USA; sub. of Los Angeles; home of many film celebrities; p. (1970) 33,416.

Beverwijk, t., nr. Haarlem, N. Holland, Neth.; agr. prods.; p. (1968) 42,008.

Bewdley, Wyre Forest, Hereford and Worcs., Eng.; mkt. t. on R. Severn; birthplace of Stanley Baldwin; residtl.; p. (1971) 7,212.

Bexhill-on-Sea, t., Rother, East Sussex, Eng.; resort; p. (1971) 32,849.

Bexley, former bor., W. Kent; now outer bor., Greater London, Eng.; inc. Chislehurst and Sidcup (N. of the A.20, Crayford and Erith; p. (est. 1976) 213,500.

Béziers, t., Hérault, France; ctr. of wine, brandy tr. and inds.; chemicals; p. (1968) 82,271.

Bezwada. See Vijayawada.

Bhadravati, t., Karnataka, India; steel; p. (1971) 61,155 (t.), 101,358 (met. a.).

Bhagalpur, t., Bihar, India; agr. tr. ctr. on R. Ganges; p. (1971) 172,202.

Bhamo, t., Upper Burma; on Irrawaddy; inland limit of steam boats; mkt. ctr.; ruby mines; p. 10,000.

Bhandara, cap. of Bhandara dist., Maharashtra, India; 48 km E. of Nagpur; cotton cloth, brass mftg.; p. (1961) 27,710.

Bhatpara, t., W. Bengal, India; on R. Hooghly; industl. t.; jute. engin.; p. (1971) 204,750.

Bhaunager, t., Gujarat, India; pt. on G. of Cambay; exp. cotton, oilseeds; p. (1971) 225,358.

Bhilai, t., Madhya Pradesh, India; steel plant; rails and rly. sleepers; p. (1961) of industl. t. 86,116; of Durg 47,114.

Bhim-Gora, sacred pool, place of Hindu pilgrimage, Uttar Pradesh, India.

Bhopal, c., cap. of Madhya Pradesh, India; impt. tr. ctr.; varied inds.; prehistoric cave paintings nearby; p. (1971) 298,022 (c.), 384,859 (met. a.).

Bhutan, kingdom, indep. mtn. st., E. Himalayas; heavy monsoon rain, rich tropical vegetation, valuable forests; N.–S. ridges and valleys result in semi-closed communities; first motor link with India opened 1962; cap. Thimbu

a. c. 46,620 km²; alt. 7,558 m (Kula Kangri); p. scattered and nomadic (est. 1969) 770,000.

Bhubaneswar, t., cap. of Orissa, **India**; 29 km from Cuttack; admin. ctr.; Hindu temples, pilgrimage ctr.; p. (1971) 105,491.

Biafra, Bight of. *See* **Bonny, Bight of.**

Bialystok, t., **Poland**; cap. of B. prov., nr. Grodno; major industl. ctr.; rly. ctr.; p. (1970) 158,500.

Biarritz, t., Pyrénées-Atlantique dep., France; on Bay of Biscay; seaside resort; p. (1968) 26,985.

Biberach, t., Baden-Württemberg, **W. Germany**; on R. Kinzig; spa; wood, metal and engin. inds.; p. (est. 1969) 25,456.

Bicester, Cherwell, Oxford, **Eng.**; anc. mkt. t., N.E. of Oxford; p. (1971) 12,340.

Biddulph, t., Staffs. Moorlands, Staffs., **Eng.**; coal mng., machin., textiles, furniture; residtl.; p. (1971) 17,372.

Bideford, Torridge, N. Devon, **Eng.**; pt. on estuary R. Torridge; mkt., boat-bldg.; resort; p. (1971) 11,766.

Biel (Bienne), t., Berne, Switzerland; nr. Lake B.; watches; impt. industl. ctr.; p. (1969) 67,800.

Bielawa, t., Wroclaw prov., S.W. **Poland**; textiles; p. (1970) 31,000.

Bielefeld, t., Rhine-Westphalia, **W. Germany**; ch. ctr. of linen industry; machin., bicycles; p. (est. 1969) 168,700.

Biella, t., Vercelli, Italy; textiles; p. (1961) (est. 1968) 53,839.

Bielsko-Biala, t., Katowice prov., **Poland**; woollens, linen, metal, chemicals; p. (est. 1969) 102,700.

Bien-hoa, t., nr. Ho Chi-minh City, S. Vietnam; sugar refining; cotton mills.

Bies-Bosch, reclaimed fenland area between N. Brabant and S.W. Neth.; sugar refining, dairying; a. 142 km².

Biggar, sm. burgh, Lanark, **Scot.**; 213 m in Southern Uplands; p. (1971) 1,637.

Biggin Hill, Greater London, Eng.; nr. Orpington; famous airfield of Battle of Britain.

Biggleswade, t., Mid Beds., **Eng.**; in valley of R. Ivel, 14 km S.E. of Bedford; ctr. of fruit-growing and mkt. gardening dist.; hydraulic machin. tools, hosiery, caravans; p. (1971) 9,598.

Big Horn Mtns., Wyo. and Mont., **USA**; Rockies; favourite film location; attractive agr. valleys; highest alt., 3,600 m.

Bihać, t., Yugoslavia; on R. Una; recent industl. development; timber processing.

Bihar, st., N.W. **India**; in Ganges basin; hilly; bulk of p. in agr. N.; irrigation; minerals in S.E.; coal, iron, mica; steelwks. at Jamshedpur, oil refining at Barauni; cap. Patna, admin. ctr. Ranchi; a. 173,882 km²; p. (1971) 56,387,296.

Bihar, t., Bihar, **India**; within middle Ganges valley nr. Patna; p. (1971) 100,046.

Biisk, c., Siberia, **USSR**; ctr. of rich agr. a.; meat packing, textiles; p. (1970) 186,000.

Bijagós, Archipelago dos (Bissagos Is.); off W. cst. Guinea-Bissau; c. 14 Is.; coconuts, rice; ch. t. Bolama on Bolama I.; a. 1,554 km².

Bijapur, t., Karnataka, **India**; cotton tr. and inds.; ruins; former cap. of B. kingdom; p. (1971) 103,931.

Bikaner, t., Rajasthan, **India**; in Thar desert; on former caravan route; wool tr., bldg. stone, handicrafts; p. (1971) 188,518 (t.), 208,894 (met. a.).

Bikini, atoll, **Pac. Oc.**; atomic-bomb tests (1946).

Bilaspur, t., Madhya Pradesh, **India**; silks, cottons; p. (1971) 98,410 (t.), 130,740 (met. a.).

Bilbao, spt., N. **Spain**; cap. Basque prov. of Viscaya; formerly famous for rapier making; iron ore, smelting; pipeline from Ayoluengo oilfield; p. (est. 1969) 369,559.

Billinge and Winstanley, t., Lancs., **Eng.**; former coal-mng. a.; p. (1971) 11,379.

Billingham, t. Cleveland, **Eng.**; on N. of Tees estuary; major petro-chemical plant.

Billings, t., Mont., **USA**; agr. tr. ctr. in irrigated a.; sulphur plant; p. (1970) 61,581.

Billingsgate, London, Eng.; old river-gate and wharf, now ch. fish mkt. of England.

Bilma (Kawar), oasis t., Niger; on caravan route from Tripoli to Agadés and L. Chad; salt tr., dates; p. c. 1,000.

Billiton I. *See* **Belitung.**

Biloxi, t., Miss., **USA**; fishing, tourist ctr.; US

Coast Guard air base; p. (1970) 47,814 (c.), 131,268 (met. a.).

Bilston, t. West Midlands, **Eng.**; part of Wolverhampton; iron and steel.

Bingen, t., Rhineland Palatinate, **W. Germany**; at S. entrance to Rhine gorge; wine; beautiful scenery; tourism; p. (est. 1967) 20,700.

Bingerville, spt., **Ivory Coast**, W. Africa; rubber processing.

Bingham Canyon, t., N. Utah, **USA**; silver, gold, lead; major open pit copper mine; p. (1970) 31.

Binghampton, N.Y., **USA**; on Susquehanna R.; boot factories, aircraft components, cameras; p. (1970) 63,229 (c.), 297,959 (met. a.).

Bingley, West Yorks., **Eng.**; mkt. t. on R. Aire, 26 km N.W. of Leeds; textiles, engin., agr.; p. (1971) 26.540.

Bintan I., lgst. island of Riouw archipelago, **Indonesia**; bauxite, tin.

Bintenne, dist., Sri Lanka; remote a., sparse p.; lge. Gal Oya reservoir; tea and rubber estates.

Biratnagar, t., S.E. Nepal, in the Tarai; jute, sugar, cotton milling, stainless steel; p. (1971) 44,938.

Birbhum, dist., W. Bengal, **India**; cap. Suri; healthy climate; rice, sugar; mnfs. silk, cotton; a. 4,550 km²; p. (1961) 1,446,158

Birkenhead, Wirral, Merseyside, **Eng.**; spt. on R. Mersey, opposite Liverpool; handles industl. goods; heavy and pt. processing inds.; shipbldg.; p. (1971) 137,738.

Birmingham, c., met. dist., West Midlands, **Eng.**; industl. cap. Midlands, second lgst. c. Gt. Britain; metal inds.; motor vehicles, components and accessories; major growth due to Industl. Revolution; univ., cath.; p. (est. 1976) 1,058,800 (dist.).

Birmingham, t. Ala., **USA**; coal, iron, limestone, steel, aircraft, chemicals, textiles; p. (1970) 297,364 (c.), 729,984 (met. a.).

Birnam, v., Perth and Kinross, **Scot.**; location of Birnam Wood in *Macbeth*; former royal forest.

Birobidzhan, or Jewish aut. oblast, RSFSR; in Khabarovsk terr.; agr., timber and mng. inds.; a° 35,988 km²; cap. Birobidzhan City; p. (1968) 174,000 (inc. 15,000 Jews).

Birr, U.D. Offaly, R.o.I.; mkt. t. on Brosna R.; observatory; p. (1966) 3,266.

Bir Tlacsin, Libya; 192 km S.W. Tripoli; oilfields.

Bisbee, t., Arizona, **USA**; very rich copper deposits, gold, silver, lead; p. (1970) 8,328.

Biscarosse, Landes dep., **France**; 72 km S.W. Bordeaux; rocket and missile testing range projected; p. (1968) 7,781.

Biscay, Bay of, stormy a. of Atl. Oc., W. of France and N. of Spain. from Ushant to C. Ortegal; the Roman Sinus Aquitanicus; heavy seas.

Bisceglie, t., Apulia, **Italy**; spt. on E. cst. 35 km N.W. of Bari; tr. in wine and olives; light inds.; cath.; p. (est. 1968) 44,317.

Bischofswerda, t., Dresden, E. **Germany**; quarrying, glass and iron inds.; rly. ctr.; p. (1963) 11,285.

Bishop Auckland, t., Wear Valley, Durham, **Eng.**; palace of Bishop of Durham; iron. lt. engin.; former coal mng.; p. (1971) 33,292.

Bishopbriggs, sm. burgh, Strathkelvin, Scot.; p. (1971) 21,684.

Bishop Rock, isolated rock, lighthouse, Scilly Is., **Eng.**; 58 km S.W. of Land's End, Cornwall; recognised internationally as E. end of trans-Atlantic ocean crossing.

Bishop's Stortford, East Herts., **Eng.**; mkt. t. on Stort R.; light inds.; Hatfield forest nearby; Norman cas.; p. (1971) 22,054.

Biskra, t., Algeria; admin. ctr., winter resort; oasis nearby; date mkt.; p. (1966) 59,052.

Bisley, v., Surrey, **Eng.**; ranges of Nat. Rifle Ass. on B. common.

Bismarck, t., st. cap. N.D., **USA**; on Missouri R.; agr. mkt. ctr.; p. (1969) 33,700.

Bismarck Archipelago, volcanic gr., S.W. Pac. Oc., off New Guinea, admin. by Australia; p. (est. 1962) 174,115.

Bisotūn, t., Iran; in ruins; monuments to Darius I (the Great).

Bissagos Is. *See* **Bijagós, Achipelago dos.**

Bissau, t., cap. of Guinea-Bissau; former ctr. of slave tr.; airpt.; p. (1970) 62,101.

Bitola, t., Macedonia, Yugoslavia; varied mnfs., recent industl. development; mosques; p. (1971) 65,851.

Bitonto, t., Apulia, on E. cst. 11 km N.W. of Bari; Italy; cath.; p. (est. 1968) 41,749.

Bitterfeld, t., Halle, E. Germany; lignite mng., engin., chemicals; p. (est. 1970) 28,964.

Bitter Lakes, Isthmus of Suez, Egypt, utilised by Suez Canal.

Biwa-ko, lgst. lake in Japan, S. Honshu; 101 m a.s.l.; canal to Kyoto provides hydroelectric power; superb scenery, historical associations; tourism; a. 675 km².

Biysk or Bisk, c., Altai terr., RSFSR; pt. on Biya R.; terminus of branch of Turk-Sib. rly.; p. (est. 1967) 181,000.

Bizerte, c., N. Tunisia; pt. and naval sta. on Med.; the anc. Hippo Zaritus; fishing, oil refining, steelwks., tyres; p. (1966) 95,023.

Björnborg. See Pori.

Blaby, l. gov. dist., Leics., Eng.; sm. a. S.W. of Leicester; p. (est. 1976) 77,300.

Black Belt, coastlands of Miss. and Ala., USA, where black soil prairie land is good for cotton.

Blackburn, t., l. gov. dist., Lancs., Eng.; once major cotton weaving ctr.; engin., lt. inds.; p. (est. 1976) 142,500 (dist.).

Black Country, Midlands, Eng.; formerly impt. iron-working and coal-mng. dist. mainly in S. West Midlands; now a. of lt. engin.; c. 130 km².

Blackdown Hills, Devon and Somerset, Eng.; sandstone hills rising over 305 m.

Black Forest. See Schwarzwald.

Blackheath, open common, S.E. London. Eng.; mustering place of Wat Tyler's (1381) and Jack Cade's (1450) revolutionary peasants; now main attraction of expensive residtl. a.; a. 108 ha.

Black Hills, mtns., between S.D. and Wyo., USA; highest, Horney Peak, 2.208 m; form part of Nat. Park.

Black Isle, peninsula, between Cromarty and Beauly Firths, Ross and Cromarty, Scot.; agr., fisheries, quarrying; a. 621 km².

Black Mtns., Powys and Dyfed, S. Wales; rise to 802 m in Brecknock Van, sandstone plateau; moorland; valleys used for reservoirs; Nat. Park.

Black Mtns., Powys, S. Wales; rise to 811 m in Waun Fach.

Blackpool, t., l. gov. dist., Lancs., Eng ; on cst. of Fylde dist.; one of major Brit. resorts; p. (est. 1976) 149,000 (dist.).

Black Prairie, region, Texas, USA; extends 560 km S.W. from Ouachita Mtns. to Austin; contains very fertile Black Waxy and Grande Prairie sub-regions devoted almost entirely to cotton growing; ch. ts., Dallas, Fort Worth, Austin; a. 77,700 km².

Blackrod, t., Gtr. Manchester, Eng.; nr. Chorley; former cotton weaving; p. (1971) 4,801.

Black Sea, bordered by 4 sts., USSR (N. and E.), Turkey (S.), Bulgaria, Romania (W.); receives waters of Danube, Dniester, Dnieper, Don, Bug; stagnant and lifeless below 146 m; fisheries in N. and W.; oil exploration by Turkey; a. 424,760 km² (exc. Sea of Azov).

Blacksod Bay, cst. of Mayo, R.o.I.

Black Volta, R., rises in Upper Volta, flows E. and S. into L Volta, Ghana; length c. 1,200 km.

Blackwater R., N. Ireland; rising in Dungannon, it forms border with R.o.I.; enters L. Neagh; 80 km long.

Blackwater R., R.o.I.; flows from Knockanefune to enter Atl. Oc. at pt. and resort of Youghal; chain of sm. ts. along course; 144 km long.

Blaenau Gwent, l. gov. dist., Gwent, Wales.; inland valley a. inc. Ebbw Vale and Abertillery; p. (est. 1976) 83,100.

Blaenavon, t., Torfaen, Gwent, Wales; former coal mng.; p. (1971) 7,182.

Blagoveshchensk, t., E. Siberia, RSFSR, on Chinese bdr. and R. Amur; wat. pl.; engin., sawmilling, flour milling; on Trans-Siberian rly.; p. (1970) 128,000.

Blair Atholl, v., Perth and Kinross, Scot.; tourist resort; cas.; seat of Duke of Atholl.

Blairgowrie and Rattray, burgh, Perth and Kinross, Scot.; at foot of Scot. Highlands; mkt. t. in Strathmore fruit growing dist.; p. (1971) 5,553.

Blakeney, v., N. Norfolk. Eng.; nr. sand spit; yachting; wild fowl.

Blandford or Blandford Forum, North Dorset, Eng.; on R. Stour; pastoral mkt. t. since 13th cent.; p. (1971) 3,643.

Blantyre, c., Malawi; in Shire Highlands; linked

by rail to Beira (Moçambique); comm. ctr.; timber processing; p. (1966) 109,795 (met. a.).

Blantyre, v., East Kilbride, Scot.; Lower B. birthplace of David Livingstone.

Blarney, v., 6 km N.W. Cork, R.o.I.; cas. and Blarney stone; p. (1966) 932.

Blasket Is., Kerry, R.o.I.; rocky Is.; uninhabited since 1953.

Blaydon, t., Tyne and Wear, Eng.; former coal mng.; p. (1971) 32,018.

Bled, glacial L., Slovenia, Yugoslavia; tourism.

Blenheim, t., S.I., N.Z.; fruit; p. (1971) 14,760.

Blenheim, v., W. Germany; scene of battle (1704) when English and Austrians under Marlborough defeated the French and Bavarians; Blenheim Palace, Woodstock, Oxon, Eng., named in honour of this victory.

Blessington, L., Wicklow, R.o.I.; glacial L., now serves as reservoir for Dublin.

Bletchley, Bucks., Eng.; expanded t.; p. (1971) 30,608.

Blida, t., Algeria; agr. tr., citrus fruits; p. (1967) 87,000.

Bloemfontein, t., cap. O.F.S., S. Africa; on plateau, alt. 1,393 m; route and tr. ctr.; univ.; p. (1970) 180,179 (met. a.).

Blois, t., cap. of Loire-et-Cher dep., France; historic t. on Loire R.; Renaissance château; wines; p. (1968) 44,762.

Bloomfield, t., N.J., USA; pharmaceuticals, metal and elec. gds.; sub. N.J. c.; p. (est. 1969) 53,000.

Bloomington, t., Ill., USA; comm. ctr. and industl. t. in rich agr. and coalmng. a.; univ.; p. (1970) 39,398 (c.), 103,308 (met. a.).

Bloomington, t., Ind., USA; electronic equipment, furniture, structural glass; univ.; p. (est. 1969) 48,000.

Bloomsbury, dist., London, Eng.; fashionable dist. with many squares; famous for B. gr. of authors in first quarter of 20th cent.; inc. Brit. Museum, Univ. of London.

Bludenz, t., W. Austria; cotton, watches; p. (est. 1965) 11,400.

Blue Grass, dist., Ky., USA; area where blue grass abundant; horse breeding.

Blue Mountains, t., N.S.W., Australia; tourist ctr.; new t. (1947); p. (est. 1968) 32,110.

Blue Mtns., Jamaica; famous for coffee; dense forest; tourism; average alt. 900–1,200 m, rising to 2,294 m in Blue Mtn. peak.

Blue Nile (Bahr-el-Azraq), R., rises in tablelands of Ethiopia, joins the White Nile at Khartoum; its seasonal flooding provides the bulk of water for irrigation in Sudan and Egypt.

Blue Ridge Mtns., S. Penn., Ga., USA; inc. Shenandoah valley; superb scenery, resorts; average alt. 600–1,200 m, rising to 1.737 m in Grandfather Mtn.

Bluff, S.I., N.Z.; 29 km from Invercargill; spt. for Southland prov.; major aluminium ctr.; p. (1971) 3,246.

Blumenau, mkt. t., Santa Catarina st., Brazil; butter, sugar; p. (est. 1968) 84,139.

Blyth, spt., Northumberland, Eng.; on coalfield; shipbldg.; now as B. Valley forms l. gov. dist.; p. (est. 1976) 69,300 (dist.).

Bo, t., Sierra Leone; gold; admin. H.Q.; p. (1963) of dist. 209,000.

Boa Vista, t., R. pt., cap. Roraima st., Brazil; p. (est. 1967) 34,659.

Bobbio, t., Emilia-Romagna, Italy, in northern Apennines; ctr. European cultural life, 9th–12th cent.; St. Columban founded monastery, 612.

Bobo Dioulassa, t., Upper Volta; agr. tr., gold mng.; p. (1967) 68,000.

Bobigny, N.E. sub. of Paris, cap. of Seine-St. Denis dep., France; varied inds.; p. (1968) 39,453.

Bobruysk, t., Belorussian SSR, USSR; pt. on R. Berezina; engin., sawmilling, paper, cellulose, grain; p. (1970) 138,000.

Bocholt, t., N. Rhine-Westphalia, W. Germany; machin., textiles, elec. gds.; p. (est. 1967) 47,200.

Bochum, t., N. Rhine-Westphalia, W. Germany; heart of Ruhr iron and steel ind.; known since 9th cent.; new (1962) Univ. of Ruhr; p. (1968) 346,805.

Boden, t., Sweden; north of Luleå R.; military and comm. ctr.; p. (est. 1970) 24,727.

Bodensee (L. Constance), S.W. West Germany and

Switzerland; 72 km long, 14 km wide.; R. Rhine flows through; fruit and horticulture on warmer slopes of L.

Bodmin, co. t., North Cornwall, Eng.; on S.W. flank of Bodmin moor; china clay, lt. engin.; p. (1971) 9,204.

Bodmin Moor, upland, N.E. Cornwall, Eng.; lower slopes cultivated, higher slopes used for sheep pastures; average alt. 300 m, highest point, Brown Willy, alt, 419 m; major ctr. of china clay quarrying.

Bodö, t., Norway; nr. Lofoten Is.; spt., fish processing; N. rly. terminus; p. (est. 1967) 14,000.

Bodrum, t., on Aegean cst., Turkey; anc. Halicarnassus; 15th cent. Crusader castle; fishing.

Boeotia, region of anc. Greece; scene of many battles; Thebes was the ch. c.; home of Hesiod and Pindar.

Bogdo Ula, massif, Sinkiang, China; forms N. perimeter of Turfan depression; 240 km wide, average alt. 4,000 m, rising to 5,479 m in Turpanat Targh.

Bognor Regis, t., Arun, West Sussex. Eng.; residtl.; seaside resort; p. (1971) 34,389.

Bogor, t., Java, Indonesia; rubber factory, textiles, footwear; p. (1971) 195,882.

Bogota, cap. and lgst. c. of Colombia; in E. Cordilleras, 2,745 m a.s.l.; univ., nat. observatory, colonial architecture; political, social and financial ctr. of rep.; p. (est. 1972) 2,680,100 (c.), 2,818,300 (met. a.).

Bohemia, historic region, former kingdom, W. ČSSR; plateau drained by R. Elbe; borders W. Germany; agr. dist.; minerals inc. lignite, graphite; textiles, sugar, pottery.

Böhmerwald (Bohemian Forest), forested range of mtns. between ČSSR and Bavaria,W. Germany; 240 km long; alt. 1,479 m at Aber; region of poor soils; sm. farms; some mng. and quarrying.

Bohol I., Philippines; maize, coconuts, rice; a. 3,864 km²; p. (1970) 674,806.

Boise, t., cap. of Idaho, USA; financial ctr.; timber mills; hot springs; p. (1970) 73,330 (c.), 109,398 (met. a.).

Bois-Colombes, sub. of Paris, Hauts-de-Seine dep., France; p. (1968) 28,934.

Boksburg, t., Transvaal, S. Africa; industl.; former coal-mng.; t. p. (1970) 104,745.

Bolama, spt., Bijagós Is., Guinea-Bissau; p. c. 4,000.

Bolan Pass, Baluchistan, Pakistan; pass from Pakistan to Afghanistan; summit 1,800 m.

Bolbec, t., Seine-Maritime, France; 19 km E. of Le Havre; textiles; elec. engin.; p. (1968) 13,053.

Boldon, t., Tyne and Wear, Eng.; coal mng.; p. (1971) 23,904.

Boleslawiec (Bunzlau), t., Lower Silesia, Poland; German before 1945; on the Bóbr R., pottery; p. (1970) 30,500.　　　　[and arsenic.

Boliden, t., N. Sweden; impt. deposits of copper

Bolivia, inland rep., S. America; land-locked, 9 deps.; cap. nominally Sucre, actual admin. H.Q. La Paz; politically unstable; much US investment but discouraged by nationalism from late 1960s; p. dispersed over wide a.; relief makes transport difficult; moves towards gaining access to cst. via internat. corridor; forests; savannahs; agr. in backward conditions; rubber, quinine, cattle, hides; ch. exp. tin; petroleum; language Spanish; a. 1,331,661 km²; p. (est. 1969) 4,804,000.

Bollington, t., Cheshire, Eng.; nr. Macclesfield; textile finishing; p. (1971) 6,610.

Bologna, c., N. Italy; cap. of B. prov. on N. flank of Apennines; impt. route ctr. commanding road and rly. across Apennines to Florence; preserved and restored in Arcadian style by Communist admin.; univ., service t.; p. (1969) 490,675.

Bologoye, RSFSR; depot and impt. junc. on Leningrad and Moscow rly.; p. 10,000.

Bolsa Island, Cal., USA; nuclear power and desalination project in progress.

Bolsena, L., Latium region, Italy; occupies lge. extinct volcanic crater in S. of Tuscan Hills 96 km N.W. of Rome; a. (approx.) 129 km².

Bolshoya Volga, t., RSFSR; 128 km N. of Moscow, at junc. of Volga and Moscow Volga Canal; Soviet Institute of Nuclear Studies.

Bolsover, t., l. gov. dist., Derbys., Eng.; limestone, coal, textiles; cas.; Hardwick Hall 6 km to S.; p. (est. 1976) 70,900 (dist.).

Bolton, t., met. dist., Gtr. Manchester, Eng.; cotton, textiles, engin.; p. (est. 1976) 261,000 (dist.).

Bolton, Abbey, North Yorks., Eng.; ruined Augustinian Priory.

Bolzano, t., Trentino Alto Adige, Italy; on R. Isarco at S. approach to Brenner Pass; resort; p. (1969) 104,699.

Boma, t., Zaïre; pt. on estuary of R. Zaïre; exp. timber, cocoa, palm prods., bananas; p. (est. 1967) 79,230.

Bombay, spt., cap. of Maharashtra st., India; harbour, docks, rly. ctr.; univ.; greatest cotton ctr. in republic; pt. handles nearly half of India's foreign tr.; oil refinery; film industry; univ., fine public bldgs.; p. (1971) 5,970,575.　　　　　　　　[7,537.

Bonaire I., Neth. Antilles; a. 287 km²; p. (1968)

Bondy, N.E. sub. of Paris, Seine-St. Denis dep., France; brewing, chemicals; p. (1968) 51,692.

Bône. See Annaba.

Bo'ness, burgh, W. Lothian, Scot.; spt. on Firth of Forth, 6 km E. of Grangemouth; foundries, timber yards; p. (1971) 12,853.

Bonifacio, spt., Corse du Sud, Corsica, France; opposite Sardinia, on Strait of Bonifacio; p. (1968) 2,433.

Bonin Is., Pac. Oc., Japan; 15 Is., volcanic; 960 km S. of Tokyo; a. 103 km²; p. (1965) 203.

Bonn, c., fed. cap. of W. Germany; at confluence of Rs. Sieg and Rhine; univ.; seat of W. German parliament; birthplace of Beethoven; founded in Roman times; varied inds. inc. printing, publishing; p. (est. 1967) 138,000 (c.); (est. 1969) 300,400 (met. a.).

Bonnet a l'Eveque, mtn., Haiti; sheer sides, flat top; site of La Ferrière fortress. alt. 900 m.

Bonneville Dam, Ore., Wash., USA; across R. Columbia 64 km above Portland (Ore.), provides irrigation to valleys in Columbia-Snake Plateau; locks permit navigation and provide hydroelectric power.

Bonneville Salt Flats, Utah, USA; remains of anc. lake; world automobile speed test, 1937–47.

Bonny, t., S. Nigeria; at mouth of R. Bonny, Niger delta; oil terminal.

Bonny, Bight of (Bight of Biafra until 1975), W. Africa; bay lying E. of the G. of Guinea between the Niger and C. Lopez.

Bonnyrigg and Lasswade, burgh, Midlothian, Scot.; 11 km S.E. of Edinburgh. p. (1971) 7,102.

Boothferry, l. gov. dist., Humberside, Eng.; lowland a. of I. of Axholme and inc. Goole; p. (est. 1976) 56,800.

Boothia, peninsula on Arctic cst., Franklin dist., Canada; separated from Baffin I., by G. of B.

Bootle, t., Sefton, Merseyside, Eng.; on E. side of entrance to Mersey estuary; shares line of docks with Liverpool; dockside inds. inc. tanning, ship-repairing; tin plant; p. (1971) 74,208.

Bor, t., Serbia, Yugoslavia; copper mng. and processing; p. (est. 1965) 20,000.

Borås, t., S. Sweden; on R. Viske, nr. Göteborg; ctr. of textile and clothing inds.; p. (1968) 70,144.

Bordeaux, spt., cap. of Gironde, France; nr. mouth of R. Garonne; cath., univ.; exp. wines, liqueurs, sugar, potatoes, pit props; oil refining nearby; p. (1968) 266,662 (c.), 555,152 (met. a.).

Borders Region, l. gov. reg., Scot.; occupies E. half of Southern Uplands; hilly cty. drained by R. Tweed and tribs.; rural a. interspersed by mkt. and mill ts.; a. 4,670 km². p. (1971) 98,840.

Bordighera, t., Italy; Riviera winter resort; p. (est. 1968) 12,172.

Boreham Wood, t., Herts., Eng.; lt. engin., computers, film studios.

Borinage, dist. around Mons, Belgium; impt. but declining coalfield.

Borislav, t., Ukrainian SSR, USSR; formerly Polish (1919–39); oilfield, natural gas; richest ozocerite deposits in Europe; oil pipeline links to Drogobych and Dashava; p. (est. 1967) 32,000.

Borisoglebsk, t., RSFSR; food processing; p. (est. 1969) 65,000.

Borisov, t., Belorussiyan SSR, USSR; defeat of Napoleon, 1812; chemicals, sawmills, hardware; p. (est. 1967) 74,000.

Borkum, I., W. Germany; off Ems R. estuary; a. 36 km²; p. (est. 1967) 5,774.

Borlänge, t., Sweden; iron, paper, engin. and chemical wks.; p. (1968) 29,060.

Borneo, lgst. I. in Malay archipelago and 3rd lgst. in world; high mtn. range extends from ctr. to N. rising to 4,180 m; low-lying swamp in S.; politically divided into Kalimantan (Indonesian B.), Sabah and Sarawak (E. Malaysia) and Brunei; jungle-covered and underdeveloped; scattered tribes inc. Dyaks; few nodes of development around oilfields (Sarawak and Brunei) as. of forest exploitation (Sabah); new settlement in Barito valley (Kalimantan); a. 738,150 km²; p. (est. 1970) 6,800,000.

Bornholm, I. in Baltic Sea, Denmark; mostly granite with poor soils; cattle rearing; kaolin; tourism and fishing impt.; cap. Rønne; a. 543 km²; p. (1971) 47,241.

Bornu, region, Nigeria; S.W. of L. Chad; former Moslem st.; a. 132,090 km²; p. (est.) 5,000,000.

Borobudur, Java, Indonesia; gr. Buddhist temple; ruins now restored.

Borrowdale, valley, Cumbria, Eng; tourist resort; former graphite mines.

Boscastle, spt., Cornwall, Eng.; resort; pilchard fishing; sm. harbour built for slate exp.

Bosnia and Hercegovina, rep., Yugoslavia; mtnous., forested, watered by R. Sava and tribs.; one-fourth cultivated; tobacco, cereals, fruit; cattle, sheep, pigs; mineral deposits in Bosnia; cap. Sarajevo; a. 51,199 km²; p. (1971) 3,742,842.

Bosporus or Strait of Constantinople (Karadeniz Boğazi), between Black Sea and Sea of Marmara; suspension bridge, first to link Europe and S.W. Asia, opened 1973.

Bossier City, t., La., USA; oil refineries, rly. wks., chemical and processing plants; p. (1970) 41,592.

Boston, t., l. gov. dist., Lincs., Eng.; sm. pt. on Witham R., agr. mkt., fruit and vegetable canning; p. (est. 1976) 50,000 (dist.).

Boston, c., st. cap. Mass., USA; fine harbour and leading pt. at head of Boston Bay; cultural, comm. and financial ctr., impt. mkt. for fish and wool; 3 univs.; leading c. in 19th cent.; varied inds. inc. leather, rubber, textiles, shoes and elec. gds.; p. (1970) 628,215 (c.), 2,730,228 (met. a.).

Bosworth or Market Bosworth, t., Leics., Eng.; battle between Richard III and Henry VII, 1485; p. (1971) 32,219 (dist.).

Botany Bay, N.S.W., Australia; inlet of Tasman Sea on E. cst., 16 km S. of Sydney; resort; first settled by Brit. in 1787; old penal colony; deep-water pt. planned.

Botaşani, t., N. Moldavia, Romania; in rich pastoral a.; p. (1968) 35,707.

Bothnia, G. of, N. of Baltic; between Finland and Sweden; shallow sea, many Is.

Botswana, Rep. of, indep. sov. st. within Brit. Commonwealth (1966), Southern Africa; stretches from Orange R. to Zambesi R., and merges W. into Kalahari desert; Bamangwato ch. tribe; cap. Gaborone; cattle-rearing; lge. potential copper and nickel ores; a. 574,980 km²; p. (est. 1969) 629,000.

Bottrop, t., N. Rhine–Westphalia, W. Germany; once a sm. t., now ctr. of Ruhr coal basin; p. (est. 1969) 108,200.

Bouches-du-Rhône, dep., S. France; covers Rhône delta and inc. the Camargue and Crau; lagoon cst.; mainly agr. but inc. industl. complex ass. with cap. of Marseilles; a. 5,270 km²; p. (1968) 1,470,271.

Bougainville, I. seceded from New Guinea to form Rep. of N. Solomons; major reserve of copper in Panguna valley; new mng. ts. of Anewa Bay and Panguna; forested; a. 10,619 km²; p. (1966) 72,490.

Bougie. See Bejaia.

Boulder, t., W. Australia; included in Kalgoorlie mun.; p. (1966) 19,892 (joint p.).

Boulder, t., Col. USA; gold- and silver-mng. dist.; univ.; resort; p. (1970) 66,870.

Boulder City, t., Nevada, USA; nr. Gr. Boulder Dam, gr. engin. project; model t., ctr. for Nat. Park services; p. (1970) 5,223.

Boulogne-Billancourt, S.W. sub. of Paris, France; car, aircraft inds.; p. (1968) 109,008.

Boulogne-sur-Mer, t., Pas-de-Calais dep., France; on English Channel; comm. and fish. pt.; Channel ferry; pt. inds.; p. (1968) 50,138.

Bounty I., N.Z., S. Pac. Oc.; uninhabited.

Bourg-en-Bresse, t., cap. of Ain dep., France; route ctr., varied inds.; p. (1968) 40,407.

Bourges, t., cap. of Cher dep., France; cath.,

univ.; industl. and transit ctr.; p. (1968) 73,998.

Bourget, L., Savoie, France; tourist a.

Bourne, t., South Kesteven, Lincs., Eng.; home of Hereward the Wake; agr. machin.; p. (1971) 6,461.

Bournemouth, t., l. gov. dist., Dorset, Eng.; on S. cst., E. of Poole Harbour; seaside resort; conference ctr.; p. (est. 1976) 144,100.

Bournville, garden sub. founded by George Cadbury (1897), 6 km S.W. of Birmingham Eng.; chocolate and cocoa wks.

Bourton-on-the-Water, v., Gloucs., Eng.; tourist ctr.

Bouvet I., uninhabited island in S. Atlantic belonging to Norway; a. about 56 km².

Bovey Tracey, v., Devon, Eng.; ball clay excavating.

Bow or Stratford-le-Bow, Tower Hamlets, E. London, Eng.; 5 km from St. Paul's.

Bow, R., Alberta, N.W. Canada; head of Saskatchewan R., flows through Banff Nat. Park; irrigation; 504 km long.

Bowdon, t., Gtr. Manchester, Eng.; p. (1971) 4,825.

Bowen, spt. N. Queensland, Australia; meat wks.; coke plant; p. (1966) 5,134.

Bow Fell, mtn., Cumbria, Eng.; at head of Borrowdale, 6 km N.W. of Wast Water, alt. 903 m.

Bowland, Forest of, W. offshoot of Pennines, Lancs., Eng.; between Rs. Lune and Ribble; designated a. of outstanding natural beauty; reservoirs.

Bowling, v., Dunbarton, Scot.; on N. bank of R. Clyde, 16 km N.W. of Glasgow; lge. oil refinery.

Bowling Green, t., Ky., USA; tr. ctr. for agr. a. producing tobacco, livestock, limestone and dairy prods.; univ.; p. (1970) 36,253.

Bowness, v., Cumbria, Eng.; W. end of Hadrian's Wall. [tourist ctr.]

Bowness, t., Cumbria, Eng.; on L. Windermere; Box Hill, nr. Dorking, Surrey, Eng.; E. of R. Mole gap through N. Downs; chalk; wooded, fine views; alt. 233 m.

Boyle, mkt. t., Roscommon, R.o.I.; on R. Boyle; dairying; p. (1966) 1,789.

Boyne, R., R.o.I.; flows to Irish Sea; Battle of the Boyne (1690) fought at Oldbridge, 5 km W. of Drogheda; salmon fishing; 128 km long.

Boyoma Falls (Stanley Falls), on Upper Zaire R., Zaïre; nr. equator; originally named after the explorer.

Bozrah, c. of anc. Edom, probably modern Buseira (Jordan), S.E. of Dead Sea.

Brabant, prov., Belgium; S. section of former Duchy; fertile and wooded; many breweries; mnfs. linen, cloth, paper, lace; cap. Brussels; a. 3,281 km²; p. (1968) 2,148,513.

Brabant, North, prov., Neth.; S. of Gelderland; N. half of former Duchy; cattle rearing; grain, hops, beetroot; cap. 's-Hertogenbosch; a. 4,972 km²; p. (1968) 1,725,292.

Brač, I., Adriatic Sea, Yugoslavia; lgst. of Dalmatian Is.; tourism, fishing; a. 393 km².

Brackley, t., South Northants., Eng.; flour milling, brewing; former prosperous wool tr.; Magdalen College School (1447); p. (1971) 4,615.

Bracknell, t., l. gov. dist., Berks., Eng.; on Thames Valley terrace, 16 km S. of Windsor; new t. designated 1949 to meet overspill needs from London; extends N. and W. of old v. of Bracknell; Meteorological Office H.Q.; engin., sealing compounds, plastics; p. (est. 1976) 71,800.

Brackwede, t. N. Rhine–Westphalia, W. Germany; iron and machin.; p. (1969) 26,448.

Bradford, c., met. dist., West Yorks., Eng.; 14 km W. of Leeds; comm. ctr. of wool-textile inds.; impt. for worsted; engin. and chem. inds.; univ.; birthplace of Delius and J. B. Priestley; p. (est. 1976) 458,900 (dist.).

Bradford-on-Avon, t., West Wilts., Eng.; on E. flank of Cotswolds from which bldg. stone derived; former ctr. of wool ind.; p. (1971) 8,001.

Bradwell, v., Essex, Eng.; at mouth of R. Blackwater; civil nuclear power-sta.; p. (1961) 1,116.

Braemar, dist. in Grampians, Kincardine and Deeside, Scot.; containing Balmoral estate.

Braeriach, mtn., Scot.; borders Badenoch and Strathspey, alt. 1,296 m.

Braga, t., cap. of B. dist. N.W. Portugal; agr. tr. ctr.; religious ctr.; cath.; p. (1970) 101,877.

Bragança, t., cap. of B. dist., N.E. Portugal; agr. tr.; p. (1970) 33,928.

Brahmaputra, one of longer Rs. in Asia; flows for much of its length through Himalayas and Assam; called Tsangpo in Tibet; fertile agr. valley subject to flooding and silting; 2,880 km long.

Braich-y-Pwll, headland, Gwynedd, Wales.

Brăila, t., Romania; R. pt. on Danube, nr. Galati; grain tr., boatbldg., reed processing; p. (est. 1969) 149,686.

Braintree, t., Mass., USA; elec. machin., rubber gds., glassware; p. (1970) 35,050.

Braintree, t., l. gov. dist., Essex, Eng.; on Blackwater; rayon mftg. metal windows, engin.; p. (est. 1976) 104,600 (dist.).

Brakpan, t., Transvaal, S. Africa; gold mng.; p. (1970) 113,115.

Brampton, t., Ontario, Canada; noted for its greenhouses; p. (1971) 41,238.

Brandenburg, t., E. Germany; on R. Havel; former cap. of prov. of B.; cath.; tractors, textiles, machin.; p. (est. 1970) 93,660.

Brandenburg. See Neubrandenburg.

Brandon, t. Manitoba, Canada; on Assiniboine R., W. of Winnipeg; comm. ctr. wheat a.; agr. equipment, oil refining; p. (1971) 30,832.

Brandon, t. Suffolk, Eng.; ctr. of Breckland; expanded t.

Brandon and Byshottles, ts., former U.D., Durham, Eng.; former coal-mng. a.; p. (1971) 16,849.

Brandywine Creek, R., Penns., USA; Americans defeated by British 1777; length 32 km.

Brantford, t., Ontario, Canada; on Grand R., S.W. of Hamilton; leading mnf. t.; farm implements, cycles, bus and truck parts; p. (1971) 62,853.

Brasilia, cap. of Brazil, Goiás st., 960 km N.W. of Rio de Janeiro; ch. of many cities designed to open up interior of rep.; modern architecture; inaugurated 1960; designed for p. 500,000; p. (1970) 272,002.

Brașov, t., Romania; at foot of Transylvanian Alps; aircraft, engin., lge. German and Hungarian p.; p. (est. 1969) 179,316 (c.); (1966) 263,158 (met. a.).

Bratislava, c. cap. of Slovakia, ČSSR; pt. on Danube 48 km below Vienna; univ.; industl. and comm. ctr.; textiles, chemicals; engin., oil refining; linked to Mozyr', USSR, by "friendship oil pipeline"; p. (est. 1968) 283,234.

Bratsk, c., central Irkutsk oblast, RSFSR; on Angara R., ship repair yards, lumber, iron-ore, wood processing chemicals; lge. hydroelectric sta.; p. (1970) 155,000.   [7,665.

Brava, spt., Somalia; leather, shoes; p. (est. 1965)

Bray, U.D., Wicklow R.o.I.; on Irish Sea cst.; popular resort; p. (1966) 12,657.

Brazil, Federative Republic of., S. America; a. 8,512,035 km²; 5th lgst cty. in world, exceeded in size only by USSR, China, Canada and USA; covers variety of land and climate; in S., gr. Brazilian plateau, in N., Amazon R. basin (thickly forested); leading industl. nation of Latin America; agr.; coffee, cotton, sugar, cocoa, rubber, fruits, hardwoods; cattle-raising; manganese, iron, gold, diamonds; admin. through 22 sts., 4 terrs., and Fed. Dist.; cap. Brasilia; lgst. industl. ctr. São Paulo; p. mainly White, Negro, Indian, Mestizo; Portuguese official language; p. concentrated in coastal belt, leaving vast a. of interior relatively underdeveloped; p. (1975) 107,145,168.

Brazos, R., Texas, USA; flows through agr. and industl. Young Co. via Waco to industl. Brazosport; length 1,520 km.

Brazzaville, c., cap. of Congo Rep.; connected by rly. with the Atlantic at Pointe-Noire; R. pt. under construction; airport; p. (1966) 156,000.

Brechin, royal burgh, Angus, Scot.; on S. Esk; cath.; linen, paper, whisky; p. (1971) 6,578.

Breckland, dist., S.W. Norfolk, N.W. Suffolk, Eng.; chalk overlain by glacial sands; heathland and coniferous plantations; a. 518 km²; lge. a. within Norfolk forms l. gov. dist., inc. Thetford, Swaffham and East Dereham; p. (est. 1976) 89,000.

Brecknock (Breconshire), former co., Wales; now mostly inc. in Powys; sm. parts in Mid-Glamorgan and Gwent; now forms l. gov. dist., within

Powys inc. Builth Wells, Hay on Wye and Brecon; p. (est. 1976) 37,400.

Brecon (Brecknock), t., Powys, Wales; on R. Usk; agr. ctr.; p. (1971) 6,283.

Brecon Beacons, mtns., S. Wales; 8 km S. of Brecon; highest peak 888 m; sandstone moorland; Nat. Park.

Breda, c. N. Brabant prov. Neth.; mnf. ctr.; machin., foundries, canneries, refineries; historic t., 13th cent. cath.; p. (est. 1969) 120,582 (c.), 146,173 (met. a.).

Bredbury and Romiley, ts., Gtr. Manchester, Eng.; paper, engin., dyeing, textiles; p. (1971) 28,472.

Bregenz, t., cap. of Vorarlberg, Austria; on Bodensee; hydroelec. power; textiles; resort nr. Bregenz Forest; p. (est. 1968) 23,600.

Breidha Fjord, lge. inlet, W. cst. Iceland.

Breman, Land, W. Germany; a. 404 km²; cap. Bremen; p. (1967) 751,800.

Bremen, c., cap. of Land B., W. Germany; old t. on right bank of Weser R., 64 km from N. Sea; new t., founded 17th cent., on left bank; leading pt., industl. and comm. ctr.; but hinterland divided by post-war division of Germany; former member of Hanseatic League; p. (est. 1969) 606,100.

Bremerhaven, c., Bremen, W. Germany; outport of Bremen at mouth of R. Weser; docks; impt. passenger and fish. pt.; shipbldg.; united with Wesermünde 1941; p. (est. 1969) 149,300.

Bremerton, t., Wash., USA; on Puget Sound; naval dockyard; elec. equipment, machin.; p. (1970) 35,307.

Brendon Hills, Somerset, Eng.; extension of Exmoor, rising to over 400 m.

Brenner Pass, lowest Alpine pass from Bolzano (Italy) to Innsbruck (Austria); used by road and rail; frequent meeting place of Mussolini and Hitler (1940–2).

Brent, outer bor., Greater London, Eng.; inc. Wembley and Willesden; p. (est. 1976) 256,500.

Brenta, R., N. Italy; rises in picturesque Alpine valley; forestry, silk, tourism; flows to Adriatic Sea; navigable in lower course; length 180 km.

Brentford and Chiswick. See Hounslow.

Brentwood, t., l. gov. dist., Essex, Eng.; residentl.; p. (est. 1976) 73,000 (dist.).

Brescia, c., cap. B. prov., Lombardy, N. Italy; industl. ctr.; iron, steel, engin., textiles; many historic bldgs.; p. (1969) 206,379.

Breslau. See Wrocław.

Bressay I., Shetland Is., Scot.; p. (1971) 251.

Brest, naval pt., Finistère dep., N.W. France; base of French Atlantic fleet; used by Germans as fortfd. submarine base 1940–4; exp. agr. prods.; impt. industl. ctr.; p. (1968) 159,857 (c.), 169,279 (met. a.).

Brest (Brest-Litovsk), c., Belorussiyan SSR, USSR; nr. Polish border; route ctr. and agr. mkt.; timber, food-processing, textiles. Captured by Germans in 1915. Treaty of Brest-Litovsk signed with Soviet Russia 1918; p. (1970) 122,000.

Bretton Woods, resort, N.H., USA; site of US monetary and financial conference, 1944, leading to establishment of the International Monetary Fund and the World Bank.

Briançon, t., Hautes-Alpes, France; in upper Durance R. valley; winter sports; p. (1968) 10,497.

Bridgend, t., Ogwr, Mid-Glamorgan, S. Wales; industl. trading estate; iron, stone, paper; coal mng.; p. (1971) 14,531.

Bridge of Allen, burgh, Stirling, Scot.; 3 km N. of Stirling; p. (1971) 4,314.

Bridgeport, c., Conn., USA; on Long Island Sound; impt. industl. c., firearms, hardware, elec. equipment, metal products, plastics; p. (1970) 155,359 (c.), 385,746 (met. a.).

Bridgeton, t., N.J., USA; founded by Quakers; glasswks., fruit; p. (1970) 20,435.

Bridgetown, t., spt., cap. Barbados; deepwater harbour opened 1961; comm. ctr.; exp. sugar, molasses, rum; tourism; p. (1970) 8,789.

Bridgewater Canal, Worsley–Manchester–Runcorn, Gtr. Manchester and Cheshire Eng.; crosses ship canal by means of Barton swing bridge; 61 km long.

Bridgnorth, t., l. gov. dist., Salop, Eng.; cas.; carpets, radio equipment; p. (est. 1976) 49,000 (dist.).

Bridgwater, t., Sedgemoor, Somerset, Eng.; on R. Parrett, 16 km from Bristol Channel; bricks and tiles, engin., wire rope, fibre fabrics, cellophane; p. (1971) 26,598.

Bridlington, t., North Wolds, Humberside, **Eng.**; on Bridlington Bay, S. of Flamborough Head; fishing; seaside resort; p. (1971) 26,729.

Bridport, West Dorset, **Eng.**; mkt. t.; seaside resort; p. (1971) 6,362.

Brie, region, Marne and Seine-et-Marne deps., France; low, level plateau of limestones and clays, S.E. of Paris; loam (limon) cover and plentiful water supply encourage agr.; grains, sugar-beet, fruit, dairy cattle; famous cheese; densely populated.

Brienz, t., Switzerland; resort on L. Brienz; wood carving; p. (1970) 2,796.

Brierfield, t., Lancs., **Eng.**; p. (1971) 7,572.

Brierley Hill, t., West Midlands, **Eng.**; on W. edge of Black Cty.; cut glass, castable metal gds., firebricks, roofing and tiling, iron and steel.

Brigg, mkt. t., Glanford, Humberside, **Eng.**; ctr. of agr. dist. between Lincoln Heights and Wolds; sugar-beet, jam, seed crushing, canning; p. (1971) 4,793.

Brighouse, t., Calderdale, West Yorks., **Eng.**; on R. Calder, 5 km S.E. of Halifax; textiles and engin.; p. (1971) 34,111.

Brightlingsea, t., Tendring, Essex, **Eng.**; on R. Colne; oysters, boatbldg., yachting; p. (1971) 6,515.

Brighton, t., l. gov. dist., East Sussex, **Eng.**; 80 km S. of London on S. cst.; seaside resort and residtl. t.; Royal Pavilion (1817), univ.; lt. inds.; birthplace of Aubrey Beardsley; p. (est. 1976) 156,500.

Brindisi, c., Apulia, **S. Italy**; spt. on Adriatic cst., sea and air connections to Middle E.; cath.; cas.; wine, olive oil, silk, petrochemicals; oil refining; p. (1969) 81,576.

Brisbane, t., cap. of Queensland, Australia; spt. 800 km N. of Sydney; fine streets and parks, univ.; pt. exp. agr. prods.; pt. processing and agr. based inds., oil refining; p. (1972) 699,371 (c.), 866,207 (met. a.).

Bristol, c., l. gov. dist., Avon, **Eng.**; pt. on R. Avon 14 km from Bristol Channel; outport at Avonmouth; cath., univ.; docks; aircraft engin., tobacco, paint, printing and lt. inds.; p. (est. 1976) 416,300.

Bristol, t., Conn., **USA**; foundries, ball bearings, clocks, bells; p. (1970) 55,487.

Bristol Channel, arm of Atl. Oc. between S. cst. of Wales and Somerset and Devon, **Eng.**; noted tidal bores.

British Antarctic Territory, Brit. col., created 1962; consists of all land and Is. S. of lat. 60° S. and between 20° and 80° W. longitude; comprising Graham Land peninsula, S. Shetlands, S. Orkneys and smaller Is., excluding S. Georgia and S. Sandwich Is.; a. 1,222,500 km².

British Columbia, W. prov. separated from rest of Canada by Rockies, borders Pac. Oc.; little lowland; parallel N.W.–S.E. ranges of Rockies crossed by Rs. Fraser, Columbia, Kootenay and Peace; vast coniferous forest and hydroelec. resources; salmon fishing on cst.; mng.; p. concentrated in S.W. around Vancouver; a. 948,600 km²; p. (1976) 2,466,608.

British Honduras *See* Belize.

British Indian Ocean Terr., Brit. col., created 1965; consists of the Chagos Archipelago (of which Diego Garcia [Anglo-American naval communications ctr.] is lgst. I.) 1,920 km N.E. of Mauritius, and formerly Is. of Aldabra, Farquhar, and Desroches in the W. Indian Oc. now part of Seychelles Rep.; p. (est. 1971) 560.

British Is., archipelago, N.W. Europe; comprising 2 lge. Is.; Great Britain, Ireland; and 5,000 sm. Is.; a. 315,029 km².

British Solomon Is. *See* Solomon Is.

British West Africa, formerly comprised Gambia, Sierra Leone, Gold Coast (Ghana), Nigeria, and parts of Togoland and Cameroons. *See* under their separate headings.

Briton Ferry, t., West Glamorgan, S. Wales; pt. at mouth of R. Neath; steel wks., engin., shipbreaking.

Brittany, region, N.W. France; penin. between Eng. Channel and Bay of Biscay; contrast between productive cst. lands (fishing, early vegetables, tourism) and barren moorland interior; economically depressed; oil refinery projected at St. Livy; p. (est. 1968) 2,468,000.

Brive-la-Gaillarde, t., Corrèze dep., France; regional mkt. in fertile basin on edge of Central Massif; p. (1968) 49,325.

Brixham, S. Devon, **Eng.**; incorporated in Torbay; fishing; resort.

Brno (Brünn), c., ČSSR; cap. of Moldavia; finely situated at confluence of Svratka and Svitava Rs., 109 km N. of Vienna; industl. and communications ctr. with mnfs. of machin., precision tools, textiles; annual tr. fair; p. (est. 1968) 335,935.

Broach, t., Gujarat, India; lowest bridging of R. Narbada; textiles. [Wales.

Broad Haven, t., new t. planned on St. Brides Bay,

Broadstairs, Thanet, Kent, **Eng.**; seaside resort; 5 km N.E. of Ramsgate; p. (1971) 19,996.

Broads, The, Norfolk, **Eng.**; series of Ls. formed by mediaeval turf cutting in lower alluvial reaches of Rs. Bure, Waveney, and Yare; yachting, fishing, tourism; plans to create a Nat. Park to help relieve pollution; lge part now forms Broadland, l. gov. dist., p. (est. 1976) 94,000.

Brockton, c., Mass., **USA**; S. of Boston; lge shoe and leather ind., machin.; annual tr. fair; p. (1970) 87,444 (c.), 186,839 (met. a.).

Brockville, t., Ontario, Canada; R. pt. on St. Lawrence R. below Thousand Is.; telephone equipment, wire cables, elec. tools; p. (1971) 19,707.

Broken Hill, t., N.S.W., Australia; major mng. industl. t., silver, lead, zinc; p. (1972) 29,743.

Bromberg. *See* Bydgoszcz.

Bromley, outer bor. of London, **Eng.**; inc. Beckenham, Orpington, Penge, and part of Sidcup; p. (est. 1976) 299,100.

Bromsgrove, l. gov. dist., Hereford and Worcs., **Eng.**; mkt. t., 21 km S.W. Birmingham; wrought ironwk., lt. engin.; p. (est. 1976) 79,500 (dist.).

Bromyard, Hereford and Worcs., **Eng.**; sm. mkt. t.; p. (1971) 8,568.

Bronx, The, one of the five bors. of New York City, **USA**; connected by bridges to bor. of Manhattan; residtl. with parks, zoological and botanical gardens, colleges and professional schools; p. (1970) 1,472,216.

Brookline, sub. of Boston, Mass., **USA**; residtl.; p. (1970) 58,689.

Brooklyn, bor., N.Y. City, **USA**; linked with Manhattan bor. by Brooklyn, Manhattan, and Williamsburgh suspension bridges across East R.; and with Staten I. by Verrazano-Narrows bridge (longest in world); mainly residtl. with numerous mftg. and comm. interests; p. (1970) 2,601,852.

Brooks Range, mtns., N. Alaska, **USA**; forms N. section of Rocky Mtns.; Eskimo p.; Arctic climate, flora and fauna; alt. 2,000 m rising to 2,818 m (Mt. Michelson). [Scot.

Broom, loch on N.W. cst. of Ross and Cromarty,

Brora, t., Sutherland, Scot.; on E. cst., 19 km N.E. of Dornoch Firth; ctr. of sm. coalfield; Harris Tweed ind.; tourism.

Brownhills, t., West Midlands, **Eng.**; former mng. t.; expanded t.

Brownsville, t., Texas, **USA**; pt. on Rio Grande nr. Mexican border; livestock, sugar-cane, fruit processing, chemicals; p. (1970) 51,080 (c.), 137,506 (met. a.).

Broxbourne, t., l. gov. dist., Herts., **Eng.**; on gravel terrace to W. of R. Lea; ctr. of very intensively cultivated dist.; lt. inds.; " dormitory " t. linked with London; p. (est. 1976) 76,800 (dist.).

Broxtowe, l. gov. dist., Notts., **Eng.**; made up of Beeston and Stapleford and Eastwood; p. (est. 1976) 102,600.

Bruay-en-Artois, t., Pas-de-Calais, France; coal mng.; p. (1968) 28,628 (t.), 126,520 (met. a.).

Bruchsal, t., Baden-Württemberg, W. Germany; tobacco, paper, machin.; p. (est. 1969) 26,506.

Brugge (Bruges), c., cap. of W. Flanders prov., N. Belgium; mediaeval t. connected by canal to its outer pt. Zeebrugge; univ.; impt. mkt. for grain, cattle, horses; engin., ship-repairing. elec. gds., glass mkg., textiles, lace; p. (est. 1967) 51,900 (c.), 113,828 (met a.).

Brühl, t., N. Rhine–Westphalia, W. Germany; 13 km S. of Cologne; cas.; lignite; p. (est. 1969) 41,475.

Brunei, intern. self-gov. Brit. prot. st., N.W.

Borneo; enclave of Sarawak (Malaysia); Seria oilfields (output now declining); underdeveloped elsewhere; rubber, natural gas, sago, pepper, timber; cap. Bandar Seri Begawan; a. 5,765 km²; p. (est. 1972) 200,000.

Brünn. *See* Brno.

Brunsbüttelkoog, pt. at mouth of R. Elbe opposite Cuxhaven, W. Germany.

Brunswick (Braunschweig), c., Lower Saxony, W. Germany; on R. Oker; formerly cap. of st. of Brunswick, now a comm. and industl. ctr.; mnfs. inc. canning, tinplate, optics, pianos, lorries; p. (est. 1969) 225,600.

Brussels (Bruxelles), cap. of Belgium and of prov. of Brabant; impt. comm., industl. and cultural ctr.; varied mnfs., inc. pharmaceuticals, electronic equipment, machine tools; lge. oil refinery at Feluy; noted for carpets and lace; occupied by the Germans 1914–18, 1940–4; univ.; mediaeval and Renaissance monuments; H.Q. of EEC; p. (est. 1969) 164,013 (c.), 1,073,111 (met. a.).

Bryan, t., Texas, USA; mkt. ctr., agr. college; p. (1970) 33,719.

Bryansk, c., cap. of B. oblast, RSFSR, on Desna R.; rly. junc.; a fortress until 19th cent.; sawmilling, engin., textiles, chemicals, steel; oil pipeline from Kuybyshev; p. inc. Bezhitsa (1970) 318,000.

Brynmawr, t., Gwent, Wales; former coal-mng. a.; industl. estate; p. (1971) 5,930.

Brzeg (Brieg), t. Silesia, Poland; on R. Oder; German until 1945; textiles, leather, chemicals; p. (1968) 29,900.

Bucaramanga, c., N. central Colombia, 900 m a.s.l. in E. highlands of Andes; ctr. of coffee-growing dist.; cigar and cigarette mkg.; p. (est. 1972) 324,400 (c.), 347,400 (met. a.).

Buchan Ness, C., nr. Peterhead, E. Scot.

Bucharest (Bucaresti), cap. and lgst c. of Romania; "Little Paris," on the Dambovita, trib. of Danube; cath., univ.; textiles, chemicals, pharmaceuticals, oil refining, engin.; 20 per cent industl. output of rep.; badly damaged by earthquake (1977); p. (est. 1969) 1,457,802.

Buckfastleigh, t., S. Devon. Eng.; wool, quarrying; nearby Benedictine abbey on site of mediaeval Cistercian abbey; p. (1971) 2,657.

Buckhaven and Methil, burgh, Kircaldy, Scot.; on N. Side of Firth of Forth, 13 km N.E. of Kirkcaldy; coal; p. (1971) 18,396.

Buckie, burgh, Moray, Scot.; boat- and yacht-bldg.; fisheries; p. (1971) 7,919.

Buckingham, Aylesbury Vale, Bucks., Eng.; mkt. t. on R. Ouse, 24 km N.W. of Aylesbury; p. (1971) 5,075.

Buckinghamshire, non-met. co., Eng.; crossed by Chilterns and Vale of Aylesbury; rural and wooded, emphasis is on dairy farming; co. t. Aylesbury; mnfs. chiefly in High Wycombe; decline in traditional handicrafts (lace-mkg. and furniture parts); a. 1,882 km²; p. (est. 1976) 256,400.

Buckley, t., Alyn and Deeside, Clwyd, Wales; sm. castings; p. (1971) 11,866.

Budapest, cap. and lgst. c. of Hungary; stands on both banks of Danube (Buda on right, Pest on left); attractive townscape; univ.; varied mnfs., inc. steel, textiles, chemicals, engin., motorbuses, oil refining; employs 40 per cent industl. workers of Hungary; p. (est. 1969) 1,934,000 (c.); (est. 1967) 2,335,000 (met. a.).

Budaun, t., Uttar Pradesh, India; agr. processing; ruins; p. (1961) 58,770.

Bude. *See* Stratton and Bude.

Budel, t., N. Brabant, S. Neth.; 19 km S. of Eindhoven; major zinc smelter project.

Budge-Budge, t., W. Bengal, India; on lower Hooghly R.; hemp, rice; p. (1961) 39,824.

Budleigh Salterton, East Devon, Eng.; resort; birthplace of Raleigh nearby; p. (1971) 4,139.

Buena Park, t., Cal., USA; agr. processing, mkt.; oilfields; p. (1970) 63,646.

Buenaventura, spt., Colombia; lumber yards, tanning, fish canning; p. (est. 1972) 102,300 (t.), 133,600 (met. a.).

Buenos Aires, c., cap. of Argentina; ch. spt. at head of Rio de la Plata, on E. edge of Pampa; connected to Uruguay, Paraguay, and Brazil by gr. R. system; industl. and tr. ctr. for outlying regions; p. (1970) 2,972,453 (c.) 8,352,900 (met. a.).

Buffalo, c., N.Y. USA; pt. on L. Erie; focus of communications on Gr. Ls. has encouraged many heavy inds.; diversified lt. inds.; univ.; p. (1970) 457,808 (c.), 1,334,485 (met. a.).

Bug R., Ukrainian SSR, USSR; known as S. or Ukrainian B.; flows from Volyno–Podolsh upland to Black Sea; navigable in lower course; 853 km long.

Eug, R., the western Bug rises in the Ukraine, USSR, not far from the southern Bug and flows N. to join the Vistula below Warsaw; forms bdy. between Poland and Ukrainian SSR; 774 km long.

Bugul'ma, t., Tatar ASSR, RSFSR; oil ctr.; p. (est. 1967) 74,000.

Buganda, prov., Uganda, E. Africa; located W. of L. Victoria largely at alt. between 1,300 and 1,800 m; intensive cultivation, cotton (ch. comm. crop), plantains, millets; cap. Kampala.

Builth Wells, t., Brecknock, Powys, Wales; on upper course of R. Wye; medicinal springs; p. (1971) 1,481.

Buitenzorg. *See* Bogor.

Bujumbura, t., cap. of Burundi; pt. on L. Tanganyika; varied inds.; airpt.; p. (est. 1970) 78,810 (met. a.).

Bukavu, t., Zaïre; cement, quinine processing; p. (est. 1972) 156,078 (met. a.).

Bukhara (Bokhara), t., Uzbek SSR, USSR; in Amu-Dar'ya valley at W. foot of Tien Shan; agr. mkt. at W. terminus of anc. caravan route from China; modern route ctr.; local natural gas, textiles; p. (1970) 112,000.

Bukittinggi, t., Sumatra, Indonesia; in Padang Highlands at 1,068 m; p. 53,700.

Bukoba, t., Tanzania; pt. midway along W. shore of L. Victoria; exp. coffee, rice and other foodstuffs to L. pts. in Kenya and Uganda.

Bukovina, Northern; terr., formerly belonging to Romania, ceded to USSR in 1940; now part of Ukrainian SSR; a. 5,542 km²; ch. t. Chernovitsy; Carpathian Mtns., forested; farming, cereals; cattle.

Bulawayo, t., Rhodesia; impt. rly. ctr.; iron and steel, brewing, agr. mnfs.; airpt.; p. (est. 1972) 295,000 (met. a.).

Bulgaria, People's Rep. of, S.E. Europe; in E. Balkans, bounded by Black Sea in E., and by Danube R. in N. which separates it from Romania; Rodopi range in S.W.; Maritsa R. basin forms central lowland a.; sharp climatic contrasts between winter and summer; fertile lowland areas organised into lge.-scale cooperative farms producing grain; impt. exp. tr. in agr. prods., inc. fruit, vegetables, tobacco; rapidly increasing industl. output; mineral and oil resources; popular tourist a. on Black Sea cst.; cap. Sofia; a. 110,911 km²; p. (est. 1974) 8,706,000.

Bunbury, t., W. Australia; spt. on cst. 179 km S. of Fremantle; comm. ctr. of lge. pastoral, fruit-growing and timber dist.; new bauxite refinery to serve Hotham R. deposits; p. (1972) 17,762.

Buncrana, U.D., mkt. t., Donegal, R.o.I.; salmon fishing; seaside resort; p. (1966) 3,120.

Bundaberg, t., Queensland, Australia; on Burnett R.; sugar factories, timber, butter, iron; p. (1972) 26,570.

Bundoran, v., Donegal, R.o.I.; fish. pt. and resort; p. (1966) 1,421.

Bungay, Waveney, Suffolk, Eng.; mkt. t. on R. Waveney; printing, malting, leather gds.; p. (1971) 3,961.

Bungosuido Channel, Japan; E. entrance into Inland Sea.

Bunzlau. *See* Boleslawiec.

Buraimi, oases lying between Oman and United Arab Emirates; rich in oil.

Buraydah (Buraida), t. Nejd., Saudi Arabia; oasis; tr. ctr.; p. (est.) 70,000.

Burbank, c., Cal., USA; airpt.; aeroplanes, film studios; p. (1970) 88,871.

Burdwan, t., W. Bengal, India; agr. processing and tr. ctr. in Damodar valley close to Raniganj coalfield; p. (1971) 143,318.

Bure, R., Norfolk, Eng.; lower course forms part of Norfolk Broads; joins Yare at Yarmouth; 93 km.

Burg, t., Magdeburg, E. Germany; on Ihle Canal; p. (est. 1970) 29,994.

Burgas, c., Bulgaria; spt. and comm. ctr. on Black Sea; ch. exp. pt. for rep.; pt. for oil tankers under construction; p. (1968) 122,212.

Burgenland, prov., **Austria;** bordered on E. by Hungary; low-lying in N., agr.; hilly in S.; cap. Eisenstadt; a. 3,962 km²; p. (1968) 267,300.

Burgess Hill, t., Mid Sussex, West Sussex, **Eng.;** bricks, tiles; p. (1971) 19,309.

Burghausen, t., W. **Germany;** chemicals, oil refining; pipeline to Munich.

Burghead, burgh. Moray, **Scot.;** fish pt., resort; p. (1971) 1,282.

Burgos, c., N. **Spain;** cap. of B. prov.; anc. cap. of Castile and cap. of Franco's regime 1936–9; cath; home of the Cid; tourism, varied inds.; p. (1967) 100,413.

Burgos, prov., Old Castile, **Spain;** cap. B.; a. 14,050 km²; p. (1970) 358,075.

Burgstädt, t., Karl-Marx-Stadt, E. **Germany;** textiles, machin.; p. (1963) 17,167.

Burgundy, former kingdom and prov., N.E. **France;** composed largely of upper valley of R. Saône; famous vineyards; strategic position on route leading between plateau of Vosges and Jura Mtns., from Rhône valley to Rhine valley.

Burhanpur, t., Madhya Pradesh, **India;** anc. walled Mogul c.; textiles, brocades; p. (1971) 105,246.

Burlington, t., S. Ontario, Canada; on L. Ontario, sub., N.E. of Hamilton; in fruit-growing a.; industl.; tourism; p. (1971) 86,125.

Burlington, t., Iowa. **USA;** on bluffs of Mississippi R.; machin., furniture; p. (1970) 32,360.

Burlington, t., Vt., **USA;** on L. Champlain; pt. of entry and ch. industl. and comm. t. in st.; numerous mnfs.; p. (est. 1969) 38,500.

Burma, Union of, rep., S.E. Asia; Irrawaddy R. basin, developed by British in 19th cent., forms major cluster of p., routeways and source of rice of which B. is one of few exporters; surrounding mtns. relatively underdeveloped, although they are a source of teak and hardwood exps.; almost self-sufficient in petroleum from deposits in N.; monsoon climate; ch. ts., Mandalay, cap. Rangoon; a. 676,580 km²; p. (est. 1975) 31,240,000.

Burnham Beeches, Berks./Bucks., **Eng.;** part of anc. forest acquired 1879 for public use; 243 ha.

Burnham-on-Crouch, t., Essex, **Eng.;** pt., yachting, boat-bldg.; p. (1971) 4,546.

Burnham-on-Sea, t., Sedgemoor, Somerset. **Eng.;** on Bridgwater Bay; resort; p. (1971) 12,281.

Burnie, spt., Tasmania, **Australia;** mnfs., paper pulp, chemicals; oil terminal; p. (1972) 20,088.

Burnley, t., l. gov. dist., Lancs., **Eng.;** textiles, engin., car accessories; p. (est 1976) 92,100 (dist.).

Burntisland, royal burgh, Kirkcaldy, **Scot.;** on F. of Forth; p. (1971) 5,699.   [595.

Burray, one of the Orkney Is., **Scot.;** p. (est. 1969)

Burrinjuck, t., N.S.W., **Australia;** on Murrumbidgee R., N. of Canberra; site of impt. dam providing irrigation in Riverina dist.

Burry Port, t., Dyfed, **Wales;** p. (1971) 5,880.

Bursa, c., N.W. **Turkey;** noted for its textiles; cap. of anc. Bithynia (3rd cent B.C.) and later of Ottoman empire; mosques; p. (1965) 211,644 (c.), 307 753 (met. a.).

Burslem. See Stoke-on-Trent.

Burton-on-Trent, t., East Staffs., **Eng.;** brewing, malting, rubber gds.; p. (1971) 50,175.

Burujird, t., **Iran;** textiles and mkt. ctr. at alt. 1,678 m; p. (1966) 71,486.

Burundi, rep., E. central Africa; high plateau on N.E. shore of L. Tanganyika; tropical climate, irregular rainfall; economy based on agr., inc. subsistence crops of manioc, sweet potatoes, and cash crops of cotton, coffee; coffee major exp.; sm. mftg. inds. developing but no rlys.; home of ruling Tutsi and rebel Hutu; cap. Bujumbura; a. 27,834 km²; p. (est. 1970) 3,340,000.

Bury, t., met. dist., Gtr. Manchester, **Eng.;** on R. Irwell to S. of Rossendale Fells; cotton, textiles; birthplace of Robert Peel; p. (est. 1976) 181,200 (dist.).

Buryat (Buryatskaya), aut. rep. **RSFSR;** borders L. Baykal; mtnous., forested; lge. mineral deposits; cap. Ulan Ude; a. 350,945 km²; p. (1970) 812,000.

Bury St. Edmunds, St. Edmundsbury, Suffolk, **Eng.;** old mkt t., on R. Lark, abbey ruins; farm implements, sugar beet processing; expanded t.; p. (1971) 25,629.

Bushey, t., Hertsmere, Herts., **Eng.;** residtl.; p. (1971) 23,729.

Bushir. See **Bandar-e-Büshehr.**

Busto Arsizio, t., Varese prov., N. **Italy;** 30 km. N.W. of Milan; cotton milling ctr., iron, steel, rayon, textile machin.; p. (est. 1968) 75,565.

Bute, Kyles of, strait, 10 km between isles of Bute and Argyll, Scot.

Buteshire, former co., now part of Strathclyde Region, Scot.

Butte, t., Mont., **USA;** mng. t. (copper, zinc, silver, manganese, gold, lead, arsenic); also a farming ctr.; p. (est. 1969) 26,000.

Buttermere, L., Cumberland, **Eng.**

Butt of Lewis, promontory with lighthouse; Lewis, Hebrides, Scot.

Buxton, t., High Peak, Derbys., **Eng.;** spa; lime-quarrying nearby; p. (1971) 20,316.

Buzau, t., Romania; rly. ctr.; cath.; wheat, timber, petroleum; p. (1968) 59,114.

Bydgoszcz, prov., **Poland;** cap. B.; drained by Rs. Vistula, Brda, and Notec; formerly called Pomorze; salt and lime deposits aid chemical inds.; a. 20,800 km²; p. (1970) 1,912,000.

Bydgoszcz (Bromberg), c., N. central **Poland;** on R. Brda; R. pt., rly. ctr.; elec. equipment. machine tools, timber mnfs.; p. (est. 1969) 275,200.

Byelorussian SSR. See **Belorussiyan SSR.**

Byron C., most E. point of Australia, Pacific cst. of N.S.W.

Bytom, c., S.W. **Poland;** formerly in Prussian prov. of Upper Silesia; ctr. of Katowice mng. a.; p. (est. 1969) 186,700.

C

Cabinda, enclave, **Angola;** separated by Zaïre R. estuary from Angola; tropical climate encourages thick forest cover; tropical crops; offshore oil production; uranium; attempts at secession; a. 7,236 km²; p. (1960) 58,547.

Cabot Strait, entrance of G. of St. Lawrence between C. Breton I. and Newfoundland, Canada.

Cáceres, c., and cap. of C. prov., W. **Spain;** in Estremadura, above Tagus valley; mkt. t. lies below the old t. topping the hill; p. (est. 1969) 56,274.

Cachar, dist., Assam, **India;** tea-growing ctr.; a. 6,961 km²; p. (1961) 1,378,476.

Cachoeira, t., Bahia, Brazil; historic c.; p. (1968) 32,432.

Cachoeira do Sul, t., Rio Grande do Sul. **Brazil;** p. (est. 1968) 98,927.

Cadarache, t., S. **France;** nr. Aix-en-Provence; nuclear research centre.

Cader Idris, mtn., Gwynedd, **Wales;** alt. 893 m.

Cádiz, maritime prov., S.W. **Spain;** cap. Cádiz; a. 7,321 km²; p. (1967) 818,847.

Cádiz, c., cap. of C. prov., S.W. **Spain;** in Andalusia; pt. on Bay of C.; fortress t., naval base; exp. sherry, cork, fruit, olive oil, tunny fish; univ., cath.; one of the most anc. ts. in Europe, built by Phoenicians, c. 1100 B.C.; p. (est. 1969) 134,815.

Caen, c., cap. of Calvados dep., **France;** church and abbey, tomb of William the Conqueror; univ.; iron ore mng. and processing; severely damaged in second world war; p. (1968) 110,262 (c.), 152,332 (met. a.).

Caerleon, t., Gwent, **Wales;** on R. Usk, 5 km N.E. of Newport; Roman Isca Silurum; remains still present; agr. machin., tools, bricks; p. (1971) 6,235.

Caernarvon, t., Arfon, Gwynedd, N. **Wales;** pt. on S. shore of Menai strait; cas. where first Prince of Wales (Edward II) was christened; bricks, plastics; p. (1971) 9,253.

Caernarvonshire, former co., N. **Wales.** See **Gwynedd.**

Caerphilly, t., Rhymney Valley, Mid-Glamorgan, S. **Wales;** cas.; lt. inds.; former coal-mng. a.; p. (1971) 40,689.

Caesar Mazaca, anc. c., Asia Minor; residence of the Cappadocian Kings; the modern Kayeri, Turkey.

Caesarea Palestinae, old c., Israel, 32 km S. Mt. Carmel; cap. of Herod the Great.

Caeté, t., Minas Gerais st., Brazil; lge. iron and steel wks.; p. (est. 1968) 36,411.

Cagliare, cap. and ch. pt. of Sardinia, Italy; univ., cath.; p. (1969) 223,002.

Caha, mtns., on bdy. of Cork and Kerry, R.o.I.; cas.; highest point 686 m.

Cahir, t., Tipperary, R.o.I.; on R. Suir; anc. cas. and abbey; salmon fishing; p. (1966) 1,740.

Cahors, t., cap. of Lot dep., France; comm. ctr.; many historic bldgs., inc. cath., palace; distilleries, shoe factory; p. (1968) 20,903.

Cairngorm, mtns., Moray, Badenoch and Strathspey, Scot.; rise to 1,310 m (Ben Mac Dhui); form part of Highlands; nat. nature reserve of arctic flora and fauna; winter sports.

Cairns, spt., Queensland, Australia; on Trinity Bay; bulk sugar pt.; p. (1972) 32,570.

Cairntoul, mtn., Kincardine and Deeside, Scot.; alt. 1,294 m.

Cairo (El Qâhira), c., cap. of Egypt; on E. bank of Nile, at head of delta; lgst. c. in rep.; univ.; mosques, palace; fortress of Babylon in old c.; p. (est. 1974) 5,384,000.

Cairo, Ill., USA; at confluence of Mississippi and Ohio; busy traffic ctr.; p. (1970) 6.277.

Caistor, t., West Lyndsey, Lincs., Eng.; site of Roman camp in Lincs. Wolds; p. (1971) 14,575 (dist.).

Caithness, l. gov. dist., former co., Scot.; most N. part of mainland; flat, with much moorland; herring fishery; poor agr.; quarrying; ch. ts. Wick, Thurso; a. 3,152 km²; p. (1971) 29,755.

Cajamarca, t., cap. of C. dep., Peru; in mtn. valley, 2,745 m; impt. in Inca times; p. (est. 1969) 27,600.

Calabar, spt., S.E. Nigeria; cap. Cross River st.; exp. palm oil, kernels, rubber, ivory, cement; p. (est. 1969) 88,621.

Calabria, region, extreme S.W. Italy; mtnous. pen.; highest point Mt. Pollino 2,234 m; ch. R. Crati; socially and economically underdeveloped; cap. Catanzaro; p. (1969) 2,057,182.

Calais, spt., Pas-de-Calais, N.E. France; cross-channel ferry pt. opposite to and 33·6 km distant from Dover; p. (1968) 74,908.

Calama, oasis, Antofagasta prov., N. Chile; in Atacama desert at foot of Andean Cordillera; water from R. Loa supplies Antofagasta and used for irrigation locally.

Calatafimi, t., Sicily, Italy; Garibaldi defeated Neapolitans, May 1860; p. (est. 1968) 9,627.

Calbayog, t., Samar, Philippines; hemp tr., fisheries; p. (est. 1968) 103,100.

Calbe, t., Magdeburg, E. Germany; on R. Saale; p. (est. 1970) 16,296.

Calcutta, c., cap. of W. Bengal st., India; pt. on Hooghly R., lgst. c. in rep. and one of most densely populated areas of world; vast tr. from Ganges plain; univ.; jute-mills, textiles, chems., engin.; exp. jute, cotton, sugar-cane, rice, tea, coal; "black hole" (1756); p. (1971) 3,148,746 (c.), 7,031,382 (met. a. covering 1,036 km²).

Calder, R., West Yorks., Eng.; trib of Aire R.

Calderdale, met. dist., West Yorks., Eng.; comprises Todmorden, Halifax, Brighouse, Hebden Royd, Ripponden and Sowerby Bridge; p. (est. 1976) 190,100.

Calder Hall, Cumbria, Eng.; first full-scale nuclear power sta. in world (1956) owned and operated by AEA, produces electricity for nat. grid.

Caldy I., off Dyfed co., Wales; lighthouse; Trappist monastery.

Caledonian Canal, from Moray Firth to Loch Linnhe, Scot., connecting North Sea with Atl. Oc.; 100 km long; opened 1822.

Calf of Man, sm. I., S.W. I. of Man, Eng.; a. 250 ha.

Calgary, ch. t., Alberta, Canada; ctr. of ranching cty.; lumber mills, tanneries, oil refining, flour milling; p. (1971) 400,514.

Cali, c., cap. of Valle del Cauca dep., W. Colombia; 1,068 m on Cauca R.; comm. and transport ctr. for rich agr. a.; p. (est. 1972) 1,003,900 (c.), 1,022,200 (met. a.).

Calicut (Kozhikode), t., Kerala, India; first pt. reached by Vasco da Gama (1498); gave its name to calico cloth; p. (1971) 333,979.

California, st., W. USA; mtnous., forested, fertile valleys; subject to earthquakes from San Andreas fault; rich in minerals, oil, natural gas, gold, silver, copper; fruits; film ind.; attractive climate and scenery; cap. Sacramento; ch. pt. San Francisco; lgst. c. Los Angeles; most populous st. in USA; a. 411,014 km²; p. (1970) 19,696,840.

California Current, E. Pac. Oc.; flows N. to S. along cst. of Ore., and Cal., USA; relatively cold water; reduces summer temp. and causes fog in cst. a. especially nr. San Francisco.

California, G. of, arm of Pac. Oc., N.W. Mexico; 1,120 km long; same rift as Imperial and Coachella valleys in S.E. Cal.

Callander, burgh, Stirling, Scot.; mkt. t. on R. Teith, 24 km N.W. of Stirling; "the gate of the Highlands," tourism; p. (1971) 1,768.

Callao, c., W. Peru; pt. of Lima; sheltered harbour; sacked by Drake in 16th cent.; p. (est. 1970) 335,400.

Calne, North Wilts., Eng.; mkt. t. on Marden R.; lge. bacon factory; p. (1971) 9,685.

Caltagirone, t., Catania, Sicily, Italy; cath.; majolica ware; p. (est. 1968) 43,455.

Caltanissetta, t., cap. of C. prov., Sicily, Italy; cath.; agr., sulphur ctr.; p. (1969) 64,048.

Calumet, v., Mich., USA; on Keweenaw peninsula, L. Superior; copper mine; p. (1970) 1,007.

Calvados, dep., N.E. France; low-lying cty. and damp climate aid dairying; butter and cheese prods.; apple orchards produce Calvados brandy; cap. Caen; a. 5,690 km²; p. (1968) 519,695.

Cam (Granta), R., Cambridge, Eng.; trib. of R. Ouse; flows through the "backs" at Cambridge; 64 km long.

Camagüey, c., Cuba; comm. ctr. in rich agr. region; cattle, sugar-cane; p. (est. 1967) 178,600.

Camargue, delta dist., Bouches-du-Rhône, France; at mouth of R. Rhône; famous col. of flamingoes; gypsies; bull-rearing; a. 777 km².

Camberley, t., Surrey, Eng.; Royal Military Staff College.

Cambodia, Democratic (Khmer Rep.), S.E. Asia; between Thailand and S. Vietnam; former associate st. of Fr. Union; cap. Phnom-Penh on Mekong R.; mainly agr., rice, rubber, maize, pepper, kapok, livestock; Gr. L., or Tonle Sap, impt. for fisheries, car assembly, cigarette-mkg., textiles, plywood, paper, tyres, cement; oil refinery nr. Sihanoukville; new constitution established after civil war 1970–5; a. 181,300 km²; p. (est. 1969) 7,000,000.

Camborne, t., Cornwall, Eng.; 18 km S.W. Truro; old tin-and copper-mines; engin., radio-television assembly; textiles, chemicals; p. (1971) 42,029 (inc. Redruth).

Cambrai, t., Nord dep., France; on R. Scheldt; textiles (gave its name to cambric), agr. processing; suffered in both world wars; p. (1968) 39,922.

Cambrian Mtns., Wales; collective name for mtns. of N. and Central Wales inc. Snowdonia and Cader Idris.

Cambridge, univ. c., co. t., l. gov. dist., Cambridgeshire, Eng.; on Cam R.; famous univ. with residtl. colleges; leading ctr. of research-based inds.; p. (est. 1976) 106,400.

Cambridgeshire, non-met. co., Eng.; low-lying, sloping from E. Anglian Heights in S.E. to Fens in N.; crossed by Rs. flowing to Wash; rich soils aid intensive agr. and mkt. gardening; inc. former cos. of Huntingdon, Peterborough and Isle of Ely; ch. t. Cambridge; a. 3,408 km²; p. (est. 1976) 185,500.

Cambridgeshire, East, l. gov. dist., Cambs., Eng.; a. N.E. of Cambridge inc. Ely; p. (est. 1976) 52,100.

Cambridgeshire, South, l. gov. dist., Cambs., Eng.; rural a. surrounding Cambridge; p. (est. 1976) 100,900.

Cambridge, c., Mass., USA; 5 km from Boston; seat of Harvard Univ. and MIT; mftg.; impt. research ctr.; now inc. in Boston met. a.

Camden, inner bor., N. London, Eng.; inc. Hampstead, Holborn, and St. Pancras; p. (est. 1976) 185,800.

Camden, c., N.J., USA; pt. of entry on Delaware R., opposite Philadelphia; comm., mftg. and residtl.; iron foundries, chemicals, shipbldg.; p. (1970) 102,551; inc. in Philadelphia met. a.

Camerino, t., central Italy; in Appennines; univ., cath.; the anc. Camerium; p. (est. 1968) 9,180.

Cameroon, United Rep. of, unitary st. (1972) W. Africa; on G. of Guinea; fed. cap. Yaoundé; timber, cocoa, palm kernels, palm oil, groundnuts, bananas, coffee; a. 475,500 km²; p. (est. 1969) 5,680,000.

Cameroon Mtn., volcano, massif, Cameroon; cstl.

mtn., hgst. in W. Africa; last eruption 1922; alt. 4,072 m.

Campagna di Roma, Latium, Italy; malarial coastal plain around Rome; now reclaimed and used for pasture.

Campania, region, S. Italy; comprising provs. Avellino, Benevento, Caserta, Naples, Salerno; admin. and comm. ctr. Naples; high p. density; fertile; intensive agr.; p. (1969) 5,159,038.

Campbelltown, t., N.S.W., Australia; dairy and poultry ctr.; proposed as satellite t. for Sydney; p. (1966) 22,812.

Campbeltown, royal burgh, spt., Kintyre, Argyll and Bute, Scot.; distilling, fishing; planned ctr. for construction of off-shore oil platforms; p. (1971) 5,960.

Campeche, spt., S.E. Mexico; on G. of Campeche; gives its name to prov. (a. 56,099 km²; p. (1969) 239,000); clothing; exp. timber, sisal hemp; p. (est. 1969) 44,000.

Campina Grande, t., Paraiba, Brazil; agr.; textiles, veg. oils; p. (1970) 163,206.

Campinas, t., Brazil; 88 km N. of São Paulo; coffee; machin.; rubber gds.; p. (1970) 328,629.

Campine or Kempenland, region in Limburg and Antwerp provs., Belgium; concealed coalfield in heathland a.

Campobasso, t., cap. of C. prov., S. Italy; agr. ctr.; famed for cutlery; 15th cent. cas.; p. (est. 1967) 33,800.

Campo Belo, t., Minas Gerais st., Brazil; impt. cattle ctr. nr. L. formed by Furnas Dam on Rio Grande; p. (est. 1968) 30,810.

Campo Duran, terr., Argentina; oil-field and refining.

Campos, c., Rio de Janeiro st., Brazil; ctr. for rich agr. region; sugar-refining; p. (1970) 153,310.

Campos do Jordão, t., Brazil; alt. 1,699 m; health resort, known as the Switzerland of Brazil; p. (est. 1968) 19,676.

Campsie Fells, range of hills, Stirling, Scot.; highest point, 578 m.

Campulung, t., Romania, in Walachia, at foot of Transylvanian Alps; summer resort; p. (est. 1970) 26,675.

Canada, indep. st., within Commonwealth; occupies N. part of N. America; enclave of Alaska (USA) in N.W.; second lgst. cty. in world, consisting of 10 provs., 2 terrs.; coastal mtns. and Rockies in W., interior plains in ctr., Hudson Bay lowlands in N., plateau a. of Quebec and Newfoundland in E.; many Is. off Arctic cst.; continental climate, severe in interior but moderated on csts.; less than 8 per cent of total land a. classified as cultivated land but agr. prods. (especially wheat) very valuable exp.; enormous forest resources but many economically inaccessible; fur trapping in N., impt. fishing inds. in both Pac. and Atl. csts.; considerable mineral resources; lgst. world producer of asbestos, silver, nickel, zinc.; major oil and gas resources in Alberta; one of most urbanised ctys. in world; p. concentrated along E.–W. axis in S. parts of W. provs. and along Gr. Ls. and St. Lawrence lowland; economy highly integrated with USA; 80 per cent of mftg. inds. based on US investment and 70 per cent of external tr. with USA; major cultural differences between English and French communities; trong separatist movements in Quebec; both nat. languages official (30 per cent p. speak French); cap. Ottawa; a. 9,976,185 km²; p. (1976) 22,992,604.

Canada Dam, Bihar, India; on R. Mayurakshi, 256 km from Calcutta.

Canadian Coast Range, mtns., B.C., W. Canada; penetrated by deep inlets (fjords) with very little cst. plain; crossed only by R. Skeena in N., R. Fraser in S.

Canadian R., S.W. USA; trib. of Arkansas R., not navigable but impt. for irrigation; 1,440 km long.

Canadian Shield (Laurentian Shield), Canada; vast region of hard anc. rock surrounding Hudson Bay, deeply eroded by ice, and lake covered; mng. and forestry.

Canal du Centre, canal, France; links Rhône–Saône valley at Chalon-sur-Saône with R. Loire at Digoin; serves Le Creusot coalfield; length 96 km.

Canal Zone, Panama; strip of land leased to USA since 1903 for Panama Canal; p. (1970) 44,650.

Canaries Current, ocean current, flows S. along

N.W. coast of Africa from El Dar-el-Belda to C. Verde; relatively cold and has very marked cooling effect on Saharan coastlands.

Canary Is., or Canaries, N. Atl. Oc.; gr. of 7 volcanic Is. belong to Spain, 96 km off cst. Africa; desires independence; inc. Tenerife (the lgst. I.), Gran Canaria, La Palma, Gomera, Hierro, Fuerteventura, Lanzarote; dry sunny climate and impressive volcanic landscape encourage tourism; intensive, irrigated agr. for bananas, tomatoes, oranges and vegetables; cap. Las Palmas, the "Fortunate Isles" of many myths and legends; a. 7,272 km²; p. (1970) 1,170,224.

Canberra, Australian Capital Territory, Australia; in Gr. Dividing Range (highest point Mt. Bimberi, 1,912 m) 317 km S.W. of Sydney; planned (1911) as seat of govt. of Commonwealth; univ.; a. 2,356 km²; p. (1972) 158,594 (met. a.).

Candia. See Iráklion.

Canea. See Khaniá.

Canna, sm. I., Hebrides, Scot.; basaltic pillars.

Cannanore, t., Kerala, India; exp. timber, coconuts; p. (1961) 48,960.

Cannes, spt., dep. Alpes-Maritimes, France; 32 km S.W. Nice; famous resort; perfumes; airpt.; annual spring international film festival; p. (1968) 67,152 (t.), 213,397 (met. a.).

Cannock Chase, upland a., Staffs., Eng.; open a. close to Midlands conurb.; now forms l. gov. dist. based on Cannock t.; p. (est. 1976) 84,800.

Canopus, c. of anc. Egypt; 19 km E. of Alexandria; here bdy. between Asia and Africa was drawn; Aboukir nr. ruins of temple of Serapis.

Cantabrians (Sierra de Cantabria), mtns., N. Spain; stretch from Pyrenees to C. Finisterre; form barrier between sea and central plateau; thick vegetation on lower slopes; coal, iron, hydroelec. power; hgst. peak Peña Vieja (2,673 m).

Cantal, dep., S.E. France; volcanic a., part of Massif Central; hgst. peak Plomb du Cantal (1,859 m); difficult agr., sparse p.; cap. Aurillac; a. 5,778 km²; p. (1968) 169,330.

Canterbury, c., l. gov. dist., Kent, Eng.; at foot of N. Downs on R. Stour; univ.; cath. founded A.D. 597 by St. Augustine; shrine of Thomas Becket; for centuries a place of pilgrimage; p. (est. 1976) 115,600 (dist.).

Canterbury, prov., S.I., N.Z.; cap. Christchurch; a. 36,104 km²; p. (1971) 398,318.

Canterbury Plains, rich grazing and wheat-growing dist., S.I., N.Z.; ch. t. Christchurch; ch. pt. Lyttelton.

Can-tho, t., Vietnam; on Mekong R. delta, tr. ctr.; rice, fish; p. (est. 1967) 61,000.

Canton. See Kuangchow.

Canton R. See Chu-kiang.

Canton, c., Ohio, USA; iron and steel, pulleys, hydraulic presses; p. (1970) 108,872 (c.), 368,876 (met. a.).

Canvey I., Castle Point, Essex, Eng.; fronting the Thames; expanded t.; resort; radio components, bookbinding, iron and wire wk., oil storage; oil refinery projected; liquid gas terminal; p. (1971) 26,462.

Cap de la Madeleine, t., S. Quebec, Canada; varied mnfs.; p. (1966) 29,433.

Cape Breton I., Nova Scotia, Canada; coalmng. steelwks.; farming, timber, fishing; ch. t. Sydney; discovered in 1497 by John Cabot; a. 9,324 km²; p. (1966) 166,943.

Cape Canaveral, E. Fla., USA; formerly Cape Kennedy; barrier I. separating Banana R. lagoon from Atl. Oc.; military base for testing missiles.

Cape Coast, t., Ghana; pt. of G. of Guinea, 96 km S.W. of Accra; cap. of Gold Coast until 1876; exp. cacao; cas.; p. (1970) 51,764.

Cape Cod, low sandy penin., Mass. Bay, USA; resort; fishing, boat bldg.; encloses C. C. Bay where Pilgrim Fathers first arrived in America 1620.

Cape Girardeau, t., Mo., USA; on Mississippi R.; footwear, clothing; p. (1970) 31,282.

Cape Kennedy. See Cape Canaveral.

Cape of Good Hope, S. Africa; famous headland, S. of Cape Town; 305 m high.

Cape Province, prov., Rep. of S. Africa; formerly Cape of Good Hope Colony; southernmost tip of Africa; cap. Cape Town; mostly plateau; inc. Transkeian terrs. in E.; sheep raising; wheat, citrus fruits, grapes, tobacco; fisheries; diamond and copper mng. in Namaqualand;

automobile assembly, textiles, food canning; a. 721,224 km²; p. (1970) 4,235,376.

Capernaüm, in time of Christ impt. place in Palestine, on N. shore of L. Galilee; the modern Tell Hum (Israel).

Cape Town, c., cap. of Cape Province, and legislative cap. of Rep. of S. Africa; spt. on Table Bay, 48 km N. of C. of Good Hope; communication by rail direct with Rhodesia, Transvaal, O.F.S., and Natal; docks; cath.; univ.; exp. wool, gold, diamonds; oil refinery under construction at Milnerton 10 km N.E., p. (1970) 1,096,257 (met. a.).

Cape Verde Is., archipelago off W. cst. Africa; former Portuguese col.; 15 volcanic Is. and islets, divided into two grs.; windward and leeward; a. 4,040 km²; cap. Praia; agr. sugar, fruit-growing; São Vicente fuelling sta. for navigation to S. America; indep. achieved 1975; irrigation and reafforestation projects; p. (est. 1969) 250,000.

Cap-Haitien, t., N. Haiti; spt., on N. cst.; exp. coffee, cacao, sugar; p. (1971) 44,123.

Capraia, I., 26 km E. of Corsica, belonging to Italy; volcanic; part of Genoa prov.

Caprera, I. off N.E. cst. Sardinia, Italy; Garibaldi buried here.

Capri, I. and tourist resort in Bay of Naples, Italy; famous Blue Grotto; celebrated in times of Augustus and Tiberius; wines; a. 10 km².

Capua, t., Campania, S. Italy; on Volturno R.; founded by Etruscans, impt. ctr. under Roman rule, sacked by Gaiseric; modern t. 5 km N. of site of anc. Capua; cath., Roman bridge; p. (est. 1968) 19,176.

Caracas, c., cap. of Venezuela; in mtn. valley 921 m a.s.l.; 13 km inland from its spt. La Guaira; modern c.; contains 20 per cent of p. of rep.; cath., univs.; oil, textile mills, sugar refining; p. (est. 1970) 2,175,400 (met. a.).

Caradon, l. gov. dist., Cornwall, Eng.; a. between Tamar and S. cst.; inc. Looe, Saltash and Liskeard; p. (est. 1976) 62,100.

Carbon County, N. Utah, USA; contains immense reserves of gd. coking coal suitable for blast furnaces; not yet developed.

Carbonia, t., Sardinia, Italy; built 1937-8 nr. lignite and barytes a.; p. (est. 1968) 32,661.

Carcassonne, c., cap of Aude dep., S. France; historic citadel guarding impt. routeway from Aquitaine to Rhône valley; old c. divided from new by Aude R.; tourism; p. (1968) 46,329.

Cardamom Hills, Kerala, S. India; highland formed where W. and E. Ghats meet; rise to over 2,400 m; hgst. land of Indian penin.; rainfall less seasonal than most of India; " China " tea plantations on middle slopes.

Cárdenas, t., W. Cuba; pt. on Cárdenas Bay; processes and exp. sugar; p. (est. 1967) 67,400.

Cardiff, c., l. gov. dist., South Glamorgan, cap. of Wales; at mouth of R. Taff on Bristol Channel, one of world's gr. coal-shipping pts; univ., cath., cas.; docks inc. Penarth and Barry; iron and steel wks., flour mills; p. (est. 1976) 281,500 (dist.).

Cardigan, t., Ceredigion, Dyfed, S. Wales; at mouth of Teifi R.; former pt., now mkt. ctr.; p. (1971) 3,800.

Cardiganshire, former co., Wales. See Dyfed.

Caribbean Sea, part of Atl. Oc., between W.I. and Central and S. America; warm sea, entirely within tropics; a. 19,425 km².

Cariboo Range, mtns., B.C., W. Canada; mass of anc. crystalline rocks inside the gr. bend of R. Fraser; widespread occurrence of lode and alluvial gold; mainly above 1,500 m; hgst. point Mt. Sir Wilfred Laurier (3,584 m).

Carinthia (Karnten), prov., Austria; cap. Klagenfurt; contains hgst. mtn. in Austria, Grossglockner, alt. 3,801 m; many Ls.; p. (1968) 522,600.

Carlisle, c. l. gov. dist., Cumbria, Eng.; on Eden R.; pt. and route ctr.; Norman cas.; cath.; textiles, plasterboard, flour, bacon, biscuits, metal boxes; p. (est. 1976) 99,600 (dist.).

Carlow, co., S.E. Leinster, R.o.I.; arable agr. and livestock; co. t. Carlow; a. 896 km²; p. (1966) 33,479.

Carlow, co. t., Carlow co., R.o.I.; cath.; mkt., agr. processing; p. (1966) 7,791.

Carlsbad, t., N.M., USA; tourist resort; impt. potash deposits; p. (1970) 21,297.

Carlsbad Caverns National Park, N.M., USA; in foothills of Guadalupe mtns.; limestone caves; 18,600 ha.

Carlton, t., Gedling, Notts., Eng.; 3 km N.E. Nottingham; hosiery; p. (1971) 45,211.

Carmarthen, t., l. gov. dist., Dyfed, Wales; on Towy R.; impt. agr. ctr.; cas. ruins; p. (est. 1976) 50,000 (dist.).

Carmarthenshire, former co., Wales. See Dyfed.

Carmiel, t., N. Israel; new t. built between Acre and Safad, in the Galilean hills.

Carmona, t., Spain; Roman walls and necropolis; p. (1970) 24,378.

Carnac, sm. t., Brittany, N.W. France; famous for its megalithic monuments.

Carnarvon, t., W. Australia; on R. Gascoyne; NASA tracking sta.; p. (1966) 2,957.

Carnoustie, burgh, Angus, Scot.; on N. Sea; 10 km S.W. of Arbroath; resort; p. (1971) 6,232.

Caroline Is., archipelago in W. Pac. Oc.; 549 in no., lying between the Philippines and the Marshall gr., former Japanese mandate now part of US Pac. Trust Terr.; ch. exp. copra; a. 1,193 km²; p. (est. 1967) 66,900.

Caroni, R., Venezuela, hydroelec. complex at confluence Orinoco R.; steelwks.

Carpathian Mtns., range, E. Europe; arc of mtns. extending from CSSR into Ukrainian SSR and Romania; major European range; 1,288 km long; contain oil fields.

Carpentaria, G. of, N. Australia; between C. Arnhem and C. York.

Carpentras, t., Vaucluse, France; on R. Auzon; antiquities; sweetmeats; p. (1968) 22,130.

Carpi, t., central Italy; 16 km N. of Modena; cath.; food processing; p. (est. 1968) 52,186.

Carrantuohill, mtn., Kerry, R.o.I.; 1,041 m, loftiest in all Ireland.

Carrara, t., Massa-e-Carrara, central Italy; famed for white marble used by Michelangelo; p. (1966) 66,592.

Carrick, l. gov. dist., Cornwall, Eng.; stretches across penin. and surrounds Fal estuary; inc. Truro, Penryn and Falmouth; p. (est. 1976) 73,000.

Carrickfergus, t., l. gov. dist., N. Ireland; pt. on N. shore of Belfast Lough; textiles, nylon fibres, tobacco inds.; p. (est. 1971) 15,162.

Carrickmacross, mkt. t., U.D., Monaghan, R.o.I.; p. (1966) 2,094.

Carrick-on-Shannon, co. t., R. D., Leitrim, R.o.I.; on flat land in Upper Shannon valley; p. of t. (1966) 1,636.

Carrick-on-Suir, mkt. t., U.D., Tipperary, R.o.I.; leather prods.; N.W. of Waterford; p. (1966) 4,830.

Carron, v., Falkirk, Scot.; nr. Falkirk; site of first ironwks. in E. Lowlands of Scot.

Carron, Loch, inlet, W. cst, Ross and Cromarty, Scot.; followed by rly. from Dingwall to Kyle of Lochalsh.

Carse of Gowrie, Perth and Kinross, Scot.; fertile coastal dist. between Perth and Dundee, S. of Sidlaw Hills; soft fruits, especially raspberries.

Carshalton. See Sutton.

Carson City, cap. Nevada, USA; smallest st. cap. at 1,427 m; tourist ctr.; p. (1970) 15,468.

Carstenz Mtns., Irian Jaya, Indonesia; major copper and base metal deposits and mng.; slurry pipeline to pts. on Tipoeka R.

Cartagena, spt., cap. dep. Bolivar, Colombia; shares with Barranquilla tr. from Magdalena R. valley; platinum, coffee, chemicals, textiles, fertilisers; oil refinery; p. (est. 1972) 315,200 (t.), 347,600 (met. a.).

Cartagena, c., Murcia prov., S.E. Spain; on Mediterranean; spt. and naval base; cath.; shipbldg., metalwkg.; p. (est. 1967) 144,316.

Cartago, t., Colombia; in Cauca valley, ctr. of rich agr. a.; p. 64,830.

Cartago, c., Costa Rica; former cap.; 1,504 m at foot of volcanic Mt. Irazu; coffee, fruits; subject to earthquakes; p. (est. 1967) 20,200.

Cartago Basin, Meseta Central, Costa Rica; alt. 5,000 ft.; a. of early Spanish settlement.

Carter Fell, mtn., a summit of the Cheviot hills, on the Eng./Scot. border, 554 m.

Carthage, anc. c., N. Africa; on Bay of Tunis; destroyed by Romans 146 B.C.; site is sub. of Tunis.

Casablanca. See El Dar-el-Beida.

Casale Monferrato, t., Piedmont, Italy; on R. Po; cath.; cement; p. (est. 1968) 43,896.

Cascade Range, USA and Canada; extends N. and S. through B.C., Wash., and Ore. between Rocky Mtns. and Pac. cst.; timber resources, hydroelec. power; hgst. peak Mt. Rainier, 4,395 m.

Cascade Tunnel, longest rly. tunnel in N. America, Wash., USA; carries trunk rly. from Spokane to Seattle through Cascade Mtns.; length 12·5 km.

Caserta, t., Italy; on N.E. edge of plain of Campania; impt. route ctr. and agr. mkt.; cath.; palace; p. (1969) 60,196.

Cashel, mkt. t., U.D. Tipperary, R.O.I.; anc. seat of kings of Munster; ruins of cath. on Rock of Cashel; p. (1966) 2,682.

Casiquiare, R., and canal, Venezuela; joins Orinoco to the Rio Negro, a trib. of the Amazon.

Casper, t., Wyo., USA; petroleum; airpt.; p. (1970) 39,361.

Caspian Sea, salt lake, USSR and Iran, between Europe and Asia; lgst. inland sea in world; a. 422,170 km² but shrinking; 28 m below sea level; maximum depth 975 m; fed by R. Volga; agr. and dense p. on S. shore; pts.; Astrakhan, at mouth of Volga, Baku (oil ctr.).

Casquets, dangerous rocks, 11 km W. of Alderney, Channel Is. Eng.; lighthouse.

Cassino, t., Frosinone, Italy; in Apennines, on Rapido R.; t. and nearby monastery destroyed 1944, now rebuilt.

Castel Gandolfo, t., central Italy; in Alban Hills; papal summer residence; p. (est. 1968) 8,044.

Castellammare del Golfo, spt., N.W. Sicily, Italy; wat. pl., tuna fishing; p. (est. 1968) 15,498.

Castellammare di Stabia, t., Campania, Italy; on Bay of Naples, at foot of Vesuvius; historic arsenal and dockyards; mineral springs; cath.; resort; p. (est. 1968) 70,287.

Castellón de la Plana, prov., Spain; on Mediterranean, part of anc. Valencia, mainly mtns. a. 6,679 km²; cap. Castellón; p. (est. 1970) 385,823.

Castellón de la Plana, t., Spain; on plain inland from Mediterranean cst.; varied agr. inds.; oil refining; p. (1967) 81,187.

Castelnaudary, t., Aude dep., France; in strategic gap between Central Massif and Pyrenees; captured by Black Prince 1355; mkt. for cereals; pottery; p. (1968) 10,844.

Castelo Branco, t., Portugal, prov. cap. Beira Baixa; agr. mkt. t.; p. (1970) 21,730.

Castelvetrano, agr. t., W. Sicily, Italy; wine-mkg.; p. (est. 1968) 31,123.

Castile, region in the high plateaux of central Spain; former kingdom; divided into Old Castile in N. (Avila, Burgos, Logroño, Santander, Segovia, Soria) and New Castile in S. (Ciudad Real, Cuenca, Guadalajara, Madrid, Toledo). Its dialect became the standard language of Spain.

Castlebar, U.D., cap. Mayo, R.O.I.; mkt. t.; pursuit of Brit. by Fr. who captured t. 1798 known as "Castlebar races"; p. (1966) 5,630.

Castleblayney, U.D., Monaghan, R.O.I.; nr. Dundalk; mkt. t.; shoes; p. (1961) 2,125.

Castlecary, v., Central Reg., Scot.; sta. on Roman wall; silica, fire clay deposits.

Castle Donington, t., North West Leics., Eng.; airpt; power sta; p. (1971) 11,851 (dist.).

Castle Douglas, burgh, Stewartry, Scot.; nr. R. Dee; nearby cas.; stock mkt.; p. (1971) 3,331.

Castleford, t., West Yorks., Eng.; 16 km S.E. of Leeds at confluence of Rs. Aire and Calder; coal mng., chemical, glass, and clothing mnfs, flour milling, brick mkg.; p. (1967) 38,210.

Castlemaine, t., Victoria, Australia; at foot of Gr. Dividing Range, 40 km S. of Bendigo; dairying, sheep; engin.; wool; p. (1972) 7,547.

Castle Morpeth, l. gov. dist., Northumberland, Eng.; based on Morpeth; p. (est. 1976) 48,100.

Castle Point, l. gov. dist., Essex, Eng.; comprises Canvey I. and Benfleet; p. (est. 1976) 82,900.

Castlereagh, l. gov. dist., N. Ireland; inc. S.E. outskirts of Belfast.

Castleton, v., Derbys., Eng.; on Hope R.; tourist ctr. for the Peak District; nearby fluorspar mines.

Castletown, t., Isle of Man, Eng.; former cap.; pt., cas. tower.

Castres, t., Tarn, France; on R. Agout; former Huguenot stronghold; cath.; textiles, soap, earthenware; p. (1968) 42,920.

Castries, t., cap. St. Lucia, Windward Is. W.I.; fine harbour; p. (1964) 5,100.

Castrop-Rauxel or Kastrop Rauxel, t., N. Rhine-Westphalia, W. Germany; part of Ruhr conurb.; industl.; coal, cement, tar prod., tiles, brandy; p. (est. 1969) 83,892.

Catalonia, region, N.E. Spain; ch. industl. a.; comprises 4 provs.; Barcelona, Gerona, Lérida, Tarragona; cap. Barcelona; hilly, drained by Ebro R.; cereals, olive oil, wines; textiles, cars; hydroelec. power stas.; nuclear power sta. projected; a. 32,185 km²; p. (1970) 5,122,567.

Catamarca, t., cap. of Catamarca prov., N.W. Argentina; in Andean foothills 128 km S. of San Miguel de Tucumán; ctr. of irrigated oasis producing vines, apricots, cherries, cotton; thermal springs; p. (1960) 42,291.

Catanduanes, I., off S. Luzon, Philippines; hilly, fertile; rice, corn, cotton, hemp, coconuts; a. 1,429 km²; p. (1970) 162,679.

Catania, c., Sicily, Italy; cap. of C. prov.; pt. on E. cst. at foot of Mt. Etna; rebuilt several times after earthquakes and volcanic eruption; cath., univ., cas.; p. (1969) 412,721.

Catanzaro, t., S. Italy; univ.; service ctr., regional cap. of Calabria; p. (1969) 82,243.

Catastrophe, C., S. extremity of Eyre Peninsula, S. Australia.

Catawba, R., S. and N.C., USA; rises in Blue Ridge Range, flows to Santee R.; extensively dammed; 480 km long.

Caterham and Warlingham, ts., former U.D., Tandridge, Surrey, Eng.; on N. Downs; residtl.; p. (1971) 35,781.

Cathay, anc. name for China and E. Tartary.

Catoche, C., N.E. point of Yucatan, Mexico.

Catskill Mtns., N.Y., USA; gr. in Appalachians, W. of Hudson R.; well wooded; resort for p. of N.Y. c.; alt. c. 900 m.

Cauca, dep., Colombia; cap. Popayán; a. 30,191 km²; p. (est. 1968) 664,003.

Cauca, R., Colombia; trib. of Magdalena; 960 km long.

Caucasia, region between Black Sea and Caspian, USSR; divided by Caucasus Mtns. into N. or Cis-Caucasia and S. or Trans-Caucasia.

Caucasus (Bol'shoy Kavkaz), mtns., separate RSFSR from Georgian SSR and Azerbaydzhan SSR, USSR; run from Black Sea to Caspian Sea; divided into 3 ranges; hgst. summits Mt. Elbruz (5,631 m) and Kasbek (5,047 m); many lofty passes and glaciers; total l. c. 1,520 km.

Caucun, t., off Yucatan penin., Mexico; developing tourist ctr.; airpt.

Causses, Les, limestone plateau, Aveyron, Tarn deps., S. France; on S.W. flank of Central Massif; caverns, gorges of Rs. Lot and Tarn; sheep provide milk for Roquefort cheese; alt. 900–1,800 m.

Cauvery, R., S. India; rises in W. Ghats, flows into Bay of Bengal through Karnataka and Tamil Nadu; length 640 km; lge. irrigation and hydroelec. power project.

Caux, region of Normandy, France; fertile loess-covered chalk plateau adjacent to English Channel; arable agr.

Cava de' Tirreni, t., Salerno, Italy; summer resort; textiles; p. (est. 1968) 46,657.

Cavaillon, t., Vaucluse, France; cath.; ctr. of mkt. gardening dist.; p. (1968) 18,544.

Cavan, inland co., R.o.I.; agr. a. with many Ls.; depopulation; borders Ulster; a. 1,932 km²; p. (1966) 53,815.

Cavan, U.D., co. t., Cavan, R.o.I.; 115 km S.W. Belfast; mkt.; cath.; p. (1966) 4,165.

Cavite, spt., Luzon, Philippines; walled t.; oil refining nearby; p. (est. 1970) 77,100.

Cavour Canal, irrigation canal, Piedmont and Lombardy regions, N. Italy; links R. Po nr. Chivassa with R. Ticino 16 km N.E. of Novara; provides water for 101,000 ha of rice-fields and meadow-land; length 128 km.

Cawnpore. See Kanpur.

Caxias, t., Maranhão, Brazil; on Itapicuru R. p. (1968) 124,403.

Caxias do Sul, t., Rio Grande do Sul, Brazil; wines; p. (1970) 107,487.

Cayambe, volcanic mtn., Andes, Ecuador; alt. 5,958 m.

Cayenne, c., cap. of French Guiana, at mouth of Cayenne R.; exp. gold; gave its name to Cayenne pepper; p. (1967) 24,518.

Cayman Is., W.I.; consists of Grand Cayman, cap. Georgetown; Little Cayman; and Cayman

Brac.; turtle and shark fishing; a. 259 km²; p. (1970) 10,652.

Ceará, st., N. Brazil; stretches from Brazilian Plateau to Atl. cst.; poor cattle rearing a. with many droughts; cap. Fortaleza; a. 148,078 km²; p. (est. 1968) 3,838,329.

Cebu, one of Visayan Is., Philippines; mtnous.; forested; coal, oil, gold; coconuts, maize; a. 4,408 km²; p. (1970) 1,632,642 (prov.).

Cebu, one of Visayan Is., Philippines; mtnous.; forested; coal, oil, gold; coconuts, maize; a. 1,702 sq. m.; p. (1970) 1,632,642 (prov.).

Cebu, t., Cebu I., Philippines; tr. ctr. of Visayan Is.; pt. for abaca and copra; p. (1968) 332,100.

Cedar Falls, t., N. Iowa, USA; on Cedar R.; p. (1970) 29,597.

Cedar Mountain, hill, Va., USA; here Stonewall Jackson defeated Banks in Civil War (second battle of Bull Run, 1862).

Cedar Rapids, c., Iowa USA; distribution and rly. ctr. for agr. a.; p. (1970) 109,111 (c.), 160,832 (met. a.).

Cegléd, t., Hungary; on edge of Central Plain in fruit growing a.; vehicle repair shops; p. (1966) 37,200.

Celaya, mkt. t., Guanajuato, Mexico; rly. junc.; ctr. of rich farming a.; many inds.; sweetmeats; p. (1970) 143,703.

Celebes. See Sulawesi.

Celje, t., Yugoslavia; industl., agr. ctr., zinc refining, fertilisers; close to Austrian border; p. (est. 1965) 30,000.

Celle, t., Lower Saxony, W. Germany; on R. Aller; cas. was residence of dukes of Brunswick-Lüneburg until 1705; oil refining, machin., textiles; p. (est. 1967) 56,500.

Celtic Sea, a. bounded by S. Ireland, Wales, Cornwall and Brittany; rich natural gas deposits 48 km S.W. of Kinsale.

Central African Empire, indep. empire within Fr. Community, Equatorial Africa; formerly Fr. colony of Ubangi-Shari; landlocked upland plateau covered by savannah grassland; cotton, diamonds; cap. Bangui; a. 616,429 km²; p. (est. 1969) 1,518,000.

Central America, stretch of land between Mexico and S. America, from the Isthmus of Tehuantepec to that of Panama; includes Guatemala, Honduras, Nicaragua, Salvador, Costa Rica, Panama, Belize; tropical climate; forests, savannahs; p. (est. 1970) 16,630,000.

Central Asia, usually applied to regions between 30° and 40° N. lat. and 55° and 85° E. long.; Soviet C.A. is the land between China and Afghanistan and the Caspian, consisting of Kazakh SSR, Tadzhik SSR, Turkmen SSR, Uzbek SSR, and Kirghiz SSR.

Central Region, l. gov. reg., Scot.; stretches from Grampian mtns. to Central Lowlands, inc. Forth valley; main ts. Falkirk and Stirling; a. 2,631 km²; p. (1971) 262,600.

Central Valley, Cal., USA; valleys of Rs. San Joaquin and Sacramento; main agr. a. of Cal.; vast scheme for irrigation, hydroelec. power, flood control and protection of wildlife.

Cephalonia (Kefalliniá), lgst. of Ionian Is., Greece; mtnous. with fertile valleys; impt. harbours of Argostólion and Lexourion; currant production; a. 751 km².

Ceram. See Seram.

Ceredigion, l. gov. dist., Dyfed, Wales; lge a. inc. Cardigan and Lampeter in S. and Aberystwyth in N.; p. (est. 1976) 58,100.

Cérignola, t., Apulia, Italy; agr. ctr.; Spanish victory over French in Italian wars 1503; p. (est. 1967) 42,200.

Cerigo (Kithíra) I., Greece; sm. I. between Crete and Peloponnesus.

Cernauti. See Chernovtsy.

Cerro de Pasco, t., Pasco dep., Peru; mng. ctr. at 4,403 m; univ.; copper, gold, lead, zinc; p. (1961) 19,354.

Cerro Rico, mtn., Bolivia; in Andes, W. of Potosí; alt. 4,782 m; rich silver, tin, tungsten ores.

Cesena, t., Emillia-Romagna, Italy; flourished in Renaissance times; cath., Malatesta library; agr. mkt. t.; p. (est. 1967) 53,300.

České Budĕjovice (Budweis), t., ČSSR; on R. Vitava, 128 km S. of Prague, major industl. ctr.; pencils, porcelain, brewing, anthracite; p. (1967) 72,000.

Ceský Tĕšin. t., ČSSR; on Olše R., trib. of Oder;

part of former t. of Teschen on Czech side of frontier with Poland; coal mng.

Cessnock-Bellbird, t., N.S.W., Australia; coalmng. declining since 1968; clothing wks.; p. (1972) 16,141.

Ceuta, spt., Spanish N. Africa, naval base; opposite to and 26 km from Gibraltar; cath.; the anc. Abyla, one of the Pillars of Hercules; p. (est. 1970) 88,468.

Cevennes, mtns., S. France; separating basins of Rhône, Loire, and Tarn; highest point Mt. Mézenc, alt. 1,767 m.

Ceylon. See Sri Lanka.

Chaco, prov., N. Argentina; farming and prairie land; cap. Resistencia; a. 99,632 km²; p. (1970) 566,613.

Chad, indep. st. within Fr. Community, Equatorial Africa; cap. Ndjamene; desert and dry savannah; cotton, livestock; a. 1,282,050 km²; p. (est. 1969) 3,510,000.

Chad, L., lge. sheet of water bordering Nigeria, Niger, Chad and Cameroon; a. 129,500 km² when in flood; varies in extent with season, and is drying up; shallow, many Is., lies between the wooded region of the Sudan and the steppes leading to the Sahara desert; joint project for devel. by neighbouring ctys.

Chadderton, t., Gtr. Manchester, Eng.; engin., chemicals, textiles; p. (1971) 32,406.

Chagos Is., 5 coral Is., Indian Oc.; admin. by Seychelles since 1965; fine harbour in Diego Garcia (Anglo-American naval communications ctr.).

Chainat, t., Thailand; on Menam Chao Phraya; major barrage for hydroelec. power and flood control.

Chalcis, t., Greece; resort for Athens; joined to mainland by swing bridge; p. (1971) 36,381.

Chalfont St. Giles, v., Bucks, Eng.; in London commuter belt; home of Milton.

Châlons-sur-Marne, t , cap. of Marne dep., N.E. France; comm. and industl; cath., churches; p. (1968) 54,025.

Châlon-sur-Saône, t., Saône-et-Loire dep., E. France; R. pt., comm. ctr. for Burgundy; historic t.; p. (1968) 52,746.

Chambal, R., trib. of R. Jumna, rising in Vindhya hills, Madhya Pradesh, India; major power, irrigation and industl. scheme; agr. in lower valley causing soil erosion, major soil conservation projection; 880 km long.

Chambéry, t., cap. of Savoie dep., S.E. France; leather gds.; tourism; p. (1968) 53,813.

Chambord, v., Loir-et-Cher dep., France; on R. Cosson, trib. of Loire; Renaissance château; p. (1968) 267.

Chamonix, t., Haute-Savoie, France; at foot of Mont Blanc, in valley of R. Arve; winter sports ctr.; road tunnel links to Aosta; p. (1968) 8,403.

Champagne, region and former prov., France; covers deps. of Aube, Marne, Haute-Marne, Ardennes, and parts of Yonne, Aisne, Seine-et-Marne, and Meuse; famous for its champagne wine; wheat, sheep; impt. tr. fairs in Middle Ages; main ctr. Reims. See Champagne Humide and Champagne Pouilleuse.

Champagne Humide, region, France; clay vale, runs 160 km N.E. from Auxerre to Bar-le-Duc; drained by Seine, Aube, Marne, Aisne, and many tribs.; heavily wooded, marshy; where cleared and drained, grain cultivation.

Champagne Pouilleuse, region, France; barren chalk plateau, extends 128 km N.E. from Sens to Reims; drained by Aisne, Vesle, Seine, Aube, Marne; dusty chalk downland pastures; sheep; vine growing on S.-facing valley sides and S.E.-facing escarpment of Falaise de l'Île de France favours production of Champagne wines; ch. producing ctrs.: Châlons-sur-Marne, Reims, Epernay.

Champaign, t., Ill., USA; close to Urbana; univ.; foundries; food processing; p. (1970) 55,976 (c.), 162,107 (met. a.).

Champigny-sur-Marne, t., Val-de-Marne dep,. France; E. sub. of Paris; varied inds.; p. (1968) 70,564.

Champlain Canal, N.Y., USA; follows gap between Adirondack Mtns. and Green Mtns. occupied by Hudson R.; links Albany with L. Champlain and allows through barge traffic between New York and St. Lawrence valley.

Champlain, L., USA; N. frontier of N.Y. st.;

discharges by Richelieu R. into St. Lawrence; flanked by trunk route from New York to Montreal; forms link between Hudson R. and St. Lawrence waterway; a. 1,126 km².

Chanaral, spt., N. Atacama, Chile; lies in gold and copper-mng. a.; p. (1960) 21,098.

Chanda, t., Nagpur, Maharashtra, India; anc. temples; p. (1961) 51,484.

Chandausi, t., Uttar Pradesh, India; cotton, hemp; rly. ctr.; p. (1961) 48,557.

Chandernagore, t., W. Bengal, India; on Hooghly R., N. of Calcutta; founded by French 1686; p. (1961) 67,105.

Chandigarh, union terr. (1966) and cap. of both Punjab and Haryana sts., India; new c. designed by Le Corbusier to replace former cap. Lahore, now in Pakistan; on plateau at foot of Himalayas, S.W. of Simla; univ.; a. of terr. 114 km², p. of c. (1971) 218,743.

Changchow (Changzhou), c., Kiangsu, China; in valley of Yangtze R., on Grand Canal 112 km S.E. of Nanking; mkt. for intensively cultivated dist.; silk; p. (1953) 297,000.

Changchun, c., Kirin, China; rly. ctr.; univ.; China's biggest motor vehicle plant, machine tools; p. (est. 1970) 1,500,000.

Changnacheri, t., Kerala, S. India; tea, cotton-spinning, silk; p. (1961) 42,376.

Changpai Shan, mtns.; form bdy. between China and N. Korea; drained by Rs. Yalu and Tumen; hgst. point Pai-t'ou-shan, 2,442 m.

Changsha, c., cap. of Hunan prov., China; pt. on Hsiang R.; univ.; tea, rice, antimony; p. (est. 1970) 850 000.

Changshu, c., Kiangsu, China; in valley of Yangtze R., 104 km S.W. of Shanghai; mkt. for local agr. prod.; p. (est. 1970) 150,000.

Channel Is., gr. of self-governing Is. belonging to the Brit. Crown off N.W. cst. France, of which the lgst. are Jersey, Guernsey, Alderney, and Sark; part of the old duchy of Normandy; vegetables, flowers, fruit, granite; two famous breeds of dairy cattle; tourist resort; impt. banking and insurance ctr. encouraged by low taxes; retirement ctr.; a. 194 km²; p. (est. 1973) 125,000.

Chantilly, t., Oise, France; famous race-course; formerly famous for lace and porcelain; p. (1968) 10,501.

Chaochow (Chaozhou), c., Kwangtung. S. China; on Han R., 32 km N. of Swatow; ctr. of cultivated plain; rice, sugar, tea; linked to Swatow by rly.; p. (1953) 101,300.

Chao Phraya. See Menam Chao Phraya.

Chapala, L., Mexico; chiefly in Jalisco st.; attractive site and climate encourage tourism; pastoral agr. on shores; a. 1,080 km².

Chapayevsk, t., Kuybyshev region, RSFSR; in Volga valley; chemicals, agr. machin.; p. (est. 1969) 87,000.

Chapelcross, nr. Annan, Annandale and Eskdale, Scot.; AEA nuclear power sta., producing electricity for nat. grid.

Chapel-en-le-Frith, mkt. t., High Peak, Derbys., Eng.; brake-linings; p. (1971) 18,689 (dist.).

Chapra, t., Bihar, India; on Ganges R.; ctr. of former saltpetre and indigo tr.; p. (1961) 75,580.

Chard, mkt. t., Somerset, Eng.; lace, engin., shirt and cotton mfg.; p. (1971) 7,905.

Charczhou, t., Turkmen SSR, USSR; inland pt. on Amu-Dar'ya R.; shipyards, textiles, chemicals; major oil refinery project; p. (1967) 85,000.

Charente, dep., S.W. France; cap. Angoulême; ctr. of distilling tr., cognac; a. 5,970 km²; p. (1968) 331,016.

Charente, R., S.W. France; rises W. of Limoges and flows into Bay of Biscay below Rochefort; valley slopes beyond Angoulême produce celebrated grapes from which brandy is made at Cognac and Jarnac.

Charente-Maritime, dep., S.W. France; cap. La Rochelle; borders Bay of Biscay; wine, wheat, oysters, pilchards; a. 7,229 km²; p. (1968) 483,622.

Charleroi, t., Hainaut, Belgium; on R. Sambre; coal mng.; glass; p. (est. 1967) 24,500 (c.); (est. 1969) 217,349 (met. a.).

Charleston, c., spt., S.C., USA; industl. and comm. ctr. on Atl. cst. founded 1670; scene of onset of Civil War; p. (1970) 64,550 (c.), 285,916 (met. a.).

Charleston, t., cap. W. Va., USA; on Kanawha R.; in bituminous coal dist.; chemicals, glass,

tools, oil, natural gas, lumber, coal processing; p. (1970) 69,531 (c.), 224,054 (met. a.).

Charleville, t., Queensland, Australia; on Warrego R., 640 km W. of Brisbane; pastoral dist.; p. (1966) 4,799.

Charleville-Méziéres, twin t., Ardennes dep., N.E. France; on Meuse R.; iron, bricks, nails, hardware; p. (1968) 55,543.

Charlotte, c., N.C., USA; key rly. junc.; machin., chemicals, textiles; p. (1970) 239,056 (c.), 405,976 (met. a.).

Charlotte Amalie, t., cap. of Virgin Is. of USA; on St. Thomas I.; excellent natural harbour; former coaling sta.; p. (1970) 12,372.

Charlottenburg, sub. of Berlin, Germany; (in W. Berlin); on R. Spree.

Charlottesville, t., Va., USA; on Rivanna R.; in apple-growing region; univ.; Monticello nearby, home of Jefferson; textiles; p. (1970) 38,880.

Charlottetown, t., ch. pt. Prince Edward I., Canada; named after Queen Charlotte, consort of George III; univ.; p. (1971) 18,631.

Charlton Kings, t., Cheltenham, Gloucs., Eng.; at foot of Cotswolds; p. (1971) 10,088.

Charnwood Forest, upland dist., Leics., Eng.; to W. of Soar valley, 19 km N.W. of Leicester; composed of anc. rocks; stone-crushing; largely forests; used for recreation by industl. ts. of E. Midlands; alt. 180–275 m; now forms l. gov. dist. of Charnwood and inc. Loughborough and Shepshed; p. (est. 1976) 133,100.

Charters Towers, t., N. Queensland, Australia; pastoral ctr.; former gold-mng. a.; p. (1972) 7,529.

Chartres, t., cap. of Eure-et-Loir dep., France; mkt. for cereals from Beauce region; famous Gothic cath.; p. (1968) 36,881.

Châteauroux, t., cap. of Indre dep., France; 96 km S.E. of Tours, on R. Indre; agr. ctr., woollens pottery; p. (1968) 51,201.

Chateau Thierry, t., Aisne, France; on R. Marne; mkt. t.; cas.; precision instruments; p. (1968) 11,629.

Châtellerault, t., Vienne, France; 64 km S. of Tours on R. Vienne; cutlery, metallurgical and aeronautical engin. Descartes lived here; p. (1968) 35,337.

Chatham, t., Medway, Kent, Eng.; on estuary of R. Medway; lt. inds.; naval dockyard established by Henry VIII; p. (1971) 56,921.

Chatham, t., spt., N.B., Canada; lumbering, fish exporting; p. (1971) 7,812.

Chatham, c., Ont., Canada; on extinct L. plain on R. Thames; agr. prods.; p. (1971) 34,601.

Chatham Is., N.Z. dependency, S. Pac. Oc.; volcanic Is.; sheep rearing and fishing; a. 963 km²; lgst. I. Wharekauri; p. (est. 1968) 500.

Chatsworth, par., Derbys., Eng.; on R. Derwent; seat of the dukes of Devonshire.

Chattanooga, c., Tenn., USA; on Tennessee R.; univ.; rly. ctr.; cottons; iron, steel, chemicals, paper, metals; p. (1970) 113,033 (c.), 293,034 (met. a.).   [(1971) 5,566.

Chatteris, Fenland, Cambridge, Eng.; mkt. t.; p.

Chaudière Falls, on Ottawa R., above Ottawa, Canada; hydroelec. sta.

Chauk, t., Burma; on R. Irrawaddy; ctr. of oilfield; oil refining; fertilisers.

Chaumont, t., cap. of Haute-Marne dep., France; on R. Marne; gloves, leather; p. (1968) 27,569.

Chautauqua, L., N.Y., st., USA; summer resort; vineyards.

Chaux-de-Fonds, La, t., can. Neuchâtel, Switzerland; ctr. of watchmkg. ind.; p. (1969) 43,200.

Cheadle, t., Staffs. Moorland, Staffs., Eng.; metal mnfs.; former coal-mng. a.; p. (1971) 4,070 (dist.).

Cheadle and Gatley, ts., Gtr. Manchester, Eng.; textile finishing and bleaching, engin.; residtl.; p. (1971) 60,648.

Cheb, t., ČSSR; nr. Bavarian frontier; comm. ctr.; machin.; p. (1967) 25,633.

Cheboksary, c., cap. of Chuvash ASSR, RSFSR; R. pt. on Volga; agr. ctr.; hydroelec. plant; p. (1970) 216,000.

Checheno-Ingush ASSR, USSR; oilfield, petro-chemicals; p. (1970) 1,065,000.

Cheddar, v., Somerset, Eng.; famous limestone caves in Mendips; cheese strawberries.

Chefoo (Yentai), c., N. Shantung prov., China; pt. on G. of Pohai; former treaty pt.; noted for its pongee silk ("shantung"); p. (est. 1970) 180,000.

Cheju (Quelpart), I., off S. Korea, E. China Sea; extinct volcano Mt. Halla, 1,968 m.

Chekiang (Zhijiang), coastal prov., S.E. China; cap. Hangchow; impt. rice-growing a.; major natural gas field; a. 102,269 km²; p. (est. 1968) 31,000,000.

Che-ling Pass, on bdy. between Kwangtung and Hunan, S. China; historic route across Nanling mtns., now followed by Wuhan to Kuangchow trunk rly.; alt. 300 m.

Chelm, t., E. Poland; nr. Lublin; cath.; flour-milling; p. (1968) 37,100.

Chelmsford, co. t., l. gov. dist., Essex, Eng.; 48 km N.E. London; cath.; agr. mkt.; p. (est. 1976) 130,000 (dist.).

Chelsea, dist., London, Eng.; fashionable residtl. dist. See Kensington.

Chelsea, t., Mass., USA; industl. sub. on Boston harbour; p. (1970) 30,625.

Cheltenham, t., l. gov. dist., Gloucs., Eng.; spa; educational ctr.; precision instruments; birth-place of Gustav Holst; p. (est. 1976) 86,500 (dist.).

Chelyabinsk, t., RSFSR; major industl. ctr. on Miass R., Siberian lowlands; steel wks.; metallurgy, machin.; on natural gas pipeline from Gazli gasfield; p. (1970) 874,000.

Chelyuskin, Cape, most N. point in Asia, in Krasnoyarsk Terr., RSFSR; named after Russian navigator who discovered it in 1742.

Chemnitz. See Karl-Marx-Stadt.

Chemulpo. See Inchon.

Chenab, R., W. Punjab, Pakistan; one of "five rivers" of Punjab; rises in Himalayas, flows S.W. into R. Sutlej; dams at Marala and Khanki; c. 1,440 km long.

Chengchow (Zhengzhou), c., cap. Honan prov., China; 24 km S. of Hwang-ho (Yellow R.), where it emerges on to N. China Plain; impt. route ctr. and rly. junc. where Peking to Wuhan rly. crosses Sian to Tunghai rly.; p. (est. 1970) 1,500,000.

Chengtu (Chengdu), c., cap. of Szechwan prov., China; ctr. of tobacco and cotton-growing a.; oil refinery; chemicals, textiles, machin.; p. (est. 1970) 2,000,000.

Chepstow, mkt. t., Gwent, Wales; on R. Wye, 3 km above confluence with R. Severn; Severn Bridge links to Aust (Avon); ruined cas.; p. (1971), 16,096.

Chequers, official residence of Brit. prime mini-sters, 3 km S. of Wendover, Bucks., Eng.; gift of Lord Lee of Fareham.

Cher, dep., France; cap. Bourges; crossed by Cher R.; chiefly pastoral agr.; a. 7,301 km²; p. (1968) 304,601.

Cher, R., central France; rises in Central Massif, joins Loire below Tours; length 320 km.

Cherbourg, spt., Manche, France; N. cst. of Contentin peninsula; opposite to and 128 km dist. from Portsmouth; naval arsenal, ship-bldg.; metals, ropes, fishing; p. (1968) 40,333.

Cheremkhovo, t., RSFSR; N.W. of Irkutsk; coal, engin., chemicals; on Trans-Siberian rly.; p. (est. 1969) 104,000.

Cherepovets, c., RSFSR; on Rybinskoye reservoir of R. Volga; steel, engin., sawmills, shipbldg.; p. (1970) 189,000.

Cheribon. See Tjirebon.

Cherkassy, t., Ukrainian SSR, USSR; nr. Kiev, on reservoir formed by Dnieper R.; sugar, engin., sawmilling; p. (1970) 159,000.

Cherkessk, t., RSFSR; rly. terminus, industl. ctr.; p. (1970) 76,000.

Chernigov, t., Ukrainian SSR, USSR; on Desna R.; caths.; univ.; flour, textiles, chemicals; p. (1970) 159,000.

Chernogorsk, t., RSFSR; 16 km N.W. of Abakan; ctr. of Minusinsk coal-mng. basin; p. (est. 1967) 63,000.

Chernovtsy, t., Ukrainian SSR, USSR; univ.; Greek cath.; wheat, dairy produce, textiles, engin., chemicals; p. (1970) 187,000.

Chernyakhovsk (Insterberg), t., Lithuanian SSR, USSR; chemicals, textiles; p. (est. 1967) 29,000.

Cherrapunji, t., Assam, India; in Khasi Hills; reputed wettest place in world, average annual rainfall 12,700 mm.

Chertsey, t., Runnymede, Surrey, Eng.; on S. bank of R. Thames, 6 km below Staines; residtl.; p. (1971) 44,886.

Cherwell, l. gov. dist., Oxon., Eng.; stretches

from Banbury to Bicester; p. (est. 1976) 104,700.

Cherwell, R., trib. of Thames, nr. Oxford, Eng.; length 48 km.

Chesapeake Bay, inlet on Atl. cst., USA; extend-ing 320 km from mouth of Susquehanna R. to C. Charles; shellfish ind.; bridge-tunnel (opened 1964) spans entrance to Bay.

Chesham, t., Bucks., Eng.; in heart of Chiltern Hills; printing, textiles, lt. engin.; residtl.; p. (1971) 20,416.

Cheshire, non-met. co., N.W. Eng.; lowland a. drained by Rs. Dee and Mersey, bounded by Pennines in E.; dairying and mkt. gardening; chemical ind. based on salt deposits around Northwich; heavy inds. in and around Warring-ton; much of co. residtl. for Liverpool and Manchester; cap. Chester; a. 2,323 km²; p. (est. 1976) 916,400.

Cheshire, t., Conn., USA; agr.; formerly copper, and barytes mined; p. (est. 1967) 42,900.

Cheshunt, t., Herts., Eng.; in Lea valley, 11 km S. of Hertford; bricks, mkt. gardening, horti-culture; p. (1971) 44,947.

Chesil Bank, Dorset, Eng.; shingle ridge en-closing the Fleet lagoon running from I. of Portland to Bridport.

Chester, c., l. gov. dist., Cheshire, Eng.; at head of estuary of R. Dee; cath., anc walls and old timbered houses; Roman c. of Deva site of legionary barracks; engin., metal gds.; p. (est. 1976) 117,200 (dist.).

Chester, t., Penns., USA; on Delaware R., S.W. Philadelphia; called Uppland by Swedish settlers 1643, renamed by William Penn; pt. of entry; shipbldg.; p. (est. 1969) 61,000.

Chesterfield, mkt. t., colly. dist., l. gov. dist., Derbys., Eng.; on Rother R.; 13 km S. of Sheffield; variety of heavy inds.; 14th-cent. church with crooked spire; p. (est. 1976) 93,900 (dist.).

Chesterfield Inlet, arm of Hudson Bay, Canada; 400 km by 40 km.

Chester-le-Street, t., l. gov. dist., Durham, Eng.; clothing, confectionery, sand wkg.; p. (est. 1976) 49,400 (dist.).

Cheviot Hills, range between Scot. and Eng.; hgst. summit, the Cheviot, 816 m.

Cheyenne, t., cap. of Wyo., USA; cattle-ranching dist.; rly. ctr.; p. (1970) 40,914.

Chiana, Val di, valley, central Italy; separ-ates Tuscan hills from central Apennines; occupied by upper course of R. Arno, middle course of R. Tiber; followed by main route from Florence to Rome.

Chiang Mai, c., cap of C. prov., and 3rd c. of Thailand; rly. terminus on Ping R.; tr. ctr.; teak; p. (1970) 89,272.

Chiapa, R., flows N. from Guatemala through Mexico to G. of Campeche; impt. routeway in lower course; length 320 km.

Chiapas, Pac. st., Mexico; mtnous., forested; bananas, tobacco, sugar and cocoa; cattle; oil reserves; close associations with Guatemala; cap. Tuxtla-Gutierrez; a. 74,408 km²; p. (1970) 1,578,180,

Chiasso, frontier t.; S. Switzerland; rly. sta. on Italian border; p. (1970) 8,868.

Chiatura, t., Georgian SSR, USSR; impt. manga-nese deposits; p. (est. 1967) 27,000.

Chiba c., cap. of C. pref. Japan; part of Keihin conurb. on Tokyo B.; tr. ctr., giant shipyard, oil refining, aluminium, chemicals, iron and steel; airpt.; p. (est. 1971) 512,000.

Chicago, c., Ill., USA; on S. shore of L. Michigan; second lgst. US c.; economic heart of Mid-West; comm. ctr. called "The Loop"; im-mense tr. by rail and Gr. Ls.; univs.; grain mills, meat packing plants, iron and steel wks., major iron-ore mkt.; electronic equipment, furniture; lgst. airpt. in world; p. (1970) 3,322,855 (c.), 6,892,509 (met. a.).

Chichester, t., l. gov. dist., West Sussex, Eng.; on S. cst. plain, 18 km W. of Arundel; cath.; yachting basin; p. (est. 1976) 93,200 (dist.).

Chickamauga Creek, USA; branch of Tennessee R. above Chattanooga, forming part of Tenn. Valley Authority scheme; Civil War battles; site of Nat. Park.

Chickerell, E. Dorset, Eng.; 5 km N.W. of Wey-mouth; site of nuclear power sta. on shores of East Fleet R.

Chiclayo, c., Lambayeque dep., Peru; mkt. ctr.

for irrigated desert a. between Andes and Pac. Oc. producing mainly rice and sugar; p. (est. 1970) 140,800.

Chicopee, t., Mass., USA; on Connecticut R. nr. Springfield; p. (1970) 66,676.

Chicoutimi, t., Quebec, Canada; pt. on Chicoutimi R.; lumber, pulp, paper; hydroelectric power; p. (1971) 32,890.

Chiemsee, L., lge. lake nr. Munich, **W. Germany**; c. 460 m a.s.l.

Chieti, t., cap. of C. prov., S. Italy; cath.; anc. Teate Marrucinorum; Europe's lgst. glass plant, using methane from Abruzzi field; p. (1969) 53,324.

Chigirk, t., Uzbek SSR, **USSR**; new t. (1963) 34 km S. of Tashkent.

Chigwell, t., Epping Forest, Essex, Eng.; on borders of Epping Forest; Hainault Estate now incorporated in Redbridge, Greater London; resdtl.; p. (1971) 53,620.

Chihli, Gulf of. *See* Pohai.

Chihauhua, lgst. st. in **Mexico**; dry climate impedes agr.; mng., cotton, cattle, Chihuahua dogs; a. 247.024 km²; p. (1969) 1,826,000.

Chihuahua, c., cap. Chihuahua st., Mexico; univ., cath.; ctr. silver-mng. ind.; p. (1970) 257,027.

Chikchi, peninsula, RSFSR; world's first Arctic nuclear power sta. being built.

Chikugo, t., N. Kyushu, Japan; lgst. coalmines in country.

Chilaw, t., Sri Lanka; ctr. of coconut plantations.

Chile, rep., S. America; extends between Andes and Pac. for 4,160 km to C. Horn, E. to W. 400 km; Atacama desert; Spanish language; Roman Catholic; similar climate to that of Argentina but lacks space for extensive agr.; dairying, sheep, wool; ch. exp. nitrates, copper, iron ore, coal, iodine, petroleum, paper; cap. Santiago; ch. pt. Valparaiso; earthquake 1960, hgst. recorded magnitude; a. 738,494 km²; p. (est. 1969) 9,566,000.

Chillán, t., cap. of Nuble prov., Chile; destroyed 1939 by one of world's worst recorded earthquakes; since rebuilt; agr. and comm. ctr.; p. (est. 1966) 77,654.

Chiloé, I. and S. prov., Chile; cap, San Carlos, earthquakes 1939 and 1960; ch. pt. Ancud destroyed 1960; heavy rainfall, tropical forest; a. 23,460 km²; p. (1970) 110,728.

Chilpancingo de los Bravos, t., cap. of Guerrero st., Mexico; ctr. of pre-Aztec culture; univ.; p. (1970) 56,904.

Chiltern, l. gov. dist., Bucks., Eng.; inc. part of C. Hills and Chesham and Amersham; p. (est. 1976) 90,100.

Chiltern Hills, chalk escarpment, Oxon., Bucks., Beds., and Herts., Eng.; cut by no. of impt. gaps used by main communications; sheep and barley; hgst. point 276 m nr. Wendover.

Chimborazo, mtn., Ecuador, 6,286 m; Andes; extinct volcano, first explored by von Humboldt (1802), first scaled by Whymper (1880).

Chimbote, spt., Peru; steel, iron-ore, coal; tinned fish fish-meal; p. (est. 1970) 102,800.

Chimkent, t., Kazakh SSR, USSR; in W. foothills of Tien Shan; nearby oasis fed by Arys R.; major industl. ctr.; lead smelting; p. (1970) 247,000.

China, People's Republic of, Asia; second lgst. cty. of world; anc. conservative civilisation overthrown by long civil war and establishment of communist régime (1949); lge. p. crowded on cultivable valleys of Hwang-ho (Yellow R.), Yangtze and Si-kiang in E.; rest of cty. either mtnous. (plateau of Tibet) or desert (Sinkiang); rapid economic growth following onset of communist régime; agr. organised on commune basis, becomes increasingly intensive in S. where climate is less extreme; vast mineral resources, many undeveloped; recent industl. growth; heavy inds. at Wuhan, Paotow and in N.E. (Manchuria); poor communications except in E.; cap. Peking; a. 11,137,000 km²; p. (est. 1975) 838,803,000, lgst. p. of any cty.

China Sea, part of W. Pacific between Korea and Philippines; divided by the narrow Formosa Strait into two areas; E. China Sea, inc. Yellow Sea, and S. China Sea.

Chinandega, mkt. t., cap. of C. dep., Nicaragua; sugar-refining; p. (1967) 36,885.

Chinchow (Jinzhou), c., Liaoning prov., China; cement, glass, bricks, tiles, paper and wood pulp, oil; p. (est. 1970) 750,000.

Chindwin, R., Burma; ch. trib. of Irrawaddy;

rises in Patkai Hills, navigable in rainy season; dense p. in power reaches; 800 km long.

Chinghai (Tsinghai), prov., W. China; between Sinkiang and Tibet, inc. C. plateau; local coal and iron-ore but exploitation hindered by isolation; two new iron and steel plants; a. 721,004 km²; p. (est. 1970) 2,000,000.

Chingola, t., Zambia; copper mng.; metal prod., printing; p. (est. 1972) 181,500 (met. a.).

Chinkiang (Zhenjiang), c., Kiangsu, China; former treaty pt., Yangtse R., 77 km below Nanking; tr. ctr.; p. (est. 1970) 250,000.

Chinon, t. Indre-et-Loire, central France; on R. Vienne, industl.; ruined cas., once a royal residency; nuclear power sta.; p. (1968) 8,035.

Chinqui, volcano, Panama; 3,480 m.

Chinwangtao (Qinhuangdao), c., spt., former treaty pt., Hopeh, N. China; on Yellow Sea cst. 240 km N.E. of Tientsin; only gd. natural harbour on N. China cst.; exp. coal from Kailan mines; p. (1953) 186,800.

Chioggia, spt., cath. t., N. Italy; on I. in G. of Venice; fishing; p. (est. 1968) 48,347.

Chios (Khios) I., in Aegean Sea, Greece; mainly agr.; wines, fruits and figs; supposed birthplace of Homer; p. (1971) 53,942.

Chippenham, North Wilts., Eng.; mkt. t. on R. Avon; rly. signal and brake equipment, bacon curing, tanning; p. (1971) 18,662.

Chipping Campden, v. Gloucs., Eng.; in Cotswold Hills; formerly impt. for woollens; tourism.

Chipping Norton, mkt. t., Oxford, Eng.; nr. Banbury; formerly impt. for woollens; p. (1971) 4,763.

Chipping Sodbury, mkt. t., Avon, Eng.; 13 km N.E. of Bristol; p. (1971) 67,040 (dist.).

Chirchik, c., Uzbek SSR, USSR; 32 km N.E. Tashkent; engin., chemicals; hydroelec. power stas.; p. (1970) 108,000.

Chiricahua Mtns., Arizona, USA; form part of Coronado Nat. Forest; long inhabited by Apache Indians; spectacular volcanic scenery; alt. 2,987 m.

Chirk, t., Clwyd, Wales; on R. Ceriog, S. of Wrexham; slate, former coal-mng. a.; cas.

Chislehurst. *See* Bromley.

Chistyakovo. *See* Torez.

Chita, c., rly. ctr. Siberia, RSFSR; on upper R.Ingoda, 640 km E. of L. Baykal; coal, engin., chemicals, sawmilling; p. (1970) 242,000.

Chittagong, c., Bangladesh; main pt. on Karnafuli R., nr. Bay of Bengal; exp. jute, tea; oil refining; steel mill; hydroelec. power; p. (1974) 416,733.

Chittaranjan, t., Bihar, India; new t. on Barakhar R., in steel ctr. of Damodar valley; rly. locomotive wks.; p. (1961) 28,957.

Chkalov. *See* Orenburg.

Choisy-le-Roi, t., Val-de-Marne dep., France; industl. sub. of Paris on R. Seine; p. (1968) 41,711.

Cholet, t., Maine-et-Loire, France; textile ctr. on R. Seine; p. (1968) 41,711.

Cholon (Cho Lon), t., S. Vietnam; 16 km S.W. of Ho Chi-minh City; ctr. of rice tr.; p. inc. Ho Chi-minh City (1968) 1,682,000.

Cholula, anc. c. of Puebla prov., Mexico; Aztec temple, pyramid of Cholula, and other remains.

Chomo Lhari, mtn., Tibet, China and Bhutan; sacred to Buddhists; part of Himalayas; alt. 7,319 m.

Chomutov, t., N. ČSSR; industl. ctr. of lignite mng. a.; coal, steel, glass; p. (1967) 38,000.

Chooz, t., Ardennes, France; pressurised water reactor; nuclear power sta. linked with Belgian grid.

Cho Oyu, mtn., between Nepal and Tibet, China; sixth hgst. in world; alt. 8,225 m.

Chorley, t., l. gov. dist., N. Lancs., Eng.; on W. flank of Rossendale Fells, 11 km S.E. of Preston; cotton, engin.; expansion as new t. with Leyland (20,200 ha); p. (est. 1976) 83,100 (dist.).

Chorleywood, t., Three Rivers, Herts., Eng.; nr. Watford; p. (1971) 8,427.

Chorrilos Pass, Argentina; in E. cordillera of Andes at alt. 4,470 m; used by rly. from San Miguel de Tucumán to Antofagasta.

Chorzów (Królewska Huta), t. Upper Silesia, Poland; coal, iron and steel, chemicals, engin.; p. (est. 1969) 151,300.

Chota Nagpur, plateau, Madhya Pradesh, India; produces lac; impt. mng. ctr.; bauxite, mica.

Chou Kou Tien, site nr. Peking, China; discovery of fossil bones of Peking man (*Sinanthropus pekinensis*).

Christchurch, t., l. gov. dist., Dorset, Eng.; on S. cst. 8 km E. of Bournemouth; holiday resort, aircraft. lt. inds.; p. (est. 1976) 36,700 (dist.).

Christchurch, c., Canterbury dist., S.I., N.Z.; comm. ctr. for lamb, wool, and grain; cath. univ.; airpt; p. (1971) 165,198 (c.); (est. 1970) 260,200 (met. a.).

Christianshåb, Danish settlement on Disko Bay, W. Greenland; meteorological sta.

Christmas I., in Indian Oc., Australian terr. since 1958; a. 161 km², healthy climate, phosphate deposits; p. (1966) 3,381.

Christmas I., lge. coral atoll in Pac. Oc., one of Line Is.; discovered by Cook 1777; a. 135 km²; nuclear test site, 1957–64.

Chu, R. Kazakh SSR, USSR; rises in Tien Shan flows N.W. for 800 km into inland drainage basin; Chumysh Dam provides hydroelectricity and water for intensive cultivation of cotton, sugarbeet, citrus fruits.

Chuanchow (Quanzhou), c., Fukien prov.; China; former pt. now silted up; p. (est. 1970) 130,000.

Chubut, R., Argentina; drains from Andes into Atl. Oc.; continual irrigation reducing soil fertility of valley; 640 km long.

Chuchow (Zhuzhou), c., Hunan prov., China; on Siang R.; rly. p. (est. 1970) 350,000.

Chudleigh, mkt. t., Devon, Eng.; on R. Teign; stone quarrying.

Chu-kiang (Canton R. or Pearl R.), Kwangtung, S. China; one of most impt. waterways of China; 176 km long, from Kuangchow to Hong Kong; fertile delta known as "land of fish, rice, and fruit"; around Kuangchow network of elec. drainage and irrigation stas., built since 1959; R. estuary now silting.

Chukotskiy, peninsula, USSR; extreme N.E.; rich gold deposit; hunting.

Chukyo, industl. area, Honshu, Japan; centred on Nagoya; textiles, ceramics, chemicals.

Chula Vista, t., Cal., USA; agr., aircraft; p. (1970) 67,901.

Chungking (Zhongqing), c., S.E. Szechwan prov., China; on Yangtze R.; comm. ctr. W. China; ctr. of rich agr. dist. of Red Basin of Szechwan; coal, iron and steel, heavy machin., lorries, vans, chemical fertilisers; former treaty pt.; p. (est. 1970) 3,500,000.

Chuquibamba Mtns., (alt. c. 6,400 m), Peru.

Chuquicamata, t., N. Chile; 3,050 m in Andes; lgst copper mine in world; p. (est. 1966) 28,786.

Chur (Coire), t., cap. Graubünden, Switzerland; in valley of upper Rhine; historic bldgs.; fruit, wine, tourist ctr.; p. (1969) 30.900.

Church, Hyndburn, sub. of Accrington, Lancs., Eng.; engin.; p. (1971) 5,310.

Churchill, R., formerly Hamilton R., flows into Hamilton inlet, cst. of Labrador, Canada; magnificent waterfall, Churchill Falls with lge. hydroelec. scheme.

Church Stretton, mkt. t., Salop, Eng.; tourism.

Chusan, I., and archipelago off E. cst. China; ch. ctr. Tinghai on Chusan I.; rich off-shore fishing grounds.

Chusovoy, t., RSFSR; in Urals; iron and steel; p. (est. 1969) 62,000.

Chuvash ASSR, aut. rep., RSFSR; in middle Volga valley; arable agr., lumbering, food processing; a. 18,407 km²; p. (1970) 1,224,000.

Chysauster, Cornwall, Eng.; prehistoric v.

Cibao, lowland a., Dominican Rep., Central America; extends along N. side of Cordillera de Cibao for 180 km; 16–56 km wide; early a. of Spanish settlement; E. part called Vega Real; richest agr. a. of Hispaniola; cacao, tobacco, maize; dense p.; ch. t. Santiago.

Cicero, t., Ill., USA; adjoins Chicago; electrical appliances, hardware; p. (1970) 67,058.

Ciechanów, t., Poland; 78 km N.W. of Warsaw; agr. inds.; p. (1970) 23,200.

Cienaga, spt., N. Colombia; p. (est. 1972) 69,100 (t.), 163,100 (met. a.).

Cienfuegos, t., Cuba; sugar, tobacco; picturesque; nuclear power sta. proposed, built with Soviet assistance; p. (est. 1967) 91,800.

Cieszyn, t., Katowice prov., Poland; part of former Teschen on Polish side of frontier with ČSSR; p. (1970) 25,200.

Cimpina, t., Romania, in Walachia; petroleum ctr.; oil pipeline links to Ploiești and Constanța on Black Sea.

Cincinnati, c., Ohio, USA; route and comm. ctr. on terraces of Ohio R.; food processing and many varied inds.; univs.; p. (1970) 448,492 (c.), 1,373,225, (met. a.).

Cinderford, t., Gloucs., Eng.; former ctr. of coalmng. a. of Forest of Dean; new lt. industl. estate.

Cinque Ports, confederation of anc. Eng. pts. on cst. of Kent and Sussex; original 5: Sandwich, Dover, Hythe, Romney, Hastings; Winchelsea, and Rye added later. *See* L23.

Cirencester, t., Cotswold, Gloucs., Eng.; the Roman Corineum; former woollen t.; p. (1971) 13,022.

Ciskei, Bantu Terr. Authority, S. Africa; established 1961 between Fish and Kei Rs. on S.E. cst.; self-gov. (1972); cap. Zwelitsha; p. (1970) 527,159.

Citta di Castello, walled t., Italy; in upper Tiber valley; impt. in Roman times; Renaissance cath., palaces; p. (est. 1968) 36,274.

Citta Vecchia (Mdina), c., central Malta; former cap.; Roman remains; cath.

Ciudad Bolivar, c., Bolivar st., Venezuela; pt. on Orinoco R.; formerly called Angostura; coffee, cattle; ctr. of new industl. development on lower Orinoco; p. (est. 1970) 109,600.

Ciudad Juarez, c., Mexico; comm. ctr. on USA border; agr. processing; tourism; p. (1970) 407,370.

Ciudad Madero, t., Mexico; styrene and detergent plants, oil refining; p. (1970) 89,994.

Ciudad Obregón, t., Sonora, Mexico; on Yaqui R.; ctr. of irrigated agr. a.; p. (1970) 114,407.

Ciudad Real, c., cap. of Ciudad Real prov., Spain; mkt. t. founded 1255; textiles; p. (1970) 41,708.

Ciudad Real, prov., central Spain; mostly at 600 m; covering la Mancha dist.; agr.; cap. C.R.; a. 19,741 km²; p. (1970) 507,650.

Ciudad Rodrigo, old fortress t., Salamanca prov., Spain; strategic position nr. Portuguese bdy.; in Peninsular War fell to Fr. (1810) and captured by Wellington (1812); p. (1970) 13,320.

Civitavecchia, t. Latium, Italy; pt. for Rome on Tyrrhenian cst. 48 km N. of mouth of R. Tiber; p. (est. 1968) 42.570.

Clackmannan, former co., l. gov. dist., Central Reg., Scot.; a. 161 km²; p. (1971) 46,340.

Clacton-on-Sea, t., Tendring, Essex, Eng.; on E. cst. 19 km S.E. of Colchester; seaside resort; lt. inds.; residtl.; p. (1971) 37,942.

Clairvaux, v., Aube, France; famous Cistercian abbey.

Clamart, t., Hauts-de-Seine, France; sub. of S.W. Paris; p. (1968) 55,299.

Clare, co., Munster, R.o.I.; cstl. co. bounded in S. and E. by R. Shannon; mainly agr. and tourism; inc. cliffs of Moher; Shannon airpt. and tax-free industl. development scheme; co. t. Ennis; a. 3,351 km²; p. (1966) 73,539.

Clare I., Clew Bay, Mayo, R.o.I.

Clarence, R., N.S.W., Australia; length 384 km.

Clarence Strait, between Melville I. and Darwin, N.T., Australia.

Clarksburg, t., W. Va., USA; industl. ctr. for coalmng. a., oil and natural gas fields; machin., glass, pottery; p. (1970) 24,684.

Clarksdale, t., Miss., USA; processing ctr. for rich farming a.; p. (1970) 21,105.

Clarksville, t., Tenn., USA; on Cumberland R.; tobacco mkt.; p. (1970) 31,719.

Clausthal-Zellerfeld, t., Lower Saxony, W. Germany in Harz mtns.; tourism.

Clay Cross, t., Derbys., Eng.; former ctr. coalmng. (first developed by George Stephenson 1838) iron, engin.; p. (1971) 10,153.

Clayton-le-Moors, t., Hyndburn, Lancs., Eng.; nr. Blackburn; textile machin., cotton and blanket weaving, bristles, soap; p. (1971) 6,760.

Clear C., southernmost point of Ireland, Clear I., R.o.I.; off S.W. cst. of Cork.

Cleare, c., Alaska, USA; site of ballistic missile early warning sta.

Clearwater, t., Fla., USA; citrus fruit, flowers, fish; resort; p. (1970) 52,074.

Cleator Moor, t. Cumbria, Eng.; former colly. t.

Cleckheaton, t., West Yorks., Eng.; nr. Bradford; woollens, blankets, asbestos.

Clee Hills, Salop, Eng.; between Rs. Severn and Teme; alt. 550 m.

Cleethorpes, t., l. gov. dist., Humberside, Eng.; 5 km S. of Grimsby; resort; p. (est. 1976) 70,600 (dist.).

Clent Hills, Hereford and Worcs., Eng.; about

16 km S.W. of Birmingham, overlooking valley of R. Stour; recreation; maximum alt. 316 m.

Clerkenwell, industl. dist., London, Eng.; immediately N. of the City; noted for watchmkg.

Clermont-Ferrand, c., cap. Puy-de-Dôme dep. central France; in Auvergne; rubber tyres, chemicals, food inds.; Gothic cath., Romanesque church; p. (1968) 148,896 (c.). 204,699 (met. a.).

Clevedon, t., Woodspring, Avon, Eng.; at mouth of R. Severn; seaside resort; quarrying, bricks, footwear; p. (1971) 14,285.

Cleveland, c., Ohio, USA; impt. Gr. Ls. pt. handling iron ore and coal which support a major iron and steel ind.; oil refining, food processing, many varied inds.; univ.; p. (1971) 738,956 (c.), 2,064,194 (met. a.).

Cleveland, non-met. co., N.E. Eng.; heavy industl. region centred around ts. of Tees estuary; chems., iron and steel mftg.; inc. part of N. York Moors to S.; a. 583 km²; p. (est. 1976) 567,900.

Cleveland Hills, North Yorks./Cleveland, Eng.; part of N. York Moors; once mined for iron ore, impt. potash deposit.

Clichy, t., Hauts-de-Seine, France; N.W. sub. of Paris; oil refining, aircraft, automobile components; p. (1968) 52,704.

Clifton, sub., Bristol, Avon, Eng.; or R. Avon; mineral springs; famous suspension bridge.

Clifton, t., N.J., USA; industl. t., nr. Passaic; p. (1970) 82,437.

Clinton, t., Iowa, USA; on Mississippi R.; iron and steel, machin.; p. (1970) 34,719.

Clitheroe, t., Ribble Valley, Lancs., Eng.; in Ribble valley; mkt. t. for rural a.; limestone quarrying nearby; p. (1971) 13,191.

Clonakilty, t., Cork, R.o.I.; nr. Bandon; sm. harbour; agr. prods.; p. (1966) 2,341.

Cloncurry, t., Queensland, Australia; in pastoral and copper-producing dist.; p. (1966) 2,174.

Clones, mkt. t., on Ulster border, Monaghan, R.o.I.; rly. ctr.; p. (1961) 2,107.

Clonmacnoise, v., Offaly, R.o.I.; ecclesiastical ruins.

Clonmel, t., Tipperary, R.o.I.; on R. Suir; agr. ctr.; fairs; cider, footwear; p. (1966) 11,026.

Clovelly, v., Devon, Eng.; seaside resort.

Clowne, t., Derbys., Eng.; coal mng.; p. (1971) 18,869 (dist.).

Cluj, c., Romania; in Transylvania on Somesul R.; univs., historic bldgs.; industl. ctr.; p. (est. 1969) 197,902 (c.), (1966) 222,491 (met. a.).

Clutha R., longest R. of S.I., N.Z., hydroelec. power; 320 km long.

Clwyd, co. N. Wales; inc. most of Denbigh and Flintshire; mtnous. to S.; N. cstl. resorts inc. Colwyn Bay, Prestatyn and Rhyl; sm. coalfield; lgst. t. Wrexham; a. 2.424 km²; p. (est. 1976) 376,000.

Clwyd, R., Clwyd, N. Wales; flows into Irish Sea at Rhyl; length 48 km.

Clydach, t., West Glamorgan, Wales; on R. Tawe, 8 km N.E. Swansea; steel wks., nickel refineries.

Clyde, R., Strathclyde Reg., S.W. Scot.; flows through industl. belt into Firth of C.; Glasgow, Greenock, Clydebank main pts.; hydroelec. stas.; twin-road tunnel under R. in Glasgow (Whiteinch–Linthouse) completed 1963; 170 km long.

Clydebank, t., l. gov. dist., Strathclyde Reg., Scot.; on Clyde adjoining Glasgow; shipbldg., sewing machin., tyres, biscuits; p. (1971) 48,300.

Clyde, Firth of, stretches from Dumbarton to Ailsa Craig, Scot.; Bute, Arran, Gr. and Little Cumbrae ch. Is.; 102 km long.

Coachella Valley, arid region, S.E. Cal., USA; part of G. of Cal.; dates and citrus fruits under irrigation from Imperial Valley irrigation system.

Coahuila, st., Mexico; 3rd st. of Mexico; lies S. of Texas, bordering Rio Grande valley; main coal deposits; mnfs. impt.; irrigated agr.; cap. Saltillo; a. 142,611 km²; p. (1969) 1,225,000.

Coalbrookdale, v., Salop., Eng.; old coal- and iron-mines; home of iron master Abraham Darby. See Bridges, Section L.

Coalville, t., North West Leics., Eng.; nr. Ashby-de-la-Zouch; coal mng., engin., elastic webbing; p. (1971) 28,334.

Coast Range, mtns., USA; along Pac. cst.; wooded ranges causing rain shadow to E. valleys; alt. up to 600 m.

Coatbridge, burgh, Strathclyde Reg., Scot., 16 km E. of Glasgow; coal, iron and steel, prefabricated houses, tubes engin.; p. (1971) 52,344.

Coats I., S. of Southampton I., Hudson Bay, Canada.

Coatzacoalcos (Puerto Mexico), spt., Mexico; on G. of Campeche; oil refinery; chemicals, fertilisers; p. (est. 1970) 108,818 (met. a.).

Cobalt, t., Ont., Canada; silver, cobalt, arsenic, nickel; p. (1971) 2,191.

Cobán, t., Guatemala, mkt. t.; coffee and Peruvian bark tr.; p. (1964) 38,426.

Cóbh (Queenstown), U.D., Cork, R.o.I.; spt. on Great I. in Cork Harbour; lge. docks; H.Q. of Royal Cork Yacht Club; seaside resort; p. (1966) 5,608.

Coburg, t., Bavaria, W. Germany; old cas.; wickerwork, furniture, metal, machines, toy inds.; p. (est. 1969) 41,456.

Cochabamba, dep., Bolivia; E. of Andes; lgst. p. concentration of Bolivia in C. basin; a. 65,496 km²; p. (est. 1969) 780,500.

Cochabamba, c., cap. of C. dep., Bolivia; second lgst. c. in rep.; alt. 2,559 m; univ., cath.; oil refining, shoes, rubber tyres, fruit-canning, modern milk plant; hydroelectric power; p. (1969) 157,000.

Cochin, spt., Kerala, India; on Malabar cst.; exp. coconut oil, tea; oil refining, silting pt.; p. (1971) 439,066.

Cochin China, region, formerly part of Indo-China; now roughly coincides with S. Vietnam; comprises the Mekong delta. See Vietnam.

Cockenzie and Port Seton, small burgh, E. Lothian, Scot.; two fishing pts. on F. of Forth; p. (1971) 3,580.

Cockermouth, t., Allerdale, Cumbria, Eng.; slate, shoe mftg., plywood, concrete prods.; birthplace of Wordsworth; p. (1971) 6,356.

Cockpit Country, upland a., W. Jamaica; classic karst landscape forming rugged upland; some cultivation in hollows; a. 500 km²; alt. 300–800 m.

Coco, R., Honduras and Nicaragua; flows to Caribbean Sea through economically impt. valley; agr., forestry, mng.; potential as routeway; 480 km long.

Cocos or Keeling Is., 27 coral atolls, Indian Oc.; since 1955 terr. of Australia; ch. prod. coconuts; strategic position S.E. of Sri Lanka, 848 km W. of Christmas I., N.E. of Mauritius; radio and cable sta.; civil aviation marine base; German cruiser Emden destroyed by Australian cruiser Sydney on N. Keeling I. in 1914; a. 13 km²; p. (est. 1970) 611.

Coesfeld, t., N. Rhine–Westphalia, W. Germany; textiles, machin.; p. (est. 1969) 21,924.

Cognac, t., Charente, France; cognac, bottles; p. (1968) 22,515.

Coiba I., off S. cst. of Panama.

Coimbatore, t., Tamil Nadu, India; commands Palghat Gap; varied inds. benefit from local hydroelec. power; p. (1971) 356.368 (c.), 736,203 (met. a.).

Coimbra, t., Portugal; cath., oldest univ. in Portugal; wine-growing; earthenware mnfs.; p. (1970) 108,046.

Colac, t., Victoria, Australia; nr. Melbourne; farming and dairying dist.; engin., and brick-mkg.; p. (1972) 10,418.

Colchester, t., l. gov. dist., Essex, Eng.; pre-Roman t. of Camulodunum on R. Colne; univ.; lt. inds., engin., oyster fisheries; pt.; p. (est. 1976) 132,400 (dist.).

Cold Fell, mtn., Northumberland, Eng.; 622 m.

Cold Harbour, v., Va., USA; battles between Grant and Lee 1864.

Coldstream, t., Berwick, Scot.; on Eng. border; agr. machin., knitwear; p. (1971) 1,278.

Coleraine, t., l. gov. dist., N. Ireland; pt. on R. Bann, 6 km from sea; univ.; linen, acrilan mftg., distilling; p. (est. 1971) 14,871.

Coleshill, t., West Midlands, Eng.; lurgi gasification plant; new colly. 1965.

Colima, mkt. t., Mexico; on Colima R. in fertile valley; univ.; agr. processing; p. (est. 1969) 44,000.

Colima, st., Mexico; on Pac. cst.; cap. Colima; pt. Manzanillo; cotton, sugar, rice, coffee; a. 5,203 km²; p. (1969) 238,000.

Colima, volcano (48 km N.E. of c.), Mexico, alt. 3,869 m.

Coll, I. off cst. of Mull, Argyll and Bute, Scot.; agr., lobster fishing.

Collie, t., W. Australia; sub-bituminous coal; p. (1972) 5,832.

Collingwood, t., Ont., Canada; on Georgian Bay, L. Huron; shipbldg., steel; p. (1971) 9,719.

Colmar, t., cap. Haut-Rhin dep., France; ctr. of Alsace textile ind.; attractive mediaeval t.; mkt. for vineyards; p. (1968) 62,341.

Colne, t., Pendle, E. Lancs., Eng.; cotton mnfs., felts; p. (1971) 18,873.

Colne, R., Eng.; trib. of R. Thames rising in Chilterns. [p. (1971) 21,188.

Colne Valley, t., West Yorks., Eng.; woollens;

Cologne (Köln), c., N. Rhine-Westphalia, W. Germany; on Rhine at N. end of Rhine gorge; cath., univ.; impt. R. pt., route and comm. ctr.; eau-de-Cologne, electro-technical ind., machin., metallurgy. paper, chemicals, cars, oil refining, textiles; p. (est. 1969) 860,800.

Colombes, t., Hauts-de-Seine dep., France; mftg. sub. of Paris on R. Seine; p. (1968) 80,616.

Colombia, rep., N.W. S. America; cap. Bogotá; Andes contain most of p.; the savannahs (llanos) to S.E. are almost uninhabited; industl. employment growing; birth and death rates high in mainly tropical climate and many diseases endemic; agr. impt.; coffee, petroleum, bananas; a. 1,139,592 km²; p. (est. 1969) 20,463,000.

Colombo, c.. cap. of Sri Lanka; on W. cst.; univ.; impt. pt. (artificial) built by British; exp. tea, rubber, coconuts; p. (est. 1968) 558,500.

Colón, t., Panama; at Atl. end of Panama Canal; free tr. zone; comm. and industl. ctr.; oil refining nearby; p. (1970) 95,308.

Colonsay, I., Inner Hebrides, Argyll and Bute, Scot.; 13 km long; ecclesiastical antiquities; p. (inc. Jura 1971) 349.

Colorado, st., USA; hgst. st. in USA; in the Rockies extending up to 4,401 m (Mt. Elbert), no land below 1,000 m; drained by headwaters of Rs. Arkansas and Colorado; major stock-rearing a.; many valuable minerals esp. uranium, radium and molybdenum; cap. Denver; a. 270,000 km²; p. (1970) 2,195,887.

Colorado, plateau, Arizona, Utah, Col., N.M., USA; arid upland with spectacular scenery, inc. Grand Canyon; alt. 1,500–3,300 m.

Colorado, R., Argentina; flows from Andes to Atl. Oc.; limited irrigation in pastoral valley; length 848 km.

Colorado, major R. of W. USA; drains 8% of USA; formed by confluence of Green and Grand Rs.; spectacular canyons inc. Grand Canyon; hydroelec. power from many dams inc. Hoover Dam; irrigation supplies intensive horticultural a. in S. section and consequent rapid decrease in volume to a sm. stream in lower course; length 2,320 km.

Colorado, R., rises N.W. Texas, USA; flows to G. of Mexico; irrigation and power; 1,552 km long.

Colorado Desert, Cal., USA; inc. Imperial Valley, a fertile irrigated a.

Colorado Springs. t. Col., USA; 102 km S. Denver; resort; p. (1970) 124,856 (c.), 228,572 (met. a.).

Colton, t., S.E. Cal., USA; fruit- and vegetable-canning; mkt. gardening; p. (1970) 20,016.

Columbia, t., Mo., USA; W. of St. Louis; st. univ.; flour, lumber; p. (1970) 58,804.

Columbia, t., st. cap. S.C., USA; in ctr. of rich farming a.; textiles, clothing; burned down in Civil War 1865; p. (1970) 111,706 (c.), 315,716 (met. a.).

Columbia, District of (D.C.); area on east bank of Potomac R., coterminus with c. of Washington, cap. of USA; a. 179 km²; p. (1970) 764,000 (c.); (1968) 2,750,700 (met. a.).

Columbia, R., major R. of western N. America; rises in Rocky Mtns., B.C., flows through Washington, USA; power sources, inc. Grand Coulee Dam, Bonneville Dam; deepwater harbour at mouth; length 2,240 km.

Columbus, c.. Ga., USA; at head of navigation on Chattahoochee R.; industl. and shipping ctr.; textile mills, food-processing; cotton-ginning machin.; p. (1970) 152,123 (c.), 234,288 (met. a.).

Columbus, t., Ind., USA; engin.; leather gds.; p. (1970) 26,457.

Columbus, t., Miss. USA; agr. prods.; p. (1970) 25,795.

Columbus, c., st. cap. Ohio, USA; rly. ctr.; st. univ.; machin., paper, aircraft machin., chemicals; p. (1970) 533,418 (c.), 904,725 (met. a.).

Colwyn Bay, t., Clwyd, N. Wales; on cst. 10 km E. of Llandudno; furniture; seaside resort; p. (1971) 25,535; as Colwyn forms basis of l. gov. dist. inc. Abergele; p. (est. 1976) 46,500.

Comayagüela, c., former cap. of Honduras; twin c. of Tegucigalpa from which it is separated by Choluteca R.; both cs. administered together as Central Dist.

Combe Martin, v., Devon, Eng.; 8 km E. of Ilfracombe; seaside resort.

Comber, t., Ards, N. Ireland; linen; p. (1966) 3,925.

Como, c., N. Italy; at foot of Alps, on L. Como; oranges, olives; textiles; cath.; tourism; p. (1969) 94,379.

Como, L., N. Italy; beautiful mtn. scenery, tourism, villas; a. 145 km².

Comodoro Rivadavia, spt., Chubut prov., Argentina; on San Jorge G., 880 km S.W. of Bahia Blanca; military zone; univ.; ch. source of oil in Argentine; oil refining; p. (1960) 40,000.

Comorin, C., most S. point of India.

Comoro Is., arch., Indian Oc.; in Moçambique channel, midway between Africa and Malagasy Rep.; cap. Moroni; total a. 2,170 km²; turtle fishing; vanilla, copra, sisal, timber, perfume plants; indep. from France declared 1975 but rejected by Mayotte Is whose future is still undecided; p. (est. 1907) 280,000

Compiegne, t., Oise, France; sugar mills, rope; Armistice signed between Allies and Germany 1918; Fr. surrendered to Hitler 1940; resort; p. (1968) 32,653.

Compton, t., Cal., USA; residtl. for Los Angeles; heavy engin., glass, oil refining; p. (1970) 78,611.

Conakry, c., cap. of Rep. of Guinea; impt. pt. on offshore islet; exp. iron ore and alumina; experimental fruit gardens; p. (1967) 197,267 (met. a.).

Concarneau, pt., Finistère, France; 19 km S.E. Quimper; fisheries; p. (1968) 18,150.

Concepción, c., prov. cap., Chile; shipping ctr. through its pt. Talcahuano; univ.; comm. and cultural t.; severe earthquakes 1939 and 1960; nr. to coalfield; p. (est. 1970) 196,317.

Concepción, prov., Chile; cap. C.; Lota-Coronel coalfield lgst. in Chile; a. 5,701 km²; p. (1970) 638,118.

Concepción, t. cap. of C. prov., Paraguay; main comm. ctr. for Chaco, pt. on R. Paraguay; p. (est. 1968) 17,200.

Conchos, R., Chihuahua prov., Mexico; flows N.E. from Madre Occidental to Rio Grande; cotton under irrigation in upper valley; hydro-elec. power; length 560 km.

Concord, t., Cal., USA; residtl. and comm. ctr. in San Francisco met. a.; rapid p. growth; p. (1970) 85,164.

Concord, t. Mass., USA; literary ctr.; textiles; p. (1970) 16,148.

Concord, t., st. cap., N.H., USA; on Merrimack R.; granite, machin., textiles; p. (1970) 30,022.

Concordia, t., Argentina; pt. on Uruguay R.; exp. agr. prod.; p. (1960) 56,000.

Condamine, R., Queensland, Australia; trib. of R. Darling; used for irrigation.

Coney I., t., N.Y., USA; on Long I., 8 km long, comprises Manhattan Beach, Brighton Beach, W. Brighton. and W. End; seaside resort.

Congleton, t., l. gov. dist., E. Cheshire, Eng.; on S.W. margin of Pennines; clothing, textiles; once impt. for silk; p. (est. 1976) 78,000 (dist.).

Congo, People's Rep. of the, indep. st. within Fr. Community. Equatorial Africa; cap. Brazzaville; agr. and forestry; hardwoods; a. 341,880 km²; p. (est. 1969) 880,000.

Congolese Republic See Zaïre.

Congo R. See Zaïre R.

Conisborough, t., South Yorks., Eng.; limestone, bricks, tiles; p. (1971) 16,800.

Coniston, t., Ont., Canada; on rly. 13 km E. of Sudbury; nickel smelting; t. built by and for nickel-mng. company.

Coniston Water, L., Cumbria, Eng.; focus of tourism in L. Dist.; 8·8 km long.

Conjeeveram. See Kanchipuram.

Connacht, prov., R.o.I.; inc. Galway, Mayo, Sligo, Leitrim, Roscommon; mtnous. in W.;

farming, fishing; a. 17,775 km²; p. (1966) 401,518.

Connah's Quay, t., Alyn and Deeside, Clwyd, Wales; p. (1971) 12,296.

Connaught Tunnel (Can. Pac. Rly.), B.C., Canada; longest in N. America (8 km) 1,500 m under mt. Sir Donald (Selkirk Mtns.).

Connecticut, R., New Eng.; **USA;** middle course forms fine agr. land; investment in navigation. irrigation and flood control; 566 km long.

Connecticut, st., New England, USA; one of original 13 sts.; humid climate; arable agr.; diversified inds.; many natural harbours on cst.; cap. Hartford; lgst. c. New Haven; a. 12,973 km²; p. (1970) 2,987,950.

Connemara, mtns., dist., R.o.I.; Co. Galway; many lakes and bogs; tourist resort.

Consett, t., Derwentside, Durham, Eng.; on edge of Pennines, 16 km S.W. Newcastle; iron, steel, coal mng.; p. (1971) 35,391.

Constance (Konstanz), c., Baden-Württemberg, **W. Germany;** on Bodensee; cath.; textiles, machin., chemicals, elec. inds.; route ctr.; tourism; p. (est. 1969) 60,821.

Constance, L. *See* Bodensee.

Constanţa, ch. spt. S.E. Romania; on Black Sea; oil pipeline to Ploieşti and Cimpina; exp. petroleum, wheat; cement, chemicals, machin.; p. (est. 1969) 170,026 (c.); (1966) 202,024 (met. a.).

Constantine, c., N.E. Algeria; stands 650 m high on gorge of Rhumel R.; planned textile and engin. wks.; p. (1966) 243,558.

Constantinople. *See* Istanbul.

Conwy (Conway), Aberconwy. Gwynedd, spt., N. Wales; mediaeval walled t.; at mouth of R. Conway; sm. seaside resort; cas.; quarrying, lt. engin.; p. (1971) 12,158.

Cook, mtn., alt. 3,764 m; hgst. point in S. Alps. N.Z.; 3 peaks.

Cook Inlet, S. cst. Alaska, **USA;** oil pipeline connects oilfields of Granite Point with marine terminal at Drift R.

Cook Is., Brit. gr. (Rarotonga, lgst.) in S. Pac., annexed to N.Z., 1901; internal self-govt. 1965; bananas, oranges, copra; a. 241 km²; p. (1966) 19,247.

Cookstown, mkt. t., l. gov. dist., N. Ireland; cement wks.; p. (1966) 5,542.

Cook Strait, channel between N. and S. Is. of N.Z.; 24–29 km wide; undersea cable completed 1965.

Cooma, t., N.S.W., Australia; mkt. t. and pastoral ctr.; tourism; H.Q. of Snowy Mts. Authority; p. (1966) 9,101.

Coonoor, t., Tamil Nadu, India; in Nilgiri Hills; sanatorium c. 1,800 m a.s.l.; p. (1961) 30,690.

Coopers Creek (Barcoo), intermittent R., central Australia; rises in Warrego Range, Gr. Dividing Range, flows S.W. into marshes of L. Eyre; provides water for livestock in semi-arid region; 1,408 km long.

Copeland, l. gov. dist., Cumbria, Eng.; cstl. a. N. of Barrow and inc. Whitehaven and Millom; p. (est. 1976) 69,600.

Copenhagen (København), ch. spt., cap. of Denmark; on E. cst. of Sjaelland I.; royal palace, univ., library; naval sta.; steel, metal, textiles, clothing, breweries; airpt.; p. (est. 1969) 643,262 (c.), 1,381,312 (met. a.).

Copiapó, t., cap. of Atacama prov., Chile; copper and iron-mng. ctr.; p. (est. 1966) 36,767.

Coquet, R., Northumberland, Eng.; rises in the Cheviots and flows into North Sea.

Coquimbo, spt., Chile; exp. iron, copper, and manganese ores; p. (est. 1966) 39,610.

Coral Sea, Pac. Oc., extends from the New Hebrides to Australia.

Coral Sea Islands Territory, Fed. terr., Australia; scattered Is., E. of Gr. Barrier Reef, off Queensland cst.; possibility of oil exploration.

Corbeil-Essonnes, t., Essonne, France; on R. Seine, 19 km S.E. of Paris; flour mills, printing, paper; p. (1968) 32,192.

Corbridge, t., Northumberland, Eng.; on R. Tyne, nr. Hexham; 17th cent. bridge; Roman t. nearby.

Corby, t., l. gov. dist., Northants., Eng.; 11 km N. of Kettering; new t.; steel wks., shoes, clothing, lamps; p. (est. 1976) 55,600 (dist.).

Córdoba, c., central **Argentina;** univ.; cultural and comm. ctr.; exp. wheat, cattle, lumber; health resort; local hydroelec. power from La Vina; p. (1970) 789,663 (met. a.).

Córdoba, t., Veracruz, Mexico; mkt. t. in coffeegrowing a.; p. (1970) 92,870.

Córdova, prov., Andalusia, Spain; cap. Córdova; olives, vines, livestock; a. 13,724 km²; p. (1970) 724,116.

Córdova, c., Andalusia, Spain; cap. of C. prov., on Guadalquivir R.; cath. originally built as a mosque in 8th cent.; tourist ctr.; p. (est. 1969) 229,407.

Corfu (Kérkira), most N. of Ionian Is., Greece; traversed by mtns. but largely lowland producing olive-oil, figs, wine, oranges; a. 637 km²; p. (1971) 92,261 (prov.).

Corinth (Kórinthos), t., cap. Corinthia prov. Greece; at end of Isthmus of C.; occupies site 5 km from anc. classic c. destroyed by earthquake 1858; raisins, wine; p. (1961) 15,892.

Corinth Canal, ship canal, S. Greece; traverses Isthmus of Corinth, links G. of Corinth and Ionian Sea with Saronic G. and Aegean Sea; opened 1893; length 5·6 km, depth 8 m.

Corinth, Isthmus of, connects the Peloponnesus with the mainland of Greece; cut across by canal

Corinto, ch. spt., N.W. Nicaragua; handles 50 per cent of cty's tr.; exp. hides, sugar, coffee; p. (est. 1970) 12,985.

Cork, co., R.o.I.; lgst. and most S.; mtns.; dairying, brewing. agr., fisheries; cap. Cork; a. 7,485 km²; p. (1966) 339,525.

Cork, spt., C.B. Cork, R.o.I.; at mouth of R. Lee; cath., univ.; woollens, butter, cattle, brewing, cars, rubber; p. (1966) 122,146 (c.), 125,283 (met. a.).

Corner Brook, c., W. Newfoundland, Canada; gd. harbour; iron foundries, cement, gypsum; one of world's lgst. newsprint mills; p. (1971) 25,929.

Cornwall, t., Ont., Canada; on St. Lawrence R.; H.Q. of Seaway Authority; textiles, pulp, paper, flour; p. (1971) 46,429.

Cornwall and Isles of Scilly, non-met. co., S.W. Eng.; penin. bordering Atl. Oc. and Eng. Channel; granite moorlands supply kaolin and tin; mild maritime climate encourages tourism, dairying, and mkt. gardening; many small fishing vs.; co. t. Bodmin; a. 3,515 km²; p. (est. 1976) 407,100.

Cornwall, North, l. gov. dist., Eng.; lge. a. on N. cst. stretching from Bodmin to Bude; p. (est. 1976) 61,500.

Coro, c., Falcón, Venezuela; on Paraguaná penin.; agr. processing; nearby oil refineries; p. (est. 1970) 55,955.

Corocoro, t., La Paz dep., Bolivia; at alt. c. 4,000 m in central Andes, 80 km S. of La Paz; impt. copper-mng. ctr.

Coromandel Coast (Carnatic region), cst. of Tamil Nadu, India; where earliest European settlements established; extensive a. of flat land built up by R. Cauvery.

Coronation Gulf, arm of Beaufort Sea; extreme point N. Canadian mainland; discovered by Franklin.

Coronel, spt., Chile; coal mng., pt. inds.; p. (est. 1966) 43,324.

Coronel Oviedo, t., Paraguay; comm. ctr.; p. (est. 1970) 59,307.

Corpus Christi, c. Texas, **USA;** cotton, oil refining, chemicals; resort; p. (1970) 201,581 (c.), 278,443 (met. a.).

Corrèze, dep., S. central France; part of Massif Central, mostly over 600 m; sparse p. based on livestock agr. and forestry; cap. Tulle; a. 5,884 km²; p. (1968) 237,858.

Corrib, Lough, Galway and Mayo, R.o.I.; drained by Corrib R. into Galway Bay; impt. brown trout fishery; a. 176 km².

Corrientes, t., Argentina; cap. t. ctr. on Paraná R.; univ.; cattle, sugar, rice, cotton; river navigation reduces isolation; p. (1970) 131,392 (met. a.).

Corryvreckan, strait and whirlpool between Jura and Scarba Is., Inner Hebrides, Scot.; whirlpool caused by tidal movement over variable sea bed.

Corsica (Corse), I. France; in Mediterranean Sea; violent history in 16th and 17th cent.; high granite peaks (Monte Cinto), mtn. torrents, fertile plains; inland and sea fishing; rapid growth of tourism with little benefit to indigeneous Corsicans; split into 2 deps. to help overcome autonomist agitation (1975); Haute

Corse, cap. Bastia, Corse du Sud, cap. Ajaccio; a. 8,721 km²; p. (1968) 269,831.

Corsicana, t., Texas, USA; site of first oil drilling in USA; p. (1970) 19,972.

Cortona, t., Tuscany, Italy; nr. Perugia; Roman remains, cath.; p. (est. 1968) 23,564.

Corumbá, pt., Mato Grosso, Brazil; on R. Paraguay; exp. agr. products; mkt. t.; p. (est. 1968) 89,199.

Corunna. See La Coruña.

Corvallis, t., Ore., USA; in fertile farming valley; lumbering; univ.; p. (1970) 35,056.

Coryton, t., Essex, Eng.; on Thames, oil refining; oil pipeline to Stanlow refinery.

Cos (Kos) I., Dodecanese, Greece; in Aegean Sea, second lgst. of gr.; gave name to Cos lettuce; birthplace of Hippocrates.

Cosenza, prov., Calabria, Italy; a. 6,646 km²; p. (1969) 716,916.

Cosenza, c., S. Italy; ctr. for figs, oranges, olive oil, wine; cath., cas.; p. (1969) 96,515.

Costa Brava, region, Catalonia, Spain; tourism.

Costa del Sol, region, Málaga cst., Spain; tourism.

Costa Rica, rep. Central America; over half p. in equable Meseta Central; forests, volcanic mtns.; agr. 40 per cent G.N.P.; coffee, bananas, cacao; high literacy and living standards; a. 50,909 km²; p. (est. 1969) 1,695,000.

Côte d'Azur, France; Mediterranean littoral E. of Rhône R.; inc. resorts of Nice, Cannes, Monte Carlo, and St. Tropez.

Côte d'Or, dep., E. France; heart of anc. Burgundy, traversed by R. Saône; cap. Dijon; wines, livestock, iron and steel; a 8,783 km²; p. (1968) 431,192.

Cotentin, peninsula, N. France; 80 km long; Cherbourg, at its extremity, 128 km from Portsmouth.

Côtes-du-Nord, dep., N. Brittany, France; rugged cst. and Is. and mild climate encourage tourism; mkt. gardens along cst.; many fishing ts.; cap. St. Brieuc; a. 7,218 km²; p. (1968) 506,102.

Cotonou, pt., Benin Rep.; new artificial pt.; fishing; lt. inds.; p. (est. 1970) 208,000.

Cotopaxi, volcano, cath. 5,982 m) in the Andes of Ecuador, nr. Quito; loftiest active volcano in the world; recent eruptions have caused great damage to Ecuador.

Cotswold, l. gov. dist., Gloucs., Eng.; lge a. covering C. Hills and inc. Cirencester and Northleach; p. (est. 1976) 67,000.

Cotswold Hills, W. Eng.; limestone escarpment; Gloucs., Oxon.; once famous for woollens; source of Thames and tribs.; highest point Cleeve Cloud, 309 m; tourism.

Cottbus or Kottbus, E. Germany; on R. Spree; rly. ctr.; textile and metal mnfs.; p. (est. 1970) 82,897.

Cottian Alps, mtn. range on border of France and Italy crossed by Hannibal; craggy; max. alt. 2,844 m (Monte Viso).

Coulsdon and Purley. See Croydon.

Council Bluffs, t., Iowa, USA; on Missouri R. nr. Omaha; rly. ctr.; farm implements, paper, machin.; p. (1970) 60,348.

Courantyne, R., Guyana; rises in Serra Acari; passes through bauxite mng. region to Atl. Oc.; navigation in lower course; 720 km long.

Courtrai. See Kortrijk.

Cove and Kilcreggan, burgh, Dumbarton, Scot.; at junc. of Loch Long and R. Clyde; p. (1971) 1,343.

Coventry, c., met. dist., West Midlands, Eng.; 29 km E.S.E. of Birmingham; ctr. of cycle, motorcycle, motor-car ind.; aircraft, tools; chemicals; projectiles, textiles; cath.; univ.; p. (est. 1976) 336,800 (dist.).

Covilhã, t., Portugal; cloth factories; p. (1970) 60,768.

Covington, t., Ky., USA; on R. Ohio, opp. Cincinnati; machin., leather, furniture; p. (1970) 52,535.

Cowbridge, t., Vale of Glamorgan, South Glamorgan, S. Wales; nr. Cardiff; p. (1971) 1,221.

Cowdenbeath, burgh, Dunfermline, Scot.; 8 km N.E. of Dunfermline; coal; p. (1971) 10,464.

Cowes, resort and pt., Medina, I. of Wight, Eng.; on estuary of R. Medina; regattas and yacht bldg.; hovercraft; p. (1971) 18,895.

Cowra, t., N.S.W., Australia; famous wheat dist. and site of state experimental farm; sm. mftg. ctr.; p. (1966) 7,082.

Cozumel I., E. of Yucatan peninsula, Mexico.

Cracόw. See Kraków.

Cradle, Mt., mtn., Tasmania, Australia; alt. 1,546 m; Nat. Park.

Cradock, t., Cape Prov., S. Africa; wool tr.; p. (est. 1967) 21,300.

Craigavon, c., l. gov. dist. N. Ireland; new "city in a garden" under construction, 16 km long, merging Portadown and Lurgan, linked by motorway, to provide major base for ind.; p. (est. 1971) 12,594.

Crail, royal burgh, North East Fife, Scot.; cstl. resort; p. (1971) 1,075.

Craiova, c., S. Romania, in Wallachia; tr. ctr.; agr. processing textiles, engin., chemicals; p. (est. 1969) 171,676.

Cramlington. t., Northumberland, Eng.; 13 km N. of Newcastle; new t., proposed p. 60,000.

Cranborne Chase, Wilts., Eng.; chalk upland of over 275 m; extension of Salisbury Plain.

Cranbrook, mkt. t., Kent, Eng.; hops and grain; former weaving t.; p. (1971) 16,022 (dist.).

Cranston, t., R.I., USA; machin., chemicals, textiles; p. (1970) 74,287.

Crater L., Ore., USA; in Nat. Park, is a body of water 600 m deep and 10 m across, set in a crater of an extinct volcano, c. 2,400 m high; varied flora and fauna on shore.

Craters of the Moon, dist., Idaho, USA; Nat. Monument of volcanic craters and cones; a. 192 km².

Crato, t., Ceara st., Brazil; ctr. of irrigated area producing cotton, sugar, rice; p. (1960) 27,649.

Crau, La, region, Bouches-du-Rhône dep., S.E. France; dry, pebbly area E. of Rhône delta; winter pasture for sheep.

Craven, dist., central Pennines, Eng.; relatively low limestone plateau, alt. mainly below 240 m; drained by R. Ribble to S.W., R. Aire to S.E.; sheep rearing in valleys, cattle for fattening, root and fodder crops; now forms l. gov. dist. based on Skipton and Settle; p. (est. 1976) 46,300.

Crawley, t., l. gov. dist., West Sussex, Eng.; on N.W. flank of Weald, 14 km S. of Reigate; new t. (1947); engin., pharmaceuticals, metal, leather, wooden gds.; p. (est. 1976) 72,600.

Crayford. See Bexley.

Creag Meagaidh, mtn., Lochaber, Scot.; alt. 1,128 m.

Crediton, mkt. t., Devon, Eng.; p. (1971) 5,144.

Cree, R., Wigtown, Scot.; flows into Wigtown Bay.

Crema, industl. and agr. t., N. Italy; S.E. of Milan; cath.; p. (est. 1968) 32,070.

Cremona, t., cap. of C. prov., Lombardy, N. Italy; famed as a ctr. of learning and later for mnf. of violins and violas; birthplace of Stradivari; cath.; pt. on new Milan-Adriatic Waterway; p. (1969) 81,061.

Crete (Kríti), I., E. Mediterranean, lgst. I. of Greece; cradle of Minoan civilisation between 1600 and 1400 B.C.; mild climate; sm. a. of cultivable land; few minerals; part of Greece since Balkan Wars (1913); cap. Khaniá; birthplace of El Greco; a. 8,379 km²; p. (1971) 456,208. (admin. reg.).

Creus, C., juts out into Mediterranean Sea, Spain; nr. Fr. border.

Creuse, dep., in Massif Central, France; soil infertile, harsh climate, limited agr.; a. 5,605 km² p. (1968) 156,876.

Crewe, t., Cheshire, Eng.; 32 km. S.E. of Chester; lge. rly. wks.; impt. rly. junc.; aircraft and refrigerator wks., clothing, engin., motor vehicles; expanded t.; p. (1971) 51,302; with Nantwich forms l. gov. dist.; p. (est. 1976) 98,100.

Crewkerne, mkt. t., Somerset, Eng.; 13 km S.W. of Yeovil; leather gds.; grammar school (1499); p. (1971) 4,819.

Criccieth, t., Dwyfor, Gwynedd, N. Wales; on N. shore of Cardigan Bay; seaside resort; p. (1971) 1,509.

Cricklade, t., N. Wilts., Eng.; on R. Thames, 13 km N.W. of Swindon; fortified township in Saxon times; p. (1971) 22,368 (dist.).

Crieff, t., Perth and Kinross, Scot.; on R. Earn; summer resort; p. (1971) 5,467.

Crimea (Krym) Peninsula, juts into Black Sea, Ukrainian SSR, USSR; wheat, tobacco, fruit; campaign 1854–55 between Russia and Allied Forces of Turkey, Britain, France, and Sardinia was chiefly fought out here (Alma, Balaclava and Sevastopol); tourism.

Crimmitschau, t., Karl-Marx-Stadt, E. Germany; nr. Zwickau; impt. textile ctr.; p. (est. 1970) 29,982.

Crinan Canal, across peninsula of Argyll and Bute, S.W. Scot.; connects Loch Gilp with Atl. Oc.; 14 km long.

Cristobal, dist., Panama Canal Zone; adjoins Colon at N. entrance to Canal; p. (1970) 11,600;

Croaghpatrick, mtns., May, R.o.I.; 766 m.

Croatia, constituent rep., Yugoslavia; stretches from Istria on Adriatic cst. to Dinaric Alps; crossed by Drava and Sava Rs.; traditional agr. being replaced by new inds.; impt. aluminium wks. based on local bauxite; chemicals, shipbldg.; new oilfields supply 70 per cent of Yugoslavia's needs; cap. Zagreb; a. 56,524 km²; p. (1971) 4,422,564.

Crocodile R. See Limpopo.

Cromarty, burgh, Ross and Cromarty, Scot.; N.E. cst. of Black Isle; p. (1971) '84.

Cromer, t., North Norfolk, Eng.; on N. cst. of E. Anglia; seaside resort; p. (1971) 5,336.

Cromford, v., Derbys., Eng.; Richard Arkwright's first waterpowered mill (1771); cotton.

Crompton, t., Gtr. Manchester, Eng.; 3 km S. of Rochdale; cotton, engin., elec. lamps; p. (1971) 17,027.

Crook and Willington, ts., former U.D., Wear Valley, Durham, Eng.; varied inds. to replace coal mng.; p. (1971) 21,485.

Crosby, t., Sefton, Merseyside, Eng.; on Liverpool Bay 5 km N. of Bootle, Seaforth container pt.; residtl.; seaside resort; p. (1971) 57,405.

Cross, R., S.E. Nigeria; rises in Cameroon Highlands, flows W. and S. into G. of Guinea at Calabar; useful inland waterway; 640 km long.

Cross Fell, mtn., Cumbria, Eng.; on E. border of co.; alt. 894 m; highest point of the Pennines.

Crotone, t., S. Italy; pt. on E. cst. Calabria; electro-chemicals and metallurgical inds.; on site of anc. Crotona founded as Greek col.; home of Pythagoras; p. (1966) 41,300.

Crowland, t., Lincs., Eng.; mkt. t. in the Fens, on R. Welland; 8th-cent. abbey ruins.

Crows Nest Pass, B.C., Alberta, Canada; southernmost pass across Canadian Rocky Mtns.; used by rly. from Medicine Hat to Syokane (USA); summit 1,360 m.

Croydon, residtl. t., Eng.; now outer bor. Greater London; inc. Coulsdon and Purley; lt. inds.; major office ctr.; p. (est. 1976) 330,600.

Crummock Water, L. Dist., Cumbria, Eng.; ribbon L.

Csepel, sub., Budapest, Hungary; iron and steel, oil refining, leather, paper; p. incorporated with Budapest 1950.

Csongrád, mkt. t., agr. dist., Hungary; at junc. of Rs. Tisza and Körös; p. (1970) 20,331.

Cuba, I., indep. rep., W.I.; cap. Havana; lies within tropics; highly fertile although half land a. is mtnous.; exp. sugar, nickel, tobacco, rum, citrus fruits; revolution (1959) reoriented economic and political connections away from USA towards USSR; 70 per cent of cultivated land in state farms or cooperatives; recent attempts to diversify economy but sugar still mainstay; a. 114,494 km²; p. (1970) 8,553,395.

Cuckfield, mkt. t., Mid Sussex, West Sussex, Eng.; p. (1971) 25,883.

Cuckmere, R., Sussex, Eng.; passes through S. Downs in beautiful gap; length 37 km.

Cúcuta, t., cap. of Norte de Santander, Colombia; close to Venezuelan border; nr. oilfield; destroyed by earthquake, 1875; new planned t.; p. (est. 1972) 219,400 (t.), 248,900 (met. a.).

Cuddalore, spt., Tamil Nadu, India; nr. Pondicherry; exp. oilseeds, cottons; p. (1971) 101 335.

Cuddapah, t., Andhra Pradesh, India; cotton, cloth factories, millet, rice; p. (1961) 49,027.

Cudworth, South Yorks., Eng.; p. (1971) 8,838.

Cuenca, t., cap. of Azuay prov., 3rd. c. of Ecuador; in fertile agr. basin of Andes; sugar, tyres, flour mills, Panama hats; p. (1970) 77,300.

Cuenca, agr. and mng. prov., central Spain; furniture, leather, paper; a. 17,063 km²; p. (1970) 247,158.

Cuenca, t., cap. of C. prov., Spain; on gorge above R. Júcar; mkt. t.; famed in mediaeval times for silver and cloth mnfs.; p. (1966) 28,173.

Cuernavaca, t., cap. of Morelos st., central Mexico;

anc. Indian t. captured by Cortes; tourist resort; univ.; p. (1970) 134,117.

Cuiabá, t. cap. of Mato Grosso st., Brazil; ctr. pastoral a.; gold and diamonds produced; galena deposit nearby; p. (est. 1968) 87,316.

Cuillin Hills. mtns. I. of Skye, Scot.; attaining 992 m in Sgurr Alasdair.

Culiacán, c., of Sinaloa, N.W. Mexico; anc. c.; Pacific pt. Altata; p. (1970) 167,956.

Culloden Moor, 10 km E. of Inverness, Scot.; defeat of Prince Charles Edward Stuart's highlanders by duke of Cumberland's forces (1746).

Culross, royal burgh, Dunfermline, Scot.; belongs to Nat. Trust; abbey; p. (1971) 523.

Culver City, t., Cal., USA; sub. of Los Angeles; lge. motion-picture plant; electronic equipment, machin., chemicals, tools; p. (1970) 34,526.

Cumaná, c., N.E. Venezuela; pt. on Caribbean; European settlement since 1510; exp. coffee, cacao; sardine canning; airpt.; p. (est. 1970) 100,500.

Cumaná, G., N. cst., Venezuela.

Cumberland, former co., Eng.; now part of Cumbria non-met. co.

Cumberland, industl. t., Md., USA; on Potomac R.; iron and steel, tyres, glassware; p. (1970) 29,724.

Cumberland Gap, Ky., USA; ch. break in high E. wall of Cumberland plateau; gives access from upper Tennessee valley to Cumberland and Ohio valleys; impt. routeway in colonisation of Ky.

Cumberland Is., off cst. of Queensland, Australia.

Cumberland Plateau, mtn. region, Ky., Tenn., Ala., USA; forms S.W. zone of Appalachian mtn. system terminating abruptly towards Tennessee valley to E., Cumberland valley to W.; drained W. by tribs. of Cumberland and Ohio Rs; composed of horizontal sandstones overlying coal; thinly populated by backward farming communities except where mng. ts. occur in valleys cut down to coal; mainly between 360-900 m.

Cumberland R., Tenn. and Ky., USA; trib. of Ohio R., rises in C. plateau; upper course forested; crosses coalmng. a. and fertile agr. valley; part of Tenn. Valley Authority scheme; hydroelec. power; 1,104 km long.

Cumbernauld, new t. (1955), l. gov. dist., Strathclyde Reg., Scot.; to house 50,000 overspill from Glasgow; adding machines; p. (est. 1974) 38,500.

Cumbrae. Gt. and Little. Is., in F. of Clyde, off cst. of Cunninghame, Scot.

Cumbria, non-met. co. N.W. Eng.; centred on L. Dist. where rugged glaciated scenery encourages tourism, sheep-farming, forestry and water storage; Cumberland coalfield on W. cst. where declining heavy inds. being replaced by new lt. inds.; major ts. Carlisle and Barrow; a. 6,809 km²; p. (est. 1976) 473,600.

Cumorian Mtns., L. Dist., Cumbria, Eng.

Cumnock, burgh, Cumnock and Doone Valley, Scot.; p. (1971) 5,714.

Cundinamarca. dep., Colombia; contains many Andean Ls. and the fed. cap Bogotá; a. 23,585 km²; p. (est. 1968) 1,165,095.

Cunene. See Kunene R.

Cuneo, prov., Italy; a. 7,433 km²; p. (1969) 541,251.

Cuneo, t., cap. of C. prov., Piedmont, Italy; mkt. for prod. of surrounding a.; withstood many sieges under the rule of house of Savoy; p. (1969) 53,233.

Cupar, royal burgh, North East Fife, Scot.; on R. Eden, W. of St. Andrews; linen; sugar beet; p. (1971) 6,603.

Curaçao, I. (Neth. Antilles), off N. cst. Venezuela; major ctr. for refining and trans-shipping Venezuelan oil; picturesque Dutch architecture in cap. Willemstad; a. 544 km²; p. (1968) 139,211.

Curepipe, t., central Mauritius; health resort; p, (est. 1968) 50,000.

Curicó, t., Chile; agr. and comm. ctr.; earthquake 1928; p. (est. 1966) 39,392.

Curitiba, c., cap. of Paraná st., Brazil; univ.; industl. and comm. ctr. at c. 900 m; coffee, maté, chemicals, pharmaceutical and forest prods., foodstuffs; p. (1970) 483,038.

Curragh, plain, Kildare, R.o.I.; turf; racecourse.

Curtis I., Queensland, Australia; low volcanic I.; wooded; cattle.

Curzola. See Korčula.

Cuttack, t., Orissa st., India; on Mahanadi R.; long famous for gold and silver filigree work; p. (1971) 194,068 (t.), 205,759 (met. a.).

Cuxhaven, spt., Lower Saxony, W. Germany; outport of Hamburg at the mouth of R. Elbe; fine harbour; p. (est. 1969) 45,383.

Cuyahoga Falls, t., Ohio, USA; industl. and residtl.; p. (1970) 49,678.

Cuzco, dep., Peru; inc. Central Cordilleras, reaching c. 5.800 m; tropical climate; agr. varies with alt.; minerals; cap. C.; a. 144,304 km²; p. (est. 1969) 742,100.

Cuzco, t., cap. of C. dep., S. Peru; in Andes at alt. 3,418 m in valley of Urubamba R.; once cap. of Incas; sacked by Francisco Pizarro 1533; cath., ruins of Inca fortress; tr. ctr. for agr. prod.; p. (est. 1970) 108,900.

Cwmamman, t., Dinefwr, Dyfed, Wales; on R. Loughor; p. (1971) 3,955.

Cwmbran, t., Torfaen, Gwent, Wales; in valley of Avon-Lwyd, 8 km N. of Newport; new t. (1949); motor accessories, wire, elec. gds., bricks, tiles, pipes; p. (est. 1974) 43,500.

Cwm Dyli, Gwynedd, Wales; hydroelec. sta.

Cyclades (Kirkádhes), gr. of about 220 Is., Greece; rugged and barren csts. conceal sheltered agr. valleys; ch. t. and pt. Hermoupolis; a. 2,650 km²; p. (1971) 86,084.

Cynon Valley, l. gov. dist., Mid Glamorgan, Wales; inland valley inc. Aberdare and Mountain Ash; p. (est. 1976) 69,300.

Cyprus, Rep. of, I., indep. federated state, E. Mediterranean, 64 km S. of Turkey; civil war between Greek and Turkish Cypriots 1974; varied cst., limestone hills in N., forested mtns. in S., central plains of Messaoris in which cap. Nicosia is situated; agr. employs 30 per cent of p.; many irrigation schemes also aid soil and water conservation; land reform programmes to reduce fragmentation of holdings; copper in Troodos mtns. but asbestos of increasing importance; lt. inds. and tourism helping to restructure economy but agr. provides over 50 per cent of exp., inc. wine, citrus fruit, vegetables exported via main pt. of Famagusta; a. 9,251 km²; p. (est. 1969) 630,000.

Cyrenaica, prov. Libya; impt. region in anc. times; Greek col. 7th cent. B.C., Roman prov. 1st cent. B.C., captured by Arabs A.D. 642, part of Ottoman Empire 16th cent.; animal grazing, dates, oil-wells; a. 854,700 km²; p. (est. 1963) 350,024.

Czechoslovak Socialist Republic (ČSSR), fed. two-rep. st. (Czech Socialist Rep. and Slovak Socialist Rep.); Central Europe; ch. ts. Prague (cap.) Brno, Bratislava, Ostrava, Plzeň; Rs. Danube, Elbe, Vltava, Oder of gr. economic importance for landlocked cty.; inds. highly developed; high standard of living; coal, non-ferrous metals, little petroleum; hydroelec. power; a. 127,897 km²; p. (est. 1969) 14,418,000.

Czeladz, t., S.W. Poland; coal; p. (1970) 31,800.

Czernowitz. See Chernovtsy.

Czestochowa, c., Katowice prov., S. Poland; on Warta R.; riy. and industl. ctr.; iron and steel, textiles; celebrated religious ctr.; monastery; p. (est. 1969) 186,200.

D

Dacca, c., cap. of Bangladesh; on Buriganga R., old channel of Ganges; jute, muslin, paper mnfs.; medical radioisotope ctr., univ.; p. (1974) 1,310,976.

Dabrowa Gornicza, t., Katowice, Poland; coal, zinc, iron ore; p. (1970) 61,700.

Dachau, t., Bavaria, W. Germany; paper, elec. gds., brewing; concentration camp during last war; p. (est. 1969) 32,713.

Dachstein, mtn., Salzkammergut, Austria; alt. 2,998 m.

Dacorum, l. gov. dist., Herts., Eng.; a. of Chilterns inc. Tring, Berkhamsted and Hemel Hempstead; p. (est. 1976) 121,900.

Dadra and Nagar Haveli, union terr., India; admin. ctr. Silvassa; a. 490 km²; p. (1962) 57,963.

Dagenham, dist. former M.B., Eng.; now forms part of Greater London bor. of Barking; on N. bank of R. Thames; motor cars, iron, drugs, chemicals; residtl.

Dagestan, Caucasian aut rep., RSFSR; mtnous.; cap. Makhachkala; cotton, orchards and vineyards; machin., engin. oil; a. 50,246 km²; p. (1970) 1,429,000.

Dagupan, t., Pangasiman, Luzon, Philippines; on Lingayen Bay; comm. ctr.; p. (est. 1970) 89,000.

Daharki Mari, t., Pakistan; 560 km N.E. of Karachi; fertiliser plant.

Dahlak Archipelago, Ethiopia; in Red Sea; only 2 Is. inhabited; noted for pearl fishing.

Dahomey. See Benin, People's Rep. of.

Daimiel, mkt. t., Ciudad Real, Spain; cheeses, oil, wine; p. (1970) 17,710.

Dakar, spt., cap. of Senegal, W. Africa; S.E. of C. Verde behind Goree I. on Atl. cst.; exp. groundnuts; some industl. development; international airport; univ. and medical ctr.; p. (est. 1969) 581,000 (met. a.).

Dakhla, oasis, Libyan Desert, Egypt; 272 km S.W. of Asyût; dates, olives; stage on caravan route from Cyrenaica to Upper Egypt; site of New Valley Project for irrigation.

Dalälven, R., S. central Sweden; length 520 km, used for timber transport.

Da Lat (Dalat), t., Vietnam; 224 km N.E. Ho Chiminh City; in Annamite hills; nuclear reactor (1963); airport.

Dalbeattie, burgh, Stewartry, Scot.; granite, dairy prod., gloves; p. (1971) 3,412.

Dalby, t., Queensland, Australia; p. likely to increase with development of Moonie oilfield; dairying, timber; p. (1972) 8,890.

Dalgety, t., on Fife cst., Scot.; new t. proposed p. 10,000.

Dalkeith, burgh, Midlothian, Scot.; 10 km S.E. of Edinburgh; mkt. t.; p. (1971) 9,532.

Dalkey, t., Dublin, R.o.I.; on E. cst.; 6 km N. of Wicklow border; resort; residtl.; p. 5,526.

Dallas, c., Texas, USA; in cotton- and grain-growing a.; machin., aircraft, petroleum prod.; univ.; scene of assassination of President Kennedy (1963); p. (1970) 836,121 (c.), 1,539,472 (met a.).

Dalmatia, region of Yugoslavia and prov. of Croatia, N.E. Adriatic cst.; high Karst plateaux; olive oil, wine; tourism; contains many resorts; a. 12,732 km²; p. 622,000.

Daltonganj, t., Bihar, India; on R. Koël; coal, cement; p. (1961) 25,270.

Dalton-in-Furness, t., Cumbria, Eng.; limestone quarrying, textiles; abbey ruins; p. (1971) 11,217.

Daman (Damão), spt., India; 160 km N. Bombay; fishing, ship-bldg., cotton; former Portuguese settlement; p. (1960) 22,388.

Damanhûr, t., Egypt; on W. margin of Nile delta, 40 km S.E. of Alexandria; mkt. for local agr. produce; p. (est. 1970) 161,400.

Damaraland, region, South-West Africa; high plateau; admin. by Rep. of S. Africa; pt., Walvis Bay; cattle rearing.

Damascus (Arabic Esh-Sham), cap. c., Syria; 91 km S.E. of its pt. Beirut; claims to be oldest continuously inhabited c. in world; metal-wk., glass, cement; univ.; p. (1970) 835,000.

Dambovitta (Dimbovita), R., Romania; rises in Mt. Omul (Transylvanian Alps), flows S. through Bucharest to R. Danube, via impt. oilfields; 320 km long.

Damietta (Dumyât), t., Lower Egypt; on main distributary of R. Nile delta; cotton; p.(est.1970) 98,000.

Dammam, spt. on Persian G. Saudi Arabia; oil pt.; planned industl. growth.

Damodar R., Bihar, India; flows through India's major coalfields; valley forms ch. industl. a. of India; multipurpose scheme for hydroelectric power, irrigation and flood control.

Dampier, spt., W. Australia; on Indian Oc.; new pt. (1965) for shipping iron ore from Mt. Tom Price and Mt. Wittenoom; pelletising plant.

Dampier Archipelago, gr. of sm. Is., off N.W. Australia, in Indian Oc.

Dampier Strait, Bismarck Archipelago, channel between W. New Britain and Umboi I.

Dampier Strait, channel between Irian Jaya and Waigeo I.

Danakil Land (Dankalia) coastal desert a., mainly in Ethiopia, but partly in Afars and Issas; includes D. depression; potash; sm. pt. and road projected.

Da-nang (Tourane), c., S. Vietnam; ch. pt. of Annam on S. China Sea; exp. agr. prod.; p. (1968) 334,229.

Danao, t., Cebu, Philippines; rice and sugar dist.; p. (est. 1970) 45,500.

Danapur, t., Bihar, India; on Ganges R., nr. Patna; p. (1961) 70,766.

Dandenong, t., Victoria, Australia; 30 km E. of Melbourne; growing industl. ctr.; p. (est. 1968) 28,700.

Dannemora, t., Sweden; 40 km N.E. of Uppsala; iron ore worked since 1579; p. (est. 1970) 4,147.

Danube (Donau), R., second longest R. in Europe; rises in Black Forest, Germany, and flows E. into Black Sea; forms comm. highway; linked by canals with Main, Rhine and Oder; Vienna, Budapest, Belgrade, and other lge. cs. on its banks; 2,706 km long.

Danube-Tisa Canal, N. Yugoslavia; irrigation, flood control, navigable; 261 km long.

Danville, t., Ill., USA; coal; mftg tr.; p. (1970) 42,570.

Danville t., Va., USA; cotton, tobacco; p. (1970) 46,391.

Danzig. *See* Gdańsk.

Dap Cau, t., Vietnam; bamboo pulp and paper factories.

Darbhanga, t., Bihar, India; rice, oil-seeds, grain, sugar tr.; univ.; p. (1971) 132,059.

Dardanelles, strait between European and Asian Turkey, connecting Aegean Sea with Sea of Marmara; (the anc. Hellespont), 64 km long.

Daresbury, v., Cheshire, Eng.; birthplace of C. L. Dodgson (Lewis Carroll).

Dar-es-Salaam, spt., cap. of Tanzania; univ.; textile mill projected; oil refining; pipeline to Ndola, Zambia; naval base and Tanzam rly. built with Chinese aid; p. (1970) 343,911.

Darien, region, Panama; tortoiseshell, pearls, gold, but agr. is basis of economy; cap. La Palma; a. 15,540 km²; p. (1968) 24,100.

Darien, Gulf of, inlet of Caribbean Sea; separates Colombia and Panama.

Darjeeling, hill t., W. Bengal, India; tea, quinine; Himalayan resort; p. (1961) 40,651.

Darkhan, new t., Mongolia, on R. Hara; industl.

Darlaston, t., West Midlands, Eng.; nuts, bolts, fabricated steel mnfs., drop forgings, car components.

Darling Downs, plateau, S.E. Queensland, Australia; grazing region; ch. t. Toowoomba.

Darling R., N.S.W., Australia; longest trib. of the Murray, forming part of the Murray-Darling Rs. scheme for irrigation and flood control; 2,723 km long.

Darlington, t., l. gov. dist., Durham, Eng.; bridge bldg., woollen yarn mnf., engin., rly. wagons, steel wks.; p. (est. 1976) 96,900 (dist.).

Darmstadt, c., Hesse, W. Germany; cas.; comm. ctr.; metallurgical prods., paper, machin., radio, chemicals, plastics; technical univ.; p. (est. 1969) 140,200.

Dart, R., Devon, Eng.; rises in Dartmoor, flows S. into English Channel at Dartmouth; picturesque estuary; 74 km long.

Dartford, t., l. gov. dist., Kent, Eng.; nr. S. cst. of Thames estuary; Dartford-Purfleet road tunnel (1963); engin., chemicals, quarrying, paper; mkt.; p. (est. 1976) 83,800 (dist.).

Dartmoor, high granite plateau, S.W. Devon, Eng.; rough moorland; sheep, cattle, and wild ponies; granite tors; Nat. Park; tourism; granite quarries, reservoirs; prison at Princetown; a. 583 km²; hgst. point High Willays, 622 m.

Dartmouth, spt., S. Devon, Eng.; on W. of estuary of R. Dart; Royal Naval College; pottery; yachting, holiday resort; p. (1971) 5,696.

Dartmouth, industl. spt. sub. of Halifax, Nova Scotia, Canada; oil refining, shipbldg.; p. (1971) 64,002.

Darton, t., South Yorks., Eng.; nr. Barnsley; coal mng.; p. (1971) 15,145.

Darvel, burgh, Strathclyde Reg., Scot.; on R. Irvine, 13 km E. Kilmarnock; birthplace of Sir Alexander Fleming, discoverer of penicillin; p. (1971) 3,209.

Darwen, t., N.E. Lancs., Eng.; on flank of Ros-

sendale Fells, 5 km S. of Blackburn; tile and glaze bricks, paint, wallpaper, plastics; p. (1971) 28,880.

Darwin, c., spt., N.T., Australia; international airpt. serves Frances Creek iron ore mines; mineral deposits; tourism; devastated by cyclone 1974; to be rebuilt; p. (1972) 35,281.

Daryal Gorge, Caucasus, Georgian SSR, USSR; deep gorge (1,800 m) cut by Terek R.; identified as the classical Caspian or Iberian Gates from which distances were reckoned; forms part of Georgian military road.

Dashava, settlement on Lvov oblast, W. Ukraine, USSR; ctr. of rich natural gas field and starting point of gas pipeline to Kiev and Moscow, built after second world war.

Datia, t., Madhya-Pradesh, India; stone-walled, palaces; p. (1961) 29,430.

Datteln, t., N. Rhine-Westphalia. W. Germany; coal, leather, iron; p. (est. 1969) 34,659.

Daugavpils, t., Latvian SSR, USSR; on Dvina R.; textiles, engin., rly. repair wks., food prods.; p. (1970) 101,000.

Dauphiné Alps, mtn. range, S.E. France; 24 peaks over 3,050 m.

Daura, t., nr. Baghdad, Iraq; oil refining.

Davangere, t., Karnataka, S. India; on 600 m plateau in Indian Penin.; p. (1971) 121,110.

Davao, t., Mindanao, Philippines; pt. for sugar; p. (est. 1968) 337,000 (met. a.).

Davenport, t., Iowa, USA; on Mississippi R. where it is spanned by bridges to Rock Island, Molise and East Molise; rly., comm. and industl. ctr.; p. (1970) 97,614 (c.), 358,917 (met. a.).

Daventry, t., l. gov. dist., Northampton, Eng.; 14 km S.E. of Rugby; boot-mkg., lt. engin.; wireless-transmission sta.; expanded t.; p. (est. 1976) 53,200 (dist.).

David, t., cap. of Chiriqui prov., Panama; timber, coffee, cacao, sugar; p. (1970) 58,827.

Davis Strait, channel between Greenland and Baffin I., N.W. Terr., Canada; connects Atl. Oc. with Baffin Bay; navigable.

Davos-Platz and Dörfli, ts., Grisons, Switzerland; Alpine winter resorts; alt. 1,478 m; p. (1970) 10,238.

Dawley, t., The Wrekin, Salop, Eng.; on S.E. flank of the Wrekin; ironwks., pipe, cement, roadstone, asphalt and brick wks., engin.; new t. (1963); p. (1971) 25,935.

Dawlish, t., Teignbridge, S. Devon, Eng.; on S. cst. between estuaries of Rs. Exe and Teign; seaside resort; flower tr.; p. (1971) 9,505.

Dawson, t., Yukon Terr., Canada; on Yukon R., nr. Klondike goldfields; asbestos mng. projected 1968; p. (1966) 881.

Dax, t., Landes, S.W. France; on Adour R.; hot sulphur spring; horse mart; p. (1968) 19,348.

Dayton, c., Ohio, USA; on Great Miami R.; univ.; aircraft, elec. machin., rubber gds.; p. (1970) 239,591 (c.), 842,157 (met. a.).

Daytona Beach, t., Fla., USA; resort; shipping, ctr.; motor speed trials; p. (1970) 45,327.

De Aar, t., rly. junc., Cape Prov., S. Africa; 500 m from Cape Town; rlys. from N.W. (Luderitz, Walvis Bay) and S.E. (Pt. Elizabeth, E. London) join Cape Town to Johannesburg trunk rly.; p. (est. 1967) 16,600.

Dead Sea, salt-water L. between Israel and Jordan; surface 392 m below level of Mediterranean; a. 881 km², length 76 km, greatest width 15 km, greatest depth 399 m; receives waters of Jordan; high mineral content, very saline.

Deal, anc. pt., E. Kent, Eng.; on S.E. cst., 11 km N.E. Dover; opposite Goodwin Sands; seaside resort; lifeboat service; p. (1971) 25,415.

Dean, Forest of, Gloucs., Eng.; between Wye and Severn Rs.; former Royal Forest; Forestry Commission plantations; former coal-mng. a.; tourism; new lt. industl. estates; now forms l. gov. dist.; p. (est. 1976) 70,300.

Dearborn, t., Mich., USA; birthplace of Henry Ford; p. (1970) 104,199.

Death Valley, depression, Cal., USA; N. of Mojave Desert, 240 km N.E. of Los Angeles; completely arid; floor covered with saline deposits; tourist attraction; depth of valley floor 84 m below sea-level.

Deauville, seaside resort, Calvados dep., N. France; on Eng. Channel; racecourse, casino; p. (1968) 5,370.

Debra Markos, t., cap. of Gojam prov., Ethiopia; vegetable oil extraction; p. (est. 1970) 27,170.

Debrecen, t., Hungary; 183 km E. of Budapest; univ.; ctr. of pastoral dist.; fairs; pharmaceutics, medical instruments, furniture; ctr. of Calvinism; p. (est. 1969) 154,000.

Decatur, t. Ala., USA; steel, textiles; industl. development after establishment of Tenn. Valley Authority; p. (1970) 38,044.

Decatur, t., Ill., USA; on Sangamon R.; industl.; rly. engin., food processing; univ.; p. (1970) 89,468 (c.), 123,926 (met. a.).

Decazeville, t., Aveyron, S. France; ctr. of sm. coalfield (no longer worked), metallurgy; p. (1968) 10,532.

Deccan, The, upland of S. India, bounded by the Narbada and Kistna Rs.; coincides with Maharashtra st.; area of very fertile lava soils; impt. cotton-growing region.

Dee, R., N. Wales and Cheshire, Eng.; 144 km long; lge. silted estuary, use for water storage planned.

Dee, R., Kincardine and Deeside, Scot.; picturesque, tourism; 139 km long.

Dehiwala-Mt Lavinia, t., Sri Lanka; on cst. S. of Colombo; p. (est. 1968) 122,500.

Dehra Dun, t., Uttar Pradesh, India; scientific research ctr.; sawmills; p. (1971) 166,073 (t.), 203,464 (met. a.).

Deir-ez-Zor, t., Syria; on Euphrates R.; on motor route between Damascus and Baghdad; p. (1962) 59,757.

Dej, t., Romania; on Somesul R., distillery; p. (est. 1970) 30,869.

Delabole, v., Cornwall, Eng.; on N.W. flank of Bodmin Moor; slate quarries.

Delagoa Bay, natural harbour, Moçambique; ch. pt. Maputo.

Delaware, st., USA; low-lying a. of Atl. cst. plain; agr., lumber; fertilisers, minerals, leather, chemicals, machin.; cap. Dover; ch. pt. Wilmington; a. 6,138 km²; p. (1970) 542,979.

Delaware Bay, inlet, Atl. cst., USA; drowned estuary of R. Delaware, extends 128 km inland from C. May into heart of highly industl. a. of Philadelphia.

Delaware R., flows between N.Y. st., USA along the Penns. border, through N.J. to Delaware Bay; 504 km long.

Delft, c., pt., S. Holland, Neth.; on Schie R. (canalised), nr. Rotterdam; technical univ.; ceramics (delft-ware), tool mftg., precision instruments; 13th cent. Old church and 15th cent. New church; p. (1968) 80,545.

Delhi, c., cap. of India; on watershed between Rs. Indus and Ganges; made up of Old Delhi with walls, palace, and fort, and New Delhi with admin. ctr.; univ.; p. (1971) 3,287,883 (c.), 3,647,023 (met. a.).

Delhi, union terr., India; hot and arid region between Indus valley and alluvial plain of Ganges; irrigation to support agr.; New Delhi and Old Delhi ch. ctrs.; a. 1,497 km²; p. (1971) 4,044,338.

Delitzsch, t., Leipzig, E. Germany; 26 km E. of Halle; sugar, chemicals; p. (est. 1970) 24,270.

Delmarva, peninsula, Del., USA; between Chesapeake Bay and Del. Bay; horticulture, poultry, forestry, fishing.

Delmenhorst, t., Lower Saxony, W. Germany; nr. Bremen; jute, woollens, linoleum, foodstuffs; p. (est. 1969) 63,068.

Delphi, anc. Phocis, central Greece, N. of G. of Corinth; famous for Delphic oracle on Mt. Parnassus.

Del Rio, t., Texas, USA; pt. of entry on Rio Grande; mkt. for agr. a.; grapes; exp. wool; border t., bridge to Mexico; p. (1970) 21,330.

Delyn, l. gov. dist., Clwyd, Wales; W. of Dee estuary inc. Holywell, Flint and Mold; p. (est. 1976) 62,300.

Demavend, dormant volcano; Iran; hgst. peak in Elburz range, c. 5,673 m.

Demerara, co., Guyana; between Essequibo and Demerara Rs.; exp. sugar, molasses, rum.

Demerara, R., Guyana; drains N. to Atl. Oc.; bauxite transport.

Denain, t., Nord dep., N. France; industl. ctr.; p. (1968) 27,988 (t.), 126,740 (met. a.).

Denbigh, former co., N. Wales; now mostly in Clwyd; sm. part in Gwynedd.

Denbigh, t., Glyndŵr, Clwyd, Wales; in Vale of Clwyd, 16 km S. of Rhyl; cas.; tourism; dairy

prods.; birthplace of Stanley the explorer; p. (1971) 8,100.

Denby Dale, t., West Yorks., Eng.; 13 km W. of Barnsley; woollen textiles; earthenware pipes; p. (1971) 11,093.

Den Haag. See Hague, The.

Den Helder. See Helder.

Denholme, t., West Yorks., Eng.; nr. Bradford; dairying, textiles; p. (1971) 2,587.

Denizli, t., Turkey; 75 km S.E. of Izmir; gardens —" the Damascus of Anatolia "; nr. site of Laodicea; p. (1965) 61,820.

Denmark, kingdom, N.W. Europe; part of Scandinavia; consists of Jutland peninsula, Is. of Sjaelland, Fyn, Falster, Lolland, and Bornholm, and 400 smaller Is., between N. Sea and Baltic; emphasis on dairy agr., producing butter, eggs, and bacon; increasing industrialisation; industl. prods. now account for 62 per cent of exp.; cap. Copenhagen; a. 42,932 km²; p. (est. 1970) 4,921,156.

Denny and Dunipace, burgh, Falkirk, Scot.; 10 km W. of Falkirk; steel castings, precast concrete, p. (1971) 9,841.

Dent du Midi, mtn. gr., Vaud can., S.W. Switzerland; rises to 10,694 ft. in Haut Cime.

Denton, t., Gtr. Manchester Eng.; nr. Manchester; felt-hat mkg.; p. (1971) 38,107.

Denton, mkt. t., Texas, USA; univs.; food processing p. (1970) 39,874.

D'Entrecasteaux Is., volcanic gr. off S.E. New Guinea, Pac. Oc., part of Papua-New Guinea.

Denver, c., cap. of Col., USA; on E. slope of Rockies, on South Platte R.; univs.; oil, electronic equipment, mng. machin., livestock, canning; tourism; p. (1970) 512,691 (c.), 1,223,142 (met. a.).

Deogarh, t., Bihar, India; temples, place of pilgrimage; p. (1961) 30,813.

Deptford. See Lewisham.

Dera Ghazi Khan, t., Pakistan; on W. bank of Indus R.; silk, brass, ivory gds.; mosques; p. (1961) 47,105.

Dera Ismail Khan, t., Pakistan; on Indus R.; admin. ctr., caravan ctr.; p. (1961) 46,100.

Derbent, c., S.E. Dagestan, RSFSR; on Caspian Sea; textiles, fish inds., glass; oil and natural gas nearby; anc. c. founded by Persians; p. (est. 1967) 59,000.

Derby, c., l. gov. dist., Derbys., Eng.; on R. Derwent; general engin., aero-engines, man-made fibres; p. (est. 1976) 213,700.

Derbyshire, non-met. co., Eng.; much of a. occupied by Pennines and Peak Dist. Nat. Park; coalfield and industl. a. in E.; forms part of Manchester met. a. in N.W.; co. t. Derby; a. 2,631 km²; p. (est. 1976) 887,600.

Derbyshire, North East, l. gov. dist., Derbys., Eng.; industl. a. of Clay Cross and Dronfield; p. (est. 1976) 92,500.

Derbyshire, South, l. gov. dist., Derbys., Eng.; a. S. of Derby and inc. Repton and Swadlingcote; p. (est. 1976) 63,200.

Derg, Lough, in basin of R. Shannon, R.o.I.; separating Galway and Clare from Tipperary.

Derg, L., Donegal, R.o.I., with cave on I. visited by R.C. pilgrims and known as " St Patrick's Purgatory ".

Derwent, lgst R., Tasmania, Australia; flows to Storm Bay; hydroelec. power; 48 km long.

Derwent, R., Derbys., Eng.; trib. of R. Trent; length 96 km.

Derwent, R., North Yorks./Humberside, Eng.; trib. of R. Ouse; length 91 km.

Derwentside, l. gov. dist., Durham, Eng.; inc. Consett Stanley and surrounding a.; p. (est. 1976) 90,400.

Derwentwater, L., Cumbria, Eng.; 5 km long.

Desaguadero, R., Bolivia; outlet of L. Titicaca; used for irrigation; 320 km long.

Desborough, t., Northants., Eng.; boot and shoe mnfs., iron mng.; p. (1971) 5,294.

Des Moines, c., cap. of Iowa st., USA; in heart of corn belt; transport and industl. ctr.; univ.; p. (1970) 198,427 (c.) 281,478 (met. a.).

Des Moines, R., Iowa, USA; trib. of Mississippi rising in Minn.; 880 km long.

Desna, R., main trib. of Dnieper R., USSR; navigable below Bryansk; 1,184 km long.

Des Plaines, t., Ill., USA; sub. of Chicago on Des Plaines; R. p. (1970) 57,239.

Dessau, t., Halle, E. Germany; at confluence of Mulde and Elbe Rs.; cas.; machin., rly. carriages, paper, sugar, chemicals; route ctr.; p. (est. 1970) 98,261.

Detmold, t., N. Rhine–Westphalia, W. Germany; cas.; paints, wood inds.; p. (est. 1969) 28,347.

Detroit, ch. c., pt., Mich., USA; busy comm. and industl. ctr.; univ.; gr. grain mart; and ctr. of the " Ford " motor-car wks., aeroplanes, military tanks, synthetic diamonds, pharmaceutics, tools, chemicals, steel; lgst exporting t. on Great Lakes; 850 murders per year; p. (1970) 1,492,914 (c.), 4,163,517 (met. a.).

Detroit, R., channel between L. St. Clair and L. Eric (40 km) separates st. of Mich., USA, from Ontario, Canada; carries more shipping than any other inland waterway in the world.

Deurne, t., Belgium; nr. Antwerp, airport; p. (1968) 77,159.

Deux Sèvres, dep., Poitou-Charentes, France; mainly agr.; vineyards; cap. Niort; a. 6,053 km²; p. (1968) 326,462.

Deventer, t., Overijssel, Neth.; on IJssel R.; industl. ctr., Hanse t. in Middle Ages; p. (1968) 62,777.

Devil's Island (I. du Diable), I., Atl. Oc. off Fr. Guiana; former penal settlement where Dreyfus was confined in 1894.

Devils Tower, N.E. Wyo., USA; tower rock of volcanic origin with fluted columns of igneous rock; alt. 264 m.

Devizes, Kennet, Wilts., Eng.; mkt. t., on Kennet and Avon canal at foot of Marlborough Downs; bricks, tiles, bacon-curing; p. (1971) 10,170.

Devonport, spt., Tasmania, Australia; 131 km from Launceston; agr. dist.; canning, foundry inds.; p. (1952) 18,150

Devonport. See Plymouth.

Devonport, bor., Auckland, N.Z.; naval base and dockyard; sub. of Auckland; p. (1971) 10,925.

Devon, non-met. co., S.W. Eng.; between English and Bristol Channels; attractive cstl. scenery, Nat. Parks of Dartmoor and Exmoor encourage tourism; mixed farming; modern lt. inds.; major ctrs. of p. at Plymouth, Torbay, Exeter; a. 6,713 km²; p. (1971) 896,000.

Devon, East, l. gov. dist., Devon, Eng.; Exmouth, Sidmouth and Seaton on cst. and inland to Honiton and Ottery St. Mary; p. (est. 1976) 104,000.

Devon, North, l. gov. dist., Eng.; inc. Exmoor and ts. of Barnstaple, Ilfracombe and Lynton; p. (est. 1976) 72,700.

Dewsbury, t., West Yorks., Eng.; on R. Calder, 13 km from Leeds; heavy woollens, shoddy, coalmng.; dyewks.; p. (1971) 51,310.

Dez Dam, over Dez R., Khurzistan prov., Iran; opened 1963.   [(1966) 105,381.

Dezfûl, t., Iran; mkt. ctr.; oil fields nearby; p.

Dhahran, spt., Saudi-Arabia; main oil pt. of S.A.; airpt.; College of Petroleum and Minerals; p. 12,001.

Dhanbad, t., Bihar, India; lead, zinc, tools, radio assembly, fertilisers; p. (1971) 79,838 (t.), 434,031 (met. a.).

Dhanushkodi, t., Tamil Nadu, India; on I. in Palk Strait; ferry pt. for passenger traffic from India to Sri Lanka.

Dhar, t., Madhya Pradesh, India; cultural and tr. ctr.; p. (1961) 28,325.

Dharmsala, hill sta., Himachal Pradesh, India; 160 km N.E. of Amritsar; sanatorium; c. 1,800 m; imposing mtn. scenery; p. (1961) 10,255.

Dharwar, t., Karnataka, India; 112 km E. of Goa; univ.; cotton mnf.; p. (1961) 77,163.

Dhaulagiri, mtn. peak, 8,172 m, Nepal, 4 summits in Himalayas.

Dhekélia, Cyprus; Brit. sovereign a. within Rep.; p. (1960) 3,602.

Dhufar, fertile prov., Oman, Arabia; sugar-cane, cattle; ch. t. Salālah; ch. pt. Mirbat.

Dhulia, t., Khandesh dist., Maharashtra, India; cotton ind.; rly. ctr.; p. (1971) 137,129.

Diamante, R., Mendoza prov., Argentina; rises in Andes. flows E. to R. Salado; irrigates oasis of San Rafael; 320 km long.

Diamantina, t., Minas Gerais, Brazil; former diamond mng. ctr.; p. (est. 1968) 34,267.

Dibrugarh, t., Assam, India; former terminus of rail communications from Calcutta; since 1965 Indo-Pakistan war river communications disrupted; p. (1961) 58,480.

Didcot, sm. t., Oxon., Eng.; 16 km S. of Oxford; ordnance depots.

Diego Garcia, I., Brit. Indian Oc. Terr.; Anglo-

American naval communications ctr.; c. 1,000 islanders evacuated to Mauritius 1966–71; major US military staging base projected 1975.

Diego Suarez, t., extreme N. of Malagasy Rep.; oxygen plant; Fr. naval base; p. (1965) 38,484.

Dieppe, pt., Seine-Maritime, France; 56 km N. of Rouen; fisheries, shipbldg., machin.; cross-Channel ferry; p. (1968) 30,404.

Differdange, t., S.W. Luxembourg; iron ore; cattle; p. (est. 1970) 17,963.

Digboi, N.E. Assam, India; oil fields and refinery; p. (1961) 35,028.

Digne, t., cap. of Alpes-de-Haute-Provence, France; nr. Aix; cath.; p. (1968) 14,661.

Dijon, c., cap. Cote-d'Or, E. France; the Roman Divonense castrum; route ctr.; Seine-Saône watershed; wine tr.; industl. ctr.; univ., cath.; p. (1968) 145,357 (c.), 183,989 (met. a.).

Dili, t., cap. of E. Timor, Indonesia; major spt.; exp. cotton, copra, coffee; p. (1970) 29,312.

Dillingen, t., Bavaria, W. Germany; on R. Danube, heavy inds.; p. (est. 1967) 11,600.

Dimitrovgrad, t., Bulgaria; founded 1947; fertilisers, chemicals, superphosphate plant, iron, thermo-electric sta.; p. (est. 1968) 44,302.

Dimitrovo. See Pernik.

Dinajpur, t., Bangladesh; comm. ctr.; univ.; p. (1961) 37,711.

Dinan, t., Brittany, France; mediaeval t. above Rance R.; hosiery, brewing; holiday resort; p. (1968) 9,901.

Dinant, t., Namur, Belgium; on R. Meuse; mkt. t., tourist resort; exported copperware (dinanderie) in Middle Ages; cath., citadel (1040); p. (1968) 9,901.

Dinard, t., Brittany, France; resort, especially for English; p. (1968) 9,162.

Dinaric Alps, mtn. range, Yugoslavia, Albania and Italy (Trieste); extend 640 km along Adriatic; hgst. peak Durmitor, 2,515 m.

Dindigul, t., Tamil Nadu, India; 40 km S. of Tiruchirapalli; cigars; p. (1971) 128,429.

Dinefwr, l. gov. dist., Dyfed, Wales; inland a. inc. Llandovery, Llandeilo, Ammanford and Cwmamman; p. (est. 1976) 35,800.

Dingle B., Kerry, R.o.I.; long inlet of sea on Atl. cst.

Dingwall, royal burgh, Ross and Cromarty, Scot.; at head of Cromarty F.; rly. junc.; cattle mkt., admin. ctr.; distilling, handloom weaving; p. (1971) 4,232.

Dinslaken, t., N. Rhine–Westphalia, W. Germany, N. of Duisburg; coal, steel, iron, footwear, timber; oil pipeline from Wesseling under construction; p. (est. 1969) 53,991.

Diomede Is., two barren granitic islets in Bering Strait between Alaska and Siberia; accepted bdy. between Soviet and US terr.

Diredawa, t., Ethiopia; 40 km N. of Harar; rly. wks.; mkt and comm. ctr.; p. (est. 1970) 60,925.

Dirk Hartog I., off Shark Bay, W. Australia.

Disko I., off W. cst. of Greenland in Baffin Bay; contains harbour of Godhavn, cap. N. Greenland; rendezvous for whalers; shrimp beds; a. 8,288 km².

Dismal Swamp, morass, S. Va. and N.C., USA; contains L. Drummond and extends 50–65 km S. from nr. Norfolk.

Diss, South Norfolk, Eng.; mkt. t. on R. Waveney, 45 km S.W. of Norwich; agr. implements; p. (1971) 4,477.

Distaghil, major peak, Gr. Karakoram, N. Kashmir, Pakistan; two summits connected by a ridge, max. alt. 7,890 m.

Distrito Federal, federal dist., Brazil; inc. cap. c. of Brasília; a. 5,815 km²; p. (1967) 142,000.

Ditchling Beacon, 10 km N. of Brighton, East Sussex, Eng.; hgst point of South Downs, 248 m.

Diu, spt., I., off S. cst. of Bombay, India; oil nearby at Kayakov; p. (1960) 14,271.

Diwāniyah, Ad, t., Iraq; cap. D. prov.; on Baghdad–Basra rly.; p. (1965) 181,000 (met. a.).

Diyarbakir, c., cap. of D. prov., central Turkey; on Tigris R.; comm. and mnf. ctr.; flour and rice mills; the anc. Amida, old walls, gates, citadel; p. (1965) 102,653 (c.), 163,691 (met. a.).

Djajapura (Sukarnapura), t., cap. of Irian Jaya, Indonesia; on Humboldt B., an inlet of Pac. Oc.

Djakarta (Batavia), c., cap. of Indonesia, N.W. Java; comm. ctr.; textiles; exps. rubber, tea; printing; airport; p. (1971) 4,576,009.

Djambi, dist., and t., Sumatra, Indonesia; on E.

cst. plain 160 km N.W. of Palembang; univ.; field; a. (dist.) 44,924 km²; p. (1971) 158,559 (t.).

Djerba, t. and I., Tunisia, at S. entrance to G. of Gabès, joined to mainland by causeway; olives, dates, textiles, pottery; a. 510 km²; p. (1966) 62,445.

Djibouti, c., cap. of Djibouti; rly. terminus; main pt. and transit ctr.; p. (est. 1970) 62,000 (met. a.).

Djibouti, Rep. of, indep. st. (1977) N.E. Africa; former French Somaliland, renamed Fr. Terr. of Afars and Issas 1967; extends inland from straits of Bab-el-Mandeb; plain, mainly below 180 m.; hot, dry climate; shark and mother-of-pearl fisheries; little cultivable land; cap. Djibouti; a. 23,051 km²; p. (est. 1967) 126,000.

Dneprodzerzhinsk, t., Ukrainian SSR, USSR; W. of Dnepropetrovsk on Dnieper R.; iron and steel, engin., chemicals; hydroelec. sta. nearby; p. (1970) 227,000 (c.), 239,000 (met. a.).

Dneproges (abbrev. Dnieper hydroelectric sta.), Ukrainian SSR, USSR; nr. Zaporoz'ye, on Dnieper; lgst dam and power sta. in Europe; destroyed by Germans, rebuilt 1944-9.

Dnepropetrovsk, c., Ukrainian SSR, USSR; on R. Dnieper; univ.; impt. rly. and industl. ctr., using iron ore (from Krivoy Rog), coal (Donbas), manganese (Nikopol) and electric power from Dnieper dam; heavy machin., chemicals; p. (1970) 863,000 (c.), 918,000 (met. a.).

Dneprorudnyy, t., Ukrainian SSR, USSR; new t. on S. shore of Kakhvota reservoir; p. (1964) 6,000.

Dneprostroy. See Zaporoz'ye.

Dnieper (Dnepr), gr. R. of Ukrainian SSR, USSR; 3rd longest R. of Europe; rises in Valdai hills, flows into Black Sea, 2,240 km long; connected by canals to Baltic; tribs. inc. Berezina, Pripet, Desna, Orel, Samara; since erection of Dneproges dam navigable for almost entire length.

Dniester (Dnestr), R., Ukraine SSR, USSR; rises in Carpathians and flows into the Black Sea; 1,403 km long.

Döbeln, t., Leipzig, E. Germany; machin., metallurgy, wood, cigar and sugar inds.; p. (est. 1970) 27,754.

Dobrich. See Tolbukhin.

Dobruja, historic region, S.E. Europe; along Black Sea cst., S.E. Romania, and N.E. Bulgaria; mainly agr.; ch. pt. Constanta.

Dobšiná, t., ČSSR; cave containing ice-field of 0·8 ha; asbestos, iron ore; p. 5,300.

Dodecanese (S. Sporades), gr. of some 20 Greek Is. (originally 12) in S. Ægean Sea; most impt. are Rhodes, Cos, and Leros; Italian 1912-46; p. (1971) 120,258.

Dodoma, proposed new cap. of Tanzania; at geographical ctr. of T. in rural a.; transfer planned for 1983.

Dodworth, t., South Yorks., Eng.; nr. Barnsley; coal; p. (1971) 4,551.

Dogger Bank, sandbank in N. Sea, between England and Denmark; depth varies from 6 to 37 m; valuable fishing ground; action between British fleet under Beatty and German fleet under Hipper; Blücher sunk Jan. 1915.

Dogs, I. of, riverside dist., formed by bend in the R. Thames off Greenwich, London, Eng.; Millwall and India docks, shipbldg. yards.

Doha, t., cap. of Qatar; spt. on E. of Qatar peninsula, Persian Gulf; internat. airpt., deep sea pt.; contains 80 per cent of p.; p. (est. 1970) 80,000.

Dokai Bay, inlet, N. Kyushu, Japan; landlocked bay on S. side of Shimonoseki straits; flanked by highly industl. zone inc. Yawata, Waka-matsu, Tobata cs.; requires constant dredging; length 6 km, width 0·8-2·4 km.

Dôle, t., Jura, E. France; on R. Doubs, nr. Dijon; industl. ctr.; anc. cap. of Franche-Comté, ceded to France in 1678; birthplace of Pasteur; p. (1968) 28,774.

Dolgarrog, sm. t., Meirionnydd, Gwynedd, Wales; site of hydroelectric sta.

Dolgellau, t., Gwynedd, N. Wales; agr. quarrying, timber; p. (1971) 2,564.

Dollar, burgh, Clackmannan, Scot.; at foot of Ochil hills; p. (1971) 2,280.

Dollar Law, mtn., nr. Peebles, Scot.; alt. 817 m.

Dolomites, gr. of limestone mtns., S. Tyrolese Alps, N.E. Italy; tourist dist.; peaks assume fantastic forms; principal peak Marmolada 3,355 m.

Dominica, W.I., most N. of Windward Is.; 25 per cent under cultivation; volcanic soils highly suitable for bananas; N.-S. mtn. range has spectacular volcanic scenery; cap. Roseau; Ass. St. within Brit. Commonwealth (1967); a. 751 km²; p. (1968) 70,177.

Dominican Rep., rep., W.I., shares I. of Hispaniola with Haiti; comprises Nat. Dist. (inc. cap. Santo Domingo) and 25 admin. provs.; mtnous. with sub-tropical climate; in path of tropical cyclones; comm. economy mainly agr.; transport system geared to exp. of sugar; govt. investment in agr. and mng.; oil refining at Nigua; exp. bauxite; tourism growing; official language Spanish; a. 48,430 km²; p. (est. 1974) 4,900,000.

Domodossola, frontier t., Piedmont, N. Italy; nr. Alpine tourist resort in Toce valley, nr. Simplon.

Don, R. South Yorks., Eng.; trib. of R. Ouse, 112 km long.

Don, R., Gordon, Scot.; flows into N. Sea nr. Aberdeen; salmon; 131 km long.

Don, major R. of southern RSFSR; falls into Sea of Azov below Rostov, its ch. pt.; navigable to Voronezh; ch. trib., Donets; access to Volga by Don-Volga canal; fisheries; 1,955 km long.

Donaghadee, t., Ards, N. Ireland; nearest point to Scot.; spt. and seaside resort; p. (1966) 3,649.

Donauwörth, t., W. Bavaria, W. Germany; bridge t. on N. bank of Danube at Wörnitz confluence; p. (est. 1968) 11,130.

Donbas, industl. region, Ukrainian SSR, USSR; in valleys of Rs. Donets and lower Dnieper; about 23,300 km²; produces 60 per cent of Russia's coal; adjoins Krivoy Rog ironfields; many lge. industl. ts.

Doncaster, t., met. dist., South Yorks., Eng.; on Don R., 27 km N.E. of Sheffield; coal mines, tractors, nylon mftg.; racecourse; p. (est. 1976) 286,500 (dist.).

Donegal, spt., Co. Donegal, R.o.I.; on W. cst. on Donegal Bay; homespun tweeds, carpets; p. (1966) 1,507.

Donegal (Tirconnail), co., N.W. R.o.I.; fishing poor agr.; cloth, hydroelectric power; co. t. Lifford; a. 4,830 km²; p. (1966) 108,486.

Donets, R., rises in uplands of central RSFSR, N.E. of Belgorod, flows S.E. to join R. Don; crosses Donets coalfield; length 1,040 km. See Donbas.

Donetsk (Stalino), t., Ukrainian SSR, USSR; industl. ctr. of Donets coal basin; iron, steel, engin., chemicals; p. (1970) 879,000 (c.), 890,000 (met. a.).

Donges, t., Loire Atlantique, France; nr. St. Nazaire; oil refinery; synthetic textiles, plastics.; p. (1968) 6,458.

Dongola (Dunqulah), t., Sudan; on left bank of Nile above Third Cataract; Old D. was 120 km to S.; p. (est. 1965) 4,970.

Donner Pass, E. Cal., USA; highway pass through Sierra Nevada at 2,176 m.

Donzère-Mondragon, Vaucluse, France; site of Rhône barrage supplying hydroelectric power.

Dora Baltea, R., N. Italy; rises in Mt. Blanc, flows E. and S. through Val d'Aosta to R. Po at Chivasso; impt. routeway from N. Italy to Switzerland (through Gr. St. Bernard Pass) and France (through Little St. Bernard Pass); 152 km long.

Dorchester, co. t., West Dorset, Eng.; mkt. t. on R. Frome; lime, agr., engin.; Roman remains; nearby prehistoric Maiden Castle; linked with the name of Thomas Hardy; p. (1971) 13,737.

Dordogne, dep., S.W. France; cap. Périgueux; crossed by Dordogne R.; fertile valleys; p. (1968) 374,073.

Dordogne, R., S.W. France; rises in Central Massif, joins Garonne to form Gironde; vineyards; upper reaches used for hydroelectric power.

Dordrecht, c., nr. Rotterdam, Neth., on R. Merwede; timber, shipbldg., seaplanes; p. (1968) 88,461.

Dorking, t., Mole Valley, Surrey, Eng.; on R. Mole to S. of gap through N. Downs; mkt., residtl.; lt. inds.; p. (1971) 22,354.

Dornbirn, t., Vorarlberg, Austria; textiles; p. (est. 1966) 32,200.

Dornoch, burgh, Sutherland, Scot.; N. of Dornoch F.; resort; p. (1971) 838.

Dorset, non-met. co., S. Eng.; borders Eng. Channel along attractive cliffed cst. formed by E.-W. limestone ridges; Portland stone quarried; many tourist resorts inc. Bournemouth; mkt. ts. serve agr. interior; a. 2,655 km²; p. (est. 1976) 575,800.

Dorset Heights hills, extend E. to W. across central Dorset, Eng.; chalk; pastoral farming, sheep; some cultivation where soil is deep enough; rise to 250-275 m.

Dorset, North, l. gov. dist., Dorset, Eng.; mainly rural but inc. ts. of Shaftesbury, Sturminster Newton and Blandford Forum; p. (est. 1976) 47,400.

Dorsten, t., N. Rhine-Westphalia, W. Germany; on R. Lippe; coal, iron, elec., chemical inds.; p. (1969) 39,354.

Dortmund, c., N. Rhine-Westphalia, W. Germany; on Dortmund-Ems Canal; industl. ctr. and pt. of Ruhr; coal, iron, steel, machin.; p. (est. 1969) 647,000.

Dortmund-Ems Canal, N. Rhine-Westphalia, W. Germany; links Dortmund on Ruhr coalfield with R. Ems 8 km above Lingen; coal, iron-ore traffic; 144 km long.

Douai, t., Nord, France; nr. Lille on Scarpe R.; coal, iron and engin. wks.; bell founding, arsenal; p. (1968) 49,187 (t.), 205,432 (met. a.).

Douala, spt., Cameroon; rly. to Yaoundé; exp. hardwoods; p. (1970) 250,00 (met. a.).

Douarnenez, spt., Finistère, N.W. France; on D. Bay; sardine fisheries; p. (1968) 20,184.

Doubs, dep., E. France; traversed by Jura range and R. Doubs; mainly agr.; watchmkg., motor vehicles; cap. Besançon; a. 5,315 km²; p. (1968) 426,363.

Douglas, t., cap. of I. of Man; 120 km W. of Liverpool, Eng.; spt.; resort; p. (1966) 19,517.

Douglas Point, on shore of L. Huron, Ont., Canada; nuclear power sta. [reactors.

Dounreay, Caithness, Scot.; fast-breeder nuclear

Douro, R., Portugal and Spain; enters Atl. Oc. below Oporto; known as Duero R. in Spain; l. 776 km; famous port wine a.

Dove, R., Derbys. and Staffs., Eng.; trib. of Trent; flows through beautiful dales; 77 km long.

Dovedale, valley, Derbys., Eng.; steeply sloping limestone ravine of R. Dove; tourism.

Dover, packet pt., l. gov. dist., Kent, Eng.; one of old Cinque pts.; nearest spt. to France the Strait of D. being only 34 km wide; ch. pt. for passenger and mail traffic with Continent; cas.; p. (est. 1976) 101,000 (dist.).

Dovey, R., Wales, flows from Cambrian Mtns. and enters Cardigan Bay by a wide estuary.

Dowlais, dist., Merthyr Tydfil, Mid Glamorgan, S. Wales; coal mng., iron founding, engin.

Down, former co.; l. gov. dist., N. Ireland; borders Strangford Lough and Dundrum Bay; agr. and fisheries; p. of former co. (est. 1971) 310,617.

Downham Market, t., West Norfolk, Eng.; on R. Ouse; flour-milling, malting, sheet-metal wks.; p. (1971) 3,608.

Downpatrick, t., Down, N. Ireland; on R. Quoile; linen; p. (1966) 4,291.

Downs, natural harbour of refuge for shipping between Kent cst. and Goodwin Sands in the English Channel.

Drachenfels, mtn. peak on the Rhine, W. Germany; the steepest of the Siebengebirge range, nr. Königswinter; alt. 325 m; ascended by lt. rly.; famous cave of legendary dragon.

Draguignan, t., S.E. France; cap. of Var. dep. until 1974; mkt. t., service ctr.; p. (1968) 18,376.

Drakensberg, mtn. chain between Natal and Orange Free State, S. Africa, and Lesotho; extending 800 km from Gt. Fish R. to Olifants R.; hgst. peak Mont-aux-Sources 3,283 m; rly. crosses range by Van Reenen Pass.

Drama, pref. Macedonia, Greece; cap. Drama; a. 3,504 km²; p. (1971) 91,015.

Drammen, spt., Norway; nr. Oslo, on the Drammen R.; shipyard; exp. timber, wood-pulp, paper; p. (1968) 47,827.

Drancy, t., Seine-St. Denis, France; N.E. sub. of Paris; p. (1968) 69,528.

Drava (Drau), R., trib. of Danube, Austria and Yugoslavia; flows from the Tyrol across Carinthia and Styria, joining Danube nr. Osijek; length 720 km; used for hydroelec. power.

Drenthe, prov., Neth.; on German frontier; cap. Assen; a. 2,663 km²; p. (1968) 354,124.

Dresden, c., E. Germany; R. pt. on Elbe, 80 km E. of Leipzig; impt. route ctr.; engin., chemicals, optical and photographic apparatus, porcelain, glass, brewing; fine art collections; scientific research; oil pipeline from Schwedt under construction; p. (est. 1969) 500.726 (c.). 635,000 (met. a.).

Driffield, t., North Wolds, Humberside, Eng.; on Yorks. Wolds 21 km N. of Beverley; oil-cake wks.; p. (1971) 7,899.

Drin, R., N. Albania, rises in Yugoslavia and flows through deep gorges into Adriatic; hydroelec. power; 288 km long.

Drina, R., trib. of Sava R., Yugoslavia; ch. source of hydroelec. power in rep.; 480 km long.

Dröbak, spt., S.E. Norway; winter pt. for Oslo; summer resort.

Drogheda, spt., Louth, R.o.I.; considerable tr. in agr. produce, salmon, etc.; stormed by Cromwell in 1649; p. (1966) 17,823.

Drogobych, t., Ukranian SSR, USSR; 64 km S.W. of Lvov; ctr. of lge. oilfields, refineries; mftg.; p. (est. 1968) 56,000.

Droitwich, t., Wychavon, Hereford and Worcs., Eng.; brine baths; lt. inds.; expanded t.; p. (1971) 12,766.

Drôme, dep., S.E. France; traversed by Alps and watered by Rs. Rhône, Drôme, and Isère; cap. Valence; agr., forestry, sericulture, textile ind.; a. 6,560 km²; p. (1968) 342,891.

Dromore, mkt. t., Banbridge, N. Ireland; on Lagan R.; linen; p. (1966) 2,081.

Dronfield, t., North East Derbys., Eng.; between Chesterfield and Sheffield; edged tools, engin. and agr. implements; p. (1971) 17,826.

Droylsden, t., Gtr. Manchester, Eng.; sub. of Manchester; chemicals; textiles; p. (1971) 24,134.

Drumochter Pass, Grampian Mtns., Scot.; carries main Perth to Inverness rly. from Glen Garry into valley of R. Spey; highest alt. reached by any main rly. in Gt. Britain, 453 m.

Dschang, t., Cameroon; quinine processing; bauxite mng.

Dubai (Dubayy), emirate, one of United Arab Emirates, Arabian Gulf; recently developed as free pt. (modelled on Singapore), major comm. ctr. of a.; offshore oil with vast underwater storage tanks; international airpt.; deepwater pt. (Port Rashid) under construction; p. (est. 1970) 70,000.

Dublin. co., R.o.I.; co. t. Dublin; a. (inc. c. of Dublin) 922 km²; p. (1966) 795,047.

Dublin (Irish Baile Átha Cliath), C.B., cap. of R.o.I.; co. t. Co. Dublin; at mouth of R. Liffey; ctr. of govt., commerce, ind., and culture; cath., univ., Abbey Theatre; brewing, distilling, food processing; Swift was buried here; p. (1966) 568,271 (c.), 650,153 (met. a.).

Dubrovnik (Ital. Ragusa), t., Yugoslavia; impt. pt. on Adriatic; retains much of its mediæval architecture; tourism; airport; p. (est. 1965) 26,000.

Dubuque, t., Iowa, USA; pt. on Mississippi R.; varied inds. inc. meat-packing; p. (1970) 62,309.

Dudinka, Arctic spt. on R. Yenisey, RSFSR; nickel.

Dudley, t., met. dist., West Midlands, Eng.; cas.; engin.; cables, chains; p. (est. 1976) 148,900 (dist.).

Duisburg, c., N. Rhine-Westphalia, W. Germany; R. pt. on E. bank of Rhine at confluence with R. Ruhr. 16 km N. of Düsseldorf; iron and steel inds., machin., textiles, chemicals, pt. inds., route and R. tr. ctr.; p. (est. 1969) 460,500.

Dukeries, dist., Sherwood Forest, Notts., Eng.; so called from ducal mansions in dist.; tourism.

Dukinfield, t., Tameside, Gtr. Manchester, Eng.; 10 km S.E. of Manchester; textiles, engin., rope and twine; p. (1971) 17,294.

Dukla Pass, anc. and easy route across Carpathians, linking Poland, Hungary and Slovakia, 497 m a.s.l.

Duluth, pt., Minn., USA; at W. end of L. Superior; gr. tr. in grain, timber and iron ore; natural gas pipeline into the Mesabi Iron Range; p. (1970) 99,761 (c.), 261,963 (met. a.).

Dulwich, residtl. sub. in bor. of Southwark, Greater London, Eng.; village character with lge. park and public school.

Dumbarton, royal burgh, l. gov. dist., Strathclyde Reg., Scot.; on N. bank of R. Clyde, 19 km below Glasgow; shipbldg., valve and tube-mkg., iron and brassware; p. (1971) 25,640.

Dum-Dum, t., W. Bengal, India; ammunition; impt. airpt.; p. (est. 1970) 195,693.

Dumfries, royal burgh, Nithsdale Scot.; on R. Nith, 16 km from Solway F.; p. (1971) 29,382.

Dumfries and Galloway Region, l. gov. reg., Scot.; occupies W. half of Southern Uplands; drained by S. flowing rivers to Solway F.; sparse rural p.; a. 6,369 km²; p. (1971) 143,295.

Dumfriesshire, former co., Scot.; now part of Dumfries and Galloway Reg.

Dunaujváros, t., Hungary; new t. built from v. of Dunapentele; iron and steel wks.; paper inds., engin.; p. (1966) 43,400.

Dunbar, royal burgh, E. Lothian. Scot.; sm. fishing pt.; Cromwell's victory 1650; p. (1971) 4,611.

Dunbartonshire, former co., Scot.; now part of Strathclyde Reg.

Dunblane, mkt. burgh, Stirling, Scot.; on Allan Water, 8 km from Stirling; Gothic cath. now used as par. church; p. (1971) 4,497.

Dundalk, U.D., cap. of Co. Louth, R.o.I.; harbour, rly. ctr.; engin., footwear, tobacco, brewing; p. (1966) 19,834.

Dundee, c., spt., royal burgh, l. gov. dist., Tayside Reg., Scot.; on F. of Tay, 80 km N. Edinburgh; jute mnf., shipbldg., engin., computers, refrigerators, clocks, watches, preserves, linoleum; univ.; p. (1971) 182,204.

Dunedin, c., Otago, S.I., N.Z.; univ.; wool and dairy produce; named after the old name of Edinburgh; p. (1971) 82,289 (c.); (est. 1970) 110,100 (met. a.).

Dunfermline, royal burgh, l. gov. dist., Fife Reg., Scot.; 22 km E. of Alloa; linen, rubber gds., synthetic fibre; birthplace of Charles I and Andrew Carnegie; cap. of Scot. 1057-93; p. (1971) 49,897.

Dungannon, mkt. t., l. gov dist., N.Ireland; linen, bricks; p. (1966) 7,335.

Dungarvan, U.D., Co. Waterford, R.o.I.; spt., mkt. t.; leather processing; p. (1966) 5,376.

Dungeness, headland of shingle, Kent, Eng.; 16 km S.E. of Rye; civil nuclear power stas.; linked by power cable to France 1961.

Dunkeld, t., Perth and Kinross, Scot.; on R. Tay at entrance to Strathmore; cath.; tourist resort.

Dunkirk, spt., Nord dep., France; strong fort; gd. harbour and tr.; fisheries, shipbldg., oil refining; steel mill; scene of evacuation of B.E.F. 1940; p. (1968) 28,082 (t.), 143,425 (met. a.).

Dun Laoghaire (Kingstown), C.B., Dublin, R o.I.; spt., mail packet sta., fishing; ferry to Eng.; p. (1966) 55,885.

Dunmanway, t., Cork, R.o.I.; on R. Brandon; tweeds, blankets.

Dunmow, Great, mkt. t., Uttlesford, Essex, Eng.; on R. Chelmer; 16 km N.W. of Chelmsford; p. (1971) 23,600 (dist.).

Dunmow, Little, v., 3 km E. of Great Dunmow; Uttlesford, Essex, Eng.; historic Dunmow Flitch (side of bacon).

Dunoon, burgh, Argyll and Bute, Scot.; on N. side of F. of Clyde. anc. cas.; holiday resort; p. (1971) 9,718.

Duns, burgh, Berwick, Scot.; agr. and allied inds.; mkt. t.; cas.; p. (1971) 1,768.

Dunsinane, hill, Sidlaws, Scot.; nr. Perth; alt. 309 m; referred to by Shakespeare in Macbeth.

Dunstable, t., South Beds., Eng.; on N. edge of Chiltern Hills 6 km W. of Luton; motor vehicles, engin., cement, rubber, and plastic gds.; p. (1971) 31,790.

Duque de Caxia, t., Brazil; oil refining; pipeline to Volta Redonda; p. (1970) 256,582.

Durance, R., S.E. France; trib. of Rhône; rapid current, 347 km long; provides irrigation and hydroelec. power.

Durango, c., cap. of D. st., Mexico; cath.; silver, gold, copper, iron-ore; p. (1970) 150,541.

Durango, st., N.W. Mexico; ming., agr., cotton, wheat; a. 109,484 km²; p. (1969) 959,000.

Durant, t., S. Okla., USA; cotton gins and compresses, cottonseed oil; p. (1970) 11,118.

Durban, c., S. Africa; on Durban Bay; ch. comm. c. of Natal; exp. coal, manganese, wool, hides; oil and sugar refining, chemicals, textiles, engin.; oil pipeline to Johannesburg; univ.; main pt. and seaside resort; p. (1970) 721,265 (met. a.).

Düren, t., N. Rhine-Westphalia, W. Germany; on R. Rur 37 km S.W. of Cologne; rly. ctr.; iron and steel wks., vehicles; p. (est. 1969) 54,745.

Durgapur, t., W. Bengal, India; site of barrage on Damodar R.; p. (1971) 206,638.

Durham, c., co. t., l. gov. dist., Durham, N.E. Eng.; sited within a meander of R. Wear; cath., cas., univ.; carpets, organ mftg., confectionery; p. (est. 1976) 88,800 (dist.).

Durham, non-met. co., N.E. Eng.; between Rs. Tyne and Tees; stretches from attractive Pennine moorland in W. to coalfield and industl. a. with many sm. ts. in E.; borders the N. Sea; a. 2,437 km²; p. (est. 1976) 610,400.

Durham, t., N.C., USA; tobacco ind., textiles; univ.; p. (1970) 93,935 (t.), 188,786 (met. a.).

Durrës (Durazzo), ch. spt., Albania; on Adriatic; pt. for Tirana; tobacco ind., plastics; tourism; p. (1967) 53,000.

Dursley, t., Gloucs., Eng.; 21 km S.W. of Gloucester; engin., agr. machin.; 18th cent. mkt. house; p. (1971) 21,149 (dist.).

Dushanbe, c., cap. of Tadzhik SSR, USSR; univ., industl. and agr. ctr.; rly. junc.; earlier called Stalinabad; p. (1970) 374,000.

Düsseldorf, c., cap. of N. Rhine-Westphalia, W. Germany; on R. Rhine, 32 km N. of Cologne; admin. and cultural ctr., art and medical academies; iron, steel, machin., soap, cars, paper, chemical inds.; impt. trans-shipment pt.; p. (est. 1969) 683,000.

Dust Bowl, region, USA; name applied to great plains on E. flank of Rocky Mtns.; subject to severe soil erosion by wind, particularly in drought years (1933, 1936) due to destruction of natural vegetation by over-grazing or by excessive ploughing.

Dutch Harbour, t., Unalaska I., Aleutian gr., N. Pac. Oc.; strategic American naval base.

Dvina or Northern Dvina, R., RSFSR; flows to White Sea at Arkhangelsk, formed by the junction of Rs. Sukhona and Vychegda at Kotlas; connected by canal with Neva and Volga; used for timber transport; 744 km long.

Dvina or Western Dvina, R., Latvian SSR, RSFSR, USSR; rises in Valdai Hills nr. sources of Volga and Dnieper, flows through Latvia to G. of Riga; connected by canal to Berezina and Dnieper; c. 1,016 km long.

Dwyfor, l. gov. dist., Gwynedd, Wales; Lleyn penin. and ts. of Pwhelli, Criccieth and Porthmadog; p. (est. 1976) 25,800.

Dyfed, co., S.W. Wales; inc. former cos. of Cardiganshire, Carmarthenshire and Pembroke; upland a. crossed by valleys of Teifi and Towy Rs.; stock rearing and fattening; tourism impt. around cst.; industl. in S.E.; a. 5,765 km²; p. (est. 1976) 323,100.

Dzaudzhikau. See Orazhonikidze.

Dzerzhinsk, c., RSFSR; R. pt. on Oka; chemicals (fertilisers, explosives); p. (1970) 221,000 (c.), 273,000 (met. a.).

Dzhalil, t., RSFSR; new t. 48 km N.E. of Almetyevsk to serve new oilfield there.

Dzhambul, c., Kazakh SSR, USSR; on Talas R. and on Turk-Sib rly.; chemicals, food-processing; p. (1970) 188,000.

Dzhezkazgan, t., Kazakh SSR, USSR; 560 km W. of L. Balkhash; copper-mines; manganese ore nearby; p. (est. 1967) 58,000.

Dzierzoniow (Reichenbach), t., Wroclaw, S.W. Poland; mnf. ctr.; textiles, machin., elec. equipment; formerly in Germany; p. (1970) 32,900.

Dzungaria, inland basin, Sinkiang prov., N.W. China; lies between Tien-Shan highlands of Soviet-Chinese frontier and Altai mtns.; former historic kingdom of Zungaria.

E

Ealing, outer bor., Greater London, Eng.; comprising former bors. of Acton, Ealing, and Southall; p. (est. 1976) 293,800.

Earl's Court, residtl. a., London, Eng.; Bor. of Kensington and Chelsea, contains E.C. exhibition hall.

Earn R., Perth, and Kinross, Scot.; issues from Loch Earn (10 km long) and flows into Tay R.; 74 km long.

Easington, l. gov. dist., Durham, Eng.; colly. v.; now part of Peterlee new t.; p. (est. 1976) 105,800 (dist.).

Easington, v., Humberside Eng.; nr. Hull; natural gas terminal.

East Anglia, comprises Norfolk and Suffolk, Eng.; former Anglo-Saxon kingdom; one of Britain's most productive agr. regions.

East Anglian Heights, hills, extend S.W. to N.E. across N.E. Hertfordshire, N. Essex, and S.W. Suffolk, Eng.; chalk overlain by glacial clays and sands; smooth, rolling surface; region of lge. farms and lge. fields, mixed farms mainly grain; rarely exceed 180 m.

East Bergholt, v., Suffolk, Eng.; birthplace of Constable.

Eastbourne, t., l. gov. dist., East Sussex, Eng.; on S. cst. to E. of Beachy Head; seaside resort; p. (est. 1976) 73,200 (dist.).

East Cape, extreme N.E. point of Asia; on Chukchi peninsula, RSFSR; Russian name Cape Dezhnova.

East Cape, extreme E. point of N.Z., named by Cook on his first voyage in 1769.

East Chicago, t., Ind., USA; L. Michigan; iron and steel wks., oil refining; p. (1970) 46,982.

East Cleveland, t., Ohio, USA; residtl.; p. (1970) 34,600.

East Dereham, t., Breckland, Norfolk, Eng.; 22 km W. of Norwich; agr. implements; p. (1971) 9 391.

Easter Island, S. Pac. Oc., 3,760 km W. of Chile; various theories to explain origin of gigantic statues; p. c. 850.

East Grinstead, t. West Sussex, Eng.; in ctr. of Weald, 14 km W. of Tunbridge Wells; agr. mkt.; famous hospital for plastic surgery; p. (1971) 18,569.

East Ham. See Newham.   [57,583.

East Hartford, t., Conn., USA; industl.; p. (1970

East Indies, name commonly applied to Is. between S.E. Asia and N. Australia, variously known as Malay archipelago, Malaysia, Indonesia.

East Kilbride, t., l. gov. dist., Strathclyde Reg., Scot.; 11 km S.S.E. of Glasgow; new t. 1947; lge. agr. machin., aero engines, engin., elec. gds. seawater distillation plant; knitwear, clothing; p. (est. 1974) 71,500.

East Lansing, t., Mich., USA; residtl.; univ.; p. (1970) 47,540.

Eastleigh, t., l. gov. dist., Hants., Eng.; rly. engin., many new inds.; p. (est. 1976) 81,300 (dist.).

East London, spt. C. Prov., S. Africa; at mouth of Buffalo R.; holiday resort; trading ctr.; inds. inc. car assembly, textiles, engin.; titanium deposits nearby; p. (1970) 123,294 (met. a.).

East Lothian (Haddington), former co., l. gov. dist., Scot.; part of Lothian Reg.

East Main R., Quebec, Canada; flows into James Bay; 432 km long.

Easton, t., Penns., USA; on Delaware R.; rly. ctr., coal, steel, machin., furniture; p. (1970) 30,256.

East Orange, t., N.J., USA; residtl. sub. of New York; p. (1970) 75,471.

East Pakistan. See Bangladesh.

East Point, t., Ga., USA; textiles, fertilisers; p. (1970) 39,315.

East Providence, t., Rhode I., USA; textiles, machin.; p. (1970) 48,207.

East Retford, t., Bassetlaw, Notts., Eng.; on R. Idle, 10 km E. of Worksop; rubber, wire ropes, engin.; p. (1971) 18,402.

East Riding, Yorkshire. See Yorkshire.

East River, tidal strait about 26 km long and from 180–1,200 m wide; separates the bors. of Manhattan and Bronx from the bors. of Queens and Brooklyn, N.Y., USA.

East St. Louis, t., R. pt., Ill., USA; on Mississippi R.; lge stockyards, meat-packing, aluminium, chemicals; p. (1970) 69,996.

East Sussex, non-met. co., S.E. Eng.; mainly rural, urban growth on cst. where resorts, retirement and dormitory ts. for London, inc. Brighton, Hastings and Eastbourne; crossed

by S. Downs in S. terminating at Beachy Head, Ashdown Forest in N.; a. 1,795 km²; p. (est. 1976) 655,600.

East Timor, prov., Indonesia; Port. terr. until 1975; mtnous; underdeveloped; cap. Dili; a. 14,693 km²; p. (est. 1968) 559,563.

Eastwood, t., Broxtowe, Notts., Eng.; birthplace of D. H. Lawrence; coal; p. (1971) 10,864.

Eau Claire, t., Wis., USA; on Chippewa R.; agr. mkt.; univ. food processing, varied mnfs.; p. (1970) 44,619.

Ebal, Mt., Israel; opposite Gerizim; alt. 911 m.

Ebbw Vale, t., Blaenau Gwent, Gwent, Wales; 27 km N.W. of Newport; coal, iron, tinplate, bricks, pipes, precast concrete; some steel wks. to close; p. (1971) 26,049.

Eberswalde, t., Frankfurt, E. Germany; N.E. of Berlin; iron, wood, and cardboard wks., chemicals; p. (est. 1970) 46,090.

Ebro, ch. R. of N.E. Spain; flows to Mediterranean from Cantabrian Mtns.; feeds hydroelectric plants, irrigation, esp. around Zaragoza; 928 km long.

Eccles, Gtr. Manchester, Eng.; 6 km W. of Manchester; chemicals, oil refining. engin.; p. (1971) 38,413.

Echo L., Tasmania, Australia; used to store water for hydroelectric power.

Echuca, t., Victoria, Australia; on R. Murray; rly. ctr.; irrigation wks.; dairy prods., timber; p. (1972) 7,510.

Écija, t., Seville, Spain; olive oil, wine, pottery; the Roman Astigi; p. (1970) 36,506.

Eckernförde, spt., Schleswig-Holstein, W. Germany; on Baltic, N. W. of Kiel; p. (est. 1969) 21,925.

Ecrins, mtn. peak, S.E. France; hgst. point of massif du Pelvoux and Dauphiné Alps; alt. 4,106 m.

Ecuador, rep., S. America; on equatorial Pac. cst., bounded by Colombia to N. and Peru to W. and S.; inc. Galapagos Is. in Pac. Oc.; lowland to E. and W. of central Andes; climate temperate in Andes and hot and humid in lowlands; comm. economy mainly agr. with impt. exp. of bananas; petroleum increasingly impt.; pipeline across Andes to pt. of Esmeraldas; communications difficult but vital for economic development; major pts. Guayaquil and Manta; official language Spanish; cap. Quito; a. inc. Galápagos Is. 454,752 km²; p. (est. 1969) 5,973,300.

Edam, t., N. Holland, Neth.; on cst. IJsselmeer; cheese, tool mftg.; p. (1967) 16,558.

Eday, I., Orkney Is., Scot.; the Ocelli of Ptolemy; p. (1971) 179.

Eddystone, rock with lighthouse, Eng. Channel; S.W. of Plymouth.

Ede, t., Gelderland, Neth.; livestock; pianos; p. (1968) 68,772.

Edea, t., pt., Cameroon; aluminium smelting based on nearby hydroelectric power plant.

Eden, Vale of, fertile belt in Cumbria, Eng.; between barren hills of Pennines and L. Dist.; occupied by R. Eden; mkt. ts. Appleby and Penrith; now forms l. gov. dist. inc. Penrith, Alston and Appleby; p. (est. 1976) 42,100.

Eder R., W. Germany; joins Fulda R. S. of Kassel; Eder dam lgst. in Germany.

Edessa (Edhessa), t., N.E. Greece; agr. tr. ctr.; the anc. Ægæ, burial place of Macedonian kings; p. (1971) 16,521.

Edgehill, ridge, 24 km S. of Warwick, Eng.; scene of first battle of civil war, 1642.

Edgewater, t., N.J., USA; sub., connected by ferry with New York; sugar refining; p. (1970) 4,987

Edgware, N. sub. of London, Eng.; inc. in outer London bor. of Barnet.

Edinburgh, c., cap. of Scot., l. gov. dist., Lothian Reg.; royal burgh on F. of Forth; univ., cas.; palace (Holyrood); printing, publishing, brewing, electronics equipment, rubber gds.; Edinburgh Festival in August; Leith, with docks is joined to E.; p. (1971) 453,584.

Edirne, t., Turkey; in Thrace, on R. Maritsa; comm. ctr. with tr. in wine, tobacco, silk, perfume; the anc. Adrianople, named after the emperor Hadrian, later cap. of Ottoman sultans 1366–1453; p. (1965) 46,264.

Edmonton, c., cap. of Alberta, Canada; fast-growing c. (119 km²) on both sides of N. Saskatchewan R.; high-level bridge links

Strathcona; major military ctr.; univ.; international air ctr.; oilfields and farming; oil and chemical inds.; p. (1971) 490,811 (met. a.).

Edremit, t., Balikesir, N.W. Turkey; cereals, opium; silverwk.; p. (1965) 25,003.

Edward, L. *See* Idi Amin Dada.

Eger, t., N.E. Hungary; mkt. t. in wine producing region; mediaeval fortress t.; p. (1968) 44,000.

Egersund pt., S. cst. Norway; fishing; mentioned in Norwegian sagas; p. (est. 1970) 10,197.

Egham, t., Runnymede, Surrey, Eng.; on R. Thames, nr. Staines; contains field of Runnymede; residtl.; p. (1971) 30,510.   [2,501 m.

Egmont, mtn., N.I., N.Z.; extinct volcano; alt.

Egremont, mkt. t., Cumbria, Eng.; 16 km S. of Whitehaven; limestone; former iron ore mng.

Egypt, Arab Republic of, indep. st., N.E. corner Africa; member of Federation of Arab Reps.; 96 per cent a. is desert except Nile valley and delta where 95 per cent of p. live; agr. depends on annual rise of Nile waters and irrigation; cereals, sugar-cane, vegetables, fruit; cotton main cash crop; phosphates; oilfield in Israeli-occupied Sinai and recent finds offshore in G. of Suez and in Western Desert; cap. Cairo; ch. spts. Alexandria, Port Said, Suez; Aswan High Dam has produced problems; (1) silting up of reservoir (L. Nasser) behind dam; (2) reduction in fertilising silt deposits in lower Nile valley; (3) erosion of Nile delta itself; (4) reduction of fish p. in E. Med.; a. 999,740 km²; p. (1976) 38,228,180 (75 per cent illiterate).

Eider, R., W. Germany; separates Holstein from Schleswig; flows into N. Sea; 125 m. long.

Eifel, plateau of volcanic rocks, W. Germany; lies N. of R. Moselle, forming W. edge of Rhine gorge between Koblenz and Bonn; formerly cultivated, now largely woodland and moorland; farming in valleys; rises to just over 600 m.

Eiger, mtn., one of the hgst. peaks of the Bernese Oberland, Switzerland; famous for steep N. wall; alt. 3,978 m.

Eigg, I., Inner Hebrides, Scot.; 24 km S.W. of Mallaig; basaltic rocks on cst.; rises to 393 m.

Eilat, new spt., Negev, Israel; on G. of Aqaba; copper at Timna; oil pipeline from Ashdod (1970).

Eildon Hills, Roxburgh, Scot.; S. of Melrose; hgst. point 422 m.

Eindhoven, c., N. Brabant, Neth.; electronic equipment, motor vehicles, tobacco and textile inds.; technical univ.; p. (est. 1969) 187,930, 331,397 (met. a.).

Eire. *See* Ireland, Republic of.

Eisenach, t., Erfurt, E. Germany; on R. Hörsel, at foot of Thuringian forest; ctr. of Werra potash field; cars, machin., textiles; birthplace of J. S. Bach; p. (est. 1969) 50,777.

Eisenerz Alps, mtn. range, Austria; most N. range of Alps, overlooking Danube valley between Linz and Vienna; impt. iron-ore deposits; alt. from 1,800–2,700 m.

Eisenhüttenstadt, t., Frankfurt, E. Germany; iron smelting; terminus of Oder–Spree canal; p. (est. 1970) 45,194.

Eisleben, t., Halle, E. Germany; machin., copper- and silver-mng. ctr.; birthplace of Luther; p. (est. 1970) 30,386.

Ekibastuz, t., Kazakh SSR, USSR; 120 km S.W. of Pavlodar; ctr. of rapidly developing mng. a., coal, gold, metals; coal-fed generating plant projected to supply power to European Russia; p. (est. 1967) 40,000.

El Aaiun, pt., Western Sahara; main pt. for exp. of phosphates.

El Alamein, v., Egypt; in Libyan Desert 96 km S.W. of Alexandria, scene of Allied victory, second world war; oilfield nearby; terminal nr. Sidi Abd el-Rahman.

Elan, R. Powys, Wales; rises on S.E. sides of Plynlimon, flows into R. Wye; lower valley contains series of 4 lge reservoirs, capacity 45,460 million litres; ch. source of water for Birmingham.

Elâzig, t., E. Turkey; dam and hydroelec. project at Keban, 48 km to N.W. at confluence of E. and W. branches of Euphrates; p. (1965) 78,899.

Elba, I., off Tuscan cst., Italy; iron ore, wine, marble, salt; ch. t. Porto Ferrajo; Napoleon's first exile here; a. 363 km²; p. (1960) 26,000.

Elbe (Labe), R., in ČSSR and Germany; rises in Riesengebirge and flows into N. Sea at Cuxhaven; navigable for 840 km of total l. of 1,160 km; connected with Rhine and Weser Rs. by Mittelland canal; forms part of border between E. and W. Germany.

Elbert, mtn., Col., USA; hgst. peak of Rocky Mtns. in USA, 4,401 m.

Elblag or Elbing, spt., Gdansk, N. Poland; shipbldg., machin., vehicles; p. (1970) 89,800.

Elbruz Mt., Caucasus, Georgian SSR, USSR; hgst. in Europe (5,636 m), over-topping Mont Blanc by 822 m; twin volcanic peaks.

Elburz, mtn. range, N. Iran; bordering on Caspian Sea; hgst. peak, Demavend, 5,642 m.

Elche, t., Alicante, Spain; palm groves; oil, soap, footwear; p. (est. 1967) 101,028.

El Dar-el-Beida (Casablanca), c., Morocco; pt. on Atl. Oc.; artificial harbour; fish canning, textiles; exp. phosphate; p. (1971) 1,371,330 (c.), 1,561,280 (met. a.).

Eldorado, radium mine, N.W. Terr., Canada; on E. shore of Gr. Bear Lake nr. Arctic Circle; produces 40 per cent of world's radium, sent to Pt. Hope, Ontario, for refining.

El Dzejair. *See* Algiers.

Electrona, Tasmania, Australia; carbide wks. based on local limestone and hydroelec. power.

Elektrenai, t., Lithuanian SSR, USSR; new township nr. Vievis, at site of thermal power sta.

Elektrostal, t., RSFSR; 56 km E. of Moscow; steel.engin.; p. (1970) 123,000.

Elephanta I., Bombay Harbour, India; Brahmanic caves with monolithic carvings.

Elephant Butte Dam, N.M., USA; on Rio Grande; built to control flood water; lake, a. 155 km² supplies irrigation water to 2,020 km² in N.M. and Texas, water also supplied to Mexico.

El Ferrol del Caudillo, spt., Spain; on N.W. cst.; fortfd., fishing; p. (1967) 84,866.

Elgin, royal burgh, Moray, Scot.; pt. Lossiemouth; woollens, whisky; ruins anc. cath.; p. (1971) 16,407.

Elgin, t., Ill., USA; watches, electrical equipment; p. (1970) 55,691.

Elgon Mt., extinct volcano, bdy. of Kenya and Uganda; 4,300 m; cave dwellings on slopes.

Elie and Earlsferry, burgh, North East Fife, Scot.; summer resort; p. (1971) 895.

Elisabethville. *See* Lubumbashi.

Elizabeth, t., S. Australia; planned t. built 1944; residtl.; chemical wks.; p. (1971) 33,389.

Elizabeth, c., N.J., USA; univ.; sewing machines, oil refining, cars, aircraft components; now inc. in Newark; p. (1970) 112,654.

Elk I., Nat. Park, Canada; animal reserve, tourism.

El Khârga, oasis, Libyan desert, Egypt, 136 km S.W. of Asyût; site of New Valley Project for irrigation.

Elkhart, t., Ind., USA; E. of Chicago; paper, machin.; elec. equipment, musical instruments; p. (1970) 43,152.

Elk Mtns., W. Col., USA; highest point Castle Peak, 4,305 m.

Elland, t., West Yorks., Eng.; on R. Calder, 5 km S.E. of Halifax; textiles; p. (1971) 17,817.

Ellesmere, agr. dist., S.I., N.Z.; on Canterbury Plain nr. Christchurch.

Ellesmere, mkt. t., N. Salop, Eng.; nearby lake; tourism.

Ellesmere I., extreme N. of Arctic Canada; barren, uninhabited; a. 106,200 km².

Ellesmere Port, t., l. gov. dist., N.W. Cheshire, Eng.; on Manchester Ship Canal and 14 km S S.E. of Liverpool; metal mftg., paper, engin., oil refineries; cars; expanded t.; p. (est. 1976) 84,700 (dist.).

Elliot Lake, t., N. Ont., Canada; ctr. of uranium mines.

Ellice Is. *See* Tuvalu I.

Ellis I., N.Y. harbour, USA; served as ch. immigration ctr., 1892–1943.

Ellon, burgh, Gordon, Scot.; on R. Ythan; p. (1971) 8,505.

Elmbridge, l. gov. dist., Surrey, Eng.; close to Gtr. London; inc. Esher, Walton and Weybridge; p. (est. 1976) 112,300.

Elmira, t., N.Y., USA; rly. gds., farm implements; burial place of Mark Twain; p. (1970) 39,945.

El Misti, mtn., S. Peru; dormant volcano with snow cap; alt. 5,846 m.

Elmshorn, t., W. Germany; N.W. of Hamburg; shipbldg.; p. (est. 1969) 40,896.

El Paso, c., Texas, USA; on E. bank Rio Grande opposite Ciudad Juárez (Mexico); natural gas distribution, oil refining, metallurgy; tourism; p. (1968) 276,687 (c.), 351,400 (met. a.).

El Salvador. See Salvador.

El Segundo, t., Cal., USA; lge oil refinery; assembly of aircraft components.

El Sharana, t., N.T., Australia; mng. base for uranium; uranium processing.

Elsinore (Helsingör), t., spt., Denmark; shipbldg.; setting of Shakespeare's Hamlet; p. (1970) 3,530.

Elstow, v., Beds., Eng.; birthplace of Bunyan.

Elstree, t., Hertsmere, Herts., Eng.; 6 km W. of Barnet; residtl.; films, lt. engin., silk hosiery; p. (1971) 33,516 (dist.).

El Teniente, Andean t., central Chile; copper mng. and smelting; p. 11,761.

Eluru, t., Andhra Pradesh, India; cotton, carpets, hosiery, oil; p. (1971) 127,023.

Elvas, mkt. t., Portugal; on Guadiana R.; plums, olives, jams; cath.; once strongly fortfd.; p. (1970) 24,510.

Ely, t., Cambridge, Eng.; on S. fringe of Fens; mkt., cath.; agr. ctr.; p. (1971) 9,969.

Ely, I. of. See Cambridgeshire.

Elyria, t., Ohio, USA; mftg.; p. (1970) 53,427.

Emba, R., Kazakh SSR, USSR; rises in Urals, flows S.W. to Caspian Sea; crosses productive Ural–Emba oilfield; 608 km long.

Emden, t., Lower Saxony, W. Germany; impt. N. Sea pt. nr. mouth of R. Ems and on Dortmund–Ems and Ems–Jade canals; exp. coal and iron from Ruhr; shipyards, fisheries; p. (est. 1967) 47,300.

Emene, t., Nigeria; nr. Enugu; steel plant; cement.

Emilia-Romagna, region, N. Italy; S. of Po R.; divided into 8 provs.; fertile agr. a.; a 22,124 km²; p. (1969) 3,834,468.

Emmen, t., Drenthe, Neth.; 48 km S.E. of Groningen; elec. machin., ball bearings, tinplate, iron wks.; p. (1968) 76,599.

Emmental, dist., Switzerland; dairy produce, especially cheese.

Empoli, t., Tuscany, Italy; on R. Arno; textile mnfs., glass; p. (est. 1968) 42,768.

Ems, R., N. W. Germany; rises in Teutoburger Wald, flows N. to N. Sea at Emden; 333 km long.

Emscher, R., W. Germany; rises in Sauerland, flows W. through heart of Ruhr coalfield to enter R. Rhine at Hamborn; canalised for most of its course; highly polluted; 88 km long.

Encarnación, pt., cap. of Itapuá dep., S.E. Paraguay; on Paraná R.; exp. timber, maté, tobacco, cotton, hides; p. (est. 1970) 47,333.

Enderby Land, Australian terr., S. of C. of Good Hope, Antarctica.

Enfield, former M.B., Middlesex, Eng.; now outer bor. Greater London; comprising Edmonton, Enfield, and Southgate; p. (est. 1976) 260,900.

Enfield, t., Conn., USA; mftg.; p. (1970) 46,189.

Engadine, Switzerland; upper valley of Inn R.; health resort; ch. t. St. Moritz; Swiss Nat. Park.

Enggano, I., Sumatra, Indonesia; sparse primitive p.; hunting, fishing, shifting cultivation.

Engels, c., RSFSR; on Volga; R. pt., mitg. and food-processing ctr.; engin., petroleum refining, textiles; p. (1970) 130,000 (c.), 151,000 (met. a.).

England, southern and lgst political div. of U.K.; bounded by Wales on W., by Scot. on N. and separated from continent of Europe by English Channel and North Sea; highly industl., circa 80 per cent of p. live in urban areas; major trading nation through main pts. London, Liverpool, Southampton; increasing contrast between prosperous S. and depressed N. and W.; very varied geology and topography produce contrasts in landscape, matched by climatic variability; increasingly attractive as tourist area although urban and agr. pressures on rural countryside cause concern in such a densely populated cty.; excellent road and rail network improved by construction of motorways and rly. electrification between London and Glasgow (Scot.); rich and varied cultural heritage and historic bldgs.; developing welfare st.; cap London; a. 130,368 km²; p. (est. 1976) 46,417,600.

Englewood, t., Col., USA; sub. of Denver; glasshouses; p. (1970) 33,695.

Englewood, t., N.J., USA; elevators, leather gds.; p. (1970) 24,985.

English Channel (La Manche), narrow sea separating England from France; extends from Strait of Dover to Land's End in Cornwall; length 480 km, greatest width 248 km.

Enham-Alamein, Hants., Eng.; rehabilitation ctr. for disabled ex-service men; 4 km N. of Andover; lt. inds.

Enid, t., Okla., USA; univ.; ironwks., farm implements; wheat mkt.; p. (1970) 44,986.

Enkhuizen, t., R. spt., Neth.; on IJsselmeer; p. (1967) 11,231.

Enna (Castrogiovanni), t., Sicily, Italy; sulphurmines; famous for its connection with the Proserpine legend; p. (1969) 28,767.

Ennepetal, t., N. Rhine–Westphalia, W. Germany; t. created 1949 with merging of Milspe and Voerde; iron, machin.; p. (est. 1969) 36,922.

Ennerdale Water, L., Cumbria, Eng.

Enniscorthy, mkt. t., U.D., Wexford, R.o.I.; cath.; p. (1966) 5,762.

Enniskillen, t., Fermanagh, N. Ireland; brewing, nylon mftg., meat processing; p. (1966) 7,154.

Enschede, c., Overijssel, Neth.; textile ctr.; technical univ.; p. (est. 1969) 138,064 (c.), 228,228 (met. a.).

Ensenada, t., Mexico; spt., exp. cotton; fishing and fish processing; p. (1970) 113,320.

Entebbe, t., Uganda; on L. Victoria; univ.; cotton ginning; airport; p. (1969) 10,900.

Entre Rios, prov., Argentina; between Paraná and Uruguay Rs.; wheat, linseed, livestock; cap. Paraná; a. 76,216 km²; p. (1970) 811,691.

Enugu, cap. of E. prov., Nigeria; coal; cloth mill; p. (est. 1971) 167,339.

Epernay, t., on S. bank of Marne, France; champagne ctr.; p. (1968) 27,767.

Ephesus, anc. Ionian c., in what is now Turkey, S. of Izmir; sacked by Goths A.D. 262; excavations.

Epinal, t., cap. of Vosges dep., France; on Moselle R.; textiles, printing, liqueur; p. (1968) 39,991.

Epirus, dist., N.W. Greece; a. 9,552 km²; p. (1971) 314,558.

Epping Forest, Essex, Eng.; forest a. N.E. of London free to public (opened by Queen Victoria 1882); formerly part of royal hunting forest; also l. gov. dist., inc. Chigwell, Waltham Cross and Ongar; p. (est. 1976) 116,200.

Epsom and Ewell, ts., l. gov. dist., Surrey, Eng.; 29 km S.W. of London; residtl., racecourse; p. (est. 1976) 70,700 (dist.).

Epworth, v., Humberside, Eng.; birthplace of John Wesley.

Equatorial Guinea, unitary state, W. Africa; former Spanish col.; indep. 1968; comprises 2 provs.; Rio Muni (mainland and Is of Corisco, Elobey Grande, Elobey Chico) and Marcias Nguema (Is. of Marcias Nguema and Pagalu); narrow coastal plain and dissected upland plateau (600 m); economy almost entirely based on agr. and timber; exploration for oil; cap. Malabo on Marcias Nguema I.; a. 45,392 km²; p. (est. 1968) 250,000.

Erbil, t., Iraq; comm. ctr.; rly. terminus; p. (1965) 134,000 (met. a.).

Erebus, mtn., active volcano, Victoria Land, Antarctica; alt. 4,027 m.

Erewash, l. gov. dist., Derbys., Eng.; a. close to Nottingham inc. Ilkeston and Long Eaton; p. (est. 1976) 101,100.

Erfurt, admin. dist., E. Germany; a. 7,322 km²; p. (1968) 1,256,034.

Erfurt, t., E. Germany; on Gera R.; cath., ctr. of mkt. gardening and seed-growing dist., textiles, machin., foodstuffs, footwear, radios, heavy engin.; p. (est. 1969) 193,997.

Ericht, loch, Scot.; in central Grampians; 25 km long; hydroelec. scheme.

Erie, c., N.W. Penns., USA; pt. on L. Erie; coal, iron, grain, petroleum; machin., domestic appliances; p. (1970) 125,941 (c.). 257,860 (met. a.).

Erie Canal. See New York State Barge Canal.

Erie, one of Great Lakes (the shallowest), N.

America, separating Canada from USA; 386 km long, 48–91 km wide; polluted waters; petroleum resources.

Erith, former M.B., Kent, Eng.; on Thames estuary; plastics, paints, varnishes, timber, concrete; now inc. in London bor. of Bexley.

Eritrea, prov., Ethiopia; tobacco, cereals, pearl fishing; demands for autonomy; cap. Asmara, a. 118,503 km²; p. (est. 1970) 1,836,800.

Erivan. *See* Yerevan.

Erlangen, t., Bavaria, W. Germany; univ.; textiles, elec. and precision engin., gloves; p. (est. 1969) 84,619.

Ermelo, t., Neth.; ctr. of agr. dist.; p. (1968) 35,434.

Ernakulam, t., Kerala, India; cotton, coffee, hides; p. (est. 1970) 213,811 (c.), 493,460 (met. a.).

Erne R., N. Ireland/R.o.I.; links Ls. in Cavan and Fermanagh; 115 km long.

Erode, t., S. Tamil Nadu, India; on R. Cauvery; p. (1971) 105,111 (t.), 169,613 (met. a.).

Erzgebirge (Ore Mtns.), mtn. range along border of ČSSR and Germany, reaching highest peak in Mt. Klinovec (1,240 m) in ČSSR; uranium; tourism.

Erzurum, t., Turkey; agr. ctr. on fertile plateau c. 1,890 m a.s.l.; formerly of gr. strategic importance; univ.; p. (1965) 105,317 (t.), 174,155 (met. a.).

Esbjerg, spt., Denmark; W. cst. of Jutland; export harbour on N. Sea cst.; exp. agr. prod.; fishing; airport; p. (est. 1970) 76,056.

Esch-sur-Alzette, t., Luxembourg; mng. ctr.; steel; p. (1968) 27,466.

Eschwege, t., Hesse, W. Germany; cas.; machin., textiles, leather, cigars, chemicals; p. (est. 1969) 22,227.

Eschweiler, t., N. Rhine–Westphalia, W. Germany; N.W. of Aachen; lignite mng., steel, iron, metallurgy; p. (est. 1969) 39,756.

Esdraelon, plain, Israel; between Carmel and Gilboa Mtns.

Eşfahān (Isfahan, anc. Aspadana), c., central Iran; prov. cap.; historic, picturesque c. noted for carpets and metal ware; tourism, airpt.; new steel mill; p. (est. 1971) 546,200.

Esher, t., Elmbridge, Surrey, Eng.; on R. Mole, residtl.; Sandown Park racecourse; p. (1971) 64,186.

Eshowe, health resort, Natal, S. Africa; 64 km from Tugela R.; p. (est. 1967) 4,800.

Esk R., Annandale and Eskdale, Scot.; Cumbria, Eng.; attractive agr. valley; flows into Solway F. from confluence of Black and White Esk Rs.; 37 km long.

Eskilstuna, t., Sweden; on R. of same name; iron, steel, machin., machin. tools; p. (1968) 173,900.

Eskişehir, t., Turkey; W. of Ankara, anc. Dorylaeum; rly. ctr.; meerschaum; p. (1965) 173,882 (t.), 243,033 (met. a.).

Esmeraldas, prov., Ecuador; cap. E. on R. of same name; cacao, tobacco; a. 14,152 km²; p. (est. 1970) 177,600.

Esmeraldas, pt., Ecuador; bananas, timber, tobacco, cacao, rubber; gold mines nearby; p. (1970) 59,000.

Esneh. *See* Isna.

Espírito Santo, st., Brazil; sugar, cotton, coffee, fruits, lumber, thorium; cap. Vitória; a. 40,883 km²; p. (est. 1968) 1,921,353.

Espíritu Santo, I., New Hebrides; volcanic I., lgst. of gr.; depopulation.

Essaouira (Mogador), spt., Morocco; cereals, almonds, gum-arabic, crude oil; p. (1960) 26,392.

Essen, c., N. Rhine–Westphalia, W. Germany; gr. industl. c., ctr. of Ruhr conurbation; coal, steel (Krupp), electric power, engin.; canal links with Dortmund–Ems and Mittelland canals and with Rhine; minster severely damaged in second world war; p. (est. 1969) 705,700 (c.); (est. 1967) 5,150,000 (met. a.).

Essequibo R.; flows N. from Brazilian border draining half Guyana; lower course navigable, rapids; timber in upper valley; 960 km long.

Essex, non-met. co., Eng.; bounded on S. by Thames, on E. by N. Sea; co. t. Chelmsford; on London clay and chalk; agr.; wheat, barley, sugar-beet; mkt. gardens; S.W. of co. forms part of Greater London with mftg. subs.; oil refineries at Shell Haven; civil nuclear power sta. at Bradwell; univ. at Colchester; a. 2,637 km²; p. (est. 1976) 1,426,200.

Esslingen, t., Baden–Württemberg, W. Germany; on R. Neckar; mach. and rly. shops; textiles, chemicals, leather gds.; Liebfrauen church (1440); p. (est. 1969) 85,350.

Essonne, dep., France; S. of Paris; cap. Ivry; a. 1,810 km²; p. (1968) 674,157.

Esteli, cap. Esteli, Nicaragua; on Inter-American Highway; p. (1963) 26,764.

Eston, t., Cleveland, Eng.; 5 km E. of Middlesbrough; shipbldg. and repairing.

Estonia (Estoniya), constituent rep., USSR; borders on Baltic, G. of Finland, G. of Riga; lowland with many Ls.; farming and dairying, fishing; oil deposits; hydroelec. power; mainly Lutheran; univ.; cap. Tallinn; a. 45,610 km²; p. (1970) 1,357,000.

Estoril, wat. pl. and thermal spa, Portugal; N. side of Tagus estuary; holiday resort.

Estremadura, maritime prov., Portugal; agr., tourism; cap. Lisbon; a. 5,348 km²; p. 1,600,000.

Estremadura, region, S.W. Spain; on the border of Portugal; largely plateau, alt. 450–900 m.; heathy moorland; sheep; less arid conditions than in remainder of central Spain allow olives, vines, cereals; irrigation in valleys of Tagus, Guadiana; govt. project to develop a. in progress.

Esztergom, t., Hungary; R. pt. on Danube; iron foundries, machine tools; mineral springs; cath.; p. (est 1966) 26,000.

Etang de Berre, lagoon, Bouches-du-Rhône, S.E. France; E. of Rhône delta; traversed by Rhône–Marseille canal; salt pans; oil refineries in a.; approx. a. 260 km².

Étaples, t., Pas-de-Calais, France; seaside resort; p. (1968) 9,108.

Etawah, t., Uttar Pradesh, India; textiles; p. (1961) 69,681.

Ethiopia (Abyssinia), indep. st. N.E. Africa; temperate climate as a result of high plateau terrain; coffee most impt. comm. crop, but poor communications inhibit economic development; low per capita income and rapid growth of p.; ch. pt. Assab; English widely spoken; univs. at Addis Ababa and Asmara; cap. Addis Ababa; monarchy abolished 1975; a. 1,221,900 km²; p. (est. 1975) 27,946,000.

Ethiopian Highlands, mtns., Ethiopia; rise over 4,500 m; source of headwaters of tribs. of R. Nile.

Etna, volcano, N.E. Sicily, Italy; most recent eruption 1971; alt. 3,276 m.

Eton, t., Berks., Eng.; on N. bank of R. Thames opposite Windsor; public school, founded by Henry VI; p. (1971) 3,954.

Etruria, anc. dist., Italy; now forms Tuscany; home of the Etruscans and part of the Roman empire by 400 B.C.

Etruria, t., Staffs., Eng.; part of Stoke-on-Trent; seat of Josiah Wedgwood's potteries (1769).

Euboea (Evvoia), lgst. of Greek Is. Aegean Sea; mtnous. (Mt. Delphi 1,746 m); vines and olives in lowlands, sheep and goats in highlands; a. 3,864 km²; p. (1971) 165,822.

Euclid, t., Ohio, USA; electrical and agr. machin.; p. (1970) 71,552.

Eucumbene Dam and L., N.S.W., Australia; major storage of Snowy Mtns. hydroelectric scheme; holds eight times as much water as Sydney harbour.

Eugene, c., Ore., USA; univ.; mkt. ctr. for rich agr. and lumbering region; fruit-canning, saw-milling; headquarters of Willamette National Forest; p. (1970) 77 284 (c.), 212,644 (met. a.).

Euphrates, lgst. R. in S.W. Asia; rises in Armenian uplands and joined by the Tigris enters Persian G. as the Shatt-al Arab; anc. ctr. of civilisation; modern irrigation, navigation, high dam opened 1973; 2,848 km long.

Eure, dep., Normandy, France; agr., fruit, livestock, textiles; cap. Évreux; a. 6,037 km²; p. (1968) 383,385.

Eure-et-Loire, dep., N. France; mainly agr.; cap. Chartres; a. 5.934 km²; p. (1968) 302,207.

Europe, continent; W. peninsula of Eurasian land mass; no well-defined bdy. with Asia but line normally accepted runs along Ural Mtns. to Caspian Sea and Caucasus to Black Sea, Sea of Marmara and Dardanelles; after Australia, Europe is smallest continent in a., but contains 20 per cent of world's p. and even more of world's economic activity; climate varies from Arctic to Mediterranean and from temperate maritime to severe continental; major physical features inc. Alps, Pyrenees in S., Baltic Shield in N.; major political div. between E. and W. Europe along Iron Curtain; W. Europe also divided into economic grs. EEC and EFTA; major concentration of p. and economic activity within Golden Triangle (q.v.), total a. c. 10,360,000 km²; p. (est. 1975) 473,000,000 (excl. USSR).

Europort, name of the post-war expansion of the port of Rotterdam, Neth.; capable of handling 100,000 tonne oil-tankers; oil refining; European oil supply ctr.; joined to Rotterdam by the New Waterway.

Evanston, t., Ill., USA., on L. Michigan, sub. of Chicago; univ.; p. (1970) 79,808.

Evansville, c., Ind., USA; on Ohio R.; shipping and comm. ctr. for agr. region; coal mng.; p. (1970) 137,997 (c.), 230,708 (met. a.).

Eveneki National Area, Siberia, RSFSR; forest and tundra covered; home of Eveneki people; cap. Tura; a. 740,740 km²; p. (1970) 13,000.

Everest, Mt. (Chomolungma = Goddess Mother of the Earth), Himlaya, on frontier of Nepal and Tibet, China, alt. 8,854 m; hgst. mtn. in the world; Hillary and Tenzing first to reach summit in 1953; within Nepal Nat. Park.

Everett, mftg. t., Mass., USA; nr. Boston; iron and steel; p. (1970) 42,485.

Everett, t., Wash., USA; on Puget Sound; harbour; comm. ctr.; timber; tourism; p. (1970) 53,622.

Everglades, Fla., USA; subtropical a., extensive marshes; home of Seminole Indians; lge. scale drainage since 1905; early vegetables.

Evesham mkt. t., Wychavon, Hereford and Worcs., Eng.; on R. Avon, in Vale of Evesham, 24 km S.E. of Worcester; fruit ctr.; tourism; p. (1971) 13,847.

Évora, t.. cap. of Upper Alentejo prov. S. Portugal; mkt. for agr. prod.; cath.; p. (1970) 47,806.

Évreux, t., cap. of Eure dep., France; mkt. ctr.; p. (1968) 45,441.

Evros, prov., Greece; borders Bulgaria and Turkey; a. 4,191 km²; p. (1971) 141,002.

Exe, R., Somerset and Devon, Eng.; rises on Exmoor, flows S. via Exeter to English Channel at Exmouth; 86 km long.

Exeter, l. gov. dist., cath. c., co. t., Devon, Eng.; former Roman Isca; E. of Dartmoor on R. Exe; mkt. t.; univ.; aircraft components; airport; p. (est. 1976) 93,300.

Exmoor, Somerset and Devon, Eng.; sandstone moorland, deep wooded valleys; Nat. Park.

Exmouth, t., East Devon, Eng.; on estuary of R. Exe; holiday resort; p. (1971) 25,815.

Exploits, R., Newfoundland, Canada; length 240 km; used for hydroelectric power.

Eye, mkt. t., Mid Suffolk, Eng.; 29 km N. of Ipswich; anc. church; p. (1971) 1,659.

Eyemouth, burgh, Berwick, Scot.; on E. cst. 14 km N. of Berwick; fishing; p. (1971) 2,530.

Eyre Lake, shallow salt L., S. Australia; 12 m below sea-level and practically dry; a. 9,065 km².

Eyre Peninsula, S. Australia; between Gr. Australian Bight and Spencer G.; iron-ore deposits; a. 51,800 km².

F

Fabriano, t., Marches, Italy; in Apennines; cath.; paper mills; p. (est. 1968) 27,252.

Faenza, t., Ravenna, Italy; at foot of Apennines; majolica, textiles; p. (est. 1968) 54,065.

Fagersta, t., Västmanland, Sweden; iron, steel smelting; p. (est. 1970) 17,054.

Failsworth, t., Gtr. Manchester, Eng.; N.E. of Manchester; textiles, elec. gds.; p. (1971) 23,233.

Fairbanks, t., Alaska, USA; univ.; sawmilling; mng.; p. (1970) 22,640.

Fairfield, t., Conn., USA; chemicals, automobile parts; univ.; p. (1970) 56,487.

Fair I., midway between Shetland and Orkney, Scot.; bird sanctuary; famous for brightly patterned, hand-knitted articles.

Fairmont, t., W. Va., USA; glass machin., coal by-products; p. (1970) 26,093.

Faiyum (El Faiyûm), t. and region, N. Egypt; oasis nr. L. Karun (anc. L. Moeris), fertilised by Nile water and silt; cereals, sugar-cane, fruits, cotton; archaeological finds; p. of t. (est. 1970) 150,900.

Faizabad, t., Uttar Pradesh, India; rly. junc.; sugar refining; p. (1971) 102,835.

Falaise, t., Calvados, France; birthplace of William the Conqueror; p. (1968) 7,599.

Falaise de l'Ile de France, low S.E.-facing escarpment, 80 km S.E. and E. of Paris, France; overlooks Champagne Pouilleuse; ch. vine-growing dist. for champagne-wine ind. of Reims, Epernay.

Falcón, st. Venezuela; bordering Caribbean Sea; cap. Coro; p. (est. 1970) 408,051.

Falconara Marittima, t.. Italy; nr. Ancona; spt.; oil refining, shipbldg.

Falkirk burgh, l. gov. dist., Central Reg., Scot., 16 km S.E. of Stirling; foundries, bricks, chemical, aluminium wks., concrete, timber yards, battles 1298 and 1746; p. (1971) 37,579.

Falkland, burgh, North East Fife, Scot.; 5 km S. of Auchtermuchty; mkt.; p. (1971) 896.

Falkland Is., Brit. Crown col., S. Atl., comprises E. and W. Falkland and adjacent Is.; sheep rearing (for wool); cap. Port Stanley on E. Falkland I.; claimed by Argentina; a. 12,173 km²; p. (1969) 2,098.

Falkland Is. Dependencies, S. Atl.; inc. Is of S. Georgia and S. Sandwich; a. 4,092 km²; p. (of S. Georgia) 11 males; now form part of Brit. Antarctic Terr.

Fall River, c., Mass., USA; on Mt. Hope Bay; pt. of entry; clothing, rubber gds., food prods., paper; p. (1970) 95,679 (c.), 148,430 (met. a.).

Falmouth, t., Carrick, Cornwall, Eng.; on W. side of estuary of R. Fal. 16 km S. of Truro; sheltered harbourage; offshore oil supply base; seaside resort; fisheries, ship repairing, mng., quarrying, lt. engin.; cas.; pt.; p. (1971) 17,883.

False Bay, inlet on E. side of C. of Good Hope peninsula, S. Africa.

Falster, I. Baltic, Denmark; cap. Nyköbing; p. (1965) 45,906.

Falun, t., Kopparberg, Sweden; paper; copper mines now exhausted; p. (est. 1970) 34,550.

Famagusta, t., spt., Cyprus; on E. cst.; resort; anc. crusade pt.; p. (est. 1970) 42,500.

Famatina, t., La Rioja prov., Argentina; in foothills of Andes, 576 km N.W. of Córdoba; copper-mines.

Fano, t.. Italy; sm. pt on Adriatic cst., N. of Ancona; seaside resort; p. (est. 1968) 45,879.

Farcham, t., l. gov. dist., Hants., Eng.; at N.W. corner of Portsmouth Harbour; p. (est. 1976) 86,300 (dist.).

Farewell (Kap Farvel), C., southernmost tip of Greenland.

Farewell, C., most N. point S.I., N.Z.

Fargo, t., N.D., USA; rly. ctr. and R. pt.; grain, farm machin.; p. (1970) 52,697 (t.), 118,555 (met. a.).

Faringdon, mkt. t., Vale of White Horse, Oxon., Eng.; Faringdon Folly.

Farnborough, t., Rushmoor, Hants., Eng.; 5 km N. of Aldershot military camp; Royal Aircraft Establishment; p. (1971) 41,233.

Farne Is., gr. of islets off Northumberland cst., Eng.; bird sanctuary; National Trust.

Farnham, t.. Waverley, Surrey, Eng.; at N. foot of N. Downs, 16 km W. of Guildford; mkt.; p. (1971) 31,175.

Farnworth, t., Gtr. Manchester, Eng.; nr. Bolton, textiles, engin., paper; p. (1971) 26,841.

Faro, spt., cap. of Algarve prov., Portugal; cork, figs, oranges; p. (1970) 30,269.

Faroe Is., 320 km N.W. of the Shetlands, Scot.; cap. Thórshavn (Strömö I.); Danish possession but not member of EEC; impt. fisheries; a. 1,399 km²; p. (1966) 37,122.

Farrukhabad, t., Uttar Pradesh, India; on Ganges R.; gold, lace, brass wk.; p. (1971) 102,768.

Fars, prov., S. Iran; agr.; cap. Shiráz; p. (1967) 1,499,472.

Fastnet, lighthouse in Atl. Oc., 7·2 km S.W.C. Clear, Irish cst. [grimage.

Fatima, v.. W. Portugal, nr. Leiria; R.C. pil-

Fatshan (Foshan), c., Kwangtung, China; S.W. of Kuangchow; iron and steel, textiles; p. (1953) 123,000.

Faversham, pt., Swale, N.E. Kent, Eng.; at head of F. creek; mkt.; fruit, hops, bricks, brushes, engin.; p. (1971) 13,807.

Fawley, t., Hants., Eng.; on W. shore Southampton Water; lge. oil refinery with pipeline to Staines and Heathrow Airpt.; synthetic rubber.

Fayetteville, t., N.C., USA; agr. processing; p. (1970) 51,606 (t.), 206,446 (met. a.).

Feather, R., N. Cal., USA; R. project for water supply irrigation, and hydroelectric power.

Featherstone, t., West Yorks., Eng.; p. (1971) 15,242.

Fécamp, sm. spt. on cst. of Normandy, France; fishing, tourism, 12th cent. abbey; p. (1968) 21,745.

Fedchenko, glacier, lgst in USSR; in Pamir-Altai mtns. of central Asia; 80 km long.

Federal German Republic. See Germany, Fed. Rep. of.

Feira de Santana, t., Bahia, Brazil; cattle, tobacco, beans, manioc; p. (1970) 127,105.

Feldberg, highest peak in Black Forest, W. Germany; alt. 1,495 m.

Feldkirch, t., Vorarlberg, Austria; on Swiss frontier; p. (1961) 17,343.

Felixstowe, pt., Suffolk Coastal, Suffolk, Eng.; dock development with container facilities; seaside resort; p. (1971) 18,888.

Felling, Tyne and Wear, Eng.; Tyneside mftg. dist.; p. (1971) 38,595.

Feltham. See Hounslow.

Fenland, l. gov. dist., Cambs., Eng.; agr. a. in N. of co. inc. Wisbech, Chatteris, March Whittlesey and North Witchford; p. (est. 1976) 66,600.

Fens, The, low-lying dist. around the Wash, Eng.; artificial drainage begun in 17th cent.; impt. agr. dist.; root crops, wheat, fruit, bulbs; a. 3,367 km².

Feodosiya, t., Ukrainian SSR, USSR; in Crimea; major Black Sea pt., tobacco, hosiery; exp. wheat; resort and sanatoria; p. (est. 1968) 59,000.

Ferghana, region, Uzbek SSR, USSR; deep basin at W. end of Tien Shan Mtns.; drained W. by R. Syr Dar'ya; semi-arid but extensive irrigation system allows intensive cultivation of cotton, citrus fruits, silk, rice; ch. ts., Kokand, Namangan.

Ferghana, c., Uzbek SSR, USSR; hydroelectric power, petroleum refining, textiles; deposits of ozocerite nearby; p. (1970) 111,000.

Fermanagh, former co.; l. gov. dist., N. Ireland; bisected by R. Erne and lakes; stock raising, dairying; p. of former co. (est. 1971) 49,960.

Fermoy, t., Cork, R.o.I.; on R. Blackwater; cath.; woollens; p. (1966) 3,207.

Fernando de Noronha, I., fed. terr., N.E. cst. Brazil; penal settlement and met. sta.; cap. Vila dos Remédios; a. 26 km²; p. (est. 1968) 2,400.

Fernando Po. See Marcias Nguema.

Ferozepore, t., Punjab st. N.W. India; rly. t.; admin. ctr.; p. (1961) 97,932.

Ferrara, c., N. Italy; nr. head of Po delta; cath., univ. palaces; mkt. for fertile plain; silk, hemp, wine; oil refinery nearby; petrochemicals; birthplace of Savonarola; p. (1969) 156,207.

Ferro (Hierro), most S. of the Canary Is., a. 275 km²; cap. Valverde; chosen by Ptolemy (A.D. 56) for his prime meridian and used by French scientists in 17th cent.; reckoned as exactly W. 20° of Paris.

Ferryhill, v., Durham, Eng.; 8 km S. of Durham, in gap through limestone ridge which separates Wear valley from Tees valley; commands main N. to S. route along lowland E. of Pennines.

Fertile Crescent, an arc of fertile land from the Mediterranean Sea, N. of the Arabian Desert, to Persian G.; home of some very early civilisations and migrations.

Fez (Fès), c., Morocco; lies inland 160 km E. of Rabat; one of the sacred cities of Islam; univ. attached to mosque (one of lgst. in Africa); comm. ctr.; p. (1971) 321,460 (c.), 379,790 (met. a.).

Fezzan, prov., S.W. Libya; desert plateau with numerous wells and inhabited oases; p. (1964) 78,326.

Ffestiniog (Festiniog), t., Meirionnydd, Gwynedd, N. Wales; at head of Vale of Ffestiniog, 14 km E. of Portmadoc; contains Ffestiniog and Blaenau Ffestiniog; slate quarries; pumped storage hydroelec. sta. (1963); cement; p. (1971) 5,751.

Fianarantsoa, t., Malagasy Rep.; rice mills, meat preserves; p. (est. 1968) 45,790.

Fichtelgebirge, mtn. range, N.E. Bavaria, W. Germany; extending into ČSSR, rising to 1,051 m in Schneeberg; forested slopes.

Fiesole, t., Tuscany, Italy; on summit of wooded hill overlooking Florence and the Arno; residtl.; 11th cent. cath.; p. (est. 1968) 13,401.

Fife, l. gov. reg., former co., E. Scot.; occupies a. between Tay and Forth estuaries; industl. dist. based originally on coalfields; a. 1,305 km²; p. (1971) 327,690.

Fiji, S.W. Pac. Oc., former Brit. col., gained independence in 1970; comprises over 800 Is.; tropical climate; agr. basis of economy, especially sugar and coconut prods.; gold an impt. exp.; forestry and tourism developing; forms ctr. of communications in S.W. Pac. Oc.; international airport at Nadi, ch. pt. and cap. Suva; a. 18,272 km²; cosmopolitan p. (1970) 513,000.

Filey, t., North Yorks., Eng.; 8 km S.E. of Scarborough; seaside resort; p. (1971) 5,337.

Filton, Bristol, Avon, Eng.; aircraft wks.

Finchley. See Barnet.

Findhorn, v., Moray, Scot.; resort; 12th cent. abbey; fishing.

Findlay, t., Ohio, USA; on Blanchard R.; agr. machin., tyres, beet sugar refining; p. (1970) 35,800.

Fingal's Cave, Staffa I., Inner Hebrides, W. Scot.; basaltic columns.

Finger Lakes, gr. of narrow glacial Ls., N.Y., USA; picturesque resorts and state parks.

Finistère (Lat. finis terrae = land's end), dep. N.W. France, in Brittany; cap. Quimper; fishing, tourism; a. 7,071 km²; p. (1968) 768,929.

Finland, rep., N. Europe; part of Scandinavia; low-lying plateau severely eroded by ice to form 60,000 Ls.; economy based on timber (forests cover 72 per cent of a.); world's leading exporter of pulp and paper; increasing importance of metal and engin. inds.; cap. Helsinki; a. 360,318 km²; p. concentrated in S.; p. (1970) 4,707,000.

Finland, G. of, E. arm of Baltic Sea, between Finland and USSR.

Finnart, Dumbarton, Scot.; crude oil terminal situated in Loch Long. N.W. Glasgow; pipeline to Grangemouth.

Finnmark, most N. co., Norway; inhabited by Lapps; whale fisheries; lge. copper deposits discovered nr. Reppan fjord; a. 48,125 km²; p. (est. 1972) 77,060.

Finsbury. See Islington.

Finsteraarhorn, highest peak in Bernese Oberland, Switzerland; 4,277 m.

Finucane I., pt. W. Australia; deepwater pt. to ship iron ore and new t. projected.

Firenze. See Florence.

Firozabad, t., Uttar Pradesh, India; glassware; agr. tr.; p. (1961) 98,611.

Fishguard and Goodwick, spt., Preseli, Dyfed, Wales; on S. of Cardigan Bay; steamer connection to Cork and Rosslare (Ireland); p. (1971) 4,933.

Fitchburg, t., Mass., USA; paper, machin., textiles; p. (1970) 43,343.

Fitzroy, R., W. Australia; flows into King Sound; dry in winter; irrigation; 560 km long.

Fiume. See Rijeka.

Flamborough Head, promontory of Yorks. cst. Eng.; steep chalk cliffs; lighthouse; anc. Brit. earthwork (Danes' dyke).

Flanders, region between R. Scheldt and cst. crossed by Franco-Belgian frontier; Dunkirk, Lille ctrs. of French F.; Belgian F. (p. (1970) 5,416,583) divided into 2 provs., E. and W.; caps. Bruges and Ghent.

Fleet, t., Hart, Hants., Eng.; 6 km N.W. of Aldershot; p. (1971) 21,362.

Fleetwood, spt., Wyre, Lancs., Eng.; at mouth of Wyre, Morecambe Bay; deep-sea fish. pt.; fish processing; lge. chemical plant nearby; p. (1971) 28,584.

Flensburg, spt., Schleswig-Holstein, W. Germany; on Baltic, close to Danish border; shipbldg., machin., chemicals, rum distilleries, fishing; p. (est. 1969) 95,488.

Flevosted, t., Neth.; admin. ctr. of new S.E. Polder.

Flinders I., Australia; lgst I. in the Furneaux gr., Bass Strait; a. 2,077 km²; p. 900.

Flinders Range, chain of mtns., S. Australia; extending 400 km N.E. from head of Spencer G., reaching 1,190 m in St. Mary's Peak; named after Matthew Flinders; uranium ore at Mt. Painter.

Flint, t., Delyn, Clwyd, Wales; viscose textile yarn, cas. ruins; p. (1971) 14,660.

Flint, t., Mich., USA; motorcars, aircraft engines; p. (1970) 193,571 (t.), 493,402 (met. a.).

Flintshire, former co., N. Wales; now part of Clwyd.

Flodden, v. Northumberland, Eng.; on R. Till; battle between James IV of Scot. and the English under the Earl of Surrey, 1513.

Flora, t., Norway; new t. 136 km N. of Bergen; p. (1965) 7,700.

Florence (Firenze), c., Tuscany, Italy; on R. Arno; univ.; leather-work; famous for art treasures, cath. and churches; ruled by Medici 1421–1737; birthplace of Dante and Machiavelli; severely affected by heavy floods Nov. 1966; plans for new EEC univ.; p. (1966) 459,058.

Florence, t., N.W. Ala., USA; on Tennessee R., nr. Wilson dam; textile, steel plants; p. (1970) 34,031.

Flores, I., most northwesterly of Azores gr.; Portuguese; cap. Santa Cruz; French to set up ballistic missiles tracking sta.; a. 142 km; p. (1960) 6,617.

Flores, I., Indonesia; mtnous.; volcanic, densely forested; a. 22,973 km²; p. (1961) 803,000.

Flores Sea, between Sulawesi and Flores, Indonesia.

Florianópolis, spt., cap. of Santa Catarina st., Brazil; comm. ctr., fishing; p. (1970) 115,665.

Florida, st., USA; between Atl. Oc. and G. of Mexico; low-lying, swampy, inc. Everglades; sea resorts on Atl. cst.; citrus fruit and subtropical agr.; agr. processing; cap Tallahassee; a. 151,670 km²; p. (1970) 6,671,162.

Florida Keys, archipelago, USA; extends in an arc from S.E. cst. Florida W.S.W. to Key West in G. of Mexico; fishing resorts.

Florida Strait, between Florida and Bahama Is.; course of Gulf Stream from G. of Mexico.

Florina. See Phlorina.

Florissant (St. Ferdinand), t., Mo., USA; sub. of St. Louis on Missouri R.; p. (1970) 65,908.

Flushing. See Vlissingen.

Fly, lgst. R. of Papua New Guinea; flows S.E. from Victor Emmanuel Range to G. of Papua; 1,280 km long.

Fochabers, v., Moray, Scot.; nr. mouth of Spey; tourist resort; food canning; p. (1971) 4,230.

Focsani, t. Romania; at foot of Transylvanian Alps; wine and grain ctr.; p. (est. 1970) 39,629.

Foggia, cath. c., S. Italy; rly. ctr. and mkt. ctr. for plain of Apulia; site of cas. of Frederick II; p. (1969) 139,981.

Foix, t., cap. of Ariège dep., S. France; historic t.; p. (1968) 9,331.

Foligno, t., central Italy; in Apennines, on Topino R.; cath., textiles, paper; p. (est. 1968) 50,237.

Folkestone, t., Shepway, Kent, Eng.; seaside resort; pt. for Folkestone–Boulogne to France 46 km; p. (1971) 43,760.

Fond du Lac, t., Winnebago L., Wis., USA; cath.; machine tools, domestic appliances; resort; p. (1970) 35,515.

Fonseca, Gulf of, Honduras; lgst indentation along Pac. cst. of Central America; sm. pt. of Amapala, US naval base, and new deepwater pt.

Fontainebleau, t., Seine-et-Marne, France; on R. Seine, 56 km S.E. Paris; in former royal forest (a. 17,200 ha); magnificent palace; p. (1968) 19,803.

Fontenoy, v., Belgium; nr. Tournai; scene of battle (1745) when the French under Marshal Saxe defeated the English and their allies; p. (est. 1969) 655.

Foochow (Fu-chou), c., cap. of Fukien prov., China; at mouth of Min R.; major comm. and industl. ctr.; became impt. with tea exp.; former treaty pt.; p. (est. 1970) 900,000.

Fordlandia. See Belterra.

Foreland, N. and S., two headlands on E. cst. Kent, Eng.; between which are the Goodwin Sands

and Pegwell Bay; lighthouses; sea battle between de Ruyter and Monk (1666).

Forest Heath, l. gov. dist., Suffolk, Eng.; part of Breckland inc. Mildenhall and Newmarket; p. (1976) 49,000.

Forest Hills, residtl. a., central Queen's bor., N.Y. USA; national and international matches played at West Side Tennis Club.

Forest of Dean. See Dean, Forest of.

Forfar, royal burgh, Angus, Scot.; jute, linen; p. (1971) 10,499.

Forli, c., Emilia-Romagna, central Italy; route ctr. in Apennine foothills; felt, textiles, footwear; p. (1969) 104,175.

Formby, t., Merseyside, Eng.; on W. cst., 10 km S.W. of Southport; residtl.; p. (1971) 23,501.

Formosa, prov., N. Argentina; bordering on Paraguay; timber; cap. Formosa; a. 72,067 km²; p. (1970) 234,075.

Formosa. See Taiwan.

Forres, royal burgh, Moray, Scot.; on Findhorn R. nr. Moray F.; agr., forestry, engin., distilleries; cas.; p. (1971) 4,718.

Forst, t., Cottbus, E. Germany; on R. Neisse; E. section of t. Polish since 1945; textiles; p. (est. 1970) 29,284.

Fortaleza, c., cap. of Ceará st., Brazil; exp. sugar cotton, hides, carnauba wax; p. (1970) 520,175.

Fort Collins, t., Col., USA; ctr. of rich farming a.; grain, sugarbeet, livestock; univ.; p. (1970) 43.337.

Fort de France, cap. of Martinique, Fr. W.I.; landlocked harbour; exp. sugar, rum; comm. ctr.; Fr. naval base; p. (1967) 99,051.

Fort Dodge, t., Iowa, USA; on Des Moines R. in rich agr. a.; grain, gypsum, coal; p. (1970) 31,263.

Fort George, R., W. Quebec, Canada; rises in Labrador and flows into Hudson Bay; 880 km long. [mines.

Fort Gouraud, t., Mauritania; modern iron-ore

Forth, R., Scot.; formed by two headstreams rising to N. of Ben Lomond which meet nr. Aberfoyle; takes meandering course to Alloa, whence it expands into Firth of Forth (q.v.); 165 km long.

Forth, Firth of, lge. inlet, E. cst. of Scot.; submerged estuary of R. Forth; navigable by lge. vessels for 64 km inland to Grangemouth; other pts., Leith, Rosyth (naval), Bo'ness; l. (to Alloa) 80 km; the Forth rly. bridge (1890) spans the F. at Queensferry; the road bridge (1964) is the longest suspension bridge in Europe.

Forth and Clyde Canal, Scot.; links F. of Forth at Grangemouth and F. of Clyde at Glasgow; 61 km long.

Fort Johnston, t., S. Malawi, on L. Malombe; new t., 1966; tobacco; airpt.

Fort Knox, Ky., USA; nation's gold bullion depository; military air-base.

Fort Lamy. See Ndjamene.

Fort Lauderdale, c., Fla., USA; on Atl. cst. N. of Miami; lge. marina; citrus fruits, mkt. garden prod.; holiday resort; p. (1970) 139,122 (c.), 612,003 (met a., inc. military personnel and families).

Fort Myers, t., Fla., USA; on G. of Mexico; resort; Eddison experimented here; p. (1970) 27,351.

Fortrose, t., royal burgh, Ross and Cromarty, Scot.; on S. cst. of Black Isle, on Moray F.; p. (1971) 1,081.

Fort Smith, c., Ark., USA; on Arkansas R.; mkt. ctr. for agr. a.; varied mnfs., inc. furniture, glass; coal and zinc mined nearby; p. (1970) 61,549 (c.), 156,750 (met. a.).

Fort Victoria, t., Rhodesia, agr. and mng. ctr., cattle, historic ruins in Zimbabwe Nat. Park; p. (est. 1970) 13,000.

Fort Wayne, c., Ind., USA; at confluence of 2 headstreams of Maumee R.; rly. repair shops; elec. machin. and domestic appliances, originally a Fr. fort; p. (1970) 175,082 (c.), 277,721 (met. a.).

Fort William. See Thunder Bay.

Fort William, burgh, Lochaber, Scot.; nr. head of Loch Linnhe, at base of Ben Nevis; aluminium factory; pulp- and paper-mill at Corpach; p. (1971) 4,214.

Fort Worth, c., Texas USA; rly. and comm. ctr, on Trinity R.; livestock and grain mkt.; oil refining, meat packing, oilfield equipment; p. (1970) 388,123 (c.), 757,105 (met. a.).

Fort Yukon, trading sta. on Yukon R., N.E. Alaska, USA.

Fos-sur-Mer, t., Bouches-du-Rhône. S. France; nr. Marseilles; new deepwater pt. and oil refinery; bauxite terminal; iron and steel plant.

Fotheringhay, v., Northampton, Eng.; on R. Nene; Mary Queen of Scots beheaded (1587) in F. Castle.

Fougères, t., Ille-et-Vilaine, France; cas.; footwear, clothing; p. (1968) 26,854.

Foulness I., S. Essex, Eng.; at mouth of R. Crouch; owned by Min. of Defence; site of projected third London airport of Maplin, now abandoned; projected container and oil pt.

Fountains Abbey, ruined 12th cent. Cistercian abbey North Yorks., Eng.; nr. Ripon.

Fowey, sm. spt., Cornwall, Eng.; nr. mouth of R. Fowey; exp. kaolin; resort; fishing; p. with St. Austell (1971) 32 252.

Foxe Basin and Channel, to N. of Hudson Bay, between Baffin I. and Southampton I., Canada.

Foyers, Falls of, Inverness, Scot.; E. of Loch Ness, nr. Fort Augustus; aluminium wks., the first hydroelectric plant erected in Britain (1896).

Foyle, Lough, inlet, N. Ireland; between Donegal (R.o.I.) and Londonderry; outlet of R. F.; Londonderry t. at head of inlet.

Foynes Is., R.o.I.; oil terminal on N. side, E. of Battery Point.

Foz do Iguaçú, t., Paraná, Brazil; highway (coffee road) from Paranaguá.

Framingham, t., Mass., USA; 32 km W. of Boston; lt. inds.; p. (1970) 64,048.

Framlingham, mkt. t., Suffolk, Eng.; N.E. of Ipswich; cas. remains.

Francavilla Fontana, t., Apulia, Italy; rly. junc.; agr. tr.; p. (est. 1968) 31,241.

France, rep., W. Europe; bounded by 3 seas: Eng. Channel, Atl. Oc., Mediterranean; variety of climate and relief; leading agr. cty. of Europe; 75 per cent under cultivation; exps. grain, fruit, vegetables, wine; industl. expansion since second world war; lgst. inds. inc. iron and steel, motor vehicles, aircraft, engin., textiles, chemicals; tourism impt.; EEC member; cap. Paris; 96 deps.; excessive social, economic, and political concentration around Paris promotes description of France as "Paris and the French Desert"; recent attempts to break this down using framework of 21 economic planning regions; a. 550,634 km²; p. (1975) 52,655,802.

Franceville, t., Gabon, Equatorial Africa; on R. Ogooué; linked to Libreville as part of the Trans-Gabon rly. project; manganese mines opened 1962; founded by De Brazza.

Francistown, t., Botswana, Southern Africa; airpt.; butter, coppermng.; p. (est. 1969) 11,000.

Frankenthal, t., Rhineland-Palatinate W. Germany; in industl. dist. of Mannheim-Ludwigshafen; engin., machin.; p. (est. 1969) 39,920.

Frankfurt-on-Main, c., Hesse, W. Germany; focal point in Rhine-Main urban region; rly. ctr., transit pt.; machin., cars, chemicals, elec. engin., publishing; airport; cath., univ.; birthplace of Goethe; p. (est. 1969) 661,880 (c.); (est. 1967) 1,520,000 (met. a.).

Frankfurt-on-Oder, c., Brandenburg, E. Germany; agr. ctr., R. pt., rail junc.; machin., chemicals; E. part of t. (Slubice) Polish since 1945; p. (est. 1967) 60,200.

Frankischer (Franconian) Jura, plateau with steep N.-facing edge, S.E. of W. Germany; runs 128 km S.W. from Fichtelgebirge; drained by Regnitz and Altmühl Rs.

Franklin, t., Tasmania, Australia; 32 km from Hobart; principal fruit-growing dist. in I.

Franklin, dist., N.W. Terr., Canada; comprising the Is. of Arctic Canada from Banks I. to Baffin I., including Boothia Peninsula and Melville Peninsula; sparsely populated; furs; a. 1,434,943 km².

Františkovy Lázne (Franzensbad), famous spa, W. Bohemia, ČSSR; 445 m a.s.l., between the the Erzgebirge and the Fichtelgebirge.

Franz Josef Land (Zemlya Frantsalosifa), RSFSR; archipelago in Arctic Oc. N. of Novaya Zemlya; a. 20,720 km²; mainly ice-covered.

Frascati, t., Italy; 19 km S.E. of Rome; summer resort; famous villas and arch. remains; nuclear research ctr.; p. (est. 1968) 18,023.

Fraser I., Queensland, Australia; low sandy I., 128 km long; timber reserve.

Fraser, R., B.C., Canada, rises at c. 1,800 m on W. slopes Rocky Mtns.; famous salmon fisheries; routeway; Vancouver nr. delta; 1,360 km long.

Fraserburgh, spt., burgh, Banff and Buchan Scot.; one of the main E. cst. herring pts.; p. (1971) 10,606.

Frauenfeld, t., cap. of Thurgau can., Switzerland; 11th cent. cas.; textiles; p. (1970) 17,576.

Fray Bentos, t., cap. of Rio Negro dep., Uruguay; pt. on R. Uruguay 80 km from mouth; meat-processing; p. (1963) 14,000.

Fredericia, t., pt., E. Jutland, Denmark; major rly. junc.; textiles, silver and electroplated gds., fertilisers; oil refinery; p. (est. 1970) 43,513.

Fredericton, c., cap. of N.B., Canada; on St. John R.; univ., cath.; timber, shoes, plastics; p. (1971) 23,612.

Frederiksberg, sub. of Copenhagen, Denmark, with indep. municipal status; p. (est. 1969) 103,621.

Frederikshaab, sm. spt. on W. cst. of Greenland; fish processing.

Frederikshavn, fish. pt., N. Jutland, Denmark, on Kattegat; p. (est. 1970) 32,826.

Frederikstad, t., Norway; at mouth of Glomma R.; ctr. of pulp and paper-producing ind.; electrotechnical inds., shipbldg., fish canning; p. (1968) 30,089.

Frederiksvaerk, t., Sjaelland, Denmark; impt. iron and steel wks.

Freetown, c., cap. of Sierra Leone; pt. on Atl. Oc.; one of lgst. natural harbours in world; humid, oppressive climate; exp. diamonds, palm oil; engin., food processing, oil refining; fishing; p. (est. 1970) 178,600.

Freiberg, t., E. Germany; S.W. of Dresden, at foot of Erzgebirge; mng. academy (silver discovered 12th cent).; metallurgy, textiles, glass, porcelain; p. (est. 1967) 49,100.

Freiburg im Breisgau, c., Baden-Württemberg, W. Germany; in Black Forest; cath., univ.; cultural ctr.; tourism; p. (est. 1969) 163,500.

Freising, t., Bavaria, W. Germany; N.E. of Munich; cath.; agr. machin., textiles, chemicals; p. (est. 1969) 29,788.

Freital, t., E. Germany; S.W. Dresden; glass, uranium ore processing; coalmines nearby; p. (est. 1970) 42,159.

Fréjus, t., Var dep., S.W. France; cath., Roman ruins; resort on Fr. Riviera; p. (1968) 25,736.

Fréjus, Col de, Alpine pass. France and Italy, 2,083 m, under which runs the Mont Cenis tunnel (13·6 km).

Fremantle, spt., W. Australia; at mouth of Swan R., 19 km S.W. from Perth, principal pt. of commerce in W. Australia and first Australian pt. of call for mail steamers; oil refining; wheat, wool; p. (1966) 32,134.

French Equatorial Africa, formerly included Gabon, Congo (Brazzaville), Ubangi-Shari and Chad, sts. which are now independent.

French Guiana, Fr. overseas dep., on N. cst. of S. America, between Surinam to W. and Brazil to S. and E.; tropical climate; little developed and thinly populated; ch. ctr. of p. and spt. at cap. of Cayenne; economy based on agr. especially sugar and forestry; some gold and bauxite mng.; a. 90,650 km²; p. (est. 1969) 48,000.

French Polynesia, Fr. overseas terr., in S. Pac. Oc., comprising several archipelagos: Society Is., Marquesas Is., Tubuai Is., Tuamotu Is. and Gambier Is; increased autonomy from 1977; cap. Papeete; a. 4,002 km²; p. (est. 1970) 109,000.

French Somaliland. See Djibouti.

French S. and Antarctic Terrs., Fr. overseas terr., comprising several grs. of Is. and Antarctic terr. of Adélie Land; a. 409,220 km²; p. 132 (mainly scientists).

French West Africa, comprised former Fr. cols. of Dahomey (Benin), Ivory Coast, Mauritania, Niger, Fr. Guinea, Upper Volta, Senegal, Fr. Soudan (Mali).

Freshwater, sm. t., I. of Wight, Eng.; at W. end of I., 13 km W. of Newport; resort.

Fresnillo de Gonzalez Echeverria, t., Zacatecas, Mexico; alt. 2,227 m; mkt. t., silver mng.; p. (1970) 101,316.

Fresno, c., Cal., USA; ctr. of vast irrigated fruit-growing dist.; p. (1970) 162,326 (c.), 407,048 (met. a.).

Fribourg (Freiburg), c., cap. of F. can. Switzerland; between Berne and Lausanne; viaduct and bridges; cath., univ.; p. (1969) 40,500.

Fribourg (Freiburg), can., Switzerland; mainly dairy farming; cereals, sugarbeet, cheese; a. 1,671 km²; p. (1969) 174,000.

Friedrichshafen, t., W. Germany; on Bodensee; machin., boat bldg., motors; resort; p. (est. 1967) 40,300.

Friendly Is. See Tonga.

Friern Barnet. See Barnet.

Friesland, prov., N. Neth.; cap. Leeuwarden; dairying, horses, cattle; natural gas on Ameland I.; a. 3,432 km²; p. (1968) 511,330.

Frimley and Camberley, ts., Surrey Heath, former U.D., Surrey, Eng.; 5 km N. of Farnborough; lt. engin., plastics; military training ctr.; p. (1971) 44,784.

Frinton and Walton, Tendring, Essex, Eng.; on E. cst., 8 km N.E. of Clacton; seaside resort; p. (1971) 20,431.

Frisches Haff, shallow freshwater lagoon, Baltic cst. of Poland; 85 km long, 6–18 km broad.

Frisian Is., chain of Is. stretching from Den Helder to Jutland, along csts. of Neth., Germany, and Denmark; ch. Is. are Texel, Vlieland, Terschelling, Ameland (West F. Is), Nordeney, Borkum (East F. Is.), Sylt, Föhr, Rømø (North F. Is.).

Friuli-Venezia Giulia, aut. reg. (created 1963), N.E. Italy; comprising 3 provs. Udine, Gorozia, Trieste; p. (1969) 1,228,927.

Frobisher Bay, inlet in S. Baffin I., N. Canada, extending 320 km between Cumberland Sound and Hudson Strait.

Frodingham, t., Humberside, Eng.; on W. flank of limestone ridge, Lincoln Edge; impt. iron-ore open-cast mines; mnfs. iron and steel; p. with Scunthorpe (1971) 70,800.

Frome, mkt. t., Mendip, Somerset, Eng.; on R. Frome, 18 km S. of Bath; p. (1971) 13,384.

Frome, R., Dorset, Eng.; flows from N. Dorset Downs into Poole Harbour.

Frontignan, t., Hérault, S. France; oil refining; pipeline under sea from Sète; produces muscat; p. (1968) 11,141.

Frunze, c., cap. of Kirghiz SSR, USSR; univ.; engin., textiles, meat-packing; p. (1970) 431,000.

Fuerteventura, I., Canary gr.; a. 1,717 km²; p. (1970) 18,192.

Fujayrah, emirate, one of United Arab Emirates, Persian G.; p. (est. 1968) 10,000.

Fujisawa, t., Honshu, Japan; bearings machin.; p. (est. 1971) 240,000.

Fujiyama, extinct volcano, Japan; 96 km S.W. of Tokyo; pilgrim resort; hgst. peak of Japan; alt. 3,780 m.

Fukien (Fujian), prov., China; cap. Foochow (Fuzhou); intensive agr., rice and sugar-cane; shellfish raised along cst.; a. 123,103 km²; p. (est. 1968) 17,000,000.

Fukui, c., cap. of F. pref., central Honshu, Japan; synthetic fibres, paper; old silk-weaving ctr.; p. (est. 1971) 216,000.

Fukuoka, c., N. Kyushu, Japan; pt. on Hakata Bay; univ. ctr., old cas. t.; textiles, dolls, shipbldg.; p. (est. 1971) 878,000.

Fukushima, c., N. Honshu, Japan; ceramics, foods, steel; publishing; p. (est. 1971) 232,000.

Fukuyama, c., S. Hokkaido, Japan; p. (est. 1971) 265,000.

Fulda, t., Hesse, W. Germany; nr. Kassel; on R. Fulda; palace, abbey; textiles, metallurgy, rubber; route ctr.; p. (est. 1967) 44,400.

Fulham. See Hammersmith.

Fulwood, t., Lancs., Eng.; 3 km N.E. of Preston; p. (1971) 21,741.

Funchal, cap. of Madeira Is., pt., winter resort; cath.; p. (1970) 105,791.

Fundy, Bay of, inlet between Nova Scotia and New Brunswick, Canada; lge. tidal range of 21 m.

Furka Pass, Switzerland; between Valais and Uri cans.; 2,433 m.

Furneaux Is., S.E. Australia; in Bass Strait, belonging to Tasmania; lgst is Flinders I.; p. (1966) 1,220.

Furness, dist., Cumbria, Eng.; between Morecambe Bay and the Irish Sea.

Fürstenwalde, t., Frankfurt, E. Germany; on R. Spree; metallurgy, leather, tyres; p. (est. 1970) 30,830.

Fürth, t., Bavaria, W. Germany; nr. Nürnberg; toy and glass inds.; p. (est. 1967) 94,800.

Fusan. See Pusan.

Fuse, t., Honshu, Japan; machin., textiles, chemicals; now part of Higashiosaka; p. (1966) 253,000.

Fushimi, c., Honshu, Japan; sub. of Kyoto.

Fushun, c., Liaoning, N. China; at foot of Changpai Shan, 35 km N.E. of Shenyang; major industl. ctr.; possesses world's thickest bituminous coal seam (127 m) worked by deep and opencast mines; oil refinery based on local oil shales; steelwks. chemicals; p. (est. 1970) 1,700 000.

Fusin (Fuxin), c., Liaoning, N. China; ctr. of lge. coalfield; p. (1953) 188,600.

Fuskiki, spt. Honshu, Japan; serves Toyama c. with metals, coal.

Futa, La, pass, Tusco-Emilian Apennines, N. Italy; used by main road from Bologna to Florence; alt. 903 m.

Futa Jalon (Fouta Djalon), upland dist., mostly in Guinea, W. Africa, with outliers in Liberia and Sierra Leone.

Futseling, t., Anhwei, China; site of lge. dam on Hwai Ho, built 1954.

Fylde, W. Lancs., Eng.; low plain behind coastal sand dunes; pig- and poultry-rearing dist.; ch. t. Blackpool; as l. gov. dist. excluding Blackpool p. (est. 1976) 71,300.

Fylingdales, ballistic missile early warning sta. on N. Yorks. moors, Eng.

Fyn, I., Denmark; in Baltic Sea; a. 3,419 km²; cap. Odense; dairying, sugarbeet; p. (1971) 433,765.

Fyne, loch on Argyll and Bute cst., W. Scot.; an arm of F. of Clyde; offshore oil platform construction; 64 km long.

Fyzabad, t., Uttar Pradesh, India; mkt. t.; sugar refineries; p. (1961) 88,296.

G

Gabès, spt., Tunisia; on G. of Gabès, 320 km S. of Tunis; dates, henna, wool; p. (1966) 76,356.

Gabon, rep., W. Africa; Cameroon to N., Zaïre to S. and E.; tropical climate, hot, humid; much tropical rain forest; forestry main ind. but mng. increasingly impt.; petroleum exp. creating increasing prosperity; manganese at Moanda (S.), iron-ore at Mekambo (N.E.); communications geared mainly to mng. areas; major pts. Libreville (cap.), Port Gentil; Trans-Gabon rly. project to promote exploitation of timber; intense forest cover makes internal air services very impt.; airport at Libreville; a. 266,770 km²; p. (est. 1970) 475,000.

Gaborone (Gaberones), cap. Botswana; formerly sm. v.; chosen as cap. for new rep.; bldg. began 1964; p. (est. 1970) 15,000.

Gadag-Betgeri, t., Karnataka, India; cotton and silk weaving; p. (1961) 76,614.

Gaeta, t., naval pt., Italy; on promontory on shore of G. of Gaeta; the anc. Caietae Portus; cath.; p. (est. 1968) 22,799.

Gafsa, t., Tunisia; phosphate mng. ctr.; p. (1966) 32,408.

Gaillard Cut, excavated channel, Panama Canal Zone; carries Panama Canal through Culebra Mtn. from L. Gatun to Pac. Oc.; 11 km long.

Gainesville, t., Fla., USA; univ.; mkt. gardening; electronics, wood prod.; p. (est. 1969) 67,000.

Gainsborough, t., West Lindsey, Lincs., Eng.; on R. Trent; agr. implements, milling, packing and wrapping machin.; some R. traffic; mkt.; George Eliot's St. Ogg's in Mill on the Floss; p. (1971) 17,420.

Gairdner, salt L., S. Australia; a. 4,766 km².

Gairloch, sea loch and v., W. Ross and Cromarty, Scot.; resort, fishing; p. (1971) 1,783.

Galapagos, volcanic Is., Pac. Oc.; 960 km W. of Ecuador (to whom they belong) on equator; flora and fauna peculiar to each I.; visited by Darwin 1835; now a wildlife sanctuary; a. 7,428 km²; p. (1967) 3,100.

Galashiels, burgh, Ettrick and Lauderdale, Scot.; on Gala Water, 3 km above confluence with R. Tweed; tweeds, woollens; p. (1971) 12,609.

Galati or Galatz, c., E. Romania; major inland pt. on lower Danube; cath.; p. (est. 1969) 172,687.

Galesburg, t., Ill., USA; engin., coal mng.; p. (1970) 36,290.

Galicia, historic region, S.E. Poland and W. Ukraine, USSR.

Galicia, region, N.W. Spain; comprising provs. La Coruña, Lugo, Orense, and Pontevedra.

Galilee, northern div. of Palestine in Roman times, containing the ts. Cana, Capernaum, Tiberias, Nazareth; the ch. scene of Christ's ministry.

Galilee, Sea of (Lake Tiberias), also known as L. Gennesaret; Biblical associations; 207 m below level of Med.; Israel plans to draw water from L. to irrigate Negev; a. 166 km².

Gallarate, t., Italy; nr. Milan; textiles; p. (est. 1968) 41,208.

Galle, c., pt. on S.W. cst. of Sri Lanka; exp. tea, rubber, coconut oil; suffered from competition with Colombo after construction of modern harbour there; p. (est. 1968) 73,000.

Gallego, R., N.E. Spain; rises in Pyrenees, flows S. to R. Ebro at Zaragoza; provides irrigation around Zaragoza; valley used by main rly. across Pyrenees from Pau (France) to Zaragoza; 176 km long.

Gallipoli. See Gelibolu.

Gällivare, dist., N. Sweden, in Norrbotton prov.; rich iron-ore deposits; p. (1968) 26,625.

Galloway, anc. dist. S.W. Scot.; inc. l. gov. dists. of Stewartry and Wigtown; dairying.

Galloway, Mull of, the extremity of the Rinns of G., the most southern pt. of Scot.

Galston, burgh, Kilmarnock and Loudoun, Scot.; on R. Irvine, nr. Kilmarnock; p. (1971) 4,239.

Galt., t., Ont., Canada; textiles, shoes; p. (1971) 38,134.

Galveston, c., spt., Texas, USA; on I. in Bay at entrance to G. of Mexico; gr. cotton and sulphur pt. with lge. exp. of agr. prod.; mills, foundries, food-processing, chemicals; univ., resort; p.(1970) 60,714 (c.), 165,669 (met. a.).

Galway, co., Galway Bay, Connacht, R.o.I.; fishery, cattle, marble quarrying; a. 6,351 km²; p. (1966) 148,190.

Galway, co. t., Galway, R.o.I.; univ.; spt., fishing; sawmills, textiles, printing; p. (1966) 24,495.

Gambia, The, rep. (1970), W. Africa, on Atl. Oc.; comprises St. Mary's I. (on which is Banjul, the cap.) and narrow mainland enclave (average width 32 km) extending 320 km inland astride R. Gambia, hot all year, summer rain, but savannah inland; agr. is basis of economy, esp. groundnuts; economic aid from Taiwan; communications developed around Banjul (spt. and airpt.); a. 10,368 km²; p. (est. 1968) 360,000.

Gambia, R., Senegal and Gambia, rises in Futa Jalon Plateau, flows N. and W. into Atl. Oc. at Banjul; forms main means of communication through Gambia, 1,120 km long.

Gambier Is., Fr Polynesia, S. Pac. Oc., 4 coral Is.; a. 31 km².

Gandhinagar, new cap. of Gujarat, India; on Sabarmati R., 21 km N. of Ahmadabad; under construction; planned initial p. 75,000 rising to 200,000.

Ganges (Ganga), sacred R. of India; rises in Himalayas and flows to Bay of Bengal via alluvial cones at foot of Himalayas and by several delta mouths, on one of which stands Calcutta; navigable for lge. ships from Allahabad; delta alone larger than Eng. and Wales; flood plain and delta very fertile and densely populated; removal of irrig. water by India causes friction with Bangladesh; 2,400 km long.

Gangtok, t., cap. of Sikkim, E. Himalayas; agr. tr. ctr.; carpets; p. (est. 1968) 9,000.

Gap, t., Hautes Alpes, S.E. France; textiles; p. (1968) 23,994.

Gard, dep., S. France; in Languedoc, on Mediterranean; cap. Nîmes; vines, olives, sericulture; a. 5,879 km²; p. (1968) 478,544.

Garda, L., between Lombardy and Venezia, Italy; variety of scenery, winter resort; a. 370 km²; greatest depth, 346 m.

Garden Grove, residtl. c., sub. S.E. Los Angeles, Cal., USA; p. (1970) 121,504.

Gardéz, t., Afghanistan; alt. 2,287 m; ctr. of comm. and transport; p. (est. 1969) 39,142.

Garforth, t., West Yorks., Eng.; coalmng., lt. inds.; p. (1971) 25,296.

Garigliano, R. and dist., S. central Italy; where Liri R. joins Gari R. below Cassino; nuclear power plant.

Garmisch-Partenkirchen, t., Bavaria, W. Germany; winter sports; p. (est. 1969) 27,267.

Garo Hills, mtnous. dist., Assam, India; a. 8,078 km²; dense forests; p. (1961) 307,228.

Garonne, R., S.W. France; rises at foot of Mt. Maladetta (Pyrenees), flows via Toulouse and agr. valley, and enters Gironde estuary 32 km below Bordeaux; 720 km long.

Garrigue, region, Languedoc, S. France; low limestone hills, run N.E. to S.W., W. of Rhône delta; semi-arid; scanty vegetation; winter pasture for sheep; olives; Montpellier, Nîmes located on S. flank.

Garut, t., W. Java, Indonesia, mtn. resort, lge. spinning mill; p. 24,219.

Gary, c., Ind., USA; on S. shore of L. Michigan; leading producer of steel, tinplate, cement; p. (1970) 174,132 (c.), 628,969 (met. a.).

Gascony, anc. prov., S.W. France; now comprises deps. along Atl. cst. and Pyrenees; Landes. Gers, Hautes-Pyrenees, and parts of Lot-et-Garonne, Tarn-et-Garonne, Haute Garonne, Gironde and Ariège. Battleground in Hundred Years War.

Gastonia, t., N.C., USA; impt. textile ctr.; p. (1970) 47,142.

Gateshead, t., met. dist., Tyne and Wear, Eng.; on R. Tyne opposite Newcastle; engin., food-processing, pumps, paper; pt.; p. (est. 1976) 222,000 (dist.).

Gatineau, R., Canada; trib. of Ottawa R., which it joins nr. Ottawa; length 480 km; hydroelec. power; forested valley.

Gatwick, West Sussex, Eng.; 40 km S. London; first airport in world where trunk road, main rly. line and air facilities combined in one unit.

Gauhati, t., India; temporary cap. of Assam being developed in E. suburb of Dispur; univ.; silk, cotton, lace, oil refinery; pipeline from Barauni; p. (1971) 123,783 (t.), 200,377 (met. a.).

Gaul (Lat. Gallia), embraced in the lands inhabited by Celtic peoples in Roman times, covering what is now modern France (Gaul proper), Belgium, N. Italy, and parts of Germany, Neth., and Switzerland. South of the Alps was known as Cisalpine Gaul, north of the Alps as Transalpine Gaul.

Gauri-Sankar, mtn. in Himalayas, Nepal and Tibet, China; 56 km W. of Mt. Everest; alt. 7,149 m.

Gävle, spt., Sweden; timber, textiles, steel, porcelain; p. (1968) 60,990.

Gävleborg, co., Sweden; ch. t., Gävle; a. 18,544 km²; p. (est. 1970) 293,377.

Gaya, t., Bihar, India; Buddhist pilgrim ctr.; cottons, silks; p. (1971) 179,884.

Gaza, t., N.E. Egypt; ch. t. of Gaza Strip (q.v.); anciently the t. where Samson brought down the temple.

Gazankulu (Machangana), Bantu Terr. Authority (1969), S. Africa; home of Shangana and Tsonga p.; cap. Giyana; p. (est. 1969) 392,000.

Gaza Strip, coastal a. under Egyptian admin. since 1949; occupied by Israeli troops, Nov. 1956–March 1957, and since June 1967.

Gaziantep, t., Turkey; S.W. of Malatya; mkt. t.; p. (1965) 160,152 (t.), 235,472 (met. a.).

Gazli, Uzbek SSR, USSR; 96 km N.W. of Bukhara; natural gas field; pipeline to Chelyabinsk opened 1963; destroyed by earthquake (1976).

Gdańsk (Danzig), c., spt., N. Poland; Baltic pt.; on branch of Vistula; annexed to Germany 1939, restored to Poland 1945; shipbldg., machin., chemicals, metals; Gdańsk, Gdynia and Sopot admin. as single c. (Trójmiasto = tri-city); p. (1970) 364,000.

Gdynia, spt., Gdańsk, N. Poland; competes with spt. of Gdańsk for Polish hinterland; impt. comm., rly. and industl. ctr.; part of the Trójmiasto; p. (1970) 190,000.

Gedling, l. gov. dist., Notts., Eng.; Basford, Carlton and Arnold and N.E. outskirts of Nottingham; p. (est. 1976) 101,600.

Geelong, c., spt., Victoria, Australia; on Corio Bay; exp. flour, wool, meat; oil refining, agr. machin., cars, carpets; p. (1972) 17,775 (c.), 121,966 (met. a.).

Gela, t., S. Sicily, Italy; in cotton-growing a.; petrochemicals; p. (est. 1968) 65,289.

Gelderland, prov., Neth.; E. and S. of Utrecht prov.; a. 5,022 km²; cap. Arnhem; cereals, tobacco; cattle rearing; p. (1968) 1,456,544.

Gelibolu (Gallipoli), pt. and penin. on the Dardanelles, Turkey; scene of unsuccessful landing by British and Anzac troops 1915; 176 km. long.

Gelligaer, t., Rhymney Valley, Mid Glamorgan, Wales; 6 km N.E. of Pontypridd; coal mng.; p. (1971) 33,670.

Gelsenkirchen, t., N. Rhine–Westphalia, W. Germany; in Ruhr conurb. on Rhine–Herne canal; collys., ironwks., glass, chemicals, oil refining; p. (est. 1969) 351,000.

Geneva, c., cap. of G. can., Switzerland; at exit of Rhône from L. Geneva; cath., univ.; former H.Q. of League of Nations; H.Q. of ILO, WHO, and Red Cross; watchmkg., jewellery, elec. gds., optical instruments; tourist resort; birthplace of Rousseau; p. (est. 1969) 169,500 (c.), 307,500 (met. a.).

Geneva (L. Léman), L., S.W. corner of Switzerland; forms a gr. crescent of water, source of poetic inspiration; 371 m a.s.l.; a. 578 km².

Génissiat, France; site of gr. barrage and hydroelec. power sta. on Rhône below Geneva; completed 1950.

Genk, t., Limburg, Belgium; stainless steel wks.. petrochemicals; p. (1968) 56,031.

Gennevilliers, t., Hauts-de-Seine France; N.W. sub. of Paris; R. pt.; p. (1968) 46,074.

Genoa (Genova), c., ch. pt. Italy; cath., univ., palaces; handles one-third of Italy's foreign tr.; pt. and airpt. expansion, shipyards, steelwks., engin., textiles, tanning; p. (est. 1970) 842,114 (met. a.).

George L., N.Y., USA; Adirondack mtns.; picturesque resort. [3,975.

Georgetown, cap., Cayman Is.; pt.; p. (1970)

Georgetown (Demerara), c., cap. of Guyana; on Demerara R.; exp. sugar, cocoa, coffee, timber, gold, diamonds, bauxite; airpt. nearby; botanical gardens; p. (1970) 99,089.

Georgetown. See Penang.

Georgia, st., S.E. USA; one of 13 original sts., on Atl. cst.; rising to Appalachians; impt. arable agr.; cotton and lumber inds.; major source of kaolin; ch. ts., Atlanta (cap.), Savannah; a. 152,489 km²; p. (1970) 4,492,038.

Georgia (Gruziya), constituent rep., USSR; rich agr., fruit, tobacco, grain; mng. inc. manganese, gold, oil; several hydroelectric power plants; coastal and mtn. resorts; active Jewish community; cap. Tbilisi; a. 69,671 km²; p. (1970) 4,688,000.

Georgian Bay, arm of L. Huron, S. Ont., Canada; separated from L. by Manitoulin I. and Saugeen peninsula; c. 160 km long, c. 80 km wide; L. pts., Owen Sound, Midland, Parry Sound; Georgian Bay Is., Nat. Park.

Gera, c., cap. of G. admin. dist., E. Germany; on White Elster R.; woollens, printing; lignite mined nearby; p. (est. 1969) 111,188.

Geraldton, spt., W. Australia; N. outlet for wheat belt; also exps. wool and manganese; early tomatoes; super phosphate; p. (1972) 15,330.

Germany, Democratic Rep. of, and E. Berlin (E. Germany), rep., Central Europe; partition from W. Germany complete by 1948; part of N. European Plain; 7th industl. nation of world; lignite field supplies 70 per cent of energy; main inds., optics, electronics and precision machin., chemicals, heavy engin.; member of Comecon; 15 admin. dists. (Bezirke); cap. E. Berlin; a. 108,267 km²; p. (1969) 17,074,504.

Germany, Fed. Rep. of (W. Germany), W. Europe; partition complete by 1948; N. half part of N. European Plain; rises in S. to Bavarian Alps; 2nd lgst. trading nation of world; mainly industl. with core in Ruhr conurb.; motor vehicles, chemicals, precision engin.; member of EEC; tourism; 10 admin. dists. (Länder) and W. Berlin; cap. Bonn; a. (inc. W. Berlin) 248,459 km²; p. (1975) 61,645,000.

Germiston, t., Transvaal, S. Africa; nr. Johannesburg; gold-mng.; rly. wkshps., engin., machin., chemicals; gas pipeline from Sasolburg, p. (1970) 281,494 (met. a.).

Gerona, c., cap. of G. prov., Spain; cath.; textiles, chemicals; p. (1970) 50,338.

Gerrards Cross, t., S.E. Bucks., Eng.; 14 km E. of High Wycombe; residtl.

Gers, dep., S.W. France; cap. Auch; grain, vines, brandy; a. 6,291 km²; p. (1968) 181,577.

Gersoppa Falls, Sharavati R., Karnataka, India; hgst. cascade 253 m; hydroelec. power.

Gezira, dist., Sudan, N.E. Africa; between Blue and White Niles; c. 12,173 km² capable of irrigation provided by Blue Nile at Sennar Dam; lge-scale growing of high-quality cotton; total a. c. 20,200 km².

Ghadames (Ghudamis), oasis, Sahara Desert, Libya; at point where Tunis, Algeria, Libya converge 480 km S.W. of Tripoli.

Ghaghara (Gogra), sacred R., India; trib. of Ganges, rises in Tibet, flows through Uttar Pradesh; lge. catchment a. but poorly developed floodplain; 960 km long.

Ghana, rep., W. Africa; indep. st., member of Brit. Commonwealth; tropical monsoon climate, but rainfall decreases inland; S. Ghana more developed than N.; agr. basis of comm. economy and cocoa (of which Ghana is world's lgst producer) major exp.; Volta R. scheme produces power from main dam at Akosombo and an aluminium smelter plant began production in 1967; oil refining and production; communications network based on Accra and Takoradi on cst., and inland ctr. of Kumasi; development of road network vital for expansion of comm. agr.; 3 univs.; pts. at Takoradi and Tema closely linked with internal economic growth; cap. Accra; a. 238,539 km²; p. (1970) 8,545,561.

Ghardaia, t., Algeria; N. of Sahara; ch. t. of Mzab valley; p. (1966) 30,167.

Ghats, mtn. ranges which border the Deccan plateau in S. India. The Eastern Ghats are broken by many Rs. and rise only to 1,362 m in Northern Circars. The Western Ghats form an almost unbroken range, reaching 2,672 m in Dodabetta in Nilgiri hills; rainfall extremely heavy; forests; hydroelectric power.

Ghaziabad, t., Uttar Pradesh, India; on R. Jumna opposite Delhi; p. (1971) 118,836.

Ghazipur, t., Uttar Pradesh, N. India; on Ganges, E. of Varanasi; p. (1961) 37,147.

Ghazni, mtn. t., E. Afghanistan; once cap. of empire of Mahmud, c. A.D. 1000; now mkt. t.; p. (est. 1969) 43,423.

Ghent, c., cap. of E. Flanders prov., Belgium; pt. at confluence of Rs. Scheldt and Lys; cath., univ.; textiles, steel, plastics, chemicals; oil refinery; p. (est. 1969) 151,614 (c.), 228,100 (met. a.).

Ghor, El, depression. Jordan and Israel between Sea of Galilee and Dead Sea 3–24 km wide; agr. resettlement scheme.

Giant's Causeway, basaltic columns on promontory of N. cst. of Moyle, N. Ireland.

Gibraltar, City of, Brit. terr. at W. entrance to Mediterranean; rocky I., 426 m. joined to Spain by sandy isthmus; few natural resources; economy depends on tourism, Admiralty dockyard, services to shipping, and entrepot tr.; Spanish govt. lays claim to terr.; a. 6·5 km²; p. (1971) 28,964.

Gibraltar, Strait of, connects Mediterranean with Atl., 13·6 km wide; of strategic importance.

Gidgelpha-Moomba, dist., S. Australia; lge. natural gas field; pipeline to Adelaide.

Giessen, t., Hesse, W. Germany; on R. Lahn; univ.; various mnfs.; p. (est. 1969) 74,380.

Gifu, t., Central Honshu, Japan; cas.; fans, lanterns, textiles; tourism for cormorant fishing; p. (est. 1971) 393,000.

Gigha, I., Argyll and Bute, Scot.; off W. cst. of Kintyre; 10 km by 3 km.

Gijón, spt., Oviedo Spain; on Bay of Biscay; gd. harbour; tobacco, petroleum, coal, earthenware; steel wks. nearby; p. (1967) 144,987.

Gila, R., N.M. and Arizona, USA; trib. of R. Colorado; used for irrigation in Imperial valley; 1,040 km long.

Gilan, prov., N.W. Iran; on Caspian Sea, bounded by USSR; sub-tropical climate; agr., inc. cotton and rice; cap Rasht; p. (1967) 754,650.

Gilbert Is., Brit. col. terr., internal self-gov. delayed by Ocean I. dispute; central Pac. Oc.; chain of coral Is. across equator; economy based on phosphate mng. and copra; cap. Tarawa; Ellice Is. separated 1976 and renamed Tuvalu Is.; full indep. by 1978; a. 956 km²; p. (1968) 53,517.

Gilgit, dist., Kashmir, India; mtnous., exceeding 6,000 m on N. and W.; with Ladakh links India with Tibet; p. 77,000.

Atlas of the World

Contents

Symbols

———— Principal Railways

════ Motorways

———— Principal Roads

▬▬▬ International Boundaries

-------- Internal Boundaries

4125 Heights in Metres

✧ Principal Airports

Height of Land

For Pages 6, 7, 8, 9

For Pages 4, 5, 12, 13, 16, 17, 18, 20, 21, 22, 26, 31, 32, 33

For Pages 10, 11, 27, 28, 29, 30, 36

For Pages 14, 15, 19, 23, 24, 25, 34, 35

© 1978 and Printed in Great Britain by George Philip & Son, Ltd., London.

WORLD : Political

Scale 1:135,000,000

EUROPE

0	100	200	300	400 miles
0	200	400	600 km	

E.E.C. members

a Greece

E.F.T.A. members

FINLAND

Honningsvag
Pechenga
Murmansk

White Sea

Mezen
Arkhangelsk

N. Dvina

Kotlas

Hammerfest

Vadso

Luleå

Kuopio

L. Onega

Tampere

Helsinki

Kronstadt

Leningrad

UNION OF SOVIET

Vyborg
L. Ladoga

Perm

Izhevsk

Sverdlovsk

Zlatoust

Kirov

REPUBLIC

Vologda

R. U. S. S. I. A. N.

S. F. S. R.

Gorki

Volga

Kazan

Ufa

Tallinn
ESTONIA

Chudskoye

Novgorod

Rybinsk Res

Yaroslavl

Ivanovo

Pskov

Kostroma

55

Ulyanovsk

Kuybyshev

Orenburg

LATVIA

Liepaja Riga

Daugavpils

W. Dvina

Vitebsk

MOSCOW

Tula

SOCIALIST

Syzran

Penza

Volga

Uralsk

Ural

Klaipeda

LITHUANIA

Kaunas

Vilnius

Smolensk

Mogilev

Orel

REPUBLICS

Tambov

Saratov

50

Kaliningrad

BELORUSSIYA

Minsk

Gomel

Kursk

Voronezh

Don

KAZAKHSTAN

Bialystok

Brest

Pripet

Chernigov

Volgograd

Volga

Guryev

WARSAW

Lublin

Kiev

Zhitomir

Dnieper

U K R A I N E

Kharkov

Voroshilovgrad

Astrakhan

45

POLAND

Lvov

Berdichev

Kirovograd

Dnepropetrovsk

Donetsk

Don

Rostov

CASPIAN SEA

Kosice

Chernovtsy

Dniester

MOLDAVIA

Krivoy Rog

Zaporozhye

Taganrog

Stavropol

Makhachkala

Debrecen

Kishinev

Nikolayev

S. of Azov

Kerch

Derbent

Cluj

Odessa

Kherson

Krasnodar

ROMANIA

Galati

Sevastopol

Novorossiysk

GEORGIA

Tbilisi

40

Timisoara

Brasov

Ploesti

Constanta

B L A C K   S E A

Batumi

AZERBAIJAN

BUCHAREST

Danube

Pleven

Varna

Sinop

Samsun

Trabzon

ARMENIA

Yerevan

A.Z.

Orekhovo

Sofia

BULGARIA

Burgas

Kastamonu

Erzurum

Tabriz

Skopje

Plovdiv

Sliven

Edirne

Istanbul

Uskudar

Ankara

Kayseri

T U R K E Y

Malatya

Diyarbakir

Mosul

IRAN

Thessaloniki

Bursa

Balikesir

A N A T O L I A

35

IRAQ

Izmir

Aydin

Konya

Adana

Iskenderun

Tigris

Piraeus

ATHENS

Antalya

Aleppo

SYRIA

Baghdad

Crete

CYPRUS

Nicosia

Homs

Euphrates

Limassol

Iraklion

30

COPYRIGHT. GEORGE PHILIP & SON. LTD.

miles
0   20   40   60
0   20   40   60   80   100 km

N O R T H   S E A

Dogger Bank

I R I S H   S E A

North Channel

S C O T L A N D

Dundee
Perth
St. Andrews
Firth of Tay
Crieff
Kinross
Dunfermline
Kirkcaldy
Firth of Forth
Bass Rock
Dunbar
FIFE
Edinburgh
CENTRAL
Stirling
Falkirk
Motherwell
Wishaw
Glasgow
Paisley
Hamilton
LOTHIAN
BORDERS
Peebles
Galashiels
Melrose
Jedburgh
Hawick
Cheviot Hills
The Cheviot
St Abb's Hd.
Berwick-upon-Tweed
Holy I.
Farne Is.

Kilmarnock
Ayr
Irvine
DUMFRIES
Dumfries
GALLOWAY
Kirkcudbright
Solway Firth
Annan
Carlisle
NORTHUMBERLAND
Morpeth
Blyth
Tynemouth
Newcastle
Gateshead
South Shields
Sunderland
Houghton-le-Spring
Durham
Hexham
TYNE AND WEAR
DURHAM
Bishop Auckland
Darlington
Stockton
Middlesbrough
Hartlepool
Redcar
CLEVELAND

ISLE OF MAN
Ramsey
Douglas
Castletown
Pt. of Ayre
Peel
Calf of Man

Whitehaven
Workington
St. Bee's Hd.
Keswick
Cumbrian Mts.
CUMBRIA
Ambleside
Kendal
Windermere
Barrow
Walney I.
Morecambe
Lancaster
Fleetwood
Blackpool
Southport
Formby Pt.
LANCASHIRE
Preston
Blackburn
Burnley
Colne
Bolton
Wigan
Warrington
Liverpool
MERSEYSIDE
Birkenhead
Wallasey
Southport

N O R T H   Y O R K S H I R E
North York Moors
Scarborough
Bridlington
Flamborough Hd.
Whitby
Northallerton
Thirsk
Ripon
Harrogate
York
Ure
Ouse
Settle
Skipton
Keighley
Bradford
Leeds
Halifax
Huddersfield
Barnsley
WEST YORKSHIRE
SOUTH YORKSHIRE
Rotherham
Sheffield
Doncaster
Worksop
Goole
Scunthorpe
HUMBERSIDE
Hull
Beverley
Hornsea
Withernsea
Spurn Hd.
Grimsby
Cleethorpes
Immingham
Gainsborough
East Retford
Lincoln
LINCOLNSHIRE
Lincoln Wold
Louth
Mablethorpe

N O R T H E R N   I R E L A N D
U L S T E R
Belfast
Lisburn
Lurgan
Portadown
Armagh
Dungannon
Coleraine
Portrush
Ballymoney
Ballymena
Antrim
Larne
Carrickfergus
Newtownards
Bangor
Ards Pen.
Strangford L.
Downpatrick
Newcastle
Mourne Mts.
Newry
Dundalk Bay
Dundalk
Drogheda
Dublin
DUBLIN
MEATH
LOUTH

ENGLAND AND WALES — SOUTH

Counties and regions

GWYNEDD · CLWYD · POWYS · DYFED · GWENT · MID GLAM. · WEST GLAM. · SOUTH GLAM. · SHROPSHIRE (SALOP) · STAFFORD · LEICESTER · NORTHAMPTON · WARWICK · HEREFORD AND WORCESTER · GLOUCESTER · OXFORD · BUCKS · BEDFORD · HERTFORD · CAMBRIDGE · NORFOLK · SUFFOLK · ESSEX · LONDON · SURREY · KENT · EAST SUSSEX · WEST SUSSEX · HANTS · BERKS · WILTS · AVON · SOMERSET · DORSET · DEVON · CORNWALL

Selected places

Great Yarmouth · Lowestoft · Norwich · King's Lynn · Ipswich · Cambridge · Peterborough · Colchester · Chelmsford · Southend · LONDON · Luton · Bedford · Northampton · Leicester · Nottingham · Derby · Stafford · Telford · Shrewsbury · Birmingham · Coventry · Worcester · Gloucester · Cheltenham · Oxford · Reading · Swindon · Bristol · Bath · Cardiff · Newport · Swansea · Port Talbot · Aberystwyth · Carmarthen · Bridgend · Weston-super-Mare · Bridgwater · Taunton · Exeter · Barnstaple · Plymouth · Devonport · Torquay · Dartmouth · Bournemouth · Poole · Weymouth · Southampton · Portsmouth · Newport (I. of Wight) · Brighton · Worthing · Eastbourne · Hastings · Dover · Folkestone · Canterbury · Margate · Ramsgate · Maidstone · Rochester · Guildford · Winchester · Salisbury · Newquay · Truro · Penzance · Land's End

Bristol Channel · English Channel · St. George's Channel · Cardigan Bay · The Wash · Strait of Dover

FRANCE · Calais · Boulogne-sur-Mer · Dieppe · Cherbourg

West from Greenwich · East from Greenwich

COPYRIGHT: GEORGE PHILIP & SON, LTD.

8

SCOTLAND

0   20   40   60 miles
0   20   40   60   80 100 km

SHETLAND

Unst
Fetlar
Yell
Whalsay
Shetland Is.
Mainland
Bressay
Foula   Lerwick

On same scale   Sumburgh Hd.

Mainland
Sumburgh Hd.

ATLANTIC

OCEAN

Fair Isle

N. Ronaldsay
Westray
Rousay   Sanday
ORKNEY   Shapinsay   Stronsay
Mainland   Orkney Is.
Kirkwall
Hoy   South Ronaldsay

Rona

NORTH

SEA

Pentland Firth

C. Wrath   Strathy Pt.
Dunnet Hd.   John
Thurso   O'Groats
Dounreay   Noss Hd.
Wick

Butt of Lewis

L. Laxford   Ben Hope
Eddrachillis Bay   971
B. More   998
Assynt   Assynt
Loch Shin
Enard Bay   Lairg   Ord of Caithness
Helmsdale

Stornoway   Broad Bay
Lewis
WESTERN
ISLES
Tarbert
Harris
Little Minch
North Minch

L. Broom   Ullapool   Oykel   Golspie
B. Dearg   Invergordon   Dornoch
Lairg   Tain   Dornoch Firth   Tarbet Ness
Ben Wyvis
HIGHLAND   Conon   1045
Fannich   Dingwall   Cromarty   Elgin   Buckie   Buchan   Kinnairds Hd.
Beauly   Nairn   Forres   Keith   Deveron   Turriff   Peterhead
Inverness   Grantown-   Huntly
on-Spey

Monach Is.
North Uist
Sound of Harris
Benbecula
B. More   619
South Uist

The Aird
L. Seaforth
Sound of Harris
L. Maddy
N. Portree
L. Snizort

N. West
Glen Affric
Glen Moriston
Loch Ness
Fort Augustus
Badenoch

Cairn Gorm
GRAMPIAN
Cairngorm Mts.
1311
Ben Macdhui   Ballater   Balmoral Castle
1309   Braemar   Banchory   Aberdeen
Lochnagar   Girdle Ness
Stonehaven

Cuillin
Hills
Cuillin Sound
Lochalsh
Kyle
Stromeferry

Canna
Rhum
Eigg
Muck   A' Mhoidart
Mallaig   L. Morar
Ardnamurchan   Loch Shiel
Point

Ben Nevis   S C O T L A N D
1342
Fort   GRAMPIAN
William   L. Arkaig
L. Rannoch
Loch Tummel   Pitlochry
Pass of   Brechin
Killiecrankie   Montrose

Barra
Barra Hd.

Tobermory
Coll   Morvern
Tiree   Loch Sunart   Ardgour   Loch Eil
Staffa   Mull   Loch Linnhe
Iona   B. More   Oban   L. Etive
966   Connel
Firth of Lorne   Inverary
Ben Cruachan   994

Aberfeldy   Blairgowrie   S. Esk
Ben Lawers   TAYSIDE   Forfar
1214   L. Tay   Brechin
Breadalbane   Sidlaw Hills   Arbroath
Crieff   Scone   Dundee   Firth of Tay
1174   Perth   Tayport
Ben More   Earn   Cupar   St. Andrews
983   Kinross   Fife Ness

Colonsay
Rudh' a' Mhail
Bowmore   Islay
Gigha

STRATHCLYDE

Loch Awe
Lochgilphead
Kintyre
Sound of Jura
Jura
Firth of Clyde

L. Lomond
Ben Lomond
983
L. Katrine
CENTRAL
Stirling   Alloa   Glenrothes
Callander   Bannockburn   FIFE   Leven
Dumbarton   Grangemouth   Dunfermline   Kirkcaldy   Anstruther
Helensburgh   Falkirk   Forth   Buckhaven
Dunoon   Clydebank   Edinburgh   Bass Rock
Greenock   Glasgow   Leith
Port Glasgow   Paisley   Coatbridge   LOTHIAN   Dalkeith   Musselburgh   Dunbar
Rothesay   Motherwell   Haddington   St. Abb's Hd.
Hamilton   Wishaw   Lammermuir Hills
Carstairs   Moorfoot   Berwick-upon-
Kilmarnock   Lanark   Hills   Peebles   Tweed
Ardrossan   Goat Fell   Saltcoats   BORDERS   Coldstream   Holy I.
Brodick   874   Irvine   Broad   Galashiels   Kelso
Arran   Prestwick   Law   Selkirk   The Cheviot
Ayr   840   Jedburgh   816   Alnwick
Southern   Hawick   Cheviot Hills

Campbeltown
Mull of Kintyre

Rathlin I.
Fair Hd.
Moville
Portrush   Ballycastle
Coleraine   Ballymoney
Sperrin Mts.   Bann   Larne
683   Ballymena   Antrim   Carrickfergus
NORTHERN   Lough Neagh   Belfast
IRELAND   Bangor

North Channel

Girvan   Sanquhar   Uplands   NORTHUMBERLAND
Merrick   Doon   DUMFRIES   Morpeth
843   AND   Gretna Green   Newcastle
Stranraer   GALLOWAY   Annan   Tyne   Blaydon
Portpatrick   Wigtown   Dumfries   Castle   Solway Firth   Hexham   Gateshead
Luce   Bay   Douglas   Carlisle   ENGLAND
Bay   Kirkcudbright   CUMBRIA   Durham
Galloway   Wigtown Bay   Maryport   Penrith   Cross Fell   Bishop
Mull of Galloway   Workington   Skiddaw   893   Auckland
731   Tees
Keswick

6   West from Greenwich   4

COPYRIGHT. GEORGE PHILIP & SON

FRANCE

0 20 40 60 80 100 miles
0 40 80 120 160 km

ENGLAND

Swansea · Newport · Swindon · LONDON · Southend
Cardiff · Bristol · Bath · Margate
Taunton · Southampton · Chichester · Brighton · Folkestone · Dover · Cala
Exeter · Exmouth · Portsmouth · Hastings · Newhaven · C. Gris Nez · Boulogne
Torquay · Weymouth · Ryde · Montreuil
St. Ives · Truro · Dartmouth · Portland · Somme
Land's End · Falmouth · Penzance · Eddystone · Le Tréport · Dieppe
Plymouth

ENGLISH CHANNEL

St. Valery
C. de la Hague · Cherbourg · Fécamp
Alderney · Pte. de Barfleur · Caux · Yvetot · S. Me.
Guernsey · St. Peter Port · Valognes · Le Havre · Bolbec · Rouen
Channel Is. · Sark · Cotentin · Trouville · Honfleur · Vexin
(Br.) · Jersey · St. Helier · Bessin · Bayeux · Lisieux · E.
Bocage · St. Lô · Caen · C. · Elbeuf · Evreux
Granville · Mt. St. · Vire · Or. · Falaise · Mantes · Versa
Michel · Avranches · M · Perche · Dreux · Y
Ushant · Morlaix · St. Malo · Dinard · Alençon · E.L.
Pte. de · Brest · Guingamp · St. Brieuc · Fougères · Mayenne · Chartres
St. Mathieu · Mts. · F. · R. · I. · C. N. · Dinan · MAINE · Beau
Bd'Arrée · Rennes · Laval · May. · Le Mans · ORLI.C.
Pte. du Raz · Mts. Noire · Quimper · I.V. · Orléa · SA
Mo. · Vilaine · Châteaubriant · Sarthe · Loir · Blois · I.
Pte. de Penmarch · Lorient · Vannes · Loire · Tours · Amboise
Quimperlé · Carnac · F. · M. · R · TOURAINE · Loches
Quiberon · Belle I. · LA · N. · U · Angers · Saumur · I.L. · Châteauroux
St. Nazaire · Loire · Nantes · Cholet · Chinon · Creuse
Ile de Noirmoutier · Ve. · Bocage · Châtellerault
Ile de Yeu · Vente · Po I T O U · D.S. · Poitiers · MAR
La Roche · Catina · Vi.
Les Sables d'Olonne · Fontenay · Niort · H.V.
Ile de Ré · La Rochelle · AUNIS · Limoges
BAY · Ile d' Oléron · Rochefort · ANGOUMOIS · LIM
Saintes · Ch.
OF · Royan · Angoulême · Uzerche
Le Verdon · Cognac · D · Périgueux
BISCAY · Médoc · Périgord
Pauillac · GI · Libourne · GUY · Sarlat
Bordeaux · Dordogne · Bergerac · Lo
Arcachon · Garonne · L.G. · Cahors
L · T.G.
Mont-de-Marsan · Agen
Gulf of · GASCONY · Ge. · Toulouse
Gijón · Gascony · Armagnac · Auch · G.H.
Oviedo · Santander · Biarritz · Pau
Llanes · Santona · Fuenterrabia · P.A.R. · Orthez
Picos de 2648 · Torrelavega · Guecho · Bayonne · Lourdes · Tarbes
Europa · Sestao · Bilbao · Guernica · BEARN · Ari
Sa. de Alba · Reinosa · Durango · San Sebastian · Roncesvalles · H.P. · Andorra
Léon · Vitoria · Tolosa · Pamplona · 2887 · La
Astorga · Pancorbo · Miranda · Ebro · 1631 · Canfranc P. · Mt. Perdu · PYRENEE
Saldaña · S P A I N · Jaca · 3355
Burgos · Logroño · Tafalla
Sahagún · Arlanzon · Aragon

West from Greenwich · 0 · East from Greenwich

FRENCH DEPARTMENTS

A.	01	Ain
Ai.	02	Aisne
Al.	03	Allier
A.H.P.	04	Alpes-de-Haute-Provence
H.A.	05	Hautes-Alpes
A.M.	06	Alpes-Maritimes
Ar.	07	Ardèche
Ard.	08	Ardennes
Ari.	09	Ariège
Aub.	10	Aube
Aud.	11	Aude
Av.	12	Aveyron
B.R.	13	Bouches-du-Rhône
Ca.	14	Calvados
Ca.	15	Cantal
Ch.	16	Charente
Ch.M.	17	Charente-Maritime
Che.	18	Cher
Co.	19	Corrèze
	20	Corse a) Haute-Corse b) Corse du Sud
C.O.	21	Côte-d'Or
C.N.	22	Côtes-du-Nord
Cr.	23	Creuse
Do.	24	Dordogne
Do.	25	Doubs
Dr.	26	Drôme
E.	27	Eure
E.L.	28	Eure-et-Loir
F.	29	Finistère Nord et Sud
G.	30	Gard
H.G.	31	Haute-Garonne
Ge.	32	Gers
Gi.	33	Gironde
H.	34	Hérault
I.V.	35	Ille-et-Vilaine
I.	36	Indre
I.L.	37	Indre-et-Loire
Is.	38	Isère
J.	39	Jura
L.	40	Landes
L.C.	41	Loir-et-Cher
Lo.	42	Loire
H.L.	43	Haute-Loire
L.A.	44	Loire-Atlantique
Loi.	45	Loiret
Lot	46	Lot
L.G.	47	Lot-et-Garonne
Loz.	48	Lozère
M.L.	49	Main-et-Loire
Ma.	50	Manche
Ma.	51	Marne
H.M.	52	Haute-Marne
May.	53	Mayenne
M.M.	54	Meurthe-et-Moselle
Me.	55	Meuse
Mo.	56	Morbihan
Mos.	57	Moselle
N.	58	Nièvre
N.	59	Nord
O.	60	Oise
Or.	61	Orne
P.C.	62	Pas-de-Calais
P.D.	63	Puy-de-Dôme
P.A.	64	Pyrénées Atlantiques
H.P.	65	Hautes Pyrénées
P.O.	66	Pyrénées (Orientales)
B.R.	67	Bas Rhin
H.R.	68	Haut Rhin
Rh.	69	Rhône
H.S.	70	Haute Saône
S.L.	71	Saône-et-Loire
S.	72	Sarthe
Sa.	73	Savoie
H.Sa.	74	Haute-Savoie
	75	Paris
S.Me.	76	Seine-Maritime
S.M.	77	Seine-et-Marne
Yv.	78	Yvelines
D.S.	79	Deux-Sèvres
So.	80	Somme
T.	81	Tarn
T.G.	82	Tarn-et-Garonne
V.	83	Var
Va.	84	Vaucluse
Ve.	85	Vendée
Vi.	86	Vienne
H.V.	87	Haute Vienne
Vo.	88	Vosges
Y.	89	Yonne
B.	90	Belfort
Es.	91	Essonne
	92	Hauts-de-Seine
	93	Seine-St. Denis
	94	Val-de-Marne
	95	Val-d'Oise

CORSICA
On same scale

NETHERLANDS

0 10 20 30 40 50 miles
0   20   40   60   80 km

East from Greenwich

SCANDINAVIA

ICELAND
On same scale
as general map

14

CENTRAL EUROPE

0   50   100 miles
0   50   100   150 km

BALTIC SEA

DENMARK

Lolland
Falster
Gedser

Flensburg
Schleswig
SCHLESWIG-HOLSTEIN

Kiel Canal
Kiel Bay
Fehmarn
Grosselbrode

Heligoland Bay
Heligoland
Wangerooge
Norderney
Borkum

Frisian Islands

NETHERLANDS

Texel
Den Helder
Terschelling
Vlieland
Ameland
Schiermonnikoog

Leeuwarden
Groningen
Assen
Meppel
Zwolle
Kampen
Deventer
Apeldoorn
Zutphen
Arnhem
Nijmegen
Enschede
Almelo
Hengelo

Haarlem
Alkmaar
Amsterdam
Leiden
The Hague
Utrecht
Hilversum
Rotterdam
Dordrecht
Gouda
's Hertogenbosch
Breda
Tilburg
Eindhoven
Turnhout

BELGIUM

Antwerp
Mechelen
Brussels
Louvain
Liège
Charleroi
Maastricht
Mönchengladbach
Maaseik

POLAND

Słupsk
Dartowo
Koszalin
Kołobrzeg
Szczecinek
Stargard
Szczecin
Gryfino

Odra (Oder)
Noteć (Netze)
Poznań
Grodzisk
Leszno
Głogów
Zielona Góra
Legnica

Wałbrzych
Jelenia Góra
Karkonosze
Kłodzko

Usedom
Wolin
Świnoujście
Haff

EAST GERMANY

Rügen
Sassnitz
Stralsund
Greifswald
Rostock
Güstrow
Wismar
Schwerin
Parchim

Neubrandenburg
Neustrelitz
Prenzlau
Eberswalde
Oranienburg
BERLIN
Potsdam

Brandenburg
Magdeburg
Stendal
Havel
Elbe
Wittenberg
Dessau
Zerbst
Bernburg
Halle
Merseburg
Leipzig
Naumburg
Gera
Jena
Erfurt
Weimar
Mühlhausen
Nordhausen

Cottbus
Spremberg
Forst
Gubin
Neisse
Görlitz
Bautzen
Dresden
Meissen
Riesa
Karl Marx Stadt
Zwickau
Plauen
Reichenbach
Hof

Thüringerwald
Erzgebirge

Brocken
Harz
Goslar
Salzgitter
Holberstadt

WEST GERMANY

Hamburg
Lübeck
Lauenburg
Lüneburg
Uelzen
Celle
Hanover
Hildesheim

LOWER SAXONY

Bremerhaven
Bremen
Verden
Nienburg
Minden
Hameln
Herford
Bielefeld
Detmold

Wilhelmshaven
Oldenburg
Emden
Lingen
Osnabrück
Münster
Teutoburger Wald
Paderborn
Kassel

NORTH RHINE WESTPHALIA

Hamm
Dortmund
Bochum
Essen
Oberhausen
Duisburg
Krefeld
Düsseldorf
Wuppertal
Remscheid
Hagen
Cologne
Bonn
Aachen

RHINE LAND

Koblenz
Taunus
Westerwald

GERMANY

Göttingen
Fulda
Giessen
Wetzlar
Vogelsberg

CZECHOSLOVAKIA

Havlíčkův Brod
Sázava
Přibram
Jablú
Třebíč
Znojmo
Plzeň
Pisek
Klatovy
České Budějovice
Böhmerwald
Třeboň
Gmünd
Zwettl
Krems
Stockerau
Baden
Wiener Neustadt
1450
Deggendorf
Passau
Freistadt
St. Pölten
Semmering 985
LOWER
Vienna
Mürzzuschlag
Eisenerz
Bruck
Kapfenberg
Maribor
Zagreb
Kupa
Karlovac
1378
Linz
Wels
Steyr
Enns
UPPER
Melk
AUSTRIA
STYRIA
Leoben
Graz
Bleiburg
Celje
Ljubljana
Rijeka
Krk
Senj
Nürnberg
Fürth
Regensburg
Ingolstadt
Landshut
Riet
Gmunden
Bad Ischl
SALZBURG
Bischofshofen
Gross Glockner 3797
Villach
2863
Klagenfurt
Drave
CARINTHIA
Karawanken
Sava
Istria
Koper
Rovinj
Erlangen
Amberg
Naab
Freising
Munich
Rosenheim
Salzburg
Kufstein
Inn
Krimml
Lienz
Tiglav 2863
Kranj
Gorizia
Trieste
Gulf of
Venice
BAVARIA
Augsburg
Donauwörth
Lech
Kempten
Innsbruck
Brenner P. 1371
Bressanone
Carnic Alps
Tagliamento
Udine
FRIULI-
VENEZIA
GIULIA
Piave
Chioggia
Heilbronn
Ludwigsburg
Stuttgart
Esslingen
Ulm
Memmingen
Bregenz
VOR-
ARLBERG
Arlberg P.
Landeck
Ötztal
Merano
Bolzano
3899
Ortles
3554
Adamello
Belluno
Vittorio Veneto
Conegliano
Treviso
Venice
Karlsruhe
Pforzheim
BADEN-
WÜRTEMBERG
Tübingen
Reutlingen
Biberach
Friedrichshafen
Bodensee
St. Gallen
LIECHTENSTEIN
Feldkirch
Chur
Davos
3797
Stelvio
ALTO ADIGE
TRENTINO
Trento
Rovereto
VENETO
Vicenza
Verona
Padua
Rovigo
Adige
Mannheim
Heidelberg
Speyer
Mainz
Karlsruhe
Rastatt
Baden
Rhine
Freiburg
Schwarzwald
Schaffhausen
Winterthur
Zürich
Zug
Schwyz
Glarus
Splügen P.
Bernina 4049
Bormio
Sondrio
Valtellina
Adda
Bergamo
Brescia
LOMBARDY
Mantua
Po
Cremona
Saarbrücken
SAAR
Kaiserslautern
Saar
Metz
Thionville
Strasbourg
Haguenau
Colmar
Mulhouse
1424
Basel
Solothurn
Aarau
Lucerne
St. Gotthard P.
Airolo 2113
Ticino
Bellinzona
Locarno
Lugano
L. Como
Lecco
Como
Milan
Pavia
Lodi
LORRAINE
Verdun
Nancy
Toul
St. Dié
Épinal
Lunéville
Belfort
Montbéliard
Besançon
La Chaux-de-Fonds
Neuchâtel
Biel
Murten
Fribourg
Berne
Bernese Oberland
Thun
Interlaken
Brienz
SWITZERLAND
Simplon P.
Domodossola
Monte Rosa 4634
Biella
Vercelli
Novara
Ivrea
Dora
Turin
Chivasso
Casale
Meuse
Bar-le-Duc
St. Dizier
Marne
Chaumont
Langres
plateau de Langres
Dijon
Saône
Dole
Doubs
Ain
Bourg
JURA
Lons-le-Saunier
Thonon
Annecy
Geneva
Lausanne
Montreux
Martigny
Great St. Bernard P.
Matterhorn 4477
Aosta
V. D'AOSTA
Mont Blanc 4810
2188
Little St. Bernard P.
Gran
Paradiso 4061
SAVOIE
Aix-les-Bains
Chambéry
Moûtiers
St. Jean
Graian Alps
Grenoble
Villeurbanne
Rhône
Voiron

East from Greenwich

46   48   8   10   12   14   46   16

16

ITALY AND
S.E. EUROPE

0   50   100   150   200 miles

0   100   200   300 km

GERMANY
Nuremberg   Plzeň   CZECHOS
Jihlava   Jablunka
Regensburg   Ostrava   Brno   Slavkov
Dijon   Augsburg   Linz   Bratislava
Belfort   Ulm   Munich   Salzburg   Vienna
Besançon   Basel   Zurich   Inn   of Constance   HU
Mâcon   Berne   Innsbruck   Bruck   Graz
SWITZERLAND   TIROL   371   Klagenfurt   Bulatar
Lyons   Geneva   Mt. Blanc   St. Gotthard   Simplon   Ortler   Ljubljana   Zagreb   Pécs
4807   Mt. (Genis Pk.)   3899   Trieste   Rijeka   YUGO
Grenoble   2083   Como   Bergamo   Brescia   Vicenza   Brod
Turin   Milan   Verona   Padua   Venice   Pula   BOSNI
Avignon   Novara   G. of   Banja Luka
Alessandria   Parma   Reggio   Ferrara   Venice
Genoa   Modena   Bologna   Ravenna
Marseilles   Monaco   Riviera   La   Rimini   San Marino   Zadar
Nice   Menton   Spezia   Florence   Dinaric Alps
Toulon   Gulf of Genoa   Pisa   Arno   Sibenik   Split
Cannes   Ligurian Sea   Leghorn   Arezzo   Anconа   Dalmatia
C. Corse   Elba   Siena   Perugia   Vis   Lastovo   Dubrovnik
2710   Bastia   Gran Sasso
Mte. Cinto   Corsica   Sabine Mts.   2914
Ajaccio   Civitavecchia   ADRIATIC SEA
Str. of Bonifacio   Tiber   ROME   Mt. Gargano   Foggia   Barletta
Caprera   Gaeta   Bari
Sassari   Olbia   Volturno   Naples   Vesuvius   Taran
Mt. del Gennargentu   1277   Capri   Salerno   G. of
1834   3719   Taranto
Sardinia   Tyrrhenian Sea   Cosenza   La Sila   1929   Io
Cagliari   Catanzaro
MEDITER   Stromboli   Lipari Is.   di
Palermo   Messina   Reggio
Skikda   Bizerta   Trapani   Egadi Is.   SICILY   Mt. Etna   C. Spartivento
Annaba   Marsala   3340   Str. of Messina
Constantine   Agrigento   Catania   Siracusa
ALGERIA   Tunis   Caltanissetta   C. Passero
Tébessa   C. Bon   Pantelleria (It.)
TUNISIA   Kairouan   G. of Hammamet   Gozo   R
Sousse   Valletta   MALTA
Lampedusa   (It.)
Sfax   4135
Tozeur   Kerkennah
Chott Djerid   Gabes   Djerba

10   East from Greenwich   15

17

COPYRIGHT. GEORGE PHILIP & SON. LTD.

SPAIN
AND PORTUGAL

0   50   100   150 miles
0   50 100 150 200 250 km

West from Greenwich 0 East from Greenwich

MIDDLE EAST

0	100	200 miles
0	100	200	300 km

East from Greenwich

ALASKA

Bering Strait

St. Lawrence I. (U.S.A.)

Wrangel I.

Chukot Sea

Gulf of Anadyr

Bering Sea

Chukot Range

O C E A N

Komsomolets I.

October Revolution I.

Bolshevik I.

De Long Is.

New Siberian Is.

Lyakhov Is.

East Siberian Sea

Beringa I.

Anadyr

Komandorskiye Is.

Kamchatka

rang Mts.

Taimyr Pen.

L. Taimyr

Laptev Sea

Nordvik

Tiksi

Yana

Nizhne Kolymsk

Kolyma

Sredne Kolymsk

Kolyma Ra.

Gizhiga

Shelakhov Gulf

Ust Kamchatsk

Nikolchevsk

Khatanga

Bulung

Verkhoyansk

Lena

Verkhoyansk Range

Petropavlovsk-Kamchatsky

Kotuy R.

Central

Zhigansk

S O V I E T

Vilyuisk

Yakutsk

Aldan

Okhotsk

Sea of Okhotsk

50

Siberian

Plateau

Olekminsk

Aldan

Stony Tunguska

S. S. R.

Dzhugdzhur Ra.

Shantar Is.

Okha

Sakhalin

Alessandrovsk

S O C I A L I S T   R E P U B L I C

Nikolayevsk

Angara

Lower Tunguska

Krasnoyarsk

Kansk

Nizhneudinsk

Taishet

Bratsk

Kirensk

Bodaibo

Stanovoi Ra.

Skovorodino

Belogorsk

Komsomolsk

Sovetskaya Gavan

Yuzhno-Sakhalinsk

Korsakov

Gulf of Tartary

Kuril Is.

Tulun

Cheremkhovo

Munku-Sardyk 3491

Minusinsk

Yenisei

Irkutsk

Angarsk

Ulan-Ude

Yablonovy Ra.

Chita

Nerchinsk

Sretensk

Blagoveshchensk

Amur

Birobidzhan

Khabarovsk

Sikhote Alin Range

Sapporo

Otaru

L. Baikal

Khilok

Oloyyannaya

Hailar

Sungari

Ussuriysk

Vladivostok

Hakodate

JAPAN

40

Kyakhta

Petrovsk

Selenga

Harbin

Sea of Japan

Dzhibkhalantu

Ulan Bator

Changchun

Mukden

Wonsan

M O N G O L I A

Antung

Yingkow

Seoul

KOREA

Pusan

Hami

Gobi or Shamo

I N N E R   M O N G O L I A

Paotow

Tatung

R E P U B L I C

Peking

Tientsin

Pyongyang

Inchon

Kunsan

Mokpo

S. KOREA

Masan

Hiroshima

Nagasaki

JAPAN

30

Lü-ta

Tsingtao

WALL

GREAT

Tsinan

Sinhailien

CHINESE

Lanchow

Hwang

Sian

Chengchow

U.S.S.R.

0   200   400   600   800 miles

0   200 400 600 800 1000 1200 km

80   70   60

100   110

S.W. ASIA

0 100 200 300 400 500 miles
0 200 400 600 800 km

COPYRIGHT GEORGE PHILIP & SON LTD.

INDIA, PAKISTAN, SRI LANKA & BURMA

0 200 400 600 miles
0 200 400 600 800 km

East from Greenwich

SRI LANKA (CEYLON)

Continuation Southward on same scale

Colombo · Kandy · Pidurutalagala 2524 · Galle · Dondra Hd. · Adam's B. · Jaffna · G. of Mannar

Tiruchirapalli · Madurai

CHINA

U.S.S.R.

SAKHALIN

Svetlaya

Sikhote-Alin Range

Iman

Mishan

Kisi

Mutankiang

Lesozavodsk

La Pérouse Strait

Rebun

Wakkanai

Sea of
Okhotsk

Spassk-Dalni

Tetyukhe
Pristan

Rishiri

Cape Soya

45

Ussuriysk

Artem

Cape
Shiretoko
Abashiri
Bay

HOKKAIDO

Rumoi

1 Mt. Asahi
2290

Abashiri

L. Kutchar

Vladivostok

Suchan

Nakhodka

Cape Kamu

Otaru

Asahigawa

HOKKAIDO

Obihiro

Kushiro

Nemuro

Yenki

Unggi

Sapporo

L. Shikotsu

L. Toya

Muroran

Mt. Horoshiri
2052

Cape Erimo

Chongjin

Okushiri

Uchiura Bay

Hakodate

Cape Esan

NORTH
KOREA

Kitchu

Cape Shiragami

Tsugaru Strait

Cape Shiriya

S E A   O F

Aomori

Cape Henashi

Hirosaki

2

Hachinohe

Noshiro

L. Towada

Mt. Iwate
2041

J A P A N

Cape Nyudo

3

Morioka

Akita

Miyako

4

Kamaishi

Ou Range

Sakata

Kitakami

TOHOKU

Ishinomaki

5

6

SOUTH
KOREA

Sado

Yamagata

Sendai

Pohang

Niigata

Mt. Azuma
2024

Fukushima

Agano

Noto

Nagaoka

8

Koriyama

Lake
Inawashiro

7

Iwaki

Wojima

Toyama

Shinano

Echigo Range

18

Utsunomiya

Oki Is.

Kanazawa

9

10

Maebashi

17

Mito

Tone

L. Kasumiga

Matsue

Tottori

Cape Kyo

11

12

Hida R.

13

14

19

TOKYO

20

Choshi
Cape Inubo

PUSAN

CHUGOKU

Chugoku Mts.

25

24

L. Biwa

N

NAGOYA

15

21

22

YOKOHAMA

Tsushima

33

32

31

KYOTO

26

Akaishi Mts.

16

Yokosuka

Boso

Hiroshima

35

34

OSAKA

28

Shizuoka

Cape Nojima

Shimonoseki

Kure

Okayama

27

Sakai

29

Toyohashi

Hamamatsu

KYUSHU

40

Matsuyama

SHIKOKU

36

37

Wakayama

Cape Iro

Fukuoka

38

39

Tokushima

30

KINKI

Nii Is.

Omuta

44

Kochi

Tosa
Bay

Cape Muroto

Cape Daio

Miyake Is.

Kumamoto

43

Nagasaki

42

SHIKOKU

Cape Ashizuri

Cape Shiono

Hachijo I.

45

46

Miyazaki

KYUSHU

P A C I F I C   O C E A N

140

goshima

Kagoshima

Osumi Strait

Tanega I.

30

Osumi
Group

1935

Yaku I.

REFERENCE TO PREFECTURES

HOKKAIDO DISTRICT	KANTO DISTRICT	CHUGOKU DISTRICT
1 Hokkaido	17 Gumma	31 Tottori
TOHOKU DISTRICT	18 Tochigi	32 Okayama
2 Aomori	19 Saitama	33 Shimane
3 Akita	20 Ibaraki	34 Hiroshima
4 Iwate	21 Tokyo	35 Yamaguchi
5 Yamagata	22 Chiba	SHIKOKU DISTRICT
6 Miyagi	23 Kanagawa	36 Kagawa
7 Fukushima	KINKI DISTRICT	37 Ehime
CHUBU DISTRICT	24 Hyogo	38 Ehime
8 Niigata	25 Kyoto	39 Kochi
9 Ishikawa	26 Shiga	KYUSHU DISTRICT
10 Toyama	27 Osaka	40 Fukuoka
11 Fukui	28 Nara	41 Saga
12 Gifu	29 Mie	42 Nagasaki
13 Nagano	30 Wakayama	43 Kumamoto
14 Yamanashi		44 Oita
15 Aichi		45 Miyazaki
16 Shizuoka		46 Kagoshima

JAPAN

0	50	100	150	200 miles

| 0 | 50 | 100 | 150 | 200 | 250 | 300 km |

East from Greenwich

130   135   140

SOUTH-EAST ASIA

600 miles
km

| 0 | 200 | 400 | 600 | 800 |

Mariana Is.

P A C I F I C   O C E A N

Guam (U.S.A.)

Caroline Islands

Trust Terr. of Pacific Is. (U.S.A.)

Yap Is.

Palau Is.

Equator

Schouten Is.

Admiralty Is.

Bismarck Sea

New Britain

Coral Sea

PAPUA NEW GUINEA

IRIAN JAYA

Torres Strait

C. York

Arafura Sea

Aru Is.

Tanimbar Is.

Kai Is.

Banda Sea

Ceram Sea

Buru

Ceram

Ambon

Obira

Halmahera

Morotai

Molucca Sea

M O L U C C A S

Celebes Sea

Sulu Sea

PHILIPPINES

Luzon

Manila   Quezon City

Mindoro

Panay

Cebu

Negros

Mindanao

Davao

Samar

Leyte

Zamboanga

S U L A W E S I

Makasar

Flores Sea

Flores

Sumbawa

Bali

Lombok

Timor

Sumba

Java Sea

J A V A

Jakarta

Bandung

Surabaya

Semarang

Yogyakarta

B O R N E O

EASTERN MALAYSIA

SABAH

Kota Kinabalu

Brunei

Bandar Seri Begawan

SARAWAK

Kuching

Pontianak

Banjarmasin

I N D O N E S I A

S O U T H   C H I N A   S E A

VIETNAM

Hanoi

Haiphong

LAOS

Vientiane

THAILAND

Bangkok

CAMBODIA

Phnom Penh

Ho Chi-minh City

Gulf of Siam

WESTERN MALAYSIA

Kuala Lumpur

Singapore

Johor Bahru

Medan

Penang

S U M A T E R A

Palembang

Padang

Bangka

I N D I A N   O C E A N

Mentawai Is.

Mergui Archipelago

Andaman Sea

Hainan Tao

CANADA

0 100 200 300 400 500 miles
0 200 400 600 800 km

120 · 110 · 100

50

C. Flatter

Kamloops · Red Deer · N. Battleford · Prince Albert

Vancouver · **Calgary** · Rosetown · Saskatoon

Victoria · Drumheller · CAN

Everett · Sandpoint · Medicine Hat · Moose Jaw · Regina · Portage la Prairie · N

Tacoma · **Seattle** · Lethbridge · Brandon

WASHINGTON · Spokane · Gt. Falls · Missouri · Minot · Grand Fork

Portland · Mt. Rainier 4392 · Missoula · Helena · MONTANA · Glendive N. · DAKOTA · Fa

Corvallis · Salem · Columbia · Walla Walla · Butte · Yellowstone · Bismarck · Aberd

Eugene · La Grande · ROCKY · Billings · S.

OREGON · Payette · Boise · IDAHO · Rapid City · DAKOTA

Medford · Klamath Falls · Snake · Idaho Falls · WYOMING · Black · Sioux

Mt. Shasta 4317 · Twin Falls · Gannett Pk. 4202 · Mou · Hills · NEBRASKA

Coast · Sierra · Elko · Gt. Salt Lake · Casper · Laramie · Cheyenne · Grand Island

Reno · Ogden · Long's Pk. 4345 · **Denver** · Platte

Sacramento · Great · NEVADA · Salt Lake City · Provo · UTAH · COLORADO · K

Oakland · Stockton · Basin · Mt. Whitney 4418 · Grand Junction · Pikes Pk. 4300 · Colorado Springs · KANS

San Francisco · Fresno · Las Vegas · Death Valley · Wasatch · Colorado · **Pueblo** · Hutchinson

Bakersfield · UNITED · Blanca Pk. 4364 · Trinidad · Arkansas · Wichit

Santa Barbara · Grand Canyon · Colorado Plateau · Santa Fé · Canadian · OKLA

LOS ANGELES · Pasadena · Winslow · Albuquerque · Amarillo · Pampa · **Oklahoma City**

Long Beach · ARIZONA · NEW MEXICO · Clovis · W F

San Diego · Gila · **Phoenix** · Rio Grande · Llano Estacado · Lubbock · **Fort Wort**

Mexicali · Las Cruces · Pecos · Odessa · Abilene

Tucson · Ciudad Juarez · **El Paso** · San Angelo · T E X

Hermosillo · Alpine · **San Antonio**

Gulf of California · SIERRA · Chihuahua · Rio Grande · Austin

Guaymas · MEXICO · Nuevo Laredo

Ciudad Obregon · MADRE

Los Mochis · Culiacan · Torreón · **Monterrey**

Tropic of Cancer

C. San Lucas · Mazatlan · San Luis Potosí

PACIFIC

OCEAN

Projection: Bonne

110 · 100

30

120

U.S.A.

0   100   200   300   400 miles
0   200   400   600 km

A   A   D   A

peg

Cochrane

Arvida

Quebec

Fredericton

MAINE

Saint John

MINNE-

Duluth

Thunder Bay

Lake Superior

Sault Ste. Marie

Sudbury

Laurentian Plateau

Trois Rivières

Montreal

Sherbrooke

70

SOTA

St. Paul

WISCONSIN

Green Bay

L. Michigan

Saginaw

Georgian Bay

Lake Huron

Ottawa

Kingston

VERMONT

N.H.

Portland

Manchester

nneapolis

Austin

Madison

Milwaukee

Grand Rapids

Toronto

Lake Ontario

Hamilton

London

Rochester

Buffalo

NEW YORK

Troy

Albany

MASS.

R.I.

Boston

C. Cod

Providence

Iowa

Des Moines

Cedar Rapids

CHICAGO

Detroit

Windsor

Lake Erie

Cleveland

Scranton

Newark

New Haven

40

Council Bluffs

ha

Peoria

Fort Wayne

Toledo

Akron

PENNSYLVANIA

Pittsburgh

N.J.

NEW YORK

Philadelphia

70

St. Joseph

ILLINOIS

INDIANA

OHIO

Columbus

Dayton

Baltimore

M.D.

Delaware B.

Washington

Kansas City

Jefferson City

Indianapolis

Cincinnati

Ohio

WEST VIRGINIA

Richmond

MISSOURI

St. Louis

Evansville

Louisville

Huntington

VIRGINIA

Norfolk

Chesapeake B.

Springfield

KENTUCKY

Lexington

Roanoke

C. Hatteras

ARKANSAS

Fort Smith

Arkansas

Little Rock

Nash-ville

Oak Ridge

Knoxville

Greensboro

Raleigh

T   A   T   E   S

TENNESSEE

Chattanooga

Greenville

Charlotte

NORTH CAROLINA

Wilmington

Memphis

Tennessee

Gadsden

Atlanta

SOUTH CAROLINA

Birmingham

MISSISSIPPI

Jackson

ALABAMA

Columbus

GEORGIA

Savannah

Charleston

Shreveport

Monroe

Montgomery

Albany

ATLANTIC

aumont

Baton Rouge

LOUISIANA

Mobile

Dothan

Jacksonville

30

OCEAN

Houston

Galveston

New Orleans

Mississippi Delta

Tampa

St. Petersburg

FLORIDA

West Palm Beach

Freeport

BAHAMAS

risti

Gulf of Mexico

C. Sable

Key West

Everglades

Miami

Nassau

Florida Strait

Connecticut
Delaware
Maryland
Massachusetts
New Hampshire
New Jersey
Rhode Island

Havana

Matanzas

Yucatan Strait

U-

B-

A

Camagüey

West from Greenwich   90   80

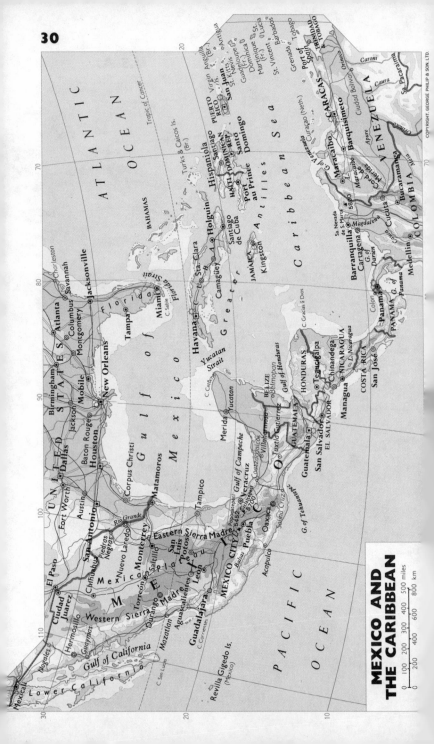

30

MEXICO AND
THE CARIBBEAN

COPYRIGHT GEORGE PHILIP & SON LTD.

ATLANTIC OCEAN

PACIFIC OCEAN

Gulf of Mexico

Caribbean Sea

Greater Antilles

Lesser Antilles

UNITED STATES

MEXICO

VENEZUELA

COLOMBIA

Charleston
Savannah
Jacksonville
Atlanta
Columbus
Montgomery
Birmingham
Jackson
Mobile
New Orleans
Baton Rouge
Houston
Austin
San Antonio
Corpus Christi
Dallas
Fort Worth
El Paso
Ciudad Juarez
Nogales
Hermosillo
Guaymas
Mexicali
Chihuahua
Piedras Negras
Nuevo Laredo
Matamoros
Monterrey
Saltillo
Torreón
Durango
Mazatlan
Culiacán
Aguascalientes
León
Guadalajara
San Luis Potosí
MEXICO CITY
Puebla
Acapulco
Oaxaca
Veracruz
Tampico
Coatzacoalcos
Villahermosa
Tuxtla Gutiérrez
Salina Cruz
Merida
Campeche

Tampa
Miami
Havana
Santa Clara
Camagüey
Holguin
Santiago de Cuba
Kingston
JAMAICA
CUBA
BAHAMAS
Turks & Caicos Is. (Br.)

HISPANIOLA
HAITI
DOMINICAN REP.
Santiago
Port au Prince
Santo Domingo
PUERTO RICO
San Juan
Virgin Anguilla
Is. (Br.)
St. Kitts-Nevis
Guadeloupe (Fr.)
Dominica
Martinique (Fr.)
St. Lucia
St. Vincent
Barbados
Grenada
Tobago
TRINIDAD & TOBAGO
Port of Spain

BELIZE
Belmopan
GUATEMALA
Guatemala
San Salvador
EL SALVADOR
HONDURAS
Tegucigalpa
NICARAGUA
Managua
Chinandega
L. Nicaragua
COSTA RICA
San José
PANAMA
Panama
Colon

CARACAS
Maracaibo
Barquisimeto
Valencia
Maracay
Bucaramanga
Cúcuta
Barranquilla
Cartagena
Medellin
Curaçao (Neth.)

Florida Strait
Yucatan Strait
Yucatan
Gulf of Campeche
Gulf of Honduras
Gulf of California
Lower California
Eastern Sierra Madre
Western Sierra Madre
Revilla Gigedo Is. (Mexico)

Tropic of Cancer
Rio Grande

SCALE
0   100 200 300 400 500 miles
0 200 400 600 800 km

31

SOUTH AMERICA

| 0 | 200 | 400 | 600 | 800 miles |
| 0 | 200 | 400 | 800 | 1200 km |

CARIBBEAN SEA

Santiago de Cuba
Sierra Maestra
Jamaica
HAITI
Kingston
Port au Prince
DOM. REP.
Hispaniola
S. Juan
PUERTO RICO (U.S.)
Leeward Is.
Windward Is.
Barbados

NICARAGUA
CANAL ZONE
COSTA RICA
PANAMA
G. of Panama
Gulf of Darién
PANAMA
Barranquilla
Cartagena
Maracaibo
G. of Venezuela
Cabimas
L. Maracaibo
Curaçao (Neth.)
Port of Spain
Trinidad

MEDELLÍN
Manizales
Pereira
Cali
Bogotá
COLOMBIA
Pasto
Popayán

Caracas
Maturin
Ciudad Bolívar
Santo Tomé
VENEZUELA
Orinoco
Bucaramanga
Sa. de Mérida
Angel Falls
Puerto Cabello
Pto. La Cruz

GUIANA
Georgetown
Demerara
SURINAM
Paramaribo
FR. GUIANA
Cayenne
Roraima 2810
Sa. Pacaraima
Casiquiare

ECUADOR
Quito
Chimborazo 6267
Cotopaxi 5897
Guayaquil
Cuenca
C. Pariña
Piura

Putumayo
Japurá
Negro
Solimões
Iquitos
Marañón
Benjamin Constant

Manaus
Amazon

Macapá
Marajó I.
Pará
Belém
São Luís
Equator
Santarém

PERU
Chiclayo
Trujillo
Pacasmayo
Huancayo
Callao
Lima
Pisco
Lomas
Cuzco
Juliaca
Arequipa
Mollendo
Tacna
Arica
Iquique

S. Antonio Falls
Purus
Madeira
Roosevelt
Guaporé
Rio Branco

BRAZIL
Plateau of Mato Grosso
Cuyabá
Goiânia
Brasília
São Francisco
Barreiras

Tocantins
Araguaia
Xingú
Tapajós
Paulistana
Teresina
Imperatriz
Parnaíba
Fortaleza
Natal
C. de São Roque
João Pessoa
Recife
Maceió
Aracaju
Alagoinhas
Salvador
Ilhéus
Vitória de Conquista
Montes Claros
Pirapora
Caravelas

BOLIVIA
La Paz
Cochabamba
Oruro
Sucre
Potosí
Uyuni

PARAGUAY
Asunción
Pilcomayo

Uberaba
Belo Horizonte
Ribeirão Prêto
Campinas
São Paulo
Santos
Niteroi
Rio de Janeiro
C. Frio
Vitória
Sa. da Mantiqueira
Campos

Ojos del Salado 6863
Tucumán
Salta
Santiago del Estero
Corrientes
Iguaçu Falls
Curitiba
Blumenau
Pôrto Alegre
Lagoa dos Patos
Rio Grande do Sul
Pelotas
Santa Maria

Tropic of Capricorn
Antofagasta
Taltal
La Serena
Aconcagua
Viña del Mar
Valparaíso
Santiago
Talca
Concepción
Valdivia
Osorno

Córdoba
Mendoza
Rosario
Santa Fé
Paraná
ARGENTINA
Buenos Aires
La Plata
Río de la Plata
Rocha
URUGUAY
Montevideo
Mar del Plata
Pta. Mogotes
Azul
Santa Rosa
Bahía Blanca

PACIFIC
OCEAN
Juan Fernández (Chile)

Temuco
Neuquén
Negro
Colorado
Viedma
G. of San Matías
Puerto Montt
Chiloé
Chonos Arch.
Chubut
Rawson
Comodoro Rivadavia
G. of San Jorge

ATLANTIC
OCEAN

Río Gallegos
Punta Arenas
Magellan's Str.
Tierra del Fuego
C. Froward
Staten I.
C. Horn
Drake Passage

Falkland Is. (Br.)
Stanley

South Georgia (Br.)

West from Greenwich

COPYRIGHT. GEORGE PHILIP & SON. LTD.

32

AFRICA

West from Greenwich 0 East from Greenwich

Tropic of Capricorn

SOUTH ATLANTIC OCEAN

INDIAN OCEAN

Ascension I.

St. Helena

Scale

0 200 400 600 800 miles
0 200 400 600 800 1000 1200 km

CONGO · GABON · ZAIRE · ANGOLA · SOUTH WEST AFRICA (NAMIBIA) · BOTSWANA · RHODESIA · MALAWI · TANZANIA · KENYA · RWANDA · MOÇAMBIQUE · SWAZILAND · NATAL · TRANSVAAL · ORANGE FREE STATE · CAPE PROVINCE · TRANSKEI

Cape Town · Port Elizabeth · East London · Durban · Johannesburg · Pretoria · Bloemfontein · Kimberley · Maputo · Salisbury · Bulawayo · Beira · Tananarive · Dar-es-Salaam · Mombasa · Nairobi · Zanzibar · Luanda · Benguela · Brazzaville · Kinshasa · Mbandaka

34

AUSTRALIA

| 0 | 100 | 200 | 300 | 400 | 500 miles |
| 0 | 200 | 400 | 600 | 800 km |

35

PAPUA NEW GUINEA
Lae
Wau
G. of Papua
Mt. Victoria 4073
Port Moresby
Riga
Torres Strait
Prince of Wales I.
Cape York
D'Entrecasteaux Is.
Louisiade Arch.
Bougainville
Choiseul
Santa Isabel
Solomon Islands
Malaita
S. Cristobal
Indispensable Str.

Coral Sea

PACIFIC OCEAN

Cape York Peninsula
Weipa
Coleman
Cooktown
Chillagoe
Mt. Bartle Frere 18 Mal.
Normanton
Innisfail
Cairns
Croydon
Townsville
Charters Towers
Bowen
Mackay
Hughenden
Chesterfield Is.

QUEENSLAND
Cloncurry
Selwyn
Winton
Longreach
Emerald
Mt. Motgano
Gladstone
Rockhampton
Bundaberg
Maryborough
Fraser I.
Gympie
Bird I.
Cato I.

Windorah
Charleville
Darling
Toowoomba
Ipswich
Brisbane
Cunnamulla
Dirranbandi
Tibooburra

NEW SOUTH WALES
Bourke
Walgett
Moree
Grafton
Coffs Harbour

AUSTRALIA
Great Dividing Range
Grey Range
Warrego

L. Callabonna
Broken Hill
Wilcannia
Menindee
Cobar
Roto
Dubbo
Newcastle
Mudgee

Murray River
Mildura
SYDNEY
Wollongong
Bathurst
Cootamundra
Goulburn
Canberra
Queanbeyan
Jervis B.
Batemans B.
Snowy Mts.
Mt. Kosciusko 2230
Bombala

VICTORIA
Horsham
Stawell
Wangaratta
Ararat
Ballarat
MELBOURNE
Colac
Geelong

King I.
Bass Strait
Furneaux Group

TASMANIA
Burnie
Devonport
Strahan
Scottsdale
Launceston
Queenstown
Hobart
P. Davey
Tasman Penin.
P. Arthur
Storm B.
S.E. Cape

NEW ZEALAND
North C.
Doubtless B.
Kaipara Harb.
Auckland
Devonport
Great Barrier I.
Thames
Hamilton
Tauranga
B. of Plenty
East C.
Rotorua
Gisborne
Hawke Bay
North Island
North Taranaki Bight
New Plymouth
Patea
Wanganui
NEW ZEALAND
Karamea B.
Nelson
Blenheim
Cook Str.
Wellington
Westport
Campbell
Ross
Waiau
South Island
Mt. Cook 3764
Mt. Aspiring
Milford Sd.
Southern Alps
Canterbury Plains
Christchurch
Lyttelton
Oamaru
Chatham Is. (N.Z.)
Kingston
Port Chalmers
Otago Harb.
Dunedin
Milford
Invercargill
Bluff
Bluff Harb.
Stewart I.
Southwest C.

NEW ZEALAND
on same scale

COPYRIGHT. GEORGE PHILIP & SON. LTD

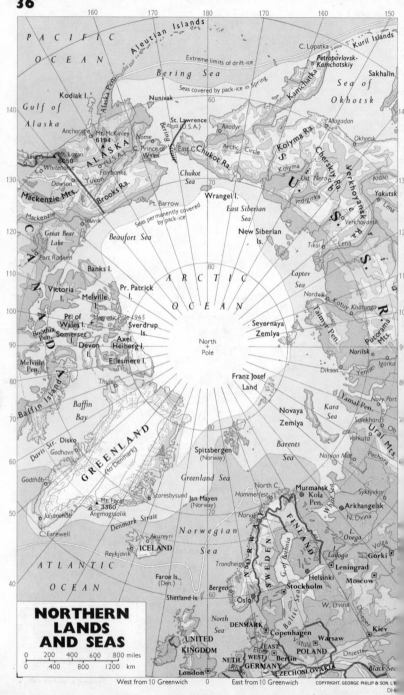

36

PACIFIC OCEAN

Aleutian Islands

C. Lopatka

Kuril Islands

Petropavlovsk-Kamchatskiy

Bering Sea

Extreme limits of drift-ice

Sakhalin

Kodiak I.

Nunivak

Seas covered by pack-ice in Spring

Sea of Okhotsk

Kamchatka

Gulf of Alaska

Anchorage

Mt. McKinley 6194

St. Lawrence (U.S.A.)

Nome

Anadyr

Magadan

Okhotsk

Mt. Logan 6050

Juneau

ALASKA (U.S.A.)

C. Prince of Wales

East C.

Chukot Ra.

Arctic Circle

Kolyma Ra.

Cherskiy Ra.

Verkhoyansk Ra.

Aldan

Whitehorse

Fairbanks

Yukon

Chukot Sea

Kolyma

Ust' Nera

Yakutsk

Dawson

Brooks Ra.

Pt. Barrow

Wrangel I.

Indigirka

Verkhoyansk

Lena

Mackenzie Mts.

Mackenzie

Inuvik

Seas permanently covered by pack-ice

East Siberian Sea

Tiksi

Lena

Great Bear Lake

Beaufort Sea

New Siberian Is.

U. S. S. R.

Port Radium

Banks I.

ARCTIC

Laptev Sea

Nordvik

Kotuy

Khatanga

Putorana Mts.

Victoria I.

Melville I.

Pr. Patrick I.

OCEAN

Taimyr Pen.

Pr. of Wales I.

Magnetic Pole 1965

Sverdrup Is.

Severnaya Zemlya

Norilsk

Igarka

Boothia Pen.

Somerset

Axel Heiberg I.

North Pole

Dikson

Yenisei

Melville Pen.

Devon I.

Ellesmere I.

Franz Josef Land

Novy Port

Baffin Island

Thule

Novaya Zemlya

Kara Sea

Yamal Pen.

Ob

Baffin Bay

Salekhard

Ural Mts.

Davis Str.

Disko

Godhavn

GREENLAND (to Denmark)

Spitsbergen (Norway)

Barents Sea

Vorkuta

Pechora

Pt. Farewell

Godthåb

Scoresbysund

Greenland Sea

Narjan Mar

Julianehåb

Mt. Forel 3360

Jan Mayen (Norway)

North C.

Hammerfest

Murmansk

Kola Pen.

Syktyvkar

Angmagssalik

Denmark Strait

Akureyri

Norwegian Sea

Narvik

Arkhangelsk

N. Dvina

Reykjavik

ICELAND

Trondheim

NORWAY

SWEDEN

FINLAND

G. of Bothnia

L. Onega

L. Ladoga

Volga

Gorki

ATLANTIC OCEAN

Faroe Is. (Den.)

Bergen

Oslo

Stockholm

Helsinki

Leningrad

Moscow

Shetland Is.

North Sea

DENMARK

Copenhagen

EAST WEST GERMANY

Berlin

Baltic Sea

Warsaw

POLAND

W. Dvina

Dnieper

Kiev

Elbe

Vistula

Dniester

Black Sea

UNITED KINGDOM

NETH.

CZECHOSLOVAKIA

London

NORTHERN LANDS AND SEAS

| 0 | 200 | 400 | 600 | 800 miles |

| 0 | 400 | 800 | 1200 km |

West from 10 Greenwich   0   East from 10 Greenwich

Gillingham, t., l. gov. dist., Kent, Eng.; 3 km E. of Chatham; on R. Medway; naval and military establishments; cement, lt. inds.; p. (est. 1976) 93,900.

Gippsland, dist., S.E. Victoria, Australia; mtnous; intensive dairying, pig-rearing, mkt. gardening; a. 36,001 km².

Girardot, t., Colombia; R. pt. and airport on upper course of Magdalena R.; linked by rly. to Bogotá; coffee, hides, ceramics; p. (est. 1968) 82,310.

Girgenti. See Agrigento.

Gironde, dep., S.W. France; vineyards, grain, fruit, wines; cap. Bordeaux; a. 10,723 km²; p. (1968) 1,009,390.

Gironde, estuary, S.W. France; formed by junc. of Rs. Garonne and Dordogne; navigable to Pauillac and Bordeaux.

Girvan, burgh, Kyle and Carrick, Scot.; on F. of Clyde, 29 km S.W. of Ayr; summer resort; p. (1971) 7,410.

Gisborne, t., spt., N.I. N.Z.; on Poverty Bay, 96 km N.E. of Napier; freezing-wks.; fishing; p. (1971) 25,709.

Giuba, R. See Juba R.

Giurgiu, t., Romania; pt. on Danube; opposite Ruse, Bulgaria; linked by oil pipelines with Ploiesti; p. (1966) 32,300.

Givors, t., Rhône dep., France; on Rhône R. 16 km S. of Lyons; mnfs.; oil refining near by at Feyzin; p. (1968) 19,048.

Giza, El, t. Egypt; on Nile. sub. of Cairo; nr. pyramids of Khufu (Cheops), Khafra (Chephren), and the Sphinx; film ind.; p. (est. 1970) 711,900.

Gjövik, t., S. Norway; on L. Mjösa; furniture, footwear, lt. inds.; p. (est. 1970) 25,164.

Glace Bay, t., Cape Breton I., Nova Scotia; Canada; coal; fishing harbour; p. (1971) 22,276.

Glacier National Park, B.C., Canada; mtn. scenery, resorts; a. 1,349 km².

Glacier National Park, Mon., USA; Rocky mtns., picturesque; a. 4,040 km².

Gladbeck, t., N. Rhine–Westphalia, W. Germany; N. of Essen; coalmng; p. (est. 1967) 82,500.

Gladstone, t., Queensland, Australia; alumina refining, oil, chemicals; p. (1972) 15,365.

Glamis, v., Angus, Scot.; G. cas. childhood home of Queen Elizabeth the Queen Mother, and featured in Shakespeare's *Macbeth*.

Glamorgan, former co., S. Wales; now divided into 3 cos., South, West and Mid-Glamorgan.

Glamorgan, Vale of. See Gwent. Plain of.

Glanford, l. gov. dist., Humberside, Eng.; a. S. of Humber and inc. Brigg and Barton; p. (est. 1976) 62,300.

Glarus, can., Switzerland; E. of Schwyz; a. 684 km²; sheep, cheese, cottons; p. (1969) 42,500.

Glarus, t., cap. of can G. Switzerland; on R. Linth. nr. Wessen; p. (1970) 6,189.

Glasgow, c., burgh, l. gov. dist., Strathclyde Reg., Scot.; on R. Clyde; leading spt. and 3rd lgst. c. in Gt. Britain; major problems of urban renewal; ctr. of industl. belt; shipbldg., iron and steel, heavy and lt. engin., electronics equipment, printing; univ. cath.; p. (1971) 897,483.

Glas Maol, mtn., Angus, Kincardine and Deeside, Scot.; part of the Braes of Angus; 1,068 m.

Glatz. See Klodzko.

Glauchau, t., Karl-Marx-Stadt, E. Germany; on R. Mulde; woollens, calicoes, dyes, machin.; p. (est. 1970) 32,127.

Gleiwitz. See Gliwice.

Glen Affric, Inverness, Scot.; drained E. to Moray F.; hydroelectric scheme.

Glencoe, Lochaber, Scot.; S.E. of Ballachulish; scene of massacre of MacDonalds 1692.

Glendalough, Wicklow, R.o.I.; scenic valley with Ls. and monastic ruins; tourism.

Glenelg, t., S. Australia; on St. Vincent G.; sub. of Adelaide; first free settlement in Australia; p. (1966) 14,800

Glen Garry, Perth and Kinross, Scot.; used by Perth to Inverness rly. on S. approach to Drumochter Pass.

Glen More, Scottish valley traversed by Caledonain canal, from Fort William to Inverness.

Glenrothes, t., Kirkaldy, Scot.; new t. (1948); coal, transistors, mng. machin., photoprecision ind.; p. (est. 1974) 32,500 .

Glen Roy, Lochaber, Scot.; 24 km N.E. of Fort

William; remarkable terraces, remains of series of glacial lakes.

Glen Spean, Lochaber, Scot.; used by Glasgow to Fort William rly.

Glittertind, mtn., Opland co., S. Norway; highest peak in Scandinavia; alt. 2,483 m.

Gliwice (Gleiwitz), c. S.W. Poland (since 1945); coal mng. and steel ctr. of Katowice region; machin., chemicals; p. (1970) 171,000.

Glomma (Glommen), R., S. Norway; lgst. R. in Scandinavia; flows to Skaggerak; timber inds.; hydroelec. power; 400 km long.

Glossop, t., High Peak, Derbys., Eng.; at foot of Pennines; paper, food-canning, textile finishing; mkt.; p. (1971) 24,174.

Gloucester, cath. c., l. gov. dist., Eng.; on R. Severn; the Roman Glevum; cath., on site of Benedictine abbey; aircraft mftg. and repair; engin., nylon; p. (est. 1976) 91,600.

Gloucester, t., Mass., USA; pt. at head of G. Harbour; resort, fish-processing; p. (1970) 27,941.

Gloucestershire, non-met. co., W. Eng.; situated around lower Severn basin, Cotswolds, Forest of Dean; sheep, dairy and fruit farming; major ctrs. of p. at Gloucester and Cheltenham; a. 2,639 km²; p. (est. 1976) 491,500.

Glyncorrwg, t., Afan, West Glamorgan, Wales; 6 km N. of Maesteg; coal-mng. dist.; p. (1971) 8,642.

Glynde, v., Sussex, Eng.; nearby Tudor manor and opera house of Glyndebourne.

Glyndwr, l. gov. dist., Clwyd, Wales; lge inland a. inc. Denbigh, Ruthin and Llangollen; p. (est. 1976) 38,900.

Gmünd. See Schwäbish-Gmünd.

Gniezno (Gnesen), c., W. Poland; E. of Poznan; first cap. of Poland (11th cent.); cath.; p. (1970) 50,600.

Goa, Daman and Diu, terr., India; former Portuguese enclaves; iron pyrites, manganese, coconuts, fish, spices, cashew nuts, salt, copra; a. 3,693 km²; p. (1971) 857,791.

Goat Fell, mtn., I. of Arran, Cunninghame, Scot.; alt. 874 m.

Gobi, steppes and stony or sandy desert, China and Mongolia; divided into two principal divs.; Shamo in Central Mongolia, and the basins of the Tarim, E. Turkestan; l. about 2,400 km (E. to W.), breadth 800–1,120 km; average elevation 1,200 m; crossed by Kalgan–Ulan Bator highway.

Godalming, t., Waverley, Surrey, Eng.; 6 km S.W. of Guildford; first public supply of elec. 1881; Charterhouse School; p. (1971) 18,634.

Godavari, sacred R., India; rises in W. Ghats, flows E. across Deccan through gap in E. Ghats to Bay of Bengal; forms lge. delta; used for irrigation and hydroelec. power; c. 1,440 km long.

Godesberg, Bad, t., N. Rhine–Westphalia, W. Germany; nr. Bonn; spa; meeting place of Chamberlain and Hitler 1938; p. (est. 1969) 73,512.

Godhavn, Danish settlement, Disco I., W. of Greenland; arctic research sta.; fish processing.

Godstone, v., Tandridge, Surrey, Eng.; nr. Reigate; p. (1971) 43,706 (dist.)

Godthåb t., admin. ctr., Greenland; first Danish col. 1721; sm. pt.; fish processing; p. (est. 1968) 6,104.

Godwin Austen, Mt. or K2, peak (8,616 m) in Karakoram between Tibet and Sinkiang, on China, after Everest highest in world; summit reached by Prof. Desio 1954; also named Chobrum.

Gogmagog Hills, Cambs., Eng.; low chalk upland, S. of Breckland; traces of Roman entrenchment

Gogra. See Ghaghara R. [47,631.

Goiana, t. Pernambuco st. Brazil; p. (est. 1968)

Goiânia, t., cap. of Goiás st., Brazil; comm. and industl. ctr.; p. (1970) 362,152.

Goiás, st., central Brazil; mtnous., forested; stock-raising. tobacco; gold, diamonds; cap. Goiânia, on Vermelho R.; a. 642,061 km²; p. (est. 1968) 2,745,711.

Gökçeada I. (Imbroz I.), off W. Turkey, in Ægean Sea at entrance to Dardanelles; a. 280 km²; p. (est. 1970) 1,856.

Golconda, fort and ruined c., nr. Hyderabad, S. India; famous for its legendary diamond troves.

Gold Coast, c. Queensland and N.S.W., Australia; tourist ctr.; p. (1972) 74,121.

Golden Gate, strait, between San Francisco Bay

and Pac. Oc., Cal., **USA**; spanned by Golden Gate Bridge, opened 1937.

Golden Horn, peninsula on the Bosporus, forming the harbour of Istanbul, **Turkey**.

Golden Triangle, a. of Britain and Europe roughly bounded by Birmingham, Frankfurt, and Paris; economic core a. of **W. Europe**.

Golden Vale, dist., Limerick, Tipperary, **R.o.I.**; drained W. to Shannon and E. to Suir; rich farming a., beef and dairy cattle, pigs.

Gold River, t., B.C., **Canada**; on W cst. of Vancouver I. at junc. of Heber and Gold Rs.; new t. 1967.

Golspie, co. t., Sutherland, Scot.; p. (1971) 3,186 (inc. Rogart and Lairg).

Gomal Pass, a pass in Sulaiman ranges, Pakistan, leading from Indus valley to Afghanistan.

Gomel', c., S.E. Belorussiyan SSR, **USSR**; on R. Sozh, trib. of Dnieper; R. pt., agr. ctr.; engin., chemicals, clothing inds.; p. (1970) 272,000.

Gomera, I., Canaries; 21 km S.W. Tenerife; cap. San Sebastian; p. (1970) 19,389.

Gondar, t., N.W. **Ethiopia**; N. of L. Tana; airport; p. (est. 1970) 35,331.

Goodwin Sands, dangerous sandbanks off E. cst. of Kent, **Eng.**; shielding the Down roadstead.

Goodwood, v., West Sussex, **Eng.**; racecourse and motor racing; home of Dukes of Richmond.

Goole, t., Boothferry, Humberside, **Eng.**; second pt. to Hull on Humber; shipbldg., flour milling, fertilisers, alum and dextrine mftg.; p. (1971) 18,066.

Goonhilly Downs, Cornwall, **Eng.**; satellite communications sta. of Post Office.

Goose Bay, t., Labrador, **Canada**; on Churchill R., international airpt.

Göppingen, t., Baden-Württemberg, **W. Germany**; between Ulm and Stuttgart; machin., iron, wood, chemicals; p. (est. 1969) 47,119.

Gorakhpur, t., Uttar Pradesh, **India**; on Rapti R., N. of Varanasi; grain, timber; fertilisers; univ.; p. (1971) 230,911.

Gore Peninsula, N.T., **Australia**; N.E. extremity of Arnhem Land; bauxite deposits and new t.; alumina plant.

Gorgān, c., **Iran**, Mazandaran prov.; nr. Caspian Sea; p. (1967) 300,878 (met. a.).

Gori, t., central Georgian SSR, **USSR**; at confluence of Bolshoy, Liakhvi, and Kura Rs.; birthplace of Stalin; p. (1968) 33,100.

Gorinchem, t., S. Holland, **Neth.**; on R. Waal; p. (1967) 24,786.

Goring Gap, Berks./Oxon., **Eng.**; where R. Thames cuts through Chilterns and Berkshire Downs.

Gorizia (Görz), c., cap. of Gorizia prov., N.E. **Italy**; on Yugoslav border; cas.; agr. mkt., fruit, wine; textile machin.; p. (1969) 43,655.

Gorki or **Gorky** (formerly Nizhni-Novgorod), c., **RSFSR**; cap. of forested G. region, on Rs. Oka and Volga; univ., churches, 13th cent. kremlin; gr. industl. ctr. with heavy engin., steel, textiles, chemicals, oil refining, cars, glass, timber inds.; birthplace of Maxim Gorky; p. (1970) 1,170,000.

Görlitz, t., E. **Germany**; on W. Neisse on Polish border; lignite mines; textile mills; religious mystic Jacob Boehme lived here; p. (1968) 88,824.

Gorlovka, t., Ukrainian SSR, **USSR**; in Donets Basin; coal, chemicals, engin.; oil pipeline connects with Grozny oilfields; p. (1970) 335,000; (1970) 362,000 (met. a.).

Gorno-Altai, aut. region, S.E. Altai terr., **RSFSR**; in Altai mtns. on Mongolian border; cap. Gorno-Altaisk; forested; pastoral agr.; mng. (gold, manganese, mercury); a. 92,567 km; p. (1970) 168,000.

Gorno-Altaisk, t., **RSFSR**; cap. of Gorno-Altai aut. region; nr. Chuya highway to Mongolia; food-processing of agr. prod. from region; p. (1970) 34,000.

Gorno Badakhshan, aut. region, S.E. Tadzhik SSR, **USSR**; in Pamirs, bordered by China and Afghanistan; mng. (gold, mica, salt, limestone); livestock; cap. Khorog; a. 63,688 km²; p. (1970) 98,000.

Gornyy Snezhnogorsk, t., **RSFSR**; new t. in Siberian Arctic on R. Hantaiki, 56 km N.W. of Komsomolsk; tin-mng.

Gorseinon, v., West Glamorgan, S. Wales; nr. Loughour estuary, 6 km N.W. of Swansea; steel-wks., zinc refineries.

Gorzów Wielkopolski (Landesberg an der Warthe), c., W. **Poland** (since 1945); industl. ctr.; lignite mines; p. (1970) 74,300.

Gosainthan (Sisha Pangma), mtn. massif, Nepal–Tibet (China) border; part of Himalayas; rises to 8,091 m.

Gosford-Woy Woy, t., N.S.W., **Australia**; 80 km N. of Sydney; resort and commuter t.; food processing, bldg. materials; p. (1972) 38,093.

Gosforth, t., sub. to Newcastle upon Tyne, Tyne and Wear, **Eng.**; coal; p. (1971) 26,826.

Goslar, t., Lower Saxony, **W. Germany**; mng. ctr. at foot of Harz mtns.; lt. inds., tourism; p. (est. 1967) 40,900.

Gosport, t., l. gov. dist., Hants., **Eng.**; naval depot W. of Portsmouth to which it is linked by ferry; marine engin.; p. (est. 1976) 82,300 (dist.).

Göta, R., **Sweden**; flows from L. Vänern to the Kattegat; also canal connecting L. Vänern with the Baltic; the G. Canal provides a popular tourist trip from Stockholm to Göteborg.

Götaland, southernmost of 3 old provs. of **Sweden**; a. 101,010 km²; name used only in weather forecasts.

Göteborg or **Gothenburg**, c., cap. of Göteborg and Bohus, S.W. **Sweden**; major spt. on R. Göta on Kattegat; second c. in Sweden for commerce and ind.; univ.; shipbldg., oil refining; deepwater tanker terminal; p. (1970) 446,875 (c.), (est. 1969) 661,308 (met. a.).

Göteborg and Bohus, co., **Sweden**; on cst. of Kattegat; a. 5.152 km²; p. (est. 1970) 699,395.

Gotha, t., Erfurt, E. **Germany**; iron, machin., engin., musical instruments, textiles, porcelain, printing, cartography; p. (est. 1967) 57,400.

Gotham, v., Notts., **Eng.**; gypsum mng. and plaster wks.

Gotland, I. in the Baltic, **Sweden**; many historic bldgs.; cap. Visby; tourism; a. 3,173 km²; p. (1968) 53,939.

Göttingen, t., Lower Saxony, **W. Germany**; univ.; scientific instruments, pharmaceutics, film studios; p. (est. 1969) 114,000.

Gottwaldov (Zlin), t., **ČSSR**; 64 km E. of Brno; footwear, leather and domestic woodware inds.; home of Bata footwear; p. (1967) 64,000.

Gouda, t., S. Holland, **Neth.**; on R. IJssel, 18 km from Rotterdam; cheese, candles, ceramics, pipes; p. (1968) 46,262.

Gough I., Atl. Oc. dependency of St. Helena; breeding ground of the great shearwater; guano.

Goulburn, t., N.S.W., **Australia**; commands route across Gr. Dividing Range; in agr. dist. W. of Sydney; cath.; wool, shoes; p. (1972) 21,568.

Goulburn Is., N.T., **Australia**; 2 sm. Is. off N. cst. of Arnhem Land; Methodist Mission sta.

Goulburn R., Victoria, **Australia**; irrigation.

Gourock, burgh, Inverclyde, Scot.; on F. of Clyde, 3 km W. of Greenock; ferry to Dunoon; resort; p. (1971) 10,922.

Gower, peninsula, W. Glamorgan, **Wales**; tourism.

Gowrie, Carse of, fertile tract N. side F. of Tay, Scot.; includes Dundee, Kinnoul, Perth.

Gozo, I. in Mediterranean, belonging to **Malta**; the anc. Gaulos; surrounded by perpendicular cliffs; a. 67 km²; p. (1961) 27,506.

Graaff-Reinet, t., Cape Prov., **S. Africa**; fruit-growing, wool; p. (est. 1967) 17,700.

Grado-Aquileia, t., Friuli-Venezia Giulia, N.E. **Italy**; pleasure resort and former Roman spt.; rich in early Christian mosaics and antiquities; Grado joined to mainland by bridge; p. (est. 1968) 10,065.

Graengesberg, dist., Kopparberg co., **Sweden**; on S. fringe of Scandinavian mtns.; iron ore.

Grafton, t., N.S.W., **Australia**; on Clarence R.; dairy prod., timber; p. (1972) 16,354.

Graham Land, Falkland Is. Dependencies, Antarctica; mtnous., icebound; discovered 1832.

Grahamstown, t., C. Prov., **S. Africa**; univ.; cath ; p. (1970) 41,086.

Graian Alps, mtns. between Savoie, France, and Piedmont, Italy; hgst. point Gran Paradiso, 4,063 m.

Grain Coast, name formerly applied to cst. of Liberia, W. Africa; "grain" refers to pepper, spices, etc.

Grammichele, t., E. Sicily, Italy; 37 km S.W. of Catania; planned settlement after 1968 earthquake.

Grampian Region, l. gov. reg., N.E. **Scot.**; inc. former cos. of Aberdeenshire, Banff, Kincardine and Moray; highland a.; rapid devel. of cst.

with N. Sea oil discoveries; a. 8,702 km²; p. (1971) 436,995.

Grampians, mtns. of Scot.; forming natural bdy. between Highlands and Lowlands; inc. Ben Nevis, the hgst. peak (1,344 m), the Cairngorms and Schiehallion.

Granada, t. W. Nicaragua; on L. Nicaragua; in rich agr. region; distilling, soap, furniture; p. (1967) 40,200.

Granada, c., cap. of G. prov., S. Spain; in Andalusia, at foot of Sierra Nevada; formerly cap of Moorish kingdom of G.; univ., cath., famous 14th cent. Alhambra; tourism; p. (est. 1969) 158,477.

Granada, prov. S. Spain; traversed by Sierra Nevada; wheat, olives, textiles, liqueurs, paper; a. 12,530 km²; p. (1970) 773,375.

Granby, t., Quebec, Canada; on Yamaska R.; sawmills, leather, textiles, rubber, plastics; p. (1966) 34,349.

Gran Chaco, extensive lowland plain, Argentina, Paraguay, and Bolivia, between Andes and Paraguay-Paraná Rs.; hot, wet, swampy region with forests containing quebracho trees, a source of tannin; potential for petroleum.

Grand Banks, submarine plateau, extending S.E. from Newfoundland, Canada; a. 1,295,000 km²; impt. cod fisheries.

Grand Bassam, t. spt., Ivory Coast; exp. bananas, palm-kernels; mnf. prefabricated houses; p. (est. 1963) 22,994.

Grand Canal, canal, N. China; c. 1,600 km long from Tientsin to Hangchow; built between A.D. 605–18 and 1282–92; rebuilt for navigation and flood control.

Grand Canary, I., Canaries; cap. Las Palmas; tomatoes, bananas potatoes; tourism; extinct volcanoes; p. (1970) 519,606.

Grand Cayman I., W.I.; a. 220 km²; coconuts; cap. Georgetown; p. (1966) 7,323.

Grand Combin, mtn. Switzerland; part of Pennine Alps nr. Italian border; alt. 4,320 m.

Grand Coulee Dam, Wash., USA; on Columbia R., 176 km below Spokane; one of lgst. concrete dams in world (1,924,000 kW); reservoir (Franklin D. Roosevelt Lake) recreational a.; supplies irrigation water to 4,900 km² between Rs. Columbia and Snake.

Grande Chartreuse, limestone massif Isère, France; brandy from monastery of La Grande Chartreuse.

Grand Falls, t., Newfoundland, Canada; newsprint; falls provide hydroelectric power; p. (1966) 7,451.

Grand Island, t., Nebraska, USA; cattle and grain t.; p. (est. 1969) 30,000.

Grand' Mère, t., Quebec, Canada; pulp and paper mills; p. (1971) 17,144.

Grand Prairie. See Black Prairie.

Grand Rapids, c., Mich., USA; on Grand R.; furniture mkg., car and aircraft parts, chemicals, paper; p. (1970) 195,892 (c.), 535,702 (met. a.).

Grand R., Mich., USA; enters L. Mich. at Grand Haven, navigable to Grand Rapids; hydroelec. power; 400 km long.

Grand Turk, I., cap. of Turks and Caicos Is.; p. (1970) 2,300.

Grange, t., South Lakeland, Cumbria, Eng.; on N. cst. of Morecambe Bay; summer resort; p. (1971) 3,627.

Grangemouth, burgh, Falkirk, Scot.; on F. of Forth; shipbldg. and repair, marine engin., oil refining, projected oil tanker terminal; petroleum prods., chemicals, pharmaceutics; electronics and elec. ind.; oil pipeline to Finnart; p. (1971) 24,569.

Granite City, Ill., USA; iron and steel, tinplate, rly. engin., chemicals; p. (1970) 40,440.

Gran Sasso d'Italia, rugged limestone highlands, Abruzzi e Molise, central Italy, in highest part of Apennines, rising to 2,923 m in Monte Corno; Mussolini was rescued from here by German paratroopers 1943; Aquila at foot of Gran Sasso winter sports ctr.

Grantham, t., S. Kesteven, Lincs., Eng.; on Witham R.; tanning, agr. machin., engin., brewing, malting basket mkg.; expanded t.; p. (1971) 27,913.

Grantown-on-Spey, burgh, Moray, Scot.; on R. Spey; resort; p. (1971) 1,600.

Granville, spt., Manche dep., France; on Golfe de St Malo; fisheries, food-processing; p. (1968) 12,715.

Grasmere, v., Cumbria, Eng.; at head of Grasmere L.; home of Wordsworth.

Grasse, t., Alpes-Maritimes dep., S.E. France, in Provence in hills above Cannes; perfumes; birthplace of Fragonard; p. (1968) 32,096.

Graubünden. See Grisons.

Graudenz. See Grudziadz.

's-Gravenhage. See Hague.

Graves, Pointe de, N. point of Médoc peninsula, France; in famous wine dist.

Gravesend, spt., Gravesham, Kent, Eng.; S. bank R. Thames facing Tilbury; pilot sta. for Port of London; paper, cement; oil refinery projected; p. (1971) 54,044.

Gravesham, l. gov. dist., Kent, Eng.; based on Gravesend and surrounding dist.; p. (est. 1976) 93,900.

Graz, c., cap. of Styria, Austria; on R. Mur at foothills of Alps; second lgst. c.; univ., cath.; machin., iron and steel, rly. wks.; p. (est. 1969) 253,800.

Great Altai, range of mtns., lying mainly in Outer Mongolia but also in Western Siberia, USSR; rising to 4,200 m.

Great Atlas (Haut Atlas), mtns., N.W. Africa; alt. c. 2,000 m; part of the Atlas mtns.

Great Australian Basin, artesian basin, Australia; underlies plains of Queensland, N.S.W., S. Australia; water supply used on sheep-farms, cattle-ranches, in a. from Normanton in N. to Renmark in S. Oodnadatta in W. to Roma in E.; a. 1,476,300 km².

Great Australian Bight, wide inlet of Indian Oc., S. cst. of Australia.

Great Barrier Reef, coral reef barrier off N.E. cst of Australia; 1,600 km long, 120–160 km from cst.; currently being eaten away by the starfish, Acanthaster planci.

Great Basin, high plateau region between the Wasatch and Sierra Nevada mtns., USA; inc. most of Nevada, parts of Utah, Cal., Idaho, Ore., Wyo.; drainage ctr. Great Salt Lake; a. 543,900 km²; much desert; sparse p.

Great Bear Lake, lge L., N.W. Terr., Canada; c. 280 km long; a. 36,260 km²; outlet through Great Bear R. to Mackenzie R.

Great Belt (Store Bælt), strait, Denmark; separates Fyn I. from Sjaelland I.; sinuous shape makes navigation difficult; rly. ferry at narrowest point (18 km) between Nyborg and Korsør; 64 km long; proposed bridge.

Great Britain. See England, Scotland, Wales, British Isles.

Great Dividing Range, mtn. system, E. Australia; extends, under different local names from Queensland to Victoria and separates E. cst. plains from interior; reaches max. alt. in Mt Kosciusko (2,230 m), in Australian Alps, on bdy. between Victoria and N.S.W.

Greater Manchester, met. co., N.W. Eng.; lge. urban a. centred on major comm. ctr. of M.. with former cotton spinning ts. to N., inc. Bolton, Bury and Rochdale; dormitory ts. to S.; former concentration on textile mftg. now reduced and inds. diversified; major industl. estate at Trafford Park; p. (1971) 2,727,000.

Great Falls, c., Mont., USA; on Missouri R.; lgst c. in st.; mkt. for irrigated farming a.; ctr. of hydroelectric power, called the "electric city"; copper- and oil-refining, flour mills; p. (est. 1969) 61,000.

Great Fisher Bank, submarine sandbank in N. Sea; 320 km E. of Aberdeen, 160 km S.W. of Stavanger; valuable fishing-ground; depth of water, from 45–75 m.

Great Gable, mtn., Cumbria, Eng.; alt. 899 m.

Great Harwood, t., Hyndburn, Lancs., Eng.; 8 km N.E. of Blackburn; textiles, aero-engin.; p. (1971) 11,000.

Great Lake, Tasmania, Australia; lgst. freshwater L. in Australia.

Great Lakes, N. America; 5 freshwater Ls.; Superior, Michigan, Huron, Erie, Ontario; glacial genesis; frozen 4 to 5 months in winter; traffic in cereals, iron, coal, etc.; major ctr. of heavy inds.; resorts; serious pollution; a. 248,640 km².

Great Plains, lowland a. of central N. America; extending E. from Rocky mtns. and S. from Mackenzie to S. Texas; stock rearing, grain, oilfields.

Great Rift Valley, geological fault system extending from S.W. Asia to E. Africa, 4,800 km in 1.; inc. L. Tiberias (Sea of Galilee), Jordan valley, Dead Sea, G. of Aqaba, Red Sea, and chain of Ls., notably L. Rudolf and L. Malawi; a branch runs through Ls. Tanganyika, Mobutu and Idi Amin Dada.

Great Salt Lake, shallow salty L., N. Utah, USA; in Great Basin plateau of N. America; remnant of L. Bonneville; alt. 1,286 m; varies in size and depth; receives Bear, Jordan and Beaver Rs.; many Is., no outlet.

Great Slave Lake, N.W. Terr., Canada; a. 28,440 km²; 496 km long; drained by Mackenzie R.; navigable.

Great Smoky Mtns., Tenn., USA; with Blue Ridge mtns. form E. zone of Appalachian mtn. system; hgst peak Clingmans Dome 2,026 m; largely preserved as Nat Park.

Great Torrington, t., Torridge, Devon, Eng.; on R. Torridge; mkt., processing of agr. prod.; p. (1971) 3,536.

Great Wall of China, wall built in N. China along S. edge of Mongolian plateau to keep out invading Mongols; length 2,400 km; begun in Ch'in dynasty by Shih Huang Ti, c. 220 B.C.; present form dates from Ming dynasty (1368–1644).

Great Whale R. (R. de la Baleine), Quebec, Canada; rises in L. Bienville, flows to Hudson Bay; difficult transport; 400 km long.

Great Yarmouth. See Yarmouth.

Greece, rep., S.E. Europe; mtnous. peninsula, between Mediterranean and Ægean Sea, inc. many sm. Is. to S., lgst. Crete; inds. increasingly impt. but agr. prods. still ch. exp. (tobacco, olive oil, cotton, citrus fruit, wine); only 25 per cent a. cultivable; economy also helped by lge. merchant fleet and tourism; deposed king in exile; executive power held by military junta 1967–74; cap. Athens; a. 132,561 km²; p. (1971) 8,736,367.

Greenland, I., between Arctic Oc. and Baffin Bay; lofty ice-capped plateau; peopled by coastal settlements of Eskimos; fisheries; whale oil, seal skins; lge. uranium deposits, potential for petroleum; some coal, lead, zinc; US base at Thule; part of Danish kingdom; cap Godthåb; a. 2,175,600 km² of which 1,833,720 km² are under a permanent ice-cap; p. (1966) 39,600.

Greenland Sea, Arctic Oc., between Greenland and Spitzbergen; ice-covered.

Green Mtns., Vt., USA; part of Appalachians reaching 1,340 m (Mt. Mansfield); Nat. Forest, tourism.

Greenock, spt., burgh, Inverclyde, Scot.; on S. shore of F. of Clyde, 40 km W. of Glasgow; container facilities; shipbldg., sugar refining, woollens, chemicals, aluminium casting, tin-plate inds.; birthplace of James Watt; p. (1971) 69,502.

Green River, Wyo., Utah, USA; rises in Wind R. Range (major watershed in Rockies); flows via spectacular scenery to Colorado R.; impt. routeway; 1,168 km long.

Greensboro', c., N.C., USA; cotton, tobacco, chemicals; regional financial ctr.; educational institutes; p. (1970) 140,672 (c.), 598,905 (met. a.).

Greenville, t., Miss., USA; on Mississippi R.; deep-water harbour; tr. ctr. for cotton, agr. prod.; chemicals, metal gds.; p. (est. 1969) 44,000.

Greenville, t., S.C., USA; univ.; industl. and comm. ctr.; textile mills, farm prod. processing; p. (1970) 61,242 (c.), 204,220 (met. a.).

Greenwich, outer bor., London, Eng.; inc. most of former bor. of Woolwich on S. bank of R. Thames; famous for its hospital, observatory (now moved to Herstmonceux) and R.N. College; longitudes conventionally calculated from Greenwich meridian; p. (est. 1976) 207,200.

Greenwich Village, lower Manhattan, N.Y. city, USA; bohemian quarter.

Greifswald, spt., Rostock, E. Germany; on Baltic inlet; shipbldg., textiles, wood inds.; p. (est. 1967) 45,800.

Greiz, t., Gera, E. Germany; paper, textiles, chemicals; p. (est. 1970) 39,058.

Grenada, W.I., most S. of Windward Is.; inc. archipelago of Grenadines; known as the "spice islands" as major exp. is nutmeg; cloves and vanilla also grown; sugar and sugar prods.; cotton-ginning; cap. St. George's;

former Brit. col., achieved indep. 1974; a. 344 km²; p. (1970) 104,000.

Grenadines, dependency of Grenada I., W.I.; gr. of over 100 sm. Is., between Grenada and St. Vincent. Windward Is.; sea-island cotton.

Grenoble, c., cap. of Isère dep., S.E. France; on Isère R. at foot of Alps; univ.; thriving cultural and scientific ctr.; impt. hydroelectric ctr.; science-based inds., joint Franco-German nuclear research reactor; gloves, paper, cement, liqueurs; p. (1968) 161,616 (c.), 332,423 (met. a.).

Gretna Green, v., Annandale and Eskdale, Scot.; on Eng. border; famous as place of runaway marriages 1754–1856.

Greymouth, spt., S.I., N.Z.; on W. cst. at mouth of Grey R.; ch. t. prov. of Westland; coal; p (1971) 7,739.

Grey Range, mtns., S.W. Queensland, Australia; forms divide between streams draining E. to R. Darling and those draining W. to L. Eyre.

Grimaldi, caves, N.W. Italy; remains of prehistoric man, late Paleolithic, found there.

Grimsby, spt., l. gov. dist., Humberside, Eng.; on S. bank of R. Humber; major distant waters fish. pt.; food-processing; chemical ind. at nearby Immingham; p. (est. 1976) 93,800.

Grindelwald, v., Bernese Oberland, Switzerland; tourist ctr.; p. (1970) 3,511.

Gris-Nez, C., N.E. France; nearest point on Fr. cst. to Dover.

Grisons (Graubünden), can., E. Switzerland; region of glaciers and magnificent peaks; ch. resorts Davos, Arosa, St. Moritz; Swiss Nat. Park; lgst can.; sparse p.; ctr. Romansch language; a. 7,112 km²; p. (1969) 153,000.

Grodno, c., W. Belorussiyan SSR, USSR; pt. on Neman R.; a Polish t. until 1939; machine parts, cloth; historic bldgs.; p. (1970) 132,000.

Groningen, c., cap. of G. prov., Neth.; univ.; impt. trading ctr.; p. (est. 1969) 168,256 (c.), 200,532 (met. a.).

Groningen, prov., N.E. Neth.; agr. and dairying; major natural gas deposits at Slochteren; a. 2,157 km²; p. (1968) 511,753.

Groote Eylandt, I., G. of Carpentaria; off cst. of N.T., Australia; manganese ore-mng.

Grosseto, t., cap. of G. prov., Tuscany, Italy; cath.; agr. mkt.; severely affected by floods 1966; p. (1969) 61,534.

Gross Glockner, mtn. (3,801 m) and pass (2,370 m), Austria, part of Hohe Tauern range; hgst. peak in Austria.

Groznyy, t., N. Caucasia, RSFSR; on R. Terek; naphtha wells, refinery, engin.; starting point of oil pipelines to Makhachkala, Tuapse and Gorlovka; p. (1970) 341,000.

Grudziadz (Graudenz), t., on R. Vistula, Bydgoszcz, Poland; mftg.; p. (1970) 75,500.

Grünberg. See Zielona Góra.

Gruyères, dist., can. Fribourg, Switzerland; cattle; cheese.

Guadalajara, c., cap. of Jalisco st., W. Mexico; c. 1,500 m high; impt. industl. and comm. ctr.; textiles, agr. processing, traditional pottery and glassware; cath.; gas pipeline from Salamanca; health resort; p. (1970) 1,196,218.

Guadalajara, c., cap. of G. prov., Spain; on Henares R., N. of Madrid; palace of Mendoza family; battle of Spanish Civil War, March 1937, fought nearby; p. (1970) 31,917.

Guadalaviar, R., E. Spain; flows into Mediterranean, below Valencia; 208 km long.

Guadalcanal, volcanic I., Pac. Oc.; lgst. of Solomon Is.; jungle and mtns.; exp. copra; ch. t. Honiara.

Guadalquivir, R. S. Spain; flows through Andalusia via Seville to Atl.; c. 560 km long; hydroelec. plants; agr.

Guadalupe Hidalgo, place of pilgrimage, N.W. Mexico City, Mexico; basilica and shrine; treaty ending Mexican–U.S. war signed here 1848.

Guadarrama, Sierra de, mtn. range, central Spain; rugged, forest covered; affects Madrid's climate; reaches 2,431 m.

Guadeloupe, overseas dep. France, W.I.; comprises most S. of Leeward gr., Basse-Terre, Grande-Terre, Marie-Galante and other Is.; economy based on sugar exports to France; rapidly rising p. aggravates process of econ. development; attempts to develop tourism and food-processing inds.; ch. comm. ctr. and pt. Pointe à Pitre (Grande Terre); cap. Basse-Terre; a. 1,748 km²; p. (1967) 312,724.

Guadiana, R., forms part of Spanish and Portuguese frontier; flows into G. of Cádiz; Estremadura valley reclamation scheme in progress; 816 km long.

Guadiana del Caudillo, new t., nr. Badajoz, Spain.

Guam, I., U.S. air and naval base in W. Pac.; developing tourist ind.; free-port and tax incentives aid investment; ch. t. Agaña; a. 541 km²; p. (1968) 58,598.

Guanabara, st., S.E. Brazil; cap. Rio de Janeiro; formerly the Fed. Dist., before Brasilia became the cap.; a. 1,357 km²; p. (est. 1968) 4,207,322.

Guanajuato, st., central Mexico; average elevation 1,800 m; mng. (silver, gold, tin, copper, iron, lead, opals); a. 30,572 km²; p. (1969) 2,326,000.

Guanajuato, cap. of G. st., Mexico; 1,990 m high in gorge; resort; p. (1970) 65,258.

Guantánamo, c., S.E. Cuba; sugar, coffee, bananas, cacao; pt. at Caimanera on G. Bay; p. (est. 1967) 135,100.

Guaporé, R., Brazil; rises in Mato Grosso st., forms Brazil-Bolivia bdy. before joining the Mamoré; length 1,440 km.

Guatemala, rep., Central America; straddles Central American isthmus; interior mtnous. with temperate climate; coastal lowlands hot and humid; economy based on agr., coffee accounting for half exp.; timber exploitation, food processing; two oil refineries; trades mainly with USA. ch. pts. Puerto Barrios, San José. Santo Tomas de Castilla; 4 univs.; cap. Guatemala City; a. 108,889 km²; p. (est. 1975) 6,000,000.

Guatemala City, c., cap. of G. rep.; cath., univ.; fruit and vegetable mkts.; coffee tr.; remains Mayan civilisation; partially destroyed by earthquake (1976); p. (est. 1970) 730,991.

Guayama, t., Puerto Rico; ctr. of agr. region; sugar-milling and food-processing; p. (1970) 36,159.

Guayaquil, ch. pt., Ecuador; cap. of Guayas prov. on Guayas R.; nr. Bay of G.; recent new pt. nearby and improvement to transport in hinterland; univ., cath.; sawmills, foundries, machin., brewing, oil refinery; p. (est. 1972) 860,600.

Gubin (Polish Guben), border t., E. Germany/Poland, on R. Neisse; comm. ctr.; textiles, machin., leather, synthetic fibre.

Gudbrandsdal, valley, S. Norway; leads S.E. from Dovrefjell towards Oslo; drained by R. Logan; used by main road Oslo to Trondheim; provides relatively lge. a. of cultivable land; hay, oats, barley, dairy cattle; 368 km long.

Guelph, t., Ont., Canada; on Speed R.; univ.; mkt. ctr. in rich farming a.; cloth, elec. equipment; p. (1971) 58,364.

Guernsey, I., Channel Is., between cst. of France and Eng., tomatoes, grapes (under glass), flowers, cattle, tourist resort. t. and ch. spt. St. Peter Port; banking; a. 6,335 ha; p. (est. 1973) 52,000.

Guerrero, st., S. Mexico; on Pac. cst.; mtnous.; cereals, cotton, coffee, tobacco; cap. Chilpancingo; ch. pt. Acapulco; a. 64.452 km; p. (1969) 1,620.000.

Guiana Highlands, platueau, S. America; extend c. 1,440 km from E. to W. across S. parts of Venezuela, Guyana, Surinam, Fr. Guiana; steep sides, rounded tops c. 900 m but rise to 2,852 m in Mt. Roraima; chiefly composed of crystalline rocks rich in minerals.

Guienne, former prov., France, partly coincides with the Aquitaine basin (q.v.); controlled by England 1154-1451.

Guildford, co. t., l. gov. dist., Surrey, Eng.; 48 km S.W. London; on gap cut by R. Wey through N. Downs, cath., univ.; vehicles, agr. implements, lt. inds.; residtl., cas.; p. (est. 1976) 121,000 (dist.).

Guinea, rep., W. Africa; climate not and humid on cst. but temperate in higher interior; 95 per cent p. engaged in agr., but bauxite dominates exp. from deposits at Boké; hydroelectric dam and aluminium smelter at Konkouré; all foreigners barred from business in G. (1968); poorly developed transport system; major spt. at cap. Conakry; socialist economic policies have been adopted since independence

from France (1958); a. 245,861 km²; p. (est. 1970) 4,000,000.

Guinea, gen. name for W. African coastlands from Senegal to Angola.

Guinea-Bissau, formerly Portuguese Guinea, W. Africa; indep. 1974; poor econ. infrastructure; no manf. inds.; depends on agr. of rice, groundnuts and stock raising; cst. edged by mangroves; offshore oil potential; a. 36,125 km² p. (est. 1969) 550,000.

Guinea, Spanish. See Equatorial Guinea.

Guinea Current, ocean current, flows W. to E. along Guinea cst., diverted away from cst. in Bight of Benin by C. Three Points.

Guinea, Gulf of, arm of Atl. Oc. formed by gr. bend of cst. of W. Africa between Ivory Coast and Gabon; Bight of Benin and Bight of Bonny are inner bays.

Guisborough, t., Langbaurgh, Cleveland, Eng.; at foot of Cleveland hills; former ctr. of iron-mng.; 12 cent. abbey ruins; p. (1971) 13,852.

Gujarat, st. India; formerly part of Bombay st.; cap. temporarily Ahmedabad; new cap. Gandhinager, 21 km N. of A. under construction; oil development in Cambay area; fertiliser plant projected; a. 187,115 km²; p. (1971) 26,661,000.

Gujranwala, c., Pakistan; N. of Lahore; power plant, engin.; p. (1969) 289,000.

Gujrat, t., Rawalpindi, Pakistan; agr. ctr., handicraft inds.; p. (est. 1969) 73,000.

Gulbarga, t., Karnataka, India; cotton, flour, paint; (1971) 145,588.

Gulfport, t., Miss., USA; pt. of entry; exp. wood, cottonseed; mnfs., textiles, fertilisers; resort; p. (est. 1969) 47,000.

Gulf Stream, warm current of the Atl. Oc., issuing from G. of Mexico by Fla. Strait. See L50.

Guntur, c., Andhra Pradesh, India; on E. cst. N. of Madras; cotton mkt.; p. (1971) 269,991.

Gur'yev, c., Kazakh SSR, USSR; pt. on R. Ural at entrance to Caspian Sea; oil refining; pipeline to Orsk; p. (1970) 113,000.

Gus-Khrustalnyy, t., RSFSR; 64 km S. of Vladimir; impt. ctr. of glass ind.; p. (est. 1969) 65,000.

Güstrow, t., Schwerin, E. Germany; S. of Rostock; cas., cath.; mkt. t.; p. (est. 1970) 37.213.

Gütersloh, t., N. Rhine-Westphalia, W. Germany; nr. Bielefeld; silk and cotton inds.; famous for its Pumpernickel (Westphalian rye bread); machin., furniture, publishing, metallurgy; p. (est. 1967) 55,200.

Guyana, rep., N. cst. S. America; former Brit. col.; largely covered by dense jungle. p. concentrated on narrow coastal belt; economy based on agr., especially sugar and rice; forestry inds. limited by lack of transport; impt. bauxite deposits; high birth-rate creates social and economic problems, especially on overpopulated coastal belt; airport at Timehri; univ. at Turkeyen; cap. Georgetown; a. 214,970 km²; p. (est. 1970) 721,098.

Gwalior, t., Madhya Pradesh, India; adjoins Lashkar (q.v.); dominated by rock of Gwalior with Jain sculptures; p. (1971) 384,722 (t.). 406,140 (met. a.).

Gwelo, t., Rhodesia; ctr. of farming dist.; shoes, glass, containers; p. (1967) 39,500.

Gwent, co., S.E. Wales; inc. most of Monmouth and sm. part of Brecon; upland in N. where coalfield and former mng. ts., lowland a. bordering Severn estuary to S. where lge. industl. ts. inc. Newport; a. 1,375 km²; p. (est. 1976) 439,600.

Gwent, Plain of (Vale of Glamorgan), lowland dist. South and Mid Glamorgan, S. Wales; lies S. of moorland of S. Wales coalfield, extends E. into Monmouth; fertile soils; mixed farming except in industl. areas of Cardiff, Barry.

Gwynedd, co., N.W. Wales; comprises former cos. of Anglesey, Caernarvon, most of Merioneth and a sm. part of Denbigh; mtnous. a. except cst. and Anglesey; inc. Snowdonia Nat. Park; sparse p. inland where hill farming; cstl. resorts inc. Llandudno; a. 3,867 km²; p. (est. 1976) 225,100.

Gympie, t., Queensland, Australia; on Mary R., 106 m. from Brisbane; former goldfield; now dairying and pastoral dist., tropical fruits, especially pineapples; p. (1972) 11,131.

Györ, t., Hungary; at confluence of Rs. Rába and Danube; cath.; textile ctr., rolling stock, chemicals, machine tools; p. (1968) 80,000.

H

Haarlem, c., cap. of N. Holland prov., **Neth.**; nr. N. Sea cst.; tulip-growing, textiles, printing; 15th cent. church; p. (est. 1969) 172,588 (c.), 239,089 (met. a.).

Hachinohe, c., Honshu, Japan; cas.; fishing, fish-processing, metal-refining; p. (est. 1971) 217,000.

Hackney, inner bor., N.E. London, **Eng.**; incorporates former bors. of Shoreditch and Stoke Newington; furniture, clothing, p. (est. 1976) 192,500.

Haddington, burgh. E. Lothian, Scot.; on R. Tyne, 26 km E. of Edinburgh; woollen mnf.; grain mkt., corn mills, lt. engin., hosiery; p. (1971) 6,501.

Haderslev, t., Denmark; tobacco, clothing, knitted gds.; p. (est. 1970) 29,647.

Hadhramaut, dist.. S. Yemen; ch. pt. and c. Al Mukallā; fertile coastal valley; frankincense, aloes, tobacco shawls, carpets; p. (1961) 240 000

Hadleigh, t., Babergh, Suffolk, **Eng.**; mkt.; flourmilling; p. (1971) 5,101.

Hadrian's Wall, part of frontier barrier, N. Eng.; stretching across Tyne–Solway isthmus, 118 km long. *See* **Roman Walls, Section L.**

Hafnarfördur, t., S. of Reykjavik, Iceland; p. (1970) 9,696.

Hagen, t., N. Rhine–Westphalia, **W. Germany;** N.E. of Wuppertal; iron, steel, chemicals, textiles, paper; p. (est. 1969) 201,500.

Hagerstown, t., Md., **USA;** machin., furniture, chemicals, aircraft; p. (1970) 35,862.

Hagersville t., Ont., **Canada;** main producer of gypsum in Canada.

Hagfors, t., Värmland, **Sweden;** site of lge. iron and steel wks. since 1878.

Hague, The or **'s-Gravenhage** or **Den Haag,** c , S. Holland, **Neth.;** seat of government; permanent court of international justice; admin. ctr.; urban inds., machin. and metal wares; engin., printing; p. (est. 1969) 557,114 (c.), 723,753 (met. a.).

Haifa, c., ch. spt., Israel; on Bay of Acre at foot of Mt. Carmel; terminus of Iraq oil pipeline; oil refining and heavy inds.; p. (1972) 217,400 (c.), 447,800 (met. a.).

Hail. t.. and oasis, Nejd Saudi Arabia; p. 30 000.

Hailsham, mkt. t., Wealden, East Sussex, **Eng.**; 8 km N. of Eastbourne; mats, rope, and twine; p. (1971) 35,502 (dist.).

Hainan, I., S. cst. of China; densely wooded; camphor, mahogany, rosewood, sugar; new rubber plantations; ch. t. Hoihow; a. 36,193 km².

Hainaut, prov., **Belgium,** adjoining N.E. border of France; industl. and agr.; coal- and iron-mines; a. 3,719 km²; p. (1968) 1,336,677.

Haiphong, c., ch. pt. Vietnam; on Red R. delta; comm. and trading ctr.; cotton, thread, soap, glass, enamel ware, fish-canning; former naval base of Fr. Indo-China; p. (1963) 369,000.

Haiti, rep., **W.I.,** W. third of I. of Hispaniola; tropical climate modified by alt.; agr. basis of economy; coffee accounts for 45 per cent exp.; irrigation scheme in Artibonite valley; unexploited mineral resources, some bauxite mng. and exp.; sm.-scale inds.; well-developed road network and international shipping services; cap. Port-au-Prince; a. 27,713 km²; p. (est. 1975) 5,400,000 (predominantly Negro).

Hakodate, c., S. Hokkaido, Japan; Seikan tunnel to Honshu (Aomori) under construction; fishing pt.; fish food processing; p. (est. 1971) 239,000.

Halberstadt, t., Magdeburg, E. Germany; cath.; metallurgy, rubber inds., engin., sugar refining; rly. junc.; p. (est. 1970) 46,774.

Halden, t., S.E. Norway; wood-pulp, paper, footwear, cotton spinning; nuclear research reactor; p. (est. 1970) 26,271.

Haldia, pt., W. Bengal, India; nr. mouth of R. Hooghly; satellite pt. for Calcutta to handle coal, ore, grain; oil pipeline to Barauni; refinery.

Hale, t., Trafford, Gtr. Manchester, **Eng.**; residtl.; p. (1971) 7,030.

Halesowen, t., S.W. of Birmingham, West Midlands, **Eng.**; weldless tubes, elec. gds., stainless steel forgings, engin.; p. (1971) 53,933.

Halesworth, t., Suffolk, **Eng;** on R. Blyth, 14 km S.W. of Beccles; p. (1971) 3,250.

Halifax, spt., cap. of Nova Scotia, Canada; univ.; naval sta. and dockyard, open in winter; machin., iron foundries, footwear, oil refining, food-processing; p. (1971) 86,290 (c.), 129,309 (met. a.).

Halifax, t., Calderdale, West Yorks., **Eng.**; on E. flanks of Pennines; carpets, textiles, machine tools; p. (1971) 91,171.

Halle, c., cap. of H. admin. dist., E. Germany; on R. Saale; univ.; lignite and potash mined nearby; engin., chemicals, food-processing; p. (est. 1969) 261.190.

Hallstatt, v., Upper Austria; in the Salzkammergut; early Iron Age culture type site.

Halmahera, I., Indonesia; mtnous., active volcanoes, tropical forests; spices. pearl fisheries, sago, rice; a. 17,218 km².

Halmstad, spt. Kattegat, Sweden; iron and steel wks., machin. engin., cycles, textiles, leather, jute, wood-pulp; p. (1968) 46,548.

Hälsingborg, spt., Malmöhus, **Sweden;** industl. ctr.; train ferry to Elsinore, Denmark; p. (1968) 80,648.

Halstead, t., Essex, **Eng.**; on R. Colne, N.W. of Colchester; rayon weaving; p. (1971) 7,621.

Haltemprice, t., Humberside, **Eng.**; p. (1971) 52,239.

Halton, l. gov. dist., Cheshire, **Eng.**; surrounds Mersey R. and inc. Runcorn and Widnes; p. (est. 1976) 113,100.

Haltwhistle, mkt. t., Tynedale, Northumberland, **Eng.**; on R. South Tyne; former coal-mng. dist.; p. (1971) 6,531 (dist.).

Hama, c., N. Syria, on R. Orontes; the anc. Hamath, ctr of Hittite culture; food tr., rural inds.; p. (1970) 137,000.

Hamadān, t., W. Iran; alt. c. 1,800 m; the anc. Ecbatana, cap. of Media; carpets, pottery; airport.; tomb of Avicenna; p. (est. 1971) 139,600.

Hamamatsu, c., S. Honshu, Japan; on cst. plain 96 km S.E. of Nagoya; ctr. of impt. cotton-mftg. region; textiles, dyeing, musical instruments, motor cycles; p. (est. 1971) 447,000.

Hamar, t., Norway; on L. Mjösa; ctr. of rich agr. dist.; tr. and mftg. inds.; p. (est. 1970) 15,189.

Hamble, Hants, Eng.; popular yachting ctr.

Hambleton, l. gov. dist., North Yorks., **Eng.**; inc. Northallerton, Bedale and Thirsk; p. (est. 1976) 73,700.

Hamburg, c., *Land* H., **W. Germany;** astride R. Elbe, nr. N. Sea; 2nd. lgst. German c. and ch. pt.; pt. to be extended by reclaiming Is. of Neuwerk and Scharhörn; diversified tr. inc. liner traffic, barge traffic down Elbe, entrepôt goods; major pt. processing inds., airpt., univ.; cultural and musical ctr.; heavily bombed in second world war; p. (est. 1969) 1,818,600.

Hämeenlinna (Tavastehus), c., cap. of Häme co., S.W. I inland; L. pt.; tourist ctr.; birthplace of Sibelius; p. (est. 1966) 36,400.

Hameln (Hamelin), t., Lower Saxony, **W. Germany;** pt. on R. Weser; iron, textiles; scene of legend of the Pied Piper; p. (est. 1967) 47,200.

Hamhung, c., **N. Korea;** industl. and comm. ctr., oil refinery, petrochemicals; coal nearby; p. (est. 1962) 125,000.

Hamilton, t., W. Victoria, **Australia;** mkt. ctr. for dairying and grazing a.; p. (1972) 9,662.

Hamilton spt., cap. of **Bermuda;** tourism, comm. and service ctr.; p. (est. 1968) 3,000.

Hamilton, c., and L. pt., S.E. Ont., **Canada;** at W. end of L. Ont.; univ.; varied metallurgical mnfs.. fruit ctr.; p. (1971) 307,473 (c.), 495,864 (met. a.).

Hamilton, t., N.I., **N.Z.;** pt. on Waikato R.; univ.; p. (1971) 74,762.

Hamilton, burgh, l. gov. dist., Strathclyde Reg., Scot.; in Clyde valley, 16 km S.E. of Glasgow; admin. ctr.; elec. gds., carpet mftg., cottons, woollens, knitwear; Rudolf Hess landed on Duke of Hamilton's estate 1941; p. (1971) 46,349.

Hamilton, t., Ohio, USA; on Great Miami R.; industl. ctr.; mnfs. metal prods., paper, machin.; p. (1970) 64,058 (t.), 218,201 (met. a.).

Hamilton, R. *See* **Churchill R.**

Hamm, t., N. Rhine–Westphalia, **W. Germany;** on R. Lippe, in Runr conurb.; rly. marshalling yards, iron and steel foundries; p (est. 1967) 72.000 (c.), 159,000 (met. a.).

Hammerfest, spt., Norway; world's most N. t., on Kvalöya I.; fishing; p. (est. 1967) 6,800.

Hammersmith, Thames-side inner bor., London

Eng.; inc. former bor. of Fulham; industl., residtl.; p. (est. 1976) 170,000.

Hammond, c., N.W. Ind., USA; on Grand Calumet R., nr. Chicago; originally slaughtering and meat-pkg. ctr., now ch. mnfs., petroleum and steel prods., soap; p. (1970) 107,108.

Hampshire, non-met. co., S. Eng.; inc. Hampshire basin of chalk covered in clay and sand; inc. infertile heath and New Forest; leading pts Southampton, Portsmouth; lt. inds.; tourism, seaside resorts; impt. planned p. growth in S. H.; co. t. Winchester; a. 3,771 km²; p. (est. 1976) 1,456,100.

Hampshire, East, l. gov. dist., Hants., Eng.; stretches from Alton to Petersfield; p. (est. 1976) 85,200.

Hampstead, former v., now inc. in Greater London, Eng.; hilltop v. with nearby heathland. *See* Camden.

Hampton, Thames-side t., Richmond upon Thames, London, Eng.; Hampton Court Palace; Hampton Wick E. of H. Court.

Hampton, t., S.E. Va., USA; oldest English community in U.S.; fishing, oyster and crab packing; p. (1970) 118,584.

Han, R, Hupeh, China; rises in S.W. Shensi prov., flows E. between Tsingling mtns. and Tapa range of N. Szechwan into Yangtze R. at Wuhan; ch. trib. of Yangtze; c. 1,280 km long.

Han, R., S. China; forms rich agr. delta nr. Swatow; c. 400 km long.

Hanau, t., Hesse, W. Germany; on Rs. Main and Kinzig; jewellery ctr., rubber and non-ferrous metals inds.; birthplace of Jakob and Wilhelm Grimm, Paul Hindemith; p. (est. 1967) 52,600.

Hanchung, c., S.W. Shensi prov., China; on Han R.; nr. Szechwan border; agr. and tr. ctr.; former Nancheng; p. (est. 1970) 120,000.

Hangchow (Hang-chou), c., cap. of Chekiang prov., E. China; picturesque setting at head of H. Bay; former treaty pt., now silted up; silk-weaving, chemicals, jute cloth; tourism; p. (est. 1970) 1,100,000.

Hankow, c., Hupeh, China; at junc. of Han and Yangtze Rs., 960 km from mouth of Yangtze but accessible to ocean-going ships; ch. comm. and mnf. ctr. of central China; former treaty pt., now part of Wuhan conurb.; machin., chemicals, cigarettes, silk. *See* Wuhan.

Hannibal, t., Mo., USA; on Mississippi R.; shoes, cement, metal gds.; boyhood home of Mark Twain; p. (1970) 18,698.

Hanoi, c., cap. of Vietnam; on Red R.; old Annamese fort, now modern comm. ctr.; univ.; cotton, silks, tobacco, pottery; super-phosphate and magnesium phosphate nearby; bricks, concrete, rubber; p. (est. 1965) 850,000.

Hanover (Hannover), c., cap. of Lower Saxony, W. Germany; route ctr.; iron, textiles, machin., paper, biscuits, cigarettes, cars, rubber-processing, chemicals; p. (est. 1969) 519,700.

Hanyang. *See* Wuhan.

Haparanda, spt., N. Sweden; salmon fishing; exp. timber, and prod. of the Lapps; p. (est. 1970) 8,963.

Hapur, t., W. Uttar Pradesh, India; tr. in sugar, timber, cotton, brassware; p. (1961) 55,248.

Harbin (Haerhpin), c., cap. of Heilungkiang prov., China; pt. on Sungari R.; tr. and comm. ctr. of N.E. China; exp. soyabeans; food-processing, machin., paper-mills, oil refining, hydro-turbines, textiles; former treaty pt.; p. (est. 1970) 2,750,000.

Harborough, l. gov. dist., S. Leics., Eng.; based on Market Harborough and Lutterworth; p. (est. 1976) 58,500.

Harburg-Wilhelmsburg, industl. pt. of Hamburg, W. Germany; oil refining.

Hardanger Fjord, W. cst. Norway; 120 km long; magnificent scenery; tourism.

Hardt Mtns., W. Germany; northward continuation of Vosges on W. of Rhine rift valley; formerly forested, now largely cleared for pasture; hgst. points reach just over 600 m.

Hardwar, t., Uttar Pradesh, India; on R. Ganges; gr. annual fair and pilgrimage; nearby dam; p. (1961) 58,513

Hargeisa, t., Somalia; comm. ctr. of livestock-raising region; airport; p. (1963) 40,255.

Haringey, inner bor., Greater London, Eng.; comprising former bors. of Hornsey, Tottenham, and Wood Green; p. (est. 1976) 228,200.

Hari-Rud, R., N. Afghanistan and Iran; the anc. "Arius"; length 1,040 km; (*Rud* = river).

Harlech, t., Gwynedd, Wales; on Cardigan Bay 16 km N. of Barmouth; farming; cas.; seaside resort.

Harlem, upper Manhattan, N.Y. city, USA; residtl. and business section of c. with lge. Negro p.; depressed economic a. with much poverty.

Harlem, R., N.Y., USA; separates Manhattan I. from bor. of Bronx; with Spuyten Duyvi Creek forms waterway 13 km long from East R. to Hudson R.

Harlingen, spt., Friesland, Neth.; natural gas; p. (est. 1970) 12,522.

Harlingen, spt., S. Texas, USA; ctr. of productive agr. a.; p. (est. 1969) 37,000.

Harlow, t., l. gov. dist., Essex, Eng.; in valley of R. Stort, 35 km N.E. of London; new t. (1947); spreads S.W. from nucleus of old mkt. t. of H.; engin., glass, furniture mkg., metallurgy; p. (est. 1976) 80,000.

Härnösand, t., Sweden; on G. Bothnia; exp. timber, wood pulp; p. (est. 1970) 27,023.

Harpenden, t., Herts., Eng.; in Chiltern Hills, 8 km N. of St. Albans; Rothamsted agr. experimental sta.; residtl.; p. (1971) 24,161.

Harr r, t., cap. H. prov., Ethiopia; unique African hilltop t. with medieval walls, towers and gates; anc. c. of Islamic learning; overlooks Rift Valley; p. (est. 1970) 45,033.

Harris, S. part of Lewis I., Outer Hebrides, Scot.; and several sm. Is.; p. (1971) 2,879.

Harrisburg, c., cap. of Penns., USA; on Susque-hanna R.; iron and steel ind.; machin., cigarettes, cotton gds.; p. (1970) 65,828 (c.) 405,387 (met. a.).

Harrogate, t., l. gov. dist., North Yorks. Eng.; in valley of R. Nidd, 22 km N. of Leeds; spa; favoured a. for retirement; p. (est. 1976) 135,500 (dist.).

Harrow, outer bor., Greater London, Eng.; public school; camera mftg.; p. (est. 1976) 200,200.

Harsprånget, t., Norrbotten, Sweden; lge. hydro-electric plant.

Harstad, ch. t., Lofoten Is., N.W. Norway; herring ind., woollen gds.; p. (1960) 4,028.

Hart, l. gov. dist., N.E. Hants., Eng.; comprises Fleet and Hartley Witney; p. (est. 1976) 71,300.

Hartebeestpoort, Dam, Transvaal, S. Africa; on R. Crocodile (Limpopo), 40 km W. of Pretoria; supplies water for cultivation, under irrigation, of cotton, maize, tobacco.

Hartford, c., cap. of Conn., USA; comm. and insurance ctr.; univ.; sm. arms, typewriters, elec. machin., aircraft engin., ceramics, plastics; Mark Twain lived here; p. (1970) 155,868 (c.), 657,104 (met. a.).

Hartland Point, Barnstaple Bay, N. Devon, Eng.

Hartlepool, spt., l. gov. dist., Cleveland, Eng.; on E. cst., 5 km N. of Tees estuary; shipbldg., lt. inds., timber, iron and steel inds., pipe making; gd. sands for holiday-makers to the S.; p. (est. 1976) 97,100 (dist.).

Harvey, t., N.E. Ill., USA; nr. Chicago; rolling stock, diesel engines, heavy machin.; p. (1970) 34,636.

Harwell, v. Oxon., Eng.; 19 km S. of Oxford; AEA nuclear power research establishment.

Harwich, spt., Tendring, Essex, Eng.; on S. cst. of estuary of R. Stour; packet sta. for Belgium, Neth., Denmark; docks, container facilities, naval base; p. (1971) 14,892.

Haryana, st., India; formed 1966 from Hindi-speaking areas of Punjab; cap. Chandigarh (also of Punjab st. until its own cap. is built); a. 45,584 km²; p. (1971) 9,971,164.

Harz Mtns., range, E. and W. Germany; between the Weser and the Elbe; highest peak the Brocken; ch. t. Goslar (W. Germany); forested slopes; rich in minerals; tourism.

Haslemere, t., Waverley, Surrey, Eng.; nr. Hindhead; mkt., residtl.; lt. inds.; p. (1971) 13,252.

Haslingden, t., Rossendale, Lancs., Eng.; on Rossendale Fells, 5 km S. of Accrington; heavy industl. textiles, waste-spinning; textile-finishing; p. (1971) 14,953.

Hasselt, t., prov. Limburg, Belgium; mkt. t.; gin distilleries; p. (1968) 38,886.

Hassi Messaoued, t., Algeria; lge. oilfield; pipe-line to Bejaia.

Hassi R'Mel, t., Algeria; lge. natural gasfield.

Hastings, t., l. gov. dist., East Sussex, Eng.; on S. cst., midway between Beachy Head and Dungeness; seaside resort; one of the Cinque Ports; cas.; p. (est. 1976) 74,600.

Hastings, t., N.I., N.Z.; on Hawke's Bay, nr. Napier; fruit-canning; p. (1971) 29,736.

Hatay (Sanjak of Alexandretta), dist., S. Turkey, comprising Antioch (now Antakya) and its pt. Alexandretta (now Iskenderun), ceded to Turkey by France 1939; p. (1960) 441,209.

Hatfield, t., Welwyn and Hatfield, Herts., Eng.; 30 km N. of London; new t. (1948) which grew around old t. of Bishops Hatfield; lt. engin., aircraft; p. (est. 1974) 26,000.

Hathras, t., Aligarh dist., Uttar Pradesh, India; sugar, cotton, carved work; p. (1961) 64,045.

Hatteras, Cape, promontory on I. and cays off N.C., USA; stormy region, marked by lighthouse.

Hattiesburg, t., Miss., USA; sawmilling, clothing, fertilisers; p. (est. 1969) 40,500.

Haugesund, spt., S. Norway; on S.W. cst., 35 m. N. of Stavanger; ch. ctr. of herring fishery; canning inds.; p. (1968) 27,294.

Hauraki Gulf, arm of Pac. Oc.; E. cst. N.I., N.Z.; forming entrance to harbour of Auckland.

Haute Garonne, dep., S. France; in Languedoc; cap. Toulouse; a. 6,366 km²; p. (1968) 690,712.

Haute-Loire, dep., France; mainly in Massif Central; cap. Le Puy; cattle, fruit, vineyards; a. 4,999 km²; p. (1968) 208,337.

Haute-Marne, dep., France; mainly in Champagne; metallurgical inds.; a. 6,268 km²; p. (1968) 214,336.

Hautes-Alpes, dep., France; mtnous.; on Italian border; sheep; cap. Gap; a. 5,641 km²; p. (1968) 91,790.

Haute-Saône, dep., France; inc. part of Vosges mtns.; mainly agr.; cap. Vesoul; a. 5,372 km²; p. (1968) 14,776.

Haute-Savoie, dep., France; borders on Italy and Switzerland; reaches highest alt. in Mont Blanc; cap. Annecy; winter sports; a. 4,595 km.; p. (1968) 378,550.

Haute-Pyrénées, dep., S. France; rises in S. to steep peaks of Pyrenees, forming bdy. with Spain; Basques live on both sides of border; cap. Tarbes; Lourdes place of pilgrimage; a. 4,533 km²; p. (1968) 225,730.

Haute-Vienne, dep., France; entirely in Massif Central; cap. Limoges; cattle-raising; a. 5,488 km²; p. (1968) 341,589.

Haut-Rhin, dep., E. France; in lower Alsace; cap. Colmar; ch. industl. t. Mulhouse; a. 3,507 km²; p. (1968) 585,018.

Hauts-de-Seine, new dep., France; W. of Paris; cap. Nanterre; a. 176 km²; p. (1968) 1,461,619.

Havana (La Habana), c., cap. of Cuba; ch. pt. of W.I., with lge. harbour; cigars, tobacco, sugar, rum, coffee, woollens, straw hats, iron-ore; oil refining on outskirts of c.; p. (est. 1967) 1,008,500 (c.), 1,557,200 (met. a.).

Havant, t., l. gov. dist., Eng.; at foot of Portsdown Hill, 10 km N.E. of Portsmouth; p. (est. 1976) 116,400 (dist.).

Havel, R., E. Germany; rises in Neubrandenburg L. region; flows to Elbe R.; partially canalised nr. Berlin; 354 km long.

Haverfordwest, t., Preseli, Dyfed, Wales; 10 km N.E. of Milford Haven; agr. mkt.; Norman cas.; p. (1971) 9,101.

Haverhill, t., St. Edmundsbury, Suffolk, Eng.; expanded t.; textiles, clothing; p. (1971) 12,430.

Haverhill, t., Mass., USA; industl.; shipping containers; p. (est. 1969) 42,000.

Havering, outer bor., E. London, Eng.; inc. Hornchurch and Romford; p. (est. 1976) 239,200.

Hawaii, I., N. central Pac. Oc.; lgst. of Hawaiian gr.; three gr. volcanic mtns., Mauna Kea (4,208 m), Mauna Loa (4,172 m), Hualalai (last erupted, 1801); ch. pt. Hilo (devastated by tidal wave, 1946); lava deserts, bamboo forests; sugar-cane, cattle, coffee; tourism; deep-sea fishing; p. (1970) 61,332.

Hawaiian Is. (Sandwich Is.), st., Pac. Oc., admitted 1959 as 50th st. of USA; chain of coral and volcanic Is.; cap. Honolulu on S.E. cst. of Oahu I.; tourism; ctr. of international shipping routes; sugar, pineapples; a. 16,638 km²; p. (1970) 748,575.

Hawarden, t., Alyn and Deeside, Clwyd, N. Wales;

steel plant; home of Gladstone; p. (1971) 42,467 (dist.).

Hawes Water, L., Cumbria, Eng.; 4 km long.

Hawick, burgh, Roxburgh, Scot.; on R. Teviot, 28 km S.W. of Kelso; hosiery, tweed, and woollens; p. (1971) 16,286.

Hawke's Bay, prov. dist., N.I., N.Z.; on E. cst.; cap. Napier; a. 11,033 km²; p. (1971) 133,814.

Hawkesbury, R., N.S.W., Australia; 528 km long.

Haworth, t., West Yorks., Eng.; nr. Keighley; home of the Brontës.

Hawthorne, t., S.W. Cal., USA; residtl.; in gas- and oil-producing a.; aircraft and electronics; p. (1970) 53,304.

Hay, t., N.S.W., Australia; situated on R. Murrumbidgee; collecting ctr. for fruit and wheat; p. (1966) 2,957.

Hay, t., Brecknock, Powys, Wales; on R. Wye; cas.; mkt.; p. (1971) 1,230.

Hay, R., Alberta, Canada; flows into G. Slave Lake; 560 km long.

Haydock, t., Merseyside, Eng.; coal mng.; inc. H. Park racecourse; p. (1971) 14,180.

Hayes and Harlington. See Hillingdon.

Hayling Island, resort, Hants, Eng.; E. of Portsmouth.

Hayward, t., Cal., USA; fruit-canning; poultry; p. (1970) 93,058.

Hayward's Heath, residtl. a., West Sussex, Eng.

Hazel Grove and Bramhall, sub. of Stockport Gtr. Manchester, Eng.; p. (1971) 39,534.

Hazleton, t., Penns., USA; anthracite region; textiles, iron and steel mnfs.; p. (est. 1969) 29,000.

Headingley, sub., Leeds, West Yorks., Eng., mainly residtl.; county cricket ground.

Heanor, t., Amber Valley, Derbys., Eng.; 11 km N.E. of Derby; hosiery, pottery, prefabricated timber bldgs. mftg.; p. (1971) 24,352.

Heard, I., S. Indian Oc.; 448 km S.E. of Kerguelen I.; Australian possession; volcanic.

Heathrow, site of London airport, Eng.; 24 km W. of central London, S. of M4 motorway; on Piccadilly tube line; residtl. a.

Hebburn, t., Tyne and Wear, Eng.; on R. Tyne 6 km below Gateshead; shipbldg., engin.; p. (1971) 23,597.

Hebden Royd, t., Calderdale, West Yorks., Eng.; cotton factories, dyewks., heavy engin., woollens and worsteds; p. (1971) 8,648.

Hebrides or Western Is., Scot.; grouped as Outer and Inner Hebrides; ch. t. Stornoway, Lewis; a. 7,382 km².

Hebron, t., Jordan; 26 km. S.W. of Jerusalem; p. (1967) 43,000.

Heckmondwike, t., West Yorks., Eng.; wool textiles; p. (1971) 9,361.

Hedon, t., Humberside, Eng.; former spt.; p. (1971) 2,600.

Heerenveen, t., Friesland prov., N. Neth.; bicycles; p. (1968) 30.282.

Heerlen, t., Limburg, Neth.; 22 km E. of Maastricht; coal mng.; p. (1968) 76,515.

Heide, t., Schleswig-Holstein, W. Germany; ctr. of Ditmarschen oilfields; p. (est. 1969) 23,352.

Heidelberg, c., Baden–Württemberg, W. Germany; on R. Neckar, nr. Mannheim; celebrated univ., cas.; tobacco, wood, leather, rly. carriages; nylon plant projected; p. (est. 1969) 122,000.

Heidenheim, t. Baden–Württemberg, W. Germany; N.E. of Ulm; textiles, machin., metallurgy, furniture; p. (est. 1969) 50,007.

Heilbronn, t., R. pt. Baden–Württemberg, W. Germany; engin., vehicles, foodstuffs; p. (est. 1969) 98,481.

Heilungkiang (Heilungjiang), prov., N.E. China; separated from USSR by Amur and Ussuri Rs.; mtnous.; crossed by Sungari R. in central plain; maize, soya beans, millets; opencast coalmines; gold; cap. Harbin; a. 466,200 km²; p. (est. 1967) 21,000,000.

Hejaz, region, Saudi Arabia; mainly desert; very poor communications; ch. t. Mecca; a. 388,500 km²; p. (est. 1963) 2,000,000, mainly Bedouin. [1,554 m.

Hekla, volcano, Iceland; erupted in 1970; alt.

Helder (Den Helder), t., N. Holland, Neth.; on strait between peninsula and I. of Texel; naval base; p. (1968) 58,356.

Helena, st. cap., Mont., USA; grew up as gold- and silver-mng. t.; bricks, pottery; resort; p. (1970) 22,730.

Helensburgh, t., Dumbarton, W. Scot.; on the Clyde; resort; p. (1971) 11,296.

Helford, R., Cornwall, **Eng.;** oysters, tourism.

Helicon, mtn. gr., **Greece;** abode of classical muses.

Heligoland (Helgoländ), sm. I., N. Sea; off mouth of Elbe: ceded by Britain to Germany 1890 in return for Zanzibar.

Hellespont. *See* Dardanelles.

Helmand or **Helmund, R., Afghanistan;** flows c. 1,360 km from mtns. of Kabul to Hamun-i-Helmand swamp on Iranian border; cultivation in valley; major irrigation project.

Helmond, t., N. Brabant, **Neth.;** on Zuid-Willem-svaart (canal); textiles; p. (1968) 56,976.

Helmsley, mkt. t., Ryedale, North Yorks., **Eng.;** cas.; p. (1971) 4,828 (dist.).

Helmstedt, t., Lower Saxony, **W. Germany;** E. of Brunswick; on E. German border; textiles, machin.; p. (est. 1969) 27,267.

Helsingör. *See* Elsinore.

Helsinki or **Helsingfors,** c., cap. of Finland; spt. on G. of Finland; harbour ice-bound Jan. to Apr., channel opened by ice-breakers; cultural ctr., univ.; timber, textiles, carpets; exp. mainly timber prods.; p. (1968) 529,091 (c.), 700,856 (met. a.).

Helston, mkt. t., Kerrier Cornwall, **Eng.;** on R. Cober, 13 km W. of Falmouth; tourist ctr.; famous for festival of floral dance (8 May); fishing, soup-canning; p. (1971) inc. Porthleven, 9,827.

Helvellyn, mtn., L. Dist., Cumbria, **Eng.;** severely eroded by ice; alt. 951 m; sharp ridge of Striding Edge.

Helwan, t., **Egypt;** 24 km S. of Cairo; sulphur springs; iron and steel complex, fertilisers, cement; car assembly; p. 51,000.

Hemel Hempstead, t., Dacorum, Herts., **Eng.;** new t. (1947), on S. slopes of Chilterns; scientific glass, elec. engin., cars; p. (est. 1974) 73,000.

Hengelo, t., Overijssel, Neth., industl. ctr.; cattle mkt.; metals, textiles; p. (1968) 68,348.

Hengyang (Hengchow), c., Hunan, **China;** on Siang R. in foothills to S. of Yangtze plain; on main Kuangchow–Peking rly.; lead and zinc mines nearby; p. (est. 1970) 240,000.

Henin-Liétard, t., Pas-de-Calais, **France;** on coalfield; p. (1968) 25,067.

Henley-on-Thames, t., South Oxfordshire, Oxon., **Eng.;** 8 km N.E. of Reading; mkt. gardening, brewing; annual regatta; p. (1971) 11,402.

Hensbarrow, upland a., Cornwall, **Eng.;** granite; kaolin-mng. dist., kaolin exp. by sea from Fowey; rises to over 300 m; a. 70 km².

Henzada, t., Burma, on Irrawaddy delta; in tobacco and rice-growing dist.; p. (est. 1962) 896,863.

Herakleion. *See* Iráklion.

Herãt, c., cap. of H. prov., N.W. **Afghanistan;** on Hari Rud R.; of historic and strategic importance, has been called "the key of India"; crude petroleum and chrome-ore nearby; tr. ctr.; textiles; p. (est. 1971) 103,915.

Hérault, dep., S.W. **France;** in Languedoc; agr.; cap. Montpellier; govt.-sponsored tourist developments along shores of Mediterranean; a. 6,221 km²; p. (1968) 596,892.

Herculaneum, anc. c., S. **Italy;** 6 km E. of Naples; buried along with Pompeii by eruption from Vesuvius A.D. 79; rediscovered 1709; site of modern Resina and Portici.

Hereford and Worcestershire, non-met. co., **Eng.;** crossed by Wye and Severn valleys, separated by Malvern Hills; mainly agr.; beef, dairy and fruit farming; major ts. Hereford and Worcester; a. 3,906 km²; p. (est. 1976) 594,200.

Hereford, c., l. gov. dist., Hereford and Worcs., **Eng.;** on R. Wye; cath.; mkt.; tiles, engin., timber, cider and preserves; furniture, brassware; p. (est. 1976) 47,800.

Herefordshire, South, l. gov. dist., H. and Worcs., **Eng.;** lge rural a. inc. Ross-on-Wye; p. (est. 1976) 44,600.

Herford, t., N. Rhine–Westphalia, **W. Germany;** on R. Werra; cotton, flax, furniture, cigars, confectionery, metallurgy; p. (est. 1967) 54,900.

Herisau, t., cap of Appenzell Ausser-Rhoden half-can., N.E. **Switzerland;** muslin, embroideries; p. (1970) 14 597.

Herm, sm. I. of Channel Is., English Channel; 6 km N.W. Sark and N.E. of Guernsey; remarkable shell-beach; a. 130 ha; p. (1971) 96.

Hermon, Mount (Jebel esh Sheikh), mtn., in Anti-Lebanon range, on Syria–Lebanon bdy., nr. Israel; alt. 2,862 m.

Hermosillo, c., cap. of Sonora st., N.W. **Mexico;** on San Miguel R.; oranges; agr. and mng. ctr.; p. (1970) 176,596.

Hermoupolis or **Hermopolis,** t., Syros I., **Greece;** cap. of Cyclades; Ægean pt. and comm. ctr.; p. (1971) 13,460.

Herne, t., N. Rhine–Westphalia, **W. Germany;** pt. on Rhine–Herne canal; industl. t. of Ruhr conurb.; p. (est. 1969) 101,500.

Herne Bay, t., Kent, **Eng.;** on cst., 19 km W. of Margate; p. (1971) 25,117.

Herning, t., Jutland, **Denmark;** knitting ind.; p. (est. 1970) 32,512.

Heröya, S. Norway; nuclear power plant; chemicals, fertilisers.

Herstal, t., **Belgium;** nr. Liège; armaments, aero-engines; p. (1968) 29,894.

Herstmonceux, v. nr. Hastings, Sussex, **Eng.;** cas.; site of Royal Greenwich Observatory.

Hertford, co. t., East Herts., **Eng.;** on R. Lea, 32 km N. of London; pharmaceutics, flour milling, rolling stock, diesels, brewing; p. (1971) 20,379.

Hertfordshire, non-met. co., **Eng.;** borders Greater London on S.; co. t., Hertford, ch. ctr. St. Albans; drained by Rs. Thames and Lea; intensive agr., lt. inds.; new ts. Welwyn, Stevenage, Hatfield, Hemel Hempstead; a. 1,637 km²; p. (est. 1976) 937,300.

Hertfordshire, East, l. gov. dist., Herts., **Eng.;** lge a. inc. Ware, Bishop's Stortford, Hertford and Sawbridgeworth; p. (est. 1976) 104,600.

Hertfordshire, North, l. gov. dist., Herts., **Eng.;** stretches from Baldock, Letchworth and Hitchin to Royston; p. (est. 1976) 104,600.

's-Hertogenbosch, t., **Neth.;** on Rs. Dommel and Aa; cap. of N. Brabant prov.; cath.; cattle mkt.; industl. development; p. (1968) 80,425.

Hertsmere, l. gov. dist., Herts., **Eng.;** a. close to London, inc. Bushey, Elstree and Potters Bar; p. (est. 1976) 87,400.

Hesse, Land, **W. Germany;** part of former Prussian prov. Hesse-Nassau; mainly upland; inds. at Frankfurt, Kassel, Darmstadt; wine produced along Rhine valley; cap. Wiesbaden; tourism; a. 21,103 km²; p. (1968) 5,333,000.

Hetch Hetchy Dam, Cal., **USA;** on R. Toulumne upstream from San Joaquin R.; ch. source of irrigation for middle San Joaquin valley; supplies water and generating power to San Francisco.

Hetton, t., Tyne and Wear, **Eng.;** 8 km N.E. of Durham; coal-mng. dist.; p. (1971) 16,871.

Hexham, mkt. t., Tynedale, Northumberland, **Eng.;** on R. Tyne, 32 km W. of Newcastle; priory; p. (1971) 9,799.

Heywood, t., Gtr. Manchester **Eng.;** 5 km E. of Bury; chemicals, engin.; p. (1971) 30,418.

Hialeah, t., Fla., **USA;** sub. of Miami; racecourse; p. (1970) 102,297.

Hidalgo, st., central **Mexico;** mtnous. with fertile valleys in S. and W.; cap. Pachuca; mng. (silver, gold, copper, lead, iron, sulphur); maguey (type of lily), tobacco, cotton, coffee; a. 20,868 km²; p. (1969) 1,282,000.

Higashiosaka, c., Japan; E. of Osaka; formed from amalgamation of Fuse, Kawachi, Hiraoka and many sm. ts.; p. (est. 1971) 485,000.

Higham Ferrers, mkt. t., East Northants, **Eng.;** 5 km E. of Wellingborough; footwear and leather dressing; p. (1971) 4,700.

Highgate, residtl. dist., N. London, **Eng.;** hilltop v. in bor. of Camden.

Highland Park, t., Mich., **USA;** sub. of Detroit; grew up with expansion of motor-car ind.; p. (1970) 32,263.

Highland Region, l. gov. reg., N. Scot.; rugged mtns. inland; p. concentrated around cst.; offshore oil development; stock raising, forestry, tourism; a. 25,128 km²; p. (1971) 172,720.

High Peak, l. gov. dist., Derbys., **Eng.;** a. of Pennines inc. New Mills, Glossop, Whaley Bridge and Buxton; p. (est. 1976) 80,100.

High Point, t., N.C., **USA;** furniture ctr., hosiery; p. (est. 1969) 64,000.   [**Eng.;** 621 m.

High Willhays, hgst. summit, Dartmoor, Devon,

High Wycombe, t., Bucks., **Eng.;** 13 km N. of Maidenhead; furniture, paper-mkg., egg processing; in London commuter belt; p. (1971) 59,298.

Hildesheim, t., Lower Saxony, **W. Germany;** at foot of Harz mtns.; cath.; machin., farm implements, textiles, ceramics; p. (est. 1967) 97,000.

Hillah, Al, mkt. t., Iraq; on R. Euphrates; nr. anc. Babylon; food tr. rugs, leather; p. (1965) 84,717 (t.), 110,795 (met. a.).

Hilleröd, t., Denmark; admin. ctr. of Frederiksborg prov.; p. (est. 1970) 23,500.

Hillingdon, outer bor., Greater London, Eng.; comprising former U.D.s of Hayes and Harlington, Ruislip and Northwood Yiewsley, W. Drayton. and former M.B. of Uxbridge; p. (est. 1976) 230,800.

Hilo, t., Hawaii; pt. of entry and main tr. and shipping ctr. of I.; tourism; Mauna Loa volcano nearby; p. (1970) 26,353.

Hilversum, t., Neth.; nr. Utrecht; radio broadcasting ctr.; noteworthy modern architecture; p. (est. 1969) 100,098.

Himachal Pradesh, st., N.W. India; bounded by Tibet on E.; forested mtns., cultivated valleys; cap. Simla; a. 56,019 km²; p. (1971) 3,424,332.

Himalayas, vast chain of mtns. along N. border of India. between the Indus and Brahamaputra Rs., and lying in Pakistan, India, Nepal, Sikkim, Bhutan, and China; made up of several parallel ranges inc. the Siwaliks, the Hindu Kush. and the Karakorams; crossed by passes, mainly in W.; 2,560 km long; hgst. peak Mt. Everest, 8,854 m.

Himeji, c., S. Honshu, Japan; mkt., ctr. on shore of Inland Sea, 48 km W. of Kobe; iron and steel ind., heavy engin.; oil refining; p. (est. 1971) 414,000.

Hinckley, mkt. t., Leics., Eng.; hosiery, cardboard boxes, dye-wks., engin.; nr. Watling Street; p. (1971) 47,982; with Market Bosworth forms l. gov. dist. of Hinkley and Bosworth; p. (est. 1976) 81,700.

Hinkley Point, Somerset, Eng.; civil nuclear power-sta.; second sta. now being built.

Hindenburg. See Zabrze. [Eng.

Hindhead, hilly common, Surrey. nr. Haslemere,

Hindiya Barrage, dam, Iraq; across R. Euphrates, 48 km above Al Hillah; provides flood control and irrigation in a. between Shatt al Hillah and R. Euphrates.

Hindley, t., Gtr. Manchester, Eng.; 3 km S.E. of Wigan; paint, knitwear, rubber, asbestos; p. (1971) 24,307.

Hindu Kush, mtn. range, mainly in N.E. Afghanistan; hgst peak Tirich Mir (7,755 m) in Chitral dist., Pakistan; Salang tunnel (opened 1964) with 2-lane motor highway cuts H.K. at height of 3,300 m, runs 240 m below mtn. top, 3·2 km.

Hindustan, former name of part of N. India between Himalayas and Vindhya ranges.

Hirfanli Dam, project on R. Kizilirmak, 144 km S.E. Ankara, Turkey, 1961.

Hirosaki, c., Honshu, Japan; mkt., lacquer-ware; cas.; p. (est. 1971) 160,000.

Hiroshima, c., S.W. Honshu, Japan; on delta of Ota R.; first c. to be destroyed by atomic bomb (6 Aug. 1945); since rebuilt; motor vehicles, shipbldg.; p. (est. 1971) 567,000.

Hirschberg. See Jelenia Góra.

Hispaniola, second lgst I. of W.I.; lies between Cuba and Puerto Rico; divided between Haiti (Fr.-speaking) and Dominican Rep. (Spanishspeaking); complex relief, climate, and vegetation, but strong cultural differences make international bdy. a sharp divide; a. 76,498 km².

Hitchin, t., North Herts., Eng.; in gap through Chiltern Hills, 56 km N. of London; lt. engin., tanning, chemicals, distilling; mkt.; p. (1971) 26,680.

Hjälmaren Lake, central Sweden; drained into L. Malaren by Esk R.; linked by canal to Arboga; a. 474 km².

Hjörring, t., Jutland, N. Denmark; biscuit and clothing wks.; p. (est. 1970) 15,699.

Hobart, cap. and ch. pt. of Tasmania, Australia; on R. Derwent; univ.; fruit exp.; zinc; cadmium, superphosphates, textiles; p. (1972) 52,425 (c.), 153,024 (met. a.).

Hoboken, t., Antwerp, Belgium; shipbldg.; refractory metals; p. (1968) 32,184.

Hoboken, t., N.J., USA; on Hudson R. above Jersey City, opp N.Y. to which it is linked by subway and ferry; pt. for ocean commerce; industl. ctr.; p. (est. 1969) 45,000.

Ho Chi-minh City (Saigon), c., spt., Vietnam; former cap. of S. Vietnam; on Saigon R. to E. of Mekong Delta; tree-lined boulevards; cath., univ., modern airport; comm. ctr.; exp. rice,

rubber; food processing; p. (est. 1968) 1,682,000.

Höchst, t., Hesse, W. Germany; industl. sub. of Frankfurt-on-Main; site of German chemical ind.

Hochstetter, mtn., S.I., N.Z.; in Southern Alps; alt. 3,416 m.

Hoddesdon, t., Herts., Eng.; in Lea valley, 6 km S. of Ware; nursery tr., tomatoes, etc.; p. (1971) 26,071.

Hodeida (Al Hudaydah), t., Yemen Arab Rep., on Red Sea; pt. and naval base; exp. dates, hides, coffee; p. (est. 1970) 90,000.

Hódmezővásárhely, t., S.E. Hungary; wheat, fruit, tobacco, cattle; natural gas pipeline from Szeged; p. (1966) 52,800.

Hof, t. Bavaria, W. Germany; on R. Saale; textiles, iron, machin., porcelain, glass, brewing; p. (est. 1967) 55,000.

Hofei or Hefei, c., cap. of Anhwei prov., China; rice-growing a.; cotton and silk, iron and steel; p. (est. 1970) 400,000.

Hoffman mtn., peak of the Sierra Nevada, Cal., USA; alt. 2,473m.

Hofuf (Al Hufuf), t., El Hasa, Saudi Arabia; dates wheat, fruit; textiles, brass- and copper-ware; oil-fields nearby; p. (est. 1967) 85,000.

Hog's Back, Surrey, Eng.; steep chalk ridge; alt. 154 m.

Hohenlimburg, t., N. Rhine–Westphalia, W. Germany; nr. Dortmund; cas.; textiles, iron, steel; p. (est. 1969) 26,176.

Hohenstein-Ernstal, t., Karl-Marx-Stadt, E. Germany; textiles, metal gds.; p. (est. 1970) 16,800.

Hohe Tauern, Alpine range, Tyrol, Austria; rugged crystalline rocks; highest point Gross Glockner, 3,801 m; traversed by rly. tunnel 8 km long.

Hoihow (Hai-k'ou), c., ch. pt. of Hainan I. Kwangtung prov., China; p. (est. 1970) 500,000.

Hokkaido, lge I. Japan, N. of Honshu; colder than other Is.; less dense p.; temperate agr.; skiing; a. 88,775 km²; p. of pref. (1970) 5,184,287.

Holbaek, t., Sjaelland, Denmark; W. of Copenhagen; engin. and motor wks.; p. (est. 1970) 17,892.

Holbeach, mkt. t. S. Lincs., Eng.; in Fens, 11 km E. of Spalding; brewing; ctr. of bulb-growing dist.

Holborn. See Camden.

Holderness, peninsula, l. gov. dist., Humberside, Eng.; between R. Humber and N. Sea; agr.; (est. 1976) 43,900.

Holguin, t., N.E. Cuba; comm. ctr.; sugar, tobacco, coffee, cattle; exps. handled by pt. Gibara; p. (est. 1967) 350,250.

Holland. See Netherlands.

Holland, N., prov., Neth.; inc. W. Frisian Is.; dairying; a. 2,629 km²; p. (1968) 2,215,876.

Holland, Parts of. See Lincolnshire.

Holland, South, t., l. gov. dist., Lincs., Eng.; fenland a. around Spalding; p. (est. 1976) 58,700.

Holland, S., prov., Neth.; crossed by R. Rhine; mkt. gardening; a. 2,927 km²; p. (1968) 2,922,450.

Hollandia, former name of cap. W. Irian, Indonesia; renamed Kota Baru by Indonesia, then Sukarnapura, now Djajapura.

Holloman, t., N.M., USA; atomic and space research ctr.; site of 1st. man-made atomic explosion.

Hollywood, t., Fla., USA; seaside resort on Atl. cst.; cement, furniture; p. (1970) 104,018; part of Fort Lauderdale met. a.

Hollywood, sub. of Los Angeles, Cal., USA; ctr. of film industry.

Holmesdale, Vale of, Kent, E. Surrey, Eng.; extends along foot of N. Downs escarpment; drained by Rs. Mole, Darent, Medway, Len, Stour; heavy clay soils; ch. ts., Dorking, Reigate, Sevenoaks, Maidstone, Ashford, which have grown up in gaps through hills to N. and S. of Vale; length 96 km, average width 2 km.

Holmfirth, t., West Yorks., Eng.; 8 km S. of Huddersfield, textiles, engin.; p. (1971) 19,319.

Holt, mkt. t., N. Norfolk, Eng.; 8 km S.W. of Sheringham; 16th-cent. school.

Holt, t., Clwyd, Wales; on R. Dee, 11 km S. of Chester; cas. ruins.

Holyhead, spt., Anglesey, Gwynedd, Wales; on Holyhead I.; mail packet sta. for Ireland;

lt. engin., woodwkg., clocks; site for aluminium smelter; pt. traffic reduced as result of damage to Menai Bridge; p. (1971) 10,608.

Holy I. (Lindisfarne), off cst. of Northumberland, Eng. [submarine base.

Holy I., Scot., in F. of Clyde, nr. I. of Arran;

Holy I., off cst. of Anglesey, Gwynedd, Wales.

Holyoke, t., Mass., USA; on Connecticut R., above Springfield; paper, machin.; p. (est. 1969) 52,000.

Holywell, mkt. t., Delyn, Clwyd, N. Wales; woollen, rayon and paper inds.; p. (1971) 8,536.

Holywood, spt., North Down, N. Ireland; on S. shore of Belfast Lough; seaside resort; p. (1966) 7,795.

Homburg (Bad Homburg), c., Hesse, W. Germany; famous spa; p. (est. 1969) 40,485.

Home Counties, term applied to the geographical counties adjoining London, i.e., Middlesex, Surrey, Essex, and Kent; sometimes Hertfordshire, Buckinghamshire, and Berkshire are included, and occasionally Sussex; (Middlesex and parts of Essex, Surrey, Kent, and Hertfordshire incorporated in Greater London 1965).

Homs, t., W. Syria; on R. Orontes; anc. Emesa; silk, textiles, cement; oil refinery; pipeline from Kirkūk oil fields; p. (1970) 216,000.

Honan (Henan), prov., N.E. China; traversed by Hwang-ho; cap. Chengchow; densely p. in fertile E.; mainly agr.; wheat, kaolin, cotton, anthracite; a. 167,172 km²; p. (est. 1968) 50,000,000.

Honda, old Spanish t., Colombia; on Magdalena R., at rapids; former comm. ctr.; p. (est. 1968) 22,315.

Honduras, rep., straddles Central American isthmus with longest cst. on Caribbean; comprises 18 deps. inc. offshore Bay Is.; coastal lowlands hot and humid, more temperate in interior highlands which rise to over 2,000 m; agr. basis of economy, especially American-owned banana plantations; bananas almost half exp.; some mng.; rlys. oriented to banana-producing areas to facilitate exp.; nationalised forests; land reform; cap. Tegucigalpa; 5 airports.; a. 111,958 km²; p. (est. 1969) 2,500,000.

Honduras, British. See Belize.

Hong Kong, Brit. Crown Col., S.E. cst. China; comprises Hong Kong I., Kowloon peninsula and New Territories (on lease from China until 1997); tunnel (1972) links H.K. with Kowloon; deepwater harbour of Victoria has lost much tr. from China; industl. development rapid since second world war yet few natural resources; dense p. aggravated by immigration from China; a. 1,031 km²; p. (1971) 3,950,802.

Honiara, t., cap. of Solomon Is.; on Guadalcanal I.; p. (1970) 11,191.

Honiton, t., East Devon, Eng.; on R. Otter, 26 km E. of Exeter; mkt.; trout-fishing; once produced lace, an ind. introduced by Flemish refugees; p. (1971) 5,058.

Honolulu, c., cap. of Hawaii; on Oahu I.; social and comm. ctr. and ch. pt. of archipelago; gd. harbour; univ.; airport; fruit-canning, sugar-processing; tourism; p. (1970) 319,784 (c.), 613,114 (met. a.).

Honshu, lgst. I. of Japan; contains most of p. along E. cst. in 320 km industl. belt; new Seikan tunnel links I. to Hokkaido; a. 230,300 km²; p. (1970) 82,569,581.

Hoogeveen, t., Drenthe, Neth.; fruit- and vegetable-canning; p. (1968) 35,375.

Hooghly, R., arm of Ganges R., India; flows into Bay of Bengal; used in jute-milling and navigable as far as Calcutta; 256 km long.

Hooghly Chinsura, t., W. Bengal, India; on Hooghly R.; rice-milling; p. (1971) 105,241 (part of Calcutta met. a.).

Hook of Holland (Hoek van Holland), spt., Neth.; packet sta. with steamer connections to Harwich, Eng.

Hoorn, old fishing t., N. Holland, Neth.; on IJsselmeer, 32 km N. of Amsterdam; cheese and cattle mkts.; birthplace of Tasman, discoverer of Tasmania and N.Z., founder of Batavia; p. (1967) 17,072.

Hoover Dam, USA; on Colorado R.; used for irrigation (parts of Cal., Arizona, and Mexico), flood control and hydroelectric power; Lake Mead, 184 km long, 2–13 km wide, one of world's lgst man-made Ls.

Hopeh (Hebei), prov., N.E. China; part of N. China plain; bounded on N. by Great Wall; cap. Tientsin; wheat, kaoliang, cotton; coal mng.; a. 194,250 km²; p. (est. 1968) 47,000,000.

Hor, unlocated biblical mtn. between Dead Sea and G. of Aqaba, the place of Aaron's death.

Horbury, t., West Yorks., Eng.; nr. Wakefield; p. (1971) 8,914.

Horeb. See Sinai. [severe gales.

Horn, C., S. Chile, most S. point of S. America;

Horncastle, mkt. t., E. Lindsey, Lincs., Eng.; at confluence of Rs. Bain and Waring at foot of Lincoln Wolds; mkt.; vegetable-processing; p. (1971) 4,096.

Hornsea, t., Humberside, Eng.; on E. cst., N.E. of Hull; seaside resort; lge. freshwater L.; p. (1971) 7,021.

Hornsey. See Haringey.

Horsens, t., Denmark, E. Jutland; on inlet of Kattegat; industl. and comm. ctr.; p. (est. 1970) 35,621.

Horsforth, t., West Yorks., Eng.; in Aire valley N.W. of Leeds; cloth, tanning, lt. engin.; p. (1971) 19,336.

Horsham, t., Victoria, Australia; on R. Wimmera; pastoral, dairying and agr. dist.; agr. machin.; p. (1972) 11,046.

Horsham, t., l. gov. dist., West Sussex, Eng.; on R. Arun at W. end of forested dist. of the High Weald; agr., timber, engin., chemicals; Horsham stone once quarried here; Shelley's birthplace; p. (est. 1976) 92,300 (dist.).

Horta, t., cap. of H. dist., Azores; on Fayal I.; excellent harbour and base for transatlantic flights; p. (1960) 7,109 (t.), 49,735 (dist.).

Horten, spt., Norway; nr. Oslo; naval base; shipbldg., mftg. inds.; p. (est. 1970) 14,050.

Horton, R., N.W. Terr., Canada; flows into Beaufort Sea, Arctic Oc.; reindeer reserve along cst.

Horwich, t., Gtr. Manchester, Eng.; on W. edge of Rossendale Fells, N.W. of Bolton; rly. t.; engin.; p. (1971) 16,433.

Hospitalet, t., Spain; sub. of Barcelona, in Llobregat valley; p. (1967) 206,512.

Hot Springs, c., Ark., USA; in Ouachita mtns. S.W. of Little Rock; Nat. Park since 1832; health resort; p. (est. 1969) 38,000.

Houghton-le-Spring, t., Tyne and Wear, Eng.; S.W. of Sunderland; former colly. t.; coal-mng. dist.; p. (1971) 32,666.

Hounslow, outer bor., Greater London, Eng.; inc. former bors. of Brentford and Chiswick, Heston and Isleworth, Feltham and Hounslow; rubber goods; p. (est. 1976) 199,100.

Housatonic, R., W. Mass., Conn., USA; falls attracted early Puritan settlement and industrialisation; dairy farming; 240 km long.

Houston, c., spt., S. Texas, USA; on Galveston Bay; gr. pt., lgst. c. of S.; univ.; oil refineries, oilfield machin., steel, chemicals, paper, processing, milling and assembling plants; NASA's manned space flight ctr. and lunar science institute; p. (1970) 1,213,064 (c.), 1,958,491 (met. a.).

Houston Ship Canal, Texas, USA; links Houston to head of shallow Galveston Bay and continues through bay to deep water; provides site for heavy inds.; opened 1915; total length 72 km.

Hove, t., l. gov. dist., East Sussex, Eng.; on S. cst., continuous with Brighton; residtl.; holiday resort; p. (est. 1976) 88,100 (dist.).

Howrah, c., W. Bengal, India; on W. bank of Hooghly R., in met. a. of Calcutta; p. (1971) 737,877.

Hoy, I., Orkneys, Scot.; lofty cliffs along W. cst.; separated from Mainland I. by Sound of Hoy; Old Man of Hoy rock 137 m high; p. (1971) 531 (inc. Walls).

Hoylake, t., Wirral, Merseyside, Eng.; on N. cst. of Wirral peninsula; residtl.; golf course; p. (1971) 32,196.

Hradec Králové, t., ČSSR; at confluence of Elbe (Labe) and Orlice Rs.; industl. ctr.; mnfs. machin., precision instruments; 14th-cent. cath. and town hall; p. (1967) 64,000.

Huancayo, t., cap. of Junin dep., Peru; in high valley of Andes, c. 3,300 m; textiles; p. (est. 1969) 91,200.

Huarás or Huaráz, cap. of Ancash dep., Peru; on Santa R., c. 3,000 m; mainly agr., some mng.; avalanche 1941 killed 6,000 inhabitants; p. (1961) 11,628 (predominantly Indian).

Huascarán, extinct volcano, Peruvian Andes, nr. Huarás, 6,773 m high; avalanche 1970 killed 20,000 people.

Hubli, c., Karnataka, India; E. of Goa; textiles, rly. engin.; p. (1971) 377,166.

Hucknall, t., Ashfield, Nottingham, Eng.; hosiery, coal; p. (1971) 26,394.

Huddersfield, t. West Yorks., Eng.; on edge of Pennines, 16 km S. of Bradford; wool, textiles, chemicals, engin.; p. (1971) 130,964.

Hudson, R., N.Y., USA; flows from Adirondacks to N.Y. harbour; with valley of Mohawk R. makes gr. highway of tr. between Great Ls. and N.Y.; scenic beauty; hydroelec. power; 560 km long.

Hudson Bay, gr. inland sea, Canada; communicates by Hudson Strait with Davis Srait (Atl. Oc.); ice-free mid-July to Oct.; salmon, cod; a. 1,398,600 km².

Hué, c., Vietnam; on Hué R., 16 km from S. China Sea; pt. and tr. ctr.; former cap. of Annam; royal palace; p. (est. 1968) 156,537.

Huelva, coastal prov., S.W. Spain; copper mng., vine- and olive-growing, stock-raising, fisheries, brandy distilling; a. 10,117 km²; p. (1970) 397,683.

Huelva, c., cap. of Huelva prov., Spain; pt. on G. of Cadiz; oil refining, chemicals, food processing; exp. of minerals from nearby Rio Tinto; p. (1967) 90,740.

Huesca, c., cap. of H. prov., N.E. Spain; at foot of Pyrenees on R. Isucla; cath.; agr. ctr.; wine and timber tr. with France; p. (1970) 33,185.

Huhehot, c., Inner Mongolia, China; diesel engines; new woollen mill; p. (est. 1970) 700,000.

Hula L. See Waters of Merom.

Hull, t., S.W. Quebec, Canada; within met. a. of Ottawa; sawmills, paper; p. (1971) 62,842 (c.), 137,759 (met. a.).

Hull or Kingston-upon-Hull, c., l. gov. dist., Humberside, Eng.; major spt. of U.K.; at influx of R. Hull in estuary of Humber; originally laid out by Edward I; lge. docks; premier distant waters fishing pt.; inds. inc. oil-extracting, flour milling, sawmilling, chemicals, engin., p. (est. 1976) 276,600.

Humber, estuary of Rs. Ouse and Trent, Eng.; fine waterway; 2–13 km wide, 61 km long.

Humberside, non-met. co., Eng.; inc. most of E. Riding of Yorks., and Humber estuary where growth of pt. processing and chem. inds. and impt. pts. of Hull and Grimsby; iron and steel at Scunthorpe; cstl. resort of Bridlington in N.E.; a. 3,512 km²; p. (est. 1976) 848,600.

Humboldt, R., N. Nevada, USA; rises in Ruby Mtns., flows for 480 km before disappearing by evaporation and percolation; impt. 19th cent. routeway.

Humboldt Bay, inlet, Cal., USA; nuclear experimental breeder reactor.

Humboldt Current. See Peru Current.

Hume Lake, reservoir, N.S.W., Australia; formed by dam where R. Murray leaves Gr. Dividing Range; supplies water for irrigation in upper Riverina dist.; capacity c. 113 million m³.

Hugh Town, cap. of the Scilly Isles, Eng.; on St. Mary's I.

Hunan, prov., central China; S. of the Yangtze; hilly in S. and W.; rice, wheat, beans; rich mineral resources, inc. mercury, tin, tungsten; cap. Changsha; Mao Tse-tung came from Hunan peasant stock; a. 205,589 km²; p. (est. 1968) 38,000,000.

Hunedoara, t., H. dist., Romania; iron and steel; p. (1966) 68,300.

Hungary, rep., E. Europe; bounded by USSR, CSSR, Romania, Yugoslavia, and Austria; lies in basin of middle Danube (Duna), with plain in E. and Carpathian mtns. in W.; mainly agr.; exp. meat, fruit, vegetables to W. Europe; inds. increasingly impt. and now account for over 50 per cent of income; plans to make R. leading exporter of buses in Europe; 19 cos., cap. Budapest; a. 93,012 km²; p. (1970) 10,314,152.

Hunsrück (= dog's back), forested highlands, Rhineland-Palatinate, W. Germany; between Mosel and Nahe Rs.; vineyards on S. slopes; hgst. point 816 m.

Hunstanton, t., West Norfolk, Eng.; S.E. shore of Wash; seaside resort; p. (1971) 3,901.

Hunter, R., N.S.W., Australia; rises in Liverpool range of Gr. Dividing Range, flows S. and E. into Tasman Sea at Newcastle; c. 400 km long.

Hunterston, Cunninghame, Scot.; civil nuclear power sta.; integrated iron and steel wks.; engin. of oil platforms and oil terminal planned.

Huntingdon, t., l. gov. dist., Cambs., Eng.; on R. Ouse; expanded t.; canning, engin., processed rubber, confectionery; birthplace of Cromwell and home of the poet Cowper; p. (est. 1976) 118,100 (dist.).

Huntingdon and Peterborough, former co., Eng.; now part of Cambridgeshire non-met. co.

Huntington, c., W. Va., USA; on Ohio R.; R. pt. comm. ctr.; rly. wks., steel; p. (1970) 72,970 (c.), 247,059 (met. a.).

Huntly, burgh, Gordon, Scot.; at confluence of Rs. Bogie and Deveron; agr. mkt.; angling resort; p. (1971) 3,645.

Huntsville, c., Ala., USA; textiles; rocket research ctr.; p. (1970) 136,102 (c.), 224,217 (met. a.).

Hupeh (Hubei), prov., central China; N. of the Yangtze; many Ls and Rs.; rice, wheat, cotton; iron ores; Hankow, Hanyang, Wuchang form tri-city of Wuhan, the major industl. region of central China; cap. Wuchang; a. 186,363 km²; p. (est. 1968) 32,000,000.

Huron, L., between Canada and USA; one of the Gr. Ls. of the St. Lawrence basin; a. 59,596 km²; 330 km long.

Husum, spt., Schleswig-Holstein, W. Germany; on N. Sea cst.; cattle mkt.; p. (est. 1969) 25,069.

Hutchinson, t., Kan., USA; salt-mng., meat-packing, flour milling, oil refining; p. (est. 1969) 40,000.

Hutt, Upper and Lower, t., N.I., N.Z.; meat-freezing, vehicle assembly textiles; p. (est. 1970) 59,400 (c.), 122,000 (met. a.).

Huyton with Roby, Knowsley, Merseyside, Eng.; sub. of Liverpool; p. (1971) 66,629.

Hwai-ho (Huai-ho), R., N. China; rises in Hwaiyang Shan, flows E. between N. China plain and lower Yangtze; subject to disastrous floods and changes of course; since 1950 flood control and irrigation canal to sea; c. 1,224 km long.

Hwainan (Huainan), c., Anhwei prov., central China; ctr. of China's ch. coalmng. region; p. (est. 1970) 350,000.

Hwang-hai (Yellow Sea), arm of Pac. Oc. between Korea and China; branches into Gs. of Pohai and Liaotung; shallow sea rapidly infilling; named after yellow silt coming from the Hwangho; length 960 km, greatest width 640 km.

Hwang-ho (Yellow R.), China; rises in Kunlun range, S. Chinghai prov.; flows c. 4,800 km into G. of Pohai; cuts through Shensi in a deep gorge; filled with yellow silt (loess) from this a.; floods frequently and changes course (once entered sea S. of Shantung); in lower part forms fertile plain; now part of multipurpose scheme for hydroelectric power, irrigation and flood control; lgst. dam in China opened at Liuchia in 1975; 4,640 km long.

Hwangshih (Huangshi), c., Hupeh prov., China; main iron and steel ctr. of central China; built since 1950; p. (est. 1970) 200,000.

Hyde, t., Tameside, Gtr. Manchester, Eng.; on R. Tame, 8 km S.E. of Manchester; paints, chemicals, food-processing, tobacco, rubber; p. (1971) 37,075.

Hyderabad, ch. c., Andhra Pradesh, India; on R. Musi; walled t. and impt. comm. ctr.; univ.; p. (1971) 1,607,396 (c.), 1,796,339 (met. a.).

Hyderabad, c., Pakistan; 5 km W. of Indus; 144 km N.E. of Karachi; old cap of Sind; univ.; noted for silk, gold and silver embroidery; now varied mnfs.; dam at nearby Kotri; p. (1969) 698,000.

Hyndburn, l. gov. dist., Lancs., Eng.; inc. Colne Valley ts. of Accrington, Great Harwood, Rishton, Clayton-le-Moors, Church and Oswaldtwistle; p. (est. 1976) 80,400.

Hythe, t., Shepway, Kent, Eng.; on S. cst., 5 km W. of Folkestone; one of the Cinque pts.; military canal passing through t., used for boating; p. (1971) 11,949.

I

Iasi (Jassy), c., Romania; former cap. of Moldavia; in fertile agr. region; univ., cath.; cultural ctr.; textiles, plastics, chems.; p. (est. 1969) 179,405.

Ibadan, c., cap. Oyo st.; S.W. Nigeria; univ.; ctr. of rich agr. a., between the savannah and forest regions; p. mainly Yoruba; crafts, small inds.; p. (est. 1971) 758,332.

Ibagué, c., cap. of Tolima dep., Colombia; transport ctr.; cotton, tobacco, sugar, leather gds.; p. (est. 1972) 194,800 (c.), 218,600 (met. a.).

Ibarra, t., Ecuador; alt. 2,226 m at foot of Imbabura volcano; on Pan-American highway; p. (est. 1970) 37,100.

Iberian Peninsula, S.W. peninsula of Europe; containing sts. of Spain and Portugal; lge. a. of high tableland; interior isolation and regionalism; historical and contemporary importance for minerals; a. 593,250 km²; p. (1968) 41,500,000.

Iceland, rep., N. Atl. Oc.; volcanic I. with ice-covered plateaux; glacier fields cover 13,000 km²; only 1 per cent of a. cultivated; cold climate; hot house cultivation using thermal springs; economy dependent on fishing and fish-processing inds.; high standard of living; tourism increasingly impt.; 7 admin. dists.; cap. Reykjavik; a. 102,846 km²; p. (1969) 203,442.

Ichang (I-ch'ang), c., S.W. Hupeh, China; on R. Yangtze; site of famous gorges; terminus for lge. vessels from Shanghai.

Ichinomiya, c., S.E. Honshu, Japan; anc. Shinto shrine; textiles, pottery; p. (est. 1971) 223,000.

Ichow. See Lin-i.

Icknield Way, prehistoric route running from near Avebury, Wilts., along the Berkshire Downs, Chilterns and East Anglian Heights into Norfolk, crossing the Thames at Streatley.

Idaho, st., USA; one of the Rocky Mtn. sts.; rich in minerals; agr. mainly in irrigated Snake R. valley; cap. Boise; a. 216,413 km²; p. (1970) 698,275.

Idaho Falls, c., Idaho, USA; on Snake R.; food-processing, lumbering; silver, lead, and gold mines nearby; nuclear experimental breeder reactor; p. (est. 1969) 36,500.

Ida Mountains, range, N.W. Turkey; volcanic, hot springs; max. alt. Mount Gargarus, 1,768 m.

Idi Amin Dada (L. Edward), on frontier of Uganda and Zaïre, one of the sources of R. Nile; occupies Gr. Rift Valley; alt. c. 900 m, 70 km long, breadth 51 km; salt, fishing, wildlife.

Idle, t., West Yorks., Eng.; in Aire valley, 5 km N. of Bradford; woollens.

Ife, t., Nigeria; ctr. of the cacao tr.; univ.; p. (est. 1971) 157,178.

Ifni, enclave, S. Morocco; ceded by Spain to Morocco (1969); cap. Sidi Ifni; a. 1,500 km²; p. (1964) 51,517.

Igarka, sm. t., Siberia, RSFSR; on R. Yenisey, 640 km from its mouth; graphite plant, nickel-mines, lumber mills; p. 15,200.

Iglesias, t., Sardinia, Italy; N.W. of Cagliari; mng. for lead, pyrites, zinc; p. (est. 1968) 28,316.

Iguaçu, R., trib. of Paraná; mostly in Brazil; famous falls where Argentina, Brazil, and Paraguay meet, excelling Niagara, height 64 m; hydroelec. power potential.

IJmuiden, c., N. Holland, Neth.; on cst. at mouth of N. Sea canal; fishing; gasification plant, major iron and steel plant; p. (1968) 67,864 (c.), 135,334 (met. a.).

IJsselmeer (Lake IJssel), freshwater reservoir, Neth., formerly Zuider Zee; separated from N. Sea by Wieringen–Friesland Barrage; active land reclamation in progress; Wieringermeer drained 1930, N.E. Polder 1942, E. Flevoland 1957, S. Flevoland 1968, Markerwaard still to be drained; when reclamation complete by end of cent. a. of Neth. will have been increased by some 6 per cent.; ch. c. on inlet (IJ) Amsterdam.

Ilchester, t., Somerset, Eng.; on R. Yeo; N.W. of Yeovil; birthplace of Roger Bacon.

Îles d'Hyères, I. gr., France; in Mediterranean off Toulon; tourism.

Ilesha, t., Nigeria; tr. ctr., cotton weaving; p. (est. 1971) 200,434.

Ilford. See Redbridge.

Ilfracombe, t., North Devon, Eng.; sm. pt. on cst. of Bristol Channel; seaside resort; p. (1971) 9,846.

Ilhéus, spt., Bahia, Brazil; exp. cacao, timber; losing tr. to lge. pts.; p. (est. 1968) 100,687.

Ili, R., Central Asia; rises in Tienshan, China, and flows into L. Balkhash in Soviet terr.;

new t. of I. at site of hydroelec. sta.; c. 1,200 km long.

Iligan, t., Mindanao, Philippines; integrated steel mill; cement; p. (est. 1969) 66,100.

Ikeston, t., Erewash, Derbys., Eng.; W. of Nottingham, iron, engin., locknit fabrics, needles, plastics; p. (1971) 34,123.

Ilkley, t., spa, West Yorks., Eng.; on R. Wharfe, N.W. of Leeds; local mkt.; p. (1971) 21,828.

Illawara dist., N.S.W., Australia; forming belt of land between S. tableland and cst.; very fertile; dairy farming; coal seams; ch. ts., Kiama, Wollongong, Bulli, Gerringong.

Ille-et-Vilaine, dep., N.W. France; on English Channel; a. 6,990 km²; agr.; cap. Rennes; p. (1968) 652,722.

Illimani, one of the high peaks of the Cordillera Real, Andes, Bolivia, 6,461 m, E. of La Paz.

Illinois, st., USA; in Middle West; named after its principal R., a lge. trib. of Mississippi; many Rs.; cap. Springfield, metropolis Chicago; rich agr.; fuel and mineral resources; major coal-mng. st.; inds. inc. meat-processing, farm implements; a. 146,076 km²; p. (1970) 10,973,986.

Illinois, R., Ill., USA; glacial valley; long history of settlement; impt. routeway; 437 km long.

Illyria, region, mainly in Yugoslavia, stretching along Adriatic Sea from Trieste in N. to Albania in S. and inland as far as Rs. Danube and Morava.

Ilmen, L., RSFSR, nr. Novgorod; drained by Volkhov R. into L. Ladoga; a. 932 km²; fisheries.

Ilminster, t., Somerset, Eng.; 16 km S.E. of Taunton; cutstone, concrete, collars, radio valves; p. (1971) 3,375.

Iloilo, c., cap. of I. prov., Panay, Philippines; ctr. of rly. network; impt. pt. exp. sugar, rice, copra, hemp; p. (est. 1968) 201,000.

Ilorin, t., N. Nigeria; on Lagos–Kano rly.; agr. and caravan ctr.; govt. sugar-growing scheme at Bacita; p. (est. 1971) 252,076.

Imabari, t., spt., N.W. Shikoku, Japan; on shore of Inland Sea; mnfs. cotton textiles, paper, canned fruits; p. (est. 1971) 111,000.

Imatra, t., Kymi, Finland; hydroelec. power sta. supplies S. Finland; electro-metallurgy; p. (1968) 35,694.

Imbroz. See Gökçeada I.

Immingham, pt., Humberside, Eng.; on the Humber, N.W. of Grimsby; lge. docks; new deep-sea oil and coal terminals; chemicals engin., refinery nearby at Killingholme.

Imola, t., Italy; S.E. of Bologna; cath.; glass, pottery; p. (est. 1968) 55,580.

Imperia, t., Italy; on G. of Genoa; sm. pt., olive-growing ctr.; resort; p. (1969) 38,831.

Imperial Valley, S. Cal., USA; extends 48 km S.E. from Salton Sea to Mexican bdy.; mainly below sea-level; hot, arid climate; irrigation from Colorado R. chiefly by All-American Canal nr. Yuma; total irrigated a. 405,000 ha; principal crops, fruit, dates, tomatoes, cotton, and dairy prod.

Imphal, cap. of Manipur, India; in rice-growing basin in hills of Assam nr. Burma bdy.; p. (1971) 100,366.

Inari L., extensive L., Lappi, Finland; outlet into Barents Sea; hydroelec. power; a. 1,774 km².

Ince-in-Makerfield, t., Gtr. Manchester, Eng.; nr. Wigan; engin.; p. (1971) 15,925.

Inchon, c., S. Korea; on Yellow Sea; pt. for Seoul; exp. soyabeans, rice; textile ctr., steel mill, glass, diesel engines; p. (1966) 525,072.

Independence, c., Mo., USA; E. of Kansas; oil refining; agr. machin.; p. (est. 1969) 112,000.

India, rep., indep. st. (since 1947), S. Asia; second cty. of world by p.; 22 sts. and 9 union terrs.; peninsula bounded by Himalayas in N. extends in wide plateau to Indian Oc. in S.; most of p. concentrated in Indo-Gangetic Plain; unpredictable monsoon climate; heavy dependence on agr.; 70 per cent of p. farmers; few cash crops except cotton (the Deccan), tea (Himalayas), and jute (W. Bengal); 854 languages and dialects impede economic development; strong caste system; high illiteracy rate (70 per cent); little industl. development except in Damodar region; cap. New Delhi; main pts. Bombay, Calcutta; a. 3,268,580 km²; p. (1976) 605,000,000 (+25 per cent since 1961).

Indiana, st., USA; in Middle West, bounded by Mich., Ohio, Ill. and sep. from Ky. by Ohio R.; agr.: coal, limestone, petroleum; steel, metal prods., machin., food prod.; cap. Indianapolis; a. 93,994 km²; p. (1970) 5,143,422.

Indianapolis, c., cap. of Ind., USA; on White R.; univ.; rly. ctr.; meat-packing, jet engines, aircraft parts, chemicals, pharmaceutics; p. (1970) 742,613 (c.), 1,099,628 (met. a.).

Indian Ocean extends from S. of Asia and E. of Africa to the C. of Good Hope and C. Leeuwin in Australia, separated from the Pacific by the Malay Archipelago and Australia; a. 75,990,600 km².

Indigirka R., Yakut ASSR, RSFSR; flows into Arctic Oc.; hydroelec. power; 1,760 km long.

Indo-China, S.E. Asia; federation in Fr. Union until end of hostilities July 1954; consisted of the three sts. of Vietnam, Cambodia, and Laos.

Indo-Gangetic Plain, India, Bangladesh and Pakistan; name applied to flat land created by the Indus and Ganges basins; densely populated a.

Indonesia, rep., S.E. Asia; former Neth. E. Indies; made up of many sm. Is. straddling equator for over 4,800 km; many Is. in W. volcanic and E. coral; lgst. Is. inc. Java, Sumatra, Kalimantan (S. Borneo), Sulawesi, and Irian (W. New Guinea); mostly underdeveloped except Java; rapidly developing oil industry; 64 per cent p. on Java, planned decentralisation to other Is.; cap. Djakarta; a. 1,907,566 km²; p. (est. 1975) 118,367,850.

Indore, c., Madhya Pradesh, India; nr. valley of Narbada R.; comm. ctr.; cotton-mills; p. (1971) 543,381 (c.), 560,936 (met. a.).

Indre, dep., central France; agr. and industl.; cap. Châteauroux; a. 6,905 km²; p. (1968) 247,178.

Indre-et-Loire, dep., central France; drained by Indre and Loire Rs.; vineyards, orchards; cap. Tours; a. 6,156 km²; p. (1968) 437,870.

Indus, R., Pakistan, rises in Tibet, flows through Kashmir, Punjab, Sind, to Arabian Sea; 5 tribs. Jhelum, Chenab, Ravi, Beas, Sutlej, form one of world's major R. systems now used extensively to irrigate the Punjab and the Sind; impt. cotton, wheat, and sugar dist.; hydroelec. power; supported Indus valley civilisation 3,000–1,500 B.C.; 2,880 km long.

Ingleborough, mtn., near Settle, North Yorks., Eng.; underground caves, stalactites; made of limestone and millstone grit; alt. 724 m.

Inglewood, t., S. Cal., USA; sub. of Los Angeles; chinchilla farms; furniture, lt. engin., aircraft parts; p. (est. 1969) 85,000.

Ingolstadt, t., Bavaria, W. Germany; on Danube, nr. Munich; cas.; machin., cars, tobacco, oil refining; pipeline from Genoa; transalpine oil pipeline from Trieste, through N.E. Italy and Austria to I.; p. (est. 1967) 69,000.

Inhambane, spt., Moçambique; sugar, copra, oil-seeds, bricks, soap, tiles; p. (1970) 745,911.

Inishboffin, I., Galway, R.o.I., sm. I. off Connemara; farming, fishing.

Inishmore, lgst. of Aran gr., Galway, R.o.I.; fishing.

Inkpen Beacon. hill. Berks., Eng.; highest point reached by chalk hills in Eng.; alt. 297 m.

Inland Sea, Japan; between Honshu on N. and Shikoku and Kyushu on S.; sheltered sea with many Is.; ch. spts. Osaka, Amagaski, Kōbe, Okayama, Hiroshima, Kure; Nat. Park; a. c. 9,500 km².

Inn, R., traversing Switzerland, the Tyrol, Austria and Bavaria; enters R. Danube at Passau; hydroelec. plants; 512 km long.

Innerleithen, burgh, Tweeddale, Scot., on R. Tweed, 8 km S.E. of Peebles; woollen cloth and knitwear; mineral springs; p. (1971) 2,218.

Inner Mongolia, Chinese aut. region, N.E. China; stretches along S. border of Mongolian People's Rep.; vast steppelands, sparse p.; st. farms for animal husbandry; peat beds; milk-processing; cap Huhehot; a. 1,177,518 km²; p. (est. 1967) 13,000,000.

Innisfail, t., Queensland, Australia; ch. sugar-producing ctr. of Australia; p. (1972) 7,475.

Innsbruck, c., cap. of the Tyrol, W. Austria; on R Inn; commands N. approach to Brenner Pass; univ.; tourism; fortfd. 12th cent.; p. (est. 1969) 112,824.

Inowroclaw, t., N. Poland; nr. Bydgoszcz; rock-salt. iron pyrites; agr. prod.; p. (1970) 54,800.

Insterburg. See **Chernyakhovsk**.

Inter-American Highway, section of Pan-American Highway system, from Mexico to Panama.

Interlaken, t., Bernese Oberland, Berne, Switzerland; on R. Aare between Ls. Thun and Brienz; tourist resort; p. (1970) 4,735.

Intracoastal Waterway, USA; toll-free waterway along Atl. and Gulf of Mexico csts.; completed 1949 using bays, rivers and canals; 4,960 km long.

Inuvik, t., Arctic, Canada; above the permafrost.

Inveraray, burgh, Argyll and Bute, Scot.; nr. head of Loch Fyne; herring fishing; p. (1971) 438.

Inverbervie, burgh, Kincardine and Deeside, Scot.; on E. cst., 13 km S. of Stonehaven; linen, rayon inds.; p. (1971) 850.

Invercargill, t., S.I., N.Z.; on S.E. cst.; sawmills, freezing wks.; aluminium smelter; served by Bluff Harbour; p. (1971) 47,092.

Inverell, t., N.S.W., Australia; 613 km N. of Sydney; wheat and lamb cty.; tin; p. (1966) 8,411.

Invergordon, burgh, spt., Ross and Cromarty, Scot.; on N. side of Cromarty F., 19 km N.E. of Dingwall; former naval pt.; whisky distillery; lge. chemical ind. and aluminium smelter projected; p. (1971) 2,350.

Inverkeithing, royal burgh, Dunfermline, Scot.; on F. of Forth, nr. Dunfermline; shipbreaking, papermkg., quarrying; p. (1971) 5,861.

Inverkip, par., v., Inverclyde, Scot.; 10 km S.W. of Greenock; par. contains Gourock; resort; car ferry.

Inverness, royal burgh, Inverness, N.E. Scot.; on Moray F.; distilling, lt. engin., tweeds; sm. pt. for coal, timber; tourism; p. (1971) 34,839.

Inverness-shire, former co., l. gov. dist., N.E. Scot.; part of Highland Reg.; a. 11,269 km²; p. (1971) 49,285.

Inverurie, royal burgh, Gordon, Scot.; on R. Don, 22 km N.W. of Aberdeen; rly. ctr., mkt. t.; tourism; p. (1971) 5,437.

Inyokern, t., E. Cal., USA; naval ordnance research sta.

Ioánnina (Janina), t., Epirus, Greece; nr. Albanian frontier; agr. tr.; embroidery; univ.; p. (1971) 39,814.

Iona, I., off cst. of Mull, Argyll, Scot.; early Scottish Christian ctr.; restored abbey; St. Columba's burial place; anc. burial place of Scottish kings.

Ionian Is., gr. in Mediterranean, belonging to Greece; comprising Corfu, Paxos, Levkas, Cephalonia, Zakinthos, Ithake; severe earthquake 1953; total a. 1,948 km²; p. (1971) 183,633.

Ionian Sea, Mediterranean; between Greece on E.; Italy and Sicily on W.

Iowa, st., USA; in Middle West; prairie cty.; watered by Mississippi and Missouri; rich farm land; maize, oats, and other grains; hogs, pigs; processing of farm prod.; flood control, reforestation; diverse inds.; cap. Des Moines; a. 145,791 km²; p. (1970) 2,789,893.

Iowa City, c., S.E. Iowa, USA; former st. cap. (1839–56); univ.; p. (est. 1969) 47,000.

Ipin (Yibin), c., Szechwan prov., China; at junc. of Yangtze and Min Rs.; p. (est. 1970) 275,000.

Ipoh, c., cap. of Perak st., N.W. Malaya; tin-mng. ctr.; Chinese rock temples; p. (1970) 247,689.

Ipswich, t., S.E. Queensland, Australia; nr. Brisbane; coalmng. ctr.; woollens; p. (1966) 53,396.

Ipswich, co. t., l. gov. dist., Suffolk, Eng.; pt. on estuary of R. Orwell; birthplace of Cardinal Wolsey; diesel engines, gen. engin.; p. (est. 1976) 121,500.

Iquique, t., N. Chile; pt. on Pac. Oc.; exp. nitrates and iodine from Atacama desert; fish-canning; p. (1966) 48,000.

Iquitos, t., N.E. Peru; on Amazon, 3,680 km from mouth; comm. ctr.; exp. timber, cotton; sawmills, oil refining; p. (est. 1969) 74,000.

Iráklion (Candia or Herakleion), t., Crete, Greece; impt. spt. on G. of I., arm of Aegean Sea; at foot of terraced hill slopes; wine, olive oil, fruit, fishing; tourism; p. (1971) 77,783.

Iran, kingdom, S.W. Asia; interior plateau at c. 900 m, ringed by mtn. ranges of up to c.

5,500 m; much of a. is desert; settled agr. limited to Caspian plain; heavy dependence on oil; oilfields centred on Abādān; high quality carpets exported, esp. to USA; cap. Tehran; a. 1,626,520 km²; p. (est. 1975) 33,019,000.

Irapuato, c., central Mexico; agr. tr. and processing; iron-founding; p. (1970) 116,651.

Iraq, rep., S.W. Asia; the anc. Mesopotamia; dominated by 2 Rs., Tigris and Euphrates; much of a. desert and semi-desert but irrigation in S. and centre enables settled agr. for barley, wheat, dates, and tobacco; only outlet to sea at N.W. end of Persian G.; oil principal source of wealth; main oilfield at Kirkūk; main oil pt. at Basra; pipelines to Lebanon and Syria; new inds. based on oil; 14 provs.; cap. Baghdad; a. 435,120 km²; p. (est. 1970) 9,465,800.

Irazú, active volcano, 3,437 m high, central Costa Rica.

Irbid, t., Jordan; comm. and agr. tr. ctr.; p. (est. 1971) 115,000.

Ireland, I., W. of Gt. Britain, separated by Irish Sea; divided politically into R.o.I. (Eire) and N. Ireland (Ulster, part of U.K.); ch. physical features, L. Neagh in N.E., Ls. of Killarney in S.W.; Rs. Shannon, Boyne, Blackwater; mtns. of Mourne, Wicklow, and Kerry; mild moist climate; called "emerald isle" because of grasslands; pastoral agr., especially dairying; tourism; a. 83,937 km²; p. (1966) 3,088,759.

Ireland, Republic of, ind. st., W. Europe; comprises 26 of 32 cos. making up I. of Ireland; remaining 6 cos. belong to U.K.; ring of highlands surround central lowland basin, much of which is peat-covered; economy based on agr., especially dairying; exps. butter, cheese, bacon; new govt.-encouraged inds.; mineral resources; tourism; cap. Dublin; a. 68,894 km²; p. (1971) 2,978,248.

Irian Jaya (formerly Dutch New Guinea, later W. Irian), prov., Indonesia; formerly W. New Guinea and Dutch col.; part of Indonesia, 1963; inaugurated as prov., 1969; primitive agr. of rice, poultry, cocoa; few oil deposits; cap. Djajapura; a. (inc. Ternate) 412,784 km²; p. (est. 1970) 957,000.

Irish Sea, Brit. Is.; between Gt. Britain and Ireland, connecting N. and S. with Atl. Oc.; 320 km long; 80–224 km wide; greatest depth 840 m; a. 18,130 km².

Irkutsk, c., cap. of I. oblast, RSFSR; on Angara R. in E. Siberia; on Trans-Siberian rly., 64 km W. of L. Baykal; univ.; engin., sawmilling, petroleum refining, chemicals, hydroelec. power sta.; p. (1970) 451,000.

Irlam, t., Gtr. Manchester, Eng.; engin., tar, soap, glycerine, margarine; steel wks. to close; overspill p.; p. (1971) 20,571.

Ironbridge, t., Salop, Eng.; scene of Darby's iron ind.; derives name from first cast-iron bridge (1779) which here crosses Severn; now inc. in Dawley new t.

Iron Country, Utah, USA; vast reserves of iron ore; undeveloped due to inaccessibility.

Iron Gate (Portile de Fier), Romania; famous rapids in R. Danube; Romanian–Yugoslavian hydroelectric and navigation project, 1964–71.

Irrawaddy, R., Burma; flows S. to Bay of Bengal; navigable for lge. steamers 1,440 km; irrigation wks.; major Asian rice bowl; 2,000 km long.

Irtysh, R., W. Siberia, USSR; ch. trib. of R. Ob'; crossed by Turk–Sib rly. at Semipalatinsk and by Trans-Siberian rly. at Omsk; hydroelectric power stas.; 2,960 km long.

Irvine, royal burgh, Cunninghame, Scot.; on mouth of R. Irvine; new t. (1966); cas.; hosiery, lt. engin., bottle wks., chemicals; p. (est. 1974) 50,100.

Irvington, t., N.J., USA; industl. sub. of Newark; machin.; p. (est. 1969) 62,000.

Irwell, R., Gtr. Manchester, Eng.; flows through Manchester to the Mersey via Manchester Ship Canal; 48 km long.

Isar, R., Austria and W. Germany; rises in Austrian Tyrol, flows N.E. to Danube; hydroelectric power stas. below Munich; 261 km long.

Isarco, R., N. Italy; rises nr. Brenner Pass, flows S. into R. Adige at Bolzano; 80 km long.

Isdud, anc. c. of the Philistines. See Ashdod.

Ise (Ujiyamada), t., Honshu, Japan; sacred c. of Shintoism; p. (1970) 103,576.

Ise Bay, inlet, S. Honshu, Japan; flanked by ch. textile mftg. a. of cty. with 5 million people centred on Nagoya; 64 km long, 24–32 km wide.

Iseo, L., N. Italy; E. of Bergamo; 124 km².

Isère, dep., S.E. France; drained by Rs. Isère and Rhône; cap. Grenoble; mtnous.; cereals; wine, butter, cheese; iron, coal, lead, silver, copper; gloves, silks; a. 8,231 km²; p. (1968) 768,450.

Isère, R., S.E. France; rises in Graian Alps, flows W. into R. Rhône nr. Valence; used to generate hydroelec. power; used, with trib. R. Arc, by main rly. from France to N. Italy through Mt. Cenis (Fréjus) tunnel.

Iserlohn, t., N. Rhine–Westphalia, W. Germany; S.E. of Dortmund; metal gds.; p. (est. 1967) 57,400.

Isfahan. See Eṣfahān.

Ishikari, t., Hokkaido, Japan; on cst. of Otaru Bay, 16 km N. of Sapporo; ctr. of second lgst. coalfield in Japan; sm. petroleum production.

Ishimbay, c., Bashkir ASSR, RSFSR; on R. Belaya; ctr. of Ishimbay oilfields; pipelines to Ufa, Orsk, and Shkaparo; p. (est. 1967) 53,000.

Isiro (Paulis), t., N.E. Zaïre; admin. offices; cotton ginneries; rly. repair shops.

Isis, R., headstream of R. Thames, Eng.; so named around and above Oxford.

Iskenderun (Alexandretta), spt., S. Turkey; recent modernisation for new Iran/Turkey rly.; new steel wks.; p. (1965) 69,259.

Islamabad, new cap. of Pakistan, to N. of Rawalpindi below Himalayas; nuclear power sta.; p. (1972) 235,000.

Islay, I. Inner Hebrides, Argyll and Bute, Scot.; a. 609 km²; farming, dairying, distilleries; p. (1971) 3,827.

Isle of Grain, Kent, Eng.; flat promontory at confluence of Thames and Medway, once separated from mainland by a tidal estuary; lge oil refinery; pipelines to Walton-on-Thames and Heathrow Airport.

Isle of Man, Irish Sea; 43 km from Eng. (Cumbria) and N. Ireland (Down); high plateau N.E. to S.W.; ch. t. Douglas; old cap. Castletown; admin. according to own laws; tourism; a. 572 km²; p. (1971) 49,743.

Islington, inner bor., London, Eng.; N. of City; incorporates Finsbury; univ.; residtl.; clocks, precision engin.; p. (est. 1976) 171,600.

Islwyn, l. gov. dist., Gwent, Wales; inland ts. of Risca, Abercarn, Bedwellty and Mynyddislwyn; p. (est. 1976) 66,200.

Ismailia (Ismā'iliya), t., Egypt; at mid-point of Suez Canal on L. Timsah; rail connections with Cairo, Suez, Port Said; declined during canal closure; p. (est. 1970) 167,500.

Isna (Esneh), t., Upper Egypt; on Nile; agr. ctr.; cottons, pottery; p. (1966) 27,400.

Ispra, t., Varese, Italy; nr. L. Maggiore; nuclear research ctr.

Israel, rep., S.W. Asia; occupies narrow corridor between Jordan valley and Mediterranean Sea; extends S. into the Negev desert (half a. of rep.); Mediterranean climate enables cultivation of early fruits and vegetables, especially citrus fruits; most highly industrialised cty. of S.W. Asia, especially for textiles and clothing; petroleum of increasing impt.; tourism; Jewish rep. since 1948; until then part of the mandate Palestine; surrounded by hostile Arab sts.; difficulties of increasing Jewish immigration; cap. Jerusalem; a. 20,850 km²; nat. a. in dispute, particularly since Arab-Israeli wars of 1967 and 1973; p. (1970) 2,995,000 (75 per cent Jewish).

Issyk Kul, mtn. L., Kirghiz SSR, USSR; in Tien-Shan mtns., alt. 1,568 m; a. 6,216 km²; ice-free in winter.

Issy-les-Moulineaux, sub. S.W. Paris, Hauts-de-Seine, France; engin.; p. (1968) 51,666.

Istanbul (Constantinople), ch. spt., former cap., Turkey; on Golden Horn peninsula on European cst. at entry of Bosporus into Sea of Marmara; divided into old "Stamboul" on S. side, and dists. of Galata and Beyoglu (Pera) on N.; the anc. Byzantium; magnificent mosque of Sta. Sophia; univ.; industl. and comm. ctr.; tourism; p. (1970) 2,312,751.

Istria, peninsula, N. Adriatic, Yugoslavia; ch. c. Pula; agr., olives, vines, oranges, maize; p. Yugoslav and Italian; a. c. 5,200 km².

Itabira, t., Minas Gerais st., Brazil; on Brazilian

Plateau, 96 km N.E. of Belo Horizonte; lgst. deposits of iron ore in Brazil; p. (est. 1968) 42,836.

Itabuna, t., Bahia, E. Brazil; cocoa, livestock; p. (est. 1968) 87,561.

Itajaí, spt., Santa Catarina, S. Brazil; exp. lumber, cement, agr. prods.; p. (est. 1968) 59,423.

Italy, rep., S. Europe; peninsula extending into Mediterranean; inc. 2 main Is. of Sicily and Sardinia; bounded by Alps to N.; central spine of Apennines; Mediterranean climate; contrast between industrialised N. and less developed agr. S. (Mezzogiorno); agr. impt., especially in Po basin; tourism attracted by Roman and Renaissance architecture and by climate; inds. based on hydroelectric power in N., inc. elec. engin., motor vehicles and textiles, centred at Milan and Turin; 19 admin. regions; cap. Rome; a. 301,049 km²; p. (1976) 56,024,000.

Ithaca, t., N.Y., USA; on Cayuga L.; seat of Cornell Univ.; elec. clocks; machin.; p. (est. 1969) 29,500.

Ithake, one of the Ionian Is., Greece; a. 96 km²; ch. t. Ithake; severe earthquake, 1953.

Itzehoe, t., Schleswig-Holstein, W. Germany; founded by Charlemagne; wood, cement, machin.; p. (est. 1969) 35,874.

Ivano-Frankovsk (Stanislav), c., Ukrainian SSR, USSR; in Carpathian foothills; industl. ctr.; oilfields nearby; oil refineries, engin.; p. (1970) 105,000.

Ivanovo, t., RSFSR; N.E. of Moscow; textiles, iron and chemical wks.; peat-fed power stas.; p. (1970) 419,000.

Iviza, I., Balearic gr. in the W. Mediterranean; Spanish; cath.; tourism.

Ivory Coast, rep., on G. of Guinea, W. Africa; formerly a Fr. overseas terr.; hot, humid climate; coastal lagoons, interior plateau (300–1,200 m); economy based on subsistence agr. although an impt. coffee and timber producer; underdeveloped mineral resources; poorly developed rail network but extensive road system; new pt. at San Pedro; Pt. Bouet outport of cap. Abidjan; a. 322,481 km²; p. (est. 1969) 4,200,000.

Iwaki, t., Honshu, Japan; ctr. of apple producing dist.; p. (est. 1971) 331,000.

Iwakuni, t., Honshu, Japan; on Inland Sea; p. (est. 1971) 108,000.

Iwo, t., Nigeria; nr. Ibadan; tr. ctr.; p. (est. 1971) 191,684.

Izhevsk, c., cap. of Udmurt ASSR, RSFSR; steel ctr., engin.; p. (1970) 422,000.

Izmail, c., Ukrainian SSR, USSR; in Bessarabia, on Danube delta, nr. Romanian border; naval base of Soviet Danube flotilla; former Turkish fortress; p. (est. 1967) 63,000.

Izmir (Smyrna), c., Turkey; at head of G. of I., Anatolia; exp. figs, raisins, tobacco, carpets, rugs; anc. and historic c.; ch. comm. ctr. of the Levant; univ.; p. (1970) 753,443.

Izmit, c., Turkey; E. end of Sea of Marmara; cereals, tobacco, oil refinery and polythene plant under construction; p. (1965) 90,061.

J

Jabalpur (Jubbulpore), c., Madhya Pradesh, India; rly. ctr.; ordnance wks.; p. (1971) 426,224 (c.), 534,845 (met. a.).

Jablonec nad Nisou. t., ČSSR; on R. Neisse; glassware ctr., inc. glass jewellery and imitation stones; p. (est. 1968) 33,722.

Jáchymov, t., ČSSR; spa; uranium mines, pitch-blende, lead, silver, nickel, cobalt.

Jackson, t., Mich., USA; on Grand R.; locomotives, motorcar accessories, electronic equipment, metal gds.; p. (1970) 45,733 (c.), 142,422 (met. a.).

Jackson, t., cap. of Miss., USA; comm. and industl. ctr.; birthplace of Harry S. Truman; p. (1970) 150,332 (c.), 252,713 (met. a.).

Jacksonville, c., Fla., USA; pt. on St. John's R.; impt. ctr. on Atl. cst.; chemicals, shipbldg. and repair, printing, lumber, cigar mftg.; tourism; p. (1970) 513,439.

Jacobabad, t., Sind, Pakistan; driest and hottest place in Indian sub-continent; p. (1961) 35,200.

Jacui, R., S. Brazil; rises in S. edge of Brazilian Plateau, enters Atl. Oc., through lagoon, Lagoa dos Patos; 560 km long.

Jadotville, t., Zaire; copper mng. and refining; p. (est. 1966) 102,187.

Jaduguda, Bihar, India; uranium plant.

Jaén, t., cap. of prov. of Jaén, S. Spain; in foothills of Andalusian mtns.; cath.; olive oil, wine, chemicals; p. (1967) 71,508.

Jaffna, spt., N. Sri Lanka; on J. peninsula; second t. of rep.; p. (est. 1968) 101,700.

Jaipur, c., cap. of Rajasthan, India; univ.; fine fabrics, jewellery; tourism; old cap. Amber is 8 km away; p. (1971) 615,258 (c.), 636,768 (met. a.).

Jajce, t., Yugoslavia; in Bosnia, at junc. of Rs. Vrbas and Pliva (hydroelectric power); Fed. People's Rep. of Yugoslavia declared here by Tito (1943).

Jakarta. See Djakarta.

Jalalabad, c., E. Afghanistan; on Kābul R., nr. Khyber Pass; univ.; agr. tr. ctr.; p. (est. 1969) 48,919.

Jalapa, c., cap. of Veracruz st., Mexico; c. 1,370 m; a.s.l.; luxuriant vegetation; agr. ctr.; tourism; p. (1970) 122,377.

Jalgaon, t., Maharashtra, India; in Tapti R. valley nr. Bhusawal; p. (1971) 106,711.

Jalisco, st., Mexico; on Pac. Oc.; traversed by Sierra Madre; well timbered, agr.; minerals; tourism; a. 80,876 km²; p. (1969) 3,344,000.

Jalón, R., Spain; rises in Iberian Mtns., flows N.E. into R. Ebro nr. Zaragoza; valley forms main rly., road route from Madrid to Ebro valley.

Jalpaiguri, t., W. Bengal, India; frontier t.; rly ctr.; p. (1961) 48,738.

Jamaica, rep., W.I.; member of Brit. Commonwealth; mtnous.; Blue Mtn. range runs E. to W. and rises to 2,258 m; tropical climate modified by alt.; economy based on agr. and mng.; major exp. crops sugar and bananas; major world producer of bauxite and alumina; tourist ind. expanding; member of Caribbean Free Trade Association; 25 per cent unemployment; major pts. Kingston, Montego Bay, Pt. Antonio; international airpt.; univ. at cap. Kingston; a. 11,424 km²; p. (est. 1975) 2,100,000, of which 45% are in Kingston.

James, R. Va., USA; hydroelec. power in upper reaches, wide estuary in lower course; outlet to Chesapeake Bay; 544 km long.

James Bay, S. arm of Hudson Bay, Canada; c. 480 km long, 224 km wide.

Jamshedpur, c. Bihar, India; W. of Calcutta; major industl. ctr. of rep.; Tata iron and steel wks.; engin.; p. (1971) 199,700 (c.), 227,640 (met. a.).

Jamestown, spt., cap. of St. Helena I.; flax; p. (1966) 1,475.

Jamestown, t., dist., Va., USA; nr. mouth of James R., where first English permanent settlement was founded 1607.

Jammu, t., J. and Kashmir, India; winter cap. of st.; univ., fort, palace; p. (est. 1970) 135,522.

Jammu and Kashmir, st., N.W. India; traversed by ranges of Himalayas; in Jhelum valley is celebrated vale of Kashmir; producing abundant crops of wheat and rice; cap. Srinagar; Muzaffarabad ch. c. of a. occupied by Pakistan (Azad Kashmir); total a. 222,823 km²; p. (1971) 4,615,176.

Jamnagar, t., Gujarat, India; on G. of Kutch; p. (1971) 199,709 (t.), 227,640 (met. a.).

Janina. See Ioánnina.

Jan Mayen I., volcanic I. between Spitzbergen and Iceland, Arctic Oc.; annexed by Norway 1929; meteorological sta.; a. 373 km²; p. (1967) 36.

Japan, monarchy, E. Asia; 4 main Is., Honshu (lgst.), Hokkaido, Shikoku, Kyushu; mtnous.; 18 active volcanoes; subject to earthquakes; only 17 per cent of land cultivable; intensive and mechanised agr.; rice, fruits, vegetables; few animals; inds. highly developed and based on imports of raw material and export of finished prods.; rapid industrialisation since second world war; inds. inc. shipbldg., motor vehicles, textiles, steel, chemicals, cheap consumer gds.; cap. Tokyo; a. 370,370 km²; p. (1975) 111,933,818 (inc. Okinawa and Ryuku Is.).

Japan Current. See Kuroshio.

Japan, Sea of, portion of Pac. Oc. between Korea, USSR, and Japan.

Japurá, R., Colombia, Brazil; rises as Caquetá in Colombian Andes, flows S.E. through Brazil to Amazon; 2,080 km long.

Jaroslaw, t., Rzeszow prov., S.E. Poland; on R. San; food-processing; founded 11th cent.; impt. tr. ctr. 16th cent.; p. (1970) 29,100.

Jarrow, t., South Tyneside, Tyne and Wear, Eng.; on S. bank of Tyne, 11 km below Gateshead; grew up as shipbldg. ctr.; hit by depression of 1930s; hunger march to London 1936; new enterprises introduced; steel and tube wks., oil storage; die-castings, knitting-wool-mkg. at Bede trading estate; the Venerable Bede lived and died here; p. (1971) 28,779.

Jasper National Park, Alberta, Canada; Rocky mtns.; tourism.

Jaunpur, t., Uttar Pradesh, India; mkt. t.; ctr. of Moslem learning and architecture in 15th cent.; p. (1961) 61,851.

Java, I., Indonesia; most developed of Indonesian Is.; traversed E. to W. by forested volcanic mtns.; fertile volcanic soils aid intensive rice cultivation; over-populated; contains 70 per cent of cty.'s p. yet only 8 per cent of land a.; exps. inc. coffee, rubber, sugar, copra, teak; noted for silver craft and batik work (anc. craft of fabric decoration); a. 130,510 km²; p. (est. 1970) 78,660,000.

Javari, R., forms bdy. between Peru and Brazil; trib. of R. Amazon.

Java Sea, part of the Pac. Oc. between N. cst. Java, Borneo, and Sumatra.

Jebba, t., Nigeria; on R. Niger; dam proposed for 1982.

Jebel Aulia, v., Sudan; S. of Khartoum; dam across White Nile R. [land.

Jebel, Arabic term for mtn., mtn. range. or high-

Jebel-Hauran, high tableland of Syria, alt. c. 1,800 m.

Jedburgh, royal burgh, Roxburgh, Scot.; on Jed Water, S.W. of Kelso; tweeds, woollens, rayon; abbey ruins; ctr. of Border warfare in Middle Ages; p. (1971) 3,874.

Jeddah. See Jiddah.

Jefferson City, st. cap. Mo., USA; on Missouri R.; univ.; comm. and processing ctr. of agr. a.; shoes, tiles, farm implements; p. (est. 1969) 29,500.

Jelenia Góra (Hirschberg), t., S.W. Poland (since 1945), formerly in Lower Silesia; mftg.; spa; p. (1970) 55,700.

Jelgava (Mitau), t., Latvian SSR, USSR; on Lielupe R.; textiles, foodstuffs, refractory materials; p. (est. 1967) 49,000.

Jemappes, t., Belgium; 5 km W. of Mons; industl.; Fr. victory over Austria 1792; battle of Mons 1914; p. (est. 1969) 12,548.

Jena, c., E. Germany; on R. Saale, 72 km S.W. of Leipzig; univ., observatory; optical glassware, precision instruments; leading cultural ctr. late 18th and early 19th cent.; defeat of Prussians by Fr. 1806; p. (est. 1967) 83,000.

Jensen, t., Utah, USA; oil refinery; on R. Green.

Jerez de la Frontera, t., Spain; in Andalusia, 22 km N.E. of Cádiz; in fertile agr. a.; sherry; p. (est. 1967) 147,633.

Jericho, v., Jordan Valley, Jordan; est. through recent excavations as one of oldest towns in the world (6000 B.C.); p. (1961) 10,284.

Jersey, I., lgst of Channel Is., 21 km W. of Fr. cst.; potatoes, tomatoes, cauliflowers, flowers, fruit, cattle; tourist resort; banking; ch. t. St. Helier; a. 117 km²; p. (est. 1973) 72,000.

Jersey City, c., N.J., USA; E. of Newark, on Hudson R.; comm. and industl. ctr.; diverse inds.; rly. ctr.; p. (1970) 253,467 (c.), 597,091 (met. a.).

Jerusalem, c., Israel and Jordan; 811 m a.s.l.; between Dead Sea and Mediterranean; the "Holy City" of the Jews and the sacred c. of the Christians and Moslems; divided between Israel and Jordan; Israeli sector cap. of Israel; Old City annexed by Israel June 1967; modern mftg.; p. (1972) 304,500 inc. E. Jerusalem.

Jervis Bay, inlet of Pac. Oc., N.S.W., Australia; acquired by Fed. Govt. as site for establishment of pt. for Canberra 1909; a. 73 km².

Jesenice, t., Yugoslavia; integrated iron and steel wks.; terminal of Brotherhood and Unity Highway.

Jesselton. See Kota Kinabalu.

Jhang Maghiana, t., Pakistan; textiles; mkt.; on R. Chenab; p. (1969) 118,000.

Jhansi, c., Uttar Pradesh, India; rly. ctr., mkt.; formerly of strategic importance; p. (1971) 173,292 (c.), 198,135 (met. a.).

Jharia, t., Bihar, India; ctr. of most impt. coalfield in India; p. (1961) 33,683.

Jhelum, R., W. Punjab, Pakistan; most W. of the five Rs. of the Punjab; forms Vale of Kashmir in upper course; Mangla Dam under Indus Waters Treaty, completed 1967.

Jhelum, t., Pakistan; on Jhelum R.; p. (1961) 52,585.

Jiddah or Jeddah, c., Hejaz, Saudi Arabia; on Red Sea, pt. of Mecca; pilgrims; steel mill projected; new King Faisal Port nearby; univ. (with Mecca); p. (est. 1965) 194,000.

Jihlava, t., Moravia, ČSSR; on Jihlava R.; 519 m a.s.l.; timber, grain, textiles; Prague Compactata signed here 1436; p. (1967) 38,000.

Jimma, t., Ethiopia; ch. prod. Jimma coffee; connected by road with Addis Ababa; Agricultural Technical School.

Jinja, t., Uganda; on N. shore of L. Victoria where Nile drains from L. over Ripon Falls; (now inundated by Owen Falls dam 2·4 km upstream); cotton mnfs., copper smelting, flour and maize milling; rly. to Kampala; p. (1961) 29,741.

João Pessoa, t., cap. of Paraíba st., Brazil; through its pt. Cabedelo expts. cotton, sugar, minerals; p. (1970) 197,398.

Joban, dist., N.E. Honshu, Japan; third lgst. coalfield in Japan; ch. t. Fukushima.

Joda, Orissa, India; ferromanganese plant.

Jodhpur, t., Rajasthan, India; ctr. of Thar desert; old fortress t.; p. (1971) 317,612.

Jogjakarta, c., Java, Indonesia; univ., cultural ctr.; handicrafts; citadel with palace; p. (1971) 342,367.

Johannesburg, c., Transvaal, S. Africa; univ.; gold-mng. ctr. of Witwatersrand; diamond cutting, engin., textiles, chemicals; oil pipeline from Durban; p. (1970) 1,432,643 (met. a.).

John o'Groat's House, place nr. Duncansby Head, Caithness, Scot.

Johnstone, burgh, Renfrew, Scot.; on R. Black Cart, nr. Paisley; machine tools, textiles, iron and brass foundry; p. (1971) 22,617.

Johnstown, industl. t., Penns., USA; on Conemaugh R.; coal-mng. and steel ctr.; machin.; p. (1970) 42,065 (t.), 260,692 (met. a.).

Johore, st., Malaysia; at S. end of Malaya; forested; cap. Johor Baharo; rubber, rice, copra, pineapples; tin, iron, bauxite; a. 18,985 km²; p. (1967) 1,297,962.

Joina Falls, Mali; dam projected for hydroelectric power and irrigation under auspices of Organisation of Riparian States of R. Senegal (Guinea, Mali, Mauritania, Senegal).

Joinville, t., Santa Catarina, Brazil; exp. timber, maté tea; textiles, machin., car parts, plastics; p. (est. 1968) 88,647.

Joliet, c., Ill., USA; on Des Plaines R., S.W. of Chicago; R. pt.; coal and limestone nearby; rly. engin., oil refining; p (est. 1969) 77,000.

Joliette, t., Quebec, Canada; textile mills, paper, tobacco-processing; p. (1970) 78,887.

Jönköping, t., cap. of J. co., Sweden; safety-matches, textiles, footwear; p. (1968) 53,815.

Jonquière, t., S. Quebec, Canada; paper and pulp mills; p. (1971) 28,080.

Joplin, t., Mo., USA; in dairy and livestock region; lead and zinc mng.; mnfs. metal and leather gds.; p. (est. 1969) 38,500.

Jordan, kingdom, S.W. Asia; bounded by Israel, Syria, Saudi Arabia, and Iraq; consists of high plateau (600 m), Jordan valley, and hill cty. to W. of R. Jordan; only 25 per cent of a. sufficiently humid for agr., much is migratory herding of animals and subsistence agr.; sm. mineral wealth; only outlet to sea Aqaba, pt. on G. of Aqaba; only one single-track rly.; cap. Amman; W. Bank of R. Jordan occupied by Israeli forces since June 1967; plan mooted (1972) to unify J. and W. Bank to form United Arab Kingdom; a. 101,140 km²; p. (est. 1969) 2,250,000 (80 per cent Moslem and 70 per cent under 24).

Jordan, R., Israel and Jordan; flows S. from Anti-Lebanon along sinuous course, mostly below sea-level to Dead Sea; its rapidity and variant depth render it unnavigable, and no t. of any importance has ever been built on its banks; Jesus was baptised in its waters; contemporary strife over use for irrigation; 368 km long.

Jos, t., central Nigeria; on Bauchi Plateau, 96 km S.W. of Bauchi; impt. tin mines; p. (est. 1969) 104,838.

Jostedalsbre, icefield, W. Norway, lgst. icefield of European mainland; a. 881 km²; rises to 2,043 m.

Jotunheimen, mtn. region, central Norway; hgst. in Scandinavia; Galdhøpiggen 2,470 m, Glitter tind 2,482 m.

Juan Fernández, two rocky volcanic Is., S. Pac. Oc., belonging to Chile; a. 98 km²; the buccaneer Alexander Selkirk marooned here 1704–9 gave idea for Defoe's *Robinson Crusoe.*

Juan les Pins, resort, Alpes-Maritimes dep., S.E. France.

Juba (Giuba), R., Somalia; narrow fertile valley, impt. agr. a.; 872 km long.

Jubbulpore. *See* Jabalpur.

Júcar, R., E. Spain; rises in Montes Universales, and flows to Mediterranean; irrigation and hydroelec. power; 400 km long.

Judaea, div of Palestine in the Roman period.

Juggernaut. *See* Puri.

Jugoslavia. *See* Yugoslavia.

Juiz de Fora, t., Minas Gerais, Brazil; textile ctr.; p. (1970) 218,832.

Julfa (Jolfa), c., N. Iran; on frontier with USSR, customs and transit ctr. on overland route from Europe.

Julian Alps, mtn. range, Yugoslavia and Italy; hgst. peak 2,865 m.

Julianehåb, t., S.W. Greenland; N.W. of C. Farewell; tr. ctr., fish. pt.

Jülich, t., N. Rhine–Westphalia, W. Germany; nuclear reactor.

Jullundur, c., Punjab, India; rly. ctr.; st. cap. until Chandigarh was built; p. (1971) 296,106.

Jumna, R., N. India; ch. trib. of R. Ganges; rises in the Himalayas and flows past Delhi and Agra to Allahabad; 1,376 km long.

Junagadh, t., Gujarat, India; agr. tr. and foodprocessing; industl. ctr.; formerly cap. of principality of J.; p. (1961) 74,298.

Jundiaí, t., São Paulo st., Brazil; industl. ctr.; nr. São Paulo; p. (1970) 145,785.

Juneau, c., former cap. of Alaska, USA; at foot of Chilkoot mtns.; lumbering; fisheries; gold settlement (1881); p. (1970) 13,556. *See* Willow South.

Jungfrau, peak, Bernese Oberland, Switzerland; height 4,161 m; electric rly. from Kleine Scheidegg to Jungfraujoch.

Junín, t., Argentina; agr. tr., rly. engin., pottery, furniture; p. (1960) 53,489.

Jura, dep., E. France; named from mtn. range on Franco–Swiss border; agr. and pastoral; cap. Lons-le-Saunier; a. 5,053 km²; p. (1968) 233,547.

Jura, I., Argyll and Bute, Scot.; off W. cst.; a. 378 km²; p. (1971) 349 inc. Colonsay.

Jura, mtn. range, Switzerland and France; folded parallel ranges separated by deep R. valleys; hgst. peak Crêt de la Neige, 1,724 m; 240 km long, breadth 48–64 km.

Juruá R., lge. trib. of Amazon; rises in E. Peru and flows through Acre and Amazonas sts., Brazil; over 3,200 km long.

Jutland (Jylland), peninsula, Denmark; intensive agr. and poultry farming; sandy heath in W.; more fertile clay in E. used for dairying; a. 29,554 km²; p. (1971) 2,193,070.

Jyväskylä, t., central Finland; pt. on L. Päijänne; pulp, paper, plywood; univ.; p. (1968) 55,328.

K

K2. *See* Godwin-Austen, Mt.

Kabardin-Balkar ASSR, aut. rep., Transcaucasia, RSFSR; cap. Nalchik; livestock, lumber, wheat, fruit; non-ferrous metals; hydro-metallurgy plant; a. 12,432 km²; p. (1970) 589,000.

Kabelega Falls (Murchison Falls), on Victoria Nile, Uganda; falls between L. Kioga and L. Mobutu Seso.

Kabinda. *See* Cabinda.

Kābul, c., cap. of Afghanistan; on Kābul R. S. of Hindu Kush; 2,104 m a.s.l.; excellent climate; univ.; comm. and cultural ctr.;

textiles, leather, timber inds.; p. (est. 1971) 318,094 (c.), 498,821 (met. a.).

Kābul, R., flows from Hindu Kush through gorges in Khyber Pass to Indus; site of dam for hydroelec. power and irrigation; length c. 480 km.

Kabwe (Broken Hill), Zambia; comm. and mng. ctr.; lead, zinc, cadmium, silver; p. (est. 1966) 44,600.

Kachin State, semi-aut. st., Burma; comprising tormer Myitkyina and Bhamo dists.; home of Kachins; a. 89,042 km².

Kadiyevka, t., Ukrainian SSR, USSR; coal, iron and steel, synthetic rubber; p. (1970) 137,000.

Kaduna, t., N. Nigeria; cap of Kaduna st.; rly. junc.; aluminium wks.; spinning and weaving; p. (est. 1971) 181,201.

Kaffa, region, Ethiopia; mtnous., forested; natural habitat of coffee plant.

Kagoshima, c., at S. end of Kyushu I., Japan; pt. on K. Bay; univs., cas.; porcelain, silk and cotton clothing, food-processing, publishing; rocket launching site nearby at Uchinoura; p. (est. 1971) 412,000.

Kahoolawe, I., Hawaiian Is.; a. 117 km²; uninhabited.

Kaieteur Falls, waterfall, Guyana; where R. Potaro leaves Guiana Highlands; among world's hgst falls (226 m).

K'ai-feng, c., Honan, China; nr. S. bank of Hwangho; one of the most anc. cities in China; cottons, chemicals; p. (est. 1970) 330,000.

Kai Islands, Is., Indonesia; between New Guinea and Timor; timber; a. 1,761 km²; p. 51,000.

Kaikoura, t., S.I., N.Z.; on E. cst., 128 km N.E. of Christchurch; in this region are the Kaikoura ranges, in which the hgst. peaks are Tapuaenuku (2,887 m) and Alarm (2,867 m); p. (1971) 1,607.

Kailas (Kang-ti-ssu Shan), range and peak, S.W. Tibet. China; unclimbed sacred mtn.; source of Indus. Ganges. Sutlej and Tsangpo (headstream of Brahmaputra).

Kainji Dam, Nigeria; power sta. transmission system and river transportation on R. Niger.

K'ai-ping, t., Hopeh, N. China; second lgst. coalmng. a. (Kailan mines) in China; coal exported through Chinwangtao.

Kairouan, holy c. of Moslems, Tunisia; 128 km S.S.E. of Tunis; founded A.D. 670; mosque; p. (1966) 82,299.

Kaiserslautern, c., Rhineland–Palatinate, W. Germany; nr. Mannheim; iron, textiles, machin., tobacco, wood; p. (est. 1969) 84,900 (c.), 107,000 (met. a.).

Kaiser Wilhelm's Land, Australian dependency, Antarctica.

Kakamega, t., Kenya; E. Africa; 48 km N. of Kisumu; ctr. of gold-mng. dist.

Kakinada, t., spt., Andhra Pradesh, India; cotton, oilseeds; p. (1971) 164,200.

Kalahari Desert, region of semi-desert, southern Africa; between Orange and Zambesi Rs.; mainly in Botswana; alt. 1,128 m; a. 51,800 km²; inhabited chiefly by Bushmen.

Kalamata, t., Peloponnesus, Greece; nr. Sparta; figs, currants, flour-milling. cigarette mftg.; p. (1971) 39,346.

Kalamazoo, c., Mich., USA; industl. and comm. ctr. in farming a.; paper, pharmaceuticals; fish hatchery nearby; p. (1970) 84,444 (c.), 199,287 (met. a.).

Kalemie (Albertville), t., Zaïre; on L. Tanganyika; rail-steamer transfer point; p. (est. 1967) 86,687.

Kalewa, t., Burma; at confluence of Irrawaddy and Chindwin Rs.; coal deposits.

Kalgan (Chang-chia-k'ou), c., Hopeh, China; nr. Great Wall, 160 km N.W. of Peking; on main route to Mongolia; tea, wool, hides; p. (est. 1970) 1,000,000.

Kalgoorlie, t., W. Australia; on transcontinental rly. route 560 km E. of Perth; semi-desert conditions; nickel, gold-mng. a.; p. (1972) 20,784 (inc. Boulder).

Kalimantan (Indonesian Borneo); straddles equator; sparse p.; poor soils; lge. areas of swamp; plans for reclamation; coal, oil, diamonds, gold in sm. quantities; rice, pepper, copra; a 539,461 km²; p. est. (1970) 626,000.

Kalinin (Tver), c., RSFSR; on upper Volga; diversified inds.; 17th cent. cath. and cas.; p. (1970) 345,000.

Kaliningrad (Königsberg), c., RSFSR; former cap. of E. Prussia; on R. Pregel, linked by canal to outer pt. Pillau; univ., cath.; shipbldg., machin., wood-pulp, chemicals, exp. agr. prods.; Kant lived here all his life; p. (1970) 297,000.

Kalisz, t., Poznan, Poland; on R. Prosna; industl. ctr., textiles; oldest Polish t.. mentioned in 2nd cent. A.D. by Ptolemy; p. (1970) 81,200.

Kalmar, t., spt., S. Sweden; on I. in Kalmar Sound; cath., cas.; matches, food inds., shipbldg.; p. (1968) 37,965.

Kalmuk (Kalmytskaya) ASSR, aut. rep., RSFSR; on Caspian Sea; harsh and infertile steppe; pastoral agr.; cap. Elista; a. 75,887 km²; p. (1970) 268,000.

Kalna, v., on Mt. Stara Planina, Yugoslavia; uranium mine and plant; nuclear power sta.

Kaluga, c., RSFSR; pt. on Oka R.; chemicals, engin., hydroelec. power plant; p. (1970) 211,000.

Kalyan, spt., Maharashtra, India; nr. Bombay; bricks, tiles; p. (1971) 168,462.

Kalymnos, I., Dodecanese, Greece; mtnous.; a. 106 km²; p. 13,600.

Kama, R., RSFSR; ch. trib. of Volga which it joins below Kazan; rises in foothills of Urals; lge. hydroelectric sta. at Perm; navigable; 2,016 km long.

Kamaishi, t., spt., N.E. Honshu, Japan; serves Kamaishi-Sennin iron-ore field, lgst. worked deposits and reserves in Japan; impt. iron and steel ind.; p. (1970) 72,923.

Kamakura, t., Honshu, Japan; on shore of Sagami Bay; tourism; p. (est. 1971) 147,000.

Kamaran I., Red Sea; Democratic Rep. of Yemen; formerly under Brit. occupation, 1915-67; a. 57 km²; p. 2,200.

Kamchatka, peninsula, E. Siberia, USSR; volcanic ranges; geothermal power sta.; mineral wealth, fisheries on cst., climate cold, wet and foggy; contains part of Koryak nat. okrug; cap. Petropavlovsk.

Kamenets-Podolskiy, t., Ukrainian SSR, USSR; on Smotrich R.; lt. inds.; mediaeval fortress t.; p. (est. 1967) 52,000.

Kamensk-Shakhtinskiy, c., RSFSR; on Donets R.; coal-mng. ctr., engin., food processing, artificial fibres; p. (est. 1967) 71,000.

Kamensk-Uralsk, c., RSFSR; aluminium, iron, steel, engin.; p. (1970) 169,000.

Kamet, Himalayan peak, on border of India and Tibet, China, 7,761 m; highest mtn. climbed (Smythe, 1931) until 1953 (Everest).

Kamloops, t., B.C., Canada; on Thompson R.; formerly Fort Thompson; on transcontinental rlys.; supply ctr. for mng. and grazing dist.; fruit and livestock mkts.; p. (1971) 25,599.

Kampala, c., cap. of Uganda; univ., ch. comm. ctr.; lt. inds., coffee-processing; p. (1969) 331,889.

Kampen, t., Overijssel, Neth.; on R. IJssel; cigar-mkg.; p. (1968) 29,041.

Kampot, t., Cambodia., spt on G. of Siam; ctr. of pepper ind.; p (1962) 12,949.

Kamyshin, t., RSFSR; spt. on Volga; textiles, mkt. gardening, grain; p. (est. 1967) 77,000.

Kan, R., S. China; rises in Nanling Shan, flows N. into L. Poyang; valley provides route for main road from Kiangsi prov. to Kwangtung prov. over Meiling Pass; c. 880 km long.

Kananga (Luluabourg), c., cap. of Kasai Occidental prov., Zaïre; on Lulua R.; comm. and communications ctr. in cotton-growing a.; p. (est. 1972) 506,033 (met. a.).

Kanawha, R., W. Va., USA; rises in Allegheny mtns., flows into R. Ohio; runs through ch. mng. a. of W. Va. coalfield nr. Charleston.

Kanazawa, c., Honshu, Japan; in Kaga plain, on Sea of Japan; machin., silk and cotton textiles; landscape gardens, No theatre; p. (est. 1971) 366,000.

Kanchenjunga, mtn., on Nepal-Sikkim bdy., N.E. India; third hgst. mtn. in world, 8,585 m.

Kanchipuram (Conjeeveram) t., Tamil Nadu, S. India; on plain S.W. of Madras; pilgrimage ctr.; textiles; p. (1971) 110,657 (t.), 119,693 (met. a.).

Kandahar, c., former cap. of Afghanistan; alt. 1,037 m; 592 km from Herāt; linked by road to Kushka (Turkmen SSR) via Herat; fruit preserving and canning; textiles; p. (est. 1971) 133,799.

Kandy, c., Sri Lanka; in mtns. in ctr.of I.; 120 km from Colombo; univ. at sub. of Peradeniya; resort in hot season; tea, cocoa; p. (est. 1968) 78,000.

Kangaroo, I., S. Australia; eucalyptus; gypsum; summer resorts; p. (1966) 3,380.

Kano, c., N. Nigeria; emporium for whole of Sudan region; impt. airport and rly. terminus; groundnut ctr.; p. (est. 1971) 357,098.

Kanpur (Cawnpore), c., Uttar Pradesh, N. India; on R. Ganges; impt. mftg. ctr.; textiles, chemicals, leather goods, foodstuffs; p. (1971) 1,154,388 (c.), 1,275,242 (met. a.).

Kansas, st., USA; called the "sunflower state"; prairie; farming, maize, wheat; cattle, dairying, pigs; coal, petroleum, natural gas, lead, meat packing, flour milling, aircraft, chemicals, machin.; cap. Topeka; a. 213,095 km²; p. (1970) 2,222,173.

Kansas, R., Kan., USA; trib. of Missouri R., confluence at Kansas City; vegetable growing in valley; periodic flooding; 272 km long.

Kansas City, Mo., USA; at confluence of Kansas and Missouri Rs.; univ.; gr. livestock mart, car and aircraft assembly, steel prods., meat-packing, food processing; p. (1970) 495,405; adjoins Kansas City, Kansas; p. (est. 1969) 172,000; 1,240,575 (joint met. a.).

Kansu (Gansu), prov., N.W. China; borders Inner Mongolia; cap. Lanchow; pastoral agr., wheat, cotton, tobacco; coal reserves; rich iron-ore deposits; a. 391,507 km²; p. (est. 1968) 13,000,000.

Kant, t., Kirghiz SSR, USSR; 19 km E. of Frunze; to be expanded to industl. c.; proposed p. 100,000.

Kanye, t., Botswana, S. Africa; lgst. t. in rep.; p. (est. 1969) 34,045.

Kaohsiung, spt., Taiwan; on S.W. cst.; industl. ctr., road and rly. terminus; oil refining, aluminium wks.; p. (est. 1970) 828,191.

Kaolack, inland pt., Senegal; 112 km up Saloum R.; groundnut ctr.; p. (est. 1969) 95,000.

Kaposvár, t., S.W. Hungary; on Kapos R.; comm. ctr.; textiles, foodstuffs; p. (1968) 50,000.

Kara-Bogaz-Gol, lge shallow bay, Turkmen SSR, USSR; an arm of Caspian Sea; rapid evaporation allows huge quantities of salt from Caspian to be deposited along its shores (world's lgst. source of Glauber's salt); a. 18,130 km².

Karabuk, t., Turkey; N. of Ankara; steel wks.; p. (1965) 47,660.

Karacheyevo-Cherkesskaya, aut. region, RSFSR; in Greater Caucasus; cap. Cherkessk; livestock, grain; coal, lead, zinc; a. 14,095 km²; p. (1970) 345,000.

Karachi, c., Pakistan; on Arabian Sea, nr. Indus delta; former cap. of Pakistan; univ.; spt., air ctr.; oil refining, industl. gases, steel mill, natural gas from Sui; nuclear power sta.; p. (1972) 3,469,000.

Karaganda, c., Kazakh SSR, USSR; on impt. coalfield developed since 1926; supplies industl. ctrs. of Urals; iron and steel wks., power sta.; p. (1970) 522,000.

Kara-Kalpak ASSR, aut. rep., N.W. Uzbek SSR, USSR; inc. Ust-Urt plateau, Kyzyl-Kum desert; irrigated agr.; cap. Nukus; a. 165,553 km²; p. (1970) 702,000.

Karakorum Range, part of Himalayas between Kashmir and China; many lofty peaks, inc. Mt. Godwin-Austen; Karakorum highway, linking Pakistan with Sinkiang prov. of China, opened 1971.

Kara-Kum, sand desert, Turkmen SSR, USSR; E. of S.E. shore of Caspian Sea; a. 349,650 km²; canal 1,440 km long across desert recently built.

Karamai (K'o-la-ma-i), t., Sinkiang, China; ctr. of lge. oilfield; pipeline to Fushantzu refinery.

Kara Sea, Arctic Oc.; E. of Novaya Zemlya; navigation to and from Siberian pts. July-Sept.

Karbala, c., Iraq; N.W. of Al Hillah; ctr. of pilgrimage; sacred c. of Moslem Shiite sect; p. (1965) 247,000 (met. a.).

Karelian ASSR, aut. rep., RSFSR; between Kola peninsula and Finland; lake-covered, coniferous forests; cap. Petrozavodsk; rich in timber, minerals, precious metals; granite and mica quarried; paper and pulp milling; a. 179,408 km²; p. (1970) 714,000.

Karelian Isthmus, RSFSR; strategic route

between Finland and USSR impt. for defence of Leningrad.

Kariba Dam, in Kariba gorge of Zambezi R., on Rhodesia–Zambia border; operated jointly by the two govts.; one of lgst. dams in world with vast artificial lake supplying hydroelectric power to Rhodesia, Malawi, and the copperbelt of Zambia; involved resettlement of Batonka peoples; completed 1960; since Rhodesian U.D.I., construction has begun on a second generating sta. on the Zambian side.

Karikal, former Fr. settlement on E. cst. of India; p. (1961) 22,252.

Karkonosze. See Riesengebirge.

Karl-Marx-Stadt (Chemnitz), c., Karl-Marx-Stadt dist., E. Germany; leading industl. ctr.; cotton, woollens, machin., cars, furniture, chemicals, engin.; nr. lignite mines; p. (est. 1969) 297,133.

Karlovac, t., Croatia, Yugoslavia; S.W. of Zagreb; chemicals, textiles, food processing; p. (est. 1965) 38,000.

Karlový Vary (Carlsbad), t., Bohemia, ČSSR; on R. Ohře; hot mineral springs; health resort; porcelain; p. (1967) 46,000.

Karlskoga, t., Sweden; E. of L. Vänern; seat of Bofors armament wks.; iron and steel, explosives, chemicals; p. (1968) 38,203.

Karlskrona, spt., S. Sweden; on Baltic Sea; main naval sta.; lighting fixtures, china; p. (1968) 37,249.

Karlsruhe, c., Baden-Württemberg, W. Germany; road and rly. ctr.; outport on Rhine; chemicals, engin., elec., tobacco inds., oil refining; nuclear reactor; oil pipeline to Lavera, nr. Marseilles; p. (est. 1969) 256,200.

Karlstad, t., Sweden; on N. shore L. Vänern; ironwks., engin., machin.; p. (1968) 53,208.

Karnak, t., Egypt; on Nile, E. of Luxor; site of the anc. Thebes; ruined temples; p. c. 11,000.

Karnal, t., Haryana, India; clothing inds.; p. (1961) 72,109.

Karnataka (Mysore), st., S.W. India; borders Arabian Oc.; inc. W. Ghats where high rainfall and hydroelec. power; rainfall decreases to E.; cap. Bangalore; a. 192,203 km²; p. (1971) 29,263,334.

Karpathos, I., Dodecanese, Greece; Aegean Sea; between Rhodes and Crete; p. 8,747.

Karroo, W. Cape Prov., S. Africa; high plateau, scrub-covered; irrigated by Verwoerd dam on Orange R.

Kars, t., N.E. Turkey; in Armenia, alt. c. 1,800 m, in strategic position nr. Soviet border; p. (1965) 41,200.

Karst, dist., Yugoslavia; in Dinaric Alps; gives name to limestone landforms which are well developed here.

Karun, R., S.W. Iran; mainly mtn. torrent; difficult access, sparse p.; 752 km long.

Karvina, t., ČSSR; on Polish border; ctr. of Ostrava-Karvina coalfield; p. (1967) 73,000.

Kasai, R., Angola and Zaïre, Central Africa; rises in Bihé Plateau (Angola) and flows over 1,920 km into R. Zaïre 192 km above Kinshasa; alluvial diamond mng. at Chicopa.

Kasai, former prov., Zaïre; agr.; impt. source of industl. diamonds; attempted secession 1960; now divided into E. Kasai (cap. Mbuji-Mayi), and W. Kasai (cap. Luluabourg).

Kāshān, c., central Iran; in agr. oasis; carpets, velvet; p. (1967) 58,500 (c.), 153,980 (dist.).

Kashgar (K'a-shih), c., W. Sinkiang prov., China; on anc. imperial silk route through central Asia; growth rapid with irrigation; visited by Marco Polo 1275; p. (est. 1970) 175,000.

Kashmir. See Jammu and Kashmir.

Kassala, t., N.E. Sudan; ctr. of cotton-growing dist.; p. (est. 1966) 68,100.

Kassel, c., Hesse, W. Germany; on R. Fulda; cas.; machin., vehicles, science-based inds.; route ctr.; p. (est. 1969) 213,100.

Kastamonu, t., N. Turkey; cap. of K. prov.; ctr. of dist. rich in minerals; textiles, copper gds.; p. (1965) 23,485.

Katanga. See Shaba.

Kathiawar, peninsula, Gujarat, India; between G. of Kutch and G. of Cambay; ch. pt. Bhaunagar; very dry a.

Katmai, Mount, S. Alaska, USA; active volcano with crater L.; alt. 2,135 m.

Katmandu (Kathmandu), cap. of Nepal; on Vishnumati R., 120 km from Indian frontier; highway to Kodari; hydroelec. sta.; brick and tile

wks.; many palaces and temples; p. (1971) 153,405.

Katoomba, t., N.S.W., Australia; holiday resort; alt. 1,006 m; p. (1972) 11,573 inc. Wentworth Falls.

Katowice, prov., S. Poland; in Upper Silesia; cap. K.; mng. and industl. a. drained by Warta R.; a. 9,516 km²; p. (1970) 3,691,000.

Katowice, c., S. Poland; cap. of K. prov.; impt. iron-mng. and industl. ctr.; heavy machin., chemicals; p. (1970) 303,000 (c.) (est. 1966) 2,010,000 (met. a.).

Katrine, Loch, S.W. Stirling, Scot.; beautiful woodland and moorland scenery; source of Glasgow water supply; scene of Scott's *Lady of the Lake*; 13 km long, c. 1·6 km wide.

Katsina, t., Nigeria; nr. Niger border; agr. tr. ctr., groundnuts, cotton; rural craft inds.; Hausa cultural ctr.; p. (est. 1971) 109,424.

Kattegat, arm of N. Sea linked with Baltic; separates Denmark (Jutland) from Sweden; 64–112 km wide.

Katwijk, t., S. Holland, Neth.; on N. Sea 24 km from the Hague; resort; synthetic resins; p. (1968) 34,730.

Kaufbeuren, t., Bavaria, W. Germany; on R. Wertach; textile mnfs.; p. (est. 1969) 39,542.

Kaunas (Kovno), c., Lithuanian SSR, USSR; on R. Nemen; R. pt. and comm. ctr.; univ.; 11th cent. c.; metal gds., chemicals, textiles, hydroelec. power; Jewish p. (circa 30 per cent) exterminated during German occupation 1941–4; p. (1970) 309,000.

Kavalla, c., E. Macedonia, Greece; on Bay of Kavalla; processes and exp. tobacco; the anc. Neapolis; nearby peat deposits; p. (1971) 46,679.

Kawagoe, c., Honshu, Japan; in Kanto plain; silk textiles; p. (est. 1971) 179,000.

Kawasaki, S. sub. Tokyo, Honshu, Japan; pt. for import of industl. raw materials; heavy inds.; p. (est. 1971) 963,000.

Kawthoolei State, st., Burma; former Karen st., extended to inc. areas in Tenasserim and Irrawaddy; a. 30,383 km².

Kayah State, semi-aut. st., Burma; on Thai border; forested plateau; tungsten mines; teak; a. 11,730 km².

Kayseri, c., Turkey; S.E. of Ankara; textiles, carpets, food tr.; anc. Hittite c.; p. (1965) 126,653 (c.); 222,699 (met. a.).

Kazakh SSR (Kazakhstan), constituent rep., USSR; in central Asia; cap. Alma-Ata; steppe with stock-raising; lge. desert areas being made fertile by irrigation; grain in N.; coal at Karaganda; asbestos at Dzhetygara; minerals inc. metaborite (richest boron mineral); oil; atomic power sta. to W. of Caspian Sea; cosmodrome at Leninsk, E. of Aral Sea; a. 2,778,544 km²; p. (1970) 12,850,000.

Kazan', c., RSFSR; cap. of Tatar ASSR; pt. on Volga; impt. tr. ctr. for E. USSR, Turkestan Bokhara and Iran; cath., univ. (where Tolstoy and Lenin were educated); engin., chemicals, synthetic rubber, textiles, paper, oil refining; natural gas pipeline to Minnibayevo; p. (1970) 869,000.

Kazanluk, t., central Bulgaria; in region famous for attar of roses; p. (est. 1968) 48,816.

Kazan-retto or **Volcanic Is.**, gr. of Is., W. Pac. Oc. S. of Tokyo; sugar plantations, sulphur; returned to Japan by USA 1968.

Kazbek, extinct volcano, N. Georgian SSR, USSR; second hgst. peak of Caucasus; alt. 5,045 m.

Kāzerūn, t., S.W. Iran; ctr. of agr. dist. where fruit, tobacco, opium, cotton grown; p. (1966) 39,758.

Kazvin or **Qazvin**, c., N.W. Iran; transit tr.; carpets, textiles; p. (1966) 88,106.

Kearsley, t., Gtr. Manchester, Eng.; chemicals, paper; p. (1971) 11,243.

Keban Dam, S.E. Turkey; at confluence of the E. and W. branches of Euphrates.

Kecskemet, c., central Hungary; fruit-canning and wine-distilling from locally grown prods.; 4th cent. c.; p. (1966) 74,400.

Kedah, st., Malaysia; on Strait of Malacca, N.W. Malaya; rice, rubber, coconuts, tungsten; cap. cap. Alor Star; a. 9,479 km²; p. (1967) 925,105.

Kediri, t., E. Java, Indonesia; food processing; p. (1971) 178,865.

Keeling Is. See Cocos Is.

Keelung (Chi-lung), c., N. Taiwan; on E. China

Sea; naval base and ch. pt.; exp. agr. prods.; chemicals; gold, sulphur, copper mined nearby; p. (est. 1970) 324,040.

Keewatin, dist., N.W. Terr., Canada; barren grounds; fur-trapping; a. 590,934 km².

Keighley, t. West Yorks., Eng.; in Aire valley, 24 km N.W. of Leeds; engin., woollen and worsteds; p. (1971) 55,263.

Keihin, vast conurb. of Tokyo, Yokohama and Kawasaki, Japan; p. (1971) 14,650,000.

Keith, burgh, Moray, Scot.; mkt. t. in agr. dist.; p. (1971) 4,177.

Kelantan, st., Malaysia; one of most fertile areas on E. cst. Malaya; cap Kota Bharu; rice, coconuts, rubber; a. 14,815 km²; p. (1967) 677,205.

Kells or Ceannanus Mor, mkt. t., Co. Meath, R.o.I.; notable for monastic remains and illuminated Book of Kells, now in library of Trinity College, Dublin; p. (1966) 2,274.

Kelso, burgh, Roxburgh, Scot.; at confluence of Rs. Teviot and Tweed; p. (1971) 4,852.

Kemerovo, c., RSFSR; S.E. of Tomsk; coalmng. ctr.; chemicals, textiles, plastics; p. (1970) 385,000 (c), 417,000 (met. a.).

Kemi, t., N.E. Finland; spt. on G. of Bothnia; sawmills; p. (1968) 30,259.

Kemi, R., N.E. Finland; used for hydroelectric power and timber transport; 480 km long.

Kempten, t., Bavaria, W. Germany; nr. Bodensee; Benedictine abbey; p. (est. 1969) 44,057.

Kendal, l. gov. dist., Cumbria, Eng.; mkt. ctr.; tourism; p. (1971) 21,572.

Kenilworth, t., Warwicks., Eng.; 6 km S.W. of Coventry; mkt.; ruined cas.; p. (1971) 20,121.

Kennet, l. gov. dist., Wiltshire, Eng.; stretches from Marlborough to Devizes; p. (est. 1976) 67,900.

Kennet, R., Wilts. and Berks., Eng.; trib. of R. Thames; followed by main rly. London to W. of Eng.; 70 km long.

Kennington, dist., in London bor. of Lambeth, Eng.; inc. the Oval cricket ground, home of Surrey C.C.

Kenosha, t., Wis., USA; on W. shore of L. Mich.; p. (1970) 78,063 (c.), 116,734 (met. a.).

Kensington and Chelsea, Royal Borough of, inner bor., W. London, Eng.; mainly residtl.; contains Kensington Palace and Gardens; p. (est. 1976) 161,400.

Kent, non-met. co., Eng.; intensive agr. mkt. gardening, orchards, hops; "Garden of England"; crossed by N. Downs and Weald; industl. zone bordering Thames and Medway estuaries; tourist resorts and cross-channel ferry pts. on cst.; London commuter hinterland; co. t. Maidstone; a. 3,730 km²; p. (est. 1976) 1,448,100.

Kentucky, E. central st., USA; in W. foothills of Appalachians and crossed by tribs. of Mississippi; "Bluegrass" st.; mainly agr.; some coal; cap. Frankfort; lgst. c. Louisville, at falls of Ohio R.; hydroelec. power; tourism; a. 104,623 km²; p. (1970) 3,160,555.

Kentucky, R., Ky., USA; flows from Cumberland plateau to Ohio R.; length 400 km.

Kenya, rep., E. Africa; member of Brit. Commonwealth; comprises 7 provs.; straddles equator but climate modified by alt.; marked contrast between sparsely populated and arid N. and well-developed S. where S.W. upland climate has attracted the European p.; economy based on prod. and processing of arable and pastoral prods., inc. dairy prod.; relatively well developed cooperative African farming; ch. spt. Mombasa, airports at Nairobi and Mombasa; famous for big game; univ.; cap. Nairobi; a. 582,646 km²; p. (1969) 10,890,000.

Kenya, Mt., volcano, Kenya; just S. of equator; snow-covered; alt. 5,197 m; 2nd hgst. peak in Africa; Nat. Park.

Kephallenia. See Cephalonia.

Kerala, st., India; cap. Trivandrum; plantations producing rubber, tea, pepper; higher proportion of literacy than in any other st.,; a. 38,855 km²,; p. (1961) 16,903,715.

Kerch, c., Ukrainian SSR, USSR; in Crimea, commanding K. strait connecting Black Sea and Azov Sea; spt. and industl. ctr.; metallurgical plant, iron and steel mills, shipbldg., fisheries; iron-ore, vanadium, natural gas nearby; p. (1970) 128,000.

Kerguelen, archipelago, S. Indian Oc.; part of Fr. Antarctic terr.; whaling, fishing; famous

for K. cabbage (Pringlea antiscorbutica) discovered by Cook.

Kerkrade, t., Limburg prov., Neth.; coal mng.; anc. abbey; p. (1968) 50,206.

Kérkira. See Corfu.

Kermadec Is., volcanic gr. Pac. Oc.; 960 km N.E. of N.Z.; a. 34 km²; met. sta. on Sunday I. (lgst of gr.); annexed to N.Z. 1887; p. (1961) 10.

Kerman, region, S.E. Iran; mtnous., much desert land; agr.; carpet-weaving; coal and iron-ore mng. being developed; recent copper find; irrigation scheme projected; p. (1967) 243,770.

Kermän, c., S.E. Iran; prov. cap.; carpet-weaving ctr.; textile mftg.; airpt.; mediaeval mosques; p. (est. 1971) 100,000.

Kermänshäh, t., N.W. Iran; cap. of Kermänshähän prov.; agr., comm. and route ctr.; airpt.; oil refinery; p. (est. 1971) 229,800.

Kern, R., E. Cal., USA; one of most impt. power-generating Rs. in st.

Kerrier, l. gov. dist., Cornwall, Eng.; a. inc. Lizard penin. and Helston; p. (est. 1976) 80,900.

Kerry, coastal co., Munster, R.o.I.; deeply indented cst.; cap. Tralee; tourism; a. 4,703 km²; p. (1966) 112,642.

Kerulen, R., N.E. Mongolia and China; flows parallel to edge of Gobi Desert; a. designated for economic development; 1,256 km long.

Kesteven, North, l. gov. dist., Lincs., Eng.; rural a. based on Sleaford; p. (est. 1976) 77,200.

Kesteven, South, l. gov. dist., Lincs., Eng.; rural a. and ts. of Grantham and Bourne; p. (est. 1976) 89,000.

Keswick, Allerdale, Cumbria, Eng.; on Greta R.; at N. end of L. Derwentwater; tourist ctr.; mkt.; pencils; p. (1971) 5,169.

Kettering, l. gov. dist., mkt. t., Northants., Eng.; nr. Wellingborough; footwear; iron mng.; p. (est. 1976) 70,500 (dist.).

Kew, dist., London bor. of Richmond-upon-Thames, Eng.; contains Kew botanical gardens.

Keweenaw, peninsula, L. Superior, USA; former impt. copper deposits.

Keynsham, t., Wansdyke, Avon, Eng.; expanded t.; p. (1971) 19,007.

Key West, c., Fla., USA; on I. c. 240 km from mainland; naval sta., coastguard base; cigar-mftg.; nearest US pt. to Panama canal; tourism; p. (est. 1969) 39,500.

Khabarovsk, c., RSFSR; cap. of K. terr., E. Siberia, on Amur R.; cath.; oil refining, aircraft engin., wood and paper inds.; pipeline links with oilfields in N. Sakhalin; transport ctr. of Far East; p. (1970) 437,000.

Khairpur, t., Pakistan; nr. Sukkur barrage; textiles; p. (1961) 34,144.

Khakass Autonomous Oblast, admin. div. of Krasnoyarsk region, RSFSR; pastoral agr., timber and mng. inds.; a. 61,784 km²; p. (1970) 446,000.

Khandwa, t., Madhya Pradesh, India; S. of Indore; cotton, oil-pressing; p. (1961) 63,505.

Khaniá, or Canea, c., cap. of Crete, Greece; in sheltered bay on W. cst.; historic sites; p. (1971) 40,452.

Khanka, L., China–USSR border; dairy farming, fishing; branch of Trans-Siberian rly. to W. shore; a. 4,403 km².

Khanty-Mansi, admin. div., RSFSR; in W. Siberian lowland; sparse p.; cap. Khanty-Mansiisk (at confluence of Ob' and Irtysh Rs.); natural gas; a. 556,850 km²; p. (1970) 272,000.

Kharagpur, c., W. Bengal, India; industl., scientific research ctr.; rly. junc.; p. (1971) 161,911.

Khärk, I., Persian Gulf, Iran; oil terminal for super-tankers, 48 km from mainland.

Khar'kov, c., Ukrainian SSR, USSR; impt. industl. ctr. in Donets coal region; cap. of K. region; univ., cath.; rly. ctr.; extensively rebuilt after second world war; p. (1970) 1,223,000.

Khartoum, c., cap. of the Sudan; at confluence of Blue and White Niles; univ.; famous siege under Gordon 1884–5; p. (est. 1971) 261,840.

Khashm el Girba, t., Sudan; new t. on Atbara R., between Khartoum and Ethiopian border; for p. of Wadi Halfa inundated by Aswan L.; sugar refinery.

Khasi Hills, Meghalaya, N.E. India; form abrupt S. edge to middle Brahmaputra valley; very heavy monsoon rains on S.-facing slopes; lower slopes forested; middle slopes impt. tea-growing region; rise to over 1,800 m.

Khaskovo, t., Bulgaria; woollens, carpets, tobacco; p. (est. 1968) 63,840.

Kherson, c., Ukrainian SSR, USSR; 24 km up R. Dnieper from Black Sea; sea and R. pt., rly. junc.; grain, oil refining, engin., textiles, shipbldg ; founded by Catherine the Great as fortress t.; p. (1970) 261,000.

Khingan, Gr. and **Little, mtn.** ranges, Inner Mongolia and Heilungkiang prov., N.E. China; rich timber resources; rise to over 1,800 m.

Khios or **Chios, I., Greece;** in Aegean Sea; wines, figs, fruits; marble; cap. Khios; supposed birthplace of Homer; p. (1972) 53,942.

Khiva, former vassal st. of Russia; now part of Uzbek SSR and Turkmen SSR, USSR.

Khiva, c., N.W. Uzbek SSR, USSR; in oasis nr. Kara-Kum desert; cottons, carpets; anc. c.; p. (est. 1967) 22,000.

Khmel'nitskiy (Proskurov), c., Ukrainian SSR, USSR; on R. Bug; machin. tools, textiles, food inds.; p. (1970) 113,000.

Khmer Republic. See Cambodia, Democratic.

Khor Abdulla, Iraq; in Persian G. nr. Basra; deepwater oil-loading island terminal (1963).

Khorāsan or **Khurasan, prov., N.E. Iran;** bounded by USSR and Afghanistan; sparsely p.; agr.; wool; turquoises; cap. Mashhad; p. (1967) 2,494,283.

Khorramshahr, spt., S.W. Iran, leading pt. on Persian G.; increased in importance in second world war when harbour facilities expanded; handles major part of foreign trade; main exp. dates; linked by pipeline to oilfields and by road and rail to Ahvāz and Tehran; p. (1967) 150,322 (met. a.).

Khotan (Ho-t'ien), c., S.W. Sinkiang prov., China; in fertile K. oasis at base of Kunlun mtns.; silk, carpets, jade-ware; on anc. Silk Road; early ctr. of Buddhism; visited by Marco Polo 1274; p. 50,000.

Khovu-Aksy, t., Tuva ASSR, RSFSR; on R. Elegest, 80 km S.W. of Kyzyl; new t. 1956; cobalt deposit being developed.

Khulna, c., Bangladesh; in low-lying a. in W. Ganges delta; p. (1974) 436,000.

Khuzestan, prov., W. Iran; frontier Iraq; leading petroleum ctr.; lge. dams; cap. Ahvāz; p. (1967) 1,614,576.

Khyber Pass, pass in Hindu Kush mtns., between Pakistan and Afghanistan; followed by route from Peshawar to Kabul; historically most famous route into India, used by many invaders, inc. Alexander the Great.

Kiamusze (Chia-mu-ssu), c., Heilungkiang prov., China; ch. pt. on lower Sungari R.; p. (est. 1970) 275,000.

Kianga-Moura, dist., Queensland, Australia; lge coalfield; coking coal exp. to Japan via Gladstone.

Kiangsi (Jiangxi), prov., S.E. China; in basin of navigable Kan R., which drains through Poyang L. to Yangtze R.; ch. cs. Shanghai, Chingkiang, Wusih, Nanchang (cap.); rice, wheat, tea, cotton; tungsten, coking coal, kaolin; a. 172,494 km²; p. (est. 1968) 22,000,000.

Kiangsu (Jiangsu), coastal prov., China; on Yellow Sea; low-lying a. N. of Yangtze delta; rich agr., densely p.; cotton, sericulture, tea, sugar, fish (many Ls.); cap. Nanking; a. 109,000 km²; p. (est. 1968) 47,000,000.

Kicking Horse Pass, mtn. pass (1,628 m), over Rocky Mtns., B.C., Canada; used by Canadian Pac. rly.

Kidderminster, t., Wyre Forest, Hereford and Worcs., Eng.; on R. Stour 6 km above its confluence with R. Severn; carpets, engin., sugarbeet refining, textile machin., elec. vehicles, drop forgings; p. (1971) 47,255.

Kidsgrove, t., "Potteries," Staff., Eng.; 5 km N.W. of Stoke-on-Trent; chemicals, metal wks., rayon, silk and nylon spinning, precast concrete, ceramics; p. (1971) 22,036.

Kidwelly, Dyfed, Wales; mkt. t.; sm. harbour; cas.; p. (1971) 3,076.

Kiel, spt., cap. of Schleswig-Holstein, W. Germany; univ.; Baltic naval pt.; shipbldg. and allied inds., elec. gds., textiles, fishing; p. (est. 1969) 269,200.

Kiel Canal (North Sea-Baltic Canal or **Kaiser-Wilhelm-Kanal) W. Germany;** connects Elbe estuary on North Sea with Baltic; 98 km long; opened 1895, reconstructed 1914; internationalised 1919 by Treaty of Versailles, but repudiated by Hitler 1936.

Kielce, c., central Poland; cap. of K. prov.; in Swietokrzyskie mtns.; cath., route ctr.; agr. machin., chemicals; minerals quarried in prov.; founded 12th cent.; p. (1970) 126,000.

Kiev (Kiyev), c.. cap. of Ukrainian SSR, USSR; on R. Dnieper; leading cultural, industl. and comm. ctr.; cath., univ.; machin., textiles; in a. of rich mineral deposits; natural gas pipeline runs from Dashava; historic c., once cap. of Muscovite empire; p. (1976) 1,974,000.

Kigali, cap. of Rwanda; comm. ctr.; airport; p. (est. 1970) 60,000 (met. a.).

Kigoma, t., W. Tanzania; pt. on E. shore of L. Tanganyika; W. terminus of Central rly. to Dar-es-Salaam; p. (est. 1967) 21,639.

Kii, peninsula, Japan; highland area and inlet of same name, S. Honshu.

Kikinda, t., Vojvodina, Yugoslavia; agr. tr.; rly. junc.; p. (est. 1965) 33,000.

Kilauea, crater, 1,112 m high, on S.E. slope of Mauna Loa, Hawaii, one of lgst. active craters in world; over 3 km in diameter.

Kildare, inland co., Leinster, R.o.I.; dairying cereals; a. 1,694 km²; p. (1966) 66,486.

Kildare, mkt. t., cap. of Kildare, R.o.I.; cath.; close by the famous racecourse, the Curragh of Kildare; p. (1966) 2,731.

Kilimanjaro, volcanic mtn., N. Tanzania; hgst. peak in Africa, 5,895 m; international airpt. at 894 m on Sanya Plain; Nat. Park.

Kilindini, spt., Kenya; adjoins Mombasa; the finest harbour on E. cst. of Africa.

Kilkenny, inland co., Leinster, R.o.I.; cap. Kilkenny; pastoral farming, black marble; a. 2,062 km²; p. (1966) 60,472.

Kilkenny, t., cap. of Kilkenny, R.o.I.; on R. Nore; local mkt., caths., cas.; p. (1966) 10,057.

Kilkieran Bay, inlet, Galway, R.o.I.

Killala Bay, Mayo and Sligo, R.o I., wide bay fed by R. Hoy.

Killaloe, v., Co. Clare R.o.I.; crossing point for R. Shannon; cath.; p. 500.

Killarney, t., U.D., Kerry, R.o.I.; local mkt.; tourist ctr. for the Ls. of K.; p. (1966) 6,870.

Killarney, Lakes of, Kerry, R.o.I.; Lower, Middle, and Upper, celebrated for their beauty; tourist resorts; Muckross on Middle L. site of anc. abbey.

Killiecrankie, Pass of, Scot.; on R. Garry; at S. approach to Drumochter Pass; used by main rly. Perth to Inverness; scene of battle 1691.

Killingworth, t., Tyne and Wear, Eng.; 6 km N.E. of Newcastle; new t.; proposed p. 20,000.

Kilmarnock, burgh, l. gov. dist., Strathclyde Reg., Scot.; on R. Irvine, 17 km N.E. of Ayr.; carpet factories, textiles; rly. ctr.; p. (1971) 48,787.

Kilo-Moto, goldfield, Zaïre; in N.E. of st., 80 km W. of L. Mobutu Seso; linked by motor road to R. Zaïre (Kisangani) and L. Mobutu Seso (Kasenyi).

Kilrenny and Anstruther, t., North East Fife, Scot.; at entrance to F. of Forth; fishing, hosiery, oilskin mnfs.; p. (1971) 3,037.

Kilrush, sm. spt., U.D., Co. Clare, R.o.I.; on R. Shannon; p. (1966) 2,734.

Kilsyth, burgh, Stirling, Scot.; at S. foot of Campsie Fells, 16 km W. of Falkirk; p. (1971) 10,165.

Kilwinning, burgh, Cunninghame, Scot.; 8 km E. of Ardrossan; to be incorporated in new t. Irvine; p. (1971) 8,290.

Kimberley, former goldfield dist., W. Australia; big deposits of bauxite discovered 1965.

Kimberley, t., B.C., Canada; on R. Kootenay; site of Sullivan mine, silver, lead, zinc; ores smelted at Trail; p. (1971) 7,441.

Kimberley, t., C. Prov. S. Africa; diamondmng. dist.; asbestos, manganese, iron, cement, engin.; founded 1871; p. (1971) 103,789.

Kinabalu, Mount, Sabah, Malaysia; in Crocker mtns.; hgst. peak in Borneo, alt. 4,104 m.

Kincardine, former co., Scot.; with Deeside forms l. gov. dist. in Grampian Reg.; a. 2,546 km²; p. (1971) 33,260.

Kinder Scout, mtn., N. Derbys., Eng.; hgst. point of the Peak dist.; alt. 637 m.

Kindia, t., Guinea; rich bauxite deposits.

Kineshma, c., RSFSR; on Volga, N.W. of Gorki; pt. for Ivanovo industl. a.; textiles; dates from early 15th cent.; p. (est. 1967) 94,000.

King George's Sound, W. Australia; nr. Albany; fine harbour and bay.

Kinghorn, t., Kircaldy, Scot.; on F. of Forth, 5 km S. of Kirkcaldy; p. (1971) 2,146.

Kingsbridge, t., South Hams, S. Devon, Eng.; at head of Kingsbridge estuary, 16 km S.W. of Dartmouth; mkt.; p. (1971) 3,535.

King's Lynn, spt., West Norfolk, Eng.; at mouth of Gr. Ouse; docks; fishing base; agr. machin., canning, chemical fertilisers, shoes; expanded t.; p. (1971) 30,120.

Kingston, t., Ont., Canada; E. end of L. Ontario; univ., military college; heavy inds.; p. (1971) 61,870.

Kingston, spt., cap. of Jamaica; ch. comm. ctr. for J.; landlocked harbour; agr.-processing; univ.; p. (1970) 117,400 (c.), (1967) 376,520 (met. a.).

Kingston-upon-Hull. See Hull.

Kingston-upon-Thames, former M.B., Surrey, Eng.; now **The Royal Borough of Kingston-upon-Thames**, outer bor. of Greater London; inc. bors. of Malden and Coombe and Surbiton; residtl. with Richmond Park, Hampton Court, Bushey Park nearby; aircraft parts; p. (est. 1976) 135,000.

Kingstown, spt., cap. of St. Vincent, **W.I.**; cath., botanic gardens; p. (1966) 20,688.

Kingswood, t., l. gov. dist., Avon, Eng.; nr. Bristol; elec. vehicles, motor cycles, boots, brushes, tools; school founded by John Wesley; p. (est. 1976) 78,800.

Kington, mkt. t., Hereford and Worcs., Eng.; 19 km W. of Leominster; p. (1971) 1,916.

Kingussie, burgh, Badenoch and Strathspey, Scot.; between Cairngorm mtns. and Monadhliath mtns., on R. Spey; summer resort; p. (1971) 1,104.

Kinki, dist., S.W. Honshu, Japan; agr., industl. and comm. complex centred on Osaka, Kyoto, and Kōbe.

Kinlochleven, v., Lochaber, Scot.; at head of Loch Leven; hydroelec. power sta.; aluminium smelting.

Kinnairds Head, promontory, nr. Fraserburgh, on N.E. cst., Scot.

Kinross, burgh, Perth and Kinross, Scot.; on Loch Leven, 26 km N.E. of Alloa; textiles; resort; p. (1971) 2,418.

Kinross-shire, former co., Scot.; now part of Perth and Kinross l. gov. dist., Grampian Reg.

Kinsale, U.D., Cork, R.o.I.; sm. fish pt. on K. harbour; tourism; p. (1971) 1,628.

Kinshasa (Leopoldville), c., cap. of Zaïre; above the cataracts on R. Zaïre; univ.; textiles, shoes; founded by Stanley 1887; p. (est. 1972) 1,623,760 (met. a.).

Kinta Valley, S.E. Perak, W. Malaysia; tin mng., rubber plantations.

Kintyre, peninsula, Argyll and Bute, Scot.; terminates in Mull of Kintyre; 67 km long, 16 km wide.

Kioga (Kyoga), L., Uganda; on R. Nile midway between L. Victoria and L. Mobuto Seso; very shallow, fringed with marsh; land reclamation.

Kiölen or **Kjölen**, mtn. range, Norway and Sweden; hgst. point Mt. Sulitjelma, 1,876 m.

Kirghiz SSR (Khirghizia), constituent rep., USSR; S.W. of Siberia; mtnous. cty., in Tienshan and Pamir systems; livestock breeding; mineral resources; food processing; cap. Frunze; a. 196,581 km²; p. (1970) 2,933,000.

Kirin (Jilin), prov., N.E. China; N. of Korea and Liaotung peninsula; crossed by Sungari R.; in fertile Manchurian plain; impt. industl. a.; soyabeans, grain, lumber, coal, gold, lead; gd. rly services; cap. Changchun; a. 186,998 km²; p. (est. 1968) 17,000,000.

Kirin (Jilin), c., Kirin, N.E. China; former prov. cap.; on Sungari R. at outlet of Sungari reservoir; impt. position on rly. from Changchun to coastal pts.; chemical fertilisers, steel, oil refinery; p. (est. 1970) 1,200,000.

Kirkburton, t., West Yorks., Eng.; S.E. of Huddersfield; woollens; p. (1971) 19,520.

Kirkby, t., Knowsley, Merseyside, Eng.; p. (1971) 59,759.

Kirkby in Ashfield, t., Ashfield, Notts., Eng.; 16 km N.W. of Nottingham; coal mng.; p. (1971) 23,638.

Kirkby Moorside, t., Ryedale, North Yorks., Eng.; nr. Vale of Pickering; mkt.-place; sailplanes, gliders; p. (1971) 4,175 (dist.).

Kirkcaldy, royal burgh, l. gov. dist., Fife Reg.,

Scot.; spt. on N. side of F. of Forth; submarine coal mng.; linoleum, potteries, engin.; birthplace of Adam Smith; p. (1971) 50,360.

Kirkcudbright, royal burgh, Stewartry, Scot.; on R. Dee at influx into K. Bay, S.W. of Dumfries; agr. ctr., hosiery; cas., abbey; p. (1971) 2,502.

Kircudbrightshire, former co., Scot.; now part of Stewartry l. gov. dist., Dumfries and Galloway Reg.

Kirkenes, t., Finnmark prov., N.E. Norway; on S. arm of Varanger fjord, nr. Soviet border; pt. for iron-mng. dist.

Kirkham, t., Kirklees, Lancs., Eng.; textiles; p. (1971) 6,422.

Kirkintilloch, burgh, Strathkelvin, Scot.; on Forth and Clyde canal; engin.; p. (1971) 25,206.

Kirklees, met. dist., West Yorks., Eng.; comprises Huddersfield, Dewsbury, Batley, Spenborough, Colne Valley, Meltham, Holmfirth, Denby Dale, Kirkburton, Heckmondwike, and Mirfield; p. (est. 1976) 372,500.

Kirkstone Pass, mtn. pass, Cumbria, Eng.; used by main road between Ullswater and Windermere Ls.

Kirkūk, t., Iraq; mart for Arab horses; oilfield with pipelines to Tripoli, Haifa and Banias; p. (1965) 175,303 (t.), 183,981 (met. a.).

Kirkwall, royal burgh, Mainland I., Orkneys, Scot.; cath.; p. (1971) 4,617.

Kirov, c., RSFSR; pt. on Vyatka R.; rly. junc.; engin., saw milling, chemicals, leather inds.; cath.; p. (1970) 332,000.

Kirovabad, c., W. Azerbaydzhan SSR, USSR; on Gandzha R.; industl. ctr.; textiles, agr. implements, wine; copper and manganese mines; aluminium plant; p. (1970) 190,000.

Kirovograd, c., Ukrainian SSR, USSR; on Ingul R.; cap. of K. oblast; agr. ctr.; engin.; p. (1970) 189,000.

Kirovsk, c., RSFSR; on Kola peninsula; apatite and nephelite mng.; chemicals; p. (est. 1967) 50,000.

Kirriemuir, burgh, Angus, Scot.; on N. margin of Strathmore, 8 km W. of Forfar; jute-weaving; birthplace of J. M. Barrie; p. (1971) 4,138.

Kirtland, t., N.M., USA; atomic and space research sta.

Kiruna, t., N. Sweden; inside Arctic Circle, N.W. of Luleå; linked by rly. to Narvik (Norway); impt. deposits of iron ore; p. (1968) 28,968.

Kiryu, c., Honshu, Japan; major textile ctr.; p. (est. 1971) 135,000.

Kisangani (Stanleyville), t., Zaïre; on R. Zaïre nr. Boyoma Falls; airpt.; univ.; p. (est. 1972) 261,496 (met. a.).

Kiselevsk, c., S.W. Siberia, RSFSR; coal-mng. ctr. in Kuznetsk basin; p. (1970) 126,000.

Kishinev, c., cap. of Moldavian SSR, USSR; on Byk R., trib. of Dniester; cath., univ.; industl. comm. ctr. in rich farming a.; tourism; p. (1970) 357,000.

Kislovodsk, c., RSFSR; in N. Caucasus; famous spa; p. (est. 1967) 84,000.   [airpt.

Kismayu, pt., Somalia; new deep-water harbour;

Kisumu, spt., cap. of Nyanza prov., Kenya; at head of Kavirondo G. on L. Victoria; handles bulk of cotton from Buganda and coffee from N. Tanzania for transhipment E. by rail; p. (1969) 30,700.

Kitakyūshū, c., N. Kyushu, Japan; one of Japan's lgst. muns. on merging (1963) of ts. Moji, Kokura, Tobata, Yawata, and Wakamatsu; sixth c. to enjoy special aut. rights; p. (est. 1971) 1,307,000.

Kitami, c., Hokkaido, Japan; mkt.; food-processing; p. (1970) 82,727.

Kitchener, c., Ont., Canada; agr. machin., tyres, hardware, agr. processing; p. (1971) 109,954 (c.) 224,390 (met. a.).

Kithira. See Cerigo.

Kitimat, c., B.C., Canada; lge. aluminium smelter powered by hydroelectricity from diversion of R. Fraser trib. through the Rockies.

Kitwe, t., Zambia; contiguous to mng. township of Nkana, ctr. of copperbelt; p. (est. 1972) 290,100 (met. a.).

Kiukiang (Chiu-chiang), c., N. Kiangsi prov., China; pt. on Yangtze R., at foot of forested mtn. of Lu-shan; entrepôt tr.; former treaty pt.; p. (est. 1970) 120,000.

Kivu, L., on border of Zaïre and Rwanda; in highlands of Gr. Rift Valley, 1,473 m high, 96 km long.

Kizel, c., RSFSR; on Kizel R., on W. slopes of Urals; coal-mng. ctr.; mng. equipment; p. (est. 1967) 55,000.

Kizil, lgst R. of Turkey; rises in Kisil Dagh, flows to Black Sea via Sivas; 1,120 km long.

Kladno, t., ČSSR; 16 km N.W. of Prague; coalmng. ctr.; iron and steel wks., machin.; p. (1967) 55,000.

Klagenfurt, t., cap. of Carinthia. Austria; winter sports ctr.; varied mnfs.; p. (est. 1969) 73,156.

Klaipeda (Memel), c., Lithuanian SSR, USSR; ice-free spt. on Baltic Sea; exp. timber, textiles, chemicals, paper; p. (1970) 140,000.

Klamath, mtns., N. Cal., S.W. Ore., USA; beautiful ranges containing Nat. Park and Indian reserve; hgst. alt. Mt. Eddy, 2,757 m.

Klamono, t., W. Irian, Indonesia; ctr. of oilfield; pipeline to Sorong harbour.

Klerksdorp, t., S. Transvaal, S. Africa; gold, diamonds; p. (1970) 75,686.

Klodzko (Glatz), t., S.W. Poland; formerly in Prussian Silesia; rly. junc.; on R. Neisse; comm. and mftg.; p. (1970) 26,100.

Klondike, R., Yukon, Canada; sm. trib. of Yukon in gold-mng. region; gold rush 1896; 160 km long.

Klyuchevskaya Sopka, one of 18 active volcanoes, RSFSR; in N.E. Siberia, on Kamchatka peninsula; alt. 4,748 m.

Knaresborough, t., North Yorks., Eng.; 5 km N.E. of Harrogate; mkt.; cas. ruins; p. (1971) 11,863.

Knighton, t., Radnor, Powys, Wales; on R. Teme; mkt.; p. (1971) 2,010.

Knockmealdown Mtns., Waterford and Tipperary, R.o.I.; highest point 796 m; tourism.

Knob Lake. *See* Schefferville.

Knossos, ruined c., cap. of anc. Crete, Greece; S.E. of Iráklion; ctr. of Cretan bronze age culture, 1800 B.C.; archaeological source of knowledge about the Minoans.

Knottingley, t., West Yorks., Eng.; on R. Aire, 19 km S.E. of Leeds; engin., glass, tar distilling, chemicals; coal mng; p. (1971) 16,360.

Knowsley, met. dist., Merseyside, Eng.; comprises Kirkby, Prescot and Huyton with Roby; p. (est. 1976) 189,700.

Knoxville, c., Tenn., USA; univ.; livestock and tobacco mkt.; textiles, marble, plastics, chemicals, aluminium; p. (1970) 169,766 (c.), 391,974 (met. a.).

Knutsford, t., N.E. Cheshire, Eng.; mkt.; home of Mrs. Gaskell, author of *Cranford*; p. (1971) 13,765.

Kōbe, c., spt., Honshu, Japan; at E. end of Inland Sea; 5th c. of Japan; developed as pt. for Osaka and Kinki plain; iron and steel, shipbldg., rubber; p. (est. 1971) 1,307,000.

Koblenz (Coblenz), t., Rhineland-Palatinate, W. Germany; at confluence of Rs. Rhine and Moselle; fine buildings; wine, paper, machin., leather, ceramics; p. (est. 1969) 105,700.

Kōchi, plain and c., Shikoku, Japan; early vegetables, double rice cropping; p. (est. 1971) 246,000.

Kodiak I., lgst. of Is. of Alaska, USA; 144 km long; forested mtns.; fur-trading, salmon-fishing, canning; earthquake 1964; p. (1970) 3,798.

Kōfu, basin and c., Honshu, Japan; rice, vineyards, orchards, silk, wine; p. (est. 1971) 189,000.

Kohat, t., Pakistan; on trib. of Indus; military t.; cement wks.; p. (1961) 49,800.

Koh-I-Baba Mtns., Afghanistan, spur of the Hindu Kush; highest point 5,380 m.

Kokand, c., Uzbek SSR, USSR; in the Ferghana Valley; mftg. ctr., textiles, chemicals, engin.; p. (1970) 133,000.

Kokiu (Gejiu), t., Yunnan prov., China; leading tin-mng. ctr. of China; p. (1953) 159,700.

Kokkola (Gamla Karleby), t. Finland; on cst. of G. of Bothnia; sulphur plant; p. (est. 1970) 20,748.

Kokomo, c., Ind., USA; on Wild Cat R.; ctr. of agr. region; car components; p. (est. 1969) 48,000.

Koko-Nor, salt L., Chinghai prov., China; at over 3,000 m in Tibetan highlands; a. 5,957 km²; no outlet.

Kokura. *See* Kitakyūshū.

Kola Peninsula, peninsula, RSFSR; extension of Lapland; rich mineral deposits; hydroelectric plants.

Kolar, c., Karnataka, India; the ctr. of the Indian gold-mng. ind.; textiles; p. (1967) 167,610.

Kolarovgrad (Shumen), c., cap. of K. prov., N.E. Bulgaria; agr. tr., leather, cloth, metal gds.; Moslem architecture; p. (est. 1968) 68,124.

Kolding, c., at head of Kolding fjord, Jutland, Denmark; spt. and fishing base; lt. inds.; p. (est. 1970) 39,609.

Kolhapur, c., Maharashtra, S.W. India; cap. of former princely st. of K.; bauxite; anc. Buddhist ctr.; p. (1971) 259,050 (c.), 267,513 (met. a.).

Kolobrzeg (Kolberg), t., N.W. Poland; spt. on Baltic cst.; comm. and fishing harbour; resort and spa; p. (1970) 25,400.

Kolomna, c., RSFSR; on Moskva R., nr. confluence with Oka R.; industl. ctr.; engin., locomotives, machin., synthetic rubber; p. (1970) 136,000.

Kolomyya, c., Ukrainian SSR, USSR; on Pruth R.; in Carpathian foothills; agr. tr., metal gds., oil refining, textiles; p. (est. 1967) 39,000.

Kolwezi, c., S. Shaba, Zaïre; comm. ctr. for mng. dist. (cobalt and copper); p. (est. 1968) 70,558.

Kolyma, R., N.E. Siberia, RSFSR; flows into Arctic Oc., via Kolyma goldfields; navigable in summer; basin largely covered with tundra, sparsely p.; 2,560 km long.

Komárno, c., ČSSR; on left bank, of Danube, opposite Hungarian Komárom, on right bank; R. pt., shipbldg., oil refining.

Komi ASSR, aut. rep., RSFSR; wooded lowland, pastoral agr.; coal from Pechora basin, oil at Ukhta and Troitsko-Pechorsk; mng. now ch. economic activity; cap. Syktyvkar, lumber ctr.; a. 415,799 km²; p. (1970) 965,000.

Komló, t., Hungary; new mng. t.; coking coal; p. (1965) 27,800.

Kompong Som. *See* Sihanoukville.

Kommunarsk (Voroshilovsk), t., Ukrainian SSR, USSR; 40 km S.W. of Lugansk; ctr. of iron, steel and coking inds.; p. (1970) 123,000.

Komsomolsk, c., RSFSR; built by volunteer youth labour, after 1932; heavy industl. development; oil refining; pipeline connects with oilfield in N. Sakhalin; p. (1970) 218,000.

Komi-Permyak, admin. div., RSFSR; forestry, cellulose, paper; cap. Kudymbar; a. 31,080 km²; p. (1970) 212,000.

Konstantinovka, industl. t., Ukrainian SSR, USSR; in heart of Donbas industl. region, 61 km N. of Donetsk; heavy engin., iron and steel, zinc smelting, fertilisers; p. (1970) 106,000.

Konya, c., Turkey; cap. of K. prov.; agr. tr. ctr.; mnfs. textiles, carpets, leather gds.; the anc. Iconium, fortress of the Hittite empire; p. (1965) 157,934 (c.), 242,414 (met. a.).

Koolan I., W. Australia; rugged I. with iron-ore deposits worked since 1960.

Koolyanobbing, mng. t., W. Australia; highgrade haematite and limonite ores; linked to rly. between Kwinana and Kalgoorlie 1968.

Kootenay or Kootenai, R., flows from B.C., Canada; through Montana and Idaho, USA, into K. L., draining it by narrow channel into Columbia R.; beautiful scenery; resort at Radium Hotsprings; upper reaches inc. K. Nat. Park; 720 km long.

Kopeysk, t., RSFSR; in Urals; lignite mng., agr. and mng. machin.; p. (1970) 156,000.

Korat Plateau, E. Thailand; headwaters of Mekong tribs.; cattle-rearing; tr. ctr. Korat.

Korcë (Koritsa), t., S.E. Albania; in infertile basin at 854 m nr. Greek border; mkt.; cultural ctr.; p. (1967) 46,000.

Korcula (Curzola), I., Yugoslavia; sm. I. in Adriatic Sea; ch. pt. K.; a. 277 km²; p. (1961) 10,223.

Korea, Democratic People's Republic of, (N. Korea); occupies N. part of Korean peninsula (N. of 38th parallel), E. Asia; bounded on N. by China and USSR; continental climate; cold dry winters, hot humid summers; predominantly mtnous. with many uninhabited offshore Is.; all inds. nationalised and collective agr.; agr. employs half working p.; development emphasis on mng. resources of coal, iron-ore and on growth of heavy inds.; most industl. resources located in N. Korea; transport network under reconstruction after devastation of Korean war; some R. transport, international airport at cap. of Pyongyang; a. 121,248 km²; p. (est. 1969) 13,300,000.

Korea, Rep. of (S. Korea), occupies S. part of Korean peninsula (S. of 38th parallel); climate and topography resemble N. Korea's; massive US aid revitalised economy after Korean war; 50 per cent work-force engaged in agr.; industl. growth hampered by lack of resources, but iron and steel ind. at Pusan; fishing is both source of subsistence and exp.; irrigation and power project (1971–81) for 4 Rs.—Hangang, Naktangang, Kum-Gang, and Yongsan-Gang; cap. Seoul; a. 99,591 km²; p. (est. 1975) 33,949,000.

Korea Bay, Yellow Sea; between N. Korea and North-East China (Manchuria).

Koriyama, Honshu, Japan; textiles, chemicals; p. (est. 1971) 251,000.

Korsör, spt., Sjaelland I., Denmark; fine harbour; glass wks.; p. (est. 1970) 13,674.

Kortrijk (Courtrai), t., W. Flanders prov., N.W. Belgium; textiles; 13th cent. Notre Dame church; battle of the Spurs 1302; p. (1968) 45,170.

Koryak, admin. div., N.E. Siberia, RSFSR; sparse p.; a. 393,680 km²; p. (1970) 31,000.

Kos, I. See Cos, I.

Kosciusko, Mount, N.S.W., in Australian Alps; highest peak in Australia; 2,230 m.

Kosi R., India; flows from Himalayas to Ganges; site of barrage for hydroelectric power and irrigation.

Košice, c., S.E. Slovakia, ČSSR; lies in fertile basin; major industl. ctr.; heavy inds., iron and steel plant; agr.-processing; univ., Gothic cath.; mediaeval fortress t.; p. (est. 1968) 119,757.

Kosovo-Metohija, aut. region, S.W. Serbia, Yugoslavia; mtnous., fertile valleys; stock raising, forestry; ch. t. Priština; a. 10,352 km²; p. (1971) 1,244,755.

Kostroma, c., cap. of K. oblast, RSFSR; at confluence of Volga and Kostroma; in flax growing a.; textiles, engin.; cath.; p. (1970) 223,000.

Koszalin (Köslin), c., cap. of K. prov., N.W. Poland; nr. Baltic cst.; paper mills, textiles, building materials; p. (1970) 64,400.

Kota, t., Rajasthan, India; on R. Chambal; textiles; p. (1971) 212,991.

Kota Kinabalu (Jesselton), t., cap of Sabah, Malaysia; on W. cst.; main rubber pt.; rly. terminal; p. (1970) 41,830.

Köthen, t., Halle, E. Germany; in former st. of Saxony-Anhalt; lignite mines, sugar-refining, machin., chemicals; p. (est. 1970) 36,587.

Kotka, spt., S.E. Finland; on G. of Finland, at mouth of Kymi R.; major exp. pt. for timber, paper, pulp; p. (1968) 33,553.

Kotor, spt., S. Montenegro, Yugoslavia; on Bay of K., inlet of Adriatic; cath.; tourism.

Kotri, t., Pakistan; on R. Indus, opposite Hyderabad; barrage N. of the t., to help irrigate Sind; p. (1961) 52,685.

Kottbus. See Cottbus.

Koulikoro, t., Mali, W. Africa; on upper course of R. Niger; mkt. for groundnuts, gumarabic, sisal; linked by R. to Timbuktu and Gao; rly. terminus, 1,216 km from Dakar.

Kovrov, c., RSFSR; on Gorki rly. line and R. Klyazma; impt. agr. exp. ctr.; engin., textiles; p. (1970) 123,000.

Kowloon, peninsula, S.E. China; on mainland opposite Hong Kong I.; pt. installations; major industl. and tr. ctr.; held by Britain on lease expiring 1998; p. (1961) 726,976.

Kozáni, dep., Macedonia, Greece; cap. K.; mainly agr.; a. 6,143 km²; p. (1971) 135,619.

Kozhikode. See Calicut.

Kra Isthmus, neck of land between B. of Bengal and G. of Thailand, linking Malay peninsula with continent of Asia.

Kragujevac, t., central Serbia, Yugoslavia; on both banks of Lepenica R. (trib. of Morava R.); cath.; arsenal and garrison; route ctr., developing agr. and industl. ctr.; p. (est. 1965) 59,000.

Krakatoa (Rakata), volcanic I., Sunda strait, Indonesia; between Java and Sumatra; greater part blown up by violent eruption 1883.

Kraków (Cracow), c., cap. of K. prov., S. Poland; pt. on Vistula; cultural ctr., univ. (Copernicus matriculated here); many historic monuments; inc. c. of Nowa Huta, lgst iron and steel ctr. of rep.; machin., chemicals, farm implements; p. (1970) 583,000.

Kramatorsk, c., Ukrainian SSR, USSR; in Donets basin; heavy engin., metallurgy; p. (1970) 151,000.

Kramfors, t., Sweden; on G. of Bothnia; papermill and sulphite pulp wks.

Krasnodar Territory, region, RSFSR; extends from Sea of Azov and Black Sea to N.W. end of Caucasus; contains Kuban steppe and Maikop oilfields; fertile black soil; main pt. Tuapse; many health resorts.

Krasnodar, c., cap. of K region, RSFSR; R. pt. Kuban R.; ctr. of industl. and agr. region; p. (1970) 465,000.

Krasnoturinsk, t., RSFSR; in Urals, 9 km N.W. of Serov; aluminium, coal; p. (est. 1969) 61,000.

Krasnovodsk, c., Turkmen SSR, USSR; pt. on Caspian Sea; oil-refining ctr.; handles agr. and oil prods.; p. (est. 1967) 48,000.

Krasnoyarsk Territory, extensive region, RSFSR; extends across Siberia to Arctic Oc.; traversed by Yenisey and tribs.; minerals, grain from Minusinska basin and timber from coniferous forests; cap. K.; a. of labour camps in Stalin era.

Krasnoyarsk, c., cap. of K. terr., E. Siberia, RSFSR; on Trans-Siberian rly. at crossing of Yenesey R.; hydroelectric sta.; industl. ctr.; local copper and iron-ore deposits; ctr. for grain and timber; p. (1970) 684,000.

Krefeld, t., N. Rhine–Westphalia, W. Germany; chemicals, steel, machin., textiles, soap; former ctr. of silk inds.; p. (est. 1969) 226,800.

Kremenchug, c., Ukrainian SSR, USSR; on R. Dnieper; timber, engin., textiles; hydroelectric sta.; oil refining; p. (1970) 148,000.

Krems, mkt. t., Austria; on R. Danube; fruit processing; founded in 10th cent. as imperial fortress; p. (1961) 21,046.

Kreuznach Bad, t., Rhineland Palatinate, W. Germany; on R. Nahe; metallurgy, leather, optical and chemical inds.; viticulture, mineral baths; p. (est. 1969) 44 139.

Krishna (Kistna), R., S. India; rises in W. Ghats, flows E. across Deccan plateau into Bay of Bengal; lower valley and delta under intensive rice cultivation; densely populated; 1,360 km long.

Kristiansand, spt., S. Norway; on Skagerrak; shipbldg., ships timber, paper, pulp, fish; electro-metallurgy; p. (1968) 53,736.

Kristianstad, c., cap. of K. prov., Sweden; on Helge R.; its pt. Ahus is on Baltic; foodprocessing, clothing, machin.; founded 1614 as fortress; p. (1968) 42,456.

Kristiansund, spt., W. cst. Norway; built on 3 Is.; trawler fleet base; exp. dried fish; heavily damaged in second world war; since rebuilt; p. (1969) 18,588.

Kristinehamn, L. pt. on L. Vänern, central Sweden; p. (est. 1970) 22,018.

Krivoy Rog., c., Ukrainian SSR, USSR; on R. Ingulets; ctr. of ch. iron-mng. a. of USSR; p. (1970) 573,000.

Krk, I., N. Adriatic Sea, Yugoslavia; S. of Rijeke; agr.; tourism; ch. t., K.; p. 14,500.

Krkonose. See Riesengebirge.

Kronshlot (Kronstadt), spt., on I. of Kotlin, RSFSR; at head of G. of Finland, nr. Leningrad; Baltic pt. and naval base; scene of naval mutiny which precipitated the Russian revolution; founded by Peter the Great 1710; p. 50,000.

Kroonstad, t., O.F.S., S. Africa; on R. Vals; rly. junc.; agr. mkt.; engin., milling; p. (1970) 50,898.

Kropotkin, c., E. Krasnodar Terr., RSFSR; foodprocessing, engin.; p. (est. 1967) 62,000.

Kruger Nat. Park, N.E. Transvaal, S. Africa; game reserve; a. 20,720 km².

Krugersdorp, t., Transvaal, S. Africa; gold mng., uranium, manganese; p. (1970) 91,202.

Kuala Lumpur, c., fed. terr., W. Malaysia; cap. of Fed. of Malaysia and of Selangor st.; univ.; ctr. of rubber and tin dist.; outport Port Kelang; p. (1968) 592,785.

Kuangchow (Kuang-chou), formerly Canton, c., cap. of Kwantung prov., S. China; industl. and educational ctr.; mnfs. inc. silk, paper, cement; univ.; former treaty pt. and major spt. of S. China but site on Chu-kiang delta results in silting and expensive harbour wks., hence Chinese interest in Hong Kong; ctr. of revolutionary movement from days of Sun Yat-Sen; p. (est. 1970) 2,300,000.

Kuantan, main t. on E. cst. W. Malaysia; linked to Kuala Lumpur; tin mng; p. (1970) 43,391.

Kuching, c., cap. of Sarawak, Malaysia; pt. on Sarawak R.; gold discovered nearby at Bau; p. (1967) 70,000.

Kuçovë (Qyteti Stalin), Albania; nr. Berat; oil prod. and refining; pipeline connects to Vlore.

Kufra, oasis, Libya; dates, barley; on caravan route.

Kuldja (I-ning), c., W. Sinkiang prov., China; on highway to Turkestan and on Ili R.; coalfield; recent industl. development inc. iron and steel; p. (est. 1970) 160,000.

Kumamoto, c., W. Kyushu, Japan; 3rd c. of K.; cas., univs.; food inds.; business ctr.; p. (est. 1971) 447,000.

Kumasi, c., cap. of Ashanti region, Ghana; univ., aerodrome; road and rly. junc.; ctr. of cocoa-producing a.; bauxite nearby; jute bags; p. (1970) 260, 286 (c.), 345,117 (met. a.).

Kumba Konam, t., Tamil Nadu, India; on Cauvery delta; silks, cotton; sacred Hindu c.; p. (1971) 113,130.

Kunene (Cunene), R., Angola; scheme to channel water from Angola to S.W. Africa; 1,200 km long.

Kungur, t., RSFSR; S.E. of Perm; oil ind. equipment; p. (est. 1967) 70,000.

Kun Lun (Kwen Lun), mtn. ranges, Tibet, China; extend 2,900 km E. from Pamirs along N. edge of high plateau of Tibet; drained N. into inland drainage basin of Lop Nor; alt. frequently exceeds 5,400 m; rising to 7,729 m.

Kunming, c., cap. of Yunnan prov., S.W. China; univ.; comm. and cultural ctr., noted for its scenic beauty; iron and steel, milling and boring machin., textiles, chemicals; p. (est. 1970) 1,700,000.

Kunsan, spt., S.W. S. Korea; on Yellow Sea, on estuary of R. Kum; p. (1966) 102,800.

Kununurra Dam, Ord R., W. Australia; opened 1963; to irrigate 81,000 ha of semi-arid land for cotton, rice, and cattle.

Kuopio, t., Finland; on L. Kalki; timber inds.; tourism; p. (1968) 55,067.

Kura, R., rises in Turkey, chief R. of Trans-caucasia, USSR, flows into Caspian Sea; agr., fishing, hydroelec. power; 1,504 km long.

Kurdistan (Country of the Kurds), includes parts of E. Turkey, Soviet Armenia, N.E. Iraq, and N.W. Iran; attempts at autonomy.

Kure, c., S.W. Honshu, Japan; spt. and naval base; engin.; shipbldg.; p. (est. 1971) 239,000.

Kurgan, c., RSFSR; on Tobol R.; impt. junc. on Trans-Siberian rly.; tr. in cattle and food-stuffs; agr. engin.; p. (1970) 244,000.

Kuria Muria Is., 5 barren Is. in Arabian Sea off cst. of Oman; admin. by U.K. until 1967.

Kurile Is., chain of volcanic Is., N. Pac., RSFSR; extend from Kamchatka to Hokkaido; mainly mtnous.; sulphur, hunting, fishing; Japan claims sovereignty over 4 Is.; a. 15,592 km²; p. 18,000.

Kurisches Haff (Kurštu Martos), shallow lagoon, Baltic cst. of Lithuanian SSR, USSR; receives water of R. Niemen; narrow entrance to Baltic Sea at N. end of lagoon commanded by pt. of Klaipeda (Memel); length 92 km, maximum width 32 km.

Kurische Nehrung, sandspit, Baltic Sea; almost cuts off Kurisches Haff from Baltic Sea; 88 km long.

Kurnool, t., Andhra Pradesh, India; agr. comm. ctr.; p. (1971) 136,710.

Kuroshio (Japan Current), ocean current, flows N.E. along Pac. cst. of Kyushu, Shikoku and S. Honshu, relatively warm water, exerts slight warming influence on this cst. in winter.

Kursk, c., cap. of K. oblast, RSFSR; on Tuskor R.; rly. junc.; in fertile fruit-growing a.; engin., textiles, synthetic rubber; p. (1970) 284,000.

Kurume, t., W. Kyushu, Japan; on Chikugo plain; comm. ctr.; p. (est. 1969) 190,000.

Kushiro, spt., S.E. Hokkaido, Japan; exp. lumber; local coal; fishing; p. (est. 1971) 201,000.

Kustanay, c., Kazakh SSR, USSR; on Tobol R.; agr.-processing, lt. inds.; p. (1970) 123,000.

Kütahya, t., cap. of K. prov., central Turkey; agr. mkt. ctr.; ceramics; p. (1965) 49,227.

Kutaisi, c., Georgian SSR, USSR; on R. Rion

(hydroelectric plant); chemicals, textiles, mng. equipment; big coal deposits being mined; mkt. gardening a.; p. (1970) 161,000.

Kut-al-Amara, t., cap. of K. prov., Iraq; on R. Tigris; agr. tr. ctr.; p. (1965) 104,000 (met. a.).

Kutch, peninsula, Gujarat st., N.W. India; bounded on N. by Pakistan; largely barren except for fertile strip along Arabian Sea; p. (1961) 696,440.

Kutch, Rann of, desert region covered with salt, but flooded during monsoons; nine-tenths belongs to India; one-tenth to Pakistan.

Kutchan, t., S.W. Hokkaido, Japan; ctr. of lge. iron-ore field; ore smelted at Muroran.

Kutno, t., Lodz, Poland; route ctr.; sm. textile ind.; p. (1970) 30,300.

Kuwait, indep. Arab st., S.W. Asia; under Brit. protection until 1971; lies at head of Persian G.; mainly desert with a few oases; imports most of food requirements; possesses 17 per cent of the proved world reserves of oil; heavily dependent on oil and natural gas exports; industl. complex of petrochemical inds. at Shuaiba projected, 48 km S. of Kuwait (cap.), which contains nearly half of p.; one of hgst. incomes per capita in world, but most of p. remains poor; a. 24,235 km²; p. (1974) 862,200.

Kuwait, c., cap. of Kuwait; pt. with natural harbour on Persian G.; univ.; p. (1970) 80,008.

Kuybyshev, c., cap. of K. oblast, RSFSR; on R. Volga; major R. pt., rly. junc. on Moscow-Siberian line, airport; hydroelectric power sta.; comm. ctr. with varied mnfs., inc. cars, aircraft, textiles, synthetic rubber; oil refining; grain and livestock exp.; p. (1970) 1,047,000.

Kuzbas (Kuznetsk Basin), industl. region, Siberia, USSR; lies S. of Trans-Siberian rly. in upper valleys of Rs. Ob and Tom; second lgst. coal output in USSR, iron and steel mftg., heavy metallurgical ind.; ch. ts., Novosibirsk, Novokuznetsk, Kemerovo, Leninsk-Kuznetsky.

Kvalöy. *See* Hammerfest.

Kwangsi Chuang (Guang Zhuang), aut. region, S. China; borders on Vietnam; cap. Nanning; drained by Si-kiang and tribs.; rice most impt. crop; timber from sub-tropical forests; home of the Chuang people (over 7 million); a. 221,321 km²; p. (est. 1968) 24,000,000.

Kwantung (Guangdong), prov., S. China; on S. China Sea; cap. Kuangchow; occupied by delta of Si-kiang and its confluents; Hong Kong in estuary; tropical monsoon climate; densely p. on R. plains and valley slopes; intensive farming of rice, sugar, fruits; a. 221,308 km²; p. (est. 1968) 40,000,000.

Kwanto Plain, S.E. Honshu, Japan; lgst. a. of continuous lowland in Japan, extends 128 km inland from Tokyo; plain devoted to intensive rice cultivation; higher, drier terraces under mulberry, vegetables, tea, tobacco; very dense rural p.; lge. number of urban ctrs., inc. Tokyo, Yokohama; a. 13,000 km²; p. (1960) 27,000,000.

Kwazulu, Bantu Terr. Authority (1970), E. S. Africa; runs 480 km from Moçambique to Cape Prov. but in 29 separate as. interspersed by white as.; cap. Nongoma in N. highland; p. (1971) 2,100,000.

Kweichow (Guizhou), inland prov., S.W. China; upland a. with p. concentrated in valley urban areas; cap. Kweiyang; cereals; tung oil; forestry; coal, mercury; a. 176,480 km²; p. (est. 1968) 17,000,000.

Kweilin (Guilin), c., Kwangsi prov., China; on Kwei R.; univ.; textiles, sugar refining, timber; noted for its beautiful setting; p. (est. 1970) 235,000.

Kweiyang (Guiynag), c., Kweichow prov., China; univ.; comm. and industl.; coal; iron and steel, textiles, chemicals; p. (est. 1970) 1,500,000.

Kwidzyn (Marienwerder), c., Gdansk, N. Poland (since 1945); cath., cas.; industl. ctr. nr. Vistula R.; p. (1970) 23,100.

Kwinana, new t., W. Australia; oil refinery and steel plant, alumina reduction, blast furnace; integrated steelwks. by 1978; p. (1972) 10,096.

Kyle of Lochalsh, v., Skye and Lochalsh, Scot.; at entrance to Loch Alsh, facing S. end of I. of Skye; terminus of rly. across Highlands from Dingwall; ch. pt. for steamers to N.W. cst., I. of Skye, Outer Hebrides.

Kymi, R., Finland; rises in L. Päijänne, flows to

G. of Finland; many Ls., timber transport, hydroelec. power; 144 km long.

Kyoto, c., Honshu, Japan; cultural and religious ctr., without lge.-scale inds.; former cap. 794–1868; univ.; shrines, old Imperial palace; p. (est. 1971) 1,424,000.

Kyushu, most S. of 4 major Is. of Japan; mtnous.; coal mng. in Chikugo basin; heavy inds.; agr. on coastal lowlands; joined to Honshu by bridge and rly.; a. 42,007 km²; p. (1960) 12,903,515.

Kyustendil, t., **Bulgaria**; in foothills of Osogovo mtns.; lge. lead and zinc deposits; combined plant for mng. and ore dressing projected.

Kzyl Orda, R. and t., Kazakh SSR, USSR; lge. dam to irrigate rice plantations.

L

Laaland I. *See* Lolland I.

Labrador, mainland a. of prov. Newfoundland, Canada; separated from I. by Strait of Belle I.; barren, severe climate; impt. cod fisheries; rich iron ore reserves nr. Quebec bdy.; Churchill R. power project; cap. Battle Harbour; a. 292,219 km²; p. (1966) 21,157.

Labrador City, t., Newfoundland, **Canada**; new t. built 1965, nr. Wabush L. to house workers of iron-ore mines.

Labuan, I., Sabah, Malaysia; rubber, rice, coconuts; cap. Victoria; a. 81 km²; p. (1960) 14,904.

Laccadive, coral Is., Arabian Sea; about 320 km off Malabar cst. joined with Minicoy and Amindivi Is. to form union terr., India; renamed Lakshadweep Is. (1974); coir, coconuts; cap. Kavaratti; a. 28 km²; p. of terr. (1971) 31,798.

Lachine, c., Quebec, Canada; on Montreal I. where St. Lawrence R. leaves St. Louis L.; iron and steel, wire, rope; Lachine canal by-passes rapids; summer resort; p. (1966) 43,155.

Lachlan, R., N.S.W., Australia; trib. of R. Murrumbidgee; irrigation; 1,472 km long.

La Coruna, spt., cap. of La Coruña prov., N.W. Spain; fishing; p. (est. 1969) 224,055.

Ladakh, dist., of the Upper Indus, India, bordering Tibet; ch. t. Leh; isolated and remote; alt. 3,600 m; p. (1961) 88,651.

Ladoga (Ladozhskoye), L., Leningrad, USSR; a. 18,389 km² (lgst. in Europe); drained to G. of Finland by R. Neva; fishing; link in new deepwater canal between White and Baltic Seas.

Ladybank, burgh, North East Fife, Scot.; 8 km S.W. of Cupar; p. (1971) 1,176.

Ladysmith, t. Natal, S. Africa; cotton mills; besieged by Boers 1899–1900; p. (1968) 32,750.

Lae, t., Papua New Guinea; pt. on Huon Gulf serving goldmng. dist;. outlet for Morobe plywood; air ctr.

Lagan (Laggan), R., N. Ireland; flows into Belfast Lough; canal link to Lough Neagh; 56 km long.

Lagôa dos Patos, L., Brazil; drained by Rio Grande do Sul; 224 km long.

Lagôa Mirim, L., on bdy. between Brazil and Uruguay; drains N.; 176 km long.

Lagos, spt., cap. of Nigeria; unhealthy and congested; cap. to be moved to Abuja by 1986; on G. of Guinea; gd. natural harbour; exp. cocoa, groundnuts, palm oil and kernels, timber, hides and skins, cotton, rubber, crude oil; mnfs. textiles, confectionery, chemicals, car assembly; univ.; p. (est. 1971) 900,979 (c.), 1,476,837 (met. a.).

La Grande Chartreuse, limestone region between Chambéry and Grenoble, France; famous monastery and liqueur.

La Grande Rivière, N. Quebec, Canada; major hydroelec. scheme; mineral and timber inds.

Laguna, dist., Durango st. Mexico; former L. bed irrigated by Rs. Nazas and Aguanaval; ch. cotton-growing region in Mexico; ch. t.. Torréon; a. 259,000 km².

Lahore, ch. c., Pakistan; univ., cath., temples, mosques; textiles, pottery, carpets, industl. gases; atomic research ctr.; second c. of Pakistan; p. (1972) 2,148,000.

Lahti, t., S. Finland; wood, plywood, brewing, textiles; p. (1968) 85,409.

Lake Champlain, N.Y., USA; forms lowland a. for main routes between Montreal and N.Y.

Lake Charles, c., La., USA; spt. at mouth of Calcasieu R.; connected to G. of Mexico by channel; exp. oil, chemicals, rice, cotton; p. (1970) 76,522 (c.), 142,288 (met. a.).

Lake District, almost circular mtnous. a., Cumbria, Eng.; 17 major and many smaller Ls. formed by glacial erosion and deposition; increasing tourist pressure on Nat. Park as motorways improve accessibility.

Lakeland, c., Fla., USA; citrus fruit ctr.; holiday resort; p. (est. 1969) 43,000.

Lakeland, South, l. gov. dist., Cumbria, Eng.; lge. a. surrounding Morecambe Bay and inc. Ulverston, Grange, Kendal and Sedbergh; p. (est. 1976) 94,000.

Lake of the Woods, L., Ont., S.E. of Winnipeg, on bdy. between Canada and USA; in pine forest; tourism.

Lakeview, t., Ont., Canada; thermal elec. power plant projected; to be lgst. in world.

Lakshadweep, union terr., India; made up of Laccadive, Minicoy and Amindivi Is.

La Linea, t., Spain; on isthmus connecting Gibraltar with mainland; p. (1970) 52,127.

La Mancha, plain, Cuidad-Real prov., S. Spain; in shallow depression on central plateau, alt. between 450–900 m, drained by headstreams of R. Guadiana; semi-arid climate with hot summers, cold winters; widespread salt deposits; Merino sheep, esparto grass; Spain's lgst. grape-growing region.

Lambaréné, t., Gabon; site of Schweitzer's hospital on Ogooué R.

Lambayeque, prov., N.W. Peru; ctr. of irrigated dists.; sugar, cotton, tobacco; cap. Chiclayo, ch. pt. Pimental; a. 11,948 km²; p. (est. 1969) 468,800.

Lambeth, inner bor., London, Eng.; L. palace. residence of Archibishop of Canterbury; p. (est. 1976) 290,300.

Lammermuir hills, E. Lothian, Scot.; highest peak Lammer Law, 529 m.

Lampang, t., Thailand; modern sugar plant; p. (est. 1969) 39,400.

Lampedusa, lgst. of Pelagi Is., between Malta and Tunisian cst., belonging to Italy; barren limestone; a. 21 km²; p. (est. 1968) 4,620.

Lampeter, t., Ceredigion, Dyfed, S. Wales; on R. Teifi; mkt.; univ. college of Wales; p. (1971) 2,189.

Lanark, former co., central Scot.; now forms several sm. l. gov. dists. within Strathclyde Reg.

Lanark, royal burgh, Lanark, Scot.; in Clyde valley 35 km S.E. of Glasgow; hosiery; ctr. of mkt. gardening a.; nr. New Lanark model t. built by Robert Owen; p. (1971) 8,700.

Lancashire, non-met. co., N.W. Eng.; major growth of p. in 19th cent. based on prod. of cotton and coal; main industl. ctrs. now outside co. in Merseyside and Gtr. Manchester met. cos.; Pennines in E.; extensive lowland in W.; admin. ctr. Preston, co. t. Lancaster; a. 2,738 km²; p. (est. 1976) 1,375,500.

Lancaster, c., co. t., l. gov. dist., Lancs., Eng.; 10 km up R. Lune; mediaeval cas., univ.; linoleum, vinyl, clothing; p. (est. 1976) 126,300 (dist.).

Lancaster, c., Penns., USA; agr. ctr., tobacco mkt.; stockyards; mnfs. linoleum, watches; birthplace of Robert Fulton; p. (1970) 57,693 (c.), 319,531 (met. a.).

Lanchow (Lanzhou), c., cap. of Kansu prov., China; on Hwang-ho; tr. ctr.; oil refining, gaseous diffusion plant, woollen mills, coal mng. nearby; p. (est. 1970) 1,500,000.

Lancing, v., West Sussex, Eng.; on S. cst., 3 km E. of Worthing; seaside resort; lt. inds.; public school.

Landau, t., Rhineland-Palatinate, W. Germany; on R. Queich; cigar mfrg., wine, iron ind.; here the carriages called Landaus were first made; p. (est. 1969) 32,094.

Landes, dep., S.W. France; on Atl. cst.; agr., vineyards, resin; cap. Mont-de-Marsan; a. 9,334 km²; p. (1968) 277,381.

Landes, Les, region, Aquitaine, S.W. France; fringes Bay of Biscay from Pointe de Grave to Biarritz; coastal sand dunes and lagoons backed by low, flat plain of alternate sandy tracts and marsh; reclaimed by drainage and afforestation, now over half a. covered by pine forests; turpentine, timber; oilfield. [cst.

Land's End, extreme S.W. point of Eng. on Cornish

Landshut, t., Bavaria, W. Germany; on R. Isar; cas.; elec. inds., glass, metallurgy, textiles, coal; rly. junc.; p. (est. 1969) 51,182.

Landskrona, spt., Sweden; on the Sound; shipping and tr. ctr.; agr.-processing; on nearby I. of Ven Tycho Brahe built his observatory; p. (1968) 32,125.

Langbaurgh, l. gov. dist. Cleveland, Eng.; a. of N. York Moors inc. Loftus, Skelton, Gainsborough and Saltburn; p. (est. 1976) 151,500.

Langdale Pikes, L. Dist., Eng ; 2 peaks Harrison Stickle (733 m), Pike-o'-Stickel (709 m); popular rambling and climbing a.; 5 km W. of Grasmere.

Langebergen, mtns., Cape Prov., S. Africa; 240 km E. to W. parallel to S. cst. of Africa; form barrier to access from cst. plain to Little Karroo, broken across by valley of R. Gouritz; max. alt. exceeds 1,370 m.

Langholm, mkt. burgh, Annandale and Eskdale, Scot.; on R. Esk; 29 km N. of Carlisle; textiles; p. (1971) 2,344.

Langreo, t., N. Spain; in Asturias, 19 km S.E. of Oviedo; coal and iron mines; p. (1970) 58,864.

Langres, t., Haute-Marne, France; cath., mediaeval fortifications; famous for its cutlery; birthplace of Diderot; p. (1968) 10,846.

Languedoc, region, former prov., S. France; inc. deps. Gard, Aude, Hérault, Lozère, Ardèche, Tarn, and parts of Haute Garonne, Tarn-et-Garonne, and Haute Loire; major govt. sponsored investment in tourist inds., along Mediterranean cst.; mono-cultural vine prod.; irrigation scheme to aid agr. diversification.

Lannemezan, region, Aquitaine, S.W. France; belt 80 km wide stretches over 160 km along foot of Pyrenees W. of Toulouse; consists of immense deltas of glacial gravel deeply cut by tribs. of Rs. Garonne and Adour; valleys liable to severe floods in summer, intervening plateau dry, bare; scantily populated.

Lansing, c., cap. of Mich., USA; on Grand R. at confluence with Cedar R.; automobiles, chemicals; p. (1970) 129,021 (c.), 373,474 (met. a.).

Lanzarote, I., Canary Is.; volcanic mtns.; developing tourist ind.; cochineal; cap. Arrecife; p. (1970) 41,912.

Laoag, t., N. Luzon I., Philippines; agr.-processing; p. (1970) 69,300.

Laoighis or **Leix Co.,** Leinster, R.o.I.; mtns. and bog; inland pasture and tillage; cap. Port Laoighise (Maryborough); a. 1,720 km²; p.(1966) 44,622.

Laon, t. cap. of Aisne dep., France; on rocky height above plain; historic fortress t.; cath.; p. (1968) 28,613.

Laos, People's Dem. Rep. of, S.E. Asia; kingdom until 1975; bordered by China, Vietnam, Cambodia, Thailand and Burma; formerly part of Fr. Indo-China; under-developed and isolated cty; economic ctr. is Mekong valley, scene of recent Mekong R. Development Project; elsewhere thickly forested mtns.; 90 per cent of p. engaged in subsistence agr. for dry rice; lge. food imports necessary; main exp., hardwoods; no rlys.; royal cap. Luang Prabang admin. cap. Vientiane; a. 231,339 km²; p. (est. 1970) 2,962,000.

La Paz, dep., Bolivia; traversed by Andes; de facto cap. La Paz, legal cap. Sucre; cocoa, coffee, rubber, tin-mng. at Catari; a. 105,377 km²; p. (est. 1969) 1,509,100.

La Paz, c., Bolivia; seat of govt.; comm. ctr.; copper, alpaca wool, cinchona, textiles; p. (1969) 525,000.

Lapland, terr., N. Europe, in Norway, Sweden, Finland, and USSR, extending from Norwegian cst. to White Sea; mainly mtn. and moorland, with many lakes; Lapps are nomadic pastoralists with reindeer herds; iron-ore at Kiruna and Gällivare; a. 336,700 km²; p. (est. 1968) 36,500.

La Plata, c., spt., Argentina; cap. of Buenos Aires prov., univ.; mftg. ctr.; iron and steel, oil refining, refrigerated meat prods.; p. (1970) 506,287 (met. a.).

La Plata, Rio de. *See* Plata, Rio de la.

Laptev Sea (Nordenskjöld Sea), inlet of Arctic Oc.; between Severnaya Zemlya and New Siberian Is., RSFSR.

Larache, spt., Morocco; on Atl. cst. 64 km S. of Tangier; exp. cork, wool; p. (1960) 30,769.

Laramie, t., Wyo., USA; univ.; industl. ctr. for cattle and timber region; rly. engin.; p. (1970) 23,143.

Laredo, t., Texas, USA; frontier t. on Rio Grande; smuggling; ctr. of Chicanos; p. (est. 1969) 73,000 (c.), 195,000 (met. a.).

Largo, v., North East Fife, Scot.; fishing, holiday resort; birthplace of Alexander Selkirk.

Largs, burgh, Cunninghame, Scot.; on F. of Clyde opposite Is. of Bute and Cumbrae; seaside resort, fishing; battle 1263 defeating last attempt by Norsemen to conquer Scot.; p. (1971) 9,771.

Larissa, dep., Thessaly, Greece; inc. infertile basin of R. Pinios; cap. Larissa; ch. pt. Volos; p. (1971) 232,157.

Larkhall, t., Strathclyde Reg., Scot.; industl. estate; foundry, hosiery. silk dye wks.

Larnaca, spt., Cyprus; the anc. Citium; grain, cotton, fruit; oil refinery; growing tourist ctr.; p. (est. 1970) 21,400.

Larne, spt., l. gov. dist., N. Ireland; at entrance to Larne Lough; cross channel service to Stranraer; tourism; p. (est. 1971) 18,242.

La Rochelle, spt., cap. of Charente-Maritime dep., France; on Atl. cst.; its deepwater pt. is La Pallice; cath.; fishing pt.; chemicals, food-processing; tourism; p. (1968) 75,497.

Larut Hills, W. Malaysia; rise to over 1,500 m; lge. tin-field.

Larvik, spt., Norway; S.W. of Oslo; seaside resort; engin., pulp, stone; former whaling pt.; p. (est. 1970) 10,376.

Las Cruces, t., N.M., USA; on Rio Grande R.; irrigated agr.; univ.; p. (1970) 37,857.

La Serena, c., cap. of Coquimbo prov., Chile; 14 km inland from its pt. Coquimbo; cath.; resort; p. (est. 1966) 48,647.

Lashio, t., Burma; on R. Salween; rly. terminus; Burma road links with China; ctr. of silver-lead mines; p. 4,638.

Lashkar, c., Madhya Pradesh, central India; modern industl. t., adjoining Gwalior.

La Skhirra, pt., on G. of Gabès, Tunisia; oil; pipeline to Edjelé.

Las Palmas, prov., Canary Is., Spain; inc. Gran Canaria, Lanzarote, Fuerteventura and smaller Is.; intensive irrigated agr. of bananas, tomatoes, potatoes; tourism encouraged by climate and volcanic landscape; a. 4,053 km²; p. (1970) 579,710.

Las Palmas. c., N.E. Gran Canaria, ch. pt. of Canary Is.; exp. agr. prods.; cath.; p. (1968) 218,072.

La Spezia, spt., Liguria, N.W. Italy; on Bay of Spezia; ch. Italian naval sta., arsenal and docks; maritime inds., elec. machin., olive oil, oil refining; p. (1969) 128,652.

Lassen Peak, Nat. Park, Cascade Range, Cal.; only active volcano in USA.

Lasswade. *See* Bonnyrigg and Lasswade.

Las Vegas, c., Nevada, USA; noted for its gambling casinos; ranching and mng. a.; p. (1970) 124,161 (c.), 270,045 (met. a.).

Latacunga, t., Ecuador; at c. 2,740 m in Andean basin, not far from Cotopaxi volcano; anc. Inca t.; tr. ctr.; p. (est. 1970) 17,300.

Latakia, spt., Syria; exp. tobacco, olive oil, sponges; p. (1970) 126,000.

Latina (Littoria), c., cap. of Latina prov., in Latium central Italy; in ctr. of reclaimed a. of Pontine marshes; mkt ctr., on which planned road system converges; built since 1932; nuclear power sta. nearby; p. (est. 1967) 45,600 (c.), 65,600 (dist.).

Latin America, the Spanish-, Portuguese- and Fr.-speaking countries of N. America, S. America, Central America, and the W.I. inc. the reps of Argentina, Bolivia, Brazil, Chile, Colombia, Costa Rica, Cuba, Dominican Republic, Ecuador, Salvador, Guatemala, Haiti, Honduras, Mexico, Nicaragua, Panama, Paraguay, Peru, Uruguay, and Venezuela; sometimes Puerto Rico, Fr. W.I., and other Is. of the W.I. are included, and occasionally Belize, Guyana, Fr. Guiana, and Surinam; p. (est. 1975) 324,000,000.

Latium (Laszio), region, central Italy; between Apennines and Tyrrhenian Sea, comprising provs. of Rome, Frosinone, Latina, Rieti, Viterbo; a. 17,182 km²; p. (1969) 4,635,528.

Latvia, constituent rep., USSR; borders on Baltic Sea; dairying, stock-raising, forestry; cap. Riga; spts. Ventspils, Liepaya; a. 66,278 km²; p. (1970) 2,365,000.

Launceston, t., Tasmania, Australia; wool, textiles, cars; p. (1792) 62,181.

Launceston, t., North Cornwall, Eng.; agr. mkt.; quarrying, lt. engin.; p. (1971) 4,725.

Laurencekirk, burgh, Kincardine and Deeside, Scot.; agr. ctr. in the Howe of Mearns; p. (est. 1976) 1,500.

Laurion or **Laurium**, pt. on Attic peninsula, Greece; lead, manganese, zinc, and silver mines; silver mined 5th cent. B.C.

Lausanne, c., cap. of Vaud can., Switzerland; nr. L. Geneva; cath., univ.; impt. rly. junc.; seat of Swiss high courts of justice; tourism; p. (est. 1969) 13,8300 (c.), 214,900 (met. a.).

Lauterbrunnen, Alpine valley, Bern can., Switzerland; famous for its waterfalls, the highest of which is Staubbach 299 m; tourist and winter sports ctr.

Laval, t., cap. of Mayenne dep., France; Mayenne R. divides old and modern parts; cotton, paper, machin., marble; cas., church; p. (1968) 49,052.

Lavenham, t., Suffolk, Eng.; a ctr. of the wool tr. in 15th cent., still preserves its mediaeval character.

Lavera, pt., nr. Marseilles, S.E. France commencement of 752 km oil pipeline to Karlsruhe, W. Germany; oil refining.

Lawrence, t., Mass., USA; on Merrimac R., N.W. of Boston; textiles, paper, footwear, engin.; p. (1970) 66,216 (c.), 229,325 (met. a.).

Lawton, t., Okla., USA; mnfs. cottonseed oil; p. (1970) 69,069 (c.), 104,504 (met. a.).

Laxey, v., I. of Man, Eng.; flour milling, woollen mills, meerschaum pipes.

Lea or **Lee**, R., Eng.; rises in Chiltern Hills nr. Luton, flows S. and E. into R. Thames through industl. zone of N.E. London; valley to become a regional park; mkt. gardening a.; 74 km long.

Leamington (Royal Leamington Spa), t., Warwicks., Eng.; on R. Leam, trib. of Avon, 3 km N.E. of Warwick; fashionable spa; engin. inds.; p. (1971) 44,989.

Leatherhead, t., Mole Valley, Surrey, Eng.; on R. Mole to N. of gap through N. Downs; residtl.; p. (1971) 40,112.

Lebanon, mtn. range, Lebanon, extending to cst. of Syria; snow-capped most of year; highest peak Timarum, 3,214 m; famous in anc. times for cedar forests.

Lebanon, rep., S.W. Asia; at E. end of Mediterranean Sea; bordered by Syria to N. and Israel to S.; narrow coastal strip backed by mtnous. interior; free mkt. a., with economy based on transit tr.; most of p. involved in tourism, finance and commerce; oil refining based on imports; cap. Beirut; strife-torn by civil war 1975–6; a. 8,806 km²; p. (est. 1972) 2,960,000. [p. (1968) 9,797.

Le Bourget, t., N.E. of Paris, France; airpt.;

Lebórk (Lauenburg), t., Gdansk, Poland (since 1945); in agr. dist.; timber and food inds.; p. (1970) 25,000.

Lebowa Territory, Bantu Terr., S. Africa; home of N. Sotho and Ndebele peoples; self-gov. Oct. 1972; cap. Seshego; p. (1970) 1,087,095.

Lecce, c., Apulia, S. Italy; agr. and route ctr. with ceramic and glass inds.; anc. Greek col.; baroque churches and palaces; p. (1969) 81,769.

Lecco, t., Italy; in Lombardy, on L. Como; iron and copper wks., agr.-processing, cheese; one of first ts. in Europe to be run by elec.; p. (est. 1967) 51,500.

Lech, R., rises in Austria and flows past Augsburg in Bavaria, W. Germany, to join Danube; 283 km long.

Le Creusot, t., Saône-et-Loire, France; ctr. of one of sm. coalfields bordering the Massif Central; steel, engin.; p. (1968) 34,109.

Ledbury, t., Hereford and Worcs., Eng.; at W. foot of Malvern hills; fruit preserving, tanning; 17th cent. mkt. hall; birthplace of John Masefield; p. (1971) 11,184 (dist.).

Leeds, c., met. dist., West Yorks., Eng.; on R. Aire; at E. margin of Pennines; univ.; lge. clothing ind., varied engin. mnfs., paper and printing; with Bradford forms conurb. of W. Yorks.; p. (est. 1976) 744,500.

Leek, mkt. t., Staffs. Moorland, Staffs., Eng.; 18 km N.E. of Stoke-on-Trent; silk mnfs., butter; expanded t.; p. (1971) 19,368.

Lee-on-Solent, t., Hants., Eng.; on Southampton Water. [4,367.

Lees, t., Gtr. Manchester, Eng.; textiles; p. (1971)

Leeuwarden, c., cap. of Friesland prov., Neth.; noted cattle mkt.; rly. junc.; p. (1968) 87,414.

Leeuwin, C., S.W. point of Australia; notorious storms.

Leeward Is., W.I., northern gr. of Lesser Antilles archipelago; so-called because winds in this a. generally blow from E.; inc. Virgin Is. of US; Fr. I. of Guadloupe, Dutch Is. of St. Eustatius and Saba, and Brit. Leeward Is. (Montserrat, Virgin Is., and former cols. of Antigua, St. Kitt-Nevis, Anguilla).

Legaspi, t., cap. of Albay prov., Philippines; spt. in S.E. Luzon; linked by rly. with Manila; p. (est. 1970) 84,700.

Leghorn. *See* Livorno.

Legionowa, t., Poland; new t. (1951) on outskirts of Warsaw; nr. artificial L. in R. Bug valley; p. (1970) 20,800.

Legnano, t., Lombardy, Italy; N.W. of Milan; textiles, machin.; p. (est. 1967) 45,900.

Legnica (Liegnitz), c., Wroclaw, S.W. Poland (since 1945); on Katzbach R., in rich agr. region; p. (1970) 75,800.

Leh, cap. of Ladakh, Kashmir, India; isolated t. in Himalayas on caravan route to Tibet; p. (1961) 3,700.

Le Havre, spt., Seine-Maritime dep., N. France; at mouth of Seine on English Channel; shipbldg., engin., chemicals, ropes, cottons, oil refining; pipeline to Grandpuits; p. (1968) 200,940 (c.), 247,374 (met. a.).

Leicester, c., co. t., l. gov. dist., Leics., Eng.; on R. Soar; univ.; footwear, hosiery, knitwear, textile machin.; Roman remains; p. (est. 1976) 289,400.

Leicestershire, non-met. co., Eng.; mainly rural, low-lying Midland co., but inc. Charnwood Forest; mixed agr., sm. coalfield; hosiery and footwear inds.; now inc. Rutland; ch. t. Leicester; a. 2,554 km²; p. (est. 1976) 837,900.

Leicestershire, North West, l. gov. dist., Leics., Eng.; inc. Ashby de la Zouch, Ashby Woulds, Coalville and Castle Donington; p. (est. 1976) 74,500.

Leiden or **Leyden**, c., S. Holland prov., Neth.; on Oude Rijn; famous univ.; printing, textiles, medical equipment; gr. weaving ctr. in Middle Ages; revolt against Spanish rule 1573–4; birthplace of Rembrandt; p. (est. 1969) 101,878 (c.), 161,341 (met. a.).

Leigh, t., Gtr. Manchester, Eng.; 8 km S.E. of Wigan; mkt.; coal mng.; textiles; p. (1971) 46,117.

Leigh-on-Sea, t., Essex, Eng.; on N. cst. of Thames estuary, 3 km W. of Southend; holiday resort, fishing.

Leighton Buzzard, t., South Beds., Eng.; at N.E. end of Vale of Aylesbury; tiles, engin., sand quarrying; p. (1971) 20,326 (inc. Linslade).

Leinster, S.E. prov., R.o.I.; bulk of recent Irish p. increase; a. 19,736 km²; p. (1966) 1,412,465.

Leipzig, c., E. Germany; comm., industl., and cultural ctr. at junc. of Rs. Pleisse, Elster, and Parthe; famous univ.; inds. inc. publishing, steel, textiles, chemicals, machin., cars; tr. fairs; Bach was organist at Thomaskirche; birthplace of Leibnitz and Wagner; p. (est. 1969) 587,761.

Leiston-cum-Sizewell, t., Suffolk Coastal, Suffolk, Eng.; on cst., 6 km E. of Saxmundham; agr. implements; nuclear power sta.; p. (1971) 4,864.

Leith, t., Edinburgh City, Scot.; shipbldg., timber, whisky; outport for Edinburgh.

Leith Hill, Surrey, Eng.; nr. Dorking; alt. 294 m; Lower Greensand crest.

Leitmeritz. *See* Litoměřice.

Leitrim, co., Connacht, R.o.I.; agr.; cap. Carrick-on-Shannon; a. 1,588 km²; p. (1966) 30,532.

Leix. *See* Laoighis.

Leixões, the modern harbour of Oporto, Portugal; oil refinery.

Lek, R., Neth.; one of the branches of the Neder Rijn; from Wijk-bij-Duurstede to Krimpen nr. Rotterdam; 64 km long.

Le Locle, t., Neuchâtel, Switzerland; ctr. of watch-mkg. ind.; p. (1969) 15,200.

Léman L. *See* Geneva, L.

Le Mans, t., cap. of Sarthe dep., N.W. France; cath.; linen, ironmongery, chemicals, motor cars, aeroplanes; motor-racing; p. (1968)｜147,651.

Lemnos, Greek I., Aegean Sea, Greece; 64 km S.W. of Dardanelles; ch. t. Kastro (the anc. Myrina); tobacco, wine; a. 466 km²; part of Lesvos dep.

Lena, one of gr. Siberian Rs., **RSFSR**; rises in Oc.; navigable; 4,480 km long.

Leninabad, c., Tadzhik SSR, USSR; on Syr Dar'ya R., S. of Tashkent; silks, cottons, fruit-preserving; hydroelectric power sta.; p (1970) 103,000.

Leninakan, c., Armenian SSR, RSFSR; nr. Turkish border; textiles, engin., rug-mkg.; p. (1970) 164,000.

Lenin Dam (Dnieper Dam). *See* Zaporozh'ye.

Leningrad, c., cap. of Leningrad oblast, RSFSR; at mouth of Neva R.; cultural ctr. with many fine bldgs., inc. winter palace, Hermitage museum, cath., admiralty bldg.; former cap. of Russia; major pt. and industl. ctr.; exp. timber, furs, and raw materials; ice-bound December–March; founded (1703) by Peter the Great as St. Petersburg; **p.** (1970) 3,513,000 (c); 4,311,000 (met. a.).

Leninogorsk, c., Kazakh SSR, **USSR**; in Altai mtns.; lead zinc, and silver mines; metallurgical plants; p. (est. 1967) 70,000.

Lenin Peak (**Mt. Kaufmann**), Trans-Altai Range, Kirghiz-Tadzhik SSR border, 2nd. hgst. mtn. of **USSR**; adjoining glacier; alt. 7,132 m.

Leninsk-Kuznetski, t., RSFSR; in W. Siberia on Inya R.; coalfield in Kuznetsk basin; heavy engin., power sta.; p. (1970) 128,000.

Lenkoran, c., pt. Azerbaydzhan SSR, USSR; on Caspian Sea, nr. Iranian border; rice, citrus fruits, tea, fisheries, food-processing; p. (est. 1967) 31,000.

Lennoxtown, t., Stirling, Scot.; alum. wks.

Lens, t., Pas-de-Calais dep., N. France; industl. ctr. in coal a.; p. (1968) 41,874 (c.), 325,696 (met. a.).

Leoben, t., Styria, Austria; lignite mng. ctr.; p. (1961) 36,257.

Leominster, mkt. t., l. gov. dist., Hereford and Worcs., Eng.; 19 km N. of Hereford; once famed for woollen ind.; p. (est. 1976) 35,900 (dist.).

León, c., central Mexico; at c. 1,700 m; comm., agr. and mng. ctr. (gold, copper, silver, lead, tin); textiles, leather; p. (1970) 364,990.

León, c., cap. of León dep., N.W. Nicaragua; cath., univ.; ctr. for agr. and industl. prods.; footwear, textiles; p. (est. 1970) 90,897.

León, cap. of L. prov., N.W. Spain; gothic cath.; craft inds.; p. (1967) 92,814.

Léopoldville. *See* Kinshasa.

Lepontine Alps, major gr., Switzerland–Italy; alt. over 3,300 m.

Le Puy, t., cap. of Haute Loire dep., France; lace, liqueurs; cath. sited on old volcanic plug; tourism; p. (1968) 29,549.

Lérida, t., cap. of L. prov., Spain; on R. Segre; 2 caths.; textiles, leather, glass; p. (1967) 75,467.

Lerwick, t., Shetland Is., Scot.; on Mainland; fishing; p. (1971) 6,127.

Lesbos. *See* Lesvos.

Les Causses. *See* Causses, Les.

Leskovac, t., Serbia, Yugoslavia; on Morava R.; in economically backward a.; textiles, soap, furniture, tobacco-processing; p. (est. 1965) 40,000.

Les Landes. *See* Landes, Les.

Leslie, burgh, Kirkcaldy, Scot.; 11 km N. of Kirkcaldy; paper, bleaching; p. (1971) 3,342.

Lesotho (Basutoland), kingdom, southern Africa; surrounded by Rep. of S. Africa; at head of Orange R. and enclosed by Drakensberg mtns.; economy mainly agr., especially pastoral farming; exp. livestock, wool, mohair, diamonds; 50 per cent revenue from U.K. grants; inds. underdeveloped; poor communications; cap. Maseru; a. 30,344 km²; p. (est. 1969) 930,000.

Lesser Antilles. *See* Antilles.

Lesvos (Lesbos, Mytilene), I., off Turkey, Aegean Sea. belonging to Greece; highest point 939 m; agr., agriculture, marbles; cap. Mytilene; a. 1,601 km²; p. (1971) 114,504 (dep.).

Leszno, t., Poznan, W. Poland; engin., distilling, tobacco; p. (1970) 33,900.

Letchworth (Garden City), t., North Herts., Eng.; at foot of Chiltern Hills, 3 km N.E. of Hitchin; first garden c., founded by Sir Ebenezer Howard 1903; engin., office equipment; expanded t.; p. (1971) 30,884.

Lethbridge, c., Alberta, Canada; in foothills of Rockies; ctr. of lge coal-mng. dist. and of irrigated wheat-growing a.; p. (1971) 40,706.

Le Touquet-Paris Plage, fashionable resort, W. cst. France, S. of Canche estuary.

Letterkenny, t., Co. Donegal, R.o.I.; on Lough Swilly; tourist ctr.; p. (1966) 4,513.

Leuna, t., Halle, E. Germany; 5 km S. of Merseburg; synthetic chemical ind.; oil pipeline from Schwedt; p. (1963) 12,702.

Levant, French and Italian name for E. cst. of Mediterranean.

Leven, burgh, Kirkcaldy, Scot.; on N. side of F. of Forth; resort; p. (1971) 9,472.

Leven, L., Perth and Kinross, Scot.; ass. with escape of Mary Queen of Scots from Castle I., 1568.

Leverkusen, t., N. Rhine–Westphalia, W. Germany; on R. Rhine, N. of Cologne; iron, machin., textiles, chemicals; p. (est. 1969) 110,800.

Levkás or Santa Maura, one of Ionian Is., off W. Greece; wine, olive oil, currants.

Lewes, co. t., l. gov. dist., East Sussex, Eng.; on R. Ouse at N. entrance to gap through S. Downs; mkt., agr. ctr.; p. (est. 1976) 75,400 (dist.).

Lewis, I ,Outer Hebrides, Scot.; fishing, tweeds; ch. t. Stornoway; a. 1,994 km²; p. (1971) 15,174.

Lewisham, inner bor., London, Eng.; inc. Deptford; residtl.; industl.; p. (est. 1976) 237,300.

Lewiston, t., Maine, USA; power for textile mill supplied by waterfall since early 19th cent.; p. (est. 1969) 40,500.

Lexington, c., Ky., USA; in heart of Blue Grass region; univ.; ch. tobacco mkt. and horse-breeding ctr. of USA; p. (1970) 107,944 (c.), 172,927 (met. a.).

Lexington, t., Mass., USA; nr. Boston; residtl.; first battle in war of independence 19 Apr. 1775; p. (est. 1969) 34,000.

Leyburn, t., Richmondshire, North Yorks., Eng.; in lower Wensleydale; mkt.; p. (1971) 5,896 (dist.).

Leyden. *See* Leiden.

Leyland, t., Lancs., Eng.; 8 km S. of Preston; motor vehicles, rubber; p. (1971) 23,391.

Leyte, one of Visayan Is., central Philippines; maize, abaca, rice; Japanese fleet defeated by US in battle of Leyte Gulf 1944; a. 7,213 km²; p. (1970) 1,340,015.

Leyton. *See* Waltham Forest.

Lhasa (Lasa), c., cap. of Tibet, China; "forbidden" c.; Buddhist ctr., temple, monasteries, shrines; caravan tr. in carpets, silk, lace, gold, tea; pharmaceutical factory, turbine pumps, fertilisers; p. (est. 1970) 175,000.

Lhotse, mtn., Tibet, China–Nepal; 4th hgst. mtn. in world; alt. 8,506 m.

Liao-ho, R., Liaoning, N.E. China; flows into G. of Liaotung, Yellow Sea; navigable for last 640 km of course; c. 1,600 km long.

Liaoning, prov., N.E. China; inc. lower course and delta of Liao-ho; part of N.E. China (formerly called Manchuria); maize, millets, soyabeans; lge. mineral reserves of coal and iron ore; cap. Shenyang; a. 150,220 km²; p. (est. 1968) 28,000,000.

Liaotung, peninsula, N.E. China; nr. G. of same name.

Liaoyang, c., E. Liaoning prov., N.E. China; in fertile valley of Liao-ho; cotton-growing; textile mills; p. (est. 1970) 250,000.

Liao-yuang, c., S.W. Kirin, China; lge. coal-mng. ctr.; p. (1953) 120,100.

Liberec, t., ČSSR; on R. Neisse; univ.; textiles, chemicals, tr. ctr.; p. (1967) 71,000.

Liberia, rep., W. Africa; tropical climate; 90 per cent of p. involved in agr.; few cash crops, inc. rubber and cocoa; rich iron deposits provide main exp.; world's lgst. merchant fleet as result of "flag of convenience"; cap. and ch. pt. Monrovia; a. 99,068 km²; p. (est. 1969) 1,134,000.

Libourne, t., Gironde, France; on R. Dordogne, 35 km N.E. of Bordeaux; wine tr.; p. (1968) 22,123.

Libreville, c., cap. of Gabon; pt. on G. of Guinea; exp. tropical hardwoods, rubber, cacao; Trans-Gabon rly. project to link L. to Booué to promote timber exploitation; p. (1965) 31,000 (c.); (1967) 57,000 (met. a.).

Libya, or Popular Socialist Libyan Arab Jamahiriyah (since 1977), rep., N. Africa; on Mediterranean cst.; desert conditions prevail; radical attitude towards oil cos., as oil accounts for 99 per cent of exp. earnings and forms basis of new-found wealth; petro-chemical inds.; over half working p. are foreigners; most of p. engaged in subsistence agr.; joint caps. Tripoli (site of government deps.), Benghazi; a. 1,759,537 km²; p. (est. 1969) 1,875,000.

Libyan Desert, part of the Sahara, Africa.

Licata, t., Sicily, Italy; spt; sulphur-processing; p. (est. 1968) 40,422.

Lichfield, c., l. gov. dist., Staffs., Eng.; cath.; agr. and lt. inds ; expanded t.; birthplace of Dr. Samuel Johnson; p. (est. 1976) 88,600 (dist.).

Lickey Hills, gr. of hills, Hereford and Worcs., Eng.; 6 km S.W. of Birmingham; reveal anc. rocks underlying younger sediments; rise to 292 m, largely wooded.

Liechtenstein, principality, between Austria and Switzerland; official language German; economy based on sm.-scale inds. and tourism in picturesque Alpine scenery aided by mild climate; wine; cap. Vaduz; a. 161 km²; p. (1969) 21,758; 20 per cent p. in Vaduz.

Liège (Luik), industl. c., E. Belgium; on R. Meuse nr. confluence of Ourthe; cath., univ.; conurb. inc. Herstal, Bressoux, Ougrée, Angleur, Grivegnée; metallurgy, armaments, vehicles, chemicals, textiles, glassware, tyres; p. (est. 1969) 148,599 (c.); 445,347 (met. a.).

Liepaja (Libau), c., Latvian SSR, USSR; ice-free pt. on Baltic Sea, second to Riga; shipyards, steel-wks., paper mills, chemicals; exp. timber, grain; p. (1969) 88,000.

Liestal, t., cap. of the half-can. Baselland, Switzerland; p. (1970) 12,500.

Liffey, R., R.o.I.; rises in Wicklow Mtns. and enters Irish Sea at Dublin; water supply for Dublin; inds. along estuary.

Liguria, region, N.W. Italy; inc. provs. of Genoa and Porto Maurizio; a. 5,411 km²; p. (1969) 1,873,039.

Ligurian Sea, Mediterranean; N. of Corsica.

Lille, c., cap. of Nord dep., N. France; on R. Deûle; mftg., comm. and cultural ctr.; former cap. of Fr. Flanders (1668); textiles (the name Lisle derived from earlier spelling of city's name), metallurgy, engin.; univ., art museums; p. (1968) 194,948 (c.), 881,439 (mct. a.).

Lilongwe, c., main ctr. of Central Region, Malawi; replaced Zomba as cap. 1975; p. (1966) 19,176.

Lima, c., cap. of Peru; 13 km from its pt. Callao; dominates comm., industl. and social life of cty.; cath., univ., imposing architecture; seaside subs. Miraflores, Barranco, Chorillos; shanty ts. on outskirts; p. (est. 1970) 2,541,300 (met. a.).

Lima, t., Ohio, USA; on Ottawa R.; rly. wks., oil, car bodies, refrigerators; p. (1970) 53,373 (c.), 170,687 (met. a.).

Limassol, t., S. Cyprus; spt. on Akrotiri Bay; new artificial harbour; ctr. of admin. dist.; wine, agr.-processing; exp. foodstuffs; tourism; p. (est. 1970) 51,500.

Limavady, t., l. gov. dist., N. Ireland; mkt.; linen; p. (1966) 4,811.

Limbach, t., Karl-Marx-Stadt, E. Germany; hosiery, textiles, machines; p. (est 1970) 25,460.

Limbe. See Blantyre-Limbe.

Limburg, prov., N.E. Belgium; bordering Neth.; mainly agr.; coal-mng. in Campine region; cap. Hasselt; a. 2,409 km²; p. (1968) 638,593.

Limburg, prov., S.E. Neth.; bordering on Belgium and W. Germany; drained by R. Maas; former coalmng.; new inds. to relieve unemployment; a. 2,191 km²; p. (1968) 985,738.

Limeira, t., São Paulo, Brazil; ctr. of orange cultivation; hats, matches; p. (est.1970) 71,690.

Limerick, co., Munster, R.o.I.; agr., livestock, fishing; a. 3,385 km²; p. (1966) 137,276.

Limerick C.B., cap. of Limerick, R.o.I.; spt. at head of Shannon estuary; bacon, tanning, shipbldg.; p. (1966) 55,885.

Limmat, R., Switzerland; trib. of R. Aare; flows through c. of Zürich; 128 km long.

Lim Fjord, shallow strait, Jutland, Denmark; connects N. Sea with Kattegat; contains I. of Mors.

Limoges, c., cap. of Haute-Vienne dep., France; to N.W. of Central Massif; anc. t., celebrated in middle ages for goldsmith's work, later for enamel ware and porcelain; cath.; p. (1968) 132,935.

Limón, spt., Costa Rica; on Caribbean; oil refining nearby; p. (est. 1968) 22,555.

Limousin, region and former prov., central France; to W. of Auvergne; now divided

into deps. Haute-Vienne, Corrèze, Dordogne; plateau, average alt. 300 m, composed of old crystalline rocks; exposed damp climate; infertile, some pastoral agr.; kaolin; ch. t. Limoges.

Limpopo or Crocodile R., S. Africa, Moçambique, and Rhodesia; lower R forms a fertile valley 1,600 km long.

Linares, prov., central Chile; thermal springs in Andes; cereals and vineyards in valleys; cap. Linares; a. 9,816 km²; p. (1970) 189,010.

Linares, t., Jaen prov., Spain; silver-lead mines; metallurgical inds.; p. (1967) 61.593.

Lincoln, c., co. t., l. gov. dist., Lincs., Eng.; on R. Witham in gap through Lincoln Edge; impt. Roman t.; cath., cas.; heavy engin., iron foundries, bricks, lime, seed milling, malting; p. (est. 1976) 73,700.

Lincoln, c., cap. of Nebraska, USA; univ.; educational ctr.; grain and cattle mkt.; flour mills, agr. machin., cars, chemicals, rubber gds.; p. (1970) 148,092.

Lincoln Edge, limestone ridge, Lincs. and Humberside, Eng.; runs N. from Ancaster through Lincoln to Humber; narrow ridge with steep scarp slope to W., broken by R. Witham at Lincoln; iron-ore deposits worked in N. nr. Scunthorpe; sheep, barley; rarely exceeds 90 m alt.

Lincolnshire, non-met. co., Eng.; between Humberside non-met. co. and the Wash; fertile soil on low-lying fenland; intensive agr., arable crops, bulbs, market gardening; food-processing; formerly divided into 3 admin. parts: Holland, Kesteven, and Lindsey; a. 5,884 km²; p. (est. 1976) 524,500.

Lincoln Wolds, low plateau, Lincs. and Humberside, Eng.; runs N. 72 km from Wash to Humber; chalk covered with glacial deposits; mixed farming, grains, roots, sheep; lge. farm units; scantily populated; rise to approx. 135 m.

Lindau, t., Baden-Württemberg, W. Germany; on I. in Bodensee; tourist resort; p. (est. 1967) 25,900.

Lindisfarne or Holy I., off cst. of Northumberland, Eng.; connected to mainland by stretch of sand at low tide; abbey founded 635 A.D. as first establishment of Celtic Christianity in Eng.

Lindsey. See Lincolnshire.

Lindsey, East, l. gov. dist., Lincs., Eng.; lge a. on E. cst. inc. Louth, Mablethorpe, Horncastle, Woodhall Spa, Skegness and Alford; p. (est. 1976) 100,100.

Line Is., Pac. Oc., coral gr. admin. by U.K., except Palmyra, Kingman and Jarvis, which belong to USA; coconuts; airfields, meteorological stas.

Lin-i (formerly **Ichow**), t, Shantung, China; at foot of Shantung Highlands.

Linköping, t., S.E. Sweden; aero-engin., pianos, furniture; cath.; p. (1968) 78,032.

Linlithgow, burgh, W. Lothian, Scot.; distilling, brewing, paper, shoes; birthplace of Mary Queen of Scots; p. (1971) 5,684.

Linnhe, Loch, Lochaber, Argyll and Bute, Scot.; 21 m. long; entrance to Caledonian canal.

Linslade. See Leighton Buzzard.

Linz, c., cap. of Upper Austria; pt. on Danube; comm. and industl. ctr. with iron and steel wks.; cath.; p. (est. 1969) 205,808.

Lipa, t., Luzon, Philippines; sugar, tobacco, cocoa, maize; processing; p. (est. 1970) 96,500.

Lipari Is. or Aeolian Is., volcanic gr. between Sicily and toe of Italy; inc. Stromboli (927 m), Lipari, Vulcano, Salina; olives, grapes, currants, pumice.

Lipetsk, c., RSFSR; on Voronezh R.; ctr. of iron-ore mng. a.; engin., steel, ferro-alloys; health resort; p. (1970) 290,000.

Lippe, R., W. Germany; trib. of Rhine; paralleled by L. canal; forms N. bdy. of Ruhr industl. dist.; 176 km long.

Lippstadt, t., N. Rhin.—Westphalia, W. Germany; on R. Lippe; metallurgy, textiles, rly. ctr.; p. (est. 1967) 40,400.

Liri, R., central Italy; rises in Alban Hills, flows S.E. to Cassino and then S.W. to G. of Gaeta; valley followed by main road from Rome to Naples; length 168 km.

Lisbon (Lisboa), c., cap of Portugal; on R. Tagus, 14 km from mouth; spt. with fine natural harbour; cas., cath., univ.; admin., comm., and industl. ctr.; expanding inds., airpt.; attracts p. from rural areas; p. (est. 1969) 830,600.

Lisburn, t., l. gov. dist., **N. Ireland;** on R. Lagan, 10 km S.W. of Belfast; p. (est. 1971) 27,405.

Lisieux, t., Calvados dep., N. France; historic t., severely damaged in second world war; cath.; Camembert cheese; p. (1968) 25,223.

Liskeard, mkt. t., Caradon, Cornwall, **Eng.;** on R. Looe at S. edge of Bodmin Moor; p. (1971) 5,255.

Lismore, t., N.S.W., **Australia;** pt. on Richmond R.; dairying, sugar refining, maize, potatoes, textiles, engin.; p. (1972) 20,901.

Lismore, mkt. t., R.D., Waterford, **R.o.I.;** on Blackwater R.; cas.; p. (1966) 894 (t.).

Listowel, U.D., Kerry, **R.o.I.;** on R. Feale; cas. ruins; p. (1966) 2,822.

Litherland, t., Sefton, Merseyside, **Eng.;** N. sub. of Liverpool; p. (1971) 23,670.

Lithuania (Litva SSR), constituent rep., **USSR;** borders Baltic Sea; agr. development on re-claimed marshland; dairy farming, stock-raising, fishing, timber inds., food-processing, ship bldg., textiles, machin.; cap. Vilna; a. 65,201 km²; p. (1970) 3,129,000.

Litoměřice, t., **ČSSR;** in Bohemia on R. Elbe (Labe); cath.; brewing, agr. ctr.; p. (est. 1968) 18,894.

Little Belt (Lille Bælt), strait, **Denmark;** separates Fyn I. from Jutland; too shallow for lge. ships; road/rly., motorway bridges cross narrow N. section nr. Frederidicia; 48 km long.

Little Bighorn R., Wyo. Mont., **USA;** Custer's last battle on ridge overlooking R. (1876); 144 km long.

Littleborough, t., Gtr. Manchester, **Eng.;** textiles and textile finishing; p. (1971) 11,987.

Littlehampton, t., Arun, West Sussex, **Eng.;** on S. cst. at mouth of R. Arun; holiday resort, sm. spt.; p. (1971) 18,621.

Little Lever, t., Gtr. Manchester, **Eng.;** 5 km S.E. of Bolton; residtl. and industl.; p. (1971) 9,124.

Little Rock, c., cap. of Ark., **USA;** N.E. of Hot Springs, on Ark. R. opposite N. Little Rock; comm. and mnf. ctr. in rich cotton and dairy farming a.; bauxite nearby; p. (1970) 128,880 (c.), 315,375 (met. a.).

Littoria. *See* Latina.

Liuchow, c., Kwangsi prov., S. **China;** on trib. of Si-kiang; route ctr. and R. pt.; p. (1958) 190,000.

Liverpool, c., spt., met. dist., **Merseyside, Eng.;** second pt. in Gr. Britain, on N. bank at entrance to Mersey estuary; deep-sea container berths at Seaforth; shipping and ship-repairing; elec. mnfs. and engin., flour milling, sugar refining, seed and rubber processing, cars; cath., univ.; second Mersey tunnel opened 1971; p. (est. 1976) 539,700 (l. gov. dist.), 1,368,630 (met. a.).

Liverpool, t., N.S.W., **Australia;** within met. a. of Sydney; mkt. and processing ctr. for dairy prod.; elec. gds., woollens; p. (1966) 60,552.

Livingston, new t. (1962), W. Lothian, **Scot.;** p. (est. 1974) 22,470.

Livingstone, t., Zambia; on Zambesi R. where rly. bridges R.; stands at c. 900 m; former cap.; sawmilling ctr.; p. (est. 1967) 41,000.

Livorno (Leghorn), spt., cap. of L. prov., **Italy;** on Ligurian Sea; shipbldg., machin., chemicals, iron and steel wks., oil refining; exp. wine, olive oil, textiles, marble; p. (1969) 173,839.

Lizard, The, c., Cornwall, **Eng.;** S. point of Eng.

Ljubljana, c., cap. of Slovenia, N.W. **Yugoslavia;** on trib. of Sava R.; industl. ctr., local coal, hydroelectric power; route ctr.; airport; univ., mediaeval fortress; ctr. of Slovene nat. movement in 19th cent.; p. (est. 1969) 172,000.

Llanberis, pass, Gwynedd, N. **Wales;** between Snowdon and Clyder Fawr; road carries heavy tourist traffic; summit 356 m; nearby tourist resort of Llanberis.

Llandaff, t., South Glamorgan, S. **Wales;** part of Cardiff; cath.

Llandarcy, v., West Glamorgan, S. **Wales;** on cst. Swansea Bay, Bristol Channel; lge oil refinery; pipeline to Angle Bay, Pembroke.

Llandeilo, mkt. t., Dinefwr, Dyfed, **Wales;** in vale of Towy, E. of Carmarthen; cas.; p. (1971) 1,794.

Llandovery, t., Dinefwr, Dyfed, **Wales;** on R. Bran, nr. confluence with Towy; mkt. ctr. for rural a.; p. (1971) 1,999.

Llandrindod Wells, t., Radnor, Powys, **Wales;** medicinal waters; p. (1971) 3,379.

Llandudno, t., Aberconwy, Gwynedd, **Wales;** between Gr. Ormes and Little Ormes headlands; resort; p. (1971) 19,009.

Llanelli, l. gov. dist., Dyfed, **Wales;** pt. on Burry inlet, 18 km. N.W. of Swansea; industl. and comm. ctr.; coal mng., steel, and tinplate wks., mng. machin.; cas.; p. (est. 1976) 76,700 (dist.).

Llanfairfechan, t., Aberconwy, Gwynedd, **Wales;** at foot of Penmaenmawr mtn.; seaside resort; granite quarrying; p. (1971) 3,430.

Llanfyllin, t., Powys, **Wales;** anc. mkt. t.; p. (1971) 1,117.

Llangefni, t., Anglesey, Gwynedd, **Wales;** in ctr. of the I.; mkt. and agr. t.; p. (1971) 3,049.

Llangollen, t., Glyndŵr, Clwyd, **Wales;** on R. Dee; vale of L., tourist ctr.; annual Eisteddfod; p. (1971) 3,108.

Llanidloes, t., Powys, **Wales;** on R. Severn; sur-rounded by hills; anc. mkt. house; p. (1971) 2,333.

Llanos, lowland region, Venezuela and Colombia, S. America; drained by R. Orinoco and tribs.; high temperatures throughout year, but rain chiefly in summer; ch. vegetation, coarse grass which withers during dry season (Dec. to May); little developed, some cattle-rearing.

Llanos de Urgel, upland region, Lérida, N.E. **Spain;** semi-arid; formerly steppe-land, now irrigated by R. Segre; vine, olive, maize, to-bacco.

Llanrwst, mkt. t., Aberconwy, Gwynedd, **Wales;** on R. Conway; tourist ctr.; p. (1971) 2,736.

Llanstephan, v., Dyfed, **Wales;** at mouth of R. Towy; ruins of Norman cas.

Llantrisant, new t., Taff-Ely, Mid Glamorgan, S. **Wales;** iron-ore quarrying; Royal Mint; p. (1971) 37,087 (dist.).

Llanwrtyd Wells, t., Brecknock, Powys, **Wales;** once a spa; resort; p. (1971) 488.

Lleyn, peninsula, Gwynedd, N. **Wales;** from Snowdonia to Bardsey I.; crystalline rocks form hills in E., otherwise low, undulating; pastoral farming, sheep, cattle; sm. seaside resorts; ch. t. Pwllheli; a. 466 km²; p. (1971) 15,200 (dist.).

Lliw Valley, l. gov. dist., West Glamorgan, **Wales;** comprises Pontardawe and Llwchwr; p. (est. 1976) 58,000.

Llwchwr, t., Lliw Valley, West Glamorgan, S. **Wales;** p. (1971) 26,845.

Llwchwr or Loughor, R., S. **Wales;** in lower course forms bdy. between Dyfed and West Glamorgan, empties into Burry inlet.

Loanhead, burgh, Midlothian, **Scot.;** 8 km S.E. of Edinburgh; coal, engin.; p. (1971) 5,963.

Lobito, spt., Angola; on Atl. Oc.; 29 km N. of Benguela; fine natural deepwater harbour; rly. terminus; varied exps.; oil-refinery under construction; p. (est. 1969) 97,758.

Locarno, t., Switzerland; on L. Maggiore; tourist ctr.; L. treaty 1925; p. (1969) 13,400.

Lochaber, mtnous. l. gov. dist., Highland Reg., **Scot.;** bounded by Loch Linnhe and Loch Leven; inc. Ben Nevis; hydroelec. power; a. 4,465 km²; p. (1971) 18,920.

Lochalsh. *See* Kyle of Lochalsh.

Lochgelly, burgh, Dunfermline l. gov. dist., **Scot.;** nr. Dunfermline; p. (1971), 7,980.

Lochgilphead, co. t., Argyll and Bute, **Scot.;** at head of Loch Gilp, 3 km N. of Ardrishaig; tourist ctr.; p. (1971) 1,184.

Lochmaben, burgh, Annandale and Eskdale, **Scot.;** in Annandale, 11 km N.E. of Dumfries; p. (1971) 1,261.

Lockerbie, burgh, Annandale and Eskdale, **Scot.;** in Annandale, 16 km E. of Dumfries; sheep mkt.; p. (1971) 3,624.

Lockport, t., N.Y., **USA;** on N.Y. st. barge canal, 38 km N.E. of Buffalo; power from Niagara falls supplies paper, metal, and other inds.; p. (1970) 25,399.

Lodi, t., **Italy;** on R. Adda, S.E. of Milan; cath.; scene of Napoleon's victory over Austrians 1796; p. (est. 1968) 42,757.

Lodore Falls, waterfalls, Cumbria, **Eng.;** in Watendlath beck at foot of Derwentwater.

Łódź, c., cap. of L. prov., central **Poland;** second c. of rep. and ctr. of textile ind.; machin., elec. equipment, chemicals, metals; univ.; cultural ctr.; problems of water-supply; p. (1970) 761,800.

Lofoten Is., storm-swept chain of Is. off N.W. cst.

Norway within Arctic Oc., stretching 240 km; cod and herring fisheries among richest in world.

Loftus, t., Langbaurgh, Cleveland, Eng.; on N.E. flank of Cleveland Hills; p. (1971) 7,706.

Logan, Mount, S.E. Yukon, Canada, E. of Alaska; alt. 6,054 m; highest mtn. in Canada and second highest in N. America.

Logroño, t., N. Spain; on Ebro R.; in wine growing a.; industl. and agr. ctr.; p. (1967) 75,157.

Loire, R., France; longest in cty., flows from Cevennes mtns. to Atl. Oc. at St. Nazaire; vineyards and many castles in attractive valley; 1,000 km long.

Loire, dep., E. central France; in part of the former provs. of Beaujolais and Lyonnais; agr., coal mng., cattle raising; cap. St. Etienne; a. 4,799 km²; p. (1968) 722,383.

Loire-Atlantique, dep., W. France; mainly agr., salt-marsh on cst.; inds. at cap. Nantes; a. 6,980 km²; p. (1968) 861,452.

Loiret, dep., N. central France; agr., vineyards, distilling, mftg.; cap. Orléans; a. 6,812 km²; p. (1968) 430,629.

Loir-et-Cher, dep., central France; contains fertile a. of Beauce; cap. Blois; a. 6,421 km²; p. (1968) 267,896.

Lokeren, industl. t., Belgium; between Ghent and Antwerp; textiles, chemicals, tobacco; p. (1968) 26,569.

Lokoja, t., Nigeria; at confluence of Rs. Niger and Benue; R. pt.; iron-ore nearby.

Lolland or Laaland, Danish I. in Baltic Sea; a. 1,241 km²; agr., forests; ch. ts. Maribo, Nakshov; p. (1965) 81,760.

Lomami, R., central Zaïre; trib. of Zaire R., rich coal-bearing strata at confluence; 1,812 km long.

Lombardy, Plain of, N. Italy; extensive lowland flanked by Alps, Apennines, Adriatic Sea; built up by alluvium from R. Po, its tribs. and R. Adige; intensively cultivated; rice, maize, flax, clover, lucerne, wheat, apples, dairy cattle; densely populated; many industl. ts., Milan, Novara, Pavia, etc.

Lombok, one of the lesser Sunda Is., Indonesia; mtnous. volcanic terrain; Wallace's Line passes between Lombok and Bali; ch. t. Mataram; p. 1,300,000.

Lomé, spt., cap. of Togo, W. Africa; on G. of Guinea; deepwater pt.; exp. cacao, cotton, palm prods.; phosphates; p. (1970) 192,745.

Lomond, Loch, Stirling, lgst. loch in Scot.; studded with Is. surrounded by hills with Ben Lomond on E. side; a. 70 km².

Lomza, t., Bialystok Poland; on Narew R., metal inds., foodstuffs; p. (1970) 25,500.

London, cap. of UK, Eng.; at head of Thames estuary; seat of govt., world ctr. of finance and communication; cultural and artistic ctr.; comprises the City, 12 inner and 20 outer bors.; Port of London one of lgst pts. in world; dockyard system expanding downstream to Tilbury; currently losing p. and inds. to outer met. a.; univs. (London, Brunel, City), caths., many historic bldgs. theatres. museums. galleries. libraries, and parks; p. (est. 1976) 6,800 (City of London), 2,744,500 (Inner London), 7,028,200 (Greater London).

London, t., Ont., Canada; on R. Thames, 104 km W. of Hamilton; industl. ctr.; univ.; p. (1971) 221,430 (c.), 284,469 (met. a.).

Londonderry, former co.; l. gov. dist., N. Ireland; borders R.o.I. and L. Foyle; Sperrin Mtns. in S.; p. of former co. (est. 1971) 130,296.

Londonderry (or Derry), c., l. gov. dist. N. Ireland; on left bank of R. Foyle, 6 km upstream from Lough Foyle; shirt mftg.; textiles; acetylene from naphtha; training ctr. for ind.; p. (est. 1971) 51,850.

Londrina, c., Paraná, Brazil; industl. and agr. ctr., coffee, maize, cotton, livestock; p. (1970) 156,670.

Long Beach, c., Cal., USA; Pac. cst. resort and industl. suburb of Los Angeles met. a.; p. (1970) 346,975.

Longbenton, t., Tyne and Wear, Eng.; 5 km N.E. of Newcastle; former coal mng.; expanded t.; p. (1971) 48,970.

Long Eaton, t., Erewash, Derbys., Eng.; on R. Trent, 8 km S.W. of Nottingham; rly. wks., lace mftg., elec. cables, flexible tubing, hosiery; p. (1971) 33,694.

Longford, co., Leinster, R.o.I.; peat bogs; dairy farming; co. t. Longford; a. 1,090 km²; p. (1966) 28,943.

Longford, co. t., Longford, R.o.I.; cas., cath.; mkt. t.; p. (1966) 3,454.

Long Forties Bank, submarine sandbank, N. Sea; 128 km E. of Aberdeen; valuable fishinggrounds; depth of water, from 45–75 m.

Long I., part of N.Y., USA; separated from mainland by East R.; contains Queens and Brooklyn bors. of N.Y. City; mkt. gardening, fisheries, oysters, holiday resorts; a. 4,356 km².

Longreach, t., Queensland, Australia; in ctr. of Gr. Australian (artesian) basin; collecting ctr. for cattle and wool; p. (1966) 3,864.

Longridge, t., Ribble Valley, Lancs., Eng.; 10 km N.E. of Preston; nails; p. (1971) 6,507.

Longview, t., Texas, USA; oil, chemicals, plastics; p. (est. 1969) 48,000.

Longwy, t., Meurthe-et-Moselle dep., N.E. France; on Belgian–Luxembourg frontier; upper part fortfd.; lower part industl. with iron and steel ind.; p. (1968) 21,087.

Lons-le-Saunier, cap. of Jura dep., E. France; saline springs; agr. ctr.; p. (1968) 18,769.

Looe, t., Caradon, Cornwall, Eng.; on Looe estuary; holiday resort; p. (1971) 4,051.

Lopburi, t., Thailand; ctr. of haematite iron deposits; former cap.

Lop Nor, marsh, Sinkiang, W. China; in Tarim Basin at foot of Altyn Tagh; ctr. of inland drainage, receives water from R. Tarim; atomic testing grounds.

Lorain, t., Ohio, USA; on L. Erie; shipbldg., steelwks., fisheries; p. (1970) 76,733 (c.), 255,612 (met. a.).

Lorca, t., Murcia, Spain; agr. prod., woollens, chemicals; bishop's palace; p. (1967) 61,445.

Lord Howe I., forested volcanic I., S. Pac. Oc., 698 km N.E. of Sydney; palm seed ind.; admin by N.S.W.

Lorient, spt., Morbihan dep., N.W. France; on Atl.; naval shipyard, fishing harbour; p. (1968) 68,960.

Lorraine, region and former prov., N.E. France; inc. deps. Moselle, Meurthe-et-Moselle, Meuse, and Vosges; ch. t. Nancy; rich iron-ore deposits; impt. but declining industl. a.; mkt. gardening, vineyards; with Alsace long disputed between Germany and France.

Los Alamos, t., N.M., USA; site of research for first atomic bomb; p. (1970) 11,310.

Los Angeles, c., S. Cal., USA; booming modern c. ("the city of angels"), busiest pt. in Cal.; fine harbour; one of world's lgst. urban areas; miles of freeway (2,400 km. planned by 1980); many prosperous inds., inc. aircraft, missiles, chemicals, machin., electronic equipment, foodprocessing, oil refining; film ctr.; p. (1970) 2,781,829 (c.), 6,974,103 (met. a.).

Looe, t., Caradon, Cornwall, Eng.; on Looe estuary; holiday resort; p. (1971) 4,051.

Lossiemouth, burgh, Moray, Scot.; on Moray F., 8 km N. of Elgin; birthplace of Ramsay Macdonald; fishing; p. (1971) 5,849.

Lot, dep., S.W. France; livestock, wine, cereals, coal, iron; a. 5,227 km²; cap. Cahors; p. (1968) 151,198. [long.

Lot, R., S. France; trib. of Garonne R., 435 km

Lota, pt., Chile; coal-mng. ctr.; ceramics, copper smelting; p. (est. 1966) 57,773.

Lot-et-Garonne, dep., S.W. France; agr. (cereals, vines, fruit); cap. Agen; a. 5,385 km²; p. (1968) 290,592.

Lothian Region, l. gov. reg., central Scot.; borders F. of Forth, and inc. a. around Edinburgh; mainly industl.; a. 1,753 km²; p. (1971) 741,275.

Lötschental, picturesque valley, Valais, Switzerland; ch. v. Kippel.

Loughborough, t., Charnwood, Leics., Eng.; on R. Soar 16 km N. of Leicester; engin., elec. gds., chemicals, textiles; univ.; former hosiery t.; bell foundry; p. (1971) 45,863. [p. (1966) 3,001.

Loughrea, mkt. t., Galway, R.o.I.; cotton mill;

Louisiana, southern st., USA; leading producer of rice, sugarcane, sweet potatoes; also cotton, maize, tobacco, oil, natural gas, lumber; cap. Baton Rouge; New Orleans major pt.; a. 125,675 km²; p. (1970) 3,564,310.

Louisville, c., Ky., USA; on Ohio R.; univ.; lgst. tobacco mkt. in world; chemicals, paints, cars, machin., elec. gds., synthetic rubber; p. (1970) 356,982 (c.), 819,057 (met. a.).

Lourdes, t., France; on R. Pau; Catholic pi grim ctr.; slate, marble; p. (1968) 18,310.

Lourenço Marques. See Maputo.

Louth, t., East Lindsey, Lincs., Eng.; on E. edge of Lincoln Wolds; abbey ruins; cattle mkt., farm implements, rope mkg., lime, malting, canning; p. (1971) 11,746.

Louth, maritime co., Leinster, R.o.I.; mtns., bog and barren land; salmon fishing; cap. Dundalk; a. 818 km²; p. (1966) 69,162.

Louvain (Leuven), c., Brabant prov., Belgium; on R. Dyle; univ. (Erasmus taught here); brewing ctr., bell foundries; p. (1968) 32,224.

Low Archipelago. See Tuamotu Is.

Low Countries, name applied to Belgium and the Neth.

Lowell, c., Mass., USA; at junc. of Merrimac and Concord Rs.; 48 km N. of Boston; textiles, machin., chemicals, carpets; birthplace of Whistler; p. (1970) 92,929 (c.), 101,048 (met. a.).

Lower California (Baja California), peninsula, N.W. Mexico; separating G. of Cal. and Pac. Oc.; isolated, arid; divided into 2 sts., Baja California (cap. Tijuana), and Baja California Territorio Sur (cap. La Paz); a. 143,963 km²; p. (1969) 1,150,000.

Lower Saxony (Nieder Sachsen), Land, W. Germany; inc. Lüneburg heath and Harz mtns.; cap. Hanover; a. 47,205 km²; p. (1968) 7,039,000.

Lowestoft, fish. pt., Waveney, Suffolk, Eng.; on E. Anglian cst. 14 km S. of Gr. Yarmouth; holiday resort, nr. Broads; food and fish processing plants; base for N. Sea gas; p. (1971) 51,182.

Lowther Hills, mtns., between Strathclyde and Dumfries and Galloway Regs., Scot.; hgst. point 733 m.

Loyalty Is., S. Pac. Oc.; included in Fr. administration of New Caledonia; copra; lgst. Is., Maré, Lifou, Uvéa; a. c. 2,100 km².

Loyang, c., Honan prov., China; industl.; ball bearing and mng. machin.; lge. car and tractor plant, oil refinery, textiles; p. (est. 1970) 750,000.

Lozère, dep., S.E. France; traversed by Cevennes mtns.; cap. Mende; a. 5,170 km²; p. (1968) 77,258.

Lualaba, R., Zaïre, central Africa; rises nr. Lubumbashi in Shaba prov., flows N. circa 800 km to Kikondja, where joined by R. Lufira to form R. Zaïre; name also applied to main stream of R. Zaïre as far downstream as Ponthierville.

Luanda, c., cap. of Angola; pt. on Atl. Oc.; exp. coffee, cotton, palm prod.; industl. ctr.; foodstuffs, tobacco, clothing, plastics; oil refining; hydroelectric power; p. (est. 1971) 346,763.

Luang Prabang, c., N.W. Laos; at confluence of Mekong and Kahn Rs.; rubber, rice, teak; former royal cap.; p. (est. 1970) 25,000.

Lubbock, c., N.W. Texas, USA; on Double Mountain fork of Brazos R.; ctr. of cotton-growing a.; p. (1970) 146,379 (c.), 175,757 (met. a.).

Lübeck, c., pt. of Schleswig-Holstein, W. Germany; on Baltic Sea at mouth of Trave R.; cath.; shipbldg., machin., chemicals, textiles, iron, foodstuffs; birthplace of Thomas Mann; p. (est. 1969) 242,900.

Lublin, c., cap. of L. prov., E. Poland; motor vehicle and elec. engin.; agr. tr. and processing; cultural ctr., univ.; cas.; p. (1970) 235,900.

Lubumbashi (Elisabethville), t., Shaba, Zaïre; copper-mng. ctr.; p. (est. 1972) 357,369 (met. a.).

Luce Bay, Wigtown, Scot.; enclosed by Mull of Galloway.

Lucca, c., cap. of L. prov., Tuscany, Italy; cath., churches, palaces; noted for olive oil, pasta, wine; silk, cotton, jute, tobacco inds.; p. (1969) 91,708.

Lucena, t., Córdoba, Spain; olive oil, ceramics, gilt metals, wine; p. (1970) 27,920.

Lucenec, t., ČSSR; on Hungarian border; magnesite, textiles, sawmilling; p. (est. 1968) 20,156.

Lucerne (Luzern), can., Switzerland; agr., pastoral, vineyards; oil refinery projected at Schötz/Ettiswil; cap. Lucerne; a. 1,492 km²; p. (est. 1969) 284,000.

Lucerne (Luzern), c., cap. of L. can., Switzerland; at N.W. end of L. Lucerne; aluminium gds., sewing machin.; tourist ctr.; p. (1969) 73,000 (c.), 148,500 (met. a.).

Lucerne, L., Switzerland; also known as L. of the Four Cantons; length 37 km; a. 70 km².

Luchon or Bagnères-de-Luchon, resort in Fr. Pyrenees, Haute-Garonne dep., S. France; warm sulphur springs; winter sports ctr.

Luchow (Luzhou), c., Szechwan prov., China; coal, iron, kaolin; synthetic ammonia plant; p. (est. 1970) 225,000.

Luckenwalde, t., E. Germany; on R. Nuthe; textiles, footwear, machin., wood and metals, chemicals; p. (est. 1970) 28 984.

Lucknow, c., cap. of Uttar Pradesh st., N. India; on R. Gumti (trib. of Ganges); educational and cultural ctr. with textile inds.; rly. ctr.; scene of 1857 mutiny; p. (1971) 749,239 (c.), 813,982 (met. a.).

Lüdenscheid, t., N. Rhine–Westphalia, W. Germany; metal mnfs., domestic hardware; supplied structures for first Zeppelins; p. (est. 1967) 57,500.

Lüderitz, t., South-West Africa; rly. pt. on desert cst.; diamonds, fishing; p. (1960) 3,604.

Ludhiana, t., Punjab st., N.W. India; S. of Sutlej R.; industl. ctr.; hosiery, knitwear; p. (1971) 397,850 (t.), 401,176 (met. a.).

Ludlow, t., South Salop., Eng.; agr. mkt.; agr. engin. cas.; p. (1971) 23,481 (dist.).

Ludwigsburg, t., Baden-Württemberg, W. Germany; N. of Stuttgart; cas.; textiles, foodstuffs, machin., toys; p. (est. 1969) 78,812.

Ludwigshafen, t., Rhine-Palatinate, W. Germany; on R. Rhine, opposite Mannheim; chemicals, marine diesel engines, metallurgy, glass; R. pt. and rly. junc.; oil pipeline from Rotterdam under construction; p. (est. 1969) 174,000.

Lugano, t., Ticino can., Switzerland; on L. Lugano; tourist resort; p. (est. 1968) 22,500.

Lugano, L., lies at S. foot of Alps between Switzerland and Italy; attractive scenery, tourism; a. 49 km².

Lugansk (Voroshilovgrad), industl. t., Ukrainian SSR, USSR; S. of R. Donets in Donbas region; impt. rly. engin. factories; textiles; p. (1970) 382,000.

Lugnaquilia, mtn., loftiest summit in Wicklow, R.o.I., 927 m.

Lugo, c., cap. of L. prov., N.W. Spain; in Galicia, on Miño R.; in fertile agr. a.; cath.; p. (1967) 67,918.

Lukuga, intermittent outlet of L. Tanganyika, Zaïre, linking with R. Zaïre.

Luleå, spt., N. Sweden, cap. of Norrbotten co.; on Lule R. at head of G. of Bothnia; iron ore; smelting plant, engin.; p. (1968) 36,296.

Luluabourg. See Kananga.

Lulworth Cove, sm. inlet, Dorset, Eng.; formed by sea breaching limestone cliffs and eroding clay behind; tourism.

Lund, t., S. Sweden; 16 km N.E. of Malmö; 11th cent. Romanesque cath.; univ.; publishing ctr.; p. (1968) 50,669.

Lundy I., Bristol Channel, N. Devon, Eng.; 19 km N.W. of Hartland Point; wildlife sanctuary; about 5 km long and 1 km wide.

Lune, R., Cumbria, Eng.; flows 72 km to Irish Sea; attractive valley.

Lüneburg, t., Lower Saxony, W. Germany; on Ilmenau R., S.E. of Hamburg; rly. junc., R. pt.; iron wks., chemicals; dates from 8th cent.; p. (est. 1967) 60,300.

Lüneburg Heath, Lower Saxony, W. Germany; lies to S. of Lüneburg; glacial outwash plain of sands and gravels; heather, scrub; some agr. but infertile acid soils.

Lünen, t., N. Rhine–Westphalia, W. Germany; in Ruhr conurb.; coal, metallurgy, glass, wood; R. pt. and rly. ctr.; p. (est. 1967) 71,000.

Lunéville, t., Meurthe-et-Moselle dep., N.E. France; in Lorraine, on R. Meurthe; 18th cent château; p. (1968) 25,367.

Lungi, t., Sierra Leone, W. Africa; nr. Freetown; only civil airport in st.

Lupata Gorge, Moçambique, E. Africa; narrow pass occupied by R. Zambesi.

Lurgan, t., Craigavon, N. Ireland; textiles, tobacco mftg.; merging with Portadown to form new c. of Craigavon; p. (est. 1971) 24,055.

Lusaka, c., cap. of Zambia; comm. and admin. ctr.; at junc. of routes to Tanzania and Malawi; motor assembly, footwear, metal prods., clothing; p. (est. 1972) 347,900 (met. a.).

Luta, special mun., S. Liaoning prov., China; comprising Port Arthur Naval Base District and the pts. of Port Arthur and Talien (Dairen); chemicals, machin., shipbldg., textiles; p. (est. 1970) 4,000,000.

Luton, t., l. gov. dist., Beds., Eng.; in Chiltern Hills nr. source of R. Lea; motor vehicles, engin., hat mkg., aircraft, gear instruments, chemicals; expanded t.; p. (est. 1976) 164,500.

Lutong, main oil pt. of Sarawak, E. Malaysia; oil refining.

Lutsk, c., Ukrainian SSR, USSR; pt. on Styr R.; one of oldest ts. in Volhynia; coal mng., machin.; architectural monuments; p. (1968) 94,000.

Luxembourg, prov., S.E. Belgium; on Fr. border; wooded and hilly; a. 2,784 km²; cap. Arlon; p. (1968) 219,368.

Luxembourg, grand duchy, W. Europe; lies between Belgium, W. Germany, and France; divided into 12 admin. cans.; official language French though German frequently used; well wooded, most of a. over 300 m; economic prosperity based upon iron and steel inds. and lge. deposits of iron-ore; agr. and cattle raising impt.; sm. size of home market makes L. keen protagonist of European economic unity and cap. of L. contains many European organisations; tourist ind. based upon scenery and cas. ts.; a. 2,587 km²; p. (est. 1969) 338,500.

Luxembourg, c., cap. of grand duchy of Luxembourg; historic t., perched above valleys of Alzette and Petrusse Rs.; cath.; seat of European Court of Justice; p. (est. 1969) 77,463.

Luxor, v., Upper Egypt; on E. bank of Nile; site of Thebes; tomb of Tutankhamun; p. (est. 1970) 84,600.

Luzon, I., lgst and most N. of Philippines; mtn. ranges; fertile Cagayan valley; rice, sugar cane, cotton, coffee, hemp, tobacco; mineral deposits; cap. Manila; a. 104,688 km²; p. (1970) 16,669,724.

L'vov, c., Ukrainian SSR, USSR; founded 13th cent.; univ., caths.; major industl. ctr.; petroleum refining; natural gas nearby; p. (1970) 553,000.

Lyalpur, t., W. Punjab, Pakistan; univ.; cotton, chemicals, fertilisers; p. (est. 1969) 854,000.

Lydd, Shepway, Kent, Eng.; anc. t. on Romney marsh, at edge of Dungeness shingle; name given to explosive lyddite mnf. here; airport; p. (1971) 4,301.

Lydda, c., Israel, S.E. of Tel-Aviv; major airport; mentioned in the Bible, and reputed birthplace of St. George; p. (est. 1967) 26,100.

Lydney, c., Gloucs., Eng.; in Forest of Dean; spt. on Severn estuary; timber imports; new lt. inds.; p. (1971) 14,447 (dist.).

Lyme Regis, spt., West Dorset, Eng.; on bdy. between Devon and Dorset; holiday resort; p. (1971) 3,394.

Lymington, ., Hants., Eng.; on the Solent; ferry to I. of Wight; abbey; p. (1971) 35,644.

Lymm, t., Cheshire, Eng.; 8 km W. of Altrincham; mainly residtl.; p. (1971) 10,458.

Lynchburg, c., Va., USA; on James R. in foothills of Appalachians; tobacco ctr.; p. (1970) 53,134 (c.), 121,832 (met. a.).

Lyndhurst, v., Hants, Eng.; recognised as cap. of New Forest; tourism.

Lynemouth, nr. Blyth, Northumberland, Eng.; aluminium smelter.

Lynn, industl. c., Mass., USA; on Mass. Bay; footwear, elec. appliances; Mary Baker Eddy lived here; p. (est. 1969) 90,500.

Lynton, t., North Devon, Eng.; 27 km W. of Minehead on Bristol Channel; tourist ctr. for Exmoor; sm. harbour of Lynmouth 130 m below; devastating flood of R. Lyn 1952; p. (1971) 1,981.

Lyons, c., cap. of Rhône dep., France; at confluence of Rs. Saône and Rhône; silk, rayon, chemicals, engin., heavy lorries; oil refinery nearby; univ.; world ctr. for cancer research; p. (1968) 527,800 (c.), 1,074,823 (met. a.).

Lytham St. Annes, t., N. Lancs., Eng.; on N. cst. of Ribble estuary, 6 km S. of Blackpool; holiday ctr.; p. (1971) 40,089.

Lyttleton, spt., S.I., N.Z., on N. cst. of Banks peninsula; ch. pt. of Canterbury plain; p. (1971) 3,277.

M

Ma'an, t., S. Jordan, terminus of rly. through Amman to Beirut; Hijaz rail line to Medina; p. (1961) 6,899.

Maas, R., Dutch name for the R. Meuse after it has entered the Neth.

Maastricht, t., cap. of Limburg prov., Neth.; on R. Maas; pottery, glass, textiles, brewing; p. (1968) 94,986.

Mablethorpe, t., East Lindsey, Lincs., Eng.; holiday resort; p. (1971) 6,156.

Macao, Portuguese col., S.E. China; increased indep. since 1975; gambling, tourism, recreation for Hong Kong; new deep water port.; oldest European col. in Far East (1557); a. 16 km²; p. (est. 1968) 250,000.

Macapá, c., cap. of Amapá st., Brazil; at mouth of R. Amazon; rubber, cattle tr.; p. (est. 1968) 74,464.

MacArthur (Ormoc), t., W. Leyte, Philippines; pt. and agr. ctr., exp. hemp, rice; p. (est. 1970) 85,900.

Macclesfield, t., l. gov. dist., Cheshire, Eng.; at foot of Pennines, 16 km S. of Stockport; on R. Bollin; mkt., textiles, clothing, paper prods., engin.; expanded t.; p. (est. 1976) 149,200 (dist.).

Macdonald Is., terr. of Australia, Antarctica.

Macdonnell Range, mtns., N.T., Australia; highest part of desert tableland, centrally situated within the continent; some gold and mica mines, but development hampered by aridity and isolation; highest alt. 1,367 m.

Macduff, spt., burgh, Banff and Buchan, Scot.; 3 km E. of Banff; fishing; p. (1971) 3,709.

Macedonia, region of Baltic peninsula, covering parts of Greece, Yugoslavia, and Bulgaria.

Macedonia, dist., Greece; mtnous.; cereals, tobacco; chromium; cap. and pt. Salonika; a. 33,945 km²; p. (1971) 1,883,156.

Macedonia, constituent rep., Yugoslavia; agr., chromium; cap. Skopje; a. 27,436 km²; p. (1971) 1,647,104.

Maceió, spt., cap. of Alagôas st., Brazil; cotton, sugar, tobacco, soap, sawmills, distilleries; p. (1970) 242,867.

Macerata, t., cap. of M. prov., Italy; cath., univ.; terracotta, glass, chemicals; p. (1969) 42,909.

Macgillicuddy's Reeks, mtns., Kerry, R.o.I.; highest peak, Carrantuohill, 1,041 m.

Machala, t., Tibet, China; hgst. coalmine in world.

Machynlleth, t., Powys, Wales; on R. Dovey; clothing; tourism; p. (1971) 1,766.

Macintyre, R., N.S.W., Australia; torms border between Queensland and N.S.W.; trib. of R. Darling; 560 km long.

Mackay, spt., Queensland, Australia; on R. Pioneer; sugar, dairying, banana ctr.; p. (1966) 24,566.

Mackenzie, R., N.W. Terr., Canada; lgst in N. America; rises in Rocky mtns. as Athabaska, flows into Athabaska L., leaves as Slave R., thence into Gr. Slave L., below which it is known as Mackenzie R., across arctic plains to Beaufort Sea; 4,000 km long.

Mackenzie Mtns., N.W. Terr., Canada; range of Rockies, still much unexplored; game preserve; max. alt. 2,760 m.

Mâcon, t., cap. of Saône-et-Loire dep., France; on R. Saône; Burgundy wines; p. (1968) 35,264.

Macon, c., Ga., USA; on Ocmulgee R.; industl. and shipping ctr. for agr. a., cotton, livestock; cotton mftg.; p. (1970) 118,764 (c.), 201,108 (met. a.).

Macquarie, I., Australian I., S. Pac.; 1,440 km S.E. of Tasmania; 34 km long, 3 km wide; meteorological and research base.

Macquarie, R., N.S.W., Australia; trib. of R. Darling; 960 km long.

Macroom, t., Cork, R.o.I.; on R. Sullane; agr. fishing; p. (1966) 2,224.

Madagascar. See Malagasy Republic.

Madang, t. and dist., Papua New Guinea; entrepôt pt. on N. cst.; international airpt.; p. of dist. (1966) 150,306.

Madeira, R., Brazil; trib. of Amazon; with Mamoré R., c. 3,200 km long.

Madeira Is., volcanic archipelago, Atl. Oc., part of met. Portugal; partial autonomy by regional gov. (1977); wine, sugar, fruits; tourism; cap. Funchal on Madeira I., lgst. of gr.; a. 790 km²; p. (est. 1970) 268,700.

Madhya Pradesh, st., India; absorbed sts. Bhopal, Vindhya Pradesh, Madhya Bharat, 1956; rice, jute, pulses, oilseeds, cotton; forests; manganese, coal, marble, limestone; cotton textile mftg.; cap. Bhopal; a. 443,452 km²; p. (1971) 41,449,729.

Madinat ash Sha'b (Al Ittihad), cap. of Democratic Rep. of Yemen; N.W. of Aden.

Madison, c., cap. of Wis., USA; educational and admin. ctr.; univ.; mnfs. agr. tools, footwear; p. (1970) 170,073 (c.), 287,501 (met. a.).

Madiun, t., Java, Indonesia; agr. and comm. ctr.; engin.; p. (1971) 136,147.

Madras, c., cap. of Tamil Nadu st., India; spt. on Bay of Bengal, on Coromandel cst.; cath., univ.; comm. and mftg. ctr.; textile mills, tanneries, potteries, chemical plants; oil refinery projected; p. (1971) 2,469,449 (c.), 3,169,930 (met. a.).

Madras. See Tamil Nadu.

Madre de Dios, R., Bolivia; trib. of R. Madeira; rises in Peru; 960 km long.

Madrid, c., cap. of Spain; and of M. prov. on Manzanares R.; stands at 665 m (highest cap. in Europe) in vast open plain; although remote with relatively few rivals, is ctr. of Spanish admin. and communications; univ., cath., Prado gallery; printing, publishing; p. (1968) 2,850,631.

Madura, I., Indonesia; off N.E. Java; dry climate, limestone soils; arable and pastoral agr.; salt; a. 4,584 km²; p. c. 2,000,000.

Madurai, t., Tamil Nadu, India; univ.; impt. textile ctr.; p. (1971) 549,114 (t.), 711,501 (met. a.).

Maebashi, c., central Honshu, Japan; N.W. Kanto plain; silk textile ctr.; p. (est. 1971) 237,000.

Maelstrom, tidewater whirlpool, in Lofoten Is., Norway.

Maentwrog, v., Gwynedd, N. Wales; in Vale of Ffestiniog, 3 km E. of Ffestiniog; ch. hydro-electric power sta. in N. Wales.

Maesteg, t., Ogwr, Mid Glamorgan, Wales; dormitory t. for steel wks. at Pt. Talbot; coal mng., cosmetics; p. (1971) 20,970.

Mafeking, t., N.E. Cape Prov., S. Africa; famous siege at outbreak of Boer War 1899-1900; p. (est. 1967) 6,200.

Magadan, spt., RSFSR; on N. side of Sea of Okhotsk; marine engin.; fishing; p. (1970) 92,000.

Magadi, L., Kenya; in Gr. Rift valley; carbonate of soda extracted.

Magdalena, R., Colombia; forms basis of inland navigation system, opening up interior; 1,600 km long.

Magdeburg, c., Magdeburg, E. Germany; on R. Elbe; cath.; beet-sugar ctr., sugar-refineries; chemicals, steel, mng. machin., heavy engin.; route ctr. and lge. inland pt.; p. (est. 1969) 269,031.

Magelang, t., Java, Indonesia; tr. ctr.; tannery; p. (1971) 110,308.

Magellan, strait, between Tierra del Fuego and Chile, separates Atl. and Pac. Ocs.

Maggiore, L., N. Italy-Switzerland; a. 212 km²; contains Borromean is.; tourist resort.

Magherafelt, l. gov. dist., centred on t. of M., N. Ireland; agr. a. bordering L. Neagh.

Maghreb, collective name given to Arabic-speaking countries bordering Mediterranean in N. Africa, inc. Algeria, Morocco and Tunisia.

Magnet Mtn., S. Urals, RSFSR; very rich deposit of magnetite iron ore; smelted at Magnitogorsk, and in Kuzbas region.

Magnitogorsk, c., RSFSR; in S. Urals, on R. Ural; sited on magnetite deposits; metallurgical ctr.; oil pipeline from Shkapovo in Bashkiria; p. (1970) 364,000.

Mahalla El Kubra, t., Lower Egypt; cotton textile ctr.; p. (1966) 225,700.

Mahanadi, R., India; flows from Orissa to Bay of Bengal; forms extensive delta; sugar and rice growing; 832 km long.

Maharashtra, st., W. India; on Arabian Sea; ch. ts. Bombay (cap.), Poona, Nagpur; fertile lava soils; impt. cotton-growing dist. of Deccan; a. 307,477 km²; p. (1971) 50,295,081.

Mahé, former Fr. prov., S. India; united with India 1954; cap. Mahé.

Mahon, spt., cap. of Minorca, Balearic Is., Spain.

Maidenhead, t., Windsor and Maidenhead, Berks., Eng.; on R. Thames, 14 km above Windsor; residtl.; p. (1971) 45,306.

Maidens, The, gr. of dangerous rocks off Larne cst., N. Ireland.

Maidstone, co. t., l. gov. dist., Kent, Eng.; on R. Medway; regional ctr.; brewing, paper, agr. tools, confectionery, timber inds.; p. (est. 1976) 126,500 (dist.).

Maiduguri, t., Nigeria; cap. Bornu st.; on rly. from Bornu; mkt.; p. (est. 1971) 169,180.

Maikop, c., cap. of Adygei aut. oblast, Krasnodar terr., RSFSR; oilfields nearby; oil-refineries, woodwkg., food-processing; p. (1970) 111,600.

Main, R., W. Germany; joins Rhine opposite Mainz; linked with Danube via Ludwig canal; 486 km long.   [to over 2,100 m.

Main Range, central mtns. of W. Malaysia; rise

Maine, st., New England, USA; mtnous., with much forest; potatoes, paper pulp, metals, woollens, shoes processed foods; c:p. Augusta; ch. spt. Portland; a. 86,027 km²; p. (1970) 977,260.

Maine-et-Loire, dep., France; agr., vineyards; cap. Angers; a. 7,280 km²; p. (1968) 584,709.

Mainland. (1) I., lgst. of Shetlands, Scot. (2) I., lgst of Orkneys, see Pomona.

Mainz, c., cap. of Rhineland-Palatinate, W. Germany; at confluence of Rs. Rhine and Main; R. pt.; cath., univ., cas.; cement, engin., optical glass, food-processing; p. (est. 1969) 174,100.

Maisons-Alfort, t., France; S.E. sub. of Paris; p. (1968) 53,761.

Maitland, t., N.S.W., Australia; on R. Hunter, nr. Newcastle; agr., pastoral ctr., coal mng., textiles; p. (1972) 24,530.

Majes, R., S. Peru; valley a. site of projected irrigation scheme; 240 km long.

Majorca (Mallorca), lgst. of Balearic Is., Spain; major tourist ctr.; ch. t. and pt. Palma; a. 3,639 km²; p. (1970) 460,030.

Majunga, t., Malagasy Rep.; second t. and pt.; meat conserves, sacks, cement; p. (est. 1970) 53,993.

Makalu, mtn., Nepal and Tibet, China; fifth hgst. mtn. in world; part of Himalayas; alt. 8,486 m.

Makasar. See Ujung Pandang.

Makasar, strait, Indonesia; separates Kalimantan from Sulawesi; 384 km wide.

Makeyevka, c., Ukrainian SSR, USSR; in Donets basin; metallurgical and coal-mng. ctr.; p. (1970) 393,000 (c.), 511,000 (met. a.).

Makhachkala, c., cap. of Dagestan ASSR, RSFSR; pt. on Caspian Sea; comm. and industl. ctr.; oil refineries linked by pipeline to Grozny fields; p. (1970) 186,000.

Makó, t., Hungary; on Maros R., nr. Romanian bdy.; comm. and agr. ctr.; p. (1966) 29,600.

Makran, dist., Pakistan and Iran; coastal dist.; lowland route between India and Middle E.

Makurdi, t., Nigeria, W. Africa; on R. Benue; mkt. for palm prod., groundnuts; rly. bridge across R. Benue.

Makwar, v., Sudan, N.E. Africa; on Blue Nile; site of Sennar Dam.

Malabar Coast, India; name applied to W. cst. of India from Goa to southern tip of peninsula at C. Comorin; sand dunes backed by lagoons; coastlands intensively cultivated, rice, spices, rubber, coconuts; ch. pt. Cochin.

Malabo (Santa Isabel), cap. of Equatorial Guinea; on Marcias Nguema I.; ch. pt. for I., exp. cacao; comm. and financial ctr.; p. (est. 1965) 37,152.

Malacca, st., S.W. W. Malaysia; originally part of Brit. Straits Settlements (q.v.); cap. M.; a. 1,658 km²; p. (1970) 403,722.

Malacca, strait, separates Sumatra, Indonesia, from W. Malaysia; 38 km wide at narrowest point; international routeway but attempts by Malaysia and Indonesia to claim it as territorial water.

Maladetta, with Pic d'Anéto, highest point in Pyrenees, Spain; alt. 3,408 m.

Malaga, c., cap. of Malaga prov., Spain; in Andalusia on Bay of M.; impt. spt.; olive oil, wine, fruit; oil pipeline from Puertollano refinery; winter resort; cath., citadel; birthplace of Picasso; p. (1968) 319,235.

Malagasy Republic (Madagascar), I. off Moçambique; former Fr. col.; distinctive evolution of flora and fauna; p. engaged in agr.; rice staple food, coffee ch. exp.; inds. based on agr.-processing; many minerals; exp. graphite, and petroleum from new refinery at ch. pt. of Tamatave; cap. Tananarive; a. 590,002 km²; p. (est. 1969) 6,600,000.

Malakoff, t. S.W. sub. of Paris, Hauts-de-Seine, France; residtl. and industl.; p. (1968) 36,297.

Malang, t., Java, Indonesia; ctr. of fertile agr. basin; p. (1971) 422,428.

Mälar, L., S.E. Sweden; connected with Baltic by Södertelge canal; 1,260 ls.; length 128 km; a. 1,235 km².

Malatya, c., cap. of M. prov., central Turkey; at foot of Taurus mtns.; ctr. of rich agr. a.; fruit, opium; p. (1965) 104,428 (c.), 174,472 (met. a.).

Malawi, rep., Central Africa; L. Malawi to S. and E.; tropical climate modified by alt.; few natural resources; economy based on agr.; lge. prod. of tung oil; exp. tobacco and tea; new cap. at Lilongwe (old cap. Zomba); a. 117,614 km²; p. (est. 1970) 4,530,000.

Malawi, L., central Africa; southward extension of the Gr. Rift valley; c. 450 m a.s.l.; 560 km by 64 km; drains by R. Shire into R. Zambesi.

Malaya. See **Malaysia, West**.

Malay Archipelago, lge. gr. of Is. extending 7,680 km from Nicobar Is. in Bay of Bengal to Solomon Is. in Pac.; inc. Sumatra, Java, Kalimantan, Sulawesi, Philippines, New Guinea, Bismarck archipelago.

Malaysa, East, part of Fed. of Malaysia; inc. Sarawak and Sabah (formerly Brit. N. Borneo); less developed than W. Malaysia; p. concentrated on cst.; hill tribes engaged in hunting in interior; oil major exp., exploration of cst.; separated from W. Malaysia by S. China Sea; a. 200,971 km²; p. (1698) 1,582,000.

Malaysia, Federation of, indep. federation (1963), S.E. Asia; member of Brit. Commonwealth; inc. W. Malaysia (Malaya) and E. Malaysia (Borneo sts. of Sarawak and Sabah); cap. Kuala Lumpur; a. 334,110 km²; p. (1968) 10,455,000.

Malaysia, West (Malaya), part of Federation of Malaysia; consists of wide peninsula, S. of Thailand; most developed in W.; world's leading producer of natural rubber, grown in plantations; oil palm and pineapples also grown; world's leading exporter of tin; nearly half p. Chinese; a. 131,588 km²; p. (1968) 8,899,000.

Malbork (Marienburg), t., Gdansk, Poland; R. pt. on Nogat R.; cas.; p. (1970) 30,900.

Malden, t., Mass., USA; mftg. sub. of Boston; rubber gds., hosiery furniture; p. (est. 1969) 54,000.

Maldive Is., indep. rep. (1968) Indian Oc.; chain of coral atolls c. 640 km S.W. of Sri Lanka; 1,067 Is., 193 inhabited; economy based on fishing (bonito and tuna); dried fish main exp.; coconuts, copra, coconut oil, coir, cowrie shells, cap. Malé; Britain to withdraw R.A.F. sta. on Gan I. in Addu Atoll; a. 298 km²; p. (1970) 114,469.

Maldon, t., l. gov. dist., Essex, Eng.; sm. pt. at head of Blackwater estuary; agr. machin., steel window-frames, flour-milling; p. (est. 1976) 44,000 (dist.).

Malegaon, t., Maharashtra, India; in Satmala Hills N.E. of Bombay; p. (1971) 191,847.

Malham Cove, North Yorks., Eng.; in Craven dist. of N. Pennines, 16 km N.W. of Skipton; semi-circular amphitheatre limestone cliffs from base of which emerges R. Aire.

Mali, Rep. of, W. Africa; landlocked st.; former Fr. col. of Soudan; dry semi-desert climate in S.; extends into Sahara desert in N.; few natural resources; nomadic pastoralist p. in N.; only 20 per cent of a. cultivable; livestock basis of inds. (hides, wool, etc.) and exps.; cap. Bamako; a. 1,204,350 km²; p. (1969) 4,929,000.

Malin Head, Donegal, R.o.I.; most N. point.

Malines (Mechelen), t., Belgium; on R. Dyle; cath.; rly. ctr.; textiles, furniture; once famous for lace; p. (1969) 65,730.

Malling, t., Kent, Eng.; 5 km W. of Maidstone; fruit, chemicals. See **Tonbridge**.

Mallow, mkt. t., Cork, R.o.I.; on R. Blackwater; agr., fishing, flour mills, tanneries, condensed milk, dehydrated foods; p. (1966) 5,539.

Malmesbury, t., North Wilts., Eng.; anc. hilltop t. in Cotswolds; mkt.; abbey; elec. engin.; birthplace of Thomas Hobbes; p. (1971) 2,526.

Malmesbury, t., Victoria, Australia; on R. Campaspe, 32 km S.E. of Bendigo; dam across R.

Malmo, c., spt., S. Sweden; on the Sound opposite Copenhagen; third lgst c. in cty.; naval and comm. pt.; shpbldg., textiles, machin.; founded in 12th cent.; proposed terminus of tunnel to Denmark; p. (1970) 258,311 (c.) (est. 1969) 435,634 (met. a.).

Malta, indep. st. within Br. C. (1964), rep. (1974); I. in Mediterranean, 93 km S. of Sicily; strategic location; British naval and military base; agr. ch. occupation with ship-repairing at dry-docks of Valletta; sm.-scale inds. growing; tourism exploits Mediterranean climate; major airport at Luqa; awarded George Cross for bravery in second world war; cap. Valletta; a. 316 km²; p. (est. 1971) 322,070 (inc. Gozo and Comino).   [14,050.

Maltby, t., Ryedale, South Yorks., Eng.; p. (1971)

Malton, mkt. t., North Yorks., Eng.; on R. Derwent. in S.W. of Vale of Pickering; brewing, p. (1971) 3,980.

Malvern, t., Hereford and Worcs., Eng.; at E. foot of Malvern hills; spa; annual dramatic festival; Elgar lived here; p. (1971) 29,004.

Malvern Hills, narrow ridge forming bdy. between Worcs. and Hereford, Eng.; rises very abruptly from Severn valley to over 300 m between Malvern and Bromsberrow; moorland, woodland on lower slopes; now forms l. gov. dist.; p. (est. 1976) 80,800.

Mammoth Cave, Ky., USA; to S. of Green R. in hilly forested parkland; spectacular limestone formations (stalactites, stalagmites), lakes and rivers (e.g., Echo R., 110 m below surface) in avenues aggregating 240 km long; included in Nat. Park.   [1,920 km long.

Mamoré, R., N. Bolivia and Brazil; rises in Andes;

Mam Soul, mtn., Kyle of Lochalsh and Inverness Scot.; alt. 1,178 m.

Manacle Rocks, dangerous reef off cst. of Cornwall, Eng.; 12 km S. of Falmouth.

Manacor, t., Majorca, Spain; artificial pearls; wine; stalactite caves of Drach and Hams; p. (1970) 23,278.

Managua, c., cap. of Nicaragua; on S. Shore of L. Managua; industl. and comm. ctr.; oil refining agr. processing, textiles, steel; univ.; 48 km from pt. Puerto Somoza; violent earthquake Dec. 1972; p. (1971) 398,514.

Managua, L., Nicaragua; second lgst. L. in Central America.

Manāmah, Al, cap. and ch. pt. Bahrain, Persian G.; free pt., comm. ctr.; declining pearl-fishing ind.; linked by causeway to internat. airpt.; p. (1971) 89,728.

Manáus (Manaos), c., cap. of Amazonas st., N.W. Brazil; on Rio Negro nr. confluence with Amazon; impt. R. pt., airpt.; oil refinery; former rubber ctr.; in free zone (10,360 km²) recently set up to encourage development in Amazonas; p. (1970) 284,118.

Manche, dep., N.W. France; on English Channel; agr. and dairying; cap. Saint Lô; ch. pt. Cherbourg; a. 6,410 km²; p. (1968) 451,939.

Manchester, c., major pt., Gtr. Manchester, Eng.; on R. Irwell; terminus of Manchester Ship Canal; ctr. of cotton and man-made fibre textile inds.; heavy, lt. and elec. engin., machine tools, petro-chemicals, dyestuffs, pharmaceutical gds.; univ.; comm., cultural, and recreational cap. of N.W. Eng.; p. (est. 1976) 490,000 (met. dist.), 2,684,000 (Greater Manchester).

Manchester, c., Conn., USA; textiles (silk); p. (est. 1969) 47,000.

Manchester, c., N.H., USA; at Amoskeag falls, on the Merrimac R.; textiles, footwear, machin.; p. (1970) 87,342 (c.), 107,675 (met. a.),

Manchester Ship Canal, ship canal, Cheshire/Merseyside/Gtr. Manchester, Eng.; joins Manchester to Mersey estuary at Eastham; can be used by ocean steamers; 57 km long.

Manchuria. See **North-East China**.

Mandalay, c., Burma; on R. Irrawaddy, 640 km N. of Rangoon; former cap.; lost importance with rise of Irrawaddy delta; many temples, palaces; p. (1969) 360,000.

Manfredonia, mkt. t., Foggia, Italy; fish. pt.; cath.; p. (est. 1968) 44,998.

Mangalore, spt., Karnataka, India; exp. coffee, coconuts, rice, spices, fertilisers; p. (1971) 165,174 (c.), 215,122 (met. a.).

Mangere, N.I., N.Z.; 21 km S. of Auckland; international airport (opened 1965).

Mangla Dam, Pakistan; world's lgst. earth-filled dam, on Jhelum R., part of Indus Basin irrigation scheme.

Manhattan, I., N.Y., USA; at mouth of Hudson R.; a. 57 km²; forms major part of bor. of Manhattan of N.Y. City.

Manila, c., S.W. Luzon, Philippines; leading c. and ch. pt. of Is.; [entrepôt tr.; modern skyscrapers; univ., cath.; major airpt.; p. (1969) 1,550,000 (c.), 2,989,300 (met. a.).

Manipur, new st. (1972), E. India; borders Burma; former princely st.; cap. Imphal; a. 22,274 km²; p. (est. 1972) 1,070,000.

Manisa, c., cap. of M. prov., W. Turkey; agr. ctr.; mineral deposits nearby; p. (1965) 69,394.

Manitoba, prov., Canada; wheat, rich mineral deposits, fisheries; diverse inds.; cap. Winnipeg; a. 650,090 km²; p. (1976) 1,021,506.

Manitowoc, c., Wis., USA; on L. Mich.; shipbldg., aluminium wks., flour mills; p. (est. 1969) 33,500.

Manizales, c., cap. of Caldas, Colombia; at 2,155 m in the Central Cordillera; in rich coffee a.; route ctr.; p. (est. 1972) 286,100 (c.), 306,500 (met. a.).

Mannar, G., with Palk Strait separates India from Sri Lanka.

Mannheim, c., Baden-Württemberg, W. Germany; between Austria and CSSR. major R. pt. at confluence of Rs. Neckar and Rhine, opposite Ludwigshafen; heavy and lt. inds., notably precision instruments, machin., vehicles; p. (est. 1969) 328,000.

Manono, t., Zaïre; ctr. for tin-mng.; foundries.

Manresa, industl. t., N.E. Spain; in Catalonia; textiles; associated with Ignatius of Loyola; place of pilgrimage; p. (est. 1965) 57,200.

Mansfield, t., l. gov. dist., Notts., Eng.; on E. flank of Pennines, 19 km N. of Nottingham; coal mng., sand-quarrying, textiles, footwear, metal boxes, machin.; p. (est. 1976) 97,200 (dist.).

Mansfield, t., Ohio, USA; machin. farm tools, paper, rubber gds.; p. (1970) 54,154 (t.), 129,162 (met. a.).

Mansfield Woodhouse, t., Notts., Eng.; 3 km N. of Mansfield; stone quarries; Roman remains; p. (1971) 24,787.

Mansûra, c., Lower Egypt; pt. on Nile; cotton mftg.; univ. proposed; p. (est. 1970) 212,300.

Mantua, c., cap. of M. prov., N. Italy; on R. Mincio; comm. and agr. ctr.; old fortfd. c.; p. (1969) 66,577.

Manukau, new t., N.I., N.Z.; in subs. of Auckland; p. (1971) 104,096.

Manukau Harbour, N.I., N.Z.; lge. shallow inlet on W. cst. of Auckland peninsula; provides additional harbour facilities for spt. of Auckland; recreational sailing; fishing.

Manych, R., RSFSR; trib. of R. Don; 480 km long; canal being built through R. to Caspian to provide through connection with Black Sea.

Manzala (Menzala), lagoon, Mediterranean cst., Egypt; extends E. from Damietta mouth of Nile to Pt. Said; fringed by salt marsh; a. 2,072 km².

Manzanillo, spt., S.E. Cuba; exp. sugar, rice, tobacco; p. (1966) 87,000.

Manzanillo, c., Colima, W. Mexico; ch. pt. on Pac. Oc.; exp. coffee, timber, minerals; p. (est. 1969) 29,347.

Maputo (Lourenço Marques), spt., cap. of Moçambique; at head of Delagoa Bay; rly. terminus; oil refining, deposits of bentonite worked nearby; ore terminal for 1976; p. (est. 1967) 90,000 (c.), 250,000 (met. a.).

Maracaibo, spt., cap. of Zulia st., Venezuela; deepwater harbour; on W. of narrow entrance to L. Maracaibo; univ.; oilfields and refineries; exp. coffee, cocoa, hardwoods; p. (est. 1970) 690,400.

Maracaibo, G., and L., Zulia st., Venezuela; brackish lake, 192 km long, 96 km wide; oilwells on fringes and drilled into lake floor.

Maracay, c., N. Venezuela; on L. Valencia, 112 km from Carácas; agr. and industl. ctr.; p. (est. 1970) 192,900.

Maragheh, t., Iran; on N. end of L. Urmia; comm. and fruit ctr.; p. (1966) 54,106.

Marajó, I., at mouth of the Rs. Amazon and Pará Brazil; a. 38,850 km².

Maralinga, S. Australia; 320 km N.E. Eucla; joint U.K.–Australian atomic testing ground, first weapon exploded here 27 Sept. 1956.

Maranhão, st., N.E. Brazil; rice, cotton sugar, tobacco, coffee, cattle, gold, copper; oil in the Barrierinhas a.; cap. São Luiz; a. 334,812 km²; p. (est. 1968) 3,497,890.

Marañon, R. See Amazon, R.

Maras, t., S. central Turkey; tr. in Kurdish carpets; p. (1965) 63,315.

Marathon, v. and plain, Greece; 32 km N.E. of Athens; here the Athenians defeated the Persians 490 B.C.

Marazion, mkt. t., Cornwall, Eng.; on Mount's Bay, nr. St. Michael's Mount; pilchard fisheries.

Marble Bar, t., W. Australia. 136 km inland by rail from Pt. Hedland; ctr. of Pilbara goldfields.

Marburg on Lahn, t., Hesse, W. Germany; univ., cas.; noted for optical instruments; p. (est. 1967) 49,900.

March, mkt. t., Fenland, Cambs., Eng.; on R. Nene, in Fens; rly. junc.; farm tools; p. (1971) 14,268.

Marches, The, region, central Italy; extending from eastern slopes of Apennines to Adriatic cst.; embracing provs. of Macerata, Ascoli-Piceno, Acona, and Pesaro e Urbino; a. 9,697 km²; p. (1969) 1,363,685.

Marchfeld, plain, Lowei Austria, between Rs. Danube and Morava which here forms bdy. between Austria and CSSR.

Marcias Nguema (Fernando Po), I., Equatorial Guinea; in Bight of Bonny; mtnous.; coffee, cocoa, bananas, timber; p. (1968) 61,000.

Mar del Plata, c., Argentina; on C. Corrientes; Atl. cst. resort; p. (1970) 299,700 (met. a.).

Maree, L., Ross and Cromarty, Scot.; 21 km long, c. 3 km wide; rocky shores; studded with wooded islets.

Maremma, coastal region along Tyrrhenean Sea, S. Tuscany, Italy; once malarial, now drained with wide fertile areas.

Mareotis or Birket-et-Mariut, L., Lower Egypt; separated from Mediterranean by ridge of sand on which stands Alexandria; 80 km long, 32 km wide.

Margam, t., in Pt. Talbot, West Glamorgan, S. Wales; on cst. of Swansea Bay; lge. new steel-wks., lgst. steel-rolling mill in Europe.

Margarita, I., in Caribbean off N. Venezuela; tourism; formerly pearl-fishing ctr.; cap. Asunción; a. 1,166 km²; p. (1961) 87,500.

Margate, t., Kent, Eng.; W. of N. Foreland, in the Isle of Thanet; seaside resort; p. (1971) 50,145.

Margelan, t., E. Uzbek SSR, USSR; in Ferghana Valley; noted for silk ind.; p. (est. 1967) 89,000.

Mari, aut. rep., RSFSR; timber, paper inds.; p. (1970) 685,000.

Mariana Is. (Marianas), chain of Is., W. Pac.; US. Trust Terr.; most impt. are Guam, Saipan, and Tinian; US Commonwealth status planned for N. Mariana Is.; a. 479 km²; p. (1968) 10,986.

Maribor, t., Slovenia, Yugoslavia; on Drava R., nr. Austrian border; metallurgical inds.; ctr. of agr. a.; p. (1971) 97,167.

Marília, t., São Paulo st., Brazil; coffee, cotton, oil peanuts; p. (est. 1968) 107,305.

Mariinsk Canal. See Volga Baltic Waterway.

Marion, c., Ind., USA; mkt. ctr. within corn belt; varied inds.; p. (est. 1969) 38,500.

Marion, t., Ohio, USA; agr. ctr. with varied agr. mnfs.; p. (est. 1969) 37,500.

Maritime Provinces, include Canadian provs. of Nova Scotia, New Brunswick, Prince Edward I.

Maritsa, R., Bulgaria and Greece; used for irrigation and hydroelectric power; 416 km long

Market Drayton, t., North Salop, Eng.; on R. Tern, 21 km S.W. of Newcastle-under-Lyme; agr. implements, nylon mftg.; p. (1971) 17,154 (dist.).

Market Harborough, t., Harborough, Leics., Eng.; on R. Welland, 13 km N.W. of Kettering; elec. engin., foodstuffs, corsetry; p. (1971) 14,527.

Market Rasen, t., West Lindsey, Lincs., Eng.; agr. ctr.; racecourse; p. (1971) 2,430.

Markinch, burgh, Kirkcaldy, Scot.; 13 km N. of Kirkcaldy; paper mftg., whisky blending and bottling; p. (1971) 2,225.

Marl, t., N. Rhine–Westphalia, W. Germany; in Ruhr; coal mng.; chemicals; p. (est. 1967) 76,100.

Marlborough, t., Wycombe, Wilts., Eng.; on R. Kennet in heart of Marlborough Downs; public school; p. (1971) 6,031.

Marlborough, prov. dist., S.I., N.Z.; pastoral; a. 10,930 km²; cap. Blenheim; p. (1971) 31,533.

Marlborough Downs, hills, Wilts., Eng.; chalk; highest point, Milk Hill, 298 m.

Marlow, t., Bucks., Eng.; on R. Thames; mkt., tourist ctr.; home of Shelley; p. (1971) 11,706.

Marmara, Sea of, separates Europe from Asia; connected with Black Sea through the Bosporus, with Aegean Sea through Dardanelles; shores belong to Turkey.

Marne, dep., N.E. France; in Champagne; ctr. of champagne ind.; cap. Châlons-sur-Marne; a. 8,205 km²; p. (1968) 485,388.

Marne, R., central France; rises in Plateau de Langres, flows across Champagne Humide, Champagne Pouilleuse, and Beauce, joins R. Seine just above Paris; with Marne–Rhine and Marne–Saône canals forms impt. inland waterway linking Seine with Rhine and Rhône valleys; c. 520 km. long.

Marple, t., Gtr. Manchester, Eng.; 5 km E. of Stockport; engin., residtl.; p. (1971) 23,217.

Marquesas Is., volcanic gr. in central Pac. Oc., part of Fr. Polynesia; lgst. Nukuhiva and Hivaoa; mtnous., fertile; exp. copra, vanilla, tobacco, cotton; a. 1,274 km²; p. (1967) 5,147.

Marrakesh, c., Morocco; tourist ctr.; leather gds., carpets; p. (1971) 330,400 (c.), 390,480 (met. a.).

Marsa el-Brega, new pt., G. of Sirte, Libya; oil pipeline from Zelten; gas liquefaction plant opened 1970; airport.

Marsala, pt., Sicily, Italy; on site of anc. Carthaginian settlement; wine ctr.; p. (est. 1967) 42,400.

Marseilles, c., spt., cap. of Bouche-du-Rhône dep., S. France; on Provence cst.; passenger and gds. traffic; pt. inds., marine engin., oil refining; oil pipeline to Karlsruhe; industl. expansion at G. of Fos; cath., univ., palace; founded as Massilia by Phocaean Greeks of Asia Minor 600 B.C.; p. (1968) 889,029 (c.), 964,412 (met. a.).

Marshall Is., gr. of coral Is., central Pac. Oc.; comprising 34 atolls; exp. copra, sugar, coffee; admin. ctr. Jaluit I.; US Pac. Trust Terr.; a. 181 km²; nuclear bomb tests; p. (1968) 18,998.

Martha's Vineyard, I., S.E. Mass., USA; state forest; summer resort; ch. ts., Vineyard Haven, Oak Bluffs, Edgartown; summer resort.

Martigny, t., Valais, Switzerland; linked by road tunnel to Aosta, Italy; p. 6,572.

Martina Franca, t., S. Italy; in Apulia; wine, olive oil; summer resort; p. (est. 1968) 38,771.

Martinique, I., Fr. overseas dep., Windward Is., W.I.; dominated by volcanic peak Mt. Pelée which erupted 1902 destroying t. of St. Pierre; hurricanes, earthquakes; economy based on sugar-cane and fruit prod.; much emigration to France; cap. Fort de France; a. 1,088 km²; p. (1970) 345,000.

Martos, t., Jaén prov., Andalusia, Spain; castled hilltop t.; wines, sulphur springs; mftg. p. (1970) 21,493.

Mary (Merv), c., Turkmen SSR, USSR; in oasis in Kara-Kum desert; anc. c. founded 3rd cent. B.C.; textile ind.; p. (1969) 61,000.

Maryborough, t., Queensland, Australia; pt. on Mary R.; exp. fruit, sugar, timber, coal; shipyards, steelwks.; p. (1972) 19,962.

Maryborough. See Port Laoighise, Ireland.

Mary Kathleen, t., Queensland, Australia; new t., nr. uranium field in Cloncurry a.

Maryland, one of original 13 sts. of USA; on shores of Chesapeake Bay; humid continental climate; arable agr. and mkt. gardening; seafishing; cap. Annapolis; lgst. c. Baltimore; a. 27,394 km²; p. (1970) 3,874,642.

Maryport, t., Allerdale, Cumbria, Eng.; former pt.; modern lt. inds. in industl. estate to S. of t.; p. (1971) 11,615.

Masaya, t., W. Nicaragua; comm ctr. in rich agr. a ; p. (est. 1970) 49,691.

Masbate, I., Philippines; gold mng.; a. 3,269 km²; p. (1970) 492,868.

Mascarene Is., collective name of Mauritius, Rodriguez and Réunion, in Indian Oc.

Maseru, t., cap. Lesotho; nr. border with S. Africa on Caledon R.; p. (1972) 17,000.

Masham, t., North Yorks., Eng.; on R. Ure; 14 km N.W. of Ripon; mkt.; p. (1971) 1,473 (dist.).

Mashhad, c., N.E. Iran; cap. of Khorassan prov.; p. (est. 1971) 530,500.

Mashonaland, dist., Rhodesia; a. inhabited by the Mashona tribe; ch. t. Salisbury.

Masjid-i-Sulamain, t., Iran; impt. oilfield and refinery.

Mask, L., Mayo and Galway, R.o.I.; 19 km long 3–6 km wide.

Mason City, t., Iowa, USA; on Sheel Rock R.; tr. ctr. of lge. agr. a.; p. (est. 1969) 30,711.

Mason–Dixon Line. See Section L.

Massachusetts, st., New England, USA; on Atl. cst.; humid continental climate; hilly interior severed by N.–S. Connecticut valley; major fishing ind.; replacement of traditional textile inds. by modern science-based inds., especially around M. Institute of Technology; impt. arable gr. a.; cap. Boston; a. 21,386 km²; p. (1970) 5,630,224.

Massa di Carrara. See Carrara.

Massawa, spt., Ethiopia, on Red Sea; fine harbour; fishing; fish meal; p. (est. 1970) 18,490.

Massif Central, upland a., France; variable geology and scenery inc. volcanic Auvergne and limestone Causses; much rural depopulation, pastoral agr.; industl. ts. inc. St. Etienne based on sm. coalfields in N.E.; other ts. inc. Limoges and Clermont-Ferrand.

Masterton, t., N.I., N.Z.; meat-packing; dairy prods., woollen mills; p. (1971) 18,556.

Masulipatam (Bandar), spt., Andhra Pradesh, India on Coromandel cst.; cotton mftg., rice; p. (1971) 129,905.

Matabeleland, dist., Rhodesia; a. inhabited by Matabele tribe; ch. t. Bulawayo.

Matadi, spt., Zaïre; on R. Zaïre; main pt.; exp. forest prod.; proposed Inga power project nearby; p. (est. 1972) 125,585 (met. a.).

Matagalpa, t., Nicaragua; ctr. of agr. a., food processing; second lgst. t. of Nicaragua; p. (est. 1967) 20,718.

Matamoros, t., Mexico; on Rio Grande; livestock tr. ctr.; p. (1970) 137,990.

Matanzas, spt., cap. of M. prov., Cuba; exp. sugar, cigars; rayon plant; p. (est. 1967) 84,100.

Matarani, new spt., S. Peru; oil refinery.

Mataró, spt., Spain; nr. Barcelona; fisheries, textiles, chemicals, paper; p. (1970) 73,129.

Matera, t., cap. of M. prov., S. Italy; stands on limestone ridge cleft by canyon; agr. ctr.; cave dwellings; 13th cent. cath. and cas.; p. (1969) 44,635.

Mathura (Muttra), t., Uttar Pradesh, India; sacred t. on R. Jumna; Hindu pilgrimage ctr.; textiles; p. (1971) 132,028 (t.), 140,150 (met. a.).

Matlock, t., West Derbys., Eng.; on R. Derwent; 24 km N. of Derby; tourist ctr., limestone quarrying, lt. inds.; p. (1971) 19,575.

Mato Grosso, st., Brazil; cap. Cuiabá; a. 1,232,081 km²; p. (est. 1968) 1,363,980.

Mato Grosso, plateau, Mato Grosso st., Brazil; average alt. 900 m, acts as divide between Amazon and Paraná–Paraguay R. systems; reserves of gold, diamonds, manganese but largely undeveloped; lge. areas of tropical rain forest.

Matozinhos, t., Portugal; fish. pt. at mouth of Leca R.; seaside resort; p. (1960) 37,694.

Matrah, t., Oman; ch. comm. ctr.; agr. tr.; site of Port Qaboos, new deep water pt.; p. 14,119.

Matsue, c., S.W. Honshu, Japan; on L. Shinji; old cas.; p. (est. 1971) 118.000.

Matsumoto, c., central Honshu, Japan; machin., food-processing, paper; once impt. for silk; remains of 16th cent. cas.; p. (est. 1971) 165,000.

Matsuyama, c., Japan; pt. based inds. of oil refining and petrochemicals; univ.; feudal cas.; p. (est. 1971) 339,000.

Matterhorn (Fr. Mt. Cervin. It. Monte Cervino); alt. 4,477 m; Pennine Alps, Switzerland.

Mauchline, mkt. t., Strathclyde Reg., Scot.; associated with Robert Burns.

Mauna Kea, volcano, Hawaii; alt. 4,208 m; now dormant.

Mauna Loa, volcano, **Hawaii**; alt. 4,172 m; one of world's lgst. volcanoes.

Mauritania, Islamic Rep. of, **W. Africa**; desert in N., S. more fertile; Senegal R. forms main artery of transport; mainly pastoral agr. (nomadic); deposits of iron ore (Fort Gouraud) and copper (Bakel Akjoujt); fishing being developed; new pt. development at Nouadhibou; cap. Nouakchott; a. 1,085,210 km²; p. (est. 1969) 1,120,000.

Mauritius, I., indep. st. within Brit. Commonwealth; Indian Oc.; volcanic I., 800 km E. of Malagasy Rep.; subtropical climate, prone to cyclones; racially mixed; dependent on sugar for 95 per cent of exps.; dense p. and unemployment cause social tension; former residents of Chagos Arch. resettled on 2 of Agalega Is.; cap. Port Louis; a. (inc. Rodrigues and Agalega) 2,038 km²; p. (1969) 798,684.

Mawson, Australian national research base, **Antarctica**.

Mayagüez, c., spt., **Puerto Rico**; ctr. of fertile region producing sugar, coffee, tobacco; cultural and educational ctr.; p. (1970) 69,485.

Maybole, burgh, Kyle and Carrick, **Scot.**; 13 km S. of Ayr; footwear, agr. implements; cas.; p. (1971) 4,523.

Mayenne, dep., N.W. **France**; pastoral and agr.; cap. Laval; a. 5,146 km²; p. (1968) 252,762.

Mayfair, dist., City of Westminster, **London, Eng.**; fashionable residtl. and comm. a., to E. of Hyde Park; clubs and hotels.

Mayo, maritime co., Connacht, **R.o.I.**; broken cst., much barren mtn. land, many lge. lakes; agr., fishery; co. t. Castlebar, a. 5,506 km²; p. (1966) 115,588.

Mayotte, ch. I., Fr. terr., Comoro Archipelago, Mocambique Channel; rejected indep. to remain Fr. dep. (1975); sugar-cane, vanilla, cacao; a. 363 km²; p. (est. 1970) 48,000.

Mazandaran, prov., N.E. **Iran**; Caspian Sea, borders USSR; subtropical climate; agr.; cap. Sari; p. (1967) 1,843,388.

Mazar-i-Sharif, c., **Afghanistan**; chemical fertilisers from natural gas; textiles, bricks, flour-milling; noted mosque; p. (est. 1969) 43,197.

Mazatlán, c., N.W. **Mexico**; major spt. on Pac. cst.; comm. and industl. ctr.; exp. metals, hides, fish prods., woods; oil refinery; fishing, tourism.; p. (1970) 119,553.

Mazzara, t., Sicily, **Italy**; cath., ruined cas.; agr. prod.; p. (est. 1968) 16,563.

M'babane, cap. of **Swaziland**; stands at c. 1,160 m; admin. ctr.; tin mng.; p. (1966) 13,803.

M'Bao, Senegal, W. Africa; oil refinery.

McMurdo Sound, ice-locked channel, **Antarctica**; base for many expeditions.

Mead, L., Cal., **USA**; on R. Colorado behind Boulder (Hoover) Dam; world's lgst. reservoir; stores water for irrigation in Imperial Valley and Yuma dist.; tourist attraction; 184 km long.

Meath, maritime co., Leinster, **R.o.I.**; pastoral; co. t., Trim; a. 2,347 km²; p. (1966) 67,279.

Meaux, t., Seine-et-Marne dep., France; on R. Marne; cath.; comm. and industl. ctr.; p. (1968) 31,420.

Mecca, holy c. of Islam, cap. of **Saudi Arabia**; birthplace of Mohammed; pilgrimage ctr.; Gr. Mosque enclosing the Kaaba; univ. (with Jidda); p. (est. 1965) 185,000.

Mechelen. *See* **Malines.**

Mecklenburg, region, E. **Germany**; part of N. European plain bordering Baltic Sea; Schwerin was cap. of former st.; a. 22,947 km².

Medan, c., cap. of N. Sumatra prov., **Indonesia**; ctr. for rubber, tobacco, tea; printing; univ.; pt. is Belawan; p. (1971) 635,562.

Médéa, t., 80 km S. of El Djezair, **Algeria**; projected industl. complex; p. (1966) 53,951.

Medellín, c., cap. of Antiquia prov., **Colombia**; at 1,533 m in Central Cordillera; second c. of rep.; univ.; cultural ctr.; coffee; textiles, steel, sugar refining, glass; coal, gold, silver mined nearby; hydroelec. power; p. (est. 1972) 1,091,600 (c.), 1,207,800 (met. a.).

Medicine Hat, t., Alberta, **Canada**; on S. Saskatchewan R.; rly. junc.; coal, natural gas, flour mills; p. (1971) 26,058.

Medina, c., Hejaz, **Saudi Arabia**; 352 km N. of Mecca; tomb of Mohammed; place of Moslem pilgrimage; univ.; harbour at Yanbu' on Red Sea; p. (est. 1965) 100,000.

Medina, l. gov. dist., I. of Wight, **Eng.**; N.E. part of I. inc. Ryde, Newport and Cowes; p. (est. 1976) 65,700.

Mediterranean, gr. inland sea, almost tideless, dividing Europe from Africa; communicating with Atl. by Strait of Gibraltar and Black Sea by Dardanelles, Sea of Marmara and Bosporus, E. part touches Asia in the Levant; total length W. to E. 3,520 km; greatest width of sea proper c. 1,120 km; water a. 2,331,000 km²; greatest depth 4,482 m; ch. Is.; Corsica, Sardinia, Sicily, Crete, Cyprus, and the Balearic, Lipari, Maltese, Ionian grs., also Greek arch.

Médoc, region, Gironde, France; extending for about 77 km along Garonne R.; noted for wines.

Medway, R., Kent, **Eng.**; flows N.E. past Tonbridge, Maidstone and Rochester (where it becomes estuarial) to mouth of Thames; 112 km long; Medway Bridge (part of London-Dover motorway) completed 1962.

Medway, l. gov. dist., Kent, **Eng.**; lower Medway estuary and ts. of Chatham and Rochester; p. (1976) 144,500.

Meekatharra, t., W. **Australia**; Flying Doctor and School of the Air ctr.

Meerut, c., Uttar Pradesh, **India**; scene of outbreak of Indian mutiny 1857; p. (1971) 270,993 (c.), 367,754 (met. a.).

Meghalaya (" Home of the Clouds "), new st. (1972), **India**; former Khasi-Jaintia Hills and Garo Hills dists. of Assam; cap. Shillong; a. 22,549 km²; p. (est. 1972) 1,000,000.

Meiling Pass, on bdy. between Kwangtung, Kiangsi, S. China; provides historic routeway across Nanling mtns., followed by old imperial highway from Nanking to Kuangchow; alt. c. 300 m.

Meiningen, t., E. **Germany**; on R. Werra; cas.; machin., chemicals, timber inds.; drama ctr. in second half 19th cent.; p. (est. 1970) 25,357.

Meirionnydd, l. gov. dist., Gwynedd, **Wales**; based on former co. of Merioneth; stretches from Ffestiniog and Bala to Tywyn and Dolgellau; p. (est. 1976) 30,600.

Meissen, t., Dresden, E. **Germany**; on R. Elbe; cath.; famous porcelain popularly known as Dresden china; p. (est. 1970) 45,571.

Meknès, t., **Morocco**; one of the caps. of M.; agr. ctr., olives; p. (1971) 244,520 (t.), 362,840 (met. a.).

Mekong, R., S.E. **Asia**; rises in Tibet, flows through China, Laos, Cambodia, and S. Vietnam, entering China Sea in extensive swampy delta; used for sm. boats but many rapids; longest R. in Asia; 4,000 km long; new R. project for flood control, irrigation and hydroelectric power.

Melanesia, archipelago, S.W. **Pac. Oc.**; inc. Admiralty, Solomon, Santa Cruz, New Hebrides, Loyalty, New Caledonian, and Fiji Is.; New Guinea is sometimes included; ethnic region; arable subsistence agr.

Melbourne, spt., cap. of Victoria, **Australia**; at mouth of Yarra R. in Hobson's Bay at N. end of Port Philip Bay; comm. ctr. of lge region; international airpt.; mnfs. inc. textiles, machin.; botanical gardens; univ., caths.; p. (1972) 74,877 (c.), 2,497,993 (met. a.).

Melilla, spt. and enclave in Morocco, on Mediterranean cst., belonging to Spain; exp. iron ore; p. (1969) 77,239.

Melitopol, c., Ukrainian SSR, **USSR**; on Molochnoy R.; ctr. of rich fruit-growing a.; heavy machin., food-processing; p. (1970) 137,000.

Melksham, t., West Wilts., **Eng.**; on R. Avon, 8 km N.E. of Bradford-on-Avon; rubber wks., engin., flour mills, creameries, rope and matting; p. (1971) 9,803.

Melrose, burgh, Ettrick and Lauderdale, **Scot.**; on R. Tweed; 6 km E. of Galashiels; ruined abbey; p. (1971) 2,185.

Meltham, t., West Yorks., **Eng.**; S.W. of Huddersfield; woollen textiles; p. (1971) 17,181.

Melton Mowbray, t., Leics., **Eng.**; on Lincoln Heights, 24 km N.E. of Leicester; mkt., hunting dist.; famous pork pies; footwear, pet foods, Stilton cheese; with surrounding a. forms l. gov. dist. of Melton; p. (est. 1976) 41,100.

Melun, t., cap. of Seine-et-Marne dep., N. **France**; on R. Seine; agr. tools and prod.; Romanesque church; p. (1968) 34,518.

Melville I., off N. cst., Arnhem Land, **Australia**; Aboriginal settlement; a. 4,350 km².

Melville I., N.W. Terr., Arctic Canada; natural gas; a. 41,958 km². [Vjosa.

Memaliaj, t., Albania; new mng. t. on banks of R.

Memel. *See* Klaipeda.

Memmingen, t., Bavaria, W. Germany; rly. junc.; machin., textiles; p. (est. 1969) 35,142.

Memphis, anc. c., Egypt; on R. Nile; 19 km S. of Cairo; nearby are Sakkara ruins.

Memphis, c., Tenn., USA; on R. Mississippi; rly. ctr., pt. of entry, lgst c. in st., mkt. ctr. for cotton and hardwoods; cottonseed oil, textiles, farm machin.; natural gas and hydroelectric power; univ.; Martin Luther King assassinated here (1968); p. (1970) 620,873 (c.), 770,160 (met. a.).

Menado, t., Sulawesi, Indonesia; second t. of I.; pt. for transit tr.; p. (1971) 169,684.

Menai Strait, separates Isle of Anglesey from mainland, Wales; crossed by Telford's suspension bridge (1825) and Britannia rly. bridge (1850).

Menam Chao Phraya, R., Thailand; main R. of cty.; dense p. in valley; lge. multi-purpose scheme for hydroelectric power and irrigation; 1,120 km long.

Mendip Hills, Avon/Somerset, Eng.; limestone range containing many karst features inc. Cheddar gorge and Wookey Hole; a. of outstanding natural beauty; quarrying; motorway; hgst. point, 325 m; now forms l. gov. dist., within Somerset inc. Frome, Wells, Shepton Mallet, Glastonbury and Street; p. (est. 1976) 82,900.

Mendoza, prov., W. Argentina, on Chilean border; Andean peaks Aconcagua and Tupungato; oilfields; alfalfa, vines, olives, fruit, peppermint; cap. M.; a. 148,783 km²; p. (1970) 973,075.

Mendoza, c., cap. of M. prov., W. Argentina; stands at c. 730 m in oasis known as "garden of the Andes"; starting point of Transandine rly.; univ.; wine; fruit; petroleum, agr. processing; p. (1970) 470,896 (met. a.).

Mendoza, R., Argentina; enters L. Guanacache; used for hydroelectric power; 320 km long.

Menin (Meenen), t., Belgium; on R. Lys on Fr. border; mediaeval cloth ctr.; tobacco tr., textiles, rubber gds., soap; scene of fierce fighting in first world war; p. (est. 1969) 22,195.

Mentawai Is., S.W. Sumatra, Indonesia; hilly and forested; primitive p.; fishing, shifting cultivation.

Menteith, Lake of, Stirling, Scot.; contains 3 Is.; 2·4 km by 1·6 km.

Menton, t., Alpes-Maritimes dep., S. France; Riviera resort; p. (1968) 25,271.

Meppel, t., Drenthe, Neth., 21 km N. of Zwolle; shipbldg.; p. (1967) 19,192.

Merauke, t., W. Irian, Indonesia; pt. on S. cst.; ctr. of livestock raising region.

Mercedes, t., S.W. Uruguay; livestock ctr., E. of its pt. Fray Bentos; p. (1963) 34,000.

Mergui, archipelago, Tenasserim cst., S. Burma; teak, rice, pearl fishing.

Mérida, c., cap. of Yucatan st., S.E. Mexico; sisal-hemp; Spanish colonial architecture; tourism; Mayan ruins; p. (1970) 212,097.

Mérida, c., Badajoz prov., S.W. Spain; on Guadiana R.; comm. ctr. of Estremadura; impt. Roman remains; p. (1970) 40,059.

Mérida, t., cap. of M. st., Venezuela; in Andes; univ., cath.; tourist ctr.; world's highest cable rly. to Espejo peak (4,690 m); p. (est. 1970) 75,634.

Meriden, t., Conn., USA; hardware mftg.; p. (est. 1969) 58,000.

Meridian, t., Miss., USA; mkt. ctr. in cotton, livestock, lumber a.; rly. and route ctr.; textiles, clothing; p. (est. 1969) 53,000.

Merioneth, former co., Wales. *See* Meirionnydd.

Merksem, industl. t., Antwerp, Belgium; p. (1968) 39,659.

Merrick, mtn., Wigtown, Scot.; hgst. peak in S. Uplands of Scot.; alt. 843 m.

Mersea, I., at mouth of R. Colne, Essex, Eng.; oysters; holiday resort; 8 km long, 3 km wide.

Merseburg, c., Halle, E. Germany; on R. Saale; ctr. of gr. lignite field; paper mills, chemical wks.; historic c.; p. (est. 1970) 55,986.

Merse of Berwick, region, S.E. Scot.; lower valleys of Rs. Tweed and Teviot; glacial clays; arable agr. for barley, wheat; dairy cattle; ch. t. Berwick-on-Tweed; a. 570 km².

Mersey, R., Cheshire/Gtr. Manchester/Merseyside, Eng.; enters Irish Sea by fine estuary at Liverpool; 109 km long.

Merseyside, met. co., N.W. Eng.; a. around lower Mersey estuary inc. N. Wirral penin. pts. of Liverpool, Birkenhead and Bootle; many chem. and pt. processing inds.; p. (est. 1976) 1,578,000.

Mersin, c., S. Turkey; spt. on Mediterranean cst.; oil refinery; dates from c. 3,600 B.C.; p. (1965) 87,267.

Merthyr Tydfil, t., l. gov. dist., Mid Glamorgan, S. Wales; in narrow valley of R. Taff, 35 km N.W. of Cardiff; coal-mng. ctr.; hosiery, aircraft, bricks, elec. domestic gds.; p. (est. 1976) 61,500 (dist.).

Merton, outer bor., Greater London, Eng.; inc. former bors. of Mitcham, Wimbledon, and Merton and Morden; p. (est. 1976) 169,400.

Meru, mtn., Tanzania, E. Africa; extinct volcano overlooking E. arm of Gt. Rift valley; coffee plantations at alt. 1,500–1,800 m, some rubber below 1,200 m; alt. summit 4,560 m.

Merv. *See* Mary.

Mesa, t., Arizona, USA; in Salt River Valley, founded by Mormons 1878; agr. ctr., helicopter mftg.; p. (est. 1969) 55,000.

Mesa Central, plateau, Mexico; part of Mexican plateau, major a. of comm. agr. (maize, wheat, agave); contains cap. Mexico City; dense p. and industl. comm. ctrs.

Mesa del Norte, plateau, Mexico; northern part of Mexican plateau.

Mesabi Range, hills, N.E. Minn., USA; vast iron ore deposits, now running out.

Mesa Verde National Park, S.W. Col., USA; Indian cliff dwellings.

Mesopotamia, anc. region, S.W. Asia; between Tigris and Euphrates Rs.; a. of early civilisation.

Messenia, anc. region, Peloponnesus, Greece; corresponding to present Messinia, densely p. agr. dep., cap. Kalamata; a. 3,406 km²; p. (1971) 172,850.

Messina, c., spt., Sicily, Italy; opposite Reggio; univ.; exp. fruit, wine, oil; p. (1969) 272,312.

Messina, strait, between Sicily and Italian mainland; length 35 km, minimum width 5 km.

Mesta, R., Bulgaria, Greece; rises in Rodopi mtns., flows S.E. into Aegean Sea 24 km E. of Kavalla; valley famous for tobacco; known in Greece as Nestos; c. 280 km long.

Mestre, t., Italy; on lagoon at landward end of causeway linking Venice to mainland.

Meta, R., Colombia and Venezuela; navigable for 640 km; trib. of R. Orinoco; 1,200 km long.

Metz, c., cap. of Moselle dep., N.E. France; on R. Moselle 40 km N. of Nancy; cultural and comm. ctr. of Lorraine; impt. iron mines; wines, preserved fruits; mediaeval bldgs.; birthplace of Verlaine; p. (1968) 107,537.

Meudon, t., Hauts-de-Seine, France; S.W. sub. of Paris; observatory; glass, linen, ammunition; p. (1968) 51,481.

Meurthe, R., N.E. France; rises in Vosges and joins Moselle N. of Nancy.

Meurthe-et-Moselle, dep., N.E. France; borders on Belgium and Luxembourg; cap. Nancy; a. 5,276 km²; p. (1968) 705,413.

Meuse, dep., N.E. France; borders on Belgium; cap. Bar-le-Duc; a. 6,237 km²; p. (1968) 209,513.

Meuse (Maas), R., France; rises in Haute-Marne, flows past Verdun into Belgium past Namur, and Liège into the Neth. and joins the Waal, left arm of the Rhine; impt. routeway; 912 km long.

Mexborough, t., South Yorks., Eng.; on R. Don, 16 km above Doncaster; potteries; p. (1971) 15,946.

Mexicali, c., Baja Cal., Mexico; border resort; p. (1970) 263,498.

Mexican Plateau, central plateau, Mexico, between the branches of the Sierra Madre; highest point over 2,400 m; impt. landform and a. of human settlement.

Mexico, fed. rep., Central America; inc. 31 sts. and fed. dist. of Mexico City; mtnous.; Sierra Madre covers most of rep.; variety of climate according to alt.; W. mostly desert; agr. requires irrigation; major world exporter of cotton, sisal, sulphur, silver; oil impt.; 14 oil refineries, new petrochemical complex at Cosoleacaque; rapid industl. expansion for consumer gds.; decentralisation of inds. from Mexico City; tourism for Americans; cap. Mexico City; a. 1,972,360 km²; p. (est. 1975) 60,145,000.

Mexico, st., Mexico; encircles fed. dist. of Mexico City; cap. Toluca; a. 21,412 km²; p. (1969) 2,803,000.

Mexico City, c., cap. of Mexico; ¹gst. c. in Latin America; on plain at 2,275 m; many noteworthy bldgs., cath., univ.; admin., comm. and industl. ctr.; nuclear reactor nearby; p. (1970) 6,874,165 (c.), 8,589,630 (met. a.).

Mexico, Gulf of, lge. inlet of Atl. Oc. (1,600 km E. to W. by 1,280 km N. to S.) lying S. of USA and E. of Mexico; communicates by Florida strait with Atl. and by Yucatan strait with Caribbean Sea; submarine oil drilling.

Mexico, Valley of, Meseta Central, Mexico; major industl. zone; over 60 per cent by value of Mexican mnfs. produced; wide range of inds.; major ctr. Mexico City; attempts to decentralise p. and economic activity throughout Mexico; once ctr. of Aztec p.

Meyrin, t., Switzerland; H.Q. of CERN, nr. Geneva.

Mezhdurechensk, t., RSFSR; W. Siberia, on R. Tom'; new coal-mng. ctr.; p. (est. 1969) 81,000.

Mezzogiorno, lge underdeveloped region, southern Italy; comprising Abruzzo and Molise, Campania, Basilicata, Apulia, Calabria and the Is. of Sicily and Sardinia; major govt. attempts to develop a.; agr. reforms and industl. growth, oil refining, iron and steel, petrochemicals; contains 40 per cent of p. of Italy, much emigration; p. (est. 1969) 19,000,000.

Miami, c., Fla., USA; on Biscayne Bay, at mouth of Miami R.; famous resort and recreational ctr.; varied inds.; international airport; M. beach across Biscayne Bay; p. (1970) 331,553 (c.), 1,259,176 (met. a.).

Miass, c., RSFSR; in Urals, 90 km S.W of Chelyabinsk; gold-mng. ctr.; cars; p. (1970) 132,000.

Michigan, st., USA; in valley of Gr. Ls.; industl.; cars, iron and steel gds., petroleum, minerals; some agr.; cap. Lansing; a. 150,779 km²; p. (1970) 8,776,873.

Michigan City, t., Ind., USA; on L. Mich.; rly. wks., furniture, hosiery; p. (est. 1969) 39,500.

Michigan Lake, 3rd lgst of Gr. Ls. and the only one wholly in USA; in basin of St. Lawrence R., enclosed by two peninsulas of the st. of Mich. and by Wis., Ill., and Ind.; a. 61,901 km²; discharges by Straits of Mackinac to L. Huron.

Michipicoten, R., Ont., Canada; flows 200 km to L. Superior; iron ore deposits in valley.

Michoacan, st., Mexico; on Pac. Oc.; mtnous., rich in minerals; cap. Morelia; a. 60,088 km²; p. (1969) 2,452,000.

Michurinsk, t., RSFSR; N.W. of Tambov; engin., textiles, food inds.; agr. exp. ctr.; p. (est. 1967) 91,000.

Micronesia, Is., S. Pac.; Carolines, Marshalls, Marianas, and Gilbert Is.; most are coral atolls.

Mid Bedfordshire, l. gov. dist., Beds., Eng.; a. N. of Luton and inc. Biggleswade, Sandy and Ampthill; p. (est. 1976) 97,600.

Middleburg, t., cap. of Zeeland prov., Neth.; on Walcheren I. nr. Flushing; margarine, timber, optical instruments; cloth ctr. in mediaeval times; p. (1968) 28,416.

Middlesbrough, t., l. gov. dist., Cleveland, Eng.; expanded t.; pt. on S. side of Tees estuary; impt. iron and steel ind., heavy engin., chemicals; p. (est. 1976) 153,900 (dist.).

Middlesex, former co., S.E. Eng.; N. of R. Thames; largely absorbed in Greater London 1964.

Middleton, t., Gtr. Manchester, Eng.; in valley of R. Irk; textiles, engin. chemicals, foam rubber; p. (1971) 53,419.

Middleton, t., Ohio, USA; on Miami R. and canal; steel, paper; p. (est. 1969) 46,500.

Middlewich, t., Cheshire, Eng.; on Rs. Dane, Wheelock and Croco, 8 km N. of Crewe; salt, chemicals, clothing; p. (1971) 7,783.

Mid Glamorgan, co., S. Wales; upland in N. dissected by deep R. valleys containing former coal-mng. settlements; lowland to S. borders Bristol Channel; a. 1,018 km²; p. (est. 1976) 540,400.

Midhurst, t., West Sussex, Eng.; on R. Rother; famous polo grounds; birthplace of Richard

Cobden; p. (1971) 18,983 (dist.).

Midland, t., Texas, USA; oilfield ctr., cotton ginning, natural gas; p. (est. 1969) 61,500.

Midlands, region, Eng.; comprises non-met. cos. of Staffs., Derbys., Notts., Leics., Warwicks., Northants., and met. co. of West Midlands; impt. a. for lt. engin.

Midlothian, former co.. l. gov. dist., Lothian Reg., Scot.; adjoins Edinburgh; a. 357 km²; p. (1971) 80,235.

Midnapore, t., W. Bengal, India; mkt. for agr. prods.; p. (1961) 59,532.

Mid Suffolk, l. gov. dist., Suffolk, Eng.; rural a. inc. Eye and Stowmarket; p. (est. 1976) 64,700.

Mid Sussex, l. gov. dist., West Sussex, Eng.; a. inc. Cuckfield and Burgess Hill; p. (est. 1976) 107,100.

Midway Island, I., Pac. Oc.; calling-place on airroutes between San Francisco and Asia, midway between Asia and USA (to which it belongs).

Mieres, t., Oviedo prov., N. Spain; in Asturias; coal-mng. ctr., iron and steel inds.; p. (1967) 68,458.

Mihoro, Gifu, Japan; power plant under construction.

Mikkeli, c., cap. of M prov., Finland; L. pt. in Saimaa L. region; p. (est. 1970) 25,188.

Milan, c., cap. of M. prov., N. Italy; route ctr. in Lombard plain; second lgst. c. in rep.; ctr. of commerce and ind.; textiles, chemicals, printing, publishing, machin., cars, aircraft, porcelain; cath.. univ.; p. (1969) 1,701.612 (met. a.).

Mildenhall, t., Forest Heath, Suffolk, Eng.; on R. Lark; 13th cent. church; R.A.F. sta. nearby; expanded t.; p. (1971) 26,613 (dist.).

Mildura, t., Victoria, Australia; on R. Murray; irrigation ctr.; fruit-canning, food-processing; p. (1972) 13,190.

Milford Haven, spt., Preseli, Dyfed, Wales; magnificent deepwater harbour recently developed; major tanker terminal (250,000 tonnes); 2 refineries; pipeline from Angle Bay to Llandarcy (nr. Swansea); major white fish pt.; trawlers built and repaired; net mkg.; p. (1971) 13,745.

Milford Sound, inlet, at S. of S.I., N.Z.; tourist resort; noted for scenery and rare birds.

Millau, t., Aveyron, France; on R. Tarn; glove mnfs.; p. (1968) 22,595.

Millom, t., Copeland, Cumbria, Eng.; on N.W. cst. of Duddon estuary; ironwks. (closed 1968 after 100 years); hosiery; declining p.; p. (1971) 14,070 (dist.).

Millport, burgh, Cunninghame, Scot.; on Gr. Cumbrae I., in F. of Clyde; resort; cath.; quarries; p. (1971) 1,254.

Milngavie, burgh, Bearsden and M., Strathclyde Reg., Scot.; 8 km N.W. of Glasgow; textiles; p. (1971) 10,741.

Milnrow, t., Gtr. Manchester, Eng.; sub. of Rochdale; cotton and waste spinning engin., brick mkg., paper and tube mftg.; p. (1971) 10,329.

Milo or Melos, I., Cyclades, Greece; cap. Plaka, nr. site of anc. c.; famous statue of Venus of Milo (now in Louvre) found here in 1820.

Milton Keynes, v., l. gov. dist., Bucks., Eng.; a. 9,000 ha; site and name of new c. for London overspill to comprise Bletchley, Wolverton and Stoney Stratford; Open University at Bletchley; p. (est. 1976) 89,000 (dist.).

Milwaukee, c., Wis., USA; lgst. c. and ch. pt. of st.; on L. Mich.; 112 km N. of Chicago; univ.; major mftg. ctr. with numerous inds., notably machin. and transport equipment, meatcanning, beer; p. (1970) 709,537 (c.), 1,393,260 (met. a.).

Min, R., Fukien, S. China; descends steeply on S.E. course to enter S. China Sea nr. Foochow, length 480 km. navigable.

Min, R., Szechwan, N.W. China; flows S., diverted at Kwanhsien into irrigation channels, joining Yangtze at Ipin; length 800 km. navigable.

Mina Hassan Tani (Kenitra), spt., Morocco; exp. grain; p. (1971) 135,960 (c.), 302, 390 (met. a.).

Minas Gerais, st., Brazil; vast iron ore reserves; gold, diamonds, manganese, uranium, aluminium; cotton, coffee; hydroelec. power sta.; cap. Belo Horizonte; plans for development of heavy inds.; a. 585,472 km²; p. (est. 1968) 11,776,817.

Minas Novas, t., Minas Gerais, Brazil; p. (est. 1968) 24,003.

Mina Sulman, free transit pt., Bahrain; deepwater pt., dry dock for OPEC super-tankers, entrepôt tr.

Minatitlán, t., E. Mexico; petroleum refineries; petrochemicals; p. 18,539.

Minch, The, channel between the mainland of Scot. and the N. portion of Outer Hebrides, 38–64 km wide; very rapid current.

Minch, The Little, channel between I. of Skye, Scot., and the middle portion of Outer Hebrides, 22–32 km wide.

Minchinhampton, t., Gloucs., Eng.; in Cotswolds, 6 km S.E. of Stroud.

Mindanao, second lgst. I. of Philippines; forested mtns., volcano Mt. Apo; exp. pineapples, hemp, coconuts, coffee; iron, gold, copper mined; plywoods and veneer, paper, pulp; ch. ts. Zamboanga, Davao; a. of govt. sponsored immigration; lge. Muslim p. seeking indep. for I.; greatest depth Mindanao Deep, off Philippines, 11,524 m; a. 94,628 km²; p. (1970) 7,292,691.

Minuen, c., N. Rhine–Westphalia, W. Germany; on R. Weser at crossing of Mittelland canal; pt., rly. junc.; cath. (12th–14th cent.) destroyed in second world war; p. (est. 1967) 51,100.

Mindoro, I., Philippines, S. of Luzon; mtnous., thickly forested; rice, coconuts grown on cst., a. 9,376 km²; p. (1970) 473,940.

Minehead, t., West Somerset, Eng.; at N. foot of Exmoor, on Bristol Channel cst.; mkt., holiday resort; p. (1971) 8,063.

Minho, R., separates Portugal from Spain in N.W.; length 272 km.

Minicoy Is., Arabian Sea; joined with Laccadive and Amindivi Is. to form union terr. of India.

Minneapolis, c., Minn., USA; on Mississippi R. at falls of St. Anthony; lgst. c. of st., pt. of entry, rly. terminus; wheat mkt., comm. and industl. ctr.; wide range of inds.; univ.; p. (1970) 431,977 (c.), 1 805,081 (met. a.).

Minnesota, st., USA; W. of L. Superior; studded with Ls., many Rs.; iron ore; maize, wheat, livestock, dairying; cap. St. Paul; a. 217,736 km²; p. (1970) 3,767,975.

Minorca (Menorca), I. off Spain; 2nd lgst. of Balearic Is.; Mediterranean agr.; developing tourism; cap. Mahón; a. 733 km²; p. (1970) 50,217.

Minsk, c., cap. of Belorussiyan SSR, USSR; lge. rly. junc.; cultural and industl. ctr.; univ.; engin., computers; rebuilt since second world war; p. (1970) 907,000 (c.), 916,000 (met. a.).

Minya, c., central Egypt; on Nile; cotton tr. ctr.; p. (est. 1970) 122,100.

Minya Konka, mtn., S.W. Szechwan prov., China; in Himalayas; highest peak in China; 7,570 m.

Mirfield, t., West Yorks., Eng.; on R. Calder, 5 km S.W. of Dewsbury; woollens; p. (1971) 16,871.

Miri, t., Sarawak, E. Malaysia; impt. oil ctr.; p. (1960) 13,350.

Mirzapur, t., Uttar Pradesh, India; on R. Ganges; carpets, brassware; p. (1971) 105,939.

Miskolc, c., N.E. Hungary; impt. industl. ctr.; iron ore, lignite nearby; varied inds., inc. textiles, porcelain, engin., bricks, refrigeration plants; p. (est. 1969) 172,000.

Mississippi, st., S. USA; in lower M. valley; bounded on S. by G. of Mexico; cotton, sweet potatoes, pecan nuts, rice, sugar-cane, sorghum-cane, fruit, livestock raising; petroleum, natural gas; cotton textiles, chemicals, fish-processing; cap. Jackson; a. 123,584 km²; p. (1970) 2,158,872.

Mississippi, principal R. of USA; rises in N. Minn. nr. L. Itasca; drains c. 3,170,000 km²; enters G. of Mexico in lge. delta nr. New Orleans; navigable, flood control problems; length 3,760 km (Mississippi–Missouri–Red Rock 6,176 km).

Missolongni, t., Greece, pt. on inlet of G. of Patras; fish, tobacco; Byron died here 1824; p. (1971) 12,368.

Missoula, t., Mont., USA; on Klark R.; univ.; rly. wks., agr.; fruit, oil refinery; tourism; p. (1970) 29,497.

Missouri, st., central USA; dominated by Mississippi and Missouri Rs.; predominantly agr.; livestock, maize; coal, iron; transport equipment; cap. Jefferson City; ch. t. St. Louis; a. 180,456 km²; p. (1970) 4,636,247.

issouri, longest R. of USA; 3,942 km; trib of Mississippi R.; main headstream Jackson R.; flood, power and irrigation schemes.

Missouri Coteau, hill ridge, N. America; runs N.W. to S.E. across prairies of Saskatchewan (Canada), N. and S. Dakota (USA); rises abruptly from 480–600 m.

Mistassini, L., Quebec, Canada; 160 km long.

Misurata, t., Tripolitania, Libya; on cst. of Mediterranean, 176 km E. of Tripoli; mkt. for local agr. produce; p. (1964) 37,000.

Mitau. See Jelgava.

Mitchelstown, t., Cork, R.o.I.; nr. Fermoy; dairy prods.; p. (1966) 2,617.

Mitidja, plain, Algeria; N. Africa; borders Mediterranean; intensive cultivation of vine; ch. ts. Algiers, Blida.

Mito, c., Honshu, Japan; cas., comm. ctr.; famous for lime trees; p. (est. 1971) 179,000.

Mittelland Canal, inland waterway system, W. Germany; system of canals and canalised Rs.; links Dortmund–Ems canal nr. Rheine through Minden, Hanover, Magdeburg, Berlin to R. Oder at Frankfurt-on-Oder; makes use of natural E.–W. troughs across the N. German plain.

Mittweida, t., Karl-Marx-Stadt, E. Germany; metallurgy, textiles; p. (est. 1970) 19,600.

Miyazaki, c., Kyushu, Japan; famous shrine; ctr. of sandy plain with lagoons; p. (est. 1971) 207,000.

Mizoram (" Land of Highlanders "), new union terr. (1972), Assam, N.E. India; former Mizo Hills dist. of Assam; 80 per cent p. Christian; 44 per cent literate, higher proportion than any other a. except Kerala; new cap. Aizawl; a. 21,238 km²; p. (est. 1971) 400,000.

Mjosa, lgst. L., Norway; 88 km long.

Mladá Boleslav (Jungbunzlau), t., Bohemia, ČSSR; vehicles, agr. machin., textiles; once ctr. of Bohemian Brethren (followers of John Hus); p. (est. 1968) 28,790.

Moanda, spt. at mouth of Zaïre R., Zaïre; oil refinery, aluminium smelter.

Mobutu Seso, L., (L. Albert), Zaïre, Uganda; on floor of Gt Rift Valley; crocodile farming; tourism; main pt. Kasenyi; 160 km long, 32 km wide; alt., 640 m; a. 5,346 km².

Mobile, c., spt., Ala. USA; on R. M.; shipbldg. pt. inds.; exp. cotton; p. (1970) 129,009 (c.), 231,105 (met. a.).

Moçambique, former Portuguese prov., indep. st. (1975), E. Africa; wide cstl. plain rising inland to 2,100 m; crossed by Zambesi R.; few exp. inc. cashew nuts, cotton, sugar, tea; deposits of coal and bauxite; Beira and Maputo (cap.) serve as import pts. for transit tr.; 40% GNP from tourism and transport; Cabora Bassa dam project in Tete dist.; border with Rhodesia closed March 1976; a. 771,820 km²; p. (est. 1969) 7,376,000.

Moçambique Channel, strait, Indian Oc.; separates Malagasy Rep. from mainland of Africa; 1,600 km long, 400–960 km wide.

Moçambique Current, ocean current, flows N. to S. along E. cst. of Moçambique and Natal, E. Africa; relatively warm water.

Moçâmedes, pt., Angola, W. Africa; ore pier; linked by rail to Cassinga mines; fishing; p. 8,000.

Mocha or Al-Mukha, t., N. Yemen; S.W. Arabia; on Red Sea; formerly noted for exp. of coffee; p. 5,000.

Modane, t., S.E. Savoie, France; commands routes via Mont Cenis Pass and tunnel; electro-metallurgy; p. (1968) 5,767.

Modena, t., cap. of M. prov. Italy; cath., univ.; textiles, leather, engin.; p. (1968) 167,810.

Modesto, t., Cal., USA; fruit (especially peaches), vegetable-processing; p. (est. 1969) 52,000.

Modica, t., S.E. Sicily, Italy; agr. ctr.; limestone grottoes, cave dwellings; Cava d'Ispica; p. (est. 1968) 44,574.

Moffat, burgh, Annandale and Eskdale, Scot.; 24 km N.W. of Lockerbie; resort; p. (1971) 2,031.

Moffat Tunnel, Col., USA; carries trunk rly. from Chicago to San Francisco under Rocky mtns. between Denver and Salt Lake City; 10 km long; alt. 2,774m.

Mogadishu, c., cap. of Rep. of Somalia; on Indian Oc.; modernised deep-sea pt., airpt.; p. (est. 1972) 230,000.

Mogador. *See* Essaouira.

Mogi das Cruzes, t., São Paulo, Brazil; agr.; bauxite mng.; p. (est. 1968) 111,554.

Mogilev, c., Belorussiyan SSR, USSR; on R. Dnieper; industl.; rly. and route junc.; p. (1970) 202,000.

Mohács, t., S. Hungary; on Danube; impt. R. pt.; strategic site; battle 1526; p. (est. 1967) 15,900.   [p. (1960) 35,010.

Mohammedia, t., Morocco, N. Africa; oil refining;

Mohawk, R., N.Y., USA; trib. of Hudson R.; followed by impt. road, rly. and canal routes across Appalachian mtns.; 280 km long.

Mojave or Mohave, S. Cal., USA; desert region of mtns. and valleys; a. 38,850 km².

Moji, spt., Kyushu, Japan; exp. coal, cement, timber; linked by bridge to Honshu. *See* Kitakyushu.

Mokpo, spt., W. cst. S. Korea; ctr. of food-processing and cotton-ginning; p. (1966) 162,322.

Mol, t., N.E. Belgium; nuclear energy research ctr.; p. (est. 1969) 28,440.

Mold, t., Delyn, Clwyd, N. Wales; on R. Alyn; chemicals, roadstone; p. (1971), 8,239.

Moldau. *See* Vltava.

Moldavian SSR, constituent rep., USSR; fertile fruit growing a. especially for vines; inds. based on fruit; cap. Kishinev; a. 34,188 km²; p. (1970) 3,372,000.

Mole Valley, l. gov. dist., Surrey, Eng.; based on Mole R. ts. of Leatherhead and Dorking; p. (est. 1976) 76,100.

Mole, R., Surrey, Eng.; rises in central Weald, flows N. into R. Thames nr. Molesey; cuts impt. gap through N. Downs between Dorking and Leatherhead; 80 km long.

Molenbeek-Saint-Jean, t., Belgium; nr. Brussels; lge mftg. ctr.; p. (est. 1967) 67,500.

Molfetta, spt., Apulia, Italy; olive oil, macaroni, wine; caths.; p. (est. 1967) 65,100.

Moline, t., Ill., USA; on Mississippi R.; agr. im-plements, ironwks., flour; p. (est. 1969) 49,000.

Mollendo, t., S.W. Peru; pt. on Pac. Oc.; former outlet for Arequipa; replaced by Matarani; wool textiles, fishing; p. (1961) 18,000.

Mölndal, t., S.W. Sweden; paper, textiles; mar-garine; p. (1968) 31,125.

Moluccas or Spice Is., prov. Indonesia; gr. of Is. between Sulawesi and W. Irian; mtnous., fer-tile; spices, sago, timber, pearls, rice, copra, ch. t. Ternate; attempts at secession by S. Moluccans; a. 496,454 km²; p. (est. 1970) 995,000.

Mombasa, spt., Kenya; ch. harbour, Killindini; rly. terminus; oil refinery; exp. tropical pro-duce (ivory, hides, rubber, etc.); p. (est. 1970) 255,400.

Mon, I., off cst. of Sjaelland, Denmark; a. 233 km²; cap. Stege; p. (1965) 12,318.

Monaco, principality, on Mediterranean cst. between France and Italy, W. Europe; economy based on tourism; benefits from climate and amenities, inc. famous casino; tax laws attract p. and shortage of land causes M. to build out into sea; much revenue derived from transactional laws, sales of tobacco and postage stamps; cap. Monte Carlo; a. 146 ha; p. (1968) 23,035.

Monadhliath Mtns., Badenoch and Strathspey, Scot.; between Spey R. and Loch Ness; hgst. peak Carn Mairg 1,216 m.

Monadnock Mt., peak, 965 m high, N.H., USA; name used as term for the geomorphological feature of an isolated hill which has successfully resisted erosion.

Monaghan, co., R.o.I.; mainly pastoral and agr.; a. 1,295 km²; p. (1966) 45,726.

Monaghan, co. t., Monaghan, R.o.I.; on the Ulster canal; cath.; p. (1966) 4,019.

Mona Passage, strait, Caribbean Sea; separates Hispaniola from Puerto Rico.

Monastir. *See* Bitola.

Mönch, peak, Bernese Alps, Switzerland; 4,101 m.

Monchegorsk, t., RSFSR; on L. Imandra; cop-per and nickel smelting; p. (est. 1969) 53,000.

Mönchengladbach, t., N. Rhine-Westphalia, W. Germany; 26 km W. of Düsseldorf; rly. ctr. textiles; p. (est. 1969) 152,200.

Monchique, t., Algarve, Portugal; spa; wine, oil, chestnuts; p. 10,000.

Moncton, t., N.B., Canada; rly. ctr., textiles; oil nearby; p. (1971) 47,781.

Mondego, R., Portugal; 208 km long.

Montalcone, t., N.E. Italy; on Adriatic; modern industl. t.; shipbldg., oil refining; p. (1968) 27,907.

Monferrato, low hills, Piedmont, N. Italy; S. and S.E. of Turin between valleys of Po and Tanaro; celebrated vineyards, produce Asti Spumante wines; alt. never exceeds 460 m.

Monghyr, t., Bihar, India; on R. Ganges; mkt. ctr.; p. (1971) 102,474.

Mongla, pt., Bangladesh; on Pussur R.; shipping pt. under construction.

Mongolia, vast elevated plateau in heart of Asia between China and USSR. *See* Mon-golian People's Rep. and Inner Mongolia.

Mongolia, Inner. *See* Inner Mongolia.

Mongolia, People's Rep. of (Outer Mongolia), central Asia; extensive plateau at 1,200 m bordering Gobi desert in S.; dry continental climate with extremely cold winters; pastoral agr. collectively organised for horses, sheep, camels, oxen, and goats; extensive state farms for cereals; 60 per cent of tr. with USSR; cap. Ulan Bator; a. 1,564,360 km²; p. (1970) 1,227,000.

Monmouth, t., l. gov. dist., Gwent, Wales; at confluence of Rs. Wye and Monnow; mkt. ctr.; timber, crushed limestone, wrought ironwk.; p. (est. 1976) 67,500 (dist.).

Monmouthshire, former co., S. Wales; mostly inc. in Gwent; parts in South and Mid Glamorgan.

Monongahela, R., W. Va., USA; joins Allegheny R. at Pittsburgh to form Ohio R.; impt. waterway.

Monopoli, spt., Apulia, Italy; oil, wine, fruit, flour tr.; p. (est. 1968) 39,746.

Monroe, t., La., USA; cotton ctr., natural gas, paper, printing ink; p. (1970) 54,647 (c). 111,527 (met. a.).

Monrovia, c., cap. of Liberia, W. Africa; pt. on Atl. at mouth of St. Paul R.; exp. rubber, palm oil; ship registration; p. (est. 1970) 96,226.

Mons, c., cap. of Hainaut prov., W. Belgium, nr. Fr. border; cath.; inds. linked with Borin-age coal-mng. dist.; varied mnfs.; scene of many battles; NATO (SHAPE) H.Q. nearby at Casteau; p. (1968) 27,680.

Montana, st., N.W. USA; in Rocky mtns. region; cap. Helena; lgst c. Great Falls; copper, silver, gold, zinc, lead, manganese; coal, petroleum, natural gas; pastoral agr.; Glacier Nat. Park, tourism; a. 377,456 km²; p. (1970) 682,133.

Montauban, t., Tarn-et-Garonne dep., France; on R. Tarn; cath.; agr. prod., wines; p. (1968) 48,455.

Montbéliard, t., Doubs dep., France; S. of Belfort; textiles, watches, typewriters, vehicles; p. (1968) 23,908 (t.), 114,670 (met. a.).

Mont Blanc, mtn., Alps; on confines of Italy and France; alt. 4,814 m; longest road tunnel in world (opened to traffic 1965) linking Cour-mayeur (Italy) and Chamonix (France), length 12 km.

Montceau-les-Mines, t., Saône-et-Loire dep., France; coal, textiles, metal-working; p. (1968) 27,421.

Mont Cenis Pass, W. Alps; on bdy. between France and Italy; approached from W. by Isère-Arc valleys, from E. by Dora Riparia; alt. 2,097 m.

Mont Cenis Tunnel, W. Alps; on bdy. between France and Italy; carries main rly. from Lyons to Turin under Col de Fréjus; approached from W. by Isère-Arc valleys, from E. by Dora Riparia; opened 1871; 12 km long.

Montclair, t., N.J., USA; residtl. sub. of N.Y.; paper gds. mnfs.; p. (1970) 44,043.

Mont-de-Marsan, t., Landes dep., France; mkt. ctr.; p. (1968) 24,458.

Mont-Dore, spa, Puy-de-Dôme dep., France; 48 km S.W. of Clermont-Ferrand; Puy de Sancy (1,887 m) hgst. peak of Mont-Dore mtn. gr.; p. (1968) 2,419.

Monte Bello Is., gr. off N.W. cst., Australia; about 136 km N. of pt. of Onslow; first Brit. atomic weapon exploded here 3 Oct. 1952.

Monte Carlo, t., Monaco; tourist resort, casino; p. (1961) 9,516.

Monte Corno, mtn., Italy; in Central Apennines; alt. 2,923 m.

Monte Cristo, Italian I., 42 km S. of Elba, in Tyrrhenian Sea; famed by novel by Dumas.

Monte Gargano, peninsula, S. Italy; projects into Adriatic Sea nr. plain of Foggia; formed by limestone plateau, alt. over 900 m; pasture on upper slopes, woodland on lower slopes; a. 1,030 km².

Montego Bay, spt., Jamaica; main ctr. tor tourism; p. (est. 1970) 42,800.

Montélimar, t., Drôme dep., France; bricks, tiles, nougat; hydroelectric barrage on R. Rhône; p. (1968) 27,483.

Montenegro, constituent rep., S.W. Yugoslavia; agr., pastoral; cap. Titograd; a. 13,812 km²; p. (1971) 530,361.

Monterey, t., Cal., USA; S. of San Francisco, resort of artists and writers; sardine ind., fruit and vegetable canneries; p. (est. 1969) 26,500.

Monteria, c., cap. of Cordoba prov., Colombia; tobacco, cacao, cotton, sugar; p. (est. 1972) 121,200 (c.), 167,600 (met. a.).

Monte Rosa, hgst. peak, 4,637 m, Pennine Alps, on border of Italy and Switzerland.

Monte Rotondo, hgst. mtn., Corsica, France; 2,767 m.

Monterrey, t., cap. of Nuevo León prov., Mexico; third lgst. c.; cath.; textiles, brewing, ironwks., minerals; thermoelec. plant; sheet metal; p. (1970) 858,107 (c.), 1,213,479 (met. a.).

Monte Sant'Angelo, hilltop t., Italy; on Gargano promontory; notable ctr. of pilgrimage; p. (est. 1968) 20,092.

Montevideo, c., cap. of Uruguay; major pt. on Rio de la Plata; dominates life of rep. as financial, comm. and industl. ctr.; fisheries, oil-refining, food-processing, tourism; cath., univ.; p. (est. 1967) 1,280.000.

Montgomery, t., l. gov. dist., Powys, central Wales; in upper Severn valley, 13 km N.E. of Newtown; agr. mkt.; cas.; p. (est. 1976) 44,500 (dist.).

Montgomery, t., W. Punjab, Pakistan; livestock; leather, cotton; p. (1961) 25,100.

Montgomery, c., cap. of Ala., USA; at head of Alabama R.; cotton, livestock, timber, dairying, fertilisers; hydroelec. power; p. (1970) 129,375 (c.), 194,522 (met. a.).

Montgomeryshire, former co., Central Wales. *See* Powys.

Montluçon, t., Allier dep., France; on R. Cher; terminus of Berry canal, linking Commentry coalfields with Loire; iron foundries, glassmaking; cas.; p. (1968) 59,983.

Montmartre, dist., N. Paris, France; on Butte de M. (101 m), commands superb view S. over Paris; picturesque square, frequented by artists; basilica of Sacré Coeur.

Montparnasse, dist., Paris, France; on left bank of Seine R.; haunt of artists and writers.

Montpellier, t., cap. of Hérault dep., France; 8 km N. of Mediterranean cst. on coastal lowland route to S.W. France; comm. and cultural ctr.; univ.; wines, fruit tr.; silk, chemicals; many anc. bldgs. inc. cath.; p. (1968) 161,910 (c.), 171,467 (met. a.).

Montreal, c., spt., Quebec, Canada; at confluence of Ottawa and St. Lawrence Rs.; caths., univs.; major industl., comm. and financial ctr.; extensive harbour installations, lge. grain exp.; diverse mnfs.; lgst c. and spt. in Canada; p. mainly French-speaking; p. (1971) 1,197,753 (c.); 2,720,413 (met. a.).

Montreuil-sous-Bois, E. sub. Paris, France; hothouse flowers and fruit for Paris mkt.; peach growing; mnfs.; p. (1968) 95,859.

Montreux, t., Switzerland; on L. Geneva; tourist ctr.; Chillon cas.; p. (1969) 19,900.

Montrose, spt., burgh, Angus, Scot.; on E. cst. at mouth of S. Esk R.; chemicals, rope wks., vegetable-canning, boat-bldg., fishing; supply base for N. Sea oil; p. (1971) 9,959.

Mont-Saint-Michel, rocky granite I., in English Channel, off Normandy cst., France; tourist ctr. with Benedictine abbey; connected to mainland by causeway; surrounding marshland reclaimed for agr.; alt. 79 m.

Montserrat, volcanic I., Leeward Is., W.I.,; chiefly agr.; exp. sea-island cotton, limes, sugar-cane and tomatoes; cap. Plymouth; a. 101 km²; p. (1968) 14,500.

Montserrat, mtn., Catalonia, Spain; Benedictine monastery, alt. 1,236 m.

Monument Valley, Utah and Arizona, USA; home of Navajo Indians.

Monza, c., Lombardy, N. Italy; 14 km from Milan; cath.; textiles, leather, hats; former royal residence; motor-racing circuit; p. (1968) 103,460.

Moonie, t., Queensland, Australia; 320 km W. of Brisbane; oilfields; pipeline to Lytton, at mouth of Brisbane R.

Moose Jaw, c., Saskatchewan, Canada; rly. junc.; agr. ctr.; agr. implements, oil refining. p. (1966) 33,417.

Moradabad, c., Uttar Pradesh, N. India; rly. junc.; cotton mills, brassware; mosque; p. (1971) 258,590 (c.), 272,652 (met. a.).

Morava, R., ČSSR and Austria; trib. of R. Danube; navigable in lower course; 339 km long.

Morava, R., Yugoslavia; formed from W. Morava and S. Morava, flows N. into Danube 80 km below Belgrade to Istanbul; 560 km long.

Moravia, region, ČSSR; part of Bohemian plateau, drained by Morava R.; inc. fertile agr. a.; mineral resources and industl. ts.

Moray, former co., l. gov. dist., Grampian Reg., Scot.; borders M. Firth; arable agr. benefiting from glacial soils; a. 2,230 km²; p. (1971) 76.595.

Moray Firth, arm of N. Sea; on Scottish E. cst., between Highland and Grampian Regs.; plans for lge.-scale industl. expansion; valuable inshore oilfield.

Morbihan, dep., N.W. France; on Bay of Biscay; agr., fishing; cap. Vannes; a. 7,094 km²; p. (1968) 540,474.

Mordovian ASSR, RSFSR; forested steppe between Rs. Oka and Volga; pastoral agr., lumbering; food processing; a. 25,493 km²; p. (1970) 1,030,000.

Morea. *See* Peloponnesus.

Morecambe and Heysham, t., N. Lancs., Eng.; on S. shore of M. Bay; M. holiday resort; H., pt. for N. Ireland and oil refinery; nuclear power sta. being built on cst. S. of M.; p. (1971) 41,863.

Morecambe Bay, between Lancs. and Cumbria, Eng.; isolates Furness dist. of Lancs.; many proposed barrages across Bay, now project increasingly probable as water shortage in N.W. Eng. grows.

Morelia, c., cap. of Michoacán st., W. Mexico; on rocky hill, 1,891 m in fertile valley; cath.; textiles, pottery; p. (1970) 161,040.

Morelos, inland st., Mexico; mtns., forested; arable agr.; cap. Cuernavaca; a. 4,962 km²; p. (1969) 597,000.

Morez, t., Jura dep., France; precision instruments, optical equipment; winter sports.

Morgan, t., R. pt., S. Australia; on R. Murray, handles transhipment of Murray and Darling R. traffic to rail for despatch to Adelaide.

Morgantown, c. W. Va., USA; univ.; coal, oil, gas fields; chemicals, heavy ind.; p. (1970) 29,341.

Morioka, c., N. Honshu, Japan; textiles, ironwks.; p. (est. 1971) 202,000.

Morlaix, spt., Finistère, France; tobacco, paper, brewing, agr.; p. (1968) 21,516.

Morley, t., West Yorks., Eng.; 5 km S.W. of Leeds; woollens, stone quarrying; p. (1971) 44,340.

Morocco, kingdom, N.W. Africa; csts. on Atl. Oc. and Mediterranean Sea; rises to Atlas mtns. inland; leading world producer of phosphates; other minerals inc. iron-ore, lead and manganese; agr. main occupation, wheat, barley, maize and livestock; fishing and tourism well developed; cap. Rabat; a. 466,200 km²; p. (1969) 15,030,000.

Morogoro, t., Tanzania, E. Africa; on E. edge of Central African plateau, alt. c. 900 m, 176 km by rail W. of Dar-es-Salaam; ctr. of sisal and cotton-growing a.

Moron, t., Venezuela; on cst. nr. Puerto Cabello; industl.; natural gas, oil refining.

Morón de la Frontera, t., S.W. Spain; agr. tr. ctr.; ruined Moorish cas.; p. (1970) 29,488.

Morpeth, t., Castle Morpeth, Northumberland, Eng.; finely situated in valley of Wansbeck; coal mng., iron-founding; mkt.; Norman cas. remains; p. (1971) 14,055.

Morriston, v., West Glamorgan, S. Wales; on R. Tawe, 3 km N.E. of Swansea; zinc. inds.

Morro Velho, gold mng. dist., Minas Gerais, Brazil; in Serra do Espinhaco; ch. t. Nova Lima.

Mors, I.. N. Jutland, **Denmark**; in Lim fjord; a. 357 km²; p. (1965) 25,739.

Morwell, t., Victoria, **Australia**; industl.; coal mng.; p. (1972) 16,327.

Moscow, c., cap. of USSR, and of RSFSR; leading cultural, political comm., industl. and route ctr. of USSR; on Moskva R.; served by several airpts., R. and canal pts.; contains Kremlin in c. ctr. with Red Square; caths., univs., palaces, many famous theatres and art galleries; p. (1970) 6,942,000 (c.); (1976) 7,632,000 (met. a.).

Moscow sea (Ucha Reservoir), artificial L., RSFSR; created behind dam on R. Volga at Ivankovo; supplies water to Moscow, maintains level on Moscow-Volga canal. and supplies water to 8 hydroelec. power-stas.; a. 329 km².

Moscow-Volga Canal, RSFSR; links R. Volga at Ivankovo with Khimki sub. of Moscow; forms part of Leningrad-Moscow inland waterway; opened 1937; 128 km long.

Moselle, dep., N.E. **France**; iron-ore, coal mng.; metal inds.; cap. Metz; a. 6,224 km²; p. (1968) 971,314.

Moselle, R., France and Germany; trib. of R. Rhine; canalised between Thionville and Koblenz (269 km); lower valley forms famous wine dist.; 525 km long.

Moshi, t., N. Tanzania; on southern slope of Mt. Kilimanjaro; ctr. of coffee-growing dist.; airpt. at 854 m (S.W. of t.).

Mosi-oa-Toenja. See Victoria Falls. The local name means " Smoke of the Thunders."

Mosjoen, t., N. Norway; recent aluminium wks.

Moskva, R., central RSFSR; trib. of R. Oka; Moscow stands on its banks; linked with upper Volga by Moscow-Volga canal (128 km long); 400 km long.

Mosonmagyaróvár, t., Hungary; aluminium wks.; agr. machin.; p. (1966) 24,100.

Mosquito Cst., lowland, E. cst. **Nicaragua**; 400 km N.-S., 192 km E.-W.; lumbering, bananas; ch. t. Bluefields; sparse p.

Moss, spt., Norway; pulp, paper, machin., textile inds.; p. (est. 1970) 24,580.

Mossamedes. See Moçâmedes.

Mossel Bay, pt. and seaside resort, Cape Prov., S. Africa; between Cape Town and Port Elizabeth; p. (est. 1967) 15,600.

Mossley, t., Tameside, Gtr. Manchester, **Eng.**; 5 km E. of Oldham; mkt. t., textiles; p. (1971) 10,055.

Most, t., ČSSR; lignite, chemicals; Druzhba crude oil pipeline extended to chemical wks.; p. (1967) 56,000.

Mostaganem, t., Algeria; spt. on Mediterranean cst., E. of Oran; exp. wine and fruits; gas pipeline from Hassi Messoud; p. (1967) 64,000.

Mostar, t., Herzegovina, **Yugoslavia**; on R. Naretva; bauxite, lignite; developing inds., wine, food-processing, aluminium plant; p. (est. 1965) 56,000.

Mosul, t., N. Iraq; on R. Tigris; in region producing cereals, citrus fruit, cattle; impt. oilfields nearby; metal work; impt. during crusades; p. (1965) 264,146.

Motala, t., on L. Vättern, **Sweden**; radio sta.; engin., woollen gds.; p. (1968) 27,887.

Motherwell and Wishaw, burgh, l. gov. dist., Strathclyde Reg., **Scot.**; in Clyde valley, 24 km S.E. of Glasgow; iron, steel, machin., engin., textiles; p. (1971) 73,658.

Moulins, c., cap. of Allier dep., **France**; on Allier R.; leather gds., clothing; cath., ruined château, art treasures; p. (1968) 27,408.

Moulmein, spt., Burma, on R. Salween; exp. teak, rice; p. (1966) 156,968.

Mountain Ash, t., Cynon Valley, Mid Glamorgan, **Wales**; in narrow valley 5 km S.E. of Aberdare; coal-mng. a.; p. (1971) 27,806.

Mount Adams, mtn., S. **Wash. USA**; beautiful volcanic scenery in Cascade Range; pine forests; alt. 3,803 m.

Mount Albert, bor., Auckland, **N.Z.**; p. (1972) 26,150.

Mount Alberta, mtn., W. Alberta, **Canada**; in Canadian Rockies and Jasper Nat. Park; alt. 3,622 m.

Mount Assiniboine, mtn., Alberta, B.C., **Canada**; " Matterhorn " of Canadian Rockies; alt. 3,620 m.

Mount Carmel, mtn., N.W. **Israel**; rises to 554 m and extends 10 km as penin. into Mediterranean Sea, forming S. limit to Bay of Acre; ass. with prophets Elijah and Elisha.

Mount Eden, bor., Auckland, **N.Z.**; p. (1972) 20,061.

Mount Goldsworthy, t., W. **Australia**; new t. being developed in iron ore mng. a.

Mount Isa, t., W. Queensland, **Australia**; in Selwyn Range 128 km W. of Cloncurry; copper mng.; p. (1972) 25,240.

Mount Lofty Range, mtn. range, S. **Australia**; forms barrier to routes leaving Adelaide; lower slopes support vineyards and outer suburbs of Adelaide; rises to over 900 m.

Mount Lyell, Tasmania, **Australia**; impt. copper mines, and refinery.

Mount McKinley, Alaska, **USA**; in Alaska Range and Nat. Park; highest point in N. America, c. 6,191 m.

Mountmellick, t., R.D., Laoighis, **R.o.I.**; p. (1961) 22,596 (R.D.).

Mount Newman, W. **Australia**; new t. built 1967 to exploit nearby iron ore.

Mount of Olives, **Jordan**; ridge (817 m), E. of Jerusalem; Garden of Gethsemane on lower slopes.

Mount Roskill, bor., Auckland, **N.Z.**; p. (1971) 33,842.

Mount's Bay, inlet, S. cst., Cornwall, **Eng.**; 32 km wide; fishery grounds.

Mount Tom Price, t., W. **Australia**; new t. being developed in iron ore mng. a.

Mount Vernon, c., N.Y., **USA**; on Bronx R.; sub. of N.Y.; residtl.; takes name from George Washington's house on Potomac, Va., 24 km S. of Washington D.C.; varied inds., notably electronic equipment; p. (1970) 72,778.

Mount Wellington, bor., Auckland, **N.Z.**; p. (1971) 20,178.

Mourenx, t., S.W. Aquitaine, **France**; nr. Lacq; new t. in oil dist.; p. (1966) 8,660.

Mourne Mtns., Newry and Mourne, **N. Ireland**; hgst. peak, 853 m.

Mouscron, t., Belgium; textile ctr. nr. Fr. border; p. (1968) 37,746.

Moyle, l. gov. dist., **N. Ireland**; borders N.E. cst.; inc. Rathlin I., Giants Causeway; main t. Ballycastle.

Mozambique. See Moçambique.

Mühlhausen, t., Erfurt, E. **Germany**; on R. Unstrut; textiles, machin., tobacco; p. (est. 1970) 45,385.

Mukden. See Shenyang.

Mulhacén, mtn., Sierra Nevada range, Spain; 3,483 m (hgst. peak Europe, outside Alps).

Mülheim-an-der-Ruhr, t., N. Rhine-Westphalia, W. **Germany**; on R. Ruhr; cas.; coal mng., iron, steel, tobacco, engin., elec., oil refining; airpt.; p. (est. 1969) 190,400.

Mulhouse, t., Haut-Rhin dep., **France**; impt. textile ctr.; potash deposits to N. supply chemical inds.; p. (1968) 116,336 (c.), 199,037 (met. a.).

Mull, I., Argyll and Bute, **Scot.**; included in Hebrides; a. 925 km²; pastoral farming, fishing, tourism; ch. t. Tobermory; p. (1971) 1,569.

Mullet, The, peninsula, W. cst. Mayo, **R.o.I.**

Mullingar, co. t., Westmeath, **R.o.I.**; on Brosna R.; mkt., agr. ctr.; cath.; p. (1966) 6,453.

Mull of Galloway, S. point of Wigtown, Scot.

Multan, t., W. Punjab, **Pakistan**; on R. Chenab; carpets, silks, pottery; steel, thermal sta.; gas pipeline to Lyallpur; p. (est. 1969) 597,000.

Muncie, t., Ind. **USA**; on White R.; iron, steel, glass and paper; p. (1970) 68,066 (c.), 127,861 (met. a.).

Munich or München, c., cap. Bavaria, W. **Germany**; on R. Isar; cultural ctr. with univ., cath., many old bldgs.; inds. varied, notably scientific instruments, brewing, elec. engin., chemicals; film studios; p. (est. 1969) 1,302,600.

Münster, c., N. Rhine-Westphalia, W. **Germany**; pt. on Dortmund-Ems canal; heavy machin. with varied mnfs.; cath., univ. and mediæval bldgs. damaged or destroyed in second world war; p. (est. 1969) 203,300.

Munster, prov., S.W. **R.o.I.**; includes cos. Waterford, Kerry, Cork, Limerick, Clare, Tipperary; a. 24,540 km²; p. (1966) 969,902.

Muonio, R., part of bdy. between **Finland** and **Sweden**; flows into G. of Bothnia.

Murano, t., Venice, **Italy**; famous since Middle Ages for glass ind.

Murchison Falls. *See* Kabelega Falls.

Murchison, R., W. Australia; length 1,280 km; near-by gold-field.

Murcia, prov. and former Moorish kingdom, S.E. Spain, on Mediterranean ("Almonds and Raisins Coast"); irrigated agr., cereals and fruit; cap. Murcia; a. 8,467 km²; p. (1970) 832,313.

Murcia, c., cap. of Murcia prov., S.E. Spain; on R. Segura; cath., univ.; textiles and food inds.; p. (1968) 274,560.

Murgab or Murghab, R., Afghanistan; flows 400 km to desert swamps.

Murmansk, spt., RSFSR; on Kola peninsula; ice-free throughout year; engin., elec. power; fishing, shipbldg.; submarine base; marine power sta. utilising tidal energy projected; p. (1970) 309,000.

Murom, t., RSFSR; pt. on Oka R.; anc. t.; textiles, engin.; p. (est. 1967) 96,000.

Muroran, spt., Hokkaido, Japan; on W. cst.; impt. iron and steel ctr.; p. (est. 1971) 170,000.

Murray, R., separates N.S.W. and Victoria, Australia; major irrigation schemes; hydro-electric power; 2,560 km long; length Murray-Darling system 3,696 km.

Murrumbidgee, R., N.S.W., Australia; trib. of R. Murray; used extensively for irrigation; 2,160 km long.

Musa Jebel, mtn., Egypt; 2,249 m; identified with the biblical Sinai.

Muscat, t., cap. of Oman, Arabia; on S. cst. of G. of Oman; gd. harbour; dates, mother-of-pearl; terminal of oil pipeline; p. (est. 1969) 9,973.

Muscat and Oman. *See* Oman.

Musgrave Range, mtns., on bdy. between S. Australia and N.T., Australia; isolated high-land in ctr. of continent; arid; rise to over 900 m.

Muskingum, R., Ohio, USA; trib. of Ohio R.; canalised for navigation; 384 km long.

Musselburgh, burgh, East Lothian, Scot.; on F. of Forth at mouth of R. Esk; wire, cables, nets, twine; paper mkg.; golf course; p. (1971) 16,790.

Mutankiang (Mudanjiang), c., Heilungkiang prov., China; pulp, paper, machin., flour milling; site of dam on R. Mutang; oil shale found locally; p. (est. 1970) 400,000.

Muttra. *See* Mathura.

Muzaffarnagar, t., Uttar Pradesh, India; N.E. of Delhi; p. (1971) 114,783.

Muzaffarpur, t., Bihar, India; in middle Ganges valley N. of Patna; p. (1971) 126,379.

Mwanza, t., N. Tanzania; pt. on L. Victoria; rly. term.; gold and diamonds mined; p. (1967) 34,186.

Mweelrea, mtn., Mayo, R.o.I.; 820 m.

Mweru, L., between Zaïre and Zambia; a. 6,993 km² at c. 900 m.

Mycenae, anc. c., N.E. Peloponnesus, Greece; excavations by Schliemann.

Myingyan, t., Burma; on R. Irrawaddy, S.W. of Mandalay; cotton spinning mill, zinc smelting, chemicals, fertilisers.

Myitkyina, t., Burma; on R. Irrawaddy; terminus of caravan route to China.

Mymensingh, t., Bangladesh; rice, jute; p. (1961) 53,200.

Mynyddislwyn, t., Islwyn, Gwent, Wales; in nar-row valley of W. Ebbw R., 11 km N.W. of port; elec. gds., kerb- and flagstones; p. (1971) 15,369.

Mystowice, t., Katowice, Poland; ctr. of coal-mng. dist.; technical porcelain; p. (1970) 44,700.

Mysore. *See* Karnataka.

Mysore, t., Karnataka, India; univ.; new inds. based on hydroelec. power; p. (1971) 355,685.

Mytilene, t. on Aegean Sea, Greece; ch. c. of I. of Lesvos (sometimes called Mytilene).

N

Naantali, t., S.W. Finland; pt. for Turku, on Baltic Sea; oil-refining, chemicals; founded 15th cent.; p. (est.) 2,778.

Naas, co. t. Co. Kildare, R.o.I.; former cap. of Leinster prov.; p. (1966) 4,528.

Nabeul, t., Tunisia, N. Africa; winter resort; p. (1966) 34,134.

Nablus, t., Jordan, N. of Jerusalem; nr. site of anc. Schechem and Jacob's Well; p. (1967) 44,223.

Nadiad, t., Gujarat, India; S. of Ahmadabad; p. (1971) 108,269.

Nagaland, st., India (1963); incorporates Naga Hills and Tuengsang; tribal a., formerly parts of Assam; cap. Kohima; a. 16,488 km²; p. (1971) 515,561.

Nagano, c., central Honshu, Japan; on R. Sinanogawa. 160 km S.W. of Niigata; cultural ctr.; publishing, machin., food-processing; textiles; p. (est. 1971) 290,000.

Nagaoka, t., N.W. Honshu, Japan; lge. oil pro-duction ctr.; p. (est. 1971) 163,000.

Nagapattinam, t., Tamil Nadu, India; spt. at mouth of R. Vettar; exp. cotton, tobacco, groundnuts; rly. terminus; p. (1961) 59,063.

Nagasaki, c., spt., Kyushu, Japan; on narrow peninsula; second c. destroyed by atomic bomb in second world war; impt. shipbldg. ctr. and associated engin.; p. (est. 1971) 427,000.

Nagercoil, t., Tamil Nadu, India; extreme S. of Indian peninsula; coconut-processing; p. (1971) 141,288.

Nagh Hamadi (Nag' Hammâdi), t., Upper Egypt; on R. Nile 256 km above Asyût; site of barrage (opened 1930) to regulate Nile flood and ensure irrigation of Girga prov.; barrage carries Cairo-Shellal rly. across Nile.

Nagorno-Karabakh, aut. oblast, S.W. Azerbay-dzhan SSR, USSR; on E. of Lesser Caucasus; forested mtns.; cap. Stepanakert; a. 4,403 km²; p. (1970) 149,000.

Nagoya, third c. of Japan; on Ise Bay, central Honshu; major pt. and industl. ctr.; univ.; textile mills, ceramic ctr., oil-refining; 16th cent. fortress t.; p. (est. 1971) 2,052,000.

Nagpur, c., Maharashtra st., India; univ.; admin. ctr.; textiles; Hindu temples; p. (1971) 866,076 (c.), 930,459 (met. a.).

Nagy Banya. *See* Baia-Mare.

Nagykanizsa, t., S.W. Hungary; industl. ctr.; heavy equipment, glasswks., beer; p. (1966) 37,800.

Nagykőrös, mkt. t., S.W. Hungary; in fruit-growing region; wine, food-processing; p. (1966) 25,400.

Naha, spt., cap. of Okinawa I., Ryuku Is.; (under 1971 treaty U.S. returns Is. to Japan); p. (est. 1971) 281,000.

Nailsworth, t., Gloucs., Eng.; in Cotswold Hills 6 km S. of Stroud; p. (1971) 3,974.

Nain, t., Iran; noted for very fine carpets; p. (1967) 40,289.

Nairn, former co., l. gov. dist., Highland Reg. Scot.; on Moray F., agr. a.; a. 420 km²; p. (1971) 9,665.

Nairn, royal burgh, Nairn, N.E. Scot.; fishing ctr.; cas.; p. (1971) 8,037.

Nairobi, c., cap. of Kenya; stands at c. 1,500 m on edge of Kenya highlands; modern c., 528 km from Mombasa; univ.; tourist ctr.; lt. inds.; wildlife game reserve; p. (est. 1970) 535,200. (met. a.).

Naivasha, L., Kenya; on floor of Gt. African Rift Valey; alt. 1,800 m.

Najaf or Nejef, c., Iraq; in Euphrates valley; Shiite Moslem pilgrimage ctr.; p. (1965) 134,027.

Nakhichevan, c., Azerbaydzhan SSR, USSR; food and wine inds.; ctr. of Nakhichevan aut. region; p. (1970) 33,000.

Nakhichevan ASSR, aut. rep., Azerbaydzhan SSR, USSR; borders Iran and Turkey; cotton, tobacco, rice, wheat in irrigated lowlands; salt and mineral deposits; a. 5,439 km².

Nakhodka, t., RSFSR; outpt. for Vladivostok on Sea of Japan; new t. 1950; p. (1970) 105,000.

Nakhon Pathom, t., Thailand; in central plain, S.W. of Bangkok; mkt. t.; p. (est. 1964) 31,746.

Nakhon Ratchasima, t., Thailand; on Mun R., in Korat plateau; rly. junc.; copper deposits nearby; p. (est. 1965) 54,310.

Nakhon si Thammarat, t., Thailand; in S. of Isthmus of Kra, on G. of Siam; anc. t.; mkt.; p. (est. 1964) 29,237.

Nakshov, spt., Lolland I., Denmark; sugar-refining; p. (est. 1970) 15,994.

Nakuru, t., Kenya rift valley (1,837 m), E. Africa; protected bird sanctuary (flamingoes) on L. Nakuru; wool-processing, fertilisers; p. (1969) 47,800.

Nalchik, c., cap. of Kabardino-Balkar ASSR, RSFSR; in foothills of N. Caucasus; food-processing; tourist resort; p. (1970) 146,000.

Namangan, c., Uzbek SSR., USSR; on Syr Dar'ya R., in Ferghana Valley; textiles, leather; p. (1970) 175,000.

Namaqualand, region, S.W. cst. of Africa; divided by Orange R. into Gr. N. in S.W. Africa, and Little N. in Cape Prov., Rep. of S. Africa; semi-arid; a. 259,000 km²; copper, diamonds.

Nam Dinh, t., N. Vietnam, nr. mouth of Red R.; cotton-spinning, silk-weaving, glass; mkt.; p. 25,000.

Namhoi. See Fatshan.

Namib Desert, desert a. along coastal strip of S.W. Africa for 1,200 km; very dry a., and almost unused.

Namibia. See South West Africa.

Namsos, spt., central Norway; on Folda fjord; lumber, fish canning; textiles; copper; p. (est. 1970) 11,223.

Nam Tso L., Tibet, China; lge. L. in ctr. of plateau of Tibet at 4,630 m.

Namur, c., cap. of N. prov., Belgium; at confluence of Meuse and Sambre Rs.; agr. processing, cutlery, glass; p. (1968) 32,418.

Nanaimo, t., B.C., Canada; pt. on Vancouver I.; timber and allied inds.; fisheries; boating and yachting; tourism; p. (1971) 14,762.

Nanchang, c., Kiangsi, China; on Kan R.; major transportation and industl. ctr.; textiles, machin., chemicals, paper; tractor wks.; dates from Sung dynasty (12th cent.); p. (est. 1970) 900,000.

Nancheng. See Hanchung.

Nancy, c., Meurthe-et-Moselle dep., France; industl. and admin. ctr.; univ., cath.; chemical ind. (based on local salt); anc. cap. of duchy of Lorraine; p. (1968) 123,428 (c.), 257,829 (met. a.).

Nanda Devi, mtn., Uttar Pradesh, India; in Himalayas, 7,822 m; first scaled, 1936.

Nanded, t., Maharashtra, India; on R. Godovari; tr. ctr.; p. (1971) 126,538.

Nanga Parbat, mtn., N.W. Kashmir, India, in W. Himalayas; alt. 8,131 m.

Nanking (Nanjing), c., Kiangsu, China; on Yangtze; cap. of China during Kuomintang régime 1928–49; famous seat of learning; tombs of founders of Ming dynasty; lge. motor vehicle plant, precision instruments, insecticides, cotton cloth, oil-refining; road-rail bridge over lowest reaches of Yangtze opened 1969; p. (est. 1970) 2,000,000.

Nanling, mtns., S. China; form divide between Rs. flowing N. to Yangtze R. and S. to Si R.; crossed by historic Cheling and Meiling Passes; alt. mainly below 1,800 m.

Nanning, c., cap. of Kwangsi prov. China; on Yu R.; ch. mkt. on S. frontier; rice transplanter factor; p. (est. 1970) 375,000.

Nan Shan, mtns., central China; branch range of Kunlun; rise to over 3,600 m.

Nanterre, N.W. sub. of Paris, France; cap. of Hauts-de-Seine dep.; aluminium mftg.; p. (1968) 90,632.

Nantes, spt., cap. of Loire-Atlantique dep., W. France; on R. Loire; ocean pt. St. Nazaire; impt. industl. and shipping ctr.; univ., cath., cas.; p. (1968) 259,208 (c.), 393,731 (met. a.).

Nantucket, I., Mass., USA; official W. end of trans-Atlantic sea-crossing; summer resort; fishing; p. (1970) 3,774.

Nantung (Nantong), c., Kiangsu, China; on N. bank of Yangtze R. estuary; cotton; p. (est. 1970) 300,000.

Nantwich, mkt. t., Crewe and N., Cheshire, Eng.; on R. Weaver, 5 km S.W. of Crewe; brine baths; clothing, food prods.; p. (1971) 11,666.

Nantyglo and Blaina, t., Blaenau Gwent, Gwent, Wales; in narrow valley 3 km N. of Abertillery; footwear, rubber prods.; p. (1971) 10,609.

Napier, c., N.I., N.Z.; pt. and ch. c. of Hawke's Bay prov. dist.; exp. frozen meat; timber processing, fishing; p. (1971) 40,181.

Napo, R., rises in Ecuador, flows S.E. into Peru where it joins the Amazon; 880 km long.

Naples (Napoli), c., Campania, S. Italy; spt. on Bay of N., at foot of Vesuvius, opposite anc. Pompeii; exp. food prods.; impt. industl. ctr.; shipbldg., oil refining, food-processing; cultural and artistic ctr.; univ., cath.; tourism; p. (1969) 1,276,824.

Nara, c., S. Honshu, Japan; anc. religious ctr. and place of pilgrimage; colossal image of Buddha (16·3 m high); cap. of Japan 710–84; tourism; p. (est. 1971) 214,000.

Nara Basin, Honshu, Japan; agr. dist. serving the Kinki plain; intensive rice and vegetable cultivation.

Narayanganj, c., Bangladesh; S. of Dacca in middle Ganges delta; p. (est. 1972) 425,000.

Narbeth, mkt t., South Pembrokeshire, Dyfed, Wales; nr. head of Milford Haven; p. (1971) 936.

Narbonne, t., Aude dep., S. France; in Languedoc; nr. Mediterranean cst.; in wine-growing a.; impt. in Roman times; cath., palace (now town hall); p. (1968) 40,035.

Narew, R., Poland and USSR; flows to R. Vistula nr. Warsaw, c. 432 km long; ch. trib. W. Bug.

Narmada, R., central India; flows W. through Madhya Pradesh and Gujarat to G. of Cambay; 1,280 km long.

Narrabri, t., N.S.W., Australia; 480 km N. of Sydney; observatory with stellar interferometer (1964); p. (1966) 5,953.

Narrandera, t., N.S.W., Australia; on R. Murrumbidgee; collecting ctr. for wool, mutton, wheat, fruits produced in irrigated a.; p. (1966) 4,897.

Narrogin, t., W. Australia; major ctr. of wheat belt; p. (1966) 4,864.

Narva, t., N.E. Estonia, USSR; textiles, machin., sawmills; hydroelectric power; founded by Danes 1223; p. (est. 1967) 49,000.

Narvik, pt., N.W. Norway; sheltered by Lofoten Is.; ice-free; linked by rly. to iron-ore fields in N. Sweden; scene of fierce sea-battles between British and Germans 1940; p. (1969) 13,422.

Naseby, v., Northants., Eng.; battle where parliamentarians under Fairfax and Cromwell beat royalists under Charles I and Prince Rupert 1645.

Nashville, c., st. cap. Tenn., USA; pt. on Cumberland R.; rly. ctr.; impt. shipping, industl. and educational ctr.; food and tobacco prods., cellophane, rayon; univs. and colleges; p. (1970) 444,489 (c.), 535,932 (met. a.).

Nasik, t., Maharashtra, India; on R. Godavari; Hindu pilgrimage ctr.; metal work; p. (1971) 176,091 (t.), 271,681 (met. a.).

Nassau, spt., cap. Bahamas, W.I.; exp. forest, sea and agr. prods.; resort; p. (1970) 3,233 (t.), 101,503 (met. a.).

Nassau, I., Cook Is., S. Pac. Oc.; N.Z. terr.; uninhabited.

Nasser City, t., Egypt; rural development at Kom Ombo, N. of Aswan, for resettlement of 50,000 Nubians before formation of Lake Nasser behind the High Dam.

Natal, spt., cap. of Rio Grande do Norte st., Brazil; above mouth of Potengi R.; exp. sugar, cotton, salt, carnauba wax, hides; new textile mills; airport on main routes from Africa to S. America; p. (1970) 250,787.

Natal, prov., S. Africa; subtropical coastal climate; sugar-cane, tea, cereals; coal; oil at Dannhauser; cap. Pietermaritzburg; a. 91,385 km²; p. (1970) 2,138,907.

Natanya or Nathania, t., Israel; resort on Mediterranean cst.; food-processing; p. (1968) 57,900.

Natuna Is., Indonesia; I. gr. in S. China Sea, N.W. of Borneo; little developed; a. 2,113 km²; p. 27,000.

Naucratis, anc. c., Egypt; between Cairo and Alexandria; excavated by Flinders Petrie and Gardiner.

Naumburg, t., Halle, E. Germany; on R. Saale; cath.; textiles, leather, toys, chemicals; p. (est. 1967) 38,300.

Nauplia (Gr. Nauplion), pt. and comm. ctr., on E. cst. Peloponnesus, Greece; the anc. Argos; first cap. of indep. Greece 1830–4, when it was superseded by Athens.

Nauru, I., indep. rep. (1968), central Pac. Oc.; formerly admin. by Australia; coral I., heavily dependent on phosphate-mng.; deposits nearly exhausted and plans to ship out new soil by UN; a. 21 km²; p. (1970) 6,664.

Navan (An Uamh), U.D., Meath R.o.I.; carpets; lead and zinc ores; p. (1971) 4,607.

Navarre, prov., N. Spain; bounded by Pyrenees; thickly wooded; cap. Pamplona; sugar-beet, cereals, cattle, hardwoods, vineyards; former kingdom; p. Basque; p. (1970) 832,313.

Naver, R., Sutherland, Scot.; flows N. to Pentland Firth; valley once densely p., cleared early 19th cent. to make room for sheep.

Naxos, I., Greece; in Aegean Sea, lgst of the Cyclades; famous for wine and fruit; a. 425 km^2; p. 19,000.

Nazareth, t., Israel; 34 km S.E. Acre; home of Jesus Christ; p. (est. 1970) 34,000.

Naze, The, C., S. point of Norway.

Nazilli, t., S.W. Turkey; on R. Menderes; agr., especially olives; p. (1965) 41,121.

Ndjamene (Fort Lamy), c., cap. of Chad Rep.; at confluence of Shari and Logone Rs.; isolated but ctr. of caravan tr.; airpt.; p. (est. 1972) 179,000. (met. a.).

Ndola, t., Zambia; nr. bdy. with Zaïre, 176 km by rail N. of Kabwe; ctr. of rich copper-mng. a., less impt. lead- and zinc-mng.; minerals despatched by rail E. to Beira and W. to Lobito Bay; oil refining nearby; international airpt. being built; p. (est. 1972) 201,300 (met. a.).

Neagh, Lough, L., N. Ireland; lgst. freshwater L. in Brit. Is.; a. 396 km^2; drained by R. Bann.

Neath, t., l. gov. dist., West Glamorgan, Wales; 10 km up R. Neath from Swansea Bay; coal, aluminium inds., oil refining; cas., abbey; p. (est. 1976) 64,900 (dist.).

Nebraska, st., USA; mainly prairie; cap. Lincoln; farming, meat-packing, wheat, maize, hay, potatoes, sugar-beet, apples, wool, livestock, petroleum, cement; a. 200,147 km^2; p. (1970) 1,468,101.

Neckar, R., W. Germany; rises between Swabian Jura and Black Forest; flows through Baden-Württemberg to Rhine at Mannheim; 384 km long.

Needles, chalk stacks in English Channel, off W. cst. of I. of Wight, Eng.

Neftyne Kamni, t., USSR; built on piles over Caspian Sea for Russian oil workers.

Negev, desert, region, S. Israel; new a. of irrigated agr.; oil and natural gas; p. (1962) c. 33,000.

Negombo, t., S.W. Sri Lanka; at mouth of Negombo lagoon; ctr. of coconut belt; metalware, ceramics; p. (est. 1968) 53,000.

Negril Beach, Jamaica; 40 km W. of Montego Bay; new resort to further Jamaica's tourist tr.

Negri Sembilan, st., W. Malaysia; on Strait of Malacca; tin and rubber; cap. Seremban; a. 6,682 km^2; p. (1970) 479,312.

Negro Rio, R., Argentina; flows into G. of St. Mathias, Atl. Oc.; used for irrigation, partly navigable.

Negro Rio, R., Brazil; one of ch. tribs. of R. Amazon; rises in Colombia, joins Amazon nr. Manaus; c. 1,520 km long.

Negro, Rio., Uruguay; flows from Brazil border to Uruguay R.; major multi-purpose project at Rincon del Bonete; 800 km long.

Negros, I., Philippines; S. of Mindanao; impt. sugar producing I.; copper deposits; a. 12,704 km^2; p. (1970) 2,307,493.

Neheim-Hüsten, t., N. Rhine-Westphalia, W. Germany; at confluence of Rs. Möhne and Ruhr; lamps, metals, chemicals; p. (est. 1969) 36,787.

Neikiang (Neijiang), c., Szechwan prov., China; on To R.; agr. ctr.; p. (est. 1970) 240,000.

Neisse or Nisa, two tribs. of R. Oder, (1) Western or Glatzer Neisse, frontier between Poland and E. Germany, 224 km long; (2) Eastern or Lausitzer Neisse, E. Silesia, Poland, 192 km long.

Neiva, t., Colombia; at head of navigation of R. Magdalena; tr. in cattle and coffee; panama hats; p. (est. 1972) 117,900 (t.), 124,700 (met. a.).

Nejd, dist., central Arabia; with Hejaz, forms kingdom of Saudi Arabia; mainly desert; impt. oil wells, horses, camels, dates, various fruits; cap. Riyadh; a. 1,087,800 km^2; p. (est.) 4,000,000.

Nellore, t., Andhra Pradesh, India; admin. ctr.; p. (1971) 133,590.

Nelson, R., Canada; drains L. Winnipeg to Hudson Bay; length (with its gr. trib. the Saskatchewan) 2,320 km.

Nelson, t., Pendle, Lancs., Eng.; on N. flank of Rossendale 5 km N.E. of Burnley; cotton, iron and brick wks., lt. engin., paper; p. (1971) 31,225.

Nelson, t., S.I., N.Z.; pt. nr. head of Tasman Bay; fishing, fruit-packing, timber; coalfield; cath.; p. (1971) 29,270.

Neman (Pol. Niemen, Ger. Memel), R., Lithua-

nian SSR and Belorussiyan SSR, USSR; rises S.W. of Minsk and flows c. 920 km into Kurisches Haff (Courland Lagoon), Baltic Sea, forming sm. delta.

Nene, R., Northants., Eng.; rises nr. Naseby and flows 144 km to the Wash.

Nepal, indep. kingdom, S.E. Asia; on S. slopes of Himalayas and inc. Mt. Everest; isolated from India by malarial forested zone of Terai; N. mostly tropical forest and jungle; home of Gurkhas; poor transport; only 1,600 km of road; agr. in fertile valleys, rice, wheat, maize; cap. Katmandu; a. 141,414 km^2; p. (est. 1969) 10,845,000..

Nerbudda. See Narmada.

Ness, Loch. L., Inverness, Scot.; occupies N.E. end of Glenmore; forms link in Caledonian Canal; very deep; 36·4 km long.

Neston, t., Cheshire, Eng.; on N. side of Dee estuary; residtl.; p. (1971) 16,848.

Nestos, R. See Mesta.

Netherlands, kingdom, N.W. Europe; bounded by N. Sea, Belgium and W. Germany; comprises 11 provs.; since second world war has taken advantage of location at mouth of Rhine, opposite Thames estuary, to develop lge.-scale coastal inds., inc. iron and steel at IJmuiden, oil refining, petrochemicals at major European pt. complex of Rotterdam–Europort; similarly major industl. growth in conurbation of Randstad Holland in steering economy far away from formerly predominant agr. basis; agr. still impt. and major sea-flood control schemes around IJsselmeer and Rhine estuary are creating valuable land for intensive agr. in a densely populated cty.; recent discoveries of natural gas in Groningen have also turned cty. into major supplier of energy for European mkts.; practises advanced policy of social welfare; cap. Amsterdam; seat of govt. at The Hague; a. 36,175 km^2; p. (est. 1970) 12,957,621.

Netherlands Antilles (Curaçao), 2 gr. of Is. in Caribbean Sea, part of Lesser Antilles; main gr. off Venezuela inc. Curaçao, Bonaire and Aruba; 2nd gr. inc. volcanic Is. of St. Eustatius, Saba, and St. Maarten (S. part only); agr. of sm. importance as a result of low rainfall; benefits from Venezuelan oil ind.; oil refineries in Curaçao and Aruba; petrochemical inds.; indep. planned for 1980; cap. Willemstad; a. 1,020 km^2; p. (1969) 216,355.

Netze. See Notec.

Neubrandenburg, c., cap. of N. admin. dist., E. Germany; fibreglass, machin., chemicals; p. (est. 1970) 45,685.

Neuchâtel, can., Switzerland; in Jura mtns.; forested with some pastures; cattle, cheese, wine; watches, cutlery, cottons, hosiery; asphalt from Val de Travers; a. 800 km^2; p. (1969) 167,000.

Neuchâtel cap. of Neuchâtel can., Switzerland; on N. slope of Lake Neuchâtel; cas.; univ.; watches, jewellery, condensed milk; p. (1969) 36,800.

Neuchâtel, L., Switzerland; at S.E. foot of Jura mtns.; drains N.E. to R. Aare; vineyards on S. facing slopes; remains of lake dwellings, anc. Celtic site of La Tène culture.

Neuilly-sur-Seine, sub., W. of Paris, Hauts-de-Seine, France; fine bridge and cas.; engin.; p. (1968) 71,215.

Neumünster, t., Schleswig-Holstein, W. Germany; rly. ctr.; leather, paper and textile inds.; p. (est. 1969) 73,175.

Neunkirchen, t., Saarland, W. Germany; iron and steel mnfs.; coal mng.; p. (est. 1969) 44,633.

Neuquen, t., cap. of N. prov., Argentina; at confluence of Rs. Limay and Neuquén, in ctr. of fruit-farming dist.; p. (1960) 17,500.

Neusalz. See Nowa Sól.

Neusandetz. See Nowy Sacz.

Neuss, c., N. Rhine-Westphalia, W. Germany; rly. junc., canal pt.; nr. Rhine, opposite Düsseldorf; metal gds., food-processing; p. (est. 1969) 116,500.

Neustadt, t., Rhineland-Palatinate, W. Germany; on R. Haardt; agr. machinery; impt. wine tr.; p. (est. 1969) 50,882.

Neustadt. See Wiener-Neustadt.

Neutitschein. See Nový Jičín.

Neva, R., RSFSR, on which Leningrad stands;

drains L. Ladoga to G. of Finland; navigable but liable to flooding; 74 km long.

Nevada, st., USA; in Rocky mtns., continental climate; mng. basis of economy gold, silver, copper, tungsten, gypsum, iron, lead; livestock agr., timber; tourism; ts. inc. Las Vegas and cap. Carson City; a. 286,299 km²; p. (1970) 481,893, grew rapidly during 1960s.

Nevers, c., cap. of Nièvre dep., France; on R. Loire; anc. iron and steel ind.; porcelain and faience; cath., historic bldgs.; p. (1968) 45,068.

Neves, t., Rio de Janeiro st., S.E. Brazil; sugar, coffee; p. (1960) 85,741.

Nevis, I., Leeward Is., W.I.; cotton, sugar; ch. t. Charlestown; desire for indep. from St. Kitts; a. 130 km²; p. (1966) 15,072.

New Albany, c., Ind., USA; on R. Ohio; domestic glassware, furniture, leather, iron and steel, car bodies; p. (est. 1969) 38,000.

New Amsterdam, spt., Guyana; on Berbice R.; processes agr. prods. from surrounding lowland; p. (1970) 18,199.

New Amsterdam, Dutch settlement, Manhattan I., USA; taken by English 1664, and renamed New York.

Newark, mkt. t., l. gov. dist., Notts., Eng.; on R. Trent 27 km N.E. of Nottingham; ball bearings, brewing and malting; cas.; p. (est. 1976) 102,800 (dist.).

Newark, c., N.J., USA; meat-packing, printing, elec. gds., paints, chemicals, cars, aircraft, leather; route ctr.; p. (1970) 378,222 (c.), 1,847,542 (met. a.).

New Bedford, c., spt., Mass., USA; on estuary of R. Acushnet; whale-fishery ctr.; mnfs. cottons, cordage, glass, shoes; resort; p. (1970) 101,262 (c.), 151,934 (met. a.).

Newbiggin-by-the-Sea, t., Wansbeck, Northumberland, Eng.; sm. seaside resort; coal mng.; p. (1971) 10,661.

New Brighton, t., Merseyside, Eng.; at entrance to Mersey estuary; residtl. dist. of Wallasey resort.

New Brighton, t., S.I., seaside resort, nr. Christchurch, N.Z.; p. (1961) 10,219.

New Britain, lgst. I., Bismarck Archipelago, Papua New Guinea; volcanic mtns.; exp. copra, cacao; a. (with adjacent Is.) 37,814 km²; p. (1966) 154,091.

New Britain, t., Conn., USA; iron and brass mnfs.; p. (1970) 82,685 (c.), 143,965 (met. a.).

New Brunswick, maritime prov., Canada; forest-clad mtns.; impt. timber inds.; fishing and fish-processing; many minerals; road and rail link with Prince Edward I.; cap. Fredericton; a. 72,481 km²; p. (1976) 677,250.

New Brunswick, t., N.J., USA; on Raritan R.; chemicals, motor lorries, leather, hosiery and hardware; univ.; p. (est. 1969) 41,000.

Newburgh, burgh, North East Fife, Scot.; on S. side of F. of Tay, 13 km E. of Perth; fish. pt.; linoleum; p. (1971) 2,062.

Newburn, t., Tyne and Wear, Eng.; on R. Tyne, 5 km W. of Newcastle; pure graphite for nuclear reactors; p. (1971) 39,379.

Newbury, t., l. gov. dist., Berks., Eng.; on R. Kennet, 27 km S.W. of Reading; engin., furniture, paper, cardboard boxmaking; mkt.; racecourse; p. (est. 1976) 115,300 (dist.).

New Caledonia, overseas terr. of France; volcanic I. in S. Pac. Oc.; nickel and chrome deposits; nickel processing; cap. Nouméa; a. 22,139 km²; p. (1970) 100,579.

Newcastle, c., N.S.W., Australia; spt. at mouth of R. Hunter, exp. agr. prod.; second c. of st.; leading industl. ctr., iron and steel, engin., shipbldg., chemicals; p. (1972) 145,718 (c.), 351,010 (met. a.).

Newcastle, spt., on Dundrum Bay; Down, N. Ireland; resort; p. (1966) 4,336.

New Castle, t., Penns., USA; tinplate, glass, steel wire, iron, coal, limestone; p. (1970) 38,559.

Newcastle Emlyn, t., Dyfed, Wales; on R. Teifi; p. (1971) 654.

Newcastle-under-Lyme, t., l. gov. dist., Staffs., Eng.; 3 km W. of Stoke-on-Trent, on Lyme Brook; coal mng.; brick and tile mnfs.; p. (est. 1976) 120,700 (dist.).

Newcastle upon Tyne, c., met. dist., Tyne and Wear, Eng.; spt. on N. bank of Tyne R., 16 km from N. Sea; shipbldg., heavy engin., iron and steel, chemicals; connected by bridges across

Tyne to Gateshead; univ., cath., many fine public bldgs., partially preserved in redevelopment of c. ctr.; airport; p. (est. 1976) 295,800 (dist.).

New Delhi. See Delhi.

New England, N.S.W., Australia; dist. of N. Tablelands; pastoral cty. for sheep and beef; ch. ts. Armidale, Glen Innes, and Tenterfield.

New England, the six N.E. Atl. sts. of USA; Me., N.H., Vt., Mass., R.I., Conn.; humid-continental climate, infertile soils, poor agr. conditions; fishing; recent industl. metamorphosis as traditional inds. are replaced by modern science-based, high-value inds.; tourism; ch. t. Boston.

Newent, mkt. t. Gloucs., Eng.; 13 km S. of Ledbury; p. (1971) 9,376 (dist.).

New Forest, forest and heathland, Hants., Eng.; relic of Royal Forest; now partly owned by Forestry Commission; pasture, ponies, tourism; residtl.; ch. t. Lyndhurst; rapid growth of p. since 1951; now forms l. gov. dist.; p. (est. 1976) 139,200.

Newfoundland, I., with Labrador, prov., of Canada; E. of the G. of St. Lawrence; in E. low; in W. rugged mtns., many Ls.; coniferous forest; fishing, cod, salmon, halibut, lobster, seal; lumber, wood-pulp, paper; iron ore, lead, zinc, copper, asbestos; hydroelec. power; climate is severe; cap. St. John's; a. prov. 404,519 km² (I. 112,300 km², Labrador 292,219 km²); p. (1976) 557,725.

New Galloway, burgh, Stewartry, Scot.; on R. Dee.; nearby Clatteringshaws hydroelec. sta.; p. (1971) 338.

New Guinea, I., S.W. Pac. Oc.; N. of Australia; equatorial climate; dense forest; central mtn. chain; lge. a. of lowland in S.; divided politically between Irian Jaya in W. (Indonesia) and Papua New Guinea in E.; economically under-developed; a. 831,390 km². See Papua New Guinea, Irian Jaya.

Newham, inner bor. Greater London, Eng.; W. of R. Lea; contains Royal group of London docks; p. and industl. decentralization from a.; p. (est. 1976) 228,900.

New Hampshire, st., New England, USA; borders on Canada; forested mtns.; agr., fruit-growing; paper and forest prods.; textiles, shoes; granite; cap. Concord; ch. spt. Portsmouth; ch. mftg. ctr. Manchester; a. 24,097 km²; p. (1970) 722,753.

Newhaven, t., East Sussex, Eng.; on S. cst. at mouth of R. Ouse, 14 km E. of Brighton; passenger pt. for Dieppe; boat-bldg. and lt. inds; p. (1971) 9,977.

New Haven, c., pt., Conn., USA; on inlet of Long I. Sound; Yale Univ.; firearms, clocks, hardware, radiators, rubber gds.; p. (1970) 133,543 (c.), 348,424 (met. a.).

New Hebrides, Anglo-French condominion, S. Pac. Oc.; between New Caledonia and Fiji Is.; strong separatist moves in Santo I.; mostly subsistence agr.; few cash crops; ch. crop coconuts; no worked minerals; thickly forested; cap. Vila; a. 14,763 km²; p. (1971) 86,084.

New Holland, v., rly. terminus, ferry pt. for crossing to Hull, Humberside, Eng.

New Ireland, volcanic I., Papua-New Guinea, in Bismarck archipelago; mtnous.; ch. pt. Kavieng; exp. copra; a. (with adjacent Is.) 9,842 km²; p. (1966) 50,129.

New Jersey, st., USA; on Atl. cst. plain, adjacent to N.Y. c.; intensive agr., mkt. gardening; heavily industrialised; oil refining, glass sand, zinc, iron ore, clay, chemicals, motor vehicles; cap. Trenton; ch. cs. Newark, Jersey City; a. 20,295 km²; p. (1970) 7,091,995.

Newmarket, t., Forest Heath, Suffolk, Eng.; at foot of E. Anglian Heights; the "racing capital of England"; p. (1971) 12,934.

New Mexico, st., USA; N. of Mexico, S. of Col. st.; traversed by Rocky mtns.; dry climate; agr. dependent upon irrigation; dry farming, arable crops, livestock; uranium, potash salts, pumice, beryllium, copper, petroleum; ch. ts. Albuquerque and cap. Santa Fé; a. 315,115 km²; p. (1970) 998,257.

New Mills, industl. t., High Peak, Derbys., Eng.; at W. foot of Pennines; textile printing, bleaching and dyeing; rayon, paper, confectionery; p. (1971) 9,165.

Newmilns and Greenholm, burgh, Kilmarnock and

Loudoun, Scot.; on R. Irvine, 19 km E. of Kilmarnock; muslin and lace curtain mnf.; p. (1971) 3,406.

New Mirpir, t., Pakistan; new t. 3 km. from old Mirpur submerged by Mangla L. 1967; planned p. 40,000.

New Orleans, c., spt., La., USA; on delta of Mississippi R.; the gr. cotton mart of America, busy comm., mftg. and cultural ctr., home of jazz; sugar refining, oil refining; p. (1970) 585,787 (c.); 1,034,316 (met. a.).

New Plymouth, t., spt., N.I., N.Z.; on W. cst. at N. foot of Mt. Egmont; sm. oil deposits; ctr. of dairy-farming dist.; p. (1971) 34,165.

Newport-on-Tay, burgh, North East Fife, Scot.; on S. side of F. of Tay, opposite Dundee; p. (1971) 3,719.

Newport, Medina, cap. of I. of Wight, Eng.; on R. Medina, in gap through central chalk ridge; mkt.; brewing, joinery, bait mnfs.; prison; p. (1971) 22,286.

Newport, mkt. t., The Wrekin, Salop, Eng.; 13 km N.E. of Wellington; p. (1971) 6,919.

Newport, spt., Vietnam; on N. outskirts of Ho Chi-minh City; lge. pt. inaugurated 1967.

Newport, t., R.I., USA; on Narragansett Bay; fashionable seaside resort; precision instruments; p. (1970) 34,562.

Newport, t., l. gov. dist., Gwent, Wales; on R. Usk, 8 km from its mouth; timber terminal and deep-water berth; engin., iron and steel, aluminium, paperboard, confectionery, chemicals, plastics; p. (est. 1976) 134,100 (dist.).

Newport News, c., spt., Va., USA; on N. shore of estuary of James R. on Hampton Roads; lge harbour; shipbldg.; outlet for Virginian tobacco and Appalachian coal; p. (1970) 137,348 (c.), 289,341 (met. a.).

Newport Pagnell, mkt. t., Bucks., Eng.; on R. Ouse; mnfs. Aston Martin cars; p. (1971) 6,337.

Newquay, t., Restormel, Cornwall, Eng.; on N. Cornish cst.; seaside resort; p. (1971) 14,963.

New Quay, t., Ceredigion, Dyfed, Wales; on cst. of Cardigan Bay; fishing; resort; p. (1971) 747.

New Radnor, t., Powys, Wales; on slope of Radnor Forest, 10 km S.W. of Presteign; p. (1971) 1,478 (dist.).

New River, artificial aqueduct, Herts. to Islington, London, Eng.; part of London's water-supply system; 58 km long.

New Rochelle, t., N.Y., USA; on Long I. Sound; residtl; p. (1970) 7 ,38 .

New Romney, t., Shepway, Kent, Eng.; nr. S. cst. to E. of Dungeness; in rich agr. dist. of Romney Marsh; Cinque pt.; old harbour silted up by shingle, now a mile from sea; p. (1971) 3,414.

New Ross, mkt. t. U.D., Wexford, R.o.I.; brewing and malting; p. (1966) 4,568.

Newry, t., Newry and Mourne, N. Ireland; pt. at head of Carlingford Lough; machin., rope, brewing, granite; p. (est. 1971) 11,393.

Newry and Mourne, l. gov. dist., N. Ireland; surrounds t. of N., borders R.o.I., Irish Sea; inc. Mtns. of Mourne.

New South Wales, st., S.E. Australia; much mineral wealth in tablelands and mtns.; climate equable and well suited to both arabie and pastoral agr.; leading agr. st. in Australia; major irrigation schemes in drier E. plains of Murray, Murrumbidgee, and Lachlan Rs.; coal mng. and heavy inds. at Newcastle, Port Kembla, Wollongong; hydroelectric power from Snowy mtns. scheme; lge concentration of p. in cap. c. of Sydney; a. 801,431 km² (excluding of Cap. Terr. of Canberra); p. (1972) 4,589,556.

Newton, t., Mass., USA; on R. Charles; in met. a. of Boston; lt. inds. p. (1970) 91,2͏3.

Newtownabbey, t., l. gov. dist., N. Ireland; sub. of Belfast, textiles, lt. inds.; p. (est. 1971) 57.908

Newton Abbot, mkt. t., Teignbridge, Devon, Eng.; at head of Teign estuary; rly. junc.; pottery, lt. engin.; agr. processing; p. (1971) 19,367.

Newton Aycliffe, t., Durham, Eng.; 10 km N.W. of Darlington; new t. (1947); engin., textiles, plastics, paints; p. (1971) 20,190.

Newton-le-Willows, t., Merseyside. Eng.; engin., printing, sugar-refining; p. (1971) 22,380.

Newton-Stewart, burgh, Wigtown, Scot.; on R. Cree, 8 km N. of Wigtown; mkt.; wool, creameries and agr. inds.; p. (1971) 1,883.

Newtown and Llanllwchaiarn, mkt. t., Powys, Wales; on R. Severn 13 km S.W. of Montgomery; precision instruments, machine tools; plan for expansion as growth-pole for central Wales; p. (1971) 6,122.

Newtownards, spt., mkt., Ards, N. Ireland; 11 km E. of Belfast; textile and engin. inds.; p. (est. 1971) 15,387.

New Waterway. See Nieuwe Waterweg.

New Westminster, t., B.C., Canada; spt. on estuary of R. Fraser; exp. timber; agr. ctr., food-processing and canning; fishing; oil refining; forms part of Vancouver met a.; p. (1971) 42,083.

New York, st., N.E. USA; one of 13 original sts., borders Canada on N., faces Atl. Oc. on S.; Adirondack mtns. in N., with lowland in E. alongside L. Ontario; Hudson valley impt. routeway; humid-continental climate; second lgst st. in p. size and despite p. movement to W., remains major a. of urbanisation (megalopolis) with comm. and industl. activity; ch. ts. inc. Buffalo, Rochester, Syracuse; st. cap. Albany, metropolis New York city; dairy farming and intensive agr. serve urban mkts.; a. 128,402 km²; p. (1970) 17,979,712.

New York, c., spt., N.Y., USA; on N.Y. Bay at mouth of Hudson R.; lgst. c. in USA and one of 3 lgst. in world; comprises 5 bors., Manhattan, Bronx, Queens, Brooklyn, Richmond; originally founded by Dutch settlers as New Amsterdam on Manhattan I.; gr. comm. ctr. and cultural cap.; univ.; fine parks, bridges, skyscrapers, and deepwater harbour; varied inds., inc. clothing, food-processing, printing and publishing, shipbldg.; despite p. and industl. decentralisation concentration of socially needy in c. causing financial difficulties to c. govt.; 2 intern. airports; p. (1971) 7,895,000 (c.); (1970) 11,572,000 (met. a.).

New York State Barge Canal (Erie Canal), N.Y. st., USA; links Tonawanda on Niagara R. with Hudson R. via the Mohawk gap through Appalachian mtns.; provides through water route from N.Y. to Gr. Ls.; opened as Erie Canal 1825, improved 1918; length 542 km (with branches 840 km), depth 4 m.

New Zealand, indep. sov. st. within Brit. Commonwealth, S. Pac. Oc.; 1,920 km E. of Sydney, Australia; consists of two major Is., N.I. and S.I., separated by Cook Strait, and several smaller Is., inc. Stewart I. to S.; mtnous., glaciated, volcanic; landscapes with superb scenery; dependent upon pastoral prods., taking advantage of equable climate and excellent grass growing conditions, but mainly reliant on Brit. mkts.; economic diversification; expansion of lt. inds., inc. car assembly, pulp and paper, textiles; hydroelec. potential being developed; oil and natural gas recently discovered; advanced social services; cap. Wellington; ch. pt. Auckland; a. 268,676 km²; p. (1971) 2,860,475 (inc. 223,300 Maoris); N.I., 2,050,208, S.I., 810,267.

Neyland, t., Preseli, Dyfed, Wales; on Milford Haven; rly. terminus and sm. pt.; p. (1971) 2,633.

Ngami, L., Botswana, S.W. Africa; swamp, the remnant of a much larger L. [2,292 m.

Ngauruhoe, mtn., N.I., N.Z.; an active volcano;

Niagara, R., forms part of boundary between Canada and USA; flows from L. Erie to L. Ontario; rapids and famous falls utilised by gr. hydroelec. power sta.; 56 km long.

Niagara Falls, waterfall, Niagara R., on bdy. of USA and Canada; in two sections, American (51 m high) and Canadian (48 m high), separated by Goat I.; major tourist attraction and hydro-elec. power sta.

Niagara Falls, t., Ontario, Canada; opposite the falls; hydroelectric power sta.; timber and agr. inds.; tourism: p. (1971) 65,271.

Niagara Falls, c., N.Y., USA; extends along summit of cliff for 5 km; paper, flour, aluminium, chemicals, hydroelectric power stas.; univ.; p. (est. 1969) 90,000; inc. in Buffalo met. a.

Niamey, t., cap. of Rep. of Niger, W. Africa; one of the termini (the other is Zinder) of the trans-Sahara motor routes; agr. tr. ctr.; p. (est. 1968) 79,991.

Nicaragua, rep., Central America; lies across isthmus with Pac. Oc. to W., Caribbean Sea to E.; sparsely populated; central mtn.

range, marshy E. cst.; tropical rain forest and climate; limited a. of fertile soils but 70 per cent. p. farmers; main exps. coffee, cotton; industl. growth based on US investment, gold and silver mng.; politically unstable; cap. Managua; a. 148,006 km²; p. (1969) 1,841,759.

Nicaragua, Lake, S.W. Nicaragua; lgst. L. in Central America; 24 km from Pac. Oc., but discharges into Caribbean via San Juan R.; fisheries; 160 km N.W. to S.E., 67 km S.W. to N.E.

Nicaraguan Depression, lowland, Nicaragua; contains Ls. Maragua and Nicaragua.

Nice, c., spt., cap. of Alpes Maritimes dep., France; on Mediterranean cst., at foot of Alps; pleasant climate and surroundings; adjoins anc. t. of Cimiez; ceded to France 1860 by Sardinia; resort; fruit and flower exp., perfume mftg.; attracting science-based inds.; major airport; p. (1968) 322,442 (c.), 392,635 (met. a.).

Nicobar Is. See Andaman and Nicobar Is.

Nicosia, c., cap. of Cyprus; agr. tr. ctr.; textiles, cigarettes, leather, pottery mnfs.; remains of Venetian fortifications; mosques; new airpt.; cap. of admin. dist. of N.; tourism; p. (est. 1969) 114,000.

Nidd, R., trib. of R. Ouse, North Yorks., Eng.; 80 km long.

Nieder Sachsen. See Lower Saxony.

Niemen R. See Neman.

Nieuwe Waterweg, ship canal, S. Holland, Neth.; connects R. Lek 11 km below Rotterdam with N. Sea cst. at Hook of Holland.

Nieuwveld Range, mtns., Cape Prov., S. Africa; part of S. terminal escarpment of African tableland; overlooks Gr. Karroo to its S.; forms impenetrable barrier to routes; mainly over 1,500 m. max. alt. 1,914 m.

Nièvre, dep., central France; traversed by Morvan mtns., forests, arable agr.; cap. Nevers; a. 6,887 km²; p. (1968) 247,702.

Nigel, t., Transvaal, S. Africa; gold mng.; industl.; p. (est. 1967) 38,400.

Niger, landlocked rep., W. Africa; 90 per cent p. dependent upon agr.; livestock (cattle, sheep, goats), cotton; exp. of groundnuts main source of wealth; rainfall diminishes to N. giving way to Sahara Desert; discovery and exploitation of uranium (1967); fishing in L. Chad; game hunting; close economic ties with France; cap. Niamey; a. 1,259,560 km²; p. (est. 1970) 4,016,000.

Niger, R., W. Africa; rises nr. sea in outer mtn. zone of W. Africa as R. Tembi, sweeps round by Timbuktu to delta in G. of Guinea, on circuitous course of 4,160 km, receiving its gr. trib., the R. Benue, about 400 km from the mouth; navigable for 1,600 km; Kainji (Nigeria) hydroelec. plant and dam opened 1969.

Nigeria, fed. rep., W. Africa; within Brit. Commonwealth; federation of 19 sts.; climate, wet, tropical in S., increasingly dry to N.; main economic development in S.; exp. agr. prods., especially cocoa; recent rapid increase in oil exp. based upon coastal deposits and European demand; cap. Lagos, lgst. c. Ibadan; cap. to be built at Abuja by 1986; a. 923,773 km²; p. (est. 1975) 62,925,000.

Niigata, c., Honshu, Japan; pt. on W. cst. exp. locally produced petroleum; chemical inds.; p. (est. 1971) 390,000.

Niihama, c., N. Shikoku, Japan; on cst. of Inland Sea, 32 km S.E. of Imabari; refines copper obtained from Besshi mines 19 km to the S.; petrochemicals; p. (est. 1971) 130,000.

Nijmegen, c., E. Neth.; on R. Waal, nr. German bdr., 18 km S. of Arnhem; Hanse t. in Middle Ages; historic bldgs., univ.; p. (est. 1969) 101,878 (c.), 201,280 (met. a.).

Nijni-Novgorod. See Gorki.

Nikko, t., Honshu, Japan; famous temples and shrines; tourist resort; p. (1966) 32,031.

Nikolayev, c., cap. of N. oblast, Ukrainian SSR, USSR; major spt. at head of Dnieper–Bug estuary on Black Sea; shipbldg. ctr.; exp. minerals, grains; founded 1784 as fortress; p. (1970) 331,000.

Nikolayevsk, lge R. pt., Khabarovsk terr., RSFSR; on R. Amur; shipyards; fishing, canning, lumbering, oil refining; p. (est. 1967) 32,000.

Nikopol, c., Ukrainian SSR, USSR; on R. Dnieper; manganese mng. ctr.; steel, machin.; p. (1970) 125,000.

Nikšić, t., Montenegro, Yugoslavia; N. of Cetinje; bauxite mng., growing industl. ctr.; p. (est. 1965) 27,000.

Nile, longest R. in Africa (see White Nile (Bahr-el-Abiad) and Blue Nile (Bahr-el-Azrek)); flows through a longer stretch of basin (over 3,920 km in a direct line) than any other R., and along all its windings measures 6,632 km; on Upper Nile navigation is hindered by sudd (floating vegetation); R. rises April, overflows Sept.; formerly cultivation entirely dependent on annual floods, but now assisted by dams, at Asyût, Aswan, Sennar, for regulating flow and navigation; Aswan High Dam completed 1970, but complex problems of delta erosion and dam-lake silting. See also Egypt.

Nilgiri Hills, Tamil Nadu, S. India; tea-growing dist.; resort a.

Nîmes, c., cap. of Gard dep., S. France; in Cevennes; Roman antiquities, notably Maison Carrée; silk, cotton, carpets, wines; tourism; p. (1968) 123,292 (c.), 124,854 (met. a.).

Nineveh, celebrated anc. c., Iraq, stood on E. bank of upper R. Tigris, opposite modern Mosul.

Ningpo (Ningbo), c., spt., Chekiang, China; 160 km from Shanghai; leading fish. pt., comm. and mnf. ctr.; exp. agr. and fish prods.; p. (est. 1970) 350,000.

Ningsia Hui, aut. region, N.W. China; bounded on N. by Inner Mongolia; dry a. but modern irrigation projects allow growth of spring wheat and rice; coal reserves, salt; cap. Yinchwan; a. 66,408 km²; p. (est. 1968) 2,000,000.

Niobrara, R., USA; trib. of Missouri R.; flows from Wyoming to Nebraska; 960 km long.

Niort, c., cap. of Deux-Sèvres dep., W. France; noted for mkt. gardens and leather gds. (gloves); birthplace of Mme de Mainteneon; p. (1968) 50,079.

Nipigon, Lake, in Thunder Bay dist., Ont., Canada; 106 km long, 74 km wide; studded with Is.; discharges by Nipigon R. to L. Superior.

Nipissing, Lake, S. Ont., Canada; 855 km²; drained by French R. to Georgian Bay.

Niš, t., Yugoslavia; on R. Nishava; route ctr.; rly. engin., developing mftg.; univ.; p. (1971) 127,178.

Nišava, R., Yugoslavia; flows N.W. into R. Morava nr. Niš; valley used by trunk rly. from Belgrade to Istanbul; length over 160 km.

Nishapur, mkt. t., N.E. Iran, S.W. of Mashhad; in fertile a.; cotton, fruits; famous turquoise mines nearby; birthplace of Omar Khayyám; impt. archaeological finds dating 9th and 10th cent.; p. (1966) 33,482.

Nishinomiya, c., S. Honshu, Japan; produces famous liquor called saké; machin., chemicals; p. (est. 1971) 378,000.

Niterói, t., cap. of Rio de Janeiro st., Brazil; shipbldg.; residtl. sub. of Rio de Janeiro c. to which it is linked by bridge; p. (1970) 291,970.

Nith, R., S.W. Scot.; flows to Solway F., S. of Dumfries; followed by main rly. from Carlisle to Kilmarnock and Glasgow; 114 km long.

Niue or Savage I., Pac. Oc.; one of Cook Is., formerly part of N.Z., self government 1974; ch. pt. Alofi; copra, plaited basketware, sweet potatoes; a. 259 km²; p. (1970) 5,302.

Nivernais, former prov. of France, now forming Nièvre prov. and part of Cher.

Nizamabad, t., Andhra Pradesh, India; road and rly. ctr. N. of Hyderabad; p. (1971) 115,640.

Nizhneudinsk, t., W. Irkutsk, RSFSR; new mftg. t.; p. (est. 1967) 38,000.

Nizhni Novgorod. See Gorki.

Nizhniy Tagil, t., RSFSR; in Ural mtns.; metallurgical ctr. using ore from Mt. Visokaya; rly. cars, iron, and steel plants, chemicals; p. (1970) 378,000.

No, Lake, Bahr-el-Ghazal prov., Sudan; N.E. Africa; vast swamp a., 906 km S.W. of Khartoum; flow of water blocked by papyrus reed and floating weed (sudd).

Nobeoka, t., Kyushu, Japan; on E. cst.; p. (est. 1971) 133,000.

Nobi Plain, S. Honshu, Japan; at head of Ise Bay; composed of: (1) low, badly drained pottery mftg. a. in Japan; inc. cs. Nagoya, alluvial plain on W. under intensive rice cultivation, (2) higher, drier, terraces on E. under mulberry, vegetables, pine-woods; very dense urban and rural p.; ch. textile and pottery mftg. a. in Japan; inc. cs. Nagoya, Gifu, Yokkaichi; a. 1,865 km²; p. (1960) 5,400,000.

Nocera Inferiore, t., Italy; nr. Naples; vegetable-canning, textile mnfs.; p. (est. 1968) 49,167.

Nogales, twin ts., Sonora, Mexico and Arizona, USA; mng. and agr. ctr.; total p. (1970) 61,811.

Noginsk, t., RSFSR; nr. Moscow; textiles, metals; natural gas pipeline from Central Asia projected; p. (1970) 104,000.

Nola, c., Italy; at foot of Vesuvius, 19 km N.E. of Naples; ctr. of fertile arable agr. a. in Campania plain; anc. c., home of Giordano Bruno; p. (est. 1968) 27,009.

Nome, c., W. Alaska, USA; on Seward peninsula; gold rush (1900); now admin. and route ctr.; airport; tourism; p. (1970) 2,488.

Noord Brabant, prov., Neth.; cap. 's-Hertogenbosch; a. 4,973 km²; p. (est. 1967) 1,700,866.

Noord Holland, prov., Neth.; a. 2,722 km²; cap. Haarlem; natural gas in Schermer Polder nr. Alkmaar; p. (1967) 2,200,062.

Noordoostpolder, Overijssel, Neth.; land reclaimed from Zuider Zee, 1942; now used for intensive agr.; a. 479 km²; p. (1967) 31,016.

Nord, dep., N. France; borders on Belgium and N. Sea; flourishing agr., mng. iron and coal, textile and chemical mnfs.; cap. Lille; a. 5,773 km²; p. (1968) 2,417,899.

Nordenham, pt. on Lower Weser R., Lower Saxony, W. Germany; lead and zinc smelting; fishing; p. (est. 1969) 16,271.

Norderney, one of the E. Frisian Is., W. Germany; low-lying sand-dunes; resort and fish. pt. at Nordseebad.

Nordhorn, t., Lower Saxony, W. Germany; nr. Neth. frontier; textiles; p. (est. 1969) 42,706.

Nordkyn, Cape, northernmost pt. of European mainland, Finnmark prov., N. Norway.

Nordland, co., N. Norway; fjord cst.; p. on cst. lowlands; fishing, livestock; iron-ore, electrochemical and metallurgical inds. based on local hydroelec. power; spt. Narvik; a. 38,146 km²; p. (est. 1972) 241,142.

Norfolk, non-met. co., E. Eng.; low-lying, fens in W.; low sandy cst. suffers from erosion; intensive arable agr. on lge farms; wheat, barley, root crops; inds. based on agr. processing and provision of agr. requisites; tourism intensively developed on Norfolk Broads; cap. Norwich; a. 5,354 km²; p. (est. 1976) 662,500.

Norfolk, c., Va., USA; naval base on Hampton Roads; fine deepwater harbour; exp. coal, industl. prods.; shipbldg., car assembly, food-processing, timber inds., fertilisers; p. (1970) 268,331 (c.), 633,142 (met. a.).

Norfolk I., remote dependency of Australia; Pac. Oc.; 1,528 km N.E. of Sydney; fertile agr.; discovered by Cook 1774; penal settlement 1788-1853; tourism; a. 34 km²; p. (1970) 1,240.

Norfolk, North, l. gov. dist., Norfolk, Eng.; cstl. a. inc. Wells-next-the-Sea, Cromer, Sheringham, Walsingham and North Walsham; p. (est. 1976) 79,700.

Norfolk, South, l. gov. dist., Norfolk, Eng.; lge. a. inc. Diss and Wymondham; p. (est. 1976) 87,700.

Noriisk, t., Krasnoyarsk terr., RSFSR; in N. Siberia; northernmost t. in Russia; mng. of coal, uranium, nickel, copper; natural gas pipeline from W. Siberia; p. (1970) 136,000.

Normandy, historic prov. of France; on English Channel; now divided into deps. Manche, Calvados, Eure, Seine-Maritime and part of Orne; Rouen was cap.; Channel Is. were part of the old duchy; conquered England 1066; allied invasion of Europe 1944.

Normanton, t., West Yorks., Eng.; 5 km N.E. of Wakefield; coal mng.; rly. wks.; p. (1971) 17,656.

Norman Wells, t., N.W. Terr., Canada; at confluence of R. Mackenzie and Gr. Bear R., 112 km W. of Gr. Bear L.; ctr. of rich oil-field.

Norrbotten, prov., N. Sweden; rich iron deposits at Kiruna; ore exp. via ice-free Narvik on Norwegian cst.; many Ls. and Rs., highest peak in Sweden, Kebnekaise; cap. Pitea; a. 105,553 km²; p. (est. 1970) 256,750.

Norris Dam, Tenn., USA; across R. Clinch at confluence with R. Tennessee, N.W. of Knoxville; lgst. dam Tenn. Valley Authority (TVA); built for flood control and hydroelectric power.

Norrköping, c., S.E. Sweden; nr. inlet of Baltic Sea; industl. and shipping ctr.; ocean-going

shipping through Lindö canal; p. (1968) 93,345.

Northallerton, mkt. t., Hambleton, North Yorks., admin. ctr., Eng.; in broad gap between Cleveland hills and Pennines; in dairy farming and agr. dist.; p. (1971) 10,508.

North America, northern continent of W. hemisphere; comprises Greenland (on N. American continental shelf), Canada, USA, Mexico; high W. Cordilleras, inc. Rocky mtns., run N. to S. from Alaska to Mexico; lower range of Appalachian mtns. in E. with vast interior basin, inc. Gr. Ls., Saskatchewan, St. Lawrence, and Miss.-Mo. R. systems; gr. variation in climate and vegetation from subtropical in S. and Mediterranean in W. to Arctic in N. and continental in interior; enormous endowment of natural resources provide basis for vast economies of USA and Canada, but contemporary public concern for natural environment of continent; formerly inhabited by Indians, now mainly occupied by a white p. with lge. European minorities, and an African-based, black p.; p. (est. 1975) 237,000,000 (inc. Hawaii).

Northampton, t., l. gov. dist., Northampton, Eng.; on R. Nene; footwear, engin., leather gds.; expanded t.; p. (est. 1976) 142,000 (dist.).

Northamptonshire, non-met. co., Eng.; E. Midlands; chiefly agr.; iron mng. and mftg.; footwear, engin., leather; co. t. Northampton; a. 2,367 km²; p. (est. 1976) 505,900.

Northamptonshire, East, l. gov. dist., Northants., Eng.; stretches from Oundle to Irthlingborough, Rushden, Raunds and Higham Ferrers; p. (est. 1976) 60,000.

Northamptonshire, South, l. gov. dist., Northants., Eng.; inc. Brackley and Towcester; p. (est. 1976) 62,400.

North Atlantic Drift, drift of surface waters of Atl. Oc. N.E. from Gulf Stream towards Europe; relatively warm; supplies prevailing S.W. winds with warmth and moisture to modify climate of Brit. Is. and countries on N.W. margin of European Continent.

Northavon, l. gov. dist., Avon, Eng.; a. N. of Bristol, inc. Sodbury; p. (est. 1976) 116,400.

North Bay, t., Ont., Canada; on L. Nipissing; air base; tourism, route ctr.; p. (1971) 49,063.

North Berwick, royal burgh, E. Lothian, Scot.; on S. of F. of Forth, 32 km E. of Edinburgh; seaside resort; golf course; fishing pt.; p. (1971) 4,392.

North Beveland, I., Neth.; in Scheldt estuary; arable agr.; a. 91 km².

North Carolina, st., S.E. USA; bounded on E. by Atl. Oc.; one of 13 original sts.; sandy, indented cst., rising in W. to Appalachian mtns.; humid subtropical climate, modified by alt.; agr. impt.; maize, cotton, tobacco; mica; textiles; ch. pt. Wilmington; cap. Raleigh; a. 136,524 km²; p. (1970) 4,961,832.

North Channel, Brit. Is.; gives access from Atl. Oc. to Irish Sea between S.W. Scotland (Galloway) and N.E. Ireland (Larne); length 96 km; narrowest width 24 km.

North China Plain, China; alluvial lowland of Hwang-ho basin; notorious floods but R. now controlled; wheat and millets; very dense p.

North Crimean Canal, USSR; links R. Dnieper with Black Sea and Sea of Azov, crossing steppes of S. Ukraine and Crimea, terminating at Kerch; first section (123 km long) opened 1963; when completed will be 352 km long, 200 km of which will be navigable.

North Dakota, st., N.W. USA; rolling prairie, rising from E.-W.; drained by Missouri R., controlled by multi-purpose Garrison Reservoir; arable agr., mainly grains, but eroded "Badlands" in S.; coal mng., petroleum; a. 183,022 km²; p. (1970) 610,648.

North Down, l. gov. dist., N. Ireland; borders Belfast Lough; main ts. Bangor, Holywood.

North Downs, Surrey/Kent, Eng.; chalk escarpment running E. to W. across S.E. Eng., flanking the Weald to N.; form "white cliffs of Dover"; followed in part by Pilgrim's Way; Box Hill 233 m.

North-East China, formerly known as Manchuria, comprises three provs.—Liaoning, Kirin, Heilungkiang, Liaopeh, Nunkiang, Hsingan, Sunkiang, Hokiang, and Antung; mtnous., N.W. and E.; drained to N. by Sungari and S. by Liao Rs.; forested; soya-beans, wheat, coal, iron;

impt. a. for iron and steel; occupied by Japanese in second world war; p. (est. 1968) 66,000,000.   [Pradesh.

North-East Frontier Agency. *See* Arunachal

North East Passage, along N. cst. Europe and Asia between Atl. and Pac. *See* **Section L.**

Northern Ireland, part of **U.K.**; occupies N.E. a. of Ireland, consisting of 26 l. gov. dists.; mild, temperate climate, exploited by dairy farming using excellent grass; arable agr. inc. barley, potatoes; traditional inds. inc. linen, shipbldg., food-processing, tobacco; modern inds. encouraged by extensive government aid inc. artificial fibres, carpets, elec. and aero-engin.; heavily dependent upon Brit. mkt.; serious social disturbance since 1969, based upon long-standing religious differences between Roman Catholic and Protestant as a result of discrimination against minority; Stormont Parliament replaced by Assembly (suspended 29 May 1974 and direct rule resumed); returns 12 members to Westminster; a. 14,121 km²; p. (1971) 1,525,187. *See also* **Section C, Part I.**

Northern Territory, st., N. Australia; variable rainfall decreasing inland from N. to S.; land rises generally N. to S. and reaches over 1,800 m in Macdonnell ranges; lge. semi-nomadic Aboriginal p.; livestock agr. dependent upon rail, road access to mkts.; mng.; ch. ts. Darwin on N. cst., Alice Springs; a. 1,356,176 km²; p. (1972) 85,519.

Northfleet, t., Kent, Eng.; on S. bank of R. Thames, adjoining Gravesend; cement, paper, rubber, tyres, cables; p. (1971) 26,679.

North Foreland, E. Kent, Eng.; chalk headland.

North Island, I., N.Z.; one of the two major Is. of N.Z.; separated from S.I. by Cook Strait; volcanic mtns.; Waikato R. drains I. Taupo; cap. Wellington, spt. Auckland; oil deposits on E. and W. csts.; a. 114,688 km²; p. (1971) 2,050,208.

Northleach, t., Cotswold, Gloucs., **Eng.**; once impt. woollen tr.; p. (1971) 7,092 (dist.).

North Little Rock, t., Ark., USA; agr. processing, engin.; p. (1970) 60,040.

North Ossetian ASSR, RSFSR; on N. slope of Gr. Caucasus; cap. Ordzhonikidze; agr. in valleys; lead, silver, zinc, and oil deposits with metallurgical and food-processing inds.; a. 8,029 km²; p. (1970) 553,000.

North Platte, t., Nebraska, USA; on N. Platte R.; in irrigated region of the Gr. Plains; grain, livestock, processed meat; p. (1970) 19,447.

North Platte R., USA; rises N. Col., flows 1,088 km through Wyo., across W. Nebraska to join S. Platte at c. of North Platte; extensive power and irrigation developments.

North Rhine–Westphalia, *Land,* **W. Germany;** highly industrialized, coal mng., iron and steel, textiles; a. 34,066 km²; p. (1967) 16,842,600.

North River (Pei-kiang), Kwangtung, S. China; rises in Nanling mtns., flows S. into Si-kiang delta; 480 km long.

North Sea, arm of the Atl., E. of Gr. Brit., W. of Norway, Sweden, and N. Germany, and N. of Holland, Belgium, and France; length 960 km, width 640 km; gd. fisheries; major natural gas, coal and oil deposits.

North Sea Canal, ship canal, N. Holland, **Neth.**; connects Amsterdam to N. Sea at Ijmuiden; depth 14 m, length 26 km.

North Shields, t., Tyne and Wear, Eng.; Tyne pt.; major new fishing pt. planned; marine engines, chain cables, anchors, rope; mkt.

North Solomons, Rep. of, formed 1975 when Bougainville I. seceded from Papua New Guinea.

North Tonawanda, t., N.Y., USA; on Niagara R.; timber tr., paper mnfs.; p. (1970) 36,012.

Northumberland, non-met. co., N. Eng.; on border of Scot. along Cheviots and R. Tweed; drained by Tyne, Blyth, Coquet Rs.; pastoral agr., especially sheep; coal mng., with former impt. exp. to London and S.E. Eng.; industl. a. now inc. in Tyne and Wear met. co.; isolation and wild landscape attractive as tourist resort; a. 5,032 km²; p. (est. 1976) 287,300.

Northumberland Straits, separates Prince Edward I. from Nova Scotia and New Brunswick; 14 km combined road and rail tunnel, bridge and causeway to link provs. projected.

Northumbria, Anglo-Saxon kingdom stretching from the Humber to the Forth; conquered by the Danes 9th cent.

North Walsham, mkt. t., North Norfolk, Eng.; 22 km N. of Norwich; former wool-weaving ctr.; p. (1971) 6,357.

North-West Passage, between Atl. and Pac. along Arctic cst. of Canada; potentially of gr. importance as a W. outlet for Alaskan oil. *See* **L.**

Northwest Territories, N.W. region and terr. of Canada; N. of 60° Lat. N., between Yukon (W.) and Hudson Bay (E.); comprises 3 dists., Franklin, Mackenzie, Keewatin; varied physical geography, inc. vast areas of lowland with with some of highest peaks in E.N. America; tree-line marks physical bdy. between N. and S.; drained in W. by Mackenzie R.; major inds. gold and silver mng. around cap. Yellowknife; petroleum, fur-trapping fisheries; a. 3,379,711 km²; p. (1976) 42,609 (two-thirds Eskimos and Indians).

Northwich, t., Cheshire, **Eng.**; on R. Weaver; impt. chemical inds. based originally upon local salt deposits, now much subsidence in a. due to salt extraction; p. (1971) 18,109.

North Wolds, l. gov. dist., Humberside, Eng.; lge. a. inc. Pocklington, Driffield and Bridlington; p. (est. 1976) 69,800.

North York Moors, limestone plateau, North Yorks./Cleveland, Eng.; lies S. of estuary of R. Tees; heather moorland; some pastoral farming on lower slopes; alt. varies from 300–450 m; formerly impt. iron-ore quarrying along N. edge in Cleveland dist.; now potential for potash mng. threatening N.Y.M. Nat. Park.

North Yorkshire, non-met. co., N. Eng.; inc. much of former N. Riding; stretches from Pennines (W.) to Vale of York (centre), N. York Moors and Yorks. Wolds (E.); crossed by R. Ouse and tribs.; mainly rural, mixed agr.; major ctrs. of p. at York, cstl. resort of Scarborough and spa of Harrogate; a. 8,316 km²; p. (est. 1976) 653,000.

Norton-Radstock, t., Avon, **Eng.**; footwear, sm. coalfield; p. (1971) 15,232.

Norwalk, t., Cal., **USA**; oil refining; p. (est. 1969) 96,000.

Norwalk, t., Conn., **USA**; gd. harbour on Long I. Sound; lt. inds., clothing; formerly impt. oyster ind. diminished by industl. pollution; p. (1970) 78,577 (t.), 118,968 (met. a.).

Norway, kingdom, W. Scandinavia, N. **Europe;** long fjord cst. stretches from Arctic to N. Sea; mtnous.; cool damp climate, influenced by prevailing W. winds; excellent conditions for hydroelectric power and electro-inds.; sm. p. makes N. heavily dependent upon foreign tr., especially exp. of aluminium, wood-pulp, paper, fish; now possesses lge. deposits of petroleum in N. Sea; arable agr. limited to fjord lowlands and a. around cap. Oslo; pastoral transhumance in mtnous. interior; a. 322,600 km²; p. (1969) 3,866,468.

Norwich, c., co. t., l. gov. dist., Norfolk, **Eng.**; on R. Wensum just above confluence with R. Yare; univ.; cath., cas.; cult. and agr. ctr.; food mnfs., footwear, printing; decentralization of office employment from London; p. (est. 1976) 119,200.

Norwich, t., Conn., **USA**; sm. pt. on Thames R.; machin., textiles; p. (1970) 41,739.

Nossi-Bé, lgst. of sm. Is., off W. cst. Malagasy; sugar, perfumery oils; ch. t. Heliville, resort and ctr. of cst. tr.; a. 337 km²; p. c. 26,000.

Notec (Netze), R., Poland; trib. R. Warta; partially navigable; 224 km long.

Notodden, t., S. Norway; nr. Tinnfoss falls which provide hydroelectric power; iron smelting, nitrates; p. (est. 1970) 13,422.

Nottingham, c., co. t., l. gov. dist., Nottinghamshire, Eng.; at bridging pt. over Trent R.; lace, hosiery, tobacco, pharmaceutical and cycle inds., all based upon local capital; univ., cas., leg. mkt. square in c. ctr.; p. (est. 1976) 280,300.

Nottinghamshire, non-met. co., Midlands, **Eng.**; contains part of productive E. Midlands coalfield serving many power stas. along Trent R.; urban growth concentrated mainly on coalfield; ch. and co. t. Nottingham; engin., hosiery; wheat, barley, cattle, roses; brilliantly characterised in writings of D. H. Lawrence; a. 2,165 km²; p. (est. 1976) 977,500.

Nouadhibar, new pt., Mauritania, W. Africa; mineral exp.; international airport.

Nouakchott, t., cap. of **Mauritania,** W. Africa;

comm. ctr. on caravan route; tr. in agr. prods.; p. (est. 1972) 55,000 (met. a.).

Nouméa (Port de France), t., cap. of Fr. New Caledonia; ch. pt. of Is.; exp. nickel, chrome; p. (est. 1969) 41,853.

Nouvelle Amsterdam, I., Indian Oc.; part of Fr. Southern and Antarctic Terrs.; volcanic; ctr. of meteorological research; a. 65 km².

Nova Friburgo, t., Rio de Janeiro, Brazil; health resort; p. (1968) 93,364.

Nova Iguaçú, t., Rio de Janeiro, Brazil; steel, tyres, chemicals; p. (1970) 331,457.

Nova Lima, t., Minas Gerais st., Brazil; in Serra do Espinhaço, 16 km S. of Belo Horizonte; adjacent to impt. gold-mines of Morro Velho; p. (est. 1968) 32,336.

Nova Lisboa (Huambo), central Angola, Africa; E. of Benguela; rly. repair shops; agr. comm. ctr.; p. (est. 1969) 49,823.

Novara, c., cap. of N. prov., N. Italy; agr. and mnf. ctr., textiles, chemicals, cheese; Romanesque church; p. (1969) 99,647.

Nova Scotia, maritime prov., Canada; mainly fertile uplands and rich valleys with agr. aided by temperate maritime climate; fruit, livestock, dairying; forested uplands along cst. nr. Bay of Fundy give rise to impt. timber inds. with many pts. along indented cst.; fishing and fish-processing; local coal supplies iron and steel ind.; cap. Halifax; a. 54,556 km²; p. (1976) 828,571.

Novaya Kakhovka, c., Ukrainian SSR, USSR; built (1951) on K. Sea nr. hydroelec. power sta. on Dnieper R.; tourism.

Novaya Zemlya, archipelago, Arctic Oc., USSR; 2 main Is.; lofty and rugged, severe climate; nuclear testing a.; a. 90,650 km².

Novgorod, c., RSFSR; on Volkhov R. nr. exit from L. Ilmen; food and timber inds., engin.; in mediaeval times gr. comm. and cultural ctr., cap. of an indep. rep.; architectural monuments; damaged by Germans in second world war; p. (1970) 128,000.

Novi Sad, c., Yugoslavia; R. pt. on Danube R., formerly royal free c.; almost destroyed by Austrians 1849; tr. in fruit, wine, vegetables, corn; p. (est. 1969) 162,000.

Novokuybyshevsk, t., RSFSR; S.W. of Kuybyshev; lge. oil processing plant; p. (1970) 104,000.

Novo Kuznetsk (Stalinsk), c., RSFSR; grew up as iron and steel ctr. of Kuznetsk Basin; engin., chemicals, aluminium, ferro-alloys; p. (1970) 499,000 (c.); (1969) 514,000 (met. a.).

Novomoskovsk (Stalinogorsk), c., RSFSR; on R. Don; lignite, fertilisers, p. (1970) 134,000.

Novorossiisk, spt., RSFSR; on N.E. cst. of Black Sea; engin., textiles; lgst. cement producer in USSR; exp. industl. prods.; p. (1970) 133,000 (c.); (1969) 146,000 (met. a.).

Novoshakhtinsk, c., RSFSR; on Rostov–Kharkov highway; coal mng., chemicals; p. (1970) 102,999 (c.); (1969) 122,000 (met. a.).

Novosibirsk, c., RSFSR; on Ob R. and Trans-Siberian rly.; lgst. industl. ctr. of Siberia, nr. Kuznetz Basin; hydroelec. power; varied inds., uranium nearby; univ.; p. (1970) 1,161,000.

Novo Troitsk, t., RSFSR; in Urals, 18 km S.W. of Orsk; cement, special steels; p. (est. 1967)82,000.

Novovoronezh, USSR; on R. Don, S. of Voronezh; nuclear power sta.

Nový Jičín (Neutitschein), t., Moravia, ČSSR; farm machin., and engin.; p. (est. 1968) 19,000.

Nowa Huta, t., Poland; 10 km S.E. Kraców on Vistula R.; newly developed Lenin metallurgical combine and modern residtl. a. within c. of Kraców; p. (1969) 112,000.

Nowa Sól (Neusalz), t., Lower Silesia, Poland; pt. on R. Oder; metal-working, food and timber inds.; p. (1970) 33,300.

Nowgong, t., Assam, India; agr. and comm. ctr.; rice, tea; p. (1961) 38,600.

Nowra-Bomaderry, t., N.S.W., Australia; on E. cst. at mouth of Shoalhaven R.; collecting ctr. for coastal agr. prod.; powdered milk, paper mill; p. (1972) 12,866.

Nowy Sącz, t., Kraków prov., S. Poland; on Dunajec R.; lignite nearby; rly. engin., mftg.; ctr. of a. renowned for beauty and tourist attractions; p. (1968) 39,300.

Nubia, anc. region, N.E. Africa, extending on both sides of Nile from first cataract at Aswan

to Khartoum, Sudan; largely desert, some irrigation alongside Nile.

Nuble, prov., Chile; borders on Argentina; comprehensive attempt to develop agr.; most industl. development and agr. mkt. at cap. Chillán; a. 14,204 km²; p. (1970) 314,738.

Nueva Esparta, st., Venezuela; consists of over 70 Is.; impt. fisheries; cap. La Asunción; a. 1,150 km²; p. (est. 1970) 112,611.

Neuva San Salvador, t., El Salvador; agr. comm. ctr. in coffee-growing and livestock region; p. (est. 1970) 38,063.

Nuevo Laredo, c., N.E. Mexico; entry point for American tourists driving to Mexico; tr. ctr. in pastoral and arable agr. a.; p. (1970) 148,867.

Nuevo Léon, st., N.E. Mexico; arable agr. needs irrigation in arid climate; impt. iron and steel inds.; cap. Monterrey; a. 65,097 km²; p. (est. 1969) 1,678,000.   [p. (1966) 15,545.

Nukualofa, cap. of Polynesian kingdom of Tonga;

Nukus, c., cap. of Karakalpak ASSR, Uzbek SSR, USSR; on Amu Dar'ya R. in Khorezm oasis; clothing inds.; p. (1970) 74,000.

Nullarbor Plain, S. Australia; low, level, limestone plateau fringing Gr. Australian Bight; arid; treeless, salt-bush scrub; crossed by Trans-continental rly. between Naretha (W. Australia) and Ooldea; rly. is dead straight, dead level for 477 km.

Numazu, t., Honshu, Japan; nr. Tokyo; ctr. of industl. dist. with varied mnfs. inc. machin.; p. (est. 1971) 196,000.

Nuneaton, t., l. gov. dist., Warwicks., Eng.; on Anker R.; coal mng., textiles, lt. inds.; mkt.; birthplace of George Eliot; p. (est. 1976) 111,100 (dist.).

Nunivak, I., Alaska, USA; lge. reindeer herds.

Nunkiang, former prov., N.E. China; crossed by Nonni R., trib. of Sungari; now part of Heilungkiang prov.

Nürnberg (Nuremberg), c., Bavaria, W. Germany; historic c. of architectural beauty; industl. ctr. with elec. mnfs., machin., heavy vehicles, precision instruments, chemicals, toys, pencils and crayons; rly. junc.; inland pt. on Rhine–Danube waterway; p. (1969) 477,783.

Nusa Tenggara, Is., Indonesia; part of Lesser Sunda Is.; p. (est. 1970) 4,752,000.

Nuwara Eliya, hill t., c. (1,800 m), Sri Lanka; health resort; p. (est. 1968) 16,000.

Nyasa, L. See Malawi L.

Nyasaland. See Malawi.

Nyiregyháza, t., N.E. Hungary; ctr. of reclaimed agr. a.; mkt. for tobacco, wine, fruits; domestic ware; p. (1968) 63,000.

Nyborg, pt., Denmark; on Fyn I.; terminal of train-ferry across Gr. Belt; shipyards; textile ind.; p. (est. 1970) 11,698.

Nykøbing, spt., Falster I., Denmark; varied inds.; admin ctr. of Storsrøms prov.; p. (est. 1970) 17,364.

Nyköping, spt., Sweden; at head of inlet on Baltic cst.; comm. and industl. ctr.; p. (1968) 31,226.

Nystad. See Uusikaupunki.

O

Oadby, t., Leics., Eng.; 5 km S.E. of Leicester; footwear; with Wigston forms small l. gov. dist., S. of Leicester; p. (est. 1976) 52,400.

Oahu, I., Hawaiian Is., Pac. Oc.; sugar, pineapples; tourist tr.; cap. Honolulu; a. 1,564 km²; p. (1970) 630,528.

Oakengates, t., The Wrekin, Salop, Eng.; 24 km N.W. of Wolverhampton; iron and steel, precast concrete, engin.; now part of new t. of Telford; p. (1971) 16,684.

Oakham, t., Rutland, Leics., Eng.; mkt.; hosiery, footwear; p. (1971) 6,411.

Oakland, c., Cal., USA; on San Francisco Bay; residtl. sub.; cars, shipbldg., fruit canning, elec. machin., clothing, tanneries, chemicals; p. (1970) 367,548 (c.); (1968) 2,999,200 (met. a.).

Oak Park Village, t., Ill., USA; now included in Chicago; birthplace of Ernest Hemingway; p. (1970) 62,511.

Oak Ridge, t., Tenn., USA; Atomic Energy Commission's major research ctr.

Oamaru, bor., spt., S.I., N.Z.; wool, frozen meat; exp. agr. prods.; p. (1971) 13,090.

Oaxaca, st., Pac. cst., S. Mexico; mtnous.,

subsistence agr. in fertile valleys; comm. prod. of coffee, cotton, tobacco; stock-raising; mng. in mtns.; cap. Oaxaca; a. 94,201 km²; p. (1969) 2,170,000.

Oaxaca, c., cap. of O. st., S. Mexico; stands at c. 1,500 m; coffee; gold and silver mines; handicraft mkt.; table linen weaving, wool zarapes; tourist ctr.; p. (1970) 116,826.

Ob', R., W. Siberia, RSFSR; one of the world's lgst. Rs., flows from Altai mtns. to G. of Ob'; crossed by Turk-Sib. rly. at Barnaul and by Trans-Siberian rly. at Novosibirsk; ch. trib. Irtysh; hydroelec. power; navigable; oilfields in middle section; outlet of Ob basin Novy-Port (Gdansk); 4,160 km long.

Oban, spt., burgh, Argyll and Bute, Scot.; on F. of Lorne; resort; ctr. for local shipping; woollens, tartans; p. (1971) 6,897.

Obed, Alberta, Canada; 240 km W. of Edmonton; major natural gas a.

Obeid, El, t., Kordofan, Sudan; economically dependent upon rly. link to Khartoum; agr. tr. ctr.; p. (est. 1969) 66,270.

Oberammergau, v., Upper Bavaria, W. Germany; scene of decennial Passion Play; winter sports; p. 4,700.

Oberhausen, t., N. Rhine–Westphalia, W. Germany; industl. ctr. of Ruhr conurb.; rly. junc., canal pt.; p. (est. 1969) 249,900.

Obidos, t., R. pt., Brazil; 800 km up R. Amazon; cacao, cotton; p. (est. 1968) 25,021.

Obihiro, t., Hokkaido, Japan; mkt; sugar-beet refining, flax, dairy prods.; p. (est. 1971) 136,000.

Obuasi, t., Ghana, E. Africa; ctr. of gold mng.; p. (1970) 31,018.

Obwalden, demi-canton, Switzerland; a. 492 km²; p. (1970) 24,509.

Ocaña, t., Magdalena st., Colombia; coffee, hides; isolated by difficult transport conditions; p. (est. 1968) 43, 481.

Ocean City, t., N.J., USA; seaside resort founded by the Methodists; p. (1970) 10,575.

Ocean I. (Banaba), Gilbert Is., Pac. Oc.; high grade phosphate (guano) worked by Brit., need for compensation and restoration of land subject of legal action 1971–76; many Banabans evacuated to Rabi I. (Fiji) 1945; future still unsettled; p. (1968) 2,192.

Oceania, name given to the Is. of the Pacific; comprising Australasia, Polynesia, Melanesia, Micronesia; p. (est. 1975) 21,000,000.

Ochil Hills, volcanic hill-range, Scot.; stretching 40 km N.E. to S.W. from F. of Tay to nr. Stirling; loftiest Ben Cleugh 721 m; beautiful glens and valleys.

Odawara, t., Japan; pt. with rail connections to Tokyo, 48 km to N.E.; p. (est. 1971) 166,000.

Odda, t., S. Norway; on branch of Hardanger Fjord; p. (1961) 7,383.

Odemis, t., Asiatic Turkey; N.E. of Aydin; tobacco, cereals, silk, cotton, flax, olives, raisins, figs; minerals; p. (1965) 30,621.

Odense, spt., Denmark; admin. ctr. of Fyn prov.; varied inds.; exp. dairy prod.; birthplace of Hans Andersen; p. (est. 1969) 103,850 (c.), 138,697 (met. a.).

Odenwald, forested hills, Hesse and Baden-Württemberg, W. Germany; highest point Katzenbuckel 626 m.

Oder (Pol. Odra), R., central Europe; flows from Moravia to Baltic through Silesia and Pomerania, forming from junc. with Neisse R. frontier between Poland and E. Germany; ch. trib. Warta R.; impt. comm. waterway below Wroclaw; 896 km long.

Odessa, t., Texas, USA; impt. oil ctr., chemicals, foundry prod., livestock tr.; p. (1970) 78,380.

Odessa, spt., Ukrainian SSR, USSR; on Black Sea; cultural, industl. ctr.; cath., univ.; gr. grain exp.; engin., oil refining, chemicals; ice-bound for a few weeks in winter; p. (1970) 892,000.

Offaly, co., Leinster, R.o.I.; much marshy land (inc. Bog of Allen), barren uplands (inc. Slieve Bloom); pastoral agr., wheat; p. mainly rural; sm.-scale domestic prods. and agr.-processing inds. in ts.; co. t. Tullamore; a. 1,999 km²; p. (1966) 51,707.

Offa's Dyke, earthwork constructed by Offa, king of Mercia (757–96) as bdy. between the English and the Welsh; still forms part of border between the two countries; long-distance footpath along the Welsh marches, 269 km.

Offenbach, t., Hesse, W. Germany; on R. Main; cas., leather museum; machin., chemicals, leather gds., metals; p. (est. 1969) 117,500.

Offenburg, t., Baden–Württemberg, W. Germany; on R. Kinzig; textiles, glass, rly. junc.; cas.; p. (est. 1969) 32,408.

Ogaden, arid region, S.W. Ethiopia; on border of Rep. of Somalia.

Ogaki, t., Honshu, Japan; route ctr. in lowland embayment, 40 km N.W. of Nagoya; p. (est. 1971) 137,000.

Ogbomosho, t., S.W. Nigeria; ctr. of agr. dist.; cotton weaving; p. (est. 1971) 386,650.

Ogden, c., Utah, USA; stands at 1,324 m, nr. Gr. Salt L.; rly. ctr.; beet-sugar, meat-packing, flour-milling, clothing, cement; p. (1970) 68,480 (c.), 124,035 (met. a.).

Ogdensburg, c., pt., N.Y., USA; on St. Lawrence R., opposite Prescott; impt. R. pt.; p. (1970) 14,554.

Ogmore and Garw, t., Ogwr, Mid Glamorgan, Wales; in narrow valley, 10 km N. of Bridgend; industl.; cas.; p. (1971) 19,415.

Ogooué, R., Gabon, Congo; site of Schweitzer's hospital at Lambaréné; 800 km long.

Ogwr, l. gov. dist., Mid Glamorgan, Wales; inc. Ogmore, Maesteg and Bridgend inland and Porthcawl on cst.; p. (est. 1976) 128,400.

Ohau, Lake, S.I., N.Z.; in Mt. Cook dist.; fed by glaciers; 19 km by 35 km; hydroelectric power potential.

Ohio, R., trib. of Mississippi R., USA; formed in Penns., by junc. of Monongahela and Allegheny Rs. at Pittsburgh, thence navigable for 1,560 km to Cairo in Ky.; an impt. comm. waterway for industl. raw materials; flood protection schemes.

Ohio, st., N. USA; agr. agr. and industl. region; maize, wheat, cattle; major deposits of coal form basis of heavy inds., especially in major ts. of Cleveland, Cincinnati, Toledo, Akron, Dayton, Youngstown; petroleum; timber inds.; cap. Columbus; a. 106,508 km²; p. (1970) 10,542,000.

Ohre (Eger), R., Bohemia, ČSSR; rises in Fichtelgebirge, flows N.E. into Labe (Elbe) and through Karlovy Vary; 224 km long.

Ohrid or Ochrida, L., forms part of bdy. between Albania and Yugoslavia; alt. c. 850 m; deepest L. in Balkans; scenic tourist a.; monasteries on shores.

Ohrid or Ochrida, t., Macedonia, Yugoslavia; on N.E. shore of L.; airport and tourist ctr.; p. (est. 1965) 19,000.

Oich, Loch, L., Gr. Glen, Inverness, Scot.; forms part of Caledonian Canal.

Oise, dep., N. France; traversed by R. Oise; fertile, forested; cap. Beauvais; a. 5,884 km²; p. (1968) 540,988.

Oise, R., trib. of R. Seine, France; canalised, navigable to Chauny; 298 km long.

Oita, c., spt., N.E. Kyushu, Japan; on Beppu Bay; wire, carbon, iron, and steel; oil refinery; p. (est. 1971) 274,000. [6,884 m.]

Ojos del Salado, mtn., N.W. Argentina; alt. 3,908.

Oka, R., Kursk, RSFSR; rises S. of Orel, flows past Kaluga, Serpukhov, Kolomna, Ryazan, Murom, to become trib. of Volga at Gorki; navigable, carrying grain and timber; 1,520 km long.

Oka, R., Irkutsk, Siberia, USSR; joins Angara R. below Bratsk; 800 km long.

Okayama, c., Honshu, Japan; textiles; lt. inds.; p. (est. 1971) 472,000.

Okazaki, t., Honshu, Japan; nr. G. of Ovari; industl. ctr.; textiles, chemicals, machin.; p. (est. 1971) 213,000.

Okeechobee, Lake, S. Fla., USA; drains to Atl. Oc. via Everglades; tourist attraction especially for fishing; also comm. fisheries.

Okefenokee, swamp, Ga./Fla., USA; forms O. Nat. Wildlife Refuge.

Okehampton, mkt. t., West Devon, Eng.; on N. flank of Dartmoor; granite quarries; p. (1971) 3,908.

Okha, spt., E. cst. Sakhalin I., RSFSR; exp. petroleum; lge. refinery; p. 50,000.

Okhotsk, Sea of, N.E. Asia; 1,600 km by 800 km; enclosed by the Siberian mainland, Kamchatka, the Kurils and Sakhalin I.

Oki Is., off cst. of Honshu, Japan; a. 350 km².

Okinawa, I., Japan, under U.S. control until 1972; lgst. and most impt. of Ryuku Is.;

US air bases at Kadena and cap. Naha; a. 1,500 km²; p. (1965) 758,777.

Oklahoma, st., **USA**; prairie, plains and mtns.; continental climate; cereals, cotton, stock-raising; petroleum, gas, zinc, coal, gypsum, lead; ch. ind. petroleum refining; cap. Oklahoma City; a. 181,090 km²; p. (1970) 2,498,378.

Oklahoma City, c., cap. of Okla. st., **USA**; univ.; livestock mkt.; tr. and processing ctr.; oil and by-prods., field machin., flour mills, meat-packing; p. (1970) 362,981 (c.), 623,592 (met. a.).

Okovango, R.; rises in Angola, flows to Ngami depression, Botswana, where it forms swampy delta; 1,600 km long.

Oktyabrsky, t., Bashkir ASSR, **USSR**; on R. Ik; in new oil-mng. dist., the "New Baku"; p. (est. 1967) 79,000.

Öland, I., Baltic Sea; off E. cst. Sweden; connected by Europe's longest bridge to mainland; agr., limestone quarries; ch. t. Borgholm; seaside resorts; a. 1,380 km²; p. (est. 1969) 26,750.

Oldbury, t., West Midlands, Eng.; N.W. of Birmingham; chemicals, bricks, glass.

Oldbury-on-Severn, Avon, Eng.; nuclear power sta.

Old Castile, historical div., Spain; now divided into Santander, Soria, Segovia, Logrono, Avila, Valladolid, Palencia, and Burgos provs.

Oldenburg, c., Lower Saxony, W. Germany; on R. Hunte nr. Hunte–Ems canal; rly. junc.; mkt. for horses and cattle; lt. inds.; natural gas nr. to cst.; p. (est. 1969) 131,200.

Old Fletton, Cambs., Eng.; on R. Nene opposite Peterborough; bricks, gen. and elec. engin.; beet sugar, fruit and vegetable canning; p. (1971) 13,660.

Oldham, c., met. dist., Gtr. Manchester, Eng.; on R. Medlock, 6 km N.E. of Manchester; man-made fibre and cotton textiles, machin.; recent industl. diversification inc. electro- and aero-engin., leather, paints; p. (est. 1976) 227,500.

Oldmeldrum, burgh, Gordon, Scot.; 6 km N.E. of Inverurie; p. (1971) 1,085.

Olenek, R., **RSFSR**; N. Siberia; flows W. of Lena R. into Laptev Sea, Arctic Oc.; abounds in fish; 2,160 km long, 960 km navigable

Oléron, Ile d', I., Charente-Maritime dep., France; lies off estuary of Charente, Bay of Biscay; oysters, early vegetables; a. 176 km².

Olifant, R., Transvaal, S. Africa; trib. of Limpopo; irrigation scheme for intensive agr. in valley.

Olinda, c., Pernambuco st., Brazil; seaside resort; phosphates; p. (1970) 187,553.

Oliva, t., Valencia, Spain; nr. Alicante; wine dist., ducal palace; p. (1970) 16,772.

Olivos, sub., Buenos Aires, Argentina.

Olmütz. *See* Olomouc.

Olney, t., Bucks., Eng.; mkt., dairy produce; annual Shrove Tuesday pancake race.

Oloibiri, S. Nigeria; oilfields; pipeline to Pt. Harcourt, 128 km W.

Olomouc (Olmütz), ČSSR; industl. ctr., steel wks., elec. equipment, textiles, food prod.; cath.; univ.; formerly one of ch. fortresses of Austria; p. (1967) 78,000.

Oloron-Sainte-Marie, t., Pyrénées-Atlantique, France; in Pyrenean foothills; caths.; p. (1968) 13,028.

Olsztyn (Allenstein), t., N.W. Poland; cap. of Olsztyn prov.; on R. Alle, 160 km N. of Warsaw; cas.; machin., wood inds.; p. (1970) 94,100.

Olten, t., N. Switzerland; rly. junc.; on R. Aare; p. (1970) 21,209.

Olympia, anc. c., Peloponnesus, S. Greece; at confluence of Alphaeus and Cladeus Rs.; site of gr. temple of Zeus and scene of Olympic games; modern v. of O. nearby; museum.

Olympia, cap. of Washington st., USA; spt. on Puget Sound; exp. timber; machin., agr.-processing inds.; p. (1970) 18,273.

Olympus, Mt., highest mtn. in Greece; on border of Thessaly and Macedonia, nr. Aegean cst.; alt. 2,975 m; regarded by anc. Greeks as home of the Olympian gods.

Omagh, t., l. gov. dist., N. Ireland; on R.; Strule agr. mkt.; tourist ctr.; p. (est. 1971) 11,953.

Omaha, c., Nebraska, USA; on Missouri R.; one of lgst. livestock and meat-packing ctrs. in US, gold and silver smelting and refining, steel fabrication, industl. alcohol prod.; univ.; p. (1970) 327,789 (c.), 538,718 (met. a.).

Oman (Muscat and Oman until 1970) sultanate, S.W. Asia; fertile coastal plain, interior desert plateau; irrigated agr., especially impt. for dates; recent oil discoveries (1964); oil now main exp.; a. 212,380 km²; p. (est. 1970) 750,000.

Oman, G. of, Arabian Sea; connected through strait of Ormuz to Persian G.; length 480 km, width 208 km.

Omaruru, t., S.W. Africa; creamery; aerodrome; p. (1960) 2,689.

Omdurman, c., central Sudan, on Nile, opposite Khartoum; site of Mahdi's tomb; here Kitchener defeated the dervishes 1898; native mkts.; p. (est. 1971) 258,532.

Ometepe, I., L. Nicaragua, Nicaragua; volcanic; alt. 1,753 m.

Omsk, c., W. Siberia, RSFSR; at confluence of Irtysh and Om Rs.; major R. pt. on Trans-Siberian rly.; in agr. region; engin., chemicals, textiles, oil refining, food processing; cath.; founded as fortress 1716; p. (1970) 821,000 (c.); (1969) 832,000.

Omuta, t., Kyushu, Japan; on Amakusa Sea; local coal at Miike giving rise to chemical inds.; pt. exp. coal; p. (est. 1971) 197,062.

Onega, Lake, RSFSR; between L. Ladoga and White Sea; second lgst. L. in Europe (L. Ladoga is lgst.); a. 9,751 km²; ch. c. Petrozavodsk; Onega canal forms part of Volga-Baltic waterway.

Onega, R., RSFSR; flows to G. of Onega; 640 kฅ long.

Onehunga, spt., bor., N.I., N.Z.; nr. Auckland; p. (1971) 15,597.

One Tree Hill, bor., Auckland, N.Z.; p. (1971) 12,963.

Onitsha, t., Nigeria; on R. Niger; agr. tr. ctr.; p. (est. 1969) 189,067.

Onstwedde, t., Groningen, Neth.; mnfs.; p. (1967) 27,666.

Ontario, prov., Canada; bounded on N. by Hudson Bay, on S. by Gr. Ls.; extreme continental climate in N., milder in S. peninsula; extensive coniferous forest in N.; temperate agr. in S.; leading mineral producer, nickel, uranium, copper, gold; well-developed inds. using plentiful hydroelectric power; agr.-processing, machin., engin.; cap. Toronto; contains fed. cap. of Ottawa; a. 1,068,587 km²; p. (1976) 8,264,465, concentrated in S.E.

Ontario, L., N. America; smallest of the Gr. Ls. of the St. Lawrence basin, separating the Canadian prov. of Ont. from N.Y., USA; navigable, carries industl. raw materials; polluted waters; a. 19,425 km²; depth 226 m.

Ontario, t., Cal., USA; aircraft components; fruit comm. ctr.; p. (1970) 64,118.

Onteniente, t., Valencia, Spain; on R. Clariano; woollen gds., paper mills; p. (1970) 23,685.

Oosterhout, t., N. Brabant, Neth.; nr. Breda; footwear, tobacco; p. (1968) 29,625.

Ootacamund, t., Tamil Nadu, India; in Nilgiri hills, c. 2,100 m; summer H.Q. of st. govt.; sanatorium; p. (1961) 50,140.

Opatija (It. Abbazia), t., Yugoslavia; tourist resort, known as the Nice of the Adriatic; p. (1961) 7,974.

Opava (Troppau), t., N. Moravia, ČSSR; nr. Polish border; industl. ctr. in agr. a.; p. (1967) 46,000.

Opladen, t., N. Rhine–Westphalia, W. Germany; on R. Wupper; metals, textiles, chemicals; p. (est. 1967) 44,700.

Opland or **Oppland**, co., central Norway; mtnous. N. inc. alpine region of Jotunheimen; forestry prods.; a. 24,885 km²; p. (est. 1972) 174,174.

Opole (Oppeln), c., S. Poland; on R. Oder; R. pt., rly. junc.; cement, metals, furniture; 3 univ. schools; cap. Prussian prov. of Upper Silesia 1919–45; p. (1970) 86,500.

Oporto, c., spt., Portugal; second c. of rep., built high above Douro R.; ctr. of port wine tr.; cath., univ., historic bldgs.; sardine fisheries, cotton and wool textiles, sugar refining, distilling, oil refining; outer harbour at Leixöes; p. (est. 1969) 325,400.

Oradea (Hung. Nagy Varad), t., W. Romania, on

Crisul Repede R., nr. Hungarian border; p.; ctr.; baroque architecture; lge. Hungarian rly p. (est. 1969) 135,400.

Öraefa Jokull, hgst. mtn., **Iceland**; alt. 1,955 m.

Orange, historic t., Vaucluse, France; title founded by Charlemagne passed to William the Silent of the house of Nassau; Roman amphitheatre; tourism; p. (1968) 25,630.

Orange, R., Cape Prov., **S. Africa**; flows from Lesotho to Atl.; part forms S. bdy. between Cape Prov. and Orange Free State; Verwoerd dam (1972) for power, irrigation, flood control; 2,080 km long.

Orange Free State, prov., **Rep.** of **S. Africa**; plateau land, Drakensberg to N.E., Rs. Orange, Vaal and Caledon; sheep, cattle, horses, wheat, maize, fruit, tobacco, coal, diamonds; cap. Bloemfontein; a. 128,586 km²; p. (1970) 1,651,610.

Oranienburg, t., Potsdam, **E. Germany**; on R. Havel; industl.; chemicals, metals, machin.; p. (est. 1970) 20,442.

Ord of Caithness, hill, headland, nr. Helmsdale, **Scot.**; alt. 366 m.

Ordos, desert region, Inner Mongolia, **China**; lies S. of Yellow R.; mean alt. 1,000 m; dry cropping, especially millets; pastoral farming.

Ordu, spt., **Turkey**; on Black Sea; exp. manganese; p. (1965) 27,307.

Ordzhonikidze, c., cap. of N. Ossetian ASSR, **RSFSR**; on R. Terek at foot of Caucasus, ind. ctr., metallurgical inds.; natural gas pipeline to Tbilisi; hydroelec. power sta.; p. (1970) 236,000.

Örebro, c., cap. of Örebro prov., **Sweden**; on R. Svartå at entrance to Hjälmar L.; anc. t., cas.; footwear, biscuits; p. (1968) 87,430.

Oregon, st., N.W. **USA**; borders Pac. Oc.; ch. physical features, Coast ranges, Cascade mtn. region, Blue mtns., Columbia R. and tribs., Willamette valley; rainy cst., drier interior (agr. with irrigation); cereals, sugar-beet, fruit, cattle; gold, silver, copper, coal, uranium; fisheries, canning, meat-packing, timber, milling; cap. Salem; a. 250,948 km²; p. (1970) 2,056,171.

Orekhovo-Zuyevo, t., **RSFSR**; E. of Moscow, on R. Klyazma; textile inds.; p. (1970) 120,000.

Orel, c., **RSFSR**; on R. Oka; univ.; rly. junc.; engin., textile mills, food prods.; birthplace of Turgenev; p. (1970) 232,000.

Orenburg (Chkalov), c., cap. of Orenburg oblast, **RSFSR**; on Ural R.; rly. junc.; food processing, agr. machin.; oil and natural gas in region; p. (est. 1967) 326,000.

Orense, t., cap. of Orense prov., **Spain**; on R. Minho; flour, leather, iron; p. (1967) 71,768.

Ore Sound, strait, between Sjaelland, Denmark, and S. Sweden; protected by agreement of adjacent countries; freezes occasionally.

Orford Ness, coastal sandspit, Suffolk. **Eng.**; cas. keep at Orford.

Oriente, prov., **Cuba**; contains mtns. of Sierra Maestra; sugar cane grown in lowlands; manganese mng.; a. 36,592 km²; p. (est. 1970) 2,998,972.

Oriente, terr., **Peru/Ecuador**; for long in dispute between the two ctys., partially settled by treaty (1942); lies E. of Andes, between Putumayo and Marañon Rs.; mainly dense forest, reputedly rich in minerals.

Orihuela, t., Alicante, **Spain**; on R. Segura; leather, textiles, wine; univ., cath.; p. (1970) 44,938.

Orinoco, R., **Venezuela**; rises in Parima mtns., flows to Atl., connected to Rio Negro and Amazofi impt. industl. development on lower O., based on hydroelec. power and iron ore; experimental scheme to reclaim delta for agr.; 2,368 km long.

Orissa, st., **India**; agr. with few ts.; Hirakud dam across Mahanadi R.; Paradeep being developed as pt.; rice; cap. Bhuvaneshwar; a. 155,825 km²; p. (1971) 21,934,827.

Orizaba, t., Veracruz, **Mexico**; textiles, paper mills, breweries; resort; p. (est. 1970) 92,728.

Orizaba, mtn., Veracruz, **Mexico**; volcanic; called Citlatepetl in Aztec times; alt. 5,704 m.

Orkney, l. gov. reg., **Scot.**; gr. of 68 Is. in N. Sea, inc. Pomona, Sanday, Westray; 29 inhabited; antiquarian remains, stone circles; farming, fishing; North Sea oil finds; cap. Kirkwall; total a. c. 932 km²; p. (1971) 17,077.

Orlando, c., Fla., **USA**; winter resort; inds. based on citrus fruit and mkt. garden prods.; p. (1970) 97,565 (c.), 426,750 (met. a.).

Orléannais, region and former prov., France; inc. deps. of Loire-et-Cher, Loiret, and parts of Eure-et-Loire and Yonne.

Orléans, c., cap. of Loiret dep., France; on R. Loire; cath., univ.; regional tr. ctr.; wine, textiles, chemicals, farm implements; statue of Joan of Arc; p. (1968) 95,828 (c.), 167,515 (met. a.).

Orleans, I., Quebec, Canada; in St. Lawrence R., nr. Quebec; resort; a. 181 km².

Ormoc. *See* MacArthur.

Ormskirk, t., West Lancs., **Eng.**; 22 km N.E. of Liverpool; in mkt. gardening a.; lt. engin., clothing; p. (1971) 27,618.

Orne, dep., N. France; agr., dairying, stock-keeping, fruit-growing, Camembert cheese; cap. Alençon; a. 6,143 km²; p. (1968) 288,524.

Orontes, R., rises in Lebanon, flows through **Syria** past Hama into **Turkey** past Antioch to Mediterranean; unnavigable but used for irrigation; part of valley followed by rly.; irrigated areas intensively cultivated; c. 400 km long.

Oroya, t., **Peru**; impt. mng. and refining ctr.; p. (est. 1969) 31,700.

Orpington. *See* Bromley.

Orrell, t., Gtr. Manchester, **Eng.**; W. of Wigan; p. (1971) 12,069.

Orsha, c., Belorussiyan SSR, **USSR**; impt. industl. and transport ctr. on R. Dnieper; textiles, metal wks., food-processing; once a frontier fortress; p. (1970) 101,000.

Orsk, c., Bashkir ASSR, **RSFSR**; in Ural mtns. on Ural R.; inds. based on surrounding mng. a.; oil pipeline terminus; oil refining; hydro-electric power sta. nearby; p. (1970) 225,000.

Orta, L., **Italy**; W. of Lago Maggiore; a. 18 km².

Orthez, t., Pyrénées-Atlantique, **France**; scene of Wellington's victory over Soult (1814); Bayonne hams; p. (1968) 10,640.

Oruro, t., **Bolivia**; cap. of O. prov. at alt. 3,709 m; once impt. ctr. for silver mng.; now other minerals impt.; p. (1967) 91,911.

Oruwala, t., **Sri Lanka**; steel rolling mill.

Orvieto, t., Umbria, **Italy**; on R. Paglia; cath., Etruscan antiquities; wines, olive oil, cereals; pottery; p. (est. 1968) 24,246.

Osaka, c., Honshu, **Japan**; ctr. of Kinki plain; built on delta in shallow O. Bay; comm. ctr.; banking, heavy industry, metals, machin., clothing; p. (est. 1971) 2,939,000.

Osasco, t., São Paulo st., **Brazil**; industl. ctr.; p. (1970) 283,203.

Osh, t., S.W. Kirghiz SSR, **USSR**; textiles, food-processing; one of oldest ts. in central Asia; p. (1970) 120,000.

Oshawa, t., Ont., Canada; pt. on L. Ont.; motor vehicles; p. (1971) 91,113.

Oshima, I., Tokyo Bay, Japan; lgst and most N. of Izu-shichito gr.; site of volcanic Mt. Mihara (755 m).

Oshkosh, t., Wis., **USA**; on Fox R.; meat packing, flour, motors; p. (est. 1969) 52,500.

Oshogbo, t., Nigeria; comm. and educational ctr.; serves agr. dist.; cotton-ginning; p. (est. 1971) 252,583.

Osijek, t., Croatia, Yugoslavia; on Drava R.; growing industl. ctr. for textiles and leather; p. (1971) 93,912.

Osinniki, t., RSFSR; W. Siberia; new ctr. of coal mng.; thermal power sta.; p. (est. 1969) 67,000.

Osipenko. *See* Berdyansk.

Oslo (Christiania), c., cap. of Norway; at head of Oslo Fjord; ch. spt., comm., industl., and cultural ctr.; ice-free harbour; cath., univ.; exp. timber, fish, matches; wood pulp, paper; occupied by Germans 1940–5; p. (est. 1969) 487,846 (c.); (1967) 685,000. (met. a.).

Osnabrück, c., Lower Saxony, W. Germany; on R. Hase; stands on a branch of the Mittelland canal; inland pt. and industl. ctr., iron and steel mills; mach., textile and paper mnfs.; p. (est. 1969) 140,400.

Osorno, t., Chile; agr. ctr.; in beautiful forested cty.; Germanic influence; food-processing; tourism; p. (est. 1966) 69,220.

Ossett, t., West Yorks., **Eng.**; 5 km W. of Wakefield; woollens, shoddy-processing, engin.; p. (1971) 17,181.

Ostend, spt., Belgium; passenger route between Britain and continent of Europe; popular resort; casino, fisheries, shipbldg., textiles, tobacco; p. (1968) 57,765.

Östergötland, co., Sweden; on Baltic cst.; rises to uplands of Småland in S. where p. declining; lowland a. crossed by Göta canal; cap. Linköping; a. 11,050 km²; p. (est. 1970) 375,947.

Östersund, t., Jämtland, Sweden; on Storsjön L.; p. (1968) 26,620.

Östfold, co., S.E. Norway; hilly a. crossed by R. Glomma; dairy prods. for Oslo; a. 4,178 km²; p. (est. 1972) 224,041.

Ostia, anc. c., Italy; once pt. of Rome, at mouth of R. Tiber, founded 4th cent. B.C.; layout revealed by excavations; modern v. of O. nearby on plain reclaimed from salt marsh.

Ostrava, c., ČSSR; at junc. of Oder and Ostravice Rs.; industl. ctr. of Ostrava–Karvinna coalmng. region; iron and steel, machin., chemicals, oil refining; p. (est. 1968) 273,280.

Ostrow Wielkopolski, t., Poznan, Poland; agr. machin., clothing; p. (1970) 49,500.

Ostrowiec Swietokrzyski (Ostrovets), t., Kielce, Poland; on R. Kamienna; ceramic and metallurgical inds.; p. (1970) 50,000.

Oswaldtwistle, t., Hyndburn, Lancs., Eng.; at N. foot of Rossendale Fells; chemicals, textiles; p. (1971) 14,015.

Oswego, t., N.Y., USA; pt. on L. Ontario; mnfs. hosiery, matches, textiles, boiler engines, paper; p. (1970) 23,844.

Oswestry, t., l. gov. dist., Salop, Eng.; at foot of Welsh mtns., cas.; engin.; p. (est. 1976) 30,500 (dist.).

Oświecim (Ger. Auschwitz), t., Kraków, Poland; at confluence of Rs. Iola and Vistula; lge. chemical wks.; German concentration camp (1940–44); p. (1970) 39,600.

Otago, prov., S.I., N.Z.; forested mtns.; gold; farming, sheep, fruit; lge. deposit of jade found at head of L. Wakatipu; coalfields; cap. Dunedin; a. 65,320 km²; p. (1971) 182,825.

Otago Harbour, Otago dist., S.I., N.Z.; Dunedin and Port Chalmers are ports on this harbour.

Otanmäki, Finland; rich deposit of magnetite-ilmenite ore.

Otaru, spt., Hokkaido, Japan; herring fisheries; coal mng., lumbering; p. (est. 1971) 192,000.

Otley, t., West Yorks., Eng.; on R. Wharfe; printing, machin., wool, paper mkg., leather, furnishings; birthplace of Thomas Chippendale; p. (1971) 13,254.

Otranto, t., S. Italy; on Strait O.; once a flourishing c., fine mosaic pavement, cath., cas.; submarine cable sta.; bauxite exp., fishing; p. (est. 1968) 4,530.

Otsu, t., Honshu, Japan; on L. Biwa; p. (est. 1971) 176,000.

Ottawa, c., cap. of Canada, Ont., on R. Ottawa; univ., caths., parliament bldgs.; hydroelec. power, lumbering, sawmills, paper, flour, leather, matches, machin., ironware; p. (1971) 298,087 (c.), 447,736 (met. a.).

Ottawa, R., Canada; trib. of St. Lawrence, forming bdy. between Ont. and Quebec; timber transport, hydroelec. power; 1,000 km long.

Ottery St. Mary, mkt. t., East Devon, Eng.; 16 km E. of Exeter; birthplace of Coleridge; p. (1971) 5,824.

Ottumwa, t., Iowa, USA; on Des Moines R.; in coalfield and agr. dist.; iron and steel, meat-packing; p. (1970) 29,610.

Ötzal, valley, Austria; longest side valley of R. Inn; tourist dist.

Ouachita or Washita, R., Ark., USA; trib. of Red R.; 880 km long.

Ouachita National Forest, Ark., Okla., USA; part of forested O. highlands.

Ouagadougou, cap. of Upper Volta; tr. and comm. ctr.; p. (1967) 79,500.

Ouahran (Oran), spt., N. Algeria; founded by Moors 10th cent.; occupied by French 1831–1962; handles wines, wool, cereals, meat, skins; fine roadstead at Mers-el-Kebir; former French naval and military sta.; p. (1967) 324,000 (c.), (1966) 328,257 (met. a.).

Oudenaarde (Audenarde), t., Belgium, on R. Scheldt; textile ctr.; scene of Marlborough's victory over French 1708; p. (1968) 22,035.

Ouenza, c., Algeria; 75 per cent of Algerian iron-ore produced in dist.

Oujda, t., N.E. Morocco; comm. ctr.; phosphate, lead and zinc-mng. dist.; p. (1971) 155,800 (t.) 317,420 (met. a.).

Oulton Broad, L., Suffolk, Eng.; nr. Lowestoft. See Broads.

Oulu, spt., cap. of Oulu prov., N.W. Finland; on G. of Bothnia at mouth of R. Oulu; univ.; p. (1968) 83,190.

Oundle, mkt. t., East Northants., Eng.; on R. Nene; public school; p. (1971) 3,741.

Ouro Prêto, old colonial t., Brazil; former cap. of Minas Gerais st.; grew as gold mng. ctr.; since p. has declined; now other minerals; school of mines; p. (est. 1968) 38,372.

Ouse or Great Ouse, R., Eng.; rises in S. Northamptonshire and flows N.E. via the Fens to the Wash; 250 km long.

Ouse, R., East Sussex, Eng.; flows to English Channel at Newhaven; 48 km long.

Ouse, R., North Yorks./Humberside, Eng.; formed by Rs. Swale and Ure, flows to Humber estuary; 208 km long.

Ovalle, t., Coquimbo prov., Chile; ctr. of fruit and pastoral dist.; p. (est. 1966) 29,377.

Overijssel, prov., Neth.; dairying, fishing; ch. ind. textiles; a. 3,364 km²; p. (1967) 887,261.

Oviedo, coastal. prov., N. Spain; agr., fruit, sardine, and other fisheries; cap. O.; a. 10,888 km²; p. (1970) 1,045,635.

Oviedo, c., cap. of O. prov., Spain; on R. Nalón; cath., univ.; industl. and comm. ctr. for agr. and mng. dists. of Asturia; p. (1968) 144,697.

Owends, pt., Liberia; deepwater pt. built to serve iron-ore mines at Belinga.

Owen Falls, Uganda; dam inaugurated 1954; converts L. Victoria into reservoir for irrigation of Egypt and Sudan; also to supply Uganda with hydroelectric power.

Owensboro', t., Ky., USA; petroleum; ctr. for stock raising and tobacco growing a.; p. (1970) 50,329.

Owens, L., S. Cal., USA; on E. flank of Sierra Nevada, 32 km S.E. of Mt. Whitney; water taken by 360 km-long aqueduct to Los Angeles; a. 311 km².

Owen Sound, t., L. pt., Ont., Canada; on S.W. cst. of Georgian Bay, L. Huron; E. terminus of lgst. wheat-carrying L. steamers; linked by rly. to Toronto (200 km) and Montreal; p. (1971) 18,281.

Oxelösund, spt., E. Sweden; on Baltic cst., S. of Stockholm; steelwks., glass; p. (1961) 10,007.

Oxford, c., l. gov. dist., Oxon., Eng.; between R. Thames and R. Cherwell; 13th cent. univ. and residtl. colleges; printing, cars, elec. engin.; p. (est. 1976) 117,400.

Oxfordshire, non-met. co., Eng.; formed by Chilterns and Cotswolds, drained by R. Thames and tribs.; mainly agr. with lge. arable farms; ch. t. Oxford; a. 2,611 km²; p. (est. 1976) 541,800.

Oxfordshire, South, l. gov. dist., Oxon., Eng.; Wallingford, Thame and Henley-on-Thames; p. (est. 1976) 140,400.

Oxnard, t., Cal., USA; citrus fruits, sugar beet, oil refining; (p. 1970) 70,128 (t.), 374,410 (met. a.).

Oxus R. See Amu Dar'ya.

Oyashio. See Bering Current.

Oyo, t., Nigeria; cotton weaving; mkt.; p. (est. 1971) 135,785.

Ozark Mtns., Okla. and Ark., USA; lead, zinc; ch. t. Joplin; forested.

Ozd, t., Hungary; iron and steel; p. (1966) 39,900.

P

Paarl, t., Cape Prov., S. Africa; summer resort extending along Gt. Berg R.; wines, fruit, tobacco; flour, saw and textile mills; p. (1970) 48,597.

Pabianice, t., Poland; nr. Lodz; textiles, farming implements, paper; cas.; p. (1969) 62,000.

Pabna, t., and dist., Bengal, Bangladesh; dist. is a fertile alluvial plain; t. serves as trading, industl. and admin. ctr. for a.; hosiery, carpets; p. (1961) 40,792 (t.).

Pacasmayo, spt., Peru; exp. rice, sugar, cotton, cacao, hides, copper, lead, zinc, silver; p. (1961) 6,000.

Pachitea, R., Peru; rises in Andes, flows N. to

R. Ucayali; sm. German immigrant colonies in upper valley; 512 km long.

Pachmarhi, Madhya Pradesh, India; summer cap., tourist ctr.; p. (1961) 6,142.

Pachuca, cap., Hidalgo st., Mexico; silver mnfs. and mng.; woollen and leather gds.; p. (1970) 84,543.

Pacific Islands, Trust Terr. of, external terr. of USA held under U.N. trusteeship; consists of Mariana Is. (except Guam), Caroline and Marshall Is., W. Pac. Oc.; inc. 2,141 Is., grouped into 6 admin. dists.; cap. (provisional) Saipan, Mariana Is.; total land a. c. 1,800 km²; p. (1970) 102,250.

Pacific Ocean, a. 176,120,000 km²; lgst. ocean in the world; extends from W. cst of America to E. cst. of Asia and Australia and the S. Ocean in the S.; enters Arctic Oc. via Bering Strait; greatest length N. to S. 1,280 km; breadth, 16,000 km; mean depth 3,830 m, 11,524 m in the Mindanao trench; many coral and volcanic Is. in S.W.

Padang, spt., W. cst. Sumatra, Indonesia; exp. agr. prods., coffee, copra, rubber and coal; cement mnfs.; univ.; p. (1971) 196,339.

Paddington. See Westminster, City of.

Paderborn, c., N. Rhine–Westphalia, W. Germany; cath. and other historic bldgs. severely damaged in second world war; foodstuffs, textiles, metals; p. (est. 1969) 64,576.

Padiham, t., Lancs., Eng.; at N. foot of Rossendale Fells, textiles, engin., gas appliances; p. (1971) 10,192.

Padstow, mkt. t., Cornwall, Eng.; on W. side of Camel estuary in which silting has caused pt. of P. to decline; lt. inds.; seaside resort; p. (1971) 17,799 (inc. Wadebridge dist.).

Padua (Padova), c., cap. of P. prov., N.E. Italy; cath., arcades, anc. bridges; univ. founded 1222 (Galileo taught here); flourished as artistic ctr.; birthplace of Livy; machin., chemicals, cloth, distilling; agr. ctr.; p. (1969) 226,244.

Paducah, c., Ky., USA; pt. on Ohio R.; saw-mills, tobacco, railway wks.; atomic energy plant; p. (1970) 31,267.

Paestum, anc. c., S. Italy; S.E. of Salerno; founded by the Greeks 600 B.C.; ruins of temples, Roman forum and amphitheatre.

Pagan, ruined c., central Burma; on Irrawaddy R.; founded circa 849, sacked 1299; in ctr. of a. covered with pagodas, place of Burmese pilgrimage; lacquer work.

Pago Pago, spt., cap. of American Samoa, S. Pac.; on Tutuila I., magnificent harbour; US naval and radio sta.; airport; p. (1970) 2,491.

Pahang, st., Malaysia, central Malaya; isolated from rest of Malaya, less economically developed; largely covered with forest; some rubber production, gold, tin mng.; cap. Kuala Lipis; a. 34,395 km²; p. (1967) 425,552.

Pahlevi. See Bandar-e-Pahlevi.

Paignton, t., S. Devon, Eng.; incorporated in Torbay; resort.

Painted Desert, Arizona, USA; a. of bare multicoloured shale and sandstones; arid; a. c. 19,400 km².

Paisley, burgh, Renfrew, Scot.; 8 km W. of Glasgow; anc. abbey; shipbldg., chemicals, engin., preserves, car bodies, cotton thread; p. (1971) 95,357.

Paita, pt., Peru; exp. cotton, wool, flax, panama hats; lge. whaling sta. to S.; p. 37,000.

Pakistan, Islamic Rep. of, forms part of Indian subcontinent, S. Asia; formerly split into two separate units, E. Pakistan (cap. Dacca) and W. Pakistan (cap. Lahore), 1,600 km apart; politically separate since 1972; W. part now forms Pakistan, E. part indep. st. of Bangladesh; dry semi-desert, irrigated by Indus R. and tribs.; cash crops, sugar, wheat, cotton; natural gas fields; new cap. Islamabad; main spt. Karachi; a. 803,944 km²; p. (est. 1975) 70,260,000 (+51 per cent. in 12 years).

Paknampoh, t., Thailand; on R. Menam, at upper limit of steam navigation; terminus of private rly.; fish breeding in L. created from swamp.

Pakokku, t., Upper Burma; pt. on Irrawaddy R.; shipping ctr. for a. producing sugar, tobacco, peanuts, teak, petroleum; Yenangyaung oilfields nearby; p. (est. 1962) 156,960.

Paktia, prov., Afghanistan; mtnous., forested;

difficult to govern, inhabited by sm. and indep. tribes, but sparse p.; livestock basis of agr.; timber exp.; a. c. 12,950 km²; p. (est. 1970) 752,779.

Palau Is., archipelago, Pac. Oc.; volcanic and coral Is.; exp. agr. prods., dried fish; p. (1968) 11,904.

Palawan I., Philippines; elongated I., rising to 1,731 m; coffee, resin, timber; sparse p.; a. 11,784 km²; p. (1970) 232,322.

Palembang, cap. of S. Sumatra prov., Indonesia; R. pt. on Musi R., 80 km from sea; terminus of S. Sumatran rly. systems; exp. coffee and petroleum prods. from nearby oilfields; inds. based on agr. processing and oil refining; p. (1971) 582,961.

Palencia, t., cap. of P. prov., N.W. Spain; industl. ctr.; rly. engin.; cath.; p. (1970) 58,370.

Palermo, spt., Sicily, Italy; cath., univ.; shiprepairing; processes agr. prod. from surrounding fertile Conca d'Oro; p. (1969) 659,177.

Palestine or The Holy Land, historic region, bounded by Syria and Lebanon on the N., Jordan on the E., the Egyptian prov. of Sinai on the S., and the Mediterranean on the W.; a. when under Brit. mandate 2,701 km²; p. (est. 1948) 782,000. See Israel.

Palghat, t., Kerala, India; commands Palghat gap through W. Ghats; p. (1961) 77,620.

Palitana, t., Gujarat, India; t. of Jain temples inhabited by priests and their servants; p. (1961) 24,581.

Palk Strait, India; separates India from Sri Lanka.

Palma de Mallorca, spt., Mallorca I. Spain; cath., palaces, varied inds.; agr. exp.; well-known tourist resort; p. (est. 1969) 177,089.

Palm Beach, t., Fla., USA; Atl. coastal resort; permanent p. (1970) 9,086.

Palmerston North, pt. and t. N.I., N.Z.; rly. junc. at ctr. of Manawatu R. lowlands; sheep and dairy prod.; univ.; p. (1971) 51,859.

Palmira, t.. W. Colombia; agr. ctr. in Cauca valley; p. (est. 1972) 154,200 (t.), 193,500 (met. a.).

Palm Springs, Cal., USA; resort; p. (1970) 20,936.

Palmyra, anc. c. in Syrian desert, 192 km N.E. of Damascus; Bible name Tadmor = city of palms; extensive ruins.

Palmyra Is. See Line Is.

Palo Alto, t., sub. development 48 km S.E. San Francisco, USA; attractive wooded site of variable relief; on shore of San Francisco Bay peninsula; Stanford Univ.; science-based inds.; p. (1970) 56,181.

Palomar, Mount, peak, 1,868 m high, S. Cal. USA; observatory with 5,080 mm reflecting telescope.

Palos de la Frontera t., Huelva, S.W. Spain; on Rio Tinto; starting point for Columbus in 1492; pt. now silted up; p. 1,900.

Palua, pt., Venezuela; pt. of shipment for iron mines at El Pao; nearby Caroni hydroelec. plant built to serve steel wks. and aluminium plant.

Pamir Mtns., high mtn. plateau ("roof of the world"), Tadzik SSR, Central Asia; Mt. Communism (7,500 m) climbed by Russo-British team 1962; name derives from high mtn. valleys known as "Pamirs."

Pampas, Argentina; vast plains stretching from the Rio Negro on the S. to the Gran Chaco in the N., and E. from the Andes to the Atl.; woodless, level country; rich pastures in E., supporting countless numbers of sheep and cattle, a major influence upon the Argentinian economy, source of livestock exps.; W. mostly barren.

Pamlona, t., Norte de Santander, Colombia; agr., comm. and tr. ctr.; inds. based on agr. processing; p. (est. 1968) 33,707.

Pamplona, c., cap. of Navarre, N. Spain; at foot of Pyrenees, anc. Basque c.; cath., fortress, univ.; industl. ctr. with varied mnfs.; p. (est. 1968) 122,005.

Panama, rep., Central America; narrow strip of terr. at S. end of isthmus separating N. and S. America; mtnous. and tropical, thickly forested; split by Canal Zone from which rep. earns 25 per cent of revenue; shipping registration impt.; subsistence agr.; exp. bananas, rice, maize; sea fisheries; rich copper deposits found 1975; poor communications; cap. Panama City; a. 74,009 km²; p. (est. 1974) 1,650,000.

Panama Canal Zone, Panama; strip of land 82 km long 16 km wide on either side of Canal, leased to USA for military base; a. 1,675 km²; p. (est. 1970) 51,400.

Panama, c. spt., cap. of Panama; free pt. at S. entrance to Canal; cath.; oil refining, steel rolling mill, cement plant, lt. inds.; contains 25 per cent p. Panama rep.; p. (est. 1974) 410,000.

Panama City, t., Fla., USA; pulp and paper mill; resort; p. (est. 1970) 418,013.

Pan American Highway, international road project, not yet fully complete, from Alaska to Chile, down W. csts. of continents; section between USA and Mexico is called Central American Inter-American Highway.

Panay, I., Philippines; between Negros I. and Mindoro I.; coconuts, maize grown in E.; fertile lowland; ch. t. Iloilo; a. 11,515 km²; p. (1970) 2,116,545.

Pančevo, t., N.E. Serbia, Yugoslavia; agr. ctr. for grain growing a., flour-milling; developing industl. ctr., fertilizers, oil refining; p. (est. 1965) 52,000.

Pangalanes Canal (Canal Des Pangalanes), Malagasy Rep.; follows E. cst. from Farafangana to Tamatave, through series of lagoons; 480 km long.

Panipat, t., Punjab, N.W. India; on Jumna R.; on route from Afghanistan to central India; scene of battles; p. (1961) 67,026.

Panjim, cap. of Goa, India; pt.; old cap. (Velha Goa) in ruins; p. (1961) 32,000.

Panjsher Valley, Afghanistan; silver and mica mines.

Pannonian Basin, major structural depression, N. and E. Yugoslavia.

Pantelleria, volcanic I., Mediterranean, Italy; midway between W. Sicily and Tunisia; figs, raisins, vines, capers, cereals; fishing; a. 150 km²; ch. t. P.; p. 10,000.

Pantin, N.E. sub., Paris, Seine-St. Denis, France; glasswks., sugar refining, tobacco factories, chemicals, leather, tallow; p. (est. 1968) 47,607.

Paoki (Baoji), c., Shensi prov., China; ctr. of arable agr. a.; cotton weaving; nearby gorge on Hwang-ho used for multi-purpose dams; p. (est. 1970) 275,000.

Paoting (Baoding), c., Hopeh prov., China; on the Yungting R.; p. (est. 1970) 350,000.

Paotow (Baotou), c., Inner Mongolia, China; on left bank of Hwang-ho, on road and rly. routes to E. China; airfield; terminus of caravan routes through Gobi desert and Tarim basin to Turkestan; tr. in non-perishable livestock prods., cereals; modern steel ind.; p. (est. 1970) 800,000.

Papakura, bor., N.I., N.Z.; p. (1971) 17,208.

Papoloa, R., Mexico; agr. and industl. development; Papaloan project for flood control and electricity generation.

Papal States, Italy; areas ruled by the Pope until 1870; comprised Latium, Umbria, the Marches, and Emilia-Romagna.

Papatoetoe, t., N.I., N.Z.; p. (1971) 21,804.

Papeete, t., pt., Tahiti I., Pac. Oc.; cap. Tahiti and of Fr. Settlements in Oceania; exp. copra, vanilla, phosphates and mother-of-pearl; p. (est. 1970) 28,000.

Paphos, admin. dist., W. cst. Cyprus; anc. c.; Old P. dates from 3000 B.C., New P. impt. spt.; rich deposits of copper and iron pyrites, sulphur in Vretsia a.; p. (est. 1970) 11,800 (t.).

Papua New Guinea, E. New Guinea, S.E. Asia; indep. st. (1974); mtnous., thickly forested; under-developed; copra, rubber and timber prods.; cap. Pt. Moresby; a. 461,693 km²; p. (1970) 2,522,890.

Pará, st., Brazil; densely forested; rubber, fruits, cacao, Brazil nuts; cap. Belem; a. 1,228,061 km²; p. (est. 1968) 1,959,756.

Paracel Is., S. China Sea; claimed by China, Taiwan and Vietnam.

Paraguay, landlocked rep., S. America; undulating cty.; swamps, forest; hot summers, warm winters, high but seasonal rainfall; sm. densely populated areas, lge. areas with no p.; most economically developed in E.; in and around cap. Asunción 25 per cent p.; economy based on agr., cereals, livestock, fruit, cotton, oil-seeds, but food imported; aid from USA for rural development; few fuel resources (a few oilfields in the Chaco Boreal) and low energy consumption; hydroelectric plants on Paraná,

Paraguay Rs. and at Guaíra Falls; some agr. based inds.; a. 406,630 km²; p. (est. 1970) 2,386,000.

Paraguay, R., S. America; rises in plateau of Mato Grosso, flows S. and joins R. Paraná nr. Corrientes; forms bdy. between Brazil and Bolivia, Brazil and Paraguay; impt. navigable waterway to Cáceres (Brazil); 1,920 km long.

Paraíba, st., N.E. Brazil; livestock, cotton, sugar cane; tin, scheelite; cap. João Pessoa; a. 56,462 km²; p. (est. 1968) 2,252,636.

Paraíba do Sul, R., S. Brazil; rises in São Paulo st., and flows between Rio de Janeiro and Minas Gerais to Atl. N.E. of Rio de Janeiro; forms routeway between São Paulo and Rio de Janeiro; 1,040 km long.

Paramaribo, spt., cap. of Surinam; on Surinam R.; exp. bauxite, timber, rubber, rice, fruit; t. built on grid pattern with canals and tree-lined streets; p. (1964) 110,867 (c.), 182,100 (met. a.).

Paraná, c., cap. of Entre Ríos prov., N.E. Argentina; pt. on Paraná R. for grain, cattle, sheep; road tunnel to Santa Fé; p. (1970) 127,836 (met. a.).

Paraná, R., S.W. Brazil; formed by junc. of Rs. Rio Grande and Paranaíba; flows W. between Paraguay and Argentina; flows into Rio de la Plata; navigable to Brazil frontier nr. Iguaçu Falls; forms part of international inland waterway system; hydroelec. power, Itaipú to be lgst. sta. in world; 3,280 km long.

Paraná, st., S. Brazil; between Paraná R. and Atl. Oc.; extensively forested; maté, timber coffee; cap. Curitiba; a. 201,287 km²; p. (est. 1968) 7,216,582.

Paranaguá, spt., Paraná st., Brazil; ch. t. for Paraná; in lagoon harbour; modern highway links with Asunción (Paraguay); p. (est. 1968) 65,178.

Pardubice, t., ČSSR; univ., cath.; rly. junc., industl. ctr.; distilling, oil refining; p. (1967) 66,000.

Paricutin, Mt., Michoacán, Mexico; volcano formed between 1943 and 1952, 2,501 m high; of great interest to scientists.

Paris, c., cap. of France; dominates rep. politically, economically, and socially, partly as result of extreme centralisation of political power in cap.; on R. Seine, 176 km from mouth, in ctr. of Paris Basin; forms major ctr. of communications; planning of Haussmann gives spacious appearance, 12 boulevards radiate from Arc de Triomphe; many historic bldgs., especially on and around Île de la Cité, an I. on R. Seine, site of cath. of Nôtre Dame; major cultural and tourist ctr.; univs.; comprises 20 admin. arrondissements; major ctr. of inds. with concentration of modern science-based inds. hindering planned attempts at decentralisation; p. (1968) 2,590,771 (c.), 8,196,746 (met. a.), representing 16 per cent of Fr. p.

Paris Basin, concentric limestone escarpments form saucer-shaped depression with Paris at ctr.; impt. agr. dist., wheat, dairy prod. and wines.

Parkersburg, t., W. Va., USA; on Ohio R.; iron- and steel-wks., oil and natural gas, coal, glassware, rayon, porcelain; p. (est. 1969) 47,000.

Parkes, t., N.S.W., Australia; mkt.; rly. junc.; radio telescope; p. (1966) 8,431.

Parma, c., cap. of P. prov., Italy; between Apennines and Po R.; tr. ctr., rly. junc.; food-processing, wine, Parmesan cheese, precision instruments, agr. machin.; Roman remains, many historic bldgs., univ., cath.; p. (1969) 172,341.

Parma, t., Ohio, USA; motor vehicle parts; residtl.; p. (1970) 100,216.

Parnaíba, spt., Piauí, Brazil; agr. comm. ctr., cotton, cattle; exp. agr. prods.; p. (est. 1968) 69,961.

Parnaíba, R., rises in Brazil; flows into N. Atl. Oc., forms bdy. between Maranhão and Piauí; 1,200 km long.

Parnassus, mtn. ridge, Greece; 133 km N.W. of Athens, nr. the anc. Delphi, the modern Liakhura; hgst. peak Licoreia 2,461 m.

Parnu or Pyarnu, spt., S.W. Estonian SSR, USSR; on G. of Riga; exp. timber, flax; health resort; p. (est. 1967) 42,000.

Páros, I., Grecian Archipelago; W. of Naxos; source of Parian marble; cap. P.; a. 163 km²; p. (1961) 7,800.

Parramatta, c., N.S.W., Australia; pt. nr. head of Parramatta R. (spanned by lgst. concrete bridge in world) in met. a. of Sydney; chemical and engin. inds.; p. (1966) 107,006.

Parrett, R., Somerset, Eng.; flows to Bristol Channel, nr. Bridgewater; 56 km long.

Pasadena, c., Cal., USA; N. of Los Angeles; in fruit-growing region, base of San Gabriel mtns.; 5,080 mm telescope on Mt. Palomar; famous for its carnival; p. (1970) 112,981; inc. in met. a. of Los Angeles.

Pasco, t., Wash., USA; on Snake R.; atomic energy plant; p. (1970) 13,920.

Pasco. See Cerro de Pasco.

Pas-de-Calais, dep., N. France; impt. heavy industl. a. based upon local extensive coal deposits; heavy inds. inc. iron and steel, but many ts. in decline as importance of coal diminishes; prosperous agr. based on arable farming; N. cst. faces English Channel and inc. pts. of Calais and Boulogne; severe devastation in both world wars; cap. Arras; a. 6,750 km²; p. (1968) 1,397,159.

Passage West, U.D., Cork, R.o.I.; declining pt., fishing; p. (1961) 2,000.

Passaic, c., N.J., USA; rubber gds., springs, steel cabinets, tin cans; p. (1970) 55,124.

Passau, c., W. Germany, at confluence of Rs. Danube, Inn and Ilz, nr. Austrian frontier; trans-shipment base, inds. inc. leather, porcelain, tobacco and brewing; cath., picturesque tourist ctr.; p. (est. 1969) 31,158.

Passchendaele, t., Belgium; strategic point in first world war; battle 31 July–6 Nov. 1917; p. (est. 1969) 3,112.

Passero I., Mediterranean Sea; off S.E. cst. of Sicily, Italy.

Passy, residtl. part of W. Paris, France; between Bois de Boulogne and right bank of Seine; residence of Balzac.

Pasto, t., cap. of Narino dep., Colombia; on flank of Pasto volcano; univ.; agr. comm. ctr.; gold nearby; p. (est. 1972) 111,100 (t.), 137,200 (met. a.).

Patagonia, extensive region, E. of Andes, Argentina/Chile; elevated plateau, arid, sterile; prin. Rs. Colorado, Rio Negro, and Chubut; impt. source of oil at Commodoro Rivadavia; lge tracts of grazing for livestock; much of p. Welsh descendants.

Patan, Gujarat, India; impt. ctr. of Buddhism; gold and silver gds.; p. (1961) 50,264.

Patani or Pattani, pt., S. Thailand; on E. cst. of Malay peninsula; spices, rubber, coconuts; tin mng.; former Malay sultanate; p. of t. (est. 1964) 19,902.

Paterno, t., Sicily, Italy; N.W. of Catania; cath., cas.; mineral springs, wines; p. (est. 1968) 42,277.

Paterson, c., N.J., USA; on Passaic R. whose falls provide hydroelectric power for gr. silk mnf. ind.; now inds. diversified; in addition to textiles and textile machin., aeroplane engines, metallurgical inds., electronic equipment; p. (1970) 142,819 (c.), 1,369,374 (met. a.).

Patiala, t., Punjab, India; metal gds., flour; univ.; p. (1971) 148,686 (t.), 151,041 (met. a.).

Patino Mines. See Uncia.

Pátmos, I., one of the Dodecanese, Greece; in Aegean Sea; a. 34 km²; p. (est.) 3,000. (According to Rev. 1. 9. the exiled St. John wrote the Revelation here.)

Patna, c., cap. of Bihar, India; univ.; rly. junc.; agr. tr., rice, oilseeds, cotton; handicraft inds.; p. (1971) 473,001 (c.), 491,217 (met. a.).

Patras (Pátrai), spt., cap. of Akhaia, Greece; citadel and cas.; exp. currants, raisins, figs, olive oil; inds. based on agr. processing; p. (1971) 111,238.

Pau, c., cap. of Pyrénées-Atlantique dep., France; on Gave-de-Pau; impt. mkt. and regional ctr.; summer and winter resort; linen, chocolate, hams, wine; natural gas nearby; p. (1968) 74,005 (c.), 110,377 (met. a.).

Pauillac, t., Gironde dep., France; pt. on Gironde estuary; ships wines, timber; oil refinery, natural gas; p. (1968) 5,691.

Paulo Affonso, falls, São Francisco R., Brazil; 79 m; Tres Marias dam and power sta. opened 1960; in Nat. Park.

Pavia, c., prov. cap., N. Italy; on R. Ticino; route ctr. and agr. mkt. in Po valley; olives, wine, Parmesan cheese; oil refining at Spineto; walled c.; battle 1525; birthplace of Lanfranc; p. (1969) 85,680.

Pavlodar, pt., Kazakh SSR, USSR; on R. Irtysh; chemicals, sulphates, agr. machin., locomotives, aluminium, oil processing; food prod.; p. (1970) 187,000.

Pawtucket, c., R.I., USA; on Pawtucket R. at head of navigation; first water-power cotton spinning factory in USA 1790; textiles remain most impt. ind.; p. (est. 1969) 76,000.

Paysandú, dep., W. Uruguay; rich pastoral a.; ranching, cattle, sheep; arable agr., cereals, mkt. gardening around c. of P.; a. 13,406 km²; p. (est. 1969) 90,800.

Paysandú, cap. of P. dep., W. Uruguay; pt. on Uruguay R. with meat-packing, soap and footwear inds.; p. (1964) 60,000.

Pazardzhik, t., Bulgaria; on main rly. line to Istanbul; industl., hemp spinning and cotton; p. (est. 1968) 59,532.

Paz de Rio, t., Boyacá, Colombia; iron and steel wks.; iron ore, coal, limestone nearby; hydro-elec. sta. projected.

Peace, R., Canada; one of ch. headstreams of Mackenzie R.; rises in Rocky mtns., and flows generally N. to Gr. Slave R. nr. L. Athabaska; a. of very mild climate in lower course, fertile agr. valley; 1,680 km long.

Peak Dist., Pennine hill dist., mid-Eng.; extends from Chesterfield to Buxton, and Ashbourne to Glossop; composed of limestone with typical karst features; within P.D. Nat. Park, tourist and recreation a. for cities to E. (Sheffield) and W. (Manchester); limestone quarrying for cement; Kinder Scout 634 m.

Pearl Harbor, landlocked harbour, Oahu I. Hawaiian Is., one of finest natural harbours in E. Pac.; US naval base; attacked by Japanese without warning 7 Dec. 1941.

Pearl Is., archipelago, G. of Panama; sea fishing, pearls.

Pearl R. See Chu-kiang.

Pechenga (Petsamo), spt., RSFSR; on inlet of Barents Sea; formerly Finnish, ceded to USSR Sept. 1944; ice-free throughout year.; exp. nickel, timber, cobalt.

Pechora, dist., RSFSR; E. of Urals; one of 4 main coalfields of USSR; coking coal; ch. ts., Vorkuta and Inta.

Pechora, R., RSFSR; rises in Urals and flows N. into Arctic Oc.; 1,120 km navigable between June and Sept. for transport of timber from its basin; fishing; 1,792 km long.

Pecos, R., N.M. and Texas, USA; trib. of Rio Grande; water control schemes provide irrigation for lge. a.; 1,482 km long.

Pécs, c., S.W. Hungary; on Yugoslav border; one of oldest and most pleasantly situated ts. of Hungary; cath., univ., airport; in coal-mng. a.; coke, chemicals, majolica, leather gds. engin., brewing; p. (est. 1969) 144,000.

Peebles, royal burgh, Tweeddale, Scot.; on upper course of R. Tweed; woollen cloth, knitwear; mkt., tourist ctr.; p. (1971) 5,884.

Peeblesshire, former co., S. Scot.; now part of Borders Reg.

Peel, t., I. of Man, Eng.; resort, fishing pt. midway along W. cst.; cas., cath.; p. (1971) 3,081.

Peel Fell, mtn., Northumberland, Eng.; 599 m.

Pegu, c., Pegu prov., S. Burma; R. pt., rly. junc.; many temples, notably Shwe May Daw Pagoda; once cap. of Burmese kingdom; came under Brit. rule 1852; p. 48,000.

Pegu Yoma, mtns., Burma; between valleys of Rs. Irrawadi and Sittang; thickly forested with teak which is comm. exploited and forms impt. exp.

Peine, t., Lower Saxony, W. Germany; N.W. of Brunswick; iron, furniture, textiles; p. (est 1969) 30,899.

Peipus, Lake, Estonian SSR, RSFSR; drained by Narva R. into G. of Finland; Pskov lies to S. scene of Alexander Nevsky's victory over the Germans 1242; a. 3,626 km².

Pekalongan, t., N. cst. Java, Indonesia; exp. sugar, rubber; p. (1961) 102,380.

Peking (Beijing), c. and mun., cap. of China cultural ctr. and c. of gr. architectural beauty for hundreds of years seat of Chinese emperor

(Mongol, Ming, Manchu regimes); formerly surrounded by walls; lge. square; seat of govt.; univ.; many sm. factories; textiles, synthetic fibres, machin., precision instruments, printing, publishing; route ctr., rly. junc., airpt.; a. 8,770 km²; p. (est. 1971) 7,570,000.

Pelagi, gr. of Italian Is., inc. Lampedusa and Linosa, between Malta and Tunisian cst.

Pelée, mtn., Martinique; active volcano, devastated town of St. Pierre 1902; alt. 1,342 m.

Pella, dep of Macedonia, Greece; mtnous.; cotton, wheat, tobacco; cap. Edessa; a. 2,802 km²; p. (1971) 126,201.

Peloponnesus (Peloponnisos), peninsula, S. Greece; separated from mainland by G. of Corinth, but joined in N.E. by Isthmus of Corinth; mtnous.; livestock agr., drought-resistant sheep and goats; ch. ts., Kalamata, Tripolis; a. 21,642 km²; p. (1971) 985,620.

Pelotas, t., Rio Grande do Sul, Brazil; pt. on lagoon S.S.W. Pôrto Alegre; meat-packing and industl. ctr.; p. (1970) 150,278.

Pemba, I., part of Tanzania; cloves, copra, coconuts; exp. mangrove bark for tannin; a. 984 km²; p. (1967) 164,243.

Pemba (Port Amelia), spt., Moçambique; sisal, coconuts, cotton, maize, groundnuts; p. (1960) 55,902.

Pembroke, mkt. t., South Pembs., Dyfed, Wales; on S. side of Milford Haven; sm. pt.; dock facilities; cas., ruins of Monkton priory; birthplace of Henry VII; p. (1971) 14,092.

Pembroke Dock, Dyfed, Wales; site of government dockyard (1814) with consequent growth of a new t.

Pembrokeshire, former co., Wales. See Dyfed.

Pembrokeshire, South, l. gov. dist., Dyfed, Wales; from Pembroke and Tenby on cst. to Narbeth inland; p. (est. 1976) 37,800.

Penang, I., st. W. Malaysia; cap. Georgetown, pt. for N. Malaya handling rubber and tin; paper mill; the first Brit. Straits Settlement (q.v.); a. 1,036 km²; p. (1967) 752,059.

Penarth, t., Vale of Glamorgan, South Glamorgan, Wales; sm. pt. on Severn estuary, 3 km S. of Cardiff; ship-repairing, seaside resort; p. (1971) 23,965.

Pendle, l. gov. dist., Lancs., Eng.; ts. of Barrowford, Colne and Nelson; p. (est. 1976) 85,100.

Pengpu (Bengbu), c., Anhwei, China; on Kwo-Ho, 168 km N.E. of Nanking; on Tientsin–Nanking rly.; p. (est. 1958) 330,000.

Penicuik, burgh, Midlothian, Scot.; on R. Esk; paper; p. (1971) 10,066.

Penistone, t., South Yorks., Eng.; on R. Don; steel; mkt.; p. (1971) 8,182.

Penki (Benqi), c., Liaoning prov., China; metallurgical ctr.; p. (est. 1970) 750,000.

Penmaenmawr, t., Aberconwy, Gwynedd, Wales; 6 km. S.W. of Conway; resort; p. (1971) 3,998.

Pennine Alps, Switzerland; div. of Alpine system; ch. peaks; Mont Blanc (4,814 m), Monte Rosa (4,637 m), Matterhorn (4,477 m); winter sports.

Pennine Range, mtn. range, "backbone of England," extends 224 km southwards from Cheviot hills to Derbyshire; limestone, millstone grit; moorland sheep, dairying in valleys, quarrying, tourism; inc. Peak Dist. Nat. Park and Pennine Way long distance route; water supply, forestry; Cross Fell, 895 m.

Pennsylvania, st., USA; originally proprietary colony of Penn family, later one of the 13 original sts. in the Union; traversed N.E. to S.W. by Appalachians; ch. Rs.: Delaware, Susquehanna, Allegheny, and Monongahela; major industl. st.; iron and steel, coal (bituminous and anthracite), natural gas, petroleum; maize, wheat, oats, rye; textiles, machin., motor cars, tobacco; cap. Harrisburg; ch. ts.: Pittsburgh, Philadelphia; a. 117,412 km²; p. (1970) 11,663,301.

Penrith, t., N.S.W., Australia; in Sydney met. a.; ctr. for mkt. gardening; p. (1966) 35,970.

Penrith, mkt. t., Eden, Cumbria, Eng.; at N. foot of Shap Fell, 29 km S.E. of Carlisle; agr. mkt.; tourist ctr.; p. (1971) 11,292.

Penryn, t., Carrick, Cornwall, Eng.; on R. Fal estuary; sm. pt., boat repairs; once ctr. of granite quarrying; p. (1971) 5,082.

Pensacola, t., Fla., USA; on N. shore of P. Bay; originally a Spanish settlement, retaining much Spanish influence in squares, bldgs., street names; fishing, sea food inds.; univ.;

naval air training school; p. (1970) 65,422 (t.) 237,995 (met. a.).

Penticton, B.C., Canada; comm. fruit ctr.; p. (1971) 17,702.

Pentonville, dist., London, Eng.; prison; birthplace of John Stuart Mill.

Pentland Firth, strait, between Orkney Is. and Caithness, Scot., connecting N. Sea and Atl. Oc.; dangerous tidal currents.

Pentland Hills, range, Scot.; extend from Lanark to Edinburgh; Scald Law, 878 m.

Penwith, l. gov. dist., Cornwall, Eng.; S.W. tip of Cornwall inc. Penzance, St. Just and St. Ives; p. (est. 1976) 52,400.

Pen-y-Ghent, peak, Pennines, North Yorks., Eng.; alt. 680 m.

Penza, c. cap. of P. oblast, RSFSR; on Sura R.; rly. junc.; agr. ctr., especially for grain tr. to Moscow; food-processing and wide range of mnfs.; oil pipeline from Mozyr'; p. (1970) 374,000.

Penzance, t., Penwith, Cornwall, Eng.; on Mount's Bay; tourist ctr.; ferry to Scilly Isles; engin.; birthplace of Sir Humphrey Davy; p. (1971) 19,352.

Peoria, t., Ill., USA; machin., domestic gds.; grain tr.; univ.; p. (1970) 125,736 (c.), 339,719 (met. a.).

Perak, st., W. Malaysia; ch. tin-dredging a., in basin of Perak R.; rubber; cap. Taiping; a. 20,668 km²; p. (1967) 1,636,605.

Pereira, t., Caldas, Colombia; cath.; comm. ctr. for coffee; p. (est. 1972) 212,200 (t.), 249,500 (met. a.). [Ukraine, USSR.]

Perekop, Isthmus of, connects Crimea with

Pergamino, t., Buenos Aires, Argentina; road and rail focus in maize-growing dist.

Périgord, dist., S.W. France; limestone plateau crossed by Dordogne R.; famous for truffles.

Périgueux, t., cap. Dordogne, France; on R. Isle; cath.; famous for pâté de foie gras; engin., china; p. (1968) 40,091.

Perim, I. in strait of Bab-el-Mandeb at S. entrance to Red Sea; part of Democratic Rep. of Yemen; former coaling sta.; a. 13 km²; p. 1,700.

Perlis, st., W. Malaysia; agr. dist. for rice and coconuts; tin; a. 803 km²; p. (1967) 117,606.

Perm, oblast, RSFSR; major mng., timber, and paper dist.; produces oil (Krasnokamsk), coal (Kizel), hydroelectricity, and potash (Solikamsh); cap. Perm.

Perm (Molotov), c., cap. of P. oblast, RSFSR; on Kama R.; machin., chemicals, oil refineries; univ.; p. (est. 1968) 811,000.

Pernambuco, st., N.E. Brazil; mtnous. interior, cst. fertile; cap. Recife; sugar, cotton, manioc, tobacco. fruits; a. 98,322 km²; p. (est. 1968) 4,728,830.

Pernik (Dimitrovo), c., Bulgaria; iron and steel inds.; p. (est. 1968) 79,335.

Pernis, t., opposite Rotterdam, Neth.; lge. oil refinery; pipeline to Wesserling (nr. Cologne). See also Terneuzen.

Perovo, t., RSFSR; nr. Moscow; engin., chemicals; agr. research institute; p. inc. in Moscow.

Perpignan, c., cap. of Pyrénées-Orientales dep., France; nr. Spanish border and Mediterranean; on Paris–Barcelona rly.; mkt. and comm. ctr. for wines and fruits; cath.; tourism; p. (1968) 102,191 (c.), 106,627 (met. a.).

Persepolis, anc. c., Iran; former cap. of Persian empire, now in ruins; tourism.

Pershore, t., Wychavon, Hereford and Worcs., Eng.; on R. Avon; ctr. of fruit-growing a.; p. (1971) 20,430 (dist.).

Persia. See Iran.

Persian Gulf, inlet from Indian Oc. through G. of Oman and Strait of Ormuz, between Iran and Arabia; oilfields in surrounding land and now in G. itself; ch. pts. Bandar-e-Bushehr, Abadan, Kuwait, Dubai; Bahrein, lgst. I.

Perth, c., cap. of W. Australia; serves lge. agr. hinterland; many inds. based upon agr. prods.; univ.; outport at Fremantle; terminus of Trans-Australian rly., airport; well planned c.; p. (1972) 97,242 (c.), 701,392 (met. a.).

Perth, c., royal burgh, Perth and Kinross, Scot.; on R. Tay; rly. junc.; cap of Scot. until assassination of James I, 1437; dyeing, textiles, whisky distilling; cath., historical associations; p. (1971) 43.030.

Perthshire, former co., Scot.; now part of Perth and Kinross l. gov. dist.. Tayside Reg.

Peru, Andean rep., **S. America**; consists of 3 N.W.–S.E. regions: Costa (cst.), Sierra (Andes, rising to over 6,100 m), and Selva (interior *montaña* and R. basins); 40 per cent p. in Costa, 60 per cent in Sierra, yet Selva covers 70 per cent total a.; ch. Rs. Ucayali, Marañon; L. Titicaca shared with Bolivia; El Misti volcano in S.; cap. Lima on Pac. cst. with 20 per cent p.; agr. diversified and being extended by irrigation schemes; fishing main single ind.; mng. impt. in Andes; major world producer of silver, phosphates potash, copper, petroleum; a. 1,249,048 km²; p. (1972) 14,100,000 (of whom 3,600,000 live in Lima-Callao met. a.).

Peru Current (Humboldt), ocean current, S. Pac. Oc.; flows N. along cst. of N. Chile and Peru; causes clouds and fog.

Perugia, spt., Umbria, Italy; on R. Tiber; univ., observatory; woollens, silks, lace; foodstuffs, furniture, pottery, chemicals, agr. machin.; p. (1969) 126,887.

Pervouralsk, t., RSFSR; in Urals; metallurgical ctr.; p. (1970) 117,000.

Pesaro, c., central Italy; on Adriatic cst.; agr. ctr., seaside resort; birthplace of Rossini; p. (1969) 81,689.

Pescadores Is., archipelago, between Taiwan and mainland China; fishing, fish-processing; a. 132 km²; p. 86,000.

Pescara, c., cap. of P. prov., S. Italy; on estuary of R. Aterno; fish. pt., olive oil, soap, pasta, pottery; resort; birthplace of D'Annunzio; p. (1969) 116,723.

Peshawar, c., cap. of North-West Frontier Prov., Pakistan; 18 km E. of Khyber pass, commanding route to Afghanistan; military sta.; univ.; handicrafts, textiles, furniture; p. (est. 1969) 296,000.

Petah Tikva, oldest modern Jewish settlement in Israel (1878); ctr. for oranges; mnfs. inc. textiles; p. (1968) 73,500.

Petaling Jaya, t., W. Malaysia; industl. estate nr. Kuala Lumpur; tyres, aluminium rolling mill.

Peter I., uninhabited I., Antarctic Oc., belonging to Norway, a. c. 243 km².

Peterborough, t., Ont., Canada; flour-milling, elec. machin., trailers, agr. equipment, plastics, textiles, paper; p. (1971) 57,498.

Peterborough, c., l. gov. dist., Cambs., **Eng.**; on R. Nene on margin of Fens; cath.; rly ctr.; ctr. of brick ind. (Oxford clay around Fletton); diesel engines, agr. machin., gen. engin.; major planned expansion as new t.; p. (est. 1976) 118,900 (dist.), (53,471 in 1951).

Peterborough, Soke oı. *See* Cambridgeshire.

Peterhead, spt., burgh, Banff and Buchan, Scot.; on E. cst., 43 km N.E. of Aberdeen; herring fisheries, fish-processing, granite quarrying; supply base for N. Sea oil; p. (1971) 14,160.

Peterlee, new t. (1948), Durham, Eng.; coal-mng. dist.; textiles, science-based inds.; p. (est. 1971) 26,500.

Petersfield, t., East Hants., **Eng.**; on R. Rother, N.W. of Chichester; mkt.; p. (1971) 8,958.

Petra, anc. c., Jordan; temples, rock tombs and Roman ruins; called Sela in Bible (2 Kings 14. 7); rediscovered by Burckhardt 1812.

Petropavlovsk, t., Kazakh SSR, **USSR**; on Ishim R.; rly. junc.; flour, leather, meat canneries, furs, engin.; p. (1970) 173,000.

Petropavlovsk-Kamchatsky, t., RSFSR; spt. on Pac. cst.; shipyard, timber mills, engin.; fishing and whaling fleet; p. (1970) 154,000 (c.); (1969) 157,000 (met. a.).

Petrópolis, t., Rio de Janeiro, Brazil; health resort, c. 700 m a.s.l.; cath.; p. (1970) 116,080.

Petsamo. *See* Pechenga.

Petten, t., Neth.; 48 km N.W. of Amsterdam, on cst.; atomic research ctr.

Petworth, mkt. t., West Sussex, **Eng.**; in Rother valley, 19 km N.E. of Chichester; associated with Turner; p. (1971) 11,070 (dist.).

Pevensey Levels, marshy a., East Sussex, Eng.; lie behind coastal sand-bars between Eastbourne and Bexhill, extend 8 km inland to Hailsham; now largely drained, cattle pastures; a. 62 km².

Pforzheim, t., Baden-Württemberg, W. Germany; S.E. of Karlsruhe; gold, silver, metal wks., jewellery; p. (est. 1969) 90,022.

Phan Thiet, spt., Vietnam; exp. dried and salt fish; p. 5,000.

Phetburi, t. and prov., Thailand; on Isthmus of Kra crossed by Phetburi R.; p. (1960) 24,654 (t.), 237,835 (prov.).

Philadelphia, c., pt., Penns., USA; on Delaware R.; comm., industl. and cultural ctr.; univ., R.C. cath., masonic temple, mint, academy of fine arts; shipbldg., locomotives, machin., surgical instruments, carpets, woollens, cottons, worsteds; sugar, and petroleum refining; ctr. of War of Independence 1790–1809; founded as Quaker col. by William Penn 1682; p. (1970) 1,927,863 (c.), 4,777,414 (met. a.).

Philae, I. in Nile R., Egypt; flooded by waters of Aswan Dam; contains anc. ruined temples which have been removed to a safer site.

Philippeville. *See* Skikda.

Philippines, Rep. of, S.E. Asia; island chain in Pac. Oc., stretching over 1,760 km; ch. Is. Luzon, Mindanao, Negros, Cebu, Mindoro, and Palawar; lie in track of cyclones; tropical climate; mtnous., agr. aided by intricate terracing system; most Is. underdeveloped except Luzon where p. concentrated; subsistence agr. rice and maize; cash crops sugar, coconuts, hemp, tobacco; close connections with USA; cap. Quezon City (admin. functions at Manila); a. 299,681 km²; p. (est. 1975) 42,513,000.

Phlorina (Florina), t., Macedonia, **Greece**; in basin at 900 m, 16 km from Yugoslav border; agr. ctr.; p. (1971) 11,180.

Phnom-Penh, c., cap. of **Cambodia**, S.E. Asia; pt. on Mekong R.; handles ships up to 2,500 tonnes; linked to Sihanoukville by modern highway; multi-purpose dam to W.; univ., royal palace; airport; p. (1971) 1,500,000.

Phoenix, c., Arizona, USA; on Salt R., ctr. of Salt River Valley irrigated region; electronics research, steel, aircraft, clothing; p. (1970) 580,275 (c.), 963,132 (met. a.).

Phoenix Group, Is., Pac. Oc.; part of Gilbert I. col.; a. 41 km²; US have some rights over Canton and Enderbury; Canton used as international airport.; p. (1963) 1,014.

Phuket I., Thailand, off Kra Isthmus; main alluvial tin-working region of Thailand; ch. t. Phuket where a tin-smelting plant is to be established; a. 534 km².

Piacenza, c., cap. of P. prov., Italy; in Emilia-Romagna, on R. Po; agr. and comm. ctr.; cath., palaces, arsenal; cars, chemicals, cement; p. (1969) 104,092.

Piatra-Neamt, t., Moldavia, Romania; timber, pharmaceuticals, soap; oil refineries; p. (1968) 48,103.

Piaui, st., Brazil; semi-arid, underdeveloped dist.; thorn scrub; livestock rearing; cap. Teresina; a. 249,319 km²; p. (est. 1968) 1,432,634.

Piave, R., N.E. Italy; flows to Adriatic, 200 km long.

Picardy, former prov., **France**; included the Somme dep. and parts of Pas-de-Calais, Aisne and Oise; old battle sites, Agincourt and Crécy; rich agr. a.; textiles.

Pichincha, prov., Ecuador; p. concentrated in Andes; many natural resources inc. lime, gypsum, silver; tropical hardwoods; cattle raising; cap. Quito; a. 16,105 km²; p. (est. 1970) 843,000.

Pickering, mkt. t., Ryedale, North Yorks., **Eng.**; on N. margin of Vale of Pickering; church with murals; cas.; gas terminal; p. (1971) 4,544.

Pickering, Vale of, North Yorks., **Eng.**, wide, flat-floored vale, once occupied by glacial lake; bounded to N. by N. York Moors, to S. by York Wolds; drained W. by R. Derwent, alluvial soils, marshy in ctr.; crop farming along margins, cattle grazing in damper meadows in ctr.; ch. ts. Pickering, Malton, Helmsley.

Picos de Europa, mtn. massif, N. Spain; hgst. massif in Cantabrian mtns., rising to 2,650 m; partially inc. in Nat. Park.

Picton, t., S.I., N.Z.; freezing wks.; tourist and fishing ctr.; pt.; p. (1971) 2,825.

Pictou, t., Nova Scotia, Canada; on Northumberland Strait; founded by Scottish settlers.

Pidurutalagala, mtn., Sri Lanka; alt. 2,530 m; hgst. peak in rep.

Piedmont, region, N. Italy; rice, wheat, vines, fruits; cottons, woollens; a. 25,416 km²; p. (1969) 4,380,508.

Pietermaritzburg, c., cap. of Natal, S. Africa;

named after Piet Retief and Gerhardus Maritz, two Boer leaders; lt. inds.; tanning; iron-ore mng. in a.; part of univ. of Natal; 2 caths.; p. (1970) 158,921 (met. a.).

Pietersburg, t., Transvaal, S. Africa; gold, asbestos, tin; comm. ctr. for cereals, tobacco, cotton, citrus fruits; p. (1968) 36,274.

Pila (Schneidemühl), t., N.W. Poland (since 1945); formerly in Prussian prov. of Pomerania; tr. ctr., lignite mines nearby; p. (1970) 43,800.

Pilar, t., Paraguay; impt. R. pt.; sawmills; textiles; p. (est. 1970) 15,324.

Pilbara, dist., W. Australia; extensive iron mng.; processing and exp. to serve Japanese mkt.; rapid growth of p.

Pilcomayo, R., northernmost R. of Argentina; rises in Bolivian Andes, flows across the Gran Chaco, to enter Paraguay, joining the Paraguay R. nr. Asunción; hydroelec. power; 1,120 km long.

Pilibhit, t., Uttar Pradesh, N. India; admin. ctr.; sugar-refining; p. (1961) 57,527.

Pilsen. See Plzeň.

Pinar del Rio, t., prov. cap., Cuba; tobacco; p. (est. 1967) 67,600.

Pinawa, t., Manitoba, Canada; 88 km N.E. of Winnipeg; nuclear research; p. (1965) 8,000.

Pindus, mtn. chain, between Thessaly and Albania, Greece; hgst. peak 2,455 m.

Pinghsiang, t., Hunan, China; supplies coking coal to Wuhan.

Pinneberg, t., Schleswig-Holstein, W. Germany; N.W. of Hamburg; rose cultivation, metals, leather; p. (est. 1969) 36,101.

Pinsk, c., Belorussian SSR, USSR; in Pripet Marshes, pt. on Pina R.; paper, wood-working inds., matches; Jewish residents exterminated during German occupation second world war; p. (est. 1967) 57,000.

Piombino, t., Italy; mainland pt. for island of Elba; steel wks.; p. (est. 1968) 39,618.

Piotrków Trybunalski, t., Poland; cas.; timber and glass inds.; new textile combine; p. (1970) 59,700.

Piqua, t., Ohio, USA; N. of Dayton; ironwks., woollens; nuclear reactor; p. (1970) 20,741.

Piracicaba, t., São Paulo, Brazil; ctr. of agr. dist.; sugar-refining, brandy, flour; p. (est. 1968) 137,184.

Piraeus, c., Greece; pt. of Athens and prin. pt. of Greece; major industl. and comm. ctr.; p. (1971) 186,223.

Pirmasens, t., Rhineland-Palatinate. W. Germany; S.W. of Mannheim; footwear, leather gds.; p. (est. 1969) 56,420.

Pirna, t., Dresden, E. Germany; on R. Elbe; textiles, paper, glass; p. (1969) 41,076.

Pirot, t., Yugoslavia; nr. Bulgarian border; in economic development a.; p. (est. 1965) 21,000.

Pisa, c., Italy; at head of Arno delta, 19 km N.E. of Livorno; famous leaning tower, cath., univ.; textiles, chemicals, engin.; airport; tourism; p. (1969) 103,011.

Pisco, spt., Peru; famous for P. brandy; p. (est. 1969) 26,700.

Pistoia, t., Tuscany, Italy; on Arno plain, N.W. of Florence; iron and steel gds., macaroni; p. (1969) 91,729.

Pit, R., Cal., USA; rises in Goose L.; cuts spectacular gorges in the Cascades; used for hydroelectric power.

Pitcairn I., E. Pac. Oc., Brit. col.; inc. atolls of Ducie and Oeno and I. of Henderson; sweet potatoes, bananas, oranges, coconuts; a. 5 km²; p. mostly descendants of mutineers of the *Bounty*; p. (1970) 80.

Pitch Lake, Trinidad, W.I.; S. of I., 16 km S.W. of San Fernando; natural deposit of asphalt; tourism; a. 86 ha.

Pitea, spt., N. Sweden; on G. of Bothnia; sawmills; p. (est. 1970) 32,365.

Pitesti, t., Romania; on Arges R.; petroleum, fruit, grain; lge. automobile plant; oil refinery under construction; p. (1968) 65,782.

Pitlochry, burgh, Perth and Kinross, Scot.; on R. Tummel, 6 km S. of Pass of Killiecrankie; summer resort; distilleries, hydros; p. (1971) 2,599.

Pittenweem, burgh, North East Fife, Scot.; at entrance to F. of Forth; fisheries; p. (1971) 1,518.

Pittsburgh, c., Penns., USA; univ.; R.C. cath.; pt. on Ohio R.; ctr. of richest American coal-

field; natural gas, petroleum, iron and steel, machin., metal gds., meat-packing, glass, aluminium, chemicals, p. (1970) 512,789 (c.), 2,383,753 (met. a.).

Pittsfield, c., Mass., USA; textiles, paper, plastics, elec. machin.; resort; p. (1966) 144,800 (met. a.).

Piura, t., N. Peru; on Piura R.; oldest Spanish t. in Peru; cotton mkt. and processing, p. (est. 1970) 111,400.

Pladju, t., S. Sumatra, Indonesia; oil refining; linked by pipeline with Tempino and Bejubang.

Plata, Rio de la (Plate R.), estuary between Argentina and Uruguay; receives waters of Rs. Paraná and Uruguay; cst. provides sites for lge. spts., Buenos Aires, La Plata, Montevideo.

Platte, R., Nebraska, USA; formed by union of N. Platte and S. Platte Rs.; total length 2,240 km; irrigation, hydroelec. power.

Plauen, t., Karl-Marx-Stadt, E. Germany; textiles, machin., cable, leather, paper, radios; rly. junc.; p. (est. 1970) 81,907.

Plenty, Bay of, N.I., N.Z.; on E. cst.; 208 km wide.

Plettenberg, t., N. Rhine-Westphalia. W. Germany; on R. Lenne; iron wks.; p. (est. 1969) 30,172.

Pleven, mkt. t., Bulgaria; many mosques; famous siege 1877; textiles, wines; p. (est. 1968) 89,814.

PlitviČka Jezera, lakes, Yugoslavia; beautiful scenery; tourism; fishing.

Ploče, new spt., Yugoslavia; on Dalmatian cst.; industl. and rly. ctr.

Plock, t., Poland; on R. Vistula, nr. Warsaw; agr.; oil refinery and petrochemical plant; food processing; agr. machin.; p. (1970) 71,700.

Ploiesti, t., Prahova dist., Romania; petroleum, engin.; p. (est. 1969) 160,011; (1966) 191,663 (met. a.).

Plovdiv (Philippopolis), c., Bulgaria; on R. Maritsa; univ., Greek cath.; second c. of rep.; agr. processing, clothing, metals, engin.; p. (est. 1969) 242,050.

Plymouth, c., spt., l. gov. dist., S. Devon, Eng.; on Plymouth Sound; comprises the "three towns" of Plymouth, Devonport, and Stonehouse; Brit. fleet faced Armada 1588; R.C. cath., guildhall, museum; shipbldg.; seaside resort; fishing and fish-canning, lt. inds.; p. (est. 1976) 259,100.

Plymouth, ch. t., Montserrat I., W.I.; p. (1970) 3,500.

Plymouth, spt., Mass., USA; on Plymouth Bay, S.E. of Boston; here Pilgrim Fathers landed 1620 from *Mayflower* to form first English col.; Pilgrim Hall, Pilgrim Rock; textiles, cordage, machin.; tourism; p. (est. 1969) 11,500.

Plynlimmon, mtn., Powys and Dyfed, Wales; alt. 753 m; source of R. Severn.

Plzeň (Pilsen), c., W. Bohemia, ČSSR; ctr. of coal-mng. region; famous for beer and Lenin (former Skoda) armament wks.; p. (est. 1968) 145,299.

Po, R., Italy; flows from Monte Viso, through Piedmont and Lombardy to the Adriatic; valley forms a major component of N. Italian lowland; natural gas deposits in valley; liable to flooding; 648 km long.

Pocklington, mkt. t., North Wolds, Humberside, Eng.; foot of York wolds, 19 km E. of York; ctr. of agr. dist.; 16th cent. grammar school; p. (1971) 15,732 (dist.).

Podolsk, t., RSFSR; on main rly. from Moscow to S.; engin., tin-smelting, food-processing; p. (1970) 169,000.

Pohai (Chihli), G. of, N. China; together with G. of Liaotung forms shallow expanse of water almost cut off from Yellow Sea by Liaotung and Shantung peninsulas; receives water and silt of Hwang-Ho; a. approx. 38,900 km².

Point-à-Pierre, Trinidad; oil refinery; natural gas pipeline from Forest Reserve field.

Pointe-à-Pitre, ch. t. and pt. Guadeloupe, Fr. W.I.; on Grande Terre I.; exp. agr. prods., bananas, sugar; p. (est. 1969) 39,000.

Pointe-des-Galets or Le Port, ch. pt. La Réunion (Fr.), Indian Oc.

Pointe-Noire, spt., Congo Rep.; airport, rly. to Brazzaville; agr. exp.; potash deposits nearby; p. (1970) 135,000.

Point Fortin, r. Trinidad; oilfield and refinery.

Poitiers, c., cap. of Vienne dep., France; many attractive bldgs., cath.; agr. tr.; mnfs. chemicals, hosiery; Black Prince defeated Fr. 1356; p. (1968) 74,852.

Poland, People's Republic, E. Europe; history dominated by constantly changing sovereignty between E. and W. powers; mainly lowland; continental climate; economy retarded by history of political fluctuation but growth of inds. and urbanisation are both proceeding rapidly; major ctr. of mng. and heavy inds. in conurb. of Upper Silesia, agr. land remains largely in private ownership, but govt. attempts to rationalise farm structure, major pts. at Gdynia, Gdansk, and Szczecin, international airport at cap. Warsaw, 17 historic provs. to be replaced by 49 large dists., a. 311,700 km²; p. (est. 1977) 34,022,000.

Polotsk, c., Belorussiyan SSR, USSR; cath.; gasoline prod., oil refining; pipeline to Latvian pt. of Ventspils; food processing; p. (est. 1967) 61,000.

Polotskiy, t. Belorussiyan SSR, USSR; 13 km W. of Polotsk; new oil workers' t. 1963.

Poltava, c., Ukrainian SSR, USSR; industl. and food-processing ctr. in rich agr. dist.; countryside described by Gogol's work; textiles, synthetic diamond plant; battle 1709 between Swedish and Russian armies; p. (1970) 220,000.

Polynesia, ethnic region, Oceania; I. grs. in Pac. Oc. within 30° N. and S. of equator; between longitude 135° E. and W.

Pomerania, former prov., N. Germany; in post-war redivision part E. of R. Oder to Poland; part W. of R. Oder incorporated in Mecklenburg, E. Germany; farming, shipbldg., fishing.

Pomona or Mainland, lgst of the Orkney Is., Scot.; Kirkwall (cap.) and Stromness on I.; p. (est. 1969) 6,674.

Pomorze. See Bydgoszcz.

Pompeii, ruined c., Italy; stood 21 km S.E. of Naples, at foot of Vesuvius; destroyed A.D. 79 by volcanic eruption, site re-discovered 1748; many interesting excavations; also modern c. nearby; fine church with famous collection of silver and gold plate.

Ponape, volcanic I., Caroline Is., W. Pac. Oc.; copra, ivory, nuts, starch, bauxite; a. 334 km².

Ponce, c., Puerto Rico; recently improved harbour on S. cst.; well connected with other ts. in rep.; ctr. of fertile, irrigated sugar-cane a.; industl. ctr.; p. (1970) 128,233 (c.), 158,981 (met. a.).

Pondicherry, spt., Tamil Nadu st., India; on Coromandel cst.; cap. of P. terr.; tr. ctr. for local prod.; p. (1971) 90,637.

Ponta Delgada, ch. t., spt., San Miguel I., Azores; attractive scenery, mild climate attract tourists; p. (1970) 69,930.

Ponta Grossa, t., Paraná, Brazil; rly. junc.; comm. ctr.; maté, rice, timber, tobacco, bananas, cattle, jerked beef; p. (est. 1968) 152,581.

Pontardawe, t., Lliw Valley, West Glamorgan, S. Wales; on R. Tawe, N.E. of Swansea; zinc smelting and refining; p. (1971) 29,431 (dist.).

Pontchartrain, Lake, shallow L., lower Mississippi flood plain, USA; connected by canal to New Orleans 10 km to S., and by deltaic channels to G. of Mexico.

Pontefract, mkt. t., West Yorks., Eng.; 11 km E. of Wakefield; coal, furniture, confectionery, mkt. gardening; cas. ruins; p. (1971) 31,335.

Pontevedra, prov., Spain; on deeply indented Atl. cst.; transatlantic pt. Vigo; scenery and fiesta attractions for tourists; agr., livestock, timber, fisheries; cap. P.; a. 4,390 km²; p. (1967) 63,315.

Pontevedra, c., cap. of P. prov., N.W. Spain; fish. pt., handicrafts, agr. tr.; p. (1967) 63,315.

Pontiac, t., Mich., USA; on Clinton R.; fishing and shooting, motor cars, rubber gds., machin., varnish; p. (1970) 85,279.

Pontianak, t., cap. of Kalimantan, Indonesia; exp. rubber, copra; rubber processing; p. (1971) 217,555.

Pontine Is., off W. cst. of Italy; in Tyrrhenian Sea; a. 11·6 km²; p. 6,000.

Pontine Marshes, region, Latium, S. Italy; coastal zone S.E. of Rome extending from Velletri to Terracina; formerly highly malarial fens, largely drained and colonised 1930–35; 3,200 new farms, 4 new ts.; ch. t. Littoria; a. 647 km².

Pontresina, t., Grisons, Switzerland; E. of St. Moritz; tourist resort; p. (1960) 1,067.

Pontypool, t., Torfaen, Gwent, Wales; coal, steel, glass, bricks, tin galvanising, nylon at Manhilad; p. (1971) 37,014.

Pontypridd, t., Taff-Ely Mid Glamorgan, Wales; on R. Taff, 19 km N.W. of Cardiff; coal, iron-founding; p. (1971) 34,465.

Pool Malebo (Stanley Pool), Congo and Zaïre; lake formed by expansion of R. Zaire; length 40 km.; width 26 km.

Poole, t., l. gov. dist., Dorset, Eng.; spt. on Poole Harbour, 6 km W. of Bournemouth; imports clay for local pottery inds.; tourism, yachting, marine engin., chemicals; p. (est. 1976) 110,600 (dist.).

Poona, c., Maharashtra, India; in W. Ghats; temperate, pleasant climate; cultural, educational (univ.) and political ctr.; military base; agr. tr. ctr.; mnfs. cotton gds., paper; p. (1971) 856,105 (c.), 1,135,900 (met. a.).

Poopó, salt L., Oruro dep., Bolivia; fed from L. Titicaca by R. Desaguadero, which flows over saline beds; no outlet; c, 3,600 m a.s.l.; a. 2,600 km².

Popayan, c., S.W. Columbia; 1,677 m above Cauca R.; cath., univ.; food processing, coffee, flour; mng. nearby; p. (est. 1972) 82,100 (c.), 103,900 (met. a.).

Poplar. See Tower Hamlets.

Popocatepetl, volcano, nr. Puebla, Mexico; alt. 5,456 m; dormant since 1702.

Porbander, spt., Gujarat, India; exp. silk, cotton; imports coal, dates, timber, machin., petroleum; birthplace of Mahatma Gandhi; p. (1971) 96,881.

Pori (Björneborg), spt., S. Finland; at mouth of R. Kokemäen; copper refinery, rolling mills, match, paper and pulp wks.; p. (1968) 70,957.

Porirua, t., Wellington, N.I., N.Z.; p. (1971) 30,345.

Porjus, t., Norrbotten, N. Sweden; on R. Luleå, hydroelectric plant supplies power to iron-ore mng. dists. of Gällivare and Kiruna, also to Narvik rly.

Porsgrunn, spt., Norway; timber, shipping, engin., porcelain, explosives; p. (1968) 31,765.

Port Adelaide, spt., S. Australia; serves Adelaide; exp. agr. prods. from hinterland; iron smelting, chemicals, cement; p. (1966) 39,747.

Portadown, t., Craigavon, N. Ireland; on R. Bann, 40 km S.W. of Belfast; linen, food processing; merged with Lurgan to form new c. of Craigavon; p. (est. 1971) 21,906.

Portaferry, spt., Ards, N. Ireland; shipping fisheries; p. (1966) 1,426.

Portage la Prairie, t., Manitoba, Canada; sm. pt. on Assiniboine R.; grain and potato tr.; p. (1966) 13,012.

Port Alberni, spt., Vancouver I., B.C., Canada; exp. timber; fisheries; timber inds.; p. (1971) 19,749.

Port Alfred, pt., Canada; upper St. Lawrence R.; imports bauxite for smelting at Arvida.

Port Amelia. See Pemba.

Portarington, mkt. t., Offaly, R.o.I.; farming; first place to have elec. power-sta. using local peat fuel; p. (1966) 2,804.

Port Arthur. See Thunder Bay.

Port Arthur (China). See Luta.

Port Arthur, t., Texas, USA; pt. on L. Sabine; exp. petroleum, chemicals, grain; p. (1970) 57,371.

Port Arzew, pt., Algeria; world's first plant to liquefy natural gas (1964); oil pipeline from Haoud el Hamra; oil refinery.

Port Assab, t., Ethiopia; oil refining.

Port Augusta, t., spt., S. Australia; at head of Spencer G.; fine harbour; salt field; exp. wheat, fruit; p. (1972) 12,095.

Port-au-Prince, c., cap. of Haiti; spt. on bay in G. of La Gonave; cultural and political ctr.; univ., cath.; iron mkt.; food processing and exp.; oil refinery; p. (est. 1975) 393,000.

Port Blair, spt., cap. of Andaman and Nicobar Is.; p. (est.) 16,000.

Port Chalmers, t., bor., S.I., N.Z.; docks, shipyards; p. (1971) 3,010.

Port Colborne, t., Ont., Canada; pt. on L. Erie; iron smelting; nickel and copper refining; power from Niagara falls; p. (1971) 21,388.

Port Elizabeth, spt., Cape Prov., S. Africa; on Algoa Bay; bilingual univ.; exp. skins, wool, ostrich feathers, mohair; foundries, soap, chemicals, car assembly, food preservation, sawmills; p. (1970) 468,577 (met. a.).

Port Erin, v., I. of Man, Eng.; on S.E. cst.; seaside resort, fisheries.

Port Essington, N. point. of Coburg peninsula. N.T., Australia; pearl culture experiments.

Port Etienne, pt., Mauritania; fish. pt.; exp. iron ore.

Port Francqui, t., Zaïre; present terminus of Zaïre rly. on Kasai R.; p. (est. 1970) 48,190.

Port Fuad, t., Egypt; N. entrance to Suez Canal.

Port Gentil, spt., Gabon, Eq. Africa; exp. palm-oil, mahogany, ebony; sawmills, fishing, oil refining; p. (est. 1970) 48,190.

Port Glasgow, burgh, spt., Inverclyde, Scot.; on S. bank of R. Clyde, 27 km below Glasgow; shipbldg. and repairing, textiles, rope, canvas mftg.; p. (1971) 22,398.

Port Harcourt, spt., Nigeria; 48 km from sea on E. branch of Niger delta; terminus of E. Nigerian rly. system; tin, palm oil, groundnuts; bitumen plant, tyres; oil refining; p. (est. 1971) 217,043.

Porthcawl, t., Ogwr, Mid Glamorgan, Wales; on cst. 16 km S.E. of Pt. Talbot; resort; p. (1971) 14,065.

Port Hedland, sm. spt., W. Australia; new t. being built 8 km inland to absorb impact of Mt. Newman ore project; twin ts. to be linked by industl. belt; exp. iron ore to Japan; p. (1972) 7,172.

Porthmadog (Portmadoc), t., Dwyfor, Gwynedd, Wales; pt. on Tremadoc Bay; terminus of Ffestiniog lt. rly.; p. (1971) 3,665.

Port Hope, t., Ont., Canada; midway along N. shore of L. Ont.; fruit, dairying, radium refining; p. (1971) 8,747.

Port Huron, t., Mich., USA; on L. Huron; summer resort, dry docks, grain elevators; motor-car parts; p. (1970) 35,749.

Portici, spt., Campania, S. Italy; on Bay of Naples; dockland sub. of Naples; p. (est. 1968) 67,888.

Potile de Fier. See Iron Gate.

Portishead, pt., Woodspring, Avon, Eng.; on Severn estuary 5 km S.W. of Avonmouth; shipping; p. (1971) 9,015.

Port Jackson, N.S.W., Australia; deep natural harbour used by Sydney and crossed by Sydney bridge.

Port Kelang (Port Swettenham), major spt. of Malaysia; 48 km W. of Kuala Lumpur; exp. primary prods. inc. tin, rubber fruit; imports mnfs.; p. 11,300.

Port Kembla, spt., N.S.W., Australia; S. of Wollongong; iron and steel wks., fertilisers.

Portknockie, burgh, Grampian Reg., Scot.; on N. Buchan cst., 8 km E. of Buckie; sm. fish. pt.; p. (1971) 1,191.

Portland, t., Weymouth and P., Dorset, Eng.; 6 km S. of Weymouth on sheltered N.E. side of I. of Portland; lge. artificial harbour; naval base, prison; p. (1971) 12,306.

Portland, t., spt., Me., USA; comm. cap. of Me.; lge fisheries; paper, pulp, lumber, processed food, clothing; p. (1970) 64,304 (t.), 139,959 (met. a.).

Portland, c., Ore., USA; gr. wheat and wool tr.; flour milling, shipbldg., fishing and canning, aluminium, lumber; p. (1970) 375,161 (c.), 992,593 (met. a.).

Portland Canal, fjord, N.W. cst. of America, forming bdy. between Alaska and B.C.

Portland, I. of, Dorset, Eng.; limestone mass, linked to mainland by shingle spit, Chesil Bank, terminates S. in Portland Bill; naval base, Borstal institution; limestone quarrying; masonry wks.

Portlaoighise, mkt. t., Laoighis, R.o.I.; flour, malting; p. (1966) 3,435.

Port Lincoln, spt., S. Australia; exp. wheat, frozen meat, wool; fertilisers; p. (1972) 9,153.

Port Louis, c., cap. of Mauritius; pt. on Indian Oc.; exp. sugar; p. (1971) 141,100.

Port Lyautey (Kenitra). See Mina Hassan Tani.

Port Macquarie, t., N.S.W., Australia; on Hastings R.; resort; p. (1972) 9,362.

Port Moresby, t., cap. of Papua New Guinea, 2,880 km from Sydney; spt., airpt.; univ.; p. (est. 1971) 76,500.

Port Nelson, spt., Manitoba, Canada; on cst. of Hudson Bay at mouth of R. Nelson; linked by rly. to trans-continental systems via The Pas; exp. wheat, minerals; closed by ice for 7 months each year.

Port Nolloth, spt., Cape Prov., S. Africa; serves copper- and diamond-mng. dists.; declining crayfish pt.

Pôrto Alegre, c., cap. of Rio Grande do Sul st., Brazil; exp. lard, preserved meats, rice, timber, tobacco; textiles, chemicals, furniture, brewing, metallurgy; oil refinery under construction; pipeline connects with Rio Grande; 2 univs.; p. (1970) 869,795.

Portobello, resort, Midlothian, Scot.; on F. of Forth, 5 km E. of Edinburgh; bricks, pottery, paper.

Port of Spain, c., cap. of Trinidad; attractive c. with squares; 2 caths., mosque; spt. exp. cocoa, sugar, asphalt, oil; natural gas pipeline from Penal; food processing; p. (1970) 11,032 (c.), 67,867 (met. a.).

Porto Marghera, spt., Venezia, N. Italy; the modern pt. of Venice, reached by ship canal dredged through shallow lagoon; oil refineries; chemicals, metal refining.

Porto Novo, t., cap. of Benin Rep.; on coastal lagoon; spt.; fishing; many old colonial bldgs.; p. (est. 1970) 87,000.

Pôrto Velho, c., cap. of Rondônia st., Brazil; in a. producing maize, rice, rubber, tin; p. (est. 1968) 83,178.

Portoviejo, t., Ecuador; mkt. and comm. ctr. for agr. dist.; p. (1966) 96,651.

Port Phillip, lge. inlet, Victoria, Australia; landlocked bay, Melbourne on N., Geelong on W.

Port Pirie, t., spt., S. Australia; smelting ores, gold refining; exp. wheat, minerals; p. (1972) 15,506.

Port Radium, t., N.W. Terr., Canada; on Gr. Bear L.; pitchblende deposits; p. 300.

Portree, spt., v., I. of Skye, Scot.; landlocked harbour on P. Bay, Sound of Raasay; fishing; tweed mill.

Portrush, spt., Coleraine, N. Ireland; 8 km N. of Coleraine; tourism; p. (1966) 4,357.

Port Said, spt., Egypt; at N. end of Suez Canal; free tr. a.; impt. fuelling sta.; entrepôt tr.; p. (est. 1970) 313,000.

Port St. Mary, v., I. of Man, Eng.; on S.E. cst.; resort; fisheries, boat-bldg.

Portsdown Hill, chalk ridge, Hants, Eng.; extends E. to W. behind Portsmouth from Havant to Fareham.

Portsea I., fortfd. I., between Portsmouth and Langston harbours, Hants, Eng.

Portslade-by-Sea, t. East Sussex, Eng.; W. of Hove; p. (1971) 18,150.

Portsmouth, c., naval pt., l. gov. dist., Hants., Eng.; opposite I. of Wight; naval establishment; Portsmouth is the garrison t.; Portsea has the naval dockyards, Landport is residtl., and Southsea is a popular resort within the bor. a.; across the harbour is Gosport; shipbldg.; gen. mnfs.; birthplace of Dickens and I. K. Brunel; p. (est. 1976) 198,500 (dist.).

Portsmouth, t., N.H., USA; summer resort, naval dockyard, cotton; the 1905 Peace Treaty between Japan and Russia was negotiated here; p. (1970) 25,717.

Portsmouth, t., Ohio, USA; iron and steel gds., aircraft, boots, shoes, bricks; p. (1970) 27,633.

Portsmouth, spt., Va.. USA; naval dockyard; farm produce, cotton, rly. wks.; p. (1970) 109,827 (c.), inc. in Norfolk met. a.

Portsoy, burgh, Banff and Buchan, Scot.; spt. 8 km W. of Banff; fisheries and meal milling; p. (1971) 1,667.

Port Stanvac, S. Australia; 24 km S. of Adelaide; oil refining.

Port Sudan, spt., Sudan; 48 km N. of Suakin; linked by rail to Atbara and Khartoum; oil refining; p. (est. 1971) 110,091.

Port Sunlight, Merseyside, Eng.; garden v. founded 1888 by Lord Leverhulme for the employees of the Port Sunlight factories.

Port Swettenham. See Port Kelang.

Port Talbot, t., Afan, West Glamorgan, S. Wales; on E. side of Swansea Bay; impt. iron and steel ind., copper, coal; new deep-water harbour serves as ore terminal; p. (1971) 50,658.

Port Taufiq, spt., Egypt; S. end of the Suez canal.

Portugal, rep., Iberia, W. Europe; mild temperate climate on cst., drier and hotter in interior; economy based on an inefficient agr. sector, located in wide fertile valleys, and associated processing inds.; major exp. of cork, but few industl. raw materials; textiles; post-war growth of tourist inds.; cap. and airport Lisbon; a. 91,945 km²; p. (1968) 8,978,800.

Portuguesa, st., Venezuela; inc. llanos plains; livestock raising; cap. Guanare; a. 15,200 km²; p. (est. 1970) 284,523.

Portuguese Guinea. See Guinea-Bissau.

Portuguese Timor. See East Timor.

Porvoo, spt., S. Finland; on G. of Finland; exp. ctr. for forest prods.; p. (1966) 13,687.

Porz, t., N. Rhine–Westphalia, W. Germany; on R. Rhine, S.E. of Cologne; glass, metals, paper; p. (est. 1967) 71,800.

Posadas, c., cap. of Misiones prov., N.E. Argentina; on upper Paraná R.; on border of Paraguay; yerba-maté, tobacco, cereals; connection for Iguaça falls; p. (1960) 70,691.

Posen. See Poznań.

Pössneck, t., Gera, E. Germany; S.E. of Weimar; porcelain, textiles, leather; p. (est. 1970) 19,074.

Postillon Is., Lesser Sunda Is., Indonesia; coco-nuts.

Postojna (Adelsberg,) t., Yugoslavia; 32 km N.E. of Trieste; extensive grotto and stalactite cavern.

Potchefstroom, t., Transvaal, S. Africa; on Mooi R.; univ.; agr.; malt, timber, engin.; p. (1970) 68,207.

Potenza, t., cap. of P. prov., Italy; on hill 220 m above Basento R.; agr. and industl. ctr.; p. (1969) 52,907.

Poti, spt., Georgian SSR, USSR; exp. manganese; fish processing, timber-milling, engin.; p. (est. 1967) 46,000.

Potomac, R., USA; divides Va. from Md.; flows past Wash. to Chesapeake Bay; 464 km long.

Potosi, dep., Bolivia; famous for silver- and tin-mines; zinc ore; cap. Potosi; a. 116,630 km²; p. (est. 1969) 850,400.

Potosi, c., Bolivia; on slope of Cerro Gordo de Potosi, 4,072 m a.s.l.; tin, silver, copper, lead mng.; p. (1967) 73,923.

Potsdam, c. cap. of admin. dist., E. Germany; on R. Havel, 29 km S.E. of Berlin; beautiful parks and gardens, many palaces; scene of conference between Allies on bdy. questions, 1945; motor and locomotive wks., engin.; precision instruments; p. (est. 1969) 110,949.

Potteries, The, dist., N. Staffs., Eng.; ctr. of earthenware ind., comprising ts. Burslem, Hanley, Fenton, Tunstall, Stoke and Longton.

Potters Bar, t., Hertsmere, Herts., Eng.; residtl.; in London commuter belt; p. (1971) 24,583.

Poulton-le-Fylde, t., Lancs., Eng.; ctr. of mkt. gardening, poultry rearing dist.; p. (1971) 16,401.

Powys, co., central Wales; mtnous. a. made up of former cos. of Radnorshire, Montgomery and most of Brecon and bordering Eng.; forestry, stockraising and water catchment for Eng.; crossed by Rs. Wye and Severn; sparse p.; a. 5,076 km²; p. (est. 1976) 101,500.

Powys, Vale of, Powys, Wales; drained by R. Severn; cattle-rearing; ch. t. Welshpool.

Poyang Hu, lge L., Kiangsi, China; on S. margin of Yangtze R. plain; surrounded by flat, intensively cultivated land, rice, sugar, mul-berry; size varies greatly with season, max. a. (in late summer) 4,662 km².

Poznań, prov., W. Poland; drained by Warta and Notec Rs.; mainly agr.; stock-raising; mnfs. inc. locomotives; a. 26,705 km²; p. (1970) 2,190,000.

Poznań, c., cap. of P. prov., Poland; on Warta R.; route ctr., industl. and educational ctr.; cath. univ.; engin., iron-founding, chemicals; anc. c., once cap. of Poland; p. (1970) 469,000.

Pozzuoli, t., Italy; 3 km W. of Naples; anc. Puteoli; mineral baths, ordnance wks.; Roman ruins; p. (est. 1968) 61,912.

Prague (Praha), c., cap. of CSSR; picturesque, anc.

c. on R. Vltava; comm. and cultural ctr.; univ. (founded 1348); outstanding architecture; extensive mnfs.; machin., sugar, leather, milling, chemicals; p. (est. 1968) 1,102,060.

Prahova, R., Walachia, Romania; rises in Transylvanian Alps, flows S. into R. Ialomita; c. 176 km long.

Prato, t., Italy; 13 km N.W. of Florence; cath., mediaeval cas. and fortifications; cottons, woollens, machin.; p. (est. 1969) 138,717.

Predeal Pass, Romania; carries main road and rly. across Transylvanian Alps from Bucharest to Brasov; alt. over 1,200 m.

Presall, t., Wyre, Lancs., Eng.; N. of Blackpool; p. (1971) 4,066.

Pregel, R., Poland; flows to Frisches Haff, nr. Kaliningrad; 200 km long.

Prek Ihnot, Khmer Rep.; power and irrigation development project on lower Mekong R.

Prerov, t., ČSSR; S.E. of Olomouc; hardware, textiles; p. (1967) 36,000.

Prescot, mftg. t., Knowsley, Merseyside, Eng.; 6 km. S.W. of St. Helens; mkt., elec. cable ind.; p. (1971) 12,590.

Preseli, l. gov. dist., Dyfed, Wales; W. penin. with ts. of Fishguard, Haverfordwest and Milford Haven; p. (est. 1976) 64,700. [40,000.

Prešov, mkt. t., ČSSR; linen mnfs.; p. (1967)

Prestatyn, t., Rhuddlan, Clwyd, Wales; on N. cst., 5 km E. of Rhyl; seaside resort; p. (1971) 14,428.

Presteign, mkt. t., Radnor, Powys, Wales; on R. Lugg, 16 km N.W. of Leominster; p. (1971) 1,214.

Preston, t., l. gov. dist., Lancs., Eng.; pt. on R. Ribble; textiles, engin., aircraft wks.; p. (est. 1976) 131,200 (dist.).

Prestonpans, burgh, E. Lothian, S.E. Scot.; on F. of Forth, 14 km E. of Edinburgh; scene of Jacobite victory 1745; p. (1971) 3,132.

Prestwich, t., Gtr. Manchester, Eng.; in valley of R. Irwell, 5 km N.W. of Manchester; cotton bleaching and dyeing, soap, furnishings; p. (1971) 32,838.

Prestwick, burgh, Kyle and Carrick, Scot.; on F. of Clyde, 5 km N. of Ayr; golfing ctr. and trans-atlantic airpt.; resort; p. (1971) 13,437.

Pretoria, c., Transvaal, admin. cap. of Rep. of S. Africa; univ., tr. ctr.; inds. inc. engin., chemicals, iron, and steel; p. (1970) 516,703 (met. a.).

Preveza, ch. pt. and t. of P. dep. of Epirus, N.W. Greece; guards G. of Arta; p. (1971) 12,816.

Pribilof Is., off S.W. Alaska, USA; seal fur; a. 168 km²; p. (est.) 550.

Pribram, t., Bohemia, ČSSR; impt. lead and silver mines, zinc, barium and antimony; p. (est. 1968) 29,689.

Prijedor, t., Bosnia and Hercegovina, Yugoslavia; on E. flank of Dinaric Alps, 104 km S.E. of Zagreb; rly. junc.; iron-ore mines.

Prilep, t., Macedonia, Yugoslavia; mkt., refractory materials, tobacco processing; p. (est. 1965) 44,000.

Primorskiy Kray, terr., RSFSR; S.E. Siberia, on Sea of Japan; coal, iron ore, and various metals in vicinity; fisheries; millet and rice; slow economic development results from isolation; wants economic links with China; ch. cs., Vladivostok (cap.), Ussuriysk; a. 168,350 km²; p. (1970) 1,722,000.

Prince Albert, t., Saskatchewan, Canada; lumber-ing, furs; p. (1966) 26,269.

Prince Edward I., prov., Canada; sm. I. in G. of St. Lawrence; physically poorly endowed; rocky, with thin soils; pastoral agr., fur-farming, fishing; cap. Charlottetown; a. 5,657 km²; p. (1976) 118,229.

Prince George, t., B.C., Canada; oil refining; lumbering, mng., fur tr.; p. (1971) 32,755.

Prince Rupert, t., B.C., Canada; Pac. pt. of Canadian National rly.; service ctr., fishing and fish-processing; p. (1971) 15,355.

Princeton, bor., N.J., USA; seat of Princeton Univ.; p. (1970) 12,311.

Principe. See São Tomé.

Pripet Marshes, Belorussiyan SSR, USSR; forested swampy region crossed by Pripet R. and its streams; greater part reclaimed; coal and petroleum; a. 46,620 km².

Pripet (Pripyat), R., Belorussiyan SSR, USSR trib. of R. Dnieper; 560 km long.

Pristina, c., cap. of Kossovo aut. region, S.W

Serbia, Yugoslavia; on Sitnic R.; admin. ctr.; many mosques; p. (1971) 69,524.

Prokopyevsk, t., S.W. Siberia, RSFSR; in Novosibirsk dist.; one of the main coalfields of Kuznetsk Basin; mng. machin., metallurgy; p. (1970) 275,000.

Prome, c., Burma; pt. on R. Irrawaddy; connected by rail and road to Rangoon; tr. in rice, cotton, tobacco; one of oldest cs. in Burma, founded 8th cent.; p. (est. 1962) 496,960.

Proskurov. See Khmel'nitskiy.

Prostejov, t., N. Moravia, ČSSR; rly. junc.; agr. machin., textiles; historic bldgs.; p. (1967) 36,000.

Provence, region and former prov., S.E. France; along Mediterranean; now embraces deps. of Var, Bouches-du-Rhône, Vaucluse and parts of Alpes-de-Haute-Provence and Alpes-Maritimes; tourism; fastest growing p. of France; mkt. gardening; intensive investment along cst.

Providence, c., R.I. USA; at head of Narragansett Bay; univ.; jewellery, textiles, silverware, rubber gds., machin., oil, coal; p. (1970) 176,920 (c.), 900,569 (met. a.).

Provo, t., Utah, USA; at base of Wasatch mtns., nr. shore of Utah L.; univ.; flour, bricks, blast furnaces; p. (1970) 53,491 (t.), 137,675 (met.a.).

Prudhoe,Tynedale, Northumberland, Eng.; former coal mng. t.; chemicals, paper; p. (1971) 11,015.

Prudhoe Bay, N.E. Alaska, USA; ctr. of recent extensive oil finds; arctic conditions make extraction and transport of oil difficult and ecologically dangerous but despite opposition from environmentalist groups 1,262 km pipeline to ice-free pt. of Valdez approved (1973).

Prussia, former kingdom (1701–1806); former st. (1806–1945), Germany; consisted of 13 provs., cap. Berlin; formally abolished 1947; E. Prussia partitioned between USSR and Poland.

Pruszkow, t., Poland; nr. Warsaw; elec. plant; engin.; p. (1970) 43,000.

Prut, R., flows between Romania and USSR; from the Carpathian mtns. to the Danube R.; 576 km long.

Przemysl, c., S.E. Poland; on San R. (trib. of Vistula) nr. bdy. between Poland and Ukrainian SSR; anc. fortress t.; sewing machin.; p. (1970) 53,200.

Pskov, c., RSFSR; on R. Velikaya, nr. entry to L. Peipus; rly. junc.; flax tr.; historic bldgs.; scene of abdication of Nicholas II, March 1917; p. (1970) 127,000.

Pudsey, t., West Yorks. Eng.; between Leeds and Bradford; woollens; p. (1971) 38,127.

Peubia de Zaragoza, c., cap. of P. st., Mexico; one of oldest and most impt. cs. of rep.; fine cath., theatre, univ.; cotton mills, onyx quarries, glazed tiles; p. (1970) 401,603.

Puebla, st., Mexico; on interior plateau at 2,400 m; fertile valleys for coffee and sugar; mng. impt.; dense p.; a. 33,991 km²; p. (1969) 2,803,000.

Pueblo, c., Col., USA; on R. Arkansas, in foothills of Rockies; iron and steel ctr.; coal and various metals nearby; p. (1970) 96,746 (c.), 117,212 (met. a.).

Puente Genil, t.. Córdoba, Spain; olive oil, quince pulp; p. (1970) 26,442.

Puerto Barrios, pt., Guatemala; rly. terminus; oil refining; p. (est. 1971) 29,425.

Puerto Cabello, spt., N. Venezuela; on Caribbean nr. Valencia; excellent harbour; linked by rail and highway to Carácas; asbestos, vegetable oils, soap, candles, meat-packing; p. (est. 1970) 70,598.

Puerto Cortés, spt., N.W. Honduras; on Caribbean; exp. bananas, hardwoods; p. (1961) 17,412.

Puerto de Santa María, spt., S.W. Spain; on Bay of Cadiz; exp. mainly sherry; p. (1970) 42,111.

Puerto la Cruz, t., Venezuela; 16 km from Barcelona; oil refining; p. (est. 1970) 82,059.

Puerto Limón. See Limón.

Puerto Montt, spt., Chile; in sheep-farming dist.; S. terminus of rlys.; devastated by earthquake 1960; p. (est. 1966) 49,473.

Puerto Ordaz. See Santo Tomé de la Guayana.

Puerto Rico, I., terr. of USA, W.I.; since 1952 free commonwealth ass. with USA; democratic economic growth aided recently by falling

birth-rate; mtnous., eroded soils, alt. modifies tropical climate; exp. mnfs., but agr. impt. internally; 80 per cent land under cultivation, sugar, tobacco, coffee; tourism; cap. San Juan; a. 8,866 km²; p. (1970) 2,712,033.

Puerto Saurez, R. pt., Bolivia; on R. Paraguay; collecting ctr. for rubber, coffee, Brazil nuts.

Puerto Varas, t., Chile; tourist ctr. in Chilean " Switzerland "; p. (1961) 26,615.

Puget Sound, Wash., USA; inlet of Pac. Oc.

Puket. See Phuket.

Pula, spt., Croatia, Yugoslavia; on Adriatic; industl. ctr. with shipyards, docks, and various inds.; ch. naval base of Hapsburg empire; tourism; Roman remains; p. (est. 1965) 45,000.

Puna, cold, bleak, and barren plateau of Andes in Peru and Bolivia, 3,600–5,500 m.

Punjab, region N.W. Indus plains, Indian subcontinent; extensive irrigation from the " five rivers "—Jhelum, Chenab, Ravi, Bias, Sutlej; now divided politically between India and Pakistan; impt. cotton, wheat, and sugar dist.; coal deposits.

Punjab (East), former st., India; partitioned on linguistic basis 1966; Punjab-speaking Punjab st. (a. 50,375 km²; p. (1971) 13,472,972 inc. 55 per cent Sikh); and Hindi-speaking Haryana st. (a. 44,056 km²; p. (1971) 9,971,165); joint cap. Chandigarh.

Punjab (West), prov., Pakistan; old prov. revived 1970; p. (1972) 37,374,000.

Punta Arenas, c., cap. of Magallanes prov., S. Chile; most S. c. in world; mutton, wool; coal nearby; natural gas pipeline from Kimiri-Aike; p. (est. 1966) 67,514.

Puntarenas, spt., Costa Rica, on G. of Nicoya; fishing; fish-processing; resort; p. (1970) 31,162.

Purbeck, I. of, sm. peninsula, Dorset cst., Eng.; anc. v. of Corfe Castle in ctr.; limestone (" Purbeck marble ") quarries; site of Britain's lgst. onshore oilfield; once a royal deer forest; now forms l. gov. dist. inc. Wareham and Swanage; p. (est. 1976) 39,500.

Puri, dist., Orissa, India; cap. P. famous for its temple and festival of the god Vishnu and his monster car, Juggernaut; p. (1961) 1,865,439.

Purley. See Croydon.

Purus, R., Peru and Brazil; rises in Andes, flows to Amazon R. through underdeveloped a.; 3,360 km long.

Pusan, main pt. of S. Korea; on Korean Strait at head of Naktong R. basin; textiles; steel mill at Pohang nearby; p. (1966) 1,425,703.

Pushkin, c., RSFSR; nr. Leningrad; summer palaces of Tsars; Pushkin museum; Pulkovo observatory nearby; p. (est. 1966) 66,000.

Puteaux, sub. Paris, France; woollens, dyes, engin., printing; p. (1968) 38,014.

Putney, sub. of London, Eng.; residtl.; Thames-side dist.

Putrid Sea. See Sivash.

Putumayo, R., trib. of R. Amazon; rises in Colombia, forming bdy. with Ecuador and Peru; here, in wild-rubber region, Roger Casement exposed cruel exploitation of native labour; 1,600 km long.

Puy-de-Dôme, extinct volcano, Massif Central, France; hgst peak of Auvergne mtns., 1,466 m.

Puy-de-Dôme, dep., France; in Auvergne; cap. Clermont-Ferrand, industl. ctr. Thiers; a. 8,003 km², p. (1968) 547,743.

Puymorens Tunnel, Pyrenees, on bdy. between France and Spain; carries main rly. between Toulouse and Barcelona.

Pwllheli, t., Dwyfor, Gwynedd, N. Wales; sm. pt. on S. cst. Lleyn peninsula; seaside resort; inshore fishing, boat-bldg.; p. (1971) 3,832.

Pyatigorsk, c., N. Caucasus, RSFSR; ctr. of Caucasian mineral water springs; Lermontov shot here in duel 1841; p. (est. 1969) 84,000.

Pylos, pt., S.W. Peloponnesus, Greece; shipbldg. and repair yard, heavy metal wks. projected; sea-battles 1827 (Navarino), 425 B.C.

Pyongyang, c., cap. of N. Korea; stands high above Taedong R.; major industl. ctr. with coal and iron ore deposits nearby; univ.; many historic relics; p. (est. 1966) 1,364,000.

Pyrenees, range of mtns., S.W. Europe; dividing France from Iberian Peninsula; 432 km long; hgst peak Pic d'Anéto (Maladetta) 3,408 m.

Pyrénées-Atlantique, dep., S.W. France; mainly agr., sheep and cattle raising; ch. ts. Pau (cap.), Bayonne, Biarritz; a. 7,713 km²; p. (1968) 508,734.

Pyrénées-Orientales, dep., **S. France;** on Mediterranean; wine, fruit, olives; cap. Perpignan; a. 4,141 km²; p. (1968) 281,976.

Pyrgos, t., Elis, S.W. Greece; has suffered from earthquakes; p. (1971) 20,380.

Q

Qarun (Karun). *See* Birket el Qarun.

Qatar, emirate, indep. st. (1971), Arabia; peninsula on Persian G.; economy based on oil; inland production declining, but increasing offshore drilling; political stability less certain after withdrawal of Brit. military protection (1971); cap. Doha; a. 10,360 km²; p. (1971) 130,000.

Qattara Depression, N. Egypt; 134 m below sea level, salt marsh produced by seepage and evaporation of artesian water; marshes; few inhabitants.

Qena or **Kene,** t., central Egypt; on R. Nile; water jars and bottles; agr. tr., cereals, dates; p. (est. 1970) 77,600.

Qisil-Qum, desert region, Central Asia; covering dried-up a. of extended Pleistocene Aral Sea.

Qizan, spt., Saudi Arabia; cereals, pearl-fishing, salt.

Qom (Qum), c., Iran; pilgrimage ctr., shrine of Fatima; rly. junction; p. (1967) 179,434 (met. a.).

Qornet es Sauda, mtn., Lebanon range, Levant, Lebanon; max. alt. 3,050 m.

Quantock Hills, Somerset, **Eng.;** S. of Bridgewater Bay; hgst. pt. 385 m; a Nat. Park.

Queanbeyan, t., N.S.W. Australia; 13 km from Canberra; pastoral, dairying dist.; mkt. and service ctr.; p. (1972) 15,368.

Quebec, c., cap. of Q. prov., **Canada;** spt. with fine harbour on St. Lawrence R. at mouth of St. Charles; cultural cap. of French Canada; inds. based on local raw materials of timber, agr. prods.; oil refining at St. Romauld; historic c. with many fine bldgs., univ., tourism; p. (1971) 182,418 (c.), 476,232 (met. a.).

Quebec, prov., **Canada;** mainly within Canadian Shield; continental climate; forests and timber inds.; agr. in S.; hydroelectric power and abundant minerals; p. mainly French-speaking; ch. cs., Quebec (cap.), Montreal; strong separatist movements; a. 1,540,687 km²; p. (1976) 6,234,445.

Quebec-Labrador Trough, Canada; geological formation extending through central Quebec prov. to Ungava Bay, Hudson Strait; immense reserves of iron-ore (locally " red-gold ").

Quedlinburg, t., Halle, **E. Germany;** at foot of Harz mtns.; cas. cath.; aniline dyes, metals, engin., horticultural mkt. t.; p. (est. 1970) 30,829.

Queenborough, sm. pt., on R. Swale, I. of Sheppey, Kent, **Eng.**

Queen Charlotte's Is., archipelago, N. of Vancouver I., off cst. B.C., Canada; halibut fishing, lumbering; p. (1966) 2.222.

Queen Charlotte Sound, strait, separating Vancouver I. from B.C. mainland, a continuation of Johnstone Strait.

Queen Elizabeth Is., Canada; I. gr. in Canadian Arctic; most N. land of N. America; a. 349,443 km²; p. (1961) 310.

Queen Mary Land, Norwegian sector of Antarctica; ice crystal mtns., 3,050 m high for 160 km along cst.

Queens, bor., N.Y. City, **USA;** residtl. dist.; lgst bor. of N.Y. c.; p. (1970) 1,973,708.

Queensbury and Shelf, t., West Yorks., **Eng.;** textiles; p. (1971) 10,603.

Queensferry, royal burgh, Edinburgh City, **Scot.;** at S. end of Forth road and rail bridges; p. (1971) 5,127.

Queensland, st., N.E. Australia; rises from E. cst. plain to Gr. Dividing Range; sub-tropical climate; p. concentrated on E. cst. where sugar-cane, pineapples, bananas, cotton; inland grassland support cattle and sheep; mng. impt for copper, lead, zinc; oil discovered at Moonie; Gr. Barrier Reef along cst.; cap. Brisbane; a. 1,736,595 km²; p. (1972) 1,823,362.

Queenstown. *See* Cobh.

Queenstown, t., Tasmania, **Australia;** mng. ctr. for copper, silver, gold; p. (1966) 4,292.

Queenstown, t., Cape Prov., **S. Africa;** in agr. region producing wool and wheat; p. (1968) 42,997.

Quelimane, pt., **Moçambique;** at head of estuary; rly. terminus; exp. copra, sisal, tea; notorious in 18th and 19th cent. as slave mkt.; p. c. 10,000.

Quelpart. *See* Cheju.

Quemoy, gr. of Is. off Chinese mainland nr. Amoy, held by Nationalist forces; p. (est.) 50,000 (plus garrison of 40,000).

Querétaro, t., cap. of Q. st., **Mexico;** site of pre-Aztec settlement at 1,881 m; cath., many colonial bldgs.; old cotton ind.; p. (1970) 140,379.

Querétaro, st., **Mexico;** in Central Plateau; arid with fertile valleys; variety of crops; mng. impt.; famous for opals; cap. Q.; a. 11,479 km²; p. (1969) 112,993.

Quetta, t., cap. of Baluchistan, **Pakistan;** at 5,000 ft., commands routes to Bolan Pass; ctr. of irrigated agr. a.; military ctr.; coal mng. nearby; damaged by severe earthquake (1935); p. (est. 1969) 130,000.

Quezaltenango, t., S.W. **Guatemala;** second c. of rep.; at 2,333 m at foot of Santa Maria volcano; univ.; comm. ctr. for rich agr. region; textiles, handicrafts; p. (est. 1971) 54,475.

Quezon City, cap. **Philippines;** new sub. 16 km N.E. of Manila; cap. since 1948; univ.; p. (est. 1968) 545,500.

Quibdó, t., **Colombia;** in forested a. on R. Atrato; platinum, gold mng.; p. (est. 1968) 46,871.

Quillon, t., Kerala, **India;** on Malabar cst., ctr. of coconut tr. and processing; p. (1971) 124,208.

Quilmes, t., Buenos Aires, **Argentina;** on Rio de la Plata estuary; English public school; resort; oil refining, textiles, chemicals, glass; p. (1960) 318,144.

Quimper, ch. t., Finistère, **France;** tourist ctr. for S. Brittany; Breton pottery; Gothic cath.; p. (1968) 57,678.

Quincy, t., Ill., **USA;** at bridging point of R. Mississippi; agr. machin., clothing, footwear, food inds.; p. (1970) 45,288.

Quincy, t., Mass., **USA;** in Mass. B., 13 km S.E. of Boston; shipbldg. ctr.; p. (1970) 87,966.

Quindio, pass, **Colombia;** provides impt. route-way through Cordillera Central; 11,099 ft.

Qui Nhon, t., **S. Vietnam;** on E. cst.; tr. in coconut prods.; fishing; p. (est. 1968) 116,821.

Quintana Roo, st., S.E. **Mexico;** on Caribbean; low-lying swamp, underdeveloped; cap. Chetumal; a. 50,344 km²; p. (1969) 80,000.

Quito, c., cap. of **Ecuador;** in Andes at 2,852 m, 24 km S. of equator; anc. Inca c., cath., univ., slower growth than coastal ts.; impt. textile ctr.; p. (est. 1972) 564,900.

Quorndon or **Quorn,** sm. t., Leics., **Eng.;** on R. Soar, 5 km S. of Loughborough; ctr. of fox-hunting dist.

R

Raake, t., N. Finland; spt.; iron wks.

Raasay, I., E. of Skye, Skye and Lochalsh, **Scot.;** 21 km long, 5·6 km wide.

Rab I., at head of Adriatic, **Yugoslavia;** tourism; a. 192 km²; p. (1961) 8,369.

Rabat, c., cap. of Morocco; spt. at mouth of Bu Regreg R. on Atl. cst.; cath., univ.; textiles, carpets, rugs; p. (1971) 435,510 (c.), 534,270 (met. a.).

Rabaul, spt., New Britain, **Papua New Guinea;** ch. pt., exp. copra; damaged by volcanic eruption (1937) former cap. of New Guinea; p. (1966) 10,589.

Racibórz (Ratibor), t., Upper Silesia, **Poland** (since 1945); on R. Oder; textiles, metals, wood engin.; p. (1970) 40,400.

Racine, c., Wis., **USA;** sm. pt. on L. Mich., 16 km S. of Milwaukee; agr. machin., tractors, car parts; p. (1970) 94,720 (c.), 171,218 (met. a.).

Radcliffe, t., Gtr. Manchester, **Eng.;** N.W. of Manchester; paper, rubber, paint, engin.; p. (1971) 29,320.

Radebeul, t., Dresden, **E. Germany;** on R. Elbe; satellite of Dresden; p. (est. 1970) 39,626.

Radium Hill, v. S. Australia; ctr. for radium mng. 1920–30 and uranium later; mines now closed.

Radnorshire, former co., Central Wales. See Powys. Now as Radnor l. gov. dist. inc. Knighton, Presteigne and Llandrindodd Wells; p. (est. 1976) 19,600.

Radom, t., Kielce, Poland; in Radomska Plain; route ctr.; metal and chemical inds.; lge. tobacco factory; p. (1970) 158,700.

Radomosko, t., Poland; on edge of Lodz Upland; metallurgical wks., food inds.; bentwood chairs for exp.; p. (1970) 31,200.

Radzionkow, t., Katowice, Poland; new t. (1951); p. (1970) 27,800.

Ragaz, Bad, spa, St. Gall can., Switzerland; at mouth of Tamina R.; hot springs from nearby v. of Pfäfers; p. (1960) 2,699.

Ragusa. See Dubrovnik.

Ragusa, t., Sicily, Italy; oil and asphalt production; p. (1969) 60,413.

Rahway, t., N.J., USA; on R. Rahway; residtl. for N.Y. business men; p. (1970) 29,114.

Raichur, t., Karnataka, India; comm. ctr.; agr. processing; p. (1961) 63,329.

Rainer, mtn., Wash., USA; 4,432 m; forms Nat. Park.

Rainford, t., Merseyside, Eng.; nr. St. Helens; former coal-mng. a.; p. (1971) 8,381.

Rainy, L., on border of Canada and Minn., USA; drained by Rainy R. to L. of the Woods.

Raipur, t., Madhya Pradesh, India; ctr. of fertile rice growing a.; p. (1971) 174, 518 (t.), 205,986 (met. a.).

Rajahmundry, t., Andhra Pradesh, India; on delta of Godivari R.; agr. tr.; p. (1971) 165,912 (t.), 188,805 (met. a.).

Rajasthan, st., India; dry a. inc. Thar desert; sparse p. where primitive irrigation; agr., millets, pulses, cotton; impt. gypsum deposits; cap. Jaipur; a. 342,274 km²; p. (1971) 25,742,142.

Rajkot, t., Gujarat, India; p. (1971) 300,612.

Rajshahi, t., Rajshahi dist., Bangladesh; on R. Ganges; univ.; silk inds.; p. (est. 1969) 76,000.

Raki-Ura I. See Stewart I.

Raleigh, c., cap. of N.C., USA; educational ctr. univ.; printing, cotton tr. and processing; p. (1970) 117,676 (c.), 225,634 (met. a.).

Ralik, W. chain of Is., Marshall gr., Pac. Oc.; lgst atoll Kwajalein; parallel with Ratak chain.

Ramat Gan, t., Israel; in plain of Sharon; univ.; lt. inds.; p. (1972) 120,100.

Rambouillet, t., Yvelines, France; nr. Versailles; anc. château; p. (1968) 14,499.

Rameswaram, t., S. India; on Rameswaram I., Palk Strait; contains Dravidian temple, Hindu holy place of pilgrimage; p. (1961) 6,801.

Ramla, t., Israel; S. of Lydda; former cap. of Palestine; ass. with crusaders; p. (est. 1970) 30,800.

Rampur, t., Uttar Pradesh, India; N.W. of Bareilly; agr. tr.; sugar refining; chemicals; cap. of former princely st. of R.; p. (1971) 161,417.

Ramree I., Burma; in Bay of Bengal, off Arakan cst.; 80 km long.

Ramsbottom, t., Lancs., Eng.; on R. Irwell, 6 km N. of Bury; engin., paper, textiles; p. (1971) 15,872.

Ramsey, mkt. t., Cambs., Eng; on edge of Fens, 11 km N. of St. Ives; engin.; abbey ruins; p. (1971) 5,646.

Ramsey, t., spt., I. of Man, Eng.; on N.E. cst.; holiday resort; p. (1971) 5,048.

Ramsgate, t., Kent, Eng.; on S. cst. of I. of Thanet; seaside resort; p. (1971) 39,482.

Rancagua, t., Colchagua prov., Chile; ctr. of fertile valley in Andean foothills; tractors, agr. processing; p. (est. 1966) 63,116.

Rance, R., Brittany, France; world's first major tidal hydroelectric power sta. (opened 1966).

Ranchi, t., Bihar, India; hot season seat of govt. in Chota Nagpur plateau; univ.; heavy engin.; p. (1971) 175,943 (c.), 255,551 (met. a.).

Rand. See Witwatersrand.

Randers, pt., Denmark; on Randers Fjord, inlet of Kattegat; machin., foundries; exp. dairy prod.; mediaeval monastery; p. (est. 1970) 41,253.

Randfontein, t., Transvaal, S. Africa; gold-mng. ctr.; uranium plant; p. (1968) 46,370.

Randstad, conurb., Neth.; Dutch " urban ring," inc. Rotterdam, the Hague, Leiden, Amsterdam

and Utrecht, contained within radius of 16 km; a. of rapid industrialisation.

Rangitaiki R., N.I., N.Z.; flows into Bay of Plenty; 192 km long.

Rangoon, c., cap. of Burma; on E. arm of Irrawaddy delta; 2 caths., many mosques, temples and pagodas; replaced Mandalay as cap. with the increasing importance of delta under the Brit. as ctr. of rice tr. and exp.; oil refining; teak collecting ctr.; p. (1970) 1,821,752.

Rangpur, t., Bangladesh; on R. Ghaghat; jute; p. (1961) 40,600.

Raniganj, t., W. Bengal, India; coalfield in Damodar basin; engin.; p. (1961) 30,113.

Rannoch, Loch, Perth and Kinross, Scot.; 14 km long, 1·6 km wide; drained to R. Tay.

Rapallo, t., Liguria, N.W. Italy; on G. of Genoa, 35 km E. of Genoa; most celebrated resort on Italian Riviera di Levante; p. (est. 1968) 25,311.

Rapanui. See Easter I.

Rapid City, t., S.D., USA; second t. of st.; comm. ctr. for agr. and mng. a.; p. (est. 1969) 43,000.

Rarotonga, volcanic I., Pac. Oc.; cap. of Cook Is.; fruit canning; ch. t. and pt. Avarua; p. (est. 1968) 10,853.

Ra's al Khaymah. See United Arab Emirates.

Rasht (Resht), c., Iran; cap of Gilan prov., in a. producing rice, cotton, silk; carpets; nearby Pahlevi serves as pt.; p. (est. 1971) 164,400.

Ras Lanug, oil terminal, on G. of Sidra, Libya; pipeline from Hofra oilfield.

Ras Tannura, spt., Nejd, Saudi Arabia; lge. oil refinery; oil exp.

Ratak, E., chain of Is., Marshall gr., Pac. Oc.; ch. I. Majuro; parallel with Ralik chain.

Rathenow, t., Potsdam, E. Germany; on R. Havel; optical and precision instruments; p. (est. 1970) 29,823.

Rathlin, I., off Fair Head, Moyle, N. Ireland; 8 km by 1·6 km.

Ratibor. See Racibórz.

Ratingen, t., N. Rhine–Westphalia, W. Germany; N.E. of Düsseldorf; textiles, machin., glass; famous for Blue L.; p. (est. 1969) 42,256.

Ratisbon. See Regensburg.

Ratlam, t., Madhya Pradesh, India; rly. junc. in Malwa Plateau; p. (1971) 106,666.

Ratnapura, t., Sri Lanka; former ctr. of gem mng.; p. (est. 1968) 24,000.

Rauma, spt., S.W. Finland; on Baltic Sea; p. (1966) 23,952.

Raunds, t., East Northants., Eng.; 8 km N.E. of Wellingborough; p. (1971) 5,945.

Raurkela, t., Orissa, India; steel, tinplate, iron, fertilisers; p. (1961) 90,287.

Ravenglass, t., Cumbria, Eng.; nr. mouth of R. Esk; old pt.; Roman remains.

Ravenna, c., cap. of Ravenna prov., Emilia-Romagna, Italy; on reclaimed plain nr. Po delta; connected to Adriatic by canal; ctr. of fertile agr. dist., agr. processing; new inds. aided by discovery of methane N. of c.; oil refineries, chemicals, fertilisers; cath., mausoleum, famous mosaics; p. (1969) 131,279.

Ravenna, prov., Emilia-Romagna, Italy; N. Italian plain rising to Apennines; fertile agr. a.; cap. R.; a. 1,852 km²; p. (1969) 352,146).

Ravensburg, t., Baden–Württemberg, W. Germany; nr. Konstanz; engin., textiles; p. (est. 1969) 31,908.

Ravenscraig, t., nr. Motherwell, Strathclyde Reg., Scot.; hot strip steelmill; cold reduction mill at Gartcosh 13 km away.

Ravi, R., Punjab, India; trib. of Chenab; used for irrigation; 720 km long.

Rawalpindi, c., Pakistan; seat of govt. until completion of Islamabad; admin., comm. and rly ctr.; foundries, oil refining, industl. gases; p. (est. 1969) 455,000.

Rawmarsh, t., South Yorks., Eng.; 3 km N.E. of Rotherham; engin.; p. (1971) 19,884.

Rawtenstall, t., Rossendale, Lancs., Eng.; on R. Irwell in ctr. of Rossendale Fells; felts; footwear, textiles; p. (1971) 21,404.

Rayleigh, t., Rochford, Essex, Eng.; 8 km N.W. of Southend; lt. inds.; dormitory for London; p. (1971) 26,265.

Ré, Ile de, I., W. cst. of Charente-Maritime dep. France; off La Rochelle; citadel (built 1681) at St. Martin de Ré is now a prison.

Reading, t., l. gov. dist., Berks., Eng.; at confluence of Rs. Thames and Kennet; univ.;

biscuits, engin., electronics, mkt. gardening, tin-box mftg. printing; p. (est. 1976) 131,200.

Reading, c., Penns., USA; on Schuylkill R.; steelwks. using local coal, optical gds.; p. (1970) 86,470 (c.), 294,104 (met. a.).

Recife, spt., cap. of Pernambuco st., N.E. Brazil; fine natural harbour; univ.; processing and exp. of sugar from surrounding a.; " Venice of Brazil " because of I. and peninsula site; lge. petrochemical wks. nearby; p. (1970) 1,046,454.

Recklinghausen, t., N. Rhine–Westphalia, W. Germany; nr. Dortmund; collieries, iron, machin., textiles, chemicals; p. (est. 1969) 125,700.

Recôncavo, dist., Bahia st., N.E. Brazil; surrounds bay at mouth of R. Paraguassu; intensive cultivation of sugar-cane, cotton, tobacco, rice, by Negro farmers; oil production; ch. ts. São Salvador, Cachoeira.

Redbridge, outer bor., E. London, Eng.; incorporates Ilford, Wanstead and Woodford, Chigwell (Hainault Estate), Dagenham (N. Chadwell Heath ward); mainly residtl.; p. (est. 1976) 231,600.

Redcar, t., Cleveland, Eng.; lge. iron and steel wks.

Redcliff, t., Rhodesia; iron-mng.; iron and steel wks.; fertilisers.

Red Deer, t., Alberta, Canada; on Red Deer R.; mkt. t. in farming a.; lge. natural gas processing plant nearby; p. (1971) 27,428.

Redditch, t., l. gov. dist., Hereford and Worcs., Eng.; 19 km S. of Birmingham; needles, fishing tackle, cycles, spring, aluminium alloys; new t. (1964); p. (est. 1976) 51,600.

Redlands, t., Cal., USA; univ.; citrus fruit packing and canning; p. (1970) 36,355.

Redonda, I., Leeward gr., Caribbean Sea; between Montserrat and Nevis; uninhabited.

Redondo Beach, t., Cal., USA; residtl.; tourism; p. (1970) 57,425.

Red R. (China and Vietnam). See Song-koi.

Red R., USA; southernmost of lge. tribs. of Mississippi R.; derives name and colour from red clay in upper course; dammed for flood control and hydroelec. power; 2,560 km long.

Red R. of the North, USA; rises in Minn., flows N. into Canada to empty into L. Winnipeg; 1,040 km long.

Redruth, t., Cornwall, Eng.; once major ctr. of tin mng.; most mines now closed, although recent revival of some; p. (1971) 42,029 (inc. Camborne).

Red Sea, arm of sea separating Arabia from Africa; connects with Indian Oc. by Straits of Bab-el-Mandeb; extension of Great African Rift Valley which further N. encloses the Dead Sea; 2,240 km long.

Redwood City, t., W. Cal., USA; timber tr.; electronics; p. (1970) 55,686.

Ree, Lough, L., R.o.I.; between Roscommon, Longford and Westmeath, an extension of R. Shannon; 27 km long.

Regensburg (Ratisbon), c., R. pt., Bavaria, W. Germany; N.E. of Munich on R. Danube; timber processing, chemicals; p. (est. 1969) 126,600.

Reggio di Calabria, spt., Calabria, Italy; on Strait of Messina; cath.; fishing, ferry to Sicily; mkt. for citrus fruit; tourism; agr. processing; rebuilt after 1908 earthquake; p. (1969) 166,022.

Reggio nell' Emilia, c., cap. of prov. of same name, in Emilia-Romagna, N. Italy; at foot of Apennines; Renaissance church of the Madonna della Ghiara; locomotives, aircraft, agr. engin.; birthplace of Ariosto; p. (1969) 127,269.

Regina, t., cap. of Saskatchewan, Canada; ctr. of wheat growing dist. of Prairies; connected by pipeline to Alberta oilfields; oil refining, chemicals, agr. machin.; p. (est. 1969) 140,000.

Rehovoth, Israel; t., in citrus fruit dist.; Weizmann Institute of Science; p. (est. 1970) 36,600.

Reichenbach, t., Karl-Marx-Stadt, E. Germany; at foot of Erzgebirge; textile ctr.; p. (est. 1970) 28,818.

Reichenberg. See Liberec.

Reigate, t., Surrey, Eng.; at foot of N. Downs, 8 km E. of Dorking; dormitory for London; with Banstead forms l. gov. dist.; p. (est. 1976) 112,400.

Reims, c., Marne dep., N.E. France; on R. Vesle; famous Gothic cath.; univ.; champagne

ctr., textiles; p. (1968) 152,967 (c.); 167,830 (met. a.).

Reindeer L., Saskatchewan, Manitoba, Canada; Indian settlement on shore; a. 6,475 km².

Rejang R., Sarawak; navigable for 72 km by ocean boats; main R. of Sarawak.

Rembang, pt., N. cst. Java, Indonesia; in dry limestone R. plateau; p. (est. 1960) 75,000.

Remscheid, t., N. Rhine–Westphalia, W. Germany; nr. Düsseldorf; iron and steel ctr.; machin. tools; p. (est. 1969) 136,400.

Renaix. See Ronse.

Rendsburg, t., Schleswig-Holstein, W. Germany; on Kiel Canal; shipbldg., elec. gds.; p. (est. 1969) 35,464.

Renfrew, royal burgh, Renfrew, Scot.; nr. R. Clyde, 8 km W. of Glasgow; p. (1971) 18,595.

Renfrewshire, former co., central Scot.; now reduced in size and forms l. gov. dist. within Strathclyde Reg.; a. of l. gov. dist. 308 km²; p. (1971) 203,995.

Renkum, t., Gelderland. Neth.; 13 km W. of Arnhem; paper mnfs.; p. (1968) 32,815.

Rennes, c., cap. of Ille-et-Vilaine dep., France; only major inland t. of Brittany, in fertile agr. basin; univ., comm. ctr.; cars, engin.; p. (1968) 180,943 (c.), 192,782 (met. a.).

Reno, lgst. t. of Nevada, USA; univ.; st. agr. college; famous for easy divorce procedure and gambling; p. (1970) 72,121 (t.), 119,965 (met. a.).

Repton, t., South Derbyshire, Eng.; famous public school in priory; former Saxon cap. of Mercia; p. (1971) 32,667 (dist.).

Resende, t., Rio de Janeiro st., Brazil; chemicals, rly. junc.; univ.; p. (est. 1968) 64,950.

Resht. See Rasht.

Resina, t., S. Italy; on Bay of Naples at W. foot of Vesuvius; nr. site of anc. Herculaneum; resort; p. (est. 1968) 51,124.

Resistencia, t., cap. of Chaco terr., Argentina; served by R. pt. of Barranqueras on R. Paraná; tr. in cattle, timber, cotton; agr. processing; p. (1970) 142,736 (met. a.).

Resita, t., Banat region, Romania; developing steel inds. based on local iron ore; heavy engin.; p. (1968) 58,679.

Restormel, l. gov. dist., Cornwall, Eng.; inc. N. and S. cst. and ts. of Newquay and St. Austell; p. (est. 1976) 75,300.

Retalhuleu, t., cap. of R. dep., Guatemala; comm. ctr. for coffee, sugar; p. (est. 1964) 36,919.

Réunion (Ile de Bourbon), I., overseas terr. of France; in Indian Oc., between Mauritius and Malagasy Rep.; volcanic I.; impt. sugar producer; cap. St. Denis; a. 2,512 km²; p. (1969) 430,000.

Reus, t., Tarragona, prov., Spain; textiles; agr. tr.; p. (1970) 59,095.

Reuss, R., Switzerland; flows N. from the St. Gotthard Pass through L. Lucerne, joining Aare R. nr. Brugg; 157 km long.

Reutlingen, t., Baden-Württemberg, W. Germany; S. of Stuttgart; textiles, metals, machin., leather; p. (est. 1969) 77,034.

Reval. See Tallin.

Revelstoke, t., B.C., Canada; rly. junc.; in timber producing a.; ctr. for R. Nat. Park; p. (1966) 4,791.

Revillagigedo Islands, archipelago, Pac. Oc., off S.W. Mexico; ch. Is., Socorro, San Benedicto (volcano suddenly arose on I. 1952).

Reykjavik, c., cap. of Iceland; on S.W. cst.; impt. fish. pt.; fish exp. and processing; water piped from geysers; airport; univ.; 2 caths.; p. (est. 1969) 81,288 (c.).

Rezayeh, c., Iran; cap. of W. Azerbaijan prov.; comm. ctr. of agr. region; p. (1966) 110,749.

Rheidol, R., Dyfed, Wales; flows from Plynlimmon in deeply incised valley (Devil's Bridge) to Aberystwyth; hydroelec. power; 38 km long.

Rheine, t., N. Rhine–Westphalia, W. Germany; on R. Ems; textiles, machin.; p. (est. 1969) 51,028.

Rheingau, dist., W. Germany; famous wine a. on right bank of Rhine from Biebrich to Assmanshausen.

Rheinhausen, t., Rhine–Westphalia, W. Germany; on left bank of Rhine opposite Duisburg; coal mng., iron, textiles; p. (est. 1969) 71,740.

Rheydt, t., N. Rhine–Westphalia, W. Germany;

twin c. of adjacent Mönchengladbach; textiles, machin.; p. (est. 1969) 100,300.

Rhin (Bas), dep., N.E. France; cap. Strasbourg;
a. 4,786 km²; p. (1968) 827,367.

Rhine, R., rises in Switzerland, can. Grisons, passes
through L. Constance, skirts Baden, traverses
Hesse, Rhineland, and the Neth., flowing to N.
Sea by two arms, Oude Rijn and the Waal (the
latter discharging finally by the Maas); famous
for its beauty, especially between Bonn and
Bingen; ch. falls at Schaffhausen; once a
natural barrier between E. and W. Europe,
spanned by 30 rly. bridges; linked to Rhône by
1985 and only 105 km incomplete of Rhine-
Danube canal; very polluted; 1,280 km long.

Rhine-Hern, canal, W. Germany; impt. Ruhr
waterway, part of Mitelland Canal; 38 km long.

**Rhineland Palatinate (Rheinland-Pfalz), Land, W.
Germany;** borders France, Luxembourg and
Belgium; drained by Rhine and Moselle, inc.
Hunsrück and Eiger mtns.; arable agr. in
Rhine valley; vineyards; cap. Mainz; a.
19,852 km; p. (1970) 3,684,000.

Rhode Island, st., New England, USA; washed
by Atl. Oc., surrounded by Mass. and Conn.;
divided by Narragansett Bay, with many
Is. lgst. being that from which the st. takes
its name; smallest and most densely populated
st.; famous for poultry; major ind. textiles;
cap. Providence; a. 3,144 km²; p. (1970)
922,461.

Rhodes (Rhodos), I., Dodecanese Is.; off S.W. cst.,
Anatolia, belonging to Greece; cap. R.; p. c.
60,000.

Rhodes, cap. of I. of Rhodes, Greece; on N.E.
cst.; picturesque; p. (1971) 32,019.

Rhodesia (Zimbabwe), Central Africa; former
Brit. col.; illegal rep. since 1965; landlocked
st.; much of land high veld above 900 m,
covered in savannah; agr., maize, cattle and
tobacco (main exp.); mng. also impt.; Wankie
coal mine lgst. in world; also asbestos, chrome
and copper; power from Kariba dam encourages
lt. inds.; cap. Salisbury; a. 389,329 km²; p.
(est. 1970) 5,310,000 (5,050,000 Africans).

Rhodope Mtns. *See* Rodopi Mtns.

Rhondda, t., l. gov. dist., Mid Glamorgan, Wales;
in narrow R. valley; coal-mng. ctr.; lt. inds.
introduced since 1930s depression; picturesque
a. in upper R. valley; p. (est. 1976) 85,400.

Rhône, dep., S.E. France; drained by R. Rhône,
and its trib. R. Saône, which unite at Lyons;
agr. grain, potatoes, wine; vine-growing, many
mnfs., silks, textiles; cap. Lyons; a. 2,859 km²;
p. (1968) 1,325,611.

Rhône, R., Switzerland and France; rises in
Rhône glacier of St. Gotthard mtn. gr., and
flows through L. of Geneva and E. France to
G. of Lyons in Mediterranean; power stas. at
Sion and Geneva; canals, dams, locks and
power stas. form part of Fr. Rhône Valley
project (1937-72); linked to Rhine by 1985; 811
km long.

Rhône-Saône Corridor, routeway, France; impt.
transport artery using Rhône, Saône R. valleys
as a means for linking Paris, Lorraine and
Rhine rift valley with Mediterranean cst.; rlys.,
roads, with major pt. of Marseilles serving the
S. terminus.

Rhuddlan, l. gov. dist., Clwyd, Eng.; cstl. a. of
Rhyl, Prestatyn and St. Asaph; p. (est.) 49,900.

Rhyl, t., Rhuddlan, Clwyd, N. Wales; at entrance
Vale of Clwyd; resort developed from sm. fishing v.; serves Lancs. conurbs.; p. (1971) 21,715.

Rhymney, t., Mid Glamorgan, Wales; on R.
Rhymney, E. of Merthyr Tydfil; former colly.
and iron founding ctr.; engin.; p. (1971) 8,051.

**Rhymney Valley, l. gov. dist., Mid Glamorgan,
Wales;** based on Rhymney and inc. Caerphilly,
Bedwas and Gelligaer; p. (est. 1976) 106,000.

Ribble, R., North Yorks., Lancs., Eng.; rises in
Pennines, flows W. to Irish Sea nr. pt. of
Preston; 120 km long.

Ribble Valley, l. gov. dist., N. Lancs., Eng.; inc.
Forest of Bowland and ts. of Clitheroe and Longridge; p. (est. 1976) 53,300.

Ribe, mkt. t., Jutland, S. Denmark; admin. ctr.
of R. prov.; impt. mediaeval c.; Romanesque
cath.; many fine bldgs.; p. (est. 1970) 8,224.

Ribeirão Prêto, t., São Paulo st., Brazil; mkt. in
rich agr. a., coffee, cotton, sugar; p. (1970)
190,897.

Richard's Bay, Natal, S. Africa; new pt. to supplement congested Durban; on natural harbour;
silting problem but designed for bulk carriers;
plans to attract ass. industl. development.

Richborough, pt., Kent, Eng.; at mouth of R.
Stour; Caesar's ch. pt., Roman remains; pt.
has been privately redeveloped; chemicals.

Richmond, t., North Yorks., Eng.; at E. foot of
Pennines on R. Swale; mkt. t., agr. tr.; 14th
cent. grammar school; Norman cas.; now as
Richmondshire forms l. gov. dist. with surrounding a. of Aysgarth and Leyburn; p. (est. 1976)
45,700.

Richmond, c., Cal., USA; deepwater pt.; oil
refining; car assembly, chemicals, electronics;
p. (1970) 79,043.

Richmond, c., cap. of Va., USA; on falls on R.
James; pt. at head of navigation; financial,
and tr. ctr.; tobacco inds., and mkt.; chemicals,
iron and steel; p. (1970) 248,074 (c.), 515,586
(met. a.).

**Richmond-upon-Thames, outer bor., Greater
London, Eng.;** inc. Barnes, Richmond and
Twickenham; industl. and residtl.; beautiful
park and riverside scenery; p. (est. 1976)
166,800. *See also* Kew.

Rickmansworth, t., Three Rivers, Herts., Eng.;
residtl. sub of London; p. (1971) 29,510.

Rideau Canal, Ont., Canada; from Ottawa R. at
Ottawa to Kingston on L. Ontario; 211 km
long.

Riesa, t., Dresden, E. Germany; R. pt. on Elbe
R. nr. Meissen; p. (est. 1970) 49,746.

**Riesengebirge, mtn. range. between Silesia
(Poland) and Bohemia (ČSSR);** highest peak
Schneekoppe (Czech Snežka, Polish Sniezka),
1,604 m.

Rieti, Latium, Italy; an anc. Sabine c. with
mediaeval townscape, in fertile Apennine
basin; route ctr. and cap. of R. prov.; chemicals, sugar refinery, textiles; p. (1969) 39,108.

Riff or Rif, mtns., Morocco, N.W. Africa; extend
along N. African cst. for 320 km from Straits
of Gibraltar; inaccessible and economically
unattractive; terr. of semi-nomadic tribes; rise
to over 2,100 m in many places.

Riga, cap. of Latvian SSR, USSR; Baltic pt.;
exp. wheat, flax, hemp, dairy produce; industl.
ctr., diesel rly. engin., furniture; univ.; local
bathing beaches; p. (1970) 733,000.

Rigi, mtn., nr. L. Lucerne, Switzerland; viewpoint reached by rack and pinion rly.; 1,801 m.

Rijeka-Susak, c., Croatia, Yugoslavia; formerly
Fiume, ceded to Yugoslavia by Italy after
second world war; rival pt. to Trieste on
Adriatic Sea; oil refining, shipbldg., tobacco,
chemicals; hydroelectric power; p. (est. 1971)
133,000.

Rimac, R., Lima dep., Peru; rises in W. cordillera
of Andes and flows W. to Pac. Oc.; provides
water for irrigation and for c. of Lima; 120 km
long.

Rimini, c., Emilia-Romagna, Italy; on Adriatic
cst. at junc. of Via Emilia and Via Flamina;
mkt. for fertile agr. a.; sm. inds.; bathing
resort; p. (est. 1969) 115,573.

Ringerike, t., Buskerud, Norway; new t. 40 km
N.W. of Oslo and inc. former t. of Hönefoss;
p. (est. 1970) 28,828.

Riobamba, t., Chimborazo, Ecuador; on R. St.
Juan; woollens, cotton gds., cement, ceramics;
Inca palace ruins; p. (1966) 61,393.

**Rio Branco, R., flows c. 560 km from Guiana High-
lands through Brazil to join Rio Negro.

Rio Branco, t., cap. of Acre st., Brazil; p. (est.
1968) 70,730.

Rio Cuarto, t., Cordoba prov., Argentina; agr.
ctr.; p. (1960) 70,000.

Rio de Janeiro, c., spt., S.E. Brazil; cap. of
Guanabara st., on G. Bay, Atl. Oc.; former
fed. cap.; beautiful natural harbour, many
fine bldgs., Sugar Loaf mtn., Copacabana
beach; flourishing tr. and inds.; mnfs. inc.
textiles, foodstuffs, pharmaceutics, china, sheet
glass; oil refining; p. (1970) 4,252,009.

Rio de Janeiro, st., S.E. Brazil; on Atl. Oc.;
consists of cst. plain, central Sero do Mar
escarpment, fertile Paraíba R. basin in W.;
coffee, sugar, fruit; cst. of heavy ind.; cement,
textiles, sugar refineries at Campos, steel wks.
at Volta Redonda; cap. Niterói; a. 42,735 km²;
p. (est. 1968) 4,505,938.

Rio Grande, headstream of R. Paraná., Brazil; Furnas dam, Estreito dam for hydroelec. power; 1,040 km long.

Rio Grande, R., flows from st. of Col. through N.M. to G. of Mexico; forms bdy. between Texas, USA and Mexico; Elephant Butte, Caballo, and Falcon multi-purpose dams; known also as Rio Grande do Norte and Rio Bravo; c. 3,016 km long.

Rio Grande do Norte, st., N.E. Brazil; cst. plain rising to S. plateau; climate semi-arid; cotton, sugar, salt, scheelite; cap. Natal; a. 53,038 km²; p. (est. 1968) 1,291,195.

Rio Grande do Sul, st., S. Brazil; grassy plains, rolling plateaux; cool climate; stock-raising, meat-processing, wheat, wine, wool; lge coal deposits at São Jeronimo; cap. Pôrto Alegre; a. 267,684 km²; p. (est. 1968) 6,560,504.

Rioja, region, N. Spain; upper Ebro valley; famous for wines and orange groves; ch. ctr. Logroño.

Riom, t., Puy-de-Dôme dep., France; former cap. of Auvergne; old bldgs. built of lava; p. (1968) 15,467.

Rio Muni, terr., Equatorial Guinea; former Spanish terr., on cst. between Cameroon and Gabon, inc. offshore Is. of Corisco, Elobey Grande, Elobey Chico; with Marcias Nguema forms Equatorial Guinea; equatorial forest; exp. tree prods. of cacao, coffee, hardwoods; ch. t. Bata; a. 26,003 km²; p. (1968) 183,000.

Rion, R., Georgian SSR, USSR; flows from Caucasus to Black Sea; lower half navigable; hydroelec. sta. at Kutaisi. (In Greek mythology the R. Phasis of the Argonauts.)

Rio Negro, prov., Argentina; in N. Patagonia; irrigated agr. in R. valley, fruits, grain crops; elsewhere stock-raising; cap. Viedma; a. 201,010 km²; p. (1970) 193,848.

Rio Negro, dep., Uruguay; livestock fattening from N. Uruguay; grain crops; ch. t. and cap. Fray Bentos; a. 8,466 km²; p. (est. 1969) 48,700.

Rio Tinto, t., Spain; at W. end of Sierra Morena 64 km N.E. of Huelva; major world ctr. of copper production.

Riouw-Lingga Archipelago, I. gr., Indonesia; S. of Malaya; Bintan lgst. I. where bauxite mng.; pepper and rubber cultivation; a. 5,905 km²; p. (1961) 278,966.

Ripley, mkt. t., Amber Valley, Derbys., Eng.; 11 km N.E. of Derby; coal, iron, heavy engin., bricks, agr. implements; p. (1971) 17,825.

Ripon, c. North Yorks., Eng.; on R. Ure; cath.; old mkt. square; old custom of wakeman; tourism; p. (1971) 10,987.

Ripponden, t., Calderdale, West Yorks., Eng.; nr. Halifax; p. (1971) 4,782.

Risca, t., Gwent, Wales; on R. Ebbw; former coal-mng. dist.; limestone quarrying; bricks, plastics; p. (1971) 15,799.

Risdon, t., Tasmania, Australia; oldest settlement in Tasmania, opposite Hobart; electrometallurgy.

Rishton, t., Hyndburn, Lancs., Eng.; at N. foot of Rossendale Fells, 6 km N.E. of Blackburn; p. (1971) 6,010.

Rive-de-Gier, t., Loire dep., France; on R. Gier, nr. Lyons; coal mng., iron and steel, glass; p. (1968) 16,855.

Rivera, dep., Uruguay; on Brazilian border; noted for cattle and sheep ranches; cap. R.; a. 9,824 km²; p. (est. 1969) 80,700.

Rivera, t., cap. of R. dep., Uruguay; on Brazilian frontier opposite Santa Ana; agr. mkt.; p. (1964) 40,000.

Riverina, pastoral cty., N.S.W., Australia; between Lachlan-Murrumbidgee and Murray Rs.; sheep, agr. with irrigation; gold, coal; ch. ts., Wagga Wagga, Albury; a. 68,894 km².

River Rouge, t., Mich., USA; ctr. of Ford car mnf.; many heavy inds.; rapidly growing t. p. (1970) 15,947.

Riverside, t., Cal., USA; ctr. for citrus fruit packing and tr.; resort; p. (1971) 139,217.

Riviera, the belt of cst. between the Alps and the Mediterranean from Spezia to Hyères, France and Italy; picturesque scenery, sheltered, mild climate; fashionable health resorts.

Riyadh, t., cap. of Saudi Arabia; 368 km inland from Persian G.; palace; univ.; route and tr. ctr., linked by rail with pt. of Zahran; p. (est. 1965) 225,000.

Rizaiyeh (Urmia), c., cap. of Azerbaijan prov.. Iran; nr. L. Urmia; comm. ctr.; birthplace of Zoroaster; p. (1966) 110,749.

Rizal, prov., central Luzon, Philippines; rapidly growing prov. in fertile Central Plain; new inds. developing; cap. Pasig; a. 2,049 km²; p. (1970) 2,781,081.

Rize, t., Turkey; nr. Trabzon, on Black Sea; ctr. of Turkish tea inds.; p. (1965) 27,069.

Road Town, spt., Tortola; cap. of the Brit. Virgin Is.; tr. in fish, poultry; p. (1960) 900.

Roanne, t., Loire dep., France; on R. Loire; château ruins; textiles; p. (1968) 54,748.

Roanoke, R., Va., and N.C., USA; flows into Albemarle Sound; hydroelec. power; 656 km long.

Roanoke, c., S.W. Va., USA; between Blue Ridge and Allegheny mtns.; rly. junc.; engin. p. (1970) 90,955 (c.), 179,352 (met. a.).

Roanoke I., off cst. N.C., USA; attempted settlement of colony by Raleigh.

Roaring Creek, Belize, Central America; site of new cap. 80 km inland, at junc. of W. highway with Hummingbird highway.

Robben I., at entrance of Table Bay, Cape Prov., S. Africa; penal settlement and former leper colony.

Robin Hood's Bay, v., North Yorks., Eng.; picturesque site in inlet; tourism, fishing.

Robson, Mt., Canada; on B.C. and Alberta border; alt. 3,956 m; in Nat. Park.

Rocha, dep., Uruguay; borders Atl. Oc.; a. of cattle and sheep rearing; cap. R.; a. 11,085 km²; p. (est. 1969) 57,800.

Rochdale, t., met. dist., Gtr. Manchester, Eng.; at S. foot of Rossendale Fells, on R. Roch; textiles, engin., asbestos; co-operative movement started here 1844; p. (est. 1976) 210,200.

Rochefort, t., Charente-Maritime dep., France; fishing pt.; former impt. naval base; p. (1968) 34,780.

Rochelle, La, t., cap. of Charente-Maritime dep., France; on Bay of Biscay; fishing pt.; shipbldg.; pt. tr. declining; p. (1968) 75,498.

Rochester, c., Medway, Kent, Eng.; on R. Medway, adjoining Chatham; cath., cas.; aeronautical, elec. and mechanical engin., paint, varnish, cement; p. (1971) 55,460.

Rochester, t., Minn., USA; famous for Mayo clinic, and Mayo medical research ctr.; p. (1970) 53,776.

Rochester, c., N.Y., USA; on Genesee R.; univ.; cameras, films, optical instruments, thermometers, electronic equipment; hydroelec. power; p. (1970) 293,695 (c.), 875,636 (met. a.).

Roche-sur-Yon, La, t., cap. of Vendée dep., France; on R. Yon; built by Napoleon I; p. (1968) 38,249.

Rochford, l. gov. dist., Essex, Eng.; cstl. a. inc. Rochford and Rayleigh; p. (est. 1976) 69,500.

Rock, R., Wis., Ill., USA; formerly home of native Indians; focus of white settlement since 1830; 456 km long.

Rockall, sm. I., Atl. Oc.; lies 320 km W. of Outer Hebrides; forms hgst. part of submarine bank which forms gd. fishing-ground; uninhabited; annexed by Britain 1955; formally incorporated into Inverness-shire (1972) to ensure control of suspected oil and natural gas deposits; rock samples aged 1,000 million years place it with some Canadian rocks.

Rockall Deep, submarine trench, N. Atl. Oc.; between N.W. Ireland and Rockall I.; suspected oil and natural gas reserves.

Rockford, c., Ill., USA; serves agr. dist.; agr. machin., machin. tools; p. (1970) 144,707 (c.), 269,829 (met. a.).

Rockhampton, t., pt., Queensland, Australia; on R. Fitzroy; comm. cap. of central Queensland; meat-preserving, fruit-canning; cotton-ginning; rly. wks.; p. (1972) 48,188.

Rock Island, c., Ill., USA; on R. Mississippi; former site of US arsenal; agr. machin., timber and agr. processing; p. (est. 1969) 52,000.

Rocky Mtns., vast mtn. chain, N. America; extend from Alaska, through Canada, USA to Mexico; made up of several parallel ranges separated by intermontane basins and plateaux; barrier to spread of settlers to W. cst. in 19th cent.; climatic barrier; extensive snow and glacier fields in N.; dry, desert landscapes in S.; many Nat. Parks; sparse p.; hydroelectric power; hgst. peak Mt. Logan (6,054 m); length 5,120 km.

Rodez, t., cap. of Aveyron dep., France; on R. Aveyron; cath.; woollens; p. (1968) 23,328.

Rodopi (Rhodope) Mtns., range S. Bulgaria; rise to 3,100 m.

Rodosto. See Tekirdag.

Rodriguez, I., Brit. dependency of Mauritius, Indian Oc.; 560 km N.E. of Mauritius; mainly agr. and fishing; cap. Port Mathurin; a. 109 km²; p. (est. 1968) 20,000.

Roermond, t., Limburg prov., Neth.; on R. Maas; minster; textiles; p. (1968) 37,011.

Roeselare. t.. W. Flanders. Belgium; on R. Lys, nr. Kortrijk, textile ctr.; p. (1968) 40,091.

Rogerstone, t., Gwent, Wales; on R. Ebbw; lge. aluminium wks.

Rohtak, t., Haryana, India; N.W. of Delhi; p. (1971) 124,755.

Roissy-en-France; 26 km N.E. of Paris, France; site of new Charles de Gaulle airpt.

Roman, t., Romania; on R. Moldava; cath.; agr. processing; p. (est. 1970) 43,188.

Romania (Rumania), Socialist Rep. of, S.E. Europe; bounded by USSR, Hungary, Yugoslavia, Bulgaria, and Black Sea; Carpathian mtn. arc., Transylvanian Alps, wide Walachian plain, Moldavian plateau; drained by Danube and its tribs.; climate predominantly continental with cold winters and hot summers; since second world war transformation of economy from agr. to industl. basis, although agr. still impt., contributing many exps.. especially timber, wine, fruit; major pt. Constanza on Black Sea; oilfields at Ploiesti; cap. Bucharest; ch. tr. partners USSR and E. Europe; Danube used for navigation; Iron Gates power and navigation system being constructed in co-operation with Yugoslavia; tourism from W. Europe and N. America encouraged; a. 237,428 km²; p. (1970) 20,040,000.

Rome (Roma), cap of Italy, and of Latium and Rome prov.; on R. Tiber, 24 km from sea; in Roman legend founded by Romulus 753 B.C.; once cap. of anc. Roman empire; inc. Vatican c., ctr. of Roman Catholic Church; situated on original " seven hills," and along the R.; leading cultural ctr.; St. Peter's church, Colosseum, Pantheon; univ.; admin. ctr.; tourism; created cap. of United Italy 1871; p. (est. 1970) 2,778,872.

Romford. See Havering.

Romney Marsh, coastal marsh, Shepway, Kent, Eng.; formed by blocking of R. Rother by shingle spit of Dungeness which extends from Rye to Hythe; largely drained; pastures for special Romney Marsh breed of sheep; a. 129 km².

Romsey, t., Test Valley, Hants., Eng.; on R. Test, 14 km N.W. of Southampton; mkt. ctr.; Norman abbey; p. (1971) 10,057.

Ronaldshay, North, most N. of Orkney Is., Scot.; p. (1971) 134.

Ronaldshay, South, most N. of Orkney Is. Scot.; p. (1971) 991.

Roncesvalles. mtn. pass in Pyrenees, Navarre, Spain; 32 km N.E. of Pamplona; defeat and death of Roland 778.

Ronda, t., Málaga, Spain; in Andalusia; anc. Moorish t., divided by deep gorge crossed by bridge; p. (1970) 30,080.

Rondônia, fed. terr., Brazil; on Bolivian border; forest covered: forest prods.; nomadic Indian tribes; cap. Pôrto Velho; a. 243,071 km²; p. (est. 1968) 116,233.

Rønne, t., Denmark; cap. of Bornholm I., fish. pt.; shipyards, ceramics; p. (est. 1970) 12,440.

Ronse (Renaix), t., Belgium; nr. Ghent; textile ctr.; p. (1968) 25,255.

Roodepoort-Maraisburg, t. Transvaal, S. Africa; ctr. Witwatersrand goldfields; p. (1970) 114,191.

Roosendaal, t., S.W. of N. Brabant, Neth., sugar-refining; p. (1968) 45,038.

Roosevelt Dam (1903–11), Arizona, USA; on R. Salt in canyon E. of Phoenix on edge of Col. plateau; used for irrigation and hydroelectric power; part of Salt river project.

Roquefort-sur-Soulzon, t.. S.E. Aveyron, France; caves in limestone cliffs used for ripening cheese; p. (1968) 1,349.

Roraima, mtn., at junc. of boundaries of Brazil, Guyana, and Venezuela; 2,852 m, hgst point of Guiana Highlands.

Roraima (Rio Branco), fed. terr., Brazil; under-developed rain forest; cap. Boa Vista; a. 214,320 km²; p. (est. 1968) 41,344.

Rosa, Monte, Pennine Alps, Swiss-Italian border; alt. 4,637 m.

Rosario, t., Santa Fé, Argentina; second t. of rep.; R. pt. on Paraná R.; agr.-processing, iron and steel, lt. inds.; univ., cath.; p. (1970) 810,840 (met. a.).

Roscommon, co. t., Roscommon, R.o.I.; mkt.; cas., priory; p. (1966) 1,659.

Roscommon, inland co., Connaught, R.o.I.; extensive peat bog and Ls.; pastoral agr., cap. R.; a. 2,458 km²; p. (1966) 56,130.

Rosetta (Rashid), t., Lower Egypt; nr. Rosetta mouth of Nile; Rosetta stone found nearby gave key to Egyptian hieroglyphs; p. (1966) 36,700.

Roskilde, t., spt., Sjaelland, Denmark; former cap.; cath. contains tombs of kings; admin. ctr. of R. prov.; p. (est. 1970) 39,984.

Ross and Cromarty, former co., l. gov. dist. Highland Reg.; Scot.; extends from N. Sea to Atl. Oc.; most of a. over 300 m, lake-covered; cattle breeding, fishing, tourism; a. 4,999 km²; p. (1971) 34,805.

Rossendale Fells (or Forest), upland, S.E. Lancs./Gtr. Manchester, Eng.; extension of Pennines between Rs. Mersey and Ribble; millstone grit moorland used for reservoirs; alt. mainly above 360 m; now forms l. gov. dist. in Lancs. inc. ts. of Haslingden, Rawtenstall, Bacup and Whitworth; p. (est. 1976) 62,400.

Ross Dependency, Antarctica; N.Z. sector; inlet of Ross Sea; a. 414,400 km²; p. (1961) 198.

Rosslare, spt., Wexford, R.o.I.; on extreme S.E. of Ireland; steamer connections to Fishguard (Wales).

Ross-on-Wye, t., South Herefordshire, Hereford and Worcs., Eng.; mkt., tourism; p. (1971) 6,399.

Ross Sea, sea extending to 85° S. in Antarctic.

Rostock, c., cap. of R. dist., E. Germany; pt. nr. Baltic cst., outport of Warnemünde; shipbldg., fish-processing, chemicals; univ.; mediaeval t.; p. (est. 1969) 193,699.

Rostov, c., RSFSR; pt. on R. Don, nr. Azov Sea (Black Sea); one of Russia's finest and oldest cs.; ctr. of agr. dist.; grain mkt.; agr.-processing; univ.; p. (1970) 789,000.

Rosyth, t., Dunfermline, Scot.; naval dockyard.

Rothamsted. v., Herts., Eng.; in Chiltern Hills, S. of Harpenden; famous agr. research sta.

Rother, l. gov. dist., East Sussex, Eng.; rural a. inc. Rye, Bexhill and Battle; p. (est. 1976) 74,300.

Rother, R., Derbys. and South Yorks., Eng.; flows to R. Don at Rotherham; 34 km long.

Rother, R., East Sussex and Kent, Eng.; rises in the Weald, flows S.E. into English Channel at Rye; 50 km long.

Rotherham, t., met. dist., South Yorks., Eng.; on R. Don, 6 km N.E. of Sheffield; iron, steel, wire, springs, glass; p. (est. 1976) 249,400 (dist.).

Rothes, burgh, Moray, Scot.; on R. Spey 19 km S.E. of Elgin; p. (1971) 1,204.

Rothesay, royal burgh, Argyll and Bute., Scot.; on E. cst. of I. of Bute in F. of Clyde; tourism; p. (1971) 6,595.

Rothwell, t., West Yorks., Eng.; on R. Aire, 5 km S.E. of Leeds; coal-mng. ctr., engin.; p. (1971) 28,353.

Rotorua, leading spa of N.Z.; on volcanic plateau, Auckland, N.I.; hot springs; p. (1971) 31,230.

Rotterdam, c., spt., Neth.; Europe's lgst spt., on Nieuwe Maas, part of Rhine-Maas-Scheldt delta; linked to outport Europoort (q.v.) by New Waterway; serves hinterland of Rhine valley and central Europe; processing of imports, especially oil refining and petrochemical inds.; badly damaged in second world war; p. (est. 1969) 692,915 (c.). 1,060,448 (met. a.).

Roubaix, t.. Nord dep.. France; nr. Lille; on Roubaix canal close to Belgian frontier; major textile ctr., especially for woollens; p. (1968) 114,547.

Rouen, c., Seine-Maritime dep., France; gr. R. pt., 125 km up R. Seine; oil refining, textiles, chemicals; cath.; Joan of Arc burned here; birthplace of Corneille and Flaubert; badly damaged in second world war; p. (1968) 120,471 (c.). 369,793 (met. a.).

Rourkela, t., Orissa, India; W. of Jamshedpur; p. (1971) 125,426 (c.), 172,502 (met. a.).

Rousay. Orkney Is., Scot.; p. (1971) 256.

Roussillon, former prov., S. **France**; now dep. of Pyrénées-Orientales; irrigated by many sm. streams; olives, wine, fruit; historical cap. Perpignan.

Rovaniemi, t., **Finland**; on Kemi R.; timber and saw mills; p. (1968) 27,832.

Rovigo, prov., Venetia, **Italy**; part of N. Italian plain extending to Adriatic; impt. agr. dist.; cap. R.; a. 218 km²; p. (1969) 225,161.

Rovigo, t., cap. of R. prov., **Italy**; on R. Adige, cath., cas. ruins, palace; p. (1969) 48,702.

Rovno, c., cap. of R. oblast, Ukrainian SSR, **USSR**; rly. junc.; industl. ctr.; ruins of mediaeval palace; p. (1970) 116,000.

Roxburgh, former co., S. **Scot.**; sheeprearing hilly cty. with wool-based inds.; now forms l. gov. dist. in Borders Reg.; a. 1,588 km²; p. (1971) 35,865.

Royal Oak, t., Mich., **USA**; residtl.; Detroit zoological park here; p. (1970) 86,238.

Royston, mkt. t., North Herts., **Eng.**; at N. foot of E. Anglian Heights, 11 km N.E. of Baldock; p. (1971) 8,272.

Royton, t., Gtr. Manchester, **Eng.**; 6 km N.E. of Manchester; textiles; p. (1971) 20,319.

Ruanda-Urundi. *See* Rwanda and Burundi.

Ruapehu, highest mtn., N.I., **N.Z.**; volcanic peak at S. extremity of central volcanic dist.; alt. 2,798 m.

Rubicon, R., central **Italy**; flows to Adriatic; crossed by Julius Caesar and his armies 49 B.C.; has been identified with the Fiumicino or the Uso. There is also a R. Rubicon (It. Rubico) a few m. N. of Rimini and S. of Cervia.

Rubtsovsk, t., W. Siberia, **RSFSR**; agr. engin.; p. (1970) 145,000.

Ruby Mines, dist., Mandalay, Upper **Burma**; hilly region of Shan plateau, once famous for rubies.

Ruda Slaska, t., Katowice, **Poland**; coal-mng. ctr.; iron and steel wks.; p. (1970) 142,400.

Rudnyy, t., Kazakh SSR, **USSR**; new t. 48 km S.W. of Kustanay; iron-ore mng. and dressing plant supplying Magnitogorsk; p. (est. 1969) 97,000.

Rudolf, L., N.W. **Kenya**; in Great Rift Valley; a. 9,065 km²; ctr. of semi-arid region.

Rudolph I., N. of Franz Josef Land, Arctic Oc.; Russian naval base; met. sta.

Rudolstadt, t., E. **Germany**; on R. Saale, in former st. of Thuringia; seat of counts of Schwarzburg-Rudolstadt (1584–1918); tourism; porcelain; p. (est. 1970) 31,539.

Rueil Malmaison, sub. of Paris, **France**; château; tomb of the empress Josephine; p. (1968) 62,933.

Rufiji, R., Tanzania; E. Africa; flows to Indian Oc.; 720 km long.

Rufisque, t., Senegal; sm. spt. nr. Dakar; growing industl. ctr. for consumer gds.; p. (est. 1967) 60,000.

Rugby, mkt. t., l. gov. dist., Warwicks, **Eng.**; on R. Avon, 18 km E. of Coventry; famous public school; elec. and gen. engin., motor and aircraft patterns; p. (est. 1976) 87,500 (dist.).

Rugeley, mkt. t., Staffs., **Eng.**; on R. Trent, 14 km S.E. of Stafford; coal, iron, tanning; expanded t.; p. (1971) 22,234.

Rügen, I., E. **Germany**; in Baltic Sea, off Stralsund; ch. t. Bergen; pt. Sassnitz, terminus of train ferry; steamer services to Trelleborg, Sweden.

Ruhr, industl. dist., W. **Germany**; lies to E. of R. Rhine, on either side of R. Ruhr; rich coalfield; impt. iron and steel, heavy engin. inds. based on local coal and iron ore from Luxembourg, Spain, Sweden; water communications to N. Sea along R. Rhine and Dortmund-Ems Canal; ch. ts. Essen, Duisburg, Düsseldorf, Dortmund, Bochum.

Ruhr, R., W. **Germany**; trib. of Rhine; flows S. of Ruhr conurb.; 232 km long.

Rukwa, L., E. **Africa**; between L. Tanganyika and L. Malawi in the rift valley; 48 km by 19 km, a. increasing.

Rum, I., Inner Hebrides, Lochaber, **Scot.**; nature reserve, highland ecology; a. 168 km².

Rumaila, Iraq; oilfield; pipeline links to the Zubair–Fao system.

Rum Jungle, N.T., **Australia**; 112 km S.E. of Darwin; uranium mng.; silver, lead and copper deposits.

Runcorn, t., Halton, Cheshire, **Eng.**; on S. side of Mersey estuary; new t. (1964); chemicals; pipeline carrying petrochemical feedstocks from Teesside; new Runcorn–Widnes bridge over Mersey and Manchester Ship Canal opened 1961 (lgst. span arch in Europe); p. of new t. (est. 1970) 48,213.

Rungis, Paris, **France**; site of major new mkt. to replace Les Halles; nr. Orly airpt.

Runnymede, l. gov. dist., Surrey, **Eng.**; comprises Egham and Chertsey; p. (est. 1976) 74,800.

Ruse, t., **Bulgaria**; on R. Danube, opposite Giurgiu in Romania; univ.; Roman t.; agr. processing; p. (1969) 142,894.

Rushcliffe, l. gov. dist., Notts., **Eng.**; a. S.E. of Nottingham inc. West Bridgeford; p. (est. 1976) 89,600.

Rushden, t., East Northants., **Eng.**; 5 km E. of Wellingborough; shoes; p. (1971) 20,156.

Rushmoor, l. gov. dist., Hants., **Eng.**; small a. of Farnborough and Aldershot; p. (est. 1976) 82,400.

Rüsselsheim, t., W. **Germany**; impt. car factory; p. (est. 1969) 55,373.

Russian Soviet Federated Socialist Republic (**RSFSR**), constituent rep., **USSR**; lgst. rep. by a. and p.; economic development; inds. centred on Leningrad and Moscow with new inds. being developed in Urals and Kuznetz basin; extends from Baltic to Pac. Oc. (8,000 km), from Arctic to Caspian Sea (4,000 km); part of N. European plain in W. and Siberian plain in E., separated by Ural mtns.; major Rs. Volga, Don, Ob, Yenisey, Lena, Amur; gr. variety in climate and p. density; major agr. region for wheat, sugar-beet, livestock; vast mineral deposits have aided economic growth; oil around Volga valley; metallic ores from Urals and Black Sea; hydroelectric power from Volga, Yenesey, and Ob Rs.; cap. Moscow; a. 16,838,885 km²; p. (1970) 130,090,000.

Rustavi, t., Georgian SSR, **USSR**; new t. 32 km S.E. Tbilisi; iron and steel; lge. metallurgical plant; p. (est. 1969) 102,000.

Rustenburg, t., Transvaal, S. **Africa**; on N.W. edge of High Veld, 96 km W. of Pretoria; local mkt. for agr. produce; agr.-processing; p. (1970) 52,657.

Rutbah, t., Iraq; on oil pipeline from Iraq to Haifa; impt. ctr. on trans-desert routes.

Rutherglen, royal burgh, Strathclyde Reg., **Scot.**; on R. Clyde, S.E. of Glasgow; chemicals, tubes, paper, wire ropes, bolts; p. (1971) 24,732.

Ruthin, t., Glyndŵr, Clwyd, **Wales**; Vale of Clwyd, 13 km S.E. of Denbigh; p. (1971) 4,331.

Rutland, former Midland co., **Eng.**; sm. co. of 394 km², now part of Leics. and l. gov. dist. based on Oakham; p. (est. 1976) 29,000.

Ruwenzori mtn. range, on **Uganda-Zaïre** border; overlooking W. arm of Gt. Rift Valley, midway between L. Mobutu Seso and L. Idi Amin Dada; hgst. peaks, Mt. Margherita (5,123 m), Mt. Alexandra (5,109 m); lower slopes covered in equatorial rain forest, coffee plantations on middle slopes above 1,500 m.

Rwanda, indep. rep., Central **Africa**; former kingdom of Ruanda, part of UN trust terr. of Ruanda-Urundi under Belgian admin. (until 1962); sm., landlocked st., S. of equator, consisting of upland plateau at 1,200 m; mainly subsistence agr.; coffee (ch. exp.), cotton, pyrethrum, cattle; tin-mng. impt.; little ind.; cap. Kigali; a. 26,338 km²; p. (est. 1969) 3,667,000.

Ryazan, c., cap. of R. oblast, **RSFSR**; on Oka R.; food inds., agr. machin., footwear, chemicals; mediaeval architecture; p. (1970) 351,000.

Rybinsk, c., major R. pt., **RSFSR**; on upper Volga; tr. and shipping ctr. since 16th cent.; site of hydroelectric power sta.; shipbldg., engin.; p. (1970) 218,000.

Rybinsk Sea (**Rybinsk Reservoir**), **RSFSR**; artificial L.; created behind dams on R. Volga and R. Sheksna at Rybinsk; part of scheme to regulate flow of R. Volga and to incorporate it in a vast inland waterway system; opened 1945; a. 3,885 km.

Rybnik, t., Katowice prov., S.W. **Poland**; ctr. of coal-mng. dist.; p. (1970) 43,400.

Rydal Water, L., nr. Ambleside, Cumbria, **Eng.**; adjacent v. contains Rydal Mount, home of Wordsworth.

Ryde, t., Medina, I. of Wight, **Eng.**; on N.E. cst.; yachting ctr. and seaside resort; boat and yacht bldg.; steamer connection across Spithead to Portsmouth; p. (1971) 23,171.

Rye, t., Rother, East Sussex, **Eng.**; at mouth of R. Rother to W. of Dungeness; one of the Cinque pts.; Ypres cas.; tourist ctr.; p. (1971) 4,434.

Ryedale, l. gov. dist., North Yorks., **Eng.**; lge a. inc. Malton, Pickering, Norton, Kirby Moorside and Helmsley; p. (est. 1976) 99,000.

Ryton, t., Tyne and Wear, **Eng.**; on R. Tyne, W. of Newcastle; p. (1971) 14,831.

Ryuku Is., archipelago, between Kyushu I., Japan, and Taiwan; ch. t. Naha on Okinawa I.; following second world war Is. S. of Lat. 30° N. occupied by USA; Amami and Tokara grs. returned to Japan 1953; American military installations on Okinawa withdrawn 1972; lge. Is. mtnous., volcanic; sweet potatoes, sugarcane, pineapples; 3 lge. oil refineries; a. 2,196 km²; p. (1969) 977,000.

Rzeszów, c., cap. of R. prov., S.E. **Poland**; at foot of Carpathian highlands; route ctr.; growing industl. t.; p. (1970) 82,200.

Rzhev, c., **RSFSR**; on Volga R.; rly. ctr. on main line to Moscow; agr. processing; p. (est. 1967) 59,000.

S

Saale, R., **E. Germany**; rises in Fichtelgebirge flows N. through Thuringia to Elbe; attractive, well wooded valley; irrigation; hydroelec. power; 360 km long.

Saalfeld, t., Gera, **E. Germany**; on R. Saale; famous cas., iron-mng.; machin., chocolate; p. (est. 1970) 33,405.

Saarland, *Land*, **W. Germany**; heavy inds. based on lge. coalfields; drained by R. Saar; cap. Saarbrücken; admin. by League of Nations 1919–35, returned to Germany after plebiscite; economic attachment to France after second world war reunited politically with W. Germany 1957; a. 2,567 km²; p. (1970) 1,127,000.

Saarbrücken, c., cap. of Saarland, **W. Germany**; on R. Saar, nr. Fr. border; cas.; rich coalfield; iron and steel wks., textiles, leather, paper, oil refining at Klarenthal nearby; p. (est. 1970) 130,765.

Saaremaa (Osel), I., Baltic Sea; at entrance to G. of Riga, Estonian SSR; low plateau, bleak and barren; ch. t. Kingisepp (Kuressaare); a. 2,720 km².

Saarlouis (Saarlautern), Saarland, **W. Germany**; on R. Saar; coal mng.; wood and metal inds.; founded by Louis XIV; birthplace of Marshal Ney; p. (est. 1967) 36,400.

Sabadell, t., **Spain**; N.W. of Barcelona; textiles, fertilisers, paper; p. (est. 1967) 145,979.

Sabah, **E. Malaysia**; attempted secession 1975; formerly N. Borneo; underdeveloped; tropical forest; forest prods., inc. rubber, the major exp.; main pt. Sandakan; cap. Kota Kinabalu; a. 76,112 km²; p. (est. 1970) 656,000.

Sabahiyah, t., **Kuwait**; new t. being built btween Ahmadi and Fahahil.

Sabara, t., Minas Gerais, **Brazil**; historic c.; museum of gold; p. (est. 1968) 26,464.

Sabine, R., Texas and La., **USA**; flows through S. Lake (an expansion of the R. 29 km long) to G. of Mexico; 936 km long.

Sable I., off S.E. cst. Nova Scotia, **Canada**; sandy I., scene of many shipwrecks.

Sacramento, c., st. cap. Cal., **USA**; on R. Sacramento; shipping and industl. ctr.; rly. wk.-shps., smelting, meat and fruit packing, flour, lumber, metal prods., rocket and missiles ind.; p. (1970) 257,860 (c.), 803,149 (met. a.).

Sacramento R., Cal., **USA**; forms N. section of Central Valley project for irrigation, hydroelectric power and flood control; 624 km long.

Saddleback (Blencathara), mtn., Cumberland, **Eng.**; nr. Keswick; alt. 868 m.

Saddleworth, t., Gtr. Manchester, **Eng.**; in Pennines, 8 km N.E. of Oldham; woollens, paper mkg., engin.; p. (1971) 20,525.

Saffron Walden, mkt. t., Uttlesford, Essex, **Eng.**; on E. Anglian heights; cas., abbey ruins; saffron crocus once cultivated here; p. (1971) 9,945.

Safi, spt., **Morocco**; on Atl. Oc.; linked by rail

to phosphate deposits at Youssoufia; pottery, fish-processing; resort; p. (1971) 129,100 (t.) 194,030 (met. a.).

Saga, c., cap. of S. pref., Kyushu, **Japan**; coalmng. ctr., textiles, ceramics; p. (est. 1971) 148,000.

Saganoseki, t., N.E. Kyushu, **Japan**; on Bungo strait; impt. gold, copper, and silver mines; smelting.

Sagar, t., Karnataka, **India**; nr. Krishna R. valley; p. (1971) 118,574 (t.), 154,785 (met. a.).

Saginaw, c., Mich., **USA**; on R. Saginaw; former fur and lumbering region; coal; beans, sugarbeet; various mnfs.; p. (1970) 90,603 (c.), 217,787 (met. a.).

Saguenay, R., Quebec, **Canada**; trib. of St. Lawrence R.; outlet of L. St. John; used for hydroelec. power; tourism; length c. 176 km.

Sagunto, t., **Spain**; nr. Valencia; integrated steelwks. projected; anc. t., sieged by Hannibal; p. (1970) 47,026.

Sahara, the gr. N. African desert between the Sudan and the Barbary sts., extending from the Atl. to the Nile, inc. Tripoli and Fezzan; a. 16,835,000 km²; numerous oases with ts. and tr. ctrs.; oil pipelines to Algerian and Tunisian csts.; p. (est. 2,500,000), nomadic Arab and Berber tribes.

Saharan Arab Democratic Rep. *See* Western Sahara.

Saharan Atlas, S. range of Atlas mtns. in Algeria; ch. peaks., Jebel Aurès, 2,331 m, J. Aïssa, 2,242 m J. Ksel, 2,011 m.

Saharanpur, c., Uttar Pradesh, N.W. **India**; woodcarving, furniture, agr.-processing inds.; p. (1971) 225,396.

Sahel, region of W. Africa, inc. Chad, Mali, Mauritania, Niger. Senegal and Upper Volta, which suffered severe famine and drought 1972–4.

Saïda (Sidon), t., **Lebanon**; on Mediterranean, S. of Beirut; terminus of oil pipeline from Saudi Arabia; refinery; p. (1963) 22,000.

Saigon. *See* Ho Chi-minh City.

Saimaa, L. system, Finland; a. of water which forms basin of R. Vuoksi; canal connects with G. of Finland and runs partly through Soviet terr.; a. 1,699 km².

Saingdin Falls, Burma; on Kaladan R.; site of new hydroelec. power sta.

St. Abb's Head, rocky promontory, Berwick, Scot.

St. Albans, c., l. gov. dist., Herts., **Eng.**; on N. margin of Vale of St. Albans, 32 km N.W. of London; faces remains of Roman Verulamium across R. Ver; lt. inds., electronics, instrument mkg.; cath.; residtl.; p. (est. 1976) 123,800 (dist.).

St. Amand, t., Cher dep., **France**; on R. Cher; Roman remains; new recreational park.

St. Andrews, royal burgh, North East Fife, Scot.; seaside resort; univ.; famous golf course; p. (1971) 11,630.

St. Anthony, waterfalls, on R. Mississippi; **USA**; predominant factor in site of Minneapolis.

St. Asaph, t., Rhuddlan, Clwyd, N. **Wales**; on R. Clwyd; p. (1971) 11,755 (dist.).

St. Austell with Fowey, mkt. ts., Restormel, Cornwall, **Eng.**; on S. flank of Hensbarrow; ctr. of Cornwall's china clay ind.; p. (1971) 32,252.

St. Barthelemy, Fr. I., **W.I.**; dependency of Guadeloupe; cash crops of sugar, bananas, cacao; cap. Gustavia; p. (1960) 2,079.

St. Bees Head, promontory, 4 km N.W. of St Bees, Cumbria, **Eng.**; freestone quarries, anhydrite.

St. Bernard Pass, Great, on Italian–Swiss bdy., W. Alps; carries main road from W. Switzerland to Plain of Lombardy; 2,477 m a.s.l.; road tunnel (5·6 km) constr. 1958–62 links Cantine de Proz (Valais can., Switzerland) and St. Rhémy (Italy); under tunnel will run projected 416 km pipeline from Genoa to Aigle.

St. Bernard Pass, Little, on French–Italian bdy., W. Alps; links Isere valley with Val d'Aosta; alt. 2,190 m.

St. Boniface, t., Manitoba, **Canada**; sub. of Winnipeg; meat-packing, petroleum prods.; p. (1971) 46,661.

St. Bride's Bay, Dyfed, Wales.

St. Brieuc, t., cap. of Côtes-du-Nord dep., N.W. **France**; sm. fish. pt.; iron and steel wks.; cath.; p. (1968) 54,763.

St. Catharines, c., Ont., **Canada**; on Welland

Ship Canal; mkt. for Niagara fruit-growing region; agr. implements, textile, paper and flour mills, vehicle components; resort; p. (1971) 109,636.

St. Chamond, t., Loire, France; nr. St. Etienne; ribbons, rayon; rly. wks.; coal mng.; p. (1968) 37,723.

St. Clair, L., Canada–USA; part of link between L. Huron and L. Erie; a. 1,191 km².

St. Clair, R., N. America; flows from L. Huron through L. of St. Clair into L. Erie; forms bdy. between Mich. (USA) and Ont. (Canada); impt. link in Gr. Ls. waterway; length 136 km, depth reduced to 6 m.

St. Clair Shores, t., Mich., USA; residtl sub. of Detroit; p. (1970) 88,093.

St. Cloud, W. sub. of Paris, France; fine park; porcelain; p. (1968) 28,560.

St. Cloud, t., Minn., USA; on R. Mississippi; granite quarries; st. college; p. (1970) 36,691.

St.-Cyr-l'Ecole, t., Yvelines, France; once famous for military school founded by Napoleon; bldgs. destroyed second world war.

St. Davids, t., Dyfed, Wales; 24 km S.W. of Fishguard; on site or anc. Minevia; cath., ruins of Bishop Gower's palace (1342); p. 1,595.

St. David's Head, promontory, Dyfed, Wales.

St. Denis, t., N. sub., Paris, France; on R. Seine; abbey, burial place of Fr. kings; chemicals., machin.; p. (1968) 100,060.

St. Denis, spt., cap. of Ile de la Réunion (Fr.), Indian Oc.; p. (1967) 85,444.

St. Dié, t., Vosges, France; on R. Meurthe; cath.; textile ctr., hosiery; p. (1968) 25,117.

St. Dizier, t., Haute-Marne, dep. France; on R. Marne; metallurgy; p. (1968) 39,034.

St. Edmundsbury, l. gov. dist., Suffolk, Eng.; based on Bury St. Edmunds and inc. Haverhill; p. (est. 1976) 81,400.

St. Elias, mtns., Alaska, USA; and Yukon, Canada; inc. Mt. McKinley (5,780 m); source of world's lgst. icefield outside polar regions.

Saintes, t., Charente-Maritime dep., France; cath.; Roman antiquities; suffered in Huguenot wars; agr. implements; earthenware; p. (1968) 26,507.

St. Etienne, t., cap. of Loire dep. France; nr. Lyons; in sm. coal basin on edge of Central Massif; famous for firearms; modern inds. inc. engin., dyes, chemicals, textiles, glass; p. (1968) 213,468 (t.), 331,414 (met. a.).

St. Gall (St. Gallen), t., cap. of can. St. G., Switzerland; founded around Benedictine monastery (7th–8th cent.); embroidered cottons; p. (1969) 80,200.

St. Gall (St. Gallen), can., Switzerland; borders L. Constance, rising to S.; mainly industl.; ch. ind. textiles; cap. St. G.; a. 2,012 km²; p. (1969) 378,000.

St. George's Channel. Brit. Isles, part of Irish Sea, separating Wales from Ireland.

St. George's, t., cap. of Grenada, W.I.; ch. spt.; built around submerged volcanic crater forming St. G. Bay; p. (1970) 7,303.

St. Germain-en-Laye, t., Yvelines, France; on R. Seine; outer sub. of Paris; residtl.; popular resort; birthplace of Debussy; p. (1968) 41,190.

Saint Gotthard, mtn. gr., Alps, S. central Switzerland; crossed by St. G. pass (2,115 m); rly. passes through St. G. tunnel (14·8 km, max. alt. 1,155 m); road tunnel (10·4 km) under pass Göschenen to Airolo projected; motorways linking pass with Zürich, Basle, and Lugano being built.

St. Gowan's Head, promontory, Dyfed Wales.

St. Helena, I., Brit. col., Atl. Oc.; 1,920 km from W. cst. Africa; spt. and only t. Jamestown; Napoleon imprisoned 1815–21, and Boer captives 1900; famous for its wirebird, species of plover peculiar to I.; a. 122 km²; p. (1967) 4,707.

St. Helens, t., met. dist., Merseyside, Eng.; 19 km E. of Liverpool; connected by canal with R. Mersey; coal, iron, alkali; copper smelting, glass, fibreglass, plastics; p. (est. 1976) 194,400 (dist.).

St. Helier, spt., Jersey, Channel Is., Eng.; resort; cas.; tr. in early vegetables; p. (1971) 28,135.

St. Hyacinthe, t., spt., Quebec, Canada; on Yamaska R.; cath.; famous for organs; st. inds.; p. (1966) 23,781.

St. Ives, t., Penwith, Cornwall, Eng.; at entrance to St. Ives Bay; fishing, holiday resort; p. (1971) 9,710.

St. Ives, t., Cambs., Eng.; on R. Ouse, 6 km E. of Huntingdon; borders the Fens; R. Ouse crossed by 16th cent. bridge containing a chapel; p. (1971) 7,130.

St. Jean, t., Quebec, Canada; on Richelieu R.; timber, grain exps.; textiles, sewing machines, p. (1966) 27,784.

St. John, c., spt., N.B., Canada; lgst. c. of N.B.; ice-free pt.; lge. dry docks; rly. terminus; impt. inds. inc. sugar- and oil-refining, paper, textiles; p. (1971) 87,910 (c.), 105,227 (met. a.). [tourism; a.971 km²

St. John, L., Quebec, Canada; on Saguenay R.;

St. John, R., Maine, N.B., Canada, USA; flows to B. of Fundy forming section of international boundary; 720 km long.

St. John's, t., cap. of Antigua, W.I.; pt., airpt.; cath.; ch. comm. ctr. of I.; p. (1963) 13,000.

St. John's, c. spt., cap. of Newfoundland, Canada; on E. cst.; first English settlement in America early 16th cent.; gr. tr. in fish with allied inds.; univ., 2 caths.; p. (1971) 86,290 (c.), 129,304 (met. a.).

St. Johns, R., USA; drains swamps of central Fla., 21 km from Atl. Oc.; 560 km long.

St. John's Wood, residtl. dist., Westminster, London, Eng.; contains Lord's Cricket Ground.

St. Joseph, t., Mich., USA; pt. on L. Mich.; ctr. of fruit-growing a.; resort; p. (1970) 11,042.

St. Joseph, t., Mo., USA; declining pt. on R. Mississippi; agr. tr. and processing; p. (1970) 72,691.

St. Just, t., Penwith, Cornwall, Eng.; nr. Lands End, 10 km W. of Penzance; former tin-mng. ctr.; p. (1971) 3,573.

St. Kilda, rocky i., most W. of the Hebrides, Scot.; 5 km long; bird sanctuary, famous for its wren, a sub-species.

St. Kitts-Nevis, Leeward gr. of Is., W.I.; asst. st. in association with Gt. Britain (Anguilla unilaterally seceded from union 1967); sugar, sea island cotton, molasses; a. 262 km²; cap. Basse-Terre; p. (est. 1967) 58,000.

St. Laurent, t., Quebec, Canada; industl. t. on Montreal I., W. of Montreal; p. (1966) 59,479.

St. Lawrence, G. of, Canada; arm of Atl. Oc., partly enclosed by Newfoundland and Nova Scotia; impt. fisheries.

St. Lawrence I., Alaska, USA; in Bering Sea; 160 km long.

St. Lawrence, R., Canada; major outlet from Gr. Lakes; forms bdy. between USA and Canada; ch. tribs. Ottawa, Richelieu, St. Maurice, Saguenay Rs.; with St. L. Seaway forms a major waterway facing Europe; grain, timber, oil, iron-ore traffic; used for hydro-electric power; total length from source (St. Louis) 3,360 km.

St. Lawrence Seaway, N. America; joint Canada-USA project links head of the Gr. Lakes with Atl. Oc.; providing channel for lge. ocean-going vessels to reach American continent; provides major source of hydroelectric power to industl. a.; opened 1959.

St. Lô, t., cap. of Manche dep., N.W. France; built on rocky hill overlooking R. Vire; cath.; p. (1968) 18,615. [(1962) 7,753.

St. Louis, t., Ile de la Réunion, Indian Oc.; p.

St. Louis, t., Senegal, W. Africa; at mouth of R. Senegal; cath.; former cap.; comm. ctr.; impt. fish. pt.; p. (est. 1969) 75,000.

St. Louis, c., Mo., USA; on R. Mississippi 16 km below confluence of Rs. Mississippi and Missouri; two univs.; impt. rly. and river junc.; mkt. for furs, livestock, grain, farm prod.; banking and fin. ctr.; varied mnfs.; machin., cars, aircraft, leather gds., beer, chemicals; p. (1970) 607,718 (c.), 2,331,016 (met. a.).

St. Lucia I., aut. st. in association with Gt. Britain, Windward Is., W.I.; volcanic, forested, fertile valleys; exp. bananas and other tropical agr. prod.; airpt.; cap. Castries; a. 616 km²; p. (est. 1968) 108,000.

St. Malo, spt., Ile-et-Vilaine dep., N.W. France; on Normandy cst.; cath.; once fortfd.; shipping, fishing, and tourist inds.; p. (1968) 43,722.

St. Martin, I., Leeward Is., W.I.; N. part Fr. dependency of Guadeloupe, S. part belongs to Neth. Antilles; divided since 1648; ch. exp. salt; total p. (est. 1969) 11,000.

St. Marylebone. See Westminster, City of.

St. Mary's I., Scilly Is., Brit. Isles.

St. Maur-des-Fossés, residtl. garden sub. of Paris, Val-de-Marne dep., France; p. (1968) 77,569.

St. Maurice, v., Valais, Switzerland; nr. Martigny; 6th-cent. abbey; once a leading Burgundian t.; p. c. 10,000.

St. Maurice, R., Quebec, Canada; trib. of St. Lawrence R.; used for timber transport and hydroelec. power; 520 km long.

St. Mawes, v., Cornwall, Eng.; on E. cst. of estuary of R. Fal; cas.; holiday resort, fishing.

St. Michael's Mt., castled rock, Cornwall, Eng.; the anc. Ictis; alt. 70 m.

St. Monance, burgh, North East Fife, Scot.; resort; p. (1971) 1,257.

St. Moritz, resort and winter sports ctr., Switzerland; in the Upper Engadine; alt. 1,857 m; p. (1970) 5,699.

St. Nazaire, t., Loire-Atlantique dep., W. France; spt. at mouth of R. Loire, outport for Nantes; growing pt. and industl. ctr.; shipyds., iron and steel, fertilisers, aircraft, oil refining; p. (1968) 64,003 (t.); 110,897 (met. a.).

St. Neots, mkt. t., Cambs. Eng.; on R. Ouse, 16 km N.E. of Bedford; brewing, milling, papermkg.; expanded t.; p. (1971) 15,137.

St. Niklaas, mftg. t., E. Flanders, Belgium; nr. Antwerp; textile ctr., carpets; p. (1968) 48,873.

St. Omer, t., Pas-de-Calais dep., N. France; ctr. of mkt.-gardening a.; textiles, food inds.; cath., abbey ruins; p. (1968) 19,957.

St. Ouen, N. sub. of Paris, Seine-St. Denis dep., France; on R. Seine at base of Butte de Montmarte; metals, chemicals, glues, tanning; p. (1968) 48,886.

St. Pancras. See Camden.

St. Paul, spt., Ile de la Réunion, Indian Oc.; p. (1968) 43,129.

St. Paul, c. cap. of Minn., USA; faces Minneapolis across Mississippi; cath.; univ.; ctr. of agr. dist.; agr. mkt. and processing; car assembly, oil refining, electronics; p. (1970) 308,686 (part of Minneapolis met. a.).

St. Paul, I., Indian Oc.; bare volcanic islet rising to 493 m; part of Fr. Southern and Antarctic Terr.; uninhabited.

St. Peter Port, spt., cap. of Guernsey, Channel Is.; exp. fruit, flowers, vegetables; resort; p. (1971) 16,303.

St. Petersburg, c., Fla., USA; resort on Tampa Bay; p. (1970) 213,189 (part of Tampa met. a.).

St. Pierre, t., Martinique I., Fr. W.I.; utterly destroyed and all inhabitants save one by eruption of Mt. Pelée 1902; tourism.

St. Pierre, t., Réunion, Indian Oc.; sm. artificial harbour; p. (est. 1971) 43,808.

St. Pierre and Miquelon, Fr. dep., consisting of 8 sm. Is. off S. cst. of Newfoundland; a. of St. Pierre gr. 26 km²; a. of Miquelon gr. 215 km²; ch. t. St. Pierre, fisheries; p. of St. P. and M. (1967) 5,235.

St. Pölten, t., Lower Austria; nr. Vienna; founded round an abbey; textiles, machin.; p. (1961) 40,112.

St. Quentin, t., Aisne dep., France; on R. Somme; impt. textile ctr.; p. (1968) 66,161.

St. Raphaël, t., Var dep., S.E. France; resort on Fr. Riviera, S.W. of Cannes; marina.

St. Rémy, t., Bouches-du-Rhône dep., France; Roman antiquities.

St. Thomas, t., Ont., Canada; ctr. of agr. dist.; rly. ctr.; lt. inds.; p. (1971) 25,062.

St. Thomas I., Atl. Oc.; main economic ctr. of USA Virgin Is.; 80 per cent of p. live in pt. of Charlotte Amalie; tourism; p. (est. 1968) 31,867.

St. Thomas I. See São Tomé.

St. Trond, t., Limburg, Belgium; impt. fruit mkt.; p. (est. 1969) 21,364.

St. Tropez, t., Var dep., S.E. France; on Fr. Riviera; popular, expanding tourist resort; marina; p. (1968) 6,151.

St. Vincent, C., S.W. Portugal; Spanish fleet defeated by British 1797.

St. Vincent, Gulf of, lge. inlet. S. Australia; penetrates 160 km inland, max. width 56 km; Pt. Adelaide is on E. side.

St. Vincent, I., aut. st. in association with Gt. Britain; one of Windward gr., W.I.; volcanic; exp. bananas, arrowroot from alluvial soils in S.W. which has majority of p.; subsistence agr. on hill slopes; cap. Kingstown; inc. 5

Is. in Grenadines; a. 389 km²; p. (est. 1967) 85,000.

Sakai, sub. of Osaka, Honshu, Japan; industl. ctr., engin., chemicals, textiles, electricity generation; p. (est. 1971) 622,000.

Sakhalin, I., off cst. of Siberia; with Kuriles forms Sakhalin oblast of RSFSR; herring fisheries, coal, naphtha, alluvial gold, oil, timber, natural gas; oil pipelines connect to Komsomolsk and Khabarovsk refineries; a. c. 63,610 km²; p. (1970) 616,000.

Sakashima Is. See Ryuku.

Sakura-jima, peninsula, S. Kyushu, Japan; former I. joined to mainland by lava flows; famed for fruit and vegetables.

Sala, t., Västmanland, Sweden; silver mine worked for over 400 years, now to limited extent; lime, bricks; p. (1961) 11,015.

Salado, R., N.W. Argentina; impt. Andean trib. of Paraná R.; 800 km long.

Salamanca, t., Guanajuato st., Mexico; oil refining; ammonia plant; natural gas pipeline to Guadalajara.

Salamanca, t., cap. of S. prov., Spain; on R. Tormes; old univ., 2 caths., many convents; p. (1970) 103,740.

Salamis, I., Greece; opposite harbour of Athens; spt. and ch. t. S.; famous naval battle 480 B.C.; p. c. 20,000.

Salar de Uyumi, windswept, dry. salt flat, S.W. Bolivia.

Salavat, t., RSFSR; in Bashkiria, 144 km S. of Ufa; ctr. cf oilfield; glass factory; became t. in 1954; p. (1970) 114,000.

Sala-y-Gomez, barren, uninhabited volcanic I., Pac. Oc.; belonging to Chile, 328 km E.N.E. of Easter I.

Salazar, Mexico; nr. Mexico City; alt. 2,897 m; nuclear reactor for radioisotopes for medical, industl. and agr. purposes.

Salcombe, t., South Hams, S. Devon, Eng.; mkt.; fishing; resort; p. (1971) 2,471.

Saldanha Bay, inlet on W. cst. C. of Good Hope, S. Africa; whaling, fishing, fish-canning at t. of S.B.; p. (1960) 2,195 (t.).

Sale, t., Victoria, Australia; ctr. of lge. agr. and pastoral dist.; food processing, plastics, engin.; p. (1972) 10,404.

Sale, t., Trafford, Gtr. Manchester, Eng.; residtl. sub. of Manchester; p. (1971) 55,623.

Sale or Salch, spt., Fez, Morocco; former pirate headquarters; fishing, fish-processing, carpets; p. (1960) 75,799.

Salekhard, t., R. pt., N.W. Siberia, RSFSR; on R. Ob; fisheries, collecting ctr. for furs; exp. timber; p. c. 22,000.

Salem, t., Tamil Nadu, India; industl. ctr., rly. junc. in picturesque valley; local iron ore, manganese mng.; mineral processing, textiles; p. (1971) 308,716 (t.), 416,440 (met. a.).

Salem, t., Mass., USA; 24 km from Boston; one of oldest New England ts.; many fine bldgs.; textiles, leather prods., machin., electronics; p. (est. 1969) 40,000.

Salem, t., st. cap. Ore., USA; on Willamette R.; univ.; fruit packing, flour milling and canning; p. (1970) 63,309 (t.), 182,569 (met. a.).

Salemi, t., Sicily, Italy; the anc. Halicyæ; famous Norman cas., terracotta vases; p. (est. 1968) 13,778.

Salerno, c., cap. of Salerno prov., in Campania, S. Italy; on G. of S.; fishing pt. and comm. ctr.; machin., textiles, food processing; univ.; Allied landing 1943; p. (1969) 150,677.

Salford, c., met. dist., Gtr. Manchester, Eng.; on R. Irwell, adjoining Manchester; inc. terminal docks of Manchester Ship Canal; varied inds.; p. and industl. decentralization; p. (1971) 130,641; p. (est. 1976) 261,100 (dist.).

Salgótarján, t., N. Hungary; coal mng., agr. machin., tools, glass; p. (1968) 35,000.

Salina, t., Kan., USA; on Smoky Hill R.; univ.; flour milling, cattle mkt., farm implements; p. (1970) 37,714.

Salinas, t., Cal., USA; comm., tr. and processing ctr. for fertile Salinas valley; birthplace of John Steinbeck; p. (1970) 58,265 (t.), 248.831 (met. a.).

Salinas, R., Cal., USA; rises in US Coast Range, flows N.W. into Bay of Monterey, Pac. Oc.; fertile valley floor irrigated to produce hard and stone fruits, mkt. garden produce (especially lettuce), alfalfa; 166 km long.

Salinas-Grandes, Las, gr. salt marsh region, Argentina; provs. Santiago del Estero and Cordoba; dry, no Rs.

Salisbury, t., South Australia; varied light inds.; p. (1971) 56,279.

Salisbury (New Sarum), cath. c., l. gov. dist., Wilts., Eng.; on S. edge of Salisbury Plain at confluence of Rs. Avon and Wily; Old Sarum to N. was the Roman Sorbiodunum and present site represents a move (1220) to a more sheltered and better watered a. in valley; cath. pure Early English with tallest spire in Eng. (123 m); ctr. mediaeval woollen ind.; regional ctr. with engin. and food-processing inds.; p. (est. 1976) 105,300 (dist.).

Salisbury, c., cap. of Rhodesia; admin. and industl. ctr. in agr. region with gold and chrome mines nearby; tr. in agr. prods., inc. tobacco; clothing, furniture, fertilisers, machin.; univ., airways ctr.; p. (est. 1972) 477,000 (met. a.).

Salisbury Plain, Wilts., Eng.; chalk upland, N. of Salisbury; Stonehenge; army training a.; a. 777 km².

Salop (Shropshire), non-met. co., Eng.; on Welsh border, crossed by R. Severn; fine pastoral cty. with hills and woodland, agr. and dairying; industl. activity at co. t. Shrewsbury; a. 3,489 km²; p. (est. 1976) 359,000.

Salpau Selka, Finland; most S. gravel ridge; forested; winter sports.

Salsette I., India; connected by bridge and causeway with Bombay; popular seaside resort at Juhu; a. 624 km².

Salt R., Arizona, USA; rises in Colorado plateau, flows into Gila R. below Phoenix; rich, irrigated fruit growing valley in lower course; many multipurpose schemes in Salt River Valley project; length 384 km. See also Roosevelt Dam.

Salta, c., cap. of Salta prov., Argentina; on R. Salta; picturesque c. with colonial atmosphere, cath.; comm. ctr. for rich agr. a.; p. (1970) 176,130 (met. a.).

Saltash, mkt. t., Caradon, Cornwall, Eng.; on W. side of Tamar estuary; lowest bridging point of Tamar by Brunel's rly. bridge (1859) and toll road bridge; p. (1971) 9,923.

Saltburn and Marks-by-the-Sea, t., Langbaurgh, Cleveland, Eng.; seaside resort; 16 km E. of Middlesbrough; p. (1971) 19,562.

Salcoats, burgh, Cunninghame, Scot.; on Firth of Clyde 3 km S. of Ardrossan; sm. harbour; hosiery; mainly residtl.; p. (1971) 14,904.

Saltillo, c., cap. of Coahuila st., Mexico; comm. industl., and mng. ctr.; p. (1970) 161,114.

Salt Lake City, c., cap. of Utah, USA; nr. Gr. Salt L., H.Q. of Mormonism; temple and univ.; agr. comm. ctr. for irrigated a.; meat packing; p. (1970) 175,280 (c.), 556,896 (met. a.).

Salto, c., cap. of S. dep., Uruguay; on Uruguay R., nr. Concordia (Argentina); rly. and tr. ctr. for agr a.; citrus fruit, grapes, wine; p. (1963) 57,958.

Salton Sea, L., S. Cal., USA; 80 m below sealevel in depression which extends N.W. from head of G. of Cal.; ctr. of inland drainage; a. 699 km². See also Imperial Valley.

Salvador, spt., cap. of Bahia, Brazil; coffee, cocoa, tobacco, hides, castor seed, sisal; oilfield and refinery at Matanipe; p. (1970) 998,258.

Salvador, El, rep., on Pac. cst. of Central America; bounded by Guatemala to W. and Honduras to N. and E.; comprises 14 administrative departments; temperate volcanic uplands, hot humid coastal lowlands; comm. economy mainly agr., especially coffee, also developing comm. fisheries and iron and steel ind.; electric power from dam across Lempa R.; well-developed transport system, inc. Pan-American Highway; pt. at Acajutla and airport at Ilopango; member of Central American Common Market; cap. San Salvador; a. 21,331 km²; p. (est. 1975) 4,100,000.

Salween, R., S.E. Asia; rises in E. Tibet, crosses Yunnan. descending into Burma to empty in G. of Martaban; many rapids; navigable to Moulmein; hydroelec. scheme; 2,880 km long.

Salzach, R., Austria; trib. of R. Inn; 208 km long.

Salzburg, c., cap. of Salzburg prov., Austria; on R. Salzach; cath., cas.; birthplace of Mozart; tourist resort; annual music festival; p. (1968) 120,204.

Salzburg, prov., Austria; adjoins Bavaria and the Tyrol, on N. slope of E. Alps; pastoral agr.; timber and some mineral wealth; hydroelectric power; cap. Salzburg; a. 7,154 km²; p. (1971) 399,000.

Salzgitter, t., Lower Saxony, W. Germany; S.W. of Brunswick; steel, engin., wagon bldg., fertilisers; p. (est. 1969) 117,300.

Salzkammergut, lake dist., Upper Austria; saline baths at Aussee and Ischl; tourist region; stock-raising, forestry.

Samar, I., Philippines; separated from Leyte by narrow strait; mainly forested mtns.; hemp, rice in lowlands; cap. Catbalogan; typhoons; a. 13,080 km²; p. (1970) 997,336.

Samarkand, c., Uzbek SSR, USSR; one of oldest cs. in world, sited in productive oasis on Zeravshan R.; many historical associations and anc. bldgs.; agr. tr. ctr.; food processing; cotton, silk; univ.; p. (1970) 267,000.

Samarra, t., Iraq; on Tigris R., N. of Baghdad; holy c. of Shiite sect; p. c. 10,000.

Sambalpur, t., Orissa, India; on Hirakud reservoir of Mahandi R.; p. (1971) 64,675.

Sambhar, salt lake, Rajasthan, India; exploited on lge. scale; a. 233 km²

Sambre, R., trib. of R. Meuse at Namur; crosses Franco-Belgian coal basin; part of N. Fr.–S. Belgian waterway system; 176 km long.

Samnan, t., N. Iran; in foothills of Elburz mtns.; iron, sulphur ores, petroleum.

Samoa, archipelago, S. Pac. Oc.; volcanic mtns., tropical climate; agr., fishing; comprises (1) American Samoa, a. 197 km²; p. (1970) 27,769; (2) Western Samoa, indep. st., cap. and ch. spt. Apia; a. 2,841 km²; p. (est. 1969) 141,000. See Western Samoa.

Sámos, I., Aegean Sea, off W. cst. Anatolia. belonging to Greece; mtnous., fine climate, fertile soils; wine, tobacco. Med. crops; ch. t. Vathy; a. 466 km²; p. (1971) 41,687 (dep.).

Samothrace, I., Aegean Sea, Greece; barren, mtnous.; sparse p.; goats, grain, olives, sponge fishing; a. 184 km²; p. c. 4,000.

Samsö, I., Kattegat, Denmark; a. 109 km²; p. (est. 1965) 5,852.

Samsun, spt., Trabzon, Turkey; on Black Sea cst.; exp. tobacco, grain, timber, wax, wool, skins, copper gds., antimony; p. (1965) 107,510.

San, R., S.E. Poland; trib. of R. Vistula; bdy. between Poland and Ukraine; navigable in lower course; 442 km long.

Sana'a, c., cap. of Yemen Arab Rep; walled c. at 2,217 m; tr. in silk, cottons, hides, grapes; handicraft inds.; Islamic cultural and educational ctr.; p. (est. 1970) 120,000.

San Andreas Fault, Cal., USA; shearing plate bdy. which extends from G. of Cal. to San Francisco; stress liable to cause sudden sharp earthquake as it did in 1906. See F9.

San Angelo, t., Texas, USA; on R. Concho; cattle, wool, mohair mkt.; dairy produce, petroleum, machine-shop prod.; p. (est. 1969) 67,000.

San Antonio, sm. coastal t., Angola, Africa; at mouth of R. Zaïre; serves as occasional pt. of embarkation for travellers from lower regions of Zaïre.

San Antonio, spt., Chile; nearest pt. for Santiago; holiday resort; agr. prods.; exp. copper; p. (est. 1966) 34,051.

San Antonio, c., most W. point of Cuba.

San Antonio, c., cap. of Bexar co., Texas, USA; in fertile San Antonio valley; serves farming and livestock a.; oil refining, food processing, meat packing; military installations in a.; warm climate attracts winter tourist tr.; Mexican atmosphere; siege of Alamo (1836); p. (1970) 650,188 (c.), 864,014 (met. a.).

San Bernardino, c., Cal., USA; founded and planned by Mormons (1852) rly. ctr.; citrus fruit packing and tr.; p. (1970) 106,676 (c.), 1,122,041 (met. a.).

San Bruno, t., Cal., USA; 16 km S. of San Francisco; site of international airpt.; printing, mainly residtl.; p. (1970) 36,254.

San Carlos, t., Luzon, Philippines; p. (est. 1968) 165,200.

San Cristóbal, c., cap. of Táchira st., Venezuela; at 830 m nr. Colombian bdy.; mng. and comm. ctr.; coffee, cacao, sugar; food-processing, cement; cath.; p. (est. 1970) 156,600.

Sancti Spiritus, t., Las Villas, Cuba; comm. ctr.

in grazing dist.; tr. in sugar, tobacco; agr. processing; p. (est. 1967) 146,450.

Sandakan, t., Sabah, Malaysia; fine natural harbour on N.E. cst.; exp. agr. prods., timber, rubber; sawmilling, fishing; p. (1960) 28,806.

Sanday, I., Barra Is., Orkney, Scot.; flat, many shipwrecks; agr. fishing; p. (1971) 592.

Sandbach, mkt. t., Cheshire, Eng.; 8 km N.E. of Crewe; salt, chemicals, comm. vehicles; p. (1971) 13,303.

Sandefjord, t., Vestfold prov., S.E. Norway; whaling pt. nr. mouth of Oslo Fjord; shipyds., whale-processing; chemicals; p. (est. 1970) 31,723.

Sandhurst, v., Berkshire, Eng.; 16 km S.E. of Reading; Royal Military Academy, National Army Museum.

Sandia, t., N.M., USA; atomic research ctr.

San Diego, c., Cal., USA; first Spanish settlement in Cal. 1542; on Pac. cst., 16 km N. of Mexican border; fine natural harbour, naval base; fish-canning, aircraft; comm. ctr. for fruit-and vegetable growing dist.; p. (1970) 675,788 (c.), 1,357,854 (met. a.).

Sandlings, The, S.E. Suffolk, Eng.; a. of glacial sands, forming heathland; difficult agr. conditions.

Sandown-Shanklin, t., South Wight, I. of Wight, Eng.; on Sandown Bay; resort; p. (1971) 15,807.

Sandringham, v., Norfolk, Eng.; Royal residence since 1861.

Sandusky, c., Ohio, USA; on S. cst. L. Erie; tr. in coal, fruit, foodstuffs; paper, farm implements, chemicals; summer resort of Cedar Point nearby; p. (1970) 32,674.

Sandviken, t., Gävleborg, Sweden; impt. steel inds.; p. (1968) 25,497.

Sandwell, met. dist., West Midlands, Eng.; comprises Warley and West Bromwich; p. (est. 1976) 312,900.

Sandwich, t., Kent, Eng.; Cinque pt. at mouth of Stour R.; harbour silted up 16th cent.; mkt., lt. inds.; p. (1971) 4,467.

Sandwich Is., dependency of Falkland Is., Brit. Crown col. S. Atlantic.

Sandy, t., Mid Beds., Eng.; 5 km N.W. of Biggleswade; mkt. gardening; p. (1971) 5,274.

Sandy Hook, peninsula, N.J., USA; projects into lower bay of N.Y.; government reservation.

San Felipe, cap. of Aconcagua prov., Chile; 72 km N. of Santiago; agr., copper and gold-mng. ctr.; p. (est. 1966) 21,979.

San Felipe, cap. of Yaracuy st., Venezuela; ctr. of agr. dist. producing coffee, sugar and other tropical prods.; p. (est. 1970) 43,402.

San Fernando, N.W. sub. of Buenos Aires, Argentina; spt. on Rio de la Plata; industl. ctr., footwear, furniture, fish canning.

San Fernando, cap. of Colchagua prov., Chile; agr. mkt. ctr.; p. (est. 1966) 25,271.

San Fernando, t., Bay of Cadiz, S. Spain; pt. has naval arsenal; salt mftg.; much of surrounding marshland now reclaimed; p. (1967) 61,330.

San Fernando, spt., Trinidad, W.I.; on W. cst. 40 km S. of Port of Spain; exp. sugar, asphalt, petrol; p. (1970) 37,313.

San Fernando, t., Venezuela; ctr. cattle ranching region of upper Llanos; oil; p. (est. 1970) 44,358.

San Francisco, c., Cal., USA; spt. on S. F. Bay; entrance spanned by Golden Gate Bridge; attractive hilly site; cosmopolitan c. with several immigrant quarters; comm. and financial ctr. with many varied inds.; univ.; sudden earthquake (1906) destroyed much of c. (*see* F9); p. (1970) 704,209 (c.), 3,109,519 (met. a.).

Sangihe Is., Indonesia; volcanic archipelago between Kalimantan and Philippines; sago, nutmeg, copra; ch. t. and spt. Tahuna; a. 813 km²; p. c. 90,000.

San Gimignano, hill t., Tuscany, Italy; overlooks Val d'Elsa; 13th cent. mediaeval t., preserved as national monument; tourist ctr.; p. (est. 1968) 8,227.

San Giovanni in Fiore, t., Calabria, Italy; agr. ctr. at 1,006 m nr. confluence of Neto and Arvo Rs.; p. (est. 1968) 22,012.

Sangli, t., Maharashtra, India; nr. Miraj on Karna-

taka border; p. (1971) 115,138 (t.), 201,597 (met. a.).

Sangre de Cristo Mtns., part of Rocky mtns. USA; name (Span. — Blood of Christ) derives from reddish hue seen at sunset; highest summit Blanca Peak 4,367 m.

San Joaquin, R., Cal., USA; forms part of Central Valley project for irrigation of farmlands of R. valley; 512 km long.

San José, prov., Costa Rica; bauxite mng. nr. San Isidro del General projected with road to Punta Uvita where sm. pt. will be built; cap. San José.

San José, c., cap. of Costa Rica; sited at c. 1,160 m in S. J. basin; cath., univ., observatory, theatre, parks; ch. industl. and comm. ctr. of rep.; oil refining, agr. processing; major route ctr., international airport; p. (1970) 436,965 (c.), 1,057,032 (met. a.).

San José, t., cap. of San José prov., Uruguay; impt. mkt.; flour-milling; p. (1963) 20,000.

San José, c., Cal., USA; in fertile Santa Clara valley; fruit and vegetable canning and processing, chemicals, paper, electronics; p. (est. 1969) 425,000 (c.); (1970) 1,064,712 (met. a.).

San Juan, prov., Argentina; at foot of Andes. gold, copper mng.; cap. S. J.; a. 89,179 km²; p. (1960) 352,000.

San Juan, c., cap. of San Juan prov., Argentina; comm. ctr. of agr. a., tr. in wine, fruit, cattle; p. (1970) 224,000 (met. a.).

San Juan, c., cap. of Puerto Rico; built in part on I.; major spt. on N.E. cst.; exp. agr. prod. to USA; agr. processing; modern inds. inc. oil refining, cement, metallurgy, pharmaceuticals; cath., univ.; p. (1970) 452,749 (c.), 820,422 (met. a.).

San Juan, R., Central America; divides Nicaragua and Costa Rica; plans made for its canalisation, which would give both countries a clear waterway from Caribbean to Pac.; 144 km long.

San Juan, R., Col., N.M., and Utah., USA; flows in goose-neck incised meanders; Navajo Dam part of Colorado River storage project, bringing irrigation to Navajo Indian reservation; 640 km long.

San Juan del Norte (Greytown), pt. on Caribbean cst. of Nicaragua; silting; sm. exp. of bananas, hardwoods; p. (1963) 599.

San Juan del Sur, spt., on Pac. cst., Nicaragua; exp. ctr. for coffee, sugar, cocoa, balsam; p. (1960) 4,223.

Sankt Ingbert, t., Saarland, W. Germany; N.E. of Saarbrücken; coal mng.; iron, glass, machin., textiles, leather; p. (est. 1969) 28,818.

Sankt Pölten, t., Lower Austria; rly. and industl. ctr.; hydroelectric power sta.; p. c. 41,000.

San Leandro, t., Cal., USA; food processing; Portuguese residents have annual religious festival; p. (1970) 68,698.

San Lorenzo, t., Argentina; 22 km N. Rosario; lge. chemical wks., oil refining.

Sanlúcar de Barrameda, pt., Cadiz prov., Spain; nr. mouth of R. Guadalquivir; wines and agr. prod.; mediaeval cas.; bathing resort; p. (1970) 41,072.

San Luis, c., cap. of S. L. prov., Argentina; ctr. of cattle, grain, wine producing dist.; rich mineral deposits in surrounding a.; hydroelectric power sta. and irrigation dam nearby; p. (1960) 38,000.

San Luis Potosí, st., Mexico; leading mng. st.; metals melting, food-processing; cap. San Luis Potosí; a. 63,235 km²; p. (1969) 1,436,300.

San Luis Potosí, t., cap. of San Luis Potosí st., Mexico; industl. and comm. ctr.; metallurgy textiles; cath., palace; p. (1970) 230,039.

San Marino, sm. indep. rep., Italy; in Apennines nr. Rimini; has kept its independence since 4th cent. A.D.; exp. wine, textiles, building stone; cap. San Marino; a. 62 km²; p. (1968) 18,360.

San Marino, t., cap. of San Marino rep.; on slope of Mt. Titano, 19 km. S.W. of Rimini; tourism; p. (1968) 4,150.

San Miguel, c., El Salvador, at foot of San Miguel volcano; sisal-fibre, coffee, cattle, cotton, indigo; cath.; p. (est. 1969) 107,658.

San Miguel de Allende, t., Guanajuato st., Mexico; picturesque hilly site; famous art institute.

San Millán de la Cogolla, Spain; oldest (6th cent.) monastic foundation in Spain; in Cárdenas valley (Logrono prov.).

San Miguel de Tucumán, c., cap. Tucumán prov., Argentina; on R. Sali; univ.; breweries, sawmills, flour, sugar; p. (1970) 365,757 (met. a.).

San Nicolas, R. pt., Argentina; on Paraná R.; cattle, flour, agr. prod., distillery, steel plant; p. (1960) 55,000.

Sanniya Hor, shallow L., Iraq; linked to R. Tigris; acts as flood control reservoir.

Sanok, t., Rzeszow prov., S.E. Poland; picturesque site on steep banks of San R.; industl. ctr., comm. vehicles, rubber gds.; p. (1970) 21,600.

San-Pedro, spt., Ivory Coast; new pt. (1970) linked with development of timber production in hinterland; p. (planned for 1980) 50,000.

San Pedro, spt., a. of Los Angeles, Cal., USA; shipyds., oil refining, fruit canning.

San Pedro de Macoris, spt., Dominican Rep.; on Caribbean; exp. sugar, sugar prods.; clothing, soap; p. (1970) 70,092.

San Pedro Sula, t., Honduras; ctr. for banana and sugar inds; food processing; p. (est. 1970) 102,516.

Sanquhar, burgh, Nithsdale, Scot.; coal mng., brick mkg.; p. (1971) 1,991.

San Rafael, t., W. Argentina; comm. ctr. for agr. a.; food processing, meat, wine, fruit; p. c. 46,000.

San Remo, sm. pt., Italy; winter resort on Italian Riviera; flower mkt., olive oil, lemons, wine; 12th cent. church; p. (est. 1968) 63,735.

San Salvador (Watling's I.), Bahama Is., W.I.; discovered by Columbus 1492, his first sight of the New World; a. 155 km²; p. (1963) 968.

San Salvador, c., cap. of El Salvador; stands c. 600 m a.s.l.; ch. comm. and industl. ctr.; food processing, textile and tobacco inds.; univ., observatory; oil refining; liable to earthquakes; p. (1971) 337,171.

Sansanding, t., Mali, W. Africa; lge. barrage across R. Niger.

San Sebastian, c., cap. of Guipúzcoa prov., N. Spain; spt. on Bay of Biscay, at foot of Mt. Urgull; seaside resort; fishing, textiles, paper, glass; captured by Wellington 1813; p. (est. 1969) 155,346.

San Severo, mkt. t., S. Italy; hilltop site, 24 km N.W. of Foggia, Apulia; cath.; wine ctr., cream of tartar, bricks; p. (est. 1968) 52,458.

Santa Ana, c., W. El Salvador; second lgst. c. of rep.; coffee, sugar, cattle; Santa Ana volcano nearby; p. (est. 1969) 168,047.

Santa Ana, c., Cal., USA; S.E. of Los Angeles; in fruit farming a.; fruit pkg., walnuts, oranges; p. (1970) 154,640 (c.), inc. in Anaheim met. a.

Santa Barbara, c., Cal., USA; resort on Pac. cst., picturesque setting, mild climate; p. (1970) 69,631 (c.), 260,299 (met. a.).

Santa Barbara Is., USA; along S. cst. of Cal.; inc. Santa Catalina I., a favourite resort.

Santa Catarina, st., Brazil; between Atl. and Argentina; tobacco, manioc, fruit, hogs; impt. coal producer; cap. Florianópolis; a. 95,830 km²; p. (1968) 2,705,394.

Santa Clara, c., Cuba; attractive site at over 360 m; agr. and comm. ctr. for sugar and tobacco; decisive victory for guerrilla army of Fidel Castro 1959; p. (1970) 213,296.

Santa Clara, c., W. Cal., USA; citrus fruit pkg.; electronics, plastics, chemicals; univ.; p. (est. 1969) 84,000.

Santa Clara Valley, Cal., USA; extends S. from San Francisco Bay; intensive fruit-growing under irrigation, prunes; ch. t. San José.

Santa Cruz, c., cap. of S.C. dep., Bolivia; alt. 457 m; agr. mkt. for sugar, coffee, rice, cattle; oil refining; international airport; impt. reserves iron ore; univ.; p. (est. 1969), 108,720.

Santa Cruz de la Sierra, t., Bolivia; on R. Piray; sugar, flour; distillery; p. (1967) 96,000.

Santa Cruz de Tenerife, spt. on Tenerife I., Canary Is.; cap. of S.C. de T. prov., Spain; gd. harbour, oil refinery; exp. agr. prods.; developing resort in attractive a. with mild climate; p. (est. 1969) 163,763.

Santa Cruz Is., volcanic gr., S. Pac. Oc.; part of Solomon Is.; exp. copra.

Santa Fé, c., cap. of S.F. prov., Argentina; impt. R. pt. on I. in Salado R.; comm. ctr. for surrounding grain and livestock a.; food processing; univ., cath.; p. (1970) 244,579 (met. a.).

Santa Fé, t., N.M., USA; at base of Sangre de Cristo range; oldest capital in US founded by Spaniards 1610; tourist and comm. ctr.; p. (1970) 41,167.

Santa Isabel. See Malabo.

Santa Maria, t., Rio Grande do Sul, Brazil; rly. junc., rly. engin., agr. tr. and processing; p. (1970) 120,667.

Santa Maria de Gerona, Spain; nr. Burgos; nuclear power plant being built.

Santa Marta, spt., cap. of Magdalena dep., Colombia; banana pt. on deep bay at mouth of Manzanares R., serving local plantations; p. (est. 1972) 141,300 (c.), 165,500 (met. a.).

Santa Monica, c., Cal., USA; W. of Los Angeles; attractive site on Santa Monica Bay; aircraft, plastics, cosmetics; p. (est. 1969) 91,500.

Santander, c., cap. of Santander prov., N. Spain; spt. and seaside resort on Bay of Biscay; exp. iron and zinc ore, agr. prods.; heavy inds., shipbldg., oil refining, chemicals; former summer resort of Spanish court; cath.; p. (est. 1969) 133,014.

Santarém, t., Pará, Brazil; rubber, cacao, Brazil nuts, sugar; p. (est. 1968) 111,706.

Santarém, t., cap. of Ribatejo prov., Portugal; on slope of hill overlooking Tagus R.; Moorish cas.; mkt. for agr. prod.; p. (1970) 57,292.

Santa Rosa, t., cap. of La Pampa terr., Argentina; p. (1960) 17,000.

Santa Rosa, c., Cal., USA; tr. and industl. ctr. for Somona Valley fruit-growing a.; p. (1970) 50,006.

Santiago, c., cap. of Chile and of S. prov.; planned t. ctr. in broad valley of Mapoche R., one of lgst. and most attractive cs. in S. America; cultural, comm., political and financial ctr., focus of routes; univ.; textiles, chemicals, paper, iron and steel; rapidly growing p.; p. (1970) 2,661,920 (met. a.).

Santiago de Compostela, c., Corunna, Spain; on R. Sar, surrounded by hills, univ., palace, cath. (with tomb of St. James); famous place of pilgrimage; agr. tr., food processing, tourism; p. (1970) 70,893.

Santiago de Cuba, c., Cuba; spt. on S. cst., exp. minerals, agr. prods., sugar, tobacco; oil refining, cigars, soap; cath., univ.; p. (est. 1967) 259,000.

Santiago del Estero, c., cap. of S. del E. prov., Argentina; transportation ctr. of Argentine Chaco; agr. tr. ctr., cattle, food processing; p. (1970) 105,209 (met. a.).

Santiago de los Caballeros, t., Dominican Rep.; comm. agr. ctr. in fertile a.; food processing, coffee, rice, tobacco; cigars, cigarettes; p. (1970) 155,151.

Santis, mtn., on border cans. St. Gallen and Appenzell, Switzerland; alt. 2,506 m, Europe's hgst. television transmitter on summit.

Santo Domingo, c., cap. Dominican Rep.; spt. on S. cst., exp. agr. prod.; food processing; 3 univs.; cath.; p. (est. 1975) 705,000.

Santo Tomé de la Guayana (Puerto Ordaz) c., S.E. Venezuela; new industl. c. nr. confluence of Orinoco and Caroni Rs.; iron mines, steel, hydroelec. power and aluminium plants in a.; vast industl. complex projected.

Santorine. See Thira.

Santos, c., spt., São Paulo, Brazil; world's ch. coffee pt.; also exp. oranges, bananas, cotton, and industl. prod. from modern harbour; p. (1970) 341,317.

San Vicente, t., cap. of S.V. dep., El Salvador; ctr. for coffee, sugar, tobacco; mnfs. leather gds., shawls, hats; p. (est. 1968) 19,314.

São Carlos, t., São Paulo st., Brazil; 192 km N.W. of São Paulo; ctr. of coffee-growing a.; textiles, refrigerators, furniture; p. (est. 1968) 73,256.

São Francisco, R., Brazil; flows from Minas Gerais prov. to Atl.; navigable for 1,440 km of middle course; used for hydroelectric power at Paulo Afonso falls and Três Marias dam; 2,560 km long.

São Goncalo, t., Rio de Janeiro, Brazil; fastgrowing t.; p. (1970) 161,392.

São Jeronimo, t., Rio Grande do Sul, Brazil; lowgrade coal; p. (1970) 36,531.

São João do Meriti, t., Rio de Janeiro, Brazil; industl. and comm. ctr.; p. (1970) 163,934.

São José dos Campos, t., São Paulo, Brazil; industl. ctr.; cattle; p. (1970) 130,118.

São Leopoldo, t., Rio Grande do Sul, S. Brazil; 32 km N. of Porto Alegre; mkt. t.; p. (est. 1968) 53,398.

São Luis, pt., cap. of Maranhão st., Brazil; on São Luis I.; noted cultural ctr. in 19th cent.; p. (1970) 167,529.

São Miguel, I., Azores; lgst. and most productive I. of archipelago; ch. t. and spt. Ponta Delgada, exp. agr. prods., pineapples; volcanic landscape a tourist attraction; p. c. 170,000.

Saône, R., France; rises in Vosges and flows to R. Rhône at Lyons; navigable, canalised; 451 km long.

Saone-et-Loire, dep., France; mtnous.; noted vineyards; cap. Mâcon; a. 8,627 km²; p. (1968) 550,362.

São Paulo, st., Brazil; on Atl. cst.; major industl. a. of S. America; coffee, cotton, sugar, rice, maize; vehicles, elec. gds., chemicals, textiles, telecomm. equipment, metal-wkg. plants; cap. São Paulo; Santos lgst pt. in Brazil; a. 247,226 km²; p. (est. 1968) 16,681,060.

São Paulo, c., cap. of São Paulo st., Brazil; fast-growing c., comm. and industl. ctr. of rep. and leading c. of S. America; vehicles, machin., elec. gds., textiles, pharmaceutics; aluminium refinery; nearby pt. Santos ships rich agr. prod. from hinterland; 2 univs., cath.; p. (1970) 5,186,752.

São Roque, Cape of, Rio Grande do Norte, N.E. Brazil; most N.E. point of S. America.

São Tomé, cap. São Tomé and Principe; p. (1960) 714.

São Tomé and Principe, former Port. col.; W. Africa; volcanic Is. in G. of Guinea; cocoa, coffee; cap. São Tomé; a. 963 km²; indep. achieved as democratic rep. 1975; p. (est. 1969) 66,000.

São Vicente, c., S.E. São Paulo, Brazil; first Portuguese settlement in Brazil (1532), on I. off mainland; sub. of Santos; fashionable beach resort; p. (1970) 116,075.

Sapele, t., Benin st., Nigeria; S. of Benin; lge. lumber mill and plywood plant.

Sapporo, c., Hokkaido, Japan; main t. of Hokkaido; planned t.; univ.; brewing, dairy processing, sawmills; p. (est. 1971) 1,031,000.

Saqqara, v., Egypt; necropolis of anc. Memphis; step pyramids; p. (1966) 12,700.

Sarajevo, c., cap. of Bosnia and Herzegovina, Yugoslavia; major route ctr., airport; ctr. of Yugoslav Moslems; mosques, caths.; diversified mnfs., metallurgy, elec. prods., textiles, tobacco, pottery; assassination 28 June 1914 of Archduke Francis Ferdinand precipitated First World War; p. (1971) 292,000.

Saransk, c., Mordvinian ASSR, RSFSR; 232 km S.E. of Gorki; univ.; elec. equipment, engin., agr. processing; p. (1970) 190,000.

Sarapul, c., RSFSR; pt. on R. Kama; radio equipment, machin., footwear, gloves; p. (est. 1967) 91,000.

Sarasota, Fla., USA; exp. fruit, veg.; resort; p. (est. 1969) 40,000 (c.), 158,000 (met. a.).

Saratoga Springs, N.Y., USA; summer resort at foot of Adirondack mtns., mineral springs; horse-racing; casino; p. (1970) 18,845.

Saratov, c., RSFSR; pt. on R. Volga; regional ctr. for agr. prod. of lower Volga valley and oil from Baku; univ.; engin., ball-bearings, textiles, oil refining, sawmilling; p. (1970) 758,000.

Sarawak, st., E. Malaysia; mtnous. inland with sparse p.; rubber, sago, pepper grown along cst.; oil; cap. Kuching; a. 121,914 km²; p. (1967) 903,000.

Sardinia, I., aut. region, Italy; mtnous., dry climate; fertile Campidano plain with fruit, wines, sheep; zinc and lead mng.; tourism; fishing; major petrochemical complex at Ottana; part of former kingdom of Sardinia belonging to house of Savoy; a. 24,002 km²; p. (1969) 1,495,383.

Sargasso Sea, zone S.W. of N. Atl. Oc.; relatively still sea within swirl of warm ocean currents; noted for abundance of gulf-weed on its surface, rich in marine life; named by Columbus.

Sari, c., cap. of Mazandaran prov., Iran; p. (1967) 206,463.

Sark, I., Channel Is.; 10 km E. of Guernsey; picturesque scenery; tourist ctr.; farming; a. 516 ha; p. (est. 1973) 580.

Sark, R., forms extreme W. bdy. between Scot. and Eng.

Sarnia, c., and pt., Ont., Canada; on St. Clair R.; connected to Port Huron by rly. tunnel; oil refineries, petrochemical inds., agr. tr.; p. (1971) 56,727.

Sarno, t., Campania, Italy; spa at foot of mtns. on E. edge of fertile Sarno plain; agr. mkt., textile ctr.; cas.; p. (est. 1968) 31,357.

Sar-Planina, Yugoslavia; nr. Skopje; impt. chrome deposits; attractive site, ctr. of mtn. tourism.

Sarpsborg, t., Norway; on R. Glommen; lgst. pulp and paper concern in kingdom; hydro-electric power sta.; p. (est. 1970) 13,165.

Sarreguemines, t., Moselle dep., France; in Lorraine; potteries based on local clay; coal mng.; p. (1968) 24,284.

Sarthe, dep., N.W. France; undulating surface; farming, apples, livestock; coal, linen, potteries; cap. Le Mans; a. 6,247 km²; p. (1968) 461,839.

Sarthe, R., France; trib. of R. Loire; 265 km long.

Sasebo, spt., Kyushu, Japan; ctr. of coalfield; engin., shipbldg.; p. (est. 1971) 262,000.

Saskatchewan, prov., Canada; coniferous forests and plains; Rs. Saskatchewan and Churchill; many lge. Ls.; extreme climate; hydroelec. power; gr. wheat prov.; livestock, dairying; oil, copper, uranium, helium plants, furs, fisheries; cap. Regina; a. 651,903 km²; p. (1976) 921,323.

Saskatchewan, R., Canada; flows from Rocky mtns. through L. Winnipeg and thence by R. Nelson to Hudson Bay; 2,320 km long.

Saskatoon, c., Saskatchewan, Canada; grew rapidly after arrival of rly. (1890); comm. ctr. for grain producing a.; meat packing and tr.; varied inds., cement, oil refining; univ.; p. (est. 1969) 129,000.

Sasolburg, t., O.F.S., S. Africa; oil from coal production; gas pipeline to Germiston a. p. (1960) 12,557.

Sassari, t., Sardinia, Italy; nr. G. of Asinara; cath., univ., palaces; tobacco and macaroni wks., cheese; p. (1969) 107,308.

Sattahip, pt., Thailand; new pt. inaugurated 1967.

Satu-Mare, t., N.W. Romania; agr. machin. handicraft inds. based on local prods., food-processing; cath.; p. (est. 1970) 78,812.

Saudi Arabia, kingdom, Arabian peninsula, S.W. Asia; mainly desert, agr. in oases and S.W. upland region of Asir; lgst. producer of oil in Middle East; oil sales account for 85 per cent govt. revenue; steel inds. and oil refinery at Jidda, petrochemicals developing at Dammam; Moslem holy cs. Mecca and Medina; cap. Riyadh (royal), Mecca (religious); main pt. King Faisal Port.; a. 2,400,930 km²; p. (est. 1969) 7,200,000.

Sauerland, dist., N. Rhine–Westphalia, W. Germany; plateau, alt. from 150–450 m E. of Rhine; agriculturally poor, largely forested; crossed by R. Wupper, with which are associated industl. ts. Wuppertal (textiles), Solingen and Remscheid (cutlery and special steel); supplies hydroelectric power to Ruhr.

Sault Ste. Marie, t., Ont., Canada; pt. on St. Mary's R., opposite Sault Ste. Marie, Mich., to which it is connected by bridge; pulp, paper. iron and steel; tourist ctr. for L. and forest region; p. (1971) 78,175.

Sault Ste. Marie, t., Mich., USA; pt. on St. Mary's R.; opposite Sault Ste. Marie, Ont.; calcium carbide; tourist ctr. for fishing, hunting a.; p. (1970) 15,136.

Sault Ste. Marie Canals (" Soo "), Canada and USA; twin canals on Canadian and American side of shallow channel linking L. Superior and L. Huron; traversed by all wheat and iron-ore traffic from L. Superior pts.; length (Canadian) 2 km; depth 5 m.

Saumur, t., Maine-et-Loire dep., France; on R. Loire, 48 km S.W. of Tours; sparkling wines, brandy; flower, vegetable mkt.; cas.; p. (1968) 23,175.

Sauternes, v., Gironde, France; name applied to white wines of dist.

Sava, R., Slovenia, Yugoslavia; joins Danube at Belgrade; used for hydroelectric power; agr. in valleys; transport axis; 928 km long.

Savage or Niue, Cook Is., Pac. Oc.; under N.Z.; ch. exp. native plaited ware, bananas, copra, and sweet potatoes; ch. pt. Alofi; a. 259 km²; p. (1968) 5,240.

Savaii I., lgst. of Samoan gr., Pac. Oc.; volcanic, mtnous., fertile; exp. bananas, copra, cocoa; a. 1,821 km²; p. c. 30,000.

Savannah, c., Ga., USA; spt. nr. mouth of Savannah R.; rly., fishing and comm. ctr. for Sea Is., Savannah valley and surrounding plantations; mkt. for naval stores; sugar refining, paper, oil refining, diverse mnfs.; tourist ind. stimulated by mild climate; p. (1970) 114,155 (c.), 182,959 (met. a.).

Savannah, R., USA; flows between Ga. and S.C. to Atl. Oc.; used for hydroelectric power; 720 km long.

Saverne, Col de, low pass, N.E. France; carries trunk rly. from Paris to Strasbourg and the East between Vosges and Hardt mtns.; gradual approach from W., steep descent to E. into Rhine valley.

Savoie (Savoy), dep., France; borders Italy in Savoy Alps; part of former duchy; dairying and vineyards; hydroelectricity forms basis of metallurgical inds.; first Fr. National Park (Vanoise Park); cap. Chambéry; a. 6,188 km²; p. (1968) 288,921.

Savona, spt., Genoa, Italy; cath.; iron, shipbldg., glass and tinplate wks.; exp. preserved fruits and tomatoes; imports coal, oil, iron ore; p. (1969) 78,748.

Savonlinna, t., Mikkeli, E. Finland; in Saimaa L. region; route ctr.; timber inds.; p. (est. 1970) 17,942.

Sawankalok, t., Thailand; impt. teak collecting ctr.

Sawbridgeworth, t., East Herts., Eng.; on R. Stort, 6 km S. of Bishops Stortford; malting, fruit preserving; p. (1971) 7,083.

Saxham, t., Suffolk, Eng.; agr. machin.

Saxmundham, mkt. t., Suffolk Coastal, Suffolk, Eng.; 29 km N.E. of Ipswich; p. (1971) 1,700.

Saxony, region, E. Germany; turbulent political and territorial history, now comprises admin. dists. of Leipzig, Dresden, Karl-Marx-Stadt, Halle and Magdeburg; inc. Erzgebirge in S., Vogtland in W. and N. European plain; drained by N. flowing Rs. Elster, Pleisse, Mulde, Elbe, Neisse, Spree; kaolin deposits basis for porcelain ind. at Meissen; industrialised in 19th and 20th cent. with notable textile ind.; coal mng. nr. Zwickau; inds. concentrated around Karl-Marx-Stadt; cap. Dresden; comm. ctr. at Leipzig; a. 16,996 km².

Sayan Mtns., range of mtns.; between Rs. Yenisey and Angra, RSFSR; form part of Sino-Soviet border; mineral resources.

Scafell Pike, mtn., Cumbria, Eng.; in N. Pennines; highest in Eng.; alt. 979 m.

Scalby, t., North Yorks., Eng.; 5 km N.W. of Scarborough; p. (1971) 8,672.

Scalloway, Shetlands, Scot.; on W. cst. of Mainland; the anc. cap.; ruined cas.; fish. pt.

Scalpay, I., off E. cst. of Skye, Scot.

Scalpay, I., Harris, Outer Hebrides, Scot.

Scandinavia, name given to lge. peninsula in N.W. Europe; comprises kingdoms of Sweden and Norway; sometimes inc. Denmark, Finland and Iceland; rugged a. of anc. peneplained rocks; climate varies from arctic (N.) to humid maritime (S.W.); rich in timber and mineral ores, esp. iron and copper; W. cst. waters valuable fishing grounds.

Scapa Flow, strait, N. Scot.; between Pomona and Hoy, Orkney Is.; surrendered German fleet scuttled 1919; Brit. battleship Royal Oak sunk at anchor 1939.

Scarba, I., Argyll and Bute, Scot.; off N. end of Jura, red deer in woods and moorlands.

Scarborough, t., l. gov. dist., North Yorks., Eng.; on E. cst.; seaside resort; cas.; former spa; p. (est. 1976) 99,000 (dist.).

Scarpanto. See Karpathos.

Schaffhausen, most. N. can., Switzerland; on R. Rhine; pastoral, forested; cereals, fruit, vegetables, wine; hydroelectric power from S. falls on Rhine; cap. S.; a. 298 km²; p. (1969) 73,000.

Schaffhausen, c., cap. of S. can., Switzerland; on Rhine below L. Constance; falls to S.W. of

c.; hydroelectricity supplies power for electro-chemical ind. and aluminium wks.; p. (1969) 38,900.

Schaumburg-Lippe, former st., between provs. of Hanover and Westphalia, Germany, now part of Lower Saxony, W. Germany; farming, coal mng.

Schefferville, t., Canada; 576 km N. of St. Lawrence estuary and connected to it (at Seven Islands) by rly.; ctr. of iron-ore mines in Quebec-Labrador trough; p. (1966) 3,086.

Scheldt (Dutch Schelde, French Escaut), R., France, Belgium, Neth.; rises in Aisne, France, flows to N. Sea forming extensive delta with Rhine (Rijn) and Meuse (Maas) in Netherlands; navigable; 432 km long; network of canals.

Schenectady, c., N.Y., USA; on Mohawk R., N.W. of Albany; electrical plants, locomotive wks.; p. (est. 1969) 71,000.

Scheveningen, seaside resort, Neth.; 3 km N.W. of The Hague; fish. pt.

Schiedam, t., Neth., on Nieuwe Maas, 4 km downstream from Rotterdam; forms part of Rotterdam–Europort; diverse pt.-based inds.; gin; p. (1968) 82,596.

Schiehallion, mtn., Perth and Kinross, Scot.; alt. 1,082 m.

Schio, t., Veneto, Italy; at foot of Alps on Leogra R.; woollens, textiles, machin.; p. (est. 1968) 32,176.

Schlei, narrow inlet of Baltic, Schleswig-Holstein, W. Germany; 40 km long.

Schleswig, t., Schleswig-Holstein, W. Germany; fish. pt. on Schlei inlet; lt. inds.; p. (est. 1969) 33,265.

Schleswig-Holstein, Land, W. Germany; occupies S. part of Jutland peninsula; a. disputed between Denmark and Prussia in 19th cent.; mainly agr.; many sm. pts.; crossed by Kiel Canal; cap. Kiel; a. 15,664 km²; p. (1968) 2,499,700.

Schneidemühl. See Pila.

Schönebeck, t., Magdeburg, E. Germany; pt. on R. Elbe; metals, chemicals, machin.; p. (est. 1970) 46,146.

Schoonebeek, v., Drenthe, Neth.; S. of Emmen; lge. oilfield; p. (1967) 7,473.

Schouten I., W. Irian, Indonesia; in Geelvink Bay; p. 25,487.

Schouwen-Duiveland, I., Zeeland prov., Neth.; cap. Zierikee; formerly 2 separate Is.

Schuylkill R., Penns., USA; flows into Delaware R.; navigable; length 208 km.

Schwäbisch-Gmünd, t., Baden-Württemberg, W. Germany; at foot of Swabian Jura, E. of Stuttgart; clocks, glass, optical, precious metal and jewellery inds.; mediaeval and baroque bldgs.; p. (est. 1969) 44,134.

Schwarzwald (Black Forest), forested mtn. range, Baden-Württemberg, W. Germany; highest peak Feldberg 1,496 m; tourism; famous for clock and toy inds.

Schwechat, t., Austria; nr. Vienna; oil refining; pipeline to Trieste; p. (1961) 13,403.

Schwedt, t., Frankfurt, E. Germany; on R. Oder; lge. oil refinery; pipeline from Mozyr' (USSR); paper, fertilisers; p. (est. 1970) 34,134.

Schweinfurt, t., Bavaria, W. Germany; on R. Main, N.E. of Würzburg; metals, machin., ball bearings, dyes, brewing; p. (est. 1969) 59,402.

Schwelm, t., N. Rhine–Westphalia, W. Germany; E. of Wuppertal; metals machin., textiles; p. (est. 1969) 32,969.

Schwenningen, t., Baden-Württemberg, W. Germany; clocks, precision instruments, optical apparatus; p. (est. 1969) 34,954.

Schwerin, c., cap. of Schwerin, E. Germany; on Schwerin L., surrounded by smaller Ls.; comm. and industl. ctr. of agr. dist.; food processing, engin., furniture; cath., cas.; p. (est. 1970) 96,949.

Schwyz, can., Switzerland; mtnous. in S.; forested; dairying impt.; original member of confederation; cap. S.; a. 907 km²; p. (1969) 85,500.

Schwyz, c., of Schwyz can., Switzerland; tourist ctr. nr. Lucerne; p. (1969) 12,500.

Sciacca, sm. pt., Sicily Italy; nr. Agrigento; mineral springs; p. (est. 1968) 33,524.

Scilly Is., archipelago, l. gov. dist., 30 m. S.W. of Land's End, Cornwall, Eng.; early flowers and vegetables benefit from mild winter climate; tourism; p. (est. 1976) 1,900.

Scioto, R., Ohio, USA; joins Ohio at Portsmouth; 400 km long.

Scone, par., Perth and Kinross, Scot.; place of residence and coronation of early Scottish kings; from here Edward I. removed Stone of Destiny to Westminster Abbey 1297; tourist ctr.; civil aerodrome.

Scoresby Sound, E. Greenland; lgst. fjord system in the world; length 304 km; fishing and hunting.

Scotland, Brit. Is., N. part of Gt. Britain; 11 Gov. Regs.; home affairs admin. by Dept. of Sec. of State for Scot.; physically divided into 3 parts: (1) the Highlands and Is., an upland a. suffering from depopulation, economically reliant on stock-rearing, tourism, hydroelec. power, whisky and fishing; intrusive impact of N. Sea oil on N.E. cst.; (2) the Central Lowlands, containing most p., based in industl. ts. on sm. coalfields, inc. lgst. c. Glasgow and cap. Edinburgh; (3) the S. Uplands, a stock-rearing a. bordering Eng.; a. 78,772 km²; p. (1971) 5,228,963.

Scranton, c., Penns., USA; on Lackawanna R.; anthracite ctr.; chemicals, shoes, textiles; univ.; p. (1970) 102,294 (c.), 231,433 (met. a.).

Scunthorpe, t., l. gov. dist., Humberside, Eng.; on Lincoln Edge, 10 km S. of Humber; iron, limestone mng. and major iron and steel ind.; p. (est. 1976) 68,100.

Scutari. See Shkodër.

Scutari (Turkey). See Üsküdar.

Seaford, t., East Sussex, Eng.; 5 km E. of Newhaven; seaside resort; declined as a pt. with shift of Ouse R. channel to Newhaven; p. (1971) 16 196.   [22 km long.

Seaforth Loch. Lewis, Outer Hebrides Scot.;

Seaham, spt., Durham, Eng.; Seaham Harbour on E. cst. 6 km S. of Sunderland; modern colly. workings extend under sea; p. (1971) 23,410.

Sea Islands, USA; chain of Is. off Atl. cst. of S.C., Ga. and Fla.; formerly impt. for sea island cotton but since 1919 infested with boll weevil.

Seathwaite, v., Cumbria, Eng.; 11 km from Keswick, close to Styhead (436 m); exceptionally heavy annual rainfall (above 3,800 mm).

Seaton, t., East Devon, Eng.; on Lyme Bay at mouth of R. Axe, seaside resort; freestone quarries; p. (1971) 4,134.

Seaton Carew, t., Cleveland, Eng.; site for nuclear power sta. nr. mouth of R. Tees; seaside resort.

Seaton Valley, t., Blyth Valley, Northumberland, Eng.; coal mng.; expanded t.; p. (1971) 32,011.

Seattle, c., Wash., USA; spt. between Puget Sound and L. Wash.; S.E. is Mt. Rainier, N.E. Mt. Baker; tr. with Far East and Alaska from wooded, agr. hinterland; fishing and fish exp.; lgst c. of Wash., a major industl. and comm. ctr.; aircraft (home of Boeing), shipbldg., food processing; univs., cath.; p. (1970) 524,263 (c.), 1,404,432 (met. a.).

Secunderabad, t., Andhra Pradesh, India; now incorporated within Hyderabad; comm. ctr., rly. junc.; p. (1961) 78,412.

Sedan, t., Ardennes dep., France; on R. Meuse; machin., metal ware, woollens, flour; Napoleon III surrendered to Prussians 1870; p. (1968) 24.499.

Sedbergh, mkt. t., South Lakeland, Cumbria, Eng.; woollen ind., public school; p. (1971) 3,547 (dist.).

Sedgefield, t., l. gov. dist., S.E. Durham, Eng.; in fertile agr. a.; cattle mkt.; racecourse; p. (est. 1976) 91,700 (dist.).

Sedgemoor, l. gov. dist., Somerset, Eng.; based on Bridgewater, Burnham and surrounding a.; p. (est. 1976) 85,100.

Sedgley. See Wolverhampton.

Sefton, met. dist., Merseyside, Eng.; comprises Crosby, Bootle and Litherland; p. (est. 1976) 306,000.

Ségou, t., R. pt., Mali; W. Africa; on R. Niger; ctr. of irrigation scheme; cotton, hides, cattle; once cap. of former kingdom.

Ségou Canal, Mali, W. Africa; leaves R. Niger 6 km below Bamako, extends 208 km N.E. to Ségou; irrigates 7,770 km² on right bank of Niger and assists navigation.

Segovia, c., cap. of S. prov., Old Castile, Spain; on rocky hill above Eresma R.; Roman aqueduct, cath.; p. (1970) 41,880.

Segovia, R., rises in N.W. Nicaragua, flows N.E. to Caribbean; forms part of S. limit of Mosquito cst., and bdy. between Honduras and Nicaragua; 480 km long.

Segre, R., Lérida, N.E. Spain; rises in E. Pyrenees, flows S.W. into R. Ebro; water irrigates the a. around Lérida, the lgst. block of irrigated land in Spain; c. 272 km long.

Segura, R., Spain; flows to Mediterranean at Guardamar; 288 km long.

Seibersdorf, Austria; ENEA experimental food irradiation project.

Seikan Tunnel, Japan; links Honshu with Hokkaido under Tsugaru strait; 37 km long.

Seine, R., France; rises in Côte d'Or dep., and flows past Paris and Rouen to English Channel at Havre; navigable, part of French waterway network; 757 km long.

Seine-et-Marne, dep., N. France; agr., stockraising, dairying; impt. source of food for Paris mkts.; Brie cheese; cap. Melun; a. 5,892 km²; p. (1968) 604,340.

Seine-Maritime, dep., N. France; undulating and fertile; grain, dairying; heavy inds. at cap. Rouen; oil refineries; beach resorts; p. (1968) 1,113,977.

Seine-Saint Denis, dep., N.E. Paris, France; mkt. gardens; cap. Bobigny; p. (1968) 1,251,792.

Seistan and Baluchistan, twin prov., Iran; co. ts. Zabol, Zahedan (rly. terminus Pakistan rly. from Quetta through Mirjaveh, the customs post on Iranian frontier).

Sekondi-Takoradi, t., S.W. Ghana; spt. on G. of Guinea; developed after construction of rly. (1903) to tap mineral, agr. and forest wealth of hinterland; deepwater harbour at Takoradi constructed 1928; fisheries, saw milling; p. (1970) 91,874 (c.), 160,868 (met. a.).

Selangor, st., central Malaya, W. Malaysia; former sultanate; economically well developed; chemicals, rubber, tin, coal, pineapples; ch. pt., Pt. Swettenham; fisheries; new st. cap. designated at Klang to relieve congestion of Kuala Lumpur; p. (1967) 1,408,881.

Selby, mkt. t., l. gov. dist., North Yorks., Eng.; on R. Ouse, 13 m. S. of York; anc. abbey church; flour milling, flax oil-cake; rich coal deposit recently found; p. (est. 1976) 71,500 (dist.).

Sele, R., S. Italy; rises in S. Apennines, flows W. into G. of Salerno; headwaters carried E. through gr. Apennine tunnel (11 km) to irrigate plateau of Apulia in S.E. Italy.

Selenga, Asiatic R., rises in Mongolia, enters USSR nr. Kiachta from where it is navigable to its delta in L. Baykal; c 1,100 km long.

Selkirk, royal burgh, Etterick and Lauderdale, Scot.; on Etterick Water; 6 km S. of Galashiels; mkt. t.; tartans, tweeds; p. (1971) 5,684.

Selkirk Mtns., B.C., Canada; run N.W. to S.E. parallel with Rocky mtns.; anc. rocks, highly mineralised; rise to over 2,700 m.

Selkirkshire, former co., S. Scot.; now part of Borders Reg.

Selma, t., Ala., USA; on Alabama R., in cotton, dairying, lumbering region; food processing, fertilisers; p. (1970) 27,379.

Selsey Bill, peninsula between Bognor Regis and Portsmouth, West Sussex, Eng.

Selukwe, t., Rhodesia; alt. 1,444 m; gold mng. chrome ore, molybdenum; ranching.

Selwyn Range, mtns., Queensland, Australia; extend 560 km W. from Gr. Dividing Range.

Semarang, spt., Java, Indonesia; exp. sugar, tobacco, tapioca, kapok; shipbldg., rly. repairs, cement, sawmills, tyres, elec. equipment; univ.; p. (est. 1971) 560,000.

Semipalatinsk, t., Kazakh SSR, USSR; on R. Irtysh; lge. meat-packing plant; textiles, engin.; rich gold deposit found in a. 1965; p. (1970) 236,000.

Semmering Pass, low pass, Austria; provides route across E. Alps for rly. from Vienna to Venice; scenic resort; alt. below 915 m.

Semnan, t., Central Prov., Iran; comm. ctr. for tobacco growing region; p. (1966) 31,058.

Sena, t., Moçambique; on R. Zambesi; iron ore mng.

Sendai, t., Honshu, Japan; cas.; univ.; metallurgy, food processing, lacquer ware; p. (est. 1971) 560,000.

Senegal, rep., W. cst. Africa; flat savannah; tropical climate with long dry season; agr. main occupation, groundnuts accounting for 72 per cent exp.; groundnut and agr. processing provide industl. basis; bauxite, phosphate, titanium, zirconium mng.; oil refinery at cap.

Dakar; a. 197,109 km²; p. (est. 1969) 3,800,000.

Senegal, R., W. Africa; flows from Kong mtns. W. and N.W. to Atl. at St. Louis, above Cape Verde; lower valley forms fertile agr. land; partially navigable; plans for economic development of valley (1972); 1,600 km long.

Senftenberg, t., Cottbus, E. Germany; inds. based on local lignite deposits; glassware, tiles; p. (est. 1970) 24,301.

Senigallia, t., Italy; resort and spt. on Adriatic; fishing and agr. ctr.; food processing, agr. machin.; p. (est. 1968) 36,730.

Senlis, t., Oise dep., France; Gallo-Roman wall; tourist ctr. in forested region, 43 km N.E. of Paris; mkt. t., furniture, rubber gds.; p. (1968) 11,169.

Sennar, t., Sudan; on Blue Nile, on rly. route to Khartoum, Suakin, Pt. Sudan; dam for irrigation, flood control and hydroelectric power; p. c. 8,000.

Sens, t., Yonne dep., France; on R. Yonne; known to Romans as Agedincum; Gothic cath.; agr. tr., food processing, farm implements, boots, chemicals, cutlery; p. (1968) 24,563.

Sensuntepeque, t., E. Salvador; pottery, distilling; p. (1968) 6,006.

Senta, t., Yugoslavia; pt. on Tisa R.; agr. ctr.; food processing, agr. machin., chemicals; p. (est. 1965) 22,000.

Seoul, c., cap. of S. Korea; in Han R. valley; food processing, textiles, rly. engin.; univs., anc. walls; international airport, connected by rly. to outport of Inchon; p. (est. 1971) 5,536,000.

Sepik, R., N. New Guinea; flows E. to Bismarck Sea; drains vast mtn. a.; very fast flow; navigable by shallow craft; 800 km long.

Sept Isles (Seven Islands), pt., on St. Lawrence, Quebec, Canada; iron brought by rail from Schefferville; airline service but no highway.

Sequoia National Park, Cal., USA; sequoia trees.

Seraing, t., Liège, Belgium; on R. Meuse; coal mng.; iron and steel heavy inds.; seat of famous Cockerill ironwks. (1817) and glasswks. (1825); p. (1968) 40,850.

Seram (Ceram), I., Moluccas, Indonesia; W.-E. mtn. range rising to 3,357 m; tobacco, sago; a. 17,148 km²; p. (1961) 73,453.

Serampore, t., W. Bengal, India; former Danish settlement; cotton and silk weaving, pottery, jute- and paper-mills; p. (1971) 102,023.

Serbia, constituent rep., N.E. Yugoslavia; lgst and most impt. rep., "bread basket" of Yugoslavia; grain, fruit; mng. copper and antimony; cap. Belgrade; a. 87,879 km²; p. (1971) 8,436,574.

Seremban, t., cap. of Negri Sembilan st., W. Malaysia; on Linggi R.; linked by rly. to Pt. Dickson; comm. ctr. for rubber and tin a.; p. (1970) 79,915.

Sereth, R., rises in Carpathians, W. Ukrainian SSR, USSR, and enters Romania to join Danube above Galati; 720 km long.

Sergipe, cst. st., Brazil; sandy cst. rising to undulating plateau in interior; est. well wooded and cropped for sugar, cotton; drier interior devoted mainly to stock-raising; oil deposits; a. 21,054 km²; p. (est. 1968) 850,603.

Sergo. See Kadiyevka.

Seria, t., Brunei; coastal t., protected from sea by 8 km dyke; oil ctr., linked by pipeline with Lutong; p. (1971) 20,801.

Serov, t., RSFSR; in Urals; iron and steel; natural gas pipeline from Ingrim; p. (1970) 100,000.

Serowe, t., Botswana, Southern Africa; seat of Bamanguato tribe; mkt. ctr.; p. (est. 1969) 34,186.

Serpukhov, t., R. pt., RSFSR; on R. Oka, planned canal link to Moscow; p. (1970) 124,000.

Serra da Mantiqueira, mtn. range, hgst. in Brazil.

Serra do Espinhaco, mtns., Brazil; highest peak, Itambe, 2,045 m; iron-ore deposits.

Serra do Mar, mtns., Brazil; form steep E. edge of Brazilian Plateau S. from Rio de Janeiro.

Serrai (Seres), dep., Macedonia, N. Greece; N. mtns. form frontier with Bulgaria in gorge of Struma R. valley; lower Struma R. basin fertile agr. a., producing cotton, tobacco; mkt. ctr. at cap. Serrai; a. 4,053 km²; p. (1971) 202,771.

Sertão, semi-arid hinterland, N.E. Brazil; stock-

raising, but drought causes migration to Amazon basin; hydroelectric power and irrigation schemes; focus of social unrest documented in Brazilian novels.

Sesto San Giovanni, sub., Milan, Italy; machin., glass, chemicals, plastics; p. (est. 1968) 85,094.

Sète, spt., Hérault dep., France; on Med. cst.; chemicals, fisheries; exp. oysters, brandy, wine; oil pipeline under sea to Frontignan; importance originally based upon canal network, now supplanted by rlys.; tourism of growing importance; p. (1968) 41,044.

Setesdal (Saetersdal), Aust-Agder, S. Norway; remote valley retaining traditional social customs; arable pastoral agr.

Sétif, cap. of Sétif dep., N.E. Algeria; agr. ctr. for surrounding plateaux; grain, livestock; phosphates in a.; p. (1967) 98,000.

Seto, t., central Honshu, Japan; porcelain ctr. (since 13th cent.); based on local deposits of kaolin; p. (1970) 92,681.

Setouchi, dist., S.W. Honshu, Japan; rice, mandarin oranges, reeds, salt, textiles; part of Japan's industl. belt.

Setté Cama, spt., Gabon, Equatorial Africa; open roadstead, landing difficult owing to swell; exp. timber; oil nearby.

Settle, mkt. t., Craven, North Yorks., Eng.; on R. Ribble in heart of Craven dist.; tourist ctr. for limestone cty. of N. Pennines; textiles; p. (1971) 13,994 (dist.).

Settsu Plain, S. Honshu, Japan; at head of Osaka Bay at E. end of Inland Sea; intensively cultivated alluvial lowlands, ch. crops, rice, vegetables, oranges; gr. industl. belt extends along cst. through Kobe, Osaka, Kishiwada; engin., chemicals, textiles; a. 1,295 km².

Setubal, t., Estremadura, S. Portugal; impt. pt. on Sado R. estuary; exp. cork, wine, oranges; fishing, fish processing, shipyds.; p. (1970) 64,531.

Sevan (Gokcha), lge L., Armenian SSR, USSR; alt. 1,934 m; never freezes; surrounded by high barren mtns.; drained by Razdan R.; several hydroelectric power stas.

Sevastopol, spt., Ukrainian SSR, USSR; built on ruins left after famous siege 1855; Black Sea resort; rebuilt after second world war; one of most beautiful Crimean cs.; p. (1970) 229,000.

Sevenoaks, mkt. t., 1. gov. dist., Kent, Eng.; in Vale of Holmesdale; residtl.; agr., lt. inds.; Knole Park; public school founded in 1432; p. (est. 1976) 102,200 (dist.).

Severn, R., Ont., Canada; flows to Hudson Bay; tr. post at mouth; 560 km long.

Severn, R., W. of Eng. and N. Wales; rises in Powys and flows to Bristol Channel; suspension bridge at estuary opened 1966; several proposals for major economic development around shores of estuary; 344 km long.

Severn Tunnel, Eng.; under estuary of R. Severn between Pilning (Avon) and Severn Tunnel Junction (Gwent); carries main rly. from London to S. Wales; longest main-line rly. tunnel in Brit. Is.; 7 km long.

Severodvinsk, t., RSFSR; on Dvina Bay, White Sea; metals, bldg. materials; p. (1970) 145,000.

Seville, c., cap. of Seville prov. and of Andalusia, Spain; spt. on Guadalquivir R., canal link with Atl. Oc.; exp. agr. prod., imports industl. raw materials; major industl., comm. and cultural ctr.; diverse mnfs.; beautiful c. with Moorish influence, prominent in narrow streets of ctr. a.; Alcázar palace; Gothic cath.; bullfighting, tourist ctr.; p. (est. 1970) 650,000.

Sèvres, t., Hauts-de-Seine, dep., N. France; S.W. sub. of Paris on Seine R.; celebrated porcelain mnfs.; headquarters of International Bureau of Weights and Measures; p. (1968) 20,288.

Seward, t., S. Alaska, USA; rly. terminal, airfield and ice-free harbour make it an impt supply ctr. for interior Alaska; p. (1970) 1,587.

Seychelles Is., indep. rep. (1976), Indian Oc.; consists of 86 Is. (37 granitic, 49 coralline), among most beautiful in world; lgst. I. Mahé; cap. Victoria; fishing, tourism; exp. copra, cinnamon bark; famous for species of nut; total a. 404 km²; p. (1968) 49,981.

Seyne, or La Seyne-sur-Mer, t., Var dep., France; nr. Toulon; shipbldg.; p. (1968) 43,783.

Sfax, spt., Tunisia; admin. ctr.; exp. phosphate, olive oil, salt, esparto grass, cereals, dates, hides; imports food, coal, textiles, soap; sponges; fishing; natural gas found in a.; surrounded by irrigated gardens and olive groves; p. (1966) 79,595 (c.), 215,836 (met. a.).

Sgurr Mor, mtn., Ross and Cromarty, Scot.; alt. 1,109 m.

Shaba (Katanga), prov., Zaïre; many varied mineral deposits inc. copper, tin, iron-ore, cobalt, radium; cap. Lubumbashi; a. 466,200 km²; (est. 1969) 2,174,404.

Shaftesbury, mkt. t., North Dorset, Eng.; Saxon hilltop t., abbey ruins; ctr. for agr. a.; p. (1971) 3,976.

Shahjahanpur, t., Uttar Pradesh, India; on Deoha R.; agr. mkt. t. and rly. junc.; grain, sugar tr. and processing; p. (1971) 135,604 (t.), 144,065 (met. a.).

Shakhty (Alexandrovsk Grushevski), t., RSFSR; anthracite mng. in Donets Basin; leather, textiles, metal wkg., food inds.; p. (1970) 205,000.

Shamaldy-Say, t., Kirghiz SSR, USSR; new t. on site of Uch-Kurgan hydroelectric power sta.

Shandakan Tunnel, N.Y. st., USA; carries water under Catskill mtns to augment water supply of c. of N.Y.; 29 km long.

Shanghai, c. and mun., Kiangsu, China; major spt. on left bank of Hwangpu (main waterway of Yangtze delta); despite marshy site its strategic location developed, largely by Brit. businessmen (1843); handles major share of Chinese shipping, but much dredging required; in part a modern W. style c., but distinctively Chinese in original Chinese site; inds. developed in response to location at transit point for major economic region of China in Yangtze basin; major educational ctr.; world's most populous c.; a. 5,799 km²; p. (est. 1971) 10,820,000.

Shanhaikwan, c., N.E. Hopei, China; on double-track rly. to N.E. China; p. (est. 1957) 598,000.

Shannon Airport, Clare, R.o.I.; N.W. of Limerick; on main transatlantic air route; ctr. of customs-free industl. estate.

Shannon, R., Ireland; separates Connaught from provs. of Leinster and Munster, flows to Atl. at Loop Head; hydroelectric power sta. at Ardnacrusha; 358 km long.

Shansi (Shanxi), prov., N. China; bounded W. and S. by Hwang-ho (Yellow R.); mainly high plateaux; fertile loess deposits, but drought conditions limit agr. potential; dry crops and livestock; coal, iron ore, petroleum; cap. Taiyuan; a. 156,420 km²; p. (est. 1967) 18,000,000.

Shan State, div., Burma; elevated plateau through which flows Salween R.; impt. mng. dist., lead, zinc, silver at Bawdwin, smelters at Namtu; also tungsten, tin, antimony, manganese; home of Shan people; former Shan and Wa sts.; cap. Taunggyi; a. 155,801 km².

Shantung, coastal prov., N. China; S. of fertile plain of Hwang-ho; dense p. but agr. potential limited by dry climate; wheat, millet, maize, soyabeans, cotton, hemp, fruits; E. mtns. contain coal, iron, bauxite, kaolin; iron and steel inds. and cotton mills at main industl. ts. of Tsinan and Tsingtao; birthplace of Confucius at foot of sacred peak Tai; cap. Tsinan; a. 146,198 km²; p. (est. 1967) 57,000,000.

Shaohing (Shaoxing), c., N. Chekiang prov., S.E. China; agr. ctr. on Hangchow Bay; rice, wheat, cotton; p. (est. 1970) 225,000.

Shaoyang, c., Hunan prov., China; coal and iron mng.; timber; p. (est. 1970) 275,000.

Shap, mkt. t., Cumbria, Eng.; nearby is Shap Fell 279 m, an impt. pass traversed by rly. and by a main road; granite quarries.

Shapinsay, Orkney Is., Scot.; p. (1971) 346.

Shari, R., central Africa; formed by several headstreams in Central African Rep., flows across Chad Rep. into L. Chad in wide delta; navigable.

Shārjah, emirate, member of the United Arab Emirates (1971), Persian Gulf; international airport at cap. Shārjah (p. 25,000); natural harbour at Khawr Fakhan; oil exploration, fishing; p. (est. 1970) 40,000.

Sharon, plain, Israel; citrus fruits, vines, poultry.

Shasi, t., S. Hupei prov., China; agr. mkt. ctr. and canalised R. pt.; tr. in cotton, grain; flour milling, textiles; p. (est. 1970) 125,000.

Shasta Dam, Cal., USA; dams water of Rs. Pit,

McCloud, Sacramento for hydroelectric power; irrigation, flood control and reclamation of lower Sacramento valley.

Shatt-al-Arab, R., Iraq; formed by union of Tigris and Euphrates, flows thence to head of Persian G.; swampy delta in rich agr. a.; deepest-water line of R.'s estuary defined (1975) as new Iraq/Iran bdy.; 192 km long.

Shawinigan Falls, c., Quebec, Canada; pulp and paper, chemicals, aluminium inds., powered by hydroelectric power from falls on St. Maurice R.; p. (1966) 30,777.

Shawnee, c., Okla., USA; rly. and tr. ctr. for rich agr. a.; electronics, aircraft components; p. (1970) 25,075.

Sheaf, R., South Yorks., Eng.; rises in S.E. Pennines, flows N.E. to join R. Don at Sheffield; 18 km long.

Shebelinka, natural gas fields nr. Kharkov, Ukrainian SSR, USSR; pipelines to Kharkov-Bryansk and Dnepropetrovsk–Odessa.

Sheboygan, t., Wis., USA; on L. Michigan; ctr. for dairy farming and resort a.; cheese, leather gds., hardware; p. (1970) 48,484.

Sheerness, Kent, Eng.; on I. of Sheppey at entrance to estuary of R. Medway; former royal dockyard and garrison; deepwater comm. pt.; electronics, furniture, coach bldg.

Sheffield, c., met. dist., South Yorks., Eng.; on cramped site at confluence of Rs. Sheaf and Don; univ.; heavy engin. ctr., famous for high quality steels, cutlery, tools; major post-war redevelopment of c. ctr. with ambitious and imaginative housebldg. programme by a socially conscious local council, taking advantage of hilly site has turned S. into a very attractive modern c.; p. (est. 1976) 558,000 (dist.).

Sheksna, R., RSFSR; rises in L. Beloye and flows S. to Rybinsk Reservoir; forms part of Volga–Baltic waterway; 160 km long.

Shellhaven, oil refineries, Essex, Eng.; on N. side of Thames estuary, nr. Standord-le-Hope.

Shenandoah National Park, Va., USA; extends along forested Blue Ridge mtns.; views of Shenandoah valley and Alleghenny mtns.

Shenandoah, R., Va., USA; trib. of Potomac R.; picturesque valley noted for rich apple orchards and pastures; scene of several campaigns in Civil War; 272 km long.

Shensi, prov., N. China; Great Wall runs nr. N. border with Inner Mongolia; from N.–S. four main regions: (1) dry, fertile loess plateau, notorious famine region, but increasingly irrigated; (2) fertile Wei R. valley, ctr. of p. and agr.; (3) Tsinling divide; (4) agr. a. of upper Han R.; grain, livestock; coal, petroleum; developing transportation network aiding economic development; cap. Sian; a. 188,860 km²; p. (est. 1968) 21,000,000.

Shen-yang (Mukden), c., cap. of Liaoning prov., N.E. China; on Hun R. in narrowest part of lowland with hilly country on both sides; impt. rly. junc. with main routes N. to Harbin and Trans-Siberian rly., S. to Peking, Luta and into Korea; comm. and educational ctr.; impt. textile ctr., heavy inds., cement, chemicals, machin.; agr. ctr.; p. (est. 1970) 3,750,000.

Shepperton, t., Victoria, Australia; ctr. of vegetable and orchard a.; fruit canning, metal and brick wks.; p. (1972) 19,409.

Sheppey, I. of, Kent, Swale, Eng.; in Thames estuary E. of mouth of R. Medway; cereals, sheep-raising; new steel wks.; ch. t., Sheerness; a. 117 km².

Shepshed, t., Charnwood, Leics., Eng.; 5 km W. of Loughborough; hosiery; p. (1971) 8,456.

Shepton Mallet, mkt. t., Mendip, Somerset, Eng.; at foot of Mendip Hills, 8 km S.E. of Wells; old woollen ctr.; bacon curling, brewing; p. (1971) 5,910.

Shepway, l. gov. dist., S.E. Kent, Eng.; cstl. a. of Folkestone, Hythe, New Romney and Lydd; p. (est. 1976) 87,000.

Sherborne, mkt. t., West Dorset, Eng.; 6 km E. of Yeovil; famous abbey and school; Norman cas. ruins; glass fibre; p. (1971) 7,265.

Sherbrook, t., S.E. Quebec, Canada; comm. and mkt. ctr. for surrounding agr. region; inds. based on local sources of hydroelectric power from Magog R.; textiles, paper mills, machin., flour milling; deposits of asbestos nearby; p. (1966) 75,960.

Sheringham, t., North Norfolk, Eng.; on cst. 6 km W. of Cromer; resort; fishing; p. (1971) 4,666.

Sherwood Forest, anc. royal woodland, Notts., Eng.; now restricted to infertile Bunter Sandstone cty.; inc. several estates and parks, notably the Dukeries.

Shetland Is., Scot.; 80 km N.E. of the Orkneys; about 100 in gr., ch. t., Mainland; lge. number of rainy days, but climate mild and tourism attracted by isolation, scenery and wildlife; Fair Isle famous for knitted clothes; fishing, livestock, agr., potatoes; offshore oil exploration; oil service bases; lge. elderly p. due to attractions as a retirement a.; ch. t. Lerwick; a. 1,427 km²; p. (est. 1971) 17,327.

Shibin el Kôm, Menûfiya, Egypt; rly. and mkt. ctr. in agr. a. of Nile delta; tobacco, textiles; p. (est. 1970) 75,600.

Shigatze, t., Tibet, China; on R. Tsangpo; tr. ctr. on main caravan routes; p. c. 20,000.

Shihkiachwang (Shijiazhuang), c., Hopeh prov., China; cotton milling, glass mftg.; grew rapidly with coming of rly.; p. (est. 1970) 1,500,000.

Shikarpur, t., N. Sind, Pakistan; tr. ctr. for grain, precious stones; engin., food processing; p. (est.1969) 62,500.

Shikoku, I., Japan; S. of Honshu; smallest of Japan's 4 main Is.; sparsely populated, mtnous. interior, heavily forested; arable agr. in lowlands; ch. cs., Matsuyama, Kochi, Tokushima; a. 18,772 km²; p. (1970) 3,904,014.

Shilka, R., E. Siberia, RSFSR; trib. of R. Amur; 552 km long.

Shillelagh, v., R.D., Wicklow, R.o.I.; oak forest, gave its name to oak or blackthorn cudgel.

Shilong, c., cap. Meghalaya, former cap. of Assam, India; at alt. 1,372 m in Khasi hills; ctr. of impt. tea-growing dist.; admin. technical education; pleasant climate attracts summer tourists; p. (1971) 87,659 (c.), 122,752 (met. a.).

Shimizu, spt., Japan; exp. tea, oranges; fishing; p. (est. 1971) 237,000.

Shimoda, spt., Honshu, Japan; between Nagoya and Yokohama; fishing; p. (1970) 30,318.

Shimoga, t., Karnataka, India; on Tunga R.; cotton-ginning, rice-milling; p. (1971) 102,709.

Shimonoseki, spt., Honshu I., Japan; at extreme S.W. of I.; tunnel and bridge links island of Kyushu; rly. ctr.; engin., chemicals based on local coal; fishing; p. (est. 1971) 264,000.

Shin, Loch, Sutherland, Scot.; 26 km long; drained by R. Shin to R. Oykell.

Shipka Pass, Bulgaria; over the Balkan mtns., 75 km N.E. of Plovdiv.

Shipley, t., West Yorks., Eng.; on R. Aire, 13 km N.W. of Leeds; worsted mnfs.; inc. model v. of Saltaire, built by Titus Salt (1851) to house his alpaca mill workers; p. (1971) 28,444.

Shiraz, c., cap. of Fars prov., Iran; beautifully sited in vine-growing dist.; textiles, rugs, metalwk., lt. elec. ind.; tourist ctr.; tombs of mediaeval poets Saadi and Hafez; known as "city of roses and nightingales"; pleasant winter climate; univ., airpt.; oil refinery projected; p. (est. 1971) 335,700.

Shire, R., flows out of L. Malawi south through Malawi and Moçambique to Zambesi; 592 km long.

Shirwa or Chilwah, shallow L., Malawi; 64 km long, 22 km wide; has 4 Is.

Shizuoka, c., cap. of S. pref., Honshu, Japan; pt. on Suruga Bay; impt. ctr. for tea and oranges; lacquerware, textiles; p. (est. 1971) 428,000.

Shkodër (Scutari), c., N. Albania; stands at foot of L. Scutari, 26 km from Adriatic; mkt. ctr., tobacco, cement, textiles; enjoyed greatest comm. prosperity after Ottoman conquest; several mosques; p. (1967) 50,000.

Shkodër (Scutari), L., on borders of Montenegro (Yugoslavia) and Albania; outlet via R. Boyana into Adriatic, 46 km long.

Sholapur, c., Maharashtra, India; between Hyderabad and Poona; rly. junc., impt. textile ctr.; p. (1971) 398,361.

Shoreham-by-Sea, t., Adur, West Sussex, Eng.; at mouth of R. Adur, 6 km E. of Worthing; spt. and mkt. t.; oil jetty; boat bldg., chemicals, soap, preserves; p. (1971) 18,804.

Shoshone Falls, on Snake R., Idaho, USA; height 61 m, used for irrigation projects.

Shott el Jerid, Algeria and Tunisia; deep depression in the desert.

Shotts, plateau, N. Africa; upland region with salt Ls., within Atlas mtns.

Shreveport, c., La., USA; industl. ctr. in cotton-growing dist.; petroleum; p. (1970) 178,061 (c.), 289,909 (met. a.).

Shrewsbury, co. t., Salop, Eng.; on R. Severn 19 km above Ironbridge gorge between the Wrekin and Wenlock Edge; agr. and dairy equipment, machin., elec. gds.; cattle and sheep mkt.; public school; with Atcham forms l. gov. dist.; p. (est. 1976) 84,800.

Shropshire. See Salop.

Shropshire, North, l. gov. dist., Salop, Eng.; a. N. of Shrewsbury and inc. Market Drayton; p. (est. 1976) 48,700.

Shropshire, South, l. gov. dist., Salop., Eng.; S. of Shrewsbury and inc. Ludlow; p. (est. 1976) 33,600.

Shusha, t., Azerbaydzhan SSR, USSR; health resort; silk spinning, rug making; Armenian p. massacred by Tatars 1926; p. c. 6,000.

Shustar, t., Iran; carpets, woollens, pottery; shallow-draught boats can reach Shaliili, nr. S. by R. Karun; p. (1966) 21,999.

Sialkot, t., Pakistan; N.E. of Lahore; sports gds., musical and surgical instruments, paper; agr. tr. and processing ctr.; p. (est. 1969) 167,000.

Siam. See Thailand.

Siam, G. of, lge. inlet, S. China Sea; sheltered with shallow water; length 616 km N.W. to S.E.

Sian (Xian), cap. of Shensi prov., China; impt. route and industl. ctr.; food processing and tr., flour, grain, tea, tobacco, iron and steel, textiles, chemicals; p. (est. 1957) 1,310,000.

Siangtan (Xiangtan), c., Hunan prov., China; on navigable Siang R.; regional tr. ctr., tea, cotton; electrical gds., machin., textiles; Mao Tse-tung born nearby; p. (est. 1970) 300,000.

Siauliai, t., Lithuanian SSR, USSR; 184 km N.W. of Vilna; impt. rly. junc.; food and leather inds. p. (est. 1969) 88,000.

Sibenik, t., Croatia, Yugoslavia; Adriatic spt.; exp. timber, bauxite; aluminium, chemical and textile inds.; p. (est. 1965) 29,000.

Siberia, terr., USSR; extends from Urals to Sea of Okhotsk and Bering Strait, bounded by Arctic on N. and by Mongolia and Turkestan on S.; climate mostly severe; ch. ts., Novosibirsk (cap. W. S.) and Irkutsk (cap. E. S.); rich in coal, iron, minerals; oil and gas in W. Siberian lowland; resources not yet fully known but Soviet economic policy is to develop S. in order to use its natural resources to the full; p. and economic activity clustered around rlys., esp. Trans-Siberian rly.; a. c. 12,950,000 km².

Sibiu, t., central Romania; picturesque site at foot of Transylvanian Alps; retains mediaeval character despite being an impt. industl. ctr.; textiles, agr. machin., chemicals, leather; lge. German minority p.; caths.; p. (est. 1969) 118,893.

Sibu, t., Sarawak, E. Malaysia; 128 km up R. Rejang; comm. ctr. at head of ocean navigation; airport; p. (1960) 29,630.

Sicily, lgst I., Mediterranean Sea; former kingdom and now aut. region of Italy; pleasant climate, mtnous.; fertile lowlands, especially plain of Catania, but agr. hampered by primitive methods, absentee landlords and need for irrigation; lge. range of Mediterranean crops; fishing; sulphur; petroleum reserves, refining and petrochemical inds.; volcanic Mt. Etna erupted in 1971; a. 25,708 km²; p. (1969) 4,876,624.

Sidi-bel-Abbès, t., W. Algeria; old fortress t., became H.Q. of Fr. Foreign Legion; agr. mkt. ctr. for region producing grain, grapes, olives, livestock; cement, furniture mnfs.; p. (1967) 101,000.

Sidlaw Hills, low mtn. range, Tayside Reg., Scot.; max. alt. 455 m.

Sidmouth, mkt. t., East Devon, Eng.; on S. cst., 24 km S.E. of Exeter; seaside resort; retirement ctr.; p. (1971) 12,039.

Sidon. See Saïda.

Siebengebirge, sm. wooded range of seven hills, W. Germany; of volcanic origin rising to 457 m on right bank of Rhine; famous for Drachenfels association with the Siegfried saga.

Siedlce, t., Poland; 88 km E. of Warsaw; rly. junc.; agr. inds.; p. (1970) 39,000.

Siegburg, t., N. Rhine–Westphalia, **W. Germany;** on **R. Sieg;** Benedictine abbey; dyes, iron, ceramics; p. (est. 1969) 33,940.

Siegen, t., N. Rhine–Westphalia, **W. Germany;** on **R. Sieg;** 2 cas.; ironmng. and smelting, machin., leather; p. (est. 1969) 57,946.

Siemianowice Slaskie, t., Poland; nr. Katowice; ctr. of mng., industl. region; iron and steel, machin.; cas.; p. (1970) 67,300.

Siena, hill-town, Tuscany, **Italy;** 51 km S. of Florence; spreads over three hilltops with Piazza del Campo in between where celebrated Palio festival (horse-races) are held; 13th- and 14th-cent. arch., cath.; agr. mkt., tanning, glass, textiles, bricks; *panforte* confectionery; tourist ctr.; p. (1969) 66,084.

Sierra Leone, rep., W. cst. Africa; mangrove swamps on cst., high plateau, with peaks over 1,800 m in interior; climate hot, humid; economy based on agr. and mng.; palm kernels, coffee, cocoa, rice, timber, iron ore; main exp. diamonds, notorious smuggling problem; fishing along cst.; cap. Freetown; a. 72,326 km²; p. (est. 1970) 2,500,000.

Sierra Madre Occidental, mtn. range, **Mexico;** volcanic, forms W. edge of Mexican plateau; average alt. 2,100 m.

Sierra Madre Oriental, mtn. range, **Mexico;** limestone, forms E. edge of Mexican plateau; average alt. 2,400 m.

Sierra Maestra, mtn. range, Oriente prov., S.E. **Cuba;** rises abruptly from cst.; rich in minerals.

Sierra Morena, mtn. range, **Spain;** between Guadalquivir and Guadiana basins, highest point 1,677 m; rich in minerals.

Sierra Nevada, mtn. range, Granada, **Spain;** highest summit Mulhacén 3,483 m.

Sierra Nevada, mtn. chain, Cal., **USA;** highest peak Mt. Whitney 4,544 m; nat. parks.

Sierra Nevada de Mérida, mtn. range, W. **Venezuela;** extends N.E. from San Cristóbal to Barquisimeto; extension of E. range of Andes, alt. over 4,880 m; impt. coffee plantations from 900–1,800 m on slopes.

Sierra Pacaraima, mtn. range, Brazil, **Venezuela;** forms part of international bdy. and watershed between Amazon and Orinoco basins.

Sighet, frontier t., N. **Romania;** on R. Tisa, on border with USSR; extreme, continental climate; timber, agr. and livestock tr.; cotton textiles; p. (est. 1970) 33,361.

Siglufjörd, spt., N. Iceland; impt. herring fisheries; p. (1970) 2,161.

Sigtuna, t., Stockholm, **Sweden;** on Mälaren L.; first cap. of Sweden; educational ctr., tourist resort; p. c. 3,300.

Sihanoukville (Kompong Som), c., Cambodia; deepwater pt. on G. of Thailand; linked to Phnom Penh by modern highway; textile mills, tractors, oil refining; p. (1962) 6,578.

Sikang, region, S.W. China; mtnous., mostly above 3,600 m; E. part in Szechwan prov., W. part in Chamdo region, Tibet; deep gorges of Salween, Mekong, Yangtze, and Hwang-ho provide severe obstacles to E.–W. communications; highest summit Minya Konka 7,570 km.

Sikhote-Alin, mtn. range, S.E. Asiatic **RSFSR;** rises to 1,800 m and extends for 1,200 km parallel to Pac. cst.; hinders access to W. basins forestry, minerals.

Si-Kiang, ch. R., S. China; headstreams rise in Yunnan plateau, form main R. nr. Sunchow; R. then flows E., enters S. China Sea through lge. delta nr. Hong Kong; lower valley intensively cultivated, rice, sugar-cane, tea; tropical climate permits continuous cultivation of most crops through year; valley very densely populated; c. 2,000 km long.

Sikkim, st., India; on S. slopes of Himalayas; incorporated as 22nd st. 1975; forest covered; economically underdeveloped; scene of rivalry between India and China; cap. Gangtok; a. 7,110 km²; p. (est. 1968) 187,000.

Sila, La, massif, Calabria, S. **Italy;** granite mass occupying full width of peninsula; alt. over 1,060 m, max. 1,930 m.

Silchester, par., Hants, **Eng.;** between Basingstoke and Reading; ruins of Roman t., Calleva Atrebatum; impt. ctr. of Roman communications network.

Silesia (Polish Śląsk, Czech Slezsko, German Schlesien), geographical region, Central Europe;

since 1945 divided between Poland, ČSSR and E. Germany; extends along both banks of Oder R.; bounded in S. by Sudeten mtns.; forested mtns., fertile arable agr. in lowlands; major concentration of economic activity based on coalfield of Upper Silesia (ceded to Poland 1922); complex territorial history; now forms highly urbanised industl. conurb. mainly in Poland, admin. by Katowice, Opole, Wroclaw, Wroclaw (c.), and part of Zielona Gora; ČSSR portion forms part of N. Moravia; E. Germany retains sm. part of Lower Silesia W. of Neisse R.; total a. 46,600 km².

Silistria, t., Bulgaria; on Danube opposite Romanian t. of Calarasi; cereals and timber tr.; mnfs. foodstuffs, ceramics, furniture; mosques; p. (est. 1968) 36,151.

Silkeborg, t., Jutland, **Denmark;** tourist resort in beautiful forest and lake region; p. (est. 1970) 26,129.

Silsden, t., West Yorks., **Eng.;** wool textiles; p. (1971) 5,588.

Silver Spring, t., Md., **USA;** sub. N. of Washington, D.C.; science-based inds. and research laboratories; p. (1970) 77,496.

Simcoe, L., S. Ont., **Canada;** several resorts; boating, fishing; 48 km by 42 km.

Simeulue, I., S.W. of Sumatra, **Indonesia;** primitive islanders; fishing and shifting cultivation.

Simferopol, t., Ukrainian SSR, **USSR;** on R. Salghir nr. Sevastopol; industl. ctr. in rich agr. a., fruit-canning, tobacco, machin.; p. (1970) 250,000.

Simla, t., Himachal Pradesh, **India;** famous hill-station c. 2,158 m high on forested ridge of Himalayas, 280 km N. of Delhi.

Simonstown, W. Cape Prov., S. **Africa;** naval sta., docks; p. (est. 1967) 8,900.

Simplon, mtn., Switzerland; alt. 3,567 m; the pass over the Simplon (alt. 2,011 m) from Domodossola, Italy, to Brig in the Rhône valley, Switzerland, was originally made by Napoleon I. The Simplon rly. tunnel leads from Brig on the Swiss side to Iselle in the Val di Vedro on the Italian and is the longest in the world, 19·7 km.

Simpson Desert, Australia; S.E. of Alice Springs, N.T., extends into S. Australia.

Sinai, peninsula, easternmost part of **Egypt;** between Gs. of Aqaba and Suez, at head of Red Sea; mainly desert in N., granitic ridges in S. rising to 2,592 m at Jebel Katrun; Jebel Musa or Mt. Sinai (2,244 m) is one of numerous peaks; mineral resources; coalmine at Maghâra; occupied by Israeli troops, Nov. 1956–March 1957, and since June 1967; a. 28,632 km².

Sinaia, t., S. Romania; health and winter sports resort in Transylvanian Alps; until 1947 summer residence of Romanian kings; palaces; p. (1966) 11,976.

Sinaloa, st., Mexico; on G. of Cal.; agr. and mng., rich in gold, silver, copper, iron and lead; cereals on uplands; sugar, cotton on lowlands; cap. Culiacán; a. 48,482 km²; p. (1969) 1,185,000.

Sind, prov. (revived 1970), **Pakistan;** lower Indus valley; dry climate; E. part reaches edge of Thar desert; agr. depends on irrigation; irrigated by Sukkur and Kotri systems; wheat, rice, cotton, oilseeds, sugar-cane, fruits; handicraft inds. in ts.; ch. ts., Karachi, Hyderabad, Sukkur, Shikarpur; a. 129,500 km² p. (1972) 13,965,000.

Singapore, rep., S.E. Asia; I. separated from Malaysian mainland by Johore Strait and linked by causeway; equatorial climate; cap. Singapore on S. cst. has fine natural harbour; major entrepôt tr. for Malaysia and S.E. Asia; world ctr. of rubber and tin mkts.; tr. in rubber, tin, petroleum, imported foodstuffs; growing industl. estates; oil refining, shipbldg.; only 20 per cent land cultivated; fruit, mkt. gardening; offshore fishing; reduction in Brit. military presence from base on N. cst. of I.; a. 580 km²; p. (1970) 2,074,507 (rep.); (est. 1969) 2,016,800 (c.).

Singhbhum, dist., Bihar, **India;** iron- and steel-wks. based on local iron mng.; a. 13,445 km²; p. (1961) 2,049,911.

Sinhailien (Xinhailion), c., Kiangsu, **China;** formed by merger of Sinput, Tunghai and Lien-yienkang; agr. comm. ctr., tr. in cereals, cotton; p. (1953) 207.600.

Sining (Xining), cap of Chinghal prov., **China;**

ctr. of spring wheat a.; woollen mills, iron and steel; p. (est. 1970) 250,000.

Sinkiang-Uighur (Xinjiang), aut. region, N.W. China; borders on USSR and Kashmir; very dry climate; remote until new roads and rlys. penetrated a.; pastoral agr., sheep, goats; new st. arable farms, wheat, maize, millet; lge oil reserves; cap. Urumchi; a. 1,646.800 km²; p. (est. 1968) 8,000,000.

Sinop, cap. of S. prov., **Turkey;** sm. pt. with gd. harbour on Black Sea but poor communications with hinterland; p. (1965) 13,354.

Sintra (Cintra), t., **Portugal;** summer resort, 29 km from Lisbon; Moorish castle, royal palace; p. (1970) 20,321.

Sinuiju, c., **W. N. Korea;** spt. at mouth of Yalu R. on Yellow Sea; linked by bridge to Antung (China); industl. ctr.; chemicals, aluminium inds., using power from Supung Dam; p. (est. 1970) 125,000.

Sinyang, t., S. Honan, **China;** regional ctr. for S. Honan and N. Hupei; p. c. 75,000.

Sion, t., cap. of Valais can., **Switzerland;** on R. Rhône; built on two castled hills; cath.; horticultural mkt. ctr.; hydroelectric power stas. and coal mines nearby; p. (1969) 21,600.

Sioux City, Iowa, **USA;** on R. Missouri; meat-packing, foundries, elec. gds. cement; p. (1970) 83,626 (c.), 113,929 (met. a.).

Sioux Falls, t., S.D., **USA;** on Big Sioux R.; in rich wheat region; machin., cars, farming implements; nuclear reactor; p. (1970) 72,488.

Siret, R., **Romania, USSR;** flows E. from Carpathians to Danube; steep forested left bank, fertile terraced right bank; hydroelectric power and irrigation schemes; 448 km long.

Sisak, t., Croatia, **Yugoslavia;** developing industl. ctr. and R. pt.; iron and steel, oil refining.

Sistan and Baluchistan, twin prov., **Iran;** bounded by Afghanistan and Pakistan; cap. Zahedan; much desert land; arid, very hot; p. (1967) 456,435.

Sitapur, t., Uttar Pradesh, **India;** rly. junc.; agr. tr. ctr.; eye hospital; p. (1961) 53,884.

Sitra, I., Persian G.; forms part of st. of Bahrain, 5 km long and 1·6 km wide; oil pipeline and causeway carrying road extends out to sea for 5 km to deep-water anchorage.

Sittang, R., **Burma;** rises in Pegu Yoma, flows S. to G. of Martaban through delta; valley intensively cultivated, delta forested; irrigation project; 976 km long.

Sittard, mkt. t., Limburg, **Neth.;** tanning; p. (1968) 33,804.

Sittingbourne and Milton, mkt. t., Swale, Kent, **Eng.;** on Milton Creek, 14 km E. of Chatham; paper-mills, brick-wks.; cement; insecticides; ctr. of fruit-growing dist.; p. (1971) 30,861.

Sittwe (Akyab), spt., **Burma;** at mouth of Kaladan R.; exp. rice; pt. suffered during war; p. (est. 1962) 86,451.

Sivas, c., cap. of S. prov., **Turkey;** impt. tr. and agr. ctr. in Kizil Irmak valley; cement, rugs; copper mng. nearby; foundations of modern Turkey laid here by Atatürk 1919; p. (1965) 108,320 (c.), 169,964 (met. a.).

Sivash Sea or **Putrid Sea,** lagoon on N.E. cst. of Crimea, **USSR;** 20 per cent salt; a. 2,590 km².

Siwa, oasis, **Egypt;** in Libyan Desert, c. 480 km S.W. of Alexandria; dates, olives; remains of temple of Zeus Ammon (visited by Alexander the Great); 32 km long, 1·6 km wide; p. (1966) 3,600.

Sizewell, Suffolk, **Eng.;** nuclear power sta.

Sjaelland, I., **Denmark;** lgst. I., separated from Fyn I. by the Gr. Belt; fertile glacial clays but rapidly spreading ts.; ch. c. Copenhagen; a. 7,356 km²; p. (1965) 2,055,040.

Skagerrak, arm of N. Sea, giving access to the Kattegat, between Norway and Denmark; 112–144 km wide.

Skagway, sm. spt., Alaska, **USA;** at head of Lynn Canal inlet, 640 km N.W. of Prince Rupert; linked by rly. to Whitehorse on upper R. Yukon; boomed in gold rush (1898), p. 15,000, subsequently declined; p. (1970) 675.

Skåne (Scania), peninsula, extreme S. of Sweden; corresponds approx. to cos. Malmöhus, Kristianstad; most favoured part of Sweden in relief, soil, climate; intensive farming, wheat, barley, sugar-beet, fodder crops, dairy cattle; ch. ts. Malmö, Lund, Hälsingborg; a. 10,360 km².

Skaraborg, co., **Sweden;** between Ls. Väner and Vätter; dairy agr.; a. 8,467 km²; p. (est. 1970) 255,964.

Skara Brae, prehistoric v., Mainland, Orkneys, Scot.; v. excavated from under sand dunes.

Skarzysko-Kamienna, t., Kielce, **Poland;** ctr. of developing metallurgical ind.; p. (1970) 39,200.

Skaw The (Grenen), C., at extreme N. of Denmark.

Skeena, R., B.C., **Canada;** rises in N. Rocky mtns., flows S.W. to Pac. Oc. at Prince Rupert; lower valley used by Canadian National Rly.; 640 km long.

Skegness, t., East Lindsey, Lincs., **Eng.;** on E. cst.; resort; lt. engin.; p. (1971) 13,557.

Skellettea, t., N. **Sweden;** on Bothnia G.; growing since discovery of Boliden ores nearby; iron and copper ore smelting; p. (1968) 61,949; (1961) 22,000.

Skelmersdale and Holland, t., West Lancs., **Eng.;** coal, bricks, drainpipes; new t. (1961); p. (est. 1970) 39,000.

Skelton and Brotton, t., Langbaurgh, Cleveland, **Eng.;** at N. foot of Cleveland hills, 16 km E. of Middlesbrough; steel flooring; p. (1971) 15,083.

Skiddaw, mtn., Cumbria, **Eng.;** E. of Bassenthwaite L.; alt. 931 m.

Skien, spt., Bratsberg, **Norway;** on R. Skien; saw-mills, timber tr.; birthplace of Ibsen; p. (1968) 44,213.

Skikda (Philippeville), t., spt., **Algeria;** exp. prods. from Saharan oases; oil pipeline to Mesdar; p. (1967) 85,000.

Skipton, t., Craven, North Yorks., **Eng.;** on R. Aire; cotton and rayon inds.; cas.; p. (1971) 12,422.

Skopje, t., cap. of Macedonia, **Yugoslavia;** anc. Scupi, one of oldest ts. in Balkans; oriental appearance; destroyed by earthquake (1963); food processing, iron and steel wks.; new oil refinery; airpt., route ctr.; p. (est. 1971) 388,000.

Skövde, t., **Sweden;** between Ls. Vänern and Vättern; garrison t., chemicals, cement; p. (1968) 28,028.

Skye, I., lgst. of Inner Hebrides, Skye and Lochalsh, Scot.; mtnous.; sheep-farming and fisheries; tourism; only t. Portree; a. 1,417 km²; p. (1971) 7,364.

Skyros, I., Sporades, **Greece;** in Aegean Sea; mainly agr.; a. 199 km²; p. (1961) 2,882.

Slagelse, t., Sjaelland, **Denmark;** food inds.; iron wks.; 11th cent. church; p. (est. 1970) 23,169.

Slave Coast, name given to the Guinea cst. of W. Africa between the Volta and Niger deltas where slaves were shipped from 16th to 19th cent.

Slave, R., N.W. Terr., **Canada;** flows into Gr. Slave L.; length 416 km.

Slavonia, historic region, **Yugoslavia;** between Drava R. (N.) and Sava R. (S.); now part of rep. of Croatia; ch. t. Osijek.

Slavyansk, t., Ukrainian SSR, **USSR;** in Donets basin; chemicals, engin.; p. (1970) 124,000.

Sleaford, mkt. t., North Kesteven, Lincs., **Eng.;** 19 km N.E. of Grantham; agr. and agr. implements; p. (1971) 7,975.

Sleat, Sound of, Lochaber, Skye and Lochalsh, Scot.; separates I. of Skye from the mainland; 11 km wide.

Slezsko. See Silesia.   [21,887.

Sliema, t., **Malta;** E. of Valletta; resort; p. (1971)

Slieve Bloom, hill range, Offaly and Laoghis cos., R.o.I.; highest point 529 m.

Slieve Donard, mtn., N. **Ireland;** highest of the Mourne mtns.; alt. 835 m.

Sligo, co., Connacht, R.o.I.; borders Atl. Oc.; rises to Ox Mtns. over 600 m; pastoral agr., fishing; co. t. S.; a. 1,909 km²; p. (1966) 51,078.

Sligo, co. t., Sligo, R.o.I.; on S. Bay; pt., exp. agr. prods.; abbey ruins; cath.; p. (1966) 13,297.

Slioch, mtn., Ross and Cromarty, Scot.; 981 m.

Sliven, t., **Bulgaria;** in Balkan mtns.; impt. woollen mnf. ctr.; carpets; p. (est. 1968) 77,458.

Slough, t., l. gov. dist., Berks., Eng.; on river terrace N. of R. Thames, 37 km W. of London; many lt. inds.; p. (est. 1976) 99,700.

Slovakia (Slovak Socialist Rep.), ČSSR; extends from Carpathians to Danube valley; pros.

perous agr.; cap. Bratislava; with Czech Socialist Rep. forms Fed. Rep. of Czechoslovakia; a. 48,956 km²; p. (est. 1970) 4,563,460.

Slovenia, constituent rep., Yugoslavia; mtnous., but many minerals inc. coal; highly developed region; cap. Ljubljana; a. 16,229 km²; p. (1971) 1,725,088.

Słupsk (Stolp), t., N.W. Poland (since 1945); formerly in Pomerania; on R. Słupia, nr. Baltic Sea; cas.; wood, metal, food processing; p. (1970) 68,300.

Småland, historic prov., S. Sweden; barren upland a. S. of L. Vättern; moorland, deciduous forest; contrasts greatly with remainder of S. Sweden.

Smederevo, t., Serbia, Yugoslavia; nr. Belgrade; pt. on R. Danube; walled t.; steel wks.; p. (1971) 27,182.

Smethwick. See Warley.

Smolensk, c., cap. of S. oblast, RSFSR; on upper Dnieper; anc. c. damaged in many wars; route ctr.; vehicles, machin., food processing; p. (1970) 211,000.

Smyrna. See Izmir.

Snaefell, highest mtn., I. of Man; alt. 620 m.

Snake R. or Lewis Fork, trib. of Columbia R., flows from Wyo. to Wash., USA; gorges; hydroelectric power; 1,680 km long.

Sneek, t., Friesland, Neth.; butter, cheese mkt.; yachting ctr.; p. (1967) 24,464.

Sneeuwbergen, mtn. range, Cape Prov., S. Africa.

Snøhetta, mtn., highest in Dovrefjell range, Norway; alt. 2,307 m.

Snowdon, mtn., Gwynedd, Wales; highest in Eng. and Wales. alt. 1,086 m; forms part of Snowdonia Nat. Park.

Snowy Mtns., N.S.W., Australia; part of Australian Alps; rise to over 2,000 m; S.M. scheme (1950) diverts water from headstreams in tunnels through mtns. to provide water for irrigation and hydroelectric power; completed 1972.

Snowy, R., N.S.W. and Victoria, Australia; rises in Mt. Kosciusko, flows S. into Bass strait 128 km W. of C. Howe; part of Snowy Mtn. scheme; 432 km long.

Soar, R., Leics., Notts., Eng.; rises S. of Leics., flows N.W. to join R. Trent; 69 km long.

Sobat, R., Sudan and Ethiopia; made up of several sm. Rs.; trib. of White Nile; 800 km long.

Soche. See Yarkand.

Sochi, t., RSFSR; on Black Sea at foot of main Caucasian range; health resort with subtropical climate and sulphur springs; developed since 1933; p. (1970) 224,000.

Society Is., Fr. Polynesia, S. Pac. Oc.; comprise Windward Is. (Tahiti, Moorea, Mehetia, etc.) and Leeward Is. (Huahune, Raiatea, etc.); discovered by Captain Cook; main prods. phosphate and copper; cap. Papeete; a. 1,647 km²; p. (1967) 61,519.

Socotra, I., G. of Aden, Indian Oc.; since 1967 part of Democratic Rep. of Yemen; under Brit. protection 1886–1967; lofty tableland; myrrh, frankincense, aloes; cap. Tamrida; a. 3,626 km²; p. (est.) 12,000.

Sodbury, t., Northavon, Avon, Eng.; former coalmng. ctr.; expanded t.; p. (1971) 67,040 (dist.).

Söderhamn, spt., Sweden; on G. of Bothnia, N. of Gavle; timber, wood-pulp; p. (est. 1970) 13,911.

Södermanland, co., Sweden; between Baltic cst. and L. Mälar; cattle-rearing; mng.; a. 6,822 km²; p. (est. 1970) 247,703.

Södertälje, t., Sweden; on S. canal linking L. Mälar with Baltic cst.; vehicles, chemicals, tobacco; p. (1968) 52,503.

Soest, c., N. Rhine–Westphalia, W. Germany; one of oldest ts., member of Hanseatic league; suffered heavily in second world war; soap, textile machin., engin.; p. (est. 1969) 35,731.

Soest, t., Utrecht, Neth.; residtl., agr. ctr.; p. (1968) 33,190.

Sofia, c., cap. of Bulgaria; Roman Serdica, and Triaditsa of Byzantine Greeks; nr. Yugoslav border; impt route ctr. and ch. industl. ctr. of rep.; machin., textiles, chemicals, elec. engin.; cath., univ., and many historic bldgs.; p. (est. 1969) 858,140 (c.); (1967) 923,400 (met. a.).

Sogne Fjord, Norway; longest fjord in Norway; length 176 km; tourism.

Sogn og Fjordane, co., W. Norway; borders

Atl. Oc., indented by Sogne Fjord; lge. hydroelectric power resources; tourism; a. 18,480 km²; p. (est. 1972) 101,740.

Sohag, t., Egypt; on R. Nile; cotton processing; p. (1960) 62,000.

Soho, dist., London, Eng.; settled by Fr. Huguenots 16th cent.; high proportion of foreign residents, sometimes known as London's "Latin quarter"; night-clubs, theatres, restaurants, filmcompany offices.

Soissons, t., Aisne dep., France; anc. Augusta Suessionum; commands N.E. approaches to Paris; cath.; agr. tr.; p. (1968) 27,641.

Sokoto, t., Nigeria, W. Africa; founded 1809 as cap. of native st. of S., p. mainly Hausa and Fulani; tr. ctr.; p. (est. 1969) 104,160.

Solent, The, strait separating I. of Wight from Hampshire mainland, Eng.

Solihull, t., met. dist., West Midlands, Eng.; 8 km S.W. of Birmingham; residtl.; motor vehicles, chemicals; p. (est. 1976) 199,600 (dist.).

Solikamsk, t., RSFSR; on R. Kama; chemicals from local potash; rapidly growing t.; p. (est. 1969) 89,000.

Solingen, t., N. Rhine–Westphalia, W. Germany; 24 km E. of Düsseldorf; cutlery ctr.; p. (est. 1969) 175,200.

Solnechnyy. See Gornyy Snezhnogorsk.

Solomon Is., S. Pac. Oc.; internal self-gov. (1976); archipelago of volcanic Is.; N. Is. form part of Papua New Guinea; remainder Brit.; dependent on exp. of copra, timber, fish; threatened by insect pests; indep. 1978; a. 29,785 km²; p. (1966) 221,290 (mostly Melanesian).

Solothurn (Soleure), can., N.W. Switzerland, crossed by Jura mtns., and R. Aare; 97 per cent cultivated; dairying; many industl. ts.; cap. S.; a. 793 km²; p. (1969) 228,000.

Solothurn (Soleure), t., cap. of S. can., Switzerland; on R. Aare; anc. t.; cath.; watches, motor mnf.; p. (1969) 19,100.

Solway Firth, arm of Irish Sea, Dumfries and Galloway Reg., Scot., and Cumbria, Eng.; 6 km long.

Somalia (Somali Democratic Rep.), E. cst. Africa; narrow cst. plain in N., widens in S., interior plateau reaching c. 2,400 m; dry, hot climate; 75 per cent. p. nomadic; livestock herding; permanent agr. in irrigated R. valleys; sugar, banana plantations in Webi Shebeli and Juba Rs. in S.; potential for mineral exploitation; cap. Mogadishu; recent conflict with Ethiopia; a. 637,658 km²; p. (est. 1969) 2,730,000.

Somaliland, French. See Djibouti.

Sombor, t., Serbia, Yugoslavia; cattle, grain tr.; textiles; p. (est. 1965) 32,000.

Somersby, v., Lincs., Eng.; birthplace of Tennyson

Somerset, non-met. co., S.W. Eng.; inc. part of Exmoor, Mendips, Quantocks and Blackdown hills; to N. is drained marshland of Somerset levels; dairying; coastal resorts; co. t. Taunton; a. 3,458 km²; p. (est. 1976) 404,400.

Somme, dep., N. France; borders Eng. Channel; crossed by R. Somme; low-lying agr. a.; textile inds.; cap. Amiens; a. 6,327 km²; p. (1968) 512,113.

Somme, R., France; flows in deps. Aisne and Somme to English Channel; scene of battles 1916; linked to Rs. Oise and Scheldt by canal; 186 km long.

Somport Tunnel, on bdy. France–Spain; carries main rly. from Pau to Zaragoza under Pyrenees; 8 km long.

Sönderborg, spt., S. Jutland, Denmark; older part of c. on Als I.; palace; textiles; p. (est. 1970) 23,069.

Sondrio, t., cap. of S. prov., Italy; commands the Adda valley, impt. routeway through Alps; agr. mkt.; textiles; p. (1969) 22,792.

Songkhla, t., Thailand; most S. t.; ctr. of rubber growing dist.; third t. of cty.; p. (est. 1964) 36,217.

Song-koi (Red R.), R., rises in Yunnan plateau, S.W. China, flows S.E. through N. Vietnam, enters G. of Tongking; Hanoi is nr. head of delta; Haiphong nr. one of R. mouths; lower valley densely populated and intensively cultivated; c. 1,280 km long.

Sonora, st., Mexico; on G. of Cal.; crossed by Sierra Madre Occidental; irrigated agr.; ch. producer of wheat, cattle; fish exp.; cap. Hermosillo; a. 182,535 km²; p. (1969) 1,249,000.

Sonoran Desert, Arizona, **USA**; alt. 900 m; enclosed basins and salt marshes.

Sonsonate, t., El Salvador; old t. with cath.; comm. ctr. of richest agr. region of rep., famed for coffee and dairy prod.; nr. Isalco volcano; p. (est. 1968) 31,435.

" **Soo** " Canals. *See* Sault Ste. Marie Canals.

Soochow (Suzhou), c., Kiangsu, **China;** nr. Shanghai; former treaty pt.; textile ctr.; p. (est. 1970) 1,300,000.

Sopot, spt., Poland; on Gdansk Bay; resort, spa; part of Trójmiasto; p. (1970) 47,600.

Sopron, t., N.W. Hungary; on R. Hunte; nr. Austrian border; textiles, chemicals; p. (1966) 44,700.

Sorau. *See* Zary.

Soria, t., cap. of prov. of Soria, Spain; on R. Duero at c. 900 m; agr.-processing; retains mediaeval appearance; p. (1970) 25,030.

Sorocaba, t., São Paulo st., Brazil; rly. wks.; textiles, cement, footwear, wines, fertilisers; p. (1970) 165,990.

Sorrento, cst. t., S. Italy; nr. S. extremity G. of Naples; popular resort, celebrated for its wines in anc. times; p. (est. 1968) 14,364.

Sosnowiec, t., Katowice prov., Poland; coal-mng. ctr., iron wks.; metal and textile inds.; cas.; p. (1970) 144,700.

Soufrière, volcano, St. Vincent, **W.I.;** alt. 1,235 m.

Sound, The, channel between Kattegat and Baltic, 5 km across at narrowest part; proposed tunnel between Denmark and Sweden.

Sousse (Susa), spt., Tunisia; exp. olive oil, phosphates; resort; p. (1966) 82,666.

South Africa, Republic of, lies in most S. part of Africa between Atl. and Indian Ocs.; comprises 4 provs., Cape Prov., Natal, O.F.S., Transvaal; narrow cst. plain, several interior plateaux (600–1,800 m) with upland grasslands (Veld) and fringed by escarpments; climate warm and sunny; most highly developed cty. in Africa, based on mineral resources of gold and diamonds, and more recent successful economic diversification; coal in Witbank and Vryheid dists. serves iron and steel ind. at Pretoria; growing textile, food-processing inds. at pts. Cape Town, Durban and rubber at Pt. Elizabeth; agr. dependent upon water supply; rich fruit growing a. around Cape Town, extensive grain growing and pastoral areas extended by irrigation; enforces practice of apartheid; caps. Pretoria (admin.), Cape Town (legislative), Bloemfontein (judicial); a. 1,224,254 km²; p. (1970) 21,300,000 (inc. 3,800,000 whites).

South America, S. continent of Western Hemisphere; inc. all ctys. S. of Panama. *See* Latin America.

Southampton, c. spt., l. gov. dist., Hants., **Eng.;** at head of Southampton Water on peninsula between estuaries of Rs. Test and Itchen; univ.; extensive docks for passenger-liners; container facilities; ship repairing, oil refining, cable mkg., electronics, synthetic rubber; p. (est. 1976) 213,700.

Southampton Water, inlet, Hants., **Eng.;** comprises drowned estuaries of Rs. Itchen and Test; gives access from Solent and Spithead to spt. of Southampton; 14 km by 1·6–2·4 km.

South Australia, st. of the Australian Commonwealth; the "desert state"; undulating interior forms part of central plateau of continent but inc. mtns. in S. and S.E. and L. Eyre basin 12 m below sea level; Nullarbor Plain in S.W.; sheep in S.E., intensive agr. in Murray R. valley; some interior mng. inds. but st. cap. of Adelaide contains most inds. and 60 per cent p.; a. 984,381 km²; p. (1972) 1,172,774.

South Bend, c., Ind., **USA;** on St. Joseph R.; ctr. of fruit and dairy region; motorcars, aircraft, agr. machin.; p. (1970) 125,580 (c.); (1968) 275,000 (met. a.).

South Carolina, st., **USA;** level in E., mtns. in W.; sub-tropical climate; part of cotton belt; pigs and maize also impt.; cotton textiles; cap. Columbia; a. 80,432 km²; p. (1970) 2,522,881.

South Dakota, st., **USA;** lies in Gt. Plains; crossed by R. Missouri; irrigated agr.; part of spring wheat belt, but now more diversified crops; agr. processing; cap. Pierre; a. 199,552 km²; p. (1970) 661,406 (inc. 25,000 Indians).

South Downs, chalk escarpment, East and West Sussex and Hants., **Eng.;** stretch from Chichester to Eastbourne; rise to over 240 m.

Southend-on-Sea, t., l. gov. dist., Essex, **Eng.;** on N. side of Thames estuary; varied lt. inds.; air ferry terminal; resort; dormitory for London; p. (est. 1976) 159,300.

Southern Alps, mtns., S.I., **N.Z.;** alt. 3,000 m.

Southern Ocean, surrounds Antarctica; pack ice.

Southern Uplands, region, S. Scot.; broad belt of hilly cty., N. part bleak moorland, S. part deeply cut by glens; sheep-rearing; dairying in valleys.

South Georgia, Brit. I., S. Atl. Oc.; dependency of Falkland Is.; former whaling ctr.; a. 4,144 km²; p. (1967) 22.

South Glamorgan, co., S. Wales; mostly lowland borders Bristol Channel; inc. lge. industl. ts. and pts. of Cardiff and Barry; a. 417 km²; p. (est. 1976) 389,200.

South Hams, l. gov. dist., S. Devon, **Eng.;** a. between Torquay and Plymouth inc. Totnes, Kingsbridge and Salcombe; p. (est. 1976) 63,900.

South I., lge. I., **N.Z.;** inc. S. Alps (highest Mt. Cook, 3,764 m), Canterbury Plains, impt. sheep-rearing dist.; cool climate; considerable hydroelectric power resources; tourism; a. 150,461 km²; p. (1971) 810,267.

South Kensington, dist., W. London, **Eng.;** contains Victoria and Albert Museum, Geological and Science Museums, British Museum of Natural History, Commonwealth Institute, Albert Hall.

South Orkney Is., Antarctica; S.W. of S. Georgia; part of Brit. Antarctic Terr. (1962); meteorological sta.

South Ossetian, aut. oblast, Georgian SSR, **USSR;** in Caucasus mtns.; goat and sheep rearing dist.; a. 3,898 km²; p. (1971) 100,000.

Southport, t., Sefton, Merseyside, **Eng.;** on S. side of Ribble estuary; 29 km N. of Liverpool; seaside resort; residtl.; p. (1971) 84,349.

South Ribble, l. gov. dist., Lans., **Eng.;** a. S. of Preston and inc. Walton-le-Dale; p. (est. 1976) 92,000.

South Sandwich Is., Antarctica; dependency of Falkland Is.; sm. volcanic Is.; a. 337 km².

South Shetland, archipelago, S. Atl. Oc.; 640 km S. C. Horn; part of Brit. Antarctic Terr. (1962).

South Shields, t., Tyne and Wear, **Eng.;** on S. bank at mouth of R. Tyne; coming holiday resort; marine engin., new lt. inds.; p. (1971) 100,513.

Southwark, inner bor., London, **Eng.;** S. of R. Thames, incorporating former bors. of Bermondsey and Camberwell; cath.; site of former Globe theatre; p. (est. 1976) 224,900.

South West Africa (Namibia), mandated terr., under U.N. responsibility but disputedly admin. by S. Africa; planned indep. for 1978; desert, scanty rainfall, part of southern African plateau; stock rearing; alluvial diamonds from Lüderitz on Orange R.; copper, lead, zinc mng. in Grootfontein dist.; ch. pt. Walvis Bay; cap. Windhoek; summer cap. Swakopmund; a. 824,296 km²; p. (1970) 746,328.

Southwick, t., Adur, West Sussex, **Eng.;** on S. cst. 6 km W. of Brighton; p. (1971) 11,850.

South Wight, l. gov. dist., I. of Wight, **Eng.;** inc. Ventnor and Sandown-Shanklin; (est. 1976) 92,000.

Southwold, spt., Waveney, Suffolk, **Eng.;** on E. cst. 13 km S. of Lowestoft; fishing; resort; p. (1971) 1,992.

South Yorkshire, met. co., **Eng.;** mainly industl. a. E. of Pennines; inc. productive coalfield nr. Barnsley and Doncaster and steel producing ts. of Sheffield and Rotherham; p. (est. 1976) 1,318,300.

Sovetsk (Tilsit), t., RSFSR (since 1945); on R. Niemen, formerly in E. Prussia; timber and paper inds.; famous for Treaty of Tilsit between Napoleon and Russia 1807; p. (est. 1967) 36,000.

Sowerby Bridge, t., Calderdale, West Yorks., **Eng.;** on R. Calder, 5 km W. of Halifax; woollens; p. (1971) 16,260.

Spa, t., Liège, Belgium; mineral springs, resort; gave name to "spas"; p. (est. 1969) 9,487.

Spain, indep. sov. st., Iberia, S.W. Europe; lge. land a. takes up 80 per cent of Iberian peninsula and helps to make climate continental;

mtnous. interior and narrow coastal strip encourages regional isolation and development of regional culture; civil war 1936–9 hindered modern economic growth; economy based on agr., but much of land is arid and although industl. raw materials in N. Spain and an oil refinery under construction at Bilbao, economic development has depended largely upon the spectacular growth of tourism; monarchy revived 1975; cap. Madrid; a. 504,747 km²; p. (1975) 35,355,039.

Spalding, mkt. t., South Holland, Lincs., **Eng.**; in Fens, 16 km up R. Welland from Wash; agr., bulb mkt. agr. machin., sugar-beet, fruit canning; p. (1971) 16,950.

Spandau, t., Potsdam, **E. Germany**; previously gr. military ctr.; at confluence of Rs. Havel and Spree; now part of Berlin.

Spanish Guinea. *See* Equatorial Guinea.

Spanish Sahara (Spanish West Africa). *See* Western Sahara.

Sparrows Point, t., Md., **USA**; situated on Chesapeake Bay; impt. iron and steel inds.

Sparta (Spárti), famous anc. c., **Greece**; on R. Eurotas in Peloponnesus; passed under Roman rule 146 B.C.; modern c. dates from 1834; p. (1971) 11,981.

Spelthorne, l. gov. dist., Surrey, **Eng.**; close to Gtr. London; inc. Staines and Sunbury-on-Thames; p. (est. 1976) 95,900.

Spencer Gulf, lge. inlet, S. **Australia**; penetrates 384 km inland, max. width 120 km.

Spennymoor, t., Durham, **Eng.**; growing industl. t. S. of Durham; p. (1971) 19,063.

Sperrin Mtns., Strabane, **N. Ireland**; peat-covered schists; Sawell, 683 m.

Spey, R., Moray, Badenoch and Strathspey, the most rapid in **Scot.**, flows N.E. to Moray Firth; used for hydroelec. power; 1,712 km long.

Speyer, t., Rhineland–Palatinate, **W. Germany**; tobacco, footwear, paper, sugar, brewing. oil refining; cas., cath.; famous Diet 1529 condemning Reformation gave rise to term " Protestant "; p. (est. 1969) 41,957.

Spitalfields, par., **E. London**, **Eng.**; formerly noted for silk weaving, introduced by Huguenots 17th cent.; name derives from spital or hospital of St. Mary, founded 12th cent.

Spithead, roadstead, between Portsmouth and I. of Wight, **Eng.**; used by ships of Royal Navy.

Spitsbergen (Svalbard), I. gr. belonging to **Norway**; within Arctic; mtnous.; sealing and whaling; coal mng.; asbestos, copper, gypsum; a. 62,021 km²; p. (1968) 2,808.

Split (Spalato), t., **Yugoslavia**; spt. on Adriatic; second spt. of rep.; airport; food processing; p. (est. 1969) 108,000.

Spokane, c., Wash., **USA**; on R. Spokane at falls used for hydroelec. power; timber tr. impt.; flour and saw mills, elec. gds.; lge. aluminium wks.; p. (1970) 168,654 (c.), 283,077 (met. a.).

Spoleto, c., Umbria, central **Italy**; cath.; many Roman remains; textiles, leather; p. (est. 1968) 37,036.

Sporades, scattered Is. belonging to **Greece** in Aegean Sea, inc. Skyros, Skiathos and Skopelos.

Spratley Is., S. China Sea; cluster of about 50 reefs and sand bars, thought to contain petroleum; ownership disputed by China, Taiwan, Philippines, and Vietnam.

Spree, R., **E. Germany**; flows W. past Berlin to the Havel at Spandau; 363 km long.

Spremberg, t., Cottbus, **E. Germany**; on R. Spree; cas., older part of t. on I.; glass, textiles; p. (est. 1970) 22,629.

Springfield, c., cap. of Ill., **USA**; in rich agr. and coal mng. a.; farming and elec. machin., food processing; home of Abraham Lincoln; p. (1970) 89,816 (c.), 159,432 (met. a.).

Springfield, c., Mass., **USA**; varied mnfs.; US armoury establ. 1794; p. (1970) 162,078 (c.), 523,502 (met. a.).

Springfield, c., Mo., **USA**; agr. ctr.; flour milling, engin.; p. (1970) 118,950.

Springfield, t., Ohio, **USA**; agr. mach., motor lorries; p. (1970) 82,188 (c.), 153,197 (met. a.).

Springs, t., Transvaal, **S. Africa**; E. of Johannesburg; gold mng., engin., machin., cars, elec. gds.; uranium plant; p. (1970) 104,090 (met. a.).

Spurn Head, Humberside, **Eng.**; sand spit at mouth of Humber estuary.

Sri Lanka (Ceylon), indep. rep. (1972) within Brit. Commonwealth (1948); in Indian Oc.; S.E.

of India; fertile plains with cash crops of coconuts and rubber (S.W.) but dry in N.; mtnous. interior ameliorates climate where tea cultivation; varied p. composition inc. Sinhalese, Tamils, Burghers (Portuguese and Dutch); dependent on exp. of primary produce; inds. growing; cap. and ch. spt. Colombo; a. 65,610 km²; p. (est. 1969) 12,240,000.

Srinagar, t., cap. of Kashmir, **India**; in vale at c. 1,600 m. on Jhelum R. in W. Himalayas; beautiful surrounding cty.; summer resorts; mnfs. silks, woollens, carpets; tourism; p. (1967) 325,000.

Srirangam, t., Tamil Nadu, **India**; on R. Cauvery; temple dedicated to Vishnu; pilgrimage ctr.; p. (1961) 41,949.

Stade, t., Lower Saxony, **W. Germany**; nr. Hamburg; pt. on R. Schwinge; leather, wood, textiles; p. (est. 1969) 31,658.

Staffa, I. in Inner Hebrides, W. **Scot.**; 10 km N. of Iona, off W. cst. Mull; grand basaltic caverns, inc. Fingal's Cave, 69 m long, 13 m wide, 20 m high.

Stafford, co. t., l. gov. dist., Staffs., **Eng.**; on R. Sow, 24 km N. of Wolverhampton; heavy elec. and other engin.; expanded t.; p. (est. 1976) 114,700 (dist.).

Staffordshire, non-met. co., W. Midlands, **Eng.**; plain drained by R. Trent and tribs.; N. Staffs. coalfield inc. a. of " Potteries "; S. Staffs. coalfield now inc. in W. Midlands met. co.; a. 2,717 km²; p. (est. 1976) 997,600.

Staffordshire, East, l. gov. dist., Staffs., **Eng.**; stretches from Uttoxeter to Burton-on-Trent; p. (est. 1976) 96,500.

Staffordshire Moorlands, l. gov. dist., Staffs., **Eng.**; borders S. Pennines and inc. Leek, Biddulph and Cheadle; p. (est. 1976) 94,300.

Staffordshire, South, l. gov. dist., Staffs., **Eng.**; a. bordering W. Midlands conurb.; p. (est. 1976) 89,000.

Staines, mkt. t., Spelthorne, Surrey, **Eng.**; on R. Thames, 6 km S.E. of Windsor; linoleum, machin.; nr. birthplace of Matthew Arnold; p. (1971) 56,386.

Stainmore, pass, North Yorks./Durham, **Eng.**; crosses N. Pennines from Greta valley into upper Eden valley; used by main road but only minor rly.; alt. 418 m.

Staithes, v., North Yorks., **Eng.**; potash mng.

Stalin. *See* Brasov.

Stalinabad. *See* Dushanbe.

Stalingrad. *See* Volgograd.

Stalino. *See* Donetsk.

Stalino. *See* Varna.

Stalinogorsk. *See* Novomoskovsk.

Stalinsk. *See* Novo Kuznetsk.

Stalybridge, t., Gtr. Manchester, **Eng.**; on R. Tame, 8 km E. of Manchester; cotton and wool, engin., plastics, rubber gds., elec. cables; p. (1971) 22,782.

Stamboul. *See* Istanbul.

Stamford, mkt. t., Lincs., **Eng.**; old bldgs., one of 5 Danelaw ts.; agr. inds., elec. gds., plastics; p. (1971) 14,485.

Stamford, c., Conn., **USA**; on shore of Long I. Sound; chemicals, engin.; p. (1970) 107,907 (c.), 204,888 (met. a.).

Stanislav. *See* Ivano-Frankovsk.

Stanley, t., Derwentside, Durham, **Eng.**; former colly. dist.; p. (1971) 41,940.

Stanley, spt., cap. of Falkland Is.; former whaling pt., contains over half p. of Falklands; p. (est. 1970) 1,098.

Stanley Falls. *See* Boyoma Falls.

Stanley Pool. *See* Pool Malebo.

Stanleyville. *See* Kisangani.

Stanlow, Ches., **Eng.**; petrol refinery, oil storage docks, chemicals.

Stanovoi Mtns., range of mtns., **USSR**; extending from N. of R. Amur to nr. Sea of Okhotsk.

Stara Zagora, t., central **Bulgaria**; textiles, agr. processing; educational ctr.; p. (est. 1969) 106,468.

Stargard Szczecinski, t., N.W. **Poland** (since 1945); formerly in Pomerania; rly. junc.; metal, chemical, and food inds.; devastated in second world war; p. (1970) 44,500.

Start Point, C., nr. Dartmouth, Devon, **Eng.**

Stassfurt, t., Magdeburg, **E. Germany**; in gr. potash mng. region; chemicals, machin., metals; p. (est. 1970) 25,695.

Staten I., the most S. point N.Y. st. **USA**; shipyds.; linked with Brooklyn by Verrazano–Narrows bridge (opened 1964); residtl.

Staten I., off Tierra del Fuego, S. America.

Stavanger, spt., cap. of Rogaland prov., S.W. Norway; comm. and industl. ctr.; fish curing and canning; oil refinery at Sola; cath., airport; p. (1968) 80,781.

Staveley, t., Derbys., Eng.; 5 km N.E. of Chesterfield; coal, iron, chemicals, concrete and iron pipes; p. (1971) 17,644.

Stellenbosch, t., Cape Prov., S. Africa; 40 km E. of Cape Town; univ.; wines, saw milling, brick and tile mkg.; p. (est. 1969) 29,000.

Stelvio Pass, between Italy and Switzerland; road pass, alt. 2,762 m.

Stendal, c., Magdeburg, E. Germany; impt. rly. junc.; sugar, metal and food inds.; cath.; Stendhal (Henri Beyle) took his name from the c.; p. (est. 1970) 36,478.

Stepney. See Tower Hamlets.

Sterlitamak, t., Bashkir ASSR, RSFSR; on S.W. flank of Ural mtns.; impt. oil refineries on "second Baku" oilfield; linked by pipeline to Togliatti; p. (1970) 185,000.

Stettin. See Szczecin.

Stettiner Haff, lagoon, E. Germany and Poland; separated from Baltic Sea by Is. Usedom and Wollin; receives R. Oder; 56 km long.

Stevenage, t., l. gov. dist., Herts., Eng.; 6 km S.E. of Hitchin; first new t. to be designated under the New Towns Act 1946; old t. known in Domesday as Stevenach; agr., lt. engin., school furniture, elec. gds., chemicals, aircraft parts; p. (est. 1976) 72,600 (dist.).

Stevenston, burgh, Cunninghame, Scot.; explosives factory; p. (1971) 12,047.

Steventon, v., Hants. Eng.; birthplace of Jane Austen.

Stewart I., off S.I., N.Z.; a. 1,735 km²; rises to over 900 m; famous for oysters.

Stewarton, burgh, Kilmarnock and Loudoun, Scot.; woollens, carpets; p. (1971) 4,492.

Steyning, v., West Sussex, Eng.; on R. Adur, 6 km N. of Shoreham at entrance to gap through S. Downs; residtl.

Steyr, t., Austria; at confluence of Rs. Enns and Steyr; industl. ctr.; historic bldgs.; p. (1961) 38,306.

Stilton, v., Cambs., Eng.; 10 km S.W. of Peterborough; famous for cheese.

Stirling, royal burgh, Stirling, Scot.; on R. Forth in gap between Campsie Fells and Ochil hills; cas., univ.; coal mng., concrete, wool, rubber gds.; p. (1971) 29,776.

Stirlingshire, former co., central Scot.; on S. edge of Grampians; now forms l. gov. dist. within the Central Reg.; a. of l. gov. dist. 2,168 km²; p. (1971) 75,520.

Stockholm, c., cap. of Sweden; on Is. at outlet of L. Malar; called the "Queen of the Baltic" for the beauty of its surroundings; comm. ctr.; machin., textiles, leather, sugar, chemicals; univ. and many academic institutions; p. (est. 1969) 747,490 (c.), 1,306,762 (met. a.).

Stockport, t., met. dist., Gtr. Manchester, Eng.; on R. Mersey, S.E. of Manchester; cotton, manmade fibres, engin.; p. (est. 1976) 292,900 (dist.).

Stocksbridge, t., South Yorks., Eng.; iron and steel; p. (1971) 13,400.

Stockton, t., Cal., USA; R. pt. on San Joaquin R.; agr. processing, farm implements; p. (1970) 102,633 (t.), 284,506 (met. a.).

Stockton-on-Tees, mkt. t., l. gov. dist., Cleveland, Eng.; 6 km W. of Middlesbrough; impt. iron and steel inds., plywood; first rly. for passenger traffic opened 1825 between Stockton and Darlington; 18th cent. town hall; racecourse; p. (est. 1976) 165,400 (dist.).

Stoke Newington. See Hackney.

Stoke-on-Trent, c., l. gov. dist., Staffs., Eng.; at S.W. foot of the Pennines; formed in 1910 by union of the "five towns" of Arnold Bennett's novels, Hanley, Burslem, Tunstall, Longton, and Fenton (with Stoke-upon-Trent); ceramics, coal, iron and steel, engin., brick and tile wks., precast concrete, rubber gds.; p. (est. 1976) 256,200.

Stolberg, t., N. Rhine–Westphalia, W. Germany; E. of Aachen; metals, glass, wood, chemicals; p. (est. 1969) 39,393.

Stolp. See Slupsk.

Stone, mkt. t., Staffs., Eng.; on R. Trent, 11 km S. of Stoke-on-Trent; footwear, tiles, porcelain,

scientific glassware; p. (1971) 10,985.

Stonehaven, t., burgh, Kincardine and Deeside, Scot.; fish. pt. on E cst., 22 km S. of Aberdeen, distilling, net mftg.; p. (1971) 4,730.

Stonehenge, prehistoric gr. of monumental stones, on Salisbury Plain, Wilts., Eng.; date of erection est. between 2100–1600 B.C.

Stornoway, spt., burgh, Scot.; on E. cst. of I. of Lewis, Outer Hebrides; ctr. Harris Tweed ind.; fishing ctr.; p. (1971) 5,152.

Stour, R., Kent, Eng.; flows past Canterbury to Pegwell Bay; 64 km long.

Stour, R., Somerset, Dorset, Eng.; trib. of R. Avon; 88 km long.

Stour, R., Suffolk and Essex, Eng.; flows E. to sea at Harwich; 67 km long.

Stour, R., Hereford and Worcs./West Midlands, Eng.; trib. of R. Severn; 32 km long.

Stourbridge, t., West Midlands, Eng.; on R. Stour; 14 km W. of Birmingham; brick and glass wks.; p. (1971) 54,331.

Stourport-on-Severn, mkt. t., Wyre Forest, Hereford and Worcs., Eng.; at confluence of Rs. Stour and Severn; carpets, iron and steel gds., porcelain, ceramics; old canal and R. pt.; p. (1971) 17,913.

Stowmarket, t., Mid Suffolk, Eng.; on R. Gipping, 18 km N.W. of Ipswich; I.C.I. paint factory; p. (1971) 8,670.

Strabane, t., l. gov. dist., N. Ireland; agr. ctr., shirt mkg.; p. (1966) 8,813.

Straits Settlements, former Brit. crown col.; Malay Peninsula; comprised Penang, Malacca, and Singapore, established 1867, dissolved 1946. See Malaysia, West.

Stralsund, spt., Rostock, E. Germany; opposite Rügen I.; grain tr., machin., metals, fish smoking, shipbldg.; p. (est. 1970) 71,551.

Strangford Lough, arm of sea, Down and Ards, N. Ireland; 29 km long, 10 km wide at entrance.

Stranraer, royal burgh, Wigtown, Scot.; at head of Loch Ryan; steamer service to Larne, N. Ireland; creameries, brewing, knitwear; cas.; mkt.; p. (1971) 9 853.

Strasbourg, c., cap. of Bas-Rhin dep., E. France; impt. pt. in Rhine valley on Ill R., 16 km S. of confluence with Rhine; terminus of Marne–Rhine and Rhône–Rhine canals; industl., comm. and cultural ctr. of economically impt. Alsace region; food processing and varied mnfs.; historic c., with many fine bldgs., inc. cath., univ., imperial palace; surrendered to Germany 1871, recovered 1919; meeting-place of European Parliament; p. (1968) 254,038 (c.), 334,668 (met. a.).

Stratford. See Newham.

Stratford-on-Avon, t., l. gov. dist., Warwicks., Eng.; on R. Avon; birthplace of Shakespeare; memorial theatre, library; many bldgs. ass. with Shakespeare; tourist ctr. in attractive setting; lt. inds.; p. (est. 1976) 100,100 (dist.).

Strathclyde Region, l. gov. reg., Central Scot.; industl. dist. formed around Glasgow, inc. ts. on Ayr and Lanarkshire coalfields; borders the F. of Clyde; a. 13,794 km²; p. (1971) 2,579,555.

Strathmore, lowland belt, central Scot.; flanked to N. by Scot. Highlands, to S. by Sidlaw and Ochil hills; drained by Rs. Earn, Tay, Isla, S. Esk; famous for cereals and small fruits; length 96 km, width 11–16 km.

Strathspey, valley of the Spey, Scot.; 112 km long.

Stratton and Bude, North Cornwall, Eng.; 19 km S. of Hartland Point; resort; p. (1971) 5,629.

Straubing, t., Lower Bavaria, W. Germany; agr. mkt. ctr.; machin.; p. (est. 1969) 37,024.

Strawberry, R., Utah, USA; on E. slopes of Wasatch mtns. 128 km S.E. of Salt Lake City; dammed to supply irrigation water led through tunnel under Wasatch mtns. to 259 km² cultivable land round L. Utah.

Street, t., Mendip, Somerset, Eng.; at foot of Polden Hills, 11 km S.W. of Wells; footwear, leather; p. (1971) 8,161.

Stretford, t., Gtr. Manchester, Eng.; borders Manchester Ship Canal; inc. Trafford Park industl. estate; residtl.; Lancashire co. cricket ground, Manchester United football ground at Old Trafford; p. (1971) 54,011.

Stromboli, I., Lipari Is., Tyrrhenian Sea, N. of Sicily, Italy; active volcano, alt. 927 m.

Stromness, burgh, Mainland, Orkney Is., Scot.; 21 km W. of Kirkwall; mkt., fish. pt.; p. (1971) 1,646.

Stronsay, Orkney Is., Scot.; p. (1971) 439.

Stroud, mkt. t., l. gov. dist., Gloucs., Eng.; on R. Frome, in Cotswolds; former ctr. of impt. cloth ind. in W. Eng.; woollens, dyes, plastics, engin.; p. (est. 1976) 80,300 (dist.).

Sturminster Newton, t., North Dorset, Eng.; impt. cattle mkt. on Stour R.; creameries; p. (1971) 10,715 (dist.).

Sturt Desert, a. N.W. of S. Australia; named after Charles Sturt, explorer.

Stuttgart, c., cap. of Baden-Württemburg, W. Germany; on Neckar R.; cas., cath., rly. junc.; industl. and comm. ctr.; publishing, science-based inds.; oil refinery nearby; p. (est. 1969) 621,000.

Styria, prov., Austria; borders Yugoslavia on S.; mtnous. with forests and pastures; lignite and iron mng., inds. around cap. Graz; grain, wine, fruit, stock-rearing; tourism; p. (1971) 1,191,000.

Suakin, former pt., Sudan, N.E. Africa; on Red Sea; now used only for pilgrim traffic to Jeddah; replaced by Pt. Sudan; plans for new pt.

Suanhwa (Xuanhua), c., Hopeh prov., China; iron mng.; p. (1953) 114,000.

Subotica, t., Serbia, Yugoslavia; univ.; agr. ctr. with Hungarian culture; agr. processing; expanding industl. ctr.; p. (1971) 88,787.

Suceava, t., S. Bukovina, N.E. Romania; mkt. t. on Suceava R.; once the residence of Mold-avian princes; p. (1968) 40,441.

Suchow (Suzhou), c., Kiangsu, China; at junc. of N. China plain and Yangtse R. basin; impt. rly. junc.; p. (est. 1970) 1,500,000.

Sucre, c., cap. of Chuquisaca dep. and *de jura* cap. of Bolivia (La Paz is *de facto* cap.); in valley of Andes at 2,600 m; agr. ctr., oil refining, 47.800.

Sucre, st., Venezuela; on Caribbean cst.; coffee and cacao; fishing impt.; fish canning at cap. Cumaná; a. 11,800 km²; p. (est. 1970) 493,840.

Sudan, The, rep., N.E. Africa; climatic transition from N. desert to rainy equatorial S.; mainly plateaux, dissected by Nile R. system; sporadic conflict between N. and S. (1955-1972); 3 southern provs. now form an autonomous reg.; long staple cotton, grown in irrigated areas, provides most valuable exp.; gum arabic from lge. forest areas; food processing; dams under construction on Atbara and Blue Nile Rs.; cap. Khartoum; a. 2,530,430 km²; p. (1970) 15,503,000.

Sudbury, t., Ont., Canada; nickel, copper mng.; refining; univ.; p. (1971) 89,898. (c.), 172,458 (met. a.).

Sudbury, t., Babergh, Suffolk, Eng.; on R. Stour, 19 km N.W. of Colchester; p. (1971) 8,183.

Sudene, terr., N.E. Brazil; government sponsored economic development.

Sudetenland, region of ČSSR bordering Germany, until 1945 German-speaking; annexed by Hitler 1938, recovered by ČSSR 1945; named after Sudeten mtns.; contains 20 per cent of p. of ČSSR.

Sudeten Mtns. or Sudetes, mtn. range along border of ČSSR and Poland; separating Bo-hemia and Moravia from Silesia; mineral resources.

Suez, spt., Egypt; the anc. Arsinoë; at head of G. of Suez (arm of Red Sea) and S. entrance of Suez canal, which crosses the isthmus of Suez to the Mediterranean at Port Said; Port Tewfiq adjoining has quay and docks; declined during closure of canal 1967-75; oil refining, fertilisers; p. (est. 1970) 315,000.

Suez Canal, ship canal, Egypt; connects Medi-terranean Sea (Pt. Said) with Red Sea (Suez) through Ls. Manzala, Timsah, and Bitter; length 162 km; closed after Arab-Israeli war of June 1967; reopened 1975.

Suez, G., Red Sea; N.W. arm of Red Sea between Arabian desert and Sinai peninsula, Egypt; southern approach to Suez canal; length 304 km., width varies from 19-40 km.

Suffolk, non-met. co. E. Anglia, Eng.; bounded on E. by N. Sea, drowned coastline; rises to 90 m in E. Anglian Heights in W.; impt. agr. a., lge farms, mixed farming; inds. based on agr.; many expanded ts. in S.; formerly divided into 2 admin. parts; co. t. Ipswich; a. 3,800 km²; p. (est. 1976) 577,600.

Suffolk Coastal, l. gov. dist., E. Suffolk, Eng.; lge

rural a. inc. ts. of Leiston-cum-Sizewell, Sax-mundham, Aldeburgh, Woodbridge and Felix-stowe; p. (est. 1976) 96,200.

Suhl, admin. dist., E. Germany; inc. Thuringian Forest; expanding inds. based on local potash and iron ore; a. 3,877 km²; p. (est. 1970) 553,020.

Suhl, t., Suhl, E. Germany; once famous for armaments; motor-cycles; p. (est.1970) 31,445.

Sui, Baluchistan, Pakistan; natural gas; pipeline to Karachi.

Sukhumi, spt., Georgian SSR, USSR; agr. processing, saw milling; resort; p. (1970) 102,000.

Sukkur, t., Pakistan; major bridging point of R. Indus; 368 km N.E. of Karachi; dam for irrigation; thermal sta.; p. (est. 1969) 131,000.

Sulaimaniya, t., Iraq; in hill dist. nr. Iran border; p. (1965) 131,000 (met. a.).

Sula Is., I. gr. in Molucca Sea, E. of Sulawesi, Indonesia; little developed.

Sulawesi (Celebes), I., Indonesia; mtnous., lge. forests; copra, coffee, gold, nickel, copper, asphalt; ch. pts. Menado, Makasar; a. 189,484 km²; p. (est. 1970) 8,925,000.

Sullom Voe, Shetland Is., Scot.; oil terminal and receiving ctr. for N. Sea oil.

Sultanabad. *See* Arak.

Sulu Is., Philippines; archipelago between Borneo and the Philippines; inc. over 400 volcanic Is. and coral islets; a. 2,461 km²; under US control 1899-1940.

Sumatra, I., Indonesia; relatively underde-veloped; sparse p.; main development in Cultuurgebied, rubber, oil palm, sisal, tobacco; impt. oil deposits and new oil refineries; a. 473,607 km²; p. (1967) 18,300,000

Sumba or Sandalwood I., S. of Flores, Indonesia; horse-breeding; rice, maize, tobacco, timber, cinnamon; cap. Waingapu; a. 11,150 km²; p. (1961) 251,126.

Sumbawa, I., Indonesia; between Flores and Lombok; wet climate, sparse p.; a. (inc. nearby Is.) 13,572 km²; p. 314,843.

Sumgait, t., Azerbaydzhan SSR, USSR; on Caspian Sea; 40 km N.W. of Baku; metal-lurgical ind.; chemicals; p. (1970) 124,000.

Sumy, t., Ukrainian SSR, USSR; engin., chemi-cals, textiles, agr. processing; p. (1970) 159,000.

Sunbury-on-Thames, t., Spelthorne, Surrey, Eng.; W. of London; residtl., water wks., gravel pits; petrol research establishment; p. (1971) 40,035.

Sunda Is., Indonesia; between S. China Sea and Indian Oc.; form two grs., Greater Sunda Is., inc. Java, Sumatra, Borneo, Sulawesi, Banka, and the Lesser Sunda Is. (renamed Nusa Tenggara 1954) inc. Bali, Lombok, Sumbawa, Timor.

Sundarbans, The, tract of forest and swamps, fringing the delta of the Ganges, India/Bangla-desh; 130 km wide; rice grown in N.; tigers and crocodiles found in S.

Sunda Strait, between Java and Sumatra, In-donesia; 21 km wide, contains the volcanic I. of Krakatao.

Sunday I., lgst. of Kermadec Is., N.Z.; 32 km in circuit and with a p. of 10 is the only one of the Kermadec Is. that is inhabited; meteorological and radio sta. established on I.

Sundbyberg, t., Sweden; adjoins Stockholm; chemicals, paper; p. (1968) 28,661.

Sunderland, spt., met. dist., Tyne and Wear, Eng.; at mouth of R. Wear; precision and aero-engin., clothing, glass, shipbldg.; p. (est. 1976) 295,700 (dist.).

Sundsvall, spt., Västernorrland, Sweden; on a wide bay of the Baltic nr. Hernösand; timber and wood-pulp inds.; p. (1968) 62,278.

Sungari, R., N.E. China; trib. of R. Amur; length 1,840 km; hydro-electric power.

Sunnyvale, t., Cal., USA; ctr. of fruit-growing a.; lt. inds.; p. (1970) 95,408.

Superior, t., Wis., USA; at head of L. Superior; tr. in grain, timber, coal; shipbldg. and flour mills; oil refining; p. (1970) 32,237.

Superior, L., N. America; lgst. sheet of fresh water in the world; lies between Canada and USA; one of chain of gr. Ls. in St. Lawrence system; outlet to L. Huron by St. Mary's R., receives waters of St. Louis, Pigeon and Nipigon; impt. waterway; a. 82,880 km².

Surabaya, spt., Java, Indonesia; ch. naval base; handles nearly half Indonesia's tr.; shipbldg., oil refining, food processing; p. (1971) 1,556,255.

Surakarta (Solo), Java, Indonesia; on Solo R.; tr. ctr. for agr. region; former sultan's palace; p. (1971) 414,285.

Surat, c., Gujarat, India; on R. Tapti; textile ctr.; notable as first English trading post 1612; p. (1971) 471,656 (c.), 493,001 (met. a.).

Surbiton, Gtr. London, Eng.; on R. Thames. inc. in Royal Borough of Kingston-upon-Thames; residtl.; lt. engin., bricks, tiles, elec. components.

Suresnes, t., Hauts-de-Seine dep., France; sub. of Paris; cars, chemicals; p. (1968) 41,263.

Surinam (Dutch Guiana), former self-gov. terr. of Neth.; indep. 1975; S. America; sub-tropical climate; p. concentrated on cst. where rice, sugar, and citrus fruits grown; main exp. bauxite (86 per cent of total exp.); cap. Paramaribo; a. 161,875 km²; p. (1967) 345,000.

Surinumu Dam, 48 km from Port Moresby, Papua New Guinea; part of hydroelectric scheme; opened 1963.

Surrey, non-met. co., S. Eng.; S of R. Thames inc. part of N. Downs; serves as dormitory a. and recreational dist. for London; mkt. gardening, dairying; co. t. Guildford; a. 1,655 km²; p. (est. 1976) 1,002,900.

Surrey Heath, l. gov. dist., Surrey, Eng.; based on Bagshot, Frimley and Camberley; p. (est. 1976) 71,900.

Susa. See Sousse.

Susquehanna, R., N.Y., Penns., and Md., USA; flows to Chesapeake Bay through highly industl. a.; routeway W. from Philadelphia and Baltimore across Appalachian mtns.; not navigable; hydroelectric power; 675 km long.

Sussex. See East Sussex, and West Sussex.

Susten Pass, alpine road, alt. 2,225 m between Hasli Tal and Reuss valley, links Bernese Oberland with Gotthard road, Switzerland.

Sutherland, l. gov. dist., former co., Highland Reg., Scot.; stretches from Atl. Oc. to Moray F.; sparsely p. reg.; a. 3,152 km²; p. (1971) 11,865.

Sutlej, R., Pakistan; rises in the Himalayas and flows to the R. Indus; used for lge. scale irrigation; 1,600 km long.

Sutton, outer bor., Greater London, Eng.; inc. former bors. of Beddington and Wallington, Sutton and Cheam. and Carshalton; residtl.; p. (est. 1976) 166,700.

Sutton Coldfield, t., West Midlands, Eng.; 10 km N.E. of Birmingham; residtl.; hardware, plastics; p. (1971) 83,130.

Sutton-in-Ashfield, t., Ashfield, Notts., Eng.; 5 km S.W. of Mansfield; lt. engin.; hosiery; coal-mng. dist.; p. (1971) 40,725.

Suva, c., cap. of Fiji Is.; on Viti Levu I.; fine harbour; exp. coconut prods., sugar; international airport; p. (1966) 54,157 (c.), 80,248 (met. a.).

Suwalki, t., N.E. Poland; nr. Lithuanian bdy.; timber, grain, woollens; p. (1970) 25,400.

Suwannee, R., Fla., and Ga., USA; flows to G. of Mexico; known as "Swanee River," 400 km long.

Svenborg, spt., Fyn, Denmark; exp. dairy prods.; textiles, machin.; p. (est. 1970) 23,149.

Sverdlovsk (Ekaterinburg), c., cap. of S. oblast, RSFSR; on R. Iset in E. foothills of Ural mtns.; on Trans-Siberian rly.; industl. expansion during second world war; heavy machin., metallurgical and chemical plants; univ.; p. (1970) 1,026,000 (c.); (1969) 1,028,000 (met. a.).

Svir, R., USSR; flows between L. Onega and L. Ladoga; hydroelectric power; navigable; 200 km long.

Svishtov (Sistova), t., N. Bulgaria; R. pt. on Danube in vine-growing dist., nr. Romanian bdr.; cath., univ.; p. (est. 1968), 22,456.

Swabia, historic region, mediaeval duchy, Germany; now forms part of Baden-Württemberg and Bavaria; contains Black Forest.

Swabian Alps, mtns., Baden-Württemberg, W. Germany; inc. the Swabian Jura range between valleys of Neckar and Danube.

Swadlincote, t., South Derbys., Eng.; 5 km E. of Burton-on-Trent; potteries, engin., clothing, coal-mng. ctr.; p. (1971) 20,235.

Swaffham, mkt. t., Breckland, Norfolk, Eng.; fruit canning; p. (1971) 4,270.

Swale, R., North Yorks., Eng.; joins R. Ure to form R. Ouse, 96 km long.

Swale, l. gov. dist., mid Kent, Eng.; nr. Thames estuary inc. Sittingbourne, Faversham and I. of Sheppey; p. (est. 1976) 106,700.

Swanage, mkt. t., Purbeck, Dorset, Eng.; on bay, E. cst. I. of Purbeck; seaside resort; stone quarries; p. (1971) 8,550.

Swanland, region, W. Australia; consists of extreme S.W. corner of W. Australia; forests of Karri and Jarrah; vines citrus and deciduous fruits, wheat; highest p. density in W. Australia; ch. ts. Perth, Fremantle, Bunbury.

Swansea, c., spt., l. gov. dist., West Glamorgan, Wales; on Swansea Bay; univ.; grew with exp. of coal; now imports minerals; copper and zinc refining; steel, aluminium, wire, plastics; p. (est. 1976) 190,800 (dist.).

Swatow (Shantou), c., spt., S.E. Kwangtung prov., China; at mouth of Han R.; mftg. and exp. tr.; sugar refineries; p. (est. 1970) 400,000.

Swaziland, indep. kingdom, S. Africa; within Brit. Commonwealth (1968), govt. based on tribal communities; bordered by S. Africa on S., W., and N. and by Moçambique on E.; four north-south regions: high, middle, low veld and Lebombo escarpment; rainfall increases with alt.; agr. basis of economy and sugar impt. exp., but iron ore major exp.; asbestos mng., food processing inds.; cattle raising main internal activity; cap. Mbabane; a. 17,363 km²; p. (1970) 451,000.

Sweden, kingdom, Scandinavia, N.W. Europe; divided for admin. purposes into 24 cos.; cap. c. Stockholm; mtnous. in N. and S. with central lowland belt containing major agr. a. and lge. proportion of p.; sm. home mkt. makes for dependency on exps., especially of minerals; inc. high-grade iron ore from Kiruna and Malmberget, N. of Arctic circle; development of high-value science-based inds.; furniture, porcelain and glass mnfs. have international reputation; social democratic st. since 1932; remained neutral in second world war; highly advanced system of social security; a. 449,792 km²; p. (1970) 8,013,696.

Swidnica (Schweidnitz), t., Poland (since 1945); formerly in Lower Silesia; metals, elec. machin., leather, textiles; p. (1970) 47,500.

Swilly, Lough, N.E. Donegal, R.o.I.; arm of Atl. Oc. between Fanad Point and Dunaff Head; extends 40 km inland.

Swindon, t., Thamesdown, Wilts., Eng.; in upper Thames Valley (Vale of White Horse), 43 km S.W. of Oxford; impt. rly. junc.; mkt. for local dist.; heavy engin., textiles, tobacco; expanded t.; p. (1971) 90,830.

Świnoujście (Swinemünde), spt., N.W. Poland (since 1945); formerly in Pomerania; on I. of Usedom (Uznam), Baltic Sea; spt. for Szczecin; spa and summer resort; fishing; p. (1971) 27,900.

Swinton and Pendlebury, ts., Gtr. Manchester, Eng.; 8 km W. of Manchester; cotton spinning, coal, engin.; p. (1971) 40,124.

Switzerland, confederation, central Europe; landlocked mtnous. st. with major physical features dominated by Alpine mtn. system; divided into 25 cantons and half-cantons for purposes of govt.; 3 official languages: German (72 per cent), French (20 per cent), Italian (6 per cent) in addition to Romansch; like Norway, major natural resource is water power; industl. specialisation on precision engin., especially watch and clock mnfs.; agr. in valleys with impt. output of dairy prod., transhumance between mtn. pastures and valley bottoms; tourism provides valuable source of income; cap. Berne; a. 41,310 km²; p. (1970) 6,269,783.

Sydney, c., cap. of N.S.W., Australia; on shore of Pt. Jackson Bay; many beautiful bldgs. and parks, stretching S. to Botany Bay; lge. comm. and active inds.; magnificent bridge, harbour and docks; ch. pt. of Australia; 2 caths., univ., oil refining, consumer gds.; wool tr.; p. (1972) 61,940 (c.), 2,799,634 (met. a.).

Sydney, spt., Cape Breton I., Nova Scotia Canada; coal mng. and exp.; steel, chemicals; p. (1971) 32,459.

Syktyvkar, c., Komi ASSR, RSFSR; R. pt. on Vychegda R.; shipyds., sawmilling, engin.; cultural ctr. of Komi people; p. (1970) 125,000.

Sylhet, t., **Bangladesh**; on Surma R. in tea growing dist.; fertilisers; p. (1961) 37,740.

Syracuse, c., S.E. Sicily, Italy; old t. on Ortygia I., off E. cst., modern t. on mainland, connected by bridge; founded c. 734 B.C.; ctr. of anc. Greek culture; exp. olive oil, oranges, lemons, wine; chemicals at Priolo; many Greek and Roman remains; p. (1969) 104,862.

Syracuse, c., N.Y., **USA**; on Erie Barge canal; impt. industl. ctr. for chemicals, electronics, machin.; formerly salt-producing ctr.; univ.; p. (1970) 192,529 (c.), 629,190 (met. a.).

Syr Dar'ya, one of main Rs. of central Asia; formed in Ferghana Valley in Uzbek SSR, USSR, flows through Tadzhik SSR and Kazakh SSR to Aral Sea; not navigable but used for irrigation and hydroelectric power; 2,400 km long.

Syria (Syrian Arab Rep.), S.W. Asia; on E. cst. Mediterranean; much of a. mtnous. and semidesert; climate hot, but cold winters in highland interior; c. 70 per cent p. engaged in agr. which provides 30 per cent nat. income; mainly pastoral, but grains, fruit and cotton grown in well watered Euphrates R. valley and along cst.; oil exp. since 1968; textiles, food processing in Aleppo and cap. Damascus; a. 184,434 km²; p. (1970) 6,294,000.

Syriam, t., **Burma**; nr. Rangoon; main oil refining ctr. of cty.

Syros or Syra, I., one of Cyclades, Aegean Sea, S. Greece; heath-covered; most populous of Cyclades; ch. t. Hermopolis; p. c. 33,000.

Syzran, c., RSFSR; impt. R. pt. on Volga nr. confluence with Syzran R.; rly. ctr.; engin., oil refining; p. (1970) 174,000.

Szazhalombatta, t., Hungary; on Danube, 24 km S. of Budapest; lgst. oil refinery in rep.; oil supplied through Druzhba pipeline.

Szczecin (Stettin), c., N.W. Poland (since 1945); formerly cap. of Prussian prov. of Pomerania; impt. spt. at mouth of R. Oder; deep-sea fishing base; shipbldg., metallurgy, engin., chemicals, technical univ.; p. (1970) 337,200.

Szczecin, prov., Poland; borders Baltic Sea; drained by R. Oder; mainly agr.; a. 31,339 km² p. (1970) 897,000.

Szechwan (Sichuan), prov., S.W. China; mostly occupied by Yangtse R., known as Red basin because of colour of its sandstone; fertile a. with mild climate; rice, tea, citrus fruit, tobacco, sugar-cane; lge. coal reserves; exp. tung oil; silk-producing a.; most populous prov.; cap. Chengtu; a. 568,997 km²; p. (est. 1968) 70,000,000.

Szeged, t., Hungary; nr. confluence of Rs. Tisza and Maros; anc. R. pt. destroyed by floods 1879, since rebuilt; univ.; tr. in cereals, paprika; textiles; p. (est. 1969) 117,000.

Szekesfehérvár, t., Hungary; nr. Budapest; mkt. t., with aluminium and metal inds., food processing; known since Roman times; once cap. of Hungarian kings; p. (1968) 68,000.

Szeping (Siping), c., Kirin prov., China; agr. distributing ctr.; cement; p. (est. 1970) 180,000.

Szolnok, t., Hungary; pt. on R. Tisa, E. of Budapest; route ctr.; machin., paper, cellulose, chemicals; p. (1968) 59,000.

Szombathely, t., W. Hungary; rly. ctr.; agr. machin., textiles, shoes; birthplace of St. Martin of Tours (c. A.D. 316); p. (1968) 60,000.

T

Tabasco, coastal st., Mexico; on Bay of Campeche; low-lying; rapid development with drainage of swamps; cash crops of cacao, coffee, sugar, tobacco; major petroleum deposits aiding industl. development; cap. Villa Hermosa; a. 25,335 km²; p. (1969) 691,000.

Table Bay, inlet of Atl., cst. of C. of Good Hope, S. Africa; site of Cape Town.

Table Mountain, Cape Prov., S. Africa; nr. Cape Town; alt. 1,082 m.

Tabor, t., ČSSR; S. of Prague, on R. Luznice; rly. junc.; textiles, tobacco; p. (1961) 20,142.

Tabora, t., central Tanzania; E. Africa; at junc. of rlys. from Dar es Salaam and L. Victoria; p. (1967) 21,012.

Tabriz, c., Iran; cap. of Azerbaijan; metal inds.,

carpets, leather, soap; famous blue mosque; univ.; p. (est. 1971) 475,600.

Tachira, st., Venezuela; mtnous. inland st. bordering Colombia; coffee; cap. San Cristobal; a. 11,100 km²; p. (est. 1970) 525,840.

Tacna, t., cap. of Tacna prov., Peru; in fertile valley of mtnous. region; agr. t.; p. (est. 1969) 30,500.

Tacna, prov., Peru; mtnous. and arid, some irrigated valleys; transferred from Chile by treaty 1929; cap. T.; subject to earthquakes; a. 12,769 km²; p. (est. 1969) 90,600.

Tacoma, spt., Wash., USA; on Puget Sound; shipping, fishing; grew with Alaskan and Pac. tr.; port inds. and agr. processing; p. (1960) 147,970 (t.); (1968) 400,800 (met. a.).

Tacuarembo, dep., Uruguay; N. of Rio Negro R., which provides hydroelectricity; mainly agr.; cap. T.; a. 15,812 km²; p. (est. 1969) 80,600.

Tadoussac, t., Quebec, Canada; on R. Saguenay, where it enters St. Lawrence R.; tourist ctr.; oldest settlement in Canada 1599; p. (1966) 1,059.

Tadzhik (Tadzhikistan) SSR, constituent rep., USSR; borders China and Afghanistan; mainly mtnous., inc. Pamirs and Turkestan and part of highly cultivated Ferghana Valley; cattle breeding; cotton main cash crop; impt. oil and hydroelec. power resources; cap. Dushanbe; a. 144,263 km²; p. (1970) 2,900,000.

Taegu, c., S. Korea; textiles, agr. processing; p. (1966) 845,073.

Taejon, t., S. Korea; S. of Seoul; fish, petroleum, p. (1966) 315,094.

Taff, R., Powys, South and Mid Glamorgan, Wales; rises in Brecon Beacons, flows S.E. across coalfield to Bristol Channel at Cardiff; 64 km long.

Taff-Ely, l. gov. dist., Mid Glamorgan, Wales; inland ts. of Pontypridd and Llantrisant; p. (est. 1976) 89,200.

Tafilalet, Morocco, N. Africa; oasis of the Sahara, E. of Atlas; dates.

Tagab, t., Afghanistan; in Panjshir R. valley N.W. of Kabul; p. (est. 1971) 102,028.

Taganrog, c., RSFSR; spt. on Sea of Azov; iron and steel, engin.; site of fortress founded by Peter the Great 1698; birthplace of Chekhov; p. (1970) 254,000.

Tagliamento, R., N.E. Italy; rises in Carnic Alps, flows W. into Adriatic; 160 km long.

Tagus, R., Spain and Portugal; rises in E. Spain and flows across the Meseta to Atl. Oc. at Lisbon where there is a magnificent new bridge; its estuary forms one of the finest harbours in Europe.

Tahiti, ch. I., Society Is., Fr. Polynesia; contains Papeete, main admin. ctr. of Fr. Oceania; fertile alluvial belt; exp. copra, phosphates, vanilla; tourism; a. 1,041 km²; p. (1967) 61,519.

Taichow (Taizhou), c., Kiangsu prov., China; rice ctr.; p. (est. 1970) 275,000.

Taichung, t., Taiwan; agr. mkt.; food processing; p. (est. 1970) 448,140.

Taif, t., Hejaz, Saudi Arabia; 80 km E. of Mecca; 1,800 m a.s.l.; summer resort; p. (est. 1963) 54,000.

Tai Hu, L., Kiangsu, China; focus of intensive system of small canals and waterways, 96 km N. of Shanghai; a. c. 260 km².

Taimyr Peninsula, N. cst., Siberia, USSR; terminates with C. Chelyuskin; occupies most of Taimyr National Area, inhabited by nomadic Samoyeds; p. (1970) 38,000.

Tainan, t., S.W. cst. of Taiwan; former cap.; univ.; p. (est. 1970) 474,835.

Taipei, c., cap. of Taiwan; on cst. plain in N. Taiwan; nucleus of major industl. a.; major transport ctr., international airpt.; 2 univs.; p. (est. 1970) 1,769,568.

Taiwan (Formosa), I., off cst. of S.E. China; beautiful I. with intensive agr.; most densely populated cty. in the world; part of Japan 1895–1945; returned to China 1945; occupied by Nationalist government (Chiang Kai-Shek) since 1949; growing political isolation; cap. Taipei; a. 35,975 km²; p. (1971) 14,833,012.

Taiyüan, c., cap. of Shansi prov., N. China; on Fen R.; walled c.; univ.; ctr. of rapid industl. development; integrated iron and steel plant; chemicals, textiles; p. (est. 1970) 2,725,000.

Taiz, t., Yemen Arab Rep.; in fertile valley; former cap.; p. (est. 1970) 48,000.

Takamatsu, t., Japan; N. cst. Shikoku; ferry terminal; univ.; tourism; p. (est. 1971) 280,000.

Takaoka, t., Honshu, Japan; ctr. of rice tr.; lacquer wk.; cars; p. (est. 1971) 162,000.

Takasaki, t., Honshu, Japan; radiation chemistry research ctr.; textiles; p. (est. 1971) 200,000.

Taklamakan, desert, W. China; basin of inland drainage; home of the Turko people; surrounded by a ring of oases.

Takoradi. See Sekondi-Takoradi.

Talara, t., N. Peru; on C. Pariñas; spt.; ctr. of petroleum refining; p. (est. 1969) 38,200.

Talaud I., Indonesia; N.E. of Sulawesi; copra; underdeveloped; a. 1,279 km².

Talavera, t., Toledo prov., central Spain; on Tagus R.; ceramics; scene of battle 1809; p. (1970) 45,327.

Talca, prov., Chile; predominantly agr.; various irrigated crops; livestock; cap. T.; a. 9,637 km²; p. (1961) 226,052.

Talca, t., cap. of Talca prov., Chile; S. of Santiago; lge. mftg. ctr.; matches, footwear, paper, and flour mills, foundries; p. (1966) 72,000.

Talcahuano, spt., Chile, nr. Concepción; naval sta.; steel plant at Huachipato; fish processing, oil refining; p. (est. 1970) 115,568.

Talien. See Luta.

Tallahassee, t., Fla., USA; univ.; timber-based inds.; p. (1970) 71,763 (t.), 102,530 (met. a.).

Tallinn, spt., cap. of Estonian SSR, USSR; on G. of Finland; diverse inds. inc. radio equipment; mediaeval architecture; p. (1970) 363,000.

Tamale, t., cap. of Kaduna st., Ghana, W. Africa; admin. ctr.; cotton milling, sheanut processing; p. (1970) 81,612.

Tamar, R., Tasmania, Australia; formed at confluence of N. Esk and S. Esk at Launceston, flows into Bass Strait nr. Georgetown.

Tamar, R., Devon and Cornwall, Eng.; flows S. to Plymouth Sound; 72 km long.

Tamatave, t., Malagasy Rep.; ch. spt. on Indian Oc.; exp. graphite, rice, chromite ore; car assembly, oil refining; p. (est. 1970) 56,910.

Tamaulipas, st., Mexico; on G. of Mexico, S. of Texas; petroleum is main resource; fishing along lagoon cst.; cotton, livestock; cap. Ciudad Victoria; a. 79,593 km²; p. (1969) 1,487,000.

Tambov, c., cap. of Tambov oblast, RSFSR; on Tsna R.; regional ctr. serving agr. dist.; engin.; p. (1970) 229,000.

Tameside, met. dist., Gtr. Manchester, Eng.; comprises Dukinfield, Ashton-under-Lyne, Hyde and Mossley; p. (est. 1976) 221,100.

Tamil Nadu (formerly Madras) st., India; on S.E. cst. of peninsula; home of Tamils; crossed by R. Cauvery; dry crops; ch. ts. Madras, Madura; a. 130,357 km²; p. (1971) 41,103,125.

Tampa, c., Fla., USA; popular winter resort, cigar factories, phosphates, electronics; fruit growing and canning; p. (1970) 274,359 (c.), 999,613 (met. a.).

Tampere (Tammerfors), t., S. Finland; on rly. between Helsinki and Vaasa; textiles, leather, paper, based on local hydroelec. power; cath.; p. (est. 1968) 151,278 (t.), 211,995 (met. a.).

Tampico, spt., Mexico; on R. Panuco, 14 km from G. of Mexico; exp. petroleum; oil refining, fish processing, chemicals; tourism; p. (1970) 179,584 (c.), 270,414 (met. a.).

Tamworth, t., l. gov. dist., Staffs., Eng.; on R. Tame, 8 km S.E. of Lichfield; anc. cas.; lt. engin.; expanded t.; p. (est. 1976) 52,800.

Tana, lge. freshwater L., N.W. Ethiopia, nr. Gondar; source of Blue Nile, surrounded by marsh, papyrus swamp.

Tana, R., Kenya; rises nr. Mt. Kenya and flows to Indian Oc.; impt. elephant habitat in valley; 800 km long.

Tanana, R. and R. pt., Alaska, USA; valley used for agr. and forestry; length of R. 760 km.

Tananarive, t., cap. of Malagasy Rep.; ctr. of commerce and communications; airpt.; lge. meat preserving factories, plastics, radios, car assembly, shoes, knitted gds., rice mills; univ.; p. (est. 1971) 347,466 (c.), 377,600 (met. a.).

Tandil, t., Argentina; resort; granite quarried in surrounding hills; p. (1960) 70,000.

Tandridge, l. gov. dist., Surrey, Eng.; S. of Gtr. London, inc. Caterham and Godstone; p. (est. 1976) 79,600.

Tanga, spt., Tanzania, E. Africa; on plateau overlooking Tanga Bay; rly. terminus; new plywood plant; p. (1967) 61,058.

Tanganyika, gr. L., E. Central Africa; lies in Gt. Rift Valley; c. 672 km long, 24–32 km wide; lgst. L. in Africa and except for L. Baykal deepest L. in world; c. 823 m a.s.l.; discovered by Burton and Speke 1858, explored by Livingstone and Stanley 1871.

Tangier, free pt., Morocco, N. Africa; on Strait of Gibraltar; no longer internationalised zone but integral part of kingdom of Morocco; summer cap.; shipyard; cigarettes, fishing; p. (1971) 185,850.

Tangshan, c., Hopeh prov., China; impt. industl. ctr.; steel, machin.; textiles, cement, oil refining; devastated by a series of earthquakes (1976); p. (est. 1970) 1,200,000.

Tanimbar Is., Indonesia; gr. of Is. in Banda Sea, S. Moluccas; forests, swamps; maize, rice, coconuts, sago; p. (est. 1965) 50,000.

Tanta, t., Lower Egypt; 55 m. N. of Cairo; impt. rly. junc.; religious fairs; cotton processing; univ. proposed; p. (est. 1970) 253,600.

Tanzania, rep., E. cst. Africa; inc. Is. of Zanzibar and Pemba, united since 1964; narrow coastal plain rises to inland plateau (Mt. Kilimanjaro, 5,895 m, hgst. peak in Africa); climate varies with alt., tropical in Zanzibar, temperate inland; predominantly subsistence agr., maize, millet, groundnuts, livestock; comm. crops inc. sisal, sugar, cotton, coffee; cloves on Is., especially Pemba; food processing, textile inds.; 5-year planning system to assist economic development; cap. Dar es Salaam; new cap. planned at Dodoma; a. 939,706 km²; p. (est. 1969) 12,926,000.

Taormino, resort, E. Sicily, Italy; 230 m above sea at foot of Mt. Etna; magnificent scenery and anc. ruins.

Tapachula, c., Chiapas st., S. Mexico; on Pac. cst. lowlands; comm. ctr. for agr. dist.; p. (1970) 108,464.

Tapti, R., W. India; flows W. to G. of Cambay from Betul dist., Madhya Pradesh; 702 km.

Tarai, marshy, jungle tract at foot of Himalayas, India, Nepal; barrier to economic development of Nepal, now much modified and reduced in area by human occupation.

Taranaki, prov., N.I., N.Z.; impt. stock rearing and dairying a.; offshore oil and gas fields; a. 9,713 km²; p. (1971) 100,668.

Taranto, t., Lecce, Italy; on G. of Taranto, inlet of Ionian Sea; maritime arsenal with gr. comm. and industl. interests; strong cas.; steel wks.; cement; oil refinery; famous for its oyster and mussel fisheries; p. (1969) 219,484.

Tarapacá, prov., N. Chile; hot, arid desert; nitrate deposits; a. 55,270 km²; p. (1970) 174,730.

Tarascon, t., Bouches-du-Rhône dep., France; connected by bridges with Beaucaire on opposite bank of R. Rhône; old cas. famous festival; p. (1968) 10,857.

Tarwera Mtn., volcanic peak, N.I., N.Z.; 305 m; in Hot Springs dist.; eruption 1866 destroyed L. Rotomahana (water later returned to form bigger and deeper L.).

Tarbes, t., cap. of Hautes-Pyrénées dep., France; on R. Adour; cath.; p. (1968) 59,432.

Targul-Mures, c., Romania; on R. Mures; ch. t. of Magyar aut. region in Transylvania; old fort, Gothic Calvinist cath.; agr. tr. and processing; p. (1968) 92,104.

Tarifa, t., Spain; on Gibraltar Strait; most S. point of mainland of Europe; fish tr., cereals, oranges, wines; p. (1970) 15,833.

Tarija, prov., Bolivia; part of Gran Chaco rising to W.; extensive agr. and forests; cap. T.; a. 64,196 km²; p. (est. 1969) 201,800.

Tarija, t., cap. of T. prov., Bolivia; alt. 1,906 m; cath., univ.; mkt. t.; p. (1967) 26,787.

Tarim Basin, depression, Sinkiang, China; desert with oases; crossed by Silk Road; anc. civilisation; state farms for wheat, millet, maize, cotton.

Tarn, dep., S. France; watered by Tarn and its tribs.; between Central Massif and basin of Aquitaine; mainly agr.; cap. Albi; a. 5,781 km²; p. (1968) 332,011.

Tarn, R., France; trib. of R. Garonne; rocky gorge 50 km long in its upper course; 376 km long.

Tarn-et-Garonne, dep., W. France; alluvial plain formed by Rs. Tarn, Garonne and Aveyron; mainly agr.; cap. Montauban; a. 3,730 km²; p. (1968) 183,572.

Tarnow, t., Poland; E. of Kraków; industl. ctr.; lge. nitrogen factory; synthetic fibres, metallurgy; cath.; p. (1970) 85,500.

Tarpon Springs, t., Fla., USA; pt.; main source of sponges in USA.

Tarragona, prov., Spain; on Mediterranean; vineyards and agr.; cap. Tarragona; a. 6,283 km²; p. (1970) 431,961.

Tarragona, spt., cap. of T. prov., Spain; at mouth of R. Francoli; exp. agr. prod. of Ebro valley; cath.; many Roman remains, inc. aqueduct; liqueur; p. (1967) 64,192.

Tarrasa, t., Barcelona, Spain; textile ctr.; p. est. (1967) 127,814.

Tarsus, anc. c., S. Turkey; nr. Adana; orange and citrus groves; ruined Roman temple; birthplace of St. Paul; p. (1965) 57,035.

Tartary or Tatary, region, Central Asia; now divided into Chinese or E. Turkestan, and W. Turkestan, USSR.

Tartu, c., Estonian SSR, USSR; pt. on Emayygi R.; rly. junc.; famous univ. founded 1632; agr. machin., tobacco ind.; p. (est. 1969) 87,000.

Tashkent, c., cap. of Uzbek SSR, USSR; cultural, industl. and scientific ctr. of central Asia; on Trans-Caspian rly. in fertile Ferghana valley; univ.; diverse inds.; terminus of gas pipeline; p. (1970) 1,385,000.

Tasman Bay, lge inlet, S.I., N.Z.; penetrates N. cst., between Separation Point and D'Urville I.; enclosed by mtns., sheltered, fertile, coastal fringe; ch. ts. Nelson, Motueka.

Tasman Glacier, S.I., N.Z.; one of the lgst. in the world.

Tasmania (formerly Van Diemen's Land), I., st., Australia; plateau with fertile valleys; temperate climate; forest and grasslands, grain, fruit, cattle-raising; aluminium, copper, zinc, lead, tin, silver; electro-metallurgical inds.; cap. Hobart; a. 67,897 km²; p. (1972) 389,874.

Tasman Sea, Australia; part of Pac. Oc. between Australia and Tasmania.

Tatabánya, t., N. Hungary; lignite mng. ctr.; aluminium refining, chemicals; p. (1968) 63,000.

Tatar ASSR, USSR; in middle Volga valley; wooded steppeland; extensive oil deposits and natural gas fields; cap. Kazan; a. 67,988 km²; p. (1970) 3,131,000.

Tatra Mtns., highest mtn. gr. of W. Carpathians, on border of ČSSR and Poland; highest peak Gerlach in Slovakia, 2,664 m; mountaineering and winter sports.

Tatung (Datong), c., Shansi prov., China; impt. coalfield; steam and diesel locomotives; p. (est. 1970) 300,000.

Taubaté, t., São Paulo st., Brazil; industl. ctr.; p. (est. 1968) 92,972.

Taunton, co. t., Somerset, Eng.; on R. Tone at W. end of Vale of Taunton; old cas.; with Wellington forms l. gov. dist. of Taunton Dean; p. (est. 1976) 82,900.

Taunton, t., Mass., USA; cotton, iron foundries, machin., plastics; p. (1970) 43,756.

Taunus, mtn. range, Hesse, W. Germany; between Rs. Lahn and Rhine and Main; forests, vineyards, and spas.

Taupo, L., N.I., N.Z.; lgst. L. in N.Z.; geysers, hot springs in vicinity; 40 km by 27 km.

Tauranga, t., N.I., N.Z.; spt. on Bay of Plenty; tourism; fishing; p. (1971) 28,120.

Taurus Mtns., range, S. Turkey; rise to over 3,660 m.

Tavastehus. See Hämeenlinna.

Tavistock, mkt. t., West Devon, Eng.; on R. Tavy; anc. stannary t.; Drake born nearby; p. (1971) 24,310 (dist.).

Tavoy, t., Burma; on Tenasserim cst.; exp. tin to Singapore; p. c. 40,000.

Taw, R., Devon, Eng.; flows from Dartmoor to Barnstaple Bay; 80 km long.

Taxco, t., Mexico; alt. 1,700 m; gold- and silver-mng.; tourist ctr.; anc. Aztec t.; p. (1970) 64,368.

Taxila, ruined c., Pakistan; nr. Rawalpindi; anc. seat of learning; ruins of Buddhist univ.; heavy machin. wks. projected.

Tay, R., Scot.; flows S.E. from Loch Tay in Perth and Kinross, to Firth of Tay; longest R. in Scot., 188 km; salmon fisheries.

Tay, Firth of, lge. inlet, E. cst. Scot.; extends inland almost to Perth.

Tayeh, t., Hupeh, China; lies to S. of Yangtze R., 67 km S.E. of Wuhan; impt. iron-ore deposits; supplies Hwangshih; iron and steel inds., heavy engin.

Tayport, burgh, North East Fife, Scot.; at entrance to Firth of Tay; opposite Broughty Ferry; linen, jute; p. (1971) 2,897.

Tayside, l. gov. reg., Scot.; inc. former cos. of Perth and Angus bordering the Highlands; a. 7,500 km²; p. (1971) 395,285.

Tbilisi (Tiflis), c., Georgian SSR, USSR; route ctr. on Kura R.; major admin., economic and cultural ctr. of Transcaucasia; machin., textiles, tanneries, furniture, food processing; power from hydroelectric power stas.; anc. tr. ctr.; some mediaeval fragments in c. ctr.; p. (1970) 889,000.

Tczew (Dirschau), t., Gdansk prov., N. Poland; pt. on Vistula; rly. junc.; agr. implements; p. (1970) 40,800.

Team Valley, Tyne and Wear, Eng.; impt. trading estate has been developed here.

Tebessa, t., N.E. Algeria; in Atlas mtns., at 851 m; mkt.; carpets; phosphate deposits nearby; p. (1966) 40,521.

Tees, R., N. Eng.; rises on Cross Fell, Cumbria, flows to N. Sea between Hartlepool and Redcar; heavy inds. in lower section; 112 km long.

Teesdale, l. gov. dist., Durham, Eng.; Pennine a. inc. Barnard Castle; p. (est. 1976) 23,900.

Teesport, oil refinery, between Redcar and Middlesbrough, Cleveland, Eng.

Teesside, former admin. dist., Cleveland, Eng.; inc. Middlesbrough, Redcar, Thornaby-on-Tees, Stockton-on-Tees, Billingham, and Eston; p. (1971) 395,477.

Tegal, spt., Java, Indonesia; textiles, sugar refining; lge. dam nearby; p. (1971) 105,752.

Tegucigalpa, c., cap. of Honduras; on R. Choluteca at 976 m; inter-ocean highway connects with Caribbean and Pac. Oc.; former ctr. of silver mng.; inc. Comayagüela, the modern part of c., where the nat. univ. is situated; p. (est. 1970) 232,276.

Tehran (Teheran), c., cap. of Iran, 112 km S. of Caspian Sea; mftg. and comm. ctr.; modern bldgs.; gas pipeline to USSR; international airpt.; univ.; car assembly, textiles, chemicals, glass; new oil refinery; p. (est. 1971) 3,639,000.

Tehuantepec, Isthmus of, separates G. of Mexico from Pac. Oc. at narrowest point of Mexico; width 200 km.

Teifi, R., S. Wales; rises in Cambrian mtns., flows S.W. to Cardigan Bay; 150 km long.

Teign, R., Devon, Eng.; flows to sea at pt. of Teignmouth from Dartmoor; picturesque estuary; 48 km long.

Teignbridge, l. gov. dist., S. Devon, Eng.; lower T. valley and ts. of Dawlish, Teignmouth, Newton Abbot and Ashburton; p. (est. 1976) 94,500.

Teignmouth, t., Teignbridge, Devon, Eng.; at mouth of R. Teign, 21 km S. of Exeter; resort; revival of pt. with ball clay exp.; p. (1971) 12,554.

Tekirdag, t., Turkey; on Sea of Marmara, W. of Istanbul; former Greek settlement; p. (1965) 26,964.

Tel Aviv-Jaffa, c., Israel; on Mediterranean; lgst. c. of cty.; financial and cultural ctr.; univ.; founded by Zionists 1909; p. (1972) 28,120.

Telemark, co., Norway; borders Skagerrak; mtnous., lake-covered, much forested; hydroelectric power forms basis for electrochemical inds.; a. 15,118 km²; p. (est. 1972) 157,553.

Telford, new t. (1963), Shropshire, Eng.; 32 km W. of Wolverhampton; p. (est. 1974) 94,200.

Tellicherry, t., spt., Kerala, India; exp. pepper; lge. college; furniture; p. (1961) 44,763.

Telok Betong, spt., Sumatra, Indonesia; exp. pepper, agr. products; p. (1971) 198,986.

Tema, pt. (opened 1962), nr. Accra, Ghana; deepwater harbour, oil refinery, aluminium smelter; impt. industl. development.

Teme, R., on border of Wales and Hereford and Worcs., Eng.; trib. of R. Severn; 112 km long.

Temir-Tau, c., Kazakh SSR, USSR; on Nura R.; industl. ctr.; iron, steel, synthetic rubber, soda; lge. thermal power sta.; p. (1970) 167,000.

Temuco, c., cap. of Cautin prov., Chile; cath.,

tr. in cereals, apples, timber; Araucanian Indian mkt.; p. (est. 1970) 104,372.

Tenali, t., Andhra Pradesh, India; nr. Guntur in Krishna delta; p. (1971) 102,937.

Tenasserim, div., lower Burma; on Thailand border; extends along Isthmus of Kra; tin and rubber; a. 92,945 km²; p. (est. 1969) 1,856,000.

Tenby, mkt. t., S. Pembs., Dyfed, Wales; on W. side of Carmarthen Bay, Bristol Channel; seaside resort; walled cas. t.; p. (1971) 4,985.

Tendring, l. gov. dist., E. Essex, Eng.; inc. cstl. ts. of Harwich, Frinton, Clacton and Brightlingsea; p. (est. 1976) 109,100.

Tenerife, I., Canary Is.; volcanic landscapes and mild climate attract tourists; cap. Santa Cruz; a. 2,025 km²; p. (1970) 500,381.

Tennessee, R., Tenn., Ky., USA; lgst. and most impt. branch of Ohio R.; valley once liable to flooding, now controlled by dams, and improved by the Tenn. Valley Authority; 1,251 km long.

Tennessee, st., USA; rises to Appalachians in E., crossed by Tennessee R. and tribs.; a. of heavy rainfall and severe soil erosion necessitated the Tenn. Valley Authority scheme of conservation, dam bldg., and afforestation; cheap hydroelectric power attracting new inds., many reservoirs attract tourists; cap. Nashville; a. 109,412 km²; p. (1970) 3,838,777.

Tenterden, mkt. t., Kent, Eng.; 13 km N. of Rye; church with famous tower; p. (1971) 5,922.

Teófilo Otoni, t., Minas Gerais, Brazil; semiprecious stone polishing; p. (est. 1968) 134,476.

Tepic, c., cap. of Nayarit st., Mexico; comm. ctr. for agr. dist.; nr. Sanguaney volcano; p. (1970) 111,344.

Teplice, wat. pl., ČSSR; N.W. of Prague; textile and hardware inds.; mineral springs; p. (1967) 52,000.

Teramo, c., cap. of T. prov., Italy; 24 km from Adriatic; route and agr. ctr.; cath.; textiles; the anc. Interamnium; p. (1969) 47,083.

Terek, R., N. Caucasia, RSFSR; flows to Caspian Sea; used for irrigation and hydroelectric power in lower course; 592 km long.

Teresina, t., cap. of Piauí st., Brazil; comm. ctr.; lt. inds.; p. (1970) 181,071.

Terezópolis, t., Rio de Janeiro, Brazil; health resort; textiles; p. (est. 1968) 69,636.

Ternate I., Moluccas Is., Indonesia; volcanic, wooded; p. 33,000.

Terneuzen, t., Neth.; on W. Schelde R.; pipeline to be constructed to carry ethylene from Pernis; p. (1967) 20,029.

Terni, t., Perugia, Italy; among the Apennines; iron and steelwks., arms factory; cath.; p. (1969) 106,062.

Ternopol (Tarnopol), t., Ukrainian SSR, USSR; E. of Lvov; rly. junc., mkt.; agr. machin., food inds.; p. (1970) 85,000.

Terre Adélie, name given to Fr. terr. and I. in Antarctic; est. a. 414,400 km².

Terre Haute, t., Ind., USA; coal, natural gas, flour, paper, glass, foundries; p. (1970) 69,247 (t.), 172,710 (met. a.).

Terreón, t., Coahuila, Mexico; ctr. of comm. agr.; oil pipeline connects to Chihuahua; thermoelec. plant; p. (1969) 243,234.

Teruel, t., cap. of Teruel prov., Spain; on R. Turia; walled t., cath.; p. (1970) 21,638.

Test Valley, l. gov. dist., W. Hants., Eng.; stretches from Andover to Romsey; p. (est. 1976) 89,800.

Tete, t., central Moçambique; on R. Zambesi; ctr. of coalfield; iron ore, graphite, radioactive materials.

Tetovo, t., Macedonia, Yugoslavia; chemicals, electro-metallurgy, textiles.

Tetuan, ch. spt., Morocco, N. Africa; walled t. p. (1971) 137,080 (t.), 273,050 (met. a.).

Teviot, R., Roxburgh, Scot.; trib. of R. Tweed; 59 km long.

Tewksesbury, mkt. t., l. gov. dist., Gloucs., Eng.; on R. Avon, close to confluence with R. Severn; Norman abbey; p. (est. 1976) 80,300 (dist.).

Texarkana, t., Texas and Ark., USA; bdy. passes down middle of main street; timber and cotton region; total p. (1970) 52,179.

Texas, st., S.W. USA; second lgst. st. by a.; borders Mexico; dry plains in W., humid cst. in E.; problems of soil erosion yet leading agr. st.; leading producer of petroleum and natural gas; cap. Austin; a. 692,408 km²; p. (1970) 10,989,123.

Texel, one of the W. Frisian Is., Neth.; scene of several naval battles; p. (1967) 11,003.

Thailand (Siam), kingdom, S.E. Asia; 4 main regions; parallel N.–S. hill ranges (2,400 m) and valleys in N. producing teak; rice growing, fertile plain of Chao Phraya R. in ctr.; thinly populated E. plateau, drained by Mekong; S. coastal strip on G. of Siam; monsoon climate; predominantly agr., accounting for over 80 per cent p. and 30 per cent nat. income; lgst. world exporter of rice; forestry, fisheries, mng., especially tin, wolfram; oil exploration; industl. development based on processing of Thai raw materials; cap. Bangkok; a. 519,083 km²; p. (est. 1975) 42,277,000.

Thal Desert, Pakistan; W. of Punjab; now irrigated for wheat and cotton.

Thame, mkt. t., South Oxford, Eng.; on R. Thame, 11 km S.W. of Aylesbury; p. (1971) 5,940.

Thames, R., Eng.; rises in Cotswold hills and flows past Oxford, Reading, Windsor, and London to the Nore; tribs. inc. Windrush, Cherwell, Thame, Kennet, Colne, Lea, and Roding; estuary impt. industl. a. with many oil refineries; flood barrier to be built at Silvertown in Woolwich; 336 km long.

Thamesdown, l. gov. dist., N.E. Wilts., Eng.; based on Swindon; p. (est. 1976) 142,700.

Thameshaven, lge. oil refinery, Essex, Eng.; on N. cst. of Thames estuary 13 km below Tilbury.

Thana, t., Maharashtra, India; textiles, chemicals, matches; p. (1971) 170,675 (t.), 207,352 (met. a.).

Thanet, I. of, lge. promontory, N.E. extremity of Kent, Eng.; formed by bifurcation of R. Stour; now also l. gov. dist. which contains Margate, Ramsgate, and Broadstairs; p. (est. 1976) 118,400.

Thanjavur, t., Tamil Nadu, India; silks, carpets, jewellery, inlaid metals; impt. Brahman ctr.; p. (1971) 140,547.

Thar Desert, on bdy. of India and Pakistan; covers slopes between N.W. Deccan and R. Indus; barren, lack of Rs. or level land prevents irrigation; crossed by caravan routes.

Thebes, c., of Boeotia, in anc. Greece; Mycenaean site; destroyed by Alexander the Great 335 B.C.; modern c. of Thívai occupies site.

Thebes, c. of anc. Egypt; on banks of Nile; site now partly occupied by vs. Karnak and Luxor; archeological discoveries in Valley of the Kings 1922, inc. tomb of Tutankhamun.

Thermopylae, celebrated pass between Mt. Oeta and the sea, N.E. Greece; heroic battle between Spartans and Persians 480 B.C.

Thessaloniki, c., Greece; spt. at head of G. of T.; with fiscal free zone; second c. of Greece; impt. route and industl. ctr.; univ.; p. (1971) 339,496.

Thessaly, prov., central Greece; fertile plain drained by R. Pinios; mainly agr.; a. 13,489 km²; p. (1971) 659,243.

Thetford, t., Breckland, Norfolk, Eng.; on Little Ouse; industl. estate for London overspill; fruit and vegetable canning, pulp mftg., engin.; p. (1971) 13,706.

Thetford Mines, t., Quebec, Canada; asbestos mng. ctr.; p. (1966) 21,614.

Thienen (Tirlemont), t., Brabant prov., Belgium; ctr. of Belgian beet-sugar refining; captured by Marlborough 1705; p. (est. 1969) 22,584.

Thiès, t., Senegal; rly. ctr. and wkshps.; aluminium, phosphate quarrying; p. (est. 1970) 91,000.

Thimbu, t., Bhutan; hydroelectric plant; 176 km road link to Phuntsholing (Sikkim) 1968.

Thionville, t., Moselle dep., N. France; in Lorraine ironfield conurb.; metallurgical and chemical inds.; p. (1968) 37,079 (c.), 136,474 (met. a.).

Thira (Santorine), volcanic I., Cyclades, Greece; wine prods.; max. alt. 567 m; a. 75 km²; p. c. 10,000.

Thirlmere, L., Cumbria, Eng.; 5 km long; furnishes part of water supply of Manchester.

Thirsk, mkt. t., Hambleton, North Yorks., Eng.; in wide gap between Pennines and Cleveland hills, 11 km S.E. of Northallerton; racecourse; p. (1971) 14,383 (dist.).

Thompson, R., B.C., Canada; trib. of R. Fraser; forms impt. routeway through Rocky mtns.; 448 km long.

Thonburi, c., Thailand; on R. Menam opposite Bangkok; second c. of T.; former cap.; "Temple of Dawn"; lt. inds.; p. (1968) 540,300.

Thorez, (Chistyakovo), Ukrainian SSR, USSR; coalmng.; p. (est. 1967) 95,000 (c.), 300,000 (met. a.).

Thornaby-on-Tees. See Teesside.

Thornbury, mkt. t., Avon, Eng.; 16 km N. of Bristol; aircraft mftg.; expanded t.; p. (1971) 42,992 (dist.).

Thornton Cleveleys, t., Wyre, Lancs., Eng.; 6 km N.E. of Blackpool; resort; p. (1971) 26,869.

Thórshavn, c., cap. of Faroe Is.; on Stromo I.; fish. pt.; anc. fortress; lighthouse; p. (1966) 9,738.

Thousand Isles, gr. of over 1,500 Is. in St. Lawrence R. which extend up-river for c. 48 km from Brockville to Gananoque, at junc. of L. Ont. and St. Lawrence R.; partly in N.Y. st. and partly in Canada.

Thrace, anc. name of terr. in S.E. Europe, part of which has been added to Greece; successively under Macedonian, Roman, Byzantine, and Turkish rule, before passing to Greece; tobacco; a. 8,586 km²; p. of dep. (1971) 329,297.

Three Rivers, l. gov. dist., S.W. Herts., Eng.; close to London and inc. Rickmansworth and Chorleywood; p. (est. 1976) 77,900.

Thule, N.W. Greenland; 1,600 km from N. Pole; American air base and site of ballistic missile early warning sta.; spt. open 2–3 months per annum.

Thumba, Kerala, India; space science and technological ctr.

Thun, L., Berne can., Switzerland; occupies valleys of R. Aare where it leaves Alpine region; separated from L. Brienz by deltaic neck of land on which is Interlaken; a. 38 km².

Thun, t., Berne, Switzerland; on N.W. end of L. Thun; cas. on hill above t.; tourism; p. (1969) 36,000.

Thunder Bay, t., Canada; formed from Port Arthur and Port William; pt. on N.W. cst. of L. Superior; grain exp. ctr.; p. (1971) 106,000 (t.), 111,492 (met. a.).

Thurgau, can., N.E. Switzerland; on L. Constance. bordered by R. Rhine; prosperous agr. a.; inds. ass. with textiles; cap. Frauenfeld; a. 1,005 km²; p. (1969) 187,000.

Thuringia, former st., E. Germany; bordered by Bavaria, Saxony-Anhalt, Lower Saxony, and Hesse; drained by Rs. Saale and Werra; crossed by Thüringer Wald and extending to Harz mtns.; fertile arable agr. a.; now comprises dists. of Erfurt, Suhl and Gera.

Thuringian Forest or Thüringer Wald, forested range of hills, E. Germany; rising to 982 m in Beerberg; famous for romantic scenery and legends; resorts.

Thurles, mkt. t., Tipperary, R.o.I.; on R. Suir; agr. processing; cath., cas.; p. (1966) 6,743.

Thurrock, t., l. gov. dist., Essex, Eng.; on Thames. nr. Tilbury; oil refining, metal refining, cement, paper board; p. (est. 1976) 127,700.

Thurso, burgh, Caithness, Scot.; nr. Dounreay; anc. stronghold of Vikings; p. (1971) 9,087.

Tiaret, t., W. Algeria; N. Africa; in strategic pass; walled; agr. mkt.; cereals, wool, cattle; p. (1966) 37,059.

Tiber, R., Italy; flows from Apennines to Mediterranean, passing through Rome; 352 km long.

Tiberias, t., Israel; on Sea of Galilee (L. Tiberias); agr. ctr.; health resort with medicinal springs; p. (est. 1970) 23,900.

Tibesti, mtns., on bdy. between Libya and Chad, Equatorial Africa; barren in spite of slight rainfall; mainly above 1,800 m, max. alt. 3,401 m.

Tibet, aut. region, China; lofty plateau, called "the roof of the world," its lowest plains being 3,660 m a.s.l.; semi-desert; network of roads being built, inc. one across Himalayas to Katmandu; pastoral agr., sheep; arable agr. in R. valleys, especially Tsangpo valley, wheat, barley, fruit, vegetables; tr. of wool, musk, gold, skins, drugs traditionally carried by yaks which can stand intense cold; salt, alluvial gold, radioactive ores; cap. Lhasa; a. 1,217,308 km²; p. (est. 1968) 1,400,000.

Ticino, R., Switzerland and Italy; trib. of Po; forms S. approach to St. Gotthard Pass; irrigation in lower course; length 240 km.

Ticino, can., Switzerland; on S. slopes of central Alps, bordering Italy; contains parts of Ls. Maggiore and Lugano; mainly pastoral agr., but wine, corn, tobacco in valleys; industl. a, in S. based on hydroelectric power, chemicals, metallurgy; many tourist resorts, inc. Locarno. Lugano; cap. Bellinzona; a. 2,813 km²; p. (1969) 242,000.

Ticonderoga, v., N.E. N.Y., USA; resort between Ls. George and Champlain; L. George falls provide hydroelectric power for paper mill; local graphite used in pencil ind.; p. (1970) 3,268.

Tideswell, t., Derbys., Eng.; tourist ctr.; limestone quarrying in a.; lge. 14th cent. church known as "cath. of the Peak." p. c. 1,500.

Tidore I., Moluccas, Indonesia; volcanic; densely populated; coffee, tobacco, spices, fruit; a. 78 km²; p. (est. 1969) 70,000.

Tien Shan (= Celestial Mtns.), mtn. chain, central Asia, along China–USSR border; highest peak 7,320 m; source of Syr-Dar'ya, Chu, Ili and many other Rs.

Tientsin (Tianjing), c., Hopeh prov., China 112 km S.E. of Peking; impt. pt. using poor harbour on Hai R.; industl. ctr., textiles. elec. instruments, steel rolling mills, machine tools, chemicals, tobacco, food processing; p. (est. 1970) 4,280,000.

Tierra del Fuego, archipelago, southernmost part of S. America; separated from Patagonia by Strait of Magellan; divided politically between Chile and Argentina; timber, pastoral agr. sheep; oilfield at Rio Grande; mng.; a. c. 47,900 km².

Tigre, st., Ethiopia; formerly an independent kingdom; cap. Adua.

Tigris, R., S.W. Asia; rises in Taurus mtns., S. Turkey, flows through Iraq where it is joined by the Euphrates and proceeds to Persian G.; comm. routeway; dam projected 56 km N. of Mosul; many of the earliest cs. located in valley; 1,840 km long.

Tijuana, t., Baja Cal. st., Mexico; resort catering for Americans; casinos, race-tracks, bull-fights; p. (1970) 277,306 (t.), 327,400 (met. a.).

Tiksi, t., USSR; Arctic spt., at mouth of Lena R.; local coal deposits; linked by air and R; to Yakutsk.

Tilburg, c., N. Brabant, Neth.; nr. Breda; woollens, textiles, tobacco, leather; p. (est. 1969) 151,897 (c.), 201,253 (met. a.).

Tilbury, pt., Essex, Eng.; on N. bank of R. Thames 32 km E. of London; within Port of London; major container terminal; p. (1961) 18,387.

Tillicoultry, burgh, Clackmannan, Scot.; on Devon R.; woollen and worsted fabrics, paper; p. (1971) 4,026.

Tilsit. See Sovetsk.

Timaru, t., S.I., N.Z.; E. cst. spt., exp. frozen foods; fishing; regional ctr. for S. Canterbury; p. (1971) 28,327.

Timbuktu, Mali, W. Africa; nr. Niger R. on border of Sahara; salt tr., handicraft inds.; flourished as comm. mart and Moslem ctr. 14th–16th cent.; p. (1967) 9,000.

Timisoara, c., W. Romania; comm., industl. and educational ctr.; univ., 2 caths., cas.; once a frontier fortress; p. (est. 1969) 189,264.

Timmins, t., Ont., Canada; gold mng. declining; vast deposits of copper, zinc, silver, discovered 1964; timber inds., brewing; p. (1966) 29,303.

Timok Basin, Serbia, Yugoslavia; industl. region; coal mng., copper smelting, chemicals, glass, food processing; arable agr., vines.

Timor, lgst. of Lesser Sunda Is., E. Indies; divided politically until 1975 into W. Timor part of Indonesia and Port. Timor; now both part of Indonesia; a. 33,748 km²; p. (est. 1970) 3,085,541.

Timor Sea, that part of the Indian Oc. N.W. of W. Australia, and S. of Timor I.

Timsah, L., Egypt; sm. L. midway along Suez Canal; formerly used for recreational purposes by Brit. garrison in Canal zone.

Tinogasta, t., Catamarca prov., Argentina; in E. foothills of Andes, 192 km N.W. of Catamarca; impt. copper mines.

Tintagel, v., Cornwall, Eng.; ruined Norman cas.; reputed birthplace of King Arthur; tourism.

Tintern, v., Gwent, Wales; Cistercian abbey.

Tinto, R., Huelva prov., S.W. Spain; in Andalusia; flows W. to Atl. Oc.; gives its name to Rio Tinto copper mng. region which it crosses; 104 km long.

Tipperary, inland co., Munster, R.o.I.; drained by Rs. Suir and Shannon; mtnous., Knockmealdown and Galty mtns.; fertile Golden Vale in S.W.; dairying, sugar-beet; divided into N. and S. Ridings; p. (1966) 53,832 (N.R.), 68,946 (S.R.).

Tipperary, t., Tipperary, R.o.I.; 46 km S.E. Limerick; dairy processing; p. (1966) 4,507.

Tipton. See Dudley.

Tiranë, t., cap. of Albania; rapid growth since becoming cap. 1920; many new inds.; agr. processing, engin., clothing, glass; univ.; airport; p. (1967) 169,300.

Tiraspol, c., S.E. Moldavian SSR, USSR; on R. Dniester; agr. processing ctr.; heat and power sta. recently constructed; p. (1970) 106,000.

Tiree, I., Inner Hebrides, Scot.; off cst. of Mull; 22 km long, up to 10 km wide; sm. freshwater lochs and prehistoric forts; p. (1971) 1,019 (inc. Coll).

Tiruchirapalli (Trichinopoly), c., Tamil Nadu, S.E. India; on R. Cauvery; rly. ctr.; textiles, cigars, goldsmithery; p. (1971) 307,400 (c.), 464,624 (met. a.).

Tirunelveli (Tinnevelly), c., Tamil Nadu, S.E. India; agr. tr. ctr. with sugar refinery; p. (1971) 108,498 (c.), 266.688 (met. a.).

Tiruppur, t., Tamil Nadu, India; nr. Coimbatore; p. (1971) 113,302 (t.), 151,127 (met. a.).

Tisa (Tisza), R., E. Europe; rises in E. Carpathians, W. Ukraine, flows across Hungary into Yugoslavia where it joins the Danube 72 km below Novi Sad; ch. tribs. Koros and Mures; length c. 960 km; navigable in part.

Titicaca, L., S. America; between two ranges of Andes, on borders of Bolivia and Peru; 3,812 m a.s.l.; highest lge. L. in world; max. depth 300 m; crossed by steamers; fishing; a. c. 8,300 km².

Titograd (Podgorica), t., cap. of Montenegro, S. Yugoslavia; nr. Albanian frontier; anc. t. but now mainly modern with growing industl. activity; agr. processing, aluminium smelting; airport; p. (1971) 54,509.

Titov Veles, t., central Macedonia, Yugoslavia; on R. Vardar, and main rly. to Belgrade; recent industl. growth; textiles; p. (est. 1965) 31,000.

Tiverton, mkt. t., l. gov. dist., Devon, Eng.; 22 km N. Exeter; once famous for lace; textiles, engin.; p. (est. 1976) 57,100 (dist.).

Tivoli, the anc. Tibur, nr. Rome, Italy; on Aniene R., magnificent situation; hydroelec. power; resort; remains of Hadrian's villa; p. (est. 1968) 40,501.

Tjirebon (Cheribon), spt., Java, Indonesia; on N. cst. 192 km E. of Djakarta; rice, tea, coffee tr.; ctr. of irrigation scheme; oil refining; p. (1971) 178,529.

Tlaxcala, smallest st., Mexico; on Mesa Central; dense p.; mainly agr.; cap. T.; a. 4,027 km²; p. (1969) 454,000.

Tlemcen, t., cap. of T. dep., N.W. Algeria; picturesque mediaeval t.; agr. ctr. in fertile region; textiles, furniture, handicrafts; p. (1967) 80,000.

Tobago, southernmost I., Windward Is., W.I.; volcanic, forested, picturesque, irregular topography; resorts utilising pleasant climate; exp. coconuts, copra, cacao, limes; ch. t. Scarborough; seeks internal self-gov.; a. 300 km²; p. (1970) 39,280. See Trinidad and Tobago.

Tobata. See Kitakyushu.

Tobermory, burgh, Argyll and Bute, Scot.; on I. of Mull at N. entrance to Sound of Mull; fish. pt., resort; p. (1971) 641.

Tobol, R., W. Siberia, RSFSR; trib. of R. Irtysh; navigable in lower course; 800 km long.

Tobolsk, t., W. Siberia, RSFSR; R. pt. on Irtysh R.; shipbldg., sawmilling, fishing; p. (est. 1967) 47,000.

Tobruk, spt., Libya, N. Africa; on cst. 352 km E. of Benghazi; exp. oil, served by pipeline from Libyan oilfields; p. (est. 1970) 28,000.

Tocantins, R., central Brazil; rises in Goiás prov., flows N. across plateau of Brazil through Pará estuary to Atl. Oc.; navigation interrupted by rapids 320 km above Pará; ch. trib. Araguaya R.; 2,560 km long.

Toce, R., N. Italy; rises in Lepontine Alps, flows

S. and S.E. into L. Maggiore; valley used by trunk rly. from Milan to Berne as S. approach to Simplon Tunnel; 86 km long.

Tocopilla, spt., Chile; exp. nitrate, copper ore, sulphates, iodine; p. (est. 1966) 23.140.

Todmorden, mkt. t., Calderdale, West Yorks., Eng.; nr. source of R. Calder. 10 km N.E. of Rochdale; cottons, machin.; p. (1971) 15,150.

Togliatti (Tol'yatti), c., RSFSR; on R. Volga 56 km W.N.W. of Kuybyshev; engin., motor wks., natural gas pipeline to Moscow; chemicals; p. (1970) 251,000.

Togo, Rep. of, W. Africa; narrow strip between Ghana (W.) and Benin (E.); N. and S. lowlands separated by mtns. (1,000 m); climate hot and humid, but drier savannah conditions in N.; coffee on slopes of central mtns., cacao, copra in S., maize in N.; phosphate mng., major iron ore deposits in N. now form ch. exp.; developing food-processing inds.; cap. Lomé; a. 54,960 km²; p. (1970) 1,956,000.

Tokaido, Japan, one of gr. feudal highways, along S. cst. Honshu, now forms main line of modern communications network.

Tokaimura, v., Ibaraki, Japan; nuclear reactor and lge. nuclear power sta.

Tokaj, t., Hungary; at confluence of Bodrog and Tisa Rs.; nearby slopes of Hegyalja produce Tokay wine; p. (1960) 5,081.

Tokat, t., cap. of T. prov., Turkey; copper refining, leather mnfs.; p. (1965) 38,006.

Tokelau or Union Isles, gr. of 3 coral atolls, S. Pac., N. of W. Samoa, belonging to N.Z.; Fakaofo, Nukunono and Atafu; natives are Polynesians; subsistence economy; copra; a. 10 km²; p. (1970) 1,687.

Tokoroa, co. t., N.I., N.Z.; kraft paper, pulp, and sawn timber; p. (1971) 15,174.

Tokushima, t., Shikoku, Japan; spt. on E. cst.; mkt. ctr., cotton mnfs.; p. (est. 1971) 236,000.

Tokyo, c., cap. of Japan; spt. with deepened harbour handling mainly S. coastal tr.; major industl. ctr. with diverse mnfs. and major problems of pollution; built on marshy site with much expensive reclamation from sea; planned decentralisation of p. and economic activity in progress; with Osaka–Kobe-Kyoto conurbs. (480 km long ribbon development) spoken of as Tokaido (q.v.) megalopolis; major educational ctr. with many univs.; p. (est. 1971) 8,841,000 (c.); 11,403,744 (met. a.).

Tolbukhin, t., N.E. Bulgaria; comm. and agr. ctr. of Dobruja; food-processing, textiles, furniture, agr. machin.; formerly Dobrich, renamed in honour of Russian soldier who took it from Germans 1944; p. (est. 1968) 61,440.

Toledo, prov., Spain; mtnous.; agr., vineyards, stock-raising; a. 15,346 km²; p. (1970) 468,925.

Toledo, anc. c., cap. of T. prov., Spain; in New Castile; on hill above Tagus R.; Gothic, Moorish, and Castillian architecture; picturesque narrow streets; Alcázar citadel; associated with El Greco; sword-mkg. still flourishes; sm. arms; tourism; p. (1970) 44,382.

Toledo, c., Ohio, USA; rly. ctr. and L. pt. with natural harbour on Maumee R.; exp. mnfs., oil, coal, agr. prod.; imports iron ore; glassmkg., shipbldg., car components and many varied mnfs.; p. (1970) 379,104 (c.), 685,455 (met. a.).

Tolentino, t., in the Marches, central Italy; on R. Chienti; mediaeval walls and houses; cath.; sm. handicraft inds.; spa and tourist ctr.; p. (est. 1968) 16,372.

Tolosa, t., Guipúzcoa prov., Spain; in the Basque cty.; mediaeval bldgs., and armour; paper mills; p. (1970) 18,766.

Tolpuddle, v., Dorset, Eng.; 11 km N.E. of Dorchester; famous for "Tolpuddle martyrs," agr. labourers condemned to transportation for trying to form a trade union (1834).

Toluca, c., cap. of Mexico st., central Mexico; stands at 2,672 m; brewing, flour, cottons, pottery; especially noted for basket weaving; p. (1970) 223,104 (c.), 322,557 (met. a.).

Tom, R., Siberia, RSFSR; flows through Kuznetsk Basin and joins R. Ob; 704 km long.

Tomaszow Mazowiecki, t., Lodz prov., central Poland; industl. t. on Pilica R., surrounded by forests; textile ind., artificial silk; p. (1970) 54,900.

Tombigbee, R., Miss., USA; flows S. to join

Alabama R. to form Mobile and Tensaw Rs.; navigable, partially canalised; length 654 km.

Tomsk, c., cap. of marshy T. oblast, RSFSR; one of few lge. ts. in N. Siberia; major pt. on R. Tom; rly. junc. on Trans-Siberian rly.; educational ctr.; univ., cath.; engin., chemicals; p. (1970) 339,000.

Tonawanda, t., N.Y. st., USA; on Niagara R. at terminus of Erie Barge Canal; steel, plastics, chemicals; power from Niagara Falls, adjacent to N. Tonawanda; p. (1970) 21,898.

Tonbridge, t., Kent, Eng.; on R. Medway; food processing; lt. inds., inc. cricket balls; Norman cas. gatehouse; public school; with Malling forms l. gov. dist.; p. (est. 1976) 94,800.

Tone, R., Honshu, Japan; flows E. across Kanto Plain to Pac. Oc., N. of Tokyo; longest R. in Japan.

Tonga, I. gr., S. Pac. Oc.; Polynesian kingdom, gained independence 1970; 158 coral and volcanic Is.; 50 per cent. p. on Tongatabu I.; exp. copra, bananas; fishing; oil discovered 1969; airport; cap. Nuku'alofa; a. 699 km²; p. (1969) 83,630.

Tongariro, volcanic peak, N.I., N.Z.; nat. park in ctr. of volcanic dist.; crater L. at summit; alt. 1,970 m.

Tongeren (Tongres), c., Limburg prov., N.E. Belgium; mkt. ctr. for fertile Hesbaye region; historic bldgs.; p. (est. 1969) 17,224.

Tonkin, region, N. Vietnam; mtns. in N. and W., alluvial plain in E. around delta of Red R., containing most p. and lge. cs.; fertile agr.; ch. t. Hanoi; ch. pt. Haiphong; a. 104,973 km².

Tonle Sap, L., Cambodia; major comm. fishing a.; L. acts as natural reservoir to control floods of Mekong R.

Tönsberg, c., Vestfold prov., S.E. Norway; one of oldest Norwegian cs., on Skagerrak at entrance to Oslo fjord; ctr. of whaling fleet; oil mills; p. (est. 1970) 11,260.

Toowoomba, t., Queensland, Australia; rly. ctr. and mkt. t. for wheat, pastoral and dairy dist.; food processing, iron foundry using local coal; p. (1972) 57,543.

Topeka, c., cap. of Kansas st., USA; on Kansas R.; impt. tr. ctr. in rich agr. region; food processing, rly. ctr. and engin.; p. (1970) 123,043.

Torbay, l. gov. dist., S. Devon, Eng.; formed by amalgamation of Torquay, Paignton, and Brixham; located around Tor Bay; tourism; p. (est. 1976) 109,900.

Torcello, I., with anc. Byzantine cath., on lagoon nr. Venice, Italy.

Torfaen, l. gov. dist., Gwent, Wales; based on Pontypool, Cwmbran and Blaenavon; p. (est. 1976) 88,700.

Torgau, t., E. Germany; R. pt. on Elbe; industl. ctr.; American and Soviet armies met here 1945; p. (est. 1970) 21,688.

Torne, R., N. Europe; rises in Sweden, drains L. Tornetrask and flows S.W. to G. of Bothnia, forming Finno-Swedish bdy.; rich in salmon; 512 km long.

Toronto, c., cap. of Ont. prov., Canada; major Gt. Ls. pt., on L. Ont.; spacious harbour; exp. lge. quantities of wheat; comm., financial, industl. and educational ctr.; many varied mnfs., univ.; notable bldgs., parks; a. 622 km²; p. (1971) 698,634 (c.), 2,609,638 (met. a.).

Torpoint, t., Cornwall, Eng.; on Plymouth Sound; p. (1971) 4,782.

Torquay, t., S. Devon, Eng.; incorporated in Torbay; on N. side of Tor Bay; seaside resort with all-year season.

Torre Annunziata, Campania, Italy; at foot of Vesuvius; spt., spa, bathing resort on Bay of Naples; arms factory, pasta mnf.; p. (est. 1968) 63,070.

Torre del Greco, t., Campania, Italy; spt. and resort on Bay of Naples at foot of Vesuvius; coral fishing; pasta mnf.; p. (est. 1968) 91,439.

Torremolinos. cst. resort, Spain; S. of Malaga.

Torrens, L., S. Australia; 208 km long, 32 km wide; varies from brackish lake to salt marsh.

Torreón, c., Coahuila, N. Mexico; developed rapidly after growth of cotton in surrounding Laguna dist.; cotton mills, rubber, smelting, food processing; rly. connection with ts. in S. Mexico; p. (1970) 257,045.

Torres Strait, between C. York, Queensland, Australia, and New Guinea; 144 km wide, dangerous navigation.

Torridge, R., Devon, Eng.; flows from Hartland dist. to a confluence with the Taw at Bideford Bay; 85 km long.

Torridge, l. gov. dist., N.W. Devon, Eng.; inc. N. cst. ts. of Northam and Bideford and stretches inland to Great Torrington; p. (est. 1976) 47,600.

Tortona, t., Piedmont, N. Italy; on Scrivia R.; textiles, metallurgy, engin., wines; cath.; the Roman Dertona; p. c. (est. 1968) 28,577.

Tortosa, c., Tarragona prov., N.E. Spain; pt. on Ebro R., 35 km from mouth; food processing, soap, pottery; cath.; impt. Moorish t.; p. (1970) 46,376.   [fertilisers.

Tororo, t., Uganda; lge. chemical wks., cement,

Tortuga or Ile de la Tortue, I., Caribbean Sea; off N. cst. Haiti; provides shelter from N.E. tr. winds for Port-de-Paix; private development to convert I. into free pt. with tax incentives for inds.; scenic attractions being tapped to develop tourist tr.; airport under construction; subsistence agr. fishing; a. c. 65 km².

Torun (Ger. Thorn), c., Bydgoszcz prov., Poland; rly. junc., pt. on Vistula; industl. ctr.; chemicals, elec. gds., clothing, metallurgy, engin., food processing; univ. bears name of Copernicus who was born here; p. (1970) 129,200.

Tory I., off N.W. cst., Donegal, R.o.I.; lighthouse; fishing; p. c. 200.

Totnes, t., South Hams, Devon, Eng.; on R. Dart, 10 km N.W. of Dartmouth; mediaeval t.; agr. mkt., food processing; p. (1971) 5,771.

Tottenham. See Haringey.

Tottori, t., Honshu, Japan; spt. on Sea of Japan, exp. lumber, raw silk, fruit; industl. ctr.; p. (est. 1971) 114,000.

Touggourt or Tuggurt, t., S. Algeria; on edge of Sahara; rly. terminus; dates; p. (1961) 26,000.

Toulon, c., Var dep., S.W. France; reinstated as cap. of Var dep. (1974); on Mediterranean cst.; base of Fr. navy; fine natural harbour; comm. pt. and industl. ctr.; many fine bldgs.; Port-Cros Nat. Park nearby; p. (1968) 174,746 (c.), 340,021 (met. a.).

Toulouse, c., cap. of Haute-Garonne dep., S. France; in Languedoc on Garonne R. and Canal du Midi, commanding route through Gate of Carcassonne; industl. and agr. tr. ctr.; food processing, varied mnfs.; many fine bldgs., notably me aeval univ., basilica, Gothic cath.; p. (1968) 370,796 (c.), 439,764 (met. a.).

Touraine, region and former prov. of France, of which Tours was the cap.; now occupied by Indre-et-Loire dep. and part of Vienne dep.; known as the " garden of France."

Tourcoing, c., Nord dep., N. France; 16 km N.E. of Lille; with twin t. of Roubaix forms major wool textile ctr.; p. (1967) 99,369.

Tournai, c., Hainaut prov., W. Belgium; on R. Scheldt, nr. Mons; historic c.; famous cath.; textiles, carpet mftg., ctr. of cement ind.; p. (1968) 33,518.

Tours, c., cap. of Indre-et-Loire dep., France; in Touraine, on R. Loire; tourist ctr. for the châteaux of the Loire; route ctr.; agr. inds.; printing, engin.; Gothic cath.; p. (1968) 128,120 (c.), 201,556 (met. a.).

Towcester, mkt. t., South Northants., Eng.; 14 km S.W. of Northampton; "Eatanswill" of Pickwick Papers; p. (1971) 20,998 (dist.).

Tower Hamlets, inner bor., E. London, Eng.; inc. former bors. of Bethnal Green, Stepney and Poplar; undergoing rapid economic and social change as p. and inds. are decentralised; site of lge. a. of London Docks with allied dockland inds.; clothing, brewing; p. (est. 1976) 146,100.

Tow Law, t., Wear Valley, Durham, Eng.; in Wear Dale, 16 km N.W. of Bishop Auckland; p. (1971) 2,547.

Townsville, spt., Queensland, Australia; on E. cst.; exp. prods. of rich dairying pastoral, and mng. terr.; copper-refining; p. (1972) 68,442.

Towton, v., North Yorks. Eng.; nearby Towton field, scene of bloodiest battle of Wars of the Roses 1461: Lancastrians under Henry VI defeated by Yorkists under Edward IV.

Towy, R., S. Wales; flows S.W. of Carmarthen Bay; 104 km long.

Toyama, c., Honshu, Japan; on Etchu plain to E. of Noto peninsula; regional admin. and comm. ctr.; patent medicines, aluminium smelting, machin.; p. (est. 1971) 275,000.

Toyohashi, t., Honshu, Japan; food processing, textiles; p. (est. 1971) 265,000.

Trabzon or Trebizond, spt., Turkey; on Black Sea; exp. tobacco, food prods., carpets; once a gr. tr. ctr. on caravan route between Persia and Europe; founded 8th cent. B.C. by Greek colonists. [famous victory 1805.

Trafalgar, C., S.W. cst., Cadiz, Spain; Nelson's

Trafford, met. dist. Gtr. Manchester, Eng.; comprises Sale, Hale, Altrincham, Urmston and Stretford; p. (est. 1976) 227,400.

Trail, t., B.C., Canada; lgst. metallurgical smelter in Commonwealth, using local non-ferrous metals; chemicals; p. (1971) 10,843.

Tralee, mkt. t., spt., Kerry, R.o.I.; on R. Lee; exp. grain, butter; p. (1966) 11,211.

Tranent, burgh, E. Lothian, Scot.; 16 km E. of Edinburgh; p. (1971) 6,281.

Trani, spt., N. Apulia, Italy; on Adriatic; mkt. t. for fertile coastal a.; fishing, food processing; cath., cas.; p. (est. 1968) 41,530.

Transbaykal, region, Siberia, RSFSR; E. of L. Baykal; mineral wealth; ch. t., Chita.

Transcaucasia, region between the Black Sea and the Caspian Sea, USSR; comprising the constituent reps. of Georgia, Armenia, and Azerbaydzhan; ch. t., Tbilisi.

Transkei, indep. Bantu Terr. (1976), S. Africa; not recognised by UN as designed to consolidate apartheid; mainly agr., maize and livestock; heavily dependent on S. Africa; p. mainly employed in mines in Transvaal and Orange Free State; cap. Umtata; a. 42,849 km²; p. (1970) 1,751,327.

Transvaal, prov., Rep. of S. Africa; high veld plateau (900-1,200 m) with Kruger Nat. Park in N.E.; hot summers, temperate winters; livestock on grasslands, grains, citrus fruits and temperate crops on irrigated land; lge. mineral wealth, especially gold in Witwatersrand; diamonds, uranium, platinum; inds. in ch. cs., Johannesburg and cap. Pretoria; a. 286,066 km²; p. (1970) 6,385,762.

Transylvania, historic region and prov., central Romania; high plateau surrounded by Carpathians; forested; mineral wealth not yet fully realised; arable agr. in valleys; ch. ts., Cluj, Brasov.

Transylvanian Alps, range of mtns., Romania; continuation of Carpathians.

Trapani, t., cap. of T. prov., W. Sicily, Italy; spt. on promontory, sheltering natural harbour; exp. wine, pasta, tuna fish caught locally; p. (1969) 76,679.

Traralgon, t., Victoria, Australia; lignite mng. nearby; p. (1972) 14,624.

Trasimeno, L., Umbria, central Italy; occupies lge. extinct volcanic crater; drained S. to R. Tiber; a. c. 155 km².

Trás-os-Montes e Alto-Douro, prov., N. Portugal; high, bleak plateau, cultivated valleys; climate cold except in S.; port wine cty. of Douro R.; remote, sparsely populated; a. 11,834 km²; p. (1960) 667,054.

Trawsfynydd, Gwynedd, Wales; within N. Wales Nat. Park; nuclear power sta.

Trebizond. See Trabzon.

Tredegar, t., Blaenau Gwent, Gwent, Wales; in narrow valley 5 km W. of Ebbw Vale; engin.; home of Aneurin Bevan; p. (1971) 17,976.

Treforest, t., Mid Glamorgan, Wales; on R. Taff; lge. trading estate established in 1930s to alleviate unemployment in primary inds. of S. Wales; aircraft accessories, electronics, chemical, pharmaceutical, rayon, metal wks.

Trelleborg, spt., S. Sweden; on Baltic Sea; most impt. rubber factory in cty.; p. (est. 1970) 36,021.

Trengganu, st., Malaysia; N.E. Malaya; rice, rubber, coconuts; tin, iron; cap. Kuala Trengganu; a. 13,080 km²; p. (1967) 378,738.

Trent, R., Eng.; rises in N. Staffs, flows round S. Pennines and joins the Ouse to form estuary of the Humber; many power stas. along its banks; polluted waterway, especially between Humber and Nottingham; 240 km long.

Trentino-Alto Adige, aut. region, N.E. Italy, between Austrian and Swiss Frontiers and L. Garda; embraces provs. Trento and Bolzano; cap. Trento; formerly called Venetia Tridentina; a. 13,598 km²; p. (1969) 839,625.

Trento, t., cap. of Trento prov. and ch. t. of Trentino-Alto Adige, N. Italy; on R. Adige and route to Brenner Pass; chemicals, cement,

elec. engin.; picturesque t.; cath.; p. (1969) 89,410.

Trenton, c., cap. N.J. st., USA; on Delaware R.; transport and industl. ctr.; noted for its wire-rope and pottery inds.; established mid-19th cent.; crockery, machin., metal and rubber gds.; p. (1970) 102,211 (c.), 299,919 (met. a.).

Tres Arroyos, t., E. Argentina; agr. and livestock ctr.; p. (1960) 40,000.

Trèves. See Trier.

Treviso, c., cap. of T. prov., Venetia, N.E. Italy; on R. Sile; agr. ctr. on fertile Venetian plain; silk mills, paper, furniture, fertilisers, pottery; p. (1969) 89,267.

Trichinopoly. See Tiruchirapalli.

Trichur, t., Kerala, India; comm. and educational ctr.; p. (1961) 73,038.

Trier (Trèves), c., Rhineland-Palatinate, W. Germany; on R. Moselle; Roman origin, (Augusta Trevorum, the Rome of the North), cath., Porta Nigra; ctr. of Moselle wine reg.; textiles, leather goods; birthplace of Marx; p. (est. 1969) 104,100.

Trieste, spt., cap. of T. prov., Friuli-Venezia Giulia, N.E. Italy; shipbldg., fishing, oil refining; pipeline to Schwechat, nr. Vienna; cath., cas., Roman antiquities; univ.; p. (1969) 278,370.

Trieste Free Territory, former free st. on the Adriatic; constituted by Peace Treaty with Italy, 1947, as compromise between conflicting Yugoslav and Italian claims; a. 743 km²; Zone A handed over to Italy, Zone B to Yugoslavia, 1954. Yugoslav/Italian agreement 1975 settled border dispute and established free industl. zone on both sides of border in region of Sezana-Fernetti.

Trikkala, t., cap. of T. dep., W. Thessaly, N. Greece; mkt. t. for pastoral prods.; damaged by earthquake 1954; p. (1971) 38,150.

Trim, co. t., U.D., Meath, R.o.I.; mkt. t. on R. Boyne; anc. seat of Irish Parliament; p. (1966) 1,467.

Trincomalee, t., N.E. cst. Sri Lanka; excellent natural harbour; formerly a British naval base; p. (est. 1968) 39,000.

Tring, mkt. t., Dacorum, Herts., Eng.; in gap through Chiltern hills, 14 km N.W. of Hemel Hempstead; p. (1971) 9,155.

Trinidad, t., cap. of Beni dep., Bolivia; exp. beef by air, but development hampered by isolation; p. (est. 1969) 17,360.

Trinidad, I., W.I.; N. of Venezuela; climate warm and humid; oil, natural gas, asphalt, sugar, rum, coconut oil, molasses, citrus fruits; tourism; cap. Port of Spain; a. 4,828 km²; p. (est. 1970) 1,010,000. See Trinidad and Tobago.

Trinidad, t., central Cuba; picturesque old t. of colonial period, declared a national monument; p. (est. 1967) 57,840.

Trinidad and Tobago, indep. st. within Commonwealth (1962), rep. (1976), W.I.; main exps. crude oil and petroleum prods. which with natural asphalt represent over 20 per cent national income; oil refining; tropical crops and food processing; sugar, molasses, rum, fruits, textiles; cap. and major spt. Port of Spain; internal self-gov. sought by Tobago; a. 5,128 km²; p. (est. 1970) 1,044,000.

Trinity, R., Texas, USA; flows S.E. to Galveston Bay; used for reservoirs; valley contains lge. p. and much economic activity; 800 km long.

Trino, Piedmont, N. Italy; 18 km S.S.W. of Vercelli; nuclear power sta.

Tripoli, c., Lebanon; spt. on Mediterranean; admin. ctr. for N. Lebanon; terminus of oil pipeline from Iraq; oil refining; exp. agr. prods.; p. (est. 1964) 127,611.

Tripoli, c., joint cap. of Libya (with Benghazi), on Mediterranean; stands on edge of palm-oasis, site of anc. Oea; tourist, comm. and mnf. ctr.; gd. harbour; p. (est. 1968) 247,365.

Tripura, new st. (1972), India; N.E. Ganges delta, bordering Assam and Bangladesh; cap. Agartala; rice, jute, cotton, sugar-cane; a. 10,360 km²; p. (est. 1971) 1,556,822.

Tristan da Cunha, sm. gr. S Is., S. Atl. Oc.; dependency of Brit. col. (t. Helena; ch. I. Tristan; evacuated 1961 volcanic eruption) but resettled 1963; a. 117 km²; p. (1970) 280.

Trivandrum, c., cap. of Kerala st., S.W. India; pt. on Arabian Sea; textiles, coconut processing; univ.; p. (1971) 409,672.

Trnava, c., W. Slovakia, ČSSR; mkt. t. in fertile agr. region on Váh R.; food processing, steel wks.; cath., monasteries, called " little Rome "; p. (1967) 36,000.

Trnovo or Tirnovo, c., Bulgaria; on Jantra R.; food processing, textiles, leather; anc. cap. of Bulgaria; p. (est. 1970) 42,344.

Trogir, t., S. Croatia, Yugoslavia; sm. pt. and seaside resort, partly sited on I. of Čiovo; mediaeval bldgs., inc. cath., palaces; p. c. 20,000.

Trois Rivières, t., Quebec, Canada; industl. ctr. on St. Lawrence R.; noted for newsprint; hydroelectric power from St. Maurice R.; p. (1966) 57,540.

Trojmiasto (Tri-City), Poland; name given to the three municipalities of Gdansk, Gdynia, and Sopot, a loosely-knit conurb.

Trollhättan, t., S.W. Sweden; on Göta R., nr. T. falls which generate power for metallurgical and chemical inds.; car and aircraft components; p. (1968) 40,803.

Trombay, I., off Bombay, India; oil refining; atomic reactor; zirconium metal produced; fertilisers.

Troms, co., N. Norway; deep fjords, offshore Is.; fishing, livestock, boat-bldg.; cap. Tromsö; a. 25,916 km²; p. (est. 1972) 138,085.

Tromsö, t., cap. of Troms prov., N. Norway; spt. on sm. I. of T. in Norwegian Sea; arctic fishing, sealing; fish processing; p. (1968) 36,340.

Trondheim, c., spt., Norway; on W. cst. on S. side of T. fjord; shipbldg., engin.; exp. timber and wood-pulp, butter, fish, copper; anc. cath., burial place of early Norwegian kings and place of coronation of recent sovereigns; p. (est. 1969) 124,870.

Troon, burgh, Kyle and Carrick, Scot.; on F. of Clyde, 10 km N. of Ayr; gd. harbour and graving docks; shipbldg., hosiery; seawater distillation research ctr. project; resort; p. (1971) 11,318.

Troppau. See Opava.

Trossachs, Stirling, Scot.; picturesque wooded glen; tourist resort.   [plant.

Troste, nr. Llanelli, Wales; steel strip mill, tin

Trouville, t., Calvados dep., N. France; popular seaside resort and fishing pt. on Normandy cst.; p. (1968) 6,577.

Trowbridge, mkt. t., West Wilts., Eng.; cloth wks., bacon curing, dairying, engin.; p. (1971) 19,245.

Troy, c., N.Y., USA; at confluence of Rs. Hudson and Mohawk; gr. shirt-mftg. ctr.; p. (1970) 62,918.

Troyes, c., cap. of Aube dep., N.E. France; on R. Seine; once cap. of Champagne; hosiery, textile machin., food processing; magnificent cath.; site of mediaeval fairs which standardised Troy weight; p. (1968) 74,898 (c.), 114,209 (met. a.).

Trucial States. See United Arab Emirates.

Trujillo, c., N.W. Peru; comm. and mkt. ctr. for irrigated agr. region, on Moche R., in foothills of Andes; sugar, cocaine; univ., cath.; p. (est. 1970) 156,200.

Trujillo, t., cap. of T. st., W. Venezuela; on Transandean highway at 805 m; agr. mkt. for region producing coffee, cacao, tobacco, maize; p. (est. 1970) 27,107.

Truro, t., Nova Scotia, Canada; on Salmon R.; hosiery, lumber mills, printing, metallurgy, machin.; p. (1971) 12,968.

Truro, c., Carrick, Cornwall, Eng.; at confluence of Rs. Kenwyn and Allen; mkt. t. and sm. pt.; admin. ctr. of Cornwall; cath.; p. (1971) 14,830.

Tsaidam, depression, Chinghai prov., China; a. of salt marsh and Ls.; rich deposits of oil; st. farms for intensive animal husbandry.

Tsamkong (Zhanjiang), c., Kwantung prov., China; spt. on Luichow peninsula; cotton milling, leather mnfs.; p. (1953) 166,000.

Tsangpo, R., Tibet, China; one of the headstreams of the R. Brahmaputra; 1,350 km long.

Tschenstokov. See Czestochowa.

Tselinograd, c., Kazakh SSR, USSR; cap. Virgin Lands terr.; on Ishim R., nr. Karaganda coalfield; chemicals, agr. machin.; p. (1970) 180,000.

Tsinan (Jinan), c., cap. of Shantung prov., China; on S. bank of Hwang-ho, 160 km from G. of Chihli; agr. ctr.; mnfs. glass, textiles,

precious stones, trucks; p. (est. 1970) 1,500,000.

Tsinghai. See Chinghai.

Tsinling Shan, mtn. range, central China; rises to over 1,830 m; watershed between Hwang-ho and Yangtze R. basins; impt. climatic divide between temperate N. China and tropical S. China.

Tsingtao (Qingdao), c., Shantung prov., China; spt. with excellent harbour at head of Kiaochow Bay; exp. soya beans, groundnuts; mnfs. locomotives, cement, textiles, machin., chemicals; p. (est. 1970) 1,900,000.

Tsitsihar (Qiqihar), c., Heilungkiang prov., N. China; on Vladivostok portion of Trans-Siberian rly.; food processing and tr., chemicals; potential oilfield; p. (est. 1970) 1,500,000.

Tskhinvali, c., N. Georgian SSR, USSR; elec. prods., lumber mills, fruit canning; p. (1970) 30,000.   [127,000.

Tsu, t., Honshu, Japan; textiles; p. (est. 1971)

Tsugaru Strait, Japan; separates Is. Hokkaido and Honshu; links Sea of Japan with Pac. Oc.; 72 km long, 24–32 km wide.

Tsuruga, spt., Japan; on W. cst. Honshu; rayon textiles, cotton, atomic power plant; p. (1970) 56,445.

Tuam, mkt. t., R.D., Galway, R.o.I.; sugar refining; p. (1961) 25,676 (R.D.); (1966) 3,621 (t.).

Tuamotu, coral archipelago, Fr. Polynesia, S. Pac. Oc.; pearl fisheries; p. of gr. (est. 1967) 6,148.

Tuapse, c., S. Krasnodar terr., RSFSR; at foot of Caucasus on Black Sea; major petroleum pt. at W. end of pipeline from Baku and Makhachkala; oil refineries; p. (est. 1967) 49,000.

Tubarao, t., Santa Catarina st., S. Brazil; on E. cst., 280 km N.W. of Pôrto Alegre; coal mines; p. (est. 1968) 59,210.

Tübingen, t., Baden-Württemberg, W. Germany; on R. Neckar; 15th cent. univ., cas.; mediaeval c. ctr.; birthplace of Hölderlin, p. (est. 1969) 55,795.

Tubuai, archipelago, Fr. Polynesia. S. Pac. Oc.; a. 163 km²; p. (est. 1967) 5,053.

Tucson, c., S.E. Arizona, USA; mkt. and distribution ctr. on Santa Cruz R.; cultural ctr. and winter resort based on Spanish heritage and warm dry climate; food processing, missile components; p. (1970) 258,303 (c.), 344,904 (met. a.).

Tucumán. See San Miguel de Tucumán.

Tudela, t., Navarre, N. Spain; mkt. ctr. for fertile fruit-growing dist. and I. of La Majana in Ebro R.; fine cath., Roman bridge; p. (1970) 20,942.

Tula, c., cap. of T. oblast, RSFSR; mnf. ctr. in Moscow industl. region; local iron and lignite mng.; Yasnaya Polyana, home of Tolstoy, nearby; p. (1970) 462,000.

Tulare, L., S. Cal., USA; ctr. of inland drainage 64 km S. of Fresno; streams feeding it used for irrigation; in drought years L. dries up completely; a. 233 km².

Tullamore, mkt. t., U.D., Offaly, R.o.I.; on Grand Canal; farming, distilling, brewing; p. (1966) 6,650.

Tulle, t., cap. of Corrèze dep., France; firearms, textiles; p. (1968) 21,324.

Tulsa, c., Okla., USA; impt. oil ctr., based on lge. local deposits; machin., aeroplanes; well laid out with many parks; p. (1970) 327,956 (c.), 471,743 (met. a.).

Tumaco, t., S.W. Colombia; spt. on Pac. Oc., on sm. I. off cst.; exp. agr. prods.; climate hot and humid; p. (est. 1968) 80.279.

Tummel, R., Perth and Kinross, Scot.; trib. of R. Tay; used by Perth to Inverness rly. as S. approach to Drumocheter Pass; hydroelec. scheme nr. Pitlochry; 88 km long.

Tunbridge Wells (officially Royal Tunbridge Wells), t., l. gov. dist., Kent, Eng.; on border of East Sussex; chalybeate waters; attractive 17th cent. promenade known as " The Pantiles "; p. (est. 1976) 96,000 (dist.).

Tunghwa, c., S.W. Kirin, China; rly. junc.; soyabean processing; local iron and coal reserves; p. (est. 1970) 275,000.

Tung Ting Hu, lge. L., Hunan, China; on S. margin of Yangtze R. plain; receives waters of Yuan and Siang Rs.. drains N. to Yangtze R.; surrounded by flat, intensively cultivated land; rice, sugar, mulberry; size varies with season; max. (in late summer) 6,500 km².

Tunguska, Upper, Stony and Lower, Rs., Siberia, USSR; all rise in Sayan mtns. nr. L. Baykal and flow N.W. through forested cty. into R. Yenisey.

Tunguska Basin, coalfield between Yenisey and Lena Rs., RSFSR; main ts., Norilsk, Igarka, Yeniseysk.

Tunis, c., cap. of Tunisia, N. Africa; spt. on inlet of Mediterranean; exp. raw materials; base for fishing fleets; univ., notable mosques; tourist ctr.; ruins of anc. Carthage to N.E.; p. (1966) 468,997 (c.), 647,640 (met. a.).

Tunisia, indep. st., N. Africa; bounded by Algeria on W., by Libya on E., indented Mediterranean cst.; Atlas mtns. penetrate into N.; temperate cst. climate, hot and dry in S. desert; agr. and mng. basis of economy; wheat, olive oil, wine, fruits, limited to wetter coastal areas and irrigated valleys; phosphates around Ghafsa; iron ore and lead in N.W.; steelwks. at Menzel Bourguiba; chemical and paper inds. based on local phosphates; cap. Tunis; a. 164,108 km²; p. (1966) 4,533,351.

Tunja, c., cap. of Boyacá dep., Colombia; route and agr. tr. ctr.; p. (est. 1972) 55,600.

Turda, t., Transylvania, Romania; local salt mines and quarrying aid chemical and ceramic inds.; p. (est. 1970) 50,113.

Turfan, depression, E. Sinkiang prov., China; on S. slopes of Tien Shan mtns.; desert a. irrigated by wells and canals for animal husbandry, fruit, cotton, grain; 275 m below sea level; ch. t. Turfan; archaeological finds.

Turgutlu (Kassaba), t., Manisa prov., Turkey; 48 km E.N.E. of Izmir; lignite, cotton, melons; p. (1965) 35,079.

Turin or Torino, c., cap. of T. prov., N. Italy; on R. Po at confluence with the Dora Riparia; former cap. of Piedmont and kingdom of Sardinia; univ., cath., many historic monuments; headquarters of Italian motor ind.; clothing, machin., furniture, chemicals; oil refinery nearby; p. (1969) 1,177,039.

Turkestan E., terr. included in Sinkiang, China; separated from W. or former Russian Turkestan by Pamir plateau; mainly desert.

Turkestan W., terr. of USSR; inc. Turkmen SSR, Uzbek SSR, Tadzhik SSR, Kirghiz SSR, and part of Kazakh SSR.

Turkey, rep., S.W. Asia; occupies mtnous. Anatolian penin.; equable climate on coastal margins, continental severity in interior; economy predominantly agr. but hampered by poor land resources; grain grown on Anatolian plateau and a Mediterranean variety of crops around cst.; noted for tobacco; industl. development based on mng. resources and oil in S.E.; cap. Ankara; a. 780,579 km²; p. (est. 1977) 39,180,000.

Turkmen (Turkmenistan), SSR, constituent rep., USSR; borders on Afghanistan, Iran, and the Caspian Sea; much of a. in Kara-Kum desert; agr. based on irrigation; fruit, cotton, wool; sulphates, petroleum; p. concentrated in oases and industl. ctrs. of cap. Ashkhabad, Mary, Chadzhou, along Trans-Caspian rly; a. 491,072 km²; p. (1970) 2,158,000.

Turks and Caicos, Is., Caribbean Sea, W.I.; about 30 sm. Is., geographically S.E. continuation of Bahamas; dry climate, poor limestone soil; exp. salt, crawfish; cap. Gran Turk; a. 430 km²; p. (est. 1970) 5,675.

Turku (Åbo), spt., S.W. Finland; on Baltic Sea; ctr. of fertile agr. a.; exp. agr. prods.; industl. ctr.; shipbldg., steel, machin., textiles; Finnish and Swedish univs.; p. (1968) 149,078 (c.); (1967) 194,464 (met. a.).

Turnhout, t., N.E. Belgium, nr. Antwerp, on Campine canal; textiles, lace, printing; p. (1968) 37,803.

Turnu Severin, c., S.W. Romania; R. pt. on Danube below Iron Gate cataracts; grain, salt, petroleum tr.; shipbldg.; p. (1968) 46,010.

Tuscaloosa, c., Ala., USA; on Black Warrior R.; rly. and industl. ctr. based on local coal, iron, cotton, timber; univ.; p. (1970) 61,933 (c.), 110,915 (met. a.).

Tuscany, region, central Italy; inc. provs. Arezzo, Firenze, Livorno, Siena, Grosseto, Lucca, Pisa, Massa and Carrara, Pistoia; mainly mtnous., drained by Arno R. system; wines, olive oil, cereals; iron ore from Elba, marble from Apuan Alps around Carrara; pt.

at Livorno (Leghorn); cap. Firenze (Florence); a. 22,989 km²; p. (est. 1968) 3,434,618.

Tuticorin, t., Tamil Nadu, S.E. India; on G. of Manaar; fertiliser plant; declining cotton and tea pt.; p. (1971) 153,310 (t.), 181,913 (met. a.).

Tuttlingen, t., Baden-Württemberg, W. Germany; on R. Danube; surgical instruments; footwear; p. (est. 1969) 26,436.

Tuva ASSR, RSFSR; bounded by Siberia and Mongolia; mtn. basin, forested; timber inds., coal mng., asbestos, pastoral agr.; cap. Kyzyl; a. c. 165,800 km²; p. (1970) 231,000.

Tuvalu Is., formerly Ellice Is., until 1975 part of Gilbert and Ellice Is., W. Pac. Oc.; indep. planned for 1978; p. mainly Polynesian; coconut cultivation in high temps.; exp. copra; a. 25 km²; p. (est. 1975) 7,000.

Tuxtla Gutiérrez, c., cap. of Chiapas st., Mexico; in fertile valley at 450 m.; ctr. for sisal, tobacco, coffee, cattle; on Inter-American Highway; Mayan ruins nearby; p. (1969) 41,000.

Tuz, L., Turkey; salt L.; a. 1,619 km² in winter much reduced in summer.

Tuzla, t., Bosnia-Hercegovina, Yugoslavia; salt, lignite, coal; hydroelectric power in a.; agr. mkt. ctr.; textiles; p. (1971) 53,825.

Tweed, R., S.E. Scot.; rises in Tweeddale, and reaches sea at Berwick; salmon fisheries; length 155 km. [R.o.I.; Benbaum, 730 m.

Twelve Pins, star-shaped mtn. range, Galway,

Twickenham. See Richmond-upon-Thames.

Tychy, t., Katowice prov., Poland; on edge of Upper Silesian industl. a.; surrounded by forest; brewing; p. (1970) 71,400.

Tyler, c., Texas, USA; oil ctr. on E. Texan field; agr. ctr. for local mkt. gardening; famous for rose growing; p. (1970) 57,700.

Tyne, R., Tyne and Wear, Durham and Northumberland, Eng.; formed by confluence of N. Tyne and S. Tyne at Hexham; flows E. to sea at Tynemouth and S. Shields; valley gives easy route across mtns. from Newcastle to Carlisle; lower course forms harbour (with shipbldg. and other wks.) from Newcastle to Tynemouth; road tunnel between Wallsend and Jarrow; 128 km long.

Tynedale, l. gov. dist., W. Northumberland, Eng.; lge. inland a. inc. Haltwistle, Hexham and Prudoe; p. (est. 1976) 54,500.

Tynemouth, t., North Tyneside, Tyne and Wear, Eng.; fishing pt. on N. bank of Tyne R.; shipbldg., engin.; ruined priory and cas.; residtl. resort; p. (1971) 68,861.

Tyne and Wear, met. co., N.E. Eng.; mainly industl. a. around lower T. and W. Rs.; inc. Newcastle-upon-Tyne, Tynemouth, Gateshead, South Shields and Sunderland; traditionally ass. with shipbldg. and cocl-mng., but inds. incr. diversified; p. (est. 1976) 1,182,900.

Tyneside, North, met. dist., Tyne and Wear, Eng.; comprises Tynemouth, Whitley Bay and Wallsend; p. (est. 1976) 202,600.

Tyneside, South, met. dist., Tyne and Wear, Eng.; comprises Jarrow, Hebburn and South Shields; p. (est. 1976) 166,800.

Tyre (Sur), Lebanon; anc. Phoenician c. and spt.; founded c. 15th cent. B.C.; now sm. comm. t., tr. in cotton, tobacco; p. 12,000.

Tyrol, Alpine region, Europe; falls within Austria and Italy, linked by Brenner Pass; embraces highest peaks of Austrian Alps, culminating in Ortler Spitz; two-fifths forest, timber inds.; mtn. pasture; tourism; Austrian prov. of Tyrol: cap. Innsbruck; a. 12,650 km²; p. (1971) 539,000.

Tyrone, former co., N. Ireland; now replaced by Strabane, Omagh, Dungannon and Cookstown l. gov. dists.

Tyrrhenian Sea, part of Mediterranean between Italy and Corsica, Sardinia and Sicily.

Tyumen, c., RSFSR; one of oldest Siberian ts., rly. ctr. on Trans-Siberian rly., R. pt. on Tura R.; many heavy inds.; ctr. of oil and natural gas region; p. (1970) 269,000.

Tywyn, mkt. t., Meirionnydd, Gwynedd, Wales; on cst. of Cardigan Bay, 5 km N.W. of Aberdovey; p. (1971) 3,818.

Tzekung (Zigong), c., Szechwan, China; petroleum, natural gas, salt wks.; p. (est. 1970) 350,000.

Tzepo (Zibo), c., Shantung, China; formed by merging 1950 coal mng. ts. of Tzechwan and Poshan and 1954 addition of Changchow; p. (1957) 806,000.

U

Ubangi, major R., Central Africa; trib. of R. Zaïre; rises on bdr. of Central African Emp. and Zaïre, flows W. and S. to join Zaïre R. at Irebu; partially navigable; 2,240 km long.

Ube, spt., S. Honshu, Japan; coal mng. and industl. ctr.; machin., synthetic petroleum; p. (est. 1971) 154,000.

Ubeda, t., Jaén prov., Spain; on plateau between Guadalquivir and Guadalimar; food processing, olive oil, soap; p. (1970) 30,186.

Uberaba, t., Minas Gerais, Brazil; ctr. of cattle rearing and arable agr. region; sugar milling, mnfs. lime; p. (1970) 108,576.

Ucayali, R., Peru; headstream of R. Amazon; over 2,240 km long, navigable for 1,600 km.

Uckfield, mkt. t., East Sussex, Eng.; 13 km N.E. of Lewes; a. ctr. of former Sussex iron ind.; p. (1971) 54,518 (dist.).

Udaipur, c., Rajasthan, N.W. India; in picturesque valley at 760 m a.s.l.; cap. of former princely st. of U.; maharajah's palace; p. (1971) 161,278.

Uddevalla, spt., S. Sweden; N. Göteborg; shipyds., prefab. houses, timber, granite quarrying, textiles; p. (1968) 36,480.

Udi, t., S. Nigeria, W. Africa; 160 km N. of Pt. Harcourt; impt. mng. ctr. on Enugu coalfield; linked by rail to Kaduna and Pt. Harcourt.

Udine, c., cap. of U. prov., Friuli-Venezia Giulia, N.E. Italy; between Alps and G. of Venice; route and industl. ctr. in agr. region; textiles, chemicals, engin., leather, woodwork; cath., many attractive bldgs., piazzas; severe earthquakes (1976); p. (1969) 96,694.

Udmurt ASSR, RSFSR; part of Urals industl. a.; two-fifths forested, timber inds.; arable agr., flax; steel inds. at cap. Izhevsk, Votkinsk, Sarapul; p. (1970) 1,417,000.

Udokan Khrebet, mtns., RSFSR; world's lgst. reserve of copper.

Ufa, c., cap. of Bashkir ASSR, RSFSR; in Urals industl. a., at confluence of Rs. Belaya and Ufa; machin., oil refineries, sawmills; p. (1970) 773,000.

Uganda, rep., E. Africa; equatorial cty., climate modified by alt.; forms part of E. African plateau (1,200 m); well-developed economy; coffee, tea, tobacco, cotton for exp.; developing pastoral economy, fishing on L. Victoria; copper at Kilembe, tin; hydroelectric power from Owen Falls, second project at Kabelega Falls; savannah areas contain abundant wildlife in Nat. Parks and Game Reserves; cap. Kampala; a. 235,887 km²; p. (est. 1970) 9,764,000.

Uist, N. and S., Is., Outer Hebrides, N.W. Scot.; indented csts.; N. Uist boggy in E., hilly in W.; S. Uist smaller but mtnous.; crofting, fishing; p. (1971) 1,726 (N.), 3,872 (S.).

Uitenhage, t., Cape prov., S. Africa; fruit, wool, rly. wks., tyres, car assembly, textiles; summer resort; p. (1970) 69,048.

Ujiji, t., in sm. terr. same name (a. 2,383 km²) on E. shore L. Tanganyika, Tanzania; where Stanley found Livingstone 1871; p. c. 14,000.

Ujiyamada. See Ise.

Ujjain, t., Madhya Pradesh, India; sacred c. and formerly cap. of Malwa; univ.; p. (1971) 203,278 (t.), 208,561 (met. a.).

Ujpest, industl. sub., Budapest, Hungary; elec. engin., leather, shoes, textiles, furniture, pharmaceuticals; p. 76,000.

Ujung Pandang (Makasar), c., Sulawesi, Indonesia; in dist. of rich volcanic soils; major spt. and airpt., entrepot tr.; p. (1971) 434,766.

Ukhta t., RSFSR; ctr of natural gas field in Pechora Basin; p. (est. 1969) 57,000.

Ukrainian SSR, constituent rep., USSR; in Eastern Europe; of dominating importance in Soviet economy; drained by Rs. Dnieper Dniester, S. Bug, Donets; Pripet Marshes in N., wooded steppes in ctr., fertile black-earth a in S.; major wheat-growing a. of Europe; highly mineralised, many industl. raw materials and ctrs. of metallurgical and heavy inds.; cap. Kiev; a. 582,750 km²; p. (1970) 47,126,000.

Ulan Bator, c., cap. of Mongolian People's Rep.; in stock-raising region; industl. ctr. of cty.; woollen gds., saddles, knitwear; new indust,

ctr. at Darkhan nearby; rly. link to China and USSR; contains one-quarter of p. of rep.; p. (1966) 250,000.

Ulan-Ude (Verkhneudinsk), t., Siberia, RSFSR; major route and mnf. ctr.; pt. on R. Ude, junc. on Trans-Siberian rly., linked by rail to Peking; engin., textiles, glass, leather; p. (1970) 254,000.

Ullapool. v., Ross and Cromarty, Scot.; sm. fish. pt. (herring landings), on L. Broom, 72 km N.W. of Inverness; attractive mtn. and cst. scenery in a.

Ullswater, L. Cumbria, Eng.; 13 km long; supplies water to Manchester; attractive tourist a.

Ulm, c., Baden–Württemberg, W. Germany; route ctr. at limit of barge navigation on Danube, although navigable limits being extended by canalisation; food-processing, metal gds., textiles, cement; p. (est. 1969) 91,852.

Ulsan, t., South Korea; oil refining, fertilisers; p. (1966) 112,858.

Ulster. See Northern Ireland.

Ulúa-Chamelhcón, R. basin, N. cst. Honduras; major banana region of Central American cst.

Ulva, I., Argyll and Bute, Scot.; off W. cst. of Mull; 8 km long.

Ulverston, mkt. t., South Lakeland, Cumbria, Eng.; nr. Morecambe Bay; antibiotics, elec. gds., tanning; p. (1971) 11,888.

Ul'yanovsk (Simbirsk), c., cap. of U. oblast, RSFSR; industl. ctr. of middle Volga region; birthplace of Lenin whose real name was Ulyanov; p. (1970) 351,000.

Uman, c., Ukrainian SSR, USSR; at confluence of Kamenka and Umanka Rs.; rly. junc.; agr.-processing; p. (est. 1969) 64,000.

Umanak, t., W. Greenland; hunting and fishing base on arm of Baffin Sea; marble mng.; p. (est. 1968) 2,348.

Umbria, region, central Italy; comprising provs. of Perugia and Terni, crossed by Apennines and upper Tiber; agr. mainstay of economy; inds. based on hydroelectric power at Terni; chemicals; developing tourist tr.; cap. Perugia; a. 8,472 km²; p. (1969) 783,048.

Ume, R., Sweden; flows S.E. to the G. of Bothnia; length 400 km.

Umeå, c., cap. of Västerbotten prov., N.E. Sweden; on G. of Bothnia at mouth of Ume R.; cultural ctr.; woodpulp; p. (1968) 51,952.

Umm-al-Quaywayn, emirate, member of United Arab Emirates; p. (est. 1968) 8,000.

Umm Qasr, t., Kuwait; on Iraq border; new deepwater port planned.

Umtali, t., Rhodesia; comm. ctr. for rich agr. a.; oil refinery at Feruka; pipeline to Beira; p. (1968) 53,500.

Umtata, t., Cape Prov., S. Africa; admin. ctr. for Transkei terrs.; cath.; p. (est. 1967) 17,200.

Uncia, t., Oruro dep., Bolivia; alt. 3,900 m in E. Cordillera of Andes, 96 km S.E. of Oruro; site of impt. Patino tin mines.

Ungava Bay, arm of Hudson Strait, projecting into Labrador, N.E. Canada; minerals abundant, recent exploitation of impt. medium and low-grade iron deposits.

Union of South Africa. See South Africa, Rep. of.

Union of Soviet Socialist Republics (USSR), E. Europe, N. Asia; major world economic and political power; ctr. of European communist bloc; extends over 9,600 km W.–E., 4,800 km N.–S.; continental climate with marked regional variations; comprises 1 fed. rep. and 14 constituent reps.; centrally planned economy emphasising development of heavy inds. at major sources of natural resources, and development of new resources in E.; timber inds. and textiles impt. with more recent developments in consumer inds.; lge.-scale, mechanised agr. with planned prod. reflecting regional variations in physical conditions; transport emphasis on rlys. to open up remote E. regions, but more recent road bldg. programme; 27 major pts. inc. Leningrad, Arkhangelsk, Riga, Murmansk, Odessa, Baku, Vladivostok; cap. Moscow; a. 22,272,290 km²; p. (1977) 257,000,000.

United Arab Emirates (Trucial Sts.), indep. sov. st. on Persian G., S.W. Asia; formed (1971) from Trucial Sts. (Abū Dhabi, Ajmān, Dubai, Al Fujayrah, Ra's al Khaymah, Shārjah, Umm-al-Quaywayn) after withdrawal of Brit. forces and termination of special defence treaty (1820–

1971); p. immigration from Middle and Far East as oil-based economic growth proceeds, esp. in Abu Dhabi; a. 82,880 km²; p. (est. 1970) 130,000 (mainly nomadic).

United Kingdom, cty., N.W. Europe; separated from continent of Europe by English Channel; consists of Gr. Britain (Eng., Wales, Scot.) and N. Ireland; a. 244,022 km²; p. (est. 1975) 55,962,000.

United States of America, fed. rep., N. America; world's major economic power and one of the 3 political " super powers "; variety of climatic and physical conditions (see N. America); economically self-supporting, but imports petroleum, coffee, machin., textiles; extremely diversified mnfs.; consists of 50 sts. and Dist. of Columbia, co-extensive with cap. of Washington; outlying dependencies inc. Puerto Rico, U.S. Virgin Is., Panama Canal Zone, Guam, American Samoa, Trust Terr. of the Pac. Is.; a. 9,363,169 km²; p. (est. 1977) 216,450,000.

Unst, I., Shetlands, Scot.; most N. of gr.; length 20 km; p. (1971) 1,127.

Unterwalden, can., Switzerland; divided into Obwalden and Nidwalden; dairying, fruit and livestock; cap. Stans; a. 767 km²; p. (1969) 50,600.

Upernavik, t., W. Greenland; on sm. I. in Baffin Bay; sealing and whaling base; meteorological sta.; p. (est. 1968) 1,930.

Upper Austria, prov., Austria; borders on W. Germany and CSSR; hilly and forested; drained by Danube R. system; inc. Salzkammergut resort a.; agr., forestry; inds. centred on Linz (cap.), Steyr and Wels; a. 11,979 km²; p. (est. 1968) 1,201,600.

Upper Hutt., c., N.I., N.Z.; p. (1971) 20,003.

Upper Volta (Voltaic Rep.), W. Africa; landlocked st.; hot dry climate, humid in S.; wooded savannah; agr. basis of economy; most of p. farmers and nomadic herdsmen; permanent agr. in irrigated R. valleys and oases, sorghum, millet, maize, yams, beans; inds. based on local handicrafts; economy hampered by landlocked location; one of poorest economies in world; rly. outlet to sea via Abidjan (Ivory Cst.); cap. Ouagadougou; a. 274,123 km²; p. (est. 1970) 5,437,000.

Uppingham, mkt. t., Leics., Eng.; 16th cent. school; p. (1971) 6,576 (dist.).

Uppsala, c. cap. of U. prov., Sweden; on R. Sala, 72 km from Stockholm; historic ctr. of anc. Sweden; cultural ctr., famous univ. (Linnaeus taught there); cath.; lt. inds.; p. (1968) 97,172.

Ur, anc. Chaldean c. Iraq; 208 km W.N.W. of Basra; ruins; flourished about 3,000 B.C.

Ural, R., RSFSR; flows S.W. and S. to Caspian Sea; used for domestic and industl. water supply; navigable; 2,400 km long.

Ural Mts., USSR; mtn. system, forms bdy. between Europe and Asia and separates Russian plain from W. Siberian lowlands; extends N.-S. for 2,400 km; highest peaks Narodnaya and Telpos-Iz; rich mineral resources have given rise to huge ctrs. of heavy ind., inc. Sverdlovsk, Chelyabinsk, Magnetogorsk.

Uralsk, N.W., Kasakh SSR; USSR; on R. Ural; grain-trading and cattle-mart ctr.; flour, leather, woollens, iron-ware; p. (1970) 134,000.

Uranium City, N. Saskatchewan, Canada; nr. N. shore of L. Athabasca, ctr. of Beaverlodge uranium-mng. a.; founded 1951; p. (1960) 3,349.

Urawa, t., Honshu, Japan; sub. of Tokyo; p. (est. 1971) 281,000.

Urbino, t., in the Marches, central Italy; agr. mkt. and route ctr.; picturesque tourist ctr.; cath., univ., palace; p. (est. 1968) 16,720.

Ure, R., North Yorks., Eng.; flows E. and S.E. to the Swale to form the Ouse; upper part of valley known as Wensleydale; 80 km long.

Urfa, t., Turkey; nr. Syrian bdr.; handicrafts, local agr. tr.; p. (1967) 72,873.

Urgench, t., cap. of Khorezm oblast, W. Uzbek SSR, USSR; pt. on Amu Dar'ya R. in Khiva oasis; cotton, food-processing; p. (est. 1967) 65,000.

Uri, can., Switzerland; S. of L. of Lucerne; forest and mtns.; traversed by St. Gotthard rly. and R. Reuss; sparse p., German speaking; cap. Altdorf; a. 1,075 km²; p. (1969) 34,000.

Urmia, L., nr. Tabriz, N.W. Iran; 136 km by 48 km; salt and shallow; no outlet.

Urmston, Trafford, Gtr. Manchester, Eng.; residtl. sub. of Manchester; inc. part of Trafford Park industl. estate; p. (1971) 44,523.

Uruapan, t., Michoacán, W. Mexico; mkt. ctr. for semi-tropical mtnous. a.; famous handicrafts; parks, gardens; p. (1970) 104,475.

Urubamba, R., Peru; rises in E. Cordillera of Andes; forms one of headstreams of R. Amazon; length 560 km.

Urubupunga, t., Brazil; new. t. for 10,000, at site of hydroelectric power sta.

Uruguaiana, t., Brazil; on R. Uruguay; cattle ctr.; jerked beef, soap, candles; p. (est. 1968) 74,581.

Uruguay, rep., S. America; smallest of S. American reps.; situated on N. bank of Rio de la Plata estuary; low hills in N.; temperate climate; 60 per cent land a. devoted to livestock rearing, especially cattle, sheep, based on extensive natural grasslands; arable land in S., grains; ch. t. Montevideo, cap. and main ctr. of inds.; food processing, leather, metallurgy, textiles, rubber; a. 186,925 km²; p. (est. 1970) 2,886,000.

Uruguay, R., S. America; rises in S. Brazil, flows 1,360 km to Rio de la Plata; forms bdy. between Argentina and Uruguay and part of bdy. between Argentina and Brazil.

Urumchi (Wulumuchi), c., cap. of Sinkiang prov., N.W. China; admin., comm. and industl. ctr.; iron and steel, cement, textiles, nitrogenous fertilisers, agr. machin.; local coal, tin, silver mng.; p. (est. 1970) 500,000.

Usak, t., Turkey; connected by rail with Izmir; noted for pile carpet-weaving; p. (1965) 38,815.

Usambara, mtns., N.E. Tanzania; scene of early European settlement (1902); lumber, tea, coffee produced on slopes; max. alt. 2,560 m.

Usedom (Uznam), I., Baltic Sea; off mouth of R. Oder; since 1945 E. part belongs to Poland, W. (the larger part) to E. Germany; a. 445 km²; p. 45,000.

Ushant, I., off cst. of Finistère, France; at entrance to English Channel; it was off Ushant that Lord Howe gained his gr. naval victory on the " glorious first of June " 1794; lighthouse, fishing; p. 2,000.

Ushuaia, t., Argentina; most S. t. in world; sheep farming, timber, furs; freezing plant; p. 6,000.

Usk, mkt. t., Gwent, Wales; 13th cent. cas.; p. (1971) 2,028.

Usk, R., Gwent, S. Wales; flows S. past Newport to Bristol Channel; picturesque, gd. fishing; 91 km long.

Usküdar (Scutari), t., Turkey; on Bosporus, opposite Istanbul; mkt. ctr.; new bridge to European side of Bosporus; Crimean memorial cemetery for Brit. troops; Muslim cemeteries; p. (1965) 133,883.

Uspallata Pass, 3,800 m high over Andes between Mendoza, Argentina, and Santiago, Chile; monument " Christ of the Andes " marks international bdy. settlement; used by Mendoza-Valparaiso rly.

Ussuri, R., rises in Maritime prov. of RSFSR, flows c. 800 km to R. Amur; final 480 km forms Sino-Soviet bdy.

Ussuriysk (Voroshilov), t., RSFSR; 112 km N. of Vladivostok; rly. junc. ot Trans-Siberian and Chinese Eastern rlys.; engin., agr. prod.; p. (1970) 128,000.

Ustica, I., Palermo, Italy; basalt; agr., fishing, handicrafts; a. 8 km²; p. c. 1,200.

Usti-nad-Labem (Aussig), c., Bohemia, CSSR; R. pt. on Elbe; route and industl. ctr.; chemicals, textiles, machin.; p. (1967) 73,000.

Ust Kamenogorsk, c., Kazakh SSR, USSR; on Irtysh R.; mng. ctr.; food processing, clothing, furniture; hydroelectric power sta. nearby; p. (1970) 230,000.

Usumbura. See Bujumbura.

Utah, st., USA; Rocky mtns. in E.; forms part of Gr. Basin in W.; Gr. Salt L. in N.W.; dry continental climate; poor agr. conditions, soil erosion; copper, gold; tourism; Nat. Parks; cap. Salt L. City; a. 219,932 km²; p. (1970) 1,060,631.

Utica, c., N.Y., USA; on Mohawk R. and Barge Canal; in rich dairying region; textiles, electronics, tools, firearms; p. (1970) 90,802 (c.), 335,809 (met. a.).

Utrecht, c., Neth.; on Old Rhine (Oude Rijn); univ.; cath.; chemical and cigar factories; printing, machin., woollens, silks, velvets; major transport and financial ctr.; picturesque; p. (est. 1969) 277,647 (c.), 451,646 (met. a.).

Utrecht, prov., Neth.; between Gelderland and N. and S. Holland; fertile agr., cattle rearing, horticulture; a. 1,362 km²; p. (1968) 768,715.

Utsunomiya, t., Honshu, Japan; ctr. for Nikko Nat. Park; p. (est. 1971) 308.000.

Uttar Pradesh, st., India; Himalayas on N. bdy., drained by Ganges and Jumna; irrigation; wheat, rice, millet, barley, maize, cotton, sugar, oil-seeds; ch. ts. Allahabad, Lucknow (cap.), Varanasi, Kanpur, Agra, Meerut; a. 293,732 km²; p. (1971) 88,299,453; (p. increasing by 2 million a year)

Uttlesford, l. gov. dist., Essex, Eng.; inc. Saffron Walden and Dunmow; p. (est. 1976) 55,800.

Uttoxeter, t., East Staffs., Eng.; on R. Dove; machin., biscuit mftg.; expanded t.; p. (1971) 9,034.

Uusikaupunki (Swed. Nystad), spt., Abo-Bjorneborg, S.W. Finland; on G. of Bothnia; p. (1966) 5,074.

Uzbek (Uzbekistan) SSR, constituent rep., USSR; crossed by Rs. Amu Dar'ya and Syr Dar'ya; contains part of fertile Ferghana Valley; intensive farming based on irrigation; rice, cotton, fruits, silk, cattle, sheep; ch. cs. Tashkent (cap.), Samarkand; alluvial gold deposits and bauxite in Kizil-Kum desert; a. 412,250 km²; p. (1970) 11,963,000.

Uzhgorod, c., Ukrainian SSR, USSR; economic and cultural ctr.; friendship pipeline from Kuybyshev; univ.; p. (est. 1967) 61,000.

V

Vaal, R., S. Africa; rises in Drakensberg mtns., flows between the Transvaal and Orange Free State to join the Orange R. nr. Kimberley. V. dam irrigates lge. a. of Witwatersrand; 896 km long.

Vaasa, c., cap. of Vaasa prov., W. Finland; pt. on G. of Bothnia; exp. timber and timber prods.; agr. ctr.; food processing, textiles, timber inds.; p. (1968) 48,679.

Vác, t., Hungary; on R. Danube; comm. ctr.; summer resort for Budapest; cath.; p. (1966) 28,700.

Vadso, cap. of Finnmark prov., N.E. Norway; ice-free Arctic pt. on N. side of Varangar fjord; whaling and fishing base; p. (est. 1970) 5,625.

Vaduz, mkt. t., cap. of Liechtenstein; nr. Rhine; sm. tourist resort; p. (1970) 3,921.

Vaigach, sm. i., between Novaya Zemlya and mainland of USSR; geological extension of Urals; low-lying reindeer pasture; seal fishing.

Valais, can., Switzerland; in upper valley of R. Rhône; surrounded by mtns., forested on slopes; vines and cereals in valleys; ch. resort Zermatt, cap. Sion; a. 5,234 km²; p. (1967) 193,000.

Valdai Hills, morainic ridges between Leningrad and Moscow, RSFSR; rise to c. 348 m and form ch. watershed of E. European Rs., Volga, Dvina and Dniester.

Val d'Aosta, aut. region, N.W. Italy; high Alpine cty., borders France and Switzerland; cap. Aosta; agr.; hydroelectric power; winter resorts; a. 3,263 km²; p. (1969) 108,848.

Val-de-Marne, dep., S.E. of Paris, France; cap. Créteil; a. 243 km²; p. (1968) 1,121,340.

Valdez, t., Alaska, USA; ice-free pt., fishing; terminal of oil pipeline from North Slope; p. (1970) 1,005.

Valdivia, c., cap. of V. prov., S. Chile; on R. Callecalle nr. the sea (pt. Corral); damaged by earthquake and tidal wave 1960; univ.; metal, wood and leather gds.; paper, flour, brewing; p. (est. 1966) 80,035.

Val d'Oise, dep., N.W. of Paris, France; cap. Pontoise; a. 1,248 km²; p. (1968) 693,269.

Valdosta, t., Ga., USA; rly. and tr. ctr. for region producing tobacco, cotton, timber; p. (1970) 32,303.

Valence, t., cap. of Drôme dep., S.E. France; on R. Rhône; silks, hosiery, vineyards; agr. mkt.; p. (1968) 64,134.

Valencia, region, E. Spain; on Mediterranean; comprises provs. of Alicante, Castellón de la

Plana and Valencia; mtnous., with densely populated, fertile coastal plain; irrigation makes a. a major producer of Mediterranean fruit and crops; a. 23,305 km²; p. (1970) 1,767,327.

Valencia, c., cap. of V. prov., E. Spain; pt. on Mediterranean at mouth of R. Turia; one of most impt. agr. ts. of cty., and active industl. and comm. ctr.; univ., cath.; resort; p. (est. 1969) 498,159.

Valencia, c., N. Venezuela; nr. L. Valencia; ctr. of agr. a., sugar-cane, cotton; leading industl. t.; cattle mart; cotton mills, meat packing; cath.; p. (est. 1970) 224,800.

Valenciennes, c., Nord dep., N. France; in Hainaut cty. on R. Escaut (Scheldt); metallurgical and chemical inds.; once famous for hand-made lace; birthplace of Froissart and Watteau; p. (1968) 46,626 (c.), 223,629 (met. a.).

Valentia, I., S.W. Kerry, R.o.I.; in Dingle Bay; agr., fishing; 10 km by 3 km.

Vale of Glamorgan, l. gov. dist., South Glamorgan, Wales; inc. cstl. ts. of Penarth, Barry and Cowbridge; p. (est. 1976) 107,700.

Vale of White Horse, l. gov. dist., Oxon., Eng.; based on Abingdon, Faringdon and Wantage; p. (est. 1976) 97,800.

Vale Royal, l. gov. dist., Ches., Eng.; a. in ctr. of co. and inc. saltfield ts. of Northwich and Winsford; p. (est. 1976) 109,900.

Valladolid, c., cap. of V. prov., Spain; on R. Pisuerga (trib. of Douro); grain tr.; route, industl. and comm. ctr.; food processing, textiles; cath., univ.; p. (est. 1969) 177,797.

Valle del General, upland, S.W. Costa Rica; pioneer subsistence agr., maize, tropical fruit, cattle; improving transport.

Vallejo, t., Cal., USA; at mouth of Napa R., on San Pablo Bay; pt. and processing ctr. for farm prod.; naval shipyard; p. (1970) 67,905 (t.), 241,332 (met. a.).

Vallenar, t., Atacama prov., Chile; agr. ctr.; dried fruit, wines; iron ore nearby; p. (1960) 30,793.

Valletta, c., cap. of Malta; ch. spt. on rocky penin. of Mt. Sceberras, E. cst.; formerly impt. British naval base; cath., univ.; p. (est. 1969) 15,512.

Valli di Comacchio, lagoon a., N.E. Italy; ctr. of an impt. eel industry; a. 259 km².

Valparaiso, c., central Chile; leading pt. on Pac. cst. of S. America; attractive c. with backdrop of steep hills; mftg., comm. and industl. cur. of rep. with textile mills, sugar refineries, paint, shoe and chemical factories; univ.; p. (est. 1970) 292,847.

Valtellina, fertile valley, Italy; in Lombard Alps above L. Como; impt. for vine cultivation; hydroelectric power resources; tourism.

Van, c., cap. of Van prov., S.E. Turkey; stands at 1,726 m on shore of salty L. Van; tr. ctr. of wheat-growing a.; new Turkish–Iranian rail link; p. (1965) 31,010.

Vancouver, c., B.C., Canada; Pac. cst. spt. with excellent natural harbour; international airport and terminus of transcontinental rly.; timber inds., shipbldg., fishing, oil and sugar refining; exp. prod. from these inds.; attractive hilly location and mild climate make c. a major tourist ctr.; univ.; p. (1971) 422,278 (c.), 1,071,081 (met. a.).

Vancouver, I., B.C., Canada; off W. cst.; mtnous., forested; woodpulp, paper; indented cst. provides many natural harbours; fishing; cap. Victoria; a. 33,797 km²; p. (1961) 290,835.

Vancouver, t., Wash., USA; spt. on Columbia R. opposite Portland (Ore.); exp. grain, timber; food processing; p. (1970) 42,493.

Vandellos, Tarragona, Spain; nuclear power sta.

Vanderbijlpark, t., Transvaal, S. Africa; on Vaal R.; ctr. for steel wks.; p. (1970) 78,745.

Vänern, lge. L. Sweden; W.N.W. of L. Vättern, with which it is connected by canal (and thence with the Baltic); a. 5,566 km².

Vänersborg, L. pt., Sweden; on tongue of land between R. Göta and the Vasobotten (southernmost bay of L. Vänern); footwear, wood and sulphite pulp; p. (est. 1970) 20,280.

Vannes, t., cap. of Morbihan dep., N.W. France; sm. pt. on S. cst. Brittany; cath.; dates from Roman times; p. (1968) 40,724.

Var, dep., S.E. France; in Provence, on Mediterranean; mainly agr. with some inds. at Draguignan and Toulon (cap. since 1974); bauxite at Brignoles; rapid growth of p.; inc.

many coastal resorts; a. 6,042 km²; p. (1968) 555,926.

Varanasi (Benares), c., Uttar Pradesh, India; famous holy c. on Ganges, 640 km N.W. of Calcutta; place of annual pilgrimage; univ.; handicrafts, brasses, brocades, embroideries, now debased; p. (1971) 466,696 (c.), 467,487 (met. a.).

Varanger Fjord, inlet of Arctic Oc. into Finnmark, Norway; iron mng. on S. shore.

Vardar, R., flows through Yugoslav and Greek Macedonia into Aegean Sea nr. Salonika; inc. V. agr. region; hydroelectric power; routeway; 448 km long.

Varde, t., W. Jutland, Denmark; agr. and route ctr.; food processing; steelwks.; p. (1960) 9,577.

Vardö, t., Finnmark prov., N.E. Norway; sm. ice-free pt. on Vardoy I. with fish and oil interests; p. c. 3,500.

Vares, t., Bosnia, Yugoslavia; iron mng.; developing mnfs.

Varese, t., Lombardy, Italy; in Alpine foothills; resort and industl. ctr.; engin., furniture, paper, textiles, wines; p. (1969) 81,620.

Värmland, prov., Sweden; agr., iron mng. and processing, timber inds.; cap. Karlstad; a. 19,236 km²; p. (est. 1970) 284,930.

Varna, t., Bulgaria; spt. on Black Sea; industl. ctr. of heavy inds.; summer resorts on cst. nearby; p. (est. 1969) 212,642.

Varnsdorf, t., ČSSR; rly. junc. on German bdr.; impt. textile ctr.; p. (est. 1968) 13,912.

Västerås, c., cap. of Västmanland prov., Sweden; on L. Mälar; impt. elec. and metallurgical inds.; power sta.; impt. mediaeval c., cath., cas.; p. (est. 1969) 113,389.

Västerbotten, prov., Sweden; forested; timber inds.; cap. Umeå; a. 59,153 km²; p. (est. 1970) 233,971.

Västernorrland, prov., Sweden; forests and timber inds.; cap. Harnosand; a. 25.706 km²; p. (est. 1970) 274,104.

Västervik, t., Kalmar prov., Sweden; on Baltic cst.; engin., wire, nails, chemicals, paper; p. (est. 1970) 23,830.

Västmanland, prov., Sweden; N. of L. Mälar; mkt. gardening in S.; iron and silver mng. in N.; iron and steel inds.; cap. Västerås; a. 6,762 km²; p. (est. 1970) 260,869.

Vasto, t., Abruzzi e Molise, Italy; agr. ctr. on steep-sided vine-producing plateau; sm. Adriatic fishing pt.; p. (est. 1968) 24,474.

Vatican City, indep. sov. Papal st., Italy; forms an enclave in Rome; inc. Papal residence, St. Peter's cath.; a. 44 ha; p. (est. 1971) 648.

Vatna Jökull, mtn., Iceland; elevated snowfield; active volcano; alt. 2,120 m.

Vättern, L., Sweden; 40 km S.E. L. Vänern; a. 1,898 km².

Vaucluse, dep. S.E. France; in Provence; cap. Avignon; a. 3,577 km²; p. (1968) 353,966.

Vand, can., W. Switzerland; N. of L. Geneva; forests and vineyards; cap. Lausanne; a. 3,209 km²; p. (1969) 509,000.

Växjö, t., S. Sweden; engin., timber wks., hosiery; p. (1968) 32,886.

Vejle, spt., Jutland, Denmark; admin. ctr. V. prov.; industl.; p. (est. 1970) 31,763.

Velbert, t., N. Rhine–Westphalia, W. Germany; N.W. of Wuppertal; metal ind., locks and keys; p. (est. 1969) 27,307.

Vélez Málaga, t., Málaga prov., S. Spain; famous for wine, raisins, sugar, olive oil; Moorish cas.; p. (1970) 42,454.

Veliki Ustyug, t., RSFSR; R. pt. on Sukhona R.; shipyards, mftg.; p. (est. 1967) 35,000.

Velletri, t., central Italy; at foot of Alban hills overlooking Pontine marshes; noted for its wine; Garibaldi routed Neapolitans here 1849; (est. 1968) 37,469.

Vellore, t., Tamil Nadu, India; agr. mkt. t.; scene of Sepoy mutiny 1806; p. (1971) 139,082 (t.), 178,554 (met. a.).

Velsen, t., N. Holland prov., Neth; nr. entrance to N. Sea Canal, inc. IJmuiden iron and steel wks.; lge. paper mill; p. (1968) 67,864.

Veluwe, dist., Gelderland, Neth.; between Arnhem and IJselmeer; low hills of glacial sands and sand-dunes; heathland and pinewoods; relatively low p. density.

Venda Territory, Bantu homeland, Transvaal, S. Africa; p. (1970) 265,129.

Vendée, dep., W. France; on Bay of Biscay; fish. pts., beach resorts, agr. pasturage, vineyards; cap. La Roche-sur-Yon; a. 6,972 km²; p. (1968) 421,250.

Vendôme, t., Loir-et-Cher dep., France; on R. Loire; leather gds., cottons; mediaeval cas.; p. (1968) 16,728.

Venetia (Veneto), region, N.E. Italy; between the Alps and the Adriatic; embraces provs. Vicenza, Verona, Venice, Udine, Treviso, Padua, Belluno, and Rovigo; mtnous. in N., inc. Dolomite Alps; fertile plain of Po R. in S.; intensive arable agr.; ch. c. Venice; a. 18,384 km²; p. (1969) 4,088,285.

Venezia Giulia. *See* Friuli-Venezia Giulia.

Venezuela, fed. rep., N. cst. S. America; wealth derived from long-established but currently stagnant oil ind.; tropical climate, with temperate uplands, tropical forests and tall grass savannah lands (llanos); most economically advanced a. around cap. Carácas and oilfield a. of L. Maracaibo; counter pole of development based on hydroelectric power resources and iron ore in Caroní R. region; growing steel inds., lge. agr. areas economically neglected and socially deprived; coffee from highlands main comm. agr. crop and exp. a. 912,050 km²; p. (est. 1971) 10,778,071.

Venice (Venezia), c., cap. of V. prov. and ch. c. of Venetia, N.E. Italy; built on gr. of islets within lagoon in G. of V., at head of Adriatic; splendid architecture, rich in art treasures and historic associations; extensive canal network, inc. Grand Canal, intensive use leading to erosion of bldgs.; gradually sinking into Adriatic, lge.-scale projects to preserve c.; industl. zone on landward side in subs. of Porto Marghera and Mestre; craft and heavy inds.; p. (1969) 367,631.

Venlo, t., Neth.; on R. Maas; agr. mkt. and rly. junc.; chemicals, optical instruments, electric lamps; p. (1967) 60,773.

Ventimiglia, t., Liguria, N.W. Italy; on Mediterranean cst. nr. Fr. border; cath.; flower mkt.; tourism; p. (est. 1969) 25,564.

Ventnor, t., South Wight, I. of Wight, Eng.; on S. cst. 18 km S. of Ryde; mild climate, tourist and health resort; p. (1971) 6,910.

Veracruz, st., E. Mexico; narrow coastal plain rising to Sierra Madre Oriental; contains volcano Orizaba; recent agr. improvements; growth of petroleum inds.; cap. Jalapa; a. 71,836 km²; p. (1969) 3,629,000.

Veracruz, c., V. st., E. Mexico; spt. on G. of Mexico; comm. and industl. ctr. of oil region; nr. site where Cortés landed 1519; p. (1970) 214,072.

Vercelli, c., cap. of V. prov. N. Italy; in Piedmont, on Sesia R.; rice mkt. for lge. irrigated plain; textiles, machin., aircraft parts; p. (1969) 56,386.

Verde, Cape, most W. part of Africa; site of Dakar, cap. of Senegal.

Verdun, t., Quebec, Canada; sub. of Montreal; p. (1966) 76,832.

Verdun, t., Meuse dep., N.E. France; in Lorraine, on R. Meuse; strategic ctr. with varied mnfs.; 12th cent. cath.; scene of famous battle 1916; p. (1968) 24,716.

Vereeniging, c., Transvaal prov., S. Africa; on Vaal R.; coal, iron and steel, bricks; Treaty of Vereeniging 1902 ended Boer War; p. (1970) 169,553.

Verkhneudinsk. *See* Ulan-Ude.

Verkhoyansk, t., Yakutsk ASSR, RSFSR; in N.E. Siberia; coldest permanently inhabited place in world; mean Jan. temp. of −59°F.; ctr. of fur trapping a.; p. c. 2,000.

Vermont, st., New England, USA; adjoining Quebec prov., Canada; traversed by the Green mtns.; farming, dairying, stock-raising, lumbering, quarrying, machine tool and textile mftg.; cap. Montpelier; famous for autumn colours; a. 24,887 km²; p. (1970) 437,744.

Verona, c., cap. of V. prov., N.E. Italy; on R. Adige; commands route from central Europe to Brenner pass and from Venice to Milan; cath. and notable monuments; active agr. tr. and inds., printing; p. (1969) 258,559.

Versailles, c., cap. of Yvelines dep., N. France; S.W. sub. of Paris; famous royal palace; mkt. gardening, distilleries; Treaty of Versailles 1919; p. (1968) 94,915.

Verviers, t., **Belgium;** nr. Liége; ctr. of textile ind. in Ardennes; p. (1968) 35,335.

Vestmannaeyjar or **Westman Is.,** archipelago, S.W. Iceland; impt. cod fishing ind. based on Heimaey I.

Vesuvius, famous active volcano, S. Italy; on shore of Bay of Naples; alt. *c.* 1,186 m; its eruption in A.D. 79 destroyed Pompeii and Herculaneum, and frequent eruptions have since been recorded; observatory founded 1844; funicular rly. from base of mtn. to rim of crater since 1880.

Veszprem, c., **Hungary;** in fruit-growing dist., 96 km S. of Budapest; cath., univ. for chemical ind.; p. (1968) 32,000.

Vevey, t., Vaud can., **Switzerland;** on N. shore of L. Geneva; beautiful situation; chocolate, watches; resort; p. (1970) **17,957.**

Viareggio, beach resort, Tuscany, Italy; on Tyrrhenian Sea, nr. Pisa; monument to Shelley; p. (est. 1968) 54,549.

Viborg, t., Jutland, **Denmark;** admin. ctr. V. prov.; comm. and route ctr.; anc. cath.; textiles, machin., food processing; p. (est. 1970) 25,468.

Vicenza, c., cap. of V. prov., N.E. **Italy;** in Venetia; mkt. ctr. for surrounding fertile agr. plain; textiles, iron and steel; many examples of Palladian architecture; p. (1969) 112,734.

Vichy, t., Allier dep., **France;** on Allier R.; famous spa; hot mineral springs; lge. exp. of V. water; seat of Pétain govt. during German occupation 1940–3; p. (1968) 33,898.

Vicksburg, t., Miss., **USA;** R. pt., on bluffs of Mississippi at junc. of Yazoo canal; shipping and mftg. ctr. in cotton and timber region; prominent in American Civil War; Confederate surrender 1863; p. (1970) 25,478.

Victoria, st., **Australia;** traversed by Gt. Dividing Range; temperate climate, modified by alt.; smallest and most densely populated st. of mainland; major industl. a.; wool, grain, dairy prod., fruit; gold, coal, tin mng., natural gas off E. cst.; cap. Melbourne; a. 227,516 km²; p. (1972) 3,496,161.

Victoria, c., cap. of B.C., **Canada;** spt. on Vancouver I.; fishing and fish-processing; sawmills, chemicals, cement; beautiful scenery; tourist ctr.; p.(1971) 60,897 (c.), 193,512 (met.a.)

Victoria, main pt. and harbour between **Hong Kong** I. and Kowloon; built on reclaimed land; admin. ctr. of Hong Kong; p. (1971) 521,612.

Victoria, t., cap. of Labuan I., Sabah, **Malaysia;** fine harbour; p. 3,213.

Victoria, t., cap. of **Seychelles,** Ind. Oc.; harbour on lgst. and most impt. I. of Mahé.

Victoria, t., S. Texas, **USA;** comm. ctr. in prosperous agr. a.; local oilfields; p. (1970) 41,349.

Victoria Falls (**Mosi-oa-Toenja**), on R. Zambesi, **Zambia;** discovered by Livingstone 1855; falls are 1,674 m wide and broken by islands and rocks.

Victoria, Lake, lgst. L. of **Africa;** bordered by Kenya, Uganda, Tanzania; in catchment of Gt. Rift Valley, at alt. 999 m, a. c. 67,340 km²; discharges into Victoria Nile; impt. fisheries; discovered by Speke 1858.

Victoria Land, region, Antactica; discovered by Ross in 1841.

Victoria Nile, R., **Uganda;** E. Africa; name of R. Nile from its source at L. Victoria until it enters L. Mobuto Seso.

Viedma, t., cap. of Rio Negro terr. of Argentine Patagonia; p. (1960) 7,000.

Vienna (Wien), c., cap. of Austria; R. pt. on branch of Danube; surrounded by Wiener Wald (Vienna forest) and Carpathian foothills; major industl., comm. and transport ctr.; many fine bldgs., inc. univ., cath., Rathaus, parliament bldgs., magnificent Prater park; influential ctr. of music, cultural and scientific ctr.; home of Haydn, Mozart, Beethoven, Schubert, Mahler, Brahms, and Freud; p. (est. 1969) 1,644,976.

Vienne, dep., W. France; drained by R. Vienne; mainly agr. dist.; cap. Poitiers; a. 7,021 km²; p. (1968) 340,256.

Vienne, t., Isère, **France;** nr. Grenoble, on R. Rhône; textiles, metallurgical inds.; Roman remains; overshadowed by Lyons 27 km to N.; p. (1968) 30,276.

Vienne, R., **France;** trib. of the Loire; rises in Massif Central; 354 km long.

Vientiane, admin. cap., Laos; pt. and comm. ctr. on Mekong R.; p. (est. 1966) 132,253 (c.); (est. 1962) 162,297 (met. a.).

Viersen, t., N. Rhine–Westphalia, **W. Germany;** S.W. of Krefeld; textiles, machin., furniture, paper ind.; p. (est. 1969) 42,576.

Vierzon, t., Cher dep., **France;** on R. Cher; bricks, tiles, porcelain from local sands, clay; agr. machin.; p. (1968) 34,421.

Vietnam, Democratic Rep. of, S.E. Asia; comprises regions of Cochinchina and Tonkin in former French Indo-China; from 1954–1976 two separate countries, N. and S. Vietnam, based on two rivers, Song-koi and Mekong respectively, and separated by the high Annamite chain of mtns.; long period of civil war resulted in reunification; intensive agr. based on rice cultivation now largely collectivised; monsoon climate and river irrigation aid high yields; coffee, tea, rubber, sugar, main comm. crops but much devastation as result of war; minerals mainly concentrated in the N. with impt. anthracite deposit at Quang-Yen; industl. devel. also mainly in N. around Hanoi and ch. pt. Haiphong; hill tribes practising subsistence agr. inhabit the intervening Annamite mtns.; a. 335,724 km²; p. (est. 1969) 39,207,000.

Viet-Tri, t., N. Vietnam; 128 km N.W. of Hanoi; chemicals, paper mill, sugar refining.

Vigevano, t., Lombardy, **Italy;** on R. Ticino; impt. agr. and industl. ctr.; footwear, plastics, textiles; cath.; p. (est. 1968) 66,443.

Vigo, spt., **Spain;** transatlantic pt. on V. Bay; processing of imports; oil refining; p. (est. 1967) 186,461.

Vijayanagar, ruined c., S.E. India; once cap. c. of Hindu empire in S. Deccan; 96 km in circumference; destroyed by Moslem forces at battle of Talikota 1565.

Vijayavada, t., Andhra Pradesh, **India;** rly. junc., comm. ctr.; irrigation dam, Kistna R.; p. (1971) 317,258 (t.), 344,607 (met. a.).

Vila Real de Santo António, pt., Faro, **Portugal;** on W. bank of Guadiana R.; exp. copper ore, fish, fruit; p. c. 6,000.

Villach, t., Carinthia, S. **Austria;** at junc. of Gail and Drava Rs.; impt. route ctr.; tourism; p. (1961) 32,971.

Villahermosa, c., cap. of Tabasco, S.E. **Mexico;** agr. mkt., sugar processing; rich local petroleum deposits; p. (1969) 52,000.

Villa Maria, t., **Argentina;** rly. junc.; ctr. of grain, timber, dairying dist.; p. (1960) 50,000.

Villarrica, t., S.E. **Paraguay;** agr. tr. ctr. for cattle, tobacco, fruit; wines, yerba-maté grown in surrounding a.; p. (est. 1970) 38,052.

Villavicencio, t., E. **Colombia;** in foothills of Andes; comm. ctr. for the *llanos*; cattle tr.; p. (est. 1968) 80,675.

Villaviciosa, t., Oviedo prov., N.W. Spain; major fishing pt. on Bay of Biscay; p. (1970) 17,213.

Villeurbanne, t., Rhône dep., **France;** sub. of Lyons; metallurgy, chemicals, leather, textiles; p. (1968) 119,879.

Vilna (Lith. Vilnius, Pol. Wilno), c., cap. of Lithuanian SSR, **USSR;** on Vilija R. (trib. of Niemen); cultural ctr., cath., univ., historic bldgs.; held by Poland 1920–39; lt. inds., food processing; p. (1970) 372,000.

Vilyui, R., Yakut ASSR, **RSFSR;** flows E. from Siberian uplands into Lena R.; R. basin impt. agr. and mng. a.; fishing; 2,400 km long.

Vimy, t., Pas-de-Calais dep., N. **France;** nearby Vimy Ridge, site of Allied victory led by Canadians 1915; p. (1968) 3,272.

Viña del Mar, seaside t., central Chile, nr. Valparaiso; fashionable S. American resort; oil and sugar refining, textiles; p. (est. 1970) 153,085.

Vincennes, t., Val-de-Marne dep., **France;** sub. of Paris; famous cas. and Bois; industl. and residtl.; p. (1968) 49,297.

Vindhya Hills, mtn. range, central India; separating the Deccan from the Ganges basin; c. 640 km long.

Vinnitsa, t., Ukrainian SSR, **USSR;** on R. Bug, 192 km S.W. of Kiev; agr. mkt. t.; engin., chemicals, textiles; p. (1970) 211,000.

Virginia, st., **USA;** one of original 13 sts.; wide Atl. coastal plain rising inland to Blue Ridge; famous for high quality " Virginia Leaf " tobacco; industl. ts. of Norfolk, Richmond, Portsmouth and Newport News; cap. Richmond; a. 105,711 km²; p. (1970) 4,543,249.

Virgin Is. (Brit.), W.I.; gr. of Is. E. of Greater Antilles; most impt. Tortola, Virgin Gorda, Anegada; water scarcity, semi-subsistence agr. economy; livestock, fish, fruit, vegetables; a. 153 km²; p. (1970) 10,500.

Virgin Is. (USA), W.I.; external terr. of USA E. of Greater Antilles, 64 km E. of Puerto Rico; 3 main Is., St. Thomas, St. John, St. Croix; bought from Denmark 1917; favourite tourist a. in Caribbean; cap. Charlotte Amalie on St. Thomas; livestock, sugar; rum distilling; a. 344 km²; p. (est. 1969) 63,200.

Vis (Lissa), I., off Dalmatian cst., Adriatic, Yugoslavia; fish-canning ctr.; a. 91 km²; anc. remains; resort; sea battle 1866 between Italian and Austrian ironclads; p. 3,000.

Visby, old spt., **Sweden;** on Gotland I. in Baltic Sea; rich in historic interest; resort; p. (est. 1970) 19,319.

Vishakhapatnam, spt., Andhra Pradesh, **India;** deepwater harbour on Bay of Bengal; exp. manganese and oilseeds from Madhya Pradesh; shipbldg.; p. (1971) 352,504 (t.), 363,467 (met. a.).

Vistula, R., **Poland;** rises in Beskids range of Carpathians, flows through Poland past Krakow to Baltic Sea nr. Gdansk; forms major link in E. European waterway system; coal and timber transport; 1,056 km long.

Vitebsk, c., Belorussiyan SSR, **USSR;** R. pt. on W. Dvina and impt. rly. junc., in agr. region; textiles, machine tools, food processing; p. (1970) 231,000.

Viterbo, c., cap. of V. prov., **Italy;** N. of Rome; agr. ctr., food-processing; 12th cent. cath. and historic bldgs.; p. (1969) 53,110.

Vitim, R., E. Siberia, **RSFSR;** flows to R. Lena; navigable for 5 months of year; coal and grain tr.; 1,400 km long.

Vitória, spt., Espírito Santo, **Brazil;** exp. coffee, cocoa, fruit, iron ore; sugar refining, shoes, textiles, cement; p. (1970) 121,978.

Vitoria, c., cap. of Alava prov., **Spain;** in Basque cty.; stands on R. at 534 m; furniture mnf.; defeat of Fr. by Wellington 1813; p. (est. 1968) 126,098.

Vitry-le-François, t., Marne dep., N.E. **France;** on Marne R.; industl., textiles, earthenware; agr. mkt. for Champagne Pouilleuse; p. (1968) 16,879.

Vitry-sur-Seine, S.E. sub., Paris, **France;** flower growing on sand and gravel terraces of Seine R., acreage being reduced by competition from housing and inds.; p. (1968) 77,846.

Vittoria, t., Sicily, **Italy;** mkt. for wine; p. (est. 1968) 46,938.

Vittorio Veneto, t., **Italy;** N. of Venice; resort; textiles; p. (est. 1968) 29,697.

Vizcaya, Basque prov., N. **Spain;** on Bay of Biscay; iron mng.; iron and steel inds.; dense p.; cap. Bilbao; a. 2,165 km²; p. (1960) 1,043,310.

Vlaardingen, t., S. Holland prov., **Neth.;** 8 km W. of Rotterdam, on Nieuwe Maas; leading fish. pt.; p. (1968) 78,654.

Vladimir, c., cap. of V. oblast, **RSFSR;** between Gorki and Moscow, on trib. of Oka R.; founded 12th cent.; caths., historic bldgs.; machine tools, agr. machin., textiles; p. (1970) 234,000.

Vladimir-Volynski, c., N.W. Ukrainian SSR, **USSR;** one of oldest Ukrainian settlements, founded 9th cent.; agr. mkt. ctr.; p. (est. 1967) 23,000.

Vladivostok, c., spt., **RSFSR;** ch. pt. and naval base on Pac.; terminus of Trans-Siberian rly. and airline from Moscow; ch. cultural ctr. of Far East; shipyards, fisheries, oil refining, engin., chemicals; economic development in hinterland hindered by distance from major ctrs. of p. and ind.; p. (1970) 442,000.

Vlieland, Friesian I., at entrance to IJsselmeer, **Neth.;** resort, nature reserve.

Vlissingen or **Flushing,** spt., Zeeland prov., S.W. **Neth.;** on Walcheren I.; shipyards, oil refining, fishing; resort; birthplace of Admiral de Ruyter; p. (1967) 38,564.

Vlonë, spt., S.W. Albania; on Strait of Otranto, Adriatic Sea; salt; oil pipeline connects from Kucovë nr. Berat; p. (1967) 50,000.

Vltava or **Moldau,** R., Bohemia, **ČSSR;** rises in Sumava mtns. (Bohemian Forest) and flows

to R. Elbe below Prague; used for hydroelectric power; c. 416 km long.

Voghera, t., Lombardy, **Italy;** rly. junc. and agr. mkt.; textiles, machin. engin.; cas., cath.; p. (est. 1968) 39,841.

Voi, t., **Kenya,** E. Africa; 144 km N.W. of Mombasa on rly. to Nairobi; branch connection with Tanzania rly. system allows agr. prod. from Arusha and Moshi dists. to pass through Mombasa as alternative to Tanga.

Voiron, t., Isère dep., **France;** on Morge R., 24 km N.W. of Grenoble; textiles, paper; p. (1968) 19,038.

Vojvodina, aut. prov., N. Serbia, **Yugoslavia;** impt. and fertile agr. dist. crossed by Danube R.; intensive agr., prosperous and dense p.; fruit, vegetables, livestock, food processing; ch. c. Novi Sad; a. 22,489 km²; p. (1971) 1,950,268.

Volcano Is., Japan; 3 volcanic Is. in Pac. Oc., S. of Japan, admin. by USA until 1968, now Japanese.

Volga, R., **USSR;** rises in Valdai hills, flows in serpentine course to Caspian at Astrakhan in wide delta; ch. tribs., Oka, Sura, Vetluga, Kama, Samara; major waterway linked to Baltic Sea, Azov, and Black Seas, and to Moscow; hydroelectric developments reducing sturgeon in Caspian Sea and caviar prod. declining; longest R. in Europe, 3,720 km.

Volga Baltic Waterway (Mariinsk Waterway), **RSFSR;** inland deepwater navigation network linking Black Sea and Caspian Sea in S. with Baltic Sea and White Sea in N.

Volgograd (Stalingrad), c., **RSFSR;** R. pt. on Volga and major rly. ctr.; exp. raw materials, fish; industl. ctr. for steel, engin., chemicals, oil refining; hydroelectric power sta.; fierce siege and successful defence 1942 turning point of second world war; p. (1970) 818,000.

Volhynia, historic region, Ukrainian SSR, **USSR;** on Polish frontier; rich agr. lowland; coal mng. at Novovodinsk; cap. Lutsk.

Volkhov, R., **RSFSR;** flows from L. Ilmen to L. Ladoga; navigable; hydroelectric power sta. and aluminium smelting plant at Volkhov (Leningrad oblast); 208 km long.

Völklingen, t., Saarland, **W. Germany;** on Saar R., 13 km W. of Saarbrücken; coal mng., iron and steel; p. (est. 1969) 40,128.

Vologda, c., **RSFSR;** R. and rly. junc. on upper Sukhona R.; in dairying a.; engin., textiles, sawmilling, paper, dairy inds.; cath., historic bldgs.; p. (1970) 178,000.

Volos, spt., **Greece;** at head of G. of V.; impt. transport, industl., comm. ctr.; exp. agr. prods.; car mnfs.; p. (1971) 51,340.

Volsk, c., **RSFSR;** R. pt. on Volga R.; cement, tanneries, metallurgy, food processing; p. (est. 1969) 71,000.

Volta (White Volta), major R., **W. Africa;** drains extensive terr. in Niger bend, flows S. through Ghana to delta on Guinea cst., 112 km E. of Accra; main means of communication but rapids make through navigation impossible; Volta R. project for industrialisation of Ghana; dam and power plant at Akosombo, aluminium smelter at Tema; 1,520 km long. *See also* **Black Volta.**

Volta Redonda, t., Rio de Janeiro, **Brazil;** state-owned steel plant; p. (1970) 120,645.

Volterra, hill t., Tuscany, **Italy;** Etruscan and mediaeval walls; alabaster, salt; p. (est. 1968) 16,558.

Volzhsky, t., **RSFSR;** new industl. t. on Volga R.; aluminium smelting, chemicals; p. (1970) 142,000.

Voorburg, t., **Neth.;** industl. ctr. E. of the Hague; p. (1968) 46,703.

Vorarlberg, prov., Austria; forestry, dairying, tourism; inds. based on hydroelectric power; textiles; cap. Bregenz; a. 2,600 km²; p. (1971) 274,000.

Vorkuta, ctr. of Pechora coal basin, **RSFSR;** beyond Arctic circle, which supplies entire European N. RSFSR; p. (est. 1967) 65,000.

Voronezh, c., **RSFSR;** R. pt. on Voronezh R. nr. junc. with Don; impt. comm. ctr. in fertile agr. dist.; machin., rubber, oil refining, food processing; nuclear power sta.; univ., cath.; p. (1970) 660,000.

Voroshilovgrad. *See* **Lugansk.**

Voroshilovsk. *See* **Kommunarsk.**

Vosges, dep., E. France; on Franco–German frontier; dairying, vineyards, stone quarrying, textiles; cap. Epinal; a. 5,970 km²; p. (1968) 388,201.

Vosges, highlands, E. France; structurally similar to Black Forest, from which they are separated by Rhine rift valley; forested slopes, vineyards; source of Meurthe, Moselle, Sarve, Ill, and Saône Rs.; highest summit Ballon de Guebwiller, 1,425 m.

Voskresensk, t., **RSFSR**; S.E. Moscow; lignite, chemicals, fertilisers; p. (est. 1969) 61,000.

Votkinsk, t., **RSFSR**; 61 km N.E. of Izhevsk; lge. engin. plant; hydroelectric power sta.; birthplace of Tchaikovsky; p. (est. 1969) 73,000.

Vranja, t., **Yugoslavia**; flax and hemp culture and mnf.; developing industl. ctr. based on handicrafts; p. (est. 1965) 19,000.

Vratsa, t., **Bulgaria**; on R. Vratcanska; jewellery, wine, silk, tanning; p. (est. 1968) 45,232.

Vrsac, t., **Yugoslavia**; milling, wine, brandy; p. (1961) 31,620.

Vulcano, I., Lipari gr., **Italy**; off N.E. cst. Sicily; active volcano; gave its name as generic title for this type of mtn.

Vyatka, R., **RSFSR**; rises in foothills of Urals, flows past Kirov into Kama R.; timber transport, fishing; c. 1,360 km long.

Vyborg (Viipuri), c., **RSFSR**; spt. on G. of Finland, occupies strategic site on Karelian Isthmus, N.W. of Leningrad; Finnish until 1945; exp. timber; shipyards, engin., food processing; p. (est. 1969) 65,000.

Vychegda, R., **RSFSR**; rises in Urals, flows W. to N. Dvina R.; timber transport; 1,120 km long.

Vyrnwy, L., reservoir, Powys, **Wales**; with dam 360 m long supplies water for Liverpool; a. 454 ha.

Vyshni-Volochek, t., **RSFSR**; 118 km N.W. of Kalinin; flour milling, textiles, glass inds. p. (est. 1969) 73,000.

W

Waal, R., **Neth.**; S. arm of R. Rhine.

Waco, c., Texas, **USA**; in Brazos valley; route ctr., airport; regional cultural ctr.; univ.; textiles, leather; p. (1970) 92,600 (c.), 142,772 (met. a.).

Waddenzee, stretch of shallow water between W. Frisian Is. and **Neth.** mainland.

Wadebridge, spt., Cornwall **Eng.**; at head of Camel estuary, 10 km N.W. of Bodmin; agr. mkt.; p. (1971) 17,799 (dist.).

Wadi Halfa, t., Sudan; on R. Nile at second cataract; rly. terminus of Sudan rlys.; inundated by Aswan L.; new t. Khashm el Girba for inhabitants.

Wad Medani, t., cap. of Blue Nile prov., Sudan; ctr. of cotton growing dist.; p. (est. 1969) 71,030.

Wagadugu. See Ouagadougou.

Wagga Wagga, t., N.S.W., **Australia**; on R. Murrumbidgee; ctr. of agr. and pastoral dist.; p. (1972) 27,636.

Wahiawa, t., Oahu I., Hawaii; pineapples; p. (1970) 37,329.

Waikaremoana, L., N.I., N.Z.; hydroelectric power.

Waikato, R., N.I., N.Z.; rises in L. Taupo and flows N.W. into Tasman Sea; coalfields, hydroelec. power stas.; 422 km long.

Wainuiomata, co. t., on Wainuiomata R., N.I., N.Z.; p. (1971) 16,670.

Wairakei, t., N.I., N.Z.; on L. Taupo; health resort; geothermal power sta.

Waitaki, t., Otago, S.I., N.Z.; Benmore hydroelectric power plant; p. (1971) 9,420.

Wakamatsu. See Kitakyushu.

Wakatipu, L. Otago, S.I., N.Z.; 83 km long, 5 km wide, 360 m deep, 320 m a.s.l.

Wakayama, spt., Honshu, Japan; textiles; new iron and steel plant; p. (est. 1971) 372,000.

Wakefield, c., met. dist., West Yorks., **Eng.**; on R. Calder; 13 km S. of Leeds; cath.; ctr. of coal-mng. a.; woollen and worsted gds., chemicals, engin.; p. (est. 1976) 306,500 (dist.).

Wakefield, t., Va., **USA**; on Potomac R., nr. Fredericksburg; birthplace of George Washington.

Wake I., coral atoll, Pac. Oc.; between Marianas and Hawaii; comm. and naval base on route to Far East, belonging to USA.

Walachia, region, S. **Romania**; wide plain bounded by Transylvanian Alps and separated from Yugoslavia by Danube; rich agr. a., "the bread-basket of Romania"; Ploiesti oilfields; inds. nr. ch. c. Bucharest; a. 76,563 km²; p. c. 7,500,000.

Walbrzych (Waldenburg), c., S.W. Poland (since 1945); formerly in Lower Silesia; industl. and mng. ctr. at 427 m; porcelain, machin., engin.; p. (1970) 125,000.

Walchensee, Lake, Bavaria, W. **Germany**; a. 16 km²; hydroelectric power sta.

Walcheren, I., Zeeland prov., S.W. Neth.; in N. Sea at entrance to Scheldt estuary; mainly agr.; ch. ts., Vlissingen, Middelburg; flooded 1944 to stop German advance; tourism.

Waldenburg. See Walbrzych.

Wales, principality, Great Britain; mostly mtnous.; Cambrian mtns. rise to 1,085 m at Snowdon; contrast between N. and Central Wales (pastoral farming, forestry, water supply, tourism, rural depopulation) and S. Wales (coalfield, metal-based inds., lge. ts.); cap. Cardiff; a. 20,761 km²; p. (est. 1976) 2,766,800 (26 per cent Welsh speaking).

Wallasey, t., Wirral, adjoining Birkenhead, Merseyside, **Eng.**; residtl., seaside resort (New Brighton); p. (1971) 97,061.

Wallensee, L., Switzerland; 18 km long.

Wallingford, t., South Oxon., **Eng.**; on R. Thames, to N. of its gap between Chilterns and Lambourn Downs; p. (1971) 6,184.

Wallis and Futuna Is., gr. of coral Is., S. Pac. Oc.; overseas terr. of France; copra; a. 275 km²; p. (est. 1969) 8,546 (mostly Polynesians).

Wallsend, t., Tyne and Wear, **Eng.**; on N. bank of Tyne, 6 km below Newcastle; Tyne tunnel links with Jarrow; shipbldg., engin., iron, plywood; at end of Hadrian's Wall; p. (1971) 45,793.

Walmer, t., Kent, **Eng.**; 3 km S. of Deal; holiday resort; cas., residence of Warden of Cinque Ports.

Walney, I., off cost. of Cumbria, **Eng.**; opposite Barrow.

Walsall, t., met. dist., West Midlands, **Eng.**; 8 km E. of Wolverhampton; leather and iron gds., engin., steel tubes; p. (est. 1976) 268,600 (dist.).

Walsingham, v., North Norfolk, **Eng.**; many old bldgs., priory ruins, abbey; mediaeval pilgrimage ctr.; p. (1971) 17,416 (dist.).

Walsum, t., N. Rhine–Westphalia, W. Germany; at confluence of Rhine and Emscher canal; R. pt. for Oberhausen steelwks.; p. (est. 1969) 48,262.

Waltham, c., Mass., **USA**; nr. Boston; science-based inds.; univ.; p. (1970) 61 582.

Waltham Abbey (Waltham Holy Cross), t., Epping Forest, Essex, **Eng.**; 21 km N.E. London, on edge of Epping Forest; glasshouses (tomatoes); Norman nave of abbey part of parish church; p. (1971) 14,585.

Waltham Forest, outer bor., E. London, **Eng.**; incorporating former bors. of Chingford, Leyton, Walthamstow; industl. and residtl.; p. (est. 1976) 223,700.

Walthamstow. See Waltham Forest.

Walton and Weybridge, ts., Elmbridge, Surrey, **Eng.**; on R. Thames, 27 km S.W. of London; engin., aircraft; p. (1971) 51,004.

Walton-le-Dale, t., South Ribble, N.E. Lancs., **Eng.**; on R. Ribble, 3 km E. of Preston; mkt. gardening, cottons, timber; p. (1971) 26,841.

Walvis Bay, spt., South-West Africa; on Walvis Bay, Atl. Oc.; fishing, fish processing; p. (est. 1965) 17,877.

Wandsworth, inner bor., S.W. London, **Eng.**; inc. Battersea; on R. Wandle at influx into Thames; oil mills, metal wks., paper, brewing; p. (est. 1976) 284,600.

Wanganui, t., N.I., N.Z.; pt. on R. Wanganui; tr. ctr. for wool, grain, meat, dairy prod.; agr. processing, steel-pipes, fertilisers; iron ore deposits; p. (1971) 35,794.

Wanganui, R., N.I., N.Z.; famous for its beauty; 256 km long.

Wangaratta, t., Victoria, **Australia**; 232 km from Melbourne; agr. dist.; nylon and woollen wks.; p. (1972) 15,535.

Wankie, t., Rhodesia; site of coal-mng. ind.; 344 km N.W. of Bulawayo; p. (est. 1970) 21,000.

Wanne-Eickel, t., N. Rhine–Westphalia, W. Germany; pt. on Rhine–Herne canal; coalmng. ctr. of Ruhr; p. (est. 1969) 100,300.

Wansbeck, R., Northumberland, Eng.; flows E. from Pennines into N. Sea 5 km N. of Blyth; 37 km long.

Wansbeck, l. gov. dist., Northumberland, Eng.; inc. Newbiggin, Ashington and Bedlington; p. (est. 1976) 62,300.

Wansdyke, l. gov. dist., S. Avon, Eng.; inland a. inc. Keynsham, Bathavon and Clutton; p. (est. 1976) 74,500.

Wantage, mkt. t., Oxon., Eng.; in Vale of the White Horse; birthplace of King Alfred; p. (1971) 8,007.

Wapping, Thames-side dist., London, Eng.

Warangal, t., Andhra Pradesh, India; textiles, carpets; p. (1971) 207,520.

Ware, mkt. t., East Herts., Eng.; on R. Lea; 3 km N.E. of Hertford; p. (1971) 14,666.

Wareham, mkt. t., Purbeck, Dorset, Eng.; on R. Frome, on N. of I. of Purbeck, 13 km S.W. of Poole; agr. machin., pipes; p. (1971) 4,379.

Warley, t., Sandwell, West Midlands, Eng.; inc. Smethwick, Oldbury and Rowley Regis; varied inds.; p. of dist. (1971) 163,388.

Warminster, t., West Wilts., Eng.; on Wylye watershed at edge of Salisbury Plain; agr. mkt., gloves; p. (1971) 13,593.

Warnemünde, spt., E. Germany; ferry pt. for rail traffic between Berlin and Copenhagen; shipbldg.; outport for Rostock; resort.

Warrego, R., Queensland, N.S.W., Australia; trib. of R. Darling; 640 km long.

Warren, t., Ohio, USA; on Mahoning R.; iron and steel mftg.; p. (1970) 63,494.

Warrenpoint, spt., Newry and Mourne N. Ireland; at head of Carlingford Lough; p. (1966) 3,579.

Warrington, t., l. gov. dist., Cheshire, Eng.; on R. Mersey and Manchester Ship Canal; metal inds. (wire-drawing), chemicals, brewing, paper; to be expanded as new c. (to take people from Manchester) with p. (1991) 205,000; p. (est. 1976) 166,200 (dist.).

Warrnambool, t., spt., Victoria, Australia; mkt., timber, plastics, engin.; p. (1972) 18,663.

Warsaw (Warszawa), c., cap. of Poland; on R. Vistula; devastated in second world war; facsimile rebuilding based on Canaletto's paintings; cath., univ.; rly. ctr.; iron, steel, engin., textiles, chemicals; p. (1970) 1,308,000.

Warsop, t., Notts., Eng.; 6 km N.E. of Mansfield; limestone, gravel; p. (1971) 13,036.

Warta, R., Poland; trib. of R. Oder; connected to R. Vistula by canal; 720 km long.

Warwick, t., Queensland Australia; sawmilling, agr. processing; p. (1966) 10,087.

Warwick, co. t., l. gov. dist., Warwicks., Eng.; on R. Avon, 13 km S.W. of Coventry; cas.; agr. implements, brewing, malting; p. (est. 1976) 113,100 (dist.).

Warwick, c., R.I., USA; on Narrangansett Bay; textile ctr.; p. (1970) 83,694.

Warwickshire, non-met. co., W. Midlands, Eng.; undulating, drained by tribs. of Rs. Severn and Trent, crossed by Cotswolds to S.; sm. coalfield to N.; much of industl. N. now inc. in West Midlands met. co.; a. 1,981 km²; p. (est. 1976) 471,000.

Warwickshire, North, l. gov. dist., Warwicks., Eng.; close to Midlands conurb., based on Atherstone; p. (est. 1976) 59,200.

Wassatch Mtns., range of Rocky mtns., Utah and Idaho, USA; alt. 3,600 m.

Wash, The, bay, N. Sea between Lincs. and Norfolk, Eng.; 35 km long, 24 km wide; partly reclaimed to form the Fens; proposed barrage to aid further reclamation and water storage.

Washington, t., Tyne and Wear, Eng.; 8 km S.E. of Gateshead; coal, iron and steel, stone quarrying, chemicals; new t. 1964; p. (est. 1974) 39,000.

Washington, c., cap. of USA; in Dist. of Columbia on Potomac R.; c. planned as national seat of Government; White House, Capitol, 5 univs.; over half p. Negro; p. (1970) 764,169 (c.), 2,835,737 (met. a.).

Washington, st., USA; in extreme N.W., stretching from Pac. Oc. into Rocky mtns.; over half a. forested; Colombia R. and tribs. provide hydroelectric power; timber, fishing, tourism; cap. Olympia; a. 176,617 km²; p. (1970) 3,352,892.

Wast Water, L. Dist., deepest L. in Eng.; 5 km long, 79 m deep.

Watchet, t., West Somerset, Eng.; sm. pt. on cst. of Bristol Channel; paper mkg., fishing; p. (1971) 2,892.

Watenstedt-Salzgitter. *See* Salzgitter.

Waterbury, c., Conn., USA; on Naugatuck R.; ctr. of brass ind. and metal gds.; p. (1970) 106,431 (c.), 206,625 (met. a.).

Waterford, co., Munster, R.o.I.; mtnous. co. in S.E.; mainly agr., dairying, pigs; fishing; co. t. Waterford; a. 1,867 km²; p. (1966) 72,986.

Waterford, co. t., spt., Waterford, R.o.I.; on R. Suir; cath.; brewing, fishing, glass mnfs.; p. (1966) 29,642.

Waterloo, t., Brabant prov., Belgium, nr. Brussels; battle nearby 1815; p. (est. 1969) 16,924.

Waterloo, t., Ont., Canada; industl. sub. of Kitchener; p. (1971) 37,245.

Waterloo, c., Iowa, USA; on Cedar R.; agr. prod. and tools; p. (1970) 75,994 (c.), 132,533 (met. a.).

Waters of Merom (L. Hula), Upper Galilee Israel; extensive drainage completed 1957; a. 14 km².

Waterton Glacier International Peace Park, Albert and Mont., Canada and USA; glacial and lake scenery; a. 596 km².

Watertown, t., Mass., USA; on Charles R.; textiles, clothing; p. (1970) 39,309.

Watertown, t., N.Y., USA; on Black R.; engin., paper; p. (1960) 33,306.

Watford, t., l. gov. dist., Herts., Eng.; on R. Colne, 26 km N.W. of London; mkt.; varied inds., inc. lt. and elec. engin., paper, printing; p. (est. 1976) 77,000.

Wattenscheid, t., N. Rhine–Westphalia, W. Germany; E. of Essen; coal, metals, footwear; p. (est. 1969) 80,527.

Waukegan, c., Ill., USA; on L. Michigan; summer resort; steel, brass, motors, sugar refining; p. (est. 1969) 65,000.

Wauwatosa, t., Wis., USA; sub. of Milwaukee; metals, concrete, chemicals; p. (est. 1969) 58,000.

Waveney, R., Norfolk and Suffolk, Eng.; 80 km long.

Waveney, l. gov. dist., Suffolk, Eng.; based on Lowestoft, Beccles and Bungay; p. (est. 1976) 96,200.

Waverley, l. gov. dist., Surrey, Eng.; inc. Farnham, Godalming and Haslemere; p. (est. 1976) 108,900

Wayatinah, hydroelectric commission v., Tasmania, Australia; dam, lagoon and power sta. at confluence of Rs. Nive and Derwent.

Wazirabad (Balkh), t., Afghanistan; anc. Bactra, cap of Bactria, called the "mother of cities", destroyed by Genghiz Khan 1221; textile plant projected; p. c. 13,000.

Weald, The, wooded and pastoral tracts S.E. Eng.; extending from Folkestone, Kent, through Surrey, Hants., and Sussex to the sea at Beachy Head; former a. of iron working; name derived from German *Wald* = forest.

Wealden, l. gov. dist., East Sussex, Eng.; stretches from Uckfield to S. cst.; p. (est. 1976) 113,500.

Wear, R., Durham/Tyne and Wear, Eng.; rises in Pennines, flows through Durham to N. Sea at Sunderland; 96 km long.

Wear Valley, l. gov. dist., Durham, Eng.; Pennine a. inc. Bishop Auckland, Crook and Willington; p. (est. 1976) 63,500.

Weaver, R., Cheshire, Eng.; industl. trib. of R. Mersey; 72 km long.

Weddell Sea, arm of S. Atl. Oc., Antarctica; whaling and sealing.

Wednesfield, t., West Midlands, Eng.; metal tubes, materials handling engin.; expanded t.

Wei, R., Shensi prov., W. China; rises in highlands of Kansu, flows E. between highlands of Shansi and Tsinling Shan to join Yellow R. nr. Tungkwan; valley contains very fertile loess soils; formed cradle of Chinese civilisation; c. 800 km long.

Weifang, c., Shantung prov., China; coal-mng.ctr.; tobacco processing; p. (est. 1970) 260,000.

Weihai, spt., Shantung prov., China; naval base; fishing; vegetable-oil processing, textiles; p. 222,000.

Weimar, t., Erfurt, E. Germany; on R. Ilm; ctr. of music and culture in 19th cent., associated with Goethe, Schiller, Nietzsche, Liszt, Herder;

scene of establishment of German rep. 1919; elec. and metal inds., textiles, musical instruments, glass; p. (est. 1970) 63,689.

Weipa, Queensland, Australia; new t., pt., and alumina plant; bauxite nearby at Aurukin.

Weisshorn, mtn. peak, **Switzerland**; alt. 4,505 m.

Wejherowo, t., Gdansk, Poland; on R. Reda; mediaeval stronghold; palace; p. (1970) 33,700.

Welkom, t., O.F.S., S. Africa; ctr. of O.F.S. goldfields; p. (1970) 131,767 (met. a.).

Welland, t., Ont., Canada; on Welland Canal; industl. t.; p. (1971) 44,222.

Welland, R., Northants. and Lincs., Eng.; rises in Northampton heights and flows N.E. into the Wash; 112 km long.

Welland Ship Canal, Ont., **Canada**; connects Ls. Erie and Ont.; 43 km long; 2-lane waterway.

Wellingborough, t., l. gov. dist., Northants., Eng.; on R. Nene, 14 km N.E. of Northampton; mkt.; footwear; expanded t.; p. (est. 1976) 62,200 dist.).

Wellington, mkt. t., The Wrekin, Salop., Eng.; brewing, sugar refining, timber, toys; name derived from " Watling Town " (stood on Watling Street); with Dawley and Oakengates forms new t. of Telford; p. (1971) 17,154.

Wellington, mkt. t., Somerset, Eng.; 10 km S.W. Taunton, anc. woollen ind. still survives; dairy prod.; p. (1971) 9,434.

Wellington, c., spt., N.I., cap. of N.Z.; univ.; impt. exp. ctr. for dairy prod., wool, meat; new inds. developing in Hutt valley with vehicle assembly, rubber, oil refineries; p. (1971) 135,515 (c.); (est. 1970) 179,300 (met. a.).

Wellington, prov., N.I., **N.Z.**; mtnous., pastoral and dairy farming; a. 28,153 km²; p. (1971) 552,640.

Wells, cath. t., Mendip, Somerset, Eng.; on S. flank of Mendip hills; cath., bishop's palace; paper mftg.; tourism; p. (1971) 8,586.

Wells-next-the-Sea, t., North Norfolk, Eng.; anc. pt. on N. cst. of E. Anglia, W. of Sheringham; whelks, cockles and mussels; p. (1971) 2,342.

Wels, t., Upper Austria; on Traun R.; mkt. for agr. a.; cas.; p. (1961) 41,060.

Welshpool, mkt. t., Powys, Wales; on R. Severn; nearby is Powys cas.; p. (1971) 6,705.

Welwyn Garden City, t., Welwyn-Hatfield, Herts., Eng.; 34 km N. of London; founded by Sir Ebenezer Howard (1920) as first satellite t. of London; new t. 1948; pharmaceuticals, plastics, radio, and electronics, lt. inds.; p. (est. 1974) 40,000.

Welwyn-Hatfield, l. gov. dist., Herts., Eng.; comprises Welwyn Garden City and Hatfield; p. (est. 1976) 91,300.

Wembley, former M.B., Middx., Eng.; now inc. in Brent outer bor. Greater London; lt. inds., sports ctr.; British Empire Exhibition 1924–5.

Wenchow (Wenzhou), c., spt., Chekiang prov., China; pt. on estuary of Wu R., E. China Sea; textiles, fishing, coastal tr.; exp. wood, tea, agr. prod.; p. (est. 1970) 250,000.

Wenlock Edge, narrow ridge, Salop, Eng.; extends 29 km S.W. from Much Wenlock to Craven Arms; limestone; moorland, mainly above 290 m.

Wensleydale, North Yorks., Eng.; valley in N. Pennines drained E. by R. Ure; cattle reared for fattening on lowland farms; some dairying (cheese); length 56 km.

Wernigerode, t., Magdeburg, E. Germany; on N. slopes of Harz mtns.; mediaeval cas.; tourism; p. (est. 1970) 32,662.

Wesel, t., N. Rhine–Westphalia, W. Germany; R. pt. at confluence of Rs. Lippe and Rhine, Ruhr conurb.; p. (est. 1969) 33,952.

Weser, R., W. Germany; formed by confluence of Fulda and Werra Rs. at Münden; flows N. to N. Sea at Bremerhaven; linked by Mittelland canal to Rhine, Ems, and Elbe; navigable for entire length of 330 m.

Wesermünde. See Bremerhaven.

Wessex, anc. kingdom, S. Eng.; inc. Berks., Hants., Wilts., Dorset, Somerset and Devon.

West Allis, t., Wis., USA; mng. machin., castings; heavy vehicles; p. (1970) 71,649.

West Bengal, st., N.E. India; W., mainly Hindu section of former presidency of B. (Muslim E.B. now Bangladesh); on Ganges delta and flood plain; humid sub-tropical climate; very dense p.; rice, jute; ch. c. Calcutta; a. 87,617 km²; p. (1971) 44,440,095.

West Bridgford, t., Rushcliffe, Notts., Eng.; at junc. of Grantham canal with R. Trent; residtl. sub. of Nottingham; p. (1971) 28,496.

West Bromwich, t., Sandwell, West Midlands, Eng.; on R. Thame, 8 km N.W. of Birmingham; heavy engin. and allied inds., chemicals, springs, oil refining; p. (1971) 166,626.

West Derbyshire, l. gov. dist., Derbys., Eng.; Pennine a. inc. Matlock, Bakewell and Ashbourne; p. (est. 1976) 66,200.

West Devon, l. gov. dist., Devon, Eng.; rural W. of Dartmoor and ts. of Tavistock and Okehampton; p. (est. 1976) 39,900.

West Dorset, l. gov. dist., Dorset, Eng.; inc. Lyme Regis, Bridport, Sherborne and Dorchester; p. (est. 1976) 78,800.

Western Australia, st. of the Australian Commonwealth; lgst. st., nearly a third of continent with only 8 per cent of p. concentrated in S.W. around st. cap. of Perth in fertile Mediterranean-like a.; diversity of relief, Hammersley range in N.W., Kimberley range in N.E., Gibson desert in interior; rich but irregularly distributed mineral deposits; intensive agr. in S.W., wheat and sheep in interior; a. 2,527,633 km²; p. (1972) 1,027,372.

Western Desert, Egypt; part of Libyan Desert; inc. Qattara depression; coastal road from Cairo to Tripoli; scene of fighting second world war.

Western Pacific High Commission Territories, inc. Solomon Is. and Gilbert and Tuvalu Is.

West Port Bay, Vic., Australia; major heavy industl. a. close to Melbourne, rapidly growing.

Western Sahara (Spanish Sahara), N.W. African cst.; comprising Rio de Oro and Sagui el Hamra; desert; rich phosphate mines at Bou Craa connected to El Aaiun pt. by rly.; upon decolonisation terr. split between Morocco and Mauritania (1976) but declared Saharan Arab Democratic Rep. by Algerians; a. 265,993 km²; p. largely nomadic (1967) 48,607.

Western Samoa, indep. sov. st., S. Pac. Oc.; member of Commonwealth (1970); gained independence from N.Z. 1962; consists of 2 lge Is. (Savai'i, Upolu) and 7 sm. Is.; 70 per cent p. in agr.; c. 30 per cent a. devoted to bananas; exp. bananas, copra, cacao beans; ch. spt. Apia on Upolu I.; a. 2,841 km²; p. (1966) 131,379.

Westerwald, plateau of old volcanic rocks, W. Germany; ending in steep slope E. of R. Rhine; fertile soil; pastureland or deciduous woodland; sm. quantities of iron ore in Siegerland.

West Glamorgan, co., S. Wales; borders Bristol Channel; inc. Gower Penin. and lge. industl. ts. of Swansea, Neath and Port Talbot; impt. metal refining and engin. inds.; a. 816 km²; p. (est. 1976) 371,900.

West Ham, former C.B., Essex, Eng.; sub. to E. of London; bordered by Rs. Thames and Lea; now inc. in Newham bor., Greater London.

West Hartford, t., Conn., USA; residtl. sub. of Hartford; metal gds., ctr. for dairying, tobacco-growing dist.; p. (1970) 68,031.

West Indies or **Antilles**, l. grs., Atl. Oc.; extend between csts. of Fla. and Venezuela, separating Caribbean Sea and G. of Mexico from Atl.; inc. Cuba, Haiti, Dominican Rep., Bahamas, Barbados, Jamaica, Leeward Is., Trinidad and Tobago, Windward Is., Guadeloupe, Martinique, Curaçao, Puerto Rico, Virgin Is.; mostly volcanic and coral Is.; former colonial terrs. developed for plantation agr. worked by W. African slaves; most of indigenous Indians killed.

West Irian. See Irian Jaya.

West Lancashire, l. gov. dist., Lancs., Eng.; N. of Merseyside, inc. Skelmersdale and Ormskirk; p. (est. 1976) 105,800.

West Lindsey, l. gov. dist., Lincs., Eng.; lge. a. N. of Lincoln and inc. Market Rasen and Gainsborough; p. (est. 1976) 74,900.

West Lothian, l. gov. dist., former co., Lothian Reg., Scot.; industl. dist. in Central Lowlands close to Edinburgh; a. 417 km²; p. (1971) 112,510.

Westmeath, co., Leinster, R.o.I.; low-lying, drained by R. Shannon, many Ls.; dairying; co. to Mullingar; ch. t. Athlone; a. 1,834 km²; p. (1966) 52,849.

West Mersea, t., Essex, Eng.; on Mersea I.; p. (1971) 4,131.

West Midlands, met. co., Eng.; mainly industl. a. centred around Birmingham and the S. Staffs. coalfield (Black Country) and Coventry and the Warwicks. coalfield; many forms of engin. and light inds. inc. vehicle mftg.; p. (est. 1976) 2,743,300.

Westminster, City of, inner bor., London, Eng.; on N. bank of R. Thames; W. of City of London; incorporates former bors. of Paddington and St. Marylebone; contains Houses of Parliament, Westminster Abbey, Government offices, Royal Palaces (Buckingham Palace and St. James's); p. (est. 1976) 216,100.

Westmorland, former co., Eng.; now part of Cumbria non-met. co.

West Norfolk, l. gov. dist., Norfolk, Eng.; lge. a. inc. Hunstanton, King's Lynn and Downham Market; p. (est. 1976) 115,700.

Weston-super-Mare, t., Woodspring, Avon, Eng.; on Bristol Channel, 32 km S.W. of Bristol; holiday resort; expanded t.; p. (1971) 50,794.

West Orange, t., N.J., USA; elec. equipment; home of T. A. Edison; p. (1970) 43,715.

West Oxfordshire, l. gov. dist., Oxon., Eng.; in Cotswolds and ts. of Chipping Norton, Witney and Woodstock; p. (est. 1976) 81,500.

West Pakistan. See Pakistan.

West Palm Beach, Fla., USA; domestic hardware; spt.; tourism; p. (1970) 56,865 (t.), 345,553 (met. a.).

Westphalia. See North Rhine–Westphalia.

West Point, military sta., N.Y., USA; on Hudson R.; military academy.

Westport, spt., S.I., N.Z.; on R. Buller; coastal shipping; coal; nearby iron fields; p. (1971) 5,008.

Westport, spt., U.D., Mayo, R.o.I.; on Clew Bay; fishing; mkt.; p. (1966) 2,927.

Westray, I., Orkney Is., Scot.; 16 km long; p. (1971) 841.

West Somerset, l. gov. dist., Somerset, Eng.; inc. Exmoor and cstl. ts. of Watchet and Minehead; p. (est. 1976) 29,400.

West Sussex, non-met. co., S.E. Eng.; crossed by E.–W. chalk ridge of S. Downs and forested Weald; diverse agr.; dormitory, retirement and tourist ts. on cst. inc. Bognor Regis and Worthing; Crawley new t. in N.; a. 2,015 km²; p. (est. 1976) 623,400.

West Virginia, st., USA; inc. Allegheny plateau; impt. mng. st. for coal; fruit farming; many industl. ts.; cap. Charleston; a. 62,629 km²; p. (1970) 1,701,913.

Westward Ho!, v., N. Devon, Eng.; named after Kingsley's novel.

West Wiltshire, l. gov. dist., Wilts., Eng.; stretches from Melksham, Bradford-on-Avon and Trowbridge to Warminster; p. (est. 1976) 94,500.

West Yorkshire, met. co., Eng.; industl. and mainly built-up a. E. of Pennines; traditionally ass. with woollen textile mftg.; inc. major ctrs. of Bradford and Leeds; p. (est. 1976) 2,072,500.

Wetar I., Indonesia; N. of Timor I.; mtns.; underdeveloped; sparse p.; a. 31,080 km².

Wetherby, t., West Yorks., Eng.; on R. Wharfe; mkt.; malting, brewing; p. (1971) 30,581 (dist.).

Wethersfield, t., Conn., USA; oldest settlement (1634) in st.; aircraft parts. agr. implements; p. (1970) 26,662.

Wetterhorn, mtn., Switzerland; alt. 3,710 m.

Wetzlar, t., Hesse, W. Germany; on R. Lahn; metallurgical and optical inds.; p. (est. 1969) 36,871.

Wexford, coastal co., Leinster, S.E. R.o.I.; mixed farming, fishing; cap. Wexford; a. 2,334 km²; p. (1966) 83,355.

Wexford, t., cap. of Wexford; Leinster, S.E. R.o.I.; on R. Slaney; agr. processing; outport at Rosslare; p. (1966) 11,533.

Wey, R., Hants., Surrey, Eng.; rises in W. Weald, flows N. into R. Thames nr. Weybridge; cuts impt. gap through N. Downs at Guildford; length 56 km.

Weybridge. See Walton and Weybridge.

Weymouth and Portland, t., l. gov. dist., Dorset, Eng.; on Weymouth Bay, 13 km S. of Dorchester; torpedo and boatbldg., bricks, tiles, engin.; holiday resort; p. (est. 1976) 57,000 (dist.).

Whaley Bridge, t., High Peak, Derbys., Eng.; textile bleaching and finishing; p. (1971) 5,232.

Whangarei, c., N.I., N.Z.; deep harbour; oil refining; natural gas pipelines from Kapuni; fertilisers, sheet glass; p. (1971) 30,749.

Wharfe, R., West and North Yorks., Eng.; trib. of R. Ouse; 96 km long.

Wheeling, c., W. Va., USA; pt. on Ohio R.; comm. and mftg. ctr. in coal and natural gas a.; iron, steel, and metal plants; p. (1970) 46,854 (c.), 180,724 (met. a.).

Whickham, t., Tyne and Wear, Eng.; nr. Gateshead; chemicals, paper; p. (1971) 28,704.

Whitburn, burgh, W. Lothian, Scot.; 32 km S.W. of Edinburgh; coal, limestone; p. (1971) 10,176.

Whitby, t., North Yorks., Eng.; at mouth of R. Esk, 27 km N.W. of Scarborough; anc. spt. and fishing t.; residtl. and coastal resort; abbey; famous for jet ornaments; potash to be mined nearby; p. (1971) 12,171.

Whitchurch, t., Salop, Eng.; 21 km S.W. of Crewe; structural steel, dairy prods.

White, R., Ark. and Mo., USA; trib. of Mississippi; hydroelectric power; 1,104 km long.

Whiteadder, R., Berwick, Scot.; trib. of R. Tweed; 54 km long.

Whitehaven, spt., Copeland, Cumbria, Eng.; on Solway F. 5 km N. of St. Bees Head; coal, methane gas, cement, chemicals; p. (1971) 26,720.

Whitehead, t., Carrickfergus, N. Ireland; at entrance to Belfast Lough; seaside resort; p. (1966) 2,740.

Whitehorse, t., cap. of Yukon terr., Canada; ctr. coal and copper mng., hunting and fur trapping; once a gold "boom town"; H.Q. Royal Canadian Mounted Police; end of Alaska highway linking Edmonton, Alberta; p. (1966) 4,771.

White Mtns., part. of Appalachian system, N.H., USA; highest summit Mt. Washington, 1,918 m.

White Nile (Bahr-el-Abiad), R., Sudan; N.E. Africa; strictly, name applied to stretch of R. Nile between L. No and Khartoum; 800 km long.

White Plains, t., N.Y., USA; on Bronx R.; residtl.; battle 1776; p. (1970) 50,346.

White Russia. See Belorussiyan SSR.

White Sea or G. of Arkangelsk, inlet of Barents Sea, USSR; frozen for 6 months of year; connected to Baltic Sea by deep-water canal; impt. fisheries.

Whitley Bay, t., North Tyneside, Northumberland, Eng.; 5 km N. of Tynemouth; seaside resort; plastics; p. (1971) 37,775.

Whitstable, spt., Kent, Eng.; on Thames estuary 10 km N. of Canterbury; holiday resort, oysters; p. (1971) 25,404.

Whittlesey, t., Fenland, Cambs., Eng.; in the Fens, 13 km W. of March; bricks, mkt. gardening; p. (1971) 10,451.

Whyalla, t., spt., S. Australia; steel and shipbldg. inds.; ironstone, pig-iron, steel from Iron Knob; p. (1972) 32,085.

Wichita, c., Kan., USA; in Arkansas valley; rly. wks., oil refineries and equipment, meatpacking ctr. in agr. and stock-raising region; univs.; p. (1970) 274,448 (c.), 385,994 (met. a.).

Wichita Falls, c., Texas, USA; oil refining, ctr. in agr. and ranching a.; p. (1970) 94,976 (c.) 124,238 (met. a.).

Wick, spt., sm. burgh, Caithness, Scot.; on E. cst., 22 km S. of John O'Groats; airport to Orkneys and Shetlands; herring fishing ctr.; p. (1971) 7,617.

Wicklow, costal co., Leinster, R.o.I.; crossed by Wicklow mtns.; pastoral agr. and tourism; cap. Wicklow; a. 2,033 km²; p. (1966) 60,281.

Wickow, t., cap. of Wicklow, Leinster, R.o.I.; on S.E. cst., 56 km S. of Dublin; mkt.; sm. seaside resort; p. (1966) 3,340.

Wicklow, mtns., Wicklow, R.o.I.; highest summit Lugnaquillia, 927 m.

Widecombe, v., Devon, Eng.; Dartmoor tourist ctr.; famous through ballad "Widecombe Fair."

Widnes, t., Halton, Cheshire, Eng.; on R. Mersey 19 km E. of Liverpool; impt. chemical inds.; expanded t.; p. (1971) 56,709.

Wiener Neustadt, t., Lower Austria; rly. and industl. ctr.; heavy machin.; founded 1192; anc. bldgs., cas., cath.; educational ctr.; p. (1961) 38,845.

Wieringermeer Polder, reclaimed a., N. Holland, Neth.; N.W. of IJsselmeer; a. 202 km².

Wiesbaden, c., cap. of Hesse, W. Germany; on Rhine, at S. foot of the Taunus; famous spa.; cas.; ctr. for Rhine wines; chemicals, metal gds.; p. (est. 1969) 259,900.

Wigan, t., met. dist., Gtr. Manchester, **Eng.**; 26 km N.E. of Liverpool; engin., chemicals, cement, food processing, paper; former coal-mng. ctr.; p. (est. 1976) 310,700 (dist.).

Wight, I. of, non-met. co., **Eng.**; English Channel, separated from Hampshire by Spithead and the Solent; crossed by chalk hills, terminating in the Needles; popular holiday resort; ch. ts., Newport, Ryde, Cowes; a. 381 km²; p. (est. 1976) 111,300.

Wigston, t., Leics., **Eng.**; 6 km S. of Leicester; engin., hosiery; p. (1971) 30,230. *See* Oadby.

Wigtown, l. gov. dist., former co., Dumfries and Galloway Reg., Scot.; along N. cst. of Solway F.; impt. dairying reg.; a. 1,712 km²; p. (1971) 29,670.

Wigtown, sm. burgh, Wigtown, Scot.; on W. Bay, Solway F.; shares admin. with Newton Stewart; p. (1971) 1,118.

Wilhelmshaven, c., Lower Saxony, **W. Germany**; on inlet of N. Sea, 64 km N.W. of Bremen; ch. German naval base until 1945; industl. ctr. with heavy machin., elec. equipment, textiles, furniture; oil pipeline; p. (est. 1969) 102,700.

Wilkes-Barre, c., Penns., **USA**; on Susquehanna R.; industl. ctr. in rich anthracite mng. a.; p. (1970) 57,946 (c.), 124,238 (met. a.).

Wilkes Land, Antarctica; featureless plateau, alt. 2,900 m; immense glaciers; U.S. base taken over by Australia 1959.

Willamette, R., Ore., **USA**; rises in Cascade mtns., flows N. into Columbia R. below Portland; valley gives rich agr. land, wheat, root-crops, dairy prod., hard and soft fruits; ch. ts. Eugene, Salem, Oregon City, Portland; used for hydroelectric power; 480 km long.

Willemstad, t., cap. of Neth. Antilles; on Curaçao I.; oil refining; tourism; p. (1964) 59,586.

Willenhall, t., West Midlands, **Eng.**; locks and keys, drop forgings.

Willesden, former M.B., Middx., **Eng.**; now inc. in Brent outer bor., Greater London impt. rly. junc., residtl. and indstl.

Williamsburg, c., Va., **USA**; between James and York Rs.; historic t., settled 1632; rebuilt in 1920s to original plan; in Colonial Nat. Historical Park; p. (1970) 9,069.

Williamsport, t., Penns., **USA**; on Susquehanna R.; rly. ctr., timber, machin.; summer resort; p. (1970) 37,918.

Williamstown, spt., sub. of Melbourne, Victoria, **Australia**; at mouth of Yarra R.; naval dockyards, shipbldg., railway wks.; p. (1966) 30,449.

Willow South, new cap. (1977), Alaska, **USA**; new t. replacing Juneau; closer to ctr. of p.; complete by 1980.

Wilmington, t., spt., Del., **USA**; on Delaware R.; shipbldg., machin., iron- and steel-wks.; chemicals; leather, cork, rubber gds.; p. (1970) 79,978 (t.), 498,977 (met. a.);

Wilmington, spt., N.C. **USA**; exp. cotton, tobacco, timber, fertilizers; shipbldg., textiles, chemicals; p. (1970) 45,067 (t.), 103,556 (met. a.).

Wilmslow, t., Cheshire, **Eng.**; on R. Bollen, 10 km S.W. of Stockport; residtl.; p. (1971) 28,982.

Wilton, t., Wilts., **Eng.**; on R. Wylye, 5 km W. of Salisbury; agr. mkt., carpets, felt; anc. cap. of Wessex; many old bldgs.; p. (1971) 3,815.

Wilton, industl. estate, Cleveland, **Eng.**; on S. side of Tees estuary; heavy organic- and petro-chemicals; nylon polymer plant.

Wiltshire, non-met. co., **Eng.**; crossed by chalk downland and Salisbury Plain; barley, wheat, dairying, pigs; co. t. Salisbury; a. 3,484 km²; p. (est. 1976) 512,800.

Wiltshire, North, l. gov. dist., Wilts., **Eng.**; rural a. inc. ts. of Calne, Chippenham and Malmesbury; p. (1976) 102,400.

Wimbledon, dist., London, **Eng.**; lge. open common; site of international tennis tournament; part of London Bor. of Merton.

Wimborne, l. gov. dist., Dorset, **Eng.**; rural a. based on W. Minster; p. (est. 1976) 61,700.

Wimborne Minster, mkt. t., Dorset, **Eng.**; on R. Stour; Roman site and home of Saxon kings; Badbury Rings earthworks nearby; p. (1971) 5,000.

Winchcomb, t., Gloucs., **Eng.**; nr. Cheltenham; old mills; pottery, paper; nearby cas.

Winchelsea, anc. t., East Sussex, **Eng.**; 3 km S.W. of Rye; once impt. walled spt. and Cinque port, now 3 km inland.

Winchester, cath. c., l. gov. dist., Hants., **Eng.**; on R. Itchen, 19 km N. of Southampton; anc. Anglo-Saxon cap.; meeting place of parliaments until time of Henry VII; magnificent cath., famous public school; p. (est. 1976) 88,900 (dist.).

Windermere, lgst. English L., in Cumbria; outlet to Morecambe Bay; supplies water to Manchester; 16 km long, 1·6 km wide.

Windhoek, t., cap. of South-West Africa; in hills at 1,700 m; comm. ctr., agr. processing; tr. in karakul (Persian lamb); p. (1970) 61,260.

Windrush, R., Oxford, Gloucs., **Eng.**; trib. of R. Thames.

Windscale, Cumbria, **Eng.**; nuclear reactors for defence purposes and prod. of elec. for national grid.

Windsor, c., pt., Ont., **Canada**; on Detroit R., linked to Detroit, USA, by tunnel, bridge and ferry; ctr. for car mftg., salt wks., chemicals, paints; univ.; p. (1971) 199,784 (c.), 255,167 (met. a.).

Windsor, New, t., Berks., **Eng.**; on R. Thames, 32 km W. of London; famous royal cas. (founded by William the Conqueror) and park, St. George's Chapel and the Royal Mausoleum; with Maidenhead forms l. gov. dist.; p. (est. 1976) 128,400.

Windward Is., W.I., extend S. from Leeward Is.; consist of Fr. Martinique and former Brit. cols. of Grenada, St. Vincent, St. Lucia and Dominica with their dependencies (the Grenadines divided between Grenada and St.Vincent) which attained associated statehood 1967; sm. limited resources, economically depressed; volcanic.

Windward Passage, channel, 96 km wide, between Cuba and Haiti.

Winnebago, L., Wis., **USA**; 43 km long; lgst. L. in Wis.

Winnipeg, c., cap. of Manitoba, **Canada**; at junc. of Red and Assiniboine Rs.; cath., univ.; rly. ctr.; ch. world wheat mkt.; meat packing and food processing; lgst. garment mnf. ctr. in cty.; oil refining; p. (1971) 243,208 (c.), 534,685 (met. a.).

Winnipeg, L., Manitoba, **Canada**; 64 km N. of Winnipeg; 416 km long, 49–96 km wide; contains several lge. Is. (Reindeer, 181 km²; Big I., 155 km²); used for hydroelectric power.

Winnipegosis, L., Manitoba and Saskatchewan, **Canada**; a. (exclusive of Is.) 5,180 km²; 80 km W. of L. Winnipeg, into which it drains.

Winsford, t., Cheshire, **Eng.**; on R. Weaver; 6 km S. of Northwich; ctr. of salt inds., chemicals; expanded t.; p. (1971) 24,791.

Winston-Salem, t., N.C., **USA**; formed 1913 from union of 2 adjacent ts.; tobacco ctr.; p. (1970) 133,820.

Winterthur, t., Zurich, **Switzerland**; on Eulach R.; rly. ctr., locomotives, machines, cottons; p. (est. 1969) 94,200 (t.), 104,600 (met. a.).

Wiri, t., N.Z.; 24 km S. of Auckland; aluminium fabricating mill.

Wirksworth, t., West Derbys., **Eng.**; in Pennines, 8 km S. of Matlock; limestone, fluorspar wks.; ctr. of Derbys. former lead-mng.; p. (1971) 5,151.

Wirral, penin., met. dist., Merseyside, **Eng.**; between estuaries of Dee and Mersey; residtl.; comprises Wallasey, Birkenhead, Bebington and Hoylake; p. (est. 1976) 348,200.

Wisbech, t., Fenland, Cambs., **Eng.**; on R. Nene, 18 km from its mouth in the Wash; mkt. gardening, fruit growing and canning, agr. implements; p. (1971) 17,002.

Wisconsin, st., **USA**; bounded by Gt. Ls.; lowlying; leading dairying st.; industl. ts. around Gt. Ls.; cap. Madison; ch. t. Milwaukee; a. 145,439 km². p. (1970) 4,366,766.

Wisconsin, R., Wis., **USA**; trib. of R. Mississippi; used for hydroelectric power; 960 km long.

Wismar, spt., Rostock, **E. Germany**; on Baltic Sea, N. of Schwerin; oil pt. and industl. ctr. with shipyards and food processing inds.; p. (est. 1970) 56,057.

Witbank, t., Transvaal, S. Africa; leading coalmng. dist. with power sta. and carbide and cyanide factories; p. (1970) 50,581.

Witham, t., Essex, **Eng.**; 14 km N.E. of Chelmsford; ctr. of mkt. gardening a.; expanded t.; p. (1971) 17,306.

Witham, R., Lincs. and Lincs., **Eng.**; flows into the Wash; cuts impressive gap through Lincoln Edge at Lincoln; 128 km long.

Witney, t., Oxford, **Eng.; on** R. Windrush, 16 km W. of Oxford; woollens, blankets, gloves; p. (1971) 12,535.

Witten, t., N. Rhine–Westphalia, **W. Germany;** on R. Ruhr; glass, machin., metals, chemicals, optical inds.; p. (est. 1969) 97,472.

Wittenberg, t., Halle, **E. Germany; on** R. Elbe; ctr. of Reformation and burial place of Luther (Schlosskirche); cas.; machin., textiles; p. (est. 1970) 47,151.

Wittenberge, t., Schwerin, **E. Germany; on** R. Elbe; rly. junc., repair wkshps., machin.; p. (est. 1970) 33,028.

Witwatersrand, dist., Transvaal, S. Africa; goldmng. dist. producing over quarter of world's gold.

Wivenhoe, t., Essex, **Eng.; on** R. Colne; boatbldg., oysters, lt. inds.; p. (1971) 5,310.

Wloclawek, t., pt., **N.** Poland; on R. Vistula; impt. paper mnfs., ceramics; p. (1970) 77,200.

Woburn, t., Beds., **Eng.;** 8 km N.E. of Leighton Buzzard; Woburn Abbey (seat of Dukes of Bedford).

Woking, t., l. gov. dist., Surrey, **Eng.;** 6 km N. of Guildford; residtl.; p. (est. 1976) 79,300.

Wokingham, mkt. t., l. gov. dist., Berks., **Eng.;** 8 km S.E. of Reading; agr. tr. and machin., bricks; p. (est. 1976) 112,600 (dist.).

Wolds, The, chalk downland, Lincs., Humberside, **Eng.;** extend S. to E. Anglian heights; traditional pastoral agr. changing to extensive arable farming; 72 km long.

Wolfenbüttel, t., Lower Saxony, **W. Germany;** on R. Oker, 11 km S. of Brunswick; noted for ducal library, founded 17th cent., of which Leibnitz and Lessing were librarians; p. (est. 1969) 40,902.

Wolf Rock, isolated rock with lighthouse, at approach to English Channel from Bay of Biscay; 14 km S.W. of Lands End, Cornwall.

Wolsburg, t., Lower Saxony, **W. Germany;** on R. Aller, N.E. of Brunswick; Volkswagen wks.; p. (est. 1969) 88,024.

Wolin, I., Baltic Sea; off mouth of R. Oder, Poland; Nat. Park; fishing, tourism; a. 344 km²; p. (est. 1966) 2,867.

Wollongong, Greater, t., N.S.W., **Australia;** coal mng., iron and steel wks., fertilisers, chemicals, bricks; inc. Port Kembla (q.v.); p. (1972) 160,902 (c.), 198,768 (met. a.).

Wolsingham, t., Durham, **Eng.; on** R. Wear; impt. steel wks.

Wolverhampton, t., met. dist., West Midlands, **Eng.;** heavy and lt. engin., boilers, rayon, elec. engin. and apparatus, iron wks., aircraft and motor components, hollow-ware, tools, strongrooms and safes, paints; p. (est. 1976) 266,400.

Wolverton, t., Bucks., **Eng.; on** R. Ouse, 24 km S.W. of Bedford; rly.-carriage wks.; p. (1971) 13,819.

Wombwell, t., South Yorks., **Eng.;** at E. foot of Pennines, 11 km N. of Sheffield; coal mng., bricks; p. (1971) 17,933.

Wonsan, spt., **N.** Korea; on Sea of Japan; major pt. and rly. ctr.; Japanese naval base in second world war; oil refining; p. (est. 1967) 300,000.

Woodbridge, t., Suffolk Coastal, Suffolk, **Eng.;** on R. Deben; engin., brush mkg.; p. (1971) 7,272.

Wood Green, former M.B., Middx., **Eng.;** now inc. in Haringey outer bor., Greater London.

Woodhall Spa, t., East Lindsey, Lincs., **Eng.;** 6 km S.W. of Horncastle; former spa, bromoiodine springs; resort; p. (1971) 2,232.

Woodspring, l. gov. dist., Avon, **Eng.;** S. of Bristol and inc. Clevedon, Portishead, and Westonsuper-Mare; p. (est. 1976) 151,100.

Woodstock, t., Ont., Canada; on R. Thames; ctr. of agr. dist.; lt. mnfs. based on hydroelectric power; p. (1971) 25,559.

Woodstock, t., Oxford, **Eng.; on** Glyme R., 11 km N.W. of Oxford; glove mnfs.; Blenheim Palace; p. (1971) 1,940.

Wookey Hole, cave, Mendip Hills, Somerset, **Eng.;** at foot of limestone hills, 3 km N.W. of Wells; R. Axe emerges from the cave.

Woolwich, dist. former met. bor., London, **Eng.;** on either side of R. Thames; impt. Tudor dockyard, now closed; now part of Greenwich and Newham bors.

Woomera, S. **Australia;** c. 432 km N.W. of Adelaide; base for joint U.K.–Australian guided-weapon testing range extending N.W.

across the continent; established 1947.

Woonsocket, t., R.I., **USA;** on Blackstone R.; textiles, rubber gds.; p. (1970) 46,820.

Worcester, l. gov. dist., Hereford and Worcs., **Eng.; on** R. Severn, 38 km N. of Gloucester; cath.; machin. porcelain, glove mkg.; birthplace of Elgar; p. (est. 1976) 73,900 (dist.).

Worcester, t., Cape Prov., S. Africa; viticultural and industl. ctr.; Goudini spa nearby; p. (1970) 175,140 (c.), 342,529 (met. a.).

Worcester, c., Mass., **USA;** univ.; cultural ctr.; machine tools, elec. engin.; p. (1970) 176,572.

Worcestershire, former Midland co., **Eng.;** now part of **Hereford and Worcs.** non-met. co. and **West Midlands** met. co.

Workington, t., Allerdale, Cumbria, **Eng.;** sm. spt. on Solway F. at mouth of Derwent R.; first Bessemer steel plant, now heavily dependent upon iron and steel wks. (soon to close); industl. diversification on nearby industl. estates, inc. bus wks.; p. (1971) 28,414.

Worksop, t., Bassetlaw, Notts., **Eng.;** 24 km S.E. of Sheffield; coal-mng. dist.; brewing, knitwear, glass, flour; p. (1971) 36,034.

Worms, t., Rhineland-Palatinate, **W. Germany;** on left bank of Rhine; historic ctr.; famous imperial diet 1521 when Luther refused to retract; scene of *Nibelungenlied;* ctr. for Liebfraumilch wines; chemical, textile, leather and metal inds.; p. (est. 1969) 77,642.

Worms Head, promontory, on West Glamorgan cst., Gower peninsula, Wales.

Worsley, t., Gtr. Manchester, **Eng.;** ctr. of coalmng. dist.; p. (1971) 49,573.

Worthing, t., l. gov. dist., West Sussex, **Eng.; on** S. cst., 16 km W. of Brighton; holiday resort, retirement ctr. in mkt. gardening dist.; p. (est. 1976) 89,100.

Woy Woy, t., N.S.W., Australia; resort and commuter t. for Sydney; clothing; p. (1966) 16,264.

Wrangel I., Arctic Oc., off Khabarovsk terr., **RSFSR;** weather sta.

Wrath, C., N.W. Sutherland, Scot.

Wrekin, hill, Salop, **Eng.;** alt. 403 m.

Wrekin, The, l. gov. dist., Salop, **Eng.;** inc. Newport, Wellington, Oakengates and Dawley; p. (est. 1976) 112,400.

Wrexham, t., Clwyd, **Wales;** 18 km S.W. Chester; tyres, synthetic fibres, clothing; as Wrexham Maelor forms l. gov. dist.; p. (est. 1976) 108,100.

Wroclaw (Breslau), c., Silesia, **Poland; on** R. Oder; impt. route ctr. and R. pt.; univ., cath.; rapid industl. development; ctr. of electronics inds.; p. (1970) 523,000.

Wroclaw (Breslau), prov., **Lower Silesia, Poland;** until 1945 part of Germany; heavy inds. based on local minerals; cap. Wroclaw; a. 24,740 km²; p. (1970) 1,937,000.

Wroxeter, v., Salop, **Eng.; on** R. Severn, 8 km S.E. Shrewsbury; Roman sta. Uriconium.

Wuchow (Wuzhou), R. pt., Kwangsi prov., China; on R. Si; tr. ctr.; exp. tung oil, hides; p. (est. 1970) 150,000.

Wuhan, c., Hupeh prov., China; formed by union of Hankow, Hanyang, and Wuchang; major metropolis on R. Yangtze; integrated iron and steel wks., machine tools, walking tractors, textiles, shipbldg.; univ.; p. (est. 1970) 4,250,000.

Wuhu, c., Anhwei prov., China; former treaty pt. on R. Yangtze; textiles; p. (est. 1970) 300,000.

Wupper, R., W. Germany; trib. of Rhine; industl. concentration along middle course; 64 km long.

Wuppertal, t., N. Rhine–Westphalia, **W. Germany;** formed by amalgamation of Barmen and Elberfeld; textiles, rubber gds., paper, metals, pharmaceuticals; p. (est. 1969) 413,000.

Württemberg-Hohenzollern, former t., **W. Germany;** since 1952 part of Baden–Württemberg.

Würzburg, c., Bavaria, **W. Germany; on** R. Main; univ., cath.; historic bldgs., engin., chemicals, printing; p. (est. 1969) 120,100.

Wurzen, t., Leipzig, **E. Germany; on** R. Mulde; cath., cas.; machin., furniture, leather, foodstuffs; p. (est. 1970) 24,164.

Wusih (Wuxi), c., Kiangsu prov., China; on N. shore of Tai L., 120 km W. of Shanghai; univ.; industl. ctr. with cotton mills, chemical wks.; former treaty pt.; p. (est. 1970) 900,000.

Wutungkiao (Wutongqiao), c., Szechwan prov.* China; 24 km S.E. of Loshan; p. (1953) 199,000.

Wyandotte, t., Mich., USA; on Detroit R.; salt deposits; chemical ind.; p. (1970) 41,061.

Wychavon, l. gov. dist., Hereford and Worcs., Eng.; inc. Vale of Evesham and Pershore in S. and Droitwich in N.; p. (est. 1976) 87,100.

Wycombe, l. gov. dist., Bucks., Eng.; close to Oxon. and inc. High Wycombe and Marlow; p. (est. 1976) 150,600.

Wye, R., Bucks., Eng.; rises in Chiltern hills, flows S.E. to R. Thames at Cookham.

Wye, R., Eng. and Wales; rises in Plynlimmon, flows S.E. into R. Severn at Chepstow; forms deeply incised valley at Symond's Yat; 208 km long.

Wye, t., Kent, Eng.; nr. Ashford; impt. agr. college (Univ. of London).

Wylfa Head, Anglesey, Gwynedd, N. Wales; nuclear power sta.

Wymondham, t., South Norfolk, Eng.; 14 km S.W. of Norwich; mkt.; Benedictine abbey founded 1107; p. (1971) 8,510.

Wyoming, st., USA; inc. areas of Rocky mtns. and great plains; Yellowstone Nat. Park; scant rainfall; irrigation; cattle and sheep ranching; petroleum; sparse p.; cap. Cheyenne; a. 253,597 km²; p. (1970) 332,416.

Wyre, R., Lancs., Eng.; rises in Pennines, flows W. into Lancaster Bay at Fleetwood; 45 km long.

Wyre, l. gov. dist., Lancs. Eng.; inc. Preesall, Fleetwood and Thornton Cleveleys; p. (est. 1976) 101,000.

Wyre Forest, l. gov. dist., Hereford and Worcester, Eng.; inc. Bewdley, Kidderminster and Stourport; p. (est. 1976) 93,000.

X

Xanthi, t., Thrace, Greece; on R. Mesta; ctr. of tobacco-growing a.; p. (1971) 25,341.

Xanthus, ruined c., Turkey; on R. Xanthus; destroyed 43 B.C.; tourism.

Xauen, t., Morocco, N. Africa; holy t. founded 15th cent.; p. (1960) 13,712.

Xingu, R., Brazil; trib. of Amazon; navigable in its lower course; 1,920 km long.

Y

Yablonovy, mtn. range, Siberia, RSFSR; E. of L. Baykal; highest peak, Sokhondo, 2,510 m; crossed by Trans-Siberian rly.

Yaila Mtns., Ukrainian SSR, USSR; form S.E. margin of Crimea penin., extend from Sevastopol to Kerch; form marked climate barrier between Black Sea littoral (Soviet Riviera) and N. part.

Yakima, t., Wash., USA; agr. ctr. of irrigated valley, noted for fruit; p. (1970) 45,588.

Yakima, R., Wash., USA; trib. of Columbia R.; used for irrigation; 333 km long.

Yakut ASSR, aut. rep., RSFSR; borders Arctic Oc.; home of Yakuts; tundra and forest region, isolated; fur trapping, diamond and gold mng., state farms; a. 3,963,355 km²; p. (1970) 664,000.

Yakutsk, t., cap. of Yakut ASSR, RSFSR; pt. on Lena R.; univ.; airport; p. (1970) 108,000.

Yallahs Valley, Jamaica; severe soil erosion; govt. improvement scheme of afforestation and new crops; a. 181 km².

Yallourn, t., Victoria, Australia; ctr. of lignite mng. a.; p. (1972) 20,764 inc. Moe.

Yalta, spt., Ukrainian SSR, USSR; sub-tropical resort on Black Sea, sheltered by Yaila mtns.; conference between Churchill, Roosevelt, and Stalin 1945; p. (est. 1969) 57,000.

Yalu, R., forms bdy. between N.E. China, and N. Korea; flows into Yellow Sea; used for hydroelectric power.

Yamagata, t., Honshu, Japan; ctr. of ricegrowing a.; cas.; p. (est. 1971) 207,000.

Yamaguchi, t., cap. of Y. prov., S.W. Honshu, Japan; cas.; comm. ctr., chemicals; p. (est. 1971) 103,000.

Yamal-Nenets National Okrug, RSFSR; inc. Yamal penin.; permafrost; hunting, fishing; cap. Salekhard; lge. natural gas finds; a. 670,810 km²; p. (1970) 80,000.

Yambol, t., Bulgaria; on R. Tunja; ruined mosque; agr. tr.; recent inds. inc. canning, farm machin., textiles, ceramics; p. (est. 1968) 67,941.

Yamethin, dist., Upper Burma; teak forests, rice; ch. t. Yamethin; site of irrigation project; p. 9,291.

Yana, R., Siberia, USSR; flows into Arctic Sea; navigable; 1,600 km long.

Yangchow (Yangzhou), c., Kiangsu prov., China; on Grand Canal; agr. mkt. ctr., historic bldgs.; p. (est. 1970) 210,000.

Yangchuan (Yangqan), c., Shansi prov., China; ironworking ctr.; p. (1953) 177,000.

Yangi-yer, t., Uzbek SSR, USSR; founded 1957 as ctr. for new irrigated cotton lands of E. Uzbekistan.

Yangtze River, China; rises in plateau of Tibet; flows E. to E. China Sea, Pac. Oc., nr. Shanghai; traverses "Red Basin" of Szechwan, a deep gorge above Ichang, and finally a broad, level plain; many lge. cs. on its banks, Chungking, Ichang, Wuhan, Nanking, Chinkiang; major water control project under construction; navigable by ocean-going vessels 2,880 km to Ichang; total length 5,600 km.

Yaoundé, t., cap. of Cameroon Rep., W. Africa; lt. inds. inc. beer, cigarettes, textiles; p. (est. 1969) 165,810 (met. a.).

Yapura, R., Brazil and Colombia, S. America; trib. of R. Amazon; length 2,400 km.

Yaracuy, st., Venezuela; crossed by Y. valley impt. agr. a. for bananas, coffee, sugar, tobacco; crossed by Pan-American Highway; cap. San Felipe; a. 7,099 km²; p. (est. 1970) 222,041.

Yare, R., Norfolk, Eng.; flows E. to N. Sea at Gorleston; forms part of Norfolk Broads navigable waterways; 80 km long.

Yarkand (Soche), c., Sinkiang prov., China; tr. ctr. in Y. oasis; tr. in wheat, rice, beans, fruit, carpets, textiles; p. (est.) 60,000.

Yarkand, R., Sinkiang prov., China; trib. of Tarim R.; 800 km long.

Yarmouth, spt., Nova Scotia, Canada; fisheries; p. (1971) 8,291.

Yarmouth, Great, pt., l. gov. dist., Norfolk, Eng.; at mouth of R. Yare; holiday resort; fish and food processing plants; base for N. Sea gas; p. (est. 1976) 77,200 (dist.).

Yaroslavl, c., cap. of Y. oblast, RSFSR; on upper Volga in Moscow industl. region; founded 1010; comm. and industl. ctr.; mnfs. inc. textiles, motor vehicles, synthetic rubber, agr. machin.; Volkov theatre, 12th cent. monastery, churches; p. (1970) 517,000.

Yasan, N., Bulgaria; lge. refinery and petrochemicals complex.

Yatsushiro, t., Kyushu, Japan; p. (est. 1971) 103,000.

Yazd, c., Isfahan prov., Iran; in desert a. at 1,190 m; fine silks, carpets; p. (1967) 280,442 (met. a.).

Yazoo, dist., Miss., USA; flood plain of R. Mississippi and R. Yazoo; very fertile alluvial soil, but subject to disastrous floods; one of ch. cottongrowing dists. in USA.

Yegoryevsk, t., RSFSR; 115 km S.E. of Moscow; lge. textile ind.; phosphorite deposits; p. (est. 1969) 65,000.

Yeletz, t., RSFSR; on R. Sosna; grain and cattle tr.; cultural ctr.; rly. junc.; p. (1970) 101,000.

Yell, I., Shetlands, Scot.; 27 km long; covered in peat moorland; p. (1971) 1,143.

Yellowhead Pass, B.C., Alberta, Canada; most N. and lowest of main passes across Rocky mtns.; carries Canadian Nat. rly. on route from Edmonton to Vancouver and Prince Rupert; summit alt. 1,130 m.

Yellowknife, t., N.W. Terr., Canada; on N. shore of Gr. Slave L.; ctr. of impt. gold-mng. dist.; linked by air to Edmonton, Alberta; p. (1966) 3,741.

Yellow R. See Hwang-ho.

Yellow Sea. See Hwang-hai.

Yellowstone, L., Wyo., USA; 32 km long, 24 km wide; alt. 2,360 m; in Y. Nat. Park.

Yellowstone National Park, N.W. Wyo., USA; volcanic scenery, geysers; a. 8,956 km².

Yemen Arab Republic (N. Yemen), S.W. Arabian penin.; climate hot and humid in semi-desert cst. strip; summer rainfall inland on high plateau; land slopes down in E. to desert of

Rub'al Khali; agr. basis of economy; irrigated, terraced, fertile land in highlands; millet, maize, sorghum, oats, fruits; Mocha coffee main exp.; expanding cotton a. in Tihama cst. a.; ch. spt. Hodeida; cap. Sana'a; proposed union with S. Yemen; a. 194,250 km²; p. (est. 1970) 5,728,000.

Yemen, People's Democratic Rep. of (S. Yemen), S.W. Arabia; comprises strategic pt. of Aden and much desert terr.; independence proclaimed 1967 when Brit. troops withdrawn; hot, dry climate; Brit. withdrawal, decline of tourism and closure of Suez Canal resulted in economic decline; subsistence agr., little comm. exploitation of rich fishing grounds; oil refinery at Aden; cap. Madinat ash Sha'b (N.W. of Aden); proposed union with N. Yemen; a. 290,274 km²; p. (est. 1970) 1,500,000.

Yenangyaung, t., R. pt., Burma; on left bank of R. Irrawaddy, 448 km N. of Rangoon; ctr. of Burma oilfields.

Yenisey, R., Siberia, RSFSR; rises in Sayan mtns., flows N. into Arctic Oc.; ch. tribs., Angara, Stony Tunguska, Lower Tunguska; hydroelectric power sta. at Krasnoyarsk; linked to Ob R. by canal; middle course navigable; 5,280 km long.

Yentai. See Chefoo.

Yeo or Ivel, R., Dorset, Somerset, Eng.; trib. of R. Parrett; 38 km long.

Yeovil, mkt. t., l. gov. dist., Somerset, Eng.; on R. Yeo; glove mnf., aero-engin.; agr. machin., dairy processing; p. (est. 1976) 124,100 (dist.).

Yerevan or Erivan, c., cap. of Armenian SSR, USSR; on Zanga R. in deep valley of Caucasus mtns.; founded 8th cent. B.C.; major science-based, industl. ctr.; p. (1970) 767,000.

Yes Tor, second highest summit, Dartmoor, Devon, Eng.; 618 m.

Yevpatoriya or Eupatoria, spt., Crimea, on Black Sea, USSR; popular resort; children's sanatoria; chemicals, leather, locks, dried fish; new pt. being built; p. (est. 1969) 75,000.

Yezd. See Yazd.

Yiewsley and West Drayton, former. U.D., Middx., Eng.; now inc. in Hillingdon outer bor. Greater London; varied lt. inds.

Yinchwan, t., cap. of Ningsia aut. region, China; on Hwang-ho; ctr. of fertile agr. a.; new lt. inds.; p. (est. 1958) 91,000.

Yingkow (Ying-k'ou), c., Liaoning prov., N.E. China; 32 km upstream from mouth of Liao R.; soyabean prods.; p. (est. 1970) 215,000.

Ynys Môn. See Anglesey.

Yokkaichi, c., spt., S. Honshu, Japan; on Ise Bay, 37 km S. of Nagoya; textiles, petrochemicals, synthetic rubber, porcelain; p. (est. 1971) 231,000.

Yokohama, leading spt., Honshu, Japan; on W. shore of Tokyo Bay; steel, chemicals, cars, oil refining, shipyards; univs.; with Tokyo and Kawasaki forms conurb. of Keihin; p. (est. 1971) 2,342,000.

Yokosuka, spt., Honshu, Japan; S. of Tokyo; holiday resort; thermal power sta.; p. (est. 1971) 359,000.

Yonkers, c., N.Y., USA; on E. bank of Hudson R.; residtl.; lt. inds., textiles; p. (1970) 204,370; part of N.Y. met. a.

Yonne, dep., France; in S.E. of Paris basin, inc. Champagne, Burgundy, Orléanais; drained by R. Yonne; cap. Auxerre; agr., Chablis wines; a. 7,495 km²; p. (1968) 283,376.

Yonne, R., France; major trib. of R. Seine; 288 km long.

York, c., co. t., l. gov. dist., North Yorks., Eng.; on R. Ouse; in central position in Vale of York; anc. part of c. enclosed by walls; minister, cas.; univ.; chocolate, confectionery, rly. wkshps.; p. (est. 1976) 101,900.

York, c., Penn., USA; ctr. of fertile agr. region; varied inds., inc. agr. tools, machin., textiles, metal gds.; p. (1970) 50,008 (c.), 326,482 (met. a.).

York, C., Queensland, Australia; most N. point on mainland of Australia.

York, Vale of, broad lowland, North Yorks., Eng.; between Pennines and N. Yorks. Moors and Yorks. Wolds; drained to Humber by R. Ouse and tribs.; glacial and alluvial soils have required draining; crop farming, wheat, barley, root-crops, associated with fattening of beef cattle; settlement mainly marginal;

ch. t. York; length 96 km, width from 16 km in N. to 48 km in S.

Yorke, penin., S. Australia; separates Spencer G. and G. of St. Vincent; 160 km long, 48 km wide.

Yorkshire, former co., Eng.; formerly divided into 3 separate admin. parts (Ridings) N., E., and W.; now split into 3 non-met. cos., Cleveland, North Yorks., and Humberside and 2 met. cos. West Yorks. and South Yorks.

Yorkshire Moors, hills North Yorks. and Cleveland, Eng.; inc. N. Yorks. Moors, Cleveland hills and Hambleton hills; bounded to N. by Tees valley, S. by vale of Pickering, W. by Swale valley, E. by sea; composed of oolitic limestone; gd. sheep pastures; impt. iron-ore deposits worked in Cleveland hills; max. alt. 454 m.

Yorkshire Wolds, hills, Humberside, Eng.; extend N.E. from Humber and terminate in Flamborough Head; chalk; gd. sheep pasture; average alt. 180 m.

Yorktown, v., Va., USA; scene of surrender by Lord Cornwallis to Washington 1781.

Yosemite National Park, Cal., USA; in Sierra Nevada; contains Yosemite creek and canyon with three famous cataracts.

Yoshkar-Ola, t., Mari ASSR, RSFSR; 128 km N.W. of Kazan; cultural ctr.; wood p.ocessing, food inds.; p. (1970) 166,000.

Youghal, spt., U.D., Cork, R.o.I.; on estuary of the Blackwater; resort; p. (1966) 5,098.

Youngstown, c., Ohio, USA; on Mahoning R.; 91 km N.W. of Pittsburgh; ctr. of one of most impt. iron and steel dists. in USA; heavy engin.; univ.; p. (1970) 139,905 (c.), 533,080 (met. a.).

Yoyang, t., Hunan prov., China; at outlet of Tung Ting L. on bank of R. Yangtze; p. 4,800.

Ypres (Ieper), t., W. Flanders prov., N.W. Belgium; textiles and textile machin.; ctr. of cloth ind. in middle ages; scene of battles 1914–17; p. (1969) 18,447.

Ypsilanti, t., Mich., USA; on Huron R.; residtl.; agr. mkt. mnfs.; univ.; p. (1970) 29,538.

Ystwyth, R., Dyfed, Wales; flows 40 km to join R. Rheidol at Aberystwyth.

Yuan, R., N.W. Hunan prov., China; flows into Tung Ting L. and Yangtze R.; rapids; 640 km long.

Yucatán, st., S.E. Mexico; limestone lowlands, poor soils; henequen (sisal hemp), chicle (resin from which chewing gum is made); cap. Mérida; a. 61,968 km²; p. (1969) 817,000.

Yugoslavia, Socialist Fed. Rep., S.E. Europe; comprises reps. of Serbia, Croatia, Macedonia, Montenegro, Slovenia, Bosnia, Hercegovina, and aut. regions of Kosovo and Vojvodina; long W. cst. on Adriatic Sea with well-developed limestone karstic topography; hilly interior; climate Mediterranean on cst., continental in interior; distinctive political development after second world war; refused to accept Soviet hegemony; well-developed links with W.; with major attempts to industrialise, based on energy, heavy and consumer inds. less p. engaged in agr.; economic decision-making increasingly freed from central control; developing tourist tr., especially with countries of W. Europe, based on climate and attractive Adriatic littoral, with many sm. Is.; cap. Belgrade; a. 255,698 km²; p. (1971) 21,500,000.

Yukon, R., Canada and Alaska, USA; flows N.W. and W. into Bering Strait; navigable for 1,920 km; 3,200 km long.

Yukon Territory, prov., N.W. Canada; mtnous. (Mt. Logan 6,050 m); gold, silver, lead, zinc; Alaska Highway links with B.C. and Alberta; ch. ts. Dawson. and Whitehorse (cap.); a. 536,327 km²; p. (1976) 21,838.

Yuma, t., Arizona, USA; at confluence of Rs. Gila and Colorado, nr. Mexican bdr.; ctr. of irrigated agr. region; p. (est. 1969) 29,000.

Yumen, c., N.W. Kansu prov., China; leading petroleum ctr.; drilling equipment, precision instruments; on Old Silk Road to Sinkiang; p. (est. 1970) 325,000.

Yunnan, prov., S. China; adjoins Burma; mtnous. a. of minority groups; rice, tobacco, tea, cotton; copper, tin; cap. Kunming; a. 420,466 km²; p. (est. 1968) 23,000,000.

Yuzhno-Sakhalinsk, t., RSFSR; at S. end of Sakhalin I.; paper, lt. inds.; p. (1970) 106,000.

Yvelines, new dep., France; W. of Paris; cap. Versailles; a. 2,271 km²; p. (1968) 853,386.
Yverdon, t., Vaud, Switzerland; typewriters; p. (1969) 20,700.

Z

Zaandam, t., Neth.; industl. dist.; rly. junc.; timber-based inds.; p. (1968) 58,312.
Zabrze, t., Upper Silesia, Katowice, Poland; impt. coal-mng. ctr. with associated heavy inds.; cultural ctr.; p. (1970) 197,200.
Zacapa, t., cap. of Z. prov., Guatemala; mkt. t. at rly. junc.; tobacco tr. and processing; sulphur springs; p. (1964) 30,187.
Zacatecas, st., Mexico; on central plateau at 2,100 m; dry, agr. dist.; sm. mng. ctrs.; a. 72,836 km²; p. (1969) 1,082,000.
Zacatecas, t., cap. of Z. st., Mexico; cath.; ctr. of silver mng., pottery, clothing; p. (1970) 56,829.
Zacatecoluca, t., El Salvador; cigar mkg., hand loom.; coffee, cotton, sugar, vanilla in a.; p. (est. 1968) 15,776.
Zadar (Zara), t., Yugoslavia; spt. on Croatian cst. of Adriatic Sea; formerly Italian (1920–47); Roman remains; cath.; car ferry to Pesaro (Italy); tourism; p. (est. 1965) 31,000.
Zagan (Sagan), t., Zielona Gora, W. Poland (since 1945); on R. Bober; cas.; textiles, paper, lignite mines; p. (1970) 21,500.
Zagazig, t., Egypt; on Nile delta; tr. ctr. of fertile agr. a. producing cotton, grains; cotton mills; p. (est. 1970) 173,300.
Zagorsk, c., RSFSR; 70 km N.E. of Moscow; woodcarving, toy mkg.; site of famous Troitse-Sergiyeva Lavra monastery, converted into museum 1920; p. (est. 1967) 85,000.
Zagreb, c., Yugoslavia; cap. of Croatia; on Sava R.; cath., univ.; tr. fair; many inds., notably petrochemicals based on local petroleum reserves, elec. engin.; airport; second c. of rep.; p. (est. 1969) 565,000.
Zagros, mtns., Iran; inc. Iran's major oilfield; highest peak Zardesh Kuh, 4,551 m.
Zahedan, c., Iran; cap. of Sistan and Baluchistan prov.; airport; terminus of rly. from Pakistan; p. (1967) 79,257.
Zahle, t., Lebanon, S.W. Asia; on slopes of L. mtn.; p. (est. 1964) 57,589.
Zaïre, Rep. of, Central Africa; comprises eight provs. (caps. in brackets): Bas-Zaïre (Matadi), Bandundu (Bandundu), Equateur (Mbandaka), Haut-Zaïre (Kisangani), Kivu (Bukavu), Shaba (Lubumbashi), Kasai Oriental (Mbuji-Mayi), Kasai Occidental (Kananga); lies in vast basin of Zaïre R., mtns. on E. and S. borders; climate equatorial in N., tropical in S.; agr. exp. inc. palm oil, cotton, coffee, but economy based on mng., diamonds (Kasai), cobalt, non-ferrous metals (Shaba), major world producer of copper; radium deposits nr. Lubumbashi; extensive navigation on Zaïre R.; main pt. Matadi on estuary linked by rail to cap. Kinshasa; a. 2,345,457 km²; p. (1971) 22,480,000.
Zaïre, gr. R. of Equatorial Africa; numerous tribs., drains 3,885,000 km²; navigable from sea to Matadi for ocean steamers, from Matadi to Pool Malebo interrupted by rapids and falls, again navigable to Boyoma Falls; proposed power project to be lgst. in Africa; estuary 11–16 km wide; c. 4,800 km long.
Zakinthos (Zante), Ionian I., Greece; cap. Zakinthos (Zante); devastated by earthquake 1953; currants, wine, olives; a. 717 km²; p. (1971) 30,156.
Zakinthos (Zante), t., Zakinthos I., Greece; spt. on E. cst.; agr. tr. and processing; p. (1971) 30,156.
Zakopane, t., Poland; in High Tatra mtns.; base for mountaineering and win.er sports; health resort; tourism; p. (1970) 27,000.
Zalaegerszeg, t., Hungary; in Göcsej dist.; oil refining; mkt. t. for grain and livestock; p. (1968) 32,000.
Zambesi, R., S.E. Africa; flows E. to Moçambique Channel, Indian Oc.; forms frontier between Zambia and Rhodesia; inc. Victoria Falls and Kariba and Cabora Bassa dams; navigable but impeded by rapids; 3,520 km long.

Zambia, rep., Central Africa; member of Commonwealth; tropical climate, modified by alt.; plateau (1,200 m); subsistence agr.; livestock on uplands free from tsetse fly; mng. basis of economy, especially in copperbelt; exp. disrupted by Rhodesian U.D.I.; need to develop alternative routes to cst.; pipeline from Ndola to Dar-es-Salaam; construction of Tan-Zam rly. financed by Chinese aid; cap. Lusaka; a. 752,618 km²; p. (1969) 4,056,995.
Zamboanga, t., Mindanao, Philippines; spt. on Basilian Strait, exp. prod. timber; p. (est. 1968) 176,800 (met. a.).
Zamora, prov., Spain; borders Portugal; drained by R. Duero; cereals, wine, merino sheep; cap. Zamora; a. 10,559 km²; p. (1970) 251,934.
Zamora, t., cap. of Zamora prov., Spain; on R. Duero; cath.; agr. tr. and processing ctr.; developing mnfs.; p. (1970) 49,029.
Zamosc, t., Lublin, Poland; Renaissance planned t. in valley of Lubianka R.; industl., comm. and cultural ctr. for E. part of Lublin prov.; p. (1970) 34,700.
Zanesville, t., Ohio, USA; textiles, pottery, machin.; p. (1970) 33,045.
Zanjan, c., Iran; cap. of Gilan prov.; cotton, woollen gds.; p. (1966) 82,350 (c.); p. (1967) 461,588 (met. a.).
Zanzibar, terr., E. Africa; comprises Is. of Z. and Pemba; joined Tanganyika to form Tanzania (1964); major world source of cloves; coconut and coconut prod. major exp. and basis of processing inds.; cap. Zanzibar; a. 2,642 km²; p. (1969) 369,000.
Zanzibar, spt., Zanzibar I., Tanzania; on W. cst. 35 km from E. Africa; outlet for clove exp., extrepot tr.; former slave mkt.; p. (1967) 68,400.
Zaporozh'ye, t., Ukrainian SSR, USSR; on R. Dnieper, nr. dam and hydroelec. power sta.; metal inds. based on Donets coal and Krivoi Rog iron ore; p. (1970) 658,000.
Zaragoza, prov., Spain; largely barren plain suffering from climatic extremes; a. 17,122 km²; cap. Z.; p. (1970) 760.186.
Zaragoza, cap. Z. prov., Spain; on R. Ebro; 2 caths., univ.; former cap. of Aragon; rly. junc.; comm. ctr.; p. (est. 1969) 387,529.
Zarate, t., Entre Rios, Argentina; paper wks., agr. ctr., meat packing; p. (1960) 52,000.
Zaria, c., N. Nigeria; founded 15th cent., old part surrounded by walls; univ., cotton ctr.; rly. ctr., p. (est. 1971) 200,850.
Zary (Soran), t., Zielona Gora, Poland (since 1945); textiles; p. (1970) 28,400.
Zawiercie, t., Poland; industl. ctr.; coal, iron, textiles, glass; p. (1970) 39,400.
Zdunska Wola, t., Poland; nr. Lodz; textiles, engin.; p. (1970) 29,100.
Zealand. See Sjaelland.
Zeebrugge, spt., Belgium; 14 km N. of Bruges; exp. coal, chemicals; oil refining; linked by canal to Bruges.
Zeeland, prov., Neth.; a. covering part of Scheldt estuary and Is.; low-lying; dairying; cap. Middelburg; a. 1,787 km²; p. (1968) 298,457.
Zeist, t., Utrecht, Neth.; chemicals, toys; p. (1968) 55,950.
Zeitz, t., Halle, E. Germany; textiles, chemicals; p. (est. 1970) 46,736.
Zelenodolsk, t., RSFSR; on R. Volga, 40 km W. of Kazan; rly. junc.; sawmills; p. (est. 1969) 76,000.
Zelten, Libya, N. Africa; oilfield; 320 km S. of Benghazi; pipeline to Mersa al-Brega.
Zenica, t., Yugoslavia; lge. iron and steel wks.; ctr. of Z. basin; rly. junc.; p. (est. 1965) 54,000.
Zeravshan, R., Tadzhik SSR and Usbek SSR, USSR; flows for 736 km before evaporating in desert region N. of Chardzhou.
Zetland. See Shetland.
Zgierz, t., Lodz. prov., central Poland; nr. source of R. Bzura; textiles, chemicals, textile machin.; p. (1970) 42,800.
Zhdanov (Mariupol), spt., S.E. Ukrainian SSR, USSR; on Sea of Azov; metallurgical ctr., chemicals; fishing and fish-processing; p. (1970) 417,000.
Zhitomir, t., Ukrainian SSR, USSR; engin., clothing; route ctr.; p. (1970) 161,000.
Zielona Gora (Grünberg), c., W. Poland (since 1945); in valley surrounded by wooded hills; admin. and industl. ctr., cap. of Z.G. prov.;

textiles, food processing, machin.; viticulture; p. (1970) 73,200.

Zielona Gora, prov., Poland; borders E. Germany; glacial sands, wooded; brown coal deposits; cap. Z.G.; a. 14,514 km²; p. (1970) 882,000.

Ziguinchor, t., Senegal; pt. on R. Casamance; exp. groundnuts; p. (est. 1967) 46,333.

Zilina, t., Slovakia, ČSSR; on R. Vah; paper, fertilisers; p. (1967) 39,000.

Zimbabwe National Park, Rhodesia; site nr. Victoria, Mashonaland, of ruined t. built c. 15th cent. A.D. by a Bantu people; discovered 1868.

Zinder, t., Niger, W. Africa; terminus of trans-Saharan motor route; tr. ctr.; former cap.; second t. of Niger; p. (est. 1969) 32,905.

Zion National Park, Utah, USA; contains Z. canyon; a. 596 km².

Zipaquirá, t., Colombia; 48 km N. of Bogotá; salt mng., chemicals; cattle-rearing a.; p. (est. 1968) 28,812.

Zistersdorf, t., Lower Austria; recently developed oilfields.

Zittau, t., Dresden, E. Germany; on R. Mandau; woollens, linens, machin., cars, chemicals; p. (est. 1970) 43,087.

Zlatoust, t., S.W. RSFSR; in Ural mtns.; metal-lurgical ctr.; steel, chemicals, sawmilling; p. (1970) 181,000.

Zletovo, terr., N.E. Macedonia, Yugoslavia; oil shales, lead, zinc deposits.

Zlin. See Gottwaldov.

Znojmo or Znaim, t., ČSSR; anc. t., cas.; ctr. of fertile agr. dist.; p. (est. 1968) 25,732.

Zomba, t., former cap. of Malawi, 884 m a.s.l. on slopes of Zomba mtn., 67 km N.E. Blantyre; Malawi's univ. t.; p. (1966) 19,616.

Zonguldak, t., Turkey; spt. on Black Sea; coal-mng. a.; p. (1965) 60,865.

Zorita De Los Canos, Guadalajara, Spain; on R. Tagus; nuclear power plant.

Zrenjanin, t., Vojvodina, Yugoslavia; pt. on R. Begej; ctr. of agr. dist.; agr. processing; p. (1971) 59,580.

Zug, smallest can., Switzerland; drained by R.

Reuss; contains part of L. Z.; dairying, fruit; cap. Z.; a. 241 km²; p. (1969) 66,700.

Zug, t., cap. of Zug can., Switzerland; on L. Z.; elec. engin., printing; p. (1969) 23,400.

Zugspitze, mtn., Bavarian Alps, on Bavarian–Austrian bdr.; highest peak in Germany, 2,965 m; connected by rack-and-pinion to Garmisch-Partenkirchen at foot.

Zuider Zee. See IJsselmeer.

Zulia, st., Venezuela; centred on L. Maracaibo, producing 70 per cent of Venezuelan oil; timber reserves; cap. Maracaibo; a. 63,902 km²; p. (est. 1970) 1,342,994.

Zululand, Bantu homeland, Natal, S. Africa; sugar on coastal plain, livestock on interior plateau; cap. Eshowe; a. 27,006 km²; p. (1970) 2,106,774.

Zürich, c., cap. of Z. can, Switzerland; on L. Z. and R. Limmat; cath., univ.; leading world banking ctr.; inds. inc. textiles, paper; p. (est. 1969) 433,500 (c.), 671,500 (met. q.).

Zürich, can., Switzerland; forested and agr. a. stretching N. from L. Z.; inds. at cap. Z. and Winterthur; a. 1,728 km²; p. (1969) 1,100,000.

Zürich, L. Z., Switzerland; drained by R. Limmat; length 40 km.

Zutphen, t., Gelderland, Neth.; on R. IJssel; textiles, paper; Sir Philip Sidney died here 1586; p. (1968) 27,290.

Zuetina, oil pt. (1968), Libya; pipeline links shore storage sta. with offshore berths.

Zweibrücken, t., Rhineland-Palatinate, W. Germany; nr. Saarbrücken; cas.; machin., foot-wear, textiles; p. (est. 1969) 32,914.

Zwickau, c., Karl-Marx-Stadt, E. Germany; on R. Mulde; cas.; coal, motors, machin., textiles; birthplace of Schumann; p. (est. 1969) 127,500.

Zwolle, t., Overijssel, Neth.; canal ctr.; cattle, mkt.; p. (1968) 73,253.

Zyrardow, t., Poland; nr. Warsaw; specialised textile ctr.; p. (1970) 33,200.

Zyryanovsk, t., Kazakh SSR, USSR; lead, zinc; p. (est. 1969) 56,090.

THE WORLD'S LARGEST CITIES

New York	(1971) 7,895,000 (c.), (1970) 11,572,000 (met. a.).
Tokyo	(est. 1971) 8,841,000 (c.), 11,403,744 (met. a.).
Shanghai	(est. 1971) 10,820,000.
Mexico City	(1970) 6,874,165 (c.), 8,589,630 (met. a.).
Buenos Aires	(1970) 2,972,453 (c.), 8,352,900 (met. a.).
Peking	(est. 1971) 7,570,000.
London	(1971) 4,234 (City of London), 7,379,014 (met. a.).
Moscow	(1970) 6,942,000 (c.), 7,061,000 (met. a.).
Los Angeles	(1970) 2,781,829 (c.), 6,974,103 (met. a.).
Chicago	(1970) 3,322,855 (c.), 6,892,509 (met. a.).
Bombay	(1971) 5,970,575.
Seoul	(est. 1971) 5,536,000.
Cairo	(est. 1974) 5,384,000.
São Paulo	(1970) 5,186,752.
Philadelphia	(1970) 1,927,863 (c.), 4,777,414 (met. a.).
Djakarta	(1971) 4,576,009.
Tientsin	(est. 1970) 4,280,000.
Rio de Janeiro	(1970) 4,252,009.
Detroit	(1970) 1,429,914 (c.), 4,163,517 (met. a.).
Delhi	(1971) 3,287,883 (c.), 3,647,023 (met. a.).

The cities shown above are ranked according to the size in terms of population of their metropolitan area.

SOME RECENT CHANGES IN PLACE NAMES

Country	Former name	New Name
Algeria	Algiers	El Djezair
	Oran	Ouahran
Belize	British Honduras	Belize
Benin	Dahomey	People's Rep. of Benin
Botswana	Gaberones	Gaborone
Cambodia	Khmer Republic	Democratic Cambodia
	Kompong Som	Sihanoukville
Canada	Port Arthur } Port William }	Thunder Bay
Central African Empire	Central African Rep.	Central African Empire
Chad	Fort Lamy	Ndjamene
Djibouti	Afars and Issas	Djibouti
Equatorial Guinea	Fernando Po	Marcias Nguema
	Annobon	Pagalu Island
	Santa Isabel	Malabo
France	Basses-Alpes	Alpes-de-Haute-Provence
Gambia	Bathurst	Banjul
Guinea-Bissau	Portuguese Guinea	Guinea-Bissau
India	North-East Frontier Agency	Arunachal Pradesh
	Mysore	Karnataka
Indonesia	Makasar	Ujung Pandang
	Port Timor	E. Timor
	Western Irian	Irian Jaya
Laos	Kingdom of Laos	People's Dem. Rep. of Laos
Malaysia	Port Swettenham	Port Kelang
Mocambique	Lourenço Marques	Maputo
Morocco	Casablanca	El-Dar-el-Beida
Nigeria	Mid West st.	Benin st.
	Northern st.	Kaduna st.
Oman	Muscat and Oman	Sultanate of Oman
Pakistan	East Pakistan	Bangladesh
Solomon Is.	Brit. Solomon Is.	Solomon Is.
Turkey	Imbroz I.	Gokceade I.
Uganda	Lake Edward	Lake Idi Amin Dada
	Murchison Falls	Kabelega Falls
United Kingdom	Conway	Conwy
	Portmadoc	Porthmadog
Vietnam	N. Vietnam } S. Vietnam }	Vietnam
	Saigon	Ho Chi-Minh City
West Africa	Bight of Biafra	Bight of Bonny
W. Pacific High Commission	Gilbert and Ellice Is.	Gilbert Is.
	Ellice Is.	Tuvalu Is.
Western Sahara	Spanish Sahara	Western Sahara
Zaire	Congolese Republic	Republic of Zaire
	Congo River	Zaire River
	Katanga	Shaba
	Lake Albert	Lake Mobutu Seso
Zambia	Stanley Falls	Boyoma Falls

METRIC CONVERSION TABLE

Kilometres		Miles	Square Kilometres		Square Miles
16·09	10	6·21	25·90	10	3·86
32·19	20	12·43	51·80	20	7·72
48·28	30	18·64	77·70	30	11·58
64·37	40	24·85	103·60	40	15·44
80·47	50	31·07	129·50	50	19·30
96·56	60	37·28	155·40	60	23·17
112·66	70	43·50	181·30	70	27·03
128·75	80	49·71	207·20	80	30·89
144·84	90	55·92	233·10	90	34·75
160·94	100	62·14	259·00	100	38·61

THE COMMONWEALTH

The British Commonwealth of Nations is a free association of independent member nations and their dependencies. The political status of the member nations listed below is clarified and given legal substance in the *Statute of Westminster* drawn up in 1931, before the Commonwealth was founded, by the United Kingdom, Canada, Australia and New Zealand.

I. MEMBERS OF THE COMMONWEALTH

Original date of member-ship	Country	Land area (km²)	Population[1]
1931	United Kingdom	244,022	55,347,000 (1971) C
	Canada	9,976,185	21,324,000 (1970)
	Australia, Commonwealth of	7,686,884	12,713,000 (1970)
	Antarctic Territory	6,044,086	—
	Christmas Island	161	3,361 (1970)
	Cocos (Keeling) Island	13	611 (1970)
	Norfolk Island	34	1,240 (1970)
	New Zealand	268,676	2,860,475 (1971) C
	Cook Islands	241	24,000 (1970)
	Island Territories (Niue, Tokelau)	502	6,871 (1970) C
	Ross Dependency	414,400	262 (1966) C
1947	India, Republic of	3,268,580	586,060,000 (1974) C
1948	Sri Lanka, Republic of	65,610	12,514,000 (1970)
1957	Ghana, Republic of	238,539	8,545,561 (1970) C
1960	Nigeria, Federal Republic of	923,773	66,174,000 (1970)
1961	Cyprus, Republic of	9,251	633,000 (1970)
	Sierra Leone, Republic of	72,326	2,500,000 (1970)
1962	Jamaica	11,424	1,861,300 (1970)
	Trinidad and Tobago, Republic of	5,128	1,044,000 (1970)
	Uganda, Republic of	235,887	9,764,000 (1970)
1963	Kenya, Republic of	582,646	10,898,000 (1970)
	Malaysia, Federation of	334,110	10,434,034 (1970) C
1964	Malawi, Republic of	117,614	4,530,000 (1970)
	Malta, Republic of	316	326,000 (1970)
	Tanzania, United Republic of	939,706	13,273,000 (1970)
	Zambia, Republic of	752,618	4,295,000 (1970)
1965	Gambia, Republic of	10,368	374,000 (1970)
	Singapore, Republic of	580	2,074,507 (1970)
1966	Barbados	429	238,141 (1970) C
	Botswana, Republic of	574,980	648,000 (1970)
	Guyana, Cooperative Republic of	214,970	721,098 (1970)
	Lesotho	30,344	1,043,000 (1970)
1968	Mauritius	2,038	834,000 (1970)
	Nauru (limited membership)	21	6,664 (1970)
	Swaziland	17,363	451,000 (1970)
1970	Fiji	18,272	513,000 (1970)
	Tonga	699	87,000 (1970)
	Western Samoa	2,841	143,000 (1970)
1972	Bangladesh, Republic of	142,776	65,000,000 (1970)
1973	Bahamas	11,406	168,838 (1970) C
1974	Grenada	344	104,000 (1970)
1975	Papua New Guinea	461,693	2,522,890 (1970)
1976	Seychelles, Republic of	430	52,000 (1970)

[1] Estimates: those countries with recent census figures, indicated by a C.

II. TERRITORIES FOR WHICH THE U.K. IS RESPONSIBLE AND WHICH ARE ADMINISTERED BY A DEPARTMENT WITHIN THE FOREIGN AND COMMONWEALTH OFFICE

(Some of the very small, or practically uninhabited islands, have been omitted)

Territory	Political Status	Land Area km²	Population[1]
Anguilla . . .	Former W.I. Ass. St., under direct Brit. rule since July 1971	91	6,000 (1971)
Antigua	W.I. Ass. St.	440	65,000 (1970)
Bermuda	Colony (internal self-gov.)	54	52,700 (1970) C
British Antarctic Territory .	Colony	1,222,500	—
Belize	Colony (internal self-gov.)	22,962	119,645 (1970) C
British Indian Ocean . . Territories	Colony	75	2,000 (1970)
British Virgin Islands . .	Colony (internal self-gov.)	153	10,500 (1970) C
Brunei	Protected St.	15,765	121,000 (1970)
Cayman Islands . . .	Colony	259	10,652 (1970) C
Dominica	W.I. Ass. St.	751	70,300 (1970) C
Falkland Islands . . .	Colony	12,173	2,000 (1970)
S. Georgia . .	Falkland Islands dependency	3,755	11
S. Sandwich Islands .	Falkland Islands dependency	337	—
Gibraltar	City	6·5	28,964 (1970)
Hong Kong	Colony	1,031	3,950,802 (1971) C
Montserrat	Colony	101	12,302 (1970) C
New Hebrides . . .	Anglo-French Condominium	14,763	86,084 (1971)
Pitcairn Islands . . .	Colony	5	80 (1970)
Rhodesia	Colony (internal self-gov.) [2]	389,329	5,310,000 (1970)
St. Helena . . .	Colony	122	5,000 (1970)
Ascension . . .	St. Helena dependency	88	1,266 (1969)
Tristan da Cunha .	St. Helena dependency	111	280 (1970)
St. Kitts-Nevis . .	W.I. Ass. St.	262	45,457 (1970)
St. Lucia	W.I. Ass. St.	616	101,100 (1970) C
St. Vincent . . .	W.I. Ass. St.	389	96,000 (1970)
Turks & Caicos Islands . .	Colony	404	6,000 (1970)
W. Pac. High Commission Terrs.:			
Solomon Is. . . .	Protectorate	29,875	160,998 (1970) C
Gilbert Is. . . .	Colony	813	50,000 (1975)
Tuvalu Is. . . .		30	7,000 (1975)

[1] Estimates: those territories with recent census figures, indicated by a C.
[2] Illegal declaration of independence 11 November 1965.

LOCAL GOVERNMENT REORGANISATION IN THE UNITED KINGDOM

In the spirit of the reorganisation of local government, the maps (6-7) and gazetteer now incorporate only the newly created local government units. This means that the distinction between the *administrative* counties (*e.g.*, Lancashire), which included all land within the county boundaries but excluded the administratively separate county boroughs (*e.g.*, Bolton), and the *geographical* counties, which were made up of both administrative counties and the county boroughs, has been discontinued.

In making their proposals for local government reform the Redcliffe Maud Commission considered that the division between administrative counties and county boroughs, originally instituted in 1888, created an entirely artificial barrier to the planning and provision of services for city regions (*see* K2). This consideration gave rise to the concept of unitary local authorities, but despite the subsequent amalgamation of boroughs and county districts and the creation of metropolitan counties the old two-tier system was preserved by the Local Government Act 1972.

The new local government structure resulting from these proposals means the disappearance of certain geographical counties (*e.g.*, Pembroke and Rutland), the appearance of completely new counties (*e.g.*, Avon and Gwynedd) and the modification of former counties (*e.g.*, Glamorgan and Yorkshire). Details of the changes are listed below.

Within the gazetteer the population figures for places now stripped of major administrative status (*e.g.*, the former County Borough of Manchester, which now becomes a metropolitan district within the new metropolitan county of Greater Manchester), relate to the former areas of the administrative units.

ENGLAND

Under the Local Government Act 1972, the English counties now number 45. They are divided into 6 metropolitan counties (met. co.) and 39 non-metropolitan counties (non-met. co.).

Metropolitan Counties

Greater Manchester	Tyne and Wear
Merseyside	West Midlands
South Yorkshire	West Yorkshire

Non-Metropolitan Counties

Avon	Isle of Wight
Bedfordshire	Kent
Berkshire	Lancashire
Buckinghamshire	Leicestershire
Cambridgeshire	Lincolnshire
Cheshire	Norfolk
Cleveland	North Yorkshire
Cornwall	Northamptonshire
Cumbria	Northumberland
Derbyshire	Nottinghamshire
Devon	Oxfordshire
Dorset	Salop
Durham	Somerset
East Sussex	Staffordshire
Essex	Suffolk
Gloucestershire	Surrey
Hampshire	Warwickshire
Hereford and Worcester	West Sussex
Hertfordshire	Wiltshire
Humberside	

WALES

The distinction between metropolitan and non-metropolitan counties does not apply to Wales The new Welsh counties created by the 1972 Act now number 8.

Clwyd	Mid Glamorgan
Dyfed	Powys
Gwent	South Glamorgan
Gwynedd	West Glamorgan

NORTHERN IRELAND

Under the Local Government (Boundaries) Act (Northern Ireland) 1971 the 6 counties and one county borough have been replaced by 26 local government districts (l. gov. dist.).

Antrim	Dungannon
Ards	Fermanagh
Armagh	Larne
Ballymena	Limavady
Ballymoney	Lisburn
Banbridge	Londonderry
Belfast	Magherafelt
Carrickfergus	Moyle
Castlereagh	Newry and Mourne
Coleraine	Newtownabbey
Cookstown	North Down
Craigavon	Omagh
Down	Strabane

SCOTLAND

Local government reorganisation in Scotland came fully into force in May 1975 (a year later than the local government reforms in England and Wales and Northern Ireland). The Scottish counties have disappeared and been replaced by nine Regions (Highland, Grampian, Tayside Fife Lothian, Central, Borders, Strathclyde, and Dumfries and Galloway) each sub-divided into districts, together with three Island Areas of Orkney. Shetland and the Western Isles. These changes are reflected in the current edition.

SOME ASPECTS OF THE SOCIAL STRUCTURE
OF THE WORLD ECONOMY

The most fundamental characteristic of the world economy is the gross inequality in economic power and income which exists between different nations and groups of nations. *See* **Section G, Part III.**

One measure of this is shown in the following table. This compares the distribution of population and of income in the world and shows that a tiny proportion of the population receives an overwhelming proportion of its income. The wealth produced by the world's labour is being systematically concentrated into the hands of the powerful within advanced capitalist countries.

Table 1. World population and income distribution in mid–1972.

	% total world population	% total world GNP	GNP per capita (US $)
Underdeveloped countries . .	49·9	14·0	280
petroleum exporters . . .	7·4	2·0	270
higher income	9·6	7·3	740
middle income	7·4	2·0	260
lower income	25·5	2·8	110
Advanced capitalist countries . .	17·9	67·0	3,670
Centrally planned economies . .	32·1	18·9	580

Source: International Bank for Reconstruction and Development (1974). *World Bank Atlas.* Washington.

Table 2 illustrates this concentration even further. It includes similar information for the ten largest countries of the world (by population), the United Kingdom and EEC.

Note: The countries shown in Tables 2–6 are arranged in descending order of population.

Table 2. Population and income of several selected countries for mid–1972.

	% total world population	% total world GNP	GNP per capita (US $)
China	21·3	3·7	170
India	15·2	1·7	110
USSR	6·7	10·4	1,530
USA	5·6	32·3	5,590
Indonesia	3·3	0·3	90
Japan	2·9	6·8	2,320
Brazil	2·7	1·4	530
Bangladesh	2·0	0·1	70
Nigeria	1·9	0·2	130
Pakistan	1·8	0·2	130
UK	1·5	4·0	2 600
EEC	6·9	20·4	2,909

Source: As for Table 1.

The concentration of income and power as shown in the above tables is closely related to social welfare. It is impossible to obtain a complete world picture in this case as statistics for individual countries are not collected on a uniform basis and are not available at all for certain countries. The following tables, however, do produce an interesting picture.

Table 3. Indicators of health and welfare for 1970.

	Expectation of life at birth (years)	Infant mortality rate per thousand	Inhabitants per physician	Inhabitants per hospital bed
India . .	52·6	140·2	4,820	2,022
USSR . .	69·5	24·4	420	91
USA . .	70·6	19·8	634	127
Indonesia .	47·0	137·0	26,069	1,388
Japan . .	72·2	13·1	890	79
Brazil .	—	—	2,067	269
UK . .	71·9	18·5	806	105
Ethiopia .	43·0	155·0	73,973	3,011
Colombia .	59·8	80·6	2,161	446
Australia .	70·8	17·9	777	84
Uganda . .	46·5	120·0	9,204	641
Iraq . .	51·6	104·0	3,266	517
Cuba . .	71·7	40·0	—	218

Source: United Nations (1975). *Compilation of development indicators for 1970.* Paris.

Table 4. Indicators of nutrition and education for 1970.

	Calorie consumption per capita per day	Protein consumption per capita per day	Literate as % of total p.	School enrolment as % age group 6–11
India . .	2,060	52·6	33·3	—
USSR . .	3,280	101·0	—	—
USA . .	3,270	97·3	99·0	99·1
Indonesia .	1,920	42·8	56·6	52·4
Japan . .	2,470	76·2	99·3	100
Brazil . .	2,600	63·8	67·0	65·7
UK . .	3,140	90·2	99·5	99·9
Ethiopia . .	2,150	68·6	—	10·0
Colombia .	2,250	50·8	73·4	57·0
Australia . .	3,050	101·0	99·5	102·4
Uganda . .	2,230	55·3	36·5	49·5
Iraq . .	2,250	62·4	28·8	53·6
Cuba . .	2,500	62·8	—	107·5

Source: As for Table 3.

Table 5. Mass media and communications for 1970

	Passenger cars per 1,000 p.	Telephones per 100,000 p.	Televisions per 1,000 p.
India	1·1	217	0
USSR	—	4,531	143
USA	433·6	58,677	413
Indonesia	2·1	228	0·8
Japan	84·1	25,239	217
Brazil	24·4	2,102	64
UK	215·7	27,006	294
Ethiopia	1·5	185	0·3
Colombia	10·8	3,665	37
Australia	310·6	31,174	227
Uganda	3·0	306	1
Iraq	7·1	1,271	37
Cuba	8·4	3,133	71

Source: As for Table 3.

Table 6. Indicators of political performance for 1970.

	Voters as % of electorate	No. of political riots 1948–67	Defence expenditure as % of GNP (1972)
India	53·1	558	3·0
USSR	99·9	44	9·6 (est.)
USA	58·7	683	7·2
Indonesia	—	82	9·6 (est.)
Japan	71·1	159	0·9
Brazil	79·6	95	42·9
UK	77·1	82	4·6
Ethiopia	88·4	16	—
Colombia	36·9	125	—
Australia	95·7	3	3·6
Uganda	66·0	104	—
Iraq	—	97	8·8
Cuba	40·0	51	7·1 (est.)

Note: Egypt spends 20·2% of GNP on defence, Israel 18·2%, Jordan 17·4%, Syria 11·5% and Korea (North) 15·8%. Much of this money is spent on arms produced in the advanced countries and it provides a profitable outlet for their industries.

Sources: US Department of Commerce (1974). *Statistical abstract of the United States* 1974. Washington, D.C.

Taylor C. L. and M. C. Hudson (1972). *World Handbook of political and social indicators* 2nd ed. Yale University Press.

GENERAL
INFORMATION

Some three thousand entries, including a number of scientific terms and explanations. Cross references direct the reader to fuller information elsewhere in the book. A list of Nobel prize winners and of symbols for correcting proofs will be found at the end of the section.

MEASUREMENTS ARE GIVEN IN METRIC UNITS

Abbreviations

mm	= millimetre	m^2	= square metre
cm	= centimetre	km^2	= square kilometre
m	= metre	ha	= hectare
km	= kilometre	m^3	= cubic metre
km/h	= kilometres per hour	s	= second
g	= gramme	min	= minute
kg	= kilogramme	h	= hour
tonne	= metric ton		

Equivalents

Length

		Reciprocal
1 cm	= 0·394 in	2·540
1 m	= 1·094 yd	0·914
1 km	= 0·621 mile	1·609

Area

1 m^2	= 1·196 yd^2	0·836
1 km^2	= 0·386 $mile^2$	2·590
1 hectare	= 2·471 acres	0·405

Volume

1 m^3	= 1·308 yd^3	0·765
1 litre	= 0·220 gallon	4·546

Mass

1 kg	= 2·205 lb	0·454
1 tonne	= 0·984 ton	1·016

Temperature

$$C = (F - 32) \div 1·8$$
$$F = (1·8 \times C) + 32$$

See also **Metric Equivalents, N8.**

L15

nate, plentifully covered with voluptuous sculpture on which draperies float rather than hang, with twisted and spiral instead of plain or fluted columns, and unnecessary windows or recesses added for ornament rather than use; (c) its emphasis on the whole at the expense of the parts such that a building's sculpture merges into its architecture and both into its painting (Baroque paintings are as closely knit as a jigsaw puzzle so that one cannot isolate individual figures as would be possible in a Renaissance one). Baroque architecture owing to its origin is found mainly in the Catholic countries; Italy, France, Austria, Bavaria, e.g., the Barberini Palace, Rome, designed by its greatest exponent Bernini and others; the Church of the Invalides, Paris. Baroque artists include Caravaggio, Guido Reni, Murillo and Rubens, the greatest Northern Baroque painter. The Baroque style merges gradually into Rococo (q.v.).

Barque, a small sailing vessel with three or four masts. A three-masted barque has fore- and mainmasts square-rigged, the mizzenmast fore- and aft-rigged.

Barrow is an ancient artificial mound of earth or stone raised over the site of a burial. In Britain barrows were built from 2500 B.C. until the late Saxon period, but the Egyptian are the earliest barrows known, the great pyramids being a spectacular development of the custom of ceremonial burial. Silbury Hill, south of Avebury, is the biggest artificial mound in Europe, 512 m in circuit at the base, 96 m at top, and 41 m high.

Bartholomew, Massacre of St., occurred in Paris on the night of 24 August 1572, when over two thousand Huguenots were massacred by order of the Catholic French Court.

Baryons, the group of heavier subatomic particles which includes the proton, neutron, lambda and omega-minus particles (and their corresponding anti-particles, called anti-baryons). Baryons interact by means of all the known forces of nature (strong, weak, electromagnetic and gravitational). However, in any closed system the total baryon number (i.e., the number of baryons minus the number of anti-baryons) is constant. This means that the proton, being the lightest known baryon, must be stable against spontaneous decay. Unlike the lighter leptons (q.v.), baryons are now thought to have internal structure reflecting the fact that they are composed of quarks (q.v.). See **F15.**

Basalt Rocks are fine-grained, dark coloured, of igneous origin and occur either as lava flows as in Mull and Staffa, or as intrusive sheets, like the Edinburgh Castle Rock and Salisbury Crags. One of the most noted examples of columnar basalt is that of the Giant's Causeway in Ireland.

Basanite, a smooth black siliceous mineral, or flinty jasper; a crypto-crystalline quartz used as a touchstone for testing the purity of gold, etc., by means of the mark left after rubbing the metal with it. Sometimes styled the Lydian stone.

Base, a substance having a tendency to accept a proton (H+). This is a wide definition and covers unconventional types of compounds. In aqueous solution bases dissolve with formation of hydroxyl ions, and will neutralise an acid to form a salt. In non-aqueous solvents, like liquid ammonia or hydrogen fluoride, compounds classically regarded as salts can be bases, e.g., sodium fluoride is a base in hydrogen fluoride solution. See **F25.**

Basilisk, is a lizard of aquatic habits, with an elevated crest (which it can erect or depress at will) down the centre of its back.

Basques, people of N. Spain and S.W. France, oldest surviving racial group in Europe, who have preserved their ancient language which is unrelated to any other tongue.

Bas-Relief ("low relief "), a term used in sculpture to denote a class of sculptures the figures of which are only slightly raised from the surface of the stone or clay upon which the design is wrought.

Bastille, a castle or fortress in Paris, built in the 14th cent., and used as a state prison, especially for political offenders. Its bad repute as an instrument of despotism excited the hatred of the populace, who stormed and demolished it

on 14 July 1789, at the beginning of the Revolution.

Bastinado, an oriental punishment, by beating with a pliable cane on the soles of the feet.

Bats. These mammals fly by means of a membrane stretched between each of the long fingers of the hand and between the fifth finger and the body. Another membrane stretches between the legs and the tail. Most British bats, including the pipistrelle, long-eared bats, noctules, belong to the family Vespertilionidae (with the exception of the horseshoe bats which belong to the family Rhinolophidae). These all feed on insects which they catch on the wing. The problem of how bats can detect their insect prey and avoid obstacles when flying in total darkness has interested zoologists for a very long time. The problem was solved with the advent of sensitive ultrasonic recording devices. Blindness does not affect this ability but deafness leaves bats comparatively helpless. One of the most interesting types of bat is the fishing bat (Noctilio) found in central America, which can detect fish by means of the ripples they make on the water surface, receiving echoes from such ripples. See also **Ultrasonics.**

Bath, Order of the, the Britain's second oldest order of knighthood. Exclusive to men since its institution by Henry IV in 1399, women became eligible for admission to the order in 1971. The order has three grades: Knight Grand Cross (G.C.B.), Knight Commander (K.C.B.), and Companion (C.B.). Women members of the order are known as Dame Grand Cross, Dame Commander and Companion.

Battery, Electric, the common term for an electric cell but really meaning a combination of two or more cells. A cell is a device for converting stored chemical energy into electricity which can then be used for heat, light, traction, or any desired purpose. A primary cell will do this until the chemical action is completed and the cell is then useless. In a secondary cell, the chemical actions are reversible and the cell can be returned to its initial condition and used again. This is done by passing an electric current through—a process called recharging. A common primary cell is the Leclanché dry cell used in torches. This works by the action of sal-ammoniac on electrodes made of zinc and carbon. About a century after it came into common use it is still the chief source of power for portable equipment in armed forces. A common secondary cell is the lead and sulphuric acid accumulator used in cars. Many other types of cell are known and some are under development because the demands of space travel, medicine, warfare, etc., call for batteries of lighter weight, greater reliability, or special properties. See **Fuel Cell, Energy Conversion.**

Bauhaus, a German institution for the training of architects, artists and industrial designers founded in 1919 at Weimar by Walter Gropius, (d. 1969). It was closed by Hitler in 1933 and re-opened at Chicago. The Bauhaus doctrine held that there should be no separation between architecture and the fine and applied arts; that art, science and technology should co-operate to create " the compositely inseparable work of art, the great building ". Thus it was an organisation with a social purpose. The original institution, at the instigation of Gropius, included on its teaching staff not only architects and technicians but also such noted artists as Paul Klee and Wassily Kandinsky.

Bauxite, the chief ore of aluminium. Chemically it is aluminium oxide. Aluminium metal is made industrially by electrolysing purified bauxite dissolved in fused cryolite. Chief producing areas: Jamaica, Australia, Surinam, USSR, Guyana, France, Greece, Guinea, USA, Hungary, Yugoslavia.

Bayeux Tapestry, a famous tapestry representing the conquest of England by William the Conqueror. It is embroidered on a band of linen 70 m long and 51 cm wide in blue, green, red and yellow, divided into 72 scenes ranging over the whole story of the conquest. The accepted view is that the tapestry was commissioned for Bayeux Cathedral, but a new interpretation is that it is an Anglo–Norman secular work of art, much influenced by the contemporary chansons de geste (songs of deeds), executed by

English embroiderers for a Norman patron. A representation can be seen in the Victoria and Albert Museum in London.

Beagle, a small hound that tracks by scent, and formerly used for hare hunting.

Bears belong to the Ursidae family of the Carnivora. They are plantigrade mammals, walking (like man) on the soles of their feet. Found in most parts of the world except Australia. The common Brown Bear was once spread over the whole of Europe; it became extinct in England about the 11th cent.; 2–2·5 m in length, and stands 1 m or more at the shoulder. The Grizzly Bear of N. America is larger, and the coat is shorter and greyer. The Polar Bear is remarkable in having a white coat all the year round; it spends much time in water, and unlike other bears is entirely carnivorous. Bear-baiting was made illegal in England in 1835.

Beaufort Scale of wind force is used to specify numerically the strength of the wind. Since the introduction of anemometers to measure the actual velocity, equivalent values of the ranges in miles per hour at a standard height in the open have been assigned to the Beaufort numbers. *See* Section N.

Beaver, a genus of mammals of the Rodentia order, with short, scaly ears, webbed hind feet, and a long broad scaly tail. They grow up to 1·2 m long, and live in communities, constructing dams and lodges where they breed. A campaign was launched in 1977 to bring back beavers to Britain where they have been extinct for several hundred years after being mercilessly hunted for their valuable pelt.

Bedlam (a corruption of Bethlehem) was a priory in Bishopsgate, afterwards converted into a hospital for lunatics. The asylum was transferred to St. George's Fields, Lambeth, in 1815. The term "bedlamite" came to be applied to any person behaving like a madman.

Beech, a deciduous tree belonging to the genus *Fagus* of some eight or nine species found in north temperate regions. The common beech, *F. sylvatica,* is believed to be native to Britain and is one of our finest trees, with massive trunk, long, pointed winter buds, and smooth, grey bark. There is little undergrowth under its dense shade. It is shorter-lived than the oak, taking about 200 years to reach full size and then declining. The timber of beech has a variety of uses, *e.g.,* spoons, handles, tools, and chairs.

Bee-eater, name of a family of brilliantly coloured birds closely related to the rollers and kingfishers inhabiting the tropical and sub-tropical parts of Africa, Asia and Europe. The European species successfully nested in Britain for the first time in 1955 and a pair nested in Alderney in 1956. With their long curved beaks they catch insects on the wing, especially bees and butterflies, and lay their eggs in dark nest tunnels.

Beefeater. *See* Yeomen of the Guard.

Beeswax, the secretion of the bee, used for the formation of the cells or honey-comb of the hive; when melted it is what is commercially known as yellow wax, white wax being made by bleaching. Being impervious to water, it acts as a good resistant and is an article of much utility.

Beetles (Coleoptera) constitute one of the biggest orders of insects, numbering over 200,000 species. There are two pairs of wings; the hind pair are used for flight, while the front pair are hardened to form a pair of protective covers (elytra). Some beetles have lost the power of flight and then the elytra are joined together.

Bel and the Dragon is the title of certain supplementary chapters to the "Book of Daniel" of an apocryphal character. First appeared in the Septuagint, but the Jewish Church did not accept it as inspired. In 1546 the Council of Trent declared it to be canonical.

Bell, a hollow body of metal used for making sounds. Bells are usually made from bell-metal, an alloy of copper and tin. Small bells used for interior functions are often made of silver, gold or brass. Ordinary hand-bells are of brass. From the 7th cent. large bells have been used in England in cathedrals, churches and monasteries. The greatest bell in the world is the "King of Bells" in the Kremlin at Moscow which weighs about 198 tonnes, is

627 cm high and 691 cm in diameter. It was cast in 1733 but cracked in the furnace (the broken part weighed 11 tonnes) and is now preserved as a national treasure. Other large bells in Russia include the 171 tonne one at Krasnogvardersk, near Leningrad, and the one of 110 tonnes at Moscow. The Great Bell (Great Paul) at St. Paul's, cast in 1881, weighs nearly 17 tonnes and is the largest in the United Kingdom. Other gigantic bells are the Great Bell at Peking (53 tonnes); Nanking (22 tonnes); Cologne Cathedral (25 tonnes); Big Ben, Westminster (over 13 tonnes); Great Peter, York Minster (10 tonnes). The Curfew Bell is rung in some parts of England to this day, notably at Ripon. The number of changes that can be rung on a peal of bells is the *factorial* of the number of bells. Thus four bells allow 24 and eight bells 40,320.

Belladonna or Deadly Nightshade (*Atropa belladonna*) a well-known poisonous wild plant found in Southern Europe and Western Asia. The alkaloid atropine it contains is valuable in medicine, although a large dose is poisonous.

Bell, Book, and Candle. To curse by "bell book, and candle" was a form of excommunication in the Roman Church ending with the words: "Close the book, quench the candle, ring the bell".

Benedicite, the canticle in the Book of Common Prayer, known also as "The Song of the Three Holy Children".

Benedictines are monks and nuns of the Benedictine Order who live under the rule of St. Benedict—the monastic code whose influence on the religious and cultural life of the West has been so powerful. The rule is marked by an absence of extravagant asceticism. The greatest of the early Benedictines was Pope Gregory I (590–604) who sent St. Augustine of Canterbury to Anglo-Saxon England. Gregorian plainsong is named after him.

Benzene. An aromatic hydrocarbon obtained from coal tar and some petroleum fractions. It is a volatile inflammable liquid with a characteristic smell. The molecule consists of a flat ring of six carbon atoms, each bound to one hydrogen atom. Benzene is the parent member of many aromatic organic compounds and is widely used in industry to synthesise intermediates for fibres, dyestuffs, explosives and pharmaceutical chemicals.

Beryl, a mineral, of which the emerald is a grass-green variety. Composed of beryllium and aluminium silicates. The pure mineral is colourless; the colour of most beryl comes from traces of impurities, notably iron and chromium. Otherwise it is yellowish, greenish-yellow, or blue, and is found in veins which traverse granite or gneiss, or embedded in granite, and sometimes in alluvial soil formed from such rocks.

Beryllium. Metallic element, symbol Be. Very similar to aluminium, it is stronger than steel and only one-quarter its weight. It is not very abundant, its main source is the mineral, beryl. Copper containing 2 per cent. beryllium is used for making springs. Because of its special properties the metal is used as a component in spacecraft, missiles and nuclear reactors. This accounts for its recent development on a technical scale. The metal powder is toxic.

Bessemer Process for making steel depends on the forcing of atmospheric air into molten pig iron to burn out the impurities. Ousted by the oxygen converter. *See* Steel.

Betel, the leaf of an Indian climbing plant, of pungent, narcotic properties. It is destructive to the teeth, and reddens the gums and lips.

Bhang, the Indian name for the hemp plant *Cannabis sativa,* the leaves and seed-capsules of which are chewed or smoked. The potent drug which comes from flowers of the female plant is called hashish in Arabia and marihuana in the United States and Mexico. *See* P23(2).

Bible (Greek *biblion* = scroll of paper; pl. *biblia* = writings) includes the Hebrew sacred Scriptures (Old Testament) and those held sacred by the Christians (New Testament). The Old Testament—the prehistoric portion—consists of 39 books, and is divided into three parts: (1) the Law, (2) the Prophets, (3) Miscellaneous Writings. The Old Testament was written in Hebrew except for parts of Ezra and Daniel, which were in Aramaic. It was not until the 9th cent. A.D. that a complete Hebrew text was made. the so-called Massoretic text. Before that the main versions were the Alexandrian Greek translation (Septuagint) made in the 2nd cent. B.C. and St. Jerome's Latin Vulgate of the 4th cent A.D. (It was Jerome who used the Latin word "testament" (formed from *testis* = a witness).) Portions were translated into the Anglo-Saxon in the 8th cent. and the Venerable Bede put the greater part of St. John's gospel into English, but it was not until 1535 that a complete printed English version appeared—the Coverdale Translation. The Authorised Version dates from 1611 in the reign of James I, and its beautiful phraseology has given it a lasting appeal. The Revised Version dates from 1885. *The New English Bible*, with the Apocrypha, was published in 1970. It is a new translation in plain English prose of the earliest Hebrew, Aramaic, and Greek manuscripts. The finding of the Dead Sea Scrolls (since 1947) has added to our knowledge of Scripture.

Biedermeier, style in interior decoration and the decorative arts developed from Empire (*q.v.*). It was created in Vienna *c.* 1815 and the name was derived from a fantasy figure in Viennese writing personifying all that which is sedate and bourgeois. Biedermeier furniture is less austere and grandiose than Empire's predecessors, more intimate and homely. A most important creation is the large circular table on a stem-like foot, which became the centre of family life, around which chairs could be grouped freely, not formally against walls as previously. In Vienna itself the style died out *c.* 1830, but in other Continental countries it survived well into the second half of the 19th cent. Its English equivalent is Early Victorian.

Billion, formerly in English usage a million million; now a thousand million, or 10^9, to conform with American and French usage.

Bill of Rights, or Declaration of Rights, was the document setting forth the conditions upon which the British throne was offered to William and Mary in 1688. This was accepted and ultimately became an Act of Parliament.

Binary Notation, for numbers, is a way of representing numbers using only two digits, 0 and 1. Electronic digital computers handle numbers in this form and many people these days are having to learn it. Many school children find it both easy and fascinating—as did the great philosopher and mathematician Leibniz. The ordinary, or decimal numbers, 0, 1, 2, 3, 4, 5, 6, 7, 8, 9, 10 are written in binary notation as follows: 0, 1, 10, 11, 100, 101, 110, 111, 1000, 1001. 1010. The reader might divide the rules from this. The point is that you "carry 1", *i.e.*, move the digit 1 a place to the left, when you reach 2. In decimal notation you move 1 a place left when you reach 10. In other words, instead of columns for units, tens, hundreds, thousands, etc.. the columns are for units, twos, fours, eights, etc. In binary notation: "1 + = 0 with 1 to carry". Since every digit in binary notation is either 0 or 1 it requires one bit of information to specify a binary digit. See Bit.

Biological Clock. All living organisms undergo cyclical changes in activity of some sort. These are linked to the changes in their environment which are produced by the alternation of night and day, the phases of the moon and the tides, and the cycle of the seasons. These cycles of activity frequently persist if the organism is put into a constant environment in which there appear to be no external clues as to what time or what season it is. A squirrel, for example, wakes up at about the same time each evening even when it is put into constant darkness. It is usual to refer to these activity patterns as being driven by a biological clock inside the organism. But very little is known about how these biological clocks work.

Biological Warfare, is the use for warlike purposes of bacteria, viruses, fungi, or other biological agents. These can be used to spread distress, incapacity, disease or death among the enemy's people or livestock. One of the strange uses to which mankind puts its science is to make naturally infective organisms even more virulent

for military use. This sort of research can be done in many countries; it is much cheaper and easier to hide than nuclear weapons development. Secret attack by biological agents is supposed to be easy and it may affect the populations without damaging buildings or bridges. In 1975 the Biological Weapons Convention, 1972, signed by Britain, the United States and Russia, came into force outlawing germ warfare. Any nation suspecting violation may lodge a complaint with the UN Security Council.

Biosphere, that part of the earth in which life exists—a very thin layer near the surface bounded by regions too hostile for life processes to occur. The upper limit is at about 9,000 m above sea level and the lower limit at about 10,000 m in the deep oceans. Ample supplies of solar energy, liquid water and places where liquid, solid and gas all meet seem to be requirements for a biosphere to exist and for all the biological cycles of water, oxygen, minerals, nitrogen, etc., to function. Whether biospheres exist elsewhere than on earth is a perennially interesting question.

Birch, a genus of deciduous trees including about 40 species and found only in northern regions. Birches native to Britain, and to Europe generally, are of two species—the silver birch. *Betula pendula*, with its graceful, drooping branches and triangular leaves, and the white birch, *Betula pubescens*, which has erect branches and soft oval leaves. Birch timber is an important plywood timber, the bark is used for tanning leather, and wintergreen oil comes from the bark of black birch, *Betula lenta*, a North American species. The birch is not a long-lived tree, few standing for more than a hundred years. The tallest recorded is at Woburn in Bedfordshire, 31 m high.

Birds, or Aves, are, next to mammals, the highest class of animal life. There are two kinds of modern birds—*Carinatae*, possessing keeled breast-bones and having power of flight; *Ratitae*, having raft-like breast-bones, and incapable of flight; and a sub-class of fossil birds, Archaeornithes, including *Archaeopteryx*. Estimates of the total number of birds breeding in the British Isles vary, but there are 229 breeding species. Of these the commonest are wrens, of which there are 10 million breeding pairs, house sparrows, blackbirds and chaffinches with up to 7 million pairs each, robins with 5 million pairs and starlings with 3·5 million pairs.

The wheatear is usually the first of the migratory birds to return, often reaching Britain at the end of February and always before the middle of March; the sand martin is the first of the "early swallows" to return, followed by the house martin. The first cuckoo arrives about the middle of April, and the whinchat, garden warbler, and sedge warbler during the last week in April. The nightjar, spotted flycatcher, and red-backed shrike are not seen until the first week in May. The swift is among the last to return from Africa and the earliest to depart. Bird-nesting is illegal in Britain. *See also* F36(2).

Birds of Paradise, over 40 species of tropical birds inhabiting the dense forests of New Guinea and neighbouring islands. The male birds are remarkable for their brilliant plumage, long tail feathers, and ruffs on wings and neck, which are displayed to advantage during courtship. Related to the Bower Birds of Australia.

Biretta, a four-cornered head-covering worn by ecclesiastics of the Roman Church and varying in colour according to the rank of the wearer. A cardinal's biretta is red, a bishop's purple, a priest's black.

Bise, a keen dry north wind prevalent in Switzerland and South France.

Bishop is a Christian ecclesiastic, a person consecrated for the spiritual government of an area, a diocese or province, to the spiritual oversight of which he has been appointed (diocesan bishops), or to aid a bishop so appointed (suffragan bishops). In the Church of England there are forty-three diocesan bishops, all nominated by the Crown. Two, Canterbury and York, are archbishops having primacy in the respective provinces. The archbishops of Canterbury and York and the bishops of London, Durham and Winchester and twenty-one other diocesan bishops in the order of seniority are spiritual peers, and sit in the House of Lords. The (Disestablished) Church of Ireland has two archbishops and twelve bishops; the (Disestablished) Church of Wales an archbishop and five bishops and the Episcopal Church in Scotland seven bishops. *See also* Cardinal.

Bismuth, metallic element, symbol Bi, in group 5 of the periodic table. Like antimony, its stable form is a grey, brittle, layer structure; electrical conductor. It is readily fusible, melting at 264°C and boiling at about 1420°C. Wood's metal, an alloy with one of the lowest melting points (under 65°C, so that a spoon made of it will melt when placed in a cup of hot tea), contains four parts bismuth, two parts lead, one part tin, one part cadmium.

Bison, a genus of wild cattle, distinguished from the ox by its shorter, wider skull, beard under the chin, high forequarters, and, in winter, a great mane of woolly hair covering head and forequarters. There are two species, the European and the American bison, both now protected in game preserves.

Bit, formerly the word often referred to the metal piece in the mouth of a bridled horse, now more likely to be a technical expression in the mouth of a computer expert. A bit is a unit of information; it is the information that can be conveyed by indicating which of two possibilities obtains. Any object that can be either of two states can therefore store one bit of information. In a technical device, the two states could be the presence or the absence of a magnetic field, or of an electric voltage. Since all numbers can be represented in the binary system (*see* Binary Notation) by a row of digits which are *either* 0 or 1, it takes one bit of information to specify a binary digit. Bit is short for binary digit.

Bittern, a bird of the heron genus, with long, loose plumage on the front and sides of the neck. It is a solitary bird inhabiting marshes, but rare in Britain.

Bivalves, shell-fish whose shell consists of two hinged valves, lying one on each side of the body, such as mussels, oysters and cockles.

Blackbird, or **Merle,** a member of the Thrush family, a familiar song bird in Britain. Male is all-black with orange bill; female is mottled brown with brown bill; the young are spotted brown.

Blackcock and Greyhen (as the female is called) are closely related to the Capercaillies but smaller. They nest on the ground and prefer wooded country to open moors. Found in northern half of northern hemisphere. Polygamous, they perform excited courtship dances; the male is a handsome blue-black bird with white undertail, the female dark brown mottled.

Black Death, the plague which swept across Europe in the years 1348–50, beginning in the ports of Italy, brought in by merchant ships from Black Sea ports. It was the worst scourge man has ever known; at least a quarter of the European population was wiped out in the first epidemic of 1348. It reached England in the winter of that year. The disease was transmitted to man by fleas from black rats, though this was not known at the time, the specific organism being *Bacillus pestis.* The disease continued to ravage Europe in recurrent outbreaks up to the late 17th cent. The epidemic which raged in England in 1665 wiped out whole villages and one-tenth of London's population of 460,000. Samuel Pepys wrote a grim account of it in his *Diary. See also* Labourers, English Statute of.

Black Hole of Calcutta, the name given to the place where a captured British garrison was confined in 1756, during the struggle for India between the French and British. Into a noisome space, about 6 m square, 146 persons were driven and only 23 were found alive the next morning. The authenticity of the story has been called into question, but after sifting the evidence Professor H. H. Dodwell, in the *Cambridge History of the British Empire,* believes it to be substantially true.

Black India. *See* Astronomy, Section F, Part I.

Black-letter, the Old English or Gothic type first used in printing blocks.

Black Power. *See* Section J.

Black Woodpecker (*Dryocopus martius*), a black

bird about the size of a rook, with slightly crested scarlet crown, found in parts of Europe.

Blenny, a group of marine fishes with spiny rays part of the fin running along the back. Several species are found around the British coast.

Blood Groups. *See* Index to Section P.

Bloody Assizes, the assizes conducted in 1685 by George Jeffreys, Lord Chief Justice, at which participants in the Duke of Monmouth's rebellion against King James II were tried. They were marked by relentless cruelty.

Bluebird, a migratory bird of North America deriving its name from its deep blue plumage. It is one of the few song birds of America, and familiar in the woods from early spring to November. In India and Malaya there is the Fairy Blue-bird; the male is black with shiny blue upper parts. Used as the symbol of happiness by Maeterlinck in his play *The Blue Bird.*

Blue Peter, a blue flag with a white square in the centre, is hoisted 24 hours before a ship leaves harbour (the letter P in the alphabet of the International Code of Signals).

Blue Ribbon, a term in general use to denote the highest honour or prize attainable in any field or competition. Thus the Derby is the blue ribbon of the turf. The expression is derived from the highest Order of Knighthood in the gift of the British Crown, the insignia of which is a garter of blue velvet.

Blue Stocking, a term used to describe a learned or literary woman, particularly if pedantic and undomesticated. It is said that the term derives from the Bas-Bleu club of Paris, which was attended by the literary savantes of the 17th cent. In England a similar literary club was formed about 1780, whose members were distinguished by their blue stockings.

" Blue " Sun, Moon, etc., a phenomenon caused by the scattering of sunlight by transparent particles suspended in the atmosphere, the effect being that blue light is transmitted and red light extinguished to direct vision. The dust from the Krakatoa eruption in 1883 and the drifting layer of smoke from the forest fires in Alberta, Canada, in September 1950 gave rise to " blue " moons and suns, phenomena sufficiently rare to be described as occurring " once in a blue moon ". In the cold climatic conditions of the Pamirs and the far north, vegetation is said to look " blue " on account of the rays of high calorific value (red, yellow, green) being absorbed, while only the blue and violet are transmitted. It was Tyndall who first explained the blue colour of the sky.

Boa, a term applied to a family of snakes of large size, some attaining a length of 9 m. They are not poisonous, but kill their prey by crushing —constriction—hence the name " boa constrictor ". They occur both in the Old World and the New, but are more abundant in the latter. Most Boas retain the eggs within the body until young are fully developed, whereas the Pythons almost all lay leather-shelled eggs.

Boar, or **Wild Hog,** an animal largely distributed over the forest regions of Europe, Asia, Africa and South America. It has a longer snout and shorter ears than its descendant the domestic hog, and is provided with tusks. Having to forage for itself, it is a more active and intelligent animal than the pig of the sty, and offers good sport to the hunter.

Boat, an open vessel, propelled by oars or sails, or both. The boats of a ship of war are the launch, barge, pinnace, yawl, cutters, jolly boat and gig; of a merchant vessel, the launch, skiff, jolly boat or yawl, stern boat, quarter-boat and captain's gig. Every ship is compelled to carry adequate, fully provisioned and equipped lifeboats.

Bode's Law, a numerical relationship formulated by Bode in 1772 (though pointed out earlier by J. D. Titius of Wittenberg), which states that the relative mean distances of the planets from the sun are found by adding 4 to each of the terms 0, 3, 6, 12, 24, 48, 96, and dividing each number by 10. The gap between Mars and Jupiter caused Bode to predict the existence of a planet there, which was later confirmed by the discovery of Ceres and other minor planets. The law breaks down however, for Neptune and Pluto.

Boer War lasted from 11 October 1899, when the

Boers invaded Natal, to 31 May 1902, when the Treaty of Vereeniging ended hostilities. At first the operations of the British troops in Cape Colony were unsuccessful and disastrous reverses were sustained. Lord Roberts was then sent out as Commander-in-Chief, with Lord Kitchener as Chief-of-Staff, and from February 1900, when Kimberley was relieved and Cronje was compelled to surrender and Ladysmith and Mafeking were relieved, the struggle was practically over.

Boiling-point is the temperature at which a liquid boils. At that point the pressure of the vapour is equal to the pressure of the atmosphere. Under increased pressure the b.p. rises and under less pressure, as on the top of a mountain, it is lower. At standard atmospheric pressure (760 mm of mercury) the b.p. of water is 100°C; alcohol 78·4°C; ether 35·6°C.

Books, Sizes of. *See* Section N.

Books, Classification of. All libraries are classified to facilitate reference, but the favourite system is the Dewey Decimal System, which divides the whole field of knowledge into ten Main Classes: General Works; Philosophy; Religion; Sociology; Philology; Natural Science; Useful Arts and Applied Science; Fine Arts; Literature; History (including geography and travel and biography). Each of these Main Classes is again subdivided into ten main divisions. As an example: the main class of Sociology receives the number 300. This range 300 to 400 (the next main class) is graduated into tens, and Economics is 330. The range 330 to 340 is again graduated, and the subject of Labour and Capital is 331. This process is carried on by decimals so that 331·2 deals with Remuneration for Work, 331·22 with Wage Scales, and 331·225 with Extra Pay.

Borax (Sodium Pyroborate) is a white, soluble, crystalline salt. It is widely and diversely used, *e.g.*, as a mild antiseptic, in glazing pottery, in soldering, in the making of pyrex glass, as a cleansing agent and sometimes as a food preservative. Borax occurs naturally in the salt lakes of Tibet, where it is called tincal, in California (Borax Lake, Death Valley), and elsewhere.

Bore. In physical geography, an almost vertical wall of water which passes upstream along certain estuaries. Its formation requires special conditions of river flow, incoming high tide, and shape of river channel. It can be spectacular and dangerous on some rivers. In Britain the best known is the Severn bore which can be over a metre high and move at 16–19 km/h. In some parts of Britain the bore is called an eagre.

Boron. A metalloid element, symbol B. There are two forms, one crystalline, the other amorphous. It is not very abundant in nature but occurs in concentrated deposits. It is best known in boric acid, which is used as a mild antiseptic (called boracic acid) and borax (*q.v.*). Boron compounds are essential to some plants, *e.g.*, beans. Used in the preparation of various special-purpose alloys, such as impact resistant steel. Compounds of boron and hydrogen are used as rocket fuels.

Borstal, an institution where young offenders between 15 and 21 on conviction may be sent for detention and reform. Emphasis is placed on vocational training in skilled trades. The Children and Young Persons Act 1969 makes provision for the minimum age to be raised to 17, if and when the Home Secretary makes an order to that effect. The first was opened in 1902 at the village of Borstal, near Rochester in Kent.

Boston Tea Party, an incident which occurred on 17 December 1773, on board some tea-ships in Boston Harbour. High taxation imposed by the British Parliament under George III had caused bitter feelings, and instigated by popular meetings, a party of citizens, disguised as Indians, boarded the tea-ships and threw the tea overboard. This incident was a prelude to the American War of Independence (1775–83).

Bounds Beating, an old Anglo-Saxon custom. The parish clergyman and officials go round the parish boundaries accompanied by boys who beat the boundary stones with long sticks of willow. The ceremony takes place on the Rogation days preceding Ascension Day.

Bourgeoisie, a term used by Marxists to indicate those who do not, like the proletariat, live by the sale of their labour. They include, on the one hand, industrialists and financiers or members of the liberal professions and, on the other, small artisans and shop-keepers who, although their standard of living may not be appreciably higher (and today is often lower) than that of the proletariat, are described as the "petty bourgeoisie". According to the Marxist view of history, the bourgeoisie arose with modern industrialism after it had overthrown the old feudal aristocracy and replaced it as ruling class.

Bow, an instrument for propelling arrows, and, in the days when it was a weapon of war, was usually made of yew or ash, and was about 2 m long, with an arrow *c.* 1 m long. It was the weapon with which Crécy, Poitiers and Agincourt were won. The cross-bow was Italian and was adopted in France, but did not become popular in Britain.

Bow Bells is the peal of the London church of St. Mary-le-Bow, Cheapside, within sound of which one must be born to be entitled to be called a "cockney". Bow Bells had not been heard since 1939, but they once again rang out over the City of London on 20 December 1961.

Bowdlerize, to expurgate a book. Derived from Thomas Bowdler (1754–1825), the editor of the Family Shakespeare, in which "those words and expressions are omitted which cannot with propriety be read aloud in a family". He treated Gibbon's *History of the Decline and Fall of the Roman Empire* in the same way, omitting "all passages of an irreligious and immoral tendency". Such prudery met with ridicule and hence the words "bowdlerism", "bowdlerist", etc.

Bower Bird, native to Australia and New Guinea and related to the Bird of Paradise, though often less striking in appearance. In the mating season the male builds a "bower" of sticks and grasses for courtship displays and as a playground. The Gardener Bower Bird of Papua makes a lawn in front of his bower and adorns it with bright coloured pebbles and flowers which are replaced as they wither. The female builds her nest away from the bower.

Boycott, a term used in connection with a person that the general body of people, or a party or society, refuse to have dealings with. Originally used when Captain Boycott (1832–97) was made the victim of a conspiracy by the Irish Land League which prevented him making any purchases or holding any social intercourse in his district. He had incurred the League's hostility by a number of evictions.

Brass, an exceedingly useful alloy of copper and zinc. Much brass is about two-thirds copper, but different proportions give different properties. It is harder than copper and easily worked. Brass in the Bible (Matt. x, 9) probably refers to bronze.

Breadfruit Tree (*Artocarpus altilis*), a native of the South Sea Islands; the fruits are a brownish green, about the size of a melon, and contain a white pulpy substance which is roasted before being eaten. The tree grows 12 m or more. Captain Bligh's ship *Bounty* was on a voyage to Jamaica carrying a cargo of 1,000 breadfruit trees when the mutiny occurred.

Breeder Reactor, a kind of nuclear reactor (*q.v.*) which besides producing energy by the fission process also produces ("breeds") more nuclear fuel at the same time. A typical reaction is: a neutron induces fission of a U-235 nucleus which breaks up into two medium-sized nuclei and some neutrons; one of the latter then enters a U-238 nucleus turning it into U-239 which then decays radioactively *via* neptunium into plutonium which is useful fuel. There are technical problems in breeder reactors which have delayed their practical use but the "breeding" principle is so valuable that experiments have gone on for many years in, *e.g.*, Scotland and Idaho, and breeder reactors will no doubt increase in importance the more the supply of natural nuclear fuel appears to become depleted. *See also* Nuclear Reactors.

Breviary (Lat. *breviarium* = abridgment), the short prayer-book of the Roman Catholic Church which gives the Divine Office, *i.e.*, the canonical hours or services. The directions for Mass are in the Missal. The modern Roman breviary is a reformed version of the 11th-cent. breviary and was produced by Pope Pius V. in 1568 in response to a decree of the Council of Trent. All Roman Catholic priests are required to recite the whole of the breviary services allotted for each day. *See also* Matins.

Bridges are structures for continuing a road, railway, or canal across a river, valley, ravine, or a road or railway at a lower level. From early times bridges were made of timber, stone, or brick, and it was not until the 19th cent. that wrought- and cast-iron were used. Today the materials mostly used are steel and reinforced concrete. Among the most famous of ancient bridges is that of S. Angelo at Rome, built by Hadrian as the Pons Aelius, A.D. 134. The Rialto bridge at Venice dates from 1588. The Ponte Santa Trinita at Florence, one of the finest Renaissance bridges and deemed the most beautiful in the world, was destroyed by German mines in 1944 but has now been reconstructed just as it was before. The first stone bridge across the Thames was begun in 1176. It had 19 arches and was lined with houses and stood until 1831 when it was replaced by the granite bridge designed by Sir John Rennie which stood until 1972. This has been replaced by a three-span concrete bridge with a six-lane carriageway and two footways. The first cast-iron bridge (recently repaired) was built by Abraham Darby at Coalbrookdale, Salop, in 1779. Telford's Menai suspension bridge (1825) has since been enlarged but the original design has been maintained. Another example of Britain's supremacy in constructional iron-work was Robert Stephenson's tubular bridge across the Menai Straits (1850), the prototype of all modern plate girder railway bridges. Other famous bridges are the Niagara (suspension), Forth railway bridge (cantilever), London Tower bridge (suspension), Tay railway bridge, Victoria Jubilee bridge across the St. Lawrence at Montreal (an open steel structure), Sydney Harbour bridge, Lower Zambesi bridge, Storstrøm bridge in Denmark, Howrah bridge at Calcutta, Volta bridge of Ghana, Auckland Harbour bridge, Verrazano-Narrows bridge spanning New York's harbour from Brooklyn to Staten I., exceeding by 18 m the centre span of San Francisco's Golden Gate bridge, Rio-Niterói bridge in Brazil. Britain has undertaken in recent years the largest bridge building programme for over a century. The bridges include the road suspension bridge across the Firth of Forth, completed 1964, the Severn suspension bridge (from which the design principles for the new bridge across the Bosphorous were taken) and the Tay road bridge, both completed 1966, the Tinsley viaduct, near Sheffield, opened 1968. When the new Humber suspension bridge is completed (1978) it will be the longest single-span bridge in the world (1,410 m).

Bridleway. In English law (sec. 27(6) of the National Parks and Access to the Countryside Act 1949) a highway over which the public have the following, but no other, rights of way, that is to say, a right of way on foot and a right of way on horseback or leading a horse, with or without a right to drive animals of any description along the highway.

Britannia Metal, an alloy of tin, antimony and copper, harder than pure tin, corrosion-resistant, used for teapots, and jugs (often electro-plated).

British Association for the Advancement of Science, The, was founded in 1831 by a group of British scientists under the leadership of Charles Babbage (1792–1871) to stimulate scientific inquiry and promote research in the interest of the nation. Its meetings are held annually in different cities of the United Kingdom. The 1978 meeting will be held at the University of Bath under the presidency of Professor Dorothy Hodgkin.

British Museum, was created by an Act of Parliament in 1753, when the Sir Hans Sloane collection, which the British Government had acquired for £20,000, was added to the Cottonian Library and the Harleian Manuscripts. It was

opened to the public in 1759 at Montagu House-Bloomsbury. The acquisition of the library of George III (known as the King's Library) in 1823 led to the construction of the present building with the new wing (1829), quadrangle (1852), domed reading room (1857), and later additions. The books and the reading room are now part of the British Library (*see* Libraries). The Natural History Department was transferred to South Kensington in the eighties. As a museum it is perhaps the most famous in the world, since it has many priceless collections of sculptures, antiquities, prints and drawings coins and medals. Its treasures include the Elgin Marbles (*q.v.*), the Rosetta Stone (*q.v.*), the Portland Vase (*q.v.*).

British Rail (British Railways). The name under which the railways of Britain were unified on 1 January 1948. Instead of the former four main railway systems six regions were formed: London Midland region (former L.M.S.R.), Western (former G.W.R.), Southern (formerly S.R.), Eastern (southern area of former L.N.E.R.), N.E. region (N.E. of former L.N.E.R.), Scottish region (Scottish system of the former L.M.S.R. and L.N.E.R.). Under the Transport Act 1962 the British Railways Board was set up to manage railway affairs. The most far-reaching change in the modernisation and re-equipment programme since 1955 has been the replacement of steam traction by electric and diesel locomotives. Under the chairmanship of Lord (then Dr.) Richard Beeching the British Railways Board planned a viable railway system by closing uneconomic branch lines, by developing new services on the liner train principle, and by utilising a more limited trunk route system. Under the Transport Act 1968 some railway passenger services are eligible for grants on social grounds, including urban railways and unprofitable rural services. High-speed inter-city passenger services linking the main centres of Gt. Britain came into operation in 1976 and in 1977 a new speed link service was launched to win freight from the roads. The name was changed to British Rail in 1964.

British Standard Time, The British Standard Time Act of 1968 put Britain an hour ahead of Greenwich Mean Time (GMT) throughout the year for an experimental 3 years. This brought Britain into line with countries in Western Europe where Central European Time is observed. In 1970 Parliament called for the restoration of the previous position—BST in the summer months and GMT in the winter months—as from 31 October 1971.

Brocken-spectre or Glory. The series of coloured rings which an observer sees around the shadow of his own head (or an aeroplane in which he is travelling) as cast upon a bank of mist or thin cloud. This effect is produced by reflection and refraction of sunlight in minute water-droplets in the air just as in a rainbow.

Bromine. A non-metal element, symbol Br, member of the halogen family (*q.v.*). It is a red, evil-smelling liquid (Greek *bromos*, a stink). It is an abundant element. In the USA bromide is extracted from sea-water on a large scale. It unites readily with many other elements, the products being termed bromides. Its derivatives with organic compounds are used in synthetic chemistry. Bromoform is a liquid resembling chloroform. Bromides are used in medicine to calm excitement.

Bronze is primarily an alloy of copper and tin, and was one of the earliest alloys known, the Bronze Age in the evolution of tool-using man coming between the Stone Age and the Iron Age. Some modern bronzes contain zinc or lead also, and a trace of phosphorus is present in " phosphor-bronze ".

Bubble Chamber. An instrument used by physicists to reveal the tracks of fast fundamental particles (*e.g.*, those produced in large accelerating machines) in a form suitable for photography; closely related to the Wilson cloud chamber (*q.v.*), but the particles leave trails of small bubbles in a superheated liquid (often liquid hydrogen) instead of droplets of liquid in a supersaturated gas; invented in 1952 by the American physicist, Dr. D. Glaser, Nobel Prizeman, 1960, and developed by Prof.

L. W. Alvarez, Univ. of California, Nobel Prize-man, 1968.

Buckingham Palace, London residence of British sovereigns since 1837. Originally built for the Duke of Buckingham (1703); bought by George III in 1762 and remodelled by Nash 1825–36.

Buddhism. See Section J.

Buntings, name of a group of finches, seed-eating birds, usually found in open country. The Yellowhammer, Reed Bunting, Corn Bunting and Cirl Bunting are resident in Britain; the Snow Bunting (which breeds in small numbers in Scotland) and Lapland Bunting are regular winter visitors, and the Ortolan is among the rare visitors.

Butane, a colourless inflammable gas made of carbon and hydrogen; formula C_4H_{10}. Found in natural gas and made as a by-product of oil refining. Butane, like propane (q.v.), can easily be liquefied and moved safely in cans and tanks. It is thus useful as a " portable gas supply "; also used in internal combustion fuels.

Byzantine Art developed in the eastern part of the Roman empire after Constantine founded the city of Constantinople (A.D. 300). It has many sources—Greek, Syrian, Egyptian and Islamic —and reached its zenith in the reign of Justinian (527–65). The major art form was ecclesiastical architecture, the basic plan of which was Roman—either basilican (symmetrical about an axis) or centralised (symmetrical about a point). Arched construction was developed, and the dome became the most typical feature, although, unlike the Roman dome which was placed on a round apartment, the Byzantine dome was placed on a square one on independent pendentives. Frequently small domes were clustered round a large one as in the case of the great church of Santa Sophia (537), the climax of Byzantine architecture. Usually the churches were small and include those of SS. Sergius and Bacchus, Sta. Irene (in Constantinople), S. Vitale in Ravenna, and the much later and larger St. Mark's in Venice. Byzantine art also took the form of miniatures, enamels, jewels, and textiles, but mosaics, frescos, and icons (q.v.) are its greatest treasures.

C

Cacao, *Theobroma cacao*, is an evergreen tree, from 4–6 m high, growing abundantly in tropical America, West Africa, the West Indies, Sri Lanka, etc., yielding seeds, called cocoa beans, from which cocoa and chocolate are manufactured. The fruit is 17–25 cm long, hard and ridged; inside are the beans, covered with a reddish-brown skin, which are first fermented, then dried. The trees mature at five to eight years and produce two crops a year.

Cactus, a family of flowering plants numbering about a thousand species adapted to living in very dry situations. The stem is usually fleshy, being composed of succulent tissue, remarkably retentive of water; commonly equipped with sharp thorns which deter animals from eating them. The roots are generally very long, tapping soil water over large area; a "prickly pear" cactus may have roots covering a circular area 7 m or more in diameter. The leaves are commonly insignificant or absent, and the stem takes over the photosynthetic leaf function and becomes accordingly flattened to expose greater area to sunlight and air. In some kinds of cactus (e.g., *Echinocactus*) the stem is shaped almost like a sea-urchin.

Cadmium. A metallic element, symbol Cd, chemically similar to zinc and mercury. Used in alloys to lower the melting point, as in Wood's metal with bismuth and tin. Alloyed with copper to make electric cables. Like zinc, it is a protective metal and is used in electroplating. The cadmium-vapour lamp gives a characteristic frequency used in measuring wavelength.

Caesium, also spelt **Cesium**, is an alkali metal element, symbol Cs, in first group of the periodic table. It resembles rubidium and potassium and was discovered by Bunsen and Kirchhoff in 1860. It was the first element whose existence was discovered spectro-scopically. The caesium atom consists of a heavy nucleus surrounded by 55 electrons, 54 of which are arranged in stable orbits, and one of which, known as the valency electron, is in a less stable orbit surrounding them. Used in the construction of photo-electric cells and as an accurate time standard (atomic clock).

Calcium, a silvery-white metallic element, symbol Ca. It melts at 810°C and is very reactive. It was discovered at 810°C by Sir Humphry Davy in 1808, but not until 1898 was it obtained pure, by Moissan. Does not occur as metal in nature, but calcium compounds make up a large part of the earth's crust. Most important calcium sources are marble, limestone, chalk (all three are, chemically, calcium carbonate); dolomite, which is the double carbonate of calcium and magnesium; gypsum, a hydrated calcium sulphate; calcium phosphate and calcium fluoride. Igneous rocks contain much calcium silicate. Calcium compounds are essential to plants and are used in fertilisers. Animals require calcium and phosphorus for bone and teeth formation; deficiency is treated by administration of calcium phosphate. Strontium is chemically similar to calcium, and the radioactive strontium 90 from atomic " fall-out " is therefore easily assimilated by the body.

Calendar, a collection of tables showing the days and months of the year, astronomical recurrences, chronological references, etc. The Julian Calendar, with its leap year, introduced by Julius Caesar, fixed the average length of the year at 365¼ days, which was about 11 minutes too long (the earth completes its orbit in 365 days 5 hours 48 minutes 46 seconds of mean solar time). The cumulative error was rectified by the Gregorian Calendar, introduced in Italy in 1582, whereby century years do not count as leap years unless divisible by 400. This is the rule we now follow. England did not adopt the reformed calendar until 1752, when she found herself 11 days behind the Continent. The Gregorian Calendar did not come into use in Russia until 1918. Old Style and New Style dates are identified as " O.S." and " N.S.".

Calends, the first day of the month in the Roman calendar.

Calorie. Unit of quantity of heat. The " small " or fundamental calorie is the amount of heat required to raise the temperature of 1 gram of water from 14·5 to 15·5 C and is equal to 4·185 joules. This is the gram-calorie used in physics and chemistry. The large Calorie (written with a capital C), commonly used in nutritional connotations, is equal to 1000 small calories and is called the kilogram-calorie.

Calvinism. See Section J.

Calypso, West Indian song in the form of a doggerel lampoon composed spontaneously and sung to a guitar.

Cambridge University had a sufficiently good teaching reputation to attract Oxford students in 1209, when lectures at their own university were suspended. In 1226 it had a Chancellor who was recognised by King and Pope. The first college to be founded was Peterhouse in 1284. The university was reorganised and granted a Charter of Incorporation by an act of Elizabeth in 1571. The colleges with their dates of foundation are Christ's (1505), Churchill (1960), Clare (1326), Clare Hall (1966), Corpus Christi (1352), Darwin (1964), Downing (1800), Emmanuel (1584), Fitzwilliam (1966), Gonville and Caius (1348), Jesus (1496), King's (1441), Magdalene (1542), Pembroke (1347), Peterhouse (1284), Queens' (1448), St. Catharine's (1473), St. Edmund's House (1896), St. John's (1511), Selwyn (1882), Sidney Sussex (1596), Trinity (1546), Trinity Hall (1350), Wolfson (1965). The women's colleges are: Girton (1869), Newnham (1871), New Hall (1954), Hughes Hall (formerly Cambridge T.C.) (1885), and Lucy Cavendish Collegiate Society (1965) (for women research students and other graduates). Women were admitted to degrees (though not allowed to sit for examination) in 1920, and to full membership of the University in 1948. A number of colleges now admit both men and women students.

Camel, a large ruminant quadruped, inhabiting Asia and Africa, where it is largely used as a beast of burden. There are two species—the

Arabian camel or dromedary, with only one hump; and the Bactrian, or double-humped camel. There are no wild dromedaries, and the only wild bactrians occur in the Gobi Desert. The camel is able to go for long periods without water, not, as was formerly believed, because it stored water in its hump, but because of the unique mechanism of its physiology which enables it to conserve water at the expense of not sweating until 40°C is reached.

Campanile, or bell-tower, is separate from but usually adjoining its parent church. The most famous are in Italy. Giotto's tower at Florence, adjoining the cathedral of Santa Maria del Fiore, is architecturally the finest in the world. Others are at Cremona, the loftiest in Italy (110 m) and Pisa (the leaning tower). The magnificent pointed campanile of St. Mark's, Venice, which collapsed in 1902 and has since been rebuilt in its original form, was begun in 902.

Canal, an artificial watercourse used for navigation which changes its level by means of locks. The completion of the Bridgewater Canal in 1761 to take coal from Worsley to Manchester marked the beginning of canal building in industrial Britain. There are over 4,000 km of navigable inland waterways in Great Britain today, c. 3,200 km of which are under the control of the British Waterways Board set up by the Transport Act 1962. The English network is based on the four great estuaries, Mersey, Humber, Severn and Thames. Under the Transport Act 1968, the Board is enabled to maintain an extensive network of amenity waterways. A number of disused canals are being restored to navigation by the Board in conjunction with local authorities and voluntary societies.

Candela unit of luminous intensity, symbol cd. An idea of the value which this unit represents may be gained from the fact that light obtained from a 40 W filament-type electric lamp or bulb is approximately the same as would be given by a point source of luminous intensity 30 cd. See S.I. units, Section N.

Candlemas, an English and Roman Church festival in celebration of the Purification of the Virgin Mary. The date is 2 February.

Canon, a term applied to signify a recognised rule for the guide of conduct in matters legal, ecclesiastical and artistic, or an authoritative ordinance: thus we have Canonical Scriptures, Canon Law, etc. A Canon is also a dignitary of the Church, usually a member of a cathedral chapter in the Anglican communion, or in the Roman Church a member of an order standing between regular monks and secular clergy.

Canonical Hours were seven in number in the Western Church; Matins and Lauds, before dawn; Prime, early morning service; Terce, 9 a.m.; Sext, noon; Nones 3 p.m.; Vespers, 4 p.m.; Compline, bed-time.

Canonisation, the entering of one of the faithful departed on the list of saints of the Roman Catholic Church. The rules governing canonisation were simplified by papal decree in 1969. The forty English martyrs, of whom Edmund Campion was one, executed between 1535 and 1679 and beatified long ago, were canonised in 1970. Beatification, by which a person is called blessed, is usually followed by canonisation, but not necessarily.

Canticles, the name given to the scriptural passages from the Bible sung by the congregation in the various Christian liturgies. They are the Benedicite, Benedictus, Magnificat, Nunc Dimittis.

Capercaillie, the largest of the grouse family, found in the Scottish highlands and the pine forests and mountainous regions of Northern and Central Europe and Asia.

Capet, the family name of the royal house of France, founded by Hugh Capet in 987, with its collateral branches. The main line of the dynasty came to an end in 1328 with the death of Charles IV when the throne passed to the related house of Valois. The direct Valois line ended in 1498 with the death of Charles VIII. The first of the Bourbon line was Henry IV whose descendants ruled France (except during the French Revolution and the Napoleonic era) until 1848.

Capitalism. See Section J.

Capuchins are members of a mendicant order of Franciscans, founded in the 16th cent. with the aim of restoring the primitive and stricter observance of the rule of St. Francis, so called from the capuce or pointed cowl worn by them.

Carat, a term used in assessing the value of gold and precious stones. In connection with gold, it represents the proportion of pure gold contained in any gold alloy, and for this purpose the metal is divided into 24 parts. Thus 24-carat indicates pure gold, and any lesser number of carats shows the proportion of gold contained in the alloy. The carat as a measure of weight is now obsolete, having been replaced by the metric carat of 0·2 grams.

Caravan, a band of travellers or traders journeying together for safety across the Eastern deserts, sometimes numbering many hundreds. There are several allusions to caravans in the Old Testament. The great caravan routes of this period from Egypt to Babylon and from Palestine to Yemen linked up with the Syrian ports and so with western sea commerce. Many wars have been fought in the past over their control.

Carbohydrates. See F26 and Diet, Section P.

Carbon, a non-metallic chemical element which occurs in crystalline form as diamonds and graphite; amorphous forms of carbon include charcoal and soot, while coke consists mainly of elementary carbon. The biochemistry of plants and animals largely hinges upon carbon compounds. The study of carbon compounds is called Organic Chemistry. Carbon 14. A radioactive isotope of carbon, with a half-life c. 6,000 years, used in following the path of compounds and their assimilation in the body. Also used in determination of the age of carbon-containing materials such as trees, fossils and very old documents. See F26 and Radiocarbon Dating.

Carbonari, members of a secret political society originated in Naples, and at one time very numerous. Their chief aim was to free Italy from foreign rule, and they exerted considerable influence in the various revolutionary movements in the first half of the 19th cent. Their name was adopted from the charcoal-burners (carbonari), and their passwords, signs, etc., were all in the phraseology of the fraternity.

Carbon dioxide. Commonest of the oxides of carbon. It is formed when carbon and its compounds are burnt with abundant supply of air, and when carbon compounds are oxidised in the respiration process of animals. The atmosphere contains carbon dioxide to the extent of about three parts in 10,000; this figure remains more or less constant because, while carbon dioxide is always being added by animal respiration and the burning of fuels, such as coal and oil by man, plants are constantly removing it in the process known as photosynthesis (F32) or carbon assimilation.

Carbon monoxide is a colourless gas with no taste or smell. It is formed when coal and coke are burnt with a restricted supply of air; the blue flame to be seen in a coke brazier, for instance, is the flame of carbon monoxide. This gas is very poisonous, forming with the haemoglobin of the blood a compound which is useless for respiration and cherry red in colour, which gives a visible symptom of poisoning by carbon monoxide. With nickel it forms a volatile compound, called nickel carbonyl, and this reaction is the basis of the Mond process for extracting nickel.

Cardinal, one of the chief dignitaries of the Roman Catholic Church who constitute the Pope's council, or Sacred College, and when the papal chair is vacant elect by secret ballot a Pope from among themselves. There are three orders: cardinal bishops, members of the Roman Curia (the central administration of the Church) and bishops of sees near Rome; cardinal deacons, also members of the Curia, holding titular bishoprics; and cardinal priests who exercise pastoral duties over sees removed from Rome, though some are members of the Curia. Their numbers were fixed by Pope Sixtus V in 1586 at 6, 14 and 50 respectively. Both Pope John XXIII and Pope Paul VI increased the number. In 1977 there were 137 cardinals, of whom no more than 120 are entitled to elect a new Pope. Their insignia was trimmed of embellishment by papal decree in 1969 with the abolition of the famous red hat (the galero) and the shoes with buckles. Cardinals must now retire at 80.

Cardinal Virtues, according to Plato these were justice, prudence, temperance, fortitude—*natural* virtues as distinct from the *theological* virtues of the Roman Catholic Church, faith, hope, charity. The phrase "seven cardinal virtues", combining the two, figures in mediaeval literature. *See* Sins, Seven Deadly.

Carmelites, a body of mendicant friars taking their name from Mount Carmel, where the order was first established in the 12th cent. The original rule of the order required absolute poverty, abstinence from meat and a hermit life. The rigidity of the rule of the order was mitigated by Innocent IV. They wear a brown habit with white mantle, hence their name of White Friars. The order of Carmelite nuns was instituted in the 15th cent.

Carolingians, dynasty of Frankish rulers founded in the 7th cent. The family was at its height when represented by Charlemagne. It ruled, with interruptions, until 987 when the Capetian dynasty succeeded.

Carp, a well-known fresh-water fish, found in plenty in most European and Asiatic still waters; reaches a length of about 60 cm and under favourable conditions lives for about 40 years. Familiar British members of the family are the roach, rudd, dace, chub, gudgeon, tench, minnow, barbel, bream and bleak. The goldfish, popular in ornamental ponds, is the domesticated variety of a Far Eastern member of the carp family.

Carthusians, an order of monks founded in 1084 by St. Bruno at the Grande Chartreuse near Grenoble, and introduced into England about a century later. They built the Charterhouse (corruption of Chartreuse) in London in 1371. The chief characteristics of the order are a separate dwelling-house in the precincts of the charterhouse for each monk, and the general assembly in the Church twice in the day and once at night. They wear a white habit, with white scapular and hood. The liqueur *Chartreuse* was invented by the order and is still their secret. For many years they have derived large revenues from its sale. The order of Carthusian nuns was founded in the 12th cent.

Casein, the chief protein in milk and cheese. It is coagulated by the action of rennet or acid. An important class of plastics ("casein plastics") are produced from it, and these plastics are converted into buttons,knitting-needles, etc. 36,000 litres of milk yield about 1 tonne of casein.

Cassowary, a genus of ostrich-like birds which, together with the emu, form a separate order found only in Australasia. All species are black with brightly coloured necks, and with a horny crest on the head. Noted for fleetness.

Castor-oil Plant (*Ricinus communis*), an African shrub now cultivated in most tropical countries. It has broad palmate leaves and bears a spiny fruit containing seeds which when pressed yield the well-known oil.

Cat, the general name for all members of the class *Felidae* of the carnivorous order, from the lion down to the domestic cat. The latter is believed to be descended from the European and African wild cats. Egypt is credited with having been the first country in which the cat was domesticated. *See* Section Z.

Catabolism, Anabolism, are the terms used to describe the two types of metabolic pathway. Catabolic pathways are routes by which large organic molecules are broken up by enzymes into their simpler constituents *e.g.*, starch into glucose. The anabolic pathways are the routes by which complex molecules are synthesised from simple sub-units, *e.g.*, proteins from amino acids.

Catalyst. A substance which speeds up a chemical reaction without being changed itself. Various aluminium and titanium compounds are catalysts in the formation of polythene from ethylene. Palladium catalyses the reaction of hydrogen with oxygen (hence its use in gas lighters). Enzymes in the body hasten the breakdown of carbohydrates and proteins by catalytic action. *See* F27(2).

Cataracts are gigantic waterfalls. The most famous are those of Niagara in North America, the Orinoco in South America, the Victoria Falls on the Zambesi in Africa, the Falls of the Rhine at Schaffhausen, and the Cascade of Gavarni in the Pyrenees.

Catechism, an elementary book of principles in any science or art, but more particularly in religion, in the form of questions and answers. There is a great variety of these, including the Lutheran, prepared by Luther in 1529, Calvin's Geneva (in 1536), and the Anglican, in the Book of Common Prayer.

Caterpillar, the larva of a butterfly or moth, worm-like in its segmented body, with 3 pairs of jointed true legs, often curiously marked and coloured, and frequently more or less hairy.

Cathedral, the chief church of a diocese, so called from its containing a Bishop's seat, or episcopal chair. The town in which it is situated is a cathedral city. Some celebrated cathedrals are St. John Lateran of Rome, Notre Dame of Paris, the cathedrals of Cologne and Milan, St. Paul's in London, Canterbury Cathedral, York Minster, and the cathedrals of Durham, Bristol, Gloucester, Peterborough, Exeter. Liverpool, and Coventry (destroyed by bombs, now rebuilt).

Catholicism. *See* Section J.

Cat's eye, a kind of quartz, much valued as a gem, opalescent, and of various shades.

Cavalier, a name adopted during the troubles of the Civil War to designate the Royalist party; it is also used generally in reference to a knightly, gallant or imperious personage.

Caves, natural hollow places in the earth, frequently found in Carboniferous limestone areas. The underground caves are formed by the action of rainwater carrying carbon dioxide, a dilute acid which slowly attacks the limestone rocks. The main caves in the British Isles are in the Mendips, Derbyshire, Yorkshire, S. Wales and in County Clare. Many British inland caves are thought to have been formed at the end of the Ice Age when there was a rise in the water table. The floods of September 1968 moved masses of débris in some of the British caves, redistributing it in a major way; new routes were blocked and old passages reopened. The scientific study of caves is known as spelaeology.

Cedar, a dark-leaved, cone-bearing, horizontal-branched evergreen tree that grows to a considerable height and girth, the best known species in Britain being the Cedar of Lebanon, which was introduced in the 17th cent.

Celluloid, one of the first synthetic thermoplastic materials, discovered by Alexander Parkes in 1865 when he was attempting to produce synthetic horn. It is made by treating cellulose nitrate with camphor and alcohol. Photographic film is made of a similar, but less-inflammable material, formed by the use of cellulose acetate instead of the nitrate.

Cellulose, a carbohydrate, and a constituent of nearly all plants. Cellulose occurs in an almost pure state in the fibres of linen (flax), absorbent cotton, jute, and filter-paper (used in laboratories).

Celsius was an 18th cent. Swedish scientist (B13) after whom the modern Celsius temperature scale is named. Since 1954, °C stands for "degree Celsius" instead of "degree Centigrade" but this is only a change in name. Both symbols refer to the temperature scale which calls the melting point of ice 0°C and the boiling point of water at one atmosphere pressure 100°C. *See* Absolute Temperature.

Celts, an ancient race found late in the third millennium B.C. in S.W. Germany, united by a common language and culture, who spread westward into Spain, northward into Britain, eastward to the Black Sea, reaching Galicia in Asia Minor. The "La Tène" iron-age Celts invaded Britain *c.* 250 B.C. After Britain was conquered by the Romans and invaded by the Angles and Saxons there remained as areas of Celtic speech only Wales (Brythonic speakers), Ireland, Scotland, Isle of Man (Gaelic speakers). The late Celtic period in Britain produced a distinctive Christian art (*e.g.*, the Lindisfarne Gospel *c.* 700, and the Irish Book of Kells, dating from about the same time). Surviving Celtic languages are Welsh, Irish, Breton and Scots Gaelic; Cornish survived until the 18th cent. and Manx Gaelic is on the point of extinction.

Centrifuge, a machine which produces large accelerations by utilising the radial force caused by rotating a body about a fixed centre. Centrifuges have found extensive application in modern science. They can be used for the separation of one size of particle from another in biochemistry or in the training of astronauts where the accelerations occurring during rocket lift-off can be simulated in a centrifuge on the ground.

Ceramics, are substances in which a combination of one or more metals with oxygen confers special and valuable properties. These include hardness, and resistance to heat and chemicals. Ceramic comes from the Greek word for pottery, and pottery materials of mud and clay were probably the first man-made ceramics. Nowadays the range is enormous and growing; apart from all the pottery materials, there are firebricks, gems, glasses, concretes, nuclear reactor fuel elements, special materials for electronic devices, coloured pigments, electrical insulators, abrasives, and many other things. The scientific study of ceramics is part of materials science (*see* **Materials Science**). The need to design ceramic objects has inspired great art, and the production of ceramics is a major industry. *See also* **China Marks, Section U.**

Cerium, a scarce metallic element discovered by Berzelius in 1803. A mixture of cerium and thorium nitrates is used in the manufacture of gas mantles, which owe their incandescent property to the deposit of cerium and thorium oxide with which they are coated.

Chain reaction. *See* **F13(1).**

Chalcedony, a mixture of crystalline silica and amorphous hydrated silica, *i.e.*, of quartz and opal. It has a waxy lustre, and is much used by jewellers for necklaces, bracelets, etc. Commonly it is white or creamy. Its bright orange-red variety is called carnelian; its brown variety, sard. Chrysoprase, plasma, bloodstone are varieties which are respectively pale apple-green, dark leek-green, green with red spots.

Chalk, a white limestone, calcium carbonate, found in the Upper Cretaceous deposits (formed from the shells of minute marine organisms). As chalk is porous, few streams form on its surface and consequently it is eroded slowly, although generally speaking it is a soft rock. Its juxtaposition with soft impervious clay in some areas results in its forming steep ridges known as escarpments, *e.g.*, N. and S. Downs and Chilterns. In contrast to the dry upland surfaces of chalk, lower levels are frequently saturated with water which emerges as springs.

Chamberlain, Lord, the senior officer of The Royal Household who is responsible for all ceremonial within the palace (levées, courts, garden parties, entertainment of foreign royalties and heads of state) but not the coronation or state opening of parliament. He is also in charge of appointments to The Royal Household. His office as censor of plays was abolished in 1968.

Chamberlain, Lord Great, one of the great officers of state whose duties are now mainly ceremonial. He attends the monarch at the state opening of parliament and at the coronation and is custodian of the Palace of Westminster (Houses of Parliament). The office is hereditary, dating from Norman times, and is held for one reign in turn by the descendants of the De Veres, Earls of Oxford. The present Lord Great Chamberlain is the Marquess of Cholmondeley.

Chameleon, a family of lizards with numerous species. Their ability to change colour is well known, but exaggerated, and is due to the movement of pigment cells beneath the skin. They are slow in movement, arboreal, and mainly insectivorous. Found in Africa, India, Sri Lanka, Madagascar and Arabia.

Chamois, a species of antelope, native of Western Europe and Asia. About the size of a goat, it lives in mountainous regions, and possesses wonderful leaping power, so that it is very difficult to capture. Its flesh is much esteemed, and from its skin chamois leather is made, although today sheep and goat skins are usually substituted. The mating season is October–November and the fawns are born in May or June. Live to be 20–25 years old.

Channel Tunnel, a scheme to bore a tunnel through 32–48 km of chalk under the sea between Dover and Calais has been a subject for discussion ever since Albert Mathieu first conceived the idea as a practical possibility in 1802. In the 1830s proposals for a bridge were made. Investigations have been undertaken from time to time, but on each occasion military doubts or cost, reinforced by the insular feelings of the English, caused the governments of the day to withhold support. However, in 1964 the British and French governments decided in principle to go ahead with a rail tunnel to link the British and European railway systems. The tunnel would provide ferry train services for road vehicles in addition to through rail services and would run from Cheriton near Folkestone, and from Sangatte, near Calais. Because of changes in the economic situation the British Government in 1975 decided to withdraw from the scheme, but, as with excavations made last century, the plans will be preserved in case the project is revived.

Chapel Royal, the church dedicated to the use of the Sovereign and Court. There are, among others, chapels royal at St. James's Palace, Buckingham Palace, Windsor, Hampton Court, the Tower, and Holyrood. *See also* **E4(2).**

Characterology. *See* **Section J.**

Charcoal, a term applied to wood that has been subjected to a process of slow smothered combustion. More generally it refers to the carbonaceous remains of vegetable, animal, or combustible mineral substances submitted to a similar process. Charcoal from special woods (in particular buckthorn) is used in making gunpowder. Bone charcoal finds use in sugar refining, as it removes dark colouring matter present in the crude syrup.

Chasuble, a sleeveless vestment worn by ecclesiastics over the alb during the celebration of Mass. It is supposed to symbolise the seamless coat of Christ.

Cheese, an article of food made from the curd of milk, which is separated from the whey and pressed in moulds and gradually dried. There are about 500 varieties differing with method of preparation and quality of milk. They used to be made in the regions after which they are named but nowadays many of them are mass-produced, *e.g.*, Cheddar is made not only in all parts of Britain but in Canada, New Zealand, Australia, Holland and the USA. Cheeses may be divided into 3 main classes: (1) soft, *e.g.*, Camembert, Cambridge, l'Evêque; (2) blue-veined, *e.g.*, Stilton, Gorgonzola, Roquefort (made from ewe's milk), (3) hard-pressed, *e.g.*, Cheddar, Cheshire, Gruyère, Parmesan, Gouda.

Cheetah or "hunting leopard", the large spotted cat of Africa and Southern Asia whose ability to run at 72 km/h for 450 m makes it the swiftest four-footed animal alive.

Chemical Warfare. This term is usually restricted to mean the use in war of anti-personnel gases, aerosols and smokes, although explosives, napalm, herbicides and defoliants are also chemical agents that are used in war. Anti-personnel chemical weapons may be classified as (a) vesicants (agents which produce skin blisters, *e.g.*, mustard gas); (b) lacrimators (*e.g.*, the original tear gas, CN, and its British-developed successor CS, now preferred for riot control); (c) sternutators (sneeze and vomiting agents, usually arsenic compounds, *e.g.*, Adamsite DM); (d) nerve gases (extremely lethal agents which incapacitate the nervous system, *e.g.*, the G-agents developed during the second world war and the more powerful V-agents developed subsequently); (e) lung irritants (*e.g.*, phosgene and chlorine). Most of these chemicals can be lethal at sufficiently high concentrations and for this reason it is doubtful whether there exists the "humane" chemical agent which instantly incapacitates but leaves no long-term side effects.

The first occasion when poison gas was used on a large scale was in the first world war: more than 100,000 fatalities resulted from the use of principally chlorine, phosgene and mustard gas. Worldwide revulsion at the hideous effects of chemical weapons and their potential as indiscriminate weapons of mass destruction resulted in the Geneva Protocol of 1925 which prohibited the use both of chemical and bacteriological weapons. It has now been ratified by over 90 nations including all the major powers (although Japan and America are only recent signatories). The Protocol has been generally well observed although notable violations have been by the Italians in Abyssinia (1935–6), the Japanese in China during the second world war and the Americans in South East Asia in the 1960s. It has however failed to prevent the continual development and stock-piling of lethal chemical agents by many nations, although recently there have been moves towards chemical weapons disarmament. *See also* Biological Warfare.

Chemistry is the science of the elements and their compounds. It is concerned with the laws of their combination and behaviour under various conditions. It had its roots in alchemy and has gradually developed into a science of vast magnitude and importance. Organic chemistry deals with the chemistry of the compounds of carbon; inorganic chemistry is concerned with the chemistry of the elements; physical chemistry is concerned with the study of chemical reactions and with the theories and laws of chemistry. *See* **F23–9**.

Chestnut, the fruit of trees of the genus *Castanea*, members of the family *Fagaceae*. *C. sativa* is the sweet or Spanish chestnut, *C. dentata* the American chestnut and *C. crenata* the Japanese chestnut. The nut is edible. The wood is used in carpentry and fencing. *See also* **Horse Chestnut**.

Chiaroscuro, a term used in painting to denote the disposition of light and shade. Rembrandt is unrivalled as a painter for his contrasts of light and shadows.

Chiltern Hundreds, three hundreds—Stoke, Burnham and Desborough—the stewardship of which is now a nominal office under the Chancellor of the Exchequer. Since about 1750 the nomination to it has been used as a method of enabling a member of Parliament to resign seat on the plea that he holds an office of honour and profit under the crown. An alternate symbolic post for an M.P. giving up his seat is the stewardship of the Manor of Northstead in Yorkshire which has been used in the same way since 1841.

Chimpanzee, a large anthropoid ape, a native of tropical Africa, of a dark brown colour, with arms reaching to the knee, and capable of walking upright. Its brain is about a third of the weight of the human brain, but is anatomically similar. The animal has considerable intelligence and powers of learning. A suitable subject for space flight experiments.

Chinchilla, a South American burrowing rodent. Grey in colour, and white underneath. It is greatly esteemed for its beautiful fur.

Chippendale Furniture was introduced in the reign of George I by Thomas Chippendale, a cabinet-maker from Yorkshire who migrated to London and set up for himself in St. Martin's Lane, Charing Cross. He was fonder of inventing designs for furniture than of making it, and in 1752 published a book of patterns; the London furniture-makers of the day soon began to model their work upon it. *See* **Section U**.

Chivalry an international brotherhood of knights formed primarily during the 13th cent. to fight against the infidels in the Crusades. For the French the major battle was against the Moslems in the Holy Land and North Africa, the Spaniards fought the same enemy in their own country, and the Germans were concerned with the heathen of Baltic lands, but Chaucer's " perfect gentle knight " had fought in all these areas. One did not easily become a knight who had to be of noble birth and then pass through a period of probation, beginning as a boy page in the castle of some great lord, serving his elders and betters humbly while he was taught good manners, singing, playing musical instruments, and the composition of verse. Probably he learned Latin, but he certainly learned French, which was the international language of knights as Latin was of scholars. At fourteen he became a squire and learned to fight with sword, battle-axe and lance, and to endure conditions of hard living while carrying out his duties of waiting on his lord, looking after his

horses, and in time accompanying him in battle Only if he showed himself suitable was he finally knighted by a stroke of the hand or sword on the shoulder from the king or lord. Knighthood was an international order and had its special code of behaviour: to honour one's sworn word, to protect the weak, to respect women, and defend the Faith. To some extent it had a civilising effect on the conduct of war (*e.g.*, knights of opposing sides might slaughter each other in battle but feast together after), but, since war was regarded as the supreme form of sport, it cannot be said to have contributed to peace.

Chlorine, a gaseous element of the halogen family, first isolated in 1774 by Scheele by the action of manganese dioxide in hydrochloric acid. It unites easily with many other elements, the compounds resulting being termed chlorides. The gaseous element is greenish-yellow, with a pungent odour. It is a suffocating gas, injuring the lungs at a concentration as low as 1 part in 50,000, and was used during the first world war as a poison gas. Has a powerful bleaching action, usually being used in form of bleaching powder, made by combining lime and chlorine. Also a valuable disinfectant; used, for instance, in rendering water of swimming baths sterile.

Chloroform, a volatile colourless liquid, compounded of carbon, hydrogen, and chlorine. It is a powerful solvent, not naturally occurring but synthesised on a large scale. When the vapour is inhaled it produces unconsciousness and insensibility to pain. It owes its discovery to Liebig, and its first application for medical purposes to Sir James Young Simpson (**F5(2)**).

Chlorophyll, the green pigment contained in the leaves of plants, first discovered by P. J. Pelletier (1788–1829) and J. B. Caventou (1795–1877) in 1818. Enables the plant to absorb sunlight and so to build up sugar. The total synthesis of chlorophyll was reported in 1960 by Prof. R. B. Woodward. This is an outstanding achievement in the field of organic chemistry. *See* **Photosynthesis, F32(1), F43(2)**.

Chouans, the name given to the band of peasants, mainly smugglers and dealers in contraband salt, who rose in revolt in the west of France in 1793 and joined the royalists of La Vendée. Balzac gives a picture of the people and the country in which they operated in his novel *Les Chouans*. They used the hoot of an owl as a signal—hence the name.

Chough, a member of the crow family, of glossy blue-green-black plumage, whose long curved bill and legs are coral red. It is used to be abundant on the cliffs of Cornwall, but its haunts are now restricted to the rocky outcrops of the western coasts and in the mountains near by. It nests in cleft rocks and caves. The Alpine chough with yellow bill inhabits the mountainous districts of Europe and Asia and is not found in Britain. It was found at *c.* 8,200 m on Everest.

Christmas means " mass of Christ " from the old English *Cristes maesse*, which is celebrated by the Western church on 25 December. The actual day on which Christ was born is not known and there is some uncertainty about the year. 25 December as the day of Nativity was not generally observed until the 5th cent. A.D., though, as the winter solstice, it had long been observed as a pagan festival of *sol invictus* (unconquered sun). The first Christmas card dates from about 1843 and the Christmas tree, of pagan origin, was introduced into England from Germany where it had been a tradition since the Middle Ages. Santa Claus is a corruption of Santa Nikolaus (St. Nicholas) patron saint of children, whose feast day properly falls on 6 December.

Chromium, a very hard, bluish-white metal element, symbol Cr, melting at a very high temperature (above 1,900°C). Its chief ore is chromite or chrome iron-ore (ferrous chromite). " Ferro-chrome " is produced by heating chromite and anthracite in an electric furnace, and chrome steels are prepared by adding the pre-calculated amount of ferro-chrome to melted steel. Best known chrome steel is stainless steel first made by Brearley in 1912 and since then developed greatly at Sheffield. A typical formula is 18 per cent. chromium,

8 per cent. nickel, 74 per cent. iron. Equally important are Stellite alloys, containing chromium, cobalt, tungsten (or molybdenum), which have made possible modern high-speed cutting tools. Dies used in manufacture of plastics are commonly of chrome steel. The elementary metal finds little use alone except in chromium-plating for motor cars, etc.

Chromosomes, the structures contained within the nucleus of every animal and plant cell by which genetic information is transmitted. The chromosome number in somatic (body) cells is constant for each species of plant and animal, e.g., man (46), cat (38), mouse (40), honey bee (16), fruit fly *Drosophila* (8), potato (48). Chromosomes are long molecules composed of deoxyribonucleoproteins (*i.e.*, proteins and DNA). Human chromosomes have been the subject of much recent research since it has been found that certain disorders are associated with chromosomal aberration, e.g., in Mongolism an extra chromosome is present. *See* **F31**.

Church Commissioners. The Church Commissioners were established in 1948 by the amalgamation of Queen Anne's Bounty (established 1704) and the Ecclesiastical Commissioners (established 1836) to administer Church revenues and to manage Church property generally. The Commissioners control funds with a book value of some £600 million (1976).

Cid, The, a famous Spanish hero of the 11th cent. Don Rodrigo Diaz de Vivar, who, before he was twenty, led a Spanish force against the Moors, and drove them out of Spain. He is celebrated in poem, play and romance.

Cilia, minute hair-like projections on the surface of some cells, which beat together in wavelike movements like the wind over a corn-field. These movements can be used as a means of locomotion as in the aquatic organism paramecium. Cilia are also found on the outer layers of the human trachea where they waft particles upwards to the throat, thus protecting the lungs. *See* **F34, P13,** *also* **Flagella.**

Cinque Ports, a number of seaport towns on the coast of Kent and Sussex, originally five; Hastings, Romney, Hythe, Dover and Sandwich. Winchelsea and Rye were added later. These ports were required to furnish a certain number of ships, ready for service, and in return they were granted many privileges. The official residence of the Lord Warden is Walmer Castle, near Dover.

Cistercians, an order of monks and nuns taking their names from Cîteaux, near Dijon, where their first monastery was established in 1098. The order was noted for the severity of its rule. They were famous agriculturists. The habit is white, with a black cowl or hood.

Civil List is the annual sum payable to the Sovereign to maintain the Royal Household and to uphold the dignity of the Crown. The amount is granted by Parliament upon the recommendation of a Select Committee and has to be settled afresh in the first six months of a new reign. The Civil List of Queen Victoria was £385,000; Edward VII and George V, £470,000; Edward VIII and George VI, £410,000; Elizabeth II £475,000. In 1972 the Civil List allowance to the Queen was increased to £980,000, in 1975 to £1·4 million, in 1976 to £1·665 million, in 1977 to £1·905 million, in 1978 to £1·950 million. Other Civil List allowances (1978) include: the Queen Mother, £175,000; the Duke of Edinburgh, £93,500; Princess Anne, £60,000; Prince Andrew £17,262 (invested apart from £600 a year while still at school); Princess Margaret £59,000; Princess Alice (Gloucester) £30,000. The Prince of Wales is entitled to tax-free revenue from the Duchy of Cornwall. Other resources available to the Queen include (1) the sums which Parliament votes to government departments each year, e.g., upkeep of palaces (Dept. of the Environment) royal yacht Britannia and the royal flight (Min. of Defence); (2) privy purse (revenues of the Duchy of Lancaster; (3) personal fortune, the size of which is not disclosed. The Queen pays no direct taxes. 80–100 per cent. of the annuities received by other members of the Royal family are treated as tax-free expenses. The system under which annual payments are made by the Government to the Queen was changed by the Civil List Act 1975: payments are now included in the annual estimates in the same way as the expenditure of a government department, and subject to scrutiny in the House of Commons. The Civil List now provides only for the Sovereign, the consort of a Sovereign, their children, and the widows of those children.

Cleopatra's Needle on the Thames Embankment is of the time of Tuthmosis III (1500–1450 B.C.). The monolith had nothing to do with Cleopatra as it only came to Alexandria after her death. It was first erected at the Biblical On (Greek Heliopolis), sacred City of the Sun. It was presented to the British Government by Mehemet Ali in 1819, but not brought to this country until 1878. Weight c. 183 tonnes; height, 208 m.

Climate is a generalised representation of the day-to-day weather conditions throughout the year, the combination of all weathers thus determining the climate of a place. Averages and extremes of temperature, variation of humidity, duration of sunshine and cloud cover, amount of rainfall and frequency of snow, frost, gales, etc., are amongst the data normally investigated. The interiors of great land masses are characterised by large ranges of temperature and low rainfall (continental climate), while proximity to oceans has an ameliorating effect with increase in rainfall (oceanic climate). Presence of mountain ranges and lakes and configuration generally produce local modifications of climate, also apparent between the centre and the outlying suburbs of a city. Latitude introduces zones of climate, e.g., tropical rain, subtropical steppe and desert, temperate rain and polar. The climate is always changing in greater or less degree. Every year, every decade, every century brings a somewhat different experience. The recent tendency between 1880 and 1940 for most parts of the world to become warmer has eased off and appears to have given way to a more prolonged cooling tendency.

Clock, a device for measuring the passage of time. The earliest timekeeper was the shadow-clock, a primitive form of sundial, used in Ancient Egypt about 1500 B.C. To find the time at night the water-clock or clepsydra was used. The sand-glass dates from the 15th cent. No one knows when the first mechanical clocks were invented, but it is known that a complicated mechanical clock driven by water and controlled by a weighbridge escapement was built in Peking in 1090. The Dover Clock in the Science Museum is not the earliest surviving clock in England, as was once believed, but early 17th cent. The Salisbury Cathedral clock dates from 1386 and that of Wells Cathedral from 1392. The pendulum clock was invented by the Dutch scientist Christiaan Huygens (1625–95). The first watches were made in Nuremberg shortly after 1500. The marine chronometer is a high-precision timepiece used at sea for giving Greenwich mean time. The quartz-crystal clocks are accurate to one thousandth of a second a day, and the improved atomic clock, developed at the British National Physical Laboratory, which makes use of the natural vibrations of the caesium atom, is said to be an almost absolute measure of time (accurate to 1 sec. in 300 years, *i.e.*, one part in 10^{10}).

Cloud Chamber, an apparatus invented by C. T. R. Wilson in which the tracks of atomic particles can be made visible. Just as the vapour trails tell of the track of an invisible aircraft high up in the air, so the vapour trails of an unseeable particle can tell of its behaviour. The rays under investigation pass through a chamber containing a gas, e.g., air thoroughly cleansed of dust, supersaturated with water- or alcohol-vapour. As the particle passes through it forms a track of tiny water droplets which can be photographed. After a long and honourable history this wonderful instrument is now virtually obsolete. A later ingenious device for tracking fast fundamental particles is the Bubble chamber (*q.v.*).

Clouds are formed by the cooling of moist air, the type depending on the way the air cools and the height at which condensation occurs. There are three main classes: (1) high cloud (about 6,100 m)—cirrus (delicate and fibrous), cirrostratus (thin white veil), and cirrocumulus (delicately rippled) consisting of ice crystals; (2) medium cloud (above 2,100 m)—altostratus (dense, greyish veil) and altocumulus (broken flattened cloudlets)—chiefly water particles, often supercooled; (3) low cloud (from near ground to 2,100 m)—cumulus (fair weather, broken, dome-topped), cumulominbus (heavy, towering to great heights), stratocumulus (layer of globular masses or rolls), stratus (like fog but off the ground), nimbostratus (low, rainy cloud). The highest clouds of all, and the rarest, are the noctilucent, seen only on summer nights in high latitudes. They form at about 80 km above the earth and consist of ice-coated dust from meteors.

Clover, plants of the *Trifolium* genus, family *Leguminosae,* with about 250 species. These are "nitrogen fixing" plants and include red clover, white clover, alsike clover and crimson clover. They are of great importance in agriculture because in a good pasture they supply directly or indirectly most of the protein available to the animals. Seed of "wild white" clover has been accepted since about 1939 as the indispensable plant of good United Kingdom grassland, largely through the efforts of pioneers like D. A. Gilchrist (1859–1927).

Coal. Until recently the most important single fuel has been coal. It is a mineral of organic origin, formed from the remains of vegetation which over millions of years has changed to coal by the effects of heat and pressure from overlying rock or water. All coal contains moisture, inflammable volatiles, mineral impurities (some of which remain as coal ash after the coal is burnt), and fixed carbon (the coke that is left after the volatiles have been driven off). The relative proportions vary—from Anthracite, a hard coal containing the highest proportion of fixed carbon, to Lignite or brown coal which is little more than a hard peat. World reserves of bituminous coal have been estimated at $7 \cdot 5 \times 10^{12}$ tonnes. If one adds the reserves of brown coal and lignite, this figure is increased by about 15 per cent. The proportion of the reserves that could be economically recovered varies from country to country and estimates vary from 50 to 100 per cent of the reserves. The reserves are highly localised—over half being located in the Soviet Union. In the United Kingdom coal has formed the basis of past industrial prosperity. Peak output occurred in 1913 when 290 million tonnes were mined one third of which was exported. At the end of the second world war production had fallen to 186 million tonnes and was far below demand. In 1947 the British coal industry was brought under public ownership and all its assets were vested in the National Coal Board. During the next ten years great efforts were made to increase coal output but, quite suddenly in 1956, demand for coal fell as oil became a popular fuel and the problem was to cut back the coal industry without causing undue social problems. The fall in demand was accompanied by increasing productivity, both mines and miners having been cut in their numbers by over half. Coal accounts for about 38 per cent. of primary energy consumption in Britain. Production is *c.* 122 million tonnes per annum. Exploration to find new reserves (including offshore drillings) is progressing. Expansion of the industry is again planned as a result of the high cost of oil since 1973.

Coat of Arms, in heraldry, a device containing a family's armorial bearings. In mediaeval times an actual coat upon which such device was embroidered; knights wore it over their armour.

Cobalt, a white metal melting at 1490°C. Two main ores are *cobalt glance* (in which the element is combined with arsenic and sulphur) and *smaltite* (cobalt arsenide). The principal sources are Ontario and Zaïre. Various cobalt alloys are important, *e.g.,* stellite, ferrocobalt and carboloy. Its monoxide is an important colouring medium, and is used for colouring glass and porcelain-blue.

Cobra, hooded and very venomous snakes. The best known species are the Indian Cobra, the Egyptian Cobra, and the Black-necked Cobra. Their food consists chiefly of small rodents. The King Cobra is almost exclusively a snake-

eater. "Spitting" Cobras (or Ringhals) of S. Africa are a related genus, capable of spitting their venom several yards.

Coca, a S. American shrub, *Erythroxylon coca,* also cultivated in Java. The leaves yield cocaine, classified as a dangerous drug: used medicinally as a local anaesthetic, especially on the eyes and in dentistry. When the natives chew the leaves they are enabled to withstand astonishing amounts of hunger and fatigue, as cocaine acts both as a mental stimulant and as an anaesthetic on the mucous lining of the stomach.

Cochineal or **Carmine,** a dyestuff consisting of the dried bodies of the female scale insect (*Dactylopius coccus*) which feeds on cacti. Of ancient origin, the dye was well known to the Aztecs, and was used widely in the Middle Ages. The famous scarlet tunics worn by the English during the Napoleonic wars owed their colour to carmine. Today it is almost entirely replaced by aniline dyes.

Cockatoo, a member of the parrot family, bearing a crest of feathers on the head, native to Australia and adjacent regions. Predominant colour is white tinged with yellow or scarlet while some species have dark plumage. The cockatoo of New Guinea is slaty black with pale red cheeks and can crack Kanary nuts which usually require a hammer to break them open.

Cockchafer (*Melolontha*), one of the most destructive of beetles, the larvae feeding on roots. It is about 2·5 cm in length, of a brownish colour, and emits a loud whirring sound when flying.

Cockle, the popular name of the bi-valve shellfish of the genus *Cardium,* found plentifully in sandy bays near low-water line.

Cockroach, inaccurately called the "black beetle"; a pest of bakeries and kitchens. In Britain two species are commonly found: the Common Cockroach (*Blatta orientalis*), resident since the time of Elizabeth I, dark brown, about 2·5 cm long, with the wing covers long in the male and short in the female; and the German Cockroach (*Blatta germanica*), now the most common, half the size, dark yellow, with both sexes fully winged. All species have long antennae and flattened, leathery, shiny bodies. They are nocturnal and omnivorous.

Coconut Palm (*Cocos nucifera*), a tropical tree, growing to a height of 30 m, with a slender, leaning trunk surmounted by giant feather-like leaves. One of the most important sources of food and raw material for people living in the tropics. The juice of the fruit, or coconut, is drunk; the kernel is eaten fresh or dried to form copra, which yields animal feeding stuffs and oil, used in the manufacture of soap, margarine, cosmetics, synthetic rubber, etc.; leaves are used for thatching; leaf stalks for canes, fence posts, needles, etc., and the trunk for houses and bridges. Main producing areas: Indonesia, Philippines, Malaysia, Sri Lanka and S. India.

Codes, a term used to designate a system of laws properly classified. The Code of Hammurabi, king of Babylon, *c.* 1751 B.C., had extensive influence over a long period. The Romans formulated several codes of historic importance including the Theodosian Code which summarised the Roman laws from the time of Constantine to 438 A.D. The final codification was made under order of the Emperor Justinian by his chief minister Tribonian and published in 529 with a new edition in 534. The most important of modern codes is the *Code Napoléon,* compiled between 1803 and 1810, and still in force. It has been used as an example for the codification of the laws of a number of countries from America to Japan. Under Frederick the Great the law of Prussia was codified. English law has never been codified, although the law on certain subjects has been gathered up into a single statute. The Law Commission Act, 1965, was passed to consolidate and codify the law wherever possible.

Codex, a manuscript volume of the Scriptures comprising the Sinaitic codex of the 4th cent., the Vatican codex of the same period, the Alexandrine codex of the 5th cent., and others. The British Museum, in 1933, purchased the *Codex Sinaiticus* from the Soviet Government for £100,000.

Coffee, a shrub found originally in Arabia and

Ethiopia, but now extensively grown in Brazil, Colombia, Ivory Coast, Uganda, Angola and Central America. It yields a seed or berry which after undergoing the necessary preparation, is ground and used in most countries as a breakfast beverage. The best coffee is the Mocha, an Arabian variety. The stimulating effect of coffee is due to the caffeine, which is also present in tea. The beverage was introduced into Europe in the 16th cent., and the first London coffee shop was opened in 1632.

Coke is the solid residue remaining when coal is carbonised and nearly all the volatile constituents have been driven off. Used as fuel, and as an agent for reducing metallic oxides to metals, e.g., iron ore to iron, in the manufacture of steel.

Colorado Beetle, a serious pest of potato crops. Both adults and larvae feed on the foliage where the orange eggs are laid. The grub is reddish, with two rows of small black spots on each side. The adults are about 1·2 cm long with yellow and black striped wing cases. The beetle is avoided by birds because of its nasty taste, and is controlled by arsenical sprays.

Colosseum, the name of the Flavian amphitheatre at Rome, begun by Vespasian and finished by Titus A.D. 80. In general outline it still remains one of the most magnificent ruins in the world. In the arena of this great building the famous gladiatorial displays and mimic naval battles used to be given, and about 50,000 spectators could be accommodated.

Colossus is the name which the ancients gave to any statue of gigantic size. The Colossus at Rhodes, which was a bronze statue of the sun god, Helios, was the most famous, and reckoned among the seven wonders of the world. It stood over 30 m high at the mouth of the harbour. There is no truth in the legend that ships could pass between its legs. It fell in an earthquake in 224 B.C.

Coluga, also known as " flying lemur ", caguan or kubuk, a remarkable mammal which may be regarded as an aberrant insectivore or an aberrant form of the earliest ancestor of the bats. It has nothing to do with lemurs. There are two genera, one inhabiting the Philippines and one inhabiting Malaya. They have a parachute-like membrane which covers them from the neck to the tip of the tail, by means of which they can glide from treetop to ground, a distance of up to 64 m.

Column, in architecture, is an upright solid body serving as a support or decoration to a building. Columns consist of a pedestal, a shaft, and a capital, over which the supported entablature rises. They are named according to the styles of architecture of which they form part, being Doric, Tuscan, Ionic, Corinthian or Composite as the case may be.

Comets are celestial bodies which generally move about the solar system in elongated elliptical or nearly parabolic orbits. Most comets are in the latter category, having extremely long orbital periods, up to millions of years, and have therefore only been seen once in recorded history. They spend most of their lifetimes at extremely large distances from the sun, far outside Pluto's orbit. Those in elliptical orbits appear periodically and a few have been observed regularly. Halley's comet, named after Edmund Halley, who first correctly predicted that this comet would reappear in 1757, was first observed in Roman times and is one of the brightest of the periodic comets. The nucleus of a comet, which appears as a faint star when the comet is very far from the sun, is believed to be a frozen mixture of dust and materials called " ices "—CO_2, H_2O, NH_3 and CH_4, frozen at the low temperatures in the outer solar system. Approaching the sun, the comet is heated by sunlight and the surface " ices " are first vaporised and later photo-dissociated and ionised by sunlight, also freeing the surface dust. The dust, gases and ions produce the fuzzy appearance of the coma of the comet. Under the influence of sunlight acting on dust, and the solar wind and interplanetary field acting on the ions, the cometary tail (often multiple) is produced. This may stretch up to 200 million km, pointing away from the sun. Donati's comet (1858) was possibly the most spectacular of all and was

visible even in daylight. Kohoutek's comet (1975) was the first to be observed from space, by the American Skylab and Russian Soyuz, and many exciting new space studies are planned for the next predicted return of Halley's comet in 1985. See also **F4(1).**

Commons are the remnants of the mediaeval open fields round villages in which the villagers had rights in common, e.g., (i) estover—the right of taking wood for house building or firewood; (ii) pasture—the right of grazing beasts; (iii) turbary—the right of digging turf; (iv) piscary—the right to fish. Many of these common lands were enclosed during the agrarian revolution which went on steadily in England from the 15th cent. onwards, and with their enclosure common rights vanished. A Royal Commission on Common Land described the commons in 1965 as the " last reservoir of uncommitted land " which provide, as far as the public is concerned, by far the largest part of the accessible open spaces of the country. Under the Commons Registration Act, 1965, it was the duty of County Councils and County Borough Councils to make a register of all common land and all town and village greens in their areas.

Commons, House of, the Lower House of the British Parliament. See **Section D.**

Commune of Paris has twice played a dramatic part in the history of France. In 1792 it was able, through its control of the administrative organisation of Paris, to override the National Assembly. In 1871, after the withdrawal of the Prussian troops, it tried to assert its authority. Public buildings were destroyed by members of the Commune and civil war raged during April and half May, but Government troops savagely suppressed the rising.

Communism. See Section J.

Compass or **Mariner's Compass.** It has been known since very early times that an iron needle, suspended freely to hang horizontally when not magnetised, comes to rest roughly along the geographical north-south line when magnetised. Further, it generally does not hang horizontally. This is the essential behaviour of the *compass,* a navigational instrument whose invention is obscure but which seems to have been known to the Chinese 4,500 years ago. That the behaviour of the compass shows the existence of a *magnetic field* associated with the Earth was first fully recognised by William Gilbert in 1600. Aircraft and ships now largely employ gyrostatic compasses which are not affected by electrical and magnetic disturbances. Sperry, Brown and Anschutz are three important types of gyroscopic compass.

Composite Materials, or more simply composites, are materials which derive useful properties by combining the virtues of two or more components. Combining clay with straw to make tougher bricks is an ancient example in which fibres (straw) are embedded in a matrix or body (the clay). A modern example is fibreglass in which glass fibres are embedded in a plastic matrix. Nature also uses composites as in bamboo in which a lignin matrix binds together the fibres of cellulose to make a light strong structure. Composites may contain flakes or particles embedded in the matrix instead of fibres—it depends on the application. Although the idea is not new composite technology has made rapid strides in the last few decades guided by scientific insight into the nature of solids and the origin of their strengths and weaknesses. The motivation has been that scientifically designed composites offer materials with exceptional strength/weight ratio, desirable magnetic properties and other technological advantages which meet the extreme demands of a variety of industries. For example, composite aluminium containing boron fibres or resin containing graphite fibres can have strength/weight ratios over twice that of high-strength solid aluminium. Composites of many kinds are now widespread in industrial use and are attracting much research and development.

Computer, a technical device for accepting an input of information, processing this information according to some prescribed programme of operations and supplying an output of processed information. Many types of operation can be performed on many types of information and computers are now indispensable in science, business, warfare, government and other activities. Early thinkers in this field were Pascal (17th cent.), Babbage (19th cent.) and Turing (1930s), but electronic computers as we know them appeared during the second world war and the first commercial machine was on sale in 1950. Computers are millions of times faster than human beings at computing; and the introduction of computers into an organisation does more than just speed up the calculations, it tends to transform the whole nature of the organisation. The possibilities for future developments seem enormous. Analogue computers and digital computers are two different kinds stemming from the difference between *measuring* and *counting*. Analogue types handle data that is repeated by physical quantities of continuously variable size such as voltages or lengths. These quantities can be made to vary like the quantities in a problem which the computer is set to solve; the problem is thus solved by analogy. A slide rule is a rudimentary analogue computer in which numbers are represented by lengths of rule. Digital computers handle actual numbers expressed in digits and the quantities in the problem are represented by discrete numbers. These can all be expressed in binary form and thus stored or handled in bits. *See* Bit, Binary Notation.

Conclave, an assembly of Roman Catholic cardinals met together to elect a pope. The last Conclave was held in the Vatican in June 1963 when Cardinal Montini, archbishop of Milan, was elected Pope Paul VI.

Concordat, an agreement or convention between the pope and a secular government regarding ecclesiastical matters. The Concordat of Worms in 1122 between Calixtus II and the Emperor Henry V was famous as decid'ng a long struggle in regard to investiture. In 1801, Napoleon concluded a concordat with Pius VII defining the restored relations between the head of the Church and the French Roman Catholics.

Condor, a large eagle of brilliant black plumage with a circlet of white feathers round its neck. It is a native of the Andes.

Confederation is a free association of sovereign states united for some common purpose It is to be distinguished from a Federation, which is a union of states with one central government, each state relinquishing its sovereignty, though retaining some independence in internal affairs.

Confucianism. *See* Section J.

Coniferae are cone-bearing trees, including firs, pines, cedars, cypresses, junipers, yews, etc., and are widely distributed in temperate regions.

Conservatism. *See* Section J.

Constitution, the fundamental organic law or principles of government of a nation, state, society, or other organised body, embodied in written documents, or implied in the institutions and customs of the country or society. The government of the USA, unlike Great Britain, works upon a written Constitution. It was framed when the USA came into existence as a sovereign body, when the Constitution built a republic out of a federation of thirteen states, based on representative government. The constitution was adopted in 1789, and its strength has been tested by the fact that, substantially unchanged, it is now the groundwork for a federation which now comprises fifty states. *See also* Sections C and D.

Continent, a word used in physical geography to denote the larger continuous land masses in contrast to the great oceans of the earth. They are: Eurasia (conventionally regarded as 2 continents, Europe and Asia), Africa, North America, South America, Australia and Antarctica. (Australasia is Australia, New Zealand and adjacent islands. Oceania is Australasia and the many islands of the S.W. Pacific).

Continental Drift. The hypothesis of drifting continents is due to F. B. Taylor, an American geologist who published his theory in 1908, and to the Austrian meteorologist Alfred Wegener in 1910. The latter was impressed by the matching coasts of South America and Africa, which seemed to him to fit together like the pieces of a jigsaw puzzle. Since then many other people have taken up and developed the

idea. According to Wegener, at one time there were two primary super-continents, Laurasia and Gondwanaland. The one in the northern hemisphere consisted of North America, Europe, and the northern part of Asia. Its southern counterpart included Antarctica, Australia, India, Africa and South America. These super-continents broke up, and their various bits moved apart In particular, the southern hemisphere continents drifted radially northwards away from the south pole, and the two Americas shifted westwards from Europe and Africa. What would have been the leading edges of the land masses on this hypothesis, are now heavily buckled up into mountain belts, such as the Cordillera and the Alpine-Himalayan chain. The resistance afforded to drifting by the strong ocean floors may well have been the cause of such structures. Despite the wealth of geological facts which have a bearing on the problem of continental drift, none of these has been able to decide the issue in a conclusive manner. Further studies of rock magnetism (*q.v.*) and of fossil climates should ultimately establish the concept of continental drift on a firm basis. *See also* Earth, F8.

Conurbation, a term used in reference to an extensive and continuous area of urban land-use. Conurbations are frequently formed by the physical coalescence of several formerly free-standing towns. They may themselves coalesce to form a higher order of physical urbanisation, known as a megalopolis. The seven conurbations officially recognised in the UK are Greater London, W. Midlands, S. E. Lancashire, W. Yorkshire, Merseyside, Tyneside and Clydeside, of which the first five are said to form the English megalopolis. In common with other old and well-developed cities throughout the capitalist world, conurbations in Britain show a marked decline in population and employment.

Convention is an assembly of delegates, representatives, members of a party met to accomplish some specific civil, social, political, ecclesiastical or other important object.

Convocation, an assembly called together to deliberate ecclesiastical affairs In the Church of England the provinces of Canterbury and York each have their convocation. The term is also applied to assemblies of the graduates of certain universities.

Coot. A very widely distributed bird of the rail family and a common resident of the British Isles. The adult is black with a conspicuous white bald shield on the forehead and a white bill. The juvenile is brownish grey with whitish breast and throat. The coot flies heavily, but swims well. It dives frequently and can remain submerged for a considerable time. It is pugnacious and in winter gregarious. The food is chiefly vegetable. The large nest is usually built among aquatic vegetation and the young are fed by both parents. Another species, the Crested Coot, occurs in S. Europe.

Copper, one of the most familiar of metals, symbol Cu, used in ancient times as an alloy with tin in producing bronze, and preceding iron as an industrial material. Copper ores are most abundant in the USA, Chile, Canada, Zambia, Zaire. All copper compounds are poisonous.

Copyright. Under the Copyright Act, 1956, copyright subsists in every original literary, dramatic musical, and artistic work if the author is a British subject or a citizen of the Republic of Ireland or resident in the United Kingdom, or if the work is first published in the United Kingdom. The Act provides that, except in certain special cases, the author of the work shall be the first owner of the copyright, and there are no formalities, such as registration or payment of fees, to be accomplished. Copyright includes the right to reproduce the work in any material form, to perform the work in public, or, if the work is unpublished, to publish the work. The Act also protects sound recordings, films and television and sound broadcasts. Literary, dramatic, musical and artistic works which enjoy the protection of the Act are automatically protected in those countries which are parties to the Berne Copyright Convention or the Universal Copyright Convention. In general, copyright in literary, dramatic, musical and artistic works is vested in the author for the period of his lifetime and 50 years following, after which it passes into the public domain and becomes freely available to any who wish to make use of it. The Copyright Libraries, entitled to receive copies of books published in the United Kingdom are given under Libraries. The Berne Copyright Convention and the Universal Copyright Convention were revised at a diplomatic conference held in Paris in 1971. The effect of the revisions allows any national of a developing country to obtain, under certain conditions, a compulsory licence to translate and publish a copyright work for the purpose of teaching, scholarship and research, upon payment of compensation to the copyright owner of the original work. The Government Department responsible for matters in connection with copyright is the Industrial Property and Copyright Department, 25 Southampton Buildings, London, WC2A 1AY.

Coral, an order of small marine animals closely related to the sea-anemone, but differing from it in their ability to develop a limy skeleton. They multiply sexually and by budding. The structure of the coral secretions assumes a variety of forms, fan-like, tree-like, mushroom shape, and so forth. Red coral (the skeleton of *Corallium rubrum*) is mainly obtained from the Mediterranean. The coral reefs of the Pacific and Indian Oceans are often many miles in extent. Living corals occur only in warm seas at about 23°C.

Cordite, a smokeless explosive adopted for small arms and heavy artillery by the British Government in the naval and military services in 1889, and composed of 58 parts of nitro-glycerine, 37 of gun-cotton, and 5 of vaseline. It is a jelly or plastic dough, and used in the form of sticks. Invented by Sir Frederick Abel and Sir John Dewar 1889.

Cork, the bark of a species of oak, *Quercus suber*, grown largely in the South of Europe and North America. The cork tree is said to yield bark every six to ten years for 150 years, and grows to a height of from 6–12 m. Its lightness, impermeability, and elasticity enable it to be used for a variety of commercial purposes, especially for stoppers of bottles.

Cormorant, a large, long-billed water-bird which captures fish by diving. The common cormorant has bronze-black plumage with white cheeks and sides and is found around the sea coasts of most parts of the world, including the British Isles. It nests in colonies on sea cliffs and rocky ledges. The Shag or Green Cormorant is a smaller bird with green-black plumage and a crest.

Corncrake. *See* Landrail.

Corn Laws were statutes intended for the benefit of British agriculture, and restricted import and export of grain. From the 14th to the mid-19th cent. such laws were in force, and were often of a stringent nature. They became so oppressive and caused corn to reach so high a price that the poorer classes were plunged into distress. A powerful anti-corn law agitation was organised of which Cobden, Bright and Villiers were the leaders, and Sir Robert Peel, in 1846, at the time of the Irish potato famine, carried through free trade. The repeal of the Corn Laws marked an important phase in the transformation of an agricultural to an industrial Britain.

Corona or Solar Corona, the outer atmosphere of the sun. This glows by virtue of light emitted by the sun and scattered by electrons and dust particles at various heights in the sun's atmosphere and also by light emitted from ionised atoms in the corona itself. Corona light is much fainter than the bright disc of the sun and is invisible against the normal blue of the sky. During total solar eclipses, the corona can be seen by the human eye as a faint glow extending irregularly outwards a few solar diameters from the sun. The sun's atmosphere extends much further than this but is invisible to the eye at large distances from the sun. The corona gases are thought to be very hot (millions of degrees) and in complex violent motion; the gross structure of the corona is connected with the sunspot cycle.

Cortes, the name of the Parliamentary assemblies of Spain and Portugal.

Cosmic Rays, a form of radiation coming from outer space, of deep penetrating power and of great scientific interest. The rays are believed to consist chiefly of fast protons, with a few α-particles and other positive nuclei. By interacting with the gas of the atmosphere, these rays initiate a complex series of events, in the course of which other particles (" secondary radiations ") are generated. The secondary rays contain virtually all the particles listed on F16; indeed, several particles were first discovered as secondary cosmic rays. Cosmic rays are investigated at and below sea-level, on mountains, in mines, in balloons, rockets and satellites. Origin still uncertain. *See* F3(2).

Cosmology is the science which studies the whole universe, its origin, its nature, its size, and evolution. At present it is a very active science partly because new techniques such as radio-astronomy are revealing more facts about distant parts of the universe and partly because of fruitful clashes between theoretical ideas. *See* F3–7.

Cotton, the name of a plant of several species bearing large yellow flowers with purple centres. These centres expand into pods, which at maturity burst and yield the white fibrous substance known as cotton. The raw cotton contains a large proportion of seeds which are removed by " ginning ". Long before the Christian era, cotton had been grown and used with great skill in India to make fabrics. The industry was not introduced into England until the middle of the 17th cent. when Protestant refugees from Flanders came to settle in the wool textile districts of East Anglia and Lancashire. With improvements in machinery and expansion of overseas trade in the 18th and 19th cent., Lancashire became the centre of the world's cotton industry but since the second world war man-made fibres have taken the place of cotton. Chief producers: USA, USSR, China, India, Brazil, Mexico, Pakistan, Egypt, Turkey.

Coulomb, a unit of electric charge, named after the French naval engineer, Charles Augustin de Coulomb (1736–1806), equal to the quantity of electricity transferred in one second by a current of one ampere.

County. The word county was introduced after the Norman conquest as an equivalent of the old English " shire ". Since the recent reorganisation of local government in the United Kingdom the distinction between *administrative* counties and *geographical* counties no longer exists. Certain geographical counties have disappeared (e.g., Rutland and Pembroke), new counties have appeared (e.g., Avon and Gwynedd), while former counties have been modified (e.g., Glamorgan and Yorkshire). *See* K186.

Coup d'Etat, a violent change in the government of a state carried out by force or illegally. Examples are the overthrow of the French Republic in 1851 by Louis Napoleon, who then became Emperor, and more recently the military *coups* in the Middle East which brought about the abdication of Farouk of Egypt in 1952 and the assassination of Feisal of Iraq in 1958.

Court Leet, a court of record held annually before the steward of any particular manor or lordship; originally there was only one court for a manor, but in the time of Edward I it branched into two, the court baron and the court leet.

Coypu or Nutria rat, a large beaver-like rodent found in S. America; now wild in E. Anglia, where it is causing damage to dykes, reeds, and crops, having escaped from farms where it is bred for its fur.

Crane, a large, graceful wading-bird with elegant long legs and neck, greyish plumage, superficially resembling the heron and related to the bustard. They migrate in V or W formation and have trumpet-like voices. There are several species, found in all continents except S. America, including the Crowned Crane with golden coronet and the Demoiselle with tuft-like crest of white feathers. The Common Crane nested in East Anglia in mediaeval times but now comes only as a rare visitor from the Continent.

Credit is an advance of money or of goods or services in consideration of a promise of payment later. Trade credit is such an advance from trader to customer; bank credit is an advance of money by a bank to a client, whether a business firm or a private person, in consideration of an interest payment by the borrower.

Creed (Latin *credo* = I believe), a formal statement of belief. The three orthodox Christian creeds are the Apostles' Creed (a summary of their teaching), the Nicene Creed (drawn up by the Church Council at Nicaea in A.D. 325 to define its theological doctrines), and the Athanasian Creed (concerning the nature and divinity of Christ). *See also* under individual headings.

Cremation, the ancient custom, revived in modern times, of burning the dead. Cremation was first legalised in Great Britain in 1885 and the first crematorium opened at Woking in that year. Application for cremation must be accompanied by two medical certificates.

Cricket, a genus of insects of the grasshopper order which move by leaps. The male produces a chirping noise by rubbing its wing-covers together. Just as the males inherit the nerve machinery for emitting the song of the species, so the females receive and respond to that song and to no other.

Crimean War (1853–56). This war between Russia and the allied powers of Turkey, England, France and Sardinia, was connected with the Eastern Question (*q.v.*) and the desire of Russia for a port on the Mediterranean. Chief engagements were the Alma, Balaclava and Inkerman, Fighting virtually ceased with fall of Sevastopol in September 1855. Treaty of Paris signed 30 March 1856.

Crocodiles and their allies (alligators, caimans and gavials) are the largest of modern reptiles. They are well equipped for a predatory life in shallow waters, having powerful tails and strong jaws. Their eggs are laid on land, in sand or decomposing vegetation.

Crow, a family of birds including many well-known species such as the rook, raven, jackdaw, carrion crow, hooded crow, magpie, nutcracker, jaw and chough.

Crusades were military expeditions undertaken by some of the Christian nations of Europe with the object of ensuring the safety of pilgrims visiting the Holy Sepulchre and to retain in Christian hands the Holy Places. For two centuries nine crusades were undertaken: First, 1095–99, under Godfrey of Bouillon, which succeeded in capturing Jerusalem; Second, 1147–49, led by Louis VII of France, a dismal failure, which ended with the fall of Jerusalem; Third, 1189–92, in which Richard I of England took part, making a truce with Saladin; Fourth, 1202–4, led by French and Flemish nobles, a shameful expedition, resulting in the founding of a Latin empire in Constantinople; Fifth, 1217–21, led by John of Brienne; Sixth, 1228–29, under the Emperor Frederick II; Seventh, 1248–54, under St. Louis of France; Eighth, 1270, under the same leadership, but cut short by his death on an ill-judged expedition to Tunis; Ninth, 1271–72, led by Prince Edward of England, which accomplished nothing. Millions of lives and an enormous amount of treasure were sacrificed in these enterprises and Jerusalem remained in the possession of the "infidels". The chief material beneficiaries were the Italian maritime cities; the chief spiritual beneficiary was the pope; but in literature and the arts both Europe and the Levant benefited enormously from the bringing together of the different cultures.

Cryogenics (Greek roots: productive of cold) is the science dealing with the production of very low temperatures and the study of their physical and technological consequences. "Very low" is often taken to mean below about −150°C. The growth of cryogenics (essentially a 20th-cent. science) is connected with the discovery of how to liquefy all gases including even helium which resisted liquefaction until 1908. Scientifically, cryogenics is important partly because special phenomena (*e.g.*, superconductivity (*q.v.*)) appear at lower temperatures and partly because more can be learned about ordinary properties by studying them in the absence of heat. Technologically, cryogenics is becoming more and more significant, for example, liquefied gases are rocket propellants, superconductors make valuable magnets, tissue-freezing techniques (using very cold liquids) have been

introduced into surgery. *See* **Absolute Temperature.**

Crystal, in everyday usage, a solid chemical substance bounded by plane surfaces which show a regular geometrical arrangement as, *e.g.*, quartz crystals, rock salt, snow flakes. In physics the term means any substance whose atoms are arranged in a regular three-dimensional array. This includes most solids, even those not particularly crystalline in appearance, *e.g.*, a lump of lead. *See also* **Glass** and **Liquid Crystals.**

Cubism, the name of a revolutionary movement in art created in the years 1907–9 by the two painters Picasso and Braque. Rejecting purely visual effects, they approached nature from an intellectual point of view, reducing it to mathematical orderliness. Its respectable grandparent was Cézanne who had once written: " you must see in nature the cylinder, the sphere, and the cone "—a concept which, together with the contemporary interest in Negro sculpture, moved the two founders of the movement to experiment with the reduction of natural forms to their basic geometrical shapes. In practice, this meant combining several views of the object all more or less superimposed in order to express the idea of the object rather than any one view of it. The name Cubism was derisive and the movement aroused the same opposition as Impressionism, Fauvism and the later Futurism. Picasso's *Young Ladies of Avignon* was the first Cubist painting and his " Head " (1909) the first Cubist sculpture. Three phases are recognised: (1) Cubism under the influence of Cézanne; (2) high or analytical Cubism (*c.* 1909–12) concentrating on the breaking-down of form to the exclusion of interest in colour; (3) synthetic Cubism (*c.* 1913) making use of *collage* in which pieces of pasted-on paper (illustrations, wallpaper, newspaper) and other materials were used in addition to paint. Amongst other early cubist painters were Metzinger, Gleizes, Gris and Léger.

Cuckoo, a well-known migratory bird which is found in Great Britain from April to July, hawk-like in shape, with a very characteristic note, uttered during the mating season only by the male. The hen has a soft bubbling call. It lays its eggs in the nests of other birds, *e.g.*, the meadow pipit and hedge sparrow, but only one egg in each nest. Feeds mainly on insects, particularly hairy caterpillars.

Cuneiform, (Latin = *wedge-shaped*), an ancient method of writing by impressing wedge like strokes into tablets of damp clay which when dried and hardened formed a permanent script. Cuneiform writing developed from its original pictographic form into a phonetic writing and can be traced back to the non-Semitic Sumerians of ancient Mesopotamia, the earliest civilisation known to us. It passed to the Semitic Accadians of Babylonia in the 3rd millennium B.C. who adapted it to their own language. Decipherment by Sir Henry Rawlinson, 1835.

Curfew (Old Fr. *covre-feu* = cover fire), a regulation common throughout Europe in mediaeval times by which, at a fixed hour in the evening, the church bell was rung as a signal that fires were to be put out and the people were to go to bed. The custom originated in the fear of fire when buildings were built of timber. Nowadays a curfew is imposed by the military in areas where riots or disturbances are expected, compelling the civilian population to remain indoors after nightfall.

Curia, the central government of the Roman Catholic Church. By the reform which came into force on 1 January 1968, its twelve Sacred Congregations or " ministries " were reorganised and reduced to nine. The aim of the reform was to streamline the Curial offices so that the Church's machinery can cope with modern problems, so favouring the desires expressed by the Ecumenical Council convened by Pope John.

Curie, a measure of the rate at which radioactive material emits radiation. One curie is a disintegration rate of $3\cdot7 \times 10^{10}$ disintegrations per second.

Curlew, a wading-bird of which there are several species. It frequents marshy places, feeds on worms, insects, molluscs and berries and possesses a very long, down-curved bill.

Currency is the name given to the types of cash money—metal or paper—in use in an area (*e.g.* pound, sterling, dollar, franc). It also designates the actual coins or notes issued. Its amount is usually subject to regulation by the Government, or by a Central Bank acting on the Government's behalf. Britain changed over to a £-based decimal currency in February 1971. *See also* **National Currencies, Section N.**

Cybernetics, the science concerned with the automatic control and communication processes in both animals and machines. Thus it is concerned with brain function, information theory, electronic computers, and automation.

Cyclone, a term usually applied to a tropical revolving storm. Cyclones often occur towards the end of the hot seasons and are mainly confined to tracks in the western areas of the oceans, being known as hurricanes (Caribbean and Pacific), cyclones (Indian Ocean) and typhoons (China Seas). The circulation of air in a cyclone is similar to that in the *depression* of temperate latitudes, but the region of low pressure is much more localised and the pressure gradients steeper. Winds of hurricane strength and torrential rain occur generally, although at the centre of the storm there is a small area, known as the " eye ", where fair, calm weather prevails.

Cyclotron, a machine for accelerating charged particles such as protons to very high energies. Devised by E. O. Lawrence in California in 1930, it uses a magnetic field to make the particles traverse nearly circular paths and an electric field to give them an additional pulse of energy each time round. The accelerated particles impinge on targets, and the resulting events are a basic source of information for nuclear physicists. The cyclotron is obsolescent and has led to the development of other machines, *e.g.*, betatrons, synchrotrons. Britain has two major national high-energy machines: a 7 GeV proton synchrotron (to be closed and replaced by a " spallation neutron source "), and a 5 GeV electron synchrotron. The European Organisation for Nuclear Resarch (CERN), to which Britain contributes through the Science Research Council (SRC), carries out research at higher energies.

D

Dactylopterus, a fish of the gurnard family, with wing-like pectoral fins; sometimes known as the flying fish, though that appellation is more generally given to *Exocaetus exiliens.*

Dadaism (French *Dada* = hobby-horse) was a hysterical and nihilistic precursor of Surrealism (*q.v.*) resulting from the shock produced by the first world war. Beginning in Zurich about 1915, it spread to other continental cities, such as Berlin and Paris, dying out in 1922. The movement was deliberately anti-art, destructive, and without meaning; it intended to scandalise by such tricks as " compositions " made out of anything that came to hand—buttons, bus tickets, pieces of wire, bits of tin, etc. Other excesses included incoherent poetry, Dada night-clubs, plays, and short-lived newspapers. Many Dadaist painters became Surrealists at a later stage, but where Surrealism is a deliberate attempt to present subconscious and dream-like images, Dadaism was sheer anarchism. Leading Dadaists were Hans Arp, Marcel Duchamp, André Breton, Kurt Schwitters and Max Ernst.

Daddy Longlegs, or Crane-fly, a slender long-legged fly of the family Tipulidae. The larvae which do damage to lawns and plants are called leather-jackets. The Americans call Harvest-men (*q.v.*) daddy longlegs.

Daguerreotype, the first practical photographic process, invented in Paris by M Daguerre during the years 1824–39. The light-sensitive plate was prepared by bringing iodine in contact with a plate of silver. After exposure a positive image came by development of the plate in mercury vapour. Even for open-air scenes the first daguerreotypes involved exposure of 5–10 minutes. The picture came in one copy only and the process was therefore of limited use. The wet collodion process (1851) rendered the technique obsolete.

Dail Eireann, the name of the national parliament of the Irish Republic.

Damaskeening, the art of inlaying one metal upon another, largely practised in the East in mediaeval times, especially in the decoration of sword blades.

Dandies, the name given to a class of exquisites prominent in early Victorian days, and who attracted attention by excessive regard for dress. Their feminine counterparts were the dandizettes.

Danegeld, a tax imposed in England in Anglo-Saxon times to raise funds for resisting the Danes or to buy them off. Edward the Confessor abolished the tax, but it was revived by the Conqueror and subsequently retained, under another name, after the danger from the Danes was past. It is the basis of all taxation in this country. Domesday Book (*q.v.*) was originally drawn up for the purpose of teaching the State how to levy the tax.

Danelaw, the law enforced by the Danes in the kingdoms of Northumbria, East Anglia, and in the districts of the five (Danish) boroughs—lands grouped round Leicester, Nottingham, Derby, Stamford and Lincoln—which they occupied during the Viking invasions of the 9th and 10th cent. The country occupied was also called the Danelaw or Danelagh.

Darter, 1. Snakebirds, a genus of the pelican family, with long, pointed bill and serpent-like neck and resembling cormorants in appearance. There are 5 species. 2. Numerous species of small freshwater fish belonging to the perch family, found in N. America.

Date Palm, *Phoenix dactylifera,* one of the oldest known food plants widely cultivated in N. Africa and W. Asia. It grows to 30 m and continues to bear for 2 or 3 centuries, its fruit being of great value as a food. From the leaves the Africans make roofs for their huts; ropes are made from the fibrous parts of the stalks; and the sap furnishes a stimulating beverage.

Dauphin, the title borne by the eldest sons of the Kings of France from 1349 to the Revolution of 1830.

Day is the most natural unit of time and may be defined as the period of rotation of the earth relative to any selected heavenly body. Relative to the sun it is called the *solar day.* Relative to a fixed star it is called the *sidereal day.* Owing to irregularities in the earth's movements, the time taken for the earth to rotate through 360° relative to the sun is variable, and so the *mean solar day* of 24 hours has been introduced, which is the average throughout the year. The *mean solar day* is our standard, used for purposes of the calendar, and astronomers use *sidereal* clocks to check mean solar time. In practice, for convenience, the sidereal day is determined by the earth's rotation relative to the vernal equinox or first point of Aries, and is equal to 23 hours 56 minutes and 4·091 seconds of mean solar time (*i.e.,* about 4 minutes shorter than a solar day). *See* **Time.**

DDT (dichloro-dephenyl-trichloroethane). A very powerful insecticide which has had wide success in the control of diseases, such as malaria and typhus which are carried by insects. Mosquito swamps are sprayed with DDT to kill the carriers. Because this toxic chemical breaks down very slowly it builds up in birds and animals and its use is now banned in Britain. Its detection in Antarctic wild life confirmed that DDT pollution was virtually world-wide.

Deacon, an ecclesiastical official, who assists in some of the smaller ministerial duties in church or chapel; in the Anglican Church he ranks below a priest.

Dead Languages are such as the ancient Greek and Roman tongues, which are no longer spoken but are preserved in literature.

Dead Sea Scrolls, a group of ancient Jewish documents, consisting of scrolls and fragments which have been recovered since 1947 in the vicinity of Qumran near the Dead Sea and which represent one of the most important finds ever made in the field of biblical archaeology and Christian origins. The scrolls written in Hebrew or Aramaic, were found in caves, the first by chance by an Arab shepherd in 1947. These consisted of biblical texts older by a thousand years than the earliest Hebrew manuscript of the Old Testament (A.D. 895). Many fragments have since been discovered, comprising the whole of the Old Testament with the exception of Esther. In addition there are commentaries and other non-biblical writings, including one called " The War of the Sons of Light with the Sons of Darkness ". The wr'ting on the scrolls indicates that they were written over a period of two centuries, the greater proportion before the birth of Christ. A nearby ruin is believed to have been the home of a religious sect called the Essenes (J18), to whom the scrolls belonged. By the aid of the latest scientific techniques, including radiocarbon tests, the age of the scrolls is being accurately determined. An account of the scrolls and their implications is given in Edmund Wilson's *The Dead Sea Scrolls: 1947–1969*.

Dean, a Church of England dignitary, ranking below a bishop, and the head of the chapter of a cathedral. A rural Dean supervises a *deanery* or group of parishes. There are also Deans of Faculties in some universities, and at Oxford and Cambridge the *Dean* is in charge of chapel services and disciplinary arrangements.

Death Watch Beetle (*Xextobium rufovillosum*), a wood-boring beetle, larger than the common furniture beetle. found chiefly in the old oak beams of churches and other historic buildings. The grub bores from 4–12 years. The name " death watch " comes from the superstition that the ticking sound, made by the beetle striking its head against the wood, is a sign of approaching death. The death watch beetle in the roof of Westminster Hall was recently smoked out by means of an insecticide called gamma benzine hexachloride. *See also* Furniture Beetle, Woodworm.

Decalogue, name given to the Ten Commandments of the Old Testament. There are two versions of them, differing in detail: Exodus xx. 2–17 and Deuteronomy v. 6–21. They are of Hebrew origin and are recognised by Jews and Christians as the divine law given by God to Moses on Mt. Sinai. Most of them are prohibitions in contrast to the beatitudes (pronounced by Christ in the Sermon on the Mount) which are positive, *e.g.*, Blessed are the merciful.

December, the last month of the year in our calendar, and the tenth in the old Roman.

Deciduous Trees are such as shed their leaves at certain seasons as distinguished from evergreens or permanent foliaged trees or shrubs.

Declaration of Independence was an Act by which the American Congress, on 4 July 1776, declared the American colonies to be independent of Great Britain. " Independence Day " is a holiday in the United States.

Defender of the Faith (*Defensor Fidei*), a title conferred upon Henry VIII by Pope Leo X in 1521 for entering the lists against Luther with his pamphlet in defence of the Seven Sacraments. After Henry assumed headship of the Church of England the Pope withdrew the title but it was confirmed to him by Parliament in 1554 and has been used ever since by English monarchs.

Deflation is a policy designed to bring down costs by reducing the supply of means of payment. It is usually advocated as a remedy for inflation, and in this connection is often referred to as Disinflation. It usually results in a fall in employment. *See* Section G.

Dehydrate, to eliminate the water from a substance. The process of dehydration is now used in the food industry, as a result of wartime research, in making such things as dried egg and packet soups. Most vegetables contain over 90 per cent. of water, and much of this can be removed under vacuum at low temperatures without appreciably impairing the flavour. The lightness of the dehydrated products is an advantage when supplies have to be transported.

Deliquescence, the process of dissolving by the absorption of moisture from the atmosphere. For instance, chromic acid crystals on exposure to the air quickly deliquesce.

Delta, a triangular tract of land between diverging branches of a river at its mouth, and so called from its general resemblance to the Greek letter Δ *delta*. The best-known examples are the deltas of the Nile, the Ganges, the Niger and the Mississippi.

Deluge, a flood, commonly applied to the story of the Deluge in the Bible, in which Noah and the Ark figure. A similar tradition lingers in the mythologies of all ancient peoples.

Democratic Party, one of the two great American political parties, originated about 1787, advocating restrictions on the federal governments and in opposition to the federalists. It was in 1825 that a group who were in favour of high tariffs seceded, later to become the Republican Party. The Democratic Party was split again over slavery before the Civil War (1861–65), and in the main the southern states have been supporters of the Democrats. The economic depression helped the Democrats to power in 1932 (*see* New Deal) and they held office until 1953 when Eisenhower became President. In 1960 Kennedy narrowly won the Presidency and in 1964 Lyndon Johnson swept in with a landslide victory over the Republican candidate. In 1968 and 1972 the Democratic candidates were beaten by Nixon. In 1976 Jimmy Carter defeated Gerald Ford who had become President after the resignation of Nixon in 1974. The symbol of the party is a donkey, invented, like the Rebublican's elephant, by the cartoonist Thomas Nast.

Dendrite, a stone or mineral on or in which tree-like tracery appears, the result of the action of the hydrous oxide of manganese.

Density, a measure of the mass per unit volume of a material, usually expressed in grams per cubic centimetre. *Specific gravity* is the ratio of the density of a material at the temperature under consideration to that of water at the temperature of its maximum density (4°C). In grams per cubic centimetre the density of gold is 19·3, silver 10·5, lead 11·3, water 0·99997, air 0·00129.

Depreciation of a currency is a fall in its relative value in terms of gold or of other currencies. The term is most often used to indicate a fall in the value of one country's money in relation to others. *See* Section G.

Depression, a region where barometric pressure is lower than that of its surroundings. These areas of low pressure are usually less extensive than anticyclones (*q.v.*) and may vary from hundreds to thousands of kilometres in diameter. The winds, often of gale force where the depression is deep, blow round the system in an anticlockwise direction in the Northern Hemisphere (in the reverse direction in the Southern Hemisphere). Well above the earth's surface the winds blow along rather than down the pressure gradient but near the surface, friction causes the winds to blow slightly (*c.* 15°) across the isobars. The depression exists only as long as more air diverges out of its upper parts than converges into its lower parts. The majority of depressions which cross the British Isles travel from the Atlantic, sometimes in series or families. at rates from a few kilometres to a thousand kilometres a day, bringing their generally unsettled weather with them.

Desalinisation, the process of removing minerals, chiefly salt, from sea or brackish water to provide pure water for drinking or industry. Small-scale desalinisation by distillation has been practised for many years on ships and small islands. By the 1960s, many large-scale distillation plants were in operation, many of them in hot dry countries as in the Middle East. Kuwait, for example, used oil revenues to buy desalinisation plant and powers the plant with natural gas. As water for large population centres becomes more precious and desalinisation techniques more efficient, the process may be more and more used though it is expensive in capital outlay and in the cost of heating required to distil the water. Methods other than distillation are under investigation but not as yet much used. Some useful by-products can be extracted from the salt.

Deserts, vast, barren, stone or sandy wastes where there is almost no rainfall and little or no vegetation. These regions are found in the interior of the continents Africa, Asia and America between 20° and 30° north and south of the equator. Europe is the only continent without deserts. The most famous are the Sahara, the largest in the world the Gobi desert of central Asia, the Kalahari desert of south-west Africa and the great Australian desert. The marginal extension of deserts (desertification) is a topic of considerable debate. The increasing size of deserts is thought to result from either climatic change or the interference by man.

Detention Centres in Britain are for young people (boys and girls) over 14 but under 21 who have been found guilty of an offence for which an adult could be sent to prison. Controlled by the Home Office.

Determinism and Free-will. *See* Section J.

Deuterium or "heavy hydrogen". The second isotope of hydrogen; the third is called tritium. Deuterium atoms have in their nuclei a neutron as well as a proton; tritium nuclei have two neutrons and one proton. In ordinary hydrogen gas about one out of every 5,000 atoms is a deuterium atom. Deuterium was discovered in 1932 by Professor Harold Urey. The oxide of deuterium corresponding to water is called "heavy water". The nucleus of the deuterium atom is called a deuteron. An anti-deuteron consisting of an anti-proton and an anti-neutron was produced at Brookhaven in 1965, the first compound anti-nucleus ever to be produced.

Devaluation is a definite, official downward valuation of a country's currency in terms of its exchange value with other currencies. The £ was devalued in 1949, when an official exchange rate of £1 = $2.8 was established, and again in 1967, to a rate of £1 = $2.4. Since 1972 there has been greater flexibility in exchange rates and national currencies have been allowed to "float". *See* Section G, Part IV.

Devonian System in geology refers to the strata between the Silurian and the Carboniferous Formations. It includes the Old Red Sandstone Formation. The fauna of the Devonian include the group of fishes known as the Rhipidistra (on the evolutionary route towards the amphibians), Actinistia (coelacanth), and the Dipnoi or lung fishes. *See* F48.

Dew, moisture deposited by condensation of water vapour on exposed objects especially during calm, cloudless nights. The loss of heat from the ground after sunset, by radiation, causes the layer of atmosphere close to the surface to be chilled below the temperature, known as the dew-point, at which the air is saturated with vapour. Part of the vapour condensed may be transpired from blades of grass and foliage of plants.

Dew Pond is a shallow artificial pond which is on high ground and rarely dries up, even during prolonged droughts, despite being used by cattle and sheep as a drinking source. The name arose from the belief that dew deposits at night provided the moisture for replenishment. Drainage of rain-water and mist condensed on neighbouring trees and shrubs are probably more important factors.

Dialectical Materialism. *See* Section J.

Diamond, a mineral, one of the two crystalline forms of the element carbon (the other is graphite), the hardest known substance, used as a gem and in industry. India was the first country to mine diamonds (the Koh-i-noor, which means "mountain of light", known since 1304, came from Golconda near Hyderabad and came into British possession when the Punjab was annexed in 1849). The celebrated diamond mines of South Africa were discovered in the 1870s. Other important diamond producing countries are Zaïre, USSR, Congo, Ghana, Sierra Leone, Namibia, Angola, Tanzania. The world's biggest diamond is the 3,106-carat Cullinan, discovered near Pretoria, South Africa, in 1905. Diamonds can be made artificially by subjecting carbon to very high temperatures and pressures; many industrial diamonds are made this way. Antwerp is the main diamond centre of the world, London the main marketing centre, Amsterdam the main diamond cutting centre.

Diatoms. One-celled algae, common in fresh and salt water. Distinctive feature is the siliceous wall which is in two halves, one fitting over the other like the lid of a box. These walls are often very finely and beautifully sculptured. The diatoms constitute a class of the plant kingdom known as the Bacillariophyta. *Diatom ooze* is a deep-sea deposit made up of diatom shells. *Diatomite* or *diatomaceous earth* is the mineral form that such diatom oozes assume (sometimes known as kieselguhr which mixed with nitroglycerine yields dynamite).

Diesel Engine, an engine in which the liquid fuel is introduced into a compressed or partially compressed charge of air, and which does not need an extraneous source of ignition. The modern oil engine has been evolved mainly from the principles enunciated by Herbert Akroyd-Stuart in his patent of 1890 and, like the steam and other inventions, represents the improvements achieved by many men, including those by Rudolf Diesel of Germany, in respect of high compression pressures and greater fuel economy.

Diet, in German history, an assembly of dignitaries or delegates called together to debate upon and decide important political or ecclesiastical questions. The most famous imperial Diets were those held at Worms (1521) Speyer (1529), and Augsburg (1530), all of which dealt with matters of religious conflict arising from the Reformation.

Diffusion is the process of mixing which occurs when two liquids or gases are in contact. It is most rapid between gases, and, as laid down by Graham's law, "the rates of diffusion of different gases are in the inverse proportion to the square roots of their relative densities". Diffusion arises through the continual movement of molecules. Even in solids diffusion can occur. If a block of gold and a block of silver are welded together, after some time particles of gold are found in the silver, and *vice versa*.

Dimensions in common speech are the magnitudes of length, breadth and thickness giving, the size of an object, thus a line has only one dimension: length; a plane surface two: length and breadth; and a solid three: length, breadth and thickness. In mathematics, hypothetical objects with any number of dimensions are considered. In physics and mechanics, dimensions are numbers which relate the units in which any quantity is measured to the so-called fundamental units. The latter are usually but not necessarily those of length, mass and time. "Dimensional analysis" is an important technique of scientific reasoning.

Dimorphism, the quality of assuming two distinct forms. For instance, carbon, which is graphite in one form, is the diamond in another.

Dinosaur, the name given to a group of extinct reptiles of the Mesozoic period, some of which were of immense size—much larger than crocodiles. *See* Diplodocus.

Dip Needle. Instrument for measuring the *dip* or inclination of the earth's magnetic field.

Diplodocus, one of the best known of the extinct mammoth dinosaurs. Fossil remains have been discovered in the Jurassic rocks of the United States. Some reached a length of over 24 m.

Dipnoi *or* **Lung Fishes.** These have the air bladder adapted to function as a lung, and they can remain alive when the stream or marsh in which they live dries up. Species of lung fish occur in Australia, Africa and S. America.

Diptera, an order of insects. Their main characteristic is that they are two-winged, and the common house-fly is the best-known example. There are at least 50,000 species of these insects, including gnats, blow-flies, mosquitoes, tsetses.

Diptych was a folding two-leaved tablet of wood, ivory, or metal, with polished inner surfaces, utilised for writing with the style by the ancient Greeks and Romans. The same term was applied to the tablets on which the names of the persons to be commemorated were inscribed in the early Church. In art any pair of pictures hinged together is styled a diptych, a set of three, a triptych.

Discus, a circular piece of metal or stone about 30 cm in diameter, used in athletic contests by the ancient Greeks and Romans. Throwing the discus was a very favourite game, which was deemed worthy of celebration in Myron's famous *Discobolus* (c. 460 B.C.–450 B.C.), the best copy of which is in Rome.

Disk, an astronomical term denoting the seemingly flat surface of celestial bodies as seen by the eye.

Distillation, a process used to separate liquids of different boiling points. This is effected by placing the mixture in a distillation apparatus and heating. The liquid with the lower boiling point distils over first, the vapour being condensed and collected, forming the first *fraction*. With continued heating the second liquid reaches its boiling point, distils over and the mixture is said to be *fractionated*. Mixtures of liquids with close very high boiling points require more elaborate apparatus. Fractional distillation is a common process in the chemical industry, particularly in the refining of petroleum.

DNA (Deoxyribonucleic acid), a polymer molecule in the form of a double-strand helix containing many thousands of sub-units. Contains the genetic information coded in sequences of sub-units called bases. The Nobel Prize for medicine was awarded in 1962 for the discovery of the structure of DNA; that for 1968 for interpreting the genetic code and its function in protein synthesis. *See* Nucleic Acids.

Docks are enclosed water spaces where ships rest while being loaded or unloaded, repaired, or waiting for cargo. There are three main types: the wet dock in which water is maintained at the level of high tide so that vessels remain afloat while loading and unloading; the tidal dock, with open entrance to permit free ebb and flow of tide (*e.g.*, Glasgow, Southampton (which has double tides)); and the dry dock, or graving dock, for overhauling and repairing vessels, so constructed that, after a ship has been docked, the water can be drawn off (*e.g.*, Southampton, Tilbury). The floating dock is a type of dry dock. The Port of London Authority operates four main groups of docks. With the closing of some of the older up-river docks, down-river docks, notably at Tilbury, have been extensively developed. Technological advances in the handling of cargo, *e.g.*, containers (sealed boxes of cargo), have led to modernisation of the docks and labour practices.

Dodo, an extinct bird, giant and flightless, which lived on the island of Mauritius up until 250 years ago. Another species, the white dodo, lived on Réunion. Some reached exceptional sizes. By the end of the 17th cent. Mauritius, Rodriguez, and Réunion had all been colonised, and the dodo along with many other birds vanished forever because of their inability to stand up to man and the animals imported into the islands.

Dog-days, a period of 40 days (3 July–11 August) when Sirius rises and sets with the sun. The ancient superstition, which can be traced back in Greek literature to Hesiod (8th cent. B.C.), was that this star exercised direct influence over the canine race.

Doge, the chief magistrate in the former republics of Venice (697–1797) and Genoa (1339–1797, 1802–5).

Dogfish, a large family of small sharks, seldom more than 1 m in length. The flesh is sold as " rock salmon ". The eggs are contained in horny cases called " mermaid's purses ". The commonest of the British dogfishes are the spur-dogs.

Doldrums, a nautical term applied to those areas of the Atlantic and Pacific within a few degrees of the Equator towards which the trade winds blow and where the weather is calm, hot and sultry. Pressure is low and the air often rises to produce heavy tropical rainfall and squalls, rendering navigation difficult.

Dolomite, a name applied to a limestone containing appreciable magnesium; also the mineral dolomite, a double carbonate of magnesium and calcium.

Dolphin, a mammal of the whale order, from 2–2·4 m long, with a long, sharp snout, and of an active disposition. They abound in most seas and swim in shoals. A few species live in large rivers (Ganges and Amazon). They can cruise for long periods at around 15 knots and produce bursts of speed in the region of 20 knots, the water apparently flowing smoothly past their bodies. Dolphins are some of the most intelligent of mammals and are currently the subject of scientific experiments in communication. Name also for the fish, dorado.

Domesday Book is the famous register of the lands of England framed by order of William the Conqueror. According to Stowe, the name was derived from *Domus dei*, the name of the place where the book was deposited in Winchester Cathedral; though by others it is connected with doom in the sense of judgment. Its compilation was determined upon in 1084, in order that William might compute what he considered to be due to him in the way of tax from his subjects. William sent into each county commissioners to make survey. They were to inquire the name of each place, the possessor, how many hides of land were in the manor, how many ploughs were in demesne, how many homagers, villeins, cottars, serving men, free tenants, and tenants in soccage; how much wood, meadow, and pasture; the number of mills and fish ponds; what had been added to or taken away from the place; what was the gross value at the time of Edward the Confessor. So minute was the survey that the Saxon chronicler of the time reports " there was not a single hide, nor one vintage of land, nor even, it is shame to tell, though it seemed no shame to do, an ox, nor a cow, nor a swine was left that was not set down ". The record, which did not take in Northumberland, Cumberland, Durham and parts of Lancashire and Westmorland, was completed on 15 November 1085, and was comprised in two volumes—one a large folio, sometimes called the Little Domesday, which deals with Essex, Norfolk and Suffolk, the other a quarto, sometimes called the Great Domesday. The first is written on 384 double pages of vellum in one and the same hand, and in a small but plain character, each page having a double column. The quarto is written on 450 pages of vellum, but in a single column and in a large, fair character. The original is preserved in the Public Record Office. *See also* Danegeld.

Dominicans, an order of mendicant preaching friars founded by St. Dominic in Languedoc in 1215 and confirmed by the Pope in 1216 The rule of the order was rigorous. The dress was a white habit and scapular with a long black mantle. This gave them the name of Black Friars. Their official name is Friars Preachers.

Donjon, the keep, or inner tower of a castle, and the strongest and most secure portion of the structure. This was the last refuge of the garrison, and there was usually a prison on the lower floor, hence the name *dungeon*.

Don Juan, the legendary hero of many famous works, supposedly based on the life and character of the unscrupulous gallant Don Juan Tenorio of 14th-cent. Seville. The first dramatisation of the legend and the most famous is Tirso de Molina's *El Burlador de Sevilla*. Don Juan was also the subject of Molière's *Le Festin de Pierre*, Mozart's *Don Giovanni*, Byron's *Don Juan*, and José Zorilla's *Don Juan Tenorio*. The latter is played on All Saints' Day throughout Spanish-speaking countries.

Don Quixote, the "night of the doleful countenance ", the hero and title of Cervantes' classic novel of 16th-cent. Spain. Don Quijote de la Mancha, a gentle country gentleman of lofty but unpractical ideals, having read many chivalric romances, believes he is called upon to redress the wrongs of the world. Mounted on his nag Rosinante and accompanied by his companion Sancho Panza, a hard-headed and practical peasant, he sets out on his journeys of knight-errantry.

Dormouse, a family of small, squirrel-like rodents widely distributed throughout Europe and Asia, and living mainly on fruit and nuts. It is of nocturnal habits and sleeps through the winter.

Dot, a French term indicating the property which a wife brings to her husband on marriage and is usually settled on the woman, being her separate property, though the income from it may go towards the general household expenses.

Dotterel, a handsome bird of the plover family found in northern Europe and Siberia. Nests in the Cairngorms, the Grampians and E. Ross. Very tame.

Doukhobors. *See* Section J.

Drachm (or **Drachma**), an ancient Greek silver coin and weight. One drachma was equivalent to six obols. The word has survived as the name of a weight: Avoirdupois, one-sixteenth part of an ounce; Apothecaries' Weight, one-eighth part of an ounce.

Drag. Term used in mechanics for resistance offered by a fluid to the passage of a body moving through it. When speed of sound is reached drag increases abruptly. The lift/drag ratio gives the aeroplane designer his measure of aerodynamic efficiency.

Dragon, a fabulous monster common to folk-lore in most countries; generally represented as a winged reptile with fiery eyes and breath of flame. A dragon guarded the garden of the Hesperides; in the New Testament there is mention of the " dragon, that old serpent, which is the devil "; St. George, England's patron saint, is supposed to have overcome the dragon; mediaeval legend abounds in dragons; in heraldry the dragon has also a conspicuous place; and in China it was the imperial emblem.

Dragonet, the name of the fish of the *Callionymus* genus, beautifully coloured, and about 30 cm in length. They are common on the British coast and in the Mediterranean.

Dragon Fly, the common name of a well-known order of insects having two pairs of membraneous wings, and often of very brilliant colours. They are swift of flight and may be seen hovering over sheets of water in the sunshine all through the summer. Their chief food is mosquitoes.

Dragon's Blood, a dark-red resinous substance obtained from the fruit of a Malay palm, and possessing medicinal virtues. In a special technique used for making line blocks in printing, dragon's blood is used.

Drawbridge, a bridge that can be lifted up so that no passage can be made across it. It was a usual feature of a fortified castle in the Middle Ages, and was raised or lowered by chains and levers. It spanned the fosse, and on the approach of an attacking party was raised and formed a special barricade to the gate. Modern drawbridges are such as are raised to allow of the passage of boats up and down a river or estuary. The Tower Bridge is a famous London bridge of this type.

Drongo. The King Crow or Indian Black Drongo is frequently seen in India perched on branches or telegraph wires, darting suddenly to catch insects and to attack crows and hawks. Other members of the family are found in Asia, Africa and Australia. Its plumage is black with steel-blue gloss.

Drosophila or Fruit Fly. More has been learnt by geneticists from breeding experiments with this insect than with any other.

Dross, the name generally applied to the refuse of molten metal, composed of slag, scales and cinders.

Drought occurs when there has been an absence of rain for a long period or a marked deficiency of precipitation over a much longer period in a climatic zone where precipitation is ordinarily adequate for vegetation or agriculture, river flow and water supplies. It is different from aridity which refers to the extreme dryness of desert or arid regions where rainless periods characterise the climatology. Hitherto in the British Isles " an absolute drought " was defined as " a period of at least 15 consecutive days without measurable rainfall ", but arbitrary definitions of this type are not now normally used. In the British Isles droughts occur from time to time but very long rainless spells at a place are rather rare. The longest recorded spell in the British Isles with no measurable daily rainfall lasted 61 days at Liss (Hants) from 16 March to 15 May 1893. Over the country as a whole the 12-month period beginning 1 May 1975 was the driest such period since records began, with less than 60 per cent. of normal precipitation in parts of the Midlands and S.W. England.

Druidism. *See Section J.*

Drupe is the scientific term for stone fruit. The stone forms the inner part (endocarp) of the fruit, and encloses a seed or kernel which is liberated after the fleshy part (pericarp) has rotted.

Dry-rot, the term was first used about 1775 to describe the fungal decay of timber in buildings. Creosote distilled from coal tar is the standard material for preservation of timber, and penta-

chlorophenol and copper naphthenate are two compounds now extensively used. Dry wood always escapes dry-rot. Chief fungi causing dry-rot are *Merulius* and *Poria.*

Duck, water bird smaller than the related goose and swan, which together form the family Antidae. Duck refers to the female, drake to the male. The duck family falls into two separate groups: the river or freshwater (surface feeding) ducks, such as the mallard, pintail, wigeon, shoveler, mandarin, teal, garganey; and the sea (diving) ducks, such as the goldeneye, pochard, scoter, eider, and the fish-eating mergansers or " sawbills ". The ancestor of all domestic breeds, with the exception of the muscovy, is the mallard.

Duckbill, *Ornithorhynchus anatinus,* also duck-billed platypus, a fur-covered, egg-laying, nest-building mammal inhabiting Australia and Tasmania. It has webbed feet and a muzzle like a duck's bill and is about 50 cm long.

Ductility is a property possessed by most metals which renders them capable of being stretched without breaking. Gold is the most, and lead the least ductile of metals, the order being gold, silver, platinum, iron, copper, palladium, aluminium, zinc, tin, lead. In animated nature the spider and the silkworm produce secretions of notable ductility.

Dugong. A marine mammal, belonging to the order Sirenia (sea-cows). Inhabits Red Sea and Indian Ocean; also found as far East as the Philippines and Australia. Lives on sea-weed. Related to the Manatee.

Duke, the highest rank in the British peerage next to that of a royal prince. Edward, the Black Prince, eldest son of Edward III, who died before his father, was the first English duke, being created Duke of Cornwall in 1337. Since then all Princes of Wales have held that title.

Dukeries, a range of English woodland and park country, mainly in Nottinghamshire, comprising the adjacent demesnes of several English dukes and nobles. The Dukeries include Sherwood Forest and the estates of Welbeck Abbey, Clumber Park, Worksop Manor and Thoresby Hall.

Dunes. Sand dunes are elliptical or crescent-shaped mounds of loose sand produced by wind action. The dune has a gentle slope on windward side; a steep slope on the leeward side.

Dunlin, very common small wading-bird of the Sandpiper family nesting in Britain. Its range extends to other areas where it also breeds.

Dunmow Flitch, a custom which originated in the parish of Little Dunmow, Essex, in the reign of Henry III, which was that the husband who was prepared to swear before the prior, convent, and townsfolk of Dunmow that he had not repented of marriage or quarrelled with his wife for a year and a day, should be rewarded with the gift of a flitch of bacon. The custom has frequently been revived.

Dunnock (*Prunella modularis*), a small bird of rich brown and dark grey plumage common in gardens and hedgerows. Sings a cheerful song all the year round. Called hedge-sparrow in southern England. Another member of the same family, the larger Alpine Accentor (*Prunella collaris*), is found on rocky mountain slopes of Europe and Asia.

Duodecimo, a sheet of paper folded into twelve leaves, written " 12mo ".

Durbar, a term used in India from the Persian word *darbár* meaning " court " or " audience ". It may be either a council for administering affairs of state, or a purely ceremonial gathering. The word was applied to great ceremonial gatherings like Lord Lytton's durbar for the proclamation of the Queen-Empress in 1877 and the Delhi durbar of 1911.

Dust, solid particles of matter floating in the atmosphere, produced chiefly by volcanic eruptions, sand-storms in desert regions, and industrial and domestic smoke. When the island of Krakatoa erupted in 1883, more than 4 km^3 of dust was thrown into the air and carried three times round the earth by the explosive wave. The particles in dust-storms are much finer than those in sand-storms and are swept up to far greater hights. The local whirlwinds which form over loose dry soils are termed dust-devils.

Dyke. A wall-like intrusion of igneous rock

which cuts across the bedding or other layered structure of the country rock; the word also signifies in alternative usage, a sea-wall and an open drain.

Dynamite, a powerful explosive whose chief element is nitro-glycerine. It was discovered by Nobel in 1867, who absorbed nitro-glycerine in kieselguhr; has a disruptive force of about eight times that of gunpowder.

Dynamo. Machine for transforming mechanical energy into electrical energy. Depends on principle of electromagnetic induction whereby a current is produced in a conductor (*e.g.,* copper wire) traversing a magnetic field. The two essential parts of a dynamo are the conductors or *armature* and the *field magnets.*

Dynasty, a succession of monarchs of the same family, as the Carlovingian dynasty, the Bourbon dynasty, the Plantagenet dynasty, etc.

E

Eagle, large bird of prey with huge hooked bill, related to the buzzard, kite, hawk, harrier, falcon and vulture, together forming the family Falconidae. There are many species to be found throughout the world, the Golden, Imperial, Tawny, Spotted and Lesser Spotted being found in Europe. The Golden Eagle, a magnificent-looking bird, nests in the Scottish Highlands, and the White-tailed Sea Eagle, which used to breed in Britain, is now only an occasional visitor. The eagle has been the symbol of royal power since the earliest times, and the American or Bald Eagle is the emblem of the United States.

Earl, a British title of nobility of the third rank, duke and marquis coming first and second. The title dates from Saxon times, and until 1337 ranked highest in our peerage.

Earl-Marshal, in England ranks as the eighth of the great officers of state, is head of the College of Arms, attends the sovereign in opening and closing the session of Parliament, arranges state processions (especially coronations) and assists in introducing newly created peers in the House of Lords. The office is hereditary in the family of the Dukes of Norfolk.

Earth, our habitable globe, is the third of the planets of the solar system in order from the sun and on an average throughout the year takes 24 hours to turn completely round relative to the sun, the whole earth revolving round the sun in a slightly elliptical orbit once in a year of 365·2564 days. The mean distance of the earth from the sun is 93,004,000 miles (149,600,000 km). The shape of the earth is that of an oblate spheroid, its equatorial and polar axes measuring 12,756 km and 12,715 km respectively. Recent earth satellite studies have shown that it is even more pear-shaped than used to be thought with the north polar region having a definite stem and the south polar region a marked depression. Why this should be is not known. The crust consists of an outer layer of surface soil of varying thickness, beneath which there is a mass of hard rock several miles deep, the percentage (by weight) of the principal elements present being oxygen 47, silicon 28, aluminium 8, sodium and potassium 5, iron 4·5, calcium 3·5, magnesium 2·2, titanium 0·5, hydrogen 0·2, carbon 0·2, phosphorus and sulphur 0·2. Mass of the earth is estimated to be nearly 6,000 million million million tonnes. Two-thirds of the earth's surface is covered with water. It has only one satellite, the moon. The earth receives more light from the sun in 13 seconds than it does from the moon in one year. Weather changes are independent of the moon. A recent estimate of the age of the earth is 4,600 million years. Recent discoveries suggest that the earth is embedded in the atmosphere of the sun and that some of the heat that reaches us from the sun gets here by direct conduction through interplanetary space. See **F8-10.**

Earthquake, a sudden violent disturbance of the earth's crust; the region of the surface immediately above the " focus ", or source where the earthquake originates, is termed the " epi-

centre ". On account of their destructive power earthquakes have attracted attention from the earliest times, but accurate study dates only from the last century and the development of a world-wide network of recording stations from the present one. The majority of severe earthquakes result from fractures, usually along existing faults, in underlying rock strata subjected to great strains, the shearing movement sometimes extending to the surface. These dislocations set up vibrations which are propagated as waves throughout the bulk of the earth or round the crust. Frequently the main shock is followed by a series of smaller aftershocks. Minor local earthquakes may be attributed to the effects of volcanic activity, but most of the larger ones originate in non-volcanic regions along well-marked lines of weakness in the earth's crust. Generally the ground is felt to tremble, undergoing oscillations which may gradually or suddenly increase to a maximum and accompanied by sounds. Where there is movement of the sea-bed a tsunami (*q.v.*) may result. One of the greatest of historic times was that which destroyed and flooded Lisbon in 1755. Among the notable shocks of the present century rank those of San Francisco (1906), Messina, Italy (1908), China (1920), Japan (1923), Napier, New Zealand (1931), N.E. Assam (1950), Ionian Is. (1953), Agadir, Morocco (1960), Chile (1960), Iran (1962), Yugoslavia (1963), Alaska (1964), E. Turkey (1966), W. Sicily (1968), Peru (1970), 1976 was a year of major earthquakes, severe in China. See also Richter Scale and **F9(2).**

Earthworm, of which there are several species, has a cylindrical body, tapering at both ends, and segmented into rings. It moves by contraction of its rings, aided by retractive bristles; is eyeless, but has a mouth, gullet and stomach. Earthworms exist in immense numbers, and perform an important part in the scheme of nature by loosening the soil and rendering it more amenable to tillage. They also form a valuable food for birds and many mammals, and are unequalled as bait for certain kinds of fish.

Earwig, a genus of insects possessing two pairs of wings and anal forceps. It is nocturnal, lives on vegetable matter, and hides by day under stones or in flowers, *e.g.,* dahlias. The old belief that it deliberately creeps into people's ears is altogether unfounded.

Easter, the annual Christian festival in commemoration of the resurrection of Christ, the English name being derived from Eostre, goddess of Spring. The date cannot fall earlier than 22 March nor later than 25 April. Many disputes arose among the early Christians as to the proper time to celebrate this day which governs all other movable feasts. It was eventually ruled at the Council of Nicaea in 325 that Easter Day should be the first Sunday after the full moon following the vernal equinox. If this happens to be a Sunday, then Easter Day is the Sunday after. It should be remembered, however, that this moon is a hypothetical moon of the ecclesiastical calendar, quite imaginary, and generally one or two days later than the real moon we see in the heavens. In fact the reverend fathers at Nicaea did us a bad turn in having anything to do with the moon but then they had no Astronomer Royal to advise them of the complications. See also **Section N.**

Eastern Question, a term formerly applied to the problems arising from the instability of the Mohammedan power of Turkey and its relations with the other nations of Europe. Later connected with other problems of the Near East, such as the possession of Constantinople and the position of the Balkan states.

East India Company was incorporated by Elizabeth in 1600. In 1613 the Company set up a factory at Surat, India, and in 1662 Bombay came under the Company's influence and developed into an important trading port. Dupleix wanted to establish French power in India and a struggle for supremacy took place. Clive gained the victory for England and thenceforward British dominion in India remained undisputed except by native princes. In 1772 Warren Hastings was appointed the first Governor-General and in 1784 Pitt's India Act established a Board of Control for the India Company. A great increase of trade resulted, and this rule continued down to 1858. when, as a result of the mutiny, the Crown assumed the sovereignty. With the passing of the Indian Independence Act of 1947, British dominion ended and India was handed back to the Indians.

Eau-de-Cologne, a popular distilled perfume first manufactured at Cologne in the 18th cent. by Johann Maria Farina, an Italian, and since made in large quantities in Cologne and elsewhere.

Ebony, a name applied to various hard black woods, the best of which are grown in Mauritius and Sri Lanka. There are also Indian and American varieties. Only the inner portions, the heartwood, of the trees are of the necessary hardness and blackness. Ebony is largely used in ornamental cabinet work, for piano keys, canes, etc.

Ecce Homo ("Behold the Man!"), used in reference to the pictures and sculptures representing Christ crowned with thorns.

Ecclesiastical Courts, courts for administering ecclesiastical law and maintaining the discipline of the Church of England. Introduced by the Normans. Originally they had jurisdiction over both clergy and laity.

Eclipse, the partial or complete obscuring of one heavenly body by another. An eclipse of the sun occurs when the moon, which is 1/400th of the diameter of the sun and about 1/390th as far away, obscures some portion of the sun as seen by an observer on the earth. A total eclipse occurs when the whole of the sun's disc is covered by the moon. Astronomers travel many thousands of miles to observe the outer layers of the sun and its corona, which is only possible when the light from the sun is totally obscured by the moon during the few minutes of an eclipse. The total solar eclipse of 7 March 1970, as seen from Mexico, was watched by millions on their television screens. Total solar eclipses have occurred over parts of the British Isles in the years 1424, 1433, 1598, 1652, 1715, 1724, 1927, 1954 (visible from the Shetland Is.), and the next will be seen only from near Land's End on 11 August 1999. *See also* **N11.**

Ecliptic is the sun's apparent path in the sky: the great circle described by the sun from west to east in the course of a year. The sun is exactly on the equator on approx. 21 March, and 23 September, and the points where the celestial equator and ecliptic intersect on these days are called the *equinoctial points.* On approx. 21 June and 22 December the sun reaches its greatest and least midday elevation and its greatest distance north and south of the equator, and the points on the ecliptic on those days are called the *solstices* (*see* Seasons, Section **N**). These four points are equidistant from each other by 90°. The equinoctial points are not fixed. The angle of inclination of the ecliptic to the equator is called the obliquity of the ecliptic which is also variable, being influenced by the gravitational action of the other planets on the earth. At present the angle is 23½°.

Ecology, a term first described by the German biologist Haeckel in the 19th cent., is the study of the inter-relationships between living organisms and their environment. Autecology is the study of the environmental relationships of *individual* plants and species. Synecology is the study of plant and animal *communities* living together as groups and the relationship of these to their environment. Since 1935 the ecosystem has been the major unit of study in synecology. *See also* **F44–7.**

Ecumenical Council, a general council of the Christian Church summoned when important questions of Church doctrine and policy are to be decided. The early councils were predominantly Greek and convoked by the emperor. Those summoned by the pope when they meet at the Lateran Palace in Rome are called Lateran Councils; others have met at Constance, Florence, Trent and the Vatican. Their decisions are not binding on the rest of Christendom. Only 21 Ecumenical Councils have been held in the history of Christendom. The first was held at Nicaea in 325 when the mystery of the Trinity was defined. The 21st (known as the 2nd Vatican Council), convened by Pope John, opened in October 1962 in St. Peter's, Rome, and ended in December 1965. Two of

the principal themes were the reunion of all Christians with the Church of Rome and the Church's place in the modern world. At the last session of the Council the Pope announced his decision to establish for the first time an international synod of bishops in Rome for consultation and collaboration in the government of the Roman Church. This Senate of Bishops will provide the balancing factor alongside the Curia, which represents the Papacy and not the episcopacy.

Edda, the name given to two important collections of early Icelandic literature—*the Elder or Poetic Edda,* poems handed down from the 9th and 10th cent., probably Norwegian in origin, and the *Younger* or *Prose Edda* of Snorri Sturluson compiled about 1230. They treat of mythical and religious legends of an early Scandinavian civilisation.

Eddystone Lighthouse, 21 km south of Plymouth, is one of the most isolated in the world. The tower is 51 m high, and its light can be seen for 28 km. The present structure is the fourth that has occupied this dangerous position. The first was of wood, completed by Winstanley in 1698, but it was destroyed by storm in 1703. In 1708 a second and stronger lighthouse was built by Rudyerd. This lasted until 1755, when it was destroyed by fire. Smeaton built the third lighthouse of granite and this withstood storm and tempest for over a hundred years, 1759–1881. The present lighthouse, also of granite. was built 1879–81 on a nearby rock by Sir James Douglass.

Eels, edible fishes of the order Apodes, with snakelike body covered with minute scales embedded in the skin. The common or freshwater eel *Anguilla anguilla* is found in the Atlantic coastal areas of N. America and Europe and in the Mediterranean, and breeds S.E. of Bermuda. The electric eel of S. America is a variety of great interest, being able to cause electric shocks.

Egghead, a term used derogatively to describe the more intelligent and thoughtful people. Frequently applied in USA to the late Adlai Stevenson, who is said to have responded with the appeal: "Eggheads of the world unite. You have nothing to lose but your brains."

Egret, a slender, graceful bird of the heron family, of pure white plumage, famed for its beautiful silky plumes (aigrettes), which appear in the breeding season, and for which it was ruthlessly hunted and would have geen exterminated had not international action been taken to protect it. The Little Egret with black bill, black legs, and yellow feet breeds in Mediterranean lands.

Eider, a large diving duck, found along the rocky coasts of northern latitudes, well known for the beautifully warm soft down, called "eider down", which the female bird plucks from her breast to line her nest. In Norway and Iceland the haunts of the eider are preserved and the birds protected by law on account of the much prized "eider down", which is collected from the nests just before the breeding season. "Eider down" is so elastic that a kilogramme of it will fill an ordinary bed covering.

Eiffel Tower, built by the French engineer Alexandre Gustave Eiffel (1832–1923) for the Paris Exhibition of 1889. The tower which is made of iron is 300 m high and weighs about 7,000 tonnes.

Eisteddfod (a sitting) was originally a congress of Welsh bards and minstrels, and dates from before the 12th cent. These assemblies, discontinued for a long period, were resumed in 1819, and have been held yearly since, each lasting three or four days. Their object is to foster the Welsh patriotic spirit; they are devoted to orations and competitions in poetry, singing and harp-playing, prizes being awarded to the successful contestants.

Eland, largest species of antelope, native of Africa; large pointed horns, stands 1·5 m high at the withers, and weighs several hundred kg.

Elder, small trees of the *Sambucus* genus, with pinnate leaves, and clusters of white flowers and, later, small purplish-black berries. The black elder, the best known, is common in most parts of Europe, and thrives in Britain. A wine is made from its berries.

El Dorado, a "golden land", was an idea much favoured in the days of the early Spanish explorers. It was believed that somewhere on the South American continent there was a country abounding in gold and precious stones. Many expeditions were fitted out to discover it. Sir Walter Raleigh also went forth on this illusive quest. The term is still used in regard to any place of rich promise.

Eleatics. *See Section J.*

Electret, a piece of solid matter which retains a permanent electric polarisation analogous to the magnetic polarisation of a permanent magnet. There are various recipes for making them; carnauba wax is a common constituent.

Electricity. *See F21, also Energy Conversion.*

Electric Light is produced in several ways, commonly by causing a tungsten wire to heat up to incandescence by passing a current through it. Current may also be forced through ionised gases, causing them to glow. Such discharges include neon lights, sodium and mercury-vapour street-lamps, and various intense electric arcs used for technical purposes. In fluorescent lights an electric discharge causes ultra-violet (invisible) light, which then excites luminosity in certain chemical substances called luminescent materials. Other forms of electric lighting are being investigated.

Electric Telegraph may be said to date from 1836, when Sir Charles Wheatstone and his co-inventor Cooke introduced their Single-Needle instrument, which was soon followed by the Double-Needle apparatus. Morse, in 1837, invented his famous recording instrument. The first electric cable was between Dover and France, and was laid in 1850. The first Atlantic cable was laid in 1858, and the second in 1866. It was in 1899 that the first Marconi wireless telegraph messages were sent between England and France.

Electroencephalograph, an instrument which records the minute voltages produced by the electrical activity of the brain by means of electrodes taped to the scalp. The record of brain waves, known as EEG, shows that there is a general cycle of activity in the brain that underlies both sleep and wakefulness. *See Q5(2).*

Electrolysis is the condition established when an electric current passes through a conducting substance, between electrodes, resulting in decomposition and separation into constituents. Water thus becomes decomposed into hydrogen and oxygen.

Electromagnetic waves. *See F14.*

Electron. *See F11, 16.*

Electronic Music, music composed of electronically generated sound, recorded on tape and played through loudspeakers. Modern technical developments mean that in theory, and to a large extent in practice, a composer can generate and record *any* sequence of sounds he likes, varying at will pitch, intensity, reverberation, rhythm, intervals and all other audible qualities. Such limitless freedom of choice imposes on him severe problems of selection, notation and intellectual and artistic organisation. Though widely composed and performed, *i.e.*, played through loudspeakers or broadcast, electronic music as an art form must still be regarded as experimental and controversial, though its use as incidental or "atmospheric" music in radio and television is well established. Among the well-known composers are Babbitt, Berio, Koenig and Stockhausen.

Electronic News Gathering (ENG), also known in the United States as Electronic Journalism (EJ) or Electronic Camera Coverage (ECC), is a system for obtaining television pictures by means of very lightweight, portable electronic cameras. ENG is highly suited to the coverage of news events. It is usually operated by a crew of two—cameraman and engineer—who are also equipped with a van or field car serving as a mobile base. Pictures from the unit can be used in three ways: they can be transmitted "live", beamed back by radio link to the studio, or recorded on to a videotape cassette on site and taken back to headquarters for editing and transmission. The chief advantage of ENG lies in its speed, as the use of electronic equipment avoids the delay which occurs in the chemical processing of film before it can be transmitted. Wastage is also reduced because new recordings can be made over unwanted or unused material. ENG is in wide use in the USA.

Electronics. The science which deals with the behaviour and control of free electrons. It started with the discovery of the electron by Sir J. J. Thomson in 1897. The practical applications, constituting electronic engineering, have given us radio, radar, photo-electric cells, cathode-ray oscillographs, electron microscopes, television. Nowadays electronics uses devices like transistors such that the electrons move inside solid matter instead of *in vacuo*. This is sometimes referred to as "solid state electronics". *See also Microelectronics.*

Electron Microscope. A microscope in which beams of electrons are focused by magnetic lenses in a manner analogous to the focusing of light beams in the ordinary optical microscope. Modern electron microscopes have very high resolving power and can magnify up to 1,500,000 times, making it possible to explore the cell and the virus. A development of the electron microscope is the scanning electron microscope (stereoscan), developed at Cambridge, which can examine an essentially thick object, giving a very large depth of focus.

Electronvolt, unit of energy used in nuclear physics. It is the amount of energy required to move one electronic charge through a potential difference of one volt. It is very small— $1 \cdot 6 \times 10^{19}$ joules—and therefore suited to atomic physics. 1 MeV = a million electronvolts; 1 GeV = a thousand million electronvolts; these larger units are used in high energy physics.

Elementary Particle, one of the basic constituents of the material universe. The idea that matter consists of tiny particles goes back to classical times but the modern concept of the atom grew out of the chemistry and physics of the 19th cent. With the discovery of the electron in 1897 and the rise of nuclear physics in the 20th cent., the chemical atom was understood to be a structure built of even more fundamental particles—the electron, the proton and the neutron. In the last few decades, many more particles have been discovered, especially in the study of cosmic rays and by the use of large accelerating machines like those at CERN (Geneva) and Brookhaven National Laboratory (Long Island, New York). Among the later discoveries are the neutrino, the positron, the antiproton, the muon, the pion. These differ in electric charge and mass and other intrinsic properties and many have only a very short lifetime before they change into something else. Whether there is a small number of really elementary particles out of which all the others can be constructed is an unanswered question at the frontier of contemporary physics. *See F15–17.*

Elements. In chemistry, substances which cannot be separated into two or more simpler chemical substances. 91 elements are found naturally on the earth, one is observed spectroscopically in the stars, and a further twelve have been made artificially. Between them these elements can appear in some 1,200 different isotopes, of which 317 occur in Nature. (There are 274 stable isotopes among 81 stable elements.) *See F6, 23, also Section F.*

Elephant, a proboscidian mammal of which only two species survive—the Asiatic, in India, and the African elephant. No other animals possess a trunk. Both males and females have large ivory tusks, of considerable commercial value. The Indian elephant is usually about 2·7 m high and weighs about 3 tonnes; African elephants are larger, weigh about 6 tonnes, and are usually much fiercer. Several fossil elephants of still larger bulk have been discovered, including the mammoth and the mastodon. The Indian elephant is domesticated and used as a beast of burden, and may live 70 years.

Eleusinian Mysteries, festivals common throughout ancient Greece, agricultural in their symbolism.

Elgin Marbles, a collection of ancient Greek sculptures and architectural fragments got together by the 7th Earl of Elgin and brought to England between 1802 and 1812. These celebrated treasures had originally formed part of the Parthenon at Athens, and were probably carved by pupils of the sculptor Phidias. Lord Elgin expended over £70,000 upon them, and they were purchased for £35,000 for the British Museum, where they can now be seen displayed.

Elk, the largest animal of the deer family, possessing enormous antlers, and standing, when mature, about 2 m high. The American moose is of the same family.

Elm, a stately, wide-spreading tree having some 20 species spread over north-temperate regions, several of which are native and peculiar to Britain. The grandest of the field elms is the English elm, *Ulmus procera*, which may reach a height of *c.* 42 m and a girth of 8 m. The wych elm, *U. glabra*, or Scots elm, is a valuable hardwood and used in boat-building. The fungus that causes Dutch elm disease is carried from tree to tree by a bark beetle. The fungus came from infected veneer logs from central Europe. Ironically the disease was named after the Dutch workers who discovered its cause!

Elzevir, the name of a celebrated family of Dutch printers, who produced editions of Latin, French and German classics, which were highly valued for their beauty of type and accuracy of printing. They flourished in the 17th cent.

Ember-days are set apart for fasting and prayer in the Western Church, at the periods appointed for ordination, viz., the Wednesday, Friday and Saturday after the first Sunday in Lent, Whit-Sunday, 14 September (Holy Cross Day), and 13 December (St. Lucia's Day); of very ancient origin.

Embossing, the art of stamping in relief, letters or designs upon pliant substances.

Emerald. The rich green variety of beryl (beryllium aluminium silicate). The colour is due to the presence of chromium oxide.

Empire, the style created in France during the reign of Napoleon in architecture and all the arts. It is austerely classical, making much use of columns, pediments and the like in buildings as well as furniture, with eagles and sphinxes, reminiscent of Napoleon's campaigns, as ornaments. The style is heavy, grandiose and with a strong element of the heroic. A typical monument is the *Arc de Triomphe* in Paris (begun 1806), almost a repetition of a Roman model. In painting Jacques Louis David interpreted the style with heroic subjects taken from classical mythology or from Napoleon's career. The style was transmitted to the rest of Europe, remaining magnificent and rich at all the Bonaparte courts. In bourgeois surroundings in Germany and Scandinavia it became simple and domesticated but retained its essence of classical dignity.

Encaenia, a festival commemorating a dedication; at Oxford University the annual commemoration of benefactors, accompanied by the conferring of honorary degrees, is held in June.

Encyclical Letters, a term used in reference to letters addressed by the Pope to his bishops upon matters of doctrine or discipline.

Encyclopaedists, a term first applied to the eminent writers who collaborated in the French *Encyclopédie* (1751–65). They included Diderot, D'Alembert, Voltaire, Helvetius; their writings generally were sceptical as to religion, destructive as to politics, and had great influence in popularising the social ideas which afterwards resulted in the French Revolution.

Energy. One of the most fundamental concepts of science. A body in motion possesses *kinetic energy* as a result of the *work* done by the forces creating the motion. But a force which does work to stretch a spring does not create motion. Instead, the work is stored up in the spring and is one example of *potential energy*. A raised body also possesses potential energy which turns into kinetic when the body falls. The *heat energy* contained in a body is the sum of the kinetic and potential energy of the constituent atoms which are vibrating all the time. Heat and motion are obtainable from electrical, magnetic, chemical, atomic, and other sources, and physicists therefore define corresponding forms of energy. The vital point is that all forms of energy are transferable into one another *without loss or gain*. This is the Law of Conservation of Energy. It is one of the most fundamental laws of science, and its general validity is the reason why energy is an important idea. Since Einstein, it has been recognised that mass also is interchangeable with energy. *See* F18, *also* Nuclear Energy.

Energy Conversion. For practical purposes it is frequently necessary to change energy from one into another of its many forms; indeed almost every activity does this in one way or another. The primary sources of energy are the sun, uranium and other elements from which nuclear energy can be drawn, and the tides. The sun is not much used *directly* because its heat is intermittent and not very intense, but solar cookers and refrigerators have been invented and solar batteries (*q.v.*) are used in spacecraft. The sun can be used *indirectly* because it has produced, *via* living processes, fossil fuels like coal and oil and still continues to generate winds, rain and rivers and hence hydroelectric and wind power. Commonly both fossil fuels and the energy of river or tidal waters are converted into electricity. Windmill type electricity generators are also quite common. The bulk of electricity production is a two-stage process: first fossil or nuclear fuel is used to create heat (*see* Nuclear Reactors); then the heat is used to raise steam and drive generators. Efforts are being made to convert heat into electricity more directly, *e.g.*, by using thermoelectric or thermionic effects (*q.v.*), but these have not been used for large-scale production. Once electrical energy is available, factories can make chemical batteries in great numbers and these can then be used as portable energy sources, as can petrol and other refined forms of fossil fuel. *See* Battery, Fuel Cell, Solar Battery.

Engraving is the art of cutting or otherwise forming designs of pictures on wood, stone, or metal surfaces for reproduction by some method of printing. Wood-engraving was the earliest in the field, dating from the 15th cent. Later, engraving on steel and copper plates was introduced, and mezzotint, lithography, stipple, aquatint, etc. Most modern methods of reproduction are based on photography.

Ensilage, a method of storing and preserving fodder, vegetables, etc., in pits dug in the ground and excluded from air or light. The system was practised in ancient Rome and revived in England in the 19th cent.

Entablature, that portion of a building which surmounts the columns and extends to the roof of the tympana of the pediments; it comprises the architrave, the frieze and the cornice.

Entomology is the study of insects. *See* Insects.

Entrepreneur. An entrepreneur or undertaker is a firm which brings together the factors of production needed for producing goods or services, undertaking the risks and uncertainties involved—though it may transfer some of them by insurance or by other methods. The entrepreneur may be either an individual or a company or corporation, private or public.

Enzymes. Organic catalysts which accelerate chemical processes occurring in living organisms. There are a large number present in the cell, and most have a high degree of specificity. Enzyme mechanisms are the key to basic biological processes. *See* F27(2), 32(1).

Epaulette, a shoulder badge fringed with cord worn by English army officers until 1855; now confined to naval officers, and varying in form and richness according to rank of wearer.

Ephemoptera or **May-flies**, an order of insects. In the larval condition they exist from two to three years aquatically, but no sooner do they arrive at maturity than their lives are hurried to a close. They rise up in pyramids on warm summer nights, take no food, propagate and perish. The Latin name expresses the fact that the adults have an ephemeral existence.

Epiphany, a church festival celebrated on January 6, Twelfth Day.

Equator, the imaginary great circle of the earth, every point of which is 90 degrees from the earth's poles, and dividing the northern from the southern hemisphere. It is from this circle that the latitude of places north and south is reckoned. The celestial equator is the circle in which the plane of the earth's equator meets the celestial sphere (the imaginary sphere, in which the observer is at the centre, used for representing the apparent positions of the heavenly bodies).

Equinox, the time when the sun crosses the plane of the earth's equator, making day and night of equal length.

Eras are distinctive periods of time associated with some remarkable historical event or personage. *The Christian era* is computed according to a 6th-cent. reckoning to begin with Jesus's birth, A.D. 1. The date is placed some years too late. Scholars now believe that Jesus was born *c.* 6 B.C. The *Jewish era* dates from 3761 B.C.; the *Julian era* from the alteration of the calendar by Julius Caesar 45 B.C.; the *Mohammedan era* from the date of the *Hejira*, or the flight of Mohammed from Mecca to Medina, which is A.D. 622, 16 July, in the Gregorian Calendar.

Erbium, belongs to the group of rare-earth metals discovered by Mosander in 1842.

Erg, the unit of work and energy in the centimetre-gram-second system; the energy involved when a force of 1 dyne moves its point of application through a distance of 1 cm.

Ernie, the name given to the " electronic random number indicator equipment ", the electronic machine which selected the prizewinning numbers in the first Premium Bond draw held June 1–2, 1957.

Eros. This asteroid is 24–32 km in diameter. It comes closer to the earth than any other member of the solar system with the exception of the moon and several very small asteroids. Determination of solar parallax based on observations of Eros in 1930–31 yielded until then the most accurate estimate of the distance of the sun from the earth (93,004,000 miles). *See* Astronomical unit.

Erse, a term used by Lowland Scottish, and English writers for the Gaelic language spoken in the Highlands of Scotland. Sometimes erroneously applied to Irish, the Gaelic language as spoken in Ireland and revived as an official language in recent times. Dr. Johnson, Sir Walter Scott, and other writers used " Erse " to signify Scottish Gaelic. The language of the Scottish Lowlands (that used by Robert Burns) is related to the English language and not to Gaelic and is variously termed Scots, Braid Scots, the Doric, the Scottish vernacular, and fashionably of late, Lallans.

Escurial or **Escorial**. Spanish monastery built in the mountains near Madrid by Philip II to commemorate the victory over the French at Saint-Quentin (1557). A palace was added later and it also includes a church, library and royal mausoleum. Built in granite in sombre style, it is one of the finest buildings in Europe.

Esperanto, an artificial international language created by L. Zamenhof of Warsaw and first published in 1887. It does not seek to replace national languages but to serve as a second language for international communication. It is based on the internationality of many words in the principal modern languages, and is entirely phonetic in spelling and pronunciation.

Estates of the Realm in Great Britain are the Lords Spiritual, the Lords Temporal and the Commons. They are the great classes invested with distinct political powers, and whose concurrence is necessary to legislation.

Esters. Organic chemicals formed by combining an alcohol with an acid. They have a pleasant smell, and occur naturally in plants as the scent of flowers. Manufactured for use in the perfumery industry, and as flavourings in food. Some esters are used as solvents, notably amyl-acetate (" pear drops ") in quick-drying paints. The polymeric fibre " Terylene " consists of chains of molecules containing many ester groups, formed by reacting an alcohol having two alcoholic (OH) groups with an acid having two acid (COOH) groups.

Etching, a technical method for producing graphic work and works of art. A plate, traditionally of copper, is covered with wax; the design or picture desired is drawn with a sharp implement which penetrates the wax. When the plate is exposed to the action of an acid this will etch into the copper where the lines have been drawn. The wax is then removed, ink is applied to the plate with its engraving, and the design or picture can be printed on to paper in many copies. Rembrandt, Goya and others made great and original works of art in the technique, but it was also widely used for reproductive purposes before the invention of photography. Hogarth painted his famous pictures in oil and

reproduced them graphically to give them a wider circulation.

Ether, in chemistry, is a volatile inflammable liquid composed of carbon, hydrogen and oxygen. It is a valuable anaesthetic obtained by heating alcohol with sulphuric acid. In physics, in the 19th cent., all space was supposed to be filled with a substance called ether, the chief property of which was to carry light waves, *i.e.*, light was supposed to be waves in this all-pervading medium known as the ether. Speculation and experiment concerned with the ether were very fruitful in advancing physics. Ultimately the attempts by Michelson and Morley to detect the motion of the earth through the ether were unsuccessful in this respect but profoundly successful in stimulating the theory of relativity. The ether concept has now been abandoned. *See also* **F17**(2).

Ethylene. A gas compounded of carbon and hydrogen, it is related to acetylene and ethane. Industrially it is obtained as a by-product in petroleum refining. It has wide uses as a starting material in the industrial manufacture of intermediates, especially alcohol. Its most important application is in the production of polythene (poly-ethylene). *See* Catalyst.

Etruscans, people believed to have come from Asia Minor who colonised Italy about 900 B.C., settled in what is now Tuscany and part of Umbria, reached the height of their civilisation about 500 B.C., and were ultimately absorbed by the Romans. They were skilled technicians in bronze, silver and goldwork, and excelled in the art of granular decoration.

Eucalyptus. This genus includes 300 species of evergreen, leathery-leaved trees native to Australia. The oils yielded by different species vary a great deal in their scent and other properties and are chiefly used in pharmacy and perfumery; about 30 species produce oils suitable for medicinal purposes. Various species produce timber.

Euro-dollar Market. An international financial market, located mainly in Britain and Europe, for lending and borrowing dollars, *i.e.*, titles to dollar deposits in United States banks. *See* Section G, Part II.

Europium, element discovered by Demarcay in 1906. A member of the rare-earth metal group.

Evaporation is the process by which a solid or liquid is resolved into vapour by heat. The opposite process is condensation. Wherever a liquid or solid surface is exposed, evaporation takes place into the space above. If the vapour is continually removed the solid or liquid vanishes into vapour; the higher the temperature the quicker the process. If the vapour is confined, then it collects, getting more concentrated until as many atoms of vapour are condensing as are evaporating. The vapour is then said to be saturated. Evaporation of water from sea, soil, plants, skin, etc., is continuously in progress, so it is a process of fundamental importance to meteorology, botany, physiology, industry, not to speak of human comfort and homely activities such as laundering.

Everest Expeditions. For many years after Mt. Everest had been shown to be the highest mountain in the world, political conditions in Nepal, lying south of the summit, and in Tibet, to the north, prevented mountaineers from attempting an ascent. At last in 1921 the Tibetan authorities gave permission, and the first expedition, organised, as were all subsequent British expeditions, by a joint committee of the Royal Geographical Society and the Alpine Club, and led by Col. C. K. Howard-Bury, was sent out. This was primarily a reconnaissance; besides mapping the northern flanks, it found a practicable route up the mountain. By 1939, six further expeditions had climbed on the northern face. Some were baulked by bad weather, others by problems previously little known, such as the effect of high altitudes on the human body and spirit. Nevertheless, notable climbs were accomplished. In 1924, for example, Col. E. F. Norton reached 8,589 m, and it was on this expedition that G. L. Mallory and Andrew Irvine were seen going well at about the same height. They never returned, however, and what disaster befell them is not known. After the war, political conditions again closed he Tibet route: permission was eventually obtained from the Nepalese Government to make the attempt from the south. In 1951 a reconnaissance expedition under Eric Shipton reached the ice-fall at the exit of the Western Cwm (a high valley lying south-west of the massif), and reported favourably on the prospects for an ascent. The first attempt from this side was made the following year by a Swiss expedition led by Dr. E. Wyss-Dunant, two members of which made an attempt on the summit, but were stopped at approx. 8,601 m by the intense cold and the very strong winds. When the British 1953 Expedition led by Col. John Hunt (now Lord Hunt), was being organised, stress was laid on three main points; proper acclimatisation of the climbers; use of oxygen for the final stages; and the establishment of very high altitude camps, so that the final assault parties would set out fresh and unencumbered. Great attention was also paid to recent developments in diet, clothing and equipment. In all these matters the 1953 expedition was able to draw on the accumulated experience of their predecessors. By the end of April, a base camp had been established below the ice-fall, and with the aid of thirty-four Sherpa porters supplies had been carried up into the Western Cwm. The next critical stage was the ascent of the steep head of the cwm, the Lhotse face, with the threat of avalanches always present. By most strenuous efforts, a camp was established on the South Col (7,869 m) on 21 May. From this camp on 26 May, T. D. Bourdillon and R. C. Evans climbed the South Peak of Everest (8,760 m), then the highest altitude ever attained. On 28 May Edmund Hillary and the Sherpa leader, Tenzing Norkey, spent the night at the highest camp (8,510 m) and on the following day, 29 May, climbed to the South Summit, negotiated the difficult final ridge, and reached the summit of Everest—the climax of a long, arduous and stirring endeavour.

Evolution, in the words of Sir Julian Huxley (d. 1975), " a natural process of irreversible change which generates novelty, variety and increase of organisation ". The theory, as laid down by Darwin, is that all existing species, genera and classes of animals and plants have developed from a few simple forms by processes of change and selection. Up to the time of Darwin a large part of the civilised world believed that life had been created suddenly at the beginning of the world which God had created, according to Archbishop Usher, on 22 October 4004 B.C. The evidence of the rocks, however, has given a more convincing theory of creation, and by studying the fossils preserved in the various layers of the earth's crust the past history of the earth's life has been pieced together. Darwin has been called the Newton of biology. *See* F29–30.

Exchequer, which derives its name from the checkered tablecloth on which accounts were calculated in early Norman times, is a term connected with the revenues of the Crown. In former times it had jurisdiction in all revenue matters. The term Exchequer is now applied to the Governmental department which deals with the public revenues, the working head of which is the Chancellor of the Exchequer.

Existentialism. *See Section J.*

Exploration. Modern exploration began in the second half of the 15th cent. with the voyages of the great Portuguese and Spanish discoverers. They were followed by sailors of other European nations, who profited from their developments in navigation and from their charts, and in less than one hundred years the coast-lines of much of the Americas, Africa and south-west Asia had been revealed and the globe circumnavigated. The motives of these early explorers were mixed: they were seeking adventure, trade, plunder, national power and the conversion of the heathen. Few if any were directly interested in advancing scientific knowledge. But from the reports of their voyages and travels, scholars at home compiled descriptions of the strange new world which stimulated their successors to undertake more systematic enquiries. One of the earliest English expeditions to be despatched for scientific research was that

of William Dampier on the *Roebuck,* which was sent out by the Admiralty in 1699 to examine the coasts of North-west Australia. In the 18th cent. British explorers were at work mainly in the Pacific Ocean, with the object of breaking the Spanish monopoly of trade. Capt. James Cook sailed thither in 1769 to observe first the transit of Venus at Tahiti, and then to search for the alleged great southern continent. On this voyage he discovered and charted much of the coasts of New Zealand and the east coast of Australia. On his second voyage he was the first to sail across the Antarctic Circle, and he showed that the southern continent was much smaller than had been supposed. By 1800 the general outlines of the continents, except for Antarctica were known, and explorers in the 19th cent. were largely engaged in opening up the interiors. In Africa British explorers solved two problems which had puzzled men for centuries: Mungo Park and Richard Lander established the true course of the River Niger, and Sir Richard Burton, J. H. Speke, Sir Samuel Baker and others revealed the true sources of the Nile. The greatest African explorer of that age was undoubtedly David Livingstone, the missionary, who in three great journeys explored the Zambesi and the region of the Great Lakes, spreading the Gospel, fighting the slave trade, and opening up the interior to settlement and trade. In North America Alexander Mackenzie was the first to cross the main breadth of the continent from sea to sea. In Asia motives were also mixed; men like Charles Doughty, who explored in Arabia, and Sir Francis Younghusband, who journeyed from China to India across the Gobi and the Himalaya, were impelled by a love of adventure and the quest for knowledge, but political considerations were often involved. In recent years, with the main features of the world's surface known, exploration has become more intensive. Teams of scientists go out to study restricted areas in detail. An Antarctic expedition can contribute to our knowledge of world weather, or by biological research into the life history of whales, can help to improve our food supplies. Similarly, expeditions in Africa can help to check the loss of valuable agricultural land through soil erosion, or to develop areas of settlement by schemes for irrigation and power. And there are still great areas to be adequately mapped. All these problems are inter-related, and in solving them the modern explorer can call on many improved techniques and instruments—the aeroplane, the aerial camera, tracked motor vehicles, radio, in fact all the resources of modern science. But the human element is still vital, and for those with the old explorers' spirit there will always be problems left to solve.

Explosives, substances which burn violently to produce gases in such volume that an explosion is induced. Gunpowder was the first explosive to be used; Roger Bacon's powder, consisting of charcoal, sulphur and saltpetre, was the only effective explosive until the 19th cent., but it was difficult to control. Nitroglycerine (glyceryl trinitrate) was first compounded in 1847 by adding glycerine to a mixture of sulphuric acid and nitric acid. In 1866 Alfred Nobel discovered how to make dynamite by absorbing nitroglycerine in the fine sand kieselguhr. Cordite was the joint invention of Sir Frederick Abel and Sir James Dewar (1889). It came into general use as a propellant. High explosives, providing bursting charge for shells and bombs, include TNT (trinitrotoluene), picric acid, cyclonite (RDX) and many others. Slurry explosives can be pumped on to the site and therefore offer advantages in transportation and safety; they are also waterproof. Chemical explosives have been eclipsed by nuclear explosives which have developed from the first atom bomb (dropped on Hiroshima 6 August 1945) to the 100-megaton hydrogen bomb.

Expressionism, a modern art movement confined primarily to the non-Latin countries of Europe which sought to give expression to intimate and personal emotions by means of distortions of line and colour and simplified style which carried a greater impact in terms of feeling. Broadly speaking, this has been characteristic of northern art in general. (*See* Gothic.) The term is usually used of the modern movement which influenced the Post-impressionists and subsequent movements in France. Tired of the naturalism of the Impressionists, such artists as van Gogh, Gauguin, Matisse and Rouault together with the Fauvists (*q.v.*) made use of simple outlines and strong colours. Apart from Toulouse-Lautrec, the principal Expressionists were Norwegian, like Munch, or German, like the painters of *Die Brücke* and *Der Blaue Reiter* groups. Individual artists were Ensor, Kokoschka, Nolde, Rouault and Soutine.

F

Fabian Society. See Section J.

Fables are fictitious narratives intended to enforce some moral precept, and may be either in prose or verse, and deal with personified animals and objects or with human beings. Aesop in ancient times and Hans Christian Andersen and the Brothers Grimm (in many of their stories) in later days, have given fables. Mention must also be made of La Fontaine's and Krylov's fables.

Fairs were established in mediaeval times as a means of bringing traders and customers together at stated periods, and formed the chief means of distribution. The great English fairs of early times were those of Winchester and Stourbridge near Cambridge. Traders from the Netherlands and the Baltic gathered there with the great merchants of London, and goods of every kind, wholesale and retail, were sold. One of the biggest trade fairs was at Nijni-Novgorod, founded in the 17th cent.; other big continental fairs were those of Leipzig (founded in the 12th cent.), Lyons and Prague. Expositions of advanced industrial products are today popular, *e.g.* Expo 67 held in Montreal.

Fairy Rings are the circles caused in grassland by certain fungi. The circles expand outwards as the fungus spreads, the fruiting bodies being at the periphery. Farther inward where the fungi are decaying the grass grows more strongly, fertilised by the nitrogen released from the rotting fungi. In olden times these rings were held to be the scene of fairy dances.

Falcon, name given to diurnal birds of prey which belong to the same family, *Falconidae,* as the hawk, eagle, buzzard, kite and harrier. They are swift of wing and feed on birds and small mammals. These birds have long, pointed wings, strong, hooked and notched bill, long, curved claws, and an eye of great power. They are found all over the world. Those that breed in Britain are the Kestrel (the most common), Hobby (one of the swiftest of European birds), Merlin and Peregrine, a swift and magnificent bird with slate-grey back, blackish crown, black "moustache" and whitish breast. Other members of the family are the Gyr Falcon from northern latitudes, Iceland and Greenland, which is a winter visitor to Britain, the Lanner, Saker, Eleonora's falcon, Red-footed falcon and the Lesser Kestrel. The Gyr Falcon and the Peregrine were used in the sport of falconry in olden times. Because of its fearlessness and larger size, the female bird was used. When the quarry was sighted, the bird was unhooded, set free, and after mounting high into the air would dart swiftly down to strike the prey. The heron was the usual victim.

Fall-out. Radioactive material produced by nuclear explosions which may cause bodily and genetic damage. (1) *Local fall-out,* due to the return to earth of larger particles, occurs locally, and within a few hours after the explosion; (2) *Tropospheric fall-out,* due to particles which remain in the troposphere and come down within a month or so, possibly all over the world, but within the altitude in which the explosion occurred; (3) *Stratospheric fall-out,* which comes from fragments taken up into the stratosphere and then deposited, in the course of many years, uniformly all over the globe. The two radioactive materials which have given rise to the greatest concern for the health of the individual are strontium-90 and iodine-131.

Both these materials are liable to become concentrated in certain parts of the human body, strontium-90 in bone and iodine-131 in the thyroid gland. Radiation exposure may produce genetic effects, that is effects which may show up in succeeding generations. An extensive survey was carried out by scientists of the US Atomic Energy Commission on the islands of the Bikini atoll, site of some 23 nuclear tests, 1946–58. Their records, published in 1969, revealed that the intensity of radioactivity underneath the point of explosion was still exceedingly high. Most of the radiation remaining was due to the radioactive isotope caesium-137. The variation in intensity from one place to another seemed to be correlated with the variations of vegetation: where there was little vegetation weathering had been rapid. (The nuclear test ban treaty, 1963, applies to all nuclear tests except those held underground.)

Fantail, a variety of the domestic pigeon; also a genus of Australian birds of the *Muscicapidae* family. A small New Zealand bird is called a fantail.

Fan Tracery, a complicated style of roof-vaulting, elaborately moulded, in which the lines of the curves in the masonry or other material employed diverge equally in every direction. It is characteristic of the late Perpendicular period of Gothic architecture, and may be seen in St. George's Chapel at Windsor and the Chapel of Henry VII at Westminster Abbey.

Farmer-General, the name given to the financiers who in the days of the old French monarchy farmed certain taxes, contracting to pay the Government a fixed sum yearly, on condition that the specified taxes were collected and appropriated by themselves. The revolution of 1789 swept Farmers-General away.

Fascism. See Section J.

Fata Morgana, the name given to a curious mirage often observed over the Straits of Messina, attributed to the magic of the fairy Morgana, half-sister of King Arthur, who was fabled to live in Calabria.

Fathers of the Church were early writers who laid the foundations of Christian ritual and doctrine. The earliest were the Apostolic Fathers (*q.v.*). The Four Fathers of the Latin Church were St. Ambrose, St. Jerome, St. Augustine and St. Gregory the Great. The Four Fathers of the Greek Church were St. Basil, St. Gregory Nazianzen, St. John Chrysostom and St. Athanasius.

Fathom, a nautical measure, the six-foot stretch (1·8 m) of a man's arms. Replaced by the metre on British Admiralty charts, but continued on yachtsmen's coastal charts.

Fatigue, a condition leading to breakage when a solid component, *e.g.,* an axle, is subjected to a large number of fluctuating repetitive stresses. Fatigue is the cause of most failures in service of metal engineering components though fatigue is not confined to metallic materials alone. Fatigue failures result from the *repetition,* not simply from the *size* of the stresses; indeed, fatigue breakage can result from stresses much lower than the material could stand if the load were applied steadily. Fatigue causes minute cracks, usually at the surface, which grow and spread. Early detection is difficult and fatigue, discovered by the railway engineers of the 19th cent., remains a severe engineering problem.

Fats are important foodstuffs. In physiology they constitute a valuable form of reserve food. They contain carbon, hydrogen and oxygen; chemically they are described as esters of glycerol (glycerine). Commonest fats are stearin, palmitin and olein, esters formed by the combination of glycerol with stearic, palmitic and oleic acid respectively. Fats are converted into soap by alkali; this process (saponification) also releases glycerol.

Fault, a term designating a breakage coupled with displacement of geological strata. *See* F9(2).

Fauvism (French *Fauve* = wild beast), a term used, at first contemptuously, to describe the work of a group of French painters who first exhibited at the Salon d'Automne in Paris in 1905. The most prominent among them was Henri Matisse. Forms are freely distorted and colours are selected and applied for their emotive power with no necessary reference to the "real" colour of the object in question. Other famous *Fauves* were Derain, Vlaminck and Rouault. By 1908 the group had lost its cohesion and its members went their separate ways.

February, the second month of the year, contains in ordinary years 28 days, but in leap years 29 days. When first introduced into the Roman calendar by Numa c. 700 B.C. it was made the last month of the year, preceding January, but in 452 B.C. the position of the two months was changed, February following January.

Federation. *See under* Confederation.

Félibrige, a movement founded in 1854 to revive the ancient glories of Provence, initiated by the French poet Frédéric Mistral.

Felspar, the name given to a group of minerals, silicates of aluminium with some calcium and sodium, or potassium, which make up probably more than half of the earth's crust. It is formed in granite and other rocks, both igneous and metamorphic.

Fenestella, the niche set apart on the south side of the altar for the piscina in Roman Catholic churches.

Fermentation, the action of chemical ferments or *enzymes* in bringing about chemical changes in the materials of living animals and plants, *e.g.*, the breaking-down of sugar by yeast into alcohol.

Ferret, a domesticated polecat. It is about half the size of a cat and is bred in captivity to hunt rats and rabbits. It has a long sinuous body and short legs which enable it to enter rabbit and rat holes and chase the quarry out to guns or into nets. Such ferreting is a popular country sport. *See* Z17.

Ferrites are compounds containing iron, oxygen, and one or two of a certain range of other possible metallic elements. Ferrites have recently become very important technically, because, unlike ordinary magnetic materials, they combine strong magnetism with electrical insulating properties. Ferrite-rod aerials are now common in portable radios, and ferrite devices are used in radar. *See* F22(2).

Feudalism. *See* Section J.

Fieldfare, the largest member of the thrush family, a regular winter visitor to Britain from Scandinavia. It is brown in colour with a lighter spotted breast and a grey head.

Field-Marshal, the highest ranking title in the British army, and only bestowed on royal personages and generals who have attained great distinction. The first British Field-Marshal was created in 1736, when John, Duke of Argyll, had the title conferred upon him by George II.

Fifth Column. When Franco, the Spanish dictator, revolted against the Spanish Republic in 1936 and attacked Madrid with four armies, he declared that a group of fascists within the city was assisting the besiegers. The term is used to describe a body of spies behind a fighting front.

Fighting-Fish, small pugnacious Siamese fish with long caudal and ventral fins. They are kept in glass globes in Siam, and when brought into contact will fight to the death, these encounters being the occasion of much gambling.

Filibuster, a name first given to pirates and buccaneers in the 17th cent. who took possession of small islands or lonely coast lands, and there maintained themselves apart from any governing authority. In later times the term was used to specify men taking part in expeditions whose object was to appropriate tracts of country, and settle upon them in disregard of international law. The most notable expeditions of this kind in modern times were those of Narcisco Lopez against Cuba in 1850–51, and of William Walker against Nicaragua, between 1855 and 1860. Both leaders were captured and executed. The term is also used to express the right of a minority in the United States Senate for unlimited debate, which is used on occasions to delay legislation.

Finches, a large family of small birds belonging to the Passerine or perching order of birds. There are about 200 species, including greenfinch, hawfinch, chaffinch, goldfinch, siskin, bullfinch, crossbill, linnet, twite and buntings.

Fir, a cone-bearing tree with small evergreen leaves and of considerable use as timber. There are two types: the Silver Firs and the Douglas Firs numbering about 25 species. All these firs attain to a considerable height, and all yield turpentine or o' her resinous material.

Fire-damp. *See* Methane.

Fire-Fly, a small winged insect of the *Eleteridae* family, is able to throw out a strong phosphorescent light in the dark. There are some remarkable specimens in tropical countries.

Fire of London, of 1666, extended from East to West, from the Tower to the Temple church, and northward to Holborn Bridge. It broke out in a baker's shop in Pudding Lane, and lasted four days, and destroyed 87 churches, including St. Paul's Cathedral, and many public buildings, among them the Royal Exchange, the Custom House and the Guildhall. In the ruins were involved 13,200 houses and 400 streets. About 100,000 people were made homeless yet in about 10 years all the houses had been rebuilt. The plague had not disappeared from London when the fire occurred.

Firkin, a former measure of capacity, the fourth part of a barrel, now only used in reference to a small cask or tub for butter, lard, tallow, etc.

Fischer-Tropsch Process. A process for making synthetic petrol from carbon monoxide and hydrogen. The synthesis is accelerated by cobalt-thoria and nickel-thoria catalysts.

Fish Louse. Parasitic crustacea found on marine and fresh-water fishes and whales.

Fission, Nuclear. A nuclear reaction in which the nucleus of an atom (*e.g.*, uranium 235, plutonium) captures a neutron, and the unstable nucleus so produced breaks into two nearly equal fragments and throws out several neutrons as well. In biology the term fission is applied to reproduction by fragmentation of a single-cell organism, as in amoeba. *See* F13(1).

Flagella, single hair-like projections found on many micro-organisms. Their sole function is, by complicated motion, to move the organism about. They are longer and less versatile than cilia (*q.v.*).

Flag Officer, a British naval officer who enjoys the right of carrying a flag at the mast-head of his ship, and is of the rank of Admiral, Vice-Admiral or Rear-Admiral.

Flagship, the ship that flies the Admiral's flag, and from which all orders proceed.

Flamingo, a strangely beautiful, extremely slender wading bird of white and rose-pink plumage with long, slender legs and neck and a long, down-curved bill with which it rakes the mud and obtains its food of worms and molluscs. The wings are bright crimson, bordered with black, and a flock in flight is a picture of singular beauty. There is a large and famous colony in the Camargue, S.E. France.

Flash-Point. This is found by heating an oil in a special cup and taking the temperature at which sufficient vapour is produced to ignite when a small flame is applied. It is an index of the inflammability of oils.

Flea. Fleas are small parasitic insects belonging to the order *Aphaniptera* (so called because these creatures have no wings). They obtain their food by sucking blood from their host. They are laterally compressed, which immediately distinguishes them from lice. The human flea (*Pulex irritans*) is able to jump vertically a distance of over 18 cm.

Fleet Prison, a noted debtors' prison that stood on the east side of Farringdon Street, London. It was notorious for the cruelties inflicted on prisoners, particularly under the wardenship of Thomas Bainbridge who took charge in 1728. It was pulled down in 1846.

Fleet Street, a famous thoroughfare in London, now the centre of journalism and newspaperdom, though it was long celebrated for its taverns where the literary coteries of the day were wont to meet. It takes its name from the Fleet stream which used to run from Hampstead through Holborn to the Thames at Blackfriars.

Flemings, the people of Flanders, whose ancestors of mediaeval times excelled in the textile arts; England owes its early eminence as a manufacturing nation to the migration of numbers of Flemings to this country in the 16th and 17th cent. *See also* Walloons.

L45

Fleur de Lis, the former national emblem of France, the flower of the lily. It was superseded by the Tricolour in 1789, but is still adhered to by the supporters of the old French royalties.

Flint, consists of granular chalcedony with some opaline silica, and occurs as nodules and bands in the Chalk. It is hard and has a conchoidal fracture, so enabling it to be used in making cutting implements in prehistoric times. Before the invention of lucifer matches, it was used along with steel for striking lights.

Flint implements are objects found in the younger geological strata, and constituting evidence of the condition and life of the period. They include knives, clubs, arrow-heads, scrapers, etc., used as weapons, tools and possibly as surgical instruments and in religious ceremonies. Similar to prehistoric specimens are the flint and obsidian implements of some of the primitive peoples of today. Ritual weapons and sacrificial knives continued to be made of stone long after the introduction of metals for practical purposes.

Flounder, one of the most familiar of the smaller flat fishes common round the British coasts, and seldom attaining a weight of over 1·3 kg.

Fluoridation, the process of adding the element fluorine, in the form of suitable compounds, to something deficient in it. Commonly met with as a proposal to add fluorides (fluorine compounds) to drinking water to combat dental decay, especially in children. Some toothpastes are fluoridated and fluoride can also be taken as tablets and in other ways. In 1976 a working party of the Royal College of Physicians recommended that water supplies should be fluoridated when the natural fluoride level is below 1 mg/litre. This recommendation drew on many investigations throughout the world giving evidence for the effectiveness of fluoride in the prevention of decay without harmful side-effects. There is, however, a body of opinion unconvinced by this and opposed to adding fluoride to drinking water, one argument being that to take or not to take fluoride should be a personal decision.

Fluorine, a chemical element, member of the halogen family, symbol F, it is found in combination with calcium in fluorspar, and occurs in minute quantities in certain other minerals. Discovered by Scheele in 1771, it was first obtained by Moissan in 1886. A pale yellow gas, it is very reactive and combines with most elements except oxygen. Its acid, hydrogen fluoride, etches glass, the fluorine combining with the silicon to form volatile silicon fluoride. Organic fluorine compounds have found use as very stable polymers which resist a wide variety of chemical actions.

Fluorescent Lamp. *See* **Electric Light** and **Ultra-Violet Rays.**

Fluorocarbons are hydrocarbons in which some or all of the hydrogen atoms have been replaced by atoms of chlorine or fluorine. They are non-toxic, non-flammable and chemically inert gases or low boiling point liquids. These properties make them very suitable for use as refrigerants, and propellants in fire-extinguishers and aerosols. The most widely used fluorocarbons are the chlorofluoromethanes (CCl_3F_2, CCl_3F and $CHClF_2$). In 1974 it was first suggested that the vast release of fluorocarbons into the atmosphere due to the greatly increased use of aerosols could cause a significant depletion of the protective ozone (*q.v.*) layer in the upper atmosphere. The mechanism for this involves the decomposition of fluorocarbons at high altitudes as a result of intense solar irradiation. The chlorine atoms so released can then catalyse the conversion of ozone into ordinary molecular oxygen. The degree of ozone depletion that will result is a matter of considerable current controversy. Similarly, opinions differ as to the detrimental effect ozone depletion might have on the incidence of skin cancer and on the climate.

Fluorspar, a mineral; chemically calcium fluoride. Can be colourless, green or yellow, but is most commonly purple. Blue fluorspar under the name of Derbyshire " blue John " has been used for ornamental purposes.

Fly, the popular name for a large number of insects with one pair of wings and a proboscis ter-

minating in a sucker through which fluid substances can be drawn up. The best-known species are the common house-fly, the bluebottle and the blow-fly. In the larval form flies are maggots, and feed upon decaying substances, animal flesh, etc. Flies are able to walk upon ceilings or upright surfaces by having suckers at the soles of their feet. *See* **Diptera.**

Flycatcher, name of a large family of small birds, the Muscicapidae. They are insect feeders, catch their food in the air, and are distributed over most countries of the world. The spotted and the pied nest in Britain, which they visit from April to September.

Flying Fish are frequently to be seen in southern waters, and are capable of gliding considerable distances without touching the water. To build up speed for its " take-off " the fish swims rapidly, to break the surface at 24–32 km/h. Maximum air speed is about 64 km/h.

Flying Fox, a member of the bat family, but of much larger size, and confined to the tropical and sub-tropical Old World. Like the bats, it is nocturnal, but it feeds entirely on fruits.

Flying Lemur. *See* **Colugo.**

Flying Lizard, or *Draco,* an Asiatic lizard, possessing wing-like projections from each side, which enable it to make flying leaps through the air, though not sufficient for continuous flight.

Flying Saucers, the name given to certain saucer-like shapes which have on occasion been seen travelling through the atmosphere. For some time speculation was rife, especially in America, but it is now believed that when not hallucinations, meteorological or cosmic-ray balloons, they are nothing more than atmospheric phenomena like mirages or mock suns caused by unusual atmospheric conditions. Described by Dr. Menzel, astrophysics professor at Harvard, " as real as rainbows are real, and no more dangerous ". It has been suggested that the study of some of the people who report the sighting of unidentified flying objects (UFOs) would be more rewarding than the investigation of what they saw! *See also* **Section J.**

Flying Squirrel, rodents of which there are several species in Europe, Asia and America. It possesses a parachute-like fold of skin by means of which it projects itself through the air. In appearance they are much like ordinary squirrels, to which they are related. The African flying squirrels belong to a different family.

Fog is caused by the presence of particles of condensed water vapour or smoke in the surface layers of the atmosphere, the term being applied meteorologically when the resulting obscurity is such as to render objects invisible at distances of up to 1 km. Fogs are frequently formed when the air near the ground is cooled below its dew-point temperature by radiation on a still, cloudless night; by flowing over a relatively cold land or water mass; or by mixing with a colder air stream. An accumulation of smoke over a large city may cause a high fog cutting off the daylight and producing gloom. *See* **Pollution** *and also* **Aerosol.**

Foliation, a geological term applied to rocks whose component minerals are arranged in parallel layers as the result of strong metamorphic action.

Folio, a printing term for a sheet of paper folded once, a half sheet constituting a leaf.

Folklore concerns itself with the mental and spiritual life of the people—both civilised and primitive—as expressed in the traditional beliefs, customs, institutions and sayings that have been handed down from generation to generation by word of mouth and with the observation, recording and interpretation of such traditions. (The word *folklore* itself was first suggested and used—as two words *Folk Lore*—by W. J. Thoms in the *Athenaeum* of 22 August 1846, and was at once absorbed into the English language.) Traditional lore of the kind included in the term folklore takes many forms and ranges from omens of good and bad luck (spilling the salt, breaking a mirror, dropping an umbrella, etc.) and the wearing of amulets or the possession of talismans (such as the horseshoe) as protection against misfortune, to elaborate ceremonial dances such as the Abbots Bromley Horn Dance, the Hobby horses of Padstow and Minehead the Northern sword-dances and the Christmas mummers' plays. Especially important are the beliefs and customs associated with birth, babyhood, marriage and death such being occasions when the individuals concerned require special protection or when unusual happenings can be used for foretelling their future. The child born on a Sunday will be the luckiest; rocking on an empty cradle will ensure the speedy arrival of a new baby; throwing an old shoe after a newly-married couple brings them luck; the bride should be carried over the threshold of the new home; on the sea-coast, death is believed to take place at the ebb-tide; the bees must be told of the death of the master of the house, or they will leave the hive. Another very large section of the subject deals with the traditional sayings and practices associated with particular days and seasons of the year—calendar customs, as they are called. The eating of pancakes on Shrove Tuesday; Mother Sunday customs and the simnel cake; Good Friday as the right day for planting potatoes, but emphatically the wrong day for washing clothes or cutting one's finger-nails; the necessity of wearing something new on Easter Sunday; the children's maypole dances and May garlands; midsummer fires; All Hallowe'en as the most favourable occasion for divining the future—especially in respect of marriage—and for games and sports such as apple-bobbing; the numerous practices accompanying the harvest. All these are examples of calendar customs; their full story would occupy several volumes. Folklorists are interested in all such oral tradition because they think that to a large extent it represents what folk have mentally stored up from the past and transmitted to their descendants throughout the centuries, and because therefore it is able to assist other historic methods—ethnographical linguistic, archaeological, etc.—in the elucidation of the early story of man. In those countries with a great diversity of peoples in all stages of culture, a knowledge of folklore and what it can teach of the mind of man is of great importance to administrators. The Folk-Lore Society was founded in 1878, and that part of the subject represented by song and dance has now its own organisation in the English Folk Dance and Song Society.

Footpath. In English law a highway over which the public have a right of way on foot only, other than such a highway at the side of a public road.

Force, as a term in physics, signifies an influence or exertion which, when made to act upon a body, tends to move it if at rest, or to affect or stop its progress if it be already in motion. In the c.g.s. system, the unit of force is the dyne; in the foot-pound-second system, the poundal; in the SI system, the newton.

Formaldehyde Chemically it lies between methyl alcohol and formic acid; oxidation of methyl alcohol yields formaldehyde, and oxidation of formaldehyde produces formic acid. It is used as a disinfectant, in silvering mirrors, and in the manufacture of phenol-formaldehyde plastics (of which bakelite is the best-known example). Solutions of formaldehyde in water, formalin, are used to preserve biological specimens.

Forme, a body of letterpress type, composed and secured for printing from; or a stereotype or electrotype. The former is used more for newspaper formes and the latter in good book work.

Formic Acid can be obtained from a colourless fluid secreted by ants and other insects and plants. It is a strong irritant. Commercially it is obtained from sodium formate, which is synthesised by the absorption of carbon monoxide in caustic soda. It is used in the electroplating, tanning and textile industries.

Fossils. Remains of animals and plants, or direct evidence of their presence, preserved in rocks. They include petrified skeletons and shells, leaf imprints, footprints, etc.

Four Freedoms, a phrase coined by President Roosevelt in January 1941, embodying what should be the goal of the Allies. They were (1) Freedom of speech and expression; (2) Freedom of every person to worship God in his own way; (3) Freedom from want; (4) Freedom from fear.

Fox, carnivorous animal of the canine family, found in considerable numbers in most parts of the world. The common fox *Vulpes vulpes* of Europe is a burrowing animal of nocturnal habits, living upon birds, rabbits and domestic poultry, in the capture of which it displays much cunning. The fox in Britain is preserved from extinction chiefly for hunting purposes. Among other notable species are the Arctic fox and the red fox of North America, of which the valuable silver fox, coveted for its fur, is a variety.

Fox-Shark, *or* **Thresher Shark,** a large species of shark common in the Atlantic and in the Mediterranean. It is very destructive to small fish, but although it attains a length of 4·5 m it is not dangerous to man.

Franciscans. *See* Friars.

Franco-German War (1870–71) was opened by a declaration of war by Napoleon III, but the Germans who were better prepared than the French, won victory after victory. In September Napoleon and the whole French army were made prisoners at Sedan, a republic was then proclaimed, and Paris sustained a four months' siege. In the end France ceded Alsace and part of Lorraine to Germany, who claimed a war indemnity of over £20 million.

Francolin, a genus of birds closely related to the common partridge, belonging to Africa. It includes the spur-legged partridge and the black partridge which ranges from Cyprus to Assam.

Frankincense is of two kinds, one being used as incense in certain religious services and obtained from olibanum, an Eastern shrub, the other is a resinous exudation derived from firs and pines, and largely used in pharmacy.

Franklin, the name given in feudal times to a country landowner who was independent of the territorial lord, and performed many of the minor functions of local government, such as serving as magistrate.

Fresco, a painting executed upon plaster walls or ceilings, a technique which has remained unchanged since it was practised by the great Renaissance artists.

Freshwater Shrimp, a small crustacean abounding in British streams, and feeding on dead fish or other decomposing matter. Although of shrimp-like form it is not closely related to salt-water shrimps. Its generic name is *Gammarus*.

Friars, members of certain mendicant orders of the Roman Catholic Church. The four chief orders are the Franciscans or Grey Friars, the Dominicans or Black Friars, the Carmelites or White Friars and the Augustinians (Austin Friars).

Friday, the 6th day of the week, named after Frigga, the wife of Odin. It is the Mohammedan Sabbath, a general abstinence day of the Roman Catholic Church, and according to popular superstition, an unlucky day.

Friends, The Society of. *See* Quakers, Section J.

Frigate-Bird, a web-footed bird widely distributed over tropical latitudes, and deriving its name from its great expanse of wing and forked tail, resembling the shape of a swift vessel. It feeds on flying fish mostly, being unable to dive and also steals from other birds. A frigate-bird was found dying on the Hebridean island of Tiree in July 1953: only twice previously had one been recorded in Europe—the first on the German coast in 1792, and the second on the coast of France in 1902.

Frog, a familiar amphibian, breathing through gills in the earlier (tadpole) part of its existence, and through lungs later. It remains three months in the tadpole stage. The frog hibernates underwater in the mud during the winter.

Frost occurs when the temperature falls to, or below, 0°C, which is freezing point. Hoar frost is applied to the needles or feather-like crystals of ice deposited on the ground, in the same manner as dew. Glazed frost is the clear icy coating which may be formed as a result of rain falling on objects whose temperatures are below the freezing point. These layers of ice, often rendering roads impassable for traffic, damaging overhead power and communication systems and endangering aircraft, can also be caused by condensation from warm, damp winds coming into contact with very cold air and freezing surfaces.

Froth-Hopper *or* **Frog-Hopper.** A family of bugs

(belonging to the insect order *Hemiptera*) which in the larval stage surround themselves with a protective mass of froth (" cuckoo spit "). These insects, which suck the sap of plants, bear a faint resemblance to frogs, and the adults possess great leaping powers.

Fuel Cells. A recent development is a type of battery into which the active chemicals are fed from external fuel tanks. This is the *fuel cell*, which is being developed in a number of versions in several countries. One was demonstrated in action when in 1959 Bacon of Cambridge University used his fuel cell to drive a fork-lift truck and a welding machine. The Bacon fuel cell consists of two electrodes of porous nickel dipping into a solution of caustic potash in water. One electrode is supplied with hydrogen gas from an outside cylinder and the other with oxygen. These gases, forming layers on the nickel, are the active chemicals. The oxygen combines with water to make two negatively charged ions, each consisting of an oxygen and a hydrogen atom joined together (a hydroxyl ion). The hydroxyl ions travel through the solution to the hydrogen electrode, where they combine with hydrogen to form neutral water Their negative charge (one electron per ion involved) has now arrived at the hydrogen electrode and is ready to flow back to the other electrode through any outside circuit that is provided. This flow constitutes the useful electric current, and it has been provided at the expense of creating water out of the original hydrogen and oxygen. The water can be removed in the form of steam. What is the advantage of all this? In the first place the fuel gases are easy to make and to store in cylinders. Supplying a new gas cylinder is easier and quicker than recharging an ordinary accumulator. Furthermore, a fuel cell is lighter for a given power than an accumulator; satellite designers have found them useful. The fuel cell is not damaged by heavy overloading, and this is valuable for application to vehicle driving. Fuel-cell-driven buses could combine the advantages of diesel buses and trolleybuses. Fuel cells are still in the development stage. It is not certain how they will compete with combustion engines or, in the oil-less future, with improved ordinary batteries.

Fulani, a non-Negro people of Hamitic stock widely distributed in N.W. Africa, chiefly in Nigeria. There are two main branches: the dark-skinned Fulani, settled farmers and city dwellers, Moslem in religion, and the light-coloured Bororo'en who are semi-nomadic herdsmen. The Fulani are different from any tribe in W. Africa though they resemble in some ways the Masai of E. Africa. The Fulani conquered the Hausa states at the beginning of the 19th cent. which passed under British suzerainty after 1903. Sokoto, built in 1810, was capital of the Fulani empire.

Fuller's Earth, a special kind of clay or marl possessing highly absorbent qualities, originally used in the " fulling "—that is, cleansing and felting—of cloth. Now used in clarifying oils. Deposits in America and in south of England.

Function. In mathematics, one quantity y is said to be a function of another quantity x, written $y = f(x)$, if a change in x results in some corresponding change in y. Thus sin$x$ or log$x$ are functions of x. If y depends not only on x but on several other quantities as well, y is called a function of many variables.

Functionalism, in architecture, a movement originated by Le Corbusier, Swiss-born French architect and town-planner, who applied the austere principles of the Purist movement in painting to his own art. From about 1924 he designed in concrete, steel and glass, buildings in which every part had a significance in terms of function on the theory that objects created to carry out their particular function to perfection cannot help being beautiful. " A house is a machine for living in." The style was in vogue between the two wars, and although its severity became somewhat modified, it is still the basis of most modern architecture.

Fungi, a class of simple plants, which reproduce from spores and lack the green colouring matter *chlorophyll*. It includes moulds, rusts, mildews, smuts, mushrooms, etc. Potato blight is a fungus disease which caused the failure of the potato crop in Ireland in 1846. 50,000 different fungi are known. *See also* **F42(1), P8(1).**

Furniture Beetle (*Anobium punctatum*). The common furniture beetle is responsible for 80 per cent of all woodworm damage and is the great pest of the comparatively modern house, causing damage in the main to softwood roofing and flooring timbers. Adults are 3 mm long. The grub tunnels for about 33 months. *See also* Woodworm, Death Watch Beetle.

Futurism, an Italian school of art and literature initiated by Marinetti, an Italian writer and mountebank friend of Mussolini at a later period. Its origin took the form of a manifesto published in Paris in 1909 in which Marinetti glorified violence, war and the machine age In its aggression it favoured the growth of fascism. One of the distinctive features of Futurist art was the use of the principle of " simultaneity " in which the same figure (*e.g.*, a woman descending a flight of stairs) is represented in successive positions like film " stills " superimposed on each other. In spite of two further manifestoes it was not until 1911 that the first examples of Futurist painting and sculpture appeared by the artists Severini, Balla and Boccioni. Apart from the principle of simultaneity, Futurism derived from Cubist and Post-impressionist techniques. The movement faded out early in the first world war.

G

Gabardine, a long, loose, coarse, over-garment, worn by men of the common class in the Middle Ages, and prescribed by law as the distinctive garment of the Jews. The name is now given to a closely woven cloth of wool and cotton used to make raincoats.

Gabbro, a kind of igneous rock, often very coarse-grained, containing a good deal of plagioclase felspar, and monoclinic pyroxene; it may occasionally also include biotite, magnetite, ilmenite and hornblende. A gabbro containing nickel at Sudbury in Canada is one of the richest sources known of that metal.

Gadfly, a widely distributed family of flies with only one pair of wings, including the horse fly. The females are very voracious, being able to bite through the skin and suck the blood of animals. The males are harmless.

Gadolinium. An element belonging to the rare-earths metals discovered in 1886 by Marignac. It is strongly magnetic.

Gaelic, relating to the Gaels and their language, a term now applied only to the Celtic people inhabiting the Highlands of Scotland, but formerly also to the Celts of Ireland and the Isle of Man.

Galago. " Bush Babies ", related to the lemur, native to Africa, large-eyed, in keeping with its nocturnal characteristics.

Galaxy or **Milky Way Galaxy** is the huge disk-shaped cloud of gas and stars (some 100,000 million, one of which is the sun) that is turning in space like a great wheel, with a diameter of about 100,000 light years. The Milky Way (that part of the heavens in Milton's words " powdered with stars ") is really only a small part of this disk, and every star in the galaxy is moving round the centre under the gravitational control of the whole. The sun and planets lie near the edge of the disk and it takes them about 250 million years to travel once round. The number of stars that can be seen with the unaided eye is about 3,000, and they all belong to the Milky Way Galaxy, as do most of the stars that can be seen with anything but the greatest telescopes. With the large modern optical and radar telescopes many other systems, similar in size and weight to our galaxy, have been discovered, scattered more or less uniformly through space, and the universe is said to include at least 10,000 million such galaxies. *See also* F4(2).

Gale, a high wind now technically defined as one of at least Beaufort force 8. Between thirty and forty gales a year occur on the north and west coasts of the British Isles and only about half of this number in the south-east. At St.

Ann's Head, Dyfed, the anemometer registered a gust of 113 mile/h (182 km/h) on 18 Jan. 1945, which is a record for these islands. Gusts exceeding 113 km/h are rarely experienced in London. Gale warnings are issued for specified areas by the Meteorological Office, the warnings taking the form of radio broadcasts and the hoisting of storm signals at certain points on the coast. *See* Beaufort Wind Scale, Section N.

Gall, abnormal vegetable growths caused by insects, mites, bacteria, or fungi, found on all parts of the plant. Oak-apples, Robin's pincushion (on wild rose), " witches' brooms " (on trees) are examples. Some are useful commercially, *e.g.*, oak apples yield tannic acid and the black oak gall is used in America as animal food.

Galleon, the name given to the old three-decked Spanish treasure vessels employed in conveying the precious minerals from the American colonies to Spain. The term is often applied to any large, especially stately, sailing vessel.

Galley, an oar-propelled sea-boat used by the ancient Greeks and Romans for transport purposes, manned by slaves. Boats of a similar class were used by the French down to the middle of the 18th cent., and manned by convicts.

Gallic Acid, obtained from gall nuts, sumach, tea, coffee, and the seeds of the mango, is used in the manufacture of inks and as an astringent in medicine. It was discovered by C. W. Scheele (1742–86), a Swedish chemist.

Gallium, a white metal, symbol Ga, related to aluminium, but which can be cut with a knife. It was discovered spectroscopically by L. de Boisbaudran in 1875. Long before Mendeleyev had predicted that an element with its properties would be found to fill the then existing gap in the Periodic Table; this gap came immediately below aluminium, so he suggested the name " eka aluminium " for it.

Gallup Poll, a system, introduced by Dr. Gallup of the United States, for testing public opinion on topical subjects by taking a test poll on questions framed to elicit opinions.

Galvanised Iron is iron coated with zinc. The name comes from the fact that such a coat protective against rust could be deposited electrolytically. Electrodeposition is sometimes used, but the cheaper and more common process depends on dipping the iron in a bath of molten zinc.

Gamboge, a resinous gum obtained from the sap of *Garcinia morella*, a tree native to Thailand, Cambodia and Sri Lanka, and used as a yellow pigment in paints and also as a purgative.

Game is the term applied to wild animals which are protected from indiscriminate slaughter by Game Laws. In the United Kingdom game comprehends deer, hares, pheasants, partridges, grouse, black game, moor game, woodcocks, bustards and certain other birds and animals of the chase. Game can only be killed (with few exceptions) by persons holding game licences. Occupiers of land and one other person authorised by them in each case are allowed to kill hares and rabbits on their land without licence. Game cannot be sold except by a person holding a proper licence. There is a " close time " prescribed for the different classes of game; for instance, the selling or exposing for sale of any hare or leveret during March, April, May, June or July is prohibited by law. Grouse cannot be shot between 11 December and 11 August; partridges between 2 February and 31 August; pheasants between 2 February and 30 September; and black game between 11 December and 10 August. In regard to foxes and stags, custom prescribes a certain law which sportsmen observe. Game reserves are legally protected areas where natural vegetation and wild life are allowed to remain unmolested by sportsmen or those who might destroy for economic ends.

Gaming, *or* **Gambling**—*i.e.*, staking money on the chances of a game—differs from betting in that it depends upon the result of a trial of skill or a turn of chance. The Betting and Gaming Act of 1959, passed by the Macmillan administration, replaced all the old laws on gaming, which went back to an Act of 1541 entitled " An Acte for Mayntenance of Artyllarie and debarringe

of unlauful games ", under which some games were unlawful if played for money in any circumstances. Roulette and any game of dice were among such games. Under the 1959 Act any game was lawful, subject to certain conditions. Since then the Betting Gaming and Lotteries Act, 1963, and the Gaming Act, 1968, have been passed, to deal with unlawful gaming and to prevent the exploitation of gaming by commercial interests. The playing of bingo is now restricted to clubs licensed for bingo only. The Gaming Board in its evidence to the Royal Commission on Gambling (1976) recommended a new Gambling Authority or Commission to ensure that any legalised gambling is not penetrated by criminals.

Gammexane, a powerful insecticide, used particularly to kill the tsetse fly and mosquito.

Gangue. Useless minerals associated with metallic ores.

Gannet, a fish-eating bird which dives on its prey from a great height, swallowing it under water, is found in large numbers off the coast of Scotland, and has breeding stations in the Hebrides, St. Kilda, Ailsa Craig, the Bass Rock, Grassholme Island and on Ortac and Les Etacs (rocks off Alderney). It is a bird of white plumage, black tips to long narrow wings and wedge-shaped tail, and weighs about 3 kg. The gannet breeds in colonies on ledges of steep, rocky, island cliffs. Related to the cormorants, pelicans and frigate-birds.

Garden Cities in England were founded by Ebenezer Howard (1850–1928), and his ideas were put forward in his book *Tomorrow—A Peaceful Path to Real Reform* (later re-issued as *Garden Cities of Tomorrow*). New towns should be so placed and planned as to get the best of town and country life, an adaptation of the model villages of certain industrial philanthropists such as Salt, Richardson, Cadbury, Leverhulme and others. The Garden City Association (later the Town and Country Planning Association) was formed in 1899, and the first garden city was begun at Letchworth in 1903 and successfully established. Welwyn Garden City was also Howard's foundation, established in 1919.

Gardener-Bird, a bird possessing many of the characteristics of the bower bird, and found only in Papua–New Guinea. *See also* Bower Bird.

Gargantua, the giant hero of Rabelais' satire, of immense eating and drinking capacity, symbolical of an antagonistic ideal of the greed of the Church.

Gargoyle, a projecting spout for carrying off water from the roof gutter of a building. Gargoyles are only found in old structures, modern waterpipe systems having rendered them unnecessary. In Gothic architecture they were turned to architectural account and made to take all kinds of grotesque forms—grinning goblins, hideous monsters, dragons and so forth.

Garlic, a bulbous plant of the same genus as the onion and the leek, and a favourite condiment among the people of Southern Europe. It possesses a very strong odour and pungent taste and its culinary use is agelong.

Garnet, a group of minerals; chemically they are orthosilicates of the metals calcium, magnesium, titanium, iron, aluminium. Garnets can be coloured yellow, brown, black, green or red; the blood-red garnet is an important gemstone.

Garrotte, a method of strangulation used as capital punishment in Spain, and consisting of a collar which is compressed by a screw that causes death by piercing the spinal marrow. Garrotting was also applied to a system of highway robbery common in England in 1862–63, the assailants seizing their victims from behind, and by a sudden compression of the windpipe disabling them until the robbery was completed.

Garter. The Most Noble Order of the Garter was founded (c. 1348) by King Edward III, and is the premier order of knighthood in Great Britain. The traditional story associating the garter and the motto with the Countess of Salisbury, who it was said dropped her garter while dancing with the King, who remarked " honi soit qui mal y pense " cannot be accepted. The order was originally limited to the

Sovereign and 25 knights, but the number has been extended, and it may now be bestowed on royal personages and leading representatives of the British peerage. The insignia of the order are the garter of dark-blue velvet with the motto in letters of gold, the mantle of dark-blue velvet lined with white silk, the surcoat and hood, and the gold-and-enamel collar. The garter is worn on the left leg below the knee and by women as a sash over the left shoulder. See Knighthood.

Gas is an elastic fluid substance, the molecules of which are in constant rapid motion, and exerting pressure. The technique whereby gases are liquefied depends on increasing pressure and diminishing temperature. Each gas has a critical point; unless the temperature is brought down to this point no amount of pressure will bring about liquefaction. Last gas to be liquefied was helium (1908) which boils at $-209°C$.

Gas from coal was first used as an illuminating agent by William Murdoch towards the end of the 18th cent. in Birmingham, and about 1807 was introduced in London, one side of Pall Mall being lighted with it. It became widely used as an illuminant. and for space heating and cooking. In the U.K. increasing attention has been paid to the use of a primary fuel—natural gas—instead of producing gas from coal or oil. See Gas, Natural.

Gas, Natural, natural mixture of gases often present with deposits of petroleum, found issuing from the ground in many parts of the world—in the oilfields of Venezuela and the Caucasus, in China, Saudi-Arabia, but chiefly in North America. Its chief component is methane. Large industrial centres have made use of this gas since the latter part of the 19th cent., but much of this valuable fuel still goes to waste. Pipelines have been constructed to deliver the gas to where it is wanted. Britain began to ship liquid methane from the Saharan oilfield in 1964. Some of the world's largest natural gas fields have recently been discovered in the North Sea and are being actively exploited. Domestic gas appliances have to be modified if the natural product is substituted for ordinary town gas because the burning characteristics are different. Oil production from the North Sea fields began in 1975 and the main single source of gas in the U.K. is now natural gas.

Gas Turbine. In this kind of engine mechanical movement is produced by a jet of gas impinging on a turbine wheel; used in aeroplanes, locomotives and ships. These engines are mechanically simple compared with internal combustion engines, and require less maintenance.

Gauge, a standard dimension or measurement applied in various branches of construction. Thus the standard railway gauge is 4 ft 8½ in (143·5 cm) in the UK, USA and most European countries. The Soviet Union uses the broader gauge of 5 ft (152 cm). Narrow railway gauges of different standards are in use on very steep inclines in various countries. Other standard gauges are fixed in building and gun-boring.

Gauls were inhabitants of ancient Gaul, the country which comprised what is now France, Belgium and parts of the Netherlands, Switzerland and Germany.

Gault, a stratum of blue clay between the Lower Greensand and the Chalk. A typical section of the Gault can be seen at Folkestone.

Gauss, a unit of magnetic induction in the c.g.s. system. named after the great German mathematician and astronomer, K. F. Gauss.

Gavelkind, an old English custom of land tenure in Kent and other places in England, whereby on the death, intestate, of a property owner his property is divided equally among his children and not according to the law of primogeniture. Abolished by the Law of Property Act, 1922, and the Administration of Estates Act, 1925.

Gazelles, a group of small, graceful antelopes which live in the drier regions of Africa and Asia. They can run very fast: speeds of over 64 km/h have been recorded.

Geiger Counter, an electrical device invented by Geiger, which can detect individual atomic particles, e.g., electrons, protons, etc. It often consists of a tube of gas at a few cm Hg pressure, fitted with two electrodes—a cylinder and an axial wire. A high voltage is kept across the electrodes, and the passage of a charged particle through the gas releases ions which permit a momentary discharge between the electrodes. Electronic circuits register this discharge as a " count ". Geiger counters are used to detect and measure radioactivity and cosmic rays both for technical and research purposes.

Gelatine, a transparent, tasteless, organic substance obtained from animal membranes, bones, tendons, etc., by boiling in water. It is of various kinds, according to the substance used in making it. Isinglass, the purest form of it, is made from air-bladders and other membranes of fish, while the coarser kind—glue—is made from hoofs, skin, hides, etc. Its constituents are carbon, hydrogen, oxygen and nitrogen. Gelatine is applied to an immense variety of purposes, from the making of food jellies to photographic materials.

Gemsbok, a large South African antelope of the open dry plains, sandy coloured with black and white markings on its face, and with long straight horns.

General, a military title next in rank to that of Field-Marshal, the highest officer in the army. Ranking below full General are Lieutenant-General, Major-General and Brigadier.

Generation, a time-measure reckoned at about 30 years when children are ready to replace parents; also the body of persons existing at the same time or period. According to a U.N. report in 1958 "one can no longer think of generations in traditional terms. Interests and activities are today changing so fast that sets of young people not more than seven or eight years apart in age may be as far apart in their thinking and behaviour as two generations once were." The generation gap is now even fewer years apart.

Generation, Spontaneous. See Abiogenesis.

Genes, the elementary units of heredity. They exist as highly differentiated regions arranged along the length of the chromosomes which the nuclei of cells carry. A chromosome may carry hundreds or even thousands of genes, each with its own particular structure and specific properties. The position of a particular gene on a chromosome is called its locus. The material of the gene is DNA (q.v.). See F34.

Genesis, the first book of the Pentateuch, compiled in the 5th cent. B.C. from earlier documents, which carries the scriptural narrative from the creation to the death of Joseph. Sometimes there is disagreement, as in the story of the creation, Gen. i and ii. Gen. i reflects the views of the ancient Greek scientist Thales (c. 640–546 B.C.) and may be said to be the first scientific account of the creation of the world. The conditions described around the figures of Abraham, Isaac, Jacob and Joseph have a genuine historical basis.

Genetic Code. The elucidation of the structure of DNA (q.v.) for which Crick, Wilkins and Watson were jointly awarded the 1962 Nobel Prize for medicine, revealed the code or chemical dictionary out of which messages serving as blueprints for living structures can be made. See Protein synthesis, F29(2).

Genetic Engineering is the name given to the introduction of human choice and design criteria into the construction and combination of genes. This refers not to breeding by selection, a traditional process, but to the biochemical alteration of the actual DNA in cells (see Section F, Part IV) so as to produce novel self-reproducing organisms. Such manipulations became possible when techniques were recently discovered for severing and rejoining DNA molecules and inserting sections into them. Many people regard this development as fraught with enormous significance. Like nuclear power, it can lead to good, to evil, and to accidental hazards, not all of which can be foreseen. Thus when biologists realised they could create new lifeforms, e.g., bacteria, with novel genes, they appreciated that, as well as medically beneficial strains, new virulent forms might by accident be produced and escape into the world. Ultimately, not imminently, men may be able to design the genes of higher animals and even of man himself and thus consciously influence biological evolution. Many scientists have been brought by these possibilities up against an old problem: is science going too far too fast?

Genetics. *See* F30(2).

Geneva Convention, an agreement made by the European Powers at Geneva in 1864, establishing humane regulations regarding the treatment of the sick and wounded in war and the status of those who minister to them. All persons, hospitals, hospital ships are required to display the Geneva cross—a red cross on a white ground. A second conference held at Geneva in 1868 drew up a supplementary agreement. An important result of this Convention was the establishment of the Red Cross Society in 1870.

Genocide is an international crime, defined by the General Assembly of the United Nations in 1948 as " acts committed with intent to destroy, in whole or in part a national, ethnic, racial or religious group as such ". The UN Convention came into force in 1951.

Genus, a term applied in biology to designate a group of similar species. A group of similar genera is called a family.

Geodesy, the science of calculating the configuration and extent of the earth's surface, and determining exact geographical positions and directions, with variations of gravity, etc. Land-surveying is a branch of geodesy.

Geography, a science concerned with the spatial organisation of natural features and life and man-made artifacts upon and immediately above the surface of the earth. It is increasingly concerned with the processes by which such patterns are generated and this concern is leading to both a greater degree of specialisation within the subject and to the merging of its constituent parts with related disciplines of economics, sociology, political science, geology, biology and meteorology.

Geology, the science which deals with the condition and structure of the earth, and the evidence afforded of ancient forms of life. The geological strata are classified in the following categories: *Primary* or *Palaeozoic* (the oldest fossil-bearing rocks including the Cambrian, Ordovician, Silurian, Devonian, Carboniferous, Permian); *Secondary* or *Mesozoic* (Triassic, Jurassic, Cretaceous); *Tertiary* or *Cainozoic* (Eocene, Oligocene, Miocene, Pliocene, Pleistocene); *Post tertiary* (most recent rocks). *See* **F48**

Geometrical Progression is a term used to indicate a succession of numbers which increase or decrease at an equal ratio—as 3, 9, 27; or 64, 16, 4.

Geometry is the branch of mathematics which demonstrates the properties of figures, and the distances of points of space from each other by means of deductions. It is a science of reason from fundamental axioms, and was perfected by Euclid about 300 B.C. The books of Euclid contain a full elucidation of the science, though supplemented in modern times by Descartes, Newton and Carnot. Of recent years non-Euclidean geometry has been developed.

Geophysics, the branches of physics which are concerned with the earth and its atmosphere. Meteorology, geomagnetism, aurora and airglow, ionosphere, solar activity, cosmic rays, glaciology, oceanography, seismology, nuclear radiation in the atmosphere, rockets and satellites—all these are geophysical subjects. The object of the International Geophysical Year, 1957–58, was to investigate the physical phenomena occurring on and around the earth by means of carefully co-ordinated observations made simultaneously all over the globe.

Geothermal Energy. Some of the heavy elements within the earth's crust are radioactive and this gives rise to a temperature rise towards the centre of the earth. The practical exploitation of this geothermal energy comes about when there are hot springs or geysers. It is believed that these are caused by rainwater slowly percolating down to the hot rocks and blowing out as steam. The homes of people living in Reykjavik are heated by geothermal steam and there are a number of small power stations in various parts of the world. Although the costs in the few cases where geothermal power has actually been exploited are remarkably low, the expense of drilling, etc., required when attempting to exploit the heat in the rocks where surface manifestations do not occur, is likely to limit the use of this source of power.

Geothermal Heating. The earth's interior is hot and in certain localities, often adjacent to volcanic or earthquake-prone regions, reservoirs of hot water or steam exist at accessible depths. Natural hot geysers occur in many such places and people, *e.g.*, the ancient Romans and present-day Japanese, use natural hot water for bathing, cooking and laundry. Occasionally the subterranean reserves permit large-scale power generation by drilling for hot steam and passing it into turbines to produce electricity. Pioneering work on this was done at Lardarello in Italy which can produce hundreds of megawatts. Other sites are in New Zealand, California, Japan and Iceland. There are possibilities in South-West England.

Germanium. A grey, hard, brittle chemical element, symbol Ge, chemically related to silicon and tin. Discovered by Winkler in 1886. Its richest ore is germanite containing 6% of the metal. Coal is also a relatively rich source. Since 1948 it has assumed great importance as a semi-conducting material for making transistors (*q.v.*). Because of this it has been so intensively studied that more is known about its physical properties than about those of any other element.

Gesta Romanorum (Latin = deeds of the Romans), a mediaeval collection of Latin stories of unknown authorship which circulated widely in Europe during the Middle Ages. First printed in the 15th cent. The stories were used by Chaucer, Shakespeare and other writers who found many romantic incidents and legends which they were able to turn to good account.

Gestation, the carrying of young in animals during pregnancy, varies considerably in its length. In the case of an elephant, the period is 21 months; a camel, 12 months; a cow, 9 months; a cat, 8 weeks; a horse, 48 weeks; a dog, 9 weeks; and a pig, 16 weeks. Hens " sit " for 21 days; geese, 30; swans, 42; turkeys, 28; pigeons, 18.

Geysers, hot springs of volcanic origination and action, are remarkable for the fact that they throw out huge streams of boiling water instead of lava as in the case of a volcano. The most famous geysers are those of Iceland, which number over a hundred, the principal one having an opening of 21 m in diameter and discharging a column of water to a height of 61 m. There are also geysers in the Yellowstone region of America, and some in New Zealand.

Ghost-Moth or **Ghost Swift,** an interesting nocturnal insect (*Hepialus humuli*), common in England, possessing in the male a white collar and known for its habit of hovering with a pendulum-like action in the twilight over a particular spot where the female is concealed.

Gibbon, the name of a long-armed ape mainly inhabiting S.E. Asia. It is without tail, and possesses the power of very rapid movement among the trees of the forests.

Gin, a well-known spirit distilled from malt or barley and flavoured with the juniper berry. The principal varieties are the English and American, known as " Gin " or " Dry Gin ", and the Dutch, referred to as " jenever " or " Hollandse jenever ". In Germany and Austria it is called " Schnapps ". The word " Gin " is an abbreviation of " Geneva ", both being primarily derived from the French geniévre (juniper).

Giraffe, the tallest of existing animals, reaching a height of from 5–6 m when full grown. Its sloping back and elongated neck seem to be the natural evolution of an animal that has to feed on the branches of trees. It is a native of Africa, is of a light fawn colour marked with darker spots and has a prehensile tongue.

Giralda, a beautiful and remarkable example of Arabian art, erected in 1195 at Seville, still in existence.

Glaciers form in the higher Alpine ranges, and are immense consolidated masses of snow, which are gradually impelled by their force down the mountain-sides until they reach a point where the temperature causes them to melt, and they run off in streams. From such glaciers the five great rivers, the Rhine, the Po, the Rhône, the Inn and the Adige, have their source. The longest of the Swiss glaciers is the Gross Aletsch, which sometimes extends over 16 km. Some of the glaciers of the Himalayas are four times as long. The Muir in Alaska is of enormous magnitude, and that of Justedlals Brae in Norway is the largest in Europe.

Gladiators were professional athletes and combatants in ancient Rome, contesting with each other or with wild beasts. At first they were drawn from the slave and prisoner classes exclusively, but so much were the successful gladiators held in esteem that men came to make a profession of athletics, and gladiatorial training schools were established. When a gladiator was vanquished without being killed in combat, it was left with the spectators to decide his fate, death being voted by holding the hands out with the thumb turned inward, and life by putting forth the hands with the thumb extended. Gladiatorial shows were the chief public displays in Rome from the 3rd to the 4th cent. A.D.

Glass is an amorphous, man-made substance, fluid when hot, solid, though fragile, when cooled. It is made of sand mixed with an alkaline flux, usually soda or potash. While hot, glass can be formed into almost any shape by moulding, blowing or, since the early 19th cent., by machine pressing. Unrefined glass normally has a greenish tinge, due to the iron content of most sands, but it is transparent or at least translucent. To make truly colourless glass is a difficult and expensive process, and such glass resembling the natural mineral, rock crystal, is given the name crystal. Glass can be tinted by the addition of various metallic oxides, cobalt producing blue, manganese mauve, etc. Because it is at once solid and transparent, glass is the perfect material for windows for which it has been used since Roman times. And since it can be made cheaply and is easy to clean, it has been used for containers in homes, shops and pharmacies, again since Roman days. Glass can also be made into things of beauty, by the use of coloured glass and by cutting, engraving, painting and gilding. The earliest vessels of glass so far found come from Egypt and date back to c. 1500 B.C. With the invention of glass-blowing in the 1st cent. A.D., the use of glass spread throughout the Roman empire. Many varieties were made, including superb art glass like the Portland vase (q.v.). The Arabs were great glassmakers from the 7th to 15th cent. During the Renaissance the Venetians created luxurious art glass, rich in colour and often manipulated into fantastic forms. Bohemia's 17th-cent. glass is wonderfully engraved with pictures and cut into glittering facets. During the 1670s in England George Ravenscroft invented a new, heavy, water-clear crystal, with an addition of lead as the magic ingredient, and English lead glass is still the basis for all modern crystals.

Glass-Snake, genus, *Ophisaurus*, of legless lizards with long fragile tails capable of re-generation when broken. Six species are known; in S.E. Europe, S.W. Asia, Indo-China and N. America. Attains a length of about 60 cm; main colouring, green, with black and yellow markings.

Glauconite. A green mineral, chemically a hydrated silicate of potassium and iron. Commonly found in marine sands (hence these rocks are known as " greensands ") and sandstones.

Glaucus is a curious genus of sea slugs often called the Sea Lizard belonging to the molluscs. It is without shell and has a soft body, with horny mouth and four tentacles. It is a native of the Atlantic, and is not more than 30 cm in length.

Glee, an unaccompanied piece for three or more voices. Glee-singing was popular in England during the 18th and early 19th cent. and glee-clubs are still in existence.

Globigerina, an oceanic unicellular animalcule with a perforated shell, and occurring in certain parts of the Atlantic in such vast numbers as to form a bed of chalk ooze with their empty shells.

Glockenspiel, an instrument composed of metal bars each of which is tuned to a note. The bars are struck by hand-hammers and give forth chiming sounds.

Glow-worm, a beetle, possessing the power (much stronger in the female than the male) of emitting phosphorescent light from the hind end of the body. The female is wingless.

Glucinium. See **Beryllium**.

Glucose, Dextrose or **Grape Sugar** is a carbohydrate (q.v.). It is produced by hydrolysis from cane sugar, dextrine, starch, cellulose, etc., by the action of reagents. It also occurs in many plants, fruits and honey. For brewing purposes glucose is prepared by the conversion of starch by sulphuric acid. Malt also converts starch into glucose.

Glutton or **Wolverine**, the biggest animal of the weasel family, inhabits the northernmost parts of Europe and America. In build it resembles the bear, and is rather larger than a badger. Its fur is of a brown-black hue, but coarse.

Glycerine or **Glycerol**, occurs in natural fats combined with fatty acids, and is obtained by decomposing those substances with alkalies or by superheated steam. It is colourless and oily and sweet, and is put to a variety of commercial uses, being widely utilised for medicaments, for lubricating purposes, and in the manufacture of nitro-glycerine.

Glycols. Organic compounds containing two alcohol groups. Ethylene glycol is the most widely known example; it is used as an anti-freeze in motor-car radiators on account of its property of greatly reducing the freezing point of water. Also used in the manufacture of " Terylene ". See **Esters**.

Glyptodon, an extinct species of gigantic armadillo, fossil remains of which have been discovered in S. America. It was some 2·7 m long, carried a huge tortoise-like shell and had fluted teeth.

Gneiss, a metamorphic rock usually containing quartz, felspar and mica. It is banded, the light-coloured minerals being concentrated apart from the dark minerals.

Gnosticism. See **Section J**.

Gnu or Wildebeest, a large antelope from Africa south of the Sahara, distinguished by its excessively short thick neck and large head with a pronounced roman nose. There are two species: the white-tailed gnu is almost extinct, the brindled gnu is still common and migrates in large herds.

Goat-Moth (*Cossus cossus*), a large moth of the *Cossidae* family, common in Britain, evil-smelling and very destructive in the larval stage to trees of the poplar and willow genus, into the wood of which the caterpillar bores during its three years' period of development.

Goats are horned ruminant quadrupeds, indigenous to the Eastern Hemisphere, but now domesticated in all parts of the world. Though related to the sheep, they are a much hardier and more active animal. The male has a tuft of hair under the chin. Many species, including those of Cashmere and Angora, are valuable for their hair, which is used for fine textile fabrics. The milk of the goat is nutritive, and goat-skins are in good demand for leather for gloves, shoes, etc.

God and Man. See **Section J**.

God and Magog, two legendary City of London giants, supposed to be the offspring of certain wicked daughters of the Emperor Diocletian and a band of demons. They were brought captive to London and made to serve as prisoners at the Palace of Brute, which stood on the site of Guildhall. Effigies of the giants have stood in Guildhall since the time of Henry V. They were destroyed in the Great Fire of 1666, replaced in 1672 and used to be carried through the streets of London in the Lord Mayor's Show. The present figures, carved in lime wood by Mr. David Evans, replaced those carved in 1708 by Richard Saunders, which were destroyed in an air raid during the last war.

Gold. Metallic element, symbol Au (Latin *Aurum*) related to silver and copper, the coinage metals. The greatest amount of gold is obtained by treating gold-bearing quartz by the cyanide process. The gold is dissolved out by cyanide solution, which is then run into long boxes filled with zinc shavings when the gold is precipitated as a black slime. This is melted with an oxidising agent which removes the zinc.

Gold-Beaters' Skin is the outside membrane of the large intestine of the ox, specially prepared and used by gold-beaters for placing between the leaves of gold while they beat them. This membrane is of great tenacity, and gets beaten to such extreme thinness that it is used to put on cuts and bruises.

Gold Standard. Under the gold-standard system which was widely prevalent up to 1914, each gold-standard country fixed the value of its currency in terms of a weight of gold of a certain fineness and was, broadly speaking, ready to exchange its currency freely for gold, which could then be exported without restriction. This involved keeping a gold reserve big enough to meet all likely demands and also to serve as a backing for the issue of notes. The gold standard had to be given up during the first world war; and though it was in substance restored in Great Britain in 1925 (when Churchill was Chancellor), the restoration was never complete, as the gold reserve remained too small for complete freedom to export to be practicable. Sterling had to be devalued in the financial crisis of 1931 (which brought about the fall of the Labour Government) and Great Britain was forced off the gold standard. Imbalance in payments between countries is financed by transfers of gold or foreign exchange. Such reserves are known as international liquidity. *See also* Section G, Parts II and IV.

Goldeneye, a species of wild duck, widely distributed over Arctic regions. It is a passage-migrant and winter-visitor to the British Isles. Has nested in Cheshire. Distinguished by a large white spot in front of each eye on a dark ground.

Golden Dawn. *See Section J.*

Golden Number, the number of any year in the metonic cycle of 19 years, deriving its name from the fact that in the old calendars it was always printed in gold. It is found by adding 1 to the number of the year A.D. and dividing by 19, the remainder being the Golden Number; or, if no remainder, the Golden Number is 19. The only use to which the Golden Number is put now is in making ecclesiastical calculations for determining movable feasts.

Goldsmiths Company, one of the richest London City Companies; the official assayers of gold and silver, invested with the power of " hallmarking " the quality of objects made from these metals. First charter granted in 1327.

Gondola, the old regulation black boats so common on the canals of Venice, propelled by a gondolier with one oar who stands at the stern, his passengers being accommodated in a covered space in the centre.

Gonfalon, the pennon affixed to a lance, spear or standard, consisting usually of two or three streamers and made to turn like a weather-cock.

Good and Evil. *See Section J.*

Gophers. Rodent mammals. The pocket gophers are stout-bodied burrowers common in the USA. The slender burrowing gophers, also called " ground squirrels ", occur in central and western USA. The sisel or suslik is a related European species. They are a great pest among grain crops.

Gordon Riots of 1780 were an anti-popery agitation fomented by Lord George Gordon. Called also " No-Popery Riots ".

Gorilla, the largest of the anthropoid apes, found in the forests of Equatorial Africa, and at maturity standing from 1·2–1·5 m high.

Goshawk (*Accipiter gentilis*), a diurnal bird of prey, fearless and extremely agile; loves wooded country and is very destructive of poultry and game-birds. It resembles the peregrine falcon in appearance, but has shorter, rounded wings. This bird was a great favourite of falconers in mediaeval times.

Gospels are those portions of the New Testament which deal with the life, death, resurrection and teachings of Christ. They are the gospels of Matthew, Mark, Luke and John, all composed in the later part of the 1st cent. The first three are called the *synoptic gospels* because of their general unity of narrative. Mark was the first to be written and John the last, and it is to Mark that one should turn for the most reliable source of knowledge of the life of Jesus. The word *gospel* comes from two Anglo-Saxon words *gode* (good) and *spell* (tidings), a translation of the Greek *euangelion* = evangel, evangelist.

Gothic, the predominant style of architecture in northern Europe from 12th–15th cent. Its most striking characteristic is the extensive use of the pointed arch, but this is really a mere external reflection of the important structural invention of the 12th cent., that of the rib vault, whereby the whole pressure of the stone vaulting is supported on slim ribs which cross each other at a rising centre. On the outside of the building, the pressure from the vaults is caught up and supported by flying buttresses. A complete Gothic construction gives a marvellous effect of airy lightness, also of something striving upwards, towards the heavens, and this is further accentuated when the churches are crowned by lofty towers and spires. The vital structural elements of Gothic architecture were first put into use in the abbey church of St. Denis in Paris *c.* 1140. The style was further developed in a glorious sequence of cathedrals in northern France: Nôtre Dame in Paris, Rheims, Amiens, Beauvais and others. When, as in Chartres, the windows are filled with stained glass of glowing colours and the doorways flanked with magnificently carved life-size figures of saints and apostles, the whole effect is one of unsurpassed solemnity and grandeur. From France the style spread to other lands in each of which it developed its own characteristics; thus the English churches tended to have massive towers and delicate spires and, as at Salisbury, were often set in open grounds surrounded by lawns; Flemish and Dutch churches were sometimes built of brick as were those in north Germany and Scandinavia; in Spain the Flamboyant style was followed. The main Gothic cathedral in Italy, that of Milan, although begun in 1386 was not completed until the early 19th cent. Late English Gothic is seen, for example, at King's College Chapel, Cambridge, Henry's Chapel at Westminster and St. George's Chapel at Windsor (all *c.* 1500). Gothic is also found in secular buildings, *e.g.* Little Wenham Hall in Suffolk, the castle at Ghent, the town halls of Louvain and Middelburg and the streets of Gothic houses in Bruges still in use today. Virtually Gothic as a style (excluding the " Gothic revival " of 19th cent. England) ended at the close of the 15th cent. Gothic art is best seen in the illuminated manuscripts of the 13th and 14th cent. and in the church sculpture. Its characteristic is a complete departure from the cool, perfectionist realism of classical times with distortion to produce emotional effects. The human figures are not ideal forms but recognisable as people we might meet in the street; yet there was also the element of wild imagination, intricate design and a wealth of feeling which might be grotesque, humorous, macabre, or even obscene. Gothic style also found expression in the decorative arts, retaining its architectural character even in small-scale works like caskets, chalices and the like in metalwork and ivory.

Goths. A Teutonic people who originally came from southern Sweden (Gotland) and by the 3rd cent. were settled in the region north of the Black Sea. They began to encroach on the Roman Empire and early in the 4th cent. split into two divisions: the " wise " Goths or Visigoths between the Danube and Dniester (referred to as the West Goths), and the " bright " Goths or Ostrogoths in southern Russia on the Dnieper (referred to as the East Goths). The Ostrogoths were conquered by the Huns *c.* 370, while the Visigoths under Alaric devastated Greece and sacked Rome in 410. Eventually the Visigoths spread to France and Spain and their last king Roderick fell in battle against the Moors in 711. The Ostrogoths regained their independence on the death of Attila in 453 and under their king Theodoric the Great conquered Italy in 493. They lost their identity after Justinian regained Italy, 525–552.

Gourd Family *or* Cucurbitaceae. This family of about 650 species of flowering plants includes the gourds, pumpkins, cantaloupes, cucumber, gherkin, water-melon and squashes. Most abundant in the tropics, the cucurbits are mainly climbing annuals with very rapid growth. The bath-room loofah is the skeleton of one cucurbit fruit, *Luffa cylindrica.* The squirting cucumber is another member of the family.

Governor. A device attached to an engine, turbine, compressor, etc., which automatically controls the engine's speed in accordance with power demand. Most governors depend upon the centrifugal action of two or more balls which are thrown outwards as their speed of rotation increases and actuate a throttle valve or cut-off. The centrifugal governor was invented by Thomas Mead, patented by him in 1787 and used on windmills. Watt adapted it to the steam engine.

Grail, Legend of the Holy, a tale of Celtic origin which became part of Arthurian legend and the subject of many mediaeval quest-romances. According to the Christian version the grail was the cup which Christ used at the Last Supper, brought to England by St. Joseph of Arimathea.

Grand Prix, the "French Derby" was established by Napoleon III, in 1863. It is the chief French race and is an international competition of three-year-olds.

Granite is a coarsely crystalline igneous rock consisting of quartz and alkali felspars plus mica or hornblende. It is a much used ornamental and building stone; it forms the high ground of Dartmoor and Bodmin Moor.

Graphite *or* **Plumbago,** commonly called black-lead, is a form of carbon occurring in foliated masses in marble, schist, etc. It is soft, will make black marks on paper or other plain surfaces, and is mainly used for lead pencils. It is also a valuable lubricant. Pure graphite has found a new use with the construction of atomic piles. Important deposits occur in Siberia, Sri Lanka, Malagasy, Canada and USA.

Graptolites, fossil animals confined to Cambrian, Ordovician and Silurian strata. Once classified as hydrazoa but now considered more likely to be hemichordates.

Grasshopper. There are many species of these leaping insects which are related to the locusts and crickets. Most are vegetarians; some eat flies and caterpillars also. The chirping sound they make is made by scraping the hind legs against the wings; in some species a noise is produced by rubbing the wings together.

Gravitation. One of the four, possibly five, types of force known to physics. The others are electromagnetic, nuclear (two types) and colour forces. Gravitational forces are an attraction that one piece of matter has for another; they dominate astronomical phenomena, but inside the atom they are negligible compared with the other types of force. Einstein's General Theory of Relativity is the only theory at present extant which attempts to interpret gravitational forces in terms of more fundamental concepts. *See* F14(2), 18(2).

Graylag, the ordinary wild grey goose of Europe, the species from which domestic geese are derived; frequents fens and marshes; breeds in Iceland, Scandinavia and Scotland; distinguished by pinkish legs and feet and lack of black markings on bill.

Grebe, a diving bird of beautiful plumage found over a great part of the world on lakes and oceans. The two species familiar in Great Britain are the Dabchick or Little Grebe and the large and handsome Great Crested Grebe, which has a feathery tuft, lost in the autumn, on each side of the head. Grebes have remarkable courtship displays. The breast feathers are of a downy softness and silver lustre, for which they were formerly much hunted.

Greek Art. *See* **Hellenic Art.**

Greek Fire, a combustible supposed to have been composed of sulphur, nitre, naphtha and asphalt, used with destructive effect by the Greeks of the Eastern Empire in their wars.

Greek Kalends, equivalent to never, as only the Romans, not the Greeks, had kalends.

Green Revolution. The "green revolution" is principally due to the American agricultural expert, Dr. Norman Borlaug, who worked in Mexico on the development of new improved strains of wheat, rice, maize and other cereals. The application of new plant varieties transformed the agricultural prospects of India, Pakistan, Sri Lanka, Mexico, the Philippines and other underdeveloped countries; food importers turned into exporters. However of late the inequity in the distribution of fertilisers has affected the grain production of these countries. For his pioneering work Dr. Borlaug was awarded the 1970 Nobel peace prize. *See* Section G, Part III.

Greenwich Mean Time. The first Nautical Almanac, for the use of navigators and astronomers, was published by the Astronomer Royal in 1767. It was based on the meridian at Greenwich, with longitude measured east and west of 0°. A master clock, which still exists, was built at Greenwich Observatory in 1852 to control the railway station clocks and Greenwich Mean Time, or Railway Time as it was sometimes called, prevailed. In 1884 Greenwich was chosen as the prime meridian of the world and GMT became known as Universal Time. *See also* British Standard Time.

Gregorian Calendar. *See* Calendar.

Gresham's Law states that if good money, *i.e.*, money with the higher intrinsic value, and bad money are in circulation together, the bad money will tend to drive out the good money from circulation. For instance, the good money is more likely to be melted down or demanded in payment by foreign creditors.

Gretna Green, a celebrated village in Annandale and Eskdale, just over the border from England, where runaway marriages were performed from 1754 to 1856, though only completely stopped during present century.

Griffin, in ancient mythology, a winged creature with an eagle's head and the body of a lion, found in ancient sculptures of Persia and Assyria. Its origin is traced to the Hittites.

Grilse, a young salmon that has only been once to the sea.

Grimm's Law, formulated by Jacob Grimm, an eminent German philologist, lays down a principle of consonantal change in the Germanic languages. For instance, Lat. *pater*, Eng. *father*, Ger. *Vater*; Lat. *frater*, Eng. *brother*, Ger. *Bruder*; Lat. *decem*, Eng. *ten*, Ger. *zehn*.

Grogram (French = *gros grain*) a kind of rough fabric made of wool and some other fibre such as silk, mohair or cotton, formerly much used for commoner kinds of wearing apparel.

Grotto, a natural or artificial cave. Among the most famous are the blue grotto of Capri and the stalactite grotto of Antiparos (Cyclades Aegean).

Ground Wave, that part of the energy emitted by a radio transmitter which travels along the ground; as opposed to the sky wave which is reflected back to earth by the ionosphere. With the lower radio-frequencies, the ground wave can be picked up over several thousand miles; in the broadcasting band, over a hundred or so miles; it is virtually useless at high frequencies.

Grouse, game bird of the northern latitudes where some 20 species occur. They are stout, compact, ground-dwelling birds, protectively plumaged (the willow grouse turns white in winter), the male usually being larger and more brightly coloured than the female. The red grouse of the British moorlands has been introduced into Belgium and W. Germany. Of the same family are the blackcock, ptarmigan, capercaillie, American prairie-hen and the common partridge. Grouse shooting begins in Britain on Aug. 12.

Guanaco, a large species of llama, common to South America, and utilised as a beast of burden.

Guano, the excrement of sea-birds, found in large quantities on the rocky islands of the western coasts of South America and Nauru Is. It forms a useful fertilising agent, being rich in phosphate and ammonia, and first came into use in 1841, since which time Peruvian guano has been a recognised article of commerce. Beds of guano from 15–18 m in thickness are not uncommon. Fish guano and bat guano from caves in South America and the Bahamas are also used as fertilisers.

Gudgeon, a small fresh-water fish of the carp family with 2 small barbels on the upper lip.

Guelph and Ghibelline, italianised forms of the German words "Welf" and "Waiblingen", the names of two rival princely families whose conflicts made much of the history of Germany and Italy during the Middle Ages. The feuds between these two factions continued in Italy during the campaigns of Emperor Frederick I, and later developed into the fierce struggles of the 13th cent. between emperor and pope. In Italy the Ghibellines supported the side of the German emperors and the Guelphs the cause of the pope. The present Royal Family of England and other Northern monarchies are descended by different routes from the Guelph George I, Duke of Brunswick-Lüneburg of the House of Hanover.

Guildhall, the place of assembly of the members of a guild, and at one time, when guilds were in full strength, was practically the Town Hall. The London Guildhall is today the hall of meeting for the City of London Corporation.

Guilds for the fostering and protection of various trades have existed in England since Anglo-Saxon times, and from the 12th to the 16th cent. exercised great influence and enjoyed many privileges. There were trades' guilds and craftsmen's guilds, and in all large cities and towns there was a guild hall. Their successes in the Middle Ages led to many monopolistic abuses, and in the end it became necessary to free the country from their restrictive power. The City Guilds (Livery Companies of the City of London) derive their name from the distinctive dress assumed by their members in the 14th cent. There are 84 Guilds in existence.

Guild Socialism. *See* **Section J.**

Guillemot, a genus of sea-birds of the auk family, common in Northern Europe, two species—the Common Guillemot and the Black Guillemot—being natives of our own sea coasts, nesting on the cliffs. Brünnich's Guillemot, an Arctic species, is a rare straggler in the British Isles.

Guinea, an English gold coin of the value of twenty-one shillings, current from 1663 to 1817, and deriving its name from the first guinea coinage having been struck from gold obtained on the coast of Guinea.

Guinea-Pig, a rodent of the cavy family about 25 cm in length and with a tail so short that it does not project outside the body. It makes an excellent pet, though easily frightened. Its ancestors were species of the wild cavy of S. America said to have been domesticated by the Incas of Peru. *See* **Z20-22.**

Gules, a heraldic term, denoting a rose of red tincture, indicated by vertical lines drawn or engraved without colour.

Gulf Stream is confined entirely to the western side of the N. Atlantic and is the warm-water current flowing through the Straits of Florida from the Gulf of Mexico parallel to the American coast up as far as Cape Hatteras. From there it continues north-eastwards as a slower, broader, cooler (yet even so, relatively warm) drift of water, merging with the North Atlantic Drift and losing its identity about 40° N. Lat., 60° W. Long. It is a common error to attribute the warmth of the British Isles and Western Europe generally to the Gulf Stream but this has no influence whatever except in so far as it feeds the North Atlantic Drift. Both the Gulf Stream and the North Atlantic Drift owe their movement to the direction of the prevailing winds, and it is the south-westerly airstream coming from warmer regions and passing over the surface waters of the Atlantic Drift that brings the warmth inland to influence the climate of Western Europe.

Gull. An extremely well-known, long-winged sea-bird with rather short legs and webbed feet. In almost all adults the body and tail are white whilst the back and most of the wings are grey or black. In the majority of cases the plumage of juveniles is partly or entirely dusky. Gulls are omnivorous, and are very useful as scavengers. They follow ships and quickly seize upon any refuse which may be thrown overboard. There are 44 species, which vary in size from moderately small to large. With certain exceptions, such as the Kittiwake in the North Atlantic, they are not found very far from land. They are sociable and mostly breed in colonies on cliff-ledges, on islands, beaches and sandhills and among vegetation in swamps, sometimes a long way from the sea. The nest is usually substantial, and the eggs generally number from two to three. Of the 29 species breeding in the northern hemisphere, 14 occur in the British Isles. The pure white Ivory Gull is the most northerly of birds. Sabine's and the Swallow-tailed Gull have forked tails. Ross's Gull has

a black ring round the neck and one species, Franklin's Gull, migrates from the North, where it breeds, to pass the winter in the Southern hemisphere.

Gums are glutinous compounds obtained from vegetable sources, soluble in cold or hot water, but not in alcohol. There are innumerable varieties. Gum Arabic is exuded from a species of acacia grown in Senegal, the Sudan, Arabia, India and other countries, and is a valuable commercial product, used in dyeing, ink-making, as a mucilage, and in medicine. India-rubber is an elastic gum. Gums are also made from starch, potatoes, wheat, etc., from seeds, bark, roots and weeds. Many so-called gums are resins.

Gun-Cotton, a powerful explosive manufactured by subjecting a prepared cotton to the prolonged action of a mixture of three parts sulphuric acid and one part of nitric acid. It burns without explosion on ignition, but by percussion explodes with a force five times greater than gunpowder does.

Gunpowder, also called "black powder", the oldest of explosive mixtures, consists of saltpetre, sulphur and charcoal, intimately mixed, the proportions being varied for different intended uses.

Gunpowder Plot was a conspiracy by a desperate band of Roman Catholics in the reign of James I to avenge the harsh treatment to which Catholics were subjected. Barrels of gunpowder were secreted in the vaults underneath the Houses of Parliament, and it was proposed to fire these when the King and his Ministers assembled on 5 November 1605. The plot was betrayed and Guy Fawkes and his co-conspirators were arrested and executed. The date serves to perpetuate the ancient custom of burning the effigy of Fawkes, a custom in which young people are the most enthusiastic participants, with bonfires, fireworks, etc.

Gurnard, a sea-fish, with large, bony head and diminutive body, of which there are some forty species. They are plentiful in British waters.

Gymnasium, originally the name given in ancient Greece to the public places where Greek youth used to exercise and receive instruction. Plato, Aristotle and other great teachers lectured there. The Greek institution was never very popular with the Romans, and it was not until the 18th and 19th cent. that the cult of combining physical with intellectual activity again found a place in educational systems. In Germany the name was applied to the classical grammar school; in this country and America to the halls where gymnastics were practised.

Gypsies, a nomadic race, believed to be of Indian origin; their language, Romany, is related to the languages of N.W. India. The Rom are spread over many parts of the world, but are most common in Europe where they appeared towards the end of the Middle Ages. The English name *gypsy* comes from the Spanish *gitano* = Egyptian; other European names are *Zigeuner* (Ger.), *zingaro* (It.), *fzigany* (Magyar), all resembling the Persian *zingar* = a saddler. Their history has been one of persecution. Hitler treated them like the Jews. In Britain since the war they have been kept increasingly on the move, but in 1968 Parliament passed a Bill to make the provision of sites a duty of local authorities. However, it is likely at the present rate of building to be many years before the 4,500 gypsy households have a site. Economic pressure has largely removed their traditional crafts of tinkering, basket-making, peg-making. The majority now deal in scrap-iron.

Gypsum, a whitish mineral consisting of hydrated sulphate of calcium. The finest gypsum is alabaster. When heated gypsum is converted into the powder called Plaster of Paris; the water it loses can be taken up when the plaster is wetted, and the reconversion of Plaster of Paris into gypsum accounts for the way in which the former sets hard. The name " Plaster of Paris " came from the location of important gypsum quarries in the Montmartre district of Paris. It was found after the flood disasters of January 1953 that gypsum could undo the effect of sea-water. By spreading it for the rain to wash into the soil, thousands of acres of farmland in Holland and Britain were made productive again.

Gyroscope is a symmetrical rapidly rotating object, typically wheel-like, which because of its mass and rotation possesses a lot of the dynamical property known as angular momentum. Basic dynamical laws tell us that angular momentum is conserved and a consequence of this is that the axis of rotation tends to stay pointing in the same direction. Disturbing influences make a gyroscope's motion complicated but the general effect of the presence of a gyroscope attached to any body is to help to stabilise the body's motion. This is made use of in reducing the rocking of ships and in compasses and control systems in aircraft, torpedoes and missiles.

H

Habeas Corpus, the name given to a writ ordering the body of a person under restraint or imprisonment to be brought into court for full inquiry into the legality of the restraint to be made. The first Habeas Corpus Act was passed in 1679, though nominally such a right had existed from Magna Carta, but some of the more despotic kings had disregarded it. In times of public peril the privilege of *habeas corpus* is sometimes temporarily suspended, many instances occurring in the history of Ireland and during the first and second world wars.

Haber Process, the important industrial process for synthesising ammonia from atmospheric nitrogen. Nitrogen and hydrogen are made to combine at high pressure (200 atmospheres or upwards) in an electric arc.

Haddock, one of the best-known fishes abounding in northern seas and averaging about 1·8 kg in weight. Related to the cod. Largely used for curing, and sold as " finnan haddies ".

Hade of veins, a mining term indicating the particular inclination that any vein, seam or strata may have from the perpendicular; thus, in Weardale the veins mainly " hade " to the north.

Hadrian's Wall. *See* **Roman walls.**

Haematite, ferric oxide, one of the principal iron ores, containing about 70% of the metal. It is usually found in kidney-shaped masses, and is specular, red or brown, in thin fragments but greyish in bulk.

Haemocyanin, the respiratory pigment of crustaceans and molluscs. It functions like haemoglobin, from which it differs in containing copper instead of iron and being blue when oxidised instead of red. *See* **F39(1).**

Haemoglobin, the pigment containing iron which gives red blood corpuscles their colour. It is a respiratory pigment, having the property of picking up oxygen when the blood passes through the lungs to produce the compound known as oxyhaemoglobin. In other parts of the body the oxyhaemoglobin breaks down, liberating oxygen, which is used in the oxidation process (respiration) that the body tissues carry on. *See* **F38(2).**

Hafiz, besides being the pseudonym of a famous Persian poet, is a title conferred upon any Mohammedan who has committed the whole of the Koran to memory.

Hafnium, a metallic element discovered by Coster and Hevesy in 1922 and important in the atomic-energy field. It occurs in most zirconium minerals to the extent of about 5 per cent.

Hagiology, a branch of literature that is wholly given up to the history of the saints, and the setting forth of the stories and legends associated with their names.

Hail, hard, roughly spherical balls of ice, consisting of white cores covered by layers of both transparent and opaque ice, frequently falling during thunderstorms. They usually do not exceed 2·5 cm in size, but hailstones as large as tennis balls have been observed. The general theory of a hailstone is that near the top of a cumulonimbus cloud a raindrop becomes frozen, grows in size by condensation and through collisions with snow particles, and eventually becomes so weighty as to overcome the ascend-

ing air currents in the cloud. Falling, it first encounters supercooled water drops, immediately freezing on it, increasing the white core, and then at lower levels ordinary water drops, freezing more slowly, producing a layer of clear ice. Before the hailstone arrives at the ground gusts and lulls may transport it several times up and down both regions, adding alternate coatings of soft white and hard clear ice.

Hake, a fish of the cod family, found in large numbers in the seas of Europe, but not in high favour for the table with fastidious feeders.

Halcyon, a term associated in olden times with the kingfisher and days of soothing calm, " halcyon days " being a frequently used expression. The legend was that the kingfisher laid its eggs on the surface of the sea at the time of the winter solstice when the sea was unruffled. (Halcyon is the Greek for Kingfisher.)

Halibut, one of the largest of the flat fishes, averaging when full grown from 1·2–1·8 m in length, and highly esteemed for the table. Specimens of still larger size occasionally occur. It is plentifully distributed. Its two eyes are on the right side of the head.

Hallmark. A mark or group of marks, impressed by an assay office on gold or silver articles (and on platinum since 1974) guaranteeing the standard of fineness of the precious metal used in them. These marks, which have been applied to silver made in London since the beginning of the 14th cent. and perhaps earlier, make it possible to establish the year and place of assay and also the name of the maker. English pieces of silver usually have not less than four marks, viz., (1) town mark; (2) maker's mark; (3) date letter; (4) sterling mark.

The town mark is rarely changed; in London a crowned leopard's head was used from the earliest days until 1820 with only minor modifications, except for the period 1697–1720 when a lion's head erased was substituted; since 1820 the crown has been omitted.

Until the late 17th cent. a symbol was often used as a maker's mark, from 1696 to 1720 the first two letters of the maker's surname, and subsequently the maker's initials. Owing to the destruction of the earlier mark plates at Goldsmiths' Hall no maker's name prior to the late 17th cent. can be identified with certainty. The London date letter is changed at the end of May each year, so each letter covers seven months of one year and five months of the following. The London date cycle has usually consisted of twenty letters: the alphabet of each cycle is of different style, and the letters are enclosed in shields of different shape.

The sterling mark, the lion passant, was introduced in 1544 and continued in use until 1697, when the higher Britannia standard was introduced in order to discourage the practice current amongst goldsmiths of melting down coin of the realm to make plate. The leopard's head crowned and the lion passant were then replaced by a figure of Britannia and a lion's head erased. Though the regulation imposing the higher standard was withdrawn in 1720, a small amount of Britannia standard silver continued to be made and still is made.

From 1784 until 1890 a plate tax was levied on all silver assayed in Great Britain and an additional duty mark, the sovereign's head, was used during this period. A Jubilee mark bearing the head of George V and Queen Mary was used between the years 1933 and 1935, and in 1953 a coronation mark with the head of Queen Elizabeth was introduced.

The tables of hallmarks in **Section U** give the London date letter cycles from 1598 to 1955. The form of town mark and sterling mark used during each cycle is given at the head of each column. Where a major alteration took place in either of these marks during a date-letter cycle, the alternative forms are also shown. The date of the change can be established by reference to the notes above. At the bottom of each page the marks used by the major provincial, Scottish and Irish assay offices are shown. Owing to lack of space, the complete date-letter cycles are not shown, but two examples only from the 17th, 18th or 19th cent. Where a provincial assay office was established in the 17th cent. or earlier, the marks of one year in the 17th and 18th cent. respectively are shown; where the office was not established until the 18th cent., the marks of one year in the 18th and 19th cent. are given.

Under the Hallmarking Act 1973 the hallmarking of platinum is now compulsory; the hallmark symbol is an orb surmounted by a cross and encompassed by a pentagon; assay offices London and Birmingham.

Halloween (31 October), the eve of All Saints' Day, a time associated, especially in Scotland, with certain pleasing superstitions attractively set forth in Burns's famous poem " Hallowe'en ". It is the night when young men and maidens are supposed, by observing certain rites, to have their future wives and husbands disclosed to them.

Hallucinogen, a drug which acts upon the brain to create sensory illusions or hallucinations with a variety of emotional effects. One of the most widely studied is LSD (q.v.) which will produce symptoms very similar to those found in some mental disorders.

Halo, a luminous circle usually of 22° radius, surrounding sun or moon, produced by the refraction and reflection of light by ice crystals of high cirrus cloud. It is a very common occurrence, in the British Isles almost one day in three. The inner side is red and the outer a whitish-yellow colour. " Mock suns ", i.e., patches of light at the same elevation as the sun are much rarer occurrences, sometimes being of great beauty and brilliance. Halo is the Greek for threshing-floor. See **Corona**.

Halogens, the group name for the four non-metallic elements fluorine, chlorine, bromine and iodine. The term " halogen " means " salt-producer ".

Halteres, the modified hind-wings of the two-winged flies or Diptera (e.g., the house-fly). The equilibrium in flight of these insects depends on the halteres, which are commonly called " balancers ".

Hampton Court Conference, presided over at Hampton Court Palace by James I in 1604 and which brought about his authorised translation of the Bible, had an important bearing on the religious differences of the time. James refused to grant tolerations to the Puritans. This sowed the seeds of civil war. Following the conference three hundred English Puritan clergy were ejected from their livings.

Hanaper Office, a former Chancery office, deriving its name from the fact that its writs and papers were kept in a hanaper (hamper). The Chancellor's office thus came to be known as the Hanaper. The Comptrollers of the Hanaper were abolished in England in 1842.

Hand, a measure of 4 in (10 cm), the average size of the palm; used in reckoning height of horses.

Handfasting, an informal marriage custom once prevalent in Scotland, whereby a man and woman bound themselves to cohabit for a year and a day, and at the end of that period either confirmed their contract by a regular marriage or separated.

Hansard, the title given to the official reports of Parliamentary debates, so named after Luke Hansard who in 1774 became partner in a firm of printers to the House of Commons. His son T. C. Hansard was first the printer and then the publisher of an unofficial series of parliamentary debates inaugurated by William Cobbett in 1803. In 1909 production was taken over by H.M. Stationery Office and today's volumes contain full, substantially verbatim, reports of what is said in both Houses of Parliament.

Hanseatic League was a confederation of North German towns established about 1241 for purposes of mutual protection in carrying on international commerce. The League became so powerful that it was able to dominate the foreign trade of Norway, Sweden, Denmark, and even to some extent of London. A branch was established in London and had its guild hall in Cannon Street for hundreds of years. The League existed down to the middle of the 17th cent. Hamburg, Lübeck and Bremen are the only cities which, as free ports, still by commercial courtesy retain the name of Hanse towns. Hansa is Old High German for Association or Merchants' Guild.

Hapsburg (Ger. **Habsburg**), the ruling house of

Austria, 1282–1918; held title of Holy Roman Emperor, 1438–1806, except for 1740–5. The aggrandisement of the Hapsburg family was mainly brought about by a series of fortunate marriages. In 1521 when the Hapsburg power was at its zenith, Charles V divided his dominions into two branches—Austrian Hapsburg and Spanish Hapsburg. The Hapsburg Danubian Monarchy dates from 1526 when the Hungarian and Bohemian crowns were united with the Austrian patrimony of the Hapsburg. The triple union lasted 400 years. The murder of the heir to the Hapsburg thrones, Francis Ferdinand, at Sarajevo in 1914, provoked the outbreak of the first world war. Francis Joseph's great-nephew, Charles, abdicated in 1918. (Prof. C. A. Macartney's authoritative work, The Habsburg Empire, 1790–1918, was published in 1969.)

Hara-kiri, the custom of suicide, as formerly practised in Japan, when in disgrace.

Hardware, the electrical, electronic magnetic and mechanical parts of a computer or data-processing system. See **Software**.

Hare, a rabbit-like animal with longer ears and legs. There are many kinds of hare distributed over the northern hemisphere and in Africa south to the Cape. They do not burrow as do rabbits but rely on camouflage, speed and mobility for safety. See **Game**.

Harleian MSS. comprise some thousands of volumes of MSS. and documents, collected by the first Earl of Oxford (1661–1724) and his son Edward. After the death of the latter, his widow handed the MSS. over to the nation for £10,000, and they are deposited in the British Museum.

Harlequin, the buffoon of ancient Italian comedy. As adapted to the British stage, however, harlequin is a pantomime character only, in love with Columbine, appearing in parti-coloured garments and carrying a wand, by which he exercises a magic influence in thwarting the fantastic tricks of the clown and pantaloon.

Harmattan, a dry wind which may blow between January and May across the Sahara to the Gulf of Guinea. Although affording relief from the tropical heat, vegetation withers because of its extreme dryness and much irritation is caused by the clouds of fine dust which it carries.

Harmonic Motion, regular periodic motion of the kind exemplified by a ball bobbing up and down at the end of a spring, and by the piston in a steam engine. It may be simple (simple harmonic motion) or composed of two or more simple harmonic motions. In simple harmonic motion the acceleration is proportional to the distance of the moving body from its original rest position.

Harp-seal, the ordinary Greenland seal, with a dark harp-shaped marking on its back, hence its name. It abounds in Newfoundland waters and further northward towards the Arctic.

Harpy Eagle, a large bird of prey named from the winged monsters of Greek mythology, inhabiting the forest regions of Central and South America. There are eight species, one with handsome grey plumage and large crest which attacks and kills animals much larger than itself, and was called by the Aztecs " winged wolf ".

Harrier, a bird of prey of the falcon family; of the various species distributed over the world, three breed in Britain: the moorland Hen harrier, the Marsh harrier and Montagu's harrier. They are large birds with long tails, long legs, long wings and gliding flight. They nest on the ground and eat small mammals, frogs, lizards and small birds.

Hartebeest, common African antelope of a grey-brown colour, with ringed and knotted horns bending backward and tapering to sharp points; gregarious, of large size. There are several species.

Harvest Bug, a very small insect, of a dark red colour, which appears in large numbers in the fields in autumn, and is peculiarly irritating to animals and man by the tenacity with which it attaches itself to the skin and burrows underneath. Probably the larvae of spinning mites (Trombido'ds). In the USA they are called " chiggers ".

Harvest Moon, the full moon that occurs nearest to the autumn equinox, in September. It rises for several nights running about the same time, and yields an unusually brilliant series of moonlight nights.

Harvestmen are, like spiders, members of the arachnid class but belong to the distinctly different order of Phalangida. They are common in the countryside in autumn and have small oval bodies and eight long slender legs which besides being mere organs of locomotion also act as sense organs. Known as "daddy longlegs" in America.

Hashish, an Arabic word for the narcotic substance prepared from the hemp plant (*Cannabis sativa*). It is known by a variety of names, *e.g.*, bhang in India and marijuana in America.

Hatchment, in heraldry, is a square board, in vertical diagonal position, placed outside a house or on the tomb at the death of a member of a family and so arranged that it indicates the sex and condition of the deceased.

Hawfinch, a well-known European bird of the finch family, having a variegated plumage, a sturdy bill and black-and-white tail. In England it is found in the Midland and Eastern counties, and locally in Scotland.

Hawk. This name is applied to almost any diurnal bird of prey other than eagle, falcon or vulture, but in its strict sense applies only to the *Accipiter* genus—the small Sparrow Hawk and the larger Goshawk, round-winged, long-tailed birds with barred under-parts. They prey upon small birds captured in flight and small mammals.

Hawk-moths, large species of moths, thick of body and strong of wing, which fly with rapid swooping motion, hence the name. There are numerous handsome species in Britain.

Hearth-Money was a tax laid on hearths (in all houses paying the church and poor rates). Charles II introduced it in 1662, and it was repealed in the reign of William and Mary.

Heat, after prolonged controversy over whether or not heat is a "substance" (formerly called "caloric"), it was established in the 19th cent. that heat is a form of energy; it is in fact the combined kinetic and potential energy of the atoms of which a body is composed. Heat can be turned into other forms of energy, *e.g.*, a red hot body loses heat by radiating it in the form of electromagnetic waves ("radiant heat"—chiefly infra-red rays). Heat may also be transferred from one place to another by conduction and, in fluids, by convection. All three processes occur when a glowing fire heats a room. A unit quantity of heat is the calorie, which is the amount of heat sufficient to raise the temperature of 1 g of water by 1°C. In general, adding heat to a body raises its temperature. The number of calories required per gram of material to raise the temperature 1°C is called the *specific heat* of the material. However, adding heat may not raise the temperature but may instead cause a change of state, *e.g.*, from solid to liquid (melting) or liquid to gas (evaporation). The amount of heat required to melt 1 gram of a solid is called the latent heat of melting. Similarly, there is a latent heat of evaporation. Strictly speaking, the specific and latent heats of a substance depend on how much its pressure and volume are allowed to vary during the measurements. Water has a high specific heat, and this makes the oceans a vast heat reservoir, a factor of great meteorological significance. The science of heat is called thermodynamics, and is of great importance in physics and chemistry. F20(1).

Heat Pump, essentially a refrigerator working in reverse, *i.e.*, a device which warms up one place, say, a house by releasing into it heat transferred from another place, say, the air or earth outside the house. The idea is attributed to Lord Kelvin (1852) and later Haldane used a heat pump to heat his house in Scotland. In summer, a house could be cooled by operating the device in reverse. As in a domestic refrigerator, the heat is transferred by a suitable fluid whose circulation has to be driven by an external supply of energy, *e.g.*, by running a mechanical compressor. With good design and favourable conditions, the energy required to run the heat pump is considerably less than would be required to produce the same warming effect directly. Since the 1930s heat pumps have

been produced commercially for domestic and industrial use but, as always, careful consideration is needed to decide whether in a particular application they are cheaper to run than alternative methods of heating.

Heath, flowering plants of the *Ericaceae* family. Heaths are widely distributed over uncultivated spaces of Europe and Africa. In Britain they are represented by heather (of which there are several species) and ling (*Calluna vulgaris*), which cover thousands of acres of moorland. Some of the African or Cape heaths are very beautiful and much prized by florists. One species of heath (*Erica arborea*) which grows in S. Europe and N. Africa has close-grained woody rootstock used for making briar pipes. In N. Europe acid heathlands, dominated by heather and ling, form one of the most widespread vegetation areas created by man through the destruction of former oak forests, grazing and burning.

Heat Wave is a spell of very hot weather, due chiefly in the British Isles to a warm southerly current of air caused by the presence of an anticyclone over western or central Europe at the same time as a depression is stationary over the Atlantic. High humidity increases the discomfort.

Hegira, an Arab term signifying departure or flight, and used in reference to Mohammed's departure from Mecca for Medina, A.D. 622, from which date the Mohammedan era is reckoned.

Helicopter, heavier-than-air aircraft which obtains its lift from blades rotating above the fuselage in windmill-fashion. The first successful helicopters were the Focke-Wulf 61, a German machine (1936), and the VS-300, designed by Igor Sikorsky, flown in 1937. Helicopters can hover, and rise and descend vertically, in addition to being capable of horizontal flight.

Heliotrope, a favourite sweet-scented flowering plant, common in tropical and sub-tropical countries; the Peruvian heliotrope is the "cherry pie" of our summer garden borders.

Helium, a gaseous element first discovered by means of the spectroscope in the sun's atmosphere. This discovery, made in 1868 by the astronomer Sir Norman Lockyer, was followed in 1895 by Sir William Ramsay's proof that the element existed on earth. He found it in the uranium ore, clevite. Later it was established that helium is formed by the radioactive decay of many elements which emit α-particles (nuclei of helium atoms) and is contained in all radioactive minerals. The largest source of helium is natural gas, the richest in helium being the gas from certain wells in Utah, USA. Next to hydrogen, helium is the lightest gas known, has a lifting power equal to 92% of hydrogen and the advantage that it is inert and non-inflammable. It is used for inflating airships. Ordinary air contains 1 part in 200,000 of helium. It was the last gaseous element to be liquefied, this being achieved by Onnes in 1908 in Leyden. Liquid helium has many remarkable properties only imperfectly understood. As well as being scientifically fascinating it is indispensable in cryogenics (*q.v.*) as a medium for cooling other substances to temperatures near absolute zero. Hydrogen fusion in the "H bomb" produces helium.

Hellebore, a plant of the *Ranunculaceae* (buttercup) family. The best-known British examples are the green and stinking varieties. There is also a garden kind which flowers in December called the Christmas Rose. Hellebore yields a bitter substance which forms a drastic purgative, but is now little used.

Hellenic Art. The art of ancient Greece may be roughly divided into three periods: the prehistoric period (c. 1500–1000 B.C.) of the bronze age Mycenaeans; the archaic period (c. 600–500 B.C.); and the classical period (c. 500–300 B.C.). Of the first period centred on Mycenae in Peloponnesus but extending to the coasts of Asia and the city of Troy we can mention only the massive stone gateways and the shaft graves of Mycenae, where the archaeologist Schliemann discovered painted vases, gold cups, bronze swords and ornaments of what had once been a great, if primitive, civilisation. During the archaic period sculpture was the principal form of art expression. The magnificent male and female figures are reminiscent of Egyptian art, but are distinctive in liveliness of facial expression. The vase-paintings of this period became more elaborate, depicting scenes from mythology or ceremonial events. Typical of classical Greek art is the representation of the beautiful and healthy human body deliberately posed and often carrying out heroic or athletic acts. The vast majority of these statues are known to us only through Roman copies. The *Hermes* of Praxiteles (born c. 385 B.C.) is possibly the only existing statue which can be assigned with any degree of certainty to an individual artist. Almost the whole of the Greek genius in architecture was expended on temples which are all basically similar in design—a rectangle with a low-pitched gabled roof resting on side walls. The three orders Doric, Corinthian and Ionic mainly referred to the type of column used, but naturally the whole building was influenced thereby. Some of the main buildings are on the Acropolis, a hill outside Athens, on which stand the Parthenon (from the outer frieze of which the Elgin marbles (*q.v.*), now mostly in the British Museum, were taken), the Erechtheum, famous for its Porch of Maidens, and the gateway known as the Propylaea with its broad flight of marble steps. Apart from that on vases, no Greek painting has come down to us, although Greek painters existed and were noted in their time. All we have are copies in mosaic and fresco made by the Romans, at Naples and Pompeii. Of Greek literature in prose, verse and the drama little can be said here. To the early period (*i.e.*, the archaic age) belong Homer's *Iliad* and *Odyssey*, Hesiod's long poem *Work and Days* and Sappho's love poems, and Pindar's Odes. The period of Pericles in the 5th cent. B.C. produced more great literature than any comparable period in history: the philosophical writings of Plato and Aristotle, the tragedies of Aeschylus, Euripides and Sophocles, the comedies of Aristophanes—all these are still part of the European tradition, and together with Greek architecture played a major part in the Renaissance (*see* Section J).

Hellenistic Art, the art of the period of Greek civilisation which began with the conquests of Alexander the Great (356–323 B.C.) and lasted until his former empire (which encompassed most of the Middle East and part of North Africa) was conquered by the Romans in 146 B.C. Culturally it was an important period because it spread Greek culture far beyond its original boundaries—even as far as the north of India, and its centres spread from Athens to the cities of Alexandria in Egypt, Antioch in Syria and Pergamum in Asia Minor. But equally Eastern culture spread to the West: democracy was replaced by absolute monarchy, cosmopolitanism took the place of the Greek tendency to believe that all who were not Greeks were barbarians, and mystical philosophies took the place of Greek rationalism. This was a sensuous, secular, pleasure-loving, rootless society and these tendencies were reflected in its art. Hellenistic sculpture was sensual, effeminate and violently emotional, yet it depicted individuals and not always noble or beautiful ones. (Classical Greek sculpture was idealistic, showed types rather than individuals and appealed to the intellect rather than the emotions.) Some of the best examples came from the school at Pergamum and later from the island of Rhodes, and the titles themselves speak of their nature: *The Dying Gaul, Gaul Slaying his Wife and Himself*, and the famous *Laocoön* (representing Laocoön and his two sons being crushed by two enormous serpents). All these date from about 240 to 50 B.C.—for the culture did not immediately end with the Roman conquest. The enormous frieze of the altar of the temple in Pergamum depicts a battle between gods and giants with tremendous realism and brutal violence far removed from the serene art of classical times. Portrait sculpture is typical of Hellenistic art, where it may almost be said to have been invented, since such ventures in the past had been idealistic rather than realistic. The great Hellenistic cities were geometrically planned and fine public buildings made their appearance in which the slender and graceful

Ionic or the ornate Corinthian columns took the place of the more austere and heavy classical ones. Alexandria was celebrated for its vast libraries and was the centre of a brilliant intellectual life (the Septuagint or Greek translation of the Bible was prepared here). Here too worked the mathematicians Euclid and Archimedes, the physicians Erasistratus and Herophilus, and the geographer Pytheas. But Hellenistic literature was a pale reflection of the glories of the past and we mention only the comedies of Menander and the pastoral verse of Theocritus of Syracuse.

Hemiptera, the order of insects to which belong the true bugs. Their wing structure is in most species incomplete, hence the term hemiptera (half-wing). This order includes the familiar water insects, the water boatman and water skater, also the aphids, cicadas, leaf hoppers, scale insects.

Hemlock, a plant of the *Umbelliferae* family, growing in all parts of Britain, and containing a strong alkaloid poison. Used medicinally, this alkaline substance is of considerable service, being a powerful sedative. According to Pliny, hemlock was the poison used by the Athenians in putting criminals to death.

Hemp (*Cannabis sativa*), name of a plant native to Asia, now cultivated widely for the valuable fibre contained in the stalk or in some species in the leaves. Hemp fibre has been replaced by cotton for textiles and by jute for sacks and is now chiefly used for cordage and twine. It contains a resinous substance from which the narcotic hashish is made. The seed yields a valuable oil. The term hemp is also used for other fibre plants, including manila hemp from the Philippines, sunn hemp from India, sisal from W. and E. Africa and phormium from New Zealand.

Henbane, a plant found in Britain and other parts of Europe and Northern Asia. It belongs to the potato family *Solanaceae*, grows mostly on waste ground and bears yellow-brown flowers veined with purple. The leaves yield a poisonous alkaloid substance which, medicinally prepared and administered, is of great use. Tincture of henbane is often preferred to laudanum.

Heptarchy, a word derived from the Greek *hepta*, seven, and denoting the seven kingdoms (*archai*) into which Anglo-Saxon England was divided before 900. The seven were Kent, Essex, Sussex, Wessex, Mercia, East Anglia and Northumbria.

Heracleum, a plant of the *Umbelliferae* family, common in southern and central Europe, though only one species, the cow parsnip, grows in England. It has a bitter root, and from the juice of the stem an intoxicating liquor is occasionally prepared.

Herald, an officer of state empowered to make formal proclamations and deliver messages from the sovereign or other high personage whom he serves. In the developments which took place in armorial bearings, the herald was the functionary charged with the duty of their proper depiction.

Heraldry, the knowledge of armorial bearings, was mainly the outcome of the love of outward distinction which prevailed in mediaeval times. "Heraldry," says Stubbs, "became a handmaid of chivalry, and the marshalling of badges, crests, coat-armour, pennons, helmets and other devices of distinction grew into an important branch of knowledge." The *shield*, or *escutcheon*, is the ground upon which armorial signs are traced, the colour of the shield being called the *tincture*, the signs recorded the *charges*. There are seven *tinctures—or* (gold), *argent* (silver), *gules* (red), *azure* (blue), *vert* (green), *purpure* (purple) and *sable* (black). The *charges* are classed as " Honourable " and " Subordinate " ordinaries, comprising lines and geometrical forms; and " Common " ordinaries, which latter includes all representations of natural objects. There is also a system of external signs, such as crowns, coronets, mitres, helmets, mantlings, wreaths and crests, each having its distinctive significance. For other distinguishing marks see **Hatchment, Quartering, Rampant.**

Heralds' College or College of Arms, was incorporated by Richard III in 1483. Its head is the Earl Marshal (an office hereditary in the family of the Dukes of Norfolk), and there are three Kings of Arms, six Heralds and four Pursuivants. The business transacted is wholly connected with the tracing of genealogies and the granting of armorial bearings. In Scotland the Heraldic functions are performed by the Lord Lyon King of Arms.

Herbarium, a systematically classified collection of preserved plants. One of the largest in the world is at the Royal Botanic Gardens at Kew.

Heredity is the study of the transmission of physical and mental characteristics from one generation to another. Gregor Mendel (1822–84), a great experimenter in the field of inheritance, established the principle embodied in Mendel's law in his work published in 1866. The ideas which he then put forward were forgotten until the early years of this century, but today they form the basis of the modern study of genetics. Genes are the units of heredity; they are contained in the chromosomes of the cell nucleus. In human cells there are 46 chromosomes—22 pairs of characteristic shape, and a 23rd (the sex chromosomes) similar in women and dissimilar in men, which unite in the process of fertilisation. An individual can only develop, even under the most favourable surroundings, as far as his inherited characteristics, *i.e.*, his genes will allow him to do. It is in the development of personality that the interplay between heredity and environment becomes most apparent. *See* **Evolution, Section F, Part IV,** *also* **Q27.**

Hermaphrodite, animals or plants possessing both male and female reproductive organs, *e.g.*, snail, earthworms, most flowering plants.

Hermit Crab, a decapod, with a soft asymmetrical body which it protects by thrusting it into an empty gastropod shell, *e.g.*, whelk, which it carries about, only abandoning it when necessary for a larger one. Found in all seas, many live in commensal relationship with sea anemones etc.

Heron, a large wading bird with long curved neck and pointed bill, is a member of the *Ardeidae* family, of which there are many species. Egrets and bitterns are included as herons. Herons are to be met with in marsh lands and near rivers and lakes, where they feed on fish and frogs. They nest in trees in large numbers, these colonies being called heronries. The common heron is native to England, and other species from the Continent are frequent visitors.

Herring (*Clupea harengus*), an important food-fish inhabiting the North Sea which has been subjected to overfishing. In Britain the herring industry is based on the Shetlands and the coastal ports of E. Scotland and N.E. England. Marine biologists have recently reported on its unique structure for hearing which makes it receptive to sound frequencies over a very wide range and able to determine distance, direction and sound of a source of sound.

Hibernation, the dormant condition in which numerous mammals, reptiles, amphibians, insects, plants, etc., pass the winter. The rate of metabolism slows down, and the body temperature drops to that of the surroundings. Work on these low temperatures and their physiological effect has led to improved surgical techniques. Animals of the torrid regions pass through an analogous period (aestivation) during the hot season, when the sources of food are dried up.

Hickory, several species of American tree of the walnut family, remarkable for its very hard, solid, heavy white wood, and bearing an edible, four-lobed nut.

Hieratic Art, a type of art (typified by the major part of the art of ancient Egypt) which is (*a*) exclusively religious and (*b*) conventionally based on earlier forms and traditions.

Hieroglyphics are the earliest form of pictured symbolic expressions, and are supposed to have been introduced by the ancient Egyptians. They consist of rude depictions of animals, plants, signs and objects, and in their later examples express, in abridged form, ideas and records from which significant historical information has been gleaned. The deciphering of Egyptian hieroglyphics long formed an ardent study, but gradually the key to the riddle was discovered, and most of the ancient records can now be understood. Besides the Egyptian there are also Hittite, Minoan and Mayan hieroglyphic scripts. *See* **Rosetta Stone.**

Hi-Fi means high fidelity and refers to gramophones, tape recorders and similar apparatus which will *faithfully* reproduce sounds. It is not too difficult these days to amplify electrical signals without distorting them much; it is more difficult to turn electrical impulses into exactly equivalent sound waves (with a loudspeaker, for example) or *vice versa* (with a microphone or gramophone pick-up). Pick-up and loudspeaker are therefore often the weak links in domestic hi-fi and faults in their design, deficiencies in the electronic amplifiers, imperfect gramophone motors can all contribute to audible results ranging from the tolerable to the execrable. Almost perfect sound reproduction is however available to enthusiasts possessing a suitable combination of discrimination, know-how and financial resources. There are periodical magazines which provide guidance.

Hindi, the official language of India.

Hinduism. *See* Section J.

Hindustani, the spoken form of Hindi (written in Devanagari script) and Urdu (written in Arabic characters).

Hippogriff, a fabulous animal like a horse in body, but with the head, wings and front legs and claws of an eagle. The monster frequently appears in the romances of the Middle Ages.

Hippopotamus or " river-horse " the largest living representative of the hog family, widely distributed over Africa, where it lives in herds. It is of immense bulk, attaining a length of 3·6 m and a weight of 4 tonnes and stands about 1·5 m high. Its skin is hairless and about 5 cm thick, and it has a pair of tusks often weighing as much as 2·7 kg. It spends most of its time in the water, and lives entirely on vegetation, both aquatic and terrestrial. The pigmy hippopotamus, which occurs in forests and swamps in W. Africa, is only half the size.

Histology is the study of the structure of plant and animal tissues. These mainly consist of groups of cells with similar functions, *e.g.*, muscle, brain tissue.

Hittites, an ancient race (often mentioned in the Old Testament) who inhabited Cappadocia (region of Eastern Asia Minor) from the third to the first millennium B.C. Excavations have revealed that they attained a high level of civilisation round about 1350 B.C. The Hittites were rivals of Egypt, disputing with the Pharaohs the mastery of the Middle East. They were the first to smelt iron successfully.

Hobby, a bird of the falcon family, 30–35 cm long. Local breeding visitor to England and Wales, April–September; irregular visitor to Scotland and Ireland. They winter in Africa.

Hog, the common name of animals of the Suina family, including the wild boar, pig and sow. The wild boar, *Sus scrofa*, is the common ancestor. The skin of the hog is covered with bristles the snout truncated and each foot has four hoofed toes. Hogs are omnivorous feeders and eat almost anything that is given them.

Hogmanay, the Scottish New Year's Eve festival and a national holiday of the country. The custom of demanding Hogmanay bread is still upheld in many parts of Scotland.

Hogshead, a cask of varying capacity, also a specific measure. In the old English measure a hogshead was 63 old gallons of wine (= 52½ imperial gallons = 238·6 litres). Of beer 54 old gallons make a hogshead.

Holly, a hardy evergreen shrub, largely grown in England. Its bright dark green prickly curved leaves and clusters of red berries are familiar in all parts of the country, and used as house decoration between Christmas Eve and Twelfth Night, probably a relic from Roman and Teutonic customs. Its wood is white and hard, valued for carved work, while its bark yields a gummy substance which is converted into bird-lime.

Hologram, a photographic record, taken under special optical conditions, of light reflected from a scene or object. The hologram is typically a piece of film. However it is nothing like a photographic negative of the ordinary kind;

for one thing it will show an unintelligible pattern of light and dark patches. Nevertheless if it is illuminated (again under special optical conditions) the light coming through it will form a *three dimensional* image of the original object. Another radical difference between a hologram and an ordinary film is that if the hologram is cut up, each fragment can be used to construct the entire image. Holography, as a method of recording and reproducing photographic information, was conceived by Gabor in 1947 but was only fully realised in practice after the invention of the laser (*q.v.*), which made available powerful sources of coherent light. The use of laser light is one of the "special conditions" referred to above. Technical applications are being explored in many laboratories. Gabor received the 1971 Nobel prize for his discovery and invention.

Holy Alliance, an alliance ostensibly for conserving religion, justice and peace in Europe, but used for repressing popular tendencies towards constitutional government. Formed by Alexander I of Russia, Francis I of Austria and Frederick William III of Prussia, at Paris on 26 September 1815. Subsequently joined by all the sovereigns of Europe, except the Pope and the King of England. It ended after the 1830 revolution in France.

Holy Coat of Treves, a garment preserved in the Cathedral of Trèves and said to have been worn by Christ. It was brought from Jerusalem by the Empress Helena in the fourth century.

Holy Rood, an annual Roman Catholic festival held on 14 September to celebrate the Elevation of the Cross in commemoration of its re-erection in Jerusalem by the Emperor Heraclius in 628 after retaking it from the Persians. Also included in the Church of England calendar.

Holyrood, the ancient royal palace at Edinburgh, dating from the 15th cent., and inhabited by many Scottish sovereigns, notably Mary Stuart, the rooms occupied by her (including the one in which Rizzio was murdered) being still shown. It is now known as Holyrood House and is still used as a royal residence.

Holy Roman Empire, the title which the German Empire received in 962 when Pope John XII crowned Otto I at Rome. It endured until 1806 when Francis II became Emperor of Austria.

Holy Water, water blessed by a priest and kept in small fonts at the entrance to Roman Catholic churches, and used by worshippers going in, and out, or by priests in sprinkling.

Holy Week is the week preceding Easter Sunday, and includes the days of the Sufferings of Christ, ending on Good Friday.

Homoeopathy. *See* Section J.

Honey, the sweet syrup formed by bees from the nectar of flowers, the sucrose in the nectar being converted into a mixture of the simple sugars, glucose and fructose. Hybla, an ancient town of Sicily, on the southern slope of Mt. Etna, was famous for its honey.

"For your words, they rob the Hybla bees
And leave them honeyless." (*Julius Caesar*).

Honey-eater, an Australian bird (of which there are many species) provided with a long curved bill and tufted tongue. It lives by sucking the "nectar" from the flowers which abound in rural parts of Australia and New Zealand.

Hookah, an Oriental pipe for tobacco smoking, the smoke being drawn through the water of a goblet (commonly a coconut shell) by means of a long flexible tube.

Hoopoe, a remarkably handsome bird with vivid black and white-barred wings and tail and black-tipped crest which opens like a fan. Ranges over Europe, Asia and Africa. It has bred in England and Wales and occurs in the British Isles in small numbers at all seasons. Other species are confined to Africa, Madagascar and India.

Hops, the female "cones" of the hop plant used in brewing; their essential oils give beer an aromatic flavour, and their tannin and resin act as a preservative as well as accounting for the bitter taste desired. The hop is a perennial climber belonging to the mulberry family. The male and female organs are on separate plants; as only the female flower-heads are commercially

useful, female plants predominate in a hop garden, only a very few male plants being grown so that the female flowers can be fertilised.

Horizon, the limit of vision, the apparent line where sea and sky, or land and sky meet. This is termed the visible horizon. An ordinary person at the height of 1·5 m can see for 4·8 km, at 6 m 9·6 km, at 15 m 14·8 km and at 305 m 67·5 km. The figures are approximate.

Hormone, a chemical substance which is released by one part of the body and produces a response in other parts after having been carried there by the bloodstream or some other transport system. Prolactin, for example, is a hormone produced by the pituitary gland of nursing mothers and serves to stimulate and maintain the milk supply.

Horn *or* **French Horn,** a brass instrument of the trumpet family (*i.e.*, played by three valves) whose tube is very thin and long (Horn in F = 12 ft). In consequence the tube is curled in a complicated manner. Owing to the sweet tone it is capable of producing, the Horn sometimes plays as part of the wood-wind.

Hornbill, large bird found in Africa and oriental regions. Some species have a casque or a horny growth above the very powerful beak. It feeds on fruits. When the female has laid her eggs in the hollow of a tree, the male bird stops up the entrance, and keeps her imprisoned until the hatching is completed and the young ones are able to fly. There are about 45 species.

Hornblende, the commonest member of the amphibole group of minerals, a silicate of calcium, magnesium, iron and aluminium, of a dark green colour. It is a constituent of numerous rocks, including diorite, syenite and hornblende schist.

Horned Viper, any of a number of species of African viper which have scales over each eye resembling horns. Their bite is usually very poisonous. The significance of the horns is not known.

Hornet, a general name for many of the bigger wasps. It usually nests in hollow trees, and despite its rather fiercesome appearance does not sting unless unduly provoked.

Horology, the science of time-measurement, including the construction and management of clocks, watches, etc. Instruments of this kind are not known to have existed before the 12th cent. and until the introduction of the pendulum in the 17th cent., clocks were ill-regulated and inaccurate. The time-recording mechanisms of the present day include (*a*) the *clock*, which shows the hours and minutes by hands, and strikes the hours, and sometimes quarters; (*b*) the *timepiece*, which is not generally a fixture and shows the time, but does not strike; (*c*) the *watch*, which is a pocket time-keeper; (*d*) the *chronometer*, which indicates the minutest portions of time; (*e*) electric timepieces, mains electric clocks; (*f*) the highly accurate quartz-crystal and atomic clocks used for astronomical purposes. *See* Clock.

Horse Chestnut, one of the large forest trees, with ample branches, and full foliage, and much esteemed for parks and ornamental grounds. The flowers, which appear in May, are white tinged with red and yellow. The tree is native to the mountainous regions of northern Greece. *See also* Chestnut.

Horse Guards, the building in Whitehall which until 1872 was the headquarters of the Commander-in-Chief of the British Army. The archway is still sentinelled by mounted guards.

Horse Latitudes, the latitudes of the sub-tropical high pressure systems, between the trade winds and the prevailing westerlies, characterised by light variable winds and low humidity.

Hospitallers, Knights, were of the order of St. John of Jerusalem, at first devoted to the aid of the sick, but afterwards military monks, who became prominent figures in the Crusades of the 12th cent. They adopted the Benedictine black habit with the eight-pointed cross worn by the modern St. John's Ambulance Brigade. In 1309 they took Rhodes, but were expelled by the Ottomans in 1522. In 1530 the emperor Charles V gave them the island of Malta, which, as Knights of Malta, they held until 1798, when they were dislodged by Napoleon. The Knights still survive as a sovereign order, with headquarters in Rome. *See* **Templars and Teutonic Order.**

Hottentots, name given to certain African natives by Dutch settlers in the 17th cent. They used to occupy the greater part of Cape Colony and though driven out a number still survive in S.W. Africa. Appear to be related to the Bushmen, though their culture is more advanced. In addition to herding, they practise some farming and know how to smelt iron.

Hounds are dogs that were originally bred and trained for hunting, such as the greyhound, foxhound, bloodhound, wolfhound, deerhound, beagle, harrier, etc., but now often kept also as domestic dogs. The greyhound, deerhound and wolfhound hunt by sight, the others, with the bloodhound first in order, track by scent.

House Flies are world-wide and prolific. Their eggs are hatched within 24 hours of being laid, and full maturity is attained in a month. They feed mainly on decayed animal and vegetable matter.

Hovercraft, or air cushion vehicle, is a craft which is lifted on a pad of air underneath it. This pad or cushion must be at a pressure higher than that of the atmosphere and it is made by sucking in air above the craft and ejecting it in a downward stream all round the lower edge. The stream is guided by a flexible skirt and the high pressure air pad is contained partly by the skirt and partly by the air stream itself which forms a continuous air curtain all round the vehicle. Hovercraft are being intensively developed and there are variations in the basic scheme just described and also in the means of propulsion which can be by air or water jets or propellers. Hovercraft were devised by Cockerell in the 1950s and a full-scale example appeared before the British public in June 1959. Craft of over 100 tonnes are made commercially and much bigger ones conceived. The air pad support means that hovercraft can move over land, water or marsh. Cross-Channel hovercraft were introduced in 1966.

Howler Monkey, a genus of South American monkey noted for a laryngeal conformation which enables it to emit a loud reverberant noise something between a yell and a howl, as the name suggests.

Huanuco-bark, a medicinal bark, brought from the Peruvian town of that name, and derived from the *Cinchona micrantha* tree.

Huguenots, a name applied to the French Protestant communities of the 16th and 17th cent. Henry of Navarre, by the Edict of Nantes in 1598, granted them religious freedom, but more than a quarter of a century before—24 August 1572—thousands had been put to death in the massacre of St. Bartholomew. The revocation of the Edict of Nantes by Louis XIV in 1685 drove thousands into exile in England, Holland, Germany and America.

Humanism. *See* **Section J.**

Humble-bee or **Bumble-bee,** the common name of the insects of the genus *bombus,* of the Hymenoptera order. They live in small communities comprising males, females and drones, their habitations being underground. They do not have one queen bee only like the hive bee, but several females occupy the same nest, and these alone live through the winter, breeding and forming new colonies in the spring. Their sting does not have a barb like the honey bee's.

Humidity, the state of the atmosphere with respect to the water-vapour it contains. "Absolute humidity" is defined as the density of the vapour present, while "relative humidity", more frequently employed indicates the degree of saturation, *i.e.,* the ratio of the actual vapour pressure to the saturation vapour pressure at the particular temperature, expressed as a percentage.

Humming Birds are so called because of the humming noise made by the vibration of their wings in flying. They are of radiant plumage, and are among the smallest birds. The smallest bird in the world is the Fairy or Princess Helen's humming bird of Cuba, whose body is only 5·7 cm long. There are from four to five hundred species, and they are confined wholly to North and South America, being most numerous in the tropical latitudes. They have long, slender bills and tubular tongues which reach down into flowers to suck up the nectar on which they feed.

Hummum, the original name for what is now called the Turkish Bath in this country. One of the first of these baths to be established in London was the Hummums in Covent Garden.

Hundred, the ancient divisional name given to a portion of a county for administration or military purposes. It is supposed to imply the territory occupied by a hundred families; or the space of a hundred hides of land, or the capacity of providing 100 soldiers. Each hundred had its hundred court, with powers similar to those of a manor court, but this was abolished in 1867 by County Court Act.

Hundred Days, the interval of time between Napoleon Bonaparte's entry into Paris after his escape from Elba and his departure after his abdication, extending from 20 March 1815 to 28 June. During this period occurred the battle of Waterloo, 18 June.

Hundred Years' War, a term applied to the almost incessant contest between England and France, lasting from 1338 to 1453, including such famous battles as Crécy, Poitiers and Agincourt, and engaging successively Edward III, Henry V and Henry VI, among English kings.

Huns, a fierce Asiatic race which swept over eastern Europe in the 4th cent. Under Attila about the middle of the 5th cent. they obtained control of a large portion of central and eastern Europe, forcing even Rome to pay tribute. Their defeat at Châlons-sur-Marne in 451 by a mixed army of Romans, Goths and Teutonic tribes, and the death of Attila in 453, terminated their empire.

Hurdy-Gurdy, an Italian rustic so-called musical stringed instrument of the lute order, the sounds of which are produced by the action of a rosined wheel turned by the left hand, the notes being made by the fingering of the right hand.

Hussites. *See* **Section J.**

Hurricane. *See* **Cyclone** *and* **Wind.**

Hydra, an aquatic animal of simple structure, whose body is in the form of a cylindrical tube, with a disc-shaped base by which it attaches itself to any shifting substance. Its mouth is surrounded by tentacles by which it catches its food. The Hydra has the power of reproducing lost parts.

Hydrates are compounds containing water of crystallisation.

Hydraulic Ram, a form of automatic pump, used to raise water to a height by the action of its own falling velocity.

Hydraulics, the science of applied hydrodynamics, or water-machine engineering, ranging from pumps to marine engines.

Hydrocarbons are compounds of carbon and hydrogen. They include the *paraffins,* which are saturated compounds (*e.g.,* methane); the ethylene, acetylene and other series which are unsaturated; compounds with ring structures, *e.g.,* benzene, naphthalene and anthracene. Petroleum is composed almost entirely of hydrocarbons. *See* **F26.**

Hydrochloric Acid, a solution of hydrogen chloride gas in water, and resulting in considerable quantities as a by-product of the soda-ash or salt-cake manufacture. Its solution forms the common hydrochloric or muriatic acid of commerce. It is present to the extent of nearly half a per cent. in the digestive juice secreted by the stomach.

Hydrocyanic Acid, cyanide of hydrogen or prussic acid; very poisonous, and of the odour of bitter almonds. It is formed by the action of acids on sodium or potassium cyanide. Used to kill wasps (and in the gas chamber in the USA). It is a very important chemical on account of the reactions of its derivatives in many synthetic fields. Discovered by Scheele in 1782.

Hydroelectric Schemes. The sun's energy has been indirectly exploited in the past by harnessing the energy of the winds and rain. The climate is due, essentially, to differential heating of the earth. The resulting convection currents in the air (the motion of which is complicated by the rotation of the earth) give rise to winds. Moisture is collected from the sea and deposited high up on mountains as rain. Some of the gravitational energy may be collected as hydropower. Simple windmills or waterwheels are so undependable that they have not been used to any extent since the beginning of the Industrial Revolution. However, the modern form of the waterwheel—the hydroelectric generation plant—is extensively used in mountainous countries and about a third of the world's electricity is produced by this means. The essential requirements for a modern hydroelectric scheme are a river with a sufficient flow of water to provide the required power, a large "head" of water so that a cheap, compact turbine can be used and a dam so that water can be stored until it is required. In some cases a hydroelectric scheme is made economic by being associated with an irrigation or drainage scheme. Such multi-purpose schemes are especially important in India and Pakistan, where most hydro projects are of this type. Other well-known examples include the Snowy Mountains scheme in Australia and the Aswan High Dam in Egypt. Although over 90 per cent of the electricity in certain individual countries, notably Norway, Sweden, Portugal, Switzerland and Uganda is produced from hydroelectric schemes, only a relatively small fraction of the total potential has been exploited. This fraction varies from about a third in Western Europe to a quarter in the United States to a very small fraction in Alaska, Canada, Africa and the hinterland of Asia.

Hydrofluoric Acid is obtained by distillation of fluorspar with sulphuric acid, and is a compound of fluorine and hydrogen. Its action is highly corrosive; a valuable agent in etching on glass, and a rapid decomposer of animal matter.

Hydrogen, symbol H, the simplest element, atomic number (q.v.) of 1, colourless, and the lightest of all substances. Cavendish in 1766 was the first to recognise that it was an element. It is 14·4 times as light as air, and is found in a free state in volcanic regions. It can be obtained by the action of metals on acids, and forms an explosive mixture with air, burning with oxygen to form water. Commercially it is used to produce the very hot flame of the oxyhydrogen blowpipe for cutting metals; to fill balloons and airships; to harden certain oils and render them suitable for margarine- and soap-production. The gas can be liquefied, and the presence of the isotope deuterium was detected by Urey in 1931 in the residue of the evaporated liquid. The third isotope, tritium, is very rare. *See also* **Deuterium, Tritium** *and* **F25, 26.**

Hydrography, the science of water measurement, as applied to seas, rivers, lakes, currents, rocks, reefs, etc., and embracing the whole art of navigation.

Hydrometer, an instrument for measuring the specific gravity of liquids, especially for ascertaining the strength of spiritous liquors and solutions. It is usually in the form of a glass bulb, to the lower end of which a smaller bulb, containing mercury, is attached which forces the instrument to sink into the liquid which it is to test. The larger bulb has a scale fixed to it, and the indication on this scale of the sinking point shows the specific gravity. There are many varieties: Twaddell's—a pear-shaped bulb containing mercury: Beaumé's, of similar construction, but applicable to liquids both heavier and lighter than water: Sykes', largely employed for determining the strength of alcohol: and Nicholson's, used for taking the specific gravities of solids.

Hydropathy, the method of treating disease with water, either by bathing or drinking. Natural springs of special chemical and therapeutic properties, such as sulphur springs, and other mineral sources, have been used since prehistoric times for this purpose. It is probably one of the most ancient methods of cure. Recently the beneficial effects of pure water treatment have been advocated. Hydropathic establishments have been set up in many health resorts.

Hydroponics, or soilless growth, is the craft and science of growing plants in liquid nutrients instead of soil. Originally a laboratory technique, hydroponics has become since the 1930s a practical method of vegetable, fruit and flower production on both small and large scale. Basically, the growing plants have their roots in troughs of nutrient solution, either in or out of doors. Advantages include: much higher

crop yields; the close control of weeds and diseases; quicker growth; and, very important, the possibilities of growing food in places where ordinary agriculture would be impracticable, *e.g.*, deserts and stony land, city roofs in houses and in remote situations like Antarctic expeditions. Hydroponics is widely practised and contributes usefully to agriculture and horticulture in many countries, including the USA, Britain, India and France. Its value in spaceships and planetary colonies has often been pointed out by technological prophets.

Hydrostatics, the science of the pressure and equilibrium of liquids that are non-elastic.

Hydrozoa are a class of water animals of the *Coelenterata phylum* to which Hydra (q.v.) belongs. In one order of the Hydrozoa, free-swimming colonies showing marked division of labour between the individual units occur; this order includes the Portuguese man-of-war.

Hyena, a nocturnal carnivore with powerful jaws. The striped hyenas inhabit N. Africa and S.W. India. The brown hyenas with long shaggy hair are natives of S. Africa. The spotted, or laughing hyena, noted for the peculiar cry from which its name is derived, is also confined to Africa.

Hygrometer, an instrument for measuring the amount of water vapour in the atmosphere. A simple form of hygrometer, known as the wet-and-dry bulb, consists of two vertical thermometers affixed to a frame. One bulb is exposed to the air, and the other is covered with muslin which dips into a water-bath to keep it moist. If the air is saturated, it takes up no moisture from the wet bulb and the two thermometers read the same. If the air is not saturated, evaporation takes place from the wet bulb, latent heat is absorbed from the air and the temperature of the wet bulb is lower than that of the dry bulb. Relative humidity and dew-point of the air can then be derived from suitable tables. Hygrometers depending upon the expansion of human hair and gold-beater's skin and the deposition of dew on a polished surface, when cooled sufficiently, are also in general use. *See* **Humidity.**

Hymenoptera, the order of insects to which bees, wasps, hornets, ants and sawflies belong. They have a well-defined waist, two pairs of membranous wings coupled together, mouth parts modified for biting or sucking; the females possess an ovipositor used for depositing eggs and is sometimes modified for stinging. There are about 70,000 species in this order and many live in highly organised communities. *See also* **Ichneumon Fly.**

Hyperbola. A curve described by certain comets that go round the sun and never return.

Hypsometer, an instrument formerly used by mountaineers to find the height above sea-level by indirectly measuring the atmospheric pressure by determining the boiling point of water at the particular height. Based on the fact that as pressure decreases with height so the boiling point is lowered. Superseded by the aneroid barometer.

I

Ibex, wild goats of several species found in the mountain regions of Europe, Asia and Africa. The male has exceedingly large curved ridged horns. The species that lives in the Alps is called the Steinbock or bouquetin.

Ibis, belongs to a family of birds related to the stork. The sacred ibis of ancient Egypt is now extinct in Egypt but is found in the lakes and swamps of the Sudan near the Upper Nile. It has white and black plumage and a long curved beak. Other species are found elsewhere, the Glossy Ibis (black plumage glossed with purple and green) occasionally visiting England.

Ibo (properly Igbo), a large tribe of S.E. Nigeria, numbering between 5 and 6 million. After the end of British rule they were active in their struggle for national independence and under their leader, Ojukwu, embarked upon the secessionist state of Biafra and the unsuccessful civil war against Federal forces. The Hausa and the Yoruba are the other main Nigerian groups.

Ice is frozen water. It is a colourless, crystalline and brittle solid. Being only 92% as dense as water, it floats on the latter; the expansion which occurs as water changes into ice causes the fracture of water-pipes, though the fracture only becomes obvious when the ice melts and leaks out through the crack. The temperature at which ice forms is 0°C, 32°F. Ice can be melted by pressure, and the ease and smoothness with which one is able to skate on ice depends on this phenomenon.

Ice Ages. Periods during which the continents were partly or largely covered by ice-sheets and glaciers. The present-day ice-sheets of Greenland and Antarctica are relics of the most recent ice age (one of the eight major ones during the past 700,000 years), which began in the Pleistocene and ended about 10,000 years ago. During this last great glaciation ice sheets covered the northern part of Europe, Asia and North America. There is strong evidence that periodic changes in the earth's orbit around the sun caused the ice ages. The earth is now in one of its warm periods though there are signs that a moderate cooling trend has begun. *See also* **Climate.**

Icebergs are detached masses of glacier which subside into the sea and float as wind or current may take them. About one-ninth of an iceberg is above sea-level. The North Atlantic is the chief home of icebergs, which reach the ocean from the ice-clad plateaux of Greenland. Some of these floating masses of ice are of enormous proportions, and constitute in the spring and early summer seasons a great menace to the safety of ships, as was disastrously shown in the *Titanic* catastrophe of 1912. For some years past these menaces to N. Atlantic shipping have been kept under close observation by vessels specially detailed for this work.

Ice-breaker, a special heavy bow-plated ship for forcing a way through ice and used especially at ports of the Baltic Sea and the Great Lakes region of Canada which freeze during the winter months. The Soviet atomic ice-breaker *Lenin*, the first of its kind in the world, launched in December 1957, was designed to cut a channel through ice of any thickness. Her icebreaking performance allowed the sea-route to the north of Siberia to be kept open throughout the year.

Icelandic Literature, the old Norse literature, centred about Iceland, which includes numerous works of poetry, mythology and history of interest and importance. Much of this literature is in the saga form. *See also* **Edda.**

Iceland Moss, a kind of lichen (*Cetraria islandica*) which grows in great quantities in the mountain regions of Iceland and other Northern countries. It possesses certain nutritive qualities and is of some value in medicine.

Iceland Spar, a colourless form of calcite (calcium carbonate), frequently found in association with metallic ores; it has the power to produce strong double refraction of light so that two images are seen of an object viewed through a piece of Iceland spar. It was formerly used in optical apparatus for producing polarised light.

Iceni, an ancient British race who in early times lived in Norfolk and other parts of Eastern England. Their most famous ruler was Queen Boadicea, who led her people against the Romans in A.D. 61.

Ice Plant, also called " dew plant " and " diamond plant ". A South African mesembryanthemum commonly grown in British gardens. Introduced in 1690.

Ice Saints, St. Mamertus, St. Pancras and St. Servatius, so called because of the legendary cold on these Saints' Days, namely, 11–13 May.

Ichneumon, the Egyptian mongoose, popularly known as " Pharaoh's Rat ". It is of great use in checking the multiplication of reptiles. It is frequently domesticated.

Ichneumon Fly, a numerous group of parasitic hymenopterous insects abounding in many lands, and all having the peculiarity of depositing their eggs in the bodies of other insects. It destroys swarms of caterpillars, which become the unwilling hosts of its progeny.

Ichthyology, the natural history of fishes.

Ichthyosaurus was a gigantic marine reptile of the Mesozoic age. The fossils are mostly found in the lias formation. Some were over 9 m.

Icon, an image of a sacred personage used in the home or in churches for devotional purposes by Christians of the Eastern Orthodox faith. Icons can be painted on wood, perhaps with the figures picked out against a golden background, or they can be cast in bronze, in the form of a crucifix, diptych (*q.v.*) or triptych with details in coloured enamels. Subjects are taken from the life of Christ or of the Saints. In churches several icons are sometimes placed together on a screen (the iconostasis, which divides the altar and sanctuary from the main body of the church). The earliest preserved icons date from the 12th cent. Icons were venerated in Russia until the Revolution and remain, still in their archaic stylised form of mediaeval origin, a characteristic feature of the Orthodox Church to this day.

Ides, in the ancient Roman Calendar, the 15th of March, May, July, October, and the 13th of all other months; always the eighth day after the Nones.

Idiom, an expression characteristic of a country, district, dialect or language, which usually gives strength and force to a phrase or sentence. The idioms of a language are its distinctive marks, and the best writers are the most idiomatic.

Idris, a famous giant belonging to the myths of Wales, commemorated by a chair of rock on the top of the Cader Idris mountain in Gwynedd.

Igneous Rocks are such as have been molten under conditions of great heat at some stage in their history: *e.g.*, granite, basalt. *See* **F9(1).**

Ignis Fatuus *or* " Will-o'-the-wisp ", a phosphorescent light which may often be seen on summer and autumn evenings hovering over marshy ground or graveyards. Its nature is hardly understood, though it is generally believed to be the result of the spontaneous combustion of gases from decaying organic matter. In olden times when marshy grounds were more common than now, this " dancing light " was very frequently visible and was regarded with superstition.

Iguana, large South American lizard, with a long tail, a scaly back and head, a thick fleshy tongue and a prominent dew-lap in the throat. Specimens of the different species average 1·2–1·5 m in length, and they live mostly in trees, though they are equally at home on land or in the water. The flesh of some species is good eating, as are also the eggs.

Iguanodon, a genus of extinct dinosaurs, whose fossils are found in the Jurassic and Cretaceous rocks. Iguanodons were 4·5–7·6 m long, and walked on their hind legs, the front legs being small and adapted for grasping the branches of trees on the leaves of which they fed.

Ilex, mentioned by classical authors, the holm- or holly-oak, which flourishes round the Mediterranean. To botanists Ilex is the genus to which the holly and maté plant belong. *See* **T9(2).**

Iliad, the great epic poem of ancient Greece attributed to Homer (*c.* 700 B.C.). It consists of ancient folk tale and saga, welded into an artistic unity, having as plot the carrying off of Helen by Paris to Troy and the subsequent siege of Troy.

Illuminated MSS. of great value and beauty of decoration exist in most public museums and in many private collections, some of them being of great antiquity, especially those of ancient Egypt executed on papyri. Greek and Latin specimens are also numerous, and the British Museum contains fine examples of all these kinds and also an extensive collection of mediaeval English MSS.

Illuminati. *See* **Section J.**

Ilmenite, a mineral widespread in igneous rocks: chemically it is an oxide of iron and titanium. Rich deposits have recently been found in the Allard Lake area of Quebec; the Travancore sands are also a source of ilmenite.

Immortality. *See* **Section J.**

Immortelles are wreaths, crosses or other designs made from what are called everlasting flowers, which are obtained from certain plants of the Composite order, and retain their colours and compactness for a long time. Immortelles are largely used as mementoes for decorating graves, especially in France.

Impeachment, a special arraignment, usually before Parliament or other high tribunal, of a person charged with some offence against the State. The custom in England was for the impeachment to be made in the House of Commons, and the trial to be before the House of Lords. The first instance occurred in 1376 when Lord Latimer was impeached. With present parliamentary procedure, impeachment is no longer necessary, since the Cabinet is responsible for the individual actions of its ministers, who, acting as a team, must carry the Commons with them, or resign, when it falls to the Leader of the Opposition to form a new Cabinet. Other famous impeachments were those of the Lord High Chancellor Francis Bacon (1621), Earl of Strafford and Archbishop Laud (1640), Warren Hastings (1788), the last being that of Lord Melville (1805). Under the constitution of the United States public officials may be impeached by the House of Representatives and tried by the Senate. A famous case was that of President Andrew Johnson who was saved from impeachment in 1868 by one vote. Had President Nixon not resigned in 1974 he would have been impeached for the affair of the tapes and his abuse of executive privilege.

Imperialism. *See* Section J.

Impressionism, the most important and influential movement in 19th cent. European painting. It gained its name, at first contemptuously, in 1874 from a picture painted by Claude Monet and named by the artist *Impression: soleil levant,* which showed the play of light on water with the observer looking straight into the rising sun. Although intended to be the ultimate form of naturalism the inspiration of the school had been the scientific study of light with an attempt to render the play of light on the surface of objects. Feeling that putting a line around a form was bound to cause it to look unnatural, they used bright colours corresponding to the spectrum and unmixed on the palette, and noted that an object of any given colour casts a shadow tinged with the complementary one (*e.g.,* red-green, yellow-blue). Hence bright sunlight was represented in clear yellows and orange with violet shadows. The first Impressionist exhibition held in Paris in 1874 aroused derision with its paintings by Monet, Renoir Sisley, Pissaro, Cézanne and Degas among others Impressionism subsequently led to the entirely artistic and anti-naturalist movement of Post-impressionism. Cézanne, who felt that he wanted to produce " something solid and durable, like the art of the museums " was only dubiously impressionist, as were also Degas and Renoir. Of course, in the wider sense of the word (*i.e.,* the recording of an ephemeral impression of a scene), Whistler, Turner and even Rembrandt used the technique.

Impressment, the forced seizure of persons for military service resorted to by many countries before the establishment of conscription. Press gangs forcibly recruited men for British warships especially during the Napoleonic wars, but such measures were abandoned after about 1850.

Imprimatur, originally an official licence to print and an important formula in the early days of printing. The term is now used in the wider significance of authority or endorsement.

Incas, an Indian people who inhabited ancient Peru, founded a great empire and reached a high level of civilisation: overthrown by the Spaniards in 1533.

Incense, an aromatic resinous substance which, under combustion, exhales a pungent odour, and is used, mixed with certain fragment perfumes, in the celebration of Mass in Roman Catholic churches. Olibanum or frankincense is ordinarily the leading ingredient.

Incisors, the sharp-edged cutting teeth at the front of mammalian jaws. Rodents have long, sharp incisor teeth. Elephant tusks are modified incisors.

Independence Day, commemorates the adoption of the Declaration of Independence on 4 July 1776. 4 July is celebrated as a holiday in the USA.

Index. The name given to a list of books, prepared by papal authority, which are declared to be dangerous to faith and morals, and therefore forbidden to Roman Catholics, called the *Index librorum prohibitorum.* One of the reforms of the Vatican Council was the closing in 1966 of the Curia office which judged writings for the Church's Index of forbidden books, though the Index itself still remains. The Pope ordered that nothing should be placed on the Index until the author had been given a chance of explaining his views. The first Index was issued by Pope Pius IV, in 1559

Indian Mutiny. This turning-point in the history of modern India occurred in 1857-58. The ostensible cause was the serving out to the native troops of cartridges greased with animal fat, for contact with this was forbidden both by the Hindu and Mohammedan faiths. A rebellious feeling, however, had long been developing, and when the Sepoys at Meerut in May 1857 refused to obey the English officers, overpowered and put them to death, the mutiny spread like wildfire. The rebels took Delhi and Lucknow, and for many months terrible massacres and atrocities were committed: men, women and children were slain in thousands. Order was re-established in the autumn of 1858 when the governing power was transferred from the East India Company to the Crown.

Indicators, substances which by a marked change in colour are used to indicate the course of a chemical reaction. Litmus paper, for instance, is red with acids and blue with alkalis. In biological work some radioactive substances are used as tracer elements.

Indigo, the substance obtained from the plant *Indigofera tinctoria,* a native of S. Asia, India being the chief producing country. The colouring matter is the result of the decomposition and fermentation of a glucoside contained in the plant. This is afterwards dried and becomes the caked indigo of commerce. Natural indigo has been eclipsed by artificial indigo, a coal-tar dye which came into commercial production at the end of the last century, and which is cheaper and more uniform in quality.

Indium, a scarce lead-coloured metal, symbol In, found in zinc blende in Saxony and certain other ores. This element was discovered in 1863 by Reich and Richter. It is an important material in the manufacture of transistors.

Indulgence. In the Roman Catholic Church the remission granted by ecclesiastical authority to a repentant sinner of the temporal punishment still due after the guilt of sin has been forgiven by God. The indiscriminate sale of Indulgences by Tetzel and other Papal agents in the 16th cent. was one of the grievances which led to the Reformation (*see* Section J); the Council of Trent made such traffic unlawful.

Indulgence, Declaration of, was the proclamation by which James II suspended the penal laws against Roman Catholics and Dissenters. It was issued in 1688, but the clergy as a body refused to obey, and the trial of the Seven Bishops and their acquittal by a jury followed. An invitation was thereupon sent to William of Orange to become King.

Industrialisation is simply a name for industrial development. It is customarily used in particular to designate the course of events in a hitherto underdeveloped country which is seeking to increase its wealth and productivity by the introduction of more advanced techniques and by the establishment of industries previously not carried on within it. The word usually covers not only the development of modern industrial production but also the provision of electric power-stations, irrigation works and transport and other developments designed to improve production in any field by methods involving large capital investments. The outstanding example in our time of rapid industrialisation has been the Soviet Union, which, unable to get the capital from abroad, had to carry it through by ruthless restriction of the people's consuming power so as to achieve an unprecedentedly high ratio of investment to total production. Industrialisation has in practice meant a high concentration on the expansion of the basic heavy industries and of power supply, coupled with much slower development of the industries supplying consumers' goods and of agricultural production; but there is no reason why this should always be the case. It may well be that in most underdeveloped countries development can but be devoted largely to the industries making consumers' goods and to measures designed to increase agricultural production and productivity.

Industrial Revolution. The name, first given by Engels in 1844, to describe the radical changes that took place in Britain during *c.* 1730–1850 to transform a mainly agricultural country into one predominantly industrial. It began with the mechanisation of the textile industry (Hargreave's spinning jenny, 1764, Arkwright's water-frame, 1769, Crompton's mule, 1770, and Watt's steam-engine, 1785), with subsequent major developments in mining, transport and industrial organisation. It was based on Britain's rich mineral resources, particularly coal and iron ore. With the use of the steam-engine as power, industry became concentrated round the coalfields and the great new industrial towns developed—Birmingham, Manchester, Newcastle and Glasgow. Britain became supreme in constructional ironwork (Telford, George and Robert Stephenson). Canals, bridges, railways and ships were built, and great advances were made in the practical application of scientific principles. Aided by colonial exploitation Britain became the most prosperous country in the world. The new industrial capitalists began to replace the country squires as ruling class. But the great accumulation of wealth at one pole of society was matched at the other by poverty and misery, for child labour, long working hours, low wages and slums were features of the industrial revolution in its infancy. As with all great technological developments, the industrial revolution produced related changes in all fields of social life—in politics, art, religion, literature and morals, and with the rise of democracy, social reforms.

Inertia, a term used in mechanics for the property of matter by which it offers resistance to a change in its state of rest or in its state or direction of motion.

Inertial Navigation, an automatic method of dead-reckoning which at present finds its chief application in guided missiles, submarines and aircraft. Navigation by this means is carried out with reference to inertial space (*i.e.*, space which is stationary with respect to the fixed stars) and not to the surface of the earth as in normal navigation (latitude and longitude). This is done by means of high-accuracy gyroscopes combined with highly sensitive accelerometers in an apparatus known as the Ship's Inertial Navigation System. The American nuclear-powered submarine *Nautilus* pioneered the new north-west passage under the polar ice pack by this method of dead-reckoning in August 1958.

Inflorescence, a flowering shoot. Many arrangements of the flowers are possible and there are many kinds of inflorescence; *e.g.*, the spike, catkin, umbel, capitulum (in composites).

Inflation. *See* Section G.

Infra-red Rays *or* **Radiation.** This is the range of rays which come between the visible red rays and the ultra-short Hertzian radiation. The wave-lengths involved range between 0·75 micron (0·75 × 10⁻⁶m) and 100 micron (1 millimetre). Infra-red rays penetrate haze; hence landscapes obscured by haze or cloud can be photographed using plates sensitive to infra-red. Many substances strongly absorb these rays and thereby become hot; this happens in toasting bread. Many industries use infra-red lamps for drying paints and lacquers. Very important to chemists, as a tool in the investigation of the structure of compounds, since various groups of elements absorb infra-red radiation at a characteristic frequency. Infra-red astronomy has developed in recent years.

Infula, a sacred fillet, of woollen material, worn on the forehead by priests, magistrates and rulers in Roman times, also by persons fleeing for protection to sanctuary. Later, each of the two lappets of a bishop's mitre.

Ingoldsby Legends, a series of whimsical metrical tales full of droll humour written by the Rev. R. H. Barham, and first published in *Bentley's Miscellany* in 1837. The best known is the *Jackdaw of Rheims.*

Ink, a liquid pigment ordinarily made from an infusion of nut-galls, copperas and gum arabic. Shumac is substituted for nut-galls for inferior inks. An acid is sometimes added to prevent oxidation, and for the blue-black inks a small quantity of solution of indigo serves for colouring. Copying ink contains glycerine or sugar, which keeps the ink moist. Lampblack used to be the leading ingredient in printer's ink but now new methods of manufacturing have been developed. Marking ink is composed of a solution of nitrate of silver, gum, ammonia and carbonate of soda. For red, blue and other coloured inks, colouring solutions are used, for example, Prussian blue. The earliest examples of ink writing (on wooden tablets) ever found in Britain were recovered from the well of a Roman villa (3rd cent. A.D.) during excavations in 1954 at Chew Stoke, Somerset.

Ink Sac, a glandular organ found in squids and other cephalopods which contains an inky solution. When roused the animal discharges the contents of the ink sac into the water, to make a cloud through which its enemies cannot see. The pigment, sepia, comes from the ink sac of the cuttlefish.

Innocents' Day, a festival day in Roman, Greek and Anglican Churches in commemoration of the killing of the children of Bethlehem by Herod, 28 December.

Inns of Court, the four bodies in London which enjoy the privilege of calling candidates to the bar after they have studied for a certain number of terms and passed certain examinations. The Inns are: the Inner Temple, the Middle Temple, Lincoln's Inn and Gray's Inn.

Inquisition, a Roman Catholic ecclesiastical court which became a formidable weapon of the Church in the 13th cent. under Pope Innocent III in dealing with charges of heresy. It was effectively set up in the various Catholic countries of the Continent, obtaining its fullest and most sweeping organisation in Spain in the days of Ferdinand and Isabella, when Torquemada was made Grand Inquisitor, and used its powers with terrible severity. *See* Auto-da-fé. In the 18th cent. its influence began to wane, and the jurisdiction of the Congregation of the Holy Office at Rome was limited to the suppression of heretical literature (*see* Index).

Insectivorous Plants, plants which trap insects with special mechanisms. Plant enzymes or bacteria digest the prey, providing the plants with nitrogen usually scarce in the soil in which they grow. The most common British species are the Sun-dew and the Bladderwort.

Insects. This huge class of invertebrate animals (*see* Arthropods (F36)) includes about 100,000 species. Insects are ubiquitous except in the sea, only a very few species being adapted to marine existence. Characteristic features are: the body is divided into three parts, head, thorax and abdomen: the head carries a pair of antennae, the thorax three pairs of legs and usually two pairs of wings. The most primitive insects constituting the sub-class *Apterygota* are wingless. The other sub-class, *Pterygota,* is divided into the *Exopterygota* (*Hemimetabola*), which have a simple metamorphosis, *e.g.*, cockroach, and the *Endopterygota* (*Holometabola*), with a complex metamorphosis, *e.g.*, butterfly, bee. Although many are parasitic on man, animals and plants, innumerable animals and some plants use them as food, and many flowering plants are dependent on a variety of insects for pollination leading to the development of seeds and fruits. *See* F36(1), 41(1).

Insignia, marks or badges of office or honour, such as stars, ribbons, crosses, medallions or other designating objects, worn by members of special Orders or holders of prominent offices.

Instinct.—*See* F40(1).

Institut de France was formed in 1795, and after various modifications was in 1832 organised on its present basis. Its five academies are—the Académie Française, Académie des Inscriptions et Belles-Lettres, Académie des Sciences, Académie des Beaux-Arts, Académie des Sciences morales et politiques. It is restricted to 40 members.

Instruments, Musical. Musical instruments may be classified in a number of ways, but in general they fall into one of the three main classes, String, Wind and Percussion, according to how the sound is produced. **Stringed Instruments** are those which produce the sound by the vibration of a string: (a) by plucking, as in Harp, Lyre, Psaltery, Zither, Lute, Guitar, Balalaika, Ukelele, Harpsichord; (b) by friction (bowed), as in Crwth, Rebec, Viol, Violin, Marine Trumpet, Hurdy-Gurdy; (c) by striking (hammered), as in Dulcimer, Pianoforte, Clavichord; (d) by wind (blown), as in the Aeolian Harp. **Wind Instruments** are those in which the air in the instruments is set in vibration: (a) by blowing into a tube (flue-voiced), as in Recorder, Pandean Pipe, Flute, Organ; (b) by means of reeds (reed-voiced), as in Oboe, Clarinet, Saxophone, Bagpipe, Cor Anglais, Bassoon, Organ reed-stops; (c) those in which the sound is produced by the vibration of the player's lips against the mouthpiece (lip-voiced), as in Bugle, Horn, Trumpet, Tuba, Trombone, Saxhorn, Flügelhorn, Cornet. In a modern orchestra these are known as the *Brass*: instruments of the flute, oboe and clarinet families as the *Woodwinds*. Then there are the **Percussion Instruments**, which include the Drums, Cymbals, Tambourines, Castenets.

Insulator, a substance that will not conduct electric current. Many solids, liquids and gases are important insulators—rubber, cotton, silk, plastics, porcelain, glass, air, oil. If the applied voltage is too high, all insulators will "break down", *i.e.*, conduct electricity perhaps with resulting breakage, puncture or charring. Thermal insulators will not conduct heat; they are usually the same kinds of substance as electrical insulators.

Insulin is a hormone which controls the supply of sugar from the blood to muscles. The breakdown of sugar provides energy. In diabetes there is a lack of insulin, causing a build-up of blood sugar which can be released by the injection of insulin. It is secreted by the islet tissue of the pancreas, from which it was isolated in 1922 by Banting and Best. Dr. F. Sanger of Cambridge won the 1958 Nobel Prize in Chemistry for isolating and identifying its amino acid components. Prof. Dorothy Hodgkin and her team at the Dept. of Molecular Biophysics at Oxford have recently succeeded in determining the structure of insulin, a task which would not have been possible without the electronic computer. The discovery may lead to a better use of insulin.

Intelligence. Intelligence has been variously defined as the innate potential of a person to learn and understand; to make appropriate judgments; to see the relationships between things; to profit from experience; or to meet adequately new problems and conditions in life. There are many lines of evidence to show that intellectual capacity is closely related to heredity and influenced by environmental factors. The idea of intelligence testing was first devised by the French psychologist Binet at the beginning of this century. He was asked by the French government to invent a test which would weed out backward children in state schools, and thus save public money and avoid holding back the work of the class by teaching children who were incapable of learning at a given standard. Briefly, a series of problems are given to a large number of children and it is thus found out which series can be solved by the average child of a given age-group; if a child of 7 can only pass the tests suitable to the average child of 6, then his mental age is 6. The intelligence quotient or I.Q. is discovered by dividing his mental age by his chronological age and multiplying by 100. A gifted child can usually be spotted at an early age. Although I.Q. tests are the standard method of estimating intelligence, they are not universally accepted as a criterion; a teacher's general judgement may be the best assessment. High intelligence may be inherited, but fail to develop to the full because facilities for education are not available. Recent research suggests that the growth of the brain may be permanently affected by undernutrition at the time of its fastest growth (the last weeks before birth, and, to a lesser extent, the first weeks after birth). At this vulnerable period even quite minor deprivation can affect

the rate and ultimate extent of growth of the brain. This has significance not only for the severely under-nourished babies in the poor parts of the world, but for babies of low birth weight in our own communities. *See also* Q28.

Interest is the payment made for the use of borrowed money over time. The rate of interest is the rate per cent per annum charged for such loans. There are many such rates, varying with the plenty or scarcity on borrowable money, with the length of time for which the loans are made, and with the degree of risk, if any, that the loans will not be duly repaid. Short-term loans are usually cheaper than long-term: the lowest rates are usually for "call money" repayable immediately on demand. These are used principally in short-term financial transactions, such as bill discounting. Bank loans, though usually made for fairly short terms, command higher rates. Long-term loans are made chiefly to public authorities, or as bonds or debentures to business concerns. The rates obtained vary with the demand and the supply of such accommodation.

Interferon, the name given to a substance discovered in 1957 by Drs. Isaacs and Lindenmann at the National Institute for Medical Research. It is produced by the interaction of viruses with living cells and has the important property of inhibiting virus reproduction. Its development may lead to a new approach to the therapy of viral diseases.

International Date Line, a line along the 180° meridian marking the difference in time between E. and W. For the westward-bound traveller crossing the line the date would be put forward one day, for the eastward-bound, back one day. To avoid difference of date in adjacent land areas, the line deviates from the 180° meridian where this crosses land.

Introit, the psalm sung by the choir as the priest approaches the altar to celebrate the Eucharist.

Invention of the Cross, a Roman Catholic festival held on 3 May, to celebrate the finding of the alleged True Cross at Calvary by the Empress St. Helena in 326. Also included in the Church of England calendar. *See* **Holy Rood.**

Iodine, a non-metal element, symbol I, member of the halogen family (*q.v.*), a substance formerly exclusively obtained from the ribbon-wrack seaweeds. These were burnt and the ashes (kelp) extracted with water. After concentrating the iodides, these were distilled with manganese dioxide and sulphuric acid to yield iodine vapour which was condensed in stoneware bottles. Nearly all iodine now in use is derived from the iodine salt present in Chile saltpetre (natural sodium nitrate). Iodine is used in photography, as an antiseptic solution in alcohol or potassium iodide (tincture of iodine), and in medicine. Discovered by Courtois in 1812.

Ionosphere, a succession of ionised layers of the earth's atmosphere lying above the stratosphere. In this region free electrically charged particles —electrons and positive ions—occur in sufficient concentration to affect substantially the propagation of radio waves through the region. It extends upwards from a height of 100 km, being most concentrated at an altitude of *c.* 300 km. The behaviour of the upper atmosphere is strongly influenced by the sun. A great deal of new information about the ionosphere above an altitude of *c.* 250 km (the topside ionosphere) has been obtained by the use of instruments carried in satellites. Normally the aurorae (*q.v.*) occur at heights between 100 and 400 km. *See also* **Atmosphere.**

Ions, electrically charged atoms, or groups of atoms. Atoms of the metals lose electrons to become positively charged ions, *e.g.*, the sodium ion (Na^+) has one electron less than the atom. The non-metal ions are negatively charged, *e.g.*, the chloride ion (Cl^-) has one electron more than the atom. Similarly, a group like the sulphate ion ($SO_4{}^{2-}$) has more electrons than the constituent atoms. Thus, the hydrogen atom without its electron is a hydrogen ion or *proton* and the helium atom without its two electrons is a helium ion or *alpha-particle*. When an electric force is applied to certain solutions, the ions into which molecules of the dissolved substance are broken up are attracted to the oppositely charged electrodes, their movements constituting an electric current through the solution. In the same way gases, including air, conduct electricity by virtue of free ions (*see* F14(1)). Combustion, radio-activity and ultra-violet and cosmic radiations produce ionisation. *See* F23.

Ipecacuanha, a flowering plant of the Brazilian forests. Various alkaloids are isolated from ipecacuanha, one is emetine, which is used in medicine to cause vomiting and so remove poisons from the stomach. Another is used as an expectorant in cough mixtures.

Iridium, a white and very hard metal, symbol Ir, discovered by Tennant in 1804. It occurs naturally as an alloy with platinum or osmium; tips for fountain-pen nibs have been made from the former native alloy. The former standard metre was composed of platinum–iridium alloy (*see* Metre) as are parts of scientific apparatus and surgical tools that must be non-corrodible.

Iris, the typical genus of the botanical order *Iridacae*, with tuberous rhizomes and sword-shaped leaves, many of the family having beautiful flowers. About 100 species of Iris are recorded from the northern temperate zone, the most common species wild in Britain being the yellow flag. Orris root, used in perfumery, comes from another iris species.

Iron is a metallic element, symbol Fe (Latin *ferrum*), occurring widely in nature in such ores as haematite, loadstone (magnetic iron oxide), spathic ore and iron pyrites. It is extracted by a process known as smelting, with coke and limestone in a furnace. Its many uses are familiar, the most important being in the manufacture of cast- and wrought-iron products and of steels, which are alloys mainly of iron with added carbon and various metals. Iron rust is formed by the action of oxygen and water, and is a coating of iron oxide. *See* Smelting.

Ironclads, ships of war cased in iron or steel plates of sufficient thickness to resist projectiles. They were first introduced (1858) in the French Navy, and in 1860 the first British ironclad, the *Warrior*, was launched.

Iron Curtain. In a speech at Fulton, USA, on 5 March 1946, Sir Winston Churchill used this phrase to describe the dividing line behind which, he said, lie all the capitals of the ancient States of Central and Eastern Europe—Warsaw, Berlin, Prague, Vienna, Budapest, Belgrade, Bucharest and Sofia. These famous cities and the populations around them, said Sir Winston, lie in the Soviet sphere and are subject " to a very high and increasing measure of control from Moscow ". The phrase is said to have had dining rather than diplomatic origins. The practice of carving at a sideboard behind a screen (an iron curtain) was called dining *à la Russe.*

Ironsides were Cromwell's special troopers, so called because of their solidity and firmness in battle.

Irrational Number, a number such as the square root of two, or pi, which cannot be expressed as the ratio of two whole numbers. *See* Rational Number, and *Pi.*

Irredentists, a political party organised in Italy about 1878 with the object of incorporating within Italy neighbouring regions. Also a person, group or party advocating policies for the restoration to their country of territory formerly belonging to it but later lost.

Irrigation, an artificial method of providing water for the growth of plants on lands where the natural supply of water is deficient. For many hundreds of years techniques of irrigation have been slow and primitive (*e.g.*, tanks, inundation canals and the Archimedes screw) and consequent inefficiencies include large water losses by evaporation and seepage, and the watering of only a small area. New developments in perennial irrigation, using barrages, large reservoirs and pumping stations, permit vast tracts of land to be irrigated. Yet these are not without their problems as witnessed after the construction of the Aswan High Dam on the Nile where complex problems of delta erosion and dam lake silting ensued. Irrigation also serves the purpose of supplying *warmth* in winter; *e.g.*, in the English water-meadows, and in the more highly

developed Italian *marcite* and winter-meadows, where the water is mostly applied in winter when there is plenty of rain. There are several other functions of irrigation; *e.g.*, washing out of excess salts and the renewing of fertility by the addition of alluvium.

Isinglass, a gelatinous substance manufactured from the swim bladders of certain fish; used to preserve eggs, to keep beer free from sediment and to make a glue.

Islam. *See* Section J.

Isobars are the lines drawn on charts linking together points of equal barometric pressure.

Isochasms, lines connecting places at which there is an equal probability of seeing an aurora, taking the average over a number of years, based on the auroral catalogue of Fritz.

Isomers are chemical compounds having the same composition but different structural arrangements, and consequently different physical and chemical properties. For example, ethyl alcohol and methyl ether are isomers, since the molecules of both are built up of two atoms of carbon, six of hydrogen and one of oxygen, *viz.*, C_2H_6O; ethyl alcohol, C_2H_5OH; and methyl ether, CH_3OCH_3.

Isotherms are lines drawn on charts through points of equal temperature.

Isotopes. When one talks of an element, say, uranium or lead, the name of the element is a generic name for a collection of uranium species and lead species. The different species are called isotopes. For any particular element, the number and arrangement of electrons around the nucleus are the same in all the isotopes, so all the isotopes have the same chemical properties. Soddy has described isotopes as " elements, the atoms of which have similar outsides but different insides ". For example, in the nucleus of the uranium isotopes U 235, U 238 and U 239, there are respectively 143, 146 and 147 neutrons, but all have 92 protons. The isotopes have different atomic weights, in this instance respectively 235, 238 and 239. But all have the same chemical properties. *See* F12(1).

Ivory, the dentine substance of which the tusks of the elephant, hippopotamus, walrus, etc., are composed. The tusks of the African elephant sometimes weigh as much as 45 kg, and reach a length of 2·4–2·7 m.

Ivory Gull, a small, beautifully shaped sea-bird with striking all-white plumage and black legs which breeds on the rocky shores of the Arctic, being found farther north than any other bird; it occasionally wanders south in the winter.

J

Jabiru, the Brazilian name for the giant stork of South America.

Jacamar, from *Jacameri*, the Brazilian name for a smallish bird with long, sharply pointed bill and brilliant plumage which inhabits the tropical regions of South America east of the Andes. These birds are seen sitting motionless on trees, darting off at intervals, like flycatchers, to catch insects on the wing.

Jacanas, small water birds with immensely long toes which enable them to walk on water lily leaves. They are sometimes called " lily-trotters " and are found in tropical Africa and America. They live in swamps and feed on seeds and insects. Sometimes brilliantly coloured.

Jack, a small schooner-rigged vessel, used in the Newfoundland fisheries; a pike; an oscillating lever; a device used in roasting meat.

Jackal, *Canis aureus*, a small wild dog related to the wolf and resembling a fox. The Common Jackal is found in S.E. Europe, India and Sri Lanka; other species inhabit Africa and Egypt. The jackal is a well-known scavenger. It hunts singly or in pairs, unlike the wolf, which usually hunts in packs.

Jackdaw, one of the smaller members of the Crow family. This European bird is typically black with grey collar. It is easily tamed, makes an amusing pet and delights in making off with and taking to its nest bright objects, such as silverware.

Jacobins, a French revolutionary club or party, formed in 1789, and accustomed to meet at a Jacobin convent, hence the name. It became a controlling force in the Revolution, especially in the movement which led to the Terror. Robespierre was its chief spokesman.

Jacobites, adherents of the Stuart cause after the abdication of James II. First James himself, then his son (the Old Pretender), and later his grandson (the Young Pretender) tried to fan the flame of rebellion in Scotland and Ireland, but after the defeat at Culloden in 1746 the cause was lost. Also the name of the monophysite heretics of Syria, so named after their leader Jacobus Baradaeus in the 6th cent. A.D.

Jade, an exquisite kind of hardstone, ranging in colour from a whitish green to a deep mauvish brown. It can be translucent or opaque and sometimes it is veined. Jade is the common name for two minerals—the rarer *jadeite* (found in Burma, Tibet and China), a sodium–aluminium silicate, and *nephrite* (found in New Zealand, China, Turkestan and Siberia), a calcium-magnesium silicate. The presence of small quantities of other chemicals accounts for the wide range of shades. In China jade has for centuries been looked upon with great veneration, magical powers have been ascribed to it, and it has been fashioned into ritual objects, also into miniature sculptures of animals or even whole landscapes, charming to look at and incredibly skilfully made. The Chinese word for jade is *yü,* used as a symbol for all that is noble, beautiful and pure.

Jaguar, a South American carnivorous animal resembling the leopard, but larger and more powerful. It preys on other animals but rarely attacks man.

Jainism. *See* Section J.

Janeite, a devotee of Jane Austen and her writings.

Janissaries, an élite band of Ottoman foot soldiers who acted as the Sultan's bodyguard. They were conscripts, raised by the "tribute of children" from conquered Christian countries, mainly Serbia and Albania. First recruited under Murad I (14th cent.). They were not allowed to marry. They gained great power under the Ottoman Empire. In 1826 the Sultan Mahmud II had them massacred.

January, the first month of the year, named after Janus, the two-faced god of the Romans. It was the *Wolf monath* and *Aefter Yule* of the Saxons.

Jasmine, a graceful climber belonging to the olive family with odoriferous blossom, originally a Persian plant, but now acclimatised in many varieties in almost all parts of the world. Two species of jasmine (the common jasmine and the Spanish jasmine) yield oils used in perfumery.

Jasper, a precious stone of the chalcedony variety, opaque and coloured red, brown, yellow and sometimes green. It was greatly esteemed by the ancients, the Bible having numerous allusions to it.

Jay, a gaily-coloured bird of the Crow family, of many species—the Blue jay of N. America, the Canada jay, sometimes called "whisky jack", the Siberian jay and the British jay, fawn-coloured with black and whitish crest and bright blue feathers in the wings. It lives in woods and like the magpie, takes the eggs and young of small nesting birds.

Jazz, a rhythmical syncopated music characterised by a strong element of improvisation in the performance, probably originating among the Negro population of the Southern States of the USA. It became popular during the first world war and, in a commercialised form, has held the popular field ever since. Modern dance music and popular songs are based on the jazz idiom, which has also had a profound effect upon contemporary music of a more serious kind.

Jean, a stout kind of twilled cotton cloth much worn in olden times, and resembling fustian. Blue *jeans,* adopted by American city youngsters from farmworkers, are now the fashion elsewhere and worn not only as overalls by workmen but by both sexes in leisure time.

Jelly-fish. The jelly-fishes, which have gelatinous, translucent bodies fringed at the margin with delicate tentacles, constitute the coelenterate order *Scyphozoa.* The mouth, with a squarish opening, is seen on the underside, and there are four horseshoe-shaped sex organs.

Jerboa, small jumping mammals of the Rodent order. These mice-like animals have long tufted tails and very long hind legs, the front legs not being used for locomotion.

Jeremiad, any utterance or writing in which sorrow or complaint is the chief characteristic, so named as recalling the style of the "Lamentations of Jeremiah", in the Old Testament.

Jerusalem Chamber, a room in Westminster Abbey, deriving its name from the circumstance of its having originally been decorated with a view of Jerusalem. Henry IV died in this chamber, and the Committee for the Revision of the Bible met there in 1870 and later.

Jesuits, members of the Roman Catholic teaching order founded by Ignatius Loyola in 1534. A long and vigorous course of study is prescribed before they are admitted into the privileges of full membership. They are required to take the vows of voluntary poverty, perfect chastity, perfect obedience and complete submission to the Pope. The Society played an important part in politics.

Jet, a deep black fossil substance admitting of a high polish and much used for jewellery, ornaments and trimming. It is a form of lignite, the most important British deposit being found near Whitby, where jet manufacture has been an established industry for a long period.

Jet Engine, an aeroplane engine which derives its thrust from the high velocity of the gases it ejects. The essential units in a jet engine are a rotary compressor and a gas turbine, the latter driving the compressor. The first reliable, high-performance jet propulsion engine for aircraft was invented by Air Commodore Sir Frank Whittle.

Jet Stream, a meteorological term coined in 1946 to describe the relatively narrow belt of strong winds (160–320 km/h) at levels in the atmosphere from 5–11 km. These winds are important in forecasting weather, and can be a valuable aid to aircraft. From the ground, where there may be little wind, the jet stream can sometimes be seen as high cirrus cloud moving across the sky at high speed.

Jew's Harp. The name is believed to be a corruption of "jaws harp". This instrument consists of a metal frame with a central tongue of spring steel. The frame is pressed against the teeth, and the tongue of the harp is twanged with the finger, the mouth acting as a resonating chamber. By altering the shape of the mouth the resonant frequency and therefore the note can be varied.

Jockey Club, the governing body that, although possessing no legal status, frames rules and laws by which horse-racing and turf matters generally are regulated. The club-house is at Newmarket.

John Bull, the typical figure of an Englishman, bluff, big and burly. Arbuthnot's *History of John Bull* is supposed to have originated the character.

John Dory, a fish found in most temperate seas and common in British waters. It is of a golden-yellow colour (*jaune doré*), has a high dorsal fin with long filaments projecting from the spines, very protractile jaws and is much valued as a table fish. According to legend the dark spot on each side of its body is the thumbprint of St. Peter who took a coin from the fish's mouth (Matt. XVII 24–7).

John o' Groat's House, W. of Duncansby Head, Caithness, popularly named as the northernmost point of Scotland. According to legend the house, which has now disappeared, was built in octagonal form by a Dutchman Jan de Groot who came to live there in the 16th cent. The site is marked and an inn was erected near it in 1876.

Jongleurs were minstrels and jesters who wandered from town to town singing songs, playing musical instruments, dancing and giving entertainments in mediaeval France and Norman England. Jongleurs were low-born in contrast to the Troubadours, who were often of the nobility.

Joule, a unit of energy in the SI system of units.

defined as the work done when the point of application of a force of one newton is displaced through a distance of one metre in the direction of the force. Named after J. P. Joule (1818–89). The relationship between mechanical energy and heat energy is called the mechanical equivalent of heat and was found by Joule to be 778 ft lbf in lb °F units, or 4·18 × 10⁷ ergs in gram °C units, or 1 Nm in SI units. *See* F20(1).

Judaism. *See* Section J.

Julian Calendar, named after Julius Caesar, who in 46 B.C., finding the Roman year 90 days in advance of the real time, was the first to adopt the calculation of time by the solar year, the average length being fixed at 365¼ days. There was still an overplus of a few minutes every year, and this was rectified by the Gregorian Calendar, introduced in Italy in 1582 and adopted in England in 1752, from which date what is called the " New Style " begins.

July, the seventh month of the year, named after Julius Caesar. It was the *Maed monath* (Mead-month) of the Saxons.

June, the sixth month of the year, containing 30 days and deriving its name from Juno. It was the *Sear* (Dry) *monath* of the Saxons.

Jungle-Fowl, birds related to the peacocks and peacock-pheasants. At least four species are known from the jungles of India, Sri Lanka and Java. The domestic chicken has been derived from the Red Jungle-Fowl (*Gallus gallus*).

Junkers, name of the ruling class of Prussia, military in spirit, who were the party of re-action and defenders of the landed interests. Supported Bismarck prior to the Franco-Prussian war and helped bring Hitler to power.

Jupiter, the largest and, after Venus, the brightest of the planets, 1,312 times the volume of the Earth but only 318 times its mass. It circles the sun in 11·86 years and its mean period of rotation is 9 h 50 min. Hydrogen, methane and ammonia have been detected in its atmo-sphere. Striking features are the coloured bands and the Great Red Spot of Jupiter's atmosphere. In 1610 Galileo made history by discovering the four major satellites of Jupiter, which he named Medicean planets after his patron Cosimo Medici; these are visible with good field-glasses. There are nine other Jovian moons. *Pioneer* 10 passed *c.* 130,000 km above the planet's surface in December 1973. *Pioneer* 11 reached the planet in December 1974 before speeding on to Saturn. It came within *c.* 43,000 km of the Jovian surface, beaming back close-up pictures and successfully passing through a belt of high-energy particles. It was thought there might be a radiation hazard (electrons and protons from the solar wind are trapped by Jupiter's magnetosphere) but it seems the spacecraft followed a path swept clean by Jupiter's moons which prevented radiation damage. The US Voyagers I and II were launched in 1977 to reach Jupiter and Saturn. *See* F8.

Jurassic Formation, a series of rocks (the evidences of which are most marked in the Jura Moun-tains) coming between the Cretaceous and Triassic groups and including the Oolite and the Lias. It is a formation rich in fauna, abounding in echinoids, lamellibranchs, ammonites and belemnites; large reptiles, marine and land, are common, as are the plants called cyads. In Britain the Jurassic outcrop extends from the Dorset coast to the Yorkshire moors and in-cludes the Cotswolds. *See* F48.

Jury, a body of private citizens chosen and sworn to hear and pass verdict upon evidence brought forward at a trial, inquest or inquiry. The origin of the English jury is obscure but it is thought to have been introduced by the Normans. The jurors are the sole judges of the true facts upon the evidence laid before them. Under the Criminal Justice Act of 1967 their verdicts in criminal courts in England and Wales no longer have to be unanimous but may be by a majority of 10 to 2. The age limit has recently been reduced from 21 to 18 and raised from 60 to 65. In Scotland 45 jurors are sum-moned in criminal cases, of whom 15 are chosen by ballot, and majority verdicts are accepted: not guilty, not proven and guilty.

Jute, the name given to the fibre of a plant grown largely in Bangladesh in the Ganges delta and used for the manufacture of coarse cloths, cordage and sacks. Calcutta is the biggest jute-manufacturing centre of the world, as Dundee was in the 19th cent.

Jutes, a Low German race who in the 5th cent. invaded the south-eastern part of England, establishing themselves in Kent and making Canterbury their capital.

Juvenile Courts. This is a special kind of Magis-trates' Court to deal with accused persons under the age of seventeen. The Magistrates chosen are specially qualified for the work, and where possible a woman is appointed as one of the magistrates who constitute the Court. The Court is held in private away from the ordinary court room. The object of the Juvenile Court is to introduce into the trial a plan to reform the offender by providing for the care and protection which he may need, by removal from undesir-able surroundings, and by subsequent education or training. In these objectives the Court has the co-operation of social workers, including Probation Officers (*q.v.*). Radical changes in methods of preventing and treating juvenile delinquency are contained in the Children and Young Persons Act, 1969, the result of the find-ings of two White Papers, 1965 and 1968. They emphasise the necessity of helping and support-ing the child as far as possible in his own family and community, with resort to formal proce-dures only where he is exposed to moral danger, or control is necessary in the interest of society or of the child. The minimum age for prosecu-tion will be raised from 10 to 12 when the Government is satisfied that " local authorities and other services have the necessary capacity to cope with this change ". Children who are below prosecutable age will be dealt with by social casework or by care proceedings. Al-though the Act places restrictions on the prose-cution of 14 to 17 year-olds, so that prosecution would be restricted to categories of offences to be prescribed and only if action by other means were inadequate, these provisions will be phased into operation.

K

Kakapo, the Maori name for the New Zealand owl-parrot, a peculiar and interesting species, possessing wings but not able to use them for flight (though it can glide); of sap-green plum-age, nocturnal in its habits and nesting in burrows. Still to be found in the larger forest areas of the South I.

Kangaroo, pouched (marsupial) mammals of Australia and adjacent islands. There are over 20 species, the smaller ones being known as " wallabies ". Kangaroos leap in a succession of springy bounds 3–6 m long, the forefeet not touching the ground. They can reach a height of over 2 m and a weight of 90 kg. First seen by white men when Capt. Cook's expedition visited Australia in 1770. Related genera in-clude the tree kangaroos, rat kangaroos and the Tasmanian Jerboa kangaroo.

Kaolin or China Clay is an essential ingredient in hard-paste porcelain (*q.v.*). It results from the decomposition of felspar, and is widely found in China, Japan and the USA. The richest de-posits in Europe are in Cornwall, near Limoges in France, and in Czechoslovakia.

Karst, geological formations typical of limestone regions in which the drainage is by underground channels. Rain water carries part of the lime-stone away in solution, leaving the surface dry and barren and pitted with innumerable hol-lows. The name comes from the Karst (Slav *Kras*) region of N.W. Yugoslavia where the rocks are massive pure limestone; the barren plateau is characterised by fissures, caves and subterranean rivers.

Kauri Pine, a large coniferous tree yielding a fine copal resin which ranges from Malaya to New Zealand. The New Zealand Kauri, *Agathis australis*, is found only in the N. Island. Some of the best Kaurigum comes from fossilised pines and is dug out of the soil far from any living trees.

Kelvin. Lord Kelvin, an important 19th-cent.

physicist, gave his name to the kelvin, symbol K, a measure of temperature on the absolute scale. The Kelvin scale is a development of the scale invented by Celsius (q.v.) for everyday use, long known as the "centigrade" scale; the degree interval on both scales is the same. The conversion formula for the absolute or Kelvin scale is $K = C + 273 \cdot 15$. See Absolute Temperature.

Kestrel, the most common British falcon, well known for its habit of hovering for minutes at a time with vibrating wings and then swooping down to attack mice and insects. The male has spotted chestnut-brown back, greyish head and tail, which has a broad black band near tip.

Ketones, a class of organic compounds, related to aldehydes, of general formula R_2CO (where R is an organic radical). The simpler ketones, especially acetone, are widely used as solvents for lacquers, synthetic rubber and polymers, such as cellulose acetate and perspex. More complex ketones occur in nature, and some are used in the perfumery industry, muscone (from the musk deer (q.v.)) is an example.

Kew Gardens, officially known as the Royal Botanic Gardens, are among the most celebrated gardens in the world. They were started in 1759 by Princess Augusta of Saxe-Gotha, widow of Frederick, Prince of Wales, and mother of George III. They remained private property until 1841, when control passed to the Commissioners of Woods and Forests. They now cover 121 hectares and are administered by the Min. of Agriculture, Fisheries and Food. Since 1841 the gardens have been open to the public, and form one of the most attractive resorts near London.

Keys, House of, is the Manx representative assembly. See Tynwald.

Keystone, the stone which occupies the centre and highest point of an arch and is usually the last to be inserted.

Khaki, a clay-coloured cloth adopted for uniforms in the British Army in the time of the war with the Boers, and used in the first and second world wars. First used by Indian regiments.

Kilderkin, once a common liquid measure in England, representing 18 gallons or 82 litres.

Kilogramme, unit of mass, defined as the mass of the international prototype kilogramme of platinum-iridium kept at the International Bureau of Weights and Measures at Sèvres. A remeasurement of Avogadro's Number (F21(2)) may lead to an atomic standard of mass (the second and the metre are already defined in atomic terms), but this will depend on the precision with which atoms can be counted.

Kilowatt. Unit of power, equal to one thousand watts. See Watt.

Kinetic Art denotes works of art which actually move or give the illusion of so doing. An early exponent of kinetic art was the American sculptor Alexander Calder (1898–1976) when he launched his famous "mobiles" in the early 1950s. Since then, constructions which rotate, jump, blink with lights, etc. have been made by many artists and the genre is being further elaborated upon today. Kinetic painters give a visual illusion of movement to their pictures by the use of particular colour contrasts or by a skilful play with spirals, squares, etc. in black and white, sometimes with colours blended in. An interesting exponent of the style is the English artist Bridget Riley (b. 1931).

Kinetic Energy, the energy (q.v.) possessed by a particle or body in virtue of its motion. If the motion is destroyed, e.g., by the impact of the body with an obstacle, the kinetic energy vanishes, being turned into some other form of energy such as heat and sound. If the body has mass m and speed v its kinetic energy (leaving out corrections due to relativity) is $\frac{1}{2}mv^2$.

King Crab, remarkable arthropods now classified separately from both Arachnids and Crustacea which they resemble, inhabiting the sea coasts of America, Japan, India and Malay Peninsula, carrying a shield-shaped shell, and having a long pointed spine projecting from the posterior. The body comprises three separate sections articulated together. These crabs—in America known commonly as the horseshoe crab because of their shape—are from 45–60 cm in length.

Fossil king crabs are found as far back as the Silurian. There are about six living species.

Kingfisher, a well-known family of brilliant-plumaged birds, found in all continents, comprising some 250 species and sub-species. The British kingfisher, Aceldo althis, haunts the rivers and streams, and is one of the most beautiful of native birds, having iridescent blue-green, white and rich chestnut in its plumage and bright-red feet. All kingfishers have long, dagger-shaped bills. In the Malayan region, New Guinea, the Moluccas and Australia the varieties are very numerous. The quaint Laughing Jackass of Australia is among the largest of the kingfisher family. The European kingfisher is the bird of the Greek legend of the Halcyon.

King-of-Arms, the name of the chief officials of the Heralds' College. There are several in England —the principal being those of the Garter, Norroy and Ulster, Clarenceux. See Heralds' College.

Kiosk, a word of Russian or Turkish origin meaning a small open pavilion of light construction much used in Eastern countries as a place of shade and rest. Similar structures are common in the streets of Paris as news and advertisement stands, and in London as telephone boxes.

Kirimon (Kiri no go Mon) and **kikumon** (Kiki no go Mon), the two Japanese imperial crests, the first a design of leaves, stems and flowers of the Paulownia plant, and the other representing the sixteen-petalled chrysanthemum.

Kite, name of several birds of prey, widely distributed, related to the hawks and eagles, graceful in flight, and distinguished by their long wings and deeply forked tails. The red kite, light chestnut brown, once the most familiar bird of prey in Britain, seen scavenging the streets of London, is now the rarest, and found only in Wales. The Egyptian kite and the pariah kite of India, notorious for their daring thefts, are closely related to the black kite, a smaller European species, with less forked tail and blackish-brown plumage.

Kittiwake, a beautiful white and pearl-grey gull with black legs, dark eyes and greenish-yellow bill. Its range is wide, and includes the British Isles, where it is a local resident. The flight of this only truly oceanic gull, which except in the breeding-season is generally found offshore, is graceful, swift and buoyant. A triangular black patch, noticeable on the ends of the wings when open, is characteristic of the species, as is the call kitti-wake, from which the bird derives its name. It nests in colonies on the ledges of caves and steep cliffs.

Kiwi, flightless, stoutly-built birds of New Zealand, now very rare and carefully protected by the Government. They are little larger than a domestic hen, and lay astonishingly large eggs for their size. Incubation and care of chicks fall to the male bird. They have rudimentary wings concealed by the plumage, and the feathers are hair-like. They are nocturnal in habit.

Knighthood is a degree of honour or title common in Europe since the Middle Ages, and was at first exclusively a military order. In Great Britain the four main orders of knighthood are those of the Garter, the Bath, the Thistle and St. Patrick; in addition to which there are several other orders, such as the Order of St. Michael and St. George, the Star of India, etc. There are also Knights Bachelors such as are not associated with any special order. The title is not hereditary, and therefore ranks below that of a baronet, though both are entitled to the prefix "Sir".

Knot, a nautical measure of speed (1 sea mile per hour), and formerly measured by a log-line, divided by knots at equal distances $\frac{1}{120}$ of a geographical mile. The number of knots travelled by the ship in half a minute corresponded to the numbers of sea miles it travelled per hour. A sea mile is equal to about $1\frac{1}{8}$ of a statute mile or 1·9 km. Also, a grey and white wading bird, usually a winter visitor to Britain found in flocks on the coast.

Knout, a whip of many thongs, often fatal in its effects, formerly used in Russia for flogging criminals.

Koala, the Australian arboreal marsupial mammal

that looks like a toy teddy-bear, with ashy-grey fur, bushy ears and rudimentary tail. It feeds on the leaves and shoots of certain eucalyptus trees, and is not more than 60 cm in length.

Kohl, a powder prepared from antimony or burnt almond shells, and in common use by the women of the East for darkening the eyelids.

Koto, a musical instrument in general use in Japan consisting of a series of 13 silken strings stretched across a curved wooden surface, and played with the fingers. Each string is 1·5 m long, and has a separate bridge so fixed as to give the vibration necessary for the note it has to produce. It is a sort of horizontal harp, and in the hands of an expert player is capable of giving forth excellent music.

Kremlin, the citadel or walled city within a Russian city which during the Middle Ages served as an administrative and religious centre and offered protection. That of Moscow, now the headquarters of the Russian government, contains the cathedral where the Tsars were crowned, an imperial palace and the " King of Bells " (*see* Bells). Its walls which are topped with towers were built in the 15th cent.

Krypton, one of the rare gases, symbol Kr, occurring in the air to the extent of 1 part in 20 million. It was discovered in 1898 by Ramsay and Travers. It is used in gas-filled electric lamps.

Kusti, the sacred cord or girdle of the Parsees, consisting of 72 threads—the number of the chapters of the *Yasna*—and two branches, each branch containing six knots, together standing for the 12 months of the year.

Kyrie Eleison (" Lord, have mercy "), the name of a common form of prayer in the Anglican, Roman Catholic and Greek Churches; also applied to the English Church responses after the recital of the commandments.

Kyrle Society, named after Pope's " Man of Ross ", John Kyrle, founded by Miss Miranda and Miss Octavia Hill in 1875, and having for its object, the decoration of workmen's clubs, hospitals, etc. and the promotion among the poor of a taste for literature, music and outdoor recreation.

L

Labarum, the standard of Constantine the Great, adopted after his conversion to Christianity, marked with his seal and represented upon the coinage.

Labourers, English Statute of, was passed 1350–51, with the object of compelling labourers to accept a certain rate of wages and not leave their employers' service, the Plague having rendered labourers so scarce that they were in great demand and had been insisting on higher pay. These enactments were bitterly opposed and led to the " Peasants' Revolt ", headed by Wat Tyler.

Labradorite, a felspar rich in calcium and of a pearly lustre on cleavage, found in masses in igneous rocks, the best samples of which come from Labrador.

Labyrinth, or Maze, a combination of roads and passages so constructed as to render it difficult for anyone ignorant of the clue to trace the way to the central part. The Egyptian labyrinth near Lake Moeris had 3,000 rooms, half of them subterranean and the remainder above ground. The labyrinth in Crete, according to Greek myth, was built by Daedalus to house the Minotaur. There was one at Lemnos, renowned for its stalactite columns; and another at Clusium constructed by Porsenna, King of Etruria, about 520 B.C. The labyrinth in which Fair Rosamond was concealed was at Woodstock. Hampton Court maze dates from the 16th cent.

Labyrinthodonts, gigantic fossil amphibians which get their name from the curious labyrinthine structure of their teeth, probably an evolutionary link between fishes and reptiles. They occur in the Carboniferous, Permian and Triassic formations, and remains have been found in Britain and other parts of Europe. Their heads were long, and their footprints, by which they were discovered, closely resemble the prints of the human hand.

Lac, a resinous matter deposited on the branches of a number of tropical trees by the females of the lac insect, the exudation including eggs and a viscous covering. At the gathering time the twigs are broken off and dried in the sun, when the insects die, and the lac that remains is termed *stick-lac.* From this, by the removal of extraneous accretions and dissolving, *seed-lac* is produced. *Shell-lac* is seed-lac after it has been melted and otherwise prepared, and this is the best known of the lacs, being used in printing and the manufacture of varnishes and sealing-wax, and for other commercial purposes.

Lace, a delicate fabric of linen, silk or cotton threads, made by hand or machinery, and worked in various ornamental designs. The kinds of lace are many, deriving their distinctive names either from the method employed in production or from the place where any special variety was originally made. The best-known makes are pillow or bobbin-lace, woven and plaited by hand; needle-point lace, worked by the needle over a traced design; and machine lace, which practically dates from Heathcote's invention of the early part of the 19th cent. Some of the most famed laces are the following: *Alençon,* a needle-point lace; *Brussels,* a very fine kind, with needle-point sprigs and flowers; *Chantilly,* a silk variety with flowers and open-work; *Cluny,* a netlace with darned stitch; *Honiton,* a delicate kind with dainty sprigs and figures; *Mechlin,* generally made in one piece and very varied in design; and *Valenciennes,* or bobbin lace, of great durability, the pattern and ground of which are made at the same time, being one of the best and most costly of laces, now manufactured mainly in Belgium. Nottingham is famous for its lace.

Lace-Wings, insects with frail, transparent and much-veined wings whose grubs eat large numbers of insect pests such as aphids. The eggs are borne at the ends of threads attached to plants.

Ladybird, the common name of a large family of beetles—the *Coccinellidae.* The insect is usually of a red or yellow colour with small black or coloured spots. Ladybirds are of good service to the gardener because their larvae feed on aphids. There are about 2,000 species.

Lady-Day, the day of the festival of the Annunciation of the Virgin Mary, 25 March. One of the four English quarter days.

Lake Dwelling, the name given to certain prehistoric habitations which were thought to have stood on platforms over lakes, like villages in certain Pacific islands. Recent excavations at the Lake of Burgäschi in Switzerland show that the prehistoric Swiss pile dwellings probably stood on the shores of lakes, not on platforms over the water. Also found at Mere and Glastonbury, Somerset.

Lakes are bodies of water collected in depressions of the earth's surface. The most notable lakes are the Great Lake series of North America, including Superior, Michigan, Huron, Erie and Ontario, all discharging into the St. Lawrence River. Africa has an enormous area of lakes, including the Mobutu Seso and the Victoria, forming the sources of the White Nile. Smaller lakes are numerous in other countries—Switzerland, Finland, Italy, England, Ireland, Scotland, all having their lake regions, where the scenery is invariably beautiful and romantic. The Kariba Dam (Rhodesia–Zambia border) and the Nasser (Egypt) are the largest man-made lakes in the world.

Lake School, the name, given, at first in ridicule, to a distinguished trio of poets—Wordsworth, Coleridge and Southey—who made their homes in the English Lake District.

Lamellibranchs (Pelecypods), the class of aquatic, bi-valve molluscs to which the oysters, cockles, mussels, clams and scallops belong. In these animals the body, which is compressed laterally, is enclosed in two hinged shells held together by muscular action. The gills are thin plates hence the name " lamellibranch ". *See* F36(2), 41(1).

Lamination, stratification on a very fine scale, as in shales.

Lammas Day is one of the oldest of the Church festivals, probably derived from the loaf-mass (*hláfmaesse*) of the Anglo-Saxons. It occurs on 1 August. In the olden times it was the day when loaves were given in place of first-fruit offerings.

Lammergeyer, the bearded vulture of alpine regions, resembling an eagle in appearance. It has a white head with black tufts at base of the bill, and its general plumage is dark brown, nearly black. It is found in the remote mountain ranges from southern Spain and parts of Africa to China, and is becoming scarce.

Lampblack, a carboniferous pigment obtained from flame-smoke, and now produced in specially constructed furnaces in which bodies rich in carbon, such as tar, resin, petroleum, etc., are burned. The smoke or soot resulting is collected from the sides of the furnace, and forms lampblack. It finds use in making printer's ink, black paint, etc. Being a very pure form of carbon, it is also utilised in the manufacture of dynamo brushes and arc-lamp carbons.

Lamprey. Eel-like fish having no scales, bones, paired fins or jaws. They attach themselves by their mouths to fish whose blood they suck. Together with the hagfishes, the lampreys are placed in a special class—the Cyclostomes. There are three British lampreys.

" Lancet ", the name of a noted English medical journal, established in 1823 by Dr. Wakley.

Land Crab, a family of crabs (*Gecarcinidae*) which live mainly on land, though migrating to the sea to deposit their eggs.

Land League, an association formed in 1879, with Parnell as president, for compelling a reduction in the rents of land, and a reconstruction of the land laws in Ireland, and in case of non-compliance refusing to pay rent. For a time this League exercised great political influence and was an important aid to the Home Rule agitation.

Landrail, popularly known as the Corncrake, was a regular summer visitor to Britain two generations ago, but no longer. Its harsh and piercing note was a familiar sound in English cornfields. It is decreasing almost everywhere.

Landslip, a sudden downward sliding under gravity of large masses of rock, soil, etc.; often set off by earthquake shock or saturation of a particular stratum with water. Many serious landslides have occurred from time to time. In 1618, an earthfall happened at Plurs, on Lake Como, involving the destruction of many buildings and the loss of numerous lives. In 1806 a portion of Rossberg mountain in Switzerland slipped from its position, and falling into the valley below buried many villages and hamlets and over 800 people. A chalk cliff 30–45 m high and 1·2 km long fell at Lyme Regis, in Dorset, in 1839, doing great damage. Over 200 people were killed by a landslip in Naini Tal, in India, in 1880; and at Quebec, in 1889, a rocky eminence called Cape Diamond gave way, many buildings being destroyed and lives lost. Notable landslips in recent times have occurred at Amalfi (Italy) in 1924, at Murchiston (New Zealand) in 1929, at Aberfan (Wales) in 1966 and near St. Gervais (France) in 1970.

Langue d'oc and Langue d'oïl, the two principal mediaeval French dialects, *oc* and *oïl* being their respective words for the affirmative particle (modern French *oui*). *Langue d'oc,* spoken south of the Loire, was the language of the troubadours. Provençal, one of its dialects had a literary revival in the 19th cent. under the influence of the poet Frédéric Mistral. *Langue d'oïl* was spoken in northern France, and it was the dialect of the Paris region which developed into modern French.

Lantern Fly, bugs belonging to the family *Fulgoridae* in which the head is drawn out to form a lantern-like structure. In no instance is the " lantern " luminous, though naturalists used to think it was.

Lanthanides, the fourteen metallic elements following lanthanum in the Periodic Table, *i.e.,* the elements cerium (no. 58) to lutetium (no. 71). They are also known as the rare-earth metals, though they are in fact all more terrestrially abundant than, for instance, mercury or arsenic (with the exception of the unstable radioactive element promethium, no. 61). The lanthanide atoms are distinguished by having an incomplete inner electron sub-shell (the 4f level), this feature giving them interesting magnetic properties. For instance, gadolinium, holmium and dysprosium are ferromagnetic (*see* **F22**) at low temperatures. Chemically, the lanthanides behave similarly, being highly reactive metals usually forming trivalent salts. *See* Periodic Table, Section **F**.

Lapis Lazuli, an azure-blue mineral, being a silicate of aluminium and sodium. The pigment ultramarine is made by grinding it, though artificial ultramarine has largely superseded it. The mineral (also called *lazurite*) has been used as a gemstone since ancient times.

Lapwing *or* **Green Plover,** familiar British bird on moors and marshlands with iridescent greenishblack plumage, white underparts and black crest. Often called " peewit " from its cry. Protected under Protection of Birds Act, 1967.

Larboard is the old nautical term indicating the left-hand side of a ship, and changed by Admiralty order to " port " in 1844. Starboard is the right-hand side.

Larch, a familiar coniferous tree in the mountain regions of northern Europe, and though not native to Britain, the Common Larch is successfully cultivated in various parts of the kingdom. It is one of the best of all turpentine-yielding trees, and the bark is valued for tanning. The larch is an unusual conifer in being deciduous.

Lark, a family of song birds (*Alaudidae*) of many species, some of which—notably the skylark—are famed for their habit of soaring into the air, singing all the while. They build their nests on the ground in the open country and, except for the black lark of Russia, have streaked brown plumage. The skylark and woodlark are the best known British species, while the crested lark and shore lark are among the occasional visitors. Africa has the greatest number of larks; America has only one species, the horned lark.

Larkspur, the common name of the genus *Delphinium,* a favourite flower introduced into British gardens from Switzerland in 1573. The common larkspur is *D. consolida.*

Larva, the undeveloped form of any animal which, before maturity, undergoes metamorphosis, usually different from the adult in structure and habits.

Laser. A remarkable kind of light source that was discovered in 1960. With the laser it is possible to probe the behaviour of matter under the influence of enormous energy densities, range and survey vast distances to microscopic accuracy and send millions of telephone and television messages between any two points that can see each other with telescopes. Laser light, in contrast to natural light, is coherent and can be expressed as a regular progression of waves carrying energy along a particular path. Thus the essential difference is that laser light is an orderly sort of wave motion in contrast to ordinary light which is inherently unsteady and therefore an inefficient carrier of information in time. The name *maser,* which is the microwave parent of the laser, derives from the expression " microwave amplification by the stimulated emission of radiation ". Upon application to light wavelengths the microwave part of the name lost its meaning and the term maser became generally descriptive of any device in which stimulated emission dominates.

Laser Fusion is a method by which it has been proposed that thermonuclear reactions may be controlled and exploited as a source of energy (*see* **Nuclear Fusion**). The idea is to irradiate a millimetre-sized pellet of a mixture of frozen deuterium and tritium with a short ($\sim$10^{-9} s) but very intense pulse of energy in the form of laser light. This has the effect of both compressing the pellet by a factor of at least a thousand and heating it to about 10^8 °C. Under these conditions, thermonuclear reactions (principally ^{2}D + ^{3}T → ^{4}He + ^{1}n) proceed sufficiently fast that a net output of energy is obtained before the pellet explosively separates. Formidable technical problems need to be solved before laser fusion can become a practical proposition. These include the development of efficient high-powered lasers and the design of a suitable reactor that can withstand up to 100 micro-hydrogen bomb explosions per second. It is still not clear whether this method of controlling nuclear fusion is more practical than the more conventional approach involving the magnetic confinement of plasmas.

Latent Heat is the quantity of heat required to convert 1 gram of a substance from one form into another. For example, when a solid changes into a liquid or a liquid into a gas, the addition of heat to bring about the change produces no rise in temperature, the energy being absorbed in the form of latent heat. An equal amount is released when the process is reversed. The latent heat of fusion of ice is about 79·6 calories per gram, that of the vaporisation of water about 539 calories per gram.

Lateran Councils were the religious conventions held in the Lateran basilica at Rome for deciding important questions of Church doctrine. The most brilliant was that of 1215 which pronounced in favour of a Crusade. *See* Ecumenical Council.

Lateran Treaty, 1929, between Italy and the Vatican established the Vatican City as an independent sovereign state.

Laterite refers to any tropical soil or soil horizon rich in hydrated ferric and aluminium oxides which harden when exposed to the atmosphere. It is difficult to cultivate and is commonly used for bricks and road metal. Laterite buildings have been known to withstand weathering for many centuries and a number of fine examples are found in India and S.E. Asia.

Latin America. The Spanish-speaking, Portuguese-speaking and French-speaking countries of N. America, S. America, Central America and the W. Indies. *See* Section K.

Latitude of a point on the earth's surface is its angular distance from the equator, measured on the surface of the earth in degrees, minutes and seconds. Thus the equator is 0° Lat. and the poles 90° Lat. (N. or S.). First determined by Hipparchus of Nicaea about 160 B.C. Latitude introduces zones of climate, *e.g.*, tropical rain, subtropical steppe and desert, temperate rain and polar.

Laughing Gas. *See* Nitrous oxide.

Launce *or* Sand Eel, a family of eel-like sea fishes found in large numbers on the coasts of North America and Europe. There are two species common to British waters. These fishes are of a bright silvery hue, and live much in the sand underneath the water. They are prized as human food and as bait.

Laurentian Shield refers to the Pre-Cambrian rocks in the region of the Upper Lakes of Canada, nearly 5 million sq km in extent. Of enormous importance to Canada on account of the mineral wealth, forests yielding valuable timber and wood-pulp, and water-power.

Lava, the molten rock which is erupted from a volcanic vent or fissure. Also the same material which has cooled and solidified.

Lawn, very fine sun-bleached linen, in olden time called " cloth of Rheims ".

Lead, a soft malleable metal, symbol Pb (Latin *plumbum*), occurring in numerous ores, which are easily smelted. Its most important source is the mineral galena which consists chiefly of lead sulphide; rarely is it found free. Lead is largely used in plumbing on account of its pliability, and in nuclear reactors as a shield against radiation because of its very high density. As an alloy element it combines in the formation of type metal, stereo metal, shot metal, pewter and many other compounds. Oxides of lead are used in some types of glass and in the manufacture of paints (red lead). All lead compounds are poisonous. Leading producers of lead are the United States (Missouri), Australia (Broken Hill) and the Soviet Union.

Leaf Miners, insect larvae which tunnel between the upper and lower skins of leaves. Most leaf miners are caterpillars of tiny moths; some sawfly larvae have the same habit.

Leagues, or combinations of kings, countries, communities, have been frequent since the kings of Canaan united against the Israelites. Among the most famous leagues may be mentioned the Holy or Catholic League, which

prevented the accession of Henry IV of France until he became a Roman Catholic; and the League of Augsburg against Louis XIV of France in 1686.

League of Nations, was founded on 10 January 1920, with the object of promoting international peace and security. The original members were the signatories to the Peace Treaties at Versailles, and membership grew to fifty-three as new nations and ex-enemy States were admitted. Two notable absentees were the United States and Soviet Russia, the latter not being represented until 1934. Germany was a member from 1926 to 1933. The League had an Assembly which met at Geneva every year and a Council which met five or six times a year. The Permanent Court of International Justice sits at The Hague. The final Assembly of the League was held at Geneva between 8 and 18 April 1946. Its place has been taken by the United Nations. The International Labour Organisation, set up by the League of Nations, met on 20 April 1944, at Philadelphia and resumed its old quarters at Geneva under the new organisation in 1946.

Leap Year *or* Bissextile, was fixed by Julius Caesar, 45 B.C., the addition of one day in every four years bringing the measure of the calendar year even with the astronomical year with three minutes per year over. The Gregorian Calendar corrected this by dropping leap year at the centuries not divisible by 400. For instance, 1700, 1800 and 1900 were not leap years.

Learning. *See* F40(2), Q16–20.

Leather was made in ancient Egypt, Greece and Rome, and has through succeeding centuries played an important part in the service of man. It consists of the dressed hides or skins of animals after the process of tanning has been gone through. Untanned skins are known as pelts. Leather is classed either according to the skins from which it is made or the system of preparation employed. The best-known kinds are morocco, kid, Russian, chamois, Cordovan, grained, patent, russet, tan, calf, Hungarian.

Leech, an aquatic blood-sucking worm, mostly found in fresh-water ponds. Each end of the body is provided with a sucker, but that at the head end has jaws and teeth. The medicinal leech has three jaws. The leech attaches itself with avidity to animal bodies and sucks until glutted. Its saliva contains an anti-coagulant.

Leeward, a nautical term, meaning the sheltered side of a vessel—that is, the opposite side to that from which the wind is blowing.

Legion, a body of Roman troops, varying in numbers at different periods. A legion was divided into 10 cohorts, and every cohort into three maniples. Three legions composed the Roman army of occupation in Britain.

Legion of Honour the French order for distinguished services, military or civil, was instituted by Napoleon I in 1802, and confirmed and modified under later rules. There are five grades—Grands Croix, Grands Officiers, Commandeurs, Officiers and Chevaliers.

Legume, the fruit typical of the pea, bean family, or *Leguminosae.*

Lemming, small light-brown rodents with dark spots, abounding in Scandinavian countries and in Siberia, about 12 cm long, with a short stump of a tail. The migrations of the lemming are famous, probably caused by overbreeding when food is plentiful. So insistent is the urge to keep moving that these animals will march on into the sea in their thousands and be drowned.

Lemur, almost the most primitive member of the primate order of mammals (to which man, apes and monkeys also belong). They are noted for having strong pliant toes enabling them to use their feet as hands, and also well-developed thumbs on the hands. They have long squirrel-like tails, fox-shaped heads and large staring eyes. True lemurs are confined to the Malagasy Rep.; closely related are the " bush-babies " of S. Africa.

Lend-Lease. During the earlier phases of the second world war the bulk of British investments in the USA had to be either sold or pledged to Americans in payment for dollar supplies. After the United States entered the war this drain was stopped by the Lend-Lease arrangement, under which Great Britain met the costs of American consumption in Great Britain, while the United States paid for British supplies from America. This arrangement was abruptly terminated on the ending of hostilities; and Great Britain and other belligerent countries found themselves without means of paying in dollars for indispensable American supplies, including the foodstuffs, materials and capital goods needed for economic reconstruction. In these circumstances Great Britain negotiated with the United States and also with Canada a large loan, which was used for buying dollar supplies and played an important part in helping the West European economies to maintain themselves and feed their peoples while they were carrying through the earlier stages of postwar reconstruction. These loans involved large charges for interest and amortisation in future years, but proved far too small to meet the dollar deficit for more than a short period. In face of this situation the United States launched the Marshall Plan.

Lenses, pieces of transparent material designed to focus an image of an illuminated object. Usually of glass, but plastic lenses are common, and quartz, etc. are used for special purposes. The surfaces of the simplest lenses are parts of spheres. Lenses which are thickest, or thinnest, at the centre are called convex and concave respectively. Lenses of complex shape are often used in microscopes, etc. Electron lenses are arrangements of electric or magnetic fields which focus beams of electrons, *e.g.,* on to television screens.

Lent, the forty days' period of fasting that precedes Easter.

Lepidoptera, the order of insects with scaly wings and bodies, to which the 90,000 butterflies and moths belong.

Leptons. A group of particles which include electrons, neutrinos and muons. All are much lighter than protons or any of the baryons (*q.v.*). *See* **F16.**

Lepus, the constellation of the Hare, situated under the Orion group, and one of the constellations with which the ancients were familiar.

Lettres de Cachet, sealed letters which the kings of France issued to their agents to secure the imprisonment of distrusted or disliked persons without trial. Abolished in 1789.

Levée, a State reception held by the Sovereign or his representative and attended by men only.

Lewis, a contrivance for stone-lifting, the principle of which was known to the ancient Romans; it consists of two dovetail tenons of iron or other metal, expanded by an intervening key in a dovetail-shaped mortice in the stone, and shackled by a ringed bolt to the hoisting chain.

Leyden Jar, the earliest form of electrical condenser. Its invention is usually credited to Muschenbroeck of Leyden (1745). It consisted of a jar coated inside and out with tinfoil for about two-thirds of its height and having its inner coating connected with the top by a brass knob and chain. The jar was charged by connecting it to an electrostatic machine.

Lias, a geological term referring to the lower section of the Jurassic group, and mainly comprising shales and limestones.

Liberalism. *See* **Section J.**

Libraries, before the invention of printing, were few, and collected together at enormous cost. At Nineveh remains of libraries, consisting of tablets of baked clay, have been discovered. There were two libraries at Alexandria containing a vast collection of rolls or volumes, founded by Ptolemy I Soter (367–283 B.C.) and established by Ptolemy II Philadelphus (309–246 B.C.). Among the great libraries of later times may be mentioned the Vatican Library at Rome, moved to its present premises in 1588; the Royal Library in Paris which later became the Bibliothèque Nationale; The Astor Library, New York; and in England, the Bodleian Library, Oxford, and the British Library (see below). Since 1850 public libraries have been established in all the chief cities and towns of the kingdom. The first lending library was opened in Edinburgh in 1726. In most villages there is a " county library centre " to which collections of books are sent by the County Library. In Great Britain there are 24,000 centres of this kind in village clubs, halls, shops,

schools and even homes. In some counties there is a library van or the bibliobus, as it has been called by a French writer. This travelling library tours on a pre-arranged time-table so that everyone knows exactly when it will arrive. The British Library in London, the National Library of Scotland, in Edinburgh, that of Wales in Aberystwyth, the Bodleian Library of Oxford and the Cambridge University Library comprise the " copyright " libraries, entitled to receive a copy of each new book and journal published in Britain. The British Library Act 1972 brought together into a single organisation (a) the former British Museum Library (the books remaining in the Museum) and the Science Reference Library in Holborn and Bayswater, the whole now being known as the British Library, Reference Division; (b) the former National Lending Library for Science and Technology and its arts and humanities counterpart, the National Central Library, together now known as the British Library, Lending Division, and located at Boston Spa, Yorkshire. Reference Division will eventually be re-housed in a single new building in London, due for completion in the early 1980s. Lending Division, which has an international reputation for rapid postal lending of journals and photocopies to institutions and libraries throughout the world, will remain in Yorkshire.

Libretto (It. booklet), the literary text of an opera or oratorio. Usually the composer and the librettist collaborate in the writing of an opera, but several composers (*e.g.*, Wagner) wrote their own librettos. Boito, librettist to Verdi for *Otello* and *Falstaff*, himself composed two operas, *Mefistofele* and *Nerone*. Most famous of Italian opera librettists was the poet and dramatist Metastasio (1698–1782). His librettos were set to music by many composers, including Gluck, Handel, Mozart, Rossini.

Licence is a permission given to do some act, which without such permission, it would be unlawful to do. Licences are required for keeping dogs, for operating a television receiving set, for driving a motor vehicle, for killing game, for setting up as a bookmaker, for selling beer, wines and spirits, tobacco, etc. and for importing certain items such as arms, ammunition, radioactive materials, animals, plants, drugs and explosives. The road fund licence on a private motor car is £50 a year.

Lichens. In every lichen, two plants are associated, one being an alga and the other a fungus. The fungus derives its food from the alga; probably the alga gains too from the association, being protected against desiccation by the fungus (an example of symbiosis). Lichens are the first plants to colonise bare rocks.

Life-Boat was invented by three men, Lionel Lukin who converted a coble into a boat for saving life in 1785; William Wouldhave, who discovered how to make a boat right herself if she capsized, and Henry Greathead, who built a life-boat, partly from Wouldhave's model, in 1789. This boat was stationed at South Shields, which was the first permanent life-boat station to be established. It was not until 1851 that the first life-boat able to self-right was built, and a motor was first installed in a life-boat in 1904. Modern motor life-boats have engines of from twin-18 h.p. to twin-80 h.p., with a speed of nearly 10 knots. All coastal life-boats in this country are maintained by the Royal National Lifeboat Institution founded by Sir William Hillary in 1824. It is supported entirely by voluntary contributions.

Light, a particular kind of electromagnetic disturbance capable of travelling through space, and some kinds of matter, and of affecting our eyes to cause vision. Its finite speed was first demonstrated by O. Römer, using observations of the eclipses of Jupiter's satellites in 1675. In 1860 Maxwell showed that light waves are electromagnetic. Since Einstein's theory of relativity (1905) it has been generally realised that the speed of light is a fundamental natural constant. Visible light with wavelengths between about 4 and 6×10^{-5} cm is only a small part of the electromagnetic spectrum. Subtle modern methods fieve the speed of light in a vacuum as $2 \cdot 997925 \times 10^8$ m/s (about 186,282 miles per sec).

Light Year. A measure of astronomical distance, equal to the distance light travels in the course of a year. A light year is thus 5.88×10^{12} miles $(9.463 \times 10^{12}$ km). *See also* **F3**(2).

Lighthouses, to warn ships of dangerous places and indicate coasts, points, harbours, etc., have existed since the building of the Pharos, a tower of white marble 183 m high, built by Ptolemy II Philadelphus at Alexandria about 280 B.C. In early lighthouses the lights were simple fires. The most famous and one of the earliest British lighthouses is the Eddystone (*q.v.*). Dungeness lighthouse, opened in 1960, is very modern in design, capable of automatic operation and the first of its kind to incorporate the xenon electric arc lamp as a source of illumination. The electric fog signal consists of sixty loud-speaker units built into the tower just below the lantern, giving a honeycomb effect. The lighthouses of England and Wales, the Channel Islands and Gibraltar are under the control of Trinity House; Commissioners of Northern Lighthouses control those of Scotland; and the Commissioners of Irish Lights control the coasts of Ireland. Particulars of lights in all parts of the world are published for the guidance of navigation in the *Admiralty Lists of Lights*, compiled annually by the British Admiralty.

Lightning, the flash of a discharge of electricity between two clouds, or between a cloud and the earth, when the strength of the electric fields becomes so great as to break down the resistance of the intervening air. With "forked" lightning the actual path, often branched, is visible, while with "sheet" lightning the flash is hidden by the clouds which themselves are illuminated. "Ball" lightning or fireballs is the name given to the luminous balls which have been seen floating in the air during a thunderstorm. The Boys camera has provided much information regarding the sequence of events in a lightning discharge. It is found that a flash consists of a number of separate strokes, usually four or five, and that the discharge of electricity to earth begins with a faintly luminous "leader" moving downwards and branching at intervals. As the ground is approached a much brighter luminosity travels back along the conducting channels, lighting up the several branches. The multiple strokes which follow in fractions of a second have the same "return" nature and are rarely branched. Lightning flashes to earth damage structures, cause loss of life and endanger overhead power systems, often interrupting electricity supply. Such storms generally affect radio transmissions and present hazards to aircraft. Thunderclouds may develop energy far exceeding the capacity of our largest power generating stations.

Lightning Conductor, a metal rod, the upper part of which is copper with a conical point, the lower portion being iron, which extends into the earth. Its effect is to gather to itself the surrounding electricity and discharge it into the earth, thus preventing its falling upon the protected building. In ships, lightning conductors are fixed to the masts and carried down through the ship's keel-sheathing. Benjamin Franklin was the first to realise the possibilities of lightning protection and, in 1752, carried out his famous experiment of drawing electricity from thunder-clouds, with the aid of a sharp-pointed conductor fixed to a kite.

Lillibulero, an old marching song composed by Purcell. With words by Wharton, it is said to have "sung James II out of three kingdoms". Used by the B.B.C. during the second world war as a station identification signal preceding news bulletins, and still in use to announce the Overseas Service programmes in English.

Lily Family (Liliaceae), one of the largest families of flowering plants, with 200 genera and 2,500 species. It includes the true lilies (*Lilium*), tulips and hyacinths. Vegetables belonging to the family are the onion and asparagus.

Limes, trees of the genus *Tilia*, including some 30 species spread over north temperate regions. The word is a corruption of "linden". Limes native to Britain are the small-leaved *T. cordata* and the broad-leaved *T. platyphyllos*. The hybrid *T. vulgaris* was introduced into Britain from the Continent during the 17th cent. and is frequently seen in streets and parks. Lime-wood was used by Grinling Gibbons for his fruit, flower and bird decorations.

Limestones, sedimentary rocks composed wholly or largely of calcium carbonate and formed by two main processes, (1) organic (skeletal remains of organisms), *e.g.,* chalk (*q.v.*) and (2) chemical (precipitation of calcium carbonate), *e.g.,* oolite (*q.v.*). Marble is limestone that will polish after cutting.

Linen, a textile fabric manufactured from flax fibre, known to the ancient Egyptians, and first manufactured in England under Henry III by Flemish weavers. The greatest linen-manufacturing region in the world is Northern Ireland (largely yarns and the lighter types of fabrics); Scotland produces coarse linens and canvas as well as household linens.

Ling, a sea-fish common on the coasts of Britain, and abounding in more northern waters. It averages about 1 m in length, and is a voracious feeder, living chiefly on small fish. Ling is also the name applied to *Calluna vulgaris*, the plant commonly called "heather".

Linseed, the seed of the flax plant, containing, apart from its fibrous substance, certain oily and nitrogenous matter of considerable commercial value. This yields linseed oil, and some of the residue is used to make cattle food.

Lion, the most impressive of the Cat family. It is chiefly found in open bush country in Africa, being comparatively rare in Asia. Its large square head, its flowing mane (in the males only) and its tufted tail distinguish it. From tip to tip it can reach a length of 3 m; a weight of 225 kg.

Lion and Unicorn, the supporting figures of the royal arms of Great Britain, date from the union of Scotland with England (1603) at the accession of James I (James VI of Scotland), the lion representing England and the unicorn Scotland.

Liqueurs are essences combined with alcoholic liquid, and are of many kinds, named according to their flavourings or place of production, and include Maraschino, Chartreuse, Curaçao, Benedictine, Noyau, Kümmel, etc.

Liquid, the name given to matter in such state that it takes its shape from the containing vessel. The volume it occupies is independent of the container, however. *See* **F20**(2).

Liquid Crystals form a special class of substance and are true liquids in that they flow easily and can be poured. However, unlike ordinary liquids, liquid crystals have their molecules arranged with geometrical regularity in one or two dimensions, so that they have a certain internal structure similar to that of solid crystals. They are fairly complicated chemicals with somewhat elongated molecules. Liquid crystals are of interest to biologists as well as to chemists and physicists, and not just because they account for the iridescence of beetles. Some body fluids are in fact liquid crystals. There are also technological applications because of their unique electrical and optical properties. They are receiving increasing attention for these reasons.

Litanies were first used in church processions in the 5th cent. The first English litany was commanded to be recited in the Reformed churches by Henry VIII in 1544.

Lithium, a soft metallic element, symbol Li, similar to sodium. It is very reactive and is stored under paraffin oil. It is the lightest metal element.

Lithography, the art of drawing on stone and printing therefrom, was discovered by Alois Senefelder about 1796, and was introduced into England a few years later. Many improvements in the art have been made, especially in chrome-lithography and photo-lithography.

Litre, a metric measure, was abolished in 1964 as a scientific unit of volume, but remains as a special name for the cubic decimetre and as an everyday unit, *e.g.,* a litre of petrol.

Liturgy, the name given to the Church ritual, though strictly applying only to the portion used in the celebration of the Eucharist or Lord's Supper. The Anglican liturgy is laid down in the Book of Common Prayer (1662). Temporary powers granted by Parliament in

1965 to the Church to make changes in the form of worship were made permanent in 1974.

Liverworts (Hepatics), a class of simple green plants related to the mosses. There is no differentiation into stem and leaves. Liverworts are most common in damp situations, such as the banks of ditches.

Lizard, the name given to a diversified order of reptiles, of which there are about 1,600 species. Included among the lizards are the geckos, chameleons, glass snakes, skinks and blind worms.

Llama, mammals related to the camels, from which they differ in small size, absence of humps, and more woolly coat. The domestic llama of S. America is used as a beast of burden, also providing wool, meat and milk. *See also* Alpaca, Guanaco.

Loadstone *or* **Lodestone,** an oxide of iron, found chiefly in Sweden and Norway. Its scientific name is magnetite. It has the power of attracting pieces of iron and served as the first magnets used in compasses. One of the class of non-metallic magnetic materials nowadays known as " ferrites " *(q.v.).*

Lobby Correspondents are political correspondents of newspapers who do not report the actual proceedings of Parliament—this is done by Parliamentary Correspondents—but interpret political news and events.

Lobsters are marine crustacean animals existing in large numbers in the northern seas of Europe and America and in fair proportion on some parts of the British coasts, especially in the neighbourhood of the Channel Islands.

Locarno, Treaty of, 1925, whereby Germany, France and Belgium undertook to maintain their present frontiers and to abstain from the use of force against each other. Hitler broke the pact by re-occupying the Rhineland, the demilitarisation of which had been recognised by Germany.

Locust, insects of the grasshopper family, but much more powerful. They are inhabitants of hot countries, and often make their appearance in untold millions, like clouds, devastating all the vegetation that comes within their course. The locust-tree (*Ceratonia siliqua*) is supposed to have furnished food to St. John the Baptist in the wilderness, and its " beans " have accordingly been styled " St. John's Bread ".

Loess, a deposit of silt or marl laid down by wind action. The biggest loess deposits are in Asia, the source of the dust of which they are composed probably being the deserts of Central Asia. Large deposits in Europe are thought to have originated from the edge of ice sheets during the Ice Age.

Logarithms, a system of calculation invented by John Napier in 1614, and developed by Henry Briggs a few years later. Thus if a number is expressed as the power of another number, *i.e.,* if $a = b^n$, then n is said to be the logarithm of a to base b, written $\log_b a$. Common logs are to base 10 and Napierian to base $2\cdot7182818\ldots$, expressed as e. Their use represents a great saving of time.

Logical Positivism. *See* Section J.

Loliards. *See* Section J.

Lombards, a German people, originating on the Elbe, who settled in Italy in the 6th cent., occupying northern and central regions, and establishing a kingdom with Pavia as capital. They were conquered by Charlemagne in 774, but left their name to the region of Lombardy. Lombard Street, London, takes its name from the Lombard merchants and bankers who came to settle there in the 12th cent.

London Clay, geological stratum which occupies much of the London Basin and part of the Hampshire Basin. It represents the lower stratum of the Eocene. Outside the metropolis, brickfields utilise the clay for brickmaking. Water held down in the Chalk by this impervious stratum is tapped by a number of artesian wells in London. The tunnels of the capital's underground railways run through the London Clay.

London University comprises nearly one-third of the academic activity of the United Kingdom, and is recognised as one of the great universities of the world. Originated in the foundation of a non-sectarian college in Gower Street in 1828.

Among the chief colleges are: University, Kings, Imperial College of Science and Technology, London School of Economics, School of Oriental and African Studies, Queen Mary, Birkbeck, Royal Holloway, Bedford, Westfield and Queen Elizabeth College. London University was the first to throw open all degrees to women (1878).

Long Distance Routes. The National Parks and Access to the Countryside Act 1949 provided for the establishment in England and Wales of Long Distance Footpaths and Bridleways. The following have been approved: Pennine Way (a magnificent hill walk of 250 miles (402 km) from Edale in Derbyshire along the Pennines over the Cheviots to the Scottish border); Pembrokeshire Coast Path Dyfed; Offa's Dyke Path (168 miles (270 km) along the marches of Wales); South Downs Way (Beachy Head to Salisbury); South-West Peninsula Coast Path (North Cornwall, South Cornwall, South Devon, Somerset and North Devon, Dorset); Yorkshire Coast and North York Moors. The Pennine Way (the first long-distance footpath), the South Downs Way (the first long-distance bridleway), Offa's Dyke (one of the most important remaining earthworks of its kind in northwestern Europe), and the Yorkshire Wolds Way have been opened. *See also* National Parks.

Longitude of a point on the earth's surface is the angle which the meridian through the poles and that point makes with some standard meridian. The meridian through Greenwich is usually accepted as the standard meridian and the longitude is measured east or west of that line. As the earth revolves through 360° in 24 h, 15° longitude represent 1 hour's difference in apparent time.

Long Parliament (1640–60), marked the end of Charles I's 11-year attempt to govern without Parliament. It carried through what has come to be called " the English Revolution " and was the parliament of the civil war (1642–49).

Lord Lieutenant is the Queen's representative in the county, and his office is now largely ceremonial. On his recommendation the magistrates or Justices of the Peace are appointed by the Lord Chancellor. The office was created in 1549 to take over the military duties of the sheriff.

Lords, House of, the Upper House of the British Parliament composed of Lords Spiritual and Lords Temporal. The former consist of the two Archbishops and twenty-four English Bishops and the latter of Peers and Peeresses. The right of the Lords to veto Bills passed by the Commons is restricted by the Parliament Acts of 1911 and 1949. The Lord Chancellor presides over the House of Lords. Under the Peerage Act 1963 a peerage may be disclaimed for life. *See* Section D.

Louse, parasitic insect found on the skin of birds and mammals. The bird or biting lice belong to the order *Mallophaga*; the true or sucking lice to the order *Anoplura*. Two species of lice parasitise man, and one of these, the body louse, is a carrier of typhus.

Louvre, one of the old royal palaces of Paris, was built in its present form partly by Francis I and added to by later monarchs, Louis XIV completing the edifice. Napoleon I turned it into a museum and enriched it with the plunder of many foreign art galleries. The great extension to the Louvre building begun by Napoleon I was completed under Napoleon III in 1857. Much injury was done to the building during the Commune of 1871. Amongst other famous treasures it houses the Venus de Milo and Leonardo da Vinci's masterpiece, *La Gioconda.*

LSD (d-lysergic acid diethylamide). This hallucinogenic drug has achieved wide notoriety because of its use by certain people to give themselves abnormal mental experiences. Doctors have frequently warned against the dangers of its use. It is active in extremely small quantities and a dose as small as a fifty-millionth part of a gram can cause marked disturbances of the mental function in man. LSD has been used in the study of mental disease because it produces symptoms very similar to mental disorders such as schizophrenia.

Luddites, a combination of workmen formed in

1811, in a period of great distress, with the object of destroying the new textile machinery then being largely adopted, which they regarded as the cause of their troubles. Their first outbreak was at Nottingham, and was stated to have been started by a young apprentice named Ned Ludd. Afterwards, serious Luddite riots occurred in various parts of the country, especially in West Yorkshire, where many people were killed, mills were destroyed and numbers of rioters were tried and executed. Charlotte Brontë used the period in her novel, *Shirley.*

Lunatic Fringe, term used by Theodore Roosevelt to characterise adherents of reform movements who refuse to recognise difficulty of practical administration and insist upon immediate fulfilment of an extreme programme.

Lutecium, element of the rare-earth metal group discovered in 1907 by Urbain.

Lutheranism. *See Section J.*

Lynx, cats of sturdy build, with tufted ears and spotted fur, inhabiting many parts of the world, including Northern and Central Europe. They commit serious ravages among sheep and goats and are very fierce.

Lyon King of Arms, the President of the Scottish Lyon Court, and head of the heraldic organisation for Scotland.

Lyre-Bird, a remarkable family of Australian birds, the males of which possess a beautiful lyre-shaped tail. The bird is not more than 38 cm long, but its tail, displayed during its remarkable courtship dance, is 58 cm in length. There are two species: the Superb and Albert's Lyrebird.

M

Macaque. A family of monkeys which include the Barbary ape (specimens of which live on Gibraltar), the Rhesus macaque (the organ grinder's monkey and the one used for experimental work in the investigation of disease), the Bonnet monkey of southern India and Sri Lanka, the Crab-eating and the Pig-tailed monkeys of south-eastern Asia.

Macaw, a genus of large parrots with brilliant scarlet and sky-blue plumage, with interminglings of green. Native to South and Central America.

McCarthyism, the term given to the wave of anti-Communist hysteria, associated with the name of Senator McCarthy (1908–57), whose campaign of vilification resulted in the loss of careers and livelihood of many innocent Americans.

Mace, originally a weapon of offence, now an ensign of authority borne before officers of state and other dignitaries. In the House of Commons the mace is handed to an official of the Crown by the Sergeant-at-Arms at the close of a parliamentary session.

Mach Number. Unit of flight speed. The ratio of speed of flight to speed of sound under same conditions of pressure and density. Speed of sound at sea-level is 762 mile/h (1,226 km/h), so flight speed of 381 mile/h (613 km/h) is equivalent to a Mach Number of $\frac{1}{2}$. At supersonic speeds the Mach Number is greater than 1; subsonic speeds, less than 1.

Mackerel, a familiar sea-fish existing in large numbers in the northern waters of both hemispheres. In May and June immense shoals are to be found round the British coasts.

Macromolecules are very large molecules about 10,000 times or more as heavy as ordinary small molecules like hydrogen. Most are built up from a large number of simple sub-units, i.e., are polymers (*q.v.*). The term macromolecule is often used in biology, *e.g.*, starch and cellulose are biological macromolecules, both built from glucose sub-units. Other important ones are proteins and nucleic acids. The properties of macromolecules depend on the sub-units of which they are composed.

Madder, one of the most important of dye-stuffs, largely used in producing Turkey-red dye, but now superseded by synthetic alizarin. Natural madder is the root of the *Rubia tinctorum.*

Maelstrom, a great whirlpool. The most famous is that off the coast of Norway, between the islands

of Moskenes and Mosken, of the Lofoten group, the power of which has been much exaggerated.

Mafia. A term which is connected with Italo-American organised crime. Historically, remoteness from the central government of Italy encouraged the growth in Sicily in the 19th cent. of *mafiosi*, key-men who gained power through fear and violence. Contemporary police records give details of *mafia* behaviour in defending their authority. Emigration of vast numbers of southern Italians to the United States led to a new type of urban *mafioso* who became connected with gangsterism and vice. Sometimes called the *Cosa Nostra*, the organisation has infiltrated city governments and is reputed to be in control of drug smuggling and other illegal operations. In Italy neo-fascist groups have made use of the *mafia* in acts of terrorism, especially in the north. An Italian parliamentary commission of inquiry into *mafia* activities set up in 1962 took twelve years to report. No legislation has as yet followed its recommendations.

Magellan, Clouds of, the name given to a pair of small galaxies, satellite systems of our own galaxy, visible only from the southern hemisphere. On account of their relative nearness to the earth (186,000 light-years), they are receiving much attention from astronomers.

Magenta, a blue-red aniline dye discovered in 1859 by Sir W. H. Perkin, and named after the great battle of that year between the French and Austrians.

Magic. *See Section J.*

Magistrates *or* **Justices of the Peace** preside over petty sessional and juvenile courts and are appointed by the Lord Chancellor on the recommendation of the Lord Lieutenant of the County. Most J.P.s are laymen and are unpaid. In certain big towns a legally-qualified, paid, full-time magistrate is appointed, known as a stipendiary magistrate. In London stipendiaries are known as Metropolitan Stipendiary Magistrates. J.P.s are no longer appointed over the age of 60 and they must retire when they reach 70. By the Justices of the Peace Act, 1968, *ex officio* J.P.s are abolished, except for the Lord Mayor and aldermen of the City of London.

Magma, molten rock material rich in volatile constituents prior to its eruption at the surface. On eruption and loss of volatiles it becomes lava.

Magna Carta was sealed by King John at Runnymede on 15 June 1215, in obedience to the insistent demands of the barons, and has been confirmed many times by later monarchs. It was not a revolutionary document. It laid down what the barons took to be the recognised and fundamental principles for the government of the realm and bound king and barons alike to maintain them. Its main provisions were that no man should be punished without fair trial, that ancient liberties generally should be preserved, and that no demands should be made by an overlord to his vassal (other than those recognised) without the sanction of the great council of the realm.

Magnesium, a metallic element, symbol Mg, first isolated in 1808 by Sir Humphry Davy, who prepared it by electrolysing the chloride. Its chief ores are magnesite and dolomite. Industrially it is obtained by electrolysis. Many important light alloys contain magnesium. The metal burns with a very bright light, and for this reason it is used in photographers' flash bulbs and also in firework manufacture.

Magnetic Storms, large irregular disturbances superimposed upon the normal magnetic field of the earth. They may occur at any time, but are most frequent during equinoctial months and in years of sunspot maxima. World-wide in extent, magnetic storms are most pronounced in the polar regions, being due apparently to intense electric currents located in the upper atmosphere near to the zones of greatest auroral frequency. One theory attributes the high ionisation of these belts to solar radiation. Magnetic storms cause radio fade-outs and interfere with telegraphic communication.

Magnetism, originally the name given to the quality of attraction for iron possessed by lodestone (*q.v.*). Now known to be a phenomenon inseparably connected with electricity (F21). Strong magnetic attraction is possessed by a comparatively small class of substances; iron, nickel and cobalt are the most common elements, but there are several less well known, *e.g.*, gadolinium. Many alloys have valuable magnetic properties which make possible numberless technical devices. New magnetic substances are always being developed (*see* Ferrite). The earth acts like a huge magnet with its axis inclined at about 11° to the axis of rotation, the magnetic poles being on the Boothia Peninsula (North Canada) and South Victoria Land (Antarctica). The magnetic field at the surface consists of the regular field of a magnetised sphere with an irregular field superimposed upon it. Variation in the magnetic forces occurs from place to place and from time to time, and maps showing the distribution over the globe of points of the same declination (*i.e.*, the angle which the magnetic meridian makes with the geographical one) are of the utmost importance in navigation. Little is known regarding the origin of the main (regular) field of the earth, but it is believed that the irregularities are due to the presence of intense electric currents in the upper atmospheres and local magnetisation of rock strata. In 1967 the discovery was claimed of isolated magnetic poles, *i.e.*, north and south magnetic poles existing separately, just as positive and negative electrical charges exist separately. If this is confirmed it will probably rank as one of the most important experimental results of the 20th cent., because of its significance for the theory of electromagnetism and fundamental particles. Magnetic field strengths are measured in gauss (c.g.s.) or tesla (S.I.) units.

Magnetohydro-dynamics. A current-carrying wire always experiences a force if it is in a magnetic field. This is the well-known electrodynamic force, and electric motors work because of it. If the current is carried in a fluid, *e.g.*, a liquid metal or a plasma, these forces cause bodily movements of the fluid, which are in general very difficult to calculate. The forces are then called *magnetohydro-dynamic forces*. Now magnetic fields are themselves produced by electric currents; so a current flowing in a fluid produces a magnetic field, which then reacts on the fluid itself by means of the magnetohydrodynamic forces. In the Harwell machine Zeta, used in studying the technical problems of thermonuclear reactions, this effect acts so as to constrict the electric discharge on to the axis of the tube and thus keeps it away from the walls. This action is assisted by an extra magnetic field produced by a separate current flowing in metallic conductors outside the tube. Thus the hot plasma is contained by magnetohydro-dynamic forces and not at all by the material tube wall. In practical devices of the future magnetic forces may have to sustain plasma pressure of 60 atmospheres—a pressure for which a thick steel wall would normally be used ! *See also* Plasma Physics.

Magnificat, the hymn of the Virgin Mary, given in Luke 1, 46 beginning in the Vulgate with the words "Magnificat anima mea Dominum" ("My soul doth magnify the Lord"), and used in the services of all Christian Churches.

Magnitude in astronomy is a measure of the apparent brightness of a star, which is inversely proportional to the square of its distance. A low number indicates a bright star, and a high one a faint star. The *absolute magnitude* is a measure of *real* brightness, *i.e.*, the brightness a star would have at a standard distance away of 32·6 light years. The distance can be calculated if the apparent and absolute magnitudes are known.

Magnolia, species of the family *Magnoliaceae* comprising many beautiful trees, and shrubs with large and fragrant flowers, and chiefly native to North America and Asia. Introduced in 1688.

Magpie, a well-known bird of the crow family, of glossy black and white plumage, famed for its mischievous propensities.

Magyars, the Hungarian race who came to eastern Europe from S.W. Asia and settled in Hungary in the 10th cent. Their language belongs to the Finno-Ugrian group.

Mahdi, an Arab leader of great influence, invested with powers akin to those of a Messiah in the Mohammedan mind. The title was taken by Mohammed Ahmed, who overran the Egyptian Sudan, and in 1885 captured Khartoum.

Maidenhair Tree *or* **Ginkgo.** This tree takes its name from the shape of its leaves, which resemble those of the maidenhair fern. Widely cultivated in China and Japan. It is the only survivor of an order of gymnosperms which flourished in Mesozoic times. Botanically interesting because the male gametes are motile.

Malmaison, château at Rueil-Malmaison, a western suburb of Paris. It derives its name from having been inhabited in the 11th cent. by the Norman brigand Odon, and afterwards, according to the tradition, by evil spirits, exorcised by the monks of St. Denis. It was the residence of Napoleon and of the Empress Josephine after her divorce. She died there in 1814 as the result of a chill caught while showing the Russian Emperor round the grounds. In 1900 it was given to the nation.

Malmsey, a strong, sweet wine originally made in Greece, but now also in Spain, Madeira and the Azores; known also as Malvoisie.

Maltose, a sugar formed in cereal grains during germination. It is produced by hydrolysis of starch, and further hydrolysis converts the maltose into glucose.

Mamluks, commonly known as Mamelukes, were originally—in the 13th cent.—a bodyguard of Turkish and Circassian slaves in the service of the Sultan of Egypt, and attained such influence that in 1250 they were strong enough to appoint one of their own body to the throne of Egypt. After that a succession of Mamluk Sultans reigned down to 1517. Then the Turks annexed Egypt, and the Mamluks were taken into the service of the Beys. They again came to the front after Napoleon's conquest of Egypt, and for a time resumed governmental sway; but in 1811 they were decoyed into the citadel of Cairo and massacred by order of Mehemet Ali.

Mammoth, extinct elephants of gigantic size. In 1799 the first perfectly preserved specimen was found in Siberia in a block of ice. It was in prehistoric times an inhabitant of Britain and other parts of Europe, as well as of Asia and America.

Mammoth Cave of Kentucky, one of the largest known limestone caverns in the world, with subterranean passages at different levels, lakes and rivers (the Echo R. flows 110 m below the surface); stalactites and stalagmites abound.

Manatee, an aquatic mammal of the sea cow (Sirenia) order of mammals, averaging when full grown from 3–3·6 m in length, with shovel-shaped tail, and forelimbs and nails which almost give the appearance of arms and hands. In spite of their ungainly aspect, these creatures are believed to have given rise to the legend of mermaids.

Manchus, the original nomadic race inhabiting northern Manchuria who invaded China early in the 17th cent. A Manchu dynasty occupied the imperial throne of China from 1644 to 1911.

Mandarin, the name given to a powerful Chinese official, civil or military, under the old régime, whose rank was shown by the wearing of a button on the cap. Mandarin is the major language of N. China.

Mandible, the lower jaw in human anatomy. The two parts of a bird's beak are known as the upper and lower mandible. The term is also used for biting jaws in arthropods.

Manganese, a metallic element, symbol Mn, discovered by Scheele in 1774. It is silver-white, not very hard (it forms a hard alloy with carbon), brittle, and tarnishes when exposed to air. Its chief ore is pyrolusite (manganese dioxide). Steels containing manganese are very tough, and used for making machine parts.

Maniple, eucharistic vestment worn over left arm.

Manna, a tree of the ash genus, *Fraxinus ornus*, growing in the South of Europe and in the East and exuding a sweet substance which is gathered, boiled and eaten.

Manometer, instrument used to measure gas

pressure. Usually a U-tube containing water or mercury, one end open to the atmosphere, the other to the gas whose pressure is to be measured. More sensitive for small pressures than the Bourdon gauge.

Manors were estates originally granted in Anglo-Saxon times as rewards for knightly service, and included the privilege of a special court with jurisdiction, criminal and civil, within the manorial territory. *See* Court-Leet.

Mansion House, the official residence of the Lord Mayor of London, stands opposite to the Bank of England, and was erected in 1739–53 from the designs of George Dance.

Mantis. Large insects belonging to the same order as the locusts and grasshoppers. The manner in which the forelegs are held, as though in suppliance, has gained for these insects the common name of "praying mantis". They are distributed throughout the warmer countries of the world.

Manx, the Celtic dialect (Manx Gaelic) of the Isle of Man, now on the point of extinction.

Maoism. *See* Section J.

Maoris, the race found in New Zealand at the time of its discovery by Captain Cook in 1769. They are believed to have migrated from Polynesia about 1350. Up to 1871 they were frequently in arms against the European settlers but their high intelligence and stamina enabled them to adapt themselves and the New Zealand laws have encouraged equal citizenship. They number 223,300 (1971). Today in New Zealand a pure Maori is a rarity.

Maple, trees native to the northern hemisphere. There are over 100 species. The sycamore is the best-known species growing in Britain. The sugar maple abounds in Canada and the eastern parts of the United States. The sugar is tapped by boring holes in the tree in February and March, and the juice that escapes is collected and evaporated. The maple-leaf is the Canadian national emblem.

Maquis, name of the dense scrub in Mediterranean France and Corsica, providing good cover for bandits and outlaws. The French resistance movement adopted the name Maquis during the German Occupation, 1940–45.

Marble is limestone in its hardest and most crystalline form. There are many varieties—33 were used in the building of the Paris Opera House—but white is the purest and rarest. White marble was used by the ancient Greeks for their temples and statues. Among the famous marbles of Italy are the Carrara and Siena marbles, which were used by Renaissance sculptors. Devonshire and Derbyshire yield some beautiful marbles and Connemara furnishes a serpentine-marble.

March, the third month of the year, and the first of the old Roman Calendar. It was named after the god Mars, and was the *Hlyd* (storm) *monath* of the Anglo-Saxons.

Mardi Gras, the last day of the Carnival in France, Shrove Tuesday.

Marionettes are puppets moved by strings. They originated in the *Fantoccini* of the 15th cent. which had such a vogue in Italy and elsewhere on the Continent. The English *Punch and Judy* is a version of Punchinello.

Marlinspike, a pointed iron tool used by sailors to splice wire. The instrument used when rope splicing is called a fid.

Marmoset, small monkeys confined to the New World. Very squirrel-like in appearance, with long bushy tails, and thick woolly fur, they are pretty little animals and the smallest of all monkeys. There are claws, not nails, on their digits, the big toe excepted.

Marprelate Tracts, seditious pamphlets written with great maliciousness by a group of Elizabethan puritans about 1586, and intended to discredit the episcopacy, caused a great sensation in their time, and led to the execution of their supposed author, John Penry.

Marquess *or* **Marquis,** the title next in precedence to that of duke. The first English marquess was Rovery de Vere, Earl of Oxford, who received the honour from Richard II, in 1385.

Marquetry, a kind of inlaying in which thin layers of coloured woods are wrought into a design, and mainly used in ornamental floors.

Mars, the fourth nearest planet to the sun (*see* F8).

There used to be much speculation among scientists about certain dark lines which some observers had seen on the surface of the planet; photographs gave no support to the theory of an artificially constructed network of canals, but it seemed possible they represented areas covered by some simple form of vegetation of the lichenous type. However, the *Mariner* probes have increased our knowledge and raised new questions. *Mariner 9* carried out an extensive study of Mars in 1971/2 covering 85 per cent of the surface in great detail. Important new findings showed that water had played an active rôle in the planet's evolution and that it was not, as scientists had concluded from the *Mariner 6* and *Mariner 7* probes, a dead and featureless planet, but one with its own distinctive character. Photographs revealed four major geological regions: volcanic; equatorial plateau marked by deep canyons, with evidence of water erosion; large cratered terrain like the moon (photographed by the 1969 probes); and a polar region with terrace-like formations and deep grooves. The 1976 *Viking* mission found no organic compounds in the soil analysed but scientists have not ruled out the possibility of life still existing on the planet. The Soviet Union has also sent spaceships to Mars to pioneer new techniques of planetary exploration. Mars has two small moons—Phobos and Deimos.

Marseillaise, the French national hymn, written and composed by Rouget de L'Isle, a French engineer officer, who was inspired to write it in 1792 to encourage the Strasburg conscripts. It immediately became popular, and received its name from the fact that it was sung by the Marseillaise troops while marching into Paris.

Marshalsea, a former prison in Southwark, London, closed 1849. It existed as early as Edward III's time and was used as a jail for royal servants convicted of offences. In its later days it became a debtors' prison. Dickens described it in *Little Dorrit*.

Marsh Gas. *See* Methane.

Marsh Tortoise, an amphibious animal of the order *Chelonia,* spread over many countries and inhabiting ponds and small rivers. There are 42 species, and they are all carnivorous.

Marston Moor, near York, was the scene of the famous battle between Prince Rupert and Cromwell on 2 July 1644. Cromwell's victory was the turning-point in the Civil War.

Marsupials, members of the order of pouched mammals. Except for the opossums of America, all marsupials occur in Australasia, and include the kangaroos, wallabies and wombats.

Martello Towers, circular forts erected on the coasts of England and Jersey early in the 19th cent. as defences against the threatened Napoleonic invasion. So called from the circular fort at Mortella (Corsica), which resisted an English sea attack in 1794.

Marten, carnivorous animals of the weasel family; one species (the Pine Marten) was once common in Britain. Most famous for their fur are the Siberian Sable and the American Marten.

Martial Law is a term loosely employed to indicate the suspension of the administration of normal civil law and its replacement by military authority when this is rendered desirable by such circumstances as war or rebellion.

Martin, a well-known bird-visitor to Britain. It belongs to the swallow family, and the two species that spend their summers here are the house-martin, which makes its nest of mud under the eaves of houses, and the sand martin, which builds in sandy banks.

Martinmas *or* St. Martin's Day, falls on 11 November, and is one of the Scottish quarter days. St. Martin was a popular Saint with our ancestors and Martinmas was a busy time for the mediaeval housewife. It was the date when "Martlemas Beef" was dried in the chimney, and enough bacon and mutton cured to last until the spring, because, owing to the scarcity of winter fodder, fresh meat could seldom be obtained. This diet of dried meat without vegetables caused scurvy. St. Martin (c. 316–400) was regarded as the patron saint of drinking and jovial meetings, as well as of reformed drunkards. The spell of fine weather sometimes occurring at Martinmas is called St. Martin's Summer.

Martyrs. People who suffer death in testimony to their faith. Stephen (Acts 6; 7) was the first Christian martyr in 39. The first English martyr was St. Alban, 286, and in Tudor times many eminent churchmen went to the stake. The Smithfield martyrs' memorial church used to be St. Peter's, St. John Street, Clerkenwell. When that church was demolished the memorial moved to the Church of St. James, Clerkenwell Green.

Marxism. *See* Section J.

Mason and Dixon Line, boundary line between Pennsylvania and Maryland, for long a source of dispute, drawn up by two English surveyors, Charles Mason and Jeremiah Dixon, between 1763 and 1767. It came to designate the boundary dividing the slave states from the free states of America, and is still used in distinguishing the " North " from the " South ".

Masques were light dramatic compositions set to music and performed on special occasions. One of the best-known examples is Milton's " Comus ", which was given at Ludlow Castle in 1634.

Mass, the service in the Roman Catholic Church in which are enacted and enshrined Christ's words and actions at the Last Supper. It is high or low, *i.e.*, performed with full choral service, or merely by the rehearsal of prayers without singing. Mass was first celebrated in Latin in the 4th cent., and was introduced into England in the 7th cent. The use of a vernacular language was sanctioned by the Second Vatican Council (1965).

Mass Spectrograph, an instrument for separating isotopes. It works by sorting electrified particles according to their masses; the particles stream through a magnetic and possibly an electric field, and the lightest particles undergo the greatest deflection.

Massorah, a collection of criticisms on the Hebrew text of the Scriptures, and rules for its correct interpretation.

Mast, a long round piece of timber or tubular steel or iron, standing upright in a vessel, and supporting the yards, sails and rigging in general. The earliest ships had only one mast, carrying a simple sail. The number increased until there were 4 or 5, or even more. Above the lower mast of a sailing-ship comes the topmast, and above that, the topgallantmast and royalmast. The position of each mast is indicated by a prefix, as foremast, foretopmast, foretopgallantmast, foreroyalmast, mainmast, maintopmast, etc. The foremast is in the fore of the ship, the mainmast in the centre and the mizzen nearest the stern. In large vessels nowadays the mast does not extend to the keel, as it formerly did, but is usually stopped at the second deck.

Master of the Revels was an important Court official upon whom devolved the arrangement of Court festivities. The office is at least as old as the time of Edward III. By 1737 it seems to have died.

Master of the Rolls, one of the English judges, formerly a judge of Chancery, but since 1881 a judge of the Court of Appeal only. In addition he has charge of the rolls or records of Chancery and ranks next to the Lord Chancellor and Lord Chief Justice.

Mastodon, an extinct order of quadruped closely resembling the elephant in structure, but larger.

Materials Science is a blend of science and technology; it is the use of scientific research methods to study and improve materials for practical use. The deeper understanding so obtained enables scientists to design new substances with hitherto unknown combinations of properties that are useful in engineering, aircraft, nuclear power, surgery, etc. Materials science institutes or university departments will usually contain an assortment of chemists, physicists, metallurgists, ceramicists, engineers and others because materials science brings to bear on materials a great many specialised techniques. The scientific study of materials is bringing continual improvement in metals, ceramics, plastics, fibres and many valuable combinations of these.

Mathematics is a body of knowledge expressed in a language of symbols. *Pure* mathematics studies the propositions that can be deduced in this language by applying definite rules of reasoning to sets of axioms. In *Applied* mathematics, the mathematical language is used, often with great effect, to discuss problems of the real world, such as mechanics, statistics and science generally. In range, subtlety, complexity and depth mathematics is unsurpassed among the intellectual disciplines and its study has attracted some of the most brilliant men in history.

Matins, the first of the canonical hours or services of the day in the Roman Catholic Church and Morning Prayer in the Anglican Church. The daily service in the Roman breviary (*q.v.*) consists of eight offices or " hours ", fixed by canon, for prayer and devotion. Formerly, Matins was recited or sung at midnight, Lauds at sunrise, Prime at 6 a.m., Terce at 9 a.m., Sext at midday, Nones at 3 p.m., Vespers at sunset and Compline before retiring for the night. Lauds are now commonly joined to Matins.

Matrix, a rectangular array of numbers considered as a single mathematical object. There are special rules for multiplying and adding matrices and they are often used in mathematics, physics and elsewhere to simplify calculations and as a notational device.

Mau-Mau, a secret, anti-European, terrorist movement which agitated the Kikuyu tribe of Kenya during the years 1953–57. Mau-mau was a symptom of native insecurity and discontent; emergency powers were lifted in November 1959, and large-scale reforms were instituted. Kenya attained independence in December 1963 with Mr. Jomo Kenyatta as Prime Minister.

Maundy Thursday, the day before Good Friday, commemorates the Last Supper. " Maundy " derives from Christ's command (mandatum) to his disciples on that day to love one another. It was the custom in the monasteries for the monks to wash the feet of the poor on this day, and for many centuries the sovereigns of England, through their almoners, have distributed money, food and clothing to " as many old men and as many old women as the Sovereign is years of age ". The Royal Maundy ceremony is still observed, maundy coins being struck from standard silver.

Mausoleum, a special place of sepulture, generally for the reception of the remains of members of a royal or other family of distinction. The name is derived from the tomb of King Mausolus at Halicarnassus, erected 352 B.C., and forming one of the seven wonders of the ancient world. Another mausoleum of antiquity is that of Hadrian in Rome.

Mauve, a colouring matter produced from lichens by Dr. Stenhouse in 1848, but in 1856 obtained from aniline by William Perkin (1838–1907), who gave it the name Mauveen. This was the first synthetic organic dyestuff ever to be produced, which led to the building up of the great synthetic dyestuffs industry (which Germany dominated before the first world war).

May, the fifth month of the year, but the third of the ancient Roman calendar. Supposed to be named after Maia, the mother of Mercury, to whom sacrifices were offered on the first day of this month. In England in former days May Day was made the occasion of many festivities, including the crowning of the May Queen, dancing round the Maypole, etc.

" Mayflower ", the name of the ship which in 1620 conveyed the Pilgrim Fathers, 101 in number, from England to America. *See* Pilgrim Fathers.

May Fly. *See* Ephemoptera.

Mazarin Bible, an edition of the Latin Vulgate, acknowledged as the masterpiece of the Gutenberg press (1456). It was the first book completely printed from movable types. It is called the Mazarin Bible because the first copy to capture the attention of scholars was found in the library of Cardinal Mazarin, in Paris. Sometimes called the Gutenberg or the 42-line Bible.

Mean. In statistics and mathematics generally understood to be the arithmetic mean. The geometric mean between two quantities is the square root of their product. *See* Average.

Mechanical Equivalent of Heat. *See* Joule.

Medals, as decorations for military service, were first issued in this country by Charles I, who ordered medals for gallantry to be distributed to certain soldiers in 1643. Medals were also issued to officers and men who were victorious against the Dutch fleet in 1653. After Lord Howe's victory in 1794 a naval medal was instituted. Medals were also struck for the victory of Waterloo, and since that time special medals have been issued in connection with all our wars. The Victoria Cross, a special reward for personal gallantry in the Navy, Army and Air Force, was instituted in 1856. The George Cross for gallantry instituted in 1940 ranks next to the Victoria Cross. The Military Cross was instituted in 1914.

Meerschaum, a white or yellow-white earthy mineral, found in beds in Asia Minor, Greece, and other places, is a silicate of magnesium allied with water. Its chief use is in making pipe-bowls.

Megalith, a prehistoric monument, consisting of a large single stone or a group of such stones, in a circle as at Stonehenge or in burial chambers as at New Grange, Ireland. Megalithic monuments have been constructed by different peoples in different parts of the world since the third millennium B.C.

Meiosis, a special type of cell division by which the gametes or sex cells are generated, resulting in the sperm or ovum receiving only half the number of chromosomes found in a somatic cell. *See* Mitosis.

Mendelian Law. The first statistical rules of inheritance, determining the ratio of variation of characteristics in the offspring of differing individuals, and the classification of characters discontinuously inherited, were first formulated by the Austrian monk Gregor Mendel. The results of his most important experiments in the crossing of peas were published in 1866, and showed that when two races are crossed, the resultant hybrids will exhibit the dominant features of one parent, but the offspring of the second generation will show those of both grandparents. *See* F30(2).

Mendicant Friars, certain religious orders which spread over Europe in the 13th cent., and comprised the Franciscans, Dominicans, Augustines and Carmelites. Originally they depended entirely on alms.

Mercator's Projection, a method of indicating meridians and parallels of latitudes on maps, introduced by Mercator in the 16th cent., and still universally used in navigators' charts.

Mercury, one of the smaller planets and the nearest to the sun, being $57 \cdot 9 \times 10^6$ km distant. It has no satellite. *See* F8.

Mercury *or* **Quicksilver,** symbol Hg (Latin *hydrargyrum*) is one of the oldest-known metals, whose chief ore is the sulphide, cinnabar, found in certain parts of Spain, China, Japan, Mexico and South America. It is liquid at ordinary temperature and is used in the construction of barometers and thermometers. Alloys of mercury are called amalgams. It is also of great value in medicine. The metal is used in the mercury-vapour (or "sunlight") lamp, since the vapour gives a bright yellow-white glow in an electric discharge.

Mercy-killing, taking the life of a person suffering from a painful and incurable disease. The killer is often actuated by a good *motive*—the desire to relieve hopeless suffering; but the *intention* is to kill, and the act, in English law, is therefore a crime. (It is not necessary for the prosecution to prove any motive.)

Meridian, an imaginary circle extending through the North and South Poles and any given place. When the sun is at its midday height at any place it is "on the meridian"; hence the terms ante-meridian (a.m.) and post-meridian (p.m.). *See also* Greenwich Mean Time.

Merino Sheep were imported into England from Spain in 1788 and had great influence in improving native breeds, especially in regard to the quality of the wool.

Merit, Order of, founded by King Edward VII in 1902 as a special distinction for eminent men and women without conferring a knighthood upon them. The Order has twenty-four British companions in addition to foreign honorary members limited in number, as the choice of members is, by the Sovereign's pleasure. Lord Kelvin was the founder companion. Dr.

Sarvepalli Radhakrishnan (1963) was an honorary member. Florence Nightingale (1907), Professor Dorothy Hodgkin (1965) and Dame Veronica Wedgwood (1969) are the only women to have received this coveted decoration.

Merovingians, the name given to the family that ruled over France from about 500 to 750. Clovis was first of the line and Childeric the last.

Mesons (from Greek *meso* = middle), a family of unstable particles of mass between that of an electron and that of a proton. Some are positive, some negative, some neutral. No stable meson is known, the longest-lived particle having a lifetime of only two-millionths of a second. The first of these particles was discovered in cosmic radiation in 1937 and called the mu-meson or *muon*. In 1947 a heavier type was discovered called the pi-meson or *pion* which behaved like the meson predicted on theoretical grounds by Yukawa in 1935. The pion is connected with the theory of nuclear forces. *See also* F15, 16.

Mesozoic. The geological era which includes the Triassic, Jurassic and Cretaceous rocks. *See* F45.

Metabolism, the general term for the physical and chemical processes occurring within a living organism. *See* 29(1).

Metalloid, an element which has properties intermediate between those of a metal and a non-metal. Arsenic is a metalloid.

Metamorphic Rocks are such geological deposits as have undergone alterations of structure and mineral reorganisation. The most active agents in producing these metamorphic changes are heat, water and pressure. *See* F9(1).

Metamorphosis, period of development from egg to adult, during which the animals have different forms, as found, *e.g.*, in the life histories of frog and butterfly.

Meteorites. The word meteor originally signified any natural phenomenon, but in modern usage meteors are small bodies coming from interplanetary space which become luminous by friction on entering the earth's atmosphere. Popularly called "shooting stars". Larger meteors are known as fireballs. Some of these reach the ground. The object which has been a meteor in flight then becomes a meteorite. In some meteorites iron and nickel are the chief metals (siderites), others are like rock (aerolites). The iron meteorites are more common amongst those which have been preserved, but falls of rock-like meteorites occur more frequently. At L'Aigle in France in 1803 from 2000 to 3000 meteorite stones fell; this fall is famous because it convinced scientists that meteorites really came from outside our atmosphere. The largest meteorite stone actually known to have fallen to earth is one which descended in Emmott County, Iowa, in 1870, weighing 197 kg. A meteorite weighing no less than 37 tonnes found in Greenland is now in New York. On 30 June 1908, an enormous object fell in Siberia in a sparsely-inhabited region. A hot blast destroyed all trees within a radius of about 8–16 km, the explosion waves being recorded by barographs as far distant as London, Washington and Batavia. For the next few nights there was in Europe in the northern sky brilliant illumination due to sunlight falling on clouds of dust at a great height in the atmosphere. Whether this dust had accompanied the object in its journey through space like the tail of a comet or whether the dust had come from Siberia is unknown. (Many Russian astronomers now believe this Siberian meteorite, as it is commonly called, was the nucleus of a small comet.) When the place where the object fell was visited in 1927 some 200 craters were found, but no considerable meteorite has been recovered. Meteorites are possibly débris from the disintegration of a body in the solar system.

Meteorology, the science of the atmosphere considered as a heat engine. Deals with weather, climate, optical phenomena, atmospheric electricity, physical processes such as radiation and precipitation, the dynamics and structure of cyclones, anticyclones, etc. Wide application to problems of aviation, agriculture, commerce and shipping. Meteorological observing stations are in operation all over the world, and on the simultaneous or synoptic reports of their instrument readings and estimates of pressure, temperature, humidity, speed and direction of wind, rain, character and amount of cloud, visibility, etc., forecasts, gale, snow and frost warnings are based. Instruments carried by earth satellites (*e.g.*, *Tiros*, *Nimbus*) outside the atmosphere can make systematic observations on a world-wide basis of the atmospheric circulation, through observation of cloud cover and of the thermal radiation into space from the atmosphere. Such observations together with the use of computers are of great importance for weather analysis and forecasting. The main communications centre for the UK is at the headquarters of the Meteorological Office at Bracknell, Berkshire, where the collection, editing and re-transmission of weather messages continue according to strict schedules day and night throughout the year.

Methane. The simplest hydrocarbon, compounded of one carbon atom and four hydrogen atoms. This gas occurs over marshes and swamps, where it is liberated in the decay of vegetable matter. It is the main constituent of natural gas, and also occurs in coal-mines, where it is called " fire-damp " because of its explosive character of its mixture with air. Formerly this natural gas was removed from the coal seams and ran to waste; now in many countries (including Britain) it is being used for commercial purposes.

Methodism. *See* Section J.

Methylated Spirit, a mixture of 90 parts by volume ethyl alcohol, 9¼ parts wood naphtha (methyl alcohol), ½ part crude pyridine, together with small amounts of petroleum oil and methyl violet dye. Industrial methylated spirit consists of a mixture of 95 parts by volume ethyl alcohol and 5 parts wood naphtha. It is used as a solvent and a fuel.

Metre, the rhythmical pattern of Verse. *See* English Verse, Section M.

Metre, unit of length in the metric system: since 1960 the wavelength of the orange-red light of krypton 86 has been adopted as the basis of the international unit of length. Before that (since 1889) the platinum–iridium bar kept at Sèvres was the international prototype metre.

Metric System, the system of weights and measures based on the gramme and the metre, smaller and larger units being decimals and multiples of the primary units respectively. A decimal currency was adopted in France in 1795 and the metric system of weights and measures in 1799. (In that year the quadrant of the earth was surveyed and the standard metre adopted.) Nevertheless the change was accepted slowly, and as late as 1837 the French Government had to pass a law forbidding the use of the old measures. Since then the metric system has been adopted in most of the continental countries and is used universally in scientific work. Although there have been many attempts to get the system adopted in Britain, it was not until 1965 that the Government encouraged the adoption of the metric system of weights and measures. The changeover to decimal coinage was made in 1971; the system of weights and measures in industry is now mainly metric. *See* N7 for SI units.

Mezzotint, a technical method for producing graphic work and works of art. A copper plate is made rough by close cross-hatching, so that a print from it produces an even black. When parts of the cross-hatching are scraped away, these areas will come out white when printed. By skilful use of his tools, the artist or technician can produce pictures finely graded from black to white and with a velvety black as background. The principles of the method were known and practised, for instance, by Rembrandt, but mezzotint became most popular for the reproduction of famous paintings from the end of the 18th cent.

Mica. The mica of commerce is a nearly transparent mineral, which has great heat-resisting power, and can be split into thin plates. The most important micas are muscovite (potassium mica), the commoner variety, phlogopite (magnesium mica) and biotite (the magnesium and iron mica).

Michael, St., and George, St., an order of knighthood originally founded for the Ionian Isles and Malta in 1818, and reorganised in 1869, so as to admit Crown servants connected with the Colonies. The Earl of Derby, Earl Russell and Earl Grey were the first of the new knights.

Michaelmas Day, the festival day of St. Michael and All Angels, 29 September, one of the English quarter days.

Microbe, a term proposed by Sédillot in 1878 to denote any microscopic organism, vegetable or animal, or found on the borderland between the two great natural kingdoms. The term is commonly used, but not by scientists.

Microelectronics, a rapidly developing technology of the 1960s which reduces entire electronic circuits to minute size and embeds them in tiny chips of solid material. These are then called integrated circuits. A circuit consisting of, say, a dozen transistors and fifty resistors can be built into a small piece of semiconductor (*q.v.*) measuring not more than a couple of millimetres in any direction. Hundreds of these circuits can be made simultaneously in penny-size wafers of silicon about one-hundredth of an inch thick. There are great advantages in cheapness, reliability, robustness and speed of electronic performance. The small size is in itself an advantage in space vehicles and medical instruments. Applications to missile control systems, computers and communications equipment are no doubt only the first fruits of this new achievement of the current technological revolution.

Micrometer, an instrument for measuring minute distances: usually attached to the eye-pieces of a microscope or telescope, and consisting of two very fine hairs or wires stretched across the field of view, one fixed, the other movable. It was invented by William Gascoigne in the 17th cent. and improved by later inventors. Sir Joseph Whitworth made one in 1858 to measure the millionth part of an inch.

Micro-organisms, the collective term applied to several types of organism, the most important of which are fungi, viruses, bacteria and protozoa. It is a classification of convenience in biological studies. These organisms are generally simple in their environmental requirements (*e.g.*, have simple nutritional needs) and in cellular organisation. This makes them very suitable for modern biological research. Much of the information on the nature of the genetic code (**F32**(2)) was obtained from experiments on these organisms.

Microphone, device for converting the acoustic energy of sound waves into waves of electrical energy, used in sound amplifying systems. Developed independently by Edison (1877) and Hughes (1878).

Microscope, invented about 1590 by Janssen, and improved by Galileo, Fontana and others, is an instrument which by a lens system magnifies minute objects. Microscopes are simple, compound and binocular. *See also* Electron Microscope.

Middle Ages (*c.* A.D. 400–1500), usually considered to be the period between the decline and fall of the Western Roman Empire and the fall of Constantinople to the Turks (*see* A4–7). The period covers (*a*) an earlier part ending with the 12th cent. (sometimes called the Dark Ages) when science was dead, when theology was the main preoccupation, and when the language of the learned West was Latin; and (*b*) a later age of Arabian influence when alchemy and astrology (at that time indistinguishable from astronomy) were central interests, technology was advancing, and Greek learning was transmitted by Arab scholars. Characteristic features of the mediaeval scene were monasticism (Sec. **J**), the Crusades (*q.v.*), Gothic art (*q.v.*), feudalism (Sec. **J**), and the supremacy of Islam in the field of learning. The period came to an end with the general decline of Christendom and the ushering in of the Renaissance (Sec. **J**). The term " Middle Ages " was coined by the 17th-cent. German historian Christoph Keller.

Midrash, name given to the homiletical interpretation of some of the Hebrew Scriptures in which allegory and legendary illustration were freely used. Compiled by Jewish rabbis from *c.* A.D. 200.

Millenary Petition was presented to James I in 1603, on behalf of nearly 1000 Puritan Ministers against certain of the rites and ceremonies of the Church of England. The Hampton Court Conference was the outcome of this petition.

Millennium, a period of a thousand years. The term is specifically used of the period of a thousand years during which, according to Rev. xx. 1–5, Christ will reign in person on earth. The Millenarians are a sect that interprets the "Millennium" as beginning with the commencement of the 6001st year from the Creation, which, according to Archbishop Ussher (1581–1650), was in 4004 B.C.

Millipede. Arthropods (**F36**) allied to the centipedes, from which they differ in having two pairs of legs to each body segment (except the first three) instead of one pair. Worm-like in shape but with a pair of antennae on the head, they can do much harm to garden plants, unlike centipedes which are beneficial.

Millstone-Grit, a series of grits and sandstones of deltaic origin underlying the coal measures of the Carboniferous system and attaining in England a thickness in parts of 1,525 m. It is from this rock that millstones have been made from time immemorial.

Mimicry, protective similarity of an animal to another animal or to inanimate objects. Examples of the former are the hover flies, which mimic wasps and bees; of the latter, leaf insects, stick insects and caterpillars that look like dead twigs.

Mink. Semi-aquatic mammals closely related to polecats. There is one American species and one European. The fur, which varies light to dark brown, is soft and thick, and is among the most valuable of commercial furs. They now live in the wild in the British Isles.

Minnesingers were minstrel poets of Germany who, during the 12th and 13th cent., composed and sang verses of heroism and love. They were of knightly rank, the counterpart of the French troubadours. *See* **E3**(2).

Minnow, a small fresh-water fish of the carp family, abounding in all the waters of Europe; it has a mottled back and silvery belly, and forms a popular bait for trout.

Minstrels were originally specially appointed instrumentalists and singers—pipers, harpers and gleemen—engaged by barons and manorial lords to amuse their tenants. Later, minstrels assumed nomadic habits, made their way into the houses of the great and were generally welcome. By Elizabeth's time, however, they were too numerous, and were classed as "rogues and vagabonds", along with actors.

Miracle Plays, popular in England in the 15th cent., were usually religious in character, representing some of the dramatic incidents of the Bible. Staging of plays was one of the many activities of the Guilds of those days. *See* **Section M, Part V.**

Mirage, an optical illusion caused by unequal temperatures in different layers of the atmosphere near the earth's surface. These temperature variations alter the refracting power of the air and cause light rays to be curved, making the air act as a huge distorting lens. This can happen at sea, in deserts and elsewhere and various types of mirage are known. A common kind in deserts curves light from the sky so that it appears to come from the ground, deceiving the observer into thinking that the sky is reflected in a lake of water. Inverted images of hills, trees, etc. also look as if reflected in the non-existent lake.

Mishna, the first part of the Talmud, setting forth the "Oral Law" of the Jews.

Missal, the name of the mass-book of the Roman Church compiled 492–96 by Pope Gelasius I, and revised by Gregory I, 590–604. The present Roman Missal was sanctioned by the Council of Trent 1546–63. In the Anglican Communion the Book of Common Prayer superseded the Missal in 1549.

Mistle Thrush receives its name from its partiality to the mistletoe-berry. Larger than the song-thrush, with spotted breast rather than speckled.

Mistletoe, a parasitic evergreen with white berries used as a decoration at Christmas-time. The familiar mistletoe of Europe is the *Viscum album,* which grows on the boughs of lime,

willow, apple, poplar, maple, ash, hawthorn but seldom on oak-trees. It was sacred to the Druids, and in Norse mythology it was a mistletoe dart that killed the god Baldur.

Mistral, a cold, dry, northerly wind peculiar to the French coast of the Mediterranean.

Mitosis, cell division whereby each daughter cell receives the same number of chromosomes as the parent cell. When the gametes (sex cells) are formed a special type of division occurs (meiosis) in which the number of chromosomes is halved. *See* **F30**(2).

Mitre, the twofold pointed head-dress of bishops and certain abbots of the Western Church and occasionally of other ecclesiastics.

Moa, the name for several species of ostrich-like extinct birds related to the New Zealand kiwi. The largest species, *Diornis maximus,* stood 2·6 m high, the smallest, *Anomalopteryx parva,* was nearer the size of a turkey. This wingless bird became extinct several centuries ago because of hunting by the Maoris from whom the name comes.

Moabite Stone, a stone of the 9th cent. B.C. containing the earliest known inscription in Phoenician characters, and discovered in the highlands of Moab in 1868. It is now in the Louvre, Paris. It records the campaign between Moab and Israel, a differing account of which is given in the Old Testament.

Moderator, a material used to slow down neutrons in an atomic pile. Examples of moderators are pure graphite and heavy water. *See* **Nuclear Reactors.**

Mohole Project, a scheme to bore through the earth's crust to take samples of the mantle rocks beneath. Drilling trials, led by an American team of geophysicists, began in 1961 near the island of Guadalupe off the Mexican coast in the Pacific. The project, however, was cancelled in 1966 on account of the escalating cost. Russian geophysicists started on a similar experiment, boring through land rocks where the digging is much deeper and higher temperatures are met with. The name "Anti-Cosmos" was given to the project. The boundary between the earth's crustal and mantle rocks is known as the Mohorovičić Discontinuity, or, more simply, as the Moho. The technology of deep sea drilling came from this project.

Molasses, sugar-cane juice in its uncrystallised form after boiling. The crystallised part is the raw sugar. Used to make rum.

Mole, a small burrowing animal with long, sensitive nose, about the size of a small rat, with short legs and forefeet armed with strong claws for digging in the earth. Their subterranean dwellings are of curiously ingenious construction, and they do not often leave them except to make raids on mice, frogs, snails, etc. The earth-worm, however, is the mole's chief item of food. Not to be confused with the vole which has a blunt nose.

Mole, or gram molecular weight. *See* **F24**(1).

Molecular Biology, a rapidly expanding branch of science mainly concerned with cell structure and function at a molecular level, in particular with genes and enzymes and the interaction between the two. Recent work in Britain has led to the unravelling of the structure of DNA, the hereditary substance of the genes, and has played a major part in uncovering the molecular mechanism of the transfer of hereditary information and the nature of the genetic code. Crystallisation of the first enzyme (urease) took place in 1929; the gene as a definite chemical entity was discovered in 1943. *See* **F29**(1).

Molecule. A group of atoms held together by chemical forces. *See* **F14, 23,** *also* **Macromolecule.**

Molybdenum, symbol Mo, a fairly hard white metal with properties resembling those of chromium. Its commonest ore is the sulphide, molybdenite. The chief use of the metals is in the manufacture of alloy steels.

Monasticism. *See* **Section J.**

Monazite, a cerium mineral containing some thorium. Occurs as grains, often as sand ("monazite sands"), derived from granites. Deposits occur in India (Travancore), Russia, Norway, Malagasy Rep., S. Africa, Brazil, USA.

Monday, the second day of the week, called by the Anglo-Saxons *Monandaeg* (moon-day).

Mongoose, species of mammals related to the civets, feeding on vermin and reptiles. These animals, which have long tails and short legs, occur in Africa and Asia (especially India). The biggest mongoose is the Egyptian ichneumon, and this has been introduced into the W. Indies because of its ability to kill large poisonous snakes.

Monitor, a family of lizards most resembling dragons. There are about 30 species widely distributed over the tropical parts of Asia, Australia and Africa.

Monroe Doctrine, a principle of American policy declining any European intervention in political affairs of the American continent, outlined by President Monroe in 1823. At the same time interference was disclaimed with existing European colonies in the Western Hemisphere. The American Civil War hampered the application of the doctrine for some time, but afterwards the United States firmly insisted on it. The Doctrine is not international law, but a national policy of the USA.

Monsoons, regular persistent winds which blow at certain seasons in middle latitudes, mainly in South and East Asia. Their occurrence is related to the great changes of pressure which take place between summer and winter over the land mass. In India the south-west monsoon (June–October) is moisture-laden from its long passage over the sea and in the higher regions, especially, there is heavy rainfall. Sudden reversal of the wind results in the cold north-east monsoon (October–March) which is dry on account of the shelter afforded by the mountain ranges to the north. Frequently the term "monsoon" is applied to denote the associated rainfall without reference to the actual winds.

Monstrance, an ornamental transparent receptacle in which the Sacred Host is carried in procession or exposed for adoration.

Month, the 12th part of the calendar year. A lunar month is the interval of new moon to new moon or full moon to full moon; mean length, 29 days, 12 hours, 44 minutes, 2·87 seconds. A sidereal month represents the time of the moon's revolution from a given star back to the same again, 27 days, 7 hours, 43 minutes, 11·5 seconds. In English law, since 1926, a month, unless otherwise expressed, means a calendar month.

Monument of London, a 202 ft (61·6 m) column, overlooking Billingsgate, designed by Wren and erected (1671–77) to mark the starting-point of the Great Fire of London (1666). The original inscription upon it ascribed the fire to "the treachery and malice of the popish faction", which stood until 1831, when the words were erased as objectionable. The black marble staircase has 345 steps (311 to the balcony).

Moon, the earth's satellite, 3,475 km in diameter and 384,400 km distant from the earth. It rotates in the same time as it revolves round the earth (27 days 7 hours 43 minutes), so that the same face is always presented to the earth. The lunar surface is pockmarked by innumerable collisions with solid particles of all sizes. Unlike the earth, it is unprotected by any atmosphere and for aeons of time it has been exposed to every kind of cosmic influence, including the parching effect of solar radiation. All moonlight derives from the sun but on the whole it is a pretty poor reflector. The exploration of the moon by means of rockets began in 1959 when the Russian *Luna* 2 crashlanded on the plains of the *Mare Imbrium*. 1969 will be remembered as the year of the U.S. *Apollo* triumphs when man first set foot on the moon. The samples of lunar rock and dust brought back to earth by the *Apollo* astronauts and the Soviet *Luna* unmanned automatic stations are being studied by lunar scientists. Samples date back further than any found on Earth as yet. The most famous, known as the Genesis Rock, is 4,100 million years old. The exploration of the moon at close range by means of spacecraft was made possible only by parallel developments in several branches of technology—rocket propulsion, long-range radio and television transmission, electronic computer control.

Moorhen, a widely distributed bird of the rail family, a common resident in the British Isles.

The adult is blackish with white under tail-coverts, a white line on the flanks and a yellow-tipped bill. The frontal shield and the base of the bill are vermilion. It bobs its head, flirts its tail and dives well. The nest is usually placed close to the water's edge or on an overhanging branch. In feeding the young the parents are sometimes helped by their offspring of a previous brood of the season. In N. America the bird is known as the Florida Gallinule.

Moors, the name given to the Moslems who live in N.W. Africa and to those who once lived in Spain. In 711 Moorish Arabs invaded Spain and spread beyond the Pyrenees into France, where they were driven back by the end of the century. Spain, however, remained virtually under Moorish domination until the 11th cent., and during that period was the most civilised and prosperous part of Western Europe. In the arts and sciences the impact of Moorish culture was profound and lasting. Examples of the brilliant splendour of Moorish architecture are still to be seen in Toledo, Córdoba, Seville and Granada. During the long struggle for the Christian reconquest thousands were killed and expelled, and in 1492 Granada, their last remaining kingdom, was forced to surrender. They were virtually exterminated by the Inquisition, and the last were expelled in 1609.

Moose, the largest members of the deer family. The N. American Moose stands 1·6–2 m high, and has huge palmate antlers. There is another New World species, occurring in Alaska. The European species is known as the elk.

Morse Alphabet, a system of dots and dashes, intended to be used in combination with the indicator in telegraphy; but usually read by sound, the receiving operator writing down the words in the system as transmitted. This system of signals was invented by the American inventor and artist Samuel Finley Breese Morse (1791–1872) of Charlestown, Massachusetts.

Mosaic, art of arranging small pieces of coloured glass, marble, or other materials in such a fashion as to produce a decorative pattern. Some of the best examples of Byzantine mosaics are to be seen at Ravenna, Rome, Venice and Sicily.

Mosque, a Mohammedan church, the greatest being that of Santa Sophia at Istanbul, now converted into a museum of Byzantine art.

Mosquito, small two-winged flies with long legs and slender body. Their larvae are aquatic. The females of some species are blood-suckers, and thus come to transmit the blood parasites which cause malaria and yellow fever, for example. *See* DDT *and* Gammexane.

Mosses. With liverworts, mosses comprise an important group of relatively simple non-vascular land plants, the bryophytes (**F39**). In the main they are small plants, the largest between 30–70 cm high, having been recorded in the Southern Hemisphere. Mosses rarely occur singly, but usually form cushions or small colonies on moist soil, bark, wood, rock or walls. The genus *sphagnum* known as "peat" or "bog moss" is of commercial value in horticulture. In Lancashire and Cheshire lowland moors in which sphagnum is common are known as "mosses". Reindeer moss is a lichen and Spanish moss a seed plant.

Moths, of the insect order, *Lepidoptera*, differing from butterflies which have clubbed antennae, in having feathery, sometimes thin, pointed antennae, rarely clubbed. Most are nocturnal, and the pupae are usually brown and enclosed in a cocoon unlike those of the butterfly, which are usually naked. *See also* **Lepidoptera**.

Motion, Laws of. According to Newton: (1) A body continues in its state of rest or uniform motion in a straight line except in so far as it is compelled by external forces to change that state. (2) Rate of change of momentum is proportional to the applied force, and takes place in the direction in which the force acts. (3) To every action there is an equal and opposite reaction. These laws are the basis of almost all engineering and everyday mechanics. Corrections to them have been made by relativity and the quantum theory. *See* **F17, 19**.

Mule, a cross between a male ass and a horse mare; a hinny is a cross between an ass mare and a horse stallion. Also the name of the spinning machine invented by Crompton in 1779 which combined the principle of Hargreaves' spinning jenny with the machine invented by Arkwright.

Mullions, the vertical bars dividing the lights in a window, forming a highly decorative feature in the Tudor period of English Gothic architecture. The cross-beam or horizontal bar of wood or stone in a mullioned window is styled a transom. *See* Windows.

Munich Agreement. In September 1938 Mr. Neville Chamberlain and M. Daladier, British and French Premiers, reached agreement with Hitler at Munich for the dismemberment of Czechoslovakia, primarily for the benefit of Germany. Czechoslovakia itself was not consulted, nor Russia who with Britain and France had jointly pledged themselves to uphold the independence of Czechoslovakia. Hitler had been threatening that country for some time, but every concession had been met by further demands. After three visits to Germany, during which Hitler raised his demands, the British and French statesmen gave way. Mr. Chamberlain declared on return that he had secured " Peace in our Time ". The Agreement was the subject of much controversy. Hitler seized Czechoslovakia in March 1939.

Muscles. *See* F37(1).

Musk Deer, a small deer of the Himalayas, standing about 51 cm high. It is grey in colour, slightly brindled, and carries a small pouch in the abdominal region, containing what is commercially known as musk, an article which is of great value in the manufacture of various perfumes. The active constituent of musk, muscone, is now made synthetically. The species was becoming rare on account of its slaughter for its musk.

Mutton Bird, an Australian name of controversial origin for a shearwater or petrel, *e.g.*, the Short-tailed and Sooty Shearwaters and the Great-winged, Kermadec, and White-headed Petrels. The young are taken by hand from their burrows for human food.

Myrrh, a resinous substance obtained from a tree of the natural order *Amyridaceae*, growing plentifully in Ethiopia and Arabia. Its use for embalming, medical and aromatic purposes may be traced back to the most remote times.

Mysteries, Greek, secret mystic ceremonies of the ancient Greeks, religious drama accompanied by dancing, the most well known being the Eleusinian and Orphic ceremonies.

Mystery Plays were mediaeval religious dramas performed at great ecclesiastical festivals, particularly in France and Bavaria, staging the Nativity, Passion and Resurrection. *See* Section M, Part V.

N

Nadir, one of the two poles of the horizon, the other being the zenith. The nadir is the pole vertically below the observer's feet.

Nahum, one of the books of the Minor Prophets of the Old Testament. It is a prophecy of doom on the approaching sack of Nineveh which fell in 612 B.C. to the Medes and Babylonians.

Nantes, Edict of, was a decree promulgated by Henry IV of France in 1598, giving full freedom of worship to the Protestants of the country. It was the revocation of this edict in 1685 by Louis XIV that drove hundreds of thousands of French Huguenots to this country.

Naphtha, a liquid combustible believed to have been one of the ingredients of " Greek fire ". Naphtha is a light, highly inflammable oil obtained by distilling petroleum, shale oil, or coal tar. The petroleum naphtha consists of a mixture of paraffins; that from shale contains olefines as well as paraffins. Coal-tar naphtha contains xylol.

Naphthalene is an aromatic hydrocarbon; it is obtained from coal tar, and its derivatives are much used in the manufacture of colours for dyers and printers. " Moth balls " are made of naphthalene.

Narcotic, a medical dictionary definition is that a narcotic is a drug that produces stupor, complete insanity or sleep. In terms of drug addiction, a narcotic has been defined as altering and distorting the user's perception of himself and of the external world, being taken primarily for that purpose. *See* P22–24.

Nardus, a genus of coarse grasses, growing on bleak upland heaths and hill slopes. *Nardus stricta*, known as " mat-weed ", is a British species.

Narghile, an oriental tobacco pipe so constructed that smoke passes through water and up a long flexible tube before reaching lips of the smoker.

Narrative Art, a type of art popular during the late 19th cent. based on the principle: " every picture tells a story "—*e.g.*, such paintings as the little Royalist boy surrounded by his anxious family and confronted across a table by the Roundheads bearing the title: " When did you last see your father? " The term, although often applied derisively, suitably describes many works of considerable artistic merit: *e.g.*, Hogarth's *Marriage à la Mode*, his series of eight engravings entitled *A Rake's Progress*, the Bayeux Tapestry, and many Babylonian and Egyptian friezes.

Naseby, Battle of, was fought on 14 June 1645, between the Royalists under the command of Prince Rupert and the King, and the Parliamentarians under Fairfax and Cromwell. It resulted in a complete defeat for Charles.

National Anthem, a musical composition with words, officially adopted for ceremonial use as an expression of patriotism and loyalty to a national cause. The national anthem of the United Kingdom, " God save the King (Queen) ", probably dates from late-17th cent. to mid-18th cent. It was sung in 1745, the year of the landing of the Young Pretender. It had no one composer and was probably a recasting of folk-tunes and plainsong. Resemblances can be traced in pieces by Purcell and John Bull.

National Assembly, the name taken by the body responsible for the opening stages of the French Revolution and subsequently by other sovereign bodies in France and elsewhere.

National Covenant, an oath and declaration subscribed to by the Scottish Presbyterians in 1638 to maintain their religion against Charles I's episcopalianising designs.

National Gallery, established in 1824 at Pall Mall, London, with the Angerstein Collection of 38 pictures, purchased for £60,000, as a nucleus. The existing building which was opened in 1838 has been enlarged several times. The National Gallery at Millbank, the Tate Gallery, was given to the nation by Sir Henry Tate in 1897.

Nationalisation is the taking over by the State of the ownership and operation of an industry or service—*e.g.*, coal-mining, railway, transport, gas and electricity. Where this is done without revolution, compensation is usually paid to the previous owners at what is regarded as a fair market price; the compensation is sometimes paid in cash, but more often in fixed-interest-bearing bonds issued either by the State or by the administration of the nationalised service, which is usually a publicly appointed Board or Corporation acting, with greater or lesser autonomy, under the direction of a Minister responsible to Parliament. In some cases the State becomes a partner with private investors in the ownership of a particular enterprise, *e.g.*, oil companies, such as the former Anglo-Iranian and some recent French examples. Nationalisation is usually brought about by a separate Act of Parliament relating to each industry or service taken over. These Acts, in Great Britain, include provision for joint consultation at all levels between the administering boards and the workers employed and their Trade Unions. When, as in the Soviet Union, nationalisation occurs as an outcome of social revolution no compensation is paid to the dispossessed owners.

National Parks. Under the National Parks Act 1949 a National Parks Commission was set up to create National Parks in England and Wales. Ten have been established: Peak District, Lake District, Snowdonia, Yorkshire Dales, Exmoor, Brecon Beacons, Dartmoor, Pembrokeshire Coast, North York Moors and Northumberland. They cover an area of some 13,618 km², or 9 per cent of the total area of England and Wales. It is not intended to change the character of these territories but to control their development so as to harmonise with the two dominant principles: (a) that the characteristic beauty of the landscape within the Park area shall be preserved and (b) that the visiting public shall have ample access and facilities for recreation and enjoyment. The establishment of a new national park has been proposed for mid-Wales. The Commission also has power to designate areas in England and Wales outside the national parks as " areas of outstanding natural beauty ". Thirty-three areas had been designated by 1977: Gower, Quantock Hills, Lleyn, Surrey Hills, Dorset, Northumberland Coast, Cannock Chase, Shropshire Hills, Malvern Hills, Cornwall, N. Devon, S. Devon, E. Devon, E. Hampshire, Isle of Wight, Forest of Bowland, Chichester Harbour, Solway Coast, Chilterns, Sussex Downs, Cotswolds, Anglesey, South Hampshire Coast, Kent Downs, Norfolk Coast, Dedham Vale, Suffolk Coast and Heaths, Wye Valley, Arnside and Silverdale, Lincolnshire Wolds, Mendip Hills, North Wessex Downs, Isles of Scilly. Under the Countryside Act, 1968, the National Parks Commission has been reconstituted as the Countryside Commission. *See also* Long Distance Routes.

National Physical Laboratory, situated at Teddington, is one of the world's largest and best-equipped laboratories. It conducts research in its three main groups: Measurement, Materials and Engineering Sciences, and maintains British primary standards and physical units. First established in 1900 and managed by the Royal Society, it is now one of the industrial research establishments under the control of the Dept. of Industry.

National Portrait Gallery, established in 1856, and now located in a building in St. Martin's Lane adjoining the National Gallery. Contains portraits of eminent people in British history and a valuable collection of medals and autographs.

National Trust, founded in 1895. " A non-profit-making organisation incorporated by Act of Parliament for the purposes of promoting the permanent preservation of lands and buildings of historic interest or natural beauty for the benefit and access of the people." As a consequence of gifts of public-spirited individuals the Trust now owns many hectares of magnificent scenery and property, including mediaeval castles, bird sanctuaries, ancient monuments, birthplaces and homes of famous men, and classic examples of domestic architecture, preserved for the enjoyment of present and future generations. Since 1946 lands and houses of interest to the nation may be given to the National Trust in lieu of death duties.

Nativity. There are three nativity festivals of the Christian Church: Christmas, 25 December, festival of birth of Christ; the birthday of the Virgin Mary (8 September); and of St. John the Baptist (24 June).

Natterjack, a curious warty, prominent-eyed, brown toad (*Bufo calamita*), having a bright yellow line down the middle of its back. It utters a muttering sort of croak, hence its name.

Natural Law. *See* Section J.

Naturalism in painting has been defined as " a direct and spontaneous approach to nature " —to landscape primarily. Constable, Turner and Boudin were among the great naturalist painters of the 19th cent. *See* Section I for naturalism in drama.

Natural Numbers, the counting numbers 1, 2, 3, 4, 5, . . .

" **Nautical Almanac** ", published under the authority of the Admiralty, is always issued four years in advance, and contains information specially prepared for the use of navigators and astronomers. It first appeared in 1767.

Nautilus, a term now applied only to the pearly-shelled nautilus, the sole surviving example of the four-gilled section of the *Cephalopoda*. Its fossil relatives are called Ammonites. The spiral shell is divided into a number of compartments, the animal living in the last and largest chamber. There are three or four species, all living in tropical seas. The Paper Nautilus is not related to the Pearly Nautilus, belonging to the same order as the octopus.

Nave is the body or main open portion of a cathedral or church, and extends from the chief entrance to the choir, or chancel, and is usually flanked by aisles. A nave, in mechanics, indicates the " hub " or central part of a wheel.

Nazism. *See* Section J.

Neanderthal, the name of the valley lying between Düsseldorf and Wuppertal, where in a limestone cave a now famous skull of a very early species of prehistoric man was discovered in 1856. Fossils of Neanderthal man have been found over a wide area, and from archaeological evidence he began to disappear from Europe during the last Ice Age, about 40,000 B.C.

Necromancy, " the black art ", was in olden times much believed in, and supposed to be an occult power by which its practitioners could converse with the spirits of the dead and learn the future.

Nekton, term used to differentiate actively swimming aquatic organisms (*e.g.*, fishes) from the " drifters " or plankton.

Nelson Column, in Trafalgar Square, London, designed by Mr. William Railton, was chosen from among a number of designs—temples, obelisks and various sculptural groups—sent in as a result of a competition held in 1839. The erection of the column was begun in 1840. Twenty-six years later the lions designed by Landseer were set up at the foot of the completed column. The statue of Nelson himself was made by E. H. Bailey and the bronze reliefs at the base executed by Carew, Woodington, Ternouth and Watson, representing the Battles of the Nile, St. Vincent, Copenhagen and Trafalgar. Height 52 m, executed in Portland stone instead of granite, as originally planned, at a cost of £46,000.

Néné or Hawaiian Goose. At the Severn Wildfowl Trust at Slimbridge Sir Peter Scott saved this bird from extinction.

Neo-Classical Style, term applied to the revival of classical logic and order after the extravagances of Rococo (*q.v.*), beginning in France in the mid-18th cent. and finding expression in architecture and the decorative arts. The style retains some of the daintiness of Rococo, furniture is on a small scale, often gilt, and silks and porcelain favour pastel shades. Straight lines take the place of the wild curvatures of Rococo and classical details like festoons and urn forms are used in many contexts and materials. Its English version is closely associated with the name of the architect Robert Adam whose light and graceful adaptations of Greek and Roman forms were introduced into English country houses. In France the style is sometimes called *Style Louis XVI,* though its dates, *c.* 1750–*c.* 1790, do not exactly coincide with the reign of that monarch. Eventually the Neo-Classical style merges into Empire (*q.v.*).

Neodymium, an element belonging to the rare earth metal group. Discovered by Welsbach in 1885.

Neo-Impressionism, a development of Impressionism (*q.v.*) by Seurat and Signac during the 1880s who devised the method of painting known as *pointillism* (the application of pure colours in minute touches to form a composite whole, based on a knowledge of the laws of colour and optics). One of the best-known examples of this technique is Seurat's *Sunday Afternoon on the Grand Jatte.*

Neon, inert gas present in air to the extent of about 1 part in 65,000. The crimson glow produced when an electric discharge passes through the gas is familiar in advertising signs.

Neoprene, generic name for a class of synthetic rubbers made from acetylene.

Nepotism, the bestowal of patronage by reason of relationship rather than of merit. It had its origin in the custom of certain Popes to enrich their families out of the offices of the Church.

Neptune. Apart from Pluto this is the most distant of the planets, estimated to be about $4,497 \times 10^6$ km from the sun, and taking about 165 years to revolve around it. Discovered by the German astronomer Galle on 23 September 1846, after its existence had been predicted by Leverrier and Adams. *See* F8.

Neptunium, element 93, one of the four new elements discovered during the progress of the atomic bomb project in the second world war

Neptunium is formed when a neutron enters a nucleus of Uranium 238, and it decays radioactively to yield plutonium.

Neutrino, a neutral particle which carries energy and spin and although possessing little or no mass plays an important part in the interaction of other fundamental particles. The discovery that there are in fact two distinct neutrinos, each with its counterpart, was discovered in 1962 as a result of an experiment made with the 30,000 million-electronvolt proton accelerator at Brookhaven. *See* F16.

Neutron, a neutral particle present in all atomic nuclei except the hydrogen nucleus which is a single proton. In the development of nuclear science and technology the neutron has played a most important role and neutrons produce the radioisotopes now widely used in medicine, agriculture and industry. Neutrons and protons are termed nucleous. *See* F11(2), 16.

Neutron Bomb, a thermonuclear fusion weapon which produces increased lethal radiation while the destructive blast and fallout are significantly less than for a fission weapon of equivalent yield: it kills organic life while sparing property, except within a small radius. In 1978 President Carter reserved his final decision on the production of this controversial weapon. *See also* F13(2) and United States, Section C, Part II.

New Deal. The measures taken by President Roosevelt in USA in 1933 to overcome the great economic crisis which broke out at the end of 1929 and to restore the social security threatened by it. The measures were drawn up by a group of experts called a Brains Trust and they provided for recovery by a programme of public works, including large-scale construction of houses and large-scale assistance to farmers. Loans were granted and authorities formed to stimulate activities which reduced the workless from 17 millions to between 7 and 10 millions. Unemployment relief was regulated and enlarged; and social insurance (which for decades had been a subject of dispute, being held to be contrary to American principles of self-help) was introduced. Many of the changes have become a permanent part of American legislation though some laws were repealed by the US Supreme Court as being unconstitutional.

Newgate Prison was situated at the western end of Newgate Street, opposite the Old Bailey, at the site of one of the old London city gates. There is a record of a prison upon this spot in the 13th cent. Later a new one was built by the executors of Richard Whittington, but this was destroyed by the Great Fire in 1666. Still another new prison on this site was erected between 1778 and 1780. In the Gordon Riots of the latter year it was destroyed by fire and re-erected. It was not used as a prison after 1880 and was demolished in 1902–3.

Newspapers. The first news-books to be published at regular intervals in Britain appeared in 1662 with news of what was going on abroad translated from German and Italian news-sheets. Licence to print was obtained from the Star Chamber, which until its abolition in 1641 allowed only the printing of foreign news. With the lifting of the ban on domestic news the Press became free. In the reign of Queen Anne English newspapers employed writers of great intellectual power and versatility. Despite the newspaper tax introduced in 1712, the number of newspapers published in London in 1776 had increased to 53, though the standard of writing was below that of earlier times. The development of the Press was greatly assisted in the 19th cent. by the abolition of the "taxes on knowledge", by the introduction of the cheap postal system and by improvements in printing, distribution, collection of news and advertising. The *London Gazette*, founded in 1665 (and still appearing twice weekly as the official organ of the Government), is the oldest newspaper living. *The Times*, known throughout the world, began as the *Daily Universal Register* in 1785, and adopted its present title in 1788. The *Manchester Guardian* (renamed *Guardian* in 1959), once a provincial but now a national newspaper with a world-wide reputation, began as a weekly in 1821, and became a daily in 1855. The *Scotsman*, founded as a weekly in 1817 and

established as a daily in 1855, and the *Glasgow Herald*, which began as the *Glasgow Advertiser* in 1783, are the leading Scottish newspapers. The London Press, which is national, publishes 10 daily, 2 evening and 7 Sunday newspapers.

Newt, amphibians of lizard shape and mottled markings. There are three British species, the largest being the Great-Crested Newt (*Triturus cristatus*), which attains a length of 15 cm.

Newton, the unit of force in the SI system of units. Under its influence a body with a mass of 1 kilogramme will accelerate at a rate of 1 metre per second each second.

Newton's Rings. Concentric circular rings, due to the phenomenon of interference, which are seen around the point of contact of a slightly convex lens with a flat plate of glass.

New Towns. Under the New Town Act 1946 and subsequent Acts 33 new towns have now been designated in Britain; 23 are in England and Wales, six in Scotland and four in Northern Ireland. They are: Basildon, Bracknell, Crawley, Harlow, Hatfield, Hemel Hempstead, Milton Keynes, Northampton, Peterborough, Stevenage and Welwyn (to relieve housing problems in the Greater London area); Aycliffe, Corby, Cwmbran, Peterlee and Washington (to serve the special needs of their areas); Newtown (to help stem rural depopulation in mid-Wales); Runcorn and Skelmersdale (to meet the over-spill needs of Liverpool and north Merseyside); Telford and Redditch (to take population from Birmingham); Warrington (expanded to take people from Liverpool and Manchester); Central Lancashire New Town (new regional city based on existing towns of Preston, Leyland and Chorley). The six Scottish new towns are Cumbernauld, East Kilbride, Glenrothes, Irvine and Livingston. In Northern Ireland Craigavon is being developed as a new city; Antrim and Ballymena are becoming centres of economic growth; Londonderry and the surrounding district have been designated as an area of special development. The population of the new towns in Great Britain is about 1·7 million. The expansion of large existing towns like Northampton, Peterborough and Warrington means that they are becoming regional centres. A major reversal in Government policy was announced in 1976: development resources in future to be directed towards inner-city areas to halt decline and to slow the growth of new and expanding towns.

New Year's Day, 1 January. The first New Year's festival of which we have record is that constituted by Numa 713 B.C., and dedicated to Janus.

Nibelungenlied, the German epic of the early 13th cent. comprising numerous mythical poems or sagas. Wagner's *The Ring of the Nibelungs* was based on Norse legends and the Nibelungenlied.

Nicene Creed, a summary of the principles of Christian faith, first issued in 325 by the Council of Nicaea (summoned by the emperor Constantine the Great) for the purpose of thwarting the Arian heresy and asserting the godhead of Christ. Date of Easter fixed at Council of Nicaea.

Nickel, silver-coloured metal, symbol Ni, fairly soft though harder than iron. Chief source of the metal is the nickel sulphide in iron–copper pyrites deposits in Ontario. Chief uses are: in electroplating, in coins, as an element in alloy steels. A novel method of making pure nickel (by treating the metal with carbon monoxide and heating the resulting liquid, nickel carbonyl) was developed in 1890 by Mond. This discovery led to many technical advances in industrial chemistry, one of which is the production of catalysts for a variety of processes.

Night Heron, a stocky, short-legged heron of black and white plumage, red eyes and yellowish legs, crepuscular except in breeding season, and an occasional visitor to Britain.

Nightingale, a familiar singing bird which visits the southern counties of England every summer, and is sometimes found as far north as Yorkshire. It is a shy, brown bird, not often seen, but the song of the male, usually heard in the late evening or at early morn, is of remarkable sweetness and variety. After its wooing period is over its song ceases.

Nightjar, nocturnal, insectivorous bird, owl-like in appearance, with mottled brown plumage of "dead leaf" pattern, and a churring song. It is a common breeding visitor to the British Isles, April to September, and lays its eggs on bare ground.

Niobium is a metal element, symbol Nb, related to vanadium. Technical development has been slow because of its rare occurrence, although niobium is now used in ferrous alloys to increase resistance to corrosion and produce steel which can be used at high temperatures.

Nitre or **Saltpetre**, is now mostly manufactured by the double decomposition of sodium nitrate and potassium chloride. Its chief use is the manufacture of gunpowder and fireworks. It has been manufactured in England since 1625.

Nitrogen, a non-combustible gaseous element, symbol N, devoid of taste or smell, and constituting nearly four-fifths of the atmospheric air. Nitrogen compounds are essential to plants and animals, and are used in fertilisers.

Nitro-Glycerine, an explosive yellow fluid produced by mixing small quantities of glycerine with a combination of one part of nitric acid and two parts of sulphuric acid. By itself it is a dangerously explosive substance to handle. In 1867, Nobel produced dynamite, a safe explosive made by absorbing nitro-glycerine in kieselguhr.

Nitrous Oxide, a compound of nitrogen and oxygen possessing mild anaesthetic power. Termed "laughing gas" on account of its exhilarating effect. It is still used in dentistry, and for minor operations and has proved useful in a new technique for finding leaks in water mains.

Nobel Prizes. The Nobel Foundation was established at the beginning of the century to give effect to the wishes expressed by Alfred Nobel in his Will. By the terms of the Will the judges are the Swedish Academy of Science, the Caroline Medico-Surgical Institute, the Swedish Academy and five members of the Norwegian Storting. The award of a Nobel Prize is accepted as the highest form of international recognition in the field in which it is given: physics, chemistry, medicine, literature, peace and, since 1969, economics. *See* end of Section.

Nones were dates of the Roman calendar which fell on the 5th of each month, excepting March, May, July and October, when they fell on the 7th.

Norman Architecture is English Romanesque (*q.v.*), which flourished from the time of the Norman Conquest and was gradually superseded through a transition period (*c.* 1175–1200) by the introduction of the pointed arch characteristic of the Early English (first Gothic style). Typical of Norman churches are the round arches, thick walls, massive cylindrical columns, with throughout the basic pattern of the square and the circle. Some churches (*e.g.*, the Temple church in London or the chapel at Ludlow Castle) are wholly circular. Roofs in the early days were flat and towers, usually placed at the "crossing", were square but occasionally round: the spires of all these towers have perished, but it seems likely that they were squat and pyramidal.

North-East Passage, from the North Atlantic to Bering Strait has been rapidly developed by the USSR in recent years as a northern sea route to render accessible vast areas of northern Siberia. Attempts to find a north-east passage were made by Englishmen and Dutchmen in the 16th cent. but they were always defeated by the ice, for the sea is completely frozen for some 4,800 km for 9 months of the year. A Swede succeeded in sailing from Europe to Japan via the Arctic in the late 19th cent. *See also* Arctic Exploration.

North-West Passage, from the Atlantic to the Pacific through the Arctic Seas, has been the dream of navigators for centuries. Attempts to find it were made in the 16th and early 17th cent. by John and Sebastian Cabot, Frobisher, Gilbert, Davis, Hudson and Baffin. Two centuries later Ross, Parry, Franklin and others made the attempt; but it was not until 1903–5 that Amundsen, discoverer of the South Pole, made the complete voyage in the *Gjoa*. The Canadian icebreaker *Labrador* was the first deep-draft vessel to traverse the North-West Passage (1954) and the US tanker *Manhattan* was the first commercial vessel to do so (1969).

Notre Dame, the famous Paris cathedral, was founded in 1163, and is one of the finest specimens of Gothic architecture in Europe. The best descriptions of the buildings are to be found in Victor Hugo's *Hunchback of Notre Dame*.

November, the 9th month of the year originally, but from *c.* 700 B.C., when Numa added January and February, it became the 11th month.

Nuclear Energy. Atomic nuclei consist of protons and neutrons joined in various proportions (**F11**). The heaviest naturally occurring nucleus contains 238 particles (92 protons, 146 neutrons) and is uranium 238 (U^{238}); the lightest is hydrogen, which consists of 1 proton. Neutrons and protons attract one another by very strong forces which are not at all well understood: they are called *nuclear forces*. Consequently it requires energy to be supplied if a nucleus is to be pulled apart into its constituent particles. The energy is required to overcome the attractions of the nuclear forces. Conversely, when the particles rush together to form a nucleus energy is released in the form of heat or radiation. The energy released when protons and neutrons coalesce to form a nucleus is called *Binding Energy*. The binding energy of a nucleus divided by the number of particles involved is called the binding energy per particle, which we will call B. It is very difficult to overestimate the importance of B to the human race. B varies from nucleus to nucleus, and the exact form of its variation is only roughly understood at the present time. But the most significant thing is that B is greatest for elements of medium atomic weight and lowest at the heavy (uranium) and light (hydrogen) ends of the periodic table. This means that if middleweight nuclei can be formed either from heavy ones or from light ones, B increases and *energy is released in either case.*

Nuclear Fission. *See* **F13**(1).

Nuclear Fusion. If light nuclei are hurled at high speeds into intimate contact they sometimes coalesce and release binding energy (*see* Nuclear Energy). This has been studied in laboratories where powerful and energy-consuming machines accelerate small numbers of particles for purely experimental purposes. If useful amounts of energy are to be gained these fusion reactions will have to occur on a bigger scale in an apparatus from which the resulting heat can be extracted in a controlled way. The one "useful" fusion device so far made is the thermonuclear bomb ("H-bomb"). Thermonuclear is the important word. If a suitable gas can be raised to a very high temperature the nuclei are stripped of their electrons and all particles move with very high speeds. The gas is then called a plasma. High enough temperatures will make speeds great enough for fusion reactions to occur and nuclear energy to be released. This is a thermonuclear reaction. For example, in deuterium gas, at temperatures over a million degrees Centigrade, the deuterium nuclei (*i.e.*, heavy hydrogen nuclei consisting of 1 proton joined to 1 neutron) interact to produce helium nuclei. To obtain a net gain in energy from this process, the temperature must be raised to about 300 million degrees C and maintained long enough; otherwise the energy released is less than that required to heat the fuel and to make up for heat losses. Many attempts to study the staggering technical problems are being made, and fusion research is very active in Britain, the USA and the Soviet Union. The joint European Torus (JET) fusion research project is sited at Culham near Oxford and aims to develop a new source of energy for the generation of electricity for the 21st cent.

Nuclear Power Stations. Britain generates about 11 per cent of her electricity for public supply in nuclear power stations. There are 11 nuclear power stations which produce electricity for the national grid controlled by the electricity authorities and five controlled by the Atomic Energy Authority or British Nuclear Fuels Ltd. Nine of the 11 nuclear power stations operated by the electricity authorities are at Berkeley, Gloucs. (1962), Bradwell, Essex (1962), Hunterston "A", Scotland (1964), Hinkley Point "A", Somerset (1965), Trawsfynydd, Wales (1966), Dungeness "A", Kent (1966), Sizewell, Suffolk (1966), Oldbury, Avon (1968),

Wylfa, Anglesey (1970). They have all been developed from the classic Calder Hall type, burning natural uranium inserted in a graphite moderator and cooled by carbon dioxide gas. They are called Magnox stations because the fuel elements of natural uranium rods are encased in magnesium alloy cans. A second nuclear power programme is based on the advanced gas cooled reactor (AGR) at Windscale, and include the reactors now under construction at Dungeness " B ", Hinkley Point " B ". Hunterston " B ", Hartlepool (Cleveland) and Heysham (Lancashire). For the third stage of the nuclear power programme the AGR has been chosen with an option open for the pressurised water reactor (PLR) in case it is needed later in the 1980s. One of the AGRs will be built at Torness in Lothian.

Nuclear Reactors are pieces of apparatus designed to permit nuclear chain reactions to occur under controlled conditions. (Uncontrolled chain reactions are dangerous, e.g. atomic bombs.) The success of a reactor depends on the neutrons reaching the U^{235} nuclei to produce more fissions and not being wasted in irrelevant processes or simply escaping through the wall of the apparatus (neutrons are quite difficult to contain). The neutrons leaving the scene of fission are rapidly moving, and they stand more chance of causing another fission if they are slowed down. Consequently a material other than the uranium has to be present to facilitate this, and it is called a moderator. A useful moderator is pure graphite. Thus a reactor may consist of alternate blocks of uranium and graphite. If the reactor is too small so many neutrons escape that there are not enough to keep the chain reaction going. The reactor must therefore be greater than a certain *critical size.* In order to intensify or damp down the chain reaction, g is arranged for pieces of neutron-absorbinit material, such as cadmium, to be inserted or withdrawn as required. While the chain reaction is proceeding countless numbers of fissions are occurring, each one liberating energy which turns into heat. The temperature therefore increases, and to prevent a catastrophic rise, cooling has to be provided. The reactor therefore has cooling pipes through which a fluid coolant is pumped. The coolant carries the heat away and, in a reactor designed to produce electrical power, the heat is taken to steam-raising boilers and the high-pressure steam is led to turbines which drive the electric generators. What has been briefly described is the type of reactor first used for serious power production at Calder Hall (1956). This is a graphite-moderated, gas-cooled reactor using as fuel natural uranium (*i.e.,* fissile U^{235} greatly diluted with U^{238}). Other thermal types of nuclear reactor are the advanced gas-cooled reactor (AGR), the high temperature reactor (HTR), the steam-generating heavy-water (SGHWR) and the light-water reactor (LWR). It is also possible to make reactors work without slowing the neutrons with a moderator: these are called *fast reactors.* The design of the prototype fast reactor (PFR) at Dounreay is based on experience gained with the Dounreay experimental fast breeder reactor (closed 1977 after 17 years' safe operation) which was the first to produce electricity on a commercial scale (1962) and achieved the highest power output of any of its type in the world. These fast reactors can produce new nuclear fuel in the course of their operation and therefore offer great economies; but they are more difficult to develop than thermal reactors. The fuel is made from the mixed oxides of plutonium and uranium and the coolant is liquid sodium metal. The Government has still to make a crucial decision whether and when to go ahead with a commercial fast breeder reactor.

Environmental considerations are likely to be increasingly topical. Most of the products of the fission process are of necessity radioactive isotopes: they could be gaseous, like krypton, xenon and tritium or solid like strontium, caesium, zirconium and ruthenium. There are also present the new radioactive elements plutonium, curium, actinium, etc. Further, in both the nuclear reactor and in the plant which is used to chemically treat and reprocess the

nuclear fuel, radioactivity will be induced in associated structural materials, to varying degrees. In this latter case, unlike the former, the radioactive waste with which one is left can to a great extent be selected and is largely overshadowed in importance by the wastes arising from the fission and breeding processes. Even if the whole of the UK electrical power was produced by nuclear means, the volumes of such wastes would be relatively small and need in principle tens of acres of storage area. Much of the activity would decay in a decade, a great deal more in a century, but that associated with the elements bred from uranium, would be present for thousands of years: Pu^{239} has a half-life of 25,000 years. Segregation of the various types of activity is feasible; their incorporation into physically and chemically stable form has received a great deal of study so that storage, readily monitored even for many generations, seems entirely possible. The radioactive properties of these wastes can only be changed by nuclear reactions. Bombardment with neutrons or other highly energetic particles can bring about such reactions so that forms of " nuclear incineration " are feasible but are not yet fully explored.

Nucleic Acids. Living matter is built up of cells each of which has a nucleus surrounded by cytoplasm. Cell nuclei are composed chiefly of substances called nucleoproteins, which consist of a protein attached to a nucleic acid (this original name is still used, although nucleic acids are found in the cytoplasm as well as the nucleus). Nucleic acids are complex organic structures made up of chains of compounds called nucleotides (**F32(2)**). Nucleotide molecules have a sugar group attached to a nitrogenous base and a phosphate group. Only two sugar groups are found in the nucleotides, ribose, giving rise to ribonucleic acids (R.N.A.s, found mainly in the cytoplasm) and deoxyribose, which forms deoxyribonucleic acids (D.N.A.s, found mainly in cell nuclei). Seven different nitrogenous bases have been isolated, so that a number of different nucleotides are possible. A repeating, regular pattern of nucleotides is linked by the phosphate groups, forming nucleic acids. The functions of nucleic acids are of fundamental importance. They are concerned in the process of transmission of inherited qualities in reproduction and in building up body proteins. *See* **F34.**

Nuremberg Trial. On 21 November 1945, an International Military Tribunal, consisting of one American, one British, one Russian and one French member, began the trial of twenty-four Nazi leaders. There were four counts: the conspiracy of Nazism; wars of aggression; war crimes; and crimes against humanity. Twelve were condemned to hanging of whom ten were hanged on 16 October 1946. Goering committed suicide; Bormann is now presumed dead; Papen, Schacht and Fritsche were acquitted. The rest received varying terms of imprisonment.

Nuthatch, name of a number of tree-creeping birds, plump, with short tail, bluish-grey plumage and black stripe under eye. Nest in holes and wedge nuts in bark of trees, hammering them to get a kernel. There are three European species, one, *Sitta europaea,* resident in England.

Nylon, a generic term for any long-chain synthetic polymeric amide which has recurring amide groups as an integral part of the main polymer chain, and which is capable of being formed into a filament in which the structural elements are orientated in the direction of the axis. The first nylon of commercial interest was made in 1935, and the world's first nylon factory—in the United States—began production in 1940.

O

Oak, a tree of the genus *Quercus,* including some 300 species distributed over the northern hemisphere and into the tropics. Two species are native to Britain, where the oak is the commonest tree (1 in 3)—*Q. petraea,* more common in the west and north on shallower, lighter soils, and *Q. robur*, more common in the south on deeper, heavier soils. Oak timber is much prized for its strength and durability, and from the time of the Spanish Armada to Nelson's day was in great demand for naval construction. It has always been used for building, flooring, furniture and cabinet work. The oak is attacked by many insects, the round nut-like oak galls, or oak-apples, being produced by the sting of certain minute gall wasps.

"Oaks," a famous race for three-year-old fillies run at Epsom two days after the "Derby".

Obelisk, a tapering monolithic column, square at the base and pyramidal at the top, regarded by the ancient Egyptians as a sacred stone and usually found at the entrance to the sun temples. Many were transported from Egypt and set up at various times: there is one in the Place de la Concorde in Paris, and one on the Thames Embankment in London—Cleopatra's Needle—originally erected at Heliopolis, centre of the sun-cult, by Tuthmosis III *c.* 1500 B.C.

Observatories. *See Astronomy and Telescopes.*

Occam's Razor. *See Section J, Q8(1).*

Ocean, comprises the great body of water which covers seven-tenths of the surface of the earth, and has an average depth of 3·2 km. The principal oceans are the Pacific, Atlantic, Indian and Arctic. The greatest ocean depth is in the Pacific, in the Mindanao Deep, 37,782 ft (11,524 m). *See* F9(2) *and* Oceanography.

Ocean Currents are well-defined streams running over certain portions of the ocean and caused mainly by wind-friction, slope of the sea surface and differences in density of the water, all movements being influenced by the deflective forces due to the earth's rotation. The climatic importance of the great ocean currents is that they constitute one of the means whereby heat is transferred from lower to higher latitudes.

Oceanography is the scientific study of the world ocean, *i.e.*, the single connected body of water that covers 70·8 per cent of the earth's surface. Modern oceanography dates from the voyage of *HMS Challenger* (1872–6) during which wide-ranging observations of the ocean were made, for the first time going well beyond what was directly required to assist shipping. Since then oceanography has matured into a highly technical and interdisciplinary science which may be roughly divided into: biological oceanography (the study of marine organisms and marine ecology); chemical oceanography (concerned with the composition of sea-water); physical oceanography (the study of ocean currents, tides and waves and the role played by the oceans in climate and weather); and geological oceanography (concerned with the formation, composition and evolution of the ocean basins). Oceanographic knowledge is essential to allow exploitation of the enormous food, mineral and energy resources of the ocean with the minimum damage to the ocean environment. However, close international co-operation (through such bodies as the Law of the Sea Conference) will also be necessary in order to avoid such hazards as overfishing and marine pollution. By 1980 it is estimated that one third of the world's oil and gas will come from offshore wells and recently vast deposits of metal-rich nodules have been located on the ocean floor. As important future sources of energy, both tidal and wave power have the attractions of being non-polluting and renewable.

Ocelot, the most common wild cat of S. America. It is about 1·2 m in length, including tail, and of a grey or tawny colour and spotted. Closely related to the Leopard cats.

Octane Number, the index of the knock-rating of petrol. It is based on the arbitrary scale in which iso-octane (which does not cause "knocking") has a value of 100, and normal heptane (which is prone to "knocking") has a value of 0. A good fuel for modern cars must have an octane number greater than 80.

Octarch, the kings of the English heptarchy, Hengist (455) being the first, and Egbert (800) the last.

October, the 10th month, but the 8th in the old Roman calendar. It was held sacred to Mars.

Octopus, a genus of marine molluscs with eight tentacles that bear suckers.

Odyssey, Homer's epic setting forth the incidents of the wanderings of Odysseus on his way back to Ithaca after the Siege of Troy.

Oersted, a unit of magnetic-field intensity in the c.g.s. system.

Offa's Dyke, largest remaining earthwork in Britain, supposed to have been built by Offa (A.D. 757–96) as a defensive boundary line between the English settlers and the dispossessed Welsh of Gwynedd, Powys and Gwent. *See also* Long Distance Routes.

Ohm's Law, propounded by G. S. Ohm in 1826, is expressed in the equation: electromotive force (in volts) = current (in amperes) × resistance (in ohms). The ohm is the unit of electrical resistance in the metre-kilogram-second system.

Oil. The great expansion in energy demand over recent years has been met to a large extent by petroleum oil. This contains a wide range of hydrocarbon molecules of varying complexity. The various components are separated from each other by making use of their different boiling points. Crude oil is heated in the base of a fractionating tower; the various components condense at different temperatures in trays at different levels of the tower. The fraction of a given composition can be increased by "cracking" or breaking down the heavier hydrocarbons into lighter ones. The total world reserves of petroleum oil are still uncertain since large parts of the world are still not fully prospected. The cutback and the rise in the price of Middle Eastern oil following the 1973 Arab-Israeli war unleashed a worldwide energy crisis which affected the economies of consumer countries. The United Kingdom can look forward to producing all her oil needs by 1980 from North Sea wells.

Okapi, nocturnal ruminant mammal, smaller than the giraffe, chestnut brown in colour with zebra-striped legs, native to the African Congo.

Olbers' Comet was discovered in 1815 by Olbers the German astronomer. Olbers also discovered the asteroids Pallas and Vesta (1802–07).

Old Red Sandstone, the continental rocks formed during the Devonian. *See* F48.

Olefines, a series of hydrocarbons, in which the hydrogen atoms are double the number of carbon. The first member of the series is ethylene.

Oléron Laws or Judgments, were a code of maritime laws, introduced into England in the reign of Richard I in the 12th cent. Oléron is an island off the west coast of France, opposite the mouth of the Charente.

Olive. This small tree, whose fruit yields olive oil, is a native of the eastern Mediterranean countries, but has been introduced into cultivation elsewhere. The green unripe fruit is pickled in brine for table olives.

Olympiads were periods of four years which elapsed between each celebration of the Olympic games, held at Olympia in honour of Zeus. These festivals included competitions in literature, art, drama, rhetoric, music and gymnastics, and they were continued, with intervals, from 776 B.C. to A.D. 394. Athletic revivals have taken place at Athens 1896, Paris 1900, St. Louis 1904, London 1908, Stockholm 1912, Antwerp 1920, Paris 1924, Amsterdam 1928, Los Angeles 1932, Berlin 1936, London 1948, Helsinki 1952, Melbourne 1956, Rome 1960, Tokyo 1964, Mexico City 1968, Munich 1972, Montreal 1976. It is planned to hold the Games in 1980 in Moscow.

Onomasticians are scientists who study the fascinating subject of names—names of places and names of people—to find out their origins. They tell us, for example, that Cambridge is an Anglo-Norman corruption of *Grantabryca* = bridge over the Granta; that Harrow-on-the-Hill was an early Anglo-Saxon settlement—"heathen temple on the hill"; that we owe the ridings of Yorkshire to the Vikings (Old Norse *thrithungr* = third part); that in Scotland *-ton* and *-toun* indicate not a town but a hamlet or village. Onomasticians are also concerned with the international standardisation of place names.

Onyx or Sardonyx, a variety of chalcedony built up of different-coloured layers, which are parallel and straight (not curved as in agate).

Oolite, a geological term for the Jurassic oolitic

limestones existing through a long stretch of country extending from Yorkshire to Dorset. It abounds in fossils of molluscs and reptiles. The term " oolite " derives from the fact that these rocks are made of egg-shaped particles of calcium carbonate.

Opal, a mineral consisting of hydrous silica, occurring in numerous varieties and colours. Opals have been prized as gems since at least 400 B.C. but the secret of their unique internal " fire " or opalescence has only recently been learned. It is a result of the diffraction of light by a regular array of tiny silica spheres, about 100 nm in diameter, of which gem opals are now known to be composed. Opal miners are called gougers. Chief source—the Andanooka and Coober Pedy fields of South Australia.

Opera. *See* Section E.

Opium was known to the ancients, and used by them as a medicine. It is obtained from the poppy (*Papaver somniferum*), the unripe " head " or seed capsule of that flower yielding a juice which when dried becomes the opium of commerce. The poppy is cultivated in India, Iran, Turkey, Macedonia and China for the sake of this juice, which yields various alkaloids, such as morphine, narcotine, codeine, etc. These days the drug is rarely used medicinally. *See also* P22(2).

Opossum, marsupial mammals found in the more southerly of the United States, South America and Australasia. They are arboreal except for the water-opossum, which eats fish.

Optics, the branch of physics which investigates the nature and properties of light and the phenomena of colour. Burning lenses were known to the ancient Greeks and Ptolemy wrote a treatise on optics A.D. 150. Lenses as visual aids were known in ancient China but eyeglasses were not in use until the 13th cent. Spectacles were in more general use after the invention of printing in the 15th cent. The camera obscura was invented in the 16th cent. and the telescope and microscope at the beginning of the 17th cent.

Oracles were in ancient times supposed to be words spoken by the gods, and it was the custom on important occasions to consult them about the future. The Greeks had the Oracles of Zeus at Dodona, and Apollo at Delphi, while the Romans consulted the Oracles of Mars, Fortune and others.

Orange, a fruit growing in most sub-tropical climates and in universal demand. It is grown on an evergreen tree that attains a height of about 6 m at maturity.

Orang-utan one of the largest of the anthropoid apes, found only in the swampy forests of Borneo and Sumatra. When full-grown it stands over 1·2 m in height and weighs about 67 kg.

Orchestra, a group of instruments and instrumentalists whose playing is under the direction of a conductor. The composition of a typical symphony orchestra is as follows: STRINGS: 1st Violin (16), 2nd Violin (16), Viola (12), Violoncello (12), Double Bass (8). WOOD-WIND: Flute (3–4), Piccolo (1), Oboe (3), Cor Anglais (1), Bass Oboe (1), Clarinet (3), Bass Clarinet (1), Bassoon (3), Contra-bassoon (1). BRASS: Horn (6), Trumpet (5), Trombone (3–4), Tuba (2). PERCUSSION: Timpani (3–6), Side Drum (1), Bass Drum (1), Cymbals (1), Harp (2).

Orders in Council are issued by the sovereign on the advice of a few selected members of the Privy Council. They must not seriously alter the law of the land. Another class of Orders in Council are issued by authority of an Act of Parliament for the carrying out of its provisions.

Ordination, the ceremony of installing ministers or clergymen in clerical offices, has existed from the earliest times. In the Anglican and Roman Catholic Churches the rites of Ordination are performed by bishops; among Nonconformists the power of ordination rests with the governing bodies of the different Churches.

Organ is a musical wind instrument of ancient origin whose tones are produced by the vibrations of air in pipes of varying length. Basically, an organ consists of a number of pipes grouped in rows or ranks according to their special tone-character. The air is fed by

bellows or, in modern organs, by a rotary fan, electrically driven. Each rank is controlled by a slider, and the knob that controls the slider is called a stop. The organist pulls out the stops to give the tones he wants, the other pipes being kept out of action by the slider. When a particular note on the keyboard is depressed the player may hear, by pulling out the appropriate stop, not only the normal pitch but the note in several octaves. A stop of which the notes are of normal pitch is called an 8-foot stop, a 16-foot stop would give an octave lower, a 4-foot stop an octave higher and a 2-foot stop two octaves higher. The hand keyboard is called a manual, and the foot keyboard the pedal board. The basic tone of an organ is its diapason tone, and is normally of 8-foot length and pitch. Most large organs have four manual keyboards and one pedal board. The most important manual is the great organ which comprises the majority of basic stops. The next in importance is the swell organ, so called because the pipes are enclosed in a box fitted with movable shutters operated by a swell-pedal. The effect provides a controlled crescendo or diminuendo. The tone of a typical English swell has a reedy character. The third manual controls the choir organ— a collection of stops suitable for vocal accompaniment. The fourth manual controls the solo organ—a group of stops which, singly or in combination, may provide a solo melody which the remainder of the organ accompanies. The pedal keyboard controls most of the bass stops. In some very large organs there is a fifth manual controlling the echo organ. This is a small group of stops usually set high in the roof of the building to give the effect of distant music. Most church organs have two or three manuals. Modern cinema organs may have some normal stops but rely chiefly on a number of effects unknown to the straight organ.

Organic Chemistry. The chemistry of compounds containing carbon and usually associated with living organisms. *See* F26–7.

Oriel Window is a window projected from the front of a building, rectangular, triangular, or pentagonal. The ordinary bay window and bow window are varieties of Oriel. When an Oriel window does not reach to the ground it usually rests upon moulded sills supported by corbels.

Oriflamme, the name of the original banner of the abbey of St. Denis, and adopted by Louis VI as his standard. It remained the national emblem of France for three centuries. The flag was of red silk, the outer edge being cut in the form of flames.

Original Sin, according to Christian doctrine the corruption that is born with us, as a result of Adam's fall.

Orioles, brilliantly coloured birds, members of the passerine family *Oriolidae,* found in the tropical regions of Asia, Africa and Australia. The golden oriole, perhaps the most beautiful of them all, with brilliant yellow plumage, black wings and tail, winters in Africa, visits England and is known to have nested here.

Orion, a famous constellation of the heavens, comprising nearly a hundred stars, all visible to the naked eye. It contains three stars of the second magnitude in a line, and these are called " Orion's Belt ".

Ormer, a shellfish (*Haliotis tuberculata*) which occurs in the Channel Islands and on parts of the French coast. It is considered a great delicacy.

Ornithology, the scientific study of birds.

Ornithorhynchus. *See* Duckbill.

Orogeny, large-scale earth movements, including faulting and folding and sometimes igneous activity, which produce a linear belt of mountains, *e.g.*, the Alpine orogeny in Europe which produced the Alps.

Orphism. *See* Section J.

Orphrey, the name of an ornamental border of gold and silver embroidered on ecclesiastical vestments.

Orrery, an instrument used in the 18th and early 19th cent. which showed the motions of the planets round the sun and the satellites round their primaries. The first orrery made was named after Charles Boyle, Earl of Orrery.

Orthodox Eastern Church. *See* Section J.

Osborne House, near Cowes, in the Isle of Wight. Queen Victoria's favourite winter-residence, and where she died. It was given to the nation by Edward VII, and is now a convalescent home.

Osier, a species of willow growing in damp soils and yielding branches utilised in basket-making.

Osmium, a very hard, bluish-white metal, symbol Os, of the platinum group and one of the heaviest known metals. It is obtained from certain sands of South America, California, Australia and Russia. The alloy of osmium and iridium (osmiridium) provides long-wearing tips for gold fountain-pen nibs.

Osmosis, the process by which absorption of liquids through semi-permeable membranes takes place. A solution exerts osmotic pressure (O.P.) or suction in proportion to concentration but also depending on kind of dissolved substance. The roots of the higher plants are covered with fine root-hairs, within the cell-walls of which the sap is normally of a higher concentration than the dissolved matter in the surrounding soil. The root-hairs, therefore, draw into themselves these weaker salt-solutions. (The explanation of water and salt exchanges is complicated by the selective ability of some cells (*e.g.*, roots) to accept or reject particular dissolved substances along with the water. The absorption of salts by a plant is selective, each plant selecting through the semi-permeable membranes of its root-hairs those substances which are most suited to itself.)

Osprey (*Pandion haliaëtus*), a large and magnificent bird of prey, dark brown above and nearly white below. The head is whitish with a dark band from eye to nape. To the British Isles it is a rare passage migrant. In 1959, thanks to the energy and vigilance of the Royal Society for the Protection of Birds, a pair nested in a Scots pine in Inverness-shire and reared three young. Since then more young ospreys have been safely fledged in this sanctuary. The food consists almost entirely of fish, which the bird seizes with its talons. The so-called osprey plumes do not come from this bird but from the egret.

Ostrich, the largest living bird, related to the rhea, emu and extinct moa, now found only on the sandy plains of Africa and parts of S.W. Asia. The male has beautiful white plumes on wings and tail. The wings are useless in flight, but the birds have a fleetness of foot exceeding that of the swiftest horse. An ostrich's egg weighs 1·3 kg.

Otary, any seal which has external ears (as opposed to the *true seals* which lack them). The eared seals make up the family *Otariidae*, which includes the Sea-Lion and the Fur-seal of the N. Pacific.

Otter, an aquatic carnivorous mammal widely distributed over Europe, and at one time very common in England and Wales. The otter averages about 60 cm in length, exclusive of tail, has web-feet and is a very expert swimmer. Otters are harmless and their hunting is a cruel and senseless blood sport. They are now protected in England.

Ounce or **Snow Leopard**, a very beautiful pale spotted cat from the Himalayas about the size of a labrador retriever but with a long furry tail.

Outcrop. Where a bed of rock appears at the surface of the ground, there is an outcrop of the particular rock. The mining of outcrop coal is called open-cast mining.

Oviparous, a zoological term referring to animals which lay eggs to be hatched outside the body of the parent.

Ovipositor, the organ by means of which female insects lay their eggs.

Owls, nocturnal birds of prey, distributed over the greater part of the world. Their forward-looking eyes, embedded in rings of feathers, give them a characteristic " owl-like " appearance, and their plumage, usually a mottled blend of browns and greys, is so soft that their flight is almost noiseless. Owls live on small mammals, reptiles, birds, insects and fish, and are very valuable birds to the farmer. British owls include the barn owl (screech owl), short-eared owl, long-eared owl, tawny owl, little owl. Snowy owls have recently nested in the Shetland Is.

Ox, the popular name of the mammals included in the genus *Bos*. They are hollow-horned ruminants and hoofed quadrupeds, and include the various classes of domestic cattle as well as the different wild species. The adult male is called a bull, the female a cow and the young a calf. The best-known breeds of domesticated cattle are the Durham or Shorthorn, the Angus, the Jersey, Ayrshire, Suffolk and Hereford.

Oxalic Acid, an organic acid obtained from numerous plants, such as sorrel and rhubarb and produced artificially for commercial purposes from sawdust, treated with caustic potash or caustic soda. It combines with metals to form oxalates; used in the manufacture of ink.

Oxford Clay, a geological formation consisting of a bed of blue clay *c*. 200 m thick, and forming the lower portion of the Upper Jurassic. It makes good bricks.

Oxford Movement. *See* Tractarianism, Section J.

Oxford University. The early history of the university is obscure. There was a school at Oxford as early as 1115 and it is known that Robert Pullen, a theologian from Paris, lectured there in 1133. Allusions to Oxford as the most celebrated centre of learning in England occurred in a work of Gerald of Wales in 1184–5. The earliest colleges to be founded were University College (1249), Balliol (about 1263), Merton (1264). In 1571 the university was reorganised and granted a Charter of Incorporation by an Act of Elizabeth. Other colleges and halls with their dates of foundation are: All Souls (1438), Brasenose (1509), Christ Church (1546), Corpus Christi (1517), Exeter (1314), Hertford (1874), Jesus (1571), Keble (1868), Linacre (1962), Lincoln (1427), Magdalen (1458), New College (1379), Nuffield (1937), Oriel (1326), Pembroke (1624), Queen's (1340), St. Anthony's (1950), St. Catherine's (1962), St. Cross (1965), St. Edmund Hall (1270), St.John's (1555), St. Peter's (1929), Trinity (1554), Wadham (1612), Wolfson (1965), Worcester (1714), Campion Hall (1962), St. Benet's Hall (1964), Mansfield (1886), Regent's Park (1958), Greyfriars Hall (1953). The women's colleges are:—Lady Margaret Hall (1878), Somerville (1879), St. Hugh's (1886), St. Hilda's (1893), St. Anne's (1952). Women were not admitted to degrees (though allowed to sit for examination) till 1920. Since 1974 a number of colleges have admitted both men and women students.

Oxygen is the most abundant of all terrestrial elements, symbol O. In combination, this gaseous element forms about 46% of the earth's crust; one-fifth of the atmosphere; eight-ninths by weight of all water. Discovered independently by Scheele (*c*. 1773) and Priestley (1774). It is colourless, tasteless and odourless, and forms the chief life-supporting element of animal and vegetable life.

Oyster, a bivalve mollusc, of the genus Ostrea, having very numerous species and abounding in nearly all seas. The shell is rough and irregular. Oysters are exceedingly prolific, spawning in May and June. In England and Scotland deep-sea oysters are not allowed to be sold between 15 June and 4 August, and other kinds between 14 May and 4 August. In Ireland, no oysters may be taken between 1 May and 1 September, except in certain waters. The Whitstable oyster beds have existed since pre-Roman times; " clocks " are dead oysters.

Oystercatcher, a wading bird with black-and-white plumage and long, orange bill, inhabiting estuaries and sea-shores. Feeds on mussels, shell fish, etc., but not oysters.

Ozone, a modified form of oxygen, containing three atoms of oxygen per molecule instead of two. It is prepared by passing oxygen through a silent electric discharge. When present in air to the extent of 1 part in 4 million parts of air it kills bacteria, and has been used for this purpose in ventilating systems, *e.g.*, that of underground railways. It is present in extremely small quantities in the lower atmosphere but is comparatively plentiful at heights between 12 and 50 km. As ozone absorbs ultra-violet light of certain wavelengths spectroscopic methods, involving the analysis of sunlight, are chiefly used in ozone determinations. *See also* Atmosphere.

P

Paca, a genus of large rodents found in Central and South America, and resembling the guinea-pig. It is of nocturnal habits, has streaked and spotted fur and lives on fruits and plants.

Pacific Ocean. The first European to recognise the Pacific as distinct from the Atlantic was the Spanish explorer, Vasco Nuñez de Balboa, who discovered its eastern shore from a peak in Panama in 1513. The first European to sail upon it was Magellan, who entered it by the strait that bears his name in 1520. Sir Francis Drake was the first Englishman to sail upon it in 1577. The world's greatest known ocean depth is in the Mindanao Trench, off the Philippines, 37,782 ft (11,524 m).

Pagan, a person who does not worship God; a heathen. The word is derived from the Latin *paganus* (a countryman or uncultivated person). In the Middle Ages the term was used largely to describe Mohammedans (Moors, Saracens, etc.).

Pagoda, the name given in China, India and other Asiatic countries to a high pyramidal tower, usually, but not necessarily, connected with a temple.

Palaeontology, the science which is devoted to the investigation of fossils: animal (palaeozoology) and plants (palaeobotany). By studying the markings and fossils of living things in the stratified rocks, palaeontologists have been able to establish with astonishing accuracy a record of the evolution of life through geological time. The geologist at the same time with the evidence of the fossils has been able to work out the order and the age of the rocks. *See also* **F48.**

Palatinate, a term formerly applied to two German electorates or provinces, the Upper and Lower Palatinates. Now provinces of Bavaria.

Pale, the name given to the part of Ireland colonised by the English and comprising portions of the counties of Louth, Dublin, Meath and Kildare. The Anglo-Norman rulers were styled " Lords of the Pale ".

Palimpsests are ancient MSS. or parchments which have been partly effaced and used for fresh writings. Many valuable MSS. were thus lost, but sometimes the second writing has been washed out, enabling the original writings to be deciphered. Among such restorations are a dialogue of Cicero's, a portion of a book of Livy, etc.

Palladium, a scarce metallic element, symbol Pd, similar to platinum, with which it is usually found. It is an expensive metal, with desirable properties as a catalyst in reactions involving hydrogen, since it has a remarkable capacity for absorbing this gas; for example, coal gas and air will inflame in the presence of palladium at room temperature. It forms a silver-white alloy with gold, and this is used in some kinds of jewellery. It is used in expensive watches to make non-magnetic springs.

Pallium, a vestmental ornamentation of white wool presented by the Pope to archbishops on their appointment, and the sign of Papal confirmation.

Palm, a large straight-trunked plant or tree common to tropical countries, and usually fruit yielding, such as dates, coconuts, etc. Many commodities useful to man are obtained from plants of the Palm family (*Palmaceae*).

Palm Sunday, the Sunday before Easter, upon which occasion it is customary to carry palms to the churches in some countries, in commemoration of Christ's entry into Jerusalem for the Feast of the Passover, when the people went forth to greet Him with palm branches.

Panama Canal. In 1903 the United States signed a treaty with Panama (which had previously seceded from Colombia) which gave the United States rights in perpetuity over a 16 km-wide strip of land extending across the isthmus for the purposes of building and running the canal. The canal connects the Atlantic and Pacific Oceans, is just over 80 kilometres long (with sea approaches) and the depth varies from 12 to 26 m. It is constructed above sea-level, with locks, and has been available for commercial shipping since 3 August 1914. Agreement was reached in 1978 for the waterway to be turned over to Panama by the end of the century.

Panda, *or* **Cat-Bear,** is related to the Raccoon. There are two kinds, the Red or True Panda, resembling a large domestic cat, which lives in the eastern Himalayas and S.W. China, and the Giant Panda, which is more like a bear in appearance and inhabits the mountains of western China. Both frequent the dense bamboo forests of those regions.

Pangolin, the scientific name of the " scaly ant-eater ", a toothless mammal, found in W. Africa and S.E. Asia. It has a long extensible tongue which it uses in catching ants and termites, its chief food. When attacked the pangolin rolls itself into a ball, and its scales assume the form of sharp spikes. Pangolins have an Order of their own—the Pholidota, the scale-bearers.

Pantagruel, the leading character in one of the satires of Rabelais.

Pantheon, the famous temple in Rome, originally consecrated to the gods, built by Agrippa in 27 B.C. and rebuilt in the 2nd cent. by Hadrian. Its splendid dome and portico make it one of the most interesting architectural monuments of ancient days. Since the 7th cent. it has been used as a Christian church.

Panther, another name for the leopard, *Panthera pardus*, related to the lion, carnivorous, active climber, found in India, and other parts of Asia, also in Africa.

Papal Infallibility. *See* Section J.

Paper has been known in one form or another from very early times. The papyrus reeds of the Nile swamps served the ancient Egyptians for sheets upon which to inscribe their records. The Chinese and Japanese, centuries later, were using something more akin to modern paper in substance, an Asiatic paper-mulberry, yielding a smooth fibrous material, being utilised. With the spread of learning in Western Europe the necessity of a readier medium made itself felt and paper began to be manufactured from pulped rags and other substances. The first known English paper-mill was Sele mill near Stevenage, built about 1490, which produced the paper for an edition of Chaucer in 1498. Other mills were set up under Elizabeth, using linen and cotton as raw material. Other papermaking staples were later introduced, such as surat, esparto grass and wood-pulp. The chief raw material in the world paper industry is wood-pulp, the main exporters being the timber-growing countries of Canada, Sweden and Finland. Canada is the world's chief producer of newsprint and supplies a large proportion of US requirements.

Papyrus, the earliest known paper made in Egypt at a very remote period from a large species of reed, *Cyperus papyrus*. This plant is to be found all over tropical Africa, especially in the " sudd " region of the White Nile.

Parachute, the umbrella-shaped safety device used in emergency by the crew and passengers of aircraft. The first parachute descent from a great height was made in 1797 by André Garnerin who dropped 915 m from a balloon. Rate of descent for a parachute jump is about 5 m/s.

Paraclete (the Holy Ghost, or Comforter), the name used in the English translations of St. John's Gospel, and adopted by Abelard to designate the convent in Champagne founded by him, and of which Héloïse became the abbess.

Paradise, a Persian word used by the translators of the Old Testament to designate the Garden of Eden, and since meaning any place of happiness.

Paraffin, a mixture of hydrocarbons of higher boiling point than petrol. Paraffin was first obtained by distillation of coal, the process being discovered about 1830. About 1848, Mr. James Young procured it from mineral oil, and Irish peat also yielded it. The main source of paraffin supply today is crude petroleum. Used in the manufacture of candles, for waterproofing and numerous other purposes.

Parakeets, various small parrots of vivid plumage native to Australia, Polynesia, Asia and Africa. One of the loveliest of the parakeets is the budgerigar of Australia.

Parallax, the change in direction of a body caused by a change in position of the observer. If the parallax is measured (in degrees of angle) and the distance between the two observation points is known the distance of the observed body can be calculated. The distance of heavenly bodies has been found this way. The first stellar distances were so obtained in 1838 by Henderson, Struve and Bessel. Stellar distances are so great that even when the two observations are made at opposite points of the earth's orbit round the sun, the parallax is always less than 1·0″ of arc. *See* **Aberration.**

Parameter, a number which is fixed for the application of a theory to one particular situation but may be different for other situations. For example, in a theory of motion near the surface of a planet the acceleration due to gravity may be regarded as a parameter constant for a particular planet but differing from planet to planet. The word is often used in a similar way in discussions of economic affairs.

Parapsychology. *See* **Section J.**

Parchment, made chiefly from the skins of animals, usually of goats and sheep, was employed in olden times before printing was invented and superseded papyrus as writing material. Vegetable parchment, invented by W. E. Gaine in 1853, though not equal in strength and durability to skin parchment, is about five times stronger than ordinary paper. Vellum is parchment made from the skins of young calves or lambs.

Paris University, of which the Sorbonne forms a part was founded in the 12th cent. and is one of the greatest educational institutions of Europe.

Parliament, is the name given to the supreme legislature of the United Kingdom. It consists of the Queen, the Lords spiritual and temporal and the Commons. It meets in two houses: the House of Lords (the Upper or Second Chamber) and the House of Commons. It derives from the Anglo-Saxon *Witans* (*see* Witan). The Statute of Westminster (1275) first uses " parlement " of the Great Council in England, which comes from the French word meaning discourse. *See* **Section D.**

Parliamentary Correspondents sit in the Press Gallery of the House of Commons and describe its proceedings for the news media either by impressions or a summary of the debate.

Parquetry, the name of a style of flooring consisting of small rectangular wooden blocks laid down according to geometrical pattern.

Parrot, the popular name of a widely distributed family of tropical birds, including the African grey parrot, the green parrot of South America —both familiar cage pets in this country—and the various parakeets, cockatoos, macaws, lories, etc. Many of these birds possess a remarkable gift of imitating sound, especially that of the human voice. *See* **Section Z.**

Parsec, unit of distance used by astronomers for expressing distances between stars; equivalent to about three and a quarter light-years.

Parthenogenesis. The development of animals from unfertilised eggs. The drones of the honey bee are parthenogenetic, and the phenomenon is also common among aphids.

Parthenon, the famous Temple of Athena on the Acropolis at Athens, was built under the rule of Pericles between 447 B.C. and 432 B.C. It was made wholly of marble without mortar. The famous sculptured friezes, known as the Elgin Marbles, are now in the British Museum.

Partridge, a well-known British game-bird. Close time: 2 February to 31 August. Two species are common in Britain.

Passeriformes, the order of perching birds which includes about half the known species.

Passport is an official document issued to a person by his own government, certifying to his citizenship and permitting him to travel abroad. Passports to British subjects are granted by the Foreign Office, authorise bearer to leave the country and guarantee him the state's protection. Passports (1977) cost £10—and are issued for a period of 10 years. Children over 16 years of age require separate passports. Parents of children under 16 who require passports should make application on form (B). A simplified form of travel document (British visitor's passport) is issued for British subjects wishing to pay short visits to certain foreign countries for a fee of £5—valid for 12 months. For those making

frequent visits abroad a 94-page passport was first issued in 1973, which now costs £20.

Patricians, the aristocracy of ancient Rome.

Paul's Cathedral, St., is the third cathedral church to be built on the site. It was preceded by a Norman building which was practically destroyed by the Great Fire in 1666. This followed a Saxon church which was burnt in 1086. The present building was designed by Sir Christopher Wren. The foundation stone was laid in 1675 and the structure was completed in 1710. It cost a little under £748,000. Its central feature is the dome, crowned by its cupola and lantern with the golden ball and cross. It escaped serious damage during the air raids of the second world war, but many of the surrounding buildings were laid waste.

*p*C Value, introduced by Dr. C. L. Whittles in 1935 as a measure of salinity of aqueous solutions (soil extract, irrigation water, etc.); defined as the negative logarithm of specific electrical conductivity in reciprocal ohms. Alone or joined with *pH* (below) is useful as an index of osmotic pressure (*see* **Osmosis**) and related hindrance to plant growth resulting from excess of fertiliser or soil salts. If manuring is balanced, growth is best about *p*C 3.3.

Peacock, a bird of large size and beautiful plumage, its characteristic feature being a tail of brilliant " eyed " feathers, which it can erect and spread out, the males possessing resplendent feathering to a much greater extent than the females. It is related to the pheasant; one species is found wild in the forests of India, and another inhabits Burma and the Malayan regions, in Africa there is the Congo Peacock.

Peanut, Ground Nut *or* **Monkey Nut.** A member of the pea family native to S. America, but now cultivated in many parts of the world. After pollination, the flower stalk bends down and buries the pod containing the peas (" nuts ") in the ground. The oil from these " nuts " can be used for margarine manufacture.

Pearl is produced by certain shelled molluscs, chiefly the oyster. The inner surface of the shells of the pearl oyster yield " mother-of-pearl ", and distinct pearls are believed to be morbid secretions, caused by some external irritation. Many fine pearls are found in the actual body of the oyster. The Persian Gulf, Sri Lanka, the north-west coast of Western Australia, many Pacific islands and the Gulf of Mexico are among the most productive pearl-fishing grounds. In ancient times Britain was renowned for its pearl fisheries, the pearls being obtained from a species of fresh-water mussel. Western Australia has produced a 40-grain pearl, the finest the world has seen. The largest pearl ever found was the " Beresford-Hope Pearl ", which weighed 1,800 grains, over six times as much as the oyster that produced it.

Peat, decayed vegetable matter found mostly in marshy positions, and common in Ireland and Scotland. Peat is coal in its first stage of development; burnt for fuel in many cottage homes.

Peccary, a pig-like animal native to the Americas. There are two species: the collared peccary and the white-lipped peccary, the latter being a vicious and dangerous animal.

Pelican, a genus of bird with long depressed bill pouched underneath, thus able to hold fish in reserve. It has immense wings and webbed feet. Eight species.

Pemmican, venison or other meat, sliced, dried, pounded and made into cakes, used by explorers and others when out of reach of fresh meat.

Penguin, a genus of flightless, fish-eating sea-birds of the southern hemisphere. They are stout-bodied, short-necked and of small, moderate or large size. The Emperor and King Penguins make no nest but protect and incubate the single egg by carrying it in the down feathers between the feet and the body. Other species brood in the usual way and may lay as many as three eggs. Penguins use their flippers for swimming under water. All 17 species are bluish-grey or blackish above and white below. They are very sociable and breed in colonies.

Penicillin. An antibiotic drug produced by the mould *Penicillium notatum*, and discovered by Sir Alexander Fleming in 1928. It is one of the most effective chemotherapeutic agents known

The mould produces a number of penicillins, all of which are effective antibiotics. *See* P4(1), 9(1).

Peninsular War lasted from 1808 to 1814. Fought in Spain and Portugal (the Iberian peninsula) by the British, Spanish and Portuguese forces, chiefly under Wellington, against the French. The latter were defeated.

Pentagon, government office in Washington (the largest in the world), housing many thousands of military and civilian workers in the War Department of the United States (Army, Navy and Air Force).

Pentateuch, the first five books of the Old Testament—Genesis, Exodus, Leviticus, Numbers and Deuteronomy. Referred to in the Gospel of Mark as " the book of Moses ".

Pepys Diary, by Samuel Pepys, was first published in 1825. It gives a picture of the social life of the period 1 January 1660 to 31 May 1669. He bequeathed the manuscript, together with his library, to Magdalene College, Cambridge.

Perch, a well-known family of fresh-water fish, with dark striped sides. The common perch of British rivers and lakes falls an easy prey to the angler because of its voracity.

Perfumes are essences or odours obtained from floral and other substances. The chief flower perfumes are those obtained from rose, jasmine, orange flower, violet and acacia. Heliotrope perfume is largely obtained from vanilla and almonds. Among the aromatic herbs which yield attractive perfumes are the rosemary, thyme, geranium, lavender, etc., while orange peel, citron peel, musk, sandalwood, patchouli and other vegetable products are largely drawn upon. In recent times chemistry has been called into play in aid of the perfumer, and many of the popular perfumes of today are chemically prepared in simulation of the scents of the flowers or other natural substances the names of which they bear. *See* Musk Deer.

Perigee, the smallest distance of the earth from any of the heavenly bodies; opposite of apogee (*q.v.*).

Perihelion. That point in a planet's orbit when it is nearest to the sun; opposite of aphelion. The earth is at perihelion (1.47×10^8 km) in mid-winter, about 3 January.

Peripatus, an animal which stands as a link between the annelid worms and the arthropods. Wormlike with short unjointed legs it breathes by a system of air tubes like those in insects. Certain other points of internal structure point to a relationship with annelid worms. There are some fifty species, the best known being the S. African *Peripatus capensis*.

Perjury, the offence of giving false evidence. The ancient Romans threw the perjurer from the Tarpeian Rock, and after the Empire was Christianised, those who swore falsely upon the Gospel had their tongues cut out. The usual punishment in England from the 16th to the 19th cent. was the pillory, fine and imprisonment.

Permian Formation, a group of rocks lying between the Trias and the Carboniferous strata. It has three subdivisions, Upper, Middle and Lower Permian. *See* F48.

Per Procurationem signature means that the subject of the correspondence has been put into the writer's care by his principal for him to use his personal judgment in the matter, and that he is authorised to sign on behalf of his principal. Normally contracted to *per pro* or *p.p.*

Peruke, the name given to the wigs worn by men in the latter half of the 18th cent. The custom of wearing wigs was gradually superseded by powdering the natural hair. Wigs are still worn by the Speaker of the House of Commons, judges and barristers.

Petrel, the name given to a member of a large, widely-distributed family of sea-birds of great diversity of size and colouring and distinguished by tube-like external nostrils. They usually skim low over the waves, and some, for this reason, are known as shearwaters. The storm petrel or Mother Carey's chicken occasionally patters along the surface, and is often called Little Peter—a reference to St. Peter walking on the water. Except when breeding, petrels are always at sea. They mostly nest in holes and crevices on islands and lay one egg, which is invariably white. The storm petrel, Leach's petrel, Manx shearwater and the fulmar petrel are resident in the British Isles. *See also* Mutton Bird.

Petroleum. *See* Oil.

Pewter, alloy of tin and lead formerly used for making household utensils and ornaments.

***p*H Value.** Introduced in 1909 by the Danish chemist Sørensen to indicate hydrogen-ion concentration on the basis of electrical conductivity and a view of ionisation since discarded; is now taken as a logarithmic scale of acidity or alkalinity of aqueous solutions: acidity 0–7, neutrality at 7·0, alkalinity 7–14. The *p*H of blood is about 7·6 (faintly alkaline). *See* F25.

Phalanger, pouched marsupial mammals. They are arboreal and superficially resemble squirrels. There are two genera of flying phalangers or flying squirrels, which have a remarkable membrane along each side of the body enabling the animals to glide through the air. The members of the phalanger family are confined to the Australasian and oriental regions.

Phalangid, a member of the arachnid family Phalangida: popularly known as " harvesters ".

Phalanx, a name applied by the ancient Greeks to a body of pike-men drawn up in close array, with overlapping shields, and eight, ten or more rows deep. The Macedonians stood sixteen rows deep. As many as 500 men could be in the front row.

Pharisees and Sadducees, two ancient Jewish sects. *See* Judaism, Section J.

Pharmacopoeia, an official publication containing information on the recognised drugs used in medicine. Each country has its own pharmacopoeia. The British Pharmacopoeia (B.P.) is published under the direction of the General Medical Council. The Pharmaceutical Society issues the British Pharmaceutical Codex (B.P.C.); there is also an International Pharmacopoeia (2 vols.) which is issued by the World Health Organisation.

Pharos, the name of the first lighthouse, built by Ptolemy II about 280 B.C., on the Isle of Pharos, at the entrance to the harbour of Alexandria. It was 183 m high, and one of the " seven wonders ".

Pheasant, game birds related to the partridges, quails, peacocks, chickens and turkeys, distinguished by their brilliant plumage and long tapering tail. First found by the Greeks in Georgia where the River Phasis flows through to the Black Sea. Close time: 2 February to 30 September.

Phillippics, the oration delivered by Demosthenes, 352–341 B.C., against Philip of Macedon—remarkable for their acrimonious invective. The word was also used for Cicero's speeches against Antony. In modern use, any impassioned invective.

Philosopher's Stone. *See* Alchemy.

Phosphorus is a non-metal element, symbol P. Most familiar as a waxy, yellow solid which is spontaneously inflammable in air. It has chemical similarities to arsenic, like which it is very poisonous. It was discovered by Brandt in urine in 1669. It is found in most animal and vegetable tissues. It is an essential element of all plants and of the bones of animals. In combination with various metals it forms different phosphates, which are largely utilised as manures. The chief commercial use of phosphorus is in the preparation of matches.

Photoelectric Cell, a device which gives a useful electrical response to light falling on it. There are several kinds depending on the different effects which light may have on a suitably chosen solid (usually a semiconductor), viz., the emission of electrons from the surface (" photoemissive cell "); change in electrical resistance (" photoconducting cell "); generation of electric current from a specially designed sensitive structure (" barrier layer " or " photovoltaic cell ", " solar battery "). Different cells respond differently to lights of various wavelength and must be chosen for each application. *See also* Solar Battery.

Photogrammetry, the science of measurement from photographs taken from an aircraft. Aerial photography has many uses and is of great value to military intelligence and for map-making.

Photon. When light behaves like a stream of discrete particles and not like waves, the particles are called photons. *See* **F14, 16.**

Photosynthesis. *See* F32(1), 43(2).

Phrenology. *See* Section J.

Phylloxera, a genus of plant-lice related to the aphids, which attacks the grape vine. Many vineyards of France, in common with the rest of Europe, were replanted with native vines grafted on immune stocks from California in 1879 after being ravaged by the insect (which came from America). Curiously enough, the remedy also came from America, the vine stocks there being immune to *phylloxera*.

Pi is the unique number denoted by the Greek letter *π* and obtained by dividing the length of the circumference of any circle by its diameter. Its value is approximately 3·14159.

Picts, inhabitants of Scotland in pre-Roman times, are held by some historians to be a branch of the old Celtic race, by others to have been of Scythian origin. They occupied the north eastern portion of Scotland, and were subdued by the Scots in Argyll in the 9th cent., Kenneth Mac-Alpin becoming king of a united kingdom of the Picts and Scots—the kingdom of Alban.

Pike, a familiar fresh-water fish abundant in the temperate regions of both hemispheres. It forms good sport for the angler in rivers and lakes, and sometimes attains a weight of from 9–13 kg. It is extremely voracious, is covered with small scales and has a ferocious-looking head.

Pilchard, a fish of the herring family, but with smaller scales and more rounded body. It appears off the Cornish coasts in vast shoals every summer.

Pilgrimage, the undertaking of a journey to a distant place or shrine to satisfy a religious vow or secure spiritual benefit, was resorted to in early Christian times. The first recorded pilgrimage is that of the Empress Helena to Jerusalem in 326. In the Middle Ages pilgrimages became common, and were undertaken by monarchs and people of rank in all Christian countries. Moslems have been making pilgrimages to Mecca since the death of the Prophet, such duty being enjoined by the Koran. Among the great centres of Christian pilgrimages are Jerusalem, Rome, the tomb of Becket at Canterbury and the holy places of Lourdes and La Salette in France.

Pilgrimage of Grace (1536), the rising in Lincolnshire and Yorkshire in the reign of Henry VIII against religious innovations and the dissolution of the smaller monasteries, which overlapped with discontents caused by taxation, rising prices, enclosures and land speculation. The insurrection was followed by many executions.

Pilgrim Fathers, the 101 English Puritans, who, after living some years in exile in Holland, to escape persecution in their own country, set sail for America in the *Mayflower*, 6 September 1620, landing at Plymouth, Mass., 4 December. They founded the settlement of Plymouth, and are regarded as the pioneers of American colonisation although 13 years earlier a small Virginian colony had been established.

Pillory, a wooden instrument of punishment in use in England until 1837. It consisted of a pair of movable boards with holes through which the culprit's head and hands were put, and was usually erected on a scaffold. While a person was undergoing this punishment the mob generally pelted him with stones and rubbish, sometimes to his serious injury. People convicted of forgery, perjury or libel were often condemned to the pillory, but from 1816 to 1837 the only offence for which it could be inflicted was perjury.

Pine, a conifer of the genus *Pinus*, which flourishes all over the northern hemisphere and includes 80–90 species, which afford valuable timber and yield turpentine and tar. The Scots Pine, *Pinus silvestris*, with its blue-green, short needles, set in pairs, and its rosy-orange branches, is native to Britain, as it is to the whole of Europe. It provides the red and yellow deal in everyday use.

Pitcairn Islanders were originally the mutineers of the *Bounty*. They took possession of the island in 1790, and it was not until 1814 that their whereabouts was ascertained, accidentally, by a passing ship. The mutineers, under their leader, Adams, had settled down to a communal existence, married Tahitian women and increased so in numbers that in the course of years they were too many for the island to support, and in 1856 they were removed to the British Government to Norfolk Island. A small number returned to Pitcairn.

Pitchblende *or* **Uraninite,** a relatively scarce mineral. It is nearly all uranium oxide, but lead, thorium, etc., are also present. Pitchblende from Joachimstal in Czechoslovakia was the material in which radium was discovered by the Curies. Other major sources are the Great Lakes region of Canada and Zaïre.

Placebo, medical treatment that the therapist uses deliberately although he knows it is without any specific effect on the condition being treated. There may be various medical reasons for using placebos, *e.g.*, for the beneficial psychological effect on people who like to feel something is being done for them; for differentiating during clinical trials of a new treatment between those persons given the real thing and a control or comparison group of persons given a placebo or inactive imitation.

Plainsong, a style of musical composition sung in unison (all voices singing the same tune without harmony), familiar in the Western Church from very early times and still performed, principally in the Roman Catholic Church. Though restrained and contemplative in spirit, it is capable of expressing deep emotion. *See* E3(2).

Planetarium, a complex optical system which projects into the interior of a dome a replica of all the phenomena of the sky that can be seen by the naked eye, *e.g.*, sun, moon, planets, stars, comets, meteors, aurora, eclipses and clouds. There is a planetarium in the Marylebone Road, London, and another (opened in 1966) at Armagh Observatory, N. Ireland.

Planets, the name given to such celestial bodies as revolve round the sun in elliptical orbits. The name was first used by the Greeks to indicate their difference from the fixed stars. There are ten planets, Mercury, Venus, Earth, Mars, Jupiter, Saturn, Uranus, Neptune, Pluto, and one discovered in 1977, not yet named. Only Saturn and Uranus are ringed. Many important questions can be answered by means of probes sent to the neighbourhood of the planets. These include the measurement of the magnetic field, if any, of the planets, the study of their atmospheres, much of which can be done without actually penetrating to the surface. With instruments landed gently on the surface it is possible to investigate surface conditions and composition by many methods. Even without a soft-landing information on these questions can be obtained by photography and subsequent transmission of the picture back to earth by some form of television scanning. The US Mars probe *Mariner IV* transmitted pictures of the Martian surface in 1965, the Russian *Venus IV* in 1967 made a soft-landing on Venus, and the US *Pioneer 11* came within 43,000 km of Jupiter in December 1974. Two US *Voyager* spacecraft were launched in 1977 to fly by Jupiter (1979) and Saturn (1980) to investigate their satellites and the interplanetary gas. *See* under their names and F8.

Plankton, a word which first came into biological use in 1886 to describe the usually microscopic plants and animals floating, swimming and drifting in the surface waters of the sea. To be distinguished from *nekton* (swimming animals like fishes and squids) and *benthos* (plants and animals living on the sea bottom, like fixed algae, sponges, oysters, crabs, etc.). Of great economic importance, providing food for fish and whales.

Plantagenets, the kings who reigned in England between 1154 and 1485 and included the Houses of Lancaster and York. More correctly they are styled Angevins, from Anjou, of which Geoffrey, father of Henry II, was Count, and whose badge was a sprig of broom (*Planta genista*).

Plasma Physics is the physics of wholly ionised gases, *i.e.*, gases in which the atoms initially present have lost practically the whole of the electrons that usually surround their nuclei, so that the gas consists of a mixture of two components, positively charged ions and negatively charged electrons. The physical properties of a *plasma* are very different from those of an unionised gas. In particular, a plasma has a high electrical conductivity and can carry large currents. *See also* **Nuclear Fusion.**

Plastics, a broad term covering those substances which become plastic when subjected to increased temperatures or pressures. The Plastics Industry is based on synthetic organic examples of this group. There are two classes of plastics: the *thermoplastic*, which become plastic every time they are heated (*e.g.* cellulosic plastics) and *thermosetting*, which undergo chemical change when heated, so that once set they cannot be rendered plastic again (*e g.* Bakelite). Plastics are composed of long-chained molecules, *e.g.*, polyethylene.

Plate Tectonics, the contemporary and by now well-developed theory of the movements of the earth's crust. The view is that the surface of the Earth consists of about a dozen rigid plates, some larger than continents, some much smaller, all in ceaseless motion relative to one another. Their separation and approach and their friction and collision are closely related to the evolution of mountain ranges, oceans and rift valleys and to phenomena like earthquakes and volcanoes. *See* **F9.**

Platinum, a metal element, symbol Pt. It is a scarce white metal generally allied with iridium, osmium, ruthenium and palladium. It can only be melted in an oxyhydrogen or electric furnace, but can be rolled out into a film-like sheet, or drawn out to the finest wire; being resistant to acids it is termed a noble metal.

Platonic Solids, five regular solid figures known to the ancient world. They are: the tetrahedron (4 triangular faces), cube (6 square faces), octahedron (8 triangular faces), dodecahedron (12 five-sided faces), icosahedron (20 triangular faces). All the faces and angles of each solid are identical.

Pleiades, famous cluster of stars in the constellation of Taurus. Of the seven principal stars in the group, one is rather faint, and many myths have sprung up about this " lost pleiad ".

Pleistocene, the geological period that succeeded the Pliocene. During the Pleistocene, also known as the *Great Ice Age*, there were four cold periods, when the ice sheets covered northern Europe and N. America, separated by warm periods when the glaciers drew back into the mountains. From recent studies based on rock magnetic measurements the transition to Pleistocene took place about 1,850,000 years ago. *See* **F48.**

Pliocene, the geological period preceding the Pleistocene, and the last major division of the Tertiary strata. It began about fifteen million years ago. *See* **F48.**

Plough Monday, the first Monday after the Epiphany, when in olden times the rustic population returned to work after the Christmas festivities.

Plover, wading birds, widely distributed over marshy places of Europe. Several species occur in Britain, including the Golden-plover, which breeds on the moors of Devon, Somerset, Wales, N.E. Yorkshire and Scotland, and the Ringed plover, Kentish plover and Dotterel.

Pluto, the last planet to be discovered: existence established by C. W. Tombaugh at the Flagstaff Observatory in Arizona in January 1930 from reckonings made by P. Lowell in 1914. It is the most distant of all the known planets; diameter about 6,000 km. Mean distance from the sun estimated at $5,900 \times 10^6$ km. *See* **F8.**

Plutonium, a chemical element, symbol Pu, capable of nuclear fission in the same way as Uranium 235. Not until after it had been synthesised in atomic piles during the second world war was it shown to occur in infinitesimally small traces in nature. Its synthesis in the atomic pile depends on the capture by Uranium 238 nuclei of neutrons; immediate product of this reaction is the element neptunium, but this undergoes rapid radioactive disintegration to plutonium. Because of its explosive power and poisonous character, an American scientist once remarked: " If ever there was an element which deserved a name associated with hell, it is plutonium."

Poet Laureate is the poet attached to the royal household, an office officially established in 1668, though its origins go back to the early Middle Ages, when minstrels were employed at the courts of English kings. Chaucer, Skelton and Spenser, though not court poets, were all unofficial poets laureate. Ben Jonson has been called the first " official laureate " (1616), but the office was not officially recognised until 1668, when Dryden was formally granted the office. It is customary for the poet laureate to write verse in celebration of events of national importance. Sir John Betjeman succeeded Cecil Day Lewis as poet laureate in 1972.

Pogrom. Russian word meaning " destruction ". First used to describe the Tsarist attacks on the Jews in 1881 in Russia. In 1938 Hitler ordered a general pogrom in Germany: all synagogues were destroyed and nearly all Jewish shops and homes, Jewish hospitals and children's homes suffered. During the subsequent war Jews of central Europe were systematically exterminated in cold blood by the Nazis.

Poitiers, Battle of, was fought on 19 September 1356, during the Hundred Years' War, when Edward the Black Prince gained a complete victory over John, King of France, who was taken prisoner and brought to London.

Polecat, an animal of a dark-brown colour, about 46 cm in length, exclusive of tail; the ears and face-markings are white or light brown. It is carnivorous and belongs to the weasel family. Like the skunk, it emits an offensive odour.

Pole-Star is of the second magnitude, and the last in the tail of the Little Bear constellation. Being near the North pole of the heavens—never more than about one degree from due north—it always remains visible in the Northern hemisphere; hence its use as a guide to seamen.

Police, a regular force established for the preservation of law and order and the prevention and detection of crime. The powers they have vary from country to country and with the type of government; the more civilised and democratic the state, the less police intervention. England, compared with countries abroad, was slow to develop a police force, and it was not until 1829 that Sir Robert Peel's Metropolitan Police Act established a regular force for the metropolis, later legislation establishing county and borough forces maintained by local police authorities throughout England and Wales. Up to that time police duties were discharged by individual constables and watchmen appointed by local areas in England and Wales. The police service in Great Britain today is organised in a number of forces (43 in England and Wales and 6 regional and 2 combined forces in Scotland). Strength *c.* 110,000. In Northern Ireland there is a single force (the Royal Ulster Constabulary). In England and Wales the forces are defined according to area of responsibility:

   1. County forces, under a police committee consisting of local councillors and magistrates.
   2. Combined forces, covering more than one county, also under a police committee consisting of local councillors and magistrates and representatives from each constituent area.
   3. The Metropolitan Police Force, covering an area within a 15-mile (24-km) radius of Charing Cross, but excluding the City of London, under the control of the Home Secretary. Strength *c.* 21,000.
   4. The City of London force operating in the area of the city, under the Court of Common Council.

In Scotland the police authority is the regional or island council. Police ranks are: chief constable, assistant chief constable, chief superintendent, superintendent, chief inspector, inspector, sergeant and constable. In the Metropolitan Police area the chief officer is the Commissioner of Police of the Metropolis. Central authority rests with the Home Secretary in England and Wales and the Secretary of State for Scotland in Scotland. In the present troubles in Northern Ireland responsibility for law and order is retained at Westminster.

Pollution of the atmosphere is due chiefly to the

incomplete combustion of fuels, especially coal, large particles of soot being deposited fairly quickly close to their place of origin and smaller particles (including smoke) remaining suspended in the air for a long time. Invisible air pollutants include sulphur dioxide from power stations and home heating, and carbon monoxide from cars. The introduction of more efficient furnaces, the washing of flue gases and the introduction of smokeless zones have assisted in the abatement of smoke and other forms of pollution. Atomic weapon tests add to the load of pollution in the atmosphere (*see* Fall-out). "Smog" (smoke-laden fog) which reduces visibility to zero and affects the respiratory organs, is liable to occur when the air near the earth is cooled below the dew-point temperature by radiation on a still, cloudless night when an accumulation of smoke over a large city cuts off daylight and produces gloom, and absence of wind or vertical currents prevents the lower layers of the air from getting away. Such conditions are associated with the smoke-laden atmosphere of large industrial towns during a winter anticyclone. During the great London smog of 1952 there were 2,000 deaths over and above those expected for the time of year. Since the Clean Air Act of 1956 pollution by smoke and sulphur dioxide has continued to diminish in London, winter sunshine has increased by 70 per cent. and fish now live in the Thames. In 1969 a special Secretaryship of State was created to deal with a wide range of functions relating to the physical environment in which people live and work, including pollution (air, waters in rivers and around coasts, noise, pesticides harmful to food and wildlife). In his 1969 Reith lectures Dr. Fraser Darling said "most pollution comes from getting rid of waste at the least possible cost". *See also* Pollution, Section F, Part VI.

Polonium, a radioactive element, symbol Po, discovered by Madame Curie in 1898, and named after her native land of Poland.

Poltergeist. *See* Section J.

Polymerisation is the linking together of small molecules to make a large long-chain molecule. The general name for polymers of ethylene is Polythene, a wax-like plastic solid which because of its special qualities is used in a variety of ways today.

Polytheism. *See* God and Man, Section J.

Pomology, the science of fruit-growing.

Pontifex, the title assigned in ancient Rome to members of the college of pontifices. "Pontifex maximus" was the official head of Roman religion. It was as "pontifex maximus" that Julius Caesar revised the calendar in 46 B.C., and when after the rise of Christianity the popes took over the title the revision fell to them.

Pope, The, the head of the Roman Catholic Church, recognised by that Church as the lawful successor of St. Peter. He is elected by the body of Cardinals. Since 1870, when the King of Italy deposed the holder from temporal power, no pope had left the Vatican between appointment and death until 1929, when peace was made between the Church and State in Italy and compensation was paid to the Holy See for the loss of temporal power. Cardinal Montini, Archbishop of Milan, was elected Pope Paul VI in 1963 on the death of Pope John XXIII.

Porcelain. The word is thought to be derived from the Italian *porcellana*, indicating the texture of a piglet. The majority of porcelain made on the continent was of "hard-paste", or true porcelain, similar to that discovered by the Chinese as early as the T'ang Dynasty (A.D. 618–907). It was composed of *kaolin* (chinaclay) and *petuntse* (china-stone) which when fired in a kiln at a temperature of *c.* 1300°C became an extremely hard and translucent material. The recipe of "hard-paste" porcelain remained a secret of the Chinese until 1709, when it was re-discovered in Europe by Johann Böttger of the Meissen factory (popularly known as Dresden). Aided by disloyal Meissen workmen, factories were later established at Vienna, Venice and in many parts of Germany. Plymouth and Bristol were the only English factories to produce this type of porcelain, from 1768 to 1781. Elsewhere, both in England and France, the material manu-

factured was known as "soft-paste" or artificial porcelain which was made by blending varying white-firing clays with the ingredients of glass. The French factory of Sèvres began to make some hard-paste porcelain by 1768 and by the 19th cent. such porcelain was the only type being made throughout the whole of the continent. In England Josiah Spode is credited with the introduction of "bone-china" about 1794. This hybrid-paste was quickly adopted by many other factories and today remains the most popular type of English porcelain. *See* Pottery and Porcelain Marks, Section U.

Porcupine, a rodent whose back is covered with long, sharp, black and white spikes, which form a powerful means of defence. There are two families of porcupines; one is confined to the Old World and the other contains the American porcupines.

Porphyry, a form of crystalline rock of many varieties that in ancient Egypt was quarried and used for the decorative portions of buildings and vessels. The term is applied generally to the eruptive rocks in which large well-formed crystals of one mineral are set in a matrix of other minerals.

Porpoise, a highly intelligent marine mammal of the dolphin and whale family, and a common inhabitant of northern seas. Porpoises travel in shoals, their progression being marked by constant leapings and plungings. Their average length is from 1·2–1·5 m. There are several species, nearly all being confined to northern oceans.

Port, a special kind of red Portuguese wine, taking its name from Oporto. It was little known in England until the Methuen Treaty of 1703, when it was permitted to be imported at a low duty.

Portcullis, a strong, movable timber or iron grating let into the wall of the gateway to a feudal castle, and capable of being lowered or raised at will. It formed an effective protection against attack in the days before firearms.

Portland Vase, one of the most renowned specimens of ancient art, long in the possession of the Portland family. In 1810 it was loaned to the British Museum. Here it was shattered in 1845 by a stone from a maniac's hand, but has been skilfully restored. It is said to have been found in the 17th cent. in an ancient tomb near Rome. It was purchased from the Barberini family in 1770 by Sir Wm. Hamilton, subsequently sold to the Duchess of Portland. The vase, which is actually a two-handled urn, stands about 25 cm high, is of transparent dark blue glass, ornamented with figures cut in relief in overlaid white opaque glass. It was purchased by the British Museum in 1945. *See also* Glass.

Portreeve in olden times was an official appointed to superintend a port or harbour, and before the name of mayor was used the chief magistrate of London was styled the Portreeve.

Positivism. *See* Section J.

Positron, the "positive electron", an atomic particle having the same mass but an electric charge equal but opposite to that of an electron. It was discovered in 1932. *See also* F16.

Post-Impressionism, a term introduced by Roger Fry to describe the exhibition of paintings sponsored by himself in London (1910–11) officially entitled "Manet and the Post-Impressionists". The exhibition included paintings by Manet, Cézanne, Gauguin, Van Gogh, Seurat, Signac, works by Matisse, Rouault and the *Fauves* (*q.v.*), and sculpture by Maillol. In a second exhibition, held in 1912, Picasso and the Cubists were also represented. The term therefore refers to the movement in modern art which reacted against the transient naturalism of the Impressionists by concerning itself primarily with colour, form and solidity. Most artists today would include Cézanne, Van Gogh and Gauguin as the main Post-Impressionists and maintain that it prepared the way for Fauvism, Cubism and Expressionism.

Potassium, a metal, symbol K (German *Kalium*). It is similar to sodium, like which it reacts violently with water. It was discovered by Sir Humphry Davy in 1807, and is now generally obtained by the electrolysis of fused potassium hydroxide or chloride/fluoride mixture. Its principal minerals are carnallite and kainte, and it is relatively common in rocks, accounting for about 2¼% of the earth's crust. An essential element for healthy plant growth; the ashes of plants are relatively rich in potassium.

Potsdam Agreement was signed by Truman, Stalin and Attlee in August 1945. By this Agreement a Council of Foreign Ministers was established, representing the five principal Powers: China, France, Soviet Russia, the United Kingdom and United States of America, with the task of drawing up the peace treaties for submission to the United Nations. It laid down, *inter alia*, that German militarism and Hitlerism should be destroyed; that industrial power should be so reduced that Germany would never again be in a position to wage aggressive war; that surplus equipment should be destroyed or transferred to replace wrecked plant in allied territories; that Germany should be treated as an economic whole; and that local self-government should be restored on democratic lines as rapidly as was consistent with military security. The Potsdam Agreement became a dead letter with the creation of a communist régime in the Russian zone of Germany, and marked the beginning of the " cold war ".

Prado Gallery, the great public picture collection of Madrid, containing a superb collection of paintings by Velasquez, Murillo, Raphael, Titian, Van Dyck, Rubens and Goya.

Pragmatism. See Section J.

Prefect, chief magistrates in ancient Rome. The title is now applied to the chiefs of administration of the departments of France.

Pre-Raphaelite Brotherhood was the name given to their school of thought by three British artists, Dante Gabriel Rossetti, J. E. Millais and W. Holman Hunt, who in 1848 revolted against the academic art of their time and advocated a return to the style of the Italian painters prior to Raphael—the simple naturalism of the Primitives, such as Botticelli, Fra Angelico and Filippo Lippi. Thus they avoided the use of heavy shadows and painted on a white ground in bright colours—a technique which aroused the ire of those used to the dark and murky canvases of the contemporary romantic artists. Although they held these principles in common the three members of the " P.R.B.", as it was popularly called, were really quite different in other respects. Thus Rossetti (who for some reason is always thought of as the typical Pre-Raphaelite) produced works of a highly romanticised mediaevalism which, apart from certain aspects of technique, bear not the slightest resemblance to the sentimental naturalism of Millais or the much more dramatic realism of Holman Hunt (*e.g.*, in *The Scapegoat*). The Brotherhood was later joined by a number of lesser artists, but its works are not commonly accepted with enthusiasm today when the general feeling is that they are sentimental and religiose rather than the product of deeply-felt emotions. Ruskin in his writings defended their work but the movement came to an end in 1853.

Presbyterianism. See Section J.

Press-Gang, a body of sailors employed to impress men into naval service, frequently resorted to in England, especially during the war with France in the early 19th cent. Press gangs were not used after about 1850.

Primitive Art. The word " primitive " has a number of different meanings: (1) the art of prehistoric communities (*e.g.*, the famous animal cave-drawings of the Aurignacians, *c.* 25,000 B.C., at Altamira in Spain); (2) the art of modern primitive communities (*e.g.*, Bushman rock-paintings); (3) child art; (4) peasant art which springs from a spontaneous desire to impart beauty to objects of daily use and shows a tendency towards abstraction. Peasant art has many features in common the world over, the woodcarving of the Norsemen being almost indistinguishable from that of the Maoris; (5) the modern school of primitive painting in which naïveté of presentation is either the aim of a highly sophisticated mind (*e.g.*, the self-taught French painter Le Douanier Rousseau (d. 1910)), or arises naturally from a simple one (the American " grandma " Moses (d. 1961) who began to paint in her seventies).

Printing by movable types was first used in Europe in 1454 by Johann Gutenberg, a citizen of Mainz. The invention is also claimed for Laurens Koster of Haarlem. It was introduced into England by Caxton, who set up a printing press in Westminster in 1476. Gothic characters were first used, being superseded by Roman letters in 1518. In 1798 Earl Stanhope replaced the wood printing press by one of iron. In 1814 Friedrich Koenig applied the principle of steam power to the press. Mr. John Walter, of *The Times* newspaper, was the first to use the steam press. Improvements were introduced by Applegarth and Cowper in 1828 and great strides were made in 1858 when the Hoe machine was put on the market. Then came the Walter press in 1866 which printed on continuous rolls of paper from curved stereotyped plates. The Monotype machine casts single letters and the Linotype whole lines. The term letterpress is used for all printing methods using plates where the characters stand in *relief.* The other main printing methods are *intaglio* and *planographic.*

The Privy Council is the Sovereign's own council, consisting of about 300 persons who have reached eminence in some branch of public affairs (Cabinet ministers must be Privy Counsellors), on whose advice and through which the Sovereign exercises his or her statutory and a number of prerogative powers. From it have sprung many organs of the constitution and many of our government departments have grown from committees of the Privy Council. For example the Judiciary or courts of justice have grown from the Sovereign's Council sitting as a Court of Justice, and today the Judicial Committee of the Privy Council is a body of distinguished lawyers acting as a Court of Appeal from courts of the Commonwealth.

Probation Officers are attached to particular Courts, sometimes a Magistrates' or a higher court. Sometimes an offender is not sentenced to punishment, but is released " on probation ", that is on the condition that he behaves well and follows directions given by the Court or by a probation officer. Such an officer is a trained man (or woman) who advises, assists and befriends people who are placed under his supervision by a court of law. The probation officer, by his assessment of the social background of the offender, can advise the court upon the wisdom of putting the offender on probation. The probation officer by his understanding can so befriend an offender as to provide a basis for his rehabilitation. He undertakes the " after care " of those released from prison or Borstal. A juvenile offender, or in need of care, may be made subject to supervision by a probation officer or local authority. *See also* **Juvenile Courts.**

Productivity. Physical productivity is the output of products during a time unit, *e.g.*, so many products per man hour, or day, or year. Total productivity is the sum of all the units of product created during the given time. Labour productivity is the part of the total that is attributed to labour as a factor of production. Productivity of capital is the element attributed to capital as a factor. Productivity of land is the element attributed to the natural powers of the soil, as distinct from what is contributed by the application to it of capital or labour. The term productivity is also used to refer not to the quantity of output, but to its money value.

Propane, a colourless inflammable gas made of carbon and hydrogen; formula C_3H_8. It is easily liquefied and transported liquid in cylinders and tanks. In this form it is familiar as a " portable gas supply " for domestic and industrial uses. It is sometimes mixed with butane (*q.v.*) for this purpose. Propane occurs in natural gas and is a by-product of oil refining.

Proteins are the main chemical substances of living matter: they are a part of every living cell and are found in all animals and plants. All proteins are basically constructed of carbon, hydrogen, oxygen and nitrogen, and some contain sulphur, phosphorus (nucleoproteins) and iron (haemoglobin). Proteins are built up of very long chains of amino-acids connected by amide linkages (the synthetic polymers such as " nylon " and casein plastics (from milk) are built up of the same linkages). The structure of protein molecules allows a variety of function. Enzymes, which bring about chemical reactions in living cells, are proteins having specific properties. See F32–3, also Diet, Section P.

Proton, a basic constituent of the atomic nucleus, positively charged, having a mass about 1836 times that of the electron. It is a positive hydrogen ion. See F10–2, 14.

Prout's hypothesis. The English chemist William Prout (1785–1850) advanced the idea that all atoms are made of hydrogen, and their weights are exact multiples of the weight of a hydrogen atom. With the modification that neutrons as well as protons occur in the nucleus, Prout's belief, though rejected for many years, has been substantially vindicated.

Provost, a Scottish official similar in rank to an English mayor. The Provosts of Edinburgh, Glasgow, Aberdeen, Perth and Dundee are styled Lords Provost. The title of provost is also given to the heads of certain colleges.

Prud'hommes (Prudent Men), Councils of, were French trade tribunals, of masters and workmen, formed to decide on disputes. Originally a mediaeval institution, they were revived by Napoleon in 1806, and were carried on by the Third Republic.

Psalms, Book of, for many years attributed to David, but present-day scholars are of opinion that the psalms were written by a series of authors at different times and for different purposes, and that few, if any, were written by David. The Holy Scriptures contain 150.

Psychedelism. See Section J.

Psychic Research. See Section J.

Psychoanalysis. See Section J.

Ptarmigan, birds of the grouse family, one species of which inhabits the Scottish Highlands. In the winter the bird assumes a white plumage.

Ptomaines, amino acids produced during the putrefaction of proteins of animal origin. Not a cause of food poisoning, as was once generally supposed, which is almost invariably due to certain specific bacteria.

Publicans, under the Roman Empire, were people who farmed the public taxes. It is this class of officials that is alluded to in the " publicans and sinners " phrase in the New Testament.

Public Corporations, statutory bodies which operate major industries and services in the public interest, e.g., UK Atomic Energy Authority, Bank of England, B.B.C., Electricity Authorities, Gas Council, National Coal Board, British Steel Corporation, British Railways Board, the Post Office, British National Oil Corporation, British Nuclear Fuels Ltd., British Airports Authority. They are accountable to Parliament but their staffs are not civil servants.

Public Schools. The Public Schools Act of 1864 named nine " public " schools: Eton, Harrow, Rugby, Winchester, Westminster, Shrewsbury, Charterhouse, St. Paul's and Merchant Taylors. Today the term embraces many more, and can be applied to all those schools which are financed by bodies other than the State and whose headmasters belong to the Headmasters' Conference as distinct from the Headmasters' Association. There are about 200 such schools in Britain, including among others: Bedford School (founded 1552); Bradfield College, Berks. (1850); Charterhouse, Godalming (1611); Cheltenham College (1841); Christ's Hospital, Horsham (1553); City of London (1442); Clifton College, Bristol (1862); Dulwich College (1619); Eton College (1440); Felsted, Dunmow, Essex (1564); Haileybury College (1862); Harrow (1571); King Edward's, Birmingham (1552); King's School, Canterbury (600); Malvern College (1865); Manchester Grammar School (1515); Marlborough College (1843); Merchant Taylors' (1561); Mill Hill (1807); Oundle (1556); Radley College, Abingdon (1847); Repton, Derbyshire (1557); Rugby School (1567); St. Albans (948); St. Paul's (1509); Sevenoaks School (1418); Sherborne (1550); Shrewsbury School (1552); Stonyhurst College (1593); Stowe School, Bucks (1923); Tonbridge (1553); Uppingham, Leics. (1584); Warwick (914); Wellington College (1859); Westminster (1560); Winchester College (1382). Public schools for girls include: Christ's Hospital, Hertford (1552), Cheltenham Ladies'

College (founded by Miss Beale in 1853), North London Collegiate School (founded by Miss Buss in 1850), Roedean (1885), Wycombe Abbey (1806). Some public schools are now co-educational.

Pulsars, cosmic objects discovered in 1967 by the radio astronomy group at Cambridge; of great scientific interest because they are probably made of highly compressed matter. Unlike quasars (q.v.) they are near objects—all are contained in the Milky Way. See F5.

Puma, mountain-lion or cougar, a large wild cat found throughout the Americas. It looks like a lean greyish lioness.

Pyramids of Egypt, on the west bank of the Nile, are vast stone or brick-built structures with inner chambers and subterranean entrances, built by the Pharaohs as royal tombs and dating from about 3000 B.C. The most celebrated are at Gizeh built during the 4th dynasty. The largest, originally 147 m high, is called the Great Pyramid, one of the seven wonders of the world, built by the Pharaoh Khufu, better known as Cheops, and there he was buried, 100,000 men, according to Herodotus, being employed for 20 years upon it. Chephren, successor of Cheops, erected the second pyramid, and the third was built by Mycerinus, a son of Cheops. The pyramid at Meidum built by King Snefru, founder of the 4th dynasty, is the most imposing of all. American and Egyptian scientists are cooperating in a project to X-ray (by means of cosmic rays) the interior of the Pyramid of Chephren.

Pythons, large snakes, non-poisonous and destroying their prey by crushing it. Some species may reach 9 m in length, and prey upon deer and other small mammals. Found in Asia, Africa and Australia. They lay eggs.

Q

Quadrant, an astronomical instrument for measuring altitudes, superseded for navigational purposes in modern times by the sextant. It consists of a graduated arc of 90° with a movable radius for measuring angles on it.

Quai d'Orsay. An embankment in Paris where the French Foreign Office is situated.

Quail, an edible bird of the partridge family, of which only one species, the Common Quail, is found in England. It is not more than 20 cm long. It is found in most of the warmer regions of the world. In England and Wales the Quail is covered by the Wild Bird Protection Acts.

Quantum Theory. The rapid development of quantum theory has been almost entirely due to the experimental and theoretical study of the interactions between electromagnetic radiation and matter. One of the first steps was taken when it was discovered that the electrons emitted from metals due to the action of ultraviolet radiation have an energy which is not related to the intensity of the incident radiation, but is dependent on its wavelength. Einstein showed in 1905 that this could only be explained on the basis that energy is transferred between radiation and matter in finite amounts, or quanta, which are inversely proportional to wavelength. See F17(2).

Quarks are hypothetical subnuclear particles recently postulated by theoretical physicists concerned with the so-called elementary particles. There may be three kinds, possibly more, all carrying electrical charges which are fractions of those carried by familiar particles like electrons and protons. This and other special properties of quarks make them suitable for explaining the existence of the large number of other particles referred to on F16–17. The physical existence of quarks may be demonstrated by experiment at any time and if this happens it will be an exciting triumph for speculative theoretical physics. See F15(2).

Quartering, in heraldry, is the disposition of various escutcheons or coats of arms in their proper " quarters " of the family shield, in such order as indicates the alliances with other families.

Quartermaster, a military officer charged with the provisioning and superintendence of soldiers in camp or barracks, and holding the equivalent rank to a lieutenant. The Quartermaster-General is an officer who presides over the provisioning department of the whole army. A Quartermaster in the Navy is a petty officer responsible to the Officer of the Watch; at sea for the correct steering of the ship and in harbour for the running of the ship's routine.

Quarto, a sheet of paper folded twice to make four leaves, or eight pages; abbreviated to " 4to ".

Quartz is a common and usually colourless mineral, occurring both crystallised and massive. In the first form it is in hexagonal prisms, terminating in pyramids. When pure its specific gravity is 2·66. It is one of the constituents of granite, gneiss, etc. Among the quartz varieties are *rock crystal* (colourless), *smoky quartz* (yellow or brown), *amethyst* (purple), *rose quartz* (pink) and *milky quartz* (white). Quartz veins in metamorphic rocks may yield rich deposits of gold. Mining for gold in the rock is termed quartz-mining.

Quasars, or in preferred terminology, quasi-stellar radio-sources, form a new class of astronomical object, first identified in the period 1960 to 1962. They have enormous energy output, and are at vast distances. Many are strong sources of radio waves and fluctuate in intensity. Their nature and cosmological significance presented the major astronomical problem of the 1960s. In the view of Professor Philip Morrison, of the Massachusetts Institute of Technology, quasars are the condensed remains of entire galaxies, while pulsars (*q.v.*) seem to be the ashes of a star that has exploded. Both, he suggests, contain a core of highly concentrated magnetised material. *See* F5.

Queen Anne's Bounty, established by Queen Anne in 1704 for the augmentation of the maintenance of the poor clergy. Since 1 April 1948, Queen Anne's Bounty and the Ecclesiastical Commissioners ceased to exist and became embodied in the Church Commissioners for England.

Queen's (or King's) Speech is the speech prepared by the Government in consultation with the Queen and delivered by Her Majesty in person or by her deputy, at the opening or closing of a Parliamentary session.

Quicksilver. *See* Mercury.

Quinine, a vegetable alkaloid obtained from the bark of several trees of the *Cinchona* genus. It is colourless and extremely bitter. The drug, sulphate of quinine, is one of the most valuable medicines, forming a powerful tonic. It is antiperiodic, antipyretic and antineuralgic. In cases of malaria it is the most efficacious remedy of natural origin known.

Quirinal, one of the seven hills of Rome.

Quisling, term which came into use during the second world war to denote traitor, collaborator or fifth-columnist. After Vidkun Quisling, who became head of the puppet government after the German invasion of Norway in 1940.

Quorum, the number of members of any body or company necessary to be present at any meeting or commission before business can be transacted. The House of Commons needs a quorum of 40, the Lords a quorum of 3.

R

Rabbi, a Jewish term applied to specially ordained officials who pronounce upon questions of legal form and ritual, and also generally accorded to any Jewish scholar of eminence.

Raccoon, plantigrade carnivorous mammals common to the American continent. There are several species. The common Raccoon (*Procyon lotor*) is about 60 cm long, with a bushy ringed tail and sharp snout. Its skin is valuable.

Race. In the old text-books anthropologists were much concerned with the differences between the various races of Man: they described the Black Man (Negro), the Yellow Man (Mongol), the Red Man (American Indian), the Brown Man (Indian), and the White Man (European). Those who study Man from this point of view further subdivide each group into others. Thus White Man may be divided into

Nordic, Alpine and Mediterranean; Black Man into Hamitic, Bushman and so on. Each of these groups tends to have physical traits which its members hold in common, although, of course, there are no *pure* racial types. All existing races have been fairly thoroughly mixed. What, in view of recent experience, is really important, is that races or even nations do not have psychological traits—at least not *innate* traits. Anthropology dismisses all theories of a superior race as unscientific: there is not the slightest evidence that one race differs in any way from another in its psychological potentialities: Jews, Irish Scots, Italians do differ (so do the inhabitants of Edinburgh and London): but their differences are due to their situation and not to anything inborn. *See* Racism, Section J.

Raceme, an inflorescence in which the main stem bears stalked flowers, *e.g.*, lupin, foxglove. The youngest flowers are at the tip of this axis.

Radar. The basic principle of radar is very similar to that of sight. We switch on a light in the dark, and we *see* an object because the light waves are reflected from it and return to our eye, which is able to detect them. Similarly the radar station *sees* an object because the invisible radio waves sent out from the transmitter are reflected from it and return to the receiver, which is able to detect them. Thus radar is the use of radio signals that man broadcasts.

The utilisation of radio waves for the detection of reflecting surfaces began with the classical experiment of the late Sir Edward Appleton in 1925, which he conducted in order to demonstrate the existence of the Heaviside layer in the upper atmosphere. During the course of the last war developments took place which tremendously improved the methods and instruments used. As in the case of so many of the inventions primarily developed for the purpose of waging war, many useful applications have been found for radar in times of peace, and, in particular, it has proved of great service as an aid to aerial and marine navigation, and in meteorology and astronomy. Radar astronomy investigates the solar system with the echoes of signals sent out from the Earth.

Radiation, energy emitted in the form of a beam of rays or waves, *e.g.*, acoustic (sound) radiation from a loudspeaker, radiant heat from a fire, β-radiation from a radioactive substance. The radiation of electromagnetic waves from a body depends on its temperature, the amount of energy radiated per second being proportional to the fourth power of the absolute temperature. The hotter the body, the shorter the wavelengths of the radiation; thus the colour of a glowing body depends on its temperature. Of paramount importance to us is radiation from the sun. Amongst other radiations, the sun sends ultra-violet, visible and infra-red (heat) waves. The principal gases of the atmosphere are transparent to practically all of the solar and sky radiation and also that which the earth re-transmits to space. Carbon dioxide and water vapour, however, strongly absorb certain types, the latter, as clouds, playing an important rôle in regulating the temperature of the globe. The cooling of the ground on a clear night is a result of the outgoing long-wave radiation exceeding that coming down from the sky; at sunrise cooling ceases as the incoming radiation becomes sufficient to compensate for the loss of heat.

Radiation, Cosmic. *See* F3(2).

Radio. The theory of electromagnetic waves—of which the radio wave is one—was originated by the British physicist James Clerk Maxwell (F14). He showed that both electrical and optical phenomena in space are essentially similar in character, and that the waves if short in wavelength are those of light, and if of longer wavelength those of radio waves. Heinrich Hertz made many useful discoveries about the waves themselves, and about their behaviour under differing conditions, and also about the apparatus for producing them. Marconi developed the use of radio waves as a practical means of communication.

Radio methods are vital for the transmission of observed data from space vehicles back to earth, a process known as "telemetering". This is done by converting the observations into electrical pulses which actuate a suitable radio transmitter so that it radiates a signal, in coded form, which can be received at a ground station and decoded. The transmission of such a signal can also be remotely controlled by means of signals from the earth. Photographic and television techniques may also be employed for obtaining the desired information and sending it back to earth, as in the case of the Russian picture of the reverse side of the moon and the American pictures of the lunar surface. The information may be stored within the spacecraft for a time, and then, upon receipt of a particular radio signal from the earth transmitted by the spacecraft at a time convenient for its reception. Soviet scientists, by a special technique, were able in the case of their *Venus IV* probe (October 1967) to parachute an instrumented canister from the spacecraft so that it could descend slowly to the surface of the planet—a feat described by Sir Bernard Lovell, who was recording the enterprise at Jodrell Bank, as " an experiment of classic elegance ". *See also* Radio Astronomy, Telemetry.

Radioactivity is the spontaneous transformation of atomic nuclei, accompanied by the emission of ionising radiations. It was discovered in 1896 by Becquerel, who noticed that salts containing uranium sent off radiations which, like X-rays, can blacken a photographic plate. Two years later Marie and Pierre Curie discovered several new chemical elements which possessed the same property, but many times more intense than uranium; the most important of these was radium. Shortly afterwards it was established, mainly by Rutherford, that three types of radiations called α-, β- and γ-rays, are emitted from radioactive substances. It was also Rutherford who, jointly with Soddy, deduced that the emission of the radiations is associated with the spontaneous disintegration of atoms which result in the transformation of one radioactive substance into another. A series of such transformations ends when a stable element is produced. All of the heavy radio-active elements can be arranged in three radio-active series, called, the uranium, thorium and actinium series. Initially, radioactivity was thought to be a property confined only to a few elements occurring in nature. In 1934, how-ever, Irene and Frederick Joliot-Curie dis-covered that ordinary elements can be trans-formed into radioactive forms by subjecting them to bombardment with α-particles. Following this, it was found that beams of other fast particles produced in accelerators can also render ordinary substances radioactive. Nowadays it is known that radioactivity is a general property of matter; any chemical element can be produced in one or more radio-active forms, or isotopes. *See* F12(1).

Radio Astronomy. The science of radio astro-nomy makes use of radio apparatus and tech-niques for the observation of events occurring in far distant parts of the universe, and, in so doing, is able to enlarge upon the observational field of optical astronomy in a remarkable way. By means of radio telescopes it is possible to observe parts of the universe so far distant that the radio waves received have taken thousands of millions of years to travel from their source to the earth, and thus to observe happenings which may have occurred near the beginning of the history of the universe. Thus radio astronomy works with signals that are broad-cast by objects in space.

There are two main types of radio telescope. The first, known as the interferometer, uses aerials spaced at large distances so as to cover a wide tract of ground. This has a high "reso-lution" but suffers from the disadvantage that it can "observe" only a very limited area of the sky overhead, as the earth turns upon its axis. The second, and "steerable", type, is that of the radio telescope at Jodrell Bank, Cheshire, which consists of an enormous concave metal bowl, with the radio aerials at its centre. This, though it has a lower "resolution", can be directed or "steered" on to any part of the sky which is above the horizon, and so can under-take a much more comprehensive observational

programme. It can be used either to receive radio waves coming from desired sources or to transmit them and then pick up the echo from, for example, the moon or a planet, as in radar.

One source of radio waves which can be detected by radio telescopes is our own sun, whose behaviour under " quiet " and " abnor-mal " conditions can be observed in this way. Some of the planets also appear to emit radio waves from parts of their surface. But much more remarkable are the waves which are re-ceived from quasars (*q.v.*).

Radiocarbon Dating is a method of dating the origin of organic materials or objects by observ-ing their radioactivity. It is of great import-ance to archaeology because it enables pre-historic dates back to about 50,000 B.C. to be established for animal and vegetable remains. It works because cosmic rays (*q.v.*) entering the atmosphere create neutrons which convert nitrogen in the air to radioactive carbon. This forms radioactive carbon dioxide and gets in-corporated into animals and vegetables through-out the world along with ordinary carbon di-oxide in a definite ratio, approximately 1 radio carbon atom to 0.8×10^{13} ordinary carbon atoms. When the tissue dies it stops inter-changing its carbon with the atmosphere, *e.g.*, by breathing, and the radioactive carbon in it gradually turns into nitrogen emitting a β-particle (*see* F12(1)). The radiocarbon con-tent decreases by about 1% in 88 years. By measuring the proportion of radioactive carbon left in, say, dead wood, and comparing it with living wood, the age of the dead sample can be calculated. This needs careful laboratory experiments. It is now believed that the pro-portion of radioactive carbon in the atmosphere varied from time to time in the past because changes in the earth's magnetic field affected the cosmic rays. This has to be allowed for in calculating the radiocarbon date. One use of radiocarbon dating has been to trace the spread of agriculture through the world from its origin in the Near East *c.* 7000 B.C. *See also* Tree-rings.

Radiosonde, a weather station in miniature carried aloft by a free balloon to heights normally in the neighbourhood of 16 km. Signals representa-tive of values of atmospheric pressure, tem-perature and humidity are transmitted sim-ultaneously by radio to ground receiving apparatus. The position of the balloon at any instant can be determined by radar, enabling the speed and direction of the upper winds to be deduced.

Radium, a radioactive metal, symbol Ra, dis-covered by Marie and Pierre Curie in 1898. Atomic weight 226. The Radium Institute, founded and equipped by Lord Iveagh and Sir Ernest Cassel, was opened in 1911 for the treatment of patients and research into the effect of radium on the human system. Radiotherapy (use of X-rays from radium) is used in the treat-ment of cancer.

Radon, a radioactive gaseous element, symbol Rn, formed by radioactive decay of radium. Its discovery completed the series of elements known as the inert (or rare) gases.

Rail, a well-known genus of the *Rallidae* family, including the Water Rail, the Moorhen, Corn-crake and Coot, resident in the British Isles.

Rain. When moist air rises into lower tempera-tures and becomes saturated, condensation takes place on the numerous hygroscopic par-ticles present in the atmosphere. If the tem-perature is above freezing a cloud of small droplets is formed. These droplets may then grow larger by coalescing with each other as they pass through the cloud until their weight is great enough to make them fall to the earth as rain. In clouds which extend above freezing level, snow and rain both form from the prefer-ential growth of ice crystals at the expense of liquid water droplets. If the resultant ice particle melts as it falls to earth, it gives rain: if not it gives snow.

Rainbow, a beautiful colour effect visible to an ob-server with back to the sun and facing a rain shower, caused by the refraction and reflection of sunlight in minute water-droplets in the air. From high in the air it would be possible to see a rainbow as a complete circle, but from the ground the most that can be seen is a semi-circle when the sun is just on the horizon; the higher the sun is, the smaller the arc of the rainbow. When conditions are suitable two bows are seen, the secondary with the colours of the spectrum reversed. The colours of the rainbow are seven: red, orange, yellow, green, blue, indigo and violet—the colours of the spectrum. *See also* Aurora.

Raingauge, an instrument consisting of a deep metal funnel whose stem dips into a graduated glass jar from which the depth of the rain water collected can be read. Continuous records of rainfall are provided by self-registering instruments.

Rain Making is a facility long desired by mankind, especially in the drought-ridden regions, and attempted throughout history by numerous non-scientific means. Since the second world war it has been proved that clouds can sometimes be made to rain or snow by dropping into them from an aeroplane very cold particles of solid carbon dioxide or by burning a solution containing silver iodide. This makes the moisture of the cloud form tiny ice crystals which grow big and finally fall out of the cloud. The process is quite complicated and not fully understood. The practical exploitation is somewhat chancy at present, but experiments have been made in many countries and the United States has a considerable programme of study. As well as scientific there are commercial and legal problems; premature commercial exploitation has resulted in disillusionment in some cases.

Rambouillet, a royal French château (14th cent., rebuilt 18th cent.), near Paris, and the official summer residence of the President of the French Republic. Also the name of the famous literary salon of the Marquise de Rambouillet (1588–1665).

Rampant, in heraldry, is a term applied to the figure of an animal with forelegs elevated, the dexter uppermost. When the animal is shown side-faced it is *rampant displayed,* when full-face, *rampant guardant;* when looking back *rampant reguardant;* and when in sitting position *rampant sejant.*

Rape, a cruciferous plant yielding coleseed or rapeseed, extensively grown in all parts of Europe and India. Rape oil is made from the seeds and as oilcake is a valuable animal feeding-stuff.

Rare Gases (also called **Inert Gases**). These are a group of elements which are chemically inert, comprising helium, neon, argon, krypton, xenon and radon. Cavendish in 1785 noticed that there was in air some gas which was not oxygen, nitrogen or carbon dioxide, but it was not until 1894 that the first of the rare gases was found by Rayleigh and Ramsay. This they called argon (inert). After the discovery of helium in 1895 Kayser, Rayleigh and Travers soon isolated the other gases except radon, which was later detected as a radioactive decay product of radium. Some of these inert gases are used to fill electric-light bulbs, and helium is used in balloons, since it is very light.

Rat, a well-known group of rodent embracing many species. The *brown rat* appeared in Europe early in the 18th cent., coming from the East and entering by way of Russia; now it is widespread and met with in Britain and all parts of the Continent. The *black rat,* which was the common rat before the arrival of the brown species, is a smaller animal and now comparatively scarce. There are numerous other kinds, all of them gross feeders, and existing in such numbers in many places as to constitute a pest. *See* Section Z.

Rational Number, a number which can be expressed as a ratio of two whole numbers. Examples are 2, ⅓, 0·3, −8. *See* Irrational Number.

Rationalism. *See* Section J.

Rattlesnake, venomous snakes which obtain their name from the possession of a rattle in the end of their tail, consisting of horny pieces so arranged that when vibrated they make a rattling sound. They are only found in N. and S. America.

Raven, a black-plumaged bird of the crow family, with raucous voice and massive bill. Occurs in many parts of Europe, Asia and America. Ravens are easily domesticated and form interesting pets. Dickens had one which he described in *Barnaby Rudge.*

Ray, fish with a very flat body and broad and fleshy pectoral fins, related to the sharks. There are about 140 species. In Britain they are generally called *skate.*

Razorbill, a sea-bird of the auk family, having a high, furrowed bill and black-and-white plumage. It inhabits rocky cliffs during the breeding season, and at other times is mostly out on the open sea.

Realism is a vague term. As a movement in art it can be said to have started with Gustave Courbet in the mid-19th cent. in his revolt against the classicism of Ingres and the romanticism of Delacroix. He was a man of strong radical views, and like Zola, Balzac and Flaubert in literature, turned to the actuality of everyday life, recording it with frankness and vigour. Some young English painters, notably Bratby, of the "kitchen sink" school, practise what some describe as social realism. In another sense, realism is an attitude concerned with interpreting the essential nature of the subject, revealing truths hidden by the accidentals of ordinary visual appearance. Thus form becomes more significant than content. Beginning with Cézanne and Van Gogh this trend passes on to Cubist and Abstract painting. *See also* Section J (philosophy), and Section I (dramatic term).

Record Office, in Chancery Lane, London, the place where the Public Records of England are preserved, including Domesday Book. More modern records are held at Kew.

Rectifier, an electrical device which will allow electric current to flow in one direction only and can therefore be used for turning alternating current into direct current. Since electricity is usually supplied in alternating form and frequently needed in direct form, rectifiers are of very common use both in industry and the home, for example in radio and television and for battery chargers. Rectifying properties are possessed by a number of different devices, one of which is a thermionic diode (*see* Valve). Very large valves filled with mercury vapour are often used for rectifying heavy currents for industrial purposes. Many other rectifiers use semiconductors in close contact with metals or with other semiconductors because such junctions have the property of passing electric current easily only in one direction.

Recusants, people who refused to attend the Anglican Church or to acknowledge the ecclesiastical supremacy of the Crown in the 16th and 17th cent.

Recycling, the process of sorting and re-using waste products. By no means a new idea, and already much used in industry and by the whole community in war-time, recycling assumes prominence when materials are scarce and prices high. There is much evidence from several countries that the public responds well to properly organised schemes for the collection, sorting and re-use of paper, plastic, glass, metals and other waste products common in industrialised countries. *See also* Section F, Part VI.

Redstart, a small bird of the Thrush family of handsome plumage and striking song. Two species visit Great Britain: the Common Redstart, with bright chestnut rump and tail, white forehead and black cheeks, favours wooded country, and the Black Redstart, with black breast and throat, chestnut tail and white wing bars, prefers rocky ground or ruins, and breeds in S. England.

Redwing, a bird of the Thrush family which finds its way to this country for the winter. Resembles the song thrush, but distinguished by smaller size, buffish-white eye-stripe, chestnut flanks and underwings. It has bred in Scotland and on Fair Isle.

Redwood *or* **Sequoia.** This genus of coniferous tree comprises two species of Redwoods occurring in N.W. America. Specimens of one species, the Giant Redwood, reach a height of over 90 m and a thickness of 11 m. The age of the largest, the General Sherman tree, is put at 3,500 years.

Referendum and Initiative, two methods by which the wishes of electors may be expressed with regard to proposed legislation. It is developed to the highest extent in Switzerland. In a *Referendum* some specific matter is referred to the electors. The *Initiative* is the means by which electors can compel their representatives to consider a specific issue. Gen. de Gaulle made use of the referendum in seeking the consent of the French nation for his policies. The British Labour Government held a referendum in June 1975, asking voters whether they felt the nation should remain in or withdraw from the European Economic Community. An Act of Parliament was required to authorise the referendum (which was something new in British constitutional history), and a further Act would have been necessary if the majority had been in favour of withdrawal. The result was for continued membership.

Reformation. See Section J.

Reform Bills. The principal Bills have been passed for the reform of the Parliamentary franchise. The first was the great Reform Bill of 1832, introduced by Lord John Russell and enacted under the Whig administration of Lord Grey. In addition to a sweeping redistribution of seats, this Act greatly extended the franchise but still left many people without the right to vote. The second Bill, passed by Disraeli in 1867, by giving the vote to workers in towns, established household suffrage. A third Bill, passed in 1884 under a Gladstone ministry, removed the distinction between borough and county franchises, enfranchised agricultural workers, and thus gave the vote to all men over 21. Women had to wait until 1918 to get the vote at the age of 30. The Representation of the People (Equal Franchise) Act, 1928, gave them the right to be registered as Parliamentary electors at the age of 21, thus making England into a true democracy. The Representation of the People Act, 1948, abolished the representation of the universities and the separate representation of the City of London and the business-premises vote. The Representation of the People Act, 1969, reduced the minimum voting age from 21 to 18 at both parliamentary and local government elections.

Refraction. The change of direction which light rays undergo when passing from one medium to another. The phenomenon is due to the fact that in different media light (and other forms of radiation) has different speeds.

Refractory, a substance capable of standing high temperatures and therefore useful for making furnaces and allied apparatus. Some insulating refractories are fire-clay, alumina, porcelain, carborundum, graphite and silica. Some refractory metals are platinum, molybdenum, tungsten, tantalum and the alloys nichrome, chromel, alumel.

Regency Style is the English version of the French Empire (*q.v.*) and approximately covers the period of the regency of Prince George, later George IV, from 1810 to 1820. It is somewhat less austere than the French style, and contains elements of the fantastic and exotic absent from Empire. The most famous monument of Regency style is the Royal Pavilion at Brighton, built for the Prince Regent by John Nash. (Regency style should not be confused with the *Régence* style in France, fashionable during the regency period between the death of Louis XIV in 1715 and the ascent to the throne of Louis XV in 1723. Here the English equivalent is Queen Anne style.)

Reindeer, a genus of deer horned in both sexes, occurring only in northerly regions. It has an average height of 1·3 m, is very fleet of foot and the Laplanders utilise it for draught purposes and for food.

Relativity. The laws of relativity have been substantially proved and have revolutionised our ideas as to the nature of space, time, matter and energy and forced us to think along new lines. In 1949 a new theory by Einstein was announced which sets forth in a series of equations the laws governing both gravitation and electromagnetism, which is said to bridge the gap that separates the universe of the stars and galaxies and the universe of the atom. At present the one is explained by relativity, and the other rests on the quantum theory. See F17–19.

Relief in sculpture is of three kinds—high relief (*alto-relievo*), in which the figures stand out to the extent of one-half of their natural proportions, low-relief (*basso-relievo*) when the figures project but slightly; and middle-relief (*mezzo-relievo*), when the projection is intermediate.

Renaissance. See Section J.

Republican Party of the United States was born by the fusion in 1854 of the group who called themselves National Republicans, having split from the Democrats over tariffs in 1825, and the northern Democrats, both of them being opposed to slavery. It came to power when Abraham Lincoln was elected President in 1860 and won 14 of the 18 presidential elections held between 1860 and 1932. It was defeated in 1932 largely as a result of the economic depression and reached its lowest ebb in the years of Roosevelt's New Deal (*q.v.*). The Party went on being defeated every four years until Eisenhower's victory in 1952. Nixon narrowly failed to defeat Kennedy in 1960 and Goldwater was decisively beaten by Lyndon Johnson in 1964. In 1968 and again in 1972 Nixon was successful in winning the Presidency. His fall from power in the aftermath of Watergate made 1974 a bad year for the Republican Party. The symbol of the Party is an elephant, the invention of Thomas Nast, a cartoonist, in 1874.

Requiem. Properly a mass for the dead, the term is extended to cover musical settings by Palestrina, Mozart, Verdi and others.

Reredos, the ornamental screen at the back of the altar or communion table. It is often of a highly decorative character and is an architectural feature in many churches in Spain. Other examples are to be found in the following cathedrals in England: Southwark, St. Albans, Winchester, Durham and Liverpool.

Resins, natural resins are vegetable compounds largely employed in the industrial arts. They comprise india-rubber, amber, mastic, copal, etc. " Synthetic resins " is a term sometimes used as a synonym for " plastics ".

Reuter, an international news agency, organised since 1941 as a trust and owned by the newspapers of Britain, Australia and New Zealand, founded by Baron J. de Reuter in 1849.

Rhea, a large flightless bird, the " ostrich " of S. America, distinguished from the ostrich proper by smaller size, longer beak, larger wings, no tail and 3 toes instead of 2. There are 2 species.

Rheology, the science of flow. See F21(1).

Rhesus Factor. See Index to Section P.

Rhinoceros, a large almost hairless animal related to the horse. Two kinds in Africa and several others in Asia. They have a horn, sometimes two, over the snout composed of modified hair. Most are leaf eaters but the largest species, the white rhino of South Africa, is a grazer. Rhinoceroses have been much hunted for their horns, which are reputed to have curative and aphrodisiac properties.

Rhodium, a metallic element, symbol Rh, discovered by Wollaston in 1804. It is found in platinum ores in small amounts, generally less than 2 per cent. With platinum it gives a very hard and durable alloy. It is also used, instead of silver, in putting the reflecting layer on a mirror.

Ribbon Fish or **Oarfish,** a deep-sea fish, deriving its name from its ribbon-like shape. Though fairly long, it is only a few centimetres thick. The ribbon fish is rarely met with because of its habitat, and most of what is known about it has been learnt from specimens occasionally cast ashore during storms.

Rice, a grain-yielding grass, of which thousands of strains are known today, extensively cultivated in China, India and certain parts of America, and forming the main food of the peoples of China, Japan, India and S.E. Asia. Some 95 per cent. of the world's rice is produced and consumed in the Orient. The grain with the husk is known as " paddy ". Arrack, an alcoholic liquor, is made from fermented rice seeds.

Richter Scale, a series of numbers used to record the relative magnitude of earthquakes. Devised by F. Richter of the California Institute of Technology. An earthquake is given a number on the scale by measuring the amplitude of earth movements, *i.e.*, the size of the to and fro motion in an earthquake wave, with a special instrument called a seismometer. The reading is corrected by calculation to allow for the distance of the instrument from the earthquake and the corrected results by observers at different places agree quite well. The scale is logarithmic, *i.e.*, earthquakes differing by one unit on the Richter scale are a factor 10 different in amplitude. An earthquake allotted zero on the scale would give a reading of 10^{-6} m on a standard seismometer 100 km from the centre of the earthquake. Smaller disturbances would have negative values on the scale. The largest known earthquakes had Richter values between $+8$ and $+9$, *i.e.*, they had 10^{+8} to 10^{+9} bigger amplitudes than earthquakes of magnitude zero. It is a widespread misconception that the scale has an upper limit of 10; there are no upper or lower limits to the scale.

Rime, a crystalline deposit of ice formed on objects exposed to wet fog at the same time as frost.

Rinderpest *or* **Cattle Plague,** is a highly contagious disease affecting cattle, sheep and other ruminants. In Europe the disease has been eradicated, but it was formerly very widespread and caused great loss of life among cattle. The disease is caused by a filtrable virus, and is attended by fever and congestion of the mucous membranes.

Ring Dove *or* **Wood Pigeon,** a blue-grey bird, distinguished from other pigeons by larger size (41 cm), white wing-bar, glossy green-and-purple neck and white half-collar. It is very common in Britain.

Rituale, the book of rites used in the Roman Catholic Church for the administration of certain sacraments and other church ceremonies. Like the Roman breviary, it dates in its present form from the Council of Trent.

RNA (Ribonucleic Acid). *See* **Nucleic Acids.**

Roaring Forties, name applied to the prevailing westerly winds over the oceans in the temperate latitudes of the Southern Hemisphere. Because unimpeded by large land areas the winds are more regular and stronger than the westerlies in the Northern Hemisphere.

Robin (or Redbreast). A small bird with olive-brown upper parts and orange-red forehead, throat and breast; both sexes look alike. The young are speckled, lacking the red breast. Its wide European distribution includes the British Isles, where it is the national bird. It also occurs in N. Africa and W. Asia. The nest is placed in a great variety of situations including holes in banks, trees and walls; in sheds, amongst ivy and sometimes in old tins. Nesting-boxes are readily adopted, but care should be taken to ensure that the entrance-hole is small enough to exclude starlings. Robins are pugnacious and defend their territories with vigour. Their attractive appearance, trustful disposition, engaging ways and sweet song make them extremely popular. The name robin is also applied to a number of very different birds, one of which, the American Robin, occasionally wanders to Europe.

Rock Dove, the grey pigeon *Columba livia* of Europe and Asia, ancestor of the domestic pigeons as Darwin was the first to show.

Rockets for use in war were first studied by Sir William Congreve early in the 19th cent., and proved very destructive in siege operations. They were invented by the Chinese as long ago as the 11th cent. The Germans devised the huge V2 rocket, carrying a ton of explosive, which was used near the end of the war to bombard London. Rockets are propelled by the burning of fuel (*e.g.*, oxygen or nitric acid), the exhaust, being ejected at high velocity, thrusts the rocket forward. For the study of the properties of the atmosphere vertical sounding rockets are used. Rocket flight in outer space was first presented as practicable by the Russian rocket expert, K. E. Tsiolkovsky, in 1903. The provision of sufficient launching velocity involves the use of rocket motors with adequate thrust. To launch a satellite into an orbit circulating within a few hundred kilometres of the surface a velocity of 29,000 km/h must be imparted. This may be done by using a multi-stage launching system. When the first-stage motor has burned out it drops off, so that, when the second-stage motor ignites, it does not have to support the weight of the first-stage, and so on. If the launching velocity is increased to 40,000 km/h the vehicle will not return to the neighbourhood of the earth but pass out of the range of the earth's gravitational pull completely. Unless the launching velocity reaches 161,000 km/h it will not escape from the sun and will become an artificial planet. *See also* **Space Research.**

Rock Magnetism. The study of naturally occurring magnetism in rocks is a subject which has gained considerable importance in recent years. There are two principal reasons for this. One is that this so-called "fossilised magnetism" may be able to tell us more about the past history of the earth's magnetic field. The other is that after many years of heated dispute between geologists rock magnetism promises to settle once and for all the controversy as to whether or not the continents have changed their relative positions in past times (continental drift theory (*q.v.*)). This branch of geophysical research, in addition to its academic interest, may well have important economic consequences. It might, for instance, become possible to locate mineral deposits once accumulated under special conditions at certain latitudes but now drifted to other places. Salt and similar deposits formed by the continuous evaporation of solutions in hot countries are one example; oil may well be another. There has been a *steady* change in rock magnetisation direction with geological time. It is now known with some accuracy that the most recent reversal took place 700,000 years ago. It has been found that the older the rock, the farther removed is its fossil magnetisation from the present field.

Rococo, an architectural style which was, in effect, the final stage of Baroque (*q.v.*). The name first came into use about 1830 to describe the period 1720–70 and means "shell-shaped" (French *Rocaille*), since the shell was a favourite motif in Rococo ornamentation. At about the beginning of the 18th cent. the heavy older type of Baroque began to show even less restraint than had characterised it in the past; it became still less utilitarian, and showed a kind of playful lighthearted vitality which manifested itself in a wealth of ornamental invention. Baroque was flamboyant and robust, Rococo dainty, graceful and smiling. Its ornaments are frequently asymmetrical, and in this Rococo is unique among the historical styles of Europe. In architecture Rococo is naturally found in those areas where the Baroque had flourished, *i.e.*, Munich, Prague, Vienna and Dresden. In painting, the best expressions of Rococo are to be seen in the works of the French painters Watteau (d. 1721), Boucher (d. 1770), a favourite of Mme de Pompadour, and famous as a decorator of boudoirs, and Fragonard (d. 1806). (As in the case of Baroque, it was typical of Rococo that the sculpture, painting and the decorative arts of a building all expressed the same spirit.)

Roe, popular name given to organs in fish which produce eggs and sperms. "Hard roe" is that of the female and consists of eggs; that of the male is the soft roe or milt.

Roe Deer (*Capreolus capreolus*) deer native to Europe and found in England and Scotland but not Ireland. "Roebuck" is the name of the male adult.

Roller, a tropical Old World bird of the *Coraciidae* family, related to the hoopoe, kingfisher and bee-eater, of strikingly brilliant blue, chestnut, greenish-blue plumage. There are fifteen species, one of which breeds in the far north and visits the British Isles on its migrations to and from its winter quarters in Africa.

Romanesque Architecture, prevailed throughout Europe from the mid-10th to the 13th cent., and implies an art which developed from that of the Romans. Notable in Romanesque style were the rounded arch and masonry vaulting. Romanesque led to the graceful and more complex Gothic (*q.v.*). The Italians never regarded Gothic highly and Romanesque churches, generally based on the basilican plan (oblong with double colonnades and a semi-circular apse at the end), continued to be built there until the beginning of the 15th cent. Some of the best examples can be seen at Pisa (11th cent.), Florence (San Miniato, 1013), Lucca (12th cent.) and Milan (the 12th cent. San Ambrogio, most famous of all). In Germany Romanesque architecture flourished longer than in France or England; the most famous churches are in the valley of the Rhine, at Cologne (completely destroyed during the second world war), Mainz and Speyer. In France Romanesque churches are found in Burgundy, Provence and Normandy. For English Romanesque see **Norman Architecture.**

Roman Roads, highways constructed by the Romans. They were of great durability. The best known British roads were Ermine Street (London, Lincoln, York), Fosse Way (Lincoln through Leicester, Cirencester. Bath, Exeter), Watling Street (Channel Ports, London to Salop).

Romanticism, a term for a movement in the arts— whether in music, painting, sculpture or literature—which seeks to give expression to the artist's feelings about his subject rather than to be concerned with form or reality. The romantic view is that art is nature seen through a temperament; the realist view is that art is a slice of life. In painting Delacroix (1798–1863) is the romantic artist par excellence with his uncontrolled expression of the passions and love of the exotic. In literature the Romantic movement reached its finest form in the works of Goethe, Schiller and Heine; in the poetry of Byron, Keats, Wordsworth, Shelley and Blake; and in the writings of Victor Hugo. Since Romanticism is partly a matter of temperament in the artist just as Classicism is, it may be found at all times and places, although whether or not it becomes predominant depends on contemporary taste. Cubism, for example, with its attention to form is classical, whereas Surrealism with its attention to content is romantic. See also **Romantic Movement, Section J.**

Roman Walls were built as frontier barriers under the Emperors Hadrian (76–138) and Antoninus Pius (86–161). Hadrian's works, linking Wallsend-on-Tyne with Bowness-on-Solway, comprised a twenty-foot stone wall, ditches, turrets, " milecastles ", fortresses and a double earthen mound, or " Vallum ". Impressive ruins are still visible at Chesters and Housesteads. Antoninus Pius, Hadrian's successor, made a further advance, but the turf wall which he built between Forth and Clyde was soon abandoned. Septimius Severus (146–211) restored Hadrian's wall after the assassination of Commodus and the subsequent civil wars. It was finally abandoned between 380 and 390. Archaeologists from Lancaster University have recently excavated the Roman fort at Ravenglass (Roman Glannaventa) on the Cumbrian coast and believe it to have been built as an extension to Hadrian's wall.

Rood Screen, an ornamental partition, separating the choir from the nave in a church, and supporting a crucifix or rood.

Rook, a member of the crow family, abounding in most parts of the British Isles and found in Europe, Asia and N. Africa. It has been introduced into New Zealand. Rooks usually nest in colonies in tall trees. They are highly intelligent birds, and their ways have long been the subject of much careful study.

Rosary, a circular chain of beads, used by Catholics when reciting a particular form of sustained prayer. Each bead represents an entire prayer, and the combined prayers constitute the Rosary.

Roses, Wars of the (1455–85), between the rival houses of York and Lancaster, for the possession of the English crown, began in the reign of Henry VI and ended with the death of Richard III on Bosworth Field. The emblem or badge of the Lancastrians was the red rose and of the Yorkists the white rose. All rivalry between The Roses ended by the marriage of Henry VII, the Lancastrian, with the Princess Elizabeth, daughter of Edward IV, the Yorkist.

Rosetta Stone, discovered in 1799 by the French at Rosetta in Egypt, and deposited in the British Museum. It is a piece of black basalt about 91 cm long, and contains a decree of the Egyptian priests of Ptolemy V Epiphanes (205–181 B.C.)

in (1) hieroglyphics, (2) demotic and (3) Greek characters. It was by means of the three different inscriptions on the same stone that hieroglyphic writing was first able to be deciphered.

Rotten Row, a corruption of route de roi (king's drive), the famous riding resort in Hyde Park.

Rouge et Noir, a well-known gambling card game played on a table divided into two sections and marked with two black and two red lozenges. Any number of players can take part, and the money is staked on the red or black spaces. The cards are dealt out, first to Noir, until the pips aggregate more than 30; then in like manner to the Rouge, and the packet coming nearest to 31 wins the stakes.

Roulette, a gambling game played on a table carrying a revolving wheel divided into 37 compartments. Each compartment bears a number, 0 (zero) and 1 to 36. The numbers are mixed and do not follow any particular order. Of these 37 numbers 18 are black and 18 are red, whereas zero is green. The players stake their money on any compartment, colour or combination of numbers they please. The wheel is whirled round and a ball is set rolling in the opposite direction, dropping finally into one of the compartments, thus deciding the winning number and colour.

Roundhead. In the reign of Charles I and later, a Puritan or member of the Parliamentary party who wore his hair cut short. It was originally a term of derision applied by the Royalists, who usually wore ringlets.

Round Towers, high circular towers with conical roof and massive masonry walls, built during the early Middle Ages (c. 10th cent.). It is believed that they served as refugees and lookouts. These buildings are numerous in Ireland, and three remain in Scotland, including that at Brechin which is attached to the church.

Royal Academy of Arts was founded in London in 1768, under the patronage of George III. The early exhibitions of the Academy were held first in Pall Mall, and after in Somerset House, where the exhibitions continued to be held until 1836, when the National Gallery being built, the Academy moved its quarters to that building. In 1869 the present Royal Academy at Burlington House was opened. The Academy numbers (1976) 64 R.A.s and 20 A.R.A.s. List of presidents: Sir Joshua Reynolds (1768), Benjamin West (1792), James Wyatt (1805), B. West (1806), Sir Thomas Lawrence (1820), Sir M. A. Shee (1830), Sir C. Eastlake (1850), Sir F. Grant (1866), Lord Leighton (1878), Sir J. E. Millais (1896), Sir E. J. Poynter (1896), Sir Aston Webb (1919), Sir F. Dicksee (1924), Sir William Llewellyn (1928), Sir E. Lutyens (1938), Sir A. J. Munnings (1944), Sir Gerald F. Kelly (1949), Sir A. E. Richardson (1954), Sir Charles Wheeler (1956), Sir Thomas Monnington (1966) and Sir Hugh Casson (1976). The Academy holds an exhibition of pictures, statuary and architectural designs every summer.

Royal Hospital, Chelsea, built by Wren, was opened in 1694 as an institution for invalid soldiers.

Royal Institution, established 1799, and incorporated by Royal Charter in 1800 for " the promotion, extension and diffusion of Science and of Useful Knowledge ". It was in the building of the Institution that Faraday conducted his experiments. Today it has extensive research laboratories. Famous also for its Christmas lectures designed for a juvenile audience. Director, Prof Sir G. Porter, F.R.S.

Royal Society was founded in 1660 and incorporated by Royal Charter in 1662. Viscount Brouncker being named the first president. Its Philosophical Transactions date from 1665. Among those who served as president of the Royal Society are Sir Christopher Wren, Pepys, Sir Isaac Newton, Sir Joseph Banks, Sir Humphry Davy, Prof. T. H. Huxley, Lord Rayleigh, Sir Archibald Geikie, Sir J. J. Thomson, O.M., Prof. Sir C. S. Sherrington, O.M., G.B.E., Lord Rutherford, O.M., Sir William Henry Bragg, O.M., Sir Henry Dale, O.M., Sir Robert Robinson, O.M., Lord Adrian, O.M., Sir Cyril Hinshelwood, O.M., Lord Florey, O.M., Lord Blackett O.M. (1965), Sir Alan Hodgkin, O.M. (1970), Lord Todd (1975).

Rubber, produced from the juice of certain trees and shrubs of tropical countries, is in such extensive demand now for tyres and other purposes that rubber plantations have been established in almost every part of the world where rubber can be grown, particularly in Indonesia and Malaysia. The Amazon is the original source of all present-day rubber. In recent years great advances have been made in the production of synthetic rubber.

Rubicon, a small river falling into the Adriatic, and forming one of the Italian boundaries, the crossing of which anciently involved decisive action and constituted a declaration of war. Thus the phrase " crossing the Rubicon ", denoting an act from which there is no withdrawal.

Rubidium, a metallic element, symbol Rb, most closely resembling potassium. It is silver-white and very soft, and was discovered in 1861 by Bunsen and Kirchhoff, using the spectroscope. It is rare, occurring in small amounts in the mica called lepidolite and in potash salts of the Strassfurt deposits in Germany.

Rubrics are instructions in regard to the ceremonies of the Church, appearing in red in the Prayer Book.

Ruby is a deep red variety of Corundum (aluminium oxide); one of the most valued of precious stones. Burma yields some of the finest, and rubies of inferior colour are found in Thailand, Sri Lanka, South Africa and Brazil.

Rudd, a fresh-water fish of wide distribution, plentiful in the rivers of Britain, and found in most other parts of Europe, also in Asia Minor. It is of a reddish-gold colour, with a greenish-blue beard.

Ruff, a bird related to the common sandpiper, at one time common in the Fen districts. The males have a ruff of feathers round the neck in the breeding season. The female is the Reeve.

Ruffe *or* **Pope**, a small fresh-water fish common in most parts of central Europe, and similar in appearance to the ordinary perch. It is found in British rivers.

" Rule, Britannia! " the national sea-song of England, was written by James Thomson (1700–48), the author of the " Seasons ", and set to music by Dr. Arne about 1740. The poet's words were " Britannia, rule the waves! " but it is usually rendered " Britannia rules the waves."

Rum, an ardent spirit distilled from molasses, and containing from 40 to 50 per cent. of alcohol. It is chiefly manufactured in the West Indies, and derives its special flavour from a volatile oil.

Ruminants, animals that chew the cud, being provided with a compartmented stomach, enabling them to swallow food, and later to bring it back to the mouth for mastication; *e.g.*, sheep, goats, oxen, etc. While in the rumen, or storage compartment, some digestion of food, especially cellulose, takes place by bacterial action.

Runcible spoon, a kind of fork used for pickles having three broad prongs. The word was used by Edward Lear about 1870 as a nonsense word and may be derived from *Rouncival* meaning large or huge from the bones said to have been dug up at *Roncesvalles* where Roland fell. Rouncival peas are the large peas called " marrowfats ".

Runes, certain characters of an alphabet found in inscriptions in the Germanic languages, found cut into buildings and implements of stone or wood in many parts of northern Europe, including Britain. The runic alphabet originally had 24 letters. Scholars agree that some of the runes derive from Greek and others from Latin.

Ruskin College, the first residential college for working people, founded at Oxford in 1899 by Mr. Walter Vrooman, an American.

Rusts, parasitic fungi, some common species of which have reddish spores which in a mass have a rusty appearance. A well-known species is the Wheat Rust (*Puccinia graminis*), which has an alternative host in the barberry.

Ruthenium, a greyish-white metallic element, symbol Ru, discovered by Claus in 1845. It is harder and more brittle than platinum, in whose ores it occurs.

Rutile, mineral titanium dioxide. It is found in many igneous rocks, and in gneisses and schists. Its commonest colour is reddish-brown.

S

Sabaoth, a Hebrew word, meaning an army or host, and applied sometimes to the Supreme Being, *e.g.*, " the Lord of Hosts " (Rom. ix. 29).

Sabbath and Sunday. Sunday, or the Lord's Day, is the first day of the week in the Christian year. It was substituted for the Jewish Sabbath in the 1st cent. A.D. as the Christian day of worship in commemoration of the Resurrection. The Sabbath, in the Jewish system, was the last day of the week (Saturday in the Christian calendar), designated as the day of religious rest in the fourth commandment of the Decalogue. It was the Puritans at the time of the Reformation who applied the term Sabbath to the Christian Sunday and the two terms have been used indiscriminately ever since.

Sabbatical Year was instituted by the Jews in ancient times for the purpose of giving the soil a rest from cultivation. This was every seventh year. In universities a sabbatical year is a year of absence from duty for the purpose of study and travel, granted to professors at certain intervals.

Sable, a furred mammal of the weasel family mainly inhabiting Siberia. It is bright brown in colour, and has a long, bushy tail. American sable is a marten.

Saccharin, a white crystalline solid manufactured from toluene, 550 times as sweet as cane sugar. It is used as a sweetening agent; as a substitute for sugar when sugar is forbidden, as in certain diseases, or when there is a shortage. It has no value as a food.

Safety Lamp, as used in coal mines, was invented by Sir Humphry Davy in 1816. The flame is enclosed in a cage of fine-meshed wire which allows air to enter and promote burning, but conducts away the heat generated in combustion so that no product of combustion escapes at a temperature high enough to ignite explosive gases in the mine.

Sainfoin, a widely cultivated forage plant, especially adapted for sheep. It is of strong, leafy growth and bears bright red flowers. It belongs to the same family of flowering plants as peas and beans.

St. Elmo's Fire, a glowing brush-like discharge of electricity which takes place from sharp-pointed objects on mountains or the masts of ships exposed to the intense electric fields of thunder-clouds.

Saints' Days. In the liturgy of the Roman Catholic church a saint is commemorated and his intercession sought on a special day (saint's day), usually the anniversary of his death. Pope Paul decreed that from 1 January 1970 the following saints were to be dropped from the calendar: Christopher, Catherine of Alexandria, Alexis, Pudenzia, Susan, Margaret, Viviana, Eustace, Martina, Venantius and Domitilla. Many others, including our own Saint George, and Nicholas (Santa Claus) have been demoted though they may be venerated locally. There are now only 153 saints' days in addition to those in honour of the Apostles, Saint Joseph and the Virgin Mary. The festival of All Saints is on 1 November.

Salamanders are amphibia superficially resembling lizards, from which they differ in having a moist skin and no scales.

Salic Law was probably instituted in France in the 5th cent. for the purpose of excluding females from inheriting the Crown. The Bourbons introduced the same law into Spain, but this was abolished by decree in 1830 to enable Isabella II to succeed.

Salmon, a fish notable for its habit of returning from the sea to spawn in the river where it was itself hatched. Their origin can be inferred from the chemical composition of certain blood proteins. Salmon from the two sides of the Atlantic migrate to communal feeding grounds off Greenland.

Saltpetre. *See* **Nitre.**

Salvarsan, the organic arsenical compound arsphenamine, which Ehrlich discovered was able to kill inside the human body the spirochaete germ that causes syphilis. Also known as " 606 ". It has been superseded by neosalvarsan.

Salvation Army. *See* **Section J.**

San Andreas Fault, is the dividing line between the North American plate and the North Pacific Ocean plate where "plate" means one of the rigid sections of the earth's crust as conceived in the theory of plate tectonics (*q.v.*). The fault runs roughly north-west—south-east in California passing near San Francisco. The Pacific Ocean bed and the North American continent are sliding past each other along this fault at about 5 cm per year. As at all plate-to-plate boundaries—another is the Western Pacific coast – the San Andreas fault is the scene of great earthquake activity. Between 1934 and 1970 there were over 7,000 earthquakes severer than magnitude 4 on Richter scale (*q.v.*) in and near southern California. Because of large population centres, the activity of the San Andreas region is studied with great care and some apprehension about a repeat of the San Francisco earthquake of 1906 which caused displacements of up to 6·4 m along the San Andreas Fault. *See also* F9.

Sanderling, small wading bird of sandpiper family; breeds in tundra regions of far north, and is seen on sandy beaches of Britain as a winter visitor. Conspicuous white wing stripe and, like Curlew, Sandpiper, Knot, Dunlin and other members of sandpiper family, has marked change of plumage between winter and summer.

Sandpiper, small- to medium-sized wading birds of several species whose migratory powers are so great that they are found in most parts of the world. They include the Common Sandpiper, a bird about 18 cm long, greenish-brown head and back, white under-parts; beak long and slender. Purple, Wood and Curlew-Sandpipers.

Sans-culottes (French = without knee breeches), a term applied by the French aristocrats to the revolutionary leaders during the French Revolution who wore long trousers instead of knee breeches.

Sanskrit is the language of ancient India, spoken by the Brahmins, and existing in early Oriental literature. It was the language of literature and government and is now confined to temples and places of learning. Its relationship to the modern Indian languages is rather like that of Latin and Greek to modern European languages.

Saponin. The term is a generic one applied to a range of organic compounds which produce frothy, soapy solutions. Saponins are extracted from the soapwort root, horse chestnut seeds, etc. Saponin is the basis of the "foam" used for fire fighting; it can be used like soap to make insecticides and fungicides adhere to the leaves of plants. Also used as detergents.

Sapphic Verse, a form of verse said to have been invented by Sappho, the lyric poetess of Lesbos, who flourished about 600 B.C.

Sapphire, a valuable deep blue variety of Corundum (aluminium oxide) found mostly in India, Sri Lanka and Northern Italy. Synthetic sapphire is often used for gramophone styli.

Saracen, the name given in classic times to the Arab tribes of Syria and adjacent territories. In the Middle Ages the current designation among the Christians for their Muslim enemies.

Sassanides were a dynasty of Persian rulers descended from Artaxerxes from 226 to 625.

Satellite Communication, the system for transmitting telephone and television signals over long distances. Satellites orbiting the earth at a height of *c.* 35,700 km above the Atlantic, Pacific and Indian oceans provide a global coverage. They take exactly 24 h to complete one orbit and so appear to stay in the same place. *Telstar*, launched in the summer of 1969, took only 2·5 h and was therefore within range of the earth stations on each side of the Atlantic for very short periods. The global satellite system Intelsat (International Telecommunications Intelsat Organisation) was founded in 1964 to establish a world-wide system on a commercial basis. The first generation of Intelsat satellites to be launched from Florida was *Early Bird*, which went into service in June 1965. Intelsat II extended coverage to more than two-thirds of the world by 1967 and by 1969 the system was completed when Intelsat III satellites were launched, making it possible to transmit all forms of communication simultaneously—television, telephone, telex,

computer data and facsimile. Further series have been introduced since then and others are being designed to meet future communications requirements. By 1978, 155 ground stations in 86 countries were being served.

Satellites are small planets revolving round the larger ones. The moon is the earth's only satellite. Jupiter has thirteen; Saturn, ten; Uranus, five; Mars, two; and Neptune, two. Earth satellite research since 1957 has yielded important scientific data.

Satin-Bird, one of the bower birds of Australia; the male is silky blue-black and the female greyish green. *See* Bower bird.

Saturday, the seventh day of the week (the Jewish Sabbath), derived its name from Saturn, or, as some hold, is called after the Saxon idol Saterne, which was worshipped on this day.

Saturn, a planet, the sixth from the sun, from which it is distant about 1427 × 10⁶ km, and around which it makes a revolution in about twenty-nine and a half years. It is about 120,000 km in diameter, or nine times as large as the earth, and rotates on its axis in ten and a quarter hours. It is surrounded by a series of rings composed of myriads of tiny satellites. It has at least ten small satellites. *See* F8.

Saturnalia, festivals held in ancient Rome in honour of the god Saturnus. They were made the scene of boisterous festivities, and were continued for several days at the end of December.

Sawfish, a large marine ray found in tropical America and Guinea, whose snout often attains the length of a metre or so, and is provided with saw-like teeth. This "saw" is swung from side to side among a shoal of fish which form the food of this ray.

Sawfly. These insects are considered to be the most primitive members of the order (*Hymenoptera*) to which the bees and wasps belong. In appearance they resemble somewhat the latter, but there is no waist separating thorax and abdomen. The ovipositor is never used as a sting; usually it is saw-like so that the female can use it to make incisions into tissues of plants where the eggs are laid. The larvae look like caterpillars of butterflies and moths.

Saxons, a Teutonic race originally inhabiting what is now Holstein. By the 7th cent. they had, with the Angles and Jutes, conquered and colonised most of England.

Scallop, marine bivalve molluscs of the genus *Pecten*, which is widely distributed. The scalloped edge to the shell results from a pattern of radiating grooves. Related to the oyster.

Scandium, a metal element, symbol Sc. It was discovered in 1879 by Nilson, and occurs in small quantities in certain rarer minerals such as wolframite.

Scapular, a vestment hanging from the shoulder to the knees, worn by members of certain Roman Catholic orders. The name is also given to two small pieces of cloth worn over the shoulders by lay members in honour of the Virgin.

Scarabaeidae, a family of beetles (Scrabs) widely distributed through Africa and Asia and the inner parts of Europe. It is to this genus that the "Sacred Beetle" of the Egyptians belongs, and numerous representations of it are found on ancient monuments.

Sceptre, the staff or rod used since ancient times to symbolise supreme authority. The sceptre used for the coronation of Queen Elizabeth II is the one made for Charles II. It is about 90 cm long and tipped with a jewelled cross.

Schism, an ecclesiastical term for division in a church. The Great Schism was the separation of the Greek Church from the Latin, finally established in 1054. The Western Schism was the division in the Roman Catholic Church from 1378 to 1417, when there were two lines of popes, one at Rome and one at Avignon.

Schist, the geological name of certain metamorphic rocks composed for the most part of minerals with thin plate-like crystals (*e.g.*, mica) so that the layers of a schist are closely parallel. Quartz occurs in schists, and where it preponderates the term "quartz schist" is applied.

Scientific Units. The International Bureau of Weights and Measures at Sèvres near Paris, is the custodian of accurate scientific measurement in terms of internationally agreed units.

Methods of measurement are continually being improved and measurements of new kinds coming into use. In defining units certain principles have evolved which can be expressed as a statement of priorities:

(i) units should be so defined that measurements made in one laboratory should be reproducible in another with as much consistency as possible;

(ii) units of all kinds should, so far as practical, form an interrelated system based on as few fundamental units as possible;

(iii) the fundamental units adopted should have a natural basis, independent of particular man-made objects such as metal bars or weights. An invariable universal natural standard was achieved for the metre in 1958 when it was defined in terms of the wavelength of a line in the spectrum of krypton–86. See **S.I. Units.**

Schoolmen, the great scholastic philosophers of the Middle Ages who devoted themselves to the study and exposition of questions of religious inquiry, and attempted to reconcile the teaching of the Church with that of Aristotle. The chief Schoolmen were Archbishop Anselm, Albertus Magnus, Thomas Aquinas, Peter Lombard, Duns Scotus. See also **Section J.**

Scorpion. The scorpions constitute an order of the arthropods. Distinctive features are the pair of powerful claws at the head and a " sting" at the tail, which curves over the back in attack or defence so that it points forwards. The poison injected by the sting is potent, causing instant death in spiders, centipedes, etc., and acute discomfort to humans. The idea that a cornered scorpion can sting itself to death is a myth; scorpions are immune to their own poison.

Scorpion Fly. The scorpion fly, of which there are less than 500 species, constitute a separate order of insects, the *Mecoptera*. They have 2 pairs of membranous wings, and gain their popular name because in some species the end of the abdomen is turned up, though it does not function as a sting.

Scree or **Talus,** the mass of loose, angular rock fragments which accumulate towards the bottom of hill-sides and mountain-sides. These fragments have been detached by weathering processes, in particular frost action.

Scythians, nomadic conquerors and skilled horsemen of ancient times (9th–3rd cent. B.C.) who inhabited much of Southern Europe and Asiatic Russia.

Sea Anemones or **Actinaria,** an order of marine animals of the coelenterate class *Anthozia.* They form a large and varied group of about 1,100 species and occur in many beautiful colours, flower-like in form.

Sea Butterfly, marine molluscs which propel themselves by two " wings", or side expansions of the foot. They constitute the order called *Pteropoda.*

Sea Cow. See **Manatee.**

Sea Cucumbers or **Holothurians.** These animals constitute the class of echinoderms called *Holothuroidea.* They are elongated and worm-like, with a ring of about twenty tentacles round the mouth. There are about 500 species.

Sea Eagle, a genus of flesh-eating birds related to the true eagles, kites and other birds of prey. Examples are the Bald Eagle, emblem of the USA, White-tailed Eagle (Grey Sea Eagle), and Steller's Sea Eagle of the Pacific coast of Asia. Last known in Britain in 1911.

Sea Elephant or **Elephant Seal,** a curious genus of seal, the males of which possess a proboscis of c. 30 cm in length that suggests an elephant's trunk. They are found on the coast of California and in certain parts of the Southern Ocean; their blubber has a commercial value.

Sea Gravimeter, an instrument to determine the density of the earth's crust beneath the oceans of the world. Designed by Dr. A. Graf of Munich and Dr. J. Lamar Worzel of Columbia University, it can detect changes of one-millionth of the value of gravity at the earth's surface and was used in the oceanographical research programme of the IGY.

Sea Hare, a genus of molluscs (*Aplysia*), so-called because of resemblance to a crouching hare. The shell is thin curved plate largely sunk in the animal's body. They have four tentacles, occur in Britain in the laminaria or ribbon wrack zone, and discharge a purple fluid when molested.

Sea Horse, a sea-fish (*Hippocampus*), very numerous in the tropics and comprising some twenty species. Their bodies are ringed and they have prehensile tails. Their heads are horse-shaped, and they swim in a vertical position.

Sea Lily. A class of echinoderms, the sea lilies may be roughly described as " stalked starfishes ". There are about 400 living species and several thousand extinct species are known. Otherwise called Crinoids.

Sea Mouse, a genus of marine worms called *Aphrodite,* oval in shape, 20–23 cm long, iridescent, covered with fine bristles.

Seasons comprise the four natural divisions of the year, and are due to the inclinations of the earth's axis to the plane of the eliptic. See **Section N.**

Sea Squirts or **Tunicates.** These animals are placed in the sub-phylum called *Urochorda;* found growing in rounded, jelly-like masses on rocks near low-water level. They get their name through the water jets they discharge.

Sea Urchin, species forming the class *Echinoidae.* The body is globular and covered with spines which may be used for both defence and locomotion. The main organs of locomotion are, however, the tube feet, as in starfishes. Much has been learnt of recent years by marine biologists from experiments with the purple sea-urchin *Arbacia.*

Secondary Sexual Characters, characters of animals which are distinctive of sex, but have no direct connection with the reproductive process. Examples are: the mane of the lion and the antlers of some deer.

Secretary Bird, so called because of the quill-like plumes about its ears, is a bird of prey related to the eagles and vultures; common in Africa, and of considerable service as an exterminator of snakes. It is a large bird about 1·2 m in height.

Sedimentary Rocks. See **F9(1).**

Seismology, the branch of geophysics devoted to the study of earthquakes and other earth movements. The instruments used for the registration of earth tremors are termed seismographs and consist in principle of a pendulum system, the supporting framework following the ground movement and the bob remaining at rest, thus setting up a relative movement between two parts. In order to record the displacements completely, at one station, three seismographs are necessary to show the two horizontal and the vertical components of the motion. Apart from detection and study of waves from earthquakes sensitive seismographs are now widely used in geophysical prospecting, particularly in the search for possible oilfields. See also **Richter Scale.**

Selenium, a non-metallic element, symbol Se; related to sulphur it is a dark red colour, and solid, found associated with sulphur, iron, pyrites, etc., though only in small quantities. It is a semiconductor (*q.v.*) and its special electrical properties have led to its use in photoelectric cells and rectifiers. Selenium is widely used in the chemical industry as a catalyst (*q.v.*) in producing aromatic hydrocarbons from less useful hydrocarbons. Also used in making some types of glass.

Semiconductors, substances with numerous special and useful electrical properties a few of which are:

(i) they conduct electricity much better than do insulators, but much less well than metals (hence their name);

(ii) their power to conduct depends strongly on their temperature—which makes them useful for temperature sensitive devices;

(iii) they are sensitive to light—hence their use in photoelectric cells and solar batteries;

(iv) when in contact with metals, or with other suitable semiconductors, they form a boundary layer which conducts electricity much better one way than the other—this is the basis of many rectifiers some of which, called crystal diodes, are an important component in radios and electronic devices;

(v) their electrical properties can be greatly influenced by putting in minute amounts of impurity, this enables semiconductor devices, especially transistors, to be made with carefully selected properties.

Semiconductors were known to Faraday, but the semiconductor age really arrived with the invention of the transistor (*q.v.*) in 1947. The ubiquitous transistor is only one of very many semiconductor devices which perform a variety of functions in technical apparatus of all kinds. Semiconductors used in technology are usually small crystals, frequently of germanium or silicon, and their robustness and small power consumption often make them superior to other devices, such as thermionic valves, which they often replace. Other semiconducting materials are cadmium sulphide, selenium. lead telluride, indium antimonide. *See also* **F22(1).**

Senate, the higher governing Assembly of a Legislature. The word, applied primarily to the Roman council, is also used to denote the upper chamber in the legislatures of France, the United States, and other countries. In certain universities the governing body is also called the Senate.

Sensitive Plant. A species of Mimosa (*Mimosa pudica*), whose leaves are extremely sensitive to touch, shaking and burning.

Sepia, the "ink" of the cuttlefish. *See* **Ink Sac.**

September, the ninth month of the year, and the seventh of the old Roman calendar; hence the name, from Septimus. The designation was several times changed by the Emperors, but none of the new names survived for long.

Septuagesima Sunday, the third Sunday before Lent.

Septuagint, the Greek translation of the Old Testament made by Alexandrian Jews between 250 B.C. and 100 B.C. from Hebrew texts now lost. There are many differences between the Septuagint and the Massoretic version (A.D. 900), and therefore it is of great value for textual criticism. The symbol for the Septuagint is LXX.

Serfs, the name given to the slaves formerly existing in Russia, who answered to the condition of the feudal " villeins " of England. They were attached to the soil and were transferred with it in all sales or leases. Serfdom existed in Prussia until 1807 and in Russia until 1861.

Serpentine, a mineral: chemically a hydrous silicate of magnesium. Green serpentine is used as an ornament stone. Fibrous serpentine is called asbestos.

Serval, a collie-dog-sized cat, long-limbed and spotted, from Africa. Preys on a variety of animals, from lizards to small antelope. Black servals occur mainly in mountainous regions.

Set, both in everyday speech (as in tea set, chess set) and in mathematics, a set is a collection of things. The members of the set can be specified by listing them or by describing the properties necessary for membership of the set, *e.g.*, the set of ginger-haired boxers. Set theory is a very important branch of mathematics founded by a great mathematician, Georg Cantor (1845–1918). Its development has influenced many other branches of mathematics. Perhaps one reflection of its fundamental nature is to be found in the fact that many schoolchildren, even of tender age, are now learning set theory and confounding parents who did not hear of it at school when they were there.

Settlement, Act of, passed in 1701, assigned the Crown to the House of Hanover in case of Anne's death without children. The decision represented the determination of the squires and the Anglican Church never again to trust themselves to a Roman Catholic king.

Seven Champions of Christendom, as set forth in mediaeval literature, were St. George of England, St. Andrew of Scotland, St. Patrick of Ireland, St. David of Wales, St. James of Spain, St. Denis of France, and St. Anthony of Italy.

Seven Churches of Asia, referred to in the Revelation of St. John, were those of Ephesus, founded by St. Paul in 57, Smyrna, Pergamos, Thyatira, Sardis, Philadelphia (Lydia) and Laodicea (Phrygia), all in W. Asia Minor.

Seven Wonders of the World were: 1, the Pyramids of Egypt; 2, the tomb of Mausolus, King of Caria (hence the word mausoleum); 3, the Temple of Diana at Ephesus; 4, the Walls and Hanging Gardens of Babylon; 5, the Colossus at Rhodes; 6, the Ivory and Gold Statue of Jupiter Olympus; and 7, the Pharos, or Watch Tower, built at Alexandria by Ptolemy Philadelphus, King of Egypt.

Seven Years War was waged by Frederick the Great and England against Austria, France, and Russia, from 1756 to 1763. It resulted in the secession of Silesia to Prussia, of Canada to England, and in the strengthening of our Indian Empire.

Severn Barrage, a barrier across the River Severn estuary proposed with a view to extracting useful electrical energy from tidal power. Essentially the idea is to let the tidal water flow into a reservoir upstream from the barrage and then to flow seaward under gravity through specially designed hydroelectric generators situated on the barrage. Tidal power has been harnessed in a French project and there is little doubt that the Severn scheme is technically feasible. However, environmental, economic and social factors enter the matter and are influencing consideration of its overall desirability. *See also* **Tidal Power.**

Sexagesima Sunday is the 2nd Sunday before Lent.

Sextant, an instrument which has superseded the quadrant as a measurer of angles between distant objects. It is of special importance in navigation and surveying, and contains 60 degrees described on a graduated arc. A small telescope is attached and there are also a couple of mirrors which reflect the distant objects so as to enable them to be accurately observed. The invention is attributed to John Hadley, and to Thomas Godfrey independently, about 1730. Even today it is still the best instrument for telling where you are at sea.

Shad, a marine fish belonging to the same genus as the herring. It is found along the Atlantic Coast of the USA, and ascends rivers to spawn.

Shagreen, shark's skin: also untanned leather of peculiar grain made from skins of wild asses, camels and horses.

Shalloon, a kind of cloth manufactured from wool and worsted, and used chiefly for women's dresses and coat linings. It gets its name from the fact that it was originally made at Châlons-sur-Marne. It was called " chalouns " by Chaucer and " shalloons " by Swift.

Shamrock, the three-leaved clover-like plant native to Ireland and its national emblem.

Shark, a large and powerful ocean fish, comprising many species, very widely distributed, but most numerous in tropical seas. They have formidable teeth and are the most carnivorous of all fishes. They usually attain a large size, the whale-shark being often of a length of 15 m. Commercially the shark yields shagreen from its skin, the fins are made into gelatine, and an oil is obtained from the liver.

Sheep, a well-known family of ruminants of great utility as wool-producers, and for food. From the earliest times sheep have been a source of wealth to England. So much were they valued in the 15th and 16th cent., that their exportation was frequently prohibited. Sheep are classified under (1) longwools; (2) shortwools; and (3) mountain breeds. Most of the longwools carry Leicester blood in their ancestry and the shortwooled Down breeds carry the blood of the Southdown. The Southdown produced the present Suffolk, one of the most popular breeds. Cheviot is an important mountain breed. Of the foreign breeds the most valued are the Merino sheep of Spain, which yield a fine long wool. Australia, USSR, China, New Zealand, India, Argentina, South Africa, Turkey, Iran, UK are the chief wool-producing countries in the world.

Shelduck, a handsome genus of surface-feeding ducks, one of which, the common shelduck, is an inhabitant of this country. It is a beautiful white-and-chestnut plumaged bird with dark-green head and neck and red bill. Another species, the ruddy shelduck, appears in Britain only occasionally.

Shellac. This resin is the secretion of the lac

insect (*Coccus lacca*), which occurs in forests of Assam and Thailand. It is used for making varnish and in the manufacture of gramophone records. *See also* Lac.

Sherardizing. Process for coating steel or iron parts with zinc to prevent corrosion; this is done by heating the parts in a closed rotating drum containing zinc dust.

Shilling has been an English coin from Saxon times, but it was not of the value of 12 pence until after the Conquest. It is interchangeable with the 5 new pence decimal piece which came into circulation in 1968.

Ships have existed from prehistoric times. There is mention of one that sailed from Egypt to Greece in 1485 B.C., and in 786 B.C. the Tyrians built a double-decked vessel. No double-decked ship was known in England, however, before the *Royal Harry* was built by Henry VII, and it was not until the 17th cent. that shipbuilding was carried on in this country as a prominent industry.

Ship-worm. *See* Teredo.

Shoddy, the name given to a kind of cloth mainly composed of woollen or worsted rags, torn up and re-fabricated by powerful machinery. It was first made at Batley in Yorkshire about 1813, and became a very important industry employing many thousands of people at Batley and the neighbouring town of Dewsbury.

Shot, the name given to solid projectiles fired from guns. In the time of Henry V stone shot was used, later leaden shot, then iron shot, and finally steel shot, introduced by Sir Joseph Whitworth.

Shrike, a large and varied family of birds of hawk-like behaviour found in all continents except S. America. The Red-backed Shrike, which winters in Africa, is a breeding visitor to England and Wales. It is commonly called the " Butcher Bird " from the way it impales its prey (small birds and insects) on thorn-twigs. The other species on the British list are the Great Grey Shrike, the Lesser Grey Shrike, the Woodchat Shrike, and the Masked Shrike.

Shrove Tuesday, the day before the first day of Lent, receiving its name from the old custom of shriving, or making confession, on that day. In England the day has always been associated with the making of pancakes.

Sicilian Vespers, the term applied to the terrible massacre of French people in Sicily in 1282. The French under Charles of Anjou were then in occupation of the island and had been guilty of many cruelties. It began at Palermo on Easter Monday at the hour of vespers and resulted in the expulsion of the French king and the introduction of Spanish rule.

Silence, Tower of, or *dakhma*, a tower about 8 m high, built by the Parsees for their dead. The corpse is taken inside by professional corpse-bearers and left to be consumed by vultures. Parsees do not burn or bury their dead, and the *dakhma* is to protect the living and the elements from defilement.

Silicon, an important non-metallic element, symbol Si, it is related to carbon. Next to oxygen, it is the most abundant constituent of the earth's crust (27% by weight). It occurs in many rocks, and its oxide occurs in many forms (*e.g.* quartz, sand, flint, agate, chalcedony, opal, etc.). Principally used as a semi-conducting material for making transistors and similar devices.

Silicones are synthetic organic derivatives of silicon which because of their high resistance to heat and moisture have special uses, *e.g.*, lubricants, heat-resistant resins and lacquers, and water-repellent finishes. Silicones are compounds in which the molecules consist of chains of atoms of silicon and oxygen alternately. Silicones were developed in the United States from discoveries first made by Prof. F. S. Kipping at Nottingham University. Manufacture began in Britain in 1950, and in the form of fluids, resins, rubbers and greases they find wide use in industry. The largest plant in Europe is in Glamorgan.

Silk, the name given to a soft glossy fabric manufactured from the fine thread produced by the silkworm. It was known to, and highly prized by the ancients, being at one time paid for, weight for weight, with gold. The manufacture

of silk was carried on in Sicily in the 12th cent., later spreading to Italy, Spain and France, where Lyons has been the great centre of production from 1450 to this day. It was not manufactured in England before 1604; but when certain French refugees established themselves at Spitalfields in 1688, the industry was developed and became of importance. In the 18th cent. the Lombes of Derby achieved great success in this industry. Japan, China, Italy, Korea and the Soviet Union are the chief silk-producing countries.

Silkworm, the larva of a species of moth, *Bombyx mori*. It is native to China, and has been cultivated with success in India, Iran, Turkey and Italy. The silkworm of commerce feeds on mulberry leaves and produces a cocoon of silk varying in colour from white to orange. The cocoon is the silken habitation constructed by the worm for its entrance upon the pupal condition, and to obtain the silk the pupa is killed by immersion in hot-water.

Sill, a sheet-like mass of igneous rock which has been intruded parallel with the stratification of the country rock, cf. a dyke.

Silurian. This geological period is one of the major subdivisions of the Palaeozoic era. Its beginning is estimated at 440 million years ago, and the period lasted about 40 million years. Maximum thickness of the Silurian strata in Britain measures 4,575 m. *See* **F48.**

Silver, a white precious metal, symbol Ag (Latin *argentum*) found in a free state, also in certain combinations, and in a variety of ores. The chief silver-producing regions are the Andes and Cordilleras. Peru, Bolivia and Mexico have yielded vast supplies of the metal since the 16th century, and Colorado and Nevada in the United States have also been very prolific in silver yield. In England standard silver (that used for coinage) formerly contained $92\frac{1}{2}$ per cent. fine silver and $7\frac{1}{2}$ per cent. alloy, but when the price rose to $89\frac{1}{2}d.$ per oz and the coins became worth more than face value, the Coinage Act of 1920 was passed, reducing the fineness to half. To provide silver bullion for industry and for a fund towards the redemption of our silver debt to America, it was decided in 1946 to replace the United Kingdom silver coinage by one made of cupro-nickel (75 per cent. copper, 25 per cent. nickel). Maundy money, however, is of the original silver standard. Silver chloride and bromide are light-sensitive compounds and are used in photography.

Simony, the offence of trading in church offices, has been contrary to English law since the time of Edward VI. Elizabeth also promulgated laws against simony. In 1879 a Royal Commission reported on the law and existing practice as to the sale, exchange and resignation of benefices. The position is now controlled by the Benefices Act 1898, the Amendment Measure 1923, and the Benefices Rules 1926.

Sinn Fein (*Irish* = ourselves alone), Irish nationalistic movement founded in 1905 which developed into a mass republican party and triumphed in the establishment of the Irish Free State. An extremist group has survived which represents politically the outlawed IRA. In Northern Ireland *Sinn Fein* was legalized in 1974.

Sins, The Seven Deadly or Capital Sins are pride, avarice, lust, anger, gluttony, envy, sloth.

Sirius, the dog-star, so called because of its situation in the mouth of the Dog (Canis Major): it is the brightest of all the fixed stars, and is also one of the nearest to us.

Sirocco, a warm, southerly, often dust-laden, wind blowing across Mediterranean lands from the Sahara, in advance of an eastward-moving depression over the Mediterranean.

Siskin, a small bird of the finch family, common in Northern regions, nesting in Britain. The common Siskin has a yellow-green colour and is a lively, swift-flying bird with a stout bill.

Sistine Chapel, the chapel of the Pope in the Vatican, renowned for its frescoes by Michelangelo.

S.I. Units (Système International d'Unités) form an internationally recognised system of metric units for scientific and technical quantities. The basic units of length, time, mass, electric current, temperature and luminous intensity are, respectively the metre, second, kilogramme, ampre, kelvin (*see* **Absolute Temperature**) and candela. The S.I. was recommended for general adoption by a number of international organisations such as the General Conference on Weights and Measures (1960). Many countries have made or are making the S.I. the only legally recognised set of units. Gt. Britain's intention to "go metric" has brought widespread use of S.I. units in its train. These units command the widespread though not absolutely unanimous support of industrialists, technologists, and scientists. Many have urged that their adoption will be a triumph of commonsense and end the confusing multiplicity of units on the world scene. *See* Section N.

Six Articles, The Statute of the, was passed in 1539 for compelling adhesion to the chief doctrines of Roman Catholic faith: transubstantiation, communion in one kind only for the laity, vows of chastity, celibacy of the clergy, private masses and auricular confession; those who refused to subscribe to the Articles were treated as heretics. The Act was repealed in 1547.

Skink. The skinks constitute a large family of lizards with large smooth scales, under each of which is a bony plate. The largest species, found in Australia, is about 61 cm long. Some skinks have adopted a burrowing habit and degeneration of the limbs is associated with this. The Common Skink is a small species c. 12 cm long, living in deserts of N. Africa.

Skua, falcon-like marine birds related to the gulls found throughout the world. Known as " Robber Birds " because they steal not only the young and eggs of other birds (including penguins) but also their food, which they force them to disgorge in mid-air. The Arctic Skua breeds as far south as Scotland. The Great Skua breeds in both Antarctica and Arctica. Other species are the Pomarine, the Long-tailed, and McCormick's Skua.

Skunk, a North American mammal of the weasel family, with short legs and long bushy tail. All fifteen species are black and white, some being striped and the rest spotted. It secretes and ejects at will a foul-smelling fluid.

Sky. The blue colour of the sky on a summer's day is the result of the scattering of light waves by particles of dust and vapour in the earth's atmosphere. Blue light having almost the smallest wavelength in the visible spectrum (0·00004 cm) is scattered laterally about 10 times as much as the red (0·00007 cm).

Skyscraper. Owing to lack of ground space, increasing cost of land, and growth of modern cities, buildings are being made higher than broader; hence the name. The structures are constructed of steel framework usually clothed in concrete or reinforced concrete. The first modern skyscraper of steel skeletal construction was the Home Insurance Building in Chicago, designed (1883) by William Le Baron. The New York skyscapers include the World Trade Center building (110 stories), Empire State building (102 stories), Chrysler (77 stories), Rockefeller Center (70 stories), and 60 Wall Tower (67 stories). The tallest building in Britain when it is completed in 1978 will be the National Westminster Bank tower, dominating the city skyline (183 m), topping the Post Office radio tower by 6 m.

Slate, fine-grained clayey rocks which have undergone metamorphism. They cleave easily, and it is this property of cleavage which makes them a valuable source of roofing material. Important quarries producing mainly green slate are in the Coniston–Ambleside area of the Lake District.

Slavery. In its earlier forms, as in the times of ancient Greece and Rome, in the feudal ages, when vassalage and villeinage existed, and in the serfdom of Russia and other northern nations, slavery was attended by many inhumanities and evils; but perhaps in the negro slavery system which prevailed in the British colonies for upwards of 200 years and in recent parts of the United States up to 1865, it attained its highest point of cruelty. In 1883 the Act of Emancipation was passed, emancipating all slaves in British territories, though slavery continued to be tolerated in northern Nigeria, Sierra Leone and in the Anglo-Egyptian Sudan long after that date. Even today slavery and

forced labour are still prevalent in some parts of the world.

Slide Rule, an instrument which consists of two logarithmic scales sliding alongside each other. By its use multiplication, division, extraction of roots, etc., are speedily carried out.

Sloth, a curious family of mammals, only found in Central and South America. They dwell almost entirely in the trees, proceeding from branch to branch with their bodies hanging downwards, their weight being supported by their large hook-like claws. They eat foliage.

Slow-Worm, a species of lizard found in Britain which lacks legs. Silver with longitudinal brown stripes, it lives almost entirely on slugs.

Smelting. The process of heating an ore with a reducing agent to convert ore into metal, and with a flux to convert rocky impurities into a slag that will float on top of the molten metal. Slag and metal can then be tapped separately. An example is iron smelting; the reducing agent is coke, and limestone is added as the flux; the smelting is carried out in a blast furnace.

Snake. The snakes constitute the important reptilian order *Ophidia*. Snakes have a scaly, cylindrical, limbless body, lidless eyes, forked tongue, and the upper and lower jaws joined by an elastic ligament. All snakes have teeth used for seizing prey, and the poisonous varieties are furnished with poison fangs in the upper jaw. These fangs are hollow modified teeth and the venom passes into them from a special gland situated behind the angle of the mouth. Some 2,500 species of snakes are known, divided into 13 families. There are 3 British species—the grass-snake, smooth-snake, and adder.

Snipe, a wading bird, long-legged, with long, slender, straight bill, brown plumage, and zig-zag flight. The Common Snipe breeds locally throughout Britain; the Great Snipe and small Jack Snipe are occasional visitors. The close season is February 1 to August 11.

Snow. When water vapour condenses at high levels at a temperature below freezing (sublimation), a cloud of ice particles is formed. If these frozen droplets are small, they fall slowly and gradually assume a feathery crystalline structure, reaching the earth as snowflakes if the temperature remains below freezing.

Socialism. *See* Section J.

Soda, carbonate of sodium, is now mainly obtained by certain processes of manufacture from common salt. It was formerly obtained from the ashes of plants. Bicarbonate of sodium is the primary product in the Solvay or Ammonia-soda method for commercial manufacture of soda; it is also formed when carbon dioxide is passed into strong soda solution. The bicarbonate is used in medicine and in the preparation of baking powder.

Sodium, a metallic element, symbol Na (Latin *Natrium*), first obtained by Sir Humphry Davy in 1807 from caustic soda by means of the electric battery. Its chloride is *common salt*; the deposits of salt (*e.g.*, in Cheshire and at Stassfurt) have come into existence through the drying up of inland seas. Salt occurs in sea-water to the extent of about 3 per cent.; the Dead Sea contains about 22 per cent. The blood of animals is maintained at a level of about 0·6% sodium chloride. That there is sodium in the sun's atmosphere was confirmed in 1859 by Kirchhoff from his spectroscopic observations. Liquid sodium metal has properties which make it suitable as a coolant in some nuclear reactors; a technique of handling this very reactive liquid has had to be developed.

Soil Erosion occurs when the soil is removed from an area at a faster rate than soil formation. This situation usually occurs as a result of man's interference with the natural balance of the environment by the removal of natural vegetation, overgrazing or by poor farming techniques. Soil thus exposed is then removed by the wind (as in the Dust Bowl in the 1930s) or by rain in the form of gully or sheet erosion (as in the Tennessee Valley, USA). Methods introduced to stop soil erosion include contour ploughing, afforestation and dry farming techniques.

Software, the internal programmes and operating procedures of a computer as opposed to its hardware. This includes system software designed to make the computer usable as well as programmes intended for particular applications such as commercial or scientific calculations. *See* Hardware.

Solar Battery, one of the innumerable devices made possible by the development of semiconducting materials, notably germanium and silicon. This device creates an electric current from light falling on it. The current can be put to use or stored in storage batteries. The energy of the current is derived from the sunlight, and the solar battery is thus an *energy converting* apparatus. Solar batteries have provided power for the instruments in satellites.

Solar Wind, a continuous stream of electrically charged particles blowing outwards from the sun, supplemented from time to time by intense outbursts from particular regions of the sun's surface. These streams of protons and electrons on encountering the earth's magnetic field distort it and cause magnetic storms and aurorae.

Soldering is a means of joining together two pieces of material, usually metals, by melting a third metal (the solder) into the joint. The solder solidifies in the pores of the other metals and holds them together. The materials to be joined are not themselves melted so the technique requires less heat than welding. Solders are alloys; there are many kinds depending on the materials to be joined and the strength of joint desired. *See* Welding.

Solstice, an astronomical term indicating the point at which the sun is most distant from the equator. *See* Seasons, Section N.

Soundings at sea, to determine depth at any point, have been taken in all seas, and with considerable accuracy. A deep reading was that of the *Challenger* expedition in 1873, near St. Thomas's in the North Atlantic, when 3,875 fathoms (7,091 m) were sounded. In 1851 H.M.S. *Challenger* recorded the then maximum ocean depth in the Marianas Trench (W. Pacific) by echo-sounding as between 5,882 and 5,950 fathoms (10,764 and 10,870 m). Another deep was located in the S. Pacific in 1952–53 of 5,814 fathoms (10,640 m) in the Tonga Trench, 290 km S. of Tonga Tabu. Since then even greater depths have been recorded, in the Marianas Trench and the Mindanao Deep. *See* Pacific Ocean.

Southern Cross, popular name of *Crux,* a constellation of the Southern hemisphere, consisting of four bright stars in the form of a Latin cross. It has been called the pole-star of the south and is indispensable to seafarers.

South Sea Bubble, the name given to a series of financial projects which began with the formation of the South Sea Company in 1711 and ended nine years later in disaster after a mania of speculation. The idea behind the parent scheme was that the state should sell certain trading monopolies in the South seas in return for a sum of money to pay off the National Debt (which stood at £51,300,000 in 1719 when the scheme started). The idea fascinated the public, fabulous profits being dreamt of, and the price of the stock rose out of all proportion to the earnings of the Company. Many dishonest speculative ventures sprang up in imitation with the inevitable result that thousands were ruined. All classes had joined in the gamble and a Committee of Secrecy set up by the House of Commons in December 1720 to investigate the affairs of the Company proved that there had been fraud and corruption on a large scale in the affairs of the Company. Sir Robert Walpole who had been an opponent of the scheme from the outset dealt with the crisis.

Space Flight. The Soviet Union was the first country to launch a man into space and bring him safely back to earth. This epoch-making event took place on 12 April 1961, when Yuri Gagarin, tragically killed in an air crash in 1968, circled the earth in a spaceship weighing about 4,826 kg. It was launched by rocket in an elliptical orbit with greatest height 300 km and least 175 km. The inclination of the orbit to the equator was 65° 4', and the period of revolution was 89 min. 6s. Since then, the Russian *Vostok* cosmonauts Titov (17 orbits), Nikolaev (64 orbits), Popovich (48 orbits),

Bykovsky (81 orbits), Toreshkova, the first woman space traveller (48 orbits), the *Voskhod* cosmonauts Komarov, Feoktistov and Yegorov (16 orbits), Belyaev and Leonov (17 orbits), the American *Mercury* astronauts Glenn (3 orbits), Carpenter (3 orbits), Schirra (6 orbits), Cooper (22 orbits), the *Gemini* astronauts Grissom and Young (3 orbits), McDivitt and White (62 orbits), Cooper and Conrad (120 orbits), Borman and Lovell (206 orbits), Schirra and Stafford (15 orbits), Armstrong and Scott (6·6 orbits), Stafford and Cernan (44 orbits), Young and Collins (43 orbits), Conrad and Gordon (44 orbits), Lovell and Aldrin (60 orbits) were among the first to complete successful missions in space. Leonov was the first to perform the extra-vehicular (EVA) experiment (1965), *i.e.,* to leave an orbiting spaceship and float freely in space. Russia was the first to achieve an automatic docking (link-up) between two unmanned spacecraft in orbital flight (October 1967), and of two manned spacecraft (January 1969.) The American *Apollo* mission was accomplished when Armstrong and Aldrin became the first men to set foot on the moon. This milestone in manned space flight took place on 20 July 1969. A joint Soviet-American project culminated in a *Soyuz-Apollo* link-up 225 km up on 17 July 1975. On 11 January 1978 two Soviet spacecraft docked with an orbiting laboratory, the first triple link-up in space.

Space Research. By space research we mean scientific research work which can only be carried to otherwise inaccessible observing locations by rocket propulsion. Such propulsion does not rely on the presence of an atmosphere to provide oxygen so that it is capable in principle of conveying objects to unlimited distances. The subject of space research is, therefore, one which is concerned with scientific applications in various fields of a single highly specialised and powerful technique. It is not a single discipline, but can provide data of great importance for many, such as the physics of the earth, the sun, moon and other bodies of the solar system, astronomy, geodesy and the study of gravitation. The prospect of investigating the biological conditions on different planets such as Mars and Venus is also opened, as well as that of experimental biological studies under conditions of zero gravity. Although the results of many aspects of space research are vital for those concerned with the practical realisation of manned travel in space, space research is largely a branch of pure science, independent of any applications which may stem from it. The major technical problems involved in space research are:

(a) Launching of the instrument-containing vehicle with the necessary velocity.

(b) Guidance and control of the vehicle so it pursues the desired path.

(c) Tracking the vehicle to determine its actual path and the position on the path at any time.

(d) Transmission of the data, recorded by the instruments, back to the earth.

(e) Satisfactory operation of scientific instruments in the environment within the vehicle.

(f) Provision of adequate power supplies to operate the equipment within the vehicle for sufficiently long periods.

It is important to distinguish three distinct types of vehicle—the vertical sounding rocket, the artificial earth satellite, and the deep space probe. The track of a vertical sounding rocket is mainly vertical, and the whole path to the highest point and back is traversed in a few minutes only. An earth satellite circulates in an orbit round the earth in the same way as does our natural satellite, the moon. If it approaches the earth at any point within 160 km of the surface the air resistance causes the path to spiral in so rapidly that the vehicle is eventually burnt up by air friction within the dense atmosphere after an orbital life of a few months only. It follows that artificial satellite vehicles are only useful as instrument containers if the distance of closest approach (the perigee distance) is not much less than 160 km. For the study of the properties of the atmosphere at lower altitudes down to the limit (32 km) attainable by balloons, vertical sounding rockets must be used. It is a great advantage for work at higher altitudes to use satellites, as it is then possible to make systematic observations for months at a time from a great number of positions relative to the earth. The successful space flights achieved by manned satellites also suggest that it should not be long before manned observatories become practicable. Deep space probes include vehicles which pass out to great distances from the earth and may leave the neighbourhood of the earth for ever to become artificial planets. Such probes may pass close to, or soft-land on, the moon or planets or may merely pursue paths well out into interplanetary space.

Spanish Civil War, 1936 to 1939. The war began with a revolt by the Fascist General Franco against the Republic which had succeeded the Monarchy in 1931. Germany and Italy aided the rebels who besieged Madrid for over 2 years. An International Brigade was formed to help the Republic, but the Spanish Government was faced by the greater part of the Army, and very effective assistance from Italy and Germany. Those powers seized the opportunity to have a curtain-raiser to the world conflict which they intended to precipitate. After a total loss of a million men the Fascists overpowered the Republic.

Sparrow, name given to finch-like birds found in most parts of the world, of which the House Sparrow *Passer domesticus,* is the most familiar of British birds. Also native to Britain is the rural Tree Sparrow, distinguished from the male House Sparrow by its chestnut crown. Other European species are the Italian, Spanish and Rock Sparrows.

Specific Gravity, defined as the ratio of the mass of a particular volume of a substance to the mass of an equal volume of water at 4°C. *See* Hydrometer.

Spectroscopy. Newton's arrangement with the prism was the first spectroscope; its function was to separate out the colour components of a source of light. Two hundred years elapsed before this apparatus was developed into a precise scientific instrument, capable of measuring both the wavelength and intensity of each colour component. In this form it is called a spectrometer. All atoms and molecules have well defined characteristic spectra which can be used to recognise them. In order to produce emission spectra it is necessary to energise the material under investigation by some means, such as by heating in a flame. The resulting radiation then consists largely of sharp bright lines, characteristic of the material. Absorption spectra are produced by interposing the experimental material between a white light source and the spectrometer. Then dark lines are seen, corresponding to absorptions of energy, in exactly the same places as the bright lines are observed in the emission spectra. Spectroscopic techniques have now been developed to such an extent that accurate measurements of wavelength and intensity are possible not only in the visible region, but over almost the whole of the electromagnetic spectrum. Not only does spectroscopy play an important rôle in probing the structure of matter, but it can be applied in the field of astronomy. The use of radio wave spectroscopy has led to the discovery of several new types of stellar object, and this data is now producing a complete reappraisal of our understanding of the universe. *See* **F14**(2).

Sphinx, in Greek mythology, a winged creature with a woman's head and a lion's body. The sphinx of ancient Egypt represented the pharaoh in a divine form.

Spiritualism. *See* Section J.

Spirituals, negro melodies with religious inspiration and which are still spontaneously created, but have also passed into art-music.

Sponge. *See* Porifera, **F36**(1).

Spoonbill, a long-legged, marsh bird, closely related to the ibis and stork, remarkable for its snow-white plumage and broad, flat, spoon-shaped bill. The European species has not bred in England since the beginning of the 17th cent., but is still a regular summer visitor from the

Netherlands, where it nests in colonies in reed-beds and islets.

Sputniks, the name of the Russian earth satellites first launched during the period of the International Geophysical Year. *Sputnik I,* launched 4 October 1957, became the first man-made earth satellite. *Sputnik II,* launched a month later carried a dog as passenger. *Sputnik III,* launched in May 1958, and weighing well over 2 tonnes, became the first fully-equipped laboratory to operate in space. The father of space travel with rockets was a Russian—Konstantin Eduardovich Tsiolkovsky—the centenary of whose birth practically coincided with the launching of the first earth satellite.

Squirting Cucumber, *Ecballium elaterium,* so named from the fact that when ripe it breaks from the stalk and ejects its seeds and juice from the hole made by the breakage.

Stainless Steel. The development of stainless steel for cutlery manufacture, etc., began with the discovery of Harry Brearsley in 1912 that steel containing 12 per cent. of chromium is rust-proof.

Stalactites are deposits of calcium carbonate formed on the roofs and sides of limestone caves, and in tunnels, under bridges, and other places where the carbonic acid of rain-water percolates through and partly dissolves the limestone, resulting in the growth of icicle-like forms that often assume groupings. The water that drops from these may deposit further calcium carbonate, which accumulates and hardens into a series of sharp mounds or hillocks called stalagmites.

Standard Deviation. In statistics it is often desirable to compare the variability or " spread " of different sets of data. For example, two kinds of light bulb could have the same average life but one kind could be more uniform or consistent than the other. The standard deviation is one of the commonest measures of spread. It is found as follows. If x is one of the data and $\bar{x}$ is the mean of all the x's, then $x - \bar{x}$ is called the deviation. Every deviation is now squared and the average squared deviation calculated. The standard deviation is then the square root of the average squared deviation. The lifetimes of the more uniform kind of light bulb would have a smaller standard deviation than those of the more erratic one.

Starch is an organic compound occurring in granules in nearly all green plants, and especially in the seeds of dicotyledonous and cereal plants, potatoes, etc. In its pure form starch is a tasteless, odourless white powder, and is a carbohydrate consisting of carbon, hydrogen, and oxygen.

Star Chamber, an ancient tribunal of state in existence in 1487 and possibly earlier, charged with the duty of trying offences against the government, unfettered by the ordinary rules of law. It was in effect a Privy Council entrusted with judicial functions. Under Charles I the Star Chamber was used by the King and his party to persecute opponents; and in 1641 a Bill carried in both Houses abolished it.

Starling (*Sturnus vulgaris*), a well-known European bird now common in many parts of the world. It has handsome iridescent blackish plumage and nests in holes and crevices. Flocks of starlings are often seen wheeling in the air; thousands roost on buildings in the heart of London. Other European species are the Spotless and Rose-coloured starlings. The latter sometimes wanders to the British Isles.

States-General, national assembly in which the chief estates of the realm were represented as separate bodies. The name, though not the institution, has survived in the Netherlands, where the two houses of parliament are known as states-general. In France the states-general consisted of three orders, clergy, nobility and commons. Philip IV first summoned it in 1302 to support him in his quarrel with Pope Boniface VIII. While absolute monarchy was establishing itself it met rarely, and not at all from 1614 until 1789, when it was convoked as a last resort by Louis XVI. But when it met it declared itself the National Assembly which marked the beginning of the revolution.

Statistics is a science that deals with the collection of numerical facts and the evaluation of their significance. The word is also used to refer to the facts themselves as in " trade statistics ". This important science gives precise meanings to words like " average " and to statements like " this set of data is significantly different from that ". In a world in which more and more information is becoming available in numerical form (I.Q.s, examination results, tax yields, health records, road accidents, etc.) the proper—as opposed to the misleading—use of statistics cannot be over-emphasised. Many young people can now study statistics at school and college, and governments and industries employ many statisticians. *See* Average.

Statute of Westminster 1931. An Act of parliament which gave a basis of equality to the British Dominions. The Dominions as well as the United Kingdom were defined by the Balfour Memorandum of 1926 as " autonomous communities within the British Empire, equal in status, in no way subordinate one to another in any aspect of their domestic or external affairs, though united by a common allegiance to the Crown, and freely associated as members of the British Commonwealth of Nations ". The Statute was the sequel. The Dominions are sovereign States governed solely by their own Parliaments and Governments. *See* K184.

Steam Engine, a machine whereby steam becomes the active agent of the working of machinery, and of very wide application. The leading types of steam engine are: (a) condensing, or low-pressure engines, where the steam is generated by a boiler; (b) non-condensing, in which the cylinder exhausts its steam into the open air. Engines of the latter type are used where portable engines are required.

Steam-hammer, invented (1839) by the Scottish engineer James Nasmyth. Consists basically of a vertical steam cylinder atop two legs with piston-rod passing through cylinder base and attached to a tup (hammer) of from 100 kg to 15 tonnes which rests on an anvil. The tup slides in V grooves on inside of legs. Length of stroke and therefore weight of blow can be accurately controlled from a light tap to a massive punch. It made possible the forging in one piece of multi-throw crankshafts for marine engines, etc. and the mass production of high-class axles and wheels, con rods and buffers, etc. for locomotives and rolling stock.

Stearin is the portion of fatty matters and oils which remains solid at an ordinary temperature, and is a compound of stearic acid with glycerine. It is largely used in the manufacture of candles. With caustic soda stearin forms a soap (sodium stearate), which is present in most commercial soaps which contain sodium palmitate and oleate in addition.

Steel, an alloy of iron and carbon, with varying proportions of other minerals. The famous blades of Damascus and steels of Toledo were made by the cementation and crucible method. The metal produced by the " Bessemer process " (*q.v.*) is of the highest value for structural purposes, rails, etc. In recent years the technique known as continuous casting has been developed which bypasses some major steps in the conventional process of steel-making.

Stereophonic Broadcasting. A person having normal hearing is able to determine the direction from which a sound reaches him by virtue of the fact that he has two ears, and, therefore, the sound will reach one of them a fraction of a second before it reaches the other. This difference in arrival time allows the brain to calculate direction. It will, therefore, be apparent that if the same person listens to, say, an orchestral concert in a large hall he will be able to determine—even with his eyes shut—the approximate position of a particular instrument with respect to the rest of the orchestra. If, however, he listens at home to a broadcast of the same concert, then, due to the fact that he hears the music after it has been picked up by a single microphone located at one point and radiated over a single-channel transmission system, he will be unable to allocate a definite position to any instrument. The aim of stereophonic broadcasting, or sound reproduction therefore, is to restore the listener's ability to locate the position in space of the various sources of sound and to follow movement. To do this it is necessary to use two microphones in the studio—to simulate the two human ears—and to transmit their outputs, through two similar, but separate, chains of equipment, to two radio receivers and their two loudspeakers, which must be placed some distance apart, in the listener's home. The fundamental work on two-channel stereophony was done by the late A. D. Blumlein of E.M.I. Ltd., his original patent being dated 1931.

Stereotype, a metal cast taken from movable type which has been set up in the ordinary way. The first to introduce the process in practical form in this country was William Ged, of Edinburgh, who made stereotype plates in 1730. An impression of the type matter is first taken by means of a mould of prepared plaster of Paris or moistened sheets of specially prepared paper, and when molten stereo metal is poured upon the mould and allowed to cool and harden, the stereo plate is formed, and can be printed from as a solid block for some time.

Steroids. A class of structurally related compounds, based on a system of condensed rings of carbon and hydrogen, which are widely distributed in animals and plants. Included in the steroid family are sterols, found in all animal cells, vitamin D, sex hormones, bile acids and cortisone, a drug used in the treatment of rheumatic fever.

Stickleback, a family of small spiny-finned fish widely distributed in both fresh and salt water. Male constructs roofed nest held together by sticky secretion from glands near kidneys. Several females deposit eggs therein which he jealously guards until after young are hatched.

Stirrup, a loop of metal U-shaped strap suspended from the sides of the saddle, used for mounting and to support the horseman's foot. Some authorities allege their use as far back as the early Iron Age, and it is generally believed that they were used in battle in A.D. 378, when the Gothic cavalry defeated the legionaries of the Emperor Valens at Adrianople. Stirrups relieved the tension of the rider's knees and so enabled him to be armed from top to toe.

Stoat, a slender, carnivorous mammal with short legs, related to the weasels. The stoat is distinguished from the latter by its longer tail, which has a black tip. The black tip is retained even in the winter when the animal turns white, the fur then being known as " ermine ". It is found in northern latitudes, and is abundant in Arctic America.

Stoma (pl. stomata), microscopic pores on the surfaces of leaves through which gaseous exchanges take place and water is lost. It has been estimated that a single maize plant bears 200 million stomata, usually closed at night.

Stone-Flies, comprise the order of insects called *Plecoptera,* which includes some 700 species, of which about thirty occur in Britain. The wings are membranous, and two long, thread-like feelers protrude at the tail end. The larvae are aquatic.

Stonehenge, a remarkable collection of Bronze Age monuments arranged in two circles, 104 m in diameter, standing on Salisbury Plain, Wiltshire. Modern archaeological research dates origin back to between 2100 and 1600 B.C. There is some evidence to suggest that the monument may have been built for astronomical purposes, providing a method of keeping a calendar for predicting the seasons and foretelling eclipses of sun and moon.

Stork, a family of heron-like birds with long bills, freely distributed over Europe, Asia, Africa and S. America. The White Stork is an occasional visitor to England, and, more rarely, the Black Stork: these are the only two European storks.

Stratosphere, a layer of the earth's atmosphere, which lies between the tropopause (c. 12 km above the earth) and the stratopause (c. 50 km). The attraction of the stratosphere as a medium for air travel rests upon the absence of storms; indeed weather phenomena as commonly understood do not occur. The ozone layer lies within the stratosphere.

Stratum (pl. strata), a bed or layer of rock.

Strontium. This silver-white metallic element was discovered by Hope and Klaproth in 1793, and isolated by Sir Humphry Davy in 1808. The chief strontium minerals are celestite (sulphate) and strontianite (carbonate). Compounds of strontium give a brilliant colour to fireworks and signal flares. Radioactive iso-topes of strontium (strontium-90) are formed as fission products in nuclear explosions and tend to collect in bone on account of the chemical similarity of strontium and calcium (*q.v.*). This genetic hazard is a cause of great alarm. *See* Fall-out.

Sturgeon, a large fish found in northern seas and rivers with five rows of bony plates along the back and sides and pointed mouth with four barbels. Caviare is prepared from sturgeon ova. The rights of the Crown to certain wild creatures, including sturgeon, caught off the coasts of Britain and held since the time of Edward II, were abolished in 1970.

Sublimation, when a solid substance is heated and turns into vapour without passing through the liquid stage and then condenses as a solid on a cold surface, it is said to "sublime" and the process is called "sublimation". Iodine be-haves in this way, and sublimation is used as a method of purifying it.

Submarine, the first submarine, the *Nautilus,* was designed by Robert Fulton and tried out in the river Seine and in the sea off Brest in 1801. The idea was too revolutionary to find acceptance and it was not until electricity for under-water propulsion became available that the submarine underwent extensive development. Britain be-came interested about 1900 and the Germans developed it and made it into an instrument of warfare. The first voyage under the North Pole was made in 1958 by the American nuclear-powered submarine *Nautilus* (*q.v.*). The Royal Navy's nuclear submarine fleet includes 4 Polaris vessels—HMS *Resolution* (1968), *Renown* (1969), *Repulse* (1969), *Revenge* (1970), each armed with 16 missiles with thermonuclear warheads—and the 8 nuclear-powered Fleet submarines—*Dreadnought, Valiant, Warspite, Churchill, Conqueror, Swiftsure, Sovereign* and *Courageous.* Britain's nuclear strategic force is assigned to NATO.

Suez Canal, connecting the Mediterranean and the Red Sea, was built by the French engineer Ferdinand de Lesseps and opened in 1869. An Egyptian company, *Canal Maritime de Suez,* was formed in 1866 with a capital of 200 million francs. The British Government acquired 176,602 shares out of a total of 400,000 for £4 million (value 31 March 1956, £28,982,544). Under the Convention of 1888 all nations were granted freedom of navigation without dis-crimination in peace or war. The right was recognised by Egypt in the Anglo-Egyptian Agreement of 1954, under which Britain agreed to give up the Suez base. The Suez Canal Company was nationalised by the Egyptian Government without warning in 1956, since when it has been widened and deepened and the average time of transit reduced. The waterway which had been barred to Israeli ships since the creation of the state of Israel in 1948, and to all shipping since the Middle East war of 1967, was reopened in 1975. Israeli civilian cargo ships are allowed through.

Suffragette, member of the Women's Suffrage Movement who in the early part of this century agitated to obtain the parliamentary vote. The movement ended in 1918, when women of 30 were given the vote. In 1928 a Bill was passed which granted equal suffrage to men and women. The leaders of the Women's Suffrage Movement were Mrs. Pankhurst and her two daughters, Sylvia and Dame Christabel, Mrs. Fawcett, Annie Kenney and others.

Sugar, to the chemist the term is a generic one covering a group of carbohydrates, including cane sugar (sucrose), glucose, fructose, and maltose. In ordinary parlance sugar means sucrose, which is obtained from the sugar cane, sugar beet or sugar maple.

Sulphur, an elementary, brittle, crystalline solid, symbol S, abounding in the vicinity of vol-canoes. It is yellow in colour. It occurs in combination with other elements, as sulphates and sulphides, and allied with oxygen, hydro-gen, chlorine, etc., is of great commercial utility. Used in its pure state it constitutes the inflammable element in gunpowder; it is also used for matches and for making sulphuric acid.

Sulphuric Acid, a compound of great commercial importance, used in a variety of manufactures,

and composed of sulphur, oxygen and hydro-gen. Extremely corrosive.

Sun, one of the millions of stars in the universe, the centre of the solar system, estimated to have a mean distance from the earth of 93 million miles ($149 \cdot 6 \times 10^6$ km), a diameter of 865,000 miles ($1 \cdot 39 \times 10^6$ km), and a volume a million times that of the earth. The gravita-tional force on the sun is almost 28 times that of the earth, *i.e.,* a body would weigh 28 times its weight on earth. It rotates on its axis from east to west, though not as a solid, the solar equator turning once in about $25\frac{1}{4}$ days and the poles in about 34 days. Large spots are ob-served on the sun which form and disappear at irregular intervals. The area of the disc covered by the spots, however, reaches a max-imum roughly every 11 years, when the sun's heat seems rather greater than usual and magnetic storms more frequent (sunspot cycle). Spectrum analysis shows that the sun is com-posed of many elements found in the earth. Its surface temperature is about 6,000°C. Observa-tions made in 1964–65 (Year of the Quiet Sun) complemented those obtained during the Inter-national Geophysical Year 1957–58, when the sun was remarkably active. The earth is in the outer atmosphere of the sun and subject to its winds and storms. The apparently inex-haustible heat of the sun, which has main-tained life on the earth for millions of years, is derived from the destruction of matter, involved in the transmutation of hydrogen nuclei into helium nuclei, in which process about four mil-lion tonnes of matter are destroyed every sec-ond. At this rate of conversion the sun will go on radiating for 30,000 million years. The Soviet space rocket *Lunik I,* fired on 2 January 1959, became the first artificial planet of the sun. *See also* **F8.**

Superconductor, a metal in a state in which its electrical resistance has entirely vanished so that electric currents can flow indefinitely with-out generating heat or decreasing in strength. The superconducting state of metals was first discovered in mercury by Onnes in Leiden in 1911. There are many magnetic and ther-mal properties associated with superconducti-vity and the phenomenon as a whole has proved to be of great scientific interest: it resisted explanation till about 1957. In the meantime many metals and alloys were found to show the property but only at very low temperatures—below $c. -260°C$. There is a growing number of practical applications, *e.g.,* coils of super-conducting wire (kept very cold by liquid helium) can be made to carry enough electric current to produce strong magnetic fields. Such fields are very constant and do not require the large supply of electrical power that ordi-nary electromagnets need.

Supersonic Speed, a speed greater than the speed of sound (in air at sea-level sound waves travel at about 1223 km/h). When a body travels at a speed which is greater than the speed at which disturbances themselves can travel, a mechan-ism exists for the generation of waves of en-hanced intensity. Thus aircraft travelling at supersonic speeds produce shock waves in the air somewhat analogous to the bow waves of fast-moving ships. These shock waves are regions of intensely disturbed air which produce the sonic boom effect so distressing to people living near supersonic routes. *Supersonic* is not to be confused with *ultrasonic* (*q.v.*).

Surface Tension. The surfaces of fluids behave in some respects as though they were covered by a stretched elastic membrane. This property is called "surface tension". The action of detergents may be attributed in part to a re-duction in the surface tension of water, allowing it to wet the surface of dirty articles.

Surrealism. The aim of the Surrealist school of painting and sculpture is to overcome the barriers between conscious and unconscious mind, the real and unreal worlds of waking and dreaming. As such it has a long and respect-able ancestry, although the term was not in use until 1922 when it was picked by André Breton from Guillaume Apollinaire who had used it in connection with certain works by Chagall. However, Bosch in the 15th cent., Fuseli and Goya in the 18th, and many other purveyors of the weird and fantastic were the forerunners of modern Surrealism. The modern movement has broadly speaking taken two different directions: the first was towards complete fantasy and absurdity which took the form of "found objects"—*e.g.* a bird-cage filled with sugarcubes and a thermometer, a bottle-dryer, a bicycle wheel, or abstract works with strange and apparently irrelevant titles such as Paul Klee's *Twittering Machine*; the second towards highly detailed and realistic paintings of objects placed in strange juxtapositions—*e.g.*, Salvador Dali's trees with limp watches drooping over their branches or Georgio de Chirico's deserted and classical-looking streets with long arcaded perspectives and a lone statue or a bunch of bananas in the foreground. On the whole Surrealism has spent its initial force and become almost respectable; its idea of strange juxtapositions, now widely commercialised, finds a place in advertisement illustrations and in the more sophisticated forms of window-dressing.

Swans, large, graceful birds which together with the ducks and geese form the family Anatidae. There are three European species with white plumage; the Mute Swan distinguished by its orange bill with black knob (less prominent in female), a familiar sight on the rivers and ornamental lakes of this country. Two wild swans are winter visitors here, the Whooper and Bewick's Swan. The "pen" (female) and "cob" (male) mate for life and the young swans are called "cygnets."

Swan-upping. The annual marking of the Thames swans which takes place during the third week of July. This ancient ceremony dates back to the 15th cent. when all the Thames swans were declared to be Royal birds owned by the Crown. Two city guilds—the Vintners' and Dyers' Companies—own one third of the 600 swans now on the Thames. This privilege was granted to them by King Edward IV in return for money grants. Vintners' birds are marked with a nick on each side of the bill, the Dyers' with a nick on the right side only. The Queen's birds are unmarked.

Sweet Potato. This plant (*Ipomoea batatas*), which is a climbing perennial belonging to the convolvulus family, has thick roots that are rich in starch, and are eaten like potatoes. A native of the W. Indies and Central America, new varieties of sweet potato have been bred which stand cooler climates and can be grown as far north as Cape Cod. The sweet potato of New Zealand is called the Kumara.

Swift, a bird so-called from the extreme speed of its flight, resembling a swallow but related to the humming-bird. It has long, scythe-like wings, sooty-black plumage and greyish-white chin. There are several species inhabiting most parts of the world, particularly the tropics. The British breeding bird is among the latest to return from Africa and the earliest to go. Swifts are the only birds to use saliva for their nests. One oriental species builds its nest entirely from saliva.

Sword, hand weapon of metal used in open combat, characterised by a longish blade. During the Middle Ages the most famous blades were those made by the Arabs at Damascus and those made at Toledo.

Symbiosis. When two organisms live together and both derive mutual benefit from the association, the partnership is known as symbiosis. An example is the symbiosis of an alga and a fungus in lichens; another is the ordinary pea plant and the bacteria which live in the nodules on the pea's roots.

Synapse is the point of association between one nerve cell and another. The nervous impulse travelling along one nerve has to be transmitted to the next across a minute gap. This is the synaptic gap. The mode of transmission is chemical though it was at first thought to be electrical. The impulse arriving at the synapse releases a chemical transmitter which diffuses across the gap and stimulates an impulse in the adjacent nerve cell. *See* Q5(2).

Syndicalism. *See* Section J.

Synod, an assembly of the clergy of a particular church, state, province, or diocese. The Synod of Whitby (664) settled the dispute between the Celtic and the Roman churches in the matter of Easter in favour of the Roman system of reckoning.

Synoptic Charts. These are meteorological charts used in forecasting on which weather conditions at a network of stations, at a standard hour of observation, are recorded, using symbols of the international weather code. Surface weather maps have been drawn regularly for more than a hundred years and the modern advance is the drawing of other maps showing conditions in the upper air. The plotting is done quickly by computer.

Synoptists. The writers of the first three Gospels whose narratives in the main agree, though Matthew and Luke add material not found in Mark (written first); all three differ from John's Gospel.

T

Taiping Rebellion, 1850–64, most famous of China's many peasant uprisings. It took place in Hunan (the province where Mao Tse-tung was born) and was savagely suppressed with the help of foreign powers.

Taj Mahal, the white marble mausoleum built at Agra by Shah Jehan in memory of his favourite wife who died 1629. Over 20,000 men were occupied for over 20 years in its erection.

Takahe or Notornis, large New Zealand bird of the rail family which for many years was believed to be extinct. Small colony found in 1948 in remote valley of mountainous part of the S. Island. The bird is strictly protected.

Take-over Bid describes an offer made to all the shareholders of a company to purchase their shares at a named price and conditional upon acceptance by the holders of a named proportion of the total share issue. If accepted the purchaser thus gains control of the company.

Tallage, in Norman times, were taxes levied by the Crown upon lands of the royal demesnes. The levying of tallage was taken away by a statute of 1340 which required the consent of Parliament for all direct taxes.

Tammany, an organisation founded in New York (c. 1786) and formed from a benevolent society named after an Indian chief. It came to exert a powerful influence over political movements in that city. The leaders of the organisation used their power when their party was successful at the polls to appoint their nominees to every prominent office, and exacted bribes for concessions and privileges, and generally Tammany rule has meant wholesale corruption. Of this there was ample evidence in the disclosures of the Tweed and other Tammany frauds, and in the fact that the "Boss" usually contrived to make himself wealthy.

Tantalum, a scarce bluish metallic element, symbol Ta, discovered by Ekeberg in 1802. Chemically related to vanadium and niobium, it is usually associated with the latter in nature. For several purposes it can be used in place of platinum, and it finds application in the making of surgical instruments. Tantalum is very hard, and resistant to acids (other than hydrofluoric acid); it is used in alloys.

Taoism. *See* Section J.

Tapestry, a fabric largely used in former times for wall decoration and hangings. It was known to the ancient Greeks, but in its modern form came into prominence in the 15th and 16th cent., when it was manufactured in a marked degree of excellence by the weavers of Flanders, especially those of Arras. The manufacture was introduced into England early in the 17th cent., and was attended by considerable success. At the present day the term is applied to worsted cloths for furniture coverings, and there are also various kinds of tapestry carpets now made. The most famous tapestries of olden times were the Aubusson Tapestry and the Savonnerie. The Gobelin Tapestry factory, originated in Paris in the reign of Francis I, is still a national establishment. *See also* Bayeux Tapestry.

Tapirs. The tapirs constitute a family close to the horse family and the rhinoceros in the Ungulate order. They have four toes on the front feet and three on the hind. The snout is drawn out into a short trunk. The largest tapir is the Malayan tapir, which stands 1 m at the shoulder. Four species occur in Central and S. America.

Tar is a dark viscid product obtained from the destructive distillation of wood, coal, peat, etc. Wood tar is acid owing to the presence of acetic acid (" pyroligneous acid "). The highest proportion of coal tar goes into road making. Distillation of coal tar yields many valuable compounds, including benzene, phenol (carbolic acid), naphthalene and creosote; the final residue after distillation is pitch. Based on the chemical manipulation of compounds from coal tar is the preparation of many perfumes, food essences, drugs, antiseptics and plastics.

Tarpeian Rock at Rome received its name from the tradition that Tarpeia, the daughter of the Governor of the Citadel who betrayed the fortress to the Sabines, was crushed to death by their shields and buried beneath the rock. From this height persons guilty of treason were hurled to death.

Tate Gallery, named after its founder, Sir Henry Tate, at Millbank, S.W., was opened in 1897; Sir Henry Tate bore the cost of the building (£80,000) and also contributed the nucleus of the present collection. " The Turner Wing ", the gift of Sir Joseph Duveen, was added in 1910. The collection is thoroughly representative of British art and has been extended several times to include modern foreign art.

Tay Bridge spans the Tay at Dundee, opened for rail traffic on 20 June 1887. A previous bridge, completed in 1877, was blown down on 28 December 1879, as a train was passing over it. A new bridge was opened on 18 August 1966 for road traffic, 2,244 m in length, the longest road bridge in Britain.

Tea was introduced into England about the middle of the 17th cent., when it was a great luxury, and fetched from £6 to £10 a pound. It is an Asiatic plant, native properly to China, Japan and India. Up to about 1885 most of the tea imported into this country came from China; the bulk now comes from India and Sri Lanka.

Teal, the smallest of the European ducks and next to the Mallard the commonest British species. It is a handsome bird and a very swift flier, but not as swift as the Garganey or Summer Teal.

Telecommunications. The sending of messages over a distance. The term is generally applied to the sending of messages by telegraph, telephone, radio, television or radar. The first submarine telegraph cable between England and France was laid in 1850 and, following Hertz's investigations into electric waves, Marconi's invention led to Britain being linked with Europe by wireless telegraphy in 1899. The first permanently successful telegraph cable across the Atlantic was laid in 1866. The first telephone service between London and Paris was opened in 1891. The electro-magnetic telephone was invented by Alexander Graham Bell, a Scottish-born American, in 1876. The first submarine telephone cable to span the Atlantic was laid in 1956 connecting Britain with Canada and the United States, and many submarine telephone cables have since been laid including the Commonwealth cable system completed in 1967. The spectacular advances in space research depended on the new tools of work provided by parallel developments in telecommunications, *e.g.*, long-range radio and television transmission, electronic computer control. *See also* **Satellite Communication, Radar, Radio, Television.**

Telemetry, measurement at remote distances by means of a radio-link from the object (missile or satellite) to the ground. The third Russian sputnik, for instance, carried apparatus for measuring, among other things, the pressure and composition of the atmosphere, and the intensity of different kinds of radiation from the sun. Its radio transmitter, powered by solar-energy batteries, sent out the information in coded form by means of uninterrupted signals at 20·005 megacycles with a duration of 150–300 milli-seconds. Radio telemetry from inside the body is being increasingly used in medical and biological research; miniature radio transmitters can be swallowed or implanted in man or animal to detect physiological conditions.

Telepathy and Clairvoyance. *See* Section J.

Teleprinter, a telegraph transmitter with a type-writer keyboard, by which characters of a message are transmitted electrically in combinations of 5 units, being recorded similarly by the receiving instrument, which then translates the matter mechanically into printed characters. The telex or public teleprinter service provides direct person-to-person transmission of written messages.

Telescope, an optical instrument for viewing objects at a distance, " the astronomer's intelligencer ". Lippershey is credited with construction of the first in 1608; Galileo constructed several from 1609 and Newton was the first to construct a reflecting telescope. The ordinary telescope consists of an object-glass and an eye-lens, with two intermediates to bring the object into an erect position. A lens brings it near to us, and the magnifier enlarges it for inspection. A refracting telescope gathers the rays together near the eye-piece and is necessarily limited as to size, but the reflecting telescope collects the rays on a larger mirror, and these are thrown back to the eye-piece. The world's largest reflectors are at Mount Semirodriki, Caucasus (600 cm), Mount Palomar, California (508 cm), Mount Wilson, California (254 cm), the McDonald Observatory at Mount Locke, Texas (208 cm), and the Victoria B.C. Observatory (183 cm). The *Hale* 508 cm telescope at Mount Palomar has revealed objects never before photographed; it is able to probe space and photograph remote galaxies out to a limiting distance of 2,000 million light years. The *Schmidt* telescope at Mount Palomar has been used to make a huge photographic map of the universe. There are plans to move the 249 cm *Isaac Newton* telescope at the Royal Observatory at Herstmonceux, Sussex, to the Canary I. of Las Palmas. The giant steerable radio telescope built by Manchester University at Jodrell Bank, Cheshire, has a 76 m reflector with a beam width of 12 minutes of arc. Early in its career it tracked the Russian earth satellites and the American lunar probes. Another instrument of radio astronomy is the interferometer which consists of spaced aerials. Recently the technique of linking radio telescopes on different continents has been developed for fine observation. *See also* F3, Astronomy.

Teletext, the system of displaying printed information and simple diagrams on domestic television screens. Two public services are available in Britain—CEEFAX (Seeing Facts), broadcast by the BBC, and ORACLE (Optical Reception of Announcements by Coded Line Electronics), by the Independent Broadcasting Authority. Teletext makes use of some of the spare lines available in the ordinary 625-line television picture, the signals being translated into written display on the screen by means of a special decoding adaptor built into the set or attached to it. User access to the information, broadcast as separate " pages ", is obtained by using a pocket calculator-sized keypad. Teletext services in Britain at present offer a wide range of subject material, including weather forecasts, news headlines, sport and financial statistics, in six colours plus white. It is also possible to superimpose news flashes over ordinary programmes. All the information is provided by specially created editorial units and the pages are transmitted in rapid rotation, a one-hundred page " magazine " taking up to 25 seconds in all. CEEFAX and ORACLE pages are made up of a maximum of 24 lines of 40 characters, the same standard format as that of Viewdata, a Post Office service planned for the general public in the 1980s. Viewdata links the television set with computerised information via the telephone and is regarded as almost limitless in application as it would be possible to make use of data offered through the global communications satellite system.

Television, or the transmission of images of moving objects by radio. To understand the problems of television it is necessary to consider the action of the human eye. Basically the eye consists of a lens which projects an image of the scene before it upon the retina, a light-sensitive screen at the back of the eye. The retina is made up of several millions of tiny light-sensitive elements, each quite separate and distinct from its neighbours, and each separately connected to the brain by an individual fibre in the optic nerve. Thus the eye is a very complex organ, and it is able to pick out numbers of tiny details from a scene and convey each detail separately and simultaneously to the brain. It does not send a blend of different points of light and shade in the same way that the ear sends a blend of different sounds; if it did the brain would receive a completely unintelligible blur. From this it is clear that a television system which transmitted a mixture of detail would be useless; it must transmit all the details in a scene separately, yet almost simultaneously, and re-assemble them at such a speed that the eye cannot observe the building-up process. A means of doing this was provided by Nipkow in 1884, when he invented his famous scanning disc, and later Weiller invented the mirror drum for the same purpose. Such mechanical devices as these held the field for many years and in 1923 Baird in this country and Jenkins in America were both using them for the experiments which, in 1925, led to the successful transmission of shadows and simple outlines. It was not until 1926, however, that the first practical demonstration of television, as we understand it, took place when Baird transmitted by radio moving pictures of living human faces over a short distance. The B.B.C. began television broadcasts in 1930; the I.T.A. in 1955. The first television exchange across the Atlantic was made in July 1962 by way of the *Telstar* satellite.

Tellurium, a relatively scarce element, symbol Te, discovered in 1782 by Reichenstein. Chemically it behaves rather like sulphur; its salts are known as tellurides. It occurs chiefly combined with metals in ores of gold, silver, copper and lead. It is a semiconductor, and some of its compounds (also semiconductors) are coming into use in technical devices.

Templars were soldier knights organised in the 12th cent. for the purpose of protecting pilgrims in their journeyings to and from Jerusalem, and obtained their name from having had granted to them by Baldwin II a temple for their accommodation. At first they were non-military, and wore neither crests nor helmets, but a long wide mantle and a red cross on the left shoulder. They were established in England about 1180. During the crusades they rendered valuable service, showing great bravery and devotion. In the 12th cent. they founded numerous religious houses in various parts of Europe and became possessed of considerable wealth. It was this that caused their downfall. Kings and Popes alike grew jealous of their influence, and they were subjected to much persecution, and Pope Clement V abolished the Order in 1312. Edward II in 1308 seized all the property of the English Templars. The English possessions of the Order were transferred to the Hospitallers of St. John, afterwards called the Knights of Malta. *See also* **Hospitallers, Knights, Teutonic Order.**

Temple, a building dedicated to the worship of a deity or deities. Those built by the ancient Greeks at Olympia, Athens and Delphi were the most famous. The Temple of Diana at Ephesus was another. The Temple of Solomon at Jerusalem was destroyed and rebuilt several times; Herod's Temple was destroyed by the Romans in A.D. 70.

Temple Bar, an historic gateway (designed by Sir Christopher Wren in 1672) that until 1877 stood at the junction of the Strand and Fleet Street, London, dividing the City from Westminster. It was re-erected at the entrance to Theobald's Park, near Cheshunt, Herts., in 1888.

Terbium, an element, symbol Tb, discovered in 1842 by Mosander, belonging to the group of rare-earth metals.

Teredo, the scientific name of the ship-worm, a peculiar bivalve mollusc, which lodges itself when young on the bottoms of wooden ships and bores its way inwards, causing much injury.

Termites, also known as *White Ants,* though they are not related to the true ants and are placed in an entirely different insect order (*Isoptera*). They abound in the tropics and also occur in temperate countries, though only two species

are common in Europe. There is no British species. They live in colonies and their nests take the form of mounds of earth and wood, cemented together with saliva, and up to 6 m in height. Five separate castes are recognised, three of them being capable of reproduction, and the other two are sterile.

Tern. This slender, gull-like bird has long pointed wings, a deeply-forked tail, pale grey and white plumage, black cap, and is a very graceful flier. There are several species, some of which are summer migrants to Britain. The Arctic tern winters in the Antarctic, returning to find a nesting place in the spring.

Terrapin, a kind of fresh-water tortoise. There are several species widely distributed in the Northern Hemisphere.

Tertiary Rocks, in geology the rocks formed during the Caenozoic era comprising the Eocene, Oligocene, Miocene and Pliocene periods. *See* **F48.**

Teutonic Order, of German military knights, was founded in the Holy Land at the end of the 12th cent. for succouring the wounded of the Christian army before Acre. They were dispersed in the 15th cent. but the Order continued to exist until 1809, when Napoleon I confiscated its properties. In 1840 the order was resuscitated in Austria as a semi-religious knighthood. *See also* **Hospitallers, Knights, Templars.**

Textured Vegetable Protein, often referred to as TVP, is an edible protein material given a fibrous texture in the course of its manufacture from agricultural products. Nutritionally the material resembles meat and the extent to which it also resembles meat in succulence, flavour, feel in the mouth, suitability for chewing, etc. depends on the sophistication of the manufacturing technique and on the skill of the cook. The common starting material is the soya bean which is rich in protein and oil. The latter is removed, also for use in the food industry, and the residue is further processed to concentrate the protein and to remove unwanted flavours. A paste of suitable consistency is then forced under pressure through small holes and solidified as fibres. Bound together with a suitable binder and appropriately flavoured, these fibres form a lump of protein substance analagous to meat. TVP is widely produced, available commercially and used domestically and in the catering industry. Meat products containing it must show it in the list of ingredients.

Thallium, a blue-grey metallic element, symbol Tl discovered by Crookes in 1861. It is obtained from the flue dust resulting from the burning of pyrites for sulphuric acid manufacture.

Thanksgiving Day, a national holiday in the United States, observed on the fourth Thursday in November; instituted by the Pilgrim Fathers in 1621 to celebrate their first successful harvest.

Theodolite. The instrument used by surveyors for measuring angles in the horizontal and vertical planes; also used in meteorology for following balloons to measure the speed and direction of wind.

Therm. The charges for gas for lighting and heating (formerly reckoned at per cubic foot) are now based on the calorific, or heat, value of the gas, and the unit used is termed a therm. The therm is 100,000 British thermal units.

Thermionic Emission is the departure of charged particles from matter under the influence of heat. The higher the temperature the greater the flow of escaping particles. The most common example is the emission of electrons from red-hot electrodes—this is the basic phenomenon made use of in thermionic valves (*see* Valve). If the hot electrode (the cathode) is enclosed in an evacuated or gas-filled bulb, the emitted electrons can be collected at another electrode (the anode) and will flow through an external circuit back to the emitter. Thus an electric current has been generated by heat.

Thermodynamics, a term first applied by Joule to designate that branch of physical science which treats of the relations of heat to work. What is called the first law of thermodynamics is thus stated by Clerk Maxwell: " When work is transformed into heat, or heat into work, the quantity of work is mechanically equivalent to the quantity of heat." In one of its many formulations, the second law asserts that " the heat tends to flow from a body of hotter temperature to one that is colder, and will not naturally flow in any other way ". See **F20**.

Thermo-electric Devices. If two wires of different materials are formed into a loop and if the two joins are kept at different temperatures a current flows in the loop. This was discovered by Seebeck in 1822, and the device is called a thermocouple. The electric current could in principle be made to drive some useful machine, and the energy comes from the heat that is absorbed by the thermocouple—if one part of the thermocouple is not hotter than the others it will not work. It has long been realised that this is a device that converts heat directly into electricity without raising steam and driving dynamos as in a power-station. However, until recently nobody has used thermocouples for much besides temperature measurement, for which they are exceedingly useful. The new development is the manufacture of semiconductors (q.v.); for the thermoelectric effects of these new materials are much greater than those of metals. A material much studied in this connection is a compound of bismuth and tellurium, bismuth telluride. It now seems practicable to generate useful electricity from suitably designed thermocouples. For example, the USSR produces a thermoelectric device which uses the heat from the chimney of a domestic oil-lamp to produce enough electricity to work a radio. Presumably this is very useful in remote parts with no electricity supply. But the possibilities do not stop there. Indeed, an eminent Russian authority has stated that thermocouples could produce electricity direct from the warmth of sunlight on a scale and at a cost comparable with conventional fuel-burning power-stations. Even if solar energy cannot be so used, it might be possible to use the heat of nuclear reactors, but this means that the thermoelectric devices would have to stand up to very heavy radioactivity and still work. It is not surprising, however, that many firms are showing great interest in thermoelectricity these days.

Thermometer, an instrument by which the temperature of bodies is ascertained. The most familiar kind of thermometer consists of a glass tube with a very small bore, containing, in general, mercury or alcohol. This expands or contracts with variation in the temperature, and the length of the thread of mercury or alcohol gives the temperature reading on a scale graduated in degrees. Various forms of thermometer are used for particular purposes. See Thermometer Comparisons, Section N.

Thermonuclear Reactions. See Nuclear Fusion.

Thirty-nine Articles. See Articles.

Thistle, Order of. See Knighthood.

Thorium, a scarce, dark grey, metal element, symbol Th, discovered by Berzelius in 1828. All substances containing thorium are radioactive. Chief source of thorium is monazite sand, big deposits of which occur in Travancore (India), Brazil and the USA. Considered important as a potential source of atomic energy since the discovery that it can be transmuted into U²³³, which is capable of fission like U²³⁵.

Thrush, a large family of song-birds of the Passeriform order, distributed all over the world. The British species include the robin, redstart, nightingale, song-thrush (or mavis), blackbird, mistle-thrush, ring-ouzel of the mountains and large numbers of migrant fieldfares and redwings from northern Europe are winter visitors.

Thunder, the sound heard after the occurrence of a lightning flash. It is due to vibrations of the air along the path of the flash, which are set up by the sudden heating (and expansion) followed by the rapid cooling (and contraction) to which the air is subjected. It is unusual for thunder to be heard more than 16 km away, the distance being estimated roughly by allowing 1 km for every 3 seconds which elapse between seeing the flash and hearing the thunder. Continued rolling of thunder results from the zig-zag nature of the flash and the multiple strokes of which it is composed, variations in the energy developed along the path, and echo effects. Thunderstorms are caused by powerful rising currents

of air within towering cumulonimbus clouds and are most frequent during the afternoons and evenings of sunny summer days.

Thursday, the 5th day of the week, named after Thor, the Scandinavian deity. To the ancient Romans Thursday was dies Jovis, or Jupiter's day.

Tidal Power. The principle of exploiting the energy of the tides is similar to hydro-power since it involves the harnessing of falling water. A barrage across a bay or estuary is filled during flow tide and closed during ebb tide creating a difference in level. When the water is allowed to fall towards the lower side of the barrage it operates a turbine which drives a generator. More sophisticated schemes would incorporate pumped storage facilities. An essential requirement is a large tidal range in order to get a sufficient head of water. Although a 240MW scheme has recently been completed on the River Rance in France, it is believed that the economics of tidal power are generally insufficiently favourable for the method to be widely used. See also Hydroelectric Schemes and Severn Barrage.

Tides, the periodical rise and fall of the waters of the ocean and its arms, are due to the gravitational effect of the moon and sun. Newton was the first to give a general explanation of the phenomenon of the tides. He supposed the ocean to cover the whole earth and to assume at each instant a figure of equilibrium, under the combined gravitational influence of earth, sun and moon, thus making and controlling the tides. At most places there are two tides a day and the times of high- and low-water vary according to the positions of the sun and moon relative to the earth. When earth, moon and sun are in line (at full moon and new moon) the gravitational pull is greatest and we get " spring " tides. When sun and moon are at right angles (first and third quarters of the moon's phases) we get the smaller " neap " tides.

Tiers Etat, the lowest of the three estates of the realm as reckoned in France—nobility, clergy and commons (tiers état)—prior to the Revolution.

Tiger, a powerful carnivorous animal of the cat family, which occurs in India and certain other parts of Asia. Its skin is of a tawny yellow, relieved by black stripings of great beauty of formation. Some tigers attain a length of from 3 to 3·6 m.

Time. The measurement of time has become of increasing importance to man with the advance of civilisation. It was at first almost inevitably based on the succession of night and day, the waxing and the waning of the moon, and on the changing seasons of the year, and the astronomical observation of these three periodic effects has served as the basis of time measurement until recent years. The precision of the observations has continually increased, and clocks have been developed for dividing the day into smaller units. The clocks were adjusted so as to keep in step with the rotation of the earth on its axis, but during recent years an atomic standard of time has been developed, and clocks are now adjusted so as to keep in step with the natural period of an atomic vibration. See Clock. Greenwich Mean Time, British Standard Time.

Tin is a white, metal element, symbol Sn (Latin Stannum), whose commonest ore is cassiterite (tin oxide), which occurs in Malaya, Indonesia, Bolivia, Zaire, Nigeria and Cornwall. It protects iron from rusting, and the tin coating on tinplate is applied by dipping the thin steel sheet in molten tin or by electrolysis. Tin alloys of importance include solder, bronze, pewter and Britannia metal.

Tit or Titmouse, a small insectivorous bird of the woodlands and forests, bright of plumage and very active and agile, often seen hanging upside down searching for food. There are over fifty species, eight of which occur in Britain: the Great and Blue Tits, familiar in gardens and countryside, the Cole Tit, Marsh Tit, Willow Tit, Bearded Tit, Long-tailed or " Bottle " Tit and the Scottish Crested Tit.

Titanium, a scarce metal, symbol Ti, difficult to extract from ores, found in association with oxygen in rutile, anatase and brookite, as well as with certain magnetic iron ores. It combines with nitrogen at a high temperature. Discovered by the Rev. William Gregor in 1791. Titanium alloys, being very resistant to stress and corrosion, and combining strength with lightness, are finding wide application not only in marine and chemical engineering but in the building of aircraft, rockets, and the nuclear-energy field. Titanium dioxide is now widely used in making paints.

Tithes, an ecclesiastical tax consisting of a tenth part of the annual produce known to the ancient Jews, and first imposed by Christian authorities in the 4th cent., although not made compulsory in England before the 9th cent. Tithes derived from land are termed " praedial ", those derived from cattle being styled " mixed ", while others are personal. After the passing of the Tithes' Commutation Act of 1836, tithes were gradually converted into rent charges, and to-day the old form of tithes exists only to a small degree. Consult Tithe Act of 1936.

TNT (Trinitrotoluene). A high explosive formed by the action of a mixture of nitric and sulphuric acids on toluene. Not highly sensitive to shock, it can be used in shells without danger, and is exploded by a time, or detonator, fuse. Apart from wartime applications, it is used in blasting in quarries and mines.

Toad, an amphibian, differing from the frog in having a dry, warty skin, a heavier, squat build and shorter limbs. It has a similar metamorphosis, is largely nocturnal, and will wander far from water after the breeding season. Two toads occur in Britain, the Common Toad and the Natterjack. The latter can be identified by the narrow light stripe running down the middle of the back.

Tobacco is made from the leaves of various narcotic plants of the *Nicotiana* family, which contain a volatile oil and an alkaloid called nicotine. Tobacco is largely grown in America, India, Japan, Turkey, Greece, Canada, Italy, Indonesia, Bulgaria, Philippines, France, Congo, China, Rhodesia, Zambia, S. Africa, S. America and other countries of a warm climate. It undergoes various processes of preparation. The leaves are first dried, then cut into small pieces, moistened and compressed, and in this form it is known as cut or " shag " tobacco; when moistened with syrup or treacle and pressed into cakes, it is Cavendish; when twisted into string form, it is " twist " or " pig-tail ". For cigars the midribs of the dry leaves are removed, and what is left is moistened and rolled into cylindrical shape. For snuff, the tobacco leaves are moistened and allowed to ferment, then dried, powdered and scented. *See* Section P (Respiratory System) for the connection between tobacco-smoking and lung cancer.

Tolls. Payments for privileges of passage were first exacted in respect of ships passing up rivers, tolls being demanded on the Elbe in 1109. Tolls for land passage are said to have originated in England in 1269, toll-bars being erected at certain distances on the high-roads in the 17th cent., where toll had to be paid for all vehicles passing to and fro. After about 1825 they began to disappear, but still linger on some country roads and bridges. Tolls on London river bridges ceased in 1878–79.

Tonic Sol-Fa, a system of musical notation in which monosyllables are substituted for notes. Thus the major diatonic scale is represented by Doh, Ray, Me, Fah, Soh, La, Te, Doh. The system was invented by a Miss Glover of Norwich in about 1840 and has proved of great assistance in the teaching of music in schools.

Tonsure, the shaven part of the head of a Roman Catholic ecclesiastic, dates from the 5th or 6th cent. In the Roman Catholic Churches only a circle, or a crown, is shaved, while in the Greek Church shaving is forbidden.

Topaz, a transparent mineral gem, being a silicate and fluoride of aluminium and generally found in granite rocks. Its colour is yellow, but it also occurs in pink and blue shades. The best kinds come from Brazil.

Topiary, the art of clipping and trimming trees, shrubs, etc., into ornamental shapes. In Britain this art goes back before Elizabethan times when gardens were formal and the shapes simple and symmetrical. By the end of Queen Anne's reign topiary had become much more elaborate, and all kinds of fanciful shapes were produced. Pliny in his *Letters* tells how box hedges were clipped into different shapes in Roman times.

Topology is a branch of mathematics which studies geometrical objects from the point of view of their general shape rather than their precise measurements. For example, from the point of view of topology a ring doughnut and a picture frame have the same shape because they both have one single hole through them. Topology is used, for example, to deduce geometrical facts about an irregularly shaped object such as the Earth from the geometry of a regular object such as a perfect sphere of the same general shape. In its more formal aspects topology is an important tool in other parts of mathematics.

Tornado, a violent whirlwind, characterised by a black, funnel-shaped cloud hanging from heavy cumulonimbus and travelling at speeds up to 60 km/h. Tornadoes vary in diameter from less than a metre to a kilometre and occur frequently in the Mississippi region of the USA where it has been estimated that the circling winds of the vortex may reach a velocity of 600 km/h. In West Africa the term is applied to thundery squalls.

Tortoises and Turtles, are cold-blooded reptiles four-footed and encased in a strong shell protection, the shells of some species being of beautifully horny substance and design, once in much demand for combs, spectacle frames and ornamental work. It is the custom to designate the land species as tortoises and the aquatic kinds as turtles. The green turtle, so called because its fat has a green tinge, is in great demand for soup. Together the tortoises and turtles make up the reptilian order called *Chelonia,* the biggest representatives of which are the giant land tortoises of the Galapagos Islands, reaching a weight of 225 kg and living a century. Some of these giant tortoises are even said to have reached 200 or 300 years of age.

Toucan, a South and Central American family of brilliantly coloured birds, remarkable for their huge bills. Toucans live on fruit, are of arboreal habits, and nest in holes. There are about 37 species.

Touchstone, a kind of jasper called by the ancients " Lydian stone ", of economic value in testing the quality of metal alloys, especially gold alloys. The testing process is very simple. The alloy is drawn across the broken surface of the Touchstone, and from the nature of the mark or streak it makes the quality of the alloy can be ascertained.

Tourmaline, a mineral occurring in different colours in prismatic crystals. It is a well-known example of a pyro-electric crystal, *i.e.,* one that has a permanent electric polarisation. A double silicate of aluminium and boron, it occurs in Cornwall, Devon, S. America and Asia.

Tournaments were equestrian contests between military knights and others armed with lances, and frequent in the Middle Ages. The Normans introduced them to England.

Tower of London was built as a fortress by William the Conqueror. It was a royal palace in the Middle Ages and later used as a garrison and prison. Many distinguished prisoners were executed there, or on the neighbouring Tower Hill, including Anne Boleyn, Catherine Howard, Lady Jane Grey, the 2nd Earl of Essex, and the Duke of Monmouth. The Chapel Royal of St. Peter ad Vincula in the Tower was built in 1105 and took its present shape in the reign of Henry VIII. The Crown Jewels are kept at the Tower, and in the Armoury a fine collection of armour is preserved. The attendant staff are called Yeomen Warders of the Tower. Their style of dress is of the Tudor period.

Trade-Mark, a mark used in relation to goods for the purpose of indicating a connection in the course of trade between the goods and some person having the right, either as a proprietor or registered user, to use the mark. Trade-marks can be registered, the registration holding good for 7 years and being renewable thereafter indefinitely for periods of 14 years. Infringement of a registered trade-mark renders the infringer liable to damages.

Trade Winds form part of the circulation of air round the great permanent anticyclones of the tropics and blow inwards from north-east (Northern Hemisphere) and south-east (Southern Hemisphere) towards the equatorial region of low pressure. Atlantic trades are more regular than those of the Pacific. The belts may extend over 2,400 km of latitude and, together with the Doldrums, move north and south in sympathy with the seasonal changes in the sun's declination, the average annual range being about 5 degrees of latitude.

Trafalgar, Battle of, was fought off Cape Trafalgar on 21 October 1805, between the British under Nelson and the French and Spanish under Villeneuve and Gravina. It was a complete victory for the British, but Nelson was killed.

Trafalgar Square. The site has often been referred to as the finest in Europe. It was conceived originally as a square by John Nash (1752–1835) when the project was considered of linking Whitehall with Bloomsbury and the British Museum. It was to be named after the new monarch as King William the Fourth's Square but on the suggestion of George Ledwell Taylor (a property owner near the site) alteration to the more popular name Trafalgar Square was agreed to by the King. On the north side the National Gallery was planned by Nash and erected by William Wilkins on the place of the Royal Mews—a work of William Kent a century before. The lay-out was the idea of Charles Barry but he did not approve the erection of the Nelson column (which see). His idea was for the square to have a grand flight of steps from the north side with sculptural figures of Wellington and Nelson but the Commons decided otherwise and the column as designed by William Railton was begun in 1840. The two fountains by Barry were supplanted in 1948 by ones designed (1938) by Sir Edwin Lutyens. Executed in Portland stone they are flanked by some bronze sculptures. In the same year memorial busts of Lords Jellicoe and Beatty were placed by the north wall.

Transept, the portion of a church which extends across the interior between the nave and the choir.

Transistor. An electronic device consisting of a small piece of semiconducting solid (usually germanium or silicon) to which contact is made at appropriate places by three wires. The three parts resemble in function (not construction or behaviour) the cathode, anode, and grid of a thermionic valve, and transistors can perform many of the operations that valves have hitherto been used for in radio, television, etc. They possess several advantages over valves since there is no need for evacuated glass bulbs nor for a heated emitter to give off electrons. This leads to much greater compactness and economy as well as to a much longer life. Nevertheless, there are certain limitations to their use, and they are not yet suitable as substitutes for valves in all cases. The device was invented by the Americans Bardeen, Brattain and Shockley in 1948.

Transubstantiation. *See* Section J.

Treasure-Trove, a legal term applying to treasure (coin, bullion, gold or silver articles) found hidden in the earth or other place, for which no owner can be discovered. The treasure legally belongs to the Crown, but it is the practice to return to the finder all articles not required for national museums and to reward him with the full market value of such as may be retained. It is the duty of the finder to report to the Coroner for the district in which the find is made who holds an inquest to find whether the discovery be treasure-trove or no. In England concealment is a criminal offence. *See also* **Wreck.**

Tree Frog, occurs most commonly in America and Australasia. The common European tree frog is a brilliant green animal, the adhesive discs at the tips of its fingers and toes enabling it to cling to trees, etc., with ease.

Tree Rings as Natural Calendar. The approximate relationship between radiocarbon dating (*q.v.*) and true calendar age for the past 7,000 years

has been established from measurements on tree-rings. Because one tree-ring is formed annually and its thickness is characteristic of the climatic conditions during its growth, it is possible, by comparing distinctive groups of rings, to date a series of trees. By using the long-lived Bristle Cone pines, tree-rings dating back to 5000 B.C. have been obtained. It has been found that the radiocarbon age around, say, 3000 B.C. is too young by c. 600 years and because of short-term fluctuations near, say, 2000 B.C., a particular radiocarbon age can correspond to more than one true calendar age. These corrections are far less than those proved necessary after the publication of the first radiocarbon dates. Tree-rings (based on the measurement of deuterium in wood) can also show the pattern of temperature fluctuations over hundreds of years and thus make it possible to trace climatic changes before written records began.

Tree Shrew, an arboreal insectivorous mammal of Asia belonging to the family *Tupaiidae*. Tree shrews are related to the shrews, though in appearance they resemble squirrels except for their sharply pointed snout. They occur in Borneo, Thailand, China and Malaya. Some zoologists classify them as primitive primates.

Trent, Council of, the longest and one of the most important in the history of the Roman Catholic Church, was convened to combat the doctrines of Martin Luther. It first sat in 1545, the last sitting being in 1563. At this Council the general policy, principles and dogmas of the Roman Catholic Church were authoritatively settled.

Triassic *or* **Trias,** the earliest geological period in the Mesozoic era, which began some 225 million years ago. Triassic formations 7,600 m thick occur in the Alps. Modern insects were appearing, and also small reptile-like mammals. Other important Triassic animals were: dinosaurs, ichthyosaurs (marine reptiles), and pterosaurs (flying reptiles). *See* **F48.**

Tribunes, name assigned to officers of different descriptions in ancient Rome. The original tribunes were the commanders of contingents of cavalry and infantry. The most important tribunes were the tribunes of the plebs, first elected in 494 B.C. as the outcome of the struggle between the patrician and the plebeian orders. They held the power of veto and their persons were sacred.

Trichoptera. This is the insect order comprising the Caddis-flies. These are moth-like insects having hairs on the wings. They are usually found fluttering weakly near water. The larvae are aquatic and are remarkable for the cases (caddis cases) which they build out of sticks, small stones, sand grains, and shells.

Tricolour, the flag of the French Republic since 1789, consisting of three nearly equal vertical bands of blue, white and red (ratio 90 : 99 : 111).

Trilobites, extinct marine arthropods, most abundant in the Cambrian and Ordovician systems. Their appearance may be roughly described as resembling that of a woodlouse, and like that animal the trilobites were capable of rolling their bodies up into a ball.

Trinity. The Christian doctrine that God exists in three persons, all co-equal, and indivisible, of the same substance—God the Father, God the Son (who became incarnate as Jesus), begotten of the Father, and God the Holy Ghost, proceeding from Father and Son. The system denying the Trinity is Unitarianism. *See* Section J.

Trinity House, on Tower Hill, London, was incorporated in 1514 as an association for piloting ships, and has ever since been entrusted with various matters connected with the regulation of British navigation. Since 1854 the lighthouses of the country have been under its supervision. The acting Elder Brethren act as Nautical Assessors in Marine causes which are tried by the High Court of Justice.

Trireme, an ancient vessel with three rows of oars of great effectuality in early naval warfare. Mentioned by Thucydides. It was a long, narrow vessel propelled by 170 rowers. The Romans copied it from the Greeks.

Tritium, a radioactive isotope of hydrogen which has three times the weight of the ordinary hydrogen atom. It is produced by bombarding an isotope of lithium with neutrons and has a half-life of 12½ years, decaying with the emission of β-particles (electrons).

Triumvirate, a term used to denote a coalition of three persons in the exercise of supreme authority. The first Roman triumvirate was that of Pompey, Julius Caesar, and Crassus, 60 B.C.; the second was that of Mark Antony, Octavus and Lepidus, 43 B.C.

Tropic-Bird, a long-tailed sea bird, of which there are 3 species (the Red-billed, the White-tailed, and the Red-tailed), frequenting the tropical regions of the Atlantic, Pacific and Indian oceans. They are commonly called Bo'sun Birds.

Troposphere. The atmospheric layer which extends from the earth's surface to the stratosphere. As a general rule the temperature in the troposphere falls as altitude increases. *See* Atmosphere.

Troubadours, lyric poets who flourished from the 11th to the end of the 13th cent., chiefly in Provence and the north of Italy. They were often knightly amateurs, and cultivated a lyrical poetry intricate in metre and rhyme and usually of a romantic amatory strain. They did much to cultivate the romantic sentiment in days when society was somewhat barbaric and helped considerably in the formation of those unwritten codes of honour which served to mitigate the rudeness of mediaeval days. *See also* Jongleurs.

Trouvère *or* Trouveur, mediaeval poet of northern France, whose compositions were of a more elaborate character—epics, romances, fables, and chansons de geste—than those of the troubadour of the south. Flourished between the 11th and 14th cent.

Truffles are subterranean edible fungi much esteemed for seasoning purposes. There are many species, and they are found in considerable quantities in France and Italy, less commonly in Britain. They are often met with under beech or oak trees, and prefer calcareous soils, but there are no positive indications on the surface to show where they are, and they are not to be cultivated. Hogs, and sometimes dogs, are used to scent them out, the former, by reason of their rooting propensities, being the most successful in the work.

Tsetse, an African dipterous fly belonging to the same family as the house-fly. It is a serious economic pest as it transmits the protozoon causing African sleeping sickness when it pierces human skin in order to suck blood, which forms its food. *See* Gammexane.

Tsunami, a seismic sea wave originating from any one of several submarine geological phenomena such as volcanic explosions, landslides or earth movements. Tsunamis are extremely long wavelength waves which travel in the open ocean at speeds up to 640 km/h. In deep water their height is only barely perceptible, but on reaching shallow coastal water they may attain heights of up to 30 m and can cause devastation to low-lying areas. The Pacific Ocean, whose rim is a seismically active area, is particularly susceptible to tsunamis. Following the damage caused by a tsunami which struck the volcanic islands of Hawaii on 1 April 1946, an early-warning system has been in operation. Tsunamis are often incorrectly referred to as tidal waves.

Tuatara or *Sphenodon punctatum*, a primitive lizard found in New Zealand. It has a rudimentary third eye on the top of the head; this is called the pineal eye and corresponds to tissue which in mammals forms the pineal gland.

Tube Foot, the characteristic organ of locomotion of starfishes and kindred animals. They are arranged in pairs along the underside of the arms, and their sucker-like ends can grip a surface very tightly. The action of the suckers depends on hydraulic pressure.

Tudor Period extends from 1485 to 1603. The first Tudor sovereign was Henry VII, descended from Owen Tudor; then followed Henry VIII, Edward VI, Mary and Elizabeth, the last of the line.

Tuesday, the third day of the week, named from the Saxon deity Tuisto, Tiw or Tuesco. To the Romans it was the day of Mars.

Tuileries, a French royal and imperial palace dating from 1564. It was attacked by insurgents during the outbreaks of 1792, 1830 and 1848, and was burned down during the Commune of Paris in 1871.

Tumulus, a mound of earth raised over the bodies of the dead. The mound of Marathon, enclosing the bodies of the Athenians who were killed in the famous battle with the Persians, is a celebrated tumulus. Such mounds were commonly raised over the tombs of the distinguished dead in ancient times, and sometimes enclosed heavy structures of masonry. The Roman " barrows " were tumuli. Evidences of such mounds are frequent in prehistoric remains.

Tuna *or* Tunny, a large marine fish belonging to the mackerel family, frequenting the warm waters of the Atlantic, Pacific and Mediterranean. Tuna fisheries are an important industry.

Tundra, the vast treeless plains lying in northern N. America and northern USSR where long severe winters and permanently frozen subsoils (permafrost) have resulted in specially adapted plant communities. The summer thaw and impervious permafrost cause waterlogging of lowland areas and marsh plants occur on these sites. In summer the ground cover of lichens and mosses with some flowering plants is distinctive. Stunted willows and birches occur in certain sites.

Tungsten, a hard, brittle metal, symbol W (it was formerly called wolfram), silver to grey in colour. Its chief ores are wolframite (iron and manganese tungstate) and scheelite (calcium tungstate). Tungsten is alloyed in steel for the manufacture of cutting tools; also in the non-ferrous alloy stellite. Electric lamp filaments are made from tungsten. Tungsten carbide is one of the hardest substances known and is used for tipping tools.

Turbines propelled by steam provide power for the propulsion of many ships, and on land steam turbines are a principal source of power, being used in large central electricity stations, for instance, to convert heat energy into electrical energy. Gas turbines have recently come into use in aeroplanes, and gas-turbine railway locomotives are being developed. The first gas-turbine ship had its trials in 1947, just half a century after the first steam-turbine ship.

Turbot, a large flat fish, highly valued as food. It often attains from 13 to 18 kg in weight. Its flesh is white and firm. It is confined to European waters, and is caught by line or trawl.

Turkey, a fowl of American origin, brought to Europe from America soon after the discovery of that country. It was a domesticated bird in England in the first half of the 16th cent.

Turpentine, an oily substance obtained from coniferous trees, mostly pines and firs. It is widely used especially in making paints and varnishes, and also has medicinal properties.

Turquoise, formerly called Turkey-Stone, is a blue or greenish-blue precious stone, the earliest and best specimens of which came from Persia. It is composed of a phosphate of aluminium, with small proportions of copper and iron. India, Tibet, and Silesia yield turquoises, and a variety is found in New Mexico and Nevada. It derives its name from the fact that the first specimens were imported through Turkey.

Turtle Dove, a summer visitor from Africa to southern England. It is a small, slender bird with reddish-brown upper parts, pinkish throat, black tail with white edges, and a repeated purring note.

Tweed. A rough-surfaced fabric of the twilled type, usually all-wool, though cheaper kinds may include cotton. Of a soft, open, flexible texture, it may have a check, twill or herring-bone pattern. Harris, Lewis, Bannockburn and Donegal tweeds are well known. " Tweeds " is said to have been written in error by a clerk for " twill ".

Twelfth Night is the eve of the feast of the Epiphany, and in olden times was made the occasion of many festivities. It was the most popular festival next to Christmas, but is now little observed.

Twilight is the light which is reflected from the upper portion of the earth's atmosphere when the sun is below the horizon (before sunrise or after sunset). The term is most usually understood to refer, however, to the evening light; the morning light we call dawn. The twilight varies in duration in different countries, according to the position of the sun. In tropical countries it is short; in the extreme north it continues through the night.

Tyburn, a former small tributary of the Thames, which gave its name to the district where now stands the Marble Arch, Hyde Park. Here public executions formerly took place.

Tycoon, the title by which the commander-in-chief of the Japanese army (virtually the ruler of Japan) was formerly described by foreigners. (In Japanese *taikun* means great lord or prince.) The term is now applied, usually in a derogatory sense, to an influential business magnate.

Tympanum is, in architectural phraseology, the triangular space at the back of a pediment, or, indeed, any space in a similar position, as over window or between the lintel and the arch of a doorway. In ecclesiastical edifices the tympanum is often adorned with sculpture.

Tynwald, the title given to the Parliament of the Isle of Man, which includes the Governor and Council (the Upper House), and the House of Keys, the representative assembly. This practically constitutes Home Rule, the Acts passed by the Tynwald simply requiring the assent of the Sovereign.

U

Uhlan, a light cavalry soldier armed with lance, pistol, and sabre and employed chiefly as skirmisher or scout. Marshal Saxe had a corps of them in the French Army; and in the Franco-German war of 1870 the Prussian Uhlans won fame.

Ultramarine, a sky-blue pigment obtained from *Lapis lazuli,* a stone found in Tibet, Iran, Siberia and some other countries. A cheaper ultramarine is now produced by grinding and heating a mixture of clay, sulphur, carbonate of soda and resin.

Ultrasonics, sound waves of frequency so high as to be inaudible to humans, *i.e.* about 20,000 Hz and upwards (Hz is SI unit for cycle per sec.). Ultrasonic waves are commonly produced by causing a solid object to vibrate with a suitably high frequency and to impart its vibrations to the air or other fluid. The object may be a quartz or other crystal in which vibrations are excited electrically, or a nickel component which is magnetically energised. There are numerous technical applications, *e.g.* submarine echo sounding, flaw detection in castings, drilling glass and ceramics, emulsification. Ultrasonic waves are an important tool of research in physics. Bats produce very loud sounds when they are flying, but at ultrasonic frequencies (20,000 to 100,000 Hz), so that we cannot ourselves hear them.

Ultra-Violet Rays. These are invisible electromagnetic rays whose wavelengths are less than 3900 Å. (Angstrom = one hundred-millionth of a centimetre.) The sun's radiation is rich in ultra-violet light, but much of it never reaches the earth, being absorbed by molecules of atmospheric gases (in particular, ozone) as well as by soot and smoke particles. One beneficial effect of ultra-violet light on human beings is that it brings about synthesis of vitamin-D from certain fatty substances (called sterols) in the skin. The wavelengths which effect this vitamin synthesis also cause sun tan and sun burn. Ultra-violet lamps (which are mercury-vapour discharge lamps) are also used for sterilising the air inside buildings, their rays being lethal to bacteria. Many substances fluoresce under ultra-violet light: for instance, zinc silicate glows green, while cadmium borate throws out red light. This phenomenon is applied practically in fluorescent lamps, the light of requisite hue being secured by judicious mixture of the fluorescent materials which coat the lamp. *See* Electric Light.

Umbra, the full shadow of the earth or moon during an eclipse; the half shadow is called penumbra.

Unciae. The Romans took over the Egyptian

cubit and divided it into 16 digits as well as into 12 parts called *unciae,* the *uncia* being the origin of the inch.

Underdeveloped Countries are those in which economic structure and development are held back, or, as some would have it, countries which are underdeveloped in the transitive sense of the word. The causes of the condition of underdevelopment are complex but two opposing sets of theories dominate discussion. On the one hand there are those theories that attribute underdevelopment to the internal characteristics of the underdeveloped countries themselves. This is the doctrine of original underdevelopment as it implies that such countries are responsible for their own underdevelopment. On the other hand there are the theories that ascribe underdevelopment directly to the distortions of economic structure and the exploitation involved in the relations between the developed and underdeveloped countries. The expansion of capitalism from its birthplace in Western Europe has created a world-wide production system and market (*i.e.,* a world economy from which no country is completely isolated) structured and determined by the imperatives of capital accumulation in the developed countries. This view implies that the state and process of underdevelopment in one part of the world is inevitable as long as there is development in another. Development and underdevelopment are then mutually interdependent. *See also* Sections **G, Part III** and **F, Part VI.**

Unicorn, a fabulous single-horned animal. In heraldry its form is horse-like, with the tail of a lion and pointed single horn growing out of the forehead. In the Middle Ages the unicorn was a symbol of virginity.

Union of Great Britain and Ireland was proposed in the Irish Parliament in January 1799 after the 1798 Rebellion and came into force on 1 January 1801. The troubled history of Ireland, associated with the question of self-government, nationalism, land and religion, culminated in the Easter revolution of 1916. A treaty giving the 26 southern counties independence in 1921, as the Irish Free State, was followed by a period of internal dissension. In 1937 a new constitution was enacted in Eire in which no reference was made to the Crown. This, however, left in force the External Relations Act of 1936 and with its repeal in 1948, Eire separated itself from the British Crown and thus severed the last constitutional link with the Commonwealth, and became an independent Republic.

Union, Treaty of, was the treaty by which Scotland became formally united to England, the two countries being incorporated as the United Kingdom of Great Britain, the same Parliament to represent both, Scotland electing sixteen peers and forty-five members of the House of Commons. Uniformity of coins, weights, and measures was provided for, Scottish trade laws and customs were assimilated to those of England, and as regards religion and the practices of the law, Scotland was to continue as before. This Act was ratified on 1 May 1707.

Universe in astronomy means not only the star system (of which the sun and planets are a small part) but all the countless star systems or nebulae which may be separated from each other by millions of light-years. *See* **F3-8.**

Universities are institutions of higher education whose principal objects are the increase of knowledge over a wide field through original thought and research and its extension by the teaching of students. Such societies existed in the ancient world, notably in Greece and India, but the origin of the University as we know it today lies in mediaeval Europe, the word *universitas* being a contraction of the Latin term for corporations of teachers and students organised for the promotion of higher learning. The earliest bodies to become recognised under this description were at Bologna and Paris in the first half of the 12th cent.; Oxford was founded by an early migration of scholars from Paris, and Cambridge began with a further migration from Oxford. Other Universities sprang up all over Europe, including three in Scotland—St. Andrews (1412), Glasgow (1451) and Aberdeen (1494)—which were followed by Edinburgh in 1582. These six bodies remained the only Universities in Great Britain until the foundation in 1826–29 of University and King's Colleges in London (resulting in the establishment of the University of London in 1836) and of the University of Durham in 1832. There are (1977) thirty-three Universities in England: Aston, Bath, Birmingham, Bradford, Bristol, Brunel, Cambridge, The City, Durham, East Anglia, Essex, Exeter, Hull, Keele, Kent, Lancaster, Leeds, Leicester, Liverpool, London, Loughborough, Manchester, Newcastle, Nottingham, Oxford, Reading, Salford, Sheffield, Southampton, Surrey, Sussex, Warwick and York. Other institutions where the work is of university standard are the University of Manchester Institute of Science and Technology; the Manchester Business School; the London Graduate School of Business Studies; Cranfield Institute of Technology; and the Royal College of Art. Formed from colleges of technology, art and design, commerce and other institutions, thirty polytechnics have been established in England and Wales as centres of higher education. Wales has one University (The University of Wales with colleges at Aberystwyth, Bangor, Cardiff and Swansea) in addition to the Welsh National School of Medicine, the Institute of Science and Technology, and St. David's, Lampeter. Scotland now has eight: Aberdeen, Dundee (1967), Edinburgh, Glasgow, Heriot-Watt (1966), St. Andrews, Stirling (1967), and Strathclyde (1964), Britain's first technological University. Northern Ireland has two: Queen's University, Belfast and the New University of Ulster at Coleraine. The Open University received its charter in 1969; it provides degree and other courses together with radio and television programmes and began its broadcasts in January 1971. The Republic of Ireland has the University of Dublin (Trinity College, Dublin), and the National University of Ireland with colleges at Dublin, Cork and Galway. The early important foundations in the British Empire were: New Brunswick (1785), McGill (1821), Toronto (1827), Queen's (1841), Laval (1852) in Canada; Sydney (1850), Melbourne (1853) in Australia; Otago (1869), Canterbury (1873), Auckland (1882) in New Zealand; Bombay, Calcutta and Madras (1857) in India; and the University of the Punjab (1882) in the present Pakistan. Since the war a number of Commonwealth Universities have been established. In the USA the development of higher education has left the Universities less sharply defined than in Europe and the Commonwealth, among the best known being Harvard (1636), Yale (1701), Princeton (1746), Columbia (1754), Cornell (1865), California (Berkeley), Massachusetts Institute of Technology. In 1973 the United Nations University was established with headquarters in Tokyo. In Britain, Universities receive aid from the State mainly in the form of direct grants from the Treasury made on the advice of the University Grants Committee. But they are self-governing institutions free from State control. In recent years students have increased their contributions to the formulation of university policy.

Uranium, a metal, symbol U, discovered by Klaproth in 1789 in pitchblende. It is a white metal which tarnishes readily in air. Great developments have followed the discovery that the nucleus of the uranium isotope U²³⁵ undergoes fission, and uranium minerals have become very important since it was found that atomic energy could be released controllably by taking advantage of fission. Before atomic energy work began to take the major part of the world's output of uranium minerals, the chief users of uranium compounds were the ceramics and textile industries. *See also* **Nuclear Reactors, Nuclear Fission, F13(1).**

Uranus. This planet was discovered by Herschel in 1781. Its diameter is *c.* 51,800 km and its mean distance from the sun is 2,869·6 × 10⁶ km. It has five small satellites and is surrounded by five very thin rings (first seen 1977). *See* F8.

Urea, the final product in mammals of the breakdown of nitrogenous waste, *e.g.*, excess amino-

acids. It is very soluble in water and is excreted in urine. In 1828 Wöhler synthesised urea from inorganic matter. This was the first laboratory synthesis of an organic substance and refuted the idea that living creatures or life force are necessary to create such substances.

Ursa Major and Ursa Minor ("Greater Bear" and "Lesser Bear"), two celebrated constellations, each of seven stars, in the northern celestial hemisphere, familiar since ancient times. Ursa Major has also been called "the Plough", "Charles's (Charlemagne's) Wain" or "the Wagon". The "Pointers" in this group of bright stars point to the brightest star in Ursa Minor, the Pole Star. Called the Big Dipper and the Little Dipper in the USA.

V

Valency. A term used by chemists to describe the combining ability of an element with respect to hydrogen. Thus oxygen, which forms water, H_2O, with hydrogen is said to have a valency of two, nitrogen (forms ammonia, NH_3) three, and carbon (forms methane, CH_4) four. Chlorine forms hydrogen chloride, HCl, and is said to be monovalent. This empirical approach cannot account for valency in such compounds as carbon monoxide, CO, which appears to require both elements to have the same valency. With the discovery of the electron it was realised that the concept of valency and chemical bonds is intimately concerned with the electronic structure of atoms, and theories have been advanced to explain why the same element can have different valencies in different compounds. Iron, for example, can have a valency of two ($FeCl_2$, ferrous chloride) or three ($FeCl_3$, ferric chloride). *See* **F11(1)** and **Table of Elements, F89.**

Valentine's Day (14 February), is a festival in celebration of St. Valentine, one of the Christian martyrs of the 3rd cent. A sweetheart or Valentine is chosen on that day and letters or tokens sent secretly to the object of affection.

Valhalla, in Scandinavian mythology, is the special Paradise to which the souls of warriors slain in battle were transported.

Valkyries, the chosen handmaidens of Odin, appointed to serve at the Valhalla banquets. Their most important office, however, according to the Norse mythology, was to ride through the air at a time of battle and point out the heroes who were to fall. It is one of these Valkyries who is made the heroine of Wagner's opera "Die Walküre".

Valve, an electronic device consisting of two or more metal plates (electrodes) usually enclosed in an evacuated glass bulb. One of the electrodes is heated causing electrons to be emitted. If a positive voltage is applied to the other electrode, the electrons will move towards it and the valve must conduct electricity. The current will only flow in one direction as the electrons are emitted only from one electrode. A valve with two electrodes is called a diode, but by putting in one or more intermediate electrodes the flow of current can be sensitively controlled and the valves are then called triodes, pentodes, etc., according to the total number of electrodes in them. Valves have found extensive applications in amplifiers, rectifiers, oscillators and many electronic devices, but have now been superseded by transistors in many applications where it is advantageous to have greater reliability, smaller power consumption and smaller size.

Vanadium, a scarce metallic element, symbol V, whose chief ores are carnotite and patronite. Some iron ores contain it. Most of the vanadium commercially produced finds its way into vanadium steels, which are used for tools and parts of vehicles, being hard, tough and very resistant to shocks. The oxide is used as a catalyst in industry, especially in making sulphuric acid.

Van Allen Belts. One of the most remarkable discoveries made during the IGY, 1957–58, was that the earth is surrounded by a great belt of radiation. Evidence came from *Sputnik II* (which carried the dog Laika) and from the American satellites, *Explorers I* and *III*. The American scientist, J. A. van Allen, was able to explain the puzzling data collected from these satellites. Subsequent observations with deep space-probes showed that there are in fact two zones of high intensity particle radiation surrounding the earth, one concentrated at a distance of about 1,600 km, the other at about 24,000 km. A close relation exists between the shapes of the zones and the earth's magnetic field. Recent evidence suggests that Jupiter also is surrounded by a dense belt of trapped energetic particles.

Vatican, the Papal residence at Rome, a famous palace on the hill adjacent to St. Peter's. Its museum is a rich treasure-house of literary and artistic objects. Works of Michelangelo glorify the Sistine Chapel.

Vauxhall Gardens, a famous London pleasure resort from the early part of the 18th to the middle of the 19th cent. It was here that many great singers appeared, where the earliest balloon ascents were made, and where there were fine displays of fireworks.

Venus, the brightest of all the planets, whose orbit lies between that of Mercury and the earth, second in order from the sun (*see* **F8**). It can approach the earth to within 40 million km. In common with all the other planets it moves around the sun in the same direction as the earth, but is the only one that rotates about its axis in the opposite direction. The planet takes just under 225 earth days to complete an orbit round the sun. In 1967 Russia succeeded in soft-landing an instrumented canister from their *Venus 4* research spacecraft. Measurements gave a picture of a very hostile environment—high surface temperature, a very high atmospheric pressure, and an atmosphere of almost pure carbon dioxide, findings very close to those obtained by later probes. *Venus 5* and *Venus 6* made twin landings in May 1969 and sent back data on the planet's mysterious veil of white clouds. *Venus 9* and *Venus 10* which made twin landings in 1975 gave data of importance to the study of Venusian geology. The pictures taken appeared to suggest volcanic activity.

Venus Fly-trap, a well-known insectivorous plant (*Dionaea muscipula*) occurring in Carolina in damp mossy places. It is related to the Sundew. The leaf is the organ that catches the insects. The leaf blade is in two halves, hinged along the centre line. Each half bears three sensitive hairs called " trigger hairs ". When an insect touches a trigger, the two halves of the leaf clap together, trapping the insect between them, when it is digested by a secretion (digestive enzymes) from the leaf, which afterwards absorbs the soluble products.

Vernalization. Seeds which, after being exposed to a low temperature, produce plants that flower earlier than usual are said to have been " vernalized ". This technique of seed treatment devised by Lysenko is called vernalization. It is claimed to have been widely used in Russia to obtain cereal crops in places where climatic conditions are favourable for only a short season.

Versailles, Treaty of. The Peace Treaty, 1919, ending the first world war. The first half was devoted to the organisation of the League of Nations. Among the territorial changes Germany ceded Alsace-Lorraine to France, Posen and the Corridor to Poland. Germany undertook to disarm, to abolish universal military service, to keep only a small army of 100,000 and a small navy. Her colonies were to be shared out among the Allies under League Mandates. Reparations were to be paid, but were gradually reduced and entirely ceased in 1932. Hitler took unilateral action against the Treaty especially in regard to rearmament and the annexation of Austria. Hitler's attempt to change the eastern frontiers was the immediate cause of the second world war.

Victoria and Albert Museum, in Kensington, London, was begun in 1852 as the Museum of Ornamental Art at Marlborough House. The present building was completed in 1909. It has the following departments: Architecture and Sculpture, Conservation, Ceramics, Paintings, Prints and Drawings, Oriental, Library Metal-work, Museum Services (inc. Information and Slide Loan Service), Textiles, Furniture and Woodwork, Education (into which the old Circulation Dept. has been absorbed), Theatre Museum. The V. & A. also administers the Wellington Museum (Apsley House, Piccadilly), Ham House (Richmond, Surrey), Osterley Park House (Middx). The Bethnal Green Museum (The Museum of Childhood) is a branch of the V. & A., opened 1872.

Victoria Cross, an order of merit for conspicuous valour, awarded to members of the Army, Navy and Air Force, was established in 1856.

Videotape recording (VTR), technique for recording television programmes on to magnetic tape. The original means of storing programmes for broadcast or library purposes was by filming productions from high-quality monitors, an expensive and slow process, since the film had to be chemically developed and edited in the conventional way. The difficulty in establishing an instant play-back system along the lines of the sound tape recording system lay in the high speed and large amount of tape needed to accommodate the picture signal. The BBC experimented with a machine called VERA (Vision Electronic Recording Apparatus), but it was an American machine, the Ampex VR100, which provided the breakthrough. This recorded the picture across a wider tape rather than along it, and moving at a slower speed. Tapes, in colour or black and white, now run for about 90 minutes and can be used many times by erasing and re-recording. accuracy of editing is achieved to the second by re-recording chosen sequences on to a second machine.

Vienna Congress, sat at Vienna from September 1814 to June 1815, and settled the delineation of the territories of the various European nations after the defeat of Napoleon. The Treaty of Vienna which resulted gave Sri Lanka, Mauritius, Cape Colony, Heligoland, Malta and part of Guyana to England; France was not permitted to hold more territory than she had possessed at the outbreak of the Revolution in 1789; Austria took Northern Italy; Russia part of Poland; and Prussia, part of Saxony and the Rhenish province. Except for one or two changes the clauses of the treaty were maintained for over forty years.

Vikings. Scandinavian pirates who from the 8th to the 10th cent. were the terror of northern waters. Sometimes the Viking raids reached south to the Mediterranean and east to the White Sea. Their leader Rurik founded the first Russian kingdom of Novgorod in A.D. 862. The Icelandic Vikings under Eric the Red discovered Greenland in A.D. 982 and a warm period in world climate allowed many to settle there. Their expeditions took them to Labrador and Newfoundland. They excelled in shipbuilding, were fine sailors and craftsmen.

Vinyl Plastics are polymers made from derivatives of ethylene, examples are polyvinyl chloride (PVC), which is used in making plastic pipes and kitchen utensils, among other things; polyvinyl acetate used in the paint industry and in bonding laminated articles like plywood; and polystyrene (poly vinyl benzene) used in making electrical fittings and for lenses.

Viper, a family of poisonous snakes in which the venom-conducting fangs hinge forward when the snake bites. One species is found in Britain the common viper or adder.

Virus. *See* **P7, F31(2).**

Visibility is defined by the distance at which the farthest of a series of objects, specially selected to show against the skyline or in good contrast with their background, can be distinguished. Visibility depends chiefly upon the concentration of water or dust particles suspended in the air. Instruments are available to measure the obscurity of the atmosphere more directly, including that at night. A large lapse rate of temperature and a strong wind are favourable to good visibility; a small lapse rate, calm or light wind favourable to bad visibility. Fog is when the visibility is less than 1,000 m; mist or haze when it is between 1,000 and 2,000 m. *See* **Pollution.**

Viscount, a title of rank coming between that of Earl and Baron. The title originally stood for deputy-earl. The first English Viscount was Viscount Beaumont, created in 1440.

Vitamins, name of a group of organic substances found in relatively minute amounts in certain foodstuffs, essential for growth and the maintenance of normal bodily structure and function. The Hungarian biochemist Szent-Györgyi, who first isolated vitamin C or ascorbic acid, defined the vitamin as " a substance that makes you ill if you don't eat it! " *See* **F32(1), P40.**

Volcanoes are vents through which magma reaches the surface as lava flows, or as the solid products, *e.g.*, ashes and bombs, of explosive eruption. The vent may be cylindrical or it may be a long fissure. The former type usually builds up cones, *e.g.*, Vesuvius. Notable active volcanoes are Etna, Vesuvius and Stromboli, in Italy; Hekla in Iceland; and Mont Pelée in Martinique. The last-named was in violent eruption in 1902, when the chief town of St. Pierre was completely destroyed. Volcanic eruptions are sometimes linked with brilliant sunset phenomena, *e.g.*, the Indonesian island of Krakatoa (1883), whose atmospheric and tidal effects were recorded all over the world, and Agung on the island of Bali (1963), which had been dormant for 120 years. A new fissure volcano (Surtsey) developed off the coast of Iceland in 1963. The 1971 eruption of Etna was a serious one, though minor compared with that of 1669.

Vole, a small rodent with blunt nose, round face and short tail. Three kinds occur in Britain: the field, the bank and the water vole.

Volt, the electromotive force unit, named after Alessandro Volta (1745–1827), and defined in terms of the coulomb, the second and the joule.

Vraic, a name for seaweed in the Channel Islands, where it is extensively used as a manure.

Vulgate, a term used to designate the Latin version of the Scriptures sanctioned by the Council of Trent. The work of St. Jerome in the late 4th cent. A.D. and still the official Bible of the Roman Catholic Church.

Vulture, a famous bird of prey of two distinctive groups; that of the Old World, whose nostrils are separated by a bony partition, and the New World vulture, which has no such division. Vultures feed on carrion and are the great scavengers of tropical regions. The European species are the Egyptian vulture, Griffon vulture, Black vulture and Bearded vulture. Vultures have no feathers on the head and neck.

W

Wading Birds, *Charadriiformes*, an order of migratory, long-legged, long-billed birds, frequenting marshes and shallow waters. They include the plovers, avocets, stilts, oystercatchers, curlews, phalaropes, godwits, dunlins, sandpipers, redshanks, greenshanks, snipe, woodcocks, the pratincole of the Mediterranean and the sun bittern of tropical America. Many species breed in Britain.

Wagtails, familiar long-tailed small birds, the most common British species being the Pied or Water (with sub-species White) Grey and the Yellow (sub-species Blue). Wagtails nest in holes and are active of habit.

Walloons, name given to the French-speaking population of the southern provinces of Belgium, in contrast to the Flemings or Dutch-speaking population of the northern provinces. The Walloon areas contain the mining and heavy industries of the country; the Flemish regions are more agricultural. Walloons number *c.* 3 million. Flemings *c.* 5 million. The *Mouvement Populaire Wallon* desires an autonomous Wallonia within the Belgian state.

Walpurgis Night, the night before 1 May, when witches and creatures of evil are supposed to have liberty to roam. Named after St. Walpurgis, an English nun, who went on a mission to Germany in the 8th cent.

Walrus, a very large marine mammal, related to the seals having in the upper jaw two large curved tusks, which average in length from 38 to 60 cm. It lives on bi-valve molluscs, and inhabits the Arctic seas. An adult walrus can exceed 4 m in length and weigh over a tonne.

Wankel Engine or Rotary Engine, is an internal combustion engine invented by Felix Wankel in the 1930s and greatly developed since by large automobile firms in several countries. The ordinary internal combustion engine has to convert reciprocating motion of the pistons into rotatory motion. In the Wankel engine the explosion of the fuel and air mixture drives a moving part (the rotor) directly into rotatory motion, and the rotor itself opens and closes the fuel inlet and exhaust ports. The three spaces between the triangular rotor and its specially shaped housing act successively as intake, compression, explosion and exhaust chambers as the rotor revolves. There are no valves and far fewer moving parts than in an ordinary piston engine. The Wankel engine is claimed to have many advantages in that it is smaller and lighter for a given horse-power, relatively simple, quieter and freer from vibration, and could contribute to pollution control. There are cars now on sale with the Wankel engine and continuous research and development will no doubt test in practice the claim of some protagonists that this engine is the agent of a technological revolution in the automobile.

Wapentake, the ancient name given in the northern counties to territorial divisions corresponding to the Hundreds of southern counties.

Warblers, a family of small, lively song-birds closely related to the flycatchers and thrushes. Represented in Britain by about 36 species, including the chiffchaff, one of the earliest spring visitors, willow-wren, wood-warbler blackcap, garden-warbler, whitethroats, sedge and grasshopper-warbler.

Water is the simplest compound of hydrogen and oxygen. It is formed when an electric spark is passed through a mixture of the gases, and is a product of combustion of all hydrogen-containing compounds, *e.g.*, petrol, coal, coal gas and wood. Water is essential to living matter, and is the medium which carries food to animals and plants. Salts in hard water may be removed by distillation of the water or by a process known as ion-exchange (water softening). Pure water freezes at 0°C and boils at 100°C and is used as a standard of temperature on this scale. it has a maximum density at 4°C. Heating water above 100°C converts it into steam which is used under pressure to convert heat energy into useful work, as in electrical power stations and steam engines. Water gas is a mixture mainly of carbon monoxide and hydrogen formed by blowing steam and oxygen through red-hot coke: it is used as a fuel. Water is one of the very few compounds which freezes from the surface down rather than from the bulk of the liquid up. This property has important consequences on the preservation of life in rivers and lakes when they are frozen over. *See also* **F26(1).**

Water Hyacinth (*Eichhornia crassipes*), a beautiful aquatic plant native to Brazil which has spread to other favourable equatorial regions of the world causing havoc on account of its abnormal rate of reproduction away from its natural environment. In recent years it has invaded the Nile and the Zaïre, forming vast floating carpets which block the channels, clog the paddles of river craft and de-oxygenate the water, killing the fish. It is being held in check by spraying with the herbicide 2,4-D.

Waterloo, Battle of, was fought on 18 June 1815. The Allies (British, German and Dutch) under Wellington and Blücher defeated the French under Napoleon. This ended Napoleon's career.

Waterloo Bridge, crossing the Thames, was built by Rennie, and opened in 1817. It had nine arches, each 120 ft (36 m) span, was built of granite, and had a length (including approaches) of 2,456 ft (749 m). The present bridge, completed in 1942, and formally opened 10 December 1945, is a fine example of reinforced concrete construction. (Architect, Sir Giles Gilbert-Scott.)

Water-Spider, an interesting little animal which spins a sac of silk on a water-plant, which it uses as a sort of diving bell. Into this bell it introduces bubbles of air one at a time; thus the spider is enabled to remain below the surface a considerable time.

Waterspout, whirling tornado-like cloud, occurring at sea. It begins as a cone of cloud tapering slowly downwards, the sea surface becoming disturbed; on reaching the centre of the cloud of spray the spout takes on the appearance of a column of water. A number of these vortices may form fairly close together at about the same time, their duration ranging up to 30 minutes.

Watling Street, the name of the old Roman road which ran from the Channel ports by way of London to Salop. *See also* **Roman Roads**.

Watt. A unit of electrical power equivalent to 1 joule of work per second, named after James Watt (1736–1819). *See* **N7**.

Wax, the name applied to certain substances or mixtures which are solids having little crystalline form and may be regarded as solidified oils. They are used for various purposes, such as the making of wax candles, bleaching and making artificial flowers and anatomical models, also in pharmacy for blending in the composition of plasters, ointment, etc. The best-known natural wax is beeswax, and there are others, such as spermaceti, obtained from the sperm whale, and Chinese wax, which is a cerotyl cerotate.

Waxbill, a small Oriental and African bird of the *Estrildidae* family, with wax-like bill and beautifully variegated plumage. The Java sparrow, and the Blue-breasted waxbill are attractive, and often find their way into cages.

Wayz-Goose, the name given to a festive gathering of people employed in printing and other works, so called from the fact that in earlier times a goose was the principal dish of the feast.

Weasel. A carnivore mammal found in Britain, smallest member of the group including the Stoat, Polecat, and Pine-marten, about 20 cm long. Its fur is reddish on the upper side of the animal, white on the under side; it may all turn white in winter with the exception of the tail.

Weather is generally accepted as being the current state of the atmosphere, particularly as regards its pressure and temperature, wind, cloud and precipitation. Many other features such as fog, sunshine duration, humidity, pressure tendency, may be added to the list, all items of which are routinely observed by specially instrumented stations usually sponsored by the national meteorological services. Day-to-day changes in the weather as experienced by the individual are due to the passage of circulation systems, many of which bring clearly recognisable areas of " good " (*i.e.*, calm and sunny) weather as frequently occurs in anticyclones and " bad " (*i.e.*, cold, windy, cloudy and rainy) weather. Clearly, the weather in any place at any time is primarily determined by the frequency and intensity of synoptic-scale weather circulation systems (*c.* 3,000 km across). Local weather (over areas of *c.* 100 km) may be heavily influenced by topography, *e.g.*, valley fogs, frost hollows, etc.

Weather Lore. Before instruments were invented to measure atmospheric conditions, man relied on his own observation of wind and sky, behaviour of birds and animals, and came to associate certain phenomena with types of weather. Many popular weather rhymes have survived the centuries, and as long as forecasting is confined to the next 24 hours there is perhaps something to be said for them, particularly those dealing with the winds. What is very unlikely is that next year's summer can be predicted from this year's winter, or that one month's weather is related to that of another. The study of past records reveals too many exceptions for such predictions to be of much use in forecasting.

Weaver Bird, the popular name for a large group of finch-like birds belonging to the family *Ploceidae*, found principally in Africa but also in Southern Asia, Australia, and Europe and remarkable for their habit of building nests formed of blades of grass dexterously interwoven and suspended from the boughs of trees.

Weaving has been practised since before any times of which we have record. The Egyptians credit the invention to Isis, the Grecians to Minerva. The main principle of the weaving loom is the same to-day as it was thousands of years ago; a warp extends lengthwise through the loom, the threads being held in separate regular order by being passed through a reed or " slay ", while the weft is crossed through alternating threads of the warp by means of a shuttle which holds the weft. Thus the fabric is built up. Weaving was done by hand up to the early part of the 19th cent., when Cartwright's steam-power loom was introduced. The Jacquard loom for weaving figured designs dates from 1801.

Wedding Anniversaries are: first, Cotton; second, Paper; third, Leather; fourth, Fruit and Flower; fifth, Wooden; sixth, Sugar; seventh, Woollen; eighth, Salt; ninth, Copper; tenth, Tin; twelfth, Silk and Fine Linen; fifteenth, Crystal; twentieth, China; twenty-fifth, Silver; thirtieth, Pearl; thirty-fifth, Coral; fortieth, Ruby; fiftieth, Golden; sixtieth, Diamond; sixty-fifth, Blue Sapphire; seventieth, Platinum.

Wednesday, the 4th day of the week, derived its name from Woden or Odin, the Norse god of war.

Weights and Measures. *See* **Section N**.

Welding is a means of joining together two pieces of material, often metals, by heating the joint until the substances melt locally, run together, and then solidify. The heating can be by burning gas (*e.g.*, oxy-acetylene welding) or electric current (electric arc welding). Techniques exist for welding anything from hair-like wires to massive steel plates. *See* **Soldering**.

Werewolf, a man or woman, who according to mediaeval belief, could be turned by witchcraft or magic into a wolf, eat human flesh or drink human blood and turn into himself again. This belief was widely held in Europe, and similar superstitions prevail among most primitive peoples, *e.g.*, the " leopard man " of certain African tribes. Lycanthropy (from Gr. = wolfman) is a form of madness in which the patient imagines himself a beast. *See* **Section J**.

Westminster Abbey stands on the site of an old church and Benedictine foundation of the 7th cent. It was rebuilt under Edward the Confessor, and again under Henry III, and important additions were made by Edward II, Edward III, Richard II, Richard III and Henry VII, the latter erecting the beautiful eastern chapel in the perpendicular style which bears his name. The western towers and front were rebuilt by Wren in the 18th cent. It contains tombs of many sovereigns, of the Unknown Warrior, and many other illustrious men are commemorated by monuments.

Westminster Cathedral, seat of the Roman Catholic Archbishop of Westminster. It was designed by J. F. Bentley and built between 1895 and 1910. It is of red brick, in early Christian Byzantine style with a domed campanile, 283 ft (86 m) high, and a decorative interior.

Westminster Hall, adjoining the Houses of Parliament, was built as a Banqueting Hall by William Rufus, and many courtly festivals were held there in succeeding centuries. King John established the Law Courts there. It now forms a gigantic hallway, leading to the Houses of Parliament. Charles I, Sir Thomas More, and Warren Hastings were tried there.

Whale, a completely aquatic mammal; the fore-limbs are modified to form fin-like paddles and there is virtually no external trace of the hind-limbs. There are two major groups of whales—the *Toothed Whales*, including the Sperm-whale (Cachalot), Dolphin, Killer-whales and Porpoises; and the *Whalebone Whales*. In the latter a series of whalebone plates grow down from the roof of the mouth, and, being frayed at their edges into a hairy fringe, together constitute a filtering mechanism. The animal takes in sea water containing minute organisms on which it feeds; the mouth is then closed and the tongue raised when the water is forced out through the filter, on which is left the food. As the tongue is lowered, the whalebone plates straighten up, flicking the food on to the tongue, which transfers it to the gut. Most whale oil is obtained from the thick layer of fat under the skin (blubber), but in the Sperm-whale there is a large reserve of oil in the head. One of the major users of sperm oil is the leather industry. Ambergris used in perfumery comes from the intestine of whales.

The number of whales that may be killed in a season is limited by International Convention. The two main whaling nations are Japan and the Soviet Union.

Whimbrel, a bird of the Curlew family, more common in Scotland than in England.

Whinchat, a small migratory bird, a breeding visitor to Britain (April to October); bright brown plumage, with prominent eye stripe.

Whiskers in physics and materials science (q.v.) are tiny rods of crystal, thinner than human hair and perhaps 1 cm long. Their importance lies in the fact that such crystals are free from the defects described on **F21.** They are also free from surface cracks and steps. This means they are immensely strong because failures of strength in ordinary solids are due to imperfections and cracks of one kind or another. Large numbers of whiskers of strong solids like graphite, silicon, or silicon carbide embedded in a matrix of softer matter such as plastic or metal would make a very strong new material. Many laboratories are developing such substances.

Whisky, an ardent spirit distilled from malt or other grain, and containing a large percentage of alcohol. It has a greater consumption than any other spirit, and is of many kinds, Scotch and Irish whiskies being chiefly consumed in this country, and being of pot still or patent still production, or a blend of the two. Whisky is the most heavily taxed product: in 1661 a duty of 4d. a gallon was imposed; today (1978) the duty on Scotch and Irish whiskies is £27·09 per proof gallon. American whiskies are mostly distilled from corn (maize), or rye. *See* Alcohol.

White Elephant, a term in common use to designate a gift that causes the recipient more trouble or cost than it is worth; derived from an old-time custom of the Kings of Thailand who presented a white elephant to a courtier whom it was desired to ruin.

Whitehall Palace, built within sight of Westminster by Hubert de Burgh, Earl of Kent, round about 1240, was the residence of the Archbishops of York until Wolsey presented it to Henry VIII in 1530. From then until 1697, when it was burned down, it continued to be the favourite town residence of royalty, and to the Stuarts especially it was a great centre of court festivities. In those days, with its grounds, it extended from the Strand to the river. The only portion of Whitehall Palace now standing is the Banqueting Hall built by Inigo Jones, on a scaffold projected from the front of which Charles I was beheaded. A block of new government buildings has recently been built on part of the site of the old Palace.

White House, the official residence at Washington of the President of the United States.

Whitsuntide, the festival celebrating the descent of the Holy Ghost and occurring seven weeks after Easter.

Whydah Bird, the widow-bird of Equatorial Africa. The Paradise Whydah is remarkable for the long tail and handsome black-and-scarlet plumage of the male during mating season.

Widow Bird, certain species of African weaver birds with predominantly black plumage. In the breeding season the male birds are strikingly beautiful, with scarlet and buff markings and long tail feathers. They are social parasites and trick other birds into rearing their young.

Wigeon, a surface-feeding duck of northern Europe, known in Britain more as a winter visitor than a nesting bird. It feeds in flocks in the muddy estuaries and has a characteristic " whee-oo " call.

Willow, a water-side-loving tree of the genus *Salix,* to which the osiers belong. The best cricket-bat blades are made from a white willow, *S. alba* var. *caerulea,* a fine tree with bluish-green leaves, mostly found in Essex. Willow is also used for polo balls. Weeping willow, *S. baby-lonica,* is native to China and is the willow seen on Old China willow-pattern plates.

Wind, air set in motion by special atmospheric conditions, is of various degrees, from a slight rustling breeze to a hurricane. Winds are *constant,* as in trade winds or anti-trade winds; *periodic,* as in monsoons and other windvisitations occurring according to influences of season; *cyclonic* and *anti-cyclonic,* when their

motion is spiral: *whirlwinds, hurricanes,* and *tornados,* when high temperature and great density induce extreme agitation. Ordinarily, a wind is named from the point of the compass from which it blows, or it may be expressed in degrees from true north. The *sirocco,* the *mistral,* and the *simoom* are local forms of winds of great velocity. A *blizzard* is a biting blast of icy temperature. *See also* Beaufort Scale, Section N.

Windmills were in use in the East in ancient times, but were not much seen in Europe before the 13th cent. Wind sawmills were invented by a Dutchman in the 17th cent., and one was erected near the Strand in London in 1633. Great improvements have been made in these mills, especially in the United States, where, by the application of the windshaft principle, much space is saved and the mills can be used for pumping, grinding and other purposes.

Windows (Old Norse *vindauga* = wind-eye), an opening in a wall of a building to admit light and air, and to afford a view of what is outside. In northern Europe windows, as the derivation of the word implies, were first used for ventilation and glass was not used in private houses before the end of the 12th cent. In early Gothic (12th cent.) windows were still small and narrow, with rounded heads. In Early English (13th cent.) they became longer and the heads pointed. In the Decorated period (14th cent.) windows were mullioned (divided by slender bars into panes) and the pointed heads often traceried. In Tudor times when the Renaissance had found its way to England, windows were larger and the bay-window (projecting from the wall) and the oriel window (q.v.) were much in vogue; in the late 18th cent. curved bays (called bow-windows) became fashionable. Sash windows (invented by the English) with wooden frames and divided into equal rectangular panes were used in Queen Anne and Georgian houses. Their design was influenced by a passion for symmetry; they were very efficient ventilators. The French window reaches to the floor and has double casements opening as doors. A Dormer window is a vertical window set on the sloping side of a roof. One of the main features of modern architecture is the large area devoted to windows, a development made possible by improved heating systems. Windows are now mass-produced in stock sizes and patterns.

Windsor Castle, the famous British royal residence on the banks of the Thames, as it now stands, was mainly built by Henry III, though a royal residence had existed there from the time of the Conqueror. Additions were made by Henry VIII, Elizabeth and Charles II. Windsor Park and Forest comprise over 5,200 ha.

Wine, the fermented juice of the freshly-gathered grape. There are innumerable varieties, each obtaining its distinctive character from the species of wine producing the grape, the locality of the vineyard, method of cultivation, etc. Wines are of three main kinds: *sparkling,* as in champagne, due to their having been bottled before fermentation is complete; *beverage,* when the must has been fermented out before bottling. Such wines include the famous red and white wines of Burgundy, Bordeaux and the Rhone valley and the white wines of the Rhine, Moselle and Loire valleys. Wines are *fortified* by the addition of alcohol either after fermentation is complete (*e.g.,* Sherry) or during fermentation (*e.g.,* Port). The principal wine-producing countries are: France, Italy, Algeria, Spain, Portugal, Rumania, Argentine, Yugoslavia, USSR, Greece, W. Germany, Hungary.

Witan *or* **Witenagemot,** the name given to the king's council of " wise men " in Anglo-Saxon times, composed of the archbishops, bishops, abbots of the greater abbeys, earldormen and influential thanes.

Witchcraft. *See* Section J.

Woad, a plant (*Isastis tinctoria*) that in olden days was largely used in England for the blue dye obtained from the leaves. It is a biennial plant belonging to the same family (*Cruciferae*) as the wallflower.

Wolves, well-known carnivorous animals still found in many parts of Europe, but not existing in Britain since the middle of the 17th cent. They usually hunt in packs.

Women's Liberation Movement. See Section J.

Woodcock, a wading bird, valued for its flesh. It is a member of the snipe family, and breeds in Britain. The parent bird is able to carry its young between its thigh and body when flying to and from the feeding spots. It is one of the birds protected by the Game Laws.

Woodpecker, a familiar tree-climbing, insectivorous bird of conspicuous plumage, of which four species are found in Britain, the green woodpecker or yaffle (because of its harsh cry), the great spotted, the lesser spotted and the wryneck. They build in the hollows of trees. Yaffle has a long sticky tongue for licking up ground insects, especially ants. The great and lesser woodpeckers obtain insects by digging into tree trunks with strong, chisel-like bills, spearing the insects with a sharp tongue. The metallic drumming sound made by the birds in spring is thought to be caused by their beaks hammering away at some hard resounding substance.

Wood's Metal, an alloy with a very low melting point (65°C, which is under 150°F) so that a spoon made of it will melt when used to stir a cup of tea. Contains bismuth 4 parts, lead 2 parts, tin 1 part, cadmium 1 part. Its use as a heat exchanger has now been largely superseded by silicone oils, which have a wider temperature range.

Woodworm. Four beetles are mainly responsible for woodworm damage: common furniture beetle (*Anobium punctatum*), powder post beetle (*Lyctus brunneus*), death watch beetle (*Xestobium rufovillosum*), and house longhorn beetle (*Hylotrupes bajulus*). Particular attention should be paid to wood in damp, dark and out-of-the-way places, and the backs and underneaths of furniture. The most frequent cause of woodworm damage is the common furniture beetle (*q.v.*).

Wool is a fibre, made up of very long protein molecules. It has been largely grown and used in the manufacture of cloth in England since before the Roman invasion. It is grown on the backs of sheep, and is of various kinds, according to the breed of sheep from which it is derived. Wool differs from hair in that it has a wavy, serrated fibre, its curl being a notable characteristic, whereas hair has a smooth surface comparatively free from serratures. Long wools are mostly used for the manufacture of worsted goods, and short wools for woollen cloths, though the improvements in machinery in recent years have enabled manufacturers to utilise short wools to a great extent for dress fabrics as well as for woollens. The finest wools are obtained from the fleece of the Spanish merino sheep. Australia, USSR, New Zealand, Argentina and South Africa are the greatest wool-producing countries.

Woolsack, the name given to the seat occupied by the Lord Chancellor in the House of Lords. It is a large square bag of wool, without back or arms, covered with red cloth. At the time when it was first used, in the reign of Edward III, wool was the great staple commodity of the country and, it is said, chosen for the seat of judges as a constant reminder of the main source of the national wealth. The Lord Chancellor is said to be " appointed to the woolsack ".

World Population. According to United Nations sources world population in mid-1975 was 3,967 million, an increase of 77 million in one year. More than half the total live in Asia (56·9 per cent). Different countries are at different stages in a demographic transition from the stability provided by a combination of high birth rate and high death rate to that provided by a combination of low birth rate and low death rate. Their recent population history and current trend of growth, the age-structure of their population, and consequently their population potential for the near future are all widely different. Most rapid growth is in Africa with rates of over 3 per cent in some countries. In most European countries the rate is less than 1 per cent. A baby girl born in Norway may expect to live the longest (77·6 years) and a baby boy in Sweden (72·1 years),

but a baby born in some African countries may not live to reach 40 years. It is estimated that about one in 25 of all human beings who have ever lived are alive today. See also Section G, Part III and Population, Section F, Part VI.

Wreck, the name given to trove found under water, usually from a maritime wreck. Finds must be brought to the notice of the Official Receiver of Wrecks, an officer of H.M. Customs and Excise.

Wren, a family of small passerine birds possessing upturned tails and most abundant in South America. The British species is an interesting singing bird with a suprisingly loud note for its size.

X

Xenon a rare gaseous element, symbol Xe, occurring in minute quantities in the atmosphere, discovered by Sir William Ramsay and M. W. Travers in 1898. See Rare Gases.

X-Rays were discovered in 1895 by Professor Röntgen, of Wurzburg, while experimenting with a Crookes vacuum tube, when the fact was accidentally revealed that a photographic plate, contained in a dark box and exposed to its rays, was affected. To the X-rays the box was transparent. X-ray photographs are now commonly taken to obtain information about objects enclosed within solid bodies; they enable bullets and any solid bodies of metal, as well as bones, etc., in the body to be perfectly located and investigated. The discovery has proved of great advantage in surgical operations. X-rays are used to determine the structure of matter; the atoms in a substance may be located and their relative positions determined by photographing reflections of the X-rays by the specimen. See **F12(2)**.

Xylem, the woody tissue of higher plants whose function is to conduct water and mineral salts upwards, and to provide mechanical support.

Y

Yacht, a light vessel now much used for pleasure trips and racing. The first yachting club was the Cork Harbour Club, started about 1720; and in 1812 the Royal Yacht Squadron was founded at Cowes. The Royal Thames Yacht Club dates from 1823. The most famous international yachting trophy is *The America's Cup* (*q.v.*).

Yak, a curious, long-haired ox, found in Tibet, used as a beast of burden, and also kept for milk and meat.

Yard, a standard measure of 36 in, the word being derived from the Saxon gyrd, or rod. The yard and pound are now defined by reference to the metre and the kilogramme: yard = 0·9144 of a metre; pound = 0·45359237 of a kilogramme. By international agreement the metre is defined by reference to the wavelength of krypton-86 light.

Yellowhammer, a common British bird of the bunting family, of lemon-yellow and brown plumage. Nests on or near the ground.

Yeomen of the Guard are a body of Foot Guards established in the reign of Henry VII for the protection of the Royal Person. Yeomen are now about 100 in number, and their duties consist in being present on ceremonial State occasions, the yearly distribution of Maundy Money, and the searching of the vaults of the Houses of Parliament on Guy Fawkes' day. " Beefeater " is the nickname of both Yeomen of the Guard and Yeomen Warders of the Tower, and they both wear the style of dress of the Tudor period, but with one distinction, the Yeomen of the Guard wear a cross belt, the Warders do not.

Yeti, opinions differ as to whether this is a mythical inhabitant of the Himalayas, a primitive primate or bear. Evidence to date is inconclusive.

Yoga. See Section J

York Minster, one of the oldest and finest of English cathedrals, is 160 m long, its nave is 73 m broad, and the central tower is 66 m high. The present edifice, in parts, dates back to the 12th cent., but a church stood on the site in the 7th cent. In 1829 it was set on fire by a lunatic named Jonathan Martin, and the destruction that then took place cost £60,000 to restore.

Ytterbium, a chemical element discovered by Urbain in 1907; one of the group of rare earth metals.

Yttrium, a chemical element discovered by Mosander in 1842. It is found in a few rare minerals such as gadolinite, xenotine, fergusonite and euxenite. One of the group of rare-earth metals.

Z

Zamboni Pile, a dry galvanic battery, which can provide small amounts of high-voltage current over a very long time. At Oxford a couple of Zamboni piles have kept a bell ringing for over a hundred years. These piles in the second world war were perfected and produced in quantity, being the most convenient source of current for infra-red signalling devices.

Zebra, an African quadruped of whitish-grey colour, with regular black stripings, perhaps the most beautiful member of the Equine family. Rather larger than an ass and smaller than the horse, it has a tufted tail, is of light build, wild and fleet of foot. The Zebra may be threatened with extinction—already the fate of the Quagga species—because of its slaughter by man for its beautiful skin.

Zen Buddhism. *See* **Section J.**

Zenith, the highest point in the heavens above an observer's head, the opposite pole to the nadir.

Zero, the cypher signifying nothing. The West is indebted to the Arabs for it, who probably got it from the Hindus and passed it to European mathematicians towards the end of the Middle Ages. The zero has also been found in Babylonian cuneiform. The Greeks had no such symbol, which hindered the development of their mathematics. The use of zero led to the invention of decimal fractions and to the later developments in astronomy, physics and chemistry. For absolute zero on the temperature scale *see* **Absolute Temperature.**

Zinc, a familiar metallic element, symbol Zn, known to the ancients, and used by them in the making of brass. It occurs as the sulphide, carbonate, etc. The ores of zinc are crushed, roasted and reduced with coal. In combination with copper it constitutes the familiar alloy called brass, and zinc itself is much used for roofing and other protective purposes. Zinc ores are mined in Canada, the USA, Mexico, Poland, Australia, Russia, Italy, Spain and many other parts of the world. Zinc smelting is carried on in most industrial countries, including Great Britain.

Zionism. *See* **Section J.**

Zirconium, metallic element, symbol Zr, was discovered by Klaproth in the sand of the rivers of Sri Lanka in 1789. The crystalline metal is white, soft and ductile; in its amorphous condition it is a blue-black powder. Zirconium is used in atomic reactors as containers for fuel elements, since it does not absorb neutrons.

Zodiac, an imaginary zone or belt of the sky enclosing the circuit over which the principal planets travel. It is divided into 12 equal spaces of 30 degrees each, comprising respectively the 12 signs of the zodiac—Aries, Taurus Gemini, Cancer, Leo, Virgo, Libra, Scorpio Sagittarius, Capricornus, Aquarius and Pisces. The idea of the zodiac originated with the Babylonians about 2000 B.C. and passed by way of the Greeks to the Western world.

Zodiacal Light, a faint cone of light occasionally seen stretching along the zodiac from the western horizon after evening twilight or the eastern horizon before morning twilight. It is believed to be due to the scattering of the sun's light by dust particles in orbit round the sun and extending beyond the earth. Recent observations at the high altitude station at Chacaltaya in the Andes suggest that the dust is travelling round the sun in regular planetary orbits.

Zonda, a warm moist wind in Argentina of great velocity blowing from the north or northwest, and, like the Sirocco in Southern Europe, causes much discomfort. It happens when a depression is moving across the pampas, bringing with it a mass of air from the humid tropics. It is followed by a refreshing wind from the south east.

Zoological Gardens of London were opened in 1828, and belong to the Zoological Society of London. They contain one of the largest and most varied collections of living animals in the world. The Society maintains an open-air zoo at Whipsnade, on the edge of Dunstable Downs; this was opened in 1931.

Zoology, the branch of science concerned with animal life, embracing many aspects such as anatomy, behaviour, classification, distribution and ecology. *See* **Section F, Part IV.**

Zoroastrianism. *See* **Section J.**

NOBEL PRIZE WINNERS (1901–1977)

YEAR.	PHYSICS.	CHEMISTRY.	PHYSIOLOGY AND MEDICINE.	LITERATURE.	PEACE.
1901	W. C. Röntgen (G).	J. H. van't Hoff (D).	E. v. Behring (G).	R. F. A. Sully Prudhomme (F).	H. Dunant (Sw), F. Passy (F).
1902	H. A. Lorentz (D), P. Zeeman (D).	E. Fischer (G).	R. Koch (G).	T. Mommsen (G).	E. Ducommun (Sw), A. Gobat (Sw).
1903	H. Becquerel (F), P. Curie (F), Marie Curie (F).	S. Arrhenius (S).	N. R. Finsen (Da).	B. Björnson (N).	Sir W. R. Cremer (B).
1904	Lord J. W. S. Rayleigh (B).	W. Ramsay (B).	I. P. Pavlov (R).	F. Mistral (F), J. Echegaray (Sp).	Institut de Droit International.
1905	P. Lenard (G).	A. v. Bayer (G).	R. Koch (G).	H. Sienkiewicz (P).	Bertha von Suttner (Au).
1906	J. J. Thomson (B).	H. Moissan (F).	C. Golgi (I), S. R. y Cajal (Sp).	G. Carducci (I).	T. Roosevelt (A).
1907	A. A. Michelson (A).	E. Buchner (G).	C. I. A. Laveran (F).	Rudyard Kipling (B).	E. T. Moneta (I), L. Renault (F).
1908	G. Lippmann (F).	E. Rutherford (B).	P. Ehrlich (G), E. Metchnikoff (R).	R. Eucken (G).	K. P. Arnoldson (S), F. Bajer (Da).
1909	F. Braun (G), G. Marconi (I).	W. Ostwald (G).	T. Kocher (Sw).	S. Lagerlöf (S).	A. M. F. Beernaert (Be), Baron d'Estournelles de Constant de Rebecque (F).
1910	J. D. van der Waals (D).	O. Wallach (G).	A. Kossel (G).	P. Heyse (G).	The Bureau International Permanent de la Paix, Berne.
1911	W. Wien (G).	Marie Curie (F).	A. Gullstrand (S).	M. Maeterlinck (Be).	T. M. C. Asser (D), A. H. Fried (Au).
1912	G. Dalén (S).	V. Grignard (F), P. Sabatier (F).	A. Carrel (A).	G. Hauptmann (G).	E. Root (A).
1913	H. Kamerlingh Onnes (D).	A. Werner (Sw).	C. Richet (F).	R. Tagore (In).	H. la Fontaine (Be).
1914	M. v. Laue (G).	T. W. Richards (A).	R. Bárány (Au.).	—	—
1915	W. H. Bragg (B), W. L. Bragg (B).	R. Willstaetter (G).	—	R. Roland (F).	—
1916	—	—	—	V. von Heidenstam (S).	—
1917	C. G. Barkla (B).	—	—	K. Gjellerup (Da), H. Pontoppidan (Da).	Comité International de la Croix-Rouge, Geneva.
1918	M. Planck (G).	F. Haber (G).	—	—	—
1919	J. Stark (G).	—	J. Bordet (Be).	C. Spitteler (Sw).	W. Wilson (A).
1920	C. E. Guillaume (F).	W. Nernst (G).	A. Krogh (Da).	K. Hamsun (N).	L. Bourgeois (F).
1921	A. Einstein (G).	F. Soddy (B).	—	A. France (F).	K. H. Branting (S), C. L. Lange (N).
1922	N. Bohr (Da).	F. W. Aston (B).	A. Hill (B), O. Meyerhof (G).	J. Benavente y Martinez (Sp).	F. Nansen (N).
1923	R. A. Millikan (A).	F. Pregl (Au).	F. G. Banting (C), J. R. Macleod (O).	W. B. Yeats (Ir).	—
1924	M. Siegbahn (S).	—	W. E. Einthoven (D).	W. Reymont (P).	—
1925	J. Franck (G), G. Hertz (G).	R. Zsigmondy (G).	—	G. B. Shaw (B).	Sir A. Chamberlain (B), C. G. Dawes (A).
1926	J. Perrin (F).	T. Svedberg (S).	J. Fibiger (Da).	G. Deledda (I).	A. Briand (F), G. Stresemann (G).
1927	A. H. Compton (A), C. T. R. Wilson (B).	H. Wieland (G).	J. Wagner-Jauregg (Au).	H. Bergson (F).	F. Buisson (F), L. Quidde (G).
1928	O. W. Richardson (B).	A. Windaus (G).	C. Nicolle (F).	S. Undset (N).	—

1929	L. de Broglie (F).	H. v. Euler-Chelpin (S), A. Harden (B).	C. Eijkman (D), F. G. Hopkins (B).	T. Mann (G).	F. B. Kellogg (A).
1930	C. V. Raman (In).	H. Fischer (G).	K. Landsteiner (Au).	S. Lewis (A).	L. O. J. Söderblom (S).
1931	—	F. Bergius (G), K. Bosch (G).	O. Warburg (G).	E. A. Karlfeldt (S).	Jane Addams (A), N. M. Butler (A).
1932	W. Heisenberg (G).	I. Langmuir (A).	C. S. Sherrington (B), E. D. Adrian (B).	J. Galsworthy (B).	—
1933	P. A. M. Dirac (B), E. Schroedinger (Au).	—	T. H. Morgan (A).	I. A. Bunin (R).	Sir Norman Angell (B).
1934	—	H. C. Urey (A).	G. Minot (A), W. Murphy (A), G. Whipple (A).	L. Pirandello (I).	Arthur Henderson (B).
1935	J. Chadwick (B).	F. Joliot (F), I. Joliot-Curie (F).	H. Spemann (G).	—	C. von Ossietzky (G).
1936	V. F. Hess (Au), C. D. Anderson (A).	P. Debye (D).	Sir H. H. Dale (B), O. Loewi (G).	E. O'Neill (A).	C. de S. Lamas (Ar).
1937	C. J. Davisson (A), G. P. Thomson (B).	W. N. Haworth (B), P. Karrer (Sw).	A. v. Szent-Dyörgyi (H).	R. Martin du Gard (F).	Viscount Cecil of Chelwood (B).
1938	E. Fermi (I).	R. Kuhn (G).	C. Heymans (Be).	Pearl S. Buck (A).	Office International Nansen pour les Réfugiés.
1939	E. O. Lawrence (A).	A. F. Butenandt (G), L. Ruzicka (Sw).	G. Domagk (G).	F. E. Sillanpää (Ff).	—
1940-42	—	—	—	—	—
1943	O. Stern (A).	G. Hevesy (H).	H. Dam (Da), E. A. Doisy (A).	—	—
1944	I. I. Rabi (A).	O. Hahn (G).	E. J. Erlanger (A), H. S. Gasser (A).	J. V. Jensen (Da).	Comité International de la Croix-Rouge, Geneva.
1945	W. Pauli (Au).	A. Virtanen (Ff).	Sir A. Fleming (B), Sir H. Florey (B), E. B. Chain (B).	G. Mistral (Ch).	Cordell Hull (A).
1946	P. W. Bridgman (A).	J. B. Sumner (A), J. H. Northrop (A), W. M. Stanley (A).	H. J. Muller (A).	H. Hesse (Sw).	Emily G. Balch (A), J. R. Mott (A).
1947	Sir Edward Appleton (B).	Sir Robert Robinson (B).	B. A. Houssay (Ar), C. F. Cori (A), G. T. Cori (A).	André Gide (F).	American and British Quaker Organisations.
1948	P. M. S. Blackett (B).	A. Tiselius (S).	P. Müller (Sw).	T. S. Eliot (B).	—
1949	H. Yukawa (J).	W. F. Giauque (A).	W. R. Hess (Sw), A. E. Moniz (Po).	W. Faulkner (A).	Lord Boyd-Orr (B).
1950	Cecil F. Powell (B).	Otto Diels (G), K. Alder (G).	E. C. Kendall (A), P. S. Hench (A), R. Reichstein (Sw).	Lord Russell (B).	Ralph Bunche (A).
1951	Sir J. Cockcroft (B), E. T. S. Walton (Ir.).	E. M. MacMillan (B), G. T. Seaborg (A).	M. Theiler (A).	P. Lagerkvist (S).	Léon Jouhaux (F).
1952	E. Purcell (A), F. Bloch (A).	A. J. P. Martin (B), R. L. M. Synge (B).	S. Waksman (A).	F. Mauriac (F).	A. Schweitzer (F).
1953	F. Zernike (D).	H. Staudinger (G).	H. A. Krebs (B), F. A. Lipmann (A).	Sir W. S. Churchill (B).	Gen. G. Marshall (A).
1954	M. Born (B), W. Bothe (G).	L. Pauling (A).	J. F. Enders (A), F. C. Robins (A), T. H. Weller (A).	E. Hemingway (A).	U.N. High Commission for Refugees.
1955	W. E. Lamb (A), P. Kusch (A).	Vicent du Vigneaud (A).	Hugo Theorell (S).	Halldór Laxness (Ic).	—
1956	W. Shockley (A), J. Bardeen (A), W. H. Brattain (A).	Sir Cyril Hinshelwood (B), N. Semenov (R).	A. F. Cournand (A), D. W. Richards (A), W. Forssmann (G).	J. Ramón Jiménez (Sp).	—

YEAR	PHYSICS.	CHEMISTRY.	PHYSIOLOGY AND MEDICINE.	LITERATURE.	PEACE.
1957	T. D. Lee (Chi), C. N. Yang (Chi).	Lord Todd (B).	D. Bovet (I).	A. Camus (F).	L. B. Pearson (C).
1958	P. A. Cerenkov (R), I. M. Frank (R), I. Tamm (R).	F. Sanger (B).	G. W. Beadle (A), E. Tatum (A), J. Lederberg (A).	B. Pasternak (R).	Father George Pire (Be).
1959	E. Segré (A), O. Chamberlain (A).	J. Heyrovsky (Cz).	S. Ochoa (A), A. Kornberg (A).	S. Quasimodo (I).	P. J. Noel-Baker (B).
1960	D. A. Glaser (A).	W. F. Libby (A).	P. B. Medawar (B), Sir M. Burnet (Aus).	A. St. Leger (F).	A. Luthuli (S.A.).
1961	R. Hofstadter (A), R. Mossbauer (G).	M. Calvin (A).	G. von Bekesy (H).	L. Andric (Y).	D. Hammarskjöld (S).
1962	L. Davidovich Landau (R).	M. F. Perutz (B), J. C. Kendrew (B).	F. H. C. Crick (B), M. H. F. Wilkins (B), J. D. Watson (A).	J. Steinbeck (A).	L. Pauling (A).
1963	Maria Goeppert-Mayer (A), J. H. D. Jensen (G), E. P. Wigner (A).	K. Ziegler (G), G. Natta (I).	A. L. Hodgkin (B), A. F. Huxley (B), Sir J. Eccles (B).	G. Seferis (Gr).	International Red Cross Committee and the International League of Red Cross Societies.
1964	C. H. Townes (A), N. G. Basov (R), A. M. Prokhorov (R).	Dorothy Hodgkin (B).	K. E. Bloch (A), F. Lynen (G).	Jean-Paul Sartre (F).	Martin Luther King (A).
1965	S. Tomonaga (J), J. Schwinger (A), P. Feynman (A).	A. B. Woodward (A).	F. Jacob (F), A. Lwoff (F), J. Monod (F).	M. Sholokhov (B).	UNICEF
1966	A. Kastler (F).	R. S. Mulliken (A).	F. P. Rous (A), C. A. Huggins (A).	S. Y. Agnon (Is), Nelly Sachs (Sw).	No award
1967	H. A. Bethe (A).	B. G. W. Norrish (B), G. Porter (B), M. Eigen (G).	R. Granit (S), H. K. Hartline (A), G. Wald (A).	M. A. Asturias (Gu).	No award
1968	L. W. Alvarez (A).	L. Onsager (A).	M. Nirenberg (A), H. G. Khorana (A), R. Holley (A).	Y. Kawabata (J).	R. Cassin (F).
1969	M. Gell-Mann (A).	D. H. R. Barton (B), O. Hassel (N).	M. Delbrück (A), A. D. Hershey (A), S. E. Luria (A).	S. Beckett (Ir).	The International Labour Organisation.
1970	L. E. Néel (F), H. Alfvén (Sw).	L. F. Leloir (Ar).	Sir Bernard Katz (B), U. von Euler (S), J. Axelrod (A).	A. Solzhenitsyn (R).	N. E. Borlaug (A).
1971	D. Gabor (B).	G. Herzberg (C).	E. W. Sutherland (A).	P. Neruda (Ch).	W. Brandt (G).
1972	J. Bardeen (A), L. N. Cooper (A), J. R. Schrieffer (A).	C. B. Anfinsen (A), S. Moore (A), W. H. Stein (A).	R. Porter (B), G. Edelman (A).	Heinrich Böll (G).	No award
1973	B. Josephson (B), L. Esaki (J), I. Glaever (A).	E. O. Fischer (G), G. Wilkinson (B).	N. Tinbergen (D), K. von Frisch (Ab), K. Lorenz (Au).	P. White (Aus).	H. Kissinger (A), Le Duc Tho (NV).

Note: The first Nobel Prize in the Economic Sciences was awarded in 1969 jointly to J. Tinbergen (D), and R. Frisch (N); 1970: P. A. Samuelson (A); 1971: S. Kuznets (A); 1972: Sir J. Hicks (B), K. Arrow (A); 1973: W. Leontief (A).

YEAR.	PHYSICS.	CHEMISTRY.	MEDICINE.	LITERATURE.	ECONOMICS.	PEACE.
1974	Sir Martin Ryle (B), A. Hewish (B).	P. J. Flory (A).	A. Claude (Be), C. de Duve (Be), G. E. Palade (A).	E. Johnson (S), H. Martinson (S).	G. Myrdal (S), F. von Hayek (B).	S. MacBride (Ir), E. Sato (J).
1975	J. Rainwater (A), A. Bohr (Da), B. Mottelson (Da).	J. Warcup (Aus), V. Prelog (Sw).	D. Baltimore (A), R. Dulbecco (A), H. M. Temin (A).	E. Montale (I).	L. V. Kantorovich (B), T. C Koopmans (A).	A. D. Sakharov (B).
1976	B. Richter (A), S. Ting (A).	W. N. Lipscomb (A).	B. S. Blumberg (A), D. C. Gajdusek (A).	S. Bellow (A).	M. Friedman (A).	Betty Williams (B), Mairead Corrigan (B).
1977	Sir Nevill Mott (B), J. Van Vleck (A), P. Anderson (A).	I. Prigogine (Be).	Rosalyn Yalow (A), R. Guillemin (A), A. Schally (A).	V. Aleixandre (Sp).	J. E. Meade (B), B. Ohlin (S).	Amnesty International (London-based)

A = American
Ar = Argentina
Au = Austrian
Aus = Australian
B = British

Be = Belgian
C = Canadian
Ch = Chilean
Chi = Chinese
Cz = Czech

D = Dutch
Da = Danish
F = French
Fi = Finnish
G = German

Gr = Greek
Gu = Guatemalan
H = Hungarian
I = Italian
Io = Icelandic

In = Indian
Ir = Irish
Is = Israeli
J = Japanese
N = Norwegian

NV = North Vietnamese
P = Polish
Po = Portuguese
R = Russian
S = Swedish

S.A. = South African
Sp = Spanish
Sw = Swiss
Y = Yugoslav

Marginal mark	Meaning	Corresponding mark in text
δΊ	Delete (take out)	Cross through
δ̲	Delete and close-up	⌐⌐ Above and below letters to be taken out
stet	Leave as printed (when words have been crossed out by mistake)	. . . . Under letters or words to remain
caps	Change to capital letters	≡ Under letters or words to be altered
s.c.	Change to small capitals	≡ Under letters or words to be altered
caps & s.c.	Use capital letters for initial letters and small capitals for rest of words	≡ Under initial letters and ═ under the rest of the words
l.c.	Change from capitals to lower case	Encircle letters to be altered
bold	Change to bold type	～～ Under letters or words to be altered
ital.	Change to italics	——— Under letters or words to be altered
rom.	Change to roman type	Encircle words to be altered
w.f.	(Wrong fount.) Replace by letter of correct fount	Encircle letter to be altered
ᘂ	Invert type	Encircle letter to be altered
✕	Replace by similar but undamaged character	Encircle letter to be altered
Ꮡ	Insert (or substitute) superior figure or sign	⋀ (Or encircle letters or signs to be altered)
ᘀ	Insert (or substitute) inferior figure or sign	⋀ (Or encircle letters or signs to be altered)
⌒	Close-up—delete space between letters	⌒ Linking words or letters
#	Insert space	⋀
eq.#	Make spacing equal	⌶ Between words
less#	Reduce space	⌶ Between words
trs.	Transpose	⌐⌐ Between letters or words, numbered when necessary
centre	Place in centre of line	Indicate position with ⌐ ⌐
⌐	Move to the left	⌶
ᒣ	Move to the right	⌶
n.p.	Begin a new paragraph	⌐ Before first word of new paragraph
run on	No fresh paragraph here	⌐→ Between paragraphs
spell out	The abbreviation or figure to be spelt out in full	Encircle words or figures to be altered
⋀	(Caret mark.) Insert matter indicated in margin	⋀
ᎭᎭ	Insert single quotation marks	⋀ ⋀
ᎭᎭ	Insert double quotation marks	⋀ ⋀

LITERARY COMPANION

This section suggests ways of approaching the poetry of the current century. It includes a guide to versification, figures of speech and literary forms.

TABLE OF CONTENTS

I. HOW TO ENJOY A POEM

References are to the *New Oxford Book of English Verse*, 1972.

Many people who enjoy listening to music and looking at pictures and sculpture find it difficult to appreciate poetry, so a few suggestions as to how we may approach a poem may be helpful. Perhaps the first thing to bear in mind is that just as we cannot fully appreciate an unfamiliar piece of music at a first hearing, nor the subtle interplay of form, line and colour in a picture at a single hasty glance, so it is equally impossible to savour the full richness of a poem in the course of one or two quick readings. A writer was once looking round an exhibition of modern paintings, fascinated by their unusual colours but utterly at a loss as to their significance and inclined foolishly to criticise what he could not understand. Sitting down to rest his aching feet, he gazed at the painting in front of him. Suddenly, as if he had put on a new pair of spectacles, the picture came into focus. It still seemed mysterious, but though he still could not fully understand it the writer now began to enjoy it. In a similar way, we can "walk around" and gaze at a poem for a long time feeling more a sense of bewildered fascination than pleasure, then, suddenly, we find a clue to the poet's vision. But how shall we seek it?

When we first meet a poem it is often helpful to read it aloud, for the poet makes use of the sound and rhythmical patterns of words and although the printed poem may seem flat as does a music score to the uninitiated, when heard it comes alive.

Then we must remember that a poet normally uses words not only literally but also figuratively and loves to speak of one thing as if it were another. When Herrick wishes to express his awareness of his mistress's exotic, yet, being mortal, inevitably transient, beauty, he speaks of her as a tulip—a highly-prized and expensive import in seventeenth-century England:

> "You are a tulip seen today,
> But, dearest, of so short a stay
> That where you grew scarce men can say."
> [OBEV 255]

When Keats describes the pleasure he has found in books he talks of them as if they were countries and he a traveller:

> "Much have I travell'd in the realms of gold
> And many goodly states and kingdoms seen;"
> [OBEV 562]

Another important point is suggested by Peter Porter's *Sanitized Sonnet 4*, which begins,

> "Much have I travelled in the realms of gold
> for which I thank the Paddington and
> Westminster Public Libraries;"
> (*The Last Of England*, p. 41).

A poem, even a contemporary poem, is an historical object. It has been affected by the poetry which preceded it—Porter expects us to recognise his quotation from Keats and to appreciate the new perspective in which he places it. A poet may write within, or in reaction from, a particular convention: in Elizabethan and Jacobean times it was a poetic fashion to speak of women as gardens, or as if their faces shone like the sun, [OBEV 158, 164, 178, 255]. A poem may be inspired by particular events and people, as are Yeats's *Easter 1916* and Dryden's *Absolom and Achitophel* (OBEV 767 and 365–366) and our enjoyment may be enhanced if we know to what and whom the writer refers. A poem always grows out of the experience of a single individual at a particular point in time. We are therefore helped to enjoy it if we know when and by whom it was written and can place it in its historical perspective.

In *The Business of Criticism* Helen Gardner quotes the case of the student who said that the poem beginning

> "At the round earth's imagined corners
> Blow your trumpets, angels,"
> [OBEV 200]

was written by a very simple man. She points out that it is indeed true that no contemporary educated Christian would use such images and we may fail to enjoy the striking originality and sophistication of the way they are employed to express a simple faith unless we know that they were conceived by a writer of the early seventeenth century and unless we have some idea of the ways in which men of that day lived, thought and wrote. We will enjoy the poem even more if we know something of the life and other work of its creator, John Donne.

We can never learn too much about a poem, but always we come back to the work itself, for it exists not only as an historical object and the product of a particular mind and vision, but also in its own right, as an enduring work of art.

Making out the "Meaning".

Remembering always that the poet normally speaks in images and that the images he uses may be influenced by the particular conventions of his day, we need to give close attention to his words if we are to appreciate their full significance. I. A. Richards in *Practical Criticism* formulated certain principles which may aid one in making out the "meaning". He distinguished four kinds of "meaning": the "plain sense" of the poem, the "feeling", the "tone" and the "intention". The "plain sense" is arrived at simply by following the words, and incidentally the punctuation, in an attempt to find out what the poet actually says. Readers do not always do this. Another aspect of the "meaning" is the poet's "feeling" for his subject—does he, for instance, express awe, tenderness, anger, amusement? Then, is his "tone" towards the reader confidential, appealing or didactic? Finally, Richards speaks of the "intention" of the poem, the whole aim that the writer is trying to pursue.

Distinguishing Subject and Theme.

Another illuminating way of looking at a poem is to distinguish between its subject and its theme, for they are seldom identical. A poet loves to transpose his experience into another setting, and below his surface narrative or description we usually find a second "meaning", the theme, which is the core of the poem. Often there are many themes subtly interwoven. In *Resolution and Independence* (OBEV 484), Wordsworth writes of a spring morning walk, but the themes of his poem are many, one being his fear of failure, poverty and ignominious death. Shelley addressed an ode to the West Wind (OBEV 549) and here one of the main themes is a plea for poetic inspiration.

The Formal Aspects of the Poem.

Other pointers to its meaning are to be found in the formal patterns of the poem, the metre and literary form in which it is cast (*see* Part II), the kind of imagery or figures of speech (Part IV). Just as all roses have a certain fundamental similarity so do all examples of, say a sonnet. With a sonnet, as with a rose, we can enjoy its beauty without ever knowing its species, but we better understand and relish the peculiar beauties of the example before us if we can recognise it for what it is.

Study of Shakespeare's Sonnet 73 [OBEV 143].

That time of year thou mayst in me behold
   When yellow leaves, or none, or few, do hang
Upon those boughs which shake against the cold,
   Bare ruined choirs, where late the sweet birds
                         sang.
In me thou seest the twilight of such day
   As after sunset fadeth in the west;
Which by and by black night doth take away,
   Death's second self, that seals up all in rest.
In me thou seest the glowing of such fire,
   That on the ashes of his youth doth lie,
As the death-bed whereon it must expire,
   Consumed with that which it was nourished by.
   This thou perceiv'st, which makes thy love
                    more strong,
   To love that well which thou must leave ere
                    long.

Kinds of Meaning.—Searching for the plain "sense", we find here three clearly defined images, the first of very late autumn.

"When yellow leaves, or none, or few, do hang Upon those boughs which shake against the cold".

Then follows an image of twilight, the brief phase after the sunset has faded and before the fall of night. The third image is of a dying fire, glowing amid its ashes. All these, says Shakespeare, "thou mayst in me behold". All three, then, suggest that phase in man's life that follows the prime, the decline towards death. The "feeling" of these first twelve lines is sombre and foreboding, and in its "tone" the poem speaks to one alone—"thou mayst behold", "thou seest". Then when we reach the concluding couplet we perceive the "intention" of the poem. It is a love poem.

"This thou perceiv'st, which makes thy love more
                   strong.
To love that well which thou must leave ere
                   long."

Subject and Theme.—We can also approach the poem trying to distinguish "subject and theme". Then we perceive more clearly the theme of the imminence of death, which gradually develops and gathers momentum. For instance, the trees are called "bare ruined choirs" where the birds no longer sing, and this poignantly suggests not only the ruined choirs of monastic churches despoiled by Henry VIII but, more generally, any ruined empty abode from which the voice has flown, the spirit departed. Then the "black night" which succeeds twilight is "Death's second self", and the fire lies on the ashes "As the death-bed, whereon it must expire".

The very colours of the poem are suggestive. A picture is painted in sombre greys and black, lit up by a dull glow soon to be engulfed in darkness, the yellow leaves on the bough, the sunset fading into twilight, the fire dying on the ashes. It is like the chiaroscuro of a Rembrandt painting.

Formal Pattern.—I now attend to the formal patterns of the poem we find how exquisitely they match the sense. The poem is a sonnet (*see* **M13**), that is a brief lyric poem of only fourteen lines,

expressing feeling in a taut and concentrated way. There is no room for digression; every word counts.

As we expect from a Shakespearean sonnet we find the rhyme scheme ABAB CDCD EFEF GG. This indicates that the poem will naturally take the design of three quatrains and a concluding couplet. Then how exquisitely and precisely each image is contained within the brief compass of its quatrain, and how apt are the metaphors in which the images are expressed.

Study of a poem by Ted Hughes.

It we now turn to another " autumnal " poem we may be helped towards appreciating the variety of ways in which a poet can use familiar material to express a personal vision.

October Dawn

October is marigold, and yet
A glass half full of wine left out

To the dark heaven all night, by dawn
Has dreamed a premonition

Of ice across its eye as if
The ice-age had begun its heave.

The lawn overtrodden and strewn
From the night before, and the whistling green

Shrubbery are doomed. Ice
Has got its spearhead into place.

First a skin, delicately here
Restraining a ripple from the air;

Soon plate and rivet on pond and brook;
Then tons of chain and massive lock

To hold rivers. Then, sound by sight
Will Mammoth and Sabre-tooth celebrate

Reunion while a fist of cold
Squeezes the fire at the core of the world.

Squeezes the fire at the core of the heart,
And now it is about to start.

Ted Hughes, *The Hawk in the Rain* (Faber, 1957).

Kinds of Meaning.—The title serves as an initial guide—the poem is about the dawn of an October day. The first three stanzas form a single sentence. It opens with a striking evocation of autumnal warmth and colour—" October is marigold "—but ends with a suggestion of the awakening of a great ice-age: the half-empty glass of wine has " dreamed a premonition of ice . . . as if/The ice-age had begun its heave ". We notice that the wine glass is gradually personified and that the vague foreboding of its " dream " remains with it now that morning has come, it has a " premonition of ice across its eye "—a glazed look. The image of the wine glass combines with the images of stanza four to suggest the morning after a lively party which has continued late into the night. The poem tells us all this is doomed. " Ice has got its spearhead into place." We notice the warlike associations of " spearhead " and that it is a primitive weapon, but poised for the kill. There follows a description of the way the ice overpowers and imprisons first " a ripple ", next " pond ", next " brook " and then even " rivers "; then comes a startling image of the great ice-age monsters, the mammoth and sabre-tooth tiger, celebrating a " reunion " while a cold fist " Squeezes the fire at the core of the world "— as if the cruel power of the ice were penetrating even to earth's molten centre.

The " feeling " changes from one of relaxed warmth through a growing sense of menace to one of fear. The "tone" is impersonal and prophetic, quite different from Shakespeare's. Hughes is speaking of a process which may affect everyone. In his poem, as in Shakespeare's, the "intention" becomes clear only in the final couplet. It suggests that Hughes is writing not simply of the way winter encroaches upon the warmth of October, but expressing a terrible sense of the imminence of a nightmare state of psychological and spiritual winter, one in which ruthless primitive forces unite to destroy one's very life. This is the theme of the poem.

ubject and Theme.—Subject and theme thus distinguished, the significance of the poem's images becomes clearer. We notice how the aural imagery of the first six lines is used to amplify the theme. At first the vowels are long and open, the consonants predominantly soft, but the sharp penultimate syllable of premoni*ti*on introduces a series of menacing hissing sounds in lines five and six. Then, as in Shakespeare, we find an image of music—"whistling" shrubbery—implying cheerful, light-hearted gaiety. The phrase may suggest a shrubbery full of whistling birds—the dawn chorus—it may also suggest cheerful guests at the party—Hughes is unspecific, perhaps because he wants us to think of both. We also notice that the sound of the word whis*tl*ing here contradicts its cheerful connotations, for it subtly echoes the menacing hisses of the earlier lines.

Hughes tells us that the shrubbery is "green" to emphasise that it is full of life—green is a traditional symbol of fertility. Later he uses other symbols of life and vitality—water and fire. All will be conquered by the "ice".

Beneath the main theme we may distinguish a subsidiary one, that of the approach of old age and death. Then we perceive that the glass of wine also symbolises life. It is spoken of as now half full—we begin to age, at first almost imperceptibly, in our prime, when we have drunk only half of life's glass.

Formal Patterns.—Turning to the poem's form, we notice that it is written in octosyllabic couplets

(M9), but that the rhyme scheme, metre and sentence patterns have been adapted so as to match and reinforce the poem's themes. We expect couplets to rhyme. These ones suggest a rhyme, sometimes almost do rhyme, yet continually frustrate our expectation and so increase the sense of unease, until in the last stanza they meet with a clinching finality all the more powerful for having been so long delayed:

> "Squeezes the fire at the core of the heart,
> And now it is about to start."

Further Suggestions: The Poems in Their Settings.—There is yet much to discover about these two poems. We will find that each time we return to them we become aware of some fresh aspect of their significance. New insights will be given if we study the poems' settings.

J. W. Lever in *The Elizabethan Love Sonnet* shows how Shakespeare took a hackneyed convention of his day and gave it new vigour. The sonnet we have read is addressed not to the poet's real or supposed mistress, as were other Elizabethan love sonnets, but is one of a series celebrating the affection between the ageing Shakespeare and his younger patron. Modern recognition of homosexuality may lead us to assume their relationship was sexual, but in Elizabethan times homosexuality was a mortal sin and when we learn more of the relation of a Rennaissance poet to his patron and of the Rennaissance ideal of Platonic friendship between educated men, we understand Shakespeare's poem differently. Further light is shed on its significance by other sonnets in the series.

The condensed elliptical style of Hughes's *October Dawn* is characteristic of twentieth-century verse. If the mode is unfamiliar to us our understanding of the poem will be enhanced by reading other modern poetry and "learning the language". We can extend our acquaintance with Hughes's poetry and learn to recognise and savour the individuality of his vigorous, sensuous style. If we read other English "nature poems" we shall be better able to appreciate and enjoy the originality of his vision.

II. ENGLISH VERSE PATTERNS

The patterns of its verse point and enhance a poem's significance. Some knowledge of the principles on which they are based can therefore help us towards a fuller enjoyment and appreciation of poetry.

The following account casts its net wide, covering verse designs as far apart in time as the Anglo-Saxon and the most up-to-date American forms. It is fully illustrated with quotations and with references to the numbered poems of *The New Oxford Book of English Verse* [OBEV] and *The Oxford Book of Twentieth Century English Verse* [OBTCV].

I. INTRODUCTION—SOME DEFINITIONS.

Verse and Prose.

The distinction between verse and prose has become blurred in our century, but we may safely say that in all verse the words are arranged so as to fall into more or less regular musical and, or, visual patterns, whereas in prose they are not. For example, if we listen carefully to a spoken sentence, we notice that some syllables are emphasised. The conventional way of indicating this in writing is by placing an acute accent over the

vowel of the stressed syllables. Unstressed syllables may be marked x as in the following sentences:

> x x /   /   x x x / x   x /
> It is some sort of a solution, after all.

> x / x /   x / x ,   x
> It is a part solution after all.

We may observe that in the first sentence the stressed and unstressed syllables fall haphazardly, while in the second they form a pattern. The first, unpatterned sentence is deemed prose, the second, patterned one, verse.

The designs of verse are almost infinitely variable and although, as it stands, alone, the unpatterned sentence is not verse, it could be incorporated into a poem and so become an element in its design. Poets are constantly modifying existing verse forms and sometimes invent entirely new ones, aural and visual.

While some reference will be made to the visual designs, this article will be chiefly concerned with the aural patterns of verse, which have been, and still are, exploited by most poets. Visual patterns, where not entirely arbitrary or whimsical, are either dependent on the musical ones or are individually determined by the poem's theme, which they are designed to reflect and enhance. They are therefore less susceptible to illustration and discussion within the compass of a short general article.

Metre.

Metre and Rhythm.

The word *metre* means a measure or rhythmical pattern. Verse originated in song, chant and invocation and its basic patterns are rhythmical. They may be founded on patterns of accent (stress), of single syllables, of cadences or lines.

Different Kinds of Metre.

Accentual verse: is written in accentual metre, a rhythmic pattern of accents or stresses.

Syllabic verse: is written in *syllabic metre*, a rhythmic pattern of syllables alone.

Accentual-syllabic or Metrical verse: is written in either *Iambic, Trochaic Dactyllic, Anapaestic, Amphibrach* or *Choriambic* metre. These metres, whose names are derived from those of Classical verse, will be further described. They are composed of regularly patterned groups of stressed and unstressed syllables, hence the name accentual-syllabic.

Quantitative Metrical verse: is usually written in one or other of six metres, also given the names *Iambic, Trochaic,* etc., quoted above. They are regularly patterned groups of long and short syllables and are the metres of Classical Greek and Latin verse. They are seldom used in English.

Free verse or *vers libre:* so called because it has no particular metre and is based on loosely patterned rhythms determined by the cadences of the speaking voice.

The Foot.

In some poetry the verse line is divided into groups of stressed and unstressed syllables, analogous to the bars in music. Such groups are known as feet. The line

" When you/shall see/me in/the toils/of Time" /
[OBTCV 2]

contains five feet, each comprising two syllables, unstressed followed by stressed.

The Caesura.

A long pause occurring at or about the middle of a line and usually indicated by a pause in the sense, *e.g.,*

" Hearing one saga,//we enact the next "
[OBTCV 493]

The Verse and the Stanza.

Some verse are divided into groups of lines, often called verses. Strictly speaking, *verse* is another name for the single line. A group of lines or verse is properly called a *stanza*. Generally the stanzas of a poem are uniform, but sometimes they are varied, as in Milton's " Lycidas " [OBEV 304].

Rhyme.

Another formal pattern is created by the use of rhyme which can be at once visual and aural, though some kinds of rhyme appeal only to the eye, others chiefly to the ear. Rhymed words normally occur at the ends of lines.

In true rhyme the last stressed vowels and the letters following them are the same, while the letters preceding the stressed vowels are different. *e.g.*, cage/page; pleasure/treasure.

Alliteration.

The repetition of the same initial consonant, as in

" Full fathom five thy father lies "
[OBEV 130].

In some verse, most notably Anglo-Saxon narrative verse, alliteration is used instead of rhyme, but the two can be, and often are, combined.

Assonance.

A similarity between vowel sounds, *e.g.* feet/creep; skin/swim.

Assonance is sometimes used instead of rhyme and occurs frequently in early folk poetry and informal verse.

II. DIFFERENT KINDS OF VERSE.

Accentual Verse.

Here the poet organises his verse according to a given number of stressed syllables in each line. The number of unstressed syllables varies.

Anglo-Saxon Verse.

This was written in an accentual metre in which each half-line contained two heavy stresses, the halves being linked by the alliteration of three of the stressed words. This kind of metrical form survived in such West Midland narrative poems of the fourteenth-century as Langland's " Piers Ploughman " and the anonymous " Sir Gawayne and the Grene Knight ", from which the following example is taken:

" There passes non bi that place so proude in his
                              armes
That he ne dynges hym to deth with dynte of
                         his honde:"

Nineteenth-Century Romantic Verse.

Coleridge experimented with accentual metre and for his " Christabel " chose a line of four stressed syllables and between three and eight unstressed ones:

×   /   ×   /   ×   /   × /
A snake's small eye blinks dull and sly
×   ×   /   ×   /   ×   ×   /
And the lady's eyes they shrank in her head
/   ×   × × /   ×   /
Each shrunk up to a serpent's eye."

Sir Walter Scott, acknowledging a debt to Coleridge, chose a similar metre for " The Lay of the Last Minstrel ".

Sprung Rhythm.

For his sonnets, Gerard Manley Hopkins devised an accentual metre which he called *sprung rhythm* and described in the preface to his *Collected Poems* (1918).

The basis of sprung rhythm, which follows the natural rhythms of speech, is a line of usually five or six feet. Each foot contains between one and four syllables and extra unstressed syllables may be added for " particular effects " and at the beginning or end of a line. The first syllable of each foot is stressed:

/ × /   ×   /   ×   /
" Gener/ations have/trod, have/trod;
× / × /   /   /   /   /
And/all is/seared with/trade;/bleared,/smeared/
                        with/toil;
×   /   /   /   ×   ×   /
And/wears/man's/smudge and shares man's/
                smell: the/soil/
/   /   /   × × /   × × /
Is/bare/now,/nor can foot/feel, being/shod. "
                        [OBEV 724].

Modern Accentual Metres.

Pound and Eliot are the modern masters of accentual metres. Examples of Pound's treatment may be found in " The River Merchant's Wife " and " Hugh Selwyn Mauberly " [OBEV 812-13]. Pound's occasional division of a line, placing the second part below and to the right of the first, so as to introduce a marked " rest ", is a practice much imitated by modern American writers of free verse (*q.v.*), and their followers. In this example Pound divides a line of six stresses:

" What thou lovest well remains

the rest is dross ".
[OBEV 814]

In poems such as " The Waste Land " [OBEV 828] and " Four Quartets " Eliot chose a basic metre of, say, four stresses, for one part of his poem, *e.g.*, the opening of " The Waste Land ", and another, of say, six stresses, for a different section. Within each section, moreover, he constantly modulated his pattern to reflect changes in the tone from one verse paragraph to another and even within each paragraph introduced occasional modifications and half-lines, the result being a metrical form of great subtlety and beauty. The following are typical examples of Eliot's use of regular and modified accentual metres:

Regular:

" Time present and time past

Are both perhaps present in time future

And time future contained in time past.

If all time is eternally present

All time is unredeemable."
" Burnt Norton ".

Modified:

" The river sweats

Oil and tar

The barges drift

With the turning tide

Red sails

Wide

To leeward, swing on the heavy spar "
[OBEV 828]

Syllabic Verse.

Writers of syllabic verse vary widely in their aims and practice. The reader is therefore referred to two issues of the magazine *Agenda*, Vol. 10 No. 4 and Vol. 11 No. 1 (double issue 1973) and Vol. 11 Nos. 2 & 3 (double issue 1974). These contain various leading British and American poets' accounts of their own understanding of syllabics. Roy Fuller's lecture " An Artifice of Versification " (*Oxford Lectures on Poetry*, 1971) is also helpful.

Basic Syllabics.

English syllabic verse was pioneered independently, but at roughly the same time, during the First World War, by the British Elizabeth Daryush and the American Marianne Moore. Its basis is a given number of syllables to the line, disregarding the number and arrangement of stresses. In the following example the lines have each six syllables:

" you've seen a strawberry
   that's had a struggle; yet
     was, where the fragments met,"
Marianne Moore: " Nevertheless ".

These lines also illustrate the common practice in syllabic verse of beginning all lines in lower case, which is felt to be less artificial than the conventional use of upper case.

Syllabic metre is natural to verse in French, but in a language such as English, where many words have feminine endings (*i.e.*, end on an unstressed syllable), it is difficult to use syllabic metres artfully.

The writer has to consider the following points:

Elision:

In spoken English some unstressed vowels are naturally elided, *e.g.*, the final " e " of learned. The poet must decide whether or not to count such elided syllables. Practice varies.

Poets such as Auden choose to make a nominal elision of certain syllables when writing but include them when the line is read aloud. Auden followed the Latin practice of eliding contiguous vowels separated by the letters " h " or " w " when counting syllables. Thus, " how elevating " would count as four syllables but be pronounced as five.

Line endings:

An obvious problem is that the strictly metrical line may end on an unimportant word, on an unstressed syllable or even in the middle of a word such as " happy " leaving the second syllable, " py ", to be carried over. Thus the line may seem boneless. Further, although on the page there is a difference between, say, three lines each of six syllables and two lines each of nine, there may be no audible difference. Poets have tackled these problems in various ways.

The first is by virtually ignoring them, usually with unhappy result. Some writers say that the reader should not pause automatically at the ends of lines, but only where the punctuation indicates a pause. This is measurement by cadence rather than by syllable and such verse is often really chopped-up free verse (*q.v.*).

Skilful practitioners such as Moore, Daryush and Auden treat the problems as a challenge and shape their verses by apt use of end-stopped lines, by carefully placing important words at the line's end and by employing rhyme. Auden used all three devices in his poem " In Memory of Sigmund Freud ", which is written in quatrains (*q.v.*) of 11, 11, 8 and 10 syllables:

" For one who lived among enemies so long;
  If often he was wrong and at times absurd
    To us he is no more a person
    Now but a whole climate of opinion."

Accentual-Syllabic or Metrical Verse.

The traditional verse of English poetry is based on regular patterns of stressed and syllables grouped into feet.

English metrical verse uses several kinds of feet, some of two syllables, or disyllabic, some of three syllables or trisyllabic, and occasionally a foot of four syllables.

Disyllabic feet are of four kinds:

The Iamb, consisting of an unstressed syllable followed by a stressed, *e.g.* " return ".
The Trochee, consisting of a stressed syllable followed by an unstressed, *e.g.*, " river ".
The Spondee, consisting of two stressed syllables, *e.g.*, " door mat ".
The Pyrrhic, consisting of two unstressed syllables, *e.g.*, in the phrase " into town ", " into " is a pyrrhic.

Trisyllabic feet are of four kinds:

The Anapaest, consisting of two unstressed syllables followed by a stressed, *e.g.* " as you wish ".
The Dactyl, consisting of a stressed syllable followed by two unstressed, *e.g.*, " archery ".
The Amphibrach, very rarely used, consisting of a stressed syllable between two unstressed, *e.g.*, " delighted ".
The Tribrach, still more rare, consisting of three unstressed syllables, *e.g.*, last three syllables of " incommunicable ".

A four-syllabled foot is very occasionally found:

The Choriambus, which may be thought of as a trochee followed by an iamb, *e.g.*, " Toll for the brave ".

Different Kinds of Metrical Line.

Based on the different kinds of feet are the different kinds of English metre, which may be compared with the " time " in music.

Disyllabic metres may be either iambic or trochaic, for it is impossible to speak at any length using only pyrrhic or spondees, and the most common trisyllabic metres are anapaestic or dactyllic. Examples of different kinds of metrical line follow.

Iambic Line.

" I stróve with nóne, for nóne was wórth my strife."
[OBEV 521]

Trochaic Line.

" Hóme art góne, and tá'en thy wáges."
[OBEV 127]

Anapaestic Line.

" With a héy, and a hó, and a héy noninó,"
[OBEV 122]

Dactylic Lines.

" Wit with his wántonness
Tásteth death's bitterness; "
[OBEV 85]

Amphibrach Lines.

" Most friendship is feigning, most lóving mere
fólly.
Then héigh-ho! the hólly!
This life is most jólly."   [OBEV 121]

Choriambic Line.

" Kéntish Sir Býng stóod for his Kíng."

Variations in Metre.

Satisfying poetry is rarely entirely regular. Mechanical regularity is soon wearisome to the ear and is a characteristic doggerel. The poet satisfies our love of rhythm in a more interesting and subtle way by introducing all kinds of variations and inversions, while at the same time maintaining the throb of the basic metre. An account of the chief variations follows.

Elision.

Elision, as explained above, is the suppression of pronunciation of a vowel or a syllable. In the anapaestic line,

" The Assýrian came dówn like a wólf on the fóld."

the second foot appears to have four syllables, but in fact the " i " of " Assýrian " is elided or dropped before the " a " as shown by the caret mark ˄. The elision of " i," which is pronounced " y " and known as " consonantal y " is especially common, and occurs in such words as " familiar ", " opinion ". Elision is often shown by the use of the apostrophe as in " heav'n ". In " heav'n " we see one of the many conventional elisions of poetry, like " 'tis ", " 'twas ", " did'st ". " o'er ". " 'gainst " and many more.

Substitution.

Substitution is the use of a foot different from that of the metre in which the poem is written. In the following examples we can see the effect on iambic verse of some common substitutions.

(i) *Of a Trochee.*

" Stiffen the sinews, súmmon úp the blóod,"
Shakespeare, " Henry V."

Here the initial trochee gives force and emphasis.

(ii) *Of a Spondee.*

" Rócks, cáves, lákes, féns, bógs, déns, and shádes of déath."

In this extraordinary line of Milton's the spondees slow down and weight the verse.

(iii) *Of a Pyrrhic.*

" They flý forgótten as a dréam "

Here the pyrrhic in the third foot gives lightness to the line.

(iv) *Of a Dactyl.*

" Shríeking his bálefull nóte, which éver dráve "
[OBEV 58]

When a dactyl replaces an iamb it is usually in the first foot as in this typical instance from Spenser where the dactyl gives emphasis and variety to the line.

(v) *Of Anapaests.*

" And the cóming wind did róar more lóud,
And the sáils did sígh like sédge; "
[OBEV 509]

The initial anapaests in these two lines from " The Ancient Mariner " give an effect of hurry and speed.

Additional Syllable.

An additional syllable may be added to either the beginning or end of a line.

(i) *Feminine Ending.*

A feminine ending is an extra unstressed syllable that is added after the final stressed syllable of a line, giving a gentle falling inflexion. It is often used in blank verse and is a marked characteristic of Shakespeare's later plays, *e.g.*,

" Be not afear'd; the isle is full of noises,
Sounds and sweet airs, that give delight, and
hurt not."

(ii) *Anacrusis.*

Anacrusis is the use of an extra syllable before the first regular foot of the line.

Dropped Syllable.

It sometimes appears that a line is a syllable, or syllables, short, until we realise that a suspense or pause occupies the time that would have been taken by the missing syllable. The dropped syllable can be indicated by the caret mark ˄. The following technical terms are used for lines that are short of syllables.

(i) *Catalectic Line.*

This leaves off in the middle of the last foot as in the trochaic line

" Éver lét the fáncy róam,"

or the dactylic line,

" Ríngs on her fíngers and bélls on her tóes,"

The catalectic line is common in trochaic and dactylic verse, for it is in keeping with the tendency of English verse to end on a stressed syllable.

(ii) *Acephalous Line.*

This omits the first syllable of the line, as in the anapaestic line,

" That hóst with their bánners at súnset were séen."

Iambic Metres.

The metre most natural to the English language is undoubtedly the iambic.

With Iambic Pentameter as Basis.

The iambic pentameter of five stresses and ten syllables, also called the iambic decasyllabic line, is more used than any other, and is the basis of the following forms.

(i) *Blank Verse.* Blank verse, consisting of unrhymed iambic pentameters, is the metre of Shakespeare's plays, Milton's " Paradise Lost ", Wordsworth's " Prelude ", and Tennyson's

"Idylls of the King". In the hands of such masters it is a most flexible instrument especially when diversified with the eleven-syllabled line with a feminine ending. Shakespeare used the metre with increasing freedom, though it must be remembered that some apparent variations are due to the different pronunciation of Elizabethan times.

The following lines of blank verse occur in Wordsworth's "Prelude", Book III. He is describing his rooms in St. John's College, Cambridge.

> And from my pillow, looking forth by light
> Of moon or favouring stars, I could behold
> The antechapel where the statue stood
> Of Newton with his prism and silent face,
> The marble index of a mind for ever
> Voyaging through strange seas of Thought,
> alone."

(ii) *Heroic Couplet.* The heroic couplet, consisting of iambic pentameters rhyming in pairs, was in Elizabethan times called "riding rhyme", possibly because it is the metre of The Prologue of Chaucer's "Canterbury Tales", and of many of the tales themselves. It became the most fashionable metre of the eighteenth century when it was used by Pope, Goldsmith and Johnson. Keats later employed it in "Lamia."

The *Closed Couplet* was, in the heyday of the couplet's vogue, considered the most polished and correct. Here the sentence form exactly coincides with the couplet and the rhyme has a clinching effect, *e.g.,*

> "True ease in writing comes from art, not chance
> As they move easiest who have learned to
> dance."

Pope was the supreme master of the closed couplet, and eschewed variations such as enjambment, or the Alexandrine.

Enjambment is a variation used by poets before Pope's time and revived by the Romantic poets. In enjambment the sentence flows over from one line or couplet to the next, and the click of the rhyme is submerged, *e.g.,* Keats's description of Lamia in her serpent form with skin of "dazzling hue".

> "And full of silver moons, that, as she breathed
> Dissolv'd or brighter shone; or interwreathed
> Their lustres with the gloomier tapestries."
> Keats, "Lamia".

The *Alexandrine,* another variation, is a line of six iambic feet. Dryden made frequent use of the Alexandrine but Pope parodied it in the brilliant line that serves as a mnemonic:

> "A needless Alexandrine ends the song,
> That, like a wounded snake, drags its slow length
> along."

The *triplet,* another variation, consists of three lines rhyming together. The third line is frequently an Alexandrine.

Other Iambic Metres.

Many of our iambic verse forms use a shorter or longer line than the pentameter.

(i) *The Octosyllabic Couplet.* The octosyllabic couplet consists of lines of four stresses and eight syllables, and the lines rhyme in pairs. English poets like Marvell have used this metre effectively, *e.g.,* "The Garden" [OBEV 338, *see also* OBEV 337, 370]. It is the metre of Masefield's "Everlasting Mercy" and "Reynard the Fox".

(ii) *Double Iambic Metre.* When we are accustomed to hearing verse we come to realise that stresses are not always of equal weight. It is possible to distinguish in these "fourteeners" of Masefield a major stress, marked ″ and a minor stress marked ′.

> "Oh sŏme are fónd of Spănish wíne, and sŏme are
> fónd of Frénch,
> And sŏme'll swăllow táy and stúff fit ŏnly
> fór a wénch."
> Masefield's "Captain Stratton's Fancy."

The lines have in fact four major stresses, and between the major stresses intervene three syllables, of which the middle has a minor stress. It is this alternation in the weight of the stress which gives its characteristic swing to such a poem as Chesterton's "The Rolling English Road" [OBEV 796].

Trochaic Metres.

Pure Trochaic Metre.

English poets seldom use a pure trochaic metre, partly because the continual feminine ending that it involves is not pleasing to the English ear. A few very short lyrics in this metre can be found, as Browne's Song "For her gait, if she be walking", but the only poem of any length is Longfellow's "Hiawatha", and the metre of this *tour de force* tends to sound monotonous. It consists of unrhymed lines, each of four stresses, *e.g.,*

> "Like a yéllow léaf in áutumn
> Like a yéllow wáter-lily."

Modified Trochaic Metre.

Ever since the Middle Ages our poets have contrived to combine the advantages of a trochaic metre and of a masculine ending by the simple expedient of shortening the last foot of the line to a stressed monosyllable. This catalectic, or shortened, trochaic line is found both in couplets and in stanza forms. *The seven-syllabled trochaic couplet, also called the trochaic tetrameter,* consists of these catalectic, or shortened, lines rhyming in pairs, and is a gay, tripping measure, as in some passages of Milton's "L'Allegro".

> "Háste thee nýmph and bríng with thée
> Jést and yóuthful jóllity."

In "Locksley Hall" Tennyson uses a fifteen-syllabled couplet, the last foot being catalectic, while a sixteen-syllabled trochaic line is used by E. A. Poe in his "Raven". Here each line is divided into halves by the caesura and the halves also rhyme:

> "Ah, distinctly I remember, it was the bleak
> December."

Lyrics in modified trochaic metre are often found. Herrick uses the seven-syllabled lines rhyming in pairs in "Cherry Ripe", Wither in "A Lover's Resolution" [OBEV 245]. Edmund Blunden, in "Forefathers" [OBEV 843], uses it in a stanza rhyming ABABCC. George Herbert in his lyric "Discipline" [OBEV 276] brilliantly combines five- and three-syllabled lines rhyming ABAB, *e.g.*

> "Thrów awáy Thy ród,
> Thrów awáy Thy wráth;
> Ó my Gód,
> Táke the géntle páth."

Further Variations in Modified Trochaic Metre.

The modified trochaic line is especially subject to further variation.

(*a*) It is often combined with a pure trochaic line, *e.g.,* in Hunt's poem "Jenny Kiss'd Me" [OBEV 600] where the catalectic and the complete trochaic line alternate regularly.

(*b*) It often has an extra unstressed syllable preceding it (anacrusis), as in the second of these lines from Keats' poem "Fancy".

> "Ín a dárk conspíracý
> To | bánish Éven fróm her sky."

The line that results might well be taken for iambic, and there are some passages in English poetry, such as lines in Milton's "L'Allegro", which can be described either as irregular trochaic or irregular iambic lines! It depends on what the hearer judges to be the *basic* stress.

Double Trochaic Metre.

Corresponding to double iambic metre there is a double trochaic metre. W. S. Gilbert effectively uses it in many of his patter songs, as in " Ferdinando and Elvira ", *e.g.*,

> " Thén we lét off páper cráckers, eách of which
>   contáined a mótto,
> Ánd she listened while I réad them, till her
>   móther tóld her nót to."

These lines, like those in double iambic metre, have four major stresses (marked ") and between the major stresses three syllables, of which the middle carries a minor stress.

A modified double trochaic metre, where the last foot is shortened to a stressed monosyllable, can be recognised in Tennyson's " Locksley Hall ", or in Lewis Carroll's verses in " Alice in Wonderland ":

> " ' Will you wálk a líttle fáster?'   sáid a whíting
>   tó a snáil."

Trisyllabic Metres Generally.

Because of the irregularities incident to verse in anapaests, dactyls, and amphibrachs, it is not easy to distinguish one trisyllabic metre from another. Swinburne, the past master of trisyllabic metres, often passes with great freedom from anapaestic to dactylic lines within the same stanza.

Anapaestic Metres.

Anapaestic metre is used only in short poems, and often conveys a sense of speed and urgency. The chief variation is the omission of one or two of the unstressed syllables at the beginning of a line. Some of the best-known examples of anapaestic verse are Byron's " Sennacherib ", Flecker's " The War Song of the Saracens ", and Lewis Carroll's parodies, " 'Tis the voice of the lobster ", and " You are old, Father William ", from *Alice in Wonderland*.

Dactylic Metres.

Pure Dactylic Metre.

Like pure trochaic metre, pure dactylic metre has a feminine ending to the line, which makes rhyming difficult and does not satisfy the English ear. Very few serious poems keep consistently to a pure dactylic verse, and Robert Graves' " In the Wilderness " is most unusual in this respect, *e.g.*,

> " Christ of His géntleness
> Thírsting and húngering
> Wálked in the wilderness."

Modified Dactylic Metre.

Normally dactylic metre is modified in that a catalectic line is frequently used, where the final foot is shortened to a trochee or a stressed monosyllable, as in Hood's " Bridge of Sighs ", the most remarkable dactylic poem in the language, *e.g.*,

> " Óne more Unfórtunate
> Wéary of bréath
> Ráshly impórtunate,
> Góne to her déath!"

Shakespeare also uses the catalectic line in the refrain to " Where the bee sucks " [OBEV 131]—

> " Mérrily mérrily sháll I live nów
> Únder the blóssom that hángs on the bóugh."

It is interesting to note how the catalectic dactylic line of the refrain is matched by the catalectic trochaic line of the verse.

Amphibrach Metres.

Pure Amphibrach Metre.

The amphibrach metre is extremely rare in English, although it occurs occasionally in a few lines, or a refrain, like that to " Blow, blow thou

Winter Wind " [OBEV 121]. Laurence Binyon's " Bablock Hythe " is one of the few poems to use amphibrachs continuously, *e.g.*,

> " Till súnset was rímming
> The Wést with pale flúshes;
> Behind the black rúshes
> The lást light was dímming."

Modified Amphibrach metre.

The pure amphibrach line can be used alternating with a catalectic line, shorn of its last syllable, as in Goldsmith's drinking song in " She Stoops to Conquer ", Act I, Scene 2, *e.g.*

> " Let schóol-masters púzzle their bráin
> With grámmar and nónsense and léarning,"

Choriambic Metres.

There are few poems in pure choriambic metre. Ruskin's quatrain " Trust Thou thy Love " is one of the few examples, *e.g.*,

> " Trúst thou thy Lóve; if she be próud, is she not
>   swéet? "

Choriambic effects are often obtained incidentally especially in blank verse, when the first foot of a line is a trochee.

Lionel Johnson frequently achieves the same kind of effect in lyric verses by substituting a choriamb for two iambs, as in the poem " By the Statue of King Charles " [OBEV 757], *e.g.*,

> " Cómely and cálm, he rídes
> Hárd by his ówn Whitehall: "

Quantitative Verse.

Since the Renaissance poets such as Spenser, Coleridge, and Tennyson have from time to time endeavoured to reproduce in English verse the complicated quantitative measures of Greek and Latin verse. The difficulty, if not impossibility, of putting the stress on the long vowel in English has for the most part rendered such experiments interesting only to the scholar.

It should always be remembered that the technical names, such as iamb and trochee, although borrowed from the classics, have in English verse a quite different meaning, referring never to quantity but always to stress.

Free Verse or *Vers Libre*.

The prosody of free verse is extremely complicated. The following note offers only a very general guide.

The free verse or *vers libre* of English and American poetry has two sources, the poems of Walt Whitman and of the French Symbolists, particularly as interpreted by Pound. It is a verse designed in the cadences and breath groups of the speaking voice and given shape by a cunning use of four rhetorical devices: repetition, parallelism—balancing one phrase or line against another, enjambment—run-on lines, and pauses.

Repetition and Parallelism.

These devices are characteristic of much ancient poetry and may be familar to the reader from the Old Testament Psalms, which are written in free verse:

> " He giveth snow like wool: he scattereth the
>   hoar-frost
>   like ashes.
> He casteth forth his ice like morsels: who
>   can stand before his cold? "
>   Psalm 147.

Whitman's verse recalls such translation of ancient Hebrew poetry in its deployment of rhetorical lists and repetitions, balancing one statement against another:

"Pleas'd with the native and pleas'd with the foreign, pleas'd
with the new and old,
Pleas'd with the homely woman as well as the handsome,
Pleas'd with the quakeress as she puts off her bonnet and
talks melodiously"
Whitman: "Song of Myself".

In "Howl" and "Kaddish" Allen Ginsberg makes similar use of parallelism and repetition.

D. H. Lawrence in "Snake" [OBEV 810] and "Kangaroo" [OBTCV 184] shows how such free verse is modified for contemplative and narrative poems, in which the parallels and repetitions are more subtly deployed:

"He reached down from a fissure in the earth-wall in
the gloom
And trailed his yellow-brown slackness soft-bellied
down, over the edge of the stone trough
And rested his throat upon the stone bottom,
And where the water had dripped from the tap, in a
small clearness,
He sipped with his straight mouth,
Softly drank through his straight gums, into his slack
long body
Silently."

[OBEV 812]

Enjambment and Pause.

We will have noticed that the lines from Lawrence's poem owe much of their effectiveness to his adroit arrangement of pauses and of run-on lines. Other writers of free verse make particular use of these two devices, and poets like George Oppen create verses in which a complex musical pattern of pauses, or rests, is indicated by the very spacing of the words:

. . . . . Who
so poor the words

would   with and   take on substantial

meaning   handholds   footholds

to dig in one's heels   sliding

hands and heels beyond the residential
lots   the plots   it is a poem

which may be sung
may well be sung
"The Winds of Downhill".

Other writers, while making some use of such spacing, or of dashes, to indicate the rests, have developed Pound's device of breaking up the lines and placing one part below and to the right of another:

This was I,
a sparrow.
I did my best;
farewell.
W. C. Williams: "The Sparrow".

III. THE DIFFERENT KINDS OF RHYME.

The most familiar division of rhyme is into masculine, feminine, and triple rhyme, but we also distinguish broken and Leonine rhyme.

Masculine, Male or Single Rhyme.

The final syllable is stressed, e.g., "cage/page", "joy/boy".

Feminine, Female or Two-syllable Rhyme.

The syllable before the last is stressed, and the final syllable unstressed, e.g., "pleasure/treasure", "bending/lending".

Triple, Tumbling or Three-syllabled Rhyme.

The antepenultimate syllable is stressed. Triple rhyme is normally found in light or comic verse, like that of W. S. Gilbert. This punning "Epitaph on a Dentist" employs it:

"Stranger! Approach this spot with gravity!
John Brown is filling his last cavity."

In "The Bridge of Sighs" Hood dares to use it in a serious poem with such rhymes as "scrútiny/mútiny".

Broken Rhyme.

Broken rhyme, where more than one word is needed to complete the rhyme, is occasionally used, e.g., "estate/their gate".

Leonine Rhyme.

Although rhyme normally occurs at the end of the line, we also find verse where the first half of the line rhymes with the second. This device, known as Leonine rhyme, is frequently used in Coleridge's "Ancient Mariner" [OBEV 509], e.g.,

"The ice did split, with a thunder-fit;"

Poetic Licence in Rhyme.

The difficulty of rhyming in English is considerable, for many words have not a single rhyming word, some have only one, others very few. Certain licences are therefore allowed to the poet in the following ways:

Eye Rhyme or Printer's Rhyme.

Here words rhyme only to the eye, as "love/move", Keats in "Meg Merrilies" uses "rushes/bushes".

Identical Rhyme.

Here the same syllable or word is used twice so that the line rhymes with itself, e.g., "universe/this verse" [OBEV 549]. The use of rhyming words spelt differently but pronounced identically is also a poetic licence, e.g., "wright, write right".

Cockney Rhyme.

Keats' use of Cockney rhymes has been much criticised, e.g., "mourn/torn", "faces/vases" "briar/attire". There is still considerable difference between regional pronunciation of English, and many eminent poets have availed themselves of a Southern pronunciation in rhyming "dawn/morn", although in some districts the "r" of "mourn" would be sounded.

Perversion of Rhyme.

Modern poets, following Wilfred Owen, have sometimes used a deliberate perversion of rhyme, which should not be confused with assonance. Wilfred Owen opens his bitter poem "A Terre" with the following stanza:

"Sit on the bed. I'm blind and three parts shell.
Be careful; can't shake hands now; never shall.
Both arms have mutinied against me,—brutes.
My fingers fidget like ten idle brats."

The deliberate falsity of rhymes like "shall/shell," and "brutes/brats" conveys Owen's horror at the disintegration and collapse of the First World War.

The Recording of Rhyme Schemes.

The conventional way of noting rhyme schemes is to call the first series a, the second b, and so on. Normally each new series is indented, e.g.,

"Joyful, joyful!   *a*
    When virginity   *b*
Seeks all coyful.   *b*
Man's affinity.   *b*
    Fate all flowery,   *c*
    Bright and bowery   *c*
    Is her dowery!   *c*
Joyful, joyful."   *a*

W. S. Gilbert, "Yeomen of the Guard."

IV. STANZA FORMS.

Two-Line Stanzas.

Couplets.

These are rhymed. Regular couplets are also closed, that is, the sense does not run over from one stanza to another.

In "The Knight and the Lady" [OBEV 20] Sir William Cornish uses a stanza of irregular octosyllabic iambic couplets, while Auden's "Roman Wall Blues" is an example of couplets written in an irregular accentual metre:

"Over the heather the wet wind blows
I've lice in my tunic and a cold in my nose."

Distiches.

These are unrhymed, but again the regular form is closed. John Wain's "Brooklyn Heights" [OBTCV 518] is an example of a poem written in distiches with an accentual metre of five stresses.

Three-Line Stanzas or Tercets.

There are various forms of which the most common are:

Triplets.

A three-line stanza with a single rhyme, AAA, BBB, etc., as in Robert Graves's "Sick Love" [OBEV 839] Roy Fuller's "The Statue" [OBEV 872].

Terza Rima.

The classic form, as used by Dante in the "Divine Comedy", has stanzas of three iambic pentameters linked by rhyme: ABA, BCB, CDC, etc., the concluding stanza having an extra line which rhymes with its middle one, *e.g.*, DEDE. A recent example of the form is Matthew Mitchell's "Printing Jenny" [OBTCV 533]. In "Ode to the West Wind" [OBEV 549] Shelley uses a modified *terza rima* in which the concluding stanza is a couplet. An interesting modification of the form is used by Auden in "If I Could Tell You" and "Miranda's Song". Each is a poem of six stanzas, the last a quatrain ending in a couplet. Only three rhymes are used throughout, ABA, the last stanzas rhyming ABAA.

In Italian the rhymes used in *terza rima* are feminine. English poets have generally preferred to use masculine rhymes.

Tercets with Short Third Lines.

These may be arranged in pairs, as in Herbert's "The British Church", where the rhyme scheme is AAB, CCB, etc., resembling the sestet of a sonnet (*q.v.*) with a strong median pause.

Unrhymed Tercets.

An example is Ted Hughes's "Thistles" [OBTCV 550] composed of four unrhymed tercets in free verse.

Four-Line Stanzas or Quatrains.

A great many variations are possible. The most common forms include:

The Ballad Stanza.

There are two main forms:

Strict ballad form.

It consists of stanzas of four iambic lines, the first and third having four feet, the second and

fourth containing three. The rhyme scheme is ABCB. Ballads such as "Sir Patrick Spens" [OBEV 357] and "The Wife of Usher's Well" [OBEV 360] are in this form. Coleridge's "Ancient Mariner" [OBEV 509] shows how flexibly the ballad stanza can be used.

Less strict ballad form.

Octosyllabic iambic stanzas with a rhyme scheme of either ABCB or ABAB. Many ancient ballads, such as "Thomas the Rhymer" [OBEV 355] are of this type.

The Envelope or "In Memoriam" Stanza.

Used by Tennyson for his poem "In Memoriam" [OBEV 604-11] the stanza resembles that of the less strict ballad form in having four iambic lines, each of four feet, but its rhyme scheme is ABBA.

Hymns.

Most English hymns are written in short iambic lines, and English hymnology refers to them according to the number of syllables in their lines.

Common measure.

8686 rhyming ABAB, *e.g.*, "O for a thousand tongues to sing" (Songs of Praise 595).

Long measure.

8888 rhyming ABAB, *e.g.*, "When I survey the wondrous cross" (Songs of Praise 133).

Short measure.

6686 rhyming ABCB, *e.g.*, "Blest are the pure in heart" (Songs of Praise 455).

The Elegiac Stanza or Heroic Quatrain.

It consists of four iambic pentameters rhyming ABAB. The form is best known from Gray's "Elegy" [OBEV 429].

The "Jabberwocky" Stanza.

Used by Lewis Carroll for his nonsense verses "Jabberwocky" [OBEV 681] the stanza consists of four iambic lines, the first three of four feet, the final line of three. The rhyme scheme is ABAB.

The "Omar Khayyam" Stanza

Named from its use by Edward Fitzgerald in translating the "Rubaiyát" [OBEV 594], the stanza has four iambic pentameters rhyming AABA.

Sapphics.

A quatrain based on the form used by the Greek poetess Sappho in her surviving ode. The first three lines are each of five feet: a trochee, a spondee, a dactyl, a trochee, a spondee. English writers generally prefer the following variation: dactyl, spondee, trochee, trochee. trochee.

The fourth line of the stanza contains but two feet. The Classic form is dactyl and spondee. In English Sapphics the line may be of a dactyl and trochee.

Isaac Watts's "The Day of Judgement" [OBEV 392] illustrates the form:

"When the fierce North-wind with his airy forces
Rears up the Baltic to a foaming fury;
And the red lightning with a storm of hail comes
                                    Rushing down;"

Another example is Sir Henry Newbolt's famous "He Fell Among Thieves" [OBTCV 52].

Other Forms.

Another particularly interesting form is the stanza used by George Herbert in "Virtue" [OBEV 271] and by Sir Richard Fanshawe in "Ode on His Majesty's Proclamation" [OBEV 297]. It consists of three lines each of four iambics, followed by a line of two feet, again iambic. The rhyme scheme is ABAB.

Five-Line Stanzas or Quintains.

Although the quintain has been used by many poets in a variety of ways no particular form has become established. The quintain's lines often vary in length, as in this example from Hardy's "Old Furniture" [OBTCV 17]:

> "I know not how it may be with others
> Who sit amid relics of householdry
> That date from the days of their mothers'
> mothers,
> But well I know how it is with me
> Continually."

Other interesting examples are the stanzas of Shakespeare's song "Who is Sylvia", Shelley's "Ode to a Skylark" [OBEV 550] Hugh Mac-Diarmid's "Cattle Show" [OBTCV 254] and Dylan Thomas's "The force . . ." [OBTCV 439].

Six-Line Stanzas or Sestets.

Again there are many examples and no definitive forms. A popular rhyme scheme is ABABCC giving the effect of a quatrain followed by a couplet. This is used with a stanza of six iambic pentameters in Marvell's "The Fair Singer" [OBEV 340] and Betjeman in "The Metropolitan Railway" [OBTCV 350]. Herbert's poem "Love" uses a more striking stanza:

> "Love bade me welcome; yet my soul drew back
> Guilty of dust and sin.
> But quick-eyed Love, observing me grow slack
> From my first entrance in,
> Drew nearer to me, sweetly questioning,
> If I lacked anything."
> [OBEV 277]

Another interesting form is that used by Auden for his menacing chorus "We are the Town" [OBTCV 379].

Seven-Line Stanzas.

The only established form is

Rhyme Royal.

A stanza of seven iambic pentameters rhyming ABABBCC, this was used by Chaucer in "Troilus and Criseyde" [OBEV 7 & 8] and by Shakespeare in "Lucrece" [OBEV 115].

Eight-Line Stanzas or Octaves.

Ottava Rima

A stanza of eight iambic pentameters rhyming ABABABCC, it was used by Byron in "Don Juan" [OBEV 543], by Keats in "Isabella" and Auden in "Letter to Lord Byron".

Other Octaves.

Many other forms exist in various combinations of metres and rhyme schemes, but none have become well known. Examples of interest include Fletcher's "Away Delights" [OBEV 223] Marvell's "The Picture of Little T. C. . . ." [OBEV 341], Hardy's "Voices from Things Growing in a Country Churchyard" [OBTCV 31] and John Berryman's "Homage to Mistress Bradstreet".

The Nine-Line Stanza.

The Spenserian Stanza.

A stanza of eight iambic pentameters followed by an Alexandrine has a rhyme scheme of ABABBCBCC. It was invented by Spenser for his "Fairie Queene" [OBEV 58–63] and used by Byron in "Childe Harold" [OBEV 536–7], Shelley in "Adonais" [OBEV 552] and Burns in "The Cottar's Saturday Night".

Other Stanza Forms.

Stanzas of ten and more lines are used in many variations. Notable ones include those in Tennyson's "Mariana" [OBEV 595], Gray's "Ode on a Distant Prospect of Eton College" [OBEV 426], and Donne's in "The Anniversary" [OBEV 195].

The Diagrammatic Stanza.

Some poets have delighted to create stanzas whose very appearance echoes their theme, as in Herbert's "Easter Wings":

> "Lord, Who createdst man in wealth and store,
> Though foolishly he lost the same,
> Decaying more and more,
> Till he became
> Most poore:
> With Thee
> O let me rise
> As larks, harmoniously,
> And sing this day Thy victories:
> Then shall the fall further the flight in me."

The second half of the poem repeats this pattern so that the whole has the shape of two pairs of wings. In the present century Dylan Thomas succeeded in creating an even more complex structure in his extraordinary "Vision and Prayer".

V. OTHER METRICAL FORMS.

The Sonnet.

A sonnet has fourteen iambic pentameters. Perfected in Italy by Petrarch, who died in 1374, it was introduced into England in the sixteenth century. There are two chief types of sonnet.

The Petrarchan, or Italian, sonnet has an "octave" of eight lines, rhyming ABBAABBA, followed by a "sestet" of six lines, where some variety of rhyme schemes is found. The strictest Petrarchan sonnets have either two "tercets" of three lines each, with rhymes CDECDE, or else three pairs of lines rhyming CDCDCD.

An example of sestet rhyming CDECDE is Milton's "On His Blindness" [OBEV 305].

Examples of sestets CDCDCD are Wordsworth's "Upon Westminster Bridge" [OBEV 486] and Keats' "On First Looking into Chapman's Homer" [OBEV 562].

Not all of these examples observe the natural pause between octave and sestet which is characteristic of the strict Italian form, and many of our finest sonnets depart from the original rhyme scheme in both octave and sestet.

A lesser-known Petrarchan sonnet by Keats:

> "To one, who has been long in city pent,
> 'Tis very sweet to look into the fair
> And open face of heaven,—to breathe a
> prayer
> Full in the smile of the blue firmament.
> Who is more happy, when, with heart's content
> Fatigued he sinks into some pleasant lair
> Of wavy grass, and reads a debonair
> And gentle tale of love and languishment?
> Returning home at evening with an ear
> Catching the notes of Philomel,—an eye
> Watching the sailing cloudlet's bright career,
> He mourns that day so soon has glided by:
> E'en like the passage of an angel's tear
> That falls through the clear ether silently."

The Elizabethan or Shakespearean sonnet consists of three quatrains with the rhymes ABAB/CDCD/EFEF/ concluded by a couplet rhyming GG. The couplet often clinches the thought.

Examples are Shakespeare's sonnets [OBEV 134–153], and Keats' last sonnet [OBEV 571].

The Limerick.

The limerick may be defined as a single anapaestic stanza, having the first two lines of three feet, the next two lines of two feet and a concluding line of three feet, with the rhyme scheme AABBA.

The origin of the limerick is uncertain, but it became popular after the appearance in 1846 of Edward Lear's "Book of Nonsense". Lear's limericks differ from the contemporary type in that his final line is normally a repetition, adding nothing to the sense and repeating one of the previous rhyme words.

Most of our modern limericks are passed on by word of mouth, but some that concisely express some intellectual attitudes have appeared in print as the following, on " Determinism "—

" There wás a young mán who said ' Damn!
   It appéars to me nów that I ám
     Just a béing that móves
     In predéstinate gróoves,
Not a táxi or bús, but a trám.' "

The Clerihew.

The clerihew is an amusing quatrain, so called after its inventor Edmund Clerihew Bentley. It disdains regular metre and depends on the simple rhyme scheme AABB. The distinctive characteristic of the clerihew is that it is concerned with some eminent person, who is named in the first line and then described in a wilfully fanciful way, the matter being dictated by the exigencies of the rhyme, as in Bentley's clerihew on J. S. Mill.

John Stuart Mill,
By a mighty effort of will,
Overcame his natural bonhomie
And wrote ' Principles of Political Economy '.

Metrical Forms of French Origin.

It became fashionable during the last years of the nineteenth century for poets to imitate certain verse forms which had long been practised in France, some of them from the time of the troubadours.

Chaucer and Gower had in the fourteenth century used some of these forms, later English poets had occasionally experimented with some of them, and Swinburne, Austin Dobson, Edmund Gosse and others did much to adapt and naturalise them, although their intricate rhyming patterns are so very difficult to construct in a language so short of rhymes as English. The most popular were the triolet, villanelle, rondeau, ballade and sestina.

Characteristic of the Anglicised versions are:

   1. Freedom as regards metre and length of line.
   2. Complicated and exacting rhyme schemes, which permit of no such poetic licence as identical rhyme.
   3. A refrain line which recurs in certain stereotyped positions without any alteration of sound, although there may be significant alteration of meaning. Only the sestina is without a refrain.

The Triolet.

A triolet is a single stanza of eight short lines. The first line is repeated as the fourth, and the first and second appear again as seventh and eighth. Only two rhymes are used, the scheme being ABAAABAB.

The triolet was re-introduced into England by Bridges in 1873. Austin Dobson's " A Kiss " is a good example of the form.

" Rose kissed me today.
   Will she kiss me tomorrow?
Let it be as it may,
Rose kissed me today,
But the pleasure gives way
   To a savour of sorrow;—
Rose kissed me today,—
   Will she kiss me tomorrow? "

The Villanelle.

The villanelle has five stanzas, each of three lines, followed by one stanza of four lines. It has a refrain which consists of the first and third lines

of the first stanza. These lines alternately form the last lines of the four middle stanzas, and re-appear as a concluding couplet to the poem. Only two rhymes are employed throughout. Stanzas one to five rhyme ABA and stanza six ABBAA.

Austin Dobson wrote several villanelles including the well-known " On a Nankin Plate ", and W. E. Henley's poem called " Villanelle " is a good example of the form. A modern example is:

A villanelle by Dylan Thomas:

    Do not go gentle into that good night

" Do not go gentle into that good night,
Old age should burn and rave at close of day;
Rage, rage against the dying of the light.

Though wise men at their end know dark is right,
Because their words had forked no lightning they
Do not go gentle into that good night.

Good men, the last wave by, crying how bright
Their frail deeds might have danced in a green
                        bay
Rage, rage against the dying of the light.

Wild men who caught and sang the sun in flight,
And learn, too late, they grieved it on its way,
Do not go gentle into that good night.

Grave men, near death, who see with blinding
                    sight
Blind eyes could blaze like meteors and be gay
Rage, rage against the dying of the light.

And you, my father, there on the sad height,
Curse, bless, me now with your fierce tears, I
                    pray.
Do not go gentle into that good night,
Rage, rage against the dying of the light."
                    [OBEV 882]

The Rondeau.

A rondeau is a short and compact verse form. It has thirteen lines, usually of eight syllables, which use only two rhymes, and in addition a refrain, usually of four syllables, which introduces a third rhyme. This refrain consists of the first half of the opening line and is twice repeated, thus giving the rondeau fifteen lines all told. The rondeau is divided into three stanzas with the following rhyme scheme: AABBA: AAB + refrain C; AABBA + refrain C.

Austin Dobson wrote many rondeaus to this exacting plan, including the ingenious " You bid me try ":

" You bid me try, Blue-Eyes, to write
A Rondeau. What!—forthwith?—to-night?
   Reflect. Some skill I have, 'tis true:—
   But thirteen lines!—and rhymed on two!
" Refrain ", as well. Ah, hapless plight!

Still, there are five lines,—ranged aright.
These Gallic bonds, I feared, would fright
   My easy Muse. They did, till you—
     You bid me try!

That makes them eight. The port's in sight:—
'Tis all because your eyes are bright!
   Now just a pair to end in ' oo '—
   When maids command, what can't we do.
Behold!—the RONDEAU, tasteful, light,
     You bid me try! "

The Roundel.

The roundel is a variation of the rondeau. Swinburne in his " Century of Roundels " wrote a hundred, and his pattern is usually followed. It consists of nine full lines, plus the refrain (consisting of the opening half of the first line), which is twice repeated, giving eleven lines all told. Only two rhymes are used throughout. The roundel is divided into three stanzas with the following rhyme scheme: ABA + refrain B; BAB; ABA + refrain B.

A Roundel by Swinburne.

The Roundel.

" A Roundel is wrought as a ring or a starbright
                      sphere,
With craft of delight and with cunning of sound
                      unsought
That the heart of the hearer may smile if to
                   please his ear
      A roundel is wrought.

Its jewel of music is carven of all or of aught—
Love, laughter, or mourning – rememberance of
                 rapture of fear—
The fancy may fashion to hand in the ear of
                 thought.

As a bird's quick song runs round, and the hearts
                 in us hear—
Pause answers to pause, and again the same
               strain caught,
So moves the device whence, round as a pearl or
                 tear,
      A roundel is wrought."

The Rondel.

The rondel is a form of verse similar to the rondeau. The modern English version consists of fourteen lines all told. Only two rhymes are used, and the initial two lines are repeated as lines 7 and 8 and again as lines 13 and 14. The rondel is frequently arranged in three stanzas with a rhyme scheme as follows: ABBA; ABAB; ABBAAB.

The rondel was revived in the nineteenth century by Bridges, Dobson, Gosse, and Henley, and Dobson's " Love comes back to his vacant dwelling " is one of the best known.

The Ballade.

There are several kinds of ballade, but the most popular modern form consists of three eight-lined stanzas followed by an envoy of four lines. Each of the stanzas and the envoy end with a refrain. The rhymes of the eight-lined stanzas are ABABBCBC and of the envoy BCBC.

Austin Dobson wrote several ballades of this kind, the best known being, " This was the Pompadour's fan ", and " And where are the galleons of Spain? "

Chaucer's " Balade ", " Hyd, Absolon, thy gilte tresses clere," is of an earlier seven-lined type without an envoy.

A ballade by Austin Dobson:

The Ballad of the Thrush.

" Across the noisy street
   I hear him careless throw
One warning utterance sweet;
   This faint at first, and low
   The full notes closer grow;
Hark! What a torrent gush!
   They pour, they overflow—
Sing on, sing on, O Thrush!

What trick, what dream's deceit
   Has fooled his fancy so
To scorn of dust and heat?
   I, prisoned here below,
   Feel the fresh breezes blow,
And see, thro' flag and rush,
   Cool water sliding slow—
Sing on, sing on, O Thrush!

Sing on. What though thou beat
   On that dull bar thy foe!
Somewhere the green boughs meet
   Beyond the roofs a-row;
   Somewhere the blue skies show,
Somewhere no black walls crush
   Poor hearts with hopeless woe—
Sing on, sing on, O Thrush!

      Envoy.
Bird, though they come we know,
   The empty cage, the hush;
Still, ere the brief day go
   Sing on, sing on, O Thrush! "

The Chant Royal.

The chant royal is a longer form of ballade. It has five stanzas of eleven lines and an envoy of five lines.

The rhyme scheme is ABABCCDDEDE, and the envoy has rhyme DDEDE.

The Sestina.

The sestina has six stanzas, each of six lines. The end words to the lines of the first stanza are repeated as end words in the other five stanzas, but in a different and stereotyped order. The poem concludes with an envoy.

The first sestina published in English was in Spenser's " Shepheardes Calender " (1579). Swinburne wrote many, including " I saw my soul at rest upon a day ".

Metrical Forms of Japanese Origin.

The Haiku.

A poem of three syllabic lines, unrhymed. The first and third lines are of five syllables, the middle one has seven. It creates a vivid pictorial image expressing an imaginative or spiritual insight. The following gives some idea of the form:

   Morning's white light, a
     new beginning heralded
       by a plump black bird.

As Japanese is a language without stresses its poetic forms are impossible to reproduce exactly in English. Most poets therefore concentrate on trying to capture the quality and spirit of the form rather than its exact structure. Pound's " Fan Piece for her Imperial Lord " is an example:

   " O fan of white silk,
     clear as frost on the grass-blade,
   You also are laid aside ."

The Tanka.

A poem similar in kind to the Haiku contains five lines. The first and third contain five syllables each, the remainder seven.

VI. CONCLUSION.

The foregoing account is no more than a description of our verse forms. It in no way implies that verse is written according to rules.

We have only to look at Shakespeare's lyrics [OBEV 117–133] to realise how brilliantly free and inventive the poet can be in devising new and delightful patterns of verse—many of them so subtle as to be very difficult to define. All that the students and critics can do is to follow in the poet's wake, endeavouring to understand and elucidate the forms that the maker has created.

III. TWENTIETH-CENTURY POETRY

INTRODUCTION.

This section does not profess to be a full account of the poetry of our century, for that would be impossible within the present compass. Its aim is, rather, to outline some of the more important trends in modern British and American poetry and to suggest ways of approaching the work of its chief writers.

Until quite recently it was—and in some quarters yet remains—usual to speak of three " masters " of twentieth-century English poetry: Yeats (1865–1939), Pound (1885–1972), and Eliot (1888–1965); but during the last twenty or so years many younger poets, especially in Britain, have come particularly to appreciate and value the work of a fourth, very different, " master ", Hardy (1840–1928).

A second important development as the century has progressed has been the division of " English " into " British " and " American " poetry. This division has been particularly noticeable since the end of the Second World War, but it had started in the 1920s.

We shall, therefore, begin by discussing the work of the four major English poets of the early twentieth century and then consider, first, some of the more important British, next some of the more important American writers who succeeded these early giants.

THE EARLY MASTERS.

Their Cultural Background.

Inevitably, poetry, like all other arts, reflects social and cultural change. During the early years of our century such change was rapid. The accelerating technological revolution and accompanying improvements in communications meant that, even in comparatively remote rural areas, people's lives were being drawn closer to those in the expanding urban and industrial centres.

The ideas of Darwin and Huxley had left many in a state of uncertainty about the ultimate meaning and purpose of life. Others were spurred to further study of man and there was an upsurge of interest in psychology, stimulated by William James's *Principles of Psychology* (1890), Bergson's work on the psychology of perception—*Matter and Memory* (1894)—and the ideas of Freud and Jung —who first lectured in America in 1909. There was a parallel growth of interest in social anthropology and comparative religion. Here William James's *Varieties of Religious Experience* (1902) and Sir James Frazer's *Golden Bough* (1922) were seminal works.

Some people regretted the increasing fragmentation of traditional culture. This sense of loss was to be intensified by the anguish of the First World War and the Depression that followed it. However, to many, and especially to the young, the period 1900–15 was a time of exhilarating intellectual and cultural excitement, its atmosphere vividly conveyed in one of the best memoirs of the period, Leonard Woolf's *Beginning Again*.

The stimulus of the new " renaissance " was reflected not only in poetry, but also in the art of the Post-Impressionists, the music of Stravinsky, the dance of the Diaghilev ballet, the novels of Proust and Joyce.

Rebelling against established values, the new young artists and writers consciously directed their work to a select minority. Sexual candour, vernacular diction, elliptical syntax, a complex organisation of imagery and erudite reference were the hallmarks of the new poetic, whose writers were as indifferent to accepted canons of beauty as they were contemptuous of bourgeois standards of success and respectability.

Hardy, by some twenty-five years the oldest of the four early masters of twentieth-century poetry, and in many ways untouched by his juniors' sense of exhilaration, nonetheless shared their scorn for the " inert crystallised opinion—hard as a rock— which the vast body of men have vested interests in supporting." He was equally tart in his dismissal of the general public's " crass illiteracy ".

Aesthetic Influences and Ideas.

(a) *The development of the Romantic aesthetic.* Social and cultural change, though very important were perhaps less immediate in their effect on poetic methods than were the aesthetic influences that came from the clarification and evolution of the Romantic concept of poetry.

As Kermode shows in his *Romantic Image*, from the time of Coleridge there had been a growing conviction among writers such as Blake, Keats, Pater and Yeats that the artist, in whom the powers of the imagination are allied with a passionate sensibility, has a special quality of apprehension and expresses his intuitions in a unique way.

According to this theory in its most extreme form, the work of art is not only original but complete in itself, an " aesthetic monad ", resisting analysis into form and content. Without ulterior purpose or utility, its only *raison d'être* is " to be ". Thus it becomes irrelevant to speak of a poem's " meaning ". The only valid question one can ask is on the lines of " Is it an organic whole? "

(b) *Problems raised by the Romantic aesthetic.* As Eliot was to point out, in its most extreme form, the Romantic aesthetic can be unhelpful and misleading, for, although it is in one sense true to say that the form and content of a work of art are always the same thing, in another sense it " always is true to say that they are different things."

One of the biggest difficulties facing the reader of an unfamiliar poem is accurately to distinguish between his or her reactions to its content and his or her reactions to its form. We often think we like, or dislike, a poem's form because we like, or dislike, its content and vice versa. Many writers who supported the Romantic aesthetic in its final extreme stage themselves fell into this trap. Their work is always mellifluous, and at its best, as in, say Swinburne's *Triumph of Time*, it is exhilarating, but it easily degenerates into the precious and sentimental verse characteristic of Dowson and Symons.

(c) *The French Symbolists.* The influence of the French school of poets on English writers is helpfully discussed in Edmund Wilson's *Axel's Castle* (1931) and Clive Scott's " Symbolism, Decadence and Impressionism " (Bradbury and McFarlane, eds.: *Modernism 1890–1930*; 1976).

Its leader, Stephane Mallarmé (1842–98), attempted to create a new idiom for poetry. Supremely disinterested, a " saint of literature ", he wrote little himself but at his modest weekly receptions gently expounded his influential views to such visitors as the painters Whistler and Dégas, the musician Debussy and writers both French and Anglo-Irish, including Wilde and Yeats.

Himself greatly influenced by an American writer of macabre genius, Edgar Allan Poe (1809–49), Mallarmé cultivated in his poetry a suggestive indefiniteness, blurring the distinctions between the actual world and that of dream and reverie. Debussy's translation into music of Mallarmé's

L'Après-midi d'un faune wonderfully conveys the poet's evocative art.

Mallarmé and his followers imitated Poe's habit of conflating the perceptions of our various senses —Poe for example had written of " hearing " the coming of darkness—and they were especially concerned to capture in verse the rhythmical flow of music (they greatly admired that of Wagner), and came even to discard the classical Alexandrine of French verse in favour of an experimental *vers libre* (see **M10**).

What was the purpose of these attempts to create a new kind of poetry? The Symbolists, preoccupied with the unique quality of individual experience and with the complex, evanescent nature of consciousness, wished to eschew anything so commonplace as a description or statement, for these " falsified " experience. Instead they sought to express unique transitory feelings by evocative images and symbols, fastidiously chosen and patterned with exquisite care. Thus, as the time-honoured rational framework of poetry was being scrapped, it became irrelevant to speak of a poem's " meaning ".

(d) *The problem of objective validity in Symbolist art.* The symbols adopted by the New French poets were not of the commonly accepted kind, such as the dove with the olive branch. Each poet deployed a highly idiosyncratic symbolism peculiar to himself, in order to express his own intensely personal feelings. Such symbols were, as Wilson says, really " metaphors detached from their subjects ". Inevitably such poetry is not easy to interpret, and the basic problem for the Symbolist poet is to find an imagery both true to his own experience and also in some way significant and communicable.

(e) *Hulme and the Imagists.* In England the Symbolists' experiments were to be fused with a new conception of poetry more Classical than Romantic in character. It was first expounded by the influential literary journalist T. E. Hulme (1883–1917).

" I object even to the best of the Romantics," he said. " I object still more to the sloppiness which doesn't consider that a poem is a poem unless it is whining or moaning about something or other." Hulme called for a tougher, more disciplined verse of a " dry hardness " that captured " the exact curve of the thing." Above all, he was asking for poets to apply a clear, cool intelligence to their art rather than to use it to indulge in the expression of warm, soft-hearted (or, as he might have said, " soft-headed ") feelings.

Taken up by a group who called themselves the Imagists, led for a time by Pound (its members included D. H. Lawrence and the influential American poetess Amy Lowell), Hulme's ideas were to have a revolutionary effect upon poetry and criticism on both sides of the Atlantic.

THE INDIVIDUAL POETS.

Thomas Hardy (1840–1928).

References are to the *Collected Poems* (Macmillan).

The fact that Hardy was unaffected by the Imagists' ideas (though Pound said he had learned much from Hardy) is the chief reason why he is sometimes thought of as either a minor twentieth-century poet or a minor Victorian one. Yet, in his best verse, though it is Romantic in character, Hardy too captures " the exact curve " of experience with a precision and " toughness " quite foreign to the Victorian poets of his youth and middle-age. It is this combination of Romantic feeling and precise, cool art, together with his rejection of the " myth kitty " so favoured by his younger contemporaries, that has led to Hardy's becoming the " master " of more recent poets such as Larkin and Gunn (*qq.v.*).

Of Dorset working-class stock, Hardy, the eldest child of a successful mason, became an architect before, in 1873, abandoning that profession to devote himself to a full-time literary career. His early verses having been rejected by periodicals, until he was verging on sixty Hardy concentrated on writing novels, though he thought of himself primarily as a poet and during the last three decades of his life was to publish nearly 1,000 poems, most of them short lyrics.

The life from which these novels and poems sprang has been vividly illuminated in Gittings's biography (2 vols. 1975 & 78). Encouraged by his parents, and by his friend Moule, the scholarson of a local parson, Hardy in his youth devoted most of his spare time to a stringent programme of self-education. However, as a talented amateur musician he also played in the " stringband " that, led by his father, provided the music for local dances, weddings and parties. Although his family's traditional role as musicians with the church choir had ended in his early childhood, Hardy was also well versed in church music, including Brady and Tate's versions of the psalms sung to traditional tunes. He also had a wide knowledge of Dorset airs and ballads, learned not only from his father's and grandfather's music books, but also from his paternal grandmother. This heritage of music, folk song and folk-lore seems to lie behind many of Hardy's most successful lyrics, such as the haunting *During the Wind and Rain* (*Moments of Vision and Miscellaneous Poems*), and much of his best work has a ballad-like simplicity and directness that stands in vivid contrast both to the lush charm of the Aesthetes' verse and to the enamelled beauty of Tennyson.

Hardy himself said he aimed to give his work " poetic texture rather than poetic veneer." The technical problems of prosody fascinated him and he sought to give his poems the spontaneous character that he felt to be the *sine qua non* of true art, by introducing " cunning irregularities " of stress and rhythm into his metres. He constantly experimented with new stanza forms.

Hardy's metrical skill is only now beginning to be appreciated, and while in weaker verses, such as *Lines to a Movement in Mozart's E Flat Symphony* (*Moments of Vision and Miscellaneous Poems*), his experiments can seem contrived, the craft of a dedicated technician rather than the art of a true poet, in other works, such as *The Voice*, *The Walk*, *After a Journey* (*Poems of 1912–13*), the form and content of Hardy's verses are united with exquisite art.

Although Hardy wrote quite a lot of " public " verse, including a fine narrative on the loss of the *Titanic* (*Convergence of the Twain*), most of his greatest work is to be found in the *Poems 1912–13*, written after the death of his first wife. Throughout his poems, however, from the time of his early, prentice work, in verses such as *Neutral Tones* (*Wessex Poems and Other Verses*) written in 1867, Hardy shows his genius for expressing the essence of a brief incident in his personal life in such a way as to give it general and lasting significance. His work is often praised for its honesty and sincerity, but while such poems do seem both honest and sincere this in itself cannot account for their power.

This power seems rather to derive from Hardy's extraordinarily penetrating awareness of the ambivalent emotions inherent in any human relationship, combined with a technical expertise that enables him to explore and express these feelings in intensely moving yet beautifully pellucid verse.

W. B. Yeats (1865–1939).

References are to the *Collected Poems* (Macmillan).

Yeats's influence is exerted not by the limp, romantic Celtic twilight verses written during his membership of the Aesthetes' Rhymers Club and published between 1889 and 1904, but by the complex, sinewy poems appearing between 1910 and 1939. Although in traditional verse forms, they established Yeats as a great master of the modern symbolic image. Indeed, there are many critics who consider him to be by far the greatest poet of our time, because the variety and range of his work far exceeds that of not only Hardy, but also of Pound and Eliot.

Brought up by a father of sceptical mind, Yeats had sought from early youth for some significance to life in " heterodox mysticism ", such as theosophy and the Kabbala, and above all in Blake. Their highly developed systems of symbols stimulated his innate sensitiveness to this intuitive form of insight and expression and encouraged him to develop his gift for waiting on images as they arose from the deeper regions of his mind. Arthur Symons, whose *The Symbolist Movement in Literature* was published in 1899, introduced him to the work of Mallarmé and other French Symbolists, and confirmed him in his poetic approach which he now realised was part of a European movement.

To give objective validity to highly subjective images he used several techniques. Following Shelley's example, he would repeat the same symbol throughout the body of his work, so that one poem illuminates another. The symbol thus seen in perspective reveals new facets of its significance, sometimes even contradictory aspects.

For example, in early poems the rose signifies not only love and, in its Rosicrucian form, a mystic union, but also Ireland, beauty both sensuous and intellectual, and the beauty of Maud Gonne, with whom Yeats remained hopelessly in love.

A ruined Norman tower which Yeats had converted into a dwelling recurs from 1919 in many poems. Its basic significance is the artist's isolation, but it also suggests Milton's Platonist, Shelley's " visionary prince ", Samuel Palmer's " lonely light ", and Yeats's own Anglo-Irish heritage. He was greatly concerned to give the symbol solidity and firm outline and stresses the tower's emblematic " winding, gyring, spiring treadmill of a stair " and the " grey stone fireplace with an open hearth " and the " fire of turf " of simple hospitality.

He juxtaposed exalted symbols with the singularly down-to-earth motifs which he deployed with increasing frequency. The indignity of age is " a sort of battered kettle at the heel," or " a tattered coat upon a stick " until in his emblematic protagonist, " Crazy Jane," he presents the ultimate in physical destitution inspired by poetic frenzy.

Yeats also relied on archetypal images from the " Great Memory," to which we respond unconsciously. In *The Two Trees* (p. 54), he follows Blake in his use of the image of the tree, which develops from the Kabbala and the Biblical Tree of Life. To Yeats it came to embody the organic nature both of all life and of the imagination, or reality intuitively perceived by the artist as whole and vital. Yeats, like Blake, contrasted this imaginative vision with the abstractions of the discursive intellect and his most perfect expression of the work of art as an organic and indissoluble unit occurs at the climax of *Among School Children*. Here in a passage of multiple import he marries the image of the tree to that of the dance.

" O chestnut-tree, great-rooted blossomer,
Are you the leaf, the blossom or the bole?
O body swayed to music, O brightening glance,
How can we know the dancer from the dance? "

Yeats's poetry was also supported by a framework of mythology, whether of Gaelic legend, Greek mythology, as in *Leda and the Swan*, or, as in much of his more mature work, that of his own private system, which he expounded in his prose *A Vision*, 1926. For instance, he saw history as opposing cycles of 2000 years, each cycle being a reversal of the previous one. He represented this diagramatically by opposing " gyres ", his gyre being the spiral traced on a cone.

But Yeats's finest poems, even when the meaning depends on his private hinterland, are still valid and intelligible in themselves. *The Second Coming* affects us through the singular clarity and force of the metaphors and the controlled energy of the rhythm:

" . . . somewhere in sands of the desert
A shape with lion body and the head of a man,
A gaze blank and pitiless as the sun,
Is moving its slow thighs, while all about it
Reel shadows of the indignant desert birds.
The darkness drops again; but now I know
That twenty centuries of stony sleep
Were vexed to nightmare by a rocking cradle,
And what rough beast, its hour come round at last,
Slouches towards Bethlehem to be born? "

Yeats is the poet of paradox and often quoted Blake, " Without contraries there is no progression." His own life was one of manifold tensions, especially between contemplation and his active participation in Irish politics and art. (He was Production Manager of the Abbey Theatre and was made a Senator.)

A dominant theme is the dichotomy between sensuous living and the creation of immortal works of art, the latter symbolised by Byzantium in two splendid poems. Here he rejects the " sensual music " of " whatever is begotten, born, and dies " or " the fury and the mire of human veins " for " monuments of unageing intellect," symbolised by Byzantium, with its gold mosaic, the starlit or the moonlit dome and the golden singing bird, a miracle, " in glory of changeless metal," (pp. 217, 280).

Yet in the contemporary *Dialogue of Self and Soul*, p. 265, the poet opts for life, however sordid.

" I am content to live it all again
And yet again, if it be life to pitch
Into the frog-spawn of a blind man's ditch,"

Paradoxically the splendour of Yeats is the unresolved conflict. In poem after poem he passionately faces his dilemmas, personal, political, artistic, metaphysical, never to rest in a complacent final solution but forging instead enigmatic and arresting images of universal experience.

Ezra Pound (1885–1972).

Born in the American mid-west, a nephew of the popular nineteenth-century poet Longfellow, Pound arrived in London in 1908 and quickly set the literary world by its ears with his confidence. Not only did he dare to " correct " the work of Yeats, even more astonishing, Yeats was prepared to accept this stripling's advice, becoming the first of several, including T. S. Eliot, who admitted their debt to Pound's acute literary judgement. Pound's incorrigible didacticism, his boundless self-confidence might, and did, make him enemies; but his exuberance, his voracious intellect, his passionate dedication to literature had magnetic power.

Pound quickly associated himself with the poets inspired by Hulme's Classical ideals, the Imagists —a name he is credited with inventing—but soon came to feel that their aims were too limited and frigid. He dismissed them as Amygists—besotted dependants of the rich American poetess Amy Lowell (in this he was—as often—less than fair).

His own catholic tastes and wide reading led Pound to find his inspiration in sources as diverse as Browning's dramatic monologues, the Romance poets of medieval Provence, Anglo-Saxon epics and not only classical Greek and Latin but even Chinese verse. Pound's renderings, or, more accurately, his re-creations of such earlier poems into modern English aroused the astonished scorn of those trained in a Classical tradition that regarded the texts as sacrosanct mummies. They assumed that he could not construe the Latin when, in his first major poem *Homage to Sextus Propertius* (1917) he rendered the Roman poet's *Cimbrorum . . . minas et benefacta Mari* (" the challenge of the Cimbrians and the services of

Marius ") as " Welsh mines and the profits Marius had out of them." His daring puns, turning *in flagrante delicto* into " fragrant delight " and *ars musica* into " bum fiddle ", outraged the critics, who, it seems, had forgotten that Augustan poets —and, even earlier, Ben Jonson—had used Classical texts in a very similar way, both as a source of inspiration and to give added point and resonance to their satires on contemporary society.

Pound's later work includes *Hugh Selwyn Mauberly* (1920), generally considered his masterpiece, and the series of poems on which he was engaged for the rest of his long life, *The Cantos.* In both, the " raw material " includes a multiplicity of references to literature, art and history and many quotations in other languages. Particularly in *The Cantos* these can involve much research for the reader, who may well feel, with Leavis, that, even when they have been tracked down, the references have " no significant effect." The value remains private to the author." Leavis contrasts Pound's " pedantic games " in *The Cantos* with Eliot's use of allusion and quotation in *The Waste Land* (**M** 20). In the latter poem they are deployed in such a way as to be effective even for the reader who may not understand their full significance.

Pound's equivalent to *The Waste Land* is *Hugh Selwyn Mauberly*, and the two poems are not dissimilar in their themes, though differing in their tone and in the poet's treatment of the themes.

Pound, like Shelley before him, seems to have been convinced that poets " are the unacknowledged legislators of the world." In *Mauberly* he offers his critique of late-nineteenth- and early-twentieth-century England in which only minor art is valued. At once satiric and tragic, the poem is a remarkable achievement, wholly original, yet firmly rooted in the great literary art of the past that Pound sought (and here succeeded) in re-creating.

The poem takes the form of a dramatic monologue divided into two parts, of which the first is the longer. Entitled " E. P. Ode pour l'Election de son Sepulchre ", it comprises thirteen short sections, the first twelve being Mauberly's meditations occasioned by E.P.'s (Pound's) decision to leave England. The thirteenth and final section inspired by Waller's *Go Lovely Rose* (OBEV 295) quotes E.P.'s exquisite " valediction ". In the second part, " Mauberly ", of five sections, the first four are Mauberly's thoughts on his own career, the fifth is his " great work " the " Medallion " in which he enshrines the face of his Venus beneath a " glaze ". Thus the two parts of the poem stand in ironic contrast one to the other. Mauberly, patronisingly dismissing E.P. as " No adjunct to the Muses' diadem ", yet, aware of the failures, shabby compromises and delusions of his immediate predecessors and contemporaries, nevertheless dooms himself to a living death as an artist.

Pound's work has attracted the attentions of a host of critics and explicators. Readers are particularly referred to Chapter IV of F. R. Leavis's *New Bearings in English Poetry* (1932), T. S. Eliot's " Introduction " to Pound's *Selected Poems* (1928) and Donald Davie's *Ezra Pound: Poet as Sculptor* (1965).

T. S. Eliot (1888–1965).

The poems referred to are contained in *Collected Poems 1909–1962* (Faber).

Eliot, by some years the youngest child of his American parents, grew up in the town of St. Louis, on the Mississippi River. The family also had a house on the New England coast, at Cape Anne. Here, the young Eliot spent his summer holidays. Many of his most vivid lines and images derive from memories of these childhood scenes. It is through the dingy backstreets of St. Louis that Prufrock makes his way to the drawing room where the local bourgoisie talk vapidly of Michelangelo. The river of *Dry Salvages*, whose rhythm was " present in the

nursery bedroom " is the Mississippi, and the Dry Salvages themselves rocks off the coast of Cape Anne. But we do not need to have seen the Mississippi to feel the force of the river which pulsates through the lines of *Dry Salvages*, nor to have seen " the ragged rock in the restless waters " to appreciate its significance as an image of abiding agony. Similarly, although Eliot was scholarly and exceptionally well-read, familiar with several languages, it is not essential that we share his scholarship in order to enjoy his poetry, any more than we need to share Milton's or Pope's knowledge of the Classics before enjoying their work, but our appreciation is greatly enhanced by some knowledge of the sources of their inspiration. Eliot draws particularly upon his reading of Dante, Shakespeare, Jacobean literature and the anthropological work of J. S. Fraser and Jessie Weston. The interested reader will find other suggestions to pursue in B. S. Southam's *A Student's Guide to the Selected Poems of T. S. Eliot.*

In Eliot's poems unity is achieved not by a framework of narrative or sensory description or even a logical sequence of thought, but by imaginative association where several layers of thought and feeling are fused. Like Milton, he is a poet who needs to be read aloud, for much of the import of his verse is expressed through its infinitely varied music.

Eliot gives his intensely subjective vision general significance by appealing not only or primarily to the literary experience of the educated, but to the general experience of twentieth-century man; to a sense of the futility and horror of the city's " strained time-ridden faces " in streets where " men and bits of paper " are " whirled by the cold wind ", images counterpointed by others of delicate beauty, evoking life's rare and unaccountable moments of ecstasy and insight,

" Whisper of running streams and winter lighting
  The wild thyme unseen and the wild strawberry ".

There were two decisive influences upon Eliot's poetic development. The first was his discovery of the French Symbolist poets, to which he was led in 1908 by his reading of Symond's *The Symbolist Movement in Literature.* The other was his meeting with Ezra Pound in 1914. Pound not only helped him to find publishers for his work, but provided the stimulus of a discerning, critical audience.

Eliot's first book of poems, *Prufrock and Other Observations* appeared in 1917. The title poem offers a good introduction both to Eliot's allusive, kaleidoscopic style and to themes and attitudes which reappear in his later work. Although *The Love Song of J. Alfred Prufrock* is a dramatic monologue owing something to Browning, it offers no clear discursive framework to guide the reader, who is required to respond to shifting scenes and moods which cohere by force of the feelings inherent in them.

The poem's title suggests something at once conventional and rather comic, while the prefatory quotation from Dante's *L'Inferno* leads us towards the poem's profounder implications. The character of Prufrock's city and of his own life is established immediately through a startling image of suspended animation—

" . . . the evening is spread out against the sky
  Like a patient etherised upon a table ".

The correlation between the exterior scene and Prufrock's interior state is made more explicit as he and " you "—possibly the reader, possibly a young woman—make their way through a maze of sordid streets

" . . . that follow like a tedious argument
  Of insidious intent
  To lead you to an overwhelming question . . .''

a question which is at once the proposal of marriage Prufrock dare not utter and a question of the very significance of his life and that of the social circle in which he moves.

Images of loneliness, futility, sensual attraction and suspended animation appear throughout the poem. The city is shrouded in fog and yellow smoke, at once sensual as a cat and yet stifling, suggestive of Baudelaire's Unreal City. "Lonely men in shirt sleeves" lean out of windows at dusk. The afternoon and evening sleep "smoothed by long fingers".

Prufrock attends a party, feeling at once nervously self-conscious, ready to run away, "I have seen the eternal Footman hold my coat, and snicker," and yet also complacent, "My necktie rich and modest, but asserted by a simple pin". He imagines himself as a modish gallant, the cynosure of all eyes, but wryly admits, "I am no Prince Hamlet". Nor is he a John the Baptist, fearlessly expressing a vital message, but a Lazarus who has not experienced the miracle of resurrection and who therefore cannot "tell you all". He has heard the bewitching song of the mermaids, "But I do not think that they will sing to me." He can only envisage himself walking, in "white flannel trousers" upon the margin of the vital sea of life and love. Drifting into a dream of sensuous bliss "we" are suddenly woken by the deadly voice of his everyday world and "drown."

The same loneliness and sense, not only of failure but of there being nothing worth succeeding in, is expressed in *Gerontion* which Eliot considered publishing as a "prelude" or preface to *The Waste Land*. This meditation on approaching death is inconclusive.

"I would meet you upon this honestly",

but if the speaker is not sure what death means he is even less sure of the meaning or value of human life. The references to "windy spaces" (line 15) and

"Gull against the wind, in the windy straits"

suggest Claudio's speech on the terrifying prospect of existence after life has ended, in *Measure for Measure*. The quotation at the head of *Gerontion* comes from the Duke's speech in that play when he tries to steel Claudio's nerve for his coming execution by proving that life is not worth having. Eliot's Old Man seems to agree, but the Duke's Christian assurance, for he is disguised as a friar, evokes no response in him for Christ, the Word, cannot communicate through the swaddling darkness. Whatever the crucifixion may have once meant has been adulterated beyond recognition and there is nothing to replace it.

The *Waste Land*, published in 1922, established Eliot as a major figure on the contemporary scene. Some reviewers thought it a literary hoax because of the elaborate use of allusion and quotation in several languages as well as the lack of any formal structure. But Sir Robert Birley has said how exciting he and his contemporaries found the poem, "no other . . . written in my lifetime has made so great and immediate an impact . . . here was someone who could give expression to our own deep, but hardly understood, doubts and uncertainties and do this in language of unforgettable beauty." Eliot himself dismissed his poem as simply "the relief of a personal and wholly insignificant grouse against life." The recent publication of the original manuscripts of *The Waste Land* together with the comments of Pound and Eliot's first wife, Vivien, and his own alterations to the drafts, give fascinating insight into the way this "piece of rhetorical grumbling" was pruned of its purely personal elements and the private vision transformed to express "the plight of a whole generation."

The poem impresses one with a sense of disillusion and anti-climax. The old pre-war Edwardian world has been destroyed, perhaps it was never very satisfactory, but there seems to be nothing to replace it. The theme is repeated at intervals throughout, in different ways; sometimes as a dead land where the sun beats, a place where the cisterns are empty, the wells exhausted, an empty chapel with dry bones. The crowds on London Bridge walking through the fog are dead, for each is locked within himself. The modern Cleopatra seated in her burnished chair is surrounded by erotic symbols, but the romantic suggestion of the gold Cupidon is disturbed by *synthetic* perfume and destroyed by recollection of the rape of Philomel. This "Cleopatra's" life is pointless and unreal; she can only look forward to a game of chess. At the other end of the social scale there is the prostitution of personal relationship to the level of having a "good time" and instead of new life, abortion. "The nymphs are departed" indeed.

But at the end there is perhaps some hope in

"The awful daring of a moment's surrender
Which an age of prudence can never retract".

In 1927 Eliot became an Anglican. His poems, *Ash Wednesday*, *Journey of the Magi*, *A Song for Simeon*, reflect his new belief and his gift for using allusion is directed towards Christian sources. Thus in *Ash Wednesday* single lines from well-known prayers and responses from the Ave Maria and The Reproaches of the Catholic Good Friday service are used technically in the same way that the repeated and echoed phrases in earlier poems are used to give unity; and as the phrases that Eliot uses are ones that are frequently repeated in the liturgy of the church, the poem provides, for some readers, a kind of ceremony, but this peculiarly Christian imagery excludes others. The generally accessible and most successful parts of the poem are not direct expressions of Christian experience but haunting, dream-like images,

"Lady, three white leopards sat under a juniper
                        tree
In the cool of the day "

and the expression of general human desire such as that for absolution and a tranquil mind,

"Teach us to care and not to care
Teach us to sit still ".

Eliot's major work after this is *Four Quartets*, where he is concerned with the philosopher poet's experience of time, language and salvation. Helen Gardner has remarked how, whereas *Ash Wednesday* moves from personal experience to "the ageless prayer of the church," in *Four Quartets* the non-Christian and Christian experiences "suddenly touch . . . we see that what the poet has been speaking of is what Christians speak of in another language." These poems, unlike *Ash Wednesday*, give *generally* meaningful expression to human experience.

Four Quartets are full of paradoxes and though a progression of thought may be traced in the four, each Quartet may be read as a unity in itself. The mood of the second Quartet, *East Coker*, is sombre and the fear of nothingness, the dissatisfaction with the "shabby equipment" of contemporary language recalls parts of *The Waste Land*; but the fourth, *Little Gidding*, named after the home of a seventeenth-century community of Anglican mystics, is more hopeful

" All manner of thing shall be well."

Considerable time needs to be spent on these poems if the complexity of the thought is to be appreciated, but the pattern of the verses, the delicate manipulation of the metre may be enjoyed by the reader who is prepared to listen carefully. Helen Gardner's study of the poems, *The Making of " Four Quartets "* (1978), is highly recommended.

LATER BRITISH POETRY.

Poets of the Thirties.

By popular tradition, the English poetic of the thirties was dominated by W. H. Auden and his trio of friends Stephen Spender (b. 1909), C. Day Lewis (1904–72), and Louis MacNeice (1907–63). As they grew older, these young writers developed their own distinctive styles and with the passage of time it became clear that Auden, who had always seemed their leader, indeed stood head and shoulders above the rest. We have also learned better to appreciate the talents of such independent and distinctive poets as the colourful Roy

Campbell (1902–54) and the highly-talented, ironic art of William Empson (b. 1906). Apart from Auden, however, the most important new poet of the thirties was his younger contemporary Dylan Thomas (*q.v.*).

Most poets of the time (Thomas was an exception) shared a desire, fostered by the Spanish Civil War and the Depression, to make poetry more explicitly concerned with contemporary issues than Eliot seemed to. They found inspiration in the posthumously published poems of the Victorian Jesuit Gerard Manley-Hopkins (1844–89), whose work showed the possibility of incorporating direct references to ethical and social ideals and dilemmas while avoiding both sententious moralising and cheap sentimentality.

Manley-Hopkins's influence was also important because his revolutionary technical innovations suggested new possibilities for using elaborate imagery and stanza forms while yet abandoning traditional prosody. He thus indicated an alternative to Eliot's free verse. Nonetheless, Eliot, and behind Eliot the metaphysical poets of the seventeenth century, remained a powerful influence on the verse of most writers of this period.

W. H. Auden (1907–73).

Collected Poems (Faber).

Auden's first book, *Poems* (1930) signalled the advent of a new voice in English poetry, at once farcical and tragic. Its target was the futility of the middle-class way of life in which Auden had been born and educated.

In his early verse, a penchant for clowning combined with an uncertain control of his material means that his poems tend to stumble uneasily between obscure private symbolism, explicit reference to public events, to Freudian and Marxist theory, erudite allusion to the history and art of the past. By the time of *Look Stranger* (1936) his style has become more disciplined and assured.

Auden's interest in politics and the violence of political struggle is reflected in much of the imagery he uses, as well as more directly in such different poems as *The Shield of Achilles* and *Alfonso to Ferdinand*. An early successful example of his political verse is *Let History Be My Judge*, inspired by the enforced collectivisation of Russian agriculture. However, this is only referred to indirectly and, were it not for the poem's date, we would not necessarily associate it with the Russian policy. It is equally meaningful as an indictment of the harsh repression of any popular uprising or of the invasion of a defenceless country. The poem ironically highlights the callous and cynical self-justification of those who hold power and impose their will upon the ignorant and defenceless.

After his emigration to the States in 1939, the character of Auden's verse gradually changes, moving away from its earlier preoccupation with social problems towards a more personal stance, influenced by his formal adoption of the Christian faith.

Some of his most successful poems date from the early 1940s. They include a beautifully-controlled meditation on suffering, *Musée des Beaux Arts*. Yet, despite the success of such poems and of the fine later sequence inspired by *The Tempest*, Auden never seemed to fulfil his early promise. The verse of his last years in collections like *About the House* is seldom more than eloquent chatter— an immensely skilled professional performance, but with little below its gleaming surface charm.

Dylan Thomas (1914–53).

Collected Poems (Dent).

In many ways Thomas's poems are the antithesis of Auden's. Politically uncommitted and hardly touched by social concerns, his work has none of Auden's intellectual force. Its kinship lies with the visionary poets such as Blake and Southwell rather than the witty metaphysicals. Thomas's immediate mentor was Yeats, yet he reserved his chief admiration for Hardy. An obsessive experimenter, who sometimes seemed as drunk on words as he was on liquor, Thomas is nevertheless a most talented and dedicated craftsman and his effects are usually carefully engineered.

His use of language, though much imitated, remains immediately recognisable. He deploys cosmic symbols: sun, heaven, stars, sea, fire, wind; organic images: womb, bird, blood; vivid colours: green, gold, red, blue, black. Much of his verse, though sometimes overloaded with images, evokes kaleidoscopic pictures, and its rhythmical metrical patterns often have an almost incantatory effect. This is intensified by his use of biblical images and the formal sound patterns of assonance and alliteration as well as rhymes.

The theme of much of Thomas's poetry is the unity of creation: human and divine intermingle, flesh and spirit are indivisible and the world we inhabit is not essentially different from ourselves:

" The force that through the green fuse drives the
                                                flower
Drives my green age; that blasts the roots of
                                                trees
Is my destroyer.

The inevitability of death is, however, the dominating theme of Thomas's work, not only incipient in birth but even in love:

" The word flowed up, translating to the heart
First characters of birth and death."

In some poems, such as *And death shall have no dominion* and *A Refusal to Mourn*, he accepts its inevitability. In others he seeks to defy it:

" Do not go gentle into that good night.
Old age should burn and rave at close of day."

At his best, Thomas produced rapturous, wholly unsentimental, celebrations of childhood: *Fern Hill*, *Poem in October*, *Over Sir John Hill*. It is on these and on a handful of occasional poems, together with his extraordinarily effective radio play *Under Milk Wood* that Thomas's literary reputation rests.

The full power of his work is best appreciated when it is read aloud, and the Caedmon group have made very good recordings of Thomas's own readings.

OTHER IMPORTANT POETS OF THE INTER-WAR PERIOD.

Standing apart from both Eliot and the talented young poets who hit the literary headlines in the thirties is a handful of distinguished older writers, Sitwell, Graves, and Muir.

Sitwell's penchant for publicity early gained her notice, but made as many enemies as friends, while the quieter, highly individual talents of Graves and Muir were so different from those of both Eliot and Auden, on the one hand, and Thomas, on the other, that, failing to catch the eye of influential critics, they had long to wait for recognition.

Edith Sitwell (1887–1964).

In *The Scarlet Tree* Sir Osbert Sitwell vividly describes his sister's early background. She was saturated in English poetry, read Baudelaire at the age of seventeen and her governess, Helen Rootham, translator of Rimbaud, became her lifelong friend.

Sitwell interprets her early verses in *Façade*, 1922, as " abstract patterns in sound " written in reaction against " rhythmical flaccidity " and " verbal deadness." She experimented indefatigably with the effect on rhythm and speed of subtle and elaborate patterns of rhyme, assonance and dissonance, successfully capturing dance rhythms. Some verses were set to music by Walton and accompany the well-known ballet.

Like the French Symbolist writer de l' Isle Adam (author of *Axel*) Sitwell also deliberately juxtaposed words that " clash in a protesting combination ". She adopted the synaesthesia practised by Poe and the French Symbolists, transferring the language of one sensation to indicate the experiences of another, as when morning light appears as " creaking " or " whining ". In later poems we find such phrases as " the dust brays ", or " purple perfumes of the polar Sun ", repeated from Rootham's Rimbaud.

Elegant and mannered, the butterfly verses of *Façade* lack inner significance yet they gave Sitwell the expertise to express intense feeling in her later poetry.

Gold Coast Customs, 1929, is the counterpart of Eliot's *Waste Land*. Both express the poet's revulsion from modern society by finding an objective parallel in primitive ritual. Sitwell, writing during the Depression, was most dismayed by the heartlessness of the city, which she images through the bygone Customs in Ashantee, where once at the death of an important person hundreds of the poor were butchered that their blood might lave his bones. This " Reeling appalling/Cannibal mart " symbolises the contemporary sacrifice of the poor demanded by the spiritually dead, epitomised by Lady Bamburger, " smart plague-cart ", massively indifferent to the destitution of the slums, where driven by " Want, a cruel rat gnawing there " the pathetic prostitutes, " The calico dummies/Flap and meet ".

The ghastly Customs, the desolate slums violently alternate and reflect each other in the kaleidoscope of nightmare, relentlessly maintained by the rhythm of savage drum beat and fevered pulse.

Although the metre and repetitive phrasing have an obsessive monotony, the impact of the poem which foretells " the sick thick smoke from London burning," is unforgettable.

In *Street Songs*, 1942, Sitwell was in command of images of arresting clarity. Two poems on the Raids are incidentally a clear vindication of Symbolist technique for both are extended " metaphors detached from their subjects ".

In the ironic *Lullaby* of despair the Pterodactyl, " the steel bird " which " fouls its nest ", has devastated the earth and only the Baboon is left to mother the surviving child.

Still Falls the Rain boldly uses the superbly simple image of rain, heavy reiteration, and a thudding, tolling rhythm, stressing the dark monosyllables:

" Still falls the Rain—
Dark as the world of man, black as our loss—
Blind as the nineteen hundred and forty nails
Upon the Cross."

It is a poem of profound and universal compassion for man and beast and also of religious faith, for the Rain is also Christ's blood shed in suffering, love and illumination.

In later publications Sitwell develops the long ode written from the vantage of the poet-seer matured by suffering. Like Yeats she was now giving her work coherence by playing variations on key symbols. Some images appear strained but the most effective are drawn from familiar sources, as the Bible, history, myth and mankind's most primitive experiences—of sun, earth, beasts, grain, fruit, metals, and of cold and warmth, always emblematic for her of evil and good. On these she sets her idiomatic stamp.

She constantly opposes two kinds of gold. In *Harvest* she celebrates the warm gold of the " laughing heat of the Sun " and " the ripe-bearded fire/Of wheat," reflecting divine energy and love. In *The Song of the Cold*, 1945, she laments the lust for the cold, destructive metal that possesses Dives and " the saints of Mammon," who

" ache with the cold/From the polar wastes of the heart", the cold of hell.

Deeply shaken by Hiroshima, Sitwell wrote *The Shadow of Cain*, 1947. The theme of the title poem is fission and envisages Mankind's migration into the Cold, from Cain's first murder up to Hiroshima, when " the Primal Matter/Was broken," and " to the murdered Sun a totem pole arose of dust in memory of Man." The crisis stirs an obscure prescience of impending calamity, of a profound fission between the two aspects of Man: Lazarus embodiment of gold corn and human suffering and Dives of money and defilement. But the two golds fight and finally unite in a new resolution and hope.

This visionary poem is sometimes declamatory and the bleak *Dirge for the New Sunrise*, with its terse antitheses, is more immediate and moving.

After *The Shadow of Cain*, " haunted ever by the shadow that fell on Hiroshima," she yet continued to write poems that are " hymns of praise to the glory of Life."

Edwin Muir (1887–1959).

Collected Poems (Faber).

Although his first poems appeared in 1925, Muir's work did not achieve any general recognition until the early fifties. One reason for this was the longish intervals between his books of verse, but more important was the fact that, like Graves, he was unaffected by the new " Franco-American modernism." Two books which cast invaluable light upon his career are his own *Autobiography* (1954) and his wife's *Belonging* (1968).

After an idyllic childhood in the Orkneys, where traditional songs, ballads and fairy-tales were still a vital part of people's everyday lives, Muir's adolescence was darkened by his parents' enforced emigration to a Glasgow flat in the winter of 1901–2. Within a year his father was dead, and by the age of eighteen Muir had also lost not only his mother, who died of cancer, but two of his older brothers, one succumbing to T.B., the other to a brain tumour.

Alone in Glasgow, working as an ill-paid clerk, first in a bottling factory and later in a Greenock bone-yard, Muir took refuge in Guild Socialism and in the writings of Heine and Nietzsche. Later, after his marriage, he and his wife were to live in Czechoslovakia, Germany and Italy both before and after the Second World War. They made friends with a number of leading writers, including the German Broch, and a major source of their income was translating, including the translation of Kafka's novels.

Thus were not only Muir's origins and early experiences—the stuff of his poetry—very different from those of other poets of his day, but his wide knowledge and love of continental literature was centred in Germany and Eastern Europe rather than in France.

A visionary poet of compelling power, though limited range, Muir drew his inspiration not only from the world of his Orkney childhood but also from the vivid dreams he began to experience after a period of psychoanalysis had enabled him to start to come to terms with the repressed horror and anguish of his Glasgow years.

His themes are the age-old conflict of good and evil, man's fall from grace and his quest to recapture visionary insight. Muir distinguishes firmly between sentimental nostalgia for the past—expressed in his poems by misty landscapes—and the clarity of the visionary " Eden " in which " all stands revealed." Personal intuitions are given general force and vigour by his use of Biblical and classical imagery as well as Orkney myth and history. One of his most successful early poems is the *Ballad of Hector in Hades*, which images Hector's tormented ghost as he relives his flight from Achilles waiting in terror for the moment when he is caught and slain. As that moment comes, he is suddenly released from fear.

" The race is ended. Far away
    I hang and do not care,
While round bright Troy Achilles whirls
    A corpse with streaming hair."

Muir's command of language is not always equal to his themes, and in some poems private intuitions have not been fully expressed and communicated, but in his best work, and particularly in the collection *One Foot in Eden* (1956), he combines the clear vision of Traherne with a compelling sense of the need to struggle in the "difficult land" of our times to retain a sense of creative love and hope.

Robert Graves (b. 1893).

Graves's early reputation was as the author of a memorable autobiographical account of life in the trenches—*Goodbye to All That* (1929)—and as a brilliantly idiosyncratic historical novelist—*I Claudius* and *Claudius the God* (both 1934).

The commercial success of these books enabled him to emigrate to Majorca, where he has mostly lived since the early thirties, following his own poetic bent with a confident disregard of fashionable opinion, rejecting " both the ornate Victorian tradition and the more recent but no less artificial Franco-American modernism."

Graves sees himself in the age-old tradition of the poetic bard, devotee of " the White Goddess ", muse of myth, of poetry and of love. He acknowledges a debt to Hardy, but his closest affinity is with the Cavalier poets of the early seventeenth century—Ben Jonson, Herrick and Marvell, lyrical poets of love who yet retain a sharply ironic eye for human foibles. He seems particularly akin to Jonson, though lacking Jonson's marvellous dramatic talent. In both an exquisite lyricism is allied with immense—often eccentric—learning, a relish for human quirkyness, belligerent self-confidence and complete dedication to his art.

Graves's later poetry is particularly concerned with themes of love, marriage and the paradoxical problems of human relationships, but his range extends from the hilarious comedy of *Welsh Incident* to the sardonic humour of *Beauty in Trouble*.

" Beauty in trouble flees to the good angel
    On whom she can rely
To pay her cab-fare, run a steaming bath,
    Poultice her bruised eye;

Will not at first, whether for shame or caution
    Her difficulty disclose;
Until he draws a cheque book from his plumage
    Asking how much she owes."

Quite different again are the wry bitterness of the prisoner's monologue *Certain Mercies*, the plangent beauty of *The Cool Web*, the highly-wrought simplicity of *The Chink*.

Like other prolific poets, Graves presents problems of selection for the reader new to his work. His own choice of his poems, published in Penguin Books, is recommended.

The " Movement " Poets.

Robert Conquest's anthology *New Lines*, 1956 (Macmillan), marks the next stage—sometimes called the " Movement "—in English poetry. In his introduction Conquest remarks that groups of poets typical of their decade were " presented to public fire by anthologies which took up definite positions." His anthology was prepared in the belief that " a genuine and healthy poetry of the new period has established itself." The main objections he makes to criticism published from the beginning of the Second World War is that it encouraged poets " to produce diffuse and sentimental verbiage or hollow technical pirouettes." The poets he chose, apart from being contemporary, have in common only the acceptance that " poetry is written by and for the whole man, intellect, emotions, senses and all," and on the technical side a " refusal to abandon rational structure and comprehensible language." However, in their reaction against the undisciplined expression of

emotion, the Movement poets tend to go to the opposite extreme. Their writing is highly intelligent and often witty, but generally seems more cerebral than truly imaginative, lacking the inspiration of passionate feeling. The wry self-mockery and hopelessness of much of Larkin's verse is typical of the work of the Movement as a whole, but some younger poets, notably Gunn and Hughes, who were early associated with the group, have gone on in another, more vigorous direction.

Philip Larkin (b. 1922).

The North Ship, 1945 (Fortune Press); *The Less Deceived*, 1955 (Marvell Press); *Whitsun Weddings*, 1964; *High Windows*, 1974 (both Faber)

After a volume of prentice-work, *The North Ship*, much indebted to Yeats, Larkin changed direction, adopting Hardy as his mentor. Compared with either of these older poets, his range is drastically limited and often characterised by a passively resigned distaste for contemporary life, the verse of the outsider now puzzled, now half-pitying half-despising the second and third-rate standards, the compromises and self-deceptions of those he watches: the dancers who " maul to and fro " in *Reasons for Attendance*, the kids " screaming for more " in the M1 café (*Going Going*), the youngsters making love in *High Windows*. "Loneliness clarifies " he says in *Here*, but the note of sour disenchantment, of having been cheated from the start in verses such as *I Remember, I Remember, This Be the Verse*, the sense that modern life is essentially a futile progression towards the emptiness of death (*Next Please, Vers de Société, High Windows*) is seldom lightened by any positive or hopeful note, even in such fine poems as *An Arundel Tomb*, where the passage of time is seen as having " transformed " the effigy—of wife and husband clasping hands—into " an untruth."

" The stone fidelity
    They hardly meant has come to be
Their blazon, and to prove
Our almost—instinct almost true:
What will survive of us is love."

Even here, the assurance of the closing line, with its confident rhythm, is undercut by the qualifications that precede it, and effectively deny its truth.

Larkin's highly accomplished verse is conventional in form, colloquial in tone. He seldom raises his voice or strives for an effect. This makes his occasional use of obscenities and four-letter words seem like assaults upon the reader.

Undoubtedly, he evokes a faithful image of aspects of modern Britain, where cows browse by " canals with floatings of industrial froth ", with its defaced posters and synthetic finery—the fake jewellery, nylon gloves and stores where " Modes for the Night "

" Lemon, sapphire, moss-green, rose
    Bri-Nylon Baby-Dolls and Shorties
    Flounce in rows."

Essentially, however, Larkin's negative vision seems minor, part of a particular generation's revolt against the changing culture of post-war Britain, a revolt Larkin shared with the Angry Young Men—his friends Amis and Wain—and also with such reactionaries as the playwright John Osborne (see Section I).

Thom Gunn (b. 1929).

Fighting Terms, 1954; *The Sense of Movement*, 1957; *My Sad Captains*, 1961; *Touch*, 1967; *Moly*, 1971 (Faber); *Jack Straw's Castle*, 1976.

At first glance Gunn's poetry seems as contemporary as the morning paper. Titles such as *On the Move*, subtitled *Man you gotta Go*, *Black Jackets*, *Elvis Presley*, suggest, rightly, that his poetry is rooted in the present, but not in such a way that it will be incomprehensible when the present has become the past. He is concerned with violence in the classical world in *The Wound* and *Helen's Rape*, in the sixteenth century in

A Mirror for Poets, and in the twentieth century in *Claus von Stauffenberg*, in personal relationships as well as public, but it is not an unthinking surrender to mere excitement or admiration of brutality, but a recognition of its necessity:

" In this society the boundaries met
  Of living, danger, death, leaving no space
  Between, ...
  . . . Yet at this point they found
  Arcadia, a fruitful permanent land."
                                    (*A Mirror for Poets*).

In *Saint Martin and the Beggar*, Martin, the saint of man, must learn to fight before he can " grow " and then without hesitating he halves his cloak to cover the beggar. He is justified because his action was natural. The tragedy of modern man lies in his inability to marry instinct, intention, and action:

" One joins the movement in a valueless world.
  . . . .
  At worst, one is in motion; and at best,
  Reaching no absolute, in which to rest,
  One is always nearer by not keeping still."
                                    (*On the Move*).

Ted Hughes (b. 1930).

The Hawk in the Rain, 1957; *Lupercal*, 1960; *Wodwo*, 1967; *Crow*, 1970, *Gaudette*, 1977. (Faber).

There is some similarity between the early poetry of Hughes and Gunn. Both worked in America; both developed a concise style to mirror the toughness of their attitude to experience, their refusal to make the rough places smooth.

This said, the differences become more apparent as their individuality becomes clearer. Hughes uses animals, in whom the primitive instinctual drives are more evident than in man, to symbolise human dilemmas, but his animals are far from being ciphers. In *Pike*, for instance, the pike exists in its own right and, since Hughes did collect animals in his boyhood, the incident

" Suddenly there were two. Finally one

With a sag belly and the grin it was born with "

is probably true. But the recollected " nightmare " at the end of the poem goes beyond a boy's terror. The pond he fished, the eye, the dream darkness are symbolic both of the violence which lay in his own subconscious and that of the human race. The human being too is potentially a killer from the egg.

In other poems Hughes is searching for an identity. In *An Otter*, the otter

" Gallops along land he no longer belongs to;
  Re-enters the water by melting."

At one level we have the hunt which loses and then finally catches the otter, but at another level there is the self, " attendant and withdrawn," the individual who " does not take root ".

In *Wodwo* Hughes moves away from naturalistic animal imagery. Here, his Ghost Crabs are the creatures of a nightmare, while the heroes of his two latest volumes *Crow* and *Gaudette* are mythical figures, the pitiful but Satanic embodiments of the poet's increasingly grim vision.

English Poetry in the 1960s and 70s.

Now the vogue for the " Liverpool sound " in pop music became a vogue for the " Liverpool sound " in pop verse. The voice of the Barrow Poet and many another itinerant bard, was raised in the pubs and cellars of the metropolis and the day of the Poet.y and Jazz Festival came upon us in the time of the Children of Albion (see the Penguin anthology of the same name, subtitled *Poetry of the Underground in Britain*, 1969).

Day Lewis became Poet Laureate and Graves, Blunden and Fuller followed Auden as the Oxford Professor of Poetry, but more people listened to reviewer and critic Alvarez as he proclaimed the eclipse of Larkin and the " genteel " Movement (*q.v.*) and extolled the greatness of the American Confessional school (*q.v.*). However, when *The*

Review, a leading poetry quarterly, recently asked some thirty-five American and British poets, critics and editors what they had found encouraging about the poetry of the last decade, the name most often referred to was Larkin's *Whitsun Weddings* and while the speakers clearly admired the work of Lowell and Plath they seemed equally impressed by that of two relatively unknown British poets, Geoffrey Hill and Peter Porter.

Geoffrey Hill (b. 1932).

For the Unfallen, 1959; *King Log*, 1968; *Mercian Hymns*, 1971. (André Deutsch).

Our understanding and appreciation of Hill's strikingly original poetry depends to some extent upon a knowledge of the Bible, of Classical and Celtic myth and of mediaeval history, but more upon a relish for the ironic ambiguities of words and a delight in sensuous imagery and verbal music, for, like Yeats and Eliot's, Hill's poetry captures our attention with its vivid word play and musical power. At first we may feel that we can glimpse only a shadow of the significance of poems like his *Funeral Hymns*, but gradually, as their images sink into our subconscious minds, their import becomes clearer, though often still tantalisingly ambiguous and elusive.

Even in his first book, *For the Unfallen* Hill's mastery of form and language strikes one immediately. He adapts and develops traditional metres, verse forms and rhyme schemes into new patterns and renews outworn metaphors, as if by a sleight of hand, sometimes altering their form, as when he writes of " the mouthy cave ", at others placing them in a context where their meaning becomes reverberatingly ambiguous, as in *The Guardians*. Here he speaks of the young who have been caught in a thunderstorm while sailing. The old watch and then " Quietly they wade the disturbed shore;/Gather the dead as the first dead scrape home."

As these brief examples also show, Hill has a vivid command of pictorial detail and verbal irony. His approach is usually oblique, as in the later poem, *September Song*, an elegy subtitled *born 19.6.32—departed 24.9.42*. It begins,

"Undesirable you may have been, untouchable
  you were not. Not forgotten
  or passed over at the proper time."

Hill's measured tone is so deceptively calm, his imagery so condensed that the full impact of his words is delayed, and thereby intensified as gradually we become aware of the multiple significance of " undesirable ", " untouchable ", " Not forgotten ", " passed over ", " proper time ", of the menace conveyed in the transition from the conditional to the indicative voice, of the clinching effect of the antithesis, enhanced by the run-on line and the counterpointed pattern of major and minor stresses, suddenly broken by the abrupt caesura following " not ".

Here, as elsewhere, Hill's work is profoundly disquieting in its effect. He writes of innocence and corruption, violence and sacrifice, suffering and abnegation of responsibility, suggesting that in these matters man is as he always has been, that past and present are one. Within the general moral concern in each book we may distinguish a particular underlying theme: In *For the Unfallen* it is " moral virtue ", in *King Log*, " matters of power and commandment".

The opening poems of *King Log* explore this theme in terms of the Classical age, of mediaeval Catholicism, sixteenth-century humanism, nineteenth-century Calvinism, twentieth-century Nazism and existentialism. The sense of the indivisibility of past and present which permeates the poems is most obvious in the opening *Ovid in the Third Reich*, more obliquely expressed in the splendid *Funeral Hymns*, a set of eight unrhymed sonnets inspired by the Wars of the Roses.

The second part of *King Log* places Hill's theme in a new perspective through a series of moving poems of rejected love, *The Songbook of Sebastian Arrurruz*. Arrurruz is an imaginary Spanish poet, his name intended to recall both St. Sebastian—martyred with arrows—and the word arrowroot, suggesting that the arrows of love which pierce the poet are centred in his own person. Arrurruz's songs are addressed to the wife who has deserted him, but even while yearning for her he acknowledges her freedom and independence.

The underlying theme of Hill's third book, *Mercian Hymns* unites the concern of the earlier volumes in an exploration of private and public morality. In this modern "epic" the mythmaking quality already apparent in *Funeral Hymns* and *The Songbook*, becomes more noticeable. Hill's hero is Offa, an eighth-century king of Mercia, here conceived of as the "presiding genius of the West Midlands, his dominion enduring" to the present day. Elements from primitive legend are used to suggest an even longer timespan by associating Offa with the British fertility god, the horned Cernunnos. The thirty stanzas of the poem, rich in pictorial detail and subtle irony and humour, cover such varied topics as childhood, money, laws, industry, war and death. Not the least remarkable aspect of this extraordinary poem is Hill's achievement in having created a completely new stanza form, inspired by the canticles of the early Christian church.

Peter Porter (b 1929).

Once Bitten, Twice Bitten, 1961; *Poems Ancient and Modern,* 1964; *A Porter Folio,* 1969. (Scorpion Press); *The Last of England,* 1970; *Preaching to the Converted,* 1972; *After Martial,* 1972; *Living in a Calm Country,* 1975. (Oxford University Press).

An Australian, Porter came to England in 1951 for "the opportunites which a common language gives to seek a wider frame of reference." He began as a satirist, but feels he is now moving towards a different position, an opinion supported by the increasingly complex and individual elegiac tone of recent poems.

In *The Sadness of the Creatures* Porter speaks of himself as "an historical cat", saying, "I run on rails". Both the forms and themes of his poems reveal his concern with "the continuity of the living and the dead . . . the only reality I can find in England". He has experimented with free verse but also uses and skilfully adapts traditional metres and verse forms.

Initially he may seem, as Eliot said of Webster, to be "much possessed by death", but he is not pessimistic and "death" has a multiple significance for him. In *Who Gets the Pope's Nose* Porter speaks of death as "God's greatest miracle" because it brings relief from suffering; in *Fossil Gathering* it is the means by which our essential nature is revealed: ". . . every feeling thing ascends from slime/to selfhood and in dying finds a face." In *There Are Too Many of Us* Porter equates death with the oblivion which should quickly descend upon the trivia of life. He suggests that it is a necessary condition of progress and that if we arrogantly complain at its inevitability oblivion comes all the sooner, for writers as for other men:

". . . we world eaters
Are eaten in our turn and if we shout
At the gods they send us the god of death
Who is immortal and who cannot read."

Evolution presents the related concept of death as the process which enables life to renew itself, and Porter here draws a vivid parallel between Resurrection, symbolised by the resurrection of the Jewish nation in the state of Israel, and evolution, symbolised by the continuous renewal of the body's tissues. In *Preaching to the Converted* the "converted" are imaged as dead, incapable of change, fixed for ever in the marble postures of memorials in the church of San Lorenzo, they have only "a *Grundrisse*" of the possibilities of life. (*Grundrisse:* a set of sketches, rough drafts; an outline syllabus; also, the title of a work by Marx.)

Porter's writing is often extremely witty and he has produced some very amusing and ingenious light verse, such as *Mort aux chats.* His work can

present unusual initial difficulties because its imagery is often allusive rather than sensuous, fragmentary rather than sustained and many poems combine esoteric references with a casual throwaway style, lacking verbal music, but in recent poems such as *May 1945, Fossil Gathering,* and the more personal *At Whitchurch Canonicorum* the imagery is sustained and the tone has a lyrical intensity.

Notes to a Biographer, Homily in the English Reading Room, John Marston Advises Anger and the more esoteric *Widow's Story* resemble Auden in the ways they show past jostling present and juxtapose learned references to music, literature and painting with references to the ephemerae of modern life. Porter also resembles Auden in the way he uses industrial and urban imagery. His other master is Pope, but in his satiric writing he generally eschews the felicitous elegance and visual immediacy of Pope's verse and his satiric juxtapositions and antitheses therefore often lack the force which Pope's command. However, in his better satiric verse, Porter applies stylistic devices learned from Auden to the subject matter of Pope and the result is powerful and individual. *The Workers* presents the young lovers Valerie and Hugues, "a torturer's and a peasant's descendants / On the broad back of money". Porter wittily describes Valerie's eye make-up in terms of industrial processes and building maintenance:

"It takes a whole Black Country
and at least one new oxidizing process
to maintain the canals in her fallen eyelids".

The fragmented style of much of his satiric writing seems to derive from an attempt to express the distorted values and incoherence of a life in which death has become the "great unmentionable" and "novel" is so often spoken of as if it were synonymous with "valuable". Porter mocks the pretentions and ephemeral fashions of contemporary pundits and versifiers and in *There Are Too Many of Us,* alluding to the "great theologian" (possibly the seventeenth-century priest and poet John Donne, *see* his *Satyre III*) Porter suggests that no-one has the sole key to wisdom and that the valuable thing in life is not anything new but man's continuing search for truth, which involves

". . . a tradition
Of mind going uphill and always
Getting steeper."

He contrasts the "lucky genius", who "refines his burden to one thing at a time" with "his passenger friends" who "are quacking in the beautiful incomprehensible languages" and ridiculously try to preserve everything on video tape—"nothing is allowed to die."

In *Elegy* he draws ironic contrasts between the advances of bureaucracy and the steady rhythms of the natural world, the discoveries of science and continuous indignity and suffering:

". . . the trees perform their ritual
leaf-shedding in the month of the setting-up
of a Ministry of Technology. A world of lasers
has millions who must be blanket bathed,
and a species of rat-like marsupial
is officially declared extinct—
the Ars Nova sound is a special
test of high-fidelity equipment."

Porter has spoken of the indelible impression of suffering he bears as a result of childhood experiences of the Depression in Brisbane and the loss of his mother, who died when he was nine. His awareness of the pain of mankind and of our inhumanity towards other people and creatures finds most powerful expression in works such as *The Sins of the Fathers, Story from Time of Disturbance.* However, some of Porter's finest writing is to be found in a handful of recent lyrical and elegiac poems. Here his gift for creating vivid precise images is used more freely and extensively and while many of his earlier poems had weak endings, as if he were afraid of being thought sententious, he now has the confidence to end boldly, as in *Thomas Hardy at Westbourne Park Villas:*

" Here, rather than in death-filled Dorset,
                              I see him,
    The watchful conspirator against the gods
Come to the capital of light on his own grim
Journey into darkness; the dazzle would tell
    Him these were the worst of possible odds—
ordinary gestures of time working on faces
                    the watermark of hell. "

Porter has said that his aim is now to " go back
deeper into English poetry . . . and at the same
time to put out feelers towards the European
imagination "—a process begun in his collections
The Last of England and *Preaching to the Converted*
taken further in the recent *Living in a Calm
Country*.

LATER AMERICAN POETRY.

The Innovators Williams, Moore and Stevens.

The American Pound and the Anglo-American
Eliot were cosmopolitan writers, as much, if not
more at home in Europe as in America. Their
poetry may, sometimes does, refer to specific
scenes and places, but in general *Hugh Selwyn
Mauberly, The Pisan Cantos, The Waste Land* and
Four Quartets express a vision of twentieth-
century man seen by poets highly cultivated and
steeped in the history of civilisation.

By contrast, most American poets of our time,
though often equally learned, have been self-
consciously American, deliberately concentrating
their attention on the immediate national, or even
provincial, setting in which they find themselves.

One reason for this emphasis stems from the
ideas of the Imagists, including Pound, who said
that the writer should strive to create poems
composed of vivid, concentrated and highly
evocative images. Americans like William Carlos
Williams (1883–1963) felt that one could best do
this by focusing one's attention on the immediate
environment.

At the same time they were eager to find ways of
expressing the specifically American experience of
life, which had hitherto found few outlets in
poetry. This was especially important to
Williams, who felt that the American spirit was
being stifled by the dead weight of English literary
forms. He said, " everything we do is tied up
with words ", but, although many Americans " no
longer speak English ", when writing they still
used the for them stultifying syntax and " the
prose or poetical rhythms which bind us to our pet
indolences and mediaevalisms." American poets,
he said, must break through the " deadness of
copied forms which keep shouting above everything that wants to get said today, drowning out
one man with the accumulated weight of a thousand voices of the past."

For Williams the writer to whom to turn for
inspiration was the nineteenth-century Whitman.
His derided free verse (*see* 6, 10) suggested the
possibility of new literary forms, within which the
Imagist techniques could be deployed.

Two of the other pioneers of twentieth-century
American poetry were more influenced by the
Symbolists' emphasis on the music of poetry
(*see* M16) than they were by Whitman. In her
search for a freer and more musical verse form
Marianne Moore (b. 1887) developed syllabic metre
(*see* 6, 7), while Wallace Stevens (1879–1955), one
of the greatest poets of our century, used Symbolist
techniques to bring new and sparkling life to
traditional verse forms. In an age when most
writers spurned the iambic pentameter and blank
verse as museum pieces Stevens shows them still
vigorously adaptable and tuneful.

None of these writers saw the development of
new techniques as an end in itself, but as the
necessary means for expressing a new vision of
life. They shared a high concept of the poet's
role which many English writers would now regard
as misguided. Auden said that nothing he had
written had saved anyone from the concentration
camps or gas chambers. These American writers
of a slightly older generation felt more optimistic.

They shared a radical humanism which led them
to rejoice in life's beauty and man's creative power
as well as to recognise the cruelty of the world.
They saw poetry as replacing religion and offering
a new, illuminating vision of life in all its joy and
sorrow.

Stevens said that poetry must be " abstract "—
that is abstracted, separated from the old visions
of life, including those offered by religion—it must
present new and original insights. It must also
give pleasure, not by encouraging the reader to
indulge in fantasies but by offering him truthful
images of reality in beautiful and illuminating
forms. Poetry must also change, that is give the
reader new insights into life, not confirm him in
his old ones. These are the recurrent themes of
Stevens's poetry and find their most complete
expression in his great work *Notes Toward a
Supreme Fiction.*

Stevens's attitude to poetry was shared by
Moore and Williams, but Williams was a less
speculative, more prophetic writer. He sought
not only to offer a clear vision, but to arouse man's
hatred for the brutal, life-denying materialism of
industrial America, exemplified in the suburb of
Paterson, where he worked as a medical practitioner. This radical strain, which he shared with
Pound, but expressed far more effectively, has been
taken up by many later American writers inspired
by Williams's poem *Paterson.*

Anyone interested in the development of
twentieth-century poetry should read the work of
Williams, Moore and Stevens. They are all highly
enjoyable as well as influential writers. Paperback editions of their poems are easily available
and selections from their theoretical prose can be
found in J. Scully's *Modern Poets on Modern
Poetry.*

The Beat Poets.

The name " Beat Generation " (*see* J7) was
applied to a group who were radical critics of
American life under the complacent Eisenhower
administration, which seemed to them to ignore
the ugliness and cruelty of life in the industrial
areas' " concrete jungles ". The distinctive protest of the Beats involved a rejection of all middle-
class ideas of respectability. They practised
communal living, often in considerable poverty,
and had a relaxed attitude towards employment,
sex and drugs. They were generally anarchic
pacifists, but uninterested in politics as such.

Their attitudes find formal expression in
Kerouac's novel *On the Road*, 1951, Burroughs's
Junkie, 1953 and *The Naked Lunch*, 1959, and in
the poetry of, among others, Laurence Ferlinghetti
(b. 1928), Gregory Corso (b. 1930) and Allen
Ginsberg (*q.v.*). A selection of their poems can be
found in *Penguin Modern Poets* 5.

The journalist John Clellan Holmes defined the
word " Beat " as " involving a sort of nakedness
of soul, a feeling of being reduced to the bedrock
of consciousness." Such " nakedness " is a
distinguishing mark of Beat verse, which may be
thought of as an extreme form of confessional
poetry (*q.v.*). Its principles, in so far as they have
been formulated by the leading Beat poet Ginsberg, take the Symbolist preoccupation with the
expression of the unique, individual consciousness
to its logical, egocentric conclusion. On the other
hand, believing that art falsifies the truth of
experience, the Beats in principle reject that
fastidious care with which the Symbolist sought to
formulate their experience. For the Beats, the
beauty of a poem's form is not the result of
artistry or talent, but is determined by the writer's
character: a good, honest man will produce a
good, honest poem, a rascal will compose bad
verse! However, like most poets, in practice,
the Beats sometimes break their own rules. The
best of their work is far from artless, though its
forms are often as unusual as its content is
unconventional.

Allen Ginsberg (b. 1926).

Howl and Other Poems, 1956; *Kaddish and
Other Poems*, 1961; *Reality Sandwiches*, 1963;

Planet News, 1968; *Ankor Watt*, 1968; *The Fall of America, poems of these states 1965-71* 1972. City Lights Books.

Ginsberg was brought up in Paterson, New Jersey, where his family was known to W. C. Williams and Williams, whose work Ginsberg is said to admire, wrote a warm introduction to the younger poet's first book, *Howl and Other Poems*. Like Williams, Ginsberg is a writer in the prophetic tradition of Whitman, Shelley and Blake. He was also early impressed by the writing of the eighteenth-century visionary Christopher Smart, but it was to Whitman in particular that he was indebted for the free verse techniques (*see* M10) which he used for many of his most impressive early poems.

It is important we should bear in mind that most of Ginsberg's work is intended to be read aloud—performed or chanted—to a sizeable audience, not quietly brooded over in solitude, although the power of such poems as " Kaddish " is clear even to the silent reader. Ginsberg himself has a charismatic personality, a theatrical flair, shrewd intelligence and a lively and amiable sense of humour, all of which add to the captivating power of his performances.

His finest work is contained in the two early collections, *Howl* and *Kaddish*. The famous—or notorious—" Howl " is a vatic lament for the way Ginsberg's talented contemporaries have, he feels, been destroyed by the inhumanity of American life. It is written in long, free verse canticles, the first sixteen pages comprising a single sentence, listing the ways in which " the best minds of my generation " have been driven to suicidal despair. It expresses a horrifying, if at times hysterical, vision of urban America.

" Sunflower Sutra ", in the same volume, is a more concentrated and powerful piece of writing, in which a skeletal grey sunflower, growing in a filthy railway siding by a San Fransisco dock, becomes a symbol of man's courageous will to survive even in the harshest surroundings. The poem vividly exemplifies Ginsberg's talent for creating precise and original pictorial images, such as that of the sunflower itself, with its

" corolla of bleary spikes pushed down and broken
     like a battered
crown . . .
 . . . sunrays obliterated on its hairy head
like a dried wire spiderweb . . ."

" America ", another poem in Ginsberg's first collection, is more self-absorbed but concludes with a flash of characteristic humour as the poet speaks of a " Reds-under-the-bed " scare:

" The Russia wants to eat us alive. The Russia's
     power mad. She
wants to take our cars from out our garages
 . . . Her make us all work sixteen hours
a day. Help.
America this is quite serious.
America this is the impression I get from looking
     in the television
set.
America is this correct?
I'd better get right down to the job.
It's true I don't want to join the Army or turn
    lathes in precision
parts factories, I'm nearsighted and
     psychopathic anyway.
America I'm putting my queer shoulder to the
     wheel."

In his later work, such as a poem addressed to the singer Bob Dylan, Ginsberg sometimes verges on the sentimental, but his earlier " Kaddish ", a lament for his unhappy mother, and " Aunt Rose ", are at once tender and objective poems, creating memorable images of these two elderly women.

In 1965, Ginsberg, who had earlier known a transcendental experience of identity with " Supreme Reality " realised that he must stop living on the memory of past visions, " which is not the actual awareness of *now*." His later work therefore takes the form of diffuse verse " diaries ", " chronicle tape recorded scribed by hand or sung condensed, the flux of car train air plane dream consciousness . . ." These verses lack the power of his early poems, although they contain still vivid images and flashes of humour.

The Black Mountain Group.

The most important poets generally referred to under this title are Charles Olson (*q.v.*), Robert Duncan (b. 1919) and Robert Creeley (b. 1926). Associated names include those of Denise Levertov (b. 1923), Ed Dorn (b. 1929) and Gary Snyder (b. 1930).

All these poets taught or studied at Black Mountain College in North Carolina, an experimental adult education centre founded during the Depression. Until its closure in 1956 it was the focal point for many who were discontented with accepted academic ideas and methods. It attracted a galaxy of talent, including the philosopher Dewey, the artist De Kooning and the musician John Cage.

Charles Olson (b. 1910).

Projective Verse, 1950 (in J. Scully, ed., *Modern Poets on Modern Poetry*, Fontana Bks., 1966); *The Maximus Poems*, 1960, *Maximus IV, V, VI*, 1968, both Cape Goliard Press.

Olson is the most influential of the poets associated with Black Mountain College. He has published a number of verse collections, including *In Cold Hell, in Thicket*, 1953, and *The Distances*, 1961, but his most important works are the two volumes of Maximus poems and the essay *Projective Verse*.

In this essay, Olson sought to define his concept of a poem. He speaks of it in terms of physics as a " high energy construct ", imagining the poet's experience as a generator which charges the battery, or poem, whose energy is then projected to another person when he plugs into it by reading or listening to the poem.

In order to construct an efficient poetic battery the writer must think of his work in terms of its energy field. Its form should be determined solely by its content. However, Olson also says, somewhat paradoxically, that the writer must consider how " to shape the energies so that the form is accomplished " and suggests that the solution to this problem can be found in the dictum " in any given poem, always one perception must MOVE, INSTANTER, ON ANOTHER! "

The writer should avoid similes and descriptive passages, which dissipate a poem's energy, and, in so far as formal considerations enter his mind, he should concentrate not on rhyme or metre, sense or sound, so much as on the syllables, which are the " figures of the dance " and the line which is its " threshing floor " (*see also* M7). The line's length is determined by the poet's sense of breathing. Pauses are indicated not only by line endings, where they should be as long as " it takes the eye . . . to pick up the next line ", they are also suggested by spacing: " space as long as the phrase before it . . . means that space to be held, by the breath, an equal length of time." Very light pauses are indicated by a diagonal line / rather than a comma, which has undesirable grammatical connotations. Varying amounts of indentation suggest the proper juxtaposition of the images.

Olson wrote his essay in the year that he composed the first of his Maximus poems and his ideas are helpful in understanding how these should be read, for, as the reader will quickly discern, they are best read aloud.

At his finest, as in the opening and closing poems of the sequence, Olson is a writer of considerable lyric power but in some poems, particularly those like " Later Tyrian Business " in the second volume, an elaborate and self-conscious typography confuses the reader and detracts from the poems' significance.

The subject of the Maximus sequence is the city of Gloucester, Massachusetts, and the treatment is heavily influenced by W. C. Williams's *Paterson*. The predominant theme, as in Williams's poem, is the way the region's inhabitants and its natural resources have from the time of the first settlers been corrupted and destroyed by capitalism and "pejorocracy". By "pejorocracy", a term coined by Pound, we are to understand a materialistic form of power based on the denial of life's essential meaning and purpose.

As in *Paterson*, passages of verse are divided by extracts from prose documents, letters and account books, etc., but the matter is generally less varied and less well chosen than that in Williams's poem. It depends heavily upon lists of long-dead settlers' names, precise accounts of their ownership of land, so on. Such a plethora of antiquarian detail might possibly be meaningful to one thoroughly versed in the documents themselves and in the local history and geography of Gloucester, but a much more rigorous selection would have concentrated the poems' energies and enhanced their significance. As it is, the work as a whole seems prolix, and self-indulgent, although it also contains powerful and beautiful passages which it would be a great pity to miss.

The "Confessional" Poets.

The term "confessional poetry" seems to have been used first by reviewers of Lowell's *Life Studies*, poems which arose from their author's suffering a mental breakdown. It has since been applied to the work of Sylvia Plath and Anne Sexton, which also derives from the immediate experience of mental illness and, like *Life Studies*, expresses feelings of guilt, bitterness and isolation, the material of the confessional or the psychoanalyst's couch.

The label "confessional" is also used in a more general, though allied sense, to denote work in which the poet makes an uninhibited confession of hatred, addiction, lust or similar experience, about which, usually, most of us are reticent.

In "confessional" writing the poet's need to objectify his experience, in order to give it artistic validity, presents itself in an acute form. Its resolution demands the rare courage and technical virtuosity that Eliot displayed in *The Waste Land* and Lowell approaches, in a very different way, in *Near the Ocean*.

Robert Lowell (1917–77). *See also Section I.*

Poems 1938–1949, 1950; *The Mills of the Kavanaughs*, 1951; *Life Studies*, 1959; *Imitations* 1961; *For The Union Dead*, 1964; *Near the Ocean*, 1967; *Notebook*, 1970; *History*, 1973; *For Lizzie and Harriet*, 1973; *The Dolphin*, 1973, *Day By Day*, 1978. (Faber).

In an interview, published in J. Scully's *Modern Poets on Modern Poetry*, Lowell records how he was early drawn to the work of Latin, Elizabethan and Jacobean poets. His own mature writing reflects the continuing influence of these early mentors, with whom he shares an anguished sense of the fragility and transience of beauty and a revulsion from the brutal, vicious materialism of the society in which he lives.

His first important work, *The Quaker Graveyard in Nantucket*, 1945, is an elegy for a cousin drowned while serving in the navy during the Second World War. The poem presents this cousin as continuing the brutal tradition of the Quaker whalers of Nantucket, and links him with Ahab, the tragic, deranged hero of Melville's *Moby Dick*. The vigour of the poem's language, the musical skill with which Lowell evokes the sounds and atmosphere of the bleak Nantucket coast and the force of his revulsion from the whalers' obscene cruelty are immediately impressive. As Hugh B. Staples has noted in his valuable reference book, *Robert Lowell—the First Twenty Years*, a central theme of the poem is "human evolution, considered as a part of God's plan". Here, as in much of his later work, Lowell shows the aggressive individualism of men bringing a return to primitive violence.

The gentle, pastoral stanza VI presents the ideal, the figure of the Virgin, who, "Expressionless, expresses God." However, this stanza lacks the force of the others. The affirmation of faith in the poem's concluding line is similarly less convincing than Lowell's expression of revulsion from the Quakers' primitive lust for power and wealth.

The poem's images have multiple significance. The whale, "IS, the whited monster," is at once a symbol of Being Itself, of the vengeful Jehovah and of *Iesu* Saviour. It is the victim of the sailors' greed and also the agent of their death and damnation, a whited sepulchre, an image of their corrupt faith. The sea is the god Poseidon, "the earth shaker", and also the primitive source of life and life itself, "hurt" and "fouled" by man.

These and allied images take on new significance in Lowell's later poems, where they replace the Catholic symbols of his early work, as he strives to achieve a more flexible, resonant style, which will give objective validity to his vision. In his mature work the sea and water continue to symbolise life, particularly the life of the spirit. Fish at times represent the primitive violence man has loosed upon the world, but the fish is also an image of vitality struggling against "the stone and bone-crushing waterfall." Monsters become "grunting" "yellow dinosaur steamshovels", possessive "dragons" and the Gorgon, a fearsome, yet beautiful and pitiful, "tyrant" and "tyrannicide."

Lowell's use of such images is linked with his frequent evocations of the language and imagery of the Bible, particularly the Old Testament and the Apocalyptic books beloved of the New England Puritans. He applies such language and imagery to the life-denying creeds of the Puritans themselves and to all those who seek to dominate their fellows, driving in "stakes" to "command/the infinite" and creating "God the Logos" in their own image, a tyrant with "bloody hands". Lowell combines such Biblical allusions with references to Classical myths—particularly that of Perseus and Medusa—to give his work wider significance and fuller perspectives. He uses American place names with religious and historical associations, Mount Sion, Concord, Carthage, and writes of contemporary life in terms of that of Ancient Israel and Rome, as in the following passage, where the insistent rhythm, the punctuation and feminine rhymes accentuate the image of the clumsy military machines irrevocably lurching toward their shattering end:

> "Hammering military splendor,
>   top-heavy Goliath in full armor—
>   little redemption in the mass
>   liquidations of their brass,
>   elephant and phalanx moving
>   with the times and still improving,
>   when that kingdom hit the crash:
>   a thousand foreskins stacked like trash . . ."
>   (*Waking Early Sunday Morning*).

In his early verse Lowell imitated the metrical forms of Elizabethan and Jacobean poetry. His middle period was a time of experiment: the dramatic monologues of *The Mills of the Kavanaughs* are written in more colloquial run-on couplets similar to those of Browning; *Life Studies* and *For the Union Dead* contain a number of poems in free verse. His volume, *Near the Ocean*, marks Lowell's return to stricter metrical forms, using a stanza based on four couplets, which he now deploys with the deceptive skill of a master. His earlier experiments with style and metre and the experience he has gained by writing plays and by recreating poems from Latin and other languages for the volume *Imitations*, now enable him to write with vigorous simplicity and haunting beauty:

> "Lost in the Near Eastern dreck,
>   the tyrant and tyrannicide
>   lie like the bridegroom and the bride;
>   the battering ram, abandoned, prone,
>   beside the apeman's phallic stone."
>   (*Near the Ocean*).

Although the autobiographical poems of *Life Studies* have been among the most widely noted of

Lowell's work, some later volumes seem or more lasting importance. They express a complex, tragic vision of life in a "black classic" world of "lost connections". We are all "tyrants". Mussolini was "one of us." Caligula is not "namesake" and "tyrannicide" itself a most arrogant form of tyranny, bringing widespread suffering and destruction:

> "I have seen the Gorgon.
> The erotic terror
> of her helpless, big bosomed body
> lay like slop.
> Wall-eyed, staring the despot to stone,
> her severed head swung
> like a lantern in the victor's hand."
> *(Florence).*

"Pity the monsters! " "Pity the planet, all joy gone/from this sweet volcanic cone."

Lowell's later poems express the anguish of our almost impossible quest for "asylum, peace". "We are like a lot of wild/spiders crying together/ but without tears." Innocence, goodness and beauty, life itself, are as fragile as "the orange and black/oriole's swinging nest! " In *For the Union Dead* he suggests we can survive only by having the "angry wrenlike vigilance" which chooses death rather than "savage servility" or the security of "a Mosler safe, the 'Rock of Ages'/that survived the blast." The ultimate test is whether we dare become "alive enough" to "die ".

Like Yeats, Lowell has come to feel that we experience innocent joy only in the creation and contemplation of art. Exploring the frightening "corners of the woodshed ", he creates from its "lumber " poems that give "darkness some control ", evoking joy even while they "sing " "despair."

Lowell's four collections beginning with *Note-book* present various stages in the composition of three sets of poems written in a fairly loose sonnet form.

The 1970, English, edition of *Notebook* differs from the first, American, one of 1969. About a hundred of the poems were modified and nearly a hundred new ones added. They were arranged according to no discernible method. Lowell said their disposition was "intuitive . . . not a pile or a sequence of related material." However, in his three subsequent volumes, the poems of the 1970 *Notebook* were further modified, in some cases drastically, and re-arranged to form three sequences.

The first, *History*, is a chronological series about people and events from Biblical and Classical times to the present day. It contains a number of new poems and also new versions of some from Lowell's earlier collections, *Near the Ocean*, *Imitations* and *Life Studies*, as well as from *Notebook*. For *Lizzie and Harriet* includes a little new work but most of it is derived from *Notebook* and forms a sequence concerning Lowell's relationship with his former wife, Elizabeth, and his daughter, Harriet. *The Dolphin* celebrates Lowell's third marriage. Most of the poems in this book are new. The three volumes whose autobiographical theme is continued in the posthumous *Day By Day*, contain many beautiful passages and throw an interesting sidelight on Lowell's methods of composition but the majority of the poems still seem rather unfinished. This may be because we have to accustom ourselves to Lowell's new development of the sonnet form.

Sylvia Plath (1932–63).

The Colossus, 1960; *Ariel*, 1965; *Crossing the Water*; *Winter Trees*, 1971. (Faber).

Sylvia Plath was an American of German ancestry. At the age of nine she suffered a traumatic shock with the death of her beloved father, a professor of biology at the University of Boston. Her adult attempts to come to terms with this overwhelming loss inspired some of her most powerful poems.

After a brilliant academic career in America and England, Plath married the English poet Ted Hughes (*q.v.*). The accounts of her premature death which were published recently by A. Alvarez have been disputed by Plath's husband and sister-in-law and, in any case, offer no new insights into her poetry.

The Colossus was the only one of Plath's books of poems to be published in her lifetime. The rest of her work has not appeared in the order of its composition. The poems of *Crossing the Water* predate those in *Winter Trees* and *Ariel*.

Plath spoke dismissively of the poems in *The Colossus*, which, unlike her subsequent ones, were not written to be read aloud and are rather monotonous in tone, although technically highly accomplished. The most important influence upon her writing was the publication of Lowell's *Life Studies* (*q.v.*). She admired these poems for the bold way they dealt with painful personal experience and she proceeded to emulate Lowell's achievement, but her work remains wholly individual in style and tone.

Like all poets, she has power to make us see the world as if for the first time, to enhance our awareness of life. She writes of poppies "wrinkly and clear red, like the skin of a mouth," and bells that "soberly bong out their names." Her world has the clarity of a primitive painting, but the poems of *Ariel* make almost intolerably painful reading, for they express the heightened vision and self-mockery, the frangible control of utter hopelessness. Their images are often grotesque and full of menace:

> "Dawn gilds the farmers like pigs,
> Swaying slightly in their thick suits,
>
> White towers of Smithfield ahead."
> *(Totem).*

The moon far from being a symbol of serene agape is a face

> "White as a knuckle and terribly upset.
> It drags the sea after it like a dark crime; it is quiet
> With the O-gape of complete despair."
> *(The Moon and the Yew Tree).*

Plath's world is starkly coloured in red, black, white and the yellow of decay. She combines these images with allied symbols of energy, death and living death: blood, the yew, moonlight, the winding-sheet and the pupa. Her poems are haunted by a black father-figure, the Nazi "panzer man " of *Daddy*. The power with which she expresses her anguished vision derives partly from the simplicity of her metres and verse forms, which often have the insistent quality of nursery rhyme.

Poems like *Daddy* and the allied *Lady Lazarus* are unlikely to be forgotten, but in future others, such as the title poem of *Ariel* and *The Arrival of the Bee Box*, *Sting*, and *Elm* may be valued more highly. Our judgment is distorted by Plath's recent death and the knowledge that the harrowing poems of *Ariel* were the prelude to her suicide.

John Berryman (1914–72).

Homage to Mistress Bradstreet, 1956; *77 Dream Songs*, 1964; *Berryman's Sonnets*, 1967; *His Toy, His Dream, His Rest*, 1969; *Love and Fame*, 1971; *Delusions, Etc.*, 1972. (Faber).

Berryman was the most distinguished of those poets to whom the label "confessional " applied in its more general sense. Technically he was most inventive and ingenious and his work expressed enormous vitality, but some critics have found it undisciplined and pretentious and it is indeed true that only in *Homage to Mistress Bradstreet* did Berryman achieve objective expression of his themes.

His earliest work includes the poems published in 1967 under the title *Berryman's Sonnets*. This sequence, written during the 1940s, deals with an unhappy love affair.

Berryman began as a disciple of Yeats. Later, before gradually finding his own voice, he was influenced by the colloquial style of Auden. His earlier experiments found fruition in the extraordinary *Homage to Mistress Bradstreet*, which the eminent American critic Edmund Wilson considers to be the finest long poem since Eliot's *The Waste Land*. It is interesting that Berryman made a conscious effort to produce a work wholly unlike Eliot's masterpiece, and gave his poem a narrative framework and composed it in regular, though unusual, metrical stanzas. The form of these stanzas was inspired by the one Yeats evolved for his *In Memory of Major Robert Gregory*. Berryman uses an iambic metre (*see* M8) and the eight lines of his stanza have respectively five, six, three, four, five, five, three and six feet. The first and last lines rhyme and the fifth and sixth form an heroic couplet (*see* M9).

The poem's theme is the frustrations of the creative writer in an hostile, life-denying environment. This is expressed through a recreation of the life and personality of the Puritan immigrant Anne Bradstreet, who is sometimes called the first American poet.

The work is divided into five sections. The brief opening prologue, or " exordium " and closing " coda " are spoken by the modern poet. The second and fourth sections are monologues by Anne Bradstreet, while in the third the two speakers engage in broken dialogue. The overall effect is of a conversation between two aspects of the same personality.

Berryman brilliantly evokes the harshness of the Puritan settlers' " barbarous " life: the rigour of its winters, " white air lashing high "; the " ruinous heat " of its summers. These exterior conditions are paralleled by the Puritans' " chapped souls " and " starched minds "; by rheumatic fever and religious fanaticism. Against these physical and spiritual limitations Mistress Bradstreet struggles to be true to her own, kindly, creative vision.

In *77 Dream Songs* and *His Toy, His Dream, His Rest* Berryman develops the techniques he used in the earlier work to present multiple facets of a protagonist called Henry, " a white American in early middle age, who has suffered an irrevocable loss." These two books form a single work of three hundred and eighty-five lyrics. Together they present a kind of open-ended *Odyssey* of contemporary American life. They are often very amusing, often intensely irritating and their allusions to American society sometimes make them difficult for the English reader to follow, but they are compulsive reading and individual Songs, the painful 29 and 53 and the grotesque 91, for example, remain fixed in our minds.

In the anecdotal *Love and Fame*, Berryman writes in his own person, composing brief lyrics on the subject of his life and loves and his pursuit of fame. The style is loose, rambling and self-absorbed, yet there are flashes of his characteristic and engaging humour here and in the lyrics and elegies, interposed with anguished prayers, which make up Berryman's last volume, *Delusions, Etc.*.

CONCLUSION.

Readers who are spurred by their study of the poets discussed here and wish to explore further will discover much to enjoy in the work of other writers to whom space precludes more than reference: Wilfred Owen, D. H. Lawrence, R. S. Thomas, Peter Redgrove, Christopher Middleton among English poets, and among the Americans Robert Frost, Carl Sandburg, Theodore Roethke, Elizabeth Bishop, George Oppen, and W. H. Snodgrass.

Penguin Books and Faber and Faber, publish useful anthologies of new poets. Readers who have difficulty in obtaining American poetry will find a comprehensive stock at the Compendium Bookshop, Camden High Street, London, N.W.1., which will send catalogues on request.

IV. FIGURES OF SPEECH

We constantly use figurative language without realising it. When we say that we are " browned off ", " fed up ", " at the end of our tether ", we do not expect to be taken literally. We are in fact employing metaphors.

An understanding of metaphors and other figurative expressions enables us to use our language with greater confidence and effectiveness. It also helps us to understand more fully what others have written. Especially is it valuable when we read a good novel, play, or poem, for to the creative writer figurative language is as natural as the air he breathes.

The following guide to our figures of speech is arranged alphabetically for ease of reference.

Alliteration. A kind of repetition. Two or more words in close succession beginning with the same letter, or sound, usually a consonant. Up to the fourteenth century much English verse was written according to an alliterative principle, as in this modernised quotation from " Piers Plowman ":

" I had *w*andered me *w*eary so *w*eary I rested me
On a *b*road *b*ank by a merry-sounding *b*urn."

A strong tendency to alliteration still survives in our poetry. Shakespeare ridicules it in the mechanical's play in " A Midsummer Night's Dream " (Act V, Scene 1) in such lines as—

" Whereat, with blade, with bloody blameful blade,
He bravely broach'd his boiling bloody breast."

Anti-climax. See Bathos.

Antithesis. A figure of speech where ideas are so set out that they are in sharp contrast to each other, *e.g.*.

" Better to reign in hell, than serve in heav'n."
Milton.

" To err is human, to forgive, divine."
Pope.

Apostrophe. A figure of speech where the speaker or writer suddenly breaks off and directly addresses some other person who may be present either in the flesh or only in the imagination. Often it is not a person but a thing, abstraction, or personification that is addressed as in Milton's famous apostrophe, " Hail, holy light " in " Paradise Lost " Book III, line 1. Apostrophe can be used with comic effect, *e.g.*,

" She turns, O guardian angels stop her
From doing anything improper."

(This couplet is also, incidentally, an example of bathos.)

Assonance. (1) Assonance is correspondence of vowel sounds. For instance, in the opening lines of the " fairy song " in " A Midsummer Night's Dream " (Act II, Scene 2) there is a play on only three vowels, and this repetition helps towards the effect of a magic charm, *e.g.*,

" Philomel with melody, Sing "

In Tennyson's poem "Break, break, break" the repetition of the "o" sound in the second line is like an outcry of grief, e.g.,

"On the cold grey stones, O Sea!"

(2) Assonance is sometimes used instead of rhyme, especially in early folk poetry. Here there is correspondence of one word with another in the accented vowel and any vowels which follow, but not in the consonants, e.g., in "King Estmere", "Spain" is rhymed with "same" and "barone" with "home".

Bathos or Anti-climax. A figure of speech that consists of a sudden and ludicrous descent from lofty to trivial things. In "The Rape of the Lock" Pope wittily used bathos to satirise the frivolity of the woman of fashion, who lacking all sense of proper feeling, casts the same "screams of horror", and "shrieks to pitying heav'n".

"When *husbands*, or when *lapdogs* breathe their last."

The careless writer may fall to bathos which is unintentionally comic in its effect. The word "bathos" in Greek means "depth".

Climax. A figure of speech where ideas are set out in such a way that each rises above its predecessor in scale. In Greek the word "climax" means a ladder. One of the finest examples is in Shakespeare's "The Tempest" (Act IV, Scene 1) when Prospero says.

"And, like the baseless fabric of this vision, The cloud-capp'd towers, the gorgeous palaces, The solemn temples, the great globe itself, Yea, all which it inherit, shall dissolve."

Epigram. A concise and pointed saying, effective by its wit and ingenuity. It often uses antithesis. S. T. Coleridge's definition of this form is in itself an epigram, e.g.,

"What is an epigram? a dwarfish whole: Its body brevity, and wit its soul."

Euphemism. A figure of speech where a harsh or distressing expression is replaced by one that is gentler, if less accurate. Thus we may call a lie a "flight of fancy", or a "terminological inexactitude". There is a striking instance of euphemism in "Macbeth" (Act I, Scene 5), when Lady Macbeth, planning the murder of her guest, Duncan, says, "He that's coming must be provided for."

Hypallage or "Transferred Epithet." A figure of speech where an adjective, or adverb, is separated from the word to which it belongs grammatically, and is transferred to some other word in the sentence, its unusual position giving it a kind of emphasis. The word "obsequious" is thus transferred in the sentence "A lacquey presented an obsequious cup of coffee".

Hyperbole. A figure of speech where there is a deliberate use of exaggeration for the sake of effect as in the phrase "tons of money". Lady Macbeth uses hyperbole when she says, "Here's the smell of blood still; all the perfumes of Arabia will not sweeten this little hand" (Act V, Scene 1).

Writers of advertisements, blurbs and film trailers frequently indulge in hyperbole.

Innuendo. A figure of speech where something is hinted at, or suggested, but not openly stated. Dickens uses innuendo to suggest Scrooge's stinginess by saying, "Darkness was cheap, and Scrooge iked it".

Irony. (1) A figure of speech where the speaker says one thing but intends the opposite to be understood. Shylock uses the word "courtesies" ironically when he says,

"Fair sir, you spit on me on Wednesday last; You spurn'd me such a day; another time You call'd me dog; and for these courtesies I'll lend you thus much moneys." "Merchant of Venice" (Act I, Scene 3).

The use of irony can clearly be seen in Shakespeare's "Julius Cæsar" in Antony's well-known speech to the citizens. They gradually realise that when Antony repeats that Brutus and the rest are "honourable men", he is speaking ironically, and intends the opposite. When they fully perceive this they cry, "They were traitors . . . villains, murderers". ("Julius Cæsar," Act III, Scene 2.)

(2) *Dramatic irony* is the use of words which have a second inner significance that is not realised by some of the actors in a scene. For instance, in Sheridan's "School for Scandal", Act IV, Scene 3, Sir Peter admires Joseph Surface's useful screen, and Surface replies, "Oh yes, I find great use in that screen." He and the audience know, but Sir Peter does not, that at that very moment the screen is concealing Sir Peter's own wife who had rashly visited Joseph.

It is helpful to remember that in Greek the word "irony" means "dissimulation."

Litotes. A figure of speech which is really a special kind of understatement (or Meiosis). Instead of making a positive statement (e.g., "This is a difficult task") we might use Litotes, and say "This is no easy task", thus expressing a positive by the negative of its opposite.

Malaprorism. An amusing inaccuracy in vocabulary. Words that have an accidental similarity in sound may become confused in the speaker's mind and the wrong word may come uppermost. Thus Mrs. Malaprop complains that the disobedience of her niece gives her, not "hysterics" but "hydrostatics." It is not surprising that Mrs. Malaprop, of Sheridan's "The Rivals", has given her name to this kind of verbal confusion, though many before her time, including humble folk in Shakespeare's plays, have uttered malapropism. Bottom, in "A Midsummer Night's Dream," says that in the wood they "may rehearse more obscenely" when he means "obscurely".

Meiosis. A figure of speech where a deliberate understatement is made for the sake of effect. English people are especially fond of Meiosis and often use it colloquially, in such an expression as "He made a very 'decent' contribution", meaning a very "generous" contribution. The full meaning of what we intend is often conveyed by the tone of voice, e.g.,

"This is *some* war."

Metaphor. It is helpful to think of the figure of speech, metaphor, as a condensed simile. In metaphor one thing is not merely *compared* to another, as in simile but is boldly spoken of as if it actually *were* that other. Thus Bacon, in the following metaphor, does not say books are *like* food, but speaks of them as if they actually *were* food, e.g., "Some books are to be tasted, others to be swallowed, and some few to be chewed and digested."

Metaphor is usually defined as the transfer of a name, or descriptive term, to some object to which it is not properly applicable, thus making an implicit comparison. Shakespeare uses nautical terms to describe our human situation when Brutus says.

"There is a tide in the affairs of men which, taken at the flood, leads on to fortune" ("Julius Cæsar," Act IV, Scene 3).

In *Mixed Metaphor* two or more inconsistent metaphors are used of the same object, as when speaking of a suspicion, someone said, "I smell a rat; I see it in the air; but I will nip it in the bud."

Metonymy. A figure of speech where a person or thing is not named directly, but by some associated thing. Instead of saying. "The prisoner addressed the magistrate". we might use metonymy and say, "The prisoner addressed the bench". Similarly, " a speech from the Lord Chancellor " is sometimes called " a speech from the Woolsack ".

Onomatopœia. The use of words which imitate or echo the sounds they suggest, *e.g.*,

" Seas half-frozen slushed the deck with slime."
Masefield.

Oxymoron. A figure of speech where words that are usually contradictory are combined in one expression, *e.g.*. " bitter-sweet ".

" I know this is a joyful trouble to you."
" Macbeth," Act II, Scene 3.

Paradox. A figure of speech where a statement is made that at first sight seems contradictory or absurd. *e.g.*.

" The rule of the road is a paradox quite:
If you keep to the left, you are sure to be right ".

and

" The Child is father of the Man;"
Wordsworth.

Pathetic Fallacy. A figure of speech where it is assumed that things of nature have feelings like those of human beings, *e.g.*,

" And daffadillies fill their cups with tears ".
Milton.

In Greek " pathos " means " feeling ".

Personification. A figure of speech where some abstraction, or some inanimate thing is represented as a person, *e.g.*

" Rule, Britannia ".
James Thomson.

" But look the dawn in russet mantle clad
Walks o'er the dew of yon high eastern hill."
" Hamlet," Act I. Scene 1.

Personification is really a special kind of metaphor.

Pun. The use of words so as to convey a double meaning, as in Belloc's couplet

" When I am dead, I hope it may be said:
' His sins were scarlet, but his books were read ' "

In the three puns that follow there is a suggestion of a banking transaction! " The Egyptians received a check on the bank of the Red Sea which was crossed by Moses." Puns, which were popular in the nineteenth century especially with Lamb and Hood, are now out of favour.

Simile. A figure of speech which makes a comparison pointing out a similarity between things otherwise unlike. It is usually introduced by " like " or " as ", *e.g.*

" Men fear death as children fear to go in the dark." Bacon.

" His own thought drove him like a goad."
Tennyson.

Spoonerism. An accidental transposition of the sound of two words, so called after Rev. W. A. Spooner, warden of New College, Oxford. *e.g.*,

" You have hissed all my mystery lectures " for
" You have missed all my history lectures ".

Synecdoche. A figure of speech where the name of a part is used for the whole, or the whole for the part, *e.g.*.

" A fleet of a hundred sail "

meaning of a hundred ships.

Synecdoche is really a special kind of Metonymy.

Transferred Epithet. See Hypallage.

V. LITERARY FORMS

Allegory. A description or story which has a second and deeper significance below the surface. The characters are really personifications, usually representing some vice or virtue. Allegory flourished in the Middle Ages, but the best-known allegory in the world is Bunyan's " Pilgrim's Progress " (1678), which has been translated into over a hundred different languages and dialects. On the surface " The Pilgrim's Progress " is the story of a journey in which the hero encounters many difficulties but at last reaches his destination. Its inner meaning is the progress of the Christian soul through life on earth. Spenser's " Faerie Queene " (1589 and 1596) is a more subtle and complex allegory, capable of several interpretations, religious, ethical, and political. Allegory has been described as extended metaphor. *See* M56.

Autobiography. The story of a man's (or woman's) own life, written by himself. The autobiography is becoming increasingly popular, recent excellent examples being Stephen Spender's *World within World*, Richard Church's *Over the Bridge* and Laurie Lee's *Cider with Rosie*.

Biography. A narrative telling the life story of some actual person, usually a well-known figure. The most famous biographer of classical times was Plutarch, who in the 1st century A.D. wrote his series of parallel " Lives " of twenty-three Greeks and twenty-three Romans. The English translation of this provided Shakespeare with some of the plots of his plays. Boswell's

Life of Samuel Johnson (1791) is our best-known English biography.

Burlesque. The aim of burlesque is to make us laugh by ridiculing the work of some other writer. Sometimes it treats his serious subject in a mocking way. Sometimes it takes the form of an absurd imitation or caricature of his style. Some of our most successful burlesques are dramatic in form, like Sheridan's " The Critic ", produced in 1779. This has a play within a play, called "A Tragedy Rehears'd ", a brilliant burlesque of the sentimental, historical plays so popular in his time.

Chant Royal. A poem of a strictly formal kind. French in origin. *See* M54.

Clerihew. A single-stanza verse form, four lines long. *See* M53.

Comedy. A play which is happy and amusing in tone, but not necessarily light or superficial. A comedy always has a fortunate conclusion. Shakespeare's " Twelfth Night " and Oscar Wilde's " The Importance of being Earnest " are typical examples.

Drama. A play in verse or prose, where the story is unfolded and the characters represented through the actions and speeches of actors on a stage. It is essential to good drama that there should be some kind of dynamic action and some conflict between the characters. In comedy the conflict is usually open and external. "As You Like It" for instance, begins with a quarrel between Orlando and Oliver. But most of the world's finest tragedies reveal also an inne conflict in the soul of man. In "Hamlet" the hero is at odds with many people, including his mother, the king, Ophelia, Polonius, and Laertes, but all these struggles are of secondary significance, compared with the conflict in his own mind. Even a play like "Waiting for Godot", which reduces incident and conflict to a minimum, must make some concession to the demand of the audience for the dynamic. Drama cannot be static. Occasionally poets have written drama which they knew were not practicable for the stage. Shelley's lyrical dramas, "Prometheus Unbound" and "Hellas", are of this kind. See Section I.

Eclogue. In classical literature a brief poem, usually in the form of a dialogue between shepherds. It was a popular form in the time of the Renaissance; Spenser's "Shepheardes Calendar" (1579) consists of twelve eclogues, one for each month of the year.

Elegy. A lyric poem of lamentation for the dead. Gray's "Elegy in a Country Churchyard" (1750) is the best-known English elegy. It reflects in a general way on the "destiny obscure" of the humble folk who are buried in a quiet churchyard, probably that of Stoke Poges, but most elegies mourn the death of only one person. Such as Shelley's "Adonais" (1821), on the death of Keats, and Matthew Arnold's "Thyrsis" (1867), commemorating his friend Arthur Hugh Clough. Tennyson's "In Memoriam" (1850) is unusual, in that it is not a single elegy, but a series of elegiac poems, inspired by the poet's grief for the death in 1833 of his friend Arthur Hallam.

Epic. A very long narrative poem, usually consisting of several books. The epic tells of the splendid deeds of some hero of history or legend and is frequently concerned with war. Some of the world's greatest epics are the Greek "Iliad" and "Odyssey", ascribed to Homer, the Latin "Aeneid" of Virgil, the Hindu "Mahabharata", and Milton's "Paradise Lost", whose hero is God himself. The epic is distinguished by its sustained dignity of style.

Essay. The word essay, derived from the French, means literally an "attempt" or "endeavour", and as a literary term it applies to a short prose composition which attempts to present the author's reflections on any subject he chooses. As a literary form the essay derives from the French "Essais" of Montaigne, first translated into English by Florio in 1603. Our first English essayist was Francis Bacon, who published between 1597 and 1625 three volumes of his essays, brief, pithy, and objective in character. In course of time the essay has become more subjective and personal, especially in the hands of Lamb, Hazlitt, and contemporary writers.

Extravaganza. A composition, musical or literary, which uses improbable and fantastic elements and incidents. A good example of narrative extravaganza is Thackeray's *Rose and the Ring* (1855), in which, for instance, Gruffanuff's husband, the footman, is, because of his rudeness, turned into a door-knocker. Extravaganzas are frequently dramatic in form, and most pantomimes may be regarded as such.

Fable. A very brief story designed to teach some lesson or moral. The characters of the story are often animals, birds, or insects, which converse like human beings. The most famous of all fables are those attributed to Aesop, and those of La Fontaine, the French writer of the 17th century.

Farce. A species of dramatic comedy whose whole aim is to excite laughter. It does not scruple to use improbable characters and incidents and absurd situations. "Charley's Aunt" is a typical farce.

Lampoon. A coarse satire (q.v.) attacking an individual. Lampoons are usually short. The word itself is derived from a French word meaning "drinking song."

Lyric. In ancient Greece a lyric was originally a poem meant to be sung to the accompaniment of the lyre, a stringed musical instrument rather like a small harp. Later the word was used for a poem with song-like qualities; short, usually divided into verses, and expressing the feelings of the poet. The lyric flourished in England in the Elizabethan age, as witnessed by the lively lyrics scattered through Shakespeare's plays. Neglected in the 18th century, it became popular again with the Romantic poets of the 19th century. Odes, elegies, and sonnets are all species of lyrics.

Mask or Masque. A dramatic entertainment performed by amateurs and originating in the court masquerade. The action or plot of the masque is of the slightest and there is little concern with portrayal of character, for the masque gives pleasure by means of its verse, music, and dancing, and its elegant costume and scenery. It was very popular in the 16th and 17th centuries, and from 1605 Ben Jonson wrote many court masques, for which Inigo Jones designed original costumes and settings. Our best-known examples are Shakespeare's masque in Act IV of "The Tempest" and Milton's "Comus."

Melodrama. There are two meanings of the word melodrama.

1. In the early 19th century a melodrama meant a play, usually of a romantic and sensational kind, in which songs were inserted, and where an orchestra accompanied the action. The musical comedy of today might be regarded as its modern counterpart.

2. Today the word melodrama is used of an inferior kind of play, which deliberately excites the emotions by its sensational and violent happenings, but which has a happy ending. We should be careful to distinguish melodrama, which uses violence for its own sake, from serious plays, like "Hamlet" or "King Lear", where violent acts are only incidents necessary to a profound interpretation of human conduct.

Miracle Plays. Mediæval verse plays produced from the late 14th to 16th centuries by the town guilds and performed in the market-place, or other suitable open space. They consisted of a series of dramatised stories from the Bible or Lives of Saints. Each scene would be allotted to one of the guilds, which was then responsible for its production on a wheeled stage. As soon as the actors of one guild had completed their scene, their stage would be trundled off, sometimes to another rendezvous, and would itself be succeeded by another stage with its scene, until a whole cycle of episodes had been performed. Four great cycles of miracle plays are still extant, called after the towns where they were probably performed, York, Coventry, Chester, and Wakefield. The Wakefield cycle is often called the Towneley cycle. The plays have not only a strong religious sense but also a lively comic spirit. The Towneley cycle has some especially racy comic scenes. One popular incident shows the noisy quarrel that results when Noah's wife refuses to go into the ark.

Mock Heroic. A species of parody (q.v.), caricaturing some play or poem written in a lofty and high-flown style. "The Rehearsal" (1672), by Villiers, is typical. It is an absurd imitation ridiculing the artificial and high falutin' heroic plays which were then in vogue.

Monody. In Greek literature an ode sung by a single voice, like our solo in music. In English literature it signifies a poem of mourning for someone's death. The elegies "Lycidas", by Milton, and "Thyrsis", by Matthew Arnold, were both called monodies by their authors.

Monologue. Originally a scene where one person of the drama spoke alone. Today it usually means a dramatic composition for a single actor, such as the well-known Lancashire monologues presented by Stanley Holloway. The word is also sometimes used as meaning soliloquy.

Moralities or Morality Plays. Mediæval verse plays of an allegorical kind, which attempted to teach lessons of virtue, the persons of the drama usually being not real people, but personifications. Most Moralities date from the 15th century, the best known being " Everyman ", which is Dutch in origin. The hero, Everyman, is summoned by Death, and vainly appeals for help to his friends, Fellowship, Kindred, Goods, Knowledge, Beauty, and Strength, but all fail him. Only his own Good Deeds will consent to accompany him on his last journey.

Mysteries or Mystery Plays. Some modern writers use the term " Mystery play " instead of " Miracle play " (q.v.). It is really an alternative title. One critic tried to distinguish between " Mystery plays ", as concerned with stories from the Gospels, and " Miracle plays ", as concerned with the lives and deeds of Saints, but this distinction is not usually followed.

Novel. A lengthy prose fiction. It is traditionally a realistic story of people and events, but in the present century many novelists have sought rather to express the fluctuating patterns of the inner life of the mind, while the chief interest of the French " new novelists " is language itself.

Some consider Thomas Nashe's picaresque romance *The Unfortunate Traveller* (1594) to be the first English novel but Samuel Richardson is more usually thought to have invented this literary form. His *Pamela* (1740–41), the first realistic novel in English, won a European reputation.

Ode. In classical literature an ode was a poem to be sung. In English literature it signifies a lyric poem, usually in rhyme, and is seldom longer than 150 lines. It is usually in the form of an address, and lofty in its feeling and style. The ode was popular with the romantic poets. Some of our best known are Shelley's " Ode to the West Wind ", and Keats' " Ode to a Nightingale ", " Ode on a Grecian Urn ", and " To Autumn ", all of them published in 1820.

Parable. A parable is an arresting simile or metaphor from nature or common life, which may be elaborated into a life-like story. It presents a situation which at a certain point implies some correspondence with ethical or religious principle. *See* C. H. Dodd's *The Parables of the Kingdom*.

Parody. A literary caricature, which mimics the themes and style of some other author in such a way as to make his faults seem absurd and laughable. J. C. Squire's *Tricks of the Trade* is an amusing collection of his skilful parodies of such writers as Byron, Wordsworth, and Masefield.

Pastoral. A pastoral poem, romance, or play is one in which the life of shepherds or of simple rustic folk is portrayed in an idealised way. Originating in Greek literature, the pastoral was revived at the time of the Renaissance. Spenser's " Shepheardes Calendar " consists of twelve pastoral eclogues. Shakespeare's " As You Like It " is a pastoral play, Milton's " Lycidas " is a pastoral elegy and his " Comus " a pastoral masque. There is usually in the pastoral a deeper meaning below the surface. A critic has said, " The shepherd's cloak was the acknowledged disguise of the lover, the poet, the courtier, the pastor of souls, the critic of contemporary life." In the pastoral form the charm of a simple setting and deeper significance are combined.

Prologue and Epilogue. Generally speaking, a prologue means a foreword, or preface, and an epilogue an appendix to a literary work, but the terms are often used more specifically when referring to a play. Here the prologue is a short speech in verse or prose spoken to the audience by one of the actors before the play begins, the epilogue a similar speech after its conclusion. The prologue endeavours to put the audience into a receptive state of mind, the epilogue to ask for a kind reception to the play. Shakespeare's " Romeo and Juliet " has a prologue, his " As You Like It " an epilogue, spoken by Rosalind, who says, " Good plays prove the better by the help of a good epilogue." In the 18th century it was customary for a leading actor to speak the prologue and for a leading actress to make a plea for the play in the epilogue.

Romance. The romance of the early Middle Ages was a fictitious tale in verse, telling the adventures of some hero of chivalry, the interest being in the incidents, sometimes of a supernatural kind, rather than in character. The most famous of these early romances is the French " Chanson de Roland " of the early 12th century. In the later Middle Ages a romance might be written in prose. In the 16th and 17th centuries a romance meant a tale in either prose or verse in which the scenes and incidents were remote from those of real life. Sir Philip Sidney's " Arcadia " (1590), written to entertain his sister, is of this type. Today the word romance is rather vaguely used of a tale of somewhat improbable events. Sir Henry Rider Haggard wrote several such romances, including *King Solomon's Mines* (1886) and *She* (1887).

Saga. The word saga, which is of Norse origin and means story, is applied to the mediæval prose narratives of Iceland and Norway, especially those concerned with the traditions of Icelandic families and Norwegian kings. William Morris, in his " Earthly Paradise ", gives in " The Lovers of Gudrun " a version of the Icelandic Laxdæla Saga.

Satire. A work in either verse or prose attacking folly and vice. Pope's " Dunciad ", in verse-published between 1728 and 1743, ridicules contemporary authors and literary follies in a massive attack on dullness and literary hacks. Swift's *Gulliver's Travels* (1726), which on the surface is a series of prose tales of travel to imaginary countries, is actually a comprehensive satire. It begins, in the first book on " Lilliput ", with incisive ridicule of the squabbles between English political parties and religious sects, and culminates, in the final book on the Houyhnhnms, in a devastating attack on all that is bestial in human nature. Samuel Butler's *Erewhon* (an anagram of Nowhere), published in 1872, also uses a prose travel tale in his satirical exposure of Victorian convention and hypocrisy. Although not precisely satires, many of Shaw's plays are satirical in spirit. " Arms and the Man " may be considered in one of its aspects as a satire on war.

Skit. A light satire, often in the form of parody.

Soliloquy. In a soliloquy a man talks to himself, or utters his thoughts aloud regardless of the presence of others who may hear him. The word is usually applied to such utterances by a character in a play. The most famous soliloquies in literature are those of Hamlet.

Squib. A brief, sharp satire (q.v.) attacking an individual.

Tragedy. A play, or other literary work, which is preoccupied with the serious and unhappy aspects of life. It is sombre in tone and deals with misfortune. Shakespeare's " Macbeth " and Ibsen's " Ghosts " are typical tragedies.

Tragi-Comedy. The word is used in two different ways:

(a) It may denote a play (or very occasionally a story) which combines both tragic and comic elements. Chekhov's " The Cherry Orchard " is a tragi-comedy of this type.

(b) It may also mean a play which is for the most part sombre in theme and tone, but which has a happy conclusion, like Shakespeare's " The Winter's Tale ".

GENERAL COMPENDIUM

A collection of useful tables and data on a variety of unrelated subjects, including SI units, weights and measures, phases of the moon, sunrise and sunset, eclipses, foreign phrases, abbreviations in common use and selected addresses of government and public offices.

TABLE OF CONTENTS

GENERAL COMPENDIUM

ENGLISH MONARCHS
(A.D. 827–1603)

Monarch	Accession	Died	Age	Reigned
I.—BEFORE THE CONQUEST.				
SAXONS AND DANES				
Egbert	827	839	—	12
Ethelwulf	839	858	—	19
Ethelbald	858	860	—	2
Ethelbert	858	865	—	7
Ethelred	865	871	—	6
Alfred the Great	871	899	50	28
Edward the Elder	899	924	54	25
Athelstan	924	939	45	15
Edmund	939	946	25	7
Eadred	946	955	32	9
Eadwig	955	959	18	3
Edgar	959	975	32	17
Edward the Martyr	975	978	17	3
Ethelred II (" the Unready ")	978	1016	48	37
Edmund Ironside	1016	1016	27	Apr.–Nov.
Canute the Dane	1017	1035	40	18
Harold I	1035	1040	—	5
Hardicanute	1040	1042	24	2
Edward the Confessor	1042	1066	62	24
Harold II	1066	1066	44	Jan.–Oct.
II.—FROM THE CONQUEST TO THE PRESENT DAY.				
NORMANS				
William I	1066	1087	60	21
William II	1087	1100	43	13
Henry I	1100	1135	67	35
Stephen, Count of Blois	1135	1154	50	19
PLANTAGENETS				
Henry II	1154	1189	56	35
Richard I	1189	1199	42	10
John	1199	1216	50	17
Henry III	1216	1272	65	56
Edward I	1272	1307	68	35
Edward II	1307	dep. 1327	43	20
Edward III	1327	1377	65	50
Richard II	1377	dep. 1399	34	22
Henry IV } Lancaster	1399	1413	47	13
Henry V } Lancaster	1413	1422	34	9
Henry VI } Lancaster	1422	dep. 1461	49	39
Edward IV } York	1461	1483	41	22
Edward V } York	1483	1483	13	Apr.–June
Richard III } York	1483	1485	32	2
TUDORS				
Henry VII	1485	1509	53	24
Henry VIII	1509	1547	56	38
Edward VI	1547	1553	16	6
Jane	1553	1554	17	9 days
Mary I	1553	1558	43	5
Elizabeth I	1558	1603	69	44

THE BRITISH MONARCHY
(1603 to the Present day)

Monarch	Accession	Died	Age	Reigned
STUARTS				
James I (VI of Scotland) . . . . . :	1603	1625	59	22
Charles I . . . . :	1625	beh. 1649	48	24
COMMONWEALTH DECLARED, MAY 19, 1649				
Oliver Cromwell, Lord Protector . . :	1653–8	—	—	—
Richard Cromwell, Lord Protector . : :	1658–9	—	—	—
STUARTS (RESTORATION)				
Charles II . . . . :	1660	1685	55	25
James II (VII of Scotland) : . . . . :	1685	dep. 1688	68	3
Interregnum Dec. 11, 1688 to Feb. 13, 1689				
William III and Mary II . . . . . :	1689	1702	51	13
		1694	33	6
Anne . . . . :	1702	1714	49	12
HOUSE OF HANOVER				
George I . . . . :	1714	1727	67	13
George II . : . . . . :	1727	1760	77	33
George III . : . . . . :	1760	1820	81	59
George IV . : . . . . :	1820	1830	67	10
William IV . . . . :	1830	1837	71	7
Victoria . . . . :	1837	1901	81	63
HOUSE OF SAXE-COBURG				
Edward VII . . . . :	1901	1910	68	9
HOUSE OF WINDSOR				
George V . . . . :	1910	1936	70	25
Edward VIII . . . . :	1936	Abd. 1936	—	325 days
George VI . : . . . . :	1936	1952	56	15
Elizabeth II . : . . . . :	1952			

SCOTTISH MONARCHS
(1057–1603)

	Monarch	Accession	Died
Malcolm III (Canmore)	Son of Duncan I	1058	1093
Donald Ban	Brother of Malcolm Canmore	1093	—
Duncan II	Son of Malcolm Canmore, by first marriage	1094	1094
Donald Ban	Restored	1094	1097
Edgar	Son of Malcolm Canmore, by second marriage	1097	1107
Alexander I	Son of Malcolm Canmore	1107	1124
David I	Son of Malcolm Canmore	1124	1153
Malcolm IV (the Maiden)	Son of Henry, eldest son of David I	1153	1165
William I (the Lion)	Brother of Malcolm the Maiden	1165	1214
Alexander II	Son of William the Lion	1214	1249
Alexander III	Son of Alexander II, by second marriage	1249	1286
Margaret, Maid of Norway	Daughter of Eric II of Norway, granddaughter of Alexander III	1286	1290
John Baliol	Grandson of eldest daughter of David, Earl of Huntingdon, brother of William the Lion	1292	1296
Robert I (Bruce)	Great-grandson of 2nd daughter of David, Earl of Huntingdon, brother of William the Lion	1306	1329
David II	Son of Robert I, by second marriage	1329	1371
Robert II (Stewart)	Son of Marjorie, daughter of Robert I by first marriage, and Walter the Steward	1371	1390
Robert III	(John, Earl of Carrick) son of Robert II	1390	1406
James I	Son of Robert III	1406	1437
James II	Son of James I	1437	1460
James III	Eldest son of James II	1460	1488
James IV	Eldest son of James III	1488	1513
James V	Son of James IV	1513	1542
Mary	Daughter of James V, by second marriage	1542	1587
James VI (ascended the Throne of England 1603)	Son of Mary, by second marriage	1567	1625

BRITISH PRIME MINISTERS

	Party	Served		Party	Served
George II, 1727-60			Earl Russell	Liberal	1865-6
Sir Robert Walpole	Whig	1721-42	Earl of Derby	Conservative	1866-8
Earl of Wilmington	Whig	1742-3	B. Disraeli	Conservative	1868
Henry Pelham	Whig	1743-54	W. E. Gladstone	Liberal	1868-74
Duke of Newcastle	Whig	1754-6	B. Disraeli	Conservative	1874-80
Duke of Devonshire	Whig	1756-7	W. E. Gladstone	Liberal	1880-5
Duke of Newcastle	Whig	1757-60	Marquis of Salisbury	Conservative	1885-6
			W. E. Gladstone	Liberal	1886
George III, 1760-1820			Marquis of Salisbury	Conservative	1886-92
Duke of Newcastle	Whig	1760-2	W. E. Gladstone	Liberal	1892-4
Earl of Bute	Tory	1762-3	Earl of Rosebery	Liberal	1894-5
George Grenville	Whig	1763-5	Marquis of Salisbury	Conservative	1895-1901
Marquis of Rocking-ham	Whig	1766			
Earl of Chatham	Tory	1766-8	**Edward VII, 1901-10**		
Duke of Grafton	Whig	1766-9	Marquis of Salisbury	Conservative	1901-2
Lord North	Tory	1770-82	A. J. Balfour	Conservative	1902-5
Marquis of Rocking-ham	Whig	1782	Sir H. Campbell-Bannerman	Liberal	1905-8
Earl of Shelburne	Whig	1782-3	H. H. Asquith	Liberal	1908-10
Duke of Portland	Coalition	1783			
William Pitt	Tory	1783-1801	**George V, 1910-36**		
Viscount Sidmouth	Tory	1801-4	H. H. Asquith	Liberal	1910-15
William Pitt	Tory	1804-6	H. H. Asquith	Coalition	1915-16
Lord Grenville	Whig	1806-7	D. Lloyd George	Coalition	1916-22
Duke of Portland	Tory	1807-9	A. Bonar Law	Conservative	1922-3
Spencer Perceval (assassinated)	Tory	1809-12	S. Baldwin	Conservative	1923-4
			J. R. MacDonald	Labour	1924
George IV, 1820-30			S. Baldwin	Conservative	1924-9
Earl of Liverpool	Tory	1812-27	J. R. MacDonald	Labour	1929-31
George Canning	Tory	1827	J. R. MacDonald	National	1931-5
Viscount Goderich	Tory	1827	S. Baldwin	National	1935-6
Duke of Wellington	Tory	1827-30			
			Edward VIII, 1936		
William IV, 1830-7					
Earl Grey	Whig	1830-4	**George VI, 1936-52**		
Viscount Melbourne	Whig	1834	S. Baldwin	National	1936-7
Sir Robert Peel	Tory	1834-5	N. Chamberlain	National	1937-39
Viscount Melbourne	Whig	1835-7	N. Chamberlain	War Cabinet	1939
			W. S. Churchill	War Cabinet	1940-45
Victoria, 1837-1901			W. S. Churchill	Caretaker	1945
Viscount Melbourne	Whig	1837-41	C. R. Attlee	Labour	1945-51
Sir Robert Peel	Tory	1841-6	Sir W S. Churchill	Conservative	1951-2
Lord John Russell	Whig	1846-52			
Earl of Derby	Tory	1852	**Elizabeth II, 1952-**		
Earl of Aberdeen	Peelite	1852-5	Sir W. S. Churchill	Conservative	1952-5
Viscount Palmerston	Liberal	1855-8	Sir A. Eden	Conservative	1955-7
Earl of Derby	Tory	1858-9	H. Macmillan	Conservative	1957-63
Viscount Palmerston	Liberal	1859-65	Sir A. Douglas-Home	Conservative	1963-4
			H. Wilson	Labour	1964-70
			E. Heath	Conservative	1970-4
			H. Wilson	Labour	1974-6
			J. Callaghan	Labour	1976-79

[handwritten annotations: "1st woman PM in GB"; "M Thatcher Conservative 1979-"]

PRESIDENTS OF THE UNITED STATES

The terms are for four years; only President F. D. Roosevelt has served more than two terms.

		Party	Served			Party	Served
1.	George Washington	Fed.	1789-97	21.	Chester A. Arthur	Rep.	1881-5
2.	John Adams	Fed.	1797-1801	22.	Grover Cleveland	Dem.	1885-9
3.	Thomas Jefferson	Rep.	1801-9	23.	Benjamin Harrison	Rep.	1889-93
4.	James Madison	Rep.	1809-17	24.	Grover Cleveland	Dem.	1893-7
5.	James Monroe	Rep.	1817-25	25.	William McKinley (assassinated)	Rep.	1897-1901
6.	John Quincey Adams	Rep.	1825-9	26.	Theodore Roosevelt	Rep.	1901-9
7.	Andrew Jackson	Dem.	1829-37	27.	William Howard Taft	Rep.	1909-13
8.	Martin Van Buren	Dem.	1837-41	28.	Woodrow Wilson	Dem.	1913-21
9.	William H. Harrison (died in office)	Whig	1841	29.	Warren G. Harding (died in office)	Rep.	1921-3
10.	John Tyler	Whig	1841-5	30.	Calvin Coolidge	Rep.	1923-9
11.	James K. Polk	Dem.	1845-9	31.	Herbert C. Hoover	Rep.	1929-33
12.	Zachary Taylor (died in office)	Whig	1849-50	32.	Franklin D. Roosevelt (died in office)	Dem.	1933-45
13.	Millard Fillmore	Whig	1850-3	33.	Harry S. Truman	Dem.	1945-53
14.	Franklin Pierce	Dem.	1853-7	34.	Dwight D. Eisenhower	Rep.	1953-61
15.	James Buchanan	Dem.	1857-61	35.	John F. Kennedy (assassinated)	Dem.	1961-3
16.	Abraham Lincoln (assassinated)	Rep.	1861-5	36.	Lyndon B. Johnson	Dem.	1963-69
17.	Andrew Johnson	Rep.	1865-9	37.	Richard M. Nixon (resigned)	Rep.	1969-74
18.	Ulysses S. Grant	Rep.	1869-77	38.	Gerald R. Ford	Rep.	1974-6
19.	Rutherford B. Hayes	Rep.	1877-81	39.	James Carter	Dem.	1976-
20.	James A. Garfield (assassinated)	Rep.	1881				

WEIGHTS AND MEASURES

Many kinds of measure now in use in the United Kingdom are gradually being converted from Imperial units to SI units. SI is short for "Système International d'Unités" and it is a system of metric units now coming into international use through the agency of such bodies as the General Conference of the International Bureau of Weights and Measures and the International Organisation for Standardisation (ISO) in whose work Britain participates. Information about SI units is available in booklets published by the British Standards Institution, Sales Branch, 101–113 Pentonville Road, London, N.1.

For a transitional period of some years, Imperial and SI units will be in use simultaneously. Important parts of the two systems are given separately below. A selection of useful conversion factors is on N8.

Unit Symbols Used in the Tables

Unit	Symbol	Unit	Symbol
metre	m	kilogramme	kg
yard	yd	gramme	g
foot	ft	pound	lb
inch	in	ounce	oz
mile	mile	hundredweight	cwt
square metre	m²	poundal	pdl
square inch	in²	pound-force	lbf
square mile	mile²	foot pound-force	ft lbf
cubic metre	m³	calorie	cal
cubic inch	in³	British thermal unit	Btu
litre	l	horsepower	hp
gallon	gal	tonne	t

I. IMPERIAL WEIGHTS AND MEASURES

Length.

1 nail	= 2¼ in	
1 link	= 7·92 in	
12 in	= 1 ft	
3 ft	= 1 yd	
22 yd	= 1 chain	
10 chains	= 1 furlong	
8 furlongs	= 1 mile = 1760 yd = 5280 ft	

Area.

144 in²	= 1 ft²
9 ft²	= 1 yd² = 1296 in²
484 yd²	= 1 square chain
1210 yd²	= 1 rood
4 roods	= 1 acre = 4840 yd²
640 acres	= 1 mile²

Volume.

1728 in³	= 1 ft³
27 ft³	= 1 yd³

Capacity.

4 gills	= 1 pint
2 pints	= 1 quart
4 quarts	= 1 gallon
2 gallons	= 1 peck
4 pecks	= 1 bushel
8 bushels	= 1 quarter
36 bushels	= 1 chaldron

The gallon, as the capacity standard, is based upon the pound.

1 gal = 277·274 in³

Weight (Avoirdupois).

1 dram	= 27·343 75 grains
16 drams	= 1 oz = 437·5 grains
16 oz	= 1 lb = 7000 grains
14 lb	= 1 stone
28 lb	= 1 quarter
4 quarters	= 1 cwt = 112 lb
20 cwt	= 1 ton = 2240 lb

Troy Weight.

1 pennyweight	= 24 grains
480 grains	= 1 ounce

The only unit of troy weight which is legal for use in trade in Britain is the ounce Troy, and weighings of precious metal are made in multiples and decimals of this unit.

The term *carat* is not a unit of weight for precious metals, but is used to denote the quality of gold plate, etc., and is a figure indicating the number of 24ths of pure gold in the alloy, *e.g.*, a 9 carat gold ring consists of nine parts of pure gold and fifteen parts of base metals.

Nautical Measures.

1 nautical mile = 6080 ft = 1853·18 m
1 knot = 1 nautical mile per hour = 1·151 mile/h

Note.—In future the international nautical mile of 1852 m will be used.

Note.—The British Pharmaceutical Code and the British National Formulary—the official works of medicinal reference—no longer contain the apothecaries' units of measurement since medicine is now measured in metric units. Prescriptions are in 5 millilitre (ml) units; medicine bottles are in six sizes from 50 to 500 ml.

II. SI UNITS

There are six base SI Units. They are:

Quantity	Name of Unit	Symbol
length	metre	m
mass	kilogramme	kg
time	second	s
electric current	ampere	A
temperature	kelvin	K
luminous intensity	candela	cd

Derived units are normally stated in terms of the base unit. Examples: the SI units of velocity and density are, respectively, the metre per second (m/s) and the kilogramme per cubic metre (kg/m³). Some important derived units have well-established names of their own. They are:

Quantity	Name of SI unit	Symbol	Expressed in terms of SI base-units or derived units
frequency	hertz	Hz	$1 \text{ Hz} = 1/\text{s}$
force	newton	N	$1 \text{ N} = 1 \text{ kg m/s}^2$
work, energy, quantity of heat	joule	J	$1 \text{ J} = 1 \text{ N m}$
power	watt	W	$1 \text{ W} = 1 \text{ J/s}$
quantity of electricity	coulomb	C	$1 \text{ C} = 1 \text{ A s}$
electric potential, potential difference, tension, electromotive force	volt	V	$1 \text{ V} = 1 \text{ W/A}$
electric capacitance	farad	F	$1 \text{ F} = 1 \text{ A s/V}$
electric resistance	ohm	Ω	$1 \text{ Ω} = 1 \text{ V/A}$
flux of magnetic induction, magnetic flux	weber	Wb	$1 \text{ Wb} = 1 \text{ V s}$
magnetic flux density, magnetic induction	tesla	T	$1 \text{ T} = 1 \text{ Wb/m}^2$
inductance	henry	H	$1 \text{ H} = 1 \text{ V s/A}$
luminous flux	lumen	lm	$1 \text{ lm} = 1 \text{ cd sr}$
illumination	lux	lx	$1 \text{ lx} = 1 \text{ lm/m}^2$

There are special prefixes for forming multiples and sub-multiples of the SI units. These are:

Factor by which the unit is multiplied	Prefix	Symbol
10^{12}	tera	T
10^{9}	giga	G
10^{6}	mega	M
10^{3}	kilo	k
10^{2}	hecto	h
10	deca	da
10^{-1}	deci	d
10^{-2}	centi	c
10^{-3}	milli	m
10^{-6}	micro	μ
10^{-9}	nano	n
10^{-12}	pico	p
10^{-15}	femto	f
10^{-18}	atto	a

Examples: one thousandth of a metre is one millimetre (1 mm); one million volts is one megavolt (1 MV). These prefixes are *recommended* but other multiples and sub-multiples will be used when convenient, *e.g.*, the centimetre (cm), the cubic decimetre (dm³).

The following is a selection of special points to note:

(i) The name litre now means 1 cubic decimetre or 10^{-3}m^3 and is a measure of volume.

(ii) Days, hours, and minutes are still used to measure time, though some scientists may prefer to use kiloseconds, etc.

(iii) The SI unit of plane angle is the radian (rad), but degrees, minutes and seconds are still used as well. $1° = \dfrac{\pi}{180}$ rad; 1 rad $= 57\cdot295\ 78° = 57°\ 17'\ 44\cdot81''$

(iv) A Celsius temperature, say 15 degrees, is written 15°C; note that 15C would mean 15 coulombs.

(v) The mole (mol) is important in science as a measure of "amount of substance" and may be adopted as a seventh basic SI unit. 1 mol is the amount of substance of a system which contains as many elementary units as there are carbon atoms in 0·012 kg of ¹²C. The elementary unit must be specified and may be an atom, a molecule, an ion, an electron, etc., or a specified group of such particles.

(vi) The SI unit of area is the square metre (m²) but the hectare (1 ha $=10^4$m²) will be the normal unit for land measure where we have previously used the acre. The are (a) $=10^2$m².

(vii) The SI unit of pressure is the newton per square metre (N/m²), but in some technical fields, notably meteorology, the unit of pressure is the bar which approximates to normal atmospheric pressure; 1 bar $= 10^5$ N/m².

II. SELECTED METRIC EQUIVALENTS FOR IMPERIAL WEIGHTS AND MEASURES

Length.

$$1 \text{ in} = 2 \cdot 54 \text{ cm} = 0 \cdot 0254 \text{ m}$$
$$12 \text{ in} = 1 \text{ ft} = 30 \cdot 48 \text{ cm} = 0 \cdot 3048 \text{ m}$$
$$3 \text{ ft} = 1 \text{ yd} = 0 \cdot 9144 \text{ m}$$
$$1760 \text{ yd} = 1 \text{ mile} = 1609 \cdot 344 \text{ m}$$

Area.

$$1 \text{ in}^2 = 6 \cdot 4516 \times 10^{-4} \text{m}^2$$
$$144 \text{ in}^2 = 1 \text{ ft}^2 = 0 \cdot 092\ 903\ 0 \text{ m}^2$$
$$9 \text{ ft}^2 = 1 \text{ yd}^2 = 0 \cdot 836\ 127 \text{ m}^2$$
$$4840 \text{ yd}^2 = 1 \text{ acre} = 0 \cdot 404\ 68$$
$$640 \text{ acres} = 1 \text{ mile}^2 = 2 \cdot 589\ 99 \times 10^6 \text{m}^2$$

Volume.

$$1 \text{ in}^3 = 1 \cdot 638\ 71 \times 10^{-5} \text{m}^3$$
$$1 \text{ ft}^3 = 0 \cdot 028\ 316\ 8 \text{ m}^3$$
$$1 \text{ UK gal} = 0 \cdot 004\ 546\ 092 \text{ m}^3$$

Velocity.

$$1 \text{ ft/s} = 0 \cdot 3048 \text{ m/s}$$
$$1 \text{ mile/h} = 0 \cdot 447\ 04 \text{ m/s} = 1 \cdot 6093 \times 10^3 \text{ m/h}$$

Capacity.

$$1 \text{ pint} = 0 \cdot 568\ l \text{ or } 10^{-3} \text{m}^3$$
$$2 \text{ pints} = 1 \text{ quart} = 1 \cdot 136\ l$$
$$4 \text{ quarts} = 1 \text{ gal} = 4 \cdot 546\ l$$
$$8 \text{ gal} = 1 \text{ bushel} = 36 \cdot 37\ l$$
$$8 \text{ bushels} = 1 \text{ quarter} = 2 \cdot 909 \times 10^3\ l$$

Weight.

$$1 \text{ oz} = 28 \cdot 35 \text{ g}$$
$$16 \text{ oz} = 1 \text{ lb} = 0 \cdot 453\ 592\ 37 \text{ kg}$$
$$14 \text{ lb} = 1 \text{ st} = 6 \cdot 350 \text{ kg}$$
$$112 \text{ lb} = 1 \text{ cwt} = 50 \cdot 80 \text{ kg}$$

$$\begin{array}{l} 20 \text{ cwt} \\ (2240 \text{ lb}) \end{array} = 1 \text{ long ton} = 1016 \text{ kg}$$
$$2000 \text{ lb} = 1 \text{ short ton} = 907 \text{ kg}$$

Note.—1 tonne (t) = 1000 kg

Density.

$$1 \text{ lb/in}^3 = 2 \cdot 767\ 99 \times 10^4 \text{ kg/m}^3$$
$$1 \text{ lb/ft}^3 = 16 \cdot 0185 \text{ kg/m}^3$$
$$1 \text{ lb/UK gal} = 99 \cdot 7764 \text{ kg/m}^3$$

Force.

$$1 \text{ pdl} = 0 \cdot 138\ 255 \text{ N}$$
$$1 \text{ lbf} = 4 \cdot 448\ 22 \text{ N}$$

Pressure.

$$1 \text{ lbf/in}^2 = 6894 \cdot 76 \text{ N/m}^2$$

Energy (work, heat).

$$1 \text{ ft pdl} = 0 \cdot 042\ 140\ 1 \text{ J}$$
$$1 \text{ ft lbf} = 1 \cdot 355\ 82 \text{ J}$$
$$1 \text{ cal} = 4 \cdot 1868 \text{ J}$$
$$1 \text{ Btu} = 1055 \cdot 06 \text{ J}$$

Power.

$$1 \text{ hp} = 745\ 700 \text{ W}$$

Temperature.

$$1 \text{ Rankine degree} = 1 \text{ Fahrenheit degree}$$
$$= 5/9 \text{ Kelvin} = 5/9 \text{ Celsius degree}$$

(The Rankine scale of absolute temperature was developed from the Fahrenheit scale, exactly as the Kelvin scale was developed from the Celsius scale.)

Note.—Figures printed in bold type are exact. Unit symbols are the same in the singular and the plural and do not carry a full point (as a mark of an abbreviation).

THERMOMETER COMPARISONS

Celsius 100°	Fahrenheit 212°	Celsius 100°	Fahrenheit 212°
95	203	20	68
90	194	15·5	60
85	185	12·8	55
78·9	174	10	50
75	167	7·2	45
70	158	5	41
65	149	1·7	35
60	140	0	32
55	131	− 1·1	30
52·8	127	− 5	23
50	122	− 6·7	20
45	113	− 10	14
42·2	108	− 12·2	10
40	104	− 15	5
36·7	98	− 17·8	0
35	95	− 20	− 4
32·2	90	− 25	− 13
30	86	− 30	− 22
26·7	80	− 35	− 31
25	77	− 40	− 40

To reduce Fahrenheit to Celsius (centigrade), subtract 32 degrees and multiply by 5/9; to reduce Celsius to Fahrenheit, multiply by 9/5 and add 32 degrees.

An alternative method, perhaps easier to remember, is to add 40 to the given figure, multiply by 5/9 (°F to °C) or 9/5 (°C to °F) and subtract 40.

SIZES OF BOUND BOOKS

Standard sizes	Size of trimmed page	
	mm	in
Metric Crown 8vo	186 × 123	7 9/32 × 4 27/32
Metric Crown 4to	246 × 189	9 11/16 × 7 7/16
Metric Large Crown 8vo	198 × 129	7 13/16 × 5 1/16
Metric Demy 8vo	216 × 138	8 1/2 × 5 7/16
Metric Demy 4to	276 × 219	10 7/8 × 8 5/8
A5	210 × 148	8 1/4 × 5 13/16
A4	297 × 210	11 5/8 × 8 1/4
Occasional sizes		
Metric Large Crown 4to	258 × 201	10 3/16 × 7 15/16
Medium 8vo . .	222 × 144	8 3/4 × 5 11/16
Old Royal 8vo . .	246 × 156	9 11/16 × 6 1/4

MAJOR NATIONAL CURRENCIES

Country	Currency
Albania	Lek
Argentina	Peso
Australia	Dollar
Austria	Schilling
Belgium/Lux.	Franc
Belize	Dollar
Bolivia	Peso Boliviano
Brazil	Cruzeiro
Bulgaria	Lev
Burma	Kyat
Canada	Dollar
Chile	Peso
China	Renminbi
Colombia	Peso
Costa Rica	Colón
Cuba	Peso
Czechoslovakia	Koruna
Denmark	Krone
Dominican Republic	Peso
Ecuador	Sucre
Egypt	Pound
El Salvador	Colón
Ethiopia	Dollar
Finland	Markka
France	Franc
Germany (E.)	Mark
Germany (Fed. Rep.)	D. Mark
Greece	Drachma
Guatemala	Quetzal
Guyana	Dollar
Haiti	Gourde
Honduras Rep.	Lempira
Hong Kong	Dollar
Iceland	Króna
India	Rupee
Indonesia	Rupiah
Iran	Rial
Iraq	Dinar
Israel	Pound
Italy	Lira
Jamaica	Dollar
Japan	Yen
Jordan	Dinar
Kenya	K. Shilling
Lebanon	Pound
Malaysia	Ringgit
Mexico	Peso
Morocco	Dirham
Netherlands	Guilder
New Zealand	Dollar
Nicaragua	Córdoba
Nigeria	Naira
Norway	Krone
Pakistan	Rupee
Panama	Balboa
Paraguay	Guaraní
Peru	Sol
Philippines	Peso
Poland	Zloty
Portugal	Escudo
Romania	Leu
South Africa	Rand
Spain	Peseta
Sri Lanka	Rupee
Sweden	Krona
Switzerland	Franc
Syria	Pound
Tanzania	T. Shilling
Thailand	Baht
Trinidad and Tobago	T.T. Dollar
Tunisia	Dinar
Turkey	Lira
United Arab Emirates	Dirham
United Kingdom	Pound
U.S.A.	Dollar
U.S.S.R.	Rouble
Uruguay	Peso
Venezuela	Bolívar
Yugoslavia	Dinar
Yemen Arab Rep.	Riyal
Yemen. South	Dinar
Zaïre	Zaïre
Zambia	Kwacha

ROMAN NUMERALS

I	1	LXX	70
II	2	LXXX	80
III	3	LXXXVIII	88
IV	4	XC	90
V	5	XCIX	99
VI	6	C	100
VII	7	CX	110
VIII	8	CXI	111
IX	9	CXC	190
X	10	CC	200
XI	11	CCXX	220
XII	12	CCC	300
XIII	13	CCCXX	320
XIV	14	CD	400
XV	15	D	500
XVI	16	DC	600
XVII	17	DCC	700
XVIII	18	DCCC	800
XIX	19	CM	900
XX	20	XM	990
XXX	30	M	1000
XL	40	MD	1500
L	50	MDCCC	1800
LV	55	MCMLXX	1970
LX	60	MM	2000

INTERNATIONAL TIME-TABLE (GMT)

Place	Time h	Place	Time h
Adelaide	21 30	Melbourne	22 00
Amsterdam	13 00	Montreal	07 00
Ankara	14 00	Moscow	15 00
Athens	14 00	Nairobi	15 00
Auckland		New York	07 00
(N.Z.)	24 00	Oslo	13 00
Belgrade	13 00	Ottawa	07 00
Berlin	13 00	Panama	07 00
Bombay	17 30	Paris	13 00
Brisbane	22 00	Peking	20 00
Brussels	13 00	Perth (W.A.)	20 00
Budapest	13 00	Prague	13 00
Buenos Aires	09 00	Quebec	07 00
Cairo	14 00	Rangoon	18 30
Calcutta	17 30	Rio de Janeiro	09 00
Cape Town	14 00	Rome	13 00
Chicago	06 00	San Francisco	04 00
Copenhagen	13 00	St. John's	
Gibraltar	13 00	(N.F.)	08 30
Helsinki	14 00	Singapore	19 30
Hobart	22 00	Stockholm	13 00
Hong Kong	20 00	Sydney	22 00
Istanbul	14 00	Tehran	15 30
Jerusalem	14 00	Tokyo	21 00
London	12 00	Toronto	07 00
Madeira	12 00	Vancouver	04 00
Madrid	13 00	Vienna	13 00
Malta	13 00	Winnipeg	06 00
Mauritius	16 00	Yokohama	21 00

GREEK ALPHABET

A	α	Alpha	N	ν	nu
B	β	beta	Ξ	ξ	xi
Γ	γ	gamma	O	o	omicron
Δ	δ	delta	Π	π	pi
E	ϵ	epsilon	P	ρ	rho
Z	ζ	zeta	Σ	σ	sigma
H	η	eta	T	τ	tau
Θ	θ	theta	Y	υ	upsilon
I	ι	iota	Φ	ϕ	phi
K	κ	kappa	X	χ	chi
Λ	λ	lambda	Ψ	ψ	psi
M	μ	mu	Ω	ω	omega

BANK AND PUBLIC HOLIDAYS

The number of public holidays in England and Wales comprise at present six bank holidays (New Year's Day, Easter Monday, May Day, Spring and Late Summer Holidays at the end of May and August respectively, and Boxing Day), with also two common law holidays (Good Friday and Christmas Day); in Scotland seven bank holidays (New Year's Day, January 2, Good Friday, May Day, Spring and Late Summer Holidays at the beginning of May and August respectively, and Christmas Day); and in Northern Ireland seven bank holidays (New Year's Day, St. Patrick's Day, Easter Monday, May Day, Spring Late Summer Holidays at the end of May and August respectively, and Boxing Day) plus two other public holidays (Easter Tuesday and the anniversary of the Battle of the Boyne).

1979   Bank Holidays in England and Wales—Jan. 1, Apr. 16, May 1, May 28, Aug. 27, Dec. 26
           Northern Ireland—Jan. 1, Mar. 17, Apr. 16, May 1, May 28, Aug. 27, Dec. 26
           Scotland—Jan. 1, Jan. 2, Apr. 13, May 1, May 7, Aug. 6, Dec. 25

Note: There are holidays in lieu of other public holidays which fall at weekends, with effect from Christmas Day and Boxing Day 1976, and New Year's Day, 1977.

THE SEASONS

	1978			1979		
	d	h	m	d	h	m
Vernal Equinox—Spring begins	Mar	20	23 34	Mar	21	05 22
Summer Solstice—Summer begins	June	21	18 10	June	21	23 56
Autumnal Equinox—Autumn begins	Sept	23	09 26	Sept	23	15 17
Winter Solstice—Winter begins	Dec	22	05 21	Dec	22	11 10

(All times are in GMT)

THE COUNTRY CODE

GUARD AGAINST THE RISK OF FIRE. Great damage is done every year to crops, plantations, woodlands, and heaths. A match or cigarette thrown away or a pipe carelessly knocked out, picnic fires not properly put out or lighted near dry crops, can quickly start a blaze.

FASTEN ALL GATES. If animals get out of a field they stray. As a result they may do serious damage to crops, suffer injury on the roads, or eat food that is harmful.

KEEP DOGS UNDER CONTROL. Animals are easily frightened, even by small, playful dogs. Stillbirths may be the result.

KEEP TO THE PATHS ACROSS FARM LAND. Crops are damaged by treading; flattened crops are difficult to harvest. Grass is a valuable crop.

AVOID DAMAGING FENCES, HEDGES, AND WALLS. If these are damaged, gaps will be caused. Where a man goes, an animal may follow.

LEAVE NO LITTER. Litter is not just unsightly, but often a danger as well. Broken glass and tins may injure animals and harm machinery.

SAFEGUARD WATER SUPPLIES. Countrymen often depend on wells and streams for water for themselves and for their animals.

PROTECT WILD LIFE, PLANTS, AND TREES. Wild animals should not be disturbed, plants uprooted, or trees treated roughly.

GO CAREFULLY ON COUNTRY ROADS. If there is no footpath, walkers are generally safer on the right, facing on-coming traffic. Care and patience are needed by motorists when passing farm animals.

RESPECT THE LIFE OF THE COUNTRYSIDE. Many of the machines and much of the business stock on which the farmer depends for his livelihood have to be kept in the open. Take care not to damage them.

THE BEAUFORT SCALE OF WIND FORCE

Beaufort number	Wind	Effect on land	Speed	
			mile/h	Knots
0	Calm	Smoke rises vertically	Less than 1	Less than 1
1	Light air	Direction shown by smoke but not by wind vanes	1–3	1–3
2	Light breeze	Wind felt on face; leaves rustle; wind vanes move	4–7	4–6
3	Gentle breeze	Leaves and twigs in motion; wind extends light flag	8–12	7–10
4	Moderate breeze	Raises dust, loose paper and moves small branches	13–18	11–16
5	Fresh breeze	Small trees in leaf begin to sway	19–24	17–21
6	Strong breeze	Large branches in motion; whistling in telegraph wires; difficulty with umbrellas	25–31	22–27
7	Moderate gale	Whole trees in motion; difficult to walk against wind	32–38	28–33
8	Fresh gale	Twigs break off trees; progress impeded	39–46	34–40
9	Strong gale	Slight structural damage occurs; chimney pots and slates blown off	47–54	41–47
10	Whole gale	Trees uprooted and considerable structural damage	55–63	48–56
11	Storm	Widespread damage, seldom experienced in England	64–75	57–65
12	Hurricane	Winds of this force only encountered in tropical revolving storms	Above 75	Above 65

SUNRISE AND SUNSET FOR LONDON, 1979

		Rise h m	Set h m			Rise h m	Set h m			Rise h m	Set h m
Jan	1	08 06	16 02	May	7	05 23	20 33	September	3	06 15	19 44
	8	08 05	16 10		14	05 11	20 44		10	06 26	19 28
	15	08 00	16 20		21	05 01	20 54		17	06 38	19 12
	22	07 53	16 32		28	04 53	21 03		24	06 49	18 56
	29	07 44	16 44	June	4	04 47	21 11	October	1	07 00	18 40
Feb	5	07 34	16 56		11	04 44	21 17		8	07 12	18 24
	12	07 21	17 09		18	04 43	21 21		15	07 23	18 09
	19	07 08	17 22		25	04 44	21 22		22	07 35	17 54
	26	06 54	17 35	July	2	04 48	21 21		29	06 48	16 40
March	5	06 39	17 47		9	05 54	21 17	November	5	07 00	16 28
	12	06 23	17 59		16	05 01	21 11		12	07 12	16 17
	19	07 07	19 11		23	05 10	21 03		19	07 24	16 07
	26	06 51	19 23		30	05 20	20 53		26	07 36	16 00
April	2	06 35	19 35	August	6	05 31	20 41	December	3	07 46	15 54
	9	06 20	19 46		13	05 42	20 28		10	07 54	15 52
	16	06 02	19 58		20	05 53	20 14		17	08 01	15 52
	23	05 50	20 10		27	06 04	19 59		24	08 05	15 55
	30	05 36	20 21						31	08 06	16 01

Note: These times are in GMT, except between 0200 on Mar. 18 and 0200 on Oct. 28, when the times are in BST. (1 hour in advance of GMT).

PHASES OF THE MOON, 1979

	New Moon d h m		First Quarter d h m		Full Moon d h m		Last Quarter d h m
Jan.	28 06 20	Jan.	5 11 15	Jan.	13 07 09	Jan.	21 11 23
Feb.	26 16 45	Feb.	4 00 36	Feb.	12 02 39	Feb.	20 01 17
Mar.	28 02 59	Mar.	5 16 23	Mar.	13 21 14	Mar.	21 11 22
Apr.	26 13 15	Apr.	4 09 57	Apr.	12 13 15	Apr.	19 18 30
May	26 00 00	May	4 04 25	May	12 02 01	May	18 23 57
June	24 11 58	June	2 22 37	June	10 11 55	June	17 05 01
July	24 01 41	July	2 15 24	July	9 19 59	July	16 10 59
Aug.	22 17 10	Aug.	1 05 57	Aug.	8 03 21	Aug.	14 19 02
Sept.	21 09 47	Aug.	30 18 09	Sept.	6 10 59	Sept.	13 06 15
Oct.	21 02 23	Sept.	29 04 20	Oct.	5 19 35	Oct.	12 21 24
Nov.	19 18 04	Oct.	28 13 06	Nov.	4 05 47	Nov.	11 16 24
Dec.	19 08 23	Nov.	26 21 09	Dec.	3 18 08	Dec.	11 13 59
		Dec.	26 05 11				

Note: All times are in GMT.

ECLIPSES 1979

1.	Total eclipse of the Sun	Feb. 26	N. America except W. Alaska, Arctic regions, Greenland except N.E., Iceland, W. Europe
2.	Partial eclipse of the Moon	Mar. 13	Asia, Australasia, Africa, Europe, the Americas
3.	Annular eclipse of the Sun	Aug. 22	Oceania, S. of S. America, part of Antarctica
4.	Total eclipse of the Moon	Sept. 6	the Americas, Australasia, Asia

Source: H.M. Nautical Almanac Office, for the Science Research Council.

UNIVERSITY DEGREES—COLOURS OF HOODS

Aberdeen

M.A.	Black silk, lined with white silk.
M.Litt.	White silk, lined with violet silk.
D.Litt.	Scarlet cloth, lined with white silk.
Ph.D.	Scarlet cloth lined with black ribbed silk the ribs running horizontally.
B.Ed.	Black silk, lined with orange silk.
M.Ed.	White silk, lined with orange silk.
B.Sc.	Black silk, lined with green silk.
B.Sc.Agr.	Black silk, edged with green silk.
B.Sc.For.	Black silk, edged with waved green silk.
B.Sc.Eng.	Black silk edged with green silk and bordered inside, within the green edging, with white cloth ($\frac{1}{4}$").
M.Sc.	White silk, lined with green silk.
D.Sc.	Scarlet cloth, lined with green silk.
B.D.	Black silk, lined with purple silk, and bordered inside with white silk (1").
M.Th.	White silk, lined with purple silk.
D.D.	Scarlet cloth, lined with purple silk.
LL.B.	Black silk, lined with pale blue silk.
LL.D.	Scarlet cloth, lined with pale blue silk.
M.B., Ch.B.	Black silk, lined with crimson silk.
M.D.	Scarlet cloth, lined with crimson silk.
Ch.M.	White silk, lined with crimson silk.
D.Mus	Scarlet cloth, lined with light brown silk.
M.Mus.	White silk, lined with light brown silk.
B.Med.Bo.	Black silk, lined with crimson silk, and bordered inside with white cloth $\frac{1}{2}$" wide.

Note.—All the hoods of this University are of uniform pear shape of a cloth or silk foundation and lined or edged with the colour peculiar to the Faculty or Degree.

Aston (Birmingham)

B.Sc.	Black, faced with 3" red silk interwoven with University crest.
M.Sc.	Like B.Sc. but fully lined.
M.Phil.	Like B.Sc. but in blue and fully lined.
Ph.D.	University red. faced as for B.Sc.
D.Sc.	Like Ph.D. but in gold and fully lined.

Bath

B.Sc. B.Pharm. B.Arch.	} Old-gold lined light olive-green taffeta.
	Old-gold lined light olive-green taffeta with medium-crimson edging.
B.A.	Old-gold lined light olive-green taffeta with yellow edging.
B.Ed.	Old-gold lined light olive-green taffeta with orange edging.
M.Sc. M.Pharm.	} Old-gold lined pale-blue taffeta.
M.Arch.	Old-gold lined pale-blue taffeta with medium-crimson edging.
M.A.	Old-gold lined pale-blue taffeta with yellow edging.
M.Ed.	Old-gold lined pale-blue taffeta with orange edging.
Ph.D.	Old-gold lined medium-crimson taffeta.
D.Sc.	Old-gold lined scarlet taffeta.
LL.D.	Old-gold lined scarlet taffeta with white edging.
D.Litt.	Old-gold lined scarlet taffeta with yellow edging.

Belfast, The Queen's University

B.A.	Black silk/stuff, rabbit-skin lining.
M.A.	Black silk, blue silk lining.
B.Ed.	Black silk, mauve silk lining.
M.Ed.	Red silk, mauve silk lining.
B.Mus.	Blue silk/stuff, white silk lining.
D.Lit.	Scarlet cloth, white silk lining.
D.Mus.	Scarlet cloth, blue silk lining.
B.Sc.	Black silk stuff, light green silk lining.
M.Sc.	Red silk, light green silk lining.
D.Sc.	Scarlet cloth, light green silk lining.
LL.B.	Black silk/stuff, pink silk lining.
LL.M.	Red silk, pink silk lining.
LL.D.	Scarlet cloth, pink silk lining.
B.Sc.(Econ.)	Black silk/stuff, light rose pink silk lining.
M.Sc.(Econ.)	Red silk, light rose pink silk lining.
D.Sc.(Econ.)	Scarlet cloth, light rose pink silk lining.

B.S.Sc.	Black silk/stuff, dark rose pink lining.
M.S.Sc.	Red silk, dark rose pink silk lining.
M.B.A.	Black silk, dark yellow silk lining.
M.B.B.Ch., B.A.O.	} Black silk/stuff, scarlet silk lining.
B.D.S.	Black silk/stuff, dove-grey silk lining.
M.D.	Scarlet cloth, scarlet silk lining.
M.Ch.	Red silk, scarlet silk lining.
M.A.O.	Red silk, purple silk lining.
M.D.S.	Red silk, dove-grey silk lining.
B.Sc.(App. Sc. and Tech.	} Black silk/stuff, dark green lining.
M.Sc.(App. Sc. and Tech.)	} Red silk, dark green silk lining.
D.Sc.(App. Sc. and Tech.)	} Scarlet cloth, dark green silk lining and facings.
B.Agr.	Black silk/stuff, light primrose silk lining.
M.Agr.	Red silk, light primrose silk lining.
B.D.	Black silk, white silk lining.
M.Th.	Red silk, white silk lining.
D.D.	Scarlet cloth, black silk lining.
Ph.D.	Scarlet cloth, violet silk lining.
B.L.S.	Black silk/stuff, dark blue silk lining.
M.L.S.	Red silk, dark blue silk lining.
B.Sc.(Food Science)	} Black silk/stuff, dark primrose silk lining
M.Sc.(Food Science)	} Red silk, dark primrose silk lining.
B.Ed.	Black silk, mauve silk lining.

Note:—Bachelors' and Masters' hoods are of spec. simple shape; Doctors' of the full (Cambridge) shape. All hoods have blue watered-silk binding, except the B.A. which has fur edging.

Birmingham

B.Sc.	Black, edged with silver-grey watered silk
M.Sc.	Black, lined with silver-grey watered silk.
D.Sc.	Scarlet, lined with silver-grey watered silk.
Ph.D.	Crimson, lined with silver-grey watered silk.
B.A.	Black, edged with electric-blue watered silk.
M.A.	Black, lined with electric-blue watered silk.
B.Ed.	Black, edged with primrose-yellow watered silk.
M.Ed.	Black, lined with primrose-yellow watered silk.
D.Litt.	Scarlet, lined with electric-blue watered silk.
Ph.D.	Crimson, lined with electric-blue watered silk.
B.Mus.	Black, edged with tangerine watered silk.
D.Mus.	Scarlet, lined with tangerine watered silk.
B.D.	Black, edged with cobalt-blue watered silk.
D.D.	Scarlet, lined with cobalt-blue watered silk.
M.B., Ch.B.	Black, edged with cardinal watered silk.
M.D.	Scarlet, lined with cardinal watered silk.
Ph.D.	Crimson, lined with cardinal watered silk.
B.D.S.	Black, edged with dark-red (Grenat) watered silk.
D.D.S.	Scarlet, lined with dark-red (Grenat) watered silk.
B.Com.	Black, edged with terracotta watered silk.
B.Soc.Sc.	Black, edged with terracotta watered silk and bound with grey silk at top edge.
M.Com.	Black, lined with terracotta watered silk.
M.Soc.Sc.	Black, lined with terracotta watered silk, edged with grey watered silk.
Ph.D.	Crimson, lined with terracotta watered silk.
D.Soc.Sc.	Scarlet, lined with terracotta watered silk and bound with grey silk at top edge.
LL.B.	Black, edged with bronze-green watered silk.
LL.M.	Black, lined with bronze-green watered silk.
M.Jur.	Black, lined with bronze-green watered silk, edged with grey watered silk.
Ph.D.	Crimson, lined with bronze-green watered silk.
LL.D.	Scarlet, lined with bronze-green watered silk.
B.Sc. B.Com.	} Black, edged with silver-grey watered silk, bound with terracotta watered silk at top edge.
B.Phil.(Ed.)	Black, lined with primrose-yellow watered silk, bound with white silk at top edge.
B.Ed.	Black, edged with primrose-yellow watered silk.

Bradford

Bachelors (B.A., B.Sc., B.Tech.)	Black, edged 3″ saffron.
Masters	Black, edged and fully lined saffron.
Ph.D.	Scarlet, fully lined saffron.
Higher Doctorates:	
Technology	Scarlet, fully lined saffron, edged on inside 1½″ violet.
Science	Scarlet, fully lined saffron, edged on inside 1½″ blue.
Literature	Scarlet, fully lined saffron, edged on inside 1½″ white.

Bristol

B.Ed.	All hoods are of the Cambridge pattern and
B.A.	made of University red stuff or silk.
M.A.	Bachelors' hoods are lined as far as the
M.Ed.	visible parts are concerned with silk of a
M.Mus.	lighter shade of University red. Hoods of
LL.B.	Bachelors of Medicine and Surgery are
LL.M.	fully lined with the lighter shade of
LL.D.	University red, the lining bound at the
M.B., Ch.B.	edge with ¾″ white silk. Hoods of
Ch.M.	Bachelors of Law are fully lined with the
M.D.	lighter shade of University red, the lining
D.Mus.	bound at the edge with ¾″ violet silk.
Ph.D.	Masters' hoods are fully lined with white
B.Sc.	silk. Hoods of Doctors of Philosophy are
M.Sc.	fully lined with dark violet silk. Hoods
D.Sc.	of Doctors in particular faculties are fully
M.Litt.	lined with salmon-coloured silk.
D.Litt.	
B.D.S.	
M.D.S.	
B.Arch.	
B.V.Sc.	

Brunel Middlesex

Bachelor	Black, lined white and faced inside 1½″ with Brunel blue velvet, reversed band showing blue in front.
Master	Brunel blue, lined silver and faced inside 2½″ with Brunel blue velvet.
Ph.D.	Mushroom, lined and edged Cardinal red, faced inside 3¼″ with Brunel blue velvet.
D.Tech. and D.U.	Cardinal red, lined and edged gold and faced 4½″ with Brunel blue velvet.

Note:—Bachelors' hoods are of a special simple shape, Masters' and Doctors' of the Cambridge shape.

Cambridge

D.D.	Scarlet cloth lined with dove-coloured silk, that is silk of a turquoise-blue shot with rose-pink.
LL.D.	Scarlet cloth lined with light-cherry silk.
M.D.	Scarlet cloth lined with mid-cherry silk.
Sc.D.	Scarlet cloth lined with pink silk shot with light blue.
Litt.D.	Scarlet cloth lined with scarlet silk to match the cloth.
Mus.D.	Cream damask lined with dark-cherry satin.
B.D.	Black corded silk lined with black silk.
Ph.D.	Black corded silk lined with scarlet cloth.
M.Chir.	Black corded silk lined mid-cherry silk.
M.A.	Black corded silk lined with white silk.
LL.M.	Black corded silk lined light-cherry silk.
Mus.M.	Black corded silk lined dark-cherry satin.
M.Sc.	Black cloth lined pink silk shot light blue.
M.Litt.	Black cloth lined with scarlet silk.
B.Ed.	Black stuff, part-lined with blue silk and an edging of white fur, the tippet edged with white fur.
M.B.	Mid-cherry silk part-lined with white fur, the tippet edged with white fur.
B.Chir.	Mid-cherry silk part-lined with white fur but with no fur edging to the tippet.
B.A.	Black stuff, part-lined with white fur, the tippet edged with white fur (or black stuff, part-lined with white, the tippet edged with white).
LL.B.	Light-cherry silk part-lined with white fur, the tippet edged with white fur.
Mus.B.	Dark-cherry satin part-lined with white fur, the tippet edged with white fur.
Vet.M.B.	Mid-cherry silk part-lined with white fur, with white fur edging (2″) to the tippet.

Note:—The neckband of the hood is of the outer colour, with no edging of the lining material. The corners of tippets are square. All hoods are of the full shape.

The City (London)

B.Sc.	Maroon cloth, lined gold taffeta, with discipline colour neckband.
M.Sc.	Maroon silk, lined and cape edged with gold taffeta, with discipline colour neckband.
M.Phil.	Maroon silk outside, edged with ¼″ gold taffeta, with discipline colour neckband.
Ph.D.	Maroon cloth, lined half maroon and half gold taffeta, with discipline colour neckband.
D.Litt.	Cardinal red cloth, lined half maroon and half gold taffeta, with gold neckband.
D.Sc.	Cardinal red cloth, lined half maroon and half gold taffeta, with grey neckband.
Disciplines: Engineering	Blue.
Science	Grey.
Management Social Science	} Green.

Note:—Bachelors' hoods are of the simple shape. Masters and Doctors' of the full shape.

Dundee

M.D.	Stewart blue, cherry lining.
Ch.M.	Black, imperial purple lining.
M.B., Ch.B.	Black, cherry lining, white fur edging.
M.M.Sc.	Black, clover lining.
B.M.Sc.	Black, clover lining, white fur edging.
D.D.Sc.	Stewart blue, ruby lining.
M.D.S.	Black, ruby lining.
B.D.S.	Black, ruby lining, white fur edging.
D.Sc.	Stewart blue, buttercup-yellow lining.
M.Sc.	Black, buttercup-yellow lining.
B.Sc.	Black, buttercup-yellow lining, white fur edging.
LL.D.	Stewart blue, old-gold lining.
LL.M.	Black, old-gold lining.
LL.B.	Black, old-gold lining, white fur edging.
D.Sc. (Eng. & App. Sc.)	Stewart blue, powder-blue lining.
M.Sc. (Eng. & App. Sc.)	Black, powder-blue lining.
B.Sc. (Eng. & App. Sc.)	Black, powder-blue lining, white fur edging.
D.Litt.	Stewart blue, smalt-blue lining.
M.A. (Soc. Sc. & Letters)	Black, tartan-green lining.
M.A. (Soc. Admin.)	Black, chartreuse-green lining.
Ph.D.	Stewart blue, eggshell-blue lining.
B.Phil.	Black, eggshell-blue lining, white fur edging.
M.Ed.	Black, tuscan-yellow lining.
B.Ed.	Black, tuscan-yellow lining, white fur edging.
B.Arch.	Black, heliotrope lining, white fur edging.
B.Sc. (Arch.) or (Envl. Studs.) or (Town and Regl. Planning).	Black, gault-grey lining, white fur edging.

Note:—Hoods have a cowl without liripipe, the cape being oblong with rounded bottom corners. All are in silk ottoman.

Durham

B.A.	Black, trimmed white fur.
B.D.	Black, lined black.
D.D	Scarlet, lined palatinate purple.
B.C.L.	Palatinate purple, bound white fur.
D.C.L. (awarded as an Honorary degree)	Scarlet, lined white.
B.Mus.	Palatinate purple, bound brocaded white silk 1″ wide.
M Mus	Black, lined white brocade, bound palatinate purple.
D.Mus.	Brocaded white satin, lined palatinate purple.
Ph.D.	Scarlet, lined scarlet, bound palatinate purple 1″ wide.
B.Sc.	Palatinate purple, bound white fur, edged scarlet ¼″ wide.
M.Sc.	Black, lined palatinate purple, bound scarlet ¼″ wide.
D.Sc.	Palatinate purple, lined scarlet.
M.Litt.	Black, lined old gold.
D.Litt.	Scarlet, lined old gold.
B.Ed.	Black, edged palatinate purple, trimmed white fur.

M.Ed. — Black, lined white, edged palatinate 1″ wide.

M.Phil. — Black, lined scarlet, bound palatinate purple ½″ wide.

Note:—Palatinate purple silk, cloth, or cassimere is peculiar to this University; it is in fact a soft lilac shade.

East Anglia

B.A. — Blue with 6″ coral outside lining in one fold.

B.Sc. — Blue with 6″ spectrum-green outside lining in one fold.

B.Phil. — Blue with 6″ red outside lining in one fold.

M.A. — Blue with coral outside lining in folds.

M.Sc. — Blue with spectrum-green outside lining in folds.

M.Mus. — Blue with Beaton-pink outside lining in folds.

M.Phil. — Blue with red outside lining in folds.

Ph.D. — Guardsman red with facings same colour.

D.Litt. — Blue with coral outside lining, draped.

D.Mus. — Blue with Beaton-pink outside lining, draped.

D.Sc. — Blue with spectrum-green outside lining, draped.

D.C.L. — Blue with crocus outside lining, draped.

Edinburgh

B.Arch. — Black silk, lined with orange-brown silk, and edged with white fur.

B.Com. — Black silk, lined with pale primrose yellow silk, and edged with white fur.

B.D. — Black silk, lined with purple silk, and bordered with white fur.

B.D.S. — Black stuff, lined crimson silk bordered ivory poplin 3″ broad, edged white fur showing 3″ crimson silk at front of neckband.

B.Ed. — Black silk, lined with pale blue silk, and edged with white fur.

B.Litt. — Black silk, lined with royal blue silk shot with maize-colour, bordered with ivory poplin 3″ broad, edged with white fur showing 3″ royal blue silk.

B.Mus. — Scarlet silk, with white silk lining, and edged with white fur.

B.Sc. — Black silk, lined with green silk, and bordered with white fur.

B.Sc.(Med.Sc.). — As B.Sc.

B.Sc.(Soc.Sc.). — Black silk, lined with deep turquoise silk and edged with white fur.

B.V.M. & S. — Black silk, lined maroon silk bordered golden yellow 3″ broad, edged white fur.

Ch.M. — Black velvet, lined with golden silk.

D.D. — Black cloth, with appended cape, lined and faced with purple silk.

D.D.S. — Black silk, lined with crimson silk bordered with white silk 3″ broad.

D.Litt. — Black cloth, lined with royal blue silk shot with maize-colour.

D.Mus. — Rich scarlet cloth, lined with rich white corded silk.

D.Sc. — Black cloth, lined with green silk.

D.Sc.Soc.Sci. — Black cloth, lined with deep turquoise silk.

D.V.M. & S. — Black silk, lined with maroon silk bordered with golden yellow 3″ broad.

LL.B. — Black silk, lined with blue silk, and bordered with white fur.

LL.M. — Black silk, lined with blue silk.

LL.D. — Black cloth, with appended cape, lined and faced with blue silk.

M.A. — Black silk, lined with white silk.

M.A.(Religious Studs.) — Black silk, lined with white silk, bordered with purple 3″ broad.

M.Arch. — Black silk, lined with orange-brown silk.

M.B., Ch.B. — Black silk, lined with crimson silk bordered with white fur.

M.D. — Black silk, with appended cape, lined and faced with crimson silk.

M.Ed. — Black silk, lined with pale blue silk.

M.Litt. — Black silk, lined with royal blue silk shot with maize colour bordered with ivory poplin 3″ broad and showing 3″ of royal blue silk.

M.Mus. — Scarlet silk lined with white silk.

M.Phil. — Black silk, lined with silver silk, bordered with blue silk shot with brown 3″ broad.

M.Sc. — Black silk, lined white silk bordered green silk 3″ broad, showing 3″ green silk at front of neckband.

M.Theol. — Black silk, lined with purple silk bordered with ivory poplin 3″ broad and showing 3″ of purple silk at front of neckband.

Ph.D. — Black cloth, lined blue silk shot brown.

Essex

B.A. — Black, lined University red taffeta.

M.A.
M.Sc. } — Black, lined University red, faced 1½″ inside with white.

M.Phil. — Black, lined University red, faced 3″ inside with white.

Ph.D. — University red, lined maroon taffeta.

Hon. Doctors — University red silk, lined and edged with white, faced with 2″ black ribbon on the inside ¾″ from the edge.

Note:—Bachelor hood is of simple shape; other hoods are of full shape.

Exeter

B.A. — Dove grey cloth edged Faculty colour silk.

M.A. — Dove grey cloth lined Faculty colour silk.

D.Litt. — Scarlet superfine cloth lined dove grey cloth, edged with Faculty colour.

LL.B. — Dove grey cloth edged Faculty colour silk.

LL.M. — Dove grey cloth lined Faculty colour silk.

LL.D. — Scarlet superfine cloth lined dove grey, edged with Faculty colour.

B.Sc. — Dove grey cloth edged Faculty colour silk.

M.Sc. — Dove grey cloth lined Faculty colour silk.

D.Sc. — Scarlet superfine cloth lined dove grey, edged with Faculty colour.

B.A. (Social Studies). — Dove grey cloth edged Faculty colour silk.

M.A. (Social Studies). — Dove grey cloth lined Faculty colour silk.

Ph.D. (all Faculties). — Dove grey cloth lined with scarlet.

B.Phil. — Dove grey cloth edged Faculty colour silk, with thin white cord sewn to leading edge of hood, edging the Faculty colour.

The Faculty colours are:—

Arts	Kingfisher blue.
Education	Ultramarine blue.
Law	Purple.
Science and Applied Science	Turquoise blue.
Social Studies	Dark blue.

Note:—All bachelors have theological college style hoods unlined, all the seams show, and the hood proper is merely edged with the Faculty colour 2″ both inside and outside the cowl portion. All Doctors' hoods (incl. Ph.D.) are very heavy, being made of cloth and fully lined with cloth—no silk. All hoods are of the full (Cambridge) shape.

Glasgow

M.A. — Black, lined and edged purple silk (colour of bell heather, *Erica cinerea*).

M.Litt.
M.Phil. } — Black, lined and edged white silk.

D.Litt. — Scarlet, lined purple silk.

B.Mus. — Black, lined azure blue silk, bordered scarlet cord.

D.Mus. — Black, lined azure blue silk.

B.Ed. — Black, lined blue silk (colour of bluebell of Scotland, *Campanula rotundifolia*), bordered scarlet cord.

M.Ed. — Black, lined and edged blue silk (colour of bluebell of Scotland, *Campanula rotundifolia*).

B.Arch. — Black, lined lime-coloured silk (colour of the lime flower, *Tilia europaea*), bordered scarlet cord.

B.D. — Black, lined light cherry silk, bordered scarlet cord.

M.Th. — Black, lined and edged light cherry silk.

D.D. — Scarlet, lined white silk.

B.L. — Black, bordered on inside venetian red silk.

LL.B. — Black, lined venetian red silk, bordered scarlet cord.

LL.M. — Black, lined and edged venetian red silk.

LL.D. — Scarlet, lined venetian red silk.

B.Acc. — Black, lined slate-grey silk, bordered scarlet cord.

M.Acc. — Black, lined and edged slate-grey silk.

M.B., Ch.B. — Black, lined scarlet silk, bordered scarlet cord.

Ch.B. — Black, lined and edged scarlet silk.

M.D. — Scarlet, lined scarlet silk.

B.D.S. — Black, lined emerald-green silk, bordered scarlet cord.

M.D.S. — Black, lined and edged emerald-green silk.

D.D.Sc. — Scarlet, lined emerald-green silk.

B.Sc. — Black, lined gold-coloured silk (colour of whin blossom, *Ulex europaeus*), bordered scarlet cord.

M.Sc. — Black, lined and edged gold-coloured silk.

D.Sc. — Scarlet, lined gold-coloured silk.

M.Eng. — Black, lined and edged gold-coloured silk.

B.V.M.S. — Black, lined terracotta silk, bordered scarlet cord.

M.V.M.   Black, lined and edged terracotta silk.
D.V.M.   }Scarlet, lined terracotta silk.
D.V.S.   }
Ph.D.   Black, lined and edged crimson silk.
M.Admin.   Black, lined and edged orange silk (colour of Slender St. John's Wort. *Hypericum pulchrum*).

Note:—All hoods are of the full shape. Bachelors who are also Masters may wear Bachelors' hoods of silk.

Heriot-Watt (Edinburgh)

Science
B.Sc.   Black, lined light blue, edged 25 mm gold.
M.Sc.   Black, lined light blue.
Ph.D.   Magenta, lined white.
D.Sc.   Light blue, lined white.

Engineering
B.Sc.   Black, lined dark blue, edged 25 mm gold.
M.Sc.   Black, lined dark blue.
M.Eng.   Black, lined dark blue, edged 25 mm white.
Ph.D.   Magenta, lined white.
D.Sc.   Dark blue, lined white.

Economic and Social Studies
B.A.   Black, lined purple, edged 25 mm gold.
M.Litt.   Black, lined purple.
M.Admin.   Black, lined purple, edged 25 mm white.
Ph.D.   Magenta, lined white.
D.Litt.   Purple, lined white.

Environmental Studies
B.Sc.   Black, lined red, edged 25 mm gold.
B.Arch.   Black, lined red, edged gold, 25 mm from edge.
B.A.   Black, lined red, edged gold, 50 mm from edge.
M.Sc.   Black, lined red.
Ph.D.   Magenta, lined white.
D.Sc./D.Litt.   Red, lined white.

Hull

B.A.   All hoods are lined throughout with the University silk, a turquoise blue taffeta.
M.A.
D.Litt.   All Bachelors' hoods (other than B.D. and
B.D.   B.Phil.) are of black ribbed rayon, of the
D.D.   improved Oxford Burgon shape. The
LL.B.   B.D. is of black superfine cloth of the same
LL.M.   shape as the Doctors'. The Doctors'
LL.D.   hoods are of the improved Oxford Doctors'
B.Mus.   shape with semi-circular cape. The Ph.D.
M.Mus.   is of claret coloured cloth and the D.Mus.
D.Mus.   of cream figured damask silk; all the other
B.Sc.   Doctors' hoods are of scarlet superfine
M.Sc.   cloth. The necks of all hoods are cut in
D.Sc.   one piece with a single central seam and no
B.Sc.(Econ.)   neck bands are let in. Edging of all
M.Sc.(Econ.)   hoods is forbidden except that Masters'
D.Sc.(Econ.)   hoods are ordered to be edged ¼" with the
B.Ed.   lining silk (turquoise blue) round the cape
M.Ed.   portion only: all Masters' hoods are of the
B.Phil. (in   London shape, with well-rounded cape.
faculties of
Arts, Social
Sciences, and
Law)
Ph.D. (in all
Faculties)

Keele

Bachelor of   Black, faced inside with gold, top edge
Arts,   piped University red.
Bachelor of
Social Science
and Bachelor
of Science
Bachelor of   Black, faced inside with silver, top edge
Education   piped University red.
Master   Black silk, lined University red and pipes gold.
Doctor of   Gold cloth, lined University Red.
Philosophy
Doctor   Purple cloth, lined University red, piped gold.

Note:—All hoods are of the full shape.

Kent at Canterbury

Bachelors   Silver.
Masters   Gold.
Ph.D.   Cardinal red.
Higher   Scarlet.
Doctorates
D.C.L.   Scarlet.

Faculty   Natural Sciences—Purple.
Colours: Social Sciences—Grey.
  Humanities—Green.
  D.C.L.—Black.

Note:—All hoods are of the special University shape i.e., flat cape effect, with the faculty denoted by a centre "V" shape panel of velvet.

Lancaster

B.A.   Black, lined with grey taffeta with ½" inside edging of red taffeta.
B.Ed.   Similar to the B.A. hood but with ¼" white ribbon sewn inside quarter of inch from red edging.
M.A.   Black, lined with red taffeta with 1½" grey border.
M.Litt.   Black, lined with red taffeta with 1½" blue taffeta border.
B.Sc.   Similar to the B.A. hood but with ¼" gold ribbon sewn inside quarter of inch from red edging.
M.Sc.   Black, lined with red taffeta with 1½" gold taffeta border.
Ph.D.   Red, lined with red taffeta.
D.Litt.   Red, lined with blue taffeta.
D.Sc.   Red, lined with gold taffeta.
LL.D.   Red, lined with grey taffeta.
D.Mus.   Red, lined with red damask.

Note:—The B.A. hood is of the simple shape: all other hoods are of the full shape.

Leeds

B.A.   Dark green.
B.Mus.   Dark green with 1" band white silk.
B.D.   Dark green with white lining and band, with 1" scarlet laid on the white silk.
B.Com.   Light green lined dark green.
B.Ed.   Dark green with 1" band light green.
LL.B.   Light green.
M.B., Ch.B.   Dark green lined light green.
M.A.   Dark green with white lining.
M.Ed.   Dark green with white lining and band, with 1" middle-green laid on the white silk.
M.Com.   Light green with white lining and band, with 1" dark green laid on the white silk.
LL.M.   Light green with white lining.
M.Sc.   Middle green with white lining.
M.Phil.   Black stuff on silk lined with middle green with narrow binding of scarlet.
B.Ch.D.   Dark green lined middle green.
Ch.M.   Dark green with white lining, edged light green.
M.Ch.D.   Dark green lined with white, edged middle green.
Ph.D.   Green lined with green with narrow bindings of scarlet.
D.D.   Scarlet lined with dark green with white binding.
D.Mus.   Scarlet lined dark green with 1" band white watered silk laid on the green 1" from edge.
Doctors of   Scarlet lined with green of the shade/
Letters,   shades appropriate to the faculty.
Laws, Science
and Medicine

Note:—All hoods are of the single or Oxford pattern and hoods of Bachelors are lined.

Leicester

B.A.   Red, lined with silver grey.
B.Sc.   Red, lined with royal blue.
LL.B   Red, lined with black.
M.A.   Red, lined with silver grey.
M.Sc.   Red, lined with royal blue.
M.Ed.   Red, lined with tartan green.
Ph.D.   Red, lined with a watered taffeta of lighter shade.
D.Litt.   Silver grey, lined red.
D.Sc.   Royal blue, lined red.
LL.D.   Black, lined red.
B.Ed.   Red, lined tartan green.
D.Mus.   Cream brocade, lined red.

Liverpool

Arts
B.A.   Black cloth, lined with apple-blossom silk, the colour of the Faculty, and bordered with white fur.

B.Ed.	Black cloth, lined with green silk and bordered with white fur.
B.Mus.	Blue silk bordered with white fur.
B.Phil.	Black cloth lined with yellow silk and bordered with white fur.
M.A.	Black silk or cloth, lined with apple-blossom silk.
M.Ed.	Black silk or cloth, lined with green silk.
D.Mus	Scarlet cloth, lined with blue silk.
Litt.D.	Scarlet cloth, lined with apple-blossom silk.

Science

B.Sc.	Black cloth, lined with slate-blue silk, the colour of the Faculty and bordered with white fur.
M.Sc.	Black silk or cloth, lined with slate-blue silk.
D.Sc.	Scarlet cloth, lined with slate-blue silk.

Medicine

M.B., Ch.B.	Black cloth, lined with lavender silk, the colour of the Faculty, and bordered with white fur.
Ch.M., M.Ch.Ortn., M.Rad., M.Ch.Otol., M.Comm.H., M.Psy.Med.	} Black silk or cloth, lined with lavender silk.
M.D.	Scarlet cloth, lined with lavender silk.
B.D.S.	Black cloth, lined with dark red silk, and bordered with white fur.
M.D.S.	Black silk or cloth, lined with dark red silk.

Law

LL.B.	Black cloth, lined with bronze silk, the colour of the Faculty, and bordered with white fur.
LL.M.	Black silk or cloth, lined with bronze silk.
LL.D.	Scarlet cloth, lined with bronze silk.

Engineering Science

B.Eng.	Black cloth, lined with orange silk, the colour of the Faculty, and bordered with white fur.
M.Eng.	Black silk or cloth, lined with orange silk.
D.Eng.	Scarlet cloth, lined with orange silk.

Veterinary Science

B.V.Sc.	Black cloth, lined with grey silk, and bordered with white fur.
M.V.Sc.	Black silk or cloth, lined with grey silk.
D.V.Sc.	Scarlet cloth, lined with grey silk.

Social and Environmental Studies

B.A.	Black cloth, lined with apple-blossom silk, the colour of the Faculty, and bordered with white fur.
B.Com.	Black cloth, lined with citron silk, and bordered with white fur.
B.Arch.	Black cloth, lined with white silk, edged with two narrow lines of black velvet, and bordered with white fur.
B.Phil.	Black cloth, lined with yellow silk and bordered with white fur.
M.A.	Black silk or cloth, lined with apple-blossom silk.
M.Arch.	Black silk or cloth, lined with white silk and edged with two narrow lines of black velvet.
M.T.D.	Black silk or cloth, lined with white silk and edged with one broad line of orange velvet.
M.C.D.	Black silk or cloth, lined with white silk and edged with one broad line of black velvet.
M.B.A.	Black silk or cloth, lined with white silk and edged with one narrow line of gold ribbon.
M.Com.	Black silk or cloth, lined with citron silk.
M.Psychol.	Black silk or cloth, lined with purple silk.
Litt.D.	Scarlet cloth, lined with apple-blossom silk.

Doctor in Philosophy

Ph.D.	Scarlet cloth or cord, lined with black silk, and trimmed with scarlet velvet.

London

	Faculty colour
Theology	
B.D.	
M.Th.	} Sarum red
D.D.	
Arts	
B.A.	
M.A.	} Russet-brown
D.Lit.	
Laws	
LL.B.	
LL.M.	} Blue
LL.D.	
Music	
B.Mus.	
M.Mus.	} White (watered silk)
D.Mus.	

Medicine

M.B., B.S.	
M.S.	} Violet
M.D.	

Medicine (Dental Surgery)

B.D.S.	} Olive green (corded
M.D.S.	

Medicine (Pharmacy)

B.Pharm.	Old gold

Medicine (Veterinary)

B.Vet.Med.	
D.Vet.Med.	} Lilac

Science, Engineering and Economics

B.Sc.	
M.Sc.	
D.Sc.	
B.Sc.(Eng.)	
M.Sc.(Eng.)	
D.Sc.(Eng.)	} Gold
B.Sc.(Econ.)	
M.Sc.(Econ.)	
D.Sc.(Econ.)	
B.Sc.(Est.Man.)	
M.Sc.(Est.Man.)	

Education

B.Ed.	} Eau-de-nil green
M.Ed.	

Education (Humanities)

B.Hum.	Pale pink.

Commerce, no longer awarded: Deep orange.

Note:—All London hoods are of identical shape (full shape with rounded cape). With the exception of B.Mus., for whom the hood is of light blue corded silk, Bachelors' hoods are of black silk or stuff faced and edged with silk of the faculty colour. Bachelors who are members of Convocation are entitled to wear hoods lined with silk and edged with silk of the faculty colour. With the exception of M.Mus., for whom the hood is of medium blue corded silk, Masters' hoods are of black corded silk, with a silk lining and edging of the faculty colour. For M.Phil. the lining is of claret colour with an edging of the colour of the faculty. Masters who are members of Convocation are entitled to wear hoods with a facing, 1½" wide, of white silk. The Ph.D. hood is of claret-coloured cloth lined with silk of a lighter shade of claret, with an edging of the faculty colour about ¼" wide. Doctors' hoods are of scarlet cloth lined with silk of the faculty colour.

Loughborough

Bachelors	Purple, lined with grey, yellow or green-grey, according to degree.
Masters	Purple, lined with grey, yellow or green-grey, according to degree, with ½" edging of degree colour.
Doctors of Philosophy	Purple, lined and edged 1" all round with maroon taffeta.
Higher Doctors	Grey (Science), yellow (Technology), green-grey (Education), green (Arts), red (Library Studies), lined and edged all round with scarlet taffeta.
Degree Colours:	Science—Grey. Technology—Yellow. Education—Green-grey. Arts—Green. Library Studies—Red.

Manchester

B.A.	Black, pale blue and fur.
B.Arch.	
B.Ling.	
B.Pl.	} Black, pale blue edging.
B.TP.	
M.A.	
M.A.(Urb. Des.)	} Black and pale blue.
M.TP.	
D.Litt.	Gold and light gold.
B.A.(Econ.)	Black, orange and fur.
M.A.(Econ.)	} Black and orange.
M.A.(E.C.S.)	
B.Ed.	Black, bluish-green and fur.
B.A. (in Education)	Black, pale blue, fur and bluish-green.
B.Sc. (in Education)	Black, salmon, fur and bluish-green
M.Ed.	Black and bluish-green.
M.Sc. (in Education)	Black and bluish-green, salmon edging.
LL.B.	Black, violet edging.
LL.M.	Black and violet.
LL.D.	Gold and light gold.
M.B., Ch.B.	Black, red edging.
B.Nurs.	Black, red and fur.
Ch.M.	Black and red.
M.Sc. (in Medicine)	Black and red, salmon edging.

M.D.	Gold and light gold.
B.D.S.	Black, fawn and fur.
M.D.S.	Black and fawn.
D.D.S.	Gold and light gold.
Mus.B.	Black and dark blue, light blue border.
Mus.D.	Gold and light gold.
B.Sc.	Black, salmon and fur.
M.Sc.	Black and salmon.
B.Sc. (in Technology)	Black, terracotta and fur.
M.Sc. (in Technology)	Black and terracotta.
D.Sc.	Gold and light gold.
B.D.	Black, heliotrope and fur.
B.A.(Theol.)	
B.A.(Relig Stud.)	Black, heliotrope edging and fur.
B.A. (in Theology)	
M.A.(Theol)	Black and heliotrope.
D.D.	Gold and light gold.
M.B.A.	Black and gold.
M.B.Sc.	
Ph.D.	Gold and light gold.

Note:—All hoods are of the simple shape, and are worn back-to-front with the tippet or liripipe outwards.

Newcastle upon Tyne

M.B., B.S.	Scarlet, Palatinate purple and white fur edging.
M.D.	Scarlet, scarlet and Palatinate purple.
M.S.	Rose and Palatinate purple.
D.Hy.	Scarlet, scarlet Palatinate purple and white.
D.Ch.	Scarlet, rose and Palatinate purple.
B.D.S.	Rose, ivory and white fur edging.
M.D.S.	Rose and ivory.
D.D.Sc.	Scarlet, rose and ivory white edging.
B.A.	Black, white fur, old gold edging.
B.Arch.	Same as B.A.
M.A.	Black and old gold.
B.Phil.	Same as M.A.
M.Phil.	Same as M.A.
M.F.A.	Same as M.A.
B.Ed.	Same as B.A.
M.Ed.	Same as M.A.
M.Litt.	Same as M.A.
D.Litt.	Scarlet, white and old gold edging.
M.Mus.	Same as M.A.
D.Mus.	Scarlet and white.
LL.B.	Maroon, Palatinate purple and white fur edging.
LL.M.	Maroon and Palatinate purple.
LL.D.	Scarlet and maroon.
D.C.L.	Scarlet and white.
B.Sc.	Black, white fur, royal blue edging.
B.Sc.(Speech)	Same as P.Sc.
B.Med.Sci.	Same as B.Sc.
M.Sc.	Black and royal blue.
D.Sc.	Scarlet, white and royal blue edging.
Ph.D.	Scarlet and scarlet.

Nottingham

Arts	Faculty colour
B.A.	
M.A.	
M.Phil.	Cherry red
Ph.D.	
D.Litt.	
B.Mus.	Pink
D.Mus.	
Theology	
B.Th.	
M.Th.	Purple
D.D.	
Law and Social Sciences.	
B.A.	
LL.B.	
M.A.	
M.Phil.	Maroon
Ph.D.	
D.Litt.	
LL.D.	
B.Arch.	Orange
Education	
B.Ed.	
M.Ed.	Lilac
M.Phil.	
Ph.D.	
Pure Science	
B.Sc.	
M.Sc.	
M.Phil.	Royal blue
Ph.D.	
D.Sc.	
B.Pharm.	Dove grey

Agricultural Science	
B.Sc.	
M.Sc.	
M.Phil.	Green
Ph.D.	
D.Sc.	
Applied Science	
B.Sc.	
M.Sc.	
M.Phil.	Light navy blue
Ph.D.	
D.Sc.	
Medicine	
B.Med.Sci.	
B.M.	
B.S.	
M.Med.Sci.	Gold
M.Phil.	
Ph.D.	
D.M.	
D.Sc.	

Note:—All hoods of this University are of the Cambridge shape. The hoods of Bachelors other than Bachelors of Divinity, Bachelors of Medicine, Bachelors of Surgery and Bachelors of Architecture are of black stuff, lined with light blue silk to a depth of 3". The lining is bound at the edges with a ribbon of the appropriate colour. In the case of Bachelors of Medicine, Bachelors of Surgery and Bachelors of Architecture the hood including the cape is bound with the appropriate colour. The hood of Bachelors of Divinity and of Masters is of black stuff or silk, lined throughout with light blue silk and bound at the edge with a ribbon of the appropriate colour. In the case of Masters of Philosophy the hood including the cape is bound with the appropriate colour. The hood of Doctors of Philosophy is of claret silk or cloth, lined throughout with light blue silk and bound at the edge with a ribbon of the appropriate colour. Hoods of Doctors other than Doctors of Philosophy are of scarlet silk or cloth, lined throughout with light blue silk and bound at the edge with a ribbon of the appropriate colour.

Oxford

B.Ed.	Black silk, lined beetle green taffeta.
B.A.	Black, half-lined and edged with white fur.
M.A.	Black silk, lined crimson or shot crimson silk.
B.D.	Black, lined fine ribbed black silk.
D.D.	Scarlet superfine cloth, lined fine ribbed black silk.
B.C.L.	Medium blue silk, half-lined and edged with white fur.
D.C.L.	Scarlet superfine cloth, lined crimson silk.
B.M., B.Ch.	Medium blue silk, half-lined and edged with white fur.
M.Ch.	Black silk, lined and edged with blue silk.
D.M.	Scarlet superfine cloth, lined crimson silk.
B.Mus.	Lilac silk, half-lined and edged white fur.
D.Mus.	Cream silk brocade, with apple-blossom embroidery, lined cherry crimson silk.
D.Litt	
D.Sc.	Scarlet superfine cloth, lined with grey silk.
B.Litt.	Light blue, half-lined and edged white fur.
B.Sc.	Same as B.Litt.
M.Sc.	Light blue silk, lined and edged with neutral grey silk.
B.Phil.	Dark blue silk, lined with white silk.
D.Phil.	Scarlet superfine cloth, lined navy-blue silk.

Note:—The Oxford Bachelors' hoods (except B.D. & B.Phil.) and the M.A. hood are either of Burgon or Oxford shape. The M.Sc. hood is always of Burgon shape. The B.Phil. and M.Ch. hoods are always of Oxford shape. The B.D. and all Doctors' hoods are of the correct full apron shape. B.A., M.A., M.Ch., and B.D. hoods are of corded black silk; the other Bachelors' hoods are of corded or ribbed silk of the colour shown, lined or trimmed with white fur. When the Burgon shape is used the hood is half-lined and edged with fur, but for the Oxford shape only an edging of fur is used.

Reading

B.A.	
LL.B.	All Reading hoods are lined with cream coloured silk. Bachelors' hoods are of dark blue lined with cream silk to a depth of 3". All hoods are full shape. All Doctors' hoods are of scarlet superfine cloth fully lined with cream silk, of the full shape, except Ph.D., which is of crimson cloth lined with cream silk (maroon Russell-Cord is generally used).
B.Ed.	
B.Mus.	
M.A.	
M.A. (Education)	
M.Sc.	
M.Sc. (Education)	
M.F.A.	
B.Sc.	
M.Sc.	
M.Agr. Sc.	
M.Agr. Eng.	

M.Phil.
Ph.D.
D.Litt.
D.Sc.

St. Andrews

M.A.	Black silk with cherry silk lining.
B.D.	Violet silk or cloth bordered with white fur.
LL.D.	Pimento silk or cloth lined with ermine or white satin.
Mus.D.	Sky blue silk or cloth lined with ermine or white satin.
Ph.D.	Blue silk lined with white satin.
B.Sc.	Purple-lilac silk or cloth bordered with white fur.
M.Sc.	Black silk lined with purple-lilac silk or cloth.
D.Sc.	Purple-lilac silk or cloth lined with ermine or white satin.
B.Litt.	Saffron yellow silk bordered with white fur.
D.Litt.	Saffron yellow silk lined with ermine or white satin.
M.Litt.	Black silk lined with saffron yellow silk or cloth.
M.Theol.	Black silk lined with violet silk or cloth.
B.Phil.	Gold silk bordered with white fur.
D.D.	Violet silk or cloth lined with ermine or white satin.

Note:—All hoods of this University are of the full shape with well-rounded capes.

Salford

Bachelors	Light University blue corded silk, lined with gold satin and faced with 2" of distinguishing colour inside.
Masters	Light University blue corded silk, the cape lined and edged with gold satin, and edged inside with 3" of distinguishing colour.
Doctors of Philosophy	Light blue, lined and edged with scarlet satin.
Doctors (other than Doctors of Philosophy)	Dark blue, lined and edged all round with gold satin.

Note:—All the hoods are of the special full shape.

Sheffield

B.A.	(Arts) Green cloth, white fur, crushed strawberry.
B.Mus.	Green cloth, white fur, cream brocade.
B.Sc.	Green cloth, white fur, apricot.
M.B., Ch.B.	Green cloth, white fur, red.
B.Med.Sci.	Green cloth, white fur, cerise.
B.D.S.	Green cloth, white fur, pale rose-pink.
LL.B.	Green cloth, white fur, pale green.
B.Jur.	Green cloth, white fur, olive-green.
B.A. (Law)	Green cloth, white fur, olive-green.
B.Eng.	Green cloth, white fur, lilac.
B.Sc.Tech.	(Engineering and Materials Technology) Green cloth, white fur, lilac.
B.Met.	Green cloth, white fur, steel-grey.
B.A.	(Social Sciences) Green cloth, white fur, lemon-yellow.
B.A.(Econ.)	Green cloth, white fur, lemon-yellow.
B.A.	(Architectural Studies) Green cloth, white fur, old gold.
B.Ed.	Green cloth, white fur, pearl.
M.A.	(Arts) Green silk, crushed strawberry.
M.Sc.	(Pure Science) Green silk, apricot.
Ch.M.	Green silk, red.
M.Med.Sci.	Green silk, cerise.
M.D.S.	Green silk, pale rose-pink.
LL.M.	Green silk, pale green.
M.A.	(Law) Green silk, olive-green.
M.Eng.	Green silk, purple.
M.Sc.Tech.	(Engineering and Materials Technology) Green silk, lilac.
M.Met.	Green silk, steel-grey.
M.A.	(Social Sciences) Green silk, lemon-yellow.
M.A.(Econ.)	Green silk, lemon yellow.
M.A.	(Architectural Studies) Green silk, old gold.
M.A.	(Educational Studies) Green silk, pearl.
M.Sc.	(Educational Studies) Green silk, pearl.
M.Ed.	Green silk, pearl.
Ph.D.	Red silk, dark green.
Litt.D.	(Arts) Red silk, crushed strawberry.
D.Mus.	Red silk, cream brocade.
D.Sc.	(Pure Science) Red silk, apricot.
M.D.	Red silk, red.
LL.D.	Red silk, pale green.
D.Eng.	Red silk, purple.

D.Sc.Tech.	(Engineering and Material Technology. Red silk, lilac.
D.Met.	Red silk, steel-grey.
Litt.D.	(Social Sciences) Red silk lemon-yellow.
Litt.D.(Econ.)	Red silk, lemon-yellow.
Litt.D.	(Architectural Studies) Red silk, old gold.
Litt.D.	(Educational Studies) Red silk, pearl.
D.Sc.	(Educational Studies) Red silk, pearl.

Southampton

Degree colour	
Arts and Lett	Mid-cerise
Music	Ivory
Science	Rich gold
Social Sciences	Light green
Education	White
Law	Blue (as the University silk
Medicine and Surgery	Crimson
Philosophy	Claret

B.A.	All hoods are fully lined with the University silk, a peacock blue. The neck portion is cut on the curve with a single central seam, no neckband is let in, and the neck is not edged. Bachelors, other than Bachelors of Music (who wear a blue hood), wear a black hood fully lined with the University silk and of the improved Oxford M.A. Burgon type. The hood proper is edged ¼" inside and out with the appropriate degree colour, except for Bachelor of Laws in which case the lining is turned over ⅜" on the outside to form the edging. Masters, other than Masters of Surgery, wear a black hood fully lined with the University silk, of the London M.A. type. The hood proper is edged inside and out with the appropriate degree colour, except for Masters of Laws in which case the lining is turned over ⅜" on the outside of the hood proper. Masters of Surgery wear a black hood fully lined with the University silk, of the Oxford Doctors' type. The hood proper is edged inside and out with crimson. Doctors of Philosophy wear a hood of claret-coloured cloth fully lined with the University silk and of the Oxford Doctors' type. Doctors (other than Doctors of Philosophy) wear a scarlet hood fully lined with the University silk of the Oxford Doctors' type.
M.A.	
D.Litt.	
B.Mus.	
D.Mus.	
LL.B.	
LL.M.	
LL.D.	
B.Sc.	
M.Sc.	
D.Sc.	
B.Sc. (Social Sciences)	
M.Sc. (Social Sciences)	
D.Sc. (Social Sciences)	
B.Ed.	
B.M.	
M.S.	
D.M.	
M.Phil. (in all faculties)	
Ph.D. (in all faculties)	

Note:—The B.Sc. (Engineering) degree is no longer awarded, but graduates who took the B.Sc.(Eng.) degree may, if they wish, wear hoods with orange edging.

Stirling

D.Univ.	Malachite green lined powder blue.
B.A.	Black lined with dove grey.
B.Ed.	Black lined with bunting azure blue.
M.Sc.	Black lined with malachite green, edged with white ribbon and bordered with fur.
M.Litt.	Black lined with malachite green, edged with white ribbon and bordered with fur.
Ph.D.	Dove grey lined with malachite green.

Note:—The hoods for Bachelors, Masters and Ph.D. are of the Edinburgh shape.
The hood for D.Univ. is of the full shape.

Strathclyde

B.A.	Blue, lined white.
B.Sc.	Blue, lined gold.
B.Arch.	Blue, lined gold, bound with scarlet cord.
LL.B.	Blue, lined white, bound with scarlet cord.
B.Ed.	Blue, lined white, bound with gold cord.
M.A.	Blue, lined white, white edging.
M.B.A.	Blue, lined white, white edging bound with black cord.
M.Litt.	Blue, lined white, white edging bound with blue cord.
M.Sc.	Blue, lined gold, gold edging.
M.Arch.	Blue, lined gold, gold edging bound with scarlet cord.
LL.M.	Blue, lined white, white edging bound with scarlet cord.
Ph.D.	As for B.A., B.Sc., B.Arch, LL.B. (as appropriate).
D.Litt.	As for B.A.
D.Sc.	As for B.Sc., B.Arch. (as appropriate).
LL.D.	Blue, lined white, bound with scarlet cord.

Note:—All hoods are of saltire blue and of the full shape.

Surrey

B.Sc.	Black cloth, lined with rayon of Surrey blue.
B.Mus.	Black cloth, lined with rayon of Surrey blue, with white brocade band.
M.Sc.	Black cloth, lined with rayon of Surrey blue.
M.Phil.	Black cloth, lined with rayon of Surrey blue, with blue rayon damask edging.
Ph.D.	Cardinal red cloth.
D.Sc.	Gold rayon satin.

Note:—All the hoods of this University are fully lined with blue rayon damask and except for the B.Sc. hood, which is modified similar to simple Oxford, are all of uniform parabolic shape.

Sussex

B.A. B.Sc. B.Ed. LL.B.	} Black cloth, lined with grey fur in squares.
M.A. M.Sc. M.S.W. (Master in Social Work) M.Ed.Psych. M.Phil.	} Black alpaca lined with dove grey.
M.Phil. (Development Studies)	} Black alpaca lined with dove grey with 1″ scarlet band over lining set quarter inch from edge.
D.Phil.	For ordinary occasions, a hood of deep royal blue lined scarlet. No hood for special occasions.
LL.D. D.Litt. D.Sc.	} As for Doctor of Philosophy.

Ulster (New University of Ulster)

B.A.	Black, lined University green, bound roy blue.
B.Sc	Black, lined University green, bound Shannon green.
M.A.	Bordeaux, lined University green, bound royal blue.
M.Sc.	Bordeaux, lined University green, bound Shannon green.
M.Phil.	Bordeaux, lined University green, bound gold.
D.Sc.	Scarlet, lined University green, bound Shannon green.
D.Litt.	Scarlet, lined University green, bound royal blue.
D.Phil.	Scarlet, lined University green, bound gold.

Note:—All hoods are of the full shape and are silk-lined throughout.

Wales

B.A. B.Sc.(Econ.) B.Sc. B.Sc.(Tech.) B.Eng. B.Eng.(Tech.) B.Ed. B.Lib. LL.B. B.Mus. B.Pharm. B.Arch. B.N. B.D.S. M.B. B.Ch. B.D. M.A. M.Sc. M.Eng. M.Sc.(Econ.) M.Ed. M.Lib. LL.M.	Bachelors' hoods are of the Oxford form, of black stuff or silk, except in the faculty of Music, in which they are dark blue silk. Except in the faculty of Medicine they are bordered with silk of the appropriate colour. In Medicine they are lined with silk of the appropriate colour and bordered with white (Medicine and Surgery) or purple (Dentistry). Masters' hoods are of the Cambridge form, of black silk, except in the faculty of Music, in which they are dark blue silk. They are lined with silk of the appropriate colour, the hood of a Master in Surgery being in addition bordered with white, and of a Master in Dental Surgery with purple. Doctors' hoods are of the Cambridge form, of scarlet cloth, except in the case of a Doctor of Philosophy, whose hood is of crimson cloth. They are lined with silk of the appropriate faculty colour, the hood of a Doctor in Medicine being in addition bordered with white.
M.Mus. M.Th. M.Pharm. M.Sc.D. M.Ch.D. M.Ch. Ph.D. M.D. D.Ch.D.	Faculty colours:— Arts—Mazarin blue shot with green. Librarianship—Mazarin blue shot with green, edged with white. Science—Bronze (yellow shot with black). B.Sc.(Tech.)—Bronze, edged with white. B.Eng.—Red shot with green. B.Eng.(Tech.)—Red shot with green, edged with white.

D.	Pharmacy—Shot silk of saxe blue.
D.Sc.	Music—Pearl (a shot silk of three hues).
D.Sc.(Econ.)	Law—Red shot with purple.
LL.D.	Theology—Mazarin blue shot with red.
D.Mus.	Medicine—Green shot with black, edged with white.
D.D.	Dentistry—Shot silk of saxe blue, edged with purple.
	Nursing—Green shot with white, edged with red.
	Architecture—Shot silk of scarlet red.
	Economic and Social Studies—Red shot with yellow.
	Education (B.Ed.)—Green shot with white

Warwick

B.A.	Black corded rayon fully lined and bound on the cowl and neckband with red taffeta.
B.Sc.	Black corded rayon fully lined and bound on the cowl and neck band with blue taffeta.
B.Ed.	Black corded rayon fully lined and bound on the cowl and neckband with green taffeta.
LL.B.	Black corded rayon fully lined and bound on the cowl and neckband with purple taffeta.
M.A.	Black corded rayon fully lined and bound with red taffeta.
M.Sc.	Black corded rayon fully lined and bound with blue taffeta.
M.Ed.	Black corded rayon fully lined and bound with green taffeta.
LL.M.	Black corded rayon fully lined and bound with purple taffeta.
M.Phil.	Black corded rayon fully lined and bound with red shot green taffeta.
Ph.D.	As Master's hood, but in maroon cloth full lined and bound with red shot green taffeta.
D.Litt.	As Master's hood, but in red cloth fully lined and bound with red taffeta.
D.Sc.	As Master's hood, but in red cloth fully lined and bound with blue taffeta.
LL.D.	As Master's hood, but in red cloth fully lined and bound with purple taffeta.

York

B.A.	Grey with white edging.
B.Phil.	Grey with red edging.
M.Phil.	Red with grey edging.
D.Phil.	Red with grey lining.
D.Univ.	Red silk with grey lining. (hon. degree)

Cranfield Institute of Technology (Bedford)

Doctor of Science	Neyron rose, lined with royal blue silk.
Doctor of Philosophy	Old gold cord, lined with neyron rose, neckband of neyron rose.
Master of Business Admin. Master of Science	} Old gold cord, lined with royal blue, neckband of royal blue.

Note:—The hoods of Doctors of Science are of the full shape, those of Masters and Doctors of Philosophy of the simple shape.

Royal College of Art

Dr.(R.C.A.)	Vermilion cloth, trimmed with white fur.
M.A.(R.C.A.)	White silk, trimmed with white fur.

The Open University (Milton Keynes)

B.A.	Light blue, faced inside with 3″ gold.
B.Phil.	Royal blue, faced inside with 3″ gold.
M.Phil.	Light blue, full lined with gold and edged with narrow band of gold.
M.A.	Gold, fully lined with royal blue and edged with narrow band of royal blue.
Ph.D.	Royal blue, fully lined with gold and edged with 1″ gold.
D.Sc.	Gold, fully lined with light blue.
D.Litt.	Gold, fully lined with royal blue.
D.Univ.	Royal blue, fully lined with light blue. The V-front to the hood is dark blue outside and light blue inside.

ABBREVIATIONS IN COMMON USE

A

a. = area; acre(s); are (100 sq. metres).
A.A. = Automobile Association; Alcoholics Anonymous.
AAA = Amateur Athletics Association.
A.A.I. = Associate of the Chartered Auctioneers' and Estate Agents' Institute.
A.A.L.P.A. = Associate of the Incorporated Society of Auctioneers and Landed Property Agents.
A. and M. = Ancient and Modern (Hymns).
A.B. = able-bodied seaman; *Artium Baccalaureus* (Bachelor of Arts).
A.B.A. = Amateur Boxing Association.
A.B.A.A. = Associate of the British Association of Accountants.
ABM = anti-ballistics missile defence system.
Abp. = Archbishop.
abr. = abridged.
ABRC = Advisory Board for Research Councils.
abs. = absolute.
a.c. (*or* A.C.) = alternating current.
A.C.A. = Associate of the Institute of Chartered Accountants.
A.C.C.A. = Associate of the Association of Certified Accountants.
A.C.I.S. = Associate of the Institute of Chartered Secretaries and Administrators.
ACT = Advisory Council on Technology.
ACTH = adreno-cortico-trophic hormone.
A.C.M.A. = Associate of the Institute of Cost and Management Accountants.
A.D. = *anno domini* (in the year of our Lord).
A.Dip. Art. Ed. = Advanced Diploma in Art Education.
A.Dip. Ed. = Advanced Diploma in Education.
A.D.C. = Aide-de-Camp.
Adm. = Admiral.
advt. (*or* adv.) = advertisement.
AEA = Atomic Energy Authority (UK).
AEC = Atomic Energy Commission (US).
AERE = Atomic Energy Research Establishment.
aet. (*or* aetat.) = *aetatis* (of age).
A.F.A.S. = Associate of the Faculty of Architects and Surveyors.
A.F.C. = Air Force Cross.
A.F.L. = American Federation of Labour.
A.F.M. = Air Force Medal.
AFRASEC = Afro-Asian Organisation for Economic Cooperation.
A.G. = Adjutant-General.
AGR = Advanced Gas-cooled Reactor.
A.H. = *anno Hegirae* (in the year of the Hegira).
A.I.A. = Associate of the Institute of Actuaries.
A.I.B. = Associate of the Institute of Bankers.
A.I.B.P. = Associate of the Institute of British Photographers.
A.I.C.E. = Associate of the Institution of Civil Engineers.
A.I.C.S. = Associate of the Institute of Chartered Shipbrokers.
AID = Agency for International Development (U.S.).
A.I.M.E. = Associate of the Institution of Mining Engineers.
A.I.Mech.E. = Associate of the Institution of Mechanical Engineers.
A.I.N.A. = Associate of the Institution of Naval Architects.
A.Inst.P. = Associate of the Institute of Physics.
A.I.Q.S. = Associate of the Institute of Quantity Surveyors.
A.L.A. = Associate of the Library Association.
A.L.S. = Associate of the Linnean Society.
alt. = altitude.
A.M. = *anno mundi* (in the year of the world); *Artium Magister* (Master of Arts); amplitude modulation.
a.m. = *ante meridiem* (before noon).
A.M.D.G. = *ad majorem Dei glorium* (to the greater glory of God).
amp. = ampere(s).
ANC = African National Congress.

anc. = ancient.
anhyd. = anhydrous.
anon. = anonymous.
ANZAC = Australian and New Zealand Army Corps.
ANZUS = Australian, New Zealand and U.S. Defence Pact (Pacific Security Treaty).
A.O.C. = Air Officer Commanding.
A.P. = Associated Press.
APT = Advanced Passenger Train.
aq. = aqueous.
A.R.A. = Associate of the Royal Academy.
A.R.A.D. = Associate of the Royal Academy of Dancing.
A.R.A.M. = Associate of the Royal Academy of Music.
A.R.B.S. = Associate of the Royal Society of British Sculptors.
ARC = Agricultural Research Council.
A.R.C.M. = Associate of the Royal College of Music.
arch. = archipelago.
A.R.C.O. = Associate of the Royal College of Organists.
A.R.C.Sc. = Associate of the Royal College of Science.
A.R.I.B.A. = Associate of the Royal Institute of British Architects.
A.R.I.C. = Associate of the Royal Institute of Chemistry.
A.R.I.C.S. = Associate of the Royal Institution of Chartered Surveyors.
A.R.P.S. = Associate of the Royal Photographic Society.
A.R.W.S. = Associate of the Royal Society of Painters in Water Colours.
A.S. (*or* AS) = Anglo-Saxon.
A.S.A. = Amateur Swimming Association.
ASDIC = Anti-submarine detector indicator.
ASEAN = Association of South-East Asian Nations (Indonesia, Malaysia, Philippines, Singapore, Thailand).
ASH = Action on Smoking and Health.
ASLIB = Association of Special Libraries and Information Bureaux.
ASPAC = Asian and Pacific Council.
A.T.C. = Air Training Corps.
A.T.D. = Art Teachers Diploma.
A.T.I.I. = Associate of the Taxation Institute Incorporated.
ATP = adenosine triphosphate.
atm. = atmospheric pressure.
at.wt. = atomic weight.
A.U.C. = *ab urbe condita* (from the founding of the City (Rome)), *or*, anno urbis conditae (in the year of the founding of the City).
av. = average.
AV = Authorized Version.
A.W.O.L. = Absent Without Leave.

B

b. = born; bowled.
B.A. = Bachelor of Arts.
B.A.A. = British Astronomical Association; British Airports Authority.
BAC = British Aircraft Corporation.
B.Acc. = Bachelor of Accountancy.
BAF = British Athletic Federation.
B.A.O. = Bachelor in the Art of Obstetrics.
BAOR = British Army of the Rhine.
B.Arch. = Bachelor of Architecture.
Bart. (*or* Bt.) = Baronet.
BAS = British Antarctic Survey.
B.B. = Boys' Brigade.
B.B.C. = British Broadcasting Corporation.
B.C. = before Christ; British Columbia.
B.Ch. (*or* Ch.B.) = Bachelor in Surgery.
B.C.L. = Bachelor in Civil Law.
B.Com. = Bachelor of Commerce.
B.D. = Bachelor in Divinity.
B.D.A. = British Dental Association.
Bde. = Brigade.
B.D.S. (*or* B.Ch.D.) = Bachelor in Dental Surgery.

B.Ed. = Bachelor of Education.
B.E.M. = British Empire Medal.
B.Eng. = Bachelor of Engineering.
BGC = British Gas Corporation.
BIM = British Institute of Management.
BIS = Bank for International Settlements.
BISRA = British Iron and Steel Research Association.
B.Litt. = Bachelor in Letters.
B.M. = Bachelor in Medicine; British Museum.
B.M.A. = British Medical Association.
B.M.C. = British Motor Corporation.
B.Mus. = Bachelor in Music.
B.N.C. = Brasenose College, Oxford.
BNOC = British National Oil Corporation.
bor. = borough.
b.p. = boiling point.
Bp. = Bishop.
B.Phil. = Bachelor of Philosophy.
Br. (or Brit.) = British.
Brit.Ass. = British Association for the Advancement of Science.
B.R. = British Railways; British Rail.
B.R.B. = British Rail Board.
B.R.C.S. = British Red Cross Society.
B.R.S. = British Road Services.
B.Sc. = Bachelor of Science.
BSC = British Steel Corporation.
B.S.I. = British Standards Institution.
BST = British summer time.
Bt. = Baronet; Brevet.
B.T.H.A. = British Travel and Holidays Association.
B.Th. = Bachelor in Theology.
Btu = British thermal unit.
B.V.M. = Blessed Virgin Mary.
B.V.M.S. = Bachelor in Veterinary Medicine and Surgery.
B.W.B. = British Waterways Board.

C

C. = Centigrade; Conservative.
c. = *circa* (about); centi- (10^{-2}).
C.A. = Chartered Accountant (Scottish Institute).
CAA = Civil Aviation Authority.
CARICOM = Caribbean Community and Common Market.
CABs = Citizens' Advice Bureaux.
Cal. = Calorie (nutritional kilogram-calorie).
cal. = calorie (gram-calorie used in physics and chemistry).
Cantab. = of Cambridge.
Cantuar. = of Canterbury.
cap. = capital letter; capitulum (chapter).
CAP = Common Agricultural Policy (Common Market).
CARD = Campaign Against Racial Discrimination.
CAS = Conciliation and Arbitration Service (took over some functions of former CIR 1974).
C.B. = Companion of the Order of the Bath.
C.B.E. = Commander of the Order of the British Empire.
CBI = Confederation of British Industry.
C.C. = County Council; County Councillor; Chamber of Commerce.
cc = cubic centimetre(s).
CCPR = Central Council of Physical Recreation.
C.D. = Civil Defence.
C.D.C. = Commonwealth Development Corporation.
C.D.S. = Chief of Defence Staff; Campaign for Democratic Socialism.
CDU = Christian Democratic Union (W. Ger.).
C.E. = Civil Engineer; Christian Era.
CEAO = West African Economic Community.
CEGB = Central Electricity Generating Board.
C.Eng. = Chartered Engineer.
CEI = Council of Engineering Institutions.
CENTO = Central Treaty Organisation.
centi = one-hundredth part (10^{-2}).
CERN = European Organisation for Nuclear Research.
CET = Central European Time; Common External Tariff (Common Market).
C.F. = Chaplain to the Forces.
cf. = *confer* (compare).
C.G.M. = Conspicuous Gallantry Medal.
C.G.S. = Chief of General Staff.

cgs = centimetre-gram-second.
CGT = Confédération Générale du Travail (French TUC).
C.H. = Companion of Honour.
Ch.Ch. = Christ Church.
Ch.M. = Master in Surgery.
C.I. = Lady of Imperial Order of the Crown of India; Channel Islands.
CIA = Central Intelligence Agency (US).
CID = Criminal Investigation Department.
C.I.E. = Companion of the Order of the Indian Empire.
Cie = Compagnie (Company).
c.i.f. = cost, insurance and freight.
C.-in-C. = Commander-in-Chief.
CIO = Congress of Industrial Organisations (US).
CIR = Commission on Industrial Relations (abolished 1974).
C.L. = Companion of Literature.
C.L.B. = Church Lads' Brigade.
cm = centimetre(s).
C.M.G. = Companion of the Order of St. Michael and St. George.
C.M.S. = Church Missionary Society.
CNAA = Council for National Academic Awards.
CND = Campaign for Nuclear Disarmament.
C.O. = Commanding Officer; Conscientious Objector.
Co. = County; Company.
c/o = care of.
C.O.D. = Cash on Delivery.
C. of E. = Church of England.
COI = Central Office of Information.
CoID = Council of Industrial Design.
COMECON = Council for Mutual Economic Assistance (East European).
Con. (or C.) = Conservative.
corr. = corrected.
COSPAR = Committee on Space Research.
CP = Communist Party.
CPAG = Child Poverty Action Group.
CPC = Communist Party of China.
C.P.R.E. = Council for the Protection of Rural England.
CPSU = Communist Party of the Soviet Union.
crit. = critical.
crystl. = crystalline.
C.S.C. = Conspicuous Service Cross; Commonwealth Scientific Committee.
C.S.E. = Certificate of Secondary Education.
C.S.I. = Companion of the Order of the Star of India.
CSP = Council on Scientific Policy.
CSU = Christian Social Union (W.Ger.).
C.T. = Civic Trust.
C.T.C. = Cyclists' Touring Club.
CTR = Controlled thermonuclear research.
cu. = cubic.
C.V.O. = Commander of the Royal Victorian Order.
cwt. = hundredweight.

D

d. = *denarius* (penny), *denarii* (pence); died; daughter.
D.A.R. = Daughters of the American Revolution.
dB = decibel(s).
D.B.E. = Dame Commander of Order of British Empire.
D.C. = District of Columbia.
d.c. (or D.C.) = direct current.
D.C.B. = Dame Commander of the Order of the Bath.
D.C.L. = Doctor in Civil Law.
D.C.M. = Distinguished Conduct Medal.
D.C.M.G. = Dame Commander, Order of St. Michael and St. George.
D.C.V.O. = Dame Commander of the Royal Victorian Order.
D.D. = Doctor in Divinity.
D.D.R. = German Democratic Republic (E. Ger.).
D.D.S. = Doctor in Dental Surgery.
DDT = Dichloro-diphenyl-trichloro-ethane.
DES = Department of Education and Science.
deca = ten times.
deci = one-tenth (10^{-1}).
del. = *delineavit* (he drew it).
D.ès L. = Docteur ès Lettres.
D.ès Sc. = Docteur ès Sciences.
D.F.C. = Distinguished Flying Cross.
D.F.M. = Distinguished Flying Medal.

D.G. = *dei gratie* (by the grace of God).
DIA = Design and Industries Association.
dil. = dilute.
Dip.Ed. = Diploma in Education.
Dip. H.E. = Diploma in Higher Education.
Dip.Tech. = Diploma in Technology.
DKP = Communist Party (W. Germany).
D.L. = Deputy-Lieutenant.
D.Lit. (*or* D. Litt) = Doctor of Literature.
D.M. = Doctor in Medicine (Oxford).
DM = Deutschemark.
D.Mus. = Doctor of Music.
DNA = deoxyribonucleic acid.
D.N.B. = Dictionary of National Biography.
do. = *ditto* (the same).
DoI = Department of Industry.
D.O.M. = *dominus optimo maximo* (To God, the best, the greatest).
D.P. = Displaced Person(s).
D.P.H. = Diploma in Public Health.
D.Phil. = Doctor of Philosophy.
D.P.M. = Diploma in Psychological Medicine.
Dr. = Doctor; debtor.
dr. = drachm.
D.Sc. = Doctor of Science.
D.S.C. = Distinguished Service Cross.
D.S.M. = Distinguished Service Medal.
D.S.O. = Companion of the Distinguished Service Order.
D.Th. = Doctor in Theology.
D.T.M. = Diploma in Tropical Medicine.
D.V. = *Deo volente* (God willing).
DVA = Dunkirk Veterans' Association.
dwt. = pennyweight.

E

EAAFRO = East African Agriculture and Forestry Research Organisation.
E. and O.E. = Errors and omissions excepted.
Ebor. = of York.
EBU = European Broadcasting Union.
EC = Electricity Council.
ECA = Economic Commission for Africa (UN).
ECAFE = Economic Commission for Asia and the Far East (UN).
ECE = Economic Commission for Europe (UN).
ECG = electro-cardiograph.
ECGD = Export Credits Guarantee Department.
ECLA = Economic Commission for Latin America (UN).
ECOSOC = Economic and Social Council (UN).
ECSC = European Coal and Steel Community.
ECTU = European Confederation of Trade Unions.
E.D. = Efficiency Decoration.
EEC = European Economic Community (Common Market).
EEG = electro-encephalogram.
EFTA = European Free Trade Association.
e.g. = *exempli gratio* (for example).
EMA = European Monetary Agreement.
EMBO = European Molecular Biology Organisation.
emf = electromotive force.
e.m.u. = electromagnetic unit.
ENEA = European Nuclear Energy Agency.
E.R. = Elizabetha Regina, *or* Edwardus Rex.
E.R.A. = Electrical Research Association.
ERNIE = electronic random number indicator equipment.
ERP = European Recovery Programme.
ESA = European Space Agency (incorporates former European Space Research Organisation (ESRO) and European Space Vehicle Launcher and Development Organisation (ELDO).
ESC = Economic and Social Council (UN).
et al. = *et alibi* (and elsewhere); *et alii* (and others).
etc. = *et cetera* (others; and so forth).
et seq. = *et sequens* (and the following).
et sqq. = *et sequentes, et sequentia* (and those following).
Euratom = European Atomic Energy Community.
ex lib. = *ex libris* (from the books of).

F

F. = Fahrenheit; Fellow.
f. = and the following page; ff. = and the following pages.

F.A. = Football Association.
F.A.L.P.A. = Fellow of the Incorporated Society of Auctioneers and Landed Property Agents.
F.A.N.Y. = First Aid Nursing Yeomanry.
FAO = Food and Agriculture Organisation (UN).
f.a.s. = free alongside.
F.B.A. = Fellow of the British Academy.
F.B.A.A. = Fellow of the British Association of Accountants.
FBI = Federal Bureau of Investigation (U.S.).
F.B.I.M. = Fellow of the British Institute of Management.
F.B.O.A. = Fellow of the British Optical Association.
F.B.S. = Fellow of the Botanical Society.
F.C.A. = Fellow of the Institute of Chartered Accountants.
F.C.C.A. = Fellow of the Association of Certified Accountants.
F.C.G.I. = Fellow of City and Guilds Institute.
F.C.I.A. = Fellow of Corporation of Insurance Agents.
F.C.I.B. = Fellow of Corporation of Insurance Brokers.
F.C.I.I. = Fellow of Chartered Insurance Institute.
F.C.I.S. = Fellow of the Institute of Chartered Secretaries and Administrators.
F.C.M.A. = Fellow of the Institute of Cost and Management Accountants.
F.D. = *Fidei Defensor* (Defender of the Faith).
FDP = Free Democratic Party (W. Ger.).
Fed. = Federation; Federal.
ff. = folios; and the following pages; fortissimo.
F.F.A.R.C.S. = Fellow of the Faculty of Anaesthetics, Royal College of Surgeons.
F.F.A.S. = Fellow of the Faculty of Architects and Surveyors.
FFI = Finance for Industry.
F.F.R. = Fellow of the Faculty of Radiologists.
F.G.S. = Fellow of the Geological Society.
F.H. = Fire Hydrant.
F.H.S. = Fellow of the Heraldry Society.
F.I.A. = Fellow of the Institute of Actuaries.
F.I.B. = Fellow of the Institute of Bankers.
F.I.B.P. = Fellow of the Institute of British Photographers.
F.I.C.S. = Fellow of the Chartered Institute of Shipbrokers.
F.I.E.E. = Fellow of the Institution of Electrical Engineers.
F. Inst.F. = Fellow of the Institute of Fuel.
F.Inst.P. = Fellow of the Institute of Physics.
F.Inst.Pet. = Fellow of the Institute of Petroleum.
F.I.Q.S. = Fellow of the Institute of Quantity Surveyors.
F.I.R.E. = Fellow of the Institute of Radio Engineers.
FIS = Family Income Supplement.
F.I.S. = Fellow of the Institute of Statisticians.
F.J.I. = Fellow of the Institute of Journalists.
fl. = *floruit* (flourished).
F.L.A. = Fellow of the Library Association.
F.L.S. = Fellow of the Linnaean Society.
FM = Frequency modulation.
FMC = Federal Maritime Commission (US).
F.N.S. = Fellow of the Newtonian Society.
F.O. = Foreign Office.
fo. = folio.
f.o.b. = free on board.
F.O.P. = Friendship Oil Pipeline (E.Europe).
f.p. = freezing point.
F.P.S. = Fellow of the Pharmaceutical Society.
F.Ph.S. = Fellow of the Philosophical Society.
F.R.A.D. = Fellow of the Royal Academy of Dancing.
F.R.A.I. = Fellow of the Royal Anthropological Institute.
F.R.A.M. = Fellow of the Royal Academy of Music.
F.R.A.S. = Fellow of the Royal Astronomical Society.
F.R.Ae.S. = Fellow of the Royal Aeronautical Society.
F.R.B.S. = Fellow of the Royal Society of British Sculptors.
F.R.C.M. = Fellow of the Royal College of Music.
F.R.C.O. = Fellow of the Royal College of Organists.
F.R.C.O.G. = Fellow of the Royal College of Obstetricians and Gynaecologists.
F.R.C.P. = Fellow of the Royal College of Physicians of London.

F.R.C.P.Ed. = Fellow of the Royal College of Physicians of Edinburgh.
F.R.C.S. = Fellow of the Royal College of Surgeons of England.
F.R.C.S.Ed. = Fellow of the Royal College of Surgeons of Edinburgh.
F.R.C.V.S. = Fellow of the Royal College of Veterinary Surgeons.
F.R.Econ.S. = Fellow of the Royal Economic Society.
F.R.F.P.S. = Fellow of the Royal Faculty of Physicians and Surgeons (Glas.).
F.R.G.S. = Fellow of the Royal Geographical Society.
F.R.H.S. = Fellow of the Royal Horticultural Society.
F.R.Hist.S. = Fellow of the Royal Historical Society.
F.R.I.B.A. = Fellow of the Royal Institute of British Architects.
F.R.I.C. = Fellow of the Royal Institute of Chemistry.
F.R.I.C.S. = Fellow of the Royal Institution of Chartered Surveyors.
F.R.M.S. = Fellow of the Royal Microscopical Society.
F.R.Met.S. = Fellow of the Royal Meteorological Society.
F.R.N.S. = Fellow of Royal Numismatic Society.
F.R.P.S. = Fellow of the Royal Photographic Society.
F.R.S. = Fellow of the Royal Society.
F.R.S.A. = Fellow of the Royal Society of Arts.
F.R.S.E. = Fellow of the Royal Society of Edinburgh.
F.R.S.L. = Fellow of the Royal Society of Literature.
FRTPI = Fellow of the Royal Town Planning Institute.
F.S.A. = Fellow of the Society of Antiquaries.
F.S.M.C. = Fellow of the Spectacle Makers Company.
F.S.S. = Fellow of the Royal Statistical Society.
F.T.I. = Fellow of the Textile Institute.
F.T.I.I. = Fellow of the Taxation Institute Incorporated.
F.Z.S. = Fellow of the Zoological Society.

G

g. = gram(s).
GATT = General Agreement on Tariffs and Trade.
G.B.E. = Knight (or Dame) Grand Cross of the Order of the British Empire.
G.C. = George Cross.
G.C.A. = Ground Control Approach.
G.C.E. = General Certificate of Education.
G.C.B. = Knight (or Dame) Grand Cross of the Order of the Bath.
G.C.I.E. = Knight Grand Commander of the Indian Empire.
G.C.M.G. = Knight (or Dame) Grand Cross of the Order of St. Michael and St. George.
G.C.S.I. = Knight Grand Commander of the Star of India.
G.C.V.O. = Knight (or Dame) Grand Cross of the Royal Victorian Order.
GDP = gross domestic product.
GDR = German Democratic Republic (E. Ger.).
Gen. = General; Genesis.
GeV = thousand million electron-volts.
G.H.Q. = General Headquarters.
G.I. = American soldier (from army term "Government Issue" applied to kit and equipment).
GLC = Greater London Council.
G.M. = George Medal.
G.M.C. = General Medical Council.
G.M.T. = Greenwich mean time.
GNP = gross national product.
G.O.C. = General Officer Commanding.
G.O.P. = Grand Old Party (US Republican Party).
G.P. = General Practitioner.
gr = grain(s).
G.R.C.M. = Graduate of the Royal College of Music.
G.R.S.M. = Graduate of the Royal Schools of Music (Royal Academy and Royal College).
G.S.O. = General Staff Officer.

GTCs = Government Training Centres.
GYP = gross domestic income.

H

ha = hectare (100 ares).
H.E. = His Excellency; His Eminence; high explosive.
hecto = one hundred times (10^2).
H.H. = His (or Her) Highness.
hhd. = hogshead.
H.I.M. = His Imperial Majesty.
H.J.S. = Hic jacet sepultus (Here lies buried).
H.M. = His (or Her) Majesty.
H.M.A.S. = Her Majesty's Australian Ship.
H.M.I. = Her Majesty's Inspector.
H.M.L. = Her Majesty's Lieutenant.
H.M.S = Her Majesty's Ship; Her Majesty's Service.
H.M.S.O. = Her Majesty's Stationery Office.
H.N.C. = Higher National Certificate.
H. of C. = House of Commons.
H. of L. = House of Lords.
Hon. = Honourable; Honorary.
hp = horsepower.
H.P. = Hire purchase.
H.R. = House of Representatives (US).
H.R.H. = His (or Her) Royal Highness.
H.S.E. = Hic sepultus est (Here lies buried).
H.T. = high tension.
HTR = high-temperature reactor (type of nuclear power station).
H.V. = health visitor.
H.W.M. = high water mark.

I

IAAS = Incorporated Association of Architects and Surveyors.
IADB = Inter-American Development Bank.
IAEA = International Atomic Energy Agency (UN).
IATA = International Air Transport Association.
ib. (or ibid.) = ibidem (in the same place).
IBA = Independent Broadcasting Authority.
IBERLANT = Iberian Atlantic Command (NATO).
IBRD = International Bank for Reconstruction and Development (World Bank) (UN).
ICAO = International Civil Aviation Organisation (UN).
ICBM = Intercontinental ballistic missile.
ICEM = Intergovernmental Committee for European Migration.
ICFTU = International Confederation of Free Trade Unions.
ICI = Imperial Chemical Industries.
ICJ = International Court of Justice (UN).
ICRC = International Committee of the Red Cross.
ICSU = International Council of Scientific Unions.
ICT = International Computers and Tabulators.
Id. = idem (the same).
IDA = International Development Association (UN).
IDC = Industrial Development Certificate system.
i.e. = id est (that is).
IEA = International Energy Agency.
IFC = International Finance Corporation (UN).
ign. = ignotus (unknown).
IGY = International Geophysical Year (1957–8).
IHS = Iesus Hominum Salvator (Jesus Saviour of men)—repr. a Greek abbrev. of the word Jesus.
ILEA = Inner London Education Authority.
ILO = International Labour Organisation (UN).
I.L.S. = Instrument Landing System.
IMCO = Intergovernmental Maritime Consultative Organisation (UN).
IMF = International Monetary Fund (UN).
Inc. = Incorporated.
Incog. = incognito (unknown, unrecognised).
inf. = infinitive; infra (below).
in loc. (in loco) = in its place.
I.N.R.I. = Iesus Nazarenus, Rex Iudaeorum (Jesus of Nazareth, King of the Jews).
Inst. = Institute; Institution.
inst. = instant (the present month).

Interpol = International Criminal Police Commission (HQ in Paris).

Intelsat = International Telecommunications Satellite Consortium.

I.O.M. = Isle of Man.

I.O.W. = Isle of Wight.

IOU = I owe you.

I.P.F.A. = Institute of Public Finance and Accountancy.

IQ = intelligence quotient.

IQSY = International Years of the Quiet Sun.

I.R. = Inland Revenue.

I.R.A. = Irish Republican Army.

IRBM = Intermediate-range ballistic missile.

IRC = International Red Cross; Industrial Reorganisation Corporation (wound up 1970).

IRDA = Industrial Research and Development Authority.

I.S.O. = Imperial Service Order; International Standardisation Organisation.

I.T.A. = Independent Television Authority; Institute of Travel Agents; Industrial Transport Association; Invalid Tricycle Association.

I.T.O. = International Trade Organisation.

I.T.U. = International Telecommunication Union (UN).

ITV = Independent Television.

IWA = Inland Waterways Association.

J

J. = Judge; Jet (aircraft).

J.P. = Justice of the Peace.

K

K = Kelvin.

K. = Köchel numeration (of Mozart's works).

KANU = Kenya African National Union.

k = kilo = thousand.

K.B.E. = Knight Commander of the Order of the British Empire.

K.C. = King's Counsel.

kc. = kilocycle(s).

K.C.B. = Knight Commander of the Order of the Bath.

K.C.I.E. = Knight Commander of the Order of the Indian Empire.

K.C.M.G. = Knight Commander of the Order of St. Michael and St. George.

K.C.S.I. = Knight Commander of the Star of India.

K.C.V.O. = Knight Commander of the Royal Victorian Order.

K.G. = Knight of the Order of the Garter.

KGB = Soviet State Security Service.

kg = kilogram(s).

kilo = one thousand times (10^3).

KJV = King James Version.

K.K.K. = Ku Klux Klan.

km = kilometre(s).

k.o. = knock out (boxing).

K.P. = Knight of the Order of St. Patrick.

K.T. = Knight of the Order of the Thistle.

Kt. = knight.

kV = kilovolt(s).

kW = kilowatt(s).

kWh = kilowatt hour(s).

L

L. (or Lib.) = Liberal.

L.A. = Local Authority.

Lab. = Labour.

L.A.C. = London Athletic Club.

LAFTA = Latin American Free Trade Association.

LAMDA = London Academy of Music and Dramatic Art.

lat. = latitude.

lb = libra (pound), librae (pounds).

lbf = pound-force.

l.b.w. = leg before wicket.

l.c. = lower case (small letter(s)).

L.C.J = Lord Chief Justice.

L.D.S. = Licentiate in Dental Surgery.

L.ès L. = Licencié ès Lettres.

L.F.B. = London Fire Brigade.

l.gov.dist. = local government district.

L.H.D. = Litterarum Humaniorum Doctor (Doctor of Humane Letters).

Lic.Med. = Licentiate in Medicine.

Lic.S. = Licentiate in Surgery.

Lit.Hum. = Literae Humaniores (Study of the Classics).

Litt.D. = Litterarum Doctor (Doctor of Letters; Doctor in Letters (Camb.)).

LL.B. = Legum Baccalaureus (Bachelor of Laws).

LL.D. = Legum Doctor (Doctor of Laws; Doctor in Law (Camb.)).

L.M. = Licentiate in Midwifery.

loc.cit. = loco citato (in the place sited).

log. = logarithm.

long. = longitude.

L.R.A.D. = Licentiate of the Royal Academy of Dancing.

L.R.A.M. = Licentiate of the Royal Academy of Music.

L.R.C.M. = Licentiate of the Royal College of Music.

L.R.C.P. = Licentiate of the Royal College of Physicians.

L.R.C.S. = Licentiate of the Royal College of Surgeons.

L.R.C.V.S. = Licentiate of the Royal College of Veterinary Surgeons.

L.S. = loco sigilli (place of the seal).

L.S.A. = Licentiate of the Society of Apothecaries.

L.s.d. = Librae, solidi, denarii (Pounds, shillings, pence).

LSD = Lysergic acid diethylamide.

L.S.E. = London School of Economics.

L.S.O. = London Symphony Orchestra.

L.T.A. = Lawn Tennis Association.

L.Th. = Licentiate in Theology.

Lt.-Gen. = Lieutenant-General.

L.W.M. = lower-water mark.

LXX = Septuagint.

M

M. = Member; Monsieur; mark (German coin); meridies (noon); mega (million times).

m = metre(s).

m. = married; masculine; million.

M.A. = Master of Arts.

MAOT = Member of the Association of Occupational Therapists.

M.A.O. = Master in the Art of Obstetrics.

max. = maximum.

M.B. = Bachelor in Medicine.

M.B.A. = Master of Business Administration.

M.B.E. = Member of the Order of the British Empire.

M.C. = Military Cross; Master of Ceremonies.

Mc = million cycles, or megacycle.

M.C.C. = Marylebone Cricket Club.

M.Ch. = Master in Surgery.

M.Ch.D. = Master in Dental Surgery.

M.Ch.Orth. = Master in Orthopaedic Surgery.

M.Com. = Master of Commerce.

M.C.S.P. = Member of the Chartered Society of Physiotherapy.

M.C.T. = Member of the College of Technologists.

M.D. = Medicineae Doctor (Doctor in Medicine).

M.D.S. = Master in Dental Surgery.

M.Ed. = Master of Education.

M.E. = Middle English.

mega = one million times (10^6).

met. co. = metropolitan county.

MeV = megaelectronvolt(s)

MFA = Movement of the Armed Forces (Portugal).

M.F.H. = Master of Foxhounds.

mg = milligram(s).

Mgr. = Monsignor.

MHD = magnetohydrodynamics.

micro = one-millionth part (10^{-6}).

M.I. = Military Intelligence.

M.I.C.E. = Member of the Institution of Civil Engineers.

M.I.Chem.E. = Member of the Institution of Chemical Engineers.

milli = one-thousandth part (10^{-3}).

M.I.M.A. = Member of the International Marine Association.

M.I.Mar.E. = Member of the Institute of Marine Engineers.

M.I.Mech.E. = Member of the Institution of Mechanical Engineers.

M.I.Min.E. = Member of the Institution of Mining Engineers.

min. = minimum.

M.I.N.A. = Member of the Institution of Naval Architects.

M.Inst.Met. = Member of the Institute of Metals.

Min. Plenip. = Minister Plenipotentiary.

M.I.Mun.E. = Member of the Institution of Municipal Engineers.

MIRV = multiple independent re-entry vehicle.

M.Inst.T. = Member of the Institute of Transport.

M.I.S. = Member of the Institute of Statisticians.

M.I.T. = Massachusetts Institute of Technology.

M.I.T.M.A. = Member of the Institute of Trade Mark Agents.

M.I.W.M. = Member of the Institution of Works Managers.

M.J.I. = Member of the Institute of Journalists.

MKS = metre-kilogram-second system.

MKSA = metre-kilogram-second-ampere (Giorgi) system.

Mlle = Mademoiselle.

MLR = Minimum Lending Rate.

MM. = Messieurs.

M.M. = Military Medal.

mm = millimetre(s).

Mme = Madame.

m.m.f. = magnetomotive force.

mmHg = millimetre(s) of mercury.

M.N. = Merchant Navy.

Mods. = Moderations (Oxford).

M.O.H. = Medical Officer of Health.

m.p. = melting point.

M.P. = Member of Parliament; Military Police.

m.p.h. = miles per hour.

M.Phil. = Master of Philosophy.

MPLA = Popular Movement for the Liberation of Angola.

M.P.S. = Member of the Pharmaceutical Society; Member of the Philological Society; Member of the Physical Society.

M.R. = Master of the Rolls.

M.R.A.S. = Member of the Royal Asiatic Society; Member of the Royal Academy of Science.

M.R.Ae.S. = Member of the Royal Aeronautical Society.

M.R.C. = Medical Research Council.

M.R.C.O.G. = Member of the Royal College of Obstetricians and Gynaecologists.

M.R.C.P. = Member of the Royal College of Physicians.

M.R.C.S. = Member of the Royal College of Surgeons.

M.R.C.V.S. = Member of the Royal College of Veterinary Surgeons.

M.R.I. = Member of the Royal Institution.

M.R. Inst. Nav. = Member of the Royal Institute of Navigation.

MRTPI = Member of the Royal Town Planning Institute.

M.S. = Master in Surgery.

Ms., Mss. = Manuscript, Manuscripts.

M.S.A. = Mutual Security Agency.

M.Sc. = Master of Science.

M.T.B. = Motor Torpedo Boat.

Mus.B. = *Musicae Baccalaureus* (Bachelor in Music).

Mus.D. = *Musicae Doctor* (Doctor in Music).

MV = million volts *or* megavolt.

M.V.O. = Member of the Royal Victorian Order.

MW = million watts *or* megawatt.

N

NAAFI = Navy, Army and Air Force Institutes.

N.A.B.M. = National Association of British Manufacturers.

NADGE = Nato Air Defence Ground Environment Organisation.

nano = one-thousand-millionth part (10^{-9}).

NASA = National Aeronautics and Space Administration (US).

NATO = North Atlantic Treaty Organisation.

NATSOPA = National Society of Operative Printers and Assistants.

N.B. = *nota bene* (note well).

NBS = National Bureau of Standards (US).

NCB = National Coal Board.

N.C.O. = Non-commissioned Officer.

N.C.U. = National Cyclists' Union.

n.d. = no date (of books).

N.D.D. = National Diploma in Design.

NEA = Nuclear Energy Agency (OECD).

NEB = National Enterprise Board; New English Bible.

NEDC = National Economic Development Council.

NEL = National Engineering Laboratory.

Nem.con. = *Nemine contradicente* (no one contradicting = unanimously).

Nem.diss. = *Nemine dissentiente* (no one dissenting = unanimously).

NERC = Natural Environment Research Council.

Net. (*or* Nett.) = free from, or not subject to, any deductions.

NHS = National Health Service.

NIBMR = no independence before majority rule.

NIRNS = National Institute for Research in Nuclear Science.

NLF = National Liberation Front (political arm of Vietcong in S. Vietnam).

NLL = National Lending Library for Science and Technology.

No. = *numero* (number).

non.seq. = *non sequitur* (it does not follow).

NPC = National Parks Commission; National Ports Council.

N.P. = Notary Public.

NPD = National Democratic Party (W. Ger.).

N.P.F.A. = National Playing Fields Association.

NPL = National Physical Laboratory.

N.R.A. = National Rifle Association.

NRDC = National Research Development Corporation.

N.S. = New Style in the calendar (in Gt. Britain since 1752).

N.S.P.C.C. = National Society for the Prevention of Cruelty to Children.

N.T. = New Testament; National Trust.

NUR = National Union of Railwaymen.

NUS = National Union of Students.

NUT = National Union of Teachers.

N.Y. = New York.

N.Z. = New Zealand.

O

OAPEC = Organisation of Arab Petroleum Exporting Countries.

OAS = Organisation of American States; Organisation de l'Armée Secrète (the clandestine army of the French colonists in Algeria).

OAU = Organisation of African Unity.

ob. = *obit* (died).

obs. = observed.

O.B.E. = Officer of the Order of the British Empire.

OBEV = Oxford Book of English Verse.

OCAM = Common African, Malagasy and Mauritanian Organisation.

OCAS = Organisation of Central American States.

OCTU = Officer Cadets' Training Unit.

ODECA = Organisation of Central American States.

OECD = Organisation for Economic Co-operation and Development.

O.E.D. = Oxford English Dictionary.

O.F.M. = *Ordo Fratrum Minorum* (Order of Friars Minor = Franciscan).

O.H.M.S. = On Her Majesty's Service.

O.M. = Member of the Order of Merit.

O.N.C. = Ordinary National Certificate.

O.P. = *Ordinis Praedicatorum* (Order of Preachers = Dominicans); opposite to prompter (stage term); out of print.

op. = *opus* (work).

op cit. = *opere citato* (in the work cited).

OPEC = Organisation of Petroleum Exporting Countries.

ORGEL = Organique et Eau Lourde (organic liquid and heavy water nuclear reactor).

O.S. = Old Style in calendar.

O.S.B. = *Ordo Sancti Benedicti* (Order of St. Benedict = Benedictines).

O.T. = Old Testament.

O.T.C. = Officers' Training Corps.

Oxon. = of Oxford.

oz. = ounce(s).

P

p = penny, pence (decimal system).
P.A. = Press Association.
PAYE = Pay as you earn (income tax scheme).
P.C. = Privy Councillor; Police Constable.
P.C.C. = People's Caretakers' Council (Nat. movement in Rhodesia).
p.c. = per cent.; postcard.
p.d. = potential difference.
pdl = poundal.
P.D.S.A. = People's Dispensary for Sick Animals.
P.E.N. = Poets, Playwrights, Essayists, Editors and Novelists (Club).
P.E.P. = Political and Economic Planning (Society).
per pro (or p.p.) = per procurationem (by proxy).
PFLP = Popular Front for the Liberation of Palestine.
Ph.D. = Philosophiae Doctor (Doctor of Philosophy).
pinx = pinxit (he painted).
P.L.A. = Port of London Authority.
PLO = Palestine Liberation Organisation.
PLP = Parliamentary Labour Party.
PLUTO = Pipe-line under the ocean.
P.M. = Prime Minister; Post master; post meridiem (afternoon); Polar Medal.
P.M.O. = Principal Medical Officer.
P.N.E.U. = Parents' National Education Union.
P.O. = Post Office; postal order; Petty Officer.
P. & O. = Peninsular and Oriental Steamship Co.
P.O.W. = prisoner of war.
pp. = pages.
P.P.C. = pour prendre congé (to take leave).
P.Q. = Parliamentary Question.
P.P.S. = Parliamentary Private Secretary.
P.R. = Proportional Representation.
P.R.A. = President of the Royal Academy.
P.R.B. = Pre-Raphaelite Brotherhood.
PRC = People's Republic of China.
Pro tem. = pro tempore (for the time being).
Prox = proximo (of the next month).
P.R.S. = President of the Royal Society.
P.S. = post scriptum (postscript).
Ps. = Psalm.
Pss. = Psalms.
P.S.W. = Psychiatric Social Worker.
P.T. = Physical Training.
Pte. = Private.
P.T.O. = please turn over.

Q

Q. = Queen.
Q = 10¹⁸ British Thermal Units (1.05×10^{21} joules).
Q.B. = Queen's Bench.
Q.C. = Queen's Counsel.
Q.E.D. = quod erat demonstrandum (which was to be demonstrated).
Q.E.F. = quod erat faciendum (which was to be done).
Q.E.I. = quod erat inveniendum (which was to be found).
q.l. (or q.pl) = quantum libet (or quantum placet) (as much as one pleases).
Q.M. = Quartermaster.
Q.M.C. = Queen Mary College.
q.s. = quantum sufficit (a sufficient quantity).
Q.S. = Quarter Sessions.
QSEs = Qualified Scientists and Engineers (i.e., skilled manpower).
QSSs = Quasars (quasi stellar radio sources).
Q.T. = quiet (slang).
Qto. = quarto (folded in four).
QTOL = Quiet Take-off and Landing.
q.v. = quod vide (which see).

R

R. = Réaumur; Rex (King); Regina (Queen); Right (stage direction).
R.A. = Rear Admiral; Royal Academy; Royal Academician; Research Association; Right Ascension (astron.).
R.A.C. = Royal Automobile Club.
RAE = Royal Aircraft Establishment.
R.Ae.S. = Royal Aeronautical Society.

R.A.F. = Royal Air Force.
R.A.M. = Royal Academy of Music.
R.A.O.C. = Royal Army Ordnance Corps.
R.C. = Red Cross; Roman Catholic.
RCD = Regional Co-operation for Development (Pakistan, Turkey, Iran).
R.D. = Rural Dean; Royal Naval Reserve Decoration; Refer to Drawer.
R.D.I. = Designer for Industry of the Royal Society of Arts.
R.E. = Royal Engineers.
Reg. Prof. = Regius Professor.
R.E.M.E. = Royal Electrical and Mechanical Engineers.
Rep. = Representative; Republican.
R.G.S. = Royal Geographical Society.
r.h. = relative humidity.
R.H.S. = Royal Humane Society; Royal Horticultural Society.
R.Hist.S. = Royal Historical Society.
R.I. = Royal Institution; Royal Institute of Painters in Water Colours; Rhode Island; Religious Instruction.
R.I.B.A. = Royal Institution of British Architects.
R.I.I.A. = Royal Institute of International Affairs (Chatham House, London).
R.I.P. = requiescat in pace (may he rest in peace).
R.M. = Royal Marines; Resident Magistrate.
R.M.C. = Royal Military College, Sandhurst.
r.m.s. = root mean square.
R.N. = Royal Navy.
RNA = ribonucleic acid.
R.N.L.I. = Royal National Lifeboat Institution.
Ro. = recto (on the right-hand page).
R.P. = Member of the Royal Society of Portrait Painters.
RRE = Royal Radar Establishment.
rpm = revolutions per minute.
R.S.A. = Royal Society of Arts; Royal Scottish Academician.
R.S.M. = Regimental Sergeant Major.
R.S.P.C.A. = Royal Society for the Prevention of Cruelty to Animals.
R.S.V.P. = Répondez, s'il vous plaît (An answer is requested).
R.S.S. = Registered Shoeing Smith.
R.S.W. = Royal Scottish Society of Painters in Water Colours.
Rt. Hon. = Right Honourable.
RTPI = Royal Town Planning Institute.
Rt. Rev. = Right Reverend (of a Bishop).
R.U. = Rugby Union.
RV = Revised Version.
R.W.S. = Royal Society of Painters in Water Colours.
R.Y.S. = Royal Yacht Squadron.

S

S. = San, Santa, Santo, or São (Saint); SS. = Saints.
s. = solidus (shilling), solidi (shillings).
S.A. = Salvation Army; Sex Appeal; South America; South Australia; South Africa; Société Anonyme (Limited).
SACEUR = Supreme Allied Commander Europe.
SACLANT = Supreme Allied Commander Atlantic.
SALT = Strategic Arms Limitation Talks.
Sarum = of Salisbury.
SAYE = Save as You Earn.
S.C. = qualified to admission to Staff College.
sc. = scilicet (namely).
Sc.D. = Scientiae Doctor (Doctor in Science).
S.C.F. = Senior Chaplain to the Forces.
S.C.M. = State Certified Midwife; Student Christian Movement.
SDLP = Social Democratic Labour Party (N. Ireland).
SEATO = South-East Asia Treaty Organisation.
SED = Socialist Unity Party (E. Ger.).
SET = selective employment tax.
S.G. = Solicitor-General; Scots Guards.
SGHWR = Steam Generating Heavy Water Reactor.
SHAPE = Supreme Headquarters Allied Powers in Europe.
SI = Système International d'Unités (International System of Units).
sic. = so written.

SINS = Ships Inertial Navigation System.
SOS = distress signal (wireless code signal, used especially by ships at sea).
s.p. = *sine prole* (without issue).
S.P.C.K. = Society for the Promotion of Christian Knowledge.
SPD = Social Democratic Party (W. Ger.).
sp. gr. = specific gravity.
sq. = square; *sequens* (the following).
sqq. = *sequentes, sequentia* (those following).
SRC = Science Research Council.
S.R.N. = State Registered Nurse.
SS. = Saints.
S.S. = Steamship.
S.S.C. = Solicitor before Supreme Court (Scotland).
SSRC = Social Science Research Council.
STADAN = Satellite Tracking and Data Acquisition Network.
STAR = Satellites for Telecommunications, Applications and Research (European consortium).
S.T.D. = *Sacrae Theologiae Doctor* (Doctor of Theology); Subscriber Trunk Dialling.
St. = Saint; Street.
Ste = *Sainte* (Saint, feminine).
Stet = Let it stand (printing term).
s.t.p. = standard temperature and pressure.
S.T.P. = *Sacrae Theologiae Professor* (Professor of Divinity, old form of D.D.)
s.v. = *sub verbo* (under the entry).

T

TAB = Technical Assistance Board (UN).
TAVR = Territorial and Army Volunteer Reserve.
T.B. = Tubercule bacillus (tuberculosis).
t.b. = torpedo boat.
T.C.D. = Trinity College, Dublin.
T.C.C.B. = Test and County Cricket Board.
T.D. = Territorial Decoration; Teachta Dála (Representative of the Dáil).
temp. = temperature.
T.F. = Territorial Force.
T.H. = Trinity House.
TNT = trinitrotoluene (high explosive).
Toc.H. = Talbot House.
tr. = transpose.
T.R.C. = Thames Rowing Club; Tithes Rent Charge.
T.T. = tubercular tested; teetotal.
TUC = Trades Union Congress.
TV = Television.
TVA = Tennessee Valley Authority.
TWA = Thames Water Authority.
TWI = Training Within Industry for Supervisors.
T.Y.C. = Thames Yacht Club; Two-year Old (*or* Thousand Yards) Course.

U

U.A.M. = Afro-Malagasy Union.
U-boat = German submarine.
UCL = University College, London.
UCS = Upper Clyde Shipbuilders.
UDEAC = Central African Economic and Customs Union.
UDEAO = Customs Union of West African States.
UEAC = Union of Central African States.
UGC = University Grants Committee.
UHF = ultra-high frequency.
U.K. (*or* UK) = United Kingdom.
UKAEA = UK Atomic Energy Authority.
ult. = *ultimo* (of the last month).
UN *or* UNO = United Nations.
UNCTAD = United Nations Conference on Trade and Development.
UNDOF = UN Disengagement Observer Force.
UNDP = United Nations Development Programme.
UNEF = United Nations Emergency Force(s).
UNESCO = United Nations Education, Scientific, and Cultural Organisation.
UNICEF = United Nations Children's Fund.

UNIDO = United Nations Industrial Development Organisation.
UNRWA = United Nations Relief and Works Agency for Palestine Refugees.
UNTSO = UN Truce Supervision Organisation in the Middle East.
U.P. = United Press.
UPU = Universal Postal Union (UN).
U.S.A. (*or* USA) = United States of America.
USAEC = US Atomic Energy Commission.
U.S.P.G. = United Society for the Propagation of the Gospel.
USSR = Union of Soviet Socialist Republics (Russia).

V

V = volt(s).
v. = *vide* (see); *versus* (against).
V.A. = Vicar-Apostolic.
VAT = value added tax.
V. & A. = Victoria and Albert Museum, S. Kensington.
V.C. = Victoria Cross.
V.C.H. = Victoria County Histories.
V.D. = venereal disease; Volunteer Officers' Decoration.
v.d. = various dates.
V.E. Day = Victory in Europe Day, 8 May 1945.
Ven. = Venerable (of an Archdeacon).
verb. sap. = *verbum sapienti sat est* (a word to the wise is enough).
Very Rev. = Very Reverend (of a Dean or a Provost).
v.g. = very good.
v.h.c. = very highly commended.
V.H.F. = very high frequency.
V.I.P. = very important person.
viz. = *videlicet* (namely).
V.J. Day = Victory over Japan Day, 15 August 1945.
V.L. = Vice-Lieutenant (of a County).
V.M. = Virgin Mary.
V.M.H. = Victoria Medal of Honour (Royal Horticultural Society).
Vo. = *verso* (on the left-hand page).
V.P. = Vice-President.
V.R. = *Victoria Regina* (Queen Victoria).
v.r. = variant, *or* various reading.
V.S. = veterinary surgeon; vital statistics.
VTOL = vertical take-off and landing (aircraft).

W

W = watt(s).
Wasps = White Anglo-Saxon Protestants.
WCC = World Council of Churches.
W.E.A. = Workers' Educational Association.
WEU = Western European Union.
WFTU = World Federation of Trade Unions.
WHO = World Health Organisation (UN).
WMO = World Meteorological Organisation (UN).
W.O. = Warrant Officer.
W.R.A.C. = Women's Royal Army Corps.
W.R.A.F. = Women's Royal Air Force.
W.R.N.S. = Women's Royal Naval Service.
W.R.V.S. = Women's Royal Voluntary Service.
W.S. = Writer to the Signet.

Y

yd = yard(s).
Y.M.C.A. = Young Men's Christian Association.
Y.W.C.A. = Young Women's Christian Association.

Z

ZANU = Zimbabwe African National Union (Nat. movement in Rhodesia).
ZAPU = Zimbabwe African People's Union (Nat. movement in Rhodesia).
ZIPA = Zimbabwe People's Army.

FOREIGN PHRASES

Fr., French. Gr., Greek. Ger., German. It., Italian. L., Latin. Sp., Spanish.

à bas (Fr.), down, down with.
ab extra (L.), from without.
ab incunabilis (L.), from the cradle.
ab initio (L.), from the beginning.
ab intra (L.), from within.
à bon chat, bon rat (Fr.), to a good cat, a good rat; well attacked and defended; tit for tat; a Rowland for an Oliver.
à bon marché (Fr.), cheap, a good bargain.
à bras ouverts (Fr.), with open arms.
absente reo (L.), the accused being absent.
absit invidia (L.), let there be no ill-will; envy apart.
ab uno disce omnes (L.), from one specimen judge of all the rest; from a single instance infer the whole.
ab urbe conditâ (L.), from the building of the city; i.e., Rome.
a capite ad calcem (L.), from head to heel.
à chaque saint sa chandelle (Fr.), to each saint his candle; honour where honour is due.
à cheval (Fr.), on horseback.
à compte (Fr.), on account; in part payment.
à corps perdu (Fr.), with might and main.
à couvert (Fr.), under cover; protected; sheltered.
ad astra (L.), to the stars.
ad calendas Græcas (L.), at the Greek calends; i.e., never, as the Greeks had no calends in their mode of reckoning.
à demi (Fr.), by halves; half-way.
a Deo et rege (L.), from God and the king.
ad hoc (L.), arranged for this purpose; special.
ad hominem (L.), to the man; to an individual's interests or passions; personal.
adhuc sub judice lis est (L.), the case has not yet been decided.
a die (L.), from that day.
ad infinitum (L.), to infinity
ad interim (L.), in the meantime.
ad libitum (L.), at pleasure.
ad modum (L.), after the manner of.
ad nauseam (L.), to disgust or satiety.
ad referendum (L.), for further consideration.
ad rem (L.), to the purpose; to the point.
ad valorem (L.), according to the value.
affaire d'amour (Fr.), a love affair.
affaire d'honneur (Fr.), an affair of honour; a duel.
affaire de cœur (Fr.), an affair of the heart.
a fortiori (L.), with stronger reason.
à gauche (Fr.), to the left.
à genoux (Fr.), on the knees.
à haute voix (Fr.), aloud.
à huis clos (Fr.), with closed doors; secretly.
à la belle étoile (Fr.), under the stars; in the open air.
à la bonne heure (Fr.), well timed; all right; very well; as you please.
à l'abri (Fr.), under shelter.
à la mode (Fr.), according to the custom or fashion.
à la Tartuffe (Fr.), like Tartuffe, the hero of a celebrated comedy by Molière; hypocritically.
al fresco (It.), in the open air; out-of-doors.
al più (It.), at most.
alter ego (L.), another self.
à merveille (Fr.), to a wonder; marvellously.
amor patriæ (L.), love of country.
amour-propre (Fr.), self-love; vanity.
ancien régime (Fr.), the ancient or former order of things.
anguis in herba (L.), a snake in the grass.
anno Christi (L.), in the year of Christ.
anno Domini (L.), in the year of our Lord.
anno mundi (L.), in the year of the world.
annus mirabilis (L.), year of wonders; wonderful year.
ante bellum (L.), before the war.
ante lucem (L.), before light.
ante meridiem (L.), before noon.
à outrance (Fr.), to the utmost; to extremities; without sparing.
à pied (Fr.), on foot.
à point (Fr.), to a point, just in time, exactly right.
a posse ad esse (L.), from possibility to reality.
ariston metron (Gr.), the middle course is the best; the golden mean.

arrière-pensée (Fr.), hidden thought; mental reservation.
au courant (Fr.), fully acquainted with.
audi alteram partem (L.), hear the other side.
au fait (Fr.), well acquainted with; expert.
au fond (Fr.), at bottom.
auf Wiedersehen ! (Ger.), till we meet again.
au pis aller (Fr.), at the worst.
au revoir (Fr.), adieu till we meet again.
aut vincere aut mori (L.), either to conquer or to die; death or victory.
a verbis ad verbera (L.), from words to blows.
a vinculo matrimonii (L.), from the bond of matrimony.
à volonté (Fr.), at pleasure.
a vostra salute (It.)
à votre santé (Fr.) } to your health.
a vuestra salud (Sp.)
bas bleu (Fr.), a blue-stocking; a literary woman.
beau monde (Fr.), the world of fashion.
beaux esprits (Fr.), men of wit; gay spirits.
beaux yeux (Fr.), fine eyes; good looks.
ben trovato (It.), well or cleverly invented.
bête noire (Fr.), a black beast; a bugbear.
bon gré mal gré (Fr.), with good or ill grace; willing or unwilling.
bonhomie (Fr.), good-nature; artlessness.
bonne bouche (Fr.), a delicate or tasty morsel.
bon vivant (Fr.), a good liver; a gourmand.
brutum fulmen (L.), a harmless thunderbolt.
canaille (Fr.), rabble.
candida Pax (L.), white-robed Peace.
casus belli (L.), that which causes or justifies war.
causa sine qua non (L.), an indispensable cause or condition.
caveat emptor (L.), let the buyer beware (or look after his own interest).
cela va sans dire (Fr.), that goes without saying; needless to say.
ceteris paribus (L.), other things being equal.
chacun son goût (Fr.), every one to his taste.
cogito, ergo sum (L.), I think, therefore I exist.
comme il faut (Fr.), as it should be.
compos mentis (L.), sound of mind; quite sane.
compte rendu (Fr.), an account rendered; a report or statement drawn up.
conditio sine qua non (L.), a necessary condition.
conseil de famille (Fr.), a family consultation.
consensus facit legem (L.), consent makes the law.
consilio et animis (L.), by wisdom and courage.
consilio et prudentia (L.), by wisdom and prudence.
constantia et virtute (L.), by constancy and virtue.
contra bonos mores (L.), against good manners.
contretemps (Fr.), an unlucky accident; a hitch.
cordon bleu (Fr.), blue ribbon; a cook of the highest class.
cordon sanitaire (Fr.), a line of guards to prevent the spreading of contagion or pestilence.
corpus delicti (L.), the body or substance of a crime or offence.
corrigenda (L.), things to be corrected.
coup de grâce (Fr.), a finishing stroke.
coup d'état (Fr.), a sudden decisive blow in politics; a stroke of policy.
coup de soleil (Fr.), sunstroke.
credat Judæus Apella (L.), let Apella, the superstitious Jew, believe it (I won't); tell that to the marines.
cucullus non facit monachum (L.), the cowl does not make the friar.
cui bono ? (L.), For whose advantage is it? to what end?
culpam pœna premit comes (L.), punishment follows hard upon crime.
cum grano salis (L.), with a grain of salt; with some allowance.
cum privilegio (L.), with privilege.
currente calamo (L.), with a fluent pen.
da locum melioribus (L.), give place to your betters.
damnant quod non intelligunt (L.), they condemn what they do not comprehend.
data et accepta (L.), expenditures and receipts.
de bon augure (Fr.), of good augury or omen.
de bonne grâce (Fr.), with good grace; willingly.

de die in diem (L.), from day to day.

de facto (L.), in point of fact; actual or actually.

dei gratia (L.), by God's grace.

de jure (L.), from the law; by right.

de mal en pis (Fr.), from bad to worse.

de novo (L.), anew.

deo volente (L.), God willing; by God's will.

de profundis (L.), out of the depths.

dernier ressort (Fr.), a last resource.

deus ex machina (L.), one who puts matters right at a critical moment; providential intervention.

dies non (L.), a day on which judges do not sit.

distingué (Fr.), distinguished; of genteel or elegant appearance.   [idleness.

dolce far niente (It.), sweet doing-nothing; sweet

double entente (Fr.), a double meaning; a play on words.

dramatis personæ (L.), characters of the drama or play.

dum spiro, spero (L.), while I breathe, I hope.

ecce homo ! (L.), behold the man !

eheu! fugaces labuntur anni (L.), alas ! the fleeting years glide by.

einmal ist keinmal (Ger.), just once doesn't count.

en avant (Fr.), forward.

en badinant (Fr.), in sport; in jest.

en déshabillé (Fr.), in undress.

en famille (Fr.), with one's family; in a domestic state.

enfant terrible (Fr.), a terrible child, or one that makes disconcerting remarks.

enfin (Fr.), in short; at last; finally.

en passant (Fr.), in passing; by the way.

en plein jour (Fr.), in broad day.

en rapport (Fr.), in harmony; in agreement; in relation.

en règle (Fr.), according to rules; in order.

entente cordiale (Fr.), cordial understanding, especially between two states.

entre nous (Fr.), between ourselves.

en vérité (Fr.), in truth; verily.

e pluribus unum (L.), one out of many; one composed of many.

esprit de corps (Fr.), the animating spirit of a collective body, as a regiment, learned profession or the like.

et sequentes, et sequentia (L.), and those that follow.

et tu, Brute ! (L.), and thou also, Brutus !

ex animo (L.), heartily; sincerely.

ex capite (L.), from the head; from memory.

ex cathedra (L.), from the chair or seat of authority, with high authority.

exceptio probat regulam (L.), the exception proves the rule.

ex curia (L.), out of court.

ex dono (L.), by the gift.

exeunt omnes (L.), all go out or retire.

exit (L.), he goes out.

ex mero motu (L.), from his own impulse, from his own free will.

ex nihilo nihil fit (L.), out of nothing, nothing comes; nothing produces nothing.

ex officio (L.), in virtue of his office.   [spective.

ex post facto (L.), after the deed is done; retro-

face à face (Fr.), face to face.

façon de parler (Fr.), manner of speaking.

faire bonne mine (Fr.), to put a good face upon the matter.

fait accompli (Fr.), a thing already done.

fama clamosa (L.), a current scandal; a prevailing report.

faute de mieux (Fr.), for want of better.

faux pas (Fr.), a false step; a slip in behaviour.

festina lente (L.), hasten slowly.

fiat justitia, ruat cœlum (L.), let justice be done though the heavens should fall.

fiat lux (L.), let there be light.

fide et amore (L.), by faith and love.

fide et fiduciâ (L.), by fidelity and confidence.

fide et fortitudine (L.), with faith and fortitude.

fidei defensor (L.), defender of the faith.

fide non armis (L.), by faith, not by arms.

fide, sed cui vide (L.), trust, but see whom.

fides et justitia (L.), fidelity and justice.

fides Punica (L.), Punic faith; treachery.

filius nullius (L.), a son of nobody; a bastard.

finis coronat opus (L.), the end crowns the work.

flagrante bello (L.), during hostilities.

flagrante delicto (L.), in the commission of the crime.

floreat (L.), let it flourish.

fons et origo (L.), the source and origin.

force majeure (Fr.), irresistible compulsion; war, strike, Act of God, etc.

forensis strepitus (L.), the clamour of the forum.

fortuna favet fortibus (L.), fortune favours the bold.

functus officio (L.), having performed one's office or duty; hence, out of office.

gaudeamus igitur (L.), so let us be joyful !

genius loci (L.), the genius or guardian spirit of a place.

gradu diverso, via una (L.), the same road by different steps.

grande parure } (Fr.), full dress.

grande toilette }

guerra al cuchillo (Sp.), war to the knife.

Hannibal ante portas (L.), Hannibal before the gates; the enemy close at hand.

hiatus valde deflendus (L.), a chasm or deficiency much to be regretted.

hic et nunc (L.), here and now.

hic et ubique (L.), here and everywhere.

hic jacet (L.), here lies.

hic labor, hoc opus est (L.), this is a labour, this is a toil.

hic sepultus (L.), here buried.

hoc genus omne (L.), all of this sort or class.

hoi polloi (Gr.), the many; the vulgar; the rabble.

hominis est errare (L.), to err is human.

homme de robe (Fr.), a man in civil office.

homme d'affaires (Fr.), a man of business.

homme d'esprit (Fr.), a man of wit or genius.

honi soit qui mal y pense (O. Fr.), evil to him who evil thinks.

honores mutant mores (L.), honours change men's manners or characters.

hors de combat (Fr.), out of condition to fight.

hors de propos (Fr.), not to the point or purpose.

hors-d'œuvre (Fr.), out of course; out of order.

ich dien (Ger.), I serve.

idée fixe (Fr.), a fixed idea.

id est (L.), that is.

il a le diable au corps (Fr.), the devil is in him.

Ilias malorum (L.), an Iliad of ills; a host of evils.

il penseroso (It.), the pensive man.

il sent le fagot (Fr.), he smells of the faggot; he is suspected of heresy.

imperium in imperio (L.), a state within a state; a government within another.

in actu (L.), in act or reality.   [last struggle.

in articulo mortis (L.), at the point of death; in the

in capite (L.), in chief.

in curia (L.), in court.

index expurgatorius } (L.), a list of books prohibited

index prohibitorius } to Roman Catholics.

in esse (L.), in being; in actuality.

in extenso (L.), at full length.

in extremis (L.), at the point of death.

in memoriam (L.), to the memory of; in memory.

in nubibus (L.), in the clouds.

in petto (It.), in (my) breast; to one's self.

in re (L.), in the matter of.

in sano sensu (L.), in a proper sense.

in situ (L.), in its original situation.

in vino veritas (L.), there is truth in wine; truth is told under the influence of intoxicants.

ipse dixit (L.), he himself said it; a dogmatic saying or assertion.

ipsissima verba (L.), the very words.

ipso facto (L.), in the fact itself.

ipso jure (L.), by the law itself.

jacta est alea (L.), the die is cast.

je ne sais quoi (Fr.), I know not what.

joci causa (L.), for the sake of a joke.

labor omnia vincit (L.), labour conquers everything.

l'allegro (It.), the merry man.

lapsus linguæ (L.), a slip of the tongue.

lares et penates (L.), household gods.

laus Deo (L.), praise to God.

le beau monde (Fr.), the fashionable world.

lector benevole (L.), kind or gentle reader.

le jeu n'en vaut pas la chandelle (Fr.), the game is not worth the candle; the object is not worth the trouble.

le mot de l'énigme (Fr.), the key to the mystery.

le point du jour (Fr.), daybreak.

lèse-majesté (Fr.), high-treason.

lettre de cachet (Fr.), a sealed letter containing private orders; a royal warrant.

lex loci (L.), the law or custom of the place.

lex non scripta (L.), unwritten law; common law.

lex scripta (L.), written law; statute law.

locum tenens (L.), a deputy.

lucri causa (L.), for the sake of gain.

magnum opus (L.), a great work.

mala fide (L.), with bad faith; treacherously.

mal à propos (Fr.), ill-timed; out of place.

malgré nous (Fr.), in spite of us.

malheur ne vient jamais seul (Fr.), misfortunes never come singly.

malum in se (L.), evil or an evil in itself.

mardi gras (Fr.), Shrove-Tuesday.

mariage de convenance (Fr.), marriage from motives of interest rather than of love.

mauvaise honte (Fr.), false modesty.

mauvais goût (Fr.), bad taste.

mea culpa (L.), my fault; by my fault.

me judice (L.), I being judge; in my opinion.

mens agitat molem (L.), mind moves matter.

mens legis (L.), the spirit of the law.

mens sana in corpore sano (L.), a sound mind in a sound body.

meo periculo (L.), at my own risk.

meo voto (L.), according to my wish.

mise en scène (Fr.), the getting up for the stage, or the putting on the stage.

modus operandi (L.), manner of working.

more suo (L.), in his own way.

motu proprio (L.), of his own accord.

multum in parvo (L.), much in little.

mutatis mutandis (L.), with suitable or necessary alteration.

nervus probandi (L.), the sinews of the argument.

nihil ad rem (L.), irrelevant.

nil desperandum (L.), there is no reason to despair.

noblesse oblige (Fr.), rank imposes obligations; much is expected from one in good position.

nolens volens (L.), willing or unwilling.

nom de guerre (Fr.), a false or assumed name.

non compos mentis (L.), not of sound mind.

non sequitur (L.), it does not follow.

nosce te ipsum (L.), know thyself.

nota bene (L.), mark well.

nudis verbis (L.), in plain words.

obiter dictum (L.), a thing said by the way.

omnia vincit amor (L.), love conquers all things.

ora pro nobis (L.), pray for us.

O tempora ! O mores ! (L.), O the times ! O the manners (or morals) !

ouï-dire (Fr.), hearsay.

padrone (It.), a master; a landlord.

par excellence (Fr.), by way of eminence.

pari passu (L.), at an equal pace or rate of progress.

particeps criminis (L.), an accomplice in a crime.

pas de quoi (Fr. abbrev. Il n'y a pas de quoi), don't mention it.

passim (L.), everywhere; in all parts of the book, chapter, etc.

pâté de foie gras (Fr.), goose-liver pie.

pater patriæ (L.), father of his country.

patres conscripti (L.), the conscript fathers; Roman senators.

pax vobiscum (L.), peace be with you.

per ardua ad astra (L.), through rough ways to the stars; through suffering to renown.

per capita (L.), by the head or poll.

per contra (It.), contrariwise.

per diem (L.), by the day; daily.

per se (L.), by itself; considered apart.

pied-à-terre (Fr.), a resting-place; a temporary lodging.

pis aller (Fr.), the worst or last shift.

plebs (L.), the common people.

poco a poco (It.), little by little. [called for.

poste restante (Fr.), to remain in the post-office till

prima facie (L.), at first view or consideration.

primus inter pares (L.), first among equals.

pro forma (L.), for the sake of form.

pro patria (L.), for our country.

pro tanto (L.), for so much; for as far as it goes.

pro tempore (L.), for the time being.

quid pro quo (L.), one thing for another; tit for tat; an equivalent.

qui m'aime, aime mon chien (Fr.), love me, love my dog. [sent.

qui tacet consentit (L.), he who is silent gives con-

quod erat demonstrandum (L.), which was to be proved or demonstrated.

quod erat faciendum (L.), which was to be done.

quod vide (L.), which see; refer to the word just mentioned.

quo jure ? (L.), by what right ? [tence.

raison d'être (Fr.), the reason for a thing's exis-

re (L.), in the matter or affair of.

reculer pour mieux sauter (Fr.), to draw back in order to make a better spring.

reductio ad adsurdum (L.), the reducing of a position to a logical absurdity.

requiescat in pace (L.), may he (or she) rest in peace.

respice finem (L.), look to the end.

respublica (L.), the commonwealth.

revenons à nos moutons (Fr.), let us return to our sheep; let us return to our subject.

re vera (L.), in truth.

sans peur et sans reproche (Fr.), without fear and without reproach.

sans rime ni raison (Fr.), without rhyme or reason.

sans souci (Fr.), without care.

sartor resartus (L.), the botcher repatched; the tailor patched or mended.

sauve qui peut (Fr.), let him save himself who can.

savoir-faire (Fr.), the knowing how to act; tact.

savoir-vivre (Fr.), good-breeding; refined manners.

semper idem (L.), always the same.

seriatim (L.), in a series; one by one.

sic passim (L.), so here and there throughout; so everywhere.

sicut ante (L.), as before.

sine die (L.), without a day being appointed.

sine mora (L.), without delay.

sine qua non (L.), without which, not; indispensable condition.

sotto voce (It.), in an undertone.

spirituel (Fr.), intellectual; witty.

stet (L.), let it stand; do not delete.

sub judice (L.), under consideration.

sub poena (L.), under a penalty

sub rosa (L.), under the rose; privately.

sub voce (L.), under such or such a word.

sui generis (L.), of its own or of a peculiar kind.

summum bonum (L.), the chief good.

tableau vivant (Fr.), a living picture; the representation of some scene by a group of persons.

tant mieux (Fr.), so much the better.

tant pis (Fr.), so much the worse.

tempora mutantur, nos et mutamur in illis (L.), the times are changing and we with them.

tempus fugit (L.), time flies.

tête-à-tête (Fr.), together in private.

tiers état (Fr.), the third estate; the commons.

to kalon (Gr.), the beautiful; the chief good.

to prepon (Gr.), the becoming or proper.

tour de force (Fr.), a feat of strength or skill.

tout à fait (Fr.), wholly; entirely.

tout à l'heure (Fr.), instantly.

tout de suite (Fr.), immediately.

tu quoque (L.), thou also.

ubique (L.), everywhere.

ubi supra (L.), where above mentioned.

ultra licitum (L.), beyond what is allowable.

ultra vires (L.), beyond powers or rights conferred by law.

urbi et orbi (L.), to the city (Rome) and the world.

utile dulci (L.), the useful with the pleasant.

ut infra (L.), as below.

ut supra (L.), as above stated.

vade in pace (L.), go in peace.

variæ lectiones (L.), various readings.

variorum notæ (L.), the notes of various commentators.

vede et crede (L.), see and believe.

veni, vidi, vici (L.), I came, I saw, I conquered.

verbatim et literatim (L.), word for word and letter for letter.

verbum sat sapienti (L.), a word is enough for a wise man.

ver non semper viret (L.), spring is not always green.

vexata quæstio (L.), a disputed question.

via media (L.), a middle course.

via trita, via tuta (L.), the beaten path is the safe path.

vice versâ (L.), the terms of the case being reversed.

videlicet (L.), that is to say; namely.

vi et armis (L.), by force of arms; by main force; by violence.

vigilate et orate (L.), watch and pray.

vita brevis, ars longa (L.), life is short; art is long.

vivat regina ! (L.), long live the queen !

vivat rex ! (L.), long live the king !

viva voce (L.), by the living voice; orally.

voilà (Fr.), behold; there is; there are.

voilà tout (Fr.), that's all.

volo, non valeo (L.), I am willing, but unable.

vox populi, vox Dei (L.), the voice of the people is the voice of God.

Embassies and High Commissions
Some useful addresses

Embassies

Country	Address of Embassy	Tel. No.
Argentina	9 Wilton Crescent, SW1X 8RP	235 3717
Austria	18 Belgrave Mews West, SW1X 8HU	235 3731
Belgium	103 Eaton Square, SW1W 9AB	235 5422
Brazil	32 Green Street, Mayfair, W1Y 4AT	629 0155
Chile	12 Devonshire Street, W1N 2DS	580 6392
China	31 Portland Place, W1N 3AG	636 5726
Cuba	57 Kensington Court, W8 5DQ	937 8226
Czechoslovakia	25 Kensington Palace Gardens, W8 4QY	229 1255
Denmark	29 Pont Street, SW1X 0BA	584 0102
Egypt	26 South Street, W1Y 6DD	499 2401
Finland	38 Chesham Place, SW1X 8HW	235 9531
France	58 Knightsbridge, SW1X 7JT	235 8080
Germany (DR)	34 Belgrave Square, SW1X 8QB	235 9941
Germany (FR)	23 Belgrave Square, SW1X 8PZ	235 5033
Greece	1a Holland Park, W11 3TP	727 8040
Hungary	35 Eaton Place, SW1X 8BY	235 7191
Indonesia	38 Grosvenor Square, W1X 9AD	499 7661
Iran	16 Prince's Gate, SW7 1PX	584 8101
Iraq	21–22 Queen's Gate, SW7 5JG	584 7141
Ireland (Rep. of)	17 Grosvenor Place, SW1X 7HR	235 2171
Israel	2 Palace Green, Kensington, W8 4QB	937 8050
Italy	14 Three Kings Yard, Davies St., W1Y 2EH	629 8200
Japan	43–46 Grosvenor Street, W1X 0BA	493 6030
Jordan	6 Upper Phillimore Gardens, W8 7HE	937 3685
Korea (S.)	4 Palace Gate, W8 5NF	581 0247
Kuwait	40 Devonshire Street, W1N 2AX	580 8471
Libya	58 Prince's Gate, SW7 2PW	589 5235
Mexico	8 Halkin Street, SW1X 7DW	235 6393
Morocco	49 Queen's Gate Gardens, SW7 5NE	584 8827
Netherlands	38 Hyde Park Gate, SW7 5DP	584 5040
Norway	25 Belgrave Square, SW1X 8QD	235 7151
Oman	64 Ennismore Gardens, SW7 5DN	584 6782
Pakistan	35 Lowndes Square, SW1X 9JN	235 2044
Peru	52 Sloane Street, SW1X 9SP	235 1917
Philippines	9a Palace Green, W8 4QE	937 3646
Poland	47 Portland Place, W1N 3AG	580 4324
Portugal	11 Belgrave Square, SW1X 8PP	235 5331
Romania	4 Palace Green, W8 4QD	937 9666
Saudi Arabia	30 Belgrave Square, SW1X 8QB	235 0831
South Africa	S. Africa House, Trafalgar Sq., WC2N 5DP	930 4488
Spain	24 Belgrave Square, SW1X 8QA	235 5555
Sudan	3 Cleveland Row, St. James's, SW1A 1DD	839 8080
Sweden	23 North Row, W1R 2DN	499 9500
Switzerland	16–18 Montagu Place, W1H 2BQ	723 0701
Thailand	29–30 Queen's Gate, SW7 5JB	589 0173
Turkey	43 Belgrave Square, SW1X 8PA	235 5252
USA	Grosvenor Square, W1A 1AE	499 9000
USSR	13 Kensington Palace Gardens, W8 4QX	229 3623
Venezuela	Flat 6, 3 Hans Crescent, SW1X 0LX	584 4206
Yugoslavia	5 Lexham Gardens, W8 5JJ	370 6105

High Commission

Country	Address	Tel. No.
Australia	Australia House, Strand, WC2B 4LA	438 8000
Bangladesh	28 Queen's Gate, SW7	584 0081
Barbados	6 Upper Belgrave Street, SW1X 8AZ	235 8686
Canada	Macdonald House, 1 Grosvenor Sq., W1	629 9492
Cyprus	93 Park Street, W1Y 4ET	499 8272
Fiji	34 Hyde Park Gate, SW7	584 3661
Gambia	60 Ennismore Gardens, SW7	584 1242
Ghana	13 Belgrave Square, SW1X 8PR	235 4142
Guyana	3 Palace Court, Bayswater Road, W2	229 7684
India	India House, Aldwych, WC2 4NA	836 8484
Jamaica	48 Grosvenor Street, W1X 0BJ	499 8600
Kenya	45 Portland Place, W1N 4AS	636 2371
Malawi	47 Great Cumberland Place, W1H 8DB	723 6021
Malaysia	45 Belgrave Square, SW1X 8QT	245 9221
Malta	24 Haymarket, SW1Y 4DJ	930 9851
Mauritius	32–33 Elvaston Place, SW7	581 0294
New Zealand	N.Z. House, Haymarket, SW1Y 4TQ	930 8422
Nigeria	9 Northumberland Avenue, WC2N 5BX	839 1244
Sierra Leone	33 Portland Place, W1N 3AG	636 6483
Singapore	2 Wilton Crescent, SW1X 8RW	235 8315
Sri Lanka	13 Hyde Park Gardens, W2 2LX	262 1841
Tanzania	43 Hertford Square, SW1X 8NT	499 8951
Trinidad and Tobago	42 Belgrave Square, SW1Y 2AB	245 9351
Zambia	7–11 Cavendish Place, W1N 0HB	580 0691

Addresses of Principal Government and Public Offices

Agriculture, Fisheries and Food, Ministry of	3–10 Whitehall Place, SW1A 2HH
British Gas Corporation	59 Bryanston Street, W1
British Railways Board	222 Marylebone Road, NW1
British Standards Institution	2 Park Street, W1
British Steel Corporation	33 Grosvenor Place, SW1
British Tourist Authority	64 St James's Street, SW1
Central Office of Information	Hercules Road, SE1 7DU
Customs and Excise Board	Mark Lane, EC3
Defence, Ministry of	Main Building, Whitehall, SW1A 2HB
Education and Science, Department of	39 York Road, SE1
Electricity Council	30 Millbank, SW1
Employment, Department of	8 St James's Sq. SW1
Energy, Department of	Thames House South, Millbank, SW1
Environment, Department of the	2 Marsham St., SW1P 3EB
Foreign and Commonwealth Office	Downing Street, SW1A 2AL
Health and Social Security, Department of	Elephant and Castle, SE1 6BY
Home Office	Whitehall, SWA 2AP
Home Office (Licensing)	Waterloo Bridge House, Waterloo Road, SE1 8UA
Industry, Department of	1 Victoria Street, SW1H 0ET
Inland Revenue, Board of	Somerset House, WC2
Meteorological Office	London Road, Bracknell, Berks.
Metrication Board	22 Kingsway, WC2B 6LE
Monopolies and Mergers Commission	48 Carey Street, WC2A 2JE
National Coal Board	Grosvenor Place, SW1X 7AE
National Trust	40–42 Queen Anne's Gate, SW1 9AS
Northern Ireland Office	Great George Street, SW1
Office of Population Censuses and Surveys	10 Kingsway, WC2
Overseas Development, Ministry of	Stag Place, Victoria, SW1E 5OH
Patent Office	25 Southampton Buildings, WC2A 1AY
Port of London Authority	World Trade Centre, E1
Post Office	23 Howland St. W1P 6HQ
Scottish Office	Dover House, Whitehall, SW1A 2AU
Trade, Department of	1 Victoria St, SW1H 0ET
Welsh Office	Gwydyr House, Whitehall, SW1

MEDICAL MATTERS

Here we give a brief summary of up-to-date medical knowledge, including some recent developments. It must not be allowed to replace your doctor, who should be consulted immediately if you are worried. An index ensures easy reference.

TABLE OF CONTENTS

An alphabetical index of diseases mentioned in the text of Part II, referring the reader to the appropriate page and column.

MEDICAL MATTERS

PART I. INTRODUCTION.

(a) HOW TO USE THE SECTION.

Diseases do not exist in watertight compartments, but doctors arrange them according either to their cause or the area of the body affected. This plan has been followed here, and at the beginning of each part an account of the group of diseases under discussion is given. Unless you know enough already, you would be wise to read it.

Here is some advice about your attitude to disease in general, and your use of this section in particular.

First of all, and obviously, no book is a substitute for the doctor, and when you are ill you must see him. There are good and bad doctors, competent and incompetent ones, just as in any other profession or trade; so choose a doctor you can trust, *and then believe what he tells you and carry out his advice.* There is no use complaining about the whole medical profession just because you are dissatisfied with your own G.P. If you are, you should sign on with another.

Secondly, *never* believe what you hear from non-medical sources. Literally millions of people are made miserable every year by taking to heart nonsense told them by others, who may well be quite unaware of the harm they do, or even have the very best intentions. In any medical matter ask your doctor, and ignore your next-door neighbour's asked-for or unasked-for advice. Doctors are sometimes wrong, but they are much less likely to be wrong than someone without a medical education. Remember, too, that the statement that there is no cure for a disease does not necessarily mean that it is deadly: and it never means that nothing can be done to make it more tolerable. There is much more to modern doctoring than simply curing the curable.

Thirdly, don't try to diagnose your own trouble or decide what treatment you think you should have. This section will have failed completely in its intentions if it puts you in the position of a character described by an English humourist, who, from a medical dictionary, discovered that he had every disease listed in it with the solitary exception of housemaid's knee. Diseases which appear to the layman to have the "same" symptoms may be vastly different in seriousness: influenza and poliomyelitis, for example, may in the initial stages, appear very similar. So also may stomach ulcer and cancer of the stomach. No human being is infallible, but it is most important that you should go to the person who is best fitted to know—your doctor.

Lastly, you should not be misled into thinking that you can always tell the seriousness of a disease by the general appearance of the patient. Children, in particular, may have a high temperature, or even be delirious, on one day, and the next be out of bed and wanting to get back to school. On the other hand, many of the most dangerous fevers (as we shall see later) are accompanied by a low temperature and do not appear particularly dramatic in the initial stages. Thus a young woman who may be aware of nothing wrong but lack of energy and getting easily tired may be seriously ill with tuberculosis of the lungs.

The best rule is to seek medical advice either when you have suddenly become ill with symptoms you don't understand or (and this is equally important) if you have gradually been feeling less fit over a period of time. Perhaps, too, it is wise to call your doctor if you have been ill with *anything* for more than three days. You should *not* call in a specialist before seeing your G.P., as is so often done in America and on the Continent. Specialists are very clever, but are naturally prejudiced in favour of their own subject; for example, an eye specialist will be predisposed to think of your headache in terms of eyestrain, an ear, nose, and throat specialist in terms of sinus trouble, and a psychiatrist in terms of mother-in-law trouble. Therefore you should first have a check from your G.P., who knows a little of all these things and probably a great deal about you and your past history. He will then advise you about a specialist if necessary.

(b) NEW VIEWS ON MEDICINE.

(1) **Body and Mind.** In former times, or at least during the nineteenth century, the body was regarded as a sort of machine belonging to you in much the same way that you own your watch. You went to your doctor and, in effect, said: "Now what on earth are you going to do about my stomach?"—and you spoke as if, somehow, your stomach didn't have anything to do with the *real* you—it was just an awkward thing that happened to be annoying you. But we know now that this is not so—that your body *is* you, that it is a fort fighting against such enemies as poisons, parasites, germs, cancer, and injuries. The defences are seriously weakened by not enough of the right kind of food, insufficient sleep, or by anxiety. Your anxieties and worries can kill you just as surely as the other agents, and can prevent recovery or retard it when you are already ill.

A stomach ulcer therefore is not just something that is happening to you, you are happening to it. Your fears, your jealousies, your hatreds, your inability to get on in life, can be (in some cases) just as harmful as germs or poisons—in fact, they act by setting free glandular poisons in your blood-stream. Scientists have discovered a reaction which they call the "stress response," and we now know that stress can ultimately lead to sickness or death without any bodily injury at all. Thus, Dr. L. J. Saul, a leading American doctor, wrote: "Emotional stress in which there is no physical damage can produce responses which lead to actual damage and even to death." Rats in the laboratory can be killed through long exposure to fear caused by loud noises or other forms of shock without even being touched.

This stress factor is emphasised not because it is more important than the other enemies of the body or mind (it would be better to say body-mind), but because, as we shall see later, it does cause serious diseases, and, secondly, as mentioned already, it influences the process of recovery. A person who is afraid or has no hope is less likely to recover from pneumonia or another disease than one who is hopeful, who has peace of mind and confidence.

(2) **New Views about Health.** A great deal of nonsense has been talked about the healthy life; at one time we were told to take eighteen chews to each bite, to do deep breathing, to take plenty of exercise, to get lots of fresh air, to eat regularly (or to indulge in peculiar diets). But more recently

eminent doctors have cast doubt on most of these fancies. Moderate exercise is necessary to health, but athletes who indulge in violent exercise have not always been noted for longevity. Fresh air is pleasant and stimulating, but, where actual breathing is concerned, it is no better than the air in most rooms. Certainly, one of the problems of our time is air pollution, but at present we are considering ordinary fresh air in comparison with the air indoors, and, in this case, the experts say there is little difference so far as health is concerned.

A balanced diet containing correct amounts of the basic food substances is essential, but there is no evidence that when, or at what intervals, you eat makes the slightest difference—unless you are a sufferer from stomach ulcer, in which case it is necessary that the intervals between meals should not be too long. The whole business of having meals at fixed intervals is nothing but a social convention, and in modern life obviously a matter of convenience. (*See* Diet, P40).

Sleep, too, is a necessity. But different people require vastly different amounts of sleep. Some manage on as little as three hours, others seem to believe that they need ten or more. The importance of the dream process is referred to in Introduction to Psychology, Q15(1).

In a number of studies of men and women who lived to a ripe old age it was found that the only factors in common between them were that they had a good balanced diet of healthy food, that they had contented minds, and that they were interested in something which gave them an aim in life. They also came of long-lived families—for living a long and healthy life depends partly upon heredity.

So the main rules of health are: (1) do not think too much about your health unless it gives you trouble; (2) have an interest in life and be prepared to sacrifice a lot for it (nothing useful has ever been done by those who are always " taking care " and being over-cautious); (3) eat a good balanced diet; (4) do not worry, and have a contented mind.

(3) **New Drugs.** A great surgeon, the first of the moderns, was Ambrose Paré, who died in 1590, and one of his best known sayings was: " I apply the dressing, but God heals the wound." He was quite right; for until about forty years ago, or even less, all the physician could do was to put the patient in as favourable a state as possible to enable his body to cure itself. That is to say, there were hardly any specific drugs—drugs that had a direct effect on the disease. There was quinine, discovered by the Spaniards in America, which was specific for malaria, and there were iron (specific for anæmia) and digitalis (specific for certain types of heart disease), but otherwise nothing until the nineteenth century, when Paul Ehrlich discovered salvarsan, which is specific for syphilis. Ehrlich died in 1914, having conceived the brilliant idea of drugs which he described as " magic bullets "—*i.e.*, drugs which, like bullets, would be aimed at the real cause of the disease. They would, that is to say, be specific.

Since then a large number of such drugs have been discovered. For example, the antibiotics, such as penicillin, discovered in 1928 by Fleming at St. Mary's Hospital, Paddington. Later, Florey and Chain in Oxford, helped in the war years by the vast resources of the American pharmaceutical industry, were able to make penicillin available to the public in sufficient quantities by new techniques of production. Penicillin is practically non-poisonous (although it is possible to become allergic to it, sometimes with serious results). It can kill some germs in a dilution of one part of penicillin to one hundred million parts of water; it is effective against streptococci, the cause of blood-poisoning, sepsis in wounds, and many other diseases; and also against the germs of anthrax, gonorrhœa, meningitis of some types, syphilis—a whole list of plagues which have troubled man for centuries. Blood-poisoning,

whether from wounds or childbirth, used to be almost incurable—now the rate of cure is 80–90 per cent.; anthrax and gonorrhœa have an almost 100 per cent. rate of cure. In pneumonia the rate is about 90 per cent., and early syphilis can be cured in a week, instead of the previous two to three years.

But that was only the beginning. Other antibiotics—streptomycin, tetracycline, erythromycin, and many others—are helping to wipe out the terrible scourges of the human race, in particular, in the case of streptomycin, tuberculosis. The sulpha group of drugs—sulphadiazine, sulphadimidine, etc.—have also proved a great boon. Then there are the new drugs which have created a revolution in psychiatry—the tranquillisers which relieve anxiety, the drugs which clear up certain types of depression, and substances such as chlorpromazine which make it possible to nurse formerly violent patients in the wards of a general hospital. The antihistamine drugs help in allergies, anticoagulants are of value after heart attacks and levodopa mitigates some of the distressing features of Parkinson's Disease.

No drug, old or new, is completely safe—if we define " safe " as meaning having absolutely no potential for harm. The household aspirin, widely used in a variety of conditions for its analgesic (pain-relieving) and antipyretic (fever-reducing) qualities, can cause bleeding from the stomach and small intestine (P23). Phenacetin, at one time a component of compound codeine tablets but now withdrawn, can—with prolonged use—damage the kidney. Chloramphenicol, a powerful antibiotic effective in typhoid fever, typhus and whooping cough, can damage the blood-forming cells of the bone marrow producing an agranulocytosis which can be fatal.

Clearly, in any one case, the doctor must weigh up the advantages and disadvantages of this or that drug before prescribing. Minor, self-limiting illnesses do not require potent, potentially toxic remedies. Chloramphenicol is rarely justified in whooping cough, but would never be withheld from a patient with typhoid fever.

Man is a unique species. A new chemical compound promising in animal experiments, for example, as an anti-inflammatory agent, apparently safe when given, say, to mice in a dose 100 times that required to produce that anti-inflammatory effect may, over a long period of time in man, not only have no effect but make his hair fall out or perhaps cause retention of urine. Nevertheless, some animal species do react like man, or vice versa, and it is possible to make reasonably accurate extrapolations from animals to man in terms of drug effect. It is also possible to estimate the toxicity of a drug for man from its toxicity in certain animal species but the ultimate test, both of the effectiveness and the toxicity of a new drug, comes only when it is given to man.

Thalidomide was unique. In every animal test used throughout the drug industry at that time—it was introduced in the late 1950s—it had a clean bill of health. It was chemically related to other drugs which had been in use for a long time. Overdosage with other sedatives such as the barbiturates was common at that time, although less so now. Overdosage with thalidomide was unlikely to prove fatal. It was marketed in Europe and in Britain as a " safe sedative ". The tragic results that followed its ingestion by women in the early weeks of pregnancy are now well known. Babies were born with severe deformities of limbs, internal organs or both. That effect could not have been foretold from any animal tests then in use. Since that date new drugs have been subjected to rigorous testing in various animal species to check the effect on foetal development as a statutory requirement, along with the older tests for toxicity which had always been undertaken by reputable drug companies.

The thalidomide disaster of the early 1960s led directly to the setting up of regulatory drug agencies in most countries of the world. In Britain the introduction and clinical testing of new compounds is controlled by the Medicines and Environmental Health Division of the Department of Health and Social Security, statutory machinery set up by the Medicines Act 1968, which followed the purely voluntary scheme of control under what was known as the Dunlop Committee after Sir Derrick Dunlop, its first chairman.

The development and introduction of new drugs is now very strictly controlled. No new drug can be marketed in Britain without the Medicines Commission being satisfied about its efficacy and its safety. We would need space in this edition almost the size of the complete Medical Section to describe fully the workings of the Commission and the limitations that the requirements of the Medicines Act inevitably place on the development and introduction of new remedies. The time from the initial synthesis of a novel compound likely to be of value to its eventual appearance in the pharmacy on prescription is now eight to 10 years. The cost is measured in millions of pounds because, for each successful drug, there will have been many thousands of unsuccessful ones.

Briefly, no new drug or modification of an old one can be sold, whether or not on prescription, unless it has been granted a product licence by the Department of Health and Social Security through its Medicines and Environmental Health Division. Many stages have to be passed to acquire that licence, from the granting of certificates to allow the drug to be tested initially in a limited way in patients in a strictly controlled manner by investigators approved by the Commission, to permission for extension of those trials at a later date to include larger numbers of patients or more investigators, to perhaps a " monitored release "—that is, to enable its use in, say, hospitals only—to the final release on the granting of a full product licence. Thus, the Medicines Commission has control at all stages.

Furthermore, all the stages are dependent on production of evidence relating to the safety and efficacy of the drug, evidence which may take the drug company months, sometimes years, to produce and which, of course, must be acceptable to the Commission. Trials may be stopped at any time, for example, if evidence of side effects of an undesirable nature come to light during clinical testing, or when evidence from some other similar compound indicates a likely risk in the use of the drug in question. Of course, " acceptable " means that the strict criteria which have been laid down by the specialist committees appointed to deal with all the various aspects of drug development, such as toxicology, adverse reactions and so forth, have been met. Experts serve on these committees which meet regularly, but the day-to-day running of the Medicines Commission is in the hands of full-time medically qualified personnel as well as pharmacists, pharmacologists and toxicologists. In addition, outside consultant opinion can be sought.

As well as all these rigid controls on development and testing in the early stages, there is also a scheme of surveillance for untoward side effects. These are the action, or actions, of a drug apart from its main one. Take the well-known side effect of drowsiness which occurs with certain antihistamine drugs: the main action, the one for which the drug is prescribed, is the mitigation of the effects of allergy, such as urticaria. Drowsiness would be an unwanted effect if the patient is not incapacitated and is able to do his usual job. On the other hand, some antihistamines have an appetite-stimulating effect which could, of course, be a useful attribute in certain situations or even allow the drug to be used solely for that purpose, the anti-allergic effect then being incidental.

An adverse reaction is a type of side effect which by definition, is unwanted and potentially harmful. The intestinal bleeding associated with aspirin, or the depressive effects of some of the earlier drugs used to lower blood pressure, such as reserpine and methyldopa, are good examples. When new drugs first become licenced for marketing and are prescribed by doctors on a gradually increasing scale it is important that adverse reactions such as those are reported. Every doctor in the National Health Service, whether in general practice or in hospital, has access to a stock of special record cards on which he can record in a standard way the details of any untoward reaction occurring in his patient during the prescribing of a new or existing drug, and which he has good reason to believe is associated with the taking of that drug. These record cards are posted to the DHSS which has a special unit to deal with them. A doctor noticing, for example, that one of his patients developed, say, double vision during treatment with a new antidepressant could not assume in the absence of other firm evidence that the two events were necessarily connected. However, if 100 cards are received by the DHSS reporting the same kind of event, there is good circumstantial evidence that those events are likely to be connected with drug administration. This adverse reaction reporting system, although voluntary, is working well and is an effective " early warning system " for drug toxicity.

We have come a long way since thalidomide, but have had to steer between the Scylla of stifling innovation in drug research by excessive control of development and the Charybdis of the free-for-all, profit-motivated bonanzas of the pre-thalidomide era. No system can be perfect, and it is fair to say that had it been necessary, for example, for aspirin, penicillin and streptomycin to be put through the system as we have set it up now they would probably never have reached the market and thence the patient.

(4) New Methods in Surgery. Only a few years before the Second World War many surgeons were saying that surgery had reached its extreme limits. It was impossible, they believed, to improve on the delicate techniques then reached. But events have proved them wrong. Operations on the heart, for example, which would have been inconceivable a short time ago are now carried out daily—the heart can be opened and defects of the all-important valves made good. " Blue babies " or adults with a heart disease which might have led to their death in a few years are now cured by surgery, and it is possible during such operations to cut off all the blood from the heart by deflecting it through tubes to an artificial heart outside the body—a machine which pumps the blood round the body whilst the real heart is at rest.

Then there are the intravenous anaesthetics, such as Pentothal, which are injected instead of breathed through a mask, as were ether and chloroform or ethyl chloride. Pentothal is much safer, and avoids the unpleasant after-effects of vomiting and nausea, which usually followed the old type of anaesthetic. Most curious of all, anaesthetists use the poison curare, used by South American Indians to poison their arrow-heads. Curare produces paralysis, but in small doses merely gives the degree of muscle relaxation which is so important to the surgeon when he is operating.

Lastly, we might mention the new techniques of plastic surgery. Thus large areas of skin which have been destroyed by severe burns can be replaced by shaving off thin layers from another part of the body. These do not need to cover completely the whole damaged area: small pieces are scattered over the wound and gradually grow together. Corneal disease (the cornea is the clear part of the eye, and when it becomes opaque the patient cannot see) is treated by removing the diseased part and replacing it by a cornea removed from a dead body, or sometimes from an eye which has had to be removed from a live patient for other reasons. There are, in fact, " cornea banks " where corneas are kept in refrigeration for future use, just as there are " blood banks " for use in blood transfusions. Other advances in surgery will be described elsewhere in the section.

(5) New Approaches in Social Medicine. Medicine has passed through many phases from the time when disease was regarded as a punishment from the gods or a sign of devil possession to the present era, when increasingly there is a tendency

to look on society as the patient. Indeed, one commonly hears doctors and sociologists nowadays talking about " the sick society."

The early primitive stage came to an end—at least in one part of the world—when in Greece, five centuries before Christ, Hippocrates and others began to teach that all diseases were due to natural causes. But after the first ray of hope the outlook began to deteriorate when, during the Middle and Dark Ages (that is, from the fall of the Roman Empire right up to the fifteenth century), there was a return to the belief in devil possession and supernatural causes.

Eighteenth-century medicine in Europe was materialistic, regarding the body as a machine. It was founded upon a sort of pseudo-science—although, of course, there were always individual exceptions, physicians such as Sydenham in England, who, avoiding all theories, based their work on observation of the patient. This mechanistic approach persisted right through the nineteenth century, but medicine became more and more truly scientific, and the century saw the most rapid advances in the field ever known until our own times: the discovery of germs by Pasteur, of antiseptics to combat them by Lister, of vaccination by Jenner and anæsthetics by the American Wells and the Scot Simpson. The use of the microscope by Virchow, who was a German, brought great advances in the understanding of disease and Ehrlich, another German, conceived, as we have already seen, the idea of "magic bullets" which would attack the germs at the root of a disease without harming the patient. But one of the greatest of all these great men is perhaps the least known. His name was Edwin Chadwick.

From the earliest period of recorded history human communities had been constantly ravaged by great plagues which swept over their lands year after year, killing untold millions. The Black Death of 1348-9 wiped out almost half the population of Europe. But, even in the first quarter of the nineteenth century, tens of thousands died from typhus, typhoid, and smallpox—and not only these, for periodically cholera would be brought into the country by travellers from abroad.

In the face of these terrible visitations the individual physician was helpless. He could not treat each one of the many sick even had he known how, and Chadwick's claim to fame rests on the fact that he was the first man to think in terms of *social* control of diseases, by so dealing with their causes that they were prevented from arising at all. In order to wipe out typhoid and cholera, he argued, we must ensure clean water supplies; for these diseases are caused by germs carried in polluted water. In order to attack typhus and plague, one must get rid of the lice which carry the germs of typhus and the rat-fleas which carry the germs of plague (including, of course, the rats, which, in turn, carry the fleas).

Chadwick was born in a Lancashire farmhouse where the children were washed every day all over, and he ruthlessly drove an obsession with cleanliness into the heads of his countrymen until, later in the century, it was possible for the German philosopher Treitschke to tell his class in Berlin: "The English think soap is civilisation." Although this remark was meant cynically, there is little doubt that soap, if it is not civilisation in itself, has played a greater part in making civilisation possible than many more elaborate remedies. A population riddled with chronic infectious illness has neither the time nor the energy to apply to the arts or sciences, and soap did a great deal to reduce infection.

One of the first Public Health measures was introduced by Chadwick and others when they brought in legislation to purify the water supply of London. Previously, the citizens had used water from the Thames (they still do, but only after it has been filtered and sterilised at the waterworks!), and from filthy, refuse-laden ponds and springs. Later, Chadwick helped to found the Poor Law Commission, and produced a Report in 1842, the principal suggestions of which were: a municipal water supply for all towns; scientific drainage both in town and country; and an independent health service with large powers for dealing with those who endangered the lives of others by polluting water or causing nuisances. He also proposed a national service for interment of the dead; for in those days bodies often remained for days in the overcrowded homes of the poor without burial.

What has the twentieth century contributed to the concept of social health? Well, of course, there has been a great deal of legislation along the lines initiated by Chadwick to control disease, and a great many other measures have been introduced concerned with the idea of positive health—not merely preventing bad health, but trying to bring about the highest possible state of good health. Orange juice, milk, and good meals for school-children have brought about a transformation in child health which has become apparent to the least observant. And the National Health Service is in the direct line of descent from early nineteenth-century legislation.

But in future years it is probable that the main achievement of the twentieth century will prove to be its extension of the term "social health" to cover every aspect of community life, not only in such subjects as bodily health and its control of social means, but also such problems as mental illness, crime, delinquency, drug addiction, and so on. What we are now asking ourselves is: how far are these problems produced by society itself, and if this is the case, how far can we go in preventing them by social means?

Community medicine takes the view that these problems can never be dealt with solely by moralising and retribution, but only by dispassionately analysing causes and dealing with them. In this century we have developed a social conscience. Not always, it is true, a very well-informed social conscience, but at least this is a good beginning. There are organisations for dealing scientifically with delinquency, for dealing with problem children, for spreading knowledge about cancer in order to show people that it can be successfully treated if taken in time. We can well say with John Donne, who died in 1631, that "no man is an island . . . every man's death diminisheth me; for I am involved in mankind." This is the attitude of twentieth-century community medicine.

Summary. Perhaps we can sum up our progress in the past hundred and forty years more dramatically in terms of hard facts.

Before the 1840s a surgical operation was never undertaken except under the gravest circumstances. There were no anæsthetics and no antiseptics, and the operation was carried out by a surgeon in a filthy tail-coat, stained with the congealed blood of countless operations (indeed the surgeons of that time took pride in the dirty condition of their coats as showing how much experience they had previously had). Germs and the part they play in producing disease were unknown, and Paul Ehrlich had not yet been born, so there were no "magic bullets" to attack syphilis, or sera for diphtheria and other diseases. The mentally ill were simply locked up with little treatment and subjected to such indignities as the strait-jacket and the padded cell; now they are given treatment which becomes more effective each year, the padded cell and strait-jacket have gone, and in very few hospitals are the ward doors locked.

Only fifty years ago you would very likely have died if you had developed pneumonia, "childbed fever" after the birth of a child, meningitis, dysentery, typhoid, or tuberculosis. With such infections as blood-poisoning you would have had practically no chance at all. Today, the sulpha drugs and the antibiotics have changed all that. Syphilis and gonorrhœa were lifelong tragedies both to the patient and his family, but now they, too, can be conquered.

The National Health Service has brought the possibility of good treatment equally to all, and other bodies—some of them privately run—deal with alcoholism and neurosis, with rehabilitation of the mentally and physically ill, with spastics, birth control, and marriage guidance. It is up to us to see that all these facilities are used to the full by all who need them.

PART II. DISEASES ARRANGED ACCORDING EITHER TO THEIR CAUSE OR THE AREA OF THE BODY AFFECTED.

THE INFECTIOUS DISEASES.
INTRODUCTION.

INFECTIOUS diseases are those which are caused by an invasion of the body by organisms from outside (the word " organism " simply means other living things, and we are using this word because, as will be seen later, it is not only what are known as " germs " which can cause infection). We know, too, that what is generally typical about this group is: (a) that the disease can be passed on from one person to another, and (b) that it is usually accompanied by a raised temperature or fever. Now (a), of course, is always true, because the definition of an infectious disease is one that can be passed on to others, but (b) is not always true, because a few infections produce little or no temperature, and also because it is possible to have a raised temperature (again in only a few cases) without any infection. For example, certain types of brain injury, tumour, or hæmorrhage can produce a raised—or lowered—temperature, and so can the injection of some foreign substance such as milk into the muscles. This is known as " protein shock," and was at one time used in the treatment of certain illnesses. Finally, solutions of dead germs, such as the anti-typhoid vaccine given to protect troops during the War, may lead when injected to very high temperatures. But, by and large, we are entitled to suppose that the patient with a raised temperature is probably suffering from an infection.

Types of Infection.

As we have seen, it is not only germs which cause infections—so from now on we shall give germs their proper name of " bacteria." Here is a list of the chief offenders which are liable to attack our bodies: bacteria, spirochætes, viruses, fungi, amœbæ, worms and other parasites. Of these, bacteria and viruses are by far the most important, but let us look at them all more closely.

Bacteria are tiny living things which can be seen only under a fairly powerful microscope. Some are grouped like bunches of grapes (staphylococci) or in strings or chains (streptococci). They are given these names because " staphylos " is the Greek word for a bunch of grapes, and " streptos " means a chain. Yet others are comma-shaped (such as the cholera vibrio), or shaped like a drumstick—a rod with a small knob at the end (the tetanus bacillus, which causes lockjaw)

It would be a mistake to think that all bacteria are harmful; for without some species we could not survive for long. Bacteriologists divide them according to their behaviour in the human body into three groups: saprophytic, parasitic or pathogenic, and symbiotic. The *saprophytic* organisms are the bacteria normally found in the skin, mouth, and intestines; they do us neither harm nor good. The *parasitic*, or as they are more usually called, pathogenic (*i.e.*, disease-producing) organisms, are the harmful ones with which we are naturally more concerned. Lastly, there are the *symbiotic* organisms, which, whilst taking something from the body, give something in return. For example, cattle would not be able to digest the cellulose of the grass they eat were it not for helpful bacteria in the lower parts of the intestines, and there are certain bacteria in the large intestine of man which produce vitamins.

Bacteria have two peculiar characteristics: each reproduces by splitting into two separate individuals as often as every twenty minutes in favourable circumstances like an open wound. If no bacterium were destroyed, one individual could produce a mass of bacteria larger than the whole world in a matter of a few weeks (since each of the offspring also divides into two, which in turn divide again—the progression goes: one gives birth to two, these two to four, the four to eight, eight to sixteen, sixteen to thirty-two, and so on—you will see, if you work it out, that in a short period the figure becomes astronomical). Fortunately, many bacteria have accidents, so for the present the world is safe! The other curious thing about bacteria is that, barring accidents, they are potentially immortal. Under ideal conditions in which no bacteria were killed, none would die; for a bacterium there is no death from old age, no corpse except when it is actively destroyed. It simply goes on dividing, dividing, and subdividing for ever.

How, then, are bacteria destroyed? Briefly, the answer is that most are destroyed by the natural defences of the body of whatever host they are preying on; others are destroyed by antiseptics and the new drugs; and many are destroyed when they are excreted from the body in the sputum or through the bowels and land in places where they are dried up and cannot survive —although some bacteria in such circumstances can form what are called " spores," rather like the seed of plants, so making it possible for them to survive in a state of suspended animation for months on end until picked up accidentally by another unfortunate host. Finally, bacteria, in addition to all these possibilities, face another danger: they may themselves develop disease. This disease is caused by even more minute organisms known as bacteriophages (viruses which affect bacteria), discovered by F. W. Twort in 1915. Attack by bacteriophage causes whole groups of bacteria (known as " colonies ") to disintegrate and become harmless.

Although bacteriophage has been used in the treatment of some diseases in human beings, this method has now been largely given up, since the new drugs are infinitely more effective.

Spirochaetes. Spirochætes, like bacteria, are minute organisms, but differ in being shaped somewhat like a corkscrew and in being able to move (which many bacteria cannot do). Their progress is produced by a sideways wriggling motion. The two main diseases caused by spirochætes are syphilis and spirochætal jaundice. Spirochætal jaundice is carried by rats, and is common in those who work in mines. It is now rare in Britain, but still occurs in Japan, Egypt, and Malaya; the infection is passed through the skin where the excreta of infected rats mingles with water on damp ground in the mine where miners kneel. Infection may also occur through eating infected food.

Viruses. Unlike bacteria, viruses are too small to be seen under an ordinary microscope. They can, however, be photographed in some cases under an electron microscope, which uses a magnetic field instead of a glass lens and a stream of electrons in place of a beam of light. Viruses cause such diseases as typhus, measles, mumps, poliomyelitis, smallpox, and chickenpox—not to mention such plant and animal diseases as tobacco mosaic disease and foot-and-mouth disease, which often have serious economic consequences. Other virus diseases are psittacosis (an infection of parrots and similar birds which can be transmitted to Man), swine fever in pigs, influenza in Man, and myxomatosis in rabbits. They also cause, it is believed, the common cold.

The main characteristics of viruses are, first, that they can only grow in living cells—unlike bacteria, which readily grow in the laboratory on plates containing a jelly made from meat broth, gelatin, milk, and other delicacies. The scientist, therefore, must keep them in portions of living tissue kept alive outside the body. Secondly, they are so small that they pass through the pores of the finest filter. Thirdly, a first attack usually produces immunity for life. Second attacks of the common virus diseases mentioned above are very rare; but unfortunately, this rule does not apply to influenza or the common cold. Fourthly, there is reason to believe that viruses represent an extraordinary intermediate stage between the living and non-living; they can, for instance, be produced in crystalline form and yet are just as dangerous when " thawed out." Lastly, the virus diseases have proved for the most part to be little affected by the new antibiotics and other drugs, although vaccination in smallpox and the injection of sera from infected patients in other infections may give immunity for longer or shorter periods.

The two great practical problems that doctors face with viruses are: (i) many viruses are unknown because of the difficulty of growing them outside the body in suitable tissue culture. They cannot therefore be conveniently identified in specimens from the patient, as bacteria can; and (ii) they are unaffected by antibiotics like penicillin. It has been a great step forward to grow viruses artificially in tissue culture, in which they are identified indirectly by the effects they have on the cultured *cells*. But since we do not know exactly how to grow some viruses (like those of infective hepatitis) they have still not been seen.

When we recover from a viral illness like chickenpox, we probably do so by producing virus-killing substances inside our own cells. Scientists are currently searching for these substances in case they can be used, like penicillin, to cure viral disease.

Fungi. Some infections are caused by fungi—that is to say organisms belonging to the same group as moulds, mushrooms, and toadstools. Penicillin and some other antibiotics are produced from moulds, so, as in the case of bacteria, some fungi are helpful; they even help to destroy each other, as bacteria do. For example actinomyces, which can cause infection of the jaw and other tissues, is destroyed by penicillin.

Most fungal infections are trivial and limited to the skin. But, although trivial, they can be unsightly and uncomfortable. Ringworm of the scalp, dhobie itch—an infection of the groin spread by infected underclothing—and so-called " athlete's foot " are caused by a fungus.

Amœbæ. Amœbæ are small, single-cell organisms, the largest of which (a harmless type found in stagnant ponds in Britain and elsewhere) is just visible to the naked eye. It is about the size of the head of a pin. Amœbæ move, in the species which are capable of moving, by pushing forward a part of the cell in the appropriate direction and causing the rest to flow into the advancing portion. Like bacteria, they reproduce by dividing into halves, each of which becomes a new amœba.

The main human disease caused by amœbæ is amœbic dysentery (not to be confused with bacillary dysentery).

Parasites. These may live on the skin like lice (which can carry typhus) or fleas (carriers of plague), or the parasites of scabies which burrow into the skin, or they may live part of their time in the blood or other tissues, like malaria. They often have complicated life-cycles involving other hosts (like mosquitoes) at certain stages of development.

Worms. Worms are intestinal parasites, but the only common types found in Britain are threadworms, the tiny thread-like worms which cause irritability and itching in the skin of children, less often in adults; round-worms, somewhat resembling the ordinary garden earthworm, which seldom lead to symptoms; and tapeworms, which may reach a length of 3 or even 6 m. Many parasitic worms (like parasites elsewhere) lead a double life—they spend part of their life in the human intestine and the other part in the muscles of another animal. The tapeworm, for example, whilst in the human intestine, lays eggs which pass out of the body in the excreta, and are then swallowed by pigs, especially in those parts of the world where human excreta are used as manure in the fields. In the pig, the eggs form cysts in the muscles—meat infected in this way is

known as " measly pork "—and when, in turn, the meat is eaten by man, the process in the intestine begins all over again.

Less common types, from our point of view, are the Russian tape-worm (which, as befits a Russian, grows to nearly 9 m!); this type is spread by caviare or undercooked infected fish. The small, leaf-shaped liver fluke lays eggs which are passed into canals or pools in tropical countries in the urine of infected people, hatch out and enter a water snail, and finally leave the snail in the form of small parasites which pierce the skin of bathers, whence they pass to the liver and subsequently the bladder and rectum. This is a serious condition, as is also filariasis (another tropical disease), for which, unlike bilharzia—caused by the liver fluke—no cure is known. The tropical disease known as loa-loa is caused by a variety of filaria.

How the Infection is Spread.

Infection is spread in many ways, some of which have already been mentioned. In the common fevers found in Europe and elsewhere one of the most frequent ways is by *droplet infection*—that is to say, by minute drops carrying the germs which are coughed or sneezed into the air by someone already suffering from the disease. Such droplets can be projected into the air for 3m or more, and when breathed in by someone within range infection may result. Next commonest mode of spread is perhaps by *infected food, water*, and the dirty hands of those who prepare food: cholera, dysentery, food-poisoning, and typhoid are spread in this way. Spread by *direct contact* is found in the venereal diseases (usually, but not always, spread by sexual intercourse with someone who already has the disease), and, of course, lice, fleas, and other parasites, including the scabies mite, are spread by contact with the infested individual—or sometimes with his clothes or bed linen. Spread through an *intermediary host*, whether it be lice, fleas, or mosquitoes carrying infection, or the various means adopted by worms, has already been described above, so no more need be said. Lastly, the infection may result from *bacteria already within the body*; for example, the bacillus coli which lives in the large intestine is there harmless, but if it gets into the bladder or the ureters (the tubes leading from kidney to bladder) a quite unpleasant result may follow in the form of cystitis or pyelitis.

How the Body Deals with Infection.

The body has many mechanisms of defence against intruders, but suffice it to say here that there are two main ones. First, substances known as antibodies and antitoxins are produced in the blood—the antitoxins to neutralise the poisons produced by the invaders, the antibodies to render them helpless, for example, by causing them to clump together so that they can more easily be dealt with by the second defence mechanism. This second mechanism is provided by the white cells in the blood, some of which (the phagocytes) act like amœbæ and swallow up and destroy the germs. Antibodies and antitoxins can be transferred from one individual to another and are used in medicine both to prevent infection and to cure it. This is known as immunisation, and can be active or passive. Active immunisation is produced by injecting either a solution of dead bacteria, as in the case of antityphoid injections, or by injecting live, but weakened, strains of the organism, as in the case of smallpox vaccination. In both cases the body is stimulated to produce its own immune substances. Passive immunisation is used either for people who have been in recent contact with infection or who are already ill, and in this case the antitoxins produced in another person who has had the illness are injected in the form of serum—*i.e.*, the liquid part of the blood without the blood cells. All these natural defences are inefficient in the ill, the underfed, the very young, and the very old.

The mechanisms of the response of the body to infection is the broad field of study of the immunologist. (*See* Part III).

Antiseptics.

The earliest antiseptic was carbolic acid, used by Lister in his operating-theatre in the form of a fine spray directed throughout the operation on the wound, or sometimes in the form of steam from a kettle containing a solution of carbolic. But carbolic is dangerous, and since Lister's time many more useful antiseptics have been discovered. Acriflavine, thymol, and other old favourites have been discarded too. The various forms of carbolic are still used to disinfect drains, but, to tell the truth, the use of antiseptics nowadays is very limited. In surgery the *antiseptic* method has given way to the *aseptic* method—instead of fighting sepsis we see to it that no possibility of sepsis is present before operating: all instruments, the surgeons' and nurses' hands, the skin, are sterilised—the instruments by boiling, the dressings by dry heat, the hands by soap and water, and almost the only antiseptic used is to clean the patient's skin in the area to be operated on.

Antiseptics are used as first-aid treatment for cuts and wounds, but should be applied only once as a general rule—that is, when the wound is first received. The trouble with antiseptics is that as well as killing germs they also kill the surrounding tissues, which antibiotics never do.

Antiseptic sprays to purify the air of a room or to destroy germs lurking in the dust on the sick-room floor—or any other floor—are practically useless. To quote the *British Medical Journal*: " There is no good scientific evidence that any of the chemical air-disinfectants can control the spread of infection in places such as schools, offices, or cinemas. Nor is there good evidence that any substantial effect on the spread of illness can be obtained by disinfection of dust."

Neither is there any good reason to believe that mouth-washes and gargles have any effect other than making the mouth feel fresher and (temporarily) removing mouth odour—by covering it up with the scent of the antiseptic. Mouth-washes are in contact with the bacteria for far too short a time to have any damaging result, and, in the case of tonsillitis and other diseases, all the important bacteria are hidden far out of any danger from gargles.

Antibiotics.

The antibiotics—penicillin, streptomycin, erythromycin, terramycin, aureomycin, and many others—have already been dealt with, and only two important practical points need to be mentioned. These are that although most of such drugs are entirely safe under ordinary conditions, it is extremely dangerous for the layman to use them without medical guidance. If, for example, people get into the undesirable habit of sucking penicillin lozenges for sore throat and keep on doing this every time the sore throat returns, they may become sensitised to penicillin so that, when they become really ill—say, with pneumonia—the serious illness no longer responds to the drug. Or the same habit may make them allergic or hypersensitive to penicillin, and an injection given later may have serious and even fatal results.

Doctors no longer use the lozenges anyway, because of this danger and another one which is that excessive use of antibiotics may kill not only the dangerous bacteria, but also the ones which are helpful to the body. When this happens, other types of organism which are not affected by antibiotics will multiply in the absence of the bacteria which normally keep them under control. Thus terramycin or aureomycin, by killing useful germs in the large intestine, may cause vitamin B deficiency, and when the non-sensitive organisms have their natural enemies removed they may step in and multiply, causing inflammation of the mouth, diarrhoea, and occasionally a fatal bowel infection.

General Treatment of Fevers.

Fevers are ordinarily heralded in by a rise in temperature which is noticeable either by a flushed face or by alternate sensations of heat and cold. A patient with a high temperature may have shivering attacks known as " rigors." Tell the doctor.

A high temperature does not necessarily (especially in a child) mean that the trouble is serious but the lay person should always treat it as such and certainly call a doctor if the patient is a child or an elderly person.

Even the trained physician finds it difficult to tell one fever from another in the early days; for most of the common fevers begin in more or less the same way. It is only when a rash or some other more definite sign becomes evident that a certain diagnosis can be made, and these may not show themselves until the patient has been feeling " run-down " and fevered for some days. Incidentally, although a clinical thermometer is a very useful thing when properly used, many a doctor must feel that, in unskilled hands, it is a menace. The " fussy " type of mother who is constantly taking her child's temperature whenever it looks in the slightest degree different from usual (probably it is simply feeling justifiably bored with its parents), not only causes anxiety to herself but also gives the habit of anxiety to her child. The child is made to feel that the world is a dangerous place, full of germs and all sorts of causes for fear—as indeed it is, but one needs a sense of proportion, and other dangers which we think much less about are at least as frightening and twice as deadly as most germs. Whatever you do, don't get the thermometer habit; your child, so far as fevers are concerned, is a good deal tougher than you.

Briefly, then, the way to treat a fever in the early stages before the doctor comes, and before one knows exactly what is wrong, is as follows:

(1) Put the patient to bed.

(2) Give little, and easily digested, food; if the patient wants none, give none.

(3) Give plenty to drink—the proprietary preparations containing lemonade and glucose are excellent, but water, weak tea with sugar, or home-made lemonade with squeezed-out lemon juice and sugar, whichever the patient likes best, are at least as good.

(4) Aspirin is useful to relieve headache or other pains and will reduce fever for two or three hours. But it will cure nothing. The patient will be more comfortable, but his illness will not be cured by aspirin except in certain very special cases. Soluble aspirin is best. Do not have special children's aspirins in the house. They are often nicely flavoured, the children are tempted to eat them like sweets, and there have been serious cases of poisoning. For small children, use suitably small quantities of ordinary adult soluble aspirin, having checked the dose with your doctor. Other methods of cooling seriously fevered patients such as bathing, tepid sponging, etc., are strictly for the doctor to prescribe. A patient as hot as that should be in a doctor's hands anyway.

THE INFECTIOUS FEVERS.

The remarks made above apply to the management of *any* fever, and we are now going to discuss particular infectious diseases, beginning with the common childhood fevers, then passing on to less common ones, tropical diseases, and worm and parasitic infestations.

The common infectious fevers are caused by bacteria or viruses, and it is useful to know the meaning of the following terms: *incubation period* is the time which elapses between being infected and developing symptoms; *prodromal period* is the time which elapses between the end of the incubation period and the appearance of a rash; *quarantine period*, the maximum time during which a person who has been in contact with the infection may develop the disease—it is usually two days more than the incubation period; *isolation period*, the time a patient is supposed to be isolated.

Views regarding the common infectious fevers have changed a good deal in recent years. Disinfection of rooms is now regarded as almost useless, and more cases are treated at home.

Quarantine in the case of the common fevers is thought by a good many doctors to be a waste of time, since all it can do is to postpone infection from early childhood to early adult life, when it is likely to be more serious. For it is a characteristic of these fevers that they affect the adult much more violently than they do the child. However, on this, and all other points, you will have to be guided by the opinion of your family doctor.

Virus Diseases.

First, we shall take the common virus diseases, measles, chickenpox, and rubella or German measles, then the other virus diseases, mumps, infective hepatitis, viral pneumonia, and some less common conditions which do not always produce a typical rash as in the case of the first three.

In nearly all of these fevers there is a long incubation period, and one infection gives immunity for life.

Measles. The incubation period is 10–11 days. The first sign is the appearance of symptoms rather like a severe cold. The eyes become red, and exposure to light is unpleasant, the nose runs, the throat becomes inflamed, and a dry, harsh cough develops. There may be headache and the temperature rises to 39°C or more. Usually the patient is a child, and especially typical is the development of so-called Koplik's spots, which are small, bluish-white, raised spots seen on the inside of the cheek at the back of the mouth. The rash begins on the fourth day of the prodomal period, *i.e.,* 14 days after the initial infection. It shows on the forehead and behind the ears, spreading within a day downwards over the whole body; in another two days it starts to disappear, but often leaves behind a sort of brownish staining which may last for one to two weeks.

Measles can be serious, especially in very young children because of its complications, such as bronchopneumonia and infection of the ear, which can now be treated with antibiotics. These drugs have no effect on the measles virus, but only on the secondarily invading bacteria which have invaded the lungs and ear during the illness. The illness can be attenuated or lessened by injection of antibodies (gamma globulin) from an immune adult, and this is often worth while in the very young. Effective vaccination is now available.

Rubella or German Measles. Incubation period 14–19 days. A mild fever, similar to measles except that the rash is usually the first sign that anything is wrong, and the temperature is rarely above 38°C. The eyes may be pink, and there are enlarged glands at the back of the neck. The rash disappears completely in thirty-six hours. There are no complications.

German measles, in itself, is harmless, but if a woman gets the disease in the early months of pregnancy malformations in the child may appear at birth. Vaccination is advised if a girl has not contracted the disease by the time she reaches puberty. There is no special treatment except the general rules for fevers given above.

Chickenpox. Incubation period 14–15 days, but may be more variable. In children chickenpox is a mild fever which begins with the appearance of tiny blisters on the chest and back. These later spread outwards to the legs, arms and face, and cause itching. Treatment is the general one for fevers already described. Calamine lotion or dusting powder will be helpful for the irritation, and the child's nails should be cut short to prevent scratching and infection of the spots. Whereas children are usually little bothered by chickenpox, young adults may be much more drastically affected—a temperature of 40°C is not uncommon, and then there may be severe headache.

Mumps. Incubation period 17–18 days. Everyone knows the typical appearance of the patient with mumps—the swelling in the salivary glands in front of the ears which makes the face look full. This causes pain later on, and it may be difficult to open the mouth. Temperature is not usually high (about 38°C). Although uncomfortable, mumps is rarely dangerous, but orchitis—swelling of the testicles—is sometimes a complication. Fluid diet should be given if eating is painful, with mouth-washes, and rest in bed.

Infective Hepatitis. "Hepatitis" means inflammation of the liver, and infective hepatitis, which is much the commonest cause of jaundice in young adults, is a viral infection of the liver. The main symptoms are fever, followed by jaundice, which is first noticed in the whites of the eyes as yellow staining, then in the skin. The urine becomes coloured also, and this is most easily noticed if, on shaking in a bottle, the froth shows coloration. If the froth remains white, no jaundice is present. Treatment is a matter for the doctor, but great care should be taken both by the patient and those in contact with him, to wash the hands thoroughly after urinating or defæcating after handling utensils from the sickroom, and both before and after eating; for the disease is very infectious.

Viral Pneumonia. Pneumonia is usually caused by bacteria, and when we speak of pneumonia, that is the type we ordinarily refer to. Viral pneumonia is known by doctors as "pneumonitis," and is believed to be closely related to influenza. There is no specific treatment so far, and since diagnosis is a specialist matter, little more need be said except that the symptoms in general resemble those of ordinary pneumonia. Psittacosis, another virus disease, can also lead to pneumonia, and although there is no specific treatment for virus infections of the lungs, it is always worth while trying the antibiotics or sulpha drugs in view of the possibility that the lung condition may be caused by a secondary invasion by bacteria.

Influenza. While serious epidemics of influenza take the form of a very dramatic and often fatal disease—for example, the epidemic of "Spanish 'flu" which followed the First World War killed more people than the actual fighting—the milder type more usually seen is difficult to distinguish from the common cold. In fact, many people who complain of "a dose of the 'flu" are suffering from simple colds.

However, a sudden onset, aching in the muscles of the back and legs, and redness of the eyes, would suggest influenza, and especially typical is the depression and weakness which follow influenza but not a cold. The measures suggested above for the general treatment of fever should be applied; but the depression and weakness which follow influenza may need special treatment by the doctor.

Colds. Although everyone thinks he, or she, knows what a "cold" is, the issue is not so simple; for the symptoms of fever, running nose, and a run-down, "headachy" feeling are found in many illnesses. They may be observed, as we have seen, in the early stages of measles before the arrival of the rash, or in a number of other fevers, such as whooping cough. Mild attacks of influenza (see above) may resemble the common cold, and blocking of the nose with discharge and fever may be due to sinusitis—although here there is usually pain above, between, or below the eyes. Colds can be caused by any one of thirty different viruses known as "rhinoviruses" as well as by others which cause influenza, or infect glands (adenoviruses). This is why a single cold does not confer immunity on the sufferer. It is probable that you will not catch a cold from the same virus, at least for the rest of the year, but there are all those others waiting to infect you with other colds in buses, tubes, and other crowded places. Like all infections, do not forget that the best way to avoid them is to keep generally well, and in a good nutritional state. Do not spend money on injections or other vaccines. They do not work, probably because of the multiplicity of viruses involved. It is unlikely that adding vitamins or mineral supplements to normal diet will do any good at all provided you are eating sensibly. The vogue for prophylactic or therapeutic treatment of colds with massive doses of vitamin C has recently received much attention from scientists attempting, with little success, to prove the effect by controlled clinical trial and to find a rational basis for its use.

Poliomyelitis

Polio, or infantile paralysis as it used to be known, is caused by a virus which has a particular affinity for the nerve cells of the spinal cord and which results in paralysis of those muscles under the control of the particular group of cells infected. Rarely, the infection is widespread in the nerve tissue causing paralysis of muscles of swallowing and respiration as well as those of the trunk and limbs. The usual pattern is for a single muscle group to be affected, for example, the muscles controlling the movements of the arm at the shoulder. Such paralysis may be transient with complete recovery, partial with some residual weakness, or total, leaving a " flail limb " which is wasted and powerless.

At one time in this country epidemics of poliomyelitis were common, mainly affecting children and young adults. There is no doubt that mild forms of the disease were always occurring in very young children, forms never diagnosed as such but conferring a natural immunity in later life.

In common with other infections, poliomyelitis begins with a mild or moderate pyrexia, with a sore throat, headache, nausea and perhaps actual vomiting, some five to 10 days after contact with the virus. There may be rigidity of the neck muscles. Paralysis, if it occurs, will become apparent about the second or third day of illness. This stage may last two or three weeks, by which time the temperature will have subsided and the paralysis started to improve. There is no specific treatment and medical care is confined to symptomatic relief. Difficulty with swallowing and breathing calls for special nursing measures. In severe cases, artificial means of maintaining respiration may have to be continued for months, or for the rest of the patient's life. Many severely paralysed polio victims of the post-war epidemics —the self-styled " responauts "—depend for their lives on artificial respirators (" iron lungs ").

With the development of the oral vaccine early in the 1960s, and its introduction into the immunisation schedule in this country, the disease has now virtually disappeared from Great Britain.

Smallpox. In previous editions we stated that " since the introduction of vaccination it (smallpox) is comparatively rare in industrialised countries." In this edition we can report that smallpox (*variola major*) has now been eradicated throughout the world. The less serious form of the disease, *variola minor*, is still found in some parts of Africa, but all the signs are that it, too, will soon be eradicated. The last case of *variola major* occurred in Bangladesh in 1975. With the disappearance of the disease vaccination will become unnecessary; however, the World Health Organisation is planning to store vaccine (which can be done almost indefinitely at a temperature of $-20°C$) in sufficient quantities to vaccinate many millions of people should the need ever arise again. We make no excuse therefore for leaving out of this edition of *Pears*, for the first time in its long history, the detailed description of the disease. The story of the discovery of vaccination should not be forgotten, and the interested reader is referred to " Immunisation " in Part III.

Glandular Fever. This is sometimes called infective mononucleosis, since one of its features is an increase in certain mononuclear white cells and an alteration in their appearance. Another feature is an apparent infectivity. Beyond this the disease is a great mystery, and although it is probably caused by a virus, it may even be related to other (malignant) diseases of white cells. This one, however, is not dangerous although it often causes a lot of trouble by dragging on for many weeks. The main symptoms are fever, enlargement of lymph glands and sore throat. The patient feels very debilitated and often very depressed. Diagnosis is often very difficult, but there is a blood test known as the " Paul-Bunnell " test which is almost specific for the disease. The patient is usually presented as a case known to doctors as " P.U.O.," meaning Pyrexia (fever) of Unknown Origin. He has often been treated with several antibiotics, one after another, without effect, because the causal agent is not affected by those drugs. He is only very mildly infective, and it is unusual to insist on isolation or quarantine.

Typhus. This disease used to be known as " jail fever," because it was frequent in prisons; but overcrowding, poverty, and bad hygienic surroundings anywhere are suitable conditions for epidemics of typhus. Improved conditions in industrialised countries have made it unusual, since typhus is carried from one person to another by infected body lice. It is due to the organism *Rickettsia prowazekii*, which displays both bacterial and viral characteristics.

Typhus comes on suddenly with a rise in temperature to about $39°C$, but within four days it may be as high as $42°C$. There may, or may not, be a rash at this time, and in the second week, when the temperature is at its highest, there is delirium, weakness, and a feeble pulse. The typical typhus rash appears about the fifth day as reddish blotches on the chest, abdomen, and wrists.

Typhus is, needless to say, very serious but responds to modern antibiotics. Preventive measures are directed towards eradicating lice.

Rabies. Finally, we shall deal very briefly with a number of less common virus diseases, beginning, as is appropriate, with *hydrophobia or rabies*, since it was in this infection that the great French scientist Louis Pasteur (1822–95) showed the possibility of prevention by vaccination. Unlike Jenner, with his ready-made cowpox virus, which we have seen to be the virus of smallpox weakened by natural passage through cows, Pasteur had to weaken the rabies virus by passing it through rabbits. The rabbits were infected, and after death the spinal cord was dried and powdered, a solution passed through another rabbit, and so on until the virus was sufficiently weakened.

Rabies is spread by the bite of infected animals, usually dogs, cats, or wolves, who are driven mad by the disease; in Trinidad, however, it has been spread by vampire bats. Those who are bitten usually show no symptoms for six weeks or more. but sooner or later convulsions and delirium arise, which within four to five days are fatal.

There is no cure once the symptoms have developed, but Pasteur's serum, if given soon after the bite, prevents illness in the majority of cases—the sooner after the bite, the better the outlook. Dogs should be muzzled in areas where the disease is common, but quarantining imported dogs has made the infection almost unknown here.

Psittacosis. This is another virus disease which is of interest mainly in that it is spread by birds of the parrot group, such as parrots, lovebirds, macaws, and the rest. It occasionally occurs here in people who have been in contact with birds of this type, and is serious both to the bird and its owner. Quarantine regulations greatly reduced the risk of infection in Britain. They were lifted a few years ago but concern over recent outbreaks, not only of psittacosis but a number of economically important diseases such as fowl pest, led to their reintroduction in 1976.

The symptoms of psittacosis are fever, cough, and bronchitis. The disease is especially dangerous to old people, but it responds to the same antibiotics as typhus.

Sandfly Fever, or phlebotomus fever, *Dengue*, or breakbone fever, and *Trench Fever* are all somewhat similar conditions in that they resemble influenza and are rarely fatal. They are all due to viruses, spread in the first case by sandflies in tropical climates; in the second by mosquitoes in tropical climates; and in the third by lice in temperate climates. They are all typical "soldiers' diseases"; the first two were common in the Middle East and Far East during the last War, the third during the First World War in France.

Yellow Fever. Of all the virus diseases, seven can now be prevented, or largely prevented, by vaccination—smallpox, measles, German measles, rabies, poliomyelitis, (if started early enough), influenza and yellow fever. Yellow fever is carried by a mosquito known as Stegomyia, common in South and Central America and in African ports. For its spread, it therefore needs: a hot climate, the stegomyia mosquito, and an infected person.

In 1898 the United States was at war with Spain in Central America, where yellow fever was a serious problem. Following this war the United States, by this time acutely aware of this terrible disease, asked a Dr. G. E. Waring to deal with it in Havana, where it was rife. But Waring died of yellow fever, as had many millions before him, without knowing its cause, and it was left to Walter Reed, who died in 1902, to prove the connection between the mosquito and yellow fever. By a vigorous war on the mosquito, the disease has been eradicated from Havana and the West Indian islands, and Reed's discovery made possible the building of the Panama Canal.

In yellow fever there is a sudden high temperature, aching of limbs and head, jaundice, and black vomit; the pulse-rate falls as the fever rises. Previous vaccination seems to be preventive if undertaken in time.

Conclusion.

All these virus diseases have this in common: that for many there is no specific cure, although some (see above) can be prevented by vaccination, or by the social control of the creatures carrying the virus. Some of the larger viruses (psittacosis) are destroyed by certain antibiotics. There is usually a long incubation period. Finally the question will sometimes arise of protecting some people from German measles or measles with gamma globulin containing another person's antibodies to the disease. This may be considered for measles in very young patients or to protect the foetus in pregnant mothers in contact with German measles.

Bacterial Diseases.

Bacterial diseases differ from virus infections in a number of respects: their incubation period tends to be shorter; having the disease once does not often confer lifelong protection; and unlike virus diseases, most bacterial diseases respond to one of the antibiotics or sulphonamides. In many cases it is possible to inoculate against the disease to prevent it occurring, as we have seen is possible with only a few of the virus diseases.

Scarlet Fever and Other Streptococcal Infections. In the days, not so long ago, before the arrival of chemotherapy (sulphonamides) and antibiotics, streptococci were very much feared and even caused a high mortality, particularly in such susceptible groups as children, and mothers and babies in maternity hospitals. They are still taken very seriously in the latter and rightly so, although one wonders how much of the mystique is simply a hangover from the days, fifty years ago, when many mothers died from "childbed fever." All signs of infection, such as fever, during the puerperium (the period following childbirth) must be promptly dealt with by a doctor, and only occasionally now is there real cause for anxiety provided treatment is prompt and rigorous.

Scarlet fever is much less common and very much less serious an illness than it used to be, partly because of the effective treatments available today, but also because of a definite but unexplained reduction in its severity. Perhaps the streptococcus has changed, and certainly the improved physical condition of people who are now much better fed and housed than they were, has helped to ward off the terrors of this disease as of so many other infections. The classical picture of signs and symptoms is now so rarely seen that it will not be further described.

The importance of streptococcal infections has shifted from the initial infection, such as a sore throat, to some serious conditions which occasionally arise as a result of some form of delayed sensitivity to the bacteria. Acute rheumatism or rheumatic fever (not to be confused with rheumatic aches and pains nor with rheumatoid arthritis) occasionally arise in people who have had a sore throat a few weeks before. Since the streptococcus is not the direct cause of the damage which may consequently occur in the heart or kidney, the antibiotics are no answer except sometimes to keep off further streptococcal invasions.

Diphtheria. This used to be an extremely serious disease, but immunisation has made it almost unknown; it is important, therefore, that all children should be immunised. There are many modern and up-to-date doctors who have qualified since the war who have never seen a case because it has become so rare, and in spite of the propaganda of certain ill-informed people, this saving of children's lives is entirely the result of nationwide inoculation during the war and since. The following description is of historic interest only, and will remain so if a high level of inoculation is kept up by parents.

In a typical case of diphtheria the incubation period is about three days; the patient is a child who becomes ill and pale-looking (*i.e.*, the onset is not sudden, as in many fevers, but insidious); the temperature is only slightly raised to, perhaps, 37° or 38°C, and although there may be no complaint of sore throat, examination will reveal inflammation with—and this is typical of diphtheria —a grey membrane spread over the tonsils, the palate, and the back of the mouth generally. The diphtheria germ does not spread within the body. It stays at the place where it entered (in this case the throat) and sends its toxins throughout the body.

Even after the acute phase is over the patient must not be allowed to walk, because the diphtheria toxin is particularly poisonous to the heart. The ordinary rule is at least one or two months in bed.

Diphtheria also occurs in the larynx—in pre-inoculation days many children choked to death with this form of the infection; in the nose; and, although this is not generally known, wounds can be infected. The so-called "Desert sores" of the North African campaign seem to have been caused by diphtheria-like organisms.

Diphtheria may lead to paralysis of the throat, with difficulty in speaking or swallowing, and paralysis of the eyes or limbs; these are due to neuritis caused by the influence of the toxin on the nerves.

Whooping Cough. For many years whooping cough has been regarded merely as a bother to the patient and a nuisance to others, as, in fact, a trivial disease. Unfortunately, this is not so: because statistics show that it caused more deaths than polio, diphtheria, scarlet fever, and measles put together.

Whooping cough begins in a child as an ordinary cold with cough and slight fever, and this stage lasts for a week or ten days. Then the " paroxysmal stage " begins as a series of coughs following in rapid succession, during which time the patient is unable to breathe. The " whoop " is caused by the noisy indrawing of breath when the fit stops. The face may become blue and congested. Bronchitis is usually present, and bronchopneumonia may result as a complication, so inoculation of all children before the disease has a chance to strike them is most important.

Once whooping cough has begun, there is no specific treatment, although modern drugs can reduce the frequency of the fits of coughing. The antibiotic chloramphenicol has been used for this disease, but the general opinion is that it is ordinarily of little benefit. Chinese physicians once described whooping cough as the " hundred-days cough," and the cough may, indeed, continue for at least a hundred days.

Food Poisoning Diseases

Strictly speaking there is no such thing as " food poisoning " if one is thinking of " poisoning " in terms of anything apart from germs. But not so long ago it used to be thought that decomposition of food in itself produced poisons known as " ptomaines " which were deadly to those who swallowed them. All food poisoning is caused by infection of food with bacteria and by no other cause—unless of course, we are thinking of the kind of poisoning which is the concern of the lawyer rather than the medical man.

Here we are considering those diseases which are commonly spread by contaminated food or drink. The classification is not scientific, but then no scientific classification has as yet been devised. First, we shall deal with typhoid, paratyphoid, and dysentery—uncommon here in Britain, although Sonné dysentery is fairly frequent. Then there is gastro-enteritis (which means irritation of the stomach and intestines), which is caused by staphylococci and the germs of the salmonella group, and lastly. botulism. which is rare.

Typhoid and Paratyphoid. These diseases are spread by infected water, food, or hands—especially uncooked food, such as milk, salads, oysters, and shellfish. Flies, too, play some part in spreading the disease. Some people are " carriers " and carry and excrete the germs without being themselves affected; for example, " Typhoid Mary," a carrier in the United States in the early years of this century, spent a large part of her life in custody as a public danger, although she did not show any symptoms of typhoid. Nevertheless, this woman caused a great deal of illness in others in her chosen profession of cook.

The influence of Chadwick's propaganda for pure water supplies is shown by the fact that deaths from typhoid, still 332 per 1,000,000 in 1870, fell to 198 per 1,000,000 at the beginning of this century. In the 1920s the death-rate was only 25 per 1,000,000, and now it is even less.

Typhoid fever begins like most fevers with headache, raised temperature, and general feeling of unwellness. This stage lasts about a week, and then the rash appears in the form of rose-red spots on the front of the chest and abdomen and on the back. In the second week there is great weakness, sometimes diarrhœa. flatulence, and mental dullness, together with dry and cracked lips and tongue. The third week is the week, in hopeful cases, of gradual decrease in temperature and other symptoms, and the fourth week is the week of convalescence.

Complications are perforation of the intestine (which needs surgical treatment), delirium, and bronchitis.

Paratyphoid fever is a milder form of typhoid (there are two forms, A and B); ordinarily it can be diagnosed only by scientific tests. The main thing is to inoculate contacts with T.A.B. vaccine and to protect food supplies; treatment is with chloramphenicol.

Dysentery. Dysentery may be caused *either* by a bacterium or an amœba; the first type is known as bacillary dysentery, the latter as amœbic dysentery (which is dealt with under tropical diseases). Infection is spread in much the same way as in typhoid. There is high fever, abdominal pain, and diarrhœa, at first consisting of fæcal matter, then blood and mucus. In severe cases the death-rate used to be over 20 per cent.

Various bacilli cause dysentery. The common tropical types are the Shiga and Flexner groups, but in this country most epidemics are due to the milder Sonné group.

However, in all these infections sulphaguanidine, ampicillin or tetracycline bring rapid relief but care must be taken to avoid infection of other people.

Diarrhœa and Vomiting. Leaving out typhoid and paratyphoid fevers and dysentery, there is a group of infections known as " D. & V.,"—diarrhœa and vomiting. In Britain D. & V. is mostly due to:

    (1) Salmonella infection.
    (2) Staphylococcal infections.
    (3) Other bacteria, ordinarily harmless, such as bacillus coli, when present in sufficient numbers.

Salmonella Infections are the most serious of this group; they affect the small intestine and produce vomiting, severe abdominal pain, and diarrhœa. These symptoms occur about one day after eating infected food and usually clear up within about two weeks. but occasionally death results. Salmonella bacteria are most likely to be found in meat, egg powder, vegetables, and ducks' eggs, but staphylococci are liable to grow in milk products, such as ice-cream and cream buns. Food poisoning from staphylococci is seldom severe, and recovery takes place in about a week. Nevertheless, it is extremely infectious, and causes a great deal of lost time in industry and temporary illness in institutions; for it is in such situations that it is most likely to occur.

Staphylococcal Food Poisoning has greatly increased in recent years, so it is important to know what circumstances are likely to cause it. The reason for its increase has nothing to do, as many people suppose, with the greater use of canned foods, but it has much to do with the greater use of communal feeding and canteen meals. It is *possible* for bacterial toxins in infected food to bring about illness even when the canning process has killed the bacteria, but it is certainly extremely rare. Canned foods, in fact. are much safer than so-called " fresh " foods in this respect—except when they have been opened, left about, and then re-heated. The same applies to the re-heating of any kind of food.

The real enemy is the canteen worker with a boil, a discharging nose, dirty hands, or a septic finger. Occasionally food may be infected in the larder by rats or mice, but the sort of canteen or restaurant where this can happen has little to commend it. Frankly, these infections are caused by dirty or stupid people who do not realise that their sore finger or boil can become someone else's diarrhœa and vomiting. Where children are concerned, the outlook is potentially more serious, and in the early part of this century the Summer-time " procession of baby coffins " was all too familiar. Infection is much more common in artificially fed babies or in older children who eat infected ice-cream. However trivial the condition may seem, diarrhœa and vomiting with fever in a child should never be ignored. Those in charge of canteens or restaurants must ensure that staff is supervised, that anyone with a septic infection is put off duty, and that all know about washing after visiting the lavatory and absolute cleanliness.

Bacilli normally present in the intestine, such

as bacillus coli, can cause infections if absorbed in large amounts, or if of a different strain from those in the patient's intestine. They are not usually serious.

Botulism. Now uncommon, this is the disease which used to be known as " ptomaine poisoning " on the theory that it was caused by poisons produced by bad food apart from germs. In the 1920s a party of picnickers at Loch Maree in the Scottish Highlands developed botulism and a number died, with the result that the disease attracted much public attention. Botulism is caused by a germ, the bacillus botulinus, which is peculiar in that, like tetanus, its poison attacks the nervous system rather than the intestines, resulting in fits, double vision, paralysis beginning in the face and spreading downwards, and difficulty in swallowing. It is found in tinned fruits or vegetables containing the toxin even when the germ has been killed, but, as we have already seen, the toxin comes from the bacilli, not from decomposition of food as such (in fact, food does not decompose in the absence of germs). Death is common in botulism, but an antitoxin is now available which, if used in time, can cure the disease.

Tuberculosis. No disease causes more public concern, and no disease is more difficult to describe, than tuberculosis; for, like the streptococcus or the staphylococcus, the tubercle germ can attack many different parts of the body and manifest itself in many ways. Furthermore, it is a widely spread disease, infecting not only humans but also cattle, birds and reptiles. But here we shall be concerned with those types common to Man—the human and bovine (*i.e.*, the type occurring in cattle which can be spread to man by infected milk).

The tubercle bacillus is particularly hardy, so that when coughed or spat out on the ground it continues to be infectious for a long time. Infection is therefore caused by: (*a*) drinking infected milk; (*b*) droplet infection through **ha**ving germs coughed in the face; (*c*) breathing in infected dust. In other words, tuberculosis is caused by absorption through either the lungs or the intestines; the former is common in adults, the latter in children.

But there is a good deal more to the problem than this: we know, for example, that over 90 per cent. of people in industrial countries have been infected with T.B. in early life and have conquered the infection. So the question arises: what conditions predispose to T.B.—why do some people get over the early infection and others not? There are two answers to this question: one is certain—that those who are impoverished and do not get enough food are liable to T.B.; the second is not so certain—that mental stress plays some part. Yet there is reasonably good evidence that such stress as a broken love-affair can cause lowered resistance to breakdown so that when germs are encountered infection will occur.

In children, lung tuberculosis is not common, but tuberculosis of the bones and glands is, as is also infection in the abdomen, the kidney or spine, and, worst of all, tuberculous meningitis. These are often of the bovine type from infected milk. Ordinarily, T.B. in children is less serious than adult infections; but tuberculous meningitis used to be almost invariably fatal until streptomycin was discovered.

Adult tuberculosis usually occurs in the lungs **or** the pleura—the thin membrane surrounding **the** lungs. In younger people military tuberculosis, which is a form of T.B. blood-poisoning or septicæmia, is a very serious condition, and the infection spreads throughout the whole body in a few weeks.

Lung infection begins gradually in someone who has previously felt unwell. There may be cough, and later blood-stained sputum (although blood which is coughed up does not necessarily prove that T.B. is present). Whatever means of treatment is used, the struggle between disease and patient is likely to be fairly long, but the outlook is now good. The closure of the Swiss sanatoria is due partly to modern disbelief that air in one place is better than that in another, but mainly to improved treatment.

Prevention depends on legal action ensuring tuberculosis-free herds of cattle; on control of spread of the disease by those " open " cases who carry germs in their sputum; on the use of vaccination in childhood with B.C.G. vaccine (which you can ask your doctor about).

Many methods are used in treatment: new drugs, such as streptomycin, isoniazid, and P.A.S., lung surgery, rest, and so on. At any rate, tuberculosis is being got under control, but anyone who is worried can get a free X-ray at the nearest Mass Radiography Centre. There are skin tests to show whether there is susceptibility to T.B.

Septicæmia. Commonly known as " blood-poisoning," is one of those diseases of which text-books prior to the Second World war used to say: " death usually occurs."

Blood-poisoning occurs generally by spread from some septic area such as a wound (or even a small prick), after childbirth, or any place where certain germs have got admission to the body. The most usual germ is the streptococcus, although the pneumococcus—which ordinarily causes pneumonia—and the staphylococcus may also cause septicæmia.

Fever comes on suddenly and rises rapidly with headaches, sweating, and shivering. The patient is obviously very ill, and later there is wasting and delirium. The white blood cells increase in number. Septicæmia sometimes occurs without any apparent local infection in those who are weak and debilitated.

Pyœmia is a type of septicæmia which leads to the formation of numerous abscesses throughout the body. Its symptoms are the same as described above, except that the causative germ is usually the staphylococcus, and abscesses are found which may need surgical treatment.

However, in both conditions the state of affairs has been revolutionised by the use of the sulpha drugs and antibiotics; cure is now the rule rather than the exception.

Septicæmia should be suspected when any small wound or cut is followed by high temperature and the symptoms described above.

The word " *Toxæmia* " is used when the germs stay in their original position and produce symptoms by spreading their toxins throughout the body. Tetanus, diphtheria, and some kinds of childbirth infection come into this category; the symptoms may vary from mild disturbance to severe illness.

Meningitis means inflammation of the meninges, the covering which, like a layer of plastic, lies over the brain and spinal cord, just as the pleura covers the lungs and the peritoneum covers internal organs in the abdomen. (Hence inflammation of the pleura is known as pleurisy, and inflammation of the peritoneum as peritonitis.)

Various germs may cause meningitis, for example, the bacillus of tuberculosis, the pneumococcus, which ordinarily causes pneumonia, and the streptococcus or staphylococcus, but ordinarily the word refers to *Cerebrospinal Meningitis* or " spotted fever " caused by the meningococcus and occurring at times as an epidemic. It is commonest in the years from infancy to the early twenties, and begins suddenly with headache, vomiting, and fever. The temperature rises quickly, and pain develops in the back and legs; on the second or third day a rash appears on the body, and particularly on the inside of the thighs. Later there is stiffness of the neck, the head may be drawn back, vomiting persists, and the headache can be so severe as to cause the patient to scream with pain.

Fortunately, this type of meningitis (and most of the others) respond to treatment with antibiotics or the sulpha drugs, so the risks are very much less than formerly.

Pneumococcal Meningitis is an unusual complication of pneumonia, and the septic types (*streptococcal* or *staphylococcal*) arise either following an infected fracture of the skull or from infection of the ear or mastoid.

Tuberculous Meningitis has already been mentioned; originally always fatal, it is now treatable with streptomycin.

All these diseases are very much a matter for

specialist and hospital treatment, but it is worth while mentioning *benign lymphocytic meningitis*, in which, although all the symptoms of meningitis are present, recovery without specific treatment is invariable. Meningitis, which was during the First World War and after what polio is to us now, is no longer common, and when taken in time is easily treated.

Tetanus is usually known as " lockjaw " because there may be difficulty in opening the mouth, although this is simply part of a spasm of all the muscles of the body. The tetanus bacillus is found in rich soil—hence the disease is less common in desert areas—and tetanus resembles rabies in that: (a) it enters at a wound; (b) it affects the nervous system; (c) it results in fits and ultimately death.

However, active immunisation with T.T. (tetanus toxoid) has resulted in the disease becoming uncommon, and even when developed, treatment with antitoxin, anæsthetics, and curare may lead to cure.

The bacillus is anærobic (*i.e.*, does not use oxygen) and is most likely to occur in such situations as when a man digging manure or working in his garden sticks a fork through his foot, or, in war-time, when he is wounded in soil contaminated with manure.

Undulant fever, also known as Malta fever or abortus fever, falls into two types: melitensis, which infects goats, and abortus, cattle and pigs. Man gets the disease by reason of close contact with or drinking the milk of infected animals. (The name abortus is given because abortion is produced in cattle and sows.)

In Undulant Fever, as one would suppose, the fever goes up and down for two to three weeks; it may then go down and rise again, persisting for many months. The disease may occur in Britain, but modern drugs are on the whole successful in dealing with it. A striking feature of the disease is the combination of a high temperature with an appearance of relative well-being.

Another disease carried by mammals is *Glanders* or *Farcy*, spread by horses. In glanders there is discharge from the nose and sometimes pneumonia. Occasionally the disease is fatal. In farcy abscesses form, usually along the lymph vessels. Both conditions are very contagious, and treatment is a matter for a specialist; infected horses should be destroyed.

Cholera. Cholera could be classified under the head of food-poisoning, because it is mainly spread by infected water (however, like typhoid, it can also be spread by flies, infected food, and carriers); it could also be classified as a tropical disease, since, although it used to be found in Europe, it is now mainly rife in India.

Also like typhoid, cholera is caused by a bacillus, and can be prevented by early inoculation and care over food supplies—boiling water and milk, washing uncooked foods in chlorinated water, and keeping flies away.

The fever begins in the usual way with a short incubation period, followed by abdominal pain, severe vomiting, and diarrhœa. Later with the loss of fluid from the body there may be cramps in the muscles, diarrhœa increases, and the motions become of the typical " rice-water " type —*i.e.*, there is no solid matter, and the appearance is that of water to which a little milk has been added. This stage is followed by collapse, with low pulse and cold hands and feet. Death, if adequate treatment is not available, results in about 70 per cent. of cases.

Anthrax. The bacillus of anthrax, like that of tuberculosis, can exist outside the body for long periods, and, like that of tetanus, then takes the form of spores or seed-like bodies. It is spread by infected cattle and horses, which get the disease from eating grass containing spores.

In human beings the form the disease takes depends on where the germ alights; sometimes it comes from infected shaving-brushes, when it causes a large sore, like a boil, on the face, known as " malignant pustule "; sometimes it develops in those who inhale the dust from infected hides or wool (hence the name " wool-sorters' disease," which is a form of bronchitis with blood-stained sputum); lastly it may arise through eating infected meat, when the result is intestinal anthrax.

In all cases the outlook is serious. Death is common, preceded by a high temperature, skin symptoms in the first instance, lung symptoms in the second, and food-poisoning symptoms in the third. Penicillin or tetracycline may be effective.

Diseases Caused by Fungi.

There are only two important groups of disease caused by fungus: the serious *actinomycosis* and the relatively harmless, if unpleasant, *ringworm*. Ringworm or tinea will be dealt with later; it affects the hair, the body, the groin (dhobie itch, already referred to), and the feet (athlete's foot). Actinomycosis is spread by a fungus in barley and grasses which may reach the human mouth, settle around bad teeth, and thence pass to the lungs, the bone of the jaw, and even to the intestines or brain. Fortunately, this unpleasant fungus, which was once difficult to eradicate, has proved susceptible to penicillin.

The Venereal Diseases.

The venereal diseases are those caused—or at least that is what the name means—by the goddess of love, Venus. Venus, of course, causes a great deal of trouble, but venereal disease is not necessarily the worst she can do. Venereal disease is spread by sexual intercourse with an infected person.

Gonorrhœa is the result of an infection by the gonococcus (*Neisseria gonorrhœa*) and ordinarily comes on after an incubation period of three to seven days. However, babies can get an infection of the eyes, known as ophthalmia, from their mother if she is infected, and gonorrhœa in young children is often the result of being in contact with infected towels or clothes. The disease in adults is evident when there is a thick, creamy discharge from the sexual organs and sometimes pain on passing water; in infants ophthalmia is prevented by the use of silver nitrate eye-drops at birth. Gonorrhœa is fairly easily cured by the use of sulpha drugs or penicillin; but unfortunately venereal disease is increasing in recent years and drug-resistant forms are becoming more common.

Syphilis is a serious venereal disease caused by a spirochete (*Treponema pallidum*). Stories about lavatory seats are simply stories, although it is occasionally possible to get syphilis by other than sexual means: for example, it has happened that a man playing football has been infected through his hand being grazed by the teeth of someone with syphilis. But this is very unusual, although kissing can spread the disease. Children, too, can be born with syphilis (the so-called congenital syphilis).

Adult syphilis begins with a sore, known as a hard chancre, at the point where the spirochete of syphilis has entered; this may be on the lips, through kissing; on the sexual organs, through intercourse; and very rarely, as explained above, elsewhere. In a short time the chancre disappears and all may seem to be well, but this primary stage is followed by a secondary stage with sore throat, a rash, headache, and enlargement of glands. This, it left alone, also clears up, but is followed by the tertiary stage, in which a chronic infection develops in some part of the body which, presumably, is most susceptible in the particular individual. Thus there may be chronic syphilis of the skin, the bones, the heart, liver, or nervous system.

In the nervous system, the commonest forms are the two diseases of *tabes dorsalis*, in which the spinal cord is infected, and G.P.I. (general paralysis of the insane), in which the brain and mind are affected. These will be discussed under Nervous Diseases.

In congenital syphilis the pregnant mother gives her child syphilis. Such infants are often stillborn or premature, they look wizened, like little old men, and amongst other symptoms are eye disease, "snuffles," a flattened nose, and when the adult teeth appear the front ones may be notched at the biting surface.

The treatment, of course, is very much a matter for a specialist, but diagnosis is usually made through the Wassermann blood test. It was for syphilis that Ehrlich produced his "magic bullet"—an arsenical drug, known as salvarsan, which could attack the organism selectively without harming the body and was the first of the modern specific drugs. Present-day treatment is with penicillin. G.P.I., was once treated with malarial therapy with some success. Penicillin alone is often adequate.

It is important to understand about venereal disease in general: (1) that it happens to many people who are no worse than anyone else; (2) that many patients believe themselves to have V.D. when, in fact, they have not; (3) that the best thing to do is to see your doctor as soon as possible—he is not concerned with your morals, and the sooner you go, the sooner you will get well; (4) every sore in the sexual area need not be V.D. There are other diseases which may be contracted as venereal infections.

Chancroid produces small septic ulcers around the sex organs, with swelling of the local glands in the groin, which may suppurate. It is caused by a bacillus, and can usually be cleared up by sulpha drugs within a week. Scabies and lice often pass from one body to another during sexual intercourse, but are not usually thought of as venereal in origin, although in many cases they are.

Tropical Diseases.

Nothing is more difficult than to define the term "tropical diseases." One might define them as the diseases which occur in tropical climates—but then measles occurs there too; and if they are defined as those diseases which are found *only* in the tropics, the solution is no easier, since leprosy, cholera, smallpox, and typhus are usually listed as tropical diseases, yet were found in this country until fairly recently—and the odd case still is.

But what a story could be told about the conquest of those infections which were—and many still are—the scourge of humanity! One day when generals and dictators are forgotten we shall remember that great international army of physicians and bacteriologists who have saved millions of lives and infinitely reduced human suffering: Koch and Ehrlich of Germany, Pasteur and Roux of France, Ross and Jenner of Britain, Reed of America, Noguchi of Japan, and many others. We shall remember how the Jesuit priests brought quinine from Peru to Europe in 1638, the first drug to save people from malaria; how in tropical heat Ronald Ross (1857–1932) peered for hours through his microscope to discover the connection between malaria and the mosquito until the sweat running from his brow rusted the instrument; how Major Walter Reed's work in Havana (1851–1902) made possible the building of the Panama Canal, and think, too, of the American soldiers who died in helping him to find the cause of yellow fever. In mentioning Jenner once more, we should recall Lady Mary Montagu (1689–1762), who brought the practice of vaccination to England from Turkey—or, rather, the practice of "variolation," which meant inoculating with the pus from smallpox cases. This was, of course, a dangerous practice, but the idea was there. Noguchi, one of the great bacteriologists of the nineteenth century, was the son of a poor peasant. He often had to steal to get enough bread even to keep alive, but was later to help in our understanding of syphilis and many tropical diseases.

Yet there is still much to do. Take, for example, the case of Egypt, one of the world's poorest countries, supporting with the help of water from the Nile about 24 million people. But if the river gives food and drink it does other things; for it carries the disease of bilharzia, which kills thousands of peasants yearly. In the villages of Egypt as many as 90–100 per cent. of the population suffer from this terrible disease. The infantile mortality rate is the second highest in the world—29·5 per cent.—seven times higher than that of Holland; the average expectation of life amongst the lower classes is thirty-one years,

of the upper classes fifty to sixty years. The country is ridden with bilharzia, ankylostomiasis, malaria, plague, amœbic dysentery, typhus, tuberculosis, and pellagra. Blindness, due to trachoma and other diseases, affects tens of thousands. Such a situation cannot be treated simply by pouring drugs into the country; what is necessary is social control, to enforce purification of the water supplies, the use of insecticides to kill the disease-bearing pests, and removal of the causes of extreme poverty (tuberculosis and vitamin deficiencies which are common in Egypt are diseases of malnutrition).

Relapsing Fever, common in India and Africa, may be louse- or tick-borne; the germ is a spirochæte, similar to that of syphilis, but the disease is non-venereal. Relapsing fever gets its name from the fact that the temperature remains high (39°–41°C) for about a week, returns to normal for a week, and rises again. There may be three to five relapses of this sort. Penicillin is effective; lice or ticks must be eradicated.

Epidemic Jaundice (also known as Weil's disease or—if you prefer it—ictero-hæmorrhagica spirochætosis), is also caused by a spirochæte, and spread by rats. Now it is rarely found in Europe, although it occurred in the trenches during the First World War, in men working in sewers, and in the women who worked in the fish market of Aberdeen, which at one time was rat-infested. It is rarely fatal, but leads to high fever and jaundice. Penicillin in high dosage or tetracycline may help.

Yaws is also a spirochætal disease, common in the tropics and particularly in children. It is unpleasant, but not serious, and tends to clear up in a year or so. There are raspberry-like growths on the skin, which disappear with the drugs used in syphilis (although the condition is non-venereal). The Wassermann reaction, positive in syphilis, is also positive in yaws.

Leprosy. Whereas syphilis, relapsing fever, epidemic jaundice, and yaws are caused by spirochætes, leprosy is caused by a bacillus resembling the bacillus of tuberculosis. Leprosy, in fact, should not be included here at all, for it is non-spirochætal, and not necessarily a tropical infection. Apart from the difficulty of classification, many popular beliefs about the disease are untrue. It is *not* the oldest disease afflicting man; *not* a disease confined to tropical countries; it is *not* very catching; *not* hereditary, *not* incurable; in leprosy the fingers and toes do *not* drop off; it is *not* a divine punishment for wrongdoing. So there are many misunderstandings about this disease, and placing it in the wrong part of the medical section is probably the least.

Leprosy is a serious disease not because of disfiguring light-coloured skin patches and lumps, but because it destroys peripheral nerves. Leprosy may disappear spontaneously, or it may progress until the face is lion-like and the hands and feet wasted and ulcerated. The disease rarely kills, but it is the world's greatest crippler.

Leprosy was once fairly common in colder Western countries, though its extent was exaggerated. The great majority of the 15 million people who suffer from leprosy live in tropical countries, but it still exists in Iceland, Japan, Korea and some of the southern states of the United States. Prolonged and intimate contact with an "open" case is said to be the main mode of infection, but only one infected husband in twenty passes leprosy to his wife.

The sulphone drugs have revolutionised the treatment of leprosy. Given early diagnosis and adequate treatment, the great majority of sufferers could be cured. Established deformity (such as claw hand, drop foot, paralysed eyelids) can be mitigated by reconstructive surgery, although lost sensation cannot be restored.

In the past, only Christian missions were concerned with the plight of the leprosy sufferer. Now, non-sectarian voluntary agencies, Governments and the World Health Organisation have joined in the fight against the disease. Enough is known to control the disease, but not enough is being done, as only one victim in five is at present getting treatment.

Plague is another disease caused by bacteria, common in Europe at one time, but now largely restricted to Asia. Nevertheless, it caused millions of deaths in Europe during the years 1348–49 and 1665 and was the "Black Death," which, indeed, changed the course of history. Interested readers may read Hans Zinnser's *Rats, Lice, and History* about this aspect of the disease. Plague is carried by the bite of the rat flea, but, once people become infected, spread may occur from one to the other by droplet infection—*i.e.*, by coughing and sneezing. After an incubation period of two to ten days, fever develops, rather like severe influenza, and in a day or two the glands in the groin begin to swell, followed perhaps by swelling of the glands elsewhere. This is the usual type of plague, but it is also possible to get disease of the lungs from droplet infection and blood-poisoning from infection of the blood-stream. Both the latter types are almost invariably fatal, and even the glandular type (bubonic plague) has a mortality of about 80 per cent. The vaccine has given place to streptomycin and sulpha drugs which are also used on contacts.

Although we have little space to discuss the subject of plagues and epidemics in general, it is worth noting that serious epidemics have almost always followed wars, revolutions, and economic and political collapse. Thus the Black Death followed the break-up of the Roman Empire, and, in the fourteenth century, accompanied the end of mediæval civilisation. The Napoleonic wars were followed by other epidemics, and the wars of the 1830s in Europe were followed by influenza. In the most widespread outburst of influenza after the First World War, more people were killed by the disease than in all the fighting of four years. It is a reflection on the peculiar mentality of Man that this devastating epidemic, which affected almost the whole world, occupies little space in his history books—we still, with few exceptions, regard history as the doings of kings, queens, and generals. Yet, in 1918, 20 million men, and women, and children died from influenza, and no cure has, as yet, been found! Later we shall see that many millions of people die yearly from starvation or vitamin deficiencies But these facts—the real facts of life—we rarely hear about.

Protozoal Diseases.

Nearly all the diseases caused by protozoa are tropical diseases, although one of the best-known protozoans is the harmless amœba found in British ponds. Protozoal diseases are caused by these organisms, large in comparison with bacteria which are really one-celled plants. Viruses are neither animals nor plants, are much smaller than the other two groups, and have some distinctive characteristics described elsewhere.

The only important diseases caused by protozoa are sleeping sickness or trypanosomiasis, malaria, and amœbic dysentery (as contrasted with bacillary dysentery), another disease, leishmaniasis—also known by the numerous names of kala-azar, dum-dum fever, and, in milder form, Delhi boil, Oriental sore, or Bagdad sore—will also be mentioned briefly. These infections are few, but important in their influence on Man; for, as Dr. Clark-Kennedy has pointed out, malaria until recently was responsible for one-fifth of all human sickness, sleeping sickness not so long ago caused a large part of Central Africa to be uninhabitable, and in some areas of the tropics there are probably more people with, than without, amœbic dysentery.

Malaria. The word, of course, means "bad air," just as "influenza" means "influence"—in Italian *influenza di freddo*—the influence of cold. Human beings have a natural tendency to suppose that, when two events occur together, then one must be caused by the other. Yet, although malaria and "bad air" may often go together, and influenza and cold, it does not follow that bad air (whatever that may be) causes malaria nor that cold causes influenza. In fact, the anopheles mosquito carries the amœba of malaria, and the mosquito prefers climates which some people might describe as "bad," but it is the amœba, not the air, which causes the disease. Anyhow, the unfortunate mosquito might well use the phrase honoured by many generations of schoolmasters: "It hurts me more than it hurts you!" For the mosquito, too, is sick, and passes on its sickness to the person it bites.

There are several types of plasmodium—which is the scientific name for this amœba—producing attacks of fever varying in severity and frequency: benign tertian, quartan, and malignant quartan. Entering the body from the mosquito bite, the parasites penetrate the blood cells, multiply there, and finally burst into the blood stream. When this happens the temperature rises, and then they return to the cells to carry out once more the same procedure. Depending on the type, the attacks of fever may be at intervals of three or four days, severe or milder. When someone with malaria is bitten by a mosquito the infection can be transmitted to the next person it meets, but malaria is not infectious from one person to another directly. Quinine, of course, is the time-honoured remedy, but many other drugs are now available: mepacrine, primaquine, chloraquine and some sulpha drugs. The drug must be taken long enough for the infection to die out, otherwise relapses can occur even after leaving a malarial country (but it is only fair to say that, just as some people continue to give themselves the title of "Major" when they have left the Army, so others long in Britain continue to describe attacks of cold or 'flu as "my old malaria again," when, to say the least of it, they are exaggerating!).

Important as are the drugs used in the treatment of malaria, even more so is the control of the parasite-bearing mosquito. The eggs of mosquitoes hatch in water, and there the young or larval forms can be attacked by pouring oil on the surface of pools so that they are unable to breathe, or by introducing small fish which have a partiality for them. Adult mosquitoes can be killed by insecticides or kept away by repellent creams or nets over beds. Prophylaxis with anti-malarials before entering and while living in known malarial zones is important.

Blackwater Fever is a sequel to malaria in tropical Africa and some parts of India. Rather illogically, it is described as "Blackwater," although the urine is red and the skin is yellow but the result is due to breaking down of the red blood cells by some malarial toxin. Possibly too much quinine may help in producing the illness. Treatment is to give plenty of fluids and no quinine or any other anti-malarial drugs in the early stages. The death-rate is about 25 per cent.

Trypanosomiasis or sleeping sickness—not to be confused with *sleepy* sickness—is essentially an African disease (although also found in tropical America) spread by the tsetse fly. Its cause is the type of protozoan known as a trypanosome, almond-shaped with vibrating membranes at the sides which enable it to move through the blood-stream, rather like a flat fish in the water.

There are three stages of the disease: first, the stage of fever with enlarged glands and a rapid pulse, which may continue off and on for three years; secondly, the stage of trembling hands, legs, and tongue, vacant expression, and slow and stumbling speech; thirdly, and lastly, the stage of low temperature, apathy, wasting of the muscles, and possibly death.

Treatment is with arsenical drugs—such as tryparsamide or Bayer 205—which give good results in early cases. Preventive measures in infected areas include the destruction of tsetse flies by insecticide, the cutting down of forests near rivers which are inhabited by tsetse flies, and some authorities have suggested the shooting of big game which may form a "reservoir" of the parasites, whence tsetse flies can carry them to human beings. For similar reasons infected people should not be allowed to move to non-infected areas.

Amœbic Dysentery, also known as *Amœbiasis, is* caused by the *Entamœba histolytica*, an amœba whose cysts are found in food, water, or spread by infected fingers or flies. There is mild fever and diarrhœa which contains blood. The disease may become chronic, and can cause abscesses, usually in the liver but sometimes in the lungs. Amœbiasis is treated with chloroquine or nitroimidazoles.

Leishmaniasis, kala-azar, or dum-dum fever, is another amœbic disease, probably spread in this instance by the bite of sandflies. It is also known as trǒpical splenomegaly—enlargement of the spleen in ordinary language—since infection results in enlargement of the spleen and liver, low, irregular fever, and death within a year or so. A milder form, affecting the skin, is known as Delhi boil, Oriental sore, or Baghdad sore, does not lead to kala-azar, and is fairly readily cured. The cure for both conditions is to give injections of antimony compounds which reduce the death-rate from kala-azar from 80 per cent. to about 5 per cent.

Diseases Caused by Parasitic Worms.

Many types of worms infest human beings and other animals. They are interesting for such reasons as their size (which may range from the almost invisible to 9 m or more), their life histories, and their serious or trivial consequences on their hosts. We shall mention only a few groups here, and mainly the ones likely to be met with in Europe—the tapeworms, the roundworms, and the threadworms—although some tropical types will be described briefly.

Tapeworms, as we have seen earlier, like many other types of intestinal worm, lead a double life. What usually happens is that the worm breeds in the human intestine, the eggs pass out in the fæces, and are then swallowed by animals eating contaminated material. In the animal the eggs hatch out into larvæ—primitive forms which penetrate the muscle, forming cysts—and Man is infected in turn by eating its meat. Thus *Tœnia solium* gets into the flesh of pigs, which, if imperfectly cooked (measly pork), causes infestation of the intestine in Man. It reaches a length of about 3 m. *Tœnia saginata*, which reaches a length of about 6 m, is spread in imperfectly cooked beef, and in Baltic countries *Dibothriocephalus latus* gets into the human intestine from caviare or undercooked fish. It reaches the awesome length of 9 m.

Now all the worms we have mentioned so far are found in the human intestine, and the cysts, which are much more dangerous and unpleasant, in the animal's muscles. But in some worms the reverse happens, with the adult in the animal's intestines and the cysts in Man. Thus in Australia the dog tapeworm (*Tœnia echinococcus*) produces cysts in both sheep and Man. This is known as hydatid disease, and may remain unsuspected until cysts in the lungs, liver, or elsewhere become infected or rupture. *Trichinella spiralis* is similar in action, being found in the intestines of pigs and getting into the muscles or other organs of Man. The main difference is that this worm migrates from the pig's intestines into its muscles, whence it reaches Man in undercooked pork meat or sausages. The muscular cysts cause swellings and sometimes pain. There are changes in the blood, swelling of the face and leg in the early stages, and fever. A minor epidemic occurred in England in 1941. *Tœnia echinococcus* and *Trichinella spiralis* are small—not more than 0·5 cm in length—but are more serious in their consequences than the large worms. Treatment is very difficult, and ordinarily all that can be done is to deal with individual cysts when they make themselves apparent.

The large tapeworms, *Tœnia solium* and *saginata* and *Dibothriocephalus latus*, produce varying symptoms or none at all. Usually they are not discovered until some segments of the worm are excreted, but there may be mild indigestion, excessive hunger, and occasionally anæmia. However, when the worm is discovered the patient, not unnaturally is likely to become anxious and uncomfortable at the thought of "having" a tapeworm; these symptoms are caused by the worry rather than the worm.

Treatment is, of course, a matter for a doctor, who now has a number of very effective drugs to choose from. One has to make sure that the head of the worm has been removed, otherwise it will continue to grow.

Roundworms are similar both in appearance and size to ordinary earth-worms and the eggs reach Man, not from an animal, but from the contaminated fingers of someone else who handles food. They give rise to no symptoms, and are noticed only when discharged in the fæces or occasionally vomited up. Piperazine is an effective treatment.

Threadworms, as the name suggests, are like small 0·5–1 cm long pieces of white thread. They are very common in children, and live mainly in the cæcum—*i.e.*, the part of the large intestine near the appendix. The males, which are the smaller ones, remain there, but the females pass down towards the rectum at night-time and lay their eggs in the area around the anus. Infection is by contaminated hands handling food—especially uncooked food—and water. Threadworms are not serious, and cause few symptoms other than itching around the anus and between the legs, but heavily infected children may show symptoms of anæmia. The nervousness often shown by such children is usually the result of the irritation produced by the worms in the anal region. Infection is not common in adults, and in children tends to disappear at puberty.

Treatment is, in theory, simple; for the worms are easily destroyed by a number of drugs, such as piperazine. Ointment is applied to the itching area, and the child should be prevented from scratching. However, since the eggs may lie about the house for some time, reinfection often happens, especially if there are several small children in the home who may pass the disease from one to another.

The idea that intestinal worms in general are likely to cause loss of weight by absorbing food eaten by the patient is largely mistaken: for, although it is true that they do live on this food, the amount taken is certainly not enough to be significant.

Tropical Worms. Bilharzia has been mentioned before in connection with its frequency in Egypt, although it is also found in other parts of Africa, Arabia, and Iraq. There are two main types: one infecting the bladder (*Schistosomum hæmatobium*), the other the rectum (*Schistosomum mansoni*). Bilharzia is more correctly known as schistosomiasis.

The parasite's fantastic life-history begins when a man bathes in infected water, and the small swimming forms known as cercariæ pierce and enter his skin—or they may enter the body by drinking infected water. From the skin they pass to the portal vein below the liver, remain there six weeks until they become adult and then swim against the blood-stream down to the pelvis, where the female lays eggs which have a sharp spine. The eggs penetrate into the bladder or rectum—depending on the type of fluke—and pass out in the fæces or urine. If they enter water they hatch out into small moving forms which seek out a water-snail, develop further in its body, and leave it in the form of cercariæ ready to find a new human victim. The female fluke is slender and round, about 2·5 cm in length, the male, flat and leaf-shaped, is about 2 cm long, and, as we have seen, their grisly courting takes place in the portal vein, whence the impregnated female passes to the bladder (hæmatobium) or rectum (mansoni) to lay her eggs.

Infection results in raised temperature and, in the urinary type, blood in the urine; in the intestinal type blood is found in the fæces, and there are symptoms resembling dysentery— e.g., diarrhœa. Treatment in both cases is with antimony tartrate or niridazole. Needless to say, attempts should be made at prevention by telling people to avoid infected canals (usually easier said than done), and by periodically cutting off the water supply to the canals to kill the snails.

Hookworm Disease, or ankylostomiasis, is found in many parts of the world, especially in miners who work on damp ground. The tiny worm enters the body usually through the feet, passes through the blood-stream to the lungs, eats through into one of the bronchial tubes, climbs the windpipe, and passes down the œsophagus into the stomach to end up in the duodenum. It causes anæmia, can be fairly readily cured, but is occasionally fatal.

Elephantiasis. Some types of parasitic worm are spread by insects. Thus in *Filiarisis* mosquitoes inject by their bites the infantile forms of a tiny worm which enters the lymphatic channels; there the blockade they cause leads to the swelling of the legs and the lower part of the body, known as elephantiasis.

PHYSICAL INJURIES.
INTRODUCTION.

In this section we shall inevitably discuss much that could be described as Principles of First Aid. You cannot learn First Aid from a book, even if you read one of the excellent first aid manuals, like those published by the St. John Ambulance Association. The only way is to join one of their many classes of practical and theoretical instruction which are held in all parts of this country and many others. There is much to be said for many more people receiving instruction, to judge by the level of general ignorance and ineffectiveness to be witnessed at most road accidents before the ambulance comes.

The most difficult thing to learn is what *not* to do. When a patient is knocked down in the road, people instinctively seem to want to drag him immediately to his feet, or otherwise pull him on to the pavement away from the traffic. Someone will have entered the nearest shop and be emerging with a chair so that the casualty can sit down. Before long a hot strong sweet cup of tea has arrived, and this or some other beverage is being poured into him. All this is instinctive, and all of it is wrong. Do *not* move the patient until you are sure he has no fracture which will be further aggravated by movement. To take an extreme case, a fractured spine clumsily moved may result in permanent widespread paralysis. Guard your patient from the traffic but only move him when you are certain it is safe to do so. If he has any injury which is likely to require a general anaesthetic on arrival in hospital (and this applies to most fractures) do not give anything at all by mouth. No anaesthetic can be given to a patient who has eaten or drunk anything in the previous three hours, in case he vomits while unconscious and dies of obstruction of his airway. Keep your patient warm (do *not* warm him up artificially) keep his head low, and unless he is bleeding severely or has stopped breathing, do nothing but protect him from the ministrations of the uninstructed until the ambulance comes.

Injuries to the Head and Back.

The head contains the brain, an organ with a number of inconvenient properties from the point of view of injury. Its very great importance is matched by its very great vulnerability as a tissue. Its consistency is that of stiff junket. It is quite incapable of repair once damaged and cannot heal by growing new parts in the way that skin and bone can. So it has to be totally enclosed by protective bone which means it cannot swell without compressing itself dangerously within its box—and this not infrequently happens after injury. Furthermore, any bleeding into the interior of the skull can only occur at the expense of compressing the brain, since the brain box is already fully occupied by the brain. There is a story in first aid known as "Concussion and Compression." It begins with a knock-out blow to the head and this is known as concussion. The patient struck a hard enough blow to the head will lose consciousness, if only for a short time, due to the brain being shaken up. Even slight knocks would do this if the brain were not cushioned by a thin layer of cerebrospinal fluid. Most concussed patients quickly regain consciousness, and for the great majority that is the end of the affair except for a sore head and a headache for a few days. Unfortunately for a minority, even though there may have been no fracture, the blow that knocked them out will also have damaged a small blood vessel on the surface of the brain. These patients may be indistinguishable from the luckier ones at first. They may have regained consciousness and will be just as anxious to go home. They will often be quite lucid for some hours. Surgeons call this the "lucid interval." However, when more than a certain amount of blood has accumulated in the head, and the brain is sufficiently compressed by it the patient loses consciousness slowly, for a second time, and from this phase of "compression" he will not recover unless something is done. The lucid interval can last some hours. Brain surgeons can relieve the compression and save the life of the patient only if they have him in their care when it occurs. This is why *all* cases of head injury who have once lost consciousness (concussion), for however short a period of time, and however lucid they may subsequently appear, *all* must be seen by a doctor and, if thought necessary, observed overnight in hospital, in case they are bleeding and proceeding to compression. There is no way of saving these avoidable fatalities other than by treating all cases of concussion seriously. Fractured skull is potentially even more serious, because the blow will have been harder and, the brain is therefore more seriously at risk.

The spinal cord can be regarded as an extension of the brain which runs down the middle of the spinal bones of the vertebral column. It has the same delicate consistency, and the same inability to recover from injury as the brain. Injury is usually the result of a fracture-dislocation of the spine. The consequences of injury are due to a permanent interruption of its two main functions. All movements of the voluntary muscles are only possible if they are connected by nerves to the brain. Except for muscles in the head, all these "motor" nerves run in the spinal cord. The nerve pathways leave the skull through a large hole in its base and run down in the spinal cord to the required level. They then emerge between the spinal bones and travel in bundles to reach the muscles. Motor nerves for the arm leave the cord between the vertebrae of the neck. Those for the leg leave the cord in the lumbar region in the small of the back. If the nerve supply is damaged in any part of its course, the muscles being supplied become paralysed and are unable to move. It follows that if the spinal cord is damaged, all muscles below the point of damage have been cut off from the brain, and will be paralysed, and this will be permanent because the cord cannot be repaired. Damage to the nerve pathway *after* it has left the cord can often be repaired. Permanent paralysis is only one of the consequences of cord damage, since there is another whole series of nerves running in the cord which carry sensations from all parts of the body to the brain. Therefore there will be loss of sensation as well as paralysis below the point of injury.

It is emphasised that fracture of the spinal bones can occur without damage to the cord taking place. It is when these bones move one over the other, or "dislocate," that permanent cord damage occurs. It is therefore extremely important that cases of back injury be moved very carefully indeed in order to avoid such a disaster, and special ways of moving such patients are taught in First Aid classes.

Haemorrhage and Shock.

Every part of the body must have a blood supply, or else it will die. It is possible to stop the blood supply to a leg, for example, by fastening a wide rubber bandage tightly around the top of the thigh. This so-called " constrictive bandage " is still mentioned in First Aid books as a desperate means of controlling haemorrhage in a limb. It should hardly ever be used, because by stopping all circulation of blood, the entire limb will die in the course of time. Besides, most haemorrhage can be stemmed by direct pressure on the bleeding point. The tissues of the leg, such as its muscle and skin and bone will begin to die in a little more than half an hour after cutting off the blood supply. The brain, however, will begin to suffer within three *seconds* of its blood supply being cut off, and will die in about three minutes. Thus it can be seen that some parts of the body are more susceptible than others to a failure of the blood supply and the brain suffers earliest of all. Since the brain is where most of the vital functions of the body are controlled, it follows that a shortage of blood to the brain is likely to lead to a " depression of the vital functions "—a state of affairs known to First Aiders as " shock."

Shock occurs in a number of conditions, but is always due to a failure of the supply of blood to the vital functions of the brain for one reason or another. Its usual causes are:

(1) haemorrhage, when there is a general shortage, but the brain feels it most;

(2) severe burns, in which much fluid is lost from the blood as will be seen later; and

(3) certain medical conditions causing acute heart failure in which there is a failure to pump blood to the brain because the pump has failed.

The treatment for shock consists basically of restoring the blood supply to the brain, and where it is caused by loss of blood or other fluid, the treatment is transfusion. Finally, it must be emphasised that treatment is always urgent, since the brain cannot function for long without its blood supply, and once damaged by the shortage, can never be repaired. No attempt is made here to describe such treatment completely, but the most important things are to keep the head low so as to reduce the work the heart must do to drive blood to the brain; and to avoid artificial heating of the body by hot water bottles, etc., which only diverts blood away from the brain where it is needed, into the skin where it is not.

The treatment of severe haemorrhage is to stop the bleeding, usually by firm, direct pressure, and then to remember above all things that even though the bleeding has stopped, there may be a dangerous state of shock from which the patient could die. This can only be prevented by restoring the circulation to the brain, usually by transfusion; so, having stopped the bleeding drive him fast to hospital for the second part of the treatment which may be as necessary to save his life as the first.

There is great confusion over the use of the word " shock." In the lay mind it is a shake-up of the nervous system caused by a fright, or some bad news, or the sight of something nasty in the woodshed. Even in the medical mind it is sometimes confused and some of the First Aid books confuse it still further. Too frequently they give the treatment as " loosen all tight clothing from neck, chest, and waist; reassure the casualty and ensure a good supply of air." All this, together with grandmother's hot strong sweet tea is perfectly good enough if the patient is only " shaken-up " by a fright or a fall, but it will be dangerously negligent and time-wasting if he is suffering from true shock due to a failure of blood supply to the brain.

Fainting is a special case which can be prevented by keeping the head low in those who feel faint. It is usually self-curing due to the patient automatically falling into a position in which the head is low. If the faint, however, is due to severe blood loss, this is the same as shock in our proper meaning of the word and must be treated accordingly.

Haemorrhage can therefore be a difficult problem. It is even more so when it is internal. This may be in *medical* cases such as in occasional cases of peptic ulceration in which the blood will be vomited and also passed in the stool. Or it may be *surgical*, in the sense of being caused by injury to internal organs. The blood may emerge from one or other of the various orifices of the body, or it may be entirely concealed within the body. Rupture of internal abdominal organs such as the spleen, kidney and liver can occur with surprisingly little to show in the way of external injury. A fractured thigh bone can pierce the main artery of the leg and cause lethal internal haemorrhage without a drop of blood being visible. In all these cases diagnosis is urgent, followed by emergency blood transfusion if the brain, and hence the patient's life, is to be saved.

Means of detecting the presence of severe haemorrhage without seeing any blood are taught in First Aid Classes as the Signs of Haemorrhage. They are in fact manifestations of the reactions of the body in its attempts to save the failing brain, and are therefore the same as the signs of shock. The main ones are a rapid, feeble pulse, getting more rapid and more feeble as time goes on in a desperate attempt to get the remaining blood to the brain; skin pallor caused by constriction of blood vessels near the surface so that the blood which remains is shunted to the brain away from the less vulnerable skin; and finally, just before death, restlessness and air hunger.

A word of warning about the First Aid treatment of shock due to heart attack (coronary thrombosis). These patients must be transported at complete rest, but many of them react very badly to being made to lie down, since they have great difficulty in breathing in this position. Transport them relaxed, in a sitting position, supported by a large comfortable back rest.

It cannot be too strongly emphasised that with haemorrhage and shock, as with so many First Aid emergencies, the importance of protecting the brain is paramount.

Asphyxia.

The previous section was concerned with maintaining an adequate supply of blood to the brain. This is needed in order to supply the brain's only possible fuel—glucose—and the oxygen with which to burn it. Many different circumstances can conspire to reduce the oxygen content of the blood, and the result in each case is asphyxia. Normally, air is taken into the lungs through the air passages and brought into contact with all the circulating blood. It diffuses from the lungs into the blood, where it enters into a special relationship with the pigment of the red cells—haemoglobin. At the same time, the waste gas carbon dioxide enters the lungs from the blood and is breathed out. The revitalised blood is passed through the heart to build up sufficient pressure to drive it into all the tissues of the body, and in particular into the brain. A special system in the brain—the respiratory centre—controls the complicated machinery of respiration and is itself, of course, kept alive by the products of the very mechanism it controls. This mechanism consists of all the muscles of respiration—those which lift the ribs, the diaphragm and many other so-called accessory muscles. They all have to be finely co-ordinated by means of nerve impulses which begin in the brain, pass down the spinal cord and out to the muscles. Information of many kinds comes along sensory nerve pathways to the respiratory centre so that breathing can be automatically adjusted to the changing needs of the moment. In order that life may continue there must be:

    (1) a functioning breathing mechanism to revitalise the blood; and

    (2) a circulation to carry the revitalised blood to the brain and other tissues.

In many cases when breathing stops and unconsciousness supervenes as brain function is depressed, the heart will go on beating for some time longer. The aim of First Aid is to restore the breathing by artificial respiration *before the heart stops*. Once the heart stops—and it eventually does so abruptly and without warning—the brain is dead within the usual few minutes unless *both* the heart and the breathing are restarted; and this is a very much more difficult proposition than artificial respiration alone.

For these reasons, a patient whose breathing has stopped must have it started again without any delay. Here, as in the case of severe haemorrhage, it is no use telephoning the doctor or even putting the patient in an ambulance. The First Aider must act himself, because he is on the spot and the only one in a position to save life. Both actions require elementary First Aid training, and even school children can accomplish them if they have been well taught.

Asphyxia is the name given to a failure of the oxygen supply to the brain and is due to a breakdown in some part of the complicated breathing mechanism outlined above. One of its chief causes is a blockage of the airway by (a) solids or (b) liquids. Any foreign body of the right shape and size will block the airway, as also will the tongue in the unconscious patient. Remember how much more easily the child's airway can become blocked because it is so much smaller. Blockage by a liquid is, of course, drowning. Remember that if a patient drowns in the entire ocean, it is only about half a cupful which is doing him any harm—as it only takes this amount to fill the airway. The same goes for the amount of tea, or vomit, required to kill an unconscious patient if it gets down the "wrong way"—as it will unless someone prevents it.

Another very common cause of asphyxia is carbon monoxide poisoning. Carbon monoxide is a lethal component of car exhaust fumes, incompletely burning and badly ventilated fires and stoves, and domestic coal gas. One of the inconvenient properties of haemoglobin is that it combines with carbon monoxide very much more eagerly than with oxygen. Prolonged contact with even a very slightly contaminated atmosphere can build up a concentration of carbon monoxide in the blood which will prevent the blood from carrying sufficient oxygen—and this is in fact how it kills. It takes a very short time for this to happen if the atmosphere is heavily contaminated. Remember the danger of even a very slight leak of the gas either in the kitchen, or into a car from a faulty exhaust pipe or silencer. Many elderly people die of coal gas poisoning every day because their sense of smell is poor and they do not detect the leak.

Other causes of asphyxia are lack of oxygen in the atmosphere, as occurs at high altitudes; crushing of the chest so that the ribs cannot move; paralysis of the muscles of breathing by interference with their nerve supply, usually in First Aid, as a result of a broken neck and consequent damage to the spinal cord (poliomyelitis can occasionally produce the same effect by attacking the nerves just before they leave the spine); and depressing the respiratory centre in the brain, most commonly nowadays by barbiturate poisoning.

The only really effective method of artificial respiration, which all members of any civilised community should be able to carry out, can be learned in half an hour at a good First Aid class. This is the direct, mouth-to-mouth method, sometimes dramatised by journalists as the "kiss of life." The method is taught with the aid of models and cannot be satisfactorily learned by only reading about it.

In discussing asphyxia, we have again had to consider the particularly vulnerable situation of the brain.

Fractures.

Broken bones are not the most serious possible consequences of injuries causing fractures. It is usually more to be feared that further damage will be done by the broken ends of the bones to tissues and organs in the neighbourhood of the fracture. The First Aid treatment of immobilising the part before transporting the casualty is designed to avoid this.

Six types of fracture are commonly taught, but some of them may co-exist in the same injury and the division is only for descriptive purposes. In addition there are two special fractures of the skull.

A "simple" or "closed" fracture is where only the bone is broken, without damage to surrounding tissues and without a wound. A "compound" or "open" fracture is one in which air, and hence germs, can get at the broken bone. This may be through a wound, in whose depths lies the broken bone; or the bone may have been pushed out through the skin; or a bullet track may lead down to the fracture. All these are examples of compound fracture and the great danger is that the bone will become infected. Even now that infections are less feared than before the days of antibiotics, it is still a grave matter for bone to get infected. However the antibiotic is given, we rely on the blood supply to carry it into the infected tissue, and bone has only a very small blood supply. If the infection is not successfully treated it can smoulder for a long time and become a "chronic osteomyelitis" which might ultimately necessitate amputation of the limb—and all because the original fracture was compound or open.

A "complicated" fracture is one in which the broken ends of the bone have damaged some important organ or tissue in the region. For example, a complicated fracture of the ribs is one in which the lung tissue, close behind the inner surface of the rib, has been pierced, and the patient will be coughing up small amounts of bright red, frothy blood. A "comminuted" fracture is one where the bone is broken into several pieces, and an "impacted" fracture is one in which the broken ends have been driven into each other and are firmly impacted. Finally a "greenstick" fracture occurs sometimes in children because their bones are not brittle and do not always break clean across. They partly break like a green stick.

"Depressed" fracture of the skull is where the vault of the skull has been struck and dinted. Many problems arise, since the brain is inevitably compressed and no dressing of the accompanying wound should be allowed to press on the brain. The dangers of infection here are not only to the broken bone, but to the meninges covering the brain, causing meningitis.

Fractured base of skull often passes through that part of the base through which the internal ear channel runs. Thus it frequently results in blood, or cerebrospinal fluid, or a mixture of both, emerging from the ear. The gravity of this fracture lies in the severity of the impact necessary to produce it, which will probably have also caused great destruction of delicate brain tissue. The outlook is usually very poor.

Remember that most casualties with fractures will require a general anaesthetic on arrival in hospital so that their fracture can be set in plaster or otherwise treated. Avoid giving them things by mouth such as drinks, which will mean a three-hour wait before anaesthetic can be administered.

Burns and Scalds.

The severity of a burn or scald depends largely on its surface area. If a patient dies of a burn, the cause of death is either infection or shock, the latter being due to fluid loss from the surface. Both hazards depend on surface area, since the bigger the surface the more germs are able to enter, and the more fluid can be lost.

It follows that the small burn on the hand or arm is seldom a threat to life, however deep the injury; and we shall therefore confine our attention to the larger burns of the whole surface of the limb or trunk.

Smaller bodies have a relatively larger surface area, and so a burn of the surface of a child's limb or trunk represents an even greater risk from fluid loss than a corresponding burn in the adult. Everyone has seen the fluid form in the blister of an ordinary small burn. It comes from the fluid part or " plasma " of the blood stream and the loss into such a blister may amount to a thimbleful. This will not hurt anyone. But the loss of similar fluid from the surface of a large burn may amount to many pints. The resultant shock will be partly due to this fluid loss from the blood stream resulting in a reduction in blood supply to the brain. Thus shock from burns has common features with shock from haemorrhage, and it is treated similarly, by transfusion. This time it is not a transfusion of blood but of plasma or some plasma substitute. In practice it is not only water that has been lost but a number of important chemicals dissolved in it as well, so that transfusion solutions have to contain sufficient of each individual substance to restore the deficit.

The arrangements for replacing the lost materials are complex and urgent; every bit as urgent as after a haemorrhage and for the same reason. The brain cannot be left too long in need. In general, the First Aid treatment of burns of large surface area is to keep them clean with a dry dressing and get the patient very quickly to hospital. Life-saving treatment by transfusion cannot start until arrival there. The only permissible delay is in the case of burns caused by corrosive chemicals which must be thoroughly washed off before transport, so that they do not continue to burn the patient on the way.

Unconsciousness.

It is not sufficiently appreciated that the dangers of being unconscious can often far outweigh the dangers from the cause of the unconsciousness. For example it is known that as many as half the deaths from head injuries are due to the airway becoming obstructed and not to the injury itself. The most important thing in managing the unconscious patient from any cause is to preserve an airway. Particularly if the patient is lying on his back it is likely to get blocked:

(a) by his own tongue as the lower jaw sags backwards;

(b) by his dentures (so remove them);

(c) by vomit; and

(d) by anything anyone may be tempted to give him by mouth.

Nothing whatever should be given by mouth in any circumstances to the unconscious patient, since he cannot swallow and it will inevitably go into his lungs.

Many of these dangers can be very much reduced by not having him on his back. Place him instead in the semi-prone position: half on his side, half on his front, with the upper leg drawn up to prevent him from rolling about. In this position the head will be inclined downwards. The jaw will tend to sag forwards and the tongue with it, away from the back of the throat. Any vomit will also come forwards. If the tongue does get in the way of the breathing the airway can usually be cleared by bending the head backwards as far as it will go and pushing the whole lower jaw forwards, by pushing from behind the angle of the jaw on both sides.

DRUG ABUSE AND DRUG DEPENDENCE.

This section of earlier editions of *Pears* was simply called " Addiction." This word is still much used, but is gradually being replaced by the terms in the present title, because ideas about the nature of the problem and methods of dealing with it are changing. Addiction is a word that conjures up rather 19th century ideas in the minds of readers: opium dens, inscrutable orientals, Sherlock Holmes injecting himself with cocaine—basically a phenomenon of foreign origin, rather frightening if its implications were not literary rather than factual, and not of great significance in Great Britain.

Drug Abuse.

It is now realised by doctors, research scientists, social workers, and the police—if still not by society as a whole—that the truth is quite different. The *abuse* of drugs in this country is at present of large proportions, increasing rapidly and showing no signs of diminishing. It is responsible each year for thousands of deaths by suicide and by accidental overdosage; for an enormous but virtually unmeasurable amount of private suffering; and for the loss to society, in terms of reduced working efficiency, of millions of man-hours every year. It has nothing to do with opium smoking which was never in any case more than the eccentricity of the few. Opium is virtually unused in medicine these days and the amount of smuggling, always small, is now negligible. The problems today arise chiefly from the misuse of drugs given by doctors for their effects on the central nervous system—the pain-killers, sleeping pills, " stimulants," and " tranquillisers."

Drugs and Medicines.

To the doctor, any substance is a drug that can be introduced into the body from outside, and that is capable of producing some detectable effect. Most such substances have a beneficial use. They are " medicines," and as such are given by doctors in suitable cases. Others, for example, nicotine (in cigarettes), alcohol (in beer, wine, or spirits), and carbon monoxide (in coal gas), are of doubtful benefit and of certain harm and are used by doctors, if at all, only under certain very special and usually experimental conditions.

Medicines may be classified under four main headings. First, there are those like quinine, or penicillin and other so-called antibiotics, that actually cure diseases by eradicating the organism (bacteria or other parasites) that cause disturbance of normal bodily function. Second, drugs such as insulin or the steroids overcome in the unhealthy the lack of some necessary substance a healthy body manufactures for itself: they must usually continue to be given for life. Third are the drugs which relieve the signs of disease—for example, there are many new drugs that lower the blood pressure or increase the output of urine—without being able to put right the disturbed basic situation which is the cause of the trouble. Fourth are drugs to relieve the patient's symptoms—which make him feel better, less breathless, take away his pain, help him to sleep, and so on—although we seldom know why they are able to do this. Indeed, in many cases we suspect that they are acting mainly as a token of help from doctor to patient, and so encouraging his body to fight a more successful battle on its own behalf.

There is no doubt that the genuine advances in beneficial drugs during the last thirty years have been enormous; but the very successes of the penicillins, tetracyclines, antimalarials, hormones, and so on have bred in the public and in the medical profession itself an attitude of uncritical wonder. There have been relatively few drugs in the first and second categories mentioned above: and in the field of mental health, the importance of which is now so rightly emphasised, there are virtually none. Yet drugs which act upon the brain are often received as if they were curative although they may pose fresh problems rather than solve the old. Thus, although there are many drugs which act upon the mind, few do this in any fundamental sense: they relieve pain and anxiety, bring sleep and lessening of stress, and may allow the patient to recuperate himself during the relief they provide. But often this deeper change does not occur—sometimes because the doctor has not clearly seen his part in helping to bring it about—and then the symptomatic relief may come to be sought for its own sake.

Dangers of Long-term Medication with Drugs acting on the Brain.

1. *Toxic effects.* Drugs which act upon the nervous system, like any others, have characteristic toxic or unwanted effects of their own (incidentally, these may become apparent rapidly; even, on rare occasions, after only a single dose). Such effects may have little or nothing to do with the desired effects for which they are being prescribed and taken. For example, it has only come to be realised quite recently that aspirin is liable to cause bleeding, which is occasionally serious, from the lining of the stomach in a large proportion of people who take aspirin regularly; or that phenacetin, another substance very frequently present in analgesics (*i.e.*, pain relievers) that can be bought from chemists without prescription, may lead (after prolonged use) to kidney damage. Some drugs may cause rashes and other allergic reactions in susceptible subjects; and jaundice, fainting, tremors, and motor disorders are known to occur in some patients taking a variety of other drugs.

2. " *Rebound.*" The body works in such a way, over a variety of its activities, that it tends to return to a " neutral " position after it has departed from this for any reason. For example, over-eating tends to be followed by a lessening of appetite, at least for a time; the runner makes up for his air-deficit during the race by breathing more deeply thereafter; and if, at rest, you breathe for a time more rapidly and deeply than you need, this period will be followed by one in which you breathe *less* often than usual until the balance is restored. These illustrations—and there are others—have nothing to do with drugs: but in a similar way, it seems that if a continued pain, or an unpleasant emotional state such as anxiety or depression is changed into its opposite, or removed altogether by the use of a drug, the prior state may return with increased force when the drug is no longer taken. The " rebound " phenomenon, naturally, encourages the patient to take another dose, and so on.

3. *Habit formation.* This alternation of mood-changed-by-drug with the disturbed mood itself leads to the habit of taking the drug. The patient comes to rely upon it and to take it anyway, even before the unpleasant state has returned. At this stage he is said to be " habituated ": he has a psychological need for the drug, and later may become disturbed at the possibility that it will not be available when he needs it. This might not matter so greatly, if it were not that continued use of drugs in this way has physical consequences as well.

4. *Tolerance and habituation.* The body also tends to restore its own balance when drugs are given, too. It " learns " surprisingly quickly how to deal with substances with which it has never before been confronted, so that it eliminates subsequent doses more and more quickly and completely. Thus the effect of each successive dose is smaller and lasts for progressively shorter periods of time. To counter this, the patient tends to increase the dose: and the vicious circle continues. At this point he has become physically dependent upon the drug: and he may suffer physically—sometimes so severely that he dies—if supplies are not continued.

As he increases the dose in this way, so his tolerance of its effects increases, to such an extent that after prolonged use he may be taking doses of a drug that are five or ten times greater than those which will kill somebody not dependent upon them in this way. It sometimes happens that a patient develops a renewed craving at some point after a course of treatment, in which the dose of drug has been reduced without removing the underlying cause of his dependence. He may then obtain and use the dose he habitually took before treatment, not knowing that his body will have lost its tolerance of such doses. That dose is now as high for him as for any other person and so may be lethal. There has been a number of deaths for this reason.

Factors in the Causation of Dependence.

The risk of becoming dependent upon a drug is governed by three main factors: the drug itself, the personality of the individual who takes it, and the circumstances in which it is taken. Most adults have taken alcohol at one time or another, unless it is against their code to do so; yet *relatively* few are dependent upon it (relatively few, but many too many: more than half a million in the United Kingdom alone). Many of us have had morphine or some other strong analgesic for medical reasons, without becoming dependent upon it (whatever so-called addicts say, it is extremely rare for anyone to become dependent on an opiate because he was introduced to it in a medical setting). On the other hand, if we start to take such a drug " for kicks "—as more and more people, particularly teen-agers and young adults are doing—it is extremely probable that we shall become dependent upon it, and sooner rather than later at that. It is also probable that each one of us would become dependent, were he obliged to take it regularly, for long enough, and in sufficient dosage. Thus, although there are personalities—psychopathic, immature, or unstable—that are more prone than others to become dependent if they are exposed to the drug, there are also drugs that are more likely than others to cause such dependence no matter to whom they are given. The extent of the dependence will vary: with some, it is never physiological but remains psychological (but not the less real or disturbing for that). Also, the rate at which dependence develops may vary; and the picture presented by the dependent subject—the extent to which his normal life is impaired, or to which he becomes dangerous to himself or others—varies as well. In a very much oversimplified way, some of these relationships will now be summarised for certain substances.

Heroin, morphine and cocaine are usually injected. Barbiturates (sleeping pills) and amphetamines (" Benzedrine ") are tablets or capsules, and marihuana (" reefers," hashish) is smoked in cigarettes. Heroin and cocaine are now usually taken together. Combinations of drugs often act differently from their individual constituents and patients dependent upon them are even more difficult to treat. Barbiturate and amphetamine, also, are often mixed (as in " purple hearts "). There is considerable *psychological* dependence on heroin, morphine, cocaine, and amphetamine, but much less with marihuana. *Physiological* dependence is great with heroin and morphine, less with barbiturates, alcohol, and amphetamine in that order, and virtually nil with cocaine and marihuana. Personality plays a greater part in initiating dependence on alcohol, marihuana, and barbiturates than with the others. Heroin, cocaine, and morphine are the cause of more antisocial tendencies in dependent people than alcohol, barbiturates, and amphetamine. The chief danger of marihuana (mere possession of which is illegal) seems to be that the search for it will lead the searcher into localities where his risk of exposure to even more dangerous influences is greatly increased. It is thus sometimes argued that if it were legal to consume marihuana, the number of young people who yearly become dependent upon the other more dangerous drugs would in fact decrease. There is as yet no evidence for or against this proposition. The number of drug dependent people in U.K. is rising fast for heroin and cocaine. This number is very large for alcohol, and is increasing in the case of barbiturates and marihuana. Very few people are dependent on morphine, and the number is not growing.

Treatment.

Exhortations, imprisonment, and other moralistic or legalistic approaches are useless. Treatment of any person dependent upon a drug is a matter for a qualified psychotherapist. It is liable to be time-consuming and frustrating for patient and doctor, and it is frequently unsuccessful. At present, there are too few specialists or centres where treatment can be obtained, although it is to be hoped that this situation will change as the problem is increasingly seen by our society to be of exceptional gravity.

When there is little or no chance of cure, prevention is certainly the best treatment. Drugs should only be taken on the prescription of a doctor: and the patient should remind him from time to time, if this be necessary, that he would like to dispense with his drugs as soon as the doctor thinks it possible. It should also be remembered that there is often no need to reach for the aspirin (or any other drug that anyone can buy from the chemist without prescription) at the first sign of a headache—or to reach for it at all to help one sleep or relax, for which purpose such drugs are in any case pharmacologically useless. A wait for ten minutes is good discipline, and will frequently resolve the problem to an extent that makes a drug unnecessary.

DISEASES OF THE BLOOD.
INTRODUCTION.

There are about five litres of blood in the adult human body. Its main function is to transport nutrient materials to all the various tissues and to carry waste products of tissue activity to organs such as the lungs, kidneys, and liver for disposal. It also helps to maintain a constant chemical environment for the body cells, some of which would be very disturbed in their function if the correct balance of organic and inorganic chemicals were not maintained. The blood also serves a protective function in fighting disease, either with certain of the white cells, or by means of immune antibodies dissolved and carried in the plasma.

A little more than half the volume of blood is the fluid plasma, in which are dissolved all the nutrient materials, organic and inorganic chemicals, hormones and large quantities of protein. The remainder consists of red cells, white cells, and some particles which are not really cells, called platelets. In every cubic millimetre of whole blood, or in every droplet the size of a pin head, there are about 5 million red cells, between 5,000 and 10,000 white cells, and 200,000 platelets as well as half a cubic millilitre of plasma. The red cells suffer a great deal of wear and tear as they are hurled round the circulation, and they only survive for three or four months. There is a red cell factory in the bone marrow which replaces them at exactly the rate they are destroyed, and you have made very many millions of new ones while you have been reading this single paragraph. The function of the red cells is to carry the oxygen from the lungs to the tissues, and to play an important part in carrying the waste gas, carbon dioxide, in the reverse direction. A shortage of red cells, and hence of their oxygen-carrying pigment, haemoglobin, is called anaemia; an excess is called polycythaemia.

There are five kinds of white cells or leucocytes: neutrophils (or polymorphonuclear leucocytes), oesinophils, basophils, lymphocytes, and mono-

cytes. The first three are quite actively motile, like amoebæ, and are capable of ingesting bacteria and other particles by "phagocytosis." There is a great increase in the number of neutrophils (a leucocytosis) during bacterial infections and other inflammatory conditions like appendicitis. Eosinophils are found in larger numbers than usual in allergic conditions like asthma, and in infestations by worms and other parasites, but we do not know why this should be. Lymphocytes are concerned with the manufacture of antibodies. In some infections, particularly tuberculosis and viral infections, there are fewer white cells than usual (leucopenia). Pus consists of the dissolved remnants of inflamed tissue and many dead neutrophils which have become casualties in the battle against infection. It also contains surviving bacteria, and as such is a source of further infection.

Platelets are curious particles, smaller than any of the cells. They are little pieces broken off certain special bone-marrow cells which produce them. They have a role in the stemming of blood loss after injury, partly because they are sticky and adhere to one another and to broken blood vessels and help to plug the open ends of damaged vessels; and partly because they contain a great deal of a substance (thrombokinase) which is necessary to the clotting mechanism of the blood.

Hæmatology, as the study of blood and its diseases is called, is a very complicated subject and only a brief general account will be given here. Diagnosis is usually made by taking small samples of blood (or of the bone marrow where blood cells are made), counting the numbers of the different cells and examining their appearance under the microscope. We shall briefly consider the main diseases involving red cells, white cells, and platelets.

Red Cell Diseases.

These are of two main groups leading to a shortage of red cells (anaemia), or an excess (polycythaemia). The former is much the more common and there are many different kinds. In all of them the shortage of red cells results in a depletion of the capacity of the blood to carry oxygen. This means that the heart must work harder to send more blood than usual to the tissues, and even so the tissues will often go short. The patient will be persistently tired and listless, and if the anaemia is severe the action of the brain and heart will be seriously impeded, even leading to fainting, cardiac pain, and breathlessness on exertion. All these symptoms, however, can be caused by many other conditions. The only way to be sure they are due to anaemia is by a proper examination of the blood, and even this will not lead to the truth if the picture has been spoilt by the patient taking iron tonics and other remedies of his own accord. Therefore do not dose yourself with tonics, in case you really have anaemia. You may make it impossible to arrive at a proper diagnosis later.

Hæmorrhagic Anæmia. Anæmia, a shortage of red cells, may be due to a variety of causes, singly or in combination. One very obvious cause is loss of blood, or hæmorrhage. Following the sudden loss of a half-litre of blood or more, the red-cell-producing bone marrow "factory" will step up its production; but even if it is adequately supplied with all the raw materials such as iron, it may well take many weeks to build up the numbers to normal. A very severe degree of hæmorrhagic anæmia is usually treated by blood transfusion. Milder degrees can be treated by taking extra iron, often over a long period of time. The supply of iron for making new red-cell pigment is nearly always the bottle-neck which limits production. Hæmorrhagic anæmia can commonly occur, however, without a sudden severe hæmorrhage. From what has been said about the constant replacement of red cells as they wear out, it must be obvious that even if there is only a slight failure to keep pace with the numbers lost, several months of such a failure can eventually deplete the numbers to the level of very severe anæmia. This situation is common when small amounts of blood are being continuously or repeatedly lost, and here again it is a shortage of dietary iron which is the usual cause of the failure to replace the lost red cells. Normal menstrual loss in women and girls whose diet is on the border-line of iron deficiency is a common cause of progressive tiredness and lack of energy. Where the menstrual flow is heavier than usual, or where it is frankly excessive in older women due to the various common gynæcological disorders, serious anæmia is surprisingly common. During pregnancy a great deal of iron is lost by the mother to the baby, and this, together with the inevitable blood loss at delivery, often makes for a very tired mother indeed, just at the time when there is an enormous amount of work to be done to manufacture milk and attend to all the extra household tasks of baby care. For these reasons it is almost routinely advisable to build up stocks of iron throughout the pregnancy by remembering to take the pills provided. Men as well as women can lose small amounts of blood continuously in later life from gastro-intestinal conditions such as piles, ulcers, and tropical infestations such as hookworm; and here again the anæmia may be just as severe in the long run as that which inevitably follows a sudden, massive hæmorrhage. One extra word of warning. Do not assume because you are pale that you are anæmic. Pallor is a very poor guide, because it is dependent on so many other things, like the blood vessels in your skin, and its thickness and translucency. Nothing but a blood test (which is so easy for your doctor to do) can really tell you if you are anæmic. And if your anæmia is due to a blood-losing condition, then that too must be treated. So do not be tempted to treat yourself, and never delay seeing your doctor about any excessive or unexplained bleeding, from any source.

Hæmolytic Anæmia occurs when for any reason, there are more blood cells than usual being destroyed in the body. This may be because the cells are abnormally fragile, or because normal cells have been attacked by something to which you are allergic, or rarely because you have become sensitive to your own red cells. Sometimes unborn babies have severe hæmolytic anæmia, due to an incompatability of blood group (Rh factor) between the mother and the baby, and the same sort of thing happens if incompatible blood is given by mistake in blood transfusion. Up to a point, in mild hæmolytic anæmia, the bone marrow can keep pace with the increased loss of cells, but beyond this point anæmia develops. After incompatible blood transfusions a very dangerous situation results from the effects of the destruction of red cells and the liberation of their products into the blood. One form of jaundice is often produced in hæmolytic anæmia, the patient becoming yellow because of the breakdown products of red cells circulating in excess as bile pigments. These latter are normally always present to a small extent due to the normal, comparatively small, rate of destruction of effete red cells

Aplastic Anæmia is the term given to anæmia due to a virtually total failure of the bone marrow red-cell factory. Sometimes this occurs for no obvious reason. It is sometimes due to a heavy dose of radioactivity or X-rays knocking out the cells of the "factory." It may even be due to cancer cells growing in the bone marrow cavity and not leaving sufficient room for the red marrow cells. It is fortunate that aplastic anæmia is very rare, because it can only be treated by blood transfusions every few weeks for the rest of the patient's life. Very occasionally there have been exceptions to this rule, when the patient's marrow has re-awakened for no apparent reason and suddenly begins to make red cells again.

Pernicious Anæmia. This is a fairly uncommon anæmia, which has a very interesting story. The processes by which red cells are manufactured are many and complex, and depend, like so many other bodily activities, on the supply of a vitamin containing cobalt, called vitamin B_{12}. This is nearly always present in more than adequate quantities in the diet, but in order for it to be absorbed from the intestine, there must also be a substance called "intrinsic factor" which is normally made by the lining of the stomach. People with pernicious anæmia have suffered a degeneration of the lining of their stomachs, probably because, for some reason, they have become "sensitive" to this part of their own tissue. This kind of civil war within the body is known as an "auto-immune" disease, and is comparable in type with some forms of hæmolytic anæmia. In other words they destroy their own stomach lining, fail to produce "intrinsic factor," and as a result fail to absorb vitamin B_{12} into the body. Faced with a failure in the supply of this essential substance, the bone marrow produces too few red cells, and the few that are produced are deformed, much too large, and very fragile. In addition to its role in blood formation, vitamin B_{12} is essential to the normal functioning of the spinal cord, and in long-standing cases of untreated pernicious anæmia, there is often a resulting neurological disability.

The cure for pernicious anæmia was discovered about forty years ago, and is a triumph for the scientific investigation of the causes of disease. While treating anæmic dogs, an American scientist named Minot discovered that eating raw liver in large quantities produced a tremendous improvement. Patients with pernicious anæmia were then made to eat vast quantities of raw liver—about one or two pounds a day—and were found to get better, whereas previously they had inevitably died. Raw liver is, of course, very unpleasant to eat, and after a few years it was found possible to prepare crude extracts for injection. Injection had the great advantage that no absorption difficulties arose, and much less liver could be used. Biochemists then began the enormous task of trying to find which of the thousands of substances in liver was the vital factor, and after many years of painstaking chemical fractionation of liver and trying out the various fractions as a cure for the disease, vitamin B_{12} was discovered. The pure substance is one of the most powerful substances known, being active in amounts as small as millionths of a gram. Nowadays pernicious anæmia is treated by small occasional injections of the vitamin, whose other name is cyanocobalamin.

Polycythæmia. Too many red cells per cubic millilitre of blood can be found without there being an increase of the total number of red cells in the body. This occurs in dehydration, when there is a loss of plasma without a comparable loss of cells, and is called hæmo-concentration. Alternatively, the bone marrow can manufacture more cells than usual as a response to living for long periods at high altitudes. The beneficial result can be that the blood can carry normal amounts of oxygen, even though the supply (in the rarefied air) is reduced. Finally there is a red cell disease, analogous to leukæmia (q.v.) in which the bone marrow factory gets out of control and produces too many cells with no beneficial results. The number in the blood can be double the normal and the blood becomes so thick that the heart has difficulty pumping it round the body. This disease (*polycythæmia rubra vera*) used to be treated by repeatedly bleeding the patient to reduce the numbers. It is now treated very successfully with carefully judged amounts of radioactive phosphorus or certain other "antimitotic" chemicals which reduce the rate of multiplication of bone marrow cells. Care has to be taken not to knock them out altogether, in which case aplastic anæmia or agranulocytosis (q.v.) could result.

White Cell Diseases.

These are fortunately much rarer than diseases involving red cells, and are usually much more to be feared.

Agranulocytosis. In this condition the number of those white cells which are responsible for phagocytosis of bacteria falls precipitously. The result is that one of the main bodily defences against infection fails, and the patient may die from an overwhelming invasion of germs and the accompanying high fever. The usual cause is abnormal sensitivity to certain drugs, often those which are in widespread use and only give trouble in the occasional case. One example among hundreds is the antibiotic chloramphenicol which specifically kills typhoid bacteria and is used for that purpose. It is believed that about one case in 60,000 becomes sensitive to it and agranulocytosis often fatally follows. The fact that almost any drug *can* do this to some people and yet be quite safe for the majority, is one good reason not to dose yourself unnecessarily with over-the-counter medicines.

Leukæmia. This is a cancer of the white cells, in which the normal rate of production of any of the white cells gets out of control, leading to a pile-up of abnormal cells at the site of production (bone marrow, lymph nodes, and spleen) or in the blood, or both. In spite of an increase in their numbers, their abnormality renders them unable to combat infection; sepsis and fever result. It is known that this kind of cancer can be caused by the effects of ionizing radiation on the white-cell factory, and it is certain at least in animals, that viruses can also be responsible. Survivors from the atomic explosions in Japan have subsequently suffered from leukæmia far more commonly than the rest of us, as have doctors, nurses, and patients who have been over-exposed to X-rays. At the time of writing, leukæmia is still a uniformly fatal disease, although patients may sometimes survive many years. Their remaining time can nearly always be made more comfortable by various forms of treatment, and one day a cure will be found by the research workers devoting their time to its study. It is difficult not to get very impatient with the slow rate of progress of these studies, particularly when caring for children and young people whose lives are inevitably ended by the disease. The solution, however, as with other forms of cancer, probably depends on the understanding of the nature of life itself, and as long as biological research remains short of the relatively small amounts of money required to tackle these problems at reasonable speed, we have no right to be impatient, except with our elected leaders who spend far more than is needed on less important things.

Hodgkin's Disease, Lymphosarcoma, and Reticulosarcoma. These are cancerous diseases in many ways similar to leukæmia, in which the cancer process involves cells of the so-called reticulo-endothelial system. Such cells are principally in lymph nodes (which used to be called lymph glands) and the spleen. Hodgkin's disease is named after one of the more illustrious pathologists at Guy's Hospital who first described it nearly a hundred years ago, and whose early specimens of affected lymph nodes are still preserved there; is an even greater puzzle than leukæmia. There are all grades of severity, and although many patients die within six months, many survive much longer, even for twenty years in some cases.

Hæmorrhagic or Bleeding Diseases.

Whenever blood vessels are damaged by injury, there is a remarkable series of mechanisms which automatically come into operation to stem the flow of blood. There is a constriction of all the smaller vessels in the locality. Platelets stick together and release substances which help the vessels to stay constricted as well as others necessary to blood clotting, and yet others which help to bind the clot tightly together. Later, materials appear to prevent too much clotting, and eventually the clot is removed altogether as healing proceeds. There are some very complicated diseases of this blood-conserving mechanism which can lead to abnormal bleeding, sometimes beneath the skin to produce bruising or even smaller leaks; sometimes leading to a greater loss of blood, par-

ticularly following a wound. In some kinds of *purpura* (bleeding tendency) the blood vessels are the cause of the trouble, having become fragile and leaky for a number of reasons. This happens in old age (*senile purpura*), in scurvy, or vitamin C deficiency, as an occasional accompaniment to infective diseases, or as an immunological effect on the lining of blood vessels when the patient becomes sensitised to certain substances (*Schönlein-Henoch* or *anaphylactoid purpura*). The latter often follows a streptococcal sore throat, just as rheumatic fever and acute nephritis do; and as well as the purpura there may be joint pains and nephritis. Just as almost any drug or chemical will cause agranulocytosis in some people, so it can also cause anaphylactoid purpura.

Purpura may also be due to a lack of platelets, known as thrombocytopenia (a shortage of thrombocytes or platelets). This can happen if the bone marrow factory is depressed, since this is where platelets too are made. It is therefore a common accompaniment of leukæmia or aplastic anæmia. Or there can be increased destruction of platelets in some diseases of the spleen. Platelets normally last eight to ten days, but their life-span can be shortened in heart failure, and following massive transfusions, or often for no apparent reason ("idiopathic" thrombocytopenia), when removal of the spleen can sometimes help.

Finally, defects of the *clotting mechanism* will lead to a bleeding tendency, and since the mechanism itself is very complex, so is the variety of things which can upset it. The liver provides the blood with many of the substances required for clotting, so it is not surprising that a clotting defect commonly accompanies liver disease. One necessary substance for blood clotting is called "anti-hæmophilic factor" and is missing from people who have inherited the disease *hæmophilia*. These unfortunate people may die of hæmorrhage from quite small cuts or minor surgical procedures like tooth-extraction, and although it is possible to prepare antihæmophilic factor, it is not yet possible to give continuous, life-long treatment with it. A new drug, aminocaproic acid, which prevents natural clots from dissolving, is now used to enable dental treatment, with the saving of much fresh blood transfusion which was formerly necessary.

DISEASES OF THE HEART AND BLOOD-VESSELS.

INTRODUCTION.

The heart consists of about 350g of muscle which makes up the walls of its four chambers. Anatomically the human heart closely resembles the sheep's hearts to be found in a butcher's shop. Indeed it would be an instructive exercise to dissect one of these in the order described below, since there is no other way of properly appreciating what the chambers, valves, etc., are really like. There are two quite separate pumps in the heart— one on the owner's right (or on your *left* if you are looking at the front of someone else), and one on his left. The right heart collects spent, deoxygenated, " venous " blood which returns there from the whole of the body, and gives it the comparatively small push required to drive it through the adjacent lungs. The left heart collects the revitalised, oxygenated "arterial" blood as it trickles away from the lungs, and gives it the enormous push required to build up the arterial blood-pressure, so that it can be forced through all the tissues of the body. As may be expected, the right heart chambers have much thinner walls than the left, since their muscle has much less work to do. This will help you get your bearings with the sheep's heart. The tip, or apex, is the lowest part. The thick-feeling side is the left, the thin right; and the great vessels are at the top.

The upper chamber on the right, or right atrium, has two large openings into it through which all the spent blood arrives from the upper and lower great veins (the superior and inferior venae cavae).

Cut open the thin wall of the right atrium with scissors between these two holes to lay open the interior of the chamber, noting the "auricle" or "dog's ear" that forms a small cul-de-sac. The whole chamber is sometimes, inaccurately, called the auricle. You should be able to push a finger downwards into the lower chamber—the right ventricle—through a communicating hole guarded by the three thin cusps of the *tricuspid valve*. These will not obstruct your finger, since they are designed to permit blood flow in the same direction. When the atrium is full of blood, it squeezes its contents through the tricuspid valve into the right ventricle; and when, a split second later, the ventricle is full and contracts, the three cusps come together to prevent the blood from flowing backwards into the atrium again. Instead the spent blood is driven onwards through the *pulmonary valve* (in the upper part of the right ventricle), through the pulmonary artery, to be delivered to the lungs. The pulmonary valve has three very well-defined cusps which prevent blood from coming back into the ventricle as it relaxes to receive more blood from the atrium before the next contraction or beat. It is possible to pass a blade of the scissors from the opened-out right atrium, through the tricuspid valve towards the tip of the heart, and cut along the right border of the heart through the thickness of the ventricular muscle. Then cut upwards again, passing the scissors blade through the pulmonary valve and open up the *pulmonary artery*. If you have done this successfully you will have followed the path taken by the spent blood through the right heart to the lungs. Notice the thick round bands of muscle lining the ventricle, and notice too that you have not entered the left heart, which has no connection with the right except in some congenital malformations (see later). The same dissection can now be made of the left heart. Open up the *left atrium*, noting its "dog's ear" or "auricle," pass the scissors down into the *left ventricle* through the two rather flimsy cusps of the *mitral valve*. Notice how much thicker is the muscle of the left ventricle, and cut upwards through the three well-formed cusps of the *aortic valve* into the main artery of the body—the *aorta*. The aorta as it leaves the left heart is distinguishable from the pulmonary artery as it leaves the right, partly by the extreme toughness of the aortic wall (it has to withstand so much more blood-pressure); and partly by the entrances or orifices of the two small branches given off by the aorta, just beyond the valve cusps, which go to supply the heart muscle itself with blood. These are the *coronary arteries* which are so necessary for the heart's own survival.

The amount of blood pumped in unit time, or the *cardiac output*, can be varied a great deal, according to the needs of the moment. This is accomplished by altering both the heart rate and the stroke volume, the amount expelled per beat. Every minute, the healthy adult man at rest shifts about 5 litres of blood through the heart—an amount equivalent to all the blood he possesses. When exercise is taken, or in response to anxiety or fear, this is stepped up many times, so that the muscles can receive a greatly augmented supply of the materials required for action. The controlling mechanisms which allow these changes to be made automatically are partly organised in the brain by the so-called *cardiac centre*; and partly by local mechanical and chemical stimuli to the heart muscle itself. The cardiac centre is continuously receiving information through nerves about the physical and chemical state of the circulation, and also from the mind; which is partly how certain emotions make the heart beat faster. All the information is integrated, and a cardiac output continuously arranged which is appropriate for current demands.

Cardiac Neurosis. In ordinary circumstances at rest, most healthy people are not conscious of their heart-beat. However, there are many perfectly healthy people whose hearts slip in an extra beat occasionally. Sometimes their owners are aware of this, and become unnecessarily alarmed. Their fear causes palpitations (a pounding of the heart) and the tension mounts. An undue anxiety about the tricks played by a healthy heart sometimes leads people to interpret minor pains in the chest, or even indigestion, as grave symptoms of heart disease, and the consequent anxiety leads to still worse symptoms. If you are one of these worried people, take your worries to your doctor, and let him decide for you whether there is anything wrong. A hundred to one there isn't, and then you will have to find something else to worry about, or better still give up the habit altogether. Many people secretly worry about heart disease and high blood-pressure for years, when very often they are worrying unnecessarily. Even if there is cause for worry, so much can be done for these conditions (as it can for cancer) provided medical advice is taken early in the course of the disease. Remember, too, that the slight feeling of giddiness when you get up suddenly from having been lying down, is often experienced by most normal people; but if you get frightened by it you will begin to breathe more quickly and deeply: and this in itself will make you feel even more faint—and so on.

Heart Failure. When the cardiac output of blood is too little for the requirements of the body, a state of *circulatory failure* has arisen, and when this is due primarily to the heart itself being at fault, it is more properly called *heart failure*. As will be seen, heart failure is not a disease, but the common result of a large number of different diseases. The signs and symptoms produced are caused by two sorts of process: (a) tissues of the body have too little blood flow through them and are therefore undersupplied; (b) blood accumulates and stagnates in tissues, causing congestion, since the failing heart cannot move forward the amount of blood presented to it in the great veins. Often the left or right side of the heart fails disproportionately. In *left heart failure* the lungs are congested because they are the territory from which the left heart is failing to move blood. The patient has great difficulty with his breathing, and in advanced cases may not be able to breathe when he lies down, because the lungs become so congested and waterlogged. In *right heart failure* the main veins are congested and other parts of the body become swollen with excess tissue fluid, mainly in the lower parts such as the legs and ankles. This swelling with fluid is called œdema, and in heart failure is only partly due to the mechanics of the failing heart. It is mainly due to a poorly understood retention of sodium in the body, a situation in which excess water is also retained. Whatever the type of heart failure it is always likely to be a changing condition, since the amount of failure will depend as much on the demands being made as on the state of the heart. For instance, in mild cases at rest when the required cardiac output is small, there may be no signs or symptoms. These may only appear on exertion. Heart failure will be referred to again later under the various conditions which cause it.

Treatment of heart failure is quite logical. It is aimed at correcting the imbalance between supply and demand of blood, and at the removal of the accumulated excess fluid. We can therefore (a) reduce the body's demand for blood; (b) increase the supply or cardiac output; and (c) promote the excretion of sodium and fluid. Demand for blood is reduced by rest, both physical and mental, and by reduction of weight, since obesity (being overweight) is an additional demand on the cardiovascular system. The cardiac output can be increased by administering a "tonic" to the heart muscle in the form of *digitalis*, which is a powerful heart stimulant derived from foxglove leaf. Fluid (and hence salt) accumulation can be helped by restricting the intake of salt and by giving drugs which promote its excretion by the kidneys (diuretics). Very occasionally, very large accumulations of fluid in the legs, abdomen, or thorax, are tapped and drained physically, with needles. These remarks on treatment, as elsewhere in the Medical Section, are of course very general and must not encourage anyone to treat himself for such a potentially serious condition as heart failure. Even such a simple measure as doing without salt can be practised quite unnecessarily by many people for years, simply as a result of reading a paragraph like the above. The most they accomplish is to make their food taste horribly dull. If you need to reduce salt intake you should be in your doctor's care, and so please let him decide.

Congenital Heart Disease. It has been estimated that of all the babies born who survive at least one month, there will be about one in every two hundred with some form of congenital heart disease; that is to say that the heart will have failed to develop properly in embryonic life. In some cases this is associated with a virus disease of the mother (commonly rubella, or German measles) or with certain drugs taken by the mother (e.g. thalidomide) at a time, very early in pregnancy, when organs are assuming their adult shape. Parents should see to it that their daughters get German measles before they grow up; and drugs of all kinds should be avoided where possible during early pregnancy. In most cases of congenital heart disease, however, there is no known cause, and it seems that the manner of formation of the embryonic heart is so delicate that it can be thrown out of gear very easily, perhaps even by chance. Scores of different types of defect occur, singly and in combination. Any of the valves may be anatomically defective—either failing to close properly (*incompetence*) or being too tight (*stenosis*); the great vessels (pulmonary artery and aorta) may be switched round, or *transposed*, so that they emerge from the wrong ventricle; there may be defects in the wall (*septum*) which separates the atria or the ventricles on each side (*septal defect*, or " hole in the heart "); or there may be a persistence of the vessel which in the fœtus normally by-passes the lungs by joining the pulmonary artery to the aorta (*patent ductus arteriosus*). This vessel normally closes at the time of birth when the first breaths are taken, and subsequently disappears, so that the whole output of the heart is then sent round the lungs. Detecting congenital heart disease is one of the purposes of routine post-natal check-up examinations of the baby. Exact diagnosis requires very complicated techniques, and sometimes the structural defect can be corrected by surgery, with almost miraculous results.

Rheumatic Heart Disease. Acute rheumatic fever is not to be confused with other forms of rheumatism. Many tissues of the body (particularly the heart) are attacked, as well as the joints, and the trouble is due to a sensitivity which has developed to certain bacteria (*hæmolytic streptococci*) which have probably caused a sore throat about three weeks before the onset of the disease. Why acute rheumatism only rarely follows streptococcal sore throat is poorly understood, but this is no consolation to the one per cent or so of the population whose hearts bear its scars. During the acute phase of the illness which usually occurs before the age of fifteen, inflammatory damage occurs to the valves, the heart muscle, and the sac in which the heart lives, the *pericardium*. So there is a *valvulitis* or *endocarditis*, a *myocarditis* and a *pericarditis*. There may be acute heart failure at this stage if the heart is severely affected. The better-known results of rheumatic heart disease, however, are caused in the ensuing years by scarring of the healed valves. The valves are thickened and deformed They may have lost their elasticity and stretch, so that they do not close properly (*incompetence*); or they may contract and tighten (*stenosis*). In both cases the heart chamber situated next to the affected valve has to work progressively harder, either because it gets no rest in between beats (in *incompetence*); or it has to force the blood through too narrow a hole (in *stenosis*). The end result is some variety of heart failure (P27). Although there are other causes of valvular heart disease which will now be mentioned, rheumatic fever is much the commonest, and much valve trouble can be blamed on rheumatic fever even when the patient has no recollection of ever having suffered from it. The other, much rarer, causes may be syphilis, congenital valvular anomaly, healed bacterial endocarditis, atherosclerosis, and mechanical injury.

The most commonly affected valve is the mitral, usually causing *mitral stenosis*, in which the opening between the left atrium and left ventricle will sometimes only admit one finger-tip instead of three fingers as it should. In time the left atrium becomes much enlarged as it overworks to force blood through this narrow orifice. Later still a back pressure develops in the lungs causing congestion and breathlessness; and even later the right ventricle is strained as it tries to force blood into the already congested lung. This is a classic example of the march of trouble backwards from the site of the damaged valve involving first the chamber " behind " it (the left atrium), then the territory " behind " that (the lungs), then the pulmonary arteries taking blood to the lungs, and finally the right ventricle trying to send blood to the pulmonary artery. This steady march of events is usually very slow, and can commonly take twenty years or longer from the initial attack of acute rheumatism to the severer symptoms of advanced mitral stenosis. Treatment is both medical and surgical. The heart failure is treated medically as already described. These days surgical reopening of the valve is almost commonplace, either by inserting a finger through the left auricle and breaking down the constriction, or by opening up the heart and re-shaping the valve under direct vision. The latter involves the additional problem of by-passing the heart by the use of some sort of external pump and poses additional problems, even though from other points of view it is obviously more convenient. As always with major surgical procedures much of the problem is in selecting the patients who will benefit from the operation and in whom it is feasible. Quite often there are other valves involved, mainly the aortic or tricuspid or both, and the hydrostatic or " plumbing " problems can be extremely complex. With luck, however, combined with good judgement and good surgery, the lives of incapacitated patients can be transformed by mitral, and other valvular, surgery. Recently a great deal of progress has been made in designing new " ball-in-basket " valves of man-made materials to replace damaged natural valves. The *aortic valve* is stenosed or narrowed by other degenerative processes besides rheumatism. *Tricuspid stenosis* is nearly always rheumatic in origin.

Coronary Heart Disease. This is the term used whenever the blood supply to the heart muscle (through the coronary arteries) is reduced to such an extent that the heart muscle suffers from a lack of supplies. It has a number of causes, but the only really common one is partial obstruction of the coronary arteries by a condition known as *atheroma* or *atherosclerosis*, and sometimes inaccurately called *arteriosclerosis*. This arterial disease is described later (P30). It takes the form of swellings or lumps on the lining of the artery which, if they become large enough to interfere seriously with the flow of blood, produce a blood starvation or *ischaemia* of the tissue being supplied. Obviously, the smaller the artery, the more easily will a lump of given size impede the flow. Equally obviously the greater the demand for blood, as in exercise, the more blood " starvation " there will be. There are two degrees of coronary artery disease: one in which the blood flow is reduced to the point where the increased demands of hard work cannot be met, and this results in *angina pectoris* due to *coronary insufficiency*; the other is when the coronary artery becomes completely blocked, preventing the flow of blood altogether, usually by a *thrombus* or clot of blood, and this is *coronary thrombosis*.

Angina Pectoris. Whenever activity is increased in any muscle, the demands for oxygen and nutriments from the blood-stream increase, and as these are used up there is an increased production of waste products known as metabolites. To meet these demands for a greater supply and a more efficient waste-disposal, the blood flow through the exercising muscle must always be increased. If sufficient increase does not occur, not only will there be a shortage of supplies, but there will also be a pile-up of metabolites in the muscle which cannot be carried away. It is mainly because of these latter that pain is caused in ischæmic, or blood-starved muscle, and pain is one of the chief symptoms when heart muscle becomes ischæmic. One important mechanism for increasing blood flow normally to exercising muscle is by automatically dilating the vessels concerned. Diseased vessels, such as coronary arteries when they are affected by atheroma, are not so easily dilated, although certain drugs which are powerful dilators of arterioles can accomplish a great deal, albeit temporarily. The measures taken to relieve the pain and blood-starvation of angina are two-fold. The patient can reduce the demands of the heart by a few minutes' rest, and a drug (usually nitroglycerin) can be taken to dilate the coronary vessels of supply. Another obvious long-term way to reduce demands is for the overweight patient to eat less, and reduce the load of extra body weight on his circulation. It is very frustrating, to say the least, that such an incapacitating and often lethal condition should be caused by the narrowing or blockage of only 5 or 8 cm of narrow piping about 3·5 mm wide. It is now possible to treat some forms of coronary artery disease by surgical means.

Heart Attack or *Coronary Thrombosis.* It should readily be understood from the above description that heart attacks will vary in their severity according to the amount of heart muscle deprived of blood; and this in turn will depend on where in the coronary artery the obstruction occurs. Most usually it is the left ventricular muscle which is cut off from supplies and dies, either in part or in all of its thickness. Since it is the left ventricle which does most of the work of pumping blood to the body, serious heart failure (P27) is to be expected. If too much muscle is killed, the heart will simply stop, and the patient will suddenly die. It is much more usual, however, for enough muscle to be left for survival, albeit with a greatly reduced cardiac efficiency. A heart attack is usually accompanied by severe pain, similar to the pain of angina but more severe, and unrelieved by rest or by the patient's usual drugs. Very occasionally the event occurs apparently without pain, or with so little that it is ignored. These so-called " silent " coronary attacks can make diagnosis extremely difficult. Since the doctor depends very considerably with heart attacks on an exact, spontaneous description of symptoms for his diagnosis, no description will be given here. There are many over-anxious people who will read these words and could be misled into an unspontaneous description of their own symptoms, and this could make the task of treating them such a problem that they could even be mis-diagnosed as a result. If you have the smallest worry that your chest pain is due to your heart, take your anxiety to your doctor without delay. He will almost certainly be able to re-assure you; and if it happens to be your heart after all, you will have taken the first sensible step towards proper treatment. Dangerous as heart attacks are, they are by no means the death warrant that many lay people think, any more than cancer is. The treatment for a true heart attack is urgent and prolonged. Patients must be at complete rest and their pain relieved quickly. The area of heart muscle they have lost must be allowed to heal with a good, firm scar, and this can take three months of rest often in hospital.

You can help to avoid a heart attack by not smoking, avoiding obesity and living a physically active life. Avoid sudden exercise, however, when you are not in training. Surgeons are getting better at replacing diseased coronary arteries with pieces of vein from elsewhere.

Blood-pressure. The blood is normally under great pressure in the arterial system, since it is this which forces it into all the tissues of the body. It is therefore no more meaningful to say you have " blood-pressure " than to say you have a temperature. You would be very badly off without. Blood-pressure which is too high, however, can give rise to problems though not always. It is another of those conditions like angina and cancer, which engender much anxiety among people even when they do not suffer from them. For this reason doctors are often unwilling to disclose a patient's blood-pressure and because of

this they unjustifiably earn a reputation for unreasonable secrecy. They are themselves to blame for the general public anxiety as the following true story shows. Twenty years ago a lady in her fifties wished to accompany her husband to a post abroad which was to last four years. All arrangements had been made—the husband resigned his previous job, sold the house, etc.—when it was discovered at a routine medical examination that she had a high blood-pressure, and she was very solemnly advised by the rather elderly doctor not to go. There was great consternation and emotional upheaval, not least because of the inconvenience involved. Eventually she was allowed to go at her own risk. The husband's job lasted eight years instead of four, during which the lady was in no way inconvenienced by her blood-pressure; except that she worried interminably about it. On returning home to retire she began to think she had angina, and elaborate hospital investigation revealed that, as might be expected, her arteries were not as young as they used to be. She was undoubtedly suffering from mild angina, but not as badly as she thought. The opportunity then arose, in her late sixties, to go abroad yet again, and this she did, living a quite strenuous life, and one which she enjoyed. At the time of writing she has returned home, and, twenty years later, at the age of seventy-three is running a home very actively, still with very little inconvenience from her blood-pressure. There is no doubt that it has been very high all this time, and it is also certain that she will die one day, although it may well not be of her blood-pressure. How much better it would have been for her not to have been told it was high twenty years ago and to have avoided all these years of anxiety. It is not being suggested here that high blood-pressure is a trivial condition, but that it is for doctors to worry about rather than patients! If you ever find out your own blood-pressure, never try to work out for yourself what the figures mean. It is much too complicated. Finally, it should be mentioned that high blood-pressure may occasionally be associated with, or " secondary to," certain kidney diseases (*nephritis*) including a strange condition known as *toxaemia of pregnancy*, which lasts only as long as the pregnancy, provided great care is taken. Most high blood-pressure is, however, " primary ", and without any known association or cause.

Low Blood-pressure. Some people seem normally to have surprisingly low blood-pressure all the time. There is nothing whatever wrong with this; indeed it may even be beneficial. At least they are unlikely ever to suffer the effects of high blood-pressure. The sudden low blood-pressure of circulatory failure or shock (P27) is another matter and must be urgently treated.

Irregularities of the Heart-beat. How quickly or how slowly the heart beats is largely under the control of the cardiac centre in the brain and the level of certain hormones in the blood. The *regularity* of the beat, however, is controlled by the so-called pace-maker in the wall of the right atrium, and by the way impulses from the pace-maker travel through specialised conducting heart cells (the bundle of His and its branches) to the ventricles. When any part of this elaborate mechanism is upset, either by altering the biochemical or electrical conditions of these specialised tissues, or by killing some of them off by deprivation of blood supply in the course of a heart attack, disordered rhythm can result. Increase (*tachycardia*) or decrease (*bradycardia*) in rate is nearly always a normal response to exercise, or anxiety. Very occasional irregularity, such as the mis-timing of an occasional beat is also quite normal in some people, although many are alarmed by it. Persistent irregularity, however, is abnormal. Its true nature can usually be elucidated by making an electrical record of the heart-beat—an electro-cardiogram. The commonest causes are varieties of coronary artery diseases or rheumatic heart disease.

Pericarditis. The heart beats inside a bag or sac. At every beat its outer surface slides against the lining of the sac, lubricated by a small amount of fluid. This is the pericardial sac, the *pericardium* being strictly the lubricated membrane which lines the sac and which also covers the outer surface of the heart. Sometimes inflammation occurs—*pericarditis*—and the sliding surfaces become roughened and even separated by a fluid effusion. Very occasionally, so much fluid accumulates that the heart's action is seriously impeded. Pericarditis may be due to infection or to rheumatic fever, and it usually overlies the area of damaged muscle after a heart attack. This illustrates something which people rarely appreciate—that inflammation is not by any means always due to infection by bacteria. The last two varieties of pericarditis are quite free from germs (sterile).

Myocarditis. A term loosely applied to disorders affecting the heart muscle. There are lots of very rare causes. The really common ones are due to acute or chronic rheumatic causes or to coronary artery disease, both of which are described above.

Endocarditis or inflammation of the lining of the heart is a term loosely applied to any disorder of the valves or heart lining. All varieties of rheumatic valvular disease (P28) are included. Bacterial endocarditis in its several forms usually involves valves already damaged by rheumatic disease. It is a complication which is still much to be feared, though somewhat less so now that antibiotic drugs are available.

Atheroma or Atherosclerosis. This is the condition referred to above in which lumps arise on the lining of arterial blood-vessels. Although it is therefore a disease of the arteries, its importance lies in the way blood flow is held up, either by the lumps themselves, or by thrombosis ultimately blocking the narrowed portion of the pipework. The effects on the body are therefore those of depriving the tissues of blood. It is an astonishing fact that in England and America, more people die of the consequences of atheroma than of any other single disease, including all forms of cancer put together. Furthermore, cancer is mainly a disease of old age, whereas many of the effects of atheroma on men occur in early middle age. If narrowing of the artery is going to do significant harm it is easy to see that it will be of more consequence in those parts of the body where small-bore vessels are supplying tissues whose functions are necessary for life. Exactly such a situation exists in the heart and in the brain. An additional factor is that the arrangement of the blood supply in these tissues is such that any particular area has only one vessel leading to it. This is unusual among the tissues generally, where several alternative, or " collateral " vessels usually supply an area, and where others can take over if one becomes obstructed. We have, therefore, a situation in which perhaps the most important tissues —the heart and the brain—run the greatest risk of deprivation, and this leads to angina and coronary thrombosis on the one hand, and cerebral thrombosis and hæmorrhage (" stroke illness ") on the other, accounting jointly for about one death in every five. In addition, the effects of atheromatous narrowing are often felt in the legs, where the blood supply to the muscles is inadequate for exercise, leading to intermittent pain comparable with that in the heart in similar circumstances. This is called *intermittent claudication*, or intermittent closing of the leg arteries. In its most severe forms, it leads to the need for amputation, although in most cases early treatment can avoid this. It is small wonder that there is intensive research into the causes of atheroma, as with cancer, but it is probably true to say that we still know rather more about cancer. A lot of attention has been given to the amounts of certain fats in the circulating blood, particularly cholesterol. This fat is found in larger amounts in the blood of sufferers from atheroma, and is also found in the arterial lumps themselves. Efforts have therefore been made to reduce blood cholesterol by modifications of the diet, but it has been extremely difficult to prove that this has done any good. Many other factors are known to contribute to atheroma, and hence to heart attacks and strokes, some of which can be reduced

and others not. Such factors are age, obesity, high blood-pressure, and smoking cigarettes. People who lead an active life, like bus conductors, seem to have less trouble than others who are less active, like bus drivers. Sudden severe exercise, however, is bad if you are not used to it. It is better, and life saving, to take regular, moderate exercise. Women have less atheroma than men, until the menopause when they begin to catch up, so that hormones have something to do with it. Serious starvation, such as occurred in the German-occupied territories of Holland and Scandinavia and in the concentration camps conferred one benefit—a freedom from atheroma, but obviously we cannot all starve, and the puzzle remains. Like many of the more important outstanding medical puzzles, there is no single factor responsible, and this is what makes it difficult to solve. *See also* **Preventive Medicine, Part III.**

Aortic Disease. The aorta, the main artery of the body, running from the left ventricle down through the chest and abdomen, also suffers from atheroma, but is too wide (about 2·5 cm across) to become obstructed. However, weaknesses occur in the thickness of its wall, sometimes due to syphilis but nowadays much more usually due to atheroma, which results in a ballooning out of a part of the vessel, rather like you sometimes see in an old bicycle inner tube. In days gone by these *aneurysms*, as the dilatations are called, reached an enormous size, and would wear away the breastbone and ribs, to appear as large pulsating masses on the chest. Now that advanced syphilis is less common, atheromatous aneurysm, with a predilection for the abdominal aorta, is the one most commonly seen; and these days it is treated by replacement of the diseased portion of vessel. *Dissecting aneurysms* of the aorta are another variety in which the blood, under high pressure, somehow finds its way in between the layers of the aortic wall and then suddenly rips up and down the whole length of the vessel, separating (or dissecting) one layer from another in its path. Sometimes it tracks back towards the heart and suddenly fills the pericardium with blood to stop the heart's action altogether.

Embolism. This term refers to any foreign object travelling in the circulation and becoming impacted when it reaches a vessel too small for it to pass through. It may be a thrombus (P31), a collection of cancer cells, a group of bacteria, a chunk of infected pus from an abscess, a collection of fat droplets or even a bubble of air. If it originates in a vein it travels to the right heart and to the lungs. If it comes from the left heart or an artery, it will impact in any part of the arterial tree. Reasonably enough an arterial embolus will commonly end up in those parts of the body with the richest blood supply, like the brain, the kidneys, the liver or the bone marrow. A thrombotic embolus will cause death of the tissue in the area previously supplied by the blocked vessel, a condition known as *infarction.* Perhaps the commonest source of thrombotic embolism is the lining of the heart chambers where a thrombus has occurred at the site of muscle damaged by a heart attack. Massive pulmonary (lung) embolism is usually the result of thrombosis of the leg veins in people kept immobile following surgery or childbirth. That is why postoperative patients are got out of bed for a while as soon as the first day after the operation. The cells of a cancer embolus usually die; but if they survive, a new cancer deposit begins to grow where the embolus impacts, and this is one of the ways cancer may spread. An infected embolus may infect the vessel wall when it impacts, producing a weakness which may give way. Air embolism, if enough insoluble gas enters the circulation, can kill by making so much froth in the heart chambers as to impede the normal pumping action. If bubbles pass the lungs and enter the brain, all sorts of neurological disorders like scores of tiny strokes arise. The same sort of thing happens all over the body in the " bends " or " caisson " disease, in which the blood literally boils. It is due to a too rapid return to normal pressure from regions of high pressure at great depths or from pressurised chambers. Fat embolism sometimes occurs after fractures due to marrow fat entering damaged veins and being carried away to the lungs.

Thrombosis. This is not quite the same as clotting. It is the mass which arises when platelets adhere to the lining of blood-vessels or heart chambers. Blood clot accumulates among layers of deposited platelets and the thrombus therefore has structure, unlike pure blood clot. Thrombosis usually occurs when the lining of the vessel or chamber is damaged by atheroma or inflammation, or when the circulation becomes very stagnant. One danger is that it will become dislodged and travel as an embolus during the first week or ten days of its existence. After this time it is usually firmly incorporated into the vessel walls by cells which migrate into it from the surrounding tissue. The other danger is, of course, that the tissue previously supplied by the blocked vessel will die before a collateral circulation can be established. As previously explained, this is called infarction. All the technical terms in this section are used elsewhere and can be looked up.

Varicose Veins. When veins become swollen they also often become tortuous (wriggly), and particularly on the surface of the leg look very unsightly. They are, however, a sign of a sluggish circulation, and are often due to disease in small valves within the veins which normally prevent the blood from pooling backwards, down towards the feet. They are often a normal maternal accompaniment of pregnancy and disappear after the child is born. If allowed to persist, the sluggish circulation allows the formation of unpleasant ulcers, mainly in elderly people. Treatment is according to severity. In the early stages they are helped by supportive stockings. Later, often as an out-patient, the sufferer may have to have them removed or obliterated by a surgeon.

Raynaud's Disease. This is a strange condition in which the finger tips and in severe cases all the fingers or the whole hand respond in an exaggerated way to cold. The vessels supplying the hand are constricted and the fingers go white as the blood drains from them. Then the capillaries dilate and become distended and filled with blood. But owing to stagnation it is venous and blue, and the fingers are therefore blue. Now we have all experienced this in very cold weather, but sufferers from Raynaud's disease, nearly always women, respond even to very slight cold, like putting their hands into cold water. Even emotional stress will start the process off. In very severe cases the fingers will be so deprived of blood for so long, that sores will develop and fingers can even be lost, but this is very rare, and can be avoided by an operation to cut the nerves which supply the circular muscle of the vessels concerned. In most cases it is sufficient to avoid getting the hands cold.

Frostbite. Strictly speaking, this is literally a freezing of the tissues. Although their freezing point might be expected to be close to that of water, it usually only occurs at temperatures below −13° C. The patient may feel a pricking feeling at first, and feel an area of firmer, pale skin on the cheeks, nose, ears, fingers or toes. If these parts are numb with cold, the onset of frostbite may not be felt, and will often only be noticed by others. In countries where extreme cold is prevalent, it is usual for complete strangers to stop each other in the street and point it out when they see it. It is important not to rub the affected part, but contrary to popular belief it must be warmed as *rapidly* as possible. Fingers should be immersed in water as hot as the normal hand can bear (43° C). Many First Aid books still quite wrongly teach that return to warmth must be gradual.

DISEASES OF THE RESPIRATORY SYSTEM.

INTRODUCTION.

When air is drawn in during the process of breathing, it is brought into very close contact with the blood passing through the lungs. In this way the air we breathe in, which contains 20 per cent oxygen, is confronted with "spent" blood returning from the tissues which contains much less, and oxygen therefore diffuses into the blood from the air. At the same time, the waste gas, carbon dioxide, passes by diffusion in the reverse direction from the blood into the air, because there is much more carbon dioxide in the returning "spent" blood than the tiny amount in the air we breathe. The blood is therefore continually circulating through the lungs and exchanging carbon dioxide for oxygen from the air we breathe in. When we breathe out, we disperse the carbon dioxide into the atmosphere.

When the air enters the nose or mouth, it passes into the windpipe or *trachea*, through the vocal cords in the pharynx. The trachea is held open all the time by rings of cartilage and is lined by a mucus-secreting membrane covered by millions of tiny "hairs" or cilia. These continuously waft a sheet of sticky mucus upwards, which traps any dust or other small particles we may have inhaled, until a collection of this material in the pharynx stimulates us to cough and expel the phlegm, usually to be swallowed. At its lower end, the trachea or windpipe divides into two, the right and left main *bronchus*. Each main bronchial tube enters a lung, one on each side, and proceeds to divide repeatedly within the lung until the air is being carried by more and more smaller and ever smaller tubes called *bronchioles*. There are many millions of these on each side, and each one ends in a collection of very small balloon-like structures —the air sacs or *alveoli*. If you were to cut across a lung and examine the cut surface in a good light, you would see that it is a spongy tissue, with many millions of tiny holes, each one just visible to the naked eye. These are the air sacs. In their walls run the blood capillaries, each one of which is a branch of the vessels carrying "spent" blood from the right side of the heart. At this stage, the blood is only separated from the air in the sacs by the walls of the capillaries and of the air sacs themselves. Both structures are extremely thin, making for easy diffusion of the gases between blood and air.

The action of breathing is accomplished by two muscular mechanisms. One is by the muscles which move the ribs, and the other by the diaphragm, a sheet of muscle which runs across the body, separating the chest cavity from the abdominal cavity. These muscles are all actuated by nerves, just as all other muscles are. Those running to the muscles of breathing are organised by a mechanism in the brain known as the *respiratory centre*. It is this centre—one of the so-called vital centres of the brain—which receives information from many different sources, and translates it into instructions for the breathing mechanism. Thus, when you run for a bus, you will automatically breathe more deeply and more quickly because the respiratory centre has been informed about all the extra carbon dioxide in your blood which has been produced by the exercising leg muscles. Even the conscious instructions involved when you blow a trumpet, inflate a balloon, or during speaking, all pass first to the respiratory centre. It is the death of the cells of this and other vital centres of the brain that is the ultimate cause of death in everyone who dies.

Bronchitis may be acute or chronic. It is an inflammation of the lining mucous membrane of the larger air passages or bronchi, and results in much more secretion than the amount normally produced, mixed with some pus. The acute form is often caused by viruses, with "secondary" infection from bacteria. It may sometimes be caused by irritant gases, like the sulphur dioxide in smog. The chronic, or long-standing form of bronchitis is often associated with *emphysema*, in which the small air sacs of the lung architecture are destroyed or distorted, leaving larger spaces than normal, often surrounded by fibrous scar tissue. Such an arrangement makes the normal gaseous exchange difficult between air and blood. While the exact cause of chronic bronchitis is difficult to discover, because it is such a mixture of causes, it is mainly associated with older age groups, particularly men, in damp foggy climates like ours in Britain, with polluted town air and especially with smoking. Smoking also makes any existing bronchitis much worse. Bronchitis can cause even more trouble than lung cancer, since instead of dying in a short time, the bronchitic lives for many years in chronic sickness. About 30,000 people die of bronchitis each year. It isn't smart to smoke. Patients cough, and produce varying amounts of sputum, or phlegm. They often wheeze like asthmatics. This may go on for many years before the right side of the heart begins to fail (P27). Gradually, during this time, the chest tends to become barrel-shaped. Treatment consists of getting the patient to stop smoking or otherwise contaminating his lungs, preventing infection, particularly during winter months, with germ-killing antibiotics, and breathing exercises. The outlook for chronic bronchitis and emphysema is nevertheless not good, although many patients continue with their disease for many years, provided they take constant care to obey instructions and stop smoking.

Bronchial Asthma is a condition in which the finer air passages become constricted due to an allergic response. In addition, an increased secretion tends to obstruct them and the patient wheezes. In many cases it can be shown that he is allergic to a particular component of dust, or, less commonly , a foodstuff. This is the same sort of thing as occurs in the upper respiratory passages in hay fever, but the effect is on a different, lower part of the respiratory system. Many other cases are due to respiratory infection of some sort, probably combined with an allergy to the bacteria causing it. A predisposition to asthma is often inherited. Once a patient has become asthmatic, his attacks will be triggered off by such additional things as emotional stress, changes in temperature (particularly sudden cold), irritating fumes or smoke, and physical exertion. These are secondary factors, and although much of the treatment is concerned with them, it is unlikely that any of them is a sole cause of the condition. Treatment is directed at the relief of the breathing difficulty and of the wheezing, as well as the control of the causative factors. Many useful drugs are available to dilate the contracted air passages and reduce the obstructing secretions. Asthma in children often gets better as the patient grows up. Asthma is another condition made much worse by smoking. Patients should avoid extremes of cold and humidity particularly out-door exertion in cold, damp weather. They should also avoid exposure to respiratory infection.

A tiny living mite about 0·3 millimetres long exists in large numbers in nearly all mattress and floor dust. This is the cause of much asthma, and in such cases it is often very helpful to vacuum-clean mattresses and floors frequently.

Bronchiectasis. In this condition the bronchial air passages are abnormally and permanently dilated, and the normal structure of the walls destroyed. It is thought to be caused by obstructions of the tubes which lead to dilatation of the parts beyond. Secretions accumulate, and since they cannot easily drain away, they become infected. The infection helps to complete the process of destruction of structures in the bronchial wall. The patient has a chronic cough which often produces large quantities of purulent sputum, and there are often recurrent episodes of pneumonia. Diagnosis is made by a special X-ray examination—a bronchogram—in which a material, opaque to X-rays, is dropped into the air passages. This shows up the dilated and distorted tubes. In some cases, where the disease is localised to one part of the lung, it is often a good idea to cut out that portion, and this is particularly true in young people. Vigorous physiotheraphy, involving drainage of the lungs by placing the patient in a suitable posture, together with antibiotic drugs for the infection, are other forms of treatment.

Cystic Fibrosis is an inborn disease which affects chiefly the lungs and the digestive system. It is sometimes called *Fibrocystic disease of the Pancreas*, and sometimes " Mucoviscidosis " Until it was medically recognised twenty-five years ago, children affected usually died from pneumonia in the first year of life. This, of course, was before antibiotics were available for the treatment of infections. Today, cystic fibrosis is known to be the commonest genetically determined disorder affecting children in Britain. One child in 2,000 receives one of the abnormal genes from each parent. Such a child therefore has a double dose of the harmful gene, and will have the disease from birth. One person in 25 of the general population carries only one of these abnormal genes, and such an individual will not have the disease, but will be a carrier of the abnormal gene. If such a seemingly normal carrier marries another carrier, there is a one in four chance of each of their children being affected. The children, therefore, who actually develop cystic fibrosis, have inherited the disease *equally* from both parents, who are carriers, but are themselves unaffected by the disease. Although much has been learned about cystic fibrosis in the past twenty-five years, there remain many unsolved problems, and we still cannot define precisely the biochemical fault which causes it. The prospects for survival into reasonably healthy adult life are steadily improving, but they depend upon early diagnosis and careful management through childhood. In cystic fibrosis most of the damage is caused by the excessive viscidity, or stickiness, of the mucus which is produced in the breathing tubes as a lubricant, and also in the ducts of the pancreatic gland which provides enzymes to help digestion. Being thick and sticky, instead of thin and slimy as in the normal, this mucus tends to block the passages instead of keeping them clear. The pancreatic cells are permanently destroyed. The gland cannot secrete pancreatic enzymes, and the food, especially protein and fat, is not properly absorbed. This deficiency can be compensated fairly well by giving pancreatic extract by mouth with every meal, and by dietary care.

The major clinical problem is in the lungs. The lung passages normally have a thin coating of mucus which is propelled steadily upwards, and is completely renewed in less than one hour. It moves more suddenly on coughing. In cystic fibrosis this upward movement is slowed down and interrupted. There is difficulty in keeping the passages clear, especially when infection with bacteria or viruses greatly increases the amount of mucus. This results in intermittent blocking of the air passages, difficulty in breathing, incomplete use of the lungs, and persistent local pockets of infection. If such infectious processes are not controlled, areas of lung will be destroyed, chronic infection will persist, and multiple lung cavities will develop. These predispose to further infection, interfering with the natural development of the lung—a process not normally complete until halfway through childhood—thus adding to the respiratory problems which the child will face in later life. Unless a correct diagnosis is made, and proper treatment instituted before the first serious lung infection has occurred, the resulting lung damage may well be permanent.

Pneumonia. This is an infection of the lung tissue, rather than of the air passages. The lung is the only internal organ which is directly exposed to the air, and since there are germs of all kinds in the air, it is a source of surprise that pneumonia is not a much more common event in all of us. The answer lies, as with all infections, in the fact that it is not simply (or even mainly) bacteria which cause disease, but our own lack of resistance to them. If we allow germs to thrive and multiply by being unhealthy or run down or undernourished, infective disease will occur. If we are fit, the entry of those same harmful germs into the body causes us no inconvenience, unless we are very young, or very old, or unless the invasion of germs is abnormally overwhelming. This helps to explain why pneumonia is so often quoted as a cause of death. In most cases it is merely a terminal event occurring in the elderly sick, whose normal resistance is so far reduced by their illness that they succumb to an invasion which they would normally not notice. There are two main kinds of pneumonia, and in both the air sacs become filled with inflammatory secretions, making the normally porous lung tissue as solid as liver. In *lobar pneumonia*, a whole segment (or lobe) of the lung becomes solid. In *bronchopneumonia*, areas of lung tissue surrounding the smaller bronchioles become consolidated, leaving normal porous lung tissue in between. Bronchopneumonia is the one which occurs in the rather stagnant lungs of people who are already ill or bedridden. Both forms respond to treatment with the appropriate antibiotics, provided any underlying debility does not interfere with the patient's own resistance. In the terminal bronchopneumonia of fatal illness, it is sometimes considered kinder not to treat the additional pneumonia. *Pleurisy* is a natural complication, and before the days of antibiotic drugs *lung abscess* was very much feared. Another form of pneumonia—*virus pneumonia*—is referred to in P10(2).

Pneumoconiosis. This is a term which refers to a large group of different diseases, all of which are caused by breathing in some form of dust over a very long period of time. It is therefore an occupational hazard of certain trades. We have already mentioned the mechanism of mucus secretion in the air passages which normally trap small particles from the air, and prevent them reaching the lung. However, in some occupations there is so much dust breathed in over the months and years that these normal barriers are defeated. About a quarter of the earth's crust consists of silicon, in quartz, flint, or sand. *Silicosis* occurs in people who have worked for many years in trades like mining, stone crushing, sandblasting, or metal grinding, who are often breathing silicon dust in high concentration. When the particles arrive in the air sacs, they set up an irritant chemical reaction which produces nodules of scar tissue. Silicosis for some reason predisposes to tuberculosis (P14(1)). Emphysema also occurs and there is a general impairment of respiratory function. Coalminer's pneumoconiosis is similar to silicosis but not identical with it. It is more prevalent in some coalfields than others, owing to the different composition of the dust to which these unfortunate men are daily exposed. It is hoped that modern mining methods will help to reduce this dread disease. Asbestos is a complex silicate of magnesium, calcium, and iron. *Asbestosis* is caused by inhaling its fine fibres. *Berylliosis* is caused by compounds of beryllium, used in the manufacture of fluorescent lamps. *Farmers lung* is a pneumoconiosis caused by inhaling hay and grain dust, and is similar to *bagassosis* and *byssinosis* caused by sugar cane and cotton dust respectively. The newest pneumoconiosis to be reported is *mushroom worker's lung*, caused by something in the compost in which mushrooms are commercially grown.

Pulmonary Embolism. This catastrophic, yet quite common condition has already been briefly referred to (P30(2)). It is a cause of tragic, sudden death in people who have had operations or have given birth to babies some days previously, or who have been bedridden for any other cause. The first event is that the blood in the veins of the legs becomes stagnant, due to the lack of exercise; and together with the tendency to clot which often follows surgery or childbirth, the whole length of a leg vein may be obstructed for twelve inches or more by an elongated clot of blood. This does little harm to the circulation of the leg, since there are plenty of other veins for returning blood to the heart. The danger is that the clot will become dislodged and be swept upwards towards the heart by the flow of returning blood. When this happens it is carried by way of the right auricle and ventricle into the pulmonary vessels which normally carry spent blood to the lungs. Here, for the first time, it enters vessels which are getting smaller as they divide, and it then impacts in the main pulmonary artery. The patient, who may have been recovering very well, suddenly collapses and not unusually dies there and then. At autopsy a long coiled-up mass of clot is found obstructing the pulmonary vessels. It often can be seen to form a cast of the leg vein and even bears the marks of the small venous valves which are

present at its site of origin. With the dramatic advances being made in chest surgery, it is now sometimes possible in selected cases to operate to remove the clot. Success clearly depends on the patient's surviving long enough to be taken to the operating theatre for the major operation of *pulmonary embolectomy*. Three quarters of all cases of pulmonary embolism die within two hours, and therefore the best hope would be to prevent the occurrence altogether. This is not at present possible, but clotting in leg veins can be discouraged by early exercise following surgery and childbirth. Patients often resent having to get up the next day because it is so uncomfortable. Herein, however, lies their best hope of avoiding pulmonary embolism.

Hæmoptysis. This means coughing up blood or blood-stained material. It must be distinguished from *hæmatemesis*, in which the blood is vomited from the stomach. It must always be taken seriously because of the underlying lung disease which may be present. No one who coughs up blood, in however small a quantity, should neglect to inform their doctor so that its source can be determined. Hæmoptysis occurs in a variety of lung disease, some of which is not serious but much of which must be treated immediately if it is not to become so. This is a suitable place to repeat our general rule that you should see your doctor without delay if you have any unexplained bleeding from any part of the body, however well you feel. And this includes hæmoptysis. *See also* **Preventive Medicine, Part III.**

Fat Embolism. Liquid fat sometimes enters the bloodstream following extensive crush injuries to soft tissue and bone. It splits up into millions of small globules which are carried to the lungs, and impact in small blood vessels there, producing obstruction of the lung circulation and consequent difficulties in breathing.

Lung Cancer. This is one of the commonest, nastiest and most incurable forms of cancer which can occur. It is also probably the easiest to prevent. In 1969, 29,768 people died of lung cancer in Great Britain, all but 5,000 of them men. Every year the toll goes up. There has been no reasonable doubt for several years now that it is associated with cigarette smoking, and the evidence is overwhelming. However, in spite of this certain knowledge, smoking continues to increase, and every year there are more and more people dying unpleasantly of lung cancer. It seems that nothing the health authorities can do is able to stop it. Intensive campaigns of public advertising of the dangers, and well organised instruction in schools have so far made no impression whatever on the smoking habits even of people who accept the evidence. The only group of people who are known to have stopped smoking are British doctors, very many of whom have given it up, and it is easy to show that giving it up has saved them from the disease. Their colleagues who have not done so have continued to die. Undoubtedly a large factor contributing to the failure of anti-smoking propaganda is the enormous expenditure by the tobacco manufacturers on very clever advertising, amounting to many millions of pounds each year. Moreover they spend a pitiful fraction of this amount on their own research into the harmful effects of their own product, which has so far discovered nothing which was not already known by research doctors many years ago. Another problem is that it takes a number of years to get cancer. It is not like an infectious disease which is caught a few days after exposure to the bacteria concerned. It may be fifteen or twenty years before the cancer begins, and many smokers are apparently unwilling to look so far ahead. Furthermore, not everyone who smokes dies this way; and so a smoker can gamble with his life and hope it will not be him. The present writer once had to perform a series of post-mortem examinations on people who died of lung cancer, and this helped him to stop smoking completely, having smoked more than twenty cigarettes a day for several years. Not everyone can have this incentive. The main encouragement to smoke probably comes from other people. Schoolboys are easily impressed when their teachers and parents stop smoking. They are not likely to fear the habit when these same people smoke openly. The smoking doctor is also a powerful stimulus to people to carry on smoking.

Lung cancer grows in the wall of a main bronchial air passage. If it grows inwards it can obstruct the air way, choking that part of the lung it is supplying with air. This causes collapse and infection of the lung and may lead to *lung abscess*. The patient will then cough up blood-stained infected and purulent material. Such a case is comparatively lucky, since the disease declares itself early by producing symptoms. In others, the lump may grow outwards into the surrounding lung and produce no symptoms at all in the early stages. Indeed, it may spread to other parts of the body, like brain or bone or liver before causing any trouble to the patient. If this happens he may go to his doctor because of fits, changes of personality, or fracture, only to discover that the origin of the trouble is in the lung.

The chances of cure are negligible, although much can be done to relieve the pain and suffering of the last stages of the illness. Not more than one in twenty cases is alive two years after it is first diagnosed. Surgery, by removing the lung, and irradiation of the growth are the standard palliative treatment. It is not the practice of the Medical Section to alarm the reader unnecessarily, but if only a few are induced to stop giving themselves such a horrible disease, then writing in this way will have been justified.

Secondary Cancer of the Lung. In nearly all forms of cancer, the big problem is that it spreads to other parts of the body. If this were not so it could be eradicated by surgical removal more often than it is. One common way in which it spreads from any part of the body is by entering the bloodstream and being carried as clumps of living cancer cells to distant parts. When these come to rest in smaller blood vessels, they begin to grow and colonise the new environment. Such new colonies are called *secondary deposits* or *metastases*. It so happens that all veins (except portal veins of the liver) lead to the right heart and thence directly to the lungs, and for this reason the lungs are a very common site of *secondary* cancer, which may have begun in the bowel, or breast, or indeed anywhere else in the body. Other common sites of secondary, blood-borne cancer are the brain, liver, bone marrow, and kidney, since all of them have an abundant blood supply, and there is therefore a high chance of the travelling cells arriving there. Secondary cancer of the lung usually consists of several lumps scattered throughout the lung. Lung cancer itself is usually only one growth. One of the main reasons for the success of early diagnosis is that treatment may be possible before blood-borne and other means of spread have occurred. Unfortunately, in the case of primary cancer of the lung, even early diagnosis is of little avail, but in many other common cancers permanent cure is possible if treatment is begun early enough.

Pleurisy. The chest is lined by one layer of a thin membrane called the *pleura*. The lungs are covered and enclosed by a second, continuous layer of this same membrane. When the lungs move during respiration, the pleura covering the lungs rubs against the pleura lining the chest, lubricated by a very thin layer of pleural fluid separating the two pleura. Whenever the pleural surface becomes inflamed, this is known as *pleurisy*. It is nearly always due to inflammatory disease of the adjoining lung, and is therefore not strictly a disease in its own right. For example, pneumonia, tuberculosis, lung cancer, or a lung infarct (P30(2)) will produce a pleurisy if the area of diseased lung adjoins the lung surface. Sometimes the area of inflamed inner pleura will tend to stick to its outer layer or rub painfully against it, producing a sharp pain when the patient breathes. Sometimes a large effusion of fluid is produced which separates the two layers and collapses the

lung by occupying space in the chest which the lung should be occupying. This latter is more usual in tuberculosis or cancer.

The lung can be collapsed by the entry of anything between the normally adjacent layers of pleura. For example, air can be introduced, or by accidental penetrating wounds of the chest wall, or by accidental rupture of the emphysematous lung (*q.v.*). This condition is called *pneumothorax* or "air in the chest." Bleeding into the cavity between the pleura is called *haemothorax*.

DISEASES OF THE DIGESTIVE
TRACT AND LARGE INTESTINE.

INTRODUCTION.

The digestive tract consists of the mouth, pharynx, œsophagus (or gullet), stomach, small intestine, large intestine (or colon), rectum, and anus. The small intestine is very long, and is subdivided into the duodenum, jejunum, and ileum. It ends at the junction of the ileum with the cæcum, where there is a small blind side-tube, the appendix. The cæcum leads into the colon. The whole tract has two main mechanical functions and two main biochemical ones. Mechanically, food has to be chewed in the mouth and further minced up by muscular squeezing, mainly by the stomach. It has also to be propelled along by an orderly series of squeezing movements known as *peristalsis*. While it is still in the digestive tract, food has to be digested. That is to say, it has to be broken down chemically into suitable materials for absorption into the system, and secondly, it has to be absorbed across the wall of the intestine into the blood stream, itself a highly complex biochemical process. The blood stream it now enters is a special part of the circulation, the "portal" system, which travels directly to the liver without first passing to the heart. In the liver the broken-down foods are processed and issued in their new form into the general, or "systemic" circulation, by which they are finally carried to all the tissues of the body.

As the food passes along the digestive tract (or, as it is sometimes called, the alimentary canal), it is mixed with various secretions which are either made in the wall of the tract, or by organs outside the wall connected to the main pathway by small tubes. Examples of the latter are bile, manufactured by the liver and sent into the duodenum through the bile ducts. Also pancreatic juice comes from the pancreas down the pancreatic ducts, also into the duodenum. These secretions are either digestive juices concerned with splitting up the foodstuffs so that they can be absorbed, or they have a lubricant function so that the gut contents slide along easily under the influence of peristalsis. Roughly speaking, it may be said that digestive juices give place to lubricant secretions at the junction between the small and large intestine.

The constituents of the diet are dealt with in a later section. The principle classes with whose digestion we are now concerned are carbohydrates, proteins, and fats.

Carbohydrates are sugars and starches. There are many sugars, which may exist alone, in pairs, or with lots of them stuck together. Alone they are such things as glucose or fructose. Common table sugar is a substance called sucrose, formed by sticking one glucose molecule to one fructose molecule. Starch is lots of glucose molecules all stuck together. Digestion of carbohydrates consists of splitting up sugars and starch into single sugars like glucose, since only single sugars can be absorbed into the system. The splitting is done by digestive *enzymes* which are found in the juices secreted into the digestive tract. Sugar-splitters are found in the saliva of the mouth, in the pancreatic juice of the duodenum, and in the duodenum's own juice from its own wall. On the face of it, you might think it would be better to eat glucose which needs no digestion and can be absorbed in this form, than to eat starch which has first to be split; and so a lot of money has been made out of a gullible public by the sale of glucose drinks and powder. In fact digesting starch is no problem whatever, even for the sick, who can obtain their carbohydrate energy just as easily (and much more cheaply) from potatoes as from expensive glucose. The end result of eating both is the same. The starch-splitting enzyme in saliva is mixed with the food as it is chewed, and it is therefore probably a good idea to chew it well. However, even if the food is bolted it does not seem to matter very much. People without teeth (neither their own nor dentures) seem to digest their carbohydrate quite well, presumably by means of their pancreatic juice at a later stage.

Proteins, which are found in meat, cheese, and eggs, have very large molecules consisting of lots of small ones strung together. Unlike starch, in which all the component glucose molecules are identical, the amino acids of which proteins are composed come in many different types. They all contain nitrogen, and there are about twenty-seven varieties. One protein differs from another in the proportions of the mixture and the order in which they are stuck together. Only single amino acids can be absorbed from the food, and so protein digestion again consists of splitting the material down into its building bricks. There is a strong protein splitting enzyme in the gastric (or stomach) juice called pepsin, whose job it is to split the long amino-acid chains into shorter chains. Several other protein-splitters in the duodenal and pancreatic juice contrive to break the smaller chains into individual amino acids which are then absorbed and sent to the liver for processing.

Fats mainly consist of glycerol to which are attached three fatty acid molecules for each molecule of glycerol. An enzyme in pancreatic juice splits the fatty acids off the glycerol, but would have some difficulty penetrating the globules of fat without the help of bile. One of the constituents of bile (bile salts) has detergent properties like washing-up powder and breaks the fat globules up into a very fine suspension so that the enzyme can get at the fat. Some fat particles of this size can even be absorbed as such, without preliminary splitting.

The processes by which all these enzymic secretions are produced are very finely controlled. They are very expensive to make in terms of energy and raw materials, and so it would be very wasteful to produce them all the time, even when there was no food to digest. And so the body has some very well designed automatic arrangements for sampling the foods as they are eaten and passed on, which ensure that exactly the right kind of juice is waiting in every part of the digestive tract for whatever food arrives. As soon as the food is digested the supply of enzymes is automatically switched off, so that there is very little waste of precious materials. It is, of course, beyond the scope of this account to describe the control mechanisms. Suffice it to say that they are operated partly by nerve reflexes which signal the imminent arrival of food, and partly by special hormones produced in various parts of the gut wall. The best secretion is affected even by psychological factors, so that pleasant company and surroundings, attractive appearance of the food, and an eager anticipation of it all make for good digestion and good health. These psychological factors are all capable of proper scientific investigation and proof. The poor health of those who habitually and irregularly bolt unpalatable food is probably due to such factors as these. So is the failure of appetite in the depressed, the anxious adult, or the scolded child.

Nearly all the digestion which has been described occurs in the stomach and upper part of the small intestine (the duodenum, jejunum, and upper ileum). Almost all absorption of the products of digestion occurs in the small intestine which is long and intricately folded to give it a large surface area for this purpose. The colon, or large intestine, is adapted for conserving water, by removing it from the residual waste material. This has then to be eliminated, and being rather dry its passage has to be lubricated by suitable secretions of mucus.

Constipation. Here, perhaps we had better mention the morbid question of constipation, about which so many people are obsessed and hold such pronounced views. First of all, what is it? For some people it is entirely normal only to pass motions about once or twice a week. For others the normal frequency is once or twice a day. What is abnormal? The answer is that the only thing worth worrying about is any pronounced change of bowel habit, particularly in middle-aged and older people. By a change is meant a change from that individual person's normal routine. Such a pronounced change—either in the direction of constipation or diarrhœa—is worth consulting your doctor about if it persists for more than a week or two. Otherwise, forget your bowels and leave them to work naturally as they know best. Many believe that constipation is the root of all evil, that it causes a mysterious condition known to them (although, alas, not to doctors) as " auto-intoxication." Sedulously fostered by the manufacturers of patent medicines, their beliefs range from the notion that headaches, spotty skin, muddy skin, and tiredness are caused by constipation, to the more extreme idea that the whole system is being poisoned and that, if the bowels do not work, the individual will shortly die. Of course, all this is the merest rubbish; for, as Professor Samson Wright, whose *Applied Physiology* is one of the most famous of medical text-books, has pointed out, there is no such thing as absorption of poisonous products from the bowel. There is no such thing as " auto-intoxication." " The symptoms of constipation," he writes, " are largely due to distension and mechanical irritation of the rectum." It has been shown that an enema removes these symptoms *immediately*, which would not be the case if they were due to poisons in the blood, and exactly the same symptoms can be produced by packing the rectum with cotton-wool. Wright mentions the case of a man who went for just over a year without a bowel motion, and at the end of that time, although his abdomen was distended and he felt some discomfort, he was not noticeably ill. Needless to say, telling these facts to the purgative addict will only make him annoyed, but it is as well to note that if no known diseases are due to constipation (although constipation may be a symptom of another disease), the regular use of purgatives *can* cause disease.

Constipation should be treated first by diet containing plenty of roughage—bran and oatmeal are excellent—plenty of stewed and fresh fruits, and at least 1½ litres of fluid should be taken daily. Failing that, one of the best things to take is a proprietary product prepared from senna pods. Never to be taken regularly are liquid paraffin, castor oil, preparations of aloes, Epsom salts, and all the other dreadful stuff that people swill down.

Œsophagus.

The œsophagus, or gullet, is more than a simple tube for taking the food from the mouth to the stomach. It is normally closed except when swallowing, and the act of swallowing is very complicated. When the material to be swallowed arrives in the back of the throat there is an automatic mechanism which opens the top end of the œsophagus to receive it, and from then onwards everything happens automatically. The next portion of the tube opens and the top closes strongly, so that the food (or drink) is propelled forcibly down the next segment. Then the part below this relaxes and the material is squeezed further downwards and so on until it arrives in the stomach. This squeezing (or milking) action is akin to the action known as peristalsis which propels contents in other parts of the gut. Thus when you see someone swallowing a glass of beer very quickly in warm weather, it is not going " down the hatch " under the influence of gravity, however much it may look like it. It is perfectly possible to swallow the same, or any other liquid, standing on your head. Getting into that position is the only difficult part. Sometimes this complicated swallowing mechanism gets out of order, leading to difficulties of swallowing, or *dysphagia*. Another disorder known as *hiatus hernia* occurs at the lower end of the œsophagus as it meets the stomach. At this point the œsophagus has to pass through the diaphragm, the sheet of muscle which separates the chest from the abdomen. The muscular fibres of the diaphragm are normally arranged in a ring around the œsophagus. These help to keep the lower end shut, so that the contents of the stomach do not regurgitate upwards, causing inflammation (*oesophagitis*) or heartburn. A hiatus hernia is when muscle fibres get slack, and the upper end of the stomach can even slide upwards into the chest. People with hiatus hernia get heartburn after meals, and particularly when they bend down or lie down. Except for very severe forms, which need surgical repair, the treatment is to eat less at a time, reduce the acidity with a suitable antacid and reduce weight, so that the weight of the abdomen does not press upwards so much. The other disease of the œsophagus, quite unrelated to the above, is *cancer of the oesophagus*, the cause of which is still unknown in most cases. When cancer occurs in the wall of any tube, it will often encircle the tube and gradually narrow the way through. This is what happens in the œsophagus, leading to difficulty in swallowing, particularly solids. It is a condition, usually, of rather elderly men, although it is sometimes associated with a special form of severe anæmia in women. Treatment is in some way to keep the passage open, either by transplanting a new tube, or more usually, by removing the constricted piece and joining up the remainder.

The Stomach and Duodenum.

By far the commonest diseases of the stomach and duodenum are *gastric ulcer* and *duodenal ulcer*. They are actually the same condition in two different sites and are often classed together as *peptic ulcer* or *acid-peptic disease*. The ulcers, which are rather like sores on the lining of the stomach or duodenum, may be "acute" or "chronic." Acute ulcers tend to be small and there are often several of them. Chronic ulcers are usually single. They may be small, or they may be several centimetres across. Chronic ulcers smoulder for months and even years, like a sore which will not heal, and a great deal of scar tissue forms in their depths. Thus they may in time erode their way right through the wall of the stomach, destroying all its layers, and begin to eat into surrounding structures like the pancreas or liver. The fact that they do not perforate more frequently is due to all the fibrous scar tissue which is formed during the slow eroding process. Healing of such a destructive ulcer is nevertheless common, and the great problem is how to help the natural healing process to win against the ulcer's tendency to erode. Better still would be to discover the cause, and prevent it happening in the first place. This extremely common affliction is confined to the human species and has been known since the earliest times. It does not vary very much with diet or with social class. Although occurring at all ages, it usually begins between the ages of twenty and forty, and is most commonly found in men between forty-five and fifty-five. Gastric ulcer is four times, and duodenal ulcer ten times more common in men than in women. It is always due to an inability of the lining to stand up to the normal digestive activity of the stomach contents. These are normally acid and contain a powerful enzyme for digesting proteins. Again it is perhaps more surprising that we all do not digest our own stomachs, rather than that some unfortunate people do digest small areas slowly. In certain abnormal conditions when the stomach stops making acid, ulcers always heal. However, some ulcers occur without excessive secretion of acid and many heal without the acid being neutralised with antacids. All this points to the main trouble being in the response of the lining to acid rather than to the acid itself. Nevertheless, the most effective treatment at present known involves regulating gastric secretion, and particularly its acidity. It is also known that peptic ulcers are more common in people whose occupations involve administrative and professional

responsibility, competitive effort and nervous tension, long periods of anxiety or frustration. Presumably the higher nervous system influences these events by the same nerves, which normally help to control secretion.

The main symptom of peptic ulcer is pain, and this usually responds well to proper doses of antacids. Many different varieties are available and a lot of money is made from selling them. When indigestion persists for longer than a few days it is always better to see your doctor so that a proper diagnosis can be made and the best remedies begun. Many other causes exist for similar pains, and you should not try to make the diagnosis yourself. It may be necessary to analyse your gastric secretions in the hospital laboratory. Almost certainly you will have a special X-ray examination, and since the stomach cannot easily be seen on a normal X-ray, they will have to show it up by making you drink a white material containing barium. This will be seen as a silhouette of the stomach and duodenal contents. Searching for an ulcer this way is a highly skilled matter and is performed by doctors specially trained in radiology.

Until recently, no drugs capable of influencing the course of peptic ulcer in any significant manner were available and the physician had to rely on general measures, such as rest, diet and the administration of antacids to relieve pain and discomfort; episodes of acute haemorrhage were not uncommon and required surgical intervention if life were threatened.

However recent advances in our knowledge of gastric and duodenal pathology have led to the development of at least two therapeutic agents of which the newest, *cimetidine*, is highly effective. Developments in fibre-optic technology have contributed greatly to progress in peptic ulcer treatment. The gastro-enterologist can now pass a *flexible* instrument, the *gastroduodenal endoscope* (the gastroscope is a *rigid* tube), under mild sedation through the patient's gullet and into the stomach and duodenum and view the lesions directly. Once an ulcer is diagnosed, the time has come to stop treating yourself with antacids from the chemist's counter, and to take the ones your doctor decides are best. Smoking should be stopped by ulcer patients (as, indeed, by everyone else, but that is another matter) because it inhibits healing. Alcohol tends to increase acid secretion and should be avoided. It is also *extremely important* to avoid taking any form of aspirin, even in quite small amounts, since this can lead to very serious bleeding from the ulcer. The ulcer patient should be warned that hundreds of proprietary preparations contain aspirin and all of them are dangerous for him. Search for the formula in small print on the label before taking any remedy, looking particularly for acetyl salicylic acid—the correct name for aspirin. Even some widely sold "hang-over" remedies which are sold for "upset-stomach" contain large quantities of aspirin. Some of the patients with "upset stomach" are, of course, ulcer patients, and some even die of haemorrhage following the ingestion of aspirin.

The main complications of peptic ulcer are bleeding, perforation, and a narrowing of the pylorus, or lower part, known as *pyloric stenosis*. Bleeding is caused by the eroding ulcer eating away at one of the many blood vessels in the stomach or duodenal wall. It leads to the passing of "altered" blood in the stool (*melaena*), or to the vomiting of blood (*haematemesis*). When the initial bleeding occurs, the patient may feel suddenly faint, and a little later will notice the black, tarry colour of his stool. This is sometimes confused with a similiar colour when the patient is taking iron. Peptic ulcer is not the only cause of this very serious hæmorrhage, which constitutes a hospital emergency whatever its cause. The treatment, like that of every large hæmorrhage, is blood transfusion which must be continued until the bleeding stops, or until the patient is sufficiently fit for surgery, should that be deemed necessary. Perforation is perhaps the most serious complication of peptic ulcer, leading to the spilling of stomach contents within the abdominal cavity. Treatment is invariably surgical, either the closure of the perforation or the partial removal of the stomach.

Surgical removal of part of the stomach is often the only way to treat a peptic ulcer which has had its chance to heal in other ways. It is tempting for the patient to "have it out and done with," but the time for surgery is a matter of fine judgment. So many ulcers heal by medical means if you give them a chance, and operations are for those which persistently refuse, or which become complicated.

Stomach Cancer. The stomach is a fairly common site for primary cancer. There is no known reason for this, and it is particularly important to stress that we know of no connection whatever between the peptic ulcers which have just been discussed and cancer. Stomach cancer used to be the commonest cancer of men, but the current rise of lung cancer has pushed it into second place. There are some strange geographical differences in its distribution. For example, it is much commoner in Japan and Scandinavia than in England or the U.S.A. It is difficult to see any reason for this in dietary habits. In Wales it causes three times as many deaths as in South-East England. All this is very puzzling, as is so much of our information about cancer generally. One of the main problems with stomach cancer is that it often causes the patient no inconvenience and thus produces no symptoms of note until the disease is far advanced and it is difficult to do much. Treatment is by surgical removal of the growth, and even in the most advanced cases a great deal can often be done to make the patient more comfortable.

The Small Intestine.

The small intestine runs from the stomach to the cæcum and comprises the duodenum, jejunum, and ileum in that order. On a more cheerful note it may be remarked that it is very rarely the site of cancer. Its main problems arise in connection with defects in absorption mechanisms, with obstructions, and with a strange inflammatory condition known as *regional enteritis*. Most obstructions are due not to blockages of the tube, but to failures of peristaltic propulsion, the process which is briefly described above under "œsophagus." Such a failure is called *ileus*. When peristalsis stops for any reason, the result is severe dehydration and loss of important chemicals like sodium and chloride from the body. This is because about 9 litres of fluid enter the small intestine each day in the form of digestive juices, and all of this has to be pushed onwards to be reabsorbed into the system at lower levels. If peristalsis fails, this bulk of fluid remains in the small intestine, or is vomited. In both cases it is lost to the body itself, leading to serious dehydration and illness. Treatment is by very careful replacement by transfusion of the fluid and the chemicals lost, and by removal of the trapped fluid within the intestine through a tube threaded down through the mouth.

Regional enteritis or *ileitis* is sometimes known as *Crohn's disease.* It is a very mysterious condition in which the normally supple wall of the small intestine becomes inflamed and gradually replaced by thick fibrous scar tissue, so that it looks and feels like a thick garden hose. Loops of inflamed gut stick together, and channels open between them, and if the disease progresses a mass of adherent, thickened intestine results to which everything in the neighbourhood also adheres. However, for some unknown reason some cases do not progress downhill in this way and get better spontaneously. Surgical treatment is necessary for the majority, however, particularly those with advanced disease leading to complications such as obstruction or perforation. Sometimes an early case can be resolved by cutting out the length of affected gut, although recurrences are unfortunately common.

Appendicitis. This must be one of the best-known surgical diseases of the intestinal tract.

The appendix is a narrow, blind-ended side tube attached to the cæcum near the end of the small intestine. Appendicitis is when it becomes obstructed, or infected, or both. From its position it is almost predictable that it will get obstructed sooner or later by pieces of fæcal matter which pass its entrance and which are normally infected. The surprising thing is that it does not happen more often. Once this has occurred, however, a closed abscess forms, and as the abscess distends the appendix, it first weakens its wall, making it gangrenous, and then bursts into the abdominal cavity causing *peritonitis* (see later). It would be useless and misleading to describe the symptoms of acute appendicitis in detail, since it is difficult even for experienced doctors to distinguish them from those of several other conditions. Suffice it to say that any severe, persisting pain in the abdomen, whether continuous or intermittent, whether associated with diarrhœa or not, should lead the sufferer to a doctor for a quick diagnosis. Germ-killing antibiotics are useless against appendicitis, and any laxative is extremely dangerous as it may cause an acutely inflamed appendix to perforate.

The Large Intestine or Colon.

The two main serious diseases of the colon are ulcerative colitis and cancer in its various forms. *Ulcerative colitis* is yet another mysterious disease in which severe ulceration of the lining of the colon gives rise most frequently to diarrhœa with the passage of blood and mucus. In fact it can be like dysentery, and it has often been considered to be due to some form of infection. Unfortunately no particular germ can routinely be found in these cases, and the situation is endlessly confused by the presence in the normal bowel of lots of different germs anyway. Nevertheless the ulcerated lining of the bowel certainly does get infected by the germs normally present, and this makes the disease worse. Therefore germ-killing antibiotics are often helpful in alleviating symptoms and can lead to an earlier settling down of the condition, although not to a cure. It has long been known that certain kinds of psychological upset are often associated, but here again the disease is so unpleasant for the sufferer that he is to be forgiven some despondency as a result of, rather than as a cause of, his troubles. It is also suspected that ulcerative colitis may be an auto-immune disease; that is it may represent rejection by the patient of his own colonic lining in a manner somewhat comparable to the tissue rejection which often follows organ transplantation. Some of the more alarming complications are perforation through the wall of the ulcerated bowel, and sometimes massive hæmorrhage occurs. The mainstay of medical treatment is the drug *sulphasalazine* together with dietary measures and the occasional use of other drugs to minimise symptoms. Surgery maybe required to relieve obstruction, deal with perforation, remove chronically affected parts of the bowel, etc.

Cancer of the Colon and Rectum. This is another very common form of cancer, which can often be completely cured by surgical removal of the growth provided it is caught in the early stages before it has spread. The commonest symptom is a change in bowel habit, either towards constipation or, more often, towards diarrhœa, in the second half of life. There may be rectal bleeding, or the passage of mucus, and there may be abdominal pain. We cannot too often repeat that any such change of bowel habit, or any unexplained bleeding from any site should lead the patient promptly to his doctor.

Diverticulitis. Some people have small pockets or sacs in the wall of the colon known as diverticula. A minority of these sometimes get inflamed, and this is *diverticulitis.* Occasionally perforation occurs.

Hernia or Rupture. This is a condition in which abdominal contents, usually a loop of intestine, protrude forwards through the muscular wall of the abdomen. The wall consists of a sheet of muscle fibres running in several directions. They normally become tense when we cough, or strain, or in getting up from a recumbent position. There are places in the groin on each side where there is a way through the muscle for the spermatic cord in the male. In many men a weakness can arise at this point, and if it persists, the way through may enlarge and allow loops of bowel to emerge from behind the muscle sheet to appear as a lump under the skin of the groin. On relaxation the lump can be made to disappear by pushing the contents back the way they came; and they will re-emerge when the patient strains. This is an extremely common complaint in men, and it should be treated by an operation in which the muscle wall is repaired. Some men, however, neglect to have their rupture treated until one day it proceeds to "strangulate." This is the term used when the muscle tightens around the neck of the protruding loop of bowel, cutting off its blood supply. From then onwards the loop becomes gangrenous and the intestine is obstructed by having a part of itself nipped outside the abdominal wall. The patient is in severe pain, vomits continously, and quickly is liable to get into such a poor condition that surgical relief is difficult. It is therefore a surgical emergency, and it would have been better to have had the relatively simple repair operation earlier and at leisure. Hernia in the region of the groin is of two types: *inguinal hernia* and *femoral hernia*, the difference between them being technical and of no consequence to the patient. They nearly always occur in men. Other types of hernia less frequently occur in both sexes. *Incisional hernia* is when the muscle wall has been weakened at the site of an old abdominal operation and has failed to heal properly. *Umbilical hernia* occurs owing to the natural weakness of the abdominal wall at the navel, and is so common in babies as to be almost normal. When a baby cries and thereby puts a strain on his abdominal wall, a lump often appears in the region of the navel, and this can be very alarming for the parents. They should of course show it to their doctor who will nearly always be able to reassure them. It is self-healing without operation in the majority of cases.

Peritonitis. The cavity of the abdomen in which the intestines and other organs lie is called the peritoneal cavity, and it is lined by a thin membrane called the peritoneum. When this becomes inflamed the condition is a serious one and is called *peritonitis.* Inflammation may be bacterial, as occurs following a burst appendix and the spillage of bacteria and pus in the cavity. It may be a sterile peritonitis as often follows perforation of a peptic ulcer, when the inflammation is caused by the acid contents of the stomach. It is always very dangerous, probably because of the large surface area afforded by the peritoneum for the absorption of inflammatory toxins.

Hæmorrhoids are simply varicose veins in the rectal and anal regions. They are very common, and are caused probably in about equal degrees by inherited weakness of the veins, strain such as heavy lifting, and constipation (this is one of the very few conditions in which constipation may do some damage, due to the mechanical pressure of hardened fæces in the rectum on the veins). Pregnant women are liable to develop hæmorrhoids or "piles," as they are commonly called, owing to the pressure of the baby's head in the pelvis. Hæmorrhoids may be external or internal, the former being in the anal region below the sphincter, the latter in the rectum; the two usually go together. There may be no symptoms, but the veins are liable to bleed, to get thrombosed (*i.e.*, a clot forms within) or to become infected. When clotting or infection occurs the piles enlarge and tend to be pushed out through the anus during defæcation, when they form extremely painful external swellings. Treatment in simple cases may be by the use of suppositories—cones of a firm grease containing suitable medicaments which are inserted in the rectum—in other cases the veins may be injected, as with varicose veins of the leg, in order to close them, but when there is

much bleeding, thrombosis, infection, or interference with bowel movements they should be removed surgically.

DISEASES OF THE LIVER.

The liver is the largest organ and has such a wide variety of known functions (to say nothing of the unknown) that it is also one of the most complicated. Nearly all of its functions are biochemical, and it is often called the laboratory of the body. Medical students, when asked to enumerate the functions of the liver, usually stick at about twenty-five, nearly all of them to do with general metabolism: that is the biochemical processing of substances taking part in structure or as body fuel. For example, the liver makes proteins from the amino-acids absorbed from the gut, and breaks down amino-acids and manufactures a waste product (urea) from them. It stores carbohydrates as glycogen, and conducts many of the processes necessary to turn carbohydrates into energy. It manufactures prothrombin with the help of vitamin K, and this is essential for blood clotting. It makes bile and secretes it into the gall bladder and bile ducts (*see later*). The three main constituents of bile (cholesterol, bile pigment or bilirubin, and bile acids) all have to be processed, or metabolised, in the liver during the production of bile. Vitamin B_{12} and iron is also stored and dealt with there, and these are involved in preventing various forms of anæmia (*q.v.*); and in addition to all these things the liver is the place where harmful substances, both from within the body and from outside it, are dealt with and rendered harmless. This last function of "detoxication" is often accomplished by making the offending molecules suitable for rapid excretion by the kidneys, or by altering their chemical shape to make them harmless.

Nearly all of these very different things are done by one single type of cell: the liver cell, and it is one of the remarkable features of the design that this cell can be so versatile. There also have to be some very efficient transport systems in the liver, in addition to the usual blood supply and venous drainage possessed by all other tissues.

One of these is the "portal venous system." Whenever a substance is absorbed across the gut wall from any part of the intestine into the interior of the body it enters the special draining blood vessels of the portal system, which are arranged throughout the length of the digestive tract. All these veins eventually unite in the main portal vein which enters the liver. Everything absorbed from the gut is therefore taken first to the liver to be processed. After this the products are carried away from the liver in the ordinary veins to the heart, and are distributed to the rest of the body by the arterial system. The liver has arteries of its own by which it receives oxygen and nutriment like any other tissue. The fourth transport system collects the bile as it is formed within the liver and delivers it to the gall bladder and bile ducts, which eventually drain it into the duodenum.

Portal Hypertension means high blood pressure in the portal venous system, and is the usual accompaniment to *cirrhosis* (*see later*). When the terminations of the portal veins in the liver are strangled and obstructed by cirrhotic disease, this tends to blow them up, or dilate them with blood. There is a natural escape route for the portal blood where the lower end of the œsophagus or gullet joins the upper end of the stomach. At this place some of the portal veins draining the stomach are connected with the ordinary veins draining the œsophagus so that when pressure rises in the portal system, blood tends to be diverted into these connecting veins, and they in turn become dilated, or varicose. Trouble begins when these dilated connecting veins, which bulge inwards into the œsophagus, are damaged by food particles passing across them and bleed severely into the stomach. The patient vomits large quantities of blood (*hæmatemesis*) or passes tarry altered blood in the stool (*melaena*). The other main cause of these is the bleeding which occasionally accompanies peptic ulcer (*q.v.*).

A second complication of portal hypertension (and hence of cirrhosis) is *ascites*, in which large amounts of a lymph-like fluid accumulate in the abdominal cavity. The fluid contains a great deal of precious protein and salt which is lost to the body economy. Ascites also sometimes accompanies cancerous deposits in the abdomen.

Jaundice means being yellow because there is too much yellow bile pigment circulating in the blood, and there are three main possible causes for this. The term "yellow jaundice," like "gastric stomach" is therefore unnecessarily redundant: there is no other kind.

Bile pigment comes from broken-down red blood cells, which normally come to the end of their time after existing for about 120 days. The breakdown products of red cells can always be found in the blood of normal people, but there is normally insufficient colour to show. Abnormal amounts of colour build up quite logically in any of the following three circumstances:

(1) If too many red cells are being destroyed and even the normal liver cannot deal with the amount of bile pigment produced, it piles up in the blood, and *hæmolytic jaundice* is the result. The expression simply means jaundice due to (abnormally large) red-cell destruction.

(2) If the liver cells are themselves sick and unable to cope even with the normal amounts of pigment from normal red-cell destruction. Here too the pigment will pile up and cause *hepatocellular jaundice*, or liver-cell jaundice.

(3) If the bile ducts carrying bile away from the liver are blocked, then bile will pile up behind the blockage and re-enter the blood stream, causing *obstructive jaundice*. In this case the rate of red-cell breakdown is normal, and the liver cells are normal: at least for a time.

It is enormously important for the treatment of jaundice for the doctor to diagnose its type correctly, since the treatment varies from surgical relief of obstruction to the medical treatment of viral infection or of excess red-cell destruction.

The so-called differential diagnosis of jaundice is often exceptionally difficult, and sometimes requires some very sophisticated laboratory tests and X-rays. At other times it is extremely easy and is obvious from a cursory glance at the urine and the stool. In any case all jaundice is a highly technical matter for the doctor who must be consulted early.

There is a special jaundice of newborn babies which resembles hæmolytic jaundice and can occasionally have serious consequences for the developing brain (*kernicterus*) if it is allowed to become too severe. When this is threatened, steps are taken to reduce the level of circulating bile pigment by replacement of the baby's blood or by other means.

The commonest cause of hepatocellular jaundice is infective or viral hepatitis. Obstructive jaundice is usually due either to blockage by gallstones (*q.v.*) or by a lump pressing on the bile ducts from an adjacent cancer. This can often be quite satisfactorily relieved by surgery.

Infective Hepatitis. There is a group of disorders affecting the liver which are caused by viruses. The incubation period is often very long, and the sickness and other debility caused is often quite severe and prolonged. One variety, known as serum sickness, is now much less common than a few years ago. It used to be transmitted by using the same needle for injections into several different people, or from transfusing contaminated blood. A greater awareness of the problem, and the use of disposable needles and syringes has cut down the incidence.

Cirrhosis. There are many different kinds of cirrhosis, the commonest of which has already

been mentioned under *portal hypertension* above. In all cases, liver cells are slowly poisoned and are killed off over a long period of time. In response to this, the surviving liver cells undergo cell division, trying to make good the numbers lost, and at the same time fibrous scar tissue replaces the damaged tissue throughout the organ. The result is a hard, knobbly liver. The many "knobs" are spherical areas of regenerated new cells, and they are separated by thickened bands of scar tissue. All of this destroys the normal architecture and leads to the portal hypertension and ascites mentioned above. In some countries (*e.g.*, France and the United States) excessive alcohol is the main cause of the original liver damage which starts it all off. In others (*e.g.*, Bantu South Africa) it seems to be nutritional starvation of the liver. In England much less than half the cases are due to alcohol, and many are thought to be due to a previous episode of infective hepatitis (*q.v.*), but this is not certain. Infective hepatitis is quite common but cirrhosis is comparatively rare. So that the great majority of people do not progress from one to the other. One day soon the treatment for advanced cirrhosis will be to replace the liver by transplantation, but there are still many problems to overcome before this can become routine.

Cancer of the Liver. Cancer of the liver is quite common, but it is nearly always cancer which has spread in the blood stream from other parts of the body. The liver is a favourite site for such secondary deposits, since it has a large blood supply and will receive a generous helping of anything being carried. It is also a very "fertile soil" for the cancer seedlings to grow in. Primary cancer of the liver is uncommon, and only occurs in a few cases of pre-existing cirrhosis.

Gallstones. These are "stones" formed by some of the major constituents of bile coming out of solution and forming solid bodies. They are very common, and often cause no trouble at all. When they do, it is usually a colicky intermittent severe pain. This is due to the muscular walls of the bile passages contracting in an effort to expel an obstructing stone into the duodenum. The second common trouble arising from gallstones is obstructive jaundice, described above. It is small consolation to gallstone sufferers that the stones are often very pretty, often being composed of beautiful cholesterol crystals coloured by varying shades of bile. If they contain calcium they will be visible on an X-ray. Otherwise they are not seen. Stones often occur in conjunction with inflammation of the gall bladder, known as *cholecystitis*. The treatment for gallstones is to remove them surgically together with the gall bladder if they are causing persistent symptoms. Ways of avoiding surgery by dissolving them in substances taken by mouth are under investigation.

The Pancreas.

This is a soft, elongated gland lying behind the stomach; it is about 12·5 cm long and 5 cm wide. Within its tissues lies the duct, which, when it leaves the pancreas, passes into the duodenum near the point of entry of the bile-duct. This duct transmits the juices containing enzymes which aid in the digestion in the small intestine. The pancreas, however, has two main functions: not only does it manufacture these important digestive juices, but in certain specialised areas, known as the islets of Langerhans, it manufactures insulin, the hormone which makes it possible for the body to utilise sugar. *Diabetes mellitus* or ordinary diabetes is a chronic disorder usually caused by a deficient secretion of insulin. The unused sugar accumulates in the blood and acts as a poison, which, in extreme cases, sends the patient into coma and may—indeed, in former times, usually did—result in death. The treatment of diabetes was revolutionised by the discovery of the hormone insulin by Banting and Best in 1921. On the whole, diabetes is more severe in young people than in the elderly, but with correct treatment it is possible for all cases to lead a perfectly normal life except for dietary restrictions and insulin injections. Not to be confused with *Diabetes insipidus* (**P43(2)**).

DIET.

When considering diet, and the effect it has on our health and well-being, there is more to it than just the things we eat. We must also know about what our body does with the food, and it would be unscientific not to acknowledge the effects of our psychological make-up and our nutritional beliefs on what we eat, what we do with it, and how well (or ill) we feel as a result.

For example, a deep-rooted conviction that brown eggs or free-range poultry are better for us than white eggs or intensively reared birds is entirely unsupported by any evidence. However, if we believe such a thing sufficiently, we will not only eat the " better " ones, but we will feel happier and more secure afterwards, and this is likely to make us healthier. Food fads can occasionally be dangerous, as when extreme vegetarians become ill through lack of certain vitamins (*e.g.* B_1) which are present only in the foods they exclude. But this is so rare, even among strict vegetarians, that such danger can virtually be ignored. On the whole (and vegetarianism is probably a good example of this) food faddism often leads to a sense of health and well-being in the believer, and should not be attacked by the rest of us for that. It is an accepted fact that personal misfortune, even when it is severe, is more easily withstood by those with strong religious conviction than by others. In the same way, a firm attachment to a theory of what is good for you can produce a feeling of well-being and genuine good health, when another person on exactly the same food intake will not feel so fit. These factors—religious belief, food faddism, or the bedside manner of a kind or persuasive doctor —are commonly dismissed by free-thinking people because they are not " true " or " real." All three, however, can materially affect our health just as can a shock, a personal tragedy or being in love. The trouble starts, and the magic ceases to work, when adherents declaim their beliefs as *ex cathedra* truths and expect the rest of us to swallow them as wholly (or holy) as they do.

Thus there are genuine *facts* about food, and fallacies too; and as well as these there is a no-man's-land between in which one man's fact is another man's fallacy (*see also* Part III)

The basic constituents of any diet are protein, fats, carbohydrates, water, vitamins, minerals, salts, and indigestible roughage. All are chemicals whose structure and function are reasonably well understood. Even the mystical differences between fine table wines, so beloved of the connoisseur and gourmet, are reasonably well understood in chemical terms. Perhaps that is a pity.

Much nonsense is talked, especially by nutritionists, about minimal daily requirements. In general terms, however, requirements can be described in terms of how many calories there are in the total intake of proteins, fats, and carbohydrates per day, and how these are distributed between the three classes of food. The other substances mentioned above are only required in trace or small amounts except for water; and roughage is only required as a mechanical stimulus to bowel movement.

During the process of digestion (described on P34–5) all proteins are split into their constituent amino acids; all carbohydrates are split into their constituent simple sugars and most fats are converted into fatty acids and glycerol. At this stage, and not until this stage, all these simpler building bricks derived from the three classes of food are absorbed into the body proper, and taken to the liver and other tissues. Here they are " metabolised." That is to say they are either burned as fuel for the various processes of the body; or they are built up again into proteins, fats, and carbohydrates of the special kinds the body needs. They will either be used to rebuild structures suffering ordinary wear and tear or they will be stored. Many of them will be converted into a different class from the one they came from when they entered the body. For example, excess carbohydrate is converted into fat; or if there is a shortage of carbohydrate, some will be made out of the protein amino-acids which would normally have been used for tissue growth and repair. Thus it is only a generalisation to say that dietary carbohydrates are fuel and proteins are for building bodily structure. The body can convert one into the other, and spoil the calculation.

There is a great deal of confusion in people's minds about *energy*, and that is why the word *fuel* has been used above in connection with carbohydrates. The lay person uses energy as a term meaning something which allows us to leap about, running and jumping and skipping and dancing, and which keeps us from getting tired and run down. Thus, the food industry tells us, we need potatoes or breakfast cereals for these activities or for a hard day's work. This is a deliberate commercial confidence trick, and the scientist is largely to blame. He originally handed out the word energy to an eager food industry and an unsuspecting public, forgetting to explain that he meant it in the strictly scientific sense of fuel for bodily processes. It simply is not true that more potatoes, or more cornflakes will make you more active. Indeed the reverse is the case, and after a certain point they will only be converted into fat and reduce your activity. The nutritionist measures energy as calories, which are units of heat, and it is certainly true that you must eat enough of these each day if you wish to remain alive, let alone active.

All the three main classes of food provide calories, and in an ordinary well-balanced diet about 15% are provided by protein. Carbohydrates produce most of the remainder. Each gram of fat contains about twice the calories of a similar quantity of carbohydrate. We simply eat less fat than carbohydrate, because fat has a " high satiety value." It takes away the appetite for more. Proteins are mostly found in meat, fish, eggs, cheese, and milk. However, there is quite a lot of protein in many predominantly starchy foods like bread, and such grains as wheat, rice, and corn. Carbohydrates are mainly found in bread, potatoes, sugar, pastry, sweets, and so forth. That is one of the words which fortunately seems to be used by both scientists and laymen in much the same sense.

Some substances are absolutely essential to the body if life is to continue, even if they are only needed in trace amounts. These are substances which the body's own factories (like the liver) cannot make for themselves, even if they are provided with the correct ingredients.

One group of such substances are the *vitamins*. Some of these are found in predominantly fatty foods (milk, butter, cheese and so on) and are known as the fat-soluble vitamins—Vitamins A, D, E and K; the others are water-soluble—the Vitamin B group and Vitamin C. All have now been chemically identified, are manufactured and can be bought over a pharmacist's counter. The myth has grown up that if a little is good for one then a lot more will be better and there are a great many vitamin enthusiasts who consume vast quantities of such manufactured products in the belief that by doing so they will induce extra vitality and energy. Unless your diet is unbalanced in some way (a vegan diet may be grossly deficient in Vitamin B12) you will not need extra vitamins—with certain reservations, *see* Part III.

Thankfully, most people buy food because they like it, not because it does them good; and provided they have normal dietary tastes they will usually get a perfectly adequate selection of the things we have spoken of as necessary for good health. The main danger in England is to have a surfeit and become overweight. In addition there are certain times of life when conscious attention should be paid to what is necessary. For example babies and nursing mothers have special dietary needs and will hear about them from their Health Visitor or from their Welfare Clinic or Doctor. Elderly people living alone are also prone to dietary deficiencies for reasons ranging from poverty to loss of appetite or inability to look after themselves properly.

Recent surveys have revealed some interesting facts about people's attitude to food and their knowledge of it. For example, half the people asked knew that meat was a source of protein, a third mentioned eggs and a fifth cheese, fish, and milk. But practically no one knew there was protein in bread. Yet in England about a fifth of our daily protein intake comes from bread, and nearly a third from cereals as a whole. Fish is well known as a source of protein, but did you know that on average we only obtain 4% of our daily protein from fish—less than we get from potatoes (5%)? No one seems to know that potatoes are an important source of vitamin C, although fruit and vegetables are well-known sources. Calcium is recognised in milk, but most people forget its presence in cheese. Most people are very confused about iron. Why does everyone think it is mainly in green vegetables, when these are really such a poor source? For our daily requirement of iron we would each have to eat 1 kg. spring greens or peas; or 2 kg. of sprouts! In fact meat provides one of our best sources, and one-fifth of our daily needs is contained in bread.

Since most of the people who read *Pears* live in England let us return finally to our commonest nutritional disease, or our commonest form of malnutrition in these islands: obesity. Call it " being overweight " if you like, but acknowledge that it means being fat. Being fat is not only unattractive and unsightly but it is dangerous to health and carries a high mortality. Ask any life insurance company how they view your chances if you are overweight and you will find they are as worried about it as if you had high blood pressure, or smoke heavily. It is a particularly important cause of heart disease. However, it is very important to know exactly what we mean by fatness. Many girls who are not at all fat think they are, and this leads them to diet unnecessarily. On the other hand there are people who do not appreciate they are overweight. Here is a table which shows what your weight should be according to your height.

If you are overweight according to these tables you need to slim, and the question is how? Answer: by will-power. There is no other satisfactory method than to decide to eat less, and to eat as little carbohydrate as possible. For the time being eat as much meat, fruit, green vegetables, and as much fat as you like, but no sugar, starch, sweets, cakes, pastry, or biscuits, and no eating between meals. And cut down on beer and other alcoholic drinks. In case you are tempted to eat " slimming " foods, be aware that there is no such thing. There is nothing you can eat which will cause you to lose weight, in spite of what the advertisement says. In special cases doctors will prescribe tablets to suppress appetite, but they are too dangerous for general use without supervision, and they do not work as well as will-power. At the same time take more exercise. Walk to work. If you make a real and genuine effort for three months without success, you should ask your doctor for advice. Almost certainly you will have to admit you have not really tried. Good luck! (*see also* Part III).

NUTRITIONAL DISORDERS.

Nutritional Deficiency and Malnutrition.—Until quite recently a consideration of malnutrition would have merely led to an account of how too

DESIRABLE WEIGHTS FOR MEN AND WOMEN ACCORDING TO HEIGHT AND FRAME, AGES 25 AND OVER

Men Height (in shoes 2·5 cm heels)	Weight in kilograms (in indoor clothing)		
	Small frame	Medium frame	Large frame
157	51–54·5	53·5–59	57–64
160	52–56	55–60·5	59–65·5
162	53·5–57	56–62	60–67
165	55–59	58–63	61–69
167	56–60·5	59–65	63–71
170	58–62	61–67	64·5–73
172	60–64	63–69	67–75·5
175	62–66	64·5–71	68·5–77
177	63·5–68	66–72·5	70·5–79
180	65·5–70	68–75	72–81
183	67–72	70–77	74–83·5
185	69–73·5	72–79·5	76–86
188	71–76	73·5–82	78·5–88
190	72·5–77·5	76–84	81–90·5
193	74·5–79·5	78–86	82·5–93

Women Height (in shoes 5 cm heels)	Weight in kilograms (in indoor clothing)		
	Small frame	Medium frame	Large frame
147	42–44·5	43·5–48·5	47–54
150	43–46	44·5–50	48–55·5
152	43·5–47	46–51	49·5–57
155	45–48·5	47–53	51–58
157	46–50	48·5–54	52–59·5
160	48–51	50–55·5	53·5–61
162	49–53	51–57	55–63
165	50·5–54	53–59	57–64·5
167	52–56	54·5–61	59–66
170	53·5–58	56–63	60·5–68
172	55·5–59·5	58–65	62–70
175	57–61	60–67	64–72
177	59–63·5	62–68·5	66–74
180	61–65·5	63·5–70·5	68–76
183	63–67	65·5–72	69·5–78·5

little food, or a deficiency of certain articles in the diet, produced deficiency diseases at the time of the restriction. For example lack of vitamins of various kinds gives rise to such diseases as rickets, scurvy, beri-beri, and pellagra; and an overall shortage of food to general starvation. These may be considered the immediate or concurrent effects of a poor diet. Modern nutritionists, however, are beginning to be concerned with two more kinds of nutritional disorders; and although the study of both kinds is in its infancy, both will be introduced in this account.

The first deals with the effects of comparatively small amounts of harmful constituents in our diet, introduced either voluntarily or involuntarily, and consumed for a long period of time; and the second with the lasting effects on our adult well-being of nutritional deficiencies in early life even though they have long since been corrected.

When viewed in this light, one or other of these three kinds of nutritional disorder may at this moment be affecting almost every individual in every part of the world, " privileged " or " underprivileged." Let us first define some terms.

Undernutrition, strictly speaking, means a state of affairs in which the quality of the diet is perfectly good. There is the correct balance of the various dietary constituents and all the necessary components are present: but there is simply too little of it. Many hundreds of millions of people throughout the underprivileged world are suffering and dying from this kind of undernutrition, and the simplicity of the problem must be appreciated: they simply need more food of the kind they are at present getting, and which can often be produced locally.

Malnutrition means an imbalance of the various constituents: a relative lack or excess of one or more of them. It usually leads to conditions which are, from the point of view of medical treatment, much more difficult to deal with. And therefore doctors often class them as " more serious."

The diseases of malnutrition range from the widespread protein deficiencies in other parts of the underprivileged world to *obesity* in our own better-off industrial countries, which is usually due to excess carbohydrate. Make no mistake about it: obesity (or being overweight) is a widespread disease of nutritional imbalance, and it kills. It is the commonest form of malnutrition in (for example) England and America today, and is a consequence of the sophistication of our diet in modern times. Between one-fifth and one-tenth of the population of the United States is more than 20% overweight, and to be 10% or 15% overweight is almost the rule nowadays in people over thirty. There are high authorities in the world of nutritional science who attribute all this overfed malnutrition to the consumption of refined sugar, or sucrose. They say it is not only the amount of refined sugar we put in our tea or on our breakfast cereals, but also the amount in sweet cakes, biscuits, drinks, chocolates and sweets, and so forth. For some people it adds up to a phenomenal quantity each day. According to this school of thought we are not so much suffering from a surfeit of carbohydrates or starches, but from this single sugar, sucrose. It is interesting to reflect on the recent banning of the artificial sweetener, cyclamate, by many governments. This substance, having been used extensively throughout the world as an apparently harmless non-fattening substitute for sugar, was suddenly banned in America because in very large doses (equivalent to the amount taken in hundreds of cups of coffee per day for a long time) it was found to produce cancer in rats. It has never been shown to do humans any harm, whereas the effects of sugar in producing an overweight population, thereby indirectly kill tens of thousands of British people each year. This is a fascinating example of the difficulties confronting our legislators in making balanced judgments when deciding to ban a foodstuff, a drug, or an artificial fertiliser.

Much the most widespread form of malnutrition, however, is a variety protein-lack which is part of a collection of nutritional diseases known as *Protein-Calorie Deficiency*. In very large underprivileged areas of the world, the childhood population receives such an inadequate diet that children live continuously on the brink of nutritional disaster. It only requires a small extra restriction or stress to topple them over into one of the clinical conditions to be described. At this stage they cease to be merely hungry. They become nutritionally ill. Sometimes the force which produces the disaster is a community catastrophe like a famine, an earthquake, or a war. Sometimes it is a family catastrophe like the loss of a lactating mother or a parental delinquency. Parents abandon young children as often in Africa as anywhere else. Sometimes the clinical nutritional disease is unmasked by a common childhood illness like measles, or gastro-enteritis which the well-fed child would have overcome. The starved child reveals his malnutrition instead and frequently dies. When the precipitating cause of the " epidemic " of malnutrition is a war or other national calamity, our newspapers and television screens carry distressing pictures of thin skeletal, pot-bellied children, and the conscience of a few is touched. It is insufficiently realised that these scenes can be witnessed anywhere in the continents of Africa and Asia, and in large parts of Central and South America any day of the week in normal times. The war has not been the cause, but is only the precipitating factor which has revealed the chronic malnutrition in more children than would normally exhibit it openly.

Protein-Calorie Deficiency is a collection of different kinds of childhood malnutrition. Some are due predominantly to deficiency of protein and are collectively called Kwashiorkor, a West African word meaning " red-haired boy " (see below). Others are mainly due to a severe deficiency of overall foodstuffs and are called *Marasmus*. But in any real-life situation the severe *mal*nutrition of Kwashiorkor exists side-by-side with all gradations between itself and the severe *under*nutrition of Marasmus, so that many intermediate forms of " marasmic kwashiorkor " are described. In kwashiorkor the child is typically listless, apathetic, whining, with a reddish discoloration of the hair, a peeling, scaly skin, and with much extra fluid in his tissues causing œdema. He is so listless as not even to be hungry. In marasmus the child is ravenously hungry. He is extremely thin and " starved " looking and is quite a different picture.

There is good reason to believe that even when protein-calorie deficiency is successfully treated, there will always be some lasting restriction of mental function, particularly if the malnutrition occurred as early as the first year of life. This is especially true in situations of appalling poverty in towns, where thousands of babies are not breastfed because their mothers are at work. Many of them die. Some of them are no heavier than their birth weight at one year of age. Breast feeding in an underprivileged community is an essential insurance for childhood health and survival.

Two new avenues of nutritional inquiry were mentioned at the beginning of this section. The impact of very long continued intake of refined sugar over many years on our bodily health is an example of one of them. Scientists and others are also becoming alarmed at the effects of modern food additives when taken, even in small amounts, over a long period. These additives include colouring matter, decolourising chemicals, taste " enhancers," and so forth, which are present in everyone's diet in a " civilised community." We are as unable to avoid a constant dosage with them as if they had been added to our water supply. It is, however, difficult to strike a balanced attitude. It is one thing to suspect that these additives are harmful and quite another to prove it. Naturally if any of them are shown to produce harm in animals given reasonable quantities they are invariably withdrawn. But in practice it is extremely difficult for animal experiments to mimic the conditions of human intake, especially as the human life span involves eating the substance concerned in small quantities for several decades. Thus it is easy to postulate the harmful effects of monosodium glutamate (a very common taste enhancer) but practically impossible to prove the question either way. It is not sufficient to condemn " chemicals." All natural foods consist of chemicals, and so do we. *See also* **Part III.**

The other new topic in nutrition is more soundly based on animal experiment. It has been repeatedly found that if animals do not grow quickly enough at certain early periods of life, they not only become small, but they remain smaller than they should be even when they are subsequently given as much as they like to eat. This is true of all animals and birds so far studied. For example, if rats are suckled in large families it is found that they are smaller by the time they are weaned (3 weeks of age) than those suckled in small families. The interesting thing is that if they are then given as much as they want to eat for the rest of their lives, the small animals from the larger families never catch up to the others. Whereas if their growth is not restricted until later in their " childhood," full " catch-up " is possible soon after normal diet is resumed. In other words there is a critical time in early life when growth can be permanently affected. At the moment it is difficult to know whether the same is true of humans and, if so, when is our period of vulnerability. There is some suggestion that the corresponding critical period in humans is during the last part of gestation in the uterus, and the first year or so of postnatal life. This new idea may turn out to be very important for world nutrition. Since there will not be enough food for all the children all the time, it may become important to concentrate our aid to underprivileged countries on certain sections of the population only. It may be a good idea to see that pregnant mothers and small babies are specially fed. In this way we may be able to put off the periods of inevitable malnutrition until a time of life when it is recoverable. Such a plan would also go a long way to safeguarding the development of the brain which also occurs mostly at the same early time of life.

We shall now describe some of the better-known nutritional deficiencies, bearing in mind that vitamin deficiencies are virtually unknown in the better-off countries. No one in England need spend money buying vitamins, as has been emphasised in the preceding section. Vitamin deficiency can still occur, however, in elderly people living alone and not having a well-balanced diet. It also occurs for similar reasons in alcoholics, vagrants, etc., and very occasionally in small children.

Beri-beri is a group of diseases usually confined to the Far East where a diet of polished rice results in a poor intake of vitamin B_1 (thiamine). In one form there is œdema (*q.v.*); in another the peripheral nerves are affected leading to tingling and numbness. A similar condition is occasionally seen in alcoholics and diabetics. Treatment is with thiamine, and with other vitamins too, since most sufferers are going short of more than one.

Pellagra is found among maize-eating populations and is due to a deficiency of several vitamins including niacin, another member of the B group of vitamins. There is dermatitis on exposed skin, and soreness of the mouth and tongue, with gastro-enteritis.

Scurvy is due to vitamin C deficiency. In children bone growth is affected. At all ages there is bleeding into the skin (bruising), impaired wound healing, mental depression, and anæmia. Most fresh fruit and vegetables contain vitamin C and a diet containing these prevents the disease.

Vitamin A deficiency is commonly found in children in some underprivileged countries. It causes permanent blindness, with thickening opacity and dryness of the whites of the eyes leading to ulceration of the eye. Beyond a certain stage, therefore, a child's sight cannot be saved. The only real hope is prevention, with an adequate diet.

Rickets, another disease of early childhood, is caused by deficiency of vitamin D. Bones are not properly calcified, and their softness leads to deformities of the legs and many other bones. Vitamin D can either be eaten in the diet or produced under the skin under the influence of sunlight. Therefore rickets commonly occurs when both the diet and the sunlight are inadequate. It was once very common in industrial England, and is still to be seen very occasionally there and in impoverished urban communities in the United States.

DISEASES OF THE ENDOCRINE GLANDS.

Glands are structures or organs which manufacture secretions (except for *lymph glands* which are not glands at all and should be called *lymph nodes*). The secretions are of two main kinds. The first are passed down tubes, or ducts, or are secreted directly into the hollow organs, and act locally. Good examples are the salivary glands which make saliva and pass it down ducts into the mouth for digestion of its contents and lubrication. These are *exocrine glands*. The second kind have no ducts, and secrete their product straight into the blood stream. This secretion is called a *hormone* and it is carried to all parts of the body by the blood where it acts at a distance on some remote part. These are the *endocrine glands* or *ductless glands*, and a number of them will be discussed in this section.

The first hormone, or "chemical messenger," was discovered by the British physiologist Starling in 1904, but the effects of removing some of the endocrine glands were known centuries before when removal of the male testes (castration) was practised to procure a form of manpower safe for the harem, to salvage a good male alto voice for the church choir, or to convert a rooster into a more eatable capon.

Anterior Pituitary.—Many of the endocrine glands do not act as separate autonomous organs in spite of their great differences. They are organised into a well-disciplined band by a "master-gland" called the anterior pituitary. Somebody once called it the "conductor of the endocrine orchestra" and the phrase is still repeated *ad nauseam* in students' examination papers. The pituitary, consisting of its two parts, anterior and posterior, is not much bigger than a pea and it sits right in the middle of the skull, centrally beneath the brain and joined to the brain by a short stalk. This astonishing tiny nodule of tissue produces at least eight important hormones.

One of these is *growth hormone*, which is necessary for normal growth, and also has an influence on insulin. An excess causes *gigantism* and *acromegaly*, often coinciding with diabetes, and too little results in a form of dwarfism. Three others, known as *gonadotrophic hormones* regulate the cyclical and other activities of the reproductive organs and lactating breast. Another, *thyrotrophic hormone*, regulates thyroid activity, *Adrenocorticotrophic hormone*, or *ACTH*, as its name implies, looks after the activities of another important endocrine gland, the adrenal cortex. And there are several others.

Hypopituitarism, including *Simmonds' disease* and *Sheehan's disease*, results from destruction of the anterior pituitary. It is extremely rare, and is usually associated with difficult childbirth involving very severe bleeding. There are disturbances of all the functions mentioned above, particularly thyroid and adrenal failure (*q.v.*) with upset sexual function. Treatment is by replacing the lost hormones.

Hyperpituitarism, including *gigantism* and *acromegaly*, results from over-activity of the anterior pituitary, and is usually due to a tumour or overgrowth of the gland. In acromegaly the growth hormone is produced in excess over a long period of time in an adult. This results in overgrowth of all the organs except the brain, and it is characteristic to find enlarged extremities—feet, hands, and jaw. In gigantism the same has occurred during childhood before the bones have stopped growing and the result is a person who may be 2 m tall or more.

Posterior Pituitary. The posterior part of the gland is really a quite separate gland. The main hormone it produces is concerned with the excretion of urine by the kidney (antidiuretic hormone). Deficiency of the hormone results in *Diabetes Insipidus*, not to be confused with *Diabetes Mellitus* or "sugar diabetes." In diabetes insipidus, the patient produces enormous quantities of dilute urine. He consequently has a prodigious thirst and consumes astonishing quantities of fluids. Treatment is by replacing the missing hormone.

Thyroid. The thyroid gland in the neck secretes an iodine-containing hormone called thyroxine. Excess of it causes *hyperthyroidism*, *thyrotoxicosis*, or *Graves' disease*. Lack of it produces *cretinism* in the growing child or *myxoedema* in the adult. Thyroxine is concerned with the metabolic rate of cells throughout the body, or the rate at which they work, as well as with the proper growth of developing tissues, especially the brain. Too much thyroxine as in thyrotoxicosis leads to over-activity, warm sweatiness in an over-excitable patient whose pulse is rapid and who is eating ravenously to try to replace the wasted energy. In spite of his appetite he is very thin, and he often has bulging eyes for a reason not understood. Treatment is by drugs which neutralise the thyroxine or by cutting out some of the gland. A *cretin* is a child usually born with insufficient thyroid. He is destined to grow poorly, and to mental subnormality of a permanent and distressing kind. If the condition is diagnosed soon after birth treatment with thyroxine can avert most of the trouble. In myxoedema, thyroxine is deficient in an adult. They become slow in all their bodily processes, the hair thins and their flesh is puffy with a dry, wrinkled skin. Treatment is by thyroid replacement. *Goitre* simply means enlargement of the gland. It may be accompanied by overactivity or underactivity, or with little functional change. One variety (Derbyshire neck) occurs in areas short of iodine in the soil and drinking water.

Adrenal Cortex. The adrenal or suprarenal glands sit, as the name implies, one on top of each kidney. There are two distinct parts: the cortex or outside which secretes steroid hormones, and the *adrenal medulla*, or core, which secretes adrenalin. There are many different steroid hormones in the adrenal cortical secretion, which look after such divers matters as sodium and potassium balance, sexual function, the reaction of the body to stress, and the regulation of sugar levels. *Addison's disease* (not to be confused with Addisonian anæmia) results from adrenal cortical insufficiency, and is often due to destruction of the gland by tuberculosis. There is weariness-malaise, pigmentation of skin creases and mucous membranes. They are short of sodium and have excess potassium. Treatment is with cortisone (replacement of the missing hormone) and by extra salt by mouth for the lack of sodium. *Cushing's* disease is due to excessive adrenal cortical function, and sometimes also occurs in patients treated with cortisone for other purposes. They have a striking redistribution of fat in the face, neck, and trunk, with stretch marks similar to those acquired by most women during pregnancy. The facial obesity makes them "moon-faced," and female patients may suffer masculinisation with deepening of the voice and hirsutism.

Testis. The male testes, as well as producing sperm are also endocrine glands producing steroid hormones known as androgens. They are mainly concerned with maintaining secondary sex characteristics. At the time of puberty the controlling secretions from the anterior pituitary begin to appear and androgens are produced. There is a whole range of rare disorders, resulting in everything from precocious puberty to delayed puberty. It should be born in mind that the normal time of puberty can vary by several years from one boy to another.

Ovary. The human ovary has two functions: to produce ova, or eggs; and to produce two hormones, oestrogen and progesterone. These functions begin at puberty, one of whose features in the female is the onset of menstruation, or menarche. Just as in boys, the timing of normal puberty is very variable, but on the average, girls achieve puberty before boys. As social conditions improve, the age of menarche is getting younger generation by generation. All the secondary sex characteristics are under the control of the ovarian hormones which are released in response to the appropriate anterior pituitary hormones. The changes which occur in the womb and elsewhere in the intervals between menstrual periods and the periods themselves are controlled by a cyclical or rhythmic secretion, first of oestrogen and then of progesterone, by the ovary. This cycle is upset by pregnancy to allow the development of the embryo. It can also be upset by taking certain combinations of the two hormones by mouth. These can prevent the formation of ova, and are a popular form of contraception. In late middle age, the ovaries lose their function, the menstrual cycles cease to occur, and reproductive life is at an end. This is called the *menopause* or "change of life," and is sometimes accompanied for a time by distressing symptoms due to a temporary imbalance between oestrogen and progesterone. Many sexual functions, however, continue well after the menopause into old age, and these can include a continuing libido or sexual desire.

Parathyroid. Four tiny parathyroid glands are buried behind the thyroid gland and are responsible for regulating the body calcium and phosphate. They are therefore particularly important for the building and maintenance of bones and teeth. Since a proper calcium level in the blood is necessary for muscle (including heart muscle) contraction, and for correct functioning of nerves, disorders of the parathyroids can give rise to muscular spasms as well as loss of bone calcium. The latter can result in fragility and fractures. Overactivity of the glands leads to too much calcium and the formation of stones especially in the kidney.

Pineal. We end this section with a mystery gland. Like the pituitary it is small—about the size of a pea—and sits well back at the base of the brain. It was endowed in ancient times with metaphysical properties all of which remain speculative. In fish and lizards and certain lower vertebrates it is a kind of third eye, and receives light. In higher mammals, like ourselves, it is so far from any source of light that it could scarcely do so. It can be removed without harm. Indeed it normally becomes calcified and inactive about the time of puberty, and its position seen on X-rays of the skull can be a good guide to whether the brain is being pushed to one side by an abnormal mass.

DISEASES OF THE URINARY SYSTEM.

Everyone knows what kidneys look like—in fact, the term "kidney-shaped" is used to describe other objects. Within the kidneys the blood vessels carrying waste materials subdivide and finally end up in little coils or glomeruli through which waste products are filtered into the other system, the system of tubes which, beginning as tiny cups around the glomeruli, become larger and larger until they join the ureter passing out at the root of the kidney, the hilum, a point at which both the veins and tubes enter and leave. The kidneys, of course, lie one on each side in the loins, so that if one puts one's hands on the hips and then slides them farther back they will cover the area over the left and right kidney. The ureters pass down on each side to the bladder, which is the storage tank of the products excreted by the kidneys, and lies in the mid-line down low in the abdomen; it is somewhat pear-shaped, and at its base in men there lies the prostate gland—a gland which apparently has few functions but can be a nuisance. Its only known function is that it adds something to the semen from the testes without which the semen would be sterile. Then, from the base of the bladder a single tube, the urethra, passes to the outside. One can, in fact, visualise the urinary system as a capital Y, in which the two upper limbs are the ureters, the place where they meet is the bladder, and the single limb at the foot is the urethra. Clearly, then, there may be diseases of the kidneys, of the ureters, of the bladder, of the prostate gland, or of the urethra.

The amount of urine may be increased or diminished. It is *increased* in the following conditions: after drinking excess of fluids; after taking drugs (known as *diuretics*) which are given to increase the flow; in diabetes of both types—mellitus and insipidus; in some types of chronic kidney disease; and finally, in emotional states of excitement. It is *decreased* in the following conditions: acute nephritis; any disease in which fluid is being lost in other ways, such as diarrhœa or sweating in fevers; when the fluid intake is small; and when both ureters are blocked by stones. Passing a great deal of urine is known as *polyuria*, passing very little as *oliguria*, passing frequent small amounts is simply called *frequency*. Normally, the urine is acid, but in infections of the bladder it may become alkaline owing to decomposition by bacteria. Abnormal substances, or normal substances in abnormal quantities, may occur in the urine and give the doctor an indication of what is wrong. In fact, urine analysis is a very important part of medical diagnosis. Thus urea is a normal content of urine which is increased in fevers, wasting diseases, or diabetes; the amount of urea is to some extent a measure of the degree of tissue breakdown. Uric acid is found in small quantities in normal urine, but the amount is increased in fevers and after an attack of gout (uric acid is important in the causation of gout, but has nothing at all to do with rheumatism in general, so one may disregard the advertisements in the popular Press showing unpleasant pictures of joints with sharp crystals of uric acid which are alleged to cause the pain of rheumatic disease). Oxalates are not ordinarily found in urine, but, since they occur in such foods as rhubarb and strawberries, and some people are unable to deal with them, such individuals may develop stones or have pain on passing urine after eating oxalate-containing fruits.

Two very important substances which ought not to be in normal urine are albumen and sugar. Albumen is a protein, and its presence in the urine indicates that the filters of the kidney are leaking —they are allowing protein to pass out which ought to remain in the body. Albumen is easily tested for, and its presence may indicate kidney disease or nephritis as it is usually called by doctors. On the other hand, small amounts of albumen occur in fevers and in nervous conditions —*functional albuminuria*. Sugar, too, should not be present, but its presence does not necessarily indicate diabetes; for small amounts may occur in nervous conditions or in some people after taking large quantities of carbohydrate.

Blood in the urine may give it an appearance which varies from bright red to a dark, smoky colour. It is found in many diseases: acute nephritis, stone, tumours, poisoning by certain drugs, infections such as bilharzia or malaria, papilloma (*i.e.*, non-malignant tumour of the bladder), after injury, in high blood-pressure, scurvy, and blood diseases. Sometimes it occurs for no known reason at all.

It will be remembered (or if it is not, you can look it up on P28 (1)) that streptococcal infection of the throat may cause in some people disease of the valves in the heart or endocarditis. In such cases, although the germ is found in the throat, it is not found in the heart or indeed anywhere else in the body. *Acute nephritis* occurs in the same circumstances, with the sole difference that the kidneys instead of the heart are affected. The disease appears to be an allergic reaction to the toxins of the streptococcus. The patient, often a child, has a sore throat (and even this may be absent or fail to be noticed) or sometimes the infection may arise in other sites: after scarlet fever, erysipelas, burns, and disease of the ear. A few days later there is headache, vomiting, pain in the loins, slight rise in temperature, and especially typical is *dropsy* or œdema. This begins in the face, first around the eyelids, and then affects the ankles; later it may become more general and affect the rest of the body. Blood and albumen are found in the urine, and the blood-pressure is slightly raised. The outlook is usually good if the kidneys are rested by reducing the amount of protein taken in and also the amounts of salt and water. When this is done, the in-flammation soon goes and no permanent harm results. In other cases, however, if treatment is inadequate or the condition severe, the symptoms may go, but the albumen found in the urine persists. This means that permanent damage has been done, and although there may be nothing else to show for many years, *chronic nephritis* develops. In this case, the blood-pressure con-tinues to rise, and since the filters of the kidneys no longer work efficiently, urea, the principal waste-product of the body to be excreted in the urine, is retained in the blood and only small amounts escape from the system. Hence chronic nephritis sooner or later leads to heart failure or hæmorrhage in the brain from the rising blood-pressure, or to the form of poisoning known as *uræmia* which results from the retention of urea in the blood. Uræmia may come on suddenly or gradually, but ends in progressive coma, drowsi-ness, and unconsciousness. There may be con-vulsions similar to those of epilepsy, high fever, and difficulty in breathing to complicate the pic-ture.

Another type of nephritis which seems to have nothing at all to do with streptococcal infections, and the cause of which is completely unknown, is *nephrosis*. Developing in early adult life, its onset is insidious, and the patient first shows signs of œdema in his white and puffy face and the swelling of his legs. (It should be said here that if you have swelling of the ankles or elsewhere, you would be foolish to jump to conclusions; for such swelling is common in many diseases—in heart disease, in allergic conditions, in neurotic illness, and even just from hot weather.) When the urine is examined in a case of nephrosis it is found to be full of albumen and, as in chronic nephritis, the blood urea starts to rise. The end-results of nephrosis are the same as those of chronic nephritis and depend upon the damage originally done.

The modern diuretics of the thiazide group help to control the œdema and, provided enough healthy tissue remains, remove both the fluid and the waste-products.

In recent years there have been considerable advances in the development of the artificial kidney. Once only used within hospital, artificial kidneys or dialysers as they are known. can now be used in patients' own homes, thus obviating in some cases long journeys to hospital twice a week for treatment. Dialysis is a relatively temporary measure; renal transplants now offer real hope to many sufferers although there are far more suitable recipients than there are potential donors.

Pyelitis is an infection of the pelvis of the kidney, that is to say, of the part where the ureter leaves the kidney. It is usually caused by the bacillus coli, which is normally present in the body, or by the streptococcus. These germs may reach the ureter through the blood-stream or may pass upwards from the bladder. Obstruction anywhere in the urinary tract which causes the urine to stagnate is liable to cause pyelitis. Symptoms come on suddenly, with high fever,

pain in the loin (the infection is usually on one side only, and is commoner in women), and pain in the abdomen. When urine is passed there is a burning sensation, and it is passed frequently and in small amounts. On examination, the urine is found to be highly acid and full of bacillus coli or whatever the causative germ may be. Pyelitis is fairly readily treated by the antibiotics or sulpha drugs. Plenty of fluids should be given and the urine made alkaline by administration of alkalis.

Cystitis means inflammation of the bladder, either acute or chronic, and its causes are much the same as in the case of pyelitis. There is pain over the lower abdomen, frequency, and sometimes slight fever. The treatment is as for pyelitis. *Urethritis* is an inflammation of the urethra, with burning pain on passing water and frequency. The most serious cause (although it can usually be easily dealt with now) is gonorrhœa. But non-specific urethritis is common, and in this case various germs or none may bring about pain and frequency; there is often a large neurotic element. Urethritis should be regarded as probably due to gonorrhœa, which has already been discussed elsewhere, when there is a thick, creamy discharge from the penis or discharge in women following sexual intercourse with an infected person.

Kidney stones or Renal calculi sometimes form, and, as in the case of gall-stones, what causes them is not certain. They may be caused by disorders of metabolism—that is, in the inability of the body to deal with calcium, proteins, uric acid, and other products; or by vitamin deficiency, obstruction in the urinary tract, and urinary infections. But when a stone or stones are formed various events may occur: thus it may remain in the kidney and cause no symptoms; or it may cause repeated attacks of pain, infection, and blood in the urine (hæmaturia); or it may completely block the passage of urine from the kidney to such a degree that it degenerates and becomes useless; or, lastly, it may pass into the ureter, and when this occurs very severe pain, known as *renal colic*, will occur. A stone passing down the ureter into the bladder may become stuck in the urethra, although this is uncommon, since a stone small enough to get down the ureters is likely to be capable of manœuvring through the rest of the tract. In fact, about 80–90 per cent. of stones are passed spontaneously. Stones not passed spontaneously may have to be removed by operation, but whether this is undertaken or not depends on various factors, such as the general health of the patient, the amount of trouble caused by the stone, and the health of the other kidney —for it is dangerous to operate on one kidney unless one is sure that the other is functioning efficiently.

If a stone blocks the passage of urine on one side for any length of time *hydronephrosis* may result, in which the part where the ureter enters the kidney swells with the retained urine. Ulti-mately much of the kidney may be destroyed by the back-pressure. The same effect may be produced by kinking of the ureter or anything else which causes obstruction. Sometimes children are born with hydronephrosis, and when the dilation is due to kinking of the tube the condition may be intermittent, with attacks of renal colic during which only small amounts of urine are passed; this is followed with relief and the passage of large quantities.

Tumours and Cysts. The kidney may also be the site of tumours and cysts which produce pain in the loins, sometimes a lump over the kidney which can be felt, and blood in the urine. Cancer of the bladder is a serious condition in which the bladder may have to be removed, so the urinary flow has then to be directed elsewhere. Either the ureters are brought out on to the skin surface, a procedure known as *cutaneous ureterostomy*, or they are implanted in the large bowel, so that the urine flows out with the fæces. This is described as *uretero-colostomy.*

There may also be benign tumours of the bladder or *papillomas*, which are soft and bleed easily; a great deal of blood is passed, but there is usually little or no pain. In this, and similar, diseases of the bladder examination of the inside of the organ is carried out by means of a cystoscope, a thin tube which is passed up the urethra and has a small electric light at the end which enables the surgeon to see what is going on. Instruments may also be passed through the tube, and simple papillomas can be cauterised. Similar instruments are used in the examination of the stomach (gastroscope) and the bronchial tubes (bronchoscope). When some obstruction in the outlet of the bladder or in the urethra occurs the bladder, of course, fills with urine, which cannot be passed, and very painful dilation occurs. In this case an attempt may be made to pass a catheter, a thin rubber tube, into the bladder to relieve the tension, or if this fails a *suprapubic cystotomy* is performed—an incision is made in the abdomen over the bladder and a tube inserted into it, through which the urine escapes. This is ordinarily a temporary expedient, and later when the patient's health has improved an attempt will be made to remove the cause of obstruction. The most common cause of such obstruction is *enlargement of the prostate gland* at the base of the bladder, which surrounds this area and the beginning of the ureter. About 40 per cent. of men over sixty have some degree of obstruction due to this cause, and about 20 per cent. of these require operation. The gland is about the size of a walnut, and, as we have seen, its function is to supply part of the fluid which makes up the semen, the male sex secretion. Enlargement of the prostate may be benign or malignant, and, although nobody knows just why, such benign enlargement tends to occur in most men in later life. There may be no symptoms, but characteristically there is frequency during the day and the need to get up at night to pass water. The flow of urine being impeded by constriction of the urethra, the passage is less forceful than normal, and there is a tendency for dribbling to occur. If the obstruction is severe and not relieved the back-pressure may be transmitted to the ureters and kidneys, resulting finally in kidney failure and uræmia. The prostate, except in cases of very mild enlargement, has to be removed either through the abdomen or through the perineum (the part of the body lying between the sex organs and the anus). Sometimes, in less serious cases, it is possible without an incision to cut away the obstructing part by an electrocautery inserted, as is a cystoscope, through the urethra. Prostatectomy was once a serious operation, all the more so because the patient was usually elderly and not in good condition, but new techniques and the use of antibiotics have greatly improved the outlook.

Cancer of the Prostate is always serious, but if discovered in time it can be operated on successfully. The gland, of course, has to be completely removed; in inoperable cases, or in patients unfit to stand operation, the tumour may be treated by means of female sex hormones, which cause it to shrink and may prolong life by some years.

DISEASES OF THE NERVOUS SYSTEM.

The nervous system consists of the Central Nervous System and the Peripheral Nervous System. The brain and spinal cord make up the former. The latter consists of the nerve fibres by which the Central Nervous System is connected to all parts of the body. Human beings have a more complicated brain than any other animal species, but it is only its complexity which makes it different from the brains of other mammals like rats and pigs and cows. We do not have the largest brains, since whales, for example, have much larger ones. Ours is not even the largest for the size of the body. Mice and dolphins and several other creatures have relatively larger brains when compared with body weight. Furthermore the cells and materials of which our brain is composed are virtually identical with those in other mammals, and its living properties are also the same.

Before describing some of the diseases of the nervous system it will be helpful to say a little about how it is made and how it works. Each human brain probably contains about ten thousand million (10,000,000,000) nerve cells and perhaps four or five times this number of supporting "glial" cells. Each nerve cell has many long thin branching projections, called dendrites, rather like the branches of a tree, leading to many thousands of "twigs" for each single nerve cell. At the end of each "twig" there is a special structure called a *synapse* by which contact is made with other nerve cells. It is through these connections that very large numbers of nerve cells give information (or send impulses) to each other so that they can be co-ordinated. As well as these dendritic branches, each nerve cell gives off one large trunk called the *axon*, down which final messages are sent as the result of all the information it receives from its dendrites. Some axons are many feet long. Some end in another synapse, by which the outgoing message is passed to yet another nerve cell. Some axons, those of the peripheral nerves, end directly on organs like muscles or glands, instructing them and making them work.

Messages are passed along dendrites and axons as electrical impulses. They are generated in the nerve cell "body." They are modified according to information received from other nerve cells and propagated down the axon. It is this superficial resemblance to a series of electrical cables which has given rise to comparisons of the brain with a telephone system or a computer, and as long as it is realised how infinitely more complicated each brain is than any known computer, the comparison is not a bad one. However, the brain generates its own electric power from the fuel brought in its own blood supply; and no spare parts or spare cables are available if the originals should get damaged, except in peripheral nerves. Furthermore the contact of one nerve cell with another through a synapse is not an electrical contact, and neither is the contact between a nerve and the muscle or other organ it is controlling. In both cases the connection is chemical. Thus when an electrical impulse arrives at the end of the nerve fibre, a chemical is released into the gap between it and the next nerve or organ, and it is this chemical which carries the stimulus forward. There is also an arrangement to neutralise the chemical transmitter when the impulse has been transmitted. So the resemblance to a telephone exchange or computer can sometimes be misleading.

Many of the nerve axons which transmit electrical impulses are clothed in fatty *myelin sheaths*, a little like the plastic insulation around an electric wire. Here again the resemblance is only partial, since the myelin sheaths are interrupted at regular intervals and these gaps in the insulation play an important role in transmitting the impulse. One of the important functions of the non-nervous *glial* cells of the brain is to manufacture and maintain the myelin sheaths.

Most of the functions of the brain are quite unknown, and even the ones we know about are very poorly understood. It is assumed to be the organ of higher mental function, of the mind and intellect; but there is surprisingly little evidence for this, and no one has any idea what physical structures or mechanisms subserve these functions. The brain is known to control all bodily functions by means of *motor* and other nerves which carry impulses from the brain outwards to all parts of the body. Sometimes these are under our voluntary control; mostly they are involuntary, reflex or automatic. Reflex actions are the result of impulses passed inwards from the body towards the brain by means of sensory nerves. Information arriving in the brain about the various sensations like heat, pain, touch, position, the need for saliva or gastric juice or even the thought or smell of food, are acted on in the various "centres" in the brain. These send out instructions down the "motor" or "secretary" nerves which instruct the muscles or glands to take appropriate action. Thus a *reflex* has a "sensory ending" which appreciates some sort of sensation. This is converted into an electrical impulse which is sent towards the brain or spinal cord along a sensory or "afferent" nerve. The impulse arrives at a "centre" in the central nervous system which co-ordinates all the relevant information and issues instructions. These travel as impulses outwards, along "efferent" nerves towards "effector" organs like muscles or glands, and an appropriate action occurs automatically. The pathway from sensory ending to effector organ is called a *reflex arc*. Many reflex activities are partly under voluntary control, although mainly automatic. If you touch something hot you will automatically withdraw your hand. But if it is a hot china cup which has cost you a lot of money, you are capable of overriding the tendency to drop it, at least for a time. Breathing is automatic, but it can also be controlled, again at least for a time.

Clearly the brain is a very delicately organised piece of machinery, and its cells are extremely specialised for their job. Achieving this kind of specialised perfection brings many difficulties, however, and the brain cells have become highly dependent on the proper functioning of the other body systems, especially the blood circulation, the respiratory system, and the systems regulating the detailed nutrient composition of the blood. Failure of these systems, even for a very short time, can damage the nerve cells. Nearly all death, from whatever original cause, is produced this way, by an ultimate interference with nerve cell function.

We have already mentioned that the brain and spinal cord are unable to repair or replace any components which get damaged. The vulnerability of the brain is even more obvious when it is realised how easily damage and destruction can occur. For example, unless a rich supply of oxygen and glucose is continuously arriving in the blood stream, brain cells will cease to function in a few seconds and will die in a few minutes, and they can never be replaced. This is in marked contrast to other tissues of the body. The leg, for example, may carry on for over half an hour without any blood at all because the muscle and other cells can find other ways of surviving. Thus the brain can be permanently damaged if the blood contains insufficient oxygen (through asphyxia), insufficient glucose, or if the blood supply is blocked or if the blood pressure falls. All these are likely to happen to any of us at any time, and so there are elaborate mechanisms trying to prevent them occurring. Most of the subject of physiology is concerned with the mechanisms designed to protect the brain, and most of us ultimately die because they eventually fail. One of the clever features of the body design is that all the mechanisms which protect the brain from a supply failure are controlled by the brain itself. Thus the brain has itself been made to control the heart beat and the breathing and the many other systems which are needed for its own survival.

In all that follows concerning disease of the nervous system it will be seen that the effects of neurological disease on the patient are the direct result of something going wrong with one of the structures or mechanisms we have described.

Diagnostic Techniques in Neurology. The doctor has many ways of testing the nervous system, most of which test its various functions as outlined in the introduction. Thus tests of sensation, muscular movement and reflexes of all kinds as well as the special functions of taste, smell, vision, hearing, speech and intellect play a part. A great deal can be learned about the brain by *arteriography*. In this test a radio opaque substance is put into the arteries supplying the brain, and an X-ray picture taken immediately afterwards shows up all the blood vessels. *Ventriculography* is an X-ray examination after gas has been introduced into the brain cavities or ventricles which are normally filled with *cerebrospinal fluid*; *myelography* is an X-ray of the spinal cord after a radio-opaque substance has been injected into the space between the spinal cord and the bony vertebral canal which houses it.

The development of the EMI Scanner, a relatively new concept in diagnostic radiology, has now made most of those "invasive" diagnostic techniques unnecessary. The equipment needed is expensive and is presently only available at a very few centres. Sometimes *radioactive isotopes* are put into the blood stream and carried into the brain where they can be detected from outside the skull by counters. *Electroencephalography* measures the electrical waves generated by the brain by placing electrodes on the scalp. *Electromyography* does the same for muscles.

Consciousness and Unconsciousness (Coma). Everyone knows what consciousness is until he

tries to define it. Full consciousness is generally taken to imply not only wakefulness but the total complement of human mental faculties. In clinical medicine, however, something less than this is usually meant. For example a demented person, or one whose memory is lost (*amnesia*), or one whose powers of speech are lost (*aphasia*) may still be "conscious." There is really a continuous gradation between full consciousness and coma, passing through drowsiness and even "stupor" in which condition a patient can be aroused from coma but sinks back into it when left alone. Many different things can cause coma ranging from swelling of the brain, compressing it in its rigid box of bone, to disorders in other body systems resulting in a failure to provide for the brain's needs. Examples of the first are bleeding within the brain or *brain tumours*, both of which occupy space and can only do so by producing compression. In the second category are asphyxia preventing oxygen from reaching the brain, lack of glucose in the blood, circulatory failure in which there is insufficient blood, or insufficient blood pressure. Fainting is a comparatively minor example.

Sleep and Insomnia. Nobody knows what causes sleep, why it is necessary, and how it helps. It is quite different from coma or even stupor, since as much oxygen and glucose is necessary asleep as awake. Insomnia is experienced by everyone at some time, and for some reason is very distressing if it persists. There are three forms: failing to get to sleep, intermittent wakefulness, and awaking early. Nearly all insomniacs sleep more than they think. They should eat light evening meals and avoid stimulants like tea and coffee after mid-day. Elderly people should realise they need less sleep. Being cold or having a full bladder can be a cause. Or simply not being tired. Sedative drugs are a last resort, but they can be useful in "breaking the habit" of wakefulness. Obviously there may be psychological factors such as anxiety and excitement. *Narcolepsy,* or a true inability to keep awake is comparatively rare. Both narcolepsy and insomnia are really extreme examples of what all normal people suffer from occasionally.

Headache is man's most common pain. Here again we must distinguish between the very common varieties of comparatively trivial significance and the rare ones due to serious causes. Some headaches are due to continuous tightness in muscles of the scalp, and are often "nervous" or psychological in origin. Others result from nose blockage and congestion, sinus problems, eye strain, toothache, etc. Migraine is a special kind and will be described below. Very occasionally indeed headache is due to serious disease like brain tumour. Most headache results from "living it up" or being "run down," or both. The headache of alcoholic hangover is probably due to dehydration. It can often be avoided by consuming a great quantity of water (a half litre or so, before going to bed), but few people are prepared to do this in the circumstances. Be careful when using aspirin, which is a useful remedy for headache, since it is very dangerous for people with stomach complaints like gastritis or gastric or duodenal ulcer. Occasionally aspirin makes the stomach bleed, and this can be so severe as to kill. A safer pain killer is paracetamol. Be particularly careful in treating "hang-over" headaches by patent fizzy remedies. They are very effective, but often contain large quantities of aspirin described in small print by its proper name as acetyl salicylic acid.

Migraine. This is a very special variety of "sick headache" and requires special treatment under medical supervision. It has many different forms, but usually there is a definite sequence of events. An attack often starts with some alteration of vision. The patient has shimmering blind spots or other visual disorders. This is followed by a well localised severe headache which may end in nausea or vomiting. The whole thing is caused by a poorly understood disorder of the blood vessels. There are special drugs, mostly derivatives of ergot, which are effective, especially if used when the first signs of an attack appear. Although there is a direct physical cause for an attack, it is also certain that some of the trouble is psychological tenseness. People with migraine are often rather anxious, striving and perfectionist people. Also it has been noticed that attacks are much less frequent when the necessary pills are not being carried available for use. However, as with all other conditions which are partly " psychological " in origin they are none the less distressing for the patient. It simply means that the treatment is also partly psychological in encouraging him to come to terms with his problems.

Menière's Disease is one of the conditions in which the organ of balance in the middle ear is affected, giving rise to *vertigo*, a form of giddiness. It usually begins in middle life in the same sort of person who sometimes has migraine. There is buzzing in the ears and some intermittent loss of hearing as well as vertigo. During an attack the patient may be unable to walk because of his loss of balance, and nausea and vomiting are common. Treatment is by special drugs, and occasionally an operation on the ear is necessary.

Epilepsy is a symptom, not a disease, which is common at all ages but especially children. It has been attributed to St. Paul, Julius Caesar, Napoleon, and (with more justice perhaps) to Dostoyevsky. Many varieties of attack occur often in the same patient, the commonest and best known being the *grand mal* or major seizure. In this the patient falls down unconscious and rigid and the jaw is clenched, so that there is danger of the tongue being bitten. This so-called tonic phase is followed, within a minute or so, by a clonic phase in which the limbs contract rhythmically. The attack ends with the patient going limp and gradually recovering consciousness, a process which may take up to an hour. Occasionally the patient has a brief warning, most often an indescribable feeling in the stomach. There are two common forms of minor seizure, one occurring mainly in children and the other more often in adults. The common minor attacks in children are often called *petit mal* or *absence*, which well describes the instantaneous and brief loss of consciousness often unaccompanied by any change in posture. Recovery is equally instantaneous. On the other hand, in the other forms of epilepsy which arise from various parts of the brain, but especially from the lobe under the temporal region, there is often a warning similar to that which may precede a major seizure. In these cases the patient shows only confusion, no definite loss of posture, but automatic activity such as fumbling with buttons, muttering, and grimacing. Following these attacks there may be a quite prolonged period of confusion in which the patient may wander away and occasionally may be violent. Criminal acts are very rarely carried out in this state.

A large number of people have had one or two fits in their lives, particularly at times of physical or psychological stress. " Fever " or " Febrile " convulsions (often called teething fits in the past) are extremely common in young children and are often thought of as something different from epilepsy since the attacks rarely continue in later years. This form of epilepsy and some cases of *petit mal* are the only forms in which hereditary factors are important in the causation, and these are the least serious forms of epilepsy. They are very rarely associated with serious physical or psychological disturbances. Most other forms of epilepsy are due to a scar or other area of brain damage. It is a proportion of these cases which develop the psychological disturbances that are occasionally very serious.

Not every patient who has had one or two fits need necessarily take regular anticonvulsant drugs; that is drugs which damp down the abnormal excessive activity of the brain that leads to the attacks. Many drugs are available of which the most important are phenobarbitone, phenytoin and clonazepam. The succinimides and troxidones are effective only against minor seizures. The choice is a matter of skilled medical judgment. Epileptics often find it difficult to get work because of the reluctance of employers to take on someone who may be more prone to ac-

cidents and whose fits may distress other workers. Obviously there are some jobs which epileptics should not do because of the danger involved (from, for example, moving machinery), and they should not drive a car. A few cases are so severe that work is almost impossible, but employers have a duty whenever possible to employ these people whose mental health may suffer greatly if they are made to feel outcasts and who ordinarily are as efficient, or even more so, as the next man. It is also hoped that employees will become less prejudiced about epilepsy as the general public become less ignorant about medical matters. In this way epileptics will come to be accepted in all those kinds of employment for which they are well suited. If some of the famous men who have suffered from this disease had had to rely on the charity of some employers today the world would have been much the poorer, although possibly we could have managed without the generals.

Congenital Malformations. The proper shape of the brain and spinal cord is achieved quite early in development by about the thirteenth week after conception. During this time very slight changes in the fœtal environment can produce disastrous malformations. The drug thalidomide, for example, operated on other body systems while they were passing through this phase of construction. Some viruses can do the same thing. Most malformations are without known cause, but it is certain that something went wrong at this very early stage, and it only needs a very minor interference with the normal process to do the permanent damage. At about this time the bones of the spine are beginning to enclose, or form a roof over the developing spinal cord. Sometimes they fail to complete the process, resulting in *spina bifida*. If the coverings of the cord protrude through the defect, this is a *meningocele*, and if the cord itself protrudes it is a *meningomyelocele*. The whole protrusion may be covered with skin but if it is not, the cord soon becomes infected. The effect on the patient is variable, according to the amount of damage to the nerve fibres in the cord, and there are varying degrees of paralysis and loss of sensation below the area involved together with loss of bowel and bladder control. Much help is often obtained from surgical repair, but many cases remain in a distressing condition always, and the only really useful attack on the problem is research to find the cause and prevent it happening. The same is true of the *malformations of the brain*. In one of these, hydrocephaly, the narrow channel is blocked which transmits the cerebrospinal fluid from the chambers within the brain where it is secreted to the outer coverings to be taken back into the blood stream. Blockage of the channel (or aqueduct) results in distension of the brain by fluid, enlargement of the head, and mental retardation. Sometimes a by-pass valve can be inserted to restore normal fluid circulation with very gratifying results. This aqueduct can also be blocked by later disease (meningitis) or injury with the same result. Sometimes the brain fails to form altogether (*anencephaly*), and the child fortunately does not survive after birth.

Cerebral Palsy is a term covering many varieties of *spastic child*. It is thought to be due to brain damage at birth or in early infancy, and is depressingly common. Although a great deal can be done for the spastic (they are often of normal intelligence) the only satisfactory approach is prevention and this means expensive research into its causes. Donations, encouragement, and offers of practical help, please, to the Spastics Society 12 Park Crescent, London W.1.

Motor Neurone Disease. This is a group of distressing diseases usually occurring in people over 40, in whom the parts of the brain and spinal cord degenerate which look after muscular movement. The group includes *Amyotrophic Lateral Sclerosis, Progressive Muscular Atrophy, Progressive Bulbar Palsy,* and *Primary Lateral Sclerosis.* The results are paralysis or weakness with wasting of the muscles of the body, including those concerned with arms, legs, breathing, speaking, etc. Nothing whatever is known of the cause, and the only treatment is that designed to alleviate the results of the disease. It is uncommon, but this is little comfort to the sufferer.

Parkinson's Disease, paralysis agitans, or the "shaking palsy" is a common condition which begins in later life over the age of 50. It has three classical features: shaking (or tremor), muscular rigidity and loss of those automatic reflexes which look after bodily posture. This results in a stooping shuffling gait. Later there is a mask-like loss of facial expression with diminished eye blinking. It is a progressive disease, but it progresses so slowly that 10 or 20 years may elapse between its onset and incapacity. A good deal can now be done to help these patients with drugs, the most recent of which at the time of writing is levodopa. Occasionally patients have benefited from surgical destruction of small areas of diseased brain. It is important to remember that many elderly people have some tremor of the head or hands called *Senile Tremor*, and this is *not* Parkinson's Disease. It is merely one of the features of achieving advanced seniority as a citizen. The Parkinson's Disease Society, of 81 Queen's Road London SW19 8NR, looks after patient welfare, supports research and publishes a regular newsletter.

Chorea. This is a group of diseases in which there is involuntary muscle movement, weakness, and emotional instability. There will be clumsiness, awkward gait, twitching of limbs, face, hands, trunk, or tongue. They include *Acute Chorea or St. Vitus' Dance* occurring in children from 5 to 15, *Hereditary or Huntington's Chorea* occurring in a well-defined genetic pattern and beginning later, between 35 and 50. *Tics* or habit spasms are not part of these diseases but are often of psychological origin. They are usually eye blinking, head shaking, shoulder shrugging, or any other sudden gesture of limbs or face.

Stroke Illness or Cerebrovascular Diseases. Strokes are due to diseases of the brain's blood vessels which either burst or get blocked. The same blood-vessel disorders cause heart attacks by blocking the coronary arteries supplying the heart. Strokes and heart attacks together kill more people than any other single cause including cancer. They account for one death in every five. Perhaps less is known of the cause of this disease than is known about cancer, and much more research is needed to find out if it is to be prevented. The cause of the commonest cancer (of the lung) is now known and it can be prevented by stopping smoking. Perhaps the prevention of strokes and heart attacks will mean an equally difficult abstinence from all those foods which make us fat. At least it is known that being overweight leads to death from these causes, just as smoking may lead to death from lung cancer.

If any artery supplying blood to any part of the brain is blocked, the territory supplied will die; and the bodily functions for which that part of the brain is responsible will cease. The process is called *infarction* of the brain, the dead area being an *infarct*. The blockage is usually due to thrombosis (*see* P31) of the blood within a vessel, a *thrombus* being a rather complicated clot with a structure of its own. The underlying cause is the arterial disease, atheroma (*see* P30) together with stagnation of the circulation. About one blockage in ten is due to a small piece of a much larger thrombus in the heart chambers being flung into the blood stream and impacting in the distant vessel in the brain. This is *cerebral embolism* (*see* P30). If the area of dead or infarcted brain is not too large the patient will recover from his unconsciousness, but will be left with permanent loss of function (paralysis, etc.) related to that part of the brain.

When a blood vessel supplying the brain bursts, this causes *cerebral haemorrhage* or apoplexy. The vessel may be on the surface (*subarachnoid haemorrhage*) or in the depths of the tissue (*intracerebral haemorrhage*). Strokes tend to occur in older people, because the associated arterial disease is a product of age and high blood pressure. Occasionally a subarachnoid haemorrhage occurs in a younger person with an unsuspected malformation of the arteries of the base of the brain known as a *berry aneurysm*. This is a small berry-sized blown-out balloon due to a defect in the wall of the vessel. Berry aneurysms can often be treated surgically. Intracerebral haemorrhage carries a very poor outlook, however, since much brain tissue is often destroyed by the escaping blood, including the deep tissues responsible for the vital functions. Haemorrhage within the brain cavity can also be caused by injury (*see concussion and compression*, P19).

Inflammatory Diseases of the Nervous System. The membranes covering the brain are called the meninges. Inflammation of these, nearly always by blood-born infection or infection following injury, is called *meningitis*. Cerebrospinal or spotted fever which used to be common and very much feared was only one variety caused by a germ called "meningococcus." It is now rare. Almost any other germ may cause meningitis, and when the germ is susceptible to one of the antibiotics it is usually treatable. It will usually be necessary to identify the germ by taking a sample of cerebrospinal fluid from a convenient space around the spinal cord in the lower back. When the disease is caused by the tubercle bacillus (*tuberculous meningitis*) the problem is more difficult because the patient is often not so obviously ill until the later, less treatable stages. *Cerebral abscess*, or abscess of the brain is very serious because it occupies space in the closed box of the skull and compresses the brain, as well as being a destructive process. It may arise due to an infected piece of tissue or pus being carried to the brain in the blood stream from a distant site in the lungs or heart. When the brain or cord tissue is itself inflamed it is called *encephalitis* (brain) or *myelitis* (cord) or *encephalo-myelitis* (both). These conditions are comparatively uncommon and are often due to infection with viruses rather than bacteria. Some have no known cause, possibly because many viruses are difficult to identify.

Herpes Zoster (Shingles) is a common viral infection of the nervous system which affects sensory nerve roots where they enter the spinal cord. The initial symptoms are of pain in the area supplied by the affected nerves—commonly one side of the trunk, the buttock or the face—followed by the appearance of blisters. Treatment is symptomatic, as there is no specific remedy. Soothing lotions may be applied to the blisters and analgesics given for the pain. The disease is fairly short-lived, but neuralgia may persist for weeks after the blisters have healed.

Shingles is interesting in that it is not a *primary* viral infection, but the result of reactivation of the varicella/zoster virus (so called because it causes *either* chicken pox or shingles) which has lain dormant in nerve root cells, probably since childhood. Primary infection with the virus at whatever age causes chicken pox, not shingles; if an adult who has never had chicken pox or shingles comes into contact with a child with chicken pox or an adult with shingles, he is likely to contract the former but not the latter.

Shingles is infectious from the time the blisters appear until they have crusted over and healed. However, it is not as infectious as chicken pox.

Multiple Sclerosis or Disseminated Sclerosis. This year Pears features a special topic on this affliction. *See* Part III.

Brain Tumours. The brain is no exception to the rule that any cell in any tissue of the body can suddenly begin to disobey the body's rules regarding its growth and multiplication. A totally unknown mechanism governs how many cells of a certain type there ought to be and calls a halt to cell multiplication when this number is reached. Every now and then one of them turns a blind eye and goes on dividing, and the result is a tumour, or lump, of anarchic cells which obey no rules. Tumours are commonest in cells which normally go on dividing throughout life, in order to replace those lost by wear and tear. Examples are the cells lining the air passages in the lung, or the alimentary tract in the stomach or large bowel. Fortunately for the brain there is little cell division once it has grown. Nerve cells cannot divide at all in adult life, and the supporting glial cells only do so in response to injury. Therefore primary brain tumours are much less common than those elsewhere. Also many brain tumours like many of those elsewhere, are benign or "innocent" tumours. They are not cancerous, and need only be removed for the patient to be completely cured. The brain, however, is at two major disadvantages compared with other tissues when it comes to tumours. One is that all tumours as they grow take up space, and space in the skull is already fully occupied. Thus even an innocent tumour can compress the brain within its rigid box of bone and become most dangerous until it is removed. The second disadvantage is due to the very large blood supply of the brain. Cancer in other parts of the body spreads partly by sending small pieces of itself to other tissues by way of the blood stream, and those tissues like liver, lung, kidney, and brain which have a big blood supply naturally receive more than their share of other tissues' tumour. These secondary deposits, or *metastases*, cause compression and other trouble in the brain much more frequently than the brain's own primary tumours. Indeed convulsions or other signs of brain disorder may be the first indication that there is a primary tumour in the lung or breast or elsewhere.

Head Injuries are dealt with in the section on Physical Injuries (P19), where a great deal of space is given to the effects of most First Aid emergencies on the proper functioning of the brain and spinal cord.

Diseases of Peripheral Nerves. Compared with the nerves of the central nervous system (brain and spinal cord), the peripheral nerves are comparatively rarely affected by disease. They have some similarities of structure with central nerve fibres in that their fibres are often covered with myelin sheaths and are arranged in bundles. A special feature, however, is that they are enclosed by connective tissue sheaths and it is probably these which allow a peripheral nerve to grow again, or regenerate, after it has been cut or damaged. Central nerve fibres are unable to do this. After *injury of a peripheral nerve* the part away from the centre is cut off from its parent cell body and it dies. All function, whether motor or sensory, is lost. But in the course of many months the central surviving part grows into the connective tissue sheaths which act like tubes to guide the new nerve to its destination. Provided the cut ends are close enough together and correctly aligned, and provided enough fibres reach their correct destination, good functional recovery is possible.

A disorder of a peripheral nerve is called a *neuropathy* and means nothing more than that. There are many kinds. One of the most distressing is *trigeminal neuralgia*, again fortunately rare. The trigeminal or fifth cranial nerve has a motor and sensory territory on the face. In this condition there are paroxysmal episodes of extremely severe pain which may resist all treatment except destruction of the nerve itself with consequent facial paralysis and loss of sensation. At the other more trivial extreme are the occasions when a leg "goes to sleep" or gets "pins and needles" after crossing it and pressing on a nerve for too long. *Bell's Palsy* is sudden loss of function of the seventh cranial nerve and there is again paralysis on one side of the face which usually recovers in time. Some bacterial diseases especially leprosy, invade the nerves themselves. Chronic alcoholism may affect the nerves, as may diabetes, probably by interfering with the nutrition of the nerve cell. So may exposure to arsenic or lead or an unpleasant nerve poison which may contaminate cooking oil known as TOCP, or triorthocresylphosphate.

Muscular Dystrophies. These are a series of diseases of muscle in which there is progressive wasting and weakness of muscle, the causes of which are entirely unknown. They are divided up according to the age of onset and the muscles involved. *Duchenne's muscular dystrophy* occurs in the first decade of life. It affects most of the muscles eventually, including the heart muscle and those concerned with breathing, and so the outlook is not good. Other forms are inherited.

Myasthenia Gravis. This is a strange disorder of the mechanism which transmits instructions from nerve to muscle at the "neuromuscular junction." There is extreme weakness of muscles after they have been used, resembling in some respects the weakness following the administration of curare, or "arrow poison." It is often associated with disorders of the thymus gland. The drug neostigmine reverses the neuromuscular disorder and removal of the thymus is also sometimes effective.

MENTAL DISEASES.

Psychosis.

Mental diseases are divided into psychoses (*i.e.*, insanity) and neuroses (*i.e.*, what is ordinarily known as "nerves"). Psychoses, in their turn, are divided into organic and functional—those due to physical disease and those in which no physical cause has been discovered. In point of fact, the distinction into organic and functional is rather meaningless; for if we accept the modern view of psychosomatic medicine which regards the body and mind as a single unit it is clear that organic disease brings out psychological defects which were already there and that functional disease must, in the final analysis, be the result of physicochemical causes, even if this is brought about by mental stress.

Organic disease results from poisoning of the nervous system by such poisons as alcohol, carbon monoxide, or lead; vitamin deficiencies, as in pellagra; infections such as syphilis; and degeneration of the brain, either primary or as a result of poor blood supply. In all cases its main symptoms are confusion, signs of other disease, and loss of memory. Alcohol leads to various conditions: in *delirium tremens* heavy bouts of drinking end in delirium (" D.T.s "), confusion, hallucination—although not necessarily of pink elephants or rats. It is a serious disease, but the outlook is much improved since it was discovered that injections of concentrated vitamins B and C can help. In more chronic cases *Korsakov's syndrome* manifests itself in the form of mental deterioration and memory defects. There can be little doubt that previously existing mental instability is a predisposing factor in these conditions. The same may be said of *general paralysis of the insane* or G.P.I., and in this case the immediate cause is syphilitic infection of the nervous system. Nevertheless, of all the patients with chronic syphilis, only a small number get syphilis of the nervous system. G.P.I. is typically associated with the usual symptoms of organic disease and delusions of grandeur; for example, a man with this disease may go out and buy several expensive cars in one day. However, it is not uncommon to find G.P.I. associated with severe depression—again the picture depends on the previous personality. The association of the above symptoms with a positive Wasserman test —which proves the presence of the spirochæte in the blood—indicates neurosyphilis. When the lower centres of the nervous system are affected the disease is known as *tabes dorsalis*, in which there is difficulty in passing urine, limb pains, inability to stand when the eyes are closed, and finally difficulty in walking. The patient becomes paralysed and ultimately bedridden. Treatment is with penicillin.

People age at varying rates, so that some are hale and hearty at eighty or ninety whereas others are old at sixty or seventy. They present the typical picture of old age: " second childishness and mere oblivion, sans eyes, sans teeth, sans everything." When this condition, which is caused by degenerative changes in the brain or by defective blood-supply resulting from arteriosclerosis, is pronounced we speak of *senile psychosis.* There is mental confusion, forgetfulness, and delusions, in which the previous personality defects which we all have are accentuated. Such patients may have to be put under special care, but the process is largely irreversible.

The functional psychoses are two in number: schizophrenia and manic-depressive insanity. In *schizophrenia,* which, when it occurs in early adult life, is known (or used to be known) as *dementia præcox,* the symptoms are bizarre. There are delusions and hallucinations, so that the patient often believes himself to be persecuted and hears voices which say objectionable things to him. Sometimes the schizophrenic is wildly excited, and in other cases he goes into a state of stupor which is described as a catatonic state. Although the disease is described as functional, recent discoveries seem to suggest that there is some derangement of the blood chemistry. Treatment by insulin and the new tranquillising drugs has revolutionised the outlook in this admittedly serious disease. Indeed, some cases of psychosis are more easily treated than neurotic patients, since the former respond to physical methods, whereas the latter may require fairly prolonged psychotherapy (psychological treatment) and are less responsive to drugs.

In cases which do not respond to other methods, the brain operation known as *leucotomy* may be performed. Leucotomy is also performed to alleviate intractable pain, as in incurable cancer, but some of the ataraxic drugs (tranquilisers) are probably equally useful for this purpose. Leucotomy involves the severing of the connecting nerve fibres between certain areas of the brain, and the results are often favourable, but in fact the operation should be performed only in cases where the outlook is otherwise very poor; chronic severe neuroses, frequent attacks of manic depressive psychosis, severe chronic depression, and schizophrenia which has not responded to other forms of treatment. The operation reduces anxiety, fear, aggressiveness, and agitation, but may result in the less-desirable symptoms of apathy, impaired judgment, lack of self-control, and loss of initiative.

Schizophrenia developing in later life is likely to be less dramatic in origin, and the delusions tend to be more systematised—that is, they take a persistent form, which does not change from day to day. This type of the disease is known as *paraphrenia.* In those beyond middle age the rare but dangerous condition described as *paranoia* may develop in which there are no hallucinations and the only symptom is a completely systematised collection of persecutory delusions, which on recital may sound entirely convincing even to the ordinary doctor. Such people are dangerous precisely because they are so plausible, and they fill the ranks of the litigious, the troublemakers, and the political and religious eccentrics. One such patient known to the writer spent his life in a mental hospital from which he had parole, employing this to form a society propagating highly eccentric sexual and political beliefs. It says little for the sanity of the general population that his meetings were invariably crowded out (although, of course, when one reads of the people who apparently believe that the various fictitious families on radio or television really exist, one need not be surprised at such examples of communal dottiness, even if one may despair of democracy).

Manic-depressive insanity is characterised by mood swings in which the emotions alternate between wild elation without obvious cause and equally causeless depression. However, the picture is not quite as simple as this; for phases of mania or excitement may occur without depression obviously following, or there may be a single attack of depression with no manic phases.

The disease may be absolutely incapacitating, or there may be periods of relative normality; typically, then, manic-depressive insanity is a disease of alternating moods. The depression responds to electroconvulsive therapy or E.C.T., but mania is less responsive to treatment. However, it ordinarily remits of itself. Sometimes in middle age *involutional depression* occurs, and this in the vast majority of cases is cured by E.C.T. As in the case of schizophrenia drugs are increasingly used for depression.

Neurosis.

The main neuroses are anxiety neurosis, hysteria, and obsessional neurosis. *Anxiety neurosis* is an illness in which the main symptom (as the name implies) is anxiety. There is fear which rationally the patient knows to be groundless; there may be anxiety attacks, in which the heart pounds, the patient feels he is going mad, is unable to sleep, and worries " for no reason at all." In hysteria, anxiety is largely absent, but there may be apparently physical symptoms ranging from paralysis of the limbs to blindness, deafness, inability to write, and lapses of memory (the so-called hysterical fugues or loss of memory). Typical of *hysteria* is the fact that the patient is less worried by his symptoms than would be expected from their apparent seriousness; this is what the early psychiatrists described as "la belle indifférence." The reason for the indifference is simple—it is that the paralysed individual *wants* to be paralysed, the blind *want* to be blind, the deaf to be deaf (there are none so blind—or deaf—as those who don't want to see, or hear), and the person who doesn't want to write conveniently finds that he cannot.

Generally speaking, neurotic people are suffering from a failure to face up to reality. They are not physically ill and are largely the end result of a faulty upbringing. It is wrong to suppose that the only bad families are those in which the children are ill-treated; much the worst ones are those in which children are spoilt, the parents possessive, and the wrong kind of love is dispensed. Neuroses are the result of a conflict between primitive desires and what the individual has been brought up to believe he should be. For example, before an examination a student may develop a nervous breakdown because he fears failure when he has been brought up to expect success. The excuse, of course, is " overwork " —an entirely non-existent condition. With his breakdown he solves his problem, he avoids the fear of failing and preserves his self-respect: he has been ill. Similarly, the soldier with " shell shock " (another non-existent condition) has a conflict between his sense of duty and his fear of death, which again is solved by becoming ill. Or, to take a final example, a woman feels the duty to look after her ageing mother. But she also wants to get married. So she unconsciously develops a neurosis which says, in effect, " I should like to do my duty in looking after my mother, but unfortunately I am unable to." There is an unconscious rebellion on the part of the mind.

Neurosis, in effect, is not a disease—it is a self-inflicted injury, a form of maladaptation to life. The neurotic, no matter how much he suffers, does not want to get well; he has found some way of getting along, even if a foolish way, and he intends to keep it. Often his symptoms are the sort of excuse that say: " If only I wasn't ill what wouldn't I be able to do! " The neurotic is a person who is different and is afraid to be himself; his problem is a conflict between being " ordinary," " like other people," and being what he was supposed to be.

Obsessional Neurosis is a more severe type of neurotic illness; for although in anxiety neurosis we find such symptoms as phobias—irrational fears of open spaces, closed spaces, animals, and so on obsessional states are characterised by compulsive feelings that certain acts must be performed or certain thoughts thought. In a mild form we all have obsessions: we feel that we must walk on the spaces between paving-stones, that we must touch lamp-posts, and so on. But when this type of compulsion gets to the stage when we must go back several times to make sure the lights have been put out, when we feel the need to wash our hands every few minutes, become obsessed with numbers on cars or dates on coins, then it becomes a nuisance and requires treatment. The obsessional neurotic is a person who feels that life must be controlled; he is "a creature who moves in predestinate grooves—he's not even a bus but a tram." His symptoms are an attempt to devise self-imposed rules which will control the unconscious desires of which he is so afraid.

All that remains to be said is that many of these conditions are treatable or, if not treatable so far as cure is concerned, they can at least be relieved. The world is full of people who are "different": there are those who are different in the right way, who should take satisfaction from their achievements, and those who are different in the wrong way, who should seek expert advice.

Lastly, although not truly appropriate to this section, we include brief notes on neurasthenia psychopathic personality, and masturbation.

Neurasthenia is an entirely imaginary condition allegedly due to exhaustion of the nervous system. Since no such condition exists, we need not bother with it. Neuroses cannot be treated by feeding the nerves (which are perfectly normal). They can be helped by such things as sedatives, but not cured. *Neurosis has nothing at all to do with disease of the physical nerves, so nerve tonics do not exist, and anyone who asserts that they do is a humbug.*

Psychopathic Personality is the term given to anyone who has different standards of behaviour from those generally accepted by society. Some of these unfortunates may be *inadequate*, that is to say, although perfectly intelligent, unable to earn their own living. Others are the *creative* people, who, as in the case of Van Gogh, did many eccentric things but also many productive things—Van Gogh was gifted, or cursed, with an intense sensitivity. Lastly, there are those who have what others regard as peculiar sexual habits. Of the first two classes nothing more need be said, and all that is necessary is to mention certain of the so-called sexual perversions. (When we say so-called the implication is not that none of these forms of behaviour is perverse but that some of them are carried out by otherwise quite ordinary people.) *Sadism* and *Masochism* refer to, in the first place, pleasure in inflicting pain and, in the second, to receiving pain. The pleasure is sexual, and it is incorrect to talk of cruelty in itself as sadism. Sadism is named after the Marquis de Sade, who suffered from this perversion, although he certainly did much less harm in his small way than numerous politicians or generals of our time, and masochism is named after the Austrian novelist Sacher-Masoch, who wrote books which, although unpleasant, were not notably more so than certain Sunday newspapers of today.

Masturbation is sexual self-stimulation. Needless to say, it produces no more *physical* harm than ordinary sexual intercourse—that is to say, none at all, although some people have the strange belief that every act of intercourse weakens the body and it has even been believed that each act shortens life by a specific length of time. This is rather illogical in view of the fact that most of the famous rakes have been noted for their longevity! Masturbation is almost universal in infancy, adolescence, or even in later life when other outlets are not available. It need only be a matter of concern: (a) when it is chosen in preference to normal sexual activity, or (b) when it is compulsive and excessive, since then it is a sign, not of sexual desire, but of severe underlying anxiety.

DISEASES OF THE SKIN.

The skin in the course of development before birth is particularly closely associated with the nervous system. It is therefore not surprising that so many skin diseases are influenced by emotional states. Other causes of skin disease are infections, glandular disorders, vitamin deficiencies, and the numerous conditions for which no cause has been discovered, but which presumably are due to metabolic disorders.

One of the commonest skin symptoms is *itching or pruritus*. It may accompany many different general diseases, for example diabetes and jaundice. It may also be troublesome during the menopause (the change of life in women), in old age, or in nervous conditions. Sedatives and sex hormones sometimes help the itching during the menopause, and there are ointments which may be useful.

Itching in the region of the anus and genital organs is relatively common. It may be caused by worms, by irritating vaginal discharge, or by sugar in the urine, as in diabetes. The alteration in the normal bacteria of the bowel which follows treatment with various antibiotics also often causes anal pruritus and soreness. In many cases however the itching has some psychological cause. In treatment it is important to avoid ointments and creams which contain a local anæsthetic, because these substances can cause severe allergic reactions if used for longer than a few days, and may thus make the condition much worse. Treatment with a local corticosteroid application is more effective and safer.

Parasites, such as the *scabies* mite or *lice* can cause severe and persistent itching. The scabies mite is very small, and since it burrows under the skin surface, is unlikely to be seen; it is the cause of itching most commonly between the fingers and on the front of the wrists. The itching is worst when the body becomes heated, as in bed. Treatment consists of painting the body from head to foot with benzyl benzoate application, followed the next day by a hot bath. Since scabies is contracted through close personal contact with an infested person it is often desirable for several or all members of a family to be treated at the same time, even though only one of them may be affected. Lice are specialists, one type of which affects the scalp, another the body, and a third the genital area. Head lice are destroyed by lethane, body lice by insecticides and genital (pubic) lice by shaving off hair and washing. Obviously, the clothes, especially in the case of body lice, should be disinfested, by using a hot iron particularly over the seams, which lice (for some inexplicable reason) seem to favour. Apart from the discomfort they cause, lice are dangerous as potential carriers of typhus fever.

Baldness, or Alopecia, is a very common condition, as is manifested by the extraordinary number of preparations advertised as curing it. When many preparations are offered for the treatment of one condition it is a fair judgment to assume that none of them is likely to be effective. There are, in fact, two types of baldness; one, which is much the commoner, is hereditary, and cannot be influenced in the slightest by any treatment, the other, *alopecia areata*, is caused by nervous stress, and would recover in most cases by itself, whether one used a solution of soot and water or the most expensive "hair food." There is no such thing as a hair food, any more than there is such a thing as a nerve food, and although it is probable that hair hygiene may delay baldness, it certainly cannot prevent it. All hair tonics and "foods" are useless, and their uselessness is only equalled by their costliness. Those who have lost their hair and find it growing again after using some alleged tonic are people who have had *alopecia areata* and whose hair would have grown back anyhow. In women the hair often thins out soon after a pregnancy, but a few months later it usually returns to normal.

Seborrhœa is a condition in which there is overactivity of the sebaceous glands. The most usual form it takes is *dandruff*. However, it takes other forms, and those who have dandruff may also have rashes on the face, shoulders, and chest. In these areas there is a patchy, greasy, and often itchy, rash which does not clear up until the primary condition in the scalp is dealt with. The scalp should be washed with one of the modern sulphur-containing shampoos at least twice a week, and the affected parts on the face and chest can be dealt with by the use of a sulphur lotion (*not* on any account by greasy ointments). Seborrhœa is not in itself difficult to treat, but, since the condition depends on over-secretion of sebum, the skin lubricant, treatment may have to be persisted in during the years of early adulthood, when it is most active.

Erythema Intertrigo is, quite simply, the sort of irritation which occurs usually from excessive sweating under the armpits, between the legs, and under the breasts in women. All that need be done is to wash frequently and to dust the affected areas after washing with powder. This is the condition which, in the tropics, is known as "prickly heat" and elswhere as a "sweat rash." In some people *hyperidrosis* or *excessive sweating* is a problem, especially when the sweating is accompanied with body odour—the sort of thing that, according to the advertisements "even your best friends won't tell you." There is little need for anyone in these days to suffer in this way: for the cosmetic firms have produced many highly efficient deodorants which not only control odour but also control the amount of sweating. Chlorophyll, which has been much advertised as removing odours, is effective when applied directly to surfaces which give off an unpleasant smell. It is however ineffective when taken by mouth, and does not prevent body odours. Stale sweat smells bad because it is decomposed by bacteria, and this type of body odour can be largely prevented by preparations containing harmless antiseptic and anti-perspirants.

Erysipelas is an infection of the skin caused by the hæmolytic streptococcus. It begins as a red, raised area anywhere on the body where the germs have been able to enter through a small crack or cut in the skin. The red area advances and spreads over the body until the disease is got under control. Erysipelas is very infectious, and those who look after the patient should wash their hands throughly after contact. At one time the disease used to spread as an epidemic throughout the hospital wards, but this is very rare nowadays. Treatment is, of course, a matter for the doctor.

Chilblains are common in cold weather, especially in those with poor circulation. Ordinarily they occur in the toes and fingers, but may appear on the nose and ears. The part affected becomes swollen, dusky, and there is pain and itching, sometimes leading to ulceration. Protection of the body, especially the hands and feet, from cold is the best and the only really effective way of preventing chilblains. Warm lined gloves and footwear, and arm stockings or trousers should be worn outdoors. Adequate heating of rooms is essential: a temperature between $18°$ and $21°$ C is recommended. Most tablets, medicines, ointments, or creams for chilblains are useless. A skin affection caused by heat is rather grandiosely described as *erythema ab igne*, and is frequently seen on the legs of ladies addicted to roasting their legs before the fire. It takes the form of red patches on the front of the legs and can be removed only by avoiding the cause.

Dermatitis means "inflammation of the skin," and therefore the word could be, strictly speaking, applied to any skin disease. In fact the term is used almost interchangeably with the term *eczema*. There are three main types of dermatitis or eczema. The first, *primary irritant dermatitis* results from injury of the skin by some powerful chemical, such as strong alkali or turpentine. The second, *contact dermatitis* is due to sensitisation of the skin to some substance which is normally liable to cause this type of allergic sensitivity; examples are nickel (in jewellery and suspender buckles), epoxy resins, rubber additives, primulas and chrysanthemums, and even ingredients of cosmetics. Contact dermatitis may continue for a long time, even after the patient is no longer in contact with the offending material. The third type is often called *constitutional eczema*. Although the skin is apt to react adversely to various irritants and sensitisers the major part is played by the personality, and there is often a history of eczema, hay fever or asthma in the family. Treatment is more difficult, but local

corticosteroids and tar, sedatives and psychological treatment can be of great help. Infantile eczema also belongs in this category, but in most patients it disappears as the child grows up.

Impetigo is an infectious skin disease caused primarily by the streptococcus, but later often infected with staphylococci. It usually occurs on the face, and takes the form of blisters filled with pus on a red base; when the blisters burst their place is taken by yellow crusts. Impetigo is very infectious and easily spread by the fingers, dirty towels, or cloths; therefore, one of the first necessities is to prevent infection of others or reinfection of oneself by avoiding scratching and using a different towel each day, which must on no account be used by anyone else. Treatment is simple with an antibacterial ointment, so the main issue is prevention of contamination.

Sycosis or "Barber's Rash" occurs in men, and is similarly treated.

Urticaria or *Nettlerash* is a familiar skin disease in which itching weals appear on the skin, usually for no obvious reason. It is not infectious, and can be caused by nervous stress, certain drugs, allergy to some foods, or even exposure of the skin to cold. In some people it is possible to write on the skin with a fingernail: the "writing" appears in the form of weals. This is known as *dermographism*; it occurs in many normal persons as well as in many patients with urticaria. The antihistamine drugs are the most useful in the treatment of urticaria. Urticarial swelling of the tongue or throat requires urgent medical attention.

Acne, or "Blackheads," is a condition found on the face and shoulders; its appearance is so familiar that no description is necessary. Acne is one of those conditions which is the end result of many factors. There is, first, a greasy skin, the result of glandular upset (which is why the disease usually occurs in adolescence); secondly, there is infection of the skin; and thirdly, there is blockage of the sebaceous ducts, which ordinarily allow the grease from the skin to pass out on to the surface. Since the condition starts with excess secretion of grease, ointments should never be used, and probably the best applications are drying lotions containing some sulphur preparation which inhibits secretion of grease. The face should be frequently washed, and it is possible now to obtain detergent solutions which are both antiseptic and prevent grease formation. In severe cases ultraviolet ray treatment may be necessary.

Rosacea. As has already been implied elsewhere, although the wages of sin may be extremely unpleasant, the wages of extreme virtue may be no less troublesome. Thus *rosacea*, in which the nose and cheeks become red and greasy and the skin coarsened, occurs alike in chronic alcoholics and elderly ladies with no vices other than a preference for strong tea. Both cases are associated with indigestion, since, regrettable as it may seem, strong tea and alcohol are about equally liable to cause the gastritis which may be at the root of this complaint. However, in many patients the chronic flushing is caused in other ways and psychological factors are important.

Lichen Planus is one of the numerous skin diseases which seem to be due to nervous states of tension. It may occur on any part of the body, but is most common on the front of the forearms and legs. The rash takes the form of nodules which are lilac in colour and have a dent on the top; when these disappear a stain is left behind. There is severe itching. Treatment is a matter for a doctor, as it also is in the case of *psoriasis*, a very common disease of largely unknown origin, which is extremely resistant to treatment. It tends to run in families. It takes the form of slightly raised papules, usually on the elbows and knees; typically the papules are covered with dry, silvery-looking scales. Apart from the rash, the patient is usually in perfectly good health and there is no itching. Many drugs have been used in psoriasis, notably chrysarobin, and while it is not difficult to cause the rash (which may occur anywhere on the body) to disappear in one area or even in all areas for a time it has a strong tendency to return.

Warts, or *Verrucae* are familiar enough. They are caused by a virus, and are, theoretically at least, contagious (although having removed many warts, the writer has never found them contagious). Most frequently they are found on the hands, but may occur elsewhere. Treatment is best carried out by a doctor, who will use a cautery, a caustic carbon dioxide frozen into "snow." A curious feature of the common wart is that it can sometimes be caused to disappear by suggestion, which is presumably why so many old wives charms are not necessarily without effect. Different altogether from the common wart is the *plantar wart*, which occurs on the soles of the feet and often causes a good deal of discomfort. It is best dealt with by a chiropodist or in bad cases by a skin specialist since it is highly infectious.

Icthyosis is a disorder of skin formation with which some unfortunate people are born. The oil and sweat-producing glands do not function well and the skin is dry and scaly like the skin of a fish. It is, however, possible to help the condition, which does not affect the general health, by frequent alkaline baths to wash off the scales, and the subsequent use of lanolin to replace the lacking oil. Large doses of vitamin A seem to help in some cases, and there have been reports in the medical Press of cases being helped by hypnosis; this, however, is very much a matter for speculation.

Cancer, Rodent Ulcer, and Cysts. Cancer of the skin occurs mostly in old people, and takes the form of what is described as an *epithelioma*. It is most common on the face or hands, and usually appears as a nodule which breaks down and produces an ulcer. The glands may later be affected, but such cancers can almost invariably be cured unless a considerable time has elapsed during which they have been neglected. *Rodent ulcer* is a form of ulcer which appears on the inner corner of the eye or the side of the nose in old people. It does not spread over the body, but acts by eating into the tissues in the area where it has started. X-ray or operation is necessary, but the outlook is good. *Cysts* on the skin are due to blockage of the sebaceous glands. They may become very large, and are best removed, as they may become infected. They do not turn into cancer, and there is no such thing as "male" and "female" cysts. It does sometimes happen that *moles*, especially of the bluish-black type, may become malignant, so it is perhaps best to have them removed surgically when they exist. *All moles which change in appearance or size should be at once referred to a doctor.*

Skin Grafts.

These are a very complex subject which can be only briefly discussed here. They are used basically for a number of conditions in which large areas of skin have been removed from the body, as in burns or serious accidents. In other cases, as in plastic surgery, grafts may be used to make a new nose, eyelids, and so on. The following are the main types:

Pinch Grafts are small, circular pieces of skin cut from some other part of the body. (The former method of using grafts from another person has been given up almost completely, since such grafts—except in the case of identical twins—never "take.") The small pieces are laid on the area without skin and gradually grow together. *Split-thickness grafts* are grafts removed from another part of the body by an instrument known as a dermatome, which cuts sections about 10 by 20 cm. containing part of the deep layers of the skin.

In *Full-thickness Grafts*, on the other hand, the whole thickness of the skin is removed from elsewhere and applied to an area which has to bear friction or heavy weights, such as the hand or the foot. Lastly, and this is largely used in plastic surgery, there is the *Pedicle graft*, which,

unfortunately, although it is certainly the most exciting type, is rather difficult to describe. Briefly, if one, for example, wants to make a new nose, one cuts an area of skin and underlying fat about 5 cm wide and 12·5–15 cm long in the abdomen. One end, however, remains attached so that it gets adequate blood-supply. The problem is how to get this tissue to the nose, and this is done by a complicated process of leap-frog. First, the free end of the graft is attached to the forearm, whilst its " root " remains in the original site, and when it begins to grow and get its blood-supply from the arm, the original " root " is cut. So we now have a " sausage " of tissue attached to the arm. The arm is then lifted to the face and kept firmly in position there until the new free part becomes attached. It is then detached from the arm, modelled to the correct shape, and grows where the nose used to be!

DISEASES OF THE JOINTS

Rheumatism is a word most doctors wish did not exist. This is partly because they do not understand it, but mainly because it is a condition which strictly does not exist: which is small comfort to the many millions of people who are more or less totally incapacitated by it. The truth is it is used for a hotch-potch of very real diseases, in all of which there is pain and stiffness of what is called the musculo-skeletal system, *i.e.*, the muscles and the joints. It may mainly involve the joints, in which case it should have been called arthritis; or it may involve other structures near the joints like tendons, muscles and fibrous tissue. Joints may either suffer from inflammation or degeneration or both, and the trouble may be acute or chronic or both; so it is easy to see what a mix-up the subject becomes, especially when we must include the joints of the spine as well as the limbs, feet and hands.

A good deal of arthritis used to be due to various germs, but these types are much less common now that the infections causing them have become rarer or better treated. They used to include gonorrhoea, tuberculosis, septic joints, syphilis, brucellosis, typhoid fever, dysentery and so on. The importance of *Rheumatic fever*, which is a reaction to an infection (streptococcal sore throat) rather than being actually caused by the streptococcus, is not because it involves the joints. This arthritis quickly clears up, but there may also be disease of the heart which may be serious and has been described on P28.

Rheumatoid arthritis is a completely different condition in which there is non-infective inflammation of connective tissues throughout the body. In the joints, the normally smooth, lubricated synovial membrane lining the joint cavity becomes scarred, leading to distortion, especially of smaller joints like those of the hand. Another characteristic feature is its capacity to vary in severity from time to time, with a strong tendency to unexplainable periods when it gets better or worse. This makes it extremely difficult to know whether any form of treatment is being useful, since any response may have occurred in any case. As in all diseases which behave like this, especially those in which medical men are also baffled, there are almost as many theories and treatments as there are doctors. It has never been satisfactorily shown to be caused by infection, faulty nutrition, " glands, " emotions, personality disturbance, nor is it convincingly inherited. The best current theory links it with an increased sensitivity reaction, perhaps to the body's own tissues, known as " autoimmunity." From the patient's point of view there is swelling and deformity of the joints with tenderness on pressure and pain on movement. Treatment involves a lengthy and complicated regime of rest, relief of pain with aspirin, exercises and the application of heat, with attention to general physical and mental health. At some stage adrenal corticosteroids (cortisone and its derivatives) are often tried, but although these can give great relief they have to be very carefully used to avoid very unpleasant side-effects.

Osteoarthritis is another completely different

condition closely related to the normal processes of aging. Therefore it occurs in older people than those with rheumatoid arthritis, and tends to be in larger, weight-bearing joints of the spine, hips and knees rather than in the hand; although the end joint of the fingers is commonly affected. Hard wear and tear, especially that caused by overweight, or injury may be the beginning of it. It is *not* due to diet, and dieting has no part in treatment except in those who need to slim. Physiotherapy, including heat, is helpful. It is not such a relentless condition as rheumatoid arthritis and patients should be reassured about this.

Fibrositis and other vague forms of "rheumatism" are very often manifestations of psychological problems. This does not make them any less real, but it directs treatment towards the mental state rather than to the joints and muscles.

EYES, EARS, NOSE AND THROAT.

Diseases of the *eyes* are very specialised and only very general information can be given here. The most common is inflammation of the conjunctiva causing redness and usually due to infection or some irritant substance or dust. If it persists and leads to hard crusts of yellow pus on waking in the morning, get it seen by a doctor for treatment probably with antibiotics. First-aiders are usually instructed how to remove small particles of grit from under the lids. It is important that these should not scratch the front of the eye—your window on the world—as this may lead to scarring and poor vision. So, above all, do not rub them in. Also, if you are fishing one out of someone else's eye, see it before removing it. Do not have a general sweep round in vague hopes of finding it. If in any doubts, obtain skilled help. Remember the eyes are part of the brain: the only visible part. Perhaps this is why people's eyes are so revealing.

Conditions such as glaucoma, cataract and disorders of vision are beyond the scope of this section.

Foreign bodies in the ears and nose are a constant minor problem with children. In these cases, whether they be peas, beads or peanuts, do *not* attempt to fish them out. They are doing no harm where they are, provided the child can be prevented from fiddling with them. Get him to a doctor who knows far better than you do about the delicate structures of the ear drum or the internal nose just behind the object, and has the proper gadget to get it out.

Sore throats are a nuisance we all have to put up with from time to time. If they last more than a few days they should be treated professionally. Persistent or recurrent sore throats are often due to over-eager treatment with antibiotics not allowing the body to learn how to fight the germs itself. Never prescribe antibiotics for yourself, especially in lozenge form, and only expect your doctor to give them when other measures have failed.

Tonsils and their inflammation may be a problem. It is comparatively rarely that they should be removed, yet every year hundreds of thousands of innocent children are subjected to this ritual cruelty to satisfy the misconceptions of their parents and the greed (or ignorance) of some surgeons. Of course there are many children who benefit so much from having tonsils out that the operation (which has real dangers) is worth doing. But please allow your doctor to decide if it is necessary, and do not pressurise him into recommending it. (The same is true of *circumcision*, for which there are no hygenic and practically no medical indications. If your reasons for inflicting this cruel assault on your little boy are religious or emotional, then please admit it: but do not pretend it is "necessary" or even medically helpful.)

DISEASES OF WOMEN.

The *internal sexual organs* of a woman, like the urinary system, can best be described as shaped like a capital Y. At the tips of the arms of the Y are the female sex glands, the ovaries: the two arms running downwards are the Fallopian tubes: the point where the arms meet is the womb or uterus: the single leg of the Y is the vagina. These are the *primary sexual organs* of a woman and they undergo regular cyclical changes in response to the control exercised over them by the pituitary gland, situated in the base of the skull. This control is mediated by chemical messengers (hormones) secreted into the circulation. The ovaries also secrete hormones, œstrogen, and progesterone, and a delicate hormonal balance is maintained between the pituitary gland and the ovaries. Each month an egg cell (ovum) matures and is released from the ovary, usually midway between two menstrual periods: the ovum is wafted along the Fallopian tubes by waves of contraction and if fertilised embeds in the lining of the uterus which has been conditioned to nourish it by the ovarian hormones. If it is not fertilised the ovum escapes from the uterus, altered hormone levels then cause the lining of the uterus to be shed (this is menstruation), usually about 14 days after ovulation. After menstruation a new cycle begins; another ovum matures and a fresh lining grows in the uterus. These cyclical changes recur from puberty to the menopause. Menstruation does not occur during pregnancy, of which a missed period is often the first sign. However, women do miss periods even though they are not pregnant, and this usually means that some minor and temporary change has occurred in the hormone balance. If three consecutive periods are missed it is wise to consult a doctor.

The *breasts* are called *secondary sexual organs* and are also under the influence of the ovarian hormones. Two conditions which need treatment are *mastitis* and *cancer of the breast*, both of which are characterised by lumps within the breast tissue. Mastitis may be uncomfortable but is not dangerous and can be treated medically, whereas cancer is more serious. The distinction between mastitis and cancer can only be made by a doctor and any woman who discovers a lump in her breast must seek medical aid *at once*.

Abscesses also occur in the breast, nearly always when the mother is feeding her child. Here again, a lump appears, the breast becomes red and very tender, and the woman may be feverish. Treatment with antibiotics is sometimes successful, especially if the mother consults her doctor quickly, otherwise treatment is by a small operation.

The Ovaries. The two commonest diseases of the ovaries are cysts and disorders arising from hormonal imbalance. The symptoms of ovarian disease are usually abdominal or low back pains, and heavy and painful loss during the periods, which may become irregular. These signs should be taken as a warning to consult a doctor.

The Fallopian Tubes. Infection of the Fallopian tubes is called salpingitis. The membrane lining the tubes is continuous with the lining of the uterus, hence an infection is rarely confined to a circumscribed area in either the tubes or the uterus, and pelvic inflammatory disease is a better name for this condition. Pelvic inflammatory disease often follows an abortion, or childbirth where part of the afterbirth (placenta) has been retained, or can spread from an infection in a nearby organ, for example the appendix. Infection is sometimes conveyed by the blood from another septic source in the body. The gonococcus is another cause of infection. The disease is characterised by pain and tenderness in the lower part of the abdomen, accompanied by fever, general malaise and frequently (but not invariably) a vaginal discharge. The treatment of pelvic inflammatory disease is usually medical and is the same irrespective of the primary site of infection. Before the introduction of antibiotics the disease often became chronic and the Fallopian tubes were frequently blocked by a cicatrising scar, a cause of subsequent sterility.

The Uterus. This is a hollow muscular organ and both its musculature and its lining membrane can be the site of disease. *Fibroids* are non-malignant muscular tumours which develop in many women. The main symptom is a heavy menstrual loss and surgical removal of the uterus (hysterectomy) is often necessary. This is a major operation, but modern anæsthesia and operative techniques minimise the discomfort. Hysterectomy does not impair sexual pleasure, but no more babies can be conceived. Infection of the lining of the uterus is usually part of a generalised pelvic inflammatory disease (*see* Fallopian tubes).

Cancer of the Uterus and Cervical Smears. The uterus is pear-shaped and consists of a body and neck. The wide end is uppermost (the body) and the narrow neck (cervix) projects into the top of the vagina. Cancer of the cervix is commonest in middle-aged women who have married young and have had a large family; cancer of the body of the uterus usually occurs after the menopause and is more common in nulliparous women. The symptoms are variable and it is sufficient to emphasise that any woman who has unexpected bleeding, especially after intercourse, whether her periods have stopped or not, *must* see her doctor at once. The treatment depends on individual circumstances, but is usually by operation. It is now possible to detect cancer of the cervix long before symptoms develop and at a stage when the disease can be eradicated by a relatively small operation. This early detection has been made possible by the development of exfoliative cytology. Cells taken from the cervix (without discomfort to the woman) are examined under a microscope. This test is popularly known as the " cancer test " or " cervical smear." A cervical smear is often taken as part of the routine gynæcological examination by consultants, general practitioners, and family planning doctors, and is also being included in some population screening programmes. It is a big step forward in preventive medicine and may ultimately solve the problem of cancer of the cervix. Every woman between the ages of 25 and 60 should seize any chance to have this test done.

Prolapse means a sagging down of the uterus into the vagina and the cervix may even appear at the outside. It is a result of frequent childbirth and laxness of the ligaments which support the uterus: weakness of the vaginal walls often occurs at the same time. The symptoms of uterine prolapse are low back pain and a heavy dragging feeling in the lower abdomen; these are often overshadowed by the distressingly embarrassing incontinence which results from lax vaginal walls. The stress of only a sneeze, a cough, or a giggle often causes the involuntary escape of urine. The cure is operative and very rewarding.

Dysmenorrhœa or pain with the periods, is very common and most women experience this symptom at some time or another. Very often a girl's first periods are troublefree, but dysmenorrhœa develops after a year or two: this suggests that a psychological element is involved. Dysmenorrhœa is a symptom which has many varying causes, and the sensible thing to do, if pain is troublesome, is to see a doctor.

Amenorrhœa means stopping of the periods in a young woman. It may signify pregnancy or glandular disease or it can be purely psychological.

Abortion, or its more acceptable name, miscarriage, describes the spontaneous or induced termination of a pregnancy before the fœtus (baby) is able to survive. A baby cannot live unless it is born after the twenty-eighth week of pregnancy, though many infants born at this time die. The two main symptoms of abortion are bleeding and abdominal pain. Any bleeding occurring during pregnancy ought to be reported at once. Pain starts in the back and lower abdomen and is usually spasmodic in character, and like colic it works up to a peak and then temporarily passes off. Any pregnant woman with pain and bleed-

ing should go to bed at once and send for her doctor. When doctors are convinced that a pregnancy should be terminated then an abortion by safe surgical means may be performed in hospital.

CONTRACEPTION.

If a couple intends to practise birth control expert advice should be obtained from their family doctor or family planning clinic. The matter of whether or not a baby is born is too important to leave to chance. The method chosen must be effective as well as acceptable to the couple concerned, and the extent of the choice only emphasises the fact that the ideal contraceptive which is best for every couple at all times has yet to be discovered. The only method which is 100 per cent. reliable is abstinence. If the male seed (sperm) fertilises the female seed (ovum) then pregnancy results. Contraception is only effective if this union is prevented. A couple can achieve a measure of contraception without the help of pills or appliances if the husband practises *coitus interruptus* or they rely on the wife's " safe period." *Coitus interruptus* (when the man withdraws before emission occurs) is a thoroughly unreliable method which often leads to psychological difficulties in both partners. The " rhythm " or " safe period " method relies on estimating the time of ovulation and abstaining from intercourse during this time. This is at best unreliable, though its effectiveness can be improved by keeping careful records of the body temperature on waking each morning as the temperature rises once ovulation has occurred. The interpretation of these temperature records needs care and couples who must rely on this method can obtain expert advice from, for example, The Catholic Marriage Advisory Council, or a family planning clinic. *Barrier methods* prevent the sperms from reaching the ovum and can be used by the man (sheath or condom) or woman (cap or diaphragm): the reliability of the barrier is greatly increased if it is used in conjunction with a spermicidal cream, jelly, or pessary. A great many women have found that the *oral contraceptive pill* is ideal for their needs: it is the most æsthetic means of contraception and offers the most complete protection against pregnancy. Oral contraceptive pills contain chemical substances (œstrogen and progestagen) which replace the hormones normally released from the ovary while an ovum is developing. Ovulation does not occur, and without an ovum there can be no pregnancy. Pills must be taken strictly as directed as the dose is the lowest that will provide effective contraception and missing a tablet may result in pregnancy. Side effects sometimes occur (for example, nausea, breast discomfort, headaches,) but usually decrease after a few cycles of medication. Newspaper reports of the deaths of young women taking the pill have caused widespread concern. These tragedies have followed blockage of a blood vessel (by thrombosis or embolism) and have been carefully investigated, and the conclusions are that the number of such deaths is small and does not differ from the number which would probably have occurred in any case. No satisfactory pill for a man has yet been developed. In the newest method of contraception a small plastic *intra-uterine device* (loop, bow, or coil) is inserted into the womb. Once inserted it can be forgotten: a tremendous advantage to many different peoples and societies. It is not as effective as the pill but is more satisfactory than barrier methods. This intra-uterine device is not suitable for all women and is usually not recommended to women who have borne no children or who have very heavy periods. However, careful selection of suitable women has resulted in a high proportion of satisfied users. The search for the ideal contraceptive continues.

Vasectomy (a form of sterilisation) may now be performed under the health service on a husband in the interests of the health of either husband or wife.

PART III. SPECIAL TOPICS

PREVENTIVE MEDICINE

" Look to your health; and if you have it, praise God, and value it next to a good conscience: for health is the second blessing that we mortals are, capable of: a blessing that money cannot buy." (" The Compleat Angler "—Izaak Walton)

Prevention is better than cure; an apple a day keeps the doctor away; the Chinese pay their doctors while they remain well. It goes without saying that keeping good health is better than falling ill, even if the best treatment is available. But money cannot buy good health, so how can it be achieved?

We cannot of course choose our parents or have much say in the way we are nourished and brought up in infancy. But we can do something about our environment and if one is born of " healthy stock " and survives the many hazards of infancy, then keeping healthy in childhood and adult life is not too difficult. The main rules have already been mentioned (P4)—(1) do not think too much about your health unless it gives you trouble, (2) have an interest in life, (3) eat a balanced diet and (4) do not worry. This article will deal generally with the first of those precepts.

What is meant by not thinking too much about health is simply that the introspective, over-anxious, am-I-all-right attitude to body function is counter-productive. Obsession with bowel function is a common example of an over-anxious attitude to health; fear of constipation leads to self-medication with over-the-counter laxatives and daily, weekly or monthly ritual purges. Self-medication is no bad thing in itself—pharmacists all over the country are happy and competent to give advice on the home treatment of simple ailments and probably save the National Health Service a great deal of money—but very often simply changing a dietary habit or a particular mode of life gives better results.

How to Keep Well.

" Do not worry overmuch about health unless it gives you trouble." This is really a plea for less daily introspection on bodily functions—e.g., studying the tongue, feeling the pulse, counting the respiration after a run up the stairs and keeping a diary of bowel movements and so on. There are three simple rules for ordinary people like us (we exclude those who have to maintain peak condition for athletic reasons) and these are summed up as :— Get enough (a) exercise, (b) food and (c) sleep.

What constitutes " enough "? As far as exercise is concerned that means simply using your locomotive powers whenever you can; for food, not overeating nor undereating—just watching your weight; and, for sleep, no slavish following of a golden eight-hour rule but getting sufficient to " recharge the batteries ". Let us look at each of these in turn.

(a) Exercise. Many people work in sedentary occupations and require to make an effort to exercise flabby bodies. There is no need to run round the block in a track suit every night. A walk of a mile or two, to and from the place of work each day; using the stairs instead of the lift; playing games at the weekend or walking or cycling or swimming—these are all that matter.

(b) Food. Many people eat and drink far too much. There is no need to buy expensive books of food tables to work out how many calories you're getting. If you are an adult and finished growing but steadily putting on weight, you are probably eating or drinking too much. " Middle-age spread " is almost an expected norm—but should not be and does not have to occur (see weight tables, P41). Obesity, even mild obesity, shortens life span and it is certainly the commonest form of malnutrition in this country today.

(c) Sleep. Sleep is a widely variable necessity. Some regularly manage happily and keep fit on anything from three to six hours a day; others may need ten. It is largely a matter of habit and there is no harm in the occasional use of sleep inducers (not hypnotics, such as barbiturates, your doctor will advise you) to restore a habit interfered with by anxiety about business or domestic matters.

How to Avoid Infection.

In recent years vaccination against influenza has become widely available and many industrial concerns offer free " shots " to their employees in the autumn. When the particular strain of virus likely to arise in a winter epidemic can be determined in advance and the appropriate vaccine produced then such schemes are undoubtedly useful. Frequently, however, vaccines are only prepared from the commoner strains of influenza virus and give no protection against new mutant strains which emerge yearly with uncanny regularity. Nevertheless, partial protection may be better than none at all. If you are a sufferer from chronic bronchitis or any other condition in which a bout of influenza would be an especial threat to your wellbeing you are entitled to such anti-flu vaccination on the National Health Service.

For the traveller to certain countries inoculation against yellow fever and cholera is available. There is no preventive inoculation against rabies. Prevention is not confined to inoculation or vaccination; drugs are used to protect against malaria, for example, and such prophylactic therapy is available to travellers working or holidaying in malarial zones. The rapid expansion of air travel since the last war has in effect brought tropical diseases within reach of all. It is possible to contract malaria on holiday or on a business trip and be back in the UK before symptoms appear. Our doctors have to be alert to such possibilities.

The other way to avoid infection is of course to keep away from potential hazards such as the crowded train or cinema when influenza is about, and behave to others as you would they behaved towards you—we have forgotten the war-time advice—" Coughs and sneezes spread diseases—trap the germs in your handkerchief ". Much has been written and spoken about avoiding the common cold and almost everyone has his or her favourite way to ward off an impending attack, from the traditional hot whisky and lemon through the mustard bath to the relatively modern idea of soaking the tissues in large doses of ascorbic acid. While Vitamin C still has its devotees (foremost among them the Nobel Prize winner Linus Pauling) the consensus of informed opinion is that after some fifteen years of clinical research we have failed to prove its efficacy either as a preventer of cold or as a modifier of its symptoms.

Environmental Medicine.

So far we have considered preventive medicine for the individual; public health is the concern of specialists in social medicine, whose quiet work behind the scenes makes a significant contribution to the health of the community as a whole. Identification of potential sources of infection, e.g., contaminated water supplies, food, defective drainage and the like, has traditionally been the concern of Medical Officers of Health since Snow stopped people taking water from the Broad Street pump in London in 1854. Certain infective diseases are statutorily notifiable, tuberculosis for example, and it has only been through the vigilance of the Public Health services together with the development of successful anti-tuberculous drugs that the disease has been virtually eliminated from this country. Tuberculosis in immigrant groups is posing a new threat in some areas, but spread to the general population is being well controlled (see also Immunisation, Part III).

Health Education.

In the last edition it was stated that a nine-membered Committee of the House of Commons (Social Services and Employment Sub-committee) chaired by Mrs Renée Short was looking into this question. The Committee's report was published after we had gone to press and is now available from HMSO as the "First Report from the Expenditure Committee," Session 1976-77, volume I.

The sub-committee heard evidence from representatives of many organisations and official bodies—from nutritionists, community physicians, dentists, family planners and health visitors; from the Royal College of Physicians, the British Medical Association, the British Dental Association, the Tobacco Research Council, the Medical Council on Alcoholism and many others. This evidence, both oral and written, is available in volumes II and III of the report.

There were ten main areas to which the sub-committee gave its attention—health education; community medicine; alcoholism; smoking; contraception and abortion; dental health; nutrition and diet; exercise; health screening; vaccination and immunisation. The conclusions and recommendations occupy four and a half pages of their report, and considerations of space preclude our dealing with them in detail. Some general comment follows.

The committee was convinced that if more stress were to be placed on preventive medicine "substantial human and financial resources" would be saved. Even in the present difficult economic climate it should be possible to switch resources from one area of relatively low priority to others where there is clearly some urgency. Top of the list of priorities comes the need for health education of *children*, for it is they in whom it is easier to lay the foundations of healthy habits which should persist into adult life. As far as specific recommendations are concerned the range is wide. Quite a number, as the report makes clear, are warnings to the ordinary citizen about what he personally can do to avoid illness and premature death. For example, on the smoking question—"There should be a much stronger health warning on packets and tins stating that smoking, especially cigarette smoking, is a major factor in the causation of lung cancer, bronchitis and heart disease." And on exercise—"The relevant Government departments, *i.e.*, DHSS and DES, should actively promote the practice of physical exercise, in a suitable form, for all age groups, as a positive contribution to preventive medicine." There is in fact little to dispute in this very comprehensive and commonsense report, and it is to be hoped that many, if not all, of the recommendations will be acted on. Education is the key in many areas and, on the alcohol question for example, it is suggested that a larger proportion of the £2,000 million raised in duty and taxation on drink should be spent on educating children and young adults in the dangers of alcohol dependence.

We have in the U.K. a *Health Education Council* which, since 1968, has striven—and continues to strive—to improve people's health, mainly by teaching them how to prevent disease before it starts. It does this on a shoe-string budget of about £2m. a year. And the whole of preventive medicine of which health education is a part receives no more than about £90m. out of a National Health Service budget of around £5000m. Many people believe that the cost of treating disease, which forms a large proportion of that huge sum, could be very greatly reduced if more were spent on prevention, especially in the form of health education.

Early Diagnosis.

Lastly, almost as good as complete prevention—and we must face the fact that having the right forebears, eating the right food, developing in the right environment and taking all the inoculations offered will still not prevent the onset of cancer, cardiovascular disease, neurological disorders and the infirmities associated with aging—is *early diagnosis*. To know the danger signs and act on them is half the battle, particularly with cancer. The danger here is that listing all the warning signs will engender mass hypochondriasis and send many healthy people scurrying to their doctors. Therefore the list is limited to a few, most of which will be obvious to anyone who takes more than a cursory interest in his bodily and mental wellbeing.

First of the warning signs is *pain*. Many people will put up with great discomfort before seeking medical advice. Of equal importance is *bleeding* from any unusual site. The coughing up of blood does not necessarily mean tuberculosis or lung cancer, nor the vomiting of blood or its passing through the rectum necessarily mean cancer of the alimentary tract—a check costs nothing but time; it is imperative to locate the site of the bleeding. Less obvious to the layman in their importance as early signs of disease are *changes* in bodily functions such as appetite and associated functions of the digestive tract. *Loss of appetite*—in the absence of an obvious cause like a dietary indiscretion, anxiety and so on—whether or not accompanied by loss of weight, persistent discomfort after food, recurrent indigestion or any change in bowel habit, are all signs not to be ignored. Weight does not have to be monitored daily or weekly and a change in the fit of one's clothes is often the only pointer to a significant loss or gain which can then be checked on the scales. Only the obsessional weight watcher uses the bathroom scales daily.

Then there are a number of seeming trivia which merit medical advice. The little spot or sore on the back of the hand or the face (common sites for skin cancer) that refuses to heal up, the "smoker's cough" that persists after giving up smoking, the piles that seem to be giving more trouble, the stairs that seem to be getting steeper (or your breath getting shorter when you climb them), the swollen ankles at the end of the day, the cold that won't clear up—all may be heralds of largely treatable diseases provided advice is sought in time. Don't get too introspective, but do treat persisting symptoms such as the brief few mentioned above with serious respect. No doctor will feel his time wasted if his patients present him with any of the symptoms we have listed. Simple investigations *e.g.*, a blood test, an electrocardiogram or a chest X-ray, are often all that are needed to reassure a patient that he is not developing a serious disease and, even if he is, then because early diagnosis has been made the chances of successful treatment are thereby greatly increased.

HEALTH FOODS AND FADS

The Concise Oxford Dictionary defines a fad as a "pet notion or rule of action, craze, piece of fancied enlightenment". Pet notions about foods, particularly "health foods", are common and may achieve a cult status—such as in some societies the Zen Macrobiotic diets. Nutrition is a relatively young science and its exponents are not among the best of communicators; messages from their researches are seldom heard and, if they are, cannot always readily be disentangled from the publicity given them by unscientifically trained journalists who ride dietary hobby-horses for the supposed benefit of a predominantly female readership.

The amount of dietary misinformation propagated in that way has never been quantified except in the USA. A National Survey in 1972 revealed, for example, that 75 per cent of the population believed that extra vitamins gave them more "pep and energy", 66 per cent believed that a *daily* bowel motion was essential to health and 20 per cent believed that arthritis and cancer were attributable to vitamin and mineral deficiencies.

It is likely that the British are not all that different in their beliefs and it is the purpose of this Special Topic article to highlight some of the more glaring items of nutrition misinformation prevalent today. The subject will be considered under three heads:—

(a) Vitamins
(b) Additives
(c) Diets

In an article of this size the topic can only be partially covered; the interested reader is referred to the bibliography at the end.

Vitamins.

In many ways the word *vitamin* is unfortunate, implying as it does that "vitality", in the sense of pep and energy, must result from the consumption thereof. If we had stuck to Hopkins' term "accessory food factors", the popular misconception that vitamins are energy-producing agents might never have arisen. Vitamins are *vital* only in the sense that they are essential to life and must be taken in small quantities in the diet because of our inability to make them for ourselves, as can plants and bacteria.

The average, adequate and mixed diet contains enough of each of the vitamins (*see* P40) to maintain health. Extra are needed only by the malnourished or undernourished by way of replacement or by those with an *increased* requirement over and above that provided in the diet, such as the pregnant, the elderly and perhaps the chronically sick. Claims have been made, even by eminent scientists, that extra large doses of certain of the vitamins—all of which can now be synthesised in pure forms—have properties not necessarily related to their normal physiological functions. Vitamin C is a good example. An average daily intake of between 10 and 50 mg is sufficient to prevent the deficiency disease scurvy. We now know that one of the functions of this vitamin (which is only a vitamin for man, the primates, the guinea-pig and one or two minor biological curiosities) is to maintain the integrity of one of the basic "cement" substances that hold cells in place—collagen. When collagen is of poor quality or insufficient in quantity one of the results is a loosening of teeth and bleeding of gums or into the skin. It is claimed that doses far in excess of the daily requirement for health— *e.g.*, 1 to 10 g—are effective in reducing the incidence and severity of the common cold. However in spite of many attempts it has never been conclusively proved in controlled clinical trials that Vitamin C has such an effect. Fortunately it is harmless because the belief in its anti-cold property is well ensconced in some countries notably in the USA and Britain, and vast quantities will continue to be bought over the counters of pharmacies and, in Europe, supermarkets, for many years.

Therapeutic claims are made, too, for each of the other vitamins but are backed by no reliable scientific data. For example, thiamine (vitamin B1) is promoted for *nervous debility*—an unjustified extrapolation from the known fact that the neuropathy of beri-beri responds (as does the disease itself of course) to replacement of that "missing" vitamin. Similarly, because it can be shown that vitamin E is a factor required for rat fertility it has been recommended for almost every human reproductive disorder from impotence to habitual abortion. The claims for vitamin A as an anti-sunburn agent and for vitamin D as a treatment for chilblains are equally without any scientific foundation.

Vitamin faddism is common, but probably harmless. There is no reliable evidence to show that extra large doses of vitamins contribute in any way to more "positive health".

Additives.

Substances added to food for human consumption during or after processing or preparation are either to replace nutrients lost or reduced in concentration during preparation (*e.g.*, vitamin B1 to white flour) or to improve the texture, appearance or keeping properties (*e.g.*, vitamin C in bacon and sausages). In general there is no discussion about the replacement of lost nutrients although the protagonists of "natural" and "synthetic" vitamins still vie one with the other. Milling of wheat to produce the whitest of white flour (overwhelmingly preferred to any other colour) gives a virtually pure starch product with little or no vitamin or mineral content because those nutrients are lost in the process. Wholemeal flour is the complete (or almost complete) ground wheat grain and is nutritionally perfect in respect of its "natural" vitamins, mineral, fat and protein content. White flour is obtained by discarding some 30 per cent of the grain in milling and, by law, requires fortification with vitamin B1, iron

and calcium before it can be sold for baking' White bread is of almost the same nutritional standard as wholemeal bread. Additionally, wholemeal bread has a much higher fibre (roughage) content. Fibre is indigestible—*i.e.*, not absorbed and utilised by the body as a nutrient is—but nevertheless it plays a part in the whole digestive process. There is epidemiological evidence linking low-fibre diets with a number of gastro-intestinal diseases, not the least of which is constipation. A greater consumption of wholemeal bread in the UK—indeed in all developed countries—would dramatically curtail the sale of bulk laxatives (*i.e.*, laxatives depending on the peristalsis-stimulating action of fibre) over the pharmacy counter.

The question therefore "Which is better— white or brown bread?" can be considered by saying that apart from the different fibre content (there are many other sources of dietary fibre anyway), it is merely a matter of taste. The addition of vitamins to breakfast cereal is not a statutory requirement but at the discretion of the manufacturer. Such additives, largely used as sales points, but probably also compensating for losses in processing, must be declared on the packet. The only other example of a statutory vitamin additive is that of vitamins A and D to margarine to bring it into line with butter. In fact, although the Vitamin A content is then the same, the Vitamin D content of margarine is about six times that of butter.

But what of the additives used to improve or preserve foodstuff? Here we are on more controversial ground. There is a very large range of substances used by the food industry, from relatively simple chemical compounds like magnesium carbonate to help the free-flowing quality of table salt and ascorbic acid (vitamin C) which is used in baking bread, to chemically complex natural substances like the plant pigments known as carotenoids which are used purely for colouring soft drinks and sweetmeats. But the manufacturer cannot add anything he chooses; he is restricted to a list of permitted substances which is revised from time to time by an expert governmental committee.

There are of course a very large number of additives which are themselves cooked or processed natural foods—*e.g.*, dried starch pastes which are incorporated in packet soups to provide the thickening, emulsifiers such as glyceryl monostearate and alginates (from seaweeds) which are important ingredients of ice-cream.

Anti-additive faddism is common and is the *raison d'être* of the health food stores. However, there is no reliable evidence that the controlled use of additives by the food industry as briefly outlined above is in any way a threat to health.

Special Diets.

Most of us have dietary likes and dislikes; taste is as individual as personality. A certain amount of faddism or fussiness is socially acceptable in a society with such a wide variety of food to choose from. Nutritionally, only five varieties of foodstuff (plus, of course, water) are required— *protein, carbohydrate, fat, vitamins* and *minerals* (*see* P40). Free-ranging man, left to himself, gets a pretty well-balanced diet; the plain English "meat and two veg" with a milk or fruit dessert as the main meal, with breakfast cereal and eggs at one end of the day and a sandwich and coffee or tea at the other, provides all that is necessary. Protein does not have to be meat protein; vegetable, dairy or nut sources are just as good. One's only carbohydrate source is usually vegetable but again, fat does not have to be animal fat (indeed there is much evidence to show that vegetable sources are preferable). Vitamins and minerals are amply provided for in a mixed diet as described above but may be taken as synthetic supplements. There are no differences between vitamins as they occur in nature (*e.g.*, vitamin B1 and vitamin E in cereal grains) and those synthesised by the chemical and pharmaceutical industries. The chemical structure of all vitamins is known and mammalian tissues utilise synthetic and "natural" vitamins with an equal facility.

Summary.

Food faddism is common but largely harmless. However, extreme forms of faddism which are propagated by nutritional quacks may acquire a cult status and be harmful to their adherents if appropriate proportions of the five basic nutrients are significantly altered.

Further reading:—

Manual of Nutrition (8th edition), Ministry of Agriculture, Fisheries and Food. HMSO, London 1976.

Food for Man, by Aykroyd, W. R. Pergamon Press 1964.

Food—Facts and Fallacies, by Cameron, A. G. Faber & Faber, London 1971.

Nutrition Reviews, Supplement No. 1, 1974 (Volume 32), " Nutrition Misinformation and Food Faddism ", Nutrition Foundation, Washington DC., USA.

MULTIPLE SCLEROSIS

Multiple sclerosis (MS), briefly described in previous editions of *Pears* in the section on " Diseases of the Nervous System," is a relatively uncommon disease in the UK. Nevertheless, it is responsible for considerable disability in our adult population, particularly among young women because they are more prone to contract the disease than men.

Charcot, a famous nineteenth-century French physician, was the first to give us an accurate description of the disease which was based on first-hand observation of a member of his household who had developed it. He studied other cases, too, and concluded that it probably followed a previous illness of some sort—typhoid and smallpox were specifically mentioned—but it was not until much later, when sufficient cases had been described elsewhere in Europe, that MS became more widely recognised as a distinct, single, multi-symptomatic disease among a whole cluster of other neurological disorders which were then rapidly filling the published medical journals and being discussed at medical meetings.

It was realised early on that MS is a *familial* disease. That is to say, while it does not follow Mendelian rules of inheritance, its occurrence among first-degree living relatives is 15 to 20 times more likely than among the general population. This may of course only mean that family members are more likely to be exposed to the same causative factors as unrelated individuals.

Causes of Mutiple Sclerosis.

In spite of a considerable research effort over the years the fact remains that the causes of MS are still unknown. The two most favoured theories today are that it is either an " autoimmune " disease or that it is a special kind of infection, probably viral. The idea of *autoimmune disease* is based on the demonstration of " autoimmunity " in patients with certain diseases hitherto not properly understood. The " autoimmunity " concept goes a long way towards explaining the hitherto puzzling nature of such diseases as *rheumatoid arthritis*. The ordinary kind of immunity—to " foreign material," *e.g.*, the infective agents (bacterial or viral) of disease—is produced as a result of development of *antibodies* to those agents by specialised body cells. Antibodies, and hence immunity, may also be acquired artificially and at will by the procedures known as immunisation and vaccination (*see also* Immunisation P62). Recovery from measles is dependent on the production of antibodies which destroy or neutralise the measles virus. The immunity so acquired is permanent, and the presence of antibody in adult blood samples, or those from a child recovering from the infection, can be demonstrated in the laboratory.

But sometimes this process takes place in the absence of infection in a way we do not understand and antibodies to *normal* body cells, or parts of cells, are produced; these antibodies fail to " recognise " such cells or cell particles as being " self " and a kind of auto-destructive process is set up which produces symptoms of disease. Again, the development of auto-antibodies can be demonstrated by laboratory tests. A disease so produced is known as an *autoimmune disease*. *Rheumatoid arthritis*, as mentioned, is an example. As far as MS is concerned there is some evidence that patients' blood contains antibodies to myelin and it is on that evidence that we adduce that it, too, is an autoimmune disorder. *Myelin*, as we shall see later, is a key substance in the normal functioning of the central nervous system (CNS), and its destruction in an apparently random way is the principal feature of MS.

The other theory is the infective one. There is much more positive evidence of a pathological, epidemiological and immunological nature to support this. It is known that measles antibody can be found in the blood of nearly all adults whether there is a definite history of exposure to the measles virus or not; but many MS patients have measles antibody in the *cerebrospinal fluid* as well. These findings, with others too technical to go into here, point to the possibility that some *part* of the measles virus, inadequately neutralised by antibody from earlier, childhood infection, may lie dormant for many years before " emerging " in some incompletely understood way to produce the first signs and symptoms of the disease.

Epidemiology.

Epidemiology is the science which studies the relationship of diseases to time and place and populations, and the epidemiology of MS has been thoroughly studied. Many intriguing facts have emerged. The most important of these is that MS is found much more often in cool and temperate climates than anywhere else and, in general, its incidence declines with *latitude*. On or near the equator it is virtually unknown. Ethiopia, at 7°N, has one case per 100,000 population. Shetland, at 61°N, has 129. The figure for Sweden is similar—120; South Australia, on the other hand, at 30°S, has only 38. It is this very striking correlation with latitude that is fascinating but puzzling and yet may ultimately prove to be the most significant factor in the elucidation of the cause of the disease.

In the UK the *prevalence rate* is between 50 and 100 cases per 100,000 population—between two or three times the world average—and at any one time there will be between 40,000 and 50,000 patients suffering from the disease.

There is good epidemiological evidence that it is a disease acquired in childhood but not manifest before early adult life. Thus it is commoner among immigrants from northern latitudes to countries like Israel (30°N) than among the indigenous population of their adopted countries. For example, the prevalence rate among central European immigrants in Israel is nearly 50 per 100,000 compared with the rate among native Israelis and immigrants from North Africa and South West Arabia of only about five per 100,000.

Current thinking, based on such epidemiological studies, is that the disease may be acquired in the teens as a viral infection in temperate climates, remain dormant for years and then only become clinically manifest in adult life whether the victim has continued to live in his country or emigrated to a lower risk area. On the other hand, it may be that early viral infection induces an immunity in the majority and it is only young adults who miss the immunising viral dose in childhood who contract the disease.

What is Multiple Sclerosis?

Multiple Sclerosis is one of the *demyelinating diseases*. Myelin is the fatty substance formed in prenatal life around nerve tissue which constitutes a protective, insulating sheath for the nerve fibres which run throughout the central nervous system (brain and spinal cord)—see P46–7. These fibres conduct the electrical impulses which are the principal characteristic of physiological activity of nervous tissue. Defects in the myelin sheath disrupt the passage of such impulses in the same way that defective insulation in domestic electrical circuits can cause leakage of current, malfunction of appliances and even blow fuses. *Demyelination* is the term given to the partial or total loss of the myelin sheath, and in MS this loss —and replacement by scar tissue, hence the name *sclerosis*—occurs randomly, both in time and place, a characteristic that earned it the original name of *disseminated sclerosis*.

Demyelination can occur in any part of the central nervous system (CNS), but it has a predilection for the optic nerves and nerve tracts in the spinal cord concerned with muscle movement and co-ordination. The loss of function, partial or complete, which occurs as a result of the demyelination process depends on its site. Thus there may be solely a change in sensation in a particular body area—the occurrence of " pins and needles," a fleeting numbness, inability to distinguish between pin prick and blunt pencil: a change in muscle power—an excessive fatigue, weakness of grip or an almost complete paralysis of an arm or leg: a loss of co-ordination—clumsiness in simple things such as picking up and using a hair brush and comb. An uncontrollable shaking of the hand may occur on going to pick up an object—the so-called " intention tremor." There may be temporary interference with vision—blurring, seeing double, uncontrollable oscillation of the eyeballs (known as nystagmus) or with micturition—urgency or retention of urine.

Diagnosis.

MS is very difficult to diagnose in its early stages. There is no test on blood or spinal fluid that can give an unequivocal answer. The real difficulty lies in the fact that not only are the early signs and symptoms bizarre and varied but they are often transient, too. If a symptom does not disappear entirely in the early stages it may become so modified that the patient learns to live with it and not bother to seek medical advice. Onset and disappearance may be subtle and pass almost unnoticed. And when medical help is sought, some of the earlier symptoms may well have been forgotten.

Essentially diagnosis is made on the history of the early symptoms—and it may be two years or more from the first symptom before a pattern is recognisable. The pattern is diverse as between individuals, but in a typical case may run something like this. There may be, out of the blue, an episode of blurred or frank double vision, leg weakness giving a slight limp or making getting upstairs difficult, or a feeling of numbness in hands or feet on one side or the side of the face. These may last only a matter of days or weeks, only to clear completely. Months may pass before other, similar symptoms occur, only to vanish again as mysteriously as the first cluster or more commonly, to last just that little longer and then to persist in one form or another. This appearance and disappearance of symptoms may be so gradual as to make it difficult to pinpoint the beginning and end with accuracy.

It is just this typical remitting and relapsing pattern of symptoms related to different areas of nervous control which makes diagnosis reasonably certain, but a thorough neurological examination is needed for confirmation. The neurologist depends on a very careful and painstaking clinical examination based on extensive knowledge of the anatomical and physiological relationship of the nervous system and its control of body functions and skill in deducing from his examination the exact site of defects in that system. Other diseases have, of course, to be excluded—such as *subacute combined degeneration of the cord* which is a sequel to untreated *pernicious anaemia* and which itself is eminently treatable and curable in its early stages. Certain blood tests have now been devised which may be useful confirmatory evidence, but it should be stressed that there is no laboratory test that will provide an unequivocal answer to the question of whether a patient has MS or not.

Prognosis.

It is commonly held that once diagnosis of MS is made it means a sentence of years of increasingly severe disablement which will progress relentlessly and inexorably and reduce the patient to a helpless vegetable state in twenty or thirty years. This may be the case, but in fact such a gloomy picture is very uncommon. Much study has gone into the " natural history " of MS, and it is clear that there are seven distinct patterns of disease. These cover a wide range of symptom patterns from that characterised by a sudden onset of symptoms as described above, with relatively few relapses after the first year, to that manifested by sudden onset followed by unremitting relapses causing progressively greater degrees of physical impairment which may indeed lead to much distressing disability and death relatively early. But between these two extremes, of which the first is far the commonest form for the disease to take and the latter relatively infrequent, there lies a whole range of disease patterns, and prediction is difficult.

The widely held belief that MS is invariably a slow, progressively deteriorating, disabling and demoralising disease must be shown to be wrong. Admittedly the outcome, once a diagnosis is established, is very uncertain indeed, but it is often much more favourable than is generally supposed.

What can be done for the MS patient? Unfortunately there is no specific cure and we are ignorant of its cause. It is a disease which is unique to man and cannot be produced in any laboratory animal. Nevertheless, research is extensive and its epidemiology and pathology have been well studied, yielding many clues which one day will lead to cracking the problem. CRACK indeed is the name given to the young arm of the Multiple Sclerosis Society (*see* P62 for address of the parent group). CRACK is " a crusade aimed at rectifying misconceptions ... about self-help, hope and single-mindedness, the determination not to be defeated by MS."

Hope for the Future.

There are many misconceptions about MS, not the least of which is that it is all to do with diet. There have indeed been very interesting discoveries about the relationship between the behaviour of the white cells of the blood and polyunsaturated fatty acids (PUFA), and it has been claimed that this behaviour, which can be studied in the test tube, is sufficiently different from that of white cells from people without the disease to enable it to be used as a diagnostic test. It is early to assess the significance of this research, and much more has to be done. However, there is even now sufficient evidence from laboratory work to point to the possibility that a deficiency of PUFA may be a contributory causal factor in MS, and clinical trials are in progress using extracts of sunflower seed or seed of the evening primrose (*Oenothera biennis*). Controlled clinical trials carried out in London and Northern Ireland over a period of two years did show that relapses were less frequent and less severe in the high PUFA supplemented diet patients compared with a control group, but there was no clear evidence that the rate of deterioration was affected. Nevertheless, it is reasonable to recommend to MS sufferers that they should reduce their animal fat intake and increase the consumption of vegetable oils and margarine, both of which are PUFA sources.

The gluten-free diet, first shown to be beneficial in 1951 by one sufferer who claimed complete recovery, has also been both the subject of much investigation and a good deal of controversy. The suggestion has been that as MS occurs predominantly in wheat-growing areas it is a " wheat related " disease. In fact there is no direct evidence, as in coeliac disease (for the control of which the gluten-free diet is mandatory), that MS has anything to do with wheat or gluten sensitivity at all.

Treatment and Management.

While there is no cure for MS, the emphasis in treatment must therefore rest on reablement, and both the hospital and Social Services rehabilitation teams are to the fore in that work. The purpose of reablement is to help the patient both mentally and physically so he can cope with life and continue to earn his own living. In that way he can keep his independence and maintain a good quality of life within the limitations of the physical disabilities produced by his disease.

Physiotherapy may help by training some muscular groups to compensate for weakness in others or by retraining those previously weakened by disease. Much can be done during remissions. *Occupational therapy* will help those still able to run their own homes by advice the therapist can give on the aids that can be provided for the performance of routine domestic tasks. She is able to advise about suitable home crafts, especially those likely to be profitable at a time when morale is low and depression may set in. Like the Parkinson's Disease Society, the Multiple Sclerosis Society exists to sponsor research and to care for patients. It was founded in the early 1950s and has more than 250 branches in the UK alone. All are run voluntarily by MS sufferers themselves or their relatives and friends, and in practical terms they see to it that fellow sufferers get visited regularly and are made aware of all the social benefits available to them. And not least, the Society raises money in various ways to finance research; in 1976 its grants totalled nearly £200,000. For more information about their activities write to 4 Tachbrook Street, London SW1V 1SJ. If you have a friend or relative who has MS see that she or he knows about the Society too.

Conclusion.

MS, while remaining a neurological enigma and apparently defying the efforts of the many researchers in the different disciplines of epidemiology, pathology, immunology and virology, is slowly yielding clues as to its identity, its cause and its relationship to infection and immunity. As with tuberculosis and many other diseases, it will eventually be cured and eradicated.

Further reading:—

"Multiple Sclerosis—a concise summary for nurses and patients," Atkinson, Jean. John Wright & Sons, Bristol.
"Multiple Sclerosis—a report," Office of Health Economics, 162 Regent Street, London W.1.
"Multiple Sclerosis—a reappraisal," McAlpine, D., *et al.* Churchill Livingston, London.
"Multiple Sclerosis, Control of the Disease," Russell, W. Ritchie. Pergamon Press, Oxford.

IMMUNISATION

When official death registration was introduced in the middle of the nineteenth century more than one-third of all deaths in England and Wales were caused by infectious diseases. In 1975 the proportion was only about a half of one per cent. Diseases such as cholera, smallpox and diphtheria, from which many thousands of people died each year have disappeared, and deaths from other nineteenth-century killers such as typhoid, measles, scarlet fever, whooping cough and tuberculosis are now relatively rare. The greater part of these changes in mortality took place in the closing decades of the last century, before most modern specific medical treatment or preventive measures had been discovered and were due to improvements in social conditions—provision of hygienic sewage and waste-disposal systems and pure water supplies, less crowded and better-quality housing, more education, and improved nutrition and child-rearing practices. Removal of sources of infection by the isolation of cases and good sanitation, and prevention of the spread of germs by good hygienic practices, particularly in relation to the production and preparation of food as well as personal cleanliness, remain the mainstay in the prevention of many infectious

diseases. Some, however, are not easily controlled in these ways. The alternative is to try to increase the resistance of people as individuals to infection. This can be achieved by general measures to promote health, such as a balanced diet or, more directly, by artificially induced resistance to specific infections, that is by *immunisation*.

In developing countries, where the improvements in food supplies and physical environment required to reduce the ravages of infectious diseases may be beyond available resources for many years to come, carefully deployed immunisation may offer a short cut to controlling some infections, though improvements may be hard to sustain in this way alone.

Principles of Immunisation.

Infection implies the colonisation or invasion of the body by microscopic living organisms—bacteria, viruses and other parasites. This may result in disease, but in many instances, even when the organism is potentially harmful, it has no apparent effect. But whether the affected person is ill or not, infection leads to mobilisation of the body's natural defences and, as a result, specific antibodies to the organism (or antigen) concerned are produced (*see* P8(2)). These antibodies not only help to combat existing infection but also persist for months or years during which the individual is relatively immune to that particular infection. In addition, however, the antibody-producing mechanism is sensitised to the organism concerned —*i.e.*, it "learns" to produce antibody to that antigen—so that in the event of future exposure to the same or a closely related species of organism a very much more rapid protective response is evoked.

The defence mechanism can be similarly primed artificially by immunisation. This involves the inoculation of vaccines prepared from the organism or its products in a form which is generally harmless, but which is nevertheless capable of stimulating the production of protective antibodies. This is not always as efficient as natural infection, and multiple doses are often needed to produce protective amounts of antibody.

Most vaccines, until recent years, were made either from whole organisms killed during the manufacturing process (*e.g.*, whooping cough and typhoid vaccines) or from the inactivated toxins (toxoids) produced by some bacteria (*e.g.*, tetanus and diphtheria vaccines). A notable exception was smallpox vaccine, which contains a live virus, not the virus of smallpox itself but a closely related one, the *vaccinia* virus. The practice of inoculating vaccinia virus into the skin to protect against smallpox owes its origin to a daring experiment by a Gloucestershire physician, Edward Jenner, in 1796. Jenner had noted that country people who had caught cowpox, a relatively mild infection, from their cattle seemed to be protected from subsequent smallpox. He sought to prove this theory by first vaccinating 8-year-old James Phipps on the arm with material from a pustule on the hand of a dairymaid, Sarah Nelmes. Seven weeks later, he inoculated the boy with matter from a smallpox pustule, but, as Jenner had forecast, the boy remained well.

Nowadays, several of the vaccines in common use are prepared from living organisms (*e.g.*, *poliomyelitis*, *rubella* (german measles), *measles* and *B.C.G.* (tuberculosis) vaccines). In most such vaccines the organism has been attenuated, that is has had its capacity to produce disease progressively weakened by growth in artificial culture media. In the case of B.C.G. vaccine the organism is an attenuated non-human strain. The main advantage of live vaccines is that the organism actively infects and multiplies in the human body, as in natural infection. In these circumstances full and lasting immunity can often be obtained with a single dose, which is obviously preferable to the multiple injections required with killed vaccines. The only snag is that the more attenuated the organism the weaker is the antibody response, and there was great difficulty, for instance, with measles vaccine in cultivating a strain capable of creating an adequate immune response without causing symptoms similar to the natural disease. There are similar difficulties in preparing killed vaccines. Sufficient antigenic material (numbers of dead organisms) must be included to produce a good antibody response, without including so much that it causes adverse (i.e., unwanted) reactions in the recipients. One way to overcome the problem is to increase the *antigenic potency* of vaccines (i.e., their capacity to stimulate antibody production) by the inclusion of small amounts of harmless chemicals known as *adjuvants*, which allow the use of smaller quantities of antigen to produce the same effect. In recent years the development of so-called " split " vaccines has offered an alternative solution. In these vaccines the critical components are split off from the rest of the organism and concentrated. Thus much unwanted protein material, which causes many of the adverse reactions, is discarded, leaving a vaccine containing only those antigens necessary to stimulate production of protective antibodies. *Influenza vaccines* prepared in this way are now in use in several countries.

Passive Immunisation.

The methods of immunisation described so far rely on stimulating the body to produce its own antibodies to a particular infection—*active immunisation*. But this can take time, particularly if multiple doses are required. So, when someone is exposed to a possibly dangerous infection, it may be necessary to give urgent temporary protection by some other means. This can be done by injecting serum or other blood products derived from human or animal donors, who, as a result of natural infection or artificial immunisation, are immune to the infection concerned and whose blood contains large amounts of the relevant antibodies. For instance, after injuries in which the wound may have been contaminated by soil, which carries a remote but real risk of causing *tetanus* (see **P15**(1)), it is usual to give the patient a dose of anti-tetanus serum if he has not been previously immunised against the disease. The main drawbacks to this method of conferring protection are that some people are extremely sensitive to animal serum, that donated antibodies disappear after a few weeks or months and that, if doses have to be repeated, with each successive dose the antibodies are lost more rapidly and, therefore, give less effective protection.

Passive immunity is also acquired naturally in the unborn baby by transfer of antibodies across the placenta from the mother's blood stream into that of the baby. As with all passively acquired antibodies, they do not last long, but they are of some help in protecting the baby against some infections for a few months after birth.

Vaccination Policy.

After Jenner's demonstration of the effectiveness of smallpox vaccination this procedure began to gain in popularity, and in 1840 when a major epidemic of smallpox was raging the State first intervened to try to control an infection by vaccination. By 1853 vaccination had become universally available and was made compulsory in Britain for infants before the age of 3 months. Nevertheless, the proportion of children who were vaccinated was never near 100% and compulsion was finally discontinued in 1946. The State did not formally promote the use of any other immunisation procedure until 1940, when diphtheria immunisation was introduced. Since then a number of other immunisation procedures have been introduced and promoted by health authorities as matters of public policy for the prevention of disease in the community.

Immunisation is valuable not only in the protection of the individual but also to prevent the spread of other infections, mainly those that spread directly from one person to another, such as *poliomyelitis*, *measles* or *smallpox*. In such cases the likelihood of spread is affected by the degree of population (" herd ") immunity in the community. If most people are immune, either because they have experienced natural infection or because they have been immunised, successful

transmission from an infected person to a susceptible person is that much more difficult. The small numbers of vulnerable individuals are, as it were, protected by being scattered among people who are incapable of catching the infection and passing it on. Part of the art of infection control lies in recognising and using this simple fact to advantage.

Specific Vaccines.

It is the policy of health authorities in Britain now to offer all infants immunisation against *diphtheria, tetanus, whooping cough, poliomyelitis* and *measles*. In order to reduce the number of seperate injections the first three are usually combined in a single preparation commonly called " triple " vaccine. This and oral *polio* (" sugar lump ") vaccine are given together in a course of three doses which is usually completed before the first birthday. Soon after this *measles* vaccine is given in a single dose. In order to maintain immunity, further doses of *diphtheria, tetanus* and *polio* vaccines should be given at about the time of school entry (age 5 years) and *tetanus* and *polio* vaccines again before leaving school.

In localities where tuberculosis incidence is high, B.C.G. vaccine is also given to infants. Elsewhere it is offered to children in their early teens who are *tuberculin negative* (i.e., those whom a skin test shows have not been previously infected). At this age too, all girls should receive *rubella* (german measles) vaccine. In this case the vaccine is necessary not to protect the girl from the disease but because there is a risk that infants born to women exposed to rubella in early pregnancy may suffer from serious birth defects such as deafness, blindness and heart deformities. About four out of five women have had rubella by the time they reach child-bearing age, but it is *impossible to be sure* from a history alone who has had it and who has not, so it is vital to ensure that all are immune by giving them the vaccine.

No other vaccine is routinely given as a matter of public policy, but it is recommended that *influenza vaccine* be given to persons at special risk from the disease, particularly tnose with chronic chest and heart diseases and elderly people.

Travellers abroad may require other vaccines, such as those against *smallpox, cholera, typhoid, yellow fever, poliomelitis* (or a booster if already immunised) and occasionally more exotic infections either because the relevant vaccination certificates are required for entry to the countries they intend to visit and/or for their own protection because the infection is currently present in that part of the world. Vaccination against *cholera* gives only limited protection for just a few months, but that for *smallpox* and *typhoid* is valid for three years or more.

Achievements of Vaccination.

The most spectacularly successful vaccination programme has been that against *smallpox*. In Britain the disease ceased to be *endemic* (i.e., persistently present) in the 1920s, though the disease has been frequently reintroduced by travellers over the years, owing to our close connections with many countries where, until recently, the disease was still highly endemic. In 1967 the World Health Organisation launched a campaign to eradicate smallpox from the world. The disease was then still endemic in 30 countries. Attempts at eradication by mass vaccination had proved inadequate, but a change in tactics which aimed at the early detection of *cases* and containment by the vaccination of immediate *contacts* soon brought success. Vigorous pursuit of this method led to the final disappearance of the major form of smallpox from the world by 1975. Now only the minor form persists in one or two remote parts of Ethiopia and adjacent territories, and it seems likely that smallpox can and will be eradicated from the face of the earth in the near future.

Another outstanding success story is the demise of *poliomyelitis* in many countries. In the 1940s and early 1950s huge epidemics of polio recurred most summers in North America, Europe and other developed countries, leaving a sad trail of death and permanently crippled children and young adults. Then, in 1949, Enders and his colleagues in the USA found a way to grow viruses which allowed the production of virus vaccines. The first such vaccine was Dr Jonas Salk's killed polio virus vaccine, produced in 1953, which made a dramatic impact on the disease in the late 1950s. It was then superseded by a vaccine containing live attenuated poliovirus produced by Dr Albert Sabin. This vaccine had the advantages, first, that it could be given by mouth in a drop on a sugar lump, which is pleasanter and simpler than injections and, second, that it created immunity to infection with natural or " wild " poliovirus in the gut. This was a particularly valuable property, since the virus commonly spreads among *carriers* (*i.e.*, people without signs of disease but capable of infecting others), and oral vaccination effectively stops this from happening as well as preventing illness in those unlucky enough to become infected. As a result, where more than about two-thirds of the population have been vaccinated the disease virtually disappears. This is the best example of the value of " herd " immunity in preventing the spread of an infectious disease.

Similar success has attended the introduction of *diphtheria immunisation*. In this case, although the action of the vaccine is to stimulate the production of *antitoxin*, which neutralises the toxins produced by diphtheria bacilli but does not directly affect the bacterium itself, extensive use of the vaccine seems to result in the disappearance of carriers of *diphtheria bacilli* as well as of the disease. *Tetanus* also has become rare. In this case the use of vaccine and anti-tetanus serum has no doubt helped, but it is probably mainly due to the replacement of horses by motorised vehicles on the road and on the farm, and thus less contamination of roads and fields with manure containing tetanus spores.

Whooping cough and *measles* vaccination has been less successful in controlling these diseases, although both vaccines can give a high degree of protection to the individual. Finally, *B.C.G. vaccine* has undoubtedly played a part in reducing the incidence of tuberculosis to very low levels in the past 20 years, though with the decline in the disease a point may soon be reached where the routine use of the vaccine will no longer be justified and a more selective approach to control will be required.

Adverse Reactions to Vaccination.

Most medical treatments and procedures involve some risk, and vaccination is no exception, but it is important to keep the risks in perspective. Where a disease is common and the risks of death or crippling after-effects are considerable, the public is likely to be more tolerant of occasional harmful reactions to vaccination than if the disease is rare or mild in its effects. Thus *smallpox*

vaccine causes relatively frequent and sometimes serious reactions, but the disease itself was so frightening that the price of vaccination was acceptable. However, a time came when the risks of introduction of smallpox into Britain become so small that in 1971 routine vaccination in infancy was no longer recommended, and it was reserved for travellers to endemic parts of the world and medical and other personnel who might have to attend cases if they occurred. In the case of *polio vaccine*, there appears to be a very small risk, in the order of 1 in 4 million, that a person vaccinated with live polio virus will develop paralysis. This tiny risk is generally accepted because of the dire consequences of the disease if it occurs. However, *whooping cough vaccine* has been the centre of great controversy because of alleged adverse reactions. The debate has been about three major issues, which are sometimes confused. The first is whether the decline in the disease during the past three decades can be credited to the vaccine. There is little doubt that vaccines in use some years ago were not as effective as people thought, but those now used seem to give good protection. The second issue concerns the association between whooping cough vaccination and serious reactions, in particular rare cases of brain damage. The evidence that the vaccine *causes* damage is at present only circumstantial. There are many causes of similar types of neurological illness in young children, and some of those who contract such illnesses for other reasons may, by chance, have been recently vaccinated. In these circumstances, obviously it would be wrong to jump to the conclusion that the vaccine was responsible for all such cases. Studies now in progress should help to resolve doubts on this matter, but in any case it is important for parents to remember that serious reactions, if they occur, are extremely rare and that whooping cough itself can be a serious illness. The third, and related issue, is whether or not children who may have been damaged by a vaccine recommended by Health Authorities should be compensated from public funds. The Secretary of State has now agreed that in principle they should.

These two examples illustrate some of the anxieties and controversies which surround any medical procedure which involves intervention in the lives of people who at the time seem healthy, in the interest of disease prevention. In most cases a judgement is involved which balances benefits against risks. Sometimes neither can be accurately measured and what is acceptable to one person is not necessarily acceptable to all. In the case of vaccines most would agree that they have saved innumerable lives and much human suffering, particularly among children. Doctors must see that the vaccines used are as effective and as safe as possible. The price of freedom is eternal vigilance, and the continued control of some diseases requires that we do not individually or as a community allow our guard to fall, but the public must make the final judgement.

PART IV. INDEX AND GLOSSARY

Abortion. The termination of pregnancy, from whatever cause, before the child is capable of independent existence, 56 (1).

Abortus fever. An infectious disease known as undulant fever, 15 (1).

Abrasion. Any injury which rubs off the surface skin.

Acidity. *See under* Peptic ulcer, 36 (1).

Acne, 53 (2).

Acromegaly. A state of excessive growth of the body caused by overaction of the pituitary gland in the base of the brain, 43 (2).

Actinomycosis, 15 (2).

Acute chorea or St. Vitus' dance, 49 (1).

Acute nephritis, 45 (1).

Addiction to drugs. *See* Drug abuse, 22.

Addison's disease, 43 (1).

Adenoids, 32 (1).

Adrenal cortex, 43 (2).

Adrenocorticotrophic hormone (ACTH), 43 (1).

Agranulocytosis, 26 (1).

Allergy. Abnormal sensitivity to any substance which does not affect normal people.

Alopecia, 52 (2).

Amenorrhœa, 56 (1).

Amnesia, 47 (2).

Amœbæ, 8 (1).

Amœbic dysentery, 17 (1).

Amphetamine, 23 (2).

Amyotrophic lateral sclerosis, 48 (2).

Anæmias, 24–25.

Anæsthetic. Any drug used by surgeons to remove pain during an operation.

Anencephaly, 48 (2).

Aneurism, 30 (2).

Angina pectoris, 28 (2).

Ankylosis. Partial or complete fixation of a joint as after some types of arthritis. In other cases deliberately produced by surgery.

Ankylostomiasis, 19 (1).

Anorexia. Loss of appetite.

Anterior pituitary, 43 (1).

Anthrax, 15 (1).

Antibiotics are drugs which act directly against the organism causing the illness by interfering with its growth or some other aspect of its living mechanisms. Of all drugs which are used against bacteria, antibiotics do least harm to the patient's own tissues; some do have unwanted side-effect, but many have none at all. *See* 4, 9, 22.

Antigens and antibodies, 8 (2).

Antihistamine drugs, 4 (2), 5 (1).

Antiseptics, 8 (2).

Anxiety neurosis, 51 (2).

Aortic diseases, 30 (2).

Aphasia, 47 (2).

Aplastic anæmia, 25 (1).

Appendicitis, 37 (1).

Arteriography, 47 (1).

Arthritis, 54 (2).

Artificial respiration (kiss of life), 21 (1).

Ascites, 39 (1).

Asphyxia, 20 (2).

Aspirin and "upset stomach", 23 (1), 36 (2); *see also* Headache.

Asthma, 32 (1).

Atheroma or Atherosclerosis, 30 (1).

Athlete's foot, 8 (1), 15 (2).

Backache. A symptom which may be caused by many different diseases—sometimes disease of the vertebræ themselves, sometimes strain of the ligaments, and sometimes inflammation or spasm of the surrounding muscles. "Lumbago" is usually due to inflammation of the muscles in the small of the back. Backache from purely local causes may be treated temporarily by applying heat in the form of a kaolin poultice or a rubber hot-water bottle and taking two aspirin tablets a day. On the other hand, many cases of backache are due to disease elsewhere. The most important thing is to find out the cause, and therefore a doctor should be consulted.

Bacteria, 7 (1). Bacterial diseases, 12–15.

Bacteriophage, 7 (2).

Baldness, 52 (2).

Barber's rash, 53 (2).

Barbiturates, 23 (2).

Bell's palsy, 50 (1).

Benzedrine. The proprietary name of a drug known as amphetamine. *See* 23 (2).

Beri-beri, 42 (2).

Berry aneurysm, 49 (2).

Bilharzia, 18 (2), 16 (1).

Birth control, 56.

Blackwater fever, 17 (2).

Bladder. *See under* Urinary diseases, 44 (2).

Bleeding diseases, 26 (1).

Blood, function of the, 24.

Blood, diseases of the, 24.

Blood Groups. Human blood plasma contains factors which clump, or agglutinate, the red cells of some other people's blood. The main blood groups are called A, B, AB, and O. The plasma of group A blood contains an anti-B factor and *vice versa*, so that people of groups A and B cannot accept each other's blood. Group AB contains neither anti-A nor anti-B factor and people with this group can therefore receive transfusions from both but can give to neither. Group O contains both anti-A and anti-B, and can therefore receive blood only from group O but can donate blood to all groups. It is important that transfused cells should not be agglutinated by the factors in the recipient's plasma. Apart from the so-called ABO system, there are several other blood groupings, one of which is mentioned under Rhesus Factor.

Blood poisoning (septicæmia), 14 (2).

Blood-pressure, 29.

Blood-vessels, diseases of the, 30.

Blue babies, 5 (2).

Botulism, 14 (1).

Brain. *See under* Nervous system, 46, Physical injuries, 19.

Brain tumour, 50 (1).

Breasts, 55 (2).

Bronchial asthma, 32 (1).

Bronchial carcinoma, 57 (2).

Bronchiectasis, 32 (1).

Bronchitis, 31(2).

Bruises and abrasions, 19 (2).

Burns and scalds, 21 (2).

Cachexia. Extreme wasting due to disease.

Cæsarean operation. When the abdomen has to be opened to remove the child, named after Julius Cæsar, who is said to have been born in this way.

AN INTRODUCTION TO PSYCHOLOGY

This section is concerned with the science and study of the human mind, a territory rich in mystery, a glimpse of which we catch through the enigma of memory, and in the misty drama of our dreams. It represents a unique guide to one of the most exciting experimental sciences of today.

TABLE OF CONTENTS

AN INTRODUCTION TO PSYCHOLOGY

The purpose of this section is to provide a general introduction to the young but expanding science of psychology. The topic itself is of course enormously broad and can only be summarised at best. However, it is hoped it will serve to give some idea of the fascinating material that psychologists study and also of their occasionally remarkable, and always interesting findings. The section also aims to dispel some of the illusions that have surrounded the subject and to define its boundaries to the extent that the reader will not only begin to understand what psychology is, but also what it isn't!

I. INTRODUCTION.

What is a Psychologist?

The popular image of a psychologist is a fairly well-defined one—he is a man who treats mental illnesses in the way that a doctor treats physical ones. His principal equipment, apart from a well-furnished "consulting room," is a leather couch for patients to lie on, a well-stocked library, and a cabinet of mysterious drugs of one kind or another to send them off to sleep. He is particularly interested in the dreams of his clients and may use some form of hypnosis to study their "repressed" thoughts and secret emotions. He is probably very wealthy, because of the enormous fees he charges, and may speak with a central European accent.

Silly though the above description may sound, it is nevertheless unfortunately true that it corresponds pretty closely to the kind of picture that most people have of a psychologist and of the kind of work he does. Remote though this description is from the truth—at least as far as the vast majority of psychologists is concerned—the average person can be forgiven for having it firmly lodged in his mind, for in literally hundreds of movies, TV and radio plays, books and novels this is the picture that has been painted. One of the first tasks of this section will be to attempt to straighten out some of these misconceptions so that a clearer idea of the nature of psychology can be given. While the mysterious and, unfortunately, rather glamorous aspect of psychology that concerns itself with mental illness and its treatment is certainly one facet of the topic, there is a good deal more to it than that. Furthermore, the part of psychology which deals not with the abnormal but with the strictly *normal* brain is the area which has best repaid scientific study and, as we hope to show, which has uncovered the most exciting raw material.

This section, therefore, begins with a clarification of the role of the psychologist, and follows with a brief introduction to his principal fields of study—the brain and human behaviour. After this we take in turn the four main areas of study which assist him in his quest for an understanding of human nature. These are Perception, Learning and Memory, Motivation, and finally Personality and Thinking.

One of the main sources of confusion in people's minds arises from puzzlement over the distinction between four commonly used words which, while differing in meaning in important respects, are almost invariably lumped together as one. These are (1) Psychiatry, (2) Psychoanalysis, (3) Psychotherapy, and (4) Psychology. The words do look and sound rather similar but it is not difficult, once the right definitions have been given, to sort the four clearly out in one's mind. Let's take psychiatry first.

(1) **Psychiatry** is the art of *treating* mental diseases or illnesses by medical means and it is a specialist branch of medicine, entered through the medical profession and taught at hospitals or universities. A psychiatrist therefore is quite invariably a doct r of medicine with ordinary medical degrees but with a postgraduate training in mental illness and its treatment. No one may call himself a psychiatrist unless so qualified, and

no one may prescribe drugs or surgery in treating mentally sick individuals unless he is medically qualified. There is an important point of issue here, for in England, and many other countries, people not trained as psychiatrists may nevertheless diagnose and treat mental illnesses—provided that they do not use drugs or surgery to do so.

(2) **Psychoanalysis** is a particular form of examination or diagnosis of an individual's mental state based on the theories of the mind and personality advanced by Sigmund Freud and his colleagues or followers, and the reader may like to turn to the entry on the subject in Section J. An interesting feature of psychoanalysis is that, unlike psychiatry, it may be practised without medical or academic qualifications on the part of the analyst. A special training analysis at a recognised institute is normally undertaken by the would-be practitioner, however this is not normally made available to individuals unqualified in medicine or psychology.

(3) **Psychotherapy** is the practice of treating mental diseases or illnesses by more or less *any* means. Thus, strictly speaking, both the psychiatrist and the psychoanalyst are psychotherapists—as are any other individuals using reputable methods who offer therapy for the mind. Once again notice that this implies that one may call oneself a psychotherapist irrespective of whether one has medical or academic qualifications, and it is a word that tends to be adopted, with impunity, by a good many "quacks" and charlatans who can of course do fearful damage in this tricky area.

(4) **Psychology** is literally the study of the mind (or soul) but its area has broadened somewhat in the last century as we have learned that one cannot consider the mind as totally isolated from the body, and it now includes the study of human personality and behaviour. Psychologists also study the behaviour and brain of animals wherever such studies throw light on human behaviour. It is important to realise that psychologists are first and foremost trained as scientists rather than as medical experts and do not necessarily take much interest in abnormalities of the brain and mental processes. Those who do, tend to take postgraduate training in what is known as "clinical psychology," and may add to their knowledge by undergoing training in psychoanalysis.

It is obvious that there is a good deal of overlap between these four aspects of the topic and in the following section we shall be entering the territory of psychiatry and psychoanalysis to some extent, but mainly concerning ourselves with psychology —the science and study of the human mind, personality, and behaviour.

1. The Brain.

From the moment of our birth and emergence from the security of the womb our body is controlled and dominated by a single but complex organ, a library, switchboard, signal-box, computer, and many other things all rolled into one—the brain (*see* F37(2), P46). Very properly encased in a hard shell of bone and equipped with instruments for detecting food or danger at a distance—eyes, ears, etc.—the brain matures slowly, unlike other bodily organs, reaching its peak of efficiency and potential approximately 18 years after birth. From then onwards, slowly and almost immeasurably at first but with remorseless steadiness, it slides into decline. Its proper functioning determines the "normality" of the behaviour of the individual and the part he can play in society, its efficiency determines to some extent his intelligence and his ability to compete, its storage capacity and information retrieval system, his potential to learn and remember. In addition its computing power determines his creativity and is the primary function which distinguishes between the mature human being and the other animals on earth. No organ or complex of organs is guarded and shielded so carefully.

The brain is the main focus of interest for the psychologist, for there can be little doubt that the key to the understanding of human personality and behaviour lies locked up within it. Its complexity of course is daunting, but thanks to physiological and anatomical studies it is possible to get at least a general idea of what's going on. In the first place the brain acts as the principal co-ordinator of messages coming in from the various sense organs, and then as the dispatch point for the appropriate responses. This co-ordinating centre is easily best developed in man, and is present in most of the "higher" animals. Simpler creatures, however, such as amoeba and certain tiny worms, get along without any important co-ordinator of nervous impulses and respond diffusely to changes in the environment—moving vaguely away from things that "annoy" or damage them and towards food or other "pleasant" things. Such animals are literally the slaves of their environment, incapable of setting up goals to achieve and with no facility for computing the consequences of any action. One important branch of the evolutionary tree shows a steady trend towards increasing brain size and, with it, freedom from this slavery.

In the second place the brain acts as the storehouse of information which the senses have gathered at some time in the individual's life. To us it may seem "obvious" that we have a memory—a device for looking at things that took place in the past—and indeed it is hard to imagine ourselves without one. However, a large number of creatures get by with only the most limited of memory systems, and some with none at all. Clearly a good deal must depend upon how long an animal is to live. If its life-span is to be brief, then it need not set aside much room to store information from its past. If it is to live for many years, survive in a changing and generally rather dangerous environment, and learn by its mistakes and its previous achievements, then this ability to refer back to the past is obviously essential. In human beings mechanisms of learning and memory are of vital importance and we will devote a good deal of this section to discussing the way in which psychologists study these.

The third primary function of the brain is to provide the computing and decision-making processes which dictate so much of human and higher animal behaviour. It is also, in the case of man, the centre of consciousness and at the same time that elusive faculty we call personality.

2. How Does the Brain Divide up its Functions?

Nowadays we rather take for granted that important things such as thinking, remembering, etc., are mediated through the brain and it comes as something of a shock to recall that early philosophers located the majority of such processes in the heart or the stomach! Even today, a good deal of controversy exists over exactly which part of the brain does what and, as we shall see when we discuss the contradictory experimental evidence later, there is even a suggestion that certain processes are dealt with by the brain *as a whole* rather than by some specific part. However, the picture is reasonably clear.

In the first place the brain is composed of a vast number of cells—the building blocks of all living systems—which in this case have become highly specialised and stretched out, rather like telephone lines. These are known as nerve or neural cells or, yet again, as neurones. They act as communication units, receiving electrical signals from other parts of the body. Comparative anatomists are able to trace the routes of whole chains of cells starting at, say, the finger tips and finishing up in a particular slab of the brain where such tactile messages are gathered and interpreted. On the whole messages from the eyes tend to finish up in the back of the brain, or occipital lobes; messages from the ears, nose, etc., on the side, or temporal lobes. In the front exists a large chunk of nervous tissue with a rather mysterious function inasmuch as it seems to be more directly related to the personality and mood of its owner than to any of his senses. In addition there are parts of the brain concerned more with output than input—the so-called motor areas which dispatch the signals commanding various parts of the body to move. Finally there are the parts principally involved in the storage of information, memory, etc.

All these areas we have been talking about up till now are known as the cerebral cortex and they are located on the outer surface of the brain itself—*i.e.*, right up against the inside of the skull. You should by now have gathered that the cortex deals largely with psychological factors closely tied up with consciousness and awareness—seeing, hearing, thinking, remembering, etc. This ties in rather nicely with its alternative name, the neocortex (or new tissue), for in evolutionary terms this part of the brain is "new." In general, the closer that an animal species approximates to man, the greater the proportion of its brain is assigned to neocortex, and the more the particular animal is capable of independent, deliberate and purposeful activity.

Tucked in beneath the cerebral cortex, growing out of the spinal cord, are the so-called lower centres—the old brain. Here in a number of specialised blocks are located the control centres which deal with the most automatic (but no less important) bodily functions such as cardiac activity, respiration, temperature, etc., and which it is unnecessary or inconvenient to keep under conscious control. Damage or injury to these centres is generally very serious, whereas damage to the outer layer of the brain, even when extensive, can have surprisingly little effect on the individual's way of life.

To sum up, we note that the brain is divided into two major functional areas in evolutionary terms—the old and the new. The former largely deals with the vital automatic processes, and the latter with the receiving and interpreting of sensory input and the decision-making processes which guide our interaction with the outside world. Clearly this is an enormously simplified picture (specific aspects of this topic are dealt with in greater detail later) and the brain and central nervous system (CNS) is complicated almost beyond description, with much of its mechanics and rules of operation still poorly understood. How then can one set out to study it properly and unravel its secrets?

3. Methods of Studying the Brain.

Psychologists and physiologists favour many approaches to finding out how the brain works, and while it won't be possible to look at them all in this section it will be worthwhile spending a bit of time on some of the most important lines of attack. These can be classed under the headings (1) comparative anatomy, (2) surgical tissue destruction, (3) electro-encephalography, (4) microelectrode recording, (5) biochemical analysis, (6) behavioural research, and (7) introspection. Some of these are really only possible with animals as the experimental subjects, and others are more suited for research on human beings.

(1) *Comparative Anatomy.*

This is perhaps the most obvious and logical method of all, but it has one serious and insurmountable drawback. Suppose that one wanted to find out how a motor-car engine worked and that one had no prior knowledge of its operation but knew what one looked like from the outside. Failing instruction booklets or advice from motor mechanics, the best method might seem to be to get hold of a complete engine and take it apart to examine its components. Given enough skill one might even be able to put it back together again. The chances are that with a relatively simple device, such as an automobile engine, an intelligent person would begin to see the principles of operation. However, until he had actually watched it at work and studied the effect of, say, depressing the accelerator or pulling out the choke, his comprehension of the device might be limited and he could well come to some funny conclusions about its function and operating habits. This approach is essentially that of the comparative anatomist who sets out to study the brain by examining a dead specimen, peering at it through a microscope, cutting out bits here and there and hoping to work out what each section contributes to the whole. Unfortunately, whereas the average motor-car engine probably contains a maximum of about 1,000 discrete and separate components, some of which are rather large and " obvious," the brain contains a conservative minimum of about *a thousand million* neurones or nerve cells and no large and obvious " moving parts " to give the anatomist useful clues. It is little wonder therefore that while students of the brain adopting post mortem dissection have, in the course of the last few centuries, acquired a pretty clear picture of the way in which the brain is laid out—an anatomical atlas so to speak—most of the principles of cerebral operation are still more or less unknown. One of the great drawbacks of this system, as you will probably have guessed, is the fact that anatomical dissection and analysis can only be done in the dead animal.

(2) *Surgical Tissue Destruction.*

To return to our rather inexact analogy with the motor-car engine, let us assume that our investigator finds himself with a working, running engine to play with. Let us also assume that he has already made himself pretty familiar with the anatomy of the " dead " engine and has perhaps formed some hypotheses as to what certain parts of it do. For example, he might have a suspicion that the carburettor and the sparking plugs were particularly important, or that a key to the complete device working was that the pistons should move up and down in the cylinders. One of the first things he might do would be to systematically remove what he considered to be important parts of the engine and note how its performance was effected. Using this technique of selective removal he might soon begin to confirm or reject his hunches and a gradual comprehension of the function and capabilities of the engine would build up in his mind. He might find that whereas the removal of one sparking plug did not stop the engine, it would lower its pulling power. Removal of the carburettor in toto would be calamitous, while twiddling with it might have unpredictable effects, making it run better or worse. On the other hand, filing bits off the iron cylinder block would make no difference whatsoever. Once again the psychophysiologist is faced with something immensely more complex when he studies the brain, but there is nevertheless obviously something to be gained by adopting a similar procedure with the working or living system. The systematic removal or destruction of parts of cerebral tissue has, in fact, been one of the most rewarding approaches adopted by brain scientists, though there are naturally severe limitations to the technique. In the first place such surgery cannot be performed on human beings, except where it is a necessary feature of therapeutic brain surgery (*e.g.*, as when removing a brain tumour) and can only be justified in living animals in the interest of serious and clearly defined scientific research. (Despite the assumptions of anti-vivisectionists, no reputable scientist enjoys performing experimental surgery on living animals and these are always conducted in such a way as to cause the creature as little distress and suffering as possible.) In the second place, the very act of surgery itself probably introduces side-effects which serve to complicate the picture. However, this technique, when skilfully used, has led to some informative experiments.

(3) *Electroencephalography.*

As we have said earlier, the principal building blocks of the brain are the neurones, specialised cells devoted to the transmission of information from one part of the body to the other. This transmission is effected by a change in the electrical potential of the cell along its long stem. The main bodies of cells tend to be pressed up against one another and when a change in potential occurs in one, this tends to trigger off a similar response in a neighbouring cell at a junction point known as a *synapse*. Incidentally, the long stems of the cells (which may be a yard or more in length in certain parts of the body) are covered by an insulating sheath which prevents the electrical " message " leaking out en route and which makes them strangely similar to the kind of electrical wires and cables we use in telecommunications. With a thousand million cells jammed up together in the head, all of them propagating electrical signals in one way or another, it should not surprise anyone to learn that sensitive recording devices can be used to get a picture of the overall electrical activity going on in the brain. Studies of this type (electroencephalography, or EEG for short) couldn't begin until suitable recording machines had been developed and thus, although scientists had been pretty confident that the brain was a potent source of electrical energy since the middle of the 19th cent., it wasn't until the 1920s that anyone was able to get a readable picture of this. The pioneers in this technique were the physiologists Berger and Adrian, who attached little electrodes to the outside of the human scalp and by hooking these up to amplifiers and then to special recording pens were able to get a kind of plot of the electrical activity going on within. To their surprise what emerged was not just a meaningless hodge-podge of electrical " noise " but rather a series of precise and elegant rhythms, the frequency and amplitude of these depending upon the part of the brain where the electrodes were applied, and also—most excitingly —on the individual's mental state at the time of the recording. As time has passed and recording technology has advanced, an immense amount of data has been gathered on these so-called brain waves, and while it is true to say that the high hopes of the pioneers who believed that they were about to unravel the brain's mysteries almost overnight with this technique have not been realised, the EEG has proved its worth in more ways than one. In medicine, for example, certain disruptions of the " normal " brain wave pattern can give clear indications to the expert of the presence of epilepsy or determine the site of otherwise totally inaccessible brain tumours. The EEG can also be enormously useful in evaluating the effectiveness and mode of operation of new drugs and is helping in our understanding of the nature of sleep—the EEG of a sleeping person differs significantly from that of a waking one. Curiously one of the most promising-looking of the many rhythms which the brain emits—and one of the first discovered by the English scientist Adrian, the so-called alpha rhythm, has turned out to be one of the most disappointing. The alpha rhythm, which is generally picked up by electrodes attached to the back of the head (over the occipital or visual cortex), is a beautifully neat and stable wave of about 14 cycles per second frequency. It is present when the individual is relaxed and has his eyes closed. Opening the eyes and looking around, or alternatively keeping them closed and doing a bit of mental arithmetic, causes the rhythm to disappear, and the hypothesis was soon advanced that alpha was a reliable index of the rather abstract mental state known as " attention." Unfortunately for this convenient idea, on further study it was found that the rhythm did not always behave as it should, sometimes doing exactly the opposite to what was expected of it. Furthermore about one in ten otherwise normal individuals show no alpha rhythm at all. The picture has been complicated even further by the publication in 1973 of a book *The Origin of the Alpha Rhythm*. In this the author, Dr. Olof Lippold of University College, London, advances the argument that alpha rhythm in fact reflects physiological tremor of the eye muscles, and therefore has very little to do with internal cerebral states. The presence of abundant alpha in the EEG, Lippold argues, is more likely to be evidence of poor vision than any special capacity to control one's attention. It's fair to say that Lippold's views are still highly controversial, but it should equally be clear that the simple view that brain waves denote complex internal processes is by no means established. All these drawbacks aside the EEG is still one of the best ways of getting some kind of index as to what is going on inside the head of a human or animal, without resorting to surgery or interfering seriously with normal thought processes.

(4) Microelectrode Recording.

For all practical purposes the record obtained by the EEG is a gross, overall view of the brain at work. The waves and rhythms encountered must, at the least, represent the sum of the activity of literally hundreds of thousands of neural cells, presumably firing more or less in synchrony. Going back once more to the motor-car analogy, the EEG could be likened to a garage mechanic listening with a stethoscope to the pulsing of an engine when running at high speed. Changes of speed, adjustments in carburation of timing, etc., would give characteristically different running sounds, but little if anything could be deduced about the state of activity of an individual component unless it were a very large one. Much the same limitations, only on a gigantic scale, surround the use of the EEG as a device for measuring specific aspects of brain activity. Quite recently, however, an interesting technological development has occurred which allows a more precise and delicate analysis of cortical cell firing to be undertaken—in fact to allow even the output from a single neural cell to be monitored. This technique involves the use of what are known as microelectrodes, tiny slivers of metal, thousandths of an inch in diameter, which when in contact with an electrical source—in this instance the body of a nerve cell or neurone—transmit a pulse of electricity to an amplifier and recording apparatus. We shall discuss the remarkable findings which have come from experiments of this kind later in the section on "Perception." Microelectrode techniques, incidentally, can on occasions be used with human subjects. In such cases, naturally the opportunity arises when an individual is undergoing brain surgery for, say, the removal of a cerebral tumour. In these circumstances with the patient's permission, the surgeon may perform experiments to study single cell responses with results which have been of great interest.

(5) Biochemical Analysis.

Scientists have recently shown increasing interest in the microstructure of cerebral tissue, not just the neural cell but in its basic constituents—in other words at the molecular level. Clearly there is not much hope or point in trying to record the behaviour of molecules by electrode recording or even by microscopic visual analysis, so some other method must be found if one is concerned with this level of analysis at all. This is where the psychologist teams with the biochemist—an example of the kind of interdisciplinary approach which is becoming common in brain research. As with much of the chemical analysis performed in other fields, scientists discover the nature of the substance they are examining by observing its behaviour when mixed with other chemicals or compounds. Crudely speaking, one mixes the unknown substance with some known chemical and simply watches what happens, the reaction which follows giving clues as to the nature of the chemical under study. Now in the case of the brain or the constituents of neurones, it is obvious that one is dealing with more than one single substance so the first problem is how to separate the constituents in order to study them individually. To achieve this biochemists use a number of techniques such as

chemical separation simple heating, and even whirling the material round at great speeds in centrifuges. The biochemical approach to brain research is a bit too complicated to deal with in detail here, but in the view of many it is one of the most promising avenues in this field.

(6) Behavioural Research.

Psychologists are interested not merely in the structure of the brain of humans and animals but also of course in their behaviour. By behaviour one means the way in which the individual interacts with its environment and its reasons for doing so. A study of what, when, and how a creature does something can tell one a good deal about the rules that govern behaviour. The way in which a bird builds its nest, a cat rears its kittens, a dog threatens another dog, frequently follow set patterns and presumably have something to do with the way in which at least a part of its brain is organised. Careful study of such behavioural patterns even allows one to make certain predictions about what an animal will do next in a given set of circumstances—and once one is able to predict accurately one has generally discovered something important. Studying animals (or people) " in the wild " is easier said than done and tends to be frustrating because of their tendency. to do unpredictable things and their general disinclination to perform to order. Furthermore the range of behaviour that one can study by such methods is limited to the so-called " instinctive " actions which are frequently simple in function and execution. The alternative is to confine the animal in a laboratory and observe its reactions to an experimentally controlled environment. In this way one can study its learning and memory processes, its sensory mechanisms, its intelligence and capacity to " reason," its behaviour under conditions of stress, its preference for various foods, etc., etc. Behavioural research of this kind has turned out to be almost the most important method employed by psychologists in their attempt to understand the brain.

(7) Introspection.

The oldest and perhaps most obvious method of studying the brain was simply to think about it! This was the method adopted by early philosophers who believed that if one was sufficiently logical and intelligent one could work out the solution to practically anything. Unfortunately, while the brain, mind, etc., might seem to be an ideal subject for its own thought processes, this method of analysis—known as introspection—just doesn't seem to work in the way that it should. The principal problem is that much of the brain's activities are exceedingly rapid and automatic, as anyone can demonstrate for themselves. For example, turn your head and look at an object on the wall. It will be " perceived " and recognised apparently instantaneously. Even if you can detect a faint lag between the act or inspection and the act of perception, it is quite impossible to describe the steps or stages in the process. Much the same applies to other important mental faculties. One cannot, merely by thinking about it, say how one actually learns something, or how one calls an item up from memory. It was realising the relative hopelessness of this quest which led philosophers interested in the brain to convert themselves, in the middle part of the 19th cent., into psychologists and adopt an experimental rather than an intellectual approach to the problem. However it should be equally clear (though many psychologists seem to have forgotten this) that there is a whole world of material which does not seem to make itself available to any of the experimental approaches (1–6) which we have described above. The study of language itself is a good example, being part of our mental life and thus of great interest. Similarly certain features of abnormal psychology ranging from the bizarre thought processes of schizophrenics to the near-mystical states of mind reported by artists and poets, or the distortions of perception and personality induced by the hallucinogenic drugs, are central to the topic of psychology and are clearly only approached in the first instance through some measure of introspection. What too of the raw material of psychoanalysis and the rich glimpse of the interior of our minds granted us through our dreams? These are merely a few examples to highlight a single point that—when studying the brain we should not ignore the mind's power to look in on itself.

This concludes our condensed survey of some of the principal methods used by psychologists and their colleagues in attempting to get to grips with their exciting and challenging field. The reader may have been surprised by a number of things, one of which must surely be how very much wider is the territory covered by psychology than is commonly believed.

4. What do Psychologists Study?

We now come to examine the main areas making up the subject matter of psychology. There are all kinds of ways of breaking this material down and as the topic is so immense (and enlarging quite rapidly) one or two important aspects will have to be left aside. We shall only refer in passing, for example, to the important sub-sections of Child Psychology, Industrial Psychology, and Ergonomics, for these need to be treated separately if they are to be properly understood. Furthermore, much of the material inherent in Sociology will have to be passed over for similar reasons. The reader will also notice some overlap between the various headings which merely confirms what one ought to suspect—that in studying human beings or living animals, it is really impossible to segment the approach completely. A person is an entity and something more than the sum of his various parts.

For the purposes of this Introduction we will consider Psychology as constituting principally the study of four major factors—

(1) Perception, which includes the study of the way information is gathered by the brain and how it is interpreted;

(2) Learning and Memory, which deals with the way the information is stored once it has been gathered and, subsequently, how it is retrieved when wanted;

(3) Motivation, which includes the vital topic of why a human or animal interacts with its environment and why it does one thing rather than another; and

(4) Personality and Thinking, which tackles the abstruse problems concerned with consciousness, self-awareness, and, naturally, disorders of both.

Anyone reading this Introduction seriously will find that in acquiring his first formal background in Psychology he will also have to think at times like a physiologist, a philosopher, an anthropologist, and a good experimental scientist, all rolled into one. This will turn out to be less complicated than one might imagine.

II. PERCEPTION.

(a) Information Gathering and Information Decoding.

The topic of perception itself breaks down into two significantly different headings and it is very important to comprehend the distinction between the two before going any further. These are the processes of *information gathering* and *information decoding*. If these words seem a bit bothersome, they need not be. Information has a meaning in science rather broader than details of train times or facts from history, and it really deals with the influence of one object, person, or thing, on another. For example, when you look at the sun or a bright light, photons from the luminous object strike the retina or sensitive layer at the back of the eye. As the result of this the retina changes its state slightly and in due course passes signals back to the brain. Now the interaction between the sun and the retina, odd though it may seem at first, constitutes an exchange of information, and when the message finally reaches the

brain and the sun is recognised for what it is, the information has flowed all the way from sun to brain. If this appears to be an odd use of the word "information," then this is probably because one has tended to think that information can only be conveyed through words or numbers and "meaningful" conversations. The more one considers this limited point of view, however, the less reasonable it seems. If one looks at a painting, which contains neither numbers nor words, but a picture of, say, a ship at sea, then most people will agree that it is conveying information (the artist originating it whenever he painted the picture). In fact we can use this analogy to add that the painting itself can be looked upon as a kind of information store since the artist who set the whole process going could easily be dead and gone, and yet his message continues to be conveyed. If one no longer feels it inappropriate to talk of the sun as an emmitter of information to the eye, then we have made a major advance and can move on into the meat of this sub-section. It is really important to get some grasp of the scientific use of words like information and information storage for they will pop up time and time again and one can make nothing of modern psychology without them. Incidentally, when we spoke of the retina sending signals up to the brain where the sun was "recognised," it should be remembered that what reaches the brain is not a kind of miniature sun but rather a pattern of impulses which need to be interpreted. This interpretation we call information decoding and it is the second important factor in perception which we will come to shortly. But first, how is the information received and gathered?

(b) The Five Senses.

Simple creatures, such as amoeba, react in a vague, generalised way to objects in their environment. The reason for this is that they have no specialised equipment to allow them to detect what is taking place, or about to take place, around them, and no computing centre capable of selecting alternative modes of behaviour. As we ascend the evolutionary scale from jellyfish to worms and up through reptiles, mammals, birds, etc., we note increasing specialisation of the body's cells, the development of devices capable of scanning the external environment and increasingly complex co-ordinating nervous centres (brains). By the time we reach Man and other advanced animals, the individual is not merely reacting to his environment but consciously aware of its flux, able to predict many of its changes before they can effect his body physically, and frequently manipulating it significantly to suit his own ends. This immense versatility is dependent upon information from the environment being fed into the nervous system for processing, and the devices which the body has developed to gather this information are known as the senses—vision, hearing, touch, taste, and smell—roughly in order of importance. Without these senses, the interface between the central nervous system and the world outside, a living creature is nothing more than a helpless vegetable, incapable of survival. For this reason if we are to get anywhere with understanding the operation of the brain we will need to know a fair bit about the sense organs that feed it. We shall spend most time on the two most important—vision and audition.

(c) The Eye.

Perhaps the most useful information from the brain's point of view would be that which concerns the detection of food or a mate at a distance or, of course, the presence of danger in the form of a predator. Consequently, the most vital and remarkably developed of our sense organs are our eyes, which are geared to detecting radiation over a frequency range which we call "light." For those who like this kind of detail, the actual spectrum detected by the eye covers light frequencies whose wavelengths range from about 380 nm to about 720 nm (1 nm = 10^{-9}m). All this means is that the distance from peak to peak of the waves which constitute the light is a very small amount indeed—far less than a thousandth of a millimetre in fact. Note, however, that not only can the eye detect the 380 nm and the 720 nm waves quite easily but it can also discriminate between them and a whole lot of other wavelengths in between as well. In fact we call the 380 nm waves " violet," the 720 nm " red," those of about 500 nm " green," etc. Remember the minute wavelengths involved and you will appreciate that whichever part of the eye handles this kind of information must be very sensitive indeed. This fabulous bit of equipment, one of the most remarkable of all biological systems, is called the retina.

The Retina.

Situated in a layer at the back of the eye the retina is a kind of screen on to which rays of light are focused by the lens after having passed through a window at the front, which is called the cornea. The question now arises as to how the retina detects the light rays and how it then signals the relevant information on to the brain. There are two ways of answering this question, one very complicated and reasonably accurate, the other quite simple and slightly less accurate. We'll choose the simpler and lose a bit of accuracy without worrying too much.

The principle employed is that of energy absorption. The retina is a densely packed mass of neural cells whose speciality is that they contain light-sensitive substances known as " pigments." These substances change their state rapidly when the photons from a light source strike them, and this change, which is really a high-speed chemical reaction, acts as the trigger which " fires " the cell. This in turn sends a pulse of electrical activity up the neurone's long stem in the direction of the brain. After it has fired, the cell then requires a brief period to recover its normal state and for the minute portion of bleached pigment to regenerate, during which time (known as the refractory period) it will not fire again. Multiply all this by one hundred million, which is the approximate number of cells in the retina, and you will get some idea of the frenzied activity contributing to the process of vision. To complicate matters there are at least two major types of visual receptors, the cones and the rods. To go into their infrastructure in detail is really the province of physiology, but it is necessary to know something about their prime function which is that the cones tend to handle the higher levels of luminance met in daytime and also mediate colour vision, while the rods, which are far more sensitive, tend to come into life in the dusk or dark. The shift from cone to rod vision, which, like most of the body's basic functions, is entirely automatic, is something we all experience regularly in our daily life. Walk out of the sun into a dark room and for a moment one is " blinded." Walk out of a dark room into the sun and again one is " blinded." Actually all that is happening is that the visual system is having to shift from one set of receptors to another and when the change is extreme and rapid, the lag in the switchover is dramatically apparent.

Colour Vision.

Psychologists have known for a long time that the cones, which tend to be packed in the centre or " more useful " part of the retina, have something to do with colour vision, but just how they do this job has been a matter of much debate and argument. One of the most likely bets would seem to be that particular types of cone are equipped with particular types of pigment, one sensitive to light in the " red " range, another to light in the " yellow," another in the " blue," etc. But how many types of cone would one need, therefore, to get the kind of colour vision we enjoy? Would one have a separate type for each subtle shade of hue for example? When thinking such things out scientists always try to see first if they can get by with the smallest possible number of hypothetical elements, and only bring in extra mechanisms when they are absolutely stumped—a principle known as " Occam's razor " and one universally revered in science and philosophy. With this in mind and with a bit of ingenuity, the general view at the moment is that

three separate types of colour receptor are all that are needed to account for human colour vision; this is known as the trichromatic theory which is all we need to know about it for the purposes of this article. But just to show how complicated things are, and yet how interesting for this very reason, we will pause to look at some experiments in human colour vision which show that no matter how neat and simple an explanation is in psychology, there is always a joker hiding in the pack.

Some Experiments in Colour Vision.

To understand these experiments, which were performed by a Swiss psychologist, Dr. Ivo Kohler, we need to know a little bit about the phenomena known as after-images. This information will come in handy again a little later on when we talk about after-images in a slightly different context. You may have observed that if you look at a bright light for longer than a second or two, when you close your eyes you see a continuing image of the object which may persist for quite a while and exhibit a nice range of rather bright colour changes. If you haven't observed this, then you can experiment yourself by just fixing with one eye on the filament of an electric light bulb—not too close to the eye. Count five slowly as you do so, then close your eyes and observe. (Don't do this with the sun, by the way, as it could be dangerous.) Now the important point at this stage is the changes in colour you will see taking place, which are generally believed to occur because the bright light has slightly overbleached the retinal pigments and they are taking longer than usual to recover. In the process of recovering they continue to send signals to the brain, which interprets this information as if there was still a light source present and thus the bulb filament is " seen " long after it has really gone. The colour changes themselves are probably due to the fact that some pigments regenerate a bit more quickly than others and thus a sequence of colours is perceived. All this involves lights of greater than average intensity and the question is whether one could get " after-images " with low intensity objects looked at for a long time. The answer is yes, and for anyone who hasn't noticed this before, another simple experiment can be tried. Take a book with a brightish colour binding—say red. Fix on it with one eye, trying to keep your head and eye as still as possible and hold it for about one minute. Now, turn the head away from the book and look at a blank, light wall or other flat surface. What one will see is a rather amorphous image of the book, but coloured green, which will linger for about half a minute before it fades away. This is another version of the first trick, with the after-image being due to the bleaching of the red pigment, and to various other changes that follow in its wake. Now the after-image, as we have noted, soon fades away and no doubt this has something to do with the intensity of the original stimulus. But what would happen if, instead of merely exposing oneself to the colour for a minute or two, one extended the time period to an hour, or a day, or a week, or even longer? This is exactly the question that Kohler set out to answer. To get over the problem of how one could possibly go on looking at something for hours or days on end, he decided on the simple expedient of wearing tinted spectacles and going about his business as usual. For the first experiment, using pink spectacles, he made a number of interesting discoveries. Number one was that although for the first few hours in his experiment the world took on a rosy hue, before the first day was over things were nearly back to normal. After a few days there was no longer any suggestion of a more than normal amount of pink about and his vision appeared to be unaffected—even though, of course, all light was being filtered through the red lenses and thus inevitably tinted. Discovery number two came when he finally took the lenses off to find the whole world tinged with green—the so-called complementary colour of red—a tint which remained for days! His next experiment, apart from doing the whole thing over again with a different set of colours—blue lenses providing a yellow world, green a red one, etc.—was to wear spectacles with one lens red and the other green. This time the position was more complicated. If he closed his right eye, which had the red filter in front of it, then he saw green through the other lens and vice versa. With both eyes open, however, the two colours would "mix" in his brain and the world appeared through a kind of bluey haze. At this point you might care to try to predict what the scientist found when, after a few weeks of this and after all the colour had washed out, he finally removed the spectacles. In the first place, if he looked at the world through both eyes he saw the complementary to blue (which is yellow) but if he looked through either of his eyes singly he saw the world tinted with the appropriate complementary colour, red or green. Once again the new tints took some time to disperse. All this of course, while exceedingly interesting, could still be reasonably explained on the theory of pigments bleaching away due to long exposure and taking some time to regenerate. Unfortunately for this simple idea, but fortunately for people who like problems, Kohler's next experiment produced a surprise result. For this he had the ingenious idea of segmenting his spectacles so that the right half of each lens was tinted red, the left half green. The position now was that if the wearer looked to the *right* with *both* eyes he saw a red-tinted world, if to the *left* a green-tinted one. Looking straight ahead produced a muddling fusion of both colours. In due course, as one might predict, all spurious colours washed out wherever one was looking. Now came the surprise. On removal of the spectacles Kohler found that when he looked ahead he saw the complementary " fused " colour, but when he looked to the right he saw the complementary of red, which was green. When he looked to the left he saw the complementary of green, which was red. To work out why this was surprising one must think about what was happening in the retina. In the early experiments, with the whole of the right visual field tinted red, say, the persisting perception of the green after-image was felt to be due to some changes in the pigmentation of the cells in the retina. But clearly this will not do in the final experiment, for in this case the same areas of retina seem to be doing two different things. After the glasses had been removed, when the subject gazed to the right he saw a green field and one might assume that this was because the pigment had been changed by overstimulation. But how could this account for the fact that when the subject turned his eyes to the left there was a change of perceived colour to red? Clearly the pigment itself couldn't have changed in that time nor could it change back when the eyes reverted to the left. Obviously, quite contrary to what one might expect, the colour changes were dependent, in this case, not on the state of the retina but rather on the direction of gaze!

No one has satisfactorily explained Kohler's intriguing results to date, but they do suggest one important point which one is always in danger of neglecting in psychology—that a living organism is not just a collection of parts acting independently of each other. In the drastic situation of wearing tinted lenses for days, or even weeks, changes were evidently taking place not just in the retina of the eye, but also in higher centres of the brain.

More About the Rods and Cones.

Returning briefly to the retina and its constituent cells we might just take a closer look at the rods which, you will recall, come largely into play in conditions of poor luminance.

The extraordinary sensitivity of the rods is the most interesting thing about them. Unlike the cones, which need the brightness of daylight to do them justice, one single rod will be triggered into action by light whose energy is as low as 100 aJ (1 aJ $= 10^{-18}$ J), and if that is a value which has no meaning one can get a graphic idea of this sensitivity when one learns that in total blackness the eye could detect the light of a single candle five miles away! Put another way, the amount of kinetic energy used in lifting a pea only two cm would, if converted to light energy, be enough to give a brief sensation of light to every person that has ever lived on earth! The clustering of

cones in the centre of the retina, the fovea, has been mentioned and the rods consequently tend to be scattered around in the periphery. You can detect this geographical distribution yourself by noticing that whereas in daytime your vision is much better directly in front of you, in very dim light you will be able to see objects on the edge of your visual field rather better. You might also care to note how the periphery of the retina, populated largely by rods and devoid of cones, is remarkably insensitive to colour. Offhand one gets the impression that the whole of one's visual field is richly endowed with colour, but this is far from true. A simple experiment will demonstrate this. Fix, with one eye closed, on a predetermined spot—a mark on a piece of paper will do. Then, slowly bring into your field of vision from the side a small piece of coloured paper drawing it closer and closer to the central spot. Now if you can manage to keep your eye really still and maintain fixation despite the tendency to peek at the incoming paper, you will be surprised how far in the latter will have to be before you can detect its colour with certainty. Try the experiment again with another colour and note that it may be recognised earlier or later. In this way it is possible to plot a simple map of one's own retina, defining the boundaries of the colour sensitive areas and nicely illustrating the division of retinal receptors into two distinct types with different jobs to do—the rods and the cones.

(d) Perception as a Dynamic Process.

Everything we have said in this particular section has reinforced the idea that creatures with complex brains are something far more than automata responding blindly to changes in the environment. Information fed in through the eyes, etc., is processed in some way by the brain, or " decoded," as we put it earlier. In fact it is this business of decoding and the possible mechanisms which help to achieve it that interest psychologists more than the raw details as to how the senses actually gather the information in the first place. Nevertheless until relatively recently there was a school of thought in psychology that made desperate attempts to deny, or at least reduce, the role of a central integrating process, implying that animal and human behaviour could ultimately be reduced to a great mass of stimulus-response networks, triggering each other into action in a totally mechanical fashion. This " Behaviourist " school, as it was known, had more impact on theories of learning and we shall look at it more closely when we come to the appropriate section, but it also influenced the thinking of psychologists interested in perception. The trouble with this point of view is that it is so obviously inadequate to explain the rich material of perceptual experience. One has only to think of the visual illusions that are experienced when information " correctly " relayed from the eye is " misunderstood " or incorrectly " decoded " in the brain itself. Clearly it is enormously interesting that all human beings fall prey to illusions, for it suggests that some common mechanism exists which is causing them.

The Gestalt Approach to Perception.

Among the first people to take this up as a general principle and use it as a frontal assault on the Behaviourist view was the so-called " Gestalt school " of psychology, founded in the early part of the century by three talented psychologists, Kurt Koffka, Wolfgang Kohler and Max Wertheimer. In point of fact they looked more closely at other common features or anomalies of perception than at visual illusions, for they believed that the introspective and experimental analysis of human perceptual experience allowed one to deduce the " laws of perceptual organisation " and that these laws must throw light on the fundamental operating procedures of the brain itself. A simple introduction to Gestalt theory is given in Section J so we will confine ourselves here to looking at a few of their more important ideas, most of which are still valid in modern psychology. The first was their insightful statement that in perception *the whole is something more than the sum of its parts.* This principle is nicely illustrated by the fact that a series of dots drawn fairly close together in the shape of a ring are perceived as having a very definite " form "— *i.e.*, that of a circle—despite the fact that all one has actually put on a paper is a collection of dots. Dots are all that are perceived by the retina, and the signals passed up to the brain can only be those arising as the result of the dot stimuli. Look at such a picture, however, and one sees a circle. But where does this come from? From the brain say the Gestalt psychologists, pointing out that the whole (*i.e.* the perception of the circle) is something over and above the sum of its parts (*i.e.* a collection of points or dots). The same thing can be applied to lines, or practically any other shape, and can even apply in the auditory sense (a " tune " is something over and above a collection of separate notes played in sequence).

Gestalt Laws of Perceptual Organisation.

The Gestalt school argued that this was clear evidence for the existence of dynamic forces in the brain whose function was to mould or *structure* the information as it was fed in by the senses. Further examples of this structuring could be seen in other types of visual phenomena, and Koffka and his colleagues formulated a number of " laws of perceptual organisation " which they held were universal and also, probably, innate or " built into " the brain at birth. These laws are a bit too involved for us to discuss in detail but one or two are worth mentioning because the reader can conduct simple experiments for himself. The first, known as " Continuity," is a rather obvious one and similar to the example of a dotted circle that we had earlier. This states that a collection of dots arranged so that they form a " continuous " line, whether straight or curved, would tend to be perceived *as a unit.* In other words, structuring forces within the brain tend to act upon such dots causing them to be perceptually linked despite the fact that they have no true continuity in the physical sense. The age-old perception of the constellations in the sky, formed out of near random stellar patterns, is a good example of the law of " Continuity " in action. Another important law is that of " Similarity." To observe this in operation, scribble on a sheet of paper about twenty small crosses at random. Now, among these crosses again scribble down about 10 small circles. Look at the composite picture and you will probably note that the circles, more or less wherever they are, tend to stand out in isolation from the crosses—the law of " Similarity " in operation. Obvious? Maybe—but why *should* similar things stand out against a dissimilar background? Obviously some important factor in perception must be at work. Yet one more Gestalt " law," that of " Closure," is worth mentioning because its operation is easy to observe experimentally. Koffka and his colleagues believed that the perceptual organising system tended to dislike incomplete or partial figures and where possible would " close " them. This was particularly true, they argued, with neat, simple figures such as circles, triangles, etc. To illustrate this, draw a small neat circle on a piece of paper but leave a small gap in it, say about a tenth of its circumference. Now close your eyes and open them very briefly to give yourself a fleeting glimpse of the figure you have drawn. The chances are that what you will see is a circle—without the gap. Try this on someone else who doesn't know that there is a gap present and it will work even better. Now one might reasonably argue that one has missed the gap because one didn't have time to see it, but that's really no explanation as to why one should see a *complete* circle. The Gestalt argument is that in such fleeting glimpses, the law of Closure within the brain overrides the rather feeble information about the gap that comes up from the retina and the result is the gap just never gets perceived. The effect, incidentally, works for longer looks at patterns viewed in dim light.

A good deal of controversy surrounded the Gestalt approach to perception, much of which has died down in recent years as the Gestalt point of view has gradually fallen out of favour. One of the most controversial facets of the theory was the belief that the so-called laws were innate, or present at birth. In other words if one could somehow question a new-born baby and get a sensible answer out of it we would find that it too had its perceptions modified according to the Gestalt laws of Continuity, Closure, etc. And this brings us to the very interesting question of just what it is that babies can see at birth—if anything.

(e) Learning to See.

Anyone who has spent any time with very young babies will realise that their powers of perception are at best poorly developed. The mother may feel greatly flattered at being " recognised " with a smile, but the harsh facts are that a young baby will produce a charming smile for practically anything—even an absolutely horrific mask—that's placed in front of it. The psychologist William James (brother of the novelist Henry James) actually stated that the world of the newborn baby was a " buzzing, booming confusion "—in other words a mass of sensory data rushing up to the brain with nothing up there to interpret it. This is probably close to the truth—at least as far as human babies are concerned, for there is very good evidence that babies do not come into the world equipped with the ability to perceive the environment in the orderly, clear-cut way that adults do. Incidentally, this is not due to any deficiency in their visual system for the new-born's eyes are physiologically mature with at least the *potential* for detailed colour and pattern vision. What seems to be happening is that in the first few months, perhaps years of life, young humans literally have to *learn to perceive,* as the brain gradually acquires the power to integrate the information sent up by the senses, into a meaningful picture of the environment. There can be no better illustration of the vital distinction psychologists draw between vision (or audition for that matter) and the act of *perception.* One concerns itself with input, the other with its interpretation. Now with animals it is a different story—somewhat. Among the primates, chimpanzees, monkeys, etc., perception at birth is better than with humans but still pretty uncertain and the lower down the animal kingdom (this is called the phylogenetic scale) one goes, in general, the better the creature is equipped at its birth to perceive the environment. Look at it another way and say that the simpler the creature and the less well equipped with cerebral cortex, the more wiring or circuitry is built into it and carried over to every member of the species. This of course is what is meant by instinct—an inherited behaviour pattern or function of some kind which appears in every member of a species at birth. *See also* F38(1)

Instincts are very useful in one sense since the creature endowed with them doesn't have to learn the instinctive task and can perform it at birth (suckling is one of the few human instinctive reflexes). On the debit side, however, is the fact that one can't *unlearn* the instincts either, so that the more of them one has, the more likely they are to get one into trouble if one is a creature likely to change its environment in any radical way. Think, for example, how powerless human beings would be if they were subject to an instinctive desire to hibernate for six months at the onset of each winter. Clearly instincts are good for creatures with limited cerebral capacity, but a big handicap if one wants to respond in a flexible way to the world around one. The big question now is, does the ability to perceive develop as a natural consequence of the maturing brain, or is it dependent upon practice and experience?

Some Investigations.

If one takes kittens and brings them up in total darkness for, say, a month, on being subjected to the light they seem to have normal perception—pretty well equivalent to that of kittens normally brought up. However, if one extends the rearing-in-the-dark for a much longer period, say a year, then the young cat never seems to achieve normal vision on its introduction to a lighted world. Post mortem examination of the brain reveals that certain parts of the visual system seem to have failed to develop in the normal way. Evidently there is a critical period, which when exceeded without visual experience, stultifies the brain so that normal perception can never be achieved. But what of humans? This may seem an impossible question to answer for how could one conduct the necessary experiment—*i.e.*, deprive new-born babies of light for up to a year—without outraging all moral and ethical values? In fact, by an odd and fortunate twist, the necessary data has come to us without the need to perform an impossible experiment. In the 1930s new techniques of surgery allowed the performance for the first time of an operation to graft the human cornea. This, you will recall, is the transparent window on the front of the eye which can, with age or disease, become clouded and opaque. Occasionally the cornea may be opaque at birth with the result that the individual can never achieve the perception of patterns or shapes. Because some light is getting through the milky window, however, he may be able to tell the difference between, say, periods of light and dark. Prior to the 1930s people afflicted with clouded corneas were consigned to a life of effective blindness—the more tragic because in all essentials they were frequently equipped with perfectly operating retinae, optic nerve, etc. With the development of corneal transplant surgery the picture dramatically changed and, while the operation is now usually performed at a relatively early age, there was an initial group of people in middle-age waiting to be treated who had *never had normal vision*. Realising that this provided a unique opportunity for an interesting observational study, the German psychologist Von Senden arranged to follow the progress of the patients with new corneas and record their reactions to the sight of objects which they had hitherto only heard described. Von Senden was set for some surprises—but nothing like the ones that he got. In the first place the newly-sighted patients, far from gazing round in wonder at the marvels of the visual world, were apparently totally incapable of making any sense out of it! This was not, incidentally, a mere failure to recognise subtle differences such as exist between people but a totally inability to tell the difference between most common, everyday objects. Showing the patients large simple drawings, such as a triangle and a square, naming them and then switching their relative position would totally confuse the patients. In order to tell the difference they would have to laboriously trace the outlines of each figure, carefully counting the corners. Notice that they could *see* the outlines, corners, etc.—their eyes were functioning properly—but they were unable to perceive the pattern. Their brains were simply not equipped to recognise shapes and, like young babies, they had to learn the whole process slowly and laboriously. Von Senden's second surprise came when he found that few of the patients seemed to find, at least in the early stages, the gift of sight at all welcome. Some, in fact, literally begged the doctors in the hospital to replace the bandages over their eyes! As with young babies, their visual world was indeed one of " buzzing, booming confusion " and it took some getting used to. There's a happy ending to Von Senden's story. All patients in due course acquired the ability to perceive, slowly at first but with increasing speed and confidence.

The moral of all this is clear, and once again emphasises all the points we have been trying to make about perception. The brain is a device designed to integrate information fed into it by its senses. In due course this integration becomes almost automatic, but this is reached only after a long period of training, which in humans occupies the greater part of infancy and early childhood. How much is actually " built into " human brains at birth in the field of perception? Probably very little, if Von Senden's work is accepted without reservation. Unfortunately there's some curious contradictory work to muddle the issue (as usual) and it concerns experiments with young babies performed by the psychologist J. J. Gibson. His strategy was to take infants and get them to crawl towards what he termed a " visual cliff." This consisted of a sheet of strong glass placed across a kind of trench or ditch in the laboratory, the bottom of which was lined with a chequer pattern. The children were tempted to cross the trench to come to their mother, this of course involving their venturing out over the glass sheet. Adults might naturally hesitate slightly, pondering perhaps the strength of the glass and the depth of the pit below it. Young babies would of course know nothing of the fragile nature of glass so should not be worried by that. Nor, if they were not equipped with proper pattern recognition mechanisms, should they be able to appreciate the " depth " of the pit or the nature of the visual " cliff " they would have to cross. Gibson found, however, that all children showed exceptional caution when reaching the " cliff " point, and many could not be tempted into apparently empty space. Common sense? Perhaps, but either they have the perceptual mechanism or they don't, and in this case it looks as though the perception of depth, and even some kind of appreciation of the gradients involved in the cliff were at least present in the babies capable of crawling. Does this contradict the work of Von Senden? Not necessarily—perhaps certain vital things (such as the ability to recognise a steep slope) are " instinctive " in humans, while matters such as the perception of patterns like faces, triangles, squares, etc., need to be learned.

(i) The Building Blocks of Perception.

To this point we have been considering (i) how the information is fed into the brain; and (ii) the evidence for the fact that dynamic integrating forces act on this information to mould it in specialised ways. We must now try to consider how this processing might take place. In other words what actually happens inside the brain when a particular pattern or shape is recognised?

Investigation of Individual Nerve Cells.

To get some insight into this we need to take a closer look at one of the latest techniques for studying the brain which we referred to earlier and which is known as microelectrode recording. The principle here is to insert an exceptionally fine electrode into the cortex of an anaesthetised animal, endeavour to place it against the body of a single neural cell and then, via a suitable amplifying system, record the pattern of electrical activity given off by the cell. This technique, which was developed in the 1950s, represents a significant advance over that of electroencephalography (the recording of brain waves from outside the head) inasmuch as instead of being faced with a rather vague pool of electrical activity, possibly coming from numerous cerebral sources, one is able to study the responses of what must surely be the brain's fundamental unit, the neural cell. Studied in this way the activity of a single cell is very interesting. Firstly cells appear to have no period of total inactivity—whether the creature is sleeping or waking and whether stimulated or not, single cells keep up a steady, periodic burst of firing at an average frequency of one burst every few seconds. This has acquired the name of " spontaneous activity," which is another way for saying that psychologists and physiologists don't know what causes it. In the normal, living brain therefore, even when the creature is in a totally relaxed state, millions of cells are bursting periodically into action, a continuous background of electrical noise. This presumably signals the presence of life itself for only with the death of the individual do the brain's cells cease their restless firing. When the animal is stimulated in some way, by light, noise, heat, cold, etc., then measurable changes take place. If the stimulus is visual, cells in the visual cortex of the brain burst into life, while those in areas subserving other senses remain at their spontaneous level. Introduce auditory stimuli, or mixtures of other stimuli and cells perk up in the appropriate areas of the brain. All this is very much as one might expect, backing up our knowledge that different sections of the cortex handle different tasks. But can one focus down rather more sharply? What happens if one studies the behaviour of cells within only one area of the cortex when different stimuli mediated by the same sense are fed in?

This experiment was first performed by the American physiologists, Hubel and Wiesel, with remarkable results. First, they located a cell in the visual cortex of the cat and began to record the output from it when the cat was shown a variety of visual patterns. At first the cell merely exhibited the normal background firing, but when the cat was shown a luminous vertical line, the cell suddenly burst into frenzied life. In the meanwhile other cells in different parts of the visual cortex continued with only background firing. When the vertical bar was slowly rotated so that it was tilted on to the diagonal, the first cell gradually relapsed into background firing but in the meanwhile, another cell began to increase its firing rate. This too " switched off " when the bar was rotated again to a new angle, while yet another cell sprang to life. In this way Hubel and Wiesel, in a memorable series of experiments in the 50s and 60s, began to systematically plot the cat's visual cortex, noting over and over again the fact that individual cells seemed to be specially " labelled " to respond only to specific stimuli. The same applied to cells in the auditory cortex and even—though these were much harder to track down—in other sensory areas. In homely terms what the two Americans had done was to isolate the building blocks of perception, the terminal points in the brain where information being fed in was categorised or classified and where the amazing process of pattern recognition was actually taking place. Similar experiments were soon being performed with a variety of animal species, and also with a range of ages from the infant animal to the totally mature. Here again evidence seemed to imply that with animals higher up the phylogenetic scale, these " perceptual units " tended to be learnt rather than built in, for they were rarely present in the very young animal or the mature animal which had been experimentally deprived of normal environment.

Recent Experiments on the Human Perceptual System.

All this tells one a good deal about the animal brain, but can one make the bald assumption that a recognition system of this kind exists in humans as well? Microelectrode recording with living humans is probably out, except in certain rare surgical cases, so one might expect this to remain an academic question for all time. However, by one of those happy chances which favour scientists from time to time, some recent experiments performed in England suggest that the human perceptual system *does* work along lines similar to that of the animals. These experiments involve a technique which has the rather daunting name of the " stabilised retinal image," but which is a good deal simpler than it sounds at first.

To see the significance of this one needs first to appreciate the relationship between movements of the eyes and the image projected on to the retina. Looking directly at a pattern of some kind, as we have learnt, leads to an image being focused on the retina at the back of the eye, much as an image is projected on to the film at the back of a camera. Now, suppose that the pattern, instead of remaining stationary, moves across the visual field, then clearly the image moves correspondingly across the retina. Conversely, if the object remains fixed, but one moves one's eyes, then the image is again displaced across the retina. Well, what happens if the object remains absolutely stationary and one keeps one's eyes fixed carefully on it? Does the projected image then lock solidly on to the retina? The answer is actually, no, but for no reason more peculiar than that it happens to be physically impossible to keep one's eyes absolutely still. No matter how hard one tries, the eyes continue to move in a fine, trembling motion, barely detectable without specialised instruments. Inevitably the image of any object in the visual field trembles rapidly on the retina at the same time. This might seem to make vision rather imprecise and blurry, but for reasons we haven't the space to go into, this tremor actually serves to *improve* vision—in particular the kind of super-detailed vision which allows us to see minute specks or very fine lines such as spiders' cobwebs. For some time psychologists have been curious about what would

happen to vision if these fine eye movements did not exist, but since they are quite involuntary and automatic the task seemed pretty hopeless. Then someone—the physicist R. W. Ditchburn—had the bright idea of tackling the problem from a different viewpoint. He simply wore a contact lens (which of course acts like a new outer layer to the eye) with a short stalk sticking out of the front of it. On the end of this stalk he fastened a little photograph and a lens to focus the image sharply on the retina. By this trick he had effectively cut out the effect of all movement made by the eye, great or small, because wherever the eye moved now, so the contact lens followed it, and the stalk and photograph followed it too. If you think for a moment you will realise that this means that the projected image of the pattern remains in one position on the retina—the stabilised retinal image. (If you find this difficult to visualise, try sketching the system on a bit of paper—eye, contact lens, stalk, pattern, and of course image on the retina. The logic will immediately be apparent.)

With this system Ditchburn made two very interesting observations. Firstly, the " stabilised " pattern disappeared, thus suggesting that the fine eye movements were essential to visual perception. Secondly, he reported that when a pattern disappeared it frequently did so *in part*, rather than washing out as a whole as one would rather expect. Furthermore, the parts that came and went tended to be neat, even sections of the pattern. For example, a cross would alternate between the vertical and horizontal bars, a triangle would break up into one or other of its three sides, etc. A number of experiments have since been performed with human subjects using this ingenious and unusual apparatus, with results which suggest to psychologists that they are dealing with the same kind of perceptual units Hubel and Wiesel found in the cat. The tendency of the lines to appear and disappear as units when viewed as stabilised images seems to imply that basic " line units " are also present in the human brain—the building blocks of perception again.

It so happens that these fascinating fragmentation effects can be observed by a simple experimental method which does not involve wearing specially fitted contact lenses. You will recall that we spoke earlier of after-images, which are temporary changes in the state of the retina caused by a bright light and these are, of course, perfectly stabilised images since they are part of the retina itself. To observe them oneself the best trick is to sit in a rather dark room and stare at the window-frame against the bright sky outside. Do this, keeping one eye closed and the other as still as you can manage, for about thirty seconds. Then close both eyes and *keep them closed.* After a second or so you will see a vivid after-image of the cross-pieces of the window frame and you will note that the vertical and horizontal bars of which it is composed come and go independently of each other. This is something far more than a trick incidentally—as you do it you will be watching your own brain at work processing the pattern locked on to the retina.

We have spent a good deal of time on vision and visual perception because (a) it is easily the most important of the sensory channels, and (b) because it is the area of perception best charted by psychologists and physiologists. We will now take a less detailed look at the other senses.

(g) The Ear.

The eyes, as we have learnt, are equipped to detect visual radiations within a fantastically fine range of wavelength—less than a thousandth of a millimetre. From the brain's point of view this takes care of a good slab of some of the most important sources of energy and radiation within the universe, but a brain equipped only with eyes would be " blind " to a good deal of important information. Therefore we find a complete set of specialised receptors handling other areas of interest, of which by far the most important are the ears. These are tuned to pick up waves and vibrations too, but of air waves rather than light, and in an entirely different range. The absolute spectrum to which the human ear responds is between about 20 and 15,000 Hz (1 Hz = s^{-1}), with a peak sensitivity between about 1,000 and 6,000 Hz. All sounds we can hear, therefore, consist ultimately of vibrations of the air occurring within this frequency range, and in the case of human speech we are dealing with a complex pattern of such vibrations. The ear's method of detecting these and translating them into an electrical code is ingenious and enormously efficient.

Auditory Perception.

The process begins with the outer ears (the flaps of skin on the side of your head!) which serve to catch sound waves coming from the most important direction, which in the case of human beings is in front of them. The importance of these directional indicators is considerable and you can note how strikingly you can change your own auditory perception by flexing the ears with your hand, or cupping your hands so that the "directional indicators" point backwards. Once channelled into the innards of the system, the sound waves are forced down an ever-narrowing tube where they come up against something called the tympanic membrane which is better known as the eardrum. Popular belief seems to be that the auditory process stops here, but from what you have learnt already you can work out that there will need to be much more than this. The translation of the physical vibration of the eardrum into electrical signals will have to take place. In fact the vibrating drum itself sets in motion a beautiful percussive machine in miniature, three tiny and elegant bones known as the hammer, anvil, and stirrup, which carry the message deeper into the ear where they come up against yet another "drum." This is the gateway to a spiral tube called the cochlea, which is filled with a densely packed fluid, and the walls of which are lined with hundreds of thousands of tiny hairs. As the last of the bones in the tiny percussive link beats up against the fluid inside the cochlea, it sets up a series of rapid shock waves which in turn induce complex patterns and rhythms of movement in the hairs linking the cochlear wall—rather like the shifting waves of motion that the sea induces in forests of seaweeds, only on a faster time-scale. These hairs are themselves hooked up to auditory nerve cells and in some way, at present uncertain to psychologists and physiologists, specific movements of the hairs tend to activate specific cells, the end product being that a series of complex but significantly different patterns of electrical activity make their way up the brain. Here the auditory centres get down to the business of interpreting these electrical signals into "meaningful" sounds.

Thinking of the immense sensitivity of the hairs in the cochlear fluid, it may have occurred to you that it ought to be possible to set them in motion by almost any kind of external vibration—and thus hear without vibrating air waves having moved into the ear. This is quite true. Sound waves can be transmitted through other media than air, including bone, and thus even if the ears are blocked one can hear certain sounds remarkably well. Try it for yourself and you will note that the quality of your hearing changes markedly —your own voice, for example, will sound deeper and barely less loud, yet if you whisper you will not hear yourself at all. The reason for this is that with ears blocked, the sound is being propagated to the cochlea by bone conduction and this acts as a filter, cutting out the high-frequency components almost totally but letting in the lower notes without too much trouble. This is why earplugs are disappointingly ineffective.

This is probably enough about the ear which, if the truth is known, is rather less well understood by psychologists than the eye. Only one major point might be briefly touched on. Why do we have two ears rather than, say, one large one on the top of our head? The answer is that a binaural system allows us to locate sounds rather better; slight differences in the time it takes for sounds to reach each ear (as when one ear is slightly closer to a sound source) cause fractional delays in the arrival of the respective signals to

the brain—enough for the magnificent computer there to deduce the sound source's rough location.

(h) Smell, Taste, and Touch.

Olfaction.

Of the remaining three senses, only one is concerned with detecting objects at a distance after the fashion of vision and audition. This is olfaction or, as we generally call it, the sense of smell. Olfaction is particularly interesting because it is concerned with the detection of chemical substances in the air, rather than with wave or vibration analysis. Animals of all kinds make much use of their ability to recognise the chemical changes taking place in plants, other animals, etc., which serve to indicate "good" (*i.e.* necessary for survival) or "bad" (*i.e.* dangerous) objects. These may range from the sweet smell of edible fruit, the characteristic odour of a mate in a sexually receptive state, or the nauseous smell of rotting flesh, riddled with dangerous bacteria. Unlike vision and audition, the olfactory sense mechanism is relatively simple in form, consisting of two small patches of cells situated rather high up in the nasal passages and not in the main line of breathing. This accounts for the animal habit of sniffing to detect smells better, the sniff being a method of pushing air up into the rather inaccessible smell receptors. As with pretty well everything else in the body the olfactory receptors are specialised nerve cells, immune of course to light or air vibration, but incredibly quick to react to a wide range of airborne molecules. The presence of particular molecules on a receptor causes a chemical change to take place in the cell, this in turn inducing an electrical signal to pass up the olfactory nerve. Psychologists have not spent too much time on this sense for it seems to be of relatively low importance to modern man, but have pondered the interesting question as to just how many different kinds of smells human beings can detect. You might try to think about this for yourself and before you say hundreds, you should realise that most smells, like most colours, are probably mixtures of a relatively small number of primaries. There is, as it happens, no definite agreement as there is on the seven colours of the visual spectrum, but an early classification by the psychologist Findley in 1924 has probably not been bettered. His "smell prism" listed six primaries which you may like to compare with your own choice. Each smell is identified with a substance which Findley thought was a typical generator of the odour. (1) fragrant (oil of jasmine), (2) etherial (oil of lemon), (3) resinous (turpentine), (4) spicy (cinnamon), (5) putrid (hydrogen sulphide or rotten eggs) and (6) burned (oil of tar).

Taste.

We now move from the distance senses to the so-called "proprioceptors" which is the name psychologists give to the senses concerned with the detection of things actually in contact with the body. Although it is not classed in this way the logical one to look at next is taste, which has much more in common with smell than most people imagine. Taste in itself is a rather feeble sense, mediated by a number of chemically sensitive receptors on the back and sides of the tongue, and the relative overemphasis of its importance is due to the fact that when people talk about great subtleties of taste they are generally talking about great subtleties of smell, for the latter is vital in any gastronomic treat. The simplest test of this is to sample some particularly good tasting substance, savour its flavour and then hold one's nose. The reduction in taste is dramatic, and one can soon realise how a bad head cold can have such drastic effects on the enjoyment of food and drink. One other remarkable feature of the sense of taste is how quickly it adapts out— a drink which tastes sweet or sour at the first taste, slips into bland neutrality before the glass is emptied. This is another experiment the reader can surprise himself with, particularly if he holds his nose while drinking, thus eliminating the vital smell component. The classification of tastes is somewhat easier it seems than that of smell, with most psychologists settling for four primaries, with which you will probably find yourself agreeing—sour, salt, sweet, and bitter. Anyway the plain fact is that the gustatory sense is a very limited tool in mankind's sensory workshop and poses few experimental questions.

Touch and Sensitivity to Pain.

The remaining sense, that of touch, includes under its heading a good deal of sub-senses such as the detection of pressure, heat, cold, and the highly enigmatic pain. Pressure, heat, and cold are fairly well-understood, probably being mediated by a number of different types of specialised cells embedded in the skin. Much controversy surrounds the number of different types of receptors involved and the matter is complicated by the fact that no one has positively identified a "pain" receptor—*i.e.* one which fires only when a potentially dangerous stimulus contacts the body. An early view held that pain was simply the signal the brain received when any kind of stimulus was excessive, but for a number of reasons this will not do. There are also some peculiar factors such as the observation that it is not all that easy for a person, without any other cues, to tell the difference between hot and cold objects. Immersing a finger in icy cold water and in very hot water briefly provokes a generally unpleasant sensation, but it is hard to tell with the eyes closed and without prior knowledge which end of the temperature spectrum is being experienced. Pain itself, the scourge of mankind (and yet his saviour in cases where it keeps him out of danger) is an incredibly mysterious phenomenon and we will not be able to say much about it here except to point out that much of its operation is determined by processes going on in the brain rather than in peripheral parts of the body. Human sensitivity to pain also varies enormously. Among certain rather neurotic people intense pain may be felt at relatively minor physical afflictions, while other people may bear (or learn to bear?) what would generally be accounted as gross physical discomfort with equanimity. The action of pain-killing or analgesic drugs is also very poorly understood. Some recent exciting studies by the physiologist, P. D. Wall, suggest however that we may be on the edge of a major advance in our understanding of pain. He has shown that in certain cases of otherwise intractable pain —following, say, serious limb injury—great relief can be achieved by the electrical stimulation of certain "inhibiting nerves" *in the site of the wound itself.* This is not counter irritation but somehow bringing into action a "damping" or inhibiting system which in the area of the wound had ceased to function properly. In extraordinary experiments patients have been taught literally to switch off their pain by stimulating these inhibitory nerves with a small electrical device at the side of their bed. Other experiments along these lines are presently taking place in various parts of the world, and brain scientists are watching their outcome with the greatest interest.

(i) Are there any Other Senses?

If we take pleasure and pain as separate senses, which might seem reasonable, then even forgetting about all other possible sub-divisions of sensory detection the traditional five senses are not enough. Most psychologists, however, are content with the traditional categorisation. One important area not particularly well covered by the present human sensory range is that of high energy radiation beyond the ultra-violet. It so happens that until quite recently few living things came much into contact with radiation of this kind—the odd cosmic particles bursting through the earth's envelope of air, while dangerous, are too rare to be worth developing special recepto s for. Within the past century, however, man has begun to work regularly with high-energy radiation sources and has suffered a good deal as a consequence. X-rays, for example, were grossly misused in the early days after their discovery, and similarly numerous deaths have been caused by the misapplication of nuclear fission devices. The problem is simply that although the radiation is doing our body mortal harm, we expose ourselves to it because we are not equipped with "radiation detectors" to warn us. Once the pain arising from tissue damage arrives—it may take decades for the damage to become apparent—it is too late to do anything about the original stimulus. This apparent digression is merely to remind one of the tremendous role the senses play in our lives, and how brief our span of life in this dangerous universe would be without them. But what of other senses? A frequently used term is that of the "sixth sense" and many people believe that humans and animals are equipped with some other major sense which allows the creature either to detect some danger at a vast distance— way beyond the range of vision or audition—or alternatively to allow one mind to communicate with another mind. We discuss this problem briefly in the section on Ideas and Beliefs, but it also has a place here since many people believe that the study of extra-sensory perception is a legitimate branch of modern psychology. The first argument against the idea of ESP (you may not feel it is particularly convincing) is that no one has been able to detect any mechanism in any part of the brain which could possibly be transmitting or receiving the messages conveyed by the sixth sense. Believers in ESP reply (*a*) that one might be discovered at any time, and (*b*) that perhaps no transmitter or receiver is necessary anyhow. The first point is of course irrefutable, but the second raises a different question and suggests that whatever mind-to-mind contact is, it cannot be looked on in the way we have been attempting to look at either sensation or its necessary complement, perception. There is an even more cogent argument, however, which the vast majority of psychologists today adopt—that there is simply no experimental evidence for the existence of telepathy anyhow. In this case it is quite unnecessary to start looking for mechanisms to mediate it. In experiments conducted to sort out the ESP controversy, psychologists *have* found that people are very much better at gathering information from each other without the use of speech than had hitherto been realised. Tiny changes in facial expression, nervous movements, shifts of eyes, even long periods of unusual silence can all serve to give the trained observer important clues as to what is going on in another person's head. Fortune tellers, detectives, and expert card players have known this for years and are only too aware that they are getting their information by clever and insightful use of their normal senses, but rely on other people's ignorance of just how good these mechanisms really are.

(j) Sensory Deprivation.

Any individual, human or animal, born without a reasonably complete complement of senses would almost certainly be doomed to an early death or a life of relying on other humans for assistance. A few startling souls, such as the late Helen Keller, fought their way out of the solitude of total blindness and deafness to lead full and useful lives, but these are golden exceptions to a fairly inflexible rule. Miss Keller in her autobiography tells of her gradually emerging realisation that the universe consisted of "other things" outside herself and states that it was only through an understanding of this that she began to form the concept of herself as an individual personality. This serves to reinforce the point of view stressed by modern psychology that the individual is a mesh between himself and his environment. True personality has no reality without constant and evolving interplay with the external world. But what would be the effect on the normal personality of inducing enforced perceptual isolation?

In the early 1950s, as scientists began to see that man would soon be able to make voyages into space, the psychologists began to ponder how well human beings could stand up to the physical and psychological isolation of a space capsule. Man is gregarious, naturally at ease among his fellows, and tends to become eccentric and unbalanced when separated from other humans for any length of time. What, they asked, would be the effect of the extended and rather dramatic isolation imposed on the astronauts of the future? To test this a number of experiments were set up in which people were isolated in sealed chambers under conditions of greatly reduced sensory input for lengthy periods. Initial studies seemed to show that the experience was unexpectedly unpleasant, and, sensing that they were on to something significant, psychologists at McGill University in Montreal where the pioneering work was done, decided to tighten up their experimental situation. Students were hired at the relatively princely sum (for students) of a dollar an hour and told that they could spend as many hours in isolation as they pleased. They were then placed in stuffed clothing rather like divers' suits, and lowered into chambers of water maintained at body temperature. The helmets of their suits were lightproof and the chamber was sealed and covered to be soundproof. The outcome of all this was that even if the student made a body movement he would feel no apparent response as his body, encased in the bulky clothing, would merely float around in the unresisting water. External vision and sound being eliminated, and with ears plugged to prevent him hearing his own breathing, the subject was in a state of almost total sensory deprivation. His only link with the outside world was a "panic button," which he could press to alert the experimenters if for some reason he wanted to terminate the experiment. What did the psychologists expect? That most students would like nothing better than to do nothing for weeks on end and get paid a solid wage for doing so? The results surprised everyone. Most subjects had had more than enough after only a few hours, and only one stuck it out for more than a day and he suffered a neurotic hangover for his pains. For human beings, total isolation from sensory input is evidently one of the most unpleasant experiences imaginable.

The experiments caused a surge of controversy and a good deal of speculation as to what the results implied. The students' principal objection was that they became oppressed with vivid and bizarre hallucinations, both visual and auditory, apparently comparable in strength and unpleasantness to the hallucinations reported by alcoholics suffering from *delirium tremens* or (more fashionable today) the worst excesses of an LSD trip. These vanished as soon as the subject was removed from the chamber and apparently did not occur again. The first hypothesis advanced was interesting—that living things have a hunger or need for sensory input, comparable, but of greater strength, to the need for food. Furthermore, when the sensory appetite was not assuaged, the brain began in desperation to create its own sensory material, hence the hallucinations. This hypothesis was unchallenged at first, but an alternative point of view has recently been put forward based on the recent discoveries in the field of sleep and dream research. Many psychologists now believe that humans need to dream and that one of the principal functions of sleep is to allow our brains to undergo a kind of sort-out of the programmes which control the central computer. In this view the hallucinations occurring during sensory deprivation would really be an example of the individual dreaming *while he was awake*, the subject's brain having been fooled into " thinking " that it was asleep by the sharp reduction in sensory input which had occurred. For various reasons the human brain carefully keeps the important process of dreaming separate from the waking state and there is some suggestion that to fully experience our dreams would be a psychologically intolerable experience. If this is correct then the McGill experiments and their successors show not a need for sensory input with consequent hallucinations to feed the sensory appetite, but rather the effects of allowing waking human beings a glimpse of the " inner space " of their minds. Similarly, incidentally, one can look upon both the LSD trip and the alcoholic hallucinations as examples of the same process occurring—except that the tripper has stimulated his dreaming mechanism into action through the drug, while in the case of the alcoholic, his excessive intake of alcohol has led to an inhibition of the normal dream process which bursts into activity when he is awake. Whatever the explanation for the strange experiences of the isolated students, there is no doubt that the human being is not psychologically equipped to face up to total loss of sensory

inflow for any sustained period. The adventures of the astronaut have in fact taken place in relatively richly-endowed sensory environments and so the expected problems have not arisen. But what of space voyages lasting for months, or even years?

(k) The Problem of Attention.

We have now really finished with the senses and perception as such, but before moving on to our section on Learning and Information storage, we need to think a little bit about the problems which are posed by the great influx of information to the brain, how it sets about coping with this and how it assigns priorities to the multitude of signals it is faced with. This involves the process which we know as Attention. To get some idea of the task facing the brain, let us take up another simple analogy, even if it isn't 100 per cent accurate to the purist's eye.

The brain can be likened to a complex communications centre, sorting vital information, rather like an air traffic control at an international airport. Information floods in from various sources, with the controller paying attention to the scene through the windows, to radio calls, to messages coming by teleprinter and by hand, etc. One way to sort out the muddle might be to assign one mode of messages to one controller, the second to another, etc., but the problem of co-ordination remains. At some stage the senior controller must select which set of signals he is to work on, switching when appropriate to other sets, and issuing instructions to the aircraft waiting to take off and land. Now there are two ways in which he might select the information. The first would be to cut off the unwanted signals at his desk by refusing to allow the stimuli to reach him, a strategy which might lead to a jam of information such as messengers, bits of paper, telephones off the hook, etc., cluttering up the control room. A second strategy would be to staunch the flow of information in the unwanted channels closer to their source, in this case at the point where they first come into the control tower. Real air traffic centres, fortunately, never get into the kind of muddle we are implying here, and nor, in most cases, does the brain. But which of the above strategies is the closest to that adopted by the brain in attending to one particular set out of a vast pool of competitive information? Until about 10 years ago psychologists tended to favour the idea that the first of the two systems was in operation with every sensory stimulus making its way to the brain to contribute to some great tangle in need of constant sorting out. Confusion and uncertainty under stress were considered to be an example of the tangle getting momentarily too complicated.

This view has now been largely rejected thanks to some brilliant experiments by the outstanding young Mexican psychologist, Raul Hernandez-Peon, who was later tragically killed in a car crash. Hernandez-Peon's experiment, which many people consider to be the first big breakthrough in the psychological study of attention, was performed first on that most useful of laboratory animals, the cat, but later repeated on other creatures. The first stage was to implant a microelectrode into the cat's brain, specifically in an area known as the cochlear nucleus. You will recall the word cochlea from our section on audition, as being the seat of the translation of the incoming sound waves into electrical signals. Now the cochlear nucleus is the first major junction box at which auditory signals meet before beginning their ascent to the brain. Prior to this there is only the network of neurones springing directly from the tiny hairs in the cochlea itself. By attaching the electrode to an amplifier and looking at the output on a TV screen, the experimenter could watch the electrical impulses from the ear as they passed through the big nucleus. The ticking of a metronome, for example, could be seen as a regular beat in time with the tick. Hernandez-Peon then set about trying to attract the cat's attention away from the metronome and did so by showing it a mouse. The cat, as predicted, gazed interestingly at the mouse whereupon—the electrical signal indicating the still-ticking metronome vanished from the TV screen! This is odder than one thinks at first. Remember that the electrode was planted in the nucleus in the region of the ear, and yet the electrical signals were no longer passing this point. If the metronome was still ticking, then its sound waves should still be activating the ear and should still be trying to send their impulses up the auditory nerve. Clearly then, a gate was being closed not in the brain but right down at the level of the ear—the message to close it, however presumably being sent down from the brain. How could this gate-shutting message get down to the ear? Evidently there must be neural fibres which send their messages downwards from brain to receptor and not just in the other direction as had hitherto been believed. These corticifugal fibres, as they are called, are now believed to run to other sensory areas, including to the retina in animals and humans, and while they are very difficult to track down by anatomical analysis they are thought to serve a very important function. The facts of the case seem to be that Hernandez-Peon had discovered one of the basic mechanisms of attention, the ability of a creature to filter relevant from irrelevant information. Thanks to his work it now looks as though the brain prevents itself from having to face a muddle of conflicting information by cutting off the unwanted signals actually at the level of the receptor, thus preventing a press of confusing and irrelevant information from flooding in. Once attention shifts again, then the appropriate gates are opened and information flows as before. If this tells us something about the selective filtering of important as against useless information, does it also say something about the way a mother will be undisturbed in the night by the flight of a jet plane and yet wake to her child's slightest cry? Perhaps this is an area which mothers know more about than psychologists ever will.

III. LEARNING AND MEMORY.

(a) How is the Information Stored?

Earlier we discussed the specialist use of the word information that psychologists and other scientists employ and remarked how important it is for an understanding of current work on the brain that one rids oneself of the idea that information can only be conveyed in the form of spoken or written messages. We now need to consider the general problem of the *storage* of information, a concept fundamental to the interesting topics of learning and memory. Most people can readily accept the idea that a book is a store of verbal information as, in a different way, is a gramophone record. In reality in neither case are words actually stored. In books the information is held in the form of coded marks, called printing which need to be decoded by the reader before he can understand the original message. Similarly in the case of the gramophone record the information, which might be the sound of a pop star singing, is coded into the form of a series of ridges on a plastic, the decoding being done by a needle plus amplifying equipment, speakers, etc. Using devices like books, films, and records, information can be held in store for very considerable periods of time, the original message sitting around more or less indefinitely until someone gets down to decoding it. Messages written on the walls of prehistoric caves by our dim and distant ancestors are still passing their information across today, and even the fossils we find in Cambrian rock formations are messages of a kind, though the senders did not consciously originate the signals. In essence then a message consists of an information source, some kind of transmitting medium and a receiver. There may also be a delay built in—storage—in which case some kind of encoding and decoding process will be added to get the message in and out of store. All this preamble leads us now to the point where, having in the previous section considered the information gathering and decoding processes in the brain, we can now consider its role as a storage device. Unlike books and records, which operate on fairly simple lines, the brain chooses immensely complicated and still rather mysterious techniques to do its job.

First, perhaps we should clear up a small point which otherwise will cause confusion—the fact that psychologists distinguish clearly between the two processes, learning and memory. In fact the distinction is simple, particularly in the light of the principles we have just been considering. Learning is the process of feeding information into store, and memory (or remembering) the process of extracting it once again. The next question is the really big one—in the case of the brain just how is this done?

Returning momentarily to gramophone records and books we can see that the process of information storage implies that the incoming signal has changed the state of the storage device, book, record, or whatever, in some way, either by covering it with marks, ridges, or, in the case of magnetic tape, altering the electrical properties of its surface. Something similar must happen in the brain. Information flows up from the receptors, is processed or interpreted by the perceptual mechanism, and then, depending upon circumstances, fed into some store where it is held until required. What kind of changes could be taking place in the neural circuitry of the brain to constitute the laying down of a memory? Psychologists have been divided on this question for decades, and there are three fairly separate competitive approaches. Without giving too much away we shall probably end up feeling that the true explanation will turn out to be some kind of mixture of all three. The three main suggestions can be summarised as (1) the neurological, (2) the biochemical, and (3) the electrical.

The first suggests that as information is fed in, causing certain patterns of brains cells to be activated, minor changes take place on the structure of these cells, modifying them in a rather gross, physical way. This would be similar in a sense to the changes that take place in the surface of a gramophone record when it is first made. The second argues that such gross changes are unlikely and that the storage must take the form of modification of the biochemical or even molecular structure of the brain, changes taking place *within* rather than on the surface of individual cells. The third view advances the hypothesis that since the brain is a mass of electrical energy, and electricity is the basis of neural activity, then the psychologist should look for changes in the electrical patterns of the brain as an index of the fact that something has been stored. We will look at each point of view in greater detail shortly, but first it will be useful to study the experimental evidence.

(b) Early Studies of Learning.

Experimental psychology started in the latter part of the 19th cent. largely as the result of pioneering work of the German physiologist and psychologist Wilhelm Wundt. No one today gets greatly excited at Wundt's experiments nor at his writings, but he was one of the first people in the world to realise that one could actually subject the raw material of mental activity to the experimental method and in this way he is memorable. Wundt concentrated on perception and similar topics and also conducted the first studies of reaction time—the delays humans make between being given the signal to start a task and actually beginning it. He had little to say about the matter of learning and memory, leaving it to a successor, Hermann Ebbinghaus, to get the ball rolling in this area.

Ebbinghaus's experiments were beautifully simple. He took human beings into his laboratory and set out to teach them lists of words, plotting the success rate (number of words in a sequence remembered) against the number of repetitions that had been given. This may all seem frightfully obvious, particularly when we say that Ebbinghaus found that the more repetitions, the better the list of words were learned. This is exactly what one would expect now, a century later, but at that time things weren't so clear cut. Furthermore, Ebbinghaus showed that when you plotted the rate of learning on a graph, a very characteristic curve emerged, common to all his normal subjects, which indicated a gentle improvement in learning with the first few repetitions of the list, followed in due course by a sharply accelerating rise which in turn tapered off. Finally a point came when the list was either completely learned, or no further improvement was made. The important factor was that while there were individual differences in the final level of achievement, and also in the time taken before the main surge of learning took place, the shape of the curve was very similar for all subjects. In other words, while there were significant differences in the ability of subjects to learn his word lists, the nature of the learning process seemed to be interestingly similar. Ebbinghaus's findings are as valid today as they were then and his learning curve fits rather well to the overall pattern of animal learning as well.

In his quest for objectivity he produced another interesting idea. It seemed to him that if one were to compare the performance of two different people in a learning task, one couldn't deduce much about their respective talents by examining the slope of the learning curve unless one knew something about their previous experience with the subject matter. For example, one person might, because of his job or something, simply have been more frequently exposed to the material featured and this would give him a built-in advantage which confused the issue. How about using foreign languages? Again Ebbinghaus felt that to get absolutely pure learning curves one would have to be certain that the subjects had not received prior exposure to the languages in question, a task almost impossible in principle. This led to his invention of a curious tool in the psychologist's workbox, the nonsense syllable, which is still used today as the standard material for many tests of learning ability. It consists of a word with a meaningful sound and look to it, but which is almost complete nonsense inasmuch as it has no obvious meaningful association. ZAT, BOK, FID, BIJ, HAB are a few examples of this strange vocabulary. Ebbinghaus-type experiments are, as you can believe, immensely boring to perform and subjects today normally have to be paid in order to persuade them to take part! However, his realisation that human learning processes could be brought into a real, if rather dull, laboratory setting was a big step forward. Furthermore he had realised the necessity of separating out performance in one task from the background of past experience, an idea which has had far-reaching consequences on the design of all psychological experiments since and which even touches on the important question of the interplay between heredity and environment which we shall look at in the final section.

(c) Learning Experiments with Animals.

The use of nonsense syllables gets over the problem of past experience in one limited area of experimental psychology only, and if one really wants to know something about the formation of the learning process from scratch then one either has to start with very young babies, or use laboratory animals. One psychologist went so far as to read aloud lengthy passages of Greek prose to his infant son at an age when the baby couldn't even understand English. Years later the psychologist gave his son, by now a young man, a number of passages of Greek prose to learn, among which were the sections the baby had previously heard. The outcome was that the sections to which the child had been exposed as a baby were found to be significantly easier than the fresh material. This odd and very tedious experiment has never been repeated, though it is generally rejected by psychologists today as having been imperfectly controlled. For example, who can say for certain what the young man had or had not learnt in the period between the two phases of the experiment? It nevertheless remains as one of a few heroic efforts to use young babies as subjects in learning experiments and it also highlights some of the great difficulties involved.

By the turn of the century more and more psychologists were beginning to follow the lead given by their physiological cousins in bringing animals into the research laboratory. One of the first and most important figures to do so was the American Edward Thorndike, who began to look at the behaviour of specially bred white rats in laboratory learning experiments. Now with humans the problem of how to get the subject to do what one wants him to—learn nonsense syllables or whatever—is met by simply speaking to him about it. With animals this won't work, so Thorndike decided that they would have to be rewarded in some way if they were to learn anything. Reward can be any one of a lot of things, and for an animal it can be getting out of a situation it doesn't like, such as some kind of maze or puzzle box in which a number of specific moves have to be made in sequence before it can get out. Thorndike found that most animals make strenuous and fairly determined efforts to get out of boxes, mazes, etc., and can follow a fairly elaborate sequence of moves in order to reach their goal. Rats, for example, will learn to press a series of levers in the right order if they will open the door to a box, and they will gradually get better and better with practice. Similarly, when placed in a complicated maze, provided they are rewarded with food or escape at the end, they will soon find their way round it. The crucial point here seemed to be the reward, and while pet owners have known for centuries that a piece of sugar presented at the proper time will make a pet do tricks, it is really not clear why it should. To say that it is because the animal " wants the sugar " is no explanation as to why this trick should be learnt rather than some other pattern of behaviour. But Thorndike found without doubt that an animal would learn a maze or similar task far better if it were rewarded in some way at the completion of the task, and he too couldn't see just why, in physiological terms, the neural events which made up the correct performance of the task should be " built in " simply because the animal was rewarded, while incorrect patterns of behaviour were rejected. Ebbinghaus had come to the conclusion that successful learning was a function of the number of times the task was repeated. Thorndike argued that while practice helped to make perfect, it needed something else as well—i.e. the successful completion of the act. How would one measure success? Well, getting out of a maze or finding sugar at the other end would presumably count, and Thorndike described this principle as the " Law of Effect," believing that he had discovered two factors necessary for learning to be successful (for the information to be placed into the store), one being frequency, the other being effect. Psychologists at the time carefully sidestepped the niggling question of how effect (something happening at the end of a sequence) could work back in time to establish the sequence in memory by arguing that the reward or reinforcement did not itself cause the sequence to be stored in the memory system. It simply made that sequence more likely to be called up on some future occasion. But, replied the critics, wouldn't that imply that all sequences were stored with both right and wrong behaviour lodged equally firmly in memory? This question is still being hotly debated today, and we will shortly be taking a look at the evidence concerning what is and isn't learnt in an experimental situation. But first a word about one of the most important concepts not only in modern psychology, but also in 20th cent. science—the conditioned reflex.

(d) Pavlov and the Conditioned Reflex.

The great Russian physiologist Pavlov reached the peak of his scientific genius in the early years following the Communist revolution in Russia, where his very physical approach to psychological phenomena found favour with his country's leaders. The reasons were ideological. To many it seemed that Pavlov could explain all behaviour in purely mechanistic terms and thus do away with mystical, metaphysical, and, to Communist thinking, totally out-of-date views of Man's nature. Pavlov, it was felt, was at last exorcising the Ghost out of the Machine. His findings in fact sent ripples across the world, and the face of psychology was changed by them—notably in injecting into it the realisation that a good psychologist must think like a physiologist at least as often as he thinks like a philosopher. On the other hand, his naïvely simple view of the machinery of mind and brain was bound sooner or later to be exposed as only partially adequate, missing many of the richly complicated facets of human behaviour which must be faced up to and not denied. What was Pavlov really saying? At rock bottom his ideas revolved around the notion of the conditioned reflex arc, a concept that all wishing to understand modern psychology must get clear in their minds sooner or later.

The experiments in question were exceedingly simple inasmuch as they confined an animal to a rather limited environment and studied its behaviour in the most fundamental kind of learning situation. Pavlov, who was enormously interested in gastric and salivary secretion, had noticed that some of the animals in his laboratory would respond to the presence of food with copious flows of saliva, while others would not. Some would even respond excitedly when a particular food pan appeared while others again would not. He reasoned that these differences were in some way a function of the particular animal's past experience and set out to study this in detail. Firstly, he devised a method of measuring saliva flow, which would normally be copious when an animal was presented with its food bowl. He then introduced, just prior to the presentation of the food, a buzzer, bell, light, or some other similar stimulus. Initially the preliminary stimulus would yield no salivary response, but after a while, provided that the pairing of the presentations was kept up, the first traces of saliva would begin to appear upon the sound of the bell. If this were reliably followed by food, soon the saliva would appear in full flood to bell alone. Failure to offer up the food, however, if persistent, would lead to a gradual falling off in the amount of saliva until it ultimately dwindled away. Pavlov declared that this must imply that a probably instinctive reflex—salivating to food—had become linked in neural terms with a stimulus which had at first been totally irrelevant, the sounding of a bell. The more frequently the two events were linked and the more closely they were associated in time, the stronger the new reflex arc would be. Lack of association between bell and food would lead to the extinction of the reflex arc. The fact that extinction was not total could be nicely shown by introducing the food again, whereupon things would come rapidly back to normal with the bell producing copious flows of saliva once more. Today this seems a fairly trivial observation, but at the time Pavlov, his co-workers, and psychologists all over the world became immensely excited about the conditioned reflex. The reason was that there seemed to be no reason in principle why the whole of an animal's behavioural responses had not been acquired in just this simple way with the same argument applying with equal force to humans. At the root of all behaviour lay a simple physiological principle. By employing this properly, all living things could have their behaviour patterns moulded in whatever direction was felt to be appropriate, all psychological malfunctions could be corrected, education made simple, the wild beast tamed, the workings of the brain fully described and comprehended. This, for a brief period, was the golden goal (if one likes to think of it in that way) of the new science of psychology—to see man for what he really was; a complex mass of inherited and conditioned reflex arcs.

If Pavlov and his followers in Russia clung to this dream for decades longer than did less politically committed scientists in other parts of the world, then this is understandable. One of the goals of scientific endeavour is simplification and an explanation of human behaviour in terms of stimulus–response units would certainly meet part of that goal. But on the other hand part of the goal of science is also objectivity—even at the risk of complicating explanations—and before long it became obvious that the animal in the experimental Pavlovian set up was *not* behaving as a complicated automaton. For example, it is possible to condition an animal to lift its foot to avoid an electric shock if a bell reliably signals the imminence of the shock. Now place the animal on its side, ring the bell and—will the animal lift its foot? Yes—but not before getting up to the standing position first. But if the animal is blindly responding to the firing of a neuro-muscular reflex arc, why does it not simply raise its foot while lying down? And how does the standing up act become incorporated into the

reflex sequence without prior training? Such experiments were simply discounted at first as being too inconvenient for the theory, but as time went on the immense oversimplification of the stimulus – response theory of behaviour became obvious. But not before a major movement sprang up in the United States which attempted to make dynamic and imaginative use of Pavlov's findings in an attempt at an all-embracing psychological theory. We now turn to look at this, the so-called Behaviourist School.

(e) The Rise of Behaviourism.

Sometime before Pavlov's ideas began to have impact in the West, a spontaneous movement had been developing among psychologists to reject the traditional methods of introspection in experimental research. The interplay of conscious thought and mental activity was felt inevitably to confuse the issue, and workers were urged wherever possible to make objective rather than subjective judgments. One of the hardest advocates of this line was J. B. Watson, who even went so far as to argue that introspective studies of consciousness, etc., were not merely misleading, but positively useless. In principle, Watson proposed, it should be possible to give a total explanation of the subject matter of psychology—whether human or animal—in descriptive, mechanical terms concerning the outward manifestations of behaviour. This implied ultimately taking such extreme points of view as declaring thinking to be merely " sub-verbal speaking," better described in terms of minor twitches of the throat, mouth, and tongue muscles than in patterns of electrical activity in the higher centres of the brain. All that was needed to give the Behaviourist school impetus was Pavlov's discovery of the conditioned reflex, and when this was published it was eagerly incorporated as the prop of Watson's argument. To Watson and his colleagues the only realistic and profitable way to look at human and animal behaviour was in terms of a strictly mechanistic model, the conditioned reflex arcs serving as the vital links in the creature's chain of activity. Now many people might agree that an animal in a highly restricted laboratory situation, trained to salivate to bells, raise its paw to avoid an electric shock, etc., might well be coming as close to a biological machine as one could imagine, but was this a really adequate way of describing its behaviour " in the wild "? Critics of Behaviourism were quick to point out certain peculiarities that they felt could not be handled by Watson's simple system. Take a dog, for example, and face it with a series of doors, behind one of which is to be found food, sometimes one door, sometimes another. Now train the dog to respond to a light switched on briefly as signalling food. Now indicate the door which has food by switching on a light above it, and the dog will soon learn to trot up reliably to the appropriate door. What has happened? Easy, say the Behaviourists —the dog has been conditioned to approach a light for food, and the reflex carries over to a light above a door. The dog is not really responding to the door, but to the light which sets the appropriate reflex arc in motion, just as pushing a button can cause a car to start. But what, the critics argued, about the fact that the light is switched on for only a few seconds, and yet even after it is off the dog still moves towards the door? Watson replied that the light caused the animal to look towards the door and it immediately adopted a particular posture, setting its musculature up so that it would set off in the appropriate direction, no longer needing the light for a guide. This might seem fair enough, but for the fact that if, just as the animal is about to set off for the door, you hold it, refusing to allow it to move, it still " shows interest " in the door. Furthermore, if you let go in five minutes time, the chances are that the animal will set off to the correct door—a bit long one would have thought for the reflex arc to have been maintained in suspended animation. Was it not simpler, Watson's critics replied, to face up to the fact that the animal was using the light as a signal and was holding the door in some mental form as a kind of goal to which it could make a delayed response if necessary? So adamant were the Behaviourists that all behaviour could be explained in terms of sequences of conditioned muscular movements that they strove to argue that even during the delay the animal was still maintaining a muscular posture—rather in the way that a hunting dog freezes to point to prey. Furthermore, Watson produced what he believed to be irrefutable evidence for the dominance of the muscular activity, even on a task as complex as learning to run a maze. In this rather cruel-sounding experiment he trained a whole lot of rats to find their way through a rather detailed maze. He then preceded to eliminate by surgery all normal sensory equipment—eyes, ears, smell, etc., leaving only the kinaesthetic, or touch, sense. These grossly deprived animals nevertheless still managed to find their way through the maze, allowing him to conclude that in line with the conditioned-reflex notion, the animals were relying predominantly on a chain of muscle reflexes. For a brief period this dramatic experiment seemed to clinch the Behaviourist case. But then came a counter-experiment, even more drastic. A psychologist called Lashley repeated Watson's experiment, but this time also removed the sense of touch by spinal surgery. The wretched creatures even now managed to stagger through the maze—though they were certainly no longer equipped with proper muscular responses. Lashley, correctly, felt this dealt with the ultra-simple Behaviourist argument and that somehow or other the animals must be retaining some kind of general directional sense, a sort of " notion " as to where the exit lay. At about this time more attacks on Behaviourism came from a rival point of view—the Gestalt school. Watson himself shortly afterwards became involved in a sensational divorce case which forced him, in those less permissive times, to resign from academic life. He ended his brilliant career in, of all things, the advertising profession.

(f) Gestalt Psychologists and Learning.

With its emphasis on such ideas as " the whole is something more than the sum of its parts " and its insistence on the idea that the brain has dynamic organising powers which serve to modify input and intervene between stimulus and response, the Gestalt point of view was clearly about as far removed from the naïve Behaviourist viewpoint as was possible. One of the principal allies of the Gestaltists in its early days was K. S. Lashley, referred to above, a brilliant experimentalist with an eye for the essentials of the problem. Throughout his long research life he remained open-minded about various schools of psychology and unconvinced on the various rival theories concerning the physiological basis of memory. He was, however, quick to see the basic weaknesses in the various brain models that fellow psychologists were always confidently erecting, and the first to feel the sharpness of his attack were the Behaviourists. Lashley swiftly realised that the attractive simplicity of the Pavlov/Watson argument was that the basic unit in learning consisted of a fundamentally simple physiological system, a neural reflex arc. In ordinary terms this could be looked on as a chain of cells connecting from, say, the retina through the higher centres of the brain (where the chain would be forged) down to the muscle or set of muscles which constituted motor output. In other words, a light would strike the retina, a number of cells would fire. These in turn would excite cortical cells which had, by prior conditioning, become linked into a reflex arc. Finally these would, quite mechanically, induce the appropriate muscular response. The memory itself constituted the connecting cells in the cortex, and this memory had been established by the learning or conditioning process. Lashley then realised that a memory unit, or an engram as he named it, must be represented by a particular set of cells in a particular part of the brain. In principle, therefore, one should be able to discover these sets of cells and find out what kind of memory is located in what part of the brain.

Lashley's technique was again that of surgical destruction of tissue and using this he performed one of the most remarkable experiments in the history of modern psychology and physiology. His findings created a shock of disbelief and con-

troversy, and their full implications are still not fully understood today—about 50 years after he performed the experiment. Taking a large number of rats, he trained them until they were highly familiar with a complicated maze. He then proceeded to remove from each rat a small portion of cortical tissue, taking a different area but an equivalent amount from each rat. In due course he had removed from his collection of rats the equivalent of one complete brain, though no individual animal had had more than 5 per cent of its cortical tissue destroyed. He then took another set of rats, trained them in the maze, and again removed the equivalent of a brain, but this time taking 10 per cent from each rat. With a further sample he went through the procedure again, but removed a quarter of each rat's brain, and in his final group he had a limited number of animals, each of which had had half its cortex removed. See if you can work out what he found. Remember that if the memory or engram consisted of a series of linked cells then one might expect that these would be found in one relatively small segment of the brain. Interrupting the chain at any point should presumably destroy or grossly handicap memory. Now from the simple behaviourist point of view, most people would have to predict that one or two rats whose hunk of cortex removed had featured the conditioned reflexes involving the maze, would be completely clueless when placed in it. The engram would have been removed. This would then tell the experimenter, as Lashley had hoped, which part of the brain dealt with such tasks as maze learning. Other animals, who had not lost their maze engram would show no detriment in their performance of this task. To his amazement, and to everyone else's for that matter, Lashley found that his first group of rats, each of whom had lost about 5 per cent of cortical tissue, were apparently totally unaffected by the surgery, running the maze just as well as they did before! The rat with bigger chunks of tissue removed were slightly more affected, but even those with only half a brain left were still able to run the maze fairly competently. The loss of memory seemed to be somewhat proportional to the amount of tissue removed, but *not in any way to the area removed!* In other words, the mysterious engram did not seem to be located in any single spot, and Lashley was forced to conclude that it looked as though learning and memory were a function of the whole brain rather than just part of it.

As could be imagined, these findings were not well received by the conditioned reflex advocates and numerous attempts made to repeat them merely served to support these first findings. They were received enthusiastically by the Gestalt psychologists, who saw them as another example of their argument that the brain must be considered as an integrated whole and not as simply a bundle of conditioned reflexes.

The next strong—perhaps the strongest—anti-Behaviourist argument came from one of the Gestalt school founders, Wolfgang Kohler. His findings were disclosed in his important book, *The Mentality of Apes*, which can be bought in paperback and which everyone interested in psychology should read. Kohler, who was one of those clever scientists who manage to find themselves work in exotic parts of the world, conducted his critical experiments at the Primate Research Station in the Canary Islands. Here he watched with great interest the considerable learning skills of the higher apes, such as chimpanzees, and quickly arrived at the conclusion that conditioned reflex theory was not adequate to explain the scope of their intellectual behaviour. His most famous observation concerned the never-to-be-forgotten chimpanzee, Sultan. Kohler had noticed that chimpanzees will play about with sticks and similar devices in their cage, which they seem to use as toys. He then began to wonder whether the monkeys could ever be induced to use them as tools, so after placing potential implements inside Sultan's cage he then put a banana on the other side of the bars just outside its reach. After a bit of fruitless stretching the ape took one of the sticks and pulled the banana in. Now this in itself is a remarkable achievement, and if the ape had actually " worked out " the solution then it would have been suggestive of very much higher thought processes in the animal than had hitherto been believed possible. However, it could be reasonably argued that the chimpanzee had seen some other person or animal using the stick as a tool and was therefore merely imitating, an action which could, with a bit of latitude, be thought of in behaviouristic terms. Kohler's next step put paid to that point of view. He placed in the cage several sticks of various lengths which could be fitted together to form a longer one, and, taking care not to show this technique to the monkey, again set a banana outside the bars but out of reach of any one single stick. After scratching round fruitlessly with various sticks and making aggrieved noises, Sultan began to play rather aimlessly with the sticks, occasionally fitting them together by chance. Suddenly Kohler, who was watching, saw the chimpanzee fit two sticks together, stare at them for a moment and then, as if making a decision, walk rapidly to the side of the cage and with this new long pole pull the banana in. The moment of comprehension when the ape "realised" what he could do Kohler wittily termed the "ah-ha reflex," a phrase which sums up beautifully a sensation we all understand and which was totally unaccounted for by the Pavlovian approach to the problem.

(g) Later Developments in Learning Theory.

You may have the feeling that Behaviourism, conditioned reflex theory, and its attendant experimental studies are more or less worthless and a hindrance rather than a help to the development of modern psychology. This is far from the truth. The point is that despite its vigorous self-confidence and contempt for "introspective" approaches to psychology, Behaviourism really only falls down through its pretentions to providing a *complete* theory of mind and brain. The Behaviourist experiments still work, and there is undoubtedly such a thing as the conditioned reflex, though one has next to no idea, from the physiological point of view, how it is laid down. Throughout the 1930s and beyond, psychologists supporting the Behaviourist position performed thousands of ingenious and often highly imaginative experiments to back up their ideas, these always being subject to counter-attack from the opposition, most of whom were followers of the Gestalt school. For years arguments raged over Kohler's "insight" study with the chimpanzees, and became even hotter when experiments claiming to demonstrate "insight" in lesser creatures, such as rats, were performed. Gradually, under intense pressure, the Behaviourist hard-line softened, the pretence that animals were no more than bundles of totally automatic reflexes was quietly abandoned. Once this occurred, and the Behaviourist method was put to work studying the functioning of living systems, then experimental psychology was set for a boom. One of the most significant features of the conditioned-reflex method, as exemplified by Pavlov's original experiments, was its usefulness for examining the nature of animal perception. Offhand one might wonder how it could be possible to tell what an animal sees, or more exactly, how fine is its capacity for perceptual discrimination. How could one find out whether a rat could tell the difference between a triangle and a square and between one colour and another? One can ask humans, but rats . . .? In the case of colours, what one could do would be to train the creature to respond to a red light, and then gradually alter its hue in the direction of another colour, say blue. If, before one had made much of a change in hue, the animal was ceasing to respond then one would know that it was detecting the change of hue. As for shape perception, the problem is even easier. In the very early days Pavlov conditioned his dogs to respond positively (*i.e.*, with saliva) to a circle, and negatively (*i.e.*, raising paw to avoid shock) when a rather angular ellipse was shown to it. Then he gradually made the circle more and more like an ellipse, and the ellipse more and more like a circle. Up to a point he got clear-cut appropriate responses, until the pattern lay somewhere in between. At this point the dog, poor creature, had a nervous breakdown, which wasn't too nice for it, but which told Pavlov a lot about its sensory and perceptual

processes. While on these slightly macabre topics it might be worth mentioning that today dogs and rats have largely been supplanted for behaviouristic studies by a rather quaint choice of animal—the pigeon. The fact is that pigeons have been found to have quite remarkable powers of sensory discrimination and will peck away at buttons to get food or avoid electric shocks for hours on end. So good is the pigeon at telling the difference between patterns that it was even once proposed for a fantastic rôle in modern warfare—not its traditional job of carrying messages from spies but, believe it or not, as the control centre for a flying bomb! In the early days of guided missiles the kind of electrical equipment available was too bulky, cumbersome and unreliable to be easily put into flying bombs. This was particularly true about the equipment necessary to allow the bomb to select the correct target at the other end. One bright psychologist argued that the pigeon would be an inexpensive, compact, and reliable "pilot" for a flying bomb. The device, complete with pigeon in a little cabin, could be launched off on course and when the bird spotted the target (say an enemy battleship) which it had been previously trained to recognise, it would peck at the appropriate button and that would be that! So far as one can tell the idea was never implemented, which is probably a good thing for us humans—to say nothing of the pigeons. The idea might be described as one of the less fruitful to come from Pavlov's original idea and serves to remind us that psychology, just as any other science, can be properly or improperly used, depending upon circumstances and the individuals involved. But let us now return to the basic question—what is the actual nature of the learning process or the memory trace?

(h) The Nature of the Engram.

Earlier we said that there were three broad approaches to the problem of the memory trace, the neurological, the electrical, and the biochemical.

(1) *The Neurological.*

This is probably the kind of model that Pavlov would put forward today if he were alive. To understand it, remember that the conditioned reflex is essentially a chain of cells running from sense organ to motor-output (finger, paw, eye-blink, whatever). The cells of course were there in the first place, built into the animal from birth. It is the connections between cells, the links in the chain that are forged in the learning process. Fine, but how *are* the connections formed? Why one chain rather than another? A number of attempts have been made to solve this one, perhaps the most ingenious in recent years coming from the Canadian psychologist D. O. Hebb, an architect incidentally of the sensory deprivation experiments, and one of the first psychologists to be elected as a Fellow of the Royal Society. Hebb had been impressed by the discovery that nerve cells were frequently adorned with tiny bumps or knobs which tended to cluster at the points where the cell made contact with other cells—the *synapse*. There was even some suggestion from microscopic studies that these synaptic knobs tended to become larger and more profuse in the brains of more mature animals. Suppose, Hebb argued, that when a nerve cell was fired, it made contact with another via a synaptic knob and thus triggered the second cell into action. Suppose also that each time a synapse was bridged via a contact knob, this knob grew a little, as though through exercise, and thus made better contact. This, as time went on, would significantly raise the likelihood of a nervous impulse crossing at this point. If one can imagine the process repeated with a whole series of cells, then one can see that repeated firings would also increase the likelihood of particular chains of cells being activated, thus wearing a kind of path through the nervous system down which the neural impulse would "prefer" to travel. This Hebb suggested, could be the basis of the conditioned reflex—simply a connection made progressively easier each time the route was travelled.

Hebb's theory attracted a good deal of attention when it was first published over 20 years ago, first because it seemed to fit the known physiological facts (such as they were) and second because it seemed to get over one of the awful difficulties facing any neurological theory of learning—the experiments of Lashley. Recapping briefly, these showed that the memory trace or engram for a particular task was not located in any one small section of the brain. Now Hebb's synaptic knob model implied that the initial path followed by a nervous impulse might be pretty random throughout the cortex, wandering here and there until, with repeated firings, it became established. This would quite possibly be a rather straggly chain and not necessarily the shortest distance between two points. Add to this the fact that the acquisition of a complex habit, such as learning a maze, would obviously depend upon thousands, possibly hundreds of thousands, of these neural links being established, and one can begin to see that Lashley's experimental results no longer seem to fly in the face of reason. Removal of any single chunk of cortical tissue would simply serve to remove a more or less random selection of the neural chains serving as the maze-memory. The more one took out, the worse the memory of the maze would be, but no single piece removed would ever eliminate the whole of the memory! To many people Hebb's theory, crude though it might be, fairly tackles the apparent paradox of Lashley's results. Others are not so sure. Its main default, the intervening years have shown, is that his nice ideas about the growth of synaptic knobs and their significance as contact points between cells are probably no longer valid. Today their function, and even their existence in the form that Hebb discussed, is questioned by many physiologists. Furthermore, for various reasons, there has been a strong shift towards the point of view that whatever form the learning process takes it is unlikely to involve changes in neural tissue—at least of such magnitude. To many psychologists and their colleagues, changes in the molecular structure of the cell must be involved. Before considering the evidence for this hypothesis, we need to examine briefly the Gestalt psychologists' attempt to account for learning and memory.

(2) Electrical Field Theory.

We have been talking of the Gestalt psychologists without pointing out an interesting fact—that the two principal founders were first trained as physicists! Jumping the broad gap between physics and psychology might seem a bit much, but Wolfgang Köhler was one who did it, and in doing so he injected into his theorising some of the ideas basic to his native topic. In the main this involved the concepts of electrical field theory. Without going into this in boring detail, it so happens that an electrical source, either in the form of a battery, a current flowing down a wire or whatever, spouts electrons in its immediate neighbourhood and these constitute an electromagnetic field. As the name implies, the most striking example of such a field is to be seen in the ordinary common-or-garden magnet, and the structure of the field can be observed by placing the magnet in a large mass of iron filings. Now Köhler and his friends argued that the brain was a potent source of electromagnetic energy and ought, therefore, to create a field within and around its tissue. The field would be powerful enough to modify incoming electrical input from the senses and to some extent impose its own pattern on it. Hence the Gestalt "laws" of perceptual organisation. This would be a two-way process, however, for sensory input, no matter how feeble, would impose at least minor changes on the structure of the cerebral field. Such changes, the Gestaltists argued, would constitute the basis of learning. It was a bold, if somewhat implausible point of view, and was treated as a serious alternative to the Pavlovian conditioned reflex ideas for at least a period. It had one or two gross defects, however, which even the Gestalt psychologists found worrying. In the first place, no kind of recording device seemed able to pick up any signs of permanent or semi-permanent electrical fields surrounding the brain. The EEG seemed to be a rhythmic picture of electrical change within, rather than of a static, powerful field highly resistant to change. Secondly, there is the odd data from electro-shock therapy. This much-maligned method of treating highly-depressed psychiatric patients relies on jolting the brain with a powerful electric shock, a not particularly pleasant process which nevertheless generally brings a notable remission in patients' symptoms. The point here is not to argue the pros and cons of ECT, as it is called, but to indicate that such tremendous shocks should be enough to seriously disturb any electrical fields, no matter how well-established, with presumably drastic effects on memory. In fact long-term memory is totally unaffected by ECT, though, as the Gestalt supporters were quick to point out, there is short-term amnesia for events immediately preceding the electric shock. Thirdly, and finally, as it happens, there is the clinching experimental work of Lashley—not his tissue-removal experiment, but yet another in the catalogue of his remarkable repertoire. Lashley's procedure was as follows. He first taught a large number of rats a particular maze. Then he inserted in their cortex very fine sheets of gold leaf—a notorious destroyer of electrical fields. He then ran the rats through the same maze again, and found no evidence of any detriment in their performance. He also taught other rats the maze after they had had the gold leaf implanted, and found that they learnt it with no undue difficulty. After this work the Gestalt battle cry never seemed so loud or so convincing again. It is doubtful, actually, whether they ever really believed the electrical field theory, but it was a nice idea while it lasted.

(3) The Biochemical Argument: Some Fresh Surprises.

The memory capacity of the human brain is absolutely enormous. It has been calculated that it is quite capable of storing all the information ever fed into it—in other words there is no need for anything ever to be thrown out of store to make room for fresh material. The real problem in this case is not finding enough room to pump in information, but in finding a sufficiently efficient system to pull it out rapidly. Not only do psychologists believe that the brain has this almost limitless storage capacity, but they also have some evidence that all the information fed in, no matter how trivial, actually is stored! Some of the most exciting evidence to back up this belief has come from studies made during human brain surgery. These studies are a trifle gruesome and the squeamish might like to jump a paragraph or two here.

For a particular type of surgery—such as the excision of a brain tumour—it is necessary to remove a portion of the cranium and for various reasons it is advisable to perform the entire operation with the patient fully conscious. This is not so horrific as all that, for the brain itself has no pain-detecting cells and the initial opening can be made with a local anaesthetic. One or two scientifically-minded surgeons, notably Dr. Wilder Penfield, have taken the opportunity presented by this surgical requirement to perform certain experiments which have turned out to be of immense interest. With the patient's permission and co-operation, Penfield stimulated selected exposed portions of their cortex with tiny electric currents. Moving round from sensory area to sensory area he found that his tiny electrical stimuli provoked characteristic sensations from the patients. In the visual areas they might "see" lights, colours, etc., in the auditory areas "hear" sounds, and in the temporal lobes, get impressions of smells, taste, etc. Stranger still, Penfield found that certain parts of the so-called association areas of cortex, when stimulated, led to the patient recalling specific memories, often of apparently forgotten items. One woman got a vivid impression of herself in a kitchen of a former home and hearing the voice of her mother, long since dead. Others reported equally specific memories, sometimes with fragments of speech or conversation attached, quite often of items which the patients reported they "hadn't thought of for years." One possible implication for this exciting work is, as we have said, that *all* information that has ever been put into the brain is stored as memory just in case it should ever be needed again. If this is so, then to most psychologists the idea that the memory trace is laid down in the form of major structural changes in the cell body (such as with synaptic knobs) is no longer tenable. There simply aren't enough cells to cope. But suppose that the engram is laid down *within* the cell, at sub-microscopic level in the form of, perhaps, the rearrangement of the specialised molecular structure. Since no one has ever got a really good look at a molecule, either in the nervous system or out of it, this might seem to be a bit of optimistic guesswork, but there is in fact some strange evidence to back the idea up. To consider this we must acquaint ourselves with one of the lowliest creatures capable of learning—the little flatworm, planaria. There is a good deal of argument about how far down the animal kingdom some form of learning can take place. Some workers even claim to have demonstrated memory mechanism in tiny single-celled creatures such as amoeba or its hairy cousin, paramecia, but you can be sure that any information stored was of the simplest and most rudimentary kind. It is when we get to the simplest form of worms, and planaria is one of these, that something closer to memory in the real sense can be clearly demonstrated. Typical of the kind of task which planaria manage, albeit with a good deal of intellectual effort, is to turn right rather than left at a little junction in order to get food or avoid an electric shock. They can also be conditioned to wince to a light being switched on when this is always followed by an electric shock—rather like Pavlov's dogs. Now planaria has the most rudimentary, almost non-existent central nervous system. It has a front end, shaped rather like an arrow with tiny light-sensitive organs in it, and which is clearly its head. It also has a back end which the charitable would call a tail. The question now is—in what part of the tiny body are memories laid down? The head would seem to be the most likely bet, though you might feel it would be hard to tell for sure. At this point the psychologist makes use of another of planaria's interesting features—its ability to regenerate tissue with ease. Take a knife and slice off planaria's tail and both ends swim away, one rather more efficiently than the other. Now in due course the head section will produce a new tail and—rather fantastically—the tail will produce a new head! Planaria can do other odd things too. Cut down the centre of its head without actually removing any tissue and in due course the two half-heads will regenerate into two full heads, producing a peculiar but rather neat looking creature. If one makes several flaps, instead of just two, you end up with lots and lots of heads on one body and get a very odd-looking planaria indeed. All this is very interesting, but the exercise has more point than this. In the first case, ask yourself a question; suppose you teach planaria a little maze and then slice the head into two. Now, of the regenerating heads, which has got the "memory" of the maze stored in it? Left; right; both; neither? Actually, the answer is both, and this should give some clue as to the answer to the next question. Cut a maze-trained planaria in half (head and tail) and let the respective sections develop again into a full creature. One would certainly expect that the head part plus its new tail would be able to perform its little task without much trouble, but what about the tail with its new head? The answer is that this too can "run" the maze. If this seems to be contradicting everything we've said about learning and the brain in general up to now, then in a way it is. We must remember that planaria is an exceedingly simple creature with no CNS to speak of and no nerve cells of the kind found in higher animals. The engram, wherever it is, certainly not formed by the development of synaptic knobs or by the modification of complex electrical fields. Furthermore, as it is evidently stored in tail as well as head section, then it must presumably be laid down in most, if not necessarily all, of the animal's body cells. This is the point where the biochemists step in

and argue that it is not the outside but rather the interior structure of the cell that is modified through learning. Odd indeed, but there is odder yet to come. Researchers got a collection of planaria and taught them a particular task—turning right in a simple maze and then took an equivalent number of planaria with no experience of this kind. They then collected the first group and whirled them round in a mixing bowl until all that was left was a homogeneous planaria soup, and repeated the process with the other, untrained group. They now fed the two kinds of soup (planaria will eat more or less anything that's hanging round) to different groups of totally untrained planaria and subsequently trained these in the original right-turn task. This produced an extraordinary result. The planaria who had been fed the soup consisting of trained planaria seemed to learn the maze task significantly quicker than those who had been fed the untrained soup! You will know enough about experimental psychology by now to realise that these results caused immense controversy, and a series of experiments were immediately launched by workers who had found the first result incredible. The controversy, incidentally, still rages as many of the attempts to repeat the experiments have not worked, but the original protagonists still maintain the validity of their results. It is not hard to see why the critics get so hot under the collar, for the implications of the findings, if valid, will throw into question just about every theoretical approach to learning to date. Since the planaria were thoroughly mashed up, no neural connections or even any formal kind of organisation within the system would remain to carry the maze information across to the cannibal planaria. Furthermore, one would have thought that the digestive processes of the cannibals would have completed the process of destruction. How then could the original maze habit, or traces of it, be possibly preserved and carried over? No one on either side of the argument has been able to offer up any convincing explanation, except that if the results are valid, then the maze habit, in the case of planaria at any rate, must be stored right down at molecular level—in other words so such a microscopic level that any mixing and digestion could have little or no effect on it. But even if the planaria results *are* valid, would the same thing necessarily apply to humans? Not necessarily, but if a process works for one living system it could in principle work for another, and we must remember our conclusion that the brain's enormous memory store suggests that modification of the neurone itself would be at too gross a level. It may well be that we shall find the brain puts down information in more than one way. There is reasonable evidence, for example, that many animals and humans are equipped with two kinds of memory store—a short-term, and possibly highly unstable one, and a long-term, more or less perpetual system. Information fed into our brains might go initially to the short-term store where it is filtered for relevance or general usefulness. If unwanted for some reason it might be eliminated, but if wanted, passed on to the longer-term system. Perhaps the short-term memory (the kind that allows you to "momentarily" remember a new telephone number) is electrical and the long-term biochemical, neurological or both. At this moment psychologists and physiologists across the world are concentrating on these exciting problems and perhaps, within the next few years, we shall have some new answers and, quite certainly, some fresh surprises.

(i) Unsolved Problems.

This section has attempted to raise some of the issues confronting psychologists in their attempt to solve one of the main mysteries of the brain—how information is stored and processed within it. Although a fair bit has been learned in the past decades, it has really served to show that the problem is much more complicated than the earlier workers ever imagined. Furthermore, you will have noticed that precious little has been said about how the information is extracted, for the very good reason that precious little is known about this. Curiously some interesting clues are beginning to come from the study of computers, man's own specially-created slave brains. These are already capable of storing quite immense quantities of information, and engineers have been working steadily at improving methods of storing information and of getting it out in a hurry. In recent years the computer engineers and the psychologists have been tending to get together and pool their ideas—with some interesting results. To more and more scientists it has become increasingly obvious that the study of the brain is real ground for interdisciplinary contact, and that contributions to its study can come equally from psychologists, physiologists, physicists, engineers, mathematicians, educationalists, and so on. The highly successful Brain Research Association, for example, is composed of scientists from practically every discipline, with psychologists and physiologists, who are traditionally the kingpins in brain science, making up no more than 25 per cent of its ranks. Perhaps the really big problems in brain research will only come from multi-disciplinary teams of this kind. But this is something of a digression and we must now pass on from learning and memory to the lesser, but no less interesting problem of motivation.

IV. MOTIVATION.

(1) Why Does an Animal Do One Thing Rather Than Another?

This question aptly sums up the problem of animal and human motivation, an important facet of modern psychological research. As is always the case with psychology, perhaps more so than with other fields of science, what initially seem to be straightforward questions, designed to elicit straightforward answers, become steadily more complicated on close inspection. The odd, almost philosophical difficulties surrounding motivation are a good example. Why *does* an animal do one thing rather than another? Because it wants to, is the stock reply—a reply which actually doesn't get anywhere at all. To say that the reason for doing something is because the doer *likes it* is no explanation, merely renaming the problem so that it comes up in a different guise. It so happens that we tend to like doing the things we do, though of course this doesn't always apply. We certainly like to eat, but do we eat principally because we like it or because the food is essential to our survival? Perhaps the key is tied up here somewhere, and the rock-bottom cause for all animal and human behaviour lies in the need to keep the individual creature alive. Well, that will certainly do for food and water, but it clearly doesn't work for other common activities, such as sex. In the long term the survival of all living things depends upon sexual activity but animals certainly don't understand this and humans only found out the link between the sexual act and conception a millennium or so ago. And anyone who believes that people indulge in sex solely to allow the human species to survive is very naïve indeed. Now the situation gets even more complicated. It seems as if we make love because we like it, with the long-term result being that the species survives. But what can be the link, in physiological terms, between liking something and it "doing us good"? And just to complicate matters even more, supposing that we accept this link, how do we explain other common patterns of human behaviour? Why do some people like going to football matches or art galleries? Why don't they go there to eat the footballers or the paintings, and how is the survival of the human species helped by such practices anyway? Having muddled the issue thoroughly—or, rather, showed it up in its true light—we can now go on to see how psychologists have set to work to try to unravel it. They have not got very far, but they have got somewhere.

(2) The Mechanical Tortoise.

The first people to face up to the problems raised above were the Behaviourists. In their gallant attempt to explain human and animal behaviour in mechanistic terms they realised that they would have to account for the tendency of animals to set out to do things rather than simply engage in random, diffuse activity, and they thought this could be fairly simply handled. They were most anxious, of course, to avoid explaining different types of behaviour in terms of different goals—to suggest that an animal had got a goal in mind was to imply that it had a mind and furthermore some kind of "picture of the future" in it. To begin with they took the simplest possible form of mechanical analogy. Imagine a clockwork mouse, which when wound up runs across the floor. What caused it to do so? The clockwork and the energy tied up in the spring, of course, with its direction determined by such matters as the orientation of its wheels, the angle of the floor, etc. Anyone saying that the toy crossed the floor because it wanted to would be being silly. Similarly, the Behaviourists stated, one should be able to avoid the same kind of inference when observing the movements of a real mouse. If the response is that the real mouse can do a good deal more than just run across a floor—can squeak, change direction, avoid cats and eat cheese—then the reply in essence is that one could build a mechanical mouse to do that as well, provided one had the time and ingenuity. The more complicated and versatile the mechanical mouse the harder it would become to tell the difference between the two, and when one had two apparently identical mice, would one still talk about one "wanting" to cross a floor and the other doing it purely automatically? Was there an important difference anyway? Critics of Behaviourism argued that indeed there was a difference. The "real" mouse ate the cheese because it satisfied a need for the food, whereas the mechanical mouse, no matter how many bogus sounds of enjoyment it made as it munched the food, was merely going through an essentially meaningless mechanical process. This is a dangerous argument, for suppose that one decided to power the artificial mouse not by clockwork but by the combustion of cheese and made it so that it would stop when its inner store of cheese ran out . . . one would now have an artificial mouse with a "need" for cheese as great as that of its biological counterpart. If this seems an unlikely step to take, consider the case of Grey Walter's mechanical tortoise. In an effort to replicate some of the conditions of behaviour, the great English psychologist, Dr. Grey Walter of the Burden Neurological Institute, constructed a tortoise which exhibited some of the paramount properties of living creatures. His tortoise—a shell on wheels with no pretensions to looking like an animal—was powered by storage batteries which drove a motor allowing it to run around on the floor. Its movements were far from aimless, for it was also equipped with photocells in its head capable of detecting areas of light or dark. A series of simple switches inside were arranged so that when the tortoise's batteries were fully charged, the device would move towards dark areas of a room, finding its way underneath chairs and tables, carefully working its way round books, human feet, etc., placed in its way. With batteries low, a different switching arrangement would come into operation and the device would now tend to avoid dark areas and seek out light ones—in particular the light inside its "hutch" where a battery charge was conveniently situated. Once inside the hutch Grey Walter's tortoise would connect up to the battery charger, later emerging "replenished" to set out for dark places again! Here the Behaviourist argument emerges most strongly. It is not, of course, that Grey Walter had manufactured a living thing—no one is making that claim—but rather a matter of whether the tortoise's tendency to seek out its battery for recharging, etc., constituted a need in the same sense as does the real mouse's need for cheese. This is a big question which you will probably have to think out for yourself. In the meanwhile let's see how the Behaviourists attempted to translate animal behaviour into similar terms.

(3) Drives and Needs.

The Behaviourist position can be summed up as an attempt at describing animal behaviour in the simplest possible way, and to do this they evolved the concept of " Drive." A drive is described as something which causes an animal to perform a particular act, and the ideal position, from the behaviouristic viewpoint, would be to find that all animal activity could be explained in terms of a limited number of drives. To begin with things looked simple and promising, for it appeared as if a drive could be thought of as something that promoted bodily well-being. For example, when an animal is short of food it is running out of power. This causes a sensation known as " hunger " which signals a bodily " need " and this in turn sets in motion a chain of activity which culminates in eating. When the food has been ingested, the need is satisfied, the hunger vanishes and the drive is reduced. The same argument applies to thirst, and, with a bit of modification, to sex. In the latter case if an animal does not engage in sexual activity for a given period of time certain substances build up in the body, the hormonal system becomes unbalanced, etc., and a need builds up in the body, which gives rise to a drive. This in turn pushes the creature towards sexual activity with a suitable mate. Carry this on just a bit more and include a " need " to escape painful situations and you've practically got the whole of animal behaviour sewn up. What's more it is sewn up in a very convincing way because the needs and drives are not vague and ambiguous, but relate directly to vital bodily processes which if not operating properly will cause the animal's death. All animal behaviour could be explained in terms of a drive to (i) reduce hunger, (ii) reduce thirst, (iii) reduce pain, and (iv) achieve sex. To those who didn't want to talk about " achievement," which seemed to imply that an animal was actually setting out to do something, then the final one could be rephrased (iv) to reduce sexual tension. An animal in a state of need would be activated by some or all of these drives and would continue to " behave " until all drives were reduced. Protagonists of this delightfully simple point of view even showed how learning theory could benefit from drive-reduction ideas; a pattern of behaviour or conditioned reflex would be established, they claimed, at its conclusion a drive was reduced. If no drive-reduction took place, then the behaviour pattern would not be learned. In the 'thirties and 'forties a number of mathematically inclined psychologists even attempted to express this in the form of sets of equations which looked enormously impressive on paper but which, alas, bore little relationship in practice to the way living animals actually behaved. For example, people soon realised that a bit of a problem emerged for an animal if all its drives were set at maximum, as it were, and all the appropriate drive-reducing stimuli were at hand. Take a rat, severely deprived of food and water, and place it in a cage with both available. What is it going to do first, eat or drink? Presumably it will be pushed in the direction suggested by the strongest drive. Using this as an idea it was decided that it ought to be possible to rank animal drives in order of strength by a simple test. Place a rat deprived of either food, water, or sexual activity in a box facing the necessary drive-reduction stimulus across an electrified grid. Now, how strong an electric shock is the rat prepared to put up with in order to fulfil its need? Experimenters found that thirst was the most effective stimulus, food next, and sex third. This was all fine until they found that rats satiated in all three modes would still occasionally cross the grid even when there was nothing on the other side! Now what kind of drive could be operating here? Furthermore, they found that an animal, again supplied with plenty of food, water, etc., would still run through a complicated maze and learn it pretty well, despite the lack of drive-reduction at the other end! Before long the theorists found themselves rather glumly proposing " exploration " or curiosity-reducing drives to account for the well-known fact that animals like to roam about all over the place. This, naturally, allows one to have a completely comprehensive theory of behaviour and learning in drive-reduction terms, but with the penalty of converting a simple, fairly sharply defined theory, tied closely to describable bodily requirements, into a complicated, diffuse,

and far less convincing one. If any activity not explained in terms of the original drives can now be accounted for in terms of a reduction of an exploratory drive, then one has an " explanation " of the behaviour. But to many people's minds it is no better than those around before the whole concept of drives and needs was introduced. Similarly, there was a certain neatness and utility to the idea that a pattern of behaviour could be learned if at its conclusion a drive such as hunger or thirst was reduced. This neatness vanishes when we are told that an animal has learnt something else because its curiosity was satisfied, or the opposite. that it was not learnt because its curiosity drive was *not* reduced! Clearly the root of all these difficulties lies in the refusal of many psychologists to admit that a creature or a person does something or learns something because it likes it. Fair enough. We have already pointed out how subjective is the idea of an animal doing something because it " wants to," and the job of the psychologist is to try to define behaviour objectively rather than subjectively. What was clearly needed was some definable describable physiological process which could correspond to " pleasure," and until this was found psychologists could proceed no further in the field of motivation. In 1954 experiments were published which gave them the green light.

(4) The Pleasure Centre.

The arrival of microelectrode recording techniques allowed numerous experimental studies of the animal and even, occasionally, the human brain in action to be made. In a prolonged assault on the inner intricacies of the cerebral cortex and lower control centres psychologists and physiologists began the elaborate job of mapping the brain, defining as rigidly as they could which areas were devoted to what function. In many cases the areas they stimulated seemed to be " silent," *i.e.*, provoking no obvious response from the animal. Others however were more dramatically active. In 1956 the American James Olds and the Englishman Peter Milner were studying the responses of rats with electrodes implanted in what is known as the septal area of the brain, a spot beneath a body known as the corpus callosum. Animals stimulated with low voltage electric currents in this area seemed to behave in an odd way—almost as if they were enjoying the experience. For many years it had been known that stimulating the area known as the hypothalamus could produce symptoms of rage in animals, the creatures responding as though angered or threatened, the " sham rage " switching off immediately the electric stimulus ceased. Similarly areas had been found which when stimulated would cause dozy, apparently sleepy behaviour. Now here was something very different and Olds and Milner began to suspect that they had hit on something akin to a " pleasure " centre. To test this they designed a weird electrical circuit. surely one of the oddest ever to be seen in a laboratory. From the electrode in the rat's septal region a wire ran to the battery providing the electrical stimulus. In the rat's cage they placed a lever, and connected this to the battery in such a way that when the lever was pressed the battery emitted a single pulse, thus allowing the rat—if it wanted to—to stimulate this particular area of the brain. Although they had half suspected that the rats might occasionally give themselves a jolt in this " pleasure area," no one had anticipated the extent of the rats' involvement. All animals, once they had discovered the trick of pushing the lever, went into a sustained surge of lever pressing, keeping the activity up for literally hours on end. In fact there was some suggestion that they might have kept it up for ever, had not physical exhaustion sooner or later intervened. Given the choice of alternative levers providing food, water, or the chance to stimulate their septal regions, all rats reliably chose the latter, even those who had been substantially deprived of opportunities to eat or drink for some time. The lack of apparent satiation of the effect was one of the really odd things about the discovery. No human or animal appetite has ever been found which cannot be satisfied, if only for short periods. Only where some severe pathology is involved, such as with a disease or brain tumour, do the normal appetites remain unquenched. But here was something quite different—an appetite which seemed to have boundless depths and which outrode any of the other paramount needs of the animal. It was for this reason that Olds and Milner hypothesised that they had hit on the centre in the brain which mediates the sensation which we humans know of as "pleasure." How surprising is it that some such centre exists? Not very. When we do something we like, be it eating, drinking, or even going to a football match, then the feeling of pleasure that we get must be matched by some parallel process in the brain, and it could well be that this is located in some convenient but specific centre. Olds and Milner, incidentally, found that their animals would very swiftly learn a task if they were rewarded by a session on the pleasure centre, and here perhaps another important point emerges. There has always been some evidence, though the matter is by no means settled, that learning was somehow improved if following the performance of the desired task, a "reward" such as food, drink, sex, etc., was given. The big question is, what kind of signal is given to the memory system to denote when something is to be permanently laid down? Olds and Milner appeared to have provided one possible answer, and one that would have greatly satisfied Pavlov, Watson, and their immediate successors, the reinforcing stimulus—the message that declares that something will be learnt—is a message that has passed through the pleasure centre. The validity of this idea is still uncertain, but it has the merit of answering an age-old question in reasonably simple fashion, and also of helping us towards the solution of an even more venerable philosophical one—the nature of pleasure itself.

(5) Emotion.

This is one of the most misunderstood words in the psychologist's vocabulary and is a source of endless confusion. The trouble is it means so many things to so many different people. To the psychologist, however, it has a fairly specific meaning and we must try to get some idea of what this is. Only by doing so can we avoid falling into such traps as to say, " Animals cannot feel emotions," or " Computers can never think because they have no emotions." First let's attempt to nail the word " emotion " to the wall and try to analyse it. When we talk of people being emotional, what exactly do we mean? That they tend to weep a lot, get easily angered? Sorrow and anger are emotions, that is clear. But is not love an emotion too? Do we mean that emotional people tend to fall in love a good deal? Or do we mean that their love is deeper than others—or perhaps shallower? Already some confusion is creeping in. Let's ask now how we know that someone is emotional, or in an emotional state. The answer is probably that they exhibit a characteristic behaviour pattern which allows us to judge. If they wave their fists, go red in the face and shout, then we might infer that they were angry. Of course they could be acting and merely pretending to be angry, in which case what is the dividing line between the real and the simulated emotion? The answer would seem to be that the latter was not accompanied by an internal *feeling* of a special kind, and this now tells us that there are at least two sides to emotion—subjective psychological state and an external, physiological one. In fact, psychologists find it convenient to consider three aspects. The first is the *behavioural*—i.e. the kind of activity in which the angry or otherwise emotional person engages. This is generally easily detected and is of the waving-arms-around variety. The second is the *physiological*, which consists of considerably more discrete behavioural signs, not always obvious to the observer but which may be detected by suitably sensitive instruments. The third is the *psychological* or introspective and this refers to the " state of mind " of the individual when he is angry or whatever. This of course cannot be directly sensed by other individuals who rely on the angry person reporting to them " how

he feels." How are these linked together, and what function do they serve?

(a) *The Behavioural.*

If you fire a pistol behind someone's back they exhibit a very characteristic response, the most common feature of which is that they jump some distance into the air. This may seem desperately obvious, but actually there is a good deal more to the response than that. High speed photography shows that all human beings respond to sudden loud noises by a highly predictable behavioural sequence, of which the jump is just one part, and which bears the name " the startle pattern." It includes a marked hunching of the shoulders, closing the eyes, baring the teeth, and raising the hands in the direction of the face. It doesn't take long to see that these actions, which occur reliably in all human beings, are not random and pointless but serve to help the individual respond rapidly to a dangerous situation. The jump is an alerting response, the eyes are closed to protect them, the hands raised in defence or perhaps to strike, the teeth bared possibly as a threatening or warning sign. Similarly, at a more common emotional level, the waving fists and loud voice of an angry man equip him to some extent for battle. And what of the tears and the cowering posture of a thoroughly frightened individual? Well, these in some way suggest to the aggressor that the battle is over and are signals to him to stop fighting. Men, being natural fighters, tend to do little in the way of crying and will generally scrap on until they are physically incapable of continuing. Women, on the other hand, who are not particularly strong or well-equipped to fight, tend to slip into weeping and submission rather easily, hence the well-known fact that tears are a woman's strongest weapon against a man. (This submissive pattern of behaviour fails dismally of course when the aggressor is a carnivore such as a tiger, when the one submitting is eaten, tears and all.) The very obvious facial expressions made by people in various emotional states led the great Charles Darwin to the view that the type of face made was a good index of what emotion the individual was in the grips of. To test this idea, psychologists took photographs of the facial expressions of people in various emotional states and then asked other people to try to name them. The results were poor, with few people doing better than chance. The only expression reliably recognised and correctly assigned to an emotion was a smile, and even this was occasionally confused with other emotional states such as pain, or even fear. The same experiment performed with movies yielded somewhat better results, and when sound was added results were again improved. The clinching thing, however, seems to be the setting in which the behaviour takes place, for people become very accurate in judging emotions when they see the surroundings in which the other people are behaving. Clearly the external signs of emotion, despite their immediate and rather obvious manifestations, are an unreliable guide to what is going on inside the individual's head. The same argument, incidentally, applies to animals, though somewhat less forcefully. Most animals give pretty explicit signs when they are angry or when they are afraid. One can even detect something suspiciously like guilt in the general pattern of behaviour of a dog which has done something it shouldn't. But can one really talk of a dog " feeling guilty "? If not—why not? Whatever answer you give will be quite as valid as any given by a psychologist.

(b) *The Physiological.*

The signs and signals we talked about above were all gross, obvious, and yet, as we pointed out, somewhat unreliable. To a large part they seem to be the outward manifestation of an internal process which at the same time serve a useful purpose, as when the startle pattern alerts the individual into a posture suitable for defensive or aggressive action. But what are the finer, physiological manifestations of emotion? These must obviously involve changes in the state of bodily and cerebral activity. Psychologists have pinned down no fewer than 11 distinct facets of human and animal behaviour which give a clear

index of changes in emotional states. To give
some idea of the complexity of emotional behaviour we will look at each of these briefly.

(1) The first, and perhaps the most obvious,
is heart-rate. The heart's job is to pump
blood around the body and the blood provides the vital organ supply to the brain.
The more intense the activity, the more
oxygen is consumed and the more blood
needs to be circulated. It should be no
surprise therefore to anyone to learn that as
activity is stepped up, so heart-rate increases
and vice versa. Furthermore, heart-rate
tends to accelerate just prior to some important or exciting piece of activity, or even
on merely thinking about it, and this means
that we have here one index of emotional
state. A device known as the electrocardiogram (EKG) can give a very precise picture
of heart fluctuations and represents one
objective way of plotting this information.

(2) We have already implied another
measure, respiration. This increases more
or less alongside heart-rate, and is a pretty
good index of most emotions. Irregularities
of breathing, including variations in the
depth of breaths, are a particularly good index
of nervousness as most people know and all
this can be detected by a suitable instrument

(3) More or less hand-in-hand with the
above come changes in local blood pressure
and volume, the facial accompaniments of
which—blanching or blushing—are only too
obvious. These can be measured by a device
known as the plethysmograph, which is
merely a version of the kind of device a
doctor uses to measure your blood pressure in
a routine medical examination.

(4) A somewhat harder emotional symptom
to measure, but very characteristic of most
emotional states, is muscle tension and its
associate, tremor. In anger, rage, and other
aggressive states muscles become tensed to
be ready for rapid action and if this is carried
too far we get trembling of the limbs—a
familiar accompaniment of great nervousness
or fright.

All the above are easily discernible indices,
amenable to instrumentation but not depending
upon it. The remaining manifestations are
harder to detect, though just as valuable once one
has caught them. Beginning with the most
obvious we have:

(5) The pilomotor response, which is a
hangover from the days when our ancestors
had a good deal more hair than we do today,
and which can be seen when a cat's fur fluffs
out in rage or fear. In humans today we call
it goose-pimples and it is often a precursor to
the feeling of full-blooded fear.

(6) Even harder to measure is salivary
secretion which is the kind of response Pavlov
studied with his dogs. In anxiety or fear
the saliva flow tends to be inhibited and we
find ourselves with "dry mouths."

(7) An index of emotion which is particularly obvious to the individual is the change
in gastrointestinal motility. Movements of
the stomach and intestine are brought to a
brief but definite halt in strong emotional
states with a complementary, and often
rather dramatic, surge back to action shortly
afterwards. There are plenty of homely and
slightly vulgar expressions to describe the
consequences of this.

(8) There has been a recent rise of interest
in the pupillary response as an index of
certain types of emotion. The pupil of the
eye tends to dilate in moments of anger or
pain with slight dilation occurring during
periods of "interest" in something. This
has led some clever psychologists who work in
the advertising profession to use this as an
index of the relative effectiveness of different
types of advertisement. All the subjects
have to do is look at the subject matter

while a recording camera photographs the
pupils of their eyes from a distance!

(9) Because the endocrine or glandular
system is active in emotional states the
chemical constitution of the blood changes
markedly as the hormones flow within it, but
this index, while potentially useful, is of
course abnormally hard to measure directly.

(10) Next we come to the so-called galvanic skin response (GSR) which is in fact
nothing more than the electrical resistance of
the skin. For various reasons, not properly
understood, the resistance of the skin to an
electrical current changes with most emotional states, tending to decrease as a function
of the intensity of the emotion. This can be
detected with a suitable instrument and
meter and is perhaps particularly interesting
because it is an automatic response which the
individual is not consciously aware of.
Connect someone up to a GSR meter, tell
him that you are going to stick a pin in him
and the needle will swing wildly. It is a
very effective demonstration of an entirely
involuntary response and is generally one of
the first experiments that fledgling psychologists perform on each other in their
laboratory classes.

(11) Finally there is the EEG, which we
referred to earlier on (see Q5). The electrical
activity of the brain does change with varying
degrees of bodily activity, though what these
changes mean is a matter for skilled interpretation.

(c) The Psychological.

You will have noticed that many of the above
indices—stomach motility, muscle tension, etc.—
have definite physical accompaniments which are
only too obvious to the individual experiencing
the emotion and it should not be too surprising
in the light of all this that an emotional state
markedly alters our physical and psychological
feelings and sensations. But is this all there is
to emotion? Can the age-old human passions of
love and hate be reduced to permutations of
salivary secretion, blood pressure, pilomotor
response and electro-cortical activity? Pu. so
baldly of course the answer is no. Love demands
a partner, a setting, a trigger and some temporal
span—as does hate. In humans these require the
active participation of the complex computer we
call the brain, and a background of education,
social activity, and some awareness of goals other
than the immediate. Nevertheless, the intense
physiological and psychological changes which
envelop us when we are in love, or when we
fight in passion, contribute the better part of
the powerful sensations we feel. But which of
the three faces of emotion, the behavioural, the
physiological, or the psychological is the real or
most significant one?

The answer is that no single one predominates
for emotion is a complex of all three. When the
object of our emotion, be it love, hate, or whatever, is first encountered then mind and body
combine to set the individual up for the optimum
pattern of responses. This involves some per-
mutation of physical change which, naturally, is
reflected in psychological changes of mood.
These in turn provoke outward changes on a
larger scale which may involve combat or the
ritual of love. If this description seems to debase
the concept of human emotional response then
this is a pity for there is no reason why it should.
The powerful forces that thrust men into the
numerous passions of the world would have no
meaning were they not accompanied by potent
changes in bodily state. The artistry that
springs from these passions is no fraction diminished because we can identify the physiological
and psychological changes that accompany and,
to some extent, determine them.

It will have occurred to you that in this section
on motivation we have drifted closer and closer to
another of the critical areas that psychologists
study—the nature of human personality. Psychologists know far less about this area than
they would like to, but their century of scientific
activity (a small span compared with the history

of the more traditional sciences, such as physics) has begun to pay off. In the next and final section we will take a look at what they have done, or have tried to do, in this most fascinating of areas.

V. PERSONALITY AND THINKING.

(1) What Constitutes a Person?

To many people this is the most important single question in psychology and indeed, perhaps, in the combined fields of science and philosophy. What is it that makes up that unique blend of psychological and physiological factors we call " personality "? The answer is, predictably, complicated and before we can even begin to consider it we must attempt to define the problems in the field. In the first place let's consider the most venerable and apparently simplest answer—a person is that thing in the head that thinks, feels, is aware of itself as an individual entity, and which controls a brain and body. This is the answer which probably fits best with the non-technical philosophy of the man-in-the-street and which matches also with a long-standing traditional view fostered by the majority of systems of religious belief. Put another way, it states that human beings are composed of essentially two parts. One of these is physical and consists of the body and its control centre, the brain. The second is non-physical, and is called the mind, soul, spirit, or some similar name. This is a separate entity which controls the body through its brain and while involved in this way must obey the laws of the physical world. It may, however, survive the death of its body (one of the most widespread of religious views or personality) and occasionally, as with telepathy, precognition, etc., may step outside to contact other similar minds in other parts of the world or even take a peek into the future. As we have said, this is an exceedingly widespread view of the nature of personality and it will be the one held by many who read this article. This is now the point where you could ask whether this view is acceptable to psychologists, and that is a fair and proper question. It requires, however, two separate answers. In the first place some psychologists, though certainly not the majority, accept this or some very similar view, but on an entirely personal plane. When they think as scientists, however, most are inclined to disagree with it. Nothing that has been uncovered in the history of experimental psychology, with the possible exception of the very dubious evidence for telepathy, suggests that the human personality is a separate entity to be considered in isolation from brain and body. Psychologists who choose to believe otherwise frankly admit that they do so on the basis of faith or hunch, and argue that even though the scientific facts appear to contradict their beliefs at the moment, perhaps in due course experimental psychology will uncover fresh new material to change the whole picture.

Does "Mind" Exist?

An increasing number of psychologists and brain scientists today take a hard-line on the " spiritual " view of personality, but does this mean that mind does not exist, as the Behaviourists strove so hard to prove? Certainly not. There is clearly a whole range of rich psychological activity which cannot be explained simply in terms of bundles of conditioned reflexes and the like. What seems to have happened in fact is that as animals have evolved via the remorseless processes of evolution, so more and more " power " has been given to the cerebral control centres. At some stage in the evolutionary ladder—it is very hard to say exactly where—the brain ceased to be a purely automatic device and some glimmerings of what we call consciousness began to appear. In the early stages, this probably merely took the form of a " switch " in the brain which allowed the creature to select from one or two alternative modes of action. This capacity would imply some system within the brain capable of making a " comparison " of the two modes and thus of " standing back from itself." Increase the complexity of the brain and its capacity to select, predict, and determine and you will see that the evolution of a higher control centre capable of

" inspecting " ongoing activity will emerge. Thus could the thing we know of as consciousness develop. Incidentally, if you feel that such an abstracting, self-inspecting system could not be conceived in purely mechanical terms then you are wrong, for the latest developments in computer technology have been devoted to achieving this. But before getting caught up in arguments about whether computers could " think " (we'll tackle this briefly later on) let us just summarise the current approach to the problem that most psychologists accept today. Mind is a phenomenon which has arisen almost inevitably as brain complexity and power have increased, and its function is to select alternative activities and compute the consequences. Just as human bodies and brains differ in countless ways, so human minds, subtly moulded over the years from infancy to adulthood, differ too. The result is that the world is populated with a large number of human beings, united as a species, but each one an individual entity, compounded of body, brain, and mind. All three are equally real, equally important—and equally helpless without each other's company. Let us now take a look at the principal forces which serve to mould these individual entities we call people, and some of the essential ways in which they differ.

(2) Interplay of Heredity and Environment.

People and animals differ in a large number of ways, and are alike in others. We share certain features—upright posture well-developed brains, etc.—with other primates, such as chimpanzees. We also share certain features—binocular vision, mammalian reproduction techniques, etc.—with white rats. We even have a limited amount in common—respiratory systems depending upon oxygen, need to ingest some kind of food, etc.—with creatures as lowly as the earwig, but nothing with cabbages or oak trees, except perhaps a dependence upon sunlight. Now what is it that determines these similarities and differences? The answer is summed up in the word heredity. Creatures of particular species mate with each other and hand on to their offspring, via the genes and chromosomes, the physical characteristics of the species (see F31). They may even hand on certain predetermined patterns of behaviour, which we have earlier referred to as instinct (see also F38). Broadly speaking, the lower down the phylogenetic scale, the more behavioural information is carried over via the genes, and the less flexible is the creature's ultimate behaviour pattern. Earwigs, for example, come into the world fully equipped to go about their simple business on this planet. They present almost identical faces to the world around them, and taking it all in all they change little from birth to death. Earwigs are largely the product of heredity, the principal forces which mould them lying in the genes of their parents and the incredible long history of their species stretching back for hundreds of millions of years. At the other end of the continuum we have human beings whose physical characteristics and a very limited number of behaviour patterns are inherited, but whose " personalities " and individualities (unlike the earwigs) change significantly throughout the span of their lives. These changes are the consequence of the impact of the environment on the flexible human brain, a flexibility which allows human beings to respond swiftly and intelligently to the changing hazards and opportunities of the world. It should be clear, therefore, that the basic differences that so obviously exist between the personalities of different people, reflect the experiences that each individual has had in his or her lifetime. See a newborn child and search for signs of its personality. You will look for a long time to no avail. But watch a child grow from infancy to adolescence and you will see the personality slowly building and emerging—more or less hand-in-hand with the young person's growing awareness of his own individuality, his strengths and his weaknesses.

Twin Studies.

Striking evidence of the immense influence that the environment has on us comes from the famous studies of identical twins performed in America by Newman in the 1930s. There is a bit of confusion in most people's minds about what actually are " identical " twins as opposed to the ordinary, born-on-the-same-day variety. In the case of the latter—known as fraternal twins—what has happened to produce the happy event is that during conception two of the eggs in the mother have been fertilised and thus two babies are born. Without going into too much detail this means that two quite separate creatures develop, each being equipped with the random genetic mix that follows the meeting of the father's sperm with the mother's egg. The children, when born, may be of different sex, different colour hair. eyes, etc., and are likely to be no more alike than would be brothers or sisters born in different years or even decades. Each, therefore, begins with a different hereditary pattern, as determined by the genes. With identical twins a curious fluke occurs. By some process, *after* conception and *after* gene mixing has taken place, the fertilised egg splits, amoeba fashion, and two babies begin to develop—but both have identical gene patterns and thus, up to the moment of birth, can be looked upon as totally identical human beings. This weird identity is, as we all know, frequently carried on throughout the twins' lifetime, even though it is generally noticeable that the similarities become less marked with age. Now to return to Newman's experiment. Nineteen pairs of identical twins were found (a good deal of research was needed) who had for one reason or another been reared apart from an early age and had grown up in different environments. Newman found that while the adult twins maintained a striking physical resemblance, the personalities of the pairs seemed in many cases to have moved apart. In one case, the first of the pair had been successful in worldly terms, had acquired a college education, and was happily married with a stable family, while the second had been less fortunate and was leading a rather unsatisfactory life in an unskilled job in a working-class neighbourhood. Twin " A " seemed optimistic, good-humoured, and more dominant a personality, while twin " B " was morose, lethargic, and lacking in self-confidence. Similar observations were in general noted with other twins, particularly in cases where one of the pair had been reared in a more stable and economically more satisfactory environment. No better illustration of the relative influence of heredity and environment on human personality can be found than in studies of this kind. But is it only physical characteristics that are genetically determined? Is none of the psychological make-up of the individual " built-in " to him at birth? We can answer this by saying that twin-studies have shown that while personality is certainly modified by the environment, there is a good deal of evidence that intelligence is relatively untouched by normal environmental differences. Newman and his colleagues, for example, found that there was a higher correlation between the IQ test scores of *identical twins reared apart* than there was between *fraternal twins reared together*—a finding which suggests that intelligence may be largely inherited. The great British psychologist, Sir Cyril Burt, also produced what seemed to be striking evidence of the inheritability of intelligence with studies made of schoolchildren in the 1930s and the 1940s. In 1976, however, Burt's work came under severe and unexpected criticism, and this led to a reopening of the whole question of the relative importance of genetic as opposed to cultural factors in determining intelligence. Part of the problem, of course, is that there is often confusion over the meaning of the word " intelligence," and for this reason it is perhaps worth looking closer at it.

(3) Intelligence and IQ Testing.

Psychologists have spent a good deal of time arguing about what exactly is meant by intelligence and it is not worth covering this battle-scarred ground again. One definition which makes a good deal of sense is " versatility of adjustment " which is another way of talking about the kind of flexible response to the environment which is so characteristic of humans. This

of course means that we can talk of animals having some degree of intelligence, and most psychologists nowadays would agree that this makes sense. The only problem arises if one considers intelligence to be inextricably tied up with consciousness, thought, language, etc., which of course it is not. Certainly the ability to communicate in linguistic terms and to think in abstract modes are signs of a highly intelligent creature, but some degree of intelligence may be present without those traits. Probably one could even talk of intelligence being present in any animal that could modify its behaviour in response to the environment and repeat this behavioural response at some later date. This means, as you will have gathered, that intelligence is present in any creature that can learn, including our little friend planaria. It is of course a *very* limited form of intelligence and planaria would not come out with much of an IQ (intelligence quotient) if submitted to human IQ tests. The structure of these tests, incidentally, becomes comprehensible if one sees them as measures of human flexibility rather than of knowledge. The standard IQ test, which forms the basis of the much-reviled 11-plus exam, is an attempt at getting some idea of an individual's general flexibility rather than how much information is actually crammed into his head. Without getting involved in the educational argument here, the point is that a test of the child's inherent capability is more likely to give some index of his fitness for higher education than is a test of his knowledge, and this is what the IQ test attempts to sort out. Hence the relative uselessness of " cramming " to prepare for the 11-plus and the surprise results it sometimes produces. You may think you see a bit of a contradiction here. On the one hand we have said that intelligence, whatever it is, seems to be built in the individual and is something to do with his basic brain power. In this case why are new-born babies not fully intelligent at birth? The paradox is solved by saying that the peak of intelligence is not reached until the brain is fully mature (at about 18 years of age in homo sapiens) after which it begins to decline remorselessly with increasing age. Thus you will find that scores on IQ tests are " weighted " according to age. For very young children considerable allowance is made for age and their " raw " score is upgraded according to a standard scale. So too is the score for older people who inevitably score lower in IQ tests than do 18-year olds. Thus we find that a university professor aged 60 would produce a far lower raw score than a young student of equivalent intelligence—even though the venerable professor's head contains far more knowledge! If this seems odd, remember that it is the individual's potential and general flexibility that the tests are all about and not the depth of his fund of knowledge. The IQ test itself is a rather arbitrary affair and was arrived at in the first place by a group of psychologists selecting a bunch of questions which they felt best tested this rather elusive faculty of flexibility. They then arrived at a scoring system which achieved the result that if you tested a large number of people, drawn randomly from the population, their average score would equal 100. In fact this is exactly what an IQ of 100 means—it is the average score of the population at large. This has led to the sarcastic observation of one psychologist that intelligence was " that faculty that is measured by intelligence tests "! This is a witticism with some truth in it, but nevertheless the IQ has a practical value, notably as a sorter out of the bright from the dull in a situation where environmental or social backgrounds might have intervened to cloud the issue. The 11-plus is one such example, as is the fact that the IQ test taken prior to university entrance is the best-known predictor of success in final degree examinations—at least in the USA. On the other hand, as you may have suspected, social and cultural factors can influence IQ scores, thus suggesting that they are not as pure as might have been hoped. Tests conducted on white and black children in America in the 1930s, for example, showed a marked difference in IQ between the two racial groups—the whites coming out pretty clearly ahead. This was greedily seized on by racialists as demonstrating the innate superiority of the white children until it was pointed out that the selection of the two samples was faulty, the black children had been drawn from rural parts of the south while the whites came from the urban north. When a repeat experiment was performed, drawing the whites from the rustic south and the blacks from the northern cities, exactly the reverse finding emerged, killing one age-old notion and at the same time highlighting the fact that IQ tests were vulnerable to social and cultural factors. Incidentally, for those who like to pursue racial arguments, it is interesting to note that the highest IQ ever recorded by standard tests, shattering 200, was scored by—a young Negro girl. When considering the world as a whole, however, the fact remains that humans are very heavily divided from each other by a barrier potentially more difficult to surmount than those of race, class, or creed—intelligence. Furthermore the gulf is one that is particularly difficult to bridge because of lack of incentive on either side. A highly intelligent person generally finds the company of a rather dull person quite unacceptable, and the reverse is also true. Also, the differences between high and low IQs are likely to become more apparent in the coming decades as the old barriers of class, etc., which used to mask intelligence, dissolve. From this important aspect of human personality we now move on to consider the nature of one of the processes most characteristic of human brains—thought.

(4) Thinking.

We have suggested that personality is an amalgam of the various faculties which are associated with cerebral activity, and that variations in personality reflect variations in the individual's environmental history. Any creature with a reasonably flexible set of responses to its environment can therefore be said to have some rudimentary personality, and many of us can detect this in our domestic pets. If this seems a peculiar notion then this is only because we have erroneously tended to think of personality as being a solely human trait, rather in the way that people dismiss animals in general as having no intelligence. But what is it that does distinguish us from other animals—do we differ merely in terms of the capacity and computing power of our brains? Probably the answer is yes, though it has to be recognised that the gulf is pretty wide. Yet if one looks at the cerebral equipment of, say, a chimpanzee one gets the feeling that there shouldn't be all *that* difference! Furthermore, if one comes closer to home and looks at some of our ancestors such as Neanderthal or Cro-Magnon Man, it is hard to account for the differences between their primitive lives and ours today. Certainly we exist 100,000 years later in time and it would be a bit pathetic if we hadn't progressed since then. But the same argument surely should apply to chimpanzees who do not seem to have developed much in the same period, and the whole thing seems even odder when we learn that the now extinct Neanderthal Man had a cranial capacity (brain size) greater than that of modern man. One might explain the vast difference between Man and his rivals on the ground that he was the possessor of an immortal soul or divine spirit. Leaving this rather unsatisfactory explanation aside, let us try to find some other approach. The key lies in the capacity of humans for abstract thought—taking a step back in their minds and "introspecting." With this marvellous facility comes a natural talent to convert the results of these introspections into a code and communicate them to other members of the species. The communicating code is what we call language, and the introspective process, with or without a linguistic component, is known as thinking. Thinking of a kind probably comes in a good deal lower down, at the level where individual animals make "decisions," such as when a dog, faced with a fence blocking it from its food ultimately gives up trying to climb over it and simply walks round it! Kohler's chimpanzee Sultan was certainly indulging in something pretty close to thought when he fitted two sticks together to reach a banana. Nevertheless, there is rather good evidence that the development of a spoken language, such as only humans have, is the trigger which allows a kind of detached, abstract processing to go on and which has allowed us to build up an immense cultural heritage over the past 10,000 years.

(a) Thought and Language.

How much is thought tied in with speech? You will remember that Watson liked to call thought "sub-verbal speech" and there is some truth in this. Open your mouth and think the word "bubble." You will probably notice a kind of catch in your throat—which shows how the two processes are tied together. On the other hand, think of some visual scene—say a polar bear sitting on an iceberg. Most people can conjure up a pretty reasonable mental picture of scenes like this without too much trouble and certainly without saying vocally or sub-vocally, either the word bear or iceberg! Incidentally, if you *can't* get a mental image of this kind, don't worry, for about a third of the world's population can't either. This facility for producing "pictures in the mind" has puzzled psychologists for a century—in particular those who can't manage the images themselves, who are inclined to be a bit sceptical about the whole thing. Twist the topic round and consider the case of visual illusions and other perceptual anomalies. For example, take the kind where two lines, objectively the same, look to be of different length. No matter how much measuring with a ruler and how much you tell yourself that the lines are similar, your erroneous percept remains. Here perception and thought are *not* inextricably tied, which disposes of any lingering arguments that thinking was merely a consequence of visual, auditory, or some other input. Incidentally, the link between thought and language is suddenly coming under close study again, almost 50 years after Watson had originally tried to explain one in terms of the other. This arises from the young sub-science known as psycholinguistics, the founder of which is the American mathematician, Noam Chomsky. His thesis, rather seriously over-simplified, is that the structure of language can be used to give us a valuable key to the inner logic of the brain's operation. We can never hope to know directly how the inner mechanics of the brain work, he says, so we must look to find them reflected in some more directly observable process. Chomsky and his followers argue that in addition to its "surface" grammar (the kind of grammar we learn at school) all human languages have a deeper set of rules, closely tied in with the programmes which handle the deepest and most fundamental thought processes. Look closely at language, state and define the logic of the "deep grammar" and you have taken a peek at the brain's deepest secrets. It is an interesting idea, shared by many scientists who hold that similar clues can come from a study of dreams, but it suggests that the problem of defining thinking is even harder than we at first imagined.

(b) Can a Machine Think?

Yet another approach comes from computer scientists, who, concerned with devising computers capable of communicating in linguistic terms with human beings, have been taking a close look at these problems. From one of the pioneers of computer science, the late British Alan Turing, came a penetrating analysis of the philosophical problems of thought which reopens the discussion again from an entirely fresh angle. He did this by posing the question. "Can a machine think?" Turing pointed out in their opinion. they were seldom able to give a really good reason for it. Typical responses, when they were asked why a machine couldn't think, included, "because you can never get more out a machine than you put into it," "because machines have no souls," and "because only people can think." None of these arguments is valid. In the first place, it is only partly true to say that you can get no more out of a machine than you put in it, and in any case what has that to do with thinking? The second and third points are equally dubious. However, Turing realised that people had a built-in inclination to assume that thinking was a property of humans only, and as a computer engineer who hoped ultimately to see "thinking computers" developed, he was anxious to correct this impression. To do so he rephrased the question this way: that the almost universal response to this question was "No," but while people felt pretty confident "Supposing that you continually built ever more clever computers, how would you know whether one had begun to think or not?" Pointing out that the only evidence we have about whether humans can think (apart from taking their word for it) is the nature of the conversation they have with us, he suggested that one would base one's decision on how well the computer was able to communicate and discourse. Assuming that the fact that the computer was a large metal object with glowing lights, reams of paper tape, etc., would bias people in their judgment of whether it was thinking or not, he proposed that the decision should be based on a simple game. Take one very clever computer which you have reason to suppose may be capable of thought and place it in a room "A." Now take a person in a room "B," and a third in a room "C." Connect up computer "A" and person "B" to person "C" by wires connected to teletypes (special typewriters which allow one to feed information into computers and allow them to respond). Person "C" doesn't know who is on the end of either teletype, "B" or the computer, but he proceeds to try to find out by asking them questions through their respective teletypes. Now if the computer was really dim it would soon give itself away by its dim answers, but if it was really clever it might easily fool "C" into thinking it was the person "B." One important rule of the game, incidentally is that both "B" and the computer were attempting to fool "C," the object being not to be identified correctly as either human or machine. Now, said Turing, if the point comes where "C" cannot reliably and certainly decide which of his two communicators is which, then to all intents and purposes the computer "A" must be said to be capable of thought! This is really a brilliant approach to the problem even if it seems to be a bit obscure at first. What Turing was really saying was that the *real* evidence that thinking is taking place is evidenced by what the individual, be it human, animal, or computer, actually does, and not what it looks like.

Before leaving this enigmatic topic, consider two recent developments in this area:

(1) In at least two centres in the United States psychologists are engaged in dramatic and apparently successful attempts at "conversational" communication with chimpanzees. The husband and wife team of the Gardners at the State University in Reno, Nevada, have taught a chimpanzee to communicate using American sign language—a series of gestures with hand and arm. Their animals apparently are able to converse in sentences at about the level of communication of a three-year-old human child. Another researcher, David Premack at the University of California, has been teaching his chimpanzees to understand the meaning of special plastic symbols or "words." Using these the monkeys form sentences by placing the symbols on a magnetised blackboard and have built up a substantial working vocabulary. They have even got to the stage of understanding and creating sentences featuring the conditional, for example " pick up the red cup *if* blue light is on," etc. Some of Premack's brightest animals are actually using a specially modified typewriter to generate their messages.

(2) Many psychologists and computer scientists believe that a breakthrough in the field of artificial intelligence—the creation of a robot or computer capable of "reason"—is imminent. Developments in this field, which have been painfully slow since the first major computers were constructed in the 1940s, have been accelerating in the 1970s. To take just one example—computers can now be programmed to play really good games of chess and can beat top-ranking club players—if not world masters yet. A game played between a Russian and an American computer for the computer chess championship of the world in Stockholm in 1974 was described as "startling" by one chess expert who watched it. The Russian computer won incidentally. The distinguished philosopher and statistician, Professor I. J. Good, himself an outstanding chess player, has evolved the concept of what he calls the "ultra-intelligent machine" (UIM). This he defines as a computer capable of performing every intellectual function at least as well as a human being. Professor Good now believes that the first UIM will be with us before the turn of the century and possibly even in the 1980s. UIMs, he points out, have one special advantage over human beings—there is no theoretical upper limit to their intelligence. He believes furthermore that one of the first tasks that scientists will give to the UIMs to perform will be to set about finding ways of making themselves even more intelligent. Incidentally, in 1976 an American computer program produced a solution to a famous mathematical puzzle, known as the "Four colour problem." Without going into details of this problem, the main point is that it had never been solved by any human brain, although mathematicians had been working on it for decades. In fact, no one was even certain whether or not it could be solved. Now a computer has done so—perhaps the first really major problem of this kind in which computer brains have shown themselves to be significantly superior to our own.

(5) The World of Inner Space.

We have constantly indicated that psychology is the study of behaviour—the activities of living creatures which respond to a meaningful nonrandom way to the vagaries of their environment. The key to understanding these patterns of behaviour is of course the brain, and within the brain itself the programmes which control and determine its actions. One important point which all who study the brain swiftly come to realise, and one which this section has attempted to emphasise, is that no living system can be considered as a mechanical assembly of different parts. Each, whether earwig, cat, or human being, is a complex, integrated system functioning as a unit. The further up the phylogenetic scale one rises, the more complex the system and the more sophisticated and elegant its mechanics. At the human level with mental activities and consciousness emerging as super-control systems, the study of psychology reaches its most fascinating point. Here too, it must be admitted, as a science it has made least headway. There are probably good reasons for this, some related to the intrinsically complicated nature of the mind, others to the attitude of the psychologists themselves. The early pioneering work of Wundt, Ebbinghaus, and others seemed to be setting psychology on course as a science in its own right. The work of Pavlov, immensely important and relevant as it was, served to weaken psychology as a discipline and shift its bias drastically in the direction of physiology. Psychologists themselves ceased to think like psychologists and instead attempted to convert themselves into second-hand physiologists, part-time mathematicians, and indifferent clinicians. This trend, which gathered strength in the 1930s, has persisted until quite recently when a growing disenchantment with the relatively meagre results stemming from the millions of behaviouristic experiments involving pigeons, monkeys, and rats has led to an inevitable swing of the pendulum. More now than at any time in this century is the principal creature for psychological study acknowledged to be man himself. Freud's fabulous and enduring insight—that the mind itself has two vitally important parts, the conscious and the unconscious, each integrated and yet strangely autonomous—is being treated with ever greater respect and understanding today. The realisation that human beings are controlled not merely by their conscious thoughts, wishes, and desires but also by dynamic forces of great power which are *not* under conscious control and barely available to linguistic analysis, is at last becoming a part of even the layman's view of mental life. The tip of the iceberg above the sea, as Freud pointed out, is that part of the mind which is under conscious control. Below the sea, massively enigmatic, lies the great bulk of the unconscious, the repository of the programmes which largely determine the behaviour of man. This is the zone, rich in mystery, which must ultimately be plotted by psychology and its researchers. This is the territory, glimpses of which we catch through the enigma of memory, the hallucinations of dementia, and in the misty drama of our dreams. The controversial English author J. G. Ballard has christened this territory "inner space," in contrast with the vast reaches of outer space that the first human astronauts are today beginning to explore.

VI. EXTRA-SENSORY PERCEPTION (ESP).

Man's Place in Nature.

Man is a tiny animal, living on a minute planet in a vast and incomprehensible universe—a universe which gives up its secrets reluctantly and which, paradoxically, seems to be getting more incomprehensible and mysterious the more we learn about it. Man himself is also more or less a total enigma. We know that he is an animal, obeying all the usual laws of biology, including those of birth, growth, ageing and death. We also suspect that he is, in some indefinable way, something *more* than an animal. He has conscious thoughts and feelings, emotions, an inner rational life, a written language and other faculties, which he appears to share with none of the other life forms on his planet. But beyond that we know very little, and therefore find it extremely hard to define his true place in nature. In fact, at the risk of slightly oversimplifying things, one could say that there are only two very broad, mutually exclusive, views of man—one cannot really call them theories—and that the world is divided up into those that hold one view and those that hold the other.

1. The first, the physicalistic view, states that man is a totally material being, composed of atoms and molecules and not much else, and no different in principle from other material facets of the universe—animals, plants and even inanimate things such as rocks and ponds.
2. The second view, the spiritual view if you like, holds that man is essentially *different* from all other things in the universe because he is really made up of two basic components—one a physical body controlled by a physical, material brain, the other a psychic or spiritual entity which, for the want of a better word, one might call a mind or soul. Mind and body are different in their nature according to this view, and while they interact at various levels, the body is temporary, destructible and must obey the laws of the material universe. The mind, soul or spirit on the other hand is permanent, indestructible and may—at times—disregard basic physicalistic laws.

Now which of these two views you hold depends largely on whether you are at heart a materialist, or are more of a religious frame of mind. But, personal belief aside, how can one decide which of the two is most likely to be correct?

Materialists argue that human beings, while marvellously complicated biological systems, nevertheless behave in an essentially mechanistic way, and that no examination of the brain or nervous system has ever revealed anything that suggests the presence of a soul or spirit. Furthermore, they argue that when brains and bodies die, all evidence of the existence of the "minds" that were once associated with them vanishes too. Non-materialists, however, argue that while the above facts seem to be correct there are occasional flashes of evidence which suggest that some part of man—his mind—can on occasions escape the shackles of the body and—if only briefly—transcend the boundaries of space and time. These flashes of evidence, glimpses of a non-materialistic aspect of the universe, go under the general heading of "extra-sensory perception" (ESP for short), and they have puzzled and intrigued scientists and philosophers for a very long time. Actually, while the word ESP is bandied around a lot and often assumed to mean any kind of supernatural experience, it has a fairly precise meaning to those scientists (they are known as parapsychologists) who study it. In studying it they draw on two main sources—(1) anecdotal evidence, and (2) laboratory experiments. At its face value the former is very impressive—people

have been recounting tales of amazing things that have happened to them (dreams about the future which come true, telepathic experiences, etc.) as far back as history extends. Some of these experiences are exceedingly strange and make fascinating reading, but to show how unsatisfying they really are let's first take a homely example. Consider the following, rather familiar type of experience: You are just thinking of a friend whom you haven't thought of for some time when the telephone rings; it is your friend, who states that he had suddenly "felt the urge to call you."

(1) Telepathy.

Now most people having an experience of this kind are considerably affected by it and, feeling that it can hardly be dismissed as coincidence, put it down to what seems to them to be a more reasonable alternative—mind-to-mind contact or "telepathy." The trouble is that this alternative explanation is only more "reasonable" when one is absolutely certain that there is such a thing as telepathy in the first place. There is a safe and good rule in science known as Occam's Razor, which says that if two explanations have to be chosen to explain some phenomenon, one should choose the simplest of the two, *provided that it fits the facts.* And calling the experience of the telephone call above "telepathy" is not actually the simplest of the two possibilities when one knows nothing at all about telepathy, and isn't even sure that it exists at all. Therefore, until telepathy is demonstrated scientifically—which really means in controlled, laboratory experiments—one has to try to find explanations of a "normal" kind to explain phenomena of this kind. Of course, some people might argue that thinking of a friend that you haven't thought of for years at the very *instant* that he picks up the phone to call you is so unlikely that it is scarcely a normal explanation. But exactly how unlikely *is* it? Certainly it's very unlikely that it will happen to *you*, but that it will happen on occasions to someone in a big country with a large population is nowhere near so unlikely. In fact one American mathematician who had just such an experience was so amazed by it that he set out to work out the odds against it happening by chance. He came to the amazing conclusion that in a country like the United States, with a population of 200 million, it would happen by chance to *hundreds of people every single day!* And, needless to say, these people would be so impressed that they would be sure to tell all their friends about it, thus spreading the news about their amazing "telepathic experience." This particular story makes two important points—firstly that anecdotal material is often less impressive and significant than it first seems, and secondly that before one can decide whether an event is "likely or unlikely," one has to have some kind of numerical value as to how frequently one would expect it to occur by chance. And this is where the laboratory experiments come in.

The first serious work looking into telepathy and other such phenomena in scientific laboratories was probably that done by Dr. J. B. Rhine, who founded a "parapsychology laboratory" at Duke University in North Carolina in the 1930s. Rhine believed that the anecdotal material had built up to such an extent that there was clearly something there worth studying, but that if it was worth studying it should be done under laboratory conditions. In this way the problem of the vagueness of the anecdotal material could be overcome and, perhaps even more important, if he did discover something significant, other scientists would know exactly how and what had been done, and—most important of all from a scientific point of view—could then set up their own independent investigations.

Rhine soon decided that the supposed paranormal powers of the mind were not simply confined to mind-to-mind contact or telepathy, and he identified four powers or faculties, coining the phrase extra-sensory perception as a blanket term for all of them. They were, in turn, (1) telepathy, (2) clairvoyance, (3) precognition and (4) psychokinesis.

Of these, the first has already been discussed and hardly needs any explanation or comment, other than to say that it implies that information is transmitted from one brain or mind to another brain or mind *without the use of the known senses.* This in turn seems to imply that physiologists probing about in the brain might some day expect to find some organ which serves to transmit the telepathic signals, and another which acts as a receiver Any transmitter or receiver, incidentally, would have to be pretty powerful or sensitive, as the anecdotal evidence often suggests that people can be in telepathic contact with each other over huge distances.

(2) Clairvoyance.

Clairvoyance, the second supposed faculty, is more troublesome from all points of view. When used scientifically, incidentally, the word does not imply fairground tricks or Spiritualist mediumship, but refers to the supposed power of the mind to know something at a d tance without the use of the normal senses, and *without receiving information from any other mind—e.g.* telepathically. For example, if someone claims they can find a lost object or read a page of a closed book, then they are claiming clairvoyant powers because the information is not known by any other mind or brain. Clairvoyance, if it were shown to exist, would, as we've indicated, be far more troublesome to science than telepathy because it is so hard to see how it could take place. With telepathy one has at least the transmitter-receiver possibility —after all we know that information can be sent quickly and invisibly from point to point through radio and TV. But in the case of clairvoyance one simply cannot imagine any mechanism, biological or otherwise, capable of reading the pages of a closed book or of hunting around finding a lost object.

(3) Psychokinesis.

The third faculty of mind which anecdotal evidence suggests might exist, and which Rhine therefore also hoped to prove in a laboratory setting, was psychokinesis—more popularly known as " mind-over-matter." Here it is supposed that by some mental effort, conscious or unconscious, the mind can reach out and move or otherwise affect objects at a distance. However unlikely this may seem, most people evidently have some kind of vague belief that they have powers of this kind. To give just one common example, notice the way in which people attempt to " will " dice to fall the way they want them to. Here again psychokinesis (generally abbreviated to PK) poses real problems for physiology and psychology— assuming that it occurs. What kind of mechanism could possibly exist in the brain with the power to move solid objects at a distance or, even more peculiarly, inside sealed containers?

(4) Precognition.

As for the fourth faculty, precognition, this is even more staggering and, if demonstrated, would throw the whole of conventional science into a spin. Here the suggestion is that the mind can sometimes glimpse events taking place in the future—as when one dreams about a forthcoming disaster, the accidental death of a friend or, on a more cheerful level, the winner of the Grand National. The problem is that classical physics is based on certain assumptions about the way in which the universe behaves, and one of these is that a cause must always precede an effect, and that time therefore always flows in one specific direction. Admittedly the notion of time itself is a rather uncertain one, but no theory of physics in current use allows one to understand how the mind could conceivably have knowledge of an event *which has not yet taken place!*

Work of Pioneer Parapsychologists.

But, despite these objections, Rhine's argument —and a point of view adopted by most other scientists seriously interested in studying ESP— was that however unlikely these phenomena might be, and however inadequate our present theories are to explain or understand them, if they exist then that's all there is to it. If the facts are such that the theories don't encompass them, then the theories must be modified accordingly. It is with this background that parapsychologists set out to turn anecdote into fact and trap the hidden powers of man's mind in the laboratory.

Their first step was to find a way of quantifying the phenomena—of measuring it numerically. The necessity for this will become obvious if one recalls the case of the telephone call from the long forgotten friend. This, at first thought, might seem to be " obviously " telepathy but, by the time one has done some sums on the total number of telephone calls received, the total number of one's friends, the total number of people on the telephone, etc., etc., one realises that it is a relatively *likely* rather than a paranormal event. Rhine therefore decided that all his experiments must be quantifiable, and with this in mind he developed a special pack of cards—the now quite famous Zener cards. Zener cards are in fact shaped like regular playing cards, but instead of the usual pictures and numbers, they each have one of five boldly marked symbols—a star, a plus sign, a triangle, a circle or a set of wavy lines. A standard Zener pack contains 25 cards in all—five of each of the above symbols. Now the point is that in doing ESP tests with these cards, one starts off with the important base of knowing exactly how many a person will guess right by chance. In fact in the average run through of a pack of 25, one will get just five right simply by guessing. Clearly, sometimes one will get more right and sometimes less, but the most likely number to get right will be five, and in all cases it is possible to deduce mathematically the odds against getting a particular number correct. Now if the person generally gets five right, but occasionally gets six or seven, sometimes three or four, and now and again a much higher number—say nine or ten—at the end of the experiment one can total up the number of guesses, look at how many of them were correct and perform a simple statistical test to determine whether the hits were more frequent than they should have been. If they were, then one could run the experiment a few more times and if the above-chance scoring continues, then one might be faced with the possibility that the guesser was somehow getting information about the test cards—possibly by telepathy. The Zener cards, by the way, were also useful in testing clairvoyance—here the guesser would try to call out the sequence of a shuffled pack of cards whose order was not known to anyone until *after the experiment was over.* Equally, they could be used in precognition experiments, simply by inviting the guesser first to call out a sequence of cards and then *a few minutes later shuffling the pack,* counting them out and comparing the guesses against the final sequence. In the case of psychokinesis, rather obviously, cards are not particularly suitable and Rhine set up experiments involving dice rolled out by a machine on to a table—the task of the subject being to try to influence the dice to come up with a particular number face upwards.

As it happens, the first results coming out of Duke University laboratory were sensational and seemed to suggest beyond all reasonable doubt that some form of ESP existed. Time and time again the card guessing tests came up with significantly " above chance " results, and it really did seem as though some information was passing from the mind of the person dealing out the cards to the individual attempting to guess them. So remarkable were the results, in fact, that scientists in other laboratories in other parts of the world rushed to repeat Rhine's experiments, realising that establishing extra-sensory perception would be one of the most important developments in the history of science, with quite profound philosophical implications about the spiritual as opposed to the materialistic view of man. Unfortunately, the positive results simply failed to show in other laboratories—time and time again other experimenters repeated the Duke studies, obtaining only chance results. Rhine defended his position by generating yet more positive results, and in response his critics suggested that his successes might have been due to the fact that his experimental procedures were not rigid enough. For example, in early experiments, the guesser was only separated from the person handling the cards by a screen, and of course it has long been known that people can unconsciously give a lot of information away by minute body movements, whispering, etc., or even by deliberate cheating in order to " help the experiments along." To meet this objection the Duke group tightened up its experiments, separating the participants in ESP tests at least by solid walls, and in some cases by placing them in different buildings. They still claimed some above chance results, but very many fewer than before.

Pro- and Anti-ESP Attitudes.

Slowly the world of science began to divide into two camps—a small but measurable minority who claimed that ESP had been demonstrated scientifically and that it was time for the fact to be faced, and a majority who felt that the topic was probably a red herring, and on the whole a waste of scientific brains and energy. Curiously, and perhaps significantly, the research groups with a pro-ESP attitude continued to produce pro-ESP results, while repeat studies in neutral or anti-ESP laboratories tended to show no evidence—a situation which prevails to the present day and which complicates the issue whenever the topic is discussed. At the heart of the problem is the fact that now and again, in apparently carefully controlled experiments, scientists come up with results suggesting telepathy, clairvoyance, etc, but that in the main these results are not repeatable in other laboratories. Because of this a basic scientific principle—that before a phenomenon is accepted into the mainframe of scientific knowledge, it must be reproducible in suitably equipped laboratories —is not met. This principle of repeatability is a quite fundamental one and is designed, among other things, to insure that research and scientific theory is not held back by having to accept every statement or premise put forward by misguided scientists or simple crackpots. If a phenomenon is a real one, it should be demonstrable to all and not just a chosen few. The strongest argument that the parapsychologists can offer to explain the non-repeatability is based on the assumption (which they claim is backed by some definite evidence) that ESP phenomena are sensitive to the attitude of mind of people taking part in ESP experiments; if they are positively disposed they somehow help the phenomena along. if sceptical or hyper-critical they damp it down. Intuitively this argument makes a kind of sense—if telepathy is real, then why should it not be " blocked " by sceptical minds or by unhelpful or aggressive attitudes? But the argument also has a terrible weakness from a scientific point of view—it allows the glib " explanation " or excuse whenever experiments fail that someone with a sceptical mind must have been present. Of course, on the other side of the coin, sceptics cannot choose to deny absolutely the evidence generated from time to time within parapsychology laboratories—it may be a great weakness that the results are not replicable, but how can one explain the positive results which *have* occurred.

If one can eliminate poor controls, incorrect statistical tests and other such variables, there doesn't seem to be much left unless one brings into the field the taboo topic of fakery and fraud. Traditionally scientists are disinclined to accuse each other of cheating—this also is a glib and unsavoury way of denying facts that one doesn't want to accept. Rhine himself once argued that when his opponents began to accuse him of cheating he would know that his battle was won—in other words, the sceptics would be implicitly acknowledging that they had no other explanation for his results. In fact accusations of cheating and falsifying data were occasionally made, but never formed a substantial part of the case against ESP, until a few years ago when a major scandal broke out in Rhine's own laboratory.

The director of research at that laboratory (Rhine had retired some time previously) was actually caught falsifying data in a major series of experiments, altering it so that it indicated ESP results where none was in fact being obtained. Perhaps it was a healthy sign that his own scientific colleagues were the ones to catch him out, and also that he immediately resigned after admitting the fraud. But the fact remains that the incident put an enormously powerful weapon in the hands of the sceptics who can now argue, with justification, that even respected scientists can be guilty of fraud and deception in their eagerness to prove the case for ESP. Since this

particular scandal, incidentally, strong suspicion has fallen on the work of the British investigator, the late Dr. S. G. Soal, whom it is now believed may have faked the results of one of his experiments—a study at one time believed to provide incontrovertible evidence for precognition.

Present Status of ESP Research.

The question now arises as to what is the status of ESP research today, and where is it likely to move in the future? In sum, it seems that contrary to the bright hopes of the pioneer parapsychologists, research in this area has moved forward very slowly, if at all, and the world of science is no more convinced of the reality of extra-sensory phenomena than it was when the Duke Laboratory opened its doors forty years ago. Worse, there is certainly a growing feeling among many scientists that if the phenomena did exist, some hard evidence really ought to have been forthcoming after so many years of diligent research. Of course, none of this disproves telepathy, clairvoyance, precognition or psychokinesis—it merely suggests that there is little scientific ground for assuming that they exist. Equally, the failure of scientific studies in this field will do nothing to shake the belief of millions of people that man is something more than a chunk of matter in a solidly materialistic universe, and that from time to time he is capable of demonstrating his spiritual nature through extra-sensory or paranormal powers. But one thing is quite certain—we don't know enough about the universe to say that ESP could or could *not* exist. No doubt one day we shall know for sure, but until that time the scientific view must remain—not proven.

VII. A QUICK GUIDE TO THE BRAIN.

In anatomical terms, the brain is the collection of nervous tissue contained inside the skull; in functional terms, it is the principal organ of the central nervous system which receives, processes and stores information from the outside world, and utilises this information to control other parts of the nervous system and the organism as a whole. The brain is the most elaborate and complicated organ in the body—in fact it would be more accurate to describe it as a set of organs, all interdependent to some degree—and any attempt at describing it has to err on the side of oversimplification. In addition, there is no absolute agreement among anatomists as to how to break it down into separate parts or units, with some workers concentrating on the physical appearance of different parts, while others lean towards the functional roles of different segments. The problem is even further compounded because, despite intensive study lasting over a period of a century, the precise function of some parts of the brain is still not properly understood. One common descriptive approach, however, divides the brain into three main units which, starting from the one closest to the spinal cord, are (1) hindbrain, (2) midbrain and (3) forebrain.

1. *The Hindbrain.* This is a cluster of structures comprising the medulla, the pons and the cerebellum. The medulla is really a kind of extension of the spinal cord and contains a mass of fibres and nuclei which serve to control the most basic of automatic bodily functions, such as respiration and blood circulation. Just behind it is the cerebellum, sometimes called the " little brain " which is heavily involved in motor co-ordination while above it is the pons which, as its Latin name implies, acts as a bridge between the two halves of the cerebellum. The hindbrain is in many ways an evolutionary primitive structure.

2. *The Midbrain.* This is a small structure, directly above the pons and buried deep inside the mass of the brain. It contains a number of substructures, including the corpora quadragemina and the tegmentum, and its principal role appears to be the control of eye movements and the vestibular system.

3. *The Forebrain.* Whereas almost all vertebrates share rather similar structuring of the so-

called lower centres—the mid- and hindbrains—the forebrain is enormously enlarged and developed in the higher animals, in particular the mammals. Anatomically the forebrain is divided into the diencephalon—consisting of the thalamus and the hypothalamus—and the telencephalon which includes the limbic system, the basal ganglia and, most significant of all in primates, the cerebral cortex. The cortex, which is in fact a convoluted layer of neurones covering the surface of the entire telencephalon, plays an important role in sensory and motor functions, though as one ascends the phylogenetic scale a greater and greater proportion of it is given over to integrative and associative functions.

To confuse matters somewhat, a large part of the forebrain and midbrain is also known collectively as the cerebrum which is itself divided into the right and left hemispheres, connected at the base by the corpus callosum. The chasm separating the hemispheres, which is the most striking single feature of the brain when seen from above, is known as the interhemispherical fissure, while other deep folds include the central and lateral fissures. These fissures tend to be useful to the neurologist in marking out the various lobes of the cerebrum—frontal, temporal, parietal, etc. and they also tend to constitute boundary lines separating out functionally different areas of the cortex—e.g. those parts concerned with receiving sensory information and those concerned with associative or integratory processes.

Without resorting to elaborate drawings, or even to some practical anatomy itself, there is little point in going into greater detail on the structure of the brain, though it is worth emphasising again that many of its functions are still extremely poorly understood. It is still not entirely clear, for example, just why the cerebrum is divided up into two hemispheres, nor why local damage may sometimes have negligible, sometimes drastic effects. The mechanism of information storage within the brain—learning and memory—is almost totally mysterious, and little is known about the relationship between cortical activity and the " higher faculties " of reasoning, imagery and consciousness. To some extent the brain appears rather more mysterious now than it did half a century ago, and we will probably do well to prepare ourselves for things to get even more puzzling before any major advances in understanding it occur.

SPORTING
RECORDS

Association Football, Athletics,
Badminton, Baseball, Bowls,
Cricket, Golf, Gymnastics, Hockey,
Horse Racing, Lawn Tennis, Motor
Racing, Rifle Shooting, Rowing
and Sculling, Rugby League, Rugby
Union, Speedway, Squash Rackets,
Swimming, Table Tennis.

SPORTING RECORDS

ASSOCIATION FOOTBALL

FOOTBALL LEAGUE CHAMPIONS

1950–1	Tottenham H	1961–2	Ipswich T	1972–3	Liverpool
1951–2	Manchester U	1962–3	Everton	1973–4	Leeds U
1952–3	Arsenal	1963–4	Liverpool	1974–5	Derby C
1953–4	Wolverhampton W	1964–5	Manchester U	1975–6	Liverpool
1954–5	Chelsea	1965–6	Liverpool	1976–7	Liverpool
1955–6	Manchester U	1966–7	Manchester U	1977–8	Nottingham F.
1956–7	Manchester U	1967–8	Manchester C		
1957–8	Wolverhampton W	1968–9	Leeds U		
1958–9	Wolverhampton W	1969–70	Everton		
1959–60	Burnley	1970–1	Arsenal		
1960–1	Tottenham H	1971–2	Derby C		

FOOTBALL ASSOCIATION CHALLENGE CUP WINNERS

1950–1	Newcastle U	1961–2	Tottenham H	1972–3	Sunderland
1951–2	Newcastle U	1962–3	Manchester U	1973–4	Liverpool
1952–3	Blackpool	1963–4	West Ham U	1974–5	West Ham U
1953–4	West Bromwich A	1964–5	Liverpool	1975–6	Southampton
1954–5	Newcastle U	1965–6	Everton	1976–7	Manchester U
1955–6	Manchester C	1966–7	Tottenham H	1977–8	Ipswich
1956–7	Aston Villa	1967–8	West Bromwich A		
1957–8	Bolton W	1968–9	Manchester C		
1958–9	Nottingham F	1969–70	Chelsea		
1959–60	Wolverhampton W	1970–1	Arsenal		
1960–1	Tottenham H	1971–2	Leeds U		

FOOTBALL LEAGUE CUP WINNERS

1960–1	Aston V	1967–8	Leeds U	1974–5	Aston V
1961–2	Norwich C	1968–9	Swindon T	1975–6	Manchester C
1962–3	Birmingham C	1969–70	Manchester C	1976–7	Aston V
1963–4	Leicester C	1970–1	Tottenham H	1977–8	Nottingham F
1964–5	Chelsea	1971–2	Stoke C		
1965–6	West Bromwich A	1972–3	Tottenham H		
1966–7	Queen's Park R	1973–4	Wolverhampton W		

SCOTTISH LEAGUE CHAMPIONS

1950–1	Hibernian	1961–2	Dundee	1972–3	Celtic
1951–2	Hibernian	1962–3	Rangers	1973–4	Celtic
1952–3	Rangers	1963–4	Rangers	1974–5	Rangers
1953–4	Celtic	1964–5	Kilmarnock	1975–6	Rangers
1954–5	Aberdeen	1965–6	Celtic	1976–7	Celtic
1955–6	Rangers	1966–7	Celtic	1977–8	Rangers
1956–7	Rangers	1967–8	Celtic		
1957–8	Hearts	1968–9	Celtic		
1958–9	Rangers	1969–70	Celtic		
1959–60	Hearts	1970–1	Celtic		
1960–1	Rangers	1971–2	Celtic		

SCOTTISH FOOTBALL ASSOCIATION CUP WINNERS

1950–1	Celtic	1961–2	Rangers	1972–3	Rangers
1951–2	Motherwell	1962–3	Rangers	1973–4	Celtic
1952–3	Rangers	1963–4	Rangers	1974–5	Celtic
1953–4	Celtic	1964–5	Celtic	1975–6	Rangers
1954–5	Clyde	1965–6	Rangers	1976–7	Celtic
1955–6	Hearts	1966–7	Celtic	1977–8	Rangers
1956–7	Falkirk	1967–8	Dunfermline A		
1957–8	Clyde	1968–9	Celtic		
1958–9	St Mirren	1969–70	Aberdeen		
1959–60	Rangers	1970–1	Celtic		
1960–1	Dunfermline A	1971–2	Celtic		

SCOTTISH LEAGUE CUP WINNERS

1950–1	Motherwell	1961–2	Rangers	1972–3	Hibernian
1951–2	Dundee	1962–3	Hearts	1973–4	Dundee
1952–3	Dundee	1963–4	Rangers	1974–5	Celtic
1953–4	East Fife	1964–5	Rangers	1975–6	Rangers
1954–5	Hearts	1965–6	Celtic	1976–7	Aberdeen
1955–6	Aberdeen	1966–7	Celtic	1977–8	Rangers
1956–7	Celtic	1967–8	Celtic		
1957–8	Celtic	1968–9	Celtic		
1958–9	Hearts	1969–70	Celtic		
1959–60	Hearts	1970–1	Rangers		
1960–1	Rangers	1971–2	Partick T		

BRITISH CHAMPIONSHIP

(81 Seasons since 1884)

	Champions	Joint Champions	Runners-up
England	30	20	24
Scotland	24	17	24
Wales	7	5	13
Ireland	1	5	9

WORLD CUP WINNERS

1930	Uruguay	1962	Brazil
1934	Italy	1966	England
1938	Italy	1970	Brazil
1950	Uruguay	1974	W Germany
1954	W Germany		
1958	Brazil		

1978 Argentina

EUROPEAN CUP WINNERS

1955–6	Real Madrid	1964–5	Inter Milan	1973–4	Bayern Munich
1956–7	Real Madrid	1965–6	Real Madrid	1974–5	Bayern Munich
1957–8	Real Madrid	1966–7	Glasgow C	1975–6	Bayern Munich
1958–9	Real Madrid	1967–8	Manchester U	1976–7	Liverpool
1959–60	Real Madrid	1968–9	A C Milan	1977–8	Liverpool
1960–1	Benfica	1969–70	Feyenoord		
1961–2	Benfica	1970–1	Ajax		
1962–3	A C Milan	1971–2	Ajax		
1963–4	Inter Milan	1972–3	Ajax		

EUROPEAN NATIONAL CUP WINNERS' CUP

1961	Florentina	1968	A C Milan	1975	Dynamo Kiev
1962	Atletico Madrid	1969	Sl Bratislava	1976	Anderlecht
1963	Tottenham H	1970	Manchester C	1977	Hamburg SV
1964	Sporting Lisbon	1971	Chelsea	1978	Anderlecht
1965	West Ham U	1972	Glasgow R		
1966	Borussia Dortmund	1973	A C Milan		
1967	Bayern Munich	1974	Magdeburg		

UEFA CUP WINNERS

1958	Barcelona	1967	Dynamo Zagreb	1975	Borussia Moenchengladbach
1960	Barcelona	1968	Leeds U		
1961	A S Roma	1969	Newcastle U	1976	Liverpool
1962	Valencia	1970	Arsenal	1977	Juventus
1963	Valencia	1971	Leeds U	1978	PSV Eindhoven
1964	Real Zaragossa	1972	Tottenham H		
1965	Ferencvaros	1973	Liverpool		
1966	Barcelona	1974	Feyenoord		

EUROPEAN NATIONS COMPETITION

1960	USSR	1972	W Germany
1964	Spain	1976	Czechoslovakia
1968	Italy		

ATHLETICS

1976 OLYMPIC GAMES (MONTREAL)

Men

100 metres H Crawford Trinidad 10·06s
200 metres D Quarrie Jamaica 20·23s
400 metres A Juantorena Cuba 44·26s
800 metres A Juantorena Cuba 1 min 43·50s
1,500 metres J Walker N Zealand 3 min 39·17s
5,000 metres L Viren Finland 13 min 24·76s
10,000 metres L Viren Finland 27 min 40·38s
Marathon W Cierpinski E Ger 2h 9 min 55·00s
4 × 100 metres relay US 38·33s
4 × 400 metres relay US 2 min 58·65s
110 metres hurdles G Drut France 13·30s
400 metres hurdles E Moses US 47·64s
3,000 metres steeplechase A Garderud Sweden 8 min 8·02s

20 kilometres walk D Bautista Mexico 1h 24 min 40·60s
High jump J Wszola Poland 2·25m
Long jump A Robinson US 8·35m
Triple jump V Saneyev USSR 17·29m
Pole vault T Slusarski Poland 5·50m
Putting the shot U Beyer E Ger 21·05m
Throwing the discus M Wilkins US 67·50m
Throwing the javelin M Nemeth Hungary 94·58m
Throwing the hammer Y Sedyh USSR 77·52m
Decathlon B Jenner US 8,618 pts

Women

100 metres A Richter W Ger 11·08s
200 metres B Eckert E Ger 22·37s
400 metres I Szewinska Poland 49·29s
800 metres T Kazankina USSR 1 min 54·94s
1,500 metres T Kazankina USSR 4 min 5·48s
4 × 100 metres relay E Ger 42·56s
4 × 400 metres relay E Ger 3 min 19·23s

100 metres hurdles J Schaller E Ger 12·77s
High jump R Ackerman E Ger 1·93m
Long jump A Voigt E Ger 6·72m
Putting the shot I Christova Bulgaria 21·16m
Throwing the discus E Schlaak E Ger 69·00m
Throwing the javelin R Fuchs E Ger 65·94m
Pentathlon S Siegl E Ger 4,745 pts

OLYMPIC RECORDS

Men

100 metres 9·95s J Hines US 1968 Mex C
200 metres 19·80s T Smith US 1968 Mex C
400 metres 43·86s L Evans US 1968 Mex C
800 metres 1 min 43·50s A Juantorena Cuba 1976 Mont
1,500 metres 3 min 34·9s K Keino Kenya 1968 Mex C
5,000 metres 13 min 20·34s B Foster GB 1976 Mont
10,000 metres 27 min 38·4s L Viren Finland 1972 Mun
Marathon 2h 9 min 55s W Cierpinski E Ger 1976 Mont
4 × 100 metres relay 38·19s US 1972 Mun
4 × 400 metres relay 2 min 56·1s US 1968 Mex C
110 metres hurdles 13·24s R Milburn US 1972 Mun
400 metres hurdles 47·64s E Moses US 1976 Mont
3,000 metres steeplechase 8 min 8·02s A Garderud Sweden 1976 Mont

20 kilometres walk 1h 24 min 40·6s D Bautista Mexico 1976 Mont
50 kilometres walk 3h 56 min 11·6s B Kannenberg W Ger 1972 Mun
High jump 2·24m R Fosbury US 1968 Mex C
Long jump 8·90m R Beamon US 1968 Mex C
Triple jump 17·29m V Saneyev USSR 1976 Mont
Pole vault 5·50m W Nordwig E Ger 1972 Mun
Putting the shot 21·32m A Barisnikov USSR 1976 Mont
Throwing the discus 68·28m M Wilkins US 1976 Mont
Throwing the javelin 94·58m M Nemeth Hungary 1976 Mont
Throwing the hammer 77·52m Y Sedyh USSR 1976 Mont
Decathlon 8,618 pts B Jenner US 1976 Mont

Women

100 metres 11·01s A Richter W Ger 1976 Mont
200 metres 22·37s B Eckert E Ger 1976 Mont
400 metres 49·29s I Szewinska Poland 1976 Mont
800 metres 1 min 54·94s T Kazankina USSR 1976 Mont
1,500 metres 4 min 1·4s L Bragina USSR 1972 Mun
4 × 100 metres relay 42·56s E Ger 1976 Mont
4 × 400 metres relay 3 min 19·23s E Ger 1976 Mont
100 metres hurdles 12·59s A Ehrhardt E Ger 1972 Mun

High jump 1·93m R Ackerman E Ger 1976 Mont
Long jump 6·82m V Viscopoleanu Romania 1968 Mex C
Putting the shot 21·16m I Christova Bulgaria 1976 Mont
Throwing the discus 69·00m E Schlaak E Ger 1976 Mont
Throwing the javelin 65·94m R Fuchs E Ger 1976 Mont
Pentathlon 4,801 pts M Peters GB 1972 Mun

1974 EUROPEAN CHAMPIONSHIPS (ROME)

Men

100 metres V Borzov USSR 10·27s
200 metres P Mennea Italy 20·6s
400 metres K Honz W Ger 45·04s
800 metres L Susanj Yugoslavia 1 min 44·1s
1,500 metres K-P Justus E Ger 3 min 40·6s
5,000 metres B Foster UK 13 min 17·2s
10,000 metres M Kuschmann E Ger 28 min 25·8s
Marathon I Thompson UK 2h 13 min 18·8s
4 × 100 metres relay France 38·69s
4 × 400 metres relay UK 3 min 3·3s
110 metres hurdles G Drut France 13·4s
400 metres hurdles A Pascoe UK 48·82s
3,000 metres steeplechase B Malinowski Poland 8 min 15s

20 kilometres walk V Golubnichiy USSR 1h 29 min 30s
50 kilometres walk C Hohne E Ger 3h 59 min 5·6s
High jump J Torring Denmark 7ft 4½in
Long jump V Podluzhniy USSR 26ft 7¾in
Triple jump V Saneyev USSR 56ft 6½in
Pole vault V Kishkun USSR 17ft 6½in
Putting the shot H Briesenick E Ger 67ft 3½in
Throwing the discus P Kahma Finland 208ft 9in
Throwing the javelin H Siitonen Finland 293ft 11in
Throwing the hammer A Spiridonov USSR 243ft 5in
Decathlon R Skowronek Poland 8,207 pts

Women

100 metres J Szewinska Poland 11·13s	100 metres hurdles A Ehrhardt E Ger 12·66s
200 metres I Szewinska Poland 22·51s	High jump R Witschas E Ger 6ft 4¾in
400 metres R Salin Finland 50·14s	Long jump I Bruzsenyak Hungary 21ft 10in
800 metres L Tomova Bulgaria 1 min 58·1s	Putting the shot N Chizhova USSR 68ft 2½in
1,500 metres G Hoffmeister E Ger 4 min 2·3s	Throwing the discus F Melnik USSR 226ft 4in
3,000 metres N Holmen Finland 8 min 55·2s	Throwing the javelin R Fuchs E Ger 220ft 6in
4 × 100 metres relay E Ger 42·51s	Pentathlon N Tkachenko USSR 4,776 pts
4 × 400 metres relay E Ger 3 min 25·2s	

1974 COMMONWEALTH GAMES (CHRISTCHURCH NZ)

Men

100 metres D Quarrie Jamaica 10·4s	3,000 metres steeplechase B Jipcho Kenya 8 min 20·8s
200 metres D Quarrie Jamaica 20·7s	20 miles walk J Warhurst Eng 2h 35 min 23s
400 metres C Asati Kenya 46·00s	High jump G Windeyer Aus 7ft 1in
800 metres J Kipkurgat Kenya 1 min 43·9s	Long jump A Lerwill Eng 26ft 0½in
1,500 metres F Bayi Tanzania 3 min 32·2s	Triple jump J Owusu Ghana 54ft 1¾in
5,000 metres B Jipcho Kenya 13 min 14·4s	Pole vault D Baird Aus 16ft 6¾in
10,000 metres R Tayler NZ 27 min 47·4s	Putting the shot G Capes Eng 68ft 0½in
Marathon I Thompson Eng 2h 9 min 12s	Throwing the discus R Tait NZ 206 ft 11in
4 × 100 metres relay Aus 39·3s	Throwing the javelin C Clover Eng 278ft 7in
4 × 400 metres relay Kenya 3 min 4·4s	Throwing the hammer I Chipchase Eng 228ft 2in
110 metres hurdles F Kimaiyo Kenya 13·7s	Decathlon M Bull NI 7,417 pts
400 metres hurdles A Pascoe Eng 48·8s	

Women

100 metres R Boyle Aus 11·3s	100 metres hurdles J Vernon Eng 13·5s
200 metres R Boyle Aus 22·5s	High jump B Lawton Eng 6ft 0½in
400 metres V Saunders Can 51·7s	Long jump M Oshikoya Nigeria 21ft 2½in
800 metres C Rendina Aus 2 min 1·1s	Putting the shot J Haist Can 52ft 10½in
1 500 metres G Reiser Can 4 min 7·8s	Throwing the discus J Haist Can 182ft 2in
4 × 100 metres relay Aus 43·5s	Throwing the javelin P Rivers Aus 182ft 0in
4 × 400 metres relay Eng 3 min 29·2s	

BADMINTON

ALL ENGLAND CHAMPIONSHIPS

Men's singles

1950–2	W P Soon (Malaya)	1966	T A Huang (Malaya)
1953–4	E B Choong (Malaya)	1967	E Kops (Denmark)
1955	W P Soon (Malaya)	1968–74	R Hartono (Indonesia)
1956–7	E B Choong (Malaya)	1975	S Pri (Denmark)
1958	E Kops (Denmark)	1976	R Hartono (Indonesia)
1959	T J Hok (Indonesia)	1977	F Delfs (Denmark)
1960–3	E Kops (Denmark)	1978	L S King (Indonesia)
1964	K A Nielsen (Denmark)		
1965	E Kops (Denmark)		

Women's singles

1950	T Ahm (Denmark)	1969	H Yuki (Japan)
1951	A S Jacobsen (Denmark)	1970	E Takenaka (Japan)
1952	T Ahm (Denmark)	1971	E Twedberg (Sweden)
1953	M Ussing (Denmark)	1972	N Nakayama (Japan)
1954	J Devlin (US)	1973	M Beck (GB)
1955–6	M Varner (US)	1974	H Yuki (Japan)
1957–8	J Devlin (US)	1975	H Yuki (Japan)
1959	H M Ward (GB)	1976	G Gilks (GB)
1960	J Devlin (US)	1977	H Yuki (Japan)
1961–4	G C K Hashman (US)	1978	G Gilks (GB)
1965	U H Smith (GB)		
1966–7	G C K Hashman (US)		
1968	E Twedberg (Sweden)		

BASEBALL (US)

WORLD SERIES WINNERS

1958	New York Yankees	1966	Baltimore Orioles	1974	Oakland Athletics
1959	Los Angeles Dodgers	1967	St Louis Cardinals	1975	Cincinnati Reds
1960	Pittsburgh Pirates	1968	Detroit Tigers	1976	Cincinnati Reds
1961	New York Yankees	1969	New York Mets	1977	New York Yankees
1962	New York Yankees	1970	Baltimore Orioles		
1963	Lost Angeles Dodgers	1971	Pittsburgh Pirates		
1964	St Louis Cardinals	1972	Oakland Athletics		
1965	Los Angeles Dodgers	1973	Oakland Athletics		

BOWLS

EBA NATIONAL CHAMPIONSHIPS
Single-handed

1960	D J Bryant	1967	W C Irish	1974	W C Irish
1961	P A Line	1968	N R Groves	1975	D J Bryan
1962	C Mercer	1969	J Davidson	1976	A O'Connell
1963	C S Graham	1970	H Kershaw	1977	C Ward
1964	P A Line	1971	D J Bryant		
1965	R E Lewis	1972	D J Bryant		
1966	D J Bryant	1973	D J Bryant		

CRICKET

TEST MATCHES

England v. Australia
(first played 1876)
Won: England 74   Australia 88   Drawn· 68
England v. South Africa
(first played 1888)
Won: England 46   South Africa 18   Drawn: 38
England v. West Indies
(first played 1928)
Won: England 19   West Indies 22   Drawn: 27
England v. New Zealand
(first played 1929)
Won: England 23   New Zealand 1   Drawn: 24
England v. India
(first played 1932)
Won: England 25   India 7   Drawn: 21
England v. Pakistan
(first played 1954)
Won: England 9   Pakistan 1   Drawn: 20

COUNTY CHAMPIONSHIP

1950	Lancashire	1960	Yorkshire	1971	Surrey
	Surrey	1961	Hampshire	1972	Warwickshire
1951	Warwickshire	1962	Yorkshire	1973	Hampshire
1952	Surrey	1963	Yorkshire	1974	Worcestershire
1953	Surrey	1964	Worcestershire	1975	Leicestershire
1954	Surrey	1965	Worcestershire	1976	Middlesex
1955	Surrey	1966	Yorkshire	1977	Kent
1956	Surrey	1967	Yorkshire		Middlesex
1957	Surrey	1968	Yorkshire		
1958	Surrey	1969	Glamorgan		
1959	Yorkshire	1970	Kent		

GILLETTE CUP

1963	Sussex	1969	Yorkshire	1975	Lancashire
1964	Sussex	1970	Lancashire	1976	Northamptonshire
1965	Yorkshire	1971	Lancashire	1977	Middlesex
1966	Warwickshire	1972	Lancashire		
1967	Kent	1973	Gloucestershire		
1968	Warwickshire	1974	Kent		

JOHN PLAYER LEAGUE

1969	Lancashire	1973	Kent	1977	Leicestershire
1970	Lancashire	1974	Leicestershire		
1971	Worcestershire	1975	Hampshire		
1972	Kent	1976	Kent		

BENSON & HEDGES CUP

1972	Leicestershire	1976	Kent
1973	Kent	1977	Gloucestershire
1974	Surrey		
1975	Leicestershire		

GOLF

OPEN CHAMPIONSHIP

1950	A D Locke (SA)	1961	A Palmer (US)	1972	L Trevino (US)
1951	M Faulkner (GB)	1962	A Palmer (US)	1973	T Weiskopf (US)
1952	A D Locke (SA)	1963	R J Charles (NZ)	1974	G J Player (SA)
1953	B Hogan (US)	1964	A Lema (US)	1975	T Watson (US)
1954	P W Thomson (Aus)	1965	P W Thomson (Aus)	1976	J Miller (US)
1955	P W Thomson (Aus)	1966	J Nicklaus (US)	1977	T Watson (US)
1956	P W Thomson (Aus)	1967	R de Vicenzo (Arg)		
1957	A D Locke (SA)	1968	G J Player (SA)		
1958	P W Thomson (Aus)	1969	A Jacklin (GB)		
1959	G J Player (SA)	1970	J Nicklaus (US)		
1960	K D G Nagle (Aus)	1971	L Trevino (US)		

GYMNASTICS

1976 OLYMPIC GAMES (MONTREAL)

Men

Combined exercises N Andrianov (USSR)
Combined exercises (team) (Japan)
Floor exercises N Andrianov (USSR)
Horizontal bar M Tsukahara (Japan)

Parallel bars S Kato (Japan)
Horse vault N Andrianov (USSR)
Pommelled horse Z Magyar (Hungary)
Rings N Andrianov (USSR)

Women

Beam N Comaneci (Romania)
Combined exercises N Comaneci (Romania)
Combined exercises (team) (USSR)

Floor exercises N Kim (USSR)
Asymmetric bars N Comaneci (Romania)
Horse vault N Kim (USSR)

HOCKEY

OLYMPIC CHAMPIONS

1908	England	1952	India	1976	New Zealand
1920	Gt Britain	1956	India		
1928	India	1960	Pakistan		
1932	India	1964	India		
1936	India	1968	Pakistan		
1948	India	1972	W Germany		

HORSE RACING

THE DERBY

	Horse	Jockey	Owner
1950	Galcador	W Johnstone	M Boussac
1951	Arctic Prince	C Spares	Mr J McGrath
1952	Tulyar	C Smirke	The Aga Khan
1953	Pinza	G Richards	Sir V Sassoon
1954	Never Say Die	L Piggott	Mr R S Clark
1955	Phil Drake	F Palmer	Mme Volterra
1956	Lavandin	W Johnstone	M Wertheimer
1957	Crepello	L Piggott	Sir V Sassoon
1958	Hard Ridden	C Smirke	Sir V Sassoon
1959	Parthia	W H Carr	Sir H de Trafford
1960	St Paddy	L Piggott	Sir V Sassoon
1961	Psidium	R Poincelet	Mrs Arpad Plesch
1962	Larkspur	N Sellwood	Mr R Guest
1963	Relko	Y Saint-Martin	M F Dupré
1964	Santa Claus	A Breasley	Mr J Ismay
1965	Sea Bird II	T P Glennon	Mr M J Ternynck
1966	Charlottown	A Breasley	Lady Z Wernher
1967	Royal Palace	G Moore	Mr H J Joel
1968	Sir Ivor	L Piggott	Mr R R Guest
1969	Blakeney	E Johnson	Mr A Budgett
1970	Nijinsky	L Piggott	Mr C W Engelhard
1971	Mill Reef	G Lewis	Mr P Mellon
1972	Roberto	L Piggott	Mr J Galbreath
1973	Morston	E Hide	Mr A Budgett
1974	Snow Knight	B Taylor	Mrs N Philips
1975	Grundy	P Eddery	Dr C Vittadini
1976	Empery	L Piggott	Mr B Hunt
1977	The Minstrel	L Piggott	Mr R Sangster
1978	Shirley Heights	G Starkey	Lord Halifax
1979	*Troy*	*W. Carson*	

THE GRAND NATIONAL

	Horse	Jockey	Owner
1950	Freebooter	J Power	Mrs L Brotherton
1951	Nickel Coin	J A Bullock	Mr J Royle
1952	Teal	A P Thompson	Mr H Lane
1953	Early Mist	B Marshall	Mr J H Griffin
1954	Royal Tan	B Marshall	Mr J H Griffin
1955	Quare Times	P Taffe	Mrs W H E Welman
1956	ESB	D Dick	Mrs L Carver
1957	Sundew	F Winter	Mrs G Kohn
1958	Mr What	A Freeman	Mr D Coughlan
1959	Oxo	M Scudamore	Mr J E Bigg
1960	Merryman II	G Scott	Miss W H S Wallace
1961	Nicolaus Silver	H Beasley	Mr C Vaughan
1962	Kilmore	F Winter	Mr N Cohen
1963	Ayala	P Buckley	Mr P B Raymond
1964	Team Spirit	G W Robinson	Mr J Goodman
1965	Jay Trump	C Smith	Mrs M Stephenson
1966	Anglo	T Norman	Mr S Levy
1967	Foinavon	J Buckingham	Mr C P T Watkins
1968	Red Alligator	B Fletcher	Mr J Manners
1969	Highland Wedding	E Harty	Mr T H McKay, jnr
1970	Gay Trip	P Taaffe	Mr A Chambers
1971	Specify	J Cook	Mr F W Pontin
1972	Well to Do	G Thorner	Capt T Forster
1973	Red Rum	B Fletcher	Mr N Le Mare
1974	Red Rum	B Fletcher	Mr N Le Mare
1975	L'Escargot	T Carberry	Mr R Guest
1976	Rag Trade	J Burke	Mr P Raymond
1977	Red Rum	T Stack	Mr N Le Mare
1978	Lucius	B R Davies	Mrs D Whitaker

LAWN TENNIS

DAVIS CUP

1950	Australia	1960	Australia	1970	USA
1951	Australia	1961	Australia	1971	USA
1952	Australia	1962	Australia	1972	USA
1953	Australia	1963	USA	1973	Australia
1954	USA	1964	Australia	1974	South Africa
1955	Australia	1965	Australia	1975	Sweden
1956	Australia	1966	Australia	1976	Italy
1957	Australia	1967	Australia	1977	Australia
1958	USA	1968	USA	*1978*	*USA*
1959	Australia	1969	USA		

WIMBLEDON CHAMPIONSHIPS

Men's Singles

1950	J E Patty (US)	1961	R Laver (Aus)	1972	S R Smith (US)
1951	R Savitt (US)	1962	R Laver (Aus)	1973	J Kodes (Czech)
1952	F A Sedgman (Aus)	1963	C R McKinley (US)	1974	J Connors (US)
1953	E V Seixas (US)	1964	R Emerson (Aus)	1975	A R Ashe (US)
1954	J Drobny (Egypt)	1965	R Emerson (Aus)	1976	B Borg (Sweden)
1955	M A Trabert (US)	1966	M Santana (Spain)	1977	B Borg (Sweden)
1956	L A Hoad (Aus)	1967	J D Newcombe (Aus)		
1957	L A Hoad (Aus)	1968	R Laver (Aus)		
1958	A J Cooper (Aus)	1969	R Laver (Aus)		
1959	A Olmedo (Peru)	1970	J D Newcombe (Aus)		
1960	N A Fraser (Aus)	1971	J D Newcombe (Aus)		

1978 B Borg (Sweden)
1979 B Borg (Sweden)

Women's Singles

1950	A L Brough (US)	1961	A Mortimer (GB)	1972	B-J King (US)
1951	D J Hart (US)	1962	J R Susman (US)	1973	B-J King (US)
1952	M Connolly (US)	1963	M Smith (Aus)	1974	C Evert (US)
1953	M Connolly (US)	1964	M E Bueno (Braz)	1975	B-J King (US)
1954	M Connolly (US)	1965	M Smith (Aus)	1976	C Evert (US)
1955	L Brough (US)	1966	B-J King (US)	1977	S V Wade (GB)
1956	S J Fry (US)	1967	B-J King (US)		
1957	A Gibson (US)	1968	B-J King (US)		
1958	A Gibson (US)	1969	A Jones (GB)		
1959	M E Bueno (Braz)	1970	M Court (Aus)		
1960	M E Bueno (Braz)	1971	E F Goolagong (Aus)		

1978 M Navratilova (Cheke/U.SA.)
1979 M Navratilova (USA)

Men's Doubles

1950	J E Bromwich & A K Quist	1966	K N Fletcher & J D Newcombe
1951	K McGregor & F A Sedgman	1967	R A Hewitt & F D McMillan
1952	K McGregor & F A Sedgman	1968	J D Newcombe & A D Roche
1953	L A Hoad & K R Rosewall	1969	J D Newcombe & A D Roche
1954	R N Hartwig & M G Rose	1970	J D Newcombe & A D Roche
1955	R N Hartwig & L A Hoad	1971	R Emerson & R Laver
1956	L A Hoad & K R Rosewall	1972	R A Hewitt & F D McMillan
1957	G Mulloy & J E Patty	1973	J S Connors & I Nastase
1958	S Davidson & U Schmidt	1974	J D Newcombe & A D Roche
1959	R Emerson & N A Fraser	1975	V Gerulaitis & A Mayer
1960	R H Osuna & R D Ralston	1976	B E Gottfried & R Ramirez
1961	R Emerson & N A Fraser	1977	R L Case & G Masters
1962	R A Hewitt & F S Stolle		
1963	R H Osuna & A Palafox		
1964	R A Hewitt & F S Stolle		
1965	J D Newcombe & A D Roche		

1978 FD McMillan + RA Hewitt
1979 J McEnroe + P Fleming.

Women's Doubles

1950	A L Brough & W Dupont	1966	M E Bueno & N Richey
1951	S J Fry & D J Hart	1967	R Casals & B-J King
1952	S J Fry & D J Hart	1968	R Casals & B-J King
1953	S J Fry & D J Hart	1969	M Court & J A Tegart
1954	A L Brough & W Dupont	1970	R Casals & B-J King
1955	A Mortimer & J A Shilcock	1971	R Casals & B-J King
1956	A Buxton & A Gibson	1972	B-J King & B Stove
1957	A Gibson & D R Hard	1973	R Casals & B-J King
1958	M E Bueno & A Gibson	1974	E Goolagong & P Michel
1959	J Arth & D R Hard	1975	A K Kiyomura & K Sawamatsu
1960	M E Bueno & D R Hard	1976	C Evert & M Navratilova
1961	K Hantze & B-J Moffitt	1977	R L Cawley & J. C Russell
1962	B-J Moffitt & J R Susman		
1963	M E Bueno & D R Hard		
1964	M Smith & L R Turner		
1965	M E Bueno & B-J Moffitt		

1978
1979 B-J King M. Navratilova

Mixed Doubles

1950	E W Sturgess & A L Brough	1966	K N Fletcher & M Smith
1951	F A Sedgman & D J Hart	1967	O K Davidson & B-J King
1952	F A Sedgman & D J Hart	1968	K N Fletcher & M Court
1953	E V Seixas & D J Hart	1969	F Stolle & A Jones
1954	E V Seixas & D J Hart	1970	I Nastase & R Casals
1955	E V Seixas & D J Hart	1971	O K Davidson & B-J King
1956	E V Seixas & S J Fry	1972	I Nastase & R Casals
1957	M G Rose & D R Hard	1973	O K Davidson & B-J King
1958	R N Howe & L Coghlan	1974	O K Davidson & B-J King
1959	R Laver & D R Hard	1975	M C Riessen & B M Court
1960	R Laver & D R Hard	1976	A D Roche & F Durr
1961	F Stolle & L R Turner	1977	R A J Hewitt & G R Stevens
1962	N A Fraser & W Dupont	*1978*	
1963	K N Fletcher & M Smith	*1979*	
1964	F Stolle & L R Turner		
1965	K N Fletcher & M Smith		

MOTOR RACING

World Champion Drivers

1950	G Farina (It)	1961	P Hill (US)	1972	E Fittipaldi (Braz)
1951	J M Fangio (Arg)	1962	G Hill (GB)	1973	J Stewart (GB)
1952	A Ascari (It)	1963	J Clark (GB)	1974	E Fittipaldi (Braz)
1953	A Ascari (It)	1964	J Surtees (GB)	1975	N Lauda (Austria)
1954	J M Fangio (Arg)	1965	J Clark (GB)	1976	J Hunt (GB)
1955	J M Fangio (Arg)	1966	J Brabham (Aus)	1977	N Lauda (Austria)
1956	J M Fangio (Arg)	1967	D Hulme (NZ)		
1957	J M Fangio (Arg)	1968	G Hill (GB)		
1958	M Hawthorn (GB)	1969	J Stewart (GB)		
1959	J Brabham (Aus)	1970	J Rindt (Austria)		
1960	J Brabham (Aus)	1971	J Stewart (GB)		

RIFLE SHOOTING

Queen's/King's Prize Winners

1950	R Greig	1961	N Beckett	1972	R P Rosling
1951	G Boa	1962	P Hall	1973	K M Pilcher
1952	A Kinnier-Wilson	1963	K Pilcher	1974	F Harris
1953	N McCaw	1964	A Harris	1975	C M Y Trotter
1954	G Twine	1965	J Allen	1976	W H Magnay
1955	L Fenwick	1966	R Hampton	1977	D A Friend
1956	G Twine	1967	J Powell		
1957	J Love	1968	A Parke		
1958	R Fulton	1969	F Little		
1959	I Mallabar	1970	G F Arnold		
1960	G Westling	1971	R M Stevens		

ROWING AND SCULLING

THE UNIVERSITY BOAT RACE

		min	s	lengths					
1952	Oxford	20	23	canvas	1968	Cambridge	18	22	3¼
1953	Cambridge	19	54	8	1969	Cambridge	18	4	4
1954	Oxford	20	23	4½	1970	Cambridge	20	22	3
1955	Cambridge	19	10	16	1971	Cambridge	17	58	10
1956	Cambridge	18	36	1¼	1972	Cambridge	18	36	9½
1957	Cambridge	19	1	2	1973	Cambridge	19	21	13
1958	Cambridge	18	15	3½	1974	Oxford	17	35	5½
1959	Oxford	18	52	6	1975	Cambridge	19	27	3¾
1960	Oxford	18	59	1	1976	Oxford	16	58*	6¼
1961	Cambridge	19	22	4½	1977	Oxford	19	28	†
1962	Cambridge	19	46	5	1978	Oxford	19	00	†
1963	Oxford	20	47	5	1979 Oxford		20	32	3½
1964	Cambridge	19	18	6¼					
1965	Oxford	18	7	4	*Record time				
1966	Oxford	19	12	3¾	†Cambridge sank				
1967	Oxford	18	52	3¼	Won: Cambridge 68 Oxford 55				

1980 Cambridge Oxford
1981 Oxford

1976 OLYMPIC GAMES WINNERS (MONTREAL)

Men

Single sculls P Karppinen Finland 7 min 29·03s
Double sculls Norway 7 min 13·20s
Coxless pairs E Ger 7 min 23·31s
Coxed pairs E Ger 7 min 58·99s

Coxless fours E Ger 6 min 37·42s
Coxed fours USSR 6 min 40·22s
Coxless quadruple sculls E Ger 6 min 18·65s
Eights E Ger 5 min 58·29s

Women

Single sculls C Scheiblich E Ger 4 min 5·56s
Double sculls Bulgaria 3 min 44·36s
Coxless pairs Bulgaria 4 min 1·22s

Coxed fours E Ger 3 min 45·08s
Coxed quadruple sculls E Ger 3 min 29·99s
Eights E Ger 3 min 33·32s

RUGBY LEAGUE

LEAGUE CHAMPIONS

1950–1	Workington T	1961–2	Huddersfield	1972–3	Dewsbury
1951–2	Wigan	1962–3	Swinton/Hunslet	1973–4	Salford
1952–3	St Helens	1963–4	Swinton/Oldham	1974–5	St Helens
1953–4	Warrington	1964–5	Halifax	1975–6	Salford
1954–5	Warrington	1965–6	St Helens	1976–7	St Helens
1955–6	Hull	1966–7	Wakefield T	1977–8	Widnes
1956–7	Oldham	1967–8	Wakefield T		
1957–8	Hull	1968–9	Leeds		
1958–9	St Helens	1969–70	St Helens		
1959–60	Wigan	1970–1	St Helens		
1960–1	Leeds	1971–2	Leeds		

CHALLENGE CUP WINNERS

1950	Warrington	1961	St Helens	1972	St Helens
1951	Wigan	1962	Wakefield **T**	1973	Featherstone R
1952	Workington **T**	1963	Wakefield **T**	1974	Warrington
1953	Huddersfield	1964	Widnes	1975	Widnes
1954	Warrington	1965	Wigan	1976	St Helens
1955	Barrow	1966	St Helens	1977	Leeds
1956	St Helens	1967	Featherstone **R**	1978	Leeds
1957	Leeds	1968	Leeds		
1958	Wigan	1969	Castleford		
1959	Wigan	1970	Castleford		
1960	Wakefield **T**	1971	Leigh		

WORLD CUP WINNERS

1954	England	1970	Australia
1957	Australia	1972	Great Britain
1960	Great Britain	1976	Australia
1968	Australia		

RUGBY UNION

COUNTY CHAMPIONS

1950	Cheshire	1961	Cheshire	1972	Gloucestershire
1951	E Midlands	1962	Warwickshire	1973	Lancashire
1952	Middlesex	1963	Warwickshire	1974	Gloucestershire
1953	Yorkshire	1964	Warwickshire	1975	Gloucestershire
1954	Middlesex	1965	Warwickshire	1976	Gloucestershire
1955	Lancashire	1966	Middlesex	1977	Lancashire
1956	Middlesex	1967	Durham/Surrey	1978	Gloucestershire
1957	Devon	1968	Middlesex		
1958	Warwickshire	1969	Lancashire		
1959	Warwickshire	1970	Staffordshire		
1960	Warwickshire	1971	Surrey		

INTERNATIONAL CHAMPIONS

1950–1	Ireland	1960–1	France	1972–3	England
1951–2	Wales	1961–2	France		France
1952–3	England	1962–3	England		Ireland
1953–4	England	1963–4	Scotland		Scotland
	France		Wales		Wales
	Wales	1964–5	Wales	1973–4	Ireland
1954–5	France	1965–6	Wales	1974–5	Wales
	Wales	1966–7	France	1975–6	Wales
1955–6	Wales	1967–8	France	1976–7	France
1956–7	England	1968–9	Wales	1977–8	Wales
1957–8	England	1969–70	France		
1958–9	France		Wales		
1959–60	England	1970–1	Wales		
	France	1971–2	Wales		

SNOOKER Prof. Champions.
1981 Steve Davis

SPEEDWAY

WORLD CHAMPIONS

1950	F Williams (W)	1961	O Fundin (Sw)	1972	I Mauger (NZ)
1951	J Young (Aus)	1962	P Craven (E)	1973	J Szczakiel (Pol)
1952	J Young (Aus)	1963	O Fundin (Sw)	1974	A Michanek (Sw)
1953	F Williams (W)	1964	B Briggs (NZ)	1975	O Olsen (Denmark)
1954	R Moore (NZ)	1965	B Knutsson (Sw)	1976	P Collins (E)
1955	P Craven (E)	1966	B Briggs (NZ)	1977	I Mauger (NZ)
1956	O Fundin (Sw)	1967	O Fundin (Sw)		
1957	B Briggs (NZ)	1968	I Mauger (NZ)		
1958	B Briggs (NZ)	1969	I Mauger (NZ)		
1959	R Moore (NZ)	1970	I Mauger (NZ)		
1960	O Fundin (Sw)	1971	O Olsen (Den)		

SQUASH RACKETS

OPEN CHAMPIONSHIP

1950–5	Hashim Khan (Pak)	1963–5	A F A Taleb (UAR)	1976	G B Hunt (Aus)
1956	Roshan Khan (Pak)	1966–7	J P Barrington (Ire)	1977	G B Hunt (Aus)
1957	Hashim Khan (Pak)	1968	G B Hunt (Aus)	1978	G B Hunt (Aus)
1958–61	Azam Khan (Pak)	1969–72	J P Barrington (Ire)		
1962	Mohibullah Khan (Pak)	1973–4	G B Hunt (Aus)		
		1975	Q Zaman (Pak)		

SWIMMING

1976 OLYMPIC GAMES WINNERS (MONTREAL)

Men

100 metres free-style J Montgomery US 49·99s
200 metres free-style B Furniss US 1 min 50·29s
400 metres free-style B Goodall US 3 min 51·93s
1,500 metres free-style B Goodall US 15 min 2·40s
100 metres back-stroke J Naber US 55·49s
200 metres back-stroke J Naber US 1 min 59·19s
100 metres breast-stroke J Hencken US 1 min 3·11s
200 metres breast-stroke D Wilkie GB 2 min 15·11s
100 metres butterfly M Vogel US 54·35s
200 metres butterfly M Bruner US 1 min 59·23s
400 metres medley R Strachan US 4 min 23·68s
4 × 100 metres medley relay US 3 min 42·22s
4 × 200 metres free-style relay US 7 min 23·22s
Highboard diving K Dibiasi Italy 600·51 pts
Springboard diving P Boggs US 619·05 pts
Water polo Hungary

Women

100 metres free-style K Ender E Ger 55·65s
200 metres free-style K Ender E Ger 1 min 59·26s
400 metres free-style P Thumer E Ger 4 min 9·89s
800 metres free-style P Thumer E Ger 8 min 37·14s
100 metres back-stroke U Richter E Ger 1 min 1·83s
200 metres back-stroke U Richter E Ger 2 min 13·43s
100 metres breast-stroke H Anke E Ger 1 min 11·16s
200 metres breast-stroke M Koshevaia USSR 2 min 33·35s
100 metres butterfly K Ender E Ger 1 min 0·13s
200 metres butterfly A Pollack E Ger 2 min 11·41s
400 metres medley U Tauber E Ger 4 min 42·77s
4 × 100 metres free-style relay US 3 min 44·82s
4 × 100 metres medley relay E Ger 4 min 7·95s
Highboard diving E Vaytsekhovskaia USSR 406·59 pts
Springboard diving J Chandler US 506·19 pts

TABLE TENNIS

WORLD CHAMPIONSHIP

Men

1950	R. Bergmann (Eng)	1959	Jung Kuo-Tuan (China)	1975	I Jonyer (Hungary)
1951	J Leach (Eng)	1961	Chuang Tse-Tung (China)	1977	M Kohno (Japan)
1952	H Satoh (Japan)	1963	Chuang Tse-Tung (China)		
1953	F Sido (Hungary)	1965	Chuang Tse-Tung (China)		
1954	I Ogimura (Japan)	1967	N Hasegawa (Japan)		
1955	T Tanaka (Japan)	1969	S Itoh (Japan)		
1956	I Ogimura (Japan)	1971	S Bengtsson (Sweden)		
1957	T Tanaka (Japan)	1973	Hsi En-Ting (China)		

Women

1950–5	A Rozeanu (Romania)	1965	N Fukazu (Japan)	1975	Pak Yung Sun (Korea DPR)
1956	T Okawa (Japan)	1967	S Morisawa (Japan)		
1957	F Eguchi (Japan)	1969	T Kowada (Japan)	1977	Pak Yung Sun (Korea DPR)
1959	K Matsuzaki (Japan)	1971	Lin Hui-Ching (China)		
1961	Chiu Chung-Hui (China)	1973	Hu Yu-Lan (China)		
1963	K Matsuzaki (Japan)	1974	M Alexandra (Romania)		

COLLECTING ANTIQUES

This section tells of the pleasures of antique-collecting and of the wide range of opportunities for learning about antiques. Practical advice is given about how antiques are bought and sold and their value and price determined. The text is accompanied by line-drawings of chairs, demonstrating the main period styles, and by tables of silver and pottery marks. An illustrated Collectors' Glossary completes the section.

TABLE OF CONTENTS

COLLECTING ANTIQUES

1. Introduction.

Until recently it was mainly the prosperous and the rich who could indulge in collecting. During the 17th and 18th centuries the English aristocracy acquired antiques with passion and avidity, or rather antiquities, for their interests were almost exclusively concentrated upon marble statues, vases and coins from the classical world. The 19th century saw an ever increasing interest in highly decorated *objets d'art*, Venetian glass, Pallissy pottery, French 18th century furniture, Dresden porcelain, elaborate clocks, arms and armour, and rich people built up vast collections. We can mention men like Felix Slade (1790–1868) and George Salting (1836–1909), who spent most of their leisure time and considerable fortunes on antique-collecting, and who have left hundreds of thousands of precious objects to our museums. Or the Fourth Marquess of Hertford (1800–70) and John Bowes (1811–85) and his wife, whose collections have been preserved in museums of their own—the Wallace Collection in London and the Bowes Museum at Barnard Castle. The early 20th century saw a great widening in the public interest in antiques, but it would still be fair to say that until recently antique-collecting was a somewhat sedate pastime for middle-aged people of comfortable means.

It was during the post-war period, and especially from the early 1960s onwards that the interest in antiques spread to every section of society. There is today a nostalgia for the past, especially among the young, for its fashions in dress, its interiors, its household goods and ornaments. In a world which changes with such confusing rapidity people find themselves turning towards the past to find some kind of continuity in life, to preserve what is so quickly disappearing and to get a feeling of stability—for the past has a way of looking stable when seen from an unstable present. The love of antiques is one expression of these needs.

What is an Antique?

As collectors have become so very much more numerous, the ideas of what is collectable have widened correspondingly. Chronological definitions have been immensely widened. The old definition of an antique as "something made before 1830" (i.e., before industrialisation began seriously to change our physical surroundings), is no longer generally accepted. The official definition of an antique, when Government has to decide for instance on questions of import and export is "what is more than a hundred years old". But for the general public, all kinds of Victoriana and objects in the styles of Art Nouveau (c. 1880–1914) and Art Deco (c. 1920–40) are eagerly and sometimes expensively collected, and even post-war objects frequently make their appearance in shops and sale-rooms. In fact, the immediate past is to many people of more absorbing interest than any period of history.

Likewise, the whole concept of objects worth collecting has expanded out of all recognition. Antiques no longer include only the old classic genres of furniture, pottery and porcelain, glass, silver, coins, ethnographica. Today, people collect everything under the sun, and the aesthetic appeal is no longer of primary importance. To mention only a few examples: grandmother's ball-dress and fur coat, old dolls, medicine-bottles, postcards, typewriters and cameras of twenty or fifty or a hundred years ago, all these and many more things are now treasured, labelled and systematised, bought and sold through the regular channels of the antique trade. Other significant additions to the world of antiques are veteran cars, boats and railway-engines, and for those who cannot handle these bulky objects in the original, pictures, old or new, will do. They

are all messengers from the past, and as such they charm, amuse and fascinate.

Why we love our Heirlooms.

Objects which have come down to us from parents, grandparents or even earlier links in the family chain are, of course, prized with special affection. Many serve us as well in daily life as they did our forbears. A mahogany chair of 18th-century design effortlessly takes its place in a modern interior as a useful piece of furniture, while at the same time it pleases us as a thing of beauty. Grandmother's tea-set is as serviceable today as when it was made, and so is what may remain of a Victorian flint dinner-service. If all that survives of it is a colourful plate or a tureen too capacious for modern family needs, they look pretty when hung on the wall or displayed on a sideboard. And even things without intrinsic beauty or modern usefulness, like a washstand with marble top, a set of tools made of brass with turned wooden handles, or a pair of old-fashioned scales, thrill us by their natural materials, the quality of their craftmanship and the simplicity of their mechanisms. Family "heirlooms", however modest, may suffer from infirmities, but we put up with them and look after them as we do our aged relatives.

Collecting—Casual or Systematic.

Many people will, however, want to add to what they may already possess by acquiring old things. Perhaps they want to cheer up a drab corner of a room with let us say "something blue", and find that an old-fashioned blue and white milk jug of Staffordshire pottery just fills the bill. A small Oriental rug, perhaps of no very great antiquity, but warm and delicious in colour and texture, will add a new charm to an interior. A bronze lion of modest size thrills us by the elegance of its lines and the energy of its movements, and we "fall for it". Perhaps we approach the antique shop or market with some purely practical purpose in mind: we go in search of a set of cut glass tumblers to match what we already have from the parental home, or we need a new armchair, and we discover that it is actually cheaper to buy an old than a new one. Living with the "new old" chair, we discover that its capriciously curved lines give a welcome element of variety to an otherwise austerely modern interior. If it needs repair and upholstery, this may be an added attraction for those with do-it-yourself talents (*see* **U17**).

Most of us are content to wander about among the welter of antiques now being offered for sale, to enjoy looking at so many things curious or beautiful (or with some luck, both), and occasionally perhaps purchase something that takes our fancy and suits our purse. But from this casual kind of buying, one is easily led on to more systematic and purposeful collecting. Having acquired something that thrills and fascinates, one's eye becomes sharpened, and one begins to look for something similar when browsing in shops and markets. One starts looking at marks on pottery, signatures on old prints, and the next purchase and perhaps the one after that again is done with greater discernment. And one day one discovers that one has become a real and keen collector—of brass candlesticks, or pestles and mortars, or old sewing-box accessories, or views of London or Norwich or Cheltenham, or memories of Queen Victoria, or whatever one finds truly fascinating among the myriads of items that are available. Having once found a subject with appeal, one is happily caught up in a hobby that will provide great enjoyment, concentrate a restless mind, and give occasion for absorbing detective work in museums and libraries.

It is a natural desire to want to create order out of what may at first look like chaos, to arrange thoughts, ideas or concrete objects in groups and series, and to want to see things, once begun, completed. Systematic collecting satisfies many of these desires. Classic examples are of course the collecting of coins and stamps. Here every item can be fairly easily identified and its date and place determined, and it is possible with application to build up complete series—whether one goes in for English postage-stamps from the Edwardian era, pennies from all ages or coins from the reign of William IV. Each item has interesting historical associations, and many are things of beauty. But people with tidy minds may find it satisfying to collect less ambitious objects, matchboxes, or figures of swans or elephants in wood or pottery or any other material or Penguin books from before decimalisation, or eggcups or eyebaths —the possibilities are virtually endless.

Collectors who concentrate for long periods, perhaps for a lifetime, on one speciality, will have the chance to build up a solid knowledge within their particular field of interest. They will find their way to dealers who are knowledgeable within their speciality and can assist in making significant additions to their collections; they will become increasingly able to distinguish between excellent, good, less good and trash, and to spot the odd fake. And they will get in touch with people who nurse the same interest, and spend enjoyable hours exchanging views and experiences, comparing and perhaps swapping. Today collectors in a large number of fields have organised themselves into societies that hold regular meetings, read papers, arrange excursions and public transactions.

Some Collectors' Clubs and Societies.

The Antique Collectors' Club.
Founded 1966.
Secretariat: Clopton, Woodbridge, Suffolk.
(With *c*. 70 affiliated regional clubs all over Britain.)

The Arms and Armour Society.
Founded 1950.
Hon. Sec.: R. J. Whittaker,
30 Alderney Street, London S.W.1.

The British Bottle Collectors' Club.
Hon. Sec.: Gregory Payne,
Greenacres, Church Road,
Black Notley,
Braintree, Essex.

The British Button Society,
Founded 1976,
Hon. Sec.: Mrs. L. M. Graham
32 Crown Hill, Rayleigh, Essex.

The Society of Caddy Spoon Collectors.
Founded 1963.
Hon. Sec.: Edward Kramer.
5 Verulam Buildings, Gray's Inn, London W.C.1.

The English Ceramic Circle.
Founded in 1927 as The English Porcelain Circle.
Reorganised under its present name in 1931.
Hon. Sec.: Mrs. E. Adams,
26 St. Paul's Place, London N.1.

The Oriental Ceramic Society.
Founded 1921.
Secretariat;
31b Torrington Square, London W.C.1.

The Commemorative Collectors' Society.
Founded 1970s.
Hon. Sec.: Steven Jackson,
25 Farndale Close, off Wilsthorpe Road,
Long Eaton, Nr. Nottingham.

The Costume Society.
Founded 1965.
Hon. Sec.: Mrs. Anne Thomas,
251, Popes Lane, London W.5.

The Decorative Arts Society 1890–1940.
Founded 1975.
Secretariat: The Royal Pavilion,
Art Gallery and Museums,
Brighton, Sussex.

The Doll Club of Great Britain.
Hon. Sec.: Mrs. Jean Palmer
2 Broomfield Road,
Oxshott,
Leatherhead, Surrey.

The Fan Circle.
Founded 1975.
Hon. Sec.: Mrs. G. Hardy,
8/8 The Paragon, Blackheath, London S.E.3.

The Fire Mark Circle.
Hon. Sec.: James Williamson
21 Winston Drive,
Bexhill-on-Sea,
Sussex.

The Friends of Blue (transfer printed earthenware).
Hon. Sec.: Robin Gurnett,
367 Liverpool Road,
London N.1.

The Furniture History Society. Founded 1964.
Secretariat: The Department of
Furniture and Woodwork,
Victoria and Albert Museum, London S.W.7.

The Glass Circle.
Founded 1937.
Hon. Sec.: Mrs C. G. Benson,
The Old Rectory, Waldershare, nr. Dover, Kent.

Goss Collectors' Club.
Hon. Sec.: Roland Ward,
21 St. Anne's Drive,
Fonce, Nr. Burnley,
Lancs.

The Heraldry Society
Hon Sec.: Mrs. Linda Biermann
28 Museum Street,
London W.C.1.

The Antiquarian Horological Society.
Founded 1953.
Hon. Sec.: Commander D. Clarke,
New House, High Street, Ticehurst, Wadhurst,
Sussex.

The National Horse Brass Society.
Founded 1975.
Hon. Sec.: J. E. C. Armitage,
Longstone Grange, Nr. Bakewell, Derbyshire.

The Islamic Art Circle.
Founded 1956.
Hon. Sec.: Mrs. P. L. Baker,
2 Tower Mansions, 134 West End Lane,
London N.W.6.

The Map Collectors' Circle.
Founded 1963.
Hon. Sec.: R. V. Tooley,
30 Baker Street,
London W.1.

The British Matchbox Label and Booklet Society.
Founded 1945.
Hon. Sec.: J. H. Luker,
The Bungalow, Pine Ridge School,
Esher Road,
Old Dean Estate,
Camberley, Surrey.

The Musical Box Society of Great Britain.
Founded 1962.
Hon. Sec.: A. R. Waylett,
"Bylands", Crockham Hill, Edenbridge Kent.

The Northern Ceramic Society.
Hon. Sec.: Michael Parkinson,
The Athenaeum,
81 Princess Street,
Manchester, 1.

The Royal Numismatic Society.
Founded 1836.
Secretariat: The Department of Coins and Medals,
British Museum, London W.C.1.

The British Numismatic Society.
Founded 1903.
(for collectors of British coins).
Hon. Sec.: Mr. W. Slayter,
63 West Way, Edgware, Middlesex.

The Pewter Society.
Founded 1918.
Hon. Sec.: C. A. Peal, The Wold, 12 Stratford Crescent, Cringleford. Norwich, Norfolk.

The Royal Philatelic Society.
Founded 1869.
Secretariat: 41 Devonshire Place, London W.1.

The Pot Lid Circle.
Hon. Sec.: A. Ball,
Garthside,
15 Arden Road,
Nuneaton,
Warwickshire.

The Scottish Pottery Society.
Secretariat: The Art Gallery and Museum, Kelvingrove,
Glasgow, 3.

The Vintage Transport Enthusiasts' Club
(Veteran Cars and Motorcycles).
Founded 1971.
Secretariat: 14 Broadway, London S.W.1.

The Wedgwood Society.
Founded 1954.
Hon. Sec.: Miss G. T. B. Brixie Jarvis,
The Roman Villa, Rockbourne, Fordingbridge, Hants.

The Wine Label Society.
Founded 1968.
Dr. Bernard Watney,
32 Upper Park Road, London N.W.3.

2. Values and Valuations.

There is also an important financial aspect. As stocks and shares are increasingly considered risky, many people invest what money they may have to spare in antiques, believing—sometimes rightly and sometimes not—that they will keep their value even when other commodities may lose theirs. Serious investors in antiques usually go in search of items of accepted excellence: silver plate from the 17th and 18th centuries, Oriental carpets, Chinese porcelain of pre-Ming vintage, good mahogany furniture of two hundred years ago or more. Sometimes such treasures are too precious and too fragile to keep on show, and they are put away in bank vaults, while their owners wait for their value to increase, so that they can be sold at a profit when the market prices are particularly favourable. This kind of speculative handling of precious and beautiful things may seem cynical to genuine lovers of what is old and excellent. But the phenomenon is not new; there have always been people to whom the monetary value of their possessions is of overriding interest, and who treat them primarily as investments. And if we are honest with ourselves, whoever owns something old will wonder about its possible monetary value. At some stage thoughts like these will cross our minds: Could the silver spoons with the sculptured heads be genuinely old Apostle spoons and something truly precious, or could the quaint porcelain figure brought home from the East by mother's grandfather be a rare Chinese piece? We find comfort in the thought that if we were ever in serious financial trouble, they might help us out.

Apart from the investment and profit motives, there are several good and sensible reasons why we should know the value of whatever we possess. For insurance purposes it is useful to know if anything old in one's possession is particularly valuable and should be separately insured. And when making a Will, everyone should see to it that one's possessions are shared out between friends and relatives with fairness, so that squabbles and disputes are avoided when the time comes. For such purposes, reputable antique dealers and auctioneers take on valuations at reasonable charges.

Below are set out rates which are currently used a a guide by members of BADA (see U9(2)) and by the big London auctioneers for these services. The exact scale of fees should cf course be agreed upon between valuer and client before the work is undertaken.

1½ per cent up to £ 10,000
1 per cent from £ 10,000 to £100,000
½ per cent from £100,000 to £200,000
¼ per cent above £200,000

(with a minimum fee of £10 plus travelling expenses).

What Determines Prices?

In the world of antiques there are no fixed standards or criteria of value, and prices are determined almost exclusively according to demand. An item made of precious metal and set with rare stones will of course have some intrinsic value, but even so this may be trifling compared to what beauty, age and style have invested it with in the eyes of a collector. Generally speaking, it is the capricious taste of the great public which determines what antiques are worth in terms of money at any given moment. And taste, as we all know, can change from love to indifference and back again, almost overnight, for reasons which are often inexplicable in rational terms. The rise and fall in the value of glass paperweights can serve as a good example of what demand can do to prices.

Glass paperweights are pretty and colourful things, and they are clever glassmakers' products. But they are not staggeringly interesting when seen in the greater perspective of the history of the art of glass, and they are not very old, the first ones having been made during the 1840s. During their time of fashion in the 19th century they became very popular and many different categories of patterns were evolved—many-coloured spirals and dots, figures of flowers and insects inlaid into the massive crystal clear glass—and some factories began to sign their best examples. Then they were forgotten for many decades, until suddenly rediscovered by collectors in a sale at Sotheby's in the early 1950s. In no time the interest exploded into wild enthusiasm, and soon a large and learned literature grew up around them: the different genres were listed and systemised into divisions and subdivisions, signatures were studied, records quoted, and for several years collectors were fighting over rare examples and paying truly fantastic prices for them. Then in 1968 came the crash. The market had been flooded, collectors' interest suddenly appeared to have been exhausted; and prices dropped sharply, the dealers who had invested heavily in paperweights finding themselves in some trouble. Glass paperweights are still very much on the collectors' map, and regular sales are still devoted to paperweights only, and, with inflation, prices for these pretty baubles are again rising to dizzy heights.

However unpredictable the value of an antique may be, and will remain, certain guidelines can be drawn up.

Generally speaking, one can say that the older an object is the greater its value will be. But the principle operates within watertight compartments: a piece of European porcelain is old at 1750, while a piece of silver of the same age is comparatively trivial, and 18th-century Chinese porcelain is young and vulgar when seen in the light of the long, long history of this most aristocratic group among antiques: it is ceramics from the T'ang and Sung dynasties (A.D. 618–1280) and bronzes from even more distant ages that hold the interest of the truly serious collectors. There are also many exceptions to the rule. Anything mediaeval will be of great interest and value, for the period is remote and its output of artefacts comparatively small. Some Roman objects—glass jars and red *terra sigillata* pottery—are on the other hand not so rare, as the period was a productive one in industrial goods, and though several hundred years older than an example of mediaeval craftsmanship, modest examples of Roman glass and pottery can be acquired fairly easily and at comparatively low prices, while almost anything mediaeval will be rare—and consequently expensive.

For rarity is a great price-raiser, in antique-dealing as in every other kind of trade. In March 1975 a chair designed by Charles Rennie Mackintosh (1868–1928) came up for sale at Sotheby Belgravia where it fetched £9,200. Why this truly staggering price for one single chair, made a mere 70 years ago? Partly because Mackintosh was a great designer, and the chair is very beautiful, with long elegant lines in an unusual rhythm and with mauve oval glass insets into the back. But also, and perhaps mainly, because Mackintosh's work is at the moment much admired, and things designed by him only rarely come on the market. This particular chair was designed for an individual patron in Glasgow, and it is believed to be unique.

Other categories of antiques, which are very attractive in themselves, but not so hard to come by, have a way of finding a kind of price level, though this will also be subject to fluctuations, some explicable, some not. An experienced dealer or collector will be able to forecast with some accuracy what the price will be at the next auction sale of an English 18th-century wineglass with a spiral stem, a piece of *famille rose* porcelain from China, a Continental silver tankard of the Baroque period or an English 17th-century silver spoon, for there are plenty of things like these about, and they regularly come on the market.

Very important in the assessment of the value of an antique is its physical condition, but here again, standards change from one group to another. Even a hair-thin beginning of a crack on a piece of pottery may reduce its value as a commercial object quite considerably, while legitimate signs of wear on an old chair may actually add to its attractiveness: the shiny surface on the ends of the arm-rest, polished by generations of users, does not detract from the beauty or solidity of the thing, but gives a charming feeling of constant use by those who came before us. In another area, that of numismatics, signs of wear are nothing but detracting. A coin in mint condition can fetch more than double the price of another example of the very same piece where the details have been blurred by wear or perhaps by polishing—for the serious coin-collector abrasive polishing materials are taboo.

Marks and Signatures Add to Value.

This seems to be one rule that has no exception. But the marks themselves must be studied carefully; some are of more interest than others, and sometimes they do not mean what they may seem to at the first rapid glance.

The assaying and consequent marking of silver and gold has been a matter of law from mediaeval times to this day. Only certain objects of very small size could be sold without marks. The rules have been enforced with greater or lesser energy at different times and in different places, but a piece of unmarked silver should always be looked at with some scepticism. And marks on silver have sometimes been tampered with, at the time when they were new, or recently. Silver marks should therefore be scrutinised with great care before they are accepted for what they at first appear to tell us. But a piece of good old silver (or even better, of gold) with clear and unproblematical marks will fetch a much bigger price among dealers and collectors than a very similar piece with questionable marks or no marks at all. *See* U20–22, and Hallmarks, L55.

From 1784 onwards, the marking of Sheffield plate (plate of silver on a copper base and made not only in Sheffield), was a right, not a duty, and the marks were put on by the makers as trademarks or advertisement. The meaning of them all has not yet been fully worked out, but even so marks will add greatly to the interest and value of an item. Indeed, unidentified marks may pose the collector with an intriguing problem. If the name in the marks has not yet been registered in printed books, one can sometimes solve the question of identity by a simple search in easily accessible records like directories or newspapers.

On ceramic wares of all kinds, marks have been put on by the makers in the great majority of cases, not because any laws told them to do so, but because they wanted to advertise their names. Here again, marks should be looked at with care, for very famous marks, like the crossed swords of Meissen or the name of Wedgwood, have been copied, perhaps with minute alterations, imitated or downright faked by other, less famous producers (*see* U19(2)). Sometimes the factory mark is accompanied by figures, emblems or letters, which to those who know, can reveal details about dating, or about the identity of individual craftsmen and painters. And, of course, the more telling the mark, the more valuable the piece. (For more details, see table of ceramic marks U23–28.)

Pewter marks have been well studied and have their own characteristics and rules. One or two on each piece normally signify the quality of the metal, others show the pewterer's name and the date when he became master of his guild. A date in a pewter mark does not therefore give the date of the piece itself, which can be several decades later than the date in the maker's mark. Apart from quality and maker's marks, pewter sometimes carries several other marks, whose meaning we do not always know. But old pewter marks have been much copied on later pieces and should be studied with great care before accepted as really being what they look like, and priced accordingly.

Until about a hundred years ago, glass was hardly ever marked, and an old glass can normally be assigned to a particular place or period only approximately, by a study of style and technique alone. Occasionally during the 17th and 18th centuries, good engravers signed their pictures, and such pieces are of course of the greatest interest and take high prices. c. 1880 the French glassmaker, Emile Gallé, began to sign every piece that left his factory with his full name. This turned out to be an enormous commercial success, and since then it has been normal practice for makers of art glass to put signatures on their works. Since the 1930s even serially produced table ware has sometimes been signed with the name of the factory and perhaps engraved or acid-etched with the initials of the designer. Glass from the last hundred years or so can at times be identified if the producer's paper label is still intact. The great interest in the glass of the 19th and 20th centuries which has recently developed must surely to a large extent be attributed to the wide use of makers' marks.

From 1751 onwards, the best Paris furniture-makers (*ébénistes*) were bound by the rules of their guild to mark their products with a stamp bearing the master's name or initials, and many Swedish furniture makers of the same period followed their example. Apart from these two groups, furniture is only rarely signed. But if a piece is found to bear the stamp of a maker, or a trade-card or maker's label is discovered glued inside it, this of course adds enormously to its value.

No scholar, collector or dealer, however learned or experienced, can have all marks within one particular area of antiques in his head; everybody is dependent on printed lists in books. When using such books it is important to find up-to-date editions, for the study of marks goes on unendingly, new marks are drawn into the world of antiques as new periods catch collectors' interest, more marks are being identified, new interpretations are constantly made possible, and monetary values fluctuate accordingly.

Look for Quality!

In the final analysis, what will give an antique whether old or not so old, its lasting value is quality. The public's interest in certain curiosities and oddities, its preference for particular periods and names, may come and go from week to week, month to month or year to year, soon to fade away again without trace. But a thing well made of good design and of attractive materials, truly representative of its period, will always retain its value, even though it may pass through short phases of neglect within the trade. Most of all, things of quality will continue to give their owner deep and genuine pleasure, unaffected by superficial changes in taste and fashion. The best advice one can give to those who want to buy antiques must therefore be: buy what you *really* like and feel a genuine desire to possess. For behind such likes and desires usually lies a true sense of the quality of the object chosen.

3. The Antique Trade in Britain.

For two centuries Britain, especially London, has held a central position in the world's antique trade. There are many reasons why this should be so.

First of all, there is in Britain an enormous stock of antiques. The British have themselves produced things of great beauty and originality—we can think of Chippendale and Hepplewhite furniture, Wedgwood table services and ornamental ware, wine glasses of lead crystal, Sheffield plate and much else. But this stock of home products has been constantly added to by British collectors, who have been active for several hundred years (*see* **U3**(1)). First royalty and the aristocracy, later also the prosperous middle classes, travelled widely in Europe, in the classic lands round the Mediterranean, and eventually all over the globe, and wherever they went, they bought whatever products of excellence and originality each country had to offer, be it old or new—French furniture, German porcelain, Venetian glass, Italian majolica, Chinese bronzes and porcelain vases, African masks and weapons, Japanese lacquer ware and ivory carvings and many many other things.

Secondly, over the years, British dealers have gained a world-wide reputation for being well stocked, experienced, knowledgeable and fair as businessmen, and collectors and fellow dealers from all over the world have come and continue to come, to buy from their shops and bid at their auctions. Apart from the commercial apparatus working smoothly and pleasantly, the British art market also offers certain advantages within the field of tax and commissions, which one must hope will be retained in spite of the present-day financial climate, for it is undoubtedly a main attraction for both buyers and vendors from abroad.

Auctioneers.

The cornerstones of the antique trade in Britain, perhaps in the world, are the two famous London auctioneers, Christie's and Sotheby's. The firm of Christie, Manson & Woods was founded by James Christie in 1766, and it has from the very beginning worked purely within the field of antiques and works of art. Its catalogues, which have been preserved from the start, have always been of a very high standard, containing much useful information, and they are today not only major sources in the history of art dealing but of art history. Christie's has been at its present address, 8 King Street, St. James's, since 1823. Sotheby's was founded in 1794, at first specialising in old books. Since 1909 the firm has been handling antiques and works of art of all kinds, and it has operated from its present address in 34–35 New Bond Street since 1917.

Both Christie's and Sotheby's hold auctions five days a week all the year round, except during holiday time summer and winter. The number of auctions per week for each firm works out at about ten, as frequently several sales run concurrently in different rooms on the same day. It is estimated that altogether some 100,000 items pass through each of these two establishments every year. Each sale is devoted to one particular category of works of art or antiques: Furniture, silver, coins, ceramics, glass etc., often with subdivisions within each category: English silver, oak chests of Tudor times, inlaid French 18th-century furniture, Oriental or Continental or English porcelain, Staffordshire figures or the like.

Apart from traditional kinds of antiques, both firms now have regular sales of old wines, photographic and scientific instruments, ethnographica toys, musical instruments, fans and costumes. Even vintage cars and steam railway engines are being sold through the two major London auctioneers.

Catalogues are published for each sale about three weeks in advance. One can buy them singly over the counter from the firm, or one can put in an annual subscription for all catalogues for the sales of one or several categories of antiques (silver and plate, Oriental ceramics, glass etc.) and receive them by post. Most of them are illustrated, and contain much learned information: the reading of potters' and goldsmiths' marks, attributions based on careful research, the detailed pedigree of single items. The high standard of the catalogues makes them much sought after, not only by prospective buyers, but by anyone interested in a particular kind of antique. In every catalogue, conditions of sale are carefully set out, and certain terms used for identification and attribution are explained in detail. Prospective clients should read it all with attention.

Some very spectacular prices are being paid for single items in the "rooms" of these two firms. In the spring of 1975 a very rare ewer of French Renaissance pottery fetched £40,000 at Sotheby's, while the sensation of 1977 was Sotheby's sale of the Earl of Rosebery's collection at Mentmore in Buckinghamshire, which lasted for nine days and where antiques changed hands to the tune of more than £6 million.

With present-day inflated prices, good examples of silver or pottery go into price ranges which ten years ago were reserved for major paintings by Rubens and Velasquez. For specially interesting sales there is admission by ticket only, and on exceptional occasions the TV cameras move in, so that millions can watch the bidding as it climbs rapidly at first, a little more slowly in the later stages, the competitors needing a few more moments for reflection as really staggering sums of money are set at risk. And when at last the auctioneer's hammer falls: "So many hundred thousand pounds to Mr. X"—viewers all over the country gasp with astonishment and excitement in company with the couple of hundred people actually present.

But the vast majority of items that pass through the great auction rooms take much lower prices. It is estimated that *c.* 60% of those sold go for less than £100. Until recently, the firm's commission on the sale of each item was higher for the cheaper things than for those fetching the bigger sums. The sinking scale in commission was reasonable enough: an 18th-century chair of anonymous make and not of the highest quality needs as much storage space and almost as much paper and print in the catalogue as a most exquisite ormolu mounted chest, made of precious woods in rich inlaid work, and signed by some famous 18th-century French *ébéniste*. The commission used to be paid exclusively by the vendor but since September 1975 the two big auctioneers, Sotheby's and Christie's, have changed that system. Under the pressure of inflation and the complexities of modern accountancy, they now charge a commission from the vendor of 10% of the final bid price (except for wines, coins and medals, where the charge is 15%) and a buyer's premium of 10% (except for wines, coins and medals, which are exempt from this premium). The new arrangement caused much dismay among the many dealers who acquire much of their stock from the great sale-rooms, but it has now been generally accepted, and other firms have followed suit.

The auctioneers do not insure things to be sold while they are in their care, but they take great security precautions. From the time of delivery of an object by the vendor, until it comes up for sale, from three to six months may pass. But the time may be shorter for silver, for instance which is being sold at quite frequent sales, than for say, Russian icons, for which there are sales only once or twice a year.

In recent years, both Christie's and Sotheby's have expanded far beyond their traditional premises in London's West End. They frequently arrange sales in the British regions; and most importantly, they have established themselves widely abroad. Christie's now organise regular sales in Geneva, Rome and Florence, in Holland and in USA and Australia, while Sotheby's have a close connection with Parke Bernet in New York. Both firms have agents in many other foreign centres. A most interesting initiative from Sotheby's side was the setting up in 1971 of a branch in Motcomb Street in London's Belgravia, exclusively devoted to the sale of art and antiques from after 1830. Sotheby's Belgravia have three to four sales per week, where pictures, furniture, silver, pottery, glass and Oriental goods, all dating from the Victorian and Edwardian ages or Art Deco items from the 1920s and 1930s, are sold and bought. Even things from the early post-war times are now being offered for sale at Sotheby's Belgravia. The establishment issues learned catalogues with many illustrations of objects that only ten or twenty years ago were spurned as "old-fashioned" and second-rate. Prices here are apt to be lower than those paid in the Bond Street mother firm, but at times they go into five figures, as when a glass vase by Emile Gallé in July 1977 fetched £22,000. Gallé's works are very numerous, and frequently come on the market. Until a sale in November 1971, a good Gallé glass used to fetch high three-figured prices. On that occasion one vase took £2,300—and six years later ten times as much was paid for another. Even under inflation, this was sensational indeed.

Sotheby's Belgravia was the first of the London auctioneers to publish advance prices in their catalogues, thus giving prospective buyers some idea of what sort of sums could be expected to be paid for each item. These forecasts are frequently found to tally quite well with the prices actually paid at the auction, but at times they are, of course way out—as when the maximum estimated price for the famous Mackintosh chair, which fetched £9,200 in the spring of 1975 (see U6) £3,000! The custom of publishing advance price estimates has now been taken up by most of the major art auctioneers in Britain.

In January 1975 Christie's opened a branch in Brompton Road in South Kensington, with a slightly different programme from Sotheby's Belgravia. Good quality antiques of Victorian and later date are still being sold at Christie's auction rooms in King Street, while the aim of the Kensington branch is to try and sell antiques in the lower price ranges as quickly as possible and with the minimum overhead expenses. Here are no soft carpets, no glossy and scholarly catalogues; the whole machinery of selling has been cut down to a utilitarian minimum, and the time from delivery of an item until it comes up for sale, has been reduced to three weeks. There are five sales a week, devoted to pictures, furniture, jewellery, silver and pottery, as well as to dolls, dresses, gramophones, photographica, etc.

There are several other auctioneers in London who handle antiques. Of almost equally venerable age as Christie's and Sotheby's are W. & F. C. Bonham's (founded 1793) of Montpelier Street, South Kensington, and King's Road, Chelsea, and Phillips Son & Neale (now Phillips for short) at Blenheim Street, off Oxford Street (founded 1796). They are smaller establishments than the two most famous firms, and the very greatest treasures do not easily find their way to their rooms, but they are excellent and reliable auctioneers, and Phillips has taken an original line in sticking to the old system of commission, and charging no buyer's premium (see U7(2)), now sometimes operates outside London and at times abroad.

There are many auctioneers outside London who handle antiques, exclusively or partly. Most of them arrange occasional sales, usually concentrating three or four in a couple of days to suit people who have to travel in order to attend. In 1973 The Society of Fine Art Auctioneers (SOFAA) was founded; in 1977 it had 29 members from all over Britain (Christie's and Sotheby's are not among them), and membership should vouch for high standards of expertise among the staff of each firm. Many collectors will also find great attraction in attending general country sales, which are not organised as "art sales" but where among

masses of trivial household goods the odd antique can be spotted by a perspicacious buyer.

Attending an Auction

Before a sale, the auctioneers and their staff willingly give advice to a client about how to go about an auction, whether as vendor or buyer. A vendor can set a reserve (minimum) price on the object he wants to sell. This protects him from seeing his treasure go at a price he considers not worth his while, but he runs the risk that if the reserve price is not reached the object is not sold at all. And the buyer who cannot or does not want to bid at a sale can arrange for the auctioneer to have bids made on his behalf, with an upper price limit agreed beforehand.

Anybody who wants to can walk in and watch an auction in progress without taking an active part, and a sale, especially at one of the great London houses, can be a fascinating spectacle. The seats immediately below the auctioneer's rostrum are usually reserved, by tacit agreement for the dealers who regularly attend particular kinds of sales and get most of their stock from the auction rooms. Round about are rows of chairs and as particularly interesting sales attract quite a crowd, many people may have to stand. On the fringe of the crowd there is a constant coming and going, and much whispered talk goes on, in a babel of foreign languages. But round the rostrum, at the heart of the sale, there is deep silence, broken only by the voice of the auctioneer as he (or, since 1976, she) in an almost rhythmical sing-song calls out the bids as they fall. By tradition these are rarely cried out in so many words and figures; the client who is "in the bidding" signifies with only a nod or a wink or a slight wave with the pencil or catalogue that he is following up with a new bid. These go in "jumps", directed by the auctioneer. For small and modest items the price may go up by only two or five pounds at a time, but when rare and coveted pieces are up for sale, and perhaps very few people, in the end two only, are left to fight it out, they may be over-bidding each other by a thousand pounds a time or more. As each item comes up for bidding, it is carried round to those nearest the rostrum by the saleroom staff, so that prospective buyers can have a last chance to look at it, check the mark, and finally make up their minds about how far to go to acquire it. Large and unwieldy pieces are held up at the back of the room and pointed out by the auctioneer as they come up for sale.

The job of the auctioneer needs intense concentration. He must have an eye on every finger to make sure that all interested get their chance, and he must be absolutely sure exactly where the bidding is standing at each precise moment—a slip may lead to disagreements, complaints and even litigation. There is a tempo and a drive about the whole procedure, a tenseness in the atmosphere, which must affect anybody present. Sometimes over 200 items are sold within the traditional hours between 11 and 1 o'clock, while some sales go on from 2.30 in the afternoon for another two hours. For those not used to the sale-room, it is easy to be carried away, and make higher bids than one had planned for, when competition becomes sharp and decisions have to be taken within split seconds.

The auction-rooms themselves have their own, very special aspect and appearance. On the walls of the room where a sale is in progress hang pictures and mirrors, and from the ceilings chandeliers are suspended, which are to be sold at some later occasion, and in the adjoining rooms people are busy inspecting what is to come up for sale in the next few days, pictures, pieces of furniture or smaller items of silver, porcelain or the like, displayed in showcases. Members of the staff go around giving assistance, answering questions and giving customers access to the locked showcases to hold and inspect items they are interested in. There is a unique atmosphere of museum-cum-salon-cum-warehouse, which has a fascination all of its own.

After the sale is over, the great auctioneers' firms give ready help and advice to people who have been buying, about packing and dispatch, payment in foreign currencies, insurance of goods in transit etc. Immediately after a sale, the prices paid are published in printed lists, which are sent out to subscribers to the catalogues.

Auction Prices.

Sales at auction are influenced by all sorts of factors, which change from place to place, from one season to another, and from day to day, even hour to hour within the particular sale. During the spring and the "London season", when customers from the country and from abroad flock to London, prices are generally higher than during the late autumn and the early part of the winter. The weather, good or bad news in the papers, the energy of the auctioneer or the intangible mood of the buying public may all influence the sale. It may be a stimulating occasion where people feel encouraged to buy at good prices, or a dull couple of hours which fail to inspire anyone to spectacular action. One sensational item in the sale catalogue may attract a larger audience than would otherwise have turned up, and have a stimulating effect on the whole auction, and one impassioned buyer in the audience, set on getting what he or she wants "at any price", can lift the price level beyond all expectations. There is, however, also much routine selling and buying going on in the auction rooms, where well-known and frequently recurring categories of antiques—English wine-glasses of the 18th century, Staffordshire pottery, certain well-established types of Chinese porcelain or Turkish Isnik plates—change hands at prices which most of those present expect and accept as reasonable.

Auction rooms, especially those of the two big London auctioneers, have a way of acting as price-setters. The prices are widely publicised through the price-lists published after every sale, and in spectacular cases through the press and even television, so that everybody involved in the trade of the particular commodity takes note of what happens at Christie's and Sotheby's, and adjusts his own prices and ideas accordingly.

Antique Shops.

It is estimated that there are some 6,500 antique shops in Britain today, and to categorise and map them out with any accuracy is an impossible task, not only because the picture is so large and complex, but also because it is constantly changing. Antique shops are to be found in considerable numbers in practically every town and city, frequently in the older quarters, and they line the High Streets of market towns and villages, where their position is often marked by attractive hanging signs with the magic word ANTIQUES in period style lettering. At the top of the quality and price range are the spacious, softly carpeted establishments of London's Mayfair and South Kensington, and their equivalents in other major cities. Many of them are old establishments, perhaps family firms, who have worked for generations in the same line of business. Here things of venerable age and of museum quality are beautifully displayed, the staff is experienced and knowledgeable to the highest degree, and they cater for an international *clientèle*. At the other end of the scale are the small, dusty shops which fade into secondhand and junk shops, mostly to be found in back streets in unfashionable areas of towns and villages. Many people find them more interesting than the big, elegant ones, partly because their prices are lower, but especially because here there may be chances of finding surprises and bargains: among the broken-down bedroom furniture, chairs and kitchen utensils, one *might* with luck come across a shimmering glass vase by Tiffany, which the owner may not have identified for what it is. and will sell at a reasonable price. Or one might see a little wooden box, offered cheaply as an anonymous "bygone", recognise it as a good example of Victorian Tunbridge work of inlaid wood, and be able to buy it "for a song". But today the chances of making such finds are small indeed, as experienced dealers early in the day comb these small and unpretentious shops for stock, and knowledge of what is sought after is spreading very widely.

In between these two extremes of elegance and shoddiness are large numbers of pleasant, middle-sized shops with a varied stock of pleasant, middle-range priced goods, where many people can enter happily, spend a fascinating half-hour, and come out with a purchase that will grace one's home or please a friend without having broken one's budget.

Within the immensely wide and varied field, there is a great deal of specialisation. Some categories of antiques like Oriental carpets, coins and stamps, books and maps, arms and armour, are to a very large extent to be found in shops which trade in these things only. And particularly in London's West End are many important antique shops, which trade exclusively in silver and plate, or in porcelain (English or Continental, Chinese or Islamic), in furniture or glass. Other dealers again concentrate on even rarer objects—long-case clocks of the 17th and 18th centuries, glass chandeliers, fireplace furnishings, Russian icons, brass locks and mounts—to mention but a few in an almost endless range.

In 1918 a group of antique dealers organised themselves into the British Antique Dealers' Association (BADA). This is not a "closed shop", many dealers operate outside the organisation, but it is considered an asset to one's reputation to be a member, and be able to display the badge of the Association in one's shop window. New members are accepted on application only. Every applicant has to obtain a proposer and a seconder among the existing membership, and at the Council meeting where an application is being considered, he or she will be accepted only if a 75% majority of the votes is obtained. When applications are considered, the main qualifications are integrity and expert knowledge, while quality of stock is also taken into account. Every membership is reviewed annually by the Council.

Today BADA has c. 500 members from all over England, Scotland and Wales and a few also in more distant English-speaking countries. It works in close cooperation with similar organisations in other countries, and all of them are affiliated to the International Federation of Antique Dealers' Associations (CINOA). Since 1958 BADA has operated with a full-time staff from its own premises in 20 Rutland Gate, London S.W.7. This makes it possible for the organisation to provide all the facilities which it wants to give to its membership and to meet the problems that face the trade in a rapidly changing world. Representations made to successive Governments by BADA have resulted in legislation which has helped to maintain London as the principal centre of the world's trade in art and antiques. If a dispute arises between a member and one of his customers, Council members of BADA will hear the case from both sides, and try and settle the argument.

In 1974 the London and provincial Antique Dealers' Association (LAPADA) came into being. Its membership now numbers c. 600, the majority of whom deal in post-1830 antiques, thus providing a useful complement to BADA. To be accepted as a member of LAPADA, one has to have been a full-time antique dealer for a minimum three years, and to be sponsored by two existing members. A Code of Practice for members has been drawn up, and anyone who does not comply faces expulsion. LAPADA operates from premises in 112 Brompton Road, London S.W.3 with a full-time secretariat.

Shop Prices.

The antique shop provides an atmosphere of peace and quiet, which is very different from the auction room with its hustle and bustle. In the shop one can browse and look around, ask questions and discuss problems with the proprietor and the staff, take one's time, perhaps go home and sleep on the question of whether to buy or not, having reserved the object in question for a day or two. The dealer will have set a price on it, which may be subject to discussion, but which provides a *point de départ* for negotiations.

When the honest dealer adds a new object to his stock and has no firm lead as to the price he should ask, he will start from what he himself paid, take into account its probable age and physical condition, use his experience and discretion and feeling for quality and set his price accordingly.

The collector who goes shopping in London's West End will most likely pay a little extra for the good name and expertise of the shop, its pleasant situation and its comfortable, even luxurious premises. But it is a fallacy to believe that the prices in London are always higher than those demanded elsewhere in the country. Prices may be just as high—and dealers just as knowledgeable and experienced—in the elegant streets of Brighton or Bath, or in the High Street of any picturesque village, where the thoughts of visitors naturally turn towards the past and their hearts are easily filled with a desire to buy something old.

Markets—Indoor and Outdoor.

Markets, whether under cover or in the open air, are becoming increasingly important meeting-places for those who want to sell antiques, and those who desire to acquire them.

The outdoor market has a long tradition in this country and some of those in modern London go quite far back in time. The Sunday morning market in Petticoat Lane in the traditionally Jewish part of East London is more than a hundred years old. The Caledonian market began its life in 1855, as a cattle-market in Highbury in North London. Eventually a more general public market grew up in parts of its grounds, much of it devoted to secondhand goods and antiques. During the second world war it was closed down and afterwards it was reopened in Bermondsey Square, near London Bridge, under its famous old name. The Caledonian market is open on Friday mornings. Portobello Road in the more bohemian part of London's West End is lined with antique shops, and on Wednesdays and Saturdays the pavements outside are invaded by stallholders, some belonging to the dealers of the area, others to people coming in from outside, many from far beyond the boundaries of London. In these and many other areas of London and other towns and cities, the municipal authorities hire out stalls and market space in certain streets on special days to anyone who wishes to sell, and who can pay the modest fees charged, and dealers queue up to get the stalls, for this is a simple and cheap way of contacting the buying public. In some street markets, the stalls containing antiques are appendages to those where food and vegetables, clothing and household wares are sold, and antiques and secondhand goods merge imperceptibly into each other.

There is an informality and directness about antique dealing in the outdoor markets, which has great appeal to both sides, and as expenses are kept down to a minimum, prices can also be kept within reasonable limits—though those days are definitely gone when one could pick up good antiques for almost nothing at the markets. Many of the stallholders have great expertise, and much of the most interesting stock is acquired early in the morning by other representatives of the trade. Especially the London markets have become important tourist attractions, and on a Saturday morning in Portobello Road and at the Bermondsey market, all the languages of the world can be heard among the clients who collect in their thousands. Bargaining is permitted, even expected, and especially towards the end of the day, stallholders may sell off some of their stock at bargain prices. On the other hand, the customer has less assurance about what he buys than if he had gone to a shop. He cannot " go back and complain " if the clock he bought in a moment of enthusiasm was sold without a key to wind it with, or if there is a crack in the Staffordshire plate that was hidden from view until the plate was brought home and examined with care.

The indoor market is a fairly recent phenomenon in the world of antique dealing in Britain. It works like this: a large number of people wishing to sell, jointly rent some large indoor space, which they pack with individual stalls, each one usually quite small. The first to adopt this kind of

sharing arrangement were the London dealers in silver and plate. In order to protect their valuable stock, they hired armoured premises in the basements in Chancery Lane, which are now popularly known as the Silver Vaults. Here the public, not least foreign tourists, crowd in to look and to buy during business hours every day of the week, while at night armoured doors protect the goods under joint security arrangements.

The first general indoor antique market in London was The Antique Supermarket, situated just behind Selfridge's, on the corner of Barrett Street and St. Christopher's Place. This charming old passage-way for pedestrians only was already lined with antique shops, and the Supermarket with its mass of stalls and its show of stock under awnings on the pavement provides a natural continuation for the prospective buyer after a walk down St. Christopher's Place. Similar markets have since sprung up all over London, and in many places up and down the country. The markets in Chelsea are cheerfully young and " with it " in atmosphere. Those in South Kensington have a slightly more traditional air, while the Bond Street Antique Centre has caught some of the glamour of this famous street for elegant shopping. And of course there is an indoor market or " Antique Centre " in Camden Passage in Islington, where antique dealers of all kinds have been congregating for many years.

Attractive and extensive antique markets are also to be found in South London, at Greenwich, in several places in the Home Counties as well as in the West Country, in the Midlands and in the North. And the picture is constantly changing. Indoor markets, antique centres and other joint trading establishments are incessantly springing up all over the country.

The indoor market offers great and obvious advantages to both buyers and sellers of antiques. Those with things to sell find an easy and inexpensive outlet for their stock by sharing accommodation in this way, while those interested in buying can see an enormous mass of varied antiques within a limited area. The indoor markets are attractive places to visit, with an easy camaraderie between stallholders, cups of coffee being passed around among dealers and customers alike and an informal atmosphere which must appeal to everyone.

Fairs.

To complete the picture of antique dealing in Britain, a mention should be made of the fairs, which are being arranged more widely and more frequently every year. The fair can be defined as a short-term market, and the most spectacular of them is the great Antiques' Fair, which has been organised in June every year (with a few exceptions) since 1934 to 1938, in the resplendent setting of the great ballroom in Grosvenor House Hotel, Park Lane, London. It lasts for two weeks, and all the c. ten thousand exhibits are carefully vetted by committees of experts within each field (most of them members of BADA, see U9(2)), to assure, as far as is humanly possible, that every item is genuine. The c. 80 exhibitors try to build up the finest of stock for the occasion, and go to great lengths to show their goods attractively and to the greatest advantage. The main fair still adheres to the old definition of antiques as being made before 1830, but in 1975 an annexe was set up in an adjoining room, where c. 30 exhibitors showed first-quality goods from the period up to 1930. Apart from the dealers, restorers and packers also have their stalls at the Antiques' Fair and so have booksellers specialising in books on antiques and the major antique magazines.

Since the war, antique fairs on a smaller and less ambitious scale than the one in Grosvenor House, but on the same general pattern, are being arranged with increasing frequency in all kinds of contexts all over the country. Some last for a week or more and have become annual events, and some are devoted to one particular category of antiques, be it coins or military effects or clocks or whatever. But most fairs produce a general showing and are informal and improvised occasions, where a handful of dealers hire premises for a couple of days and make a local event of it.

With the present hunger for antiques, they collect a good public and business is brisk.

4. How to Learn about Antiques.

The enjoyment of antiques is greatly increased the more one knows about one's possession. Indeed, one of the fascinating aspects of antique-collecting is the way it has of making one first look at things, then speculate and eventually try and find answers to at least some of the questions that have begun to pose themselves. If the contemplation of music boxes gives one a genuine thrill, the collector will soon begin to wonder why music boxes were invented, and where, and why the invention happened just then and there, and little by little one small corner of the history of human skill and endeavour will reveal itself to one's fascinated eyes.

It is not too difficult to acquire quite a detailed knowledge within some limited field, to master the history of glass paperweights or Goss pottery, or thimbles or dolls, without troubling too much about the wider historical context. But few people will become collectors at all unless they already possess some feeling for the passing of time and some knowledge of a few fixed points in the great flow of history. In order to enlarge and deepen one's understanding of history, it is not necessary, perhaps not even desirable, to read thick books on political events, wars and conquests. One can gain an easier access to the past, and acquire more relevant historical knowledge by reading biographies and books on social customs and on technology.

Very useful, in fact indispensable to anyone who wants to try and identify things old, is some familiarity with the period styles.

Some Knowledge of Period Styles is Useful.

The existence of period styles is a strange phenomenon within the great framework of history.

Any artefact of the past will tell us something about the practical needs of its time, about the technical ability of its people and the tools and materials available to them. What is extraordinary is that the shape of the artefact—if it goes at all beyond the most sober, utilitarian functional form—in many cases reflects, not only the superficial fashions of the day, but the deeper thoughts and mental attitudes of its time.

Innumerable works have been written on the history of styles, and it is not too hard to acquire a basic knowledge of the chief characteristics of each, and how they follow one another in a historical sequence. The logical Renaissance and the exuberant Baroque cover the 16th and 17th centuries, while the styles of Queen Anne, of Chippendale and Adam (*Régence*, Rococo and Neo-Classicism, to mention the corresponding Continental styles) dominate the 18th century in turn. The English Regency style is a variant and a close relation of French Empire, and covers a period which goes somewhat beyond the regency of Prince George, who became King in 1820. (It should always be kept in mind that the period of a style named after a reigning monarch (Queen Anne) or an individual person (Chippendale), never coincides *exactly* with the dates of that person.)

From the early years of the 19th century industrialisation had widened its impact on the methods of production of most European artefacts. One result of this was a great confusion of stylistic ideas with a revival of all the historic styles of the past, Neo-Gothic, Neo-Rococo, Neo-Renaissance and all the others. It is hard to map out the revival styles with exactitude, and modern art historians now discuss the whole period under the general name of Historicism.

With the ideas of John Ruskin (1819–1900) and William Morris (1834–96) as guiding stars, reformers began to see the futility of much of this often clumsy copying of styles created for people of times long past, and began to try and find their way back to basic principles of form and ornament in the light of the capacities of modern production methods and the real needs of modern people.

The Art Nouveau of the *fin-de-siècle* (or Jugend-Stil as it was called in many parts of the Continent) reflected the spirit of the age in applying to the products of craftsmen and industry alike the principles of natural growth and organic form. The style reached its climax at the Paris Exhibition of 1900 and lingered on in the design of many commercial goods until the outbreak of the first world war.

Earlier in the 19th century a few pioneers had propagated ideas of pure construction and sober, functional form, especially for industrial goods. After the end of the first world war these ideas were generally accepted as suitable for the brave new world of speed, jazz and efficiency that was rapidly taking form.

Functionalism and its somewhat more mondaine and coquettish sister, Art Deco, remained the dominating styles in progressive circles between the two wars. So much for the bare bones of the history of styles.

But the history of styles must not be accepted as a simple " grammar " but should be used with discretion. It must always be remembered that there is no clear division between each style. The one grew naturally and gradually out of the one that went before, and in time merged imperceptibly into the next. Another point to keep in mind is that styles took on new faces under differing circumstances. The great period styles first emerged in the important cultural centres of their time, in Florence and Rome, Venice and Augsburg, Paris and London. But as the ideas and impulses moved from the places of origin to other countries, the style often changed its character quite fundamentally: the Baroque style of Italy is very different from that of France, and this again differs in an easily recognisable way from the English equivalents of Stuart and Jacobean. And as the great styles reached provincial centres and remote country districts, there was sometimes a considerable time-lag, and in these outlying areas styles survived perhaps for decades after their original inception.

Finally, period styles have constantly been repeated and revived by men of later times. The great example of a recurring style is of course that of classical Greek and Roman antiquity, with its columns and pediments and the rest. It has been revived over and over again for over 2000 years and always in slightly varying versions. Classical forms have been used not only in architecture, but in furniture, silver and many other products of crafts and industry.

We have already mentioned how the Victorian age saw a welter of revivals of all the historic styles of Europe. During that period, some of them came back several times, and it needs experience and sensitivity to distinguish the Neo-Rococo of the 1830s from that of the 1890s, and both from the 18th century originals.

These are just some indications of how the history of styles is more complex and subtle than would appear at first approach, and has to be applied with care and perspicacity by anyone who is trying to identify the date and place of origin of his or her antiques by its criteria.

Chairs in Different Styles.

Among all things old the chair is our most sensitive barometer of the changing period styles. Its dimensions have remained the same from its invention hundreds of years ago to this day, dictated as they are by the proportions of the human frame, and its basic function, to support a sitting person, is the same today as at any time in its long history. The following diagrams of chairs from the last 300 years should give some idea of how access to new materials and techniques and the changes in mental climate of differing periods have altered its appearance and construction.

Baroque, c. 680

This chair is made of walnut, a favourite kind of wood for the richly carved types that became fashionable in England after the Restoration. The cane-work of the seat and the panel back is another novelty of the age. The arm-rests make it a truly luxurious example, a fitting seat for some high-ranking servant of the King and Court, for armchairs were until then somewhat rare. With its majestic contours and splendid carving, the chair reflects the new prosperity of the age and its love of grandeur and extravagance.

Queen Anne, c. 1700

A direct descendant of the previous chair, this example is also made of walnut, richly carved, with cane-work for the seat and back. Standing tall, it retains some of the dignity of the Baroque style, but there is a restraint about it that makes it representative of the austere and logical Queen Anne style in its early stages. Carved ornamentation is sparingly used and concentrated on important points of the construction, top and bottom of the back, legs and stretchers, the front member being particularly fine. Considerable areas have been left plain and unadorned.

Wing-chair, c. 1720

An English invention of the late 17th century, the wing-chair became a favoured piece of furniture in prosperous homes during the early part of the 18th century. It is the earliest fully upholstered chair in history, the first real easy-chair. Its solid sides and back gave protection against draught, and in its capacious interior one could lean back, even curl up, be alone and take a nap. No wonder the type has remained popular and been in constant production in versions almost unchanged from the original ones to this day.

Chippendale, c. 1760

One of a set of six, this chair is made of mahogany which from c. 1720 became the most sought-after material for fine furniture. The chair is simple, sturdy and practical, all ornamentation being concentrated on the back with its gently curving outline and its finely carved splat. When chairs of this type are called " Chippendale ", it does not of course mean that they are known to have been made in the workshops of Thomas Chippendale (1718–79), merely that they are in the style which became popularised through his famous book of furniture designs, *The Gentleman and Cabinet Makers' Director*, first published in 1762.

Hepplewhite, c. 1775

With its simple closed outlines and its neat gracefulness, this chair has caught much that is essential in the Neo-Classical style. It is more subtly elegant than the Chippendale example, having tapering legs that make it look as if it stands on tip-toe, and a shield back with exquisitely carved splat. A special refinement is provided by the curved supports that attach the back to the seat. The name Hepplewhite also needs comment. No piece of extant furniture can be ascribed to George Hepplewhite (d. 1786), but his design-book, *The Cabinet Maker and Upholsterer's Guide* (2nd ed., publ. 1794, after his death) is so representative of the Neo-Classical style in English furniture that the whole stylistic phase has become associated with his name.

Sheraton, c. 1810

With its pleasantly flowing lines, the Sheraton chair is somewhat more relaxed than the Hepplewhite example. It has obviously been made for comfort as well as for beauty. It is made of beechwood that has been painted and gilded. Thomas Sheraton (1751–1806) is the last in the great triumvirate of English furniture-makers and his fame, like his predecessors', is based not on any important body of extant furniture, but on a book of designs, *The Cabinet-Maker and Upholsterer's Drawing-Book*, publ. between 1791 and 1794. It is doubtful whether Sheraton ever made furniture at all, but his book seems to epitomise the general taste in furniture of the Regency style.

Early Victorian—Neo-Gothic, 1847

When in 1847 a royal lodge was being built for the King of Sweden and Norway, this chair was designed by the building's Danish architect. The Gothic features, the pointed arch and its decoration, were borrowed from cathedral architecture, for there were no direct models for upholstered chairs from real Gothic times. Neo-Gothic was the first of the revival styles of the 19th century. In England it can be traced back into the 18th century, while on the Continent its vogue began somewhat later.

Mid-Victorian—Neo-Rococo, c. 1850–60

The wooden framework of this chair with its curves and pretty ornaments goes back to the original 18th-century Rococo style. But though traditional in form, it contains a couple of technical innovations that are very much of the age. The seat has steel springs that make the chair more comfortable and give the characteristic domed appearance to the seat. And the upholstery is much more elaborate than anything made in the 18th century. The new technique of folding the covering material and fixing it to its background with buttons, made it possible to cover the back firmly, solidly and with beautiful precision despite its complicated curvature.

Rocking-chair, c. 1890

The rocking-chair is an American invention, the earliest examples dating from c. 1840. They are simple wooden chairs with four legs put on rockers, and the type became popular all over the world. This chair, also American, was invented c. 1890 and remained popular for a couple of decades. It has the advantage of saving the floorboards, as the rockers rest upon a construction of firm legs. Its mechanism is fairly complex, with steel springs holding the rockers in place and regulating their movements. The chair itself has a seat with steel springs, it is covered with plush, and the woodwork is elaborately turned and polished.

Art Nouveau, c. 1900

With its subtly curved lines, its exquisite materials (palisander and silk), its fine detail and gentle and sweet appearance, this chair is typical of the *fin de siècle* in Paris. Tired of the pomp and over-decoration of many 19th-century products, artists in many countries had begun to grope their way back to basic principles of design and decoration, simplicity of line, good workmanship and a close marriage between form and ornamentation. The designer of this chair, Eugène Gaillard (1862–1933), was among the finest furniture-makers of his time, and one of a circle of young artists who collected round the fashionable shop, " L'Art Nouveau " of Samuel Bing (opened in 1896). It became such a centre for the promotion and sale of fashionable articles of quality that its name came to be given to the whole style.

Bent-wood furniture, 1860

When this chair was made in 1860 it represented something revolutionary in construction. It was the work of a German carpenter, Michael Thonet (1796–1871), who shortly before had invented a completely new method for making chairs. Instead of joining rigid pieces of wood together in complex constructions strengthened with glue and pegs, he bent specially prepared pieces of beechwood into the desired curves and angles, thus saving much work and complicated craftsmanship. His chairs became cheap to buy, light in weight and handsome to look at. From his factory in Vienna (which was active until after the first world war) millions of chairs went out all over the world. His rocking-chair is the most exciting of his models. It remained in production for a long time after its invention.

Functionalism, 1928

When cold hard shiny steel was first introduced into furniture-making it represented an almost brutal break with tradition. This chair is one of the earliest of its kind. It is made of chromium-plated steel tube, and is covered with calf's skin. The designer is the famous French architect Le Corbusier (1887–1965), who produced it for a villa he built for a private client in 1928–29. It is a real luxury product, with a clear, intellectual construction that has not been camouflaged in any way, and it is also comfortable to sit in. In 1965 it was put into production again in Britain and in Italy.

Line-drawings by courtesy of H. Aschehoug & Co. (W. Nygaard), Oslo, Norway.

Facilities Offered by Museums.

Those interested in increasing their understanding of antiques have many aids and facilities at their disposal.

Of primary importance are our museums. Here we can walk in, without paying any entrance fee, and look at things old, usually of good quality and frequently well documented, for museums of repute try to admit nothing else to their collections. Where finance and staffing make it possible, the objects are attractively displayed, in their contexts, either together with other things of the same period or as part of systematical series of silver, pottery or whatever it may be. Usually the objects are accompanied by labels, which give basic information about date, place of origin and the reading of marks. The visitor who wants to pursue his quest into a particular subject beyond what he can gather from the display, may ask for further information from the museum offices, where detailed catalogues and original documents are kept, containing all available knowledge about each object in the museum's care.

In the professional staff of museums is lodged an enormous body of learning, based on a wide experience in handling and analysing things old, and backed by general academic training. Many curators have done extremely valuable original research into particular subjects. A generation or two back, much of the research into antiques in Britain was done by amateurs: it is to the patient and imaginative work by non-professionals that we owe our basic understanding of what marks on English silver and pewter mean, and many old books, still useful and valuable, on subjects like Oriental pottery and English glass, were written by collectors. But today, as art history has become a regular subject in our universities and as the museum services have become more highly organised, it is largely to the men and women working inside these institutions that we owe the most valuable research work. They have established many of those criteria for the dating and identification of things old that help us to answer the questions of "Made when and where, by whom and for whom?", asked by us all when we get fascinated with an antique. They have made it possible to come closer to the artistic personalities of important designers and decorators of different periods, and they are constantly assisting us in learning to distinguish what is good, what is not so good and what is merely repetitious.

The learned men and women of our museums share their knowledge with the greater public in a variety of ways, most importantly through the books and articles they write. Most museums have libraries and reading-rooms, where reference books and specialised literature on many subjects are available to the general public for consultation, and where current issues of relevant periodicals are on display. But few museums allow home loans of their books.

Museum staff also help the public to understand the objects in their care by demonstrations in the collections. The larger institutions have people who work on education only, giving lectures in front of the objects, guiding schoolchildren in their first approach to museums, and assisting teachers in understanding how to interpret the collections to their pupils as part of history courses within the normal school curriculum. To art students, the museum collections and libraries are of course treasure houses for visual inspiration.

Members of the public can also bring their own antiques to museums, where the staff will inspect them and to the best of their abilities give opinions on date, origin and quality. Most of the larger public museums provide this kind of service, and it has become so popular that in many places it has become necessary to limit the times for such visits to certain hours of certain days of the week. Museum staff will give opinions on objects brought in by the public free of charge, but they cannot take any legal or other responsibility for what they say on these occasions, and they will not discuss monetary values.

Facilities Offered by Auctioneers and Dealers.

The great auctioneers in London now have a highly organised service for giving opinions on things brought in to them in advance of sales. At special counters for each category of antiques members of their staff look at what is shown to them, give an on-the-spot opinion and suggest what price the thing might fetch in a sale. As thousands of objects are brought in to them every year, the inspection will at times have to be somewhat summary, but if there is any possibility of something of real value or rarety having turned up, higher grade members of the staff are called in for closer examination. For at the heart of the great auctioneering firms sit a small band of extremely learned men and women, who over the years have built up a vast experience, and who keep abreast of whatever new research is being made within their special field; some contribute to such research themselves. These specialists are of course of vital importance to the firm, not only to their prestige, but in the most direct and commercial way: a piece of enamelled glass will fetch a very, very much higher price if a perspicacious member of the staff can identify it as a fine example of Islamic 13th-century work, when it could have been presented for sale as a pretty 19th-century ornament and no one to tell the difference. Or suppose a drinking horn with silver mounts is brought in, and the silver expert remembers to have seen the mark on the rim on a dated piece of Bergen silver that passed through the firm years ago. From this he can identify the horn as an undoubted piece of Norwegian Renaissance silver, and its interest and value are greatly enhanced.

Whoever is in doubt about the identity and value of an antique can find good assistance also from a dealer—if he finds his way to the right one. Specialised dealers, like the members of auction-room staff, are experienced and knowledgeable people, and—this is important—through their hands pass many more objects than most museum curators normally handle, and the dealers get an experience in eye and fingertip that is of inestimable value. Naturally, the serious dealer will also keep himself informed on what scholarly research is going on within his chosen field—and, most importantly, he will be able to set a price to the object brought in for his inspection.

The collector who wants to get as close as possible to a true identification of his treasure and find out its monetary value, should first ask for the impartial opinion of a museum curator. Then, with what he has been told in mind, he should approach a good dealer, ask for *his* opinion—and if this doesn't precisely coincide with what the museum has said an interesting discussion may arise, before the dealer finally estimates the price.

Books and Periodicals.

There is today available an enormous literature in English on every possible aspect of antiques, from the most learned treatise containing original scholarly discoveries, to the simplest compendium of what is known, or some of what is known, on any general or particular subject. If well written and attractively presented, these simpler publications can be extremely useful to the beginner in the field: there is a constant demand for such " primers " and they come and go in the shops. Some of the more learned books remain cornerstones of basic knowledge, and may not be superseded for decades. At the moment there is a vogue for information to be presented in dictionary or encyclopaedia form, and the best of these books are of course extremely useful tools for whoever works with antiques. So are exhibition catalogues and sale catalogues, where sometimes leading authorities in their special fields have documented and described important items in a scholarly way.

One thing that strikes one when trying to survey the available literature is what fantastically detailed studies have been conducted into the most esoteric corners of the world of antiques. To mention some examples: books have been written, not only on English silver of the Huguenot period, on Biedermeier furniture, on almost every ceramic factory in Britain and on the Continent, on Islamic glass and Art Nouveau posters, but also on pins and pin-cushions, buttons, toy-soldiers, on dolls and jigsaw puzzles on bottle seals and very much else—there seems to be no limit to the specialisation, and there is a public for it all.

Whoever wants to keep up to date with what goes on in the world of antiques should keep an eye on at least some of the periodicals devoted to the subject that are being published in Britain. The periodicals contain articles on antiques. some written for beginners, some presenting original research of great interest to those really advanced within the special field. Added to this, most periodicals also comment on current exhibitions and fairs, and publish reviews of new books and reports on recent sales, with prices. Not the least valuable are the advertisements, many beautifully illustrated, giving details about forthcoming auction sales, and about specially fine objects that specific dealers have to offer at this particular moment.

Here is a list of some of the most useful and well-established periodicals on antiques:

The Connoisseur. Monthly.
Chestergate House. Vauxhall Bridge Road, London S.W.1.

Apollo. Monthly.
22 Davies Street, London W.1.

The Antique Collector. Monthly.
Chestergate House. Vauxhall Bridge Road, London S.W.1.

The Antique Collector's Guide. Monthly.
1–3 Wine Office Court, Fleet Street, London E.C.4.

More informal publications act as direct links between buyers and sellers of antiques, advertising specific antiques to be bought or sold. and listing current fairs of interest to dealers and collectors alike:

Antique Collecting. Monthly.
Founded 1966.
5 Church Street, Woodbridge, Suffolk.

The Antiques and Art Weekly.
Founded 1961.
181 Queen Victoria Street, London E.C.4.

Collectors' Bazaar. Monthly.
Founded 1975.
14 Broadway, London S.W.1.

5. Upkeep and Repairs.

To keep one's antiques in good condition demands constant vigilance and attention. and the problems one meets are as extensive and varied as the world of antiques itself. Let it be said at once and emphatically : for the handling of things of some age and technical complexity, one should seek the advice and assistance of professional restorers, for much damage can be done if an amateur tackles the finer points of upkeep and repair in enthusiastic ignorance. The mechanism of an old clock is to the serious clock collector as valuable an antique as the handsomest clockcase, and these fine examples of old skill and craftsmanship may be seriously and irreparably damaged by clumsy repairs by someone who takes one in hand with the only purpose of " making it go ". The beautiful joints of a drawer of an 18th-century chest can be masterpieces of traditional cabinetmaking, and should not be touched except by those who really know the old methods by which they were made, and can repeat them. And, of course, one should never apply modern chemicals (perhaps camouflaged in detergents or paints) to fragile old materials without first conferring with a restorer, who will know exactly what does which to what, whether beneficial of destructive. Most antique dealers are in regular touch with professional restorers, and will advise their clients on where to get the best assistance when questions of repair arise—and this goes for specialised areas like musical instruments, book-bindings, carpets and chair covers, as well as for the more conventional categories of antiques.

All we can do here is to touch upon some of the problems most frequently met with by those who own antique furniture, silver, pewter, glass and pottery.

Looking after Furniture.

Old furniture will always need quite **regular** repair, for much of it still has to stand the wear and tear of daily use. Many pieces are complex constructions, and the problems faced here are more manifold than those of almost any other category of antique.

It is a well-known fact that old furniture often responds unhappily to modern home-heating methods. The high, even temperatures in centrally heated rooms have made old glues dry up and crack, and old woods contract and expand in unexpected ways. Fine veneers and inlaid work have often suffered particularly badly and here one should always consult experts if one wants to obtain good and lasting improvements.

All pre-19th century furniture and many things of later make will need regular polishing to preserve the beautiful texture of the old " naked " wood, and today special polishes suitable for antique furniture are easily available, if not in one's household shop, then at good dealers in old furniture. French polishing was an invention of the early 19th century, and consists in layers of fine shellac lacquers applied to the surface and producing a brilliant gloss. Good French polishing is long and patient work, and should not easily be undertaken by the amateur. It should of course not be applied to furniture of earlier periods than is correct. The removal of old paint or polish should also be tackled with great care, and preferably under the guidance of an expert. Valuable information about what the original paint really was can be lost for ever by heavy-handed removal work, and it will be impossible to bring the piece back to its original appearance.

Locks, hinges and handles are subjected to heavy wear, and will often need replacement or repair. It is very important to the appearance of an old piece of furniture that these details be correct in period-style materials and techniques. Today many firms specialise in selling old locks, hinges and handles, or good reproductions, suitable for replacements on furniture in any period style.

Upholstery on seating furniture in regular use will frequently need renewal, and here it is very important that one should follow the style of the relevant historical period as closely as possible. There is now a big choice of materials available in all period styles, both as to texture and pattern; real horsehair is still being produced, but it is very costly. It is worth remembering that in the development of upholstery, quite a revolution happened at the beginning of the 19th century. It is important that chairs made before the invention of interior springs (or, of course, of foam rubber) should be given the hard flat seats that were used up till then. The restoration of 19th-century upholstery may be quite complicated and expensive to undertake, for it is a difficult process to cover a Victorian chair or a sofa neatly with all the necessary folds and buttons, the correct interior springing (or at least the appearance of it, to give the right curves and angles to the seats), and finish off with adding the full and rich set of trimmings, fringes and tassles in the materials and colours right for the period.

Chair seats and backs with cane-work or rush-work should be cleaned gently with warm soapy water on a soft sponge, then carefully dried and left for twenty-four hours before use. Most antique shops will be able to advise on how to get such work professionally repaired, when that is needed.

Old leather covers on chairs and tables or indeed on books need constant " feeding " not to dry up and crack. Saddle-soap will do for pieces that are not too old or precious, but in the case of things of truly venerable age or with rich decorations one should seek the advice of a museum or responsible dealer for a more subtle polish. The cleaning of really old leather and its repair when torn should also be done on expert advice only.

Looking after Gold and Silver.

Gold presents few problems to its owner for it neither rusts nor tarnishes. Any visitor to our museums will have seen gold objects made hundreds of years ago appearing as bright and shiny as if they were made yesterday. But their silver neighbours may show signs of tarnish, if the museum staffs have not very recently been doing their polishing round, and the same goes for Sheffield plate.

For centuries the only way of removing tarnish was by polishing with abrasive, and much old silver has suffered badly at the hands of over-zealous housewives and their maids: engraved ornaments have all but disappeared, the profiles of chased ornaments have lost their precision and marks have been worn away and become undecipherable. Undecorated silver can take a lot of cleaning with soft modern abrasives and soft modern silver cloths. Some of these silver cloths are impregnated with cleaning-material, and are fine for day-to-day upkeep. And now we have the fluid "dips" that remove tarnish by chemical means and work miraculously, though a few seconds in the dip is enough. Longer immersion will remove some of the real silver surface, and produce a dead and unattractive appearance. The dip method is particularly useful for objects of filigree or silver with other kinds of rich and detailed decoration. Dipped objects should be rinsed afterwards in warm water; soap or detergent is unnecessary. It is very important that silver should be meticulously dried after washing, for moisture is one of the enemies of silver. The tarnish it produces is particularly hard to remove.

In the old days, green baize was the standard protective material for storing away cleaned and polished silver. Today plastic provides perfect protection.

Looking after Pewter.

Rule one concerning the upkeep of old pewter is that it should not be over-polished. A certain matting of the surface is part of its natural ageing-process, indeed this patina represents some of the charm of this popular kind of antique. Pewter is easily contaminated by contact with salts and other chemicals, and if left for a long time in very cold surroundings, the surface will develop dark spots and bubbles; if this process is left to develop, the surface will eventually dissolve into a sort of powder. Day-by-day cleaning should be done with a soft polishing cloth, and if something stronger is needed, an oily rag with a gentle abrasive can be applied, but not too often or for too long. Pewter is very soft and the surface highly susceptible to scratches and knocks. Dents and other accidental imperfections should preferably be corrected by experts. A clumsy amateur can do much damage by well-meaning efforts to try and "do it oneself", just because the material is so soft. Engraved ornaments should of course be polished with particular care, so that the sharpness of the lines is not destroyed.

Looking after Glass.

To keep old glass is not difficult, for it is corrupted neither by rust nor moths. Undecorated glass can take a lot of cleaning in strong soapy warm (not hot!) water, and spots and impurities can be attacked with abrasives, but the fragility of the glass itself must of course always be kept in mind. Glass with cut or engraved decoration should be handled more gently, and here one can try and remove obstinate spots or marks by soaking the object concerned in a strong solution of household detergent for some hours. But glass decorated with enamelling or gilding should of course not be submitted to cleaning with abrasives nor to very strong soapy solutions. In all cases careful drying is essential to a good result.

If glass should break, which it does all too easily, it is hard to repair in a way that looks well, especially where the glass is colourless and transparent. In most cases the best one can do is to try and make the repairs look as neat and tidy as one can, for to make them invisible is very rarely possible. The broken stem of a precious wine-glass may be joined again with silver, and in such cases care should be taken that the original proportions of the glass are not unduly disturbed. Work like this should of course be entrusted only to specialists. In many cases one must resign oneself to the fact that a glass is broken beyond repair and write it off as lost, however reluctantly. Only when glass of great age or rarity is at stake is it worth trying to save it by joins and repairs with glues and rivets.

To repair old glass by replacing decayed or missing parts with new glass, is to all intents and purposes not possible. Glass is made by melting its various ingredients in furnaces at extremely high temperatures, and then submitting it to a long and gradual cooling process. Any contact between the old "cold" glass and the new hot one will involve the greatest risks of breaks and bursts in the old glass, and the method, though it has been tried with some success in a few cases, is not to be recommended

Decanters are among the most popular types of antique glass. They were normally made with stoppers, and when acquiring an old decanter, it is important to see that the original stopper is still there. Usually, a wrong stopper is easily recognised: it will differ from the decanter in the colour and consistency of the glass, as well as in patterns of decoration and the proportions of decanter and stopper may not harmonise. A decanter which has lost its stopper is a better antique than a decanter with a wrong one added. Naturally, similar problems pose themselves with glass goblets and other glasses with covers. To clean a decanter that has become stained inside, fine silver sand and water should be swilled around the inside to act as a gentle abrasive, or one can use a mixture of tea leaves and vinegar in the same way. The decanter should then be rinsed and drained by inverting it in a vase or jug until absolutely dry.

Glass sometimes suffers from what is called "glass disease". The symptoms are, first, the appearance of shades of matting, which look like dirt or impurities, but cannot be removed by rubbing. They occur most frequently where there are natural marks of use, for instance round the inner rim of a wineglass. For the weakness inherent in the glass is affected by contact with moisture of every kind, first of all by the contents which it has been filled with. But the ordinary moisture of the air will also have its effect. The disease usually develops slowly, but inexorably. In the later stages the glass will take on a "crizzled" aspect like cracked ice, and if unchecked, the process will end in total collapse.

Glass disease is caused by an imbalance in the original mixture of the ingredients that make up the glass, and it cannot be cured. All one can do is to try and stop its progress, by insulating the glass from any moisture of the air by putting it in an airtight case, or by covering the surface with some protective and invisible kind of lacquer; expert advice is necessary for the application of such remedies. Venetian glass of the 18th century, Potsdam and Bohemian glass and English glass of the late 17th century are particularly prone to glass disease. But even some 19th- and 20th-century glass can be found to suffer from glass disease. It is of course not infectious.

Looking after Pottery.

Generally speaking, glazed pottery (which of course includes porcelain), is fairly resistant to cleaning, even scrubbing with abrasives—that is, if the decorations, whether printed or enamel-painted, were properly fixed to the surface by firing when the things were first made. "Cold" (i.e., unfired) paint is very fragile, but fortunately also very rare. But gilding should be handled with some care when submitted to cleaning.

Simple, clean breaks in ceramic wares can usually be repaired at home with the help of the excellent modern glues now available. The instructions printed on the packing should be followed meticulously But when it comes to more complicated breaks and cracks, where perhaps some of the original ware has been broken "into smithereens" and has to be repaired with replacement material then expert hands and experience are needed.

It is only a generation or two since modern glues

came on to the market, and in many cases old, heavily repaired examples of ceramic ware can with advantage be re-repaired. Old, discoloured glues and ugly rivets can be removed, and the necessary repairs done much more neatly.

6. Fakes.

Whatever kind of antique one takes an interest in, one stands in danger of meeting fakes, and anyone can fall into a trap. Even learned academics and experienced dealers will at some time or another have been deceived by a skilful fake. Books and articles have been written on the subject, unveiling famous examples of fakes in the past, and many others are undoubtedly at this moment on the market. But when one handles antiques, one soon discovers that there is no neat dividing line between good honest things on the one hand, and wicked fakes on the other. The world of fakes is a complex one, full of gliding values and transitional cases.

Let us first define what we mean by a " genuine fake "—it is an object made to look like something much older and rarer than it really is, a counterfeit offered for sale as the genuine article, with the express purpose to deceive. A flagrant example is the case of the " Billies and Charlies ". They were lead figures, crudely and " primitively " made by two illiterate labourers, at the middle of the last century. They had invented these figures with their own hands and out of their own heads, and distributed them generously into various sites under excavation. For a short time the figures were accepted as products of mediaeval craftsmanship, but they were fairly soon recognised by specialists as the naïve fakes they were—though they continued to puzzle less sophisticated diggers until quite recent times.

But let us consider some less clear-cut cases. What is a " real " Chippendale chair?

If one want to be pedantic, one must say that no such thing exists for none have been preserved which are known for certain to have been made by Thomas Chippendale himself. The nearest we can come to " real " Chippendale are chairs made during his period and in his style as we know it from his pattern-book (*see* line drawing **U**13), in solid mahogany and of first-class workmanship. What makes the problem really knotty is that chairs in the style of Chippendale have been made continuously through long periods during the Victorian age, not as fake antiques, but in order to satisfy a never-ending demand for these neat and handsome chairs, and it needs a trained eye to distinguish Victorian from 18th-century Chippendale. And then we have the frank copies, made as " period furniture " from late Victorian into modern times, when the Chippendale style had become historical and attractive as such. None of these varieties are wicked fakes, but if inexperienced people are asked to pay " real " Chippendale prices for these later versions, the element of faking must be laid at the door of the vendor whose aim it has been to deceive for personal monetary gain.

Honest copies, made in admiration for the craftsmanship of past ages, may lead to misunderstanding. Philippe-Joseph Brocard (d. 1896) of Paris went to enormous trouble to learn to master the difficult technique of enamelling on glass, practised in such a masterly way by Islamic decorators of the 13th–16th centuries. He succeeded so well that some of his works can only with difficulty be distinguished from the Islamic masterpieces, especially the copies of mosque lamps with Cufic inscriptions. Fortunately he signed much of his work, and to the sharp observer the smoother quality of the 19th-century glass he used will reveal even his unsigned works as modern copies. Brocard was a fine craftsman, who surely never worked with any intention of faking.

Repairs are of course perfectly legitimate means of keeping valuable and much-loved antiques from the natural decay brought on by heavy use and the passing of time (*see* **U**17). But sometimes restorations may be so extensive that they take us into the borderland of faking.

Tudor furniture has for long been greatly admired by collectors, but it is, oh!, so easily counter-

feited, wholly or partly. It is constructed by a rich combination of framed panels, supported by bulbous feet and columns, and it is fairly easy to substitute one or two—or five or ten—parts with " restorations ". If in the end one is left with only one or two original pieces of carving, combined with a multiplicity of modern copies and variations of old carved work and with new supports added, there is not really much left of the original Tudor piece. One also finds old parts of such furniture combined with new in ways that were never dreamt of by our Tudor forefathers; the very constructions are fruits of the modern restorer's—or faker's—imagination.

All porcelain figures are made from moulds. A clever person can reproduce things moulded, like coins and certain kinds of jewellery, without too much difficulty: he can make a cast from the original and then a new mould, from which he can draw as many copies as he likes. Such copies can usually be recognised for what they are from a certain crudity of detail. But porcelain figures can pose more difficult problems than that. In some cases old moulds from one or two hundred years back have been preserved and used again. These later copies will usually be painted in a different and more varied colour-scale than those of the original period, and it may have been necessary to make small repairs to the moulds which will show in the finished product. If figures made in modern times from 18th-century moulds are presented as 18th-century work and sold at correspondingly high prices, faking is taking place. But if they are being offered for what they are—repeats, reproductions—and sold at suitably lower prices, this is of course perfectly honest—and incidentally, the figures can still give great pleasure, preserving as they do the major sculptural qualities of the original models.

Finally a word about the faking of marks. This has been done extensively on silver and pewter as well as on pottery. The famous mark of two crossed swords has from 1724 to this day been the mark of Meissen porcelain, and over the centuries a number of less exalted factories have been tempted to adopt marks so similar to the Meissen one, that at a quick glance they could be mistaken for it. Apart from these imitations, there has been quite a lot of downright faking of the Meissen mark. The most famous of English potteries is that founded by Josiah Wedgwood during the 1750s and still, of course, very much alive and active. From 1771 to this day every piece of pottery that has left the Wedgwood factory has been marked with the name WEDGWOOD, sometimes in solitary grandeur, sometimes accompanied by emblems or names of individual decorators, and from 1860 onwards often with a date-mark in the form of a single letter, that changes from one year to another. All these details can easily be checked in any up-to-date book on pottery marks, or on the firm of Josiah Wedgwood & Sons Ltd., which is the correct trade-name of the firm. But c. 1825 an indifferent producer of pottery in Stockton, called Willam Smith, began to put the word **Wedgwood**, or more frequently **Wedgewood**, after his own name or initials, on his products. In 1848 the real Wedgwood firm fought a lawsuit to prevent this misuse of their name, and the practice was stopped. But from c. 1860 until quite recently, a firm in Tunstall has been calling itself Wedgwood & Co. and marked its ware with this name, sometimes combined with the figure of a unicorn. Only a sharp observer will notice the difference between " & Co " and " & Sons "—at a quick glance. More details on the faking of ceramic marks can be found adjoining the tables of marks on **U**23-28. On faked silver marks, *see* **U**6.

These brief remarks will give the reader some indication of what kind of problems face the unwary, or for that matter even the most vigilant, when moving about the world of antiques.

How can one protect oneself? Absolute guarantees against fakes and counterfeits do not exist, as fakers and irresponsible traders use their imagination and wicked skills in ever new ways. But one can guard against being taken in by being constantly sceptical, by acquiring whatever knowledge there is about known fakes, and by using one's imagination about what can technically and financially be worthwhile for anyone to try and counterfeit.

THE LONDON

Letter	Year	Letter	Year	Letter	Year	Letter	Year	Letter	Year	Letter	Year
A	1598	a	1618	A	1638	A	1658	A	1678	A	1697
B	9	b	19	B	39	B	59	b	79	B	97
C	1600	C	20	C	40	C	Chas. II. 60	C	80	C	98
D	1	d	21	D	41	D	61	D	81	D	99
E	2	e	22	E	42	E	62	E	82	E	1700
F	Jas. I. 3	f	23	ff	43	F	63	F	83	ff	1
G	4	g	24	O	44	G	64	G	84	O	Anne. 2
h	5	h	Chas. I. 25	H	45	H	65	h	Jas. II. 85	B	3
I	6	i	26	H	46	I	66	I	86	O	4
K	7	k	27	K	47	K	67	k	87	K	5
L	8	l	28	E	48	L	68	I	88	L	6
M	9	m	29	N	Cmwth. 49	M	69	m	W. & M. 89	M	7
N	10	n	30	N	50	N	70	n	90	N	8
O	11	O	31	O	51	O	71	O	91	O	9
P	12	P	32	P	52	P	72	P	92	P	10
Q	13	q	33	O	53	Q	73	q	93	Q	11
R	14	r	34	R	54	R	74	r	94	R	12
S	15	s	35	O	55	S	75	S	Wm. III. 95	O	13
T	16	t	36	T	56	T	76	t	96	T	Geo. I. 14
V	17	v	37	B	57	W	77			B	15

PROVINCIAL SILVER MARKS

BIRMINGHAM	. .	1800		1900	
CHESTER	.	1701		1800	
EXETER	. .	1601		1800	

See also **Hall-mark**, Gen. Information.

SILVER MARKS

Letter	Date	Letter	Date	Letter	Date	Letter	Date	Letter	Date	Letter	Date
A	Geo. i. 1716	a	1736	A	1756	a	1776	A	1796	a	1816
B	17	b	37	B	57	b	77	B	97	b	17
C	18	c	38	C	58	c	78	C	98	c	18
D	19	dd	39	D	59	d	79	D	99	d	19
E	20	e	40	E	Geo.III 60	e	80	E	1800	e	Geo. IV. 20
F	21	f	41	f	61	f	81	F	1	f	21
G	22	g	42	G	62	g	82	G	2	g	22
H	23	h	43	H	63	h	83	H	3	h	23
I	24	i	44	J	64	i	84	I	4	i	24
K	25	k	45	K	65	k	85	K	5	k	25
L	26	l	46	L	66	l	86	L	6	l	26
M	Geo. II 27	m	47	m	67	m	87	M	7	m	27
N	28	n	48	N	68	n	88	N	8	n	28
O	29	o	49	O	69	o	89	O	9	o	29
P	30	p	50	P	70	p	90	P	10	p	Will.IV. 30
Q	31	q	51	Q	71	q	91	Q	11	q	31
R	32	r	52	R	72	r	92	R	12	r	32
S	33	s	53	S	73	s	93	S	13	s	33
T	34	t	54	T	74	t	94	T	14	t	34
V	35	u	55	u	75	u	95	U	15	u	35

PROVINCIAL SILVER MARKS

NEWCASTLE	1702		1800
SHEFFIELD	1800		1900
YORK	1700		1800

THE LONDON SILVER MARKS

A	1836	X	1856	A	1876	a	1896	A	1916
B	Vic. 37	b	57	B	77	b	97	b	17
C	38	c	58	C	78	c	98	c	18
D	39	d	59	D	79	d	99	d	19
E	40	e	60	E	80	e	1900	e	20
F	41	f	61	F	81	f	Ed. VII. 1	f	21
G	42	g	62	G	82	g	2	g	22
H	43	h	63	H	83	h	3	h	23
J	44	i	64	I	84	i	4	i	24
K	45	k	65	K	85	k	5	k	25
L	46	l	66	L	86	l	6	l	26
M	47	m	67	M	87	m	7	m	27
N	48	n	68	N	88	n	8	n	28
O	49	o	69	O	89	o	9	o	29
P	50	p	70	P	90	p	Geo. V. 10	p	30
Q	51	q	71	Q	91	q	11	q	31
R	52	r	72	R	92	r	12	x	32
S	53	s	73	S	93	s	13	s	33
T	54	t	74	T	94	t	14	t	34
U	55	v	75	U	95	u	15	u	35

A	Ed. VIII. 1936
B	Geo. VI 37
C	38
D	39
E	40
F	41
G	42
H	43
I	44
K	45
L	46
M	47
N	48
O	49
P	50
Q	51
R	Eliz. II. 52
S	53
T	54
U	55

SCOTTISH AND IRISH SILVER MARKS

EDINBURGH	.	1700		1800
GLASGOW	. .	1700		1800
DUBLIN	. .	1700		1800

MARKS ON ENGLISH POTTERY AND PORCELAIN

Many of the marks found on ceramics are merely the marks of painters and workman. Even when identified, they are not a sure guide to the place of manufacture, as these people would work in many different factories in the course of their careers. The throwers or "repairers" (the workers who assembled the various parts of figures, etc.) invariably used a mark scratched in the body of the ware prior to the biscuit-firing. These marks when *under* the glaze can safely be treated as genuine. A mark which has been ground in after

firing, in order to deceive, will not have the characteristic burr or raised edge produced when soft clay is scratched.

Painters and gilders would generally use one of the colours in their palette or gilt to mark the wares upon which they worked. This was probably for the benefit of the management as payment was often on a piecework basis.

The marks used on English wares were applied in several different ways—by incising, impressing, painting, or by transfer-printing *under* the glaze in blue (also in green after 1850). Marking by painting, transfer-printing, or stencilling *over* the glaze in enamel colours is always liable to be fraudulent as these types of mark can be added at any time after the piece has been made.

From 1842–83 many manufacturers' wares were marked with the "diamond-mark", illustrated above. This was an indication that the design had been reg stered with the British Patent Office. Ceramics was Class **IV**, indicated in the topmost section of the mark. This gave copyright protection for three years. After 1883 the mark was written as a number, *e.g.*, Rd. No. 12345.

A further indication of late wares is the inclusion of the word "England" in the mark. This was necessary to comply with the American McKinley Tariff Act of 1891. The full term "Made in England" is an indication of 20th century manufacture.

MARKS ON CONTINENTAL POTTERY AND PORCELAIN

FRANCE

Saint-Cloud
c.1678 ~ 1766

early incised mark

St.C
T
c.1722 - 66
in blue

Chantilly
1725 ~ 1800

'hunting-horn' mark

red on early wares

blue & other colours from c.1750

Mennecy
1734 - 1806

'D.V.' mark for duc de Villeroy

·D·V· in red

in black D·V

D.V. incised

Sceaux
c.1763 ~ 94

S·X incised

c.1775 ~

Lille 1784 - 1817

stencilled in red

Sèvres

First established at Vincennes c.1738, moved to Sèvres c.1756 ~

early Vincennes marks

mark with date-letter for 1753
letters were used from 1753 until 17th July 1793 to show year of manufacture

A ~ 1753	V ~ 1774
B ~ 1754	X ~ 1775
C ~ 1755	Y ~ 1776
D ~ 1756	Z ~ 1777
E ~ 1757	AA ~ 1778
F ~ 1758	BB ~ 1779
G ~ 1759	CC ~ 1780
H ~ 1760	DD ~ 1781
I ~ 1761	EE ~ 1782
J ~ 1762	FF ~ 1783
K ~ 1763	GG ~ 1784
L ~ 1764	HH ~ 1785
M ~ 1765	II ~ 1786
N ~ 1766	JJ ~ 1787
O ~ 1767	KK ~ 1788
P ~ 1768	LL ~ 1789
Q ~ 1769	MM ~ 1790
R ~ 1770	NN ~ 1791
S ~ 1771	OO ~ 1792
T ~ 1772	PP ~ 1793
U ~ 1773	

(until 17th July)

in blue 1793 - 1804
Jéures

M.Nᵉ in red
Sèvres 1803 - 11 - 1804
Consular period

Paris factories

rue Thiroux
c.1775 ~ 19th. Cent.

A blue   A red

GS red

LEVEILLE
12 Rue THIROUX

rue de Crussol
1789 ~ 19th.Cent.
Christopher Potter

B
Potter
42

E.B   PB
all in blue

rue de Charonne
1795 - c.1840

DARTE
FRERES   in red
A PARIS

rue de Bondy
1780 - 1829
gold

Pont-aux-Choux
1743 ~ c.1785
gold

La Courtille 1771 ~ c.1840

in blue

incised.

Clignacourt
1771 - c.1798

in gold

M stencilled in red.

marks on reproductions made by:-

Samson & Co.
1845 ~

ε··· on so-called 'Chinese-Lowestoft'

Japanese and Chinese wares
Persian and Hispano~ Moresque
Limousin enamels, Italian wares

Sèvres and terra-cotta

Meissen

French, Italian, Spanish, English porcelain, European enamels

---

It was not until the adoption on Meissen porcelain in 1723 of the " K.P.M." and in 1724 of the cross-swords (from the arms of Saxony) that marks began to be used at all regularly in Europe. The placing of the mark underneath and the use of blue are clear indications that the Chinese model was being followed. The Meissen practice was then adopted by other German and, indeed, by most porcelain factories of repute.

Throughout the 18th century the practice was never regularised, and except for a brief period in France from 1766, and two years later in the Dutch town of Delft, there was no compulsory marking of wares. The factories of repute, proud of their productions, added a recognised mark and even used it, as at Nymphenburg, as part of the decoration. Their imitators left their wares unmarked or employed a mark likely to be mistaken for a more famous one: Weesp and Tournay both adopted a version of the Meissen crossed-swords;

MARKS ON CONTINENTAL POTTERY AND PORCELAIN

GERMANY
Meissen 1710~

K.P.M

'Königliche Porzellan Manufaktur 1723-24.

'caduceus-mark' c.1723

blue

cipher (for 'Augustus Rex') of King of Poland, generally 1725-1730. Common on forgeries

c.1724~

'Dot period' c.1763-1774

'Marcolini Period' 1774-1814

19th Cent

all in blue

Vienna 1719-1864
Du Paquier period (1719-1744)

in blue c.1720-30

State period (1744-1784)

---

red and other colours

impressed

blue

Sorgenthal period (1784-1864)

blue, 1820-27

blue, c.1850-64

Höchst c.1750-96

1750-c.1765 red

1762-96 blue

c.1765-1774 blue

Fürstenberg 1753~ present

F   F

F   all in blue

Frankenthal 1755-99

PH

PHF
impressed marks of Paul Hannong. c.1755-c.59.

in blue c.1756.

---

c.1756-59 in blue

Nymphenburg 1753~ present

impressed 1754-65

impressed c.1850-62

1763-67

'hexagram mark'

Ludwigsburg 1756-1824

in blue 1758-93

in blue c.1775-1810

marks of factories in imitation of Meissen

Freiwaldau H. Schmidt 1842~

Gräfenroda Dornheim, Koch & Fischer 1860~

DKF

Kloster-Veilsdorf modern mark

Limbach 1772-88

Plaue-on-Havel Schierholz 1817~

ITALY Florence
Medici porcelain 1575-87

in blue.

Venice
Vezzi factory c.1719-1727

Ven. incised

Ven; red, green or blue

Cozzi factory c.1764-1812

in red.

Capodimonte 1743-59

impressed

gold   blue
similar marks on Buen Retiro of Spain 1760-1808.

Naples 1771-1806

in blue

1772 in blue or incised

N incised

Doccia, 1735~

in blue   impressed

---

the torches of La Courtille, the hooks of Rauenstein, the hayforks of Rudolstadt, the "L"s of Limbach, and the "W" of Wallendorf, were all drawn in such a way as to resemble the Meissen mark.

The firm of Samson & Co. was established in Paris in 1845, claiming to make "Reproductions of Ancient Works emanating from the Museums and from Private Collections". When imitating the true hard-paste porcelain of the Far East or the Continent, Samson's wares are difficult to detect, due to their being made from similar materials, whereas his reproductions of such English factories as Bow, Chelsea, and Derby are more easily recognised as fakes. Unfortunately the range of Samson's marks, illustrated above, do not appear to have been regularly used, or, as is sometimes the case, the original mark has been removed by grinding or by etching away with acid, and a replica of a known genuine mark added.

CHINESE REIGN MARKS   MING DYNASTY

洪武 年製 — Hung Wu (1368~1398)

建文 — Chien Wên (1399~1402)

Yung Lo (1403~1424) In archaic script

永樂 年製 — Yung Lo (1403~1424)

洪熙 — Hung Hsi (1425)

大明宣 德年製 — Hsüan Tê (1426~1435)

In seal characters

正統 — Chêng T'ung (1436~1449)

景泰 — Ching T'ai (1450~1457)

天順 — T'ien Shun (1457~1464)

大明成 化年製 — Ch'êng Hua (1465~1487)

成化 — In seal characters

大明弘 治年製 — Hung Chih (1488~1505)

大明正 德年製 — Chêng Tê (1506~1521)

大明嘉 靖年製 — Chia Ching (1522~1566)

大明隆 慶年製 — Lung Ch'ing (1567~1572)

大明萬 曆年製 — Wan Li (1573~1619)

泰昌 — T'ai Ch'ang (1620)

大明天 啟年製 — T'ien Ch'i (1621~1627)

崇禎 年製 — Ch'ung Chêng (1628~1643)

Factory marks in the Western sense are practically unknown on Chinese porcelain wares, while those purporting to record the period of manufacture are so liable to be "commemorative", or even deliberately fraudulent, as to be a frequent cause of dispute among students. Marks of the Ming Chinese Emperors, Hsüan Tê, Ch'êng Hua and Chia Ching are commonly found on wares of the reign of the Ch'ing Emperor K'ang Hsi, while the reign name of K'ang Hsi himself, rare on the abundant porcelain of his period, is chiefly found on 19th- and 20th-century wares.

Under the rule of the Ming Emperors (1368-1644) the Sung ideals in pottery were largely rejected in favour of the vogue for fine-grained white porcelain heralding the beginning of a new period in Chinese ceramic history with its centre in the town of Ching-tê Chên in Kiangsi province where a new Imperial factory was started in 1369 with a prolific output of early Ming blue-and-white

CHINESE REIGN MARKS   CH'ING DYNASTY

Shun Chih
(1644~1661)

In seal characters

In seal characters

Ch'ien Lung
(1736~1795)

K'ang Hsi
(1662~1722)

In seal characters

In seal characters

Chia Ch'ing
(1796~1821)

Yung Chêng
(1723~1735)

In seal characters

Tao Kuang
(1821~1850)

In seal characters

Kuang Hsü
(1874~1908)

In seal characters

Hsien Fêng
(1851~1861)

In seal characters

Hsüan T'ung
(1909~1912)

T'ung Chih
(1862~1873)

Hung Hsien
(1916)
(Yüan Shih-kai)

Drawn by J. P. Cushion, Victoria and Albert Museum.

and fine enamel-painted porcelain both for the court and later for general use and export.

Following the fall of the Ming Dynasty in 1644 their declining culture was revived by the Ch'ing Emperor K'ang Hsi (1662—1722) who was a great patron of the arts. The European influence of the French and Netherlandish Jesuits at his courts is seen in the Baroque character of the early Ch'ing porcelain.

There was a backward-looking tendency during the reigns of Yung-Chêng (1723–35) and Ch'ien Lung (1736–95) when exact copies of the classical Sung wares and the early Ming painted porcelain were made.

The Imperial porcelain of the 19th century was as a rule carefully and weakly correct in following earlier styles and models. The factory was burnt in 1853 by the T'ai-ping rebels and hardly recovered before the 1911 revolution ended the Dynasty.

COLLECTORS' GLOSSARY

Acanthus, a thistle-like plant which grows abundantly in the Mediterranean countries, and which has inspired decorators from classical antiquity to modern times to fine leaf ornaments. The acanthus appears on Corinthian columns on Greek and Roman temples, it lends its rhythm to stone carvings on medieval cathedrals, and runs in friezes on innumerable Renaissance buildings and art objects. During the Baroque, it appears, rich and majestic, handled with particular grandeur in England by Grinling Gibbons (1648–1721). In the revival styles of the 19th cent., the acanthus appears in all kinds of connections.

One reason for the never-ending popularity of the acanthus is that it can be adapted to almost any shape, to fit the capital of a column as well as a frieze or an "un-ending" flat pattern. And it can be interpreted in any material, carved in stone or wood, printed and painted, woven in silk, wrought in iron—the possibilities are endless.

Acanthus ornament in wrought iron. Paris, 17th cent.

Animaliers (Fr. = " animal makers "), term used to describe the group of French 19th cent. sculptors who specialised in the modelling of animals. They made them singly or in pairs to form a group and the animals are described in much naturalistic detail and always in vigorous movement, leaping, running, fighting. They are cast in bronze, in dimensions small enough for them to be used as table ornaments. The originator of the genre was Antoine-Louis Barye (1796–1875). The quality of the works of *les animaliers* can vary greatly, and there has been much recasting of good models, with results which are inevitably imperfect.

Aquamanile (Lat. *aqua* = water and *manus* = hand), an ewer of brass or bronze used for ceremonial handwashing for church or lay purposes during the Middle Ages. One popular and picturesque version has the shape of a standing lion. Its body contains the water, which can be poured out through a spout concealed in its tongue, while the tail is twirled up to serve as handle.

Arabesque, a decorative motif consisting of curved and interlacing lines, symmetrically arranged; a stylised interpretation of branches, tendrils and leaves as seen in nature. As the name suggests, the motif was invented by the Arabs, who used it for hundreds of years, partly because the representation of beings, animal or human, were not permitted by their culture. Arabesques were used most impressively to cover large areas, like tiled walls and carpets. From the Renaissance onwards, the Europeans adapted the arabesque to decorate inlaid furniture, ceramic plates and tiles and textiles.

Aquamanile bronze, 14th cent.

Arita, see **Imari.**

Automobile mascots, sculptured ornaments affixed to the bonnet of motor-cars. They came into fashion immediately after the first world war, when fast cars became symbols of the modern age of streamlined speed. The mascots have been made in a variety of materials, silver or silver plate, brass and bronze, cast glass. The figures usually suggest speed (girls' heads or figures facing the oncoming wind with ecstatic joy) or power (prancing horses, falcons' heads). Today they are becoming increasingly collectable.

Biscuit (Fr. = " twice baked "), porcelain (*see* L98) which has been fired but not glazed. This gives a matted marble-like surface, and *biscuit* has been widely used for porcelain sculpture.

Blanc-de-Chine, a kind of Chinese porcelain, made into vessels or figures, covered with a fine, milky-white glaze and otherwise unornamented. Within the great ceramic history of China, *blanc-de-Chine* represents a distinctive and strictly limited group. It was made during the 18th, 19th and 20th centuries in Tê-Hua in Fukien province. Much of it was exported to Europe. The serene figure of the female deity Kuan-Yin has always been very popular in the West, and many models have been made, varying from the exquisite to the clumsy and angular. Of great interest are also the groups of Europeans with their Chinese servants, made in Tê-Hua for the Western market.

Boulle (Buhl) furniture, a luxurious kind of case furniture, first made in Paris by the Court cabinetmaker André-Charles Boulle (Buhl is the Germanised form) (1642–1732). Cupboards, chests, clocks, etc. are veneered with tortoiseshell and inlaid with patterns in bronze. The technique was practised in Paris throughout the 18th cent. by the sons and successors of André-Charles Boulle, and later by imitators in many countries. Boulle furniture has been made right up to recent times.

Britannia Metal, a soft variety of pewter compounded of tin, antimony and copper. It was first made in S' effield during the late 18th cent. under the name of White Metal, and used as a cheap substitute for pewter. The name Britannia Metal was introduced in 1817. By the 1840s it was increasingly being electroplated (*q.v.*) with silver. Such wares are frequently marked EPBM = Electro Plated Britannia Metal, the letters being placed in separate oval frames to simulate hallmarks on silver. The metal and its markings have been in use well into the 20th cent.

Brocard, Philippe-Joseph, see **U19.**

Bullet teapot, a modern collectors' term for silver teapots, as first made by Huguenot goldsmiths in London at the time of Queen Anne, with the body and its cover made in the form of a sphere, with a low foot and a spout of silver and a black wooden handle. Bullet teapots were also made after the reign of Queen Anne, and the shape was eventually translated into porcelain and earthenware, in England and on the Continent.

Cameos are cut from stones or from shells which have natural layers of different colours, so that the ornaments stand in high relief as well as in a contrasting colour against the background. The Italians have always been masters in cameo-cutting. During the 19th cent. they had a large production of shell cameos with white figures on a brown ground, the whole mounted in gold or silver and used as brooches. Today cameos are being mass-produced in man-made materials in imitation of the genuine articles.

Shell cameo brooch with white figures on a brown background. Italy, c. 1860.

Candlesticks have of course been household necessities as long as candles were main means of lighting. Over the ages people have rigged up all kinds of cheap and simple candleholders, but the handsome tall candlestick on a steady foot has existed since the late Middle Ages. They have been made in brass and pewter, silver or Sheffield plate in ever-varying forms. The drawings show a few examples from different periods.

Cased glass, a technique whereby clear or coloured glass is covered by a layer of glass in a different shade; when patterns are cut through the top layer the inner core will be revealed and interesting colour effects and contrasts result.

The most famous piece of cased glass in history is the Portland Vase, of Roman make (1st cent. A.D.) now in the British Museum (see Section L).

Plate of ruby red glass cased with milky white cut through to the red base. Bohemia, c. 1850.

Celadon, a soft greyish-green coloured glaze, widely used on Chinese pottery and porcelain from the Sung period (960–1279) and well into the 19th cent. The name was given it by the Europeans: in Honoré d'Urfé's 17th cent. pastoral romance " L'Astreé " a shepherd called Celadon wore a costume of this subtle and beautiful colour. The French imported a lot of Celadon ware from China during the 18th cent., and the best pieces were mounted in elaborate bronze.

Champlevé see Enamel.

Ching-tê Chên, see U27.

Engraving after Figures chinoises et tartares, by Watteau c. 1719.

Chinoiserie, ornamentation used in 7th, 18th and early 19th cent. Europe, which made wide

16th cent.   17th cent.   c. 1790.   19th cent.

Candlesticks from different periods, all of brass, except the one in the middle, which is of Sheffield plate.

use of Oriental themes " chinamen ", pagodas, bells, parasols, dragons and the like. Chinoiserie was preferably used on porcelain, silks and lacquered furniture, materials which were admiringly associated with China and the East. It was also expressed in architecture. in garden houses in pagoda and pavilion style, the Pagoda in Kew Gardens, built in 1762 by Sir William Chambers, being a famous example. Chinoiserie was based on an incomplete knowledge of the Oriental models, and this gave full scope for imagination and caprice on the part of the European designers The best examples date from early and mid 18th cent., the rococo versions being particularly charming and suggestive of " the dream of Cathay ".

Chippendale, Thomas, see B15, U13 and 19.

Cloisonné, see Enamel.

Clutha glass, decorative vessels of tinted glass, made during the 1890s by the Glasgow firm of James Couper & Sons to designs by Christopher Dresser. The glass, usually amber or green, is made purposely rough and " primitive " with bubbles and striations. and formed into free, furnace-worked shapes. Occasionally other colours are added. The more elaborate examples are marked underneath in acid-etching with CLUTHA and name of producer and designer.

Cranberry glass, a modern collectors' term for Victorian glass of a deep red colour. It is reminiscent of the famous 17th-cent. ruby glass, but it is less brilliantly red and was cheaper to make. It had its great vogue during the latter part of the 19th cent., and was used for all manner of objects, often combined with clear glass in handles, stems and the like.

Creamware, a ceramic material which has a cream-coloured glaze over a solid and resistant body, the clay usually containing calcined flint. Creamware was developed in Staffordshire during the middle years of the 18th cent.. and brought to perfection in the course of the 1760s by Josiah Wedgwood. He formed the new ware into shapes which were at the same time practical and handsome, suitable for every household, and with a distinctive touch of the Neo-Classical style which was just coming into fashion. When his product was complete and perfect, he appealed to Royalty for patronage and received permission to call his invention Queen's Ware.

Soon creamware was put into production by most Staffordshire firms, and, most importantly, by the factory at Leeds, who became a major producer. Because of its excellent ceramic qualities, its elegant appearance and reasonable price, creamware became the standard material for plates, dishes and the like all over the world and by the beginning of the 19th cent. it was being widely produced on the Continent. The rise of creamware meant the decline of faience (q.v.). Until quite recently, English creamware was still the basis for most of the ceramic tableware used in the world.

Cymric silver, jewellery, table-silver and plate in a " Celtic " variety of the Art Nouveau (see **U15**), made by various designers and producers to the orders of Liberty's of Regent Street and sold in their shop. The objects were serially produced, but looked hand-made, with a wide use of enamelling, stones and " hammered " surfaces. Many examples have the word CYMRIC struck next to maker's mark. The best period for Cymric silver was c. 1900–12, but the genre was not finally given up until 1927. Cf. Tudric pewter.

Davenport, a special type of writing desk, originally made for travelling, small in size, with a sloping top and three or four drawers opening to the side. According to tradition, it got its name from one Captain Davenport, who ordered such a desk from Gillow's in Lancaster in the early 19th cent. This is, however, apparently apocryphal, for the type has now been traced back to the late 18th cent. The early examples

are compact in shape and devoid of ornamentation. But as the 19th cent. proceeded, the type became popular as a lady's desk, and it was provided with pigeon-holes on top and richly ornamented in Neo-Rococo. Most of the extant examples are veneered with mahogany. Davenports remained in regular use until the end of the Victorian age.

Davenport early 19th cent.

" Diamond-mark ", see **U24**.

Dolls have for some time been important collectors' items. Christie's have regular doll sales at their South Kensington rooms, and rare examples can on occasion fetch sums of four figures. Connoisseurs distinguish expertly between dolls with heads of wax or bisque (= biscuit, q.v.), eyes, wigs and of course clothes also influence prices, and so do marks and makers' signatures. The dolls which change hands date almost exclusively from the 19th and 20th cents. Related material like doll's-house furniture and toys is normally included in the sales. Anybody interested in this highly specialized branch of collecting is advised to study the Christie catalogues and the literature that has grown up around the subject.

Electroplating. The process of coating one metal with another by the use of an electric current was invented during the early years of the 19th cent., but became widely used, especially in Sheffield and Birmingham, after 1840 when the Birmingham firm of Elkington patented their method for coating copper with silver in this manner. Eventually nickel silver, compounded of nickel, copper and zinc, was increasingly employed as a base for the silver plating, and the products were marked EPNS = Electro Plated Nickel Silver, the letters being sometimes placed in separate oval frames to simulate hall-marks on silver. This ware was widely used until the 1920s and 1930s.

Enamel, is glass, usually brilliantly coloured, which has been crushed to powder and mixed with oily fluids. It is applied to metal, pottery and glass for decorative purposes.

When applied to faience (q.v.) or porcelain (see **L98**), the enamels are painted on to the glazed surface, the object is fired at a moderate temperature and the colours will be permanently fixed. Similar methods are used for enamelling on glass, both vessels and windows, and for enamelling on enamelled surfaces, as practised so charmingly in Birmingham and Bilston during the 18th cent.

When applied to the hard, smooth surfaces of metals, special methods are needed to prevent the colours from running. Among the most important are:

Champlevé: the outlines of the pattern are engraved or cut into the surface, and the enamel is poured into the grooves.

Cloisonné: the outlines of the pattern are drawn up by tiny dividing walls which are soldered on to the surface, and the enamels are poured into the spaces in between.

Plique-à-jour: enamels are filled into the empty spaces in a carefully prepared net of metal threads.

Enamelling has been practised with mastery in ancient, medieval and modern times. The Chinese and Japanese have used enamels on copper and brass in complex combinations for several hundred years. During the 19th cent., French artist-craftsmen used all techniques most delicately, while Russian enamelling of the same period is picturesque and robust, and became widely influential.

Épergne, centrepiece for the luxuriously laid table, carrying baskets and bowls for sweets, nuts, fruit, macaroons and the like. It is an 18th-cent. invention, and was at first made in silver, later in colourful porcelain or earthenware, in glass and eventually in Sheffield plate. Its purpose was always more to be ornamental than useful, and in the making of épergnes, goldsmiths, potters and glassmakers let their fancy roam freely, whether making them in rococo or neo-classical form or as Chinoiserie (*q.v.*).

Etagère, *see* **Whatnot.**

Fabergé, Peter Carl (1846–1920), Russian goldsmith. From 1870 onwards his firm in St. Petersburg produced great quantities of luxury goods, mostly miniature objects such as gold boxes, picture frames, cigarette cases, umbrella handles, all finely wrought, richly enamelled and some even set with precious stones. Famous are his Easter eggs, which, when opened, are found to contain a tiny model of a carriage, a string of miniature pictures framed in gold and skilfully folded, and the like. The firm also made miniature figures of animals carved in semi-precious stones such as agate and neo-phryte, and other varieties of super sophisticated luxury trinkets.

Fabergé's products had a rich, aristocratic and international clientèle, with the Imperial family as the keenest patrons of all. He employed a large staff of first-rate goldsmiths, and had a phenomenal commercial success, running branches in Moscow, Odessa, Kiev and for a time also in London. The whole structure collapsed with the revolution in 1917. Fabergé products are sometimes marked with his name in Russian characters and the mark of the workmaster, under whose supervision the object was made.

Faience, a ceramic ware of porous, lightweight, fired clay covered with a milky-white, non-transparent tin glaze. It began as an imitation of Chinese porcelain, and was usually decorated with coloured ornamentation As the painted motifs have to be applied directly on to the wet glaze to be fired with it. the colours are absorbed into the damp surface as if it were blotting-paper, and the painter has to work fast, without changing his mind or correcting his work. This gives to faience painting an imminence, at times a nonchalance, which is its greatest charm.

The name faience is derived from Faenza, the name of a north Italian town, which has had a large and important output from the 15th cent.

to this day. But Faenza was only one of many centres in Italy to produce this kind of ware during the Renaissance, which in some contexts is described as Maiolica (*q.v.*). The word faience is applied more specifically to tin-glazed ceramic ware made in northern Europe during post-Renaissance times.

Fairings (lit. a gift bought from a fair), small porcelain groups telling simple stories of a sentimental or gross kind, with titles painted on the base like " The Orphan " or " The Wedding Night ". They were made for the English market in Germany from late 19th cent. until 1914, the firm of Conta & Böhme in Saxony being particularly productive. They were cheap to buy at the time, today they are collectors' items at modest prices. They are now being made in modern copies.

Friggers, objects made by glassblowers outside working hours. Some were made by apprentices in training, others by highly-skilled and experienced men, who could display their personal fancies and idiosyncracies more freely when " friggering " than when working on instructions to produce commercial goods.

Furnace-work, the forming and decorating of vessels by the glassblower in front of his furnace, while the glass is still hot and pliable.

Gallé, Emile (1846–1904) of Nancy in Lorraine, maker of art glass, decorative pottery and luxury furniture, and a main exponent of Art Nouveau (*see* **U15**) in Europe. Gallé began making decorative glass during the 1870s, and at the Paris exhibition in 1889 he created a world sensation with his imaginative and technically complex art glass. In that year he began the production of carved and inlaid furniture, while he went on developing his glass-making to ever greater heights of intricacy and sophistication. Flowers, leaves and insects were the chief decorative themes, and texts from contemporary poets were sometimes integrated into the patterns. He invented endless variations and combinations of coloured glass, many models being produced in a personal version of the cased glass technique (*q.v.*). The output of his factories was enormous, and while the standardized cased glass models made for the commercial market may become monotonous, those composed for individual clients in one to five copies are marvels of beauty and originality. Every item that left the works in Nancy were marked with his name (*see* **U6**). Pottery production, which was never very important, seems to have ended in 1892 and furniture making finished with his death. But the glassmaking plant carried on until 1935, making standardized cased glass in an ever more repetitious manner, and still signed with his name. This long posthumous production of indifferent glass has done much to lower his reputation.

Goss, ware from the Staffordshire pottery, founded by W. H. Goss in 1858 and active until the Second World War. Its fame is mainly built on the masses of miniature models in porcelain of objects of local fame or association, with the arms of the locality printed in colours, like the Coronation Chair with the arms of Westminster or the gold cup in Dorchester Cathedral with the arms of Dorchester. Goss mementoes have been collected systematically since before the First World War, and are today sold by the handful at modest, but steady prices. The

E. Gallé à Nancy.

Gallé

Cristallerie de Gallé à Nancy

firm also produced statuettes in Parian (*q.v.*), models of the houses of famous men and many other small, toy-like objects.

Hepplewhite, George, *see* **B31** and **U13.**

Imari, a port on the Japanese island of Kyushu, whence porcelain made at the nearby production centre of Arita was exported in large quantities. The name applies particularly to the wares made from the 17th cent. and until recently, with red and dark blue ornaments on a white ground, accompanied by plenty of gilding; in essence the style changed little over the long period when Imari porcelain enjoyed its great popularity in the West. The best examples are very fine, while other pieces made in the later stages can be somewhat crude.

Isnik pottery, a kind of faience (*q.v.*), made in Isnik in Anatolia between *c.* 1550 and 1700. Characteristic are the bold floral designs in brilliant blues, greens and tomato reds, which decorate plates and dishes, bowls, ewers and tiles. Isnik pottery was made in great quantities, and good examples are frequently changing hands within the antique trade in Britain.

Kelmscott Press, a printing press set up in 1890 by William Morris (*see* **B43**) in a cottage in Hammersmith. Here he produced *c.* 50 books from handcut and specially designed type, on handmade paper, every page being most carefully laid out with exquisite borders and vignettes. Medieval illuminated manuscript books and early printed books were his chief sources of inspiration. The Kelmscott Press finished working in 1896, two years after Morris's death. Morris's work sparked off a revival in fine book production at home and abroad, which has lasted until today. The press was named after Kelmscott Manor in Gloucestershire, which Morris had aquired as a summer home in 1871. He is buried in the village church, and the Manor, which contains many Morris memories is open to the public.

Vignette from the Kelmscott Press, 1897.

Macdonald, Margaret, *see* **Mackintosh, Charles Rennie.**

Mackintosh, Charles Rennie (1868–1928), Scottish architect and designer. From the late 1890s until the First World War he designed several important buildings in Glasgow and elsewhere in Scotland, and he also composed complete interiors, including the furniture, clocks, light-fittings, etc. His taste for what was simple and rectilinear was remarkably advanced for his time, and perfectly attuned to the new sober intellectual style that was emerging on the Continent. At exhibitions in Vienna in 1900 and in Turin in 1902 he gained enthusiastic international recognition. (For sale of sensational chair, *see* **U6.**) He married Margaret Macdonald (1865–1933), an important artist and designer in her own right.

Mahogany, a very hard wood with a fine grain and distinctive markings. Because it is so hard, carved work retains its precision even after years of wear. Mahogany can also be polished to a wonderfully high gloss and sparkle. Because of these qualities it has been widely used for fine furniture ever since it was first imported into Europe early in the 18th cent. The dark Cuban mahogany (Swietenia) was first used

most widely, later much fine mahogany (Khaya) from Africa was in demand. The English were the first to use mahogany for furniture, and it gave distinctive character to many of their finest 18th cent. products, like the chairs in the styles of Chippendale and Hepplewhite (*see* **U13**) and, as veneers, on chests and cupboards.

Maiolica, a ceramic ware with a white tin glaze and decorated with painted figures, often with a metallic lustre sheen. The name itself appears to have been derived from Majorca because ware of this kind by Hispano-Moresque potters was largely imported into Italy, the ships arriving by way of this island. The name has been retained for tin-glazed ware with painted decoration made in various Italian centres during the Renaissance, but it can also be defined as Faience (*q.v.*).

Majolica, a ceramic ware of the 19th cent., invented at the Minton factory in 1849, and imitated all over Europe within a short time. It is a kind of earthenware, suitable for bold modelling on a large scale, and when covered with colourful glazes in greens and browns, particularly well suited for outdoor goods, *jardinières* on tall stands or decorative sculptures. Majolica tiles became extremely popular for covering halls, kitchens, etc. Some of them are handsomely provided with relief decoration, while the fact that they could easily be washed down with water added to their popularity.

Marquetry, inlaid work of woods in constrasting colours. The patterns can be geometrical (and this is particularly suitable when marquetry is used for floors), but the technique can also be applied to veneered furniture, with delicate motifs of flowers, animals or human figures with lively curves and much fine detail.

Mary Gregory glass, an imprecise but generally accepted term used to describe a group of 19th-cent. coloured glass decorated in opaque white enamels with pretty pictures of children playing and the like. The genre probably originated in Bohemia, but it was widely produced also in Britain and in the USA. Mary Gregory is believed to have been an American glass painter, but nothing is known of her life or personality, and no existing piece of glass can be ascribed to her.

Netsuke, a clasp or sliding toggle, used on the sash of the Japanese kimono, to carry a small bag or box for the little necessities of daily life. Netsuke can be made in a variety of materials, wood, horn, ivory, bamboo, etc.; and carved into sculptured form or covered with black lacquer ornamented with pictures in gold. The subjects of the decorations are usually taken from Japanese folklore or mythology. Netsuke have been collectors' items for many decades.

Niello, a method for decorating silver. A line pattern is engraved into the silver surface, and the lines are filled with an alloy of metals, which produces a black colour. The black makes a handsome contrast to the whiteness of the silver, and niello has been one of the most ancient ways of ornamenting the precious metal, having been used in classical antiquity as well as in pre-Christian and medieval Europe. Later, it gave way to more sophisticated methods of decoration.

Opaline, modern collectors' word used to describe an important group of French 19th cent. ornamental glass. *Opaline* is made of opaque, usually milky-white glass with an opalescent sheen. The best *opaline* is the earliest, which dates from the Napoleonic period and the Restoration. It comes in vases, urns, ewers and the like, severely Neo-Classical in shape and frequently mounted in brass or bronze. After *c.*1830, the shapes become less austere, and the glass is sometimes tinted into pastel shades. *Opaline* became widely used for dainty flacons for ladies' boudoirs and decorated with gilding and pretty painted flowers. After *c.*1860 the whole genre degenerated; the opalescent glass was replaced by a grey and dull kind of material, and decorations in relief were produced by machine-pressing. *Opaline* with painted decorations was also made in England.

Ewer and basin of *opaline* glass mounted in brass. France c. 1830.

Papier-maché (French literally: "chewed paper"), one of the earliest man-made materials, produced from pulped paper, rags, chalk, sand and glues. After mixing and preparation, it becomes plastic and can be pressed and formed into any variety of shapes. When covered in black varnish, inlaid with mother-of-pearl, gilt and painted, it becomes very attractive. *Papier-maché* was invented in England in the late 18th cent., and Birmingham become an important centre of production. It was particularly well suited for trays, covered boxes and other small and medium-sized objects, but by the middle of the 19th cent. whole pieces of furniture of *papier-maché* were also being made. By this time, the taste for it had spread to the Continent, and it was soon being widely produced in Europe. The fashion for *papier-maché* declined towards the end of the century, when the market was being flooded by so many new inventions of materials and processes.

Parian ware, a kind of opaque white porcelain with a surface that gives an illusion of marble. It was invented in England c.1845, and used by many porcelain factories for the production of statuettes, groups and busts in sculptured forms for use as ornaments for parlours; it was sometimes called "statuary porcelain". Parian ware was imitated, name and all, in many European countries and in the USA.

The name is derived from Paros, a Greek island which in classical antiquity provided a particularly fine marble, much sought after by sculptors.

Pastille burners, miniature models of buildings, made of Staffordshire earthenware, glazed and painted, and often of fantastic shapes, with plenty of window openings. When a pastille was burned inside, the windows lit up prettily. These Victorian pieces of amusement were made in quantity from c. 1835 onwards. In their period they cost a few shillings, today they fetch good prices at auctions and in shops.

Plique-à-jour, *see* Enamel.

Porcelain, *see* Section L.

Prayer carpet, a small portable rug, used by Mohammedans when they perform their daily prayers demanded by Islam of its adherents. The carpet, usually knotted in several colours, is rectangular with the figure of a niche woven in. When the carpet is rolled out for use, the niche is made to point towards Mecca. Above it is an ornamental strip where the praying man should touch his forehead, while a pair of small ornamental panels on either side are provided for supporting the palms of his hands. The individual prayer carpets are the most usual, but there are bigger ones, with five or more niches, for use in family prayers.

Printed decoration on pottery, the most usual kind of ornamentation for table-services of earthenware throughout the 19th cent. and into modern times. In its simplest form the process worked like this: The pattern or motif desired was engraved into a steel or copper plate, printed on to a piece of thin paper, and from there transferred on to the piece of pottery (thence the expression transfer printing). In the kiln the colour was fixed to the surface. The method was perfected by a Liverpool printer, John Sadler, and put into commercial use on Wedgwood creamware (*q.v.*) c. 1760. Sadler & Green, as the firm became in 1763, executed printing on ware from many potteries in the Midlands. It was active until 1799, but by that time most potteries had acquired their own printing equipment.

During the 19th cent. printing was constantly improved upon, to give richer and more finely shaded colours. While early printing is usually done in black, blue became the favourite colour of the 19th cent. By 1840 it was possible to produce multi-coloured printed patterns. Printing on pottery was practised outside Britain from the late 18th cent., *see* Willow pattern, **U36**.

Puzzle-jug, a ewer or tankard facetiously made with a perforated neck and other unexpected leakages, so that whoever drank from it would find the contents spilling down his clothes. The type was made in pottery during the 17th and 18th cents., and reflects the robust love of practical jokes of the period.

Roemer, the wineglass with the most ancient history. It has a rounded bowl, a broad hollow stem with "strawberries" or prunts, and a tall foot made of coiled-up glass thread. The basic shape is known from classical antiquity as well as from southern and eastern Europe during the mediaeval period. During the Renaissance it was revived in the Rhine area and became the classic vessel for the drinking of Rhenish wines, a role it has retained to this day. The early examples are made of rough green glass, but during the 17th cent., *Roemers* were sometimes made from fine, crystal-clear glass or from glass purposely tinted into a bright green. The tradition of the green glass for German wines dates from this period. The 19th cent. saw a revival of the ancient form, in a number of new varieties. Modern *Roemers* have the rounded bowl, the prunts and the tall stem with horizontal lines. They are usually made of tinted glass in green or mauve or brown, and sometimes vine-leaves are engraved on the bowl.

Roemer of green glass, Germany or Holland, 17th cent.

Satinwood, an exotic kind of wood, blond in colour, with a fine grain and a silky sheen. From c.1770 until c.1800 it was widely used for small and exquisite pieces of furniture in the Adam Style (*see* **U11**). Rarer than mahogany, satinwood was used mainly for veneering and throughout the 19th cent. for small inlaid motifs on less expensive woods. During the 18th cent. satinwood was imported mainly from the West and East Indies, though it has also been found in Tasmania and Florida. During the Edwardian period satinwood furniture enjoyed a brief revival.

Sewing table, came into fashion c. 1820. It usually stands on a pedestal with three feet, the table itself being oval, octagonal or of some other interesting shape, prettily made with a lift-up lid covering neat little compartments for silks, thimbles etc., usually a pin-cushion and perhaps a mirror. Underneath is a bag to hold the work in hand. Much fine work of inlay, painting and upholstery was lavished on these charming pieces of ladies' furniture.

Sewing table, prob. of German make, c. 1830.

Shaving bowl, of the approximate shape of a large soup plate with a segment cut out of the edge so that the barber could hold it comfortably under the chin of his client while applying lather to his face. Shaving bowls date mainly from the late 17th and 18th cents. Some are made of pewter, but the majority are of faience or porcelain, occasionally with painted decorations in the form of barbers' requisites, like combs, scissors, knives, saws and lancets, barbers of the period acting also as surgeons.

Shaving bowl of English faience, made in London or Liverpool, early 18th cent., with blue painted barber's tools.

Sheffield plate, a substitute for solid silver, consisting of a copper base coated on both sides with silver, the whole fused into one indissoluble whole and rolled into plate from which the desired objects are formed. The method was invented in Sheffield by Thomas Bolsover c. 1742. The new, cheap, silverlike plate became very popular, and was soon being widely produced not only in Sheffield, but in Birmingham, London, Edinburgh and elsewhere, also by firms outside Britain. The special character of the fused plate imposed certain limits on the makers. The normal goldsmith's methods of decorating by engraving and chasing were not suitable, while wirework came out beautifully, as did ornamental borders and ornaments, cast separately and soldered on to the plated body.
Sheffield plate had its finest period from c.

1780 onwards, when technical methods had been perfected and aesthetic possibilities exploited to the full. By c. 1840 it was ousted by even cheaper silver substitutes (see Britannia Metal **U**29 and Electroplating **U**31). Today objects of old Sheffield plate are sought-after antiques. The old methods have, however, been revived in modern times in traditional shapes.
For marks on Sheffield plate, see **U**16.

Candelabrum 'of Sheffield plate with ornamental borders soldered on. The model was first made c. 1830 and has been repeated throughout the 19th cent.

Sheraton, Thomas, see **B**55 and **U**13.

Ship-bowls, made of faience (q.v.) in sea-ports like Bristol, Liverpool and Hamburg, were made for sale to visiting sea-captains. The bowls are usually decorated in blue with the picture of a sailing-ship in the centre, and with the name of the captain and his vessel on the rim. The ship pictures are conventional, and should not be accepted as "portraits" of the ships named. The genre belongs mainly to the 18th cent.

Snuffers, used for snuffing candles and formed like a pair of scissors with a small, square box positioned on one of the blades to catch the glowing, smoking wick-end. Examples survive from late 17th cent., and they remained in use as long as candles were a normal kind of lighting in the home. Snuffers were usually made of brass or steel.

Thonet, Michael, see **U**15.

Transfer printing, see **Printed decoration on pottery.**

Tudric pewter, was made by the Birmingham firm of Haseler to designs by various artists under the sponsorship of Liberty's of Regent Street, who sold it in their shop. The style is a "Celtic" variety of the Art Nouveau (see **U**15), and many of the preserved examples are stamped TUDRIC. The best period was c. 1800–1914, but the production lingered on until well into the 1930s. Cf. Cymric silver.

Tunbridge ware, small wooden objects, some turned (cups, bowls and dishes), most of them joined and inlaid (boxes, gaming boards and the like), made mostly from local woods by local craftsmen in Tunbridge Wells and sold in quantity to visitors who flocked to take the waters at the spa. Tunbridge work is mentioned in documents from the late 17th cent., but the most productive period was from c.. 1820 to 1870. Occasionally products bear makers' labels. Some London firms produced woodwork in the Tunbridge style in the 18th cent., and called it "Tunbridge Ware" in their advertisements.

Wedgwood, Josiah, *see* Creamware, *also* B63.

Whatnot, a piece of furniture made of three to five shelves or trays, placed one above the other between four corner-supports. The whatnot, which in France is called an *etagère*, became fashionable during the early part of the 19th cent. for the display of ornaments. Today it seems to epitomise one aspect of Victorian life, the love of fancy objects.

Willow pattern, the most popular of all printed (*q.v.*) motifs for table-ware. It consists of a **chinoiserie** (*q.v.*) island landscape with a bridge with figures and a willow-tree bending over it, on the islands pavilions, on the water a house-boat, in the air flying birds. It was probably invented in late 18th cent., nobody knows by whom. The only dated example is from 1818. With small variations it has been used to this day, usually printed in blue, occasionally in mauve and more rarely in yet other colours. Various romantic anecdotes which it is supposed to illustrate are all inventions from this cent.

Wing-glass, an ornamental glass with freely furnace-worked "wings" added to the stem. The ornaments may be formed as ropes twisted into fantastic curves and convolutions, or as figures of eight or related forms. The details are frequently made in bluish-green against otherwise clear and colourless glass. Wing-glasses were made most expertly by Italian glass-makers at work in northern Europe from c. 1550 to 1650. They have been widely copied in German and Belgian factories within the last hundred years. The shapes may have been very faithfully reproduced, but the faultless perfection of the modern material give them away as modern copies.

Arabesque in black and white marble, from the floor of the Cathedral at Siena, dated 1372.

PETS
AND
PONIES

The most important factors in maintaining a pet in health and comfort are regular care and attention, cleanliness, wise feeding, and knowing what to do if it becomes ill or out of condition. This section has been compiled to give this guidance and contains suggestions for further reading. A special topic examines zoonosis and some other diseases associated with animals.

TABLE OF CONTENTS

DOMESTIC PETS

By ALASTAIR N. WORDEN, M.A., Ph.D. (Cantab); D.Vet. Med. (London) F.R.C. Path. (Chairman Huntingdon Research Centre; Co-ordinator of Environmental Studies, University College, Cambridge; Professor of Toxicology, University of Bath).
SARAH E. M. WORDEN
(Addenbrookes Hospital, Cambridge).

Introduction.

This section attempts to deal not with all the many hundreds of species and varieties of animal that may be kept as pets, but mainly with those that are best suited to average homes in Great Britain. The maintenance of monkeys, squirrels, bats, mongooses, and snakes while quite feasible to those with experience and facilities, requires considerable time and—in some instances—expense. Those who contemplate such exotic pets should consult works of reference, study the methods adopted in zoological gardens, and discuss the matter with experts. Even in the case of the more common animals the information provided in the following pages is to be regarded only as a beginning, to be supplemented so far as possible by practical experience, discussions with more knowledgeable owners, and the study of more detailed writings.

Certain considerations are basic. Never keep a pet unless you are really interested in it and are prepared to give it due—and regular—care and attention. Do not keep a pet you cannot afford to maintain in health and comfort. Scrupulous attention to cleanliness is essential, and wise feeding is one of the most important factors in avoiding illness and loss of condition.

The choice of species is nowadays restricted—perhaps as well from the standpoint of animal welfare—on account of stringent import regulations. The Rabies (Importation of Dogs, Cats and Other Mammals) Order 1974 controls the landing in this country of all mammals of the orders Carnivora (dog and cat families, bears, racoons, mink, stoats, civets, mongooses, etc.) and Chiroptera (bats), and of certain members of the orders Dermoptera (gliding or "flying" lemurs), Edentata (sloths, armadillos, etc.), Hyracoidea (hyraxes or "conies"), Insectivora (moles, shrews, hedgehogs and other insect-eating mammals), Lagomorpha (hares and rabbits) and Marsupialia (opossums, kangaroos, wallabies bandicoots and other pouched mammals). Animals subject to control may only be landed at specified ports and airports, and must be moved as soon as practicable after landing to authorised quarantine premises—except vampire bats, which must be quarantined for life. Licences are not, however, required for animals coming from Northern Ireland, the Republic of Ireland, the Channel Islands and the Isle of Man provided that they have not been outside the British Isles within the previous 6 months. Animals landed illegally, or in breach of a licence, may be destroyed. There are other legislative measures that control the importation of monkeys, various kinds of birds and other animals, and these are unlikely to be relaxed.

Since the passing of the Veterinary Surgeons Act of 1948 it has been illegal for anyone but a veterinary surgeon (or whose name has been placed upon a special register) to practise the diagnosis and treatment of animal diseases. Not even a pharmacist may do so. Anyone may, of course, render "first aid" and an owner may—at his own risk—apply treatment. It is, of course, a wise precaution to seek veterinary advice for any ailing animal, and the sooner it is sought the more likely is it to prove beneficial. Nowadays, veterinary surgeons take a keen interest not only in diseases but also in animal husbandry and good practices and can prove of help to the owners of a vast variety of animals. There are, for example, branches of the B.V.A. such as the British Small Animals Veterinary Association and the British Veterinary Zoological Society. Their interests extend even to fish, and the current editor of *Fish Biology* is a veterinarian.

The maintenance of animals in or near the house is not free from medical hazard. There are various infections and parasites that can be passed from animals to man, and vice-versa. Rabies is not the only potential hazard from imported stock although one should heed the advice given by Dr. Ethelward Vella in a letter to the *Lancet* in December 1975: "It would be a great help to doctors if holidaymakers, before going abroad, were to learn not to befriend any animal whatsoever. If they do get bitten by a domestic animal such as a dog, the name and address of the owner should be taken, the vaccination status of the animal should be ascertained, and local medical assistance should be sought." In this country, any person bitten or scratched by an animal should seek medical advice promptly and, in all appropriate instances, request an anti-tetanus injection. The infection known as psittacosis in members of the parrot family, and as ornithosis in other birds—including pigeons—is quite easily transmitted to human beings through the inhalation of dust that contains faecal material from infected birds. Although the pneumonia that often results is usually susceptible to treatment it can be severe and sometimes fatal. Other hazards of pet-keeping include asthma or allergic sensitivity, which may become progressively severe in susceptible persons. "Small furry animals" are regarded with suspicion by many clinicians who seek the cause of childhood asthma —and, of course, larger animals may also produce a dander that provokes severe reactions. "Bird fancier's lung" is usually regarded as an allergic alveolitis resulting from the inhalation of dust from pigeon lofts or bird cages. More mundane hazards include the simple contamination of food and water by animal excretion. Nor should it be forgotten that some species of animal can contract diseases from man.

Against such risks one has to balance the enjoyment, education and companionship to be derived from a healthy association with pets. Most children, and very many adults, benefit from an association with animals and from the responsibilities of maintaining them properly. There are some restrictions placed upon flat-dwellers and some other owners and tenants of urban properties, but it would be a sad day if some at least of the animals referred to in this section did not form part of the British home background.

There are many recommendations to follow regarding further reading. One of the authors was privileged to edit, in 1947, the first edition of the *Handbook on the Care and Management of Laboratory Animals* produced by the UFAW (the Universities' Federation for Animal Welfare). There have been several subsequent editions and the latest, edited by the UFAW staff is a mine of information, much of it applicable to pets as distinct from laboratory animals. It is published by Churchill Livingstone (London and Edinburgh). Still valuable, although written just before the second world war, is the work produced from the Zoological Society of London by Margaret Shaw and James Fisher (London: Dent), *Animals as Friends (and how to keep them)*, which deals with several species not included here. The late James Fisher, incidentally, shared with one of the present authors in the production of the first-ever section on Domestic Pets to appear in *Pears Cyclopaedia*.

DOGS.

Description.

"Man's best friend" has been associated with man, in many parts of the world, for thousands of years. There has always been considerable scientific debate over the exact origin—or origins—of the domestic dog, and Darwin himself, over a century ago, reviewed the evidence then available for and against the polyphyletic origin of the different domesticated races and suggested that: "We shall probably never be able to ascertain their origin with certainty." The northern wolf, the coyote and Asiatic jackal have been among the several wild canids that are thought to have been the progenitors, and although most of the evidence favours the first of these, there are contrary thoughts. From whatever species the domestic dog may have been derived, it is highly probable that its ancestors were pack hunters and strictly monogamous. The fidelity of the dog fox and his excellent manners towards his vixen are models of male behaviour and constitute a problem for the fox breeder. Domesticity appears to have relaxed the dogs' attitude, and the dog breeder does not find himself faced with the same problems as the fox breeder in breaking the monogamous habit. Nevertheless, as the great animal behaviourist, Konrad Lorenz, has emphasised, male dogs behave with great chivalry towards bitches and puppies. He states that in the wolf this chivalrous self-control is extended to females of the same pack, whereas in certain breeds of dogs that he believes to be predominantly jackal in origin, it applies to every bitch even though she may be a complete stranger. He states that the Chow Chow holds an intermediate position, and that if the male lives with own breed it may behave loutishly towards strange bitches, though he has never known one that actually bit one.

There are more than 100 breeds of domesticated dog (*Canis familiaris*) and the weight range varies between a few kg for the toy breeds to 70 kg or more for St. Bernards and Wolfhounds. Pets should be selected carefully on the grounds of temperament and size, and may, of course, either be purebreds or crossbreds, the latter usually being described as mongrels, while the former are, of course, the only suitable animals for dog-breeding in the usual sense of that term.

Dog breeding and showing have become highly specialised during the present century, and average persons cannot be expected to take them up without adequate time, resources and knowledge. Any amateur who wishes to breed for profit should seek expert advice before attempting to do so.

The General Committee of the Kennel Club, 1 Clarges Street, London, W.1 (01-493-6651), maintains a breed register for each pure breed recognised by it. For the purposes of competition between dogs of different breeds, the grouping of breeds—see accompanying table—is held to define Sporting (Hounds, Gundogs and Terriers) and Non-Sporting (Utility, Working and Toys). Full details of registration, including some new regulations dating from 1 January 1976 that relate to the progeny of certain purebred dogs of different breeds within the same category, are available on application to the Kennel Club. Before an imported dog can be accepted for registration, the applicant must give the date of importation, the address of the quarantine station at which it had been detained, and the name and the address of the importer.

SPORTING BREEDS
Hound Group

Afghan Hounds	Dachshunds (Miniature
Basenjis	Wire-Haired)
Basset Hounds	Deerhounds
Bassets Griffons Ven-	Elkhounds
deen	Finnish Spitz
Beagles	Foxhounds
Bloodhounds	Greyhounds
Borzois	Ibizan Hounds
Dachsbracke	Irish Wolfhounds
Dachshunds (Long-	Otterhounds
Haired)	Pharaoh Hounds
Dachshunds (Miniature	Portuguese Warren
Long-Haired)	Hounds
Dachshunds (Smooth-	Rhodesian Ridgebacks
Haired)	Salukis
Dachshunds (Miniature	Sloughis
Smooth-Haired)	Swedish Foxhounds
Dachshunds (Wire-	Swiss Laufhunds (Jura)
Haired)	Whippets

Gundog Group

English Setter	German Wirehaired
German Longhaired	Pointers
Pointers	Gordon Setters
German Shorthaired	Hungarian Vizslas
Pointers	Irish Setters

Italian Spinones
Large Munsterlanders
Pointers
Pointing Wirehaired Griffons
Retrievers (Chesapeake Bay)
Retrievers (Curly Coated)
Retrievers (Flat Coated)
Retrievers (Golden)
Retrievers (Labrador)
Small Munsterlanders
Spaniels (American Cocker)
Spaniels (Clumber)
Spaniels (Cocker)
Spaniels (English Springer)
Spaniels (Field)
Spaniels (Irish Water)
Spaniels (Sussex)
Spaniels (Welsh Springer)
Weimaraners

Terrier Group

Airedale Terriers	Lakeland Terriers
Australian Terriers	Manchester Terriers
Bedlington Terriers	Norfolk Terriers
Border Terriers	Norwich Terriers
Bull Terriers	Scottish Terriers
Bull Terriers	Sealyham Terriers
(Miniature)	Skye Terriers
Cairn Terriers	Soft-Coated Wheaten
Dandie Dinmont	Terriers
Terriers	Staffordshire Bull
Fox Terriers (Smooth)	Terriers
Fox Terriers (Wire)	Welsh Terriers
Glen of Imaal Terriers	West Highland White
Irish Terriers	Terriers
Kerry Blue Terriers	

NON-SPORTING BREEDS
Utility Group

Boston Terriers	Lhasa Apsos
Bulldogs	Mexican Hairless
Canaan Dogs	Miniature Schnauzers
Chow Chows	Poodles (Standard)
Dalmations	Poodles (Miniature)
French Bulldogs	Poodles (Toy)
Giant Schnauzers	Schipperkes
Iceland Dogs	Schnauzers
Japanese Akitas	Shih Tzus
Keeshonds	Tibetan Spaniels
Leonbergers	Tibetan Terriers

Working Group

Alaskan Malamutes	Hungarian Kuvasz
Alsatians (German	Hungarian Pulis
Shepherd Dogs)	Huskies
Anatolian (Karabash)	Komondors
Dogs	Maremma Sheepdogs
Australian Kelpies	Mastiffs
Bearded Collies	Newfoundlands
Beaucerons	Norwegian Buhunds
Belgian Shepherd Dogs	Old English Sheepdogs
(Groenendaels)	Polish Sheepdogs
Belgian Shepherd Dogs	Portuguese Water
(Malinois)	Dogs
Belgian Shepherd Dogs	Pyrenean Mountain
(Tervuerens)	Dogs
Bernese Mountain	Rottweilers
Dogs	St. Bernards
Bouviers Des Flandres	Samoyeds
Boxers	Shetland Sheepdogs
Briards	Siberian Huskies
Bullmastiffs	Tibetan Mastiffs
Collies (Rough)	Welsh Corgis
Collies (Smooth)	(Cardigan)
Dobermanns	Welsh Corgis
Great Danes	(Pembroke)

Toy Group

Affenpinschers	Italian Greyhounds
Bichons Frises	Japanese Chin
Cavalier King Charles	King Charles Spaniels
Spaniels	Lowchen
Chihuahuas (Long	Maltese
Coat)	Miniature Pinschers
Chihuahuas (Smooth	Papillons
Coat)	Pekingese
Chinese Crested Dogs	Pomeranians
English Toy terriers	Pugs
(Black and Tan)	Silky Terriers
Griffons Bruxellois	Yorkshire Terriers

There are many valuable books upon the dog, among which may be cited *The Book of the Dog*, edited by Brian Vesey-FitzGerald (London: Nicholson & Watson), *Dogs in Britain* by Clifford

Hubbard (London: Macmillan), *Feeding Our Dogs* and *The Natural Method of Dog Training*, both by Dr. Leon Whitney (London: Macmillan, and Nicholas Vane, respectively), *The Genetics of the Dog* by Marca Burns (Technical Communications No. 9 of the Commonwealth Bureau of Animal Breeding and Genetics, Edinburgh) and *The Natural History of the Dog* by Richard and Alice T.-W.-Fiennes (London: Weidenfeld & Nicolson). There is also a chapter in the *UFAW Handbook*, already referred to, by Dr. Malcom Hime. Works on individual breeds are too numerous to mention, but there have been several excellent series of individual booklets, including, for example, those issued in the USA, by All-Pets Books of Fond du Lac, Wisconsin. Douglas and Carol Appleton provide much valuable information in their *Beagles and Beagling* (London: Kaye & Ward), which contains sections by Dr. Ralph Heywood on the abnormalities that are not uncommon in this—as in almost every other breed of long standing—and other veterinary matters. Those who wish to maintain a Husky or other sled dog should contact the Husky Club of Great Britain, the present secretary of which is Mrs. Stella Colling-Mudge. The editor of its publication, *The Sled Dog*, is Mrs. Janet Ward, 3 Turpins Close, Oaklands, Welwyn, Herts., AL6 OQ2 (048-871-5413).

There are important breed differences in the way in which young dogs become adapted to man. Thus, there is evidence that the Basenji has much greater shyness at 5 weeks compared with, say, the Cocker Spaniel, and that this difference is inherited on Mendelian lines, there probably being two genetic factors involved. Similar differences are often found to exist in respect of crouching, which appears to represent the " setting " that has survived in Cocker Spaniels since there has now been no selection against it. Modern setters are really pointers.

Some understanding of agonistic, sexual and territorial behaviour and of dominance relationships is of considerable importance not only for professional training breeding and showing but also for successful maintenance of dogs as pets. When puppies are left together in groups, a tendency to fighting may be noticed from a very early age. It occurs during the play periods and appears to be a response to unusual roughness on the part of a particular member of the litter, when there will be a slight flare up of tempers, a bit of a fight, and then all will settle down again. So far as is possible, this tendency should be checked at an early age if it is intended to run dogs together subsequently. Real fighting comes later, and is usually linked with defence of owner or of territorial, or with sexual considerations. In household dogs, there may be evidence of real male aggressive behaviour as early as 4–5 months of age, before there is any sign of sexual activity. Fighting in the female usually starts at a later stage. At about 6–7 months of age, the first signs of sexual maturity will appear, and is manifested in the male by the typical lifting of the leg at urination and by some degree of interest in the odours outlining the animal's own territorial area.

Dominance orders are clearly manifest among dogs within litters or colonies maintained together, and in the animals of a neighbourhood. In some groups of dogs, there is real persecution of an individual by other members. In dog breeding and training, aggressiveness is usually regarded as valuable only if limited, although in the past some breeds were selected for their ability to fight. Dr. J. P Scott, who with his colleagues has made many contributions to dog behaviour, states that all of the terriers are fighting breeds: they are easily excited and relatively insensitive to pain with tough skin on their necks and shoulders and strong jaws and teeth. On the other hand many breeds are selected for the opposite kind of behaviour. Hounds work in packs to find game, and fighting is highly undesirable. Beagles—which make docile pets and are good animals for laboratory studies—get along peaceably together, and even strange adult males can be put in the same kennel with little more than some growling and barking.

To a domesticated dog, a human being is his pack leader, and Konrad Lorenz has suggested that the failure of the adult male wolf to accept this situation is basically the reason why it, with the exception sometimes of the wolf bitch, is usually impossible to train as a pet, even from an early age. Dominance is usually shown by the taking of the other dog by the scruff of its neck, and indeed the most effective means of punishment is to mimic this by shaking the animal by its scruff. Lorenz pointed out that since dogs, like monkeys, do not hit, but bite each other during their ranking order disputes, a blow is not really an adequate or intelligible form of chastisement. One can imitate the penal methods of the pack leader, and involve one's own personal feelings much less, by lifting the dog up by the neck and shaking him. Although this form of punishment seems to us to be much less severe than beating with a cane or whip, we must be very chary of using it, even on adult dogs, if we do not wish to intimidate them altogether.

Marking out of territory by urination is an inborn habit that has to be suppressed for satisfactory domesticated relationships in the average household, but will be revived at once if that territory is invaded by a strange dog. Lorenz considers it unfair to take one's dog to a household where another dog is kept, if only in regard of the housewife's feelings at the effects upon her soft furnishings.

Within the age range corresponding to the period of socialisation indicated in the paragraphs on training, the vast majority of puppies will, in appropriate circumstances, begin a form a strong attachment to an individual human being. This may persist or wane according to type, but there is often a phase of adolescent independence when the dog will become disobedient and defiant. Discipline must be persisted with during this period, and patience must also be shown and the animal will normally become more obedient again at the age of 18 months to 2 years.

Dogs are equipped with good senses of hearing and smell and their sound localisation has been shown to be about twice as accurate as that of a human. The capacity of the dog to detect an individual odour of human beings is quite remarkable. This individual odour is perceived by the dog even when it is mixed with the odour of another person or with other strongly smelling substances. In tracking experiments, dogs have been found able to distinguish even between the odours of identical human twin sisters. Sight is of much less importance, although it has been suggested that the Greyhound, Whippet, Borzoi, Saluki, Afghan, Irish Wolfhound, Scottish Deerhound and Dachshund all hunt by sight, and that the smallness of the optical angle suggests that the dog may have good binocular and stereoscopic vision. It is extremely difficult to detect blindness from simple observation in domestic or laboratory animals that know their quarters well.

With advancing age, hearing fails frequently, and the first sign of this may be an inability to detect the direction the sound is coming from, though it obviously can be heard. This may lead gradually or suddenly to total deafness. Such animals can be taught to respond to signs, but, of course they become an increased responsibility as they have to be watched in relation to traffic and other hazards. Sight, on the whole, remains good as does the sense of smell.

All domestic dogs over six months of age must, of course, be licensed, the licences being available from Post Offices. Since the Control of Dogs Order of 1930, it has been obligatory for every domestic dog while in a highway or any place public resort to wear a collar with the name and address of the owner inscribed on the collar or on a plate or badge attached thereto. It is also within the power of Local Authorities to make regulations requiring that dogs of any class shall be kept under control between sunset and sunrise with a view to the prevention of worrying cattle—the expression " cattle " including not only cows but also horses, mules, asses, sheep, goats and swine. There are also many local regulations that request the use of leads in the street or other public places, so making it an offence to allow a dog to foul the pavement.

Accommodation.

Up till comparatively recently most dogs were kennelled down out of doors. This practice has its advantages, but today the majority of pet dogs are allowed more or less the run of the house. A warm sleeping-place, such as a box or basket, should be provided, and should contain removable bedding. Newspaper is an excellent non-conductor of heat. It is a very useful material to place at the bottom of a dog's box; and on two or three thicknesses may be placed a rug or blanket on which the animal may lie. It is astonishing the amount of grit and dust a dog can bring into a house on his limbs and the lower part of his body. His bedding will require frequent shaking out and renewal, and paper is easily changed. The box or basket in which the dog lies should be allowed a place free from draughts, and requires airing daily when the dog leaves its bed in the morning. Wood-wool makes excellent bedding in outhouses or where a special structure is provided by way of dog-kennel, but is inclined to be messy about the house, as a dog will draw portions of it about the room as he leaves his bed. If straw is used, it is best stuffed into a sack and made into a kind of mattress. An odd piece of linoleum forms an excellent foundation to the dog's sleeping-box or kennel; it does not strike cold to the skin, is a slow conductor of heat, and has the advantage of being easily kept clean, particularly during illness where there may be discharges and messes to be frequently cleaned up, until the animal can once more go out of doors.

Exercise.

Every dog should be exercised regularly, but there is no need to over-exercise, and the practice of allowing a dog (other than a large and athletic animal) to run behind a bicycle for mile after mile cannot be too strongly deprecated. Two or three fairly short walks a day are sufficient for a small terrier, always provided that there is a garden in which he can play on fine days and some open space where he can run freely for a short time. While still in the puppyhood stages, a dog should be trained to walk to heel and to beware of traffic. Even so, it is usually safer to put him on a lead in busy thoroughfares. One point which, to the annoyance of the public, many dog-owners fail to realise, is that their animals would show much less tendency to fight if allowed to investigate one another off the lead. A dog naturally feels aggressive if put on the lead immediately a rival hails in sight. There are, of course, certain dogs which attack others at sight; these are a public nuisance, and should never be allowed loose on the streets.

The practice of allowing a dog to take his own exercise is to be deprecated, especially in towns and suburbs. The animal will be tempted to sniff into dustbins, and, if a male, will tend to follow a bitch in season or to take part in the unsavoury " dog parties " which are so often to be seen. Furthermore, such an animal is usually responsible for the disgusting habit of fouling the pavements and gateways. In this connection, it should be emphasised that dogs may quite easily be trained to defaecate in the gutter, or on the grass verge, and so avoid contamination of the pavement or carriage-way. In some districts owners are liable to a fine if their dogs foul the pavement.

Training.

Patience combined with the gift of putting yourself in the dog's place is the chief requisite for successful education. It is most important to encourage regularity of habit, as an animal will obviously learn very much more quickly if his daily walks, meals, and grooming take place at fairly constant times. A quiet firmness is the ideal method, and a puppy should learn early that a command *is* a command, and must be obeyed. There is no need to shout and make an exhibition of oneself, or to race in circles after a disobedient puppy; if these things are done, the animal will never become so well trained as it otherwise would. Again, it is rather ridiculous to chastise a puppy *after* he has somewhat belatedly decided to come to heel: quite obviously, he will then be liable to think that he has done wrong in actually coming to heel. Whatever happens, it must never be that the dog becomes master; there is no more unbecoming sight than that of a person with a frankly disobedient dog, and if the animal be large and powerful it may prove a menace to its owner and to the public.

Puppies should be house-trained at an early stage. If care and thought are given to the matter, the animal will soon learn not to make messes in the house. However, it is very stupid to forget all about a puppy or dog for many hours, and then, out of sheer vexation, chastise it for having made a mess. If puppies are let out every two hours or so at first, they will soon learn not to make a mess. Encourage them for performing in the right place rather than scold them for doing so in the wrong one. Physical punishment should be administered only where strictly necessary, and then in a sensible fashion.

It is important to realise that the puppy has its own pattern of infant behaviour, that of sleep, feeding and play and to base training upon the subsequent normal developmental processes. During the first 1–2 weeks of life, sleep takes precedence and newly-born pups (and kittens) probably sleep for up to 90% of the time, wakening only to be fed and cleaned by the dam. Gradually the sleep periods will become slightly less and feeding periods rather more prolonged, and, by about the 3rd or 4th week of life, some slight evidence of a play pattern will be noted. Very shortly after the play pattern is noticed there is obvious sexual activity in that puppies at the age of 3–4 weeks will frequently make copulatory movements. This phase lasts only about two weeks and subsequently disappears until sexual maturity. The sucking instinct is very persistent indeed and, when puppies are 3–4 weeks old and the dam is leaving them for longer periods at a time, during the waking part of the time puppies will frequently suck the preputial orifice of other males in the litter.

Observation of puppies in the nest makes it clear that excretory activity follows a certain pattern. From the age of about 3–4 weeks, when some locomotor activity is possible, it will be noticed that immediately on waking puppies attempt to leave the sleeping area and immediately urinate. They will then feed and, having fed, will be cleaned by the dam and will then indulge in a play period. Midway through the play period it will be noted that one puppy after another suddenly becomes pensive and will again urinate and probably defaecate. Considerable use can be made of this pattern of behaviour in the house training of young puppies. Nearly all books on the training of puppies recommend that, in order to instil habits of cleanliness, puppies should be put out immediately after feeding. This would seem to be absolutely wrong. A puppy should be put out immediately after waking, should be allowed to empty the bladder, should then be brought in to feed and should be carefully watched during the subsequent play period and, immediately there is a cessation of play activity, it should be transferred to the place intended for toilet purposes, when it will probably relieve itself again. Persistence of this popular fallacy that a puppy should be clean after feeding is not based on observation of normal behaviour.

Over the first few weeks of life, sleep periods will gradually decrease and be replaced by longer and longer periods of activity. It is essential that during the immediate post-weaning period long periods of sleep should be allowed. Far too many people, on obtaining a new puppy, make no allowance for the enormous infant requirement of sleep.

Dr. Scott refers to the habit in puppies, from about 3 weeks of age, of tasting various odorous substances combined with mouthing of pieces of wood or pebbles, as well as the bodies of other puppies, and states that stronger reactions are given to raw meat and to the vomit of the mother, both of which are eaten without hesitation if the pup is hungry.

Dr. Scott and his colleagues have divided the developmental period in puppies into four periods, which vary from one individual to another within relatively narrow limits: viz. a neonatal period from birth until the eyes open; a transition period from then until the animal first appears to respond to sound, at about 20 days of age; a period of socialisation lasting until a final weaning at 7–10 weeks of age; and a juvenile period from then until the animal is first capable of mating behaviour proper—as opposed to the juvenile activities already mentioned—at any time from 6 months onwards. Until the end of the transition period the puppy cannot be made to develop conditioned reflexes or to indicate other evidence of learned responses. Electroencephalograms first indicate a difference between sleeping and waking waves at about 20 days of age and the adult form of electroencephalogram is attained between 7–8 weeks. Similar development appears to be the case in wolf puppies, which can readily be socialised to human beings if taken just before the eyes open, but which if taken a few weeks later have become extremely difficult to handle. The majority of dog puppies raised under kennel conditions with but little human contact to 5 weeks of age will show fear reaction which, however, will gradually disappear within the next two weeks if the pups are handled regularly. Puppies taken from the litter at 3–4 weeks of age, and raised by hand, do not show fear reactions at 5 weeks, but those allowed to run wild without handling to about 12 weeks of age become increasingly timid and may be extremely difficult to catch. Such puppies can be trained, but will always be more timid and less responsive than those socialised earlier.

Grooming and Washing.

Whilst short-haired breeds need little or no attention to the coat, bar an occasional brisk rub down with a brush or rough towel (which incidentally puts a pleasant gloss on the smooth-haired breeds), yet with the long-haired breeds grooming should be carried out regularly, and if the habit is made a daily one it will not be forgotten so readily. Nearly all dogs love this procedure, and most dogs will actually ask for their daily groom by jumping on the table or bench on which it is carried out. Steel combs and brushes are sold by many shops, principally corn chandlers, though some store chemists also provide a suitable range of grooming kit for all breeds. There is a curious fetish current among many breeds that dogs should not be washed. There is no reason why, with a few simple precautions, a dog should not be washed whenever it is socially necessary. The first precaution is to use a soap that does not contain an excess of soda. The strong washing-up soaps, excellent as they are for certain purposes, are too irritant for a dog's skin. While some of the toilet soaps suitable for human use may be employed for dogs, the special dog soaps and shampoos are much better for the purpose. They are more suited to the dog's skin and coat and have better detergent properties. It is important not to have water that is too hot—as with a baby's bath, it should be possible to dip the point of one's elbow into the water and find that it gives a pleasantly warm sensation but is easily bearable, i.e., it should not be above 35–38 °C. On emerging from a bath a dog will shake himself thoroughly, and then, if not curbed will roll on the floor or ground and speedily cover himself with dust or dirt! It is therefore necessary to give him a brisk rub down with old (but clean) towelling, whereupon he may be allowed to dry off in a warm place free from draughts or, in good weather, put on a lead and taken for a brisk walk. In the case of many of the long-coated breeds it is customary to have them trimmed at the beginning of summer, and this is a sensible precaution that may avoid a good deal of distress during hot weather. The smaller long-haired dogs in particular, such as Scottish Terriers, suffer unduly from the heat if their coats are grown too long.

Feeding.

Nowadays many domestic dogs are fed on canned or "dry" diets that are intended to be nutritionally complete. In the laboratory, the dry diets or "dog chows" do seem to be able to provide for long and active life over many years, although in the laboratory of one of the authors there is also a daily allowance—for Beagles and for the other relatively small breeds, e.g., Scottish Terriers, Cocker Spaniels and Pembrokeshire Corgis used in the past—of ¼ pint (c. 20 ml) of cow's milk, and vitamin tablets were also given while there was some doubt about the effective vitamin content of that kind of diet. It is important to distinguish between "complete" dry diets and dog biscuits, although the latter, as indicated below, many be safely incorporated in mixed diets. Canned foods have varied considerably in the past, but some are almost certainly capable of maintaining animals in health with few additions. In the authors' view it is probably best to give the household dog the advantage and variety that is possible, i.e. to use "complete dog" or canned foods on some days and so-called "scraps" on others. The following paragraphs discuss the subject in terms of suitable non-processed foodstuffs.

Meat, usually beef, is generally regarded as the staple article of the dog's diet. It must be pointed out, however, that although the dog is naturally a carnivore (flesh eater) ordinary meat (muscle or "flesh") is not a completely adequate diet, and lacks certain factors which the wild dog would find in the blood, bones, liver, and other organs of his prey. The ratio of calcium: phosphorus in lean meat is quite unsuitable for dogs, and indeed for all the carnivora kept in domestication or captivity, and a diet consisting solely of this has led to serious problems in Zoological gardens, where nowadays extra calcium is fed to balance the deficiency. Furthermore, it has been proved scientifically that dogs can thrive on a meatless diet. In spite of these reservations however, meat must be regarded as an excellent article of food, and if properly supplemented will prove very satisfactory. In recommendations made in America, Dr. S. R. Speelman, of the US Department of Agriculture, suggested that meat (beef, lamb, mutton, or horseflesh, providing that the last was fed regularly and not spasmodically) or meat substitutes (fish, milk, eggs, etc.) should constitute ⅓ of the daily ration, and that the remainder should comprise approximately equal parts of cereal substances (bread, biscuits) and of vegetables (carrots, spinach, onion, beet, etc.). He pointed out that many dogs do not accept the vegetable material readily. On this basis, the approximate quantities of food required by adult dogs—expressed in metric terms—were calculated as follows:—

Weight of dog	Total food/day
500 g	60 g
5 kg	400 g
10 kg	750 g
20 kg	1 kg
35 kg	1.5 kg
50 kg	2 kg
70 kg	2.5 kg

(Weights of up to 5 kg would include the toy breeds, 10 kg would correspond to a Fox Terrier; Airedale Terriers and Retrievers would fall into the 25–35 kg class, and the larger weights would be those of the very big breeds, such as the St. Bernard.) The quantities given are, of course, an approximation and no more. Dogs which lead a very active life will require more, while those which take little exercise, or which tend to put on fat easily, will require less. Common sense is necessary, and great care must be taken not to over-feed or to under-nourish.

Meat is probably best fed raw, or lightly cooked, but many animals appear to have a preference (probably through habit) for well-cooked meat. In any event, the meat should not be "over-done," as there is substantial evidence that prolonged heating destroys much of the food value of the meat protein. Fish is an excellent substitute. There need be no anxiety about the greed with which a dog swallows lumps of meat and also neglects to masticate them. The teeth of the dog are for tearing meat, he is not concerned with biting his food up small; indeed, his salivary glands contain no digestive ferments, as is the case with some other animals.

Milk is almost essential during pregnancy and lactation and may well be included in normal dietaries. Whether or not bones should be fed is a matter which has been hotly debated, but for mature household dogs the evidence suggests that they are unnecessary. (The teeth of racing greyhounds, which receive a "sloppy" diet, are quite as good as those of the average household dog). Bone-feeding is responsible for much trouble, including constipation, actual impaction of the rectum, and lodgement of pieces of bone in the mouth or throat. The value of bones is, of course, that they contain large quantities of essential mineral substances, and for this reason the inclusion in the diet of bone-meal, or of steamed bone-

flour, or, preferably, a mineral supplement. is recommended. Only very small quantities of these substances are required.

Bread is an article of food which is often overlooked in the case of the dog, but there is no doubt that wholemeal bread is very suitable indeed, provided it is not fed to excess.

The answer to the question whether a dog requires vegetables is, in the main, no. From the Vitamin C standpoint they are quite unnecessary, since it has been shown that a dog manufactures this vitamin for itself, but the fact remains that many dogs, particularly of the toy variety, enjoy a few slices of banana or apple, and there is no harm in letting them pander to their taste. Vegetables do help, however, to provide roughage, and cooked (*not* raw) *potatoes* may be used in place of bread or biscuits. The dog—like many other animals—cannot digest raw starch properly. *Flaked maize* and *oatmeal* are other substitutes, but it must be remembered that the energy value of maize is high and that the dogs must never be overfed. *Dog biscuits* were long in disfavour with some professional people on account of their often having been made from agenised white flour, but now that this factor has been overcome, and the biscuits themselves are being improved in other ways, their use for the non-meat portion of the diet may be recommended.

Clean fresh *water* must be provided at all times.

In addition to the diets recommended above there are on the market several tinned dog food which claim to be complete, or almost complete diets for the dog. It must be said that many dogs (including those of the writer) have remained in excellent health when receiving one of these foods as a large part of the diet over long periods. There is, therefore, little that may be said against the widespread use of the better varieties of such products. Again, it is a matter for common sense; if an owner finds that his animal is thriving on such a diet, he is wise to continue to use it.

It is customary to give dogs two meals a day. There is no need to give more than two to healthy adults, for the dog's stomach is exceedingly capacious and adapted to long gaps between meals. Many dogs thrive on only one meal in twenty-four hours. Whatever plan is decided on, regularity should be adhered to, and a meal or meals given at the same times every day. Dogs require vitamins A and D and B complex. There are several ways of administering these, but the special commercial preparations, including the modern form of condition-powder tablet, are the most convenient.

The *pregnant* and *lactating bitch* require special consideration. The food requirements are very much increased in a bitch which is carrying puppies, especially towards the end of the period. Normally, appetite is not a complete guide to a dog's food requirements, but in pregnancy and lactation the bitch must not be allowed to go hungry. It is quite normal for a heavily pregnant bitch to require over one and a half times her normal amount of food, and in lactation her requirements will increase still further. Milk is a most excellent article of diet at this time; indeed, there is no better way (apart from commercial preparations) of replacing the milk which the bitch is giving to her own puppies.

Up to the age of three weeks or so, *puppies* need have mother's milk only, but at any time after this it is a sound policy to give them additional food, and so spare the mother and also render weaning (at from six to eight weeks) a *gradual* process. At first a little cow's milk or one of the commercial "dog-milk" preparations may be given, and gradually the puppies should be encouraged to eat solid food. Eggs (if they can be spared), wholemeal bread in milk, or even finely minced meat may be given, at first in very small amounts but later in larger quantities. If this process is carefully carried out, there will be far less trouble at and after weaning time. After weaning, puppies should receive five or six meals a day, and this number may be cut down gradually until two or three only are given to the fully grown dog. (The smaller breeds are fully grown at about a year.) *More* meat or meat substitutes and milk, and *less* cereal or vegetable matter, should be fed to the growing dog as compared with the adult. This fact is important, as the substances present in meat and milk are required for laying down the growing tissues. Nevertheless, the energy portion of the ration is important, and the cereal or vegetable should be nutritious and not fibrous. It is possible to rear puppies by hand from birth if the bitch for any reason should die. It requires great patience for the first two or three weeks, as naturally the puppies will require feeding once or twice during the night. Special milks for puppies are to be recommended. Cow's milk requires enriching with fat and sugar to approximate to the composition of bitch's milk. Feeding will have to be done at every two or three hours, and a very useful gadget is a fountain-pen filler attached to cyclo-valve tubing. Very small quantities are required for the first two or three days, and a level teaspoonful of milk is more than sufficient for the average terrier at first. Even with the best care in the world hand-fed puppies tend to be weaklings and do not grow as fast as those naturally fed. A foster bitch. if obtainable, is much to be preferred.

A summary by one of the authors on the feeding of dogs (and cats) is given in *Canine and Feline Nutritional Requirements*, edited by O. Graham-Jones (Oxford: Pergamon).

Breeding.

It is natural for adult dogs of both sexes to wish to breed, and in the case of the female especially it is an excellent thing if one can arrange for a suitable mating to take place. Bitches come "into season" or "on heat" (lay terms for oestrus) at approximately six-monthly intervals, but it is not advisable to breed from the first season which occurs usually at about eight to nine months of age, but over a wide range of age according to breed and other factors. The periods of season often occur between January and March and in early autumn, but there is no fixed rule. Each season lasts for three weeks. For the first seven days, approximately (pro-oestrus), a bitch does not permit mating, though during this time she is a source of strong attraction to all males in the neighbourhood. At about the seventh to the tenth day the blood-stained discharge, which ushers in the heat, stops; this is usually taken by the breeder as an indication that the bitch will stand to service. If possible, it is always better when puppies are wanted to allow mating to occur more than once. Under natural conditions a dog and bitch are usually strictly monogamous and mate for life, and during the period of oestrus will mate many times. A dog and bitch that are kept together all the time will probably behave naturally, but under domestication both dogs and bitches usually become promiscuous. Many bitches will in fact accept service from different males on different days, and the phenomenon of superfecundation, *i.e.*, the production of a litter that is fathered by *two* males, may occur. It is therefore wise to retain strict control of the bitch throughout the whole of the three weeks or so she is in season. At the end of season the bitch passes into a state of "metoestrus" if she has not conceived.

If a bitch conceives, she carries her puppies for a period of about nine weeks. There is, however, a normal variation of fifty-eight to seventy days, and puppies born before the fifty-eighth day sometimes live. The number of puppies born varies with breed; in the smaller terriers it is usually from four to six, but in Airedales and Alsatians the number may be eight to ten, and the larger breeds tend to have even more offspring at a time. Birth usually takes place fairly easily in the larger breeds, but there is often much difficulty in the case of the short-legged breeds, such as Scottish and Sealyham Terriers, Pekingese and Dachshunds. In some breeds, in fact, the problem is one that is giving serious concern to veterinary surgeons and breeders.

A short while before her puppies are due, a bitch will "make her bed." Owners are often amazed at the destruction of soft furnishings, or even of wall-paper, that a previously well-behaved bitch may carry out at this time; it is therefore by far the best to provide a suitable box (if the animal has not one already). A smooth flooring such as a strip of linoleum serves for the bitch to give birth to her puppies. Her instinct to tear up everything given to her for bedding may lead to suffocation of the puppies by pieces of bedding. Provided labour occurs in a warm room, it is some-times better—according to the temperament of the bitch—to remove each puppy as it is born, placing a warm bottle underneath, and bring it back to the mother when the last birth has occurred. At this time the bitch should be watched carefully for any discharge from the vulva or for any evidence of straining. If either of these occurs without results, it is advisable to send for help as early as possible, especially in the case of the smaller breeds. Many hundreds of bitches are lost through neglect at this time, and usually because it was not suspected that any-thing was wrong. If the discharge becomes bloody, or green, help should be obtained at once if no puppy is delivered. Similarly, any great delay between births is a matter for concern. The afterbirth usually follows the puppy within a few minutes, but puppies are sometimes delivered in their foetal membranes, and in this case the latter should be gently but quickly removed. It is quite normal for the umbilical cord to remain attached to the puppy, but the bitch will normally break it by biting through it.

The mother will wash and attend to the new-born puppies, and after the last is born it is a good idea to burn all the mess and to provide clean newspaper, but do not worry or frighten the bitch more than is necessary. Puppies, like kittens, are born with their eyes closed, but open them after about nine days—there again being considerable variation.

The phenomenon of pseudopregnancy is com-mon in bitches, and indeed to a minor degree it is probably present in most bitches following an oestrus without conception. In some bitches, however, presumably those with strong maternal drives, the changes in the ovary, may be accom-panied by external signs of "phantom" or "ghost" pregnancy. These may include not only enlargement but actual functioning of the mammary glands, and the making of a "nest" by the bitch just as if her puppies were really due. The average duration of pseudopregnancy is usually given as about two months, and although variable, it is often sufficiently near to the correct time after oestrus that everyone suspects the bitch to be truly pregnant. The condition may be suppressed with the aid of modern drugs, but in some instances it is not realised that the condition is not real. In many cases only professional advice can solve the mystery, and radiographical examinations have often proved necessary to ascertain the truth, particularly in fat bitches of the heavier breeds. It might be well to note, at this point, that there is another condition of the older bitch that is known as Pyometra. This condition usually reveals itself at the same time as the ghost pregnancy (and is sometimes a patho-logical extension of it) but is accompanied by considerable disturbance of health, coupled in many instances with purulent discharge from the vagina. A bitch which is off-colour in the weeks following pregnancy, or which develops a discharge from the vulva (especially one which is dark in colour), may well be a pyometra subject. The disease is most serious, and often requires surgical intervention. As the best chance of success is to operate or otherwise deal with early, a veterinary surgeon should be consulted immediately.

Diseases and Injuries.

Since the days when one of the authors took a veterinary qualification, shortly before the second world war, there has been a tremendous advance in the understanding of disease in dogs. Except as indicated below, it is wise to seek prompt veterinary advice whenever a dog is "off colour". As in human beings, the pattern of disease may change quite markedly with the years, and there is always the risk of the emergence of new or modi-fied strains of organism that can create havoc, especially among large kennels or packs.

Canine Distemper and "Para-distemper" (In-cluding so-called "Hard-pad").

It has long been recognised that the commonest and most serious disease of dogs throughout the world is canine distemper. Dogs of all ages and breeds are susceptible, and no dog is free from the risk of infection unless it has recovered from the disease or has acquired an immunity for other reasons. The disease is caused primarily by a minute agent known as a filterable virus, which may be of varying type in that it will attack the body in different ways. Thus some strains of the virus are known as "neurotropic" because they show an affinity for the nervous system. Some-times a dog will apparently recover from an attack of distemper, only to succumb later to "fits" or other nervous manifestations due to permanent damage to the central nervous system by the virus. Often, however, the virus is not fatal in itself, but will lower the dog's resistance and per-mit the entry or the activity of bacteria that may lead to pneumonia or other serious effects. These so-called "secondary invaders", as the bacteria are termed, may prove as harmful as the original virus. Indeed, once these bacteria have set to work it is too late to expect the best results from the use of serum, and whether or not the dog will live through will depend upon the severity of the attack, the dog's powers of resistance, and good nursing. It is therefore most important either to prevent the disease by vaccination or to be able to send for veterinary attention (and hence for an injection of serum) immediately an attack is suspected. Any puppy which is listless or off its food, or which may throw a fit, or which is obviously unwell with other symptoms (e.g., cough or diarrhoea) may well be in the early stages of distemper, and it is then (not the next day) that help should be sought. Many thousands of puppies (and older dogs) that have been injected with serum in the early stages of the disease have become perfectly normal within forty-eight hours. On the other hand, the number of dogs that die in Great Britain alone from distemper and distemper-like infections must assume enormous proportions. Distemper is a highly infectious disease, and it is important that the owner of an infected animal should do his best to avoid contact with other dogs, ferrets, or mink. Ferrets and mink are very susceptible to canine distemper. On the other hand, human beings and cats are not susceptible to canine distemper, and the so-called distemper of cats is quite a distinct disease.

A highly satisfactory means of vaccinating puppies against distemper was worked out about 1926–30, and this—named the "Laidlaw–Dun-kin" after its two inventors—has since afforded protection to thousands of animals. Modern vaccines are based on a virus which has been modified by growth on developing egg embryos; or, more recently, in tissue culture. Puppies should be vaccinated when they are 10–12 weeks; prior to this age the immunity induced by the vaccine may not develop satisfactorily. After vaccination the puppy requires some time, pos-sibly 2 weeks, before an immunity is established. Sometimes vaccinated dogs suffer distemper or distemper-like signs due to "secondary invaders" causing disease on their own account; or because they were already infected when vaccinated. Variants of distemper, of which "hard pad" was an example, may also overwhelm a vaccinated dog's immunity, although this is uncommon with modern vaccines, since several distemper strains are used in their production. Hyperimmune serum, which is collected from animals previously hyperimmunised against distemper, is available and can immediately aid the dog suffering from distemper but its effect is short-lived (7–10 days).

Infectious Hepatitis or Rubarth's Disease.

Another virus disease of dogs (and foxes) is known as Rubarth's disease, after one of its dis-coverers, now known as infectious hepatitis. This disease has been recognised in Sweden ever since the 1930s, but in Great Britain only since the end of the second world war. The condition is extremely sudden in onset, and an infected dog may be found dead. Many cases are, however, mild, and in some instances only one or two out of a large group of dogs have been affected. The changes seen after death vary, but the findings in the liver cells are usually characteristic. Speci-fic treatment is not yet available, as in the case of the distemper-like conditions, although the administration of antibiotics may prevent the effects of secondary infection. An effective vaccine is often combined with distemper vac-cine. A dog is thereby protected against both these diseases. (It has recently been established that canine hepatitis is due to an adenovirus, and that while it predominantly attacks the liver it can—even in some vaccinated animals—sometimes spread by droplet infection. After causing relatively little trouble for nearly 20 years, fresh outbreaks became evident in the 1970s).

Canine Hysteria.

Called "fright disease" or "running fits" in the USA this is an alarming but not necessarily serious condition (in that it can often be cured very readily) which appears to arise from a variety of exciting causes. The affected animal rushes around wildly, often screaming and howling, and obviously loses all sense of whereabouts or ability to recognise people. After a more severe attack (and there are all degrees up to a full epileptiform fit) the dog may appear quite exhausted but returns to normal. Sometimes there are many attacks in one day. The dog will not wilfully attack people during a bout of hysteria—at least that has been the experience of the writers—but is very difficult to control. Apart from ensuring that the dog does itself no grievous bodily harm, there is little that can be done until the attack has subsided. Then the animal should be kept as quiet as possible and given a tranquilliser

Hysteria may arise from a hereditary taint, derived from one or other parent. In certain circumstances, however, it may arise in apparently normal animals. There are several possible causes (including parasites), but a definite one is the bleaching agent—nitrogen trichloride or "agene" once employed in the manufacture of flour, and hence present in white bread and certain dog biscuits. Indeed, the clear demonstration that agene could set up hysteria in dogs, and subsequent scientific work, resulted in its abandonment as a bleaching agent in favour of other methods which have been found not to cause hysteria. There has since been an almost total reduction in the incidence of hysteria due to dietary factors.

Rabies.

Rabies is a fatal disease of dogs, and is also due to a "filterable virus." It is transmissible to the human being and to many other species, but has fortunately been absent from Great Britain for many years. Stringent precautions are taken to prevent its entry, and dogs which are brought into Great Britain must spend a long period in quarantine. A vaccine is available and people taking dogs to countries where rabies occurs should have their animals protected. Many countries insist on this procedure.

Tonsillitis.

Tonsillitis appears quite frequently in dogs, and seems in many cases to be part of a more generalised infection. It demands expert treatment, but although it may persist for a long time, it usually yields to treatment.

Nephritis.

Inflammation of the kidneys is unfortunately all too common in dogs, and in adult males in particular there is a high incidence of chronic kidney damage. One of the symptoms is a marked thirst. Sometimes this condition is a sequel to an infection known as leptospirosis, which calls for prompt veterinary treatment if death or permanent damage is not to follow. It is always worth while seeking professional advice for a dog that drinks excessively or has a somewhat characteristic type of bad breath. A vaccine which gives a good immunity against the two common forms of leptospirosis is available.

Anal Glands.

Anal glands which are found in the dog and in other carnivora, often give rise to trouble. Animals which "rub themselves along the ground" are not necessarily affected with "worms," but with impaction of these two little glands, which are situated one on each side of the anus. They secrete a peculiar dark-coloured, very offensive fluid, which sometimes is not discharged properly and causes the animal great discomfort. The glands in such cases should be relieved periodically. Those who do not mind this somewhat dirty task may perhaps learn how to do it themselves. Occasionally, segments of tapeworm are responsible for the impaction, but usually the trouble has nothing to do with worms. Whenever a dog pays considerable attention to his anus, this impaction should be suspected. Actual infection of the glands is also fairly common, and demands expert attention.

Diseases of the Ear.

Diseases of the ear, especially of the outer ear, are very common in dogs. The dog's outer ear is somewhat more complicated than is our own, and the drum is set more deeply. Hence it is easy for wax and dirt to accumulate, for various parasites to establish themselves, and for inflammatory conditions to result. The word "canker" (which has no precise scientific meaning) is sometimes applied by lay people to the more serious or chronic forms of inflammation of the outer ear canal. It is not difficult to diagnose "ear trouble," as the affected animal usually shakes its head or worries or scratches its ear and rubs it along the ground. The ears should be inspected regularly to see that there is no great accumulation of wax or dirt. Cotton-wool twisted on to the end of a match-stick or orange-stick is quite satisfactory for cleaning out the ear, providing care is taken. A dog which is continually worrying its ear, or which has ears which are obviously diseased, should not be neglected, as the sooner expert treatment is begun the more readily will the condition be cured. Even if the lining of the ear is greatly thickened through inflammatory reaction, and the lumen nearly occluded, it is still possible for a plastic operation to be performed. Many hundreds of such cases have been successfully treated in this way. A percentage of inflammatory conditions of the outer ear is associated with ear mange mites. In such an event treatment with modern anti-mange preparations should be carried out.

Deafness.

Deafness in certain white dogs (e.g., in some Bull Terriers) appears to be hereditary, and is quite incurable. Old dogs often become deaf, and deafness has been produced experimentally in young puppies by feeding them on a deficient diet.

Diseases of the Eye.

Diseases of the eye are very common in dogs, and are often the result of injury. Except for minor discharges from the corners of their eyes (and in younger dogs especially it must be ascertained that these are not a symptom of distemper) any eye disease is sufficiently serious to merit professional advice. Boracic lotion is not suitable for the eyes of dogs. It is slightly irritant, and dogs are apt to scratch and make the eyes raw after application. Colloidal silver eye lotions and ointments are far more suitable pending the advice of a veterinary surgeon. In eye inflammation avoid sunlight and wind. For some days in the early stages of inflamed eyes, the light in the room should be subdued. Pekingese seem to be especially prone to eye disease, but the remarkably unwholesome appearance of some affected eyes in this breed is not necessarily evidence that recovery is unlikely. Steps should be taken to ensure that the dog does not inflict further injury on an already diseased eye. Cat scratches are a frequent source of inflammatory conditions of the dog's eye. Eyes must never be neglected, for the consequences are serious. Hereditary eye defects are well known in some breeds.

Skin Diseases.

Skin diseases are common in dogs, and may be contagious. Among the common contagious causes of skin disease are lice, mange mites and fleas. Lice and mange mites (except for demodex) are killed by modern insecticides although two applications at a 10–14 day interval are required to destroy the young stages which are within the insecticide-resistant eggs at the first dressing.

The flea actually on the dog is only one of four stages in the life cycle of the flea; the others are in the house or dog's bedding. Insecticides used for flea control should therefore be applied every week or 10 days during the summer to kill the young fleas as they hatch and infest the dog. The dog's bedding should be discarded or cleaned. The dog also suffers from other skin diseases caused by systemic disorders for which expert attention is required.

Diseases of the Teeth and Gums.

Diseases of the teeth and gums are very common in household dogs. A serious systemic disease, such as distemper, may leave the enamel of the teeth permanently pitted, hence " distemper teeth." More serious than this, however, is a form of pyorrhœa, which is really a disease of the gums rather than a primary disease of the teeth themselves. The margins of the gums become red and swollen, and may bleed easily. As the condition progresses the teeth may become loosened. Particles of food become lodged between the teeth or between teeth and gums, and add to the inflammation and to the smell of the breath.

This disease may, if unchecked, become very serious. In many cases extraction of one or more teeth is indicated, but unfortunately it is not always possible to do this. The condition demands expert attention.

Another common condition of dogs' teeth is the deposition around them of " tartar." This should be removed by scaling or by special use of dental forceps. Some breeders and others may themselves have learnt how to carry out these operations with the requisite skill and care, but they are not easy to the amateur, and it is essential that no harm be done to the animal's soft tissues by injudicious use of the instruments. Ordinary dog-owners are strongly advised to take their dogs to a veterinary surgeon in order to have the " tartar " removed.

Most puppies lose their first or " milk " teeth quite regularly between the ages of three and five months, but sometimes there is difficulty and the primary teeth are not shed properly. These cases should be treated by a veterinary surgeon before the permanent teeth are thrown out of their proper alignment.

One hears very much about " teething fits " in puppies, and while these occur, owners should be *very* careful to ensure that a " teething fit " is not a sign of distemper, which often starts with a fit. As puppies of this age are so susceptible to distemper, it is advisable to seek professional advice should any form of fit occur. It may save much time, money and trouble, and even the animal's life.

Internal Parasites: " Worms."

It is probable that more nonsense has been talked and written about " worms " in dogs than about any other canine subject. According to some people " worms " are the root of nearly all doggy evil, and so long as a dog is regularly " wormed " all will go well with him. These beliefs are frankly absurd. The real facts are very different, and are stated in as brief a fashion as possible in the following sentences. In this country dogs are infested by a species of " roundworm " (a creature which is a dirty-white colour and in shape somewhat resembles the common earthworm) and by several species of " tapeworm," which are also whitish but which are flat and are made up of many small segments joined to a little " head " which is attached to the lining of the gut. In spite of all that is said, tapeworms as such are rarely responsible for much harm to the dog, although they can, of course, prove debilitating and should be removed. They are a nuisance, and attempts to remove them should be made by administration of the appropriate drug. Occasionally, segments of worm are responsible for impaction of the ducts of the *anal glands* (see above).

The roundworms may be extremely serious in young puppies, in which they cause stunting, " pot-belly," harshness of coat and dangerous or fatal illness. Fortunately, modern anti-roundworm preparations are available for animals of this age. Once over the age of 4–8 months, dogs rarely suffer serious illness from roundworms, although these may cause occasional vomiting, or even diarrhœa, and some loss of coat and bodily condition. It is now known that puppies are infected before birth from their mother. It is therefore desirable to keep down the incidence of roundworms in the mother—and in dogs generally—and fortunately the modern preparations are—unlike some of the old-fashioned ones—safe in use and unlikely to cause digestive disturbances. From all that has been said above owners will realise the necessity of taking professional advice about young dogs which are ill, and any signs of " worms " in young puppies—either in the stools or by some obvious intestinal upset or bloated appearance of the belly—should be acted upon. One last word about this aspect of worms—do not assume that your adult dog has " tapeworms " unless you see some evidence in his stools. There are so many "signs of worms " that veterinary surgeons must at times get a little tired of being assured that " My dog has worms " because of some trivial habit connected with appetite.

There is, however, another side to the study of tapeworms, and one which is not generally realised. The tapeworm which is found in the dog represents one stage in the life-cycle. The eggs, which are present in the ripe segment passed by the dog, develop, not in the outside world, but in another animal altogether. Thus one of the commonest tapeworms in this country has an intermediate stage, as it is called, in the flea, and it is when the flea is eaten by the dog that this intermediate stage develops further to become a tapeworm. Another tapeworm has an intermediate stage which develops in the sheep, and a third has one which develops in the ox. There is a fourth tapeworm which has an intermediate stage which *may* develop in man, to set up serious diseases in certain cases. Children may become infected through handling the dog, and so picking up the eggs, which may then be eaten through putting the hands in the mouth. The dogs which are most likely to be infested are those which have the opportunity to eat freshly killed sheep and other food-animals. An ordinary household dog is not likely to be infested, and people should not worry unduly in this connection, provided they do not allow their dogs to stray into the wrong places. It is illegal to allow dogs to enter a slaughter-house, but unfortunately one often sees dogs in such places. The routine worming of dogs is justified if evidence of infection exists, and certainly in country areas where opportunities of tapeworm re-infection may be plentiful.

Tumours.

Tumours, including malignant tumours (" cancers ") are relatively very common in the dog—almost as common as in the human subject. Space does not permit of a detailed account, but the following examples of growths may be mentioned: a proliferation of warts on the lips of puppies (usually disappear spontaneously); a true cancer of the tonsil in middle-aged and older dogs of both sexes; cancer of the mammary glands in bitches (both incurable); fatty growths of the vagina of bitches (amenable to operation).

Space does not allow of the discussion of other diseases, but it should be pointed out that dogs are susceptible to human and bovine forms of *tuberculosis*, especially the former. In a household which contains a tubercular person, the dog should be watched for any signs of illness, and the thought entertained that he might be responsible for the further spread of the disease. In the late 1960s, it was reported that a virus of the herpes group could cause the death of pups at 3–4 weeks of age. The infection is transmitted from dam to young *in utero*. For a discussion on ringworm see the appropriate heading in the section on the cat.

Accidents and Injuries.

In these days of swiftly moving motor transport, street accidents to dogs are extremely common. Many could be prevented by training the animal to walk to heel, by the use of a lead in busy thoroughfares, and by not allowing dogs to roam the streets unaccompanied—a thoroughly bad habit. Sometimes the victim escapes with a scare and a few bruises, and at others death is mercifully swift. In the vast majority of accidents, however, a more or less serious injury is incurred, and if the animal is unable to move, the police should be notified immediately. The dog is best left quiet, and it is not recommended that attempts be made to administer brandy or other supposed "stimulants" unless help is markedly delayed. Excessive haemorrhage may in some instances be prevented by common-sense application of principles learnt in first-aid courses.

One of the commonest accidents to dogs, especially to young dogs, is a fracture involving the head of the femur, or thigh-bone. Inability to put one of the hind legs to the ground, or to bear any weight on this limb, is an indication of such an injury. (This injury may occur also from falling off a chair or wall.) Professional help is, of course, required in such cases.

Cuts and Bruises.

Cuts and bruises, if not serious, may be treated at home as in the case of human beings. The indiscriminate use of tincture of iodine is not to be recommended, and spirit alone makes a more satisfactory dressing in most cases. Simple washing and removal of dirt are usually sufficient, combined, perhaps, with modern antiseptic ointments or other preparations. The dog (and also the cat) are very liable to sepsis, and it is best in such cases to send for proper assistance early, or there may be grave trouble. It is probable that in nature many of the flesh-eating animals end their lives as victims of the sepsis following wounds.

Injuries from cat-scratches are exceedingly common, as are bites from other dogs. These are serious, as they more readily result in septic places. The scratch or bite sometimes penetrates quite deeply, leaving a pocket which fills up with pus. This pus may spread under the skin to form sinuses. Never neglect such places.

Conclusion.

There are a few concluding remarks on the treatment of the diseases of the dog:—

(1) It is not correct that "water should be withheld from a sick dog." It is true that an animal which is using water only to vomit, or which is drinking excessively, should have its water intake restricted, but it is wrong to deprive a dog altogether. It may be suffering from diabetes and should be taken to the vet for testing.

(2) There have been such wonderful advances in the field of veterinary anaesthetics that there is nowadays little to fear in this connection from operations to dogs and cats. The records over the past years at the Royal Veterinary College, London and at other centres have been most encouraging, and the anaesthetic risk is now small indeed.

(3) When a dog's life is a burden to him, it is unfair to keep him alive, and he should be put to sleep. It must be realised, however, that putting a dog to sleep is a very skilled task. It is made much easier if an owner will allow his veterinary surgeon to administer an anaesthetic and not allow the animal "to come round," and shooting is also straightforward and painless if *skilfully* carried out. There are no "magical ways" of destroying human or animal life, and an owner must not expect his veterinary surgeon to be able to bring about death merely by holding a pad to the dog's face. It is usually better that the task be carried out at a veterinary surgeon's own premises, where there is skilled assistance.

CATS.

Description.

Many of the general remarks in the preceding section apply equally to cats, and will not be repeated unnecessarily in the following paragraphs.

The domestic cat (*Felis catus*) is one of the smallest members of the genus *Felis*, a group of predatory carnivorous mammals that includes lions and tigers. They have characteristic rounded skulls with small incisor teeth, prominent sharp canine teeth and large molars. They can climb, leap and move rapidly for short periods, and cheetahs are the fastest runners of all animals, but do not need or benefit from prolonged exercise. Indeed, a fully grown, healthy cat may be unable to follow the leisurely pace of a strolling human being for even half an hour without showing signs of exhaustion.

Dr. Patricia Scott, of the Royal Free Hospital School of Medicine, and perhaps the world's leading scientific authority on cats, has written a valuable chapter on them in the *UFAW Handbook*.

Most authorities subscribe to the view that the European domestic cat probably originated from crossing between 2 wild species, *Felis sylvestris* and *F. lybica*, and certainly it has been domesticated for thousands of years. (The wild cat of Scotland is a sub-species of *F. sylvestris*). The tabby markings of *F. catus* appear in 2 distinct forms: the first, "torquata" with narrow vertical stripes on the body, and the second, "catus" with 3 dorsal stripes running to the root of the tail and a looped or spiral arrangement of blotched stripes on the side.

Konrad Lorenz, whose observations have already been referred to, has provided beautiful descriptions of the play of kittens, which, in fact, provide evidence for the existence of inborn hunting behaviour. Kittens and other cats are attracted by almost any moving object. Since the majority of cats are neutered at an early age, while entire males indulge in sexual behaviour out of doors, the development of certain forms of adolescent behaviour are often absent or unseen in domestic pets.

Cats will defend their homes against neighbouring or intruding cats, and also possess a fairly large hunting territory which they will guard against trespassers. There may, of course, be partial overlap between neighbouring territories. Encounters between strange cats are enacted according to what seem to be fixed rules. The territory "owner" usually has the better of it. The superior cat attempts to smell the nose and anus of the intruder as the latter tries to explore the strange territory. Even quite young cats will attempt a thorough exploration of a new room. A true submissive attitude does not, however, appear to be usual in adult cats, which as solitary animals do not establish rigid social orders if several of them are kept together in a fairly large room. One or two "despots" and one or more " pariahs " may emerge but the rest of the crowd appears to be on equal footing.

The reaction of cats to dogs and to man has received considerable study. Most people look upon cats and dogs as sworn enemies, but the kitten does not seem to have any inborn understanding of the facial expressions of the dog. It would seem that cats, without previous experience do not understand the expressive movements of dogs, even though these are so similar to their own. Cats which are on friendly terms with dogs in the same house may display a trustfulness towards strange dogs with disastrous results. It is equally unusual, incidentally, for a cat-friendly dog to understand the threatening of a cat unless it has already learnt to do so from bitter experience.

Many cat owners are proud of the independence of their charges, and Lorenz has emphasised the dual role of the cat that hunts and fights out of doors but becomes a peaceful pet within. He said that, in spite of their well-defined private lives in the wild which often kept them from home for days on end, his most temperamental and virile cats were at the same time the most affectionate.

Some animal behaviourists say that cats, alone among mammals below the primates, are capable of true imitative behaviour, *i.e.*, can copy a novel or otherwise improbable act, or some act for which there is clearly no instructive tendency. Cats will spontaneously copy the begging of dogs at table and one of the authors, when young and with plenty of time to spare, succeeded in teaching young kittens to play " hide and seek " both ways, and even to learn to box one another.

Cat showing and pedigree breeding are not so extensive as comparable activities for dogs, but there exists a Governing Council of the Cat Fancy. The secretary is Mrs. W. Davis, Dovefields, Petworth Road, Witley, Surrey GU8 5QW and the receptor for all registration, transfers and export pedigrees is Mr. R. Loveys, 28 Brendon Road, Watchet, Somerset (Watchet 395). There are separate secretaries for the many different Cat Groups, and the Honorary Secretary of the National Cat Club is Mrs. Rosemary Gowdy, Porlock House, Haw Lane, Bledlow Ridge, Bucks. (024-027-463). The objects of the Council are to provide for the registration of cats and cat pedigrees, to classify cat breeds, to provide cat shows, to improve cat breeding, to protect the welfare of cats and the interests of cat owners generally, to exercise disciplinary powers and to concern itself with publications.

The accompanying table lists the different breeds by the numbers that have been registered by the Council.

There is an up-to-date book by Dr. R. Robinson, *Genetics for Cat Breeders* (Oxford: Pergamon). For those who wish to make a scientific study, further information can be found in the issues of *Carnivore Genetics Newsletter*, obtainable from P.O. Box 5, Newtownville, Massachusetts 02160, USA.

BREED NUMBERS

Long-Haired Cats

1	Black.
2	White (Blue Eyes).
2a	White (Orange Eyes).
2b	White (Odd Eyes).
3	Blue.
4	Red Self.
5	Cream.
6	Smoke.
6a	Blue Smoke.
7	Silver Tabby.
8	Brown Tabby.
9	Red Tabby
10	Chinchilla.
11	Tortoiseshell.
12	Tortoiseshell-and-White.
12a	Bi-Coloured.
13	Blue Cream.
13a	Any Other Colour.
13b/1	Seal Colourpoint.
13b/2	Blue Colourpoint.
13b/3	Chocolate Colourpoint.
13b/4	Lilac Colourpoint.
13b/5	Red Colourpoint.
13b/6	Tortie Colourpoint.
13b/7	Cream Colourpoint.
13b/8	Blue Cream Colourpoint.
13b/9	Chocolate Cream Colourpoint.
13b/10	Lilac Cream Colourpoint.
13c	Birman.
13d	Turkish.

Short-Haired Cats

14	White (Blue Eyes).
14a	White (Orange Eyes).
14b	White (Odd Eyes).
15	Black.
16	Blue British.
16a	Blue Russian.
17	Cream.
18	Silver Tabby.
19	Red Tabby.
20	Brown Tabby.
21	Tortoiseshell.
22	Tortoiseshell-and-White.
23	Abyssinian.
23a	Red Abyssinian.
23b	Cream Abyssinian.
23c	Blue Abyssinian.
23d	Chocolate Abyssinian.
23e	Lilac Abyssinian.
23x	A.O.C. Abyssinian.
24	Seal-Pointed Siamese.
24a	Blue-Pointed Siamese.
24b	Chocolate-Pointed Siamese.
24c	Lilac-Pointed Siamese.
25	Manx.
25a	Stumpies.
25b	Tailed.
26	Any Other Variety.
27	Brown Burmese.
27a	Blue Burmese.
27b	Chocolate Burmese.
27c	Lilac Burmese.

27d	Red Burmese.
27e	Tortie Burmese.
27f	Cream Burmese.
27g	Blue-Cream Burmese.
27h	Chocolate-Tortie Burmese.
27j	Lilac-Cream Burmese.
28	Blue Cream.
29	Havana.
29c	Foreign Lilac.
30	Spotted.
31	Bi-Coloured.
32	Tabby-Point Siamese.
32a	Red-Point Siamese.
32b	Tortie-Point Siamese.
32x	A.O.C. Siamese.
33	Cornish Rex.
33a	Devon Rex.
35	Foreign White.
32c	Cream Point.
34	Korat.
36	Smoke.

Although there are, as noted above, many varieties of cat, most people are content to accept an ordinary kitten, and for them the chief points to consider will be: (a) whether to have a long-haired or a short-haired animal, (b) whether to have a male or female, (c) whether or not to have the kitten "doctored" (i.e., castrated or spayed). As a general rule, short-haired cats are probably more suitable for the average household, since their fur does not become shed so noticeably and they probably suffer less from "fur-balling." Nevertheless, many long-haired cats are so attractive that they will obviously be preferred, and there is no reason why they should not be chosen. Sex is a rather more important question, although, as may be seen in the section on management, it is possible to have both males and females "doctored." Male cats which are kept as entires are often a nuisance in that they make abominable smells in the house and spend much of their time in fighting. These characteristics are by no means invariable; but they are so common as to justify the castration of the majority of males. Siamese males in particular may be a liability. Females are generally credited with a greater attachment to the home (although they wander when "in season") and with being better mousers. The principal objection to females is that they seem to be bearing kittens almost continuously. In normal circumstances it is, of course, quite impossible to prevent cats from mating by keeping the female in confinement during her season, a practice which is frequently adopted in the case of the dog. For one thing, most people are never aware when their female cats are in season.

Whatever animal is chosen, it is essential to pick a healthy and preferably a fairly young—but *not* too young—kitten. It is best not to accept a kitten under about eight weeks of age.

For those who are prepared for additional responsibilities, Siamese cats make excellent and highly intelligent pets. Siamese kittens are born white, but gradually develop their even pale fawn colour, with cream on belly and chest and with "seal brown" mask, ears, legs, feet, and tail. The coat is very short, and the eyes are blue. There has long been a popular belief that Siamese cats are delicate creatures, but the present writers have seen healthy specimens, kept under ordinary household conditions, living to a mature age. It is not wise to keep a male Siamese as a household pet. The male is a fierce fighter, and is generally a worse offender in the house than the males of other breeds, and should therefore be castrated if it is to be kept as a pet.

Many people find Manx cats attractive. Instead of the normal large number of tail bones, they have but three, and hence appear almost tailless. One should beware against fraudulent amputation of the tail of ordinary cats, which are then described as "Manx."

Accommodation and Management.

The cat is an independent creature, so much so that one may say that to a large extent it manages its own affairs. This, however, is not true of all cats, and every reasonable attempt should be made to provide the cat with a comfortable and friendly home. Cats are highly intelligent, and if sufficient patience is exercised they will respond to a very great degree to human attention. Kittens should not be neglected, but should be talked to and played with just as are puppies. Many cats, especially young cats make excellent playmates for children.

In order to prevent to a large extent their nocturnal wanderings, many cats of both sexes are castrated or spayed (the popular lay expression for this is " doctored "). In the male cat the testicles are removed by an operation which is almost always safe and simple if carried out skilfully. From three to four months is a good age at which to have this done. Female cats may also be " doctored." As the female glands or ovaries lie within the body cavity, this operation is a major one, but it is nevertheless quite a straightforward, though a more expensive, procedure, if conducted at the right age (about five months). Very many thousands of female cats have been so operated upon and the subsequent health of these cats has been excellent. Indeed, it has been said that a spayed female makes one of the best of all household cats.

Cats may choose to sleep in a variety of places, and will often lie on beds, chairs, mats, and other warm places. It is a sound policy to provide them with a box or basket, and to encourage them to use newspaper as a bedding. Most cats will take well to newspaper. The bed should be placed in a warm site—it is of little use putting it in a cold corner of a room and expecting the cat to lie in it.

Owing to the fact that, even in play, a cat's claws may inflict serious injury, dogs and cats do not always make the best of house companions. Nevertheless, the traditional enmity of cat and dog is often overcome, and if the two are brought up together they often make firm friends, sharing the same basket or hearth-rug and feeding together without serious consequences.

A cat normally attends to its own toilet, and everyone must be aware that a cat devotes long periods each day to cleaning and washing itself. Except in special cases, therefore, bathing is quite unnecessary, while in short-haired cats especially grooming, too, is superfluous (this does not apply to show-cats). For some reason (and sometimes, apparently, because an owner attempts to assist in the daily grooming) an occasional cat may cease to wash or care for itself. Such an animal is a dejected sight, and should be taken to a veterinary surgeon to have its matted fur cut or combed, and its dirt removed. Such animals (unless they completely re-acquire their self-respect) must be groomed regularly if they are to be kept at all.

All household cats are accustomed to take their own exercise, and it is advisable (except in any special circumstances) to allow them free access to and from the outer world. Do not shut your cat in the house for a long period and then blame it for making a mess. Cats are clean creatures; they normally dig small holes in which to defaecate or urinate, and subsequently cover the deposit with earth. If, therefore, they are for some reason debarred temporarily or permanently from access to a garden, they should be provided with a box or tray containing soil or cinders. Indeed, in many types of houses it is a good plan to encourage kittens to use such a device. (Note the corresponding remarks about puppies.)

It is generally stated that " cats never forget a blow," and for that reason it is recommended that cats are not chastised. It may be said that, if a cat (or dog) be brought up conscientiously and well, it should never, or very rarely, require such punishment. An animal which has been brought up properly seems to develop a fair sense of what is right and what is wrong.

For pedigree cats, or those kept in confinement for other reasons, see the relevant remarks in the section on breeding.

Feeding.

Cats are true carnivores, and wild or feral cats eat rodents, frogs, insects and occasionally birds, supplementing these by raids on human food-stores and waste-bins. Both large and small members of the cat family consume all their prey, i.e. they eat the skin, bones and viscera as well as the lean meat or muscle, and thus obtain adequate supplies of all essential foods. The well-nourished

adult cat is an occasional feeder, and usually has a considerable body reserve of fat and protein. It can generally withstand periods of fasting remarkably well, as has been shown by the survival of cats that have been accidentally shut in outhouses. Dr. Scott states that cats differ from rodents in that they will starve to death rather than eat a diet they dislike. The first criterion of satisfactory diet, therefore, must be that the animal will eat sufficient of it to supply enough calories for maintenance, growth and—in the case of breeding stock—reproduction. Cats can very easily be put off their food by anything which frightens them or which affects their general health, and some who are used to being fed by one person will refuse food offered by others.

The taste of food is very important: meat flavours—especially fresh, raw meat but also meat extracts—are appreciated, as are sweet-tasting foods such as milk powder, condensed milk or chocolate, while most cats like butter, margarine and other fats. For good acceptance of food it must be fresh and free from bacterial decay, and this applies especially to fish. If food has been overcooked, or has been overheated in processing to above about 120°C, it is likely to be rejected.

At weaning, a kitten can be trained to like one particular food in preference to another or to eat a variety of foods, but once the cat's tastes have become fixed it may prove difficult to persuade it to eat a different diet.

The cat requires a greater proportion of protein to ensure satisfactory maintenance and growth than does the dog, and good diets for cats usually contain 12–14% or so of protein on a wet basis. Fat is a valuable source of energy, and especially when canned or dried foods are fed it is important to ensure an adequate intake of vitamin A. As was indicated in the section on dogs the ratio of calcium to phosphorus is much too low in lean meat, and indeed calcium deficiency is by no means uncommon in cats. Iodine intake may also be low.

Weaned kittens require a total of about 100g of wet diet daily at first, and this should be about 200g at 10 weeks, while a cat feeding 4 kittens may eat up to 500g of meat a day. The fluid requirements of cats are usually met by giving liquid milk, but access to a clean water supply is always desirable. Fluid requirements are greatly increased during lactation.

Although most cats are capable of supplementing their diet by catching small rodents or birds, it is unwise to rely on this as a regular source of food. The idea that hungry cats make the best mousers is by no means always correct. Indeed, animals that are in poor condition are less likely to be successful hunters. Moreover, while the riddance of pests is an excellent matter from the human point of view—and one of the reasons why the keeping of cats is economically justified—the " cruel " fashion in which most cats tackle their prey is repulsive to most of us.

It is therefore necessary and desirable to provide regular daily feeding. Kittens should receive several meals a day, but by the time they are six months old the number of daily feeds should be reduced to one or at most, two. Most cats (many Siamese are exceptions) are extremely fond of milk, especially if it is creamy, and the cat's love of fish is well known. Many meats, especially rabbit meat, are relished, and a diet high in " animal protein " is indeed the aim, always provided that it contains sufficient " dietary energy," and is balanced in the ways indicated above. It is significant that cat's milk has a higher content of fat and sugar than cow's milk, i.e., it is a richer source of energy. Some of the proprietary bitch-milk substitutes are nearer to cat's milk in composition than is cow's milk.

Many hundreds of cats have been reared and bred successfully in experimental laboratories on a diet consisting, in the main, of one part of fish or meat and two parts of cooked potatoes. This is relatively inexpensive, and may be supplemented by milk and by some of the proprietary cat foods.

Cats are also extremely fond of liver. Some of the proprietary cat foods—the better ones of which are excellent—and vitamin tablets contain liver, which is a rich source of the vitamin B complex.

Within reason a healthy kitten should be fed to appetite, always provided good-quality foods are available. The amount should be restricted when they are adult, however, except for pregnant and lactating cats, which are sometimes referred to as "queens" as opposed to the male "toms."

Cats are, as noted above, fastidious eaters; they usually sniff and examine carefully any strange or doubtful food. At the same time they are often greedy, especially with relished food to which they are accustomed, but fortunately they can, like dogs vomit very readily. Here, incidentally, is one very good tip—an excellent emetic for both cat and dog is a small crystal of washing-soda, given as a pill. People are usually amazed at the way this simple device results in a dog's or a cat's bringing up undesirable food.

It is important not to overfeed cats, and it is almost equally important to prepare all food in a clean manner, and to make it as attractive as possible. Cats will greatly appreciate this care. While milk is an excellent food for kittens (see under breeding), and is relished by most adult cats, it must be supplemented by solid food.

As already indicated, clean fresh water should be provided at all times even if the cat appears to drink it but little.

Breeding.

Pedigree animals are normally confined, and their breeding is strictly controlled. Ordinary household cats are at the opposite extreme, and there is little that can be done to prevent their mating. The length and scope of this article does not permit of a discussion of controlled mating.

Scientifically, there is as yet a good deal to learn about the reproductive behaviour of the cat. As an American physiologist has succinctly put it in a description of the reproductive cycle of the female cat, "no two authors agree." In Northern Europe there are two main heat periods a year, in spring and early autumn, but some animals may appear in heat at any time from January to July, and those who keep female cats in confinement describe their charges as "calling" quite frequently if not mated. A cat which is "in season" or "on heat" is often observed to be behaving in a quite characteristic fashion, rolling about on the floor and making peculiar sounds. The periods of heat, which commence usually at about eight months of age, may last for several days, and during this time the female will make every attempt to find a mate.

Gestation lasts about nine weeks, as in the case of the bitch but here again there is a considerable variation. As most owners are quite unaware of the time at which their cats were mated, it is difficult to talk of "going overtime," but if there is any evidence of trouble during pregnancy, or at birth, veterinary advice should be obtained. As soon as a cat is obviously pregnant, her food allowance should be increased, and she should be allowed plenty of milk. It is highly important to increase her food and milk ration still further after the kittens are born, as lactation is a great drain on the mother.

Cats sometimes choose strange, out-of-the-way places in which to litter, and many healthy litters are born and reared out of doors. Rats are a source of danger, and will often destroy very young kittens during the mother's absence. For this and other reasons it is better in town and suburban areas to have the litter comfortably housed indoors. A wooden box containing newspaper is ideal, provided it is kept in a fairly warm place and out of the way of draughts. An average litter consists of three to six kittens, which are born blind, but which normally open their eyes after eight or nine days. There is no need to be alarmed if the eyes remain closed for a few days longer. Kittens which are born dead should be removed and buried or burnt. If the whole litter is born dead, the mother's food supply should be cut down considerably, and little milk given for a few days. If the mammary glands become inflamed, they may be bathed in a cold solution of alum. The glands normally return to their former size within a short space of time if they are not milked, but if there is persistent trouble veterinary advice should be sought.

While many pedigree owners wean kittens at four to five weeks of age, it is strongly advised that the household cat be allowed to continue to feed her family for a longer period, and eight weeks is not too long if the mother is still in good bodily condition. She *must*, however, be well fed and be allowed plenty of milk. As in the case of puppies, it is an excellent idea to provide the kittens with a little solid food as from a few weeks of age. It is very wrong to remove a kitten from its mother too early, and such an animal is often weakly, develops an intestinal infection, and dies as a miserable bedraggled creature. Moreover, during the period following weaning the mother educates her offspring in the art of living, including mousing.

As many litters are unwanted, some people get rid of all the kittens as soon as possible after birth. Drowning is frequently practised, but it is not recommended as a merciful death. Indeed, a hard blow on the back of the head is more humane if given accurately. It is much better to take the kittens to a veterinary surgeon or clinic.

Diseases.

A normally healthy cat, which is unafraid, has an alert bearing and moves about readily with head held straight, showing interest in its surroundings. It is able to spring to the floor from a table or window sill with an easy controlled movement. Its skin is clean and free from blemishes, and there is in most instances a thick bushy undercoat with either short or long silky guard hairs according to variety. Its eyes are shining, its teeth are white and free from tartar, and its tongue and gums are clean and pinkish. The ear holes are also clean. It grooms itself frequently and has a sleek appearance. On the back of a well-fed cat, the lumbar muscles form a firm bundle on either side, and the vertebrae should not be felt easily in the adult. A cat that remains in its box or resting place at mealtimes and that displays little interest in food, may not be well. Watery or purulent discharges from the eyes, discharges from the nose or ears, excessive salivation, vomiting and diarrhoea are all indications of possible infection, including that which may result from accidents or fighting.

The principal infectious diseases of cats are still in need of much scientific study. It is now clear, however, that there are at least two major cat plagues. Both have been given many names, and there is much confusion between them.

Feline Enteritis or Panleucopenia.

This is a highly infectious disease, due to a filterable virus. The symptoms include loss of appetite, sometimes accompanied by a rise in body temperature, followed by listlessness, usually vomiting, sometimes diarrhoea, and a marked tendency to show tenderness or pain on being handled. This tenderness or pain is due to a developing peritonitis. The poor animal may become seriously ill, with loss of water from the tissues or dehydration, prostrate and dead within 48 hours or less from the time of the first symptoms. The incubation period of the disease is believed to be from 4 to 8 days, or sometimes longer. There is a fall in the white-cell count of the blood, hence the term "panleucopenia." Some cats recover, the recovery rate in different outbreaks that have been studied ranging from 30 to 80 per cent., and recovered animals are probably immune to further attacks. Cats that are able to take a little food during the early stages of recovery have the best chance of recovery, but require careful nursing. There may be complications during the convalescent stage due to secondary bacterial infections or to vitamin deficiency, and a light nourishing diet, combined with vitamin preparations, is recommended. Fleas may transmit the disease to other cats, as may contact with infected materials. It has been shown that bedding and dirt trays from sick cats were infectious for other cats for up to 16 days. The disease is not transmissible to dogs or to human beings. There is nowadays a protective vaccine, and it is a wise precaution to have your pet vaccinated.

Feline Pneumonitis.

This disease is sometimes called "cat distemper"—as indeed is feline enteritis—but it has no connection with dog distemper, and is not transmissible to dogs or to human beings. Both mild and severe forms occur, and the incubation period varies from 5 to 8 days. The mild form may seem like a cold, and there is a weeping from the eyes and a varying degree of conjunctivitis. There is a thin, clear discharge from the nose, with a characteristic sneezing. Provided that the animals can be made to continue eating, and are kept in warm and dry but ventilated conditions, recovery may be rapid and not entail serious loss of condition. The eyes should be treated with a suitable preparation, such as silver vitellin. There may be secondary bacterial infection in cases that are neglected.

The severe form of the disease has similar, although more severe, commencing symptoms, but the nasal discharge becomes purulent and there is often profuse salivation, with much spreading of the long ropes of saliva. The cat is listless, dislikes strong light, and seems to resent being disturbed. It loses its appetite, and rapidly becomes thinner over a period of from 2 to 5 days or so. Breathing becomes laboured, and a bronchopneumonia develops. There may be a high death rate in young kittens, and pregnant females may abort. Recovery tends to be slow, and is often complicated by bacterial infection. Some of the modern antibiotics appear to be highly effective in the treatment of many cases of this disease, but they must, of course, be given under veterinary supervision.

Tuberculosis.

The cat, like the dog, can contract tuberculosis, but so far as is known only the bovine form has been known to infect it. The infection usually comes, of course, from milk, and the elimination of bovine tuberculosis from this country will stop the incidence of the disease in cats. The disease commences in the abdomen, but may spread to the lungs. There is general wasting.

Skin Diseases.

As in the case of the dog, skin disease in the cat is usually of parasitic origin, and fleas and mange mites are again the chief source of trouble in Great Britain. Cats do so much of their own toilet that the average household cat has probably a cleaner skin than its canine counterpart. When skin disease does develop, it is strongly advised that the animal be taken to a veterinary surgeon for appropriate treatment. As a rule cats greatly resent the interference which must accompany any attempt to bathe or dress an affected place, and for this reason it is usually unwise for an owner to attempt to do other than make an inspection. Very small patches of skin eruption may clear satisfactorily if the surrounding hair is clipped away with curved scissors, but generally speaking skin disease calls for professional attention. The cat flea has a similar life cycle to the dog flea.

Diseases of the Ear.

The outer ear of the cat is frequently affected, and in a great many cases a form of mange mite is responsible. The animal provides evidence of the trouble by scratching and shaking its ear and generally showing its discomfort. It will not always be possible, for an owner to make a thorough examination, as in many cases the cat objects, but if it is possible to look inside the ear it will be seen that there is a dirty and usually brownish mess of tissue, sometimes mixed with dried blood or pus. Not all cases are as bad as this, of course, but if a cat persistently worries its ear it should be taken to a veterinary surgeon. There are satisfactory dressings for this condition, and owners will be able to dress their cats if the latter are docile. Otherwise it is necessary to have the ears dressed by a veterinary surgeon or by one of his staff.

A cat's ear is frequently the site of a blood blister, or haematoma. This is usually the sequel to a blow, such as a slamming door, and shows itself as a large, tense swelling, which when opened by the surgeon proves to be an accumulation of serum usually tinged with blood. Some cases become infected at the time of injury, some after with the patient's rubbing. With the greatest surgical skill in the world one must expect a slight deformity, and the cat develops a puckered ear, much the same as the human boxer.

Disease of the Urinary tract.

The bladder is a common seat of disease in cats and is frequently affected through the blocking of the natural water-passage by small sand-like calculi. Neutered male cats are more often affected, as the terminal end of the urinary tracts is wider and more dilatable in females. The urine is unable to escape, and the bladder becomes filled with a mixture of urine and the sandy calcular matter. The condition may be diagnosed quite readily, as the cat usually collapses, or partially collapses and one may easily feel the distended bladder through the walls of the abdomen (belly). It is necessary to send for professional help immediately, and, while no relief can be guaranteed it is often possible to relieve the condition by judicious manipulation. Owners should not attempt to do this themselves (unless help cannot be obtained), as they may easily burst the bladder. As the animal is usually in a state of collapse when the condition is discovered, it makes a bad risk for actual operation, and relief by *skilled* pressure is usually to be recommended.

Ringworm.

There are two common kinds of ringworm in the cat (a third, which may also infect the dog, is more rare; it is the trichophyton which is usually found on cattle). The first kind is acquired from rats and mice, and is most commonly to be found at the bases of the claws, from where it may spread to the ears and face. The individual lesions are circular and yellow in colour, and consist largely of a scabby material. This kind of ringworm is known as " favus."

The second type of ringworm (microsporon) is more important, because it is more readily transmissible to human beings. Whereas this form usually sets up circular scaly lesions in the dog, it often infects cats without there being much naked-eye evidence of its presence. Indeed, in the cat the condition is often unsuspected until the owner himself becomes infected and consults his doctor.

Ringworm should be treated or dealt with by a veterinary surgeon, who will also confirm or refute by special methods the presence of microsporon in cats.

Intestinal Parasites—" Worms."

The cat also is subject to both roundworms and tapeworms. The roundworm which parasitises cats in this country is similar to that of the dog (although a different species) and is also much more harmful to the young than to the adult animal. In kittens the symptoms are a general unthriftiness, staring coat, and in some cases diarrhœa and a " pot-bellied " appearance.

The commonest cat tapeworm in this country is one which passes its intermediate stage in the rat or mouse, or sometimes in other rodents. The tapeworm, which, as mentioned under the section on dogs, is dangerous to man, is sometimes found in the cat also.

Accidents and Injuries.

Despite their sagacity and alertness in many ways, cats seem curiously unable, in many instances, to acquire road-sense. They are dazed by a car's head-lights, while if a motorist sounds his horn they tend to stop still in their tracks.

Injuries from traps, *e.g.*, gin-traps, are very common, and it is probable that many thousands of cats annually are maimed in this fashion. Cats suffer injury from shooting, from stoning, and from blows with sticks. Since they are predatory animals, they have often to pay the penalty inflicted on them by wrathful people. Needless to say, cats which survive to return home usually require expert treatment.

Poisoning may be included under this heading. Although there are doubtless many deliberate attempts to poison marauding cats, alleged " poisoning " is often no more than a case of feline enteritis, and owners should not claim glibly that their cats have been poisoned until they have expert evidence to back their judgment.

Fur-balling, as it has been termed, may be mentioned here. Cats, especially the long-haired varieties, must often ingest hair during their toilet, and occasionally serious trouble (a stoppage of the bowels) is brought about by a mass of such hair which has collected in a part of the bowel. There is constipation, loss of condition, and often evidence of considerable pain. Such cats should be taken to a veterinary surgeon.

Bites and scratches are even more common in the cat than they are in the dog and subsequent sepsis is equally likely.

FERRETS.

Description.

The ferret (*Mustela putorius furo*) is a carnivore of the mustelid group to which belong otters, weasels and mink. In their chapter in the *UFAW Handbook*, Doctors J. Hammond Jr. & F. C. Chesterman report that it has been domesticated for at least 2000 years and that it is generally held to be a form of the European polecat, with which it will interbreed, although some consider it to be a hybrid between the polecat and other species. As a domesticated animal it has been used principally for hunting rabbits and other prey, and has thus gained a reputation for ferocity which Dr. Hammond suggests is quite undeserved. One of the authors has employed ferrets for nutritional studies, and is well aware of the fact that they must be handled with care especially by strangers. They are most easily rendered completely docile so far as human beings are concerned, by handling them while still young, and in this respect they may be compared with the "finger-tamed" mink. Most tame ferrets have pink eyes and yellowish-white fur, but there are darker forms believed to have resulted from crossing in previous generations with wild polecats. Indeed, these darker forms are popularly termed "polecat ferrets." They are of two main kinds, the first having creamy under-fur and black guard hairs, and the second being a chocolate-brown colour, with brown upper-parts and black under-parts, and a few scattered light hairs on the face.

Ferrets are long creatures in relation to their body weight, and when fully grown may have a body 36 cm long or more and a tail of 13 cm. Some strains grow appreciably larger.

Accommodation.

Ferrets must have dry, clean accommodation in a room free from draughts but well ventilated. Wood is warmer than metal, but more difficult to clean, and is best lined with hard asbestos sheeting, which is resistant to water. The most suitable accommodation comprises a sleeping compartment of similar proportions to a small kennel, leading by a small doorway or "pop-hole" to a wire-netting exercising run, which should be as large as possible compatible with cleanliness. It is a good idea to have a means of closing the doorway so that the ferret or ferrets may be confined within the sleeping-compartment if necessary. Wood-wool makes an excellent bedding, but if difficult to obtain newspaper may be provided for the ferret to lie on. The floor of the run may have a false bottom or may be sprinkled with sawdust. It is imperative to keep the whole of the accommodation clean and dry, not only to avoid smell but also to prevent the ferrets from developing a very serious necrotic infection of the feet known as "foot-rot", see below.

Feeding.

Many ferrets are unfortunately not fed adequately. It must be appreciated that basically they are carnivorous animals, and that their food requirements are more similar to those of the dog and cat than those of rodents. Indeed, many of the general remarks made about the principles of feeding dogs and cats apply to ferrets also.

Most ferrets like bread-and-milk, and while this is an excellent article of diet, it is in itself inadequate. Up to about 125 g of raw meat (minced for younger animals) daily is an excellent basis, and this may be replaced by fish. Liver,

especially raw liver, is an excellent source of many factors, and there is good reason to provide some at least weekly if it can be obtained. Failing this, it is advisable to add 1–2 per cent. of whole dry liver to the diet. Once ferrets are grown, one feeding daily—at a fixed time— is sufficient. The female (jill) should have ample supplies of milk just prior to the birth of her young and while she is suckling them.

Breeding.

In the northern hemisphere the female ferret usually comes into oestrus (season) in early March of the year following that in which it is born. If the jill does not conceive during this oestrus she will have a further oestral period in July or August. The desire of the jill to mate is very strong, and if not allowed to do so, some animals sometimes have been found to waste and pine. The act of mating is prefaced by very vigorous behaviour on the part of the male (hob), and anyone not appreciating the performance might think that he was out to kill his mate! The mating act itself is usually prolonged, and may take up to three hours. If left together the hob and jill will probably mate from two to four times during the course of a couple of days. As in the cat and rabbit, ovulation or the shedding of the egg from the ovary takes place as a result of mating, and not spontaneously. The period of gestation is forty-two days, and the numbers of young born usually varies from five to thirteen, the average litter being six to eight. Pseudo-pregnancy occurs if the jill is not mated, and may become outwardly obvious as in the case of certain bitches.

Males also have a seasonal rhythm, their capacity to fertilise being greatest from early March to August. Young hobs seem to be active about a month earlier than older ones. The length of daylight or, rather, the incrementation in light from day to day, has an important bearing on breeding capacity in both sexes, and by the use of artificial light it has proved possible to induce either oestrus or male activity at different times of the year.

The young are hairless and blind, and weigh on the average under 15 g at birth. Their eyes open at about four weeks, and they can then commence to eat small pieces of solid food to supplement their mother's milk. They may be weaned at from six to eight weeks.

Diseases.

Ferrets are extremely susceptible to the virus of *canine distemper*, which is capable of wiping out a whole colony. The disease is transmitted by contact or by droplet infection, with the incubation period of about 10 days. The usual first signs include a watery discharge from the eyes and nose and later there may be muscular tremors, twitching and convulsions. Routine vaccination is, of course, highly desirable. Ferrets are susceptible also to some of the strains of influenza virus that affect man, and cross-infection between staff and ferrets has been described in medical laboratories.

In the days when unpasteurised milk was widely used, ferrets sometimes contracted the bovine strain of *tuberculosis*. Foot-rot is a form of mange and should on no account be neglected, the feet becoming swollen, scabby and eventually clawless. *Mange* or "scabies" of the back and tail region should also be dealt with promptly, employing modern preparations. Ear mite (*Otodectes cynotis*) may produce inflammation and irritation, with resultant scratching of the ears. Following any of these ectoparasitic conditions, the bedding should be burnt and quarters treated with a blow-lamp or treated with a hot, strong solution of washing soda and, of course, thoroughly washed and dried out before the animals are reinstated. *Abscesses* of the neck region are often encountered and should receive treatment if they do not clear up rapidly, as they are likely to spread, with dire consequences. Such abscesses may sometimes arise from perforations from fish bones in the diet. Abscesses of the groin region and of the scent glands are sometimes seen.

Many other diseases of the ferret have been described, and veterinary advice should be sought in the case of any sick animal.

RATS.

Description.

Tame rats are domesticated varieties of the wild Norway or "brown" rat (*Rattus norvegicus*). Such rats are usually albinos or black-and-white, although other colours have been bred. The hooded varieties are those in which the head and foreparts are mainly black or chocolate and the remainder of the body, apart from small patches the same colours as the hood, is white. Tame rats differ materially from wild ones in disposition, and properly managed are extremely tractable. Healthy specimens accustomed to handling bite only when frightened, *e.g.* when a sudden movement is made in front of them. Males appear to live longer than females, but three years is a good age.

"Black" rats, *i.e.* the species (*Rattus rattus*) sometimes known as the ship or Alexandrine rat, have been bred in captivity, but tame strains are not generally available.

Housing.

Tame rats require a warm, even temperature 18–21 °C all the year round—and draughts or lowered temperature may precipitate lung disease or other disorders. It is best to have a complete spare set of boxes or cages, and to change to fresh quarters weekly except when the females have unweaned young with them. Empty cages should be cleaned and disinfected thoroughly before being used again. Provided the temperature conditions are suitable—and this is essential—metal cages of the types employed in scientific laboratories are best with wire-mesh false bottoms and trays containing sawdust to catch the droppings. Accommodation should be ample, and

1·25 cm WIRE MESH

SOLID TRAY TO CATCH DROPPINGS AND SPILLED FOOD, ETC.

CORNER LEDGES TO HOLD EDGES OF WIRE TRAY.

even for a pair of pet rats the cage should measure about 75 cm × 45 cm × 45 cm. If wooden boxes are employed it maybe desirable to line them with hard asbestos sheeting or galvanised metal to prevent damage from gnawing.

Small, dark "shelters" and exercising devices, *e.g.*, wheels or ladders, are appreciated by the rats, but must be kept clean. Wood-wool makes the best bedding.

Feeding.

Rats may take a wide variety of foods, including many of our own, and there are several successful ways of feeding them, including the provision of specially formulated "rat-cubes," of the same type as that described below for mice. A good daily diet is wholemeal bread, mixed creals (*e.g.*, oats, wheat, hempseed), with about 5 per cent. dried brewers' yeast and milk either fed separately or mixed with the rest of the food. Twice weekly each rat should be given up to 15 g or more of meat, liver, fish, or other "animal protein." A little fresh greenfood (even grass) is appreciated, and in winter especially some supplement containing vitamins A and D is desirable. Expectant and nursing mothers should have as much milk as they require. Never overfeed or allow uneaten food residues to remain in the cage. Fresh water (preferably in bulbs or bottles) should be available at all times. Far cleaner than open dishes are the special but simple type of water

bulbs suspended on or in front of the cage or box so that the rat can drink from the rounded end of the spout. A simple substitute is a medicine "flat" bottle—or even a ¼- or ½-pint milk-type bottle. This should be fitted with a cork—or, better, a rubber bung—pierced for a piece of

opening→

WATER BULB SUITABLE FOR USE WITH PET RODENTS.

bent glass tubing. Provided that the free end of the glass tubing is not sharp, and is chosen so that the aperture is considerably smaller than that of the tube itself, the water will not run out unless sucked out by the rat. The spout should, of course, be within easy access of the rat, which will soon learn to drink from it.

Breeding.

Rats can breed at quite a young age (usually being capable of mating when fifty to sixty days old), but it is better to separate the sexes within a fortnight or so of weaning (weaning being usually at twenty-one days of age) and to mate at about 100 to 120 days of age onwards, the female rat has an oestrous cycle lasting just over four days. One male (buck) may be mated to one female (doe)—this is probably best in the case of pet rats—or with two or three females if preferred, but it is unwise to keep more than one adult male in the presence of females. The gestation period is twenty-one to twenty-two days or occasionally a few days longer. The number born varies considerably, but often it is best to try to rear only six to eight young. The young have their ears open at 2¼ to 3¼ days, cut their incisor teeth at eight to ten days, can find their way to their mother at about the same time, open their eyes at fourteen to seventeen days, and may leave the nest at twenty-one days. In the case of pet rats it is probably best to leave the young with the mother for up to a week or so longer. Breeding can occur all the year round, but takes place less readily in winter.

Handling.

Rats should not be "tailed," or the skin may slough off. Regular handling after weaning is excellent and promotes docility. The weight of the body should be supported.

Diseases.

Since many tame rats are derived from laboratory stocks or from breeders who provide laboratories, it is possible for pet animals to suffer from the same infections and parasites. Generally speaking, rats in domestic conditions are much less prone than are mice, provided that temperature conditions are suitable. The commonest infection is a form of *broncho-pneumonia*, carried by some of the animals and precipitated either by the introduction of additional stock or by conditions of cold. *Mange,* especially of the ear, and *infestation of lice* may occur, and should be dealt with promptly by means of modern insecticides.

Those who are interested in the diseases of the rat may follow the references of Dr. W. Lane-Petter in the chapter in the *UFAW Handbook.*

The most important principle in preventing disease in tame rats is to avoid contact with wild rodents and the use of food or bedding that may have been contaminated by wild rats or mice.

MICE.

Description.

Tame mice are descended from the common wild or house mouse (*Mus musculus*), and it is believed that they may have been domesticated for over 3000 years. The wild house mouse exists in very many parts of the world, and is commonly found in places that are inhabited by man, including dwellings, warehouses, food stores and farms. It is quite often found in habitats apart from man where there is plentiful food and shelter. The fur of the wild mouse is agouti, lighter on the under surface, while the eyes are black and the skin is pigmented. Dr. W. Lane-Petter in his comprehensive chapter in the *UFAW Handbook*, states that wild mice are somewhat variable in size but are likely to weigh 18–20 g by 4 weeks of age and may reach 30–40 g by six months or so, when they are fully mature. (Newborn mice weigh about 1 g). They are omnivorous, daring to eat many things that are edible and many things that are not, although they begin tentatively with unfamiliar substances. They are capable of penetrating small holes, wall cavities and roof spaces, and are often able to travel considerable distances in pipes of only 2·5 cm diameter. They can also climb brick walls quite easily. Although they prefer warmth, they have been found able to survive and to breed at low temperatures, and during the second world war they showed themselves capable of breeding in refrigerated meat stores. The animals that did this successfully laid down a great deal of body fat, and had well-developed coats.

Tame mice are similar in size to wild mice, but they have been bred so extensively for scientific and other fancy purposes that there is now a very wide range of coat colours, while both large and small strains exist. Most laboratory, and many tame mice, are albinos.

Laboratory and tame mice are timid, gentle and easily handled. They tend to avoid strong light, and are more active by night than by day. They are gregarious creatures but most of them are determined escapers. Males of some strains tend to be pugnacious when mature, but females are usually docile and seldom fight except when they have young and are disturbed by strangers. Males that are kept in the same cage or box may attack each other fiercely, especially when the weaker cannot escape or seek refuge in bedding, and this is one of the situations in which the characteristic "mousey" odour of acetamide is given off. Provided that they remain healthy, mice may live up to 30 months or more and some to over 3 years.

Housing.

Although strains vary, most tame mice require a warm even temperature and the same general remarks concerning temperature range, bedding, and wooden or metal cages apply as in the case of rats. If a solid floor is used, this should be covered with clean sawdust, wood shavings, cellulose webbing, peat moss, treated wood chips or even sugar beet. It is a good plan to change to a clean cage regularly, except when the female (doe) is nursing her young. If the cage is large (as in the case of pet mice it should be, with a floor space of say 60 cm × 30 cm × 30 cm for a group of mice), inner nesting boxes should be provided—one for each doe if breeding is taking place, although two does will often share the same nest box. (In changing to fresh cages the nest box, with mother and young inside, may, of course, be moved over.) A "two-storey" cage, with a ladder or "staircase" to the upper part, is an attractive variation, although difficult to keep clean. Mice should be kept well out of reach of wild rodents, from which they may all too readily contract disease.

Feeding.

The wild house-mouse is, as already stated, omnivorous, but its preferred foods appear to be cereals, seeds and many types of other substances that are capable of being stored. Mice, like most rodents, have a simple digestive tract, and it has been found that a female in full lactation may eat her own body weight of food and water in 24 hours. The easiest diets to feed are those of the kind employed in laboratories, and sold either as compressed or expanded pellets some 8–12 mm in diameter. Many are in use but all basically contain a large cereal element, sometimes of one kind and sometimes a mixture. Most of the protein is derived from fish meal, meat meal, dried milk or a combination of these. Fat is usually of vegetable origin but may include tallow. Yeast is often included, but there is usually a guaranteed supply of vitamins and minerals that have been added during manufacture in the form of a premix.

Needless to say, there is a considerable variation and the owner should be able to utilise pellets that appear to suit his stock. The pellets should be reasonably hard, especially if fed through a wire hopper, since mice will gnaw at them to the base and pull them through when small enough, then dropping them in the cage to go back for more, thus wasting partially eaten pellets. There should be a supply of pellets in the hopper at all times.

There are, of course, many other ways of feeding mice, and some owners rely upon such items as bread, biscuit and vegetables. Wholemeal bread is excellent if not allowed to become stale but it should not form the sole article of diet, and it is a good plan to feed it alternatively with a grain mixture made up of rolled oats and other cereal grains or mixed bird seed. Cheese is relished, but may smell if not fed carefully. Mice sometimes like the occasional pinch of marmalade, and it is not a bad idea to offer them fresh lettuce or other green food every week or so, always with care to remove eaten and soiled food. It is perhaps worth emphasising that cod-liver oil should not be fed in excess—¼% of the total diet is quite sufficient to provide vitamins A and D—or it may prevent breeding and possibly have other harmful effects.

There should be a constant supply of fresh water preferably from bulbs or bottles as described for rats.

Breeding.

Young mice may be weaned at twenty-one days, although it is usually preferable to leave them with their mother for a further week. The age at which mice are capable of mating varies considerably from one strain or individual to another, and while the average is six to eight weeks, it may be much younger. It is therefore desirable to separate the males from the females at or shortly after weaning. Mice may be mated up at at two to three months of age, and the best arrangements are one male (buck) to one or two females. A pair of mice or a "bigamous trio" makes a successful combination. The oestrus cycle is similar to that of the rat, but its length appears to vary with coat colour, being longest in the brown mice and shortest in blacks and albinos. The gestation period is usually from eighteen to twenty days, but may be prolonged if the female was still suckling her previous litter when she conceived. There may be up to twelve or more young in a litter, but the average litter size is from five to seven. The second litter is usually the largest, and subsequent litters tend to decrease in numbers, so that the sixth is usually smaller than the first. Breeding may take place all the year round, although, as with rats, fertility is higher during the summer months.

Handling.

Any rapid or rough movement may frighten mice and cause them to bite through fear. Mice should be lifted by the tail—not too near the tip—and may be held in the palm of the hand, where they may be suitably restrained by keeping the tail between two fingers.

Diseases.

Mice are, unfortunately, prone to a considerable number of diseases, among them being the virus infections, ectromelia and infantile diarrhoea. Like other rodents, they are susceptible to *salmonellosis*, while susceptible also to what is probably another bacterial infection known as *Tyzzer's disease*.

The risks of diseases are greatly reduced if the mice are kept in suitable surroundings, with avoidance of contamination from other rodents including that from bedding. The quarters should not be accessible to wild house-mice, and it is a good practice to keep the house or building completely free from wild rodents and birds. Dr. Lane-Petter points out that anything that places an extra burden on the animal's metabolism is likely to predispose to disease and that poor nutrition, overcrowding, lack of hygiene, inadequate ventilation, bad handling and exposure—direct or indirect—to mice suffering from disease will all favour an outbreak of disease in a colony. A large colony of high density offers a more favourable environment for the spread of infection than a smaller colony. Infrequent changes of bedding may also favour the development of disease as will poor general standards of cleanliness. Poor ventilation is another adverse factor.

The accurate diagnosis of important diseases of mice calls for expert opinion and even for special laboratory examinations. Most owners should, however, be able to recognise signs of ill-health or departure from normal, one of the commonest being loss of appetite. In young mice the coat should be smooth and glossy. As mice get older there may be loss of pigmentation (in coloured mice) or even loss of fur. A sick mouse usually sits hunched up and has a ruffled coat, while the eyes may be partially closed or have some discharge. A healthy mouse will usually catch on to suitable objects when held by its tail and is capable of pulling quite hard, whereas the pull of a sick mouse is much weaker. If one or more mice die it is best to destroy at once any cage-mates that appear seedy. As in the case of rats, external parasites should be dealt with promptly with the aid of modern insecticidal preparations.

GOLDEN HAMSTERS.

Description.

There are at least 54 different species, varieties or sub-species of hamster, all being rodents of the family Cricetidae: the general description is that they are "mouse-like animals with thick-set bodies, short tails and cheek pouches." They are distributed throughout many parts of Europe, Africa and Asia as far east as China. Most of them appear to be active in the evening and early morning, and possibly throughout the night, and some species are known to hibernate in winter. There is an excellent chapter on hamsters in the *UFAW Handbook* by Dr. Michael Festing. Not a great deal is known about the habits of wild hamsters, but most of them are solitary territorial animals that live in extensive burrows in which they store food consisting of seeds and vegetable matter. This habit of hoarding food causes some of them to be classified as pests.

The common pet hamster is the Golden—sometimes referred to as the Syrian-Hamster (*Mesocricetus auratus*), a delightful little creature of which the full-grown female—females being larger than males—rarely exceeds 18 cm in length.

The history of the domestication of the golden hamster is quite remarkable, for prior to 1930 only museum specimens were known. In that year a mother and her twelve young were dug up in a field near Aleppo and were taken to the Hebrew University Jerusalem, and from that one family have been bred the hundreds of thousands of golden hamsters now employed as pets or as laboratory animals in many parts of the world. The species has taken well to captivity and, although capable of inflicting a nasty little bite if frightened or handled roughly, becomes docile and friendly when properly cared for. Characteristic features are the soft, smooth fur, the large black eyes, the "cheek pouches" in which food is stored and which may become enormously distended after a meal, the short, stumpy tail, and the extremely loose skin, inside which the hamster can turn round to a considerable degree.

Housing.

The same remarks about accommodation, environmental temperature, freedom from draughts, fittings, and other general considerations (including cleanliness) apply as in the case of rats and mice. For breeding purposes a dark inner chamber or nest-box is desirable. Several hamsters may be kept together, but the introduction of a stranger (or even the re-introduction of a former cage-mate that has been removed for some time) may lead to fighting.

Feeding.

Satisfactory diets include the following: (1) rat cubes, carrots, greenfood and milk; (2) cereal grains and/or wholemeal bread, carrots, greenfood and milk; (3) steamed Rangoon beans, wheat, maize meal bread, a little Marmite and milk. Care must be taken not to allow storage of excess food, which will deteriorate and cause a smell. Grass is a suitable source of greenfood during its growing season. Apples and other fruits are often relished. Water, preferably in bulbs or bottles as described for rats, should always be available.

Breeding.

Golden Hamsters attain puberty at from ten to fifteen weeks of age, or even younger, males being usually earlier. Generally speaking, it is best to defer breeding until after fifteen weeks of age. There is an oestrus cycle of about four days, and the gestation period is very short, averaging sixteen days, although sometimes up to nineteen days. Mating not followed by conception results in phantom or pseudopregnancy. Litter size varies from one to fifteen, but the average is six to seven. Not many females have more than four litters and although both sexes may live up to two years, breeding by the female is rare after nine months. The young are naked and blind at birth. Hair first appears at five days, and covers the whole body at eight days. The eyes open at about eleven days, and soon after this the young begin to take food for themselves and may be weaned at three to four weeks. Care must be taken that the female does not injure the male, and for safety's sake it is probably better to keep only one female and one male together and to remove the male before the young are born.

Handling.

Gentleness is essential, and sudden movements should be avoided. The tail is much too short to use, and the easiest way is to lift them by the loose skin over the back and shoulders. As already noted, they can twist easily within their skins, unless a substantial amount is taken in the hand. After picking up they may be allowed to sit on the palm of the hand.

Diseases.

Like most rodents, hamsters are susceptible to *Salmonella* infections but probably the most serious disease is known as "wet tail", a diarrhoea that is usually fatal and has been known in some cases, to destroy whole colonies. The exact cause has not been established with certainty, but the intestines of affected animals frequently contain large numbers of coliform bacteria, and Dr. Festing refers to the effective prophylactic use of neomycin sulphate. There are several spontaneous diseases which appear to be due to nutritional deficiencies, and in one large colony that was studied over a 15-year period there was a high incidence of cirrhosis of the liver.

CAVIES (GUINEA-PIGS).

Description.

Cavies or guinea-pigs (*Cavia porcellus*) are rodents descended from one of the several kinds of wild South American cavy, probably *Caviae cutleri*, still to be found in Peru. It used to be thought that the name "Guinea" was a corruption of Guiana, but the *O.E.D.* regards this as unlikely; more probably it relates to a former designation for an unknown distant country, or because the animal was thought to resemble the young of the river-pig (*Potomochoerus pictus*) of W. Africa. Detailed information is provided in the *UFAW Handbook* by Dr. J. Stuart Paterson, who had unrivalled knowledge of this species in health and disease. Three main varieties are recognised. The *English* is the commonest, is short-haired (3·8 cm) and may be self-coloured (*e.g.*, white, black, agouti, sandy, red, chocolate, cream) or a combination of either two or three colours, described as bicolour or tricolour respectively. The fancy recognises such descriptions as Himalayan or Dutch, which denote colourings similar to those of the relevant varieties of rabbit. The *Abyssinian* is also short-coated, but one that is rough and radiates as rosettes. The *Peruvian* is long-haired (15 cm).

Guinea-pigs, which are thought to have been domesticated by the Incas long before the advent of Europeans, are extremely tame, and are easily frightened; they should always be treated gently and quietly. The males (boars) tend to fight, and should be kept apart from one another, but they do not usually attack females (sows), nor is fighting between females common.

Cavies make safe and reliable pets which breed prolifically if allowed to do so. Many regard them as relatively unresponsive to human affection. They speedily distinguish their owners, or those who feed and tend them, from strangers, and greet the former with a characteristic chirruping noise, especially at feeding times! Their short legs and heavy bodies prevent them from climbing or jumping, and it is, therefore, possible to keep them in open pens or runs, but this is inadvisable in most cases, since they are helpless against a variety of would-be predators.

In health, this is an alert animal, with a smooth, silky coat unsoiled by faeces or urine. The flesh should be firm, and the animal should not feel "light." There should not be any obvious discharge from the nose or ears, nor any evidence of slobbering or diarrhoea and breathing should be regular and quiet.

The life-span is variable, but the authors have maintained individuals for up to eight years. At birth the average weight of the English variety is about 90 g for males and 85 g for females although with single births, up to 150 g has been recorded, by weaning, body weight may average nearly 250 g, and maturity is attained by about five months when the average weight lies between 700 and 750 g. A further weight increase may take place until the animals are about fifteen months, by which time really heavy males may be 1000 g and females 850 g.

Housing.

This may be outside or inside, or a combination of both. For individual animals, the authors have found the most successful system to consist of a movable hutch with a floor—approximately 100 cm × 50 cm and covered, except over the sleeping area, by an impervious tray—raised (on legs or wheels) some six inches above the ground. The sides (approximately 40 cm at front, and 30 cm at back), back and roof (with a 5 cm overhang at the front) are made of solid wood and roofing-felt. The interior is divided, by a wooden partition, allowing free access from a smaller sleeping-quarter, with solid door, into a larger living area fronted by framed chicken wire. To the hutch is attached a run, comprising a frame with sides, top and end of strong, small-mesh, chicken wire. Such a hutch, with its run. may be kept outdoors, on grass, throughout a good deal of the year. Except on wet or inclement days, the guinea-pig may be allowed into its run for up to several hours, and be permitted to graze freely. These animals are good grazers and it is necessary, therefore, to move the hutch and run on to a new patch every 2–3 days or so. The floor of both the sleeping and living quarters should be covered with several layers of newspaper or other absorbant bedding which should be changed and destroyed at least weekly, and there should be abundant, additional bedding in the sleeping quarter, the best being shavings from seasoned soft wood, or woodwool which provides a cosy resting place. This too should be changed every few days. In severe weather, the hutch and, if space permits, the run may be kept in a shed or indoors.

There are several types of indoor housing including floor pens and cages. If there is any danger from cats, dogs or other predators, the pens should have a top of some kind. Peat moss may be used instead of newspaper to cover the floors. Some persons prefer to have two separate pens for each animal or group of animals, moving them from one to the other to permit of cleaning and resting between use. Cages or wooden boxes may have solid floors in which case they should be covered as indicated for outside hutches, or they should be fitted with wire-mesh bottoms. If the animals are to be bred, however, great care should be taken with wire bottoms for the new born can easily break their legs or strangle themselves. Dr. Paterson states that if losses are to be avoided, guinea-pigs must be brought up to live on wire so that they learn to walk on it without trouble, and if they have been reared on solid bottomed cages and transferred to wire-floor cages in later life, it is wise to keep the wire well covered with hay for the first week or two. The size of the wire is important: the rigid welded floor of 7·62 cm × 1·27 cm mesh is ordinarily satisfactory.

Feeding.

Guinea-pigs are vegetarians. Like human beings, apes and monkeys, they require a dietary source of vitamin C or ascorbic acid. A growing animal weighing 250 g requires 3 mg, a fully grown one at least 10 mg and pregnant females 20 mg daily to prevent the occurrence of scurvy and to maintain natural resistance to disease. They also have a requirement for vitamins E and K, and for an unknown but apparently essential factor or factors in hay. Provided that these necessary vitamins are in adequate supply, a wide variety of diet has been found satisfactory. Unless ascorbic acid is provided in some other way, liberal amounts of fresh green food are essential throughout the year. As Dr. Paterson states, the term "green food" should not be taken too literally: certain roots are a valuable source of vitamin C during the winter months and sprouted green has been employed with success. All members of the cabbage and kale family are suitable, as are chicory and lucerne. Carrots are excellent but mangolds, although relished, have a relatively low vitamin C content. Dr. Paterson suggests that while the type of green food should not be suddenly changed he has found that guinea-pigs flourish well when different types of green food are offered in rotation on successive days. All green food should be given as fresh as possible and any spoiled material should be rejected. Soil should be washed off. and in frosty conditions, greens should be thoroughly thawed out before being fed. Even when the guinea-pig is in an outdoor run, additional fresh greens are necessary during the winter months.

Hay should be given *ad libitum*. Most suitable is fine meadow hay of good quality free from weeds and particularly from thistles, the spines of which may injure the mouth. If young, actively-growing stock are deprived of hay, illness and death may ensue, and in suckling females deprived of hay, there may be a severe and rapid dental overgrowth.

The rest of the food should comprise mash or pellets. The simplest mash consists of 2 parts crushed oats mixed with 1 part broad bran fed dry or slightly dampened. Another suitable mixture comprises bran and sugar beet pulp in the ratio of 2:1. the beet being soaked overnight the surplus water drained off and the bran mixed to form a moist crumbly mass. Only the required amount of mash should be prepared at one time as it quickly goes sour. These simple mashes require the addition of protein concentrate and minerals in order to promote reproduction and good growth. Pelleted diets have been used for many years in laboratories and can be obtained from pet shops and corn chandlers. They are of several kinds and some even contain declared amounts of vitamin C. For pet animals, however, it is probably wise always to provide fresh green food throughout the year. For breeding stock, a pelleted diet is advisable. and one known as Diet S.G.1. after Short & Gammage, comprises white fish meal (67% protein) 10; grass meal (18% protein) 20; finely ground oats 12; medium bran 18 and coarse bran 40. Pellets may be fed from small bowls or from specially constructed hoppers that permit free access and supplies that will last for several days. It is wise however, not to leave such food unchanged for more than a few days at a time owing to the possibility of contamination by moulds. Although guinea-pigs normally derive moisture from fresh green food, and may appear to take little or no water for long periods, it is a mistake not to provide a fresh supply, either from bowls (washed and replenished regularly to prevent contamination) or from inverted bottles or from troughs fed with special drinking spouts (these lessen contamination but should still be kept clean and freshly supplied).

Diseases.

The most important and probably the most lethal of all guinea-pig diseases is *salmonellosis* or "paratyphoid." This is caused by organisms of the *Salmonella* group, usually *S. Typhimurium* and sometimes by *S. Enteritidis* or *S. dublin*. Infection takes place by mouth, usually from food or water being contaminated by wild rodents. Where guinea-pigs are kept in groups, it usually begins in one or two deaths, followed by the loss of almost all the colony. There is also a more chronic form in which the animals may survive for two weeks. The animals that recover may remain as " carriers " of the disease and are liable to infect guinea-pigs with which they are placed. Cold or other environmental variations, including faulty feeding, can help to set off an outbreak. There is, unfortunately, no completely successful treatment for this disease, attempts to immunise breeding stock have not, as yet, been successful.

Another disease is *Pseudotuberculosis* usually a chronic infection caused by *Pasteurella pseudotuberculosis* characterised by the development of cheese-like nodules particularly in the lymph nodes and internal organs. This, again, is usually acquired by eating material contaminated by wild rodents or rabbits. There are three forms of the disease. The first is an acute septicaemia, which is rapidly fatal The second, and by far the most common, is characterised by progressive emaciation (" going light ") and death in 3–4 weeks. In the case of breeding stock, the young of infected animals may be congenitally affected or may become infected soon after birth. The third form is not usually fatal since the lesions are confined to the lymph nodes of the head and neck, and the danger lies in the risk that these lesions may burst externally and spread infection. It has been claimed that infection of breeding stock can be controlled but Dr. Paterson regards such claims as unconfirmed. In the case of large colonies, the disease may be controlled under veterinary supervision by making use of the fact that some of the enlarged glands can be palpated in the early stages, before the animals become infectious to others, with the weeding out of others that are affected.

Coccidiosis is common, but is usually much less of a threat than in the case of rabbits. It is developed in infected stocks through feeding inadequate diets, and provided that nutrition and hygiene are adequate, there is little serious trouble from this disease. In the case of larger colonies, control may be based upon the regular and adequate cleaning and sterilisation of cages, since the oocysts responsible take a minimum time of six days to sporulate and to become infectious.

Respiratory infections, due to a variety of organisms are usually uncommon except when there is overcrowding or when guinea-pigs are kept in draught, damp, poorly-ventilated or cold houses In the case of large colonies, it may be necessary to adopt fairly rigorous culling of affected animals.

Middle ear disease is not uncommon especially in large colonies, and is characterised by the tilting of the head to one side. This may become so severe that the animal is unable to walk in a straight line. In the case of individual animals veterinary attention should be sought promptly. With large colonies, prompt culling is often necessary to prevent spread.

External parasites of the guinea-pig, including *lice*, which live on skin debris, cause the animals to scratch themselves, especially at the backs of the ears, and if infestation is heavy, the animals show loss of condition and a harsh coat. Aerial insecticidal vapours are said to be more effective than dusting powders.

Non-parasitic skin disorders may occur when the diet is too dry or is lacking in sufficient fresh green food of good quality and will clear up when this is put right.

RABBITS.

Description.

Domesticated varieties of the wild European rabbit (*Oryctolagus cuniculus*) are now kept in many countries. The wild rabbit is believed to have been introduced into Great Britain in the 12th cent., and a full description of its biology is given in *The Rabbit* by Harry V. Thompson & Alastair N. Worden (London: Collins, New Naturalist " Special " Volume). Tame rabbits have been bred for centuries, and the breeds and strains produced differ appreciably in size, colour, and habits from the common wild form. Some breeds have been specially bred for table purposes, while others (*e.g.* the Angora, Sitka, and Argente de Champagne) have been developed for their fur. In addition, many varieties are produced for show purposes by the extensive rabbit " fancy. " The small hardy Dutch rabbit (usually black and white) is one of the kinds suitable for beginners. Among well-known categories are the English, Japanese, Himalayan, Belgian Hare (really a rabbit), Flemish Giant, Beveren, Blue Imperial, Polish, Havana, Lop, Half-Lop, Chinchilla and New Zealand White. The Copenhagen rabbit appears to be identical with the New Zealand White. The smaller breeds weigh only 2–3 kg when fully grown, whereas some specimens of some of the giant breeds attain a weight of 9 kg or more.

Rabbits and hares were formerly classified with the rodents, but are now placed in a separate Order of mammals, known as the Lagomorphs. Young rabbits (in contrast to leverets or young hares) are blind and helpless for some time after birth. Tame specimens may live for 4–5 years, individuals have lived for up to 13 years.

Housing.

Since rabbits are kept for commercial purposes, various systems have been devised, including the use of movable ark-huts, with covered runs, that can be moved regularly to fresh ground. If kept indoors rabbits do not need special heating, but freedom from draughts, damp, excessive cold and access by wild rodents is most desirable. A garage is regarded as an unsuitable place, owing to the susceptibility of rabbits to exhaust or engine fumes. One of the great difficulties of rabbit-keeping is coccidiosis, which is a serious disease in rabbits and hares. (European hares could never be bred successfully in captivity until means of overcoming coccidiosis were discovered.) With young rabbits especially (*i.e.*, those that have left the nest and are able to run about freely) it is a sound principle to move them to a clean floor or fresh ground every two days, so as to " break " the life-cycle of the coccidial parasite. One way of doing this is to have " back-to-back " cages or hutches, from one to the other of which the rabbits may be transferred easily. The empty cage or hutch may then be cleaned and disinfected thoroughly and allowed to dry out before the rabbits are returned to it. Wood-wool makes a suitable bedding material, although the female (doe) will pluck her own fur to line the nest when her litter is due to be born. Wire-mesh floors with a tray beneath are convenient, but if solid floors are used these should be sprinkled with fresh sawdust daily or every other day. Provided the standard of hygiene can be maintained, cages or hutches and their runs should be large. The absolute minimum is " 1 sq. ft of floor space for each 1 lb weight of rabbit " *i.e.*, if there are two rabbits totalling 12 lb in weight there must be at least 12 sq. ft of floor space. In metric terms one can refer to approximately 200 cm^2 for each 500 gm of rabbit, this being a slightly more generous allowance but still on the low side.

Feeding.

The wild rabbit grazes at dusk and dawn, and it is preferable to feed tame rabbits twice daily, while pregnant or lactating does and young rabbits benefit from three meals a day. As in the case of guinea-pigs, the ratio may be thought of as consisting of two parts, a concentrate portion and a portion consisting of greenfood and other succulent material. The concentrate portion consists usually of a mixture of cereal grains or of some other form of mash. Successful mashes, of which there are many, include: (1) a mixture of 4 parts cereal grains and 1 part dairy cake; (2) equal parts of bran, weatings, flaked maize—or barley meal—and fish meal. This second is useful for breeding. If materials for the mash are in short supply they may in part be replaced by cooked potatoes. An average daily food allowance for a resting (non-breeding) adult of medium size would be: greenfood (grass, clover, weeds, lettuce, etc.) and/or roots 350–450 g; hay (good quality) 60–90 g; and concentrates (cereal grain or meal mash), 60 g. If cooked potatoes are used they should be fed at the rate of 4 parts to each 1 part of cereal that they replace. For a doe nursing her litter a suitable diet would comprise: greenfood to appetite, hay (good quality and preferably containing clover or other legume), 60–120 g; concentrates (preferably with fish meal or some other suitable source of "animal protein"), 120–180 g; and common salt at the level of up to 1% of the ration. A mineral mixture is preferable to salt alone. Excessive greenfood, especially in the form of cabbage and other Brassica plants, may cause polyuria, i.e., the passage of excessive quantities of urine. No matter how much fresh greenfood rabbits may have available, a supply of fresh water should always be provided. The daily water requirement of the rabbit is quite high, and certain bad habits such as urine drinking or even cannibalism may result from an inadequate supply of water. Pots that cannot be overturned or, preferably, water bulbs or bottles as described for guinea-pigs, are the most suitable means of providing water.

Cubed diets, as described for guinea-pigs, are suitable for rabbits. Although the rabbit is capable of synthesising its own vitamin C, fresh greenfood is preferably fed in addition as a source of other nutrients, while the water requirement with diets of this kind is considerable.

Breeding.

The age of puberty varies with the breed, and also with the time of year at which the individual rabbit was born. Rabbits born in spring are usually capable of breeding at a younger age than those born in the autumn. In Great Britain the wild rabbit has a fairly sharply defined main breeding season, lasting from January to June, but some degree of "out-of-season" breeding may take place at almost all other times. Tame rabbits may not breed freely during the winter months, especially if environmental conditions are cold. Mating may take place as early as four months of age, and although this does not often result in pregnancy, it is accompanied by competition and fighting between individuals of the same sex. Males (bucks) and females should therefore be separated at weaning or at least before they are four months old. Fertile matings may occur at from about 5½ months of age onwards, but it is wise to defer breeding until later—say seven to eight months for most breeds. The female does not ovulate or shed her eggs from the ovary spontaneously as do most domestic mammals, but, like the cat and ferret, does so in response to the act of mating or some other strong stimulus. Even playing between two does may precipitate ovulation, in which case a so-called "phantom pregnancy" (pseudopregnancy) may result, the doe that has ovulated appearing pregnant and even developing lactating mammary glands. There is not therefore an obvious regularly recurring oestrus cycle as in the domestic rat, mouse, and guinea-pig, and in summer at least the doe may be ready to mate at almost any time. Observation suggests, however, that there are fluctuations in the desire to mate. The act of mating in rabbits sometimes causes alarm that all is not well to those that have not hitherto witnessed it, for the buck usually emits a peculiar cry and loses his balance to fall over sideways. It is usually best to separate the buck from the doe before the young are born. The gestation period is usually thirty to thirty-two days. In wild rabbits a high percentage of embryos die and are "resorbed," and are therefore never born. In some populations it appears that about two-thirds of all rabbits conceived (including about 60 per cent. of total litters) are lost before birth in this way. Losses from this cause are probably much less common in domesticated rabbits, especially when the standards of feeding and management are high. Litter size is variable, and depends in part on the breed or strain. In some strains mean litter sizes up to eight or nine have been obtained, but a mean of four or so is more common. Does that do not prepare the nest or rear their young properly should not be selected for further breeding. The doe with her new-born litter should not be disturbed unduly, or she may desert her young, which are blind and helpless at birth and are entirely dependent on her for at least three weeks, after which they begin to nibble food to supplement the milk that they receive from her. The eyes open at about fourteen days. Weaning should be carried out at between six and eight weeks of age, by which time the young should be able to fend for themselves completely.

Handling.

Rabbits should never be lifted by the ears alone. One good way of lifting them is to grip the ears firmly but gently with one hand and to place the other hand under the rump to take the weight of the rabbit's body. Alternatively, one hand may be placed flat under the rabbit's belly, but this requires more care, and may be a risky procedure with pregnant does. Another convenient way to handle rabbits, especially young ones, is to lift them by the loose skin over the shoulders. Rabbits can inflict quite nasty scratches with the nails of the hind feet. It is incidentally a good plan to examine the nails of all four feet and to trim them if they are too long. Care should be taken not to cut back as far as the "quick," i.e., the bluish portion at the base of the nail that contains blood vessels.

Diseases.

In his chapter in the *UFAW Handbook*, Dr. C. E. Adams refers to a survey conducted on over 30,000 laboratory rabbits, which showed that in breeding colonies about one-fifth of all those that were born, died before they were fully mature, and that approximately half of these deaths occurred before weaning. Some 5% of bought-in rabbits also died. The most commonly reported diseases were intestinal ones and included enteritis, mucoid enteritis, impaction, scours and diarrhoea. Coccidiosis and respiratory diseases (snuffles and pneumonia) were also significant.

Coccidiosis is highly important in young animals. It may be either of the "hepatic type", affecting principally the liver, or the "intestinal type" affecting principally the gut. Even in the case of the hepatic type, however, the coccidial parasites are picked up by the mouth and after penetrating the intestinal walls make their way via the blood-stream to the liver. Hygienic measures are the best means of preventing the disease (see under Housing), but should it break out, prompt treatment with certain sulphonamides or other anti-coccidial drugs may prove effective. In certain rabbitries in which coccidiosis is a constant problem, protection has been obtained by feeding a dilute solution of one of the soluble sulphonamides in place of drinking-water. There are certain types of digestive disturbance that may resemble cocciosis, and one of these, the cause of which has not yet been established with certainty, is known as *mucoid enteritis*. Some such cases are probably variations of "bloat" ("the blows") a condition the cause of which is again not fully established, although there may in fact be several factors. A rabbit may, of course, "blow" after eating fermentative food but cases of "bloat" can occur independently of this, and some may be due to a virus.

Snuffles is characterised by a nasal discharge, and is not always associated with the same organism. In its milder forms it is not a severe disease, but with the more chronic forms the nasal discharge becomes marked and gives rise to a typical snuffling noise. Severe chronic cases become progressively worse and die of a terminal pneumonia. There is also a severe acute form in which the rabbit dies so rapidly that the condition is sometimes not recognised. Acute cases that are treated in time with certain sulphonamides may respond well but chronic snufflers are difficult to treat and go on spreading the infection, and hence are better destroyed. Correct environmental conditions are a great help in preventing this disease.

A chronic type of infection is known as *pseudo-tuberculosis*, which is usually acquired from eating material contaminated by wild rodents or by other infected rabbits. It is caused by quite a different organism from that of true tuberculosis, which is much rarer in rabbits. Clinical cases should be killed, and prevention lies in hygienic measures.

Infected wounds or skin abscesses may lead to a disease caused by the "necrosis bacillus" (*Fusiformis necrophorus*) and known sometimes as *necrobacillosis*. It is usually characterised by subcutaneous swellings distributed irregularly over the head and body. Although in the early stages the affected rabbit may remain in apparently good health, the spread of the disease is insidious and usually fatal, and in most instances it is kinder and safer to destroy a case before it progresses too far. There are, unfortunately, several other infectious conditions occurring in rabbits, but all call for expert help in diagnosis and treatment.

Among non-infectious conditions *pregnancy toxaemia* is not uncommon in does during the very late pregnancy, and usually proves fatal within two to three days. It is a "metabolic disorder" *i.e.*, it is associated with some functional derangement of the endocrine or ductless glands or with the inability to control properly the utilisation of its food. Faulty feeding is probably a contributory cause.

Ringworm is not common among external parasites but may be acquired from rodents. Affected rabbits that are to be treated must be isolated. *Ear mange* (known usually as *ear canker*) is common, and may be treated by strict attention to hygiene, with thorough disinfection of the hut or cage, and by dressing with a modern anti-mange preparation. *Body mange* is much less common but far more difficult to treat.

So-called "*bladder worms*," *i.e.*, the larval stages of two dog tapeworms (*Taenia pisiformis* and *Taenia serialis*) are quite common among internal parasites although rarely fatal. The feeding of grass or other greenstuff to which dogs have had access should be avoided, as well as the contamination of the drinking-water with dog faeces.

Myxomatosis has not died out completely in this country, and it is probably a wise precaution to vaccinate stock against it as recommended in suitable instances for all animal diseases. This, and other forms of prophylaxis and treatment should be carried out by, or with the advice of, a veterinary surgeon.

GERBILS.

Description.

Gerbils, also known as jirds, sand rats and desert rats, are members of the sub-family *Gerbillinae* of the rodent family *Cricetidae*. There are some fourteen genera comprising some 50 species. The genera *Meriones* and *Gerbillus* are the most widely represented (about 14 and 10 species respectively). Virtually unknown in Britain until the mid-1960s, a few species have now been introduced from Asia, Africa and the Middle East, initially as laboratory animals.

Gerbils have now become immensely popular pets, both in schools and in the home, and provided one ensures that a docile species is acquired, one has perhaps the ideal pet mammal. They are virtually odourless, easy to handle and to breed, and pleasing to watch, both in appearance and antics.

Species differ widely in both size and disposition and hence one must take care when acquiring specimens. The Indian gerbil *Tatera indica* is, for example, large, aggressive and virtually untameable. Species recommended include *Gerbillus pyramidum*, *Meriones libycus* and *Meriones unguiculatus* (the Mongolian gerbil). The following advice applies to these species and particularly to the Mongolian gerbil—which is by far the most popular species available in Great Britain and hence the one most likely to be offered. There is a valuable chapter on this species by Dr. J. H. Marston in the *UFAW Handbook*.

Housing.

Gerbils appear to tolerate a wide range of temperature conditions. Petter has bred several species (though not *M. unguiculatus*) in outdoor conditions in Paris. There is no evidence to suggest that the Mongolian gerbil is less hardy, though indoor conditions are advised. Precautions against escape should be exercised since gerbils could become feral, and a pest.

Metal cages comprised largely of bars are recommended. Two-storey hamster cages are suitable and these enable one to watch the gerbils' complex and fascinating behaviour. Provide plenty of hay, straw or wood shavings and white paper. The animals shred material to make bedding and "nests." Since the animals are virtually odourless, as too are their urine and faeces, they need cleaning out less frequently than other rodents: once per two weeks suffices.

Either a pair of gerbils may be kept, or two males with two or three females. It is important, however, to introduce only young animals from separate litters into the same cage. Adults unused to one another are frequently hostile and aggressive.

Since the animals are burrowers in their natural state, they may be kept in a deep container, *e.g.*, a large aquarium, and supplied with a good depth of peat or a similar material. This method of housing, however, has the drawback that one sees little of the animals.

Pieces of wood provide a gnawing surface: very necessary for most rodents.

Feeding.

Virtually nothing is known of the gerbil's natural foods; still less their nutritional requirements. One must simply provide a range of foodstuffs from which the animals select what is adequate for their needs. Gerbils will take insects, spiders and meat, though they thrive on an entirely vegetarian diet.

Satisfactory foodstuffs include rodent pellets or a coarse seed mixture such as that sold for parrots or for wild birds. Sunflower seeds are taken with avidity as too is germinating grain (*i.e.*, soaked and allowed to grow for a few days to seedling stage). Pieces of raw fruit and vegetable are also consumed.

Water should be provided, though the animals drink little, particularly if vegetables are available.

Breeding.

As indicated under Housing, several adults may be run together.

Mating is rarely observed, though it is said to occur most usually in the late afternoon. Little is known about the breeding cycle.

The duration of pregnancy is about 25 days and the average litter number is about 6. Not infrequently the first litter is small in number and the young may be killed by the parents. Second and subsequent litters are usually reared successfully. Hair develops in 6–10 days and the eyes open at about 3 weeks. Varieties of gerbils have been reported since the late 1960s.

Handling.

Recently weaned specimens up to some 8 weeks of age require firm "cupping" in the hands since they are prone to jump with little regard for their own safety.

Regular handling over this age ensures a tame yet ever-inquisitive pet. Grasping by the base of the tail is usually necessary to enable one to remove the animal from a cage. Thereafter cupping is to be preferred.

Careless or over-enthusiastic handling of a timid individual sometimes produces a "fright reaction" where the animal lies trembling though otherwise almost inert for a minute or two. However, this soon passes.

Diseases.

Apart from the vulnerability of the first litter these animals are remarkably healthy. The result of fighting between adults from different cages is the only likely injury encountered apart from occasional skin infection around the nose and lips—possibly due to burrowing activity. This condition responds to a mild antiseptic cream.

Old animals may develop a condition where the eyeball tends to protrude. Neither cause nor cure has been investigated.

Any unwanted or infirm animal may be quickly and painlessly killed by the following procedure: put a little ether (diethyl ether) on a generous pad of cotton wool. Introduce this into a screw-cap jar, place the animal in, and fix the cap on firmly. Leave for 20 minutes.

HEDGEHOGS.

Description.

The European hedgehog (*Erinaceus europaceus*), found throughout Great Britain, belongs to the Order Insectivora, of which moles and shrews are also members. Its diet is, however, by no means restricted to insects, although in nature a considerable portion is probably made up of small invertebrates. There is a good deal of prejudice against them as pets, owing to the fact that freshly caught specimens are usually infested with fleas or other external parasites. The spines of the hedgehog, being well-spaced, make the presence of external parasites more obvious than is the case in animals with a coat of close fur. The hedgehog's spines form its defence, and its capacity to roll up into a prickly ball at the threat of danger is well known. This defence reaction is unfortunately of no avail to it when the danger is an oncoming car or lorry, and thousands of hedgehogs die every year as a result of being killed by vehicles on the roads. Many other species of mammals wander on to the roads, but most attempt to flee when they sense the approach of a vehicle. The capacity to roll up is not secure defence even against animal enemies. There are some foxes, dogs, and cats that have learned to "uncurl" a hedgehog, and subsequently eat it.

Provided that care is taken, a hedgehog makes an excellent pet, especially if given a suitable enclosure in the garden. For a variable time during winter hedgehogs hibernate, and during this time they must not be disturbed. Should they emerge at any time however, food must be provided. Some specimens have lived for five years or more in captivity.

Accommodation.

The most satisfactory way to maintain a pet hedgehog is to provide it with a large "run" in part of the garden. If wire-netting is employed it should be sunk under the ground to a depth of several inches, or the hedgehog will burrow underneath and escape. The top of the run must be wired in, or alternatively there must be a "baffle board" or wire-frame (at least 23 cm wide) near the top of the sides to prevent escape that way, for hedgehogs can scale wire-netting—and some other types of fence—with ease. There should be a warm, dry box for shelter, containing wood-wool or other bedding material. A simple but suitable shelter may be made out of a soap-box, preferably lined with asbestos sheeting or some other material impervious to water. A shallow sunken bath in the enclosure may be of interest, for hedgehogs take well to water, but the edges should be such that the hedgehog can get out easily.

If it is decided to keep a hedgehog indoors, then the best accommodation is probably similar to that described for ferrets.

Feeding.

The simplest diet consists of milk, some bread, and minced lean meat. Cooked meat is preferred to raw, but raw liver should be given occasionally. Another satisfactory diet comprises meat offals, "root" vegetables (*e.g.*, carrot, potato, and swede), and wheaten wholemeal biscuit, steamed together until cooked, and then mixed and minced with a small proportion of raw liver. A small quantity (say 1–2 per cent.) of mineral mixture is also desirable, and milk should be given freely. Although hedgehogs appear to drink but little water, a fresh supply should always be provided.

Breeding.

During the breeding season marked changes occur in both males and females, and the structures associated with reproduction increase enormously in size from about March onwards. The female is capable of having two litters a year,

the first in May or June and the second in August or September. The period of gestation has not been determined exactly, but is believed to be thirty-five days, possibly with variations of up to well over forty days. During the breeding season the males are very pugnacious towards each other if females are with them, and may do each other considerable damage. (The mixing of strange hedgehogs is often a difficult procedure anyway, for they often fight and inflict nasty bites on one another's feet.)

The litter size is usually four to six, and the young, which have "soft" spines, are suckled by their mother for nearly six weeks. The young can partake of some solid food at about three weeks, and there is some evidence that if left with their mother for longer than six weeks she may compete unfairly with them for food!

Diseases.

Hedgehogs in captivity are susceptible to *respiratory infections*, and can sometimes contract certain strains of *human influenza*. They are susceptible also to *Salmonellosis* (see under mice and guinea-pigs). Fleas and other external parasites have been mentioned; these often disappear spontaneously as the hedgehog begins to thrive in captivity, but if not they should be dealt with by modern methods. The nails of a hedgehog may need trimming.

LAND TORTOISES.

Tortoises are popular pets, but although many have been kept with great success in Great Britain, the majority of those imported have never been looked after adequately, or have failed to thrive for other reasons.

Most land tortoises imported into Great Britain for sale through dealers have been:

(1) The Spur-thighed Mediterranean Land Tortoise (*Testudo graeca*), commonly known as the "Moroccan tortoise" and sometimes as the "Iberian" or "Algerian"; or

(2) Hermann's Tortoise (*Testudo hermanni*). The second is distributed in Southern France, Southern Italy, the larger islands of the Western Mediterranean and parts of Yugoslavia, Albania, and Greece. There is a species found in Greece, the Margined Tortoise (*Testudo marginata*), but while adaptable to life in Great Britain, it is more difficult to acquire. The two common species differ in several ways, the "Moroccan tortoise" having a small bony spur on the back of the thigh. (The upper part of the shell is termed the carapace and the ventral portion the plastron.)

In selecting a tortoise one should ensure that the animal appears healthy. It should be active and withdraw quickly into its shell on being disturbed. Its legs should be firm and not limp, and there should be no abnormal discharge from the eyes or nostrils. The shell and limbs should be uninjured. Females are generally larger and have a shorter tail than the male. The shield above the tail is flat in the former and curved in the male. It is a good idea to obtain a pair or more of tortoises, but not more than can be looked after with care. On being purchased they should be washed in tepid water.

Many tortoises are given free range in gardens, but this is not advised with all, as they eat a wide variety of vegetables and young plants, and being wandering animals are liable to get lost if the garden is not completely fenced or walled. They should be provided with as large a "pen" or "run" as possible, the walls or wire-netting of which should be high enough to prevent their climbing over. The practice of tethering tortoises by a hole in the shell should be discouraged. They should always be provided with a box or shelter, the cheapest form being a wooden soap box turned on one side and with a sufficiently wide entrance, the wood being creosoted and covered with roofing felt. It can be lined with asbestos sheeting if desired, and have its floor covered with dry leaves or other bedding material. Some other shelter should also be provided in the run. The tortoises should be bathed during the hot weather. The occasional appliction of olive oil will keep the shell polished.

Land tortoises must be fed daily, and it is important to allow them to build up good reserves to enable them to hibernate through the winter successfully. Suitable foods include lettuce, young cabbage, peas, clover, dandelions, and a wide variety of green plants and ripe, sweet fruits. Generally bread and milk should be avoided. For young tortoises especially, it is recommended that once weekly or so the food should be sprinkled with powdered cuttlefish bone, or better still a small quantity of powdered calcium gluconate or cod-liver oil. Fresh water in a shallow tray, or even a saucer, should always be provided.

One of the most difficult problems in tortoise keeping is hibernation. Some persons avoid allowing their pets to hibernate by transferring them to a warm place, such as a heated greenhouse; if this is done they must be kept well fed and their place maintained at a summer temperature. It is imperative to do one thing or the other—the half-torpid tortoise that is neither hibernating nor kept at summer temperature will die. Moreoover, a tortoise that is allowed to hibernate must not be disturbed.

Signs of pending hibernation, including sluggishness and lowered appetite, are usually evident late in September or early in October. Tortoises living in the garden may commence to bury themselves. If this is allowed they must be well covered, else they may be killed by the ensuing frost. It is, though, more convenient and perhaps provides a greater chance of survival, due to the changeable winter conditions in Britain, to place the animal in a large box, which should be packed with straw, leaves, or hay. The box should be stored in a cool but frostproof place, such as out-building, cellar, or attic. It is important not to create conditions that will awaken the tortoise or tempt it to emerge before the following spring. Rats have been known to attack hibernating tortoises, and so precautions should be taken.

On emerging from hibernation the eyes and nostrils are somewhat sealed, and should be released by bathing with a 4 per cent. boric acid solution and warm water.

Recently imported female tortoises frequently lay eggs, but it is not a common occurrence for pairs to breed freely in Britain. During the early part of the summer the male is sometimes seen butting the shell of the female, this being a courtship action. If eggs are laid it is unlikely that they will be fertile, and less likely that they can be hatched. They have been hatched by placing them on damp sand and storing them in a warm place—a heated greenhouse or airing cupboard. The eggs should not be disturbed or "turned" once incubation has commenced.

Tortoise ticks are often present on freshly imported specimens, and may best be removed by damping the tick with paraffin or methylated spirits and then removing it gently with tweezers. Round worms are very numerous in tortoises, and should they be seen in the faecal matter the remainder may be eliminated by sprinkling up to one grain of powdered santonin on the food once a week for six weeks. Possibly, some of the newer, safe anthelmintic preparations including piperazine derivatives may be equally effective. Eye infections are common, and are usually remedied by bathing the eye well with a 4 per cent. boric acid solution or warm cod-liver oil. Continuous discharge from the nose indicates lung infection, and as a primary measure the animal should be kept warm. Bleeding can be stopped by using Friar's Balsam, and care should be taken to prevent insects settling on open wounds.

WATER TORTOISES (TERRAPINS).

In Great Britain the tortoises that have become adapted to life in ponds and rivers are usually termed "terrapins," the name turtle being applied to marine forms. In the U.S.A. and Canada, however, not only the marine species but also terrapins and tortoises are all termed "turtles."

Several kinds of terrapin are available and capable of thriving in Great Britain. These include several American species, the European Pond Tortoise (*Emys orbicularis*), the Spanish Terrapin (*Clemmys leprosa*), the Caspian Terrapin (*Clemmys caspica*), and the Reeves' Terrapin (*Chinemys reevesii*), which hails from China and Japan.

The ideal place in which to keep terrapins is a garden pond within an enclosure. The pond should contain an "island" of dry ground on to which the animals can climb easily. The water should vary in depth, and at one point be at least 0·6 m deep. Provided that there is a suitable "island" the boundary walls of the pond can be upright to prevent escape. The final coat of cement should be smooth and mixed with a waterproofing agent. Shade should be available, not only on the island but also in some parts of the water. This may be provided by suitable plants.

Terrapins are almost entirely carnivorous, although the young of some species may take a little lettuce or other vegetable food. Suitable foods include *small* pieces of raw meat, raw liver (this should certainly be given from time to time), fish, and earthworms. Terrapins prefer to take their food in the water, and it is best to feed them individually if there are several, to ensure that each receives his proper share.

Water tortoises also hibernate. Some bury themselves in mud or sand at the bottom of their ponds, others will dig themselves into the earth in the island or banks of their pond, while others again may go to sleep in the box that, as in the case of land tortoises, should preferably be provided for them on part of their "land." Should they sleep at the bottom of the pond, it is as well to prevent freezing of the water. One means of doing this is to leave a log or logs floating on the surface. Moving these logs on cold mornings will help to break any ice formed and to prevent total freezing.

There is a valuable chapter on reptiles by Dr. D. J. Ball and Professor A. d'A. Bellair in the *U F A W Handbook*.

AQUARIUM FISH.

There are two types of aquaria—the cold-water for fish from this and other temperate countries and the heated, for tropical varieties of fish. Apart from the fact that a suitable heating mechanism—usually electric, with thermostatic control—has to be maintained for tropical aquaria, the general principles governing the two types are much the same. There is a certain amount of additional initial expense in setting up a heated aquarium—the running costs are not high—but in some respects tropical fish are easier to maintain than many of the cold-water varieties.

It should be emphasised at the outset that those who want to keep fish should invest in a proper aquarium and not in a "goldfish bowl," unless the latter be very large in relation to the fish to be kept. Far too many fish suffer from overcrowding or from lack of sufficient water surface. In the case of cold freshwater fish such as carp and goldfish (which need quite different conditions from tropical fish) it has been calculated that every " 1 inch of body " (*i.e.*, 2·5 cm) requires 1 sq ft (*i.e.*, 930 cm²) of water surface in order to obtain sufficient oxygen for respiration. Thus a fish the body of which (*i.e.*, the length minus the tail fins) is 10 cm will require at least an area of 60 cm × 60 cm. Two such fish will require twice this area, and so on. In *The Right Way to Keep Pet Fish* by R. Dutta, it is pointed out that a goldfish should normally live for twenty-five years in a suitable pond, and grow to its full length of over 35 cm. There are few indoor aquaria capable of supporting many full-grown goldfish in adequate conditions, and indeed it is recommended that domestic varieties of goldfish such as shubunkins, fantails, veiltails, and orandas, which grow more slowly, are far better adapted to cold-water aquaria. Tropical fish of the varieties kept in aquaria are usually much smaller, differ in their oxygen requirements, and can be kept in more crowded conditions. Many have an average body length of only about 3 cm, and eighteen such fish may be maintained in a suitably heated tank with an area of water surface of 45 cm × 30 cm.

A beginner should not only read good books on the subject (including *Water Life* publications) *e.g.*, *Guide to Tropical Fish-keeping* by J. H. P. Brymer) but also consult experts and his local aquarist or dealer. There is a useful chapter by Dr. H. G. Vevers in the *U F A W Handbook*, while a symposia on *Diseases of Fish*, edited by the late Dr. Lionel Mawdesley-Thomas, was published for the Zoological Society of London by Academic Press. Whatever aquarium is chosen, the conditions should be correct *before* any fish are introduced. Should fish be suddenly acquired, before a proper aquarium has been fitted up for them, they should be kept in some temporary (but sufficiently capacious) quarters until the aquarium is ready.

The instructions for installing and fitting up an aquarium are usually supplied, and should be followed carefully. The sand that is usually placed on the bottom should be thoroughly washed, and is best put in a little at a time. Make sure that the inside of the aquarium is thoroughly clean before anything at all is put into it. Ornamental rocks may next be introduced, and great care should be taken to ensure that these are of the correct type, unlikely to harm the fish physically or chemically. Water is then added very gently indeed, and suitable plants set. In the case of large tanks the planting is best done when the tank is only partly filled with water, but in any event the plants themselves should be kept wet all the time, or they may quickly shrivel up. In the case of cold-water aquaria everything may now be left for a few days—preferably a week or more—to ensure that all is well, and to allow certain micro-organisms that help form the food of the fish to develop. In the case of heated aquaria it is necessary also to ensure that the thermostat is working correctly and that the temperature is remaining constant or within very narrow limits. Here again it is advisable to wait at least a week before introducing any fish. Should conditions " go wrong " before or after the fish are introduced, it is best to start filling the tank all over again.

Fish should not be overfed, although regular feeding is essential. Attention must be paid to the feeding instructions issued with prepared fish foods, and to details given by the supplier of " live " foods. Provided fish are neither overcrowded nor overfed, the amount of sediment that accumulates in the tank will not be excessive, but it should be siphoned away gently every month, or more often if necessary. Water lost by evaporation should be replaced, and in the case of heated tanks especially, it is most desirable that the added water be of the same temperature as that already in the tanks.

Certain species of water snail are often placed in aquaria to act as scavengers. It is necessary to ensure that, if snails are kept, they are of the right type, and it is important to consult experts on this matter.

Breeding is an interesting topic, there being both egg-laying and viviparous or " live-bearing " fish. The beginner is well advised to learn first how to keep fish in healthy condition in his aquarium before indulging in any planned breeding, and he should study the relevant information in books on the subject.

An aeration plant is often recommended on the grounds that it will increase the fish-carrying capacity of the aquarium. This is true up to a point, but overcrowding may bring other troubles besides those connected with lack of sufficient oxygen, and the golden rule is never to keep too many fish for the size of aquarium in question. Another factor to be remembered is that should the aerator break down it may leave the fish with less oxygen than their proper requirement. It has been recommended that an aerator is best thought of as a stand-by, to be employed only in emergencies, *e.g.*, when for some reason extra fish have to be added to a tank already holding all or almost all its proper capacity.

There are unfortunately many diseases of fish, and as yet scientific knowledge concerning many of them is far less detailed than it should be. It is clear, however, that environmental factors are responsible for many deaths or cases of unthriftiness, and among the factors concerned may be listed: overcrowding, overfeeding, the provision of a diet that is qualitatively inadequate, lack of " balance " in the aquarium leading to unsuitable conditions, dirt, too strong light, lead paint and noxious substances, that may somehow have come into contact with the water (*e.g.* from the hands of the person tending them) or been absorbed from the atmosphere. One must be careful of such things as disinfectants, soaps, petrol, etc. In the case of tropical fish the temperature of the water may be incorrect. Should fish troubles occur, therefore, it is as well to consider these

various possibilities although one should not hesitate to seek professional advice where there appears to be a case of infectious disease. An ailing fish should certainly be removed from the tank (assuming that there are other fish present) and given separate quarters of its own if such a course is feasible.

It is not intended to provide a description of the separate diseases, although it may be mentioned that such signs as the appearance of material resembling cotton-wool (actual fungal growths) and " rotting " of the tail or fins, are among those that should lead the owner to isolate affected fish and to seek help immediately.

No attempt is made here to describe any of the many different species and varieties of fish suitable for private aquaria. Some of the " points "

LATERAL LINE — DORSAL FIN — CAUDAL OR TAIL FIN — ANAL FIN — PECTORAL FINS (PAIRED) — PELVIC OR VENTRAL FINS (PAIRED)

of a fish are shown in the accompanying illustration. Great care must be taken in mixing species, *e.g.*, " hard mouthed " and " soft mouthed " kinds should not be kept together. The temptation to put other species (*e.g.*, newts) with aquarium fish must likewise be avoided.

CAGE-BIRDS.

Many species and varieties of birds are maintained successfully in captivity and there exists in Great Britain a general fancy that caters for a high proportion of the smaller adapted for cage or aviary life. The increase in the numbers of budgerigars after the end of the second world war was phenomenal, and by the peak year of 1957 it was estimated that there were over 6 million in the country, and that the corresponding figure for the USA, where the popular name for this species is " parakeet," exceeded 18 million.

There are various restrictions on the importation of certain types of cage bird but the following notes refer to species that have, generally speaking, been available from breeders or dealers.

The different types and sizes of birds have different requirements, and in the space available it is not possible to do more than cover the general principles and to deal briefly with the special characteristics of the management of the more easily maintained species. The beginner is advised to restrict his attention to one of the better-known species, *e.g.*, canaries or budgerigars, and not to attempt to maintain exotic varieties until he has acquired considerable experience.

Most species thrive best in aviaries, which may be indoor, outdoor, or of the combined " outdoor-indoor " type. An indoor aviary is usually all-wire and portable. The criticism of many such aviaries is that they tend to be high and narrow, whereas a fairly large floor-space is desirable. They should not be placed in cold or draughty places, nor too near a fire. If sited so as to receive much direct sunlight they must have adequate shelter. The wires must be close together, especially if smaller species are kept, a distance between them of about 10 mm being generally suitable. An outdoor aviary—suitable only for some species or at certain times in the case of others—should occupy a sunny position, although it too must include shade, and must be protected from winds. There ought in fact to be a sheltered portion, dry and well protected from the elements. The aviary must be strongly made and safe from all predators, including rats and mice. While it is often considered desirable to allow herbage to protrude through the wire-mesh floor, it is essential that the birds are never in close contact with wild rodents or their droppings. Most birds are highly susceptible to some forms of *Salmonellosis* (see under mice and guinea-pigs), and can contract them in this way. It is advisable also that the roof of the aviary is solid: corrugated asbestos sheeting, projecting well clear of the edges of the uprights so as to prevent water and other matter from entering the interior, is excellent. The droppings of wild birds may be a potent source of bacterial infection or of internal parasites. To prevent close contact otherwise with wild birds, the wire or wire-netting " walls " of the aviary may be double. If an " outdoor-indoor " aviary is employed, there is usually an indoor flight cage, separated from the external portion either by a very light hanging door of suitable size, through which the birds can easily push their way, or by a sliding partition that the owner can operate as required.

SECTION THROUGH CAGE.

If an aviary is out of the question, then a suitable cage should be purchased or constructed. The cage need not be ornate—indeed simplicity of design usually facilitates the highly important task of keeping everything clean—but it must be large enough. A cross-section through a breeding-cage suitable for canaries, and for many other species, is shown in the accompanying illustration. Such a cage should measure about 100 cm in length × 30 cm × 45 cm high. It is constructed of wood or some suitable sheeting except for the front, which consists of vertical wires with horizontal stays and can be divided into two parts by means of a suitable partition containing a removable section made of wire. By this means the cock and hen canaries can be introduced into the separate sections and develop a courtship

PERCH.

NESTING-BOX WITH PLAIN WOOD BOTTOM.

before being allowed to be together for actual mating. The cross-section indicates the site and size of the removable portion of the partition, and it shows also the removable tray that is such an excellent fitting for almost any type of cage, and which greatly facilitates cleaning.

Whether an aviary or a cage is employed, it is essential to have proper fittings, including conveniently placed drinking-troughs, feeding-trays and bird-baths, and good perches. Much unnecessary discomfort is brought about through the use of unsuitable perches, or ones that are incorrectly situated or not sufficiently " firm."

A suitable type of perch, of which there should be several in the cage or aviary, is shown in the accompanying illustration, and it should be of the appropriate dimensions for the size of bird. In the case of the larger canaries (Norwich and

BIRD BATH.

Yorkshire), *e.g.*, the sectional measurements should be 16 mm × 20 mm, whereas for a smaller canary (Border) they should be 13 mm × 20 mm. The type of perch shown is easy to clean and does not possess awkward corners in which parasites may be harboured. The dimensions of a nesting box a bird-bath, and a feeding-tray suitable for canaries are also given in the accompanying illustrations.

SEED TROUGH.

While wood is a convenient material for aviary and cage construction, it has, of course, several disadvantages. Out of doors it is best creosoted (lead paint must never be used for places in which birds or other small animals are kept), and indoors it is better lined with hard asbestos sheeting. Metal is suitable—provided that it does not rust or corrode and that the environmental conditions are warm enough.

In all cases a supply of clean, fresh water should be available. Strict cleanliness should be observed, and professional advice taken immediately if a bird is not thriving.

Canaries (Serinus canarius).

These are domesticated forms of the race of wild serin found in the Canary Islands, and may live up to twenty-five years. Many varieties are known, and although most individuals are "canary yellow," other colours have been developed by fanciers. Many books have been written about the canary, although there is still much to be learned concerning its feeding and diseases—as is indeed the case with almost all cage-birds. The system of feeding generally recommended is based upon a mixture of 2 or 3 parts of canary seed (which is rich in energy, and which is sometimes mixed with a little millet seed) to 1 part of summer rape seed, which is high in fat and protein. There seems to have been some difficulty in obtaining suitable rape seed in some areas since the war. The best is German summer rape or Rübsen rape. Other seeds are employed as substitutes, or for special purposes, e.g., niger is usually added at breeding time, and linseed if there is any indication of premature or soft (out-of-season) moult. Good proprietary seed mixtures are available. A little greenfood should be provided twice weekly, and a piece of cuttlefish bone placed between the wires is a suitable source of calcium. Soft-bill food (containing boiled egg, dried egg yolk, dried flies, and ants' pupæ) is also recommended by many breeders, while others give chopped egg alone. Others again favour milk, especially for young birds.

Breeding is usually started late in March or early in April, but not unless the daily shade temperature is at least 10° C. The pairs should be selected earlier than this and transferred to breeding-cages, with the partition in position. By the middle of February the wire partition may be installed so that the two birds can see one another. A little niger seed is usually added to the diet, while finely ground oystershell or eggshell may be sprinkled on the floor. (Otherwise the floor may be covered with washed sand that is not too fine and is free from dust.) When the birds begin to feed one another through the wire they are ready for mating, and the partition may be removed. The nest-box can then be inserted and suitable nesting materials, e.g., cow hair and moss, placed in the cage. The incubation period is thirteen to fourteen days. After the eggs are laid some owners prefer to separate the cock and the hen, but allow him to rejoin her after the young are all about eight to nine days old and have opened their eyes. If it is desired that all the chicks be hatched together then one can remove the first three eggs that are laid—usually one egg is laid daily—and keep them in a box at room temperature, substituting dummy eggs for them in the nest-box. On the afternoon of the third day of laying they are returned to the nest-box in place of the dummies.

When the young chicks are able to feed themselves they should be provided with special food, such as egg and bread crumbs and a little cracked canary seed. If the cock bird interferes with them, or causes the hen to neglect them, he must be returned to his own section. Usually, however, all goes well, and the hen will go to the nest again when the first chicks are almost sixteen days old. Some three or four broods may be raised in a season. There is a useful chapter on the canary by Dr. I. F. Keymer in the UFAW Handbook. Crosses between the canary and other birds and indeed cross breeds in general, are dealt with by V. A. Carr in Mule and Hybrid Birds (London: Cage Birds).

Waxbills, Finches, and Other Seed-eaters.

The canary is of course a finch, but most of the other "foreign finches" are considered by dealers and writers together with other types of seed-eating birds. Well over 30 species of Avadavats, Buntings, Mannikins, Cardinals, Why-

dahs, Weavers, and Finches of various descriptions have been maintained successfully in captivity in Great Britain. One of the most popular is the Zebra finch (Taeniopygia castanotis), from Australia, which has bred so successfully in this country that supplies no longer depend upon fresh importations and which appears in several varieties. The native bird, and many of its descendants, are grey and white, with red beaks. The male bird has orange cheek-patches, and orange flanks with white markings. The throat has black barring on a white background, and indeed the characteristic markings of the male have been the subject of interesting behaviour studies. The female lacks these special markings. The species is hardy, and is capable of living in outdoor aviaries all the year round, so long as it has shelter from draughts or strong winds and adequate facilities for roosting. If provided with nest-boxes, the birds will attempt—often successfully—to breed all the year round, so to avoid overbreeding it is better to remove these boxes in winter. A mixture of millet and canary seed forms the basis of their diet, which should be supplemented with fresh greenfood, millet sprays, fine grit, and cuttlebone—and, of course, fresh water should be available. A useful introduction is Zebra Finches by C. H. Rogers (London: Iliffe). Another bird suitable for the relatively uninitiated bird-keeper is the Bengalese (a domestic variety of Munia striata). It seems that these birds are the result of careful breeding by the Japanese, and may be regarded as fertile hybrids. Three main forms, the Chocolate-and-White, the Fawn-and-White, and the White, have been developed. These birds will thrive in cages or in aviaries. As in the case of Zebra Finches, they will attempt to breed all the year round if provided with nest-boxes. Bengalese are sociable birds, sometimes known in the USA as Society Finches. They appear to require less additional food than most species, thriving on a mixture of canary and millet seed, together with grit, cuttlebone and an occasional millet spray or item of greenstuff.

For details of these birds, and of the many others from which a selection may be made, works of reference should be consulted. Three very useful books, all published by Cage Birds, London, are Foreign Bird Keeping, by Edward J. Boosey; Foreign Birds for Beginners, by D. H. S. Risdon; and Foreign Birds for Garden Aviaries, by Alec Brooksbank.

Budgerigars.

The increase in the popularity of this bird has been phenomenal, although to those who have experience of other birds as pets the reasons are soon fairly obvious. Apart from the capacity to talk, shown by many birds—especially males kept alone and trained, there is a liveliness, almost a "cheekiness," and an apparent like of human companionship. The wild green budgerigar (Melopsittacus undulatus) exists in large numbers in the grassland and desert shrub regions of Australia. The usual colour is grass green—it is frequently known as the Grass Parakeet—with a yellow mask, with three black spots on either side. As a result of intensive breeding, a considerable number of colour varieties has been produced and the genetics of colour are a constant source of interest to budgerigar breeders. A vast budgerigar "fancy" has been built up in the United Kingdom, the USA, and other countries, and World Budgerigar Congresses are held every few years. Budgerigars will thrive in outdoor aviaries all the year round, but the vast majority are kept as indoor pets in cages or small aviaries. The cages can be similar to those used for canaries and care should be taken that the perches are of the correct diameter. If nest-boxes are put up, and the environmental conditions are suitable, budgerigars suitably paired will breed at almost any time of the year. It is customary, however, to restrict breeding to the spring, summer, and early autumn. Overbreeding may lead to difficulties, including the production of "runners" or "French moult." The sexes may normally be distinguished, at any rate in mature individuals by the colour of the cere at the base of the beak, which is blue in males and brown in females. Males may lose their colour if not in good condition and for other reasons.

There are now many proprietary seeds mixtures, but some owners prefer to make up their own mixtures of millet (usually mixing small yellow and large white varieties) and canary seed. Millet sprays, fresh greenfood, good grit, and cuttlebone are all desirable, and it is important that the correct size and consistency of grit be chosen. Variety in " extras " to the basal seeds diet is probably important, for the captive bird has not the same opportunities as its wild ancestors for ranging widely for, possibly, important trace items of food. Breeding birds secrete a " milk," comparable with the crop milk of pigeons and some other birds, and this is of importance in the early feeding of the young.

Most healthy budgerigars seem to live to the age of 5-7 years or more, and considerably greater ages have been attained in captivity.

Such is the development of the budgerigar fancy that most equipment as well as food can be obtained ready for use. The playful habits of budgerigars have led to their being given table-tennis balls or a variety of small toys to play with, while some forms of food are supplied as budgerigar bells or otherwise in special shapes that seem to amuse the birds as they take the constituent seed from them.

The study of budgerigar diseases is in its infancy, but already some important facts have become realised. *French moult* is certainly reproducible by overbreeding, and may be linked with deficiencies in the ability of the parent birds to feed their young—or to hand over to them at the time of laying sufficient nutritional reserves to carry them through hatching and parental feeding until the time that they can fend for themselves. A deficiency in the " milk " has been shown in some cases, and may be generally true. Large chicks can be produced by killing off or removing all but a single member of the clutch, and allowing the parents to deal with it alone.

A mite infestation, due to *Cnemidocoptes pilae*, may give rise to *Scaly face, Scaly beak,* or *Scaly leg,* for which veterinary treatment is now available. Another condition, known as *Brown hypertrophy of the cere,* is characterised by thickening and darkening of the surface of the cere. In the early stages it is sometimes thought that the bird is changing its sex. There is no known successful treatment at the time of writing, and if the overgrowth is cut away it will only reform. These are various disturbances of the *digestive tract,* and some of these may be associated with inability to stand properly.

There are many treatises on the budgerigar, including the chapter in the *UFAW Handbook* by Dr. I. F. Keymer. Still a very useful work is *The Cult of the Budgerigar* by W. Watmough (London: Cage Birds) as is *Genetics for Budgerigar Breeders* by T. G. Taylor & Cyril Warmer (London: Iliffe).

Lovebirds and Parrotlets.

These birds are also members of the parrot family, and while they are unlikely to equal the budgerigar in popularity, they are nevertheless interesting birds that are being kept in increasing numbers as pets. Lovebirds, of the genus *Agapornis,* are African in origin, and some six species are commonly kept in captivity. Parrotlets derive from South America, the commonest species being the Guiana Parrotlet, *Forpus passerinus.* Both types of bird are relatively simple to maintain in aviaries or large cages, and their basal diet (which should be supplemented widely) is a mixture of millet and canary seed. They are hardy and vigorous creatures, many details of which are to be found in condensed form in *Guide to Lovebirds and Parrotlets* by E. N. T. Vane (Cage Birds). There are many works on the larger parrots, one that is still useful being *Parrots and Parrot-like Birds* by the Duke of Bedford with a section on diseases by David L. Coffin (Fond du Lac, Wisconsin All-Pets Books).

PONIES
Introduction.

As indicated for pets in general, it is necessary before acquiring any animal to consider carefully the time, expense and work involved: these factors are especially apt when contemplating the purchase of a child's riding pony. Doubtless every child, at some time or another, dreams of owning his or her own pony but it is not every family that can afford one in terms of space, time and cost.

Ponies are not machines to be ridden at one's whim: they require kindness, companionship and sensible treatment. Also one should never consider buying a pony without having acquired some background knowledge of equitation, saddlery and horsemastership. These skills can only be learnt by practical experience, and the best method is to enrol for a full course of instruction at a Riding School which has British Horse Society approved instructors. The address of the B.H.S. is 35 Belgrave Sq., London S.W.1 (01-235-6431). Horsemanship is a subject about which even the experts are still learning, but a valuable grounding for any child with a pony or with access to one is membership of the Pony Club which competently promotes better horsemanship for young people and which is associated with the B.H.S.

It is impossible in a few paragraphs to give a full outline of every aspect of horsemanship. The authors attempt only to cover the very basic management of a child's riding pony and leave the more expert matters, such as breaking-in, breeding and veterinary care, to be studied under the guidance of the appropriate professionals. Children wishing to keep ponies should, even after becoming competent riders, seek expert advice and read widely on the subject. An extremely valuable reference book to have is *The Manual of Horsemanship of the British Horse Society and The Pony Club* (London; The British Horse Society).

Description.

Ponies are, by definition horses who attain a height of not more than 15 hands (152 cm) at the highest point of the withers. (A " hand " is 4 inches, or approximately 10 cm). Larger children or young adults may require a horse, but a pony is suitable for a child in terms of size and temperament.

In the British Isles there are 9 breeds of native ponies which are renowned for their hardiness, sure-footedness and kind temperament: all are comprehensively described in *British Native Ponies* by Daphne Machin Goodall (London: Country Life). The 9 breeds are Connemara, Dales, Dartmoor, Exmoor, Fell, Highland, New Forest, Shetland and Welsh. These breeds of pure, or crosses between them, form the basis of the pony stock of this country and will be seen all over the British Isles, and in many other countries as well. The most usual colours are, depending on breed, black, brown, bay, chestnut, various greys, various roans, dun, piebald (black with white) and skewbald (any colour except black with white).

A pony at birth is a foal—either a colt (male) or a filly (female). After the age of 3, a filly is known as a mare and a colt, if left uncastrated, a stallion or entire. However, most colts—unless being kept for breeding purposes—will be castrated and are then called geldings. A gelding is considered more serene and manageable, and hence more suitable for riding.

Feeding and Accommodation.

The feeding of a pony will depend, to a great extent, on whether it is kept out at grass or in a stable, or by a combination of the two. The amount of food a pony requires will depend on the season of the year, the quality of the grass and the amount of work being undertaken.

For a pony kept at grass, there may be more than enough for it in rich pasture during the summer months, especially in some parts of the country, about which there will be local knowledge. Some ponies, especially those with a tendency to gain weight easily, may contract *laminitis* if grazing on lush grass, especially in May, is not restricted. This same pasture may have little or no feeding value from September through to April, again according to locality. A grass-kept pony requires, depending upon the quality of grass, a minimum of 1 acre, and 2 acres is more generous.

Preferably, a single pony should have up to 4 acres divided into sections. They are selective grazers, unlike cattle, and are best moved from one section to another periodically. This allows the grass to rest and is more economical in the long run. The land should be conserved by removing dung daily by barrow and shovel, or by harrowing periodically to spread the dung.

A very dry summer may make the grass bare and if the pony cannot be moved to better pasture, it will need supplementary feeding with hay.

During the winter months, extra feed will be needed. An average 13·2 hands high pony will need about 10 pounds (4·5 kg) of hay daily. Hay must be of good quality; mouldy or musty hay should never be fed. Sainfoin and meadow hay are probably the best two types for feeding. An average-sized pony will probably need two feeds of hay daily, fed either from the ground or from a hay-net tied high enough so that the pony cannot get his feet in it, even when it is empty. Hay-nets are economical methods of feeding as there is less wastage. It will take about 25 cwt (c. 1,275 kg) of hay to last the winter. If being worked daily, the pony will need about 3 pounds (c. 1·5 kg) of bruised or rolled oats and 1 pound (c. 0·5 kg) of bran mixed together, slightly dampened and fed in 2 feeds. For variety, boiled turnips, sliced carrots, beetroots, parsnips, mangels or swedes may be added. Manufactured horsecubes can also be incorporated into the feeds: these have proved very successful but must not, of course, be fed to excess.

Fresh, clean water should be available at all times and a mineral " salt lick " should be placed in the paddock or stable. A shelter should also be provided in the paddock, either by a thicket, coppice or high hedge on the north side, or a built shelter shed. Ponies are fairly resilient to the elements but a shelter is appreciated, particularly during the summer months in order to escape heat and flies. If the field is sectioned, the provision of water and shelter to cover all parts must be considered.

A stabled pony will require a loose box of about 10 feet (c. 3 m) × 12 feet (c. 4 m) with a door, in two parts, of about 4 feet (c. 1·25 m) in width. The floor must be non-slippery and impervious to moisture. Stable bricks are undoubtedly the best. Adequate ventilation is very important, and the stable should have a window, best when it opens inwards so that fresh air enters in an upwards direction and so goes over rather than on to the pony's back.

The floor needs to be covered with bedding—wheat straw, wood shavings or peat moss being the best—which will have to be " mucked out " each morning and " bedded-down " each evening.

A stabled pony will require more food—probably 3 feeds daily and a continual supply of water.

Food should be adjusted accordingly if the pony is kept by a combination of indoor and outdoor methods.

Grain foodstuffs must be stored in a dry, cool place, preferably in special bins with vermin-proof lids. Hay should be kept in a dry place, under cover.

General Management.

Ponies must be treated kindly, sensibly but firmly at all times. Shouting and sudden jerky movements of the arms will frighten them and should, therefore, be avoided. Always speak to a pony before approaching to handle it and before moving: this will warn and prepare it. Approach a pony at his shoulder, speak and then pat it on the neck or shoulder. Lead a pony from its near (left) side with one's right hand close to the bridle or head-collar and the left hand holding the slack of the rope. If a pony does not follow readily, persist patiently using the voice all the time: do not stare the pony in the eye or it will usually stop dead in its tracks. In order to turn a pony, push its head away rather than pull it towards one, as this will help it to remain better balanced and more co-ordinated.

A pony at grass should not be forgotten but visited daily, caught and checked over. When catching a pony, one should approach gently, offering a tit-bit in a feed-tin or bucket. If caught at feeding time, a pony soon associates the two and comes readily to its owner's call.

Grooming.

As well as improving the appearance and ensuring cleanliness, grooming helps to promote health and prevent disease. It is important that it should be carried out regularly, but not too frequently on a grass-kept pony as this may remove the insulating and waterproofing grease from the coat. A healthy pony should have a sleek, shiny coat indicative of good condition.

The basic grooming kit should consist of:

(i) a hoof pick for cleaning out the feet;
(ii) a dandy brush for removing caked mud and dust;
(iii) a body brush for removing dust and scurf from the coat and from the mane and tail;
(iv) a curry comb for cleaning the body brush;
(v) a water brush to use, slightly dampened, on the mane, tail and feet;
(vi) a stable sponge for cleaning the eyes, muzzle and dock and
(vii) a stable rubber to add a final polish.

The feet must be picked out daily—a stone left in the foot will probably lead to lameness—with a hoof pick and this should be done downwards from the heel towards the toe. This prevents any risk of the pick's penetrating the soft part of the " frog ", which is nature's anti-slipping device for ponies.

Shoeing.

" No foot—no horse " is a wise saying. Shoeing is necessary for ponies who are worked on roads or other hard surfaces which, without shoeing, would wear the wall of the foot away at a faster rate than it is replaced. The wall of the foot will grow whilst the shoes are on and so regular attention by a farrier or blacksmith is essential. Unshod ponies need their feet trimmed regularly, so that every pony should be seen by a farrier at least every 4–6 weeks or so. Shoeing is carried out either " hot " or " cold," and great care must be taken to ensure that the shoes fit correctly.

Saddlery.

The harness or " tack " for a pony should be well-fitting and clean. There are a great many items of saddlery available and the following are only the very basic ones:

Saddle
Girth
Stirrup irons
Stirrup leathers
Bridle
Headcollar and rope

Great care must be taken to ensure that a saddle does not pinch on the withers and that the girth is not likely to cause sores or " galls."

The " bit " of the bridle must be suitable for the pony's mouth, and most ponies can be ridden in a smooth-jointed snaffle.

All saddlery must be kept scrupulously clean, as this will improve appearance and keep the leather soft. Tack should be cleaned regularly, preferably every time it has been used. Leather should be cleaned with glycerine saddle soap, and metal washed, dried and then cleaned with metal polish (except the mouthpiece of the bit).

Saddlery should be stored in a dry place, the saddle itself put on a special purpose bracket and covered, and the bridle hung on a round or " half-moon " shaped hanger.

Saddlery is a vast and expert subject and an excellent book available is Saddlery by Captain E. Hartley Edwards (London: Country Life).

Diseases and Injuries.

These, almost without exception, call for prompt veterinary attention and any sign of lameness should not be neglected. A pony in good health is alert, has a shiny coat, quiet, regular breathing and a keen appetite. Any signs of it being " off-colour " should not be ignored. However, a useful reference book in which diseases and injuries are illustrated is the TV Vet Horse Book by " The TV Vet " (Ipswich: Farming Press).

SPECIAL TOPIC

This special article looks at zoonosis and other diseases associated with animals. Topics covered include fleas, mites, toxocariasis, hydatid disease, ringworm, tetanus and salmonella, cat-scratch disease and other allergies.

ZOONOSIS.

Introduction.

The word zoonosis is applied to a disease of lower animals transmissible to man, and at least 100 such diseases have been recognised. Some e.g., psittacosis or "parrot disease" and—especially during recent years—rabies, have attracted considerable public attention or scare. Generally speaking, the infections and parasites of one's own kind constitute a much more frequent and dangerous hazard, and it is only comparatively rarely that serious disease and infestation results from other animal sources. Adaptation and change through many generations have generally favoured this situation, and it is possible that infections once common to several species, including man, have become more restricted. Thus there are no modern records of distemper in man or of measles in the dog, yet the two viruses are so alike that a preparation made from measle virus has been used to protect dogs against distemper.

On the other hand, there seems a strong likelihood that some strains of influenza may be carried in lower animals and in certain circumstances undergo genetic recombination with a human strain to form a virulent virus capable of setting up widespread infection in man. It has already been shown that new "recombinants" can arise when groups of pigs or turkeys deliberately infected with different strains of influenza virus are herded together.

Although not strictly zoonoses, there are some, mainly allergic, conditions of man that are attributable to contact with animals or to the inhalation of dust containing animal dander or other material. Susceptible individuals who develop asthma or other problems as a result of such sensitivity should not of course keep or be in close contact with the animal or animals concerned, but it is important to secure help through one's doctor in determining the exact cause: it is easy to blame the cat or budgerigar when in fact other components of household dust may be responsible: in such instances the condition may persist after the suspected offender has been removed. On the other hand, it is important to deal firmly and effectively with the situation in those happily uncommon instances in which the animal poses a real threat to health.

It is impracticable to deal with all the possible zoonoses and "allergies" that may arise from pet animals and ponies—let alone with the important zoonoses that arise from other animal sources (e.g., anthrax, bovine turberculosis, cysticercosis from pork tapeworm, anaemia from fish tapeworm, trichinosis from partially cooked infective pork, bile duct disease from sheep liver fluke, virus B and Marburg disease from monkeys, brucellosis from cattle and goats, etc.) or that no longer occur in the UK (e.g., glanders from horses). The areas selected are of potential practical importance and require a sensible and balanced outlook should they ever arise or be suspected. One should never take chances, and always seek both medical and veterinary advice if a disease or infestation associated with one's animals is suspected.

There have of course been many allegations—often shown to have been unfounded—that pet and other animals are incriminated in human diseases, e.g., cancer was once reported to occur twice as frequently in households where canine cancer had occurred, but careful re-examination of the data did not confirm this. More recently it has been suggested that there is a significant association between multiple sclerosis and the ownership of small dogs. Again, however, re-examination of the data has not provided confirmation, while subsequent surveys conducted in places as distant as the Orkney and Shetland islands and Lower Saxony have proved negative (see, e.g., Prof. H. J. Bauer and Dr. J. Wikström, Lancet, 12 November 1977, p. 1029).

Fleas.

There are very many species of flea and, while most are host-specific, it must be borne in mind that most of their life-cycle is passed off the host, their larvae feeding on organic dust and on the semi-digested blood excreted by the adult fleas. The human flea, Pulex irritans, was once commonly found in pig-sties, but it is not prevalent in many parts of the UK today. Adult fleas can often "cross-infect" other hosts, e.g., the cat flea (Ctenocephalides felis) can infest the dog and the dog flea (C. canis) the cat, while both can infest man—as can the hen flea, Ceratophyllus gallinae. When flea infestation is suspected it is a good plan to brush the dog and cat over a sheet of black polythene and to take the brushings or hair for examination. Dog and cat fleas are characterised by the large spines or "combs" on the head and thorax. Treatment of donor or pet must be supplemented by stringent dealings with the bed, nest or other favourite haunt of the animal—disposal by burning being best and a thorough clean up of all the surroundings. Unfed fleas do not live long in dry surroundings, but may live for several months in a humid environment if debris in which they can hide is present. Specimens of the rat flea (Ceratophyllus fasciatus) were once maintained alive for 17 months at a temperature of 15·5 °C and a 70% R.H.

Mites.

Man has his own species of sarcoptic mange mite (Sarcoptes scabei)—producing scabies, which is widespread and which becomes very common in times of national disaster, e.g. after the Chilean earthquake—but several animal mites can infest him. The dog mange mite (S. canis) causes a transient infestation in man, unpleasant but amenable to modern acaricides. A site of attack in man is frequently the wrist, as with human scabies. S. cuniculus of pet rabbits and S. equi of horses may infest man, the latter causing "cavalryman's itch," but the condition never develops into true scabies and sometimes resolves spontaneously. Dog mange can, of course, be due to other mites, which probably are not pathogenic for man, but when S. canis is believed to have infested the owner, medical advice for him and veterinary advice for the dog should be sought, and the infestation eradicated.

Toxocariasis.

Toxocara canis is a roundworm that occurs in the small intestine of the dog and fox, and Toxocara cati is similarly found in the cat and its wild relations. Young animals are chiefly affected, and the intra-uterine infection of pups or kittens by worm larvae, which pass through the lung capillaries of the mother, is an important factor. These larvae remain in the liver of the foetal animal until the latter is born and begins to breathe, when they continue their migration through the lungs, eventually passing up the trachea and down the oesophagus to the intestine, where they grow into adults. The infective eggs if swallowed by other vertebrate species, including man, are capable of hatching out in the intestine with migration of larvae through the lungs and elsewhere (" larva migrani "), but subsequent growth into adult worms takes place only in suitable hosts. Children who are in close contact with infected animals or their excreta are particularly liable to ingest eggs, which then hatch out and are able to migrate through the body and can cause allergic phenomena, e.g., asthma, oesinophilia and enlarged spleen. Rarely, the worms may actually mature in the human host. Occasionally a granuloma develops around a dead larva in the eye, causing an obstruction to vision, or the brain, causing epilepsy. (It has even been suggested that the larvae could convey poliomyelitis virus from the intestine to the nervous system.) Until the early 1960s only some seven cases of toxocariasis in man had been reported in Britain, all affecting the eye. Studies since carried out mainly at the London School of Hygiene and Tropical Medicine have established, however, that there is not uncommon transmission to man of these common dog and cat parasites, which constitute a large reservoir of potential infection. About 2% of the apparently healthy UK population show immunological evidence of past infection, although in the vast majority of instances the parasite produces few if any symptoms " . . . and in all but a few cases questioning discloses no past illness which can clearly be identified as toxocaral in origin." Only about half of the fifty eye cases seen at the London School of Hygiene gave a clear history of having had a dog or cat in their household, and a subsequent survey showed that almost 25% of 800 specimens of soil collected from public parks in widely separated areas of Great Britain contained *T. canis* or *T. cati* eggs. About 4% of children living near the parks gave a positive reaction to the toxocaral skin sensitivity test (Dr. O. A. Borg and Prof. A. W. Woodruff, *British Medical Journal*, 1973, ii, 470). Handwashing after playing on contaminated soil or sand, or handling soil when gardening is clearly desirable.

It was once thought that toxocara infections played an important part in the transmission of another disease, toxoplasmosis, but this view now seems to have been discarded.

Hydatid Disease (Echinococcosis).

Echinococcus granulosus is a tapeworm found in the small intestine of the dog, fox and several wild carnivores. (It sometimes infests the cat, but in this host the parasites die before reaching sexual maturity.) It is only a small tapeworm, from 2·5 to 9 mm in length and has usually only four segments or proglottides, or which the most posterior is gravid and frequently as large as the rest of the body, and the head or scolex has two rows of hooks for attachment to the intestinal wall. The tapeworm itself is comparatively harmless to the dog unless present in very large numbers, when it can cause varying degrees of enteritis, from a simple catarrh to a haemorrhagic form. The eggs are passed out in the faeces and are ingested by the intermediate host, which may be man or almost any domestic or one of many wild animals. The eggs hatch in the intestine and the embryos migrate in the blood stream to various organs, where they grow slowly into large vesicles, 5 cm or more in diameter—in man sometimes exceeding 25 cm. Each vesicle is known as an echinococcus or hydatid cyst, is filled with relatively clear fluid, and has a fairly thick concentrically laminated cuticle—resembling sheets of fine tissue paper, outside which there is an inflammatory reaction on the part of the host—and from which daughter cysts may " bud "—and an internal germinal layer that produces numerous small vesicles or brood capsules about 5–6 months after infection. These brood capsules may become detached from the wall of the vesicle and float freely in the vesicular fluid, and are referred to as " hydatid sand." They may rupture and turn inside out. (The dog or other final host acquires the infection by ingesting fertile hydatids, and develops adult worms in 6–7 weeks.)

In man a hydatid cyst is typically acquired in childhood—often from eating the eggs that have inadvertently been picked up from the dog's coat—and it may take many years for pressure symptoms to develop. In nearly 75% of patients the right lobe of the liver is invaded and contains a single cyst, but other tissues affected include the lung, brain and orbit of the eye. The cyst may burst into the peritoneal or other body cavity, and the liberated brood capsules, scolices and germinal epithelium are all capable of forming new cysts or " bladders." It is therefore dangerous to puncture a cyst and allow the fluid to escape. Sometimes the original implantation occurs in bone, where it penetrates the canals and marrow cavity and may cause erosion and result in fracture: the affected long bones may necessitate amputation.

There is a third pattern of localisation in man in certain parts of Europe and Asia, known as the alveolar hydatid or " echinococcus alveolaris."

This consists of a fibrous stroma containing numerous small bladders, some of which may be fertile. The whole mass grows like a tumour, infiltrating the liver, entering the blood vessels and giving rise to " secondaries " in other organs. Very serious disease may of course result, depending upon the location of the hydatid within the body, but almost always taking many years to develop—it may appear primarily as affecting the liver, lung, central nervous system or bone. Impingement upon blood vessels may cause clots and local death of tissue; bronchi may be eroded; pressure may be exerted in vital centres in the brain; or the bile ducts may become obstructed. Primitive man may have trephined the skull of an affected fellow in an attempt to remove the cyst or to relieve the pressure caused by it.

The sheep appears to be the most " natural " intermediate host, for over 90% of cysts in it are fertile, compared with some 80% in pigs and only 10% in cattle. (In Bangladesh, however, where there are few sheep, cattle appear to be the main intermediate host.) Particular attention should be given to sheep dogs, and persons handling sheep must remember that the *Echinococcus* eggs tend to stick to the fleece, whence they may be transferred to human beings.

Drs. R. C. A. Thompson and J. D. Smyth of the Imperial College of Science and Technology, London, pointed out (*British Medical Journal*, 1974, ii, 807) that human hydatid disease originating from the sheep-and-dog combination was fortunately uncommon in Britain and largely confined to Wales. They drew attention to veterinary references to a dramatic increase in the occurrence of hydatid disease in the horse since the end of World War II, probably associated with the practice of feeding raw meat and offal, including horse offal, to foxhounds. They found over 25% of hounds from 21 kennels to be infected. They believe that the horse-and-dog combination produces strains that may be less infective to man, but one that should nevertheless be watched for, especially as development might be even slower than for the sheep-and-dog strains.

Toxoplasmosis.

The protozoan parasite, *Toxoplasma gondii*, was originally discovered in a small North African rodent, but now at least 150 mammalian or avian hosts have been reported, including man. Infection is cosmopolitan, but more prevalent in hot, humid climates. Its life cycle eluded investigators for many decades, although it was long realised that congenital transmission could occur in man. It was found, however, that *T. gondii* is a coccidian parasite of the domestic cat, in which all five stages of its life cycle occur—only two of them take place in man and other animals. Other members of the cat family are believed to be responsible for maintenance of the disease in areas where the domestic cat is absent.

There is evidence that toxoplasma infection is widespread, and in some communities more than 60% of the population are serologically positive. The prevalence increases with age, and this is believed to reflect continued exposure to the risk of infection either by eating raw or uncooked meat (from cattle, sheep or pigs carrying the parasite) or through the ingestion of the encysted eggs introduced into the environment by cats. These oocysts as they are termed can remain viable in soil for long periods and can be transported by flies and cockroaches. Contrary to opinions that have often been expressed, dogs do *not* excrete oocysts and " . . . the family dog would not appear to be important in the transmission of toxoplasmosis to man" (Dr. M. B. Morris, *British Medical Journal*, 1973, i, 666). Dogs themselves do pick up the parasite, either from meat or, probably, from flies which they have succeeded in catching and swallowing after snapping at them.

The parasite is apparently capable of surviving and replicating within virtually any cell type in the human body. The oocysts lodge in the mucosa of the bowel, germinate and release organisms which are spread widely via the bloodstream. The vast majority of human infections are symptom-free or mild. When acute infections occur, they are characterised by a rash, involvement of the lungs, heart, skeletal muscles, liver, brain and parts of the eye, sometimes with a fatal outcome.

Human infants may be infected *in utero*, but it is generally believed that a woman transmits the disease only when the primary infection has occurred during that pregnancy.

There are so many possible sources of infection that control is difficult. Oocysts freshly passed by the cat are not infective, and may safely be disposed of by flushing the excreta down the lavatory or by burning. In soil, however, the oocysts " sporulate. " Raw or undercooked meat should be avoided by man, dog or cat. Protection of children's sandpits or sand boxes is advisable, as cats generally have access to play areas. Special care should be taken when a cat shows signs of an enteric infection.

Ringworm.

In Britain most of the ringed lesions due to fungal infection are cattle ringworm. Some, however, are due to *Microsporon canis*, which is found on both dogs and cats, especially young ones. Ringworm of the scalp may be due either to *M. canis* or to *M. audovini*, derived from human beings. An irregular bald area dotted with distorted broken stumps of hair appears, and ranging from slight scaling to scanty pustules. An interesting inflammatory immune response occurs in some cases derived from dogs or cats. When examined with potash the hair stump is found to be packed with spores, and the infected hair (human or animal) gives a characteristic turquoise fluorescence when examined under Wood's light (330–360 nm).

Although *M. canis* infections usually clear spontaneously in man in about 3 months, medical advice and treatment should be sought, and it is imperative to seek veterinary advice on the incriminated animal.

Tetanus, Salmonella and other bacterial infections.

Despite the general statement in the introduction, there are of course many bacteria that can produce disease in man and in other animals, and animal sources of human infection should always be borne in mind. Fortunately, infections that derive from non-exotic pet animals and ponies are not numerous.

Tetanus is not acquired directly from animals, but the causal organism, *Clostridium tetani*, forms spores that can survive for an almost unlimited period of time outside man, *e.g.*, in soil. The spores do not germinate in the gut after being ingested with plants and vegetables, and they are passed out in the excreta. They may contaminate soil or herbage or other material in this way, and horses—perhaps because they are prone to develop tetanus themselves—are regarded with particular suspicion as a source of contamination.

The disease is usually contracted by the contamination of wounds with the spores. The spores require conditions of low oxygen tension in order to germinate, and hazardous wounds are those that are penetrating and permit the development of deep-seated infections, which become sealed off at the surface. The spores appear to require also some nutrients from contamination or from dead tissue, and it seems that they are entirely harmless in clean, debrided wounds devoid of tissue necrosis. It is usual therefore to tidy up all tissue injuries, removing the dead tissue and to " lay open " a deep wound suspected of harbouring spores.

The usual incubation period is 1–2 weeks—although thought spores may remain dormant for a long time—and the onset is characterised by stiffness of voluntary muscles, often just in the jaw, and this leads to difficulty in opening the jaw, known as trismus or lockjaw, and followed by difficulty in breathing. All persons should be actively immunised with tetanus toxoid, and a " booster " should be given whenever an accident or injury occurs that might lead to contamination and spore development.

Salmonella and related organisms give rise to a variety of diseases in man, including typhoid and enteric fevers, gastroenteritis or " food poisoning " and febrile septicaemia. There are many types of Salmonella, some of which cause disease only in man, some only in lower animals and some in both. Persons who " carry " Salmonella may contaminate food during cooking or handling, or water, and fleas may be a vector in transmitting some forms. Infection is by mouth. Some foods are contaminated, and during World War II many Salmonella organisms were recovered from dried egg. Dr. H. Williams-Smith, then of the Animal Health Trust Farm Livestock Research Centre at Stock, published in 1959 a survey on the isolation of Salmonella organisms from apparently healthy animals and recorded that some 12% of the pigs, 4·5% of the dogs and 2·5% of the cats he examined were carrying the infection. He wrote (*Journal of Hygiene*, 1959, **57**, 266–273) that the part played by cats and dogs in spreading salmonella infection to man was not fully understood, adding, " However, their relatively high rate of infection with salmonellae, their close association with man, and the fact that they have been shown to have been responsible for some cases of human infection, indicates that they should be considered as possible sources of infection whenever outbreaks in man are being investigated." He made special mention of the recovery of a particular organism, *Salmonella heidelberg*, from 4 out of 200 dogs, since this following its original isolation in Britain in 1953, had become the second most important of the salmonellae causing food poisoning in man.

Ornithosis (" Psittacosis ").

For many years since the first reported human case in Switzerland in 1879 this was known as psittacosis or " parrot disease ", and indeed most cases in the outbreaks that occurred in many countries in 1929–30 were attributed to birds of the parrot family, in which it causes diarrhoea, shivering, weakness and apathy. In man the disease was once described as resembling typhoid fever in many respects, often complicated by pneumonia—actually an acute interstitial pneumonitis. Often, however, it takes the form only of a mild influenzal-like illness. The incubation period is usually from 6 to 15 days, followed by a relatively sudden onset of fever and chills, malaise, headache, sore throat and cough. The responsible agent is one of the group of organisms lying intermediate between bacteria and viruses and collectively known as the Chlamydiae or Bedsoniae, and is transmitted by handling the bird or—less often—by its bite or by the inhalation of infective material such as faeces in the dust. Some workers have given it the specific name *Chlamydia psittaci*. Spread may occur from person to person during the height of active disease, at which time there may be drowsiness, delirium or stupor.

Some authorities still retain the use of the term psittacosis, or employ it for those human infections traced to psittacine birds. It is now recognized, however, that strains of the infection—often perhaps less virulent—occur in other avian species, hence " ornithosis. " In the South Somerset clinical area between 1964 and 1971 Dr. J. P. Anderson (*Postgraduate Medical Journal*, 1973, **49**, 533) recorded 70 patients who by complement fixation testing were found to have ornithosis. Of these, 47 fulfilled strict diagnostic criteria and 33 presented at a chest clinic, usually for " post-influenzal " surveillance: in most, cough was a prominent symptom, while the general appearance mimicked major chest disease. In none was the disease life-threatening, but 14 who were hospitalised were quite severely affected. Acutely ill patients obtained clinical benefit from tetracyclines. Bird contacts were not traced in 11 instances, but the remaining 36 confirmed cases showed an interesting variety, viz.: budgerigars 10, hens 6, pigeons 5, wild birds 4, finches 3, parrots 3, " pet shop " 2, turkey 1, dove 1 and owl 1. The three cases infected by parrots were all quite severely infected, which is in accord with other observations that cases contracted from parrots are usually more severe and have a higher death rate. Also, contrary to views hitherto held British budgerigars seem not infrequently to cause human infections (see also Dr. N. R. Grist, *British Medical Journal*, 1972, **i**, 378). Pigeons are probably a fairly significant source of low-grade infections, as well as occasional more serious ones, for surveys have indicated quite widespread infection rates among this species—and often serological evidence of infection among those who work with them.

There is some evidence that ornithosis may be responsible for acquired valvular heart disease. Heart-valve involvement in birds dying from the infection is recognised, and there have been reports in man, especially in cases of " rheumatic heart disease " not associated with a history of rheumatic fever. Drs. C. and A. M. Ward in Sheffield (*Lancet*, 1974, ii, 734) found evidence of previous ornithosis infection in 7 out of 27 patients with acquired valvular heart disease. They pointed out that permanent cardiac damage can result from mild influenza in as many as 5% of persons and query whether the same may not be true in mild cases of ornithosis.

Cat-scratch Disease.

It is undecided whether this benign infectious disease is due to a virus or to a chlamydial infection. Almost invariably the disease in man is associated with a cat, but there are instances in which inoculation has been associated with splinters or thorns. The local injury is usually trivial, but sometimes there forms an erithrematous papule or crust. After 1–2 weeks, but sometimes several months, the regional lymph glands draining the area become painfully enlarged, *e.g.*, in the armpit, head, neck or groin. The glands may swell to as much as 8–10 cm in diameter, and in about 50% of cases become soft and suppurate. Rarely there is a high fever (100° F) and, extremely uncommonly, encephalitis develops, but generally the disease is mild and is important only in that it may be mistaken for glandular fever, tuberculosis or other more severe conditions.

There is a means of diagnosing exposure to infection, using cat-scratch disease skin-test antigen.

Allergies.

Bronchial asthma—to be distinguished from asthmatic bronchitis—is an allergic disorder associated with wheeziness or repeated attacks of bronchospasm. There is a history of infantile eczema in about half the patients, and it has been said that at the age of 2 years the child may exchange his eczema for asthma. Sometimes asthma commences later in life, especially in middle age. The allergens responsible are inhaled and are derived from organic material such as pollen, house dust containing mites (*Dermatophagoides pteronyssinus*), feathers, animal dander and fungal spores. House dust mites thrive in the superficial layers of mattresses. Much less frequently, the allergens are ingested from certain foods. Feathers are considered to be a frequent precipitating cause, and these may of course derive not only from pillows, cushions and other soft furnishings but also from birds kept in the house, especially the budgerigar.

It is very important that medical advice for asthmatics should be sought anyway, and it is important also that the allergen or allergens responsible be tracked down and, so far as practicable, removed from the environment. If it is the pet bird that is incriminated, then that has to go elsewhere. It must be remembered, however, that most allergic asthmatics are sensitive to more than one allergen, and that some allergens, *e.g.*, pollen or moulds, are seasonal. Paediatricians and allergists recognise that the symptoms are often aggravated by non-specific factors such as bronchial irritation from dust, tobacco smoke, acrid fumes or cold air, bacterial infection in the respiratory tract, emotional stress and even strenuous exertion.

Episodes of nasal congestion, watery nasal discharge and sneezing are characteristic of *hay fever*, or " seasonal " *allergic rhinitis*, associated with grass and other pollens. Similar symptoms may occur perennially when the allergen is derived from other sources such as those indicated for bronchial asthma, and among which animal danders are important. (One of the authors used to suffer from the dander of cattle and of several other ruminants.) Among these danders are those of the pony, while cat epithelium may also be responsible (see *Clinical Allergy*, 1976, 6, 147).

It is nowadays usual to be able to identify the cause or causes of the allergy and, when a pet is definitely involved the only rational procedure is to remove it. Desensitisation is effective in some but by no means all instances. As with bronchial asthma—which may develop or co-exist—it is important to bear in mind that an individual may be sensitive to more than one allergen—and that often there is a family history of some form of allergy.

Sensitivity—manifested by allergic respiratory and skin symptoms—has been reported in up to 10% of persons working with rats and mice in laboratories (*Journal of Occupational Medicine*, 1974, 16, 465), and Drs. A. N. Taylor, Joan L. Longbottom and J. Pepys of the Cardiothoracic Institute, London, have recently confirmed (*Lancet*, 1977, ii, 847) that the urine of these species may be an important source of allergenic protein. Sensitisation to these proteins can occur following inhalation of airborne dust contaminated with urine, and there has been one reported case of an alveolitis (similar to that described under bird fancier's lung). Dr. Taylor and colleagues described sensitivity in five laboratory workers—one of whom was an asthmatic and the others hay-fever sufferers—to protein isolated from rat and mouse urine.

Some experts are a good deal more cautious than others in removing the suspected source of the allergies from the immediate environment. Thus Dr. R. A. L. Brewis in the 1976 edition of his *Lecture Notes on Respiratory Disease* (Oxford: Blackwell) writes that, " It is rarely necessary to advise patients to move to a different house or climate or to dispose of pets or change employment on account of asthma unless the indications are particularly compelling and treatment is unsatisfactory."

Bird Fancier's Lung.

This is one of several forms of what is known as extrinsic allergic alveolitis, in which the inhalation of certain types of organic dust produces a diffuse allergic reaction in the walls of the alveoli and bronchioles of the lung. Continued exposure to the offending material may lead to permanent lung damage with severe respiratory disability, and fatal cases have been recorded.

Other forms include farmer's lung (from mouldy hay), mushroom worker's lung (from compost) and a condition in those working in factories producing " biological " washing powder.

Bird fancier's disease is associated with the inhalation of avian protein, usually from pigeon or budgerigar droppings. Dr. D. Lane (*British Medical Journal*, 1977, ii, 1066) has pointed out that there are differences between the illnesses produced by exposure to pigeons and budgerigars: exposure to pigeons—kept outside and cleaned out once a week—is usually intermittent and the onset acute, whereas exposure to budgerigars—kept in cages in the living room—is virtually continuous and the onset insidious. Up to 40% of pigeon fanciers have avian precipitin but no evidence of lung disease, whereas it is unusual for budgerigar fanciers to have the precipitin without the disease. (One of the authors, however, recently saw an 8-year-old boy who had developed the acute disease from a pigeon that was kept inside the house.) The incidence from budgerigars must be quite rare, since up to 7 million budgerigars are kept in the UK, with one in seven households possessing one.

Allergic alveolitis should be suspected when a person regularly exposed to a concentration of the offending dust complains, a few hours after re-exposure to the same dust, of general malaise, dry cough and dyspnoea without wheeze, and help should be sought through one's medical practitioner to determine whether there is evidence of avian protein through the precipitin test. If so, the cause must of course be removed. Mild cases usually recover rapidly when this has been done.

It is of great interest that a small proportion of persons who have bird fancier's lung may have atrophy of the interstinal villi indicative of coeliac disease, although the relationship is by no means clear as yet. Another feature is that non-smokers are far more likely than smokers to develop an antibody response.

INDEX

Each section has a letter and, where appropriate, the column is given in brackets after the page number, *e.g.*, F8(1), G25(2). Some of the sections are alphabetically arranged and index themselves. Their contents are not included here except where it is anticipated some special difficulty may arise. The sections "Medical Matters" and "The World of Music" have each a separate index and glossary.

1981. Steve Davis
1980. Cliff Thorburn
1979. Terry Griffiths
1978